BOOK AUCTION RECORDS

BOOK AUCTION RECORDS

A PRICED AND ANNOTATED ANNUAL RECORD

OF INTERNATIONAL BOOK AUCTIONS

Part I

Printed Books & Atlases

Part II

Printed Maps Charts & Plans

VOLUME 78

For the Auction Season August 1980–July 1981

EDITOR: Wendy Y. Heath

DAWSON

Published by Dawson Publishing

Cannon House

Folkestone, Kent CT19 5EE

©Wm Dawson & Sons Ltd., 1981

ISBN 0 7129 1018 2

Printed in Great Britain by
Unwin Brothers Limited, The Gresham Press,
Old Woking, Surrey.

Contents

Publisher's Note

Throughout this year one of our main preoccupations has been to find ways and means of maintaining the published price of Book Auction Records at its previous level in the face of escalating manufacturing and editorial costs.

Our editorial team have undoubtedly made considerable efforts to increase their productivity without sacrificing their standards of accuracy.

By altering the typographical lay-out in the Records Section of the Volume it has been possible to include more entries per page without adversely affecting legibility. This has resulted in a smaller increase in manufacturing costs than otherwise would have been the case, and it has been possible to hold the price of Volume 78 at the same level as that of the two previous volumes *in respect of standing orders and orders received before 31st January 1982*; thereafter a modest price increase will apply.

Volume 78 contains well over 33,000 record entries covering 324 auction sales conducted by 52 auction houses throughout the world, thus maintaining the international character of Book Auction Records.

As a comprehensive reference work, B.A.R. is consulted largely by antiquarian booksellers, collectors and librarians and its main purpose is to provide the maximum spread of accurate information to enable readers to follow international price movements of antiquarian books. For this reason we have deleted some extraneous preliminary matter which does not further this objective, and can be found in other types of publication. The savings effected by this change have been utilised to increase the number of entries in the record section.

We hope that the measures outlined above will meet with the approval of our readers and that they will be seen as a determined effort on our part to ensure that Book Auction Records retains its position as a leading guide to prices of antiquarian books and represents the best buy in its field.

Readers will have noted that we have reduced the time-lag in publication and the Volumes are now being published within five months of the end of the relevant auction season; it is our intention to maintain this timetable.

The explanatory notes which follow describe the changes which have been made in this volume to achieve legibility and ease of reference compatible with economical setting.

December, 1981.

Explanatory Notes

BOOK AUCTION RECORDS VOLUME 78 is marked by a number of changes and improvements in the arrangement. The most important of these changes is in the order of description within entries, these now being arranged in an order which is closer to current bibliographical practice. Another change we have made is to revert to our former custom of using dashes to ditto both Author and Title, followed where necessary by 'Anr. Copy', 'Anr. Edn.' or 'Anr. Run' to indicate another copy/set/run/volume and another edition/issue/impression. Brackets when used to indicate anonymity are placed around the dash dittoing the Author, but are otherwise used in the normal manner in the entry. The volume as previously is in two parts, Part I, Printed Books & Atlases, Part II, Printed Maps, Charts and Plans.

The Book entries are arranged alphabetically by author (personal or corporate), or where there is no known author, by title, by private press or other obvious association. Often, official reports, directories and similar publications are listed geographically. Authors' names frequently take different forms, for instance those which are commonly Latinised, and for these we have endeavoured to use the form by which they are most generally known. As an exception to this rule, pseudonymous authors, although often better known by their pseudonyms, are entered under their real names, when known. The pseudonyms are cross-referenced. Anonymous works are indicated by enclosing the Author dash in brackets. Brackets are also used elsewhere in the usual manner to indicate notes, translations, interpolations etc. that do not appear in the original work, but have been added by the Editor or the Auctioneers' cataloguer.

Certain large categories are listed under subject headings. These are Almanacs, Bibles, Breviaries, Costume, Horae, Hymnals, Magna Carta, Missals, New Testament, Prayerbooks, Psalms, Statuta and Trials. The individual works listed under these large subject categories and under certain prolific authors such as Shakespeare and Cervantes are not always arranged alphabetically, but are often arranged chronologically or by language.

In the listings of individual works, ample bibliographical detail is given for ease of identification. After the author and title, these details include editor, translator, illustrator, place of publication, Press if important, and date. Then follow details of edition/issue, number of volumes if more than one, format, description of binding and, when applicable, important ownership marks, presentation inscriptions, annotations or extraneous material such as letters, notes or other inserts. Information is also given on imperfections, damage or defects that might possibly affect the price. Where no place or date of publication appears in a work this also, if known, is given, enclosed in brackets; otherwise the fact is indicated by the usual abbreviation n.p. or n.d. Where no place is shown it may be assumed that the place of publication is London.

The bibliographical description is followed by the auction sale record, which gives the auction house (in code, see our 'Key to Sales'), date of sale, sale lot number, buyer's name (when given and published by the auction house) and the price made, which is the hammer price, thus not including any buyer's premium that may apply. In addition cross-references are made for pseudonyms, joint authorship, nobles, important books bound together, compound names (in cases where confusion may arise) and also for the more important illustrators, editors and translators. Bibliographical abbreviations used in the records are those which appear in the list of abbreviations. Non-bibliographical abbreviations in general use are not listed.

It is not our policy to include in Book Auction Records lots of two or more unrelated works, single engravings, prints and photographs etc., but important books bound together may appear. Volume 78 records only those lots which realised £50.00 and over (U.K.), $100.00 and over (U.S.A., Canada & Australia), or the European equivalent of £100.00 and over (see our 'Currency Conversion Rates'). For lots 'sold with all faults' (w.a.f.) only those which realised at least £100.00 and $200.00 are included.

The map entries are generally arranged alphabetically by Author or Cartographer followed by the title, place and date of publication, size, description and sale record. The description includes details of decoration, whether coloured, framed and glazed or mounted, and also any imperfections that might possibly affect the price.

Book Auction Records is compiled from the season's auction catalogues and we are constantly faced with the problem of variant, abridged, obscure and even faulty descriptions of titles, this inevitably causing much additional time to be spent on bibliographical research and checking. Therefore whilst every endeavour is made to avoid mistakes and correct faulty information, some errors will unavoidably have crept in. Certain entries in Book Auction Records may appear to be incomplete but this is usually due to lack of information in the auction catalogue.

The more obvious value of Book Auction Records to booksellers, collectors and librarians, is a unique record of international auction prices over a long period of years, but with its vast number of incidental references to anonymous and pseudonymous authors, editors, translators, illustrators, private presses, societies and ownership etc., it is also invaluable for general bibliographical reference.

Abbreviations

A.D.(s).	= autograph document (signed)	fore-e. pntg.	= fore-edge. painting	plt(s).	= plate(s)
advt(s).	= advertisement(s)	Fr.	= French	pol.	= polished
A.L.(s).	= autograph letter (signed)	frontis.	= frontispiece	port(s).	= portrait(s)
Amer.	= American	gt.	= gilt	portfo.	= portfolio
A.N.(s).	= autograph note (signed)	hf.	= half	pp.	= pages
annot(s).	= annotation(s)	histor.	= historiated	Pr.	= Press
anr.	= another	H.M.P.	= hand-made paper	prelims.	= preliminary pages
bd(s).	= board(s)	ill(s).	= Illustrator/illustrated/ illustration(s)	pres.	= presentation
bdg.	= binding	imp.	= impression	priv. ptd.	= privately printed
bkd.	= backed	impft.	= imperfect	pt(s).	= part(s)
bkplt.	= bookplate	incompl.	= incomplete	ptd.	= printed
bnd.	= bound	inscr.	= inscribed/inscription	publd.	= published
brkn.	= broken	Iss.	= Issue/issued	qtr.	= quarter
C.	= century	Jnr.	= Junior	rebkd.	= rebacked
ca.	= circa	jnt(s).	= joint(s)	rebnd.	= rebound
card.	= cardboard	leath.	= leather	reprd.	= repaired
cf.	= calf	lev.	= levant	russ.	= russia leather
chromo(s).	= chromolithograph(s)	lf.	= leaf	s.-c.('s)	= slip case(s)
cl.	= cloth	lge.	= large	sig(s).	= signature(s)
col(d).	= colour(ed)	liby.	= library	sigd.	= signed
coll.	= collected	litho(s).	= lithograph(s)	sm.	= small
compl.	= complete	ll.	= leaves	Soc.	= Society
cont.	= contemporary	L.P.	= Large Paper	spr.	= sprinkled/speckled/ spotted
decor(s).	= decorated/ decoration(s)	lr. (cover)	= lower (cover)	stp(d).	= stamp(ed)
		Ltd.	= Limited	str.-grd.	= straight-grained
defect.	= defective	marb.	= marbled	supp(s).	= supplement(s)
detchd.	= detached	mntd.	= mounted	thro.-out.	= throughout
disbnd.	= disbound	mod.	= modern	T.L.(s).	= typed letter (signed)
doubls.	= doublures	monog(s).	= monogram(s)	trans.	= Translator/translated/ translation
dtd.	= dated	mor.	= morocco		
dupl.	= duplicate	mott.	= mottled	unbnd.	= unbound
d.-w.('s)	= dust wrapper(s)	MS(S).	= manuscript(s)	unc.	= uncut
Ed.	= Editor/edited	mus. notat.	= musical notation	unif.	= uniform
Edn(s).	= Edition(s)	n.d.	= no date	upr. (cover)	= upper (cover)
elab.	= elaborately	no(s).	= number(s)	v.d.	= various dates
Engl.	= English	n.p.	= no place	vell.	= vellum
engr(s).	= engraving(s)	ob.	= oblong	vig(s).	= vignette(s)
F.	= framed	orig.	= original	vol(s).	= volume(s)
facs.	= facsimile(s)	outl.	= outline	v.p.	= various places
F. & G.	= framed & glazed	p.	= page	w.a.f.	= with all faults
fo.	= folio	panel.	= panelled	wrap(s).	= wrapper(s)
		parch.	= parchment	wtrmkd.	= watermarked
		pict.	= pictorial		

ABBREVIATIONS FOR PLACE NAMES

Amst.	= Amsterdam	Copen.	= Copenhagen	Nuremb.	= Nuremburg
Antw.	= Antwerp	Edinb.	= Edinburgh	N.Y.	= New York
Balt.	= Baltimore	Flor.	= Florence	Phila.	= Philadelphia
Bg'ham.	= Birmingham	L.	= London	Pittsb.	= Pittsburgh
Camb.	= Cambridge	L'pool.	= Liverpool	San Franc.	= San Francisco
Chic.	= Chicago	Mich.	= Michigan	St. Petersb.	= Saint Petersburgh
Cinc.	= Cincinatti	N.O.	= New Orleans	Wash.	= Washington

ABBREVIATIONS FOR PRIVATE PRESSES

Ash. Pr.	= Ashendene Press	Grol. Soc.	= Grolier Society	Roxb. Cl.	= Roxburghe Club
Bannat. Cl.	= Bannatyne Club	Kelms. Pr.	= Kelmscott Press	Shakes. Hd. Pr.	= Shakespeare Head Press
Gold. Cock. Pr.	= Golden Cockerell Press	Ltd. Edns. Cl.	= Limited Editions Club	Straw. Hill Pr.	= Strawberry Hill Press
Gregy. Pr.	= Gregynog Press	Nones. Pr.	= Nonesuch Press		
Grol. Cl.	= Grolier Club				

Auction Houses

B	J.L. BEIJERS Achter Sint Pieter 14 Utrecht NETHERLANDS		DWB	DREWEATT, WATSON & BARTON Donnington Priory Donnington Newbury Berkshire RG13 2JE ENGLAND
BS	BONHAMS Montpelier Galleries Montpelier Street Knightsbridge London SW7 1HH ENGLAND		GM	GEORGE MEALY & SONS 2 & 3 Proby's Lane Dublin 1 EIRE
C	CHRISTIE, MANSON & WOODS LTD 8 King Street St. James' London SW1Y 6QT ENGLAND		GT	GARROD TURNER 50 St. Nicholas Street Ipswich IP1 1TP ENGLAND
CB	CANADA BOOK AUCTIONS 35 Front Street East Toronto M5E 1B3 CANADA		H	HAUSWEDELL & NOLTE D–2000 Hamburg 13 Pöseldorfer Weg 1 WEST GERMANY
CE	CHRISTIE'S & EDMISTON'S LTD 164 Bath Street Glasgow G2 4TG SCOTLAND		HD	HOTEL DROUOT 9 Rue Drouot 75002 Paris FRANCE
CNY	CHRISTIE, MANSON & WOODS INT INC 502 Park Avenue New York NY 10022 U.S.A.		HK	HARTUNG & KARL D–8000 München 2 Karolinenplatz 5a WEST GERMANY
CR	CHRISTIE'S (INTERNATIONAL) S.A. Piazza Navona, 114 00186 Roma ITALY		HL	HARMERS 41 New Bond Street London W1A 4EH ENGLAND
CSK	CHRISTIE'S SOUTH KENSINGTON LTD (London) 85 Old Brompton Road South Kensington London SW7 3JS ENGLAND		HSS	HENRY SPENCER & SONS 20 The Square Retford Nottinghamshire DN22 6DJ ENGLAND
D	F. DORLING Neuer Wall 40–42 2000 Hamburg 36 WEST GERMANY		HY	HARVEY'S AUCTIONS LTD 22–23 Long Acre London WC2E 9LD ENGLAND
			JL	JAMES R. LAWSON PTY LTD 236 Castlereagh Street Sydney AUSTRALIA
DS	DURAN SUBASTAS DE ARTE Serrano, 12 Madrid 1 SPAIN		JN	JAMES, NORWICH AUCTIONS, LTD 33 Timberhill Norwich ENGLAND

KH	KENNETH HINCE 140 Greville Street Prahan Victoria 3181 AUSTRALIA		PNY	PHILLIPS SON & NEALE INC 525 East 72nd Street New York NY 10021 U.S.A.

KH   KENNETH HINCE
140 Greville Street
Prahan
Victoria 3181
AUSTRALIA

LA   W.H. LANE & SON
Central Auction Rooms
Penzance
ENGLAND

Central Auction Rooms
Trelawney Lane
Plymouth
ENGLAND

LC   T.R.G. LAWRENCE & SON
South Street
Crewkerne
Somerset
TA18 7JU
ENGLAND

LM   LOUIS MOORTHAMERS
Rue Lesbroussart 124
1050 Bruxelles
BELGIUM

MMB   MESSENGER, MAY & BAVERSTOCK
93 High Street
Godalming
Surrey
ENGLAND

O   OLIVERS
23/24 Market Hill
Sudbury
Suffolk
ENGLAND

P   PHILLIPS SON & NEALE
Blenstock House
7 Blenheim Street
New Bond Street
London
W1Y 0AS
ENGLAND

PD   PHILLIPS SON & NEALE
65 George Street
Edinburgh
EH2 2JL
SCOTLAND

PG   PHILLIPS SON & NEALE
98 Sauchiehall Street
Glasgow
G2 3DQ
SCOTLAND

PJ   PHILLIPS & JOLLYS
1 Old King Street
Bath
BA1 1DD
ENGLAND

PL   PHILLIPS SON & NEALE
17a East Parade
Leeds
LS1 2BU
ENGLAND

PNY   PHILLIPS SON & NEALE INC
525 East 72nd Street
New York
NY 10021
U.S.A.

867 Madison Avenue
New York
NY 10021
U.S.A.

PWP   PHILLIPS WARD-PRICE
76 Davenport Road
Toronto
Ontario
M5R 1H3
CANADA

480 St. François Xavier
Montreal
Quebec
H2Y 2T4
CANADA

R   REISS & AUVERMANN
Zum Talblick 2
6246 Glashütten im Taunus 1
WEST GERMANY

RBT   RICHARD BAKER & THOMSON
9 Hamilton Street
Birkenhead
Merseyside
ENGLAND

S   SOTHEBY PARKE BERNET & CO
Grosvenor Saleroom
Bloomfield Place
New Bond Street
London
W1A 2AA
ENGLAND

SBA   SOTHEBY BERESFORD ADAMS
Booth Mansion
Watergate Street
Chester
CH1 1NP
ENGLAND

SD   SOTHEBY BEARNE
Rainbow
Torquay
TQ2 5TG
ENGLAND

SG   SWANN GALLERIES INC
104 East 25th Street
New York
NY 10010
U.S.A.

SH   SOTHEBY PARKE BERNET & CO
Hodgson's Salerooms
Bloomfield Place
New Bond Street
London
W1A 2AA
ENGLAND

SI   SOTHEBY PARKE BERNET ITALIA S.R.L.
Via Montenapoleone 3
20121 Milan
ITALY

SKC   SOTHEBY, KING & CHASEMORE
Station Road
Pulborough
West Sussex
RH20 1AJ
ENGLAND

SM   SOTHEBY PARKE BERNET MONACO S.A.
P.O. Box 45
Sporting d'Hiver
Place du Casino
Monte Carlo
MONACO

SPB   SOTHEBY PARKE BERNET INC
171 East 84th Street
New York
NY 10021
U.S.A.

SSA   SOTHEBY PARKE BERNET SOUTH AFRICA
(PTY) LTD
P.O. Box 31010
Braamfontein 2017
Johannesburg
SOUTH AFRICA

TA   TAVINER'S AUCTION ROOMS
Prewett Street
Redcliffe
Bristol
BS1 6PB
ENGLAND

TRL   THOMSON, RODDICK & LAURIE
24 Lowther Street
Carlisle
ENGLAND

TW   THOMAS WATSON & SON
Northumberland Street
Darlington
County Durham
ENGLAND

VA   VOLKS RARE BOOK AUCTIONS
222–224 Schubart Street
Pretoria
P.O. Box 2144
Transvaal
SOUTH AFRICA

VG   A.L. VAN GENDT & CO
96–98 Keizersgracht
1015 CV Amsterdam
NETHERLANDS

WW   WOOLLEY & WALLIS
The Castle Auction Mart
Castle Street
Salisbury
Wiltshire
SP1 3SU
ENGLAND

Key to Sales
August 1980-July 1981

1980
B = J.L. BEIJERS (*Utrecht*)
Dec 10/11   The Library of the late Dr. W.C. van Unnik

1980
BS = BONHAMS (*London*)
Sep 17   Printed Books
Nov 26   Prints & Printed Books

1981
Feb 25   Prints & Printed Books
May 13   Prints & Printed Books
Jun 11   Printed Books

1980
C = CHRISTIE, MANSON & WOODS LTD (*London*)
Oct 22   Valuable Autograph Letters, Historical Documents & Music Manuscripts
Nov 5/6   Fine Natural History & Topographical Books & Atlases
Nov 19/20   Valuable English Literature, Early Printed Books & Manuscripts
Nov 26/27   Important Books from Chetham's Library, Manchester

1981
Feb 4   Printed Books
Feb 25   Valuable Printed Books
Mar 18   Valuable Natural History & Travel Books
Apr 1   Early Printed Books, Books on the History of Science, Economics, Literature & Theology
Apr 15/16   Books from the Library of the late Eric Sexton, F.S.A.
May 20   Printed Books, including Travel, Topography & Natural History
Jun 10   Venetian Illustrated Books of the Eighteenth Century: The Collection of John A. Saks
Jul 15/16   Valuable Printed Books
Jul 22   Art Reference & Modern Printed Books

1980
CB = CANADA BOOK AUCTIONS (*Toronto*)
Sep 24   Ornithology & Natural History, Voyages, Travel & Exploration . . .
Nov 12   Books on the Indian & Eskimo, Canadiana, Antiquarian Books . . .
Dec 9   The Stephen Leacock Collection, Arctica, Canadiana . . .

1981
Feb 18   Americana, Antiquarian & Plate Books, Maps & Atlases . . .
Apr 1   The Wilson MacDonald Literary Archives, Canadiana, Books about Books . . .
May 27   The Arthur W. Wallace Collection of Architecture, Canadiana & Canadian Architecture . . .

1980
CE = CHRISTIE'S & EDMISTON'S LTD (*Glasgow*)
Aug 28   Antiquarian & Scots Law Books
Oct 24   Antiquarian Books
Nov 20   Valuable Antiquarian Books, mainly Scottish
Dec 4   Antiquarian Books

1981
Feb 19   Scots Law & Antiquarian Books
Mar 19   Antiquarian Books
Apr 23   Antiquarian Books
Jun 4   Antiquarian Books
Jul 9   Important Antiquarian Books

1980
CNY = CHRISTIE, MANSON & WOODS INT INC (*New York*)
Oct 1   Early Printed Books & Manuscripts
Oct 1   Printed Books & Manuscripts
Oct 9   An Important Collection of Judaica

1981
Feb 6   The Prescott Collection of Printed Books & Manuscripts
Apr 8   Fifteenth Century Books Illustrating the Spread of Printing: The Collection of the late Eric Sexton, F.S.A.
May 22   Printed Books & Manuscripts

1981
CR = CHRISTIE'S (INTERNATIONAL) S.A. (*Roma*)
Mar 19   Libri d'Arte di Viaggi ed Atlanti
Jun 11/12   Libri d'Arte Antichi ed Autografi

1980
CSK = CHRISTIE'S SOUTH KENSINGTON LTD (*London*)
Aug 1   Printed Books
Aug 15   Printed Books
Aug 22   Printed Books
Aug 29   Printed Books
Sep 5   Printed Books
Sep 12   Printed Books
Sep 19   Printed Books
Sep 26   Printed Books
Oct 3   Printed Books
Oct 10   Printed Books
Oct 16/17   The Remaining Contents of North End House, Rottingdean
Oct 17   Printed Books
Oct 24   Printed Books
Oct 27   Books from Manton Hall, Rutland
Oct 31   Printed Books
Nov 7   Printed Books
Nov 14   Printed Books
Nov 21   Printed Books
Nov 28   Printed Books
Dec 10   The Remaining Contents of the Studios of the late Sir W.R. & F.M.R. Flint
Dec 12   Printed Books

1981
Jan 9   Printed Books
Jan 16   Printed Books
Jan 23   Printed Books
Jan 30   Printed Books
Feb 6   Printed Books, Atlases & Maps
Feb 13   Printed Books
Feb 20   Printed Books
Feb 27   Printed Books
Mar 6   Printed Books
Mar 13   Printed Books
Mar 20   Printed Books

1981	**O = OLIVERS** (*Sudbury*)
Jun 3	Books . . .

1980	**P = PHILLIPS SON & NEALE** (*London*)
Sep 11	Printed Books, Atlases & Maps
Oct 2	Printed Books, Atlases, Maps & Important Manuscripts
Oct 23	Printed Books, Atlases & Maps
Nov 13	Printed Books, Atlases & Maps
Dec 1	Edward Ardizzone: Autographed Illustrated Books
Dec 11	Printed Books, Atlases, Maps & Manuscripts
1981	
Jan 22	Printed Books, Atlases, Maps & Manuscripts
Feb 19	Printed Books, Atlases & Maps
Mar 12	Printed Books, Atlases, Maps & Manuscripts
Apr 9	Printed Books, Atlases & Maps
Apr 30	Printed Books, Atlases & Maps
May 14	Printed Books, Atlases & Maps
Jun 11	Printed Books, Atlases, Maps & Manuscripts
Jul 2	Printed Books, Atlases, Maps & Manuscripts
Jul 30	Printed Books, Atlases & Maps

1980	**PD = PHILLIPS SON & NEALE** (*Edinburgh*)
Aug 20	Books
Oct 22	Books
Nov 26	Books & Postcards
1981	
Feb 18	Books, Postcards, Maps
Apr 1	Books . . .
May 20	Books & Postcards

1980	**PG = PHILLIPS SON & NEALE** (*Glasgow*)
Sep 3	Books
Dec 12	Books

1980	**PJ = PHILLIPS & JOLLYS** (*Bath*)
Mar 7	Books
Jun 6	Books
Dec 5	Books

1980	**PL = PHILLIPS SON & NEALE** (*Leeds*)
Sep 18	Books, Maps, Prints
Nov 27	Books, Maps, Prints & Ephemera
1981	
Jul 9	Books, Maps, Prints & Ephemera

1980	**PNY = PHILLIPS SON & NEALE INC** (*New York*)
Oct 1	Printed Books & Autographs
Dec 3	Printed Books
1981	
Mar 3/4	The Collection of the late Elizabeth Fuller Chapman
Mar 26	Printed Books
May 21	Printed Books, Autographs, Manuscripts & Literary Art

1981	**PWP = PHILLIPS WARD-PRICE** (*Toronto & Montreal*)
Apr 9	Books, Maps & Prints
Jun 4	Arts Québécois

1980	**R = REISS & AUVERMANN** (*Glasshütten im Taunus*)
Oct 14–18	Wertvolle Bücher, Dekorative Graphik
1981	
Mar 31–Apr 4	Wertvolle Bücher, Dekorative Graphik

1981	**RBT = RICHARD BAKER & THOMSON** (*Birkenhead*)
Jan 22	Antiquarian & other Books

1980	**S = SOTHEBY PARKE BERNET & CO, GROSVENOR ROOMS** (*London*)
Sep 29	Printed Books
Sep 30–Oct 1	The Contents of Much Hadham Hall
Oct 17	Ephemera from the Sixteenth Century to the Present Day
Oct 20/21	Printed Books
Nov 3/4	Atlases, Maps & Printed Books
Nov 10/11	The Honeyman Collection, Part VI (N-Sa)
Nov 17/18	The late Dr. Yeshayahu Sachar's Collection of Hebrew Books
Nov 24/25	Valuable Printed Books
Dec 1–3	Printed Books relating to Science & Natural History
Dec 8/9	Printed Books
1981	
Jan 26/27	Printed Books
Feb 9/10	Printed Books
Feb 23	Printed Books mainly relating to Medicine & Science
Mar 16/17	Printed Books
Mar 30/31	Atlases, Maps & Printed Books, relating to Travel & Exploration
Apr 6/7	Printed Books, including Medicine & Science
Apr 28/29	Fine Oriental Miniatures, Manuscripts & Printed Books
May 5	Printed Books
May 18	Printed Books & Manuscripts relating to Wine & Food
May 19/20	The Honeyman Collection, Part VII (Sc–Z & Addenda)
Jun 1	Valuable Printed Books relating to Natural History
Jun 9	Printed Books & Manuscripts
Jun 15–17	An Important Collection of Medical Books of the Fifteenth to the Twentieth Century
Jun 22/23	Valuable Printed Books
Jun 29	Atlases, Maps & Printed Books
Jul 22	Modern First Editions & Presentation Copies
Jul 27	Printed Books
Jul 31	English Illustrated & Private Press Books, Related Drawings

1980	**SBA = SOTHEBY BERESFORD ADAMS** (*Chester*)
Jul 22	Printed Books
Oct 21/22	Printed Books
Dec 16	Printed Books
1981	
Mar 4	Printed Books
May 27	Printed Books
Jul 14	Printed Books

1981	**SD = SOTHEBY BEARNE** (*Torquay*)
Feb 4	Antiquarian & Modern Books

1980	**SG = SWANN GALLERIES INC** (*New York*)
Aug 7	Theater History, Natural History, Literature, Sets & Bindings . . .

1981			1980	**VA = VOLKS RARE BOOK AUCTIONS**

1981
Jan 22   Printed Books & Related Ephemera
Feb 19   Atlases, Travel & Exploration, Maps &
             Prints
Feb 19   Printed Books & Related Ephemera
Mar 19   Art Reference & Bibliography
Mar 19   Printed Books & Related Ephemera
Apr 16   Printed Books & Related Ephemera
May 21   Atlases, Travel & Exploration, Maps &
             Prints
May 21   Printed Books & Related Ephemera
Jun 18   Natural History & Allied Subjects
Jun 18   Printed Books & Related Ephemera
Jul 16   Printed Books & Related Ephemera

1980   **TRL = THOMSON, RODDICK &**
           LAURIE (*Carlisle*)
Dec 10   Antiquarian & other Books, Maps & Prints

1980   **TW = THOMAS WATSON & SON**
           (*Darlington*)
Sep 19   Books
Nov 26   Books . . .

1980   **VA = VOLKS RARE BOOK AUCTIONS**
           (*Pretoria*)
Aug 29   Africana & General Literature, Autographs
Oct 31   The Denis Godfrey Africana Library,
             Part I (A–J)

1981
Jan 30   The Denis Godfrey Africana Library,
             Part II (K–Z)
May 8   Africana, General Literature & Illustrated
             Books

1980   **VG = A.L. VAN GENDT & CO**
           (*Amsterdam*)
Oct 13   Fine Books
Oct 28   General Topography, Maps, Plans, Views &
             Prints
Nov 17/18   Miscellaneous Books
Dec 15–17   Miscellaneous Books, Autographs, etc

1981   **WW = WOOLLEY & WALLIS** (*Salisbury*)
May 20   Books, Sporting & other Prints

Currency Conversion Rates

To enable readers to establish the approximate Sterling equivalent of foreign currency prices quoted in this volume we list below the exchange rates prevailing at the end of July 1981.

AUSTRALIA	Aus.$	1.63		ITALY	Lire	2,266
BELGIUM	B.Frs.	74.85		NETHERLANDS	Fls.	5.05
CANADA	Can.$	2.27		SOUTH AFRICA	R	1.77
FRANCE	Frs.	10.81		SPAIN	Pts.	183.70
GERMANY	DM	4.55		USA	$	1.86

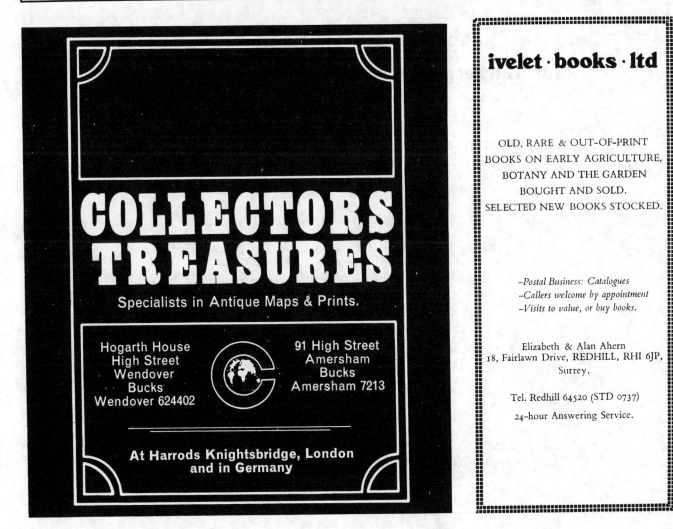

Eighteenth ~ Century British Books

A
SUBJECT
Catalogue

extracted from the

British Museum General Catalogue
of Printed Books

by

G. AVERLEY, A. FLOWERS,
F.J.G. ROBINSON, E.A. THOMPSON
R.V. *and* P.J. WALLIS

Prospectus available on request from

DAWSON PUBLISHING

CANNON HOUSE
FOLKESTONE
KENT CT19 5EE

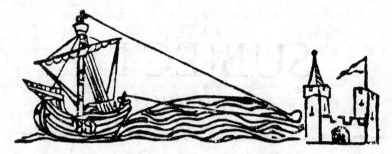

xxvi

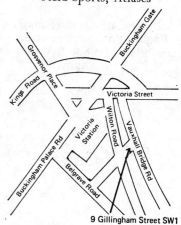

Eighteenth ~ Century British Books

An
AUTHOR UNION
Catalogue

extracted from the
British Museum General Catalogue
of Printed Books
and the
Catalogues of the Bodleian Library
and of the
University Library, Cambridge

by
F.J.G. ROBINSON, G. AVERLEY
D.R. ESSLEMONT and P.J. WALLIS

Prospectus available on request from
DAWSON PUBLISHING

CANNON HOUSE
FOLKESTONE
KENT CT19 5EE

Part I

Printed Books & Atlases

A.E. (Pseud.)
See–RUSSELL, George William

AA, A.J. Van der
– Ons Vaderland en Zijne Bewoners. Amst., 1857. Some staining thro.-out affecting some plts., 1 plt. defect. & reprd. No bdg. stated, upr. wrap. bnd. in. As a collection of prints w.a.f. (BS. Jun.11; 407)
£200
– – Anr. Copy. Some slight foxing. Cont. hf. cf. (VG. Oct.13; 1)
Fls. 2,800

AA, Pieter van der
– La Celèbre Ville d'Amsterdam ... Leiden, ca. 1700. Fo. 2 plts. in smaller size, 2nd. state of etching by Romein de Hooghe, with his address scratched out in the plt. Orig. paper wraps., worn, unc. (VG. Dec.17; 1155)
Fls. 2,850

AA, VV.
– Gli Ornati de Coro della Chiesa di S. Pietro dei Monaci Cassinesi di Perugia. Ill.:– Stefano da Bergamo. Rome, 1845. Fo. Hf. cf. (CR. Jun.11; 2)
Lire 260,000
– Italie Pittoresque. Paris, 1834. 4to. Hf. cf. (CR. Mar.19; 353)
Lire 200,000

ABANO, Petrus de
– Medices. Legatus de Exsilio ... Venice & Mense, Dec. 1522. 4to. Old cf., gt. roulette border, centre arms, decor. spine raised bands. (HD. Apr.24; 3)
Frs. 2,100

ABARBANEL, Don Yitzhak
– Ma'ayanei Ha'yeshuah. Amst., 1647. 2nd. Edn. 4to. Lacks Latin title, worming, stained. Part of orig. leath. mntd. on wood, rebkd., severely worn, torn. (SPB. May 11; 17)
$600
– Peirush Al Ha'Torah. Hanau, 1710. 3rd. Edn. Fo. Title pp. defect., discolouration, torn, some repairs. Cl., faded. (SPB. May 11; 18)
$225
– Rosh Emanah. Venice, 1545. 2nd. Edn. 4to. Lacks 1 lf. between sigs. 3 & 4, cropped, stained, reprd., owners' sigs. on title. Mod. cl. Bkplt. of Samuel Dresner. (SPB. May 11; 19)
$600

ABBEY, Maj. John Roland
– Life in England. 1953. (400) numbered. 4to. Orig. buckram. (S. Jul.27; 170)   *Subunso.* £100
– – Anr. Copy. (SH. Mar.6; 479)   *Lenton.* £95
– Scenery in Great Britain & Ireland. 1952. Ltd. Edn. 4to. Orig. cl. (SH. Mar.6; 480)
Dawson. £110

ABBING, C.A.
– Geschiedenis der stad Hoorn, ged. het Grootste Gedeelte der XVII end XVIII Eeuw (1630-1773), of Vervolg op Velius Chronyk. Hoorn, 1841-42. 2 vols. Slight staining. Orig. bds., new cl. spines. (VG. Dec.15; 386)
Fls. 480

ABBOT, John & Smith, J.E.
– [–] [The Natural History of the Rarer Lepidopterous Insects of Georgia]. [1797]. Fo. Plts. numbered 1-12, 22, 25-6, 32-4, 36, [40], 44-7, 49, 55, 60-1, [62], 65, 76, 89, 94, 101-03, only, together 37 plts. (of 104), plts. wtrmkd. 1822-25, 17 plts. with added imprint 'Sold by R. Martin' (not present in book itself), slight soiling to plt. 6, light dust-soiling in fore-edges of a few plts. Cl.-bkd. bds., spine defect., covers soiled, contents loose or detchd. (S. Dec.3; 876)   *Marshall.* £390

ABC BEITRAGE ZUM BAUEN
Ed.:– H. Schmidt, M. Stam, H. Meyer. Basel, 1924-29. Series 1, pts. 2, 5 & 6, Series II, pts. 1-4. Fo. Some sm. tears. Orig. wraps. (H. Dec.9/10; 1908)
DM 1,200

ABC DES KINDES, ERSTER UNTERRICHT IN BILD UND WERT
Stuttgart, ca. 1870. Orig. bds. (SH. Mar.19; 1)
Hackhofer. £90

ABDICATED Prince, The
1690. 1st. Edn. 4to. Mor. by Sangorski, partly unc. [Wing A71] (C. Nov.19; 43)   *Quaritch.* £400

A'BECKETT, Gilbert Abbot
– Table-Book. Ill.:– George Cruikshank. L., 1845. 1st. Edn. Cf., triple gt. fillet borders, spine gt. with sm. gt. figures, by Root, bkplt., buckram s.-c. (SG. Mar.19; 57)
$130

ABEILLE, L.P. & MONTAUDOUIN, J.G.
– Corps d'Observations de la Societé d'Agriculture ... Années 1757-58-59-60. Rennes; Paris, 1760; 1772. 2 vols. 1 vig. torn away. Cont. marb. cf., arms of Brittany in centre of covers, spines decor. with raised bands. (HD. Jun.24; 77)   Frs. 1,200

ABEL, Clarke
– Narrative of a Journey in the Interior of China. 1818. 1st. Edn. 4to. 3 (of 4) folding maps mntd. on linen, 8 plts. hand-cold., margins finger-marked. 19th. C. hf. mor. From Chetham's Liby., Manchester. (C. Nov.26; 1)   *Elstein.* £120

ABELA, Giovanni Francesco
– Malta Illustrata. Malta, 1772-80. 2 vols. Fo. Both vols. wormed thro.-out, mainly in inner margins, sm. repairs to a few plts., some ll. very browned. 19th. C. hf. cf., wormed & defect. (S. Dec.8; 232)   *Harlinghausen.* £130

ABELIN, Johann Philipp 'Johann Ludwig Gottfried'
– Historische Chronica. Ill.:– Matthew Merian. [Frankfurt], 1674. Sm. fo. Cont. blind-stpd. pig over wood bds., worn, lacks clasps. (SG. Oct.9; 1)
$1,200
– Neuwe Archontologia Cosmica ... Ill.:– M. Merian. Frankfurt, 1638? Fo. Lacks text, lge. faults in 3 lge. views, many maps & views bkd., sm. tears, slightly soiled, lacks copper engraved title. 19th. C. vell. (HK. Nov.18-21; 1190)
DM 23,000
– Newe Welt und Americanische Historien. Frankfurt, 1631. 1st. Edn. Fo. 172 (of 175) hf.-p. text. copper engrs. Old bds., very defect. & loose. W.a.f. (R. Oct.14-18; 1668)   DM 2,200

See–MERIAN, Matthias

ABERCROMBIE, John
– Inquiries concerning the Intellectual Powers & the Investigation of Truth. Edinb., 1830. 1st. Edn. Hf. cf., worn. Pres. copy, inscr. (S. Jun.15; 3)
Thoemmes. £80
– Pathological & Practical Researches on Diseases of the Brain & the Spinal Cord. Edinb., 1828. 1st. Edn. New qtr. cf., unc. (S. Jun.15; 2)
Quaritch. £100

ABERCROMBY, Patrick
– The Martial Achievements of the Scots Nation. Edinb., 1711 & 1715. 1st. Edn. 2 vols. Fo. Considerably age-browned, etc. Disbnd., ex-liby. (SG. Feb.5; 1)
$100

ABERDEEN, Lady
See–CHAMPLAIN Society

ABERNETHY, John
– The Surgical & Physiological Works. 1830-1817. 4 vols. (vol. 2 Surgical works from anr. Edn.). New bds., unc. (S. Jun.15; 4)   *Cooke.* £55

ABOAB, Yitzhak
– Nehar Pishon. Constantinople, 1538. 1st. Edn. Sm. 4to. 76 ll. only (of 80, lacks ll. 5-6, 27 & 50),

inner & outer margins of title reprd. with loss of portion of border & some words, worming affecting some letters, cropped, lightly stained. Mod. cl. (SPB. May 11; 77)
$2,900

ABOU'LKASIM FIRDOUSI
– Histoire de Minoutchehr selon le Livre des Rois. Ill.:– Simonidy. Paris, 1919. (75) on Jap. 4to. Mor. by Affolter, red more. doubls. with gt. arms, orig. wraps, bnd. in, s.-c. (SM. Oct.8; 2312)
Frs. 4,200

ABOUT, Edmond
– Tolla. Ill.:– Felicien de Myrbach & Adolphe Giraldon. Paris, 1889. Lge. 4to. Wd.-engraved plts., each in 3 states. Lev., multiple gt. fillet borders, spines gt., elab. dentelles by Lortic, s.-c. (SG. Oct.9; 2)
$275

ABRACADABRA
Ed.:– [C.G. Neale] Goodliffe. B'gham, 1946-79. Vols. 1-68. 1st. 7 vols. in cl., rest orig. wraps. as iss. (SH. Oct.23; 1)   *O'Dowd.* £70

ABRAHAM Ben Alexander, of Cologne
– Keter Shem Tov. Amst., 1810. 1st. Edn. 4to. Outer margins reprd. without text loss. Hf. cl. Bkplts. of Rabbi Nachum Friedman of Sagadur & Jacob Klatzin. (SPB. May 11; 21)
$275

ABRAHAM DOV BER, of Ovrutch
– Bat Ayin. Jerusalem, 1847. 1st. Edn. 4to. Hf. leath. (S. Nov.17; 134)   *Rock.* £180
– – Anr. Edn. Zhitomir, 1850. 2nd. Edn. 4to. Hf. leath. (S. Nov.17; 135)   *Quaritch.* £90

ABRAHAM Ha'levi
– Meshare Kitrin. Constantinople, 1510. 1st. Edn. Sm. 4to. 13 ll. only (of 19, lacks ll. 14-19), margin of 1 lf. torn with loss of some words, staining, worming. Mod. buckram, torn. (SPB. May 11; 76)
$4,000

ABRAHAM NOAH Ha'Levi Heller, of Dolino
– Zrizuta De'Abraham. Lvov, 1900. 1st. Edn. 4to. Bds. (S. Nov.17; 138)   *Maggs.* £70

ABRAHAM ZACUTO
– Sepher ha 'Yuhasin. Cracow, 1580. 2nd. Edn. Sm. 4to. Some staining thro.-out, liby. stp. of 'Seminar Fraenckelsche Stiftung', Breslau, on title. Mod. mor. (C. Jul.16: 302)   *Stein.* £480

ABRAVANEL, Isaac
– Rosh Amana. Cremona, 1557. 2nd. Edn. Sm. 4to. Stp. of Fraenckelsche Stiftung on title. Later marb. bds. (C. Jul.16; 303)   *Stern.* £260

ABREGE   HISTORIQUE   ET ICONOGRAPHIQUE De la Vie de Charles V., Duc de Lorraine; dedié à son Altesse Royale Leopold I
Ill.:– after J. Waldemann by J.U. Kraus, J. Müller & others. Nancy, 1701. Fo. Partly lightly browned, 2 Ms. stps. on title, lacks plts. 2, 4, 26, 27, 29 (ports.) Cont. hf. leath. (R. Oct.14-18; 2059)   DM 1,100

ABSTRACT OF THE RETURNS of Charitable Donations for the Benefit of Poor Persons made by the Ministers & Church-Wardens of Parishes & Townships in England & Wales, 1786-88
1816. 2 vols. Fo. Cont. hf. cf. (SH. Oct.10; 407)
Bunsei. £50

ABUDRAHAM, David
– Abudraham-Peirush Al Hatefilot. Venice, 1546. 4th. Edn. Fo. Mod. hf. vell. (SPB. May 11; 23)
$850

ACADEMIE DES DAMES
Venise [Paris], ca. 1750. Red mor., by David, inner gt. dntelles, partly unc. (SM. Oct.8; 2101) Frs. 8,500
– – **Anr. Edn.** Venise, ca. 1780. Some ll. at beginning & end reprd., frontis., title & last blank lf. soiled. Hf. leath. (HK. May 12-14; 1501) DM 800

ACCADEMIA Pubblica di Venezia
– **Statuto e Prescrizioni . . . di Pittura, Scultura ed Architettura.** Ill.:– Marco Pitteri after Pietro A. Novelli (frontis.). Venice, 1782. 4to. Cont. mott. cf. gt., buckram s.-c. From the collection of John A. Saks. (C. Jun.10; 1) *King.* £120

ACCORAMBONI, Girolamo
– **Tractatus de Lacte.** Venice, Jun. 1536. 1st. Edn. A few cont. marginal notes (cropped), liby. stp. removed from title & last lf. Cont. limp vell. (C. Apr.1; 1) *Hopper.* £130

ACCUM, Friedrich
– **Culinary Chemistry Exhibiting the Scientific Principles of Cookery.** 1821. Hf. cf., rebkd. (S. Dec.1; 8) *Quaritch.* £130
– **Description of the Process of Manufacturing Coal Gas for the Lighting of Streets, Houses & Public Buildings.** 1819. 1st. Edn. 1 lf. of preface misbnd. New cl. (S. Dec.1; 6) *Phelps.* £80
– **Elements of Cristallography after the Method of Hauy.** 1813. 1st. Edn. New cl., unc. (S. Dec.1; 4) *Walford.* £90
– **Guide to the Chalybeat Spring of Thetford.** 1819. 1st. Edn. New cf. gt., unc. (S. Dec.1; 7) *Phelps.* £55
– **Practical Treatise on Gas-Light.** 1815. 2nd. Edn. Slightly offset. Mod. cl. (S. Dec.2; 664) *Phelps.* £60
– **A System of Theoretical & Practical Chemistry.** Priv. ptd. 1803. 1st. Edn. 2 vols. Orig. bds., rebkd., unc. (S. Dec.1; 2) *Quaritch.* £60

ACERBI, Joseph
– **Travels through Sweden, Finland & Lapland.** 1802. 1st. Edn. 2 vols. 4to. Some offsetting & foxing, 1 plt. dampstained. Old tree cf., slightly worn. (BS. Jun.11; 135) £120
– **Travels through Sweden, Finland & Lapland . . . 1798 & 1799. – Vues de la Suède, de la Finlande, et de la Lapponie . . .** Ill.:– J. Merigot after L. Belanger. L., Paris, 1802; 1803. 1st. Edn. 2 vols. & supp. vol. Ltd. printing (150) numbered, together 3 vols. Cont. tree cf. & cont. mott. cf. 1st. 2 vols. with armorial bkplt. of Jonathan Pytts, 2nd. with later armorial bkplt. (PNY. Oct.1; 5) $950
See–BISSELIUS, Johannes–ACERBI, Joseph

ACHARISIO, Alberto
– **Vocabolario, Grammatica, et Orthographia de la Lingua Volgare . . . con Espositioni di Molti Luoghi di Dante, Petrarca, et del Boccaccio.** Cento, Jun. 1543. 4to. 19th. C. hf. vell. (SI. Dec.3; 4) Lire 420,000

ACKERMAN, Phyllis
See–POPE, Arthur Upham & Ackerman, Phyllis

ACKERMANN, B.R.
– **Rheingegenden Von Mainz bis Cologn.** 1823. Fo. 22 cold. plts. (of 24). Paper, worn, some spotting. (CE. Jul.9; 66) £920

ACKERMANN, Richard
– **Poetical Magazine.** Ill.:– after Thomas Rowlandson. 1809-10. Vols. I, II & pt. III in 2 vols. Cont. hf. cf. (Ta. Oct.16; 349) £70

ACKERMANN, Rudolph
– **Drawing Book for 1824.** 1824. Ob. 4to. Slight foxing. Mod. qtr. mor. (P. Feb.19; 62) *Marlborough.* £80
– **Furniture Designs. [Extracted from 'Repository of Arts'].** V.d. 139 hand-cold. engraved plts., no text. Mod. hf. cf. (S. Mar.17; 397) *Longmire.* £180
– – **Anr. Copy.** 82 hand-cold. engraved plts., mostly mntd., some loose, no text. Mod. cl. (S. Mar.17; 398) *Quaritch.* £80
– **Historical Sketch of Moscow.** 1813. Orig. bds., worn. (SH. Feb.5; 191) *De Velasco.* £460
– **The History of the Abbey Church of St. Peter's Westminster.** L., 1812. 1st. Edn. 2 vols. Lge. 4to. Engraved port. & plan, 80 (of 81) hand-cold. aquatint plts., foxed, browned, heavy offsetting to text, ink inscr. on hf.-titles. Cont. str.-grd. mor. gt., spines gt., watered silk endpapers with gt. borders, by C. Hering with his ticket, very worn,

vol. 1 upr. cover nearly detchd. (CNY. May 22; 13) $280
– – **Anr. Edn.** 1812. 1st. Edn., 1st. Iss. 2 vols. 4to. Slightly browned & foxed. Cont. cf. qt. (TA. Nov.20; 435) £325
– – **Anr. Copy.** 2 vols. 4to. With the Valence plt. sigd. by Mackenzie, 1st. title offset & browned, occasional offsetting & spotting in text. 19th. C. hf. roan, gt., vol. 1 rebkd. preserving orig. spine. (S. Jun.23; 311) *Kershaw.* £160
– – **Anr. Edn.** L., 1812. 1st. Edn., 2nd. Iss. 2 vols. 4to. Occasional light foxing & stains in margins of text. Qtr. leath., rebkd., portion of orig. spines preserved, bkplt. (CB. Feb.18; 227) Can. £700
– – **Anr. Edn.** 1812. 2 vols. in 3. Lge. 4to. Extra-ill. with 184 plts. Mod. lev. mor., gt. From the collection of Eric Sexton. (C. Apr.16; 202) *Traylen.* £280
– – **Anr. Copy.** 2 vols., lacks plt. list. Crimson mor., sides with gt. & blind tooled borders, spines gt., by Bayntun. (C. Mar.18; 157) *Traylen.* £220
– – **Anr. Copy.** Parts of text browned. Hf. cf., rebkd. (TA. Mar.19; 601) £200
– **The History of the Colleges of Winchester, Eton & Westminster.** 1816. [1st. Edn.?]. Lge. 4to. 48 cold. plts. Cont. cf., gt. & blind-stpd. borders on sides, rebkd. (C. May 20; 97) *Davidson.* £600
– – **Anr. Copy.** 48 Hand-cold. plts., lacks plt.-list. Cont. diced cf. gt., rebkd. (SG. Oct.9; 7) $1,600
– – **Anr. Copy.** Red mor. gt., spine gt., partly unc., silk doubls. & endpapers by Morrell. (CNY. May 22; 14) $1,000
– – **Anr. Edn.** 1816. L.P. Lge. 4to. Cont. hf. mor. gt., Lord Grenville, Chancellor of Oxford's seal in gt. on covers. (C. Mar.18; 5) *Rostron.* £1,500
– – **Anr. Copy.** 48 hand-cold. plts., Abbey's plt. No.23 in 1st. state, 26 in 3rd. state, text wtrmkd. 1816, plts. 1812. Cont. str.-grd. mor. gt. (S. Nov.24; 2) *Symonds.* £600
– **A History of the University of Cambridge, its Colleges, Halls & Public Buildings.** Ill.:– after W. Westall, R. Pugin & others. 1815. [1st. Edn.?]. 2 vols. 4to. Plts. wtrmkd. 1812-39, some plts. offset on text. Cont. cf., lr. covers detchd. (C. Feb.25; 21) *Allison.* £1,200
– – **Anr. Copy.** 79 hand-cold. aquatint plts., lacks founders ports. Hf. cf., reprd., partly loose. (SG. Oct.9; 3) $1,700
– – **Anr. Copy.** Offsetting from plts. on text. Cont. hf. russ. gt., spines very defect. (SPB. Oct.1; 175) $1,500
– – **Anr. Edn.** 1815. (50) on L.P. 2 vols. Lge. 4to. Cont. hf. mor. (C. Mar.18; 4) *Rostron.* £2,500
– **A History of the University of Oxford.** 1814. L.P. 2 vols. Lge. 4to. Lacks hf.-title. Cont. cf., sides with gt. borders & Grenville, Chancellor of Oxford's seal in gt., spines gt., rebkd. 2-pp. A.L.s. from Edward Cardwell to Charles W. Williams Wynn pasted in. (C. Mar.18; 3) *Rostron.* £2,000
– – **Anr. Copy.** Port., 114 hand-cold. plts. including Founders ports., 3 plts. very foxed, pp. 69/70 in vol. 2 from smaller copy, ex-liby. Orig. bds., worn, 1 cover & 1st. few ll. of vol. 1 detchd., unc. (SG. Oct.9; 6) $3,200
– – **Anr. Edn.** 1814. 2 vols. Lge. 4to. Cont. diced cf. From the collection of Eric Sexton. (C. Apr.16; 203) *Old Hall.* £800
– – **Anr. Copy.** Light offsetting, occasional insignificant spotting, with plts. 1 & 50 in 1st. state, rest in 2nd. state. Pold. cf., qt., by Rivière. (S. Nov.4; 539) *Marsden.* £750
– – **Anr. Copy.** 113 (of 114) plts., offsetting from plts. on text. Cont. hf. russ. gt., very worn. (SPB. Oct.1; 176) $1,200
– **The Microcosm of London.** L., [1808-10]. 1st. Edn., early iss. 3 vols. Lge. 4to. 104 full-p. hand-cold. plts. (wtrmkd. 1807 & 1808), 7 in 1st. state, all but one of errata uncorrected. Late 19th. C. str.-grd. mor. gt. by Broca, rebkd., orig. qt. spines preserved. (CNY. May 22; 15) $2,800
– – **Anr. Copy.** 104 full-p. hand-cold. aquatint plts. (wtrmkd. 1807 & 1808), 6 in 1st. state, all but one of errata uncorrected, offsetting to text, some staining. Cont. mott. cf. gt., worn, rebkd. (CNY. May 22; 16) $1,600
– – **Anr. Edn.** [1808-10]. 1st. Edn. 3 vols. Lge. 4to. 104 hand-cold. plts. wtrmkd. J. Whatman 1801-08, plts. 8, 11 & 28 in 1st. state. Cont. red str.-grd. mor. gt., sides with triple gt. fillet & blind-tooled borders, Hugh Walpole's bkplt. (C. Mar.18; 164) *Courage.* £1,500
– – **Anr. Copy.** Plts. wtrmkd. 1808-09, 1 text lf. torn & reprd. Cont. hf. russ. qt., rebkd. (SBA. Oct.21; 1) *Cumming.* £1,300

– – **Anr. Copy.** Engd. titles, 104 hand-cold. aqua. plts., plts. wtrmkd. 1806, 1807 & 1808, 3 plts. in 1st state. Tree cf., rebkd. (SG. Oct.9; 5) $3,200
– – **Anr. Edn.** n.d. 4to. 66 ll. of text only. Disbnd. W.a.f. (CSK. Jan.9; 17) £150
– [Oxford & Cambridge] **Portraits of Founders.** L., [1814-15]. L.P. Lge. 4to. 49 hand-cold. ports. Old bds., mod. cf.-bkd. (SG. Oct.9; 4) $600
– **Repository of Arts.** 1807. 2nd. Series, vols. 7-8 only. Cont. hf. cf., worn, 1 cover detchd. W.a.f. (SH. Jul.9; 49) *Crossley.* £150
– – **Anr. Edn.** 1809-28. Series 1-3 in 40 vols. & 2 index vols. General index to 1st. series & facs. general index to 2nd, series (previously unrecorded). Hf. mor. gt. (P. Sep.11; 271) *Hammond.* £6,000
– **Sketches of Russia.** 1814. 1 plt. ink-marked, 1 music lf. bnd. in at rear. Loose in cont. qtr. mor., worn. (Ta. Nov.20; 406) £55
– **Tom Raw, The Griffin: A Burlesque Poem . . . Descriptive of the Adventures of a Cadet . . . by a Civilian & an Officer on the Bengal Establishment.** 1828. 10 pp. publisher's advts. bnd. in at rear. Recently rebnd. in three-qtr. mor. (TA. Feb.19; 316) £74

ACOSTA, Jose de
– **Histoire Naturelle et Morale des Indes, tant orientalles qu'occidentales.** Trans.:– Robert Regnault. Paris, 1598. 1st. Edn. in Fr. Occasional light browning & staining. 19th. C. mor.-bkd. bds. [Sabin 125] (S. Nov.4; 618) *Fleming.* £400
– **Historia Naturale e Morale delle Indie.** Venice, 1596. 1st. Edn. in Italian. 4to. Sm. hole in title, liby. stp. Cont. limp vell. From Chetham's Liby., Manchester. (C. Nov.26; 2) *Tzakas.* £90
– – **Anr. Copy.** Light stain at end, some spotting. [Sabin 124] (SPB. May 5; 53) $325
See–BRY, Theodore de & others

ACROYD, A.(?)
[–] **Tables of Leasses & Interest, with their Grounds Expressed in Foure Tables of Fractions . . .** 1628. 1st. Edn. Slight marginal staining. Cont. cf., worn. The Kenney copy; from Honeyman Collection. [NSTC 23638] (S. May 19; 2952) *Lewin.* £100

ACT [An] for Improving & Rendering More Commodious the Port & Harbour of Bristol
1803. 5 acts in 1 vol. Fo. Lge. folding linen-bkd. engraved map, bnd. with 4 other similar Acts, 1803-22. Cont. cf. (TA. May 21; 492) £85

ACT for Making a Navigable Cut or Canal from the River Dee, within the Liberties of the City of Chester, to or Near Middlewich & Nantwich, in the Country of Chester
1772. Fo. 2 maps both slightly torn, 2nd. strengthened. Cont. hf. cf., slightly worn. (SBA. Oct.22; 291) *Catherine L. Turpin.* £65

ACTA ofte handelingen des Nationalen Synodi . . . gehouden door Authoriteyt van Staten Generael des Ver. Nederlandts tot Dordrecht anno 1618 & 1619
Dordrecht, 1621. 1st. Edn. in Dutch. 3 pts. in 1 vol. Fo. Lr. margins stained towards end. Cont. cf. over wood (rebkd.), wood of lr. cover brkn., chased brass clasps, corner & centrepieces & strip (lacking 1). (VG. Dec.17; 1156) Fls. 450

ACTA SANCTORUM
Paris etc., Jan. 1863-Nov.4 1902 only. 66 vols. Fo. Cont. hf. mor., with fitted bookcase. (SH. May 28; 1) *Howes Books.* £300

ACTON, Harold
– **This Chaos.** Paris, Hours Pr. 1930. (150). 4to. Orig. mor.-bkd. bds., sm. pt. missing from backstrip. Sigd. (SH. Dec.19; 404) *Maggs.* £55

ACTON, John
[–] **An Essay on Shooting . . .** L., 1791. 2nd. Edn. Later hf. cf. (SG. Apr.9; 327) $150

ACTS OF PARLIAMENT
– **Anno Regni Georgii III, Regis Magnae Britanniae, Franciae & Hiberniae.** L., 1763-64. Sm. fo. Cont. panel. cf., worn, gt. coat-of-arms on covers. (SG. Jun.11; 354) $210
– **Bank of England & the South Sea Company . . . 59 Acts of Parliament.** 1697-1820. Fo. Some browned or soiled. All disbnd. (SH. Mar.5; 175) *Bunsei.* £200
– **Canals (A Collection of 18 Acts).** 1783-97. Fo. All disbnd. (SH. Mar.5; 34) *Bunsei Books.* £95

ACUÑA, Cristobal
– **Relation de la Rivière des Amazones.** Trans.:– M. de Gomberville. Paris, 1682. 4 vols. Sm.

engraved vig. by Corneille pasted onto A2 of vol. 1, facs. of folding engraved map, some discolouration. Qtr. cf. (SPB. May 5; 54) $225

ADAIR, A.H.
See–TOYE, Nina & Adair, A.H.

ADAIR, James
– **The History of the American Indians.** 1775. 1st. Edn. 4to. Some ll. slightly spotted. Cont. cf., worn, rebkd. From Chetham's Liby., Manchester. [Sabin 155] (C. Nov.26; 3) *Arader*. £220
– – **Anr. Copy.** 1st. 3 ll. reprd. affecting a few letters of text. Cont. cf. rebkd., crude cl. tape reinforcement at inner hinges, folding hf. leath. s.-c. From liby. of William E. Wilson. (SPB. Apr.29; 2) $1,300
– – **Anr. Copy.** Ex-liby with sm. stp. on title & verso, very foxed thro.-out. Mod. red three-qtr. mor. by Worsfold, spine gt. (SG. May 14; 3) $600
– – **Anr. Copy.** Lacks map, ex liby. Mod. buckram. (SG. Jun.11; 3) $375

ADAM
[–] **Raziel Ha'malach [Kabbalah & Amulets].** Amst., 1701. 1st. Edn. 4to. Cl. (S. Nov.18; 386) *James*. £260

ADAM
– **Tribulations Parisiennes et Campagnardes.** n.d. Bds., worn. (CE. Nov.20; 201) £62

ADAM, Juliette Lamber
– **La Chanson des Nouveaux Epoux.** Paris, 1882. (400); (100) on Jap., numbered. Lge. 4to. Etchings in 2 states. Mor. by Chambolle-Duru, decor. spine & covers, inside dentelle, wrap. preserved, s.-c. (SM. Feb.11; 141) Frs. 11,000

ADAM, Robert
– **Ruins of the Palace of the Emperor Diocletian at Spalatro in Dalmatia.** 1764. 1st. Edn. Fo. Cont. cf., gt., rebkd., few sm. repairs. (S. Nov.25; 424) *Weinreb*. £480

ADAM, Robert Borthwick
See–SMITH, Harry B.–ADAM, Robert Borthwick

ADAM, V.
– **Combat du Taureau.** Paris, ca. 1830. Ob. fo. Fr. & Spanish Captions. Later hf. leath. (R. Mar.31-Apr.4; 1520) DM 1,500

ADAM, Victor
– **Collection des Costumes Militaires, Armée Française ...** [Paris], [1940]. Ob. fo. Three-qtr. lev., raised bands, by Atelier Bindery, unc. (SG. Oct.9; 8) $1,800

ADAM, William
– **Vitruvius Scoticus.** Edinb., [1810]. Fo. Cont. hf. russ., cover detchd. (C. Nov.6; 182) *Traylen*. £3,200

ADAMS, Ansel
– **Images 1923-1974.** Boston, 1974. (1,000) sigd., with orig. photograph sigd. in pencil by Adams. Ob. 4to. Orig. cl., d.-w., folding box, box worn. (SPB. May 6; 137) $650

ADAMS, George
– **Essays on the Microscope.** 1787. Plt. vol. only. Ob. fo. 32 engd. plts., some stained, few detchd., lacks text vol. Orig. bds., unc., lacks back-strip. W.a.f. (C. May 20; 1) *Zeitlin*. £100
– – **Anr. Edn.** 1798. 4to. Old. cf. (P. Nov.13; 300) *Dartmoor*. £110
– **Geometrische und Graphische Versuche ...** Trans.:– J.G. Geissler. Leipzig, 1795. 1st. German Edn. 2 vols. 4 to. Stained thro.-out, stpd. on title recto & all plts. Cont. leath. gt. (R. Mar.31-Apr.4; 1205) DM 600
– **Micrographia Illustrata: or the Microscope Explained.** 1771. 4th. Edn. Slight spotting & offsetting. Cont. cf.-bkd. bds., worn, unc. (S. Apr.6; 2) *Phelps*. £100

ADAMS, H.G.
– **Favourite Song Birds.** 1851. 1st. Edn. 16mo. Browned. Mod. hf. cf. (SH. Jun.18; 169) *Frick*. £60
– – **Anr. Edn.** 1856. 2nd. Edn. 12mo. Orig. Cl. (SH. Jun.18; 170) *Frick*. £50

ADAMS, J.Q.
– **Discurso del Ex-Presidente de los Estados Unidos en la Camara de Representantes de Washington, Mayo 25 de 1836.** Mexico, 1836. 12mo. In Spanish. Ptd. self-wraps., upr. wrap. loose, minor foxing. (SG. Jan.8; 284) $160

ADAMS, John
– **Index Villaris.** Priv. Ptd., 1680. 1st. Edn. Fo. With the lge. engraved hand-cold. map. Cont. red mor., gt. panels on covers. Bkplts. of the Duke of Beaufort, Viscount Mersey & Sir C.E.H. Chadwyck-Healey, lately in the collection of Eric Sexton. [Wing A479] (C. Apr.16; 206) *Traylen*. £340

ADAMS, Joseph
– **Memoirs of the Life & Doctrines of the late John Hunter.** 1818. 2nd. Edn. Advt. lf. Hf. cf. (S. Jun.15; 6) *Quaritch*. £80

ADAMS, Richard
– **Watership Down.** 1972. 1st. Edn. Orig. cl., d.-w. Inscr. by author. (CSK. Nov.28; 109) £100
– – **Anr. Copy.** (SH. Dec.10; 76) *Kendall*. £90

ADAMS, Robert
– **Narrative of a Sailor who was wrecked on the Western Coast of Africa.** 1816. 4to. Slightly spotted. Cont. hf. mor. (SH. Nov.7; 269) *K. Books*. £72
– – **Anr. Copy.** Some spotting. Orig. bds., worn. MS. note on front free endpaper from Rev. G.G. Stonestreet, Secretary & Treasurer of the 'Cambrai Club'. (CSK. Jan.16; 14) £65

ADAMS, W.H.D.
– **The History, Topography, & Antiquities of the Isle of Wight.** 1856. 4to. Portion cut from title. Orig. cl. (SH. Mar.5; 1) *Crowe*. £80
– **The White King: or Charles the First.** 1889. 2 vols. Fo. Text mntd. in fo., extra-ill. with approximately 250 plts., most engraved ports., with a few views. Cont. mor., gt. (SH. Oct.10; 408) *Fogg*. £180

ADAMSON, M.
– **A Voyage to Senegal, The Isle of Goree, & the River Gambia.** 1759. Folding engraved map slightly torn, edges untrimmed. Cont. qtr. cf., worn. (TA. Feb.19; 23) £60

ADAMUS, Melchior
– **The Life & Death of Dr. Martin Luther.** Trans.:– Thomas Hayne. L., 1645. 4to. With errata lf. Mod. hf. cf. [Wing A508] (SG. Feb.5; 218) $120

ADANSON, Michel
– **Histoire Naturelle du Senegal.** Paris, 1757. 1st. Edn. 2 vols. in 1. 4to. Title dust-soiled & slightly torn. 19th. C. cl., both covers detchd. From Chetham's Liby., Manchester. (C. Nov.26; 4) *Weldon & Wesley*. £90

ADDISON, Charles G.
– **Damascus & Palmyra.** 1838. 2 vols. Cont. cf., gt. Bkplt. of Duff Cooper. (C. Nov.5; 1) *Hossains*. £85

ADDISON, Joseph
[–] **Days with Sir Roger de Coverley.** Ill.:– Hugh Thomson. 1892. Orig. cl., unc. Pres. copy from artist to William Heighway. (SH. Mar.27; 510) *Illustrated Antiques*. £130
– **A Poem to his Majesty.** 1695. 1st. Edn. Fo. Lacks final blank, sm. piece torn from upr. corner of title affecting border, some browning. Disbnd., several ll. detchd. [Wing A511] (S. May 5; 340) *Quaritch*. £100
– **Remarks on Several Parts of Italy. &c. in the Years 1701-03.** L., 1705. 1st. Edn. Cont. gt. cf. Armorial bkplt. of Agnew of Locknaw & mod. bkplt. of Walter T. Shirley 11. (PNY. Oct.1; 7) $120
– **Works.** Bg'ham., 1761. 1st. Edn. 4 vols. 4to. 19th. C. cf., rebkd., Henry Abel bkplt. in each vol. (SG. Sep.25; 3) $225

ADDISON, Joseph & Steele, Sir Richard
– **The Guardian.** L., Mar.12, 1713-Oct.1, 1713. Nos. 1-175 (all publd.) in 2 vols. 1 frontis. reprd. in margin. Cont. cf., vol. 1 rebkd., upr. cover of vol. 2 detchd. (CB. Apr.1; 226) *Can*. $150

ADDY, Gulielmus
– **Bible in Shorthand.** 1687. 12mo. Cont. cf. (Ta. Sep.18; 214) £70

ADELPHUS, J. [i.e. J.A. Muelich]
– **Barbarossa.** Strassburg, 1535. 3rd. Edn. Fo. Slight browning & soiling. Mod. limp. leath. (R. Oct.14-18; 11) DM 6,300

ADELUNG, Johann Christoph
– **Geschichte der Schiffahrten und Versuche welche zur Entdeckung des Nordostlichen Weges nach Japan und China ...** Halle, 1768. 4to. Cont. hf. cf., worn. (TA. Feb.19; 29) £260

ADELUNG, Theodor
– **Risunki k Puteshestviyu po Rossii ... Barona Meyerberga ...** St. Petersb., 1827. Leath.-bkd. bds., cover detchd. (SG. Oct.9; 9) $275

ADEY, John
See–REPTON, Humphrey & Adey, John

ADLER, Elkan Nathan
– **Catalogue of Hebrew Manuscripts.** Camb., 1921. 4to. Hf. cl. (S. Nov.17; 47) *Quaritch*. £110

ADLIVANKIN
See–MAYAKOVSKY, Vladimir & others

ADLUNG, J.
– **Anleitung zur Musikalischen Gelahrtheit.** Ed.:– J.E. Bachs. Erfurt, 1758. 1st. Edn. Cont. hf. leath. (H. Dec.9/10; 1032) DM 2,000

ADMONITIO de Profectu Animae
See–ISIDORUS, Hispaliensis–ANON

ADOLPHUS, John
See–HUME, David & others

ADONIAS, Isa
– **Mapos e Planos Manuscritos Relativos ao Brasil Colonial.** [Rio de Janeiro], 1960. 2 vols. Ptd. wraps. (SG. Mar.26; 108) $120

ADRIANI, Giovanni Battista
– **Istoria de Suoi Tempi.** Venice, 1587. 2 vols. 4to. Cont. red mor., gt. pointillé fillet, cipher of Peiresc in centre, decor. spine. (HD. Mar.18; 1) Frs. 4,500

ADRICHOMIUS [VAN ADRICHEM], Christian
– **Theatrum Terrae Sanctae et Biblicarum Historiarum.** Cologne, 1682. 6th. Edn. Pp. 113/114 with restored tears, map & plan bkd. Cont. vell., spine pasted with vell. (R. Mar.31-Apr.4; 2524) DM 3,800

ADVENTURES of a Post Captain
Ill.:– C. Williams. L., [1817?]. Plts. hand-cold., minor tears, some foxing. Mor. gt. (SPB. May 29; 2) $125

ADVERTISING Cards
[France], ca. 1900. Ob. fo. Album containing over 800 cards, cold, ills., many chromolitho., some heightened with gold. Orig. cl, spine & covers loose. (SH. Apr.10; 545) *Hackhoffer*. £300

AEGIDUS, Columna Romanus
– **Expositio Super Libros Posterior Aristotelis.** Venice, Bonetus Locatellus for Octavianus Scotus. 29 Dec. 1495. Fo. Sm. hole in 1 lf., reprd., affecting text, cont. M.S. notes cropped, upr. & outer margins of title reprd., liby. stp. removed from title. Mod. vell. bds. [Hain 138*; BMC V p. 446; Goff A 66] (C. Apr.1; 2) *Metzdorf*. £240
– **Quodlibeta.** Ed.:– [Simon de Ungaria]. Bologna, Dominicus de Lapis, May 22, 1481. 1st. Edn. Fo. Spaces for capital initials, 8-line initial U on a2r, painted blue on gold ground with purple & green flower & purple ascender, central margin decor. in green, purple, brown, blue & gold with flower bouquet at foot, other initials thro.-out in alternating red & blue, rubricated in red & blue, 1st. 2 ll. browned & inner margins with sm. patches, some sm. stains or worming to extreme lr. blank margins, early owner's inscr. erased leaving stain, many early ink marginal annots. Mod. hf. vell. From the collection of Eric Sexton. [BMC VI, 814, Goff A85, H 113*] (CNY. Apr.8; 28) $3,600

See–HIBERNIA, Thomas de–AEGIDIUS, Columna Romanus

AELIANUS, Tacticus
– **De Militaribus Ordinibus Instituendis More Graecorum.** Venice, 1552. Title in Greek & Latin, text in Greek, slight worming affecting a few letters. Later cf., worn. (CSK. May 29; 148) £75
– **The Tactiks of Aelian.** Trans.:– J. Bingham. 1616. 1st. Edn. in Engl. Fo. Mod. mott. cf. [STC 161] (C. Jul.16; 343) *Taylor*. £340
– – **Anr. Copy.** Cont. cf., rebkd. [STC 161] (S. Mar.16; 139) *Maggs*. £190

See–VEGETIUS, Flavius Renatus; Aelianus Tacticus; Frontinus, Sextus Julius–Modestus

AELURIUS, Georgius
- Glaciographia, Oder Glätzische Chronica. Leipzig, 1625. 1st. Edn. 4to. Plt. reprd. Cont. blind-stpd. pig, rebkd. with cf. (S. Jan.27; 302)
Wenner. £140

AEMYLIUS, Paulus
See–CAESAR, Caius Julius–AEMYLIUS, Paulus

AENIUS SILVIUS
See–HIERONYMUS PADUANUS–BEROALDUS, Philippus Bononiensis–ANSONIUS MATUTINA–AENIUS SILVIUS–LACTANTIUS

AEROPLANE Supply Company, The
- First Aviation Catalogue. Ed.:– Bernard Isaac. Oct. 1909. Orig. cover. (P. Oct.2; 26)
Skenson. £50

AESCHYLUS
-[Oeuvres]. Trans.:– Leconte de Lisle, Paris, 1872 (100) on Hollande. Red mor. by Zaehnsdorf, mor doublrs., decor. mor onlay in centre, orig. wraps preserved. (SM. Oct.8; 2313) Frs. 1,000
- Prometheus Bound. Ed.:– [Elizabeth Barrett Browning]. L., 1833. 1st. Edn. 12mo. Orig. patterned cl., bds. lightly spotted, unc. Many corrections in Browning's hand at pp. 104-107, 2 compl. stanzas (each corrected) inserted between stanzas 20/21 & 22/23 of the ptd. text; owner's inscr. of Henrietta Barrett on front fly-lf., lately in the Prescott Collection. (CNY. Feb.6; 29) $3,500
- Tragoediae VII. 1557. Sm. 4to. In Greek. Old stpd. vell. initialled H.R., & with initials of orig. owner, 'J.D.' & date 1576 stpd. on upr. cover. From the liby. of J.R. Abbey, with his bkplt., sig. of Joannes Ducarus on title. (BS. Jun.11; 228) £320
- - Anr. Copy. Early 19th C. Engl. red mor., blind-tooled gt. fillet, blind-tooled border of fleurons & drawer-handles, spine gt., s.-c. Bkplt. of Jean Furstenberg. (HD. Mar.18; 66) Frs. 2,800
- Tragoediae Sex. Graece . . . Venice, Feb. 1518. 1st. Edn. Liby. stp. on verse of last lf. Mod. bds. (HD. Apr.24; 18) Frs. 6,300

AESOP
- Esopus in Europa. Ill.:– Romain de Hooghe. Amst., 1701-02. 1st. Edn. 40 Pts. in 1 vol. 4to. Cont. vell. bds. (S. Nov.25; 379) *Quaritch.* £380
- Esopus Moralisatus cum bono commento. Deventer, Jacobus de Breda. 30 Jul. 1494. 4to. Lacks g4 (blank) & c5-6, present in photocopy, sm. tears in blank margins of title reprd. Mod. mor. [HC 312; BMC IX p. 68; Goff A 137] (C. Apr.1; 3) *Corby.* £220
- Et Aliorum Fabulae Latinus. Lima, 1752. Owners' stp. of the Franciscans at Tarija, Bolivia, some spotting. Cont. limp vell. (SPB. May 5; 56) $250
- Esope en Bel Humeur, ou Fables d'Esope en Vaudevilles. Paris, ca. 1800. 16mo. Later white silk, covers & spine decor. with twines of gold thread with wtrmks. of different cold. spangles, lge. oval medallion with miniat. in centre of each cover, wtrd. silk doubls. & end-ll., unc. (HD. Apr.9; 463) Frs. 1,300
- Fables. 1687. 3 pts. in 1 vol., with his life. Fo. Text in Engl., Latin & Fr., 30 (of 32) full-p. engraved plts., 1 slightly torn, anr. with perforation, a few margins strengthened but barely affecting text, 1 lf. just torn, a few other minor defects. Later diced cf. gt., very worn, covers detchd. [Wing A703] (SBA. Mar.4; 22) *Duran.* £200.
- - Anr. Edn. Ed.:– Sir Roger L'Estrange. Ill.:– William Hollar & others. 1692. Fo. Extra-ill. with 134 plts., 1 bnd. as frontis. with engraved port. of John Ogilvy mntd. on verso, a few ll. cleanly torn. Old cf., worn. [Wing A706] (CSK. Jan.9; 141) £150
- - Anr. Copy. Old cf., cover detchd. (SG. Feb.5; 6) $100
- - Anr. Edn. Ill.:– Francis Barlow. 1703. Cf. (DWB. May 15; 302) £350
- - Anr. Edn. L., 1793. 2 vols. Slight spotting. Recently rebnd. in hf. cf. (TA. Sep.18; 315) £85
- - Anr. Copy. Cont. diced cf. gt., rebkd. (SH. Apr.9; 177) *Bayley.* £75
- - Anr. Copy. Some spotting. Cont. diced russ., spines worn, upr. cover of vol. 2 detchd. (CSK. Feb.6; 186) £55
- - Anr. Edn. Ill.:– T. Bewick. Newcastle, 1818. Cont. hf. leath. gt., decor. (HK. May 12-14; 1570) DM 1,300

- - Anr. Edn. Trans.:– Thomas James. Ill.:– Sir John Tenniel. L., 1848. 1st. Edn. Mor. gt., worn, some spotting. (SG. Sep.4; 435) $130
- - Anr. Edn. Ill.:– Julius Bien after Henry L. Stephens. N.Y., 1868. L.P. Fo. Three-qtr. mor., back gt.-tooled with floral designs, by Stikeman. (SG. May 21; 316) $200
- - Anr. Edn. L., 1894. Kelliegram bdg. of mor., gt. panel spine, upr. cover with gt. & blind panel design, inlaid corner ornaments of scenes from the fables, centre ornament. (SPB. Nov.25; 139) $1,300
- - Anr. Edn. Ill.:– Edward J. Detmold. 1909. (750) numbered, sigd. 4to. Orig. pict. cl. gt. (S. Jul.31; 199) *Jones.* £160
- - Anr. Edn. Ill.:– Arthur Rackham. L., 1912. (1450) numbered, sigd. by artist. 4to. Mor. qt., slightly discold. (SKC. May 19; 53) £190
- - Anr. Copy. Orig. buckram, gt., soiled. (SH. Dec.11; 435) *Schierenberg.* £95
- - Anr. Copy. Orig. cl., soiled. (SPB. May 29; 355) $550
- - Anr. Copy. Some foxing. Gt.-pict. cl. Raymond M. Sutton, Jr. copy. (SG. May 7; 4) $425
- - Anr. Copy. Publisher's cl., unc. (HD. Jun.25; 239) Frs. 1,350
- - Anr. Edn. Ill.:– Charles Folkard. 1912. (250) sigd. by publishers. 4to. Orig. pict. cl., marked. (SH. Dec.10; 205) *Reisler.* £70
- - Anr. Edn. Ill.:– Arthur Rackham. Paris, 1913. (55) numbered on papier du Japon, sigd. by artist. Lge. 4to. Gt.-pict. vell., spine buckled & warped, lacks ties, cl. box. Raymond M. Sutton, Jr. copy. (SG. May 7; 6) $1,000
- - Anr. Edn. Trans.:– Roger L'Estrange. Ill.:– Celia Fiennes. Gold. Cock. Pr., 1926. (350). Orig. cl.-bkd. bds., unc., unopened, d.-w. torn. (SH. Feb.19; 149) *Goolden.* £70
- - Anr. Edn. Ed.:– Sir Roger L'Estrange. Ill.:– Alexander Calder. Paris, 1931. (50) with orig. Calder drawing, sigd. by artist. 4to. This copy unnumbered. Orig. wrap., folder & box. Title-p. sigd. by artist. (SPB. Nov.25; 233) $1,800
- - Anr. Edn. Ed.:– Sir Roger L'Estrange. Ill.:– Alexander Calder. Paris, [1931]. (595) numbered on Auvergne H.M.P. Tall 8vo. The 'paper knife for Fables of Aesop' laid in. Bds., pict. paper covers, bd. folder. (SG. Apr.2; 38) $220
- - Anr. Edn. Trans.:– William Caxton. Ill.:– Agnes Miller Parker, William McCance. Gregy. Pr., 1931. (250) numbered. 4to. Orig. sheep, rubbed & faded, affecting lettering on spine, fore-e.'s of covers slightly stained, unc. (S. Jul. 31; 129) *Jonathan.* £240
- - Anr. Edn. Ed.:– Sir Roger L'Estrange. Ill.:– Alexander Calder. 1931. (615). Orig. bds., unc., unopened, folder, s.-c. (SH. Nov.21; 253) *Monk Bretton.* £60
- - Anr. Edn. Ed.:– Victor Scholderer. Trans.:– Samuel Croxall. Ltd. Edns. Cl., 1933. (1500) numbered. 4to. Marb. bds., vell. spine, orig. box, partly untrimmed. Sigd. by Bruce Rogers. (SG. Jan.15; 110) $110
- - Anr. Edn. Ed.:– Sir Roger L'Estrange. Ill.:– Stephen Gooden. 1936. (525) numbered, sigd. by artist. Sm. 4to. Decor. vell., s.-c. (PJ. Jun.6 (80) 53) £150
- - Anr. Copy. Orig. vell. gt., warped. (SH. Mar.26; 260) *Schrire.* £125
- - Anr. Edn. Ed.:– Sir Roger L'Estrange. Ill.:– Stephen Gooden. 1936. (533) numbered, sigd. by artist. Orig. vell. gt., s.-c. (SH. Mar.26; 261) *Maggs.* £220
- - Anr. Edn. Ill.:– Anna Bramanti. Verona, 1973. (160) numbered. 2 vols. Orig. mor. gt., s.-c. (S. Jul.31; 160) *Marks.* £320
- - Anr. Edn. Ill.:– Edward J. Detmold. N.d. (750) numbered, sigd. by artist. 4to. Orig. buckram gt. (PJ. Dec.5; 87) £95
- Les Fables et la Vie. Paris, 1578. 16mo. 19th. C cf.-bkd. bds. (S. Apr.7; 232) *Forum.* £180
- Fabulae Elegantissimis Eiconibus veras Animalii Species. Leiden, 1570. 12mo. Text in Greek & Latin, some pp. reprd., a few cont. annots. & underlinings. Old vell., rebkd. (TA. Dec.18; 402) £95
- Twelve Fables. Ed.:– Glenway Wescott. Ill.:– Antonio Frasconi. N.Y., 1954. (1000) numbered. 4to. Cl.-bkd. pict. bds., boxed. Sigd. by Frasconi, Wescott & Joseph Blumenthal, the printer. (SG. Oct.23; 131) $110
- Vita et Fabulae. Trans.:– [Francesco del Tuppo]. Naples, [for] Francesco del Tuppo. Feb.13, 1485. Fo. 126 ll. only (of 168), 68 (of 88) woodcuts,

spaces for capital initials with guide letters, inlaid thro.-out & enlarged, 2 woodcuts defect., most of woodcut border on fo. 45 in facs., some letters lost on fo. 123, most of the fable woodcuts with ink inscrs. & some crudely cold., stained, holes in folios 110, 122, & 153. Maroon mor. gt., ornamental gt.-panel. covers, by Leighton. W.a.f. From the collection of Eric Sexton. [BMC VI, 870, Goff A155, HC(+Add) R 353] (CNY. Apr.8; 110) $4,800
- - Anr. Edn. Trans.:– [A.P. Manutius]. Basle, Jan. 1518. Single wormhole from q4 to end, slightly affecting text, sm. piece torn from lr. outer corner of m1, a few inscrs. in text, slight browning. 17th C. cf. rebkd. (S. May 5; 19) *Maggs.* £140
- The Fables of Aesop, & others. Ill.:– Thomas Bewick. Newcastle, 1818. 1st. Bewick Edn. on imperial paper. Engraved receipt-plt. with Bewick's sig. & thumb-print, slight spotting. Cont. diced russ., gt. (S. Feb.10; 405) *Quaritch.* £160
- - Anr. Copy. Some offsetting to text, slight spotting, 'thumb mark' receipt without purchaser's name. Lev. mor., spine gt.-lettered. (CNY. Oct.1; 135) $320
- - Anr. Edn. Ill.:– Thomas Bewick. Newcastle, 1823. 2nd. Edn. Cont. hf. mor. gt. (SBA. Oct.22; 436) *Duill.* £60

AESOP & Others
- Select Fables of Esop & other Fabulists. Ed.:– [Robert Dodsley]. Bg'ham., 1764. 2nd. Edn. Cont. red mor. by Derome le Jeune with his ticket, wide dentelle border, spine gt. in compartments, floral inner gt. dentelles, silk liners. (SM. Oct.7; 1527) Frs. 28,000

AEULIUS, Caesar
- De Divinis Attributis quae Sephirot ab Hebraeis Nuncupantur. Venice, 1689. Sm. 4to. Later hf. cf. & bds., cf. worn. (PNY. May 21; 306) $150

AEVOLUS, Caesar
- Delle Ordinanze et Battaglie. Rome, 1586. Fo. Cont. cf., spine gt. (C. Jul.16; 232) *Rodgers.* £80

AFANAS'EV-SOLOV'EV, I. & others
- V Kibitke Vdokhnoven'ya [In the Carriage of Inspiration]. Petrograd, 1923. (500). Orig. wraps. Pres. copy from Shmerel'son (joint author). (SH. Feb.6; 375) *McVay.* £120

AFANASIEV, A.N.
- Maria Morevna. Ill.:– I. Ya. Bilibin. St. Petersb., 1903. 4to. Orig. pict. wraps., neatly rebkd. (SH. Mar.19; 27) *Fletcher.* £65
- Peryshko Finista Yasna-Sokola [The Plume of Finist Bright-Hawk]. Ill.:– I. Ya. Bilibin. St. Petersb., 1902. 4to. Orig. pict. wraps., neatly rebkd. (SH. Mar.19; 25) *Fletcher.* £65
- Sestritsa Alenushka i Bratets Ivanushka, Belaya Utochka [Sister Alenushka & Brother Ivanushka, The Little White Duck]. Ill.:– I. Ya. Bilibin. St. Petersb., 1903. 4to. Orig. pict. wraps., neatly rebkd. (SH. Mar.19; 28) *Fletcher.* £100
- Skazka ob Ivane-Tsareviche [The Tale of Ivan Tsarevich, Fire-Bird & the Grey Wolf]. Ill.:– I. Ya. Bilibin. St. Petersb., 1901. 4to. Orig. pict. wraps., neatly rebkd. (SH. Mar.19; 23) *Fletcher.* £75
- Tsarevna Lyagushka [The Frog Princess]. Ill.:– I. Ya. Bilibin. St. Petersb., 1901. 4to. Orig. pict. wraps., neatly rebkd. (SH. Mar.19; 24) *Fletcher.* £85
- Vasilisa Prekrasnaya [Vasilisa the Beautiful]. Ill.:– I. Ya. Bilibin. St. Petersb., 1902. 4to. Orig. pict. wraps., neatly rebkd. (SH. Mar.19; 26) *Fletcher.* £65

AFBEELDINGE VAN DE VERSCHEYDE VERGROOTINGE VAN AMSTERDAM ... Representation de Plusieurs Agrandissemens d'Amsterdam [Amst.], ca. 1670. Ob. 4to. Some slight soiling or spotting. Cont. cf., gt., upr. cover detchd. As a collection, w.a.f. (S. Apr.7; 235) *Marriot.* £350

AFFAIR of the Diamond Necklace, a Collection of Contemporary Publications concerning this ... 1786. 24 pieces in 2 vols. 4to. Engr. & 26 mezzotint ports. bnd. in. Cont. cf., lettered 'Historie du Collier', 1 backstrip loose, Gomez de la Cortina & Schuhmann bkplts., as a collection, W.a.f. (SM. Oct.8; 2382) Frs. 3,500

AFFAIRE du Collier
Paris, 1785-87. 4to. Bnd. vol. comprising 26 tracts on the affair, & 20 aquatint ports. & lge. folding engr. Later hf. cf. (SG. Feb.5; 115) $400

AFFICHES Etrangers Illustrées, Les
Ill.:– Lautrec, Beardsley, Bradley, J. Pennell, & others. Paris, 1897. 1st. Edn., (1000) numbered on Velin paper. Lge. tall 4to. Gt.-pict. mor. by Brentano, upr. hinge brkn. Sigd. Pres. Copy, from Nikola Tesla to E. de L. Havemeyer, with Havemeyer's armorial bkplt. (PNY. May 21; 352)
$1,700

AFRICAN WILD LIFE–Magazine of the Wild Life Protection Society
Oct. 1946-Dec. 1970. Vol. 1, no. 1-vol. 4, no. 3; vol. 5, no. 1-vol. 24, no. 4. Wraps. As a periodical, w.a.f. (VA. May 8; 396)
R.220
– – **Anr. Run.** Johannesburg. 1946-70. Vols. 1-24. Wraps. (SSA. Jun.18; 36)
R. 90

AFRICANA Collectanea Series
Cape Town, 1962-75. (50). 40 vols. Hf. mor. (SSA. Jun.18; 34)
R. 550

AFRICANUS (Pseud.)
See–LEO, John 'Africanus'

AGASSIZ, Jean Louis Rodolphe
– **Etudes sur les Flaciers.** Neuchatel, 1840. Atlas vol. only. Fo. Without title, most plts. mntd. on versos. Roan-bkd. cl. (S. Jul.27; 274)
Russell. £300
– **Recherches sur la les Poissons Fossiles.** Neuchatel, 1833-43. Text: 5 vols. in 2, Atlas: 5 vols. in 2. 4to. & ob. fo. Most plts. cold., some foxing to text, occasional soiling & creasing of plts. 19th. C. hf. mor., 2 covers detchd. From Chetham's Liby., Manchester. (C. Nov.26; 5)
Weldon & Wesley. £1,000

AGATHA: OR A NARRATIVE of Recent Events. A Novel
Priv. ptd. 1796. 1st. Edn. 3 vols. Advt. leaf in vol. 3. Cont. marb. bds., paper spines defect., unc. (S. Oct. 20; 1)
Temperley. £140

AGGRAVII VENETIANI, & c., or the Venetian & other Grievances, together with a Proposal for Raising the Price of Tin in the Counties of Devon & Cornwall
1697. 1st. Edn. Pt. 1 (All publd.) 4to. Slight foxing. Recent cf.-bkd. bds. [Wing A62] (C. Apr.1; 186)
Lawson. £90

AGHION, Janine
– **The Essence of the Mode of the Day, Paris 1920.** Paris, [1920]. (150) numbered, on Arches Paper. Loose as issued in ptd. wraps. (SG. Oct.23; 1)
$350

AGIN, A.
– **Sto chetyre risunka [104 Drawings to Gogol's 'Dead Souls'].** Ill.:– Berdadsky after Agin. St. Petersb., 1892. 3rd. Edn. 4to. Slightly soiled, last few ll. wormed. Cont. cf.-bkd. cl., worn. (SH. Feb.6; 289)
Lempert. £50

AGLIONBY, William
– **Painting Illustrated in Three Dialogues.** 1685. 1st. Edn. 4to. Cont. cf. (SH. Jul.16; 157)
Ars Artis. £50

AGNELLINI, Timoteo
– **Proverbi Utili, e Virtuosi in Lingua Araba, Persiana, e Turca.** Padua, 1688. 1st. Edn. Some soiling & foxing. Later cl.-bkd. bds., slightly soiled. (S. Apr.29; 358)
Brill. £200

AGNEW, Thomas & Sons
See–COLNAGHI & CO., P. & D., Agnew, Thomas & Sons

AGOSTINI, Giovanni Degli
– **Notizie Istorico-Critiche intorno la Vita, e le Opere degli Scrittori Viniziani.** Venice, 1952-54. L.P. Edn. 2 vols. 4to. Cont. mor., blind-stpd. fillets, later gt. Ed. stpd. on upr. covers, flat spines gt. in compartments inner gt. dentelles. Ragley hall bkplt. (SM. Oct.7; 1528)
Frs. 2,500

AGOSTINI, Leonardo
– **Le Gemme Antiche.** Rome, 1686. 2nd Edn. 2 vols. 4to. Slight dampstaining. Cont. cf., rather worn. (S. May 5; 415)
Cristani. £130
– **Gemmae et Sculpturae Antiquae Depictae.** Frankfurt, 1694. 2 pts. in 1 vol. 4to. Old cf., rebkd. (TA. Feb.19; 450)
£95

AGOSTINI, Nicolo degli
See–BOIARDO, Matteo Maria–AGOSTINI, Nicolo degli

AGOSTINO, Antonio
– **Dialoghi . . . Intorno alle Medaglie.** Trans.:– Dionigi Ottaviano Sada. Rome, 1592. Fo. Some browning, spotting & staining. 17th. C. sheep. (S. Jul.27; 218)
Drury. £90

AGRICOLA, Franciscus
– **Gründtlicher Bericht, ob Zauber und Hexerei die argste und grewlichste sünd auff Erden sey.** Dillingen, 1613. Slightly spotted in pts. Cont. spr. cf., blind-stpd. arms of a bishop on sides. (S. Jan.27; 303)
Schwing. £70

AGRICOLA, Georgius
– **De Re Metallica.** Basle, 1556. 1st. Edn. Fo. Last lf. with sm. portion excised, affecting device, inner & lr. margins of title reprd., a few minor stains. Cont. German blind-stpd. vell. over wooden bds., owner's name 'Senat. Hayn' & date 1556 blind-stpd. on upr. cover, brass clasps. (C. Apr.1; 97)
RTZ. £6,000
– – **Anr. Edn.** 16th. C. 9¼ × 5⅓ ins. Comprising plts., with Latin text, only, most plts. with mod. hand-colouring, 1 or 2 plts. with minor stains, some age-darkened. Unbnd. (SG. May 21; 161)
$150
– – **Anr. Edn.** Basel, 1657. 1st. [& only] Coll. Edn. Fo. Title woodcut, 2 folding woodcut plts. & 270 text woodcuts, 67 full-p, some worming. Cont. vell., slightly stained, lacks ties. (R. Oct.14-18; 223)
DM 5,800
– – **Anr. Edn. Trans.:** H.C. & L.H. Hoover. 1912. Fo. Orig. vell. (SH. Jan.30; 397)
Subunso. £130
– – **Anr. Copy.** Reproductions of many woodcuts, slight worming to inside upr. cover & prelim. blanks. Vell., unc. (C. Feb.4; 107)
Lloyd. £100
– – **Anr. Copy.** Vell. bds. Sigd. by Pres. H.C. Hoover. (SG. Oct.9; 10)
$350
– – **Anr. Copy.** Some browning, foxing, tears. Orig. vell., stained, red mor.-bkd. cl. s.-c. (SPB. Jun.22; 69)
$150
– – **Anr. Copy.** 4to. Cl., unc. Pres. copy from H.C. Hoover. (SSA. Jan.22; 62)
R. 330
– – **Anr. Copy.** Fo. Lacks top right hand corners of end-papers. Parch., worn. (VA. Jan.30; 559)
R. 230
– **Vom Bergwerck XII Bucher.** Trans.:– P. Bechius. Basel, 1557. 1st. German Edn. Fo. 2 sm. pen drawings on title, dtd. 1616. Cont. blind-stpd. vell. on bds., clasps. (P. Apr.30; 61)
Quaritch. £2,100

AGRICOLA, Johannes
– **Deutliche und wolgegrundete Anmerckungen uber die chymischen Artzneyen Johannis Poppii.** Ed.:– J.H. Jungkens. Nuremb., 1686. 4to. Vell. (S. Dec.1; 15)
Quaritch. £160

AGRICOLA, Johannes of Spremberg
– **Die Zwelff Artickel unsers Christlichen Glaubens sampt der heiligen Aposteln Ankunfft.** Ill.:– Lucas Cranach. Wittenberg, 1561. 4to. Lr. & inner margin of title strengthened with some repairs in lr. woodcut border, lr. section of title under imprint strengthened slightly affecting woodcut on verso, sm. tear & hole in following lf. & last lf., C1 & C2 reprd., a few stains at beginning. Red mor. by Rivière. (S. Dec.1; 16)
Rota. £180

AGRIPPA, Camillo
– **Trattato di Scientia d'Arme.** Rome, Antonio Blado, 1553. 1st. Edn. 4to. Lacks last blank. Cont. vell. bds. Dyson-Perrins copy, with bkplt. & number. (S. Nov. 25; 360)
Abrams. £700

AGRIPPA, Henricus Cornilius
– **Three Books of Occult Philosophy.** 1651. Cont. cf.-bkd. bds., jnts. cracked. [Wing A789] (CSK. Nov.7; 228)
£110
– **The Vanity of Arts & Sciences.** 1684. Cont. panel. cf. [Wing A791] (S. Jun.15; 10)
Maggs. £55

AGUADO DE CORDOVA, A.F. & others
– **Bullarium Equistris Ordinis S. Jacobi de Spatha.** Ill.:– P. de Villafranca [frontis]. Madrid, 1719. Fo. Cf. (DS. May 22; 829)
Pts. 34,000

AGUILON, François d'
– **Opticorum libri sex.** Ill.:– Rubens. Antw., 1613. 1st. Edn. Fo. Hf.-title slightly soiled with liby. stp. of St. John's College, Waterford, hf.-title & title reprd., f2G1 ptd. only on recto, 2G6 only on verso, both missing pp. of text inserted in photostat. Cont. panel. cf., rebkd. (S. Apr.6; 206)
Quaritch. £260

AGUSTIN, Antonio, Archbp. of Tarragona
– **Dialogos de Medallas Inscriciones Y Otras Antiguedades.** Tarragona, 1587. 1st. Edn. 4to. 1 lf. reprd. Cont. Fr. mor., gt., arms of Aymar Duperier, on covers, gt. panel with acorn corner sprays, double gt. fillet, flat spine gt. with double panel. Bkplts. of Jean Jobert & Hadrian Beverland. (SM. Oct.7; 1530)
Frs. 6,000

AHLES, Dr.
– **Allgemein Verbreitete Essbare und Schaedliche Pilze mit Einingen Mikroskopischen Zergliederungen** Esslingen, 1876. 1st. Edn. Sm. fo. Orig. cl.-bkd. pict. bds. (PNY. May 21; 295)
$100

AHMAD Ibn Muhammad
– **Historia Tamerlanis Arabice.** Ed.:– Jacobus Golius. Leiden, 1636. 1st. Edn. 4to. Text entirely in Arabic. Cont. vell. (C. Nov.20; 173)
Hosains. £420

AHRTAL, Das
Bonn, ca. 1840. Orig. bds., s-c. (VG. Nov.18; 898)
Fls. 750

AIKEN, Conrad
– **Priapus & the Pool.** Camb. Massachusetts, 1922. (50) numbered, on H.M.P., sigd. Sm. 4to. Orig. bds. (SG. Jun.4; 1)
$160

AIKIN, Dr. John
– **A Description of the Country from Thirty to Forty Miles Round Manchester.** 1795. 4to. 1 map slightly torn. Cont. diced russ. gt. (SBA. Oct.22; 376)
Newby. £180
– – **Anr. Copy.** Cont. hf. russ. gt., worn. W.a.f. (SBA. Oct.22; 375)
Child. £140
– – **Anr. Copy.** 1 vol. in 2. Folding map & plan detchd. Mod. buckram. From the collection of Eric Sexton. (C. Apr.16; 207)
Chesters. £110
– **England Delineated.** 1790. Cf. (P. May 14; 334)
Martin. £75

AIME MARTIN, L.
– **Lettres à Sophie sur la Physique, la Chimie et l'Histoire Naturelle.** Ill.:– after Massard & Boquet (frontis). Paris, 1811. 4 vols. 16mo. Some foxing. Cont. red str.-grd. mor., spines decor., covers gt.-decor., lge. floral roulette inner dentelle, inscrs. on upr. covers. (HD. Apr.9; 388)
Frs. 1,000

AINSLIE, Sir Robert & Mayer, Luigi
– **Interesting Views in Turkey.** L., 1819. 4to. Cl., worn. (S. Mar.17; 388)
Symonds. £70
– **Views in Egypt.** 1801. 2 vols. (text & plts.). Fo. Recent hf. cf. with old marb. bds. (TA. Nov.20; 393)
£350
– – **Anr. Copy.** Cont. hf. russ., covers detchd. (C. Nov.5; 106)
Asmail. £320
– – **Anr. Copy.** Lacks 10 plts. Bdg. defect. (HY. Jan.14; 84)
£85
– – **Anr. Copy.** 48 hand-cold. plts., lacks port., liby. bkplt. with release stp. Cont. str.-grd. mor. (SG. Oct.9; 163)
$1,600
– – **Anr. Copy.** Plts. in 2 states, in sepia before the letter & cold. Publisher's str.-grd. red hf. mor., spines decor. with special tools, sm. corners, unc. (HD. Mar.18; 118)
Frs. 9,000
– **Views in Egypt, Views in the Ottoman Empire.** 1801-03 [plts. wtrmkd. 1794 & 1801]. 2 pts. in 1 vol. Fo. Lacks the un-cold. frontis. port. Cont. diced russ., gt. panel on covers, spine gt., upr. cover detchd. (C. Feb.25; 116)
Cucci. £620
– **Views in the Ottoman Dominions, Europe, in Asia & some of the Mediterranean Islands.** L., 1810. Slightly browned. Cont. hf. leath., spine defect. (R. Mar.31-Apr.4; 2513)
DM 2,800
– – **Anr. Copy.** Lge. fo. 68 (of 71) plts., slightly soiled in parts. No bdg. (R. Oct.14-18; 1799)
DM 2,700
– **Views in the Ottoman Empire, chiefly in Caramania, a Part of Asia Minor.** L., 1803. Lge. fo. Cont. leath. gt. (R. Mar.31-Apr.4; 2512)
DM 900
– **Views in Palestine.** 1804. Fo. Text in Engl. & Fr. Cont. mor.-bkd. cf., gt. (SH. Nov.7; 427)
Max. £410
[-] **Views in Turkey, in Europe & in Asia . . .** 1811-12. 2 pts. in 1 vol. Fo. 56 cold. aquatints & 8 views. Cont. hf. mor. (C. Jul.15; 74)
Zanzotto. £550
– **Views of Turkey in Europe & Asia.–Selection of the most interesting of . . . collection of views in Egypt, Asia Minor, & c.** L., 1811; 1812. 2 works in 1 vol. Fo. Very slight browning, 1st. work: 8 more plts. than called for in list of plts. Cont. hf. cf., worn, spine crudely reprd. with tape. (SPB. Nov.25; 118)
$1,000
[-] **Views in Turkey . . . Syria, Sicily, the Eolian Islands . . . & c.** 1811 [plts. wtrmkd. 1809]. Fo. 16 hand-cold. aquatint plts. after Mayer only, lacks 8 plts., occasional spotting, a few light marginal stains. Hf. mor., limp covers, soiled. (CSK. Jan.30; 147)
£120

AINSWORTH, W.F.
– **All Around the World.** N.Y., Ca. 1870. 4 vols. Orig. linen, defect. (R. Oct.14-18; 1464) DM 430

AINSWORTH, William Harrison

- **Jack Sheppard.** Ill.:– George Cruikshank. 1839. 1st. Edn. 3 vols. 12mo. Some tears & spotting. Later hf. cf. (SH. Jun.4; 203) *Blanks.* £60
- **[Works].** 1878-82. 31 vols. (? only). Cont. hf. cf., spines gt. W.a.f. (CSK. Jan.23; 18) £110

AIRY, Osmund

- **Charles II.** 1901. Ltd. Edn. 4to. Red mor. gt. with coat of arms, by Bumpus. (CE. Jun.4; 129) £55

AITZEMA, Lieuwe van

- **Historie of Verhael van Saken van Staet en Oorlogh.–Verhael van de Nederlandsche Vreede Handeling.** The Hague; Amst., 1657-71; 1653. 1st. Edn. (1st. work). 14 vols. only (of 15, lacks vol. 7); 2 vols. in 1. 4to. 2nd. work dampstained. Unif. old cf., worn & brkn., ex-liby. (SG. Feb.5; 7) $400
- **Saken van Staet en Oorlogh.** Ed.:– L. Sylvius (supps.). The Hague, 1669-72, 1685 & 1688. 6 vols. in 7, & 2 supp. vols. Fo. Some age-browning, etc., old liby. label on all title-pp. Cont. vell., ex-liby. (vols.), & old vell. (supps.). (SG. Feb.5; 8) $1,700

AITZINGER, or Eyzinger, Michael

- **Novus de Leone Belgico eiusque Topographica atque Historica Descriptione Liber.** Cologne, 1588. [1606]. 2 pts. in 1 vol. 4to. Light worming at beginning, some plts. browned. 18th. C. leath. (R. Oct.14-18; 1824) DM 23,000

AKADEMIE DES BAUWESENS

- **Karl Friedrich Schinkel.** Berlin, 1941. Pt. 1. 4to. Orig. linen, spine defect. (D. Dec.11-13; 531) DM 550

A'KEMPIS, Thomas, Saint

- **Closter Pratic.** Trans.:– F.A. Neumayr. Thierhaupten, 1599. Lightly browned & soiled, owner's mark. Cont. blind tooled gt. leath-bkd. wood bds., lightly rubbed, lr. cover with hole, 2 clasps. (HK. May 12-14; 171) DM 460
- **[-] De Imitatione Christi [with De Meditatione Cordis & other works of Johannes Gerson].** Luneberg, Johann Luce, May 22, 1493. Spaces for initial capitals, most with guide letters, capitals, paragraph marks, underlines & initial strokes supplied in red, lacks Q4 & 5, title-p. soiled, sm. tear to inner margin of B1 slightly affecting text, lr. & outer margins of N1 reinforced, light dampstains to some margins, extensive marginalia & notes in ink at 1st. 6 ll. & 7 others toward end. Vell. Bkplt. of A. de Saint Ferriol, lately in the collection of Eric Sexton. [BMC III, 698, Goff I29, HC 9105] (CNY. Apr.8; 85) $2,500
- – **Anr. Edn.** Trans.:– P.F. Coelestino. Rome, 1663. 1st. Edn. in Arabic. Slight browning. Cont. vell., soiled, inside hinges brkn., s.-c. (S. Apr.29; 360) *Jazmaian.* £100
- – **Anr. Edn.** Trans.:– Gerson. Nuremb., ca. 1942. Lacks title lf., paginates beginning at lf. ii as: (6) & 182 ll., ll. 172 & 173 paginated in Roman numerals & tipped-in, rubricated thro.-out (lf. 1 with some bleeding). Early 18th. C. cf., sm. wormholes at 1st. 4 ll. of Tabulae. [Goff 27; Hain-Copinger 9103] (PNY. Oct.1; 296) $380
- **Imitatio Christi.** Rome, 1674. Text in Turkish, wood-engraved device on hf.-title verso. Later bds. gt. (SBA. Jul.23; 540) *Brian.* £90
- **Of the Imitation of Christ.** L., 1905. (500) on L.P. 4to. Crushed mor., gt.-stpd. with ruled borders, surrounded by a border of leafy sprays at gt.-panel. spine inner dentelles gt., by C. McLeish at Doves Bindery. (PNY. Dec.3; 113) $260
- **Tractatus de Ymitatione Cristi Cum Tractatulo de Meditatione Cordis (By Johannes Gerson).** Ulm, Johann Zainer. 1487. Lacks title, 3 blanks & folios 13, 14, 54 & 55, the last 4 supplied in early MS., initials & chaptermarks supplied in red & blue, some initials with penwork extending into margins, initial strokes supplied in red, slightly browned & spotted, natural flaw in a few ll. slightly affecting text, 1 marginal tear, 1 lf. soiled, sm. hole in margin of 1 lf., sm. hole & scribbles on anr. Red stained blind-stpd. sheep over wooden bds., rebkd. using old spine, lacks clasp. [HC (+Add) 9091*; BMC II, 530; Goff I, 13] (S. Apr.7; 291) *Dr. Kubicek.* £260

A'KEMPIS, Thomas Saint–Holcoth, Robert

- **De Imitatione Christi.–Heptalogus.** Ed.:– Joannis Gerson. Antwerp; [Paris], 8th. May, 1518; [1517]. 2 works in 1 vol. 1st work: title slightly damaged, slightly affecting print, owners inscr. on both titles deleted, some ll. slightly soiled, some

old marginalia. Cont. blind-stpd. cf., spine worn, lacks ties. (S. Oct.21; 444) *De Graaf.* £200

AKENSIDE, Mark

- **The Pleasures of Imagination.** Ed.:– Mrs. Barbauld (critical essay). Ill.:– after Thomas Stothard. L., [1794]. 16mo. Cont. crimson str.-grd. mor. gt., slightly worn. Fore-e. pntg.; from the liby. of Zola E. Harvey. (SG. Mar.19; 106) $220

AKHMATOVA, Anna

- **Anno Domini MCMXXI.** Petrograd, 1921. 1st. Edn., (2000). Orig. wraps., reprd., slightly soiled. (SH. Feb.6; 290) *Nijhoff.* £95
See–BLOK, Alexander & others

ALADDIN & THE WONDERFUL LAMP

N.Y., ca. 1885. 4to. Orig. pict. bds., backstrip worn. (SH. Mar.19; 208) *Fletcher.* £70

ALAIN-FOURNIER, Henri

- **Grand Meaulnes (Le).** Ill.:– Jean Frelaut. 1946. (225) on vell. & Lana. 4to. In sheets, s.-c. Sigd. by artist. (HD. Feb.27; 134) Frs. 2,500

ALAMAN, Lucas

- **Disertaciones sobre la Historia de la República Mejicana, desde le Epoca de la Conquista.** Havana, 1873. 3 vols. & Appendix in 1 vol. Sm. 4to. A few light stains, 1 ptd. wrap. bnd. in. Later qtr. cf. (SPB. May 5; 57) $425

ALAMANNI, Luigi

- **La Coltivatione.** Parigi, 1546. 1st. Edn. 4to. Margin of title reprd. 18th. C. red Fr. mor., triple gt. fillet, spine gt. in compartments, 2 wormholes, 2 corners worn. (SM. Oct.7; 1533) Frs.2,300

ALASTAIR (Pseud.)

See–VOIGHT, Hans H. 'Alastair'

ALBANI, F.

See–DORIGNY, Nicolaus–BERETTINI, Petro –ALBANI, F.–BERETTINI, Petro–BERTOLUS, P.S.

ALBANIS DE BEAUMONT, Jean François

- **Travels from France to Italy, through the Lepontine Alps.** 1806. Fo. Title detchd., contents lf. defect. Cf.-bkd. bds., worn. (CSK. Aug.29; 100) £110
- **Travels through the Maritime Alps.** L., 1795. Fo. Lacks 3 plans. Cont. hf. cl. (SM. Oct.8; 2166) Frs.3,000
- **Travels through the Rhaetian Alps–Travels through the Maritime Alps.–Travels from France to Italy, through the Lepontine Alps ... L.,** 1792-1800. 3 vols. Fo. Ex-liby. Unif. mod. buck. (SG. Oct.9; 11) $2,000

ALBELDA, Moshe Ben Yakov

- **Shaarei Dim'ah.** Venice, 1586. 1st. Edn. Sm. 4to. Mod. blind-stpd. cf. Bkplt. of Dr. Samuel Dresner. (SPB. May 11; 24) $600

ALBEMARLE, George [Monck], Duke of

- **Observations upon Military & Political Affairs.** 1671. 1st. Edn. Fo. Cont. sheep, front free end-paper sigd. in cont. hand. [Wing A864.] (S. Sep.29; 1) *Fletcher.* £60

ALBER, Erasmus

- **[-] L'Alcoran des Cordeliers.** Ill.:– Bernard Picart. Amst., 1734. 2 vols. 12mo. S3 & S4 of vol. 11 misbnd., in place of R3 & R4 of vol. 1 & vice versa, sig. of A.A. Renouard on titles, vell. end ll. inserted in each vol. 18th. C. red mott. Spanish mor., triple gt. fillet, flat spines gt. with design in each compartment, inner gt. dentelles, pink silk liners. Book labels of Mortimer Schiff & J.R. Abbey, 3 pp. notes by E. Gordon Duff loosely inserted. (SM. Oct.7; 1534) Frs. 2,400

ALBERS, Josef

- **Interaction of Colors.** New Haven, 1963. 3 vols. Fo. 80 text pp., with portfo. of 80 lge. folders & 48-p. Commentary. Wraps. & bd. folder & cl. s.-c. (SG. May 14; 4) $1,400

ALBERTANUS Causidicus Brixiensis

- **De Arte Loquendi et Tracendi.** Ingoldstadt, [Printer of the Celtes], ca. 1492. 4to. The variant 'lingua' in line 4 of fo. 1r, & the reading 'causidico' in colophon, spaces for initial capitals, in red with flourishes, paragraph marks, initial strokes & underlines in red, foxed, erased liby. stp. at fo. lr. Recent vell. Bkplt. of Boies Penrose, lately in the collection of Eric Sexton. [BMC III, 677, Goff A206, H 398*] (CNY. Apr.8; 78) $2,500

ALBERTI, Giuseppe Antonio

- **La Pirotechnia.** Venice, 1749. 1st. Edn. 4to. Some foxing & staining, corner torn from plt. 17. Orig. bds., worn, unc. From Honeyman Collection. (S. May 20; 3163) *Simonin.* £240
- – **Anr. Copy.** Some scattered light foxing. Cont. vell. bds. From the collection of John A. Saks. (C. Jun.10; 2) *Lyon.* £80

ALBERTI, Leon Battista

- **L'Architettura.** Trans.:– Bartoli. Venice, 1565. 2nd. Edn. of this translation. 4to. 2 ll. (?from anr. Edn.) inserted in 1st. gathering, 1 corner torn away, some worming barely touching text, some browning & soiling. Later vell., upr. hinge brkn. (SPB. Jul.28; 2) $225
- **Della Architettura, Della Pittura, Della Statua.** Trans.:– C. Bartoli. Bologna, 1782. Fo. Vell. gt. (P. Dec.11; 122) *Balbi.* £190
- – **Anr. Copy.** Orig. hf. cf. (BS. Feb.25; 255) £65
- **Descrittione di tutta Italia.** Vinegia, 1551. 4to. Hf. cf. (CR. Mar.19; 360) Lire 380,000
- – **Anr. Edn.** Venetia, 1561. Cont. vell. (P. Mar.12; 92) £60
- – **Anr. Edn.** Venice, 1577. 2 pts. in 1 vol. 4to. Lacks a8 of 1st. 'Tavola', 1st. title defect. & mntd., sm. hole in n4, a few ll. with marginal repairs several ll. stained & browned. 18th. C. vell. bds., slight wear. Edward Gibbon's copy, with his 1st. bkplt. (S. Jun.9; 32) *Blackwells.* £140
- – **Anr. Edn.** Venice, 1588. 2 pts. in 1 vol. Sm. 4to. Slight browning. 18th. C. vell. bds., soiled. Bkplt. of John Conyers, Copt Hall, Essex; from liby. of André L. Simon. (S. May 18; 10) *Quaritch.* £75
See–DOLCE, Lodovico–DONI, Anton Francesco –ALBERTI, Leon Battista

ALBERTI, Rafael

- **La Amante.** Malaga, 1926. 1st. Edn. Orig. wraps. (DS. Apr.24; 915) Pts. 24,000

ALBERTINUS CAUSIDICUS BRIXIENSIS

- **Tractatus de Arte Loquendi et Tacendi.** Cologne, [Heinrich Quentell]. 1487. 4to. Rubricated, cont. notes in red thro.-out, (natural paper fault in 1 lf. affecting 3 words). Mod. vell. bds. [Hain 403; BMC I p. 271; Goff A 199] (C. Apr.1; 4) *Branners.* £320

ALBERTUS, Erasmus

- **Von den Zeichen des Juengsten Tags: Ein Schon Lied von Johannes Walter.** [Wittenberg]. 1548. 1st. Edn. Sm. 4to. Tear in blank portion of last lf. reprd., some staining & browning thro.-out. Mod. buckram, 18th. C. wraps. bnd. in. From the collection of Eric Sexton. (C. Apr.15; 1) *Quaritch.* £1,150

ALBERTUS MAGNUS, Bp. of Ratisbon

- **De Aludibus Beatae Virginis Mariae.** Milan, Uldericus Scinzenzeler, 17 Apr. 1488. 4to. 111 ll. (of 112), lacks last blank, upr. inner corner reprd. thro.-out, few wormholes reprd. 19th. C. blind-stpd. sheep, spine gt. [BMC VI, 763] (S. Mar.17; 266) *Norton.* £220
- **De Animalibus.** Venice, 21 May 1495. Fo. Some later MS. notes on verso of title & recto of last lf., slight browning & soiling. 17th. C. cf., rebkd., liby-stp. on some ll. [Hain 547; BMC V 346; Goff A225.] (S. Sep.29; 87) *Duran.* £420
- **Opus Tripartitum.** Cologne, 29 III. 1503. Fo. Old Ms. notats. thro.-out, a little soiled. 19th. C. bds. (HK. Nov.18-21; 99) DM 650
- **Philosophia Pauperum.** Brescia, Baptista de Farfengo. 10 Sep. 1490. Initials in red & blue. Mod. vell. [BMC VII, 985] (SG. May 14; 5) $1,400
- **Secreta Mulierum et Virorum.** [Geneva], [Louis Cruse]. [not before 1487]. 4to. Unrubricated, lr. margin of b1 renewed, trifling marginal repair to a8. Mor., gt.-lettered spine. From the collection of Eric Sexton. [BMC VIII, 366, C 186] (CNY. Apr.8; 69) $7,000
- – **Anr. Edn.** [Rouen], [Laurent Hostingue?]. [after 1500?]. 12mo. Lr. corner of C1 renewed, portion of upr. margin of E4 renewed, with some letters shaved. Mor., gt.-lettered spine, by Sangorski & Sutcliffe. Stp. of the Collection Munaret, lately in the collection of Eric Sexton. [Goff A317] (CNY. Apr.8; 149) $2,600
- – **Anr. Edn.** Liptzk, 1502. Marginal notes thro.-out in early hand, initials blank. Later vell. bds. (SG. May 14; 6) $325
- **Sermones de Tempore et de Sanctis.** Ulm, ca. 1478-80. Fo. Lacks 1 blank lf., some old marginalia, lightly soiled. 16th. C. vell. (HK. Nov.18-21; 98) DM 4,200

– Suma Prelucidissima de Mirabli Eucaristie Sacramto ... [Ulm], [J. Zainer]. 1474. Fo. Slightly browned. Rebnd. in vell., slightly soiled. [Goff A335] (TA. Oct.16; 186) £625

ALBIN, Eleazar
– Insectorum Angliae Naturalis Historia. Ed.:– G. Derham. L., 1731. Text vol. & plt. vol. 4to. Cont. cf., spines gt. (VG. Oct.13; 4) Fls. 3,700
– A Natural History of Birds. 1738. 3 vols. 4to. Many plts. offset on to facing p. 19th. C. hf. mor. From Chetham's Liby., Manchester. (C. Nov.26; 6) *Unterberger.* £2,600
– A Natural History of English Insects. 1720. 1st. Edn. 4to. 100 hand-cold. engd. plts., 1 almost detchd. Cont. cf., rebkd., worn. (C. Mar.18; 6) *Dillon.* £580
– – Anr. Copy. Some internal spotting, margins of plts. 3 & 4 reprd. Orig. qtr. cf. W.a.f. (TA. Aug.21; 302) £525
– – Anr. Copy. 99 (of 100) plts. Cont. Engl. red mor., gt., orange & gt. end-papers, some wear, probably the Pembroke copy, binding & label on spine being typical of the Wilton books. (S. Dec.3; 877) *Dillon.* £380
– – Anr. Copy. Ex-liby. 19th C. hf. mor. (SG. Oct.9; 12) $1,500
– – Anr. Edn. Ed.:– W. Derham. 1724. 4to. Plts. hand-cold. Cont. cf., gt., slightly worn. From the collection of Eric Sexton. (C. Apr.15; 2) *Roberts.* £380
– – Anr. Edn. Ed.:– W. Derham. 1749. 3rd. Edn. 4to. Some plts. a little spotted. 19th. C. hf. mor. From Chetham's Liby., Manchester. (C. Nov.26; 7) *Junk.* £400
– – Anr. Copy. A few brownings. Cont. cf., slightly defect. (H. May 21/22; 163) DM 2,600
– Natural History of English Song Birds. N.d. 4to. Child's pencil markings thro.-out, lacks title. Hf. mor., worn. As a collection of plts. (P. Apr.9; 93) *Kubricele.* £140
– A Natural History of Spiders & Other Curious Insects. 1736. 4to. Some minor spotting. Recent hf. cf. (TA. Mar.19; 595) £230

ALBINUS, Bernardus Siegfried
– Explicatio Tabularum Anatomicarum Bartholomaei Eustachii. Leiden, 1744. 2 vols. Fo. 90 engraved plts. including dupls. of each plt. in outl. & for 7 plts. an additional folding outl. plt., slightly spotted. Cont. bds., corners & spines slightly worn. (S. Feb.23; 2) *Jenner.* £380
– – Anr. Copy. Slight soiling & marginal stains. Cont. cf., worn & defect. (S. Apr.6; 4) *Hildebrand.* £240
– – Anr. Edn. Leiden, 1761. [2nd. Edn.?]. Fo. Lower portions dampstained thro.-out, 2 plts. slightly torn, lacks port. Cont. cf. gt., worn, upr. cover defect. (CNY. Oct.1; 1) $600
– – Anr. Copy. Cont. leath., old corners, spines renewed later. (R. Oct.14-18; 298) DM 2,000
– Tables of the Skeleton & Muscles of the Human Body ... Edinb., 1777-78. 2 vols. Lge. Fo. No port., some browning & soiling. Cont. hf. cf., worn, 1 cover detchd. (S. Apr.6; 5) *Schuster.* £160
– Tables of the Skeleton & Muscles of the human body.–A Complete System of the Blood Vessels & Nerves. 1749-50; 1754. 2 pts. in 1 vol. Fo. Plts. 4 & 3 in 1 misbnd., some stains. Hf. cf., not unif., text vol. unc. (S. Jun.15; 11) *Driscoll.* £160
– Tabulae Sceleti et Musculorum Corporis Humani. –A Compleat System of the Blood-Vessels & Nerves. Ill.:– Charles Grigion, Scotin, & others. 1749-50. 2 works in 1 vol. Elephant fo. Lacks lf. of dedication. 19th. C. hf. mor. From Chetham's Liby., Manchester. (C. Nov.26; 8) *Lester.* £600

ALBION, L.
– Histoire Naturelle des Oiseaux. The Hague, 1750. Vol. 1 (of 3). 4to. Some plts. slightly stained. Cont. leath., gt., fillets, arms, slightly worn, upr. cover loose. (R. Mar.31-Apr.4; 1315) DM 4,200

ALBO, Josef
– Sefer Haikkerim. Soncino, [Joshua Solomon Soncino]. Tebet 21, 5246 [Oct.3-Dec.29, 1485]. Fo. 7 woodcut initial letters, some 12 ll. probably supplied from anr. copy, last lf. cut round & mntd., 1st. 2 ll. remargined affecting some letters at bottom of fo. 2, following lf. with repairs to extreme inner margin, penultimate lf. hinged, upr. outer corners of folios 104-107 with loss of several letters, several marginal tears reprd., some scattered marginal worming. Mor., gt.-lettered spine. From the collection of Eric Sexton. [Goff Heb 64, HC 606] (CNY. Apr.8; 157) $22,000

ALBRECHT, Butters & others
– Bilder aus den Neuen Reichslanden und aus dem Südwestlichen Deutschland. Leipzig, 1880. Cont. hf. leath. (R. Oct.14-18; 2141) DM 850

ALBRIZZI, Isabella Teotochi de
– Ritratti. Padua, 1808. 2nd. Edn. Cont. mor., gt. spine, inner & outer dentelles, & end-papers of silk & cold. paper. (H. May 21/22; 961) DM 520

ALBRIZZI, J.B.
– L'Etranger plainement Instruit ... de la Ville de Venise. Ed.:– F. Calvert, Lord Baltimore. Venice, 1771. Cf., worn. (P. Jul.30; 203) *Davis.* £380

ALBUMASAR, Abu Ma'shar
– De Magnis Coniunctionibus ... Ed.:– Johannes Angelus. Augsburg, Erhard Ratdolt. 31 Mar., 1489. 1st. Edn. Sm. 4to. 19th. C. hf. roan. [BMC II, 383] (S. Nov.25; 338) *Riley Smith.* £2,000
– – Anr. Copy. Some dampstaining, mainly to 1st. & last ll., rest mostly marginal, 2 ink stps. on A2. Old qtr. vell. & paper bds., worn. [BMC II, 383, Goff A360, HC 611*] (CNY. Oct.1; 79) $4,000
– – Anr. Copy. Some ll. sigd. 19th C. mor., double fillet around covers, arms of Prince d'Essling in centre. (HD. Jun.24; 2) Frs. 15,000

ALBUMS
– L'Album. Ed.:– Jules Tallandier. Ill.:– Job, Guillaume, Forain, Ferdinand Bac, Gerbault & others. Paris, 1902/03. Nos. I–XIX. Fo. Orig. litho. wraps., loosely contained in mod. solander box, wraps. on 1st. no. detchd. (SPB. May 6; 139) $400
– Album Amicorum. N.d. Ob. 4to. Romantic Lavallière mor., blind & mosaic decor. dentelle à la cathédrale, limp decor. spine, inner dentelle. (HD. Apr.24; 112) Frs. 1,000
– Album Amicorum Deliciae Batavicae. Pays-Bas, 1625. Interleaved with white paper. Cont. vell., 2 arms. (LM. Mar.21; 2) B.Frs. 72,000
– Album de Pomologie. N.p., ca. 1860 Ob. 4to. Some text ll. with slight tears. Cont. leath. (HK. May 12-14; 196) DM 1,400
– Album der Interessantesten und Schönsten Ansichten von Carlsruhe. Karlsruhe, ca. 1840. Loose in orig. wraps. (R. Oct.14-18; 2160) DM 1,200
– Album of 30 Primitive Style Watercolour Drawings, Dutch Costume & Trades. Ca. 1800-30. 4to. Hf. mor., covers detchd. (TA. Sep.18; 231) £100
– Album Officiel de la Fête des Vignerons Vervey 1889. Lausanne & Vervey, 1889. Ob. 8vo. Spotted, a few margin stains. Orig. cl.-bkd. bds., slightly soiled. (SH. Nov.6; 183) *Crete.* £55
– Album Pittoresque de Stockholm. Copen., ca. 1870. Liby. stp. on 1st. plt. Orig. bds., brkn. As a collection of prints, w.a.f. (BS. Nov.26; 198) £150
– Album publié par l'Association des Aquafortistes Anversois sous le Patronage du Cercle Artistique. Antw., 1883. Fo. Unbnd. in orig. wraps., torn. (CSK. Sep.5; 198) £70
– [European Scenery]. 1882-1908. 2 vols. 19½×15 inches, & 15×21 inches. Containing approx. 130 watercolours in amateur hand, some full-p. (LC. Oct.2; 2) £110
– [Topographical Views]. 1870's-80's. 4to. Containing about 175 photographs of various sizes, most titled, including albumen print of F.M. Sutcliffe's 'The Water Rats' (initialled on negative with reference number), 1 or 2 other photographs initialled 'R.E.' & 'W.G.P.', some photographs with stp. of R.W. Thrupp, B'gham. Hf. mor. gt. (LC. Oct.2; 51) £190

ALCALA, Pedro de
– Arte Para Ligermaente Saber la Lengua Arauica. Granada, Juan de Varela, 1505. 2 Pts. in 1 vol. 4to. Mod. vell. (S. Nov.25; 342) *Willow.* £5,000

ALCEDO, Antonio de
– Diccionario geográfico-histórico de las Indias Occidentales ó América: es a saber: de los Reynos del Perú, Nueva España, Tierra Firme, Chile y Nuevo Reyno de Granada. Madrid, 1786-89. 5 vols. Sm. 4to. Cont. mott. cf. [Sabin 682] (SPB. May 5; 58) $750
– The Geographical & Historical Dictionary of America & the West Indies. Ed.:– G.A. Thompson. L., 1812-15. 1st. Edn. in Engl. 5 vols. 4to. Lacks hf.-titles, vol. 5 apparently lacks prelims., some liby. hand-stps., some foxing & hand soiling. Later liby. buckram. (SG. Jan.8; 7) $120

ALCIATUS, Andreas
– Los Emblemas ... traducidos en Rhimas Espanolas. Lyon, 1549. 1st. Edn. in Spanish. Lacks O1, a little thumbed at beginning, inner margin of title torn. Cont. Fr. (?) mor., blind-stpd. double panels on covers, spine in 5 compartments, lacks ties, new end-papers. (C. Apr.1; 124) *Torras.* £200
– Emblemata ... Lyon, 1548. Some tears, stains, slight worming. Old cf., worn, wormed. (SPB. May 29; 4) $175
– – Anr. Edn. Passau, 1621. Thick sm. 4to. Cont. panel. cf., jnts. brkn. (SG. Sep.25; 9) $170
– [Emblemata]. Diverse imprese accomodate a diverse moralita ... Translated from the Latin. Lione, 1579. 1st. Rovillio Edn. Allegorical woodcuts sigd. 'P.V.' (PNY. Oct.1; 13) $160
– Emblemata.–Diverse Impresse ... Tratte da gli Emblemi.–Liber Emblematum. Ed.:– J. Amman & Virg. Solis (3rd. vol.). Leiden; Lyons; Frankfurt, 1548; 1551; 1566 [colophon: 1567]. 1st. Edn. (1st. vol.). 3 vols. 4to. & 8vo. Liby. stps. on verso of title-pp. inked out, staining & foxing, occasional tears & repairs. Various bdgs., 1 brkn. (SPB. May 6; 140) $650
– In D. Andreae Alciati Emblemata Succinta Commentariola ... Lyons, 1556. 24mo. Sigs. of De La Reynie & F. Parkes Weber. Early 17th. C. red mor. in Jansenist style, cipher HD surrounded by 4 S fermés, gt., on covers. (SM. Oct.7; 1535) Frs. 1,400
– Notitia utraque cum orientis tum occidentis. Basle, 1552. Fo. Old cf., rebkd. (P. Mar.12; 232) *Cambridge.* £200
– Omnia Emblemata, cum Commentariis. Ed.:– C. Minoes. Paris, 1589. 2 pts. in 1 vol., 18th. C. paper bds. (R. Oct.14-18; 53) DM 520
See–BUDAEUS or Bude, Guilielmus–ALCIATUS, Andreas
See–LE JEUNE, S. Adrian–ALCIATUS, Andreas

ALCOCK, Sir Rutherford
– Capital of the Tycoon. 1863. [1st. Edn.?]. 2 vols. 1 folding map mntd. on linen. Mod. cf.-bkd. cl. (SH. Nov.7; 332) *Fine Books Oriental.* £110
– – Anr. Copy. Few ll. dampstained at edges. Cl. (SH. Apr.9; 131) *Dawsons.* £90
– – Anr. Copy. 2 vols. Cont. linen, defect. & loose. (R. Oct. 14-18; 1787) DM 600

ALCOTT, Louisa May
– Little Women.–Little Women, Part Second. –Little Men. Boston. 1868-69; 1871. 1st. Edns. Together 3 vols. 12mo. 1st. & 3rd. works with 1st. iss. points cited in 'Peter Parley to Penrod', 2nd. work later iss., & with 8 pp. of advts. All gt.-lettered cl., worn & loose, in hf. mor. s.-c. (SG. Apr.30; 9) $200
– Little Women.–Little Men.–Jo's Boys, & How They Turned Out. Boston, 1868 & 1869; 1871; 1886. 1st. Edns., 1st. States (except 2nd. work; 1st. Amer. Edn.). 2 pts. in 3 vols.; 1 vol.; 1 vol. 12mo. All orig. cl., upr. cover of 2nd. work stained, 1st. work in qtr. mor. gt. case, 2nd. in cl. s.-c., 3rd. in cl. folding case. From the Prescott Collection. (CNY. Feb.6; 2) $600

ALDAM, W.H.
– A Quaint Treatise on 'Flees & the Art a Artifichall Flee Making'. Ill.:– After James Poole. 1876. 4to. 6 bds. carrying specimen flies, hackles & thread on sunken mounts, slightly spotted, sigd. photograph of author on verso of dedication lf. Orig. cl. gt. W.a.f. (SBA. Oct.21; 137) *Petersfield Bookshop.* £550
– – Anr. Copy. Some spotting. Orig. cl. Mntd. port. photograph of Aldam sigd. by him below. (CSK. Jul.3; 142) £420
– – Anr. Copy. Gt.-pict. cl. (SG. Apr.9; 279) $1,300
– – Anr. Edn. 1880. 4to. 11 pp. with examples of flies, but some flies lacking, especially toward end. Orig. mor. gt. W.a.f. (C. Jul.22; 174) *Thorpe.* £150

ALDAY Y ASPEL, Manuel de
– Synodo Diocesana, que Celebró et Ilustrissimo Señor Doctor ... Obispo de Santiago de Chile.
– Synodo Diocesana con la Carta Pastoral Convocatoria para ella: y otra, en Orden a la Paga de los Diezmos. Celebróla el Ilustrissimo ... Don Fray Bernardo Carrasco y Saavedra, Obispa de Santiago de Chile. Lima, 1764; 1764. 2 pts. in 1 vol. Fo. Limp vell. (SPB. May 5; 59) $475

ALDIN, Cecil–FIFE
- Time I was Dead-Ratcatcher to Scarlet. -Scarlet, Blue & Green. Ill:– Cecil Aldin. 1934; (1932); 1932. 1st. Edn., (100) numbered. (1st work). 3 works in 3 vols. Aldin's obituary inserted in 1st. work., some light foxing. Hf. mor. (1st. work). (SG. Dec.11; 158) **$130**

ALDINGTON, Richard
- Images of War. Ill.:– Paul Nash. Beaumont Pr., 1919. 1st. Edn., (200) numbered. Prospectus loosely inserted. Orig. cl.-bkd. bds., unc. (SH. Mar.27; 353) *Phillips.* **£85**

ALDINI, Tobias
- Exactissima Descriptio Rariorum Quarundam Plantarum. Rome, 1625. 1st. Edn. Fo. Cont. vell. From Chetham's Liby., Manchester. (C. Nov.26; 9) *Wagner.* **£170**

ALDRICH, Thomas Bailey–GREENSLET, Ferris
- Works.-Life of Thomas Bailey Aldrich. Camb., 1897; 1908. (250) sigd.; (500), both L.P. 9 vols.; 1 vol. Unif. bnd. in hf. mor. gt., gt. panel spines. (SPB. May 6; 282) **$200**

ALDROVANDUS, Ulysees
- De Animalibus Insectis libri Septem cum singulorum Iconibus ad vivum Expressis. Bologna, 1602. 1st. Edn. Fo. Cont. vell. sides stained, spine slightly defect. (C. Nov.6; 196) *Wagner.* **£320**
- De Quadrupedibus solidid Pedibus. -Quadrupedum Omnium Bisolcorum Historia. Bologna, 1616; 1621. 1st. Edns. 2 works in 2 vols. Fo. Cont. vell.; cont. vell., spine wormed. (C. Nov.6; 197) *Wagner.* **£320**
- Monstrorum Historia cum paralipomenis Historiae omnium Animalium Bartholomaeus Ambrosinus ... Marcus Antonius Bernia ... edidit. Bologna, 1642. 1st. Edn. 2 pts. in 1 vol. Fo. Lacks last lf. (blank?), last 60 ll. of pt. II slightly defect., affecting some text, 1st 4 ll. reprd in inner margin, a few marginal tears. 18th. C. mott. Sheep, top of spine & corners worn. (S. Feb.23; 3) *Korn.* **£190**
- Ornithologiae. Ill:– J. Thaller (engraved title border). Frankfurt, 1610-10-35. 3 vols. in 2. Fo. 1st. engraved plt. at F2 in cancelled & uncancelled states, former with running title 'Ornithologiae Liber II', lacks final blank ll (?), sm. flaw to each title, sm. repair to P2 in vol. II, sm. rust holes in V5 in vol. I, & 3G2 in vol. II, affecting a few letters, some ll. lightly stained in inner margins, or browned, occasional spotting. 17th. C. cf., gt. spines gt., with arms of Henri Loyens gt.-stpd. on covers, both spines with repairs, slight wear. (S. Dec.3; 878) *Broseghini.* **£640**
- - Anr. Edn. Frankfurt, 1630. 3 vols. in 1. Fo. Vol. III with some plts. pasted on blank versos of text ll., lacks plts. 13 & 14 (not issued in this edn.?), sm. holes affecting a few letters in C6, slight browning, a few other minor flaws. Cont. vell. bds., upr. cover stpd. GWD/1651, soiled. (SPB. May 6; 141) **$275**
- Serpentum et Draconum Historiae Libri duo. Bologna, 1640. 1st. Edn. Fo. Hf. title & engraved title slightly stained. Cont. vell., slightly wormed, endpapers wormed. (C. Nov.6; 195) *Israel.* **£190**

ALEMAN, Mateo
[–] Ortografia Castellana. [Mexico], [1609]. 1st. Edn. Sm. 4to. Lacks title-p. & final blank, piece torn from 1st. lf., short tear in G4. Cont. limp vell., ties. [Sabin 715.] (S. Mar.16; 110) *Rosenburg.* **£130**
- The Rogue. Trans:– James Mabbe. 1622. 1st. Edn. in Engl., 1st. Iss. 2 pts. in 1 vol. Mor. gt. by Rivière, cl. case. Bkplt. of J.P.R. Lyell. [STC 288] (C. Nov.19; 1) *Engel.* **£240**

ALEMANNIA, Conradus de
- Concordantiae Bibliorum. [Reutlingen], [Michel Greyff], [before 1482]. Fo. Capital spaces, capital initials, initial strokes & paragraph marks in red & blue thro-out, lge. initials with red penwork tracery, MS. headlines & quiring in red, all by cont. hand, lacks final blank lf., slight staining in some places. Cont. blind-stpd. cf.-bkd. wood bds., brass fittings for clasps, rebkd., badly worn, upr. cover detchd. with some leath. missing, lacks bosses. Bkplt. of Dr. Georg Kloss, bkplt. of the General Theological Seminary Liby. [BMC II, 577; Goff C850; HC 5630] (CNY. Oct.1; 50) **$2,200**

ALEMBERT, Jean Le Rond d'
See–DIDEROT, Denis & ALEMBERT, Jean Le Rond d'
See–MARPURG, Friedrich Wilhelm –ALEMBERT, Jean le Rond d'

ALESSANDRI, Innocente & Scattaglia, Pietro
- Animali Quadripedi dal Naturale dissengnati. Venice, 1771-72. Pt. 1-2 only, of 4. Fo. 2 title-pp defect. with lower portion cut away & tipped to following plts. Unbound sheets. W.a.f. (CNY. Oct.1; 129) **$1,500**
- Descrizioni degli Animali. Ed:– Lodovico Laschi (text). Venice, 1771-75. 4 vols. in 2. Fo. Additional titles & plts. hand-cold., head-pieces uncold. Mod. hf. mor. From the collection of John A. Saks. (C. Jun.10; 3) *La Fiera del Libro.* **£4,200**

ALESSIO, Piemontese
See–RUSCELLI, Girolamo 'Piemontese Alessio'

ALEXANDER, Sir James Edward
- An Expedition of Discovery into the Interior of Africa. 1838. 2 vols. Orig. cl. (SH. May 21; 1) *Mitton.* **£75**
- Transatlantic Sketches, Comprising Visits to the most interesting Scenes in North & South America & the West Indies. L., 1833. 1st. Edn. 2 vols. Some spotting, stains, slight browning. Hf. cf., rebkd., recased. [Sabin 735] (SPB. May 5; 60) **$175**
- - Anr. Copy. Lacks 'Arrawaaks' plt., some foxing. Old hf. cf. (SG. Mar.5; 3) **$170**
- Travels to the Seat of the War in the East through the Crimea, in 1829. 1830. 1st. Edn. 2 vols. Orig. bds. rebkd. & with old labels, slightly worn. (S. Jun.29; 275) *Minerva.* **£50**

ALEXANDER, William
- The Costume of China. L., 1805. 1st. Edn. Fo. Cont. red mor., elab. gt.-stpd., cf. rebkd., outer corners worn. (PNY. May 21; 133) **$550**
- - Anr. Edn. 1805. 4to. Wtrmkd. 1794 & 1802, occasional slight spotting, 1 p. publisher's advt. at end. Cont. cf., rebkd. (CSK. Feb.20; 46) **£130**
- - Anr. Copy. 47 hand-cold. aquatint plts. only (lacks no. II), without subscribers list & dedication, a few marginal tears, some reprd., 1 with loss of a few letters, soiling thro.-out. Later hf. cf. (CSK. Jan.16; 107) **£75**
[–] Costume of the Russian Empire. L., 1803. 1st. Edn. Fo. Very little foxing. Cont. gt.-stpd. russ., new spine, corners reprd. (VG. Oct.13; 49) *Fls.* **1,500**
- Picturesque Representations of the Dress & Manners of the Chinese. 1814. 4to. Hf. leath. (S. Jan.27; 494) *Lyon.* **£95**
- - Anr. Copy. 37 cold. plts. (of 50), a few frayed. Orig. hf. cf., worn. (SH. Jun.18; 143) *Elliott.* **£60**
- - Anr. Copy. Tall 4to. Mod. mor.-bkd. marb. bds. (SG. Oct.30; 17) **$425**
- - Anr. Copy. Fo. Maroon hf. mor., spine gt. (CNY. May 22; 19) **$300**
- - Anr. Edn. L., [1814]. 2nd. Edn. Later hf. leath., worn, unc. (H. Dec.9/10; 533) **DM 700**
- - Anr. Copy. Cont. str.-grd. garnet mor., decor. spine, gt. blind-tooled fillets & roll-stps. on covers. (HD. Dec.5; 1) **Frs. 1,000**
- Picturesque Representations of the Dress & Manners of the Chinese.- ... of the Austrians.- ... of the English.- ... of the Turks.- .... of the Russians. 1814. Together 5 vols. Unif. cont. str.-grd. mor., sides panel. in gt. & blind, spines gt. (C. Mar.18; 7) *Traylen.* **£750**
[–] Picturesque Representations of the Dress & Manners of the Turks. N.d. Lacks plt. 34. Cont. hf. mor., worn, lacks spine. (SH. Jul.16; 92) *J.S. Gimesh.* **£70**
See–MASON, George Henry & Alexander, W.

ALEXANDER, William–HOME, Robert
- The Costume of China.-Select Views in Mysore. 1805; 1808. 2 works in 1 vol. 4to. 1st. work: lacks subscribers' list & advt. lf.; 2nd. work: without the 4 maps (as issued?). Cont. diced russ., gt. (C. Nov.5; 2) *Quaritch.* **£220**

ALEXANDER, Sir William, Earl of Stirling, 1580-1640
- The Mapp & Description of New-England. L., 1630. 3rd. Edn. Sm. 4to. Mor. by Rivière. Boies Penrose bkplt. [STC 342] (CNY. May 22; 18) **$2,200**
- Recreations with the Muses. Ill.:– Marshall (port. frontis.). 1637. 1st. Edn. Fo. Cont. cf., cont.

owner's inscr. of 'Rich. Beauchamp'. [STC 347] (C. Feb.25; 147) *Quaritch.* **£420**

ALEXANDER Carpentarius
- Destructorium Vitiorum. Nuremb., Anton Koberger. Sep.20, 1496. Fo. Initials & rubrics supplied in red, several wormholes at beginning & end, slightly affecting text, cont. owner's inscr. at foot of a2r, & repeated once. Cont. blind-stpd. pig over wood bds., slightly worn, lacks clasps & piece from head of spine. [BMC II, 443, Goff A393, HC 652*] (S. Feb.10; 213) *Fletcher.* **£350**

ALEXANDER de Ales
- Super Tertium Sententiarum. Venice, Johannes de Colonia & Johannes Manthen. 1475. 1st. Edn. Fo. Spaces for capital initials with guide letters, illuminated hf.-border on 1st. p, of white vine-scroll design on blue ground incorporating lge. gold N, capitals, paragraph marks & initial strokes supplied in red & blue, lacks preliminary blank, some ll. slightly spotted, 1st. lf. slightly cropped, 2 quires with slight worming at inner margin. 18th. C. vell. [BMC V, 226, Goff A385, HC 647*] (CNY. Oct.1; 115) **$1,100**

ALEXANDER, de Villa Dei
- Doctrinale. Ed.:– [Maturinus de Barda; & M. Lombardus (commentary)]. Paris, Pierre Levet. Aug.31, 1489. 'Partes I-IV'. Fo. Lge. capital initials supplied in red with pen & ink floral & foliate grounds with extensions, rubricated, some dampstaining to upr. inner portions, particularly at end with restoration to some upr. blank margins, some early MS. annots. in text. Cont. blind-stpd. cf. over wood bds., lge. central ruled panel of lozenges with binder's stps. of Saint Lawrence (repeated 8 times) & the crowned double-headed eagle (repeated 4 times) on each cover, vell. fly-ll. comprising 2 nearly compl. bifolia of a late 13th. C. Engl.(?) MS., by the Bat binder, spine, corners & a tear in lr. cover restored, lacks clasp & catch, new endpapers. [H 763] (CNY. Apr.8; 118) **$14,000**

ALEXANDER ZISKIND, Zusha Ha'Cohen of Siedlec & Plozk
- Torat Cohen. Warsaw, 1939. 1st. Edn. 2 pts. in 1 vol. 4to. With notes by Joseph Weiss. Cl. (S. Nov.17; 141) *Rock.* **£50**
- Yakar Mi'paz. Warsaw, 1932. 1st. Edn. Hf. cl. (S. Nov.17; 142) *Rock.* **£50**

ALEXANDRE, Arsène
- L'Art Decoratif de Leon Bakst. Ed.:– Jean Cocteau. Ill.:– Leon Bakst. Paris, 1913. 1st. Edn. on L.P. Tall fo. Gt. hf. vell. & cl. (PNY. Oct.1; 88) **$425**
- - Anr. Copy. Port., 77 mntd. plts., 50 cold., many wrinkled, lacks orig. watercolour. Orig. hf. vell., very worn, crudely reprd. (SG. Oct.23; 10) **$300**
- The Decorative Art of Leon Bakst. Ed.:– Jean Cocteau. 1913. Fo. A few creases. Orig. hf. vell. bds., gt., partly unc. (S. Jun.9; 20) *Lord Perth.* **£240**
- - Anr. Copy. Orig. hf. vell., slightly stained, worn. (SH. Nov.20; 130) *Salinas.* **£180**

ALEXANDRE, Arsène–MORICE, Charles
- Paul Gauguin, sa Vie et le Sens de Son Oeuvre.- Paul Gauguin. Paris, 1930; 1919. 2 works in 2 vols. 4to. Orig. ill. wraps., unc. (1st. work); & cl., orig. wraps. bnd. in, partly unc. (C. Jul.22; 129) *Sims & Reed.* **£100**

ALEXANDRE, Vicente
- Ambito. Málaga, 1928. 1st. Edn. 4to. Orig. wraps. (D5. Apr.24; 984) **Pts. 35,000**

ALEXIS of Piedmont
- The Thyrde & Last Parte of the Secretes ... Trans:– Wylliam Warde. 1566. 4to. A few stains. Hf. mor. [STC 306] (S. Dec.1; 24) *Claridge.* **£70**

ALFASI, Yitzhak Ben Yakov
- Rav Alfas. Frankfurt a. M., 1699. Vol. III only. 12mo. Repairs to folding plt., minor tears, foxing, browning. Hf. vell., soiled. (SPB. May 11; 26) **$225**
- - Anr. Edn. Vienna, 1804. 6 pts. in 3 vols. Lge. fo. Vell.-bkd. bds., spotted. (SPB. May 11; 25) **$150**

ALFIERI, Vittorio
- Il Misogallo: Prose, e Rime. Londra (i.e. Flor.), 1799. 1st. Edn. Slight wear to fore-edges & corners. Cont. flowered paper wraps., worn, paper

spine added, unc. From the collection of John A. Saks. (C. Jun.10; 4) *Quaritch.* £60
- **Tragedie.** Paris, 1788-87. 2nd. Edn. Some stains. Cont. sheep, gt. spine, unc. (SI. Dec.3; 11) Lire 220,000

ALGAROTTI, Francesco
- **Opere.** Ed.:- F. Agletti. Ill:- R. Morghen & Bianconi after Novelli & others. Venice, 1791-94. New Edn. 17 vols. Port. with reprd. tear in margin. Mod. cf.-bkd. bds. From the collection of John A. Saks. (C. Jun.10; 6) *Taylor.* £60
*See-*FRUGONI, Carlo Innocenzo & others

ALGAROTTI,   Francesco-MICHELESSI, Domenico
- **Il Newtonianismo per le Dame Ovvero Dialoghi Sopra la Luce e i Colori.-Memorie Intorno alla Vita ed agli Scritti del Conte Francesco Algarotti.** Ill.:- Pitteri after Piazzetta (frontis.) (1st. work). Napoli (i.e. Venice); Venice, 1737; 1770. 1st. Edn. (1st. work). 2 works in 2 vols. Sm. 4to.; sm. 8vo. Mod. mor.-bkd. bds. (1st. work); & cont. vell. gt. From the collection of John A. Saks. (C. Jun.10; 5) *Rota.* £100

ALGREN, Nelson
- **A Walk on the Wild Side.** N.Y., [1956]. 1st. Edn. 2-tone bds., d.-w. Sigd. Pres. Copy, to F.W. Eppling. (PNY. May 21; 4) $120

ALHAZEN [i.e. HASAN ibn Hasan or Ibn Al-Haitham]
Opticae Thesavrus Libri Septem . . . Basel, 1572. 1st. Edn. Fo. Cont. blind-tooled pig-bkd. decor. wd. bds., 2 clasps. (HK. Nov.18-21; 100) DM 10,000

ALHOY, Maurice (Ed.)
*See-*MUSEE POUR RIRE

ALHOY, Maurice & Huart, L.
[-] **[Les Cent et un Robert-Macaire.]** Ill.:- H. Daumier. [Paris], [1839.] 4to. Some ll. browned, slightly soiled thro-out, lacks titles. Cont. hf. leath. (HK. Nov.18-21; 2327) DM 2,250
- - **Anr. Edn.** Ill.:- H. Daumier. Paris, 1839-40. 1st. Edn. 2 vols. in 1. 4to. Soiled. Cont. hf. leath., gt. spine. (R. Oct.14-18; 2558) DM 2,200
- - **Anr. Edn.** Ill.:- Honoré Daumier. Paris, 1840. Reduced & inverted lithos. after 1836-38 Edn., 1839 title. 2 vols. in 1. 4to. Lacks 1 litho. plt. 31, soiled & slightly browned. Cont. hf. leath. gt. (R. Mar.31-Apr.4; 1543) DM 2,400

ALI BEY
- **Travels . . . in Morocco, Tripoli, Cyprus, Egypt, Arabia, Syria & Turkey.** 1816. 1st. Edn. 2 vols. 4to. Slight spotting. 19th. C. hf. mor., rebkd. (S. Sep.29; 184) *Hawley.* £340

ALISON, Sir Archibald
- **History of Europe.** 1789-1815; 1815-52; Index 1854-59. 14 vols.; 9 vols. including Index. Unif. tree cf. a. set. 1st. set: bnd. into vol. I is correspondence between author & Blackwoods comprising:- 6 A.L.s., 15pp., 1832-56, in vol. II is 3pp. A.L.s. from author to W. Young, vol. XIV has attached copyright certificate. 2nd. set: in vol. I, 3 A.L.s. bnd. in, 13½pp., 1851-52, vol. VIII has bnd. in a copy letter from Earl of Derby, Index has attached a further copyright certificate. (CE. Jul.9; 54) £120
- - **Anr. Edn.** 1849-59. 23 vols. (2 Series). Cf., gt., T.C.D. prize bdg. (S. Dec.8; 68) *Alasonatti.* £130

ALKABAZ, Solomon
- **Manot ha-Levy.** Venice, 1585. 1st. Edn. Sm. 4to. Title in woodcut border, reprd. Old. vell. (C. Jul. 16; 304) *Landau.* £200

ALKEN, Henry
- **The Beauties & Defects in the Figure of the Horse.** L., [1816]. 1st. Edn. 4to. Slight offsetting, minor defects. Cf. gt. with equine decor., orig. wraps. bnd. in. (SPB. Jul.38; 3) $200
- - **Anr. Edn.** L., n.d. [plts. wtrmkd. 1815]. 1st. Edn. 4to. Orig. bds., unc., spine renewed. (CNY. May 22; 184) $100
- **A Collection of plates depicting scenes from a foxhunt.** [L.], [1818?]. Ob. 4to. 7 hand-cold. plts., all but 1 plt. dtd. Jan.1, 1818, last dtd. Mar.15, 1818, slight foxing. Hf. red mor., slightly worn. (SPB. May 6; 143) $500
[-] **Comparative Meltonians.** L., [1823.] Ob. fo. Wtrmkd. J. Whatman 1823, lacks ptd. title-page. Red hf. mor. gt. (SPB. Oct.1; 78) $750
[-] **[Hunting, or Six Hours Sport.]** [L.], [1823.] Red hf. mor. (SPB. Oct.1; 79) $500

- **Ideas, Accidental & Incidental to Hunting & Other Sports.** L., [1826-30]. Orig. Iss. Fo. Cont. (orig?) red hf. mor. gt., stitching brkn., cl. case. (SPB. Oct.1; 82) $2,200
- **Illustrations to Popular Songs.** 1822. Sm. Ob. fo. Occasional light spotting. Cont. hf. roan, spine torn with loss. (CSK. Jun.26; 92) £200
- - **Anr. Edn.** 1826. Ob. 4to. 41 (of 43) cold. plts. Three-qtr. lev. by Root. (SG. Sep.4; 5) $260
[-] **[Leicestershire Covers].** Ill:- Sutherland after Alken. [L.], [1824]. Spotted, formerly framed. Red str.-grd. mor. gt. by Rivière. The William Hartmann Woodin Set. (SPB. Oct.1; 80) $750
- **The National Sports of Great Britain.** 1820. 1st. Edn., 1st. Iss. Fo. Extra cold. aquatint title with sm. tears reprd., 50 cold. aquatint plts. wtrmkd. 1816-18. Cont. str.-grd. mor., gt. panel. sides with elab. blind & gt. tooled borders & central gt. ornament. (C. Mar.18; 8) *Sawyer.* £3,500
- - **Anr. Edn.** L., 1821. 1st. Edn. Fo. 2nd state of ptd. title, offsetting from text on most plts. Orig. red str.-grd. mor. gt. (SPB. Oct.1; 75) $4,600
- - **Anr. Edn.** L., 1821 [1823 or later]. Fo. Text wtrmkd. 1818-19. Cont. mor. gt., spine tooled in compartments, covers with arabesque border & lge. centre vig. (S. Nov.24; 4) *Niedbardt.* £3,500
- - **Anr. Edn.** 1825. Red mor., sides with gt. fillet borders & floral cornerpieces, spine gt. in compartments, by Rivière. (C. Mar.18; 9) *Schuster.* £1,000
- - **Anr. Copy.** 1 plt. reprd. with adhesive tape, portions torn away from margins of 2 others, occasional spotting. Orig. cl., worn & disbnd. W.a.f. (CSK. Dec.12; 117) £220
- - **Anr. Copy.** L.P. Fo. Few light stains. Cont. hf. red mor., stitching brkn. (SPB. Oct.1; 81) $2,600
- - **Anr. Edn.** 1903. Fo. Orig. cl., dampstained lr. edges. (SH. Jan.30; 368) *Walford.* £170
- - **Anr. Copy.** Hf. leath. gt. (R. Mar.31-Apr.4; 1661) DM 2,800
[-] **Qualified Horses & Unqualified Riders.** L., 1815. Ob. fo. Orig. ptd. wraps., unc., cl. case. (SPB. Oct.1; 74) $1,000
- **Studies of the Horse.** L., 1830. Ob. 4to. Mod. mor gt. (P. Jun.11; 5) *Porter.* £120
- **Symptoms of Being Amused.** L., 1882. [1st. Edn.?]. 40 plts. (of 41), some soiled & with marginal tears. Cont. hf. roan, rebkd., worn. (S. Dec.8; 9) *Way.* £100
- - **Anr. Copy.** Vol. 1. Ob. fo. Cont. (?orig.) qtr. roan bds., very worn. (CSK. Oct.1; 77) $950
- - **Anr. Copy.** In 7 pts. Ob. 4to. Slight marginal staining, offsetting. Orig. wraps., some tears, worn, loss to 1 lr. wrap., in mor.-bkd. s.-c. (SPB. May 6; 142) $600
- - **Anr. Edn.** 1822. Vol. 1 only. Ob. 4to. Hf. cf. (P. Apr.30; 271) *Schapiro.* £170
- **Tutor's Assistant.** 1823-24. Ob. fo. Generally foxed. Orig. wraps., some wear. (Ta. Sep.18; 251) £70

ALKEN, Samuel
*See-*GILPIN, William & Alken, Samuel

ALL ENGLAND LAW REPORTS
1948-78. 81 vols. only. Orig. cl. (SH. Jan.30; 398) *Barnett.* £300

ALLA MAESTA DI NAPOLEONE I, Imperator de Francesi Coronato Re dell'Italia . . . Visione del Professore V. Monti
Milan, 1805. Lge. 4to. Italian long-grd. red mor., sm. tool border, crown in corners & centre eagle round Lombardy crown, wtrd. silk doubls. & gds. Napoleon arms. (HD. Oct.10; 277) Frs. 3,500

ALLARD, C.
- **Nieuwe Hollandse Scheeps-bouw.** Amst., 1695. 4to. Slightly browned. Cont. cf., worn. (SH. Jun.4; 178) *Forum.* £480

ALLASON, Thomas
- **Picturesque Views of the Antiquities of Pola.** 1819. 1st. Edn., L.P. Fo. Engraved frontis., 9 plts., 4 vigs., all on India Paper. 19th C. hf. str.-grd. mor., ptly unc., worn. (S. Sep.29; 201) *Pinto.* £110

ALLEMAGNE, Henry René d'
- **Les Accessoires du Costume et du Mobilier.** Paris, 1928. 3 vols. Bds., jnts. worn. (BS. Jun.11; 413) £110
- - **Anr. Copy.** (HD. Feb.27; 63) Frs. 3,200
- **Les Cartes à jouer du XIV au XXe Siècle.** Paris, 1906. 2 vols. 4to. Hf. more. (SM. Oct.8; 2174) Frs. 4,500

- **Histoire des Jouets.** Paris, priv. ptd., [1902.] 4to. Publisher's cl. s.-c., multicold. decor. on spine & covers. (HD. Dec.5; 58) Frs. 3,300
- **La Maison d'un vieux Collectionneur.** Paris, 1948. Ltd. Edn. 2 vols. 4to. Orig. stiff wraps. (C. Feb.4; 210) *Diba.* £65
- - **Anr. Edn.** Ed.:- Guillaume Janneau. Paris, [1948]. (600) numbered. 2 vols. 4to. Vol. I text in ptd. wraps., vol. II plts. loose in folding portfo. (SG. Dec.4; 8) $180
- **Sports et Jeux d'Adresse.** Paris, ca. 1900. Lge. 4to. 100 plts., 29 hand-cold. Cold. pict. bds. (SG. Apr.30; 10) £425
- - **Anr. Copy.** Three-qtr. mor., orig. wraps. bnd. in. (SG. Dec.11; 162) $280

ALLEMAND, Comte
*See-*HERMANT, Godefroy-ALLEMAND, Comte

ALLEN, A.H.
*See-*McMURTRIE, Douglas C. & Allen, A.H.

ALLEN, Charles Dexter
- **A Classified List of Early American Book-plates . . .** N.Y., Grol. Cl., 1894. (3) on vell. Unbnd. folded sheets, 1st. gathering unopened, cl. case. (CNY. May 22; 415) $600

ALLEN, George H.
- **The French Revolution.** Phila., [1922]. 4 vols. 4to. Crimson mor. gt., gt. medallion design in each corner. (SPB. May 6; 283) $150

ALLEN, J. Romilly
- **The Early Christian Monuments of Scotland . . .** Edinb., 1903. (400). 4to. Hf. mor., rebkd., upr. cover slightly soiled, front & back endpapers slightly torn. (PD. May 20; 128) £160

ALLEN, James Lane
- **A Kentucky Cardinal & Aftermath.** Ill.:- Hugh Thomson. 1901. Orig. cl. gt. Pres. copy from artist to William Heighway. (SH. Mar.27; 516) *Donnithorne.* £250

ALLEN, John
- **Modern Judaism, or a brief account of the opinions, traditions, rites & ceremonies of the Jews in modern times.** L., 1816. Cf. (S. Nov.18; 634) *Laine.* £80

ALLEN, Thomas
- **A New & Complete History of the County of York.** Ill.:- after Whittock. L., 1828. 6 vols. Hf. cf., marb. bds. (HSS. Apr.24; 320) £110
- - **Anr. Edn.** Ill.:- Nathaniel Whittock. 1829-31. 3 vols. 4to. Plts. on india paper & mntd., extra plt. at p. 175 in vol. II, titles slightly soiled. Cont. diced russ. gt., vol. 3 rebkd. preserving orig. spine. (C. Nov.6; 279) *Kidd.* £180
- **Pacific Railroad Commenced: Address to the Board of Directors of the Pacific Railroad Company, January 31, 1850 . . .** St. Louis, 1850. 1st. Edn. Mod. hf. mor. (PNY. Mar.26; 242) $220
- **Picturesque Beauties of Great Britain . . . Kent.** 1828. 4to. Browned. Hf. cf., defect. (P. Apr.30; 275) *Cummings.* £110

ALLEN, Capt. William
- **Picturesque Views in the Island of Ascension.** Priv. ptd. 1835. Ob. fo. Spotted, some repairs. Cont. limp cl. (SH. Nov.7; 499) *Proud.* £240
- **Picturesque Views on the River Niger.** 1840. Ob. 4to. Orig. wraps., holed & slightly dampstained, backstrip worn. (CSK. Jun.12; 153) £85

ALLEN, Capt. William & others
- **Narrative of the Expedition . . . to the River Niger.** 1848. 2 vols. Mod. hf. cf. (SH. Nov.7; 270) *Enfield.* £100
- - **Anr. Copy.** Occasional spotting. Orig. cl., soiled. (CSK. Mar.13; 107) £55

ALLENDYER, R.
*See-*WHITE, A. & others

ALLESTREE, Richard
- **The Causes of the Decay of Christian Piety.** L., 1671. 4th. Edn. Cont. Engl. mor. by Queens' Binder A (?William Nott), spine tooled in compartments, elab. pattern on covers. [Wing A1100] (S. Nov.24; 5) *Breslauer.* £380
[-] **The Gentleman's Calling.** L., 1671. 9th. Edn. Cont. Engl. mor. by Queens' Binder A (?William Nott), spine tooled in compartments, elab. pattern on covers. [Wing A1115] (S. Nov.24; 6) *Breslauer.* £380

ALLEZARD, J.J.
– Recueil . . . Plans des Ports et Rades de la Mediterranée. 1833. Ob. 4to. Some staining. Qtr. cf., worn. (P. Jul.30; 121)   *Finney.* £200

ALLGEMEINE OECONOMISCHES FORST-MAGAZIN
Ed.:– J.F.Stahl. Frankfurt & Leipzig. 1763-69. Vols. 1-12 in 6 vols., all publd. Title pp. stpd. Cont. leath., gt. (R. Oct.14-18; 2757)   DM 1,500

ALLG. SAMMLUNG, Historischer Memoirs
Ed.:– Fr. Schiller. Jena, 1790-1806. 33 vols. Cont. hf. cf. gt., decor. W.a.f. (HK. May 15; 4860)   DM 2,600

ALLGEMEINES MAGAZIN DER NATUR, Kunst und Wissenschaften
Ed.:– J.D. Titius & others. Leipzig, 1753-56. Pts. 1-7 in 6 vols. 10 copperplts., most foldg. Cont. vell. (R. Oct.14-18; 172)   DM 2,400

ALLGEMEINE ZEITSCHRIFT
Ed.:– Schelling. Nuremb., 1813. Vol. 1 pts. 1-4, all publd. Lacks hf.-title to pts. 3 & 4, mispaginated, lf. 1 pref. paper fault reprd. slightly soiled, old Ms entries, ex-lib. Cont. bds. gt. (HK. May 15; 4819)   DM 900

ALLIACO, Petrus de
– Imago Mundi et Tractatus Alii. [Louvain], [Johann de Paderborn (Westphalia)], [ca. 1483]. Fo. 166 ll. (of 172, lacks 1st. 6 ll. including 1 blank, text supplied in facs.), a few marginal repairs, portion of hh5 verso smudged. 19th. C. hf. cf. [HC 836; BMC IX 146; Goff A477] (SPB. May 6; 144) $350
– Concordantia Astronomiae cum Theologia. Augsburg, Erhard Ratdolt, Jan. 2, 1490. 1st. Edn. 4to Paper bds. [BMC II, 383, Goff A471, Hain 834*] (CNY. Oct.1; 80) $3,800
– Libellus Sacramentalis. Louvain. Aegidius van der Heerstraten, Apr.14, 1487. 4to. 91 ll. (of 92), lacks initial, initials written in red & blue, few cont. Ms. notes, liby. stp. on first 2 ll. 18th. C. cf., rebkd. Heber Liby. stp. [BMC IX, 166] (C. Jul.16; 233)   *Quaritch.* £1,100
– [Tractatus et sermones] Tractatus De Anima. Brussels, Brethren of the Common Life, Not after 1483. Fo. Lacks all before f. 148, A4 & final blank, rubricated in red & blue with calligraphic initials thro.-out, some repairs to blank margins, a few minor stains. Recent mott. sheep. [Hain 850; BMC IX p. 174; Goff A487] (C. Apr.1; 5)   *Corby.* £200

ALLIBONE, Samuel Austin
– Critical Dictionary of English Literature, & British & American Authors, Living & Deceased, from the Earliest Accounts to the Latter Half of the Nineteenth Century. 1859-71. 3 vols. in 6. Cont. hf. cf. gt. (TA. Sep.18; 45)   £52

ALLIES' FAIRY BOOK
Ed.:– Edmund Gosse. Ill.:– Arthur Rackham. L., 1916. (525) numbered, sigd. by artist. 4to. Gt.-stpd. cl. Raymond M. Sutton, Jr. copy. (SG. May 7; 7) $300
– – Anr. Edn. Ill.:– Arthur Rackham. L. & Phila., [1916]. (525) numbered, sigd. by Rackham. 4to. Cl. gt. (SG. Oct.9; 201) $475

ALLINGHAM, William
– In Fairyland, a Series of Pictures from the Elf World. Ill.:– Richard Doyle. 1870. Fo. Slightly spotted. Lacks upper end-lf., loose in orig. cl. gt. (SKC. Sep.9; 1424)   £160
– – Anr. Copy. Margins soiled. Orig. cl., soiled, disbnd. (CSK. Apr.24; 38)   £80
– – Anr. Edn. Ill.:– Richard Doyle. 1875. 2nd. Edn. Fo. Some ll. detchd. Orig. cl., slightly soiled. (CSK. Oct.17; 39)   £100
– – Anr. Copy. Marginal staining, occasional spotting. Orig. cl., worn, disbnd. (CSK. Jul.31; 83)   £95
– The Music Master. Ill.:– Dante Gabriel Rossetti & others. 1855. 1st. Edn. Orig. cl. (SH. Mar.27; 471)   *Swales.* £85

ALLIONI, Carlo
– Flora Pedemontana. Ill.:– P. Peiroleri. Turin, 1785. 3 vols. Fo. Without the port. (often lacking). Cont. hf. vell., worn. (S. Jul.27; 275)   *Pilo.* £400
– Rariorum Pedemonto Stirpium. Turin, 1755. Specimen Primum (all publd.). 4to. 19th. C. cl., stitching brkn., covers detchd. From Chetham's Liby., Manchester. (C. Nov.26; 10)   *Junk.* £80

ALLIX, Peter
– Judgement of the Ancient Jewish Church against the Unitarians. L., 1699. 1 lf. torn, bkplt. mntd. on verso of title. Blind-tooled cf. [Wing A1224] (S. Nov.18; 635)   *Rock.* £240

ALLOM, F. & Reeve, E.
– Character & Costume in Turkey & Italy. ca. 1840. Fo. Lacks 3 plts., 1 loose & trimmed. Orig. cl., worn, crudely rebkd. (SH. Nov.7; 500)   *Fairburn.* £80

ALLOM, Thomas
– Ansichten von Tyrol. ca. 1830. A few plts. slightly spotted. Cont. roan. (S. Nov.4; 592)   *Maggs.* £100
– Forty-Six Views of Tyrolese Scenery. N.d. 4to. Some spotting. Orig. embossed cl., worn. (S. Dec.8; 214)   *Traylen.* £100
– France Illustrated. L. & Paris, ca. 1850. 4to. Lacks ptd. title. Cont. hf. leath. gt. (D. Dec.11-13; 1308)   DM 480
– [–] – Anr. Edn. N.d. 3 vols. in 1. 4to. Some slight soiling. Cont. diced cf. gt. (SD. Feb.4; 238)   £95
– Views in the Tyrol. L., ca. 1830. 4to. Lightly soiled. Cont. cf. gt. (R. Mar.31-Apr.4; 2685)   DM 950
– – Anr. Edn. L., ca. 1835. 4to. Lightly soiled in parts, mostly at margin. Cont. mor. gt. (HK. Nov.18-21; 1285)   DM 600
– – Anr. Edn. [1836]. 4to. Orig. cl. gt. (SBA. Jul.22; 70)   *Baer.* £150
– – Anr. Copy. 2 plts. defect. Decor. cl. (GM. Apr.30; 706)   £105
– – Anr. Copy. Spotted, dampstains. Cont. hf. cf., worn. (CSK. Feb.6; 44)   £70
– – Anr. Edn. Ca. 1840. 4to. Some foxing. Cont. hf. cf., gt. decor. spine. (TA. Dec.18; 384)   £95
– – Anr. Edn. L., ca. 1850. 4to. Cont. leath., defect., lacks spine. (R. Oct.14-18; 1968)   DM 600
– – Anr. Edn. Ill.:– after Allom. N.d. Spotted. Stitched. (CSK. May 15; 76)   £95

ALLOM, Thomas
*See–*BEATTIE, William
*See–*BRAYLEY, Edward Wedlake & Britton, John
*See–*CARNE, John
*See–*NOBLE, Thomas & Rose, Thomas
*See–*ROSE, Thomas
*See–*WALSH, Rev. Robert
*See–*WRIGHT, Rev. George Newnham

ALLOM, Thomas & Bartlett, William Henry
– Devonshire Illustrated. 1829. Many views not collated. Rebnd., foxed. (LA. Mar.5; 59)   £135
– – Anr. Copy. 4to. Vig. title defect. Cont. bds. with leath. backstrip, worn. (TA. May 21; 493)   £56

ALLOM, Thomas & Reeve, Emma
– Character & Costume in Turkey & Italy. [1839]. 4to. Cont. mor., covers blind-tooled, gt. ornament. Signet Liby. bkplt. (C. Jul.15; 1)   *Taylor.* £150

ALMA ESPAÑOLA
Madrid, 1903-4. 23 issues. Linen. (DS. Apr.24; 1045)   Pts. 20,000

ALMAIN Armourer's Album
Ed.:– Viscount Dillion. 1905. Fo. Vell., gt., dampstained. (CE. Nov.20; 30)   £90
– – Anr. Copy. Orig. vell. gt. (SBA. Jul.22; 168)   *Way.* £50

ALMALIK, Abraham
– Likutei Shikcha U'Peah. Ferrara, 1556. 1st. Edn. 4to. Stained, worming, owners' sigs. on title. Hf. cl. (SPB. May 11; 20) $2,300

ALMANAC OF TWELVE SPORTS
*See–*KIPLING, Rudyard

ALMANACS (Chronologically)
– Almanach Royal. Paris, 1727. Cont. red mor., gt., gt. arms. (SM. Oct.8; 2102)   Frs. 1,900
– – Anr. Edn. Paris, 1729. Cont. red mor., gt., wide borders round Louis XV arms. (SM. Oct.8; 2383)   Frs. 1,200
– Almanach Royal. Année Bissextile. Paris, 1764. 1 lf. detchd. Cont. red mor., triple gt. fillet around covers, spine with raised bands & fleurs-de-lys, gold paper end-papers, arms of Marquis de Villevault, bdg. slightly defect. Bkplt. of Larcher. (HD. Feb.27; 2)   Frs. 1,550
– Almanachs Iconologiques. Ill.:– after Gravelot et Cochin. Paris, 1764-81. 12 vols. (of 17). 18mo. Cont. red mor., decor. spines, inner dentelles, 3

fillets, some bdgs. worn. (HD. Apr.8; 39)   Frs. 4,500
– Almanach Royal. 1767. Cont. red mor. by Dubuisson, gt. plaque & arms of Rouillé de Jouy on covers, spine with raised bands & fleurs-de-lys, gold paper end-papers, minor repairs. (HD. Feb.27; 3)   Frs. 5,800
– Almanach Royal 1769. [1768]. Sm. 18mo. Cont. red mor., covers decor. with mor. spangles, gt. semé, central medallion with coat of arms of Noailles, doubls. & watered silk end-ll. (HD. Apr.8; 30)   Frs. 2,100
– Almanacks for 1769. L., 1769. 17 Pts. in 1 vol. Cont. Engl. mor. gt., spine tooled in compartments, covers with elab. pattern. (S. Nov.24; 7)   *Traylen.* £140
– Almanach Géographique, ou Petit Atlas Elémentaire. Paris, 1770. 18mo. Cont. red mor., decor. spine, 3 fillets, inner dentelles. (HD. Apr.8; 19)   Frs. 1,400
– Almanach Royal. Paris, 1773. Cont. mor., gt. plaque, centre arms, decor. spine raised bands, fleurs-de-lys. (HD. Apr.24; 24)   Frs. 13,000
– – Anr. Edn. Paris, 1780. Cont. red mor., back decor. with fleurs-de-lys, gt. roll-stp., arms in centre of covers, inside dentelle. (HD. Dec.5; 2)   Frs. 4,500
– – Anr. Edn. Paris, [1781]. Light foxing & spotting, later owner's inscr. Cont. red mor., gt. fleurs-de-lys in spine panels & corners, gt. arms. (SM. Oct.8; 2384)   Frs. 3,000
– Almanach Anacréontique, ou Les Ruses de l'Amour. Ill.:– Queverdo. Paris, [1783]. Sm. 18mo. Cont. decor. cl. From the liby. of Henri Lavedan. (HD. Apr.8; 7)   Frs. 2,600
– Almanach Royal. Année Bissextile. Paris, 1784. Cont. red mor., gt. plaque by Dubuisson on covers, spine with raised bands & fleurs-de-lys, watered silk end-papers, inside dentelle. Bkplt. of Larcher. (HD. Feb.27; 4)   Frs. 5,800
– Almanach Royal. Paris, [1784]. Cont. red mor., covers decor. with lge. gt. plaque, mosaic arms of Reynaud de Monts, fleurs-de-lys on spine, inside dentelle, stain on upr. cover. (HD. Mar.18; 2)   Frs. 3,300
– Almanach Royal. Année 1785. Paris, [1784]. 18mo. Cont. red mor., lge. gt. motif on covers with central medallion of mor. decor. with sm. flower. (HD. Apr.8; 31)   Frs. 3,000
– Almanach Royal. Paris, 1786. Cont. red mor. gt., stpd. with plaque arms of Mesdames de France in centre of covers, fleur-de-lys in corners & compartments of spine, silk liners, 1 corner torn. (SBA. May 27; 137)   *Davisson.* £230
– Almanach Royal, année 1787. Paris, [1786]. 18mo. Cont. red mor., decor. spine, 3 fillets on covers, centre arms of the Duke of Penthièvre, doubls. & end-papers watered silk. (HD. Apr.8; 32)   Frs. 1,900
– Almanach Royal. Paris, 1787. Cont. red mor., gt. plt. by Dubuisson on covers, spine with raised bands & fleurs-de-lys, watered silk end-papers. Bkplt. of Larcher. (HD. Feb.27; 5)   Frs. 4,800
– – Anr. Edn. Paris, [1788]. 18mo. Cont. Fr. red mor., gt. sides with plaque central medallion, silk liners. (SM. Oct.8; 2386)   Frs. 1,300
– Almanach. [1788]. Cont. kid, gt. decor. covers in rocaille style, lge. centre motif on each cover. (HD. Apr.10; 187)   Frs. 1,800
– – Anr. Edn. Amst., 1789. 3½ × 3 inches. 3½ × 3 inches. Orig. wallet-type vell., ptd. in red on upr. & lr. covers. (CSK. Oct.17; 184)   £70
– [–] – Anr. Edn. Ill.:– Queverdo. [1790]. Lacks title. Cont. kid, covers gt. & painted in var. cols. (HD. Apr.8; 5)   Frs. 2,400
– Almanach Royal. Paris, 1790. L.P. red mor., gt. fillet borders, angle fleurs-de-lys, centre arms, limp decor. spine, wtrd. silk end-ll. (HD. Apr.24; 28)   Frs. 5,000
– Almanach National de France, année 1793. Paris, [1792]. 18mo. Cont. red mor., gt. decor. covers, watered silk end-ll., doubls., inner dentelles. (HD. Apr.8; 23)   Frs. 1,300
– Almanach Pacifique, ou l'Ecole de la Vertu. Paris, [1792]. Sm. 18mo. 11 cold. figures. Cont. red mor., plts. covers decor. with lge. frame gt. with central medallion surrounding ribbon representing a heart with 'Agréable à tous' motto. (HD. Apr.8; 25)   Frs. 2,300
– – Anr. Copy. Cont. kid, spine & covers decor. gt. and cold. (HD. Apr.8; 24)   Frs. 1,000
– – Anr. Edn. Paris, [1795]. 18mo. Cont.silk, covers & spine gt. decor. (HD. Apr.8; 26)   Frs. 3,300

– Berlinischer Almanach. Ill.:– M.S. Lowe. Berlin, [1795]. 32mo. Considerable foxing. Loose in pict. wraps., spine torn. (SG. Feb.5; 36) $100

– Almanach des Folies de l'Amour ou le Tribut de l'amitié au Beau Sexe. Ill.:– Dorgez. Paris, [1796]. 18mo. Cont. mor., gt. decor. (HD. Apr.8; 15) Frs. 2,400

– London Almanack for the Year 1807. [1806]. 57 mm. × 31 mm. Orig. red mor. gt., in similarly decor. s.-c. (SH. Mar.19; 190) *Till.* £85

– – **Anr. Copy.** 2.25 × 0.6 inches. Cont. red mor. with leath. onlays on covers, stpd. & ruled in gt., in matching s.-c. (CSK. Jun.26; 96) £70

– Almanach Impérial. 1809. Cont. str.-grd. red mor., gt. roll-stps. around covers, smooth decor. spine, watered silk end-papers, inside dentelle, arms glued on lr. cover, stain on upr. cover, slightly disbnd. (HD. Feb.27; 64) Frs. 2,000

– Almanachs de la Cour, de la Ville, et des Départements. Paris, 1810-1848. 26 vols. Most in cont. cold. paper bds., s.-c.'s. (HD. Apr.8; 35) Frs. 2,400

– Almanach Impérial. 1811. Cont. str.-grd. red mor., gt. roll-stps. around covers, arms of Savary, Duc de Rovigo, smooth decor. spine, watered silk end-papers, inside dentelle, bdg. slightly defect. (HD. Feb.27; 65) Frs. 8,500

– – **Anr. Edn.** Paris, 1811-1824. 5 vols. 18mo. Cont. red str.-grd. mor., fillet on covers, s.-c. (HD. Apr.8; 34) Frs. 1,000

– – **Anr. Edn.** 1812. Cont. str.-grd. red mor., gt. roll-stps. around covers, crowned cypher of Eugène de Beauharnais, smooth decor. spine. (HD. Feb.27; 66) Frs. 4,000

– Longworth's American Almanack, New-York Register, & City Directory. N.Y., 1812-1842. 31 vols. 16mo. & 12mo. Unif. linen, ex-liby. (SG. Mar.5; 281) $1,600

– Almanach Impérial. Paris, 1813. L.P. Cont. long-grd. mor., gt. fillets & roulettes border, centre arms, limp decor. spine, inner dentelle, watered silk end-ll. (HD. Apr.24; 116) Frs. 3,000

– London Almanack for the Year 1814. [1813]. 58mm.×31mm. Orig. red mor. gt. with onlays, in similarly decor. s.-c. (SH. Mar.19; 191) *Fletcher.* £140

– Almanachs dédiés aux Dames. Paris, 1816-18-19-23. 4 vols. 16mo. Each vol. contains several engrs. & pp. of music. Cont. cfs., spines decor., gt. fillet on covers, inner dentelles. (HD. Apr.8; 36) Frs. 1,300

– Almanach des Modes, suivi de l'Annuaire des Modes. Ill.:– Blanchard. Paris, 1817. 4th Year. 16mo. Cont. red str.-grd. mor., gt. decor. spine & gt. roulettes on covers, s.-c. (HD. Apr.8; 16) Frs. 1,100

– Almanach Royal. Paris, 1817. Cont. red mor., gt. roll-stp. around covers, crowned cypher, smooth decor. spine. (HD. Feb.27; 67) Frs. 2,000

– Almanach Royal d'Hayti pour l'Année 1818. Sans-Souci, [1817]. Lacks blank at end. Parch.-bkd. bds. [Sabin 29567] (SPB. Jun.22; 66) $125

– Almanachs Lilliputiens. Ca. 1820. 5 vols. 128mo. Cont. unif. red or green mor., 1 with s.-c. (HD. Apr.8; 40) Frs. 2,000

– Almanach des Spectacles, par K.Y.Z. Paris, [1823]. 32mo. Engraved title with cold. vig., 9 hand-cold. engraved plts. Orig. decor. bds., s.-c. (SG. Oct.9; 15) $250

– Almanach de Gotha. 1824-28, 1830, 1832-36, 1838, 1842, 1844, 1849, 1850, 1852-55, 1857-61, 1863-68. 31 vols. Publisher's cl. & bds. (HD. Jun.29; 79) Frs. 2,250

– Almanach Royal. Paris, 1828. Cont. red mor., gt. roll-stp. & fillets around covers, fleurs-de-lys in corners, arms of Duchesse de Berry, smooth decor. spine, watered silk end-papers, inside roll-stp., bdg. slightly defect. From liby. of Palais Royal. (HD. Feb.27; 68) Frs. 4,000

– Almanak, Overijsselsche, voor Oudheid en Letteren. Deventer, 1836-55. 19 vols. Mod. hf.-cl. Not collated, w.a.f. (VG. Nov.18; 779) Fls. 850

– Schloss English Bijou Almanack. [1837]. 20mm. × 14mm. Sm. hole in 1 lf. Orig. roan gt. with onlays, in similarly decor. s.-c. with onlays, in orig. roan fitted case. (SH. Mar.19; 182) *Till.* £120

– – **Anr. Edn.** Ill.:– L[etitia] E[lizabeth] L[ondon]. [1838]. 20mm. × 14mm. Orig. roan gt. with onlays, in similarly decor. s.-c., in orig. roan fitted case with magnifying glass. (SH. Mar.19; 183) *Till.* £170.

– – **Anr. Edn.** [1839]. 20mm. × 14mm. Orig. roan gt. with onlays, in similarly decor. s.-c., in orig.

roan fitted case, with magnifying glass. (SH. Mar.19; 184) *Till.* £140

– – **Anr. Copy.** 0.8 × 0.6 inches. Orig. bds., rebkd., s.-c., magnifying glass, in fitted silk & velvet lined mor. box. (CSK. Nov.7; 63) £120

– – **Anr. Copy.** 20 × 15 mm. Orig. roan gt., roan onlays, orig. roan s.-c., lacks magnifying glass. Miniature Book. (SH. Dec.12; 546) *Till.* £70

– – **Anr. Copy.** 20 × 14mm. Orig. red roan gt., onlaid centrepieces on covers, decor. s.-c., worn. Miniature Book. (SH. Dec. 12; 547) *Till.* £50

– – **Anr. Edn.** [1840]. 20 × 14mm. Orig. red mor. gt. with onlays, lacks s.-c., in orig. roan fitted case with magnifying glass. (SH. Mar.19; 185) *Till.* £120

– – **Anr. Edn.** [1844]. 28 × 17mm. Orig. ptd. wraps., upr. cover loose, metal case. Miniature Book. (SH. Dec.12; 544) *Till.* £80

– London Almanack. [1854]. 58mm × 33mm. Orig. mor. gt., onlays, in similarly decor. s.-c. Inscr.: 'To the beloved Queen, from her true and devoted Friend and Cousin, Victoria, January 1st 1855'. (SH. Mar.19; 193) *Till.* £190

– – **Anr. Edn.** [1855]. 58mm. × 32mm. Orig. red mor. with mor. onlays, in similarly decor. s.-c. (SH. Mar.19; 194) *Fletcher.* £130

– Almanach. N.d. Sm. 18mo. Lacks title. Cont. mor., covers decor. with gt. motif, central motif of red mosaic in medallion. (HD. Apr.8; 6) Frs. 1,400

See–GREENAWAY, Kate

ALMEIDA, Manoel Angelo
– Declamacaõ Moral, que na occasiam da Rogativa, que fez a Veneravel Ordem Terceira do Carmo da Bahia. Lisbon, 1736. Sm. 4to. Some worming affecting text. Mod. qtr. cf. (SPB. May.5; 62) $125

ALMON, John
– The Remembrancer, or Impartial Repository of Public Events. L., Priv. ptd., 1775-1780. Vol. 1 from 2nd. edn. 10 vols. (I-X). 8vo.; vol. I larger. Disbnd., ex-liby. (SG. Mar.5; 5) $180

ALPHABET & Image–IMAGE
1946-52. Nos. 1-8; nos. 1-8. 4to. Orig. wraps., few slightly worn. (SKC. May.19; 124) £70

ALPHABET-FLORE . . . composé des plus belles fleures.
Ed.:– Fleur Chavant. Ill.:– P.J. Redoute & Chirat. Paris, n.d. Sm. fo. Some soiling & spotting. Cont. mor.-bkd. cl., recased, orig. wrap., title bnd. in but cropped. (CSK. Sep.12; 207) £120

ALPHABETICAL LADDER
ca. 1815. 16mo. Lacks title, presumably on orig. upr. cover., 1 short tear reprd. Paper wraps., fitted case. (SH. Mar.19; 10) *Cetus.* £120

ALPHABETUM HEBRAICUM Utilissima Hebraice Discere Cupentibus
Venice, Aldus Manutius, 1500-01. Slight soiling. Mod. vell., soiled. (SPB. May 11; 27) $2,200

ALPHABETUM IBERICUM, sive Georgianum, cum Oratione Dominicali Salutatione Angelica
Rome, 1629. Some browning. 19th. C. bds., unc., s.-c. (S. Apr.29; 362) *Brill.* £130

ALPHAND, A.
– Les Promenades de Paris. Paris, 1867-1873. 2 vols. Fo. Some ll. spotted. Loose in orig. mor.-bkd. cl. portfo. (SH. Mar.5; 3) *Weinreb.* £250

ALPHEN, P. von
– Kaert-Boek, waer in de XVII Nederlandse Provincie, door 47, curieuse Kaerte verthoont word. Rotterdam, 1691. Ink writing on verso of 1st. 5 maps, lacks 1 map. Cont. leath. (R. Oct.14-18; 1522) DM 1,800

ALPHERAKY, Sergius
– The Geese of Europe & Asia. Ill.:– P.P. Sushkin (frontis), F.W. Frohawk (plts.). 1905. 4to. Title & preface loose. Orig. cl. (S. Jun.1; 55) *Old Hall Books.* £180

ALPINE PLANTS
Ed.:– David Wooster. 1874. Vol. 1: 2nd. Edn; vol. 2: 1st. Edn. 2 vols. 4to. Orig. cl. (CSK. Oct.3; 139) £85

ALPINUS, Prosperus
– De Medicana Aegyptiorum . . . & Iacobi Bontii . . . De Medicina Indorum. Paris, 1646. 4to. Several ll. stained in inner margins. 18th. C. vell. bds., sig. of Richard Frewin on front free end-paper. (S. Jun.29; 307) *Weiner.* £65

– De Plantis Aegypti. Venice, 1592. 2 pts. in 1 vol. 4to. Cont. vell. From Chetham's Liby., Manchester. (C. Nov.26; 11) *Junk.* £350

– De Plantis Exoticus. Venice, 1656. 3rd. Edn. 4to. Engraved title slightly soiled. 19th. C. hf. mor. From Chetham's Liby., Manchester. (C. Nov.26; 12) *Junk.* £340

– Medicina Aegyptiorum accessit . . . Liber de Balsamo et Rhapontico ut et Jacobi Bontii Medicina Indorum. Leiden, 1745. New Edn. 2 pts. in 1 vol. 4to. A few ll. slightly dampstained. Cont. mott. cf., spine gt. (S. Feb.23; 4) *Frick.* £50

ALTEN, Johann Wilhelm von
– Systematische Abhandlung uber die Erd–und Flussconchylien welche um Augsburg . . . Augsburg, 1812. Ex-liby copy, stps. on verso of title-p. & plts. Recent cl. (TA. Sep.18; 28) £60

ALTMANN, J.G.
[–] **L'Etat et Délices de la Suisse.** Basle, 1776. New Edn. 4 vols. Later mott. cf. gt., Rosebery monogs. in gt. on covers. (SBA. Jul.23; 422) *Maurer.* £2,200

[–] – **Anr. Copy.** 12mo. Directions to binder bnd. in at end of vol. 4, slight offsetting. Cont. mott. cf. gt., worn. (SBA. Dec.16; 46) *Baer.* £1,600

ALTWOOD, G.
– Treatise on the Rectilinear Motion & Rotation of Bodies; with a Description of Original Experiments. Camb., 1784. 1st Edn. Some spotting. 19th C. hf. mor. Bkplt. of Sir Andrew Noble. (S. Apr.6; 207) *R.E. & G.B. Way.* £100

ALUNNO, Francesco
– Le Ricchezze della Lingua Vulgare. Venice, 1544. 1st. Edn. Fo. Slight browning & soiling, inscrs. on title. Early 19th. C. parch.-bkd. bds., soiled. From liby. of André L. Simon. (S. May 18; 16) *Zeitlin.* £180

ALVAREZ, Francisco
– Noticia del Establecimiento y Poblacion de las Colonias Inglesas en la America Septentrional. Madrid, 1778. Sm. 4to. Owner's inscr. on p. 7. Cont. cf., slightly worn. [Sabin 975] (SPB. May 5; 63) $325

ALVAREZ, R. & Grediaga, I.G.
[–] **Guia de Neuva York para Uso de los Espagnoles e Hispano-Americanos . . .** N.Y., Priv. ptd., 1863. 1st Edn. Lge. folding map (copyrighted 1857 by Humphrey Phelps) tipped-in at hf.-title, imprint has advt. for Spanish hotel mntd. over it. Orig. gt. cl. (PNY. Mar.26; 232) $160

ALVAREZ DE ABREU, Antonio Joseph
– Victima Real Legal . . . sobre que las Vacantes Mayores y Menores de las Iglesias de las Indias Occidentales. Madrid, 1769. Fo. Recent inscr. on title, sm. marginal stain. Cont. cf., worn. [Sabin 76] (SPB. May 5; 64) $100

ALVAREZ DE COLMENAR, Juan
– Annales d'Espagne et de Portugal. Amst., 1741. 4 vols. 4to. Slightly soiled. Cont. hf. leath. (R. Oct.14-18; 2047) DM 1,700

– Les Delices de l'Espagne & du Portugal. Leiden, 1707. Vols. I & II in 1 vol. Lightly browned, 1 copper engr. reprd., 2 with sm. tears. Cont. cf., spine torn. (H. Dec.9/10; 636) DM 520

– – **Anr. Edn.** Leiden, 1715. New Edn. Plts. mostly browned, 1 plt. with sm. hole. Cont. leath., 1 cover loose. (R. Oct.14-18; 2046) DM 1,700

ALVORD, Thomas G., Jnr.
– Paul Bunyan, & Resinous Rhymes of the North Woods. 1934. (332) numbered, & sigd. Gt.-decor. cl. Full-p. inscr. in upr. cover by H.G.P., & laid in is rhymed Xmas card from Susan & Harold Pickering. (SG. Dec.11; 209) $500

– – **Anr. Edn.** 1934. (166) numbered. Gt.-decor. cl., writing & crayon drawing in upr. cover. (SG. Dec.11; 208) $110

AMADIS des Gaules
Amst., 1750. 4 vols. 12mo. Some spotting. Cont. marb. cf., decor. spines. (SM. Feb.11; 41) Frs. 1,200

AMALGAMATED COTTON MILLS Trust Limited
– Concerning Cotton, a Brief Account of the Aims & Achievements . . . 1920. (6) specially bnd. 4to. Red lev. mor., covers with gt. scroll panel & rose cornerpieces enclosing elab. gt. inner foliate border, spine gt. in compartments with mor. onlay centrepieces, raised bands, inner dentelles, silk doubls. & end-papers by Zaehnsdorf for The Rt.

AMALGAMATED COTTON MILLS Trust Limited . . .-contd.
Hon. Sir Henry Dalziel Bart. (C. Jul.22; 185)
Joseph. £160

AMAT Y JUNIENT, Manuel de
- Ordenanzas del Monte Pio de Militares del Perú . . . Ordenanzas de S.M. sobre Prohibicion des Casamientos de Oficiales. [Lima], [1772]. Sm. 4to. Wormhole just touching surface of woodcut coat of arms. Disbnd. (SPB. May 5; 65) $200
- Reglamento para el Gobierno de la Aduana de esta Cuidad, y el Metodo de Recaudación, y Administración de los Reales Derechos de Almoxarifazgo, y Alcabala del Reyno del Peru. Lima, 1773. Sm. 4to. Limp vell. (SPB. May 5; 66) $300

AMATEUR BOOK COLLECTOR, The
Sep., 1950-Jul./Aug., 1976. Vol. I, no. 1-Vol. XXVI, no. 6; 26 vols. (compl.) & some indices. Fo. & 4to. 7 or 8 ll. flecked, 1 severely. Vols. I-XV bnd. in 12 in hf. (artificial?) mor., rest in wrappered pts. as iss. (KH. Mar.24; 59) Aus. $240

AMATI, Carlo
- Regole del Chiar-oscuro in Architettura. Milan, 1802. Fo. Slight spotting. Cont. bds. (S. Jun.22; 1) *Quaritch.* £65

AMATI, G.
- Ricerche Storico-critico-scientifiche sulle Origini, Scoperte, Invenzioni e Perfezionamenti fatti nelle Lettere, nelle Arti e Nelle Scienze con alcuni Tratti Biografici. Mailand, 1823-30. 5 vols. 4to. Cont. red mor., gt. spine, cover & outer dentelle, marb. paper end-ll. (HK. Nov.18-21; 1440) DM 850

AMBRONN, L.
- Handbuch der Astronomische Instrumentenkunde. Berlin, 1899. 4to. Orig. linen. (H. Dec.9/10; 298) DM 500

AMBROSE, Saint, Bp. of Milan
- Liber de Helia et Jeiunio. In q[uo] Ieiunii ac Sobrietatis Virtute[m] Execllenter com[m]e[n]dat: Ebrietatisq[ue] et gule Vitium arguta Disputatione condemnat: feliciter incipit. [Cologne], [Probably after 1500]. 1st. Edn. Sm. 4to. Slight browning, sm. wormhole slightly affecting text. Mod. pol. cf. by Rivière, spine gt. Bkplt. of Michael Tomkinson, Franche Hall, Worcestershire; from liby. of André L. Simon. (S. May 18; 17) *Otto.* £1,100

AMEDEO, H.R.H. Luigi of Savoy
- On the 'Polar Star' in the Arctic Sea. 1903. 2 vols. Orig. bdg. (TRL. Dec.10; 19) £58

AMERBACH, V.
- Libri Sex, de Philosophia Naturali. Basel, [1549]. Title stpd., MS owner's mark. inside cover of Marcus Fugger. Cont. blind-tooled cf. gt., corner fleurons, centrepiece, upr-cover loose, slightly defect. (HK. May 12-14; 70) DM 700

AMERICAN ART-UNION
See-APOLLO Art-Union-AMERICAN Art-Union

AMERICAN BOOK PRICES Current
N.Y., 1923-71. 47 vols. (including indexes for 1916-22 & 1933-40). Cl. (SG. Jan.22; 10) $550
- - Anr. Edn. N.Y., 1929-31; 1939; 1964; 1965; Index 1933-40; 1950-65. Together 9 vols. (6 & 3) Orig. cl. (CNY. May 22; 21) $320
- - Anr. Edn. N.Y., 1943-65. Together 23 vols. Buckram, d.-w.'s. (SG. Oct.2; 6) $350
- - Anr. Edn. N.Y., 1979. Vol. 84. Orig. cl. (CSK. Apr.10; 99) £55

AMERICAN ENCYCLOPAEDIA OF PRINTING
Ed.:– J. Luther Ringwalt. Phila., 1871. 1st Edn. 4to. Gt-pict. cl., torn, loose. (SG. Oct.2; 9) $140

AMERICAN ETCHERS
N.Y., [1929-31]. De Luxe Edn., (75) with orig. sigd. etching. 12 vols. 4to. Cl., orig boxes brkn. Notarized certificate of authenticity sigd. by Winifred Day loosely inserted in most vols. (SG. Oct.9; 16) $2,400

AMERICAN FISTIANA
N.Y., [1873]. Pict. wraps. (SG. Dec.11; 163) $160

AMERICAN INDUSTRIAL SOCIETY
Documentary History of Ed.:– John R. Commons, U.B. Phillips & others. Cleveland, 1910-11. 11 vols. Cl. (SG. Apr.9; 91) $190

AMERICAN INSTITUTE of Electrical Engineers
- Catalogue of the Wheeler Gift of Books, Pamphlets & Periodicals in the Library. Ed.:– William D. Weaver. N.Y., 1909. 2 vols. Red three-qtr. mor. Inscr. by Weaver. (SG. Jan.22; 20) $150

AMERICAN MAGAZINE & Monthly Chronicle for the British Colonies
[Phila.], 1757. Vol.1, No.2. Disbnd. (SG. Jun.11; 21) $150

AMERICAN Military Pocket Atlas
L., [1776]. 1st. Edn. 6 lge. folding maps, cold. in outl. Unbnd. (SG. Oct.9; 17) $1,200

AMERICAN NUMISMATIC SOCIETY
- Museum Notes. N.Y., 1946-76. Nos. 1-21. Orig. wraps. (SH. Mar.6; 307) *Trade Art.* £220
- Numismatic Literature. N.Y., 1947-77. Nos. 1-98. Unbnd. & orig. wraps. (SH. Mar.6; 308) *Trade Art.* £60
- Numismatic Notes & Monographs.–Annual Meetings. N.Y. 1920-78. Nos. 1-160; 24 vols; together 184. Orig. wraps., a few spines torn. (SH. Mar.6; 309) *Trade Art.* £1,150

AMERICAN PAINTER ETCHINGS
- Ten Original Etchings by the Best American Artists. Ed.:– Walter Rowlands. Boston, [1888]. (215) numbered. Lge. fo. Cl., worn, ex-liby. (SG. May 21; 321) $400

AMERICAN STAR, The
Mexico City, Sep. 23, 1847-Oct. 31, 1847. Vol. I, no. 2-Vol. I, no. 27. 20 issues. Newspaper fo. Some ageing & marginal fraying. Loose as iss. (PNY. Mar.26; 210) $1,300

AMERY, L.S.
- The Times History of the War in South Africa. 1899-1900. L., 1900. 7 vols. Lacks map in vol. 4. Orig. bdg. (VA. Oct.31; 44) R.210
- - Anr. Edn. 1900-1909. Vols. I-VII. Cl. (SSA. Jun.18; 39) R.160

AMES, Joseph
- Catalogue of the Genuine & Entire Collection of Scarce Printed Books & Curious Manuscripts. Langford, 1760. B4 misbnd. after C4, about half of prices & buyers' names in MS. Cont. hf. sheep. (SM. Oct.7; 1302) Frs. 1,800

AMES, Joseph & Herbert, William
- Typographical Antiquities. 1785. 3 vols. 4to. Frontis. re-mntd. Later hf. mor. (TA. Sep.18; 48) £120
- - Anr. Edn. 1785-90. 3 vols., 4to. No list of subscribers. 19th. C. hf. cf. (S. Sep.29; 2) *Quaritch.* £120
- - Anr. Edn. Ed.:– Thomas Frognall Dibdin. L., 1810-19. 1st. Edn. 4 vols. 4to. 19th C. hf. mor., spines gt. (S. Nov.24; 8) *Dawson.* £450

AMES, Richard
- The Search After Claret; or, a Visitation of the Vintners . . . 1691. 1st. Edn. Sm. 4to. Slight browning & soiling. Mod. pol. hf. cf. by Rivière, spine gt. From liby. of André L. Simon. [Wing A2989] (S. May 18; 18) *Overton.* £500

AMICI, Domenico
- Nuova Raccolta dei Monumenti Antichi dell' alma Citta di Roma. 1823. Ob. fo. Last 2 plts. cleanly cut, spotting. Orig. wraps. (CSK. Jun.5; 155) £50
- Raccolta delle Principali Vedute di Roma. Rome, 1835. Ob. 4to. Light foxing, mostly marginal. Vell. gt., soiled, bkplt. (SG. Dec.4; 15) $400
- - Anr. Copy. Cl., spine brkn. (CR. Mar.19; 285) Lire 480,000

AMICIS, Edmondo de
- Holland & Its People. Ill.:– Samuel Colman, & others. N.Y., 1885. Zuyder-Zee Edn. (600) numbered. 4to. Some foxing. Gt.-pict. cl. (SG. Nov.20; 360) $200

AMINSON, Henrico
- Bibliotheca Templi Cathedralis Strengnesensis. Stockholm, 1863. 2 vols. Ptd. wraps., unc., unopened, a little worn. (SG. Oct.2; 12) $150

AMIS
- Of the Friendship of Amis & Amile. Trans.:– William Morris. Kelms. Pr., 1894. (500). 16mo. Orig. holland-bkd. bds., unc. (SH. Feb.19; 5) *Pickering.* £65
[-] - Anr. Edn. Trans.:– William Morris. [Kelms. Pr.]. [1894]. [(515)]. 16mo. Orig. cl.-bkd. bds. (CSK. Apr.3; 76) £100

AMMANN, Johann
- Stirpium Rariorum in Imperio Rutheno. St. Petersb., 1739. 4to. Lacks plt. no. 16. Cont. cf., rebkd. From Chetham's Liby., Manchester. (C. Nov.26; 13) *Weldon & Wesley.* £70

AMMAN, Jost
- Kunst-Buchlein. [1599]. Sm. 4to. 222 woodcuts inlaid to size, slightly worn, lacks title. Mor. gt., Stirling Maxwell arms on covers, slightly worn. As a collection of prints, w.a.f. (BS. Jun.11; 302) £600

AMMAN, Jost & Modius, Fr.
- Cleruis Iotius Romanae Ecclesiae subiecti. Frankfurt, 1585. 4to. Hf. leath., defect., leath. very brkn., cover loose. (HK. Nov.18-21; 102) DM 800

AMMIANUS Marcellinus
- The Roman Historie . . . Trans.:– Phileman Holland. 1609. 1st. Edn. in Engl. 3 pts. in 1 vol., Fo. Slight browning & soiling, 1 or 2 sm. holes slightly affecting text. Cont. limp vell. [NSTC 71311] (S. Sep.29; 54) *Fletcher.* £100

AMMIRATO, Scipione
- Opuscoli. Flor., 1640-37-42. 1st. Edn., L.P. 3 vols. 4to. Bibliotheca Colbertina inscr. on titles. Early 18th. C. red mor., arms of Count Hoym, triple gt. fillet, later 'ED.' gt. above arms, spine compartments gt. with Hoym cipher. Bkplt. of Marquess of Hertford. (SM. Oct.7; 1537) Frs. 3,800

AMORIS DIVINI EMBLEMATA, Studio et Aere Othonis Vaeni Concinnata
Antw., 1660. 4to. 1 plt. reprd. Old vell., soiled. (TA. Feb.19; 448) £62

AMOS, William
- Minutes in Agriculture & Planting. 1804. Fo. Slight browning. Cont. mott. cf., spine gt. (S. Jun.1; 56) *Traylen.* £110

AMOURS (Les) de Messaline cy-devant Reine de l'Isle d'Albion
Cologne, 1689. 2nd. Edn. 12mo. Red mor., gt., by Duru. (SM. Oct.8; 2229) Frs. 1,000

AMPERE, André Marie
- Mémoire de l'Action Mutuelle de deux Courans électriques. Pans, 1820. 1st. Edn. In Annales de Chimie et de Physique Vol. XV., minimal soiling in parts. Cont. leath., very worn. (HK. May 12-14; 295) DM 780
- Mémoire sur la Determination de la Surface Courbe des Ondes Lumineuses dans un Milieu dont l'Elasticité est Different Suivant les trois Directions Principales. 1828. 1st. Separate Edn. Orig. wraps., unc., inscr. in wrap. Pres. copy, explanatory note in John Carter's hand on envelope. (S. Dec.2; 669) *Quaritch.* £180

AMPUDIA, Pedro de
- El Ciudadano General Pedro de Ampudia ante el Tribunal Respetable de la Opinion Publica, sobre los Primeros Sucesos Ocurridos en la Guerra a que nos Provoca, Decreta, y Sostiene el Gobierno de los Estados-Unidos de America. San Luis Potosi, 1846. 1st. Edn. Ptd. self-wraps., slight wear. (SG. Jan.8; 278) $500

AMPZING, S.
- Beschryvinge ende Lof der Stad Haerlem in Holland. Mitsg. P. Scriverii Laure-Kranz voor Laurens Koster, eerste Vinder vande Boek-Druckerye. Ill.:– J. van Velde after P. Saenredam. Haarlem, 1628. 2 pts. in 1 vol. 4to. Browned, some foxing in places, a few marginal stains. Cont. vell., gt. arms of Haerlem on covers, loose, lacks ties. (VG. Dec.17; 1169) Fls. 3,400

AMSINCK, Paul
- Tunbridge Wells, & its Neighbourhood. 1810. 1st. Edn. 4to. Slight spotting & offsetting. Cont. hf. cf. (S. Jun.22; 2) *Dupre.* £100

AMSINCK, Paul–LEWIS, John
- Tunbridge Wells, & its Neighbourhood.–The History & Antiquities . . . of the Isle of Tenet in Kent. 1810; 1736. 2 works in 2 vols. 4to. 1st. work: some spotting, mainly affecting frontis. & margins of some plts.; 2nd work: slight spotting & staining. 1st. work: cont. cf.; 2nd. work: cont. diced russ. From the collection of Eric Sexton. (C. Apr.16; 208) *Foyle.* £130

AMSTELDAM en Zijne Geschiedenissen in 't kort
Ill.:– Vinkeles after Buys. Amst., 1788-92. L.P. 6

vols. Orig. hf. cf., spines gt. (VG. Oct.13; 8)
Fls. 650

AMSTERDAM
– Verzameling der fraaiste Gezigten van Amsterdam. Amst./Harlingen, 1782. Fo. Lacks plts. 44 & 74. Cont. hf. cf., back gt. (VG. Dec.17; 1580) Fls. 800

AMUNDSEN, Roald
– The North West Passage. 1908. 2 vols. Bdg. not stated. (TRL. Dec.10; 31) £55
– The South Pole. 1913. 2 vols. Orig. cl. (SH. Nov.7; 470) Plant. £100

ANACREON
– Anacreon done into English. Trans.:– Abraham Cowley. Ill.:– Stephen Gooden. Soho, Nones. Pr., 1923. (725) numbered. Vell.-bkd. bds., gt., gt. d.-w., unc. (SG. Jan.15; 59) $140
– Anacreonte tradotto in versi Italiani da varj ... e della Versione Latina. Trans.:– Giosue Barnes. Venice, 1736. 4to. Cont. red mor., triple gt. fillet, flat spine with horizontal gt. borders, inner gt. dentelles of acanthus & fleur-de-lis. Lamoignon copy, bkplt. of Edward Davenport. (SM. Oct.7; 1538) Frs. 1,400
– Odaria. Parma, 1785. (50) on fine paper. 4to. Cont. red mor. by Derome le Jeune with his ticket, gt. border of single fillet terminating with star, spine gt. in compartments, purple silk liners, wide inner dentelle borders. (SM. Oct.7; 1540) Frs. 1,500
– – Anr. Edn. Parma, Bod. Pr., 1791. 16mo. Cont. Italian red mor. gt., covers with ornaments at corners, rounded spine gt. in 6 compartments, hf. mor. s.-c. (CNY. Oct.1; 152) $420

ANACREON–KALLIMACHOS
Ed.:– J.F.Boissonade. Paris, 1823; 1824. 2 works in 2 vols. 24mo. Greek text, Latin notes. Red str-grd. mor. 2 fore-e. pntgs. (SG. Aug.7; 318) $300

ANACREON & others–MUSAEUS
– Traduction Nouvelle en Prose, Suivie de la Veillée des Fêtes de Vénus.–Hero et Léandre; on y a joint la Traduction de Plusieurs Idylles de Théocrite. Trans.:– [Moutonnet Clairfons]. Ill.:– Eisen. Paphos & Paris; Sestos & Paris, 1773; 1774. 1st Printing; on thick paper. 2 works in 1 vol. Red mor. by F. Bedford, lge. dentelle on covers, decor. spine, inside dentelle, watered silk doubls. (HD. Mar.18; 5) Frs. 2,700

ANBUREY, Thomas
[–] **Travels Through the Interior Parts of North America ... By An Officer.** L., 1789. 1st. Edn. 2 vols. Slight foxing, liby. stp. of Middleton Park. Cont. cf.-bkd. bds., worn. From liby. of William E. Wilson; bkplt. of Sarah Sophia Child. [Sabin 1366] (SPB. Apr.29; 6) $500

ANCHAR [Antiar]
Ed.:– [D.G. Chisliev]. St. Petersb., 1906. No. 1 only (of 3). Fo. Unbnd. (SH. Feb.5; 46) De la Casa. £60

ANCIENT IRISH Histories–BOURKE, Ulick, Marquis of Clanricarde
– The Works of Spencer, Campion, Hanmer & Marleburrough.–Memoirs ... Dublin; L., 1809; 1722. L.P. (2nd. edn). 2 vols.; 1 vol. Irish str.-grd. red mor., covers with broad gt.-tooled borders, spines gt. in 6 compartments, silk end-papers, by George Mullen with his ticket (1st. work); & red antique-style mor., gt., with the Gosford crest on covers by Lewis. From the collection of Eric Sexton. (C. Apr.15; 160) Quaritch. £420

ANCILLON, Charles
[–] **Eunuchism Display'd.** 1718. 12mo. Advt. ll., lacks 1st. (?blank) lf., some ll. spotted. Later cf. (SH. Mar.5; 195) Murray Hill. £100

ANCONA, Paolo d'
– La Miniatura Fiorentina. Flor., 1914. (300) 2 vols.: text & plts. Sm. fo. Orig. bd. portfo. & orig. bds. (R. Oct.14-18; 504) DM 700

ANDERSEN, Hans Christian
– The Complete Andersen. Trans.:– Jean Hersholt. Ill.:– Fritz Kredel. Ltd. Edns. Cl., 1949. (1500) numbered & sigd. by Hersholt & Kredel. 6 vols. Tall 8vo. Patterned bds., box. (SG. Apr.2; 163) $150
– – Anr. Copy. Cl.-bkd. patterned bds., orig. box (defect.). (SG. Jan.15; 113) $110

– Contes d'Andersen, Calendrier pour 1912. Ill.:– Heinrich Lefler & Joseph Urban. Vienna, [1911]. 4to. Orig. wraps., decor. d.-w. (SH. Mar.19; 15) Fletcher. £150
– Fairy Tales. Trans.:– Harry Leigh Douglas Ward & Augusta Plesner. Ill.:– Eleanor Verge B[oyle]. 1872. 4to. 1 plt. loose. Orig. red decor. cl. gt., dampstained. (SH. Dec.10; 110) Till. £55
– – Anr. Edn. Ill.:– W. Heath Robinson. 1913. 4to. Orig. pict. cl. gt. (SH. Mar.27; 463) Magee. £70
– – Anr. Edn. Ill.:– W. Heath Robinson. 1913. (100) numbered, sigd. by artist. 4to. Orig. vell. gt. (SH. Mar.27; 462) Joseph. £480
– – Anr. Copy. This copy unnumbered? Stained. (SH. Dec.11; 465) Joseph. £350
– – Anr. Copy. Soiled. (S. Jul.31; 306) Joseph. £280
– – Anr. Edn. Ill.:– Harry Clarke. [1916]. 4to. Cl., preserving orig. pict. label. (SH. Dec.10; 131) Jones. £125
– – Anr. Edn. Ill.:– Kay Nielsen. [1924]. (500) de Luxe, sigd. by artist. 4to. Limitation sheet slightly spotted. Orig. vell. gt. (SBA. Jul.14; 419) Black. £530
– – Anr. Copy. Mor. (SG. Oct.9; 177) $950
– – Anr. Copy. Cl. (SG. Oct.23; 236) $750
– – Anr. Edn. Ill.:– Kay Nielsen. [1924]. 4to. Orig. pict. cl. gt., d.-w. (SH. Mar.27; 383) Fletcher. £250
– – Anr. Edn. Ill.:– Arthur Rackham. 1932. (525) sigd. by artist. 4to. Orig. vell. gt., unopened & unc., s.-c. (C. Jul.22; 96) Wood. £650
– – Anr. Copy. Orig. parch. gt., s.-c. (SH. Mar.27; 443) Black. £490
– – Anr. Copy. Vell., triple fillet gt. border, wrinkled, partly unc. & unopened, orig. publisher's box worn. Raymond M. Sutton, Jr. copy, Gregory Schapiro bkplt. (SG. May 7; 9) $650
– – Anr. Edn. Ill.:– Arthur Rackham. [1932]. 1st. Amer. Trade Edn. 4to. Cl., d.-w. Raymond M. Sutton, Jr. copy. (SG. May 7; 10) $300
– – Anr. Edn. Ill.:– Kay Nielsen. N.d. Ltd. Edn., sigd. by artist. 4to. Orig. vell. gt. (P. Dec.11; 206) Thorp. £320
– – Anr. Copy. Cl. gt., box. (P. Dec.11; 212) Thorp. £210
– – Anr. Copy. Mntd. cold. plts., some spotting in text. Orig. cl. (CSK. Nov.14; 45) £95
– Die Prinzessin und der Schweinhirt. Ill.:– Heinrich Lefler. Vienna, 1897. Fo. Outer title dust-soiled. Lacks ptd. wraps. & portfo. (C. Jul.22; 42a) Maggs. £50
– The Red Shoes. Ill.:– Willi Harwerth. Bristol, 1928. (10) numbered, on H.M.P., sigd. by artist. 12mo. Hand-cold. wood-engrs., 2 extra suites of engrs., cold. & uncold., & orig. watercolour sigd. by artist. Vell., unc. (SG. Oct.23; 157) $850
– La Reine des Neiges, et Quatre Autres Contes. Ill.:– Edmund Dulac. Paris, 1911. (500) numbered, sigd. by artist. 4to. Cont. hf. mor., spine decor. with onlays, slightly worn, orig. wraps. bnd. in, by Samblanx. (S. Jul.31; 205) Mirdam. £190
– Sämmtl. Märchen. Trans.:– J. Reuscher. Ill.:– L. Richter & others Leipzig, 1878. Orig. linen, gt. (HK. May 15; 5050) DM 500
– Sein oder nicht sein. Leipzig, 1857. 3 pts in 1 vol. Soiled. Orig. linen, gt., spine slightly defect. MS. dedication. (HK. May 15; 4064) DM 480
– Stories. Ill.:– Edmund Dulac. 1911. 4to. Mor. gt. (SKC. May 19; 24) £60
– – Anr. Copy. Orig. cl. gt. (SH. Dec.10; 184) Subunso. £50
– – Anr. Edn. Ill.:– Edmund Dulac. 1911. Ltd. De Luxe Edn. sigd. by ill. 4to. Orig. vell. gt., 1 tie detchd. (SBA Jul.22; 190) Jones. £300
– – Anr. Copy. (750) numbered sigd. by ill. (SH. Mar.26; 169) Mirdan. £190

ANDERSEN, Hendrik Christian
– Creation of a World Centre of Communication ... Ernest M. Hébrard, Architect. Paris, 1913. Fo. Occasional spotting. Orig. cl., gt., unc. (S. Jun.9; 68) Quaritch. £90

ANDERSON, Adam
– An Historical & Chronological Deduction of the Origin of Commerce. Ill.:– D. Orme after Stothard (frontis.). 1787-89. 4 vols. 4to. Cont. tree cf. (C. Jul.22; 175) Traylen. £90
[–] **– Anr. Copy.** A few ll. near end of vol. III slightly stained, 1st. map slightly soiled in outer edge, light offsetting. Cont. spr. cf., gt., slight

wear. [Sabin 1382] (S. Jan.26; 230) Traylen. £80

ANDERSON, David
– Canada. 1814. 1st Edn. Folding engraved hand-cold. map torn & neatly reprd. Cont. cl.-bkd. bds., unc., slightly worn. [Sabin 1391] (S. May 5; 238) Crete. £100

ANDERSON, George William
– New Authentic, & Complete Collection of Voyages round The World. Ca. 1780. Fo. 1 plt. torn. Cont. reversed cf., some wear. (TA. Dec.18; 106) £190
– – Anr. Edn. [1784-86]. Fo. Sm. hole in 1 plt. Cont. reversed cf. (SBA. Jul.22; 78) Duran. £280
– – Anr. Copy. Some browning & soiling. Cont. cf., rebkd., worn. (S. Sep.29; 89) Lester. £200
– – Anr. Edn. ca. 1790. Fo. Lacks 1 plt. & has 1 dupl. plt. Diced cf., defect. (P. Sep.11; 296) Walford. £210
– – Anr. Edn. L., ca. 1810. Fo. Lacks final lf., frontis. reprd., title wrinkled, folding map defect., other minor tears & wear at some plt. & text edges. Bdg. not stated, but nearly disbnd. W.a.f. (PNY. May 21; 143) $400
– – Anr. Edn. N.d. Fo. Engraved port., 152 plts. & 1 folding map only. Cf., rebkd., upr. cover detchd. W.a.f. (CSK. Sep.26; 92) £140
– – Anr. Copy. Port. & title preserved, some plts. torn, soiling & browning, a few ll. detchd. Spine only. W.a.f. (CSK. Dec.12; 140) £100

ANDERSON, J. C.
– English Landscape & Views. 1883. Ob. fo. 24 engrs. on India paper. Orig. cl. gt. (P. Mar.12; 39) Henderson. £170

ANDERSON, James
– An Account of the Present State of the Hebrides & the Western Coasts of Scotland. Dublin, 1786. Cont. tree cf., slight wear. (S. Dec.9; 441) Crowe. £140
– Recreations in Agriculture, Natural-History, Arts & Miscellaneous Literature. 1799-1801. 6 vols. Cont. cf., spines gt. (C. May 20; 2) Brooke-Hitchings. £120
– Selectus Diplomatium & Numismatum Scotiae Thesaurus ... Edinb., 1739. Fo. Slight staining on a few ll. Cont. cf., worn. (PD. Aug.20; 74) £80

ANDERSON, John
– Zoology of Egypt. 1898. Vol. 1-Reptilia & Batrachia. 4to. Orig. cl. (TA. Mar.19; 571) £65

ANDERSON, Melville B.
See–DANTE ALIGHIERI–ANDERSON, Melville B.

ANDERSON, Sherwood
– Windy McPherson's Son. N.Y., 1916. 1st Edn. Cl. Sigd., A.L.s. (SG. Jun.4; 5) $240

ANDERSON, William
– Pictorial Arts of Japan. Ca. 1885. Fo. Title-p. & last lf. soiled. Orig. decor. cl. with mor. backstrip, covers detchd. (TA. Sep.18; 138) £60
– – Anr. Edn. L., 1886. 4to. Orig. mor.-bkd. cl. gt. (P. Mar.12; 28) Miles. £75
– – Anr. Copy. Orig. mor.-bkd. cl., rebkd. (SH. Jan.29; 67) Walford. £65
– – Anr. Edn. Boston, 1886. Fo. Disbnd., ex-liby. (SG. Mar.12; 208) $150

ANDERSSON, Charles John
– Notes on the Birds of Damara Land & the Adjacent Countries of South-West Africa. L., 1872. 1st. Edn. Cl. (SSA. Jan.22; 145) R. 160

ANDERTON, Laurence (Pseud.)
See–BRERELEY, John 'Laurence Anderton'

ANDRADE DE FIGUEIREDO, Manuel Carlos de
– Luz da Liberal e Nobre Arte da Cavallaria. Lisbon, 1790. 1st. Edn. 2 Pts. in 1 vol. 4to. 19th. C. cf., sides elab. gt., spine gt. (C. Mar.18; 10) Neidhardt. £3,000
– – Anr. Copy. Fo. Errata lf. Cont. cf. (SPB. Oct.1; 218) $5,250
– Nova Escola para Aprender a Ler, Escrever, e Contar. Lisbon, [1722]. Fo. Cont. mott. cf., spine gt. (SG. May 14; 8) $750

ANDRAL, Gabriel
– Essai d'Hematologie Pathologique. Paris, 1845. 1st. Edn. Later cl. From the Brooklyn Academy of Medicine. (SG. Jan.29; 18) $170

ANDRASY, Emmanuel, Count Mano & others
– Les Chasses et le Sport en Hongrie. Pest, [1857].
Fo. Plts., some spotted. Maroon hf. mor. The
Comte de Beaufort-Schwerdt copy. (SPB.
Oct.1; 84) $1,400

ANDRE, Maj. John
– Andre's Journal: an Authentic Record of the
Movements & Engagements of the British Army in
America, June 1777-November 1778. Ed.:– Henry
Cabot Lodge. Boston, Riverside Pr. 1903. (487).
1st. printing. 2 vols. 4to. Gt.-decor. vell., bkplts.
removed from front free end-papers. Etched plts.
sigd. by artists. (SG. Jan.8; 21) $200

ANDREAE, Antonius
– Quaestiones de Tribus Principiis Rerum
Naturalium (with other tracts). Ed.:– [Thomas
Penketh]. [Padua,] [Laurentius Canozius, de
Lendenaria,] [1475.] 1st Edn. fo. 60 ll. only (of
66), illuminated initial on fo. 1 in green, violet,
gold & blue on burnished ground with decoration
extending into margin, initials & paragraph marks
in red & blue, a few wormholes running thro.-out,
cutting some letters, some ll. marginally stained.
Mod. vell. bds., upr. cover defect. [BMC VII, 908;
HC 990; Goff A588] (S. May 5; 4)   Thorp. £240

ANDREAE, Joannes
– Arbor Consanguineitatis. Ill.:– Hans Baldung
Grien. Nuremb., 18 Jun. 1505. 1st. Edn. 4to.
Some ll. lightly soiled or stained. Incunable wraps.
(HK. Nov.18-21; 103)   DM 1,500
– Hieronymianus. [Cologne], [Conrad Winters de
Hormborch], [9 Aug., 1482]. 1st. Edn. Fo. Lacks
final blank, some stains, sm. holes in 3 ll. 18th. C.
cf., spine gt., worn. Bibliotheca Heberiana stp.
[BMC 1, 249]. (SG. May 14; 9) $900
– Lectura Arboris Diversis . . . Nuremb., Friedrich
Creussner, before 1476. Fo. Initials supplied in
red, initial-strokes supplied in parts in red. Mod.
vell.-bkd. bds., lined with fragments of incunabula
ll. Alfred Ehrman's copy, with his stp. & number.
[BMC II, 448]. (S. Nov.25; 312)   Abrams. £260
– Lecture . . . Super Arboribus Consanguinitatis
. . . Commentary by Henricus Greve. [Leipzig],
[Marin Landsberg], [1492]. Fo. 50-51 lines
commentary round text, 5 woodcuts, 2 full-p. cold.
by cont. hand, initials in red & blue, rubricated
thro.-out. 18th. C. marb. bds., spine & corners
worn. Inscr. by Johannes de Breitenbach of
Leipzig, dtd. 1492. [Hain 1041] (S. Nov.25; 313)
                 Fletcher. £320
– Super Arboribus Consanguinitatis, Affinitatis et
Cognationis Spiritualis. Nuremb., Friedrich
Creussner, 1481. Fo. 3 full-p. woodcuts, 1 chopped
at foot, rubricated thro.-out. Vell. bds. [Goff
A726] (C. Jul.16; 234)   Andreae. £160

ANDREAS
See–BURCHIUS, Lambertus van der–ANDREAS
–JONSTON, John

ANDREAS Ferrariensis
– Exposition Ingeniosa et Accomodata a Nostri
Tepi del xiiii. xv. et xvii Psalmo. Ferrara, 11 Feb.
1513. With 2 last ll. (colophon & blank). 19th. C.
hf. mor. (SI. Dec.3; 20)   Lire 250,000

ANDREINI, Giovanni Battista
– L'Adamo Sacra Rapresentatione. Milan, 1613.
Sm. 4to. Staining thro.-out, some lr. margins
reprd. & some upr. margins trimmed. Mod. cl., cf.
spine. (BS. Jun.11; 15)   £85

ANDRELINUS, Publius Faustus
– De Obitu Caroli Octavi Deploratio. Paris,
[Michel Tholoze], [after 1500?]. 4to. Sm.
woodcut initial capitals. Mor. gt., cover with gt.
arms, by W. Pratt. From the collection of Eric
Sexton. [BMC VIII, 210, C 465, Goff A706]
(CNY. Apr.8; 128) $550

ANDRESEN, Andreas
– Die Deutschen Maler-Radierer d. 19.
Jakrhunderts. Unveranderte Band-Ausg. mit gen.
Register. Leipzig, 1878. 5 vols. Orig. cl. (VG.
Dec.16; 539)   Fls. 480

ANDREW, W.J.
– A Numismatic History of the Reign of Henry I.
1901. Some ll. soiled. Cont. hf. mor. (SH.
Mar.6; 311)   Spink. £50

ANDREWS, Henry C.
– [Coloured Engravings of Heaths]. 1794-98. Fo.
30 hand-cold. plts. only. Hf. russ., covers detchd.
(S. Jun.1; 58)   Carr. £200
– – Anr. Edn. 1802-09. 3 vols. Fo. 212 (of 216)
hand-cold. engraved plts. Cont. Engl. red str.-grd.

mor., sides with gt. & blind-tooled borders &
cornerpieces, gt. arms, spines gt. (C. Jul.15; 164)
                Henderson. £2,100
– Roses, or a Monograph of the Genus Rosa. 1805.
1 vol. only. 4to. 73 hand-cold. engraved plts. (of
129). Cont. cf., gt., rebkd., preserving orig. gt.
spine. W.a.f. (C. Mar.18; 11)   Davidson. £1,900

**ANDREWS, Henry C.–SMITH, Sir James
Edward & Sowerby, James–ANON**
– The Botanist's Repository.–A Specimen of the
Botany of New Holland.–[Spicilegium Botanicum].
1797; 1793; [1792]. 1st. work 1st. Edn. 3 works in
1 vol., 1st. work pt. I (of 10). A few ll. & plts.
loose, 2nd. work: 8 hand-cold. plts. (of 16, lacks
plts. 5-8 & 13-16), lacks text accompanying plts.
5-8 & all text after p. 38; 3rd. work: 23 hand-cold.
plts. (of 24, lacks plt. 8), lacks title. 19th. C. hf.
roan, spine & corners slightly worn. (S. Jun.1; 59)
                McCormick. £300

ANDREWS, J.
– A Collection of Plans of Capital Cities etc.
[1771]. 4to. 41 maps (of 43?), lacks prelims.,
some tears. Cont. cf., worn. W.a.f. (SH.
Jun.18; 181)   Fairburn. £250
– Flower Painting. [1835]. 4to. Hf. cf. (P.
Sep.11; 59)   Nagel. £110

ANDREWS, John & Dury, Andrew
– A Map of the Country Sixty-Five Miles round
London. 1809. Ob. fo., (600 × 870mm).
Hand-cold. engraved key map-frontis. map in 20
engraved sheets, sm. holes in blank surface of last
2 sheets. Orig. stiff wraps., 1 or 2 holes in lr.
wrap., latter soiled, unc., folded. W.a.f. (S.
Nov.4; 327)   Clark. £170
– Topographical Map of the County of Kent. 1769.
Fo. Red hf. mor. gt., stained. W.a.f. (C.
Nov.6; 237)   Cumming. £260
– A Topographical Map of Hartfordshire. ca. 1766.
Fo. Sectional maps cold. in outl. Hf. cf. (P.
Sep.11; 123)   Crowe. £440

ANDREWS, William Loring
– An English XIX Century Sportsman . . . N.Y.,
1906. (32) on Imperial Japan Paper. Bds., d.-w.
J.A. Spoor bkplt. (SG. Apr.9; 330) $260
– New York as Washington Knew It after the
Revolution. Ill.:– Sidney L. Smith. N.Y., 1905.
(135) on Fr. H.M.P. Bds., Spoor bkplt. (SG.
Jan.8; 23) $100
– Paul Revere & his Engravings. Ill.:– E.D.
French (etched title), & Sidney L. Smith. N.Y.,
1901. (135) on Van Gelder paper. Two-tone bds.,
partly unc. Spoor bkplt. (SG. Mar.26; 10) $150

ANDRIVEAU-GOUJON, E.
– Atlas Classique et Universel de Géographie
Ancienne et Moderne. Paris, 1843. Fo. Cont. hf.
leath., a little loose. (SI. Dec.3; 21)   Lire 400,000
– – Anr. Edn. Paris, 1858. Fo. 49 maps, lacks 1, 15
& 27, with 2 additional maps, ob. double-p. ill. of
races, all hand-tinted & cold. in outl., ca. 21×27
inches, a few maps loose. Marb. bds., upr. cover
loose, backstrip reprd. (PWP. Apr.9; 150)
                Can. $140
– Atlas Usuel. Géographie Moderne. Paris, [1850].
Fo. Some maps torn. Hf. cf., defect., loose. W.a.f.
(CR. Mar.19; 286)   Lire 320,000

ANDROUET DU CERCEAU, Jacques
– Livre d'Architecture. Paris, 1648. 2 vols. in 1. Fo.
129 (of 130?) plts. Cont. vell., gt., worn. (S.
Nov.25; 412)   Weinreb. £450
– Les Plus Excellent Bastiments de France. Ed.:–
H. Destailleur. Ill.:– Faure Dujarric. Paris,
1868-70. New Edn. 2 vols. Fo. Cont. hf. mor. (S.
Nov.25; 400)   Duran. £250

ANDRY, Nicolas
– De la Generation des Vers dans le Corps de
l'Homme. Amst., 1701. 12mo. Lge. folding plt.
slightly torn. Cont. cf. (CB. Nov.12; 141)
                Can.$110

ANDUEZA, J.M. de
– Isla de Cuba pintoresca. Ill.:– Aragon after R.
Weis. Madrid, 1841. 1st. Ill. Edn. Spotting, a few
liby. stps. not affecting plts., sm. marginal stain.
Cont. qtr. cf. (SPB. May 5; 68) $750
– – Anr. Copy. Sm. 4to. Lr. corner portion of title
replaced, not affecting text, 3rd. lf. reprd. at
portion of inner margin, light damp-soiling at lr.
blank corners. Mod. cl. gt. (PNY. May 21; 158)
                $220

ANEAU, Bartholomy
[–] Picta Poesis ut Pictura Poesis Erit. Lyons,
1552. 1st. Latin Edn. 19th. C. cf., upr. cover
detchd. (S. Apr.7; 236)   Quaritch. £550

ANECDOTES of Mary; or, the Good Governess
1795. 1st. Edn. 12mo. Last 2 advt. ll. Cont. sheep,
worn. (SH. Jun.4; 105)   Quaritch. £65

ANGAS, George French
– The Kafirs Illustrated. Ed.:– F.R. Bradlow. Cape
Town, 1974. Facs. of Orig. 1849 Edn., De Luxe
Edn., (100) sigd. by ed. Lge. fo. Publisher's hf.
leath. (VA. May 8; 270)   R.220
– – Anr. Copy. (VA. Oct.31; 50)   R.180
– – Anr. Edn. Cape Town, 1974. (950). Lge. fo.
Orig. bdg. (VA. Aug.29; 223)   R.130
– New Zealanders Illustrated. 1846-47. 2 vols. Fo.
Slight tear in plt. 47. Hf. mor. gt. (P. Jul.30; 8)
                Crowe. £1,800
– – Anr. Edn. Wellington etc., 1966. Ltd. facs.
Edn. Fo. Orig. hf. mor., gt. (SH. Nov. 7; 451)
                Way. £70
– South Australia Illustrated. 1967. Facs. Edn.
(1000) numbered. Fo. Orig. qtr. mor. (KH.
Nov.18; 9)   Aus. $450
– – Anr. Copy. Hf. mor., marb. bds., case. (JL.
Jul.20; 706)   Aus. $370
– – Anr. Copy. Bds., hf. mor. (KH. Mar.24; 4)
                Aus. $280

ANGELIS, Paulus de
– Basilicae S. Mariae Maioris de Urbe . . .
Descriptio et Delineatio. Rome, 1621. fo. 36
engraved plts. & plans (of 38, lacks nos. 3 & 35),
3 engraved plts. of a different, slightly smaller
work inserted, ? lacks a1 & b4 (? blank), title
slightly soiled, a few ll. or plts. slightly soiled.
Cont. cf., spine worn. British Museum's stp. &
cancellation stp. on verso of title BM stp. at end.
(S. May 5; 169)   Weinreb. £80

ANGELO, Domenico, 1716-1802
[–] Armes . . . Paris, n.d. 40 engrs., lacks title.
Mor. gt. (P. Jun.11; 341)   Schuster. £200
– The School of Fencing. Ill.:– Hall, Ryland &
others after J. Gwyn. 1765. 1st. Edn. Fo. Reprd.
tear to upr. margin of plt. 28, numeral on plt. 14
altered in ink, light soiling & occasional light
foxing to edges. 19th. C. red hf. mor. From
Chetham's Liby., Manchester. (C. Nov.26; 15)
                Map House. £950
– – Anr. Copy. Ob. fo. Text in Engl. & Fr., lacks 3
plts., Engl. title reprd., a few plts. with sm. holes,
minor marginal tears, some soiling & marginal
staining. Mod. hf. cl. (S. Jan.26; 147)
                Nagel. £320
– – Anr. Edn. 1787. Ob. 8vo. Cf. gt. (P. Nov.13; 8)
                Goddard. £190
– – Anr. Copy. Diced cf., cover detchd. (P.
Sep.11; 297)   Nagel. £130
– – Anr. Copy. Old cf. (HD. Dec.5; 4)   Frs. 1,100

ANGELO, Malevolti
– L'Ecole des Armes. L., 1763. 1st. Edn. Lge. ob.
fo. Cont. style leath. (R. Oct.14-18; 2502)
                DM 4,250

ANGELUS, de Clavasio
– Summa Angelica de Casibus Conscientiae. Ed.:–
[Hieronymous Tornielli]. Chivasso, Jacobinus
Suigus, de Suico, 13 May, 1486. 1st. Edn. 4to.
Spaces for capital initials with guide letters, initials
supplied in red & blue, rubricated in red & blue,
lacks initial blank, R1 torn across & defect.,
some severe dampstaining at end with lr. margin
of fo. 379 restored, v6 torn, paper darkened &
brittle thro.-out. Old qtr. vell. gt. From the
collection of Eric Sexton. [BMC VII, 1111,
A713, HC 5382] (CNY. Apr.8; 36) $1,600
– – Anr. Edn. Nuremb., 28 Aug. 1488. Sm. fo.
Lge. illuminated initial A, painted in gold & cols.
& with extensions to 2 margins on 1st. text lf.,
alternate red & blue rubricated initials thro.-out.
Old vell. (VG. Oct.13; 10)   Fls. 1,600
– – Anr. Edn. Alost, Thierry Martens, 4 Jul. 1490.
Fo. Spaces for initial capitals, at fo. 6r an 8-line
capital A supplied in blue with penwork
elaboration in red, other capitals, initials strokes,
& paragraph marks in red, 1st. p. soiled, & with
inner margin reinforced, 1st. 10 ll. with lr. blank
margins renewed, minor repairs to corners of
folios 89-94, 56 ll. with portion of inner margin
renewed, light dampstains to lr. inner margins
toward end, marginal dampstains to final ll.,
monastic inscrs. on paste-down, fo. 1r & 2r. Cont.
cf. over wood bds., very worn, rebkd. From the

collection of Eric Sexton. [BMC IX, 127, Goff A720, HC 5389] (CNY. Apr.8; 5) $4,400
– – **Anr. Edn.** Venice, Georgius Arrivabenus, 2 May, 1495. 538 ll. (of 540), lacks [-]8 & X8, liby. stp. on title & first few ll. Vell. [HC 5398] (C. Jul.16; 235) *Amman.* £70

ANGER, G.
– **Illustrirte Geschichte der k.k. Osterreichischen Armee.** Vienna, 1888. 3 vols. in 2. Slightly browned, 3 pp. loose vol. 3. Orig. pict. linen. (R. Oct.14-18; 2830) DM 580

ANGHIERA, Pietro Martire d'
– **De Orbe Nouo Decades.** Alcala, 1516. 1st. Compl. Edn. Fo. Iss. without the 'Legatio Babylonica', margin of title reprd. slightly affecting text, sm. wormhole in a2 infilled affecting initial, sm. rust hole in b7 affecting text. Spanish cf., rebkd., covers slightly worn. [Sabin 1550] (C. Nov.20; 174) *Wisbech.* £1,800

ANGLE, Edward H.
– **The Angle System of Regulation & Retention of his Teeth** ... Phila., 1895. 4th. Edn. 11 p. catalogue at end. Cl. From Brooklyn Academy of Medicine. (SG. Jan.29; 118) $150

ANGLERIUS, Petrus Martyr
– **The Historie of the West-Indies, Containing the Actes & Adventures of the Spaniards.** L., [1625]. Title in facs., some staining, soiling. Reversed cf., slightly stained. [STC 651] (SPB. May 5; 69) $375

ANGLO-SAXON Review, The
Ed.:– Lady Randolph Spencer Churchill. 1899-1901. Vols. I-X. (all publd.) Fo. Orig. mor. gt. (SBA. Jul.23; 217) *Maggs.* £70
– – **Anr. Copy.** 4to. (SH. Oct.10; 410) *Van der Peet.* £55

ANGUS, William
– **Seats of the Nobility & Gentry in Great Britain & Wales.** 1787. Ob. 4to. Mor. gt., slightly worn. (BS. Jun.11; 136) £130
– – **Anr. Copy.** Some foxing. Cont. hf. cf. gt. (TA. Nov.20; 431) £110
– – **Anr. Copy.** 62 (of 63) plts., nos. 15, 16, 17, 19, 20 reprd. Cl.-bkd. bds. (P. Sep.11; 285) *Edistar.* £90
– – **Anr. Edn.** 1787-[1815]. Ob. 4to. Some spotting. Cont. hf. cf., worn, upr. cover & spine loose. (S. Apr.7; 446) *Elliott.* £70

ANIANUS, Magister
– **Copotus Novissime Ampliatus (by N. Bonaspes).** Paris, ca. 1512. Lr. fore-corner torn from title-p. with some loss of device, sm. hole & tear in B4, margins of C3 & 4 cut down slightly. 19th. C. vell., slightly soiled. (S. Jul.27; 126) *Rota.* £140

ANIMAUX ENSEIGNEMENT par les yeux, Nouvelles Images à l'usage des Ecoles Maternelles et des Ecoles Elementaires
Paris, n.d. Ob. fo. 50 cold. litho. plts., no titles or text. Orig. ptd. pict. bds., cl.-bkd. W.a.f. (C. Jul.15; 165) *Schuster.* £190

ANIMAUX MUSICIENS, Les
Paris, ca. 1900. 4to. Cl-bkd. bds., lge. pict. label incorporating title on upr. cover. Moving Picture Book. (SH. Dec.12; 580) *Arts Anciens.* £55

ANKER, Jean
– **Bird Books & Bird Art.** Copen., 1938. 4to. Orig. wraps., unc. (C. Mar.18; 165) *Hill.* £90

ANLEY, Heriot
[–] **Collection of 31 botanical Water-Colour Drawings.** Ca. 1830. Ob. 4to. Later hf. cf. (TA. Nov.20; 455) £110

ANNALEN des Wiener Museums der Naturgeschichte
Vienna, 1835-36. 2 vols. 4to. Cont. hf. cf. (S. Mar.17; 232) *Schierenberg.* £85

ANNALES DU MUSEE
1815. 19 vols. including 2 vols. of Paysages, in ll. Cont. hf. cf. (SH. May 21; 3) *Studio Books.* £70

ANNALES DE POMOLOGIE Belge et Etrangère
Brussels, 1860. Year 8. Fo. Some text ll. & approx 10 plts. loose. Liby. linen. (R. Oct.14-18; 2965) DM 3,500

ANNALES des Voyages, de la Géographie et de l'Histoire ...
Ed.:– Conrad Malte-Brun. Paris, 1808-13. Vols. 5-20, together 16 vols. bnd. in 8. Cont. leath.-bkd. hf. cf. (SG. Oct.30; 236) $200

ANNALS of Ireland
Ed.:– John O'Donovan. Dublin, 1856. 2nd. Edn. 7 vols. 4to. Cont. mor., ornamental gt. panel on covers with shamrock cornerpieces, abrasions to some covers. From the collection of Eric Sexton. (C. Apr.16; 321) *Staricoff.* £250

ANNALS OF SPORTING & Fancy Gazette; a magazine entirely appropriated to sporting subjects & fancy pursuits
Ill.:– after Alken, Herring, Cruikshank, Landseer & others. Jan. 1822-May 1828. 13 vols. Occasional minor discolouration & spotting, lacks most hf.-titles & 6 plts. Cont. cf., worn, many covers detchd. W.a.f. as a periodical. (C. Feb.4; 109) *Walford.* £500

ANNAN, Thomas
– **The Old Closes & Streets of Glasgow.** Ed.:– William Young (introduction). Glasgow, 1900. (100) ptd. for Corporation of Glasgow. Fo. Cl., gt. arms, worn. (SG. Apr.23; 12) $2,200

ANNAN, Thomas & R.
– **University of Glasgow, Old & New.** Glasgow, 1891. (350) numbered. Fo. Cl. (SG. Apr.23; 11) $475

ANNE, of Brittany
– **Le Livre d'Heures de la Reine Anne de Bretagne.** Trans.:– L'Abbé Delaunay. Paris, 1841. Facs. reproduction of orig. MS. 2 vols. Fo. Slightly spotted. Mor. (S. Jun.23; 266) *Traylen.* £200

ANNENKOV, Yury
– **¼ Devyatova [Quarter to Ten].** Petrograd, n.d. Orig. wraps. by author. (SH. Feb.6; 378) *Quaritch.* £270

ANNESLEY, George, Viscount Valentia
See– **VALENTIA, George Annesley, Viscount**

ANNIUS, Johannes, of Viterbo
– **Antiquatū variarū volumina.** XVII. [Paris], 10 Oct. 1515. Fo. Slight browning, brief later inscriptions on title. Mod. bds. (S. Oct.21; 519) *D. Vine.* £70

ANNUAL REGISTER, The
1758-1921. 165 vols., including index for years 1758-1819. Hf. cf., most vols. worn, some covers detchd., lacks some labels. W.a.f. (SBA. Jul.23; 424) *Dawson.* £520
– – **Anr. Run.** 1758-1829. Vols. 1-71 with index, lacks vols 6 & 15, together 70 vols. Cont. cf. (SH. Jun.25; 191) *Bunsei.* £180
– – **Anr. Run.** 1758-1826. Vols. 1-68 & General Index for 1758-19. A few minor defects. Cont. tree cf. gt., some worn, a few jnts. torn. As a periodical, w.a.f. (SBA. Jul.14; 89) *Hyde Park Bookshops.* £110
– – **Anr. Run.** 1758-99. 42 vols. including index. Cont. cf. gt. (P. Dec.11; 255) *Georges.* £120

ANNUAIRE DE LA NOBLESSE DE BELGIQUE
Brussels, 1848-1900. 64 vols. Mod. unif. bdg. (LM. Nov.8; 150) B. Frs. 28,000

ANNUNZIO, Gabriele d'
– **Laudi del Cielo, del Mare, della Terra e degli Eroi.** Milan, 1903-04. 1st. Edn. 2 vols. 4to. Orig. vell. gt., unc. Both vols. inscr. to Federico Balestra. (SI. Dec.3; 172) Lire 280,000
– **Tutte le Opere.** Verona, 1927-36. (209) numbered. on Imperial Jap. 50 vols. including plt. vol. 4to. Mod. hf. red mor., last vol. in mod. russ. orig. wraps. bnd. in, partly unc. (SI. Dec.3; 180) Lire 2,200,000

ANQUETIL, Louis Pierre
– **Histoire de France** ... Paris, 1818-31. 15 vols. Slight worming. Cont. str.-grd. red mor., gt. roll-stp. around covers, crowned cypher of Marie-Louise Duchesse de Parme. smooth decor. spines, watered silk end-papers. (HD. Feb.27; 70) Frs. 9,800

ANSELME de Sainte-Marie, Père
– **Histoire Généalogique et Chronologique de la Maison Royale de France** ... Paris, 1712. 1st Edn. 2 vols. Fo. Cont. cf., upr. cover of vol. 1 defect. (HD. Jun.29; 81) Frs. 1,350

ANSELMUS, Abp. of Canterbury
– **[Opera].** Nuremb., 1491. 1st. Edn. Fo. Lacks title-lf. & last blank lf., initial spaces, MS. notes on several ll., 3 stps., old notes & owner's mark on 1st. lf., slightly stained & soiled in parts. Cont. hf.-leath. wood bds., defect., lacks spine & 1 clasp. (H. Dec.9/10; 1332) DM 820

ANSICHTEN Von Heidelberg
Ill.:– after Charles de Graimberg. [Heidelberg], ca. 1821. 2 vols. Ob. sm. 8vo. 2 ll. of privilege but no other text. Cont. leath., gt., slightly worn. (S. Jan.27; 581) *Robinson.* £320

ANSON, George Lord
– **Reise um die Welt.** Göttingen, 1763. Cont. panel. cf., spine gt. [Sabin 101188] (SPB. May 5; 73) $375
– **Voyage Autour du Monde Fait dans les Années 1740 à 1744** ... Amst. & Leipzig, 1749. Orig. Edn. of Fr. Trans. 4to. Some browning. Cont. marb. cf., decor. spine raised bands. (HD. Apr.24; 30) Frs. 2,500
– – **Anr. Edn.** Geneva; Lyons, 1750; 1756. 2 works in 1 vol. 4to. Cont. cf [Sabin 1637; 1639] (SPB. May 5; 72) $650
– **A Voyage Round the World.** 1748. 1st. Edn. 4to. 1 folding map slightly torn, some other very minor defects. Cont. spr. cf. (SBA. May 27; 268) *Brooke-Hitching.* £900
– – **Anr. Copy.** Title & dedication slightly wormed. Mod. cf., spine gt. [Sabin 1625] (C. Nov.6; 198) *Arader.* £260
– – **Anr. Copy.** Title-p. detchd., slight browning. Cont. mott. cf., worn. [Sabin 1625] (S. Jun.22; 162) *Remmington.* £220
– – **Anr. Copy.** 2 maps torn, stitching brkn., slight soiling & marginal worming. Orig. bds., very worn. [Sabin 1625] (S. Jun.22; 163) *Remmington.* £170
– – **Anr. Copy.** Lacks subscribers list. Cont. red mor., gt. floral borders, spine gt. (SG. Oct.30; 22) $575
– – **Anr. Copy.** Lacks plt.-list. Old cf., rebkd. (SG. Feb.26; 22) $300
– – **Anr. Edn.** 1748. 3rd. Edn. Cf. gt. (P. Oct.23; 1) *Burden.* £50
– – **Anr. Edn.** 1749. 5th. Edn. 4to. Old cf., worn. (BS. Nov.26; 186) £85
– – **Anr. Edn.** 1756. 9th. Edn. 4to. Some margins slightly torn or soiled, some other very minor defects. Cont. spr. cf. gt., worn. (SBA. May 27; 269) *Duran.* £80
– – **Anr. Edn.** 1757. 9th. Edn. 3 folding maps torn, soiled. Cont. cf. (SH. Apr.9; 132) *Makiya.* £50
– – **Anr. Edn.** 1776. 15th. Edn. 4to. Cont. russ., rebkd. [Sabin 1629] (S. Mar.31; 441) *Reddui.* £220
– **Atlas for Voyage around the World.** 1848. 4to. Cf., covers detchd. (P. Nov.13; 97) *Burr.* £70

ANSONIUS MATUTINA
See– **HIERONYMUS PADUANUS–BEROALDUS, Philippus Bononiensis–ANSONIUS MATUTINA–AENIUS SILVIUS –LACTANTIUS**

ANSTIS, John
[–] **The Register of the Most Noble Order of the Garter.** L., 1724. 1st. Edn. 2 vols. Some foxing, etc. Disbnd. (SG. Feb.5; 15) $100

ANSTRUTHER, G. Elliot
– **The Bindings of Tomorrow.** L., Guild of Women-Binders, 1902. (500). 4to. Mod. hf. mor. & bds., unc. (CNY. May 22; 123) $350

ANTHING, Johann Friedrich
– **Collection de cent Silhouettes des Personnes Illustres et Célèbres.** Gotha, 1791. A few plts. slightly spotted. Cont. cf., spine slightly worn. (S. Oct.21; 473) *Braeklen.* £780

ANTHOLOGIA GRAECA
Ed.:– Janus Lascaris. Flor., Laurentius [Francisci] de Alopa, Venetcs. 11 Aug. 1494. 1st. Edn. 4to. Lacks title, last quire (sig. *) & last blank. Mod. vell. [Goff A-765; BMC VI, 666] (SPB. Nov.25; 68) $550
– – **Anr. Edn.** Flor., 1519. Some staining. Cont. limp vell., strengthened with vell. Ms., lacks ties, unc. (C. Jul.16; 236) *Maggs.* £260

ANTHONY, Susan B.
See– **STANTON, Elizabeth Cady, Anthony, Susan B. & Gage, Matilda Joslyn**

ANTICHITA di Ercolano
Napoli, 1755-71. 7 (of 9) vols. Fo. Some vols. with light, mainly marginal stains. Cont. hf.-cf., spines gt., defect. W.a.f. (VG. Nov.18; 986) Fls. 900

ANTI-GUISART, imprimé nouvellement
1586. Lacks last lf. (blank?), Méon number in red on flylf., Mortimer L. Schiff & J.R. Abbey book labels. 18th. C. red mor., by Mouillié with his ticket, triple gt. fillet, flat spine gt. with single

ANTI-GUISART, imprimé nouvellement *-contd.* roundel in compartments, inner gt. dentelles. Méon–Schiff–Abbey copy. (SMC. Oct.7; 1800) Frs. 1,400

ANTICHITA DELLE LONGOBARDICO-MILANESI . . .
Milan, 1792-93. 4 vols. 4to. Some light staining. Cont. hf. sheep. (SI. Dec.3; 23) Lire 400,000

ANTIQUE GEMS from the Greek & Latin
Phila., [1901-02]. (1,000) on Japan vell. 13 vols. Text in Greek or Latin & Engl., liby. blind-stp. on titles. Red mor. gt., floral gt. inlays on spines, silk end-papers. (SPB. May 6; 284) $700

ANTIQUITIES OF GREAT BRITAIN
[vol. 2 dtd. 1807]. Vols. 1 & 2 in 1 vol. Ob. fo. 1 plt. reprd. Cont. cf., worn, spine reprd. (SKC. Feb.26; 1621) £150

ANTIQUITY
1927-72. Vols. 1-46 in 164. Cont. cl. & orig. wraps. (SH. Mar.5; 165) *Fox & Co.* £200

ANTI-SLAVERY ALPHABET, The
Phila., 1847. 12mo. Orig. decor. wraps., device on lr. cover hand-cold., stained, backstrip worn. (SH. Mar.19; 17) *Schiller.* £85

ANTI-SLAVERY Monthly Reporter Commencing June 1825 & ending December 1830
L., 1827-31. Nos. 1-72 in 3 vols. Some spotting. Hf. cf., not unif. (SPB. May 5; 74) $275

ANTOLINI, Giovanni
– Foro-Bonaparte in Milano. Milan, 1801-02. Fo. No title, some light staining. Cont. hf. cf., rather worn. (SI. Dec.3; 24) Lire 650,000

ANTONELLI, G.
– Nuova Raccolta delle Principali Vedute Antiche e Moderne dell'alma Citta di Roma . . . Rome, ca. 1830. Ob. 8vo. Engraved title & 94 views. Cont. hf. russ., worn. (C. Jul.15; 2) *Woodruff.* £100

ANTONINI, Carlo
– Manuale di Vari Ornamenti componenti la Serie de' Vasi Antichi. Rome, 1821. [1st. Edn.?] 3 vols. Fo. Slight marginal spotting. Cont. vell. bds., gt. spines, 1 label defect. (S. Jun.22; 3) *Ars Artis.* £80
– – Anr. Copy. 2 vols. in 1. 4to. Spotted. Cont. hf. cf., worn. (SH. Jun.11; 64) *Sims & Reed.* £50
See–**SPAMPANI, Giambattista & Antonini, Carlo**

ANTONINUS, Saint, Archbp. of Florence
– Chronicon. Nuremb., 31. VII. 1484. 1st. Edn. 3 vols. Fo. Vol. 1 stained thro., rest soiled in parts, reprd., some old Ms. annots. 17th. C. vell. (HK. Nov.18-21; 104) DM 2,000
– Confessionale it S. Johannis Chrystostomi Sermo de Penitentia . . . Venice, Johannes de Colnia & Johannes Manthen, 1474. Fo. Few wormholes thro.-out. Later old style panel. cf. W.a.f. (TA. Aug.21; 187) £280
– Opus Historiale. Basle, Nicolaus Kesler, Feb.10, 1491. 3 vols. Fo. Capital spaces, capital initials, underlinings, initial strokes & paragraph marks supplied in red thro.-out with blue in the prelims., by cont. hand, lacks 4 ll. register at end of vol. 3 & 5 blank ll. thro.-out, 1st. quire of vol. 2 detchd., some ll. loose, some ll. browned, especially at beginning & end. Cont. oak bds., blind-tooled pig spines, brass clasps, upr. cover of vol. 2 detchd. Bkplts. of Dr. Georg Kloss & the General Theological Seminary Liby. [BMC III, 769, Goff A780, HC 1161] (CNY. Oct.1; 11) $1,200
– Summa Confessionale [Defecerunt Scrutantes Scrutino . . .]. [Cologne], [Peter Ther Hoernen], ca. 1486. 4to. Spaces for initials, lge. initial at a1r in blue with red penwork tracery extending into margin, other initials, paragraph marks & line strokes supplied in red by cont. hand, 1st. 5 ll., r1 & 6 strengthened at inner margins, last lf. with fore-edge strengthened, dampstained. Old vell., pastedowns & free end-paper brkn. Bkplt. of the General Theological Seminary Liby. [BMC I, 298, C 493, Goff A819] (CNY. Oct.1; 18) $600
– [Summa Confessionum] Defecerunt Scrutantes Scrutinium. [Cologne], [Ulrich Zel], [not after Aug.29, 1468]. 1st. Edn. 4to. Rubricator's note at colophon, spaces for initial capitals, supplied in red, as are paragraph marks, initial strokes & underlines, MS. catchwords preserved, lacks 1st. & final blanks, portions of lr. margins of 1st. 3 ll. renewed, 2 ll. with minor reprd. tears at inner margins, ink stp. at blank margin of 1st. p. Early stpd. pig over wood bds., recased, covers worn & wormed, spine extensively restored. From the collection of Eric Sexton. [BMC I, 181, Goff A786, HC(Add) 1162a] (CNY. Apr.8; 44) $6,000
– – Anr. Edn. [Cologne], [Ulrich Zell], ca. 1470. 4to. Initials in red, rubricated, old marginalia & ownership inscrs., marginal tear reprd. Cf. by Petit [BMC I, 183] (S. Nov.25; 314) *Rota.* £450
– – Anr. Edn. [Esslingen], Conrad Fyner, [not after 1474]. 4to. Spaces for initial capitals, supplied in red with pen-work flourishes, paragraph marks, underlines & initial stroke in red, lr. margin of fo. 1 renewed, tear to lr. margin of fo. 2, sm. liby. stps. at 1st. & last pp. Cont. German cf. over wood bds., upr. cover divided into 2 concentric panels & frame, central panel with repetitions of diamond tool with dotted centre, outer panel with repeated stp. of griffon in lozenge, frame with lge. flowers, open foliate tools & a 'maria' scroll, lr. cover with fillets intersecting at centre, flowers & open foliate tools, spine with 2 raised bands, lacks clasps & catches, spine reprd. at extremities. The copy of the Royal Liby., Munich & E.P. Goldschmidt, lately in the collection of Eric Sexton. [BMC II, 513, Goff A799, H 1171*] (CNY. Apr.8; 57) $3,000

ANTONINUS, Marcus Aurelius Emperor
– Thoughts. Ill.:– William Russell Flint. L., Riccardi Pr. 1909. (17) on vell. 4to. Plts. in 2 states. Mor. gt., gt. panel. spine, by Bumpus. (SPB. Nov.25; 389) $1,900

ANTONIUS (de Balocco), de Vercellis
– Sermones Quadragesimales de XII Mirabilibus Christianae Fidei Excellentiis. Ed.:– [Ludouicus Brognolo]. Venice, Joannes & Gregorius de Gregoriis, de Forlivio, Feb.16, 1492/93. 4to. Spaces for initial capitals, with guide letters, worming at beginning & end, catching text in some places, minor repairs to inner margin of fo. 2. Cont. qtr. pig & wood bds., worn & reprd. Partly defect. bkplt. of Dr. George Kloss, lately in the collection of Eric Sexton. [BMC V, 343, Goff A918, H 15949*] (CNY. Apr.8; 192) $800

ANTONIUS DE BITONTO
– Expositiones Evangeliorum Dominicalium. Venice, Johannes Hamman for Nicolaus de Frankfordia, 15 Aug.1496. 1st. Edn. Cont. Ms. index at end, liby. stp. on title. Cont. blind-stpd. cf.-bkd. wooden bds., spine reprd., clasp. F.S. Ferguson bklabel. (C. Jul.16; 237) *Rota.* £160

APEL, Johann August 'Septimus Globus'
– Der Freischütz Travestie. Ill.:– George Cruikshank. 1824. Cont. hf. mor. Bkplt. of Thomas Gaisford. (S. Nov.24; 82) *Simeone.* £85
– – Anr. Copy. Foxing. Mor. gt. by E. Riley, orig. wraps. bnd. in, s.-c. (SPB. Jul.28; 97) $150

APHRODITE, A Mythical Journey in Eight Episodes
Ed.:– William Blake, D.H. Lawrence, Guillaume Apollinaire & others. Ill.:– Ann Brunskill. 1970. (75) numbered, sigd. by artist. Fo. 8 etchings by Brunskill, each captioned & sigd., prospectus inserted. Unsewn as Iss., wraps., cl. portfo., ties. (S. Jul.31; 191) *Forster.* £90

APIANUS, Petrus
– Astronomicum Caesareum. Ingoldstadt, [Priv. Ptd.]. May 1540. 1st. Edn. Lge. fo. 36 full-p. woodcuts (21 with a total of 53 volvelles, of 83), cold. thro.-out by cont. hand, 3 orig. silk threads partly remaining, some minor stains & defects in volvelles, sm. pt. of 1 lf. facs?, volvelles on G3v detchd. from lf., some margins slightly stained mostly not affecting text or ills. Cont. German cf., covers with blind-stpd. historiated & crested rolls, rebkd. & recornered. Sold (as usual) w.a.f. on account of defects in or lack of movable pts., armorial bkplt. of Count Schaffgotsch of Silesia, bkplt. & accession number of J.R. Abbey. (C. Nov.20; 175) *Zeitlin.* £8,000
– – Anr. Edn. Ed.:– D. Wattersberg. Munich, 1967. Facs. of 1540 Ingolstadt Edn., (200) hand-cold. 2 vols. (text & commentary). Lge. fo & lge. 4to. Orig. leath. & orig. hf.-linen in hf.-linen box. (HK. Nov.18-21; 3128) DM 1,100
– Cosmographia . . . Ed.:– Gemma Frisius. Cologne, 1574. Sm. 4to. Lacks mappemonde, with volvelles on O3r, lacks those on C2v & 1 each from D1r & H2r, C3r lacks thread, without the 2 separate diagrams, last few ll. slightly stained, title frayed, endpapers from early Justinian. Cont. cf., worn, upr. cover detchd. From Honeyman Collection. [Sabin 1750] (S. May 20; 3166) *'Hughes'.* £300
– Cosmographicus Liber. Ed.:– Gemma Frisius. Antw., Feb.1529. 1st. Frisius Edn. Sm. 4to. Lacks volvelles & all but remnant of 2 separate diagrams ill. Instrumentum Syderale, slight soiling. Old limp vell. From Honeyman Collection. [Sabin 1739] (S. May 20; 3165) *Simonin.* £170
– Cosmographie . . . Ed.:– Gemma Frisius. Antw., 1581. Sm. 4to. D1v with 2 volvelles only, threads missing from latter & from C3v, without 2 separate diagrams, a few woodcuts & initials hand-cold. at beginning, title & following lf. slightly defect. in lr. inner corners & reprd., text cropped at foot of map. Mod. cf., gt. spine, covers slightly marked. From Honeyman Collection. (S. May 20; 3167) *Quaritch.* £480
See–**FINE or Finé, Oronce–APIANUS, Petrus**
See–**SCHWENTER, Daniel–APIANUS, Petrus –URSINUS, P.**

APOCALYPSE (L') Selon Saint Jean
Ill.:– Waroquier. Paris, 1954. (76) numbered on vell. d'Arches. Fo. With suite of all ills. Wraps., portfo. & s.-c. (SM. Oct.8; 2302) Frs. 1,400

APOCRYPHA
[Edinb.], [1822]. Tall 4to. Extracted from a Bible ptd. by Blair & Bruce, blank inter-ll. between each 2 ll. Cont. cf., gt. borders with lge. blind-stpd. arabesque central design. Double fore-e. pntg. (SG. Mar.19; 108) $550
– – Anr. Edn. Ill.:– Hughes-Stanton, Gooden, etc. Cresset Pr. 1929. (450). Fo. Orig. vell. bds. (SH. Jun.11; 88) *Schriver.* £60

APOLLINAIRE, Guillaume
– Alcools. Ill.:– Picasso. 1913. Sewed. (HD. Oct.10; 4) Frs. 2,500
– Le Bestiaire, ou, Cortège d'Orphée. Ill.:– Raoul Dufy. Paris, 1919. 2nd. Edn, (50) numbered on vieux japon. 4to. Bds., orig. wraps. bnd. in. (SH. Nov.21; 309) *Baron.* £80
– L'Enchanteur Pourissant. Ill.:– André Derain. Paris, [1909]. 1st. Edn., (106); (75) numbered on thick laid-paper in the style of Arches factories, sigd. by author & artist. Sm. 4to. Parch. wrap., sewed. (HD. Dec.5; 5) Frs. 35,600
– Ombre de mon Amour. Ill.:– Vertes. 1956. (172) on special paper. 4to. Ll. in s.-c. (HD. Feb.18; 205) Frs. 1,000
– Poèmes Secrets. Ill.:– Salvador Dali. Paris, 1967. (135) numbered on Arches blanc with artist's sig. Lge. 4to. Loose ll. Wrap., s.-c. & publisher's box, special tools. (LM. Nov.8; 3) B. Frs. 16,000
– Le Poète Assassiné. 1916. Sewed. (HD. Oct.10; 5) Frs. 1,000
– – Anr. Edn. Ill.:– Raoul Dufy. 1926. (470) on special vell. 4to. Sewed, pict. wraps. (faded). (HD. Feb.18; 206) Frs. 2,600
– – Anr. Copy. Sewed. (HD. Oct.10; 177) Frs. 2,400
– Sept Calligrammes. Ill.:– O. Zadkine. [Paris], Priv. ptd. 1967. (7). Fo. Loose ll. in orig. wraps., linen cover & s.-c. Every etching sigd. by artist, printer's mark sigd. by artist & editor. (H. Dec.9/10; 2399) DM 2,500

APOLLINARIS, Q.
– Kurtzes Handtbüchlein unnd Experiment viler Artzneyen. Strassburg, 1583. Slightly soiled. Hf. linen. (HK. Nov.18-21; 721) DM 1,400

APOLLO Art-Union–AMERICAN Art-Union
– Transactions & c. N.Y., 1839-43; 1844-46. Old mor., richly gt.-tooled border enclosing owner's name: Prosper M. Wetmore, Esq., spine torn. (SG. Dec.4; 11) $300

APOLLONIUS Pergaeus
– Conicorum libri IV . . . Ed.:– Claud Richard. Antw., 1655. Marin Marsenne's Latin version, on cream-P. Fo. Orig. bdg., unc. (HD. Feb.18; 2) Frs. 1,500
– Conicorum Lib. V. VI. VII . . . Ed.:– Abraham Echellensis. Trans.:– Alfonso Giovanni Borelli. Flor., 1661. 1st. Latin Trans. Fo. Hf.-box, decor. spine, unc. (HD. Feb.18; 1) Frs. 1,500

APOLLONIUS, of Rhodes
– Argonautica (with the Scholia of Lucillus, Sophocles & Theon). Flor., [Laurentius (Francisci) de Alopa Venetus], 1496. 1st. Edn. 4to. Spaces for initials, some slight browning, mostly to edges, faint ink inscr. on 1st. p. 18th. C. Italian mor. gt., borders of alternating ovals & rectangles enclosing flower cornerpieces, spine gt. with vase & flower ornaments & gt.-lettered. Inscr. of

Sebastian Tergasely(?), pencilled shelf-mark of Sir George Holford, lately in the collection of Eric Sexton. [BMC VI, 667, Goff A924, HC 1292*] (CNY. Apr.8; 65) $9,500

– Argonauticon. [Geneva], 1574. 4to. Cont. vell. bds. (S. Nov.25; 361) *Maggs.* £150

– – Anr. Edn. Paris, 1574. 4to. Some foxing, fol. 3 torn at top. 17th. C. cf. gt., arms of a member of Nicolai family with garland of the Ordre de St. Michel, spine gt. (CNY. May 22; 24) $120

– Argonotica . . . Graece. Venice, Apr.1521. 16th. C. havanna cf., blind-stpd., worn. (HD. Apr.24; 21) Frs. 3,800

APPELL, J.W.

– Der Rhein und die Rheinlande in Original-Ansichten. Darmstadt, 1850. Pt. 1. Lacks 2 steel engrs. Cont. linen. (R. Mar.31-Apr.4; 1893) DM 8,000

– – Anr. Edn. Darmstadt, 1852. Slightly soiled in parts, lacks 30 steel engraved plts. Hf. linen portfolio. (HK. May 12-14; 727) DM 4,800

– – Anr. Edn. Darmstadt, 1856. Pt. 1. Slightly soiled. Cont. hf. leath., defect. & loose. (R. Oct.14-18; 2143) DM 8,000

– Le Rhin et ses Bords depuis les Alpes jusqu'à Mayence. Trans.:– Le Belley-Hertzog. Darmstadt & Paris, 1854. Orig. hf. roan, slightly worn. (S. Nov.4; 593) *Brown.* £1,600

APPERLEY, Capt. Charles James 'Nimrod'

– The Chace, the Turf, & the Road. L., 1870. All plts. etc. hand-cold. 2-tone cl., worn. (SG. Dec.11; 164) $100

– Hunting Reminiscences. Ill.:– after Wildrake, Henderson & Alken. L., 1843. 1st. Edn. Later red mor., double gold-stpd. cover fillet, gt. spine, outer dentelle & wide floral inner dentelle, worn. (D. Dec.11-13; 2141) DM 500

– Life of the late John Mytton. L., 1835. 1st. Edn. Some offsetting. Red mor. gt., s.-c. (SPB. Nov.25; 119) $950

– – Anr. Copy. Plts. slightly spotted, 3 plts. which were not included in subsequent editions. Orig. cl. gt., unc., rebkd., cl. case. (SPB. Oct.1; 85) $700

– – Anr. Edn. Ill.:– Henry Alken & T.J. Rawlins. L., 1837. 2nd. Edn. 1 plt. reprd. & bkd., stains, 6 extra plts. Red mor. by Rivière. (SPB. Oct.1; 86) $325

[–] – Anr. Edn. 1851. 3rd. Edn. Orig. cl., rebkd., old spine preserved. (CSK. Sep.5; 111) £180

– – Anr. Copy. Slight foxing. Red mor. gt. by Birdsall. (SPB. May 6; 145) $600

– – Anr. Edn. Ill.:– After Henry Alken & T.J. Rawlins. 1869. 4th. Edn. Spotting. Orig. cl., soiled & recased. (CSK. Oct.27; 88) £100

– – Anr. Copy. Cont. style hf. leath. gt., pict. gt. orig. lines of upr. cover & spine bnd. in. (R. Mar.31-Apr.4; 1668) DM 1,400

[–] – Anr. Edn. Ill.:– H. Alken & T.J. Rawlins. 1870. 5th. Edn. Orig. cl., worn. (CSK. Oct.3; 35) £130

– – Anr. Edn. Ill.:– Alken & Rawlins. 1877. Hf. mor. gt. (CE. Nov.20; 125) £100

– – Anr. Edn. Ill.:– Alken & Rawlins. ca. 1890. Cf., gt. fillet borders with sm. gt. cornerpieces, spine decr. gt., gt. dentelles, by Rivière. (SG. Dec.11; 165) $150

[–] – Anr. Edn. Ill.:– Henry Alken. 1899. (50) on L.P., sigd. by Ed. 4to. Orig. buck-bkd. bds. gt., unc. (SBA. Jul.23; 425) *Way.* £55

– The Life of a Sportsman. Ill.:– Henry Alken. L., 1842. 1st. Edn., 1st Iss. Pt. 33 in 2nd. state, 5 ll. of advts. Orig. cl. gt., worn, end-papers restored, mor. pull-off case. (SPB. Oct.1; 87) $1,200

– – Anr. Copy. 1 plt. detchd., 10 p. publisher's catalogue at end. Orig. cl. gt., spine & corners worn, inner jnts. brkn., qtr. mor. box. Bkplt. of Arthur W.H. Hay Drummond, lately in the Prescott Collection. (CNY. Feb.6; 4) $1,100

– – Anr. Edn. Ill.:– after Henry Alken. 1842. 1st. Edn., 2nd. Iss. Orig. cl. gt. (SBA. Mar.4; 5) *Kent Nielson.* £390

[–] – Anr. Edn. Ill.:– after H. Alken. L., 1874. 2nd. Edn. 2 new plts., plts. lightly browned in parts. Cont. hf. leath., gt. spine, orig. linen bnd. in. (HK. Nov.18-21; 1727) DM 1,600

– – Anr. Edn. Ill.:– after Henry Alken. 1903. Orig. cl. gt., slightly soiled. (SBA. Mar.4; 6) *Fletcher.* £100

– Sporting . . . L., 1838. Fo. Mor. gt. by J. Mackenzie. (S. Nov.24; 10) *Niedhardt.* £130

APPIANUS ALEXANDRINUS

– Historia Romana.–De Bellis Civilibus. Trans.:– Petrus Candidus Decembrius. Venice, Bernhard Maler (Pictor), Erhard Ratdolt & Peter Löslein. 1477. 1st. Compl. Edn., Pt. 1, 1st. Edn., Pt. 2, 2nd. Edn. Fo. Pt. 1, 131 ll. (of 132) lacks 1st. blank, pt. 2, 212 ll., woodcut borders & 20 lge. initials cold. by cont. hand, running headlines in red thro.-out, rubricated & ruled in red. Vell., spine gt., bnd. for William Brown of Edinb. [BMC V 244] (CNY. May 22; 25) $3,200

– – Anr. Edn. Trans.:– [Petrus Candidus Decembrius] (both works). Scandiano; Reggio Emilia, Peregrinus de Pasqualibus; Franciscus de Mazalibus, Jan.10, 1495; Oct.22, 1494. 2 works in 1 vol. Fo. 1st. work: spaces for initial capitals, some with guide letters, slight wear to fore-edges of 1st. few ll., 1st. lf. with sm. tear to lr. margin, 2 wormholes to 1st. 20 ll.; 2nd. work: spaces for initial capitals, most with guide letters. Hf. mor., gt. spine. Bkplt. of Frederick Spiegelberg, lately in the collection of Eric Sexton. [BMC VII, 1118 & 1088, Goff A930 & A932] (CNY. Apr.8; 154) $2,800

– Historia Romana [– De Civilibus Romanorum Bellis.] Venice, Bernadus Pictor, Erhard Ratdolt & Petrus Loslein, 1477. 1st. Edn. 2 pts. in 1 vol. Fo. 211 ll. (of 212, lacks 1st blank), 2nd pt. bnd. before 1st, some ll. at beginning of pt. II & end of pt. I defect. & reprd. in outer edges, some ll. at beginning of pt. II with very slight worming, cutting some letters, some ll. stained from outer edges, marginal annot. and foliation in cont. hand on some ll., blank c1v, & c2r in pt. I with MS. notes in 18th. C. hand. Old vell. bds., pt. of spine & lr. cover defect. From High Legh liby., front free end-paper with 18th. C. shelfmark, & monog. 'SMR'. [BMC V, 244; H 1307 (II, I)] (S. May 5; 5) *Quaritch.* £1,300

APPIANUS, Constantius

– Soliloquia de Humani Arbitrii Libertate et Potestate. Cremona, Carolus de Darleriis, Oct.4, 1496. 4to. Spaces for capital initials with guide letters, a1 & 12 & 11 & 10 rehinged, some inner margins slightly restored, some ptd. & early ink MS. marginalia cropped. Mod. vell. From the collection of Eric Sexton. [BMC VII, 959, Goff A933, HC 1313*] (CNY. Apr.8; 50) $980

APPLETON'S CYCLOPAEDIA of American Biography

Ed.:– James Grant Wilson & John Fiske. N.Y., 1894. 6 vols. 4to. Cl. (SG. Jun.11; 30) $180

APPLETON'S EUROPEAN GUIDE BOOK

L. & N.Y., [1872]. Orig. limp leath., defect. & loose. (R. Oct.14-18; 1826) DM 460

APPLICATION OF IRON TO RAILWAY STRUCTURES

– Report of the Commissioners. 1849. Fo. 1 plt. loose, some ll. soiled. Disbnd. (SH. Mar.5; 166) *Weinreb.* £340

– – Anr. Copy. 2 vols. Some ll. slightly soiled. Mod. hf. cf. (SH. Oct.9; 280) *Weinreb.* £260

APPOLONIUS OF TYRE

– Historia. Ill.:– Mark Severin. Gold. Cock. Pr. 1956. (300), this number 6 of 75 specially bound. 4to. With an additional suite of 7 plts. & a prospectus loosely inserted. Orig. mor. (CSK. Oct.31; 70) £70

APRES DE MANNEVILLETTE, Jean Baptiste Nicolas Denis d'

– Le Neptune Oriental. Paris & Brest, 1775. Fo. 1 map slightly torn, 1 with sm. hole, lacks. supp. Cont. mott. cf., worn, covers detchd. (S. Nov.4; 478) *Feldman* £400

APULEIUS, Lucius

– L'Amour de Cupido et de Psiché. Trans.:– C. Chappuy, A. Heroet, M. de Saint-Gelais. Ill.:– Leonard Gaultier. [Paris], [1586?]. Sm. 4to. 19th. C. marb. roan, fillet, decor. spine, inside dentelle. Sigd. by artist. (HD. Mar.18; 6) Frs. 5,600

– Asinus Aureus. Ed.:– [Philippus Beroaldus]. Bologna, Benedictus Hectoris, Aug.1, 1500. Fo. Spaces for initial capitals with guide letters, initial capitals supplied thro.-out in red & blue, illuminated coat-of-arms at foot of A1, bnd. without Tabula (issued later), title-p. slightly soiled, slight wormholes to initial ll., defect in lr. corner of D3 reprd. Vell.-bkd. bds. [BMC VI, 845, Goff A938, HC 1319*] (CNY. Oct.1; 82) $850

– Cupid & Psyche. Trans.:– J.H. Mason. Ill.:– Vivien Gribble. Priv. ptd. 1928-35. (130?) numbered. 4to. Orig. Linson vell., unc. (C. Feb.4; 197) *Tzakas.* £50

– De Cupidinus et Psyches Amoribus. Ill.:– Charles Ricketts. Vale Pr., 1901. (310). Orig. linen-bkd. bds., unc., unopened. (S. Jul.31; 49) *Warrack & Perkins.* £110

– – Anr. Copy. Sm. fo. Orig. holland-bkd. bds., unopened. (SH. Feb.19; 51) *Ayres.* £100

– Dell'Asino d'Oro. Trans.:– M. Angelo Firenzuola Fiorentino. Venice, 1567. Lr. corner of H8 restored with 10 letters in facs., some browning & a few inner margins reprd. near text, slight dampstaining. Old vell. Bkplt. of William Morris, later the copy of Richard Bennett & John A. Saks. (CNY. Oct.1; 133) $180

– The Golden Asse. Chelsea, Ash. Pr., 1924. (16) on vell. Fo. Orig. mor. gt., hf. mor. drop-box. (CNY. May 22; 295) $8,000

– – Anr. Edn. Trans.:– William Aldington. Ash. Pr., 1924. (165). 4to. Orig. cl.-bkd. bds., unc. (SH. Feb.19; 19) *Pickering.* £100

– L. Apuleii Metamorphoseos Libri XI. Ed.:– Joannes Pricaeus. Ill.:– Persyn. 1650. Early 19th C. str.-grd. red mor. (by Bozérian?), border of 2 fillets, lozenge-rectangle decor. in fillet, spine decor. with emblematic tooling, Greek inside. Bkplt. of Docteur Danyau. (HD. Mar.18; 7) Frs. 1,250

– The Marriage of Cupid & Psyche. Trans.:– William Adlington. Ill.:– Charles Ricketts. Vale Pr., 1897. (210). Orig. buckram, unc. (S. Jul.31; 41) *Warrack & Perkins.* £90

– – Anr. Copy. Slightly soiled, unc. (SG. Jan.15; 101) $260

– – Anr. Edn. Ed.:– Walter Pater. Ill.:– Edmund Dulac. N.Y., Ltd. Edns. Cl., 1951. (1,500) numbered, sigd. by artist. 4to. Vell., boxed. (SG. Oct.23; 97) $120

APUSHKIN, Yakov

– Kamerny Teatr. Moscow & Leningrad, 1927. (5,000). Title cut. Orig. wraps. by 2-Stenbert-2. (SH. Feb.6; 293) *Kent University.* £55

AQUINAS, Saint Thomas

– Cathena Aurea Angelici . . . nuper redacta super omnia Euangelia Dominicalia et Ferialia . . . per Religiosum Patrem Fratrem Petrum de Vincentia. Venice, Johannes Rubeus Vercellensis, 29 Apr.1494. 4to. 2 sigs. misbnd., lr. outside corners stained, frayed at beginning & end affecting text on last lf. only. 16th. C. spr. cf., gt. spine, head & foot of spine chipped. [Hain 1337*; BMC V p. 418; Goff T 224] (C. Apr.1; 91) *Stewart.* £220

– Commentaria in octo Physicorum Aristotelis Libros. Venice, 1566. Fo. Lacks last blank, browned, slight worming. Mod. bds. (SH. Jun.11; 198) *Gennadins Library.* £60

– De Periculis Contingentibus circa Sacramentum Eucharistiae [with De Suffragiis Missae]. Ghent, Arend de Keysere, [between 1483 & 1489]. 2 capital initials supplied in blue & red, rubricated in red, blue & yellow. Late 19th. C. Belgian sheep gt. The copy of J.-F. vande Velde, P.P.C. Lammens, C.-A. van Coetsem, & the Duke of Arenberg, lately in the collection of Eric Sexton. [Goff T314, HC 1382] (CNY. Apr.8; 71) $40,000

– Expositio Super Libros De Generatione et Corruptione Aristotelis. Ed.:– [Eugenius Venetus]. Venice, Bonetus Locatellus, for Octavianus Scotus, Dec.22, 1498. Fo. Ornamental white on black woodcut initials, short tear at foot of A4, some slight stains, some early marginal Ms. annots. Mor. gt. to a 16th. C. Italian design, s.-c., by Gozzi of Modena. From the collection of Eric Sexton. [Goff T244] (CNY. Apr.8; 196) $1,700

– Libellus de Viciis et Virtutib [US] Numero Quaternario procedens. [Cologne], ca. 1495. 4to. Rubricated, washed. Bds. (HK. Nov.18-21; 309) DM 420

– Opus Aureum . . . super quatuor Euangelia. Venice, Bonetus Locatellus, for Octavianus Scotus. 4 Jun. 1493. Fo. Some dampstaining, a few ll. torn or wormed, with slight loss of text. 17th. C. limp vell., soiled. [Hain 1336*; BMC V, 441; Goff T232] (S. Jan.27; 359) *Hendricks.* £240

– Opuscula. Venice, 7.ix.1490. 4to. Stained thro.-out in parts, 1st. part & end-ll. soiled with defects., some text loss in 1st. 2 ll., some also with worming. Cont. blind-tooled wood bds., blind-tooled pig spine, 2 clasps. [BMC V, 358] (HK. Nov.18-21; 307) DM 1,400

– Prima Pars secunde partis sũme Theologie. Venice, Franciscus Renner & Petrus de Bartua. 1470 [1478]. 4to. 279 ll. (of 280, lacks last blank), on f. 1 lge. illuminated initial on gold background with narrow border in colours extending into 2

AQUINAS, Saint Thomas -contd.
margins, other initials supplied in red or blue with red ornamental penwork slightly extending into margins, red or blue chaptermarks, f. 273 1st. lf. of index cut shorter but with same ornamentation, 1st. & last lf. reprd. slightly affecting text, wormhole in 1st. few ll., some ll. slightly soiled or spotted. Mod. antique-style sheep spine, wooden bds., 1 clasp defect. [BMC V, 194; Goff T204; HC 1448] (S. Jun.23; 209) *Duran.* £580
- **Quaestiones de Duodecim Quodlibet.** Ulm, Johann Zainer, 1475. Fo. 232 ll., additional blank ll. inserted, initials painted in red, 1 red & blue, paragraph marks & initial strokes in red, titles & chapter numbers added in red, wormed, sm. stp. of Buxheim Lib. Cont. German blind-stpd. pig. on wooden bds., bnd. in the Carthusian House at Buxheim, 2 clasps, some worming. [BMC II, 524] (S. Nov.25; 327) *Harper.* £800
- **Questiones de quodlibet Sancti Thome de Agno Ordinis Fratum pdicatarum incipiut feliciter.** Venice, 1476. 4to. Initials supplied thro.-out in red & blue, margins discoloured & a few wormholes. Recent vell. by Gray, Camb. [H 1404] (TA. May 21; 367) £750
- - **Anr. Edn.** Ed.:- Th. de Susteren. Cologne, 1500. Fo. Lacks ll. 9 & 10, bnd. in in facs., some old Ms. notes, slightly soiled & stained in places or wormed. Cont. blind-tooled leath.-bkd. wood bds., 4 (of 8) brass bosses, 2 clasps, lacks ties, spine reprd. in 18th. C. [Hain 1418; BMC I, 292; G T178] (HK. May 12-14; 170) DM 800
- **Scripta super Quatuor Libros Sententiarum.** Strassburg, 1490. Fo. 1655 Ms. liby. mark on 1st. lf., this lf. lightly soiled, 1st. 15 ll. browned & last hf. of work. 19th. C. hf. leath., gt. spine. (HK. Nov.18-21; 310) DM 1,600
- **Scriptum . . . Super Secundo Sententiarum.** Ed.:- Cornelius Sambacus. Venice, Bonetus Coctellus, 22 Dec.1488. Fo. 157 ll. (of 158), lacks f. 78, used as fly-ll., 2 Ms. ll. from Italian Sacramentary on vell. ca. 1100 with headings & incipits in hf.-anial letters with 22 lge. initials in red. Cont. Venetian mor., blind-stpd., lacks clasps. [BMC V, 451] (S. Nov.25; 337) *Parikian.* £1,300
- **Summa Theologica Tertia.** Venice, Bernardinus Stagninus de Tridino, 1486. Fo. Initial letters not supplied, a few wormholes to text. Cont. wood bds., clasps defect., with recent leath. backstrip. (TA. Feb.19; 461) £380
- **Super Epistolas Sancti Pauli.** Venice, 1498. Fo. Old vell. recovered. [Hain 1341] (LM. Mar.21; 153) B. Frs. 20,000
- **Super Libros Aristotelis de Generatione et Corruptione.** Salamanca, Leonhard Hutz & Lupus Sanz. 26 Feb. 1496. 2nd. Edn., but the 1st. ptd. in Spain. Fo. Wanting final blank lf., annots. thro.-out by an early hand, title lf. reprd., not affecting text, a few sm. stains. Mor., gt., by Rivière. (SPB. Nov.25; 61) $5,000

AQUINO, Carlo d'
- **Sacra Exequialia in Funere Jacobi II Magnae Britanniae Regis.** Rome, 1702. Fo. Some plts. reprd. Marb. bds., spine worn. Liby. label 'Bibliothecae Petri Buoninsegni Senis 1814' at foot of title. (S. Jun.22; 4)
Marlborough Rare Books. £120

ARABIAN NIGHTS
- **Adventure of Hunch-back & the Stories connected with it.** Ill.:- William Daniell after Robert Smirke. 1814. Fo. 17 hand-cold. plts. mntd. on India paper, last few ll. with 12 unrelated mntd. plts. Cont. hf. mor., worn. (CSK. Nov.21; 222) £55
- - **Anr. Copy.** 4to. Frontis. detchd., light foxing to some text pp. Three-qtr. leath., upr. cover & free end-paper detchd., worn. (SG. May 21; 325) $110
- **Ali Baba & the Forty Thieves.** Trans.:- Edward Powys Mathers. Ill.:- Edward Ardizzone. 1949. (2,500) numbered, sigd. by artist. Fo. Orig. Hf. bds. with line drawing, orig. cold. litho. endpapers. (P. Dec.1; 102) £170
- **Arabian Nights.** Ed.:- J. Scott. Ill.:- Robert Smirke. 1811. 6 vols. Leath., gt. (HY. Jan.14; 8) £55
- - **Anr. Edn.** Ed.:- R.F. Burton. 1897. De Luxe Edn. Plts. in orig. portfo. (P. Jan.22; 304) *Hosain.* £75
- - **Anr. Edn.** Ed.:- Kate D. Wiggins & Nora A. Smith. Ill.:- Maxfield Parrish. N.Y., 1909. 1st. Parrish Edn. Sm. 4to. Cl. (PNY. Mar.4; 205) $120

- - **Anr. Edn.** Ill.:- E.J. Detmold. Ca. 1924. (100) sigd. by artist. 4to. Orig. vell. gt., partly unc., s.-c. (C. Jul.22; 54) *Joseph.* £360
- - **Anr. Edn.** Ill.:- Adolphe Lalauze, Albert Letchford, & others. N.d 8 vols. 4to. Ills. only (some in proof state) from various edns. 1 vol. full, the rest hf. mor. Bkplts. of Dyson Perrins, w.a.f. (CSK. Aug.1; 51) £140
- - **Anr. Edn.** Ill.:- E.J. Detmold. N.d. 4to. Orig. cl., gt., publishers box. (CSK. Nov.28; 110) £80
- **The Book of the Thousand Nights & a Night.** Ed.:- R.F. Burton. Benares, Grol. Cl. 1885. De Luxe Edn., (20) numbered. 12 vols. Plts. in 3 states. Orig. vell. gt., in glazed bookcase. (SH. May 28; 4) *Hosain Books.* £520
- - **Anr. Edn.** Ed.:- Leonard C. Smithers. Trans.:- Sir Richard F. Burton. L., 1894. Liby. Edn. 12 vols. Elab. gt.-stpd. cl., each fore-edge with brass lock (key provided). (SG. Mar.19; 6) $250
- - **Anr. Edn.** Ed.:- L.C. Smithers. Trans.:- Sir R.F. Burton. Ill.:- Albert Letchford. 1897. Liby. Edn. 12 vols. Cl., gt. (CE. Aug.28; 177) £50
- - **Anr. Edn.** Trans.:- [Sir Richard Francis Burton]. Burton Club. n.d. (1,000) numbered. 17 vols. Orig. cl. (SH. Mar.5; 167) *Domê.* £60
- **Book of the Thousand Nights & a Night [with Supplemental Nights].** Trans.:- Richard Burton. Burton Club. [1888]. Ill. Benares Edn., (1000). 17 vols. Hf. russet mor., gt. (SBA. Oct.21; 5) *Laywood.* £150
- - **Anr. Edn.** N.p., Burton Cl., n.d. Medina Edn., (1000). 17 vols. Hf. red mor., gt. (SPB. May 29; 63) $325
- - **Anr. Edn.** Ed.:- Sir Richard Francis Burton. N.p., Burton Cl., n.d. Bassorah Edn., (1000). 18 vols. Slight browning. Hf. cf. gt., some stains. (SPB. May 29; 61) $125
- **Contes des Mille et Une Nuits.** Ill.:- Edmund Dulac. Paris, n.d. 4to. Cont. hf. mor., spine decor. with onlays & gt. tooling, slightly worn, orig. wraps. bnd. in, by Samblanx. (S. Jul.31; 208) *Salinas.* £110
- **The Entertainments.** Ed.:- Henry Torrens, Edward Lane, & John Payne. Trans.:- Richard F. Burton. Ill.:- Arthur Szyk. Ltd. Edns. Cl. 1954. (1500) numbered. 4 vols. 4to. Cl. gt., orig. box. (SG. Jan.15; 116) $170
- **Histoire d'Aboulhassan Ali Ebn Becar et de Schemselnihar . . . Conte Tiré des Mille et Une Nuits . . .** Trans.:- A. Galland. Ill.:- M.A.J. Bauer. Harlem, 1929. (33), numbered. 4to. Orig. watercolour on hf.-title. Mor. by Michèle Miron, covers & spine decor. with fillets interlaced in waves, wrap. preserved, s.-c. (SM. Feb.11; 232) Frs. 8,500
- **Die Inseln Wak Wak.** Trans.:- F.P. Greve Ill.:- Max Slevogt. Berlin, [1921]. (300) on Bütten. Fo. 57 lithos. (title gives 54). Orig. pict. silk, lightly cockled, endpaper slightly soiled. Printer's mark sigd. by artist. (H. May 21/22; 1809) DM 2,000
- - **Anr. Edn.** Trans.:- F.P. Greve. Ill.:- M. Slevogt. N.p., n.d. (360) on Bütten. Orig. linen. Printer's mark sigd. by artist. (H. Dec.9/10; 2351) DM 1,700
- **Little Hunchback.** 1817. 1st. Edn. 16mo. Orig. wraps. (S. Feb.9; 27) *Gross.* £60
- **Le Livre des Mille Nuits et une Nuit.** Ed.:- Dr. Joseph Charles Mardrus. Paris, n.d. 8 vols. bnd. in 4. Hf. mor., spine & corners, 4 lge. spine raised bands, decor. motif between, unc., box. (LM. Jun.13; 194) B.Frs. 12,000
- **Les Mille et Une Nuits.** Ill.:- after Westall (frontis.). Paris, 1822-25. On vell.; frontis. on India paper. 6 vols. Some sm. stains. Hf. cf. by Bauzonnet, spines gt. (SM. Feb.11; 13) Frs. 1,600
- - **Anr. Edn.** Trans.:- A. Galland. Paris, 1834. 6 vols. Cont. hf.-mor., decor. spines. (HD. Feb.18; 126) Frs. 1,900
- - **Anr. Edn.** Trans.:- M. Galland. Ill.:- after Wattier, Laville, Demoraine & Marville. Paris, [1840]. 3 vols. Lge. 8vo. Mod. str.-grd. red hf. mor., decor. spines, wraps. (HD. Dec.5; 150) Frs. 2,000
- - **Anr. Edn.** Ed.:- Antoine Galland. Ill.:- Lalauze. Paris, 1881. (10) on Japon, L.P. 10 vols. 21 engd. plts. in 3 states. Mor. gt., gt., by Dupré. (SM. Oct.8; 2335) Frs. 17,000
- - **Anr. Edn.** Paris, ca. 1899. 8 vols. Lge. 4to. Cold. plts. reproducing illuminations from Oriental Ms., decor. cold. borders. Hf. mor. (SH. Apr.9; 291) *Kauffman.* £150
- - **Anr. Edn.** Trans.:- Dr. J.C. Mardrus. Paris, n.d. 8 vols. Lge. 4to. Cl.-bkd. bds., gt. & decor. spines. (SM. Oct.8; 2353) Frs. 2,000

- **A Plain & Literal Translation of the Arabian Nights' Entertainment . . . with Supplemental Nights.** Trans.:- Sir Richard F. Burton. [1885-88]. Benares Edn. 16 vols. Cl., ornamented in gold & silver, 2 spines torn. (SG. Dec.18; 66) $230
- - **Anr. Edn.** Trans.:- Richard F. Burton. [Denver], [1900-01]. Facs. of orig. Benares Edn., (1000) numbered. 16 vols. Gt. & silver-decor. cl. (SG. Dec.18; 11) $140
- **Princess Badoura.** Ill.:- Edmund Dulac. N.d. Ltd. Edn., sigd. by artist. 4to. Orig. cl. gt., slightly worn. (P. Jan.22; 239) *Renard.* £95
- - **Anr. Copy.** 1st. quire loosening. Orig. decor. buckram, partly unc. (LC. Jun.18; 21) £50
- **La Princesse Badourah.** Ill.:- Edmund Dulac. Paris, 1914. (500) numbered, on Japon paper, sigd. by artist. 4to. Cont. lev. mor., spine tooled in gt., orig. wraps. bnd. in. (SH. Mar.26; 172) *Henderson.* £240
- **Sinbad le Marin, et d'Autres des Mille et Une Nuits.** Ill.:- Edmund Dulac. Paris, [1919]. (1,000) numbered. 4to. Mor., spine gt. with fleurons. (SG. Oct.23; 104) $150
- **Sinbad the Sailor.** Ill.:- Edmund Dulac. N.d. 4to. Orig. cl. (P. Jan.22; 240) *Welby.* £60
- **Sinbad the Sailor & Other Stories.** Ill.:- Edmund Dulac. [1911]. (500). 4to. Orig. vell. gt., lacks ties. Sigd. by artist. (SH. Dec.10; 188) *Welby.* £220
- **Sindbad Der Seefahrer.** Ill.:- M. Slevogt. 1908. (300). Sm. fo. Orig. pict. vell., slightly soiled, sm. tear. Printer's mark sigd. by artist. (H. May 21/22; 1812) DM 500
- **Stories from the Arabian Nights.** Ed.:- Laurence Housman. Ill.:- Edmund Dulac. 1907. 4to. Some ll. of text loose. Orig. cl. gt., worn. (SH. Dec.10; 178) *Duran.* £50
- - **Anr. Edn.** Ed.:- Laurence Housman. Ill.:- Edmund Dulac. [1907]. 4to. Cl. (SG. Oct.23; 105) $110
- - **Anr. Edn.** Ed.:- Laurence Housman. Ill.:- Edmund Dulac. [L.], n.d. 4to. Cl. gt., d.-w. with mntd. cold. plt. (SG. Oct.23; 99) $100

ARAGO, François
- **Le Daguerréotype [Séance du Lundi 19 Août 1839].** Paris, 1839. 1st. Edn. in Comtes Rendus . . . de l'Académie des Sciences, vol. IX. 4to. 1 quire loose. Orig. wraps., unopened. (S. Oct.21; 361) *Walford.* £170

ARAGO, Jacques Etienne Victor
- **Narrative of a Voyage Round the World.** 1823. 1st. Edn. in Engl. 4to. Lacks hf. title. Mod. hf. cf. [Sabin 1865] (S. Mar.31; 442) *Maggs.* £380
- **Souvenirs d'un Aveugle: Voyage Autour du Monde.** Paris, 1839. 4 vols. Cont. cf., needs rebdg. (SG. Oct.30; 24) $120

ARAGON, Louis
- **Les Chambres.** Ill.:- Man Ray. Paris, [1969]. (60) numbered on velin de Rives, sigd., & with orig. sigd. & numbered etching laid in. 4to. Loose as iss. in wraps., bd. folder & s.-c. (SG. Apr.2; 187) $250

ARBEAU, Thoinot (Pseud.)
See-TABOUROT, Jehan 'Thoinot Arbeau'

ARBER, Prof. Edward
- **An English Garner.** 1909. Ltd. Penshurst Edn. 12 vols. Cont. hf. mor. (SH. May 28; 5) *Howes Books.* £55
- **The Term Catalogues, 1668-1709 A.D.** 1903-06. 1st. Edn. 3 vols. 4to. Orig. cl., slightly worn. (S. Feb.23; 325) *Thorp.* £100

ARBORETUM, Arnold
- **Catalogue of the Library of . . .** Ed.:- Charles S. Sargent & Ethelyn M. Tucker. Camb., 1914-33. 3 vols. 4to. Crudely rebnd. in brown paper. (SG. Jan.22; 36) $400

ARBUTHNOT, John
- **A Postscript to John Bull Containing the History of the Crown Inn [-Continuation of the History of the Crown-Inn].** Ca. 1720. 2 pts. in 1 vol. Slightly soiled or spotted. 19th. C. cf.-bkd. bds. (S. Apr.7; 237) *Bickersteth.* £80
See-GAY, John, Pope, Alexander & Arbuthnot, John

ARCAMBEAU, Edme
- **The Book of Bridges.** Ill.:- Jessie M. King. 1911. (1000). 4to. Orig. cl. Cold. pict. title sigd. by artist. (SKC. Feb.26; 1288) £90
- - **Anr. Copy.** (SH. Mar.26; 312)
Hatchards. £75

– – **Anr. Copy.** Cl. (SH. Jul.16; 128)
D. White. £50
See–KING, Jessie M. & Arcambeau, Edme

ARCHAEOLOGIA: Or, Miscellaneous Tracts Relating to Antiquity
1779-1846. Vols. 1-31 (including 2 vols. Indices, unbnd.) & vols. 33-34. 4to. Some dampstaining. Cont. hf. cf., spines worn, vol. 34 unbnd. (TA. Apr.16; 291) £150
– – **Anr. Edn.** 1898-1961. Vols. 56-98 in 50. 4to. Orig. cl. (SH. Mar.5; 168) *Landry.* £160

ARCHAEOLOGICAL Album (The)
Ed.:– Thomas Wright. 1845. 4to. Some ll. slightly spotted. Orig. vell. gt. (SBA. May 27; 133)
Hoare. £54

ARCHAEOLOGICAL ASSOCIATIONS
Edinb., 1878-99. Ltd. Edns. 17 vols. Cl., soiled. (CE. Nov.20; 15) £80

ARCHER, Sir Geoffrey & Godman, Eva M.
– **The Birds of British Somaliland & the Gulf of Aden.** L. & Edinb., 1937. 2 vols. 4to. Orig. cl. (CB. Sep.24; 7) *Can.* $500
– – **Anr. Edn.** Ill.:– Λ. Thorburn & H. Grönvold. 1937-61. 4 vols. 4to. 3 folding maps (of 4, lacks map at end of vol. II). Orig. cl., gt., vols. I & II soiled. (S. Jun.1; 60) *Hill.* £240

ARCHER, Lieut. J.
– **Statistical Survey of the County Dublin.** Dublin, 1801. Soiled & dampstained. Orig. bds., defect., unc. (GM. Apr.30; 279) £55

ARCHER, John Wykeham
– **Vestiges of Old London.** L., 1851. Fo. Ex libry. Hf. mor. (SG. Oct.30; 25) $120

ARCHIMEDES
– **Opera .** Trans.:– Nicolaus Tartaglia [William of Moerbeke?]. Venice, 1543. 1st Latin (partial) Edn. Sm. 4to. Marginal tear reprd. in 1st. quire. Mod. vell. From Honeyman Collection. (S. May 20; 3169) *Zeitlin & Verbrugge.* £450
– **Opera: Apolloniis Pergaei Conicorum . Theodosii Sphaerica.** Ed.:– Isaac Burrow. 1675. 1st. Edn. 3 pts. in 1 vol. 4to. Without separate title to Archimedes, errata lf. to Apollonius, or lf. 'Brevitatis gratia . .', slightly soiled. Old cf., worn, rebkd. Bkplts. of J. Beever & R. Pandelbury. [Wing A3621] (S. Apr.6; 208) *Faurre.* £60

ARCHITECTURAL REVIEW (The)
[1896]-1909. Vols. 1-25. 4to. Some plts. mntd. Orig. cl. (CSK. Jul.10; 84) £320
– – **Anr. Edn.** 1931-70. Together 86 vols. & issues, vols. 69-147; with duplicates for vols. 113-144. 4to. 7 vols. orig. wraps., rest publisher's cl. (SH. Oct.9; 111) *Weinreb.* £630

ARCHITEKTONISCHE RUNDSCHAU
Ed.:– L. Eisenlohr & C. Weigle. Stuttgart, 1888-99. Year 4-13 & 15 in 11 vols. Fo. Orig. hf. linen, slightly soiled. W.a.f. (HK. Nov.18-21; 3257) DM 500

ARCHIVES de la Commission Scientifique du Mexique
Paris, 1865-67. 3 vols. Foxing. Cont. qtr. mor. (SPB. May 5; 76) $400

ARCHIVO DELLA R. SOCIETA ROMANA DI STORIA PATRIA
[1878-1977]. Years I-C. 1st. 62 hf. cl., rest orig. wraps. (CR. Mar.19; 370) Lire 750,000

ARCONATI VISCONTI, G.
– **Diario di un Viaggio in Arabia Petrea.** Torino, 1872. 2 vols. 4to. Cl., gt. Autog. ded. (CR. Mar.19; 371) Lire 190,000

ARDIZZONE, Edward
– **Lucy Brown & Mr. Grimes.** 1937. 1st. Edn. Fo. Orig. paper pict. bds., d.-w. Sigd. (P. Dec.1; 6) £75
– **Nicholas & the Fast Moving Diesel.** Ca. 1936. 1st. Edn. Fo. Orig. paper pict. bds. Sigd., also sigd. by Nicholas Ardizzone. (P. Dec.1; 8) £60
– **Sarah & Simon & No Red Paint.** 1965. 1st. Edn. 4to. Orig. pict. paper bds. Sigd. (P. Dec.1; 11) £75

AREL'SKY, Graal
– **Leteisky brag.** St. Petersb., 1913. Orig. wraps., slightly soiled. (SH. Feb.6; 379) *Quaritch.* £80

ARENE, Paul
– **Jean des Figues.** 1870. Three quarter mor., by Carayon, wrap, lacks spine. (HD. Oct.10; 6)
Frs. 800

ARETIN François (L') par un Membre de l'Académie des Dames
Ill.:– Borel, engraved by Elluin. L. [Paris], 1787. 18mo. Mod. vell., renewed, unc. Bnd. at end 'Les Epices de Venus, ou Pièces diverses du même Academicien', L. [Paris], 1787, engraved by Borel. (HD. Apr.10; 316) Frs. 3,500
– – **Anr. Edn.** Ill.:– after Borel. N.p., ca. 1850. 18mo. Jansenist cf., inner dentelle, by Pagnant. (HD. Apr.10; 317) Frs. 2,700

ARETINO, Pietro
– **Capriciosi et Piacevoli Ragionamenti [La Puttana Errante].** [Leiden]. 1660. 1st. Iss. 2 pts. in 1 vol. 18th. C. mor., triple gt. fillet, spine gt. in compartments, inner gt. dentelles. Renouard copy. (SM. Oct.7; 1544) Frs. 1,200
– **Quattro Comedie.** [L.], 1588. 1st. Edn. 18th. C. mor., triple gt. fillet, spine compartments gt. à la grotesque, inner gt. dentelles, corners worn. Bkplt. of Girardot de Préfond & Lord Rivers. [STC 19911] (SM. Oct.7; 1545) Frs. 4,000
– **Ragionamenti . . .** [L.], ca. 1597. 3 Pts. in 1 vol. Lacks S7 in Pt. 2, single wormhole from title to end, tear in D7. 17th. C. Continental vell. bds., gt. arms on covers, worn, lacks ties. (S. Nov. 25; 450)
The Italian. £160
– – **Anr. Edn.** Ed.:– Agresto da Ficarvolo. Np. [The Continent], ca. 1651. 3 pts. in 1 vol. With the 'MeDICata ReLabor' & blank [2A1], lacks final blank, 1st title & 2 ll. reprd., 1st title soiled, some ll. stained. Cont. cf., some wear. (S. May 5; 60)
Cristani. £90
– **Les Ragionamenti.** Ill.:– Paul-Emile Becat. 1944. 2 vols. Sm. 4to. Chagrin, mosaic backs, 2 gt. fillets on covers, unc., wraps & spines, s.-c. (HD. Dec.5; 6) Frs. 1,000

ARGENS, Jean Baptiste de Boyer, Marquis d'
[–] **Mémoires Historiques et Secrets, concernant les Amours des Rois de France.** Paris, 1739. 12mo. 18th. C. mor. by Derome le Jeune with his 1785 ticket, triple gt. fillet, flat spine gt. with fleuron in compartments, inner gt. dentelles. (SM. Oct.7; 1546) Frs. 1,000
– **Ocellus Lucanus . . . avec des Dissertationes sur les Principales Questions de la Metaphisique . . . des Anciens.** Berlin, 1762. Cont. mor. by Derome le Jeune with his 1785 ticket, concentric narrow gt. borders & fillets, flat spine gt. in compartments with single fleuron, inner gt. dentelles. (SM. Oct.7; 1547) Frs. 1,400

ARGENSOLA, Bartolomé Leonardo de
– **Conquista de la Islas Molucas.** Madrid, 1609. Fo. Engraved title preserved, imprint cropped, final lf. preserved with scribblings on verso, old inscrs. on title deleted, hole in last lf. of prelims. affecting several ll., some light marginal stains. Later cf., head of spine defect. [Sabin 1946] (SPB. May 5; 77) $400

ARGENSON, Mr. le Marquis d'
– **Considérations sur le Gouvernement Ancien et Présent de la France.** Amst., 1764. Red Bibliothèque Royale stp. on title, old sig. on flylf., pr. marks F. 4812 & L. 1917. A.8 on verso of hf.-title. Cont. red mor., gt., arms of Louis XV, triple gt. fillet, cipher, spine gt. in compartments, inner gt. dentelles. Bkplt. of Henry Terry. (SM. Oct.7; 1548) Frs. 2,800

ARGENTI, Philip P.
– **The Costumes of Chios.** 1953. 1st. Edn. (500). 4to. Orig. cl. (S. Nov.25; 496) *Crete.* £150

ARGENTRE, Bertrand d'
– **L'Histoire de Bretagne . . .** Paris, 1588. 2nd. Edn. Fo. Slight dampstaining. Mod. marb. roan, triple gt. fillet around covers, spine decor. with raised bands. (HD. Jun.24; 78) Frs. 4,200
– – **Anr. Edn.** Rennes, 1681. Fo. Cont. cf. (HD. Jun.29; 141) Frs. 3,550

ARGENVILLE, Antoine Joseph Dezallier d'
See–DEZALLIER D'ARGENVILLE, Antoine Joseph

ARGNANI, Federico
– **Le Ceramiche e Maioliche Faentine.** Faensa, 1889. (285). 4to. Hf. cl. (CR. Jun.11; 21)
Lire 380,000
– **Il Rinascimento delle Ceramiche Maiolicate in Faenza.** Ed.:– C. Malagola. Faenza, 1898. 2 vols. 4to. Sewed, 1st. vol. loose. (CR. Jun.11; 20)
Lire 600,000
– – **Anr. Copy.** Hf. mor. Ernesto Pagnoni ex-libris. (SI. Dec.3; 26) Lire 320,000

ARIA, Mrs.
– **The May-Book.** Ill.:– Randolph Caldecott & others. 1901. 4to. Orig. pict. cl., worn. Max Beerbohm's copy. (SH. Mar.26; 69)
Baldur. £160

ARIAS, P.E.
– **Greek Vase Painting.** N.Y., [1961]. 1st. Edn. in Engl. Cl., d.-w. (PNY. May 21; 203) $150

ARIAS Montanus, Benedictus
– **Dictatum Cristianum.** Antw., 1585. 19th. C. mor., covers stpd. & ruled in gt., with strapwork in black, red, green & white, spine gt. (CSK. May 29; 100) £75

ARIEL POEMS
N.Y., 1927. 1st. Amer. Edns. (27). Nos. 1-8. Orig. wraps., unc. (S. Jul.22; 2) *Waterfield.* £370
– – **Anr. Copy.** (SH. Dec.18; 40) *Quaritch.* £260
– – **Anr. Edn.** 1927-31. 1st. Edns. Nos. 1-28 (lacks nos. 7, 13, 14, 26 & 29). Orig. decor. wraps. (S. Jul.22; 1) *Hawthorne Bks.* £65
– – **Anr. Edn.** 1927-54. 1st. Edns., (200-500), some unnumbered. Numbers 1-38, new series, numbers 1-8, compl. set. Numbers 1-8 in orig. decor. limp bds., 9-38 in orig. bds., rest in orig. wraps. & envelopes. (SH. Dec.18; 34)
Subunso. £780
– – **Anr. Copy.** Orig. wraps., all but 1 of new series in orig. envelopes. (SH. Dec.18; 35)
Connelly. £130
– – **Anr. Edn.** [1929]. Proof copies. Nos. 18-31, together 14 vols. No. 25-31 without the number of poem on lr. cover. Orig. wraps., ills. & wraps. of a few with different col. to 1st. Edns. (S. Jul.22; 4)
Waterfield. £130
– **Ubi Ecclesia.** (No. 21). Ed.:– G.K. Chesterton Ill.:– Diana Murphy. 1929. 1st. Edn. (400). Self-caricature of author. Orig. bds., unc. This copy unnumbered. (SH. Dec.18; 74)
Donnithorne. £125
– **The Wonder Night.** (No. 5). Ed.:– Laurence Binyon. Ill.:– Barnett Freedman. 1927. 1st. Edn. Orig. pink wraps. Ink & wtrcolr. drawing inserted, proof copy of 1st. Edn. (SH. Dec.18; 62)
Waterfield. £50

ARIOSTIS, Alexander de
See–SAVONAROLA, Girolamo–ARIOSTIS, Alexander de

ARIOSTO, Lodovico
– **Comedia . . . Intitulata li Sopposti.–Comedia . . . Intitulata Cassaria.** Venice, 1542; 1536. 2 vols. Running-title & foliation on most ll. of 2nd. vol. shaved or cropped. Mod. paper bds.; mod. paper bds. (C. Apr.1; 6) *Walton.* £80
– **Comedie.** Ed.:– T. Poracacchi. Venice, 1562. In 5 pts. Mod. pig. gt. (P. Apr.9; 322) *Duran.* £50
– **Opere.** Ill.:– B. Castelli, G. Filosi, & G. Giampicoli (plts.). Venice, 1730. 2 vols. Fo. Lr. margin of 1 plt. reprd., some ll. spotted, traces of light dampstains at front of vol. 2. Cont. vell. bds., soiled. From the collection of John A. Saks. (C. Jun.10; 9) *Greindl.* £180
– **Orlando Furioso.** Venice, 1544. 4to. Ruled. Cont. cf., decor. with scrolls, gt. fillets & various fleurons, beaten gold title on upr. cover, owner's name on lr. cover, spine remade, end-papers renewed, interlaced with wax, ex-libry. (HD. Mar.18; 8) Frs. 8,500
– – **Anr. Edn.** Venice, 1568. 4to. Sm. tear in f. Z2, some pp. lightly stained or browned. 18th. C. vell. (SI. Dec.3; 27) Lire 200,000
– – **Anr. Edn.** Venice, 1580. Cont. vell., soiled. (CSK. Mar.20; 37) £100
– – **Anr. Edn.** Ill.:– Girolamo Porro. Venice, 1584. 3 pts. in 1 vol. 4to. 1 plt. repeated, f.A reprd. 18th. C. red mor., triple gt. fillet, spine gt. in compartments, inner gt. dentelles. (SM. Oct.7; 1549) Frs. 5,500
– – **Anr. Copy.** 2 pts. in 1 vol. Upper margins torn in places with slight text loss, some staining. 19th. C. hf. vell. (SI. Dec.3; 28) Lire 500,000
– – **Anr. Edn.** Ill.:– Eisen (port.), Cipriani, Cochin, Eisen, Greuze, Moreau & Monnet. Bg'ham, 1773. 1st. Printing. 4 vols. Red mor., triple fillet decor., inner dentelle, by Derome. From André Langlois libry. (HD. Jun.10; 2) Frs. 23,000
– **Orlando Furioso.** [Osservationi by A. Lauezuola with commentary by G. Ruscelli]. Venice, 1584. 4to. Lacks final blank lf, some headlines just cropped, edges & some ll. slightly browned. 18th. C. Fr. mor. gt., broad gt. border of stem & interlaced leaf tool, spine gt. in 6 compartments with 5 raised bands with flower ornaments in 5

ARIOSTO, Lodovico -contd.
compartments, gt.-lettered, cl. s.-c. Bkplt. of John A. Saks. (CNY. Oct.1; 134) $1,500
– – **Anr. Edn.** Venice, 1609. 24mo. Slight browning. Cont. limp vell., spine defect. (S. May 5; 52) *Greindl.* £65
– – **Anr. Edn.** Ill.:– G. Zuliani & others after P.A. Novelli. Venice, 1772-73. 4 vols. 4to. Cont. mott. cf., gt. spines. From the collection of John A. Saks. (C. Jun.10; 8) *Breslauer.* £520
– – **Anr. Copy.** Cont. vell., gt. & blind-stpd. borders. (R. Oct.14-18; 826) DM 770
– – **Anr. Edn.** Bg'ham, 1773. 4 vols. 4to. Cont. red str.-grd. mor. gt. (C. Jul.16; 328) *Beck.* £400
– – **Anr. Copy.** Cf., spines worn. (SG. Sep.25; 31) $150
– – **Anr. Edn.** Ill.:– Eisen, Cipriani, Cochin & others. Bg'ham., 1773. (100). 4 vols. Cont. cf. gt. (SI. Dec.3; 30) Lire 420,000
– – **Anr. Edn.** Ill.:– Boily (port.). L., 1783. 4 vols. 18mo. Red mor., by Cazin. (HD. Apr.8; 210) Frs. 1,400
– – **Anr. Edn.** Ill.:– Doré. Milan, 1881. Fo. Cont. vell. gt. (SI. Dec.3; 31) Lire 300,000
– **Orlando Furioso** [–I Cinque Canti]. Venice, 1572. 4to. Lacks r4-5, 1st. title defect. & reprd., some other sm. repairs, some ll. marginally wormed & stained at foot, occasional browning & staining. Cont. sheep, spine gt. & defect., worn. (S. Feb.10; 260) *Erlini.* £65
– **Roland Furieux.** Trans.:– D'Ussieux. Ill.:– After Baskerville & Cochin. Paris, 1775-83. 4 vols. Name & sm. stp. on titles. Cont. tree cf., gt., 2 spines slightly worn, a few wormholes. (S. Oct.21; 295) *Mendez.* £220
– – **Anr. Copy.** Cont. pol. cf. gt., by Lesné. (SM. Oct.8; 2314) Frs. 1,600
– – **Anr. Edn.** Trans.:– Lre Comte De Tressan. Ill.:– Queverdo. Paris, 1796. 6 vols. 12mo. Cont. dyed cf., decor. spines, roulette, inner dentelle. (HD. Apr.9; 574) Frs. 1,300
– – **Anr. Edn.** Trans.:– V. Filipon de La Madelaine. Ill.– T. Johannot, Baron, Français & C. Nanteuil. Paris, 1844. 1st. Edn. 2 vols. 1st. printing of ills., plts. on China. Later hf. mor., corners, spines decor. with raised bands. With extra ills. from other edns. (including that of François Meissonier, 1839). (HD. Feb.27; 72) Frs. 1,800
– – **Anr. Edn.** Ill.:– Gustave Doré. Paris, 1879. Lge. 4to. Orig. pict. cl. gt. Pres. Copy, to George A. Sala from Doré, lately in the collection of Eric Sexton. (C. Apr.15; 66) *Henderson.* £140
See–BOIARDO, Matteo Maria & Ariosto, Lodovico

ARISI, F.
– **Felice Boselli.** Rome, 1973. (285). 4to. Cl. (CR. Jun.11; 22) Lire 260,000

ARISTOPHANES
– **Lysistrata.** Ill.:– Norman Lindsay. Fanfrolico Pr. [1926]. (725) numbered, sigd. by Jack Lindsay. Fo. Orig. hf. mor., boxed. (CSK. Feb.20; 8) £140
– – **Anr. Edn.** Ill.:– Pablo Picasso. N.Y., Ltd. Edns. Cl. 1934. (1,500) numbered, sigd. by artist. 4to. Pict. bds., lacks box. (SG. May 14; 10) $1,100
– – **Anr. Copy.** Spine worn, orig. box. (SG. Jan.15; 117) $650
– **Lysistrata.–Women in Parliament.** Trans.:– Jack Lindsay. Ill.:– Norman Lindsay. L., Franfrolico Pr. [1926]; [1929]. (500); (725); both numbered on Batchelor's H.M.P. 2 works in 2 vols. Fo. Leath.-bkd. gt.-decor bds., partly unc. (SG. Apr.2; 176) $300
– **Lysistrate.** Trans.:– Lucien Dhuys. Ill.:– François Kupka. Paris, 1911. Ltd. Edn., this copy specially ptd. for A. Barthelemy. 4to. Frontis. & many cold. text etchings, with additional plt. in 3 states, prospectus bnd. in. Lev., elab. inlaid mor. decors., upr. cover with inlaid port., gt. dentelles, doubls. & end-ll. of satin, by Fluchaire, orig. wraps. bnd. in. (SG. Oct.9; 19) $500
– **Women in Parliament.** Ill.:– Norman Lindsay. Fanfrolico Pr. [1929]. (500) numbered. Fo. Orig. hf. mor., boxed. Sigd. by artist. (CSK. Feb.20; 9) £150
– – **Anr. Copy.** Orig. three-qtr. cf. gt., partly untrimmed. (TA. Nov.20; 118) £100

ARISTOTELES
– **De Natura, aut de Rerum Principiis Lib. VIII. –De Caelo Libri IIII.–Liber de Mundo.–De Ortu & Interitu Libri duo.–Meteorologicorum Libri Quatuor.–De Animo Libri III.–Libelli, qui parva naturalia vulgo appellantur.** Paris, 1559; 1559;

1559; 1558; 1558; 1558; 1558. 7 works in 1 vol. 4to. Heavily annotated thro.-out, 1st. title soiled & with owners' inscrs. of [Joannes] Tixier & B.M. Piperus, 4th. work: C3v & C4r soiled. Cont. panel. cf., gt. ornaments on sides, owner's name erased, worn, rebkd. & reprd. (S. Jan.27; 383) *Poole.* £70
– **Ethica Nicomachea.** Ed.:– Jacob E.T. Rogers. L., 1865. 2nd. Edn. Portion of final advt. lf. torn away. Orig. mor.-bkd. cl. bds., worn, spine torn, mor. gt. solander case. Oscar Wilde's copy, with his sig. on title-p., interleaved with some 200 pp. of notes in Wilde's holograph, lge. portions of text with underlining, & many pp. with marginalia, lately in the Prescott Collection. (CNY. Feb.6; 413) $7,500
– **Ethicorvm ad Nichomachum Libri Decem ...**
– **Decem Libroru Moralium ...** Paris 1555; 6.xi.1542. Cont. blind-tooled pig-bkd. wood. bds., decor., 2 clasps. (HK. Nov.18-21; 106) DM 600
– **The Metaphysics.** Trans.:– Thomas Taylor. L., Priv. Ptd. 1801. 1st. Edn. Tall 4to. Mod. panel. hf. cf. (PNY. May 21; 24) $150
– **La Morale.** Trans.:– [Catel]. Toulouse, 1644. 4to. Hole in title. 17th. C. velvet embroidered bdg., with appliquée satin lobed medallion on each cover, bearing on front, the cipher HVH surmntd. by ducal coronet, surrounded by laurel wreath, & on rear arms of Châtillon, Comte de Blois, surrounded by laurel wreath, remains of silk ties, worn & stained. (SM. Oct.7; 1550) Frs. 11,500
– **[Opera].** Ed.:– Immanuel Bekker. Berlin, 1831-70. 5 vols. 4to. Cont. gt., filigree hf. vell. & cl. (CB. Apr.1; 208) Can.$ 160
– **Opera Omnia.** Paris, 1619. 2 vols. in 4. Fo. Latin & Greek text, vol. I slightly dampstained in margin. 17th. C. spr. cf., slightly worn. (S. Dec.3; 133) *Maggs.* £160
– **Organum.** Ed.:– Jul. Pacius. Morgiis, 1584. 4to. Cont. owner's inscr. at head, text in Greek & Latin, a few stains, mainly marginal. Cont. vell., worn. (CSK. Jun.12; 73) £50
– **Rettorica d'Aristotile fatta in Lingua Toscana.–I tre Libri della Retorica d'Aristotele.** Venice, 1570; 1571. Together 2 vols. 4to. Cont. vell. (C. Jul.16; 238) *Maggs.* £80
– **Thextus Ethicorum . . .–Politicon Libri Octo . . . (with the commentary of Jacob Faber Stapulensis).** Trans.:– Johannes Bur(idani) (1st. work). Paris, [Andre Bocard for] Jean Petit (1st. work). 26 Sep., 1500; 1506. 2 works in 1 vol. Fo. 1st. work: title & 1st. lf. rubricated, upr. corner torn from title & folios a2 & r1 with loss of text, owner's inscr. on title; 2nd. work: initials supplied in red or blue, some extending into margins, lacks folios A1 & 2; both works with some marginal tears reprd. 16th. C. blind-stpd. vell. over wood bds., slightly worn, ex-liby. (with some sm. stps.). [Goff A990; H 1758] (S. Jul.27; 100) *Abad.* £240
See–SAVONAROLA, Hieronymus–PAULUS Pergulensis–ARISTOTELES

ARISTOTELES–RIVIRIUS, J.N.
– **[Organon]. Logica . . .– Repertorium in Liboros Aristo.** Lyon, [1530]; Apr. 1530. 2 works in 1 vol. Cont. pig-bkd. wd. bds., 2 clasps. (HK. Nov.18-21; 108) DM 550

ARITHMETICA
Paris, 1562. 1st. Edn. A few stains. Vell. bds. From Honeyman Collection. (S. May 20; 3170) *Hughes.* £75

ARITHMETICE LILIU TRIPLICIS PRACTICE
[Cologne], 1511. Sm. 4to. Slight staining. Mod. bds., unc. Lge. copy; from Honeyman Collection. (S. May 20; 3171) *Maggs.* £240

ARKHITEKTURA SSSR [Architecture of U.S.S.R., designed by El Lisitsky]
Moscow, 1933-36. Nos. 1 & 2 of 1933; nos. 3, 5, 7 & 9 of 1934; nos. 2 of 1936, 7 Iss. only. 4to. Orig. wraps., slightly soiled. (SH. Feb.6; 294) *Ex-libris.* £160

ARKSTEE, H.K.
– **Nymegen, de Oude Hoofdstad der Batavieren.** Ill.:– J. Ruyter after C. Pronk. Amst., 1733. 1st. Edn. Cont. blind-stpd. vell. (VG. Oct.13; 11) Fls. 2,600

ARLAND, Marcel
– **Maternité.** Ill.:– Marc Chagall. Paris, 1926. 1st. Edn.; (35) of (75) on Jap. Square 8vo. Sewed, wraps. (HD. Dec.5; 7) Frs. 6,800
– – **Anr. Edn.** Ill.:– Marc Chagall. Paris, 1926. 1st. Edn., (765) numbered, on Lafuma de Voiron. Orig. ptd. wraps. (PNY. Mar.4; 124) $475

– – **Anr. Copy.** 5 orig. etchings. Sewed. (HD. Jun.24; 129) Frs. 1,500
– – **Anr. Edn.** Ill.:– Marc Chagall. Paris, 1926. (960) numbered. 4to. Orig. wraps., unc. (SH. Nov.21; 261) *Frumpkin.* £260

ARMENO-VENETO
– **Compendio Storico e Documenti delle Relazioni degli Armeni coi Veneziani.** Venice, 1893. 2 vols. Preface sigd. 'M', slight browning. Orig. ptd. wraps. (S. Apr.29; 410) *Loman.* £60

ARMIN, Th.
– **Das Heutige Mexico.** Leipzig, 1865. Gt-pict. cl., worn. (SG. Aug.21; 395) $100

ARMITAGE, Albert B.
– **Two Years in the Antarctic.** 1905. No bdg. stated. (TRL. Dec.10; 40) £68

ARMORIAL D'ABRY – TABLE DES MEUBLES HERALDIQUES
Ed.:– Guy Poswick & Pierre Delrée. Liège, 1956-57. 2 vols. 4to. Publisher's bds. (LM. Nov.8; 202) B. Frs. 8,500

ARMROYD, George
[–] **A Connected View of the Whole Internal Navigation of the United States, Natural & Artificial ...** Phila., 1826. 1st. Edn. Some text foxing. Orig. bds., covers loose, spine worn, folding cl. s.-c. From liby. of William E. Wilson. (SPB. Apr.29; 7) $750

ARMS, Dorothy Noyes
– **Churches of France.** Ill.:– after John T. Arms. N.Y., 1929. 1st. Edn., (200) numbered on H.M.P., & sigd., with orig. sigd. etching as frontis. 4to. Two-tone cl., unc. & unopened. Letter from Arms' secretary tipped in, presenting this book to the Grolier Club, with their bkplt. (SG. Mar.12; 10) $300

ARMSTRONG, John, Physician & Poet
[–] **The Art of Preserving Health.** 1744. 1st. Edn. 4to. Cont. mott. cf. (S. Sep.29; 124) *Hannas.* £75

ARMSTRONG, Col. John
– **History ... of the Navigation of the Port of King's-Lyn & of Cambridge.** 1725. Fo. 2 maps hand-cold., some staining, sm. hole in H2 affecting text. Mod. hf. cf. (S. Jan.27; 594) *Crowe.* £150

ARMSTRONG, Mostyn John
– **A Scotch Atlas.** Ill.:– H. Ashby. 1 Oct. 1787. 4to. Cf. s.-c. (CE. Dec.4; 228) £70
– – **Anr. Edn.** L., 1794. Sm. 4to. Bdg. not stated, lacks upr. cover. (P. Jun.11; 206) *Map House.* £160

ARMSTRONG, Robert B.
– **Musical Instruments.** 1904. 4to. Decor. cl., gt. Pres. copy with letter from author in 2nd. vol. (CE. Jul.9; 229) £230

ARMSTRONG, W.G.
– **Industrial Resources of the ... Tyne, Wear, & Tees.** 1864. Hf. mor. gt. (P. Oct.2; 78) *Crowe.* £50

ARMSTRONG, Walter
– **The Thames from its Rise to the Nore.** Ill.:– J.A. McNeil Whistler, F. Slocombe & others. L., n.d. 2 vols. 4to. Hf.-titles slightly dampstained, publisher's advts. Orig. pict. cl. (CB. Feb.18; 202) Can. $120

ARMY MEDICAL DEPARTMENT
– **Anatomical Drawings from Preparations in the Museum of the Army Medical Department at Chatham.** Ed.:– Sir James McGrigor (pts. 2-5). 1824-50. 5 pts. Fo. Orig. ptd. bds., cl. spine. (S. Jun. 15; 16) *Norman.* £220

ARMY MEDICAL LIBRARY
– **Index-Catalogue of the Library of the Surgeon-Generals Office, United States Army, First Series. – Fourth Series. – Fifth Series.** Wash., 1880-95; 1936-55; 1959-61. 16 vols.; 11 vols.; 3 vols. 4to. All orig. cl. (S. Feb.23; 327) *Whitehart.* £220

ARMY & NAVY GAZETTE, The
– **Types of the British Army.** Ill.:– after R. Simkin. 1889-90. Cl. gt., 3 vols. rebnd. with orig. cl. bds. (HSS. Apr.24; 262) £80

ARMYANSKY Sbornik [Armenian Collection]
Moscow, 1911. Orig. wraps. by N. Goncharova, very slightly soiled. (SH. Feb.6; 380) *National Art Centre.* £160

ARNALDUS DE VILLANOVA
[-] Regimen Sanitatis . . . Strassburg, 1513. Sm. 4to. Some dampstaining. 19th. C. limp vell., slightly soiled. From liby. of André L. Simon. (S. May 18; 21) *Quaritch.* £380

ARNAUD, Baculard d'
- Fanni, ou la Nouvelle Paméla, Histoire Anglaise. –Clary ou le Retour à la Vertu Récompensé, Histoire Anglaise.–Lucie et Melaine, ou les Deux Soeurs Généreuses, Anecdote Historique. Ill.:– Eisen. Paris, 1767. L.P. 3 works in 1 vol. Cont. red mor., 1 fillet, fleurons in corners, decor. spine. Bkplt. of Deschamps-Scrive. (HD. Mar.18; 10) *Frs. 1,200*

ARNAULT, Antoine Vincent, Jay, A. & others
- Biographie Nouvelle des Contemporains. Paris, 1827. 20 vols. Some ll. loose, slightly spotted in places. Orig. ptd. wraps., 1 upr. cover detchd., unc. (SH. Jul.27; 203) *Hartinghausen.* £60

ARNETH, A
- Prinz Eugen v. Savoyen. Vienna, 1858. 3 vols. Cont. linen gt., slightly soiled. (HK. May 12-14; 616) *DM 420*

ARNOLD, Christoph
- Wahrhaftige Beschreibung dreyer Mächtiger Königreiche, Japan, Siam, und Corea . . . Nureemb., 1672. Some staining. Disbnd. W.a.f. (C. Nov.20; 176) *Kossow.* £130

ARNOLD, Edwin
- The Light of Asia or the Great Renunciation, being the Life & Teaching of Gautama, Prince of India & the Founder of Buddhism. Ill.:– F. Bourdin. L., 1879. Orange mor., sigd. by Rivière, gt., floral stp. on spine, quadruple fillets & corner fleurons, inner & outer gt. dentelle, silk end-ll., orig. wraps. bnd. in, box. (D. Dec.11-13; 627) *DM 2,200*

ARNOLD, G.
- Waare Afbeelding der Eerste Christenen. Ill.:– J. Mulder & Jan Luyken. Amst., 1700-01. 2 pts. in 1 vol. Fo. Lacks 3 plts. Cont. blindstpd. russ. over wood, brass clasps & catches, spine reprd., new fly-ll. (VG. Nov.18; 992) *Fls. 750*

ARNOLD, Matthew 'A'
- The Strayed Reveller & other Poems. 1849. 1st. Edn. 12mo. Slight browning, inscr. on title. Orig. cl. Inscr. on front free end-paper 'W. Allingham from A.H. Clough . . .'. (SH. Jul.27; 97) *Maggs.* £220
- The Works. L., 1904. De Luxe Edn., (750). 15 vols. Hf. burgandy mor. gt., gt. panel. spines. 2-pp. A.L.s. tipped in. (SPB. May 6; 285) *$700*

ARNOLD, Sir Thomas W. & Grohmann, Adolf
- The Islamic Book. Pegasus Press. 1929. (375) numbered copies. 4to. Gt-decor. cl. (SG. Oct.2; 14) *$400*

ARNOLD, Sir Thomas W. & Wilkinson, J.V.S.
- The Library of A. Chester Beatty. A catalogue of the Indian Miniatures. Priv. Ptd., 1936. 3 vols. Fo. Orig. buckram, unc., d.-w.'s. (C. Jul.22; 35) *Maggs.* £650

ARNOLDUS, Abbot of Vetus Mons
- Oratio Contra Monasteriorum Commendas. [Rome], [Eucharius Silber], ca. 1500. 4to. 3-line white on black woodcut capital initial in 1st. p., some slight marginal wormholes, old inscr. erased from 1st. p. Mor. gt., gt. arms of Eric Sexton on covers, by Sangorski & Sutcliffe. [BMC IV, 125] (CNY. Apr.8; 147) *$300*

ARNOULD, E.J.
- La Genèse du Barbier de Séville. Dublin & Paris, 1965. (543). 4to. Orig. cl. (SH. Mar.5; 170) *E. & J. Stevens.* £230

ARON BEN ISRAEL, of SADAGUR, Friedman
- Kdushat Aron Al Ha'torah. Warsaw, 1913. 1st. Edn. 4to. Hf. cl. (S. Nov.17; 249) *Zysblat.* £65

ARON HA'COHEN, of Apta
[-] Or Ha'ganus. Zolkiev, 1800. 1st. Edn. Hf. cl. (S. Nov.17; 180) *Zysblat.* £55

ARON HA'GADOL, of Karlin
- Bet Aron. Brody, 1875. 1st. Edn. 4to. Leath. (S. Nov.17; 153) *Zysblat.* £130

ARON, HA'LEVI, of Barcelona
- Sefer Chinuch. Venice, 1600. 2nd. Edn. Sm. 4to. Title reprd., stained. Mod. leath., s.-c. (SPB. May 11; 32) *$700*

ARON HA'LEVI, Frumkin, of Staroselye
- Avodat Ha'levi [on Genesis, Exodus, Leviticus & Haftrorot]; Likutim; She'eilot U'teshurog. [Johannesburg], 1842. 1st. Edn. 5 pts. in 1 vol. 4to. Bds. (S. Nov.17; 184) *Low.* £120
- Avodat Ha'levi-Drushim [on Numbers & Deuteronomy]. Warsaw, 1866. 1st. Edn. 2 pts. in 1 vol. 4to. Bds. (S. Nov.17; 185) *Zysblat.* £100

ARON ISAIAN FISCH
- Kdushat Aron. Debreczen, 1938. 1st. Edn. Hf. cl. (S. Nov.17; 152) *Maggs.* £65

ARON, OF ZHITOMIR
- Toldot Aron. Berditchev, 1817. 1st. Edn., on blue paper. 4to. Title torn affecting text of approbation, reprd., some worming, without loss of text. Hf. cl. (S. Nov.17; 157) *Zysblat.* £70
- - Anr. Edn. Lvov, 1864. 2nd. Edn. 4to. Cl. (S. Nov.17; 158) *Goldberg.* £55

ARP, Jean
- Dreams & Projects. N.Y., [1951-52]. (25) numbered, & sigd., with extra suite of ills. in sigd. sleeve. 4to. Loose as iss. in ptd. wraps., bd. s.-c. (SG. Apr.2; 5) *$1,400*
- Vers le Blanc Infini. Lausanne & Paris, 1960. (499) numbered on grand velin de Rives, & sigd. Fo. Loose in gt.-decor. bds., vell. spine, boxed. (SG. Apr.2; 6) *$550*
- - Anr. Copy. Fo. (SG. Oct.23; 4) *$350*
- - Anr. Edn. Lausanne, 1960. (600) copies, sigd. by Arp. 4to. Orig. wraps., unsewn, folded & box, slight soiling of case. (SPB. Nov.25; 216) *$1,100*

ARP, Jean, Delaunay, Sonia, & others
- [10 Lithographs]. Paris, 1950. (15) hors commerce, numbered, sigd. 4to. Unsewn, unc., in orig. folder & s.-c. (SH. Nov.20; 207) *Givaudon.* £120

ARRAIS, Edward Madeira
See– BACON, Roger & Arrais, Edward Madeira

ARRIGONI, Paolo
- Milano nelle Vecchie Stampe. Milan, 1969. 2 vols. Ob. 4to. Hf. mor., orig. wraps. bnd. in, boxes. (SI. Dec.3; 33) *Lire 300,000*

ARRIGONI, Paolo & Bertarelli, Achille
- Le Stampe Storiche . . . conservate nella Raccolta del Castello Sforzesco. Milan, 1930-32. 3 vols. 4to. Mod. red. hf. mor., orig. wraps. bnd. in. (SI. Dec.3; 34) *Lire 200,000*

ARROWSMITH, Aaron
- A New General Atlas. 1817. 4to. Engraved title & 53 maps, hand-cold. in outll., occasional spotting, prospectus for Arrowsmith's Geographical dictionary bnd. in. Orig. hf. mor. (CSK. Apr.10; 35) *£120*
- - Anr. Edn. Ca. 1830. 4to. Maps hand-cold. in outll., including frontis. Orig. cf.-bkd. bds. (S. Nov.4; 464) *Schuster.* £75
- - Anr. Edn. N.d. Maps hand-cold. in outll., 1st. few ll. detchd. Cont. mor.-bkd. cl., worn. (CSK. Aug.22; 16) *£55*
- Outlines of the World. 1825. Fo. 44 maps cold. in outll., engraved port. Hf. cf., defect. Ded. (P. Oct.23; 106) *Whatley.* £110

ARROWSMITH, John
- The London Atlas of Universal Geography. 1842. Fo. Cont. russ. gt. W.a.f. (C. Nov.6; 238) *Antipodean.* £900

ARROWSMITH, Joseph
[-] The Reformation. 1673. 1st. Edn. 4to. 1 p. stained. Mor. by Sangorski. [Wing A3780] (C. Nov.19; 44) *Pickering & Chatto.* £90

ARS TINCTORIA FUNDAMENTALIS, oder Gründliche Anweisung zur Farbekunst . . . Erstlich auss dem Frantzosischen ins Teutsche ubersetzt.–Ars Tinctoria Experimentalis. Frankfurt & Leipzig, 1683; 1685. 2 works in 1 vol. Browned thro.-out, slight marginal staining. Bds., worn, hf. mor. case. From Honeyman Collection. (S. May 20; 3172) *Rota.* £110

ART, L'
Paris, 1875-94. 57 vols. Fo. (last 2 vols. 4to). Many sm. stains & other minor defects. Orig. cl., most vols. slightly worn. (SM. Feb.11; 18) *Frs. 20,000*

ART D'AUJOURD'HUI
[Paris], 1924-29. 1st. Edns. Vols. I-VI, separately iss. Lge. 4to. Text & plts. loose, as iss., 4 vols.

retaining tissue guards. Cl.-bkd. ptd. bd. folders, ties. (PNY. Mar.4; 96) *$375*

ART DE CHASSE et de Peche
Lyon, 1719. Orig. Edn. 2 vols. Cont. leath. gt., 1 spine slightly defect. at head. (HK. Nov.18-21; 1729) *DM 420*

ART DE FRANCE
Ed.:– P. Berès & A. Chastel. Ill.:– Max Ernst & others. Paris, 1961-64. Fo. Orig. bds. (HK. May 12-14; 1774) *DM 420*

ART DE VOYAGER DANS LES AIRS, OU LES BALLONS
Paris, 1784. Lacks plts. Orig. wraps., rebkd., unc. (S. Dec.8; 152) *Bart.* £55
- - Anr. Copy. 14 pp. supp, 11 MS. pp. Orig. bds. (HD. Jun.24; 1) *Frs. 3,900*
- - Anr. Copy. 2 pts. in 1 vol. Cont. marb. wraps. (R. Oct.14-18; 454) *DM 1,400*

ART DECORATIF aux Expositions des Beaux-Arts (L')
1903-06. 6 vols. Sm. 4to. Later mor.-bkd. cl. (SH. Apr.9; 31) *Fogg.* £140

ART GALLERY (The)
N.d. Vols. 1-3. 4to. n.d. W.a.f. (CSK. Jun.12; 3) *£150*

ART in Australia
Sydney, 1923-24. 3rd. Series. Nos. 3-7. No. 3 lacks 3 cold. plts. Orig. wraps., corners bent. (JL. Jul.20; 607) *Aus. $110*
- - Anr. Run. Sydney, 1941-42. Series 4. Nos. 2-4 4to. Orig. wraps., marked, spines chipped. (JL. Jul.20; 605) *Aus. $210*
- - Anr. Run. N.d. 1st. series: Nos. 3, 4, & 6-11; 2nd. series: no. 2; 3rd. series: nos. 1-20, 22-24, 26, 27, 29-53, 55-59, 62, 64-69, 75, & 77-81. Wraps, or stiffened wraps. as iss., lacks 1 lr. wrap., severe defects to 4 others. W.a.f. (KH. Mar.24; 10) *Aus. $3,100*

ART JOURNAL, The
1849-54. New series, vols. 1-6 only. Fo. Orig. cl., slightly soiled. (CSK. Aug.1; 160) *£150*
- - Anr. Run. 1849-56. Vols. 11 & 12, New Series vols. 1-6, together 8 vols. Fo. A few minor defects. Cont. mor. gt., stained. (SBA. Mar.4; 234) *Hyde Park Bookshop.* £180
- - Anr. Run. 1849, 1852, 1854, 1857-59, 1862. 8 vols. 4to. Hf. cf., worn. As a periodical, w.a.f. (BS. Nov.26; 172) *£220*
- - Anr. Run. 1850 etc. 13 vols. Orig. bdgs. (DWB. Mar.31; 1) *£110*
- - Anr. Run. 1853-74. 8 vols., various. 4to. Hf. mor. W.a.f. (CSK. Jun.12; 78) *£240*
- - Anr. Run. 1854-80. 7 vols. various, including 1 dupl. Fo. Various bdgs. W.a.f. (CSK. Mar.27; 21) *£170*
- - Anr. Run. Ill.:– after Turner. 1862-64, 1866. 4 vols. 4to. Cont. hf. cf., some wear. (TA. Oct.16; 111) *£100*
- - Anr. Run. 1862-66. 5 vols. only. 4to. Cont. hf. mor., gt. spines. (SH. Oct.9; 156) *Walford.* £130
- - Anr. Run. 1869-76. 8 vols. only. 4to. Occasional spotting. Cont. hf. mor., spines gt. (CSK. Nov.21; 44) *£120*

ART OF ANCIENT EGYPT
- Series of Photographic Plates. Priv. ptd. 1895. 4to. 27 mntd. photographs slightly faded. Orig. cl., soiled. (CSK. Jan.30; 132) *£55*

ART OF DRAWING & PAINTING in Watercolours
1735. Some spotting. Mod. bds. (P. Apr.9; 25) *Edmunds.* £50

ART OF SAIL-MAKING, The
1796. Cont. cf. (SH. Jul.9; 112) *Libris.* £90

ART REVUE Hebdomadaire Illustrée
Paris, 1875-88. Vols. 1-45 only. Fo. Vols. 1-16 hf. mor., rest orig. bds., backstrips worn. (CSK. Nov.28; 161) *£780*
- - Anr. Edn. Ill.:– F. Goya. Paris & L., 1875-93. Year 1, Vols. 2 & 3 (of 3) & Year 2-19 together in 54 (of 55) vols. Fo. Orig. linen, some orig. wraps. bnd. in, plts. loose, slightly soiled. W.a.f. (HK. Nov.18-21; 3258) *DM 6,200*

ART UNION/Art Journal
1848-52. Vols. 10-14. 4to. Cont. gt. decor. crimson mor. (TA. Jun.18; 337) *£80*

ARTE E MANIFATTURE ANTICHE E MODERNE IN ORNAMENTI DI LUSSO
Milan, 1842. Fo. 1 sm. reprd. tear. Mod. hf. red mor. (SI. Dec.3; 38)   Lire 1,100,000

ARTE of Angling
See–SAMUEL, William, Attrib. to

ARTE VENETA, Rivista Trimestrale di Storia dell, Arte
Venice, 1947-71. Compl. coll. to year XXV inclusive. 4to. Orig. wraps or publisher's bdg. (DR. Mar.19; 6)   Lire 2,200,000

ARTE Y VOCABULARIO en la Lengua General del Peru llamada Quichua, y en la Lengua Espanola
En los Reyes [Lima], 1614. Inner margin of title guarded obscuring letters, a few ll. at end with loss of text. Old cf. (SPB. May 5; 78) $2,500

ARTHAUD, (J.)
– De la Vigne et de ses Produits. Bordeaux, 1858. 1st. Edn. Cont. red mor.-bkd. marb. bds., spine gt. Pres. copy; from liby. of André L. Simon. (S. May 18; 22)   Clark. £60

ARTHUR, E.R.
– Small Houses of the Late 18th & Early 19th Centuries in Ontario. Ca. 1928. 4to. Orig. wraps. (CB. May 17; 284)   Can. $120

ARTICLES & REGULATIONS of the Friendly Assocation in Beith
Glasgow, 1784. Bds., soiled. (CE. Dec.4; 110)   £240

ARTIS AURIFERAE, quam chemiam vocant volumina duo quae continent rubam philosophorum aliosque antiqu. auctores. Basle, 1610. 1st complete Edn. with Pt III. 3 pts. in 1 vol. Owner's inscr. Limp vell. with ties. Bkplt. Bibliotheca Lindesiana. (S Dec.1; 31)   Quaritch. £600

ARTIST (The)
1931-43. Vols. 1-24. 4to. Orig. cl. (SKC. Jul.28; 2434)   £65

ARTIST & THE BOOK (The): 1860-1960
Boston, [1961]. 4to. Cl., d.-w. (PNY. Mar.4; 101) $130

ARTISTS DEPOSITORY
– Illustrations For Scrap Books. Ob. 4to. Later hf. mor. W.a.f. (TA. Aug.21; 317)   £105

ARTOIS, le Comte d'
– Catalogue des Livres du Cabinet. Paris, 1783. (15) L.P. 4to. Cont. bds., unc. (SM. Oct.7; 1304)   Frs. 4,200

ARUBAS, Yitzhak Ben Chananiah (Ed.)
See–EMET VE'EMUNAH

ARUNDELL, Francis V.J.
See–CONDY, Nicholas & Arundell, Francis V.J.

ARYE OF LANZHUT
– Arbra'a Charashim. [Lvov], 1849. 1st Edn. Hf. cl. (S. Nov.17; 159)   Zysblat. £80

ARYE LEIB MOCHIACH of Polonnoye
– Kol Arye. Koretz, 1798. 1st Edn., on blue paper. 4to. Hf. cl. (S. Nov.17; 160)   Low. £175

ASBJØRNSEN, Peter Christen
– Norge, Fremstillet Tegninger. Christiana, 1846-48. 17 pts. in 10. Ob. fo. Orig. ptd. wraps. (S. Oct.20; 16)   Temperley. £200

ASBJØRNSEN, Peter Christen & Moe, Jorgen I.
– East of the Sun & West of the Moon. Ill.:– Kay Nielsen. [1914]. 4to. Orig. cl. gt. (SH. Mar.27; 378)   Rios. £280
– – Anr. Copy. Gt.-decor. cl. (SG. Apr.2; 213) $900
– – Anr. Copy. Orig. cl., gt., bds. slightly warped. (SPB. Nov.25; 366) $400
– – Anr. Copy. Cl. (SG. Oct.23; 238) $100
[–] – Anr. Edn. Ill.:– Kay Nielsen. N.Y., [1927]. Contains extra plt. Orig. cl., d.w. torn. (SH. Dec.11; 373)   Hatchard's. £130
[–] – Anr. Copy. Orig. cl., worn. (SH. Dec.11; 374)   Jones. £75
[–] Anr. Edn. Ill.:– Kay Nielsen. Ca. 1930. Orig. cl., spine slightly soiled. With bkplt. of Neville Main. (S. Jul.31; 266)   Ross. £50
– – Anr. Edn. Ill.:– Kay Nielsen. L., n.d. 4to. Orig. cl. gt. (P. Jun.11; 107)   Steenson. £180
– – Anr. Copy. Orig. pict. cl. (PL. Nov.27; 64)   Berry. £80

[–] – Anr. Copy. Orig. cl. (SKC. Feb.26; 1292)   £60
– – Anr. Copy. Some spotting of text, foxing, stitching loose. Orig. cl. gt., slight warping, tears. (SPB. May 29; 320) $425

ASBJØRNSEN, Peter Christen & Tönsberg, Christian
– Norge Fremstillet i Tegninger. Christiania, 1848. Ob. 4to. 82 tinted litho. plts. Hf. mor. gt. (P. Jun.11; 307)   Bailey. £180

ASCENSIUS, Jodocus Badius (Ed.)
See–EPISTOLAE Illustrium Virorum

ASCHAM, Roger–DEMOSTHENES
– The Scholemaster.-A Report & Discourse . . . of the Affairs & State of. Germany.-The Three Orationes. 1570; [1570]; 1570. 1st. Edn.; 1st. Edn.; 1st. Edn. in Engl. 3 works in 1 vol. 4to. Cont. cf., rebkd., worn. [STC 832; 830; 6578] (C. Nov.20; 216)   Carnegie. £2,000

ASCONIUS PEDIANUS, Quintus
– Commentarii in Orationes Ciceronis. Ed.:– Hieronymus Squazaficus. Venice, Johannes de Colonia & Johannes Manthen, after 2 Jun., 1477. 1st. Edn. Fo. Initials, chaptermarks & initial strokes supplied in red, last lf. reprd., slightly affecting text, owner's inscr. Mod. mor.-bkd. bds. [BMC V, 232] (S. Nov.25; 334)   Abrams. £480

ASEEV, Nikolai
– Oksana. Moscow, 1916. Orig. wraps. (SH. Feb.6; 381)   Quaritch. £50

ASEEV, Nikolai & Mayakovsky, V.
– Odna golova vsegda bedna, a potomu i bedna, chto zhivet odna [One Head is always not enough, but that is why it is poor to live alone]. Moscow, 1924. Orig. wraps. by Mayakovsky. (SH. Feb.6; 382)   Quaritch. £260
– Pervy Pervomai [The First of May]. Leningrad, 1926. Orig. wraps. by B. Titov. (SH. Feb.6; 383)   Kazinkas. £200
– Rasskaz o tom, putem kakim s bedoi upravilsya Akim [Tale of how Akim delivered himself from Trouble]. Moscow, 1925. Orig. wraps. by I. Manati, tear in upr. cover. (SH. Feb.6; 384)   Quaritch. £360

ASELLI, Gaspard
– De Lactibus. Leiden, 1640. 3rd Edn. 4to. Plt. 4 bnd. inverted, title & last p. dust-soiled. Hf. cf. (S. Jun.15; 18)   Rota. £160
– – Anr. Copy. Liby. stp. on title. New cl. (S. Dec.2; 442)   Phelps. £140

ASH, Edward C.
– Dogs: their History & Development. L., 1927. 2 vols. 4to. Vol. 2 title reprd. Cl. (SG. Apr.9; 334) $180
– – Anr. Edn. N.Y., Derrydale Pr., 1931. Buckram, d.-w. (SG. Apr.9; 347) $200

ASHBEE, Charles Robert
– American Sheaves & English Seed Corn. L., Essex House Pr., 1901. (300). Orig. vell., unc. (CNY. May 22; 308) $120
– An Endeavour towards the Teaching of John Ruskin & William Morris. Ill.:– George Thomson. Essex House Pr., 1901. (350) numbered. 2 ll. badly opened. Orig. limp vell., slightly stained, unc., mostly unopened. (S. Jul.31; 56)   Foyles. £80
– – Anr. Copy. Vell.-bkd. patterned bds., unc. & unopened. (SG. Jan.15; 26) $120
– The Last Records of a Cotswold Community. L., Essex House Pr., 1904. (75) on Essex House paper. 4to. Orig. buckram, unc., unopened. (CNY. May 22; 312) $250
– Modern English Silverwork. 1908. Ltd. Edn. 4to. Orig. cl. (SH. Jul.23; 254)   Sims & Reed. £300

ASHBEE, Charles Robert & others
See–LONDON County Council

ASHBROOK, Stanley B.
– The United States One Cent Stamp of 1851-1857. N.Y., 1938. 2 vols. Buckram, d.w.'s. Sigd. (SG. Feb.12; 307) $120

ASHE, Thomas
– Travels in America, Performed in 1806, for the Purpose of Exploring the Rivers Alleghany, Monongahela, Ohio & Mississippi . . . L., 1808. 1st. Edn. 3 vols. 12mo. Cont. cf., gt., worn, upr. cover of vol. I detchd. From liby. of William E. Wilson. (SPB. Apr.29; 8) $175

ASHENDENE PRESS
– Descriptive Bibliography of Books Printed at . . . Ash. Pr., 1935. (390) sigd. by C.H. St. J. Hornby. Fo. Orig. cf., upr. cover with gt. device. Pres. Copy from C.H. St. J. Hornby to Eric G. Millar, prospectus for this book & A.L.s. from Hornby to Millar loosely inserted. (SH. Feb.19; 22)   John. £520
– – Anr. Copy. With the 2 errata slips & a sigd. note tipped in or loosely inserted. Partly unc., mor., s.-c., in marb. bds. (KH. Nov.18; 19)   Aus. $980

ASHMOLE, Elias
– The Antiquities of Berkshire. Ill.:– Van der Gucht (frontis.) & W. Hollar (view). 1719. 3 vols. Last 6 ll. of vol. 1 & 1st. 5 ll. of vol. 2 with dampstain to inner margin. Cont. cf., panel on covers with gt. cornerpiece of an oak wreath enclosing a shell ornament, spines gt., bnd. for Richard Rawlinson, worn, sm. abrasions. From the collection of Eric Sexton. (C. Apr.16; 209)   Traylen. £120
– The Institution, Laws & Ceremonies of the Most Noble Order of the Garter. Ill.:– Sherwin (port.) & W. Hollar. 1672. 1st. Edn. Fo. Cont. cf., rebkd. Pres. Copy, to Nicholas Oudart, later note by Narcissus Luttrell, & his MS. additions to the list of the Knights-Companion, lately in the collection of Eric Sexton. [Wing A3983] (C. Apr.15; 161)   Murray-Hill. £300
– – Anr. Edn. Fo. Cont. cf., worn. (SG. Sep.25; 25) $280
– – Anr. Edn. Ill.:– Hollar. 1693. 2nd. Edn. Fo. Port. & 2 ll. torn, some ll & a few plts. stained in margins, offsetting to 1st. title, a few rustholes & short tears. 19th. C. str.-grd. mor., gt., Chesterfield arms on covers, detchd., very worn. [Wing A3984] (S. Dec.9; 290)   Hyde. £55

ASIATIC SOCIETY OF BENGAL
– Asiatic Researches. 1799-1803. Vols. 1-7 only. 4to. Cont. cf., worn. (SH. Jun.18; 201)   Makiya. £55

ASIATISCHE KUNST
Ed.:– Alfred Salmony, & Paul Pelliot (notes). Munich, [1929]. Fo. Loose as iss. in linen folder (stained). (SG. Mar.12; 15) $160

ASPIN, Jehoshaphat
– Cosmorama. [1827]. 1st. Edn. 12mo. Later roan gt. (S. Feb.9; 3)   Quaritch. £85
– The Naval & Military Exploits . . . 1820. 12mo. Frontis. & plts. hand-cold., & with the 2 additional plts. 'Vittoria' & 'Pampeluna' not called for in the plt. list. Cont. tree cf., gt., by W. Appleby, with his ticket. From the collection of Eric Sexton. (C. Apr.15; 23)   Maggs. £240
– – Anr. Copy. Lacks the 2 extra plts. Cont. red mor., gt. title & emblem on upr. cover, gt. borders & spine, buckram s.-c. (C. Nov.6; 281)   Spencer. £80

ASPLUND, Dr. Karl
– Anders Zorn, His Life & Work. 1921. 4to. Cont. vell.-bkd. bds., gt. (P. Mar.12; 20)   Fenton. £55

ASSIETTE AU BEURRE, L'
Apr. 1901-Jan. 1902. Nos. 1-40 in 1 vol. 4to. Qtr. mor. (P. Feb.19; 55)   Lipman. £360

ASSOCIATION of Edison Illuminating Companies
– Edison Honored Throughout the Entire World. N.Y., 1929. 4to. Leatherette, with gt. medallion on cover, in orig. 2 pt. card. box. T.L.s., by Edison laid in (May 19, 1911, 4to., 1 p.). (SG. Jan.29; 147) $240

ASTELL, Mary
– Essay in Defence of the Female Sex. 1696. Frontis. bnd. in (not called for). Cf. (P. Sep.11; 71)   Traylen. £90

ASTESANUS de Ast
– Canones Poenitentiales. [Vienna], [Johann Winterberg], ca. 1496. 4to. Woodcut initial capital at fo. 2r, some slight stains. Recent vell. From the collection of Eric Sexton. [BMC III, 812, Goff A1159, H 4343] (CNY. Apr.8; 203) $2,200
– Summa de Casibus Conscientiae. Ed.:– Bartholomaeus de Ballatis & Gometius de Ulixona. Nuremb., Anton Koberger, 11 May, 1482. Fo. Some initials in blue or red with ornamental background in col. & penwork, other initials in red or blue, red chaptermarks & initial stroke. Cont. German blind-stpd. cf. on wooden bds., rebkd., spine worn & damaged, corners

worn, lacks clasps. [BMC II, 423] (S. Mar.17; 235)   *Fletcher.* £650

ASTLE, Thomas
– The Origin & Progress of Writing. L., Priv. Ptd., 1784. 1st. Edn. 4to. Disbnd. (SG. Mar.26; 15) $120
– – Anr. Edn. 1803. 2nd. Edn. Fo. Cont. cf., gt., spine lacquered. (SG. Oct.2; 17) $220
See–GROSE, Francis & others

ASTLEY, Philip
– System of Equestrian Education. Dublin, 1802. 8th Edn. Vol. 1 only (all publd.). Orig. bds., rather worn. (SKC. Jul.28; 2506)   £50

ASTLEY, Thomas
– New General Collection of Voyages & Travels. 1745-46. 1st. Edn. Vols. 1-3 only. 4to. Cont. cf. W.a.f. (CSK. Jan.30; 83)   £100
– – Anr. Edn. L., 1745-47. 1st. Edn. 4 vols. 4to. Cont. cf., rebkd., new endpapers. Clinton copy, with Rolle bkplt. replaced, as an atlas, w.a.f. (SPB. Oct.1; 178) $700

ASTRONOMIA. Teutsch Astronomei
Frankfurt a. M., 1545. 1st. Edn. Fo. Some browning, paper flaw in E2 slightly affecting text. 19th. C. bds., worn. From Honeyman Collection. (S. May 20; 3173)   *Hill.* £550

ASTRUC, Jean
– De Morbis Venereis. Paris, 1736. 1st. Edn. 4to. Slight browning & soiling. Cont. mott. cf., spine gt., slightly worn. From liby. of Dr. E. Ashworth Underwood. (S. Feb.23; 139)   *Guice.* £55

ASTRUC, Dr. John
– Memoires pour l'Histoire naturelle de la Province de Languedoc. Paris, 1737. 1st. Edn. 4to. With approbation leaf at end, sig. of Carl Gustaf Tessin on title. Cont. cf., gt. spine, worn & eroded. (S. Oct.20; 18)   *R. E. Kessow.* £130
– – Anr. Edn. Paris, 1738. 4to. 19th. C. hf. mor. From Chetham's Liby., Manchester. (C. Nov.26; 19)   *Lester.* £60

ASTRY, Thomas
– True Relation of a Young Man about Seventeen . . . struck Dumb . . . Twenty Four Hours . . . Priv. ptd., 1671. 4to. Title & last lf. stained. Disbnd. [Wing A4085] (SH. Apr.10; 474)   *Quaritch.* £55

ATAR, Chaim Ibn
– Or Ha'chaim. Zolkiev, 1799. 2nd. Edn. 4to. Some discolouration. Bds. (S. Nov.18; 393)   *Low.* £60
– – Anr. Copy. Cropped, stained & soiled. Cf. (SPB. May 11; 34) $300

ATGET, Eugene
– Photographe de Paris. Ed.:– Pierre Mac-Orlan (preface). Ill.:– Berenice Abbott (port.). N.Y., [1930]. 4to. Some plts. with liby. stps., separate pamphlet of captions laid-in. Gt.-lettered cl., minor spotting. (SG. Jul.9; 30) $300
– A Vision of Paris. N.Y., 1963. 1st. Amer. Edn. 4to. Owner's sig. on front endpaper. Cl., upr. spine bumped, d.-w. defect. (SG. Apr.23; 18) $200
– – Anr. Copy. Cl., d.-w. (PNY. May 21; 29) $160

ATHENAEUS
– Deipnosophistarum. Trans.:– Comitum Natalis. Basle, 1556. Cont. vell. (P. Dec.11; 117)   *Georges.* £50
– Deipnosophostarum Libri quindecim.–Les Quinze Livres des Deipnosophistes. Ed.:– I. Casaubon (1st. work). Trans.:– J. Dalechamps (1st. work). Lyons; Paris, 1657; 1680. 2 vols. Fo.; 4to. 1st. work with some browning; 2nd. work with slight dampstaining. Cont. vell. bds., soiled; cont. cf., worn. From liby. of André L. Simon. (S. May 18; 23)   *Poole.* £50
– Les Quinze Livres des Deipnosophistes. Trans.:– [Michel de Marolles]. Paris, 1680. 4to. Port. with biographical notes under in 18th. C. hand, cropped by bdg. 18th. C. mor., borders composed of fillets, leaves entwined with dots, sm. ovals & lozenges joined by dots, spine gt. in compartments, inner gt. dentelles. Bkplt of Baron Northwick. (SM. Oct.7; 1552)   *Frs.* 5,800

ATHERTON, William
– Narrative of the Suffering & Defeat of the North-Western Army Under General Winchester . . . Frankfort, Ky., 1842. 1st. Edn. 16mo. Lightly foxed. Orig. sheep-bkd. marb. bds., head & foot of spine worn. From liby. of William E. Wilson. (SPB. Apr.29; 9) $125

ATKINS, John
– A Voyage to Guinea, Brasil, & the West-Indies. L., 1735. Publisher's advts. at front & back, errata, browning, some tears, chipping, ex-liby. with liby. stp. on title & p. 121, inner margin of title strengthened. Cf. [Sabin 2274] (SPB. May 5; 79) $300

ATKINS, S. E. & Overall, W.H.
– Some account of the Worshipful Company of Clockmakers of the City of London. Priv. ptd., 1881. Orig. hf.-mor. (CSK. Sep.12; 229)   £50

ATKINSON, C.T.–GROVES, Lieut.-Col. Percy
– History of the Royal Dragoons.–History of the 2nd Dragoons. 1934; 1893. 2 works in 2 vols. 4to. Both cl. gt. (C. Jul.22; 177)   *Browning.* £60

ATKINSON, Capt. George Francklin
– Curry & Rice. N.d. Some tears. Later hf. cf. (SH. Jun.4; 124)   *Pigeonhole.* £80

ATKINSON, James
– Medical Bibliography A & B [all publd.]. Churchill, 1834. Liby. stp. on title. Orig. cl., hinges reprd., label worn. (S. Jun.15; 20)   *Talerman.* £170

ATKINSON, John Augustus
– Sketches in Afghaunistan. 1842. Fo. Margins frayed, not affecting plts. Cont. mor.-bkd. cl. (CSK. Oct.10; 78)   £130
– – Anr. Copy. 23 (of 25) tinted litho. plts., lacks nos. 7 & 13. Orig. qtr. mor. (TA. May 21; 231)   £70
– – Anr. Edn. [1842]. Fo. Loosely inserted are 11 dupl., hand-finished, cold. litho. plts. Cl. (C. Nov.5; 4)   *Petcher.* £600
– – Anr. Copy. Orig. mor.-bkd. cl. (C. May 20; 98)   *Quaritch.* £380
– – Anr. Copy. Some spotting. Worn, disbnd. (CSK. Mar.6; 111)   £100
– – Anr. Copy. Soiling & staining, 1 lf. of letterpress. Worn & disbnd. (CSK. Nov.7; 181)   £70

ATKINSON, John Augustus & Walker, James
– A Picturesque Representation . . . of the Russians. 1803-04. 3 vols. in 1. Fo. Lacks port., a few ll. slightly spotted. Disbnd. (SH. Feb 5; 195)   *Dimsdale.* £200

ATKINSON, Thomas William
– Oriental & Western Siberia. 1858. 1st. Edn. A few plts. slightly loose & with frayed margins, some foxing. Orig. cl., gt., unc., loose. (S. Jun.29; 274)   *Brown.* £60

ATKYNS, Sir Robert
– The Ancient & Present State of Glostershire. Ill.:– Kip. 1712. 1st. Edn. Fo. Old cf. gt., worn. Bkplt. of the Earl of Cork & Orrery. (LC. Jun.18; 131)   £340
– – Anr. Copy. Antique-style panel. cf. From the collection of Eric Sexton. (C. Apr.16; 210)   *Traylen.* £320
– – Anr. Edn. 1768. 2nd. Edn. Fo. Cont. cf., panel of floral roll tool border on covers enclosing gt. arms, upr. cover detchd. (C. Feb.25; 22)   *Crowe.* £380
– – Anr. Copy. Cont. cf., rebkd. W.a.f. (TA. Aug.21; 293)   £280
– – Anr. Copy. 63 double-p. engraved plts. only (of 64, lacks Broadwell), some plts. creased at fold. Cf., rebkd. (LC. Jun.18; 132)   £180

ATL, Dr.
– Iglesias de Mexico. Ill.:– Kahlo & Atl. Mexico, 1924-25. Vols. I-IV. Tall fo. Cl.-bkd. pict. bds., spines torn, liby. bkplt. (SG. Mar.12; 255) $130

ATLANTE Di Botanica Popolare
Ill.:– Raimondo Petraroja after Longobardi & others. Italy, ca. 1870. 140 hand-cold. lithos. from the work, each with publisher's blindstp., foxed. (SG. Sep.18; 23) $130

ATLANTIS. Volksmärchen und Volksdichtungen Afrikas. Veröffentlichungen des Forschungsinstit-uts Für Kulturmorphologie
Ed.:– L. Frobenius. Ill.:– F.H. Ehmcke. (cover). Jena, 1921-28. Vols. 1-12. Orig. linen. (D. Dec.11-13; 853)   DM 500

ATLASES
– The American Military Pocket Atlas . . . British Colonies . . . L., ca. 1776. 1st. Edn. Mod. gt. hf. cf. & cl. (PNY. Oct.1; 40) $2,000
– [Atlas]. Ill.:– De Lisle, Visscher & others. [Amst., Regnier & Josua Ottens], ca. 1731-50? Fo. (sheets 620 × 535 mm). 97 double-p. or

folding engraved hand-cold. maps, 6 torn, others with marginal tears, lacks title-p. & text. Cont. mott. cf. gt., very worn, covers detchd. W.a.f. (CNY. May 22; 30) $5,000
– Atlas de la Monarchie Prussienne. Ill.:– P.F. Tardieu after Mentelle. L., 1788. Fo. Cont. hf. cf. (S. Jan.27; 305)   *Schuster.* £190
– – Anr. Copy. 10 double-p. maps, 93 plts. Bds. (P. Mar.12; 177)   *Kestrel.* £140
– Atlas de toutes les Parties Connues du Globe Terrestre. Geneva, 1781. 4to. Bds. (LM. Nov.8; 6)   B. Frs. 10,000
– – Anr. Edn. [Paris], ca. 1840 4to. Slightly soiled in parts, title stpd. Cont. hf. leath. (H. Dec.9/10; 442)   DM 720
– Atlas des Voyages et Cartes des Découvertes faites dans l'Océan Atlantique Sud par le Capitaine Cook. Carte d'Amérique, Mer Pacifique, etc. N.p., n.d. 4to. 65 plts., folding. Hf. cf., worn. (LM. Nov.8; 7)   B. Frs. 10,000
– Atlas en Miniature, ou Leger Aperçu de Géographie Physique et Politique, à la Jeunesse Curieuse et que Desire s'Instruire. Paris, ca. 1825. Ob. 8vo. All but 2 maps outlined in colour. Orig. wraps, slightly worn & stained, orig. bds , cover of pt. 2 loose, orig. pict. s.-c., worn. (SH. Mar.19; 18)   *Schierenberg.* £100
– Atlas Encyclopédique. Paris, 1787. 4to. 73 double-p. maps by Bonne, 16 loose. Bdg. not stated. (P. Mar.12; 179)   *Cambridge.* £190
– Atlas Moderne. Ca. 1771. Fo. 44 partly cold. double-p. maps by Bonne, Zannonni, etc., 8 in Atlas, others loose. Bdg. not stated. (P. Mar.12; 178)   *Fairburn.* £150
– – Anr. Copy. Pt. 11 (of 2), separately issued. Cont. mott. bds., worn. Cont. owner's inscr. (PNY. Oct.1; 42) $850
– – Anr. Edn. Paris, [1773]. Fo. All maps with MS. notes in margins, lacks 7 maps. Cont. hf. leath. gt., spine defect. (R. Mar.31-Apr.4; 2297)   DM 2,400
– Atlas National Portatif de la France.–Précis Elémentaire et Methodique de la Nouvelle Géographie de la France. Paris, 1792; 1791. 2 works in 1 vol. Ob. 4to. Maps hand-cold. in 1st. work. 19th. C. hf. mor. W.a.f., from Chetham's Liby., Manchester. (C. Nov.26; 20)   *Ginsberg.* £220
– Atlas [Nouvel]. Amst., n.d. Ob. fo. Cold. borders. Old hf. roan, corners, blind-stpd. spine, bdg. slightly defect. (HD. Feb.27; 6)   Frs. 6,500
– Atlas Russicus, Atlas Russien. St. Petersb., 1745. Fo. Some dampstains, especially on title, last map & endpapers, cont. outl. colouring. Old paper bds., very worn & defect. (S. Oct.20; 19)   *Bjorck & Borjesson.* £1,600
– Atlas van alle de Zee-Havens der Bataafsche Republiek. Ill.:– M. de Sallieth, D. de Jonq, after D. de Jong, G. Groenewegen & Kobel. Amst., [1802]. 1st. Edn. Fo. Some plts. lightly soiled. Cont. hf. leath., defect., lacks upr. cover. (R. Oct.14-18; 1892)   DM 11,500
– Collection of 26 engraved maps. Ill.:– after N. Sanson & others. Paris, Priv. ptd., maps dtd. 1684-1732. Fo. Maps hand-cold. in outl., some with crude repairs. Canvas covered cont. sheep. (C. Feb.26; 67)   *Burgess.* £700
– French Atlas of the Ancient World (unidentified). Paris, ca. 1760. Marked at spine as the Atlas (Vol. 4). Fo. (16¼ × 13½). Maps engraved on heavy wtrmkd. laid paper. Cont. mott. cf., worn. (PNY. Oct.1; 41) $700
– Théâtre de la Guerre en Flanders. 1744-47. Ob. 4to. General map, 24 plans. Wraps. (P. Jun.11; 205)   *Maggs.* £70
– [The World from the Best Authorities]. [Edinb.], ca. 1780. 35 double-p. or folding copper engraved maps & 6 copperplts., 2 folding. Cont. hf. leath., defect. (R. Oct.14-18; 1523)   DM 700

ATMOSPHERIC RAILWAYS
– Report from the Select Committee. 1845. Fo. Disbnd. (SH. Mar.5; 173)   *Weinreb.* £130

ATTEMPT TO VINDICATE THE AMERICAN CHARACTER, being Principally a Reply to the Intemperate Animadversions of Thomas Moore Esq.
Phila., 1806. 1st. Edn. Foxed, annots. Disband. (SG. Mar.5; 19)   £130

ATTORNEY-General's charges against the late Queen
Ill.:– George Cruikshank, Robert Cruikshank & others. L., n.d. Fo. Hf. red mor., discold. The Sir

ATTORNEY-General's charges against the late Queen -contd.
William Augustus Fraser-Clarence S. Bemens Copy. (SPB. Oct.1; 192) $2,800

ATWATER, Caleb
- **Remarks Made on a Tour to Prairie du Chien . . .** Columbus, 1831. 1st. Edn. 12mo. Browned, inner margin of title reprd. Hf. mor., head & foot of spine chipped. From liby. of William E. Wilson. [Sabin 2335] (SPB. Apr.29; 10) $150

ATWOOD, George
- **A Treatise on the Rectilinear Motion & Rotation of Bodies: with a description of original experiments relative to the subject.** 1784. 1st. Edn. Verso of errata lf. stained, slightly affecting 1 plt., a few short tears, slight browning. Cont. spr. cf., slightly soiled. Bkplt. of Sir John Trollope. (S. Jun.23; 269) *Quaritch.* £350

AUBANEL
- **Li Fiho d'Avignon.** Mount-Pélié, 1885. (300). Parallel Fr. trans. Jansenist mor., wrap., by Cretté. (HD. Oct.10; 7) Frs. 1,150

AUBER, D.F.E.
- **La Muette de Portici.** Paris, [1828]. 1st. Edn. 2 vols. Fo. Slightly soiled thro.-out. Hf. leath. (H. Dec.9/10; 1039) DM 750

AUBERT DE GASPE, Philippe
- **Les Anciens Canadiens.** Quebec, 1864. 2nd. Edn. Mor. gt., upr. cover gt.-lettered 'Offert a Son Altesse Royale le Prince Arthur par la Province de Quebec'. (SG. Mar.5; 103) $200
- **Memoires.** Ottawa, 1866. 1st. Edn. Mor., upr. cover lettered in gt. 'Offert à son Altesse Royale le Prince Arthur par la Province de Quebec'. (SG. Mar.5; 102) $300

AUBERY, Jacques
- **Histoire de l'Execution de Cabrières et de Mérindol et d'Autres Lieux de Provence . . .** Paris, 1645. 4to. Cont. cf., arms & cipher (repeated on spine) of J.-A. de Thou & Fasparde de la Chastre. (HD. Mar.18; 12) Frs. 4,200

AUBLET, Jean Baptiste Christophe Fusée
- **Histoire des Plantes de la Guiane Françoise.** L. & Paris, 1775. 1st. Edn. 4 vols. 4to. Dupl. of plt. 375. Cont. cf., worn, rebkd. From Chetham's Liby., Manchester. (C. Nov.26; 21) *Cucchi.* £600
- - **Anr. Copy.** 352 (of 392) plts. only. Cont. hf. russ. W.a.f. From collection of Massachusetts Horticultural Society, unstpd. (SPB. Oct.1; 99) $475

AUBREY, John
- **The Natural History & Antiquities of the County of Surrey.** 1719. 1st. Edn., L.P. 5 vols. Both folding plts. with sm. tears, folding map slightly torn, slight browning & spotting. Late 19th. C. red mor., gt., covers slightly worn. Bkplt. of Alfred Harmsworth. (S. Jun.22; 5) *Traylen.* £200

AUBRY, Charles
- **Histoire Pittoresque de l'Equitation Ancienne & Moderne.** Paris, 1833-34. Fo. Lightly soiled. Cont. hf. leath. (H. Dec.9/10; 362) DM 2,000

AUBUSSON de la Feuillade, F.
- **Journal de l'Expedition pour le Secours de Candide.** Lyon, 1669. Folding plan dampstained. Cont. cf., worn. (SH. Jun.11; 187) *Galen.* £65

AUCASSIN & Nicolette
L., 1887. Orig. cl., slightly worn. Aubrey Beardsley's copy with his sig. (SPB. Jul.28; 21) $275
- - **Anr. Edn.** Ill.:– Lucien Pissarro. L., Eragny Pr., 1903. (230). Bds., unc. (SG. Oct.9; 88) $250

AUDEBERT, Jean Baptiste
- **Histoire Naturelle des Singes et des Makis.** Paris, 1798-99. 1st. Edn. Fo. 62 only (of 63) plts., with 60 ptd. cold. & hand-finished, occasional foxing & some light staining at edges. Cont. diced russ., gt. borders on covers. From Chetham's Liby., Manchester. (C. Nov.26; 22) *Isley.* £1,200

AUDEBERT, Jean Baptiste & Vieillot, Louis Jean Pierre
- **Histoire Naturelle et Générale des Grimpereaux et des Oiseaux de Paradis.** Paris, 1802. Fo. 105 plts., col. ptd., hand finished with titles in gold. Cont. diced russ., covers detchd. (C. Mar.18; 11a) *Rostron.* £2,800

- **Oiseaux Dorés ou à Reflets Metalliques.** Paris, An XI [1802]. 1st. Edn. 2 vols. Fo. Occasional light foxing to plts. Cont. Fr. red mor., sides with wide fillet borders of foliage sprays enclosing figures of birds, spines gt. in 7 compartments with figures of birds, by Bozerian, & sigd. at foot of spines. (C. Nov.5; 5) *F.A.M.* £10,00
- - **Anr. Edn.** Paris, 1802. Vol. II only (of 2). Fo. 105 plts., ptd. cold. & hand-finished, occasional light foxing, mostly marginal. Cont. diced russ., gt. borders on covers, jnts. brkn. From Chetham's Liby., Manchester. (C. Nov.26; 23) *Taylor.* £1,800

AUDEN, Wystan Hugh
- **The Dance of Death.** 1933. 1st. Edn. Unbnd. Page proofs for 1st. Edn., some autograph corrections & revisions by author. (SH. Dec.18; 46) *Quaritch.* £200
- **Poems.** 1930. 1st. Edn. 4to. Orig. wraps., unc. (SH. Dec.18; 42) *Blackwell.* £100
- - **Anr. Edn.** L., [1930]. 1st. Edn. 4to. Wraps. (SG. Jun.4; 7) $180
- - **Anr. Edn.** 1933. 2nd. Edn. End-ll slightly spotted. Orig. plain paper wraps. Proof Copy, 7 poems substituted, 4 pencil autograph corrections. (SH. Dec.18; 43) *Rota.* £90

AUDEN, Wystan Hugh & Garrett, John
- **The Poet's Tongue.** 1935. Trade Iss. 2 vols. in 1. Orig. cl. Inscr. by Auden to Cecil Beaton. (SH. Dec.19; 331) *Ross.* £65

AUDIFFRET, J.B.
[-] **La Géographie Ancienne, Moderne et Historique.** Paris, 1689-94. 3 vols. 4to. Cont. leath., gt. spine, spine partly defect. (R. Oct.14-18; 1524) DM 1,500

AUDIN, Marius
- **Essai sur les Graveurs de Bois en France au Dix-Huitième Siecle.** Paris, 1925. Sq. 8vo. Ptd. wraps., unc. & unopened. (SG. Mar.26; 22) $100
- **Histoire de l'Imprimerie par l'Image.** Paris, 1929. 4 vols. Sq. 8vo. Ptd. wraps., unc. (SG. Mar.26; 23) $300

AUDOIT, Edmond
- **Atlas de l'Herbier des Demoiselles.** Ill.:– Belaife frontis. Paris, n.d. Ob. 4to. Hf. red chagrin, decor. spine. (HD. Jun.10; 116) Frs. 1,000

AUDOT, Louis Eustache
[-] **L'Italie, La Sicilie, Les Isles Eoliennes, l'Ile d'Elbe . . .** Paris, 1834-47. 1st. Edn. 7 vols. Liby. stp. on titles, few ll. partly detchd. Cont. mor.-bkd. bds. (S. Nov.25; 497) *Broseghini.* £400

AUDRAN, J.
See–DUERER, Albrecht–AUDRAN, J.

AUDSLEY, George Ashdown
- **The Art of Chromolithography.** 1883. Fo. Loose in bdg., 1 outer margin defect. Cl. (BS. May 13; 282) £110
- **The Art of Organ-Building.** N.Y., 1905. 1st. Edn. 2 vols. Fo. Buckram, ex-liby. (SG. Dec.4; 22) $200
- **Gems of Japanese Art & Handicraft.** 1913. Fo. Cf. gt. by Worsall. (P. Mar.12; 225) *Cambridge.* £200
- - **Anr. Copy.** Orig. cl. portfo., worn, ties. (SH. Jan.29; 204) *Walford.* £85
- **The Ornamental Arts of Japan.** 1882. 2 vols. Fo. Cont. hf. mor., gt. spines. (SH. Oct.9; 159) *Fine Books Oriental.* £210
- - **Anr. Edn.** 1882-84. 2 vols. Fo. Occasional spotting. Orig. mor., jnts. worn. (CSK. Jun.26; 102) £170
- - **Anr. Copy.** Sm. embossed liby. stps. on titles. Three-qtr. mor. (SG. Mar.12; 209) $275
- - **Anr. Edn.** 1882-84. (50) artist's proof copies for Engl. subscribers. 2 vols. Fo. Orig. mor. gt., upr. covers with red & green onlays, 1 cover detchd. (C. Jul.22; 130) *Joseph.* £190
- **The Practical Decorator & Ornamentalist.** N.d. 15 orig. pts. Fo. A few plts. slightly soiled, revised plt. descriptions to pts. 1-4 with the publisher's ptd. advice that 'The Original descriptions should be destroyed'. Unbnd. as Iss. in orig. wraps., some slightly soiled & torn. (CSK. Jul.10; 69) £290

AUDSLEY, George Ashdown & Bowes, James Lord
- **Keramic Art of Japan.** 1875. 2 vols. Cont. red mor., gt., vol. 2 lr. cover very burnt. (SH. Oct.9; 142) *Fine Books Oriental.* £190
- - **Anr. Copy.** Fo. Cont. cl.-bkd. bds. (SH. Jan.29; 168) *Ars Artis.* £110

- - **Anr. Copy.** Cont. mor. (SH. Jan.29; 167) *Ars Artis.* £105
- - **Anr. Copy.** Plts. in cold. litho. gold & silver ptd., some plts. slightly stained on verso. Orig. leath. vol. 2 cover loose. (R. Oct.14-18; 713a) DM 650
- - **Anr. Edn.** L'Pool. & L., 1875-[80]. 2 vols. Fo. Many plts. cold. Orig. cl. gt. (SBA. Jul.22; 128) *Chesters.* £120

AUDUBON, John James Laforest
- **The Birds of America.** Ill.:– Endicott & J.T. Bowen after Audubon. N.Y. & Phila., Priv. Ptd., 1840-44. 1st. 8vo. Edn., 2nd. iss of Pts. 1-13. 100 orig. pts. in 7 vols. Fo. Plt. 347 in pt. 70 supplied from anr. copy, scattered text foxing, some tissue guards foxed, a few plts. with traces of light foxing or browning, subscriber's lists, tables of contents & introduction bnd at back of pts. 14, 28, 42, 56, 70, 85 & 100. Orig. ptd. paper wraps., pts. 1-70 with spines & sewing renewed, some wraps. spotted, some pts. with cont. inscrs. on upr. wraps. with date & price paid. As a periodical, w.a.f. (CNY. Oct.1; 130) $17,000
- - **Anr. Edn.** N.Y., 1840-44. 1st. 8vo. Edn. Minor spotting, a few ll. misbnd., 1 or 2 just touched by binder, 1st. title with bkplt. of Dr. P. Tidyman. Cont. Amer. hf. red mor., gt. (S. Dec.3; 880) *Arader.* £2,400
- - **Anr. Copy.** 7 vols. Lacks subscribers list. Three-qtr. mor., rebkd. (SG. Oct.9; 21) $14,000
- - **Anr. Copy.** 6 vols. (of 7). Foxing, some staining, ex-liby., with seal on end-papers. Orig. red mor. gt. (SPB. Nov.25; 84) $8,750
- - **Anr. Copy.** 7 vols. Some slight browning, some plts. trimmed. New hf. mor. (SPB. May 6; 146) $7,000
- - **Anr. Copy.** 7 vols. List of subscribers in each vol., foxing & staining. Hf. mor., 1st 5 vols. bnd. uniformly, last 2 in different colour mor. (SPB. Oct.1; 180) $4,750
- - **Anr. Edn.** N.Y., 1859. 7 vols. Shaken, some plts. loose, severely foxed. Publisher's blind-stpd. mor., several vols. loose in bdg. (SPB. Nov.25; 86) $3,000
- - **Anr. Edn.** N.Y., 1861. 7 vols. Some foxing. Hf. mor., worn. (SPB. May 6; 148) $3,500
- - **Anr. Edn.** N.Y., [1870-71]. A few minor stains. Cont. hf. mor., gt. Large copy. (S. Jun.1; 62) *Arader.* £1,500
- - **Anr. Copy.** 8 vols. Orig. mor., sides panel. in blind central lozenge. (CNY. May 22; 189) $4,500
- - **Anr. Edn.** Ill.:– J.T. Bowen after Audubon. N.Y., ca. 1870. 8 vols. Blind-stp. of Paul Pratt Memorial Liby., Mass. on titles. Cont. hf. mor. (C. Nov.6; 199) *Arader.* £2,000
- - **Anr. Edn.** Ariel Pr., 1973. Ltd. Edn. Vol. 2. Lge. fo. Hf. cl. (SH. Jul.16; 211) *C.A. Burden.* £110

- **The Birds of America. A selection of Plates.** Ariel Pr., [1972-3]. (1,000) numbered sigd. by the Publisher. 2 vols. Lge. fo. Orig. hf. cl. (CSK. Aug.15; 112) £140
- **Ornithological Biography.** Edinb., 1831-39. 5 vols. Occasional spotting. Cont. hf. mor., spines gt. in compartments with bird motifs. (CSK. Sep.26; 54) £240
- **Original Water-colour Paintings . . . for the Birds of America.** Ed.:– Marshall B. Davidson. 1966. [1st. Edn.?]. 2 vols. Lge. 4to. Orig. buckram. gt., s.-c. (C. Mar.18; 13) *Howard.* £80
- - **Anr. Copy.** Cl. gt., box. (CE. Oct.24; 259) £50
- - **Anr. Copy.** Bdg. not stated. (JL. Mar.2; 588) Aus. $100
[-] - **Anr. Copy.** Cl., s.-c. (SSA. Jan.22; 9) R. 160
- **Prospectus for Birds of America.** L., 1831. 6th. Edn. 1st. & last ll. torn at fold. Unbnd., stitching brkn., cl. case. (CNY. May 22; 186) $500

AUDUBON, John James & Bachman, Rev. John
- **The Quadrupeds of North America.** N.Y., 1849-51-54. 1st. 8vo. Edn. 3 vols. Maroon mor. gt. (SPB. Oct.1; 181) $2,700
- - **Anr. Copy.** Foxing, some browning, ink inscr. on titles. Hf. mor. (SPB. Nov.25; 87) $2,000
- - **Anr. Edn.** N.Y., ca. 1850. 3 vols. Cont. mor., blind-stpd. scroll panel on covers. (C. Jul.15; 166) *Taylor.* £900
- - **Anr. Edn.** N.Y., 1852-51-54. 3 vols. Foxing, mainly to text, spotting affecting several plts. Publisher's red mor., gt., gt. spines. (CNY. Oct.1; 132) $1,800

- - **Anr. Edn.** N.Y., 1854. 3 vols. Plts. guarded, a few trimmed. Mor. gt., red mor. gt. inlays on covers & spines. (SPB. May 6; 149) $2,600
- - **Anr. Copy.** Three-qtr. mor., rebkd. (SG. Oct.9; 22) $2,100
- - **Anr. Copy.** Vol. II only. Gt.-stpd. mor., worn & brkn. [Sabin 2368] (CB. Feb.18; 275) Can. $500
- - **Anr. Edn.** N.Y., 1854-n.d. 3 vols. 155 cold.plts. Mor. (SPB. Jun.22; 6) $1,000
- **The Viviparous Quadrupeds of North America.** N.Y., 1845-46-48. 1st. Edn. 3 vols. Atlas fo. All titles with sm. tears reprd., 2 plts. with sm. tears reprd. Mod. mor.-bkd. cl. bds., spines gt., cl. s.-c.'s. (C. Mar.18; 12) Sabin £28,00
- - **Anr. Copy.** 3 vols., lacks text vols. Title & contents ll. of vols. 2 & 3 creased, stained in vol. 3, plt. 46 foxed, plt. 49 sm. piece chipped away, plt. 141 with 3-inch reprd. tear. Cont. hf. purple mor. gt., spines & extremities worn, jnts. breaking. Pierpont Morgan Liby. copy. (CNY. May 22; 190) $65,000
- - **Anr. Copy.** 3 vols. Minor spotting to plts. 67, 95 & 102, lacks text vols., 3 ll. of contents, sm. ink stp. on titles of S.H. Green. Cont. mor. gt. with gt. borders. (CNY. Oct.1; 131) $58,000

AUDUBON, John James–AUDUBON, John James & Bachman, John
- **The Birds of America.–The Quadrupeds of North America.** N.Y., 1840-44; 1849-54. 1st. 8vo. Edns. Together 10 vols (7 & 3). 2nd. work lacks hf.-title in vol. 2, vols. 1 & 3 with few ll. loose. Cont. mor. gt., spines gt., for Raynor's Bookstore. with tickets in 2nd. work. head of spine of vol. 1 of 1st. work torn & loose. (CNY. May 22; 187) $9,000

AUDUBON, John Woodhouse
- **The Drawings ... Illustrating his Adventures through Mexico & California, 1849-50.** Ed.:– Carl S. Dentzel. San Franc., Grabhorn Pr., 1957. (400). Fo. Qtr. cl. & decor. bds., d.-w. (PNY. Dec.3; 160) $110

AUER, A.
- **Die entdeckung des Naturselbstdruckes oder die Erfindung.** Vienna, 1854. Fo. Slight browning. Cont. hf. roan, worn. (S. Jun.1; 64) Marlborough Rare Books. £180

AUERBACH, Shmuel Ben David
- **Chesed Shmuel.** Amst., 1699. Bds. (S. Nov.18; 394) Waters. £55

AUGSBURG – Insignia & Elogia ... episcopi, et rr. Concoicorum Sanctae Ecclesiae Augustae Vindelorum
[Augsburg], 1607. 1 plt. torn affecting text. Cont. vell. bds. (S. Jan.27; 306) Quaritch. £150

AUGURELLUS, Joannes Aurelius
- **Jambicus Liber Primus ...** Venice, Apr. 1505. Long-grd. mor., spine raised bands. (HD. Apr.24; 7) Frs. 1,100

AUGUST, d. J. Herzog von Braunschweig Luneburg (Ed.)
See–SELENUS, Gustavus

AUGUSTINUS, Saint Aurelius, Bishop of Hippo.
- **Les Confessions.** Trans.:– Arnauld d'Andilly. Paris, 1676. Cont. red mor., fillet, crowned cypher in corners, repeated on spine, sm. stains on covers, ex-liby. (HD. Mar.18; 14) Frs. 2,800
- **De Arte Praedicandi.** [Mainz], Johann Fust [& Peter Schoeffer], [before Mar., 1467]. Fo. One 2-line & one 6-line capital initial supplied in red, rubricated, verso of last lf, soiled. 19th. C. European mor. gt., lge. inlaid recessed panels of black glass-paper with onlaid oval centrepieces of mor. gt. (with gt.-lettered title on upr. cover). From the collection of Eric Sexton. [BMC I, 21, Goff A1227, H 1957] (CNY. Apr.8; 92) $14,000
- **De Civitate Dei.** Ed.:– [Thomas Waleys & Nicolaus Trivet] (commentaries). [Strassburg], [Johann Mentelin], [not after 1468]. 2 pts. in 1 vol. Fo. 1st. pt.: spaces for initial capitals, supplied in red, 7-line capital G at p. 1 illuminated in red, blue & green with penwork flourishes, a few larger capitals in blue, incipits, chapter numberings & initial strokes in red; 2nd. pt.: spaces for initial capitals, 8-line capital F at 1st. p. illuminated in red, blue & green with penwork flourishes, rubricated as pt. 1; reprd. tears & slight fraying to fore-margins of folios 251-253, intermittent worming to folios 238-252 & folios 253-269, catching some letters of text, scattered foxing. Red lev. mor., covers ruled & decor. in gt. & blind, gt. spine, by Rivière & Son. From the collection of

Eric Sexton. [BMC I, 52, Goff A1239, H 2046*] (CNY. Apr.8; 161) $14,000
- - **Anr. Edn.** [Venice], [Antonio di Bartolommeo (Miscomini)], ca. 1476-78. 1st. Edn. in Italian. Fo. Spaces for initials left blank, lacks blank before the tavola, quires n & u interchanged by binder, & the tavola bnd. at end, marginal tear to s8, long reprd. tear to z6, some light staining & spotting in the tavola. Early 19th. C. Italian sheep, gt. & blind-stpd. with neo-classical decor. The copy of George John Warren, 5th. Baron Vernon, lately in the Pierpont Morgan Liby. [BMC VII, 1136, Goff A1248, HC 2071] (CNY. Apr.8; 185) $4,000
- - **Anr. Edn.** Ed.:– Thome Valois & Nicolai Triveth. Lyon, 1520. Fo. A few wormholes running thro-out, browned & stained, stitching brkn. in middle. Cont. limp vell. (S. Jan.27; 361) Hendricks. £85
- - **Anr. Edn.** Ed.:– C. Weymann. Munich. Bremer Pr., [1924]. (385) on Bütten. Fo. Orig. hf. linen. (H. Dec.9/10; 1787) DM 520
- - **Anr. Edn.** Ed.:– [C. Weymann]. [Munich], Bremer Pr., [1925]. (385) on Bütten. Fo. Lacks printers mark. Mor., gt. spine & upr. cover, inner fillet dentelle, linen box, silk end-ll. not bnd. in, slightly soiled. (HK. Nov.18-21, 2454) DM 900
- **De Civitate Dei.–De Trinitate.** Ed.:– [Thomas Waleys & Nicolaus Trivet] (commentary) (1st. work). [Basle], Johann Amerbach, 13 Feb., 1490; 1490. 2 works in 1 vol. Fo. Both works with spaces for initial capitals, with guide letters, capitals, paragraph marks & initial stroke of 2nd. work supplied in red, slight repair to corners, 1st. lf. torn at inner margin, 2 long tears to B1 of 1st. work, reprd. without loss, J4 with portion of outer margin renewed, corners of a3, b1 & g4 in 2nd. work renewed, l1 & l6 with reprd. tears to text, some 20 ll. with slight defect to outer corners. Bnd. at the Benedictine Monastery of Saints Peter & Paul at Abinghof at Paderborn, in cont. cf. over wood-bds., central panels of covers with floral diaper & repetitions of stylized thistle, sm. lozenges of heart pierced by arrow lge. Virgin & Child lozenge & anr. depicting a saint, lr. cover with border of circular Agnus Dei & griffin tools, at bottom the monastery's sig. stp. of Saints Peter & Paul. From the collection of Eric Sexton. [BMC III, 752 & 753, Goff A1244 & A1345, H 2066 & 2039*] (CNY. Apr.8; 20) $3,200
- **De Consensu Evangelistarum.** Lauingen, 12 Apr., 1473. 1st. Edn. Fo. Spaces for some initial capitals, others ptd. in outl., capitals & initial strokes supplied in red, some with flourishes incorporating grotesques, sm. portion of extreme inner margin of fo. 2 renewed, fo. 24 with sm. strip torn from fore-margin, last blank with slight repair & some wormholes, scattered foxing. 16th. C. blind-stpd. pig over wood bds., rebkd. preserving orig. spine (with mor. labels), brass clasps & catches. From the collection of Eric Sexton. [BMC II, 545, Goff A1257, HC 1961*] (CNY. Apr.8; 79) $3,200
- **Enchiridion de Fide, Spe et Caritate.** [Cologne], [Ulrich Zel], ca. 1466-67. 1st. Edn. 4to. Initials painted in red, other rubrication, 1st. & last blanks removed. 19th. C. marb. bds., cf. spine & tips, gt. mor. s.-c. From liby. of J. Pierpont Morgan, with his bkplt. [Goff A1265; BMC I, 181] (PNY. Mar.26; 29) $4,500
- - **Anr. Edn.** [Cologne], [Ulrich Zel], ca. 1467. 4to. Spaces for initial capitals, lge. capital L at fo. 1r & anr. capital D at fo. 7r illuminated in cols. with pen-work elaboration, other capitals supplied in red or blue, underlines & initial strokes in red, light dampstaining to some margins. Mor., gt.-lettered spine. The copy of W. Lyon Wood, Esq., lately in the collection of Eric Sexton. [BMC I, 181, Goff A1265, H 2028*] (CNY. Apr.8; 41) $6,500
- **Epistolae.** [Strassburg], [Johann Mentelin], [not after 1471]. 1st. Edn. Fo. Spaces for initial capitals, supplied in red, 7-line capital D at p.1 illuminated in pink & green on broad gold ground with foliage sprays extending the length of the column, similar sprays in lr. margin incorporating arms of Hilprand Brandenburg, fo. 70 with 1 column of text on recto only, the blank portion here excised, sm. worm-holes to last few ll., 4 ll. guarded, orig. conjugate folios 111 & 120 detchd. but present. Cont. Strassburg bdg. of blind-tooled pig over bevelled wood bds., covers divided by quintuple fillets into a frame & 2 concentric panels, frame with 2 rows of a sq. quatrefoil tool, inner panel with row imps. of an elongated tool of 3 stylized plants, central panel with 2 rows of a sq.

floral tool & 1 row of a lettered scroll reading 'meister', 4 pp. of binder's blanks at end bearing cont. MS. table, top of spine torn. Hand-cold. woodcut bkplt. of Hilprand Brandenburg von Biberach, & 4-line inscr. recording the gift of the book to the Carthusian Charterhouse at Buxheim, later the copy of Paul Schmidt, bkplt. of E.P. Goldschmidt, recently in the collection of Eric Sexton. [BMC I, 55, Goff A1267, H 1966*] (CNY. Apr.8; 163) $19,000
- - **Anr. Edn.** Basle, [14]93. 2nd. (1st dtd.) Edn. Fo. Wormholes at beginning & end, some reprd., stp. of Vienna Hofbibliothek on f.2. 18th. C. mor., gt., arms of Prince Eugene of Savoy on covers, triple gt. fillet, spine gt. in compartments with alternate arms & cipher of Prince Eugene, inner gt. dentelles, some wormholes in spine, liby. label on inner upr. cover. [BMC 111 755; HC 1969; Goff A1268] (SM. Oct.7; 1553) Frs. 9,100
- **Libri XIII Confessionum.** Leyden, 1675. Elzevier Edn. 12mo. Early 18th C. red mor., fleuron in corners, angel in centre holding a garland in an oval of leaves, decor. spine, end-papers renewed. Sigd. by Charles Nodier on end-paper. (HD. Mar.18; 13) Frs. 1,400
- **Manuale de Aspiratione Animae ad Deum.** [Alost], [Thierry Martens], [not after Feb.28, 1487]. 4to. Spaces for initial capitals, supplied in red, rubricated, folios 1-4 with sm. reprd. wormhole, touching some letters of text on folios 2-4. Mor. gt., arms of Eric Sexton in gt. on covers, by Sangorski & Sutcliffe. [BMC IX, 126, C 756=757, Goff A1287] (CNY. Apr.8; 2) $3,500
- **Meditationes.** [Milan], [Johannes Antonius & Beninus de Honate], ca. 1480-82. Spaces for capital initials, some with guide letters, some capitals supplied in red, otherwise unrubricated, 2 prelims. misbnd., ink stps. at 1st. & last pp. Cf. over wood bds., blind-stpd., covers divided into central panel & 2 frames by multiple fillets extending to edges, centre panel divided by triple fillets into lozenge & triangular compartments, each filled with a rosette or palmated leaf, outer frame with repetitions of scroll lettered 'hilf maria', outermost frame with repeated imps. of sm. open foliate stps., spine with 3 raised bands, each cover with 5 brass bosses, clasps & catches, bnd. at the Benedictine Monastery of Saint Georgenberg, with inscr. at folios 2 & 185. The copy of the Allen Liby., cancelled ink stps. of the London Liby., lately in the collection of E. Sexton. [BMC VI, 740, Goff A1292] (CNY. Apr.8; 104) $4,200
- **Meditationes [with other Tracts].** Venice, Andreas de Bonetis, 23 Jul., 1484. 4to. Lacks 1st. blank, 1st. text lf. & last lf. reprd. in lr. margin just affecting last line, some pp. in 1st. quire ptd. askance with 1st. line of a8r cropped, some headlines cropped, slightly spotted & soiled, old lf. (1st. blank?) reprd. in margin & bnd. in at end with MS. index, old marginalia. 19th. C. vell. bds. [BMC V, 361, Goff A1217, HC 1947*] (S. Jul.27; 101) Hamilton. £300
- **Of the Citie of God.** Trans.:– John H[ealey]. 1610. 1st. Edn. in Engl. Fo. Most margins lightly stained. Cont. Engl. cf., rebkd. [STC 916] (S. May 5; 292) Ohern. £300
- - **Anr. Edn.** Trans.:– J. H[ealey]. 1620. 2nd. Edn. in Engl. Fo. Some minor staining. Cont. cf., rebkd. From the collection of Eric Sexton. [STC 917] (C. Apr.15; 82) O'Hern. £80
- **Opera.** Ed.:– S. Benedictus & S. Maurus. Antw., 1700-03. 12 vols. in 6. Fo. Vell., some stains, sm. defects. (B. Dec.10/11; 965) Fls. 850
- **Sermones.** 1520. 3 pts. in 1 vol. 4to. Recent qtr. cf. (TA. Feb.19; 445) £76
- - **Anr. Edn.** Ed.:– J. Vlimmerius. Louvain, 1564. 4to. Blind-tooled cf., bds. removed, some defects. (B. Dec.10/11; 967) Fls. 450
- **Soliloquia.** Winterberg, Johannes Alakraw, 1484. 1st. Dtd. Edn. 4to. Spaces for initial capitals, lacks final blank, extreme inner margins wormed, last 3 ll. with sm. repair at inner margin. Old qtr. pig & paper bds. From the collection of Eric Sexton. [BMC III, 814, Goff A1326, H 2013*] (CNY. Apr.8; 206) $3,000

AUGUSTINUS [Pseud.]
- **De Vita Christiana.** [Mainz], Johann Fust & Peter Schoeffer, ca. 1460-65. 1st. Edn. 4to. Spaces for capital letters, faint traces of crossed shields ptd. red at fo. 17v, faint traces of rubrication (effaced by washing & pressing), sm. clean tear at exteme lr. inner margin of fo. 4, similar tear to fo. 17, repairs to several blank fore-margins. Lev.

AUGUSTINUS [Pseud.] – De Vita Christiana.
-contd.
mor., gt. & blind-tooled, spine gt.-lettered, by R. de Coverly. The copy of Rev. William Makellar, lately in the collection of Eric Sexton. [BMC I, 20, C 768, Goff A1354] (CNY. Apr.8; 91) $15,000
– – **Anr. Edn.** [Mainz], Peter Schoeffer, ca. 1470-75. Reprint of the 1st. Edn. 4to. Spaces for capitals, rubricated, 1st. lf. browned, occasional marginalia (bleached). 19th. C. crushed mor., by Cape, upr. cover rehinged. The copy of Richard Bennett, lately in the Pierpont Morgan Liby. [BMC I, 37, Goff A1356, H 2093] (CNY. Apr.8; 93) $6,000

AUMONT, [Louis Marie Augustin], Duc de
– Catalogue des Livres. Paris, 1782. Index at end, old stp. with cipher 'EL' in oval on title. Cont. cf.-bkd. bds., gt. (SM. Oct.7; 1307) Frs. 1,600

AURBACH, Johannes
– Summa de Sacramentis. Augsburg, Gunther Zainer, 1469. 1st. Edn. Fo. Spaces for initial capitals, supplied in red. paragraph marks & initial strokes in red, light dampstain to blank upr. corners, sm. wormhole to blank fore-margins of final 10 ll., cont. ink table on blank recto of fo. 1. Vell. From the collection of Eric Sexton. [BMC II, 315, Goff A1381, H. 2124*] (CNY. Apr.8; 12) $5,000

AURELIUS Antoninus, Marcus
– Golden Boke. Trans.:– [Antonio de Guevara]. 1546. 5th. Edn. Lacks colophon lf. Late 18th. C. qtr. cf., worn. [STC 12440] (S. Mar.16; 118) *Sotheran.* £130
– The Thoughts. Ill.:– Sir William Russell Flint. Riccardi Pr., 1909. (517) numbered. 4to. Orig. limp vell., silk ties, s.-c. (SH. Mar.26; 199) *Marks.* £110

AURIC, Georges
See–BRAQUE, Georges, Cocteau, Jean & others

AUSMO, Nicolaus de
See–NICOLAUS de Auximo

AUSONIUS, [Decius Magnus]
Omnia [Opera] Ill.:– Eliam Vinetum. Bordeaux, 1580. 2 pts. in 1 vol. 4to. Some browning, 1 or 2 tears & rust-holes slightly affecting text. 18th. C. Fr. mott. cf., spine gt. Bkplt. of Joseph-Chrisostome Lemoine; from Liby. of André L. Simon. (S. May 18; 25) *Hill.* £120

AUSTEN, Jane
[–] Emma. L., 1816. 1st. Edn. 3 vols. Hf. roan gt. (P. Jul.2; 1) *Hosain.* £420
– – **Anr. Copy.** Foxing thro.-out, sm. tears on outer margin of B2 in vol. 2. Cont. cf., soiled, worn. (PD. Oct.22; 91) £240
[–] – **Anr. Copy.** 12mo. Lacks hf.-titles & last advt. lf. in vol. III, fo. H7 in vol. I misbnd., some ll. spotted. Later cf., rebkd. (SH. May 28; 112) *Korn.* £160
– – **Anr. Copy.** Lacks hf.-titles, sig. of Lady Beresford, dtd. 1816, on endpapers, some foxing, staining. Cont. hf. cf., some stains on bds. (SPB. Nov.25; 148) $1,300
[–] Mansfield Park. 1814. 1st. Edn. 3 vols. 12mo. Occasional staining thro.-out, lacks pts. of 3 blank margins in vol. 1, natural paper fault affecting catch-word. Cont. hf. russ. (C. Feb.4; 111) *Quaritch.* £280
– – **Anr. Copy.** 3 vols. Inner margin of 1st. few ll. of each vol. strengthened, pp. 335-8 in vol. 1 reprd., some spotting thro.-out. Recent qtr. cf. (TA. Jul.16; 53) £65
[–] Northanger Abbey: & Persuasion. 1818. 1st. Edn. 4 vols. 12mo. Hf.-titles misbnd. before general titles in vols. 2-4, slight discolouration. Cont. hf. cf., rebkd. (C. Feb.4; 112) *Quaritch.* £260
[–] – **Anr. Copy.** Vol. 3 lacks hf.-title. Mod. hf. cf. (P. Jul.2; 95) *Sotheran.* £210
[–] – **Anr. Copy.** Cont. russ., lacks some labels. (C. Jul.16; 366) *Taylor.* £180
– – **Anr. Copy.** Text spotted. Orig. drab paper bds., jnts. restored, qtr. mor. gt. s.-c.'s, unc. From the Prescott Collection. (CNY. Feb.6; 6) $2,200
– Novels. 1911-12. Winchester Edn. 12 vols. Hf. cf., gt. (P. Sep.11; 102) £190
– – **Anr. Edn.** Edinb., n.d. Winchester Edn. 10 vols. Gt.-ruled three-qtr. maroon mor., by Bayntun, upr. hinge brkn. at 2 vols. (PNY. Dec.3; 31a) $170

[–] **Pride & Prejudice.** 1813. 1st. Edn. 3 vols. 2 hf.-titles with sm. marginal tear reprd., slight spotting. 19th. C. pol. cf., gt., upr. cover of vol. I weak, bkplt. of John Croft Deverell. (S. Dec.8; 56) *Boyle.* £820
– – **Anr. Copy.** 12mo. Spotting. Cf. by Sangorski & Sutcliffe, upr. jnt. of Vol. 1 crudely reprd., 1 cover detchd. (SPB. Nov.25; 147) $700
[–] – **Anr. Edn.** 1813. 2nd. Edn. 3 vols. 12mo. Cont. hf. mor. (CSK. Jul.10; 91) £120
[–] – **Anr. Edn.** 1817. 3rd. Edn. 2 vols. 12mo. Slight browning. Cont. hf. cf., spine of vol. I loose (S. May 5; 377) *Sanders.* £65
– – **Anr. Edn.** Ill.:– Hugh Thomson. L., 1894. Maroon mor. gt., covers with cold. mor. onlays, mother-of-pearl ornaments, mor. doubls. & free endpages with designs gt.-tooled in outl., silk fly-ll. gt., red mor. velvet-lined box with orig. pencil sketches for bdg. sewn together & laid in, by Sangorski & Sutcliffe. (CNY. May 22; 351) $1,100
– Sense & Sensibility. L., Priv. Ptd., 1811. 1st. Edn. 3 vols. Some text browned or spotted. Orig. bds., spines reprd. with portions restored, cont. owner's ink inscr. on upr. covers, mor. gt. folding box (by Sangorski & Sutcliffe). From the Prescott Collection. (CNY. Feb.6; 5) $13,000
– – **Anr. Copy.** 12mo. Lacks hf.-titles, some discolouration. Cont. hf. cf., gt. spines. (SPB. Nov.25; 146) $1,500
[–] – **[Works].** Ill.:– Hugh Thompson & Charles Brock. 1908-13. 5 vols. Hf. mor., spines gt. (SKC. Dec.4; 1535) £75

AUSTEN, John
– Original Drawings for Martin Secker's 'A National Gallery'. 1933. Fo. Title & 42 (on 31) drawings in ink, on thick paper. Loose in mor.-bkd. buckram box. Sigd. on title. (C. Jul.22; 43) *Steenson.* £420

AUSTEN, Ralph
– A Treatise of Fruit Trees. – Observations upon some Part of Francis Bacon's Natural History. Oxford, 1653; 1658. 2 works in 1 vol. Sm. 4to. Stains. Cont. sheep, worn, 1 cover detchd. (SH. Jun.11; 156) *Lawson & Co.* £55

AUSTIN, S. & others
– Lancashire Illustrated. Ill.:– After Allom & others. 1831. 4to. Slight spotting. Cont. hf. red mor. (SBA. Oct.22; 377) *Okell.* £260
– – **Anr. Copy.** Some margins slightly browned. Cont. hf. cf., slightly worn. (SBA. Mar.4; 169a) *Dauncy.* £170

AUSTRALASIAN Antique Collector (The)
Sydney, 1966-81. Vols. 1-21. Vol. 1 stained. No bdg. stated. (JL. Jul.20; 611) Aus. $120

AUSTRALIAN KEEPSAKE
– Landscape Scenery illustrating New South Wales. 1855. Ob. 4to. Few plts. spotted. Orig. cl. (SH. Apr.9; 137) *Quaritch.* £340

AUTHENTICATED TARTANS OF THE CLANS & Families of Scotland
Mauchline, 1850. 4to. Hf. roan, worn. (CE. Nov.20; 71) £80

AUTOMOBILE ENGINEER, A Technical Journal Devoted to the Theory & Practice of Automobile & Aircraft Construction
1920-26. 7 vols. 4to. Cl. (TA. Mar.19; 376) £64

AUVERT, A.
– Selecta Praxis Medico-Chirurgicae . . . Paris, 1848. 2 vols. Lge. fo. Three-qtr chagrin, decor. spine raised bands, crowned cypher. (HD. Apr.24; 118) Frs. 2,100

AVEDON, Richard
– Observations. Ed.:– Truman Capote (text). N.Y., [1959]. 1st. Edn. Fo. White ptd. bds., lightly foxed, orig. ptd. bd. s.-c. stained & worn. (SG. Apr.23; 23) $120

AVEDON, Richard–LIBERMAN, Alexander
– Observations.–The Artist in His Studio. Ed.:– Truman Capote (text) (1st. work). N.Y., 1959; [1960]. 1st. Edns. 2 works in 2 vols. Fo. & sm. fo. Bds., glassine d.-w. (1st. work); & cl., d.-w. last work a Sigd. Pres. Copy, & also sigd. by Frank Finocchio. (PNY. May 21; 71) $280

AVEIRO, Pantaleao d'
– Itinerario de Terra Sancta. Lisbon, 1596. Sm. 4to. Title & some ll. at beginning & end reprd. at times with slight loss, slightly soiled (especially title), old marginalia. 19th. C. antique-style

blind-stpd. cf. (S. Jul.27; 136) *Ad Orientem.* £280

AVENDANO, Fernando de
See–VILLAGOMEZ, Pedro de–AVENDANO, Fernando de

AVENTINUS, Joh. Thurmair
– Annalivm Boiorvm. Libri Septem. Ed.:– H. Lautensack. Ingolstadt, 1554. 1st. Edn. Fo. Title slightly soiled, old MS. note, 1 lf. stained. Cont. leath., spine renewed, endpapers renewed. (HK. Nov.18-21; 111) DM 1,600

AVERMAETE, Roger
– La Gravure sur Bois Moderne de l'Occident. Paris, 1928. (1000) numbered on Papier Chiffon by Montgolfier. 4to. Mor.-bkd. marb. bds., orig. wraps. bnd. in. (SG. Dec.4; 24) $240

AVERNUS, William, Bp. of Paris
– Postille Maiores Totivs Anni cum Multis Historibus sive Figuris . . . Lyon, 1525. Fo. (mostly in 8's). Some ll. with minor marginal defects, slight soiling & staining. Old cf., reprd., new end-papers, lacks clasps. W.a.f. (KH. Mar.24; 15) Aus. $280

AVERY, Milton
– Paintings 1930-1960. Ed.:– Hilton Kramer. N.Y. & L., [1962]. 4to. Cl., slightly worn. (SG. Dec.4; 25) $160

AVERY Architectural Library
– Catalogue. N.Y., 1895. (1000). 4to. Three-qtr. mor., worn, partly unc. (SG. Jan.22; 43) $400

AVER'YANOV, Vecheslav
– Gavan' [Harbour]. Ill.:– D. Zagoskin, P. Utkin, K. Polyakov, K. Krasovsky, V. Yustitsky & V. Perel'man. Saratov, 1922. (50). Lithographed MS. Orig. wraps., slightly soiled, spine torn. (SH. Feb.6; 385) *Quaritch.* £100

AVICENNA
– Liber Canonis. De Medicinis Cordialibus Cantica. – Index in Avicennae libros. Ed.:– 1st. work Andreas Alpagus Belluensis & Benedictus Rinius; 2nd. work Julio Palamede. Venice, 1562. 2 works in 1 vol. Fo. Inkstain at extreme outer edge of margins at end, a few light stains. Vell., rebkd. (S. Jun.15; 22) *Jenner Books.* £280

AVILA ET ZUNNIGA, Ludwig de
– Commentariorum de Bello Germanico a Carol V. gesto Libri Duo. Antw., 1550. 18th. C. hf. vell., cold. spr. paper-bkd. (D. Dec.11-13; 2628) DM 1,600

AVILER, C.A. d'
– Cours d'Architecture . . . l'Art de batir . . . Paris, 1710. 2 vols. Liby. stps. on titles. Cont. marb. cf., decor. spines. bdg. reprd. (HD. Feb.18; 8) Frs. 1,100
– – **Anr. Edn.** Paris, 1756. New Edn. 4to. Minor foxing & hand-soiling. Cont. cf., worn. (SG. Dec.4; 26) $120

AVOGARO, Giovan Battista Birago
– Mercurio Veridico, overo Annali Universali d'Europe. Venice, 1648. 1st. Edn. 4to. Old Fr. red mor., elab. gt. borders & spine. (SG. Sep.25; 44) $300

AXIS
Ill.:– Picasso, Kandinsky, Miró, Moore & others. 1935-37. Nos. 1-8 in 2 vols. 4to. Cont. cl. (SH. Nov.20; 209) *Fogg.* £70

AYER, Edward Everett
– Reminiscences of the Far West 1861-1918. Chic., after 1918. Ltd. Edn. for private distribution. Fo. Mimeographed typescript, about 135 ll., printed on rectos only. Binder's cl., gt., some wear. Pres. copy. (SG. Jan.8; 28) $650

AYLIFF, J. & Whiteside, J.
– History of the Abamdo. 1912. Wraps. (VA. Oct.31; 66) R. 190

AYME, Marcel
– Images de l'Amour. Ill.:– Vertès. Paris, 1957. 1st. Edn., (34) on Rives vell. Lge. 4to. In sheets, publisher's s.-c. (HD. Dec.5; 9) Frs. 1,400

AYRES, John
– The Baur Collection: Chinese Ceramics. Geneva, 1968-74. Ltd. Edn. 4 vols. 4to. Orig. cl., d.-w., s.-c.'s. (S. Sep.30; 369) £750

AYRES, Philip
– Emblemata Amatoria. 1863. Text in Latin, Engl., Italian & Fr., 44 (of 46) full-p. ills. & 44

(of 46) text ll., a few ll. slightly wormed or torn with only slight loss. Later tree cf. qt., worn. (SBA. Jul.14; 92) *Amiklartat.* £95
– **Emblems of Love.** [1683]. 2nd. Edn. Title & 1st. lf. in facs., the 1st. torn & reprd., lacks 1st. & final blanks, sm. repair to plt. 15, occasional spotting & browning. Red mor., gt., by Lewis & Harris. Brent Gration-Maxfield's copy. [Wing A4309] (S. May 5; 329) *Russell.* £100

AYROUARD, Jacques
– **Recueil de Plusieurs Plans des Ports et Rades . . . de la Mer Méditerranée.** 1746. 4to. Cont. cf. (P. May 14; 137) *Fisher.* £120

AYTON, Richard
See–DANIELL, William & Ayton, Richard

AZARA, Félix de
– **Voyages dans l'Amérique Méridionale . . . Contenant la Description Géographique, Politique et Civile du Paraguay et de la Rivière de la Plata.** Paris, 1809. 5 vols. 8vo. & atlas 4to. Orig. bds., unc., slightly worn. [Sabin 2541] (SPB. May 5; 80) $1,600

AZAREVICH, Valentin & Te, M.
– **Serdtse Zaplate** [Heart in Patches]. St. Petersb., 1920. Dupl. typescript, browned. Orig. wraps., loose. (SH. Feb.6; 386) *Quaritch.* £130

AZARIA OF FANO, Menachem
See–BEN SHNEUR of Lubavitch, Dov Ber
–AZARIA OF FANO, Menachem

AZULAI, Chaim Joseph David (Chida)
– **Kise Rachamim.** Livorno, 1803. 1st. Edn. Fo. Cf. (S. Nov.18; 397) *Goldberg.* £80
See–SCHNEUR Salman of Liadi–MENDEL of Lisko–AZULAI, Chaim Joseph David

B., C.
– **Metodo per fare, Migliorare e Conservare il Vino che Felicemente puo riuscire nella Collina e nel Piano di Lombardia.** Bergamo, 1823. 2nd. Edn. Some spotting. Orig. wraps., covers with fleuron decorations, slightly soiled, unc. Pres. copy to Count Girolamo Grumelli; from liby. of André L. Simon. (S. May 18; 26) *Facchi.* £85

B., J.L.
– **The Butterfly's Funeral.** Jun., 1808. 1st. Edn. 16mo. Orig. ptd. wraps., cl. case. (S. Feb.9; 4) *Rota.* £220

BA'AL SHEM, Joel, of Poznan
– **Mif'alot Elohim.** Turko, 1767. 3rd. Edn. Some discolouration. Bds. (S. Nov.18; 398) *Stern.* £50

BAALDE, S.J.
– **Nieuwe Astronomische, Geographische en Historische Zak en Reis Atlas.** Amst., 1770. 27 (of 39) outl. cold. copperplt. maps, 3 copperplts., 2 cold. Cont. hf. leath. (R. Oct.14-18; 1525) DM 1,500

BABBAGE, Charles
– **A Comparative View of the Various Institutions for the Assurance of Lives.** 1826. 1st. Edn. Cont. cf. (SH. Oct.10; 286) *Shaw.* £140
– **On the Economy of Machinery & Manufactures.** 1832. 1st. Edn. Title & dedication spotted. Orig. cl. (CSK. Nov.14; 158) £95
– – **Anr. Copy.** Orig. cl., rebkd., worn. (SH. Jun.11; 144) *Quaritch.* £65
– – **Anr. Edn.** 1832. 1st. Edn. L.P. Orig. cl., rebkd. (SH. Jun.11; 143) *Quaritch.* £170

BABCOCK, Philip H.
– **Falling Leaves.** Ill.:– Aiden L. Ripley. [1937]. (950) numbered. Leatherette. (SG. Dec.11; 211) $130

BABELON, J. & Lafaurie, J.
– **Congres International de Numismatique. 1953.** Paris, 1953-57. 2 vols. Orig. wraps. (SH. Mar.6; 313) *Spink.* £85

BABES in the Wood (The)
1849. Etched title & 9 pp. text, with ills. & borders, hand-cold. Orig. bds., rebkd. (SH. Apr.9; 181) *Quaritch.* £65

BABSON, Grace K.
– **A Descriptive Catalogue of [her] Collection of the Works of Sir Isaac Newton.** N.Y., 1950 & 1955. (750) & (450). 1 vol., & Macomber's supp., together £155) Cl. (SG. Jan.22; 313) $120

BACCI, Andreas
– **Del Teuere libri tre.** Venice, 1576. 1st. Edn. 4to. Some dampstaining. 17th. C. limp vell., soiled,

detchd. From liby. of André L. Simon. (S. May 18; 27) *Facchi.* £200

BACCI, Pietro Giacomo
– **Vita di S. Filippo Neri.** Ill.:– I. Alessandri after P.A. Novelli. Venice, 1794. Fo. Secondary engraved title dtd. 1799, & plts. dtd. 1786-93, ptd. title slightly discold., & with reprd. tear. Cont. Roman 'imitation' mor. gt., cardinal's armorial device gt. on sides. From the collection of John A. Saks. (C. Jun.10; 12) *Taylor.* £60

BACH, Johann Sebastian
– **Grosse Passionsmusik.** Berlin, [after 1830]. Ob. fo. Stained & soiled thro.-out. Leath. (H. Dec.9/10; 1042) DM 820
– **Motetten in Partitur.** Leipzig, [1803]. 1st. Edn. Pts. 1-2. Fo. Slightly soiled. Cont. paper bds. (H. Dec.9/10; 1041) DM 660
– **Passio Domini Nostri J.C. secundum Evangelistam Matthaeum.** [Leipzig], [1922]. (500) Facs. of MS. Fo. Hand-bnd. orig. marb. cf. gt. (H. Dec.9/10; 1045) DM 520

BACHAUMONT, Louis Petit de
– **Mémoires Secrets.** L., 1777-89. 36 vols. 12mo. Lacks to vol. 36, dupl. title to vol. 20 bnd. in by mistake. Cf. gt. by Simier., sigd. at foot of spines, lacks some labels. W.a.f. (SBA. Jul.23; 428) *Meister.* £320

BACHELARD, Gaston
See–CHAGALL, Marc

BACHELIN-DELORENNE, A.
– **La Decoration Polychrome d'après les Etoffes Anciennes.** Paris, 1890. Fo. Hf. cl., partly unc. (SI. Dec.3; 42) Lire 260,000

BACHMAN, Rev. John
See–AUDUBON, John James & Bachman, Rev. John

BACHMANN, C.
See–CRAMER, D. & Bachman, C.

BACK, George
– **Narrative of the Arctic Land Expedition.** Ill.:– E. Finden & others. 1836. [1st. Edn.?]. 4to. Slight foxing to plts. Cont. embossed cl. (C. Feb.25; 68) *Bowes.* £250
– – **Anr. Copy.** Folding map slightly torn, some very minor defects. Cont. hf. cf., faded. Owner's inscr. of Will Colbeck. (SBA. May 27; 272) *Hutchinson.* £75

BACKHOUSE, James
– **A Narrative of a Visit to the Australian Colonies.** Ill.:– James Wyld & others. L. & N.Y., 1843. 1st. Edn. Some foxing to maps & 2 plts. Orig. cl. (C. Jul.15; 5) *Ball.* £65
– – **Anr. Copy.** Partly unopened. (SKC. Oct.8; 1459) £50
– – **Anr. Copy.** In 2 vols. Prelims. but not the frontis. repeated in 2nd. vol., slight foxing of the plts. Old hf. cf. (KH. Nov.18; 24) Aus. $260

BACON, Edward R.
See–GETZ, John

BACON, Sir Francis, Baron Verulum
– **Cases of Treason.** 1641. 1st. Edn. Sm. 4to. Stitched as issued, unc., cl. portfo. & qtr. leath. s.-c. [Wing B272] (S. Mar.16; 135) *Maggs.* £160
– – **Anr. Copy.** Title & contents lf. soiled & reprd. Cf., gt., spine chipped. (SPB. May 29; 13) $250
– **Considerations Touching a Warre with Spaine.** 1629. 1st. Edn. 4to. Cf. gt. by Zaehnsdorf. [STC 1126] (C. Nov.19; 26) *Monash.* £140
– [–] **A Declaration of the Practises & Treasons . . . Committed by Robert late Earle of Essex . . .** L., 1601. 1st. Edn. Sm. 4to. Lf. A1 (?blank) lacking. Later hf. cf., reprd., Signet Lib. gt. arms on covers. [STC 1133] (SG. Oct.9; 23) $425
– **Essaies.** 1612. 6th. Edn. Cont. vell. Early sig. of John Breame. [STC 1141] (S. May 5; 264) *Quaritch.* £1,100
– – **Anr. Edn.** 1613 [probably later]. 8th. Edn., Iss. with 'Aturney' in title. Lacks first & last blanks. Early 20th. C. red mor. by David. [STC 1143] (S. Mar.16; 133) *Maggs.* £80
– – **Anr. Edn.** 1624. Lacks 1st. & final blanks, occasional browning, some inscrs. in text. Cont. cf., slight wear to spine. [STC 1146] (S. Feb.10; 406) *Waterfield.* £70
– – **Anr. Edn.** L., 1632. 4to. Slight occasional spotting, inscr. on fly-lf. Very early cf. (SG. Feb.5; 25) $180

– **Historia Vitae et Mortis.** L., 1623. 1st. Edn. Cont. Fr. cf., arms of Leonor d'Estampes de Valencay, Archbishop of Rheims, 1589-1651, gt. on sides. [STC 1156] (S. May 5; 265) *Thomas.* £265
– **The History of Life & Death.** 1638. 1st. Edn. in Engl. 12mo. Initial imprimatur lf. detchd. Cont. cf., gt. fleur-de-lys on upr. cover, rebkd. [STC 1157.] (S. Mar.16; 134) *Rota.* £55
– – **Anr. Edn.** Ed.:– William Rawley. L., 1638. 1st. Authorized Edn. in Engl. 24mo. Disbnd. [STC 1158] (SG. Sep.25; 29) $200
– – **Anr. Edn.** 1638 [Imprimatur lf. dtd. Dec.29, 1637]. 1st. Edn. in Engl., 2nd. Iss. 12mo. Ex-liby. copy with stps. to title-p. & some others, some dampstaining thro.-out, 2nd. Imprimatur lf. bnd. in at end. Old cf., spine worn. (TA. Jan.22; 174) £65
– **Instauratio Magna.** Ill.:– Simon Passe. L., 1620. 1st. Edn., 2nd. Printing. Fo. With errata lf. & changed printer's mark, MS. note on copper engraved title, stp. on verso, slightly soiled in parts. Cont. vell., spine renewed. (HK. Nov.18-21; 372) DM 2,700
– **The Naturall & Experimentall History of Winds, & c.** Trans.:– R[obert] G[entili]. Ill.:– T. Cross. (engraved port.) 1653. 1st. Edn. in Engl. 12mo. Slight soiling, owner's inscrs. on title-p. Cont. sheep, worn. [Wing B305] (S. Jan.26; 264) *Claridge.* £70
– **Of the Advancement & Proficience of Learning.** Ed.:– Gilbert Wats. Oxford, 1640. 1st. Edn., 2nd. Iss. Fo. Title sigd. 'Samuel Ladyman'. Cont. cf., rebkd. [STC 1167] (S. Sept.29; 4) *Lindsay.* £80
– **Of Gardens, an Essay.** Ill.:– Lucien Pissarro. Eragny Pr., 1902. (226). Orig. bds., unc. With wood-engraved pict. bkplt. of William A. Pye, by T. Sturge Moore, & that of Major Abbey. (S. Jul.31; 23) *Foyles.* £150
– **Opera Omnia.** Ed.:– J. Blackbourne. 1730. 4 vols. Fo. Mallet's 'Life of Bacon', 1760, bnd. at end of vol. IV, slight soiling & offsetting. 19th. C. cf., gt. From liby. of Dr. E. Ashworth Underwood. (S. Feb.23; 140) *Goldschmidt.* £90
– **Sylva Sylvarum . . .** 1627. 1st. Edn., 2nd. Iss. Fo. Aa 2 soiled, inner margin of port. strengthened. Cont. cf., spine defect. [STC 1169] (S. Dec.1; 36) *Claridge.* £50
– **Sylva Sylvarum; New Atlantis.–Of the Advancement & Proficience of Learning.** Oxford [3rd. work], 1627; [1658?]; 1640. 1st. 2 works in 1 vol., together 2 vols. Fo. A few sm. tears, most reprd., 1st. work lacks 2M1 (Blank), ll. dampstained, 3rd. work lacks port. Mod. hf. mor. [STC 1169; Wing B307; STC 1167] (SH. Jan.30; 402) *Blundell.* £55
– **The Twoo Bookes . . . of the Proficience & Advancement of Learning.** 1605. 1st. Edn. 4to. Lacks the 2 errata ll., title stained, staining towards end. Cl.-bkd. bds. [STC 1164] (C. Nov.20; 217) *Carnegie.* £340
– – **Anr. Copy.** Without 2 errata ll., sm. repair to A4, a few marginal repairs, inscr. on title-p. of [William] Hepworth Dixon. Mod. red mor. From Honeyman Collection. [STC 1164] (S. May 20; 3174) *Zeitlin & Verbrugge.* £320
– – **Anr. Copy.** 2 vols. in 1. Title-p. cut & mntd., cont. annots. on final blank lf. Old spr. cf. (TA. Nov.20; 201) £170
– – **Anr. Copy.** 2 vols. in 1. Title cut & mntd., cont. annots. on final blank lf. Old spr. cf. (TA. Apr.16; 210) £65
– – **Anr. Copy.** Title completely bkd. with old paper & with old name, lightly soiled in parts, mostly only in edges, lacks blank lf. Hhh-2 & both errata ll. at end. Leath. (R. Mar.31-Apr.4; 259) DM 1,800
– **The Works.** Ed.:– J. Blackbourne. 1730. L.P. 4 vols. Fo. Lacks subscribers list, offsetting to titles, slight spotting. Cont. diced russ., gt., worn at head & foot. (S. Jan.26; 105) *Whitby.* £60
– – **Anr. Edn.** L., 1740. 4 vols. Fo. Damp damage thro.-out. Spr. cf. (GM. Apr.30; 554) £60
– – **Anr. Edn.** 1857-68. 11 vols. Cont. hf. cf. (SH. May 28; 6) *Howes Books.* £100

BACON, Mary Ann
– **Fruits from the Garden & Field.** Ill.:– Owen Jones & E.L. Bateman. 1850. 4to. Orig. blind-stpd. cf., lacks part of spine. Pres. copy from Jones to his cousin. (SH. Mar.26; 302) *Slade.* £85

BACON, Roger
– **The Mirror of Alchimy . . .** 1597. 1st. Edn. in Engl. 4to. 2 ll. (preface & pp. 1-2 of text) in pen

BACON, Roger – The Mirror of Alchimy ...
-contd.
facs., title slightly soiled & cleaned, cut less round
& mntd., last lf. roughly remargined & with a few
sm. tears, sm. tear in L3, extreme lr. blank
margins of a few ll. at end damaged by a burn.
Old cf., rebkd., new endpapers. [STC 1182] (S.
Dec.1; 40) *Fletcher*. £280
See-PECKHAM, Joannes, Archbp. of Canterbury
-BACON, Roger

BACON, Roger & Arrais, Edward Madeira
– The Cure of Old Age & Preservation of Youth
... also a Physical Account of the Tree of Life.
1683. 1st. Edn. in Engl. 2 Pts. in 1 vol. Lacks last
lf. (?blank). Cont. spr. sheep., rebkd. [Wing B372]
(S. Mar.16; 109) *Thorp*. £160
– – **Anr. Copy.** Lacks(?) last lf. (blank?). Early
19th. C. str.-grd. mor. gt. (S. Mar.16; 171)
Fletcher. £120

**BADEN-POWELL, Maj. Gen. Robert Stephenson
Smyth**
– The Matabele Campaign. 1897. Orig. cl. (SH.
Jun.25; 17) *Allsop*. £55

BADER, J.
– Badische Volkssitten und Trachten. Karlsruhe,
[1843-44]. Cont. bds. (R. Mar.31-Apr.4; 1895)
DM 3,400

BADESLADE, Thomas
– The History of the Ancient & Present State of
the Navigation of the Port of King's-Lyn, & of
Cambridge. 1725. 1st. Edn. Fo. A few ll.
marginally stained. Cont. cf., worn. (S. Dec.9; 418)
Weinreb. £200

BADESLADE, Thomas & Toms, Willliam Henry
– Chorographia Britanniae. 1742. Slightly
browned, 1 map spotted. Cf., worn, bds. almost
detchd. (CSK. Feb.6; 98) £300
– – **Anr. Edn.** Ca. 1745. Title detchd. & worn.
Cont. cf., covers detchd. W.a.f. (S. Nov.3; 19)
Gibbons. £320
– – **Anr. Edn.** N.d [plts. dtd. 1742]. 1 map loose,
title & some ll. cropped affecting text, title stained.
Orig. bdg., lacks upr. cover. (SKC. Dec.4; 1622)
£210

BADGER, Mrs. C.M.
– Floral Belles from the Greenhouse & Garden.
N.Y., 1867. Fo. Orig. mor., upr. cover gt. with
title amid hanging fuchsia flowers in a border in
Egyptian taste, gt. spine, slightly worn. (S.
Jun.1; 65) *Joseph*. £290
– Wild Flowers Drawn & Colored from Nature.
Ed.:– Mrs. L.H. Sigourny. N.Y., 1859. 1st. Edn.
Fo. Text heavily foxed, plts. occasionally affected.
Cont. hf. mor. (SG. May 21; 327) $400

BADIANUS MANUSCRIPT
See-CODEX BARBERINI

BADMINTON LIBRARY of Sports & Pastimes
– Fencing, Boxing, Wrestling.-Riding; Polo.
-Mountaineering.-Archery.-Big Game Hunting.
-The Poetry of Sport. L., 1889-96. (250)
numbered on L.P. 7 vols., 5th. work 2 vols. 4to.
Hf. mor., worn. (SG. Dec.11; 170) $130

**BADMINTON MAGAZINE of Sports &
Pastimes**
Ed.:– Alfred E.T. Watson. L., Jul., 1897-Jun.,
1902. Vols. 5-14. Hf. cf., last 3 vols. in hf. mor.
(worn). (SG. Dec.11; 171) $110

BAEDEKER, Karl
– Indien. Leipzig, 1914. Orig. linen. (R.
Mar.31-Apr.4; 2497). DM 450
– Rheinreise von Basel bis Düsseldorf mit Ausflügen
in das Elsass und die Rheinpfalz. Koblenz, 1849.
Slightly soiled. Orig. bds. (D. Dec.11-13; 1369)
DM 850
– Russia; with Teheran, Port Arthur & Peking.
Leipzig, 1914. 16mo. Flexible cl. (SG. Feb.26; 42)
$180
– – **Anr. Copy.** Cl. (SG. Oct. 30; 320) $150

BAGATELLA, A.
– Regole per la Costruzione de' Violin, Viole,
Violoncelli e Violoni ... Padova, 1786. 4to.
Browned thro.-out. Newer hf. linen. (H.
Dec.9/10; 1046) DM 620

BAGATTI-VALSECCHI, Fausto
– Felice Calvi ed Altri. Famiglie Notabili Milanesi.
Milan, 1774. 4 vols. Fo. Cont. mor. (SI. Dec.3; 43)
Lire 620,000

BAGE, Robert
[-] Hermsprong; Or, Man as He Is Not. A Novel.
1796. 1st. Edn. 3 vols. Titles ptd. off-centre,
therefore closely cropped to right-hand margin,
publisher's advts. to rear of vols. 1 & 2, some
spotting. Cont. tree cf., rebkd. (TA. Feb.19; 574)
£50

BAGLIONE, Giovanni Romano
– Le Vite de'Pittori, Scultori, Architetti, ed
Intagliatori. Naples, 1733. 4to. With life of
Salvator Rosa Napoletano by G.P. Passeri, 2pp.
unnumbered. Cont. bds. (CR. Mar.19; 375)
Lire 400,000

BAGLIVI, Giorgio
– Opera omnia medico-practica et anatomica ...
Lyons, 1704. 6th. Edn. 4to. Tear in margin of 4P3
affecting a few letters. Cf., hinges reprd. (S.
Jun.15; 27) *Dillon*. £50
– The Practice of Physick reduc'd to the Ancient
way of Observations ... together with several new
& curious dissertations, particularly of the
Tarantula & the nature of its poison ... 1704. 1st.
Engl. Edn. A few stains, inscr. on title-p. New hf.
cf. (S. Jun.15; 28) *Dawson*. £160

BAGROW, Leo
– History of Cartography. 1964. 4to. Orig. cl.
(SH. Jun.4; 43) *Fisher*. £50

BAIF, Jean Antoine de
– Les Amours.-Euvres [sic] en Rime. Paris, 1573.
2nd. Edn.; 1st. Edn. 2 vols. 2nd. vol lacks 2 prelims.
18th. C. mor., triple gt. fillet, spines gt. in compartments, inner gt. dentelles, spines defect., corners
worn. (SM. Oct.7; 1555) Frs. 2,000

BAILEY, Harold H.
– The Birds of Florida. Ill.:– George M. Sutton.
Baltimore, 1925. Ltd. Edn. 4to. Orig. buckram.
(CB. Sep.24; 10) Can. $130

BAILEY, Nathan
– Universal Etymological English Dictionary.
1726-27. 2 vols. Cont. cf. gt. (P. Dec.11; 258)
Jarndyce. £65
– – **Anr. Edn.** 1731; 1735. 2nd. Edn.; 7th. Edn. 2
vols. 2nd. edn. with 'Vol. II' title-page. Old cf.,
covers loose, ex-liby. (SG. Aug.7; 240) $120
– – **Anr. Edn.** Ed.:– Joseph Nicol Scott. L., 1764.
New Edn. Fo. Cont. russ. gt., jnts. split. Bkplt. of
Nonsuch House. (S. Nov.24; 12) *Frost*. £85

BAILEY, Percival
See-CUSHING, Harvey & Bailey, Percival

BAILLIE, Matthew
– The Morbid Anatomy ... of the Human Body.
Albany, 1795. 1st. Amer. Edn. Orig. mott. cf.
(SG. Sep.18; 27) $100
– A Series of Engravings ... to Illustrate the
Morbid Anatomy of Some of the Most Important
Parts of the Human Body. 1799-1803. 1st. Edn.
4to. 1st. sectional title at beginning, general title,
hf.-title & dedication bnd. in front of 10th.
section, some plts. foxed & dampstained. Cont. hf.
cf., worn, upr. cover detchd. 2-p. A.L.s. by author
tipped in at end; from liby Dr. E. Ashworth
Underwood. (S. Feb.23; 141) *Jenner*. £360
– – **Anr. Edn.** Ill.:– William Clift. 1812. 2nd. Edn.
Lge. 4to. Bds., mor. spine, unc. (S. Jun.15; 29)
Pratt. £170
– The Works. Ed.:– James Wardrop. 1825. 2 vols.
in 1. Hf. cf. (S. Jun.15; 30) *Jenner Books*. £80

BAILLIERE, F.F.
– South Australian Gazetteer & Road Guide ...
with map. Ed.:– Robert P. Whitworth. Adelaide,
1866. Light stain in lr. margins, map (with 2 short
tears) re-inserted, outer margins of early ll.
dust-stained. Old hf. roan. Pres. copy. (KH.
Nov.18; 639) *Aus*. $200
– Victorian Gazetteer & Road Guide. Ed.:–
Robert P. Whitworth. Melbourne, 1865. Folding
map reprd. with tape, several paper clippings
preserved on rear end-papers. Hf. roan, cl. bds.
(KH. Nov.18; 640) *Aus*. $250

BAILY, Francis
– Journal of a Tour Through Unsettled Parts of
North America in 1796 & 1797 ... L., 1856. 1st.
Edn. Owner's stp. of R.L.C. White on title &
front pastedown, MS. notation 'from Miss Baily,
Tavistock Place.' Orig. blind-stpd. cl., slightly
soiled, chipped at head & foot of spine. From liby.
of William E. Wilson. (SPB. Apr.29; 14) $350

BAILY's Magazine of Sports & Pastimes
1860-1910. 94 vols. (some dupl.). Cont. hf. cf. gt.
W.a.f. (SBA. Jul.22; 80) *Dawson*. £180

BAINBRIDGE, George C.
– The Fly Fisher's Guide. L'pool., Priv. Ptd., 1816.
1st. Edn. Plts. & frontis. hand-cold., captions to
plts. & full-p. MS. 'Index to Plates' added by
previous owner, extra engr. 'Fly Fishing for Trout'
tipped onto title verso. Crude hf. cl., ex-liby. (SG.
Dec.11; 9) $400

BAINBRIDGE, Henry Charles
– Peter Carl Faberge. Ed.:– Sacheverell Sitwell. L.,
[1949]. (350) De Luxe Edn. on H.M.P. &
specially bnd. 4to. Buckram, with gt. arms, lev.
spine & tips, boxed. (SG. Dec.4; 136) $200

BAINES, Edward
– History of the County Palatine & Duchy of
Lancaster. 1824-36. 5 vols., including a folder. 4to
& 8vo. Engraved maps & tables from an earlier
edn. Cont. cf., gt., & orig. hf. cl. folder. (SH.
Mar.5; 8) *Crowe*. £260
– – **Anr. Edn.** 1836. 4 vols. Hf. mor. (RBT.
Jan.22; 241) £230
– – **Anr. Copy.** 4 vols. 4to. Later hf. mor. (SBA.
Dec.16; 154) *Rochdale Book Co*. £160
– – **Anr. Copy.** Vols. 2-4 only. Engraved double-p.
map, hand-cold. in outl., plan of Manchester
slightly torn. Cont. hf. cf. (SBA. Mar.4; 170)
Birch Books. £120
– – **Anr. Copy.** 4 vols. Offset to title of vol. I,
minor occasional foxing. Cont. hf. mor. From the
collection of Eric Sexton. (C. Apr.16; 211)
Kidd. £90
– – **Anr. Edn.** Ed.:– John Harland. 1868-70. 2 vols.
4to. Folding map slightly torn at fold. Orig. cl.
(CSK. Apr.3; 112) £65

BAINES, J.T.
[-] Nature & Art. L., 1886-87. 2 vols. in 1. 4to.
Cont. hf. mor., upr. cover loose. (SSA. Jun.18; 46)
R. 150

BAINES, Thomas, Explorer & Artist
– The Birds of South Africa. Johannesburg, 1975.
Pres. Edn. (marked A-Z). 4to. Orig. bdg., s.-c.
(VA. Oct.31; 74) R. 170
– – **Anr. Edn.** Johannesburg, ca. 1975. Pres. Edn.
(marked A-Y). Lge. fo. In orig. box. (VA.
Oct.31; 73) R. 110
– – **Anr. Edn.** Johannesburg, 1975. (500). 4to.
Orig. bdg., s.-c. (VA. May 8; 272) R. 200
– – **Anr. Copy.** Rexine, s.-c. (SSA. Jun.18; 45)
R. 140
– Explorations in South-West Africa. 1864. Advts.
Mod. hf. cf., unc. (S. Jun.29; 211) *Adelson*. £110
– – **Anr. Copy.** Some marginal tears reprd., some
browning of edges. Mod. cf. (VA. Oct.31; 75)
R. 290
– The Gold Regions of South Eastern Africa. 1877.
1st. Edn. Folding facs., folding map in pocket, 26
pp. advts. Orig. pict. cl. (S. Nov.4; 633)
Traylen. £75
– – **Anr. Copy.** Some light foxing. Orig. bdg.
Bkplt. of William Jardine. (VA. Oct.31; 77)
R. 160
– The Victoria Falls ... L., 1856. Fo. Outer edges
of some plts. reprd. Orig. cl., recased. (SSA.
Nov.5; 193) R. 2,800
– Watercolours. Ed.:– R.F. Kennedy.
Johannesburg, 1967. De Luxe Edn. Lge. fo.
Leath., orig. case. (VA. Oct.31; 79) R. 90

BAINVILLE, Jacques
– Napoléon. 1931. On Japon. Sewed. (HD.
Oct.10; 8) Frs. 550

BAINVILLE, Théodor de
– Odes Funambulesques. Alençon, 1857. On Vergé
fin. Orig. bdg. A.L.s. (HD. Oct.10; 10) Frs. 500
– Les Princesses. Ill.:– Decisy after Georges
Rochegrosse. Paris, 1904. (130) advance copies on
Japon or vell d'Arches. 4to. Ills. in 3 states, orig.
watercolour by Rochegrosse at beginning. Hf.
mor. by Flammerion, silk doubls., orig. wraps.
preserved, s.-c. (SM. Oct.8; 2318) Frs. 6,000

BAIRD, Spencer F.
– The Birds of North America. Phila., 1860. [1st.
Edn.?]. 2 vols. 4to. Slight soiling. Orig. cl., worn,
ex-liby. (SPB. Oct.1; 182) $1,000
– – **Anr. Copy.** (CNY. Oct.1; 133) $750

BAISER, Le
Nancy, 1888. (15) on imperial Japon, numbered.
Lge. 8vo. Mor. by Canape, mosaic flower on upr.

cover, silk doubls., s.-c. (SM. Feb.11; 142)
Frs. 11,000

BAKER, Charles H.
- The Gentleman's Companion. 1939. (1250)
numbered. 2 vols. 2-tone cl., unopened. (SG.
Dec.11; 212) $100

BAKER, Charles Henry Collins
- Lely & the Stuart Portrait Painters. 1912. (375)
numbered. 2 vols. 4to. Orig. bds. (SH. Jun.4; 219)
Baker. £140

BAKER, David Erskine
[-] The Companion to the Play-House. 1764. 4 vols.
12mo. Mod. hf. cf., rebkd. (CSK. Nov.14; 104)
£50

BAKER, David Erskine & others
- Biographia Dramatica; or, A Companion to the
Playhouse. 1812. 4 vols. Mod. hf. cf. (CSK.
Nov.14; 103) £50

BAKER, Edward Charles Stuart
- The Fauna of British India, including Ceylon &
Burma: Birds. Ed.:- Arthur E. Shipley. L.,
1922-30. Vols. I-[VIII]. Orig. buckram. (CB.
Sep.24; 11) Can. $110
- Game Birds of India, Burma & Ceylon. 1921.
2nd. Edn. Vol. 1 only. Additional title & 33 plts.
Later hf. mor., slightly soiled. (CSK. Jan.23; 182)
£80
- - Anr. Edn. Ill.:- after Gronvold, Lodge,
Keulemans. Bombay, 1921-30. 3 vols. Vols. 1 & 2
cont. hf. mor., vol. 3 in similar cl. (TA. Jun.18; 53)
£120
- - Anr. Copy. 4to. Various bdgs. (SH. Jul.9; 156)
Bookroom. £110
- Indian Ducks & their Allies. 1908. Hf. mor. gt.
(P. Nov.13; 178) *Burr.* £140
- - Anr. Edn. Ill.:- Gronvold & others. 1908. Ltd.
Edn. Cont. hf. mor. (C. May 20; 190) *Hill.* £95

BAKER, Ezekiel
- Remarks on Rifle Guns. 1825. 9th. Edn. Spotted.
Cont. hf. mor., soiled. (CSK. Feb.20; 25) £65
- - Anr. Edn. 1829. 10th. Edn. Cont. hf. roan.
(SH. Jun.18; 156) *Henderson.* £75

BAKER, George
- The History & Antiquities of the County of
Northampton. Ill.:- after Edward Blore (plts.),
hand-cold. litho. plt. by L.G. Scharf. 1822-30. 5
pts. in 2 vols. Fo. Most. plts. slightly dampstained.
Cont. mor., gt.-panel. spines, inner dentelles, by
Zaehnsdorf. (C. Feb.25; 23) *Maggs.* £300

BAKER, Henry
- Beyträge zu Nutzlichem und Vergnügendem
Gebrauch und Verbesserung des Microscopii, in
zwey Theilen. Augsburg, 1754. 1st. German Edn.
2 pts. in 1 vol. Slightly browned. Cont. leath.,
wormed, especially spine. (R. Oct.14-18; 463)
DM 700
- Le Microscope à la Portée de Tout le Monde . . .
Paris, 1754. 1st. Fr. Edn. Mod. hf. chagrin. (HD.
Jun.24; 6) Frs. 1,100

BAKER, Sir Samuel White
- The Albert N'Yanza.-Ismailia. 1866; 1874. 1st.
work 1st. Edn. Each 2 vols. Cont. hf. cf. (SH. May
21; 193) *Francis.* £50

BAKEWELL, Robert
- An Introduction to Geology. L., 1813. 1st. Edn.
Cont. qtr. leath. & marb. bds. (CB. Apr.1; 212)
Can. $160
- - Anr. Edn. 1823. 2 vols. in 1. Cont. cf., worn.
(SH. Nov.6; 188) *Baird.* £95
- - Anr. Copy. Hf. mor. (P. Jul.30; 65)
Nightingale. £65

BAKST, Léon
- L'Oeuvre pour la Belle au Bois Dormant. Paris,
1922. (500) numbered on L.P., sigd. by Bakst. Fo.
Orig. wraps. (SH. Apr.9; 131) *Mackenzie.* £220
- - Anr. Copy. Fo. Mod. qtr. mor., orig. upr.
wrap. bnd. in, unc. (PNY. May 21; 72) $750
- - Anr. Copy. Fo. Sewed, s.-c. (HD. Jun.10; 117)
Frs. 3,800

BALBINUS, Bohuslav
- Epitome Historica Rerum Behemicarum. Prag.,
1677 & 1673. 1st. Edn. 2 pts. in 1 vol. Fo. Cont.
vell., paper covered spine. (D. Dec.11-13; 1603)
DM 1,000

BALBUS, Joannes
- Catholicon. Mainz, [Johann Gutenburg?]. 1460.
Fo. 1 lf. only, rubricated; laid in at end of
Margaret Bingham Stillwell's 'Gutenburg & the

Catholicon of 1460' (N.Y., 1936, orig. buckram
gt., chemise & s.-c. (worn)). From the collection
of Eric Sexton. [BMC I, 39, Goff B20, HC 2254*]
(CNY. Apr.8; 89) $2,500
- - Anr. Edn. Augsburg, Günther Zainer, 30 Apr.
1469. 2nd. Printing. 2 vols. Fo. 2 initials on f.1r &
f.89v. illuminated, the first histor., with borders
extending into 3 & 2 margins, 30 cold. initials,
some with extensions, other initials in red, some
with penwork extensions, rubric. 18th. C. russ., gt.
arms of Duke of Devonshire on sides, his cypher at
top of spines, rebkd. using old spine. Chatsworth
bkplt. [BMC II, 315] (S. Nov.25; 329)
Abrams. £10.00

BALDAEUS, Phillipus
- Naauwkeurige Beschryvinge van Malabar en
Chromandel . . . en het Machtige Eyland Ceylon.
Amst., 1672. 1st. Edn. 3 pts. in 1 vol. Fo. Lacks 2
ports. & 1 plt., 2 engrs. tipped in, pt. II with the
gathering *4 inserted between fo.'s F3 & F4, sm.
marginal tear, a few maps & plts. slightly spotted.
Cont. vell. bds. (S. Jan.27; 544) *Chester.* £280

BALDAEUS, Philippus-SAAR, J.J.
- Wahrhaftige Ausführliche Beschreibung der
Berühmten Ost-Indischen Kusten Malabar und
Coromandel, als auch der Insel Zeylon.
-Ost-Indianische Funfzehn-jährige Kriegs-Dienste
. . . Amst.; Nuremb., 1672; 1672. 1st. German
Edn.; 2nd. Edn. 2 works in 1 vol. Fo. Slightly
soiled. Cont. vell., spine defect. (R.
Oct.14-18; 1771) DM 2,400

BALDESANO, Giuglio
- La Sacra Historia dis. Mauritio Anciduca della
Legione Thebea, et de suoi Valorosi Campioni . . .
Torino, 1604. 4to. Cont Italian red mor., double
border of 2 fillets, fleurons in outside corners,
bouquets of leaves in inside corners, arms of
Charles Emmanuel, Duke of Savoy, spine decor.
in fanfare style. Dedication copy. (HD.
Mar.18; 15) Frs. 1,500

BALDUINUS (or Balduin), F.
- Iustinianus, sive de Iure Novo, Commentariorum
Libri IV.-Disputationes Duae de Iure Civili, ex
Papiniano. Basel; Heidelberg, 1560; 1561. 1st.
Edn. 2 works in 1 vol. Many old MS. marginalia.
Cont. pig. (R. Oct.14-18; 1386) DM 620

BALDWIN, Thomas
- Narrative of the Massacre, by the Savages, of the
Wife & Children of Thomas Baldwin . . . N.Y.,
1835. 1st. Edn. Folding plt. with partial later
colouring, text lightly foxed & stained, some
repairs. Mod. buckram, gt. spine. From liby. of
William E. Wilson. (SPB. Apr.29; 15) $100

BALDWIN, William
See-KNAPP, Andrew & Baldwin, William

BALDWIN, William Charles
- African Hunting . . . L., 1863. 2nd. Edn. Cf. gt.
(VA. Oct.31; 81) R. 110

BALE, John, Bp.
- The First Two Partes of the Actes or Unchaste
Examples of the Englysh Votaryes, gathered out of
their owne Legenades & Chronycles. 1551. 2 pts.
in 1 vol. Dampstained, slight browning & soiling.
Old cf., rebkd. [STC 1273] (S. Dec.9; 277)
Booth. £60

BALEN, Matthias
- Beschryvinge der Stad Dordrecht. Ill.:- R. de
Hooghe. Dordrecht, 1677. 4to. Cont. blind-stpd.
vell. (VG. Dec.17; 1185) Fls. 1,600
- - Anr. Copy. 2 plts. seriously defect., some short
tears, a few ll. loose, stained at beginning & end.
Cont. marb. cf., back gt., some defects. (VG.
Dec.17; 1186) Fls. 550

BALESTRIERI, Domenico
- Rime Milanesi. [Milan], ca. 1744. 4to. Mod.
antique style hf. cf. (SI. Dec.3; 45) Lire 320,000
- Rime Toscane e Milanesi. Milan, 1774. Thick
paper. Hf.-title. Cont. mor. gt. (SI. Dec.3; 44)
Lire 420,000

BALFOUR PAUL, Sir J.
- Scots Peerage. 1904-14. 9 vols. Cl. gt., marked.
(CE. Feb.19; 115) £155

BALGDON, F.W.
See-WILLIAMSON, Capt. Thomas & Balgdon,
F.W.

BALL, F. Elrington
- The Judges in Ireland, 1221-1921. N.Y., 1927.
1st. Edn. 2 vols. 2 errata slips. Cl. (GM.
Apr.30; 25) £55

BALLADS & SONGS OF LOVE
Munich, Bremer Pr., 1930. (280) numbered. Fo.
Orig. vell. (SKC. Feb.26; 1249) £100

BALLANTYNE, John, publisher
- Novelist's Library Series. 1821-24. Vols. 1-10.
Old bds. & cf. corners with recent leath.
backstrips. (TA. Mar.19; 242) £54

BALLANTYNE, Robert Michael 'Comus'
- Hudson's Bay. Edinb., 1848. 1st. Edn., for
private circulation. 12mo. Cont. hf. calf., recent
qtr. mor. fall-down-back box. [Sabin 2952] (CB.
Feb.18; 284) Can. $1,550

BALLARD, Christophe
- Nouvelles Parodies Bachiques, mélées de
Vaudevilles ou Rondes de Table. Paris, 1700-02. 3
vols. 12mo. Slight browning, sig. 'P. Moreau'.
Cont. cf. Bkplt. of H.B.H. Beaufroy, F.R.S.; from
liby. of André L. Simon. (S. May 18; 29)
Smith. £90

BALLARD, R.
- Recueil des Chansons à Danser et à Boire de
Denis Macé. Paris, 1643. With annots. in early
hand on some ll. Vell.-bkd. bds. (BS. Jun.11; 230)
£260

BALLARDINI, G.
- Corpus della Maiolica Italiana Rome, 1933-39. 2
vols. 4to. Publr's. hf. vell. (CR. Jun.11; 28)
Lire 950,000

BALLESTEROS, Tomas de
- Ordenanzas del Peru. Lima, 1685. 1st. Edn. Vol.
1 (all publd.). Fo. Sm. wormhole affecting text.
19th. C. hf. roan. (SPB. May 5; 82) $750

BALLETS Russe
- Programme Officiel des Ballets Russe. Ill.:-
Leon Bakst. Paris, 1912. 4to. Pict. wraps., upr.
cover detchd. (SG. Feb.12; 81) $120

BALLING, F.A.V.
- Die Heilquellen und Bäder zu Kissingen. Bad
Kissingen, 1876. 8th. Edn. Cont. hf. linen. (R.
Mar.31-Apr.4; 1948) DM 1,400

BALLOU's Pictorial Drawing Room Companion
Boston, Jan.-Jun.10 1856. Vol. X. Fo. Gt.-pict. cl.,
rebkd. in leath. (SG. May 21; 328) $100

BALOG, P.
- The Coinage of the Mamluk Sultans of Egypt &
Syria. N.Y., 1964. Orig. wraps. (SH. Mar.6; 315)
Klat. £170

BALS DE L'OPERA
- Costumes du Quadrille Historique. Paris, [1834].
Fo. Some slight soiling & foxing thro.-out. Bds.,
defect. (BS. Jun.11; 304) £130

BALTHASAR, P.
- Les Généalogies et Anciennes Descentes des
Forrestiers et Comtes de Flandres. Antw., [1580].
3 vols. in 1. Sm. fo. Some ll. browned, 1 plt. reprd.
Old vell. (BS. Jun.11; 305) £75

BALTHAZAR, Andre
- A Bras le Corps. Ill.:- Pol Bury. Belgium, n.d.
(100) sigd. by author & artist, numbered. 4to.
Unsewn in orig. wraps., s.-c. (SH. Nov.20; 249)
Ayres. £55

BALTIMORE, Lord Frederick Calvert
- Coelestes et Inferi. Venice, 1771. 4to. Frontis.
slightly cropped, 4 ll. with light dampstain, 1 quire
sprung. Cont. Italian cf. gt; gt. dentelles, worn,
rebkd. Pres. Copy, to Antonio Maria Zanetti,
lately in the collection of John A. Saks. (C.
Jun.10; 32) *Quaritch.* £150
[-] Gli Abitatori del Cielo e dell' Inferno. Trans.:-
[Gianfrancesco Giogetti]. Venice, 1771. Thick
paper. Fo. Cont. Italian cf., silk end-papers.
Bkplt. of Sir Edward Sullivan, disposal label of Ely
Cathedral Liby., lately in the collection of John. A.
Saks. (C. Jun.10; 33) *Quaritch.* £190
- A Tour to the East . . . L., 1767. 1st. Edn. Cont.
red mor. gt. (S. Nov.24; 13) *Riley Smith.* £280
- - Anr. Copy. Cont. mott. cf. (SG. Feb.26; 45)
$140

BALZAC, Guez de
- Aristippe ou De la Cour. Paris, 1658. 12mo. Red
Jansenist mor. by Belz-Niedrée, Inside dentelle.
Bkplt. of Alfred Piat. (HD. Mar.18; 16)
Frs. 1,400

BALZAC, Honoré de
– César Birotteau. Ill.:– Boullaire. Paris, 1929. (1075); (40) on holland. Sm. 4to. Mor. by Trinckvel, decor. spine, gt. border on covers, gt. silk doubls. wrap. preserved, s.-c. (SM. Feb.11; 175) Frs. 1,100
– Comédie Humaine. Ed.:– George Saintsbury. L., 1896-1901. 40 vols. Hf. mor. gt., gt. panel. spines, by Sangorski & Sutcliffe, slightly worn. (SPB. Nov.25; 428) $600
– Les Contes Drolatiques. Ill.:– Doré. Paris, 1855. 2 vols. Mor., gt., by Chambolle-Duru, partly unc. Blacque & Poor copy. (SM. Oct.8; 2230) Frs. 3,200
– – Anr. Copy. Slight foxing. Publisher's buckram. (HD. Jun.24; 138) Frs. 1,900
– Le Curé de Village. Ill.:– Paul-Louis Guilbert. Paris, 1946. (270); (1), numbered. 2 vols. 4to. 2 states of engrs. with comments, 1 unique proof, 2 proofs of rejected plts. Red mor. by Lambert, covers of vol. I with geometric motif, wrap. preserved, s.-c. (SM. Feb.11; 176) Frs. 12,000
– Facino Carse. Ill.:– Decisy after Léandre. Paris, 1910. (100) advance copies. 4to. Ills. in cold. & uncold. states. Mor., ornate gt. & gt.-stpd., by H. Blanchetiere, mor. doubls., orig. wraps inserted. A.L.s. by binder loosely inserted. (SM. Oct.8; 2316) Frs. 2,800
– La Femme de Trente Ans . . . Ill.:– Robaudi. Paris, 1902. (500) on Jap. numbered. Mod. hf. red mor., gt. spine, orig. wraps, bnd. in, partly unc. (SI. Dec.3; 46) Lire 300,000
– Un Grand Homme de Province à Paris . . . –Histoire de . . . César Birotteau . . . Paris, 1839; 1838. 1st. Edns. 2 works in 4 vols. 1st. work: p 352 of vol. II reprd., lacks table lf. & advt. ll. of vol. II; 2nd. work: lacks pp. 17-32 of 2nd. vol. 1st. work: mod glazed violin hf. cf., corners, smooth spines; 2nd. work: Bradel bds., wraps., lacks wrap. of vol. 2. (HD. Jun.24; 136) Frs. 1,300
– Grandeur et . . . Décadence de César Birotteau. Paris, 1838. 1st. Edn. 2 vols. Advts., some foxing. Cont. cased bdg., combed paper, unc. (HD. Dec.5; 12) Frs. 1,350
– Le Lys dans la Vallée. 1 Jun. 1836. Orig. Edn. 2 vols. Cont. hf. roan. Ex-lib. Eugène Scribe. (HD. Jun.30; 4) Frs. 3,600
– Das Mädchen mit den Goldaugen Trans.:– E. Hardt. Ill.:– M. Behmer. Leipzig, 1904. 1st. Edn. (500). Orig. vell., gt. upr. cover, end-paper by M. Bohmer. (HK. Nov.18-21; 2428) DM 900
– Le Médecin de Campagne. Paris, Feb. 1833. 1st. Edn. 2 vols. Advts. Violin hf. cf. by Bernasconi, decor. spine, unc. (HD. Dec.5; 11) Frs. 1,350
– Menschliche Komödie. Ed.:– H.V. Hofmannsthal. Trans.:– F.P. Greve. Ill.:– E. Gill (decor.). Leipzig, 1908-11. Orig. red mor. (HK. May 15; 4093) DM 500
– Oeuvres. Houssiaux, 1855-1863. 20 vols. Cont. red hf.-roan. (HD. Feb. 18; 92) Frs. 2,600
– Oeuvres Complètes. 1874. 20 vols. Cl., spine gt. (CE. Feb.19; 121) £52
– – Anr. Edn. Paris, 1912-14. (100). 38 vols. 4to. Hf. mor. gt., head of 1 spine defect. (SPB. Nov.25; 429) $550
– – Anr. Edn. Paris, n.d. 48 vols. Cont. hf. cf., gt. spines (SH. Mar.5; 174) *Wade.* £130
– Oeuvres Illustrées. Ill.:– T. Johannot, Stael, Bertall, H. Monnier, Daumier & others. Paris, 1852. 8 vols. in 4. 4to. Later hf. chagrin, spines decor. with raised bands. (HD. Feb.27; 74) Frs. 1,400
– Les Paysans. Ill.:– Georges Jeanniot. Paris, 1911. (125), numbered. 4to. Orig. drawing, 5 states of printing. Red mor. by Meunier, mor. border in spine compartments & on covers, mor. doubls. with mosaic flowers in multi-cold. mor. in corners, wrap. preserved, s.-c. (SM. Feb.11; 177) Frs. 14,000
– Les Paysans.–Traité des Excitants.–Voyage à Java. Paris, [1855.] 1st work; 1st. Fr. Edn.; 3rd. work: 1st. Edn. 3 works in 5 vols. Mod. Bradel marb. paper s.-c., unc. wraps. (HD. Dec.5; 15) Frs. 2,300
– La Peau de Chagrin. Ill.:– Gavarni & others. 1838. 1st. printing. Browning. Mor., decor., inner border, silk doubls. & end-ll., unc. (HD. Jun.30; 5) Frs. 1,800
– – Anr. Copy. 4to. Lightly browned, title stpd. Cont. leath. A.N. Dernidow Fürst von San Donato ex-lib. (H. May 21/22; 984) DM 560
– – Anr. Edn. Ill.:– Paul Gavarni & others. Paris, 1838. 1st. Ill. Edn. Slightly spotted. Cont. hf. mor. (SH. Nov.20; 158) *Lelievre.* £55
– Le Père Goriot . . . Ill.:– Lynch. Paris, 1885. (100) on Jap. Sm. 4to. 10 engraved etchings in 2 states. Mor. by Gozzi, gt. blind-tooled fillets on covers, spine decor. with raised bands, watered silk end-papers, wrap. & spine preserved, s.-c. (HD. Jun.24; 140) Frs. 1,500
– Petites Misères de la Vie Conjugale. Ill.:– After Bertall. Paris, ca. 1845. 1st. Edn. Bnd. from 50 pts. 4to. Cont. hf. mor. (SH. Apr. 9; 182) *Duran.* £60
– Physiologie du Mariage. Paris, 1830. 1st. Edn. 2 vols. Cont. hf. sheep., smooth decor. backs. (HD. Dec. 5; 10) Frs. 1,850
– Revue Parisienne. 1840. 3 publd. nos. (HD. Oct.10; 9) Frs. 1,050
– Romans et Contes Philosophiques. Paris, 1833. 4th. Edn. 2 vols. Cf., monog., marb. covering & end-ll. (D. Dec.11-13; 754) DM 1,200
– Scènes de la Vie de Province. 1837. 1st. pt. in Orig. Edn., 1st. 2 vols. are reprints. 4 vols. Later. hf.-calico, unc. Ex liby. MS. of M. Lemarchand on 1st. vol. (HD. Feb.18; 91) Frs. 3,000
– Scènes de la Vie Politique. Le Député d'Arcis. Paris, [1854.] 1st. Trade Edn. 4 vols. Mod. Bradel cased bdg., marb. paper, unc., wraps. & spine. (HD. Dec.5; 13) Frs. 1,350
– Ursule Mirouet. Paris, 1842. 1st. Edn. 2 vols. Mod. hf. cf., corners, spines decor. with raised bands. (HD. Jun.24; 137) Frs. 1,300
– Works. Ill.:– De los Rios & others. Phila., [1896-1900.] (1,000) numbered. 53 vols. Maroon three-qtr. mor., partly. unopened., spines gt., by Oldach. (SG. Oct.9; 25) $400
– Works, in English. Ed.:– George Saintsbury. L., ca. 1900. (410) numbered. 40 vols. Three-qtr. leatherette, spines gt, (SG. Dec.18; 16) $160

BALZAC, Honoré de & others
[–] L'Excommunié. Paris, 1837. 1st. Edn. 2 vols. Slight foxing. Mod. hf. cf., spines decor. with raised bands, unc., wraps. Bkplt. of Serrigny. (HD. Jun.24; 134) Frs. 1,700
– Scènes de la Vie Privée et Publique des Animaux. Ed.:– P.-J. Stahl. Ill.:– after Grandville. Paris, 1842. 2 vols. Hf. mor. gt., hinges strengthened. (SH. Nov.20; 193) *Droller.* £80

BANCROFT, Hubert Howe
– The Book of the Fair. Chic. & San Franc., 1893. Columbian Edn. In the 10 orig. pts. Fo. Pict. wraps., some torn. (SG. Dec.4; 103) $120

BANCROFT, John
[–] Henry the Second, King of England. 1693. 1st. Edn. 4to. Natural paper fault in 1 lf. affecting a few words. Mor. by Sangorski. [Wing B634] (C. Nov.19; 45) *Blackwell.* £90

BANDELLUS de Castronovo, Vincentius
– De Singulari Puritate et Praerogativa Conceptione Salvatoris Nostri Jesu Christi. Ed.:– [Antonius Faventius & M.L.]. Lubeck, [Matthaeus Brandis], ca. 1486. 4to. Spaces for initial capitals, supplied in red, 9-line capital C at fo. 4v with penwork ornamentation extending into margins, other rubrication in red, MS. quiring preserved in many places, marginal repairs to folios, 1, 51, & 90, with loss of some letters at fo. 90v, paper flaw at fo. 19 with some letters unptd., occasional soiling. 16th. C. blind-stpd. pig over wood bds., rebkd. From the collection of Eric Sexton [BMC II, 556, C 823=1479, Goff B50, H 2351=2355] (CNY. Apr.8; 84) $2,800

BANDINI, Ralph
– Veiled Horizons. [1939]. (950) numbered. 4to. Gt.-pict. cl., unopened. (SG. Dec.11; 213) $100

BANDURI, Domni Anselmi
– Imperium Orientale sive Antiquitates Constantinopolitane. Paris, 1711. 2 vols. Fo. Cont. cf., worn. (TA. Jan.22; 97) £75
– Numismata Imperatorum Romanorum . . . Paris, 1718. 2 vols. Fo. Some ll. very slightly spotted or soiled. Cont. vell. bds., ornamental centrepiece on covers, jnts. reprd. (S. Jul.27; 219) £170

BANKES, Thomas
– A Modern, Authentic & Complete System of Universal Geography. L., ca. 1801. Fo. 1 world map & added plt. at p. 476 not called for in plt. list. Early reversed cf. (KH. Mar.24; 20) Aus. $350
– A New, Royal, Authentic & Complete System of Universal Geography. [L.], [1790]. 2 vols. Fo. 109 (of 110?) engraved plts. Mor. gt. (P. Dec.11; 4) *Burgess.* £410
– – Anr. Copy. 2 vols. in 1. 109 (of 110) plts. & maps, frontis. detchd. & frayed, some early plts. & maps with minor defects, mainly in folds. Cont. cf., disbnd. As an atlas, w.a.f. (SBA. May 27; 273) *Bailey.* £325
– – Anr. Copy. Cont. cf., worn. W.a.f. (C. Nov.6; 240) *Solder.* £280
– – Anr. Copy. 2 vols. 109 (of 112?) engraved maps, some badly folded & torn, foxing. Old mor. worn. W.a.f. (VA. Aug.29; 11) R. 180
– – Anr. Edn. N.d. 4to. 2 maps badly torn, some ll. soiled. Cont. cf., worn, covers loose. W.a.f. (SD. Feb.4; 241) £260
– – Anr. Copy. Fo. 72 plts. only, some loose, torn, browned, foxed. Hf. cf., worn. (SPB. May 29; 15) $300

BANKS, John
– Cyrus the Great. 1696. 1st. Edn. 4to. Sm. natural paper fault in 1 lf. affecting 1 word. Mor.-bkd. bds. [Wing B656] (C. Nov.19; 46) *Blackwell.* £90
[–] The Innocent Usurper. 1694. 1st. Edn. 4to. Lacks A4 (blank?), natural paper faults in 2 ll. slightly affecting text, sigs. & catchwords occasionally shaved, some foxing & staining. Hf. cf. [Wing B658] (C. Nov.19; 47) *Blackwell.* £90
– The Island Queens. 1684. 1st. Edn. 4to. Natural paper fault affecting 1 word. Mor.-bkd. bds. [Wing 659] (C. Nov.19; 48) *Quaritch.* £200
– Vertue Betray'd. 1682. 1st. Edn. 4to. Some minor stains. Mor.-bkd. bds. [Wing B667] (C. Nov.19; 49) *Blackwell.* £90

BANKS, Sir Joseph
– An Epistle from Oberea. Ill.:– Ray Crooke. Fern Tree Gulley, 1955. (250) sigd. by artist. Decor. cl. (KH. Mar.24; 21) Aus. $140

BANKS, Sir Joseph & Solander, Dr. Daniel
– Illustrations of Australian Plants collected during Captain Cook's Voyage round the World . . . L., 1900-05. 3 pts. Fo. Some marginal defects, occasional dust-staining. Orig. bds. & qtr. cl. (KH. Mar.24; 22) Aus. $2,300

BANKS, Sir Thomas Christopher
– An Analytical Statement of the Case of Alexander, Earl of Stirling & Dovan. L., 1832. Orig. bds. Bkplt. of John Roche Dasent. (CB. Feb.18; 6) Can. $500

BANNERMAN, David Armitage
– Birds of the Atlantic Islands. 1963-68. 4 vols. Orig. cl., d.-w.'s (P. Nov.13; 181) *Graham.* £150
– The Birds of the British Isles Edinb., 1953-63. [1st. Edns.?]. 12 vols. Cl. (S. Jun.1; 67) *Rickwood.* £300
– – Anr. Copy. 4to. Orig. cl., all but vol.5 in d-w.'s. (TA. Feb.19; 541) £260
– – Anr. Copy. Orig. buckram, d.-w.'s, a few reprd. with sellotape. (S. Jun.23; 292) *Baynon.* £240
– Birds of Cyprus. 1958. Cl., d.-w.'s. (P. Nov.13; 182) *Traylen.* £75
– The Birds of Tropical West Africa. 1930-31. Vols. 1 & 2 only (of 8). 2 wormholes running through a few final ll. of vol. 1. Orig. cl., slightly stained (SBA. Jul.14; 216) *Wheldon & Wesley.* £140
– – Anr. Edn. L., 1930-49. 7 vols. (of 8). 4to. Orig. cl. (P. Jun.11; 308) *Graham.* £120
– – Anr. Edn. 1930-51. 8 vols. A quire & 1 plt. loose in vol. I. Orig. cl., partly unc. (LC. Jun.18; 94) £250
– – Anr. Copy. Orig. cl. (CB. Sep.24; 12) Can. $700
– The Birds of West & Equatorial Africa. 1953. 2 vols. Cl., d.-w.'s. (P. Nov.13; 180) *Hill.* £50

BANNERMAN, David Armitage–HALL & Moreau–ROSEVEAR, D.S.
– The Birds of West & Equatorial Africa.–An Atlas of Speciation in African Passerine Birds. –The Bats of West Africa. Edinb. & L.; L.; L., [1953]; 1970; 1965. 3 works in 4 vols., 1st. work 2 vols. 8vo.; fo.; 4to. All in orig. cl. (CB. Sep.24; 13) Can. $190

BANNERMAN, Helen
– Sambo & the Twins. N.Y., 1936. 1st. Edn. 16mo. Orig. cl., d.w. Pres. copy to her brother Charles Bannerman, further note loosely inserted. (SH. Dec.10; 99) *Reisler.* £135

BANNET, Ivor
– The Amazons. Ill.:– Clifford Webb, maps by Mina Greenhill. 1948. (80) numbered, sigd. by artist & author, specially bnd. Fo. Orig. mor., d.-w., by Sangorski & Sutcliffe. (CSK. Apr.3; 57) £110

– – **Anr. Edn.** Ill.:– Clifford Webb. Gold. Cock. Pr. 1948. (80) specially bnd., sigd. by author & artist. 4to. Orig. mor. gt., s.-c. (SH. Feb.19; 185)
Matthews. £90

BANNINGH, Janus Bodecheer
– **Epigrammatic Americana.** Leiden, 1639. Fo. Wraps., preserved in fold-over case. (SPB. May 5; 84) $500

BANNISTER, S.
– **Humane Policy, or Justice to the Aborigines of New Settlements essential to a Due Expenditure of British Money** . . . L., 1830. Orig. bds., front hinge brkn. Pres. copy. (SSA. Jan.22; 153)   R. 350

BANVILLE, Théodore de
– **Odes Funambulesques.** Ill.:– Bracquemond. Alençon, 1857. Orig. Edn. Cont. hf. Bordeaux chag., decor. spine, lr. wrap. L. to Millet, MS. note. (HD. Jun.10; 119)   Frs. 1,100
– **Les Princesses.** Ill.:– Rochegrosse. Paris, 1904. (400); (130) on Jap., numbered. 4to. Figures in 2 states. Mor. by Bernasconi, decor. spine, border of 3 fillets on covers, wrap. preserved. (SM. Feb.11; 179)   Frs. 5,000

BAPTISTA MANTUANUS
– **Parthenice Secunda.** Venice, Jacobus Pentius de Leuco, 14 July, 1499. Mod. cf. [Goff B71] (C. Jul.16; 240)   *James.* £50

BAR, Jacques-Charles
– **Recueil de Tous Les Costumes des Ordres Religieux et Militaires.** Ill.:– Bar. Paris, Priv. ptd. 1778-85. 5 vols. only (of 6). Fo. Vols. I-IV in cont. cf., sides with roll tool gt. borders & gt. floral festoons, spines gt., vol. V in cont. cf.-bkd. bds., unc., worn. W.a.f. (C. Feb.25; 215)
Traylen. £850
– – **Anr. Copy.** Vols. I-IV (of 6). 24 Lacks vol. 1 engraved cold. title & end lf. vol. IV, vols. 1 & IV lack 1 copper engraving, some text ll. slightly defect., some copper engrs. torn, slightly soiled in parts. Cont. hf. leath., worn. Not collated. (H. Dec.9/10; 736)   DM 2,400

BARANTE
– **Historie des Ducs de Bourgogne** . . . Ill.:– Boulanger, Delacroix, Déveria, Grandville, T. Johannot & others. Paris, 1839. 103 vigs. on China. Cont. hf. chagrin, smooth decor. spines. (HD. Feb.27; 75)   Frs. 2,300

BARASORDA, Panfilo
– **Pedimentos Presentados a la Exma. Primera Sala del Supremo Tribunal de la Guerra y Marina en la Causa formada al E. Sr. gral. Don Mariano Arista, por la Perdida de las Batalles de Palo-Alto y la Resaca de Guerrero.** Mexico, 1849. Ptd. wraps., light marginal chipping & stains, corner torn from blank corner of upr. wrap. (SG. Jan.8; 279) $120

BARATTIERI, Giovanni Battista
– **Architettura d'Acque.** Piacenza, 1656. 1st. Edn. Fo. 10 unnumbered pp., 1 unnumbered p. Cont. vell. (CR. Mar.19; 244)   Lire 380,000

BARBA, Alvaro Alonso
– **Arte de los Metales** . . . nuevamente ahora anadido con el Tratado de las antiguas Minas de Espana.** Lima, 1817. 1st. Amer. Edn. 4to. A few ll. stained. Cont. vell. From Honeyman Collection. (S. May 20; 3178)   *Hughes.* £190
– – **Anr. Edn.** Lima, 1817. 1st. Peruvian Edn. 4to. Ex liby. Cont. vell., soiled & buckled. [Sabin 3253] (SG. May 14; 13) $375
– – **Anr. Copy.** Stains, final lf. with sm. repair & wormholes affecting letters, minor repair to title. Later vell. bds., lr. cover defect. (SPB. May 5; 85) $300
– **A Collection of Scarce & Valuable Treatises upon Metals, Mines & Minerals.** 1740. 2nd. Edn. 12mo. New qtr. mor. (S. Dec.1; 41) *Detroit.* £60
– **Metallurgie ou l'Art de tirer et de Purifier les Metaux** . . . avec les Dissertations les plus rares sur les Mines.** Paris, 1751. 2 vols. Orig. marb. bds., unc. From Honeyman collection. (S. May 20; 3177)   *Rogers Turner.* £140
– **Verhandeling over de Metalen, Mynen en Mineralen.** Leiden, 1740. Later hf.-vell. (VG. Nov.18; 1003)   Fls. 500

BARBA, Alvaro Alonso–[VALLEMONT,P.L. de]
– **Berg-Büchlein.–Der Heimliche und Unerforschliche Natur-Kündiger.** [bnd. 1st.]. Hamburg; Nuremb., 1776; 1694. 1st. German Edn. (1st. title). 2 works in 1 vol., 2nd. title bnd. at front. Slightly browned, some underlining, 1st.

lacks pp. 345-8, wormhole in 2nd. Cont. leath. Oct.14-18; 225)   DM 2,200

BARBADICUS, Nicolaus
See–INGRESSO del Procurator di San Marco Alessandro Albrizzi

BARBADOS
– **Acts of Assembly, Passed in the Island of Barbados, from 1648 to 1718.–Part II. Acts of Assembly** . . . **1717-18 to 1738.** L., 1732; 1739. 2 pts. in 1 vol. Fo. 47 ll. of MS. extension at end containing acts passed from 1739 to 1751, lacks title to Pt. II, indices, & lf. preceding title, worming, browning G2 in 1st. pt. loose, ptd. indices have been removed & MS. index substituted, of which only 2pp. (A-E) are present. Old cf., rebkd. Jonathan Blenman, Attorney General of Barbados' copy. [Sabin 3260] (SPB. May 5; 86) $300

BARBARO, Ermolao
See–DIOSCORIDES, Anazarbei Pedacius
–BARBARO, Ermolao

BARBAULD, Anna Letitia
See–EDGEWORTH, Maria & Barbauld, Anna Letitia

BARBAULT, Jean
– **Les Plus Beaux Monuments de Rome Ancienne.** Rome, 1761. Fo. Lacks title-p., minor soiling & dampstaining. 19th. C. leath. (SG. Dec.4; 29) $250

BARBEDOR, L.
– **Traité de l'Art d'Escrire** . . . Paris, priv. ptd. 1655. Ob. fo. Cont. vell. (HD. Jun.24; 7)   Frs. 1,100

BARBER, James
[–] **Tom K-g's: or, the Paphian Grove.** [1738]. 1st. Edn. Cont. red str.-grd. mor. gt. (S. Nov.24; 14)   *Quaritch.* £85

BARBER, Joel
– **Wild Fowl Decoys.** N.Y., Derry. Pr. [1934]. (55) on L.P. 4to. Red mor. gt., partly unc. & unopened, s.-c. Sigd. on fly-lf. (CNY. Oct.1; 163) $4,000

BARBER, John W. & Howe, Henry
– **Historical Collections of New Jersey, Past & Present.** New Haven, 1868. Updtd. Edn. New cl. (SG. Mar.5; 333) $100

BARBER, Mrs. Mary
[–] **Poems on Several Occasions.** 1736. 1st. Edn. 4to. Cont. cf., gt. spine. From the collection of Eric Sexton. (C. Apr.15; 83)   *Hannas.* £70

BARBER, Thomas
– **Picturesque Illustrations of the Isle of Wight.** Ill.:– Barber & W.H. Bartlett. L., ca. 1835. Orig. cl. (SG. Nov.20; 292) $120

BARBEY d'Aurevilly, Jules
– **Le Bonheur dans le Crime.** Ill.:– A. Rassenfosse. Paris, 1920. (125), numbered. Lge. 8vo. Hf. mor. by Brisson, spine with mosaic motif in multi-cold. mor., wrap. preserved. (SM. Feb.11; 180)
Frs. 2,800
– **Le Chevalier des Touches.** Paris, 1864. Orig. Edn. 12mo. Cf., decor. Border, blind & gt. plaque, inner dentelle, wrap., by de Samblanx, some defects. (HD. Jun.10; 120)   Frs. 2,100
– – **Anr. Copy.** Three-quarter mor., wrap., lacks spine, by Farez. (HD. Oct.10; 15)   Frs. 1,500
– **Les Diaboliques.** Ill.:– Lobel-Riche. Paris, 1910. (250) on vell., numbered. 4to. Some sm. stains, final state of all plts., with the 3 plts. not offered for sale. Red mor. by Lanoë, sm. figure of devil in centre of covers, wrap. preserved. (SM. Feb.11; 182)   Frs. 5,500
– **Mémorandum.** Caen, 1856. 1st. Edn., (36). Square 16mo. Sewed. Sigd. autograph dedication to Baronne de Maistre, author's marginal annot. to p. 83. (HD. Feb.27; 78)   Frs. 8,500
– **Oeuvres Complètes.** 1926-28. 1st. Coll. Edn.; 1st. Edn. of 'Lettres a Trébutien'; on laid paper. 17 vols. in 14. Hf. roan, corners, spines with raised bands. (HD. Feb.27; 79)   Frs. 2,300
– **Poésies.** Caen, 1854. 1st. Edn., (36). 12mo. Sewed. Sigd. autograph dedication from author to Baronne de Maistre, author's autograph corrections to pp. 39 & 45. (HD. Feb.27; 77)   Frs. 4,500

BARBIANI, Marcello Vestrio–DONDE, Antoine
– **Pontificale Romanum Clementis VIII.–Les Figures et l'Abbregé de la Vie, de la Mort, et des Miracles de St. François de Paule.** Rome; Paris, 1611; 1671. 2 works in 2 vols. Fo. 1st. work; title soiled & restored, last lf. backed & soiled; 2nd. work: lacks final blank, some ll. browned. Both 19th. C. str.-grd. mor., 1st. work with some wear. (S. Feb.10; 279)   *Thomas.* £90

BARBIER, Antoine Alexandre
– **Dictionnaire des Ouvrages Anonymes et Pseudonymes.** Paris, 1806-09. 1st. Edn. 4 vols. Cont. cf., spines worn. (SH. Jul.9; 161)
Talerman. £55
– – **Anr. Edn.** Paris, 1822-27. 2nd. Edn. 4 vols. Cont. hf. cf. (SG. Jan.22; 47) $130

BARBIER, George
– **Le Bonheur du Jour** . . . Paris, [1920]. (300) on thick vell. Ob. fo. In sheets, ill. wrap. (HD. Jun.24; 143)   Frs. 7,800
– – **Anr. Edn.** Paris, [Plts. dtd. 1920-24]. Ob. fo. Cover ill. by H. Reidel after Barbier, hand-cold., very sm. tear in corner of upr. wrap., unsewn in orig. wraps., unc. (SH. Nov.20, 210)   *Rios.* £610
– **Dessins sur les Danses de Vaslav Nijinsky.** Paris, [1913]. 1st. Edn., (340). Lge. 4to. 1 vig. sigd. Orig. bds., spine torn. MS. ded. (D. Dec.11-13; 1157)   DM 1,800

BARBIERI, Giovanni Francesco, called Il Guercino
– **Eighty-two Prints.** Ill.:– Bartolozzi. 2 vols. in 1. Fo. 155 plts. Hf. mor. (P. Jul.2; 218)
L'Aquaforte. £900
– **Raccolta di Alcuni Disegni.** Ill.:– Bartolozzi, Nevray, Ottaviani & Piranesi, after Barbieri. Rome, 1764. Fo. 26 (? of 33) plts., additional double-p. plt. loosely inserted at end, stain in upper margin of some ll., touching several plts. 19th. C. bds., slightly worn. W.a.f. (S. Oct.21; 329)   *Broseghini.* £710

BARBOZA DU BOCAGE, J.V.
– **Ornithologie D'Angola.** Lisbon, 1881. Hf. cf., orig. wraps. bound in. (P. Nov.13; 183)
Quaritch. £200

BARBUSSE, Henri
– **L'Enfer.** Ill.:– Edouard Chimot. Paris, 1921. (355) numbered on Arches vell. 4to. 1 state of etchings. Red mor. by Bruel, author's name in mosaic mor. on spine, & title on both covers, silk doubls., wrap. preserved, s.-c. (SM. Feb.11; 183)   Frs. 3,100
– **Le Feu (Journal d'une Escouade).** Ill.:– Eugène Dété after Renefer. Paris, 1918. (70) numbered on Rives. 4to. Bordeaux mor. by Blanchetière. (SM. Feb.11; 184)   Frs. 2,800
– **Quelques Coins du Coeur.** Ill.:– Frans Masereel. Geneva, 1921. (26) with extra set of ills. on chine. Orig. wraps., slightly soiled. (SH. Nov.21; 408)   *Schwing.* £70

BARBUT, Jacques
– **The Genera Insectorum of Linnaeus Exemplified.** 1780-81. 4to. 2 folding plts. trimmed. Cont. russia, covers detchd. (S. Dec.3; 885)   *Quaritch.* £170
– – **Anr. Edn.** 1781. 4to. 2 folding plts., 20 hand-cold. engd. plts. Cont. red mor., sides with gt. tooled borders, spine gt. (C. Jul.15; 167)
Henderson. £380
– – **Anr. Copy.** Text in Engl. & Fr. Bds. (P. Apr.30; 202)   *Dillon.* £200
– **The Genera Insectorum of Linnaeus.–The Genera Vermium.** 1781; 1783. 2 works in 1 vol. (the 2nd. work is Pt. 1 only, of 2). 4to. Plts. in both works hand-cold. (excepting the 2 folding plts. in the 1st. work), Ms. index at end of 1st. work. Cont. diced russ. gt. From the collection of Eric Sexton. (C. Apr.15; 3)   *Traylen.* £300
– **Genera Vermium Exemplified by Various Specimens of the Animals.** 1783. 4to. Mott. cf. gt. (P. Dec.11; 2)   *Stern.* £130
– **The Genera Vermium [The Genera Vermium of Linnaeus Part 2d].** Priv. Ptd. 1783-88. 1st. Edns. 2 pts. in 1 vol. 4to. Frontis. & plts. hand-cold. in 1. 19th. C. hf. mor., covers detchd. From Chetham's Liby., Manchester. (C. Nov.26; 25)
Taylor. £120
– **Les Genres des Insectes de Linne.** 1781. 1st. Edn. 4to. Frontis. & 19 only (of 20) hand-cold. plts. Cont. cf., worn, rebkd. From Chetham's Liby., Manchester. (C. Nov.26; 24)   *Wagner.* £100

BARCHUSEN, Johann Conrad
- Pyrosophia Succincte atque breviter iatrochemiam pervestigans, Prem Metallicam et Chrysopopoeiam. Leiden, 1698. 4to. Old vell. (S. Dec.2; 445) *Rota.* £280

BARCIA, Andreas Gonzales
See–GARCILASSO de la Vega

BARCLAY, Rev. James
- A Complete & Universal Dictionary. N.d. New Edn. MS. note on engraved title. Cont. hf. cf., rebkd. (SBA. Jul.22; 197) *Hulme.* £500
- – Anr. Copy. Cf. (P. Jul.30; 216) *Martin.* £340
- Universal English Dictionary. Ed.:– Henry W. Dewhurst. Ca. 1840. 4to. Occasional staining. Cf., worn. W.a.f. (CSK. Apr.10; 47) £160

BARCLAY, John
- An Inquiry into the opinions . . . concerning Life & Organization. Edinb., 1822. Cf. (P. Dec.11; 259) *Rickerstone.* £60

BARCLAY, Robert
- An Apology for the True Christian Divinity. Bg'ham., 1765. 8th Edn. in Engl. 4to. Inscr. on fly-lf. Cont. cf., rebkd., 1 cover detchd. (SG. Feb.5; 27) $150

BARCLAY-SMITH, Phyllis
See–POLLARD, Hugh B.C. & Barclay-Smith, Phyllis

BARD, Samuel
- A Compendium of the Theory & Practice of Midwifery . . . N.Y., 1808. 1st. Edn. 12mo. Foxed. Orig. mott. cf., rebkd., 1 cover detchd. 26-line MS. poem by Sally Bard tipped-in. (SG. Sep.18; 30) $200

BARGONE, Frédéric Charles Pierre Edouard 'Claude Farrère'
- La Bataille. Ill.:– Charles Fouqueray. Paris, 1925. (350) numbered on Arches vell. 4to. Red mor. by Marot Roddé, gold mosaic title on spine, 4 Chinese motifs on upr. cover, mor. doubls., wrap. preserved Mntd. A.L.s. by author. (SM. Feb.11; 213) *Frs.* 7,500
- Boui Bouis. Ill.:– Boris Grigorieff. Petropolis, 1924. 1st. Edn. ptd. on heavy L.P. Fo. Contains orig. pencil drawing sigd. by Ill., mntd. at upr. fly. Gt.-pict. wraps. Pres. Copy. (PNY. Oct.1; 252) $225
- Les Civilisés. Ill.:– Henri Le Riche. Paris, 1926. (200) numbered on Arches vell. 4to. 2 states of ills. (black-&-white & cold.) & 3 states of plts. Decor. mor. by Kieffer. (SM. Feb.11; 214) *Frs.* 2,800
- Fumée d'Opium. 1904. Jansenist mor., wrap., lacks spine, by Marius Michel. N. (HD. Oct.10; 47) *Frs.* 1,400
- – Anr. Edn. Ill.:– Georges Jauneau. Paris, 1921. (250) numbered on Arches vell. Lge. 8vo. Orig. gouache by H. Lehaye, name of collector gummed on hf. title. Mor. by L. Loir, mosaic on upr. cover, wrap. preserved. Sigd. by binder. (SM. Feb.11; 156) *Frs.* 10,500
- Thomas l'Angelet. Ill.:– Guy Arnoux & Raoul Serres. Paris, priv. ptd., 1927. (175) on Arches vell. Lge. 4to. 21 additional essay plts., 1 orig. lge. cold. drawing. Red mor., title gt., inside fillets gt. & blind-tooled, unc., wrap. & spine. Sigd. by artist & dedicated to Simone Berriau. (HD. Dec.5; 77) *Frs.* 1,000

BARHAM, Henry
- An Essay upon the Silk-Worm. 1719. 1st. Edn. Stp. on title. Cont. panel. cf., covers detchd. (S. Mar.17; 317) *Lawson.* £55

BARHAM, Rev. Richard H. 'Thomas Ingoldsby'
- The Ingoldsby Legends. Ill.:– G. Cruikshank & J. Leech. 1840-42-47. 1st. Edn., 1st. Iss. 3 vols. (1st.-3rd. Series). Orig. pen & ink design for title inserted in vol. I, without the correction slip opposite blank p. 236 in vol. I, 4 pp. of advts. at end of vol. II. Lev. mor. gt. by Rivière, orig. cl. covers & spine bnd. at end of each vol. From the collection of Eric Sexton. (C. Apr.15; 84) *Edmonds.* £240
- – Anr. Edn. Ill.:– Arthur Rackham. L., 1907. 4to. Foxed. Orig.-pict. cl., d.-w. reprd. Raymond M. Sutton Jr. copy. (SG. May 7; 17) $120
- – Anr. Copy. 1 p. cut away, slight soiling. Orig. vell. gt., slight warping, soiled. (SPB. May 29; 357) $100
- [–] – Anr. Edn. Ill.:– Arthur Rackham. L., 1907. (50) for America, sigd. by artist. Lge. 4to. Gt.-pict. vell., lacks ties, partly unc. & unopened.

Raymond M. Sutton Jr. copy. (SG. May 7; 16) $800
- [–] – Anr. Edn. Ill.:– Arthur Rackham. 1907. (560) numbered, sigd. by artist. Lge. 4to. This copy unnumbered? Orig. vell. gt., lacks ties. (SH. Dec.11; 417) *Black.* £230
- – Anr. Copy. Orig. vell. gt., slightly spotted, plts. loosely inserted. (S. Jul.31; 278) *Beetles.* £220
- [–] – Anr. Copy. Gt.-pict. vell., lacks ties. Raymond M. Sutton Jr. copy (SG May 7; 15) $475
- – Anr. Copy. Defect. plt. following p. 254. Upr. cover & upr. hinge defect., lacks ties. (PNY. Oct.1; 93) $375
- – Anr. Edn. 1909. Hf. ribbed mor. gt., by Ramage. (CE. Feb.19; 273) £50
- – Anr. Edn. 1929. 4to. Cont. mor., gt. (SH. Jun.25; 62) *Fairburn.* £55
- The Jackdaw of Rheims. Ill.:– Charles Folkard. L., 1913. (100) numbered, & sigd. by artist. Fo. Gt.-pict. vell., slightly soiled, partly unc. (SG. Apr.2; 113) $210

BARING, Daniel Eberhard
- Clavis Diplomatica. Hanover, 1737. 1st. Edn. 4to. Browned. Cont. hf. vell. (SH. Jun.18; 26) *Thorp.* £55

BARING-GOULD, Sabine & Fisher, J.
- Lives of the British Saints. 1907-13. 4 vols. Cl. gt. (PJ. Dec.5; 114) £58

BARKER, Benjamin
- Landscape Scenery Principally Views in & Near Bath. Ill.:– Theodore Fielding. Bath, 1824. Ob. 4to. 44 cold. aquatints cut round & mntd. on paper framed with ink rule, numbered title slips pasted below, MS. index tipped in. Hf. cf., rebkd. (C. Mar.18; 15) *Taylor.* £520
- – Anr. Copy. 48 cold. aquatints. (C. Jul.15; 6) *Quaritch.* £450
- – Anr. Copy. 2 vols. Aquatint views cut round & mntd. with ruled borders on brown paper, ptd. captions pasted beneath, titles laid down. Cont. mor., lettered in gt. W.a.f. From the collection of Eric Sexton. (C. Apr.16; 212) *Taylor.* £360
- – Anr. Copy. 2 vols. 40 cold. aquatints, cut round & mntd. with ruled borders, ptd. captions pasted beneath, titles laid down. Cont. mor. W.a.f. (C. Jul.15; 7) *Henderson.* £320

BARKER, George
- Elegy on Spain. Manchester, 1939. 1st. Edn. Orig. cl., d.-w. Inscr. to Richard de la Mare. (SH. Dec.18; 56) *Blackwell.* £55
- [–] – Anr. Copy. Inscr. to Walter de la Mare. (SH. Dec.18; 55) *Rota.* £50

BARKER, George T.
- Instructions in the Preparation, Administration, & Properties of Nitrous Oxide. Phila., 1866. 1st. Edn. Price-list of Rubencame & Stockton at end, wood-engrs. stpd. on versos. Cl. From Brooklyn Academy of Medicine. (SG. Jan.29; 121) $125

BARKER, Matthew Henry
- Greenwich Hospital. Ill.:– George Cruikshank. 1826. [1st. Edn.?]. 4to. Plts. in 2 states (cold. & uncold.). Later hf. mor., gt. (C. Nov.6; 284) *Fairburn.* £150
- – Anr. Copy. 19th. C. hf. mor. gt. Bkplt. of Thomas Gaisford. (S. Nov.24; 65) *Way.* £90
- [–] – Anr. Copy. Three-qtr. mor. (SG. Oct.30; 114) $350

BARKER, Thomas
- Forty Lithographic Impressions. Bath, Dec.1813. 'No more than two hundred'. 4to. Some plts. ptd. on tinted paper, all mntd. Orig. bds., cl. spine brkn., unc. From the collection of Eric Sexton. (C. Apr.15; 59) *Traylen.* £420

BARKHATOV, M.E. & Funke, V.V.
- Istoriya Russko-Yaponskoi Voiny [History of the Russo-Japanese war]. St. Petersb., n.d. 6 vols. 4to. Cont. hf. mor., gt. spines. (SH. Feb.5; 196) *Flegon.* £170

BARLACH, Ernst
- Der Findling. Berlin, 1922. (80) Privilege Edn. on Zandersbütten. 4to. 2nd. series of woodcuts on Jap., woodcuts under passepartouts. Hand-bnd. orig. vell., box. Printer's mark & all ll. of separ. series sigd. by artist. (H. May 21/22; 1495) DM 10,000

BARLAEUS, Caspar
- Brazilianische Geschichte. Cleve, 1659. Old vell. (BS. Jun.11; 137) £400

- Rerum per Octennium in Brasilia . . . Amst., 1647. 1st. Edn. Fo. 16 double-p. engraved maps, lacks 8 maps, 31 plts., port. & lf. preceding A1, title & following lf. torn, some worming & repairs. 17th. C. cf. [Sabin 3408] (S. Mar.31; 443) *Fletcher.* £220
- – Anr. Copy. Atlas fo. 25 maps & 31 plts., all double-p., engraved & hand-cold., 3 plts. very spotted & browned, all detchd., lacks port., text incompl. Orig. Dutch vell., gt. panel. sides, brkn. (CNY. May 22; 28) $8,000
- Triumphus super captâ Olinda, Pernambuci Vrbe, Brasiliae Metro poli, fasti ducibus, Viris fortissumus, Lonckio, Waardenburgio, armis opibusque Societaris Indiae Occidentalis. Leiden, 1630. 1st. Edn. Fo. Wraps., preserved in fold-over case. (SPB. May 5; 88) $800

BARLANDUS, Adrian
- Chroniques des Ducs de Brabant. Ill.:– J. Colaert. 1603. Sm. fo. Lacks parts of pp. 76 & 109. Mod. hf. roan. (HD. Feb.27; 8) *Frs.* 1,500
- Ducum Brabantiae Chronica. Antw., 1600. Sm. fo. 1 engr. slightly defect. Old bds., new cf. spine. (BS. Jun.11; 100) £65

BARLANDUS, Adrian–MARTIN, Corneille
- Chroniques des Ducs de Brabant.–Généalogies des Forestiers et Contes de Flandres . . . Ill.:– J. Colaert. Antw., 1612. 2 works in 1 vol. Fo. Some browning. Cont. red mor., 2 fillets, cypher of Peiresc in centre, decor. spine, hinges & corners reprd. (HD. Mar.18; 17) *Frs.* 5,500

BARLOW, Thomas
- The Gunpowder-Treason. 1679. Some ll. spotted. Cont. cf., worn. [Wing B833] (SH. Mar.5; 176) *Jarndyce.* £55

BARMANN, G.N.
- Hamburg und Hamburgs Umgegend. Hamburg, 1822. Orig. bds. (R. Mar.31-Apr.4; 2099) DM 480

BARNABAS, Saint & Clement, Saint
- Zwey Send-Schreiben aus der Ersten Apostolischen Kirchen . . . Trans.:– M. Gottfried Arnold von Annaberg. 1695. 1st Edn. in German. 2 pts. in 1 vol. 24mo. Old vell., lev. solander s.-c. Sig. & bkplt. of H.A. Muglenberg. (SG. Sep.25; 23) $500

BARNARD, A.
- Noted Breweries of Great Britain & Ireland. N.d. 3 vols. Orig. cl., reprd. (P. Jul.30; 217) *Weston.* £60

BARNARD, George, Artist
- Trees from Nature. 1868. Fo. Orig. hf. mor. Pres. copy to Archbishop Temple. (SH. Mar.26; 47) *Marks.* £55

BARNARD, George N.
- Photographic Views of Sherman's Campaign. [N.Y.], [1866]. Ob. fo. (15½ × 20½ inches). Lacks title-p. & descriptive text, foxed thro.-out. Leath., title in gt., rebkd. (SG. Apr.23; 26) $4,000

BARNAUD, Nicolas 'Eusebius Philadelphus'
[–] Le Cabinet du Roi de France, dans lequel il y a trois Perles précieuses d'inestimable Valeur. 1581. 1st. Edn. Sig. of A.A. Renouard, 1786, on title, & accession number 1039 on fly-lf. & name stpd. in gt. on red mor. label on inner upr. cover. 18th. C. mor., by Derome le Jeune, narrow gt. borders with sm. fleurs-de-lis in a row, circles in squares divided by vertical lines, lozenges & ovals joined by dots, flat spine gt. in compartments, inner gt. dentelles, pink silk liners. (SM. Oct.7; 1558) *Frs.* 3,200
[–] Dialogi ab Eusebio Philadelpho Cosmopolita in Gallorum . . . Gratiam Compositi. Edinb. [?Strassb.], 1574. Cont. Oxford cf., blindstpd. arabesque on covers, later ties. [STC 10577] (S. Mar.16; 125) *Rota.* £70

BARNERUS, Jacob
- Chymia philosophica perfecte delineata. Nuremb., 1689. 1st. Edn. Vell. (S. Dec.1; 42) *Rota.* £110

BARNES, Djuna
- Night Wood. L., [1936]. 1st. Edn. Cl., d.-w. Pres. copy from Barnes as the 'Memoires of Dog Boy' (followed by pencil sketch of dog's head). (PNY. Mar.4; 103) $220
- – Anr. Copy. Cl., worn. Inscr. (SG. Nov.13; 9) $160

BARNES, Lieut.-Commander J.S.
- **Submarine Warfare Offensive & Defensive** ...
N.Y., 1869. 1st. Edn. Cold. litho. front., 19 plts.,
ex-liby. Cl. (SG. Oct.30; 39) $110

BARNES, Joseph K., Surgeon Gen.
- **Medical & Surgical History of the War of the
Rebellion.** Wash., 1870-88. 6 vols. 4to. Cl. (SG.
Sep.18; 31) $650
-- **Anr. Edn.** Ill.:– Bell, Ward, French & others,
& American Photo-Relief Printing Co. Wash.,
1870; 1877; 1883. Vol. II, pts. I, II, & III,
together 3 vols. 4to. Cl., disbnd., ex-liby. (SG.
Apr.23; 128) $275

BARNETT, P. Neville
- **Pictorial Bookplates.** Sydney, 1931. (100) sigd.
Tears to 2 blank lr. margins. Cl. gt. (KH.
Mar.24; 23) Aus. $480
-- **Anr. Edn.** Ed.:– Lionel Lindsey (foreword). Syd-
ney, 1934, De Luxe Iss., (70) numbered & sigd.
Papered bds. & qtr. imitation vell. (KH.
Mar.24; 24) Aus. $600

BARNEY, Nathalie Clifford
- **Quelques Portraits-Sonnets de Femmes.
-Eparpillements.-Pensées d'une Amazone.** Ill.:–
1st. work: Carolus Duran (port.-frontis.); Alice
Barrey. Paris, 1900; 1910; 1921. 1st. 2 works: 1st.
Edns. 3 works in 3 vols. 12mo. Hf. mor., smooth
spines, wraps. Sigd. dedications & letter to Pierre
Louys, Franck Arris & Vincent O'Sullivan. (HD.
Jun.24; 144) Frs. 2,500

BARNUM, Phineas T.
- **Struggles & Triumphs.** Buffalo, 1882. Hf. cf.
Pres. copy to James A. Bailey. (SPB. Jun.22; 8)
$250

BAROCIUS, Franciscus
See–BAROZZI or Barocius, Franciscus

BARON, Robert
[-] **Mirza.** [1655]. 1st. Edn. Running title &
pagination occasionally shaved or cropped. 18th.
C. cf., rebkd. preserving orig. gt. spine. [Wing
B891] (C. Nov.19; 50) Blackwell. £90

BARON, Salo W.
- **A Social & Religious History of the Jews.** N.Y.,
Phila., 1952-76. 2nd. Edn. 16 vols. Cl. (S.
Nov.18; 578) Spiro. £100

BAROZZI or Barocius, Franciscus
Cosmographia in Quatour Libros Distributa.
Venice, 1585. [1st. Edn.?]. Title slightly soiled,
some margins lightly stained, title with 2 sm.
wormholes. Recent hf. cf. (S. Jul.27; 107)
Morton-Smith. £100
-- **Anr. Copy.** Cont. blind-tooled pig., 2 centre
ports. (HK. Nov.18-21; 113) DM 460

BAROZZI de Vignalo, Giacomo
See–VIGNALO, Giacomo Barozzi de

BARRATT, Thomas James
- **Annals of Hampstead.** 1912. (550) sigd. 3 vols.
4to. Some plts. mntd. & cold. Orig. cl. (CSK.
Feb.6; 166) £80
-- **Anr. Copy.** (SH. Jun.11; 149) Norman. £60
-- **Anr. Copy.** Orig. gt. decor. cl., slightly
dampstained. (TA. Dec.18; 75) £62

BARRE
- **Catalogue des Livres.** Paris, 1743. 2 vols. Errata
lf. & table of authors in vol. II, MS. priced thro.-
out. Cont. cf., charges from the Soubise arms, gt.,
on spine, covers detchd. (SM. Oct.7; 1310)
Frs. 2,400

BARRE, P.-FERRERAS, Jean de
- **Histoire Générale D'Allemagne.-Histoire
Générale D'Espagna.** Paris, 1748; 1742-51. 11
vols.; 10 vols. 4to. Cf. gt., minor defects, worn.
(SPB. May 6; 287) $425

BARREIRA, Isidoro de
- **Tractado das Significacoens das Plantas, Flores,
e Fructos que se Referem na Sagrada Escriptura.**
Lisbon, 1622. 1st. Edn. 2 pts. in 1 vol. Sm. 4to.
Slight dampstaining, some browning. Cont. limp

vell., soiled. From liby. of André L. Simon. (S.
May 18; 30) Hill. £320
-- **Anr. Copy.** 1 engraved title detchd. (S.
only (of 334, lacks final plt.). 19th. C. hf. mor.,
worn. From Chetham's Liby., Manchester. (C.
Nov.26; 26) Broseghini. £300

BARREME, François
- **Compte-fait ... ou Tarif Général dédié à
Monseigneur Desmaretz.** Paris, 1708. 12mo. Advt.
of contents & armorial plt., letterpr. 'Avis' &
publications list before title, 2-lf. Table de
Augmentation at end, old inscr. on flylf., sig. of
Paul Laplagne-Barris, 1853. Cont. red mor., gt.,
arms of Nicolas Desmaretz, triple gt. fillet, spine
compartments gt. in pointillé, inner gt. dentelles.
Dedication copy to Nicolas Desmaretz. (SM.
Oct.7; 1559) Frs. 1,400

BARRERE de Vieuzac
- **Le Point du Jour ...** Paris, 1789-1791. 27 vols
Cont. marb. roan, smooth decor. spines, bdgs.
defect. (HD. Feb.27; 9) Frs. 7,600

BARRES, Maurice
- **En Italie.** Ill.:– A.-H. Thomas. Paris, 1911.
(250); (180). 4to. 1 state of etchings, ills. in 2
states (black-&-white & cold.), set of those ready
for press at end. Mor. by Kieffer, wrap. preserved,
s.-c. (SM. Feb.11; 185) Frs. 1,800

BARRETT, C.G.
- **The Lepidoptera of the British Islands.** Ill.:– by
& after R. Morgan. 1893-1904. 11 vols. Cl. (HSS.
Apr.24; 225) £210

BARRETT, E.S.
- **The Heroine.** 1813. 3 vols. 12mo. Mod. qtr. cf.
Pres. Copy, name of recipient shaved by binder.
(S. May 5; 374) Quaritch. £190

BARRETT, H.J.
- **Fifteen Years Among the Zulus & the Boers ...
Circumstances ... led to the Present War ...**
Hull, 1879. Stp. erased on title & 2 sm. wormholes.
Qtr. cf. (VA. May 8; 402) R. 220

BARRETT, William
- **The History & Antiquities of the City of Bristol.**
Bristol, [1789]. 1st. Edn. 4to. Some spotting.
Cont. tree cf., upr. cover detchd. (S. Jul.16; 129)
£62
-- **Anr. Edn.** Bristol, 1789. 4to. Folding map torn
& reprd., spotting to many folding plts. Cont. tree
cf. From the collection of Eric Sexton. (C.
Apr.16; 213) Elliott. £50
-- **Anr. Copy.** Bristol, [1789]. 4to. Cont. hf. cf.
(SH. Mar.5; 10) Marlborough Rare Books. £65
· -- **Anr. Copy.** Some spotting. Cont. tree cf., upr.
cover detchd. (TA. Jun.18; 253) £56
-- **Anr. Copy.** 29 (of 30) copperplt. engrs. Orig.
bdg., brkn. (TA. Mar.19; 319) £52

BARRI, Giraldus de
- **The Itinerary of Archbishop Baldwin through
Wales.** Ed.:– Sir Richard Colt Hoare. 1806. L.P. 2
vols. 4to. Cont. cf., gt., inner gt. & blind-tooled
dentelles. Bkplt. of Edward Herbert, lately in the
collection of Eric Sexton. (C. Apr.15; 180)
Lloyd-George. £160

BARRICATE (Le) DI MILANO
Ill.:– Bonatti, Donghi e Luzzi. Milan, [1848]. Ob.
4to. 8 aquatint plts. hand-cold. Red mor. sigd. by
Torriani, orig. wraps. bnd. in. (SI. Dec.3; 51)
Lire 1,000,000

BARRIE, Sir James Matthew
[-] **The Allahakbarrie Book of Broadway Cricket
for 1899.** N.p. [Priv. Ptd.], [1899] Ltd. 1st. Edn.
12mo. Ill. with drawings & photographs. Orig.
ptd. vell. wraps., mor. solander case. Autograph
sigs. of the cricket team (including Barrie, A.
Birrell, & A.E.W. Mason) on verso of last p., but
lacks 3 sigs. for completeness; from the Prescott
Collection. (CNY. Feb.6; 8) $350
- **George Meredith.** L., [1909]. 1st. Edn. 12mo.
Orig. cl., sm. stain on upr. cover, qtr. mor. s.-c.
Pres. Copy, to Ellen Terry, lately in the Prescott
Collection. (CNY. Feb.6; 9) $120
- **Ibsen's Ghost.** Cornivus Pr., Jan.1939. 1st. Edn.,
(16) numbered. Orig. buckram-bkd. linen, s.-c. (S.
Jul.31; 149) Green. £240
-- **Anr. Copy.** (S. Jul.22; 72) Rota. £150
- **Peter Pan in Kensington Gardens.** Ill.:– Arthur
Rackham. N.Y., 1906. 4to. Orig. cl. gt. (SH.
Dec.11; 412) Faustus. £75
-- **Anr. Edn.** Ill.:– Arthur Rackham. [L.,] 1906.
[1st. Edn.?] (500) sigd. by artist. 4to. Orig. vell.
gt., lacks tie. (C. Feb.4; 203) Joseph. £200

-- **Anr. Copy.** Lge. 4to. 1st. Edn. (500)
numbered, sigd. by artist. Gt.-pict. vell., warped &
spotted, orig. silk ties replaced with ribbons.
Raymond M. Sutton Jr. copy. (SG. May 7; 19)
$1,100
-- **Anr. Copy.** Linen ties, number of sm. holes in
upr. cover, hf. mor. s.-c., partly unc. (SG.
Apr.30; 265) $850
-- **Anr. Edn.** Ill.:– Arthur Rackham. 1907. 4to.
Orig. cl. pict. gt., worn. (PL. Sep.18; 127)
Smith. £60
-- **Anr. Copy.** 4to. Mor. gt., slight wear. (P.
Sep.11; 194) Kent. £55
-- **Anr. Edn.** Ill.:– Arthur Rackham. 1910. 4to.
Cont. mor. (SH. Dec.11; 416) Mundy. £50
-- **Anr. Edn.** Ill.:– Arthur Rackham. L., 1912. De
Luxe Edn. Lge. 4to. Gt.-decor. vell., spotted,
warped, lacks ties. Raymond M. Sutton Jr. copy.
(SG. May 7; 20) $750
-- **Anr. Edn.** Ill.:– Arthur Rackham. L., ca. 1920.
Sm. 4to. Foxed. Gift bdg. of pict. stpd. limp suede.
Raymond M. Sutton Jr. copy. (SG. May 7; 21)
$425
-- **Anr. Edn.** Ill.:– Arthur Rackham. N.d. 4to. Cl.
gt. (P. Oct.23; 133) Roberts. £60
- **Peter Pan Portfolio.** Ill.:– Arthur Rackham. N.d.
Ltd. Edn. sigd. by Publisher & Engraver. Fo.
Lacks 1 cold. plt. (of 12). Hf. vell. gt. (P.
Sep.11; 181) Wellby. £190
- **Quality Street.** Ill.:– Hugh Thomson. N.d.
(1,000) numbered, sigd. by artist. 4to. Orig. vell.,
gt., slightly soiled, silk tie torn. (CSK. Feb.20; 153)
£88
- **Scotland's Lament.** L., Priv. Ptd. Dec.3, 1894
(1895). 1st. Edn., Wise Piracy, (12). Stitched as
iss., qtr. mor. gt. s.-c. Telegram from Lloyd
Osbourne to Edmund Gosse laid in (San Franc.,
Dec. 22, 1894), & with 2 A.L.s.'s (1 with initials)
to Gosse from Barrie (Jan. 24 & Sep. 19, 1925,
12mo., 3 pp.); from the Prescott Collection.
(CNY. Feb.6; 7) $800
- **When a Man's Single.-An Edinburgh Eleven.-
Peter & Wendy.** L., 1888; 1889; [1911]. 1st.
Edns. [2nd. work 1st. Iss.]. 3 works in 3 vols.
12mo. & 8vo. Orig. cl. or wraps., covers of 2nd.
work soiled, qtr. mor. gt. s.-c. All Pres. Copies,
lately in the Prescott Collection. (CNY. Feb.6; 10)
$600
- **Works.** N.Y., 1929-31. (1030) numbered. Vols.
1-14. Linen.-bkd. bds., with gt. medallion, unc. &
mostly unopened. Unsigd., the limitat. having
written over it 'This is one of the thirty copies for
Presentation'. (SG. Nov.13; 11) $120

BARRIFFE, William
- **Military Discipline.** 1656. 5th. Edn. 2 pts. in 1
vol. Sm. 4to. Some worming, running-title shaved
on 2 pp. Mott. cf. gt. by Rivière. (C. Jul.16; 344)
Maggs. £200

BARRIN, J.
See–BAYLE, P. & Barrin, J.

BARRINGTON, Daines
- **The Anglo-Saxon Version, from the Historian
Orosius ... English Translation from the
Anglo-Saxon.** 1773. J.R. Forster's notes on
Anglo-Saxon version of Orosius ptd. at end of this
vol. with footnote that he was 'now with the vessels
sent upon discoveries in the southern hemisphere'.
Orig. bds., unc., some paper missing from spine,
light stains. Pres. copy, inscr. on flyleaf 'For Mr
Professor Ihre at Upsala from Mr John Reinhold
Forster now on a Voiage to the South Sea by Mr.
Charles G. Woide'. (S. Oct.20; 21)
Quaritch. £130
- **Miscellanies.** 1781. 1st. Edn. 4to. Cf. gt., spine
defect. (P. Jul.30; 150) Georges. £120
-- **Anr. Copy.** Later hf. cf. gt. (SBA. Oct.21; 10)
Quaritch. £110

BARRINGTON, George
- **The Life of ...** [L.], ca. 1791. 8th. Edn. Cl.,
mor. backstrip. (KH. Mar.24; 28) Aus. $200
- **The Memoirs.** L., ca. 1790. Sm. paper defect to
1 lf., some slight foxing or discolouration, stp.
erased from title-p., slightly affecting imprint.
Later roan or mor. (KH. Mar.24; 27) Aus. $180
- **Voyage to New South Wales.** L., 1795. Mod. qtr.
cf. gt. (P. Jan.22; 107) Thorp. £140
-- **Anr. Edn.** Phila., 1796. 12mo. Advt. lf.,
browned thro.-out. Mod. buckram. (S. Nov.4; 621)
Rota. £80

BARRINGTON, Sir Jonah
- **Historical Memoirs of Ireland ... & The Union.**
L., 1835. New Edn. 2 vols. 4to, 34 ports. (of 35).

BARRINGTON, Sir Jonah – Historical Memoirs of Ireland . . . & The Union. -contd.
Hf. mott. cf., marb. end-papers by H. Young, L'pool., Trabolgan bkplt. (GM. Apr.30; 428)
£140

BARRON, Albert Stewart 'Sabretache'
- **More Shires & Provinces.** Ill.:– Lionel Edwards. 1928. 4to. Orig. cl., gt. (P. Mar.12; 249)
Holmes. £90
- **Shires & Provinces.** Ill.:– Lionel Edwards. 1926. Orig. bdg. (DWB. Mar.31; 170)
£98
- – **Anr. Copy.** Fo. Orig. cl. (SH. Jan.30; 370)
Way. £85
- – **Anr. Edn.** Ill:– Lionel Edwards. L., 1926. (100) numbered on L.P. 4to. Gt.-decor. vell., very soiled. Sigd. by author & artist. (SG. Dec.11; 396)
£120

BARROS ARANA, D.
- **Historia Jeneral de la Independencia de Chile.** Santiago, 1854-58. 4 vols. Qtr. cf., gt. (SPB. May 5; 91)
$325

BARROUGH, Philip
- **The Methode of Phisicke.** L., 1583. 1st. Edn. Fo. Index misbnd. at beginning, lacks title-lf. & M5, some ll. loose, fraying at some edges. Loosely bnd. in cont. vell., worn. [STC 1508] (SG. Jan.29; 33)
$2,100

BARROW, John
- **Dictionarium Polygraphicum, or the Whole Body of Arts.** 1735. 1st. Edn. 2 vols. Old cf. gt. (BS. Jun.11; 118)
£65

BARROW, Sir John
- **Travels in China.** 1804. 1st. Edn. 4to. Frontis. cropped at foot, marginal tear in C3, slightly soiled in places. Cont. hf. cf., covers worn. (S. May 5; 239)
R. Lyon. £70
- – **Anr. Edn.** 1806. 4to. Some offsetting. Cf., brkn. (BS. Jun.11; 138)
£60
- **Travels into the Interior of Southern Africa.** 1801. [1st. Edn.?] 4to. Cf. gt. rebkd. (P. Oct.23; 4)
Enfield. £110
- – **Anr. Copy.** 4to. Bds. (RBT. Jan.22; 73)
£68
- – **Anr. Edn.** 1801-04. 1st. Edn. 2 vols. 4to. 1 map reprd. in margin. Cont. cf., rebkd. (S. Nov.4; 630)
Schire. £80
- – **Anr. Edn.** L., [1801]-1806. 1st. Edn.; 2nd. Edn. 2 vols. 4to. Lacks last lf. in vol. 2, some foxing & offsetting. Hf. mor. & marb. bds. (VA. Oct.31; 87)
R. 90
- – **Anr. Edn.** L., 1806. 2nd. Edn. 2 vols. 4to. Cf. (SSA. Apr.22; 97)
R. 600
- – **Anr. Copy.** 9 folding maps & charts, some reprd. at folds, Military Plan of the Cape Peninsular torn in hf., reprd. at hinges, some pencil notes in margins, browned & stained. Cont. cf., rebkd. (SSA. Jun.18; 52)
R. 280
- **A Voyage to Cochinchina . . .** 1806. 1st. Edn. 4to. Folding engraved map cold. in outl., occasional light browning in text. Cont. cf., gt., rebkd. with orig. spine preserved. (S. Jun.29; 239)
Maggs. £420
- – **Anr. Copy.** Plan of Harbour & preceding lf. p. 135 dampstained, plt. at p. 162 torn across. Orig. bds., rebkd., unc. (C. Nov.6; 285)
Clark. £220
- – **Anr. Copy.** Browning, tears, repairs. Mod. hf. cf. (SPB. May 5; 93)
$375
- – **Anr. Copy.** Folding engraved chart, 20 cold. aquatint plts., 2 folding both torn at folds, some staining & offsetting. Old cf., rebkd. (CNY. May 22; 32)
$180
- – **Anr. Copy.** Cont. cf., rebkd.
R. 610

BARROW, John Henry
See–LANDSEER, Thomas & Barrow, John Henry

BARRY, Sir Edward
- **Observations Historical, Critical, & Medical, on the Wines of the Ancients.** L., 1775. 1st. Edn. 4to. Plt. at p. 160 used as frontis? Cont. cf., needs rebdg. (SG. Jan.29; 34)
$280

BARRY, Martin
- **Ascent to the Summit of Mont Blanc.** [1835]. Orig. bds., lacks spine. (SH. Mar.5; 11)
Astill. £135
- – **Anr. Copy.** 2 litho. plts. on India paper. Soiled. Inscr. (SH. Nov.6; 189)
Enfield. £130

BARTH, Henry
- **Travels & Discoveries in North & Central Africa.** 1857-58. 5 vols. 2 plts. loose, a few ll. slightly browned. Orig. cl. (SH. Nov.7; 277)
House. £250

- – **Anr. Copy.** 5 vols. Vol. 1 hf.-title detchd. Vol. 1 cf-bkd. bds., covers detchd., vols. 2-5 orig. cl., inner hinges broken., vol. 5 stitching brkn., ex-liby. copies. (CSK. Jul.10; 118)
£90

BARTH, K.
- **Die Kirchliche Dogmatik.** Zürich, 1947-70. 4 vols. & index in 14 vols. Orig. linen. (B. Dec.10/11; 1455)
Fls. 475

BARTHELEMY, Abbé Jean Jacques
- **Travels of Anacharsis the Younger in Greece.** 1793-94. 2nd. Edn. 8 vols. Cont. cf. (SH. May 21; 6)
Nicholas. £60
[-] **Voyage du Jeune Anarcharsis en Grèce.** Paris, 1789 [1790]. 5 vols. & atlas. 8vo. & 4to. Cont. paper bd. (atlas) & cont. hf. leath., slightly defect. & worn. (H. Dec.9/10; 1395)
DM 420

BARTHELEMY & Mery
- **Napoléon en Égypte, Waterloo et le Fils de L'Homme . . .** Ill.:– after H. Vernet & H. Bellangé. Paris, [1842.] 1st. Printing. Lge. 8vo. Mor. by Mazère, decor, covers & spine, decor., inside border, watered silk end-papers, wrap., s.-c. (HD. Jun.24; 148)
Frs. 1,200

BARTHOLINUS, Erasmus
- **Experimenta Crystalii Islandici disdiaclastici quibus mira & insolita refractio detegitur.** Amst., 1670. Sm. 4to. Slight dampstaining. 18th. C. mott. cf., covers warped, bkplt. of Gaddesden Park liby. (S. Apr.6; 209)
Phelps. £170

BARTHOLINUS, Thomas
- **Anatome.** Leiden, 1673. A few plts. with clean tears, 1 reprd., some marginal soiling. Cont. cf. W.a.f. (CSK. Nov.14; 151)
£100
- – **Anr. Copy.** Without port., engraved title dtd. 1674. Old cf., brkn. (SG. Jan.29; 36)
$130
- **Anatome ex Omnium Veterum Recentiorumque Observationibus.** Leiden. 1686. Lacks Waller port., slightly soiled in parts & lightly browned at margins, frontis. cut top & bottom, old owner's mark on title. Cont. vell., super-ex-lib. (H. May 21/22; 182)
DM 900
- **Anatome quartum renovata . . . Caspari Bartholini, . . . cum Iconibus Novis et Indicibus.** Lyons, 1677. 2 sm. tears, very slightly dampstained at beginning & end, lacks frontis. (?). Cont. mott. cf. (S. Feb.23; 9)
Nagel. £80
- **Anatomia.** Hagae-Comitis, 1666. Lf. with port. defect. Old cf., worn. (SG. Jan.29; 35)
$200
- **Opuscula Nova Anatomica de Lacteis Thoracicis et Lymphaticis Vasis.–De Pulmonum Substantia et Motu diatribe accedunt Cl. V. Marcelli Malpighi de Pulmonibus Observationes Anatomicae.** Copen., 1670; 1663. 2nd. work 2nd. Edn. 2 works in 1 vol. 2nd. work paper browned. Cont. vell. (S. Jun.15; 40)
Norman. £460
See–PECQUET, Jean–BARTHOLINUS, Thomas

BARTHOLOMAEO, P. Paulino A. S.
- **Musei Borgiani Velitris Codices Avenes Peguani Siamici Malabarici Indostani.** Rome, 1793. 4to. Cont. vell., soiled. (TA. Mar.19; 215)
£54

BARTHOLOMAEUS Anglicus
- **De Proprietatibus Rerum.** [Basle], [Berthold Ruppel], ca. 1480? Fo. Lacks 1st. blank, wide margins, capital-spaces, slight browning, some worming affecting text. Cont. blind-stpd. mor., upr. cover with border of running stags & hounds, lr. cover including scroll with name 'Maria', rather worn, metal clasps. From liby. of André. L. Simon. [BMC III, 716; HC 2499; Goff B130] (S. May 18; 32)
Riley-Smith. £2,400
- – **Anr. Edn.** Nuremb., Anton Koberger. May 30, 1483. Fo. Spaces for initial capitals, paragraph marks, capitals, underlines & initial strokes supplied in red, lacks final blank, minor marginal tears to some ll., last 2 ll. rehinged, scattered dampstains & spotting, occasional browning. Cont. blind-stpd. cf. over wood bds., central panel of upr. cover with lge. floral tools, the outer border with repeated imps. of double & single headed eagle & double fleur-de-lys tools, lr. cover with overall lozenge & triangular pattern filled with the eagle tools, lge. rosette & a thistle stp., spine with 4 raised bands, bnd. at the Benedictine Abbey at Ebersberg, with their arms at top of upr. cover, cl. s.-c. The copy of Major J.R. Abbey & Martin Breslauer, lately in the collection of Eric Sexton. [BMC II, 425, Goff B137, H 2505*] (CNY. Apr.8; 112)
$5,500
- – **Anr. Edn.** [Heidelberg], [Printer of Lindelbach [Heinrich Knoblochtzer?]], 21 May, 1488. Fo. Capitals supplied in red, wide margins,

some dampstaining, a few short tears, portion torn from head of q2 & r5, with slight loss of text. Cont. blind-stpd. cf., spine & covers tooled with floral patterns, lacks clasps, very worn. From liby. of André L. Simon. [BMC II, 670; HC 2507*; Goff B139] (S. May 18; 33)
Harper. £480
- – **Anr. Edn.** Strassburg, [Printer of the 1483 Jordanus de Quedlinburg [Georg/Husner]]. 11 Aug., 1491. Fo. Lacks final blank, capital spaces with guide-letters, slight dampstaining. 18th. C. Fr. mott. cf., worn. From liby. of André L. Simon. [BMC I, 142; HC 2509*; Goff B140] (S. May 18; 34)
Gurney. £320
- – **Anr. Edn.** Nuremb., Anton Koberger, Jun.20 1492. Fo. Lacks last blank, prelim. ll. stained & reprd. in margins at end, x2 & x5 possibly inserted from anr. copy, inscr. on title 'Del convento de Religiosos descalcos de nuestra senora del Carmen'. 19th. C. mor., panel. in blind, hf. red mor. case. From Honeyman Collection. [BMC II, 435; Goff B141; HC 2510] (S. May 20; 3179)
Elstein. £320
- – **Anr. Edn.** Trans.:– [Vicente de Burgos]. Toulouse, Henricus Mayer, Sep. 18, 1494. Fo. Spaces for initial capitals with guide letters at head of books, woodcut Lombard capitals elsewhere, folios 170, 255-300, & 309-320 possibly from anr. copy with gutter margins renewed, title-p. heavily restored with portions probably in facs., many ll. with repairs & restorations to margins, some headlines cropped, folios 30-38, 293-300, & 310 with slight worming, catching text on some pp. & woodcut border at fo. 310, scattered spotting, finger-soiling & other defects. Red lev. mor., spine gt.-lettered, by Rivière & Son, corners worn. Bkplt. of Edward J. Bullrich, lately in the collection of Eric Sexton. [BMC VIII, 360, Goff B150] (CNY. Apr.8; 174)
$5,000
- **Van den Proprieteyten der Dinghen.** Haarlem, Jacob Bellaert, Dec.24, 1485. 1st. Edn. in Dutch. Fo. Spaces for initial capitals, supplied in red, larger capitals at beginning of each book illuminated in red, blue & green with penwork ornamentation, woodcuts cold., lacks blank folios 1, 246, & 466, lacks woodcut at A1, fo. 465 (with printer's device), & text lf. W8 (A1 & fo. 465 supplied in facs.), 1st. 3 & final 2 ll. stained, reprd. marginal tears at b1, p2-3, u3 & y8, tears affecting text at c5, m8 & Q3, portion of margin renewed at 5 ll., scattered staining & soiling. Vell., slightly worn. Bkplts. of Augustus Frederick, John Duncanson, & Edmund McClure, lately in the collection of Eric Sexton. [BMC IX, 102, Goff B142, HC 2522]. (CNY. Apr.8; 75)
$7,500

BARTHOLOMAEUS DE CHAIMIS
- **Interrogatorium Siue Confessionale.** Venice, Reynaldus de Novimagio, 28 Sep. 1486. Sm. 4to. Lacks 1st. blank, some later MS. p. numberings, slight browning & soiling, sm. blank corner cut from cl. 19th. C. mor. From liby. of André L. Simon. [BMC V, 258; Goff B162; HC (Add) 2488*] (S. May 18; 36)
Univ Place. £250

BARTHOLOMAEUS Sybilla Monopolitanus
- **Speculu[m] Peregrinaru[m] Questionu[m].** Lyons, 26 Nov. 1510. Slight browning & soiling. Cont. blind-stpd. Camb. cf. by Nicholas Spierinck, covers with his stp. & ornaments of griffins, wiverns, & lions, worn, head & foot of spine defect., reprd., lacks ties. (S. Jun.29; 354)
Maggs. £80

BARTHOLOMEW, John
- **The Times Atlas of the World.** Boston, 1955-59. 5 vols. Fo. Orig. cl. gt., d.-w.'s. (P. Jul.2; 232a)
Harmers. £50

BARTHOLOMEW, John George
- **The Royal Atlas & Gazetteer of Australasia.** 1890. Fo. Orig. cl. gt. (SBA. Jul.23; 225)
Mason. £85

BARTISCH, Georg
- **Opthalmodouleia [Greek].** Dresden, 1583. 1st. Edn. Fo. Some ll. browned, a few sm. stains. Cont. limp vell. bds. slight soiling, lacks ties. Stps. of the University Liby. of Tübingen on title, on front pastedown is cont. purchase inscr. dtd. 1585 in the hand of Adreas Laubmairius, Doctor of Canon & Civil Law at Tübingen. (S. Jun.23; 268)
Brooke-Hitching. £4,500

BARTLETT, Henrietta C. & Pollard, Alfred William
- **A Census of Shakespeare's Plays in Quarto.** New Haven, 1939. Revised Edn. 4to. Gt. cl., d.-w. (SG. Oct.2; 23)
$100

BARTLETT, John Russell
- The Literature of the Rebellion. Boston & Providence, 1866. (60). 4to. Contents partly loose in bdg. Crude hf. cf., ex-liby. Inscr. to S.C. Eastman. (SG. Jan.22; 48) $110
- Personal Narrative of Explorations & Incidents in Texas, New Mexico, California, Sonora, & Chihuahua, Connected with the U.S. & Mexican Boundary Commission, 1850-'53. N.Y., 1854. 1st. Edn. 2 vols. in 1 (as issued). Orig. cl. (SG. Jan.8; 32) $280
- - Anr. Copy. 2 vols. Map with pasted tear, lightly soiled. Orig. linen. [Sabin 3746] (R. Mar.31-Apr.4; 2440) DM 900

BARTLETT, William Henry
- History of the United States of North America. Ed.:– B.B. Woodward. N.Y., [1856?]. 3 vols. Lightly soiled in parts, title & plts. stp. on verso. Cont. hf. leath. gt. [Sabin 1,3788] (HK. May 12-14; 501) DM 520
- Mountain, Lake, & River. Ed.:– N.P. Willis. Boston, 1884. 4to. Occasional light foxing. Orig. decor. cl. (CB. Sep.24; 160) Can. $100
- Vues de la Hollande et de la Belgique. Ed.:– Prof. N.G. VanKampen. L., n.d. Lacks map. Hf roan, limp spine, decor. (LM. Jun.13; 263) B.Frs. 10,000
- Walks about the City & Environs of Jerusalem. [L.], ca. 1845. 2nd. Edn. Sm. 4to. Cont. hf. cf., worn, stitching breaking, some ll. coming loose. (C. Mar.18; 167) English. £55
- - Anr. Copy. Orig. gt.-decor. cl. (SG. Feb.26; 50) $110
See-ALLOM, Thomas & Bartlett, William Henry
See-BEATTIE, William & Bartlett, William Henry
See-STEBBING, Henry & Bartlett, William Henry
See-VAN KAMPEN, Prof. N.G. & Bartlett, William Henry
See-WILLIS, Nathaniel Parker & Bartlett, William Henry

BARTLEY, G.C.T.
- The Rhine from its source to the sea. L., 1878. Lge. 4to. Decor. cl. (PJ. Mar.7(80); 22) £220

BARTOLI, Cosimo
- Del Modo Di Dividere l'Alluuioni l'Isole, & gl'Alvei. Rome, 1587. Some ll. browned. Old hf. vell., wormed. (TA. Nov.20; 217) £55

BARTOLI, Pietro Santo
- Colonna Traiana. Rome, [1700]. Ob. fo. 1 unnumbered text p., 1 index lf. Cont. vell. (CR. Mar.19; 288) Lire 320,000
- - Anr. Edn. Rome, n.d. Ob. fo. With privilege of S. Pontifice, margins browned. Cont. hf. mor. (CSK. Nov.28; 21) £95
- Le Pitture Antiche delle Grotte di Roma, e del Sepolcro de' Nasoni ... Ill.:– Pietro Bellori & Michelangelo Causei dela Chausse. Rome, 1706. Fo. Tear in F2, a few ll. marginally stained. Cont. hf. vell., spine soiled. (S. Oct.21; 325) Duran. £110
- - Anr. Copy. Vell. (DS. May 22, 874) Pts. 34,000

BARTOLOCCI, Julio
- Bibliotheca Magna Rabbinica. Rome, 1675-94. 5 vols. Fo. Vols. 1 & 5 facs., 1966-68. Hf. leath. (S. Nov.17; 53) Valmadonna. £140

BARTOLOZZI, Francesco & others
- Eighty-Two [& Seventy-Three] Prints ... from the Original Drawings of Guercino [& others]. Ca. 1800. 2 vols. in 1. Fo. With 7 additional plts. (6 dupls.), 1 trimmed & mntd., others loosely inserted, 1 imprint cropped, some plts. slightly spotted, contents slightly loose. Cont. hf. russ., lacks spine, covers detchd. Bkplt. of Ditton Park, note in the hand of Mary Montagu on front free end-paper, as a collection of plts., w.a.f. (S. Feb.10; 332) Mistrali. £1,700
- - Anr. Copy. 2 vols. Lge. fo. 145 engraved plts. of 155. Orig. bdg., defect., 2 covers detchd. Apr.30; 727) £1,600
- Italian School of Design, a Series of Select Studia. 1842. Fo. Soiled. Cont. hf. mor. (SH. Jan.29; 69) Platemark. £100
- Seventy-Three Prints ... from the Original Pictures & Drawings ... in the Collection of His Majesty. Ill.:– Bartolozzi, Gandolfi, Du Bosc, Mariette & others after Guercino, Carracci, da Cortona, Parmigiano, Michelangelo & others. Ca. 1800. Vol. II only (of 2). Fo. Lacks 1 plt., 1 with tear, imprint cropped, 1 crudely reprd., piece torn

from outer margin of anr., occasional spotting, title & several ll. detchd. Cont. hf. russ., upr. cover detchd., very worn. As a collection of plts., w.a.f. (S. Jan.27; 454) Broseghini. £850

BARTOLUS, P.S.
See-DORIGNY, Nicolaus-BERETTINI, Petro -ALBANI, F.-BERETTINI, Petro-BARTOLUS, P.S.

BARTOLUS DE SAXOFERRATO
[-] [Ordo Iudich]. Incipit Tractatus de Renūciationib. [Vienna], [1478]. [1st. Edn.] 4to. Lacks 29 ll., 1st. lf. reprd. 18th. C. mor. by Derome le Jeune with his ticket, triple gt. fillet, flat spine gt. with longitudinal title, inner gt. dentelles. [HC 3608] (SM. Oct.7; 1561) Frs. 2,400

BARTON, William P.C.
- A Flora of North America. Phila., 1821-23. 1st. Edn. 3 vols., separately issued. 4to. 1 plt. reprd. Orig. gt.-ornamental hf. roan & patterned bds. [Sabin 3858]. (PNY. Oct.1; 96) $1,800
- Vegetable Materia Medica of the United States. Phila., 1817-18. 2 vols. 4to. 1 plt. affected by damp, some spotting. Cont. hf. mor., slightly soiled. (CSK. May 22; 128) £120

BARTRAM, William
- Travels through North & South Carolina ... Phila., 1791. 1st. Edn. Folding map, 8 plts., frontis. mntd., rehinged thro-out, pt. of 1 lf. supplied in photostat, ex liby. Old mott. cf., scorched, rebkd. (SG. Oct.30; 47) $320
- - Anr. Edn. L., 1794. Later hf. cf., unc., worn, upr. cover detchd., spine torn. (SPB. Jun.22; 9) $275

BARTSCH, Adam
- Le Peintre Graveur. Vienna, 1803-43. 23 vols. including supp. & atlas of plts. 8vo. & 4to. Plts. spotted. Cont. vell., atlas in hf. vell., soiled. (SH. Jan.29; 70) Schwing. £350
- - Anr. Edn. Leipzig; Vienna, 1854; 1805-21. Vols. I-III; Vols. IV-XXI. Browning, minor tears. Unif. bnd. in mor.-bkd. bds., chipped, lacks label on 1 vol. (SPB. May 6; 151) $500

BASAN, Pierre François
- Catalogue Raisonné des Differens Objets de Curiosités dans les Sciences et Arts. Ill.:– after Guercino, Cochin & Moreau. Paris, 1775. Margins of final lf. slightly dampstained. Later cf.-bkd. bds. Liby. stp. of Edward Cheney. (SBA. May 27; 140) Temperley. £55
- - Anr. Edn. Trans.:– Moreau. Ill.:– Jean Michel le Jeune & Cochin. Paris, Priv. Ptd. 1775. (12) on Holland paper. Priced thro-out in MS., 2 loosely inserted proofs of frontis. before letter, dampstained. Cont. red mor., gt., arms of Marquis de Nicolai with central oval of field & charge onlaid, gt. fillets, spine gt. in compartments, inner gt. dentelles, end-papers stained. (SM. Oct.7; 1445) Frs. 1,100
- Collection de Cent-Vingt Estampes Gravées d'Apres les Tableaux et Dessins qui Composoient le Cabinet de M. Poullain. Paris, 1781. 4to. Text bnd. in at end. Later mor.-bkd. bds., spine torn. (SBA. May 27; 141) Barker. £230
- - Anr. Copy. 4to. Old red mor., reprd., gt. fillets. (HD. Dec.5; 16) Frs. 4,300
- - Anr. Copy. 4to. Lightly soiled in places. Cont. red leath. gt., gold fillets & outer dentelles. (R. Mar.31-Apr.4; 1577) DM 3,500
- Dictionaire des Graveurs anciens et modernes. Paris, 1789. 2nd. (1st. ill.) Edn. 2 vols. Bkplt. & a few initial-stamps in vol. I. Cont. mott. cf., gt., not unif. (S. Oct.21; 294) C. Mendez. £170
- Recueil d'Estampes Gravées d'après les Tableaux du Cabinet de Monseigneur le Duc de Choiseul. Paris, 1771. 4to. Engraved title, dedication, port., table of contents & 124 plts. only, lacks 44, 45, 64 & 118, browning & spotting, mainly marginal. Hf. mor. W.a.f. (CSK. Nov.14; 58) £380
- - Anr. Copy. 4to. Some foxing & browning. Cont. str.-grd. red mor., thick & thin gt. fillets, spine decor. with fillets & fine dentelles, Greek inside. Bkplts. of Charles Whibley & Lord Berwick. (HD. Mar.18; 18) Frs. 6,000

BASANOFF, Anne
- Itinerario della Carta dall' Oriente all' Occidente, e sua Diffusione in Europe. Milan, [1965]. (200) unnumbered on heavy paper. Fo. Cl.-bkd. batik bds., unc. 2 p. A.L.s. laid in. (SG. Mar.26; 349) $190

BASEDOW, Herbert
- The Australian Aboriginal. Adelaide, 1925. Orig. cl. (KH. Mar.24; 29) Aus. $100
- Collection of offprints & reprints ... South Australia. Adelaide, 1901, 1905, etc. 1 vol. Old hf. mor. Bnd. in is Basedow's 'Catalogue of Minerals in the Technological Museum of South Australian School of Mines & Industries', Adelaide 1907. (KH. Nov.18; 34) Aus. $220
See-SCHIDLOFF, B. & others

BASEDOW, Jean B.
- Clementarwerke. Berlin & Dessau, 1774. Ob. Introduction in Fr., German & Latin. Hf. mor., worn. W.a.f. (CE. Feb.19; 192) £125
- Für Cosmopoliten etwas zu lesen, zu denken und zu thun. Leipzig, 1775. 1st. Edn. Mod. bds. (R. Mar.31-Apr.4; 260) DM 750

BASEILHAC, Jean, called le Frère Cosme
- Nouvelle Methode d'Extraire la Pierre de la Vessie Urinaire ... Brussels & Paris, 1779, 12mo. Cont. wraps., worn. (SG. Sep.18; 33) $260

BASILE, Giambattista
- Stories from the Pentamerone. Ed.:– Edward F. Strange. Ill.:– Warwick Goble. 1911. (150). 4to. Orig. vell. gt., lacks ties. (SH. Dec.10; 216) Joseph. £90
- - Anr. Copy. (S. Jul.31; 233) Ralph. £60

BASILIUS Magnus, Saint
- Opera.-Hexameron. Trans.:– Raphaelis Volaterranus; Joannes Argyropulus. Rome, 15 Sep.1515; 12 Dec.1515. 1st. Edn. 2 works in 1 vol. Fo. Many underlinings & cold MS. marginalia, a few ll. browned. Cont. limp vell., slightly soiled, spine defect. (R. Oct.14-18; 20) DM 680

BASILY-Callimaki, Mme de
- J.-B. Isabey. Ill.:– Loewy, Chauvet & Porcabeuf. Paris, 1909. (550) on velin à la cuve. 4to. Crushed mor., gt. panel on sides with cornerpieces of rose sprays enclosing a fleur-de-lys, panel on upr. cover with gt. centrepiece of rose wreath enclosing Isabey's initials in cold. mor. on floral spray ground, spine gt. in compartments with Napoleonic emblems of bees & fleur-de-lys, inner dentelles, partly unc., by Sotheran. (C. Jul.22; 76) Sawyer. £170

BASKERVILLE, Margaret
- Margaret Baskerville, Sculptor. Melbourne, [1929]. (250) sigd. 4to. Vell. gt. (KH. Mar.24; 32) Aus. $130

BASNAGE, Jacques de Beauval
- Histoire des Juifs. 1716. 15 vols. Titles in red & black. Cont. vell. (P. Oct.23; 84) Piermont. £70
- Histoire du Vieux et du Nouveau Testament. Ill.:– After Romeyn de Hooghe; Jacob Gole. Amst., 1704. 2 pts. in 1 vol. Fo. 1 blank fore-e. reprd. 18th. C. mor., triple gt. fillet, spine gt. in compartments, inner gt. floral dentelles. (SM. Oct.7; 1562) Frs. 6,000
- History of the Jews from Jesus Christ to the Present Time. Trans.:– Thomas Taylor. L., 1708. 1st. Edn. in Engl. Fo. Some staining. Leath. (S. Nov.18; 641) Kingsgate. £320
- - Anr. Copy. Fo. Cont. panel. cf., covers detchd. (SG. Sep.25; 32) $170

BASOLI, A.
- Collezione di Varie Scene Teatrali. Bologna, 1821. Fo.; 38 × 141 cm. Cont. hf. vell. (CR. Jun.11; 456) Lire 750,000

BASON, Frederick T.
- Bibliography of the Writings of William Somerset Maugham. L., 1931. (50) numbered on Mould-made paper, sigd. by Maugham. Buckram. (SG. Jun.4; 368) $110

BASS, Sabtai
- Siftei Chachamim. Frankfurt a. M., 1712. 1st. Edn. 4to. Cropped, lightly stained. Mod. leath., s.-c. (SPB. May 11; 36) $225
- Siftei Yesheinim. Amst., 1680. Slightly browned. Nathaniel Weill's sig., some titles underlined in red. Orig. bdg. (S. Nov.17; 54) Kingsgate. £260

BASSANI, Israel Benjamin
- Ottave Ebraiche, colla Versione Italiana. Venice, 1750. Wraps. (C. Apr.1; 7) Quaritch. £260

BASSERMANN-JORDAN, F.
- Geschichte des Weinbaus unter besonderer Berücksichtung der Bayerischen-Rheinpfaz. Frankfurt, 1907. Orig. linen. (R. Oct.14-18; 2742) DM 510

BASSI, Martino
- **Disparei in Materia d'Architettura, et Perspettiva.** Brescia, 1572. 1st. Edn. 4to. Some browning, sm. wormholes in last 5 plts. barely touching etched surface, title. stp. on verso of title-p. Later bds. (SPB. May 6; 152) $550
- **Anr. Copy.** Stain on title & last p., 1 plt. slightly defect. 19th. C. hf. red mor. (SI. Dec.3; 52) Lire 950,000

BASSOMPIERRE, François de
- **Mémoires ... contenant l'Histoire de sa Vie.** Cologne, 1666. 2 vols. 12mo. 18th. C. mor. by Derome le Jeune with his ticket, triple gt. fillet, flat spine gt. with single fleuron in compartments, inner gt. dentelles. Bkplt. of Laurence Currie, Roger du Nord copy. (SM. Oct.7; 1564) Frs. 2,500

BASTA, G.
See—UFANO, Diego–BASTA, G.–ERRARD de Bar-le Duc, J.

BASTELAER, René van
- **Les Estampes de Peter Bruegel l'Ancien.** Brussels, 1908. 4to. Later hf. cl. (SH. Oct.9; 62) Antico Ltd. £70
- **Anr. Copy.** 4to. Orig. wraps., soiled. (SH. Jun.4; 14) Phillips. £50
- **Anr. Copy.** 4to. Three-qtr. cf., orig. wraps. bnd. in. (SG. Mar.12; 45) $350

BASTIAN, Henry Charlton
- **Paralyses Cerebral, Bulbar & Spinal.** 1881. 1st. Edn. Orig. cl. (S. Jun.15; 42) Jenner Books. £70
- **A Treatise on Aphasia & other Speech Defects.** 1898. 1st. Edn. Cl. (S. Jun.15; 43) Pratt. £75

BASTIDE, J.-F.
- **La Petite Maison.** Ill.:– Lalauze. Paris, 1905. (150), numbered. 4to. Ills. in several states (4-8, with proofs), set of orig. drawings. Red hf. mor., decor. spine, wrap preserved. (SM. Feb.11; 186) Frs. 12,000

BATAILLE, Georges
- **Histoire de l'Oeil.** Ill.:– Bellmer. Seville, 1940. (199); (100) on vell. 6 orig. engrs. Sewed, folder, s.-c. (HD. Jun.24; 147) Frs. 4,900

BATAILLE, Henry
- **Têtes et Pensées.** Paris, 1901. (50) numbered. Fo. Ports. each in 3 variant states, a few very slightly spotted. Loose in portfo., very slightly worn. (SH. Nov.20; 220) Henderson. £50

BATEMAN, James
- **The Orchidaceae of Mexico & Guatemala.** Ill.:– M. Gauci after Holden, George Cruikshank, & others. Priv. Ptd. [1837]-43. Elephant fo. Plts. hand-cold., slight foxing & dust-soiling affecting about 10 plts. 19th. C. hf. mor., very worn, covers detchd. From Chetham's Liby., Manchester. (C. Nov.26; 27) Isley. £5,200

BATES, Alfred
- **The Drama.** L., 1903. The Aeschylus Edn., (26). 20 vols. Puce mor. gt., lge. sword of inlay & gt. on upr. covers, rose inlay on spine, elab. mor. doubl. with inlaid panel of roses, silk free endpapers. (SPB. May 6; 288) $650
- **The Drama & Opera.** L., 1903. Beaux Arts Edn., (500). 12 vols. Red mor., elab. gt. (SPB. May 6; 289) $400

BATES, Henry Walter
- **The Naturalist on the River Amazons.** 1863. 1st. Edn. 2 vols. Orig. cl., gt., slightly soiled. (S. Apr.7; 479) Quaritch. £90
- **Anr. Copy.** 2 vols. Orig. cl., slightly chipped, Bibliotheca Lindesiana bkplt. (SPB. May 5; 95) $250

BATES, Herbert Ernest
- **The Beauty of the Dead ...** Corvinus Pr., 1941. 1st. Edn. (25) numbered, sigd. Orig. buckram-bkd. bds. (S. Jul.22; 74) Jon Ash. £160
- **Anr. Copy.** Orig. buckram-bkd. bds., s.-c. (S. Jul.31; 152) Bertram Rota. £130
- **I am Not Myself.** Corvinus Pr., Jun.1939. 1st. Edn., (38) numbered, reserved for Mrs. Everard Gates, sigd. 4to. Orig. mor.-bkd. linen, slightly stained at top of spine, s.-c. (S. Jul.31; 150) Bertram Rota. £110

BATESON, Edward & others
- **History of Northumberland.** Newcastle, 1893-1940. 15 vols. 4to. Occasional spotting. Orig. cl. (CSK. Sep.26; 125) £100

BATESON, William
- **Materials for the Study of Variation treated with especial Regard to Discontinuity in the Origin of Species.** 1894. 1st. Edn. Advt. lf. Orig. cl. (S. Jun.15; 47) Rota. £55

BATH SOCIETY
- **Letters & Papers on Agriculture, Planting, etc., Selected from the Correspondence Book of the Society Instituted at Bath.** 1788-1810. 12 vols. Some slight spotting. Cont. diced cf. gt., slight worming. (SD. Feb.4; 267) £80

BATSCH, A.J.C.
- **Le Nouveau Jardin à Fleurs.** Weimar, 1802. 2nd. Edn. German & Fr. text, some plts. & text ll. slightly soiled. Bds. (R. Oct.14-18; 2911) DM 1,600

BATTARRA, Antonio
- **Fungorum Agri Ariminensis Historia ...** Faenza, 1759. 2nd. Edn. 4to. 19th. C. hf. mor. From Chetham's Liby., Manchester. (C. Nov.26; 28) Israel. £220

BATTIE, William
- **A Treatise on Madness.** 1758. 1st. Edn. 4to. Marb. paper bds., new cf. spine. (S. Jun.15; 48) Rota. £270

BATTISS, W.W.
- **Art in South Africa.** Pretoria, 1939. (200). 4to. 33 loose ills. Orig. bdg., wraps. (SSA. Jan.22; 154) R. 130
- **Bushman Art, Portfolio No. 1.** Pretoria, n.d. Fo. With an extra plt., 'Rock Painting from Barrowhill, O.F.S.'. Orig. bdg., decor. wraps. Introduction sigd. by author. (VA. Jan.30; 5) R. 100
- **South African Paint Pot.** Pretoria, n.d. (500). 4to. Stiff wraps. & d.-w., spine slightly defect. Plt. 1 sigd. by Battiss. (VA. May 8; 403) R. 145

BATTY, Elizabeth Frances
- **Italian Scenery.** 1820. [1st. Edn.?] 4to. Light spotting. Hf. mor. (CSK. Feb.13; 5) £180
- **Anr. Copy.** Stained. Cont. cf., worn, lacks upr. cover. (CSK. May 29; 142) £160
- **Anr. Copy.** Tears, marginal stain, foxed. Mor. gt., worn at corners & spine. (SPB. May 29; 22) $130

BATTY, Capt. Robert
- **French Scenery.** L., 1822. 4to. Stained thro.-out, ded. lf. misbnd. Str.-grd. mor. gt. by Simier, arms of Duchesse de Berri on sides. (S. Nov.24; 15) Chaponniere. £220
- **Anr. Copy.** Some foxing. Mor. gt. (SPB. Jul.28; 19) $250
- **Anr. Copy.** Some foxing, soiling. Hf. red mor., very worn. (SPB. May 29; 23) $200
- **German Scenery.** 1823. Slightly soiled. Orig. cl., worn, lacks spine, loose. (SH. Mar.5; 12) Omniphil. £720
- **Anr. Copy.** Foxed. Mor. gt., corners worn. (SPB. May 6; 153) $1,100
- **Hanoverian & Saxon Scenery.** L., 1829. 4to. Cont. leath., gt., cover loose & spine defect. (R. Oct.14-18; 2306) DM 8,800
- **Scenery of the Rhine, Belgium & Holland.** L., 1826. 4to. Frontis. & title slightly soiled. Cont. leath., gt. & blind-tooled. (R. Oct.14-18; 2394) DM 3,500
- **Welsh Scenery.** Ill.:– Edward Finden after Batty. 1823. L.P.? 4to. Slight spotting. Cont. str.-grd. mor. gt. (SBA. Dec.16; 173) Crete. £82
- **Anr. Edn.** 1823. Mod. mor.-bkd. bds. (SH. Nov.6; 73) Crete. £60

BAUCHART, Ernest Quentin
- **Les Femmes Bibliophiles de France.** Paris, 1886. (300) numbered copies. 2 vols. Mod. 4to. buckram, unc. (SG. Oct.2; 25) $200

BAUDELAIRE, Charles
- **Les Epaves.** Ill.:– Félicien Rops. Amst., 1866. (250) on L.P. vergé de Hollande. Cont. hf. mor. (HD. Oct.10; 17) Frs. 1,300
- **Fleurs du Mal.** Paris, 1857. 1st. Edn. 12mo. Some foxing, mostly at beginning & end. Cont. hf. chagrin, square blind-tooled fillets on spine. (HD. Dec.5; 17) Frs. 10,700
- **Anr. Edn.** Paris, 1861. 2nd. Edn. Lacks port., light foxing & spotting. Early 20th. C. mor.-bkd. bds., partly unc. & orig. wraps. bnd. in, loose s.-c. (SM. Oct.8; 2231) Frs. 2,000
- **Anr. Edn.** Ill.:– Georges Rochegrosse & Denis Volx. Paris, Priv. Ptd., 1910. On Whatman L.-P. 4to. Plts. in 3 states, extra suite of port. & 10 plts.

on Japon by Volx. Mor., silk doubls., orig. wraps bnd. in s.-c. (SM. Oct.8, 2320)
- **Anr. Edn.** Ill.:– Mariette Lydis. Paris, 1928. (50) numbered on imperial Jap. 4to. 2 orig. watercolour drawings (1 with 4 states of plt.), 2 orig. copper-engs., 10 etchings in 2 states. Mor. by Trinckvel, orig. wrap., s.-c. Plts. sigd. by artist. (SM. Feb.11; 187) Frs. 26,000
- **Anr. Edn.** Ill.:– Mariette Lydis. Paris, 1928. (290) numbered, on Pannekoek Holland paper, with each plt. sigd. in pencil by artist. Lge. 4to. Red mor., orig. wraps bnd. in. (SG. Oct.23; 200) $150
- **Anr. Edn.** Trans.:– C. Bower Alcock. Ill.:– Beresford Egan. Sophistocles Pr., 1929. (500) numbered, sigd. by artist. 4to. Orig. bds. (SH. Mar.26; 184) Drummond. £52
- **Anr. Edn.** Ill.:– H. Matisse. 1947. On vell. de Rives. 4to. Ll. in box. 1 orig. etching on China, sigd. by artist. (HD. Jun.30; 6) Frs. 2,100
- **Les Fleurs du Mal.–Flowers of Evil.** Ill.:– Auguste Rodin; Jacob Epstein. N.Y., Ltd. Edns. Cl., 1940. (1,500) numbered. Together 2 vols. 4to. Wraps. & cl., 1st. vol. unc. & unopened, orig. boxes. (SG. Apr.9; 466) $100
- **Flowers of Evil.–Les Fleurs du Mal.** Trans.:– James Laver. Ill.:– Jacob Epstein & Auguste Rodin. Ltd. Edns. Cl., 1940. (1500) numbered. 2 vols. 4to. Cl., partly untrimmed (1st. work); & wraps., unc. boxed together. (SG. Jan.15; 119) $150
- **Les Paradis Artificiels Opium et Haschisch.** Paris, 1860. 1st. Edn. Mor. by Aussourd. (SM. Oct.8; 2232) Frs. 4,200
- **Poèmes.** Ill.:– Charles Despiau. Paris, 1933. (5) on hollande reserved for collaborators, sigd. by artist, numbered. 4to. Unsewn in orig. wraps., unc., folder & s.-c., latter slightly defect. (SH. Nov.21; 299) Jamieson. £320

BAUDELOCQUE, Jean Louis
- **L'Art des Accouchements.** Paris, 1796. 3rd. Edn. 2 vols. Some folding plts. detchd., 1 plt. torn. Cont. marb. roan, jnts. split. (HD. Feb.18; 9) Frs. 1,400
- **A System of Midwifery.** Trans.:– John Heath. Priv. ptd., 1790. 3 vols. New bds., cf. spine. (S. Jun.15; 49) Norman. £140

BAUDIAU, J.F.
- **Le Morvand ...** 1865-67. 3 vols. Cont. hf. chagrin, spines with raised bands. (HD. Feb.27; 80) Frs. 1,100

BAUDOIN, Comte de
- **L'Exercice de l'Infanterie Française ...** 1757. Fo. Reprs. to frontis. & plts. Havana mor., centre arms, spine raised bands, by Hardy-Menil. (HD. Apr.24; 31) Frs. 3,200

BAUDU, René
- **Les Après-midi de Montmartre.** Ill.:– E. Chimot. Paris, 1919. (170); (100) on vell. 4to. Hf. mor., corners, spine decor. with raised bands, wrap. & spine preserved. (HD. Jun.24; 149) Frs. 1,150

BAUER, Dr. Max
- **Precious Stones ... with an Appendix on Pearls & Coral.** Trans.:– L.J. Spencer. 1904. 1st. Engl. Edn. 4to. Some annots. to margins. Recent cl. (TA. Mar.19; 75) £65
- **Anr. Copy.** 4to. Hf. mor. (SSA. Jan.22; 10) R. 130

BAUERLE, A. (Ed.)
See—THEATER-ZEITUNG

BAUERNFEIND, C.M.
- **Karte der Koenigl. Bayer. Eisenbahnen.** Nuremb., 1845. Cont. hf. linen. (HK. May 12-14; 272) DM 650

BAUGH, Robert
- **Maps of Shropshire.** [Final map with imprint of Robert Baugh, Llanymynech (Shrops.) 1808]. Lge. fo. Engraved title with inset view, maps partly hand-cold. in outl. & with marginal MS. notes. Hf. cf. (SKC. May 19; 387) £50

BAUHAUS. Zeitschrift für Gestaltung
Dessau, 1928 & 1929. Yrs. II & III, 8 issues in 7 pts. in 1 vol. 4to. 2 ll. loose, some ll. with tears. Old hf. leath., orig. wraps. bnds. in. (H. Dec.9/10; 1946) DM 1,000

BAUM, Lyman Frank
- **[-] Babes in Birdland.** Ill.:– Maginal Wright Enright. Chic., [1911]. 4to. Pict. bds., crudely

rebkd., lacks front free end-paper. (SG. Apr.9; 32)
$100
- **The Daring Twins.–Phoebe Daring.** Ill.:– P.M. Batchelder & J.P. Nuyttens. Chicago, [1911; 1912]. 1st. Edns. Together 2 vols. 'Times Union' stp. on some pp. of 1st. work. Cold. pict. stpd. cl. in 1st. state, shaken. (SG. Apr.9; 35) $160
- **Dorothy & the Wizard in Oz.** Ill.:– John R. Neill. Chic., [1908]. 1st. Edn., 1st. Iss. Cl. (SG. Apr.9; 25) $160
- **Dot & Tot of Merryland.** Ill.:– W.W. Denslow. Chic., 1901. 1st. Edn. 4to. Pict. cl. gt. (SG. Apr.9; 6) $150
- **The Emerald City of Oz.** Ill.:– John R. Neill. Chic., [1910]. 1st. Edn., 1st. State. Prelims. & title border hand-cold. by previous owner. Cl. (SG. Apr.9; 30) $110
- **Glinda of Oz.** Ill.:– John R. Neill. Chic., [1920]. 1st. Edn., 1st. Iss. Advts., 1 plt. loose, lacks front free end-paper. Cl. (SG. Sep.4; 24) $110
- **John Dough & the Cherub.** Ill.:– John R. Neill. Chic., [1906]. 1st. Edn., 1st. Iss. Pict. cl. (SG. Apr.9; 20) $250
- **Juvenile Speaker.** Ill.:– John R. Neill & Maginel Wright Enright. Chic., [1910]. 1st. Edn. 4to. Pict. cl., loose. (SG. Apr.9; 31) $180
- **Little Wizard Series.** Ill.:– John R. Neill. Chic., [1913]. 1st. Edns. Together 5 vols. (of 6). Sm. 4to. Cold. pict. bds. (SG. Apr.9; 38) $650
- **The Lost Princess of Oz.** Ill.:– John R. Neill. Chic., [1917]. 1st. Edn., 1st. State. Cl., shaken, early d.-w. (SG. Apr.9; 48) $375
- **The Magic of Oz.** Ill.:– John R. Neill. Chic., [1919]. 1st. Edn., 1st. Iss. Advts. Cl. (SG. Sep.4; 23) $160
- – **Anr. Copy.** Cl., later d.-w. (SG. Apr.9; 52) $130
- **The Marvellous Land of Oz.** Ill.:– John R. Neill. Chic., 1904. 1st. Edn., 2nd. State. Pict. cl. (SG. Apr.9; 11) $140
- – **Anr. Copy.** Pict. cl. (SG. Apr.9; 12) $100
- **Mother Goose in Prose.** Ill.:– Maxfield Parrish. Chic., [1897]. 1st. Edn., 1st. State. 4to. Cold.-pict. cl., soiled & spotted. (PNY. Dec.3; 34) $450
- – **Anr. Edn.** Ill.:– Maxfield Parrish. Chic., [1901]. 2nd. Edn. 4to. Pict. cl. (SG. Apr.9; 1) $120
- **A New Wonderland.** Ill.:– Frank Verbeck. N.Y., 1900. 1st. Printing. 4to. Pict. cl. (SG. Apr.9; 3) $450
- **Ozma of Oz.** Ill.:– John R. Neill. Chic., [1907]. 1st. Edn., 1st. State. Cold. pict. cl., shaken. (SG. Apr.9; 23) $140
- **The Patchwork Girl of Oz.** Ill.:– John R. Neill. Chic., [1913]. 1st. Edn., 1st. State. Pict. cl. (SG. Apr.9; 41) $120
- [–] **Prairie-Dog Town.** Ill.:– Maginel Wright Enright. Chic., [1906]. 1st. Edn. Pict. cl. (SG. Apr.9; 17) $160
- **Queen Zixi of Ix.** Ill.:– Frederick Richardson N.Y., 1905. 1st. Edn., 1st. State. 4to. Pict. cl. (SG. Apr.9; 14) $130
- **The Road to Oz.** Ill.:– John R. Neill. Chic., [1909]. 1st. Edn., earliest Iss. Advt. lf., perfect type in words 'Toto on' page 34, line 4 & in numeral '121' on page 121, numeral & caption present beneath ill. on page 129. Cold. pict. cl., primary bdg. (SG. Sep.4; 21) $110
- **The Scarecrow of Oz.** Ill.:– John R. Neill. Chic., [1915]. 1st. Edn., 1st. Printing. Cl. (SG. Apr.9; 43) $100
- **Tik-Tok of Oz.** Chic., [1914]. 1st. Edn., 1st. State. Cl. (SG. Apr.9; 42) $175
- **The Wishing Horse of Oz.** Ill.:– John R. Neill. Chic., [1935]. 1st. Edn. Cl., lr. cover stained. (SG. Apr.9; 61) $130
- **The Wonderful Wizard of Oz.** Ill.:– W.W. Denslow. Chic., 1900. 1st. Edn., 2nd. State. Pict. stpd. cl., shaken. (SG. Apr.9; 5) $450

BAUME, Antoine
- **Elemens de Pharmacie . . .** Paris, 1762. 1st. Edn. Slightly soiled. Cont. leath. gt., worn. (HK. Nov.18-21; 379) DM 650

BAUMGÄRTNER, Karl Heinrich
- **Kranken-Physiognomik.** Stuttgart, 1842. 2nd. Edn. Some plt. numbers cropped, some ll. slightly spotted. Cont. patterned bds. (S. Feb.23; 10) *Robinson.* £170

BAUR, Johann Wilhelm
- **Iconographia.** Augsburg, 1670. Ob. fo. Engraved title torn & reprd., 2 plts. torn & reprd., 1 outer margin holed, 1st. few ll. creased. Early 19th. C.

red mor., stpd. & ruled in gt. & blind, slightly soiled. (CSK. Jan.23; 71) £520
- [–] **[A Series of Engravings Illustrating Scenes from Ovid's Metamorphoses].** [Vienna], [1641]. Ob. 4to. 149 (of 150?) etched plts. only, without dedication(?), some margins slightly soiled or stained, some cont. marginal notes. Later hf. cf., very worn. (SBA. May 27; 9) *Edistar.* £180

BAUR COLLECTION
See–COULLERY, M.T. & Newstead, M.S.

BAXTER, George
- **The Pictorial Album.** [1837]. 4to. Title slightly browned, some spotting. Orig. roan gt., rubbed. (C. Jul.22; 44) *Rostron.* £100

BAXTER, William, Botanist
- **British Phaenogamous Botany.** 1834-37. Vols. 1, 2, 3 & 6. Hf. mor., worn. W.a.f. (P. Dec.11; 87) *Fairburn.* £230
- – **Anr. Edn.** Oxford, Priv. Ptd., 1834-43. 3 vols. in 6. Cont. hf- cf., gt. (C. Nov.5; 8) *Hener.* £450
- – **Anr. Copy.** 6 vols. Early cl. (S. Dec.3; 886) *Varekamp.* £360
- – **Anr. Edn.** Oxford, [1834]-43. 6 vols. in 3. Lacks title & prelims. to vol. 1. Hf. leath., very worn. W.a.f. (S. Dec.3; 887) *Varekamp.* £320

BAYAN, Vadim & others
- **Iz Batarei serdtsa [From the Battery of the Heart].** [Moscow], 1922. 4to. Orig. wraps. (SH. Feb.6; 389) *Quaritch.* £100
- **Obvaly Serdtsa [Crumblings of the Heart].** Sebastopol, 1920. 4to. A few ll. slightly stained. Orig. wraps., soiled, spine torn. (SH. Feb.6; 390) *Quaritch.* £120
- **Srublenny Potselui [Curtailed Kiss].** [?Petrograd], [1920]. 4to. Orig. wraps. (SH. Feb.6; 388) *Quaritch.* £90

BAYARDI, Ottavio Antoine & others
- **Le Antichita di Ercolano Eposte.–Catalogo degli Antichi Monumenti di Ercolano.** Naples, 1757-92; 1755. 7 vols. only (of 8, lacks vol. 7); Vol. 1 (all publd.). Fo. Some prelims. in 1st. work creased, slight marginal staining in vol. 5. Cont. mott. cf., gt. spines, some wear. Vol. 1 of 1st. work inscr. 'The Gift of Princess Franca Villa to Robert Adair'. (S. Jul.27; 212) *Duran.* £240

BAYER, F. Perez
- **Numorum Hebraeo-Samaritanorum Vindiciae.** 1790. Sm. fo. Cont. red mor., lge. gt. Greek Key pattern. & dentelle border, decor. spine, silk end-ll. (HD Jun.30; 7) Frs. 3,300

BAYLE, Pierre
- **Dictionaire Historique et Critique.** Rotterdam, 1697. 2 vols. in 4. Fo. A few ll. slightly soiled. Cont. sheep-bkd. bds, worn. (S. Oct.21; 451) *Saracen.* £110
- – **Anr. Edn.** Ill.:– Simonneau after Verdie (engraved frontis.), Chevreau (engraved port.). Rotterdam, 1720. 3rd. Edn. 4 vols. Fo. Engraved port. mntd., a few ll. spotted or browned, with the verses on the Regent by H.P. Limiers on fly-lf. in a cont. hand in vol. I. Cont. red mor., triple gt. fillets, spine gt. in compartments on ground semé with gt. stars, dots & fleur-de-lis, inner gt. dentelles. (S. Apr.7; 349) *Fletcher.* £500
- – **Anr. Copy.** Some verses on Regent by H.P. Limiers in cont. hand, in vol. 1. (SM. Oct.7; 1566) Frs. 3,000
- – **Anr. Edn.** Trans.:– Des Maizeaux. Amst./Leiden, 1740. 5th. Edn. Fo. Orig. leath. spines gt. (VG. Dec.17; 1192) Fls. 1,600
- **Historical & Critical Dictionary.** Ed.:– Des Maizeaux. L., 1734-38. 5 vols. Fo. Hf. cf. gt. (P. Jul.2; 70) £50
- **Oeuvres Diverses.** La Haye, 1727-31. 1st. Edn., L.P. 4 vols. Fo. Some margins dampstained in vol. ll, pres. label on verso of titles from W. Whewell, 1853, to Trinity College. Cont. red mor., triple gt. fillet & floral corner sprays, with fleuron, spine gt. in compartments, floral inner gt. dentelles. Bkplt. of Charles Campbell. (SM. Oct.7; 1567) Frs. 5,000

BAYLE, Pierre & Barrin, J.
- **Nouvelles de la République des Lettres.** Amst., 1684-1718. 40 vols. Cont. cf. (P. Jan.22; 51) *Fairburn.* £95

BAYLES, F.H.
- **Race Courses Atlas of Great Britain & Ireland.** 1903. Ob. fo. Slightly spotted. Orig. hf. mor., spine torn. (CSK. Nov.28; 47) £50

BAYLEY, Frank W.
- **Five Colonial Artists of New England.** Boston, Priv. Ptd., 1929. (500). Fo. Cl., gt. (SG. Dec.4; 33) $130

BAYLEY, Frederick W.N.
- **Gems for the Drawing Room.** 1852-n.d. 4 vols. Fo. 1 ill. mntd., publishers advts. at end of vols. 2-4. Orig. cl., upr. endsht. with hand-cold. litho. treated paper panel, lr. covers stpd. in gt. & blind, slightly soiled, vols. 2-4 disbnd. (CSK. Feb.13; 176) £550

BAYLEY, Harold W.
- **The Lost Language of Symbolism.** L., 1912. 1st. Edn. 2 vols. Cl. (SG. Dec.18; 386) $130
- **A New Light on the Renaissance displayed in Contemporary Emblems.** 1909. 1st. Edn. 4to. Gt-decor. buckram, worn. (SG. Oct.2; 27) $130

BAYLEY, John
- **The History & Antiquities of the Tower of London.** 1821-25. 2 vols. 4to. Some spotting & offsetting. Hf. cf., slightly marked. (S. Jul.27; 44) *Subunso.* £70

BAYLEY, Richard
- **An Account of the Epidemic Fever which Prevailed in the City of New York during part of the Summer & Fall of 1795.** N.Y., 1796. Inscr. 'Peter Forrester', New York, 1831 on hf.-title & title. Cl.-bkd. bds. (S. Jun.15; 50) *Tait.* £60

BAYLY, Thomas
- **Herba Parietis.** 1650. 1st. Edn. Sm. fo. Spr. cf. gt. by Rivière. [Wing B1511] (S. Mar.16; 154) *Reich.* £280

BAYRER, Leonard
- **Huelfsbuechlein zum Unterrichte der Proselyten aus dem Judenthume, und Protestantism.** Augsburg, 1794. 2 pts. in 1 vol. 12mo. Bds. (S. Nov.18; 642) *Honig.* £55

BAYROS, Franz von
- **The Divine Comedy.** [Vienna], [1921]. 60 mntd. cold. plts. only, lacks text. Cl. portfo., ties. (SG. Oct.23; 17) $210
- **Einundzwanzig Exlibris, mit einem Geleitwort.** Leipzig & Berlin, [1926?]. (500) numbered, with 10 additional bkpltds. 2 vols. 4to. Unsewn as iss., cf. boxes, locks, lacks keys. (SH. Nov.20; 222) *Fine Art Soc.* £160

BAZ, Gustavo & Gallo, E.L.
- **History of the Mexican Railway, Wealth of Mexico.** Trans.:– G.F. Henderson. Mexico, 1876. 1st. Engl. Edn. Fo. Title & some text ll. with lge, stp., plts. with sm. light stp. in margin, lacks hf.-title(?). Linen, spine renewed. (R. Mar.31-Apr.4; 2441) DM 2,400

BEADLE & Co.
- **Beadle Dime No.3, Book of Fun.** N.Y., [1866]. 1st. Edn. 12mo. Staining to margins of 1st. few ll.; contains 3 works by Samuel L. Clemens. Orig. pict. wraps., hf. of spine chipped away affecting lettering, sm. stain on upr. cover, mor.-bkd. s.-c. From the Prescott Collection. (CNY. Feb.6; 48) $1,200

BEALE, Anne
- [–] **Gladys of Harlech; or, The Sacrifice. A Romance of Welsh History.** 1858. 3 vols. 12mo. Errata slip in vol. 1, pencil note by William Wynne also in vol. 1 about accuracy of the history, slightly spotted. Orig. cl. (SBA. Jul.23; 303) *Laywood.* £42

BEALE, Joseph Henry
- **A Bibliography of Early English Law Books.** Camb., Mass., 1926. 4to. Buckram. (SG. Jan.22; 26) $110

BEALE, Thomas
- **The Natural History of the Sperm Whale . . . to which is added, A Sketch of a South-Sea Whale Voyage.** 1839. Slight browning. Mod. hf. cf. (CSK. Mar.6; 67) £65

BEAMISH, North Ludlow
- **History of the German Legion.** 1832-37. 2 vols. Hf. cf. (P. Oct.23; 265) £110

BEAN, C.E.W. & others
- **[Official History of Australia in the War of 1914-1918].** Sydney, 1921-42. 7 vols. Orig. cl., some vols. slightly stained. (CB. Dec.9; 110) Can. $100

BEARD, Charles R.
- Catalogue of the Collection of Martinware formed by Mr. Frederick John Nettlefold. 1936. Fo. Cl. gt., s-c. (P. Oct.23; 159) *Volpe.* £200

BEARDMAN, Thomas
- A Dictionary of the Veterinary Art. 1805. 4to. Cont. hf. cf. (SBA. Jul.23; 228) *Comben.* £60

BEARDSLEY, Aubrey
- A Book of Fifty Drawings.–A Second Book of Fifty Drawings. 1897-99. (550); (1050). 2 vols. 4to. Orig. pict. cl. gt. (S. Jul.31; 182) *Jones.* £80
- The Early Works. Ed.:– H.C. Marillier. L., 1912. Tall 4to. Decor. cl. (SG. Mar.12; 20) $100
- Under the Hill & other Essays. 1907. 4to. Orig. cl. gt. (P. Sep.11; 300) *Hatchards.* £50

BEARDSLEY, Aubrey
See–AFFICHES Etrangers Illustrées
See–BRIGHTON Grammar School
See–MALORY, Sir Thomas
See–POE, Edgar Allan
See–POPE, Alexander
See–THE SAVOY
See–WILDE, Oscar
See–THE YELLOW BOOK: An Illustrated Quarterly

BEASLEY, Robert E.
- A Plan to Stop the Present & Prevent Future Wars . . . Rio Vista, California, Priv. ptd., 1864. 1st. Edn. Orig. ptd. wraps., sewed, slightly soiled. [Sabin 4143] (PNY. Mar.26; 75) $160

BEATON, Cecil
- Scrapbook.–Ashcombe.–Time Exposure.
-Beaton's New York. L.; N.Y., £1937]; [1949]; 1941; [1938]. 1st. & 1st. Amer. Edns. 4 vols. 4to. & 8vo. Hf. cl. & cl., 1st. 3 in d.-w.'s. (PNY. Mar.4; 106) $140

BEATTIE, James
- The Minstrel. L., 1817. 12mo. Crimson str.-grd. mor., gt. borders & spine. Two fore-e. pntgs. side-by-side; from the liby. of Zola E. Harvey. (SG. Mar.19; 109) $400

BEATTIE, William
- Caledonia Illustrated. N.d. 2 vols. 4to. Hf. mor., worn. (PD. Nov.26; 206) £70
- – Anr. Copy. Some plts. spotted. Cont. hf. mor. (CSK. Jul.24; 99) £60
- The Danube. Ill.:– William Henry Bartlett. 1842. 4to. Some lr. margins just stained. Cont. red hf. mor. gt. (SBA. Oct.21; 103) *Schuster.* £190
- – Anr. Edn. 1844. [1st. Edn.]. 4to. Lacks 2 plts., slight spotting. Cont. hf. cf. (SBA. Oct.21; 94) *Schuster.* £190
- – Anr. Copy. Orig. mor. gt. (C. Feb.4; 165) *Amann.* £180
- – Anr. Edn. Ill.:– William Henry Bartlett. [1844]. [1st. Edn.]. 4to. Pol. cf., sides with elab. gt. borders enclosing blind-stpd. ornam., spine gt. with raised bands. (C. Nov.5; 9) *Petscher.* £350
- – Anr. Copy. slight soiling to additional title. Orig. pict. cl., gt., worn. (S. Sep.29; 209) *Dupont.* £210
- – Anr. Copy. 78 plts. (of 80), slight spotting. Recent hf. cl., unc. (S. Dec.8; 227) *Schuster.* £150
- – Anr. Edn. Ill.:– after W.H. Bartlett. Ca. 1850. 4to. Cont. hf. cf. (TA. Jun.18; 504) £180
- – Anr. Copy. Cont. leath., cover loose. (R. Oct.14-18; 2193) DM 1,600
- – Anr. Copy. Lightly soiled. Cont. hf. leath., lacks upr. cover. (HK. May 12-14; 606) DM 1,300
- – Anr. Edn. Ill.:– William Henry Bartlett. N.d. 4to. Cont. hf. cf., very worn. (TRL. Dec.10; 181) £210
- – Anr. Copy. Some spotting. (CSK. Feb.6; 107) £190
- – Anr. Copy. 4to. Orig. cl. gt., 'The Bosphorus and Danube' blocked on spine, corners & extremities of spine worn. (LC. Feb.12; 167) £170
- – Anr. Copy. Some staining, foxing. Hf. red mor. (SPB. May 29; 30) $325
- Le Danube Illustré. Ed.:– H.L. Sazerac. Paris, Ca. 1850. 2 vols. Soiled. Cont. linen. (R. Oct.14-18; 2192) DM 1,350
- Scotland. Ill.:– William Henry Bartlett & others. 1838. [1st. Edn.]. 2 vols. 4to. Hf. cf. gt. (P. Jan.22; 69) *Cambridge.* £120
- – Anr. Copy. Some spotting & staining. Cont. hf. cf. (CSK. Sep.12; 208) £80

– – Anr. Copy. Mor., worn & soiled. (PD. Nov.26; 27) £65
– – Anr. Copy. 4 vols. Slightly foxed. Decor. cf., worn. (CE. Jun.4; 59) £50
– – Anr. Copy. 2 vols. Some stains, foxing. Hf. maroon mor. gt. (SPB. May 29; 28) $100
– – Anr. Copy. 2 vols. Lacks 5 steel engrd. plts. Cont. hf. leath. (R. Oct.14-18; 1879) DM 450
– – Anr. Edn. Ca. 1840. 2 vols. in 1 4to. Some marginal dampstaining. Cont. cf. gt., upr. cover detchd.. (TA. Nov.20; 414) £65
– – Anr. Edn. Ill.:– after Allom, Bartlett & M'Culloch. 1842. 2 vols. 4to. 117 (of 188) engraved titles & plts., some spotting. Cont. hf. cf., worn. (TA. Mar.19; 628) £54
– – Anr. Edn. Ill.:– after Bartlett, Allom & others. Ca. 1860. 2 vols. in 1. 4to. Some foxing. Cont. cf., upr. cover detchd. (TA. Mar.19; 593) £50
– – Anr. Edn. N.d. 2 vols. in 1. 4to. Some staining. Cf. gt. (P. Jul.30; 43) *Brazier.* £75
- Switzerland. Ill.:– W.H. Bartlett. L., 1834. 4to. A few plts. soiled. Cl. (GM. Apr.30; 791) £190
[–] – Anr. Copy. Some spotting. Disbnd. (TA. May 21; 75) £75
– – Anr. Edn. 1834-36. 2 vols. 4to. Short tear in map. Cont. diced cf. gt. (SD. Feb.4; 237) £190
– – Anr. Copy. 2 vols. in 1. Vol. 1 lacks ptd. title. Lacks bdg., part of leath. preserved. (R. Mar.31-Apr.4; 2731) DM 1,500
– – Anr. Edn. Ill.:– after W.H. Bartlett. 1835. Vol. I only. 4to. Some ll. slightly spotted. Orig. cl., worn. (SBA. May 27; 277) *Crete.* £100
– – Anr. Edn. Ill.:– W.H. Bartlett. L., [1835]. Vol. 1. 4to. Fragment, lacks ptd. title, some end pp. & probably 9 other plts., soiled. Cont. leath., worn. (R. Oct.14-18; 1996) DM 650
– – Anr. Edn. Ill.:– W.H. Bartlett. 1835-36. 2 vols. 4to. 2 engraved titles, folding map, 108 engraved plts., lacks ptd. title & plt. list in vol.1, some foxing. Cont. hf. cf. gt., not unif. (C. Mar.18; 158) *Wazzau.* £260
– – Anr. Copy. Slight tears, slight spotting. Mor. gt. (P. Feb.19; 195) *Arts Anciens.* £250
– – Anr. Edn. Ill.:– W.H. Bartlett. F. Salathe after G. Lory, Sperli & Hegi. 1836. 2 vols. 4to. Extra-ill. with 20 views from the 'Voyage Pittoresque aux Glaciers de Chamouni', 1 unsigd. aquatint, trimmed & mntd., 1 sm. watercolour sigd. 'G. Charlton', some plts. stained in lr. edges, occasional spotting, a few of the additional ills. loose or detchd. Cont. hf. roan, slightly worn, unc. As a collection, w.a.f. (S. Nov.4; 487) *Crete.* £500
– – Anr. Copy. Folding map torn, some spotting, slight marginal staining. Cont. embossed leath. (S. Jun.22; 164) *Gal Iris Wazzeau.* £280
– – Anr. Copy. Spotted, a few ll. loose. Cont. mor., covers loose, lacks spines. (SKC. Feb.26; 1626) £180
– – Anr. Copy. Red mor. (HSS. Apr.24; 340) £100
– – Anr. Copy. Vol. 1 only Hf. mor., defect. (P. Jul.30; 68) *Chelsea.* £60
– – Anr. Edn. Ill.:– William Henry Bartlett. ca. 1836. Vol. 1 only. 4to. Mor. gt. (RBT. Jan.22; 4) £95
– – Anr. Edn. Ill.:– W.H. Bartlett. L., ca. 1838. 4to. Port. stained. Cont. hf. leath. (H. Dec.9/10; 622) DM 1,600
– – Anr. Edn. Ill.:– W.H. Bartlett. L., 1839. 2 vols. 4to. Cont. leath. gt., gold fillets. (R. Oct.14-18; 1995) DM 1,800
– – Anr. Edn. Ill.:– W.H. Bartlett, L., n.d. 2 vols. 4to. Cf., 5 decor. spine raised bands, lge. gt. border, inr. dent. (LM. Mar.21; 306) B.Frs. 40,000
- The Waldenses. 1836. 2 vols. 4to. A few minor defects. Cont. hf. cf., worn, spines slightly torn. (SBA. Jul.14; 15) *Salinas.* £100
– – Anr. Copy. Cont. mor. gt. (TA. Jun.18; 502) £70
– – Anr. Edn. Ill.:– after William Henry Bartlett & W. Brockendon. 1838. 4to. MS. numerals in some margins. Orig. mor.-bkd. cl. gt., worn. (SBA. Oct.21; 105) *Dallai.* £110
– – Anr. Copy. Some foxing. Cont. hf. mor. (TA. Jan.22; 406) £80
– – Anr. Copy. Orig. roan, blind-stpd. spines & jnts. very worn. (SG. Oct.30; 46) $200
– – Anr. Copy. Some ll. loose, some tears, foxed. Hf. mor., worn. (SPB. May 29; 29) $125
– – Anr. Copy. Soiled in parts. Cont. leath., gold-stpd., upr. cover loose. (R. Mar.31-Apr.4; 2608) DM 480

– – Anr. Copy. Cont. hf. leath., gt., loose, spine defect., slightly soiled. (R. Oct.14-18; 1855) DM 430

See–PARDOE, Julia–BEATTIE, William

BEAUCHAMP, Alphonse de
- Histoire de Bresil. Paris, 1815. 3 vols. Some spotting. Hf. cf., worn. (SPB. May 5; 97) $250

BEAULIEU, Sébastien de Pontcault, Chevalier de
[–] Plan et Cartes des Villes D'Artois. [Paris], ca. 1670. Cont. spr. cf., spine gt., crowned cypher XS on covers, slightly worn, jnts. brkn. As a collection, w.a.f. (S. Apr.7; 240) *Quaritch.* £250
[–] – Anr. Copy. Ob. 4to. Cont. cf., spine gt. As a collection, w.a.f. (S. Apr.7; 241) *Quaritch.* £200
- Les Plans et Profils des Principales Villes du Comte D'Alost ou Flandre. Paris, ca. 1670. Ob. 4to. Cont. cf., spine gt., slightly worn. As a collection, w.a.f. (S. Apr.7; 238) *Quaritch.* £600
– – Anr. Copy. Cont. spr. cf., spine gt., gt. cypher XS on covers, slightly worn. As a collection, w.a.f. (S. Apr.7; 239) *Quaritch.* £550
– – Anr. Copy. Cont. cf., spine gt., slightly worn. As a collection, w.a.f. (S. Apr.7; 244) *Quaritch.* £480
– – Anr. Copy. Title-p. slightly wrinkled. Cont. spr. cf., spine gt., crowned cypher XS on covers. As a collection, w.a.f. (S. Apr.7; 243) *Quaritch.* £350
- Les Plans et Profils des Principales Villes et Lieux Considerables de la Principauté Catalogne. Paris, ca. 1670. Ob. 4to. Cont. cf., spine gt., slightly worn. As a collection, w.a.f. (S. Apr.7; 242) *Quaritch.* £550
- Plans et Profilz (sic) des Principales Villes du Duche de Lorraine et Bar. [Paris], ca. 1670. Ob. 4to. Cont. cf., spine gt., slightly worn. As a collection, w.a.f. (S. Apr.7; 245) *Quaritch.* £900

BEAUMARCHAIS, Pierre Auguste Caron de
- La Folle Journee. Ill.:– Halbou & others after Saint-Quentin. [Kehl], 1785. 19th C. Engl. red mor. gt. (S. Nov.24; 16) *Maggs.* £75
– – Anr. Copy. With errata lf. Cont. leath., gt. spine. (R. Oct.14-18; 836) DM 650
- Mariage de Figaro.–Lettre sur la Folle Journee. -Eugénie.–Les Deux Amis.–Le Barbier de Séville. Ill.:– Gravelot (3rd. work). Paris & Seville, 1785; 1784; 1767; 1770; 1775. 1st. Edns. 5 works in 2 vol. 1st work: parodies & pamphlets relating to Mariage de Figaro. Cont. cf., gt. fillets around covers, spines decor. with raised bands. (HD. Feb.27; 10) Frs. 2,800
- Oeuvres Choisies. Ill.:– Bovinet, Simonet, Manceau & Adam. 1818. 4 vols. 18mo. Very slight browning. Cf., blind & fillet decor. border, decor. gt. & blind spines, inner dentelles, by Thouvenin-Jeune. (HD. Feb.18; 94) Frs. 2,000
- Oeuvres Complètes. Ill.:– Tony Johannot & Deveria. 1826. 6 vols. Cont. hf. cf. (HD. Oct.10; 217) Frs. 1,600

BEAUMONT, Albanis de
- Travels through the Maritime Alps from Italy to Lyons.–Select Views in the South of France. L., 1795; 1794. 2 works in 1 vol. Fo. Cont. hf. cf., unc. (SI. Dec.3; 56) Lire 1,400,000

BEAUMONT, Cyril
- The Art of Stanislas Idzikowski . . . Ill.:– after Vera Willoughby. 1926. (350) numbered. 4to. Cont. mor. with tooled & onlaid design with some hand-colouring of Harlequin on upr. cover after a plt. by Vera Willoughby in the book. (SH. Nov.20; 135) *Henderson.* £70
- The History of Harlequin. Ed.:– Sacheverell Sitwell. Ill.:– Claudia Guercio. Beaumont Pr., 1926. (325). Sm. 4to. Orig. parch.-bkd. pict. bds. unc. (SH. Feb.20; 416) *Mackenzie.* £50

BEAUMONT, Cyril W. & Sitwell, Sacheverell
- Romantic Ballet. 1938. 4to. Orig. cl. (SH. Apr.9; 15) *Fleming.* £200
– – Anr. Copy. Orig. cl., d.-w. (SH. Oct.10; 412) *J. Mackenzie.* £120

BEAUMONT, Francis & Fletcher, John
- Comedies & Tragedies. 1647. 1st. Edn. Fo. Engraved port. frontis. in 1st. state. Cont. panel. cf., rebkd. preserving orig. spine. [Wing B1581] (C. Nov.19; 51) *Sharples.* £320
– – Anr. Copy. Port. re-margined, tear in title reprd., minor paper fault in 4H3, other minor tears & repairs. Mor., gt. by Rivière. [Wing B1581] (C. Apr.1; 190a) *Hannas.* £220

– – Anr. Copy. Title & port. soiled & restored. Cont. cf., rebkd. [Wing B1581] (S. Mar.16; 152) *A.G. Thomas.* £170

– Dramatic Works. 1778. 10 vols. Old cf. gt. (P. Dec.11; 261) *Quaritch.* £220

– – Anr. Copy. 50 engraved plts. only, occasional browning or spotting. Cont. tree cf. (CSK. Nov.14; 35) £55

– Fifty Comedies & Tragedies. 1679. 1st. Compl. Edn. Fo. Cont. cf., rebkd. Late 17th. C. sig. of 1st. Earl of Dartmouth on title verso. [Wing B1582] (C. Nov.19; 52) *Waddingham.* £55

– – Anr. Edn. 1679. 2nd. Coll. Edn. Fo. Lacks final blank, port. & some ll. spotted, a few stains. 18th. C. cf., spine gt., rebkd., some wear. Bkplt. of Joseph Knight. [Wing B1582] (S. Dec.9; 293) *Quaritch.* £130

– The Prophetess. Ed.:– [Thomas Betterton]. 1690. 1st. Separate Edn. 4to. Sigs. & catchwords occasionally shaved or cropped, some stains. Mor. by Sangorski. [Wing B1605] (C. Nov.19; 53) *Blackwell.* £110

– The Wild-Goose Chase. 1652. 1st. Edn. Fo. With cancel slip on a1v. Cont. cf., rebkd. Bkplts. of the Earl of Jersey & H. Buxton Forman. [Wing B1616] (C. Nov.19; 54) *Brett-Smith.* £300

– – Anr. Copy. Slight spotting. Lev. mor. by Rivière, mor.-bkd. solander case. [Wing B1616] (SPB. Nov.25; 70) $350

BEAUMONT, G.
– Maps & Terrier of Estates in the Lordship of Plumtree Nottinghamshire, the property of W.E. & J. Elliott. 1818. Fo. Cf. gt. (HSS. Apr.24; 264) £90

BEAUMONT, Jean François Albanis de
See–ALBANIS DE BEAUMONT, Jean François

BEAUMONT, John, Geologist & Spiritualist
– Historisch-Physiologisch- und Theologischer Tractat von Geister, Erscheinungen, Hexereyen . . . Trans.:– Theodor Arnold. Halle, 1721. 4to. Slightly browned thro.-out, heavier in parts, slightly soiled in parts. Cont. leath. (D. Dec.11-13; 3) DM 800

BEAUMONT, William
– Experiments & Observations on the Gastric Juice & the Physiology of Digestion. Plattsburgh, 1833. 1st. Edn. Orig. cl.-bkd. bds., lacks most of spine label. Tipped-in pres. from James P. Andrews to James Black, Colerain, P.A., Jan. 14, 1863. (SG. Sep.18; 36) $900

– – Anr. Copy. Spotted. (CNY. Oct.1; 2) $600

– – Anr. Edn. Boston, 1834. 1st. Edn., 2nd Iss. Inscr. 'Samuel Thompson, Reigate' on title-p. Orig. cl.-bkd. bds., spine torn, unc. (S. Jun.15; 52) *Shecter.* £140

BEAUNTER, F. & Rathier, L.
– Recueil des Costumes Françaises. [Paris], 1809-13. Pts. 1-36 in 2 vols. Fo. Lacks title ll., slightly soiled. Later hf. leath. (H. Dec.9/10; 738) DM 850

– – Anr. Edn. Paris, 1810. 2 vols. in 1. Fo. Some slight foxing thro.-out. Hf. mor., brkn. (BS. Jun.11; 307) £70

BEAUTIES of Nature & Art Displayed in a Tour through the World . . .
1763-4. 14 vols., Some worming in vol. 12., text & plts affected. Cont. cf., scuffed & worn. (PD. Aug.20; 105) £100

– – Anr. Copy. 14 vols. 12mo. Cf. gt. (P. Oct.23; 243) £65

BEAUTIFUL BIRDS
N.d. 3 vols. A few plts. detchd. Orig. cl., slightly dampstained. (CSK. Nov.7; 17) £65

BEAUVILLIERS, Antoine
– L'Art du Cuisinier. Paris, 1814. 1st. Edn. 2 vols. in 1. Some spotting. Hf. sheep. Sigd. (P. Nov.13; 264) *Clarke.* £160

BEAUX & BELLES OF ENGLAND
L., Grolier Society, n.d. Connoisseur Edn., (150). 14 vols. Hf. mor. gt. (SPB. May 6; 290) $350
See–JACKSON, Lady Catherine–ANON

BECCADELLI, Antonius
– Alfonsii V Regis Dicta et Facto. Pisa, Gregorius de Gente, Feb. 1, 1485. 1st. Edn. 4to. Spaces for capital initials, the 6 initials supplied in gold with painted backgrounds of blue, red & green, rubricated in blue & gold, lacks 1st. blank & fo. 6 (supplied in facs.), some slight worming, mostly marginal, other marginal defects, mostly restored, faint staining. Cont. Italian blind-stpd. mor. over

oak bds., leath. covers with double rules & leaf-tool ornament, spine ruled to lozenge design, lacks 1 brass clasp, spine restored. From the collection of Eric Sexton. [BMC VII, 1096, Goff(Supp.) B290a] (CNY. Apr.8; 138) $3,000

BECCARIA, Giambatista
– Elettricismo Artificiale.–Nuovo Sperimenti Della Ellectricità Terrestre Atmosferica Cielo Sereno. Turin, 1772-80. Lge. 4to. Slightly soiled in parts. Cont. hf. leath. (HK. Nov.18-21; 478) DM 550

BECHAYEI, Ben Joseph Ibn Pakuda
– Chovat Ha'levavot. Mantua, 1559, 4th. Edn. Outer margins of title & 1st. 3 ll. reprd., sig. of former owners on title, some staining. Hf. leath. (S. Nov.18; 400) *Tedesco.* £550

BECHAYEI, Ben Joseph Ibn Paduka–GABIROL, Shlomo Ibn
– Chovot Ha'levavot.–Tikun Midot Ha'nefesh. Trans.:– Judah Ibn Tibbon. Constantinople, 1550. 3rd. Edn.; 1st. Edn. 2 works in 1 vol. Sm. 4to. 1st. work: mispaginated; 2nd. work: margins reprd., staining, owner's sig. on 2nd. lf. Mod. cl. (SPB. May 11; 79) $5,000

BECHAYEI, Ben Joseph Ibn Pakuda–NORZI, Raphael
– Chovot Halevavot.–Se'ah Solet-Marpe La'nefesh, & Orach Chaim. Mantua; Venice, 1559; 1579. 4th. Edn. (1st. work). 2 works in 1 vol. Initial ll. loose or detchd., some worming. Cf., cover & spine detchd., torn, worming. (SPB. May 11; 37) $1,500

BECHER, Joannes Joachim
– Experimentum Chymicum Novum quo Artificalis et Instantanea Metallorum Generatio & Translutatio . . . demonstratur. Frankfurt, 1671. 1st. Edn. Cont. cf., rebkd. Dupl. from Duveen collection with bkplt. (S. Dec.1; 45) *Quaritch.* £140

– Institutiones chimicae prodomae i.e. . . . Oedipus chimicus. Frankfurt, 1664. 1st. Edn. 12mo. Spotted, stp. & name on title. Mod. hf. mor. (S. Oct.21; 363) *Brosseghini.* £130

– Natur-Kündigung der Metallen. Frankfurt, 1705. Browned thro.-out, slightly stained at foot. Hf. leath. (HK. Nov.18-21; 391) DM 540

– Physica Subterranea . . . & Specimen Beccherianum . . . subjunxit Georg. Ernestus Stahl. Leipzig, 1703. Nailhole thro. 1st. few ll., owner's inscr. on fly lf. Cont. vell. bds., soiled, upr. cover slightly defect. (S. Dec.2; 674) *Barnet.* £220

– Physica Subterranea Profundam Subtarraneorum. Leipzig, 1738. Latest Edn. 2 pts. in 1 vol. 4to. Complete with 3 Supplements & Stahl's 'Specimen', some worming to front. & title. Cont. bds. (R. Oct.14-18; 185) DM 640

BECHSTEIN, Johann Matthias
– Cage & Chamber Birds. 1853. Orig. cl. (CSK. Mar.20; 102) £75

– Gemeinnützige Naturgeschichte Deutschlands. Leipzig, 1795. Vol. IV. Slightly soiled in parts. Cont. hf. leath., very worn. (HK. Nov.18-21; 796) DM 460

– Getreue Abbildungen Naturhistorischer Gegenstaende . . . Nuremb., 1805. Lacks plts. 98 & 99, text browned thro.-out, some plts. browned. Cont. hf. leath., lacks spine. (H. May 21/22; 247) DM 500

BECHSTEIN, Ludwig
– Die Donau-Reise. Hildburgh, 1838. 2 pts. in 1 vol. Ob. 4to. Lightly soiled, plts. minimal browning. Hf. mor. ca. 1860, gt., initials under crown on spine. (HK. May 12-14; 607) DM 2,400

– – Anr. Edn. Ed.:– J. Meyer. N.p., n.d. 2 pts. in 1 vol. Slightly soiled in parts. Cont. hf. leath. gt. (HK. Nov.18-21; 1147) DM 1,800
See–BLUMENHAGEN, W.–BECHSTEIN, Ludwig

BECHTELN, Johannes
– Kurzer Catechismus vor etliche Gemeinen Jesu aus der Reformirten Religion in Pennsylvania. Phila., [Benjamin Franklin], 1742. 1st. Edn. 24mo. Cf. antique, qtr. cf. case. (CNY May 22; 114) $300

BECK, Matthias Fridericus
– Ephemerides Persarum per totium Annum. Augsburg, 1695-96. 1st. Edn. Fo. Errata lf. at end, 1 p. torn & reprd., foxing Cont. cf., gt. spine. (CNY. Oct.1; 3) $380

BECKER, T.A.
– Prospector of Danske Herregarde. Ill.:– Hellesen, Grove & others. Copenhagen, 1850. 4to. & ob. 4to. Slightly soiled. Hf. leath. (D. Dec.11-13; 1339) DM 2,200

BECKER, Wilhelm Gottlieb
[–] Miscellen f. Gartenfreunde, Botaniker U. Gärtner. Leipzig, 1802. 5 vols. Slightly soiled, ex-liby. Cont. bds. (HK. Nov.18-21; 1676) DM 420

BECKETT, Samuel
– All Strange Away. Ill.:– Edward Gorey. [1976]. 1st. Edn. (26) sigd. by author & artist. Mor.-bkd. pict. bds., boxed. (SG. Jun.4; 40) $325

– Comment C'Est. Paris, [1961]. 1st. Edn. 12mo. Wraps., partly unopened. Inscr. to Mr. & Mrs. George Reavey. (SG. Jun.4; 27) $160

– Le Depeupleur. Paris, 1970. 1st. Edn., (7) Hors-commerce. 16mo. Wraps. Inscr. to Mr. & Mrs. George Reavey. (SG. Jun.4; 31) $160

– Echo's Bones & Other Precipitates. Paris, Europa Pr., 1935. 1st. Edn. (250) numbered. 4to. Wraps. (SG. Jun.4; 18) $350

– Fin de Partie. Paris, [1957]. 1st. Edn. 12mo. Wraps., unc., unopened. Inscr. to Mr. & Mrs. George Reavey. (SG. Jun.4; 24) $190

– From an Abandoned Work.–Not I. L., 1958; 1973. Together 2 vols. Wraps. Each inscr. to Mr. & Mrs. George Reavey. (SG. Jun.4; 36) $110

– Happy Days. N.Y., Grove Pr., 1961. 1st. Edn. Wraps. Inscr. to Mr. & Mrs. George Reavey. (SG. Jun.4; 26) $170

– L'Innommable. [Paris], [1935]. 1st. Edn. Orig. wraps. Inscr. to George Reavey. (SG. Jun.4; 21) $220

– Malone Meurt. Paris, [1951]. 1st. Edn. 12mo. Wraps. Inscr. to George Reavey. (SG. Jun.4; 20) $220

– Mercier et Camier Paris, [1970]. 1st. Edn. 12mo. Wraps. Inscr. to Mr. & Mrs. George Reavey. (SG. Jun.4; 32) $110

– The North. Ill.:– Avigdor Arikha. L., Enitharmon Pr., 1972. 1st. Edn., (12) Ad Personum. Fo. 3 orig. etchings. Loose as issued in blind-stpd. wraps., linen s.-c. Inscr. to Mr. & Mrs. George Reavey, each etching sigd. by artist. (SG. Jun.4; 33) $550

– Poèmes. [Paris], [1968]. 1st. Edn., (100) numbered hors-commerce. Sm. 4to. Wraps., unc., unopened. Inscr. to Mr. & Mrs. George Reavey. (SG. Jun.4; 28) $260

– Poems in English. L., [1961]. 1st. Edn. Cl., d.-w. Inscr. to Mr. & Mrs. George Reavey. (SG. Jun.4; 25) $200

– Pour Finir Encore et Autres Foirades. [Paris], [1976]. 1st. Edn. 16mo. Wraps. Inscr. to George & Jean Reavey, in orig. envelope addressed by Beckett. (SG. Jun.4; 35) $160

– Proust. L., 1931. 1st. Edn. 12mo. Pict. bds., d.-w. Inscr. to George Reavey, dtd. 26.3.31. (SG. Jun.4; 17) $400

– – Anr. Edn. N.d. 1st. Edn. Publisher's advt. for the book loosely inserted. Orig. decor. cl., d.-w. (CSK. Jul.24; 64) £50

– Sans. [Paris], [1969]. 1st. Edn., (100) numbered Hors-commerce. Sm. 4to. Wraps. Inscr. to Mr. & Mrs. George Reavey. (SG. Jun.4; 29) $160

– Waiting for Godot. N.Y., Grove Pr., 1954. 1st. Edn. in Engl. Cl., d.-w. Inscr. to George Reavey, Barney Rosset's business card laid in. (SG. Jun.4; 22) $750

– Whoroscope. Paris, Hours Pr., 1930. (100) sigd. Wraps. George Reavey copy. (SG. Jun.4; 16) $1,100

– – Anr. Copy. Orig. wraps. & ptd. band. (SPB. Nov.25; 220) $800

BECKETT, Thomas A', Saint, Archbp. of Canterbury
– Vita et Processus S. Thomae Super Libertate Ecclesiastica; [Petri Bertrandi Libellus de Jurisdictione Ecclesiastica]. Paris, Johann Philippi. 27 Mar., 1495. 2 pts. in 1 vol. 4to. Spaces for capital initials, some with guide letters, initials supplied in alternating red & blue, rubricated, faint dampstaining thro.-out. Early 18th. C. Fr. sheep, spine gt., covers & corners worn. Cont. inscr. on title of P.A. Aurelius, lately in the collection of Eric Sexton. [BMC VIII, 148, Goff T159, HC 15510] (CNY. Apr.8; 119) $2,500

BECKFORD, William of Fonthill Abbey
[–] Azemia. 1797. 1st. Edn. 2 vols. 12mo. Lacks hf.-titles, browned thro.-out. Mod. cl. (SH. Mar.5; 185) *Murray-Hill.* £120

BECKFORD, William of Fonthill Abbey -contd.
[-] **Biographical Memoirs of Extraordinary painters** 1780. 1st. Edn. A few ll. soiled. Later hf. mor. (SH. Mar.5; 186)   *Scott.* £95
[-] – **Anr. Copy.** Cont. tree cf., slightly worn, bkplt. of Earl of Normanton. (S. Dec.9; 455)   *Quaritch.* £60
[-] **The Hamilton Palace Libraries. Catalogue of the First [Second, Third, Fourth] Portion.** –**Catalogue of the Hamilton Library.** 1882-84. 4 pts. in 2 vols., 1 vol. Ptd. list of prices (& buyers' names 1st. 2 vols.) at end of each vol., William Cooke bkplt. & pres. bkplt. of Selwyn College, Cambridge & stp. in 1st. 2 vols. 1st. work cont. cf. by Rivière, rebkd., old spines laid down; 2nd. work orig. wraps. bnd. in, cont. hf. red mor. (SM. Oct.7; 1315)   Frs. 1,700
[-] **Italy; with Sketches of Spain & Portugal.** 1834. 1st. Edn. 2 vols. Engraved plt. tipped in, offset. Cont. hf. cf., lacks 1 label. (S. Oct.1; 502)   £55
– **Italy.**–**Recollections of an Excursion to the Monasteries of Alcobaca & Batalha.** 1834; 1835. 1st. Edns. 1st. work 2 vols. Cont. hf. cf. (SH. Mar.5; 188)   *Quaritch.* £90
– **Library of Books in Fonthill Abbey.** 1823. Cont. hf. mor., rebkd. (SH. Mar.5; 189)   *Quaritch.* £100
[-] – **Anr. Copy.** Catalogue for 37 days sale (of 39), lacks separate catalogue of Furniture, Wines & Miscellanies. Cont. hf. red roan, spine worn. (SM. Oct.7; 1316)   Frs. 1,500
[-] **[Vathek]. An Arabian Tale.** Trans.:– Samuel Henley. 1786. 1st. Edn. in Engl. Some spots. Mott. cf., gt., by Bedford. (S. Feb.10; 408)   *Waterfield.* £200
[-] – **Anr. Copy.** Slight browning. Cont. mott. cf., rebkd., spine gt. Bkplts. of Edward Winnington 1766 & Vivien L. Henderson. (S. Jun.23; 409)   *Traylen.* £160
[-] – **Anr. Copy.** Some ll. slightly browned. Cont. cf. (SH. Mar.5; 179)   *George's.* £140
[-] – **Anr. Copy.** Cont. mott. cf., armorial bkplt. (PNY. Mar.26; 36) $100
[-] – **Anr. Edn.** 1809. 2nd. Edn. in English. Orig. bds., front hinge torn, unc. (SH. Mar.5; 182)   *George's.* £100
[-] **Vathek, Conte Arabe.** Paris, 1787. 1st. Paris Edn. Lacks last advt. lf., some ll. spotted. Later hf. cf. (SH. Mar.5; 181)   *George's.* £100
[-] **Vathek.–A quoi sert un Titre si l'Ouvrage est Bon.** Lausanne; A Tout, 1787; 1789. 1st. Fr. Edn. (1st. work). 2 works in 1 vol. 2nd. work lacks 1st. lf. (hf.-title?), 1 lf. torn. Later hf. cf. (SH. Mar.5; 180)   *Quaritch.* £240

BECKFORD, William, of Jamaica
– **A Descriptive Account of the Island of Jamaica.** 1790. 2 vols. Lacks hf.-titles. Cont. cf. (SH. Mar.5; 178)   *Dawson's.* £190

BECKMANN, Johann Christoph
– **Anleitung zur Technologie . . .** Göttingen, 1787. 3rd. Edn. Cont. vell., lightly worn. (HK. Nov.18-21; 380)   DM 480
– **Beyträge zur Geschichte der Erfindungen.** Leipzig, 1783-1805. 5 vols. Slightly browned, some ll. loose. Cont. hf. leath., very defect. (R. Mar.31-Apr.4; 1211)   DM 1,300
[-] **Historia Orbis Terrarum.** Frankfurt & Leipzig, 1698. 2 pts. in 2 vols. Sm. 4to. Interleaved, with extensive annots. & notes, liby. stps. on verso of title. Cont. vell., slightly wormed. [Sabin 4255] (SPB. May 5; 99) $100

BECON, Thomas
– **The Reliques of Rome.** 1563. 2nd. Edn. Title slightly repaired at fore-e., lr. blank margin torn from f.B4, some side-notes & a few catchwords cropped, title & a few ll. slightly soiled. 19th. C. blind-tooled cf. [STC 1755] (S. Apr.7; 246)   *Laywood.* £95

BECQUEREL, Alexandre-Edmond
– **La Lumière: ses Causes et ses Effets.** Paris, 1867-8. 1st. Edn. 2 vols. Several ll. in vol. II badly ink-stained. Orig. wraps., spines strengthened, unc., cl. case (S. Apr.6; 210)   *Sir G. Porter.* £160

BECQUEREL, Antoine Henri
– **Recherches sur une Propriété Nouvelle de la Matière Active Radiante Spontanée ou Radioactivité de la Matière.** Paris, 1903. In: Memoires de l'Academie des Sciences de l'Institut de France, tome 46ième. 4to. Hf.-title & title of journal, 13 plts. Hf. mor., orig. wraps. of journal bnd. in. (S. Dec.1; 49)   *Rota.* £60

– – **Anr. Edn.** Paris, 1903. 1st. Edn. 4to. Offprint with hf.-title & separate title-p. Cl. (S. Dec.1; 48)   *Rota.* £100
– **Sur les radiations émises par phosphorescence;** (& 5 other papers on the discovery of Radioactivity. Paris, 1896. Together 6 papers in Comptes Rendus . . . de l'Académie des Sciences vol. 122. 4to. Orig. wraps., unopened. (S. Oct.21; 364)   *Barnett.* £220

BECQUEREL, Edmond
– **La Lumière, ses Causes et ses Effets.** Paris, 1867-68. 1st. Edn. 2 vols. Hf. cf., worn, hinges cracked & roughly reprd. (S. Dec.1; 47)   *Dr. Pike.* £65

BEDDEVOLE, Dominique
[-] **Essays of Anatomy . . . according to the New Hypothèses.** 1696. 2nd. Edn. in Engl. Advt. lf., slight browning. Cont. sheep, worn. From liby. of Dr. E. Ashworth Underwood. [Wing B1664] (S. Feb.23; 143)   *Lawson.* £90

BEDDOES, Thomas
– **Contributions to Physical & Medical Knowledge Principally from the West of England.** Bristol, 1799. 1st. Edn. Advt. & errata lf. at end. Mor.-bkd. bds. (S. Jun.15; 53)   *Maggs.* £320
– **Essay on the Causes, Early Signs, & Prevention of Pulmonary Consumption.** Bristol, 1799. 1st. Edn. Cont. cf. (S. Jun.15; 54)   *Phillips.* £120

BEDE, The Venerable
– **The History of the Church of England.** Trans.:– Thomas Stapleton. Shakes. Hd. Pr., 1930. (475). Sm. fo. Orig. cf.-bkd. bds., unc., unopened. (S. Jul.31; 127)   *Ralph.* £70
– – **Anr. Copy.** 2 vols. 4to. Mor. gt., partly unc., by Mansell. (CNY. May 22; 338) $200
– **Venerabilis Bedae Presbyteri Ecclesiasticae Historiae Gentis Anglorum.** Louvain, 1566. 12mo. Cont. cf., worn, rebkd. Pres. Copy, from Sir Robert Cotton to Francis Tate, & MS. notes by them (many cropped), lately in the collection of Eric Sexton. (C. Apr.15; 85)   *Quaritch.* £150
– – **Anr. Edn.** 1644. 3 pts. in 1 vol. Fo. Some slight dampstaining, a few short tears & sm. holes, scarcely affecting text, inscr. on front free end-paper. Cont. mott. cf. Bkplt. of W.W. Greg. [Wing B1662] (S. Jun.29; 355)   *Thorpe.* £50

BEDNY, D.
See–BLOK, Alexander

BEDOUKAIN, P.Z.
– **Coinage of Cilician Armenia.** N.Y., 1962. Orig. wraps. (SH. Mar.6; 317)   *Azezian.* £55

BEDOYA, B.F.G.
– **Historia del Toreo.** Madrid, 1850. Hf. cf., some soiling. (BS. Jun.11; 18)   £100

BEDWELL, W.
See–BUTCHER, Richard–BEDWELL, W. –PILKINGTON, G.

BEDWELL, W.–PILKINGTON, G.
– **Briefe Description of the Towne of Tottenham Highcrosse in Middlesex.–The Turnament of Tottenham.** 1631. Orig. bdg. (P. Sep.11; 256)   *Quaritch.* £180

BEEBE, Charles William
– **Galapagos: World's End.** N.Y., 1924. 1st. Edn., (100) numbered on L.P., & sigd. Tall 4to. Gt.-ptd. cl., gt.-ptd. cl. d.-w. Author's copy, with bkplt. (PNY. May 21; 84) $300
– **A Monograph of the Pheasants.** 1918. (600) numbered. Vol. 1 only. Fo. 1 lf. detchd. Orig. cl., soiled. (CSK. Apr.10; 137)   £120
– – **Anr. Edn.** Ill.:– Archibald Thorburn & others. 1918-22. (600). 4 vols. Fo. Cl. gt. (C. Mar.18; 122)   *Goldfoot.* £750
– – **Anr. Copy.** 4 vols. Fo. Orig. buckram. (CNY Oct.1; 134) $1,500
– **Pheasants: Their Lives & Homes.** Ill.:– Louis A. Fuertes & others. Garden City, 1926. 1st. Trade Edn. 2 vols. 4to. Gt.-decor. cl., orig. d.-w's. (SG Sep.18; 303) $110
– – **Anr. Edn.** 1926. Ltd. Edn., sigd. 2 vols. Unc. bds. gt. (P. Oct.23; 210)   £80
– – **Anr. Copy.** 4to. Parch. paper bds., with gt. medallion, & green bands & tips. (SG. Jan.29; 46) $100

BEECHEY, Frederick William
– **Narrative of a Voyage to the Pacific & Beering's Strait . . .** 1831. 2nd. Edn. 2 vols. 2 litho. plts., 3 folding engraved charts, 1 torn. Cont. hf. cf. [Sabin 4347] (S. Mar.31; 444)   *Remington.* £130

– **A Voyage of Discovery towards the North Pole . . .** L., 1843. 1st. Edn. 1 plt. reinforced at fold. Cont. hf. cf., rebkd. (PNY. May 21; 86) $290

BEECHEY, Capt. Frederick William & Henry William
– **Proceedings of the Expedition to Explore the Northern Coast of Africa from Tripoly Eastward.** 1828. 1st. Edn. 4to. Advt. slip at end, slightly spotted in places, title reprd. in margin. Cont. hf. cf., worn, rebkd. with cl. (S. Jan.27; 570)   *Schierenberg.* £130

BEEDHAM, R. John
– **Wood Engraving.** Ed.:– Eric Gill. Ill.:– David Jones & Desmond Chute. St. Dominic's Pr., 1929. 2nd. Edn. Orig. buckram-bkd. bds., unc. (SH. Feb.19; 79)   *Donnithorne.* £55

BEELDENAER OFTE FIGUUR-BOECK dienende op de Nieuwe Ordonnantie van der Munte The Hague, 1622. 4to. Vell. (LM. Mar.21; 241)   B.Frs. 7,000

BEER, Georg Joseph, M.D.
– **Lehre von den Augenkrankheiten.** Vienna, 1813-17. 2 vols. Slightly soiled in parts, title-lf. stpd. Cont. bds. (R. Mar.31-Apr.4; 940)   DM 850
– **Praktische Beobachtungen über Verschiedene, vorzüglich aber über jene Augenkrankheiten.** Vienna, 1791. Cont. wraps. (R. Mar.31-Apr.4; 941)   DM 460

BEERBOHM, Max
– **Observations.** 1926. (280) numbered, sigd. by artist. 4to. Orig. cl., d.-w. Additional plt. initialled by artist in pocket at end. (SKC. Feb.26; 1245)   £70
– – **Anr. Copy.** Stained. 1 cold. plt. sigd., loosely inserted in pocket. (SH. Mar.26; 73)   *Tate Gallery.* £60
– – **Anr. Copy.** Cl. (SG. Oct.23; 31) $130
– **The Poet's Corner.** 1904. 1st. Edn. Fo. Orig. pict. bds., lacks spine, worn. Pres. copy. (SH. Mar.26; 70)   *Baldur.* £55
– **Rossetti & His Circle.** [1922]. De Luxe Edn. (380) sigd. Cl. (SG. Oct.23; 33) $130
– **The Works.** Ed.:– John Lane. 1896. 1st. Edn. Orig. cl., unc. (S. Jul.22; 24)   *Baldus.* £55
– – **Anr. Edn.** 1922-28. (780) sigd. & numbered by author. 10 vols. Orig. cl. (C. Feb.4; 1)   *Kenyusha.* £230
– – **Anr. Copy.** Sm. 4to. Unc. (C. Jul.22; 2)   *Thorpe.* £70
– **Zuleika Dobson.** 1911. 1st. Edn. Orig. cl. (S. Jul.22; 25)   *Maggs.* £50

BEERS, F.W.
– **Atlas of New Haven County, Connecticut.** N.Y., 1868. Fo. Disbnd., ex-liby. (SG. Aug.21; 245) $120
– **New York & Vicinity.** N.Y., 1867. Westchester Atlas. Fo. Folding maps on special paper, some foxing. Cl., crudely rebkd., worn, ex-liby. (SG. Aug.21; 266) $250

BEETHOVEN, Ludwig van
– **Christ am Oelberge.** Leipzig, [1811]. 1st. Edn. Fo. Soiled thro-out, stp. on title. Cont. paper bds., defect. (H. Dec.9/10; 1050)   DM 600
– **Sonata per il Piano-forte ed un Violino Obligato . . . dedicata al suo Amico R. Kreuzer.** Bonn, [1805]. 1st. Edn. Ob. fo. Cont. hf. leath., mod. linen box. (H. Dec.9/10; 1058)   DM 1,600
– **Studien im Generalbasse, Contrapuncte und in der Compositions-Lehre.** Ed.:– I. von Seyfried. Vienna, [1832]. Slightly soiled, port., title & 1st. ll. slightly browned. 1st. Edn. With supp. Slightly soiled, port., title & 1st. ll. slightly browned, title stpd. Cont. liby. hf. linen. (R. Oct.14-18; 1291)   DM 260
– – **Anr. Copy.** Lightly browned in parts. Cont. hf. leath., orig. wraps., spine very defect. & torn. (H. Dec.9/10; 1063)   DM 460
– **Wellingtons-Sieg.** Vienna, [1816]. Orig. Edn. 4to. Slightly soiled & browned thro-out. Cont. paper bds. (H. Dec.9/10; 1061)   DM 520

BEETON, Mrs Isabella
– **Book of Household Management.** 1859-61. 24 (in 23) orig. pts. (incomplete). 12 plts. only (of 13), some ll. spotted, 1 torn. Orig. wraps., slightly torn & soiled, some loose. (SH. Oct.10; 413)   *Segal.* £90

BEEVER, John
– **Practical Fly Fishing.** 1893. (56) numbered on Dutch H.M.P. Mor. gt., arms. stpd. on covers, decor. corners, silk end-papers with monog., lion

on fly-lf., by Zaehnsdorf. (CE. Nov.20; 175)
£140
– – **Anr. Copy.** Cl., unc. J.G. Heckscher's copy, with 2 bkplts. (SG. Oct.16; 9)　　　　　$160

BEEVERELL, James
– **Les Délices de la Grand' Bretagne & de l'Irlande.** Leiden, 1706-07. 1st. Edn. 8 vols. in 9. 12mo. Cont. cf., decor. spines. (HD. Feb.18; 10)
Frs. 5,200
– – **Anr. Edn.** Ill.:– J. Goeree & others. Leiden, 1707. [1st. Edn.?]. 8 vols. in 9. A few plts. with short tears in folds. Cont. spr. cf., spines gt. (C. Feb.25; 73)　　　　　　　　　*Douwma.* £400
– – **Anr. Copy.** 9 pts. in 8 vols. 12mo. Sig. of Guyon de la Sardière on ptd. title & at end of each vol. Cont. red & olive mor. with yaps, border & corner sprays, gt., in pointillé, flat spines gt. in compartments with sm. pointillé decors. & titles, inner gt. dentelles, some worming. Bkplt. of Marquess of Bath. (SM. Oct.7; 1570)　Frs. 3,800
– – **Anr. Edn.** Leiden, 1727. 8 vols. in 6. Errata notice & advt.-lf. Later mott. cf. gt., gt. monogs. of Earl of Rosebery on covers. (SBA. Jul.23; 434)
Baer. £420
– – **Anr. Copy.** 8 vols. Some ll. loose in vols. 1 & 6, worming to inner margins of vols. 1 & 4, slight dampstaining to some plts. & text pp. Cont. cf., spines gt., worn, lacks some labels. Bkplt. of J.L. Mazuel; as a collection of plts., w.a.f. (LC. Feb.17; 169)　　　　　　　　　　　£130
– – **Anr. Copy.** 12mo. Old cf., 5 spine raised bands, 1 cover of vol. VII detchd. (LM. Jun.13; 77)
B.Frs. 12,000

BEGG, Alexander
See–CHAMPLAIN Society

BEGIN, Emile
– **Voyage Pittoresque en Suisse en Savoie et sur les Alpes.** Ill.:– Rouargue brothers. Paris, 1852. Cont. hf. leath. gt. (D. Dec.11-13; 1271)　　DM 600

BEGIN ENDE VOORTGANG vande Vereenigde Needer Iandtsche Geoctroyeerde Oost-Indische Compagnie 't Tweede Deel
1646. Sm. ob. 4to. Browned. Later qtr. vell. (TA. Jan.22; 181)　　　　　　　　　　　　　£160

BEGUIN, Jean
– **Les Elemens de Chymie, Revues ... par I.L.D.R.B. IC.E.M.** Paris, 1620. Lf. following F1 inserted, marginal tear in B6, hole in C1 at end affecting letters, title scribbled on & inner blank corner torn, some worming affecting letters. Limp vell. (S. Dec.1; 51)　　　　　*Grammers.* £50

BEGULE, Lucien
– **Monographie de la Cathédrale de Lyon.** Lyon, 1880. (385). Fo. Loose in cl.-bkd. bd. folder, linen ties. Inscr. to Grasset. (SG. Mar.12; 23)　　$220

BEHAN, Brendan
– **The Hostage.** N.Y., Grove Pr., [1958]. Pict. wraps. Inscr. to George Reavey & his wife. (SG. Jun.4; 42)　　　　　　　　　　　　$130

BEHMER, Marcus
– **Der Prophet Jona nach Luther.** Leipzig, 1930. (300). 4to. A few pp. at front lightly foxed. Orig. cl.-bkd. paper bds., unc., boxed. Each full-p. plt. sigd. in pencil, & again at colophon, by artist. (CNY. Oct.1; 148)　　　　　　　　$320

BEHN, Aphra
– **The Dutch Lover.** 1673. 1st. Edn. 4to. Some foxing & a few marginal tears, 1 affecting text. Mor. by Sangorski. [Wing B1726] (C. Nov.19; 55)
Pickering & Chatto. £100
– **The Forc'd Marriage.** 1671. 1st. Edn. 4to. Tear in last lf. reprd. Mor. by Sangorski. [Wing B1734] (C. Nov.19; 56)　　　　　*Quaritch.* £300

BEIL, J.A.
– **Stand u. Ergebnisse d. Europ. Eisenbahnen.** Vienna, 1845. Lge. 4to. Cont. hf. leath. (HK. May 12-14; 273)　　　　　　　　　　　DM 900

BEILER, Christoph
[-] **Schau-Platz Dess Niederlandes oder: ... Beschreibung der siebenzehen Provincien desselben.** Vienna, 1673. Fo. Engraved folding map reprd. in fold, folding plt., slightly torn in fold, slightly dampstained, a few wormholes, very slightly affecting plts. Cont. cf.-bkd. bds., worn. (S. Jan.27; 309)　　　　　　　*Forum.* £450

BEKKER, Balthasar
– **Die Bezauberte Welte.** Amst., 1693. 1st. German Edn. 4 pts. in 1 vol. 4to. 1 lf. slightly torn at

margin, title stpd. on verso. Cont. vell. (HK. Nov.18-21; 1909)　　　　　　　　　DM 650

BELCHER, Capt. Sir Edward
– **Narrative of the Voyage of H.M.S. Samarang.** L., 1848. [1st. Edn.]. Orig. cl., faded, unc. (KH. Mar.24; 36)　　　　　　　　　Aus. $300

BELCHER, Henry
– **Illustrations of the Scenery on the Line of the Whitby & Pickering Railway.** Ill.:– G. Dodgson. 1836. Orig. cl., soiled. (CSK. Oct.17; 50)　£55

BELENSON, Aleksandr
– **Vrata Tesnyya [Narrow Gate].** Ill.:– N. Kul'bin (port.), D. Burlyuk (mark). St. Petersb., 1922. (300). Orig. wraps. by Yu. Cherkesov, slightly soiled. (SH. Feb.6; 391)　　　*Kazinikas.* £50

BELGIUM
– **La République Belgique.** Rome, 1789-90. 3 vols. Added at end of vol. 1 Dialogue entre Guillaume Premier, Alexandre Farnèse et Marie Thérèse aux Champs Elysées. N.p., n.d. Cont. hf. cf., limp decor. spine. (LM. Jun.13; 27)　　B.Frs. 7,500

BELGIUM & Nassau; or the Continental Tourist
N.d. L.P. 4to. Orig. cl., rebkd. (P. Jul.30; 63)
Dupont. £160
– – **Anr. Edn.** N.d. Dampstains. Cl. soiled. (P. May 14; 202)　　　　　　　*Walford.* £150

BEL'GYSKY Sbornik [Belgian Collection]
Petrograd, 1915. 4to. Orig. wraps., upr. wrap. detchd. (SH. Feb.6; 392)　　　　*Nijhoff.* £65

BELHOMME, Lt. Col.
– **Histoire de la Infanterie en France.** Paris & Limoges, ca. 1900. 5 vols. Hf. leath. (SG. Oct.30; 50)　　　　　　　　　　　$270

BELIDOR, Bernard Forest de
– **Architecture Hydraulique.** Ill.:– Riguad. Paris, 1737-53. 1st. Edn. 2 pts. in 4 vols. 4to. A few plt. numbers cropped, 1 plt. slightly torn affecting number, very slightly spotted in places. Cont. cf., slightly worn & reprd., not uniform. (S. Oct.21; 339)　　　　　　　　*Barretto.* £670
– – **Anr. Copy.** 2 pts. in 4 vols. 4to. A few plt. numbers cropped, 1 plt. slightly torn affecting number, very slight spotting in places. Cont. cf., slightly worn & reprd., not unif. (S. Apr.6; 211)
Weinreb. £600
– – **Anr. Edn.** Ill.:– Rigaud. Paris, 1737-53. Vols. 1, 2 & 4 (of 4). 4to. Title stpd., minimal soiling. Cont. cf., gt. spine, inner & outer dentelle, gold-stpd. arms on all covers, cover fillets. (HK. May 12-14; 207)　　　　　　　　　DM 700
– – **Anr. Edn.** Paris, 1750-82. Various Edns. 2 pts. in 4 vols. 4to. 217 (of 219) folding plts. Cont. mott. cf. (SH. Oct.10; 414)　　　　*Vine.* £170
– **Le Bombardier François.** Paris, 1731. 1st. Edn. 4to. Cont. cf., spine gt. (CNY. May 22; 152)
$120

BELISARIO, I.M.
– **Sketches of Character in Illustration of the Habits, Occupation & costume of the Negro Population, in the Island of Jamaica.** Kingston, 1837. 2 pts. in 1 vol. Fo. Some browning, stains. Cl., orig. ptd. wraps. bnd. in, stained, some tears, repairs. Accompanied by 4 litho. plts. by Belisario. (SPB. May 5; 100)　　　　　　　$6,000

BELL, Mrs. A.
– **Thomas Gainsborough.** 1897. Lev. mor. by Bayntun, gt., with miniature by F. Gassiez inlaid, 8 semi-precious stones inset, 1 loose, cl. box. (SH. Jan.29; 75)　　　　　　　　　　*Way.* £95

BELL, Acton (Pseud.)
See–BRONTE, Anne

BELL, Benjamin
– **Instituzioni di Chirurgia.** Venice, 1788-91. 1st. Edn. in Italian. 6 vols. Cont. decor. paper bds., gt. spines, slight wear. From the collection of John A. Saks. (C. Jun.10; 14)　　　*Quaritch.* £85
– **Lehrbegriff d. Wundarzneykunst.** Leipzig, 1784-90. 1st. German Edn. Cont. hf. leath., lightly soiled in parts. (HK. Nov.18-21; 385)　　DM 700

BELL, Sir Charles
– **The Anatomy of the Brain explained in a Series of Engravings.** 1802. 1st. Edn. 4to. Inscr. on title. Hf. cf. (S. Jun.15; 56)　　　　　*Norman.* £650
– – **Anr. Copy.** Publisher's catalogue at end, stitching defect, slightly soiled. Cl.-bkd. bds., worn. (S. Apr.6; 11)　　　　　　　　*Canale.* £530

– **Engravings from Specimens of morbid parts preserved in the Author's Collection now in Windmill Street.** 1813. Fasciculus I (all publd.). Fo. Browned thro.-out. Old bds., cl. spine. Dr. J.G. Crosse's copy with sig. on title-p. (S. Jun.15; 58)
Phillips. £260
– **Essays on the Anatomy of Expression in Painting.** 1806. 1st. Edn. (L.P.) 4to. Advt.-lf., ?lacks last blank, F4 torn. Cont. hf. roan, spine defect., worn, contents loose or detchd., unc. (S. Sep.29; 218)
Rota. £60
– **An Exposition of the Natural System of the Nerves of the Human Body with a Republication of the Papers delivered to the Royal Society.** 1824. Light stain in upr. margins at beginning, last p. dust-soiled. New bds., unc. (S. Jun.15; 61)
Rota. £160
– **The Hand ...** L., 1833. 1st. Edn. Mod. cl., ex liby. (SG. Sep.18; 39)　　　　　　　　$300
– **Illustrations of the Great Operations of Surgery, Trepan, Hernia, Amputation, Aneurism & Lithotomy.** 1821. Ob. fo. Name written on title. Cl.-bkd. bds., loose, unc. (S. Jun.15; 59)
Phillips. £400
– **Institutes of Surgery.** Edinb., 1838. 1st. Edn. 2 vols. Advt. lf. in vol. I, liby. stp. & label on title-pp. Cl., loose, unc. (S. Jun.15; 64)　*Phillips.* £100
– **The Nervous System of the Human Body; embracing the papers delivered to the Royal Society on the Subject of Nerves.** Wash., 1833. Cl. Stp. of J. Carson M.D. on title & bkplt. of Walter Edward Dandy. (S. Jun.15; 63)　　*Carmel.* £70
– **The Nervous System of the Human Body embracing the papers delivered to the Royal Society ...–On the functions of some parts of the Brain & on the Relations between the Brain & Nerves of Motion & Sensation (with continuation).** 1830-34. 2 works in 1 vol.; 2nd. work 2 pts. 4to. Orig. cl. (S. Jun.15; 62)　　　　*Phillips.* £320
– **Observations on injuries of the Spine & of the Thigh Bone in Two Lectures delivered in the school of Great Windmill Street.** 1824. [1st. Edn?]. 4to. Advt. lf., liby. stp. in text & on all plts. Qtr. cf. (S. Jun.15; 60)　　　　　　　*Phillips.* £170
– – **Anr. Copy.** Many margins frayed, foxed & stained. Completely disbnd. (SG. Jan.29; 49)
$170
– **A Series of Engravings Explaining the Course of the Nerves.** 1803. 1st. Edn. 4to. Advt. lf. Qtr. cf. (S. Jun.15; 57)　　　　　　　*Canale.* £130

BELL, Currer (Pseud.)
See–BRONTE, Charlotte 'Currer Bell'

BELL, Ellis (Pseud.)
See–BRONTE, Emily

BELL, H.I. & Roberts, C.H.
– **Descriptive Catalogue of the Greek Papyri in the Collection of W. Merton.** 1948. 2 vols. 4to. Cl., gt. (P. Jan.22; 317)　　　　　　　　*King.* £60

BELL, James F.
– **Jesuit Relations & Other Americana in the Library of ...** Ed.:– F.K. Walter & Virginia Doneghy. Minneapolis, [1950]. 1 vol., & the 4 vols. of additions. 4to. Cl. (SG. Jan.22; 227) $110

BELL, John, of Antermony
– **Travels from St. Petersburg in Russia to Diverse Parts of Asia.** Priv. Ptd., 1763. 1st. Edn. 2 vols. Sm. 4to. Cont. diced cf. gt. Bkplt. of Arthur Annesley, lately in the collection of Eric Sexton. (C. Apr.15; 24)　　　　　　　*Dawson.* £180
– – **Anr. Edn.** Edinb., 1788. 2 vols. Cont. cf., worn. (TA. Feb.19; 53)　　　　　　　　　£75
– – **Anr. Copy.** Cf. gt. (P. Oct.23; 5)
Quaritch. £65

BELL, John, Publisher
– **Collection of Illustrations from ... British Theatre, Shakespeare & Johnson's Lives of the Poets.** 1773-78. 4 vols. 8vo. & 4to. 201 engraved plts. Late 18th. C. Engl. red str.-grd. mor., gt., spines tooled in compartments, covers with elab. borders & frames, each vol. similar but not unif. Bkplt. of William Douglas, as a collection, w.a.f. (S. Nov.24; 17)　　　　　　*Maggs.* £3,500

BELL, John, Surgeon
– **Engravings explaining the Anatomy of the Bones, Muscles & Joints.** Edinb., 1794. 1st. Edn. 4to. Upr. margin of title renewed, some notes in ink on plts. by a student, frontis. cut round & mntd., owners' inscr. 'Archibald M.D. 1831 & Robin N. Revill Clarke 1946'. Hf. cf., worn. Bkplt. of Stewart Beauchamp Gwatkin 1888. (S. Jun.15; 65)　　　　　　　　　　　*Rota.* £180

BELL, John, Surgeon -*contd.*
- **The Principles of Surgery.** Edinb., 1801-08. 1st. Edn. 4 pts. in 3 vols. 4to. 12 plts. hand-cold., title of vol. 2 detchd. some ll. & plts. slightly browned. Cont. hf. mor., covers of vols. 2 & 3 detchd., lacks 2 spines. From Chetham's Liby., Manchester. (C. Nov.26; 29) *Riley-Smith.* £500

BELL, John & Sir Charles
- **The Anatomy of the Human Body.** Edinb.; L., 1797; 1803-04. Vols. 2-4 1st. Edns., vol. 1 2nd. Edn. 4 vols. Old marb. bds., cf. spine. (S. Jun.15; 66) *Rota.* £80
- – **Anr. Edn.** 1811. 3rd. Edn. 3 vols. Paper flaw in Aa2 of vol. 3. Cf., rebkd. (S. Jun.15; 67) *Jenner Books.* £80

BELL, Thomas
- **A Monograph of the Testudinata.** Ill.:– Edward Lear after J. de C. Sowerby. [1836-42]. 8 orig. Pts. in 1 vol. Fo. Later hf. cf., orig. upr. wraps. bnd. in. (C. Mar.18; 16) *Goldschmid.* £1,700
See-OWEN, Prof. Richard & Bell, Thomas

BELL, Thomas, Naturalist & Dentist, 1792-1880
- **Anatomy, Physiology & Diseases of the Teeth.** Phila., 1831. Very foxed, lacks fly-lf. Orig. sheep, worn. (SG. Sep.18; 40) $130
- – **Anr. Edn.** L., 1835. 2nd. Edn. Upr. edges of plts. browned, plts. stpd. on versos. Disbnd. From Brooklyn Academy of Medicine. (SG. Jan.29; 123) $190

BELL, W.D.M.
- **The Wanderings of an Elephant Hunter.** L., 1923. 4to. Cl.-bkd. bds. (SG. Apr.9; 337) $180
- – **Anr. Copy.** Three-qtr. lev., spine gt. (SG. Dec.11; 172) $160

BELL'S WORLD OF FASHION & Continental Feuilletons
Jan.-Dec. 1837. Vol. XIV. Square 4to. 7 plts. defect. Orig. hf. mor. (TA. Dec.18; 381) £90

BELLAMY, Edward
- **Looking Backward, 2000-1887.** Boston, 1888. 1st. Edn., 1st. Iss. Orig. cl. gt. Montague bkplt. (SH. Dec.19; 410) *Barry Scott.* £110

BELLAMY, George Anne
- **An Apology for the Life of.** L., Priv. ptd., 1785. 1st. Edn. 6 vols. in 3. 12mo. 8pp. of J. Bell's advts. & index in vol. VI. Cont. spr. cf. (SG. Aug.7; 29) $100

BELLARMINE, Cardinal Robert
- **Institutiones Linguae Hebraicae.** Rome, 1580. 2 pts. in 1 vol. 16 cont. annots., some browning. Vell-bkd. bds., worn, s.-c. (S. Apr.29; 366) *Brill.* £200
See-SCULTET, Abraham-BELLARMINE, Cardinal Robert

BELLASIS, George Hutchins
- **Views of Saint Helena.** 1815 (1 plt. wtrmkd. 1811). Ob. fo. A few short marginal tears. Buckram-bkd. wraps., orig. ptd. label pasted to front wrap., in folding hf. mor. case. (S. Nov.4; 613) *Way.* £350

BELLAY, Joachim du
- **Les Oeuvres Françoises.** Rouen, 1592. 12mo. Mod. vell. (HD. Dec.5; 72) Frs. 1,400

BELLE ASSEMBLEE (La) or Bell's Court & Fashionable Magazine ...
L., 1806-24. 26 vols. Hf. mor., bds. W.a.f. (SSA. Jun.18; 2) R. 610
- – **Anr. Run.** 1809-10. 4 vols. only. Some spotting Cont. hf. cf., worn. (CSK. Aug.1; 173) £110
- – **Anr. Run.** Ill.:– Austin. 1810-1815. New Series. Vols. 1-12. A few minor defects. Cont. tree cf. gt., a few covers detchd. As a periodical, w.a.f. (SBA. Dec.16; 215) *Hyde Park Bookshop.* £160

BELLENDEN, John
- **Works.** Edinb., 1821-22. 3 vols. Hf. mor. gt. (CE. Nov.20; 127) £180

BELLEVILLE, Philippe de
- **Théâtre d'Histoire ...** Brussels, 1613. 4to. 19th. C. linen. (DS. May 22; 873) Pts. 130,000

BELLEVILLE COUNTRYMAN, The
Ed.:– J.P. Osterhout. Belleville, Texas, 1862-65. Vol. 31. No. 1-vol. 6 no. 2; lacks 14 numbers. Newspaper fo. Many iss. with browning & staining, perhaps a 4th. suffer paper loss. (PNY. Mar.26; 316) $600

BELLEW, Capt. F.J.
- **Memoirs of a Griffin.** L., 1843. 1st. Edn. 2 vols. 12mo. Orig. cl., rebkd., spines laid down, buckram folding case. Inscr. (SG. Oct.30; 51) $100

BELLIER de Villiers, A.C.E.
- **Les Déduits de la Chasse au Chevreuil.** 1870. (550). 4to. Some slight foxing. Cont. hf. mor., spine with raised bands. (HD. Feb.27; 81) Frs. 1,350

BELLIN, Jacques Nicolas
- **Description Géographique des Isles Antilles possedées pars les Anglois.** Paris, 1758. 4to. Some browning, stains, slight tears, lacks front free endpaper & a2. Mott. sheep, worming. [Sabin 4553] (SPB. May 5; 101) $500
- **Hydrographie Françoise Recueil des Cartes Marines.** Paris, 1773. Vol. 2. Fo. Cont. cf. (P. Jul.2; 229) *Heald.* £1,800
- **Le Neptune François.** Paris, 1754. Fo. 2 charts inlaid to size, ink-stain on verso of 1 frontis., blank top edges of both frontis. slightly stained, 1 chart loose & unnumbered, front end ll. stained. 19th. C. cl.-bkd. bds. As an atlas, w.a.f. (SPB. Oct.1; 271) $7,500
- **Le Petit Atlas Maritime.** [Paris], 1764. 5 vols. 4to. Vol. 1: map no. 102 torn & reprd., no separate vol. title; vol. 2: map no. 8 inverted, 2 maps numbered 39; vol. 3: maps nos. 3, 92 & 95 appear twice; vol. 4: maps nos. 50 & 109 appear twice; vol. 5: title foxed. 19th. C. hf. mor. & cl., covers detchd. As an atlas, w.a.f., from Chetham's Liby., Manchester. (C. Nov.26; 30) *Burdon.* £2,800
- – **Anr. Edn.** N.d. Tome IV. 4to. Cf., worn. (CE. Mar.19; 207) £190

BELLINCINUS, Bartholomaeus de
- **De Caritativo Subsidio et Decima Beneficiorum.** Ed.:– [Aurelius Bellincinus]. Modena, Dominicus Rocociolus & Antonio Miscomini, May 9, 1489. 1st. Edn. Fo. Capital initial space with guide letter on fo. 1, b4 & A1 soiled, some light dampstaining to upr. portions of some ll., inkstain at fore-edge, slightly affecting some blank margins. Vell., from 15th. C. antiphonal. From the collection of Eric Sexton. [BMC VII, 1061, Goff B302, HC 2671*] (CNY. Apr.8; 106) $1,800

BELLINGER, A.R.
- **Essays on the Coinage of Alexander the Great** N.Y., 1963. Orig. wraps. (SH. Mar.6; 318) *Trade Art.* £55
- **The Syrian Tetradrachms of Caracalla & Macrinus.** N.Y., 1940. Orig. wraps., spine torn. (SH. Mar.6; 319) *Trade Art.* £140

BELLINI, Laurentius
- **Opuscula aliquot ... in quibus ... agitur de Motu Cordis ... de Motu Bilis ... de Fermentis et Glandulis.** Leiden, 1737. 4to. Cont. cf., Fr. royal arms on sides. (S. Jun.15; 69) *Veulemane.* £80

BELLOC, Hilaire
- **The Highway & its Vehicles.** 1926. (1250) numbered. 4to. Orig. buckram. (SKC. Feb.26; 1628) £65
- **Verses & Sonnets.** 1896. 1st. Edn. 12mo. Orig. cl. Inscr., 2 MS. poems (also by author?) on front free endpaper. (CSK. Aug.22; 221) £70

BELLORI, Giovanni Pietro
- **Veteres Arcus Augustorum Triumphis Insignes.** Ill.:– P.S. Bartoli. Rome, 1690. Fo. Slight spotting. Cont. vell. bds., slight wear. (S. Feb.10; 315) *Mistrali.* £60

BELLORI, Giovanni Pietro & Causeus, Michelangelo
- **Picturae Antiquae Cryptarum Romanarum.** Ill.:– Bartoli. Ca. 1700. Fo. Hf. cf. (P. Mar.12; 43) *Cambridge.* £75

BELLOW, Saul
- **Humboldt's Gift.** N.Y., [1975]. 1st. Edn. Qtr. cl., d.-w. Sigd. (PNY. Mar.4; 105) $110

BELLOY, Marquis A. de
See-BALZAC, Honoré de & others

BELOE, William
- **Anecdotes of Literature & Scarce Books.** 1808-14. Mixed Edns. 6 vols. Slight spotting. Cont. cf., gt., slight wear & staining, bkplt. of Holland House. (S. Dec.8; 40) *Forster.* £50
- **De Aquatilibus.** Paris, 1553. 1st. Edn. Ob. 8vo. Some browning & soiling, some ll. slightly defect. reprd., lacks last lf. 19th. C. mor. From liby. of Dr. E. Ashworth Underwood. (S. Feb.23; 146) *Rota.* £240

BELON du Mans, Pierre
- **L'Histoire de la Nature des Oyseaux, avec leurs Descriptions.** Paris, 1555. 1st. Edn., Chavallat Iss. Fo. Pages 149-50, 159-60, 279-80, & 355-6 inserted from a slightly shorter copy of Corrozet Iss., MS. notes on recto of blank A6, slight browning. 18th. C. vell., gt., rebkd., old spine preserved, cl. s.-c. From Honeyman Collection. (S. May 20; 3181) *Simonin.* £780
- **Les Observations de Plusieurs Singularitez et Choses Memorables, Trouvées en Grèce ...** Paris, 1588. 4to. Minor dust-soiling & staining. Cont. limp vell., lacks ties. From Chetham's Liby., Manchester. (C. Nov.26; 31) *Quaritch.* £550

BELTON, William
- [-] **The Angler in Ireland.** L., 1834. 2 vols. Orig. cl.-bkd. bds., unc. (GM. Apr.30; 251) £55

BELTRAMI, Giacomo Constantino
- **La Découverte des Sources du Mississippi et de la Rivière Sanglante.** N.O., 1824. With errata slip, liby. stp. on 1st. & last ll. Cont. qtr. leath. [Sabin 4604] (CB. Sep.24; 174) Can. $550
- **A Pilgrimage in Europe & America, Leading to the Discovery of the Sources of the Mississippi & Bloody River; with a Description of the Whole Course of the Former, & of the Ohio.** L., 1828. 1st. Edn. in Engl. 2 vols. Tipped in errata slip in vol. I, considerable foxing. Cont. mor., gt.-tooled, armorial bkplt. of Earl Nelson. (SG. Jan.8; 34) $190
- – **Anr. Copy.** Lacks 1 plan. Mod. hf. roan, loose. From liby. of William E. Wilson. [Sabin 4605 & 4604] (SPB. Apr.29; 16) $150
- – **Anr. Copy.** 2 vols. Cont. hf. mor., rebkd. preserving mor. spines. (CB. Feb.18; 112) Can. $170

BELTRAMI, Luca
- **Opuscoli.** Milan, 1882-1932. 10 boxes, orig. wraps. W.a.f. (SI. Dec.3; 62) Lire 520,000

BELY, A.
See-BLOK, Alexander & others

BELZONI, Giovanni Battista
- **Plates illustrative of the Researches & Operations in Egypt & Nubia.** 1820. Fo. Lacks 1 plt. Orig. bds. (C. Feb.25; 74) *Cucci.* £260
- – **Anr. Edn.** Ill.:– after Belzoni. 1820-22. Including supp. 4to. 46 plts. hand-cold., marginal tears to some plts., sm. liby. stp. on each plt. Cont. hf. cf. From Chetham's Liby., Manchester. (C. Nov.26; 32) *Remington.* £110
- – **Anr. Edn.** 1821. Atlas vol. only. Fo. Cont. hf. cf., worn, upr. cover detchd. (LC. Jun 18; 136) £160

BEMBO, Cardinal Pietro
- **Della Historia Vinitiana ...** Venice, 1552. 1st. Edn. in Italian. 4to. Sig. on title of Ballesdens & 'Bibliotheca Colbertina'. Late 16th. C. mor., central wreath, gt., on covers, gt. foliate cornerpieces with angel's head, double gt. fillet, sm. lozenge in spine compartments, blind-stpd. arms of Lord Bagot on covers. (SM. Oct.7; 1572) Frs. 2,100
- **Historiae Venetae Libri XII.** Venice, 1551. 1st. Edn. Fo. 18th. C. hf. vell., spine worn. (S. Nov.25; 359) *Crete.* £380
- **Opere.–Della Istoria Viniziana.** Ill.:– Zucchi & Bartolozzi (frontis. in each work). Venice, 1729; 1790. 1st. Coll. Edn. (1st. work). 4 vols. in 2; 2 vols. Fo.; 4to. Cont. vell. (1st. work); & cont. marb. paper bds. From the collection of John A. Saks. (C. Jun.10; 15) *Lyon.* £130
- **Prose, nelle quali si ragiona della volgar Lingua scritte al Cardinale Medici.** Vinegia, 1525. 1st. Edn. Fo. Hf. cf. (CR. Jun.11; 491) Lire 200,000

BEMMEL, Abraham van
- **Beschryving der Stad Amersfoort.** Ill.:– Paul van Liender. Utrecht, 1760. 1st. Edn. 2 vols. Cont. cf., spines gt., worn, ex-liby. (SG. Feb.5; 35) $700

BEMROSE, W.
- **Life & Works of Joseph Wright.** 1885. (100) on L.P. Fo. Orig. hf. mor., cl. box. (S. May 5; 170) *Subunso.* £70

BEN ABRAHAM Ashkenazi of Dobromil, Shimon
- **Nachlat Shimon.** Polonnoye, [1820]. 2nd. Edn., on blue paper. 4to. Cl. (S. Nov.18; 325) *Maggs.* £65

BEN ABRAHAM OF KOSSOF, Baruch
– Yesod Ha'emunah-Yesod Ha'ta'amim, Likutei Shass-Likutei Amarim. Czernowitz, 1853. 1st. Edn. 4 pts. in 1 vol. 4to. Hf. leath. (S. Nov.17; 164) *Valmadonna.* £120

BEN ASHER Hurwitz of Ropschitz, Menasseh
– Lechem Shmone. Lvov, 1876. 1st. Edn. 12mo. Orig. wraps. (S. Nov.18; 300) *Maggs.* £80

BEN BER of Mezritch, Abraham, 'The Angel'
– Chesed le'Abraham. [Czernowicz], 1851. 1st. Edn. 4to. Bds. (S. Nov.17; 131) *Maggs.* £160

BEN DAVID SOSES OF STANISLAV, Pinchas
– Pardes Ha'melech. Buczacz, 1907. 4to. Hf. cl. (S. Nov.18; 318) *Maggs.* £75

BEN ELKANA of Zbarev & Zalozhitz, Joseph Mashe
– Be'er Maim (a Chasidut commentary on the Passover Haggadah). [Medziboz?], 1817. 1st. Edn. 4to. Lacks last lf., 1 torn, slightly browned. Bds. (S. Nov.18; 269) *Bloch.* £180

BEN EZRA, Juan Josafat (Pseud.)
See–LACUNZA, Manuel 'Juan Josafat Ben-Ezra'

BEN GEDALIA of Zloczev, Braham Chaim
– Orach Le'Chaim. [Zolkiev?], 1817. 1st. Edn., on blue paper. 5 pts. in 1 vol. 4to. Wanting title & approbation lf., some worming, without loss of text. Bds. (S. Nov.17; 133) *Elberg.* £120

BEN IEHUDA, Elieser
– Milon Halashon Ha'ivrit. Jerusalem–Tel-Aviv, 1948, 17 vols. 4to. Hf. vell. (S. Nov.18; 538) *Israel.* £75

BEN JOSEPH OF Rosenau, Jonathan
– Zurat Ha'aretz. Offenbach, 1730. 4to. Slight worming. Hf. vell. (S. Nov.18; 706) *Rosen.* £65

BEN MENACHEM Mendel Hager of Kassof, Chaim
– Torat Chaim. Lvov, 1855. 1st. Edn. 4to. Cl. (S. Nov.17; 233) *Low.* £50

BEN MOSHE of Vitebsk, Menachem Mendel
– Pri Ha'aretz. Kopyst, 1814. 1st. Edn. 4to. Title reprd., wormed, without loss of text. Cl. (S. Nov.18; 298) *Bistrisky.* £75

BEN SABTAI of Kosiniec, Israel–[Anonymous]
– Or Israel.–Lehon Chasidim. Czernowitz; Lvov, 1862; 1876. 2 works in 1 vol. 4to. Hf. leath. (S. Nov.18; 264) *Elberg.* £80

BEN SHLOMO CHARIF of Sanatow, Israel
– Tiferet Israel Al Ha'torah. Lublin, 1875. 1st. Edn. 4to. Bds. (S. Nov.18; 265) *Elberg.* £50

BEN SHNEUR Salman of Lubavitch, Dov Ber, 'Der Mitteler Rabbi'
– Ateret Rosh. Kopyst, 1821. 1st. Edn., on blue paper. Hf. cl. (S. Nov.17; 186) *Rock.* £350
– – Anr. Edn. Johannesburg, [1860]. 3rd. Edn. Bds. (S. Nov.17; 187) *Quaritch.* £55
– Kuntras Ha'hitpa'alut Sha'ar Ha'bchira. [Konigesberg], [1831-48?]. 1st. Edn. Notes by Joseph Weiss. Cl. (S. Nov.17; 190) *Lews.* £140
– Ner Mitzvah Ve'torah Or-Kuntras Ha'yichud [i.e. Ha'hitbonenut]. Kopyst, 1820. 1st. Edn., on blue paper. Orig. leath. (S. Nov.17; 192) *Rock.* £160
– Sha'ar Ha'teshuva Ve'hatefila-Chinuch. Shklov, 1818. 1st. Edn., on blue paper. Pt. II only. 4 inserted ll. with typographic changes. Leath., Gerschom Scholem's bkplt. (S. Nov.17; 194) *Rapport.* £200
– Shaarei Teshuvah-Chinuch. Zhitomir, 1864. 3rd Edn. 2 pts. in 1 vol. Hf. cl. (S. Nov.17; 196) *Low.* £70
See–SHNEUR SALMAN of Liadi & Ben Shneur Salman of Lubavitch, Dov Ber

BEN SHNEUR Salman of Lubavitch, Dov Ber -AZARIA OF FANO, Menachem
– Ma'amarim Yekarim.-Yonat Elem. N.p.; Lvov, 1846; 1859. 1st. Edn.; 3rd Edn. 2 works in 1 vol. Orig. bdg. (S. Nov.17; 191) *Zysblat.* £80

BEN YEHUDA Leib Segal, Shmuel
– Likutim Yekarim. Lvov, 1792. 1st. Edn. 4to. 1st. 2 ll. reprd., without loss of text, slightly browned, notes by Joseph Weiss. Hf. cl. (S. Nov.18; 329) *James.* £130

BEN YEHUDA of Ostroho, Yakov Joseph
– Rav Yeivi. Brody, 1874. 3rd Edn. Fo. With notes by Joseph Weiss. Cl. (S. Nov.18; 344) *James.* £85

BEN YITZHAK of Marypol, Gedalyahu
– Teshu'ot Chen. Berditchev, 1818. 1st. Edn., blue paper. 4to. With notes by Joseph Weiss, lacks title-p., slight worming, without loss of text. Hf. cl. (S. Nov.18; 256) *Friedman.* £55

BENARD, Johannes
– Theologica Responsio de Indulgentis. [Poitiers], [Jean Bouyer], [not after Mar. 1483/84]. 1st. Edn. 4to. Unrubricated, faulty inking at a2r with some letters unptd., portion of lr. blank margins of b3 & 4 trimmed away, reprd. marginal tear to bl. Sheep, cover blind-tooled, gt.-lettered spine. Inscr. of Casparus Gueldischourg(?), lately in the collection of Eric Sexton. [C 942, Goff(Supp.) B304a] (CNY. Apr.8; 139) $4,500

BENAVEN, Jean-Michel
– Le Caissier Italien. N.d. 2 vols. Fo. Hf. cf., 6 lge. spine raised bands. (LM. Mar.21; 212) B.Frs. 15,500

BENAVIDES, Fray Alonso de
– The Memorial of, 1630. Ed.:– F.W. Hodge & C.F. Lummis. Trans.:– Mrs E.E. Ayer. Chic., Priv. ptd., 1916. (300) numbered. Cl., soiled. Sigd. inscr. by husband of trans. (SG. Jan.8, 35) $130

[BENAVIDES], Marco, Mantovano
– Opereta Nova Utile et Dilectevole de l'Heremita. Milan, 1523. 2nd. Edn. 16mo. Some marginalia. 18th. C. mor., triple gt. fillet, flat spine gt., inner gt. dentelles, corners worn. (SM. Oct.7; 1573) Frs. 1,000

BENDIRE, Charles
– Life Histories of North American Birds. Wash., 1892-95. 2 vols. 4to. Hf. cf. gt. (P. Nov.13; 184) *Bookroom.* £50

BENEDETTI, Jo. Bapt.
– De Gnomonum Umbrarumg. Solarium Usu Liber. Turin, 1574. 1st. Edn. Fo. 17th. C. leath., worn, spine reprd. (HK. Nov.18-21; 755) DM 1,600
– Die Kunst, gute Sonnen-Uhren zu Machen. Ulm, Frankfurt & Leipzig, 1762. Slightly soiled, MS. note on title & sm. hole. Cont. leath. (HK. Nov.18-21; 756) DM 600

BENEDICT, Saint
– Beatissimi Patris Benedicti ... Trans.:– Dominus Guidones. Paris, 10 Sep. 1521. Slight browning, a few early (cont.?) MS. notes, later inscrs. on title including 'Bellelay' & 'A. Secretan'. Late 19th. C. red mor., gt., arms of Marquis de Trans et de Flayosc on covers. From liby. of André L. Simon. (S. May 18; 37) *Elstein.* £400
– Regula Sanctissimi Patris Benedicti, ad usum Congregationis SS. Vitoni et Hydulphi Accommodata. Paris, 1769. 12mo. Bkplt. of R.P. Aubert, Doctor of Sorbonne, mntd. on verso of title. Cont. mor., vig. incorporating word 'Pax' & Sacred Heart on title-p. repeated, gt., on covers with rococo dentelle border, flat spine gt. in compartments with sm. H. at ft., inner gt. dentelles, gt. & white starred endpapers, 1 corner worn. (SM. Oct.7; 1574) Frs. 1,200

BENEDICTUS, Edouard
– Relais 1930, préliminaires de Y. Rambosson. Paris, 1930. Fo. Loose in orig. cl.-bkd. portfo., ties. (SH. Nov.20; 227) *Monk Bretton.* £110
– Variations: Quatre-Vingt-Six Motifs Decoratifs. Ill.:– Jean Saude. Paris, ca. 1925. Tall fo. Loose as issued in 2 bd. folders, lacks ties, bds. & cl. spine worn. (SG. Oct.9; 28) $450

BENEDITE, L.
– Théodore Chassériau ... Paris, 1931. Ltd. Edn. 2 vols. 4to. Sewed, wraps. (HD. Dec.5; 19) Frs. 2,000
– – Anr. Copy. Slightly soiled. Hf. leath. (HK. Nov.18-21; 3308) DM 550

BENESCH, Otto
– The Drawings of Rembrandt. 1954-57. 1st. Compl. Edn. 6 vols. Fo. Orig. buckram, 5 vols. with d.-w.'s. (S. Jul.27; 188) *Nakajima.* £160

BENET, Stephen Vincent
– The Devil & Daniel Webster. Ill.:– Harold Denison. Weston, Vt., [1937]. (700) numbered, sigd. by author & artist. Linen, boxed. Stpd. 'Editorial copy', inscr. by publishers. (SG. Jun.4; 44) $170
– The Drug Shop. [New Haven], Priv. Ptd., 1917. 1st. Edn., (100) sigd. Orig. ptd. wraps., qtr. mor. gt. s.-c. From the Prescott Collection. (CNY. Feb.6; 16) $280

– John Brown's Body. Garden City, 1928. (201) numbered on L.P., & sigd. Orig. ptd. bds., spine spotted, qtr. mor. gt. s.-c. 5 lines of verse from the book written out on front fly-lf. by Benet, sigd., & dtd. 1931; from the Prescott Collection. (CNY. Feb.6; 17) $280

BENEZIT, Emanuel
– Dictionnaire Critique et Documentaire des Peintres Sculpteurs, Dessinateurs, etc. Paris, 1911-15. 3 vols. Hf. cf., spine defect. (CR. Mar.19; 19) Lire 300,000
– – Anr. Edn. Paris, 1924. 3 vols. Cl. (CSK. May 29; 62) £50
– – Anr. Edn. Paris, 1948-55. 8 vols. Cont. cl. (SH. Jan.29; 76) *Baer.* £155
– – Anr. Copy. Later hf. mor., ex liby. (SH. Apr.9; 54) *Bayley.* £110
– – Anr. Edn. France, 1948-55. Ltd. Edn. 8 vols. Orig. cl. (SM. Oct.8; 2289) Frs. 1,400
– – Anr. Edn. 1955. 8 vols. Cl., worn. (P. Mar.12; 360) *Duran.* £80
– – Anr. Edn. 1955-61. 8 vols. Orig. cl. (SKC. May 19; 140) £95
– – Anr. Edn. Paris, 1956-61. 8 vols. Orig. cl., slightly worn. (SII. Oct.9; 64) *Bloom.* £75
– – Anr. Edn. Paris, 1959-62. 8 vols. A few ll. loose. Orig. cl., 2 spines worn. (SH. Mar.6; 484) *Lund.* £80
– – Anr. Edn. 1960. 8 vols. Hf. mor. by Frost. (S. Jul.22; 132) *Maggs.* £200
– – Anr. Copy. Cl. gt. (VG. Nov.17; 138) Fls. 750
– – Anr. Edn. 1960-56-61. New Edn. 8 vols. Orig. cl., slightly warped. (CSK. Jan.30; 56) £95
– – Anr. Edn. 1960-61. 8 vols. Cl. gt. (P. Apr.9; 244) *Duran.* £70
– – Anr. Edn. Paris, 1966. 8 vols. Orig. cl. (S. May 5; 171) *Duran.* £140
– – Anr. Copy. Orig. cl. gt. (LC. Feb.12; 67) £90
– – Anr. Copy. 8 vols. Cl., glassine d.-w.'s. (SG. Mar.12; 26) $250

BENJAMIN, L.N.
– The St. Albans Raid; or, Investigation into the Charges against Lieut. Bennett H. Young & Command, for their acts at St. Albans ... Montreal, 1865. Red hf. mor., bkplt. (CB. Feb.18; 56) Can. £110

BENJAMIN, of Tudela
See–MENASSEH, David–LOCHMAN–BENJA-MIN, of Tudela
See–MESSANAH Ben Israel–BENJAMIN, of Tudela

BENNET, Christopher
– Theatrum Tabidorum or the nature & cure of Consumptions. 1720. 1st. Engl. Edn. 4 pp. advts. Cf., rebkd. (S. Jun.15; 70) *Quaritch.* £110

BENNETT, Mrs. Agnes Maria
– The Beggar Girl. 1797. 1st. Edn. 7 vols. 12mo. Cf. gt. (P. Dec.11; 263) *Quaritch.* £220

BENNETT, Charles H.
– The Fables of Aesop & Others. Ill.:– Charles Bennett. 1847. 4to. Hf.-cf., upr. cover detchd. (SH. Dec.10; 104) *Gamble.* £50

BENNETT, Charles H. & Brough, Robert B.
– Shadow & Substance. Ill.:– After Charles Bennett. 1860. Cont. red str.-grd. mor. gt. (SH. Dec.10; 103) *Reisler.* £75
Some browning. Mor. gt. by Rivière, s.-c. (SPB. Jul.28; 26) $125

BENNETT, Douglas
– Irish Georgian Silver. [1972]. 4to. Orig. cl., d.-w. (CSK. Oct.10; 94) £65

BENNETT, Geoffrey D.S.
– Famous Harness Horses. 1926-32. (600) numbered, sigd. by the author. 2 vols. 4to. Orig. cl., slightly soiled. (SH. Oct.9; 206) *Way.* £95

BENNETT, George
– Wanderings In New South Wales, Batavia, Pedir Coast, Singapore & China. L., 1834. 2 vols. Foxing in 1st. vol., 1 frontis. defect. at gutter. Early hf. cf., unc. Pres. copy to author's sister. (KH. Nov.18; 50) *Aus.* £230
– – Anr. Copy. Some ll. with marginal fraying, frontis.'s foxed & offset onto titles, slight soiling, bnd. without advts., & directions lf. in vol. 2. Mod. bds. & qtr. mor., unc. (KH. Mar.24; 37) *Aus.* £150

BENNETT, James
– The American System of Practical Book-Keeping, adapted to the Commerce of the United States in its Domestic & Foreign Relations. Ill.:– Willard & Rawdon. N.Y., 1820. 1st. Edn. Title-lf. loose. Later hf. linen, ex-liby. (SG. Mar.5; 27) $110

BENNETT, John Whitchurch
– A Selection from the Most Remarkable & Interesting Fishes found on the Coast of Ceylon. 1834. 4to. Mor.-bkd. bds., contents detchd. from bdg., spine torn. (C. Mar.18; 17)
Schierenberg. £750

BENNETT, Whitman
– American Collectors' Practical Guide. N.Y., 1941. (100) bnd. in hf. mor. Hf. mor. Pres. copy. (SPB. Jul.28; 27) $125
– A Practical Guide to American Nineteenth Century Color Plate Books. N.Y., 1949. 12mo. With the 8 p. supp. No. 1 laid in. Cl. (SG. Jan.22; 54) $120

BENOIST, Felix & Lalaisse, Hippolyte
– Galerie Armoricaine. Costumes et Vues Pittoresque. Nantes, 1848. 3 pts. only (of 5) in 1 vol. Fo. Cont. mor.-bkd. bds. (SH. Nov.6; 226)
Coltman. £600
– – Anr. Edn. Nantes, [1848]. Fo. A few plts. slightly foxed. Hf. mor., worn. (BS. Jun.11; 358) £780
– – Anr. Edn. Nantes, 1858. 4to. Some spotting, stains, tears. Hf. roan, very worn, end-papers detchd. & torn. As a collection of plts., w.a.f. (SPB. May 29; 254) $900
– La Normandie Illustrée. Nantes, 1854. 2 vols. in 1. Fo. Severe damage to last section of vol., tears, foxing, stains. Red hf. mor., very worn, defect. As a collection of plts., w.a.f. (SPB. May 29; 253) $700

BENOIST, René
– Traicté des Dismes ... Paris, 1564. Cf. by Simier, fillet, spine decor. with sm. tooling, inside dentelle. (HD. Mar.18; 19) Frs. 1,000

BENOIT, Pierre
– L'Atlantide. 1919. (50) on Japan. Red mor., 5 fillets, mor. doubls., fillet, wrap., s.-c., by Maylander. (HD. Oct.10; 18) Frs. 3,300
– Eclatement. Ill.:– Gianni Pertini. Ales, 1961. (5) (together 40) numbered & sigd. by artist, Priv. Edn. Supp. series of 3 etchings, sigd. Orig. wraps. bnd. in, cf., sigd. by Leroux 1963, decor., inner dentelles, gold fillets, hf. cf. s.-c., suede lined, wood decor. cover. (D. Dec.11-13; 1131)
DM 8,000
– Le Puits de Jacob. Ed.:– A. De Monzie (preface). Ill.:– Arthur Szyk. Paris, 1927. (300) numbered on velin d'arches. Fore-edge slightly soiled. Cl. (SPB. May 11; 240) $300
– Voyage à Surinam. Brussels, 1839. 1st. Edn. Fo. Spotted, hf.-title detchd., upr. hinge brkn. Cont. hf. roan, worn. [Sabin 4737] (S. Nov.4; 656)
Maggs. £120

BENSON, Arthur Christopher & Weaver, Sir Lawrence
– Book of the Queen's Doll's House. 1924. Ltd. Edn. 2 vols. 4to. Orig. linen-bkd. bds., unc. spare lettering pieces, d.-w.'s, s.-c. (MMB. Oct.8; 61)
Waley. £90
– – Anr. Copy. Orig. cl.-bkd. bds., 1 spine slightly worn, unc., s.-c. (SKC. Jul.28; 2437) £60
– – Anr. Copy. Linen-bkd. bds., unc. (SG. Apr.30; 260) $275
– – Anr. Copy. Linen-bkd., gt.-armorial bds., outer corners slightly worn. (PNY. Dec.3; 55) $100

BENSON, Robert
– Sketches of Corsica. 1825. [1st. Edn.?]. Vig. title, 5 cold. aquatint plts., lacks 'directions to binder'. Mod. hf. cf. gt. (C. Jul.15; 10)
Taylor. £240
– – Anr. Copy. Cont. cf. (SH. Jun.11; 2)
Thorp. £60

BENTHAM, James
– History & Antiquities of the Conventual & Cathedral Church of Ely. 1770. 1st. Edn. 4to. Slight foxing. Cont. cf. gt., rebkd. (TA. Nov.20; 84) £90
– – Anr. Edn. Camb. & Norwich, 1771 & 1817. 3 vols. in 2 (including supp. to the 2nd. edn.). 4to. Cont. spr. cf., spines gt. From the collection of Eric Sexton. (C. Apr.16; 215) *Traylen.* £100

BENTHAM, Jeremy
– Chrestomathia: being a Collection of Papers, explanatory of the Design of an Institution. 1816. 1st. Edn. Hf.-title, slightly browned. Cont. hf. cf., worn, lacks spine, cover detchd. (SH. Oct.10; 289)
Drury. £85
– Defence of Usury. Phila., 1796. 1st. Amer. Edn. 12mo. Slight browning, blank portion torn from head of title, advt. lf. at end. Cont. sheep, slightly worn. (S. Jan.26; 231)
University College Library. £100
– Théorie des Peines et des Recompenses ... Trans.:– M. et Dumont. L., 1811. 2 vols. With final advt. lf. Old cf. (KH. Mar.24; 38) Aus. $240

BENTHAM, Sir Samuel
– Services rendered in the Civil Department of the Navy. 1813. Bound with 4 other pamphlets (V.d.), 3(?) separately paginated, & 2(?) separately titled. Cf. gt., Marquis of Bute's armorial bearings surrounded by collar & badge of the Order of the Bath in gt. on both covers. Marquis of Bute's copy, inscr. by author 'To Sir Charles Stuart K.B. . . . (LC. Oct.2; 205) £60

BENTIVOGLIO, Cardinal Guido
– Della Guerra di Fiandra. Cologne, 1633-39. 3 vols. 4to. Sig. of D.P.? de St. Aignan Episc. Belvai on title, Ragley Hall bkplt. 18th. C. red mor., triple gt. fillet, spine gt. in compartments with label with crest of Joseph Gulston & date of each vol., inner gt. dentelles. Marquess of Hertford's copy. (SM. Oct.7; 1575) Frs. 4,200
– The History of the Warrs of Flanders. –Historicall Relations of the United Provinces of Flanders. Trans.:– Henry, Earle of Monmouth. 1654; 1652. 1st. Edns. 2 wrks. in 1 vol. Fo. Slight browning & soiling. Cont. cf., rebkd., slightly worn. [Wing B1910; 1911] (S. Sep.29; 7)
Van Haverberge. £120

BENTLEY, Richard
– Designs for Six Poems ... 1753. Fo. Cont. cf. (SH. Jul.9; 113) *Swales.* £90

BENTZON, T.
– Jacqueline. Ill.:– Albert Lynch. Paris, 1893. 4to. Plts. engraved on India paper, 5 orig. drawings & 2 orig. watercolours mntd. at beginning & end, 6 proofs & 1 prospectus loosely inserted. Red mor., decor. spine, border of 2 fillets & 2 gt. corner fleurons, wrap. preserved. (SM. Feb.11; 188)
Frs. 4,500

BENVENUTO
– The Passenger. 1612. 1st. Edn. 4to. Slight foxing on titles. 17th. C. cf., rebkd. [STC 1896] (C. Nov.20; 218) *A. Thomas.* £300

BENZO, Hugo, Senensis
– Consilia ... que a vertice ad plantam pedis omnium egritudinum materias causas, signa & remedia copiosissime discutiunt. Ed.:– C. Astarius. Flor., Feb. 1523. Fo. Minor stains on title & a few other ll., sm. holes in blank margin of title. Antique-style cf. (C. Apr.1; 8) *Corby.* £65

BENZONI, Girolamo
– La Historia del Mondo Nuovo. Venice, 1572. 2nd Edn. Some browning. Later vell. bds., slightly soiled Bkplt. of F.W. Dahlgren. [Sabin 4791] (S. May 5; 43) *Elliot.* £220
– Novae Novi Orbis Historiae, id est, Rerum ab Hispanis in India Occidentali hactenus Gestarum. [Geneva], 1578. 1st. Latin Edn. Mor. by Lortic with his ticket. [Sabin 4792] (SPB. May 5; 102) $1,100

See– BRY, Theodore de & others

BEOWULF
– Tale of Beowulf. Hammersmith, Kelms. Pr. 1895. (300). 4to. End-papers slightly soiled. Vell., worn & discold. (SPB. Nov.25; 318) $350
– – Anr. Edn. Trans.:– William Morris & A.J. Wyatt. [Kelms. Pr.]. [1895]. [308]. 4to. Orig. limp vell., silk ties. (CSK. Apr.3; 79) £280

BÉQUET, Etienne
– Marie ou le Mouchoir Bleu. Ill.:– Sta. Paris, 1884. (1200). 18mo. Some pp. spotted. Mor. by Dervois, mosaic & gold rose bud in corners of covers & spine, border of 4 fillets, 2 with gold dots, inside dentelle, wrap. preserved. (SM. Feb.11; 189)
Frs. 1,000

BERAB, Yakov
– Zimrat Ha'aretz. Livorno, 1829. 2nd. Edn. In Hebrew & Ladino, slight discoloration. Bds. (S. Nov.18; 584) *Rapoport.* £70

BERACHIA BEIRACH
– Zera Beirach Shlishi. Halle, 1714. 1st. Edn. Fo. Cl. (S. Nov.18; 585) *Rock.* £90

BERALDI, H.
See– PORTALIS, Baron Roger & Beraldi, H.

BÉRANGER, Pierre Jean de
– Les Chansons ... Ill.:– Devéria (vigs.); Henri Monnier (drawings). Paris, 1828. 3 vols. Hf. mor. by Lortic, corners, spines decor. with raised bands, s.-c. (HD. Jun.24; 151) Frs. 1,300
– – Anr. Edn. Ill.:– Deveria, Bellanger, Tony Johannot, etc. Paris & Brussels, 1829-33. 5 vols. Plts. mntd. on cold. paper. Cont. cf., decor. spines, covers decor. with blind, roulettes between gt. fillets, inner dentelle. (HD. Apr.9; 396)
Frs. 1,300
– Oeuvres Complètes. Ill.:– after Grandville & Raffet. Paris, 1836. 3 vols. Slightly spotted. Cont. cf.-bkd. bds. (SH. Nov.20; 152) *Droller.* £50
– – Anr. Edn. Ill.:– Grandville & Raffet. Paris, 1837. 3 vols. Hf.-titles. Cont. hf. cf., partly unc. (SI. Dec.3; 67) Lire 220,000

BERCKENMEYER, P.L.
– Vermehrter Curieuser Antiquarius. Hamburg, 1711-[1712]. 2 vols. in 1. 29 (of 30), most folding, copperplts., 2 defect. Cont. vell., browned & soiled. (R. Oct.14-18; 1831) DM 830

BERENGER, Baron de
– Helps & Hints how to Protect Life & Property. Ill.:– George & Robert Cruikshank. 1835. 19th. C. hf. mor., spine gt. (S. Nov.24; 66) *Way.* £60

BERENSON, Bernhard
– The Drawings of Florentine Painters. Chic., 1938. 3 vols. 4to. Orig. cl. (SH. Jan.29; 77)
Phillips. £60

BERESFORD, Capt. G. de la Poer
– Twelve Sketches in double tinted lighography of Scenes in Southern Albania. 1855. Fo. Dampstained thro-out, marginal tears, soiled. Unbnd. (CSK. Jan.9; 132) £270

BERESFORD, James
– The Miseries of Human Life. 1807. 8th. Edn. 2 vols. A few plts. torn & reprd. Cont. cf., worn. (CSK. Mar.13; 18) £50

BERETTINI, Petro
See– DORIGNY, Nicolaus–BERETTINI, Petro –ALBANI, F.–BERETTINI, Petro–BARTOLUS, P.S.

BERG, Johann August
– Sverige Framstaldt i Taflor, nittiosex Lithografier tontryck med beskrifvande text. Goteberg, 1850-56. 24 pts. Ob. fo. Orig. ptd. wraps. (S. Oct.20; 25) *Lind.* £380

BERG, J.S.
– Bilder ur Svenska Folklifvet. Ill.:– Nordenberg, Zoll & others. Gotheborg, 1855. Fo. 12 chromolitho. plts., stained thro.-out. Leath.-bkd. bds. (SG. Oct.30; 100) $200

BERGAMIN, José
– El Arte de Birlibirlogue. Ill.:– Maruja Mallo, Rafael Alberti. Madrid, 1930. 1st. Edn. 4to. Linen, wraps. Ills. sigd. & dtd., A. dedication (DS. Apr.24; 1026) Pts. 50,000

BERGE, F.
– Schmetterlings-Buch. Ed.:– H.V. Heinemann. Stuttgart, 1876. 4to. Orig. linen gt. (HK. Nov.18-21; 732) DM 800

BERGENGRUEN, W.
– Die Drei Falken. Ill.:– Felix Hoffmann. Frankfurt, 1956. (350) numbered, sigd. by author & artist on printer's mark. Mor. Orig. hf. vell. gt., by W. Pingel, s.-c. (D. Dec.11-13; 997) DM 450

BERGERAC, Cyrano de
– Les Ouvres Diverses. Amst., 1710. 2 vols. Cont. diced cf., decor. spines, slightly worn. (SM. Feb. 11; 124) Frs. 1,200

BERGERET, Jean Pierre
– Phytonomatotechnie Universelle. Paris, 1783-84. Vols. I & II (of 3). Fo. Some outer margins stained &/or strengthened in vol. I. Hf. cf., worn. W.a.f. (S. Jun.1; 70) *Carr.* £350

BERGERON, L.E.
– Manuel du Tourneur. Ed.:– P. Hamelin-Bergeron. Paris, 1816. 2nd. Edn., sigd. by Ed. 3 vols. including the plt. vol. 4to. 1 plt. cleanly torn, 1 detchd., occasional slight damp

staining. Cont. marb. cf. (CSK. Feb.13; 102)
£130

BERGHAUS, Hans
– Physikalischer Atlas. Gotha, 1845-48. Fo. & lge. ob. fo. Slightly soiled in parts. Cont. hf. leath., worn. (HK. Nov.18-21; 388)   DM 1,400

BERGMAN, Torbern.
– A Dissertation on Elective Attractions. Trans.:– [Thomas Beddoes]. 1785. 1st. Engl. Edn. Some wormholes, mostly marginal, bookblock brkn., slightly spotted in places. Orig. bds., worn, covers detchd. (S. Dec.2; 677)   Phelps. £70
– – Anr. Edn. 1788-91. 3 vols. Some slight browning. Cont. cf., spines gt. (S. May 5; 417)
Hannas. £150

BERGOMENSIS Forestus, Jacobus Philippus
– De Claris Selectisque Mulieribus. Ed.:– [Albertus de Placentia & Augustinus de Casali Maiori]. Ferrara, Laurentius de Rubeis, de Valentia. Apr.29, 1497. 1st. Edn. Fo. Very sm. hole in last. lf., last gathering rehinged. Cont. oak bds., blind-stpd. mor. spine, vell. & brass clasps, mor. restored at edges but with some slight worming, qtr. mor. gt. folding case. Etched bkplt. with initials MB, later the copy of Fritz Kreisler & John A. Saks. [BMC VI, 613, Goff J204, HC 2813] (CNY. Oct.1; 86) $16,000
– De Plurimis Claris Sceletisque Mulieribus. Ferrara, Lorenzo Rossi, 29 Apr. 1497. 1st. Edn. Fo. Sm. wormhole in woodcut border of A1 verso, which also has sm. ink scribbles over some figures. Mod. mor. in buckram case. [Hain 2813*; BMC VI-613; Goff J-204] (C. Apr.1; 9)
Mediolanum. £4,000
– Nouissime Hystoriarum omnium Repercussiones. Venice, May 1503. Fo. 3 full-p. woodcuts (of 4, lacks b1-2), occasional severe staining at beginning, title partly detchd. 17th. C. cf., lr. jnt. & corners reprd. (C. Nov.20; 177)   Watson. £700
– Supplementum Chronicarum ... Venice, Bernardinus Benalius. Dec.15, 1486. Fo. 263 ll. (of 274, lacks all before quire c, save 1 lf. which is loose), woodcut ills. & initials cold. by early hand as far as 18v, many tears, several wormholes at end, slightly affecting text, upr. fore-corners dampstained thro.-out with the last 2 ll. defect. Cont. South German blind-stpd. pig over wood bds., worn, lacks lge. portion of pig on upr. cover & smaller amount on lr. cover, lacks clasps. [BMC V, 371, Goff J210, HC 2807*] (S. Feb.10; 210)   Sinistri. £360
– Supplementum Supplement Chronicarum. Venice, 20 Aug. 1513. Fo. Worming in upr. margins at end affecting text slightly, a few wormholes in text at beginning & end. Mod. vell. (S. Jun.23; 202)   Staley. £320

BERGSTRASSER, J.A.B.
– Ueber sein am 21. Dezember, 1784. angekündigtes Problem einer Korrespondez in ab- und unabsehbaren Weiten der Krigsvorfälle, oder über Synthematographik. Hanau, 1785. 1st. Edn. 5 vols. Cont. bds. (R. Oct.14-18; 482)   DM 1,600

BERICHT, Kurtzer und gründlicher
– Wie sich jeder meniglich für der erschröcklichen Seuche der Pestilentz praeservieren ... und recht curirt werden soll ... jetzo aber wider übersehen, gemehret, und in den Truck gegeben. Regensburg, 1599. 4to. Slightly soiled in pts., a few marginal tears. Disbnd., spine strengthened with black paper. (S. Jan.27; 310)   Goldschmidt. £160

BERINGER, L.A.
– Hans Thoma. Rudierungen. Munich, 1923. 4to. Orig. hf. vell. (HK. Nov.18-21; 2970)   DM 680

BERINGTON, Joseph
– Letters on Materialism & Hartley's Theory of the Human Mind Addressed to Dr. Priestley. 1776. New cl., cf. spine. (S. Dec.1; 345) Blackwell. £60

BERKELEY, George
– Alciphron: or, The Minute Philosopher. 1732. 1st. Edn. 2 vols. Cont. panel. cf., rebkd. (S. Oct.21; 440)   Thoemmes. £55
– An Essay Towards a New Theory of Vision. Dublin, 1709. 2nd. Edn., Thick paper. Errata slip pasted on b4v, sm. tear to 4 ll. Cf. gt., upr. cover detchd. Inscr. on title 'From the library of the Rt. Honb. Joseph Addison at Bilton near Rugby'. (LC. Jun.18; 242)   £140
– A Treatise Concerning the Principles of Human Knowledge. 1734. Mod. hf.cf. (S. Dec.8; 155)
Lawson. £60

– Works. Ed.:– Rev. A.A. Luce & T.E. Jessop. 1948-57. 1st. Edns. 9 vols. Cl., some with wraps. (HSS. Apr.24; 425)   £90

BERKENHOUT, John–HAMILTON, Robert M.D., of Ipswich
– Symptomatology.–Remarks on the means of obviating the Fatal Effects of the Bite of a Mad dog or other Rabid Animal. 1st. work priv. ptd. 1784; 1785. 1st. work 1st. Edn. 2 works in 1 vol. Liby. stps., 1st. work with advt. lf. New cl. (S. Jun.15; 73)   Whitehart. £50

BERKOWITZ, David Sandler
– In Remembrance of Creation; Evolution of Art & Scholarship in the Medieval & Renaissance Bible. Waltham, Massachusetts, 1968. 4to. Cl. (S. Nov.17; 56)   Kingsgate. £90

BERLIN Olympic Games, 1936
– Die Olympischen Spiele 1936 in Berlin und Garmisch-Partenkirchen   Altona Cigaretten-Bilderdienst. 1936. 2 vols. Fo. Ill. with tipped in photographs. No bdg. stated, d.-w. (JL. Jul.20; 881)   Aus. $100

BERLINER, Rudolf
– Die Bildwerke d. Bayer. National museum. Augsburg, 1926. Pt. 4. Orig. linen. (HK. Nov.18-21; 3452)   DM 600

BERLINER, Rudolf & Borchardt, P.
– Silberschmiedearbeiten aus Kurdistan. Berlin, 1922. Fo. Orig. cl.-bkd. bds. (SH. Jul.23; 255)
Ad Orientem. £60

BERLIOZ, Hector
– Episode de la Vie d'un Artiste. Paris, [1845]. 1st. Edn. Fo. Slightly soiled thro.-out, liby. stp. Hf. leath. (H. Dec.9/10; 1070)

BERLYN, Mrs. Alfred 'Vera'
– Sunrise-Land; Rambles in Eastern England. Ill.:– Arthur Rackham & others. L., 1894. 1st. Edn., 1st. Iss. Advts. Cl. Raymond M. Sutton Jr. copy. (SG. May 7; 27) $130

BERMAN, E.
– Art & Artists of South Africa ... Cape Town, 1970. 4to. Orig. bdg., d.-w. (VA. May 8; 276)
R. 90
– – Anr. Edn. Cape Town, 1973. (200). 4to. Hf. mor., d.-w. (SSA. Jan. 22; 160)   R. 95

BERMONDSEY Book, The
Dec., 1923-Mar./Apr./May, 1930. Vol. I no. 1-Vol. VIII no. 2 (compl.). 4to. Orig. ptd. wraps. (LC. Feb.12; 300)   £100

BERNANOS, Georges
– Journal d'un Curé de Campagne. 1936. (50) on pur fil Lafuma. Sewed. (HD. Oct.10; 20)
Frs. 900

BERNARD, Saint, Abbot of Clairvaux
– Epistola melliflui Bernardi ... de Regimine Domus. [Leipzig], 1509. Sm. 4to. Many cont. MS. notes glossing the text, browned, sm. wormholes, slightly affecting text. Mod. vell. bds., slightly soiled. From liby. of André L. Simon. (S. May 18; 38)   Schaeffer. £65
– Flores. Venice, 31st. Aug., 1503. Owner's inscr. on title, very slightly dampstained at end. Cont. blind-stpd. cf., worm, neatly reprd., lacks clasps. (S. Dec.8; 116)   Bart. £70

BERNARD, Auguste
– Geofroy Tory ... an account of his life & works ... Trans.:– George B. Ives. Ill.:– After Bruce Rogers. Boston & N.Y., River. Pr. 1909. (370). Orig. bds., buckram spine, gt., unc., publisher's s.-c. The John A. Saks copy. (CNY. Oct.1; 149) $280

BERNARD, Charles
– Gerfaut. Ill.:– Manesse after Weisz. Paris, 1889. (50) on Jap., numbered. 4to. Hf. mor. by Charles Meunier, mosaic olive tree on spine, wrap. preserved. (SM. Feb.11; 190)   Frs. 1,200

BERNARD, Claude
– Leçons de Physiologie Experimentale Appliquée a la Médecine. Paris, 1855-56. 1st. Edn. 2 vols. Loose. Orig. wraps., with some of lr. cover advts. referring to works publd. in 1857, slightly worn, spines split, unc. From liby. of Dr. E. Ashworth Underwood. (S. Feb.23; 149)   Quaritch. £90
– – Anr. Copy. A few spots, no advt. ll. New cl. (S. Jun.15; 74)   Rota. £50
– – Anr. Copy. 2 vols. in 1. Some notes on fly-lf. Hf. mor., worn. (SG. Jan.29; 54) $275

– Leçons de Physiologie Operatoire. Paris, 1879. 1st. Edn. A little spotting. Cl., lacks spine. From liby. of Dr. E. Ashworth Underwood. (S. Feb.23; 150)   Quaritch. £100
– – Anr. Copy. Orig. ptd. wraps., unc. & unopened. (S. Jun.15; 77)   Zeitlin & Verbrugge. £80
– Leçons sur la Chaleur Animale, sur les Effets de la Chaleur, et sur la Fièvre. Paris, 1876. 1st. Edn. A little spotting. Mod. buckram-bkd. bds., slightly marked. From liby. of Dr. E. Ashworth Underwood. (S. Feb.23; 151)   Quaritch. £65
– Leçons sur la Physiologie et la Pathologie du Systéme Nerveux. Paris, 1858. 1st. Edn. 2 vols. Cont. red mor.-bkd. marb. bds. From liby. of Dr. E. Ashworth Underwood. (S. Feb. 23; 153)   Quaritch. £130
– – Anr. Copy. No advt. ll. Fr. qtr. cf., leath. at top of vol. II scraped. (S. Jun.15; 75)   Pratt. £75
– – Anr. Copy. 2 vols. in 1. Orig. bdg., cl. spine, ex-liby. (SG. Jan.29; 55) $180
– Leçons sur la Diabète et la Glycogenèse Animale. Paris, 1877. 1st. Edn. Orig. wraps., spine gt. From liby. of Dr. E. Ashworth Underwood. (S. Feb.23; 152)   Quaritch. £100
– Leçons sur les Effets des Substances Toxiques et Médicamenteuses. Paris, 1857. 1st. Edn. A little spotting. Cont. red mor.-bkd. marb. bds. From liby. of Dr. E. Ashworth Underwood. (S. Feb.23; 154)   Quaritch. £65
– Leçons sur les Propriétés des Tissus Vivants. Paris, 1866. 1st. Edn. A little spotting, some underlinings in text. Mod. mor.-bkd. marb. bds. From liby. of Dr. E. Ashworth Underwood. (S. Feb.23; 156)   Quaritch. £60
– Leçons sur les Propriétés Physiologiques et les Alterations Pathologiques des Liquides de l'Organisme. Paris, 1859. 1st. Edn. 2 vols. Cont. red mor.-bkd. marb. bds. From liby. of Dr. E. Ashworth Underwood. (S. Feb.23; 157)   Asherson. £100
– Rapport sur les Progres et la Marche de la Physiologie Générale en France. Paris, 1867. 1st. Edn. Hf. mor., orig. ptd. wraps. bound in. (SG. Sep.18; 41) $150
– Sur une Nouvelle Fonction du Foie chez l'Homme et les Animaux. Paris, 1850. In: Comptes Rendus de l'Académie des Sciences, Vol. XXXI. 4to. Some dampstaining. Wraps., unc. From Honeyman Collection. (S. May 20; 3182)   Dixon. £200

BERNARD, Claude & Huette, Charles
– Précis Iconographique de Médecine operatoire et d'Anatomie Chirurgicale. Ill.:– Davesne after J.B. Leveillé. 1848. Text slightly browned. Mor.-bkd. bds. (S. Jun.15; 79)   Preidel. £90

BERNARD, P.P. & Couailhac, L.
– Jardin des Plantes. Ill.:– Jacque, Daubigny, Marvy, Daurnier Gavarni etc. Paris, 1842. 1st. Printing. 2 vols. Hf. mor., corners, unc., part. wraps., by Assourd. (HD. Jun.10; 123) Frs. 3,800

BERNARDUS, Trevisanus
– De Chymico Miraculo, quod Lapidem Philosophiae Appellant. Dionys. Zecharius Gallus de eodem. Ed.:– Gerardus Dorn. Basel, 1583. 1st. Edn. Lacks 2 blank ll. at end, stained thro.-out, title soiled. Cont. vell., hf. mor. case. From Honeyman Collection. (S. May 20; 3183)   Ritman. £180

BERNARD, Tristan
– Amants & Voleurs. Ill.:– Dignimont. Paris, 1927. (420); (350) on Rives vell., numbered. 4to. Etchings in 2 states (black-&-white & cold.), orig. water-colour. Hf. mor. by Ersé, decor. spine, orig. wrap. (SM. Feb.11; 191)   Frs. 1,800
– Tableau de la Boxe. Ill.:– A. Dunoyer de Segonzac. [1922]. Orig. ill. added. (HD. Oct.10; 178)   Frs. 3,200

BERNARDIN de Saint Pierre, Jacques Henri
See–Saint Pierre, Jacques Henri Bernardin de

BERNARDUS Claravallensis Abbatis, Saint
– De Concordantia Statuum Religiosorum. –Meditationes de Interiori Homine ... [Paris], ca. 1495. 2 works in 1 vol. Initials in red, rubricated, stained. 16th. C. vell. [BMC VIII, 107] (1st. work only). (S. Mar.16; 38)   Smith. £170
– De Consideratione ad Eugenium Papam. [Utrecht], [Nicolaus Ketelaer & Gerardus de Leempt]. ca. 1473. Fo. Spaces for initial capitals with guide letters, capitals, paragraph marks & underlines supplied in red, 1st. lf. with lr. corner resized, & slight wear at fore-edge margin. Mor. gt. by Sangorski & Sutcliffe. From the collection

BERNARDUS Claravallensis Abbatis, Saint -contd.
of Eric Sexton. [BMC IX, 7, Goff B367] (CNY. Apr.8; 181) $8,500
- Epistolae. Brussels, [Fratres Vitae Communis]. Apr.11, 1481. Fo. Spaces for initial capitals, supplied in red, as are paragraph marks, initial strokes & underlines, some minor marginal wormholes to final 2 ll. Cont. blind-stpd. cf. over wood bds., worn, rebkd. & reprd. From the collection of Eric Sexton. [BMC IX, (IB 49511), Goff B384, HC 2871] (CNY. Apr.8; 33) $4,800
- Meditationes de Interiori Homine. Barcelona, Pedro Posa. 1499. 4to. Woodcut Lombard initial capitals, unrubricated, sm. rust-hole at fo. 12 just catching 2 letters of text, minor dampstain to corner of last few ll. Mor., covers ruled in blind, by Rivière. Bkplt. of William Cole of Gray's Inn, lately in the collection of Eric Sexton. [Goff B409] (CNY. Apr.8; 18) $4,800
- Sermones Bernardi In Duytssche. Zwolle, Pieter van Os. May 27, 1495. Fo. Spaces for initial capitals, some with guide letters, most capitals supplied in red, some in blue, rubricated, all except 1 hf.-p. woodcut flanked by floral or architectural borders, sm. stain to fore-margin of 1st. 50 ll., larger stain at fo. 44 touching a portion of woodcut on verso, last p. soiled. Cont. blind-tooled cf. over wood bds., covers divided by triple fillets into lge. central panel, narrow frame & a border, panel divided into lozenge & triangular compartments each filled with lozenge stps. of an eagle or stylized garland, the same tools repeated in borders, narrow inner frame with end to end repetitions of an elongated stylized foliage tool, orig. brass clasps & catches, lacks 1 clasp, rebkd., slight repair to 2 corners. Bkplt. of Vincent Van Gogh (engraved by Marius Bauer), later the copy of Carl J. Ullmann, recently in the collection of Eric Sexton. [BMC IX, 88, Goff B435] (CNY. Apr.8; 211) $58,000
- Sermones Super Cantica Canticorum. Rostock, Fratres Horti Viridis Ad S. Michaelem, Jul.28, 1481. 1st. Edn. Fo. Spaces for initial capitals, capitals, paragraph marks & initial strokes supplied in red, with 4 lf. table bnd. at rear, 2 ll. with portion of corner torn away, tear to fo. 167 affecting 8 lines of text, last 4 ll. hinged & slightly frayed at edges, minor worming to last 12 ll., some margins with minor dampstains. Cont. blind-stpd. pig over wood bds., clasps & catches, rebkd. in vell., portions of covers reprd. with vell., new end-ll. From the collection of Eric Sexton. [Goff B427, HC 2856] (CNY. Apr.8; 148) $4,800

BERNERS or Barnes, Dame Juliana
- [Book of Saint Albans] The Book containing the Treatises of Hawking, Hunting, Coat-Armour, Fishing & Blasing of Arms ... Ed.:- Joseph Haslewood. 1810. Sm. fo. Armorial ills. partly hand-cold. Hf. pig. (C. Jul.22; 119) Thorpe. £70
- - Anr. Edn. Ed.:- Joseph Haslewood. Wynkn de Werd, 1820 [1811]. (150). 4to. Slight offsetting. 19th. C. str.-grd. mor. gt. Inscr. by Haslewood to Thomas Park, later Graham Pollard's copy. (S. Jul.27; 273)   Bow Windows Bookshop. £130
- The Treatyse of Fysshynge wyth an Angle. 1827. Cont. hf. mor., bkplt. of Henry B. Humphrey. (S. Apr.7; 428)   Blackwell. £100
- - Anr. Edn. Ed.:- William Loring Andrews. N.Y., 1903. (150) H.M.P. Gt.-lettered vell., linen ties, partly unc. (SG. Dec.11; 12) $140
- The Treatise of Fyssynge wyth an Angle, & Three other works. L., 1827. 1st. Pickering Edn. 4 works in 1 vol. 12mo. Gt.-tooled mor. (SG. Dec.11; 10) $160

BERNIA, Francesco
See-TANSILLO, Luigi & Bernia, Francesco

BERNIER, François
- Voyages Contenant la Description des Etats du Grand Mogol. Amst., 1699. 2 vols. 1 plt. torn. Cont. vell., soiled. (SH. May 21; 8)   Baxter. £85
- - Anr. Copy. 2 vols. in 1. Old vell. (BS. Feb.25; 349)   £60

BERNIS, Cardinal de
- Oeuvres Complètes. L., 1777. Latest Edn. 2 vols. in 1. 24mo. Cont. mor., fillet, decor. spine, 1st. owner's name (Dauger) in beaten gold on spine. (HD. Mar.18; 20)   Frs. 1,200

BERNOULLI, James & others
- Doctrine of Permutations & Combinations, being an Essential & Fundamental Part of the Doctrine of Chances ... together with some other useful mathematical tracts. 1795. Lacks final lf. (blank?). 19th. C. hf. cf., upr. cover detchd. (S. Dec.2; 679)   Quaritch. £160

BERNSTEIN, Julius
- Untersuchungen ueber den Erregungvorgang im Nerven und Muskelsysteme. Heidelberg, 1871. 1st. Edn. Title torn in inner blank margin, 1 prelim. lf. loose. Cl. (S. Jun.15; 80)   Jenner Books. £55

BERNT, Walther
- Die Niederländischen Zeichner des 17. Jahrhunderts. Munich, 1957-58. 2 vols. Cl. gt., ties. (P. Oct.23; 148)   £65

BEROALDE de Verville, François
- Le Moyen de Parvenir. Ill.:- after Martinet (frontis.). [Paris], [1757]. 2 vols. 12mo. Cont. red mor., fillet, spine decor. with grenades. (HD. Mar.18; 21)   Frs. 1,600

BEROALDUS, Philippus
- De Felicitate Opusculum. Bologna, 30 Jun. 1502. Sm. 4to. Early (cont.?) MS. notes on title & in text, some browning & soiling. Mod. marb. bds. From liby. of André L. Simon. (S. May 18; 41)   Lyle. £60
- De Felicitate.-De Optimo Statu et Principe. Paris, Thielman Kerver, for Jean Petit, Mar.28, 1500; Apr.10, 1500. 2 works in 1 vol. (probably issued together). Both works with Lombard initials, & rubricated in red & blue. Late 19th. C. mor. gt., watered silk linings. The copy of the Diocese of Portsmouth, Virtue & Cahill Liby., lately in the collection of Eric Sexton. [BMC VIII, 219, Goff B485 & B488, H 2972* & 2979*] (CNY. Apr.8; 127) $1,600
- - Anr. Edn. Paris, 1507. 2 pts. in 1 vol. Sm. 4to. Slight browning & soiling. Mod. pol. hf. cf. by Wood, spine gt. From liby. of André L. Simon. (S. May 18; 42)   Goldschmidt. £110
- Declamatio Lepidissima Ebriosi Scortatoris Aleatoris uitiosítate Disceptantium. Bologna, Benedictus Hectoris, 1499. 1st. Edn.? Sm. 4to. Slight browning & soiling, worming at foot of a few ll., scarcely affecting text. 19th. C. cf.-bkd. marb. bds., splits in jnts., reprd. From liby. of André L. Simon. [Goff B471] (S. May 18; 39)   Facchi. £300
- - Anr. Edn. Bologna, B. Hectoris, 1499. 2nd. Edn.? Sm. 4to. Slight browning & soiling, title possibly inserted from anr. copy. Mod. pol. hf. cf. by Wood, spine gt., slightly marked. From liby. of André L. Simon. [BMC VI, 845; Goff B472] (S. May 18; 40)   Schaeffer. £190
See-HIERONYMUS PADUANUS-BEROAL-DUS, Philippus Bononiensis -ANSONIUS MATUTINA-AENIUS SILVIUS -LACTANTIUS -LACTANTIUS

BEROSUS, the Chaldean
- Antiquitatum Italiae ac totius orbis libri Quinque. Antw., 1552. Errata-lf. at end, some browning & soiling. Cont. (German?) blind-stpd. cf. over oak bds., with a roll sigd. WG, rebkd., worn, bkplt. of Bibliotheca Elseghemensis. (S. Oct.21; 520)   Pearson. £60
- De his quae praecesserût Inundatione Terrarû [etc]. N.p. [probably Strassburg], 1511. 4to. Slight browning & soiling. Mod. cf.-bkd. bds., bkplt. of the Baron Landau liby. (S. Oct.21; 521)   Quaritch. £140

BERQUIN, Arnaud
- Romances. Paris, 1776. 1st. Edn. 12mo. Short marginal tear in 1 plt., sig. & stp. on title, slight offsetting. Cont. hf. cf., spine gt. (S. Jun.9; 55)   Flower. £55
- - Anr. Edn. Ill.:- after Marrillier. Paris, 1976. 1st. Edn., 1st. Iss., L.P. 12mo. Red mor. by Wallis with elab. gt. covers & gt. panel. spine, unc. (SPB. Jul.28; 28) $550

BERQUIN-DUVILLON
- [-] Travels in Louisiana & the Floridas, in the Year, 1802 ... Trans.:- John Davis. N.Y., 1806. 1st. Amer. Edn. 12mo. Portions of text browned & lightly foxed, bottom of title tape reinforced on verso. Later hf. cf., gt. spine, upr. cover loose. From liby. of William E. Wilson. (SPB. Apr. 29; 17) $650

BERRETTINI, Pietro da Corotona
- [-] Tabulae anatomicae. Rome, 1741. 1st. Edn. Fo. Plts. only, slight soiling. Bds., worn. (SPB. Nov.25; 97) $1,100

BERRY, William
- The History of the Island of Guernsey. 1815. 1st. Edn. 4to. Some ll. spotted, folding map torn in fold. Cont. cf., worn, upr. cover detchd., spine loose. (S. Sep.29; 134)   Grosvenor Prints. £120
- - Anr. Copy. Lge. folding map slightly torn but neatly reprd. Orig. bds., rebkd. & cornered, new end-papers, unc. (SBA. Oct.22; 762)   Chesters. £52
See-SANSON, Nicholas & Berry, William

BERTARELLI, Achille
See-ARRIGONI, Paolo & Bertarelli, Achille

BERTARELLI, Achille & Monti, Antonio
- Tre Secoli di Vita Milanese nei Documenti Iconografici 1630-1875. Milan, 1927. 4to. Mor. by Torriani, gt., worn, box. (SI. Dec.3; 71)   Lire 380,000

BERTARELLI, Achille & Prior, Henry
- Il Biglietto di Visita Italiano. Bergamo, n.d. 4to. Orig. cl. (SI. Dec.3; 72)   Lire 320,000

BERTELLIUS, P.
- Diversarum Nationum Habitus. Patavii, 1594. [Pt. I]. 94 engraved plts. (of 106), 4 plts. in facs. Mod. vell. (BS. Jun.11; 310)   £75

BERTHELOT, Pierre Eugène Marcellin
- Collection des Anciens Alchimistes Grecs.-La Chimie au Moyen Age. Paris; Paris, 1888; 1893. 1st. work: 3 vols. in 2, 2nd. work: 3 vols. 4to. Cont. hf. vell., gt. (SH. Oct.10; 416)   Music Market. £260

BERTHOLDUS, F.
- Horologium Devotionis. [Basle], [Johann Amerbach], [not after 1490]. 1st. few ll. rubricated, several woodcuts touched with pale yellow wash, lacks final blank, slight marginal stains to some ll. 19th. C. crushed mor., pointellé gt. tooling, by Thompson. The Robert Hoe copy, lately in the Pierpont Morgan Liby. [Goff B506, H 2990(I)œ2993œ8928] (CNY. Apr.8; 21) $9,000

BERTHOLLET, Claude Louis
- Eléments de l'art de la Teinture. Paris, 1791. 1st. Edn. 2 vols. A few ll. slightly spotted. Mod. tree cf., gt. (S. Oct.21; 367)   Artico. £120
- Researches into the Laws of Chemical Affinity. Trans.:- M. Farrell, M.D. 1804. Lacks hf.-title, liby. stps. Cl. (S. Dec.1; 61)   Gurney. £60

BERTHORIUS, Petrus-NAUSEA, Fredericus, Bp. of Vienna-GREGORIUS Nyssenus
- Morale reductorium super tota Bibliam. -Sermones Adventvales.-Libri octo. Ill.:- Urs Graf (1st. work). Basle; Cologne; Strassburg, 1517; 1536; 1512. 3 works in 1 vol., 2nd. work Pt. I (of IV). Fo. A few light stains, 1st. work: pp. 2-5 short & inserted from anr. copy; 3rd. work: long inscr. on 12 by Georgius Piensis recording his academic career in Prague 1511-42, a few red inkstains. 16th. C. qtr. vell. over wooden bds. (S. Jun.23; 223)   Filsell. £130

BERTINATTI, Francesco
- Tavole Anatomiche Annesse agli Elementi di Anatomia Fisologica Applicata alle Belle Arti. Torino, 1838. Fo. 27 plts. (of 33). Hf. cl. (SI. Dec.3; 76)   Lire 220,000

BERTIUS, Petrus
- Commentariorum Rerum Germanicarum. Amst., 1616. Ob. 4to. Cont. vell. (HK. Nov.18-21; 1114)   DM 20,000
- Commentariorum Rerum Germanicarum Libri III. Amst., 1616. Ob. 4to. Heavily browned in places, lacks engraved title & unnumbered end lf. & pp. 373/376 with 1 map, pp. 553/560 with 1 view, pp. 661/662 with view & pp. 731/732 & end-lf., errata, 1 lf. with margin tear. Cont. vell., lacks end-lf. (HK. May 12-14; 578)   DM 17,000
- - Anr. Edn. Amst., 1635. 3 pts. in 1 vol. 12mo. Cont. vell. (R. Oct.14-18; 2067)   DM 950
- Geographischer eyn oder Zusammengezogener Tabeln. Frankfurt, 1612. Engraved title, 168 engraved maps, all but one hand-cold. Cont. vell. As an atlas, w.a.f. (C. Jul.15; 11)   Burgess. £1,500
- Tabularum Geographicum Contractarum. Libri Quinque. Amst., 1602. 2nd. Edn. Ob. 8vo. Some ill. loose, text short in upr. margin in places. Old cf. (LM. Jun.13; 23)   B.Frs. 64,000

BERTOLONI, G.
– **Illustrazione di Piante Mozambigesi.** Bologna, 1850-55. 4 pts. in 1 vol. Fo. Cont. leath., gt. Offprints from Mem. Accad. Sci. (S. Dec.3; 890) *Asher.* £100

BERTONIO, Ludovico
– **Libro de la Vida y Milagros de Nuestro Senor Iesu Christi en dos Lenguas, Aymara, y Romance.** Trans.:– Licenciado Alonso de Villegar. [Lima], 1612. Sm. 4to. Old owner's inscr. relating to Lima on title partly erased, later liby. stps., wormholes affecting letters, particularly at end, lacks pp. 389-396, 501-08, a proof-p. for an Aymara dictionary (letter A) inserted as final free endpaper. Cont. limp vell., detchd. (SPB. May 5; 103) $750

BERTORELLI, A. & Prior, H.
– **Il Biglietto di Visita Itatiano.** Bergamo, 1911. Publisher's cl. (CR. Jun.11; 493) Lire 320,000

BERTOTTI-SCAMOZZI, Ottavio
[–] **Il Forestiere Istrutto delle Cosepiu' Rare di Architettura** ... Ill.:– Cristoforo dall' Acqua. Vicenza, 1761. 1st. Edn. 4to. Mod. paper wraps., unc. From the collection of John A. Saks. (C. Jun.10; 16) *King.* £300
[–] – **Anr. Edn.** Ill.:– Cristoforo dall' Acqua. Vicenza, 1780. Early owner's inscr. on title. Cont. cf. gt., gt. spine. From the collection of John A. Saks. (C. Jun.10; 17) *King.* £240

BERTRAM, Anthony
– **Contemporary British Artists: Paul Nash.** 1923. 4to. Orig. cl.-bkd. bds., d.-w. defect. Desmond Coke copy, with his inscr. & bkplt., John Carter bkplt., A.L.s. from Nash to Coke, A.L.s. from Albert Rutherston. (SH. Mar.27; 356A) *Music Sales.* £130

BERTRAND, Aloysius
– **Gaspard de la Nuit.** Ill.:– Max Dutzauer. Paris, 1904. (125); (110) on vell., numbered. 4to. Mor. by Blanchetière, decor. spine, covers with cathedral border & bats in corners, inside dentelle, wrap. preserved. (SM. Feb.11; 194) Frs. 8,000

BERTRAND DE MOLEVILLE, Antoine François
– **The Costume of the Hereditary States of the House of Austria.** 1804. Fo. Cont. red hf. mor. (S. Nov.25; 434) *Robinson.* £450
– – **Anr. Copy.** Wtrmkd. 1811 & 1817, text in both Fr. & Engl. cont. mor., slightly dampstained. (CSK. Sep.19; 56) £290
– – **Anr. Copy.** Cf., worn. (S. Dec.9; 517) *Hyde.* £230
– – **Anr. Copy.** Text wtrmkd. 1811, plts. 1817, advt. lf. dtd. Apr. 1818 tipped in after titles, some light offsetting to some plts. & text ll., a few spots. Cont. str.-grd. mor. gt., spine gt., covers, stained, some wear. (S. Oct.21; 513) £200
– – **Anr. Copy.** Hf. cf. worn. (BS. Jun.11; 374) £140
See–COSTUME–BERTRAND DE MOLEVILLE, Antoine François

BERTUCH, C.
– **Bilderbuch z. Nutzen u. Vergnügen d. Jugend. Sammelband. Insekten.** Vienna, ca. 1810. 4to. Many inter-ll. with cont. MS. notes, very worn & soiled. Cont. linen. (HK. Nov.18-21; 484) DM 900

BERTUCH, Friedrich Justus
– **Bilderbuch für Kinder.** Weimar, 1810. Vol. 7. 4to. Lacks 1 copperplt., slightly soiled in parts. Cont. hf. leath. (R. Oct.14-18; 2490) DM 850
– **Bilderbuch zum Nutzen und Vergnügen der Jugend.** Vienna, 1808 & 1802. New Edn. Vols. 3 & 4 in 1 vol. 4to. Lacks 1 old cold. copperplt. Cont. hf. leath. (R. Mar.31-Apr.4; 1478) DM 1,200
– – **Anr. Edn.** Vienna, [1808-15]. Vols. 1-4, 7-14 in 6 vols. 4to. Bds., worn. W.a.f. (S. Jun.1; 71) *Koch.* £800

BERZELIUS, Jon Jacob
– **An Attempt to Establish a Pure Scientific System of Mineralogy.** Trans.:– J. Black. 1814. Mod. cf.-bkd. cl. (SH. Jan.30; 407) *Walford.* £85
– **The Use of the Blowpipe in Chemical Analysis & in the Examination of Minerals.** Trans.:– M. Fresnel. 1822. 1st. Edn. in Engl. New cl. (S. Jun.15; 81) *Maggs.* £55

BESANT, Sir Walter
– **The Survey of London.** 1903-25. 10 vols. 4to. Orig. cl. gt. (P. Sep.11; 315) *Crowe.* £90
– – **Anr. Edn.** 1906-12. 10 vols. 4to. Orig. cl., gt.

From the collection of Eric Sexton. (C. Apr.16; 216) *Pisan.* £85

BESENVAL, Baron de
– **Contes.** Ill.:– Paul Avril. Paris, 1881. Ltd. Edn. Ills. in 2 states. Mor. by Pagnan, decor. spine, inside dentelle. Bkplt. of Francis Kettaneh. (SM. Feb.11; 143) Frs. 4,000

BESLER, Basilius
– **Hortus Eystettensis.** Ill.:– Wolfgang Kilian & others. [Eichstatt & Nuremb.], 1613. 1st. Edn. 2 vols. Atlas 4to. Engraved general title (bnd. in vol. 2), 3 (of 4) engraved architectural titles, 367 engraved plts., titles & plts. cold. by cont. hand, general title laid down, lacks port., other prelims. & indexes. Cont. blind-stpd. vell. on wooden bds., spines reprd., lacks ties. Maria Theresa Earle bkplt., as a collection of plts., w.a.f. (C. Jul.15; 164a) *Quaritch.* £82.00
[–] – **Anr. Edn.** [Nuremb. & Eichstätt], 1713 [–ca. 1750]. Latest Edn. 3 vols. Fo. Lacks author's port. Cont. bds., slightly soiled. (R. Oct.14-18; 2912) DM 150,000
See–KLEPPISIUS, Gregorius–BESLER, Basilius

BESLER, Michael Rupert
– **Rariora Musei Besleriani.** Ed.:– J. Heinrich Lechner. [Nuremb.], 1716. Fo. Lacks 1 port? Cont. vell. From Chetham's Liby., Manchester. (C. Nov.26; 33) *Wheldon & Wesley.* £100

BESSARION, Cardinal Johannes
– **Adversus Calumniatorum Platonis.** Rome, Conradus Sweynheym & Arnoldus Pannartz, [before Sep. 13, 1469]. 1st. Edn. Fo. Spaces for 6 initial capitals, which are illuminated in red, green, purple & gold, some with floral sprays extending into margins, some 20 ll. reinforced at extreme inner margins, 1st. blank with some slight repairs, light dampstain to portions of upr. margins, scattered light marginal foxing. Cont. blind-stpd. cf. over wood bds., covers divided by rows of 5 fillets into 4 narrow concentric panels, each filled with repetitions of an 'Ihs' stp., 2 rectangular tools & a floral tool, spine compartments with repeated rosettes, covers slightly wormed. Sm. ink stps. of the K.K. Hofbibliothek, Vienna, lately in the collection of Eric Sexton. [BMC IV, 7, Goff B518, HC 3004*] (CNY. Apr.8; 142) $30,000

BESSEL, Friedrich Wilhelm
– **Abhandlungen.** Ed.:– Rudolf Engelmann. Leipzig, 1875-76. 3 pts. in 1 vol. 4to. Mod. cl. (S. Mar.17; 319) *Weiner.* £52
– **Tabulae Regiomontanae Reductionum Observationum Astronomicarum ab Anno 1750 usque ad Annum 1850 Computatae.** Konigsberg, 1830. 1st. Edn. Some ll. slightly spotted or soiled, stp. of Royal Astronomical Society on title. Cont. roan-bkd. bds. (S. Dec.2; 680) *Quaritch.* £220

BESSON, Jacques
– **Théâtre des Instrumens Mathématiques & Méchaniques** ... Trans.:– Fr. Beroald. Lyon, 1578. Fo. Light browning, 2 fragments bnd. at end; Chereau, Paris, 1728; Fr. Vitruvius pp. 285-354 with many copperplts., part of bk. IXX bk. compl., 1 text p. torn, lightly soiled in parts. 18th. C. leath., some worming, worn. (HK. Nov.18-21; 402) DM 3,500
– – **Anr. Copy.** Sm. title fault., 1 lf. torn without loss, old staining. Cont. limp vell. (LM. Jun.13; 196) B.Frs. 18,000

BEST, R.I. & MacNeill, Eoin
– **The Annals of Inisfallen.** Dublin, 1933. 4to. Cl.-bkd. bds. (GM. Apr.30; 411) £60

BEST BOOKS of the Season, 1935-36
Ill.:– Arthur Rackham. [L.], [1935]. 4to. Cold. pict. wraps. Raymond M. Sutton Jr. copy. (SG. May 7; 28) $160

BEST PLAYS of the Old Dramatists
Ed.:– Havelock Ellis. L., 1888. 22 vols. Some browning. Hf. mor. (SPB. May 29; 38) $100

BESTE, John R.
– **The Wabash: Or Adventures of an English Gentleman's Family in the Interior of America** ... L., 1855. 1st. Edn. 2 vols. Orig. cl., blind-stpd. covers, gt. spine, endpapers. glue-strained. From liby. of William E. Wilson. (SPB. Apr.29; 18) $225

BÉTANCOURT, Augustin de
See–LANZ, Phillipe Louis & Betancourt, Augustin de

BETHEL, Slingsby
[–] **The Present Interest of England Stated.** 1671. 1st. Edn. 4to. Mod. cf. [Wing B2072] (C. Apr.1; 174) *Mahler.* £70

BETHUNE, Baron Jean
– **Meraux des Familles Brugeoises.** Bruges, 1890-94. 2 pts. in 1 vol. 4to. Mod. bdg. (LM. Nov.8; 166) B.Frs. 24,000

BETJEMAN, Sir John
– **Continual Dew.–New Bats in Old Belfries.** 1937; 1945. 1st. Edns., 2nd. work Ltd. on special paper, sigd. Together 2 vols. 1st. work orig. cl. gt., d.-w. by E. McKnight Kauffer inserted, 2nd. work; orig. cl., d.-w. (S. Jul.22; 29) *Rota.* £55
– **Mount Zion, or In Touch with the Infinite.** [1931]. Orig. bds. Sigd. by author. (P. Jul.30; 320) *Henderson.* £120
– **An Oxford University Chest.**–: Osbert Lancaster & others. 1938. 1st. Edn. Orig. cl.-bkd. bds. (S. Jul.22; 28) *Mimpriss.* £80
[–] **Sir John Piers, by Epsilon.** Mullingar, [1938]. 1st. Edn. (140). Orig. wraps. 5 MS. corrections. (SH. Jul.9; 128) *Minerva.* £110

BETRUEBTER BILD-SAAL Ungcluecklicher Verliebten
Frankfurt & Leipzig, 1769. Some foxing, etc. Disbnd. (SG. Feb.5; 244) $110

BETTI, Zaccaria
– **Del Baco da Seta. Canti IV.** Ill.:– Domenico Cunego after Francesco Lorenzi. Verona, 1756. 4to. Orig. paper bds., rebkd., unc. From the collection of John A. Saks. (C. Jun.10; 18) *Goldschmidt.* £100

BETTINA, Arnim v.
[–] **Die Günderode.** Grünberg, 1840. 1st. Edn. 2 vols. Both titles stpd., slightly soiled. Cont. linen gt., blind-tooled decor. (HK. May 15; 4067) DM 550

BETTINELLI, Saverio
– **Il Mondo della Luna.** Venice, 1754. Early 19th. C. hf. mor. gt. From the collection of John A. Saks. (C. Jun.10; 19) *Quaritch.* £160
See–FRUGONI, Carlo Innocenze & others

BETTONI, Eugenio
– **Storia Naturale degli Uccelli che Nidificano in Lombardia.** Ill.:– Oscar Dressler. Milan, 1868. 2 vols. Fo. Hf.-title, 1 loose plt., some light stains. Early 20th C. hf. mor., partly unc. (SI. Dec.3; 79) Lire 12,000,000

BEUGNOT, Auguste
– **Essai sur les Institutions de Saint Louis.** 1821. Cf. gt., gt. border, by Deforgue. (HD. Oct.10; 219) Frs. 1,150
– **Mémoires du Comte Beugnot ancien Ministre (1783-1815).** Paris, 1866. 2 vols. Cont. hf. chagrin, spines decor. with raised bands. Autograph dedication from author's son to Madame la Maréchale Duchesse d'Albufera. (HD. Feb.27; 85) Frs. 1,200

BEUVE, Paul
– **Iconographie de A. Willette.** Paris, 1909. (200) numbered. 4to. Cont. red mor. (CSK. May 29; 30) £60

BEVAN, Philip
[–] **America. A Poem.** Cinc., 1848. 1st. Edn. Staining & foxing. Disbnd., cl. case. From liby. of William E. Wilson. (SPB. Apr.29; 19) $300

BEVERIDGE, Erskine
– **Coll & Tiree.** Edinb., 1903. Ltd. Edn. Mor. spine, worn. (CE. Dec.4; 206) £70

BEVERLEY, Robert
[–] **Histoire de la Virginie, contenant l'histoire de son etablissement, de son gouvernement d'aprésent, ses productions** ... Amst., 1712. 3rd. Edn. in Fr. 12mo. Cont. cf., qt. spine. [Sabin 5117] (S. Nov.4; 650) *Lawford.* £60
– **The History of Virginia.** L., 1722. 2nd. Edn. Old cf. gt., worn, some staining, in qtr. mor. gt. s.-c. [Sabin 5113] (CNY. Oct.1; 75) $180

BEVERWIJCK, Jan van
– **Van de Wtnementheyt des Vrouwelicken Geslachts. Met verssen van C. Boy.** Dordrecht, 1639. 1st. Edn. Title & 1st. few ll. stained. Cont. vell. (VG. Dec.17; 1198) Fls. 750

BEVIER, R.S.
– **History of the First & Second Missouri Confederate Brigades** ... St. Louis, 1879. 1st. Edn. Decor. cl. (SG. Jun.11; 106) $120

BEVY, Abbé Charles Joseph de
[-] Histoire des Inaugurations des Rois, Empereurs, et autres Souverains de l'Univers. Paris, 1776. 2-lf. privilege & approbation at end. Cont. red mor., gt., arms of Comtesse de Provence & Signet arms on covers, latter de-gilded, triple gt. fillet & corner sprays, spine gt. in compartments, inner gt. dentelles. (SM. Oct.7; 1579) Frs. 1,200

BEWICK, Thomas
– British Land Birds.–British Water Birds. Newcastle, 1825. Both (100). 2 vols. 4to. 1st. work: lr. margin of 1st. 15 ll. affected by damp, some spotting. Cont. cl., rebkd. & cornered, old spines preserved. (CSK. Apr.10; 129) £140
– British Water Birds. Newcastle, 1825. 4to. 19th. C. hf. mor. gt. by Stones of Manchester. (LC. Feb.12; 614) £110
– A Cabinet of Natural History. Alnwick, 1809. 7 pts. in 1 vol. Each pt. with orig. wraps., hf. cf., a little worn. (S. Dec.3; 892) Dr. Pike. £150
– Figures of British Land Birds. Newcastle, 1800. Vol. 1 (all publd.). Hf. cf. gt. (P. Nov.13; 185) Steedman. £140
– A General History of Quadrupeds. Ill.:– Bewick. Newcastle, 1790. 1st. Edn. Title slightly dust-soiled. Orig. bds., unc., covers detchd., lacks most of label. (C. Feb.25; 2) Quaritch. £100
– – Anr. Edn. Newcastle, 1791. 2nd. Edn. Hf. cf. (CB. Dec.9; 129) Can. $260
– – Anr. Copy. Cont. hf. cf. (CB. Apr.1; 286) Can. $200
– – Anr. Edn. 1800. 4th. Edn. Panel. cf. gt. (BS. Sep.17; 60) £90
– General History of Quadrupeds & History of British Birds. 1820 & 1832. Hf. mor. gt. (CE. Nov.20; 112) £100
– Gleanings. Ed.:– Julia Boyd. Newcastle-upon-Tyne, 1886. Sm. paper copy, sigd. by Ed., this numbered 115. 4to. 1 facs. letter. Hf. mor. (CSK. Feb.20; 156) £65
– The History of British Birds. Newcastle, 1797-1804. 1st. Edn., on imperial paper. 2 vols. Slight spotting. 19th. C. cf., gt. (S. Feb.10; 409) Temperley. £230
– – Anr. Edn. Newcastle, 1797-1804. 1st. Edn. 2 vols. Occasional spotting, engraved port. of Bewick tipped in at front of vol. 1, advt. Cont. cf., 1 cover detchd. (CSK. Sep.12; 222) £170
– – Anr. Copy. Slight spotting. Late 19th. C. pol. cf. by W. Pratt, spines gt. (S. Jun.1; 256) Traylen. £130
– – Anr. Copy. 2 vols. Advt. in vol. II Hf. cf. (PG. Sep.3; 69) £85
– – Anr. Edn. Newcastle, 1797-1804; 1821. 1st. Edn. 2 vols. & supp. in 2 pts. Pol. cf., gt., by Rivière. (C. Nov.5; 13) Gibbs. £280
[-] – Anr. Edn. Newcastle, 1804. Vol. 1 3rd. Edn. 2 vols. Occasional spotting. Cf. (CSK. Sep.26; 105) £65
– – Anr. Edn. Newcastle, 1804. 2 vols. in 1. Hf. mor. (SKC. Feb.26; 1571) £85
– – Anr. Edn. Newcastle, 1804 [1805]. Cont. cf. gt., spines faded. (SBA. May 27; 169) Damms. £70
– – Anr. Edn. Newcastle, 1805. 2 vols. Cont. hf. mor., recased. (TA. Sep.18; 70) £75
– – Anr. Copy. Occasional slight soiling, corner cut from each title-p. Cont. cf., slightly defect. (KH. Nov.18; 63) Aus. $150
– – Anr. Edn. Newcastle, 1821. 7th. Edn.; 5th. Edn. 2 vols., including supp. Some spotting, heavy towards end of vol. 1. Cont. cf. (CSK. Nov.7; 169) £70
– – Anr. Copy. 2 vols., including supp. Some spotting. Later cl. rebkd. (CSK. Oct.31; 2) £50
– – Anr. Edn. Newcastle, 1826. 8th. Edn.; 6th. Edn. 2 vols. Cont. hf. cf. (CSK. Nov.14; 8) £70
– – Anr. Edn. Newcastle, 1826. 2 vols. Cont. hf. mor. (C. May 20; 192) Titles. £80
– – Anr. Copy. Slight staining. Mor. gt., repeating floral design. (SPB. Nov.25; 88) $150
– – Anr. Edn. Newcastle, 1847. Cont. tree cf. (CSK. Jul.24; 29) £70
– – Anr. Edn. Newcastle upon Tyne, 1885. Ltd. Edn. 5 vols. Hf. cf., worn. (SH. Jul.9; 110) Thorp. £100
– A Memoir of Thomas Bewick. 1862. 1st. Edn. Orig. cl. gt., unc., unopened. (SH. Mar.26; 83) Music Sales. £105
– – Anr. Copy. Cont. hf. mor. gt., neatly rebkd., preserving the orig., hinges strengthened. (SBA. Oct.22; 441) Jones. £55
– – Anr. Copy. Cl. (SG. Dec.11; 14) $100

– A Natural History of British Quadrupeds . . . Alnwick, 1809. 7 Pts. in 1 vol. 12mo. Late 19th. C. pol. cf. by Rivière, spine gt., orig. wraps. preserved. (S. Nov.24; 20) Steedman. £300
– – Anr. Copy. Some browning. Cont. cf., orig. wraps. bnd. in, covers detchd. (CSK. Jan.9; 225) £65
– – Anr. Edn. Alnwick, 1814? 7 vols. 12mo. Occasional light spotting & browning. Orig. decor. paper wraps., each with lge. woodcut on lr. cover, several spines defect., some light staining. (S. May 5; 93) Cristani. £100
– A Portfolio of Thomas Bewick Wood-Engravings. Ed.:– James M. Wells (intro.). Chic., 1970. 3 vols. 4to. Orig. qtr. cl., s.-c. (S. Jul.27; 276) Stirling. £60
– [Vignettes]. N.d. Ob. tall 8vo. 81 woodcut vigs. for head & tall pieces, on thin paper, apparently in proof state, in preparation for publication of 'Vignettes'. Later gt. hf. mor., unc., sm. piece missing from spine. (PNY. Mar.26; 37) $350
– Works. Newcastle, 1885-87. Memorial Edn., (750). 5 vols. Orig. hf. mor. gt. (SH. Mar.26; 84) Joseph. £150

BEWICK, Thomas (Ill.)
See–CONSETT, Matthew
See–GOLDSMITH, Oliver & Parnell, Thomas
See–SOMERVILLE, William
See–THORNTON, Robert John

BEWICK, Thomas–BEWICK, Thomas & John
– [The Works].–Select Fables. Edinb. (2nd. work), 1885-87; 1879. Memorial Edn., (750) sigd. by publishers; (100). 5 vols.; 1 vol. Unif. hf. mor., spines gt. (CSK. Jun.5; 49) £150

BEWICK, Thomas & John
– Descriptive & Critical Catalogue of Works. 1851. (100). 4to. Subscribers list inserted. Orig. cl., worn. Thomas Bell's copy, with sig. (SH. Mar.26; 82) Hatchard. £170
– Emblems of Mortality. L., 1789. 12mo. Early 19th. C. red mor. gt. (S. Nov.24; 19) Bickersteth. £95
– – Anr. Copy. Later hf. leath., worn. (SG. Feb.5; 107) $150
– – Anr. Edn. Ill.:– after Hans Holbein. 1795. 19th. C. mor. (SH. Dec.10; 27) Gamble. £125
– Select Fables. 1820. 1st. Coll. Edn. L.P. Red mor. gt. by Bedford, bird motif in 5 compartments of spine. Bkplt. of J.L.D. Stewart of Gleonogil. (S. Nov.24; 21) Steedman. £280
– – Anr. Copy. Sm. 4to. Later gt.-floral & gt.-ruled mor., unc. (PNY. May 21; 92) $190
– – Anr. Copy. Mor. gt. by Bickers & Son. (SKC. Feb.26; 1247) £120
– – Anr. Copy. Hf. cf., worn. (CE. Jun.4; 119) £70

BEYER, J.H.
– Conometria Mauritiana.–Kurtzer Bericht von Zubereytung einer Visier-Ruthen, auz e. geeichten Weinfass.–Logistica Decimalis . . . Frankfurt, 1619; 1620; 1619. 3 works in 1 vol. 4to. Slightly wormed, title defect. & mntd. Cont. vell., lacks ties. (HK. Nov.18-21; 403) DM 950

BEYER, J.S.
– Musicalischer Vorrath neu-variirter Fest-Choral-Gesänge . . . Freyberg, [1716-19]. 1st. Edn. 3 vols. in 1. Very browned & stained thro.-out. Hf. vell., cover very defect. (H. Dec.9/10; 1074) DM 1,000

BEYER, Jan de
[-] Sammelband mit 186 Kupfertafeln. Kirchen, ca. 1732-50. Slightly soiled in parts, 1 plt. stained. 19th. C. Engl. hf. leath., unc. (R. Oct.14-18; 1893) DM 5,200

BEYLE, Marie Henri 'Stendhal'
– Histoire de la Peinture en Italie. Paris, 1817. 1st. Edn. 2 vols. A few marginal stains, slight spotting. Cont. cf.-bkd. bds., slightly worn. (S. Jun.23; 263) Tzakas. £220
– Promenades dans Rome. Ill.:– Couché fils after Civeton (frontis.'s). 1829. 1st. Edn. 2 vols. Folding plan in 2 states. Cont. Bradel bds., unc. (HD. Feb.27; 234) Frs. 2,500
[-[Le Rouge et le Noir. Paris, 1831. 1st. Edn. 2 vols. Cont. hf. cf., worn. (S. Mar.17; 294) Quaritch. £850
– – Anr. Edn. Ill.:– H. Dubouchet, L. Chapron (Pref.) 1884. (500). 3 vols. Red mor., gt. fillets, decor. spine raised bands, gt. fillets, wraps. & spine preserved, s.-c., by Chambolle Durie. 19

A.L.s.'s, 11 pp. MS. of Chapron pref. 113 orig. ills. (HD. Apr.24; 186) Frs. 4,900
– – Anr. Edn. Ill.:– P.E. Vibert. Paris, 1912. On Rives. 2 vols. Hf. red mor., corners, gt. fillet, decor. & mosaic spines, unc., wrap., by Affolter. (HD. Jun.10; 209) Frs. 1,200
– Vie de Henri Brulard. Paris, 1890. Orig. Edn. 12mo. Pol. chagrin, 5 fillets, decor. spine, inner fillet, silk doubl., unc., wrap. (HD. Jun.10; 210) Frs. 1,050

BEZA, Theodore
– A Briefe & piththie sum of the Christian Faith. L., 1572. Engraved port. (inserted?). Cont. limp vell. [STC 2010] (SPB. Nov.25; 71) $200
– Ecclesiastes . . . [1588?]. Some browning & soiling. 19th. C. mor. [STC 2764] (S. Jun.29; 356) Van den Tol. £120

BEZALEL OF KOBRIN
– Amudeha Shivah (Sermons, with Approbation of Council of Lithuania, & Council of Four lands). Lublin, 1666. 1st. Edn. 4to. Lacks title & last lf. of index, slight staining. Orig. bdg. (S. Nov.18; 403) Honig. £140

BEZOUT, Etienne
– Cours de Mathematiques . . . Paris, 1775. 4 vols. Liby. stp. on titles. Cont. cf. (S. Mar.17; 320) Booth. £50

BHAGVAT-GEETA, or Dialogues of Kreeshna & Arjoon . . . with Notes
Trans.:– Charles Wilkins. 1785. 1st. Edn. in Engl. 4to. Orig. cl-bkd. bds., slightly worn, unc. (S. Oct.21; 428) Quaritch. £140
– – Anr. Copy. Fo. L.P. heavily foxed. Disbnd., unc. (SG. Feb.5; 38) $130

BIANCHI, L.
See–CUCINIELLO, Domenico & Bianchi, L.

BIANCHINI, Francesco
– Il Palazzo de Cesari. Ill.:– Marco Pitteri, Giuseppe Scolari & others. Verona, 1738. Fo. Some ll. lightly foxed. Cont. cf. gt., gt. arms on covers of Jean-Jacques Amelot de Chaillou, jnts. reprd. From the collection of John A. Saks. (C. Jun.10; 21) Elstein. £280

BIANCHINI, Giuseppe
– Dei Gran Duchi di Toscana della Real Casa de' Medici. Ill.:– G. Filosi, M. Pitteri, A. Halvech, & others. Venice, 1741. Fo. Cont. mott. cf., gt. spine. From the collection of John A. Saks. (C. Jun.10; 22) Pompelmo. £190

BIANCO, Margery Williams
– Poor Cecco. Ill.:– Arthur Rackham. N.Y., [1925]. 1st. Trade Edn. 4to. Gt.-pict. cl., d.-w. Raymond M. Sutton Jr. copy. (SG. May 7; 31) $220
– – Anr. Edn. Ill.:– Arthur Rackham. N.Y., [1925]. 1st. Edn. Deluxe, (105) numbered, sigd. 4to. Vell.-style bkd. bds., orig. d.-w. & box, both worn. Raymond M. Sutton Jr. copy. (SG. May 7; 30) $8,600

[BIARD, A.] Sieur de Sonan
– Chriserionte de Gaule, Histoire Memorable. Lyon, 1620. Old sig. on title, bkplt. of Girardot de Préfond & his name, gt., stpd. on front doubl. 18th. C. mor., triple gt. fillet, spine compartments gt. à la grotesque, inner gt. dentelles. Meon copy with red ink accession number on flylf. (SM. Oct.7; 1581) Frs. 2,000

BIBAUD, Jeune
– Dictionnaire Historique des Hommes Illustres du Canada et de l'Amérique. Montreal, 1857. 1st. Edn. Mor. gt., upr. cover gt.-lettered 'Presented to H.R.H. Prince Arthur by the Province of Quebec.' (SG. Mar.5; 104) $220

BIBELOT, The
Portland, 1895-1915. Orig. Edn. 21 vols. including index. 16mo. Bds. unc., partly unopened. (SG. Oct.2; 31) $110

BIBLES
(Arranged alphabetically by language, each language chronologically).

BIBLES [Danish]
– Biblia, det er, den gantske Hellige scrifft, paa Daske. Copen., 1589. 2nd. Edn. in Danish. 3 pts. in 1 vol. Fo. Lacks general title, but with port. of Frederick II mntd. on flyleaf, ff. 2C6 & 2D2 of 3rd pt. supplied in old MS., lacks 1st. & last ll. f5, (blanks?), lge. pieces torn from 6 ll. with text supplied in MS. facs., sig. 1617, on f.A, trimmed, book label of E. Egeberg. Old cf., over bds., stpd. on upr. cover 'P.V. 1741' embossed brass cornerpieces, apparently lacking an in-set stone, 1 slightly damaged, brass clasps. 1 detchd., spine

rather worn. [D. & M. 3156] (S. Oct.21; 277) *Barrington.* £460

BIBLES [Dutch]

– **Bible.** Delft, Jacob Jacobszoen van der Meer & Mauricius Yemantszoen. Jan.10, 1477. 1st. Edn. of the Bible in Dutch. Fo. 204 ll. (only, of 319), comprising 39 ll. of vol. I (quires 30-33 & colophon, from a shorter copy) bnd. after 165 ll. of vol. II (quires 1-17, lacks folios 1, 32, 39, 40 & 170, supplied in facs.), spaces for capital initials, supplied in red, rubricated, last lf. of vol. I laid down, marginal restoration to ll. of vol. I, some lr. margins dampstained. Cont. blind-stpd. cf. over bevelled wood bds., covers with lge. rectangular panel with triple rules to a lattice design, rebnd. with mod. cf. preserving upr. cover, two-thirds of lr. cover, & some of orig. backstrip, brass clasps. [BMC IX, 16, Goff B648, HC 3160] (CNY. Apr.8; 51) $2,600

– **Biblia cum Concordantiis Veteris et Novi Testamenti.** Nuremb., 1501. 1st. Edn. Fo. Liby.-stp. on title & last lf., some marginal annots., last lf. reprd., lacks endpapers, 1st. 20 ll. badly stained, a few other stains, mainly towards end. 17th. C. cf.-bkd. wooden bds., lacks clasps, loose in bdg. [D. & M. p.909; STC German p.85] (VG. Nov.18; 1012) Fls. 3,200

– **Den Bibel Oude en Nieuvve Testament.** Antur, 14 Aug., 17 Aug. 1532. Fo. Title & 1st. 4 ll. defect. without text loss, restored & remntd. Mod. cf. (LM. Jun.13; 28) B.Frs. 26,000

– **Bibel, den, Inhoudende dat Oude ende Nieuwe Testament.** [Emden], 1560. 3 pts. in 1 vol. 17th. C. vell. (VG. Dec.17; 1104) Fls. 3,500

– **Biblia: dat is, de gantsche H. Schrift . . .** Leyden, 1589. A few marginal stains, outer margins of a number of ll. short, with loss of some text of the ptd. marginal annots. 17th. C. mott. cf., spine gt., corners slightly defect. (VG. Nov.18; 1017) Fls. 475

– **Biblia, dat is, De Gantsche Heylige Schrift, . . .** Ill.:– Maps after P. Plancius, engraved by Bapt. v. Doetechem. Leyden, 1590. The 'Deux-Aes' Bible. 4 pts. in 1 vol. 4to. Cut short, stains, maps worn in folds, 1 reprd. 18th. C. hf. cf., defect. (VG. Dec.17; 1107) Fls. 1,800

– **Bibel, den, Inhoudende dat Oude ende Nieuwe Testament.** N.p. [Harlingen?], 1598. Biestkens bible. Fo. Stained thro.-out, hole in 3 ll., marginal wormholes at beginning. Cont. blind-stpd. cf. over wooden bds., 1 brass clasp (of 2) & brass central & corner-pieces, rebkd. (VG. Dec.17; 1106) Fls. 2,400

– **Biblia, dat is, de Gantsche H. Schrifture . . .** Trans.:– Martin Luther. Amst., 1648. 3 pts. in 1 vol. Fo. Cont. vell., slightly soiled, lacks ties. (VG. Dec.17; 1110) Fls. 800

– – **Anr. Edn.** The Hague, [1649]. 3 pts. in 1 vol. Fo. Short thro.-out, some margins reprd., mainly at beginning, affecting text in places, some stains, without the usual maps. Cont. cf. over wood, initials H.L. on upr. cover, orig. brass cornerpieces & strips, new clasps, catches & centrepiece, new spine. (VG. Nov.18; 1020) Fls. 1,300

– – **Anr. Edn.** Amst., 1661. Biestkens' bible. 2 pts. in 1 vol. Fo. Upr. corners of 1st. ll. stained. Cont. blind-stpd. & panel. cf. over wood, old brass clasps, catches (reprd.) & cornerpieces. (VG. Dec.17; 1112) Fls. 1,900

– – **Anr. Edn.** Ill.:– N. Visscher. Leyden, 1663. 3 pts. in 2 vols. Fo. 5 (of 6) double-p. engraved maps, lacks World map. Cont. cf., double gt. lines round sides, with gt. crowns in corners, spines gt., raised in compartments, some repairs. [D. & M. 3321] (VG. Nov.18; 1021) Fls. 1,550

– – **Anr. Copy.** 3 pts. in 1 vol. Some lr. corners worn, badly frayed & defect., with loss of text several ll. with holes & loss of text, title stained, defect. & reprd. Cont. russ. over wood with orig. brass clasps, corner & centrepieces, spine reprd. (VG. Dec.17; 1114) Fls. 850

– – **Anr. Edn.** Dordrecht & Amst., 1688. 3 pts. in 1 vol. Fo. Without usual maps. Mod. leath. over orig. wooden bds., old clasps catches & cornerpieces. With hand-written family register of the van Breeman family covering the years 1669-1728 (Utrecht, Rotterdam, Bodegraven) on end-papers. (VG. Nov.18; 1022) Fls. 1,300

– **Biblia.** Amst., 1702. Fo. 2 engraved ports, & 6 maps, 2 torn, some stains. Cont. cf., spine worn, clasps & cornerpieces. (SH. Jun.18; 221) *Burgess.* £240

– **Biblia, dat is De gantsche H. Schrifture . . .** Dordrecht/Amst., 1704. 3 pts. in 1 vol. Fo. Engraved title reprd., some marginal repairs, worn & stained, lacks maps. Cont. blind-stpd. russ. over wood, old brass clasps & cornerpieces, 1 cornerpiece new, new spine, corner of upr. cover reprd. (VG. Nov.18; 1023) Fls. 1,400

– – **Anr. Edn.** Dordrecht & Amst., 1714. 3 pts. in 1 vol. Lge. fo. Wide margins. Cont. blind-stpd. russ. over wood, orig. brass clasps & cornerpieces, foot of spine & 1 corner brkn., 1 inner hinge strengthened. (VG. Dec.17; 1117) Fls. 2,800

– – **Anr. Copy.** Lacks 4 maps, 3 ll. partly torn out, corners of ca. 100 ll. badly frayed with some loss of text in places. Cont. blind-stpd. russ. over wood, orig. brass clasps & cornerpieces, sm. pt. of top of spine clumsily reprd. W.a.f. (VG. Dec.17; 1118) Fls. 975

– – **Anr. Edn.** Ill.:– W.A. Bachienne (extra-engraved maps). Dordrecht, 1729. 3 pts. in 1 vol. Lge. fo. 12 extra-engraved maps ca. 1750, light foxing, wide margins. Cont. blind-stpd. russ. over wood, orig. brass clasps & cornerpieces, mod. end-papers. Bnd. up with plts. by J. Luiken, which also appeared in 'Afbeeldingen der Merkwaardigste Geschiedenissen v.h. Oude en Nieuwe Testament'. (VG. Dec.17; 1122) Fls. 5,250

– – **Anr. Edn.** Dordrecht/Amst., 1729. 4 pts. in 1 vol. Fo. Lacks all maps, title & 2 ll. of text in facs., several ll. reprd. in upr. margin, some stains thro.-out, also several pp. at end dampstained & badly soiled in margins. Cont. blind-stpd. cf. over wood, rebkd., brass clasps, catches & cornerpieces. W.a.f. (VG. Nov.18; 1026) Fls. 1,200

– – **Anr. Edn.** Dordrecht, 1730. 3 pts. in 1 vol. Fo. Cont. blind-stpd. russ. over wood, orig. brass clasps & cornerpieces, cf. on upr. cover with some tears, foot of spine renewed. (VG. Dec.17; 1123) Fls. 2,000

– **Biblia, dat is De Gantsche H. Schrifture. – De CL Psalmen des Propheten Davids, en eenige andere Lofsangen.** Dordrecht, 1738-39. 3 pts. in 2 vols. 4to. Title & some ll. frayed, marginal staining in places, a few plts. slightly defect. in folds. Cont. blind-stpd. russ., brass clasps & cornerpieces. Extra-ill. (VG. Dec.17; 1124) Fls. 1,300

– **Bybel Dat Is, De Gansche H. Schrift . . . Ouden & Niewen Testaments . . . Staaten Generaal . . .** Gorinchem, 1748. Thick fo. 1st. gathering detchd., some loosening. Cont. stpd. cf., brass corner pieces, 1 clasp, lacks spine. (VA. Aug.29; 15) R. 310

– – **Anr. Edn.** Ill.:– W.A. Bachiene (maps). Gorinchem, 1748. 2 vols. Fo. Foxed & browned in places. Cont. marb. cf., spines gt., spines & corners reprd., some scratches on sides. (VG. Nov.18; 1030) Fls. 750

– **Biblia, dat is de gantsche H. Schrifture . . .** Amst., 1777, 1774. 3 pts. (including Psalms) in 1 vol. 4to. Cut short, in places affecting ptd. marginal notes, several corners reprd. with loss, some staining. Cont. blind-stpd. & panel. russ. over wood, brass clasps & catches (not cont.), inscr. in gt. lettering beginning on upr. cover & continuing on lr. cover, some imperfections to corners of bdg. (VG. Nov.18; 1032) Fls. 450

– – **Anr. Edn.** Ill.:– S. Fokke, P. Tanje & others. Amst., [1892]. 'Compagnie Bijbel', H.M.P. Fo. Orig. woven cl., decor. with embroidery in colours & with gold thread, brass clasps & cornerpieces, back defect., a few other defects. (VG. Dec.17; 1129) Fls. 1,150

– – **Anr. Edn.** Leyden, n.d. 3 pts. in 1 vol. Fo. A made-up copy, with engraved title of 1st. Edn., sig. on verso of B. van Langenes & date 1637, but with different collation & lf.-numbering for the other books (except for the Apocrypha) from the 1st. Edn. & without the colophon with date 1636 at end of both Old & New Testament, stains, worn. 18th. or 19th. C. roan. W.a.f. (VG. Nov.18; 1019) Fls. 850

BIBLES [Dutch & Malay]

– **Boeck Mosis, het eerste, genaemt Genesis/Genesis, Attau kitab deri miarahan, kitab Mosis, Nang Bermoula.** Trans.:– D. Brower. Amst., 1697. 4to. Wormholes, (neatly reprd.), soiled & stained. Mod. cl., soiled. (VG. Dec.17; 1137) Fls.700

BIBLES [English]

– **Bible.** L., 1539. 1st. Edn. of the Great Bible. Fo. Lacks 1st. & 3rd. titles, *2-4, & 6 of prelims., blank Q4 & Nn8 at end, general title & 3rd. divisional title in facs., 2nd. & 4th. titles cut-round & inlaid, with letterpress to latter in facs., 5th. title in facs. with orig. letterpress inlaid, *2-4, & 6 & Nn8 in facs., *5 with all margins renewed & portions of 8 lines in facs., some 50 ll. with margins or corners renewed, with slight text loss or slight loss of marginal notes on 39 ll., minor repairs to other ll., soiling & scattered spotting. Mor., covers diapered & panel. in blind, gt.-lettered spine, by W. Pratt, worn, upr. cover detchd. Bkplt. of the General Theological Seminary Liby. (CNY. Oct.1; 22) $4,800

– – **Anr. Edn.** L., Apr. 1540. 2nd. Edn. of the Great Bible. Fo. Lacks blank Q4, 1st. quire detchd., 1st. title cut-round & mntd. with slight loss to border at inner margin, lr. fore-edge & 2 lines of letterpress, the defects in facs., 2nd. title with reprd. tear affecting border, 4th. title with sm. hole to border reprd., 5th. title with reprd. tear & sm. portion of border at upr. fore-edge in facs., 24 ll. with corners or portions of margins renewed, with loss of some letters at DD6 & Kkk3, reprd. tears to some 20 ll., 11 affecting text without loss, reprd. rust-holes at e2 & Nn7 with loss of some letters, other minor defects, minor spotting & wear to corners. 19th. C. mor., covers diapered & panel. in blind with gt.-lettered title, repeated on spine, vell. end-ll., by Rivière, worn, upr. cover detchd. Bkplt. of the General Theological Seminary Liby. (CNY. Oct.1; 23) $7,000

– – **Anr. Edn.** Trans.:– Thomas Mathew. L., 1551. 2 vols. Thick sm. fo. Old Testament lacks first 12 prelim. ll., including title, bnd. in at end of 2nd. vol. is incompl. copy of early Psalter, lacks title, many tears & stains. Later cf., worn. W.a.f. (SG. Sep.25; 34) $220

– – **Anr. Edn.** L., 1568. 1st. Edn. Fo. Incompl., containing the O.T. & Apocrypha only, & lacking all but last 7 prelims. 18th. C. cf., rebkd. W.a.f. (SG. Feb.5; 39) $600

– – **Anr. Edn.** L., 1578. 1st. lge. Fo. Edn. of Geneva version. Lge. Fo. Prelim. lf. laid onto title verso, lacks last 5 ll., early ink scribblings, 4-pp. 18th C. MS. records of Collman family at end, some outer ll. soiled, some margins reprd. Old cf., disbnd. (SG. Sep.25; 35) $375

– **The Bible: That is, The Holy Scriptures Contained in the Old & Newe Testament. – Book of Psalms.** 1587. 3 pts. in 1 vol. 4to. Margins ruled in red thro.-out, a few sm. margins wormed, owner's inscr. of Mary Jones of Shrewsbury at front dtd. 1696, earlier MS. entries regarding same family at end. 17th. C. red panel. mor. gt., spine torn. (SBA. Jul.14; 151) *Mortens of Manchester.* £110

– **The Holy Bible translated according to the Ebrew & Greeke.–Whole Booke of Psalmes collected into English Meetre by Thomas Sternbold etc.** 1589; 1588. 2 works in 1 vol. 4to. A few upr. margins just cropped, 1st. work: 3 pts. in 1 vol., 1st. title with margins strengthened, 2nd. work: margins of final lf. strengthened, lacks C8. 17th. C. spr. cf. gt., slightly worn, hinges strengthened. [STC 2148; 2475; D. & M. 152] (SBA. Oct.21; 14) *Stourton.* £90

– **Bible.** Ed.:– [Tomson]. 1597. [Geneva version]. Fo. Title slightly defect & bkd. with lge. hand-cold. wooodcut, 1st. title & several following ll. loose, tear in 2V1, some ll. marginally wormed affecting sidenotes, with Metrical Psalms (1597) bnd. in at end. 17th. C. cf., 1 hinge brkn., worn. [STC 2168; D. & M. 235] (S. May 5; 278) *Canale.* £100

– – **Anr. Edn.** 1599. Geneva Version. 2 Pts. in 1 vol. 4to. Red ruled thro.-out. 19th. C. blind-stpd. cf. [STC 2177] (S. Mar.16; 130) *Maggs.* £110

– **The Bible, that is the Holy Scripture.** 1599 [1633?] 4 pts. in 1 vol., Apocrypha from anr. edn. 4to. Slight staining. 19th. C. cf. [STC 2179; D. & M. (H) 253] (S. Dec.9; 295) *Armstrong.* £55

– **The Holy Bible.** 1601. Geneva Version. 4to. Mor. gt., decor. spine, gt. (CE. Jul.9; 149) £72

– – **Anr. Edn.** 1602. Fo. Engraved title trimmed & mntd. Later panel. cf. [STC 2188; D. & M. 206] (SBA. Jul.22; 199) *Thomas.* £320

– **The Holie Bible Faithfully Translated into English . . .** Douai, 1609. Sm. 4to. Title & a few prelims. loose, some other ll. slightly stained. Cont. cf., very worn. (SBA. Jul.14; 154) *Smith.* £60

– – **Anr. Edn.** Douai, 1609-10. 1st. Edn. in Engl. 2 vols. 4to. Errata lf. bnd. in at end of Vol. I, short tear in 6T4 of vol.II, affecting text, other short tears, some ll. loose, slight browning, slight dampstaining to a few ll. Cont. cf., gt., rather worn. [NSTC 2207, D. & M. (Herbert) 300] (S. May 5; 418) *Maggs.* £220

BIBLES [English] *-contd.*

– – Anr. Edn. L., 1619. 4to. Book of Common Prayer, L., & Genealogies Recorded in the Sacred Scriptures . . . by J.S. (n.d.), bnd. in. Restoration bdg. in mor., gt. & blind-tooled central panel on covers with initials M[ary] C[arnarvon] & coronet, spine gt. Bkplt. of Sir William Abdy of Chobham Place, sig. of 'A.S. Carnarvon' 1st. Countess of Carnarvon. (SG. Oct.9; 29) $650

– Bible, with the Book of Common Prayer, & the Whole Book of Psalms . . . Thomas Sternhold, John Hopkins & others. Edinb.; Edinb.; L., 1633; 1633; 1633. 1st. Edn. of the Compl. King James Vers. (A Vers.). 3 works in 1 vol., Bible in 2 pts. Engraved title to N.T. reprd. affecting text, 'Carkases' reading, rubricated thro.-out. Cont. velvet, Dutch silver decor., 16 oval engraved plaques, 4 with figures burnished away, plaques mntd. 7 per side, & 2 on clasps. marb. paste-downs, slightly wormed, cl. box. Bkplt. of J.R. Abbey, with his arms on cl. box. [STC 2311] [STC 16394] (SM. Oct.8; 2428) Frs. 20,000

– The Holy Bible containing the Old Testament & the New . . . 1640-39. [Authorised Edn.]. 2 vols. in 1. Fo. Corner of a few ll. strengthened, causing very slight loss, stab marks in some inner margins, a few other minor defects, mainly marginal. Cont. cf., rebkd., new endpapers. [STC 2339] (SBA. Jul.14; 152) *Smith.* £170

– The Holy Bible. Ill.:– Lombart (engraved title), W. Hollar (coat of arms), Visscher & Hollar (plts.). Camb., 1659-60. 2 vols. Fo. Old mor. gt., worn. W.a.f. (SKC. Feb.26; 1731) £320

– Bible. Ill.:– Lambert, W. Hollar & Visscher after Rubens & others. Camb., 1660-59. Authorized Version, Ogilby's Ill. Edn. 2 vols. Fo. Late 17th. C. red mor., panel. in gt. [D. & M. 668] (S. Nov.24; 24) *Broseghini.* £1,100

– The Holy Bible, Containing the Old & New Testament. Ill.:– Visscher. Amst., 1672. Fo. Extra-ill. with 116 double-p. plts., many cropped or stained, or otherwise imperfect, many by Visscher, & 5 double-p. maps, most slightly stained, 2 with sm. tears just affecting print area. Cont. cf. over wooden bds., rebkd., upr. cover loose, metal clasps & cornerpieces. W.a.f. [Wing B2284] (C. Apr.1; 192) *Faupel.* £650

– Bible . . . with The Whole Book of Psalms. 1674. 12mo. Slight browning. Cont. black mor., covers tooled with outer gt. roll enclosing panel with red mor. onlays in corners, maroon mor. onlays on covers, & natural mor. onlays in centre, onlays & intervening spaces with gt. tooling, spine in gt. tooled, panels with later lettering, upr. cover slightly wormed, a few onlay pieces missing, split in spine, gauffered with flowers with painted petals. Bkplt. of Charles Butler. [Wing B2290] (S. Jun.9; 41) *Thomas.* £90

– The Holy Bible containing the Old Testament & the New . . . Ill.:– Van Hove. L., 1678. Cont. mor., tooled gt. panel & decor., with initials W.S. (GM. Apr.30; 628) £80

– English Shorthand Bible L., [1687]. 1st. Edn. in Engl. Shorthand 3 engraved titles/frontis., one stained, red ruled thro.-out., port. darkened. Cont. black mor. gt., gt. fillet border on covers. gt.-tooled spine. [Wing B2802] (CNY. May 22; 34) $400

– The Holy Bible, Containing the Old & New Testaments. 1715. Fo. 1 map torn with loss. Cont. blind-stpd. cf., worn. (CSK. Aug.22; 49) £120

– The Holy Bible, containing the Old & New Testaments . . . [with the Book of Common Prayer]. Oxford, 1715. 2 vols. Fo. Ruled in red thro.-out, a few spots. Cont. black mor., gt. (S. Oct.21; 522) *Thomas.* £170

– The Holy Bible. 1738. Fo. Red mor. gt., tooled border with thistles & Crowns & eagles, central lozenge of intertwining branches & geometric designs & decor. spine in 8 compartments. (CE. Jul.9; 150) £200

– – Anr. Edn. Edinb., 1756. 4to. Cont. red mor., tooled edge of stylized ll. & central decor. cross, & tooled spine of stylized flowers in 6 compartments, lacks front & back free end-papers. (CE. Jul.9; 147) £80

– The Holy Bible Containing the Old Testament & the New. Camb., 1763. Fo. Cont. black mor., gt. roll-tooled triple-panel. covers, wide centre panel & outer panel tooled with volutes, gt. panel spine tooled with crowns etc., head & foot of spine worn. (C. Apr.1; 193) *Traylen.* £280

– – Anr. Copy. 2 pts. in 1. Subscription list in 3rd. state, prelims. slightly spotted. Cont. red mor. gt., neatly rebkd., preserving orig. spine. (SBA. Oct.22; 540) *Stoughton.* £190

– – Anr. Copy. Cont. reversed cf., neatly rebkd. & cornered, new end-papers. (SBA. Oct.22; 540a) *Temperley.* £52

– – Anr. Copy. Cont. red mor. gt., JHS & Cross gt. stp. on covers in onlaid mor. frames, gt. border, spine in 8 compartments, 7 raised bands. (CNY. May 22; 298) $2,200

– – Anr. Edn. Bg'ham., 1769-71. 2 vols. in 1. Lge. fo. Continuous sigs., 10 engraved plts. Cont. Irish red mor. gt., spine tooled in compartments with ornaments & mor. onlays & inlays, elab. decor. covers. (S. Nov.24; 23) *Lyon.* £23,00

– – Anr. Edn. Bg'ham., Baskerville Pr. 1772. 2 pts. in 1 vol. Fo. A few ll. slightly spotted. Cont. mor. gt., neatly rebkd., preserving orig. spine. (SBA. Oct.22; 541) *Stoughton.* £90

– Bible. Phila., 1782-81. 12mo. Stained & browned, title defect., some ll. frayed. Cont. cf., worn, upr. cover detchd., cl. box. (CNY. May 22; 33) $750

– The Holy Bible, containing the Old & New Testaments; together with the Apocrypha. Ill.:– J.H. Seymour. Worcester, 1791. 4to. Considerably foxed. Old cf., spine heavily gt., covers loose. (SG. Jan.8; 37) $140

– – Anr. Edn. 1793. Title soiled at edges, foxed. Cont. ruled cf., upr. cover loose. (PNY. Dec.3; 38) $110

– – Anr. Edn. Ill.:– James Fittler. 1795. 2 vols. Red mor. gt. (CE. Jul.9; 148) £50

– – Anr. Copy. 3 vols. 4to. Cont. str.-grd. mor., gt. with lozenge designs, spines gt., slightly worn. (SG. Feb.5; 43) $200

– The Holy Bible, containing the Old & New Testament & the Apocrypha. Ill.:– F. Bartolozzi & others after Sir J. Reynolds others. 1800-16. 8 vols. Lge. 4to. Occasional minor spotting. Cont. red str.-grd. mor., covers with stylized gt. greek-key panel (tooling on vol. VIII non-unif.), spines gt., by L. Staggemeier with his ticket, upr. cover of vol. I detchd., slight abrasions to some covers. From the collection of Eric Sexton. (C. Apr.15; 60) *Fogg.* £200

– The Holy Bible, Containing the Old & New Testaments. Oxford, 1815. L.P. 9 vols. Lge. 4to. Extra ill. with over 1,500 engraved plts. Early mor., gt. floral borders & spines, gt. dentelles. (SG. Oct.9; 30) $1,800

– Bible, with the Book of Common Prayer. L. & Oxford, 1822. 2 vols. 16mo. Old maroon str.-grd. mor. gt., broad gt. borders & decor. spines, orig. unif. mor. gt. flap-box (slightly worn). With fore-e. pntg. in each vol.; from the Prescott Collection. (CNY. Feb.6; 115) $550

– The Holy Bible. Camb., 1825. Early black str.-grd. mor., jnts. crudely reprd. Fore-e. pntg. of old Philadelphia; from the liby. of Zola E. Harvey. (SG. Mar.19; 112) $325

– The Illuminated Bible, containing the Old & New Testaments . . . also Apocrypha. Ill.:– from designs by J.G. Chapman. N.Y., 1846. Bnd. from pts. 4to. Hf. mor., wraps. of 6 pts. bnd. in, liby. bkplt., brkn. (SG. Mar.5; 28) $500

– – Anr. Copy. Orig. elab. gt.-stpd. mor., upr.-cover detchd. (SG. Sep.4; 39) $350

– Bible. Ca. 1890. Silver bdg. in 18th. C. Dutch style, elab. embossed, clasps. (S. Mar.16; 197) *Smith.* £280

– The English Bible. Ed.:– Rev. F.H. Scrivener. Doves Pr. 1903-05. (500). Fo. Orig. limp vell., unc. Engraved bkplt. of John Raymond Danson by Stephen Gooden. (SH. Feb.19; 39a) *Fletcher.* £900

– – Anr. Copy. 5 vols. Orig. vell., slight shrinkage to vols. 1 & 4. vell.-tipped s.-c.'s. & spine guards. (CNY. May 22; 377) $1,800

– – Anr. Copy. Prepared for rebinding, in stitched bds. (SPB. Nov. 25; 255) $900

– The Holy Bible. L., [1911]. 3 vols. Tall 8vo. Orig. frontis. etchings on Japan vell., text ptd. on india paper. Gt. & blind-ruled crushed rust mor. (PNY. Dec.3; 33) $130

– – Anr. Edn. Ill.:– Stephen Gooden. L., Nones. Pr. 1924-27. (75) on Arnold rag paper. 5 vols. Fo. Orig. stiff vell., gt.-lettered, unc., qtr. mor. s.-c.'s, bkplt. of Stuart W. Jackson. The John A. Saks copy. (CNY. Oct.1; 197) $1,600

– – Anr. Edn. Ill.:– Bruce Rogers. Oxford, 1935. (180). Lge. fo. Lev. mor. on heavy bds., double-ruled in blind, outer border of onlaid mor. blindstpd. with sm. tool & gt. stpd., upr. cover with mor. onlay of cross, lr. cover with sm. panel matching outer border, spine in 6 compartments ruled as covers, 5 raised bands, sm. brass cornerpieces, clasps & 2 sm. square bosses on each cover, by Douglas Cockerell & Son, sigd. & dtd. 1939, orig. shipping box also preserved, corduroy-lined, braided thongs, orig. hand-written label, cl. case. (CNY. May 22; 361) $15,000

– – Anr. Edn. Designed by Bruce Rogers. Oxford, 1935. (200). 2 vols. Fo. Stitched, unbnd., unc. (SH. Feb.20; 369) *Appleton.* £4,200

– The Jerusalem Bible. Ill.:– Salvador Dali. Garden City, 1970. 4to. Gt.-lettered leatherette, marb. endpapers. Sigd. by Dali on hf.-title. (SG. Apr.2; 84) $160

– Holy Bible–Illustrated Family Bible. Ed.:– John Kitto. Ill.:– John Martin. N.d. 2 vols. 4to. 19 (of 20?) mezzotints, 1 loose & with margin slightly frayed. Orig. mor. gt. (SBA. Oct.21; 229) *Kawamatsu.* £160

– The Holy Bible. Camb., n.d., New Testament title dtd. 1638. Rubricated thro.-out, titles with various pen & ink decors. Late 17th. C. black mor., covers panel. & elab. tooled in gt., spine similarly tooled to form 2 main panels, later end-papers. W.a.f. (CSK. Apr.24; 122) £440

BIBLES [English]–PRAYER BOOKS [English]

– The Bible.–Book of Common Prayer. 1615. 2 works in 1 vol. 4to. Last work with some serious defects. Later cf., slightly worn. (SBA. May 27; 64) *Cresswell.* £55

– – Anr. Edn. L.; Oxford, 1826; 1825. 2 vols. 24mo. Str.-grd. mor., multiple gt. fillet borders, spines gt. Each vol. with fore-e. pntg. (SG. Mar.19; 113) $450

BIBLES [English]–PRAYER BOOKS [English] –PSALMS, PSALTERS & PSEUMES

– The Bible.–Book of Common Prayer.–The Whole Book of Psalmes.–Concordances. L.; Camb.; L.; L., 1602; 1630; 1598; 1602. 4 works in 1 vol. 4to. Some ll. reprd., some remargined towards end, occasional minor staining, some cont. MS. markings. Cf., rebkd. (CB. Nov.12; 144) Can. $150

BIBLES [English]–PRAYER BOOKS [English] –PSALMS, PSALTERS, & PSEUMES–SPEEDE, John

– Bible.–The Book of Common Prayer.–The Whole Book of Psalms.–The Genealogies.–A Description of Canaan . . .–Concordances. L.; n.p.; L.; n.p.; n.p.; L., 1614-15; n.d.; 1619; n.d.; n.d.; 1615. 4to. 2nd. work lacks title-p., last lf. of N.T. with lr. hf. cut-out (no text loss), occasional minor staining, some dust soiling, some cont. MS. markings. 18th. C. panel. cf., lacks sm. piece from head of spine. (CB. Nov.12; 145) Can. $150

BIBLES [English]–PSALMS, PSALTERS & PSEUMES

– Bible.–Whole Booke of Psalmes. L., 1644; 1641. 2 vols. in 1. 12mo. Cont. needlework bdg. of cold. wools on silver thread background, spine in 4 compartments, 18th. C. brass clasp, endpapers renewed with old marble paper, silver thread slightly tarnished, loose in old cold. cl. bag, qtr. red mor. gt. box. [1st. work Wing B 2205] (CNY. May 22; 364) $2,000

– – Anr. Edn. Oxford; L., [1682]; 1684. 2 works in 1 vol. 17th. C. Engl. mor., fillet compartments, gt. decor. with sm. pointillé tools formed of flowers, spine similarly decor., inside dentelle, cover. (HD. Mar.18; 145) Frs. 4,000

BIBLES [French]

– Bible. Trans.:– [Jacques Lefevre d'Etaples]. Antw., Dec. 10, 1530. 1st. Edn. of the Compl. Translation. 2 vols. in 1. Fo. 1st. 5 ll. & 2 at end mntd. on guards, lacks last blank, & blank at end of Psalms, marginal tears touching text at fo. 224 of O.T. & 1 lf. of table at front of N.T. with marginal soiling or fraying, some sections worn. Cont. blind-stpd. black cf. over wood bds., covers with fleurons in lozenges at central panel, brass bosses, cornerpieces & clasps, worn, rebkd. folding cl. case. The copy of Rev. William Makellar, bkplt. of the General Theological Seminary Liby. [D. & M. 3708] (CNY. Oct.1; 1) $8,500

– – Anr. Edn. Ed.:– John Calvin (privilege & intro.). Trans.:– [Pierre Robert Olivetan]. Neuchatel, Jun. 4, 1535. 4 pts. in 1 vol. Fo. Sm. puncture to lr. margins of folios 42-50 of N.T., last lf. creased & lightly soiled, slight occasional dampstaining to margins. Cont. blind-stpd. cf., covers with lge. central lozenge & borders of fillets & floral rolls, worn, rebkd. with portions of orig. spine preserved. The copy of Rev. William Makellar, bkplt of the General Theological

Seminary Liby. [D. & M. 3710] (CNY. Oct.1; 29) $16,000

– **La Saincte Bible.** Paris, 1616. Fo. Cont. cf., gt., very worn. (S. Mar.16; 51) *Hendricks.* £85

– **La Saincte Bible; Contenant le Vieil et le Nouveau Testament Enrichie de Plusieurs Belles Figures.** Cologne, 17th. C. Ob. 4to. 246 (of 269) copper-plts., occasional staining to plts. Old. cf. (SG. May 21; 334) $475

– **La Sainte Bible.** L., 1811. 12mo. Cont. red str.-grd. mor. gt. Fore-e. pntg. of Bellini's 'Madonna of the Meadow'. (SG. Mar.19; 111) $260

– **La Sainte Bible selon la Vulgate.** Ill.:– Gustave Doré. Tours, 1866. 2 vols. Fo. Some slight foxing. Cont. red hf. mor. (SM. Feb.11; 282) Frs. 2,800

BIBLES [German]

– **Bible.** Augsburg, [Gunther Zainer], [1475-76]. 4th. Edn. of the Bible in German. 2 vols. Fo. All but 1 capital initial cold., 1st. initial with hf.-border of stylized floral design of red, green & blue, all colouring by cont. hand, rubricated, some slight wormholes at beginning & end of each vol., some very slight marginal worming, 3 marginal tears in vol. 2 reprd., inserted at front of vol. 2 is a single column sheet in cont. MS. repeating the final 50 lines of vol. 1. Late 19th. C. pol. cf., spine gt.-lettered, in 2 mor.-tipped s.-c.'s. Bkplt. of William Morris, with his long (about 500 words) note on fly-lf., later the copy of Marsden J. Perry, bkplt. of John A. Saks. [BMC II, 323, Goff B267, H. 3133] (CNY. Oct.1; 78) $60,000

– – **Anr. Edn.** Augsburg, [Günther Zainer], 1477. 2 vols. Fo. F.2 recto with cont. illumination in 2 margins, 74 lge. histor. initials, 73 cold. by later hands, cold. woodcut device at end of each vol., some ornaments, woodcut initials partly cold., other initials supplied in red, rubricated in parts, f.1 mntd, some wormholes, sm. 19th. C. liby. stps. at beginning of each vol. 17th. C. German blind-stpd. pig. on wooden bds., 3 (of 4) clasps. [BMC II, 324] (S. Nov.25; 335). *Niedhardt.* £8,000

– – **Anr. Edn.** Nuremb., Anton Koberger, 17 Feb., 1483. 2 vols. Fo. 109 woodcuts with orig. col., 3 with gold lf., 4 initials painted in blue & white on gold ground in painted frame borders, chief initials in red & blue, others red or blue, rubricated thro.-out. Orig. blind-stpd. Nuremb. cf. elab. decor., sm. metal bosses, cornerpieces & clasp-holders on vol. 2, missing on vol 1. Bkplt. of Alfred Pfeiffer. [BMC II, 424] (S. Nov.25; 328) *Breslauer.* £23,00

– – **Anr. Copy.** Vol. I only (of 2). Spaces for initial capitals, 2 capitals illuminated in cols. & gold, capitals at head of each book supplied in red, blue & green, others in red or blue, paragraph marks & initial strokes added in red, all 88 woodcuts cold. by cont. hand, lacks final blank, many ll. at front with marginal tears affecting text on 14 ll. & woodcuts on 5 ll., some margins heavily frayed, marginal dampstaining touching text in some places, light worming to extreme inner margins of some ll., soiling & traces of use. Cont. Nuremb. bdg. of blind-stpd. cf. over wood bds., upr. cover with central panel of floral tools & stylized foliage flanked by lge. rosettes & foliage tools, lr. cover panel. & with lozenge stps. enclosing a griffin & double-headed eagle, brass centre & cornerpieces, worn, upr. cover detchd., lacks spine, folding cl. case. Bkplt. of the General Theological Seminary Liby. [BMC II, 424, Goff B532, HC 3173*] (CNY. Oct.1; 36) $5,000

– **Bibel.** Ed.:– Johan Ecken. [Ingolstadt], 1537. 1st. Edn. Fo. Lacks last lf., penultimate lf. laid down, soiled & browned, stained in parts. Cont. blind-tooled pig-bkd. wood bds., 2 clasps, 1 brkn. (HK. Nov.18-21; 119) DM 3,600

– **Catholische Bibell.** Ed.:– D.J. Dietenberger. Ill.:– V. Solis (woodcuts); A. Woensam v. Worms (cold initials). Cologne, 1564. 2 pts. in 1 vol. Lge. fo. 1st. & last ll. soiled & stained, some slight tears. Cont. blind-tooled pig-bkd. wood bds., 2 clasps. (HK. May 12-14; 77) DM 10,000

– **Bibell.** Trans.:– J. Dietenberger. Cologne, 1587. 2 vols. in 1. Fo. 2 repeated woodcut title borders, slightly browned & stained, 1. 392 defect with some text loss. Cont. blind-stpd. pig-bkd. wood bds., clasps brkn. [D. & M. 4211] (R. Oct.14-18; 26) DM 2,200

– – **Anr. Copy.** Title backed, old owner's mark, last & 1st. ll very soiled, browned thro.-out & slightly soiled. Cont. leath.-bkd. wood-bds., very worn. (HK. Nov.18-21; 120) DM 1,000

– **Biblia.** Trans.:– M. Luther. Wittenberg, 1618. Kurfürstenbibel, probably 2nd. printing. Fo. Lengthy MS. note on pref.; some underlining, lightly browned, new endpapers. Later cf., renewed spine, lacks clasps, lacks lr. bosses, defect., reprd. (H. Dec.9/10; 1397) DM 2,600

– **Biblia Germanica.–Biblia Sacra, das ist die gantse Heilige Schrifft.** Trans.:– C. Vlenbergirs. Cologne, 1630. Fo. 1st. sig. slightly soiled. Cont. blind-tooled leath.-bkd. wood bds., & decor. brass bosses, 2 lge. brass clasps, spine & cover defect. (HK. Nov.18-21; 1500) DM 3,000

– **Biblia.** Nuremb., 1644. Fo. Some defects to folding plts., etc. Cont. stpd. pig over wood bds., lacks 1 metal clasp. W.a.f. (SG. Feb.5; 45) $400

– – **Anr. Edn.** Trans.:– M. Luther. Ill.:– Ph. Kilian & others. Lüneburg, 1672. Fo. Lacks frontis., lightly soiled. Cont. blind-tooled pig-bkd. wood bds., lacks 2 clasps. (HK. May 12-14; 959) DM 3,600

– – **Anr. Edn.** Trans.:– Martin Luther. Lüneburg, 1684. 3 pts. in 1 vol. Fo. Additional engraved title, cut down & mntd., slightly spotted. Blind-stpd. German cf. over wooden bds, with 7 (of 8) bosses, initials I.B.B. & date 1802 on upr. cover, worn, upr. jnt. reprd., lower jnt. brkn., lacks clasps. (S. May 5; 67) *Quaritch.* £260

– **Biblia, Das ist: Die Gantze H. Schrift . . .** Trans.:– Dr. Martin Luther. Ill.:– after Richter by Dürr & others. Nuremb., 1692. Kurfürstenbibel. Lge. fo. Some plts. bkd., slightly soiled in parts. Cont. pig-bkd. wood bds., blind-tooled, ports. in centre covers, 7 raised bands, 8 brass bosses, 2 clasps. (D. Dec.11-13; 4) DM 2,000

– – **Anr. Copy.** Lacks copper engraved title, 2 ll. at beginning, ports. 2, 7, 8 & 9, left half of plan, & PP. 665-686, several ll. & copper engrs. with tears, mostly at beginning, some plt. & text loss. 1st. ll. wormed. Cont. blind-tooled vell., upr. cover loose, spine defect. (HK. Nov.18-21; 1501) DM 700

– – **Anr. Edn.** Trans.:– M. Luther. Ill.:– M. Merian. Frankfurt, Merians Heirs. 1704. Fo. Pt. 1 lacks 1 lf., pp. 3/4 with sm. tear at foot, pt. 2 some pp. lack lr. corner, pt. 1 some pp. with lge. hole in text, other pp. with loss or tears at foot or margin, slightly soiled thro.-out, browned in parts, several ll. loose at beginning & end. Cont. blind-tooled pig-bkd. wood bds., worn, spine old restored at foot, upr. cover with fault, 8 brass bosses, lacks 3, 2 clasps. (HK. May 12-14; 966) DM 1,600

– – **Anr. Edn.** Ill.:– Elias Porzel after J.J. v. Sandrart. Nuremb., 1710. 2 pts. in 1 vol. Fo. Lightly soiled in parts, some tears at edges, 1 copper title torn. Cont. leath.-bkd. wood bds. gt. clasps brkn., brass bosses, 1 corner defect. (R. Mar.31-Apr.4; 212) DM 2,050

– – **Anr. Edn.** Ed.:– Chr. M. Pfaff. Trans.:– M. Luther. Tübingen, 1729. 2 pts. in 1 vol. Fo. Lacks 1 port. & probably 1 plt., 1st. ll. soiled, lower corner defect., soiled in parts, plts. slightly frayed. Cont. blind-tooled pig-bkd. wood bds., 2 clasps, lacks 1 clasp & 1 boss, defect. & worn. (HK. Nov.18-21; 1502) DM 800

– – **Anr. Edn.** Ed.:– J.J. Ulrich. Trans.:– M. Luther. Basel, 1729. Fo. Cont. blind-tooled pig-bkd. wood bds., lacks brass bosses & clasps, fault in upr. cover leath. (HK. May 12-14; 960) DM 1,000

– – **Anr. Copy.** 1 copper engr. with lge. tear in centre fold, 1 lf. with tear & slight text loss, last lf. loose, some browning. Cont. cf., with added later cf., spine defect. (H. Dec.9/10; 1398) DM 720

– – **Anr. Edn.** Ed.:– F. Battier & T. Gernier. Trans.:– Martin Luther. Basel, 1736. 2nd. Edn. 2 pts. in 1 vol. Fo. Slightly browned thro.-out & mostly slightly soiled edges. Cont. pig-bkd. wood bds., 6 (of 8) corner bosses, ties brkn., upr. cover defect. (R. Mar.31-Apr.4; 216) DM 1,100

– – **Anr. Edn.** Ed.:– J. Fricke (Pref.) Trans.:– Dr. Martin Luther. Ulm, 1742. Cont. leath., wide floral gold stpd. borders on both covers, gt. spine, gt. inner & outer dentelles, pink silk end-papers. (D. Dec.11-13; 6) DM 500

– – **Anr. Edn.** Nuremb., 1747. Fo. Cont. blind-stpd. vell. on wooden bds., brass cornerpieces & clasps, lacks 1 clasp. (C. Jul.16; 217) *Amman.* £80

– – **Anr. Edn.** Ed.:– J. Chr. Klemm. Trans.:– M. Luther. Tübingen, 1748. 2 pts. in 1 vol. Fo. Lacks both copperplts., slightly browned & lightly soiled. Cont. leath.-bkd. wood bds., lacks hf. lr. cover, lacks clasps. (HK. Nov. 18-21; 1504) DM 570

– – **Anr. Edn.** Ed.:– J.M. Dilherrn. Nuremb., ca. 1750. Fo. Some ll. stained, 1 torn, reprd. Cont. blind-tooled pig-bkd. wood bds., 7 (of 8) corner bosses, clasps defect., some worming in upr. cover. [D. & M. 4225] (R. Oct.14-18; 1267) DM 2,700

– – **Anr. Edn.** Ed.:– J.M. Dillhern & A. Rehberger. Trans.:– Martin Luther. Nuremb., 1765. 2 pts. in 1 vol. Fo. Slightly browned or soiled in parts. Cont. blind-stpd. pig-bkd. wood bds., 7 (of 8) corner bosses, clasps. (R. Mar.31-Apr.4; 213) DM 2,600

– – **Anr. Copy.** Lacks 2 or 3 ll. & 1 frontis. & several copperplts., soiled thro.-out. Foot of spine defect., 8 brass bosses, lacks 2 clasps. W.a.f. (HK. May 12-14; 961) DM 650

– – **Anr. Edn.** Ed.:– J. Sauberti & S. Glassens, J.M. Dilherrns. Trans.:– M. Luther Nuremb., 1770. Fo. Lightly soiled in some upper margins, heavily soiled at beginning, 2 engraved frontis. torn at edge, 1 loose, port. with sm. tear. Cont. blind-tooled pig-bkd. wood bds., 1 (of 2) clasps, end-ll. renewed. (R. Mar.31-Apr.4; 215) DM 900

– – **Anr. Edn.** Ed.:– F. Battier & T. Gernier. Trans.:– Martin Luther. Basel, 1798. 2 pts. in 1 vol. Slightly browned or soiled. Cont. leath.-bkd. wood bds., 10 brass bosses, ties brkn., defect. & reprd. (R. Mar.31-Apr.4; 218) DM 750

See–NEW TESTAMENT [German]

BIBLES [German & Latin]

– **Biblia Sacra.** Ed.:– G. Cartier. Konstanz, 1763. Vulgate Edn., 2nd. Edn. 4 pts. in 2 vols. Slightly soiled. Cont. leath., spine slightly torn. (HK. Nov.18-21; 1507) DM 700

BIBLES [Greek]

– **Sacrae Scripturae Veteris Novae que Omnia.** Venice, Feb. 1518. 1st. Publd. Edn. of the Bible in Greek. Fo. Spaces for initials with guide letters, title slightly soiled, sm. wormhole through 1st. eleven ll. Black mor. gt. by F. Bedford, rebkd. with orig. back-strip preserved, cl. s.-c. Bkplt. of the General Theological Seminary Liby. (CNY. Oct.1; 75) $12,000

–[–] **Anr. Edn.** Ed.:– Philip Melanchthon. Ill.:– after Holbein. Basle, 1545. 4th. Edn. Fo. Old marginal annots. & underlinings, stains towards end, a few other stains. Blind-tooled pig.-bkd. wooden bds., rebkd., reprd., clasps. [D. & M. 4614] (VG. Nov.18; 1016) Fls. 750

See–NEW TESTAMENT [Greek]

BIBLES [Hebrew]

– **[Bible]. Neviim Rishonim: Joshua, Judges, Samuel & Kings.** Ed.:– David Kimchi (commentary). Soncino, Joshua Solomon, Oct. 15, 1485. Sm. fo. 157 ll. only (of 166), biblical text in sq. type with nikud written in, some inner margins strengthened & reprd., 1 tear not affecting text, 1 line censored but legible, p. containing colophon torn not affecting text, sigd. by censors in 1601, 1613 & 1626, slight staining. Mod. bds., leath. spine. s.-c. [Goff (Hebrew) 22, H 13408] (SPB. May 11; 14) $11,000

– **Magna Biblia Rabbinica-Mikraot Gedolot.** Ed.:– Felix Pratensis. Venice, 1516-18. 1st. Edn. 4 pts. in 2 vols. Fo. Lightly stained, worming. Leath. mntd. on wood, in s.-c.'s, rebkd., worming. (SPB. May 11; 40) $17,000

– **Biblia Hebraica.** Venice, 1521. 4to. Inscr. on title, some marginal annots., a few stains at beginning. 17th. C. blind-tooled russ., rubbed. [D. & M. 5084] (VG. Nov.18; 1015) Fls. 4,100

– **Old Testament, with the Targum of Jonathan, the Commentaries of Rashi & Kimchi, the Masora Magna & Masora Parva.** Ed.:– Jacob b. Chayim of Tunis. Venice, 1524-25. 2nd. Edn. 4 vols. Fo. Lacks final blank in vol. 2, blank ll. 8 in vol. 4, ll. 31 & 8 & last 2 ll. of table in vol. 4, sm. piece torn from upper margin of ll. 97 in vol. 4 with loss of about 20 letters in 1 column, dampstaining to margins, affecting some text, 5 ll. with reprd. marginal tears, 8 ll. in vol. 3 with reprd. wormhole to upr. margin. 18th. C. cf.-bkd. wood bds., covers with lge. armorial stps. in gt., rebkd., worn. Bkplt. of the General Theological Seminary Liby. [D. & M. 5085] (CNY. Oct.1; 76) $18,000

– **Bible.** Paris, 1544-46. 13 vols. 16mo. Browned. Orig. cf., slightly rubbed. (SPB. May 11; 41) $4,000

– – **Anr. Edn.** [Paris], [1544-46]. 13 pts. in 8 vols. 16mo. 18th. C. panel. cf., 2nd. vol. not uniform. W.a.f. (C. Jul.16; 306) *Tareave.* £2,200

– **Old Testament.** [Paris], [1544-48]. 17 vols. 32mo. 17th. C. red mor. gt., gt. spines & dentelles. (SG. Oct.9; 31) $6,200

– **Bible.** Antw., 1566. 4to. Wormholes affecting some letters, tears, browning, lge. stp. on title.

BIBLES [Hebrew] *-contd.*
Blind-stpd. mor., worn, stained & torn. (SPB. May 11; 42) $1,400
-- **Anr. Edn.** Antw., 1573. 16mo. Cropped, tears, stains & browning. Velvet, defect., stitching loose. (SPB. May 11; 43) $1,100
-- **Anr. Edn.** Amst., 1705. 4 pts. in 1 vol. 12mo. Cropped, browning, staining. Mod. leath. (SPB. May 11; 44) $300
-- **Anr. Edn.** Ed.:– J.H.M. & G. Chr. Burklin. Frankfurt a. M., 1716. 4to. Lightly stained, some ll. loose. Cf., rebkd., worn, spine torn. (SPB. May 11; 45) $225
-- **Anr. Edn.** Ill.:– Griselini. Venice, 1739. 4to. Some ll. loose or detchd., slight soiling on some ll. Cf. gt., slight worming. (SPB. May 11; 227) $1,300
- **Bible-Minchat Shai.** Ed.:– Shlomo Norzi (critical glosses). Mantua, 1742-44. 1st. Edn. 4 pts. in 3 vols. 4to. Margins reprd. Mod. vell. (SPB. May 11; 46) $550
- **Bible.** Pisa, 1803. 4to. Some staining, ll reprd. without text loss. Hf. vell. (SPB. May 11; 47) $225
- **Biblia Hebraica.** Ed.:– Johannes Leusden. Phila., 1814. 2 vols. Lacks title in 1st. vol., some ll. stained & detchd. Orig. bds., cl. covered folding box. Bkplt. of the Boston School of Theology Liby. (SPB. May 11; 48) $1,600

BIBLES [Icelandic]
- **Biblia Pad Er, Oll Heilog Rit-ning, Vtlgod a Norraenu.** Ed.:– Gudbrandur Thorladsson, Bishop of Holar, M. Luther. Holum, 1584. 1st Edn. Fo. Marginal stains & worming in 1st. & last quires occasionally touching text, old repairs obscuring 2 lines, inner corner torn from B6 & sm. repair to F6 in New Testament, some old stains thro.-out., lacks final blank, loosely inserted is a slip of paper with notes sigd. by John Ihre. Cf. over beech bds., panel. with rolls, initials PES on upr. cover & GVD on the lower with date 1625, raised brass cornerpieces & central boss, remains of clasps, worn. Textual corrections stpd. by hand in margins after sheets had been ptd. [D. & M. 5489] (S. Oct.20; 28) *Solnes.* £7,500

BIBLES [Italian]
- **La Sacra Bibbia.** Trans.:– Antonio Martini. Ill.:– Doré. Milan, 1877-79. 2 vols. Fo. Mod. red hf. mor. (SI. Dec.3; 203) Lire 240,000

BIBLES [Latin]
- **Bible.** Mainz, Johann Fust & Peter Schoeffer. 14 Aug., 1462. 2 vols. Fo. Many Lombard initial capitals ptd. red or blue, spaces for others, headlines, initial strokes, some chapter nos. & capitals supplied in red, fo. 239 of vol. I lacks colophon, fo. 242 of vol. II lacks explicit to Apocolypse & bears the 7-line colophon (De Ricci's 3rd. form), 28 ll. in vol. I with reprd. tears, 8 affecting text (that at fo. 157 crossing both columns) slight replacements to 5 ll. of vol. II, with loss of 2 letters at fo. 51, 31 ll. in vol. II with reprd. tears, 9 affecting text, scattered spotting, soiling, several sm. rust-holes & light worming at beginning & end, catching some text at end of vol. I. Maroon lev. mor. gt., covers with triple gt. fillet borders & central panel with fleurons at corners, spines gt. & gt.-lettered, by F. Bedford, late 19th. C. mor. solander cases. Bkplt. of the General Theological Seminary Liby. [BMC I, 22, D. & M. 6080, Goff B529, HC 3050*] (CNY. Oct.1; 26) $75,000
-- **Anr. Edn.** [Strassburg], Heinrich Eggestein. ca. 1468-70. 2 vols. Fo. Spaces for initial capitals, 95 lge. capitals supplied in 2 or 3 cols., some with gold highlights (oxidized), many with scrollwork ornamentation extending into margins, other capitals in red or blue, many with flourishes, incipits, chapter numbers, headlines & initial strokes added in red, without the 4 ll. of rubrics found in some copies, minor worming to some ll. at beginning & end of each vol., slight browning at margins, folios 1 & 319 of vols. 1 from anr. copy (the former lf. with marginal repair), some ll. on guards, sm. portions of lr. margin torn-away from folios 229, 289 & 298 of vol. 2, some minor dampstains. Cont. blind-stpd. German pig, central panels of vol. 1 divided into lozenges & triangular compartments by triple fillets, diapered with sm. rosette in a square, outer frame with repeated circular rosette tools, vol. 2 with concentric panels of triple fillets, central one decor. with a bird in a square, outer frame with repeated circular rosette tools, rebkd., some repair to edges & corners, rubbed, lacks clasps. Bkplt. of the General Theological Seminary Liby. [BMC I, 66, Goff B533, HC 3035*] (CNY. Oct.1; 56) $18,000
-- **Anr. Edn.** [Strassburg], [Heinrich Eggestein], [before 1469]. 2 vols. Fo. Spaces for incipits, explicits & initial capitals, 1st. p. of each vol. illuminated, vol. 1 with 8-line initial F depicting a bishop & elab. full-borders, 66 initial capitals illuminated in cols. & gold, all with marginal extensions of foliage, 26 with elab. marginal decors., other capitals supplied in 2 or 3 cols. or red & blue, incipits, explicits, headlines, chapter numbers & initial strokes in red, lacks folios 178-227, 249 & last blank in vol. 1, & 2 final blanks in vol. 2, 19 ll. with tears touching text, reprd. without loss, 57 other ll. with reprd. marginal tears, 1st. lf. of vol. 2 & 24 other ll. with corners or sm. portion of margin replaced, slight marginal worming at beginning & end of each vol., & to inner margins of some ll., traces of use & occasional spotting. Mod. mor., gt. spines, mor.-tipped s.-c.'s. Bkplt. of William Morris, later the copy of Richard Bennet, bkplt. of the General Theological Seminary Liby. [BMC I, 66, Goff B531, HC 3036] (CNY. Oct.1; 55) $12,000
-- **Anr. Edn.** [Basle], [Berthold Ruppel], ca. 1471. 2 vols. Fo. Spaces for initial capitals, supplied in red, many with penwork flourishes, chapter numbers & initial strokes in red, incipits, headlines & chapter summaries supplied in brown ink, with the 4 ll. of directions to the rubricator, lacks blank fo. 110 in vol 1, folios 134-182 supplied from anr. copy, tear affecting text at fo. 10 of vol. 1 reprd. without loss, clean tear to lr. margins of folios 152-155, folios 11 & 134 spotted, fo. 134 to end with several punctures, vol. 2 with similar punctures thro.-out (both without loss), last lf. with reprd. tear & portions of margins strengthened, 1 lf. of cont. MS. table added at end of vol. 2. Mod. pig, covers blind-panel., pig-tipped s.-c.'s by Gerhard Gerlach. Bkplt. of the General Theological Seminary Liby. [BMC III, 714, Goff B532, HC 3045*] (CNY. Oct.1; 5) $30,000
-- **Anr. Edn.** Mainz, Peter Schoeffer, 24 Feb. 1472. Fo. Spaces for initial capitals, lge. capitals at head of each book supplied in red & blue, many with elab. penwork embellishments, other capitals in red or blue, chapter numbers, headlines & initial strokes in red, some ll. at beginning & end with stains in upr. & fore-edge margins, occasionally touching some MS. headlines, some sm. wormholes at early & last ll., fo. 259v & fo. 260r soiled. Mod. maroon lev. mor., covers with blind-tooled borders, gt. spine, mor.-tipped s.-c. Bkplt. of the General Theological Seminary Liby. [BMC I, 28, D. & M. 6080, Goff B536, HC 3052*] (CNY. Oct.1; 27) $15,000
-- **Anr. Edn.** [Basle], [Berthold Ruppel (pt. 1), & Bernhard Richel (Pt. 2)], [before 1475]. 2 pts. in 1 vol. Fo. 1st. pt.: spaces for initial capitals, supplied in red or blue, incipits, chapter numbers, headlines & initial strokes in red; 2nd. pt.: 83 lge. woodcut initial letters, spaces for sm. capitals, supplied in red or blue, incipits, chapter numbers, headlines & initial strokes in red; partially untrimmed, with MS. quiring at lr. corners & MS. rubricator's directions at upr. & lr. edges preserved (but without the 4 ll. of rubrics), portion of 7 lines in 1 column worn away at fo. 207r, lr. corner of 1st. lf. reinforced, folios 431-436 reinforced at corners, slight worming at beginning & end, folios 112 & 113 with light dampstaining to corners, last 150 ll. with light stain, & some minor fraying to lr. outer corner, scattered light foxing, mostly marginal. Cont. undecor. pig over wood bds., worn, lacks clasps. Augustus Frederick's copy, bkplts. of George Livermore & the General Theological Seminary Liby. [BMC III, 714 & 736, Goff B538, HC 3044] (CNY. Oct.1; 6) $8,500
-- **Anr. Edn.** Venice, Franciscus Renner, de Heilbronn & Nicolaus de Frankfordia, 1475. Fo. Spaces for capital letters, some of which are supplied in brown (faded), unrubricated, light worming to some ll. at beginning & end reprd., repair to paper flaw in fore-edge margin at fo. 116, staining thro.-out, darkening at early ll. 18th. C. cf., covers with gt. floral borders with rosettes at corners & floral sprays at inner corners, gt. arms on upr. cover of Pope Pius VI, gt. spine, lr. cover detchd., qtr. mor folding case. Bkplt. of the General Theological Seminary Liby. [BMC V, 193, Goff B541, HC 3054] (CNY. Oct.1; 66) $1,500
-- **Anr. Edn.** [Cologne], [Conrad Winters de Homborch], ca. 1475. 2 vols. Fo. Spaces for initial capitals, lge. initials at head of each book supplied in 3 cols. with floral decor. & penwork flourishes extending into margins, smaller capitals in red or blue, chapter numbers, headlines, paragraph marks & initial strokes in red, MS. quiring & catchwords preserved in many places at extreme lr. edges, 20 smaller ll. bnd. in at various places bearing the prologues of St. Jerome in brown ink by cont. hand, prologue to proverbs added to verso of 1st. blank in vol 2, 1st. 3 & last 2 ll. of vol. 1 with repairs to blank margins with some paper loss, similar repairs to last 2 ll. of vol. 2, some sm. wormholes, scattered dampstaining occasionally touching text. Cont. blind-stpd. German cf. over bds., cover panels divided into lozenge & triangular compartments by diagonal double fillet, compartments decor., upr. covers with vell. label in brass frame, 2 (of 4) brass clasps only, 1 detchd., vell. pastedowns & end-ll., rebkd., rubbed, hf. mor. folding boxes (worn). Bkplt. of William Bateman, Middleton Hall, bkplt. of the General Theological Seminary Liby. [Goff B539, HC 3039] (CNY. Oct.1; 13) $12,000
-- **Anr. Edn.** Basle, Bernhard Richel, 1475 & 1477. 3 vols. Fo. Lge. capital F at 1st. p. illuminated in red, green & blue with scrollwork extending into margins, some capitals supplied in 2 cols., many woodcut capitals touched with red, foliation, paragraph marks & initial strokes in red, with rubricator's date 1475 at end of vol. 2, 1st. lf. of vol. 1 with lr. margin reinforced & sm. hole, some worming, affecting a few letters on some pp., occasional light foxing & scattered dampstaining, 1st. 40 ll. of vol. 1 stained, register lf. in early German hand added at front of vol. 2, some cont. marginalia, cont. monastic owner's inscr. in vol. 2. Mod. red lev. mor. & unif. hf. red mor., gt. spines, mor.-tipped s.-c.'s, by Semet & Plumelle. The copy of Rev. William Makellar, bkplt. of the General Theological Seminary Liby. [BMC III, 736 & 737, Goff B540 & B553, HC 3053* & 3064*] (CNY. Oct.1; 7) $4,800
-- **Anr. Edn.** Venice, Nicolaus Jenson, 1476. Fo. Spaces for initial capitals, opening of Genesis illuminated with a miniature of God the Creator with the sphere of the universe on a blue ground with gold stars, the initial letter I illuminated in green, blue & purple on a gold ground with marginal ornamentation, a wreath with an unidentified coat-of-arms at foot of p., some initial capitals & paragraph marks supplied in brown, now faded, lacks preliminary blank, 1st. 9 ll. with repair at corners, 1st. lf. stained, with sm. repair to fore-edge margin, fo. 260 with lge. tear reprd. without loss, slight repairs to margins of some additional ll., stained & cleaned but with paper still crisp. Mod. hf. mor., gt. spine. Bkplt. of the General Theological Seminary Liby. [BMC V, 176, Goff B547, HC 3061*] (CNY. Oct.1; 67) $3,000
- **Bible [with additions by Thomas Taqui & Biagio Romero].** Naples, Mathias Moravus [& Biagio Romero], 1476. 2 vols. Fo. Spaces for initial capitals, supplied in red, paragraph marks & some initial strokes also in red, some 100 ll. reinforced at gutter margin without loss, many inner margins browned, fo. 1 with blank recto bkd., reprd. tear to upr. margin of fo. 84 touching 1 column of text, anr. clean tear at fo. 103 in vol. II touching 1 column of text, last lf. with lr. corner torn-away & portion of gutter margin renewed, minor worming to inner margins of final ll. reprd. 18th. C. cf., covers gt. panel., rebkd., upr. hinge of vol. I brkn., spine gt., mor.-tipped s.-c.'s. Ink pressmarks of Charles Spencer, 3rd. Earl of Sunderland on front fly-ll., later the copy of Rev. William Makellar, bkplt. of the General Theological Seminary Liby. [BMC VI, 862, Goff B545, HC 3059] (CNY. Oct.1; 28) $4,000
- **Samuel II, Chapters XIV & XV.–Psalms, Chapter LXXII.** Venice; Nuremb., Nicolaus Jenson; Anton Koberger, 1476; 1480. Fo. 2 single ll. only; 1st. with initials at beginning in red or blue; 2nd. heavily rubricated. (SG. Feb.5; 180) $120
- **Bible.** Paris, Ulrich Gering, Martin Crantz & Michael Friburger, [between Jul.22, 1476 & Jul.21, 1477]. 2 vols. Fo. Spaces for initial capitals with guide letters, 1st. p. of vol. 1 with 7-line initial F illuminated in blue, red & gold, the margins with hf. border of floral sprays, 1st. p. of vol. 2 with illuminated initial P & similar border, other capitals & some paragraph marks supplied in red or blue, headlines in red & blue, lacks preliminary blank in vol. 1, & preliminary final

blanks in vol. 2 1st. 10 ll. with portion of margin reinforced with slight paper loss at extreme top of 6 ll. & lr. gutter of 2 others, folios 48-53 slightly wormed at upr. gutter margins, 1st. lf. of vol. 2 with extreme lr. margin reinforced, fo. 161 with clean tear extending across 1 column of text, reprd. without loss, some wormholes to last 5 ll. catching some letters, verso of last lf. soiled & with slight reinforcements to portion of gutter margin, some marginalia in 16th. C. Engl. hand. 18th. C. red mor. gt., broad onlaid borders of mor. gt. with flowers & foliate tools, gt. crest & motto 'Nobilis ira' of William Stuart on upr. covers, spine in 7 compartments with 6 raised bands, rebkd. with old spines preserved, corners & edges restored, qtr. red mor. gt. folding cases. The copy of Sir Guy Fairfax & Rev. William Makellar, bkplt. of the General Theological Seminary Liby. [BMC VIII, 8, Goff B550, H 3058] (CNY. Oct.1; 41) $56,000

– – **Anr. Edn.** Basle, Bernhard Richel, Sep. 8, 1477. 2 vols. Fo. Spaces for initial capitals in Genesis through Psalms, many with guide letters, Proverbs through Revelations with 7 sets of woodcut initial capitals, 1st. text p. of vol. I with 10-line capital F illuminated in green on red ground decor. with gold foliage, foliate sprays in red, blue & green with gold highlights extending into margins, partially rubricated, many capitals supplied in red, some woodcut capitals touched with red, occasional chapter numbers, paragraph marks & initial strokes added in red, lacks blank at end of N.T., staining to upr. & lr. edges thro.-out, touching some text, folios 117, 221 & 246 of vol. II with clean marginal tears. 19th. C. red lev. mor. gt., gt. spine, by Henderson & Bisset, brkn. The copy of Rev. William Makellar, bkplt. of the General Theological Seminary Liby. [BMC III, 737, Goff B553, HC 3064*] (CNY. Oct.1; 8) $3,000

– **Bible [with Additions by Monardus Monachus].** Nuremb., Anton Koberger, Apr. 14, 1478. Fo. Spaces for initial capitals, 1st. p. with lge. capital I supplied in red & blue with gold highlights, next p. with 13-line capital F in the same style, other capitals supplied in red, many with flourishes, paragraph marks also in red, dupls. of folios 234 & 239 bnd. at rear, folios 1-2 & 10-13 on guards, slight marginal repairs to 1st. & last ll., corner of fo. 98 renewed, puncture to lr. margin of last few ll. with slight loss at last lf., some traces of soiling. Cont. German blind-stpd. cf. over bevelled wood bds., covers panel. with strapwork rolls & fillets, central panels with repeated sm. rosette stps., outer panels with eagle in square, circular owl tool & the Agnus Dei in square, outermost frame with scroll stp., brass centrepiece, cornerpieces & clasps, rebkd., edges restored, clasps & straps renewed, folding cl. case. Bkplts. of Walter A. Copinger, F. Perkins & the General Theological Seminary Liby. [BMC II, 415, Goff B557, HC 3068*] (CNY. Oct.1; 32) $4,000

– – **Anr. Edn.** Nuremb., Anton Koberger, Nov. 10, 1478. Fo. Spaces for initial capitals, 1st. text p. with 14-line capital F illuminated in blue on a ground of red & green foliage penwork with ornamentation extending the length of inner margin, capitals at head of each Book similarly decor., others in red or blue, paragraph marks & initial strokes in red, sm. pieces torn from lr. margins of folios 5 & 6, strip cut from fore-edge margin of fo. 61, light dampstaining to some margins, some traces of soiling, inscr. cut from upr. margin of 1st. lf. Cont. blind-stpd. cf. over wood bds., brass cornerpieces, worn, folding cl. case. Bkplt. of the General Theological Seminary Liby. [BMC II, 416, Goff B559, HC 3069*] (CNY. Oct.1; 33) $3,000

– **Bible.** Venice, Nicolaus Jenson, 1479. Fo. Spaces for initial capitals with guide letters, 1st. p. with capital F illuminated in cols. & gold & with floral sprays extending into margins, in lr. margins a partly erased coat-of-arms, fo. 4r with a miniature, 62 illuminated capitals in cols. & gold, most with marginal decoration, those at head of Gospels historiated, smaller capitals & paragraph marks in red or blue, lacks preliminary blank, 1st. 8 ll. on guards, restorations & reprd. tears at lr. margins of folios 1-3, clean tear reprd. at I10, anr. at E7 affecting some letters, some minor wormholes, staining to inner & lr. margins of some quires, heavier at end. Mod. lev. mor., gt. spine, mor.-tipped s.-c. Bkplt. of the General Theological Seminary Liby. [BMC V, 180, Goff B563, HC 3073*] (CNY. Oct.1; 70) $4,800

– – **Anr. Edn.** Ulm, Johann Zainer, Jan. 29, 1480. Fo. Woodcut initials cold., other capitals supplied in red, lacks preliminary blank, several ll. at beginning & end wormed, light stains to inner margins of early quires, other minor marginal stains & scattered spotting, fo. 2r with 7 lines of 1 column & 12 lines of the other ptd. on separate piece of paper pasted to sheet before printing, folios 33, 51, 241 & 384 with sm. pieces torn from margin. 16th. C. blind-stpd. pig, covers with blind-stpd. panel with centre medallion & cornerpieces, worn & wormed, with 3 old patches to covers & spine. Bkplt. of the General Theological Seminary Liby. [BMC II, 526, Goff B567, HC 3079] (CNY. Oct.1; 64) $4,600

– **Bible [with Additions by Monardus Monachus].** Nuremb., Anton Koberger, Apr.14, 1480. Fo. Spaces for initial capitals, text opening at p. 2 with 14-line capital F illuminated in blue on a gold impressed ground with a frame of purple, red & green, with floral sprays extending into side margin, the 2 columns divided by a gold staff, lr. margin with elab. foliate sprays in green & red with blue & yellow flowers & gold highlights, other capitals supplied in alternating red or blue, some larger capitals in 3 cols. with flourishes, initial strokes in red, light soiling & slight foxing, mainly at beginning & end, slight dampstaining to extreme inner margins of last ll. Cont. German blind-stpd. cf. over wood bds., covers divided by groups of fillet into panel & 3 frames, borders & central panel of upr. cover with ornate stylized floral roll, borders of lr. cover with strapwork roll, central panel with alternate strapwork & floral rolls flanked by alternate fleur-de-lys & rosette stps., rebkd., worn at edges & corners, lacks clasps. Partly defect. bkplt. 'Bibliotheca Novacellensis', bkplt. of the General Theological Seminary Liby. [BMC II, 418, Goff B568, HC 3076*] (CNY. Oct.1; 34) $2,800

– **Bible.** Cologne, [Nicolaus Gotz], May 9, 1480. 2 vols. Fo. Spaces for initial capitals, supplied in red, as are paragraph marks & initial strokes, MS. quiring preserved at lr. edges in many places, tear crossing line of text & sm. piece torn away at lr. margin of fo. 292 of vol. 2, some ll. slightly soiled or browned, some slight marginal stains, light worming at beginning & end of each vol., monastic inscr. in each vol. Mod. red lev. mor., gt. spines, mor.-tipped s.-c.'s, by Gerhard Gerlach, cl. folding case preserving orig. bdgs. of cont. goat over wood bds., covers divided into lozenge & triangular compartments & diapered with lge. & sm. rosette stps., worn. Bkplt. of the General Theological Seminary Liby. [C 1025, Goff B569] (CNY. Oct.1; 16) $3,000

– **Bible [with the glossa ordinaria of Walafridus Strabo & interlinear notes of Anselm of Laon].** [Strassburg], [Adolf Rusch for Anton Koberger], [before 1481]. 1st. Edn. 6 vols. Fo. Spaces for initial capitals, 1st. p. of vol. 1 with ll-line capital F in red & blue with floral sprays added in brown ink extending the length of inner margin, capitals at head of Prologues & Books generally supplied in red & blue, many with elaborate flourishes, other capitals in red or blue, paragraph marks & initial strokes added in red thro.-out, lacks the 2 blanks at end, slight worming at beginning & end of each vol., some ll. lightly browned, 1st. lf. of vol. 3 & vol. 6 on guard, some upr. margins in vols. 5 & 6 with light stain touching headline & several lines of text in 1 column, a very few ll. with slight soiling to margins or minor spotting, monastic inscr. on 1st. p. of each vol. Hf. pig, gt. spines, pig-tipped s.-c.'s (1 split), by Zaehnsdorf. The copy of Rev. William Makellar, bkplt. of the General Theological Seminary Liby. [BMC I, 92, Goff B607, HC 3173*] (CNY. Oct.1; 60) $10,000

– **Biblia cum Postillis Nicolai de Lyra, et Expositionibus Guilleloni Britonis in omnes Prologoo S. Hieronymi et Additionibus Pauli Burgensis replicisque Matthiae Doerung . . .** Venice, 31. VII. 1481. 1st. Edn. Fo. Cont. blind tooled vell.-bkd. wd bds., 2 clasps, lacks 1 tie, stained at ends, lacks lr. endpaper, upr.-endpaper loose, 2 line owners note on vell. endpaper. (HD. Nov.18-21; 122) DM 1,600

– **Bible.** Basle, Johann Amerbach, 1481. 2nd. Edn. of the 'Fontibus ex Graecis' Edn. Fo. Spaces for initial capitals, with guide letters, lge. capitals supplied in red & green, smaller capitals in alternate red or green, underlines & initial strokes added in red, lacks final blank, last quire loosening, slight dampstaining to lr. inner margins of early quires, other slight dampstains to some ll., minor worming at beginning & end, sm. portion of inner margins of 2 ll. reinforced. Cont. blind-stpd. pig over wood bds., covers with central panels of floral rolls & fleurons, brass clasps, worn, spine torn. Bkplt. of Dr. I.L. Porter, pencilled note of W.A. Copinger, bkplt. of the General Theological Seminary Liby. [BMC III, 745, Goff B571, HC 3081*] (CNY. Oct.1; 9) $1,700

– – **Anr. Edn.** [Lyons], Marcus Reinhart & Nicolaus Philippi, 1482. Fo. Spaces for initial capitals with guide letters, 1st. p. with lge. capital F in blue, others supplied in red & blue alternately, underlinings, paragraph marks & initial strokes added in red, lacks preliminary & final blanks, last lf. on guard, restorations to gutter margins of 3 ll., minor worming at beginning & end, some light marginal stains or soiling, browned, inscr. on 1st. p. Cont. blind-stpd. pig over bevelled wood bds., cover panel. with intersecting fillets & fleurons in centre panel, rebkd., lacks clasps. Bkplt. of the General Theological Seminary Liby. [BMC VIII, 245, Goff B574, HC 3085] (CNY. Oct.1; 24) $3,400

– – **Anr. Edn.** [Lyons], [Mathias Huss], 1483. Fo. Spaces for initial capitals with guide letters, 1st. p. with 13-line capital F illuminated in blue on red foliage ground with gold highlights & incorporating the monog. M.F.I., other capitals added in red &/or blue, initial strokes supplied in yellow, lacks preliminary blank, staining to inner margins of many ll. at front & back, touching text in places, other stains to upr. & fore-edge margins of some ll., sm. repairs to margins of folios 101 & 507, some other minor marginal defects, fo. 270 heavily stained, worming to upr. margin of table at end, portion of 1 column of last lf. worn & reprd. with loss of some letters, inscr. on 1st. p. 19th. C. black mor., worn, upr. cover detchd., spine loose. Bkplt. of Walter Arthur Copinger, bkplt of the General Theological Seminary Liby. [Goff B576] (CNY. Oct.1; 25) $1,600

– **Bible [with Postilla of Nicolaus de Lyra & exposition of the Prologues of Jerome by Guillelmi Britonis, & additions by Paulus Bergensis of the Prologues of Jerome by Guillelmi Britonis, & additions by Paulus Bergensis].** Nuremb., Anton Koberger, Dec. 3, 1487 (pt. 1), May 7, 1485 (pts. 2-4). 4 pts. in 4 vols. Fo. Spaces for initial capitals, most with guides, capitals supplied in red thro.-out, many with flourishes, paragraph marks & initial strokes in red, lacks blank at end of 1st. section of pt. 2 & 1 blank at end of pt. 4, light worming at beginning & end of each vol., wormhole thro.-out vol. 2 between text columns but catching a few letters in some places, upr. portion of most ll. in vol. 1 dampstained, sm. dampstain to upr. inner margins at front of vol. 2, scattered ll. browned, some minor marginal tears & some corners defect. Cont. oak bds., pig spines blind-stpd. with floral rolls & lozenge tools, covers of vol. 4 detchd., lacks some clasps. Bkplt. of the General Theological Seminary Liby. [BMC II, 427 & 432, Goff B613 & B614, HC 3166* & 3167*] (CNY. Oct.1; 38) $3,800

[–] **Biblia Latina** [Basel], [1487]. Fo. Lacks 4 ll., some margin defects. reprd., especially at beginning & end, last lf. defect. with text loss, slightly soiled & stained in parts, some old MS. notes. 19th. C. hf. linen. [Hain 3100; BMC III, 765] (HK. May 12-14; 74) DM 900

– **Biblia Latina cum Postillis Nicolai de Lyra.** Venice, [Bonetus Locatellus, for] Octavianus Scotus, 1489. 4 vols. Fo. 1094 ll. (of 1107, lacks 11 ll. of text & 2 blanks), 3 histor. initials & woodcut in gold & colours at beginning of vol. I, other initials supplied in red & blue alternately in vols. I-III, some dampstaining & worming affecting text, 1st. gathering torn & loose in vol. II. Cont. blind-stpd. cf., vol. IV not unif., vol. I with defect. spine & upr. cover detchd., others worn. W.a.f. [BMC V, 437, Goff B616; HC 3168] (S. Jun.23; 213) *Cohen.* £350

– **[Biblia Latina].** Basel, Johanem Frobem de Hammelburk, 1491. Hand-drawn illuminated initials thro.-out, lacks 4 prelims., pi4, last lf. of gathering a8 & final 5 gatherings (A-E8), cropped at head & edges with occasional partial loss at headings & marginal references, occasional minor stains. Cont. vell. over bds., vell. spine, lacks clasps. [BMC II, p.789; Goff B592; Hain 3107] (CB. Nov.12; 143) Can. $900

BIBLES [Latin] *-contd.*
- Bible. Basle, [Johann Froben]. 27 Oct. 1495. 456 ll. (of 508), lacks 12 prelims., 1 blank & 39 index ll. at end, initials in red or blue, rubricated. Cont. cf. blind-stpd., flap & brass clasp, tear in spine & jnts. [BMC III, 791] (S. Nov.25; 315) *Marriott.* £220
- Biblia Latina. Nuremb., Anton Koberger, 1497. 2 vols. Fo. Worming affecting text, staining, some repairs, S3 in Book IV badly torn, tears, browning. Blind-stpd. vell., wormed, torn, lacks clasps, folding boxes. [BMC II, p.443; HC 3171] (S. May 6; 203) $950
- - Anr. Edn. Basle, [1498]. Pts. IV & V only (of 6). Fo. Sm. tear to lf. N4 in vol. IV & some minor marginal dampstaining, ll. N1-P8 in vol. V loose, many initials supplied in red to both vols. Cont. leath.-covered oak bds. with tooled panels, detchd. or almost detchd. (TA. Jul.16; 230) £300
- Bible [with table of Gabriel Brunus]. Venice, Simon Bevilaqua, May 8, 1498. 4to. Spaces for capital initials with guide letters, folios 218, 227, 238, & 239 inserted from anr. copy, title & final lf. rehinged, some dampstaining, mostly to 1st. ll., but also to some upr. portions & some margins, early ink annots. in some margins, & a few pencil marks. 19th. C. hf. vell., spine gt. The copy of C.W. Dyson Perrins, lately in the collection of Eric Sexton. [BMC V, 522, Goff B603, HC 3124*] (CNY. Apr.8; 195) $2,000
- - Anr. Copy. Some MS. marginalia & underlining, slightly soiled at front, lacks 36 ll. of interpretations. Bds. (HK. Nov.18-21; 123) DM 2,000
- Biblia cum Pleno Apparatu Summariorum Concordantiarum . . . [Lyons], Nov. 10, 1506. Fo. Woodcut initials, others in red or blue, many cont. annots. in red & blue, lacks folios A8 & B8 (title & prelims., including blank) & other 2 blanks X6 & 2d6, marginal tears. 19th. C. striped silk with embroidery on upr. cover. [D. & M. 6091] (S. Mar.17; 237) *Lamm.* £110
- Biblia . . . Quinta pars Huius Operis in se Continens Glossam Ordinariam . . . Glossam Ordinariam . . . Ed.:- Nicolaus de Lyra. [Basle], 1507. Vol. 5 only (of 7). Fo. Slight marginal staining at beginning. Blind-stpd. cf. over wood bds., covers with broad intersecting blind rolls enclosing a diaper panel of fillets & pineapples, by John Reynes, rebkd. with most of orig. spine preserved, covers rubbed & scuffed, lacks clasps. As a bdg., w.a.f. (C. Nov.20; 178) *Middleton.* £380
- Bible. Venice, May 28, 1511. 4to. 1st. 2, final & some other ll. rehinged, some staining, tightly bnd, with some loss of marginalia. 16th. C. blind-stpd. mor. over wood bds., 2 gt. lozenges in central panel, 4 gt. stylized cornerpieces, coat-of-arms of the Conventus Magnus, Mexico City at centre, & 17 smaller gt. stars overall (this design on both covers), spine similarly gt., rebkd. preserving orig. backstrip, qtr. mor. gt. s.-c. The copy of John A. Saks. (CNY. Oct.1; 127) $1,500
- Biblia cum Concordantiis Veteris et Novi Testamenti . . . . . . Lyons, [1520]. Thick fo. Lacks last lf. of glossary, 1st and last ll. reprd. Old stpd. cf. on wood bds., brkn. (SG. Sep.25; 38) $425
- Biblia Biblicorum Opus Sacrosanctum Vulgati . . . Lyons, 1536. Fo. Browned. Cont. vell. (HD. Apr.24; 33) Frs. 1,100
- Biblia Sacra ex Santis Pagnini Tralatione. Ed.:- [Michael Servetus]. Lyon, 1542. Fo. 2 flaws in blank margins of final errata lf. reprd. on verso, 'Ex lib Descorbiac' inscr. on title, 1 or 2 ll. stained. 18th. C. mor. by Derome le Jeune with his ticket, wide gt. rococo dentelle borders, spine gt. in compartments, inner floral dentelles, pink silk liners. (SM. Oct.7; 1583) Frs. 27,000
- Biblia Sacronsanta Testamenti Veteris & Novi. Lyons, 1546. Fo. Some ll. reprd., fo. A2 misbnd., some wormholes, sm. hole in last lf., soiled & stained. Cont. blind-stpd. cf. on wooden bds., lacks some leath., mainly on upr. cover, jnts. brkn, lacks clasps. (S. Mar.17; 270) *Panadero.* £90
- Bible. Paris, 1546. Fo. Unif. light browning, slight dampstain to lr. corners of 1st. quire. Cont. cf., covers panel. in blind with central scroll-work device in gt., worn, rebkd. Bkplt. of Walter Arthur Copinger, bkplt. of the General Theological Seminary Liby. (CNY. Oct.1; 46) $700
- Biblia Sacra ad Optima Quaque Veteris, ut Vocant Tralationis Exemplaria. Exemplaria. Lyon, 1550. 3 vols. in 2. Hebrew glossary in vol. II, sigs. of Argidius de Maypeou & Martin Ffolkes & John Quicke. Cont. red mor., lge. gt. openwork centrepiece, ground semé with dots, lge. gt. arabesque cornerpieces surrounded by gt. & blind fillets, cipher of 0 & X (or 0 & 2 Ys) at each corner, central oval replaced with 18th. C. arms, gt., on red mor., flat spine gt. in compartments with same cipher divided by arabesque borders, lacks ties. (SM. Oct.7; 1582) Frs. 5,000
- Biblia Sacra. Ill.:- Bernard Salomon. Lyon, 1556. Fo. Light staining. Mod. qtr. sheep. [D. & M. 6138] (S. Jul.27; 120) *Armstrong.* £140
- Biblia ad Vetustissima Exemplaria . . . Venice, 1576. Fo. 8 unnumbered pp., 1 blank. Old cf., gt. tooled decor. (CR. Mar.19; 246) Lire 420,000
- Biblia Sacra Veteris et Novi Testamenti. Basle, 1578. 3 Pts. in 1 vol. Cont. blind-stpd. pig on wooden bds., dtd. 1580 on covers, lacks clasps. (S. Nov.25; 363) *A. Stewart.* £190
- Sacra Biblia acri Studio . . . Venice, 1588. 4to. Old marginal pen notes, 8 unnumbered pp., 1 blank, 2 engraved frontis., 244 xylographs. Cont. limp vell. (CR. Mar.19; 245) Lire 300,000
- Biblia Sacra. Ill.:- J. Th. de Bry, J.D. Zetter after C. Keller (titles). Mainz, 1609. Vulgate Edn. 4to. Lacks N.T. title, browned. & reprd.) bnd. in from orig. bdg. Leath., end-ll. (defect. & reprd.) bnd. in from orig. bdg. (HK. Nov.18-21; 1506) DM 620
- Biblia Ad Vetustissima Exemplaria Castigala . . . Antw., 1665. Cont. mor., decor. tools. (HD. Apr.24; 34) Frs. 1,800
- Biblia Sacra. Paris, 1666. Vulgatae Edn. 4to. Margins browned. Later mor. gt. (TA. Dec.18; 413) £52
- Biblia Sacra Vulgatae Editionis Sixti V Pont. Max. iussu recognita et Clementis VIII auctoritate. Parallel Latin German, some footnotes, stained and slightly browned. Cont. leath., gt. spine, spine & corners reprd. [D. & M. II, 4245] (R. Oct.14-18; 1268) DM 1,600
- Biblia Sacra. Ill.:- Francesco Bartolozzi after G.B. Tiepolo (frontis.). Venice, 1763. Fo. Minor spotting to margin of frontis. Cont. vell. bds. From the collection of John A. Saks. (C. Jun.10; 23) *Robison.* £110
- Bibliorum Sacrorum . . . Paris, 1785. Vulgate Edn. 2 vols. 4to. Approbation lf. in vol. 1. Cont. red mor., gt. concentric roll borders with filled ovals, fleurs-de-lis & fillets entwined with leafy branch, spine gt. in compartments with repeated lozenges of zig-zag intersecting lines, inner gt. dentelles, silk liners. (SM. Oct.7; 1584) Frs. 1,000
- Biblia Sacra, Veteris et Novi Testamenti. Ill.:- Anton Klauber. Augsburg, 1835. Ob. sm. fo. (9¼ × 15 inches). Later mor., cover detchd. (SG. Sep.4; 38) $180
- Biblia Sacra Vulgatae Editionis Sixti V Pont. Max. iussu recognita et Clementis VIII auctoritate. Ill.:- Salvador Dali. Milan, 1967. (199) De Luxe Edn., numbered. 5 vols. Fo. Mor., etched floral decor. on back, inner cover with gt. stpd. border, inner lined, satin doubls., mor. & satin boxes. With guarantee certificate from publisher. (CR. Mar.19; 290) Lire 3,000,000
See-**NEW TESTAMENT [Latin]**
See-**GUTENBERG, Johann**

BIBLES [Latin & French]
- Sainte Bible. Ill.:- Devéria. Paris, 1828-34. 13 vols. Cont. roan, gt. roll-stp., around covers, blind-tooled plaques in centre, smooth decor. spines. (HD. Feb.27; 225) Frs. 1,700

BIBLES [Latin & Hebrew]
- Hebraica Biblia Latina. Trans.:- Sebastian Munster. Basel, 1534-35. 2 vols. Fo. Both vols. somewhat wormed with 1 or 2 wormholes thro.-out, some light stains. Cont. blind-stpd. pig over wood bds., lacks clasps, some worming, vol. I rebkd. preserving orig. spine. [D. & M. 5087] (S. Jul.27; 134) *Lunzer.* £550

BIBLES [Low German]
- De Biblie. Ed.:- Nicholas de Lyra & others (Glosses). [Lübeck], [1494]. Vol. 1. Fo. 99 woodcuts (some repeated) in old col., some with gt., 2 multi-cold. initials gt., 6 painted blue, many partly figurative woodcut-initials, on ll. 3v & 7r on gold ground in red, blue, yellow, green with multi-cold. flourishes, 40 ll. with reprd. corners or margins, slightly soiled in parts. Old cf., blind-tooled, slightly torn & worn, clasps leath., renewed, restored. (H. May 21/22; 912) DM 40,000

BIBLES [Polyglot]
- Bible. Ed.:- [Benedictus Arias Montanus]. Antw., 1569-73. 1st. Plantine Edn. 8 vols. Fo. Hf.-title to vol. 3 & 1st. quire of vol. 5 loose, marginal dampstaining to several vols., occasionally affecting text, worming in upr. margins of several quires in vols. 6 & 7, catching headlines & some lines of text, liby. inscr. on title-pp. Cont. German blind-stpd. pig over wood bds., covers with panels of fillet & floral rolls, centre panel with gt. coat-of-arms, brass clasps, worn, 2 covers detchd. Bkplts. of W.A. Copinger, bkplt. of the General Theological Seminary Liby. [D. & M. 1422] (CNY. Oct.1; 3) $6,000
- - Anr. Edn. Hamburg, 1596. 4 pts. in 1 vol. Fo. Lacks ptd. title, some MS. notes, slightly browned in parts, light stain towards middle & end, 1st. ll. reprd. at margin, some sm. tears & worming, last lf. defect. with some text loss, 2 borders on engraved title cold. Hf. linen. (H. May 21/22; 914) DM 800
- The Polyglot Bible. N.d. Engl. version. Cont. mor., elab. blind-stpd., gt. metal clasps & corners, with painted pious exhortations intertwined with stylized foliage, boxed. (CSK. Jun.5; 91) £70

BIBLES [Swedish]
- Thet är all then Heliga Skrift pa Swensko . . . Stockholm, 1703. Fo. No errata & front fly-ll. loose. Cont. spr. black cf. (?by Georg Ihle of Stockholm), richly gt. panel., orig. brass clasps, 1 corner defect., with worn limp leath. fitted cover. [D. & M. 8817] (S. Oct.20; 27) *Bjorck & Borjesson.* £300

BIBLIANA
(Chronologically by Language)

BIBLIANA [Dutch]
- Historie des Ouden en Nieuwen Testaments. Ill.:- after Goete & others. Amst., Pieter Mortier, 1700. 2 vols. Fo. Cont. gt.-ornamental mott. cf. (PNY. Oct.1; 102) $375
- - Anr. Copy. 5 maps at end of 2nd. vol. Cont. vell. (LM. Jun.13; 167) DM 45,000
- Afbeeldingen der Voornaamste Historien, soo van het Oude als Nieuwe Testament. Amst., ca. 1720. 3 pts. in 1 vol. Fo. Cont. mott. cf., spine gt., head of spine defect. (VG. Dec.17; 1138) Fls. 1,150
- Histoire des Ouden en Nieuwen Testaments . . . Ill.:- Jan Luyken. Amst., 1722. 2nd. Edn. of the 'Kleinen Bybel van Mortier'. 2 vols. in 1. Fo. Mod. blind-stpd. cf., antique-style. (VG. Dec.17; 1141) Fls. 850

BIBLIANA [English]
- [Ihesus. The floure of the commaundements of god with many examples & auctorytees]. [1521]. Sm. fo. Title & last lf. in facs., tears reprd. in B6 & O6, marginal repairs & other sm. imperfections. Mott. cf., by Rivière, rebkd. preserving earlier labels. W.a.f. [NSTC 23877] (S. Jun.23; 363) *Smith.* £500
- The Book of Ruth. [1611]. Fo. Extracted from the 1st. iss. of the King James Bible of 1611, with a hand-lettered & hand-illuminated title-p. Gt.-ptd. cf., boxed. (PNY. May 21; 95) $250
- In Sacre Biblia Graeca Ex Versione LXX Interpretum Scholia . . . L., 1653. Slight browning. Late 17th.-early 18th. C. red mor. gt. [Wing I122] (SPB. May 29; 221) $100
- Biblia 1727. 1¾ × 1¼ ins. (in 8's). Engraved frontis., engraved title, & 12 other plts. only, lacks sectional title. Cont. red mor. gt., border of double fillets with cornerpieces, central stp. with 4 acorns, spine with raised bands, marb. endpapers. (LC. Feb.12; 288) £140
- The Bible in Miniature. 1771. 1¾ × 1¼ ins. (in 8's). Cont. cf. gt., double fillet border. (LC. Feb.12; 286) £60
- - Anr. Edn. 1780. 41 × 26mm. Orig. red roan gt., black oval centrepieces. Miniature Book. (SH. Dec.12; 541) *Vincent.* £60
- - Anr. Edn. Ca. 1802. 43mm.×29mm. Orig. roan gt., black oval centre-pieces, mod. roan box. (SH. Mar.19; 177) *Fletcher.* £80
- - Anr. Edn. L., 1809. 1¾×1½ ins. Cont. cf. (SG. Mar.19; 250) $160
- The Self-Interpreting Bible. Ed.:- Rev. John Brown. Bungay, 1815. Fo. Additional engraved title-p. dtd. 1812, ink stain at head of 1st. few ll. Cont. cf. (CB. Nov.12; 146) Can. $100
- The Pictorial Bible . . . L., 1836-38. 3 vols. 4to. Cont. mor., gt. borders & spines. Fore-e. pntg. in each vol. (SG. Mar.19; 161) $750
- The Book of Ruth. Ill.:- Henry Noel Humphries. 1850. Orig. embossed leath., s.-c. (CSK. Jul.3; 100) £95

- **The Book of Ruth & the Book of Esther.** Ill.:–
Lucian Pissarro. Eragny Pr., 1896. (155). Errata
slip loosely inserted, 4 ll. slightly spotted. Orig.
bds., slightly worn, unc. (S. Jul.31; 16)
Marks. £120
- **A Book of Songs & Poems from the Old
Testament & the Apochrypha.** Ash. Pr., 1904.
(175), (50) on paper. Orig. limp vell., unc. (S.
Jul.31; 63) *Marks.* £270
- - **Anr. Copy.** (SH. Feb.19; 18) *Quaritch.* £250
- **Book of Genesis.** Ill.:– F. Cayley Robinson.
Riccardi Pr., 1914. (512) numbered. 4to. Orig.
cl.-bkd. bds., d.-w. (SH. Mar.27; 459)
Ralph. £60
- - **Anr. Edn.** Ill.:– Paul Nash. Nones. Pr., 1924.
(375) numbered. 4to. Orig. bds., unc., d.-w. worn.
(S. Jul.31; 109) *Marks.* £130
- **Book of Ruth.** Flansham, Tintern Pr., 1934. (50)
sigd. by printer. 4to. Orig. cl.-bkd. bds., unc. Pres.
copy from Vincent Stuart to Sylvia Marshall.
(SH. Feb.20; 261) *Nolan.* £110
- **Book of Job.–Book of Ruth.** Ed.:– Mary E.
Chase (prefaces). Ill.:– Arthur Szyk. Ltd. Edns.
Cl., 1946; 1947. Each (1950) numbered, & sigd.
by artlst. 2 works in 2 vols. Both leath.-bkd.
gt.-pict. bds., gt. boxes. (SG. Apr.2; 284) $250
- - **Anr. Copy.** Fo. Gt.-pict. bds., leath.-bkd., gt.
bd. s.c.'s (SG. Oct.23; 321) $130
- **Book of Job.** Ill.:– Frank Brangwyn.
Leigh-on-Sea, 1948. (110) numbered. 4to. Gt.
three-qtr. vell. by Sangorski & Sutcliffe, cl. box,
partly untrimmed. (SG. Apr.2; 31) $600
See–NEW TESTAMENTIANA [English]

BIBLIANA [French]
- **Histoire du Vieux et du Nouveau Testament (L').**
Ed.:– Sieur de Royaumont. Ill.:– Sebastien Le
Clerc. Paris, 1670. 1st. Edn. 4to. With pp. 21 &
331, & 4 ll. numbered CCXCIX-CCCVI inserted
between pp. 296 & 297, some pp. restored. Mor.
by Capé, fillets around covers, blind-tooled arms
in upr. corner, gt. motif, spine with raised bands,
inside roll-stp. Bkplt. of Berryer. (HD. Feb.27; 54)
Frs. 1,800
- **Figures de la Bible.** La Haye, 1728. Fo. Hf. cf.
(LM. Mar.21; 174) *B.Frs.* 16,000
- **Office de l'Eglise en François et en Latin.** Paris,
1754. 12mo. Cont. bookseller's ticket of J.P.
Labottière, Bordeaux. Cont. Fr. inlaid bdg., lge.
double flower on each cover inlaid in mor., gt.,
smaller cinqfoil inlaid on mor. in each corner, gt.,
roll-tooled border, alternate spine compartments
onlaid with mor., with fleurons, gt., inner gt.
dentelles, Dutch & white & gt. endpapers, 1 lr.
corner slightly worn, mor. case by Rivière. (SM.
Oct.8; 1892) *Frs.* 16,000

BIBLIANA [German]
- **Biblia Historica, oder, Kurtz verfasste
Historia[n]-Bibel.** Schwabisch Hall, 1670. 2 pts. in
1 vol. Title to NT missing, a few scribbles in some
margins, some ll. slightly soiled or dampstained.
19th. C. cf. (S. Dec.8; 96) *Hyde.* £80
- **Bilder-Beuchlein.** Magdeburg, 1691. Ob. 8vo.
Some ll. misbnd., 1 or 2 lacking? Later three-qtr.
cf. (SG. Feb.5; 47) $250
- **Die Heiligen Schriften des Alten [und Neuen]
Testaments in [je] Hundert Biblischen Kupfern
dargestellt.** Frankfurt, ca. 1820. 2nd. Edn. 2 vols.
Slightly soiled in parts. Cont. bds. (R.
Mar.31-Apr.4; 1480) DM 550
- **Buch Ester.** Trans.:– Dr. Martin Luther. Ill.:–
F.W. Kleukens. Leipzig, 1908. (300). Orig. cf.,
gold stpd., silk end-ll. (D. Dec.11-13; 1011)
DM 1,600
- - **Anr. Copy.** Ex-liby. Orig. leath., silk end-ll.,
worn. (HK. Nov.18-21; 2536) DM 750
- **Das Buch Judith.** Trans.:– M. Luther. Ill.:– L.
Corinth. Berlin, 1910. (250). Fo. Orig. linen. (HK.
Nov.18-21; 2487) DM 1,700
- - **Anr. Edn.** Ill.:– O. Becker. [Darmstadt.],
[1923]. (50) numbered, Priv. Edn. on Gelder. 4to.
Ex-liby. Orig. vell., fillet covers, inner & outer
dentelles, by Ernst Rehbein, Darmstadt, bd. s.-c.
(HK. Nov.18-21; 2538) DM 1,250

BIBLIANA [Greek]
- Lucian. Hexamplorum Origenis quae Supersunt
[Containing the Varieties of the Greek Versions of
the Old Testament made by Aquila, Symmachus, the
Septuagint, etc.]. Ed.:– Montfaucon. Paris,
1714. 2 vols. Fo. Lacks 1st. blank in vol. I, final
blank in vol. II, some browning. Cont. vell., soiled,
labels defect. (S. Jun.9; 44) *Thomas.* £160

BIBLIANA [Hebrew]
- **Megillat Esther U'peirush.** Ed.:– Yitzhak Arama
[commentary]. Constantinople, 1518. 1st. Edn. of
commentary. Sm. 4to. Inner margins of title
reprd. without loss of words, tears affecting text,
staining, worming. Mod. bds. (SPB. May 11; 85)
$9,000
- **Job im Pierush.** Ed.:– Yitzhak Cohen
[commentary]. Constantinople, 1545. 1st. Edn.
Sm. 4to. Last 2 ll. of register with outer margins
reprd., without text loss, staining. Mod. cl. (SPB.
May 11; 81) $3,700
- **Torah Pentateuch [Tikun Sofrim].** Sabionetta,
1553-55. 12mo. Some sigs. loose, tears, stained,
browning. Vell., worn, wormed & stained. (SPB.
May 11; 49) $2,100
- **The Five Books of Moses & the Five Migoloth.**
Venice, 1590. 6 vols. 12mo. Bk. 1 lacks title & 1st.
lf., 2nd. Bk. lacks title, 3rd. Bk. has title glued to
following lf. 18th. C. marb. bds., spines crudely
reprd. (PNY. Oct.1; 103) $110
- **Torah-Pentateuch [only Numbers & Deuteron-
omy, with Targum Onkelos, Jonathan & Rashi's
commentary], & Five Megillot.–Haftorot.**
Venice, 1590-91; 1591. 2 works in 1 vol. Cropped,
discolouration. Mod. hf. leath. (SPB. May 11, 50)
$750
- **Torah-Pentateuch, Five Megillot & Haftorot.**
Mantua, 1785. Marginal tears, slight staining.
Vell., worn. Inscr. by Israel Casis, Rabbi of
Mantua on title & 1 lf. (SPB. May 11; 51) $850

BIBLIANA [Latin]
- **Historiarum Veteris Testamenti Icones ad
Uiuum Expressae [with French Verses by Gilles
Corrozet].** Ill.:– Hans Holbein, the Younger.
Lyons, 1539. 2nd. Edn. 4to. Variant iss. with
colophon in cartouche on N3v, sm. wormhole at lr.
inner margins, some staining & marginal repairs
thro.-out. Crimson mor., spine gt.-lettered, by
Cape. The copy of John A. Saks. (CNY. Oct.1; 94)
$4,000
- **Typi in Apocalypsi Ioannis Depicti ut Clarius
Vaticinia Ioannis Intelligi Possint.** Ill.:– Hans
Sebald Beham. Frankfurt, 1539. 1st. Edn. 4to.
Rebnd. in old vell., wraps., cl. s.-c., slightly soiled.
Bkplt. of John A. Saks. (CNY. Oct.1; 88) $3,000
- **Historiarum Veteris Testamenti.** Paris, 1544.
Counterfeit of 1538 Treschel Edn. Sm. 4to. Sm.
marginal loss to title. 19th. C. roan, blind-stpd. Du
Seuil decor., gt. spine with cypher, 1 cover detchd.
(HD. Jun.10; 41) *Frs.* 1,800

BIBLICA. Revue Trimestrielle
Ed.:– L'Institut Biblique Pontifical de Rome.
Rome, 1947-78. 31 vols. in pts. Orig. bdgs. (B.
Dec.10/11; 1332) *Fls.* 650

BIBLIOGRAFIA ESPANOLA de Arqitectura (1526-1850)
Madrid, 1947. (200) numbered. 4to. Ptd. wraps.,
unc. (SG. Jan.22; 32) $150

BIBLIOGRAFIA OD ELENCO RAGIONATO delle opere contenute nella Collezione de'Classici Italiani, Milan, Dalla Societa Tipografica de'Classici Italini
1814. Cont. red mor. by 'Lefebrer', elab. tooled in
gt. (CSK. Apr.3; 36) £90

BIBLIOGRAPHIA
1895-97. 12 pts. 4to. Orig. wraps., torn. (SH.
Jan.29; 3) *Edrich.* £65

BIBLIOGRAPHICA: Papers on Books, their History & Art
L., 1895-97. 12 iss. in 3 vols. Lge. 4to. Lev.,
multiple gt. fillet borders & central panels,
gt.-panel. spines, gt. dentelles, by Rowfant
Bindery, Cleveland, orig. wraps. bnd. in (SG.
Oct.9; 32) $475
- - **Anr. Edn.** [1895-97]. Pts. I-XI only (of 12).
4to. Orig. wraps., unc. (C. Jul.22; 104)
Forster. £60

BIBLIOPHILE, Julien le (Pseud.)
See–LACROIX, Paul 'Julien le Bibliophile'

BIBLIOTHECA AMERICANA
- **Catalogue of the John Carter Brown Library in
Brown University, 1569-1674.** Providence,
1919-1931. Orig. Edn. 5 vols. Linen-bkd. buckram
bds., liby. bkplt. in each vol., unc. (SG. Oct.2; 34)
$425

BIBLIOTHECA LINDESIANA
- **Bibliography of Royal Proclamations,
1485-1714.–Handlist of Proclamations,
1714-1910.** Ed.:– Robert Steele (1st. work).

Oxford; Wigan, 1910; 1913. Fo. Both orig.
buckram. (C. Jul.22; 106) *Quaritch.* £180
- **A Bibliography of the Writings . . . Forming the
Literature of Philately.** Ed.:– [Earl of Crawford].
Aberdeen, 1911. Fo. Orig. buckram. (C.
Jul.22; 108) *Quaritch.* £70
- **Handlist of Proclamations, 1509-1901.
–Catalogue of English Broadsides.** Ed.:– Earl of
Crawford (1st. work). Aberdeen (1st. work), Priv.
Ptd. (2nd. work)., 1893-1901; 1898. (50)
numbered; (100) numbered. 4 vols.; 1 vol. Fo.; 4to.
Both orig. cl. (C. Jul.22; 107) *Quaritch.* £220

BIBLIOTHECA PHILLIPPICA
1886-1938. 22 vols. in 4. Sale cat., priced. Cl.
(SH. Mar.6; 486) *Forster.* £560
- - **Anr. Copy.** (SH. Mar.6; 487) *Thomas.* £500

BIBLIOTHECIS POLONIAE
- **Incunabula quae in Bibliothecis Poloniae
Asservantur.** Wratislaviae, 1970. 2 vols. 4to. Cl.
(SG. Mar.26; 269) $100

BIBLIOTHEQUE DU ROI
- **Catalogus Codicum Manuscriptorum
Bibliothecae Regiae.–Catalogue des Livres
Imprimés de la Bibliothèque du Roi.** Paris,
1739-44; 1739-50. 4 vols; 6 vols. (all publd.) Fo.
Unif. bnd. cont. red mor., gt. Louis I arms, triple
gt. fillet, gt. compartment spines, lge. central
fleur-de-lis & smaller one at corners, sunflowers
on spine of 1st. 4 vols., inner gt. dentelles. (SM.
Oct.7; 1322) *Frs.* 4,200

BIBLIOTHEQUE PORTATIVE du Voyageur
Paris, 1802-03. 15 vols. 32mo. Various, mainly
old, bdgs. (HD. Apr.9; 402) *Frs.* 1,100

BIBLIOTHEQUE UNIVERSELLE et Historique
Amst., 1686-1700. 26 vols. 12mo. Cont. mott. cf.
(GM. Apr.30; 747) £120
- - **Anr. Edn.** Amst., 1687-91. 20 vols. 12mo. Vell.
(P. Mar.12; 74) *Fairburn.* £60

BIBLIOTHEQUE UNIVERSELLE des Voyages . . .
Trans.:– M. Albert-Montémont. Paris, 1833-36.
46 vols. Spotted thro.-out. Cont. hf. cf., decor.
spines. (SM. Feb.11; 19) *Frs.* 4,000

BIBLISCHE EMBLEMATA
Nuremb., 1626. 4to. Soiled. Cont. vell. (SH.
Jun.11; 134) *Fairburn.* £110

BICHAT, Marie François Xavier
- **Anatomie Générale, Appliquée à la Physiologie et
à la Médecine.** Paris, 1801. 1st. Edn. 4 vols. A few
stains, minor worming in vols. II & IV, hole in last
lf. of vol. I. Cont. cf.-bkd. bds. From liby. of Dr. E.
Ashworth Underwood. (S. Feb.23; 158)
Meyer. £180
- - **Anr. Edn.** Paris, 1812. New Edn. 4 vols.
Disbnd., ex-liby. (SG. Aug.21; 287) $110
- **Anatomie générale appliquée à la Physiologie et
à la Médecine.–Traité d'Anatomie descriptive.
–Traité des Membranes.** Paris, 1821; 1823; ca.
1827. 4 vols.; 5 vols.; 1 vol., together 10 vols. Lacks
a few last ll. (?), (blank?). Cont. hf. cf., some
corners slightly worn. (S. Feb.23; 13) *Korn.* £60
- **General Anatomy, applied to Physiology & to
the Practice of Medicine.** Ed.:– George Calvert.
Trans.:– Constant Coffyn. Priv. ptd., 1824. 1st.
Edn. in Engl. 4 vols. in 2. Hf. cf. (S. Jun.15; 83)
Gurney. £90
- **Physiological Researches on Life & Death.**
Trans.:– F. Gold. L., ca. 1805. Hf. mor., worn.
From Brooklyn Academy of Medicine. (SG.
Jan.29; 57) $200
- - **Anr. Edn.** Trans.:– Tobias Watkins. Phila.,
1809. 1st. Edn. in Engl. Foxed. New buckram, ex
liby. (SG. Sep.18; 45) $150

BICKHAM, George, the Elder
- **The British Monarchy.** 1748. Fo. Mod. pol. cf.,
gt. (S. Nov.25; 428) *Traylen.* £340
- **The Universal Penman.** 1741. Fo. Frontis. & last
lf. torn without loss. Cont. cf., covers detchd. (TA.
Jul.16; 265) £145
- - **Anr. Edn.** Priv. ptd., [1741]. Subscribers Edn.
Fo. Title trimmed & mntd., lacks a few ll., some
slight defects. Cont. hf. cf., slightly worn. W.a.f.
(SBA. Dec.16; 5) *Petersfield Bookshop.* £125
- - **Anr. Edn.** 1743. Fo. Plt. 84 torn & reprd. Red
lev. mor., by Sangorski & Sutcliffe. (C.
Nov.6; 200) *Taylor.* £340
- - **Anr. Edn.** [1743]. Fo. Title & 5 plts. reprd.
Mod. mott. cf., elab. gt. (S. Nov.24; 25)
Traylen. £240

BICKHAM, George, the Younger
- The Musical Entertainer. Ca. 1739. 2 vols. Fo. Panel. cf. gt., by Rivière. (S. Nov.24; 26)
Fenyves. £1,400

BICKNELL, Clarence
- Flowering Plants & Ferns of The Riviera. 1885. Some slight foxing thro.-out. Cl., mor. spine. (BS. Jun.11; 22)
£65

BIDLOO, Govard
- Anatomia Humani Corporis. Ill.:– after G. de Lairesse Amst., 1685. Fo. Plt. 11 inverted, plt. 28 slightly cropped affecting plt. no., tear reprd. in fold of plt. 23. 19th. C. hf. mor. From Chetham's Liby., Manchester. (C. Nov.26; 35)
Lester. £750
- De Oculis et Visu Variorum Animalium Observationes Physico-Anatomicae. Leyden, 1715. 1st. Edn. Sm. 4to. Later vell.-bkd. marb. bds. (SG. May 14; 19)
$700

BIE, J.P. de & Loosjes, J.
- Biographisch Woordenboek van Protestantsche Godgeleerden in Nederland. The Hague, 1907-49. 5 vols., all publd. Cl. (B. Dec.10/11; 1567)
Fls. 1,100

BIE, Oskar
- Holländisches Skizzenbuch. Ill.:– Liebermann. Berlin, 1911. (450). Ob. 4to. Soiled, lightly browned. No bdg. stated. (H. May 21/22; 1703)
DM 460

BIEDERMANN, Wilhelm
- Electro-physiology. Trans.:– Frances A. Welby. 1896-98. 1st. Engl. Edn. 2 vols. Orig. cl. (S. Jun.15; 85)
Whitehart. £60

BIENFAIT, A.G.
- Oude Hollandsche Tuinen. The Hague, 1943. Text 8vo., atles ob. fo. Cl. (VG. Dec.15; 113)
Fls. 480

BIERBAUM, Otto Julius
- Das Schöne Mädchen von Pao. Ill.:– P. v. Bayros. Munich, [1910]. De Luxe Edn. (600) numbered on Holland. Lge. 4to. Orig. leath., gt. spine, inner & outer dentelle, by P. Renner. (HK. Nov.18-21; 2421)
DM 1,050

BIERCE, Ambrose
- The Collected Works. N.Y., 1902-12. 12 vols. Orig. cl. (SPB. Jul.28; 29)
$225

BIERMANN, Georg
- Der Zeichner Lovis Corinth. Ill.:– L. Corinth (etched frontis.). Dresden, 1924. Ltd. Edn. numbered. 4to. Cont. mor. gt. Etched frontis. sigd. by Corinth. (SH. Nov.21; 284)
Reed & Sims. £58

BIGELOW, Henry Jacob
- Dr. Harlow's case of Recovery from the Passage of an Iron Bar through the Head. Phila., 1850. Orig. ptd. wraps., unc., in cl. case. (S. Jun.15; 86)
Jenner Books. £70

BIGELOW, John Jr.
- The Campaign of Chancellorsville: a Strategic & Tactical Study. N.Y., [1910]. (1,000) numbered. 4to. Sig. of Brig. Gen. G.P. Borden. Cl. (SG. Jan.8; 86)
$140

BIGOT, Georges
- Croquis Japonais. Tokyo, 1886. Tall fo. Bnd. in is Bigot's 'Le Jour de l'An au Japon'. Hf. lev., orig. Japanese wraps. bnd. in. Bkplt. of the Grolier Club. (SG. Mar.12; 205)
$600

BIJOU de Société (Le), ou l'Amusement des Grâces
Paphos, ca. 1785. 2 vols. 18mo. Cont. marb. roan, decor. spines. (HD. Apr.10; 321)
Frs. 2,700

BIJOU Pocket Book & Fashionable Remembrancer for 1861
L., [1860]. 2¾×1½ ins. Orig. mor. with wallet edge (rather worn), spine defect. (SG. Mar.19; 251)
$150

BILDERBUCH FUR KLEINE WISSBEGIERIGE KNABEN
Nuremb., 1825. Lacks 2 pp., slightly browned in parts & soiled, 3 ll. heavier. Cont. paper bds., slightly defect. (H. Dec.9/10; 1704)
DM 420

BILDERGALLERIE f. d. Jugend
Gotha, 1835. 12 pts. Ob. 4to. A few plts. browned. Orig. wraps. (HD. Nov.18-21; 1116)
DM 1,100

BILIBIN, Ivan
- Perishko Finista Yasna Sokola [The Feather of Finist the Bright Falcon]. St. Petersb., 1902. 4to. Orig. pict. wraps. (CSK. Jun.12; 124)
£85

- Sestritsa Alenyshka in Bratets Ivanushka. Belaya Utochka [Sister Alenyshka & Brother Ivanushka. The Little White Duck]. St. Petersb., 1903. 4to. Orig. pict. wraps. (CSK. Jun.12; 123)
£85
-- Anr. Copy. Fo. 2 ills. slightly defect., Engl. translations inserted. Orig. wraps. (SH. Feb.5; 198)
De la Casa. £60
- Vol'ga. 1904. Fo. Wraps., torn. (SH. Jul.23; 4)
Quaritch. £80

BILLED-GALLERI af Beromte Maleres Vaerker . . .
Copen., 1874. 2 pts. in 1 vol. 4to. Slightly soiled. Orig. hf. leath. gt. (D. Dec.11-13; 1272) *DM* 600

BILLIG, G.
- Deutschlands Verhängnisvolles Jahr 1866. Dresden, [1866]. Sm. 4to. Soiled. Cont. hf. leath. (R. Oct.14-18; 2068)
DM 1,100

BILLINGS, Robert William
- Baronial & Ecclesiastical Antiquities of Scotland. 1845-52. 4 vols. Mor. gt. (CE. Nov.20; 135)
£130
-- Anr. Copy. 4to. Slight foxing. Hf. mor., worn. (CE. Jul.9; 168)
£60
-- Anr. Edn. Edinb., 1901. 4 vols. 4to. Cl. (PD. Feb.18; 173)
£75
-- Anr. Copy. Some minor spotting. Orig. qtr. mor., spines worn. (TA. Jan.22; 435)
£50
-- Anr. Edn. N.d. 4 vols. 4to. Cont. cf., gt. spines. (SH. Nov.6; 76)
Cavendish. £50

BILLMARK, C.J.
- Pittoresk Resetur fran Stockholm till Neapel. [Stockholm], [1852]. Lge. fo. Later hf. leath., ca. 1900, spine slightly defect. (R. Oct.14-18; 1832)
DM 19,000
-- Anr. Copy. Cont. hf. leath., spine restored. (R. Mar.31-Apr.4; 2588)
DM 13,500

BILLY, André
- Adieux aux Fortifications. Ill.:– Jouas, Chahine, Dauchez, Bouroux & others. Paris, 1930. (127), numbered. 4to. 2 proofs at end. Red mor. by Cretté, silk doubls., wrap. preserved, s.-c. (SM. Feb.11; 195)
Frs. 3,600
- Route Cavalière de la Solitude. Ill.:– Madrassi (port.); de Pidoll (woodcuts). Paris, 1928. (1) on imperial Jap., numbered. Sm. 4to. Lacks cancelled copper-engr. of port., this dry point in 2 states, proof of cancelled copper-engr., woodcuts on Jap. Red mor. by Kieffer, spine & covers gt., wrap. preserved, s.-c. 2 unpubld. autograph pp. (SM. Feb.11; 196)
Frs. 1,800

BING, Samuel
- Artistic Japan. [1889-91]. 6 vols. 4to. Some browning. Cont. hf. cf., orig. upr. covers of wraps. bnd. in. (CSK. Nov.28; 5)
£170
- Le Japon Artistique. Paris, [1888]. 3 vols. Fo. A few ll. detchd., stitching loose. Orig. hf. cl. & decor. bds., stained, worn. (SPB. Jul.28; 46) $125

BINION, Samuel Augustus–YOUNG, Thomas
- Ancient Egypt or Mizrai'm.–Hieroglyphics. N.Y. (1st. work), Priv. Ptd. (2nd. work), 1887; 1823. Ltd. Deluxe Edn. (1st. work). 2 vols. in 4; 1 vol. Lge. 4to.; lge. fo. Hf. mor., wood case (1st. work); & cont. mor., gt., arms of the Duc de Blacas? gt. on covers, crest on spine, by Lewis, covers slightly spotted. From the collection of Eric Sexton. (C. Apr.15; 26)
Quaritch. £180

BINNS, Edward
- The Anatomy of Sleep or the Art of Procuring Sound & Refreshing Slumber at will. 1842. 1st. Edn. Orig. cl., loose. Bkplt. of Ambrose Lisle Phillipps of Garendon. (S. Jun.15; 89)
De Lisle. £80

BINNS, Lewis John
- Forty Theatrical Celebrities, Authors etc., (sketchbook). Ca. 1910. Ob. 8vo. Orig. linen. (SH. Apr.10; 623)
Drummond. £100

BINS de Saint Victor
- Tableau Historique et Pittoresque de Paris . . . Paris, 1808-11. 1st. Ill. Edn. 3 vols. 4to. Cont. glazed cf., gt. fillets & roll-stps. around covers, smooth decor. spines. Author's MS. bkplt. (HD. Feb.27; 86)
Frs. 4,000

BINYON, Robert Laurence
- The Art of Botticelli. Ill.:– Muirhead Bone (frontis.). L. & Glasgow, 1913. (275). Fo. Hf. vell., soiled, worn at edges. Frontis. sigd. by artist. (SG. Dec.4; 38)
$150

- Catalogue of Drawings by British Artists in the British Museum. 1898-1907. 4 vols. Orig. cl. (SH. Jul.23; 24)
MacKinnon. £90
- Drawings & Engravings of William Blake. L., 1922. Lge. square 8vo. Bds., qtr. vell. (KH. Nov.18; 67)
Aus. $130
-- Anr. Edn. 1922. (200) numbered. Fo. Orig. vell. gt., cl. case, ties. (SH. Mar.26; 92)
Quaritch. £90
-- Anr. Copy. Gt.-lettered heavy vell., soiled. Review Copy. (SG. Dec.4; 52)
$130
- Dream-Come-True. Ill.:– Lucien Pissarro. Eragny Pr., 1905. (185). Orig. bds., unc. (S. Jul.31; 32)
Warrack & Perkins. £150
-- Anr. Copy. Partly unopened. (S. Jul.31; 31)
Bolton. £90
- The Followers of William Blake . . . 1925. 4to. Orig. cl. gt. Sir Cecil Beaton copy. (SH. Mar.26; 29)
Down. £70
- Poems. Daniel Pr., 1895. (200) numbered. Dark red mor. gt., lge. centre panel on upr. cover with repeated rose spray, similar decor. on spine & inside covers, silk doubls. & end-ll., by Schulze, orig. wraps. bnd. in. (S. Jul.31; 2)
Monk Bretton. £160
-- Anr. Copy. Orig. wraps. (CSK. Apr.3; 67)
£50

BINYON, Robert Laurence (Ed.)
See–ARIEL Poems

BINYON, Robert Lawrence & Sexton, J.J. O'B.
- Japanese Colour Prints. 1923. Ltd. Edn. sigd. by authors. 4to. Orig. pig. (SH. Jan.29; 78)
George's. £120

BIOGRAPHIE UNIVERSELLE, ANCIENNE ET MODERNE
1811-44. Vols. 1-75 only, including supp., lacks vol. 46. Cont. sheep, worn. (SH. Mar.6; 489)
Wade Gallery. £110

BIOGRAPHISCHES LEXIKON DER HERVORRAGENDEN ARZTE
Munich & Berlin, 1962. Facs. reprint. 8 vols. including index to vol. I–V. Orig. cl. (S. Feb.23; 329)
Phillips. £140

BION
See–ANACREON & others–MUSAEUS
See–THEOCRITUS, Bion & Moschus

BION, Nicolas
- The Construction & Principal Uses of Mathematical Instruments. Trans.:– Edmund Stone. 1723. 1st. Engl. Edn. Fo. Edge of last plt. dust-soiled, plts. slightly dis-cold., some foxing at end. Cont. panel. cf. (C. Feb.25; 3) *Maggs.* £240
-- Anr. Copy. General soiling. Recent cf. (TA. Jan.22; 88)
£75
-- Anr. Copy. Some plts. torn, 3 heavily. Cont. hf.-leath., reprd. (R. Mar.31-Apr.4; 1214)
DM 500
- Neu-eröffnete Mathematische Werck-Schule. Frankfurt & Leipzig, 1712. 1st. German Edn. 4to. Lacks plt. 16, several ll. bkd., slightly soiled in parts. Hf. leath. (HK. May 12-14; 222) *DM* 600
-- Anr. Edn. Nuremb., 1726-28. 3rd. German Edn. 3 Pts. in 1 vol. 4to. Cont. leath., gt. spine. (R. Oct.14-18; 269)
DM 1,150
- Traité de la Construction et des Principaux Instrumens de Mathématique . . . Paris, 1709. Cont. roan, gt. fillets on covers with fleurons in corners, arms of Abbey of St. Chéron, Chartres, spine with raised bands, ink-stain on edge. (HD. Feb.27; 12)
Frs. 1,700
-- Anr. Edn. Ill.:– D. Coster. The Hague, 1723. New Edn. 4to. Cont. leath., gt. spine, lightly worn. (HK. Nov.18-21; 405)
DM 720
- L'Usage des Globes Céleste et Terrestre et des Sphères. 1710. 3rd. Edn. Cont. marb. cf., spine decor. with raised bands. (HD. Feb.27; 13)
Frs. 1,700

BIONDI, Giovanni Francesco
- Donzella Desterrada. Trans.:– James Hayward. 1635. 1st. Edn. in Engl. Fo. Lacks final blank, & blank portion of 1 margin. Cont. cf., gt. spine. [STC 3074] (C. Nov.19; 27)
Sharples. £240

BIONDO, Michelangelo
- Angoscia. Venice, 1542. 2 vols. 19th. C. hf. mor. (SI. Dec.3; 80)
Lire 300,000

BIRCH, George H.
- London Churches of the XVIIth & XVIIIth Centuries. L., 1896. Fo. Plts. & text loose. Cont. hf. leath. & buckram, hinges brkn. (CB. May 27; 34)
Can. $130

BIRCH, Thomas
- The Heads of Illustrious Persons of Great Britain. the Dwellings of the Poor in Large Towns. 1747-52. [1st. Edn.?]. Fo. Extra-ill. containing 140 plts. (4 dupl.), cut round & mntd. to lge. fo. size, 1 imprint cropped, no title or text. Red mor. panel. in gt., by F. Bedford. (S. Apr.7; 451) *Nolan*. £130
- - Anr. Copy. 19th. C. mor., elab. gt. (S. Nov.24; 27) *Erlini*. £90
- - Anr. Edn. 1756. Fo. Title reprd. & guarded in inner margin. 19th. C. russ., rebkd., preserving orig. spine, slightly worn. Lge. copy. (S. Sep.29; 254) *Maggs*. £90
- - Anr. Edn. Ill.:- Houbraken & Vertue. 1813. New Edn. [2nd. Edn.?]. Fo. Some offsetting onto text, hole in 3G2 affecting text, title creased & with slit below vig. Hf. mor., worn. (S. Dec.9; 487) *Mistrali*. £160
- - Anr. Copy. 107 (of 108) ports., lacks Ben Jonson. Linen-bkd. mod. bds., bkplt. (SG. May 21; 370) $160
- - Anr. Copy. Cont. hf. heath., upr. cover loose. (R. Oct.14-18; 2669) DM 1,100
- - Anr. Edn. 1833. Fo. Hf. mor., worn, some ll. stained. (BS. May 13; 219) £60

BIRCH, William
- Délices de la Grande Bretagne. Ill.:- Birch after Reynolds, Gainsborough & others. 1791. Ob. 4to. Occasional light dampstaining. Cont. diced cf., gt. From the collection of Eric Sexton. (C. Apr.16; 217) *Traylen*. £150

BIRCH, William R.
- The Country Seats of the United States of North America. Springland, near Bristol, Pa., 1808. 1st. Edn. Ob. 4to. Ex-libry. Cont. red hf. mor. gt., worn, boxed. Bkplts. of Frederic R. Kirkland & William Loring Andrew. (SPB. Jun.22; 10) $10,000

BIRD, Isabella L.
- Unbeaten Tracks in Japan. 1880. 2 vols. Hf. cf., worn. (CE. Apr.23; 54) £155

BIRD, John
- Grounds of Grammer Penned & Published. Oxford, 1641. 2nd. Edn., re-iss. of the 1639 Edn. Outer blank margin torn & reprd. Cont. sheep, worn, upr. cover detchd. [Wing B2953] (C. Feb.25; 148) *Lawson*. £150
See-YOUNG, George, & Bird, John

BIRD, Robert Montgomery
- Nick of the Woods, or the Jibbenainosay ... Phila., 1837. 1st. Edn. 2 vols. Mod. mor., gt. spines & panel., floral & hunting motifs, orig. wraps. & ptd. labels bnd. in each vol. From liby. of William E. Wilson (SPB. Apr.29; 21) $300

BIRGITTA, Sancta
- Orationes. [Rome], [Stephen Plannck], ca. 1495. Sm. wormhole on some ll. affecting woodcut, ff. 3-8 possibly from anr. copy, liby. stp. removed from verso of f. 10. Mod. mor. [H. Add. 3209; Goff B 679] (C. Apr.1; 10) *Hopper*. £6,000
- Reuelationes. Nuremb., 21 Sep. 1500. 2nd. Latin Edn. Fo. 1 initial painted, lacks last blank lf., heavily browned in parts, the 1st. 2 ll. with browning, stained in parts, especially at beginning & end, sm. pen ill. under printer's mark, old entry on last lf. Old vell., slightly soiled, sm. wormholes, 2 sm. tears in spine. (H. Dec.9/10; 1334) DM 8,500

BIRINGUCCIO, Vanuccio
- De la Pirotechnia. Venice, 1540. 1st. Edn. 4to. Sm. tear affecting border of title, reprd., some ll. a little browned. 19th. C. mor.-bkd. bds. (C. Apr.1; 98) *Goldschmidt*. £3,000
- - Anr. Edn. Venice, 1559. 4th. (1st. 8vo.) Edn. Lightly browned at beginning & end. Cont. limp vell. (R. Mar.31-Apr.4; 1239) DM 1,050
- La Pyrotechnie ou art du feu ... traicte de toutes sortes ... de Minières, Fusions, et Separations des Metaux ... des Distillations, de Mines etc. ... Trans.:- Jacques Vincent. Rouen, 1627. 4to. Some dampstains. Limp vell., worn. (S. Dec.1; 65) *Music Mart*. £110

BIRKBECK, Morris
- Notes on a Journey in America, from the Coast of Virginia to the Territory of Illinois.-Letters from Illinois. L., 1818. 2nd. Edn. of 1st. work. 2 vols. in 1. 1st. 2 ll. loose in bdg., old liby. stp. on verso of titles, 1st. work with the map. Hf. cf. (SG. Jan.8; 39) $140

BIRNBAUM, Solomon A.
- The Hebrew Scripts. L.; Leiden, 1954-57; 1971. 2 vols. Fo. Cl. (S. Nov.18; 732) *Kingsgate*. £60

BISANI, Alessandro
- A Picturesque Tour through Part of Europe, Asia & Africa. 1793. 1st. Edn. 4to. Lacks 1st. lf. (?blank). Cont. red str.-grd. mor. gt. Bkplt. of George Gostling. (S. Nov.24; 29) *Howes*. £70

BISHOP, John
- Beautiful Blossomes. 1577. 1st. Edn. Sm. 4to. 1 lf. torn & reprd., cont. owners' motto on title. Cont. limp vell. [STC 3091] (C. Nov.19; 2) *Terry*. £420

BISHOP, William Warner
- A Checklist of American Copies of 'Short-Title Catalogue' Books. 1950. 4to. Orig. cl. (LC. Feb.12; 69) £60

BISSELIUS, Johannes-ACERBI, Joseph
- Argonauticon Americanorum.-Reise durch Schweden und Finland. Trans.:- C. Weyland (2nd. work). Munich; Berlin, 1647; 1803. 1st. Edn. in Latin (1st. work). 2 works in 2 vols. 12mo.; 8vo. Liby. stps. on title of 1st. work. 1st. work: cont. vell. bds., lacks portion of spine; 2nd. work: orig. wraps., lacks spine, unc. [Sabin 99443] (S. Jul.27; 30) *Remington*. £190

BISSET, Major-General
- Sport & War ... in South Africa. L., 1875. Occasional light foxing. Orig. bdg. (VA. Oct.31; 118) R. 95

BISSET, R.
- Modern Literature. 1804. 3 vols. Cf. gt. (P. Dec.11; 264) *Laywood*. £80

BITAUBE, [Paul Jérémie]
- Joseph. Ill.:- Saint Aubin after Charles Nicholas Cochin, Née after Marillier. Paris, 1786. 4th. Edn. Privilege lf., old inscr. on flylf. Cont. red mor. by Derome le Jeune with his ticket, gt. arms of Dauphin Louis-Joseph-Xavier-François (1781-89) on covers, triple gt. fillet, flat spine gt. in compartments, inner gt. dentelles, cl. chemise & mor.-bkd. s-c. (SM. Oct.7; 1586) *Frs*. 5,200

BITTING, Katherine Golden
- Gastronomic Bibliography. San Franc., 1939. Buckram. (SG. Jan.22; 63) $200

BIVORT, A.
- Album de Pomologie. Brussels, 1847-50. Vols. 1-3 in 1 vol. Ob. 4to. A few ll. at beginning & end silked. Mor. by the Wigmore Bindery. Due to uncertainty of collation, w.a.f. (S. Jun.1; 72) *Quaritch*. £1,500

BIZOT, Pierre
- Histoire metallique de la Republique de Hollande. Paris, 1687. 1st. Edn. Fo. Browning, marginal staining. Old cf. (SPB. Nov.25; 109) $200
- Medalische Historie der Republyk van Holland. Amst., 1690. 4to. Engraved frontis. reprd., some spotting. Recent cf. by Period Binders, Bath. (TA. Apr.16; 243) £75
- - Anr. Copy. 14 (of 15) plts. Cont. cf., back gt., upr. jnt. brkn. (VG. Dec.15; 461) Fls. 700

BJORNSON, Bjornstjerne
- Works. L., 1884. Author's Edn. 7 vols. Hf. cf. by Root. (SPB. May 6; 291) $375

BLAAUW, F.E.
- A Monograph of the Cranes. Ill.:- after H. Leutemann & J.G. Keulemans. Leiden & L., 1897. (170). Fo. 1st. lf. removed. Publisher's mor., gt. title on upr. cover, gt. inner borders, a few slight scratches, bkplt. removed from inside upr. cover. (S. Jun.1; 73) *Wheldon & Wesley*. £850

BLACK, Adam & Charles
- General Atlas. Edinb., 1850. Fo. 54 of 60 maps, cold. (JN. Apr.2; 819) £70

BLACK, Joseph
- Experiments upon Magnesia Alba. Edinb., 1777. 12mo. Lacks hf.-title & last blank. Cont. cf., rebkd. (SH. Jun.11; 14) *Rota*. £100
- Lectures on the Elements of Chemistry. Edinb., 1803. 1st. Edn. 2 vols. 4to. Cont. tree cf., worn. (S. Dec.2; 681) *Stanley*. £80

BLACK, W.H.
- History & Antiquities of the Worshipful Company of Leathersellers. Priv. ptd. 1871. Fo. 2 plts. folding & mntd. on cl. Orig. mor., worn. (CSK. Jun.26; 142) £50

BLACK, William, Physician, 1771-1811
- An Historical Sketch of Medicine & Surgery. L., 1782. 1st. Edn. Errata/advt. lf. Cont. vell.-bkd. marb. bds., torn. (SG. Sep.18; 48) $120

BLACKALL, John
- Observations on the Nature & Cure of Dropsies. 1814. 2nd. Edn. Errata slip tipped in near beginning, occasional spotting, advt. ll. Orig. paper bds., spine defect., unc. (S. Feb.10; 366) *Laywood*. £50

BLACKBURN, Mrs. Hugh
- Birds Drawn from Nature. 1862. Fo. Plts. hand-cold. Orig. roan-bkd. bds., worn. (SH. Jun.18; 98) *Quaritch*. £120
- - Anr. Copy. Orig. ptd. bds. with linen backstrip. (TA. Jun.18; 124) £85
- - Anr. Edn. Glasgow, 1868. Fo. Orig. gt. decor. cl., some wear to spine. (TA. Jun.18; 125) £60

BLACKBURN, Philip C.
See-LANGFELD, William R. & Blackburn, Philip C.

BLACKBURNE, Francis
[-] The Confessional ... L., 1766. Lower hf. of last lf. verso covered to conceal advts., 10-p. review bnd. in. Red mor., bnd. for Thomas Brand-Hollis with gt.-stpd. olive branch & owls. Thomas Brand-Hollis stps. on blank ll., armor. bkplt. of Dr. John Disney, note by Richard Heber. (SG. May 14; 20) $425

BLACKER, J.F.
See-GORER, Edgar & Blacker, J.F.

BLACKER, Valentine
- Memoir of the Operations of the British Army in India, during the Manratta War of 1817, 1818 & 1819. L., 1821. 1st. Edn. 2 vols. in 1. 4to. Cont. hf. cf. & marb. bds., covers loosening. (PNY. Oct.1; 298) $320

BLACKER, William
- Art of Fly Making ... L., 1855. 18mo. Orig. cl. (SG. Apr.9; 281) $425

BLACKIE, W.G.
- The Imperial Atlas. [1872]. 4to. Hf. cf., defect. (P. Apr.9; 143) *Shaffar*. £55

BLACKLOCK, Dr. Thomas
- Poems together with an Essay on the Education of the Blind. Edinb., 1793. L.P. 4to. Later hf. cf. (SH. May 21; 258) *Bickersteth*. £100

BLACKMANTLE, Bernard (Pseud.)
See-WESTMACOTT, Charles Molloy 'Bernard Blackmantle'

BLACKMORE, Sir Richard
[-] The Kit-Cats. 1708. 1st. Edn. Fo. Several inscrs. & corrections in a cont. hand, slight browning. Disbnd., some ll. detchd. (S. May 5; 345) *Frost*. £110

BLACKMORE, Richard Dodridge
- Fringilla: Or Tales in Verse. Ill.:- Will H. Bradley. Cleveland, 1905. (600) numbered on lge. H.M.P. Tall 8vo. Occasional foxing. Cl.-bkd. pict. bds. (PNY. Mar.26; 54) $300
- Lorna Doone. L., 1869. 1st. Edn. 3 vols. Some text slightly soiled, publisher's catalogue at end. Orig. watered cl. (Carter's 'A' bdg.), spines & corners worn, bdgs. tightened, qtr. mor. gt. s-c. From the Prescott Collection. (CNY. Feb.6; 19) $350

BLACKSTON, W.A. & others
- The Illustrated Book of Canaries & Cage-Birds. Ca. 1880. 4to. Cl. (S. Dec.3; 896) *Gilberts*. £55

BLACKSTONE, Sir William
- An Analysis of the Laws of England. Oxford, 1771. 6th. Edn. Disbnd. (SG. Sep.25; 51) $180
- Commentaries on the Laws of England. Oxford, 1766-68. Var. Edns. Vols. 1-3 (of 4). 4to. Cont. cf. (SBA. Jul.22; 45) *Laywood*. £85
- - Anr. Edn. Oxford, 1766-69. Vol. 1: 2nd. Edn.; Vols. 2, 3, 4: 1st. Edns. 4 vols. 4to. Cont. mott. cf., worn. (SPB. Nov.25; 150) $400
- - Anr. Edn. 1778. 4 vols. Red mor. gt., wormholes, worn. (CE. Jul.9; 152) £120
- - Anr. Edn. 1778-87. 8th. & 10th. Edns. 8 vols. Some ll. soiled. Cont. cf., worn, some covers detchd. (SH. May 28; 151) *Pharos*. £65
- - Anr. Edn. L., 1795. 12th. Edn. 4 vols. Slight foxing, slight worming to title-p, vol. 4, vol. 2 contains table of descents facing p. 239. Rebnd. buckram. (JL. Dec.15; 734) Aus. $150

BLACKSTONE, Sir William *-contd.*
– – **Anr. Edn.** 1800. 13th. Edn. 4 vols. Cont. cf. (SH. May 21; 9) *Pharos.* £85
– **The Great Charter.** Oxford, 1759. 1st. Edn. 4to. Cont. cf., rebkd. (SH. Jun.25; 31) *Frognal.* £260
– – **Anr. Edn.** Oxford, 1759. 1st. Edn., L.P. on thick paper. Lge. 4to. Old cf., disbnd. (SG. Sep.25; 50) $500

BLACKWALL, John
– **A History of the Spiders of Great Britain & Ireland.** 1861. 2 pts. in 1 vol. Fo. Hf. leath., worn. (S. Jun.1; 1) *Allsopp.* £220
– – **Anr. Edn.** 1861-64. 2 pts. in 1 vol. Fo. Slight spotting. Mod. cl. (P. Apr.30; 203) *Quaritch.* £100

BLACKWELL, Elizabeth
– **A Curious Herbal.** 1739. 2 vols. Fo. Some offsetting, short tear in plt. 496, plt. 205 soiled, text plt. 99 holed & torn in margin. Late 19th. C. panel. cf., worn. (S. Jun.1; 257) *Traylen.* £2,600
– – **Anr. Copy.** 496 (of 500) hand-cold. plts., lacks nos. 230, 233, 251 & 252, some soiling. Cont. Dutch cf., gt., rebkd. with mor. (S. Jun.1; 74) *Cucchio.* £1,800
– **Herbarium Blackwellianum.** Ed.:– C.J. Trew & C.G. Ludwig. Nuremb., 1749-60. 4 vols. (of 6). Fo. Vol. 1 frontis. mntd. previously, title of 6th. pt. bnd. in for ptd. vol. 1 title. Cont. hf. leath. (R. Oct.14-18; 2913) DM 21,000
– – **Anr. Edn.** Ed.:– Christoph Jacob Trew. Ill.:– N.G. Eisenberger. Nuremb., 1750-73. 6 vols. in 3. Fo. Vols. 1 & 2 stained on upr. pts. of text & most plts., 8 plts. torn without loss, plts. 253-288 in vol. 3 with stain & loss from decay, vol. 2 engraved title with lge. pt. torn away, text quire in vol. 6 sprung. Cont. vell., worn. W.a.f. (CNY. May 22; 192) $3,800
– – **Anr. Edn.** [Nurnberg], [1750-73]. 6 vols. Fo. 596 hand-cold. plts. (of 615), lacks all text, extra illustrated by insertion of approximately 200 hand-cold. plts. from Kreb's Vollständige Beschreibung und Abbildung der sämmtlichen Holzarten, 1826, & other works, the whole rearranged according to genera. 19th. C. qtr. cl. As a collection of plts., w.a.f., from collection of Massachusetts Horticultural Society, plts. unstpd. (SPB. Oct.1; 100) $8,500
– – **Anr. Edn.** Ed.:– C.J. Trew. Ill.:– N.F. Eisenberger. Nuremb., 1757-54-73. 6 vols. Fo. Hand-cold. engraved titles & plts., fore-margins slightly discold. 19th. C. hf. mor., worn, covers detchd., spines defect. From Chetham's Liby., Manchester. (C. Nov.26; 37) *Schmidt.* £2,600

BLACKWOOD, Lady Alicia
[–] **Scutari, Bosphorus, Crimea.** [Ventnor, Isle of Wight], 1857. 2 vols. Fo. Dampstained thro.-out, 1 plt. torn cleanly, marginal soiling. Orig. wraps., soiled. (CSK. Jan.9; 133) £85

BLACKWOOD'S Edinburgh Magazine
1828-74. Vols. 23-116. Cont. hf. cf. (SH. Apr.9; 191) *Wade Gallery.* £230

BLAES, Gerard
– **Anatome Animalium Terrestrium Variorum.** Ill.:– Jan Luyken (frontis.). Amst., 1681. 1st. Edn. 4to. 1 plt. torn to plt. mark. 19th. C. hf. mor. From Chetham's Liby., Manchester. (C. Nov.26; 38) *Weldon & Wesley.* £100

BLAEU, Johannes or Jan
– **Atlas of England, Scotland, Wales & Ireland.** Ed.:– R.V. Tooley. Ca. 1970. Facs. reprint, (500) numbered. Tall fo. Orig. hf. mor. with brkn. s.-c. (TA. Jun.18; 466) £60
– **Collection of 153 Engraved Maps & an Engraved Chart.** [Amst.], ca. 1700, or later. Fo., (528mm × 315mm). All but 1 map hand-cold. in outl., pict. & other title-cartouches, vigs., coats-of-arms, etc., fully cold., ptd. 'Catalogue of the Mapps', numbered 1-151, plus 3 unnumbered maps listed in MS., without other text or prelims., numbering thro.-out written in rectos of top fore-corners, the 93 Blaeu maps consist of 54 of Engl. counties etc., from the 1662 Fr. Edn. of the Atlas Major & 42 maps from other Edns. with Latin, Fr. or Dutch text on versos, all of these latter cut round & mntd., sm. hole in heading of 1 map, Blaeu's Wiltshire separated in fold, 1 or 2 maps loose. Cont. mor., gt. spine. W.a.f. (S. Nov.3; 15) *Pescetti.* £8,500
– **Géographie Blaviane. Bd. 2: [Nord-Ost-U. Südost-Europa].** Amst., 1667. 2nd. Fr. Edn. Lge. fo. Lightly browned in parts, title ll. heavier. Orig. vell. gt. (R. Mar.31-Apr.4; 2299) DM 12,500
– **Géographie Blaviane. Bd. 3: [Belgien, Niederland, Luxemburg].** Amst., 1667. 2nd. Fr. Edn. Lge. fo. Lightly browned in parts, 2 maps, with minimal tears in lower margin. Orig. cont. vell. gt. (R. Mar.31-Apr.4; 2300) DM 28,000
– **Géographie Blaviane. Bd. 4: [England].** Amst., 1667. 2nd. Fr. Edn. Lge. fo. Slightly browned in parts, mostly only in margins, 2 maps with sm. tears in lower margin, wormed in 2nd. part. Orig. vell. gt. (R. Mar.31-Apr.4; 2301) DM 17,000
– **Geographiae Blavianae.** Amst., 1662. Books XII & XIII. Orig. bdg. (CE. Nov.20; 37) £1,300
– **Le Grand Atlas ou Cosmographie Blaviane . . .** Amst., 1667-63-67. Vols. 6 & 11 1st. Edn., rest 2nd. Edn. Compl. in 12 vols. Fo. With Brahe's plts. of astronomical instruments, all vigs., maps, plts., & c. cold. by cont. hand, engraved titles & vigs. heightened in gold, mntd. on guards thro.-out, lacks dedication to pt. 4 of vol. 2, 'Regions Orientales', not in index, occasional light soiling, some maps creased, 1 loose, very light worming at end of vol. 3. Unif. cont. vell., panel. gt., with centre & cornerpieces, spines gt., slightly soiled. As an atlas, w.a.f., from Chetham's Liby., Manchester. (C. Nov.26; 39) *Neidhardt.* £54,00
– – **Anr. Edn.** Amst., 1667. 2nd. Edn. in Fr. 12 vols. Lge. fo. 3 unindexed plts., lacks 'Partie meridionale de la Jutie septentrionale'. Publisher's ivory vell. with gt. decor. cover, 2 borders of roll-stps., corner-pieces, lozenge motifs in centre, decor. spine, silk ties. (HD. Mar.18; 23) Frs. 670,000
– – **Anr. Edn.** Amst., 1967. (1,000) numbered. Vols. I–VII only, of 12. Fo. Facs. of Amst. 1663 Edn., engraved plts. & double-p. maps, some cold. Orig. gt. decor. mock cf. (TA. Oct.16; 184) £250
– **Groot Stedeboek van Geheel Italie . . .** The Hague, 1724. 3rd. Edn. (2nd. with Dutch text). 4 vols. Lge. fo. Pt. IV lacks number 43, last 8 plts. of this vol. unnumbered & bearing address of Alberts, some weak spots & sm. tears in centre folds of a few plts. (especially in 1st. vol.), due to rebdg., some folds strengthened, a few traces of use & stains in places, sm. pt. of explanatory text & a few plts. a little browned, some older plts. in weaker impressions. Late 18th. C. hf. mor., spines richly gt., raised in compartments, gt. tools of empire-style motives, corners strengthened with vell. 19th. C. bkplts. of J.B. Powis. (VG. Dec.17; 1176a) Fls. 20,000
– **Het Nieuw Stede Boek van Italie.** Amst., 1704-05. 4 vols. Fo. Orig. vell. from workshop of Blaeu-Mortier, smooth decor. spines, 2 borders on covers with gt. decor. in angles & lozenge piece in centre, rather soiled. (SM. Feb.11; 121) Frs. 87,000
– **Novum et Magnum Theatrum Urbium Belgicae Foederatae; . . . Urbium Belgicae Regiae.** Amst., [1649]. 3rd. Edn. 2 vols. Lge. fo. Armorial engraved titles, 220 (of 223) engraved plts., 1 title detchd. & frayed, some plts. partly separated in centre fold, 1 defect., some torn, some stained or creased. Orig. vell. gt., roll-tooled borders, inner panel, cornerpieces & centre ornament, vol. 1, detchd. from bdg., lacks spine & ties, very worn. W.a.f. (S. Mar.31; 270) *Span.* £6,000
– **Theatrum Civitatum et Admirandorum Italiae.** Amst., 1663. Pt. 2 only. Fo. Title with woodcut device, 43 engraved plts., plt. 11 bis, but lacks plts. 33 & 18, without frontis. & possibly 8 pp. text & index, plt. 7 torn & reprd., some worming. Cont. mott. cf., spine gt. in 7 compartments. W.a.f. (S. Mar.31; 285) *Gal San Giorgio.* £1,100

BLAEU, Willem or Guilielmus Janszoon
– **Atlas of England, Scotland, Wales & Ireland.** N.d. Ltd. Edn., Facs. Reprint. Fo. Orig. hf. mor., bd. case. (SH. Jul.16; 160) *Book Room, Cambridge.* £50

BLAEU, Willem or Guilielmus Janszoon & Johannes or Jan
– **Atlas Major.** Amst., 1662. Latin Edn. Vol. 11 [America]. Fo. 23 double-p. engraved maps, hand-cold. in outl., principal features fully cold., lf. 3M in dupl., later guards thro.-out. 18th. C. panel. cf., gt. spine, worn. W.a.f. (S. Mar.31; 283) *Waterloo Inn.* £3,500
[–] – **Anr. Edn.** [Amst.], ca. 1662. Spanish Edn., L.P. Fo. Engraved title, 23 (of 26) engraved maps, cartouches, etc., text engrs., contents lf. torn, loosely inserted, wormed. Cont. parch., spine defect. W.a.f. (S. Mar.31; 284) *Rayleigh.* £700
[–] **Collection of Maps of Spain, France, Switzerland, the Low Countries, Austria & Germany.** [Amst.], ca. 1670, or later. Fo. 131 engraved maps, mostly double-p., histor. & other cartouches, coats of arms, etc., versos blank, numbered in Ms., lacks some numbers, 1 map defect., a few torn, reprd., frayed or stained, 1 dupl., some underscoring thro.-out, few maps detchd., without title, text, or prelim. ll. Cont. mott. cf., spine gt., very worn. W.a.f. (S. Mar.31; 286) *Schmidt.* £3,000
– **Derde Stuck der Aerdrycks-Beschryving, welck vervat de Nederlanden.** Amst., 1664. 2 pts. in 1 vol. Lge. fo. Orig. blind-stpd. & panel vell., lacks ties. (VG. Oct.13; 12) Fls. 37,000
– **Geographiae, Volvmen Septimvm.** Amst., 1662. 2 vols. in 1. Lge. fo. Added map bnd. in, lacks 10 pp. & 5 maps, cont. vell. gt., lightly browned thro.-out & slightly soiled in parts, 2 worm holes. Cont. vell. gt., spine with sm. tear. (H. Dec.9/10; 443) DM 7,000
– **Grooten Atlas oft Werelt-Beschryving. (Eerste deel).** Amst., 1642. 2 pts. in 1 vol. Lge. fo. Engraved title for 2nd. pt. in cont. hand-colouring, all maps (118 of 120) with cont. hand-colouring, cartouches fully cold., lacks map of the world & general map of Europe, several maps from anr., smaller, copy of edn., 1 folding map torn in folds, some short tears, several maps creased in inner parts, a few sm. stains in blank margins, last 2 maps in rather poor condition. Cont. gt.-stpd. vell., defect., spine gone & clumsily pasted with strip of old vell. (VG. Dec.17; 1174) Fls. 28,000
– **[Italy].** Ca. 1650. Double-p. fo. A collection of 44 maps from a Blaeu atlas, cold. in outl. Cont. cf. rebkd., gt., 2 fine 17th. C. views of Genoa & Parma, double-p. fo., loosely inserted. (SPB. Oct.1; 262) $3,100
– **Novus Atlas: China.** Amst., 1655. Vol. 6. Fo. Hand-cold. title, 17 hand-cold. maps. Cont. vell. gt. (P. Jul.2; 231) *Weiss.* £1,600
– **Paises Bachos, o Belgia, dividida en dos Partes.** Amst., 1663. Vol. IV of Spanish Atlas Mayor. 2 pts. in 1 vol. Lge. fo. All maps in old, but probably not cont., hand-colouring, including cartouches, lge. initials in text hand-cold., lacks title to pt. II, engraved title of a different atlas bnd. in. 18th. C. hf. roan. (VG. Dec.17; 1176) Fls. 24,000
– **Russia, quae est Europae Liber Quartus.** [Amst.], [1662]. Fo. 8 double-p. engraved plts. hand-cold. in outl., cartouches, coats of arms, figures, vigs., etc., fully cold. Mod. marb. bds. W.a.f. (S. Mar.31; 407) *Terry.* £120
– **La Théâtre du Monde ou Nouvel Atlas.** Amst., 1640. Pt. 3. Fo. Hand-cold. engraved title with ptd. overslip, 66 double-p. engraved maps, hand-cold. in outl. with cold. borders, pict. cartouches & inset plans, arms, etc., mntd. on guards thro.-out. Cont. gt. panel. vell., gt. cornerpieces & central arabesque, lacks ties. (C. Jul.15; 12) *Taylor.* £3,200
– – **Anr. Copy.** Pt. 3. Fo. Hand-cold. engraved title with ptd. overslip, 66 hand-cold. engraved maps with cold. borders, pict. cartouches & inset arms, etc., mntd. on guards thro.-out. Cont. gt. panel. vell., gt. cornerpieces & central arabesque. (C. Jul.15; 13) *Taylor.* £2,800
– – **Anr. Copy.** Engraved title with ptd. overslip, mntd. on guards thro.-out. Cont. gt. panel. vell. with gt. cornerpieces & central arabesque, slightly worn, covers slightly stained. W.a.f. (C. Nov.6; 241) *Cooper.* £2,400
– – **Anr. Edn.** [Amst.], [1640]. 2nd. Pt. 19½ × 335 inches. Gt.-ruled vell., rebkd. (JN. Apr.2; 806A) £6,500
– – **Anr. Edn.** 1654. Vol. 5 only, Scotland & Ireland. 52 uncold. maps, 8 with dampstains, 1 cold. map of Connaught inserted, lacks title. Cont. vell., defect. (P. Mar.12; 76) *McLean.* £1,000
– **[Le Theatre du Monde vol. VI] Novus Atlas Sinensis a Martino Martinio.** [Amst.], [1655]. Fo. 17th. C. mott. cf. (C. Apr.1; 125a) *Weiss.* £1,900
[–] **Theatrum Orbis Terrarum.** [Amst.], ca. 1650, or later. Fo. 35 (of 58) engraved maps, hand-cold. in outl., histor. & other cartouches, coats of arms, etc. fully cold., lacks title, lf. to reader & index lf. 19th. C. maroon hf. mor. gt., worn. W.a.f. (S. Mar.31; 282) *Burgess.* £2,600
– **Theatrum Orbis Terrarum sive Atlas Novus.** Amst., 1640. Vol. 1. Fo. 109 maps, most double-p. Cont. vell., worn. (P. Jun.11; 201) *Burgess.* £4,800
– – **Anr. Edn.** Amst., 1645. 1st. Latin Edn. Vol. 4. Lge. fo. Lightly browned in parts, 1 map with sm. margin tear. Orig. vell. gt. (R. Mar.31-Apr.4; 2305) DM 18,000

– **Toonneel des Aerdrijcx ofte Nieuwe Atlas.** Amst., 1635. Vol. 2. Lge. fo. Engraved title in old hand colouring & 103 + 4 engraved maps, but for 2, all double-p. & hand-cold. in the period, the four maps inserted from a later edn. of Blaeu's Atlas: Aragon, Navarre, De Groote Mogol, & Florida, 2 maps were originally ptd. on the wrong sheets, these are pasted over with the right maps, 5 or 6 maps have slit in fold, naked figure cut out from cartouche of 2 maps, some sm. wormholes in lr. margin, 1st. few ll. loose & frayed. Cont. panel & gt. vell., badly worn & defect. (VG. Dec.17; 1173)
Fls. 22,500

– – **Anr. Edn.** Amst., 1642. Fo. Architectural engraved title, ptd. label in centre, 66 engraved maps, hand-cold. in outl., histor. & other cartouches, arms, etc. fully cold., title heightened with gold, sm. rust-hole in V1. Cont. mott. cf. gt., roll-tooled borders & panel, gt. spine, worn. W.a.f. (S. Mar.31; 275) *Marshall.* £3,200

– – **Anr. Copy.** Vol. 3. Title & maps with cont. hand-colouring. Cont. panel. & gt. vell., worn, spine a little defect. (VG. Dec.17; 1175)
Fls. 10,000

– – **Anr. Edn.** Amst., 1646. Thick Paper. Pt. IV. Fo. Engraved title, 60 engraved maps, cold. by cont. hand in outl., histor. cartouches, vigs., etc. fully cold. 3 text engrs. hand-cold. Orig. vell. gt., roll borders, inner panel, cornerpieces, centre ornam., lacks ties. W.a.f. (S. Mar.31; 276)
Map House. £5,200

– – **Anr. Edn.** Amst., 1650. Vol. 3. Fo. Engraved title, 60 (of 62) engraved maps, all hand-cold. in outl., histor. cartouches, arms etc. & title fully cold., 4Z1 torn, some staining, later guards thro.-out. 19th. C. parch. W.a.f. (S. Mar.31; 281)
Mistrali. £2,800

BLAGDEN, Charles Otto
See–SKEAT, Walter William & Blagden, Charles Otto

BLAGDON, Francis William
[–] **An Historical Memento representing the different Scenes of Publick rejoicing in St. James's & Hyde Parks in celebration of the Glorious Peace of 1814.** Ill.:– J.H. Clark. L., 1814. [1st. Edn.?] 4to. Aquatint plts. hand-cold. Mor.-bkd. bds., head of spine worn. From the collection of Eric Sexton. (C. Apr.16; 218) *Henderson.* £350

– – **Anr. Copy.** Fo. Orig. leath.-bkd. bds., unc., worn. (SG. May 14; 21) $550

BLAGDON, Francis William, Daniell, William & others.
– **A Brief History of Ancient & Modern India.** 1805. 3 Pts. in 1 vol. fo. 2 extra hand-cold. engraved titles, 64 (of 66) hand-cold. engraved plts., plts. wtrmkd. 1827-28, first engraved title & some following ll. detchd. Hf. roan, both covers detchd., spine defect., very worn. (S. Nov.25; 429)
Symonds. £400

BLAINE, Delabere P.
– **An Encyclopaedia of Rural Sports ...** Ill.:– Branston after Alken, Landseer, Dickes, & others. L., 1840. 1st. Edn. Early mor., gt.-tooled with scrolls enclosing fish, flies, etc., spine gt. with sporting emblems, worn. (SG. Dec.11; 177) $180

BLAINVILLE, M. de
– **Travels through Holland, Germany, Switzerland & Italy.** Trans.:– Dr. Turnbull, Mr. Guthrie & others. 1767. 3 vols. 4to. Lacks hf.-titles (?), plt. at p. 323 vol. II torn, a few other plts. with marginal tears, occasional stains or browning, a few minor defects to text. Cont. vell. bds. (S. Jun.22; 6)
Fairburn. £260

BLAIR, Eric Arthur 'George Orwell'
– **Homage to Catalonia.** 1938, 1st. Edn. Orig. cl. (SH. Jul.22; 290) *Hossain.* £75

BLAIR, Robert
– **The Grave.** Ill.:– Schiavonetti after William Blake. 1808. [1st. Edn.?]. Lge. 4to. Late 19th C. str.-grd. mor. by F. Bedford, partly unc. Subscriber's copy. (S. Nov.24; 31) *Traylen.* £350

– – **Anr. Copy.** Occasional minor spotting, fore-edge of frontis. & engraved title partly dampstained. Cont. hf. cf. by Whitman Bennett, rubbed. From the collection of Eric Sexton. (C. Apr.15; 62) *F.A.S.* £250

– – **Anr. Copy.** Fo. Three-qtr. red mor. (SG. Oct.9; 34) $400

– – **Anr. Edn.** Ill.:– Louis Schiavonetti after William Blake. 1813. 4to. Prelims. spotted. Cont. hf. cf., covers detchd. (TA. May 21; 286) £75

– – **Anr. Copy.** 4to. Light spotting to some plts.

Cont. hf. mor. gt., worn, covers detchd., spine defect. (LC. Feb.12; 8) £65

BLAKE, Edward Warren
See–BANKES, Rev. Thomas & others

BLAKE, W.H.
– **Brown Waters.** Ed.:– Lord Tweedsmuir. Ill.:– Clarence Gagnon. Toronto, 1940. Square 4to. Name of orig. owner inked-in on fly-lf. Orig. buckram covers. (PWP. Apr.9; 184) Can. $200

BLAKE, William
– **All Religions are One.** Trianon Pr., 1970. (36) numbered. 4to. Mor., mor.-edged bd. s.-c. (C. Jul.22; 45) *Traylen.* £100

– **Auguries of Innocence.** Ill.:– Leonard Baskin. [Northampton, Massachusetts], Gehenna Pr., 1959. (250) numbered, on H.M.P. sigd. by Baskin, also dupl. set of ills. each sigd. by Baskin. Wraps., mor.-bkd. bd. portfo. (SG. Oct.23; 14) $260

– **The Book of Urizen.** Trianon Pr. 1958. (526) numbered. 4to. Orig. mor.-bkd. bds., s.-c. (SH. Jan.29; 4) *Subunso.* £175

– **Europe, A Prophecy.** Trianon Pr., 1969. (20) numbered. Fo. Mor., mor.-edged bd. s.-c. (C. Jul.22; 46) *Marks.* £190

– **The Gates of Paradise.** Trianon Pr., 1968. (50) numbered. 3 vols. & supp. vol. Sm. 4to. & sm. fo. Mor., supp. vol. in cl., cl. s.-c. (C. Jul.22; 47)
Fine Arts Society. £80

– **Illustrations of the Book of Job.** L., Mar. 8, 1825 [i.e. Mar. 1826]. (65) on Fr. paper. Fo. Engraved title & 22 plts. on wove paper, the word 'Proof' distinct, guarded & interleaved, some foxing thro.-out. Bds., spine defect., qtr. mor. gt. s.-c. Inscr. 'Copy of proofs presented to G. Wythes Esqr. by John Linnell Decr. 1863'. (CNY. May 22; 35) $9,500

– – **Anr. Edn.** 1902. Facs. Edn., (1000). Fo. Orig. wraps. (TA. Jun.18; 312) £52

– – **Anr. Copy.** Ptd. stiff wraps. (SG. Dec.4; 43) $100

– **Jerusalem.** [1877]. (100). 4to. Monochrome facs. Cl., soiled, orig. wrap. (numbered '90') bnd. in. (CSK. Oct.27; 86) £70

– – **Anr. Edn.** Trianon Pr., [1951]. (516) numbered. 4to. Orig. cl., box. (CSK. Feb.13; 41) £350

– – **Anr. Copy.** This copy unnumbered? Orig. buckram gt. over bevelled bds. (KH. Nov.18; 69) Aus. $1,150

– **The Marriage of Heaven & Hell.** Ca. 1868? 4to. Hf. mor., worn, unc. (SG. Mar.19; 24) $120

– – **Anr. Edn.** [Paris], [Trianon Pr.], [1960]. (526). Fo. Mod. qtr. mor., s.-c. (S. Jun.9; 10)
Thomas. £150

– **Milton, A Poem.** Trianon Pr., 1967. Rosenwald MS. Facs. Edn., (20) numbered. 4to. Mor., mor.-edged bd. s.-c. (C. Jul.22; 48) *Marks.* £250

– – **Anr. Edn.** [Clairvaux], Trianon Pr., [1967]. Standard Iss., (380) numbered on Arches pure rag paper. Bds., qtr. mor., card s.-c. (KH. Nov.18; 70) Aus. $290

– **Pencil Drawings.** Ed.:– Geoffrey Keynes. Nones. Pr., 1927. (1550) numbered. 4to. Hf. cl. over bds., unc. (SG. Dec.4; 47) $100

– – **Anr. Edn.** Ed.:– Geoffrey Keynes. Nones. Pr., 1956. 2nd Series, (1440) numbered. 4to. Orig. cl., unc., d.-w. (S. Jul.31; 119) *Reid.* £50

– **Poems.** Ed.:– John Sampson (preface). L., Florence Pr., 1921. L.P. Mor., gt.-stpd. at sides & at panel spine with decor., mor. doubls., gt.-stpd. by C. & C. MacLeish at the Doves Bindery, thin line from knife at upr. cover. (PNY. Dec.3; 109) $140

– **Reproductions of Twelve Water-Colour Drawings Illustrating Milton's Paradise Lost.** L'pool., 1906. Loose in buckram folding case. (SG. Dec.4; 50) $110

– **The Song of Los.** [Paris], [Trianon Pr.], [1975]. (458). 4to. Mod. qtr. mor., marb. covers, s.-c. (S. Jun.9; 11) *Lord Eccles.* £100

– **Songs of Innocence & Experience ...** [L.], 1789-94. 4to. Compl. set of later imps. of orig. copperplts., including 'A Divine Image', 3 in 2 forms, together 57 sheets cut to 4to. size, 280×190 mm., some slightly smaller, mntd. in album, all on Whatman paper, 9 wtrmkd. 1831-32. Maroon mor., unc., by Rivière. H. Buxton Forman bkplt. (CNY. May 22; 36) $15,000

– – **Anr. Edn.** L., 1839. 1st. Typographical Edn. 12mo. Slight tears & foxing. Orig. cl., faded. (SPB. May 29; 43) $300

– – **Anr. Edn.** [Clairvaux], [Trianon Pr.], [1955]. (500) for sale. Orig. mor., bd. s.-c., slight soiling. (KH. Nov.18; 72) Aus. $300

– **Visions of the Daughters of Albion.** Ed.:– Geoffrey Keynes. Trianon Pr., 1959. (20) with set of hand-cold. plts. Fo. Orig. mor., s.-c. (SH. Mar.26; 96) *Illustrated Antiques.* £280

– **The Writings.** Ed.:– Geoffrey Keynes. Nones. Pr., 1925. (1,500) numbered on Vidalon H.M.P. 3 vols. 4to. Vell.-bkd. bds., unc. 2 page A.L.s. by Keynes, 1935, laid in. (SG. Sep.4; 66) $350

– – **Anr. Copy.** Vell.-bkd. marb. bds., unc., last vol. unopened. (SG. Apr.9; 535) $100

– – **Anr. Edn.** Nones. Pr., 1925. (1575) numbered. 3 vols. 4to. Orig. parch.-bkd. bds., unc. (S. Jul.31; 110) *Down.* £90

– – **Anr. Edn.** Nones. Pr., 1925. 3 vols. Vell. & marb. bds. (CE. Nov.20; 134) £140

– **Works.** Ed.:– Edwin John Ellis & William Butler Yeats. 1893. 3 vols. Advts., a few ll. slightly spotted. Orig. cl. gt. (SBA. Oct.21; 208)
Sunbun-so. £220

– – **Anr. Copy.** Some spotting. Orig. hf. mor. (CSK. Sep.26; 56) £200

BLAKE, William (Ill.)
See–WOLLSTONECRAFT, Mary

BLAKE, William Hume
– **Brown Waters.** Ed.:– Lord Tweedsmuir. Ill.:– Clarence A. Gagnon. Toronto, 1940. (1000). Orig. canvas, d.-w. (reprd.). (CB. Sep.24; 282)
Can. $450

BLAKEWAY, J.B.
See–OWEN, Hugh, of Shrewsbury & Blakeway, J.B.

BLAKISTON, Maj. John
[–] **Twelve Years' Military Adventure in Three Quarters of the Globe.** L., 1829. 1st. Edn. 2 vols. Sheep., worn. (SG. Feb.26; 57) $110

BLAKSTON, W.A. & others
– **Illustrated Book of Canaries & Cage-Birds, British & Foreign.** Ca. 1860. 4to. Disbnd. (TA. Dec.18; 346) £50

BLANCARD or Blankaart, Stevan
– **Anatomia Reformata.** Leiden, 1687. 2 pts. in 1 vol. Slightly soiled, last & 1st. ll. with sm. traces of worming in margin. Cont. vell. (HK. May 12-14; 224) DM 1,300

– – **Anr. Edn.** Leiden, 1688. Cont. leath. (R. Oct.14-18; 314) DM 800

– – **Anr. Edn.** Leyden, 1695. 1 sm. hole, lacks port., slightly soiled. Cont. vell. bds., soiled, spine worn. (SH. Jun.4; 126) *Nagel.* £120

– **Theatrum Chemicum oder Eroffneter Schauplatz und Thur zu den Heimligkeiten in der Scheide-Kunst nebenst einer Vermehrung wie die geringen Metallen ... zu verbessern sind durch Kenelm Digby.** Leipzig, 1700. 2 pts. in 1 vol. 1 plt. divided into 2, title mntd., a few rust marks & tiny rust holes. Cf., worn, spine reprd. (S. Dec.1; 67)
Grammers. £100

[–] **Theatrum Chimicum ofte geopende Deure der Chymische Verborgenheden ... met een vervolg over de Chymische Verborgentheden ... door den Ridder K. Digby.** Amst., 1693. 2 pts. in 1 vol. Lacks plt. 7. Hf. cf. (S. Dec.2; 448)
Haverbeke. £120

BLANCHARD, E.
– **Histoire Naturelle des Insectes.** 1851. Hf. cf., worn. (P. Apr.30; 204) *Bookroom.* £50

BLANCHARD, Jerrold
See–DORE, Gustav & Blanchard, Jerrold

BLANCHET, François
[–] **Variétés Morales et Amusantes, tirées des Journaux Anglois.** Paris, 1784. On Holland paper. 2 vols. 12mo. Port. in vol. 1 mntd. in oval with engraved inscr. mntd. beneath, folded sheet of notes tipped into vol. 1. Cont. mor., gt., border of fillets & lozenges, flat spine gt. in compartments with single ovals, inner gt. dentelles (row of concentric circles). Pixérécourt bkplt. (SM. Oct.7; 1588) Frs. 1,000

BLANCK, Jacob
– **Merle Johnson's American First Editions.** N.Y., 1942. 4th. Edn. Orig. cl., worn, hole in spine. (SPB. Jul.28; 49) $100

– **Peter Parley to Penrod ... the Best-Loved American Juvenile Books.** N.Y., 1938. (500). 12mo. Buckram. (SG. Apr.30; 30) $130

BLANCKLEY, T.R.
– **A Naval Expositor ...** 1750. 1st. Edn. 4to. Slight browning. Cont. hf. cf., rebkd. (S. Apr.7; 394) *Foyles.* £350

BLANCO, Manuel
- Flora de Filipinas. Manila, 1877-80-[83]. 5 vols., including Appendix. 4to. Plts. numbered 1-477 in pencil. Cont. red hf. mor. gt., unc. From collection of Massachusetts Horticultural Society, stps. on plts. (SPB. Oct.1; 101) $7,000

BLANE, William N.
- [-] Travels Through the United States & Canada ... L., 1828. 2nd. Edn. Frontis. map torn. Orig. mott. cf. bds., rebkd., later endpapers. From liby. of William E. Wilson. [Sabin 5872] (SPB Apr.29; 25) $250

BLANFORD, W.T.
- Observations on the Geology & Zoology of Abyssinia. 1870. Orig. cl. (P. Sep.11; 225) Way. £85
- - Anr. Copy. Orig. cl. gt. (P. Dec.11; 10) Thorp. £80
See-GOLDSMID, Sir F.J. & Blanford, W.T.

BLANKAART, Stephen
See-BLANCARD or Blankaart, Steven

BLANKENBURG, Fr. von
- Litterarische Zusätze zu J.G. Sulzers Allgemeiner Theorie der Schönen Künste. Leipzig, 1796-98. 3 vols. Cont. hf. leath., spine gt., worn. (H. Dec.9/10; 1401) DM 580

BLASI e Gambacorta, Giovanni Evangelista di & others
- [-] Funerali per Carlo III Re delle Spagne e per l'Infante de Napoli D. Gennaro Borbone. Palermo, 1789. Fo. 1 folding plt. with tear reprd. Cont. vell.-bkd. bds., slightly worn & stained. (S. Jun.22; 7) Goldschmidt. £120

BLASIUS, Joannes Martinus
- Arithmetica. Ed.:- T. Rhaetus. Paris, 1526. Fo. Lacks final blank, a few ll. stained, fl with minor repair, cont. marginalia, owners' inscrs. of Franciscan convent, the Brothers Minor Giovanni Pucelli & Francesco Demayo, & Giovanni Rezia. Old vell. bds. From Honeyman Collection. (S. May 20; 3185) Nador. £130

BLAST
Ed.:- Wyndham Lewis. 1914. No. 1. 4to. Orig. wraps., spine worn. (SH. Mar.26; 317) Thomson. £75
- - Anr. Edn. Ed.:- Wyndham Lewis. 1915. 4to. Orig. pict. wraps., spine worn. (S. Jul.22; 204) Sims & Reed. £90

BLATHWAYT, William
- Atlas. Ed.:- Jeanette D. Black. Providence, 1975. 2 vols. Fo. & 4to. Loosely contained in cl. covered folding box, cl., d.-w. (SPB. May 5; 105) $250

BLAUE REITER (Der)
Ed.:- W. Kandinsky & Fr. Marc. Munich, 1914 4to. Torn & soiled at margins. Orig. bds. with cold. woodcut by Kandinsky, linen strip pasted on spine. (HK. Nov.18-21; 2697) DM 1,400

BLEGNY, Etienne de
- Les Elemens ou Premières Instructions de la Jeunesse. Paris, 1702. 2 pts. in 1 vol. Browned. Cont. cf., worn. (SH. Jun.11; 50) Quaritch. £50

BLELOCH, W.
- The New South Africa. L., 1901. 1st. Edn. Cl., edges badly dampstained. Pres. Copy, from Kipling (with his bkplt.) to Alfred Baldwin (with his bkplt.). (SG. Nov.13; 402) $125

BLES, Joseph
- Rare English Glasses of the XVII & XVIII Centuries. 1925. 4to. Orig. cl. (SBA. Mar.4; 240) Tallerman. £90
- - Anr. Edn. Ed.:- G. Bles. [1925]. 4to. Orig. cl., worn. (P. Sep.11; 263) Sims & Reed. £75
- - Anr. Edn. N.d. 4to. Occasional spotting to text. Orig. buckram, d.-w. (CSK. Sep.26; 202) £90

BLESSINGTON, Joseph P.
- [-] The Campaigns of Walker's Texas Division. N.Y., 1875. 1st. Edn. Cl. (SG. Jun.11; 107) $120

BLEW, William C.A.
- Brighton & its Coaches. 1894. 1 cold. ill. detchd., a few minor defects. Orig. cl. gt., worn. (SBA. Mar.4; 103) Quaritch. £60
- - Anr. Copy. Fo. Cont. hf. mor. gt. by Root & Son, L., orig. cl. covers bnd. in, partly unc. (TA. Oct.16; 297) £52
- A History of Steeple-Chasing. Ill.:- after Henry Alken. 1901. Occasional spotting. Orig. cl., soiled. (CSK. Oct.27; 80) £65
- - Anr. Copy. Pict. cl. (SG. Dec.11; 179) $100

BLEYSWIJK, D. van
- Beschryvinge der Stadt Delft. Ill.:- C. Decker. Delft, 1667[after 1680]. 2 vols. 4to. With mezzatint port. of author. & separate part 'Delftsche Broertgens-Kermis'. Cf., gt. spines, 1 slightly defect. (VG. Oct.13; 24) Fls. 2,200

BLIGH, [William]
- Bligh's voyage in the Resource from Coupang to Batavia. [L.], [Gold. Cock. Pr.]. [1937]. [1st. Edn.], (350) numbered. Fo. Cl., slightly soiled. (KH. Nov.18; 75) Aus. $200
- Log of H.M.S. Bounty, 1787-89. [Surrey], 1975. [1st. Edn. thus] (50) copies, from (500). Fo. Main text a facs. of Bligh's hand. Mor. by Zaehnsdorf with gt. inner dentelles, silk end-papers & raised bands, preserved in buckram box, gt. Tipped-in lf. of limitation sigd. by Earl Mountbatten of Burma. (KH. Nov.18; 76) Aus. $500
- Log of H.M.S. Providence, 1791-1793. [Surrey], 1976. [1st. Edn. thus], (50) sopies from (500). Fo. Main text is facs. of Bligh's own log. Mor. by Zaehnsdorf with gt. inner dentelles & silk end-papers, raised bands, preserved in a buckram box. Tipped in lf. indicating the limitation, sigd. by Earl Mountbatten. (KH. Nov.18; 77) Aus. $500
- - Anr. Edn. [Surrey], 1976. (500). Fo. Cl. & hf. cf. (KH. Mar.24; 46) Aus. $320
- A Narrative of the Mutiny on board His Majesty's Ship Bounty. L., 1790. 1st. Edn. 4to. Offsetting. Cf.-bkd. bds. by Bumpus, Philip Gosse's bkplt. (SPB. May 6; 157) $1,400
- - Anr. Copy. Slight foxing. Mod. hf. mor. (KH. Nov.18; 78) Aus. $2,250
- A Voyage to the South Sea for the Purpose of Conveying the Bread-Fruit to the West Indies in His Majesty's Ship the Bounty. 1792. 1st. Edn. 4to. Slightly spotted, slight offsetting onto title. Cont. cf. (S. Jul.27; 2) Brook-Hitching. £900
- - Anr. Copy. Slight offsetting, minor tears & stains, some repairs. Old sheep, rebkd., reprd., new endpapers. [Sabin 5910] (SPB. May 5; 106) $1,900
- - Anr. Copy. Foxing & offsetting. Cont. russ. gt., spine worn. (SPB. May 6; 158) $1,200
- - Anr. Copy. Some foxing & offsetting, lacks thin section round fold of chart at p. 179. Later hf. cf. (KH. Nov.18; 79) Aus. $700

BLISS, Douglas Percy
- A History of Wood-Engraving ... L. (etc.), 1928. Orig. cl., d.-w. (slightly worn). (CB. Feb.18; 204) Can. $100

BLISS, Robert Wood
- Collection of Pre-Columbian Art. Phaidon, 1957. Sm. fo. Orig. cl. (CSK. May 22; 87) £75

BLITH, Walter
- English Improver. 1649. 1st. Edn. Sm. 4to. ? lacks 1st lf. (? blank), title slightly soiled. 18th C. hf. cf. [Wing B3193] (S. May 5; 309) Thorp. £140

BLOCH, Jean-Richard
- Dix Filles dans un Pré. Ill.:- Marie Laurencin. Paris, 1926. (35) on japon imperial with 2 extra suites of the etchings. Mor.-bkd. bds., orig. wraps. bnd. in, unc., unopened. Etched bkplt. of Edward Wassermann by Marie Laurencin loosely inserted. (SH. Nov.21; 372) Kawamatsu. £250

BLOCH, Marcus Elieser
- Ichthyologie ou Histoire Naturelle, Générale et Particulière des Poissons. Trans.:- [Jean Charles] Laveaux. Ill.:- Berger after Rosenberg. Berlin, 1785-97. 12 vols. Fo. Plts. hand-cold., occasional light foxing & offsetting. Cont. hf. russ., several covers detchd. From Chetham's Liby., Manchester. (C. Nov.26; 41) King. £8,500
- Naturgeschichte der Fische. [Berlin], ca. 1790. Ob. 8vo. 2 copperplts. uncold., a few slightly browned plts. Cont. hf. leath. (H. May 21/22; 158) DM 6,000
- Systema Ichthyologiae. Ed.:- J.G. Schneider. Ill.:- J.F. Henning. Berlin, 1801. 17 copper engrs. uncold., 2 of these folding, slightly soiled in parts. No bdg. (H. Dec.9/10; 272) DM 4,600

BLOCIUS, Johannes
- Collegium Martinale: de quibusdam hodie Bibentium & Moribus Gestis. Magdeburg, 1618. 1st. Edn. Sm. 4to. Slight browning. Mod. pol. hf. cf. by Rivière, spine gt., slightly rubbed. From liby. of André L. Simon. (S. May 18; 45) Offenbacher. £50

BLOEMWERK, NEDERLANDSCH, door een Gezelschap van Geleerden
Amst., 1794. 4to. All plts. hand-cold., title slightly defect., thumbed. Later hf. cl., soiled, some defects. (VG. Dec.17; 1208) Fls. 4,750

BLOK, Aleksandr
- Dvenadtsat'. Skify [The Twelve. Scythians]. Ed.:- Ivanov-Razumnik (preface). St. Petersb., 1918. 1st. Edn. Browned. Orig. wraps., spine torn, loose. (SH. Feb.6; 395) Bjorck. £100
- Liricheskiya Dramy [Lyrical Dramas]. St. Petersb., 1908. 7 pp. of music by M.A. Kuzmin. Orig. bds. by K.A. Somov, rebkd. (SH. Feb.6; 396) Rosenthal. £50
- Nechayannaya Radost' [Unexpected Joy]. Ill.:- V. Milioti. Moscow, 1907. A few ll. slightly spotted. Mod. bds., orig. wraps. preserved, soiled. (SH. Feb.6; 397) Quaritch. £50
- Stikhi o Prekrasnoi Dame [Verses on A Beautiful Lady]. Moscow, 1905. 1st. Edn. 4to. Mod. cf.-bkd. bds., orig. wraps. (reprd.) by V.V. (SH. Feb.6; 400) Bjorck. £120

BLOK, Aleksander & others
- Pro: Kozlov, sobak Veverleev (About Goats, Dogs & Veverleys). Kiev, 1925. Later cl., orig. upr. wrap. by Vs. Averin mntd. (SH. Feb.6; 298) Flegon. £55

BLOME, Richard
- Britannia. 1673. 1st. Edn. Fo. Cont. cf. As an atlas, w.a.f. (C. May 20; 101) Villers. £1,200
- - Anr. Copy. Old cf., covers detchd., lacks one. W.a.f. (C. May 20; 102) Burgess. £650
- A Description of the Island of Jamaica; With the other Isles & Territories in America to which the English are Related. L., 1678. Some tears, lacks port., marginal worming, slight soiling, spotting. Sheep, spine torn, worming, stains. [Sabin 5967] (SPB. May 5; 107) $200
- The Gentleman's Recreation. 1710. 2nd. Edn. Fo. Cont. panel. cf. (TA. Jan.22; 98) £425
- - Anr. Copy. 3 Pts. in 1 vol. 77 engraved plts. (of 80). Late 18th. C. russ. gt. (S. Nov.24; 33) Schuster. £100
- A Geographical description of the World. [2nd. pt. dtd. 1680]. Fo. Lacks title & 1st. few ll. of text, 21 engraved maps only, hand-cold. in outl., some soiled or torn. Hf. cf., worn, bds. detchd. W.a.f. (CSK. Apr.10; 5) £220
See-COX, Nicholas & Blome, Richard

BLOMEFIELD, Francis & Parkin, Charles
- An Essay towards a Topographical History of the County of Norfolk. 1739-75. 1st. Edn. 5 vols. Fo. 32 plts. only (of 37), lacks the List of Subscribers in vol. 1, end of vol. V. slightly browned. 18th. C. russ., gt. (C. Feb.25; 24) Adams. £160

BLOMFIELD, Sir Reginald
- A History of French Architecture from the reign of Charles VIII till the death of Mazarin [1494-1661].–A History ... from the death of Mazarin till the death of Louis XV, 1661-1774. L., 1911-21. 4 vols. Orig. cl. (CB. May 27; 35) Can. $110

BLONDEEL, Valentyn Jan
- Beschryvinge der Stad Utrecht. Utrecht, 1757. Old vell., ex-liby. (SG. Feb.5; 49) $120

BLONDEL, David
- A Treatise of the Sibyls ... Trans.:- J.D. [Davies]. L., 1661. 1st. Edn. in Engl. Fo. Ex-liby. Mod. buck. (SG. Sep.25; 52) $130

BLONDEL, François
- L'Art de jetter les Bombes. Amst., 1699. 4to. Cont. Dutch grd. cf., blind decor., double border of 2 fillets, angle fleurons, centre losenge plaque, reprd. (HD. Jun.10; 10) Frs. 3,800
- Resolution des quatre principaux problemes d'architecture. Paris, 1673. 1st. Edn. Fo. 7 (of 8) engraved plts. only. Cont. mott. cf. gt., arms of Louis XIV on sides & his cypher on spine. (C. Feb.25; 174) Laget. £350
- Thermarum Aquisgranensium et Porcenatarum Eluciatio & Thamaturgia. Aachen, 1688. 3rd. Edn. 4to. Title & dedication loose, copper engraved title & typog. title with lge. stain, 2nd. half with light browning. Cont. wraps., unc. (D. Dec.11-13; 190) DM 800

BLONDEL, Spire
- Histoire des Eventails ... Paris, 1875. Bradel vell. (HD. Jun.24; 153) Frs. 1,100

BLONDUS, Flavius
- **Historiarum Romanarum Decades.** Venice, Octavianus Scottus, 16 Jul. 1483. 1st. Edn. Fo. Some wormholes at beginning & end, a few wormholes slightly affecting a few letters, ff. H9 & 10, I1 & 2 torn & reprd. affecting text, some old marginalia, some ll. slightly spotted. 17th C. blind-stpd. cf., wormed & worn. [BMC V 277; HC 3248] (S. Jun.23; 212)   *Fletcher.* £260
- – **Anr. Copy.** 369 ll. (of 372, lacks 1st. blank, q4 & q7 supplied in facs.), initial on a2 supplied in blue & decor. with scroll-work extending to the inner margin, other initials supplied in red or blue, tear in i1 affecting 2 letters, marginal repair to final lf. touching 1 letter. 19th. C. hf. cf., worn. Lr. margin of 1st. lf. contains a cont. owner's inscr. of the monastery of Santa Justina, Padua with their inventory no. 4017. [HC 3248; BMC V 277; Goff B698] (SPB. May 6; 159) $500

BLOOMFIELD, Robert
- **The Fakenham Ghost, a True Tale.** [1813, from imprint of last p.]. 16mo. Orig. wraps., last ill. & verse on lr. cover. (SH.   Mar.19; 31)   *Quaritch.* £380
- [–] **The Farmer's Boy.** 1800. 1st. Edn. 4to. Name on title. Red. hf. mor. Pres. Copy from Leonard Clark to Walter de la Mare, & inscr. photograph by Clark loosely inserted. (S. Oct.1; 507)   £70

BLOUNT, Sir Henry
- [–] **A Voyage into the Levant.** 1636. 1st. Edn. 4to. Cont. cf., rebkd. Bkplt. of Lord Capell of Hadham, bkplts. of Boies Penrose, lately in the collection of Eric Sexton. [STC 3136] (C. Apr.15; 27)   *Hammond.* £320

BLUCHER, H.
- **Moderne Technik.** Leipzig & Vienna, 1912. 2 vols., text & plts. Fo. Owner's mark on title. Orig. linen. (HK. Nov.18-21; 407)   DM 1,100

BLUMBERG, H.D.
See–FIELD, C. & Blumberg, H.D.

BLUME, Karl Ludwig
- **Rumphiae.** Leyden, 1835-48-[49]. 4 vols. in 3. Fo. Hf. mor. gt. From collection of Massachusetts Horticultural Society, stps. on plts. (SPB. Oct.1; 102) $4,600

BLUME, Karl Ludwig & Fischer, J.B.
- **Flora Javae.** Brussels, 1828-62. 3 vols. Fo. With an additional 23 unpubld. hand-cold. plts, 1 double-p. (shaved, just affecting caption). Mod. str.-grd. mor., gt., by Jeanne Benoist-Gazel of Nice, unc. (C. Nov.5; 14)   *Studio.* £120
- – **Anr. Edn.** Brussels, Leiden & Amst., 1828-59 & n.d. Pt. 1, new series, vol. 1, (all publd.) & supp. Fo. Together 99 lithos., 79 cold., frontis. soiled, some sm. tears. Loose in orig. hf. linen portfol., wraps & orig. paper bds., very defect. (H. Dec.9/10; 370)   DM 3,400

BLUMENBACH, Johann Friedrich
- **Abbildungen Naturhistorischer Gegenstande.** Gottingen, 1796-99. Nos. 1-10 (complete in itself). Title-p. soiled, misbnd. Later bds. (TA. Nov.20; 362)   £56
- **Decas (prima-sexta) Collectionis suae Craniorum Diversarum Gentium Illustra.–Nova pentas Collectionis suae Craniorum Diversarum Gentium.** Göttingen, 1790-1820; 1828. Together 7 pts. in 1 vol. 4to. A few ll. very slightly spotted, long inscr. on Blumenbach in German on fly-lf. Cont. bds., slightly worn. (S. Oct.21; 368)   *Quaritch.* £210
- **Elements of Physiology.** Trans.:– Charles Caldwell. Phila., 1795. 1st. Amer. Edn. 2 vols. in 1. Old cf. (SG. Sep.18; 50) $130

BLUMENHAGEN, W.
- **Wanderungen durch den Harz.** Ill.:– after L. Richter. Leipzig, [1838]. 29 (of 30) steel engraved plts., stained in parts. Cont. hf. leath. (D. Dec.11-13; 1288)   DM 500

BLUMENHAGEN, W.–BECHSTEIN, Ludwig
- **Wanderungen durch den Harz.–Wanderungen durch Thüringen.** Leipzig, ca. 1840. 1st. Edn. 2 vols. in 1. Lacks 1 steel engr., slightly soiled. Cont. linen. (R. Oct.14-18; 2321)   DM 850

BLUNDEN, Edmund
- **The Barn.** Uckfield, 1916. 1st. Edn. 16mo. Orig. wraps. Pres. copy to J. Isaacs, 1920. (S. Jul.22; 135)   *Rota.* £320
- [–] **On Several Occasions, by a Fellow of Merton College.** Corvinus Pr., Dec. 1938. (63) numbered, sigd. Orig. buckram-bkd. linen, s.-c. (S. Jul.31; 147)   *Monk Breton.* £100

- **The Silver Bird of Herndyke Mill** . . . Uckfield, 1916. 1st. Edn. 16mo. Orig. wraps. Pres. copy to J. Isaacs, 1920. (S. Jul.22; 136)   *Quaritch.* £260

BLUNT, Anthony
- **Nicolas Poussin.** Phaidon, 1966-67. 3 vols. 4to. Orig. cl. in d.-w.'s, last vol. in s.-c. (TA. Mar.19; 135)   £58

BLUNT, Cmndr. David Enderby
- **Elephant.,** L., 1933. Cl., soiled. (SSA. Jan.22; 165)   R. 170

BLUNT, Wilfred
- **Georg Dionysius Ehret (1708-1770).** 1953. Fo. 2 plts. slightly spotted. Mor., gt., by Zaehnsdorf, upr. cover onlaid with red mor. roses at corners, slightly warped & stained. (S. May 5; 94)   *Crete.* £60
See–SITWELL, Sacheverell & Blunt, Wilfred

BLUNT, Wilfred (Ed.)
See–JONES, Paul

BLUNT, William Scawen
- **The Love Lyrics & Songs of Proteus.** Kelms. Pr., 1892. (300). Vell. gt. with ties, unc. (P. Apr.9; 118)   *Schriver.* £140
- – **Anr. Copy.** 4to. Slight browning. Orig. vell., slight soiling, ties torn. (SPB. Jul.28; 202) $225

BOAISTUAU, Pierre & others
- **Histoires Prodigieuses.** Antw., 1594 [colophon: 14 Mar., 1595]. 12mo. 19th. C. hf. cf. (S. Mar.17; 239)   *Maggs.* £120

BOBANUS, P. Phil
- **Recreatio Mentis et Oculi in Obseruatione Animalium Testaceorum.** Rome, 1684. 4to. A few plts. at end stained. Old vell. (D. Dec.11-13; 283)   DM 2,000

BOBINSKI, Capt. Kazimierz & Zamoyski, Stefan
- **Family Tables of Racehorses II, 1953-59.** L., 1960. Ltd. Edn. numbered. With 3 supps. Fo. Map. Orig. bdg., gt. s.-c. (JL. Dec.14; 478)   Aus. $300

BOBRINSKY, A.A.
- **Narodnyya Russkiya Derevyannyya Izdeliya [Folk Russian Wooden Articles].** Moscow, 1913. 2nd. Edn. Pts. 4, 5 & 7 only. Fo. Orig. portfo.'s, worn. (SH. Feb.5; 200)   *Smith.* £80

BOBROV, Sergei
- **Lira Lir [Lyre of Lyres].** Moscow, 1917. Inscr. on title. Orig. wraps. after the author. (SH. Feb.6; 405)   *Quaritch.* £65
- **Liricheskaya Tema [Lirical Theme. XVIII Digressions in that Province].** Moscow, Tsentrifuga, 1914. Export stp. on title & upr. cover. Orig. wraps., spine slightly torn. (SH. Feb.6; 300)   *Quaritch.* £100
- **Vertogradari nad Lozami [Gardeners on Vines].** Ill.:– N. Goncharova. Moscow, 1913. Orig. wraps., slightly torn, loose. (SH. Feb.6; 407)   *Carus.* £400

BOBROVSKY, P.O.
See–KHRESHCHATITSKY, B.P. & Bobrovsky, P.O.

BOCCACIO, Giovanni (attributed to)
- **Die Gantz Römisch Histori auffs Fleissigst . . . Begriffen. Eine Oration M.T. Ciceronis für Marcellum . . .** Trans.:– Christophorus Bruno von Hyrtzwail. Ill.:– H. Schaeufflein & Burgkmair. Augsburg, 1542. Fo. Mod. hf. vell. Dedication sigd. by author, 2 plts. sigd. with cypher of Schaeufflein. (HD. Mar.11; 24b)   Frs. 4,000

BOCCACCIO, Giovanni
- **Ameto.** Milan, 1520. Sm. 4to. Soiled, title wormed. Vell. bds. (SH. Jun.4; 121)   *Ayres.* £55
- – **Anr. Edn.** Venice, 1526. Lacks blank M8, some dampstaining. 18th. C. mor., triple gt. fillet, flat spine gt. with longitudinal title, inner gt. dentelles. (SM. Oct.7; 1589)   Frs. 1,400
- **Amorosa Visione.–Laberinto d'Amoredi.–Poetae tres egregii nunc primum in lucem editi.** Venice, 1549; 1558; 1534. 3 works in 1 vol. 18th. C. cf. (CSK. Apr.24; 54)   £65
- **The Amorous Fiammetta.** Ed.:– K.H. Josling. Trans.:– Barth. Young. Ill.:– M. Leone. L., Mandrake Pr., 1929. (500). Orig. vell., gold-stpd. vig. (D. Dec.11-13; 1002)   DM 5,000
- **Les Cent Nouvelles Nouvelles.** Ill.:– Vander Gouwen after Romain de Hooge. Cologne, 1701. 2 vols. Red mor. gt. by Derome le Jeune, with his ticket. (SM. Oct.8; 2392)   Frs. 2,200
- **Comedie.** Venice, Dec. 1503. Fo. Liby. stps. removed from title & last lf., light staining in upr.

blank margin, a few other minor stains, sm. wormhole thro. most of text. Mod. cf. (C. Apr.1; 11)   *Mediolanum.* £200
- **Contes.** Ill.:– Vidal after Boucher, Eisen & Gravelot. L., [Paris], 1779. Reprint of 1757 Edn. Slightly soiled in parts. Cont. marb. leath. gt., slight worming. (HK.   Nov.18-21; 2315)   DM 1,100
- – **Anr. Edn.** Ill.:– Gravelot engraved by Vidal. L., [Paris], 1791. 10 vols. Sm. 12mo. Imitation 18th. C. porphyr cf., decor. spines, 3 gt. fillets, inner dentelle, hf. bnd. s.-c. (HD. Apr.9; 408)   Frs. 3,200
- – **Anr. Edn.** Trans.:– A. Sabatier de Castres. Ill.:– Gravelot. Paris, 1801. 11 vols. 16mo. Cont. grd. roan, decor. spines. (HD. Apr.9; 409)   Frs. 1,800
- **Contes et Nouvelles.** Ill.:– Romain de Hooghe. Amst., 1697. 1st. printing. 2 vols. Sm. 8vo. Red mor. by R. Petit, fillet, decor. spine, inside dentelle, s.-c.'s (HD. Mar.18; 25)   Frs. 4,200
- **The Decameron [English].** 1620. 1st. Edn. in Engl. Fo. Slight staining. Mor. by Zaehnsdorf. [STC 3172] (C. Nov.19; 3)   *Wisbech.* £1,300
- – **Anr. Edn.** Ed.:– [Ugo Foscolo]. Ill.:– Thomas Stothard. L., 1825. L.P. 3 vols. Proofs on india paper loosely inserted, blank endpapers spotted. Citron mor. gt. by Bedford. (C. Nov.20; 179)   *Klusmann.* £450
- – **Anr. Edn.** Trans.:– Antoine Le Maçon. L. Tice. N.Y., Priv. ptd., 1925. (2,000) numbered on L.P., sigd. by publisher. 2 vols. 4to. Gt.-pict. cl., wallet-edged. (PNY. Dec.3; 50) $100
- **Le Décameron [French].** Trans.:– Antoine Le Maçon. Ill.:– Gravelot. Rouen & Paris, 1670. 2 vols. 12mo. 1 frontis. & 18 figs. for 1757. Edn. bnd. in. Cf., decor. spines, 3 fillets on covers, inner dentelle, imitation 18th. C. bdg. (HD. Apr.10; 323)   Frs. 2,000
- – **Anr. Edn.** Trans.:– Antoine Le Maçon. L. [Paris], 1757-61. 5 vols. Slightly soiled in parts. Cont. leath., floral gt. spine, triple cover fillets, inner gt. dentelle, rubbed. (D. Dec.11-13; 637)   DM 3,000
- – **Anr. Edn.** L., 1779. 10 vols. Cont. cf. (P. Jan.22; 52)   *Weston.* £70
- – **Anr. Edn.** Ill.:– Wagrez. Paris, 1890. De Luxe Edn. 3 vols. 4to. Hf. mor., gt. spines. (SI. Dec.3; 85)   Lire 380,000
- **Il Decamerone [French & Italian].** Ill.:– mostly after Gravelot. L. [but Paris], 1757. 1 engraved title in Fr. Late 19th. C. red hf. mor., gt. (CSK. Jan.30; 49)   £130
- – **Anr. Copy.** 5 vols. Late 19th. C. Fr. mor. gt. Harry & Caresse Crosby bkplt., their names on gt. shield on all covers. (CNY. May 22; 38) $1,400
- **Das Dekameron [German].** Trans.:– A. Wellelski. [Leipzig], [1912]. (825). 4to. Cont. leath., gt., spines slightly defect. (R.   Oct.14-18; 945)   DM 420
- **Decamerone. [Italian].** Venice, 5 Dec. 1498. Fo. Lacks title & 1st. text lf., 1st. lf. browned, 1st. 2 sigs. also slightly torn, slightly wormed. Cont. vell., loose, soiled. (HK.   Nov.18-21; 126)   DM 15,000
- – **Anr. Edn.** Flor. [Venice], 14 Apr. 1527 [1729]. Facs. reprint of 1527 Giunta edn., (300) L.P. Sm. 4to. 19th. C. diced cf. From liby. of Sir Edward Sullivan. (S. Jun.9; 47)   *Duran.* £100
- – **Anr. Copy.** Cont. mor., cf. rebkd., spine gt. (S. Mar.16; 111)   *King.* £55
- – **Anr. Copy.** Stain on title & last p. 19th. C. hf. cf., gt. spine. (SI. Dec.3; 83)   Lire 200,000
- – **Anr. Edn.** Venice, 1587. 4to. A few tears, browned. Later vell., worn. (SH. Jun.11; 169)   *Duran.* £90
- – **Anr. Edn.** Amst., 1665. 12mo. Late 18th C. Engl. mor., gt. fillet border, Engl. arms., decor. spine, inner guarland. (HD. Jun.10; 11)   Frs. 1,500
- – **Anr. Edn.** Ill.:– after Gravelot, Boucher, Cochin & Eisen. Londra [Paris], 1757. On Papier Hollande. 5 vols. Additional title bnd. into vol. I, 4 plts. of 'Estampes Galantes' bnd. into vol. II. Cont. red Fr. mor. gt., spines elab. tooled. (C. Nov.20; 208)   *Klusmann.* £1,500
- – **Anr. Copy.** Cont red mor., fillet border & dentelle, decor., decor. spine raised bands, inner dentelle. From Falquet de Planta & Vautier liby. (HD. Jun.10; 12)   Frs. 20,000
- – **Anr. Copy.** Mod. vell., unc. (HD. Feb.18; 13)   Frs. 2,600
- – **Anr. Edn.** Ed.:– Fernando Palazzi. Ill.:– Boccasile. Milan, 1955. Fo. Mor., orig. wraps. bnd. in, boxed. (SI. Dec.3; 88)   Lire 600,000

BOCCACCIO, Giovanni -contd.

- **Della Genealogia de gli Dei** . . . Ill.:– Honervogt. Venice, 1627. 4to. Owner. lf. with engraved floral border by Honervogt inserted, central compartment left blank, inscr. on title & fly-lf., some pr. marks on title & front free end-paper. 17th. C. Parisian mott. cf. bnd. for John Evelyn, his cipher, gt., on covers intersected by palm fronds in wreath. gt. panel, smaller version of cipher at corners in wreath of palm & laurel, spine gt. in compartments with same cipher. (SM. Oct.7; 1590) Frs. 3,000
- **Le Fiancée du Roy de Garbe.** Trans.:– Anthoine le Maçon. Ill.:– Leon Lebegue. Paris, 1903. (40) **Effgiacionibus cuiusq[ue] Gentilis Dei.** Paris, 22 on China paper. Tall 4to. Crimson crushed lev., gt.-tooled & inlaid, gt. dentelles, satin end-papers by Zaehnsdorf., orig. cold. wraps. bnd. in, s.-c. (SG. Oct.9; 146) $1,400
- **Il Filocolo.** Venice, Peregrinus de Pasqualibus, Dec.24, 1488. Fo. 139 ll. (of 140), lacks prelim. blank, illuminated arms in colours & gold on f.a2, 6 illuminated initials in colours & gold, many in red & blue. 19th. C. mor. [Goff B744]. (C. Jul.16; 320) Maggs. £850
- **Florio und . . . Bianceffora.** Metz, Caspar Hochfeder, Aug.2, 1500. Fo. 84 ll. only (of 130, the missing ll. supplied in facs.), most woodcuts with heavy late colouring, some ll. badly stained & with severe repairs. Hf. vell. W.a.f. Pencil inscr. of A.W.M. Mensing, bkplt. of Boies Penrose, lately in the collection of Eric Sexton. [BMC III, 664, Goff B747, H 7191*]. (CNY. Apr.8; 103) $1,500
- **Genealogie . . . cum Micantissimis Arborum Effgiacionibus cuiusq[ue] Gentilis Dei.** Paris, 22 Aug. 1511. Fo. Title slightly soiled, a few ll. slightly spotted, 2 sm. wormholes at beginning, slightly affecting a few letters. Cf.-bkd. bds. (S. Jan.27; 311) Handricks. £140
- **Genealogie Deorum.** Venice, Bonetus Locatellus for Octavianus Scotus, Feb.23, 1494/95. 4th. [1st. Ill.] Edn. Fo. Inner portions stained, mostly marginal, some marginal worming. Old vell. Dupl. from the Vollbehr Incunable Collection, with bkplt., bkplt. of John A. Saks. [BMC V, 444, Goff B753, HC 3321] (CNY. Oct.1; 120) $1,300
- **Las Muyeres Illustres.** Saragossa, Paul Hurus. Oct.24, 1494. 1st. Edn. in Spanish. Fo. Lacks final lf. (supplied in facs.), margins of h6, o8 & p6-7 reprd., some holes in p7 slightly affecting text reprd., marginal slits in some other ll. reprd., sm. tear to 13, slight defect to woodcut border on p4, some staining thro.-out, particularly to inner portions & with some inner margins reprd., ink stp. on title. 17th. C. cf., gt.-stpd. arms on covers of Louis-Archille-August de Harlay, rebkd., corners reprd. Bkplt. of D.D. d'Archambault, bkplt. of Lessing & Edith Rosenwald, LJR label at front & Liby. of Congress gift label, lately in the collection of Eric Sexton. [Goff B723, H(Add) 3337a] (CNY. Apr.8; 153) $25,000
- **Nouvelles.** Trans.:– Mirabeau. Paris, 1803. 8 vols. 16mo. Cont. grd. roan, decor. spines, & cover roulettes. (HD. Apr.9; 410) Frs. 1,100
- **Nymphs of Fiesole.** Verona, 1952. (225) numbered. Fo. 1 facs. Orig. vell.-bkd. bds., s.-c. Inscr. by William Russell Flint. (CSK. Dec.10; 1) £300

BOCCHI, Francesco

- **Le Bellezze della Citta di Firenze.** Firenze, 1677. Old vell. Sig. of Thomas Bludworth, 1690, on title. (SG. Mar.12; 150) $325

BOCCHIUS, Achille

- **Symbolicarum Quaestionum.** Ill.:– Giulio Bonasone. Bologna, 1555. 1st. Edn. 4to. Some ll. stained from lr. margins, touching some plt. surfaces, slight browning & spotting. Cont. vell. bds., upr. cover slightly wormed, bkplt. of Graf zu Leininging-Westerburg. (S. Feb.10; 410) Plate Mark. £320
- – **Anr. Edn.** Bologna, 1574. 2nd. Edn. Sm. 4to. 149 engraved plts. Cont. limp vell., gt. stp. on covers. (C. Jul.15; 218) Watson. £85

BOCCIONI, Umberto

- **Pittura, Scultura Futuriste (Dinamismo Plastico).** Milan, 1914. Tear in title reprd., slightly discold. Cont. cl. (SH. Nov.20; 196) Tate Gallery. £80

BOCCONE, Paolo

- **Museo di Fisica e de Esperienze Varatio.** Venice, 1697. 1st. Edn. 4to. Lf. Y1 torn across. 19th. C. qtr. mor., unc. From Chetham's Liby., Manchester. (C. Nov.26; 42) Weldon & Wesley. £80

- **Museo de Piante Rare della Sicilia, Malta, Corsica, Italia, Piemonte e Germania.** Venice, 1697. 4to. Plt. 90 with strip of browning at fore-e., occasional light offsetting, unobtrusive ink notations to most plts., without port. present in some copies, with additional 20 ll. index at back. Cont. vell. The Arpad Plesch copy. (CNY. Oct.1; 136) $700

BOCHART, Samuel

- **Geographiae Sacrae.** Caen, 1646. 1st. Edn. 2 vols. in 1. Fo. Old vell., worn. (SG. Sep.25; 53) $200
- **Hierozoicon** . . . L., 1663. 1st. Edn. Fo. Cont. vell. (SG. Jan.29; 63) $110

BOCHER, Edouard & Emmanuel

- **Nos Livres: Catalogue de la Bibliothèque de** . . . Paris, 1896. 4to. Cont. hf. lev. by Rivière, partly unc. Pres. Copy. (S. Nov.24; 35) Breslauer. £80

BOCHIUS, Joanne

- **Historica Narratio Profectionis.** Antw., 1602. Fo. Sm. fault on 1st. title, plt. bnd. inverted, typog. mark on last plt. verso. Marb. cf., F decor. spine raised bands. (LM. Jun.13; 66) B.Frs. 65,000

BOCK, Benedict

- **Oetinger Brack, Bey des** . . . **Joachim Ernst** . . . **Grafen zu Oetingen** . . . **Leich-Begängnüs in der Schlosskirchen zu Harburg.** Nuremb., 1661. Fo. Name on fo. 2 corrected in ink, lacks additional engraved title-p., slightly dampstained & spotted. Old bds., slightly worn. (S. Jan.27; 312) Quaritch. £110

BOCK, Carl

- **The Head-Hunters of Borneo.** 1882. 2nd. Edn. Orig. pict. cl. gt., slightly worn. (S. Jul.27; 14) Maggs. £130

BOCK, Elfried

- **Adolph Mensel. Verz. s. Graphischen Werkes.** Ill.:– O. Bangemann. Berlin, 1923. 4to. Orig. hf. vell., end-papers lightly soiled. (HK. Nov.18-21; 3442) DM 440

BOCK, Hieronymus

[-] [**Kreuter Buch**]. Ill.:– D. Kandel. [Strassb.], [1551?]. Fo. Ll. 22, 25-30, 32-76, 78-288, 290-300, soiled especially at beginning & end, faults, reprd. thro.-out, partly with text loss, some later MS. ll. bnd. in. 19th. C. hf. linen. (HK. May 12-14, 226) DM 900
[-] [-] **Anr. Edn.** [Strassburg], [1560]. Enlarged Edn. Fo. Lacks title & 1 blank pref. lf., 2 ll. near end with loss, MS. completion, 1st. lf. of pref. with tear backed, ll. 1-4 slightly stained or soiled, some ll. slightly browned. 17th. C. Leath., worn. (HK. Nov.18-21; 410) DM 9,000
- – **Anr. Edn.** Ill.:– D. Kandel. Strassburg, 1565. Fo. Ll. at beginning & end very soiled, some misbnd., old notes, port. cold., pagination ptd. Arabic & MS. Roman, slightly soiled. Cont. blind-tooled pig bkd. wood bds., defect. & reprd. (HK. May 12-14; 227) DM 3,200

BÖCKLER, Georg Andreas

[-] **Architectura Curiosa Nova.** Nuremb., ca. 1660. 1st. Edn. Pts. 2-4 (of 4). Fo. Pt. 3 lacks plts. 1-4, 7, 8 & 33-35 & 3 plts. slightly defect. Cont. leath., gt. spine, covers, inner & outer dentelle, oxidized. (HK. May 12-14; 977) DM 650
- – **Anr. Edn.** Nuremb., [1664]. 1st. Edn. in Latin. 4 pts. in 1 vol. Fo. Some discolouration generally affecting letterpress. Vell. bds., lettering piece chipped. (SPB. May 6; 160) $1,200
- – **Anr. Copy.** 196 (of 200) plts., last 4 plts. torn, 2 severely, some foxing, stains. Vell.-bkd. bds., stained. (SPB. May 6; 161) $650
- – **Anr. Copy.** Lightly browned in parts, pt. 3 plt. 120 with loss, pt. 4 lacks plt. 35, 5 plts. backed at corner & 1 torn. Cont. style hf. leath. (R. Mar.31-Apr.4; 1215) DM 1,750
- – **Anr. Edn.** Nuremb., 1701. 4 pts. in 1 vol. Fo. Lacks engraved title present in earlier Edns. (missing?), some discolouration. Mod. qtr. mor. (SPB. May 6; 162) $325
- **Theatrum Machinarum Novum.** Trans.:– H. Schmitz. Cologne, 1662. 1st. Edn. in Latin. Fo. Margins a little stained. 19th. C. hf. mor. From Chetham's Liby., Manchester. (C. Nov.26; 43) Mediolanum. £600
- – **Anr. Copy.** Without engraved title, 153 plts. only (lacks plt. 154), plt. 153 torn & preserved with loss, a few plts. slightly torn & reprd., title & preface soiled. With engraved title, 4 plts. & text of the 1st. pt. of Architectura Curiosa Nova by

Bockleri bnd. in, cont. vell. W.a.f. (CSK. Oct.24; 217) £230
- – **Anr. Edn.** Nuremb., 1673. Fo. Lacks plts. 146 & 147., slightly soiled, last 8 plts. with sm. tear bkd., plt. 154 mntd., browned in pts. Cont. vell., worn, spine with sm. defect. (HK. Nov.18-21; 414) DM 1,200

BOCKLER, Georg Andreas–FELIBIEN, Andre –WALLHAUSEN, Johann Jacob von

- **Architectura Curiosa Nova.–Tapisseries du Roy. –Kriegs-Kunst zu Pferd.** Nuremb.; Auguburg; Frankfurt, [1664]; 1687; 1670. 1st. Edn.; 1st. German Edn.; Unknown Edn. 3 works in 1 vol. Fo. Slightly soiled or spotted in places, slightly dampstained; 1st. work: 1 plt. slightly torn & 1 corner torn away slightly affecting engr., 1 folding plt. reprd.; 2nd. work: engrs. by J.U. Krauss after Charles Le Brun; 3rd. work: 1 folding plt. slightly torn, some slightly frayed, browned. 18th. C. cf. over wood bds., worn, covers detchd., lacks clasps. (S. Feb.10; 197) Mistrali. £850

BODDAERT, Pieter

- **Natuur-Beschouwer of Verzameling van de Nieuwste Verhandelingen over de drie Ryken der Natuur.** The Hague, 1779-81. 2 Pts. in 1 vol. Cont. hf. cf., lacks top of spine. (S. Mar.17; 321) Phelps. £50

BODE, Johann Elbert

- **Allgemeine Beschreibung und Nachweisung der Gestirne, nebst Verzeichniss der geraden Aufsteigung und Abweichung von 17240 Sternen** . . . **(pour servir de suite à son Uranographie).** Berlin, 1801. 1st. Edn. Fo. Many corrections & annots. in ink thro.-out, also a degree conversion table on pastedown, & index on endpaper in hand of Caroline & J.F.W. Herschel. Cont. tree cf., jnts. brkn. Inscr. on title by Caroline Herschel, Sir J.F.W. Herschel & later Sir Wm. James Herschel (the last dtd. 1889) (C. Apr.1; 99) Johns. £550

BODE, W. von

- **Frans Hals. Sein Leben und seine Werke.** Berlin, 1914. (200) on Bütten. 2 vols. Fo. Orig. hf. vell. (H. May 21/22; 117) DM 850

BODE, Dr. Wilhelm & Hofstede de Groot, C.

- **Complete Work of Rembrandt.** Paris, 1897-1906. Ltd. Edn. 8 vols. Fo. Orig. wraps., spines defect. (SH. Apr.9; 55) Mangold. £60

BODE, Dr. Wilhelm von & Knapp, F.

- **Meister Werke de Malerei, Alte Meister.** Berlin, ca. 1900-1910. Lge. fo. Orig. box, elab. embossed leath. spine & corner pieces set with 'jewels', the upr. cover with elab. peacock feather design. In gold, rebkd. as a bdg., w.a.f. (VA. May 8; 192) R. 170

BODENEHR, Gabriel

- **Europens Pracht u Macht.** Augsb., Ca. 1700. Ob. 4to. Lacks 1 folding copperplt., some margins frayed or torn, lightly soiled. Cont. leath., wormed. (HK. Nov.18-21; 1117) DM 36,000

BODENSCHATZ, Johann Christoph Georg

- **Aufrichtig Teutsch Redender Hebraer.** Frankfurt, 1756. 2nd. Edn. Pts. 1 & 2 only (of 4). 4to. Some foxing. Later leath. (SG. Feb.5; 193) $300
- **Kirchliche Verfassung der Heutigen Juden Sonderlich derer in Deutschland.** Frankfurt am Main–Leipzig, 1749. 4 pts. in 1 vol. 4to. Lacks 6 plts., slight discolouration. Leath., rebkd. (S. Nov.18; 643) Waechter. £420
- – **Anr. Edn.** Frankfurt a. M. & Leipzig, 1757. 2nd. Edn. 4 pts. in 1 vol. Cf., cover detchd., spine torn, worn. (SPB. May 11; 63) $1,800

BODENSTEDT, Friedrich

- **Die Lieder des Mirza-Schaffy mit einem Prolog.** Ill.:– Loeillot. Berlin, 1875. Fo. Orig. ornately gt. cl., disbnd. (SG. Sep.4; 71) $210

BODIN, Jean, Angevin

- **De la Demonomanie des Sorciers.** Paris, 1581. 2nd. Edn. 4to. 1 or 2 ll. stained, some old MS. marginalia, trimmed, ?18th. C. inscr. on rear end-paper. 17th. C. spr. cf., arms of Auget de Monthyon, gt., on covers, spine gt. Bkplt. of Lord Crewe. (SM. Oct.7; 1591) Frs. 2,500
- – **Anr. Edn.** Paris, 1582. 4to. Many old MS. notes. Cf. by Koehler, decor. spine, 3 fillets, inside dentelle, slightly worn. (HD. Dec.5; 20) Frs. 1,800
- **De Republica Libri Sex.** Lyons & Paris, 1686. Fo. 18th. C. cf., gt. ornament in centre of covers, rebkd. & reprd. (S. Dec.8; 149) Quaritch. £160

BODLEIAN Library–HOUSE of Commons
- Catalogi Librorum Manuscriptorum.–Report from the Committee Appointed to View the Cottonian Library. Oxford; L., 1697; 1734. 2 works in 2 vols. Fo. Staining to 1st. 20 ll. of 1st. work. 1st. work: cont. cf., rebkd.; 2nd. work: cf. gt. by Sangorski. From the collection of Eric Sexton. (C. Apr.15; 88) *Morton-Smith.* £190

BODMER, C.
- Ansichten aus Nordamerika. [Koblenz], ca. 1840. Ob. fo. 32 ll. of aquatint etchings & 1 outl. cold. engraved map, plts. I-XVIII & XX-XXXIII, all ll. blind-stpd., slightly soiled in parts, with litho. by Honegger after Bodmer ca. 1840, slightly stained. (H. Dec.9/10; 498) **DM 2,400**

BODONI, Giovanni Battista
- Cimelio Tipografico-Pittorico. Parma, 1811. (ca. 100). Fo. Orig. bds., worn, loose. (SH. Jun.4; 1) *Maggs.* £170
- Manuale Tipografico. Parma, 1818. 2nd. Edn. 2 vols. 4to. 19th. C. vell. (C. Jul.16; 319) *Appleton.* £3,000

BOECKLIN, Arnold
- Eine Auswahl der hervorragendsten Werke. Munich, n.d. [Vols. III & IV]. Lge. fo. Prelims. to vol. III slightly foxed. Loose in portfo. cases as Iss. (SPB. Jul.28; 51) **$150**

BOEHME, Jacob
- XL Questions concerning the Soule. L., 1647. 1st. Edn. in Engl. Sm. 4to. Folding copperplt. torn, title margin trimmed with loss of last number in date. Old qtr. cf. Engraved bkplt. of Ethan Allen Hitchcock. [Wing B3408.] (SG. Sep.25; 62) $700
- Theosophia Revelata ... Ed.:– Johan Georg Gichtel. [Hamburg], 1715. 3 Pts. in 1 vol. Cont. cf. on wooden bds., upr. cover detchd., lacks brass clasps. (C. May 20; 5) *Goldschmidt.* £160
- Works. L., 1764-81. 4 vols. Lge. 4to. 1st. vol. early cf., others orig. bds., worn & brkn. unc., last vol. unopened. Joseph Were booklabel, 1810. (SG. May 14; 23) **$1,050**

BOEHN, Max von
- Die Mode Menschen und Moden. Munich, 1923-25. 8 vols. Orig. cl. (SH. Jun.4; 191) *Lenton.* £55

BOEK DER PSALMEN
See-NEW TESTAMENT [Dutch]

BOEKENOOGEN, G.J.
See-HEURCK, Emile H. van & Boekenoogen, G.J.

BOER, L.J.
- Abhandlungen u. Versuche Geburtshilfl. Inhalts ... Vienna, 1791-1804. 1st. Edn. 4 pts. in 2 vols. Slightly soiled in parts, browning at beginning vol. 2 at head. Cont. hf.-leath., worn, spine slightly defect. (HK. Nov.18-21; 528) **DM 750**
- – Anr. Edn. Vienna, 1810. 2nd. Edn. 3 vols. in 1. Old hf. linen. (R. Oct.14-18; 315) **DM 530**

BOER WAR
- An Album of Photographs. 4to. About 55 orig. photographs, most inscr. Bdg. brkn. As a collection, w.a.f. (VA. Oct.31; 168) **R. 200**
- Operations of General Hutton ... 1900. N.d. 4to. Buckram. Inscr. 'For Private Circulation Only To L. Colonel Parrott ... General Edward Hutton ... (VA. Oct.31; 171) **R. 135**

BOERHAAVE, Hermann
- Academical Lectures on the Theory of Physic being a genuine Translation of his Institutes & Explanatory Comment. 1742-46. 6 vols. Slight worming in lr. margins at beginning of vol. 6. Cont. cf. (S. Jun.15; 93) *Quaritch.* £90
- – Anr. Edn. 1751-43-46. Mixed edns. 6 vols. Cont. cf., gt., slightly worn. From liby. of Dr. E. Ashworth Underwood. (S. Feb.23; 160) *Bickersteth.* £130
- De Usu Ratiocinii Mechanici in Medicina Oratio. –Libellus de Materia Medica.–Aphorismi de Cognoscendis et Curandis Morbis.–Libellus de Materie (sic) Medica.–Institutiones Medicae. Leiden; Leiden; Paris; Paris; Paris, 1709; 1727; 1728; 1720; 1735. 2nd. Edn.; 2nd. Edn.; New Edn.; New Edn.; 6th. Edn. 4 vols. (3rd. & 4th. works in 1 vol.). 2nd. work with title dust-soiled. Bds.; cf.; cont. cf.; cont. cf. (S. Dec.1; 77) *Whipple.* £60
- De Viribus Medicamentorum or a Treatise of the Virtue & Energy of Medicines. 1720. 1st. Edn. in Engl. Cont. cf., rebkd. (S. Dec.1; 70) *Bickersteth.* £80

- Elementa Chemicae. Leiden, 1732. 1st. Authorized Edn. 2 vols. 4to. Foxing. Cont. hf. cf. Author's sig. of authentication on verso of title in vol. 1. (SPB. Nov.25; 98) **$850**
- Institutiones et Experimentae Chemicae. Paris [Leiden?], 1724. Unauthorised Edn. 2 vols. in 1. Some ll. wormed in lr. margins. Cont. cf. (S. Dec.1; 71) *Gurney.* £65
- Institutiones Medicae in Usum Annuae Exercitationes Domesticos.–Aphorismi de Cognoscendis et Curandis Morbis. Leiden, 1708; 1709. 1st. Edns. 2 works in 1 vol. 1st. work: title-p. mended in inner margin, 2nd. work: sm. stain on a few ll. towards end, marginal MS notes in both works. Cf., rebkd, new end-papers, armorial bkplt. of William Greene, M.D. (S. Dec.1; 69) *Gurney.* £800
- A New Method of Chemistry Including the Theory & Practice of that Art ... Trans.:– P. Shaw & E. Chambers. 1727. 1st. Edn. in Engl. 3 pts. in 1 vol. 4to. Liby. stps. of Chemical Society. Cont. cf., worn, rebkd. (S. Dec.1; 72) *Gurney.* £110
- – Anr. Edn. Ed.:– Peter Shaw. 1753. 3rd. Edn. 4to. Cont. cf., very worn, spines defect. (S. Dec.1; 76) *Musch.* £75
- – Anr. Copy. Some spotting, vol. II lacks 1st. lf. (?) (blank?). Rebkd., spines gt. From liby. of Dr. E. Ashworth Underwood; bkplt. of Institute of Chemistry. (S. Feb.23; 162) *Kurzer.* £70
- Praxis Medica Boerhaaveana, being a Compleat Body of Prescriptions adapted to each Section of the Practical Aphorisms.–Aphorismi de Cognoscendis et Curandis Morbis; Institutiones Medicae. Paris [2nd. work], Leiden & Rotterdam [3rd. work], 1716; 1720; 1746. 3 vols. 12mo. & 8vo. Slight browning. Cont. cf. From liby. of Dr. E. Ashworth Underwood. (S. Feb.23; 164) *Bickersteth.* £50

BOERMAN, Thomas
- A Description of Above Three Hundred Animals, with a Particular Account of the Manner of Catching Whales in Greenland. Edinb., 1782. 12mo. Folding plt. reprd., frontis. preserved, a few ll. mntd. on stubs. Mod. cf.-bkd. bds. (SH. Mar.19; 32) *Quaritch.* £90

BOERSCHMANN, Ernst
- Chinesische Architebtur. Berlin, [1925]. Lge. 4to. Orig. linen. (HK. Nov.18-21; 3460) **DM 760**

BOETHIUS, Anicius Manilius Torquatus Severinus
- De Consolatione Philosophiae. Paris, 1783. On vell. 3 vols. 12mo. F.a2 of vol. 1 repeated as *a2 in vol. 11. Cont. mor., triple gt. fillet, fleuron in each corner, flat spine gt. in compartments, inner gt. dentelles, pink silk liners. (SM. Oct.7; 1592) **Frs. 45,000**
- De Consolatione Philosophiae cum Optimo Commento Beati Thomas [Pseudo-Thomas de Aquinus]. Cologne, 2 Sep. 1500. Stained slightly, some old MS. marginalia at beginning, one third rubricated. Hf. Vell. (R. Oct.14-18; 84) **DM 1,500**
- De Consolatione Philosophica. Lyon, ca. 1515. 2 pts. in 1 vol. 4to. Sm. ink stains on title, 1st. ll. restored, worming in middle of 1st. pt., lightly browned in parts. Cont. style cf., blind-tooled. (R. Mar.31-Apr.4; 8) **DM 530**
- De Trinitate [De Hebdomadibus, Carmen de Trinitate]. [Venice], [Paganinus de Paganinis], [Nov. 1489]. 4to. Slight spotting, mainly in margins. Recent mor. [Hain 3427; BMC V 455; Goff B 830] (C. Apr.1; 12) *Laughton.* £170
- Divi Severini Boetii arithmetica, duobus discreta libris (with Commentary by Girardus Ruffus). Paris, 1521. Fo. Some cont. MS. marginalia. Hf. mor. (SPB. Oct.1; 219) **$400**
- Five Books of Philosophical Comfort. 1609. Lacks ll. blank. Mod. bds. (SH. Jul.23; 87) *Burgess.* £80
- – Anr. Copy. Lacks A1 (?front blank), first few ll. slightly spotted. Mod. cf. [STC 3202] (CSK. May 29; 97) £60
- Opera. Venice, Joannes & Gregorius de Gregoriis, 26 Mar., 1491. 1st. Edn. Fo. 19th. C. vell. [BMC V, 341] (SG. May 14; 24) **$550**
See-HILARIUS, Saint-BOETHIUS, Anicius Manilius Torquatus Severinus

BOETHIUS, Anicius Manilius Torquatus Severinis –SIXTUS IV, Pope
- De Consolatione Philosophiae.–De Sanguine Christi. Ed.:– [J.P. de Lignamine] (2nd. work). Pinerolo; Nuremb., Jacobus Rubeus; Friedrich Creussner, Oct.25, 1479; 1474. 2 works in 1 vol.

Fo. Both works with spaces for initials (supplied in red in 1st. work). 1st. work: last line of text on a4r supplied by cont. hand, inscr. on fo. 1v; 2nd. work: dampstained with some printing faint, some supplied initials washed out, last lf. torn & reprd. with loss of some letters, lacks k10 & 11 (both blanks) & 12-10. 19th. C. Irish mor. gt. by James Adam for F.W. Conway, with stp. on upr. turn-in. From the collection of Eric Sexton. [Goff B770 & S581, H 3358 & 14798*] (CNY. Apr.8; 137) **$4,000**

BOETTGER, Adolf
- Die Pilgerfahrt der Blumengeister. Ill.:– A.H. Payne, after Grandville's 'Fleurs Animées'. Leipzig, 1851. Orig. gt-lettered & decor. mor., foxing. (SG. Sep.4; 234) **$350**
- – Anr. Copy. Orig. mor. (SG. Apr.9; 185) **$140**

BOFA, Gus
- La Symphonie de la Peur. 1937. (25) on Japon. Sewed. Orig. lge. ill. (HD. Oct.10; 179) **Frs. 1,300**

BOGENG, G.A.E.
- Die Grossen Bibliophilen. Leipzig, 1922. 3 vols. Orig. cl. (SH. May 28; 153) *Dawson.* £70

BOGORODSKY, Fedor
- Daesh' [Come on as though Poetry, with postscripts by V. Kamensky, V. Khlebnikov, S. Spassky & Worker Rodov]. [Moscow], 1922. (1,000). Orig. wraps. by the author, stained. (SH. Feb.6; 408) *Quaritch.* £90

BOGOTA
- Constituciones del Colegio Mayor de Nuestra Señora del Rosario en la Cuidad de Sante Fe de Bogota ... Madrid, 1666. Fo. Stains. Cont. vell., soiled. (SPB. May 5; 108) **$250**

BOHM, A.
See-SEPP, Anton & Bohm, A.

BOHN, Henry George
- Italian School of Design. Ill.:– Bartolozzi & others. 1842. 4to. Hf. mor. gt. (P. Feb.19; 219) *Hawkins.* £55

BOHN, Johann
- Circulus Anatomico-Physiologicus seu Oeconomia Corporis Animalis. Leipzig, 1686. 1st. Edn. Sm. 4to. Paper discold. New bds. (S. Jun.15; 95) *Dawson.* £160

BOIARDO, Matteo Maria
- Orlando Innamorato. Ed.:– Francesco Berni. Milan, 1542. 4to. Lacks 2 final blanks, 2 sm. wormholes in title & 3 prelims., A1 & 2 reprd., some dampstaining, some pen markings on title & inscr. 'A Delio nomen'. 18th. C. red mor., triple gt. fillet, flat spine gt. with floral motif & corner-pieces in compartments, inner gt. dentelles. (SM. Oct.7; 1594) **Frs. 2,000**

BOIARDO, Matteo Maria & Ariosto, Lodovico
- Orlando Innamorato ... Orlando Furioso. Ed.:– Antonio Panizzi. 1830-34. 9 vols. Cf. gt. by Hayday. (S. Nov.25; 493) *Thorp.* £90

BOIARDO, Matteo Maria–AGOSTINI, Nicolo degli
- Orlando Innamorato. I Tre Libri–Il Quarto, Quinto, 'E Sesto Libri dell'Innamoramento. Venice, 1539; [1544]. 2 works in 1 vol. 4to. 1st. work: slight soiling; 2nd. work: lacks 2X1 & final blank, sm. repair to final lf., several ll. slightly stained or marginally wormed, slight soiling. 18th. C. mott. cf. rebkd., worn. (S. May 5; 28) *Symonds.* £60

BOIELDIEU, F.A.
- La Dame Blanche. Paris, [1826]. 1st. Edn. Fo. Soiled thro.-out. Cont. leath. gt. (H. Dec.9/10; 1076) **DM 920**
- Jean de Paris. Paris, [1812]. Fo. Slightly soiled. Hf. vell. (H. Dec.9/10; 1077) **DM 900**

BOILEAU-DESPREAUX, Nicolas
- Oeuvres. Ill.:– Bernard Picart. Amst., 1729. 2 vols. Fo. Cont. mott. cf., spines gt., jnts. worn. (SG. Sep.25; 63) **$140**
- – Anr. Edn. Ill.:– Dupin. (port.). L., 1780. 2 vols. 18mo. Red mor. by Cazin. (HD. Apr.8; 220) **Frs. 1,250**
- – Anr. Edn. Ed.:– M. Amar. Ill.:– Rigaud engraved by Lignon (port.) & Desenne (figs.). Paris, 1821. 4 vols. Some browning. Cf., gt. fillets, decor. spine raised bands, by Héring. (HD. Apr.24; 122) **Frs. 1,250**

BOILEAU-DESPREAUX, Nicolas -contd.
- The Works. 1712-11. Vols. 1 & 2 only (of 3)
Cont. Engl. mor. gt., spines tooled in
compartments, covers with 2-line roll border &
ornamental panel & frame. Bkplt. of Charles,
Lord Halifax in each vol. (S. Nov.24; 36)
Way. £60

BOILLEREE, S.
- Nieder-Rhein. Munich, 1842. Fo. Marginal tears
& soiling. Unbnd., orig. wraps., soiled. (CSK.
Feb.6; 45) £210

BOILLOT, Joseph Langrois
- Modelles Artifices de feu et divers Instrumes de
Guerre avec les Moyés de s'en prevaloir ...
Chaumont en Bassigny, 1598. 1st. Edn. Fo. A few
pp. left blank, except for headline, etc., marginal
tear to H4, corner torn from K6, slight browning,
a few ll. marginally soiled. Cont. limp vell.,
slightly soiled, bkplt. of John Ehrman. (S.
Apr.7; 316) *Rota.* £950

BOISARD, Jean-Jacques François Marin
- Fables. Ill.:– Saint-Aubin & Schmits after
Monnet. [Paris]. 1777. L.P. 2 vols. Cont. red.
mor., gt. (SM Oct.8; 2391) Frs. 3,500

BOISGELIN, Louis de
- Travels through Denmark & Sweden, to which is
prefixed a journal of a voyage down the Elbe. 1810.
[1st. Edn.?] 2 vols. in 1. Some ll. spotted,
offsetting onto text. Cont. diced cf., gt., rebkd.
preserving old spine, worn. (S. Dec.8; 212)
Mason. £120
– – Anr. Copy. 2 vols. 4to. Heavily browned in
parts. Mod. hf. leath., rubbed. (H. May
21/22; 454) DM 750

BOISSARD, Jean Jacques
- Habitus Variarum Orbis Gentium. [Frankfurt],
1581. Ob. 4to. Engraved title & 63 (of 67)
engraved plts., many reprd., mostly marginal. Old
blind-stpd. vell., reprd. W.a.f. (BS. Jun.11; 412)
£440
- Icones Virorvm Illustrium. Frankfurt, 1597-99.
1st. Edn. 4 vols. in 2. 4to. Engraved port. repeated
197 engraved full-p, ports., all ports in decor.
borders, lightly browned in places, especially in 1,
some sm. stains, sm. burn hole in 2. Cont. vell. (H.
May 21/22; 915) DM 6,200
- Pars Romanae Urbis Topographiae. Ill.:–
Theodore de Bry. Frankfurt, 1597-1602. 1st. Edn.
6 pts. in 2 vols. Fo. Lacks engraved titles in pt. 6,
lacks plts. 121-149 in pt. 4, inscr. on fly-lf. 18th.
C. mott. mor., gt. panel on covers, spine gt. with
lozenge of fleurons in each compartment. Osterley
Park bkplt of Earl of Jersey & Henry J.B.
Clements; E.G. Stanley copy. (SM. Oct.7; 1597)
Frs. 1,800
- Topographia Urbis Romae. Dar ist, Eygentliche
Beschreibung des Statt Rom. Frankfurt, 1603. Fo.
Engraved title with sm. tear, several plts. with
short tears, some soiling & browning, stitching
brkn. Bds., worn. (S. Jun.23; 236) *Erlini.* £80

BOISSEAU, Jean
- Promptuaire Armorial Général ... Paris, 1658.
2nd. Edn. 4 pts. in 1 vol. Fo. Cont. cf., decor. spine.
(HD. Jun.29; 89) Frs. 3,050

BOISSIER, Edmond
- Voyage botanique dans le midi de l'Espagne.
Ill.:– After Jean Cristoph Heyland & Alfred
Riocreux. Paris, 1839-45. (120-130) 2 vols. 4to.
Some text lightly browned. Cont. hf. cf. From
collection of Massachusetts Horticultural Society,
stps. on plts. (SPB. Oct.1; 103) $3,000

BOITET, R.
- Beschryving der Stadt Delft. Ill.:– C. Decker
after P. Smith. Delft, 1729. Fo. Pp. 181-196
misbnd., lr. parts of a few quires stained. Cont. hf.
cf., slightly defect. & worn, unc. (VG.
Dec.17; 1219) Fls. 2,600

BOIZARD, Jean
- Traité des Monoyes, de leurs Circonstances &
Dépendances. Paris, 1692. 1st. Edn. 12mo. Some
browning. Cont. cf., worn. (S. Jan.26; 232)
Subunso. £120

BOKHART, Jacob
- Neben d. Heerstrasse. Ill.:– E.L. Kirchner.
Zürich & Leipzig, 1923. 1st. Kurchner Edn. Orig.
bds. (HK. Nov.18-21; 2702) DM 520
– – Anr. Copy. Orig. hf. linen. (D.
Dec.11-13; 1004) DM 450

BOLAFFI, G.
- Catalogo Bolaffi della Grafica Italiana. Turin,
1970-78. Vol. 1-8. 4to. Each vol. with orig. etching
inserted. Orig. cl. (SH. Jan.29; 81)
Ars Artis. £70

BOLDONIUS, Octavus
- Theatrum Temporaneum ... Ill.:– Giovanni
Bianchi. Milan, 1636. 1st. Edn. Fo. Marginal
wormholes in 1st. 4 ll., just affecting imprint. Old
vell. bds. (S. Feb.10; 198) *Parikian.* £200

BOLIVAR, Simon
[-] Documentos para la Historia de la Vida Publica
del Libertador de Colombia, Peru y Bolivia,
Publicados por Dispocion del General Guzman
Blanco. Caracas, 1875-77. 14 vols. 4to. Cl., leath.
spines, worn. (SG. Jan.8; 43) $100

**BOLLETTINO D'ARTE DEL MINISTERO
DELLA EDUCAZIONE NAZIONALE**
Rome, 1920-30. 2nd. Series. Years I-X. 4to. 120
loose pts. (DR. Mar.19; 25) Lire 500,000

BOLONGARO-CREVENNA, Pierre Antoine
See–CREVENNA, afterwards BOLONGARO–
CREVENNA, Pierre Antoine

BOL'SHAKOV, Georgy Zolutukhin
See–BAYAN, Vadim & others

BOL'SHAKOV, Konstantin
- Solnstse na izlete [Setting Sun]. Moscow, 1916.
4to. Orig. wraps. by El Lissitsky, slightly soiled.
(SH. Feb.6; 409) *Lempert.* £75

BOLTON, Arthur T.
- Architecture of Robert & James Adam
(1758-1794). 1922. 1st. Edn. 2 vols. Fo. Orig. cl.
(S. Nov.4; 557) *Traylen.* £100
– – Anr. Copy. Cl., slightly worn. (BS.
Nov.26; 141) £70
– – Anr. Copy. Many clippings relating to the
Adams laid in loosely. Orig. cl., d.-w. slightly
tattered. (CB. May 27; 38) Can. $400

BOLTON, James
[-] Harmonia Ruralis; or, ... a Natural History of
British Song Birds. 1824. 2 vols. 4to. Slight
spotting. Recent hf. cf. (S. Dec.8; 156)
Way. £300
– – Anr. Edn. L., 1830. 4th. Edn. 2 vols. in 1. 4to.
Mod. hf. mor. gt., partly unc. (CNY. May 22; 193)
$500
– – Anr. Edn. 1845. 2 vols. in 1. 4to. Cont. hf. mor.
(C. Mar.18; 169) *Henderson.* £850
– – Anr. Copy. Cont. hf. mor., rebkd., orig. gt.
spine preserved. (C. Jul.15; 168)
Henderson. £720
– – Anr. Copy. Cont. hf. mor., rebkd., orig. gt.
spine preserved. (C. Mar.18; 19) *Lloyd.* £700
– – Anr. Copy. Hand-cold. frontis. & 79 (of 80)
hand-cold. plts., lacks plt. XXV & pp. 39-40. Cf.
gt. rebkd., Kenneth Rae bkplt. by R. Whistler. (P.
May 14; 200) £240
- An History of Fungusses, Growing About
Halifax. Huddersfield, 1788-89. 1st. Edn. 3 vols.
in 1, lacks later supp. 4to. Errata slip pasted on
recto of (G4) in vol. I, introductory matter to vol.
II-III bnd. out of order after main title, lacks
hf.-titles(?) to vol. II-III, occasional offsetting to
text & browning. Cont. mott. cf., gt., spine gt.,
jnts. split, some wear, bkplt. of T.F.G. Dunston of
Burltons. (S. Dec.3; 900) *W. & W.* £330
– – Anr. Edn. Halifax/Huddersfield, Priv. Ptd.,
1788-91. 1st. Edn. 4 vols., including supp. 4to.
Some spotting & foxing on text ll. Cont. diced
russ., worn, most covers detchd. From Chetham's
Liby., Manchester. (C. Nov.26; 44)
Pickering. £650

BOLTON, Sol.
- Geographia Antiqua. Ill.:– Thomas Jefferys. L.,
1775. 4to. Title of each map written on verso by
former owner. Old bds., disbnd. (SG. Aug.21; 246)
$225

BOLUS, H.
- The Orchids of the Cape Peninsula. Cape Town,
1918. 2nd. Edn. Orig. bdg. (VA. May 8; 6)
R. 170

BON GENRE (Le)
Paris, [1931]. Ltd. Edn. Fo. Orig. ptd. folder,
worn, lacks ties. (BS. Jun.11; 360) £140
- Trente-neuf Aquarelles Originales. Ill.:– Lanté,
Garnerey & others. Paris, 1930. (500). Fo. In
sheets, publisher's portfo. (HD. Dec.5; 22)
Frs. 3,200

BON-ACCORD MAGAZINE
Aberdeen, 1880-1914. 30 vols., incompl. run.
Bound. (CE. Oct.24; 65) £75

BONAFOUS, Mathieu
- Histoire Naturelle, agricole, et economique du
Mais. Ill.:– after Redoute. Paris & Turin, 1836.
Fo. Port. of author not mentioned by any of usual
authorities, not present in pres. copy in Plesch
Collection. Hf. mor. From collection of
Massachusetts Horticultural Society, stps. on plts.
(SPB. Oct.1; 104) $3,000

BONANNI, Filippo
- Catalogo degli Ordini Religiosi della Chiesa
Militante.–La Gerarchia Ecclesiastica.–Catalogo
degli Ordini Equestri, e Militari. Rome, 1712-23;
1720; 1724. Together 6 vols. 4to. Some text pp.
browned. Cont. cf., not unif., gt. spines. (SI.
Dec.3; 92) Lire 550,000
- Museaum Kircherianum ... Rome, 1709. 1st.
Edn. Fo. Port. of Kircher inserted, some plts.
inverted. Cont. cf., worn, rebkd. From Chetham's
Liby., Manchester. (C. Nov.26; 45)
Pickering. £650
- Numismata Pontificum Romanorum. Rome,
1699. 1st. Edn. 2 vols. Fo. Cont. spr. cf., spine
slightly worn. (S. May 5; 172) *Seaby.* £450
- Ordinum Religiosorum in Ecclesia Militanti
Catalogus. Rome, 1706-10. 1st. Edn. 3 vols. 4to.
Latin & Italian text, slightly soiled & browned in
parts. 19th. C. mor., blind-tooled. (H. Dec.
9/10; 743) DM 700
– – Anr. Edn. Rome, 1722-24. 3rd. Edn. 4 vols.
including Catalogo degli ordini Equistri, e Militari.
4to. Cont. vell., spine soiled (CSK. Apr.24; 50)
£170
- Recreatio Mentis et Oculi in Observatione
Animalium Testaceorum Curiosis Naturae
Inspectoribus. Italico Sermone Primum Proposita,
nunc denuo Latine Oblata, centum additis
Testaceorum Iconibus. Rome, 1684. 4to. Frontis.
cut to plt. & mntd. Cont. cf., spine slightly defect.
(VG. Dec.17; 1220) Fls. 1,000
- Recreatio Mentis, et Oculi in Observatione
Animalium Testaceorum.–Icones Testaceorum.
Rome, 1684. 4 pts. in 1 vol. 1st. 34 pp. dctchd.
19th. C. cl., cover & spine detchd. From
Chetham's Liby., Manchester. (C. Nov.26; 46)
Antiqua Libri. £220
- Verzeichnis der Geistlichen ordens-Personen in
der Streitenden Kirchen. Nuremb., 1711. 2 pts. in
1 vol. Cont. vell. (LM. Mar.21; 90) B.Frs. 10,000
See–GIUSTIANUS, Abbé Bernardus, Bonanni,
Filippo & others

BONAPARTE, Prince Charles Lucien
- Iconografia della Fauna Italica per le quattro
Classi degli Animali Vertebrati. Rome, 1834-41. 3
vols. Fo. Cont. Italian vell., spines gt. (S.
Jun.1; 76) *Sobisa.* £3,000
– – Anr. Copy. Cont. hf. cf. (SI. Dec.3; 90)
Lire 10,000,000
– – Anr. Copy. 3 vols. in 2. Hf. vell. (CR.
Jun.11; 554) Lire 3,200,000
- Iconographie des Pigeons. Ill.:– Lemercier after
Oudart, Willy & Blanchard. Paris, 1857. Fo.
Mod. hf. mor., orig. wraps. bnd. in, wraps. torn &
reprd. (C. Mar.18; 123) *Duran.* £1,100
– – Anr. Copy. Some plts. slightly soiled. Loose in
orig. wraps., defect. (HK. Nov.18-21; 797)
DM 4,200
See–WILSON, Alexander & Bonaparte, Prince
Charles Lucien

BONAPARTE, Prince Napoleon-Louis
- Etudes sur le Passé et l'Avenir de l'Artillerie.
Ill.:– Lemaitre. Paris, 1846; 1851. 2 vols. 4to.
Later cf., spines gt. Booklabel in each vol. of
the Biblioteka Grigoriya Ivanovicha Chertkova.
(SG. Oct.30; 262) $200
- Memoirs. Ed.:– Somerset De Chair. Gold. Cock.
Pr., 1945. (500) numbered. 2 vols. Fo. Orig. cl.
(CSK. Apr.3; 59) £100
- Supper at Beauclaire. Trans.:– Somerset De
Chair. Gold. Cock. Pr., 1945. (100) on H.M.P.,
sigd. by translator, & specially bnd. 16mo. Orig.
vell., by Sangorski & Sutcliffe. (CSK. Apr.3; 59A)
£50

BONARELLI Della Rovere, G.–GUARINI, G.B.
- Filli di Sciro, Favola Pastorale.–Compendio della
Poesia Tragicomica, Tratto dai Duo Verati.
Ferrara; Venetia, n.d.; 1603. 2 works in 1 vol. Sm.
4to. Cf. Rockford Liby. copy. (BS. Jun.11; 232)
£110

BONAVENTURA, Saint [Giovanni Fidanza], Bp. of Albano
- **Biblia Pauperum.** [Venice], [Georgius Walch], ca. 1480. 1st. Edn. Sm. 4to. 100 ll. (of 102) lacks 2 prelims., rubricated thro.-out. 19th. C. hf. cf. [Goff B850] (C. Jul.16; 321) *Taylor.* £160
- **Breviloquium.** Augsburg, Anton Sorg, before 1476. Fo. Cont. blind-stpd. cf.-bkd. wooden bds., clasp. (S. Nov.25; 316) *Abrams.* £600
- **Centiloquium.** Ed.:– [Marchesinus de Regio]. Zwolle, Pieter van Os, ca. 1479-80. 1st. Edn. 4to. Spaces for initial capitals, supplied in red, as are paragraph marks, initial strokes & underlines, lacks 1st. blank. Paper bds., worn. Bkplt. of P.P.C. Lammens, lately in the collection of Eric Sexton. [BMC IX, 81, Goff B869, HC 3496] (CNY. Apr.8; 210) $11,000
- **Doctrina Cordis.** Baeca, 1551. 4to. Occasional foxing, 1 lf. with sm. ink-stain. Blind-stpd. cf. (C. Apr.1; 13) *Laughton.* £160
- **In Primum [-Quartum] Librum Sententiarum elaborata dilucidatio.** Ed.:– J. Balainius Andrius. Venice, 1574. 4 pts. & Index Generalis in 4 vols. Cont. limp vell., 1 spine slightly defect. (R. Oct.14-18; 31) DM 500
- **In Quatuor Libros Sententiarum Disputata.** Lyon, 1515. 4 pts. & Index in 2 vols. Fo. Partly wormed & soiled. Cont. blind-stpd. pig-bkd. wd. bds., lacks clasps. (HK. Nov.18-21; 129) DM 750
- **[Legenda Maior S. Francisci] Vita e Fioretti di Santo Francisco.** Milan, Uldericus Scinzenzeler, Dec. 1, 1495. 4to. Slight repair to fore-margin of fo. 2, some other minor repairs. Red mor., covers gt.-ruled, gt. arms on covers of Victor Massena, gt. spine with monogs., by Lortic. From the collection of Eric Sexton. [Goff B892, H 7329] (CNY. Apr.8; 105) $6,000
- **Liber ... Qui Incendium Amoris Dicitur ...** Montserrat, Johannes Luschner, 27 May, 1499. Blind-stpd. mor., sigd. & dtd. Brugalla, 1949, s.-c. [BMC X, 78] (S. Nov.25; 341) *Breslauer.* £1,700
[–] **Meditationes Vitae Christi.** Augsburg, Gunther Zainer, Mar. 12, [14]87. 1st. Edn. Fo. Spaces for initial capitals, supplied in red with ornamental flourishes, initial strokes & underlinings in red, lacks initial blank, minor foxing to some margins. Red mor., spine gt.-lettered, by Rivière & Son. Ink stp. of the Royal Liby., Munich at fo. 3r, bkplts. of Roderick Terry & Lucius Wilmerding, lately in the collection of Eric Sexton. [BMC II, 315, Goff B893, H 3557*] (CNY. Apr.8; 11) $20,000
– – **Anr. Edn.** [Paris], [Gaufridus de Marnef], ca. 1500. 94 ll. (of 96) lacks title & M2, some worming & staining. Cont. blind-stpd. cf. on wooden bds., upr. cover reprd. (C. Jul.16; 245) *Quaritch.* £50
- **Opus super primo [& secondo] Libro Sententiarum [Petri Lombardi].** Ill.:– Johannes Beckenhaub. Nuremb. [& Lyon], [1515]. 3 pts. (of 5). Fo. Some slight worming. Cont. blind-stpd. hf. pig. over wooden bds., clasps. [Goff B292] (VG. Nov.18; 1072) Fls. 500
- **Opuscula.** [Cologne], [Bartholomaeus de Unkel; Johann Koelhoff, the Elder], after Jun. 28, 1484; ca. 1485. 2 pts. in 1 vol. Fo. Capital spaces (with guide letters in pt. 2), 5-line initial E in blue on green ground with red penwork tracery on a2 of pt. 1, other initials & paragraph strokes of pt. 1 in red, pt. 2 unrubricated, title torn & mntd., marginal repair to last lf., dampstaining to lr. portions of some ll. Pol. niger mor. gt. by Sangorski & Sutcliffe. Bkplts. of Dr. Georg Kloss & the General Theological Seminary. [Goff B924, H 3463 & 3497] (CNY. Oct.1; 17) $1,000
– – **Anr. Copy.** George Kloss bkplt., bkplt. of the General Theological Seminary Liby. (CNY. May 22; 40) $650
- **Sermones Mediocres de Tempore [with others].** Strassburg, [Printer of the 1483 Jordanus de Quedlingberg (Georg Husner)]. Mar. 12, 1496. 4to. Spaces for initial capitals, paragraph marks, capitals, initial strokes & underlines supplied in red. Cont. German blind-stpd. pig over wood bds., brass clasp & catch. Hand-cold. woodcut bkplt. of Hilprand Brandenburg von Biberach, & 8-line inscr. recording the gift of the book to the Carthusian Charterhouse at Buxheim, lately in the collection of Eric Sexton. [BMC I, 145, Goff B942, HC(+Add) 3523*] (CNY. Apr.8; 170) $6,500
- **Sermones Mediocres de Tempore [with others].** [Johann Otmar], 'Autumn' 1484. Fo. Spaces for initial capitals, unrubricated, reprd. tears at g8 &

C5, inner margin of U4 reinforced, some minor marginal tears, early quires wormed, light worming to some ll. at rear, occasional light dampstains to margins. Cont. blind-stpd. pig over wood bds., brass clasp & catch, worn, covers wormed. Inscrs. of Casparus Gueldischourg(?) & the Capuchin Brothers, lately in the collection of Eric Sexton. [BMC II, 585, Goff B950, H 3515*=3514] (CNY. Apr.8; 140) $1,900
- **Tabula super Libros Sententia [rum].** [Nuremb.], ca. 1491. Fo. Margins slightly soiled. Cont. antiphonar-MS. vell. [BMC 11, 433, H 8540, C 1159, Goff B-292] (HK. May 12-14; 79) DM 420

BOND, Francis
- **An introduction to English Church Architecture from the Eleventh to the Sixteenth Century.** L., 1913. 2 vols. 4to. Orig. gt.-stpd. cl. (CB. May 27; 39) *Can.* $120

BONE, Muirhead
- **Set of Six Original Lithographs 'On the Clyde, 1917-18'.** Colnaghi, [1918]. Fo. Orig. ptd. wrap. Sigd. in pencil. (S. Nov.24; 37) *Cumming.* £110

BONELLI, Georgio & Martelli, Niccola
- **Hortus Romanus.** Ill.:– Maddalena Bouchard. Rome, 1772-80. 6 vols. only (of 8). Fo. Plts. hand-cold., occasional stains to blank margins in vol. I, natural fine crease at centre of paper thro.-out (only noticeable on a few plts.). Cont. hf. vell., soiled. From Chetham's Liby., Manchester. (C. Nov.26; 47) *Baskett & Day.* £7,800

BONETUS, Theophilus
- **Medicina Septentrionalis Collatitia ... exhibens Observationes Medicas.** Geneva, 1686. 2 vols. Fo. Engraved port. of author loosely inserted, reprd. Cont. cf., spines gt. (S. Feb.23; 16) *Primrose.* £50
- **Sepulchretum sive Anatomia Practica.** Ed.:– J.J. Mangetus. Geneva, 1700. 3 vols. Fo. Some foxing. Cont. vell., soiled. (S. Apr.6; 14) *Gurney.* £110

BONGIOVANNI, A.
See-ZANETTI, Antonio Maria, the Younger & Bongiovanni, A.

B[ONHOMME], J[ean] Baptiste
- **Traité de Céphalatomie ou Description Anatomique des Parties que la tête renferme.** Avignon, 1748. 4to. Stain on frontis. & 1st. few ll., plt. 19 very discold. New bds., cl. spine, unc. (S. Jun.15; 96) *Phelps.* £280

BONI, Albert
- **Photographic Literature: an International Guide to General & Specialized Literature on Photographic Processes; Techniques; Chemistry; Physics; Apparatus; Materials & Applications; Industry; History; Biography; Aesthetics.** N.Y., [1962]. 4to. Cl. (SG. Apr.23; 34) $140

BONI, Mauro
[–] **Lettere sui Primi Libri a Stampa di Alcune Citta' e Terre dell'Italia Superiore.** Venezia, 1794. 1st. Edn. 2 pts. in 1 vol. 4to. Cont. limp bds., torn, unc. (SG. Jan.22; 68) $110

BONIFACCIO, Giovanni
- **Istoria di Trivigi.** Venice, 1744. New Edn. Sm. fo. Cont. marb. paper bds. From the collection of John A. Saks. (C. Jun.10; 24) *Bozzolato.* £220

BONIFACE, A.
- **Introduction à l'Etude de la Géographie.** Paris, 1826. 12mo. Text foxed. Mosaic Citron mor., elab. gt. borders round gt. arabesque with red mor. inlays, spine gt. to match, gt. dentelles. Mortimer Schiff bkplt. (SG. Sep.4; 43) $190

BONN, Andreas
- **Tabulae Anatomico-chirurgicae Doctrinam Herniarum illustrantes ... Ontleed-en heelkundige Platen.** Ed.:– Gerardus Sandifort. Leiden, 1828. Fo. Latin & Dutch text, slightly spotted. Cont. hf. cf., slightly worn. (S. Feb.23; 17) *Gurney.* £55

BONNAFFE, A.A.
- **Recuerdos de Lima. Album.** Ill.:– E. Prugue after Bonnaffe. Lima, 1856. Lge. fo. Slightly soiled. Cont. hf. linen. (R. Oct.14-18) DM 1,400

BONNARD, Camille
- **Costumes Historiques des XIIe, XIIIe, XIVe et XVe Siècles.** Ill.:– P. Mercurius. Paris, 1860-61. 3rd. Fr. Edn. 3 vols. Lge. 4to. Slightly soiled in parts. Cont. hf. leath. (H. Dec.9/10; 745) DM 1,100

BONNARD, Camille [& Mercuri, Paolo]
- **Costumi de' Secoli XIIIe, XIVe, e XVe.** Rome, 1827. 1st. Edn. Vol. I only. 4to. Italian & Fr. text, subscribers' list, plt. 24 detchd., sm. marginal stain to plt. 28, lacks plt. list. Cont. hf. cf., spine gt. & worn. (S. Oct.21; 334) *C.E. King.* £100

BONNATERRE, Pierre Joseph, Abbé
- **Tableau Encyclopedique et Methodique des Trois Regnes de la Nature ... Ichthyologie.** Paris, 1788. 4to. Text wormed, plts. lightly browned & soiled in parts. Cont. paper bds., very defect. (H. Dec.9/10; 273) DM 1,200

BONNE, Rigobert
- **Atlas de Toutes les Parties connues du Globe Terrestre.** [Geneva], ca. 1780? 4to. Lacks maps nos. 29, 33 & 34, slight spotting & dampstaining. Cont. cf.-bkd. bds., worn. W.a.f. (S. Nov.3; 23) *Map House.* £140
- **Atlas Maritime ... de France.** Paris, 1778. Title with old MS. owner's mark. Cont. red mor., floral gt., gt. cover & inner & outer fillet, lr. cover stained. (HK. May 12-14; 549) DM 700
- **Petit Tableau de la France.** 1764. 2 Pts. in 1 vol. Cont. Fr. red mor., gt. spine, worn (S Mar.16; 213) *Symonds.* £120

BONNEAU, [du Chesne Pierre]
- **Catalogue des Livres.** Paris, 1754. Priced thro.-out in MS., table of authors at end. Cont. red mor., floral cornerpieces, triple gt. fillet, spine gt. in compartments, inner gt. dentelles. Comte de Lignerolles copy, bkplt. of Lucius Wilmerding. (SM. Oct.7; 1326) Frs. 3,300

BONNEFONS, Nicolas de
- **Les Délices de la Campagne. Suitte de Iardinier Francois.** Paris, 1656. 2nd. [3rd.] Edn. 12mo. Some browning & soiling, inscr. on ptd. title, lacks last 3 ll. Cont. limp vell., soiled. From liby. of André L. Simon. (S. May 18; 46) *McKirdy.* £110
[–] **The French Gardiner ... annexed, The English Vineyard Vindicated by John Rose.** Trans.:– John Evelyn. Ill.:– Hertochs (additional title). 1669. 2nd. Edn. in Engl. 2 pts. in 1 vol. Some ll. slightly spotted or soiled. 19th. C. cf., gt., bkplt. of John Evelyn. [Wing B3600] (S. Dec.8; 157) *Quaritch.* £360
[–] – **Anr. Copy.** Most top margins cut rather close, some spotting & staining thro.-out. Later cf., worn. (S. Dec.3; 901) *Blackwell.* £160

BONNEFOY, Yves
- **Anti-Platon.** Ill.:– Joan Miro. [Paris], [1962]. (25) numbered, on Auvergne paper, sigd. by author & artist, with extra suite of all etchings. Lge. 4to. Orig. sheets loose in pict. wraps., cl. folder, new buckram, s.-c. (SG. Oct.23; 224) $1,300

BONNEMAISON, [Féréol]
- **Galerie de son Altesse Royale Madame la Duchesse de Berry. Ecole Française. Peintres Modernes.** Paris, 1822. 1st. Edn. 2 vols. Fo. Plts. on india paper, lacks title to vol. II, occasional spotting, sm. blind-stpd. liby. stp. on each lf., occasionally touching india surface. Cont. hf. roan, spines defect., covers detchd., worn. (S. Jan.27; 455) *Lester.* £650

BONNET, Charles
- **Considérations sur les Corps Organisées où l'on Traite de leur Origine, de leur Développement, de leur Reproductions.** Amst., 1762. 1st. Edn. 2 vols. in 1. Hf. vell. (S. Jun.15; 97) *Dillon.* £80
- **La Palingénésie Philosophique ...** Münster, 1770. 2 vols. Cont. cf., 2 fillets, fleuron in corners, crowned cipher of Marie Anne Sophie, Princess of Bavaria, decor. spines. (HD. Mar.18; 26) Frs. 1,400
- **Recherches sur l'Usage des Feuilles dans les Plantes.** Göttingen & Leiden, 1754. 1st. Edn. Some browning of text, stp. on title. Cont. mott. sheep, worn. (S. Jun.1; 79) *Schierenberg.* £100
– – **Anr. Copy.** 4to. Cont. marb. cf., spine gt. (VG. Oct.13; 26) Fls. 650

BONNEVILLE, Alphonse
- **Nouvelle Encyclopedie Monétaire.** Paris, 1849. Fo. Hf. cl. (LM. Mar.21; 215) *B.Frs.* 10,000

BONNEVILLE, Pierre-Frederic
- **Traité des Monnaies d'Or et d'Argent.** Paris, 1806. Fo. Old cf. (LM. Mar.21; 216) B.Frs. 8,000

BONNEVILLE de Marsangy, L.
- **La Legion d'Honneur 1802-1900 . . .** Paris, 1900. Fo. Hf. mor. (HD. Jun.29; 90)   Frs. 1,050

BONNEY, Thomas George
See–WALTON, Elijah & Bonney, Thomas George

BONNOT DE MABLY, Gabriel
[–] **Translations from the French,** by D.Y. [Observations on the Greeks . . .]. Lynn, Priv. Ptd., 1770. 4to. Cont. hf. cf. (C. Jul.16; 371)   *Rota.* £50

BONPLAND, Aime J.A.
See–HUMBOLDT, Alexander von & Bonpland, Aime J.A.

BONS EXEMPLES: Alphabet Moral
Paris, ca. 1840. 3¾ × 2¾ ins. Orig. bds. & s.-c. (SG. Apr.30; 225) $400

BONTEKOE, W. Y.
- **Journaal ofte Gedenkwaardige Befchryvinge van de Oostindiesze Reize van Willem Ysbrantsz.** Amst., n.d. Orig. pict. wraps. bnd. in. (SSA. Apr.22; 108)   R. 110

BONTOUS, Jacques Joseph
- **L'Auguste Pieté de la Royale Maison de Bourbon . . . de l'appareil fait à Avignon pour la reception de Monseigneur Le Duc de Bourgogne et de Monsieur Le Duc de Berry.** Ill.:– L. David, & others after P. Perru, L. Cotel & others. Avignon, 1701. Fo. Some browning & light spotting. Cont. mott. cf., gt. spine. (CNY. Oct.1; 79) $380

BONWICK, James
- **The Last of the Tasmanians.** L., 1884. Occasional wear thro.-out. Mod. hf. cf. (KH. Mar.24; 57)   Aus. $100

BOODT, Anselme Boece de
- **Gemmarum et Lapidum Historia.** Hanover, 1609. 1st. Edn. 4to. Liby. stp. on title. Later bds. (SH. Jan.29; 209)   *Rota.* £50
- **Le Parfaict Joaillier.** Lyon, 1644. Ownership inscr. 18th. C. mor., triple gt. fillet, spine gt. in compartments, inner gt. dentelles, trimmed. (SM. Oct.7; 1600)   Frs. 1,800

BOOK AUCTION RECORDS
1903-66. Vols. 1-62, & dupl. of vol. 36, in 64 vols. Orig. cl., a few worn. (SH. Oct.9; 43)   *Quaritch.* £340
- - **Anr. Edn.** 1905-53. Vols. 3, 7-36, 43, 45, 47-49, 36 vols. only. Orig. cl. & cont. hf. cf., 2 spines worn. (SH. Jan.29; 6)   *Lawton.* £110
- - **Anr. Edn.** From 1908. Vols. 5-57, 36 vols. Orig. bdgs., some covers stained. (JL. Mar.2; 744)   Aus. $300
- - **Anr. Edn.** 1919-1964. Vols. 16-60, 45 vols. Red cl., ex-liby., worn. (SG. Oct.2; 42) $170
- - **Anr. Edn.** 1928-54. Vols. 25-50. Orig. cl. (SH. Jul.9; 70)   *Elliott.* £60
- - **Anr. Edn.** 1947-72. Vols. 42-68. Orig. cl. (LC. Jun.18; 59)   £75
- - **Anr. Edn.** 1947-79. Vols. 42-75 with General Indexes 7 & 8, together 36 vols. 8vo. & 4to. Orig. cl. (SH. Mar.6; 492)   *George's.* £200
- - **Anr. Edn.** 1956-80; 1902-48. Vols. 54-5, 58, 65-70, 72, 74-7; Indexes 1-5, together 19 vols. Orig. cl. (SH. Jul.16; 96) *Brooke Hitching.* £420
- - **Anr. Edn.** 1957-78. Vols. 53, 58-74, together 18 vols. 8vo. & 4to. Orig. cl. (SH. Mar.6; 493)   *Domé.* £90
- - **Anr. Edn.** [1966-80]. Vols. 62, 63, 68, 71-73, 75-76, together 8 vols. 8vo & 4to. Orig. cl. (SKC. Feb.26; 1417)   £150
- - **Anr. Edn.** [Folkestone], [1975-79]. Vols. 71-75. 8vo & 4to. Orig. cl. (CSK. Apr.10; 98)   £130
- - **Anr. Edn.** Folkestone, 1977. Index vol. 66-69 for (1968-72). Orig. cl. (CSK. Nov.7; 199)   £50

BOOK CLUB of California
- **Keepsakes: Attention Pioneers.–Pictorial Humor of the Gold Rush.–Treasure of California Collections.–Early California Resorts.** San Franc., 1952-57. Ltd. Edns. 4 series. Each in hf. mor. s.-c. (SG. Jan.15; 5) $100
- **Keepsakes: Gold Rush Steamers.–California Sheet Music Covers.–Early California Mailbag. –Early California Firehouses . . .–Portfolio of Book Club Printers.** San Franc., 1958-62. Ltd. Edns. 5 series. Each in hf. mor. s.-c. (SG. Jan.15; 6) $110

BOOK OF THE CLUB of True Highlanders
N.d. Fo. Some damage to top corners of pp. Cl., worn. (CE. Jul.9; 206)   £55

BOOK COLLECTOR, The
1952-72. Orig. Iss. Vols. 1-21, with indexes to most vols., & 3 dupls. Orig. wraps. As a periodical, w.a.f. (C. Jul.22; 109)   *Monk Bretton.* £130
- - **Anr. Edn.** 1952-80. Complete run from Vol. 1, no. 1-Vol. 29, no. 2., plus yearly indices, lacks Vol. 14, 1965 (never issued?). Orig. wraps. (TA. Sep.18; 160)   £310
- - **Anr. Edn.** 1965-80. 61 orig. quarterly iss. in 14 vols., except for last 5 iss. which are unbnd. Cl. (TA. Sep.18; 95)   £70

BOOK OF COMMON PRAYER
See–PRAYER BOOKS

BOOK of the Dead, The
See–BUDGE, Sir Ernest Alfred Thompson

BOOK OF DURROW: Evangeliorum Quattuor Codex Durmachensis
Switzerland, 1960. Ltd. numbered Edn. 2 vols. Fo. Vol. 1 orig. Celtic design pig, vol. II pig-bkd. bds., d.-w., in s.-c. (GM. Apr.30; 394)   £480

BOOK OF ENGLISH TRADES
L., [1824]. Cont. leath. (R. Mar.31-Apr.4; 1535)   DM 1,100
- - **Anr. Edn.** 1835. Lacks hand-cold. engraved frontis. Cl., defect. (P. May 14; 75)   *Elliott.* £85

BOOK OF GEMS (The)
Ed.:– S.C. Hall. 1837. 1st. Edn. Vol. II only (of 3). Engraved vig.-headpieces, with a number in proof before letter state inserted, facs. sigs. at end, several ll. stained or spotted. Red mor., gt., by Hampstead Bindery, covers elaborately tooled with gt. fillets to overall mosaic pattern, vari-cold. mor. inlays & pointillé decoration, spine similarly gt., mor. doubls., vell. end-papers, partly unc. Mexborough bkplt. (S. May 5; 388)   *Ponder.* £70

BOOK OF KELLS
Bern, 1951. (500) numbered. 2 vols. Fo. Vell. (SG. May 14; 25a) $4,400

BOOK of the Old Edinburgh Club
1908-33. Vols. 1-19. Orig. cl. (CSK. Sep.12; 157)   £50
- - **Anr. Edn.** 1908-69; 1974-79. Vols. 1-33, plus pts. 1 & 2 of vol. 34. Wraps. (PD. Nov.26; 57)   £75

BOOK OF SPORTS: British & Foreign
Ed.:– C. J. Apperley, Wildrake & others. Ill.:– Alken, Landseer, Howitt, Cooper, & others. 1843. 4to. Lacks? 1 plt. in vol. I, some spotting. Cont. hf. mor., worn. (C. Nov.6; 286)   *Wagner.* £220

BOOKANO STORIES [The Story of Vulcan the Smith, etc.]
Ca. 1930. 4to. Orig. pict. bds. (SH. Mar.19; 209)   *Fletcher.* £80

BOOKBINDER
1888-89. Vols. 1 & 3 only. Orig. cl. (SH. May 28; 154)   *Talerman.* £100

BOOK-COLLECTOR'S Quarterly
1930-35. Nos. 1-15 & 17 only. Orig. wraps., soiled. (SH. May 28; 155)   *Landry.* £50

BOOKMAN SPECIAL CHRISTMAS NUMBERS plus Portfolio
Ill.:– after Rackham, Dulac, Thomson, Wilcox Smith, Hudson & others. 1911-13, 1915-16, 1919-23, 1926, portfo.: 1914. Fo. Cold. ills. tipped in. Orig. decor. wraps. (TA. Dec.18; 136)   £52

BOOKS ABOUT BOOKS SERIES
- **Great Book-Collectors.–Book-Plates.–Books in Manuscript.–Early Printed Books.–Early Illustrated Books.–Bindings of Books.** 1893-94. 6 vols. Unif. orig. cl. gt. (TA. Sep.18; 106)   £76

BOOLE, George
- **An Investigation of the Laws of Thought.** 1854. 1st. Edn., 2nd. Iss. Lacks final 'Note' & publisher's catalogue, prelims. loose. Orig. cl., worn, rebkd. (S. Jul.27; 252)   *Nador.* £95

BOON, K.G.
See–WHITE, Chr. & Boon, K.G.

BOORDE, Andrew
- **The Breviarie of Health for all Maner of Syckeness & Diseases.** 1552. 2nd. Edn. 2 pts. in 1 vol. Sm. 4to. Title-p. to pt. I in pen facs. on parch., the words 'The second boke of' on 2nd title-p. erased causing a tiny hole, a few stains mainly towards end, marginal tears & holes in last 3 ll. with loss of letters. Antique style cf., rebkd. [STC 3375] (S. Jun.15; 98)   *Rix.* £110

BOOTH, Edwin Carton
- **Australia.** Ill.:– after Skinner, Prout, Chevalier, & others. Ca. 1870. Vol. II only. 4to. Some foxing. Cont. mor. gt. (TA. Feb.19; 670)   £115
- - **Anr. Edn.** [1873-76]. 8 orig. pts. 4to. Some plts. loose. Orig. cl., worn. W.a.f. (BS. Nov.26; 222)   £460
- - **Anr. Copy.** 8 orig. vols. 1 engraved title only (?), some ll. slightly spotted, some loose. Orig. cl. gt., slightly faded. (SBA. May 27; 280)   *Bailey.* £280
- - **Anr. Edn.** Ill.:– after Skinner, Prout, Chevalier & others. Ca. 1875. 2 vols. 4to. Some foxing. Orig. mor. gt., worn. (TA. Feb.19; 669)   £340
- - **Anr. Edn.** N.d. 2 vols. 4to. 7 (of 8) maps, 97 (of 111) engrs. Mod. hf. cl. W.a.f. (P. Apr.30; 262)   *Trevor.* £320

BOOTH, Edward Thomas
- **Rough Notes on the Birds Observed . . . in the British Islands.** Ill.:– E. Neale. 1881-87. 3 vols. Lge. 4to. Titles to orig. 15 pts. bnd. at end vol. 3. Cont. hf. mor., gt. (C. Mar.18; 124)   *Pillar.* £1,300

BOOTH, Henry
- **An Account of the Liverpool & Manchester Railway.** L'pool., [1830]. Owner's names on title. Cl., ?orig. wraps. bnd. in, unc. (SKC. Feb.26; 1750)   £85

BOOTH, Gen. William
- **In Darkest England & the Way Out.** [1890]. 1st. Edn. Orig. cl. Inscr., 3 photos. loosely inserted. (S. Nov.25; 495)   *Stewart.* £150

BOOTH, William Beattie
See–CHANDLER, Alfred & Booth, William Beattie

BOOTHBY, Mrs. Francis
- **Marcelia.** L., 1670. 1st. Edn. 4to. Recent mor. [Wing B3742] (C. Nov.19; 57)   *Brett-Smith.* £140

BOOTT, Francis
- **Illustrations of the genus Carex.** L., 1858-67. 4 vols. 4to. Orig. cl., worn, liby. marks on spines. Pres. copies, variously inscr., from collection of Massachusetts Horticultural Society, stps. on plts. (SPB. Oct.1; 105) $300

BOR, Peter Christian
- **Nederlantsche Oorloghen.** Ill.:– Jan Luyken, C. Decker & G. vander Gouwen. Leyden & Amst., 1621-[34]. 1st. Compl. Edn. 5 vols. bnd. in 6. Fo. Plts. from 2nd. Edn. bnd. in, probably lacks 1 prelim lf. in vol. III, pt. 1; hf.-title vol. II & index vol. IV (Bks. 28-32) if Publd. Cont. blind-stpd. vell., gt. spines & raised in compartments, ties. (VG. Oct.13; 175)   Fls. 8,500
- **Oorsprongk, Begin en Vervolgh der Nederlandsche Oorlogen, Beroerten en Borgerlijke Oneenigheden.** Ill.:– Jan Luyken & C. Decker, Blooteling (frontis.) Amst., 1679-84. Lge. fo. Wide margins. Cont. blind-stpd. vell., orig. ties preserved, upr. pt. of spine of vol. I a little defect. (VG. Dec.17; 1222)   Fls. 4,300

BORCHARDT, P.
See–BERLINER, R. & Borchardt, P.

BORCHARDT, Rudolf
- **Gartenphantasie.** Ill.:– Anna Simons (title & initials). Munich, 1925. (300), on Bütten, hand-ptd. Hand-bnd. orig. mor., by Frieda Thirsch. (H. May 21/22; 1378)   DM 1,200

BORDE, Andrew
- **The Breviary of Healthe, for all Manner of Syckenesses & Diseases the which may be in man or woman.** 1556-57. 2 pts. in 1 vol. 4to. Slight damp staining, a few wormholes slightly affecting text, cont. owner's inscr. on fly-lf. Cont. cf., slightly worn & reprd. [STC 3375] (S. Dec.2; 685)   *Rota.* £300

BORDERIEI, Arthur de la (Etude Historique)
See–POITIER DE COURCY, Pol.–RECUEIL DES BLASONS DE BRETAGNE

BORDES, Charles
- **Parapilla . . .** Flor., 1776. 1st. Edn. Hf.-title & title marbled. Red mor. by Lortic elab. gt. (SPB. Jul.28; 58) $325
- - **Anr. Edn.** Flor., 1782. 18mo. Red mor. by Cazin. (HD. Apr.8; 221)   Frs. 5,000
[–] - **Anr. Copy.** 16mo. Cont. Engl. str.-grd. red mor., decor. spine, gt. fillet border, pointille angle motifs, inner gt. fillet. (HD. Apr.10; 324)   Frs. 1,600

BORDEU, Théophile de
– Idioma Natural de el Cuerpo Humano Indagaciones sobre el Pulso en que se adelantan ... las Ideas de Solano de Luque ... Trans.:– Joseph Ignacio Carballo. Madrid, 1768. 4to. Spanish limp vell. (S. Jun.15; 99) *Quaritch.* £90

BORDIGNE, Count de
– Légitimité Portugaise. Paris, 1830. 4to. Occasional spotting, a few ll. browned, inscr. on front free end-paper 'A sa Majesté l'Empereur de toutes les Russies, Hommage respecteur de l'auteur. Le Bon de Bordigne. Str.-grd. mor., Imperial Russian arms on sides, borders & spine gt. by Simier, with his ticket. (SPB. May 5; 112) $175

BORDONA, J. Dominguez
– Spanish Illumination. Paris, 1930. 2 vols. 4to. Orig. hf. mor. gt.-panel. spine, spine faded. (C. Jul.22; 133) *Ars Artis.* £70

BORDONE, Benedetto
– Isolario. Venedig, 1547. Fo. Marginalia in old hand in 1st. hf., some worming at end. Cont. vell., newly hinged. (R. Oct.14-18; 1527) DM 5,000

BORDSWELL, Monica
See-TRISTRAM, Ernest William & Bordswell, Monica

BORELLI, Giovanni Alfonso
– De Motu Animalism. Leiden, 1710. 2 vols. in 1. 4to. Later hf. reversed cf., disbnd. (SBA. Oct.21; 132) *Durham University.* £220
– – Anr. Edn. The Hague, 1743. 2 pts. in 1 vol. 4to. Some browning. Cont. cf., rebkd. & reprd. (S. Apr.6; 15) *Phelps.* £90

BORGNIS, Guiseppe Antonio
– Traité de Mécanique appliqué aux Arts ... Composition des Machines. Paris, 1818-20. 2 pts. in 1 vol. (Plts. bound separately, together 2 vols.). 4to. Slightly spotted, stp. of Mersey Docks Harbour Board, repeated. Mod. hf. mott. cf., preserving cont. marb. bds. (S. Oct.21; 340) *Walford.* £85

BORLASE, Edmund
– The History of the Execrable Irish Rebellion. 1680. Fo. old cf., defect. (P. Apr.9; 267) £65
[–] – Anr. Copy. Some browning & spotting. Cont. cf., rebkd. [Wing B3767] (CSK. May 29; 136) £55

BORLASE, William
– Observations on the Antiquities Historical & Monumental of the County of Cornwall. Oxford, 1754. Fo. Cont. cf., rebkd. preserving orig. gt. spine. Bkplt. of John Gordon, lately in the collection of Eric Sexton. (C. Apr.16; 219) *Maggs.* £75
– – Anr. Edn. 1769. Fo. Engraved maps & plts., folding map stained. Later hf. mor. (C. May 20; 103) *Mann.* £140
– – Anr. Copy. Folding map stained. 19th. C. hf. mor. (C. Jul.15; 14) *Elliott.* £55

BORN, Ignaz von
– New Process of Amalgamation of Gold & Silver Ore, & other Metallic Mixtures. Trans.:– R.E. Raspe. 1791. 4to. Some margins dust-soiled. Orig. bds., rebkd. with cl., worn, upr. cover detchd., w.a.f. (S. Dec.2; 686) *Gurney.* £100
– Testacae Musei Caesarei Vindobonensis. Vienna, 1780. Fo. Plts. hand-cold., hf.-title & edges of plts. lightly browned. Cont. red str.-grd. mor., gt. fillet borders on sides, gt. panel. spine, rubbed. From Chetham's Liby., Manchester. (C. Nov.26; 48) *Weldon & Wesley.* £460

BOROWSKI, G.H. & Herbst, J.F.W.
– Gemeinnuzzige Naturgeschichte des Thierreichs. Berlin, 1780-89. 8 vols. only. 357 plts. only, some spotting. Cont. hf. roan, spines worn. W.a.f. (CSK. Nov.7; 27) £550
[–] Gemeinnützige Naturgeschichte des Thierreichs. Bd. 5: Von den Fischen. Ill.:– after D.F. Sotzmann. Berlin & Stralsund, 1784. Cont. leath., worn. (R. Mar.31-Apr.4; 1353) DM 1,100

BORRA, Luigi
– L'Amoroso Rime. Milan, Dec. 1542. 1st. Edn. 4to. Title preserved, 1st. few ll. & last lf. a little stained, corner of a few ll. reprd. affecting a few letters on D4-5. 16th. C. vell. bds., spine wormed. Harvard liby. bkplt. (C. Apr.1; 15) *Schweitzer.* £140

BORRICHIUS, Olaus
– Docimastice Metallica.–De Somno et Somniferis Maxime Papavereis Dissertatio. Copen., 1677; 1681. 2 works in 1 vol. 4to. Bkplt. of Thomas South & sig. of A.J. & M. Atwood, 1859, on fly-lf. 18th. C. mor., triple gt. fillet, spine gt. in compartments, inner gt. dentelles. (SM. Oct.7; 1604) Frs. 1,600
See–NEANDER, Jean–BORRICHIUS, O.–PETIT, P.

BORROW, George 'Ellis Wyn'
– Axel Thordson & Fair-Valborg.–Signelil, a Tale from the Cornish. Priv. ptd. 1913; 1913. Each (30). Together 2 vols. 4to. Orig. wraps. 2nd. work inscr. by T.J. Wise & with 2 A.L.s.'s from him concerning the pamphlets. (SH. Jan.30; 320) *Quaritch.* £110
– Tales of the Wild & the Wonderful. L., 1825. 1st. Edn. Occasional foxing. Old hf. cf. Armorial bkplts. of T.M.B. Baskerville & E.H. Litchfield. (SG. Mar.19; 29) $130
– The Zincali.–The Bible in Spain.–Lavengro.–The Romany Rye. 1843; 1843; 1851; 1858. 3rd. work 1st. Edn., rest 2nd. Edns. 2 vols.; 3 vols.; 3 vols.; 2 vols. Unif. hf. mor. by R. de Coverley. (SKC. Feb.26; 1489) £210
– Works. Ed.:– Clement Shorter. 1923-24. Norwich Edn., (775) numbered. 16 vols. Orig. cl., partly untrimmed. (TA. May 21; 371) £155

BORY de Saint Vincent, J.B.G.M.
See–DESMAREST, N. & Bory de Saint Vincent, J.B.G.M.

BOS or Bosch, Lambert van den 'Lambert Wood'
[–] Leeven en Daden der Doorluchtighste Zee-Helden en Ontdeckers van Landen. Amst., 1676. 2 pts. in 1 vol. Slightly soiled in some margins. Cont. vell. (R. Mar.31-Apr.4; 1786) DM 750
– Toonel des Oorlogs. Amst., 1675. 4 pts. in 2 vols. 4to. Slightly soiled in parts. Cont. hf. leath. (D. Dec.11-13; 2753) DM 1,400
– – Anr. Copy. Pts. 1 & 2 (of 4) in 1 vol. Engrs. browned. Cont. vell. W.a.f. (VG. Nov.18; 1076) Fls. 500

BOSCOVICH, Roger Joseph
– Abhandlung von den Verbesserten Dioptrischen Fernrohren, aus den Sammlungen des Instituts zu Bologna, sammt einem Anhange des Ubersetzers C[arl] S[cherffer] S.J.. Vienna, 1765. Partially obscured liby. stp. on last lf. & last plt. Cl.-bkd. bds. (S. Dec.2; 687) *Quaritch.* £150
– De Centro Gravitatis Dissertatio. Rome, 1751. 1st. Edn. 4to. Slight staining. Mod. bds. From Honeyman Collection. (S. May 20; 3186) *Howell.* £110

BOSMAN, William
– New & Accurate Description of the Coast of Guinea. 1721. 2nd. Edn. Cf. gt. (P. Sep.11; 51) *Ad Orientem.* £120
– – Anr. Copy. Cont. cf. (SH. May 21; 10) *Shaw.* £90

BOSSCHERE, Jean de
– The Closed Door. Ed.:– May Sinclair. Trans.:– F.S. Flint. 1917. (50) on H.M.P. Orig. parch.-bkd. cl. Inscr. to Ed. (SH. Mar.26; 102) *Illustrated Antiques.* £100
– Joo le Pauvre. 1922. (50) with 2nd. suite of ills. Bds., worn, unc., partly unopened. Pres. copy to May Sinclair. (SH. Mar.26; 104) *Illustrated Antiques.* £60
– 12 Occupations. Trans.:– Ezra Pound. 1916. 1st. Edn. Orig. wraps., worn. Pres. copy. (SH. Mar.26; 101) *Illustrated Antiques.* £75
– Weird Islands. 1921. Orig. cl. Pres. copy to May Sinclair. (SH. Mar.26; 103) *Illustrated Antiques.* £95

BOSSE, Abraham
– Manière Universelle de Mr. Desargues, pour Pratiquer la Perspective par petit-pied, comme le Géometral. Paris, 1648. 1 folding plt. creased & frayed, title slightly soiled, ink-stain in fore-margins at end. Cont. cf., worn. From Honeyman Collection. (S. May 20; 3188) *Maggs.* £95
– – Anr. Edn. Paris, 1648. L.P. Without the port., some browning & spotting. Mod. vell. From Honeyman Collection. (S. May 20; 3189) *Simonin.* £90

BOSSERT, H. & Guttmann, H.
– Aus der Fruehzeit der Photographie, 1840-70. Frankfurt a. M., 1930. 1st. Edn. 199 (of 200)

reproductions. Orig. cl. stained. (SG. Jul.9; 44) $200

BOSSERT, Dr. Helmuth Theodor
– Geschichte des Kunstgewerbes aller Zeiten und Völker. Berlin, 1928-35. 6 vols. 4to. Orig. hf. leath., 1 spine slightly defect. (H. Dec.9/10; 204) DM 750
– – Anr. Copy. (HK. Nov.18-21; 3300) DM 700
– Ornament. Two Thousand Decorative Motifs in Colour, Forming a Survey of the Applied Art of All Ages & All Countries. 1924. 4to. Orig. cl. in d.-w. (TA. Mar.19; 55) £110
– Peasant Art in Europe. 1926. Cl. gt. (P. Jan.22; 276) *Thorp.* £50

BOSSEWELLE, John
– Workes of Armorie. 1597. 2nd. Edn. 4to. Most woodcuts cold., running title on 2 ll. cropped, sm. rust-hole in 1 lf. affecting 1 letter. Cont. diced cf., gt. spine, rebkd. preserving orig. spine. From the collection of Eric Sexton. [STC 3394] (C. Apr.15; 162) *Henderson.* £220

BOSSHART, J.
See–BOKHART, Jakob

BOSSIUS, Donatus
– Chronica Bossiana. Milan, Antonius Zarotus for the author, 1 Mar. 1492. Fo. Some staining, mostly in blank margins, lr. outside corner on a1 a little soiled, minor worming in last 4 ll. of text. 19th. C. cf.-bkd. bds. [Hain 3667*; BMC VI p. 722; Goff B 1040] (C. Apr.1; 16) *Pilo.* £750

BOSSOLI, Carlo
– The Beautiful Scenery & Chief Places of Interest throughout the Crimea. 1856. Fo. Some plts. spotted, title loose & marginally torn. Cont. hf. mor., spine worn. (SH. Feb.5; 201) *Lester.* £210
– Guerra d'Italia scritta dal Corrispondente del Times. 1859. Paris & Torin, 1860. Ob. 4to. Many margins lightly stained. Mod. hf. mor. (SI. Dec.3; 96) Lire 800,000
– War in Italy with a descriptive Narrative by the author of 'The Times' Letters from the allied camp. Ill.:– after Bossoli. 1859. 3 plts. torn with slight marginal loss, spotting. Orig. cl., gt. by Robert Dudley, slightly soiled. (CSK. Nov.28; 114) £240
– – Anr. Copy. 4to. Tinted litho. title & 35 plts. only (of 39), 2 maps, loose. Worn. (SH. Apr.9; 195) *Pramaggiore.* £150

BOSSU, Jean Bernard
– Travels Through that Part of North America formerly called Louisiana. Trans.:– J.R. Forster. 1771. 1st. Edn. in Engl. 2 vols. 19th. C. hf. mor., 1 upr. cover detchd. From Chetham's Liby., Manchester. [Sabin 6466] (C. Nov.26; 49) *Burdon.* £160

BOSSUET, Jacques Benigne
– L'Apocalypse. Paris, 1689. 1st. Edn. Red mor., decor. spine, 3 fillets, inside dentelle. (HD. Dec.5; 23) Frs. 1,500
– Défense de l'Histoire des Variations ... Paris, 1691. 1st. Edn. 12mo. 19th C. mor., Du Seuil decor., decor. spine, inside dentelle. (HD. Mar.17; 27) Frs. 1,300
– Defensio Declarationis Celeberrimae, quam de Potestate Ecclesiastica sanxit Clerus Gallicanus XIX Marth MDCLXXXII. Luxemburg, 1730. 1st. Edn. 2 vols. in 1. 4to. Lacks port., old initials 'A.A.' on title & number 60 on title. Cont. red mor., gt., arms of Armand Gaston de Rohan-Soubise, triple gt. fillet, spine gt. in compartments with charges from arms, inner gt. dentelles, upr. cover stained. (SM. Oct.7; 1606) Frs. 2,000
– Discours sur L'Histoire Universelle. Paris, 1681. 1st Edn. 4to. Cont. cf. (S. May 5; 65) *Ker.* £50
– – Anr. Edn. Paris, 1682. 2nd Edn. L.P. 12mo. Lacks cancels, sig. of A.A. Renouard, 1782, on title, & his number 331 on free end-paper, sig. of Fanny Anne Burney on fly-lf. Cont. red. mor. bnd. for Renouard by Derome le Jeune with his ticket, triple gt. fillet, Renouard's name gt. at foot., inner gt. dentelles. SM. Oct.7; 1608) Frs. 2,800
– – Anr. Edn. Paris, 1732. New Edn. Pt. 1. 4to. Cont. spr. cf., spine gt. Edward Gibbon's copy. (S. Jun.9; 34) *Quaritch.* £200
– – Anr. Edn. Paris, 1784. 4to. Some ll. yellowed. Cont. red mor., triple gt. fillet around covers, spine decor. with raised bands. (HD. Feb.27; 17) Frs. 1,300
– – Anr. Edn. 1784. (200) on Vélin paper. 4to. Cont. red mor. by Derome le Jeune with his 1785

BOSSUET, Jacques Benigne -contd.
ticket, triple gt. fillet, spine gt. in compartments, inner gt. dentelles. Bkplts. of Lord Gosford, John Naylor & Henry J.B. Clements. (SM. Oct.7; 1609) Frs. 3,500
- - **Anr. Edn.** Paris, 1814. Fine paper copy. 2 vols. Violin cf. by Purgold, decor. spines, gt. fillets & blind-tooled roll-stps. on covers. (HD. Dec.5; 24) Frs. 1,100
- **Maximes et Reflexions sur la Comédie.** Paris, 1694. 1st Edn. 12mo. Jansenist red mor. by Hardy, inside dentelle. (HD. Mar.18; 28) Frs. 2,400
- **Oeuvres.** Ill.:– after G.B. Piazzetta & Tiepolo. Venice, 1736-58. 10 vols. 4to. Mod. hf. cf., old spines preserved, unc. From the collection of John A. Saks. (C. Jun.10; 25) Taylor. £170
- **Oraison Funèbre de Marie-Thérèse d'Autriche** . . . Paris, 1683. 1st Edn. 4to. Jansenist red mor. by Trautz-Bauzonnet, raised bands on spine, inside dentelle. Bkplt. of J. Lemaitre. (HD. Jun.24; 11) Frs. 3,900
- **Traitez du Libre-arbitre, et de la Concupiscence.** Paris, 1731. 1st. Edn. 12mo. Red mor. by Trautz-Bauzonnet, crowned cypher of Baron de Lurde in corners & repeated on spine, inside dentelle. Bkplts. of Barons de Ruble & de Lurde. (HD. Mar.18; 29) Frs. 2,500

BOSSUS, Matthaeus
- **Recuperationes Faesulanae.** Ed.:– Philippus Beroaldus. Bologna, Franciscus (Plato) de Benedictus, 20 Jul. 1493. Fo. 178 ll. (of 184, lacks 6 ll., supplied in facs.), a few stains. 19th. C. qtr. cf., worn. [HC 3669; BMC VI 826; Goff B 1045] (SPB. May 6; 164) $275

BOSTON Medical & Surgical Journal
Boston, Feb.4; 1846-Jan.26; 1848. Vols. 34-37 in 2. Cont. hf. sheep, worn. (SG. Sep.18; 13) $1,000

BOSWELL, Henry
[–] **Historical Descriptions . . . of the Antiquities of England & Wales.** [1786]. Fo. Lacks prelims. & plts. Cont. hf.-cf. W.a.f. (SBA. Jul.22; 131) Hulme. £480
- - **Anr. Copy.** Fo. Some offsetting. Cont. cf. (S. Sep.29; 141) Bailey. £380
- - **Anr. Edn.** Ca. 1790. Fo. Cont. hf. cf., spine reprd., very rubbed. W.a.f. From the collection of Eric Sexton. (C. Apr.16; 220) Kentish. £320
- - **Anr. Edn.** N.d. Fo. Extra-ill. with 12 plts., 9 preserved, 2 folding maps mntd. on end-papers, title torn with loss, preserved, some ll. detchd., soiled. Cont. cf., worn. W.a.f. (CSK. Feb.20; 72) £420

BOSWELL, James
- **An Account of Corsica.** Glasgow, 1768. 1st. Edn. Folding map in state with imprint, lacks final blank, Z3 uncancelled, port. of Boswell mntd. on verso of hf.-title. Mod. bds. (S. Dec.8; 221) Thomson. £55
- **The Journal of a Tour to the Hebrides.** Dublin, 1785. 1st. Irish Edn. Slight spotting, advt. lf. at end. Cont. mott. cf. Bkplt. of John D'Arcy. (S. Jul.27; 49) Scott. £80
- **The Life of Samuel Johnson.** 1791. 1st. Edn. 2 vols. 4to. With the reading 'gve' on p. 135 in vol. 1, & the cancels listed by Rothschild, lacks final blank in vol. 2, slight spotting. Cont. panel. cf., spines gt. Bkplt. of the Marquess of Donegall. (S. Feb.10; 411) Quaritch. £1,100
- - **Anr. Copy.** 2 vols. 4to. Lacks initial blank in vol. II, s4r in 1st. state with 'gve' in line 10, cancels as listed by Rothschild, title, port, & 2 plts. slightly foxed, minor worming in lr. blank margin of vol. II, 'The Principal Corrections & Additions . . .' bnd. at end of vol. II. Recent hf. cf. (C. Nov.20; 222) Joseph. £400
- - **Anr. Copy.** 2nd. state, with reading 'give' on p. 135 of vol. I, & the 7 cancels as listed by Rothschild. Orig. bds., covers detchd. & worn, spines defect., inscr. cut-away from upr. free end-paper of vol. II, qtr. mor. gt. drop box, unc. From the Prescott Collection. (CNY. Feb.6; 20) $4,500
- - **Anr. Copy.** With the reading 'gve' on p. 135. Cont. cf.-bkd. marb. bds., spines worn. (SG. May 14; 26) $2,400
- - **Anr. Copy.** With the reading 'gve' on p. 135. Early cf., rehinged. Ports. of Boswell & others bnd. in, tog. with early MS. copy of John Bacon's letter describing his design for Johnson statue. (SG. Oct.9; 39) $1,100
- - **Anr. Edn.** 1791. 1st. Edn., 2nd. Iss. 2 vols. 4to. Gateshead Public Liby. stp. on a few outer

margins. Cont. cf., worn. (SBA. Mar.4; 1) Symonds. £125
- - **Anr. Edn.** L., 1793. 2nd. Edn. 3 vols. The lf. 'Additional Corrections' after p. xxxvi & numbered xxxviii. Cont. tree cf. (CB. Apr.1; 215) Can. $260
- - **Anr. Edn.** N.Y., 1922. Temple Bar Edn., (685). 10 vols. Cf., gt. spine. (SPB. Nov.25; 430) $550
- - **Anr. Edn.** Ed.:– H.L.T. Piozzi & E.G. Fletcher. Ltd. Edns. Cl., 1938. (1500) numbered. 3 vols. Cl., orig. box (worn). (SG. Jan.15; 127) $160
- - **Anr. Edn.** Oxford, 1943-50. 6 vols. Extra-ill. with approximately 100 plts. Mod. hf. mor. With empty bdg. entitled 'Letters'. (SH. Mar.5; 201) Thorp. £170
- **The Life of Samuel Johnson . . . With two Supplementary Volumes of Johsoniana.** Ed.:– John Wilson Croker. L., 1857. New Edn. 10 vols. 16mo. Three-qtr. cf., spines gt., by Macdonald., rubbed. (SG. Sep.4; 77) $100
- **The Principal Corrections & Additions . . . (to the) Life of Samuel Johnson.** L., 1793. 1st. Edn. 4to. Title & final p. browned. Stitched, unc. & unopened as iss., cl. case. From the Prescott Collection. (CNY. Feb.6; 21) $1,500
- **The Private Papers of James Boswell from Malahide Castle** . . . Ed.:– Geoffrey Scott & Frederick Pottle. [Mount Vernon], [1928-34]. (570) on laid paper. 18 vols. 4to. & fo. With the prospectus, & 2 indexes (dtd. 1931 & 1937). Orig. paper bds., s.-c.'s, unc. & mostly unopened, prospectus in paper wraps., indexes in orig. cl. & orig. buckram, 2nd. index unc. From the Prescott Collection. (CNY. Feb.6; 22) $1,000
- - **Anr. Edn.** Ed.:– G. Scott. 1928-37. 18 vols. & Index. Various sizes. Orig. cl. (SH. Apr.10; 329) Rhys-Jones. £150
- - **Anr. Edn.** Ed.:– Frederick A. Pottle. 1951-60. Ltd. & numbered Yale Edn. 6 vols. Orig. vell.-bkd. buckram gt., all but 1 in s.-c.'s, unc. (SKC. Dec.4; 1539) £130

BOTALLUS, Leonardus
- **Opera Omnia Medica & Chirurgica.** Ed.:– J. van Horne. Leiden, 1660. Vell. (S. Dec.2; 454) Dawson. £110

BOTANIC Garden, The
See–MAUND, Benjamin

BOTERO, Giovanni
- **Delle Relationi Universali.** Venice, Pts. 2-4 dtd. 1596. 4 pts. in 5 vols. Lacks title-p. to pt. 1. Later cf. W.a.f. (CSK. Jun.26; 10) £140
- **Le Relationi Universali.** Ill.:– Hans Burgkmair. Venice, 1617-18. Pts. I-V & with the Aggiunta alla Quarta Parte dell'Indie (of 8, lacks pt. VI & the Saggio dell'Opera). 4to. Sm. piece torn from outer edge of Africa map, America map with a few short tears, 2nd. & 10th. woodcuts defect. & reprd., several trimmed or slightly cropped at upr. & lr. edges & with sm. repairs, 1st. title holed, piece torn from lr. edge affecting imprint, hole in A1, piece torn from blank, some spotting, a few rustholes. Cont. limp vell., covers loose, worn & reprd. [Sabin 6806] (S. Jun.22; 165) Crossley. £360
- - **Anr. Edn.** Venice, 1622. 8 pts. in 1 vol. A few ll. washed at beginning & end, minor marginal repairs, some discolouration. Old limp vell., upr. cover with later decor. (SPB. May 5; 114) $1,500

BOTHMER, Freiherr Carl von
[–] **Betrachtungen und Einfalle Uber die Bauart der Privatgebaude in Teutschland.** Augsburg, 1779. 1st. Edn. Cont. hf. cf., corners & spine slightly worn. (S. Feb.10; 199) Marlborough. £180

BOTHWICK, J.D.
- **Three Years in California.** 1857. Orig. cl. gt. (P. Sep.11; 293) Traylen. £55

BOTTA, Charles
- **Histoire de la Guerre de l'Indépendance des Etats-Unis d'Amérique.** Ed.:– L. de Sévelinges (introduction). Paris, 1812-13. 4 vols. 200 ports., lacks plans & maps. Str.grd. hf. mor. by Hering & Muller, corners, spines decor. with raised bands, unc. (HD. Jun.24; 155) Frs. 1,100

BOTTEGHE OSCURE–BOTTEGHE OSCURE READER
Ed.:– Marguerite Caetani. Naples, Rome, etc., 1948-60. Together 26 vols. (25 & 1). Wraps., many issues unc. & unopened. (SG. Jun.4; 50) $200

BOUCHE, Henri
See–DOLLFUS, Charles & Bouche, Henri

BOUCHER, Jean
[–] **Histoire Tragique et Memorable, de Pierre de Gaverston.** N.p., 1588. Old inscr. on title, some staining in lr. inner margin. 18th. C. mor., triple gt. fillet, flat spine gt. with longitudinal title, inner gt. dentelles. (SM. Oct.7; 1610) Frs. 2,800

BOUCHER, Jonathan
- **A View of the Causes & Consequences of the American Revolution in Thirteen Discourses** . . . L., 1797. 1st. Edn. Some foxing. Cf., worn, covers detchd. From liby. of William E. Wilson. [Sabin 6839] (SPB. Apr.29; 27) $200

BOUCHET, Jean
- **Les Triomphes de la Noble et Amoureuse Dame** . . . Paris, 1541. Gothic 8vo. Mor. by E. Thomas, fillet on covers & spine, inside dentelle. (HD. Mar.18; 31) Frs. 3,800
[–] **Von den Losen Füchsen dieser Welt** . . . Frankfurt, 1546. Orig. Edn. 4to. 84 ll., various papers & wtrmrks., ex-liby. MS. notes. Vell. (D. Dec.11-13; 10) DM 12,800

BOUCHETTE, Joseph
- **The British Dominions in North America.** Ill.:– J. Thomson, L. Haghe & others. 1832. 2 vols. 4to. Cont. tree cf. gt., rebkd., orig. spines preserved, corners reprd. [Sabin 6848] (C. Jul.15; 15) Dawson. £320
- **A Topographical Description of the Province of Lower Canada.** L., Priv. Ptd., 1815. Minor foxing to frontis. Late 19th. C. hf. leath. & buckram. (CB. Apr.1; 39) Can. $450
- - **Anr. Edn.** L., 1832. 4to. Occasional light foxing & sm. stains. Cont. cl., recently rebkd. in leath. [Sabin 6851] (CB. Sep.24; 71) Can. $150
- - **Anr. Copy.** 4to. Cont. buckram, unopened. (CB. Apr.1; 40) Can. $130

BOUCHOT, Henri
- **La Miniature Française.** Paris, 1907. (200). 5 pts. 4to. In sheets, in publisher's decor. embroidered silk wraps. (HD. Dec.5; 25) Frs. 2,100

BOUDOIR d'Amaranthe (Le), ou Les Nouveaux Plaisirs de l'Isle de Cythère
Paris, 1803. 16mo. Cont. bradel paper bds., unc. (HD. Apr.10; 325) Frs. 1,000

BOUFFLERS, Stanislas de
- **Contes.** Ill.:– Lalauze (port.); Poirson (ills.). Paris, 1878. Ltd. Edn. Ills. in 2 states. Mor. by Pagnan, decor. spine, inside dentelle. Bkplt. of Francis Kettaneh. (SM. Feb.11; 144) Frs. 4,500
- **Oeuvres.** Ill.:– Marillier. Paris, 1828. New Edn. 2 vols. Cont. red mor., triple gt. fillet around covers, crowned cypher of Prince Demidoff, spines decor. with raised bands, inside dentelle. (HD. Feb.27; 89) Frs. 2,600

BOUGAINVILLE, Louis Antoine de
- **The History of a Voyage to the Malouine Islands** . . . L., 1773. 2nd. Edn. 4to. Later hf. cf. (SG. Oct.30; 57) $300
- **Reis Rondom de Weereldt in de Jaren 1766-60.** Trans.:– P. Leuter. Dordrecht, 1772. 1st. Edn. of Dutch trans. Lge. 4to. Large margins. Mod. hf. cf., unc. [Sabin 6872] (VG. Oct.13; 27) Fls. 650
- **Traité du Calcul Integral** . . . Paris, 1754-56. 1st. Edn. 2 vols. 4to. Cont. mott. cf., some splitting at jnts. (SG. Sep.18; 53) $130
- **Voyage Autour du Monde.** Paris, 1771. 1st. Edn. 4to. With final advt. lf., title & 1st. ll. loose. 19th. C. hf. cf., upr. cover detchd. From Chetham's Liby., Manchester. (C. Nov.26; 50) Tzakas. £360
- - **Anr. Copy.** Cont. mott. cf., worn. Ham Court Bkplt. (SG. Oct.9; 40) $1,300
[–] - **Anr. Copy.** Cont. stained & gt. (SG. Oct.30; 56) $1,000
- - **Anr. Copy.** Cont. mott. cf., gt.-panel. back. Bkplt. of the Marquise de Chauvelin. (PNY. May 21; 107) $500
- - **Anr. Edn.** Paris, 1772. 2nd. Edn. 2 vols. Worming, not affecting text. Cont. mott. cf., gt.-panel. backs. (PNY. May 21; 108) $300
- **A Voyage round the World.** Trans.:– John Reinhold Forster. 1772. 4to. Cont. mor., triple blind-stpd. fillet, title, gt., in spine compartments, inner blind-stpd. dentelles. Bkplt. of George Wilbraham. (SM. Oct.7; 1611) Frs. 5,500

BOUGARD, R.
- **The Little Sea Torch.** Trans.:– J.T. Serres. Priv. Ptd., 1801. Fo. Plts. cold. & charts hand-cold. Cont. hf. roan. Bkplt. of William Carlyon, lately

BOU

in the collection of Eric Sexton. (C. Apr.15; 28)
Maggs. £900
– – **Anr. Copy.** 20 cold. aquatint plts. & 22
hand-cold. charts on 11 sheets only, lacks one
sheet with 2 charts, title laid down. Cont. hf. cf.,
rebkd. W.a.f. (C. May 20; 104)   *Taylor.* £220
– – **Anr. Copy.** 20 cold. plts. & 22 hand-cold.
charts on 11 sheets only, lacks one sheet with 2
charts, title laid down. Cont. hf. cf., corners reprd.,
rebkd. W.a.f. (C. Jul.15; 16)   *Cash.* £190

BOUGUER, Pierre
– De la Manoeuvre des Vaisseaux . . . Paris, 1757.
1st. Edn. 4to. Cont. cf., hinges & spine worn. (C.
Nov.6; 287)   *Rota.* £100
– Traité du Navire. Paris, 1746. 1st. Edn. 4to.
Foxed. Cont. cf. gt., rebkd., worn. (CNY. May
22; 154) $220

BOUILLAUD, Jean Baptiste
– Recherches Clinique propres à démontrer que le
Sens du Langage articulé et le principe coordinateur
des Mouvements de la Parole resident dans les
Lobules Antérieures du Cerveau. Paris, 1848. Orig.
ptd. wraps., upr. wrap. defect. at corner, hinge
torn, s.-c. (S. Jun.15; 104)   *Norman.* £90
– Traité Clinique du Rhumatisme Articulaire et de
la Loi de coincidence des Inflammations du Coeur
avec cette Maladie. Paris, 1840. 1st. Edn. Cont.
bds., unc. (S. Jun.15; 103)   *Gurney.* £110

BOULANGER, Nicolas, Antoine
– L'Antiquité devoilée par ses Usages. Amst., 1766.
L.P. 4to. Fly-lf. inscr. 'il faut joindre à traité au
Christianisme devoilé' & initialled 'P', bkplt. of
Arthur Edward Waite. Cont. mor. in Jansenist
style, title, gt., on spine, inner gt. dentelles. 'Paris
d'Illens' copy. (SM. Oct.7; 1614)   *Frs.* 1,300

BOULGER, Prof. George S. & Perrin, Ida S.
– British Flowering Plants. 1914. (1000). 4 vols.
4to. Orig. buckram. (SH. Dec.18; 6)
Argyll Etkin. £55

BOULLANGER, Charles Joseph
– Catalogue des Livres de la Bibliothèque. Paris,
1741. 12mo. Priced in MS., stp. on title of
Lenormand de Coudray. Cont. sheep-bkd. bds,
some wormholes in spine. (SM. Oct.7; 1327)
Frs. 2,300

BOULTON, D'Arcy
– Sketch of His Majesty's Province of Upper
Canada. 1805. 4to. Cold. map (some stains).
Wraps. (P. Nov.13; 335)   *Traylen.* £240
– – **Anr. Copy.** Lacks map, supplied in facs. Qtr.
mor. (CB. Sep.24; 185)   *Can.* $320

BOULTON, Samuel
– Medicina Magica tamen Physica Magical, but
Natural Physick or a Medical Tractate of
Diastatical Physick. 1656. 1st. Edn. Advt. lf., title
browned & written on, bad inking on pp. 51, 62 &
63 affecting text. Cont. cf. [Wing B3833A] (S.
Dec.2; 455)   *Music Mart.* £90

BOURCARD, Francesco de
– Usi e Costumi di Napoli e Contorni. Naples,
1853-58. 2 vols. Orig. bds., litho. Sigd. (SI.
Dec.3; 98)   Lire 4,100,000
– – **Anr. Edn.** Naples, 1857-66. 2 vols. Some
foxing thro.-out, 1 plt. defect. Mor. gt., worn. (BS.
Jun.11; 312)   £730

BOURCET, Lt. General Pierre Joseph
– Principes de la Guerre de Montagnes. Paris,
1888. 1st. Edn. Lge. 4to. Three-qtr. mor., spine gt.
(SG. Oct.30; 59) $125

BOURCHIER, John, Lord Berners
– The History of the Valiant Knight Arthur of
Little Britain. 1814. New Edn. 4to. Cont. str.-grd.
mor. gt. (SBA. Mar.4; 23)
Rochdale Bookshop. £80

BOURDALOUE, Louis
– Oeuvres Complètes. 1821-22; 1825-26. 16 vols.
Cont. grd. cf. (HD. Oct.10; 222)   *Frs.* 1,300
– Sermons. Paris, 1712-40. 2nd Edn. 18 vols.
(lacks the 2 vols. of Tables). Sm. 8vo. Cont. red
mor., decor. spines, 3 gt. fillets & fleurons. (HD.
Dec.5; 26)   *Frs.* 3,300

BOURDILLON, F.W.
– Ailes d'Alovette. Daniel Pr., 1890. (100)
numbered. Sm. 4to. Red mor., slightly discold. &
stained, orig. wraps. bnd. in, by Zaehnsdorf.
Bkplt. of Charles Plumptre Johnson. (S. Jul.31; 1)
Sanders. £75

BOURDON, Pierre
– Livre Premier [Deuxième et Troisième]. Paris,
1703. 3 pts. in 1 vol. 4to. Lacks title & last blank,
title-lf. of second series replaced with anr. lf.
Marb. leath., floral gt. (D. Dec.11-13; 638)
DM 2,000

BOURGEOIS, Constant
– Recueil de Vues Pittoresques de la France. Paris,
1818-20. Fo. Lacks title, some browning. Cont. hf.
red mor., corners, decor. spine. (HD. Jun.10; 127)
Frs. 5,000

BOURGET, Paul
– Le Disciple. 1889. (100) on Hollande. Mor. by
Marius Michel, mor. doubls., wrap. (HD.
Oct.10; 23)   *Frs.* 2,100
– Pastels: Dix Portraits de Femmes. Ill.:– Robaudi
& Giraldon. Paris, 1895. (200) numbered copies
on Japan vell., initialled by publisher. Mor.,
multiple gt. fillet borders, spine gt. with mor.
inlays, gt. dentelles, doubls. & end. ll. of Marius
Michel, orig. pict. wraps. bnd. in. (SG. Oct.9; 41)
$300

BOURGEVILLE, Charles de
– Les Recherches et Antiquitez de la Province de
Neustrie . . . Caen, 1588. Jansenist red mor. by
Chambolle-Duru, raised bands on spine, inside
dentelle. From liby. of La Germonière. (HD.
Jun.24; 83)   *Frs.* 2,200

BOURGOGNE, Sargent
– Memoirs. Ed.:– Paul Cottin & Maurice Henault.
Ill.:– Reymond after Alfred Paris. Paris, 1900. 4to.
Leath.-bkd. gt.-pict. cl., orig. cold. pict. wraps.
bnd. in. (SG. Oct.30; 60) $140

BOURGOING, Baron Jean François
– Atlas to the Modern State of Spain. 1808. 4to. 1
plt. reprd., several stained. Hf. cf., brkn., spine
defect. 16 plts. of Spanish Costume, by Juan de la
Cruz, inserted. (BS. Jun.11; 141)   £80
– Die Franzos Bildnisminiatur. Vienna, 1928.
(1000) on Esparto-Bütten. Lge. 4to. Hf. leath.
(HK. May 12-14; 2323)   DM 420
– Tableau de l'Espagne Moderne. Paris, 1803. 3rd.
Edn. 3 vols. Cf. (DS. May 22; 941)   Pts. 28,000
– – **Anr. Edn.** 1807. 4th. Edn. 2 vols. Cont. cf. gt.
(SBA. Jul.23; 446)   *Shapero.* £85

BOURGUET, Louis
[–] Memoires pour sevir à l'Histoire Naturelle des
Petrifications dans les Quatre Parties du Monde.
The Hague, 1742. 1st. Edn. 4to. 19th. C. hf. mor.
From Chetham's Liby., Manchester. (C.
Nov. 26; 51)   *Wheldon & Wesley.* £75

BOURIENNE, Louis Antoine Fauvelet de
– Mémoires sur Napoléon et le Directoire, le
Consulat, l'Empire et la Restauration. Paris, 1829.
10 vols. Hf. cf., by Masquillier. (HD. Oct.10; 223)
Frs. 2,600

BOURKE, Ulick, Marquis of Clanricarde
See–ANCIENT Irish Histories–BOURKE, Ulick,
Marquis of Clanricarde

BOURKE-WHITE, Margaret
– [U.S.S.R. Photographs]. [Albany] [1934]. 1000).
Fo. Lacks title & text. Loose as iss. in cl., leath.
spine. (SG. Apr.23; 35) $425

BOURNE, John C.
– The History & Description of the Great Western
Railway. 1846. [1st. Edn.?] Lge. fo. Mod. mor.
(C. May 20; 6)   *Taylor.* £1,100
– – **Anr. Copy.** Some plts. spotted, several plts.
dust-soiled in fore-edges. Cont. bds., anr. frontis.
trimmed & mntd. on upr. cover, spine defect.,
contents disbnd. & loose. (S. Nov.4; 549)
Traylen. £520

BOURNE, Samuel
– Scenes of India. Ca. 1866. Ob. fo. 90
photographs, mostly sigd. & numbered in the
negative, mntd. in album. No bdg. stated. (BS.
Jun.11; 1)   £1,500

BOURRET
– Catalogue de la Bibliothèque. [Paris, Boudot &
Guerin], 1735. 12mo enlarged to 8vo. Priced in
MS. in margins, many cont. bibliographical notes
on interleaved sheets, lacks title, 2 ll. of books
omitted at end. Cont. mott. cf., triple gt. fillet &
corner sprays, spine gt. in compartments. Worn.
(SM. Oct.7; 1328)   *Frs.* 1,100

BOUSSUET, François
– De Natura Aquatilium Carmen. Lyon, 1558. 1st.
Edn. 2 pts. in 1 vol. 4to. Occasional light spotting

BOW

& discolouration. early sig. on title-p. Early 20th.
C. vell. (S. Jul.27; 279)
Dekker & Nordemann. £650

BOUTELL, Charles
– The Monumental Brasses of England. Ill.:– R.B.
Utting. L., 1849. Cl., worn. (SG. Mar.12; 36)
$130

BOUTET, Henri
– Almanach pour 1899, 1900.–Les Heures de la
Parisienne La Parisienne et les Fleurs. Paris,
[1898-99]. (1,051) numbered. Orig. pict. wraps.,
worm. (SH. Nov.20; 235A)   *Whiteley.* £80

BOUTET de Monvel
– Jean d'Arc. Paris, [1896]. Ltd., numbered
Subscriber's Proof Copy, on China paper. Ob. fo.
Loose as iss. in gt.-ornamented bd. folder, linen
ties. (SG. Apr.30; 31) $1,600

BOUVELLE, Charles de
– Tractatus Varii. 1510. Fo. 4 MS. ll. on vell. at
beginning & end, 1 lf. torn, lacks q8., some
dampstaining. Cont. vell., slightly defect. (HD.
Feb.27; 15)   *Frs.* 1,000

BOUZOUNET, Claudine
See–STELLA, Jacques & Bouzounet, Claudine

BOWDITCH, Nathaniel
– The New American Practical Navigator.
Newburyport. [1811]. 3rd. Edn. Some
dampstains, etc. Orig. leath., worn, advt. mntd. in
upr. cover. (SG. Jan.29; 67) $220

BOWDITCH, Sarah [Mrs. Thomas Edward]
– The Fresh-water Fishes of Great Britain. 1828.
4to. 44 orig. watercolour drawings heightened
with silver & gold, & 1 uncold. drawing, all sigd.
Cont. str.-grd. mor., elab. gt., by White. Marquess
of Lansdowne's Bkplt. (C.   Jul.15; 141)
Henderson. £5,400
– – **Anr. Copy.** 4to. Cont. mor., elab. gt. borders
on covers, rebkd. (C. Mar.18; 21)   *Taylor.* £4,500

BOWEN, Emmanuel
– [Atlas] The Maps & Charts to the Modern Part
of the Universal History. 1766. Fo. A trifle
discold., on guards thro.-out. Cont. mott. cf. gt.,
roll-tooled border, spine gt. in compartments. (S.
Jun.29; 176)   *Kentish.* £500
See–OGILBY, John & Bowen, Emmanuel
See–OWEN, John & Bowen, Emmanuel

BOWEN, Emmanuel & Kitchen, Thomas
– Atlas Anglicanus. Ca. 1770. Ob. fo. 44 uncold.
maps, Surrey loose. Qtr. mor. (P. Mar.12; 173)
Kidd. £580
– The Large English Atlas L., [1753]. Fo. Maps,
plans, on guards thro.-out. stain on maps of
England & Essex, a few other minor stains, also
includes 3 additional doublepage engraved maps:
Andrew Rutherford: An exact plan of . . . Roads
through the Highlands of Scotland, 1 Dec. 1745;
P. Elphinston: Map of North Britain, 6 Mar.
1745; T. Jeffrys: Map of the Kingdom of Ireland,
13 Nov. 1759, last hand-cold. in outl. 18th C. qtr.
cf., paper bds. As an atlas, w.a.f. (SPB. Oct.1; 272)
$5,000
– – **Anr. Edn.** 1763. Lge. fo. 46 hand-cold. maps
(of 47), lacks Devonshire. Hf. cf. (P. Apr.9; 147)
Burgess. £1,600
– – **Anr. Edn.** 1767. Fo. Lacks 1 double-p. map, on
guards thro.-out, maps hand-cold. in outl., title
detchd., some minor defects. Cont. hf. cf., very
worn, upr. cover detchd. (SBA. Dec.16; 49)
Nicholson. £1,900
– – **Anr. Edn.** N.d. (some imprints 1756). Lge. fo.
(560mm.×390mm.). Maps hand-cold. in outl., 1
map reprd., some dampstaining of title, 1st. map
& several maps at end, a few paint stains, 1 map
misbnd. Cont. hf. russ. gt., 1 cover detchd., very
worn. W.a.f. (S. Jun.29; 3)   *Kidd.* £1,500
– – **Anr. Edn.** V.d. Fo. Made-up copy: with 25
double-p. engraved maps from the Hinton &
Tinney edn. of 1749-55, 18 double-p. engraved
maps from the Bowles edn. of 1760, & 2 maps
from the Bowles edn. of 1763, lacks text, some
paper deterioration at edges. Cont. hf. cf., worn &
defect. W.a.f. (C. Nov.6; 244)   *Kentish.* £1,300

BOWEN, Thomas
[–] An Historical Account of the Origin, Progress
& Present State of Bethlem Hospital founded by
Henry the Eighth, for the cure of Lunatics. 1783.

BOWEN, Thomas State of Bethlem Hospital founded by Henry the Eighth, -contd.
Sm. 4to. Bds. (S. Jun.15; 106) *Jenner Books.* £60

BOWERS, G.
- Hollybush Hall. Or Open House in an Open Country. N.d. Ob. 4to. Some slight spotting. Orig. cl., slightly wormed, largely disbnd. (CSK. Jun.26; 90) £50

BOWES, James Lord
- Japanese Pottery. L'pool, 1890. Cont. hf. mor. Inscr. (S. Sep.30; 375) £60
-- Anr. Copy. 4to. Cont. hf. cf. (SH. Jul.16; 45) *C. Frost.* £55
See-AUDSLEY, George Ashdown & Bowes, James Lord

BOWLES, William
- Introduzione alla Storia Naturale e alla Geografia Fisica de Spagna. Ed.:– Giuseppe Niccola d'Azara. Trans.:– Francesco Milizia. Parma, 1783. 1st. Edn. in Italian. 2 vols. Slight foxing. Cont. Italian red mor., decor. borders, mor. onlays on covers, unidentified arms of a cardinal gt.-stpd. & gt. initials D.B. at foot of upr. cover, slight worming & wear to head of spine of vol. 2. The John A. Saks copy, bkplt. of Cortlandt F. Bishop. (CNY. Oct.1; 150) $250

BOWLKER, Charles
- The Art of Angling: And Compleat Fly-Fishing. 1786. Cont. cf., worn. (PD. May 20; 168) £160
-- Anr. Copy. 12mo. Browned. Cont. leath.-bkd. marb. bds., very worn. (SG. Apr.9; 282) $400
-- Anr. Edn. B'gham, 1788. 12mo. Frontis. trimmed & mntd. Later three-qtr. mor. (SG. Dec.11; 19) $210

BOWMAN, Sir William
- The Collected Papers. Ed.:– J. Burdon-Sanderson & J.W. Hulke. 1892. 2 vols. 4to. Orig. cl. (S. Jun.15; 107) *Jenner Books.* £90

BOWNAS, Samuel
- An Account of the Life, Travels & Christian Experiences of ... L., 1756. 1st. Edn. Title & early ll. slightly stained, slight foxing & soiling, advts. Later hf. cf., scarred. From liby. of William E. Wilson. [Sabin 7097] (SPB. Apr.29; 28) $250

BOWND, Nicholas
- The Vnbeleefe of S. Thomas ... with a Comfortable Treatise for all that are Afflicted. 1608. 1st. Edn. 2 pts. in 1 vol. 1st. pt. lacks (?) last lf. (blank?), 2nd. pt. lacks (?) ¶4 (also blank?), 2nd. pt. with short tear in title, not affecting text, & hole in K3 with loss of a few letters of text. Early 19th. C. hf. cf. [STC 3441 [2nd. pt.]] (S. Jun.29; 364) *Lachman.* £75

BOWRING, John
- Specimens of the Russian Poets. L., 1821. Soiled, minor tears. Red mor. gt., slight worming, end-papers browned. Double fore-e. pntgs. of ports. of Mikhail Lomonosov & Ivan Krilov, & a 4-part Novogorod ikon depicting the raising of Lazarus, the Old Testament Trinity, the Evangelist John dictating his gospel to Prochrus, & the presentation in the Temple, sold as fore-e. pntgs., w.a.f. (SPB. May 6; 192) $750

BOWYER, Robert
- An Illustrated Record of the Important Events in the Annals of Europe ... L., 1816. Fo. Appendix with 4-pp. text & 2 plts. bnd. in, ex-liby. Cont. red mor., gt.-tooled. Pres. mor. bkplt. dtd. 1817 to Rev. Robert Holt Butcher from George Greaves. (SG. Oct.9; 42) $1,600
-- Anr. Edn. 1820. Fo. 1 aquatint torn, some dampstaining. Mod. hf. cf. (S. Apr.7; 454) *Hyde Park Books.* £420
-- Anr. Copy. Cont. hf. cf., spine worn & defect. W.a.f. (C. Jul.15; 17) *Walford.* £350
- An Illustrated Record of Important Events in the Annals of Europe ...-The Campaign of Waterloo. 1815-16. 2 works in 1 vol. Fo. 2 engraved maps, 2 uncold. plts. of ports. only (of 3), plt. of facs. autographs, & 23 cold. aquatints. Cont. hf. mor. (C. May 20; 105) *Lancey.* £900
[-] -- Anr. Copy. 25 hand-cold. aqua. plts. on 23 ll., 5 folding, 2 engraved. plts. of ports., 1 of facs., 1 map, 1 plan, lacks medallion plt. & ?Hague lf. in 1st. work & 'Appendix' in 2nd. with 2 uncold. plts. Cont. hf. russ., cover detchd. (S. Nov.24; 39) *Schwarz.* £700
- An Impartial Historical Narrative of those Momentous Events ... 1816 to 1823. 1823. 1st.

Edn. Fo. 2 plts. of facs., offsetting to title & some ll., some spatting. Cont. mor., spine defect., upr.-cover detchd. (S. Sep.29; 165) *Primrose Hill Books.* £170
-- Anr. Copy. Title slightly soiled. Mod. hf. mor. (BS. Jun.11; 32) £95
-- Anr. Copy. Fo. Title detchd., some offsetting & spotting to text & a few plts. Cont. bds., spine defect., upr.-cover detchd. (S. Sep.29; 172) *Elliot.* £50

BOWYER, William
See-NICHOLS, John & Bowyer, William

BOYCE, E.
- The Second Usurpation of Bonaparte. L., 1816. 2 vols. Red mor. gt., Napoleon monog., spine raised bands, gt. inner & outer dentelle, by Hatchards. (D. Dec.11-13; 2694) DM 1,300

BOYCE, W.B.
- Notes on South African Affairs. L., 1839. Mod. leath., unc. (VA. Oct.31; 183) R. 120

BOYD, Nancy (Pseud.)
See-MILLAY, Edna St. Vincent

BOYDELL, John & Josiah
- A Collection of Prints from ... the Dramatic Works of Shakespeare. 1803. 2 vols. in 1. Fo. Both engraved frontis. bnd. before vol. 1 title, plt. 48 of vol. 2 preserved & misbnd., some marginal spotting. Cont. bdg., gt. W.a.f. (CSK. Jun.12; 44) £360
-- Anr. Copy. 2 vols. Cont. str-grd. mor., gt. panel. sides, worn, rebkd. (C. May 20; 7) *Barker.* £350
- Graphic Illustrations of the Dramatic Works of Shakespeare. [1802]. Fo. Lacks frontis., 1 plt. loose, some plts. spotted, mainly in margins. Cont. cf., worn, covers detchd. (S. Jan.27; 456) *Mistrali.* £220
- An History of the River Thames. Ill.:– Joseph Farington. 1794-96. [1st Edn.?] 2 vols. Fo. Lacks general titles & dedication to King George III. Cont. str.-grd. mor., gt. Orig. wash drawing by Farington pasted in vol. 1, bkplts. of Coningsby Disraeli & Hermann Marx. (C. Mar.18; 22) *Taylor.* £2,400
[-] - Anr. Copy. 1 plt. wtrmkd. 1794, 14 plts. slightly offset, a few ll. in middle of vol. I spotted. Cont. russ., gt., rebkd., corners slightly defect., George Morgan's bkplt. (S. Nov.4; 534) *Young.* £1,700
-- Anr. Copy. 76 hand-cold. aquatint plts., lacks frontis. & folding map, some text pp. & margins of 3 plts. heavily foxed, some offsetting. Red mor. gt., worn, hinges brkn., spines defect. (CNY. May 22; 46) $1,300
-- Anr. Edn. 1794-96. L.P. 2 vols. 4to. Aquatint plts. hand-cold. Mod. hf. mor. From the collection of Eric Sexton. (C. Apr.16; 221) *Taylor.* £950
- Select Views in Great Britain . Ill.:– S. Middiman. Ca. 1790. Ob. 4to. Text in Engl. & Fr., some staining. Mor. gt. (P. Jul.30; 102) *Lamb.* £120

BOYDELL, Josiah
- A Set of Prints Engraved after ... Paintings in the Collection of ... the Empress of Russia, lately in the Possession of the Earl of Orford. 1788. 2 vols. Lge. fo. Lacks 19 plts. from vol. 1 & 11 from vol. 2, some spotting, lacks last lf. of vol. 1 plt. list. Unbnd. W.a.f. (CSK. Jun.12; 117) £700

BOYER, Alexis, Baron
- Traité des Maladies Chirurgicales et des Operations qui leur conviennent. Paris, 1814-26. 1st. Edn. 11 vols. Cont. cf.-bkd. bds., a few spines slightly worn at head & foot. (S. Feb.23; 20) *Brienx.* £50

BOYLE, Hon. Robert
- Certain Physiological Essays & other Tracts. 1669. 2nd. Edn. 4to. Lacks last blank. Cont. cf., slightly worn. [Wing B3930] (S. Jun.15; 111) *Murray-Hill.* £160
- Chymista Scepticus vel dubia et paradoxa Chymicophysica circa Spagyricorum Principia. Rotterdam, 1668. 12mo. Cont. sheep. (S. Dec.2; 690) *Dawson.* £80
- Chymista Scepticus vel dubia et Paradoxa Chymico.–Physica Circa Spagyricorum Principia Vulgo dicta Hypostatica. Geneva, 1680. 4to. Inner lr. blank corners of ll. towards end wormed & reprd. New cf. (S. Dec.1; 79) *Quaritch.* £50

- An Essay on the Great Effects of Even Languid & Unheeded Motion whereunto is annexed an Experimental Discourse on ... the Insalubrity & Salubrity of the Air. 1690. Lacks last blank. Cf., rebkd. (S. Jun.15; 114) *Murray-Hill.* £90
- An Essay about the Origine & Virtues of Gems. 1672. 1st. Edn. Cont. cf., unpressed copy. Near cont. sig. of Thomas Hawes B.A. on fly-lf. (S. Jun.15; 112) *Edwards.* £480
[-] The Excellency of Theology. 1674. 1st. Edn. 2 pts. in 1 vol. Cf. [Wing B3955] (C. Nov.20; 223) *A. Thomas.* £50
- Exercitationes de Atmosphaeris Corporum Consistentium. Geneva, 1677. 4 pts. in 1 vol. Sm. 4to. Each pt. separately paginated, browned. Recently bnd. in cf. (TA. Dec.18; 185) £78
- Experiments & Considerations about the Porosity of Bodies. 1684. 1st. Edn. Some ll. marginally wormed, cutting several letters, several ll. stained from head. 19th. C. cf., rebkd. [Wing B3966] (S. Feb.10; 413) *Thomas.* £140
-- Anr. Copy. 1 lf. holed with loss of a few letters. Cont. cf., upr. cover detchd. (CSK. Mar.20; 90) £55
[-] A Free Enquiry into the Vulgarly Receiv'd Notion of Nature ... 1686. 1st. Edn. Lacks advt. lf. after a4, later sigs. on title. Cont. cf., rebkd. Sig. of John Middleton. [Wing B3979] (C. Nov.20; 224) *A. Thomas.* £150
- The General History of the Air ... 1692. 1st. Edn. 4to. 1-p. advt., slight browning. Mod. cf., spine gt. [Wing B3981] (S. Jun.23; 271) *Hammond.* £300
- Hydrostatical Paradoxes. Oxford, 1666. 1st. Edn. Occasional browning & spotting. Cont. cf., rebkd., worn. Bkplt. of Edward Waple, dispersal stp. of the Sion College Liby. [Wing B3985] (S. Feb.10; 414) *Thomas.* £320
- Memoirs for the Natural History of Humane Blood, Especially the Spirit of that Liquor. 1683/4. 1st. Edn., 1st. Iss. Some browning & staining, a few sm. holes & marginal tears with slight loss of text, pres. inscr. in Latin on fly-lf. to Henry Lee from S.B.W. Cont. mor., panel. in gt., slightly worn, 19th. C. bkplt. of Javez Watson, Magd. Coll., Camb., with his crest added on upr. cover. From liby. of Dr. E. Ashworth Underwood. (S. Feb.23; 166) *Dawson.* £620
-- Anr. Edn. 1684. 1st. Edn., 2nd. Iss. Cont. cf., rebkd. (s. Jun.15; 113) *Norman.* £850
- New Experiments & Observations Touching Cold. 1683. 2nd. Edn. 2 pts. in 1 vol. 4to. With the additional ll. 2L1 & 2 at the beginning. Cont. cf., spine gt., bkplt. of John Rutherfurd of Edger ton. [Wing B3887] (S. Jan.26; 270) *Rademaker.* £110
- New Pneumatical Experiments about Respiration. L., 1670-71. 4to. Disbnd. (SG. Sep.18; 55) $210
- Occasional Reflections on Several Subjects whereunto is premis'd a discourse about such kind of thoughts. 1665. 1st. Edn. Slight worming in outer lr. corners & some extreme inner upr. corners, sig. O etc. affecting letters. New mor. Sir Irvine Masson's copy, given by Professor E. Bowden. [Wing B4005] (S. Jun.15; 110) *Murray-Hill.* £100
- Of the Reconcileableness of Specific Medicines to the Corpuscular Philosophy. 1685. 1st. Edn. Occasional browning & spotting, with the inserted lf. 'Pag. 137' near beginning, advt. ll. at end, some pencil marks in margins. Early 18th. C. Engl. mor., gt.-decor. border incorporating crowns & sm. bird-heads, spine gt. in compartments with 1 crown over letter 'O', slight rubbing. The Earl of Orrery's copy. [Wing B4013] (S. Feb.10; 415) *Temperley.* £550
-- Anr. Copy. With 'Pag. 137' used as divisional title to 'Simple Medicines', divisional title frayed in outer edge, tear in E2, advt. ll. at end. Mod. cf., faded. (S. Feb.10; 412) *Thomas.* £280
- The Origine of Formes & Qualities. Oxford, 1666. 1st. Edn. Slight browning. Mod. cf., spine faded. [Wing B4014] (S. Feb.10; 416) *Lawson.* £220
-- Anr. Copy. Sm. hole affecting some letters in several gatherings, S8 crudely reprd., browning. Later cl., faded. (SPB. May 29; 47) $125
- The Philosophical Works. Ed.:– Peter Shaw. 1725. 3 vols. 4to. Slight browning & soiling, a little worming in vol. I, not affecting text. Cont. cf., worn, covers detchd., bkplts. of John Gough, & Harry Arnold, Arnbarrow. From liby. of Dr. E. Ashworth Underwood. (S. Feb.23; 168) *Rademaker* £65

- The Sceptical Chymist. Oxford, 1680. 1st. Compl. Edn. Cont. cf., rebkd. (SG. Oct.9; 43) $750
[-] - **Anr. Edn.** Oxford, 1680. 2nd. Edn. 2 pts. in 1 vol. A few ll. slightly soiled. Cont. cf. [Wing B4022] (S. Apr.7; 247) *Frank Hammond.* £1,600
[-] - **Anr. Copy.** Slight dampstaining to a few ll. Cont. mott. cf. (S. Jun.23; 270) *Hammond.* £1,000
- Some Considerations touching the Usefulness of Experimental Philosophy. Oxford, 1664-71. 2nd. Edn., Iss. B. of vol. I. 2 vols. in 1. 4to. Tiny wormhole through some inner margins in the middle. Cont. panel. cf. (S. Jun.15; 109) *Murrey-Hill.* £190
- - **Anr. Copy.** 2 tomes (8 pts.) in 1 vol. Hf.-title to tome II (not called for in tome I), lacks 1 blank lf. Cont. cf., spine gt., slightly worn. [Wing B4030] (S. Jan.26; 269) *Rademaker.* £120
- Tracts. 1674. 1st. Edn. 6 pts. in 1 vol. With the 'Advertisement to the Bookbinder', preface to the Animadversions' misbnd. at end of 'New Experiments' & preface to 'Cause of Suctions' misbnd. before 'Suspicions', lacks 1st. & final blanks, 1st. title holed & stained, tear in C2 of 'Animadversions', occasional spotting & browning. Cont. cf., some wear. [Wing B4054] (S. Feb.10; 417) *Thomas.* £140
- Tracts . . . containing New Experiments Touching the Relation Betwixt Flame & Air. -Essays of the Strange Subtility, Determinate Nature, Great Efficacy of Effluviums. 1672; 1673. 1st. Edns. 6 pts. & 4 pts. in 1 vol. Cont. cf., upr. hinge brkn. [Wing B4060; 3951] (C. Nov.20; 226) *A. Thomas.* £300
- Works. L., 1744. 5 vols. Fo. Recent hf. cf. (TA. Mar.19; 598) £240
- The Works, with a life of the Author. Ed.:- Thomas Birch. Ill.:- after T. Kessebohm (port.). 1772. 6 vols. 4to. Cont. tree cf. gt. From the liby. of Edward Gibbon with his bkplt. in vol. 1, later in the liby. of John Hely Hutchinson with his bkplt. (S. Jun.15; 108) *Murray-Hill.* £420
- - **Anr. Copy.** Cont. vell. bds. (SH. Jan.30; 412) *Walford.* £360
- - **Anr. Copy.** Marginal tear in 4B1 vol. III, slight spotting & browning. Cont. cf., arms of Duke of Northumberland gt. on covers, spines very worn, lacks some labels. From liby. of Dr. E. Ashworth Underwood. (S. Feb.23; 167) *Weiner.* £150

BOYLESVE, René
- La Leçon d'Amour dans un Parc. 1902. Mor. by Marius Michel, pink mor. doubls., wrap., lacks spine. N. (HD. Oct.10; 26) Frs. 1,300
- - **Anr. Edn.** Ill.:- after Brunelleschi. Paris, 1933. (375) numbered on Arches. 4to. Mor. by Bruel, lge. mosaic vase of flowers in multi-cold. mor. on upr. cover, wrap. preserved, s.-c. (SM. Feb.11; 198) Frs. 3,200
- Leçon d'Amour dans un Parc.-Nouvelles Leçons d'Amour dans un Parc. Ill.:- Carlègle. Paris, 1929-30. On Jap., with separate sets of ills. 2 works in 2 vols. Jansenist mor. by Trinckvel, inside gt. fillet, unc., wraps. & spines, s.-c. (HD. Dec.5; 27) Frs. 2,600

BOYNE, William
- Trade Tokens Issued in the Seventeenth Century. Ed:- G.C. Williamson. 1889. (25) numbered. 2 vols. 4to. Orig. mor.-bkd. cl. (SH. Apr.9; 58) *Seaby.* £65

BOYS, William
- Collections for a History of Sandwich, in Kent. '1892' [i.e. 1792]. 1st. Edn. 2 vols. 4to. Some spotting & discolouration. Cont. tree cf. (C. Feb.25; 25) *Crowe.* £140

BOY'S Own Book, The
1829. 3rd. Edn. Hf.-cf. (SH. Oct.23; 110) *Walker.* £52

BOZ (Pseud.)
See–DICKENS, Charles

BOZIERE, A.F.J.
- Tournai Ancien et Moderne. Tournai, 1864. Hf. chagrin, decor. spine. (LM. Jun.13; 268) B.Frs. 10,500

BRAAK, M. Ter
- Verzameld Werk. Amst., 1950-51. 1st. Coll. Edn., India paper. 7 vols. Orig. cl. (VG. Nov.17; 57) Fls. 450

BRABANT
- Généalogie des Ducs et Duchesses de Brabant. -Les Nouvelles Chroniques de Brabant. Antw., 1546; 1565. 2 works in 1 vol. Fo. 1st work: borders of ports. touched by binder's knife; sm. tears & wormholes. Cont. vell. (HD. Mar.18; 31b) Frs. 7,000
- Le Grand Théâtre Sacré du Duché de Brabant. La Haye, 1729. 3 vols. Fo. Lge. margin. Old marb. cf., 7 decor. spine raised bands, gt. border. gt. frame, worn. (LM. Mar.21, 59) B.Frs. 90,000
- Den Luyster ende Glorie van het Hertogdom van Brabant. N.p., n.d. 3 pts. in 1 vol. Fo. Old cf., 5 spine raised bands, worn. (LM. Nov.8; 25) B.Frs. 7,500

BRACCIOLINI, Poggius
[-] **Historia Florentina.** Trans.:– [Jacobus Poggius]. Flor., Bartolommeo di Libri, 3 Sep. 1492. 2nd. Edn. Fo. Spaces for initials with guide letters, initials supplied in red by cont. hand, 2 slight wormholes affecting last 66 ll., many ll. browned. Late 18th. C. qtr. cf., worn. Bkplt. of Dr. Georg Kloss, bkplt. of the General Theological Seminary Liby. [BMC VI, 649, Goff P874, HC 13173] (CNY. Oct.1; 20) $850

BRACKENBURY, H.
- The Ashanti War. 1874. 2 vols. 1 map torn, a few ll. spotted. Cont. hf. cf. (SH. Nov.7; 280) *Cookey.* £65

BRACKENRIDGE, H[enry] M.
- Views of Louisiana . . . Pittsburgh, 1814. 1st. Edn. Slight soiling & staining. Orig. tree cf., spine weak at foot & top, upr. cover loose. From liby. of William E. Wilson. (SPB. Apr.29; 29) $250

BRADBURY, Frederick
- History of Old Sheffield Plate. 1912. 4to. Mor. gt. (C. Feb.4; 228) *Basket & Day.* £80

BRADBURY, John
- Travels in the Interior of America in the Years 1809, 1810, & 1811; Including a Description of the Upper Louisiana, Together with the States of Ohio, Kentucky, Indian, & Tennessee . . . L'pool., 1817. 1st. Edn. Advts., slight foxing. Orig. cf.-bkd. bds. From liby. of William E. Wilson. (SPB. Apr.29; 31) $650
- - **Anr. Copy.** Orig. bds. Pres. copy. (SPB. Jun.22; 11) $600

BRADBURY, Ray
- The Martian Chronicles. Ill.:– Joseph Mugnaini. Ltd. Edns. Cl., 1974. (2000) sigd. by author & artist. 4to. Cl., boxed. (SG. Jan.15; 128) $110

BRADFORD, Duncan
- The Wonders of the Heavens. Boston, 1837. 1st. Edn. 4to. Some foxing. Orig. marb. bds., rebkd. in buckram. (SG. Jan.29; 68) $100

BRADFORD, J.J.C.
- Report on the Proposed Electric Railways for the City of Sydney. Sydney, 1916. Foolscap fo. Orig. bds. Ingleton bkplt. (JL. Dec.15; 685) Aus. $100

BRADFORD, Mrs. Sarah H.
- Grandmama's Search, or Tommy Lost & Found, for Little Children. Dresden, 1869. Ob. 4to. Some short tears around most flaps of ills. Orig. cl.-bkd. pict. bds., neatly rebkd. (SH. Mar.19; 35) *Fletcher.* £130

BRADFORD, Rev. William
- The Arctic Regions illustrated with photographs taken on an art expedition to Greenland . . . 1873. Lge. fo. 90 albumen prints only, varying in size from 2½×3½ to 11×15½ inches, a little light spotting & staining in the text, some ll. detchd. Orig. mor., gt., worn. (CSK. May 15; 43) £250
- Sketches of the Country, Character & Costume in Portugal & Spain . . . 1810. 1st. Edn. Fo. Plts. dtd. 1809. Mod. red hf. mor. (C. Nov.5; 18) *Marshall.* £240
- - **Anr. Edn.** [1810?]. 2 pts. in 1 vol. 4to. Text in Engl. & Fr., 52 hand-cold. plts. (of 54), dtd. 1809. Hf. mor. W.a.f. (P. Apr.9; 285) *Reid.* £360
- - **Anr. Edn.** N.d. Fo. Plts. (dtd. 1809-10) only, plus list. Loosely contained in mod. purpose-made box with crimson mor. backstrip. (TA. May 21; 232) £250
- - **Anr. Edn.** 1813. Fo. 48 (of 50) hand-cold. plts. Cont. hf. cf. W.a.f.(C. Mar.18; 23) *Duran.* £260
- - **Anr. Edn.** [1813]. 2 pts. in 1 vol. Fo. Text in 1st. pt. in Engl. & Fr., 1 text lf. torn, a margin strengthened. Cl., spine slightly torn. (SBA. Oct.21; 106) *Santos.* £320

- - **Anr. Copy.** Lacks title, some offsetting. Mor. gt. As a collection of prints, w.a.f. (BS. Jun.11; 313) £180
- - **Anr. Edn.** [1814]. Fo. Title & text in Engl. & Fr., some offsetting onto text. Hf. mor., slightly worn. (BS. Nov.26; 236) £320
- - **Anr. Edn.** Ca. 1822. Fo. Some plts. wtrmkd. 19th C. hf. mor. (S. Sep.29; 214) *Dennistown.* £370

BRADLEY, John W.
- A Dictionary of Miniaturists, Illuminators, Calligraphers, & Copyists. 1887-89. 3 vols. Orig. qtr. mor. (TA. Feb.19; 414) £80

BRADLEY, Richard
- The Country Housewife, & Lady's Director. 1753. 6th. Edn. Advt. lf., cont. MS. recipe on fly-lf., some margins slightly soiled or stained. Cont. cf., worn. (SBA. Jul.14; 100) *Lawton.* £85
- The Gentleman & Farmer's Guide for the Increase & Improvement of Cattle . . . Also the best Manner of Breeding, & Breaking Horses. 1729. Cont. cf., rather worn. (SH. Oct.10; 290) *Brooke-Hitching.* £170
See–FURBER, Robert & Bradley, Richard
See–WILDMAN, Thomas–BRADLEY, Richard

BRADLEY, Will H.
- His Book. Ill.:– Bradley, Edward Penfield, Maxfield Parrish & others. Springfield, Ma., 1896. 1st. printings. Vol. I, numbers 1, 2, & 4; Vol. II, number 1, together 4 vols. Sm. 4to. & 4to. Prospectus for Vol. 1, number 1 inserted in Number 1. Pict. wraps., minor chipping of 3 numbers. (PNY. Mar.26; 52) $350
- - **Anr. Copy.** Vol. I, no. 1. Narrow 8vo. Pict. wraps. (SG. Mar.26; 107) $150

BRADSHAW, George
- Railway Companion. Manchester, 1840. 16mo. Some loosening near upr. hinge. Orig. cl. (LC. Jun.18; 246) £80
- Railway Time Tables, & Assistant to Railway Travelling. 1839. 32mo. Orig. cl. gt. (SKC. Feb.26; 1752) £80
- Tables of the Gradients to Bradshaw's Map of the Railways of Great Britain. 1839. Lge. cl.-bkd. folding engraved map, hand-cold. Orig. mor., worn, ties. (SKC. Feb.26; 1754) £55

BRADSHAW, Percy V.
- The Art of the Illustrator. Ca. 1918. 20 orig. pts. Fo. Orig. wraps., orig. cl. box gt., worn. (SBA. Mar.4; 242) *Duran.* £80
- - **Anr. Edn.** Ill.:– after Heath Robinson, Russell Flint & others. N.d. 20 vols. Fo. In orig. folders, text bnd. in. (SBA. Mar.4; 241) *Duran.* £120

BRADSHAW, T. & Rider, William
- Views in Mauritius. L., 1832. Nos. 2-10. Fo. No 3 incompl., plts. loose, Plt. 'The Barracks of Mahebourg' torn, not affecting surface. Wraps., some torn. (SSA. Jan.22; 106) R. 210

BRADWARDINE, Thomas
- De Causa, Dei, Contra Pelagium, et de Virtute Causarum. Ed:– Sir Henry Savile. 1618. 1st. Edn. Fo. Lacks 1st. blank, a few rustholes. 18th. C. str.-grd. red mor., gt. floral borders on covers, spine gt. in compartments, by (Richard Weir, at Toulouse). From liby. of Count Justin MacCarthy Reagh; the Bp. W. van Mildert–F.M.C. Currer–Canon H.P. Liddon–College of St. Peter & St. Paul, Dorchester, Oxon–Keble College, Oxford, copy. (S. Jun.9; 36) *Quaritch.* £300
- Geometria Speculativa. Paris, Guy Marchant, May 20, 1495. 1st. Edn. Fo. With the reading 'impresse' for 'impressa' in the last line of the colophon & with C3v ptd., spaces for initial capitals with guide letters, tear in blank portion of title reprd. on verso with tape, upr. margins of some ll. lightly dampstained, extremities of some woodcut diagrams cropped. Mod. wraps., cl. case. [BMC VIII, 61, Goff B1072] (CNY. Oct.1; 101) $6,500

BRAGHT, Thielem Jans
- Het Bloedig Tooneel of Martelaers Spiegel der Doopgesinde of Weereloose Christenen. Ill.:– Jan Luiken. Amst., 1685. 2nd. Edn. 2 vols. Fo. Large margin. Cont. blind-stpd. vell. (VG. Oct.13; 28) Fls. 3,800
- Der Blutige Schau-Platz oder Martyrer-Spiegel der Tauffs Gesinnten oder Wehrlosen-Christen. Ephrata, 1748-49. 1st. Edn. 1 vol. Fo. Frontis. browned & mntd., foxed, ex liby. Cont. cf. on wood bds., covers detchd., worn, lacks clasps. (SG. Jun.11; 55) $220

BRAGITSKY, Eduard & others
– Serebryanyya Truby [Silver Trumpets]. Odessa, 1915. 4to. Orig. wraps. by Fazini, slightly soiled & torn. Inscr. to Georgi Ivanov from the authors on title. (SH. Feb.6; 387) *Quaritch.* £75

BRAHE, Tycho
[–] L'Historia Coelestis. Ill.:– Ph. Kilian [frontis]. Augsburg, 1666. 1st. Edn. 2 pts. in 1 vol. Fo. Engraved port. plt. Cont. blind-tooled leath.-bkd. wood bds., worn, fault in upr. cover, 2 clasps. MS. ded. (HK. May 12-14; 229) DM 7,000

BRAIM, Thomas Henry
– A History of New South Wales. 1846. 1st. Edn. 2 vols. Tinted litho. frontis. foxed. Cont. cf., spines gt. (C. Jul.15; 18) *Walford.* £80

BRAITHWAITE, R.
– The British Moss-Flora. 1887-1905. 3 vols. Ex-libris, hf. cf. gt. (PL. Jul.11; 50) *Wheldon & Wesley.* £75

BRAIVE, Michel F.
– L'Age de la Photographie. Brussels, 1965. 1st. Edn. 4to. Cl., d.-w. (chipped). (SG. Jul.9; 52) $100
– The Photograph: A Social History. N.Y., [1966]. 4to. Cl., d.-w., boxed. (SG. Apr.23; 37) $140

BRAMHALL, John
– The Works of ... Dublin, 1677. Fo. A few stains & soiling. Rebkd. cf. (GM. Apr.30; 93) £95

BRANCA, Giovanni
– Manuale di Architettura. Rome, 1718. 12mo. Vell. Armorial bkplt. of Patrick Hume, Earl of Marchmont. (PNY. May 21; 21) $140

BRAND, John
– The History & Antiquities of the Town & Country of Newcastle upon Tyne ... 1789. 2 vols. 4to. Cont. hf. cf., slightly stained & worn. (PD. Aug.20; 66) £130
– – Anr. Copy. Fo. Slight foxing & browning. Mod. hf. cf. with marb. paper-covered bds. (TW. Nov.26; 236) £100

BRANDER, Gustavus
– Fossila Hantoniensa Collecta. Ed:– Daniel Solander. 1766. 1st. Edn. 4to. 19th. C. qtr. mor. From Chetham's Liby., Manchester. (C. Nov.26; 53) *Weldon & Wesley.* £65

BRANDT, Bill
– Shadow of Light: A Collection of Photographs from 1931 to the Present. Ed:– Cyril Connolly (introduction). N.Y., [1966]. 4to. Cl., writing on front end-papers. (SG. Apr.23; 38) $175

BRANDT, F.J. & Ratzeburg, J.T.C.
– Medizinische Zoologie oder Getreue Darstellung und Beschreibung der Thier die in der Arzneimittellehre in Betracht kommen. Berlin, 1829-33. 2 vols. 4to. Cont. hf. cf., vol. II rebkd. using old spine. (S. Feb.23; 21) *Robinson.* £170

BRANDT, Gerard
– Leben und Thaten des Fuertreflichen und Sonderbahren Herrn Michaels de Ruiter. Amst., 1687. 1st. Edn. in German. Fo. Age-browned thro.-out. Cont. vell., ex-liby. (SG. Feb.5; 294) $180
– Het Leven und Bedryf van den Heere Michiel de Ruyter. Amst., 1701. Fo. 1 plt. loose, 2nd. hf. slightly stained at head. Cont. hf. vell. (D. Dec.11-13; 2322) DM 1,000
– – Anr. Edn. Ill.:– D. Stoopendaal. Amst., 1746. 4th. Edn. Sm. fo. Some tears badly reprd. Cont. blind-stpd. vell. (VG. Oct.13; 137) Fls. 870
– – Anr. Copy. Traces of use, slightly foxed, some stains. Cont. cf., slightly worn, slightly defect. (VG. Nov.18; 1354) Fls. 850
– – Anr. Copy. Slightly browned in parts. Cont. leath. gt. (R. Oct.14-18; 2887) DM 1,750
– – Anr. Edn. Amst./Rotterdam/The Hague. 1732. 3rd. printing. Fo. Plts. partly misbnd. Cont. blind-stpd. vell. soiled. (VG. Dec.17; 1515) Fls. 1,000

BRANDT, Herbert–GABRIELSON, Ira N. & Lincoln, Frederick
– Alaska Bird Trails.–The Birds of Alaska. Cleveland/Harrisburg, 1943; [1959]. 2 works in 2 vols. 4to.; 8vo. Both orig. cl. (CB. Sep.24; 17) *Can.* $100

BRANDT, Sebastian
– Aff-Ghebeelde Narren Speel-Schuyt. Trans.:– A.B. Leyden, 1610. 4to. Lacks ll. 10-11 (D 2-3) with 2 woodcuts, title cut short & mntd., corner of 1st. prelim. torn off & reprd., missing text in pen & pencil, blank outer margin of same & next lf.

reprd., some tears reprd., some light stains & wear. Old hf. vell. (VG. Oct.13; 29) Fls. 1,700
– In Laudem Gloriose Virginis Marie Multorumque Sanctorum. Ill.:– Albrecht Durer & others. [Basle], [Johannes Bergmann de Olpe], [1494]. 1st. Edn., 1st. Iss. 4to. Without the later supplementary quire of 8 ll. containing a poem by Brandt to Saint Bruno, minor repairs at inner margin of title lf. Mor. janseniste by B. Niedrée, 1847, upr. cover rehinged. The copy of F.S. Ellis & Clarence S. Bement, lately in the Pierpont Morgan Liby. [BMC III, 795, Goff B1077, H 3733] (CNY. Apr.8; 23) $22,000
– Das Narrenschiff.. Ed:– [Thomas Beccadeli]. Trans.:– [Jacobus Locher]. [Lyons], Jacobus Sacon, 28 Jun. 1488 [i.e. 1498]. 4to. Lacks final blank, woodcut on 1st. lf. slightly defect. & with lr. blank portion renewed, sm. wormhole from folios 1-21 affecting 15 text ll. & touching 5 woodcut borders, upr. margins with sm. patches from fo. 75 to end touching 7 headlines & 9 text lines, final lf. badly worn & slightly defect. Mor., spine gt.-lettered, by Lloyd. From the collection of Eric Sexton. [BMC VIII, 336, Goff B1093, HC 3752] (CNY. Apr.8; 86) $3,200
– – Anr. Edn. Trans.:– [Jacobus Locher 'Philomusus']. Ill.:– [Albrecht Durer] & others. Basle, Johannes Bergmann de Olpe, 1 Mar. 1498. 2nd. Latin Edn. 4to. Title-p. woodcut & 1st. text woodcut cold. with yellow, brown & green washes, rest uncold., 2nd. printer's device, with date 1497, on x4v, title-p. weakened & soiled by acid, & with sm. tear to woodcut, without loss, occasional light staining to margins, several ll. slightly browned. Mod. three-qtr. mor. & marb. bds. 17th. C. inscr. of Wilhelm Hegers, later the copy of Richard Bennett, recently in the Pierpont Morgan Liby. [Goff B1091, H 3751] (CNY. Apr.8; 24) $7,800
– Navis Stultifera ... Trans.:– Jacobus Locher. Basle, 1507. 4to. Title slightly defect. & reprd., piece lacking from fore-margin of i6, sm. hole in last 5 ll., some staining. Mor. gt. by W. Nutt, rubbed. (S. Feb.10; 214) *Wolfgang.* £850
– Das Neue Narrenschift. Augsburg, Johann Schonsperger, 29 May 1498. Unauthorized Edn. 4to. Some woodcuts cold., lacks final blank, some worming affecting 1st. ll & last 64 ll., sm. tear at lr. margin of fo. 13 touching 1 letter, cl with sm. hole, some staining. Old vell. From the collection of Eric Sexton. [BMC II, 372, Goff B1085, HC 3745*] (CNY. Apr.8; 16) $6,400
– Stultifera Navis. Basel, 1 Mar. 1497. 1st. reprint of 1st. Latin Edn. Lightly soiled in parts, loose, lacks 10 hf.-p. text wdcts., 135 (of 145) ll., some text loss, some old MS. marginalia. Cont. wood bds., clasps brkn. [Hain 3747; BMC II, 471; Goff B-1087] (R. Mar.31-Apr.4; 55) DM 2,500
– – Anr. Edn. Trans.:– [Jacob Locher Philomusus]. Ill.:– after Albrecht Durer. Basel, Johann Bergmann, 1 Mar. 1497. 1st. Edn. in Latin. 4to. Some slight dampstaining, particularly to upr. inner portions, 6 ll. rehinged at inner margins, some foliation numerals cropped, lr. corner of g3 creased. Cont. oak bds., blind-stpd. pig spine, brass clasp, qtr. mor. gt. s.-c. [BMC III, 795, Goff B1086, Hain 3746] (CNY. Oct.1; 81) $8,200
– – Anr. Edn. Basle, Mar. 1572. Lacks s8 (blank?), slight dampstaining. Early 19th. C. cf. From liby. of André L. Simon. (S. May 18; 47) *Frankel.* £150
– Welt Spiegel ... Basel, 1574. 1st. Edn. Title & last lf. reprd. at margin, lacks penultimate lf. Leath. ca. 1900 gt. (HK. May 12-14; 81) DM 620

BRANDT, Sebastian–[DURANDUS, W.]
– Der Richterlich Clagspiegel.–Speculator Abbreviatus, alias Speculum Abbreviatum Joannis de Stynna. [Strassburg], [1516]; 1511. 1st. Edn. (1st. work). 2 works in 1 vol. Fo. 1st work: Some old Ms. marginalia, 1st. 2 ll. with repairs; 2nd. work: 7 ll. bnd. in 1st. with old Ms. indexes, notes etc., including 1 on vell; 2nd. title stpd. & soiled, some ll. with corrections some old Ms. marginalia. Cont. blind-stpd. cf.-bkd. wd. bds. 2 clasps. (HK. Nov.18-21; 130) DM 2,100

BRANGWYN, Frank
– Catalogue of the Etched Work. L., 1912. 4to. Hf. vell., torn & loose. (SG. Mar.12; 38) $110
– The Etchings of Frank Brangwyn. L., 1912. 4to. Mor., slight foxing to end-pp. (JL. Mar.2; 831) *Aus.* $160
– Work. [?1914]. (70) proof copies, sigd. Ob. fo. Orig. cl.-bkd. bds. portfo. (SH. Mar.26; 112) *Sherlock.* £70

– Zwanzig Graphische Arbeiten. Ed.:– A.S. Levetus. Vienna, [1921]. (100) with prints sigd. Fo. Orig. box. (SH. Mar.26; 116) *Reed & Sims.* £120

BRANGWYN, Frank & Sparrow, Walter Shaw
– A Book of Bridges. Bodley Head, 1916. (75) numbered, on L.P. Fo. Orig. litho. frontis. sigd. in pencil, cold. plts. tipped in. Orig. hf. parch., slightly soiled. (TA. Mar.19; 50) £100
– A Book of Bridges.–The Bridge. 1915; 1926. 2 vols. 4to. Cont. hf. mor.; orig. cl. (SH. Jun.18; 99) *Makiya.* £60

BRANNON, George
– Vectis Scenery . . . a Series of . . . Views . . . of the Isle of Wight. 1824. 2nd. Edn. Ob. 4to. Some spotting. Orig. cl.-bkd. bds., slightly soiled. (S. Apr.7; 498) *Maggs.* £55
– – Anr. Edn. Southampton, 1825. Ob. 4to. Soiled. Cont. hf. cf., worn, lacks spine. (SH. Mar.5; 20) *Schuster.* £70
– – Anr. Edn. 1828. Ob. 4to. Hf. mor. (BS. Jun.11; 142) £70
– – Anr. Edn. Isle of Wight, 1829. Ob. 4to. Orig. hf. mor., worn. (TA. Oct.16; 296) £110
– – Anr. Edn. 1835. Ob. 4to. Some foxing. Hf. mor. (P. Apr.9; 287) £70
– – Anr. Edn. Wootton Common, Isle of Wight. 1839. 4to. Cont. hf. mor., lacks spine. (C. May 20; 106) *Maggs.* £60
– – Anr. Edn. Wooton Common, 1847. 4to. Lacks 1 plt. Hf. leath., worn. (S. Jan.27; 597) *Academy.* £95
– – Anr. Edn. 1855. 4to. Spotted. Orig. cl., rebkd. (SH. Mar.5; 13) *Crowe.* £95

BRANT, Sebastian
See–BRANDT, Sebastian

BRANTEGHEM, Guilhelmus de
– La Vie de Nostra Seigneur Jesus Christ par Figures Selon le Texte . . . Paris, 1540. Chipping, affecting title & final lf., worming. Old vell. (SG. May 21; 344) $160

BRANTOME, Pierre de Bourdeille, Seigneur de
– Oeuvres. 1740. 15 vols. Sm. 12mo. Cont. mor., gt. fillet. (HD. Jun.30; 9) Frs. 4,500

BRANTOME, Pierre de Bourdeille, Abbé de
– Les Sept Discours Touchant les Dames Galantes. Ill.:– Edouard de Beaumont. Paris, 1882. (20) on China paper. 3 vols. Double proof of engrs. Mor. by Ruban, mosaic compartments on spines, mosaic frames on covers, s.-c. (SM. Feb.11; 145) Frs. 20,000

BRAQUE, Georges
– Cahier. 1916-1947. Paris, 1948. 1st. Edn. (750/845) on Vel de Marais. Fo. Orig. pict. bds., linen box. Jean Paulhan's copy with MS. ded. on end-paper from Braque & orig. ill. (D. Dec.11-13; 1005) DM 8,500
– Catalogue de l'Oeuvre. Montrouge, 1959-60. 2 vols. only. 4to. Orig. pict. cl. binders. (S. Jul.27; 186) *Nakajima.* £80
– Intimate Sketchbooks of. Ed:– Will Grohmann & Antoine Tudal. N.Y., [1955]. Fo. Pict. bds., cover design by Braque. (SG. Oct.23; 43) $160
– – Anr. Copy. D.-w. (sm. piece torn from top). (PNY. Mar.4; 110) $100

BRAQUE, Georges, Cocteau, Jean, & others
– Les Facheux. Paris, 1924. (500) numbered. 2 vols. 4to. Orig. wraps. with cold. design by Braque, s.-c. (SH. Nov.20; 236) *Henderson.* £180
– Theatre Serge de Diaghlew; Les Facheux. Ill.:– Cocteau (port. plt.). Paris, 1924. 1st. Edn. (385) on Velin d'Arches. 2 vols. 4to. Unif. cold. pict. wraps., tissue wraps., designed by Braque. (PNY. Mar.4; 111) $400

BRASAVOLA, Antonius Musa
– In Octo Libros Aphorismorum Hippocratis et Galeni, Commentaria et Annotationes ... Basle, 1551. Fo. Dampstained. Mod. hf. cf. (HD. Jun.24; 12) Frs. 1,100

BRASHER, Rex
– Birds & Trees of North America. Kent, Conn., 1929-32. (100) sigd. on each title. 12 vols. Ob. fo. 867 cold. plts. Orig. hf. goat. binders, hardboard sides, with hand-painted figure. (C. Jul.15; 169) *Taylor.* £4,000
– – Anr. Copy. 3 vols. 303 (of 867) hand-cold. plts., numbers 417-631 disbnd., most plts. with accompanying text lf., a few plts. with liby. stp. on verso. Orig hf. mor. (SG. Sep.18; 58) $2,400

- - Anr. Edn. Kent, 1930-31. 7 vols. (of 12) a duplicate of the Game Birds of North America. Fo. Orig. bdg., worn, chipped. As a collection of plts., w.a.f. (SPB. May 6; 165) $1,800

BRASSEUR dE BOURBOURG, Charles Etienne
- Dictionnaire, Grammaire et Chrestomathie de la Langue Maya. Paris, 1872. 2 vols. in 1. Cont. red hf. mor., orig. ptd. wraps. bnd. in, slightly soiled. (SPB. May 5; 115) $650

BRATHWAIT, Richard
- The English Gentleman . . . 1630. 1st. Edn. 4to. Lacks corner of B4, affecting pagination, sidenote & 3 other words, some stains, most minor, some worming in blank margins towards end, many ll. & sigs. loose, a little worn at edges. Cont. cf., slightly worn. [STC 3563] (C. Apr.1; 196) *Carloe.* £90
- - Anr. Edn. Ill.:– Marshall (engraved vig. title). 1641. 3rd. Edn. Fo. Folding table torn & bkd., engraved title trimmed & mntd. Cont. L. mor., gt., tooled with semé of suns in broad border, initials 'EW' in sm. oval in centre, worn & reprd. The Ashburnham–Michael Tompkinson–J.R. Abbey copy; as a bdg., w.a.f. [Wing B4262] (S. Jun.9; 38) *Maggs.* £110
- Times Treasury: or, Academy for Gentry . . . with A Ladies Love-Lecture; & . . . The Turtles Triumph. 1652. 1st. Edn. under this title. Fo. 2 sm. holes in 2F3 cutting a few letters, several ll. stained from foot, some ll. marginally wormed, a few rustholes, sig. on title. Cont. spr. cf., rebkd. [Wing B2476] (S. Jun.23; 384) *Maggs.* £190

BRAUER, Erich
- Malerei des Phantastischen Realismus. Ed.:– Herbert Gleissner. Munich, [1968]. (250) numbered, with 8 orig. graphics on Japan paper, each sigd. Gt.–decor. cl., boxed. (SG. Oct.23; 45) $200

BRAUER, H. & Wittkower, R.
- Die Zeichnungen des Gianlorenzo Bernini. Berlin, 1931. 2 vols. 4to. Publisher's cl. (CR. Mar.19; 382) DM 380,000

BRAUN or Bruin, George
- Civitates Orbis Terrarum . . . Ill.:– F. Hogenberg & Simon Van den Noevel. Cologne, 1572-1618. 6 vols. in 3. Lge. fo. Marginal dampstaining in vols. 3 & 4, some touching engrs., some plts. in bad condition, especially at end, Cont ivory vell. with bands. (HD. Jun.24; 12b) Frs. 160,000

BRAUN, Georg & Hogenberg. Franz
- Civitates Orbis Terrarum. Cologne, [1575]-1588. Vols. 1-4 in 1 vol. Fo. 17th. C. leath., gt. spine. (R. Oct.14-18; 1464a) DM 100,000
- - Anr. Edn. Ed.:– R.A. Skelton [Intro.]. Kassel & Basel, 1965. Facs. Edn. of Cologne 1572-1618 Edn. 6 pts. in 3 vols. Lge. fo. Orig. linen. (HK. May 12-14; 594) DM 600

BRAUN, Johannes
- Bigde Cohanim – Vestitus Sacerdotum Hebraeorum. Leiden, 1680. 1st. Edn. 2 pts. in 1 vol. 4to. Lacks 3 blank ll., 1 lf. loose. Vell. (S. Nov.18; 644) *Rock.* £320
- Vestitus Sacerdotum Hebraerum. Amst., 1701. 2 vols. in 1. 4to. Cont. blind-stpd. vell., slightly worn & soiled. (SG. Feb.5; 194) $325

BRAUNER, J.J.
- Der Treu-meinende Teutsche Weiber-und Kinder-Arzt. N.p., n.d. 4to. Cont. vell. (D. Dec.11-13; 192) DM 700

BRAUNS, E.L.
- Das Liberale System, oder das Freie Bürgerthum . . . Nordamerika . . . Potsdam, 1831-33. Slightly soiled. Cont. leath., gt. spine. (R. Oct.14-18; 1656) DM 1,300

BRAUNSCHWEIG, Hieronymus
- Das Buch zu Distillieren. Strasbourg, 1519. Fo. Title torn & partly reprd. on verso, portion torn from Zz1 with some text loss, worming thro.-out, affecting text at beginning & end, some browning, owners' inscr. on endpaper. Cont. blind-stpd. pig over wood bds., bevelled edges, lacks 1 clasp, wormed & worn. (C. Nov.20; 180) *Carnegie.* £1,800

BRAVO, F.
See–BUZETA, M. & Bravo, F.

BRAY, Anna Eliza
- The Life of Thomas Stothard. 1851. 3 vols. Fo. Pages inlaid into L.P., with 2 lge. engraved ports. & over 600 orig. engraved ills., all inlaid or mntd.

Mor. gt. by Chatelin, orig. paper covers mntd. From the collection of Eric Sexton. (C. Apr.15; 78) *Traylen.* £520

BRAY, François Gabriel, Comte de
- Voyage Pittoresque dans le Tyrol. Ill.:– Rösel. Paris, 1825. 3rd. Edn. Fo. Orig. bds. (SBA. Jul.22; 72) *Temperley.* £500

BRAY, William
See–MANNING, Owen & Bray, William

BRAYLEY, Edward Wedlake
- Delineations, Historical & Topological of the Isle of Thanet & the Cinque Ports. 1817-18. L.P. 2 vols. in 1. Cont. diced cf. (CSK. Aug.1; 212) £90
- Londiniana. 1829. 4 vols. Cont. hf. vell., slightly soiled. (S. Oct.1; 512) £110
- - Anr. Copy. Hf. cf., gt., by Bayntun. (C. Nov.6; 201) *Bateman.* £55
- A Topographical History of Surrey. 1841. 5 vols. 4to. Lacks a few plts., some loosely inserted. Cont. hf. vell., bds. worn. (SKC. May 19; 439) £85
- - Anr. Edn. Ill.:– after T. Allom & others. 1850. 5 vols. 4to. Occasional minor spotting, sm. liby. blind-stp. on titles & last 2 pp. Cont. hf. mor. by Harrison. From the collection of Eric Sexton. (C. Apr.16; 223) *Traylen.* £150
- - Anr. Copy. Orig. cl. (C. May 20; 107) *Traylen.* £100
- - Anr. Copy. 4to. Some foxing, lacks 1 plt. from vol. 1 – Subjects in Fresco in St. John's Chapel. Orig. blind-stpd. cl., worn. (TA. Mar.19; 289) £62
- - Anr. Edn. Ed.:– Edward Walford. N.d 4 vols. 4to. Hf. mor. (MMB. Oct.8; 66) £175
- - Anr. Copy. 3 vols. Orig. cl. (SKC. Feb.26; 1630) £100
See–NASH, John & Brayley, Edward Wedlake
See–NEALE, John Preston & Brayley, Edward Wedlake

BRAYLEY, Edward Wedlake & Britton, John
- The Beauties of England & Wales. 1801-15. 1st. Edn. 18 vols. in 25. Without Brewers Introduction. Cont. cf., worn. (SH. Mar.5; 23) *Burden.* £260
- - Anr. Copy. 17 (of 18) vols. in 25 pts. Old cf., all bdgs. worn. W.a.f. (SG. Oct.30; 48) $480
- - Anr. Edn. 1801-16. 17 vols. in 24. Slight foxing & offsetting. Mor. gt., some covers detchd. (PL. Sep.18; 229) *Forbes.* £280
- - Anr. Edn. 1801-18. 25 vols., various, including Brewer's Introduction. Cont. hf. cf. W.a.f. (CSK. Mar.20; 127) £280
- - Anr. Copy. 18 vols. in 25 & Introduction, together 26 vols. Some browning & spotting. Cont. cf. gt., rebkd., worn, 1 cover detchd. W.a.f. (S. Jun.22; 8) *Burden.* £260
- - Anr. Copy. Vols. 1-9, 11-15 (each in 2 vols.) & 18, together 20 vols. With J. Norris Brewer's Introduction to the entire work. Old hf. leath., all bdgs. completely brkn. W.a.f. (SG. May 21; 333) $350
- - Anr. Edn. 1801-25. 18 vols. in 25. Cont. hf. cf., worn (SH. May 21; 14) *Kidd.* £160
- - Anr. Edn. 1807 etc. 25 vols. Orig. bdgs. (DWB. Mar.31; 133) £260
- Devonshire Illustrated. 1832. 4to. Some plts. spotted. Cont. mor.-bkd. cl. (SKC. Jul.28; 2525) £65
- Devonshire & Cornwall Illustrated. Ill.:– Allom & Bartlett. 1829-31. 2 vols. in 1. 4to. A few minor defects. Cont. hf. cf., slightly soiled. (SBA. Jul.14; 290) *Moorland.* £100
- - Anr. Edn. 1832. 2 vols. in 1. 4to. Some ll. spotted, 2 ll. torn & mntd. Mod. cl. (SH. Mar.5; 21) *Price.* £150
- - Anr. Copy. Some spotting thro.-out. Mod. hf-mor. W.a.f. (S. Sep.29; 147) *Postaprint.* £110
- - Anr. Copy. Spotted. Cont. hf. cf., worn. (SH May 21; 15) *Price* £80
- - Anr. Edn. Ill.:– after Allom & Bartlett. [1832]. 2 vols. in 1. 4to. 118 (only) engraved plts., some very minor defects. Cont. hf. mor. gt. (SBA. May 27; 358) *Temperley.* £105
- - Anr. Edn. 1833-31. 2 works in 1 vol. 4to. Hf. mor. gt., worn. (P. Sep.11; 196) *Hughes.* £160
- - Anr. Edn. Ed.:– Edward W. Brayley. 1837. 4to. Dampstains. Cover detchd. (P. Oct.2; 287) *Whatmore.* £130

BRAZER, C.W.
See–WATERHOUSE, N.E.–BRAZER, C.W.

BREASTED, James Henry
- The Edwin Smith Surgical Papyrus published in facsimile . . . with Translation. Chic., 1930. 1 vol.

text, 1 vol. facs. plts. 4to. & fo. Cl. (S. Jun.15; 121)
- - Anr. Copy. 1 vol. text, & atlas, together 2 vols. 2-tone buckram. From the Brooklyn Academy of Medicine. (SG. Jan.29; 71) $190

BRECHT, Berthold
- Die Drei Soldaten. Ill.:– Georg Grosz. Berlin, 1932. 1st. Edn. Sewed. (D. Dec.11-13; 1007) DM 600

BREDERODE, G.A.
- Alle de Wercken. Amst., 1638-37. 11 pts. in 1 vol. 4to. Upr. margins with slight staining, a few blank margins with light staining, a few annots. Cont. vell. (VG. Dec.17; 1228) Fls. 1,400

BREE, Charles Robert
- History of the Birds of Europe . . . 1859-63. 1st Edn. 4 vols. Some slight marginal spotting. Cont. hf. cf. (S. May 5; 98) *Cristani.* £380
- - Anr. Copy. Orig. cl. (CSK. Sep.19; 51) £280
- - Anr. Edn. L., 1860-63. 4 vols. 177 (of 238) hand-cold. plts., vols. 1 & 3 lack titles. hf. mor. As a collection of plts., w.a.f. (P. Jul.2; 13) *Weston.* £200
- - Anr. Copy. Vols. II, III & IV. A few plts. affected by damp. Cont. hf. cf., some wear. (TA. Jun.22; 431) £90
- - Anr. Edn. 1863. 4 vols. Cl., worn. (S. Dec.3; 905) *Westwood.* £230
- - Anr. Edn. 1863-64-63. 4 vols. Occasional light foxing. Recent hf. mor., gt. ornaments on spine, partly unc. (S. Jul.27; 280) *Midwest Galleries.* £280
- - Anr. Edn. 1866-67. 4 vols. A few ll. slightly spotted. Orig. cl., gt. spines, worn. (SH. Oct.9; 207) *Way.* £170
- - Anr. Copy. 3 vols. (of 4, lacks vol.3). Cont. mor., worn, spines gt. (SKC. Jul.28; 2400) £100
- - Anr. Edn. 1875-76. 2nd. Edn. 5 vols. Orig. cl., gt., spines worn. (S. Jan.26; 272) *Libris.* £420
- - Anr. Copy. Slight spotting. (S. Jun.1; 82) *Traylen.* £340
- - Anr. Copy. 4to. Apparently lacks 1 egg plt. in vol. I. Orig. pict. cl. (S. Dec.3; 906) *W. & W* £260

BREES, Samuel Charles
- Pictorial Illustration of New Zealand. L., n.d. 4to. Slight staining. Hf. mor. (P. Jul.30; 119) *Walford.* £150
- Railway Practice. A Collection of Working Plans & Practical Details of Construction in the Public Works of the Most Celebrated Engineers. 1837. 4to. Most plts. dampstained at corners, some foxing. Recent cf. (TA. Feb.19; 648) £80
- - Anr. Copy. Corners dampstained, some foxing. (TA. Mar.19; 408) £65

BREHM, Alfred Edmund
- Cassell's Book of Birds. Ed.:– Thomas Rymer Jones. L., ca. 1880. 4 vols. in 2. 4to. 37 (of 40) cold. lithos., text engs. Hf. mor., worn, loose. (SG. Sep.18; 77) $100
- Thierleben. Leipzig, 1882-84. 10 vols. 4to. Hf. mor. (P. Apr.9; 136) *Thomas* £65
- - Anr. Edn. Ed.:– Pechuel-Loesche. Leipzig – Wien, 1893-1900. 3rd. Edn. 10 vols. & index vol. Orig. hf. leath. & orig. linen (index). (D. Dec.11-13; 285) DM 500
- - Anr. Edn. Ed.:– O. zur Strassen. Leipzig, 1925-30. 4to. Orig. linen. (HK. Nov.18-21; 421) DM 520

BREITKOPF, J.G.I.
- Uber Bibliographie. Leipzig, 1793. 4to. Probably lacks 1 lf. (hf.-title?) Bds. (HK. Nov.18-21 3097) DM 480

BRELAGUE, Marquis de
- Memoirs & Adventures of Marquis de Brelague. Trans.:– William Erskine. 1743. 3 vols. Cf. gt. (P. Dec.11; 310) *Jarndyce.* £85

BREMNER, Benjamin
- Memories of Long Ago. – An Island Scrap Book, historical & traditional. Charlottetown, 1930; 1932. 2 vols. Orig. wraps. 1st. vol. sigd. (CB. May 27; 290) *Can.* $130

BRENCHLEY, Julius L.
- Jottings during the Cruise of H.M.S. Curacoa . . . L., 1873. 1st. Edn. Cl., worn, rehinged. Loosely inserted are 3 orig. photos. from which the text cuts were made. (SG. Oct.30; 64) $325
See–REMY, Jules & Brenchley, Julius

BRENTANO, Clemens
- **Der Goldfaden.** Ill.:– L.E. Grimm. Heidelberg, 1809. 1st. Edn. Cont. Style hf. leath. gt. (HK. May 15; 4114) DM 850
- **Victoria und Ihre Geschwister, mit Fliegenden Fahnen und Brennender Lunte.** Berlin; 1817. 1st. Edn. Heavily soiled in parts, mus., supps. soiled, 1 lf with sm. hole. Newer bds. (H. May 21/22; 1005) DM 460

BRERELEY, John 'Laurence Anderton'
- **The Lyturgie of the Masse.** [Birchley Hall, Lancs.], 1620. 4to. Lacks. prelim blank (?), title stained. Later cf.-bkd. bds. [STC 3607] (SBA. Oct.22; 382) McVey. £140
- **The Protestant's Apologie for the Roman Church.** [St. Omer], 1608. 2 pts. in 1 vol. 4to. Lacks blank before table of contents. Cont. cf. qt. [STC 3605] (SBA. Oct.22; 383) J. Webb. £60

BRES
- **Mythologie des Dames.** Paris, [1823]. 16mo. Cont. cf., decor. spine, lge. gt. fillet on covers & central lozenge in blind. (HD. Apr.8; 46) Frs. 1,100

BRESSANI, Francesco Giuseppe
- **Breve Relatione d'alcune Missioni ... della Compagnia de Giesu nella Nouva Francia.** Macerata, 1653. 1st. Edn. 4to. Recent mor. gt., gt. spine. [Sabin 7734] (CNY. Oct.1; 38) $1,600

BRETON, Lieut.
- **Excursions in New South Wales, Western Australia, & Van Dieman's Land.** L., 1834. 2nd. Edn. Several ll. slightly stained, occasional foxing. Early hf. cf. (KH. Nov.18; 123) Aus. $130

BRETON, André
- **Position Politique du Surréalisme.** Paris, [1935]. 1st. Edn. 12mo. Wraps. Inscr. to George Reavey. (SG. Jun.4; 472) $110
- **Second Manifeste du Surréalisme.** Ill.:– Salvador Dali. Paris, 1930. 1st. Edn., (60) numbered with triple frontis. 4to. 1 p. slightly soiled in margin. Bds. with orig. wraps on upr. & lr. cover. (D. Dec.11-13; 1010) DM 1,500

BRETON, André (Ed.)
See–SURREALISME EN 1947

BRETON, André & Legrand, Gerard
- **L'Art Magique.** Paris, 1957. (3,626) numbered. 4to. 1st. gathering loose. Orig. cl. (SH. Nov.20; 92) Tate Gallery. £50

BRETON DE LA MARTINIERE, Jean Baptiste Joseph
- **China: its Costume, Arts, Manufactures.** 1813; 1813; 1812; 1813. 'Mixed Edns'. 4 vols. Literary 'puff' on recto of G2 in vol. I, lacks hf.-titles, plt. & contents ll., & advt. lf. in vol. III, many ll. spotted. Cont. str.-grd. red mor., gt., spine gt. (S. Nov.4; 607) Grossmith. £95
- – Anr. Copy. 4 vols. Lacks hf.-titles, plt. & contents ll., & advt. lf. in vol. 3, spotted. (S. Mar.17; 377) A.G. Dorme £85
- – Anr. Edn. 1824. 4 vols. 12mo. Mod. bds., unc. (BS. Jun.11; 144) £130
- – Anr. Copy. Margins soiled, contents slightly loose. Orig. bds., crudely rebkd. (TA. Dec.18; 48) £90
- **La Chine en Miniature, ou Choix de Costumes, Arts et Metiers de cet Empire.** Paris, 1811. 4 vols. 16mo. Cont. marb. cf., spines decor. with repeated pagodas, inner dentelles, decor. covers. (HD. Apr.9; 413) Frs. 4,100
- – Anr. Copy. 16mo. cont. roan. (HD. Apr.9; 414) Frs. 2,500
- **L'Egypte et la Syrie, ou Moeurs, Usages, Costumes et Monuments des Egyptiens, des Arabes et des Syriens.** Paris, 1814. 6 vols. 16mo. Publisher's decor. paper bds., unc. (HD. Apr.9; 417) Frs. 2,000
- **L'Espagne et le Portugal, ou Moeurs, Usages et Costumes des Habitans de ces Royaumes.** Paris, 1815. 6 vols. 16mo. Cont. publisher's decor. paper bds., unc. (HD. Apr.9; 418) Frs. 3,800
- **Le Japon, ou Moeurs, Usages et Costumes des Habitans de cet Empire.** Paris, 1818. 4 vols. 16mo. Cont. bradel paper bds., unc. (HD. Apr.9; 423) Frs. 1,150
- **Les Marattes, ou Moeurs, Usages et Costumes de ce Peuple.** Trans.:– Thomas Duer Broughton. Paris, 1817. 2 vols. 16mo. Cont. cf., decor. covers, inner dentelle. (HD. Apr.9; 420) Frs. 1,400
- **La Russie, ou Moeurs, Usages et Costumes des Habitans des Provinces de cet Empire.** Paris, 1813. 6 vols. 16mo. Cont. Bozerian style red str.-grd.

mor., decor. spines, gt. decor. covers, inner dentelle, lge. border of roulettes between gt. fillets. (HD. Apr.9; 415) Frs. 8,300
- – Anr. Copy. Cont. cf. (HD. Apr.9; 416) Frs. 4,100
- **Tableau du Royaume de Caboul et de ses Dépendances dans la Perse, la Tartarie et l'Inde.** Trans.:– Mountstuart Elphinstone. Paris, 1817. 3 vols. 16mo. Cont. cf., spines decor., roulette decor. covers, inner dentelle. (HD. Apr.9; 422) Frs. 1,700

BRETT, A.B.
- **Catalogue of Greek Coins.** Boston, 1955-64. 2 vols. with supp. 4to. Orig. cl. & wraps. (SH. Mar.6; 322) Trade Art. £260

BRETTINGHAM, Mathew
- **The Plans, elevations & sections of Holkham in Norfolk.** 1761. 1st. Edn. Fo. Cont. cf.-bkd. bds., spine defect. (C. Feb.25; 175) Marlborough. £220

BREUER, Joseph
See–FREUD, Sigmund & Breuer, Joseph

BREVAL, John Durant
- **Remarks on Several Parts of Europe.** 1726 & 1738. 1st. & 2nd. Series. Together 4 vols. Fo. Some dampstaining to vol. II of 2nd. series. Cont. panel. cf. From the collection of Eric Sexton. (C. Apr.15; 29) Dawson. £220

BREVIARIES (Arranged chronologically irrespective of use)
- **Breviarium Cartusianum.** Venice, Andreas Torresanus, de Asula, May 5, 'M.CCC.iCi' [i.e. 1491]. 1st. Edn. of the Carthusian Breviary. Gt. & illuminated capitals & full floral borders on 6 pp., foliated in red by cont. hand, from the beginning of the Psalter to the end of the vol., lacks title-p. (verso blank) & final blank, title-lf. supplied in facs., 2nd. lf. rubbed, with marginal paper repair not touching text, lr. margin of final 3 ll. stained. 19th. C. crushed black mor. gt., by Rivière & Son. The copy of Richard Bennet, lately in the Pierpont Morgan Liby. [Goff B1134] (CNY. Apr.8; 191) $2,800
- **Breviarium Bambergense.** Bamberg, Johann Pfeyl, Nov.23, 1498 & Jan.24, 1499. 2 pts. in 2 vols. Spaces for some major capitals, supplied in blue, dampstaining to fore-margins of some quires at beginning & end of vol. 1, 1st. 8 & final 13 ll. frayed at fore-margins, not affecting letterpress, wormhole to margin of final 2 ll. in vol. 2, light soiling & traces of use. Cont. blind-stpd. cf. over bevelled wood bds., worn & reprd., lacks clasps & bosses, end-papers with cont. MS. prayers, including at front of vol. 1 a series of prayers 'Pro Peste'. Inscrs. of Andreas Rochomerius Norimbergensis & Bernardus Pfost(?), lately in the collection of Eric Sexton. [BMC I, 176, Goff B1148, H 3799] (CNY. Apr.8; 17) $6,800
- **Breviarum Chorum Patuiensis Ecclesie ...** Venice, 1508. 12mo. 18th. C. vell.-bkd. bds. (S. Jun.23; 221) Quaritch. £190
- **Breviarum secundum ... Ecclesie Parisiensis ...** 1529. Cont. decor. cf. (HD. Jun.30; 10) Frs. 1,000
- **Portifiorum seu Breviarium, ad Insignis Sariburiensis Ecclesiae Usum.** 1556. 2 vols. in 1. 4to. Lacks P4, short tear in R3 affecting text, other short tears, slight browning. 18th C. cf., covers detchd., lacks spine. [NSTC 15842] (S. May 5; 283) Thomas. £100
- **Breviarum Romanum.** Venice, Jun. 1560. 16mo. Mor., blind fillet border, Charles Louis de Bourbon arms & crowned cyphers at angles & spine, inner dentelle, by Lortic. From Duc Robert de Parme liby. (HD. Jun.10; 15) Frs. 5,500
- **Breuiarium vna cum Psalterio.** Tegernsee, 1576. 2 vols. Fo. Slightly browned in parts & slightly stained, worm. Cont. pig-bkd. wood bds., blind-tooled, slightly worn & soiled, lacks bosses & clasps. Charles Louis de Bourbon Exlibris in cover. (H. Dec.9/10; 1335) DM 2,200
- **Breviarium Romanum ex Decreto Sacrosancti Concilii Tridentini Restitutum. Pii V. Pont. Max. Iussu Editum.** Venice, 1584. Lacks 5 ll., including 3 with lge. woodcut, 1 repeated, stained at end, slight worming. Late Renaissance / late 16th. C. leath., probably Italian, rich gt. spine, clasps brkn., narrow double gold fillet decor. border, arabesque decor., oval centrepiece with monog., spine reprd. at head & foot, end-papers renewed, recased, 4 raised bands. (R. Oct.14-18; 51) DM 580

- **Breviarium Romanum ...** Antw., 1764. 4 vols. Cont. cf., spines decor. with raised bands, s.-c. (HD. Feb.27; 18) Frs. 1,700

BREWSTER, David
- **Treatise on New Philosophical Instruments for Various Purposes in the Arts & Sciences. With Experiments on Light & Colours.** Edinb., 1813. 1st. Edn. A few ll. slightly spotted, lacks hf.-title, owner's inscr. on title. 19th. C. hf. cf. (S. Dec.2; 693) Quaritch. £100

BREWSTER, John
- **The Parochial History & Antiquities of Stockton-upon-Tees.** Stockton. 1796. 4to. Compl. with advt. & errata, slight stain on frontis. Mod. hf. cf. (TW. Sep.19; 52) £50

BREYDENBACH, Bernhard von
- **Peregrinatio in Terram Sanctam.** Mainz, Erhard Reuwich, 11 Feb. 1486. 1st. Edn. Fo. Ornamental woodcut initials on folios 2r & 4v, spaces for capital initials elsewhere, the capitals supplied in alternating red & blue, rubricated, lacks final blank, cleaned thro.-out with some ll. resized, folding maps with some restoration, including some repair. tears & facs. work. Blind-stpd. & ruled mor., spine gt.-lettered, by Rivière, doubls. of early 19th. C. str.-grd. mor. with gt. crest of the Rt. Hon. Francis Henry Egerton. Bkplt. of Lucius Wilmerding, lately in the collection of Eric Sexton. [BMC I, 43, Goff B1189, HC 3596*] (CNY. Apr.8; 95) $17,000
- – Anr. Copy. Lacks 1st. lf. with woodcut, last blank, 8 ll. of 4 of panoramas & 4 ll. with views of Parenza & Corfu, lacks hand-cold. woodcut, f.a6 reprd., panorama reprd., some old marginalia. 18th. C. red mor., triple gt. fillet, spine gt. in compartments, inner gt. dentelles. Lord Egerton of Tatton copy. (SM. Oct.7; 1617) Frs. 17,000
- – Anr. Edn. Speier, Peter Drach, 29 Jul. 1490. Fo. 83 ll. (of 120, lacks ll. in most signatures), double-p. woodcut view of Corfu defect. at fold, stained thro.-out, many woodcuts lacking or torn. Hf. cf., bds. defect. at lr. outside corner. W.a.f. [Goff B 1190] (C. Apr.1; 17) Valmadonna Trust. £170

BREYN, Jacob
- **Prodromi Fasciculi Rariorum Plantarum primus et secundus.** Danzig, 1739. 4to. Cont. cf., ducal cypher & arms on sides, rebkd., corners worn. From Chetham's Liby., Manchester. (C. Nov.26; 56) Potter. £320
- **Prodromus Fasciculi Rariorum Plantarum Secundus.–Prodromus Fasciculi Rariorum Platarum anno 1679 in hortis ...** Danzig, 1689; 1680. 2 works in 1 vol. 4to. 19th. C. hf. mor. Owner's inscr. of Robert Gray on 1st. title, lately in Chetham's Liby. (C. Nov.26; 54) Quaritch. £380

BREYN, Jacob & Rhyne, W. ten
- **Exoticarum Plantarum Centuria Prima.** Ill.:– Isaac Saal after Andreas Stech. Danzig, 1678. 1st. Edn. Fo. Occasional minor spotting & slight discolouration, sm. liby. stps. thro.-out. 19th. C. hf. mor. From Chetham's Liby., Manchester. (C. Nov.26; 55) Potter. £750

BREZE, Argenterio, Marquis de
[–] **Essais sur Les Haras.** Turin, 1769. Cf. gt. (P. Apr.30; 323) Henderson. £65

BREZE, Jacques de
[–] **Le Livre de la Chasse du Grand Seneschal de Normandye.** Paris, 1858. (10) on 'papier de couleur'. Cont. red mor., slightly stained, party unc. C.F.G.R. Schwerdt's copy; bkplts. of Comte de Beaufort & Joseph Nouvellet. (S. Jun.9; 64) Maggs. £55

BRICKER, Charles
- **A History of Cartography.** Ed.:– R.V. Tooley, & Gerald R. Crone (preface). L., [1969]. Tall fo. Cl., d.-w. (SG. Mar.26; 438) $100
See–TOOLEY, Ronald Vere & Bricker, Charles

BRIDGENS, Richard
- **Costumes of Italy, Switzerland & France.** 1821. 4to. Hf. mor. gt. (P. Feb.19; 159) Thorp. £210
- **Furniture with Candelabra & Interior Decoration.** 1838. Fo. Mod. qtr. leath., unc. (S. Mar.17; 400) Traylen. £450

BRIDGES, John
- **The History & Antiquities of Northamptonshire.** Ill.:– G. Vertue after G. Kneller (frontis. port.). Oxford, 1791. 2 vols. Fo. Occasional minor foxing. Cont. mott. cf., gt. panel. spines, inner dentelles,

by Rivière. From the collection of Eric Sexton. (C. Apr.16; 224) *Old Hall.* £220

BRIDGES, Robert
- **Eros & Psyche.** Ill.:– after Burne-Jones. Gregy. Pr., 1935. 4to. Orig. pig, spotted, s.-c. (SH. Jul.23; 6) *Schrire.* £210
- – **Anr. Copy.** Orig. pig. gt., s.-c. (SH. Feb.20; 213) *George's.* £150
- **Lord Kitchener.** [L.], [June 14, 1916]. 1st. Separate Edn., (20). 4to. Wraps. (SG. Jun.4; 54) $100

BRIDGEWATER Treatises
1833-40. 13 vols. only. Cont. cf. (SH. May 28; 11) *Walford.* £60

BRIEL, Yehuda Ben Elieser
- **Shefer Klalei Ha'dikduk.** Mantua, 1724. 1st. Edn. Title reprd. without loss, worming, slightly stained. Wraps., worn. (SPB. May 11; 64) $500

BRIERRE DE BOISMONT, A.
- **Des Hallucinations ou histoire raisonnée des Apparitions, des Visions, des Songes, de l'extase, du Magnetisme et du Somnambulisme.** Paris, 1845. 1st. Edn. Mod. cl.-bkd. marb. bds. (S. Oct.21; 369) *Maggs.* £55

BRIGGS, Henry
- **Arithmetica Logarithmica.** 1624. 1st. Edn. Fo. With additional 6 ll. of logarithmic numbers over 100,000 inserted at end. Cont. cf., armorial gt.-stp. in laurel wreath on sides, rubbed, rebkd. From Chetham's Liby., Manchester. [STC 3739] (C. Nov.26; 57) *Rota.* £600
- **Arithmetique Logaritmetique ou la Construction et Usage d'une Table contenant les Logarithmes de tous les Nombres depuis l'Unité jusques à 100000 . . .** Trans.:– Adriaen Vlacq. Gouda, 1628. 1st. Edn. in Fr. Fo. Some browning & marginal staining, short tear in errata lf., rust-hole in S1, wormhole in 3R3-4, a few ll. sprung. Wraps., worn & soiled, hf. red mor. case. From Honeyman Collection. (S. May 20; 3190) *Whitehart.* £50

BRIGGS, Martin Shaw
- **Muhammadan architecture in Egypt & Palestine.** Oxford, 1924. 4to. Orig. cl. (CB. May 27; 46) *Can.* $190

BRIGGS, Richard
- **English Art of Cookery.** 1788. Cf. gt. (P. Sep.11; 62) *Grove.* £140

BRIGHT, J.S.
- **A History of Dorking . . . - The History of Guildford . . .** Dorking & L.; Guildford, 1884; 1801. Together 2 vols. 1st work: engraved frontis. port., plts., folding map & table, table torn; 2nd. work: hf.-title, engraved plt., folding hand-cold. MS. plan, MS. additions, plt. inverted. 1st work: cont. gt.-panel. cf., spine gt.; 2nd. work: orig. paper-bkd. bds., unc., pieces lacking from spine. (C. Jul.15; 19) *Traylen.* £60

BRIGHT, Dr. Richard
- **Reports of Medical Cases, selected with a View of Illustrating the Symptoms & Cure of Diseases by a reference to Morbid Anatomy.** 1827-31. 1st. Edn. 2 vols. in 3. 4to. Dupl. hf.-title in vol. II. Pt.1 orig. bds., unc., hf. cf. 1 & 3 rebkd., labels worn, label on vol. 2 new. From Dr. Gilpin's liby. (S. Jun.15; 122) *Norman.* £4,600
- **Travels from Vienna through Lower Hungary.** 1818. 4to. Cf. gt. (P. Oct.23; 6) *Brooke-Hitching.* £95

BRIGHT, Timothy
- **A Treatise of Melancholy.** 1586. 1st. Edn., 2nd. Iss.(?). Some stains to text. 19th. C. hf. mor. gt. [STC 3748] (C. Nov.20; 227) *Clarke.* £480

BRIGHTON Grammar School
- **Annual Entertainment at the Dome, containing the Comic Opera 'The Play of the Pied Piper'. - Past & Present, the Magazine of the Brighton Grammar School.** Ill.:– Aubrey Beardsley. Brighton, 1888; 1889. 2 works in 1 vol., 2nd. work vol. 14. Cl., orig. wraps. bnd. in. (S. Jul.31; 180) *Sawyer.* £140

BRIK, O.M.
- **Ne poputchitsa (Not a Fellow-traveller).** Moscow & Petrograd, 1923. (3,000). Orig. wraps. by Alavinsky, unopened. (SH. Feb.6; 301) *Lempert.* £65

BRILLAT-SAVARIN, Jean Anselme
- **Physiologie du Goût.** Ill.:– Bertall. Paris, [1848]. 1st. Edn. ill. by Bertall. Some ll. soiled at beginning,

endpaper oxidized. Cont. hf. leath gt. (HK. May 12-14, 1027) DM 600
- – **Anr. Edn.** Ed.:– Ch. Monselet. Ill.:– Lalauze. 1879. (210) on L.P., (170) on Holland paper. 2 vols. Hf. chagrin, corner, cover lacks backs., unc. (HD. Feb.18; 105) *Frs.* 1,600
- – **Anr. Edn.** Ill.:– Charles Huard. Paris, 1930. (30) on Jap. with orig. watercolour & separate sets of ills. 2 vols. 4to. Sewed, publisher's s.-c. (HD. Dec.5; 28) *Frs.* 1,500

BRINDLEY, J.
- **Theatre of the Present War in the Netherlands & upon the Rhine.** 1745. 2 pts. in 1 vol. Sm. hole in title. Cont. cf. gt. (P. Dec.11; 269) *Traylen.* £70

BRINE, Frederic
See–COLBORNE, John & Brine, Frederic

BRINKLEY, Capt. Frank
- **Japan.** Boston, [1897]. Orient Edn., (500) numbered. 10 vols. Fo. Ptd. prospectus for De Luxe Edn. Ea. vol. in different patterned cl., laced, bnd. in Japanese manner, in 2 orig. bd. boxes, soiled & worn, ex-liby. (SG. Apr.23; 112) $275
- – **Anr. Edn.** [1897-98]. In 14 (of 15) orig. pts., lacks pt. 1. Fo. Pict. wraps., cl. spines. (SG. Dec.4; 191) $160
- **Oriental Series: Japan & China.** Boston & Tokyo, [1901-02]. On Japan vell. 15 vols. Orig. watercolour paintings on silk, sigd., on upr. & lr. blanks of each vol., extra-ill. with ca. 250 ills., many orig. watercolour drawings on silk, many photographic plts., many orig. watercolour marginal decors. & scenes. Elab. mor. gt., gt. panels. with decors., mor. gt. inlays surrounding panels, mor. gt. doubls., silk endpapers. (SPB. May 6; 292) $7,500
- – **Anr. Edn.** Boston & Tokyo, [1901-02]. Artists' Edn., (500) numbered. 12 vols. Three-qtr. mor., bdgs. dried & brkn. (SG. Jul.9; 55) $110
- – **Anr. Edn.** Boston & Tokyo, [1901-02]. Satsuma Edn., (500) numbered. 12 vols. Three-qtr. mor., gt. & red floral design, unc. & mostly unopened. (SG. Mar.12; 40) $160
- – **Anr. Edn.** L. & Edinb., 1903-04. De Luxe Edn., (35) numbered on Japan vell. 12 vols. 4to. Buckram gt. (SBA. May 27; 453) *Quaritch.* £280

BRINLEY, George
- **Catalogue of [his] American Library.** Hartford, 1878-93. Pts. I-V (compl.) & Fletcher's index, all bnd. in 1 vol. 4to. Priced thro.-out. Cont. three-qtr. mor., worn, orig. wraps. bnd. in. (SG. Jan.22; 74) $140
- – **Anr. Edn.** Hartford, Conn., [1878-97]. 6 vols. in 5. Index bnd. in vol. I, prices realized in each vol. Orig. wraps., unc. & unopened. (CB. Nov.12; 127) *Can.* $130

BRINSLEY, John
- **Ludus Literarius.** 1612. 1st. Edn. 4to. Lacks sm. portion of margin of title affecting 1 word, slight staining towards end. 19th. C. cf. [STC 3768] (C. Nov.20; 228) *Money.* £220

BRION de la Tour, Louis, the Elder
- **Atlas Portatif d'Italie.** Venice, 1783. Fo. Slightly stained thro.-out. Cont. paper bds. From the collection of John A. Saks. (C. Jun.10; 11) *Romano.* £55

BRIQUET, Charles-Moïse
- **Les Filigranes.** Leipzig, 1923. 2nd. Edn. 4 vols. Fo. Orig. linen-bkd. bds. (SM. Oct.7; 1332) *Frs.* 2,000

BRISSON, Mathurin Jacques
- **Ornithologia.** Ill.:– Martinet. Paris, 1760. 1st. Edn. 6 vols., including supp. bnd. at end of vol. 6. 4to. Some plts. slightly discold. Cont. cf., rebkd. From Chetham's Liby., Manchester. (C. Nov.26; 58) *Lange.* £500

BRISSOT de Warville, Jacques-Pierre
- **New Travels in the United States of America . . .** L., 1794. 2nd. Edn. 2 vols. Cont. pol. cf., end-papers slightly browned. [Sabin 8027] (CB. Apr.1; 130) *Can.* $200

BRISTED, John
- **The Resources of the United States of America.** N.Y., 1818. 1st. Edn. Slight foxing. Orig. bds., spine & label slightly worn, largely unopened. From liby. of William E. Wilson. [Sabin 8050] (SPB. Apr.29; 32) $100

BRISTOL & Gloucestershire Archaeological Society
- **Transactions.** 1876-1944. Vols. 1-65, 8 extra vols. & 4 index vols. All except for 12 bnd. in orig. cl., rest in ptd. wraps. As a periodical, w.a.f. From the collection of Eric Sexton. (C. Apr.16; 225) *Koffler.* £120

BRITANNIA DELINEATA
1822. Fo. Title lightly foxed. Cont. hf. cf. (C. Nov.6; 289) *Cumming.* £160
- – **Anr. Edn.** Ill.:– W. Westall, Charles Hullmandel & J.D. Harding. 1822-23. Fo. Cont. hf. mor. (C. May 20; 108) *Marlborough.* £420

BRITANNICUS, Johannes
- **In Persii Satiras Commentarii.** Brescia, Gabriele [di Pietro] Tarsivinus, Nov. 14, 1481. 1st. Edn. Fo. 4-line capital initial C on 1st. p. of text in gold on blue ground, with purple, green & penwork ornament, in lr. margin a laurel wreath enclosing coat-of-arms in cols. & silver, spaces for other capital initials mostly with guide letters, A1 & 2 detchd., slight marginal tear in h6, final blank lf. pasted down at end, slight worming, cont. coat-of-arms on fo. 2. Cont. Italian blind-stpd. sheep over wood bds., central panel of 3 connected knotwork lozenges in plain frame except for flower tool repeated 8 times, surrounded by broad border of continuous knotwork pattern, rebkd. & worn, lacks clasps. From the collection of Eric Sexton. [BMC VII, 966, Goff B1213, HC 12729] (CNY. Apr.8; 29) $5,000

BRITISH BIRDS
Ed.:– Harry Forbes Witherby. 1907-64. Vols. 1-57 (lacks vols. 35 & 49) together 55 vols. Buckram. (C. May 20; 256) *Langmead.* £300

BRITISH BUTTERFLIES
Ca. 1820-30. 4to. 28 prints, each with several insects amid flowers, latter in watercolours, with MS. text, several ll. wtrmkd. 1817. Recent hf. mor. (S. Dec.3; 909) *Broseghini.* £300

BRITISH COLUMBIA
- **Reports of the Provincial Museum of Natural History, for 1914 through 1955.** Victoria, 1915-1956. 3 vols. Bnd. in is Guide to Anthropological Collection, 1909. Buckram. (SG. Mar.5; 54) $100

BRITISH Essaists, The
Ed.:– Alexander Chalmers. 1803. 45 vols. 12mo. Some ll. spotted. Later hf. cf. (SD. Feb.4; 98) £100
- – **Anr. Edn.** Ed.:– J. Ferguson. 1819. 44 vols. (of 45). Cf. gt. (BS. May 13; 239) £80
- – **Anr. Edn.** Ed.:– Alex. Chalmers. Boston, 1855-1857. 38 vols. 16mo. Ex-liby., with bkplt. & sm. stp. on title of each vol. Hf. cf., spines gt. (SG. Aug.7; 272) $160

BRITISH GALLERY OF PICTURES, Selected from the Most Admired Productions of the Old Masters, in Great Britain
1818. 4to. Orig. hf. mor. gt. (TA. Oct.16; 109) £90

BRITISH GAZETTE
Ed.:– Winston S. Churchill. 1926. Nos. 1-8 (all publd.). With 19 duplicates etc. of all issues except no. 1. Loose as iss. (S. May 5; 400) *Rawlings.* £50

BRITISH HUNTS & HUNTSMEN
1910. 3 vols. Hf. cf. & cl. (HSS. Apr.24; 203) £62

BRITISH INSECTS
N.d. Cont. cf.-bkd. marb. bds., slightly soiled, spine worn. (CSK. Nov.7; 35) £65

BRITISH ISLES depicted by pen & camera, The
Ca. 1910. 5 vols. Cl. (HSS. Apr. 24; 249) £60

BRITISH MILITARY LIBRARY
Oct. 1798-Mar. 1801. 2 vols. 4to. Lacks a few plts. & ll. Cl., soiled. W.a.f. (SKC. Feb.26; 1421) £200
- – **Anr. Copy.** 3 plts. torn. Hf. cf., spines gt. (CNY. May 22; 155) $600

BRITISH MUSEUM
- **Catalogue of the Birds in the British Museum.** 1883-86. Vols. 7, 8, 10 & 11 only. Orig. cl. (P. Apr.9; 204) *Dartmoor.* £65
- **Catalogue of Books printed in the XVth Century now in the British Museum.** L., 1908-1930. Pts. 1-6 only, 6 vols. Fo. Linen-bkd. ptd. bds, some soiling. (SG. Oct.2; 190) $190

BRITISH MUSEUM -contd.
- **Catalogue of the Harleian Collection of Manuscripts.** 1769. 2 vols. Fo. Later cf. (SH. Oct.9; 44) *Symonds.* £60
- **– Anr. Edn.** 1808-12. 4 vols. Fo. Some foxing, margins untrimmed. Cont. bds., soiled. (TA. Oct.16; 106) £56
- **A Catalogue of the Works of Linnaeus preserved in the British Museum.** L., 1933. 2nd. Edn. 4to. Cl. shelf number on spine. (SG. Jan.22; 245) $100

BRITISH NEW GUINEA
- **Report for the Year 1887 (4th. Sept. 1888-30th. June 1891; 1st. July 1892-30th. June 1893).** Brisbane, 1888-94. 5 blue-books in 1 vol. Fo. 29 plts. & maps (of 30), a few torn, some ll. slightly spotted or browned. Cont. hf. cf. (SH. Nov.7; 455) *Cawthorn.* £65

BRITISH NOVELISTS (The)
1810-20. 50 vols. Most vols. with some spotting. Cont. hf. cf., spines gt. (SKC. May 19; 283) £240

BRITISH NUMISMATIC JOURNAL
1905-61. 1st. Series, 10 vols.; 2nd. Series, 10 vols.; 3rd. Series, vol. 4, pts. 1-3, vol. 5-6, vol. 7, pt. 2, vol. 8-10 only, together in 33 vols. 4to. & 8vo. Cont. cl. & orig. wraps. (SH. Mar.6; 323) *Spink.* £440

BRITISH POETS (The)
See–POETS

BRITISH TAX REVIEW & Indices
1956-79; 1956-75. 24 pts.; 2 pts. Cl. (CE. Feb.19; 29) £50

BRITO, Bernardo Gomez de
- **Monarchia Lusytana.** Lisbon, 1690. 1st. Pt. Fo. A few ll. browned or spotted, sm. liby. stp. partly erased from title. Cont. cf., spine wormed. (SPB. May 5; 118) $150

BRITTANY
- **Recueil des Arrests de Règlement du Parlement de Bretagne ...** Rennes, 1769. New Edn. Cont. spr. cf. (HD. Jun.29; 165) *Frs.* 1,600

BRITTEN, Frederick James
- **Old Clocks & Watches & their Makers.** [1932]. 6th. Edn. Orig. cl. (CSK. Sep.5; 79) £60
- **– Anr. Copy.** (S.H. Mar.6; 495) *Laskaris.* £55
- **Old English Clocks [The Wetherfield Collection].** 1907. (320). Fo. Cl. (PD. Oct.22; 20) £70

BRITTON, John
- **Architectural Antiquities of Great Britain.** 1806-26. 5 vols. 4to. Some spotting. Cont. hf. mor. (CSK. Nov.21; 178) £65
- **– Anr. Edn.** 1835. [2nd. Edn.?]. 5 vols. 4to. Hf. mor., worn. (BS. May 13; 244) £60
- **– Anr. Copy.** Cont. hf. mor. & marb. bds. (CB. May 27; 49) *Can.* $320
- **Architectural Antiquities of Great Britain.** –**Cathedral Antiquities.** 1835; 1836. 5 vols.; 5 vols. 4to. Spotted & offset in pts., some ll. & plts. loose. Cont. hf. roan, spines gt., worn. (S. Jan.27; 474) *Dunn.* £120
- **Bath & Bristol, with the Counties of Somerset & Gloucester.** Ill.:– after Thomas Hosmer Shepherd. 1829. 4to. A few margins reprd., some discolouration. Orig. hf. cf. (TA. Dec.18; 353) £120
- **The Beauties of Wiltshire.** 1801-25. 3 vols. Occasional minor spotting. Cont. red str.-grd. mor., gt. From the collection of Eric Sexton. (C. Apr.16; 226) *Heraldry Today.* £85
- **Cathedral Antiquities.** 1836. 5 vols. 4to. Some plts. slightly spotted, liby. stp. on some pp. & verso of plts. Cont. hf. mor., gt. spines. (SH. Mar.5; 22) *Crowe.* £60
- **The History & Antiquities of the Cathedral Church of Salisbury.** L., Priv. ptd., 1814. 1st. Edn. 4to. Dampstain in lr. margin of 1st. & last few ll. Orig. bds., lacks backstrip, unc. (CB. May 27; 234) *Can.* $110
- **History & Antiquities of the Cathedral Church of Salisbury, [Winchester, York, Lichfield, Canterbury, Oxford, Wells, Exeter, Peterborough, Gloucester, Bristol, Hereford & Worcester].** Ill.:– After Mackenzie, Le Keux, Clarke & others. 1814-35. 13 vols. 4to. Some spotting & offsetting, mostly in margins of plts. Cont. pol. cf., spines ornately gt., gt. border round sides. (S. Nov.4; 540) *Schuster.* £100
- **– Anr. Copy.** Together 14 vols. in 5. Fo. Occasional offsetting. Cont. mor. gt., gt. spines, covers with lge. central gothic cathedral stps. & gt. borders, gt. spines, by Hering, jnts. & extremities worn. (CNY. Oct.1; 4) $1,200

- **Picturesque Views of the English Cities.** 1828. 4to. Some plts. spotted. Cont. hf. mor. (SH. Apr.9; 138) *Nolan.* £140
- **– Anr. Edn.** 1830. 4to. Some spotting, a few ll. detchd. Orig. cl., worn. (CSK. Oct.31; 209) £150
- **– Anr. Edn.** Ill.:– W.H. Bartlett. L., 1836. 4to. Sm. liby. stp. Disbnd. (SG. Oct.30; 41) $190
- **[–] The Pleasures of Human Life.** Ill.:– Thomas Rowlandson. L., 1807. 1st. Edn. Frontis.'s reset. Orig. 2-tone bds., back & edges worn, bkplt. (PNY. May 21; 363) $100
- *See*–BRAYLEY, Edward W. & Britton, John
- *See*–GODWIN, George & Britton, John

BRITTON, John & Pugin, Augustus Welby
- **Illustrations of the Public Buildings of London.** L., Priv. ptd., 1825-28. 2 vols., no Supp. Plts. foxed. Mod. hf. cf. & marb. bds. (CB. May 27; 50) *Can.* $170

BRITTON, John, Bp. of Hereford
- **[On the Laws of England].** [1540]. 1st. Edn. Marginal annots. in several 16th. C. hands. Cont. cf., covers with roll-tooled panels, spine reprd., lacks ties, 4 end-ll. from Pynson's 1502 Processional. [STC 3803] (C. Nov.20; 229) *Bennett.* £620

BRITTON, Nathaniel Lord & Rose, J.N.
- The Cactaceae. 1937. 4 vols. 4to. Orig. buckram gt. (PL. Sep.18; 191) *Chilton.* £90

BRIUIN, Ui
- **Ui Briuin na h Eirann. The White Wild Flame.** Cuala Pr., 1937. (10). Orig. linen-bkd. bds., unc. (S. Jul.22; 84) *Quaritch.* £170

BROADBENT, Rev. S.
- **A Narrative of the First Introduction of Christianity amongst the Barolong Tribe of Bechuanas South Africa ...** L., 1865. Orig. cl. (SSA. Jan.22; 172) *R.* 90

BROCKEDON, William
- **Illustrations of the Passes of the Alps.** 1828. Vol. 1 only. 4to. Spotting. Cont. cf., upr. cover detchd., lacks spine. (CSK. Jan.30; 78) £120
- **– Anr. Edn.** 1828-29. [1st. Edn?]. 2 vols. 4to. Sm. marginal blind-stps. 7 stains. Cl., 1 spine reprd. (SH. Jul.9; 7) *Wilson.* £190
- **– Anr. Copy.** 2 vols. 4to. Pol. cf. gt. (C. Jul.15; 123) *Marks.* £280
- **– Anr. Copy.** Cont. mor., gt. (C. Mar.18; 25) *Mediolanum.* £220
- **– Anr. Copy.** Cont. mor., gt. spine & inner & outer dentelle. (HK. Nov.18-21; 987) DM 1,400
- **– Anr. Copy.** All steel engrs. with publisher's dry stp., lightly browned & soiled in parts, vol. 2 more heavily browned. New hf. leath. (H. May 21/22; 390) DM 900
- **– Anr. Edn.** L., [1828-29]. 2 vols. 4to. Soiled. Cont. hf. leath. (R. Oct.14-18; 1997) DM 1,000
- **– Anr. Edn.** 1838. 2 vols. 4to. Many ll. becoming loose in gutta-percha bdg. Cont. hf. mor. (C. Mar.18; 159) *Ediston.* £240
- **Italy.** Ca. 1847. Fo. Cont. hf. mor., rebkd. (C. Jul.15; 20) *Dallai.* £300
- **– Anr. Edn.** N.d. Fo. Title & 53 plts. on india paper, occasional light soiling. Later red mor., elab. gt. (CSK. Nov.14; 122) £260
- **– Anr. Copy.** 1 plt. detchd., a few spotted. Cont. hf. mor. W.a.f. (CSK. Oct.24; 192) £110

BROCKHAUS, A.
- **Netsuke.** Leipzig, 1905. 4to. Orig. cf., worn. (SH. Jan.29; 213) *Eskenazi.* £300
- **– Anr. Edn.** Leipzig, 1909. 2nd. Edn. Orig. mor., gt. (VG. Dec.15; 123) *Fls.* 2,400

BROCKHAUS, F.A.
- **Allgemeine Deutsche Real-Encyclopädie für die Gebildeten Stände.** Leipzig, 1820-29. 5th. Edn. 12 vols. in 14 & 2 supp. vols., together in 16 vols. Vols. 11 & 12 also called New Series Vols. 1 & 2. Not collated, slightly stained, supp. vol. 2 very stained. Cont. hf. leath. (R. Oct.14-18; 494) DM 950
- **– Anr. Edn.** Leipzig, 1827. Slightly soiled in parts, not collated. Cont. leath., spine defect. (R. Oct.14-18; 495) DM 600
- **Bilder-Atlas: Ikonographische Encyklopaedie der Wissenschaften und Kuenste.** Leipzig, ca. 1880. 8 vols. Ob. fo. Qtr. mor. (SG. May 21; 335) $325
- **Conversations-Lexikon der Neuesten Zeit und Literatur.** Leipzig, 1833-39. 13 vols. Not collated. Cont. hf. linen. (R. Oct.14-18; 497) DM 950
- **– Anr. Edn.** Berlin, Leipzig, 1843-44. 4 vols. Not collated. Cont. leath. (R. Oct.14-18; 496) DM 200

- **– Anr. Edn.** Leipzig, 1898. Jubiläums Edn. 17 vols. Not collated. Orig. hf. leath. (R. Oct.14-18; 501) DM 600
- **Die Gegenwart.** Leipzig, 1848-56. 12 vols. Not collated. Cont. hf. leath., gt. spine, 4 spines defect., 1 upr. cover loose, 2 vols. not uniform. (R. Oct.14-18; 498) DM 550

BRODIE, B.C.
- **Pathological & Surgical Observations on Disease of the Joints.** 1818. 1st. Edn. New hf. cf. Pres. copy. (BS. Feb.25; 333) £55

BRODRICK, William
See–SALVIN, Francis Henry & Brodrick, William

BROGLIE, Charles François, Comte de
- **Histoire Plaisante et Singulière d'un Arrière-petit Fils d'Oui-Dire, surnommé Imbroglio.** Paris, 1779. 20 pieces. 4to. 5 pieces in cont. MS., ptd. piece mntd., loosely inserted note in cont. hand. Cont. red mor., fleuron, gt., in each corner, triple fillet, spine gt. in compartments, inner gt. floral dentelles. (SM. Oct.7; 1618) *Frs.* 1,800

BROINOWSKI, Gracius J.
- **Cockatoos & Nestors of Australia & New Zealand.** 1888. Vol. 3 only. 4to. Mor. gt. (P. Sep.11; 20) *Arnold.* £500
- **– Anr. Copy.** Fo. Sm. ink stain on plt. 19. Publisher's gt.-decor. mor., some sm. defects. Inscr. on title-p. (KH. Mar.24; 76) *Aus.* $2,400

BROMFIELD, William
- **Chirurgical Observations & Cases.** 1773. 2 vols. Hf.-title in vol. II only (? not called for in vol. I), liby. stps. Cont. cf. (S. Jun.15; 126) *Joslen.* £70

BROMHALL, Thomas–FIELDING, Henry
- **A Treatise of Specters.–An Enquiry into the Causes of the late Increase of Robbers etc.** L., 1658; 1751. 1st. Edn.; 1st. Edn. 2 vols. in 1. Some soiling, repairs, gathering A in 1st. vol. has 3 ll. only, foxed. Old cf., very worn, covers detchd. [Wing B4886] (SPB. Nov.25; 72) $175

BROMLEY, George W. & Walter S.
- **Atlas of Westchester County.** Phila., 1907. Atlas fo. All double-p. maps linen-mntd., extra-ill. with some 25 plans, prospectuses, etc. Orig. bdg. (SG. Jun.11; 307) $275

BROMME, Traugott
- **Illustrirter Hand-Atlas der Geographie und Statistik.** Stuttgart, 1862. Fo. Slightly soiled, especially 1st. & last ll. heavily, lacks flag plt. Cont. hf. leath. (R. Oct.14-18; 2069) DM 2,500

BROMMY, R. & Littrow, H. von
- **Die Marine.** Vienna, 1878. 3rd. Edn. Some ll. slightly soiled. Orig. linen. (H. Dec.9/10; 476) DM 420

BRONTE, Anne 'Acton Bell'
- **[–] The Tenant of Wildfell Hall.** 1848. 3 vols. 12mo. Minor marginal staining & foxing. Mod. hf. cf. (C. Feb.4; 3) *Traylen.* £240

BRONTE, Charlotte 'Currer Bell'
- **Jane Eyre.** L., 1847. 1st. Edn. 3 vols. 32 p. publisher's catalogue at end of vol. I, without the preceding fly-title dtd. Jun. 1847 & following 1 p. advt. Orig. blind-stpd. cl., covers discold., head & foot of spines strengthened, qtr. mor. gt. folding box. From the Prescott Collection. (CNY. Feb.6; 27) $4,000
- **– Anr. Edn.** Ill.:– Ethel Gabain. Paris, 1923. (20). Fo. Loose as iss. in ptd. wraps., buckram folding case with linen ties. This copy specially ptd. for the Grol. Cl. on wtrmkd. Arches paper, 2 p. A.L.s. presenting this copy laid in, bkplt. of the Grol. Cl. (SG. Apr.2; 119) $190
- **– Anr. Edn.** Ill.:– Ethel Gabain. Paris, 1923. (460) numbered, on specially wtrmkd. paper. Fo. Ptd. wraps., unc. bd. folder & s.-c. (SG. Oct.23; 135) $140
- **[–] The Professor.** 1857. 1st. Edn. 2 vols. 2 pp. advts. in vol. I, 16 pp. advts. in vol. II. Orig. cl., soiled. (P. Jul.30; 314) *Yablon.* £80
- **– Anr. Copy.** Some ll. soiled. Worn, loose. (SH. May 28; 116) *Primrose Hill Books.* £50
- **– Anr. Copy.** Lf. of advts. in vol. I, imprint lf. at end vol. II. Crimson three-qtr. mor., spines gt., by Bayntun. (SG. Nov.13; 27) $160
- **[–] Shirley, a Tale.** 1849. 1st. Edn., early Iss. 3 vols. Advts. dtd. Oct. 1849 in vol. I, spotting. Orig. cl., loose, spine on vol. II torn. (C. Feb.4; 114) *Sotheran.* £140

[–] – **Anr. Copy.** Ex-liby. copy, 2 stps. in vol. 2, 1 lf. reprd. in vol. 1, margins soiled. Hf. mor. (TA. Jan.22; 294) £85
– **Villette.** 1853. 1st. Edn. 3 vols. Publisher's advts. bnd. in at end of vol. 1 (12pp.). Orig. blind-stpd. cl., vol. 1 rebkd., some wear to tops & bottoms of spines. (TA. Sep.18; 285) £200
– – **Anr. Copy.** With 12 pp. of advts. Orig. cl. (SH. Jul.23; 56) *Thorp.* £190
– – **Anr. Copy.** (C. Feb.4; 115) *Cooper.* £120
– – **Anr. Copy.** (C. Feb.4; 116) *Primrose Hill Books.* £50

BRONTE, Emily 'Ellis Bell'
– **Wuthering Heights.** Ill.:– Clare Leighton. N.Y., 1931. (450) numbered, & sigd. by artist. 4to. Cl. (SG. Apr.2; 174) $110

BRONTE, Charlotte, Emily & Anne 'Currer, Ellis & Acton Bell'
– **Life & Works.** Ed.:– Mrs. Humphrey Ward (preface). Ill.:– after W.R. Bland. [1899-1900]. De Luxe Thornfield Edn., (150) numbered & sigd. by publisher. Cl.-bkd. bds. (SG. Mar.19; 32) $220
– **Novels.** Ill.:– Edmund Dulac. 1905-11. Together 10 vols. Orig. cl. gt. (SH. Mar.26; 162) *Mirdan.* £90
– – **Anr. Edn.** Ed.:– Temple Scott. Edinb., 1924. [Thornton Edn.]. 12 vols. Cl., d.-w., unc. (PD. Nov.26; 163) £85
– – **Anr. Copy.** (PD. Aug.20; 12) £50
– – **Anr. Copy.** Hf. cf. gt. by Sangorski & Sutcliffe. (SPB. Nov.25; 431) $600
– **Poems.** 1846 [1848]. 1st. Edn. 2nd. Iss. Lacks errata. Orig. cl. (SKC. Feb.26; 1491) £50
– **The Works.** 1893. 12 vols. A few plts. slightly dampstained. Hf. mor., spines gt. (SKC. Feb.26; 1490) £140
– – **Anr. Edn.** 1905-10. Haworth Edn. 7 vols. Cont. hf. mor. (SH. Jul.16; 62) *Walford.* £90

BRONTE, Charlotte, Emily, Anne, & Branwell
– **Works.** Oxford, 1931. (1000). 13 vols. only. Hf. mor. gt., spines faded. (SPB. May 29; 52) $150

BRONWICK, James
– **Rides Out & About; Rambles of an Australian School Inspector.** L., n.d. Orig. decor. & gt. cl. (KH. Nov.18; 108) Aus. $160

BROOK, Lord
– **Life of Sir Philip Sidney.** Kent, 1816. (100). 2 vols. in 1. Text in ruled borders, slight discolouration. Cont. red mor. gt. (SPB. Nov.25; 153) $150

BROOK, Richard
– **New Cyclopaedia of Botany & Complete Book of Herbs.** N.d. 2 vols. 1 plt. detchd., some browning & spotting. Orig. cl., worn. (CSK. Feb.13; 108) £50

BROOK, Sir Robert
– **La Graunde Abridgement.** 1576. 2 Pts. in 1 vol. 4to. Early 17th. C. cf., rebkd. [STC 3828] (S. Mar.16; 82) *Cresswell.* £220

BROOKE, Sir Arthur de Capell
– **Winter Sketches in Lapland.** 1826. 1st. Edn. 4to. Occasional minor foxing. Orig. ptd. bds., spine torn. Inscr. on title. (C. Nov.6; 290) *Cash.* £320

BROOKE, Lord Fulke Greville.
– **Caelica.** Gregy. Pr., 1936 [1937]. (225). Orig. mor.-bkd. bds., gt. (SH. Feb.20; 215) *Maggs.* £85
– **The Life of the Renowned Sir Philip Sydney.** Ill.:– H.G. Webb. Caradoc Pr., 1906. (271), (11) numbered on vell. Orig. limp vell., silk ties, unc. Etched frontis. sigd. in pencil by artist. (S. Jul.31; 172) *Sawyer.* £110

BROOKES, Richard
[–] **The Art of Angling.** L., 1740. 1st. Edn. 12mo. Disbnd. (SG. Dec.11; 20) $110

BROOKS, H.C.
– **Compendiosa Bibliografia** Flor. 1927. [1st. Edn.]. Bds., unc. (BS. Jun.11; 31) £100
– – **Anr. Edn.** Flor., 1927. (50) numbered on Fabriano H.M.P. 4to. Orig. bds., unc., box. (SI. Dec.3; 105) Lire 320,000
– – **Anr. Edn.** 1927. 1st. Edn., (700) on laid paper. 4to. Orig. bds., unc. (SM. Oct.7; 1334) Frs. 1,200

– – **Anr. Edn.** Firenze, 1927. (700) numbered. 4to. Ptd. bds., unc. & unopened. (SG. Jan.22; 65) $425

BROOKSHAW, George
– **Groups of Fruit [Flowers] accurately drawn . . .** 1817-19. 2 vols. 4to. 12 engraved plts. in 2 states, plain & hand-cold. Cont. hf. roan. (S. Jun.23; 293) *Studio Books.* £300
– **Groups of Fruit.–Groups of Flowers.–Six Birds.** 1817. 1st. Edns. 3 works in 1 vol. Fo. Cont. str.-grd. mor. gt., rebkd. with orig. gt. spine preserved, slightly worn. (C. Nov.5; 20) *Walford.* £700
– **The Horticultural Repository.** [1820]-23. 2 vols. Cont. maroon hf. mor., gt. (C. Mar.18; 26) *Map House.* £900
– – **Anr. Edn.** 1823. 2 vols. in 1. Mod. hf. mor. (S. Dec.3; 910) *Varekamp.* £560
– **Pomona Britannica.** Priv. Ptd., 1812. 1st. Edn. in Book Form. Lge. fo. With the slip 'Before the first numbers . . .'. Cont. red str.-grd. mor., sides panel, in gt. & blind, slightly worn, rebkd. with orig. spine preserved. (C. Nov.5; 21) *Arader.* £8,500
– – **Anr. Edn.** L., 1812. 4to. Contains slip explaining that 3 pineapple plts. were never publd., plt. XCII oxidised, plt. LI slightly so. Cont. russ. gt., rebkd. From collection of Massachusetts Horticultural Society, stps. on plts. (SPB. Oct.1; 106) $1,400
– – **Anr. Edn.** 1817. 2 vols. in 1. Lge. 4to. Cont. mor., gt. borders, spine gt. (C. Jul.15; 170) *Henderson.* £1,400

BROTUFF, Ernst
[–] **Chronica von den Antiquitäten des Keiserlichen Stiffts. der Römischen Burg und Stadt Marsburg an der Salah [Merseburg a.d. Saale].** Bautzen, 1556. 1st. Edn. 4to. Slightly spotted, some old marginalia. Cont. blind-stpd. pig over wooden bds., crudely rebkd. with stiff paper, lacks clasps. (S. Jan.27; 315) *Wenner.* £95

BROUAUT, Jean
– **Traité de l'eau de Vie.** Paris, 1646. 1st. Edn. 4to. Title slightly soiled, some staining affecting text. Cont. cf., rebkd. (C. Nov.20; 181) *Rota.* £350

BROUERIUS van Nidek, Matthaeus
– **Kabinet van Nederlandsche en Kleefsche Outheden.** Ill.:– Abraham Rademaker. Amst., 1727-33. 6 vols. Sq. 4to. Lacks title-p. to vol. II, old liby. stps. on title-pp. Orig. bdg., covers detchd., some lacking. (SG. Feb.5; 55) $1,000
– – **Anr. Edn.** Trans.:– J.H. Reisig & A.B. Strabbe. Ill.:– A. Rademaker. Amst., 1792-1803. 8 vols. A few marginal stains in places, mainly in text. Orig. limp bds., spines slightly defect., unc. (VG. Nov.18; 1084) Fls. 4,800
– **Het Zegenpralent Kennemerland . . .** Ill.:– H. de Leth. Amst., ca. 1730. 2 pts. in 1 vol. Fo. Tears in maps reprd. with sellotape. Cont. blind-stpd. vell. (VG. Dec.17; 1230) Fls. 1,350
– – **Anr. Copy.** 99 (of 100) engraved views, lacks folding map & plt. 51, some ll. cut into 2 pts. Cont. wraps., lacks loose lr. cover. (VG. Nov.18; 1083) Fls. 1,100
See–HALMA, François & Brouerius van Nidek, Matthew
See–STOPENDAAL, Daniel & Brouerius van Niedek, M.

BROUGH, Robert B.
See–BENNETT, Charles H. & Brough, Robert B.

BROUGHTON, Sir Delves L.
– **Records of an Old Cheshire Family.** 1908. (110) numbered. 4to. Orig. cl., gt. (SBA. Oct.22; 288) *Chesters.* £50

BROUGHTON, Thomas Dyer
– **Costume, Character . . . of the Mahrattas.** 1813. 4to. Cf. gt. (P. Apr.30; 3) *Bookroom.* £60
– **Letters Written in a Mahratta Camp during the Year 1809.** 1813. [1st. Edn.?] 4to. Some minor spotting. Cont. tree cf., rebkd. (TA. Feb.19; 33) £85
– – **Anr. Copy.** Lacks 1 (of 10) hand-cold. aquatint plts. Hf. mor. (C. Nov.5; 22) *Hosain.* £60
– – **Anr. Copy.** Bds., crude leath. back, worn, unc. (SG. Feb.26; 61) $160

BROUGHTON, U.H.R.
– **The Dress of the First Regiment of Life Guards in Three Centuries.** 1925. (300) numbered. 4to. Orig. pig. (SH. Jan.29; 214) *Baldur.* £90

BROUN, Heywood (Ed.)
See–CONNECTICUT NUTMEG

BROUSSAIS, François Joseph Victor
– **Examen des Doctrines Medicales et des Systemes de Nosologie.** Paris, 1821. 1st. Edn. 2 vols. A little slight dampstaining. Cont. mott. cf., spines gt. (S. Apr.6; 18) *Gurney.* £80
– **On Irritation & Insanity, a work wherein the relations of the physical with the moral conditions of man, are established on the basis of physiological medicine.** Trans.:– Thomas Cooper. Columbia, Mar. 1831. 1st. Amer. Edn. [? & 1st. Edn. in Engl.]. Content ll. at beginning misbnd. Hf. cf. (S. Jun.15; 127) *Cooper.* £50

BROUWER, C. & Masen, J.
– **Antiquitatum et Annalium Trevirensium Libri XXV.** Ill.:– Ph. Killian (frontis.). Lüttich, 1670. 2nd. Edn. 2 vols. Fo. Cont. vell., both spines slightly defect. (R. Oct.14-18; 2473) DM 2,500
– – **Anr. Edn.** Lüttich, 1671. 2 vols. Fo. Lightly browned, sm. stain in places, 3 ll. loose, 2 ll. with sm. MS. correction, title verso with erased stps. Cont. paper bds., defect. (H. Dec.9/10; 705) DM 720

BROWN, Abbie Farwell
– **The Lonesomest Doll.** Ill.:– Arthur Rackham. [1928]. 1st. Edn. Sm. 4to. Cold. pict. cl. Raymond M. Sutton Jr. copy. (SG. May 7; 34) $110

BROWN, C.
– **Narrative of the Expedition to South America . . .** L., 1819. 1st. Edn. No hf.-title. Three-qtr. lev., spine gt. (SG. Jan.8; 51) $140

BROWN, E.
– **Durch Niederland, Teutschland, Hungarn . . .** Nuremb., 1686. 4to. Cont. vell. (R. Oct.14-18; 1834) DM 600
– **Reysen door Nederland, Duytsland, Hongaryen, Servien, Bulgarien, Macedonien . . .** Ill.:– Jan Luyken. Amst., 1682. L.P. 4to. Browned. Mod. blind-stpd. & panel. cf., antique style. (VG. Dec.17; 1231) Fls. 550

BROWN, Frank
– **Frost's Drawings of Ipswich & Sketches in Suffolk.** 1895. (105) numbered, sigd. Fo. Spotted. Orig. cl. (SH. Nov.6; 41) *Doncaster.* £50

BROWN, J.E.
– **The Forest Flora of South Australia.** [1882-90]. Lge. fo. Plts. only, some margins slightly soiled. Orig. ptd. bds., some wear. (TA. Jun.18; 120) £65

BROWN, John
– **Description of the Use of the Triangular Quadrant.–Horologiographia.–Appendix to the Use of the Triangular Quadrant in Navigatio.** 1671. 3 pts. in 1 vol. 48 engraved plts., a few still pasted to the fore-margin but mostly loose, advt. lf., some wormholes in lr. margin of pts. II & III, slightly affecting corners of a few plts., slight spotting. Cont. cf., head & foot of spine worn. Harrison D. Horblit's bkplt. [Wing B4041-2] (S. Nov.4; 464) *Bozzolato.* £400

BROWN, John
– **North West Passage.** L., 1858. 1st. Edn. Some spotting. Orig. cl., worn. (SPB. May 29; 55) $100

BROWN, John Carter
– **Bibliotheca Americana: A Catalogue of Books . . . in the library of . . .** Ed.:– John Russell Bartlett. Providence, 1875 & 1882. (20) L.P. 2 pts. in 2 vols. 4to. Orig. hf. mor. & cl., worn. (SG. Jan.22; 49) $500

BROWN, Louise Norton
– **Block Printing.** 1924. Orig. cl.-bkd. bds. (CSK. Jun.19; 138) £85

BROWN, M.P.
– **Supplement to the Dictionary of Decisions.** Edinb., 1826. 5 vols. Hf. cf., worn. (CE. Aug.28; 29) £110

BROWN, P.L.
– **Narrative of George Russell of Golf Hill.–Clyde Company Papers.** Melbourne, 1935-71. [1st. Edns.]. 8 vols. Buckram gt., with d.-w.'s, a few wraps. only with slight defects. (KH. Nov.18; 127) Aus. $150

BROWN, Paul
– **Aintree Grand Nationals–Past & Present.** N.Y., Derry. Pr. 1930. (50) L.P. 4to. Red mor. gt., partly unc. With a sigd. reproduction of an ink

BROWN, Paul – Aintree Grand Nationals–Past & Present. -contd.
drawing, with some pencil work by author. (CNY. Oct.1; 160) $1,200
– – **Anr. Edn.** Ed.:– Henry G. Vaughan. 1930. (850). 4to. Gt.-decor. cl., light wear, owner's blind-stp. on endpaper. (SG. Dec.11; 217) $110
– **Hits & Misses.** [1935]. (950) numbered. 4to. 2-tone pict. cl. Sigd. (SG. Dec.11; 218) $220
– **Spills & Thrills.** N.Y., 1933. (780) numbered & sigd. Ob. 8vo. Cl., owner's inscr. & stp. on endpaper. (SG. Dec.11; 184) $120

BROWN, Percy
– **Indian Painting under the Mughals.** Oxford, 1924. 4to. Orig. cl. gt., unc., d.-w. (SKC. May 19; 147) £90

BROWN, Peter
– **New Illustrations of Zoology.** Trans.:– [Thomas Pennant]. 1776. 4to. Plts. hand-cold. 19th. C. hf. mor. From Chetham's Liby., Manchester. (C. Nov.26; 59) Fletcher. £1,600
– – **Anr. Copy.** 50 plts., pen & ink sketches on versos. Cont. hf. cf., worn. (SH. Jul.16; 99) Gregory. £90

See–EDWARDS, George–BROWN, Peter

BROWN, R.
– **The Countries of the World.** L., Paris & N.Y., ca. 1880. 6 vols. 4to. Orig. hf. leath. (D. Dec.11-13; 1258) DM 600

BROWN, R.N. Rudmose & others
[–] **The Voyage of the 'Scotia'.** Edinb., & L., 1906. 1st. Edn. 1 map slightly torn, occasional slight spotting. Orig. cl. (CSK. Feb.27; 146) £70

BROWN, Richard
– **Domestic Architecture: Containing a History of the Science & the Principles of Designing Public Edifices, Private Dwelling Houses . . .** 1842. 4to. Some spotting. Orig. hf. cf., some wear. (TA. Oct.16; 131) £52

BROWN, Robert
– **History of Paisley.** Paisley, 1886. 4to. Cl., worn. (CE. Nov.20; 14) £52

BROWN, Robert, Botanist 1773-1858
– **The Miscellaneous Botanical Works.** 1866-68. 3 vols. 8vo. & fo. Orig. embossed cl., gt., partly unc., ex-liby., vol. 3 cl.-bkd. bds. (PL. Jul.11; 73) Wheldon & Wesley. £90

BROWN, Samuel R.
– **The Western Gazeteer; or Emigrant's Directory . . .** Auburn, N.Y., 1817. 1st. Edn., 1st. Iss. Foxed, lacks errata slip. Mod. hf. mor., stained, worn at head & foot of spine, gt. spine & borders. From liby. of William E. Wilson. (SPB. Apr.29; 34) $100

BROWN, Stewardson
– **Alpine Flora of the Canadian Rocky Mountains.** Ill.:– Mrs. Charles Schaffer. N.Y. & L., 1907. Orig. cl., lacks front free endpaper. (CB. Feb.18; 40) Can. $130

BROWN, T. Allston
– **A History of the New York Stage.** N.Y., 1903. 1st. Edn., (358) numbered sets ptd. from type. 3 vols. Buckram, partly unc. (SG. Aug.7; 48) $160

BROWN, Capt. Thomas
– **Illustrations of the American Ornithology of . . . Wilson & . . . Bonaparte . . .** Edinb., Dublin & L., [1831]-35. Lge. fo. Engraved title, engraved dedication, 3pp. 'Systematic Index', 124 hand-cold. engraved plts. Cont. hf. cf. by John McKendrick of Glasgow, rebkd., orig. gt. backstrip preserved. Frederick Ducane Godman bkplt. (C. Jul.15; 172) Ibarcord. £13,00
– **Illustrations of the Conchology of Great Britain & Ireland.** 1827. 1st. Edn. 4to. Some minor spotting. Orig. ptd. bds., mor. backstrip, worn. (TA. Jul.16; 150) £200
– **Illustrations of the Fossil Conchology of Great Britain & Ireland.** 1849. 1st. Edn. 4to. Cont. roan-bkd. cl. (S. Dec.3; 912) Garvey. £80
– **Illustrations of the Fossil Conchology of Great Britain & Ireland.–Illustrations of the Recent Conchology of Great Britain & Ireland.** [1837]-49; [1837]-44. 2nd. Edn. (2nd. work). 2 works in 1 vol. 4to. Most plts. hand-cold. in each work. 19th. C. hf. mor. gt. From Chetham's Liby., Manchester. (C. Nov.26; 60) Gilbert. £380
– **Illustrations of the Land & Fresh Water Conchology of Great Britain & Ireland.** 1845. Later hf. leath. (S. May 5; 99) Cristani. £60

– **Illustrations of the Recent Conchology of Great Britain & Ireland.** 1844. 2nd. Edn. 4to. Cont. roan-bkd. cl. (S. Dec.3; 911) W. & W. £260

BROWN, Thomas, of Musselburgh
– **An Enquiry into the Antivariolous Power of Vaccination.** Edinb., 1809. 1st. Edn. Liby. inscr. on title. Orig. paper bds., unc. (S. Feb.10; 367) Bicker. £55

BROWN, Thomas, Satirist
– **Lectures on the Philosophy of the Human Mind.** Edinb., 1820. 4 vols. Cont. cf. (P. Dec.11; 271) Brooke-Hitching. £120

BROWN, William Robinson
– **The Horse of the Desert.** N.Y., 1929. De Luxe Edn., (75) numbered. 4to. Mor. gt., partly unc. Sigd. copyright p. (CNY. Oct.1; 159) $1,700
– – **Anr. Edn.** N.Y., 1929. (750). 4to. Orig. cl. gt., partly unc. (CNY. May 22; 196) $180

BROWNE, Christopher
– **Geographia Classica.** 1712. Slight soiling. Cont. cf.-bkd. bds. (CSK. Jan.16; 120) £75
– **Nova Totius Angliae Tabula.** Ill.:– J. Harris. Ca. 1765. Ob. fo. Map, in 13 linen-bkd. sheets, Latin title bnd. at end, Engl. title in engraved vig., slightly soiled thro.-out. Cl. bds., worn, poorly rebkd. W.a.f. (C. Nov.6; 245) Kentish. £150

BROWNE or Brown, Edward
– **A Brief Account of some Travels in divers Parts of Europe.** 1685. 2nd. Edn. Fo. Advt. lf., slight browning & soiling. Cont. mott. cf. [Wing B5111] (S. Sep.29; 8) Lamm. £120

BROWNE, Hablot Knight 'Phiz'
– **Racing & Chasing.** L., ca. 1870. Various series. Ob. fo. Cold. pict. bds., leath. spine & tips, very worn. (SG. Dec.11; 185) $110

BROWNE, Hablot Knight & Young, Robert
– **Four Plates . . . to Illustrate the Cheap Edition of 'The Old Curiosity Shop' . . . –Four Plates . . . to Illustrate the Cheap Edition of 'Barnaby Rudge'.** L., 1848; 1849. 2 vols. Sm. 4to. Plts. as proofs. Loose, as iss., in ptd. wraps., inserted in 4-way cl. folder, mor. bookplts. of Barton Currie, & Thomas A. McGraw. (PNY. Mar.26; 95) $200

BROWNE, John
– **History of the Metropolitan Church of St. Peter, York.** 1847. 2 vols. 4to. Some ll. slightly spotted. Cont. mor., gt. (SH. Nov.6; 79) Fairburn. £110

BROWNE, Dr. John
– **A compleat Treatise of the Muscles as they appear in the humane body.** 1681. 1st. Edn. Fo. Port. frontis. torn affecting plt., sm. hole in 1 plt., some early plts. torn & stained, staining in upr. inside corner, especially at beginning, stains in text ll. at beginning. Cont. mott. cf., corners & head & foot of spine worn. Cont. owner's inscr. of William Salmon. [Wing B5126] (C. Feb.25; 4) Stern. £300
– – **Anr. Copy.** 36 (of 37) copperplts. Cont. cf., worn. (SG. Sep.18; 65) $450

BROWNE, John Ross
– **Reisen u. Abenteuer im Apachenlande.** Trans.:– H. Hertz. Gera, 1874. Slightly soiled. Cont. hf. linen. (HK. May 12-14; 504) DM 550

BROWNE, Maggie
– **The Book of Betty Barber.** Ill.:– Arthur Rackham. Boston, [1910]. 1st. Amer. Edn. 4to. Cl., d.-w., publisher's box. Raymond M. Sutton Jr. copy. (SG. May 7; 36) $475
– **The Surprising Adventures of Tuppy & Tue.** Ill.:– Arthur Rackham. L., 1904. Pict. cl., worn. Raymond M. Sutton Jr. copy. (SG. May 7; 35) $450

BROWNE, Nina E.
See–LANE, William Coolidge & Browne, Nina E.

BROWNE, Patrick
– **The Civil & Natural History of Jamaica.** Priv. Ptd., 1756. 1st. Edn. Fo. Hf. cf. & marb. bds. (C. Jul.15; 21) Maggs. £400
– – **Anr. Copy.** 2 pts. in 1 vol. 1st. title stained, some plts. slightly discold. 19th. C. hf. mor. From Chetham's Liby., Manchester. (C. Nov.26; 61) Soames. £150
– – **Anr. Copy.** Slight browning, staining on a few ll. Cont. cf., worn. [Sabin 8670] (SPB. May 5; 119) $275
– – **Anr. Edn.** L., 1789. Fo. Slight browning, spotting, tears, ex-liby. with stps., not on plts. New hf. mor. (SPB. May 5; 120) $650

BROWNE, Sir Thomas
– **Certain Miscellany Tracts.** 1684. 1st. Edn., 2nd. Iss. Some ll. near end slightly wormed, cutting a few letters. Cont. mott. cf., some wear, spine gt. [Wing B5152] (S. Feb.10; 418) Lawson. £110
– **Christian Morals.** Camb., 1716. 1st. Edn. 12mo. Later bds., worn & loose. (SG. Sep.25; 68) $150
– – **Anr. Edn.** Ed.:– Samuel Johnson. 1756. 2nd. [3rd.] Edn. Lacks hf.-title, very sm. stain at extreme outer edge of blank margins at beginning. New mor. (S. Jun.15; 132) Bickersteth. £90
– – **Anr. Copy.** Slight browning. Cont. spr. cf., rebkd. (S. Oct.1; 514) £50
– **Hydriotaphia, Urne-Buriall . . . Garden of Cyrus.** 1658. 1st. Edn. 2 engraved plts., text engr., publisher's advt. lf., lacks errata lf. & O8 with longitudinal label. first gathering nearly detchd. Cont. sheep., worn, upr. cover detchd. [Wing B5154] (S. Nov.25; 453) Thomas. £75
– – **Anr. Copy.** Plts., lacks O8 & errata, wormed. Cont. cf. [Wing B5154] (SH. Jul.16; 210) Pickering & Chatto. £55
– **Pseudodoxia Epidemica.** 1646. 1st. Edn. Fo. 2nd. state of imprint, piece torn from outer margin of b2, occasional browning & spotting, some underlinings in text. Cont. spr. cf. Bkplt. of Antoine Lavoisier. [Wing B5159] (S. Feb.10; 420) Traylen. £140
– – **Anr. Copy.** Wormed. Cont. cf., rebkd. [Wing B5159] (SH. Jul.16; 209) Pickering & Chatto. £85
– – **Anr. Copy.** Fo. Browning, stains, tears. Old cf., worn. (SPB. Jul.28; 64) $100
– – **Anr. Edn.** 1658. 4th. Edn.; 1st. Edn. (Hydriotaphia). Bnd. in: Hydriotaphia Urne-Buriall, with the 3 ll. usually missing, Statement to the Reader, Books printed for Mr. Browne & Garden of Cyprus. Hf. cf., worn. (CE. Dec.4; 231) £150
– – **Anr. Edn.** 1672. 6th. & last Edn. 4to. Engraved port. mntd. New antique-style cf. [Wing B5165] (S. Dec.2; 798) Beaver. £50
– **Religio Medici.** 1669. 6th. Edn. A few spots. Cont. cf., slight wear. [Wing B5175] (S. Dec.9; 298) Quaritch. £240
[–] – **Anr. Edn.** 1678. '7th.' [11th.] Edn. Some browning. Cont. cf. [Wing B5177] (S. Apr.7; 382) Blackwell. £80
– **The Works.** 1686. 1st. Edn. Fo. Slight browning, inscrs. on title. Cont. cf., worn, rebkd. & reprd. [Wing B5150] (S. Oct.1; 516) £110
– – **Anr. Copy.** Slight marginal staining towards end. Recent cf.-bkd. bds., upr. cover almost detchd. Bkplt. of John Carter. [Wing B5150] (C. Nov.20; 230) Vine. £70
– – **Anr. Edn.** 1720. 5 vols. 12mo. Cont. red mor. gt., spines worn. Bkplt. of John Ludford. (S. Nov.24; 42) Bennett. £70
– – **Anr. Edn.** 1836-35. 4 vols. 2 plts. dampstained. Mod. hf. cf., gt. From liby. of Dr. E. Ashworth Underwood. (S. Feb.23; 171) Canale. £58
– – **Anr. Edn.** Ed.:– Geoffrey Keynes. 1928-31. (210) sigd. by Ed. 6 vols. Orig. parch. (S. Oct.1; 517) £55

BROWNE, William
– **Circe & Ulysses.** Ill.:– Mark Severin. Gold. Cock. Pr., 1954. (100) sigd. by artist, specially bnd. Orig. mor. gt. (SH. Feb.19; 197a) May. £105

BROWNING, Elizabeth Barrett
– **The Battle of Marathon.** L., 1820. 1st. Edn., (2?) unc. Repairs to blank margins of 1st. lf. (partly separated from its conjugate) & to blank fore-margin of last lf., title & last lf. stained & brittle, sm. portion of lr. corner of title torn-away. Stabbed & sewn, unbnd., as iss., mor. solander case. Ink corrections to text at 40 places 'presumably in the hand of the author'. From the Prescott Collection. (CNY. Feb.6; 28) $12,000
– **Complete Works.** N.Y., 1901. Autograph Edn., (275), sigd. by eds. 6 vols. Mor. gt., floral inlays on spine & corners, mor. doubls. (SPB. Nov.25; 432) $950
– **Napoleon III in Italy, & other Poems.** N.Y., 1860. 12mo. Orig. pebbled cl., slight wear at corners & head of spine, qtr. red mor. gt. folding case. 16 corrections to the preface in author's hand; Pres. Copy, to Robert Browning, with his initials, & his note on title-p., lately in the Prescott Collection. (CNY. Feb.6; 30) $4,800
– **Poems.** L., 1844. 1st. Edn. 2 vols. 8 pp. of advts. dtd. Jan.1, 1845, p. 141 in vol. II with revised reading '. . . let your flood of bitter scorn dash on me'. Cl. with blind-stpd. arabesques on covers

(Carter's A bdg.), yellow endpapers, hf. mor. s.-c. (SG. Nov.13; 28) $270

- - **Anr. Copy.** Tall 12mo. Orig. cl., mor. & cl. s.-c., sm. snag at head of vol. 2. (PNY. Mar.4; 112) $130

- **Religious Opinions.** L., 1896. (30) copies. 4to. Orig. paper bds., slightly soiled, folding mor. box, worn, upr. cover detchd. Accompanied by an A.L.s. by Thomas J. Wise, dtd. 17 Mar. 1897, to Mr. Charles Letts discussing some of his works. (SPB. Nov.25; 172) $150

- **Seraphim & other Poems.** L., 1838. 1st. Edn. Slight browning. Orig. cl., worn. Pres. copy to Annie E. Roberts. (SPB. Nov.25; 171) $400

- **Sonnets from the Portuguese.** Montagnola, 1925. (225). 4to. Orig. vell., vell. s.-c. (HK. May 12-14; 2000) DM 2,000

- - **Anr. Edn.** [Inscr. dtd. 1937]. (30) on vell., St. Dunstan Edn. Sm. 4to. This copy unnumbered. Orig. mor., s.-c. defect. (SH. Feb.20; 417) *Thorp.* £60

BROWNING, Robert
- **Dramatis Personae.** Hammersmith, Doves Pr., 1910. (15) on vell. Sm. 4to. Lev. mor., gt.-tooled, spine in 6 compartments, 5 raised bands, gt.-tooled & panel., sigd. by Doves Bindery 1912, qtr. mor. s.-c. Inscr. by T.J. Cobden-Sanderson. (CNY. May 22; 390) $6,500

- - **Anr. Edn.** [Hammersmith], [Doves Pr.], [1910]. (250). 4to. Rust mor., gt.-stpd. with leaves & acorns, inner dentelles gt., by C. & C. McLeish at the Doves Bindery. (PNY. Dec.3; 114) $550

- **Men & Women.** Ill.:- Edward Johnston. Hammersmith, Doves Pr., 1908. (12) on vell. 2 vols. 4to. Crushed lev. mor., covers with gt.-ruled border enclosing lge. central panel of double gt.-rules, gt. cornerpieces, spines in 6 compartments, 5 raised bands, gt.-panel., sigd. by Doves Bindery, 1914, qtr. mor. s.-c. H. Alfred Fowler & Cortlandt Field Bishop bkplts. (CNY. May 22; 385) $8,500

- - **Anr. Edn.** Ill.:- Edward Johnston. Hammersmith, Doves Pr., 1908. (250), sigd. & dtd. by artist. 2 vols. Orig. limp vell., spines gt., unc. (CNY. May 22; 303) $550

- - **Anr. Edn.** Ill.:- Edward Johnston. Doves Pr., 1908. (250). 4to. Orig. limp vell., cl. folder, s.-c. (SH. Feb.19; 43) *Appleton.* £270

- - **Anr. Edn.** Ill.:- Edward Johnston. [Hammersmith], [Doves Pr], [1908]. (250) sigd. by artist. 2 vols. 4to. Crushed mor., gt.-stpd. at covers & panel. spine in multiple rules of both continuous & broken lines, inner dentelles gt., by C. & C. McLeish for the Doves Bindery. (PNY. Dec.3; 115) $850

- **Pacchiarotto ... with other Poems.** L., 1876. 1st. Edn. 12mo. Orig. cl., qtr. mor. gt. s.-c. Pres. Copy, to Fanny Haworth, lately in the Prescott Collection. (CNY. Feb.6; 33) $500

- **The Pied Piper of Hamelin.** Ill.:- Kate Greenaway. L., [1888]. 1st. Edn., 1st. Iss. 4to. With Glasgow, Manchester & N.Y. included in imprint, & 'Published by arrangement . . .' on title verso. Cl.-bkd. pict. bds., upr. cover wrinkled. (SG. Apr.30; 160) $160

- - **Anr. Edn.** Ill.:- Kate Greenaway. L., [1888]. 4to. Proof imp. Orig. glazed pict. wraps., bnd. in buckram. From the Prescott Collection. (CNY. Feb.6; 137) $750

- - **Anr. Edn.** Ill.:- Arthur Rackham. L., [1934]. 1st. Trade Edn. Cold. pict. wraps., d.-w. Raymond M. Sutton Jr. copy. (SG. May.7; 38) $120

- - **Anr. Edn.** Ill.:- Arthur Rackham. 1934. (410) numbered, sigd. by artist. Vell., s.-c. (PJ. Jun.6 (80); 51) £155

- - **Anr. Copy.** Limp vell., s.-c. Raymond M. Sutton Jr. copy. (SG. May 7; 37) $600

- **Poetical Works.** L., 1888-94. 17 vols. Cf., triple gt. fillet borders, spines gt., gt. dentelles, by Zaehnsdorf. (SG. Mar.19; 37) $450

- **So Here Then is The Last Ride.** East Aurora, Roycroft Pr., 1900. (940) numbered, sigd. by Elbert Hubbard, & illuminer, Fanny Stiles. Mor., lge. stpd. design on upr. cover, sigd. M.R.P. (SG. Apr.9; 551) $100

- **Some Poems.** Ill.:- Lucien Pissarro. Eragny Pr., 1904. (226). Orig. bds., unc. (S. Jul.31; 28) *Warrack & Perkins.* £140

- **Strafford.** 1837. 1st. Edn. Mor. gt., cover elab. gt. with floral corner & centrepieces, spine gt., by Sangorski, buckram box. Pres. Copy, to John Kenyon. (C. Jul.22; 3) *Sawyer.* £380

- - **Anr. Copy.** 4 pp. publisher's advts. bnd. in. Orig. wraps. untrimmed, spine reprd. with tape, in

---

mor. s.-c. by Rivière & Son. (TA. May 21; 382) £85

- **The Complete Works.** Ed.:- Charlotte Porter & Helen A. Clarke. N.Y., 1899. Connoisseurs Edn., (45) numbered, sigd. by editors & publisher. 12 vols. Each vol. with frontis. in 2 states. Red crushed lev., gt. tooled, inlaid doubls., silk free end-papers, raised bands. (SG. Sep.4; 80) $125

- **Works.** N.Y., [1910]. Assisi Edn., (100). 12 vols. Plts. in 2 states. Hf. mor. gt., gt. floral inlays on spine. (SPB. May 6; 293) $1,100

- - **Anr. Edn.** 1912. 10 vols. Orig. cl. (SH. May 28; 13) *Walford.* £80

BRUCE, James
- **Travels to Discover the Source of the Nile.** Edinb., 1790. 1st. Edn. 5 vols. 4to. Lacks hf.-titles, some browning. Cont. tree cf., gt. spines, worn. (S. Mar.31; 446) *Keiffer.* £220

- - **Anr. Copy.** 1 folding map (of 3), slight foxing, a few sm. holes & repairs, each vol. inscr. 'Jane Carr the gift of Miss [Janet Maitland] Bruce of Kinnaird 1803'. Cont. cf., jnts. worn. (S. Jan.27; 571) *Schmull.* £150

- - **Anr. Copy.** Slight foxing. Cont. tree cf., spines worn. (TA. Dec.18; 105) £100

- - **Anr. Copy.** Lacks port., some stains & discolouration, repairs. Mott. cf., rebkd., worn. (SPB. Nov.25; 152) $200

- - **Anr. Edn.** Dublin, 1790-91. 6 vols. Hf. cf. (SH. May 21; 16) *Tooting.* £55

- - **Anr. Edn.** 1804-5. 2nd. Edn. 8 vols., including Atlas. 4to. Cf. gt. (P. Oct.23; 7) *Rogers.* £180

- - **Anr. Copy.** 7 vols, & plt. vol. 8vo. & 4to. 3 charts reprd. some staining to 4 text vols. Early cf. & early hf. cf., upr. cover of plt. vol. detchd. (KH. Mar.24; 78) *Aus.* $350

- - **Anr. Edn.** Edinb., 1805. 2nd. Edn. Atlas vol. only (vol. VIII). Fo. 1 map torn along folds, some slight spotting. Cont. hf. cf., upr. cover detchd. (S. May 5; 240) *Byrne.* £65

- - **Anr. Copy.** Vol. VIII only. Some damp staining. Cont. cf., worn. (TA. Sep.18; 324) £62

- - **Anr. Copy.** Atlas vol. only. Engraved port., 78 plts., 3 folding maps, 1 cropped & detchd. Cont. tree cf. (S. Mar.31; 447) *Schuster.* £50

BRUCE, Peter Henry
- **Memoirs of a Military Officer.** L., 1782. 1st. Edn. Lge. 4to. Mod. three-qtr. cf. (SG. Oct.30; 69) $180

BRUE, A.H.
- **Atlas Universal.** 1822. Fo. Double-p. maps, cold. in outl. Hf. leath. (HY. Jan.14; 87) £65

- - **Anr. Copy.** Lacks plt. 18, double-p. maps, hand-cold. in outl., some dampstaining to lr. margin, not affecting maps. Cont. hf. mor., worn. (TA. Nov.20; 293) £60

- - **Anr. Edn.** 1828. 2nd. Edn. Fo. Cont. hf. mor., worn. (SH. Apr.9; 139) *Kauffman.* £120

BRUEHL, Anton
- **Photographs of Mexico.** N.Y., [1933]. 1st. Edn. (1,000), this copy unnumbered. Fo. Linen, leath. spine, bkplt. (SG. Apr.3; 42) $190

BRUEL, François-Louis
- **Histoire Aéronautique ...** Paris, 1909. (325) on laid paper. Fo. Ills. mntd. on guards, 1 on silk, with Montgolfière day poster (30 Jun. 1951). Red hf. mor., spine decor. with raised bands, wrap. & spine preserved. (HD. Feb.27; 91) Frs. 13,500

BRUGGE
- **Kueren ende Costumen. Mitsgaders den Deelbouck vanden Lande vanden Vryen.** Brugghe, 1619. [1620 at end]. Fo. Limp vell. (LM. Mar.21; 69) B.Frs. 10,000

BRUGIS, Thomas
- **The Marrow of Physicke. Or, a Learned Discourse upon the Severall Parts of Man's Body.** 1640. 1st. Edn. 2 pts. in 1 vol. 4to. Lacks last blank, title soiled, inscr. & with sm. repair, repairs to B4, D1-4 & P4, with loss of several letters, sm. repairs to table & a few ll., some ll. stained from inner margins, inscrs. in text, some browning. Mod. cf., gt., spine gt. [STC 3931] (S. Dec.2; 695) *Phelps.* £300

BRUGNATELLI, Luigi Vincenzo
- **Memorie sull Elettricita Animale.** Pavia, 1972. Some ll. stained, title browned. Mod. bds., unc., cl. case. From Honeyman Collection. (S. May 20; 3193) *Gurney.* £130

BRUIN, W.R.A. & C.
- **Bybelische Tafereelen des Ouden en Nieuwen Testaments ...** Amst., 1740. 4to. 214 (of 215) engrs. in text, slightly stained at beginning. Mod. blind-stpd. & panel. cf., antique style. (VG. Dec.17; 1139) Fls. 500

BRUMOY, Pierre
- **Théâtre des Grecs.** Ill.:- Borel & others. 1785. L.P. 13 vols. 4to. Lacks pts. 441-8 vol. III & 443-40 vol. VII. Cont. cf., dentelle. (HD. Jun.30; 11) Frs. 2,400

- - **Anr. Edn.** 1820-25. 2nd. Compl. Edn. 16 vols. Cf., gt. & blind border, by Purgold, vol. 1 jnts. split. (HD. Oct.10; 224) Frs. 2,800

BRUNET, Gustave
- **Etudes sur la Reliure des Livres et sur les Collections Bibliophiles célèbres.** Bordeaux, 1891. 2nd. [3rd. Edn.], 225 on H.M.P. 2 pp. with prices added in margin in cont. hand. Later red mor.-bkd. bds., orig. wrap. bnd. in, partly unc. (SM. Oct.7; 1335) Frs. 1,200

BRUNET, Jacques Charles
- **Manuel du Libraire.** Paris, 1842-44. 5 vols. Cont. hf. mor. (SH. Jan.29; 9) *Baer.* £110

- - **Anr. Edn.** Paris, 1860-65. 5th. Edn. 6 vols. Foxed at beginning & end of vol. Cont. hf. mor., partly unc. (S. Feb.23; 330) *Licini.* £170

- - **Anr. Edn.** Paris, 1860-80. 5th. Edn. 8 vols. including Supp. Lacks hf.-titles to vols. 1-6, stpd. on titles, few in text. Liby. cl. (S. Nov.25; 505) *Weinreb.* £160

- - **Anr. Copy.** 8 vols. in 7, including Supp. Cont. hf. mor. (C. Jul.22; 110) *Quaritch.* £140

- - **Anr. Copy.** Cont. roan-bkd. bds., 1 worn. (SH. May 28; 14) *Duran.* £80

- - **Anr. Copy.** 6 vols. & 3 supp. vols. Orig. linen. (HK. May 12-14; 2200) DM 900

- - **Anr. Copy.** 8 vols., including 2 supps. Cont. hf. red mor., 1 spine loosening, partly unc. (SI. Dec.3; 106) Lire 400,000

- - **Anr. Edn.** Berlin & Paris, 1922-1878. 8 vols. including 2 vol. supp. Cont. & mod. hf. mor. (SH. Oct.9; 45) *Bunsie.* £130

- - **Anr. Edn.** Copen., 1966-68. 9 vols. Reprint. Orig. cl. (SH. Mar.6; 497) *Thorp.* £120

BRUNFELS, Otto
- **Herbarum Vivae Eicones ... with Novi Herbariii Tomus II.** Strassburg, 1532-31. 2nd. Edn., 1st. Edn. 2 vols. only (of 3). Fo. Lacks blank lf. at end. 1st. title soiled & slightly defect. (laid down, detchd.), some stains to upr. margins, just touching text. 19th. C. hf. mor. From Chetham's Liby., Manchester. (C. Nov.26; 63) *Weldon & Wesley.* £1,200

BRUNHOFF, Jean de
- **Histoire de Babar.–Le Voyage de Babar.–Le Roi Babar.** Paris, [1931]; [1932]; [1933]. 1st. Edns. 3 works in 3 vols. Fo. All pict. bds., cl. spines, some remains of home-made protective wraps. (SG. Apr.30; 32) $170

BRUNO, Giordano
- **De Umbris Idearum (& Ars Memoriae).** Paris, 1582. 1st. Edn. 2 pts. in 1 vol. With the blank lf. u4, very minor stain in blank upr. margin of 1st. few ll. Cont. limp vell. (C. Apr.1; 18) *Lyon.* £3,400

BRUNO, Saint, Bp. of Würzburg
- **Expositio ... in o[mn]es Divi Pauli Epistolas.** Paris, 16 Feb. 1509. 4to. Some wormholes, slightly affecting a few letters. Cont. vell. bds., slightly worn. (S. Apr.6; 295) *Dr. Kubicek.* £90

BRUNSCHWIG, Hieronymus
- **Das Buch zu Distillieren.** Strassburg, 28 Aug. 1519. 2nd. Edn. Browned, approx. 20 ll. reprd. at corners, title-lf. reprd., some marginalia. Cont. blind-tooled hf. pig-bkd. wood bds., reprd. (R. Oct.14-18; 317) DM 10,000

- **Distilierbuch ...** Frankfurt, 1555. Sm. 4to. Bds. covered with old vell. MS. (SG. Oct.9; 45) $1,200

See-TURNER,   William-BRUNSCHWIG, Hieronymus

BRUNSCHWIG, Hieronymus–VOGTER, Bartholomeus
- **Distilierbuch der rechten Kunst, Newe und gemein Distilier und Brennöfen.–Wie man alle gebresten und Kranckheiten des Menschlichen Leibs ... vertreiben soll mit aussgebranten Wassern; Gart der Gesundtheyt.** Frankfurt, 1554; 1550; 1556. 3 works in 1 vol. Sm. 4to.

BRUNSCHWIG, Hieronymus–VOGTER, Bartholomeus – Distilierbuch der rechten Kunst, Newe und gemein Distilier -*contd.*
Dampstained thro.-out, 1st. work with owner's inscr. of Johann Zacharias Paden von Creytzenstein, title stained & with short tear at upr. inner corner, lacks B1, a few ll. badly wormed, corner of A4 reprd. with slight loss of text, lr. margins of C4 & D1 reprd., Z4 torn & frayed, a few minor tears; 2nd. work with lr. fore-corners of R4 & S4 reprd.; 3rd. work is an impft. copy. Bnd. in vell. lf. from 15th. C. German liturgical MS. over bds., hf. red mor. case. Bkplt. of Ignaz Dominik Graf von Chorinski; from Honeyman Collection; w.a.f. (S. May 20; 3194)
Quaritch. £170

BRUNUS ARETINUS, Leonardus (Trans.)
See–PROCOPIUS of Caesarea

BRUSCAMBILLE (Pseud.)
See–DESLAURIERS 'Bruscambille'. Comedian

BRUSONIUS, Lucius Domitius
– **Facetiarum Exemplorumq. Libri VII.** Rome, 1518. 1st. Edn. Fo. Old. sig. on title, some marginal dampstains. 18th. C. red mor., triple gt. fillet, spine gt. in compartments, inner gt. dentelles, Heber liby. stp. on fly-lf. (SM. Oct.7; 1621) Frs. 3,000
– – **Anr. Edn.** Basle, 1559. 4to. Some slight soiling. Cont. vell., soiled. (CSK. Feb.13; 73) £85
– – **Anr. Edn.** Basle, [1559?]. 4to. 1st. few ll. slightly damp stained. Vell., soiled. (TA. Dec.18; 181) £56

BRUSSIUS [BRUCE], W.
See–NATHAN BEN KALONYMUS, Isaak
– CAMERARIUS, Joachim–BRUSSELS [BRUCE], W.

BRUTUS, Petrus
– **Victoria Contra Judaeos.** Vicenza, 1489. 1st. Edn. Fo. 126 (of 130) ll. Mod. pig. [Goff B1264] (SG. Oct.9; 46) $425

BRUUN, L.E.
– **Catalogue of the Collection of Coins.** 1925. 2 vols. 4to. Orig. wraps. (SH. Mar.6; 325)
Weinreb. £50
– **Gave til den Kongelige Møntd- og Medaillesamling.** Copen., 1928. 2 vols. 4to. Plts. loose as iss., mod. cl. & orig. wraps. (SH. Mar.6; 327) *Spink.* £140
– **Sammlung. Schwedische Munzen.** Frankfurt am Main, 1914. 2 vols. 4to. Cont. hf. roan. (SH. Mar.6; 328) *Schneider-Henn.* £70

BRUYERE, Louis
– **Etudes à l'Art des Constructions.** Paris, 1823. 2 vols. Fo. Hf. cf., worn. (CE. Oct.24; 197) £50

BRUYERES, H.
– **La Phrénologie, le Geste et la Physionomie.** Paris, 1847. 4to. Hf.-title & title with inscr., spotted. Cont. hf. roan, some wear, contents loose. (S. May 5; 163) *Cooper.* £80

BRUYN, Abraham
– **Diversarum Gentium Armatura Equestris.** N.p., ca. 1580. 4to. Lacks probably 8 text ll., 2 plt. versos with ink scrawl, 1 plt. with sm. hole. 17th. C. vell. (R. Oct.14-18; 2763a) DM 3,500
– **Habits de Diverses Nations de l'Europe, Asie, Afrique et Amérique.** [Antw.], [1610]. Ob. fo. Title & several plts. defect. & preserved. No bdg. stated. As a collection of prints, w.a.f. (BS. Jun.11; 316) £300

BRUYN, C. de
– **Reizeri over Moskovie, door Persie en Indie** . . . Ill.:– B. Picart (frontis.). 1714. Fo. Cont. blind-tooled vell. (HK. Nov.18-21; 1025)
DM 2,000

BRUZEN DE LA MARTINIERE, Antoine-Augustin
– **Le Grand Dictionnaire Géographique et Critique.** Paris, 1768. 6 vols. Fo. Old marb. cf., 6 spine raised bands, decor. (LM. Jun.13; 75)
B.Frs. 18,000
– **Histoire de la Vie et du Règne de Louis XIV** . . . The Hague, 1740. 5 vols. 4to. Some ll. yellowed. Cont. red mor., triple gt. fillets around covers, spines decor. with raised bands, bdgs. slightly defect. (HD. Feb.27; 20) Frs. 3,500
– – **Anr. Copy.** Cont. marb. cf., 5 decor. spine raised bands, worn. (LM. Mar.21; 76)
B.Frs. 12,000

[–] **Reise nach Norden, worinnen die Sitten, Lebens-Art und Aberglauben derer Norweger, Lappländer, Kiloppen, Borandier, Moscowiter** . . . Leipzig, 1706. 2nd. German Edn. 12mo. Later hf. leath. (R. Oct.14-18; 2040) DM 1,000
See–PUFENDORF, Baron Samuel & Bruzen de la Martinière, Antoine-Augustin

BRY, Johannes Theodore de
– **Florilegium Novum** . . . **New Blumbuch.** Oppenheim, 1612. Fo. 1 plt. torn & reprd., many stained. Cont. vell. W.a.f., from Chetham's Liby., Manchester, cont. sig. of Roger Bradshawe on title. (C. Nov.26; 102) *Schmidt.* £800
– [–] **Florilegium Renovatum.** [1644, etc.]. Fo. 112 plts. only, lacks some, some from anr. work. Old bds., worn. W.a.f. (S. Nov.25; 416)
Niedhardt. £480
See–BRY, Theodore de & others

BRY, Johann Theodore de & Johann Israel de
– **Emblemata Saecularia** . . . Ill.:– after Pieter Brueghel & others. Frankfurt, [Priv. Ptd.], 1596. 1st. Edn. 4to. Some ll. (mostly text) discold. Cont. cf., gt. borders & lge. rectangular panel of gt. cornucopia tools enclosing gt. coat-of-arms of Frederick William I, Duke of Saxony-Altenberg on upr. cover, & those of his consort Anna Maria van Neuberg on lr. cover, spine gt. with fleuron ornaments & 4 raised bands, rebkd. with orig. backstrip preserved, corners reprd., lacks ties, qtr. red mor. gt. s.-c. The copy of John A. Saks. (CNY. Oct.1; 89) $10,000

BRY, Theodore de & others
– **Admiranda Narratio Fida Tamen, De Commodis et Incolarum Ritibus Virginiae** . . . **anglico scripta sermone à Thoma Hariot.** Frankfurt am Main, 1590. 1st. Edn. Fo. Lacks engr. of Adam & Eve. Mod. vell. [Sabin III, pp. 24 et seq.] (S. Dec.8; 256) *Arader.* £850
– – **Anr. Edn.** 1590. 2nd. or counterfeit edn., iss. with imprint on title-p. Fo. Late 19th. C. hf. mor. [Sabin III, pp. 24 et seq.] (S. Dec.8; 208)
Crossley. £740
– – **Anr. Edn.** [1590]. 2nd. or counterfeit edn., iss. without imprint on title-p. Pt. 1. Fo. All but 1 or 2 of map & 28 plts. mntd. Mod. limp vell. [Sabin III, pp. 24 et seq.] (S. Dec.8; 207)
Crossley. £760
– [America]. Frankfurt, 1590-1630. 12 (of 13) pts. in 5 vols., lacks pt. 13. Fo. 1 plt. & 14 maps misbnd., paper often browned, occasional liby. blind-stps. Cont. cf., rebkd., & 19th. C. hf. mor., all worn, most covers detchd. W.a.f., from Chetham's Liby., Manchester. [Sabin 8784] (C. Nov.26; 103) *Arader.* £2,000
– **Americae Nona** . . . **Pars.** Frankfurt, 1602. 1st. Edn. Fo. Engraved coat of arms with another tipped in as overlay, full-p. engraved map, 39 lge. engraved text ills., some cold., Henry Stevens note tipped in. Mor., arabesque stps. on sides, by Pratt. (SPB. Jun.22; 19) $550
– **Americae Pars Quarta.** Frankfurt, 1594. 1st. Edn. Fo. Hand-cold. engraved titles, full-p. engraved plts., 26 lge. hand-cold. engraved text plts. (of 27). Disbnd., preserved in hf. mor. s.-c. (SPB. Jun.22; 20) $650
– **Americae Pars Quinta.** [Frankfurt], 1595; ca. 1617. Fo. Henry Stevens descriptive note tipped in. Mor., arabesque stp. on sides, by Pratt. (SPB. Jun.22; 20) $550
– **Americae Pars Septem.** [Frankfurt], 1625. Fo. Henry Stevens descriptive note tipped in. Mor., arabesque stp. on sides, by Pratt. (SPB. Jun.22; 21) $250
– **Der Ander Theyl der Newlich erfundenen Landtschafft Americae** . . . **Frantzosen in Floridam** . . . Frankfurt on Main, 1591. Fo. 2 engraved titles, 42 copperplts., almost every plt. reprd., some inlaid, lacks map. Mod. qtr. vell. W.a.f. (SG. Jun.11; 61) $400
– [**Reisen nach Amerika**]. Frankfurt, 1594-[1617]. 2nd. Latin Edn. Vols. 1, 3-6 in 5 vols. Fo. Lacks 1 engraved title & 4 engraved maps & 41 copper engrs., loose & browned in parts, text in vols. 1, 3 & 6 incompl. Very defect., spine partly brkn., lacks bdg. (H. May 21/22; 350) DM 1,350
– [–] **Anr. Edn.** Ill.:– Matthias Merian. Oppenheim & Frankfurt, 1603-28. Pts. 1, II, IV, X-XIII in 6 vols. Fo. 17 (of 26) engraved maps, ll text copper engrs., 120 (of 136) copperplts., with 10 ll. copper engrs. from same work, very defect., browned & partly loose, text incompl., 1 copper engr. with lge. reprd. hole, others with browning, title of vol. 1

stpd. 1 cont. paper bds. & no bdgs. [Sabin 8784] (H. Dec.9/10; 491) DM 2,600
– **Das VII Theil America. Zehender Theil Americae.** [Frankfurt]; Oppenheim, 1597; 1618. Together 2 pts. Fo. Disbnd. W.a.f. 1st. pt.: [Sabin vol. 3 p. 54]; 2nd. pt: [Sabin vol. 3 pp. 56-57] (CNY. Oct.1; 39) $850
– **Minor Voyages (India & Far East).** Frankfurt, 1598-1613. 1st. Edns. thro.-out. 10 (of 12) pts. in 3 vols., lacks pts. 11 & 12. Pt. 1 without the appendix (publd. later), some ll. creased, many plts., maps & c. with liby. blind stps. 19th. C. hf. mor., worn, lacks 2 covers, rest detchd. W.a.f., from Chetham's Liby., Manchester. (C. Nov.26; 104) *Remington.* £1,000
– – **Anr. Edn.** Frankfurt, 1601-07. 1st. Edns. Pts. 4, 5, 6 & 8 only (of 12). Fo. Pt. 5: plts. 4, 8 & 20 from anr. copy (2 cropped in fore-margin), lge. wormhole in plts. 9-19 affecting some headlines; pt. 6: plts. 18, 25 & 26 from anr. copy & loosely inserted, edges of fore & lr. margins of text extended with blank paper, flaw in heading of plt. 4; pt. 8: plts. 13 & 18 from anr. copy & loosely inserted. Pt. 5 in 19th. C. cl., remaining pts. disbnd. & loose. As a collection, w.a.f. (S. Jul.27; 52) *Schuster.* £120

BRYAN, Daniel
– **The Mountain Muse: Comprising the Adventures of Daniel Boone** . . . Harrisonburg, 1813. 1st. Edn. 12mo. Owner's notation on hf.-title, portions of text slightly foxed. Cont. cf., worn. From liby. of William E. Wilson. [Sabin 8787] (SPB. Apr.29; 35) $200

BRYAN, [Michael]
– **Dictionary of Painters & Engravers.** 1903-05. 5 vols. 4to. Cont. hf. mor. (SH. Jan.29; 84)
Stirling. £80
– – **Anr. Copy.** Orig. buckram-bkd. cl. (SKC. May 19; 148) £50
– – **Anr. Edn.** Ed.:– George C. Williamson. 1909-10. New Edn. 5 vols. 4to. Orig. cl., soiled. (CSK. Jan.30; 55) £70
– – **Anr. Edn.** Ed.:– George C. Williamson. 1919-20. 5 vols. 4to. Cont. hf. mor. (TA. Oct.16; 120) £90
– – **Anr. Edn.** 1920-21. 5 vols. 4to. Orig. cl. (SH. May 28; 223) *Subunso.* £70
– – **Anr. Edn.** Ed.:– George C. Williamson. L., 1920-26. 5 vols. 4to. Some pp. damp-wrinkled. Two-tone cl. (SG. Mar.12; 48) $180
– – **Anr. Edn.** 1920-30. 5 vols. 4to. Orig. cl. (SH. Oct.9; 66) *Prince.* £60
– – **Anr. Edn.** Ed.:– G.C. Williamson. 1925. 5 vols. Orig. cl. (P. Mar.12; 361) *Gonzalez.* £55
– – **Anr. Edn.** 1925-27. 5 vols. Cl. gt. (P. Feb.19; 224) *Myer.* £60
– – **Anr. Edn.** 1930-34. New Edn. 5 vols. Orig. cl., d.-w. (CSK. May 8; 96) £55
– – **Anr. Edn.** Ed.:– G.C. Williamson. Port Wash., [1964]. 5 vols. Orig. cl. (CSK. Nov.14; 184) £50

BRYANT, G.E.
– **Chelsea Porcelain Toys.** 1925. (650) sigd. 4to. Cl. (P. Oct.23; 169) *Tallerman.* £90
– – **Anr. Copy.** Orig. cl. (LC. Jun.18; 61) £55

BRYANT, William Cullen
– **Picturesque America.** N.Y., [1872]. 2 vols. in 4. 4to. Cont. hf. leath. (R. Oct.14-18; 1657)
DM 600
– – **Anr. Copy.** (R. Oct.14-18; 1658) DM 550
– – **Anr. Copy.** 2 vols. Cont. leath., slightly worn. (R. Mar.31-Apr.4; 2392) DM 450
– – **Anr. Edn.** N.Y., 1872-74. 2 vols. 4to. Orig. embossed gt. decor. mor. (TA. Oct.16; 279) £95
– – **Anr. Copy.** Orig. gt. & blind-stpd. mor., worn & scuffed. (SG. Nov.20; 392) $170
– – **Anr. Edn.** N.Y., [1872-74]. 2 vols. Lge. 4to. Orig. mor. (SG. Jun.11; 359) $200
– – **Anr. Copy.** Vol. I heavily dampstained in part. Orig. gt.-lettered three-qtr. mor. (SG. May 21; 416) $140
– – **Anr. Copy.** Some foxing, etc. Orig. mor., worn. (SG. May 21; 339) $110
– – **Anr. Edn.** N.d., ca. 1875. 4 vols. 4to. Publisher's hf. mor., spines gt. with fleurons. (SG. Jan.8; 361) $120
– – **Anr. Edn.** N.d. 4 vols. 4to. Cont. hf. mor., gt. spines. (SH. Mar.5; 24) *Sekuller.* £75
– – **Anr. Copy.** 2 vols. A few light marginal stains. Orig. leath., ex-liby. (CSK. May 15; 31) £65
– **Poems.** Camb., 1821. 1st. Edn. Orig. drab ptd. bds., edges worn, qtr. mor. gt. s.-c., unc. A.L.s. laid in (Apr. 13, 1878, 12mo., 1 p.); from the Prescott Collection. (CNY. Feb.6; 34) $950

BRYDEN, Henry A.
- **Great & Small Game of Africa.** L., 1899. 1st. Edn., (500) numbered. 4to. With the unnumbered advt. lf. at end. Cl., ex-liby. Sigd. by the publisher. (SG. Dec.11; 186) $900
- – Anr. Copy. Some foxing. (SSA. Jan.22; 175) R. 690

BRYDGES, Sir Egerton Bertram
- **A Poetical Tale.** Lee Priory Pr., 1814. (100), ptd. on India Paper. Slight spotting. Cont. mor. by Reeve, stpd. & ruled in gt., slightly rubbed and soiled. Lowndes states that 1 copy was printed on India Paper. (CSK. Aug.1; 210) £120

BRYNE, W.
See–HEARNE, Thomas & Bryne, W.

BRYUSOV, V.
See–BLOK, Alexander & others

BUACHE, Philippe
[-] **Atlas.** Ca. 1740. 4to. No title-p., 13 uncold. maps, some folding. Bds. (P. Dec.11; 160) *Chelsea.* £80

BUBER, M.
- **Jüdische Künstler.** Berlin, 1903. 1st. Edn. 4to. Orig. linen, soiled. (H. May 21/22; 1523) DM 420

BUCELINUS, Gabriel
- **Germania Topo-Chrono-Stemmatographica, Sacra et Profana.** Augsburg & Ulm, & Frankfurt (vol. 3). 1655-62 & 1671. Vols. 1-3. Cont. blind-tooled pig-bkd. wood bds. & 2 mod. linen. (R. Oct.14-18; 1212) DM 1,100

BUCER or Butzer, Martin
- **Apologia qua Fidei sua atque Doctrina, circa Christi Caenam.** [Strassburg], 1526. 1st. Edn. Mod. hf. vell. (R. Oct.14-18; 33) DM 900

BUCH DER ERFINDUNGEN
Ed.:– F. Releaux. Leipzig & Berlin, 1884-88. Orig. hf. leath., gt. spine. W.a.f. (HK. Nov.18-21; 426) DM 720

BUCH DER KUNST Dadurch der Weltlich Mensch mag Geistlich Werden
Augsburg, Johann Bamler, Dec.9, [14]78. 4to. Woodcut initial capitals, 93 ll. (only of 110, lacks initial & final blank & 15 text ll, all except blanks supplied in facs.), 84 (of 104) woodcuts, a3-5 with margins renewed without loss, 12 ll. with sm. portions of margins or corners renewed or restored, several reprd. marginal tears, sm. tear affecting woodcut at glr reprd., sm. wormhole from 16 to end, catching some text & 12 woodcuts. Red mor. gt., covers gt. & blind-tooled, by W. Pratt. Bkplts. of Charles Inglis & Charles Butler, lately in the collection of Eric Sexton. [Goff B1266, H. 4037] (CNY. Apr.8; 14) $4,500

BUCH DER WELT
Stuttgart, 1859. 4to. Text soiled. Orig. linen. (R. Mar.31-Apr.4; 1482) DM 800
- – Anr. Edn. Stuttgart, 1861. 4to. Cont. hf. leath. (HK. May 12-14; 979) DM 800

BUCHANAN, George
- **Opera Omnia . . .** Leyden, 1725. 2 vols. 4to. Cont. vell. (VG. Nov.18; 1092) Fls. 450
- **Poemata quae extant.** Leyden, 1628. Latest Edn. 24mo. (4¼×2½ inches). Red str.-grd. mor., gt., gt. spine, gt. dentelles, satin doubls. & end-ll., by Bozerian Jeune, erroneous date (1638) beneath his name. (SG. Sep.4; 44) $275
- **Rerum Scoticarum Historia.** Edinb., 1582. 1st. Edn. Fo. Cont. blind-stpd. cf. [STC 3991] (S. Nov.25; 448) *Armstrong.* £130
See–HILL, David Octavius & Buchanan, George

BUCHANAN, George (Trans.)
See–PSALMS, PSALTERS & PSEUMES (Latin & Greek)

BUCHANAN, Handasyde
See–SITWELL, Sacheverell & others

BUCHANAN, William
- **Historical & Genealogical Essay on the Family of Buchanan.** Glasgow, 1723. Free end paper with Coat of Arms. Tooled crimson mor., with 4 Coats of Arms, silk linings, box. (CE. Nov.20; 111) £130

BUCHDRUCK DES 15. JAHRHUNDERTS
Berlin, 1929-36. (500) numbered. 5 orig. pts. Orig. wraps. (R. Mar.31-Apr.4; 769) DM 550

BUCHENAU, S. (Ed.)
See–IMPRIMATUR

BUCHER, Bruno
- **Die Glassammlung des K.K. Oesterreich.** Wein, 1888. Fo. Later buckram, ex-liby. (SG. Dec.4; 159) $130

BUCHNER, Georg
- **Lenz. Ein Fragment.** Ill.:– Walter Gramatté. Hamburg, 1925. (150) numbered. Fo. Stained thro.-out in upr. part. Orig. bds., end-ll. soiled, spine defect. (D. Dec.11-13; 1012) DM 480
- **Leonce und Lena.** Ill.:– K. Walser. Berlin, 1910. (250). Lge. 4to. Sm. hole in inner margin. Orig. pict. vell., lightly soiled. (HK. Nov.18-21; 3004) DM 480
- **Sämmtl. Werke.** Ed.:– K.E. Franzos. Frankfurt, 1879. 1st. Coll. Edn. Cont. hf. leath. gt. (HK. May 15; 4120) DM 1,500
- – Anr. Copy. Lightly browned in places. Hf. linen. (H. May 21/22; 1008) DM 700

BUCHOLZ, Carl August
- **Actenstuekke die Verbesserung des Buergerlichen Zustandes der Israeliten Betreffend.** Stuttgard-Tuebingen, 1815. Leath., gt. (S. Nov.18; 645) *Hirschler.* £50

BUCHON, J.A.C.
- **Atlas Géographique, Statistique, Historique et Chronologique des Deux Amériques et des Iles Adjacentes.** Paris, 1825. 1st. Edn. Atlas fo. (22×15 inches). Late 19th. C. hf. cl., edges worn. (PNY. Mar.26; 27) $1,700

BUCHOZ, Pierre Joseph
- **Collection precieuse et enluminée des Fleurs . . . que se cultivent tant dans les Jardins de la Chine que dans ceux de l'Europe.** Paris, 1776. 2 pts. in 2 vols. Fo. Many plts. in 1st. vol. identified in ptd. Chinese characters, marks in upr. margins (probably where tissues were once attached). Cont. Fr. red mor., spines & borders gt. (SPB. Nov.25; 89) $19,000
- **Les Dons Merveilleux et Diversement Coloriés de la Nature.** Paris, 1782. Fo. 87 (of 90) hand-cold. plts., last plt. badly torn & some sm. marginal tears. Old bds., worn. (TA. May 21; 525) £475
- **Herbier colorié de l'Amérique.** Paris, 1783. 2 vols. Fo. Engraved titles & 206 hand-cold. plts., each bnd. according to a ptd. list in vol. 1 without regard to ptd. plt. numbers, new numbering inserted in cont. hand, last 6 plts. (not included in ptd. list) are preceded by a further copy of the engraved title, light stain affecting plt. 118, a few others slightly spotted or discold. Cont. Fr. red mor., spine & borders gt. (SPB. May 5; 120a) $11,000
[-] **The Toilet of Flora.** 1779. 12mo. Frontis. spotted. Cont. sheep, rebkd. (SH. Jun.11; 16) *Thorp.* £60
[-] – Anr. Copy. 12mo. Some marginal staining & early discolouration, margins of 2 or 3 ll. frayed. Cont. mor., blind-stpd. & gt. (KH. Mar.24; 80) Aus. $120
[-] **[Traité Historique des Plantes que croissent dans la Lorraine].** [Paris & Nancy], ca. 1770. 4to. 197 (of 203) engraved plts., lacks text. Cf., worn. W.a.f. (S. Jun.1; 85) *Shapero.* £140

BUCHOZ, Pierre Joseph & La Marquise de Sillery
[-] **Le Porte-Feuille du Botaniste ou Connoissance des Plantes . . . mise à la Portée de Tout le Monde.** [Paris], ca. 1780. Fo. 18 other engraved plts., many of grafting, bnd. at end. Hf. cf., worn. W.a.f. (S. Dec.3; 913) *Varekamp.* £240

BUCHSENMEISTEREI Von Gschoss, Büchsen, Pulver . . . und Feuerwerck
Frankfurt, 1534. 4to. Wraps. (S. Jan.27; 316) *Goldschmidt.* £500

BUCK, G.H. & Co.
- **Botanical Fine Art Weekly Wild Flowers of America.** N.Y., 1894. Ob. 4to. Title torn & reprd., slight browning. Cont. hf. cf., worn. (CSK. Jul.10; 14) £70

BUCK, Sir George
- **The Great Plantagenet.** 1635. 2nd. Edn. Sm. 4to. Sm. holes in woodcut caused by stab-marks, reprd., sm. hole in last lf. affecting 2 letters. Spr. cf. gt. by Rivière. Bkplts. of W.H. Hagen & M.C. Lefferts, lately in the collection of Eric Sexton. [STC 3997] (C. Apr.15; 164) *Quaritch.* £50

BUCK, Samuel & Nathaniel
- **Views of Ruined Abbeys & Castles in England & Wales.** [Plts. dtd. 1740-42]. Ob. fo. 83 engraved views only, lacks title, a few reprd., 1

mntd. Later hf. mor. (SH. Mar.5; 26) *Williams.* £420

BUCKINGHAM, E.B., of Vauxhall
See–CHANDLER, Alfred & Buckingham, E.B. of Vauxhall

BUCKINGHAM, George Villiers, Duke of
- **The Rehearsal.** 1672. 1st. Edn. 4to. Mor. by Sangorski. [Wing B5323] (C. Nov.19; 58) *Blackwell.* £120

BUCKINGHAM, James Silk
- **Travels in Assyria, Media & Persia.** 1830. 2nd. Edn. 2 vols. A few ll. slightly dampstained. Cont. hf. cf., gt. spines. (SH. Nov.7; 400) *Diba.* £85
- **Travels in Mesopotamia. Including a Journey from Aleppo to Bagdad.** 1827. 1st. Edn. 2 vols. Cont. hf. cf. (S. Jun.29; 245) *Ghani.* £160
- **Travels in Palestine.** 1821. 4to. Slight spotting, some ll. soiled. Mod. hf. mor. (CSK. Nov.21; 185) £110
- – Anr. Edn. 1822. 2nd. Edn. 2 vols. Cont hf. cf., lacks labels. (C. May 20; 109) *Maggs.* £90

BUCKINGHAM, L.F.A.
See–WRIGHT, George Newnham & Buckingham, L.F.A.

BUCKINGHAM, Nash
- **Blood Lines.** Ed.:– H.P. Davis. [1938]. (1250) numbered. Leatherette, with cold. circular medallion by Dr. Edgar Burke on cover. (SG. Dec.11; 222) $260
- **De Shootinest Gent'man; & other Tales.** Ed.:– Col. H.P. Sheldon. [1934]. (950) numbered. Leatherette, cold. medallion on cover, bkplt. (SG. Dec.11; 219) $325
- **Mark Right Tales of Shooting & Fishing.** [1936]. (1250). Leatherette, cold. medallion by Dr. Edgar Burke on upr. cover. (SG. Dec.11; 220) $220
- **Ole Miss'.** Ed.:– Paul A. Curtis. [1937]. (1250) numbered. Leatherette, with cold. medallion by Dr. Edgar Burke inset on upr. cover, bkplt. (SG. Dec.11; 221) $240

BUCKLAND, William
- **Geology & Mineralogy.** L., 1836. 1st. Edn. 2 vols. Three-qtr. mor., spine gt. (SG. Sep.18; 68) $100

BUCKLE, Henry Thomas
- **Library Illustrative of Social Progress.** [L.], ca. 1890? Vols. 1-7. 12mo. Hf. cl., endpapers damp-soiled. (SG. Feb.12; 187) $150

BUCKLER, John & J.C.
- **Views of Eaton Hall in Cheshire.** 1826. L.P.? Fo. Plts. on India proof paper, a few ll. slightly spotted. Orig. hf. mor., very worn. (SBA. Dec.16; 169) *Chesters.* £62

BUCKLER, William
- **The Larvae of the British Butterflies & Moths.** Ed.:– H.T. Stainton & G.T. Porritt. 1886-1901. 9 vols. A few ll. & plts. in vol 1 loose. Orig. embossed cl., gt., ex-liby. (PL. Jul.11; 87) *Miles.* £260

BUCKLEY, Arabella B.
- **Winner's in Life's Race.** L., 1892. Cf. gt. Fore-e. pntg. (SG. Mar.19; 116) $220

BUCKMASTER, Ernest
- **The Art of . . .** Melbourne & c., [1951]. Orig. bdg. (KH. Mar.24; 82) Aus. $140

BUCKNILL, Sir John Charles & Tuke, Daniel H.
- **A Manual of Psychological Medicine containing the History, Nosology, Description . . . of Insanity.** 1858. 1st. Edn. Erratum slip, 32pp. of advts. dtd. Nov. 1859. Orig. cl., spine gt., unc. (S. Jun.15; 137) *Sargeant.* £120

BUCKTON, G.B.
- **Monograph of the British Aphides.** 1876-83. 4 vols. 2 litho. plts. loose & 2 soiled. Orig. embossed cl., gt., ex-liby. (PL. Jul.11; 84) *Wheldon & Wesley.* £80

BUDAEUS or Bude, Guillaume
- **Annotationes Priores in Pandectas.–Altera Aeditio Annotationum in Pandectas.** Cologne, J. Soter, Apr. 1527; Feb. 1527. 2 works in 1 vol. 18th. C. vell. (S. Nov.25; 351) *Erasmus.* £65
- **Commentarii Linguae Graecae.** Paris, 1529. 1st. Edn. Fo. Lacks final blank lf., some dampstaining, wormed, particularly at front & back & thro.-out pp. 160-215, some margins brittle & just frayed. Qtr. maroon mor., gt.-lettered, by Zaehnsdorf.

BUDAEUS or Bude, Guillaume -*contd.*
Bkplt. of the General Theological Seminary Liby.
(CNY. Oct.1; 45) $600

BUDAEUS or Bude, Guilielmus–ALCIATUS, Andreas
– De Asse et Partibus Eius ...; De Studio
Literarum ...–Libellus de Ponderibus et Mensuris
[& other works]. Cologne; Basle; Hagenau, Aug.,
1528; Mar., 1533; Oct., 1530 [Mar., 1531]. 3
works in 1 vol. 1st. work: some ll. soiled, MS. notes
in margins; 2nd. work: title soiled & detchd., sm.
hole in title not affecting text, Q1v & Q2r badly
soiled; 3rd. work: lacks plts., folding table & final
colophon lf., some shaving affecting headline of
last lf., slight damp-staining; all works with slight
browning. 17th. C. mott. cf., slightly worn. (S.
Jul.27; 130) *Bozzolato.* £160

BUDAEUS, J.F.
– Allgemeines Historisches Lexicon. Leipzig &
Frankfurt, 1709-14. 1st. Edn. 5 vols. in 3. Fo.
Cont. cf., gt. spines. (H. Dec.9/10; 843) DM 860

BUDDHA
– Auswahl aus dem Palikanon. Trans.:– Paul
Dahlke. Ill.:– Marcus Behmer. Berlin, 1922. (225)
numbered on Zanders H.M.P. Fo. Orig. vell., gt.
borders enclosing gt. wheel on mor. inset, spine gt.,
partly unc., by P. Demeter, Hellerau. (SG.
Jan.15; 10) $140

BUDGE, Sir Ernest Alfred Thompson
– The Book of the Dead. Facsimile of the Papyrus
of Ani. 1890. Fo. Cont. hf. mor. (SH. Jan.29; 8)
Mathews. £105
– – Anr. Copy. (SH. Apr.9; 59) *Duran.* £65
– – Anr. Edn. 1894. 2nd. Edn. Fo. Cont. hf. mor.,
worn. (CSK. Sep.5; 134) £55
– – Anr. Edn. 1913. 2 vols. Orig. cl., d.-w.'s. (SH.
Jul.16; 161) *Trocchi.* £55
– The Life of Takla Hâymânot. Priv. Ptd., 1906.
(250). Fo. Cl. on bds. (P. Oct.2; 316)
Rees-Jones. £60
– – Anr. Copy. 2 vols. 4to. Orig. cl. (SH.
Mar.6; 499) *George's.* £50
– – Anr. Copy. 2 vols. Fo. Cl. (SG. May 14; 29)
$350
– Osiris & the Egyptian Resurrection.–The Gods
of the Egyptians. L.; Chic., 1911; 1904. 1st. Edn.,
1st. Amer. Edn. 2 vols.; 2 vols. 4to. Orig. gt. pict.
cl. (PNY. Dec.3; 59) $130

BUDGETT, H.M.
– Hunting by Scent. Ill.:– L. Edwards. N.d. (50)
sigd. by author & artist. Orig. vell.-bkd. cl. (SH.
Oct.9; 210) *Head.* £70

BUDIL'NIK [Alarm Clock]
Moscow, 1896. 50 Iss. only in 1 vol. Fo. Some sm.
tears, some ll. slightly soiled. Orig. cold. wraps.,
lacks 1, disbnd. (SH. Feb.6; 304)
De la Casa. £70

BUEK, F.G.
– Hamburg und seine Umgebungen im 19.
Jahrhundert. Hamburg, 1848. Pt. 2. Slightly
browned & very soiled in parts. Later linen. (H.
Dec.9/10; 666) DM 5,200

BUESCHING, A.F.
– Nuova Geografia ... Trans.:– Guadioso
Jagemann. Venice, 1774-82. 35 vols., including
index & supp. to vol. 25. Orig. ptd. paper wraps.,
unc. From the collection of John A. Saks. (C.
Jun.10; 27) *Breslauer.* £70

BUFFET, Bernard
– Naples. Ed.:– Text:– Montesquieu, Charles de
Brosses, Chateaubriand, Gerard de Nervar,
Lamartine, Theophile Gautier, Stendhal,
Alexandre Dumas Père, Charles Baudelaire,
Taine, Anatole France, André Gide, Valéry
Larbaud, pref.:– Gino Doria. N.p., 1959 (300) on
papier pur fil d'Arches, numbered & sigd. by
artist. 4to. Loose ll. Wrap. & publisher's box.
(LM. Nov.8; 34) B.Frs. 9,000

BUFFON, Georges Louis Leclerc, Comte de
– Cours Complet d'Histoire Naturelle. Paris,
1801-03. 774 (of 785) mostly cold. copperplts.
Cont. marb. leath., gt. spine & inner & outer dent.
(HK. Nov.18-21; 430) DM 12,000
– Encyclopédie Méthodique. Histoire Naturelle,
Planches. [Paris], ca. 1790. Pts. 1 & 2 in 2 vols.
4to. Slightly stained in margin, lacks 1 copperplt.
Cont. bds., stained & worn, unc. (HK.
Nov.18-21; 801) DM 650
[–] Histoire Naturelle, Générale et Particulière,
avec la Description du Cabinet du Roi. Ed.:–

[L.J.M. Daubenton]. Paris, 1749-67. 1st. Series.
15 vols. (of 36). 4to. Cont. marb. cf., spines richly
gt., top of 1 spine defect. (VG. Nov.18; 1095)
Fls. 1,050
– – Anr. Edn. Paris, 1749-78. Vols. 1-15, vols. 1-5
of Supp. only. 4to. Cont. cf., worn. W.a.f. (CSK.
Feb.27; 23) £280
– – Anr. Edn. Paris, 1749-89. 40 vols. 4to. Cont.
cf., decor spines. (HD. Jun.29; 264b) Frs. 16,800
[–] – Anr. Edn. Paris, 1750-67. 1st. Edn., vols.
I-III 2nd. Edn. 15 vols. 4to. Slightly browned or
soiled in parts, vol. II, heavier thro.-out. Cont. cf.,
gt. spine, slightly worn & soiled. From Blome
liby., engraved ex-lib. & MS. owner's mark. (H.
May 21/22; 152) DM 1,900
– – Anr. Edn. Amst., 1778-79. New Edn. Vols.
1-15 bnd. in ll, & 1-6 of supp., together 21 vols.
Cont. hf. cf. (LM. Jun.13; 90) B.Frs. 22,000
– – Anr. Edn. Bern, 1784-91. 40 vols. Slightly
soiled & browned in parts, many ll. & plts. loose.
Cont. paper bds., worn. (H. Dec.9/10; 269)
DM 640
– – Anr. Edn. Paris, 1725-91. 28 vols. 'Oiseaux' 14
(of 18) vols., lacks vols. 4, 5, 6 & 10,
'Quadrupedes', compl. series, vols. I-XIV, 284
engraved col. heightened plts. Sewed, wraps. (LM.
Jun.13; 89) B.Frs. 18,000
– – Anr. Edn. Ed.:– Sonnini. Paris, 1800-19. 127
vols. plus 5 vol. supp. Hf. russ., worn. W.a.f. (S.
Dec.3; 918) *W. & W.* £420
– – Anr. Edn. Paris, 1801. 31 vols. (of 80) only.
12mo. Lf. cut away from front of some vols., slight
browning. Cf., gt., worn. (SPB. May 29; 57) $225
[–] Histoire Naturelle des Osieaux. Paris, 1770-83.
1st. Edn. 9 vols. 4to. Cont. mott. cf., rebkd. (S.
Dec.3; 914) *Waters.* £500
– Histoire Naturelle, Générale et Particulière,
[Oiseaux]. [Minéraux].–[Quadrupeds]. Paris,
1785-91. Various Edns.? Vols. 1-18 (lacks vols. 3
& 17); vols. 1-13 (lacks vol. 10); vols. 1-14 (lacks
vol. 2), together 41 vols. Lacks a few plts., some
dampstains & offsetting. Cont. sheep, slightly
soiled. W.a.f. (SBA. Jul.14; 221) *Shapiro.* £105
– Keepsake d'Histoire Naturelle, Description des
Oiseaux. Paris, n.d. Some staining. Hf. cl. gt. (P.
Nov.13; 16) *Graham.* £55
– Natural History. 1781. 8 vols. Piece cut from
blank portion of title. Cont. cf., gt., worn. (S.
Dec.3; 915) *Erlini.* £50
– – Anr. Edn. 1797-1808. 16 vols. Vol. 8 lacks
title-p. & list of contents. Orig. bds. worn, vol. 8
lacks upr. cover, unc. (P. May. 14; 273) £95
– – Anr. Edn. Trans.:– J.S. Barr. 1806-16. 10 vols.,
& 6 supp. vols. 128 hand-cold. plts. (of
approximately 140), 1 plt. loose, some foxing &
cropping. Cf. gt., worn. (PL. Sep.18; 151)
Hyde Park Books. £78
– – Anr. Edn. Trans.:– J. Barr. 1810-15-07. Slight
browning. Cl.-bkd. bds. (S. Jun.1; 87)
Bevan. £70
– – Anr. Edn. 1820. 20 vols. Some ll. spotted.
Cont. cf., 2 spines worn. (SH. May 21; 263)
Lynch. £75
– – Anr. Edn. Trans.:– W. Smellie. 1820. 2 vols.
4to. Hand-cold. plts. misbnd., some stains. Sheep.
(P. Mar.12; 246) *Cambridge.* £55
– Natural History, containing a Theory of the
Earth. - Natural History of Birds, Fish, Insects &
Reptiles. Trans.:– J.S. Barr (2nd. work).
1797-1807; 1808. 10 vols.; 6 vols. 12mo. 1st. work:
a few plts. hand-cold. by a previous owner; 2nd.
work: some spots. Unif. cont. hf. cf. (SBA.
Jul.22; 83) *Cuenca.* £55
– Naturgeschichte der Vögel. Trans.:– F.H.W.
Marlini. Berlin, 1772-1809. 1st German Edn.
Cont. marb. leath. gt., marb. end-papers. (HK.
May 12-14; 464) DM 15,000
– – Anr. Edn. Trans.:– B. Chr. Otto. [Berlin],
[1789-91]. Plt. vols. 13-17 in 1 vol. Cont. hf. leath.
(HK. Nov.18-21; 798) DM 3,600
– – Anr. Edn. [Berlin], [1794-95]. Plt. vols. 21-22
in 1 vol. Cont. hf. leath., worn. (HK.
Nov.18-21; 799) DM 2,300
– – Anr. Edn. [Berlin], [1803-07]. Plts Vol. 31-33
in 1 vol. Cont. hf. leath., worn. (HK.
Nov.18-21; 800) DM 1,700
– Oeuvres Complètes. Paris, 1770-89. 56 vols.
12mo. Cont. vell., 5 spine raised bands. (CR.
Mar.19; 291) Lire 2,700,000
– – Anr. Edn. Paris, 1774-82. 24 vols. 12mo. Cont.
mott. cf., spines gt., spine of 1 vol. stained & torn.
W.a.f. (C. Jul.15; 136) *Amman.* £100
– – Anr. Edn. Paris, 1774-89. Reprint of 1749 Edn.
36 vols. 4to. Slightly browned, 1 schematic plt.

torn. Cont. leath., spine defect. in 3 vols. (R.
Mar.31-Apr.4; 1323) DM 6,000
– – Anr. Edn. Ed.:– M. Flourens. Paris, 1853-55.
12 vols. 4to. Hf. mor., 4 spine raised bands. (CR.
Jun.11; 557) Lire 800,000
– – Anr. Edn. Ed.:– Flourens. Ill.:– Travies & H.
Gobin. Paris, [1853]. 12 vols. Lge. 8vo. Cont. hf.
chagrin, spines with raised bands. (HD.
Feb.27; 93) Frs. 4,200
– Oeuvres Complètes avec les Extraits de
Daubenton et la Classification de Cuvier. Paris,
1839, 1841. 7 vols. Lge. 8vo. Some ll. yellowed,
foxed. Cont. hf. chagrin, smooth decor. spines.
(HD. Feb.27; 92) Frs. 1,400
– Oeuvres Complètes. – Histoire des Quadrupeds.
Paris, 1774-78; 1775-85. Vols. 1-13; vols. 1-10.
12mo. Cont. mott. cf. (GM. Apr.30; 580) £80
– – Anr. Edn. Paris, 1775-77. 9 vols. 12mo. 266
engraved plts. (of 267), 2 plts. & 2 ll. detchd.
Cont. mott. cf. (S. Mar.17; 241) *Faupel.* £160
– – Anr. Edn. Brussels, 1828-29. 14 vols. Cont. hf.
roan, worn. W.a.f. (C. Mar.18; 187)
Schierenberg. £400
– – Anr. Edn. Ed.:– M. Flourens. Paris, n.d. 12
vols. 4to. Hf. chagrin, worn. (LM. Mar.21; 77)
B.Frs. 17,000
– Sämtl. Werke samt den Ergänzungen nach der
Klassifikation von Cuvier. Trans.:– H.J.
Schaltenbrand. Cologne, 1837-40. 8 vols. Slightly
soiled. Orig. bds. (D. Dec.11-13; 287) DM 600

BUGENHAGEN, Johann
– Psalteruim Davidis. Frankfurt, after 1544. 4to.
Titler restored, last ll. wormed & bkd. Cont.
pig.-bkd. wood bds., blind-tooled decor., slightly
soiled & worn. (H. May 21/22; 916) DM 800
– Unterrichtung ... Wittenberg, 1526. 1st.
German Edn. Slightly browned. Mod. hf. vell. (R.
Oct.14-18; 34) DM 640

**BUILDER'S Magazine (The), or a Universal
Dictionary for Architects, Carpenters, Masons,
Bricklayers, etc.**
1779. 2nd. Edn. 4to. Cont. cf., some wear. (SKC.
Oct.8; 1437) £50
– – Anr. Edn. L., 1788. New Edn. 4to. Plts. 162 &
163 misnumbered cxiiii & clxiv. Cont. qtr. cf., bds.
(CB. May 27; 53) Can. $450

BUILDER'S PRACTICAL DIRECTOR (The)
N.d. 4to. A few plts. slightly cropped, spotted.
Orig. cl. (SKC. May 19; 149) £75

BUKET [Bouquet]
Ed.:– [E.M. Narusbek]. St. Petersb., 1906. Nos.
1-6. 4to. Unbnd. (SH. Feb.5; 51)
De la Casa. £180

BUKSIR [Tug]
Ed.:– [Yu. V. Gol'dberg]. St. Petersb., 1907. No.
1. 4to. Unbnd. (SH. Feb.5; 52) *Quaritch.* £65

BULKELY, John & Cummins, John
– A Voyage to the South-Seas in the Years
1740-41. L., 1743. 1st. Edn. Browning, minor
defects. Later buckram, ex-liby. [Sabin 9108]
(SPB. Jul.28; 65) $125

BULKELEY, Peter
– The Gospel-Covenant. 1651. 4to. Worming
towards end affecting running titles & pagination,
staining to upr. hf. of text. Cont. cf., gt.
fleur-de-lys in corners of covers, initials KG gt. in
centre, worn, recornered. From the collection of
Eric Sexton. [Sabin 9097, Wing B5404] (C.
Apr.15; 86) *Burgess.* £50

BULLART, Isaac
– Academie des Sciences et des Arts. Ill.:–
Larmessin & others. Brussels, 1682. 2 vols. in 1.
Sm. fo. Early vell. (SG. May 14; 32) $1,000

BULLEIN, William
– Bulleins Bulwarke of Defence Against all
Sicknesse, Soarenesse & Woundes that do Daily
Assault Mankind. 1579. 4 pts. in 1 vol. Fo. Light
stain on inner portion of 1st. pt., some inkstains on
L1 verso & L2, sm. hole in last lf. affecting
numeral, lacks last blank lf. Cont. limp vell., worn,
ties torn. [STC 4034] (S. Jun.15; 141)
Maggs. £650
[–] A Newe Boke of Phisicke called ye Government
of Health ... whereunto is added a sufferain
regiment against the pestilence. [?1559]. 126 ll.,
title & Index in photostat facs., hole in A78 & lr.
outer portion of C1 torn away, both with loss of
text. Marb. bds., sheep spine. [STC 4041?] (S.
Jun.15; 140) *Rix.* £95

BULLER, Sir Walter Lawry
– A History of the Birds of New Zealand. 1873. 1st. Edn. 4to. Frontis. stained & foxed, some very slight foxing. Orig. cl., badly stained. (BS. May 13; 294) £360
– – Anr. Edn. Ill.:– J.G. Keulemans. 1888. 2nd. Edn. 2 vols. Lge. 4to. Hf. mor., richly gt., partly unc. (S. Jun.1; 89) *Traylen.* £620
– – Anr. Copy. 4to. Lf. of index torn & reprd. without loss. Mod. hf. mor. (TA. Jun.18; 116) £425

BULLETIN DE L'INSTITUT ARCHEOLOGIQUE LIEGEOIS
Liège, 1852-1935. Vol. 1-19. in 48 vols. Vols. 1-16 hf. cl., rest hf. chagrin. (LM. Jun.13; 115) B.Frs. 45,000

BULLIALDUS, Ismael
– Opus Novum ad Arithmeticam Infinitorum libris sex Comprehensum. Paris, 1682. 1st. Edn. Fo. A few stains in upr. margins. Cont. cf., worn, upr. cover detchd. Pres. copy to Abbe Carlo Antonio Gondi; from Marquess of Bute's liby.; from Honeyman Collection. (S. May 20; 3195) *Quaritch.* £65

BULLIARD, Jean Baptiste François, called Pierre
– Herbier de la France ou Collection Complette des Plantes Indigènes de ce Royanne. Paris, 1780 [1785], [completed 1798]. Vols. 1-5 (of 13). Fo. 240 plts. (of 602), nos. 1-48 not numbered (apart from no. 1), rest numbered 49-240, most plts. slightly foxed at edges, a few plts. browned. Cl. (VA. Jan.30; 579) R. 1,000

BULLINGER, Henry
– A Hundred Sermons upon the Apocalipse of Jesu Christ. 1561. 1st. Edn. in Engl. 4to. Woodcut decors. detchd., Ll3 & 4 misbnd. after Ll6, 1 lf. cleanly torn, some worming & dampstaining. Later hf. cf., worn. W.a.f. [STC 4061] (CSK. Mar.27; 108) £200
– – Anr. Edn. 1573. 2nd. Edn. in Engl. 4to. Title & margins soiled. Later hf. cf., covers detchd., lacks spine. [STC 4062] (CSK. Mar.27; 109) £140
– Zwo Predigen uber den CXXX auch CXXXIII Psalmen Davids. Zurich, 1574. Last lf. torn & reprd. without loss, some soiling. Mod. wraps., stitching shaken. (CSK. Mar.27; 111) £50

BULLITT, Thomas W.
– My Life at Oxmoor: Life on a Farm in Kentucky before the War. Louisville, Priv. ptd., 1911. (100) numbered. Cl. This copy presented to Haley Fiske by Bullitt's son. (SG. Jan.8; 232) $120

BULLOCK, John G.
– Jolts & Scrambles: or, We Uns & Our Doin's. Ill.:– Bullock & Strickland L. Kneass. Phila., Priv. ptd., 1884. 1st. & only Edn. Ob. sm. 8vo. Mntd. albumen prints by Bullock, 8 orig. etched plts. by Kneass titled in pencil & sigd. in plt. Orig. gt.-ptd. cl. (PNY. Dec.3; 60) $900

BULLOCK, William
– Six Months Residence & Travels in Mexico. 1824. 1st. Edn. Some ll. misbnd., a few slight offsets on text, no hf.-title. Cont. hf. cf., spine worn. [Sabin 9140] (S. Apr.7; 248) *Remington.* £150
– – Anr. Copy. A few maps tattered. Near cont. cl. (CSK. May 1; 111) £50
– Sketch of a Journey Through the Western States of North America, . . . L., 1827. 1st. Edn. 12mo. Folding map torn & detchd. at some folds, silked on verso, text lightly foxed. Mod. hf. mor., gt. spine & borders. From liby. of William E. Wilson. (SPB. Apr.29; 36) $425

BULLOT, M.
See–HELYOT, Pierre & Bullot, M.

BULTEAU, Charles de, Conseiller du Roy
– Bibliotheca Bultelliana: sue Catalogus Librorum. Paris, 1711. 2 vols. Index in vol. 2. Cont. cf., lacks labels. (SM. Oct.7; 1338) Frs. 1,500

BULWER-LYTTON
See–LYTTON, Edward George Lytton Bulwer, Baron

BULYUK, N. & D.
See–KHLEBINIKOV, V. & others

BUMALDI, J.A.
See–SEGUIERIO, J.F. & Bumaldi, J.A.

BUNBURY, Henry
– Twenty-Two Plates illustrative of Various Interesting Scenes in the Plays of Shakespeare. Ill.:– Bartolozzi & others after Bunbury. [Plts. dtd. 1792-95]. Fo. Some plts. with captions cropped, 1 caption torn. Cont. hf. cf., rebkd. preserving orig. spine. (C. Jul.22; 51) *Fletcher.* £550

BUNBURY, Henry William 'Geoffrey Gambado'
– An Academy for Grown Horsemen. L., 1787. 1st. Edn. Fo. 1st. lf. of dedication & 1 plt. cropped, prelims. with marginal tears, some marginal stains. Cont. cf., covers detchd., spine worn. (CB. Dec.9; 130) Can. $260
– – Anr. Edn. Ill.:– W. Dickinson. L., 1796. 2nd. Edn. Fo. Rather foxed thro.-out. Mod. cl., unc. (SG. Dec.11; 187) $120
– – Anr. Edn. Ill.:– Rowlandson. 1809. Lr. blank corner of title reprd. Mor. gt. by Rivière. (C. Jul.22; 4) *Maggs.* £120
– – Anr. Copy. Hf. cf. & marb. bds., worn. (CE. Dec.4; 215) £60
– – Anr. Edn. 1825. 12mo. Loosely inserted is newspaper cutting suggesting book was gift of Prince of Wales to Lancelot Lowther. Mod. cf., gt., unc. (S. Dec.8; 8) *Quaritch.* £150
– Academy for Grown Horsemen . . . the Annals of Horsemanship. Ill.:– Th. Rowlandson after H. Bunbury. L., 1809. Later cf., triple gold stpd. fillet, gt. spine, gold-stpd. outer fillet, wide floral inner gt. dentelle. (D. Dec.11-13; 2134) DM 720
– Annals of Horsemanship. L., 1796. Fo. Some foxing, stains & marginal tears. Mod. cl., unc. (SG. Dec.11; 188) $120
– – Anr. Edn. L., 1808. 3rd. Edn. 2 vols. in 1. Fo. Foxed, with some marginal stains, edges of 1st. frontis. reprd. New marb. bds., leath. spine & tips. (SG. Dec.11; 189) $160
– – Anr. Edn. 1811. 1 copperplt. loose & trimmed. Orig. bdg. (DWB. May 15; 95) £50

BUNDETO, Carlos
– El Espejo de la Muerte. Ill.:– after Romain de Hooge. 'Antw.' [Amst.], 1700. 4to. Some ll. slightly browned or stained. Later panel. mor. gt. by Winstanley, Manchester. (SBA. Dec.16; 7A) *Duran.* £240

BUNIN, L.
– Sinodik ili Pomyannik. N.p., mid-18th. C. 3rd. Edn. Fo. 40 engraved ll., crudely hand-cold., with following MS. ll., soiled thro-out. Cont. gt.-stpd. cf., rebkd. (SH. Feb.5; 202) *Burrows.* £250

BUNN, Alfred
– The Stage, both before and behind the Curtain. 1840. 1st. Edn. 3 vols. Errata slip in vol. 1. Orig. cl., 1 upr. hinge split, faded, unc. (SH. Apr.10; 386) *Crete.* £60

BUNN, Matthew
– Narrative of the Life & Adventures . . . in an Expedition Against the North-Western Indians in the Years 1791, 2, 3, 4 & 5. Batavia, 1818. 7th. Edn. 12mo. Soiled. Later wraps., folding cl. case, unc. From liby. of William E. Wilson. (SPB. Apr.29; 37) $325

BUNNY, Rupert
– The Art of . . . Ed.:– Clive Turnbull. Ill.:– Tristan Buesset. Sydney, n.d. (1200). 4to. Orig. cl. (JL. Jul.20; 621) Aus. $100

BUNSEN, Robert
– Gasometrischen Methodern. Braunschweig, 1857. 1st. Edn. Slightly soiled. Cont. hf. leath. (HK. Nov.18-21; 431) DM 720
– Gesammelte Abhandlung. Ed.:– W. Ostwald & M. Bodenstein. Leipzig, 1904. Coll. Edn. 3 vols. Lge. 8vo. Orig. linen. (R. Oct.14-18; 271) DM 500

BUNTING, Edward
– The Ancient Music of Ireland. Dublin, 1840. Fo. Cl., decor., gt. (GM. Apr.30; 101) £55

BUNTING, H.–PLINIUS, Caius Secundus,–The Elder–HERBSTEIN, Sigmund von
– Itinerarivm Sacrae Scriptvrae. – Des Weitberumbten . . . Philosophi . . . Bücher vnd Schrifften, von Natur, Art vnd Eygenschafft aller Creaturen.–Rervm Moscoviticarum Commentarij. Ill.:– J. Amman. Wittenberg [& Magdeburg]; Frankfurt; Basel, 1588; 1584; [1556]. 3rd. Edn. (3rd. work). 3 works in 1 vol. Fo. 2nd. title lacks 14pp., 3rd. work bds. maps soiled, folding genealogical table defect. with loss, lacks last index. lf., slightly soiled, old MS. underlining.

Cont. hf. pig., heavily soiled & defect., partly wormed. (HK. Nov.18-21; 131) Frs. 10,000

BUNTING, H.
– Itinerarium Sacrae Scripturae Trans.:– J.G. Leuckfeld. Magdeburg, 1718. 2 pts. in 1 vol. Fo. Slightly browned, little soiled, owner's mark on title, title marked Cont. hf. vell., 19th. C. new bkd. (HK. May 12-14; 528) DM 480

BUNYAN, John
– The Holy War made by Shaddai upon Diabolus. L., 1782. 12mo. Orig. spr. sheep. (SG. Apr.30; 33) $100

BUNYAN, John
[–] The Pilgrim's Progress. [1678]. 2nd. Edn. 12mo. Without the added lf. of 'Conclusion' (not called for), lacks title, but with photstat loosely inserted, some stains & soiling, prelims. & some ll. frayed, sm. tear in I3, loose. Cont. sheep, worn, cl. case. [Wing B5558] (S. Jul.27; 67) *Ponder.* £400
– – Anr. Edn. 1680. 4th. Edn., 2nd. Iss. 12mo. With corrected reading 'London' on title-p. & 6-line advt. on verso, 2 or 3 letters erased of A4v & A5r, printing flaw on C2r. Cont. mott. cf., cl. case. [Wing B5561] (S. Jul.27; 68) *Quaritch.* £1,300
– – Anr. Edn. 1823. Pts. 1-3 in 2 vols. Ob. 12mo. Orig. wraps. (SH. Mar.19; 36) *Alderson.* £200
– – Anr. Edn. Ill.:– Thomas Stothard. L., 1893. Lev. gt., gt. dentelles, by Ramage. Fore-e. pntg. (SG. Mar.19; 117) $180
– – Anr. Edn. L., Essex House Pr., 1899. (750). Niger mor. gt., central medallion ornament, gt. decor., gt.-ruled, spine in 6 compartments, 5 with gt. ornaments, 5 raised bands, by Douglas Cockerell, sigd. 'DC 1900'. Cortlandt Field Bishop bkplt. (CNY. May 22; 360) $1,300
– – Anr. Copy. Orig. vell., unc. (CNY. May 22; 306) $120
– – Anr. Edn. Ill.:– Blair Hughes-Stanton & Gertrude Hermes. Cresset Pr., 1928. (205) numbered. 2 vols. Fo. Orig. parch., slightly marked. (S. Jul.31; 239) *Lam.* £130
– – Anr. Edn. L., Cresset Pr. 1928. (195). 2 vols. Fo. Orig. cl., slightly worn. (SPB. Nov.25; 241) $250
– – Anr. Edn. Ed.:– G.B. Harrison & G. Keynes. Ill.:– after William Blake. Ltd. Edns. Cl., 1941. (1500) numbered. 4to. Buckram. Blind-stpd. on limitation p. 'This is one of 15 presentation copies', & marked 'A.J.'. (SG. Jan.15; 133) $110
– – Anr. Copy. Orig. box. (SG. Apr.9; 473) $100
– Works. L., 1736. 2nd. Edn. Fo. Last lf. defect., & silked. Mod. mott. cf. (SG. Feb.5; 57) $100

BUONAIUTI, B. Serafino & others
– Italian Scenery. 1806. 1st. Edn. Fo. Cont. cf.-bkd. bds., reprd. (SH. Mar.5; 28) *Vitale.* £260
– – Anr. Copy. Fo. Cont. leath. gt. (HK. May 12-14, 1149) DM 1,600

BUONANNI, Filippo
– Musaeum Kircherianum sive Musaeum A.P. Athanasio Kirchero in Collegio Romano Societatis Jesu. Rome, 1709. 1st. Edn. Fo. Cont. vell. (HK. Mar.12-14; 351) DM 2,000
– Ricreatione dell'Occhio e della Mente. Rome, 1681. 1st. Edn. 4to. 19th. C. vell. From Chetham's Liby., Manchester. (C. Nov.26; 64) *Antiqua Libri.* £500

BUONAROTTI, Filippo
– Osservazioni Istoriche Sopra Alcuni Medaglioni. Rome, 1698. 4to. Folding plts. with short tears. Cont. vell., slightly worn. (S. Jul.27; 220) *Duran.* £75

BUONARROTI, Michelagniolo
– Poesie. [Montagnola], [1923]. (175) on vell. 4to. Orig. vell., orig. vell. s.-c. (HK. Nov.18-21; 2835) DM 2,200

BURAVCHIK [Gimlet]
Ed.:– [K.G. Borman & V.V. Zhukov]. St. Petersb., 1906. Nos. 1, 3-4 only (of 4). Unbnd. (SH. Feb.5; 54) *De la Casa.* £100

BURBIDGE, Frederick William Thomas
– The Narcissus . . . Ed.:– J.G. Baker. 1875. Some ll. loose in gutta-percha bdg. Orig. cl. gt. (C. May 20; 193) *Jean.* £250

BURCHARDUS de Biberach
– Historia Friederici Imperatoris Magni. [Augsbourg], ca. 1477. Fo. Rubricated, red & blue hand-painted initials, hand-painted blason on

BURCHARDUS de Biberach – Historia Friederici Imperatoris Magni. -contd.
1st. lf., lacks 1 blank lf. Mod. vell., arms. [Hain 8768] (LM. Nov.8; 90) B.Frs. 53,000

BURCHELL, William J.
– **The South African Drawings . . . Volume One.** Johannesburg, 1938. (300). 4to. Hf. mor., d.-w. (SSA. Nov.5; 310) R. 160
– **The South African Drawings . . . Volume Two.** Johannesburg, 1952. (300). 4to. Hf. mor., d.-w. (SSA. Nov.5; 311) R. 100
– **Travels in the Interior of Southern Africa.** 1822-24. 2 vols. 4to. Slight spotting, a few margins soiled. Cont. cf. (TA. Nov.20; 395) £925
– – **Anr. Copy.** Cf. gt. (P. Apr.9; 117) Maggs. £920
– – **Anr. Copy.** Foxing, stains, some repairs. Mod. hf. red mor. gt. (SPB. May 6; 168) $1,600
– – **Anr. Copy.** Some foxing, pp. 12 & 51 of vol. 1 slightly torn, but not affecting text, including 'Hints on Emigration to the Cape of Good Hope' at end of Vol. 1. Hf. mor., marb. bds. (SSA. Jan. 22; 179) R. 1,900
– – **Anr. Edn.** Cape Town, 1967. Facs. Reprint, (900) in cl. 4to. Cl. (VA. May 8; 293) R. 120
– – **Anr. Edn.** Cape Town, 1967. Facs. Reprint, (1000). 2 vols. 4to. Orig. bdg. (VA. Oct.31; 231) R. 100

BURCHIUS, Lambertus van der–ANDREAS Bp. of Ratisbon–JONSTON, John
– **Sabaudorum Ducum . . . Historiae Gentilitae Libri duo.–Chronicon de Ducibus Bavariae . . . cum Paralipomenis Leonhard Bauholtz. –Inscriptiones Historicae Pregum Scotorum.** Ed.:– Marquardi Freheri (2nd. work). Leyden; Amberg; Amst. & Edinb., 1599; 1602; 1602. 1st. Edns. 3 works in 1 vol. 4to. Slightly spotted or soiled in pts., last work lacks plts. 18th. C. vell. bds., lacks ties. [3rd. work: NSTC 14787] (S. Jan.27; 317) Loibl. £90

BURCKHARDT, C. Jacob
– **Kleinasiatische Reise.** Munich, 1925. Mor. gt., cover, spine & inner dentelle, marb. end-ll., by W. Gerlach, Berlin. (H. May 21/22; 1382) DM 620

BURCKHARDT, John Lewis
– **Arabic Proverbs.–Travels in Nubia.** 1830; 1822. 1st. Edn.; 2nd. Edn. 4to. Unif. cont. cf. (C. Feb.25; 78) Ad Orientem. £400
– **Notes on the Bedouins & Wahabys.** 1830. 1st. Edn. 4to. Cont. cf. (C. Feb.25; 77) Kossow. £420
– – **Anr. Copy.** Map loose. Orig. bds., covers detchd. (SH. May 21; 18) Hosain. £150
– **Travels in Arabia.** 1829. 1st. Edn. 4to. Slight offsetting. Cont. cf., a little worn. (S. Sep.29; 189) Bucherkabinet. £280
– – **Anr. Copy.** 2 vols. 1 folding map stained, some foxing, preliminary advts. in vol. I, final advts. in vol. II. Orig. bds., stains to covers of vol. I, both vols. crudely rebkd. (LC. Jun.18; 141) £80
– **Travels in Nubia.** 1819. 1st. Edn. 4to. Occasional light spotting. Cont. hf. cf. (S. Jun.29; 243) Maggs. £190
– – **Anr. Copy.** Hf. cf. gt. (P. Feb.19; 106) Hatchards. £90
– **Travels in Syria & the Holy Land.** 1822. 1st. Edn. 4to. Slightly spotted. 19th. C. cl., spine defect., cover detchd. From Chetham's Liby., Manchester. (C. Nov.26; 65) Taylor. £120

BURDETT, William
See–CIBBER, Colley–BURDETT, William –FARLEY, J.–ANON

BURELOM [Wind-fallen Wood]
Ed.:– [G.P. Erastov]. St. Petersb., 1905-06. Nos. 1-3 & extra no. 1 dtd. 18 Dec. 1905, & Christmas no. (all publd.). Fo. Unbnd. (SH. Feb.5; 55) Landry. £190
– – **Anr. Copy.** Nos. 1-3 & Christmas Iss. only. Unbnd. (SH. Feb.5; 171) Quaritch. £60

BUREVAL
Ed.:– [V.E. Turok]. St. Petersb., 1906. Nos. 1, 2 & 4 (of 4). 4to. Unbnd. (SH. Feb.5; 56) Landry. £130

BURGER or Burgher, Gottfried August
[–] **Des Freih. v. Münchhausen Wunderbare Reisen und Abentheuer zu Wasser und zu Lande.** Ill.:– Hosemann. Göttingen & Berlin, 1840. New Orig. Edn., 1st. Edn. ill. Hosemann. Slightly soiled. Orig. wraps., soiled, sm. tears, 1 pasted. (H. May 21/22; 1212) DM 500

– – **Anr. Edn.** Ill.:– Walter Klemm. Weimar, 1923. (100). 4to. Hf. vell. Orig. woodcuts sigd. by artist. (D. Dec.11-13; 1014) DM 700
– **Leonora.** Trans.:– W.R. Spencer. Ill.:– Lady Diana Beauclerc & Bartolozzi. 1796. L.P. Fo. Cont. str.-grd. mor. gt., silk linings, by Staggermeier, with his ticket. Bkplt. of Earl Lanesborough. (S. Nov.25; 484) Lyon. £140

BURGERMEISTER, Johann Stephan
– **Thesaurus Juris Equestris. – Bibliotheca Equestris. – Codex Diplomaticus Equestris . . . oder Reichs Ritter-Archis.** Ulm, 1718-21. Each 2 vols., together 6 vols. 4to. 1 title frayed affecting imprint. Cont. vell. bds., soiled. (S. Jun.1; 17) Way. £200

BURGESS, Anthony
– **The World of William Shakespeare.** Arcadia Pr., 1971. (265) sigd. 4to. Orig. red mor., upr. cover centrepiece of mor. onlays & gt. tooling, cl. box. (SH. Feb.20; 344) Downing. £50

BURGESS, Henry W.
– **Eidodendron, views of the general character & appearance of trees, foreign & indigenous, connected with picturesque scenery.** L., 1827-31. Fo. Contains the slip 'Several valuable letters . . .' at plt. 29, margins spotted. Cont. hf. red mor., worn. From collection of Massachusetts Horticultural Society, stps on plts. (SPB. Oct.1; 107) $900

BURGESS, Walter W.
– **Bits of Old Chelsea. A Series of Original Etchings.** L., 1894. (110). Fo. 36 etchings (lacks 5). Orig. decor. cl., spine torn, unc. (JL. Mar.2; 809) Aus. $120

BURGHER, Gottfried August
See–BURGER or Burgher, Gottfried August

BURGKARD, Fr. [i.e. Erstenberger]
– **De Anatomia.** Munich, 1586. 1st. Edn. Pts. 1 & 2 (of 3) in 1 vol. 4to. Cont. blind-tooled pig-bkd. wd. bds., 2 clasps. (HK. Nov.18-21; 132) DM 620

BURGKMAIR, Hans
– **Le Triomphe de l'Empereur Maximilien I.** Ill.:– Burgkmair, Altdorfer, Springinklee, Durer & others after Burgkmair. L. & Vienna, 1796. Lge. fo. Ptd. from orig. blocks cut in 1516-19, wtrmkd. IDM thro.-out, slight fold marks on a few plts. Hf. cf. (BS. Jun.11; 210) £4,200

BURGOYNE, Gen. John
– **A Letter . . . to his Constituents, upon his late Resignation; with the Correspondences between the Secretaries of War & him, relative to his Return to America.** L., 1779. 1st. Edn. Disbnd., unc. (SG. Mar.5; 46) $130
– **A State of the Expedition from Canada . . .** L., 1780. 1st. Edn. 4to. Frontis. map reprd. & rebkd., advt., text browned. Mod. hf. red mor., gt. spine & borders. From liby. of William E. Wilson. (SPB. Apr.29; 38) $700
– **The Substance of . . . Speeches on Mr. Vyner's Motion, & upon Mr. Hartley's Motion, 1778; with an Appendix, containing General Washington's Letter to General Burgoyne, &c.** L., 1778. 1st. Edn. Liby. stp. on verso of title. Disbnd., unc. (SG. Mar.5; 45) $100

BURGOYNE, Gen. John–VENAULT DE CHARMILLY, Col.
– **A State of the Expedition from Canada . . . with the appendix.–Lettre à M. Bryan Edwards . . .** 1780; 1797. 1st. Edns. 2 works in 1 vol. 4to. 1st. work: 2 maps with overslips, 'advt' lf., 2nd. work: wanting 3D1-2. Disbnd. W.a.f. [Sabin 9255; 98838] (S. Nov.4; 652) Traylen. £380

BURKE, Edmund
– **An Account of the European Settlements in North America.** L., 1757. 1st. Edn. 2 vols. Cont. cf., spines gt. (SG. Oct.9; 47) $400
[–] **A Philosophical Enquiry into the Origin of our Ideas of the Sublime & Beautiful.** 1757. 1st. Edn. Some ll. browned from margins, sig. on title. Cont. spr. cf., gt., some wear, 1 cover loose. (S. Feb.10; 421) Finch. £70
– **Reflections on the Revolution in France.** 1790. 1st. Edn. Slight browning. Orig. bds., unc. (S. Jun.23; 411) Quaritch. £220
– – **Anr. Copy.** Mod. hf. mor. A.L.s. taped onto front free end-paper, 1 p. 4to, n.d., on a political matter, split at folds. (SPB. Jul.28; 66) $275
– **Works.** 1826-39. 17 vols. Cont. cf. (SH. May 28; 15) Pharos. £75

– – **Anr. Edn.** Boston, 1884. 12 vols. Roseberry liby. stp. on titles. Orig. cl., unc. (SBA. Jul.23; 452) Subunso. £55

BURKE, Edmund–PRIOR, James
– **The Works.–Memoir of the Life & Character of . . . Edmund Burke.** 1801-27; 1826. 16 vols.; 2 vols. Vol. 2 of 2nd. work with facs. MS. frontis. (offset on title). Both in cont. diced russ. (C. Jul.22; 5) Chelsea Rare Books. £100

BURKE, H. Farnham
– **The Historical Record of the Coronation of Their Majesties King George the Fifth & Queen Mary, 1911.** Ill.:– after A. Pearse. L., [1911]. Lge. 4to. 4-p. Official Programme for Princess Mary's Wedding, 1922, laid in. Maroon lev., multiple gt. fillet borders enclosing royal monogs. & crowns, moire satin end-ll. (SG. Apr.9; 147) $130

BURKE, John
– **A Genealogical & Heraldic History of the Commoners of Great Britain & Ireland.** L., 1936-38. 1st. Edn. 4 vols. Some light foxing. Qtr. cf. (CB. Dec.9; 111) Can. $190
See–LODGE, John–COLLINS, Arthur–BURKE, John

BURKE, Sir John Bernard
– **Visitation of Seats & Arms.** 1852-55. 4 vols. Orig. cl. gt., 1 vol. not unif. 2 A.L.s. loosely inserted. (SBA. Jul.23; 308) Temperley. £65

BURKE, William
– **Histoire des Colonies européennes dans l'Amérique.** Paris, 1780. 2 vols. 12mo. Cont. cf., worn. [Sabin 9284] (SPB. May 5; 123) $325

BURKILL, I.H.
– **A Dictionary of the Economic Products of the Malay Peninsula.** 1935. 2 vols. Orig. cl. (SH. Mar.5; 29) Ad Orientem. £70

BURKILL, John
– **Bolton Illustrated.** 1848. Lge. fo. 6 (of 7) cold. litho. views, cut round & mntd. on card, text & plts. loose in gutta-percha bdg. Cont. mor.-bkd. cl. bds., worn. W.a.f. (C. Mar.18; 27) Taylor. £300

BURLAMAQUI, J.J.
– **Principes du Droit Naturel.–Principes du Droit Politique.** Geneva, 1747-51. 1st. Edns. 2 vols. 4to. Cont. mott. cf., spines richly gt., spine & upr. cover of 2nd. work with a few wormholes. (VG. Nov.18; 1098) Fls. 600

BURLINGTON, Charles & others
– **The Modern Universal British Traveller.** 1779. Fo. Cont. hf. cf., worn upr. cover detchd. W.a.f. (CSK. Aug.29; 161) £320
– – **Anr. Copy.** Maps and plts., some torn, soiling. Cont. cf., worn, covers detchd. W.a.f. (SH. Jun.25; 36) Orde. £190
– – **Anr. Edn.** L., [1786]. Fo. Cont. leath., spine reprd. (R. Oct.14-18; 1880) DM 1,700

BURLINGTON Fine Arts Club
– **Exhibition of Book Bindings.** Ed.:– S.T. Prideaux. 1891. 4to. Hf. mor. (C. Jul.22; 111) Kamph. £320
– **Exhibition of Illuminated Manuscripts.** 1908. Orig. cl. (SH. Jan.29; 10) Forster. £65
– **Exhibition of Portrait Miniatures. – Illustrated Catalogue of Pictures by the Masters of the Milanese. – Exhibition of English Mezzotint Portraits.–Exhibition Illustrative of Early English Portraiture.–Exhibition. of Early English Earthenware.** 1889; 1899; 1902; 1909; 1914. 4to. & fo. Orig. cl. (SH. Jan.29; 215) Barra Books. £70

BURLINGTON MAGAZINE for Connoisseurs
1903-04. Ltd. Edns. Vols. I-IV plus Supps. in 5. 4to. Cont. hf. lev. mor. by Root, gt. (SH. Oct.9; 162) Quaritch. £65

BURLYUK, David
– **Desyaty Oktyabr' [October 10th].** N.Y., 1928. Orig. wraps., rebkd., slightly soiled. (SH. Feb.6; 413) Kazinikas. £120

BURLYUK, David, & others
– **Buke Russkoi Literary [Bogeyman of Russian Literature]** Ill.:– I. Klyun. Moscow, 1923. (2,000). Orig. wraps by Nagorskaya. (SH. Feb.6; 414) National Art Centre. £100

BURMANN, Johannes
– **Rariorum Africanorum Plantarum . . .** Amst. 1738-39. 1st. Edn. 4to. Minor spotting. Cont. vell. From Chetham's Liby., Manchester. (C. Nov.26; 67) Marshall. £650

- Thesaurus Zeylanicus, with [Catalogi duo Plantarum Africanarum]. Amst., 1737. 4to. Engraved port., 111 engraved plts. Cf., spine gt. (C. Jul.15; 171) *Taylor.* £550
– – Anr. Copy. With additional plt. 18. 19th. C. cl., upr. cover detchd. From Chetham's Liby., Manchester. (C. Nov.26; 68) *Soames.* £500

BURMANN, Nicolaas Laurens
- Flora Indica ... Leiden & Amst., 1768. 4to. With an extra plt. 21. 19th. C. hf. mor. From Chetham's Liby., Manchester. (C. Nov.26; 69) *Wheldon & Wesley.* £420

BURN, Richard
See–NICOLSON, Joseph & Burn, Richard

BURNABY, Rev. Andrew
- Travels Through the Middle Settlements in North America in 1759 & 1760 ... L., 1775. 1st. Edn. 4to. Advt. lf., washed. Mod. hf. mor., worn at head & foot of spine. From liby. of William E. Wilson. [Sabin 9359] (SPB. Apr.29; 40) $325

BURNABY, Rev. Andrew–GOWER, Foote
- Travels through the Middle Settlements in North America.–A Sketch of the Materials for a New History of Cheshire ... L.; Chester & L., 1775; 1771. 1st. Edn. (1st. work). 2 works in 1 vol. 4to. Without Postscript to 2nd. work (not called for?). Cont. hf. cf. & marb. bds. (LC. Jun.18; 142) £55

BURNACINI, L.O. Maschere
- Denkmaeler des Theaters. Muenchen, n.d. 1st. portfo., (300) numbered. Ob. fo. Descriptive pamphlet of text by Joseph Gregor laid in. Loose in orig. marb. bd. covers, linen-bkd. (SG. Feb.12; 165) $150

BURNARD, R.
- Les Alliés dans la Guerre des Nations. Ill:– E. Burnand. Paris, 1922. (12) on Whatman, with orig. cold. pastel. 4to. Mor., worn. (SH. Jul.9; 219) *Burnand.* £70

BURNE-JONES, Edward
- The Beginning of the World. 1902. Fo. Orig. cl.-bkd. bds., unopened & unc., d.-w. (frayed). (C. Jul.22; 52) *Joseph.* £50
- The Flower Book. 1905. (300). 4to. Mor. gt. (SH. Mar.26; 125) *Maggs.* £440

BURNE-JONES, Sir Edward (Ill.)
See–BRIDGES, Robert
See–CHAUCER, Geoffrey
See–DALZIEL, George & Edward
See–DEGREVAUNT, Romance of Sire ...
See–MORRIS, William
See–PAGEANT, The

BURNES, Alexander
- Cabool. 1842. 1st. Edn. Orig. cl. (SH. Mar.5; 30) *Sherlock.* £105
- Travels into Bokhara. 1834. 3 vols. Lacks hf.-titles, & map (iss. separately), some light browning & a few spots. Cont. hf. cf. (CSK. Mar.13; 120) £90

BURNET, Jacob
- Notes on the Early Settlements of the North-Western Territory. Cinc., 1847. 1st. Edn. 4to. With the frontis. port., port. & title foxed, text slightly foxed. Cont. hf. mor., worn, scarred, marb. bds. & endpapers. From liby. of William E. Wilson. [Sabin 9373] (SPB. Apr.29; 42) $100

BURNET, John
- The Discourses of Sir Joshua Reynolds. L., [1842]. 4to. Some plts. cropped in margins, some light foxing. Orig. cl. (CB. Feb.18; 207) Can. $100
- Practical Treatise on Paintings. 1827. 3 pts. in 1 vol. 4to. Hf. mor. (P. Apr.9; 94) *Kubricele.* £65
– – Anr. Edn. 1837. [1839]. 4 pts. in 1 vol. 4to. Mor. gt. by James Toovey. (S. Nov.24; 45) *Traylen.* £75

BURNETT, Gilbert Thomas
- An Encyclopaedia of Useful & Ornamental Plants. L., 1852. 2 vols. 4to. Orig. qtr. mor. gt., worn. From collection of Massachusetts Horticultural Society, stps. on plts. (SPB. Oct.1; 108) $1,100

BURNETT, M.A.
- Plantae Utilores; or Illustrations of Useful Plants. 1842-49. 4 vols. in 2. 4to. 2 plts. detchd., 1 with margins just frayed. Orig. cl., slightly faded. W.a.f. (SBA. Oct.21; 145) *Varekamp.* £320

BURNETT, William
See–DUGDALE, Thomas & Burnett, William

BURNEY, Dr. Charles
- General History of Music. Ill.:– Bartolozzi & others. L., 1782 & 89. 1st. Edn. (vol. II–IV), 2nd. Edn. (Vol. 1). 4 vols. 4to. Lightly browned in parts & some soiling, port. stained. Cont. cf., very defect. & worn, spine renewed. (H. Dec.9/10; 1079) DM 1,300
– – Anr. Copy. Cont. hf. leath. (HK. Nov.18-21; 1863) DM 700
– – Anr. Edn. L., 1819. 1st. Edn. 2 vols. Slight browning & soiling. Later mor., gt. decor., heavily worn, some soiling. (H. Dec.9/10; 1083) DM 440
- Present State of Music in France & Italy. 1771. 1st. Edn. Advt. & Errata lf., pp. iii-iv loose. Cont. cf. (P. Jul.30; 60) *Georges.* £150
– – Anr. Copy. 'Advt.' lf. before introduction, lacks last blank lf. (?). Cont. sheep., spine gt. (S. Dec.9; 445) *Baron.* £110
- Present State of Music in Germany, the Netherlands, & United Provinces. 1775. 2nd. Edn. 2 vols. Lacks 1st. blank in vol. 2. Cont. cf. (P. Jul.30; 61) *Georges.* £55
– – Anr. Copy. 19th. C. three-qtr. mor., unc. (SG. Sep.4; 83) $225
- Present State of Music in Germany, the Netherlands, & The United Provinces.–Present State of Music in France & Italy. 1773; 1773. 2nd. Edns. 2 works in 3 vols. Occasional browning, advt. lf. in vol. II. Cont. sheep, very worn, 1 cover detchd. (S. May 5; 407) *Simeone.* £200

BURNEY, Frances
See–D'ARBLAY née Burney, Frances 'Fanny Burney'

BURNEY, James
- History of the Buccaneers of America. 1816. 4to. Cont. cf., gt. (S. May 5; 376) *Traylen.* £120

BURNS, Allan
- Observations on some of the most Frequent & Important Diseases of the Heart. Edinb., 1809. Title written on. Hf. cf., worn. From the Liby. of the Medico-Chirurgical Society, Aberdeen. (S. Jun.15; 143) *Norman.* £170
- Observations on the Surgical Anatomy of the Head & Neck. 1811. 1st. Edn. Some stains & thumb-marks, liby. stps. on plts. New cf. From the liby. of the Medico-Chirurgical Society, Aberdeen, inscr. on title. (S. Jun.15; 144) *Norman.* £100

BURNS, Edward
- The Coinage of Scotland. 1887. Ltd. Edn. 3 vols. 4to. Cont. hf. mor. (SH. Mar.6; 330) *Spink.* £200

BURNS, Robert
- Complete Writings. Ed.:– John Buchan (intro.). Ill.:– after C.S. Alcott & others. Boston, 1926. (750) numbered on L.P., with extra plts. & hand-cold. frontis.'s. 10 vols. Three-qtr. lev., spine gt. with thistles, by the Riverside Pr., unopened. (SG. Mar.19; 40) $130
- Letters Adressed to Clarinda, & c. Glasgow, 1802. 1st. Edn. 16mo. Str.-grd. mor. by Rivière. (SG. Nov.13; 33) $120
- Poems, chiefly in the Scottish Dialect. Kilmarnock, 1786. 1st. Edn. 1st. 4 ll. stained, some other internal staining, slight tears to blank margins of Q2 & 3, sm. defects. to p. numerals in pp.139 & 167/8, early owners' sig. on title, preface, & on fly-lf. Cont. sheep, spine gt., head of spine & corners worn, early inked price of $1.50 on paste-down, poem 'Scots wha Hae' written in ink on verso of final free endpaper. From the Prescott Collection. (CNY. Feb.6; 39) $8,000
– – Anr. Edn. Ill.:– Buego after Nasmyth (frontis. port.). Edinb., Priv. Ptd., 1787. 2nd. Edn. [1st. Edinb. Edn.]. With the readings 'Duke of Boxburgh' on p. xxxvii, & 'skinking' on p. 263. Pol. cf. gt. extra, spine in compartments, by Rivière & Son. Bkplt. of O.N. Chadwyck- Healey. (LC. Feb.12; 430) £300
– – Anr. Copy. With the readings 'Boxburgh' & 'skinking', lacks hf.-title. Red. mor. gt., by Rivière, partly unc. (S. Nov.25; 480) *Cumming.* £140
– – Anr. Copy. With the misprint 'Boxburgh', but 'skinking' correctly spelled, offsetting to hf.-title, slight browning. Cont. cf., gt. Stp. of Middleton Park. (S. Feb.10; 425) *Hauer.* £120
– – Anr. Edn. Ill.:– Beugo after Nasmyth. Edinb., Priv. Ptd., 1787. 2nd. (1st. Edinb.) Edn., 1st. Iss. With the readings 'stinking' on p. 263 & 'Boxburgh' in subscriber's list, lacks hf.-title. Later crushed cf., rebkd. & reprd. Fore-e. pntg. in 2 panels; from the liby. of Zola E. Harvey. (SG. Mar.19; 118) $1,000
– – Anr. Edn. 1787. 1st. L. Edn. Hf.-title spotted, faint pres. inscr. on hf.-title. Red mor. gt. by Rivière. (S. Jul.27; 90) *Bickersteth.* £150
– – Anr. Edn. Edinb., 1793. 2 vols. 12mo. Red crushed lev. mor., flat spines in 6 compartments, 5 raised bands, by Doves Bindery, sigd., & dtd. 1894. Robert M. Mann bkplts. (CNY. May 22; 341) $280
- Poetical Works. L., 1826. 16mo. Early str.-grd. mor., wide gt. floral borders, spine gt. Fore-e. pntg.; from the liby. of Zola E. Harvey. (SG. Mar.19; 120) $240
- Songs, chiefly in the Scottish Dialect.–Poems, chiefly in the Scottish Dialect. L., 1824. 2 vols. 12mo. Cont. mor. with gt. lyres on all covers, by J. Morton, slightly worn. Each vol. with fore-e. pntg. (SG. Mar.19; 119) $275
- Tam O'Shanter. Ill.:– William Strang. Essex House Pr., 1902. (150) numbered on vell. Orig. vell., slightly soiled & warped. (CSK. May 29; 21) £70
- Works. L., 1834. 8 vols. Slight browning. Hf. cf. gt., gt. panel. spines, by Sangorski & Sutcliffe, slightly worn. (SPB. Nov.25; 434) $150
- The Works–The Gentleman's Diary. L., 1801; [1826 & 1828]. 4 vols.; 2 vols. 1st. work. cont. str.-grd. mor. gt.; 2nd. work: cont. str.-grd. mor. gt., s.-c.'s. Both works with fore-e. pntg. in each vol.; from the Prescott collection. (CNY. Feb.6; 114) $850
– – Anr. Edn. Ed.:– William Scott Douglas. Edinb., 1877. 6 vols. Extra-ill. with some 200 steel-engrs., some hand-cold. Crushed three-qtr. lev., gt.-panel. spines, by Bayntun. (SG. Mar.19; 39) $220

BURNS, Rev. Thomas
- Old Scottish Communion Plate. 1892. (175) numbered, & sigd. 4to. Orig. hf. cf. (SH. Jul.23; 259) *Sims & Reed.* £50

BURR, Aaron
- The Private Journal. Rochester, 1903. (250) numbered, for private distribution. 2 vols. Three qtr. lev., spines gt., by the Atelier Bindery. Initialled by W.H. Bixby of St. Louis, owner of orig. MS. (SG. Jan.8; 54) $160
- Reports of the Trials of ... for Treason, & for a Misdemeanor. Taken in Short Hand by David Robertson. Phila., 1808. 1st. Edn. 2 vols. Foxed. Cont. bds., rebkd. in mod. buckram. (SG. Jan.8; 53) $100

BURR, David H.
- An Atlas of the State of New York. N.Y., 1829. Atlas fo. Mod. buckram. (SG. May 14; 33) $2,300

BURROUGHS, Edgar Rice
- Thuvia, Maid of Mars. Chic., 1920. 1st. Edn. Orig. cl., lr. hinge separated, d.-w. (PNY. Oct.1; 122) $160

BURROUGHS, John
- The Writings. Ill.:– Clifton Johnson & Others. Boston, 1904-1922. (750) numbered sigd. by author & publisher. 23 vols., Three qtr. lev., spines gt. in compartments, partly unc. (SG. Sep.4; 86) $300

See–HARRIMAN Alaska Expedition

BURROWES' PIANO-FORTE PRIMER ... Calculated either for Private Tuition, or Teaching in Classes
Ed.:– W.C. Peters. Richmond, 1864. 1st. Edn. 12mo. Ptd. wraps. (SG. Mar.5; 150) $250

BURROWS, C. Acton
- The Annals of the Town of Guelph, 1827-1877. Guelph, 1877. Orig. ptd. wraps. (CB. Nov.12; 70) Can. $100

BURROWS, George Man
- An Inquiry into Certain Errors relative to Insanity. 1820. 1st. Edn. Cont. bds., unc. (S. Jun.15; 145) *Phillips.* £130

BURTIN, François Xavier de
- Oryctographie de Bruxelles. Brussels, 1784. Tall fo. Mod. cf.-bkd. old marb. bds. (SG. May 14; 34) $400

BURTON, A.
See–MITFORD, John, Journalist 'A. Burton'

BURTON, John, Classical Scholar, 1696-1771
- Monastican Eboracense. 1758. Vol. 1 [all publd.]. Fo. 1 folding engraved map reprd. Orig. tree cf., rebkd., ex-liby. (PL. Jul.11; 133) *Holmes.* £95

BURTON, John, Classical Scholar, 1696-1771 – Monastican Eboracense. -contd.
– – **Anr. Copy.** 1 double-p. plan slightly torn, a few margins slightly dampstained. Cont. cf. gt., neatly rebkd. & cornered. (SBA. Oct.22; 576) *Vernon.* £52

BURTON, Sir Richard Francis
– **Abeokuta & the Camaroons Mountain.** 1863. 2 vols. Orig. cl. (SH. Nov.7; 284) *Bowden.* £210
– **The City of the Saints.** 1861. 1st. Edn. With folding plan of Salt Lake City. Maroon hf. mor., by Sangorski & Sutcliffe. (C. Nov.6; 203) *Ludgrove.* £110
– – **Anr. Copy.** Cont. hf. mor., slightly marked. [Sabin 9497] (S. Jun.29; 186) *Maggs.* £60
– **Explorations of the Highlands of the Brazil.** 1869. 1st. Edn. 2 vols. Slight spotting, owner's inscr. cut away from head of hf.-titles. Orig. cl., gt. [Sabin 9498] (S. Apr.7; 476) *Foyles.* £110
– – **Anr. Copy.** Folding map slightly torn, slightly soiled. Orig. cl., rebkd. (SH. Nov.7; 367) *Cookey.* £95
– – **Anr. Edn.** 1869. 1st. Edn., 2nd. Iss. 2 vols. Spotted. Orig. cl. (SH. Nov.7; 368) *Bowden.* £60
– **Falconry in the Valley of the Indus.** 1852. 1st. Edn. Orig. cl., worn. (BS. Nov.26; 227) £100
– **First Footsteps in East Africa.** 1856. 1st. Edn. 1 lf. of 4th. Appendix only, a few ll. loose & slightly soiled. Later cl., soiled. (SH. Nov.7; 283) *Edwards.* £120
– – **Anr. Edn.** 1856. 1st. Edn., 2nd. Iss. 26pp. publisher's advts. bnd. in at rear. Cont. blind-stpd. cl. (TA. Nov.20; 412) £100
– **Goa, & the Blue Mountains.** 1851. 1st. Edn., 1st Iss. Some ll. dampstained. Orig. cl. (SH. Nov.7; 282) *Kossow.* £85
– **The Gold-Mines of Midian.** 1878. [1st. Edn.?] Orig. cl., soiled. (SH. Nov.7; 401) *Kossow.* £130
– – **Anr. Copy.** (SG. Feb.26; 65) $270
– **The Guide-Book. A Pilgrimage to Mecca & Medina.** 1865. 1st. & only Edn. Orig. wraps., slightly soiled, spine torn. (SH. Nov.7; 402) *Walford.* £320
– **The Kasidah of Haji Abu El-Yezdi.** L., Priv. Ptd., [1880]. 1st Edn., 1st. Iss. 4to. Orig. ptd. wraps., partially faded, mor. solander case. From the Prescott Collection. (CNY. Feb.6; 41) $1,300
[–] – **Anr. Edn.** L., Priv. Ptd., [1880]. (250). 4to. Wraps., cl. folding case. (SG. May 14; 35) $850
– – **Anr. Edn.** Ed.:– D.G. Mukerji (intro.). Ill.:– Willy Pogany. Phila., [1931]. (250) numbered, & sigd. by Pogany & Mukerji. 4to. Three-qtr. mor., spine gt. with crescents & stars, by Bennett. (SG. Apr.2; 242) $130
– – **Anr. Edn.** Ill:– Valenti Angelo. Ltd. Edns. Cl., 1937. (1500) numbered, & sigd. by artist. 12mo. Cf., orig. box. (SG. Jan.15; 134) $100
– **The Lake Regions of Central Africa.** 1860. 1st. Edn. 2 vols. Publisher's advts. at end vol. 2. Mod. buckram. (C. Nov.6; 202) *Harcourt-Williams.* £150
– – **Anr. Copy.** Folding map reprd. & badly creased. Cont. hf. mor., inner jnts. reprd. (TA. Feb.19; 9) £75
– **A Mission to Gelele, King of Dahome.** 1864. 1st. Edn. 2 vols. Cont. hf. cf., jnts. split, reprd. (S. Mar.31; 448) *Mitchener.* £110
– **Personal Narrative to El-Medinah & Meccah.** 1855-56. 1st. Edn. 3 vols. 1 plt. detchd. with slight loss, last few ll. of vols. 1 & 3 detchd. Hf. cf., worn, some covers detchd., ex-liby. (CSK. Jul.10; 114) £88
– – **Anr. Copy.** Errata lf. in vol. 1, plt.-list in vol. 3 only, lacks hf.-titles. Three-qtr. mor. (SG. Oct.30; 71) $380
– – **Anr. Edn.** 1893. Memorial Edn. 2 vols. Orig. pict. cl. gt. Bkplt. of O.N. Chadwyck-Healey. (LC. Feb.12; 172) £60
[–] **Wanderings in West Africa.** 1863. 2 vols. A few ll. slightly wormed. Mod. hf. cf. (SH. Nov.7; 285) *Enfield.* £120
– **Wit & Wisdom from West Africa.** 1865. 1st. Edn. Orig. cl., unc., recased. (TA. Jul.16; 292) £58
– **Zanzibar.** 1872. 1st. Edn. 2 vols. Orig. cl., gt. design of Indian on upr. covers, worn & disbnd., ex-liby. (CSK. Jul.10; 113) £70
– **[Works].** 1851-1901. Mostly 1st. Edns. 20 works in 32 vols. Unif. hf. mor., gt. (SH. Mar.5; 31) *Sawyer.* £1,400

BURTON, Sir Richard Francis & Cameron, Verney Lovett
– **To the Gold Coast for Gold.** 1883. 1st. Edn. 2 vols. Last 16 advt. pp. in vol. I loose. Orig. bdg. (SH. Mar.5; 32) *Dawson's.* £210

BURTON, Sir Richard F. & Drake, C. F. T.
– **Unexplored Syria.** 1872. 2 vols. Orig. cl. (SH. May 21; 201) *Hosain.* £70

BURTON, Robert 'Democritus Junior'
[–] **The Anatomy of Melancholy.** Oxford, 1621. 1st. Edn. 4to. Lf. of errata mntd. 19th. C. mor. [STC 4159] (C. Nov.20; 233) *Carnegie.* £2,300
– – **Anr. Edn.** Oxford, 1624. 2nd. Edn. Fo. Some later MS. notes, some browning & sailing. Cont. cf., worn. [STC 4160] (S. Sep.29; 10) *Fletcher.* £240
– – **Anr. Copy.** 4to. Cont. hf. cf., covers loose. (SH. Oct.10; 363) *Thorp.* £160
– – **Anr. Edn.** Oxford, 1632. 4th. Edn. Fo. Lacks 1st. lf., some browning & soiling, portion torn from 3×1 with slight loss of text, a few rust holes. Cf., spine defect., lacks covers. [STC 4162] (S. Sep.29; 11) *Berman.* £50
[–] – **Anr. Edn.** 1676. 8th. Edn. Fo. Sig. on title, 'Argument' lf. creased. Old black-stained vell. bds., painted arms on covers, very worn. Bkplt. of H.J.B. Clements. [Wing B6184] (S. Jun.9; 48a) *Subunso.* £60
[–] – **Anr. Edn.** L., 1827. 13th. Edn. 2 vols. Cf. gt., by Rivière, 1 free endpaper creased. Fore-e. pntg.; from the liby. of Zola E. Harvey. (SG. Mar.19; 121) $475
– – **Anr. Edn.** Ill.:– E. McKnight Kauffer. L., Nones. Pr., 1925. (750) numbered on Dutch paper. 2 vols. Tall 4to. Qtr. vell. & patterned bds., light soiling at edges, unopened. (PNY. May 21; 302) $100
– – **Anr. Edn.** Ill.:– E. McKnight Kauffer. Nones. Pr., 1925. (790). 2 vols. Fo. Orig. parch.-bkd. bds., unc. (SH. Feb.19; 121) *Sherlock.* £85
– – **Anr. Edn.** Ill.:– E. McKnight Kauffer. Nones. Pr., 1925. (790) numbered, (40) of single vol. Edn. on japon vell. Fo. With some ills. hand-cold. Tree cf. gt. (S. Jul.31; 111) *Campus.* £140
– **The English Empire in America . . .** L., 1728. 6th. Edn. 16mo. MS. index added on back free endpaper, browned. 19th. C. hf. cf., gt., gt. spine. From liby. of William E. Wilson. [Sabin 9499] (SPB. Apr.29; 45) $275

BURTON, William
[–] **An Account of the Life & Writings of Hermann Boerhaave.** 1743. 1st. Edn. Cont. cf. (S. Jun.15; 94) *Maggs.* £55
– **A Commentary on Antoninus his Itinerary.** Ill.:– Wenceslaus Hollar. 1658. 1st. Edn. Fo. Slight browning. Cont. sheep, worn. [Wing B6185]. (S. Sep.29; 12) *Scott.* £55

BURY, Lady Charlotte
– **The Three Great Sanctuaries of Tuscany, Valambrosa, Camaldoli, Laverna.** Ill:– after Edward Bury. 1833. Ob. fo. Mntd. engraved port., etched additional title detchd., some spotting, mostly marginal. Orig. cl. (CSK. Jan.30; 109) £60

BURY, Mrs Edward
– **A Selection of Hexandrian plants belonging to the Natural Orders Amaryllidae & Lilacae.** L., 1831-34. Fo. Prelims. preserved apparently before bdg. Cont. mor.-edged marb. bds. gt. From collection of Massachusetts Horticultural Society, stpd on plts. (SPB. Oct.1; 109) $21,000

BURY, Thomas Talbot
– **Coloured Views on the Liverpool & Manchester Railway.** L., 1831. 1st. Edn. Fo. Orig. marb. bds., roan spine, worn. (SG. Oct.9; 48) $4,000
– – **Anr. Copy.** 4to. 7 full-p. hand-cold. aquatint engrs. Hf. str.-grd. mor., spine gt. (CNY. May 22; 50) $900
– – **Anr. Edn.** 1832. Lge. 4to. 16 hand-cold. plts., 3 folding, text & single plts. wtrmkd. 1832. 1st. folding plt. 1834, last folding plt. 1836. Recent cl. (S. Mar.16; 203) *Quaritch.* £1,900
– – **Anr. Edn.** 1837. Pt. 1 only (all publd.). 4to. Plts. without watermark, some spots & stains. 19th. C. marb. bds., orig. wraps. preserved. (S. Feb.10; 349) *Rostron.* £3,000
– – **Anr. Edn.** Oldham, 1977. Facs. of orig. Edn. of 1831, (250) numbered, De Luxe Edn. 4to. Cf., s.-c. by Zaehnsdorf, facs. ptd. paper wraps. bnd. in at rear. (TA. May 21; 435) £65
– – **Anr. Copy.** 4to. (TA. May 21; 436) £60

BURYA [Storm]
Ed.:– [G.P. Erastov]. St. Petersb., 1906. Nos. 4-5. 4to. Unbnd. (SH. Feb.5; 57) *Landry.* £170

BUSBY, Thomas Lord
[–] **Costume of the Lower Orders in Paris.** [1820?]. 12mo. No text, occasional minor discolouration. Pol. cf., by Root. Sigd. by author. (C. Feb.4; 176) *Davidson.* £150
– **Costume of the Lower Orders of London.** [1820]. 4to. Mott. cf. gt., upr. cover detchd. (S. Nov.24; 46) *Quaritch.* £170

BUSCA, Gabriello
– **Della Espugnatione et Difesa delle Forezze.** Turin, 1585. 1st. Edn. 4to. Short tear on title, spotting. Later cl.-bkd. bds. (SPB. Jul.28; 67) $375

BUSCH, J.
– **Abhandlung von d. Geldsumlauf.** Hamburg & Kiel, 1780. 1st. Edn. 2 vols. Slightly soiled in parts, MS. owner's note on title. Cont. marb. bds., worn. (HK. Nov.18-21; 1776) DM 1,100
– **Sämtliche Schriften über Banken und Münzwesen.** Ed.:– C.D. Ebeling. Hamburg, 1801. Bnd. with G.H. Sieveking: Über den Hamburg 1789. Cont. hf. leath., gt. spine. (R. Oct.14-18; 1440) DM 1,850

BUSCH, J.H.M.
– **Bilder aus dem Orient.** Trieste, 1864. 1st. Edn. Fo. Spotted, 30 plts. (of 32). Orig. bds., worn. (SH. Jun.18; 78) *Walford.* £65

BUSCH, Wilhelm
– **Bilderbogen.** Munich, ca. 1880-90. 2 vols. Soiled in parts. Orig. hf. linen, very defect & loose. (R. Mar.31-Apr.4; 1483) DM 650

BUSCHING, A.Fr.
– **Erdbeschreibung.** Hamburg, 1787-92. Very browned in parts, title with sm. name stp. Cont. cf., 1 spine reprd. at head. (H. Dec. 9/10; 456) DM 720

BUSE, G.H.
– **Vollständiges Handbuch der Geldkunde.** Erfurt, 1800-03. 3 vols. Soiled & slightly browned in parts. Cont. hf. leath. (HK. Nov.18-21; 1777) DM 420

BUSENELLO, G.F.
– **L'Incoronatione di Poppea . . . Opera Musicale.** Venetia, 1556. Old cf. (BS. Jun.11; 235) £260

BUSHELL, Stephen W.
– **Oriental Ceramic Art illustrated by examples from the collection of W.T. Walters.** N.Y., 1897. (500). 10 vols. Fo. Etched frontis. port, plts. inlaid on Japan vell. Orig. cl.-bkd. ill. bds., unc., in 5 Chinese silk & cl. portfos., most retaining orig. silk ties. (C. Feb.4; 230) *Quaritch.* £1,100

BUSSATO, Marco
– **Giardino di Agricoltura.** Venice, 1599. 4to. Light brown stain in lr. margins at beginning. Cont. limp vell. Bkplt. of André Simon. (S. Jul.27; 281) *Duran.* £150

BUSSEMECHER, J.
See–QUAD, Matthew & Bussemecher, J.

BUSSINGIUS, Caspare
– **Einleitung zu der Herolds-Kunst . . .** Hamburg, 1694. 3 pts. in 1 vol. Ob. 12mo. Book worming, 1 lf. reprd. Cont. tree cf., spine decor. with raised bands, bdg. defect. (HD. Jun.24; 14) Frs. 1,000

BUSSIUS, I.
See–NEANDER, M.–BUSSIUS, I.–GLOCERUS, G.

BUSSU, N.
– **Nouveaux Voyages aux Indes Occidentales.** Paris, 1768. 2nd. Edn. 2 pts. in 2 vols. 12mo. Cont. mott. cf. [Sabin 6465] (SPB. May 5; 113) $475

BUSSY-RABUTIN, Roger, Comte de
– **Histoire Amoureuse des Gaules.** L., 1781. 6 vols. 18mo. Wormholes in vol. 3, vol. 5 bnd. inverted. Marb. cf. by Cazin. (HD. Apr.8; 225) Frs. 1,650

BUTCHER, Richard–BEDWELL, W.–PILKINGTON, G.
– **The Survey & Antiquity of the Town of Stamford.–A Brief Description of Tottenham.–The Turnament of Tottenham.** 1718. Old cf., rebkd. (P. Sep.11; 257) *Schapiro.* £55

BUTEO, Joannes
– **Opera Geometrica.** Lyons, 1559. 2nd. Edn. 4to. Light marginal dampstains. Cont. limp vell., gt.

eliptical centre piece on covers, lacks ties, hf. red mor. case. (S. Oct.21; 372) *Pearson.* £80

BUTKENS, F. Christophe
- Trophées tant Sacrés que Profanes du Duché de Brabant. La Haye, 1724, 1726. 2 vols & 2 vols. supp. Fo. Spr. cf., 6 spine raised bands, (LM. Nov.8; 23) B.Frs. 60,000

BUTLER, Dr. Arthur Gardiner
- Birds of Great Britain & Ireland. Order Passeres. Ill.:– after H. Gronvold & F.W. Frohawk. [1904-08]. 2nd. Edn. 2 vols. 4to. Slight spotting. Cont. roan-bkd. bds., some wear. (S. Dec.3; 925) *Demetzy.* £50
- – Anr. Edn. Ill.:– H. Grönvold & F.W. Frohawk. L., [1904-08]. New Edn., new iss. Orig. linen. (R. Oct.14-18; 2918) DM 900
- – Anr. Edn. N.d. 2 vols. 4to. Cl. gt., slight wear. (P. Nov.13; 190) *Quaritch.* £100
- British Birds with Their Nests & Eggs. Ill.:– F.W. Frohawk. L., [1896-98]. 6 vols. 4to. Pict. cl., gt. (GM. Apr.30: 455) £57
- Foreign Finches in Captivity. Ill.:– F.Q. Frohawk. [1894-96]. 1st. Edn. 4to. Orig. cl. gt., slightly soilcd. (SBA. Jul.14; 222) *Hillman.* £340
- – Anr. Copy. 4to. Slight soiling. Cont. hf. cf., worn. (S. Jun.23; 294) *Fletcher.* £260
- – Anr. Edn. Ill.:– F.W. Frohawk. [1896]. 4to. 58 (of 60) hand-cold. litho. plts., lacks plts. of the Indigo Bunting & Napoleon Weaver but Yellow-Shouldered Weaver in dupl., loose. Orig. cl., gt., slightly worn. (S. Jun.1; 90) *Carr.* £220
- – Anr. Edn. 1899. 2nd. Edn. 4to. Cont. hf. cf. (S. May 5; 87) *Vitali.* £90
- – Anr. Copy. Orig. cl. gt. (P. Dec.11; 11) *Bass.* £75

BUTLER, Charles
- The Feminine Monarchie. Oxford, 1634. 3rd. Edn. Sm. 4to. Sm. hole in last lf., rather stained. Cont. cf., rebkd., worn. [STC 4194] (S. May 5; 301) *Sanders.* £220

BUTLER, F.J.
- Old Clocks & Watches 1904. 2nd. Edn. Orig. cl. (CSK. Sep.19; 198) £55

BUTLER, Capt. Henry
- South African Sketches ... 1841. Fo. Mod. hf. leath. (S. Jun.29; 210) *Arader.* £240
- – Anr. Copy. Mod. maroon lev. mor. (C. Nov.5; 22a) *Walford.* £130
- – Anr. Copy. 4to. Hf. mor. (SSA. Apr.22; 124) R. 320
- – Anr. Copy. Lge. 4to. Hf. mor. (VA. May 8; 294) R. 200

BUTLER, J.
- Travels & Adventures in the Province of Assam. 1855. 1st. Edn. Early 20th. C. hf. cf. by Morrell. (S. Mar.31; 450) *Crete.* £65

BUTLER, Mann
- A History of the Commonwealth of Kentucky. Louisville, 1834. 1st. Edn. Browned, foxed & soiled, slight worming. Orig. cf., warped, gt. spine. From liby. of William E. Wilson. (SPB. Apr.29; 47) $150

BUTLER, Rev. R.
- Registrum Prioratus Omnium Sanctorum Juxta Dublin. Dublin, 1845. 4to. Cl. (GM. Apr.30; 369) £55

BUTLER, Samuel, Bp. of Lichfield
- Alps & Sanctuaries of Piedmont & the Canton Ticino. 1882. 1st. Edn. Orig. pict. cl. gt., rebkd., old spine laid down. A.L.s. from author 1½ pp., Apr.25, 1882 to Mr. Daniel. (SH. Dec.19; 420) *Rota.* £60
- An Atlas of Modern Geography. 1844. Hf. roan, defect. (P. Apr.9; 145) *Shaffer.* £55
- Ex Voto: An Account of the Sacro Monte or New Jerusalem at Varallo-Sesia. 1888. 1st. Edn. 3 pp. advts. Orig. cl. Inscr. to C.P. Pauli, Roger Senhouse bkpl. (SH. Dec.19; 421) *Rota.* £85

BUTLER, Samuel, Philosopher
- Erewhon. Ill.:– Blair Hughes-Stanton. Gregy. Pr., 1933. Orig. sheep., unc. (SH. Feb.20; 209) *Reading Univ.* £50
- Erewhon Revisited. 1901. 1st. Edn. Advts., errata slip. Orig. cl. Inscr. to Harry Quilter. (SH. Dec.19; 428) *Temple.* £55
- – Anr. Copy. Page of advts. at end. Cl., cl. s.-c. Pres. Copy, to F.B. Bickley. (SG. Mar.19; 42) $180

BUTLER, Samuel, Satirist, 1612-80
- Hudibras. Ill.:– William Hogarth. L., 1726. 12mo. Disbnd. (SG. Sep.25; 165) $130
- – Anr. Edn. 1793. 3 vols. including Supp. vol. of notes. 4to. Unif. cont. cf., decor. spine, gt. (CE. Jul.9; 226) £90
- – Anr. Copy. 3 vols., including the 2 vols. of Nash's Notes in 1. Cont. russ. gt. (C. Jul.22; 7) *Taylor.* £65
- – Anr. Edn. 1819. 2 vols. Crimson mor. gt. (CE. Nov.20; 123) £110
- – Anr. Copy. Cf. by Zaehnsdorf., triple gt. fillet borders, spine gt. in 6 compartments, inner dentelles. (SG. Sep.4; 89) $300
- Works. L., 1923. Shrewsbury Edn. 20 vols. Tree cf. gt., decor. gt. spines, slightly worn. (SPB. Nov.25; 435) $700

BUTLER, Rev. Weedon, Attrib. to
- The Indian Vocabulary. L., 1788. 16mo. Interleaved thro.-out. with 14 pp. of advts. Mod. hf. lev. (SG. Feb.5; 184) $180

BUTOR, Michel & Rosenburg, Harold
- Saul Steinberg: Le Masque. Paris, 1966. (300) numbered, with orig. numbered & sigd. litho. laid in. Ob. 4to. Cold. pict. wraps., boxed. (SG. Apr.2; 280) $850

BUTTERFLY Quarterly
Ed.:– M.H. Scott, A. Màrgaret, A.R. Smith & G. Plank. [Phila.], Autumn 1907-Summer 1908. (500) numbered. Nos. 1-4. 4to. Hf. vell., very soiled, orig. stiff wraps. bnd. in. (SG. Mar.26; 118) $230

BUTTERWORTH, Benjamin
- The Growth of Industrial Art. Wash., 1892. Lge. fo. Some plts. torn. Cont. linen, defect. & loose. (R. Oct.14-18; 2556) DM 1,900
- – Anr. Copy. Linen. (R. Mar.31-Apr.4; 1537) DM 1,400

BUTTNER, David Sigismund
- Coralliographia Subterranea seu Dissertatio de Corallis Fossilibus, in Specie de Lapide Corneo Horn-oder Gemeinem Feuer-Stein. Leipzig, 1714. 4to. Bds. (S. Dec.2; 459) *Lindahall.* £130

BUTTNER, J.H.
- Genealogie oder Stamm-und Geschlecht-Register der Vornehmsten Adelichen Patricien-Geschlechter. Lüneburg, 1704. Fo. Some ll. stained, defect. & reprd. Hf. vell. ca. 1900. (R. Oct.14-18; 1213) DM 600

BUXBAUM, Johann Christian
- Plantarum Minus Cognitarum Centuria I (–V). St. Petersb., 1728-80. 5 pts. in 2 vols. 4to. Some plts. slightly discold., 1 torn & reprd. in margin. Cont. cf., worn, rebkd. From Chetham's Liby., Manchester. (C. Nov.26; 70) *Israel.* £450

BUXTON, Thomas Fowell
- The African Slave Trade & its Remedy. 1840. Orig. cl. [Sabin 9686] (SH. Jun.18; 6) *Lawson.* £50

BUXTORF, Johannes, The Elder
- De Abbreviaturis Hebraicis & Bibliotheca Rabbinica. Basel, 1640. 2nd. Edn. Title slightly torn, slight browning. Orig. bdg. (S. Nov.17; 61) *Waechter Town.* £70
- Lexicon Chaldaicum Talmudicum et Rabbinicum. Basle, 1639-40. 1st. Edn. Fo. In Hebrew & Latin. Cont. vell. decor. with geometric designs. (S. Nov.18; 540) *Selig.* £220
- Magna Biblia Rabbinica. Basel, 1618. 4 books in 2 vols. Fo. Stp. on title, owner's sigs. on flylf. Leath., spine defect. (S. Nov.17; 44) *Low.* £380
- Synagoga Judaica. Frankfurt a. M., 1738. 2nd. Edn. Browning, stitching brkn. Cf., disbnd., covers detchd., very worn. (SPB. May 11; 228) $850

BUXTORF, Johannes, The Younger
- Florilegium Hebraicum Continens Elegantes Sententias, Proverbia, Apophthegmata. Basle, 1648. 1st. Edn. In Hebrew & Latin, slight discolouration. Hf. leath., bkplt. of Jacob Klatzkin. (S. Nov.18; 646) *Rock.* £60

BUY DE MORNAS, Claude
- Atlas Historique et Géographique. Paris, 1762. Vol. 2 only. Fo. 69 (of 70) double-p. ll., including title, introducltion & definitions, 46 maps, plan, plts. & tables, many maps hand-cold. in outl., the principal areas fully cold., lacks plt. 59. Cont. mott. cf., spine gt., worn. W.a.f. (S. Mar.31; 298) *Marshall.* £200

- – Anr. Copy. Ob. atlas fo. 2 sm. holes at top of title-p., sm. hole through top of 1st. 23 ll., not affecting maps. Cont. cf.-bkd. dyed bds., cf. tips (very worn). (PNY. May 21; 31) $230

BUZETA, M. & Bravo, F.
- Diccionario Geográfico, Estadistico Histórico de la Islas Filipinas. Madrid, 1850-51. 2 vols. Cont. hf. leath., 1 spine slightly defect. (R. Mar.31-Apr.4; 2538) DM 750

BYAM, Lydia
[–] A Collection of Exotics from the Island of Antigua. Priv. ptd., [1797]. Fo. Hf. cf., reprd. (S. Dec.3; 927) *Quaritch.* £1,300
- A Collection of Fruits from the West Indies. L., 1800. Fo. Title & 4 ll. of text, 9 hand-cold. engraved plts., disbnd., the plts. matted. Mor. folding box. (SPB. May 5; 124) $2,100

BYBLIS, MIROIR DES ARTS DU LIVRE ET DE L'ESTAMPE
Ill.:– Bonfils, L. Boucher, Favorsky, Hermann-Paul, & others. Paris, 1927-30. Vols. VI-IX. 4to. Unsewn as iss., cl.-bkd. folders, worn, ties. (SH. Nov.20; 19) *Ayres.* £60

BYERLY, A.E.–TEMPLIN, Hugh
- Fergus of the Fergusson-Webster Settlement; A History of Lower Nichol.–Fergus & the Rebellion of 1837. Elora; Guelph: n.p., 1932-34; 1930; [1937]. 3 works in 3 vols. 8vo; 8vo; 12mo. All orig. bdgs. (CB. Dec.9; 40) Can. $130

BYERLEY, T.
See–ROBERTSON, J.C. & Byerley, T.

BYLINY [Legendary Tales]
Ill.:– Ivan Bilibin. St. Petersb., 1904. Lge. 4to. Orig. pict. wraps., slightly worn. (CSK. Jun.12; 126) £150

BYNG, Adm. John
- An Appeal to the People Containing the Genuine & Entire Letter of ... –An Appeal to the Sense of the People ... –An Appeal to Reason & Common Sense.–A Letter to Rt. Hon. William Pitt ... L., 1756. 4 titles in 1 vol. Cont. cf. [Sabin 1787] (SG. Oct.30; 72) $360

BYNNER, Witter
- Grenstone Poems. N.Y., [1917]. 1st. Edn. 12mo. Cl. Author's copy, with owner's annot. & many pencil alterations. (SG. Jun.4; 59) $260
- The New World. N.Y., 1915. 1st. Edn. 12mo. Cl., disbnd. Author's copy, many pencil annots. (SG. Jun.4; 58) $160
See–FORD, Julia Ellsworth & Bynner, Witter

BYRD, William
- Songs of Sundrie Natures, some of Grautitie, & others of Myrth, Sextus.–Liber Secundus Sacrarum Cantionum, Sextus. L., 1589; 1591. 2 works in 1 vol. 4to. Slight staining at end. Cont. limp vell. [STC 4256; 4248] (C. Nov.20; 209) *Engel.* £380

BYRNE, Letitia
See–HEARNE, Samuel–POUNCY, B.T.–Byrne, Letitia–GILPIN, William & Alken, Samuel

BYRNE, J. Patrick
- Consubstantial. Cuala Pr., 1939. 1st. Edn., (20). Orig. linen-bkd. bds., unc., unopened. (S. Jul.22; 87) *Figgis.* £140

BYRNE, Julia Clara
- Twelve Years' Wanderings in the British Colonies. 1848. 2 vols. Folding litho. map, mntd. on cl. in wallet at end of vol. 2. Mod. cf.-bkd. cl. (CSK. Jan.9; 18) £80

BYRNE, Oliver
- The First Six Books of the Elements of Euclid, in Which Coloured Diagams & Symbols are Used Instead of Letters for the Greater Ease of Learners. 1847. 4to. Some foxing, top right-hand corner of title cut off to remove previous owner's name. Cont. hf. cf., hinges reprd. (TA. Feb.19; 462) £110

BYRNE, W.
See–HEARNE, Thomas & Byrne, W.

BYRNES, Thomas
- Professional Criminals of America. N.Y., [1886]. 4to. Rebnd. in buckram. (SG. Jan.8; 55) $180

BYRON, Lord George Gordon Noel
- Age of Bronze. 1823. 1st. Edn. Advt. lf. inserted at end. slight browning. Orig. wraps., unc. (S. Oct.1; 526) £65

BYRON, Lord George Gordon Noel -*contd.*
- **Beppo, a Venetian Story.** 1818. 1st. Edn. 4pp. advts. Orig. wraps., unc., cl. folding case. (C. Feb.4; 6) *Roseu.* £280
- **Childe Harold's Pilgrimage.** L., 1857. 16mo. Mor., gt. borders enclosing flower-bedecked harp. Fore-e. pntg. (SG. Mar.19; 122) $240
- **Childe Harold's Pilgrimage [cantos I-II].–Childe Harold's Pilgrimage, canto the third.–Childe Harold's Pilgrimage, canto the fourth.** 1812; 1816; 1818. 1st. Edn.; 1st. Edn. 2nd. Iss.; 1st. Edn. 2nd. Iss. 3 vols. 4to; 8vo; 8vo. 2nd. work: 5 pp. advts., slight spotting, orig. wraps. bnd. in; 3rd. work: 2 pp. advts. Unif. mor. gt. by Rivière, partly unc. (C. Feb.4; 7) *Levis.* £250
- **The Corsair; Lara.** L., 1817. 16mo. Comprising vol. III of the Works. Str.-grd. mor., spine gt. Fore-e. pntg. (SG. Mar.19; 123) $150
- [–] **Don Juan (Cantos 1-5).** Ill.:– I.R. Cruikshank. L., [1821]. Frontis. & engraved title with the G. Smeaton imprint, foxed. Orig. bds., lettered spine, jnts. crudely reprd., red str.-grd. mor. solander s.-c. (SG. Mar.19; 46) $110
- [–] **Don Juan [cantos I-II].–Sardanapalus, a tragedy, The Two Foscari, a tradegy, cain, a mystery.–Manfred, a dramatic poem.** 1819; 1821; 1817. 1st. Edn.; 1st. Edn.; 1st. Edn. 3rd. Iss. 3 vols. 4to.; 8vo; 8vo. 1st. work: 3 words erased on 1 p.; 3rd. work: orig. wraps. bnd. in. Unif. mor. gt. by Rivière, partly unc. (C. Feb.4; 11) *Elstein.* £130
- [–] **English Bards & Scotch Reviewers.** [1809]. 1st. Edn. 12mo. Inscr. on hf.-title 'Charles Skinner Matthews Esqr' with his notes & comments in the margins thro.-out. Hf. mor. (C. Feb.4; 12) *Sawyer.* £260
- **Hebrew Melodies.** 1815. 1st. Edn. 1st. Iss. Orig. wraps., unc., in cl. folding case. (C. Feb.4; 14) *Maggs.* £90
- **The Island, or Christian & his Comrades.** 1823. 1st. Edn. Orig. wraps., unc., in cl. s.-c. (C. Feb.4; 16) *Jarndyce.* £85
- – **Anr. Edn.** L., 1823. 3rd. Edn. Pp. 92+(ii) inc. Foreign wraps., circulating ticket of Cheadle Book Society. (KH. Nov.18; 136) Aus. $190
- [–] **Lara, a Tale; Jacqueline, a Tale.** 1814. 1st. Edn. Orig. bds., unc., in cl. folding case. (C. Feb.4; 18) *Cosser.* £50
- **Letters & Journals.** Ed.:– Thomas Moore. L., 1830. 4 vols. Lge. 4to. Extra-ill. with approx. 550 engd. plts. Lev., triple gt. fillet borders, spines gt., gt. dentelles. by Jenkins & Cecil. 5 A.L.s by R.B. Sheridan, J.P. Kemble, James Montgomery, Maria Foote & Capel Lofft, hf.-title inscr. 'From the Author', Francis Hodgson, Provost of Eton sig. (SG. May 14; 36) $900
- [–] **The Liberal.** 1822-23. 1st. Edn. 4 pts. in 2 vols. 19th. C. hf. cf. (C. Feb.4; 35) *Rogers.* £70
- **Life & Works.** L., 1833. 17 vols. Slight browning. Hf. mor. gt., 1 cover detchd. (SPB. Jul.28; 68) $100
- **Ode to Napoleon Buonaparte.** 1814. 1st. Edn. Last 2 advt. ll. Cf. by Rivière, gt. (SH. Jun.18; 164) *Joughin.* £280
- **Poems–Monody on the Death of the right honourable R.B. Sheridan.** 1816; 1816. 1st. Edns., 2nd. Iss. 2 vols. Mor. gt. by Rivière, partly unc. (C. Feb.4; 25) *Chelsea Rare Books.* £55
- **Poetical Works.** 1855. 6 vols. Extra-ill. with about 140 engrs. from an 1833 edn. Mor. gt. by Bayntun. (C. Feb.4; 33) *Traylen.* £200
- **The Prisoner of Chillon.** L., 1816. 1st. Edn. 1st. Iss., with E8 recto blank. Orig. wraps., orig. bookseller's label on upr. cover, slight stain on covers, qtr. mor. gt. s.-c. From the Prescott Collection. (CNY. Feb.6; 42) $350
- **Sardanapalus, a tragedy. The Two Foscari, a tragedy, Cain, a mystery.** 1821. 1st. Edn. Orig.[?] paper bds., unc. Pres. copy. (C. Feb.4; 28) *Blackwell.* £110
- [–] **Uriel, a Poetical Address to the Right Honourable Lord Byron.** 1822. Probably lacks hf.-title. Hf. cf. by Rivière. (C. Feb.4; 38) *Shaw.* £120
- **Works.** 1823-25. 14 vols. Cont. mor. (SH. Jun.25; 210) *Wolfson.* £60
- – **Anr. Edn.** L., 1828. 4 vols. 16mo. Cont. red str.-grd. mor. gt., buckram s.-c. With fore-e. pntg. in each vol.; from the Prescott Collection. (CNY. Feb.6; 116) $550
- – **Anr. Copy.** 17 vols. Slight spotting. Cf. gt. by Rivière, slight rubbing. (SPB. May 29; 64) $150
- **Works . . . with Letters, Journals & his Life.** L., 1832. 17 vols. Slight foxing. Cf., some wear. (SPB. Nov.25; 436) $400

- **Works.** Ed.:– Thomas Moore. 1832-33. 17 vols. Cont. mor., gt. (C. Feb.4; 32) *Elstein.* £190
- – **Anr. Copy.** Maroon str.-grd. mor., triple gt. fillets on covers, spines gt., by Zaehnsdorf. (SG. Feb.12; 136) $350
- – **Anr. Edn.** 1851. 16 vols. Hf. mor. gt. (P. Mar.12; 34) *Kay.* £80
- – **Anr. Copy.** 10 vols. Str.-grd. mor. gt. by Rivière (DWB. Mar.31; 141) £50
- – **Anr. Edn.** 1854. 10 vols. Str.-grd. mor. gt. by Rivière (P. Oct.23; 301) *Hersworth.* £65
- – **Anr. Edn.** L., 1855-56. 6 vols. Extra-ill. with 115 plts. Three-qtr. mor. Bkplt. of Rodman Wanamaker in each vol. (SG. Apr.9; 125) $130
- – **Anr. Edn.** Ed.:– R.E. Prothero. 1898-1904. 13 vols. Extra-ill. Hf. mor. gt., Byron's crest in compartments on spines. (C. Feb.4; 34) *Traylen.* £280
- – **Anr. Edn.** 1898-1904. (250) numbered. 13 vols. 4to. Orig. cf.-bkd. cl. (SH. May 28; 18) *Dawson.* £140
- – **Anr. Copy.** Orig. mor.-bkd. cl. (CSK. Jun.12; 17) £50

BYRON, John
- **A Voyage Round the World.** 1767. 1st. Edn. Mod. mor.-bkd. bds. (C. Nov.5; 23) *Remington.* £50
- – **Anr. Edn.** L., 1767. 2nd. Edn. Advt. lf. at end. Cont. cf. rebkd. [Sabin 9732] (SBP. May 5; 125) $200

BYRON, May
- **Featherweights.** Ill.:– Arthur Rackham. L., n.d. 12mo. Cold. decor. wraps. Raymond M. Sutton Jr. copy. (SG. May 7; 41) $220

BYSTANDER, The
1908-13. Vols. 20-40 only. 4to. Cont. cl. (SH. Oct.9; 3) *Landry.* £105

C., L. V., Keyserlicher Stallmeister
- **Ritterliche Reutter Kunst Darinen Ordentlich begriffen . . . Ubung der Reutterey . . . Ritterspiel, Mumerey . . . Dessgleichen . . . Underricht der Marstallerey und Rossartzeney.** Ill.:– Jost Amman. Frankfurt, 1584. 1st. Edn. Fo. 18th. C. vell. bds. (S. Jun.1; 18) *Joseph.* £1,000

CABALA Sive Scrinia Sacra
L., 1691. 3rd. Edn. 2 pts. in 1 vol. Fo. Cont. cf., rebkd. (SG. Feb.5; 61) $130

CABEO, Nicolao
- **Philosophia Magnetica in qua Magnetis Natura Penitus explicatur . . . nova etiam Pyxis construitur.** Ferrara, 1629. 1st. Edn. Fo. Lacks ptd. title & dedication lf., some ll. slightly spotted, dedication supplied in Xerox copy. 18th. C. stained vell. (S. Oct.21; 373) *Brookfield.* £170
- – **Anr. Copy.** Stained thro.-out, Slightly wormed, stp. on title verso. Cont. leath., gold-stpd. arms supra libros. (HK. Nov.18-21; 432) DM 1,200

CABINET d'Amour et de Vénus (Le)
Cologne, n.d. Sm. 12mo. Cont. red mor., decor. spine, 3 fillets, inner dentelle. (HD. Apr.10; 326) Frs. 3,300

CABINET DES FEES, Ou Collection Choisie des Contes de Fées et autres Contes Merveilleux
Ill.:– Marillier, Berthet, Biosse, Borgnet, Choffard Delignon, Delvaux, Fessare & others. Amst., ca. 1785-89. 41 vols. Vol. 29 lacks hf.-title & title & 2 (of 3) ills. Cont. hf. leath., gt., sm. floral stps. rubbed, 1 vol. newer but unif. style, vol. 1 leath., 1 vol. slightly differing decor. (D. Dec.11-13; 642) DM 1,700

CABINET-MAKER'S Assistant
Glasgow, 1853. Fo. 101 engraved plts., & 3 unnumbered plts., some foxing. Hf. leath., covers detchd. (SG. Mar.12; 56) $110

CABINET-MAKERS London Book of Prices, The
Ill.:– Towes after Shearer. 1788. 4to. Lacks 1st. lf. of dedication, tear in F1, title defect. & detchd. some staining. Cont. qtr. cf., worn. (S. Mar.17; 401) *Warwick Univ.* £60

CADEAU des Muses
- **Etrennes utiles et agréables pour l'An XIII.** Falaise, Paris, Rouen, [1804-05]. 32mo. Cont. red mor., covers decor. with gt. motifs, garland, central medallion, etc. (HD. Apr.8; 51) Frs. 1,100

CADIK, Dr. Jindrich
- **Dilo Josefa Drahonovskeho.** Prague, 1933. De Luxe Edn. Lge. 4to. Frontis., 64 plts. Crimson mor., raised bands, each cover with circular onlay

under glass, upr. cover with crystal gem, lr. cover with initials R.B. [Rudolf Beran], mor. & satin end-ll., hf. leath. d.-w. & s.-c. (SG. Oct.9; 109) $650

CAESAR, Caius Julius
- **C. Julii Caesaris Quae Extant.** Ill.:– Huijberts & others after Mantegna & others. 1712. (25) L.P. Fo. Text below plt. 77 slightly cropped. Cont. cf., rebkd., fault in lr. cover. (C. Nov.20; 234) *Dutt.* £290
- – **Anr. Copy.** Cont. diced cf., gt. roll-tooled panels on sides, gt. Spine. (C. Feb.25; 176) *Maggs.* £240
- **Commentaria . . .** Lyons, 1519. Ink drawing by former owner on title verso. Later bds., liby. bkplt. (SG. Feb.5; 65) $325
- **Commentaries.** Ed.:– W. Duncan. 1753. Fo. Old cf., brkn. (BS. Jun.11; 35) £130
- – **Anr. Copy.** Cont. cf., rebkd., worn, upr. cover detchd. (S. Jul.27; 87) *Crossley.* £100
- – **Anr. Copy.** Plt. 3 sigd. three/four, port. slightly chewed in lr. outer corner, 2 plts. reprd., 2 shaved or slightly cropped, a few short tears. Cont. spr. cf., gt., worn, Baron Carbery's bkplt. (S. Jan.26; 133) *Erlini.* £80
- – **Anr. Copy.** Cont. cf. (SG. May 14; 37) $600
- – **Anr. Edn.** Ed.:– Somerset de Chair. Ill.:– Clifford Webb. Gold. Cock. Pr., 1951. (70) numbered, sigd. by translator & artist, specially bnd. Fo. Orig. mor., d.-w., by Sangorski & Sutcliffe. (CSK. Apr.3; 58) £120
- – **Anr. Edn.** Ed.:– Somerset de Chair. Ill.:– Clifford Webb. Gold. Cock. Pr., 1951. (320), numbered. Fo. Orig. cl. (CSK. Oct.31; 40) £55
- **Commentarii.** Ed.:– Hieronymus Bononis. Treviso, Michael Manzolus, 30 Jun., 1480. Fo. F.1 reprd., old marginalia, few wormholes. 18th. C. vell. bds., spine wormed. [BMC VI, 899] (S. Nov.25; 336) *Fletcher.* £480
- **Commentariorum Libri VIII.** Basel, 1575. Partly lightly browned & slightly soiled, some sm. MS. notes. Cont. blind-stpd. pig-bkd. wood bds., 1 (of 2) clasps. (HK. Nov.18-21; 133) DM 660
- **Commentarium de Bello Gallico.** Venice, 1519. Lack B8 & 2K8 (blanks?), a few sm. wormholes but mainly marginal, some ll. washed? Later cf. gt. (SBA. Oct.21; 23) *Ponder.* £95
- **The Complete Captain, or an Abridgement of Casars Warres, with Observations upon them [etc.] . . . & A Particular Treatise of Modern War . . . by . . . the Duke of Rohan.** Trans.:– T. C[ruso]. 1640. 2 pts. in 1 vol. Slight browning & soiling. Cont. sheep, rebkd. [STC 4338] (S. Jun.29; 365) *Murray-Hill.* £150
- **La Guerre des Suisses.** Trans.:– Louis XIV. 1651. 1st. Edn. Fo. Lacks 1st. & final blanks. Cont. cf., some wear, letter 'F' stpd. on covers. The Phillipps copy with shelfmark &, . 'Fletcher 1843' on front free endpaper. (S. Jun.9; 39) *Quaritch.* £150
- **[Opera] Quae Extant.** Ed.:– Samuel Clarke. Ill.:– Vertue after Kneller. 1712. Lge. fo. Cont. russ. gt. (S. Mar.16; 176) *Erlini.* £260

CAESAR, Caius Julius–AEMYLIUS, Paulus
- **Rerum ab se Gestarum Commentarii.–De Rebus Gestis Francorum.** Paris, 1543; 1544. 2 works in 1 vol. Fo. 17th. C. cf., panelled in gt., orig. spine preserved. (S. Dec.8; 146) *Stopp.* £110

CAETANI, Marguerite (Ed.)
See-BOTTEGHE OSCURE . . .

CAFMEYER, Petrus de
- **Hooghweirdighe Historie van het Alderheylighste Sacrament van Mirabel.–Eerste Vervolgh van de Hogweerdige Historie.** Brussels, 1720. 1st. Printing. 2 works in 1 vol. Fo. 2 added MS. pieces bnd. in. Mod. grd. cf., 5 decor. raised bands, double border each with triple fillet & gt. guarland, inner dentelle. (LM. Jun.13; 37) B.Frs. 14,000

CAHIERS D'ART: Revue d'Art Paraissant Dix Fois par An
Ed.:– Christian Zervos. Paris, 1933-52. 9 numbers from the 8th. to 30th. years. Sm. fo. Numbers 3-4 vol. has full-p. Man Ray photographic port. of Leger. Orig. lithographic & ptd. wraps. Inscr. & sigd. by Leger. (PNY. Mar.4; 113) $550
- **23e Année, 1948. Containing the Works of Pablo Picasso for 1946-48 . . .** Paris, [1948]. 1st. Edn. Sm. fo. Ptd. wraps., tissue guard, publisher's box. Pres. copy from Picasso, 'A Bobsy' [Goodspeed]. (PNY. Mar.4; 217) $260

CAHIERS NOBLES (Les)
Paris, 1954-[1970]. (333) 1st. issues, other issues

various. No. 1-37, 34 pts. of 37., lacks no. 27-28-29 & 30. 4to. (LM. Nov.8; 232) B.Frs. 22,000

CAILLARD, A.B.
- Catalogue des Livres. Paris, 1805. (25) on L.P. Bkplts. of Gomez de la Cortina & Maurice Escoffier. Later mor., gt., with arms of Gomez de la Cortina, spine partly detchd. (SM. Oct.7; 1339)
Frs. 1,300

CAILLAU, J.M.–CULLEN, William–HALLER, Albrecht–COSTE, M.
- Tableau de la Medecine Hippocratique. –Physiologie de . . .–Dissertation sur les Parties Irritables et Sensibles des Animaux.–Traité des Maladies du Poumon. Trans.:– Bosquillon (2nd. work); M. Tissot (3rd. work). Bordeaux; Paris; Lausanne; Paris, 1806; 1785; 1755; 1767. 4 works in 1 vol. 12mo. 4th. work: p. xi mispaginated x, last 7 ll. stained. Cont. cf. (CB. Nov.12; 148)
Can. $260

CAILLIE, Rene
- Travels through Central Africa to Timbuctoo; & Across the Great Desert, to Morocco . . . in the Years 1824-28. 1830. 2 vols. Some spotting. Cont. hf. cf. (TA. Apr.16; 419) £75

CAIRNIE, J.
- Essay on Curling & Artificial Pond Making. Glasgow, 1833. 1st. Edn. Orig. cl., unopened. (PNY. Dec.3; 100) $150

CAIUS or Kay, Joannes
- De Canibus Brittannicis Liber unus.–De Rariorum Animalium et Stirpium Historia, Liber unus.–De Libris Propriis, Liber unus. 1570. 1st. Edn. 3 pts. in 1 vol. Lacks folding table after f. C3. 18th. C. mor., triple gt. fillet, spine gt. with 5 sm. roundels in each compartment, inner gt. dentelles. [STC 4346] (S. Jun.1; 91) Way. £180

CALATAYUD, Pedro P. de
- Juizio de los Sacerdotes, Doctrina Practica y Anatomia de sus Conciencias, dispuestas en seis platicas, que suele hazer el Gremio Eclesiastico en sus Misiones. Lima, 1752. Sm. 4to. Liby. stp. of the Franciscans at Tarija on title, some discolouration. Cont. limp vell. (SPB. May 5; 126) $150

CALBET, Antoine
- [Original Drawings]. N.d. 2 vols. Sm. fo. 52 orig. pastels, mntd. on pastebds. Chagrin. (HD. Dec.5; 30) Frs. 31,500

CALDANI, Leopoldo M.A. & Floriana
- Icones Anatomicae. Ill.:– after Franciscus Ambrosi, C. Bosa, & others. Venice, 1801-14. 5 vols. text, 4 vols. plts. Fo. & elephant fo. Cont. hf. cf., 1 text vol. with upr. cover detchd. From Chetham's Liby., Manchester. (C. Nov.26; 71)
Arader. £850

CALDECOTT, Randolph
- The Complete Collection of . . . Contributions to the 'Graphic'. Ed.:– Arthur Locker (preface). L., 1888. (1250) numbered. Fo. Orig. cl. covers, rebkd. in buckram. (SG. Apr.30; 44) $150
- The Complete Collection of Pictures & Songs. 1887. (800). Fo. Orig. cl., 2 corners dampstained. (SH. Dec.11; 278) Seaton. £70
- 'Graphic' Pictures. L., 1889. Compl. Edn. Ob. 4to. Cl., worn. (SG. Sep.4; 92) $100
- The House that Jack built.–The Diverting History of John Gilpin.–The Babes in the Wood. –The Milkmaid . . . [1878-1885]. 16 vols. 4to. Orig. wraps., some backstrips reprd. (SH. Dec.11; 277) Johns. £80
- Picture Books. L., ca. 1878-84. 1st. Edn. of 12 vols., later Edn. of rest. 16 vols. 4to. & ob. 4to. Some slight offsetting. Orig. cold. pict. wraps., 2 spines worn, sm. early owner's ink initials on most covers. From the Prescott Collection. (CNY. Feb.6; 44) $420

CALDER, Alexander
- Stabiles. Ed.:– James Jones & Michel Ragon. Paris, 1963. Edn. de Tête, (150) numbered on velin de Rives, sigd. Tall fo. Loose as issued in pict. wraps., bd. folder & s.-c. (SG. Oct.23; 50) $220
- Three Young Rats & Other Rhymes. Ed.:– James J. Sweeney. N.Y., 1944. 1st. Edn. (700) numbered (this copy unnumbered) on Arnold Paper. Tall 4to. Cl.-bkd. pict. bds., d.-w. (PNY. Mar.4; 114) $240
-- Anr. Copy. Sigd. Pres. Copy. (PNY. May 21; 118) $170

CALDER, J.E.
- Some Account of the Wars . . . of the Native Tribes of Tasmania. Hobart, 1875. With 4 prelims. not listed by Ferguson. Orig. cl. (KH. Mar.24; 86) Aus. $160

CALDERINUS, Johannes
See–MOLLENBECKE, Petrus–CALDERINUS, Johannes

CALDERON DE LA BARCA, Frances Erskine
[–] Life in Mexico. Ed.:– W.H. Prescott. L., 1843. 1st. Edn. Orig. cl. (SG. Jun.11; 208) $100
[–] – Anr. Edn. Ed.:– H.T. & M.H. Fisher. Garden City, 1966. 2-toned cl. (SG. Mar.5; 306) $140

CALDERON DE LA BARCA, Pedro
- Autos Sacramentales, Alegóricos y Historiales. Ed.:– D. Pedro de Pando y Mier. Madrid, 1717. 1st. Coll. Edn. 6 vols. 4to. Orig. vell. (DS. May 22; 809) Pts. 28,000

CALEDONIAN CANAL
- Reports of the Commissioners for making & maintaining an Inland Navigation, commonly called the Caledonian Canal, from the Eastern to the Western Sea . . . 1804-58. Vols. 1-53. Orig. cl. (SH. May 21; 147) Weinreb. £780

CALEDONIAN HORTICULTURAL Society (The)
- Memoirs of. Edinb., 1814. Vol. 1 (?only). Cont. str.-grd. mor. by Thomson of Edinb., stpd. & rubbed in gt. & blind, gt. inner dentelles, watered silk doubls. (CSK. Jun.19; 93) £50

CALENDARS
- A Rosary Calender, 1931. Ill.:– David Jones. St. Dominic's Pr., 1930. Orig. wraps. (SH. Feb.19; 67) Quaritch. £165
- Thomas Aquinas Calendar, 1926. Ill.:– Eric Gill & David Jones. St. Dominic's Pr., [1925]. Fo. Mod. cl., orig. upr. wrap. bnd. in. (SH. Feb.19; 66a) Chapman. £85

CALENDRIER de Belgique, curieux et utile pour l'année 1789
Gand, [1788]. 18mo. Cont. silk, covers & spine decor. with gold embroidery with different cold. spangles, watered silk fly-ll. & doubls. (HD. Apr.8; 74) Frs. 3,400

CALENDRIER de la Cour
Paris, 1725. 18mo. Later red mor., gt. fillet on covers, decors., ca. 1780. (HD. Apr.8; 52)
Frs. 1,700
-- Anr. Edn. Paris, 1767. 18mo. Cont. kid, covers decor., red mor. cut-outs, gt. decor., doubls. & end-ll. watered silk. (HD. Apr.8; 54) Frs. 3,900
-- Anr. Edn. Paris, 1774. 18mo. Cont. red mor. gt. decor. border, centre motif. (HD. Apr.8; 55)
Frs. 1,000
-- Anr. Edn. Paris, 1777. 18mo. Cont. kid, covers decor. with red mor. cut-outs, spangles, & gold or silver motifs with 2 paintings in centre. (HD. Apr.8; 56) Frs. 3,700
-- Anr. Edn. Paris, 1778. Sm. 18mo. Cont. red mor. decor. spine, fillet on covers, Arms of France, doubls. & end-ll. watered silk. (HD. Apr.8; 57)
Frs. 1,100
-- Anr. Edn. Paris, 1780. Sm. 18mo. Cont. mor. gt. decor. covers, doubls. & fly-ll. watered silk. (HD. Apr.8; 58) Frs. 2,400
-- Anr. Edn. Paris, 1784. 18mo. Cont. red mor., lge. gt. plaque on covers, central Arms of France. (HD. Apr.8; 60) Frs. 1,100
-- Anr. Edn. Paris, 1786. 32mo. Cont. mor., gt. borders enclosing, on both covers, royal arms in gt., spine gt. Irwin Laughlin bkplt. (SG. Oct.9; 49) $175
-- Anr. Copy. 18mo. Cont. mor., covers gt. decor., central medallion. (HD. Apr.8; 61)
Frs. 1,400
-- Anr. Edn. Paris, 1787. Sm. 18mo. Cont. red mor., gt. fillet, royal Arms of France. (HD. Apr.8; 63) Frs. 1,100
-- Anr. Edn. Paris, 1788. 18mo. Cont. red mor., gt. decor., central motif, inner dentelle. (HD. Apr.8; 64) Frs. 1,000
-- Anr. Edn. Paris, 1790. 18mo. Cont. kid, gt. border, crowned initials, centre devise, watered silk doubls. & end-ll. From the liby. of Mortimer Schiff. (HD. Apr.8; 67) Frs. 2,800
-- Anr. Copy. Cont. kid, covers decor with red & olive mor. cut-outs, motifs of pewter or silver, central medallion on each cover, silk doubls. & fly-ll. (HD. Apr.8; 68) Frs. 1,600

-- Anr. Copy. Cont. mor., gt. decor. covers, border & centre motif. (HD. Apr.8; 69)
Frs. 1,400
-- Anr. Edn. Paris, 1791. 18mo. Cont. red mor., gt. decor. covers with central motif. & wide border. (HD. Apr.8; 71) Frs. 1,100

CALENDRIER de la Flandre (Le) pour l'année bissextile 1780
Lille, [1779]. Sm. 18mo. Cont. red mor., covers richly decor. (HD. Apr.8; 75) Frs. 1,600

CALENDRIER de Toulouse pour l'Année 1789
Toulouse, [1788]. Sm. 18mo. Cont. red mor., lge. gt. decor. on covers with central motif. From the liby. of the Marquis de Biencourt. (HD. Apr.8; 76)
Frs. 3,000

CALENDRIER pour l'An Sixième de la République Française
Paris, [1797]. Sm. 18mo. Frontis. entitled 'Etrennes des neuf soeurs, dédiées a l'amour'. Cont. red mor., gt. decor. covers, central medallion with knot of ribbons with motif on upr. cover & engraved device on lr., watered silk fly-ll. & doubls. (HD. Apr.8; 77) Frs. 2,000

CALERIUS, Aegidius
- Sporta Fragmentorum; Sportula Fragmentorum [with other tracts]. Brussels, [Frates Vitae Communis], [1478] & 1479. 1st. Edn. 2 pts. in 1 vol. Fo. Spaces for initial capitals, supplied in red (as are paragraph marks & initial strokes), some MS. headlines, MS. foliation, MS. quiring preserved in many places, 1st. p. soiled, fore-margins of some 20 ll. at front with 2 sm. wormholes. Mor., spine gt.-lettered (faded). From the collection of Eric Sexton. [BMC IX, 171, Goff C200] (CNY. Apr.8; 32) $7,500

CALIFORNIA
- The Act Passed by the Legislature of California, at the Session of 1877-8, incorporating the Town of Berkeley, Alameda County. Berkeley, 1878. Ptd. wraps., some writing & liby. stps. on upr. wrap. (SG. Jan.8; 57) $100

CALLAGHAN, Morley
- No Man's Meat. Paris, 1931. 1st. Edn. Orig. bds., canvas spine, glassine d.-w., bd. s.-c. (CB. Apr.1; 4) Can. $220

CALLAHAN, Harry
- Photographs. Santa Barbara, [1964]. 1st. Edn. 4to. Cl., owner's label on front free endpaper, unif. bd. s.-c. (SG. Apr.23; 47) $600

CALLCOTT, Sir Augustus Watt
- Italian & English Landscape. Ill.:– Dibdin after Callcott. 1847. Fo. 24 (of 25) plts., title & contents loose & spotted. Orig. mor.-bkd. cl. (SKC. Sep.9; 1678) £120

CALLIMACHUS or Callimaco
- Epigrammata. Glasgow, 1755. Fo. Cont. cf., rebkd. (TA. Mar.19; 565) £50
- Hymnes. Trans.:– La Porte du Theil. Paris, 1775. New Edn. Parallel Fr. & Greek text. Cont. red mor., fillet, decor. spine, wtrd. silk doubls. & end-ll., inner dentelle, stpd. arms, ex-liby. on verso of 1st. fly-lf. From Choppin & Blumenthal libys. (HD. Jun.10; 16) Frs. 1,500

CALLOT, Jacques
- Capricci di varie Figure. Ca. 1700. Ob. 12mo. Mott. cf. (BS. Jun.11; 318) £160
- Costumes de la Noblesse Lorraine. [Nancy], 1624? Ob. 8vo. Engrs. cut at borders & remntd., stained. Hf. mor., ca. 1860. (HD. Dec.5; 31)
Frs. 1,350
- De Droeve Ellendigheden Van Den Oorloogh. Ca. 1630-40. Ob. fo. Engraved title-p. & plts. closely cropped & remntd. on 19th. C. art paper. Hf. mor. (TA. Sep.18; 215) £140
-- Anr. Edn. Ca. 1640. Approximately 10cm.×20cm. Stitched & unbnd. (TA. Oct.16; 182) £85
-- Anr. Edn. Ca. 1700. Ob. 8vo. 17 plts. mntd. on close-wove cream paper. Old hf. mor. (TA. Jan.22; 180) £125
- Twelve Engravings of Costume, on India Paper. Ca. 1760. Sm. 4to. Plts. trimmed & preserved. No bdg. stated. (BS. Jun.11; 319) £55

CALMET, Augustin
- Dissertations sur les Apparitions des Anges . . . Paris, 1746. 1st. Edn. 12mo. With 4 pp. of advts., title backed. Mod. vell. (SG. Feb.5; 344) $100
- Dissertations sur les Apparations . . . et sur les Revenans et Vampires de Hongrie. Paris, 1746.

CALMET, Augustin -contd.
12mo. Marginal wormhole, some browning. Cont. mott. cf. (SPB. May 29; 65) $150
– **Gelehrte Verhandlung der Materi, von Erscheinung der Geistern** . . . Augsburg, 1751. 1st. German Edn. 2 vols. in 1. Double-p. title. Later bds. (R. Oct.14-18; 187) DM 950

CALMET, Austin
– **Dictionnaire Historique** . . . **de la Bible.** 1730. 4 vols. Fo. Cf. (P. Apr.9; 228) *Cohen.* £220
– **Histoire Ecclésiastique et Civile de Lorraine** . . . **1690.** Nancy, 1728. 1st. Edn. 3 vols. Fo. Cont. marb. cf., decor. spines. (HD. Jun.10; 17) Frs. 4,800
– **Histoire Généalogique de la Maison du Chatelet** . . . Ill.:– Humblot, Aveline, Ravenal. Nancy, 1741. Fo. 19th. C. marb. roan, decor. spine arms. (HD. Jun.10; 18) Frs. 3,400

CALOT, F.
See–PREVERT, Jacques & Calot, F.

CALPURNIUS SICULUS, Titus
– **Laendliche Gedichte.** Trans.:– Friedrich Adelung. St. Petersb., 1804. 1st. Edn. 4to. Cont. red str.-grd. mor., gt. floral borders, satin end-papers, by A. Buehler. (SG. Sep.4; 93) $170

CALPURNIUS SICULUS, Titus & Olympius Nemesianus, Marcus Aurelius
– **Bucolica.** Parma, Angelus Ugoletus, [1491?]. Sm. 4to. Slight browning. 19th. C. hf. roan. From liby. of André L. Simon. [BMC VII, 944; Goff C65] (S. May 18; 51) *Harper.* £320

CALVERT, Alfred A.
– **Moorish Remains in Spain.–The Alhambra.** 1906. 2 vols. Orig. cl. (SH. Oct.9; 114) *Reed & Sims.* £55

CALVERT, Frederick, Lord Baltimore
See–BALTIMORE, Lord Frederick Calvert

CALVERT, James
– **Vazeeri Rupi, the Silver Country of the Vazeers in Kulu.** 1873. Orig. cl. gt. (P. Jul.1; 206) *Hosain.* £75

CALVIN, John
– **A Commentarie upon S. Paules Epistles to the Corinthians.** 1577. 1st. Edn. in Engl. 4to. Later hf. cf., reprd. [STC 4400] (C. Jul.16; 247) *Duffield.* £50
– **Commentarij in Epistolam Pauli ad Romanos.** Strassburg, 1540. Early Edn. Old owner's note on title, title & 1 lf. with stp., lacks last blank lf., last text lf. loose, lightly browned, many notes & underlinings in 1st. part. Bds. (H. Dec.9/10; 1336) DM 750
– **Institution de la Religion Chrestienne.** Genf, 1562. 4to. About 400 MS. marginalia. Early 19th. C. mor., gold-stpd. title & blind-stpd. fillets, gt. inner & outer dentelles, marb. end-papers, sigd. by Gruel. Maximilien de Bethune's copy, MS. note on 1st. end-paper, early 19th. C., black mor. box. (D. Dec.11-13; 14) DM 130,000
– **Wtlegginghe** . . . **op alle de senttriebeven Pauli des Apostles.** Leiden, 1601. Fo. Stained thro.-out, some ll. at beginning & end loose & a few defect. Cont. Dutch blind-stpd. cf. over wooden bds., defect. Sig. of William Bradford on title-p. (SPB. Nov.24; 4) $8,000

CALVIN, John–PETRUS LOMBARDUS
– **Institutio Christianae Religionis.–Sententiarum Textus.** Strassburg; Basel, 1539; 1516. 2nd. Edn. 2 works in 1 vol. Fo. Wormed at beginning & upr. cover. Cont. blind-tooled pig-bkd. wood bds., 2 clasps. (R. Mar.31-Apr.4; 11) DM 9,000

CALWER, C.G.
– **Deutschlands Obst- und Beerenfrüchte.** Stuttgart, 1854. 4to. Text browned. Orig. hf. linen, spine defect. (R. Oct.14-18; 2966) DM 800

CAMBINI, Andrea
– **Two Very Noble Commentaries.** Trans.:– John Shute. 1562. 4to. Cont. cf., armorial stp. of Thomas Wotton in laurel wreath gt. on covers, rebkd. preserving orig. spine with raised bands. The copy of the Britwell liby., bkplt. of J.R. Abbey, lately in the collection of Eric Sexton. [STC 4470] (C. Apr.15; 87) *Maggs.* £2,000

CAMBRIDGE
– **Gratulato Academiae Cantabrigiensis de Reditu Serenissimi Regis Guilielmi III post Pacem & Libertatem Europae** . . . Camb., [1697]. 1st. Edn. Fo. Slight dampstaining to 1st. few ll. Early 19th. C. limp blindstpd. pig with stp. of Frederick

Walpole. Bkplt. of Robert Walpole Earl of Orford. [Wing C332] (S. May 5; 341) *Quaritch.* £60

CAMBRIDGE, R.O.
– **Scriberiad.** 1751. 4to. Old cf. (P. Apr.30; 36) *Bickersteth.* £60

CAMBRIDGE BIBLIOGRAPHY of English Literature (The)
Ed.:– F.W. Bateson & George Watson. 1940. 5 vols. Orig. bdgs. (WW. May 20; 41) £50
– – **Anr. Edn.** Ed.:– F.W. Bateson & George Watson. Camb., 1940-57. 1st. Edn. 5 vols. (including supp.). 4to. Orig. buckram. (S. Apr.7; 467) *Talerman.* £65

CAMBRIDGE Medieval History–CAMBRIDGE Modern History
Camb., 1911-36; 1907-11. 13 vols.; 8 vols. in 13 (only, lacks maps for vols. 3-5). Cont. hf. mor. (1st. work); & portfos., worn, faded. (SH. Jul.23; 107) *Lipton.* £60

CAMBRIDGE POETRY
Ed.:– Christopher Saltmarshe & others. L., Hogarth Pr., 1929. 12mo. Errata slip inserted. Decor. bds. Sigd. by many contributors, George Reavey's copy with sig. (SG. Jun.4; 67) $220

CAMBRIDGE UNIVERSITY
– **Epicidium Cantabrigiense, in obitum immaturum, Semperq; deflendum, Heinrici, illustrissimi principis Walliae, & c.** Ed.:– George Herbert & Matthew Wren (contributors). 1612. 2nd. Edn. 4to. Slight browning. Limp vell., slightly soiled. [STC 4482] (S. Jun.29; 366) *Quaritch.* £110
– **Irenodia Cantabrigiensis: ob Paciferum Serenissimi Regis Caroli e Scotia reditum Mense Novembri 1641.** Ed.:– Cleveland, Cowley, & Cudworth (contributors). 1641. 1st. Edn. Sm. 4to. Slight browning, a few ll. cropped at foot with loss to catchwords, etc., a few ll. from anr. work, a Latin disputation, inserted at end. Later limp vell., slightly soiled. [Wing C340] (S. Jun.29; 368) *Kingsgate.* £110
– **Lacrymae Cantabrigiensis in Obitum Serenissimae Reginae Mariae.** 1695. 1st. Edn. Sm. 4to. Slight browning, lacks front free end-paper. Cont. panel. cf., worn. Bkplt. of Thomas Brooke, F.S.A. Armitage Bridge. [Wing C342] (S. Jun.29; 369) *Kingsgate.* £110
– **Musae Cantabrigiensis, serenissimis principibus Wilhelmo et Mariae (etc.).** 1689. 1st. Edn. Sm. 4to. Blank lf. inserted between b2 & b3, with MS. additions (by author?) to poem in Engl. by P. Sayve of Trinity College, some dampstaining, lacks? 1st. lf. (blank?). 18th. C. cf., worn. [Wing C344] (S. Jun.29; 371) *Kingsgate.* £110
– **Musarum Cantabrigiensium luctus & gratulation: ille in Funere Oliveri** . . . **Protectoris; haec de Ricardi successione felicissima, ad eundem.** 1658. 1st. Edn.? Sm. 4to. Slight browning & soiling. Early 19th. C. hf. cf., worn. [Wing C345] (S. Jun.29; 372) *Pickering & Chatto.* £50
– **Rex Redux, sive Musa Cantabrigiensis Voti damnas de Incolumitate & felici reditu Regis Caroli post receptam Coronam, comitiaq; peracta in Scotia.** Ed.:– Richard Crashaw, Thomas Fuller, Edward King, Matthew Wren & Edmund Waller (contributors). 1633. 1st. Edn., iss. with 88 pp. Latin & Greek text. Sm. 4to. A few spots. Orig. vell., gt., a Camb. pres. bgd. by Henry Moody, covers with 2-line roll-border & panel, panel with tulip & other ornaments at corners & covers, centre-piece painted in red, slightly rubbed & soiled, lacks ties. [STC 4491] (S. Jun.29; 373) *Quaritch.* £320

CAMBRY, Jacques
[–] **Voyage dans le Finistère** . . . Ill.:– Valentin. Paris, An VII [1799]. 1st. Edn. 3 vols. Some foxing. Cont. hf. cf., corners, smooth decor. spines. (HD. Jun.24; 84) Frs. 1,400
– – **Anr. Edn.** N.d. 3 vols. Cont. cf., decor. spine, dentelle on covers. (HD. Jun.29; 148) Frs. 2,000

CAMDEN, William
– **Britain.** Trans.:– Philemon Holland. 1610. 1st. Edn. in Engl. Fo. 57 maps & frontis. with map of Britain, all later hand-cold., from p. 161 to end is rodent damage in lr. fore-e., text slightly soiled & spotted. Old cf. with ribbed spine, worn. (CE. Jul.9; 29) £2,000
– – **Anr. Copy.** Engraved title slightly soiled & with lr. margin strengthened, map of Ireland slightly torn in folds and reprd., a few others very

slightly dampstained. Later mor.-bkd. cl. As an atlas, w.a.f. (SBA. Mar.4; 2) *Broadbent.* £1,250
[–] [–] **Anr. Copy** Lacks ptd. title, Dedication to King James & 1st. lf. of Latin verses, Anglo-Saxon alphabet bnd. at end, engraved title soiled & bkd., several maps slightly cropped in outer edges, some repairs, mostly on blank sides of maps with sellotape, occasional spotting. Cont. cf., rebkd., worn. [STC 4509] (S. Jun.22; 157) *Burgess.* £950
– – **Anr. Copy.** Cont. cf. gt., rebkd. As an atlas, w.a.f. .[STC 4509] (S. Nov.25; 411) *Schuster.* £800
– – **Anr. Copy.** Lge. gt. arabesque on covers, reprd. ex-liby. (SG. Oct.30; 75) $3,300
– – **Anr. Edn.** Trans.:– Philemon Holland. Ill.:– Hole & Kip after Norden, Saxton & Owen. 1637. Fo. Lacks map of Yorkshire, West Riding, clean tear in map of Camb. 18th. C. diced russ., rebkd. & reprd. W.a.f. [STC 4510] (C. Nov.6; 246) *Grant.* £1,200
– **Britannia.** 1587. 2nd. Edn. 18th. C. cf., rebkd. Pres. Copy, Edward Bulkeley (inscr. slightly cropped), lately in the collection of Eric Sexton. (C. Apr.15; 165) *Thorp.* £150
– – **Anr. Copy.** About 215 MS. coats of arms in pen & cold. ink, some staining & soiling, blank lr. corner of G2 torn away, 1 of the free endpapers inscr. in a mid-18th. C. hand, at end is a 2-p. MS. in anr. hand, the title bears 2 earlier inscrs. (in different hands), engraved arms of Charles Tounley, York Herald, with an inscr. in same hand as that on front free endpaper bnd. in, front pastedown bears bkplt. of George Hay Drummond, Prebendary of York, the back that of Edward Auriol Hay Drummond D. D., whilst one of the other free endpapers bears the 19th. C. owners' inscrs. of the same family. Late 18th. or early 19th. C. red mor. [STC 4504] (CSK. Dec.12; 102) £80
– – **Anr. Edn.** 1600. 4to. Lge. piece torn from X6, some staining. Cont. cf., rebkd. [STC 4507] (S. Feb.10; 356) *Potter.* £60
– – **Anr. Edn.** Trans.:– Edmund Gibson. Ill.:– Robert Morden. 1695. 1st. Gibson Edn. Fo. Marginal soiling thro.-out. Cont. mor., jnts. worn. (CSK. May 8; 31) £800
– – **Anr. Copy.** 50 engraved maps, 9 plts., text engrs., lacks port./frontis., title worn, some tears & worming. Cont. panel. cf., rebkd. W.a.f. (S. Mar.31; 294) *Tooley.* £650
– – **Anr. Copy.** Engraved port./frontis., 49 (of 50) engraved maps, 9 plts., text engrs., 1 map torn, 1 reprd., a few torn, F4 torn. 1 cover detchd., worn. W.a.f. (S. Mar.31; 292) *Map House.* £620
– – **Anr. Copy.** Some maps reprd., 1 detchd., Saxton's map of Caernarvon loosely inserted. Cont. cf., worn. W.a.f. [Wing C359] (SBA. Jul.22; 48) *Burgess.* £520
– – **Anr. Copy.** 48 (of 50) engraved maps, lacks maps of Saxon Britain & Surrey, maps of Hertfordshire & Herefordshire transposed, 1 or 2 maps torn, a few wormed in margin, map of Scotland loose & frayed, slit in B1, piece torn from 2E4, touching side-note, title frayed, port. & lf. of appendix torn & defect., tear in inner margins of last 4 ll. of index, affecting text, title & port. detchd. W.a.f. (S. Jun.29; 17) *Orde.* £450
– – **Anr. Copy.** Most maps bkd. with blank paper (as iss.?), 5 plts. only (of 9), lacks port., title & some other ll. defect., maps slightly soiled, a few with sm. tears. W.a.f. (S. Apr.7; 468) *Burgess.* £420
– – **Anr. Copy.** Title, port. & prelims. loose, 48 maps, (of 50), lacks Scotland & Rutland, many maps frayed or torn. Old cf., defect. (P. Jul.30; 51) *Burgess.* £360
– – **Anr. Edn.** Ill.:– Robert Morden. 1722. 2nd. Gibson Edn. 2 vols. Fo. Cont. panel. cf, rebkd. (SBA. Jul.22; 84) *Wragg.* £900
– – **Anr. Copy.** Cont. cf. (P. May 14; 138) *Kidd.* £650
– – **Anr. Copy.** Title & port. in vol. 1 slightly stained, a few other minor defects. Cont. cf. gt., worn. As an atlas, w.a.f. (SBA. Jul.14; 21) *Shapiro.* £520
– – **Anr. Copy.** Lacks map of Huntingdon. Old cf. gt., worn. (LC. Jun.18; 144) £420
– – **Anr. Edn.** Trans.:– E. Gibson. Ill.:– Robert Morden (maps). L., 1725. Fo. Lacks title & all after column 678 (4R2). Disbnd. W.a.f. (SG. May 21; 18) $350
– – **Anr. Edn.** Ed.:– Ed. Gibson. Ill.:– R. Morden (maps). 1753. 2 vols. Fo. 38 (of 50) uncold. maps. Cf. (P. Apr.30; 92a) *Kidd.* £360

CAM

91

CAM

– – Anr. Edn. Trans.:– Edmund Gibson. 1772. 4th. Gibson Edn. 2 vols. Fo. Cont. cf., jnts. worn, spines gt. (SKC. Feb.26; 1545) £750
– – Anr. Copy. Short tear in England map, sm. natural flaw in anr., 1 with short tear along plt.-line, very slight offsetting, sig. in title-margins. Rebkd. (S. Jun.22; 158) *Burgess.* £360
– – Anr. Edn. Trans.:– Richard Gough. Ill.:– J. Cary. 1789. 1st. Edn. of this translation. 3 vols. Fo. 90 engraved plts. (of 97), 1 map browned, sm. marginal hole in anr., a few margins cropped, 1 other reprd., a few text ll. slightly spotted. Cont. russ. gt., worn, rebkd. As an atlas, w.a.f. (SBA. Jul.14; 20) *Orde.* £420
– – Anr. Copy. 54 engraved maps only, a few ll. slightly wormed, mainly marginal. Cont. bds., very worn. As an atlas, w.a.f. (SBA. Mar.4; 25) *Stirling.* £320
– – Anr. Edn. Trans.:– R. Gough. 1806. 2nd. Edn. of this translation. 4 vols. Fo. Slight browning. Cont. cf., covers almost detchd. Letter from R. Gough to Mr. Cockfield mntd. on front free endpaper. (CSK. Feb.6; 25) £350
– – Anr. Copy. Engraved port., plts. & maps, some double-p., hand-cold. in outl., title, port., index & a few ll. of vol. 1 detchd. Orig. bds., lacks 2 covers, other covers detchd. W.a.f. (C. May 20; 110) *Burgess.* £280
– – Anr. Copy. Orig. cf.-bkd. bds. (SH. Jul.16; 124) *Smith.* £190
– – Anr. Edn. N.d. 4to. 49 (of 50) double-p. maps, some torn & soiled, a few badly, lacks title pp. & last few pp., some ll. torn & loose. Cont. cf., worn. W.a.f. (SD. Feb.4; 244) £480
– Britannia abridg'd. 1701. Vol. 1 (of 2). 22 folding maps only, 1 loose. Cont. cf., rebkd. (SH. May 21; 266) *Green.* £140
– – Anr. Copy. Vol. II only (of 2). Lacks 2 maps, title mntd., slightly soiled. Later cf., recased. (SH. Nov.6; 80) *Burden.* £120
[–] The History of the Most Renowned & Victorious Princesse Elizabeth. Trans.:– [R. Norton]. 1630. Fo. Cont. cf., rebkd. From the collection of Eric Sexton. [STC 4500] (C. Apr.15; 166) *Morton-Smith.* £60
[–] Reges, Reginae, Nobiles et Alii. 1600. 1st. Edn. Sm. 4to. Title dust-soiled, some cont. MS. notes. Stab-sewn in old limp vell. From the collection of Eric Sexton. [STC 4518] (C. Apr.15; 167) *Field.* £90
[–] Remaines concerning Britaine . . . 1614. Sm. 4to. Cont. vell., mor.-bkd. s.-c. Bkplt. of Harold Greenhill, lately in the collection of Eric Sexton. [STC 4522] (C. Apr.15; 168) *Morton-Smith.* £100

CAMDEN SOCIETY
– Publications. 1838-53. Ca. 57 vols. in 33. Cont. cf. (SH. May 28; 21) *Wade Gallery.* £160
– – Anr. Edn. 1838-1975. 92 vols. only. Orig. cl. (SH. Oct.10; 338) *Bunsei.* £340

CAMERA WORK
Ill.:– Steichen; Rodin. N.Y., 1911. Number 34/35. 4to. Orig. ptd. wraps., spine torn, partly unopened. Inscr. from Stieglitz to Waldo Frank. (SG. Apr.23; 49) $300

CAMERARIUS, Joachim
– Eclecta Georgica (Greek), sive Opuscula Quaedam de Re Rustica. Nuremb., 1596. Some browning, plt. slightly torn. Cont. cf., gt., arms of J.A. de Thou on covers, monog. of de Thou & his 1st. wife on spine. Bkplt. of Biblioteca de Meaux; from liby. of André L. Simon. (S. May 18; 52) *Hill.* £350
– Symbolorum & Emblematum. Ill.:– Hans Sibmacher (engraved title). Nuremb., 1590 [i.e. 1593]. 1st. Edn. Sm. 4to. 70 only (of 100) engraved circular ills. Cont. kid leath., silver-tooled double fillet border & cornerpieces on covers, gt. stp. on upr. cover of a mounted knight, & lettered 'Petr Wok Wolff Zrozmberka, MDXXCV', surrounded by a circular wreath, unif. silver stp. on lr. cover of arms of Peter Wok dtd. 1585, silver tooling blackened, spine worn & reprd., lacks ties, in buckram case. As a bdg., w.a.f. Bkplt. of J.R. Abbey, lately in the collection of Eric Sexton. (C. Apr.15; 5) *Maggs.* £400
[–] Symbolorum et Emblematum ex Re Herbaria. **–ex Animalibus . . .** Ill.:– Hans Siebmacher. [Frankfurt], [1661]. Pts. 1-3 (of 4) in 1 vol. 4to. Lacks pt. 1 title, pt. 2 copper engrs. 5-7, 10 & 24 in pt. 2, stained. Cont. vell., worn. W.a.f. (HK. Nov.18-21; 1564). DM 460

– Symbolum et Emblematum ex Re Herbaria.–[Ex Animalibus Quadrupedibus.–Ex Volitatibus et Insectis.–Ex Acquatilibus et Reptilibus]. Nuremb., 1590-1604. 1st. Edns. 4 vols. in 1. 4to. 1st. title rehinged, uniform browning. Cont. blind-stpd. & gt.-stpd. cf. over wooden bds., covers with gt. panels & central device, 7 of 8 brass clasps, brass cornerpieces. (CNY. Oct.1; 137) $2,600
– Vier Hundert Wahl-Sprüche vnd Sinnen-Bilder. Mainz, 1671. 1st. German Edn. 4 pts. in 1 vol. Cont. vell. (H. Dec.9/10; 1459) DM 650
See–MELANCHTHON, Philip–NIGRUS, A. –CAMERARIUS, Joachim.–CONFESSIO Doctrinae Saxonicarum Ecclesiarum, . . .
See–NATHAN BEN KALONYMUS, Isaak –CAMERARIUS, Joachim–BRUSSIUS [BRUCE], W.

CAMERON. A Novel
1832. 3 vols. 12mo. Orig. moire cl. (CSK. May 8; 106) £50

CAMERON, P.
– A monograph of the British Phytophagous Hymenoptera. 1882-93. 4 vols. 1 plt. & 1 lf. shaken. Orig. embossed cl., gt., ex-liby. (PL. Jul.11; 86) *Wheldon & Wesley.* £80

CAMERON, Verney Lovett
See–BURTON, Sir Richard Francis & Cameron, Verney Lovett

CAMERS, J.
– Commentaria in C. Iullü Solini Polyhistora, et Lucii Floride Romanorum Rebus Gestis Libros . . . Praeterea Pomponii Melae de Orbis Situ Libri Tres, cum Commentariis J. Vadiani . . . Basel, 1557. Coll. Edn. 2 pts. in 1 vol. Fo. Lightly browned in parts, title slightly soiled with torn corner bkd. 17th. C. limp bds. (R. Mar.31-Apr.4; 12) DM 600

CAMFIELD, Benjamin
– A Theological Discourse of Angels. L., 1678. 1st. Edn. With final lf. of advts. & separate title-p. Mod. three-qtr. cf. Sig. of Gulielmi Bolton on title. (SG. Feb.5; 345) $100

CAMILLI, Camillo
– Imprese Illustri di Diversi. Ill.:– Girlamo Porro. Venice, 1586. 1st. Edn. 3 pts. in 1 vol. 4to. Loose in cont. vell. (SG. Sep.25; 74) $200

CAMMAS, Henry & Lefevre, André
– La Vallée du Nil. Paris, 1862. Lge. 8vo. Cont. hf. chagrin, smooth spine. (HD. Feb.27; 94) Frs. 18,000

CAMMERLANDER, J.
[–] Phisionomi und Chiromanci. Strassburg, 1540. Lightly browned in parts, 1 lf. torn with text & plt. loss. Later hf. vell. (D. Dec.11-13; 15) DM 1,200

CAMPAIGN of Waterloo
1816. Fo. Later hf. mor. Copy of Times newspaper dtd. Thursday 22nd June tipped in, w.a.f. (TA. Aug.21; 10) £120

CAMPAN, Jean-Louise Henriette, Madame
– Mémoires sur la vie Privée de Marie-Antoinette. Ill:– Boisson da Lalauze. Paris, 1910. (200) on vell. du Marais numbered. 2 vols. Mor., sigd. by Torriano, mostly unc. (SI. Dec.3; 113) Lire 220,000

CAMPANA CONTRA LOS AMERICANOS DEL NORTE. Primera Parte. Relacion Historica de los Cuarenta Dias que Mando en Gefe el Ejercito del Norte el E. Sr. General de Division Don Mariano Arista, escrita por un official de infanteria
Mexico. 1846. 1st. Edn. All publd. Ptd. wraps, light wear & soiling, covers curled. (SG. Jan.8; 280) $450

CAMPANELLA, Tommaso
– Realis Philosophiae Epilogisticae Partes Quatuor. Frankfurt (-a.-M.), 1623. 1st. Edn. 2 pts. in 1 vol. 4to. 1st. iss.(?), without the woodcut border round general title, some browning & dampstaining. Mod. mor.-bkd. marb. bds. (S. Feb.10; 286) *Bjorck.* £1,400

CAMPANUS, Johannes Antonius
– Oratio Funebris pro Baptista Sfortia. Cagli, Robertus de Fano & Bernardus de Bergamo, 1 Mar., 1476. Spaces for capital initials, supplied in ink, some inner marginal staining & repair, old marginal MS. annots. cropped. Mor. gt., to a Padeloup design, vell. paste-downs, s.-c., by Gozzi of Modena. From the collection of Eric Sexton.

[BMC VII, 1069, Goff C77] (CNY. Apr.8; 34) $4,000

CAMPBELL, Alexander
– A Journey from Edinburgh through Parts of North Britain. 1802. 1st. Edn. 2 vols. 4to. Cont. diced russ. gt. (S. Nov.24; 48) *Dunsmuir.* £110
– – Anr. Edn. 1802. 2 vols. in 1. 4to. Cont. hf. cf. (SH. May 21; 19) *Ayres.* £60

CAMPBELL, Alfred W.
– Histological Studies on the Localisation of Cerebral Function. Camb., 1905. Cl., ex-liby. (S. Jun.15; 147) *Tait.* £50

CAMPBELL, Lord Archibald
– Records of Argyll. Ill.:– Charles Laurie. Edinb. & L., 1885. Ltd. Edn. 4to. Some minor defects. Orig. cl. gt., unc. (SBA. May 27; 396) *Argyll Etkin Ltd.* £80

CAMPBELL, Bruce
– The Bird Paintings of Henry Jones. Ed.:– H.R.H. The Duke of Edinb. (foreword); Prof. Lord Zuckerman (preface). L., 1976. (500) numbered. Ob. 4to. Orig. hf. cf. with s.-c. by Hunter & Foulis of Edinb. (TA. Jun.18; 129) £170

CAMPBELL, Colin
– Vitruvius Britannicus. 1715-17. 5 vols. Fo. Plts. in vol. IV ptd. in sepia, minor dampstain in some upr. margins of vol. I. Antique-style hf. cf. Bkplts. of Lord Polwarth, lately in the collection of Eric Sexton. (C. Apr.15; 63) *Laget.* £1,600
– – Anr. Edn. 1715-25. Vols. 1-3. Fo. Cont. blind & gt.-stpd. cf., bkplt. of Lord Willoughby de Broke. (SH. Jan.29; 220) *Barnett.* £310
– – Anr. Edn. 1715; 1725. Vols. 1 & 3. Fo. Cf., not. unif., 1 defect., 1 rebkd. As a collection of prints, w.a.f. (BS. Jun.11; 121) £170
– – Anr. Edn. [1715]-31. 1st. Edn. Vols. I-III only (of 5). Fo. Some marginal worming in vols. I-II, cutting surface of several plts., a few sm. repairs & tears, slight spotting. Cont. mott. cf., spines gt., worn. Bkplt. of Sir James Graham, of Esk & Netherby. (S. Jun.22; 117) *Weinreb.* £150
– – Anr. Edn. [1715-31]. Vols. 1-3. Fo. Lacks plt. 70, often not found, some discolouration to vol. 3. Cont. cf., worn. (TA. Apr.16; 343) £95
– – Anr. Edn. [1715?-1727?]-1731-67-71 5 vols. Fo. Very occasional spotting. 19th. C. hf. mor., slightly worn. (C. Nov.5; 24) *Traylen.* £1,000
– – Anr. Edn. 1717-25. Vols. 1 & 3 only (of 5). Lge. fo. Cont. cf., spines very worn. W.a.f. (S. Nov.25; 413) *Weinreb.* £140
– – Anr. Edn. 1731. Vols. 1-3. Fo. Old hf. russ., jnts. brkn. (BS. Jun.11; 120) £200
– – Anr. Edn. 1767. Vol. 4 only (of 5). Fo. Title & text in Engl. & Fr. Cont. hf. cf., upr. cover torn. (C. Feb.25; 177) *Laget.* £150
– – Anr. Edn. L., n.d., 1767; 1771. 5 vols. Atlas fo. Cont. leath.-bkd. marb. bds., unc. (SG. May 14; 38) $3,300
– – Anr. Edn. Ill.:– Inigo Jones & Ors. N.d., n.d. & 1731. 3 vols. Fo. Cf., worn. (CE. Nov.20; 39) £300
– – Anr. Copy. Vols. 1-3. Text in Engl. & Fr. Old cf. (P. Mar.12; 40) *Cambridge.* £170

CAMPBELL, John LL.D. 1708-75
[–] Candid & Impartial Considerations on the Nature of the Sugar Trade, the Comparative Importance of the British & French Islands in the West Indies. 1763. Cont. red mor., gt. border of crowns, flowers, etc & other sm. tools, spine gt. [Sabin 10231] (S. Dec.1; 86a) *Lawson.* £120
[–] The Military History of the Late Prince Eugene of Savoy & of the Late John, Duke of Malborough. Ill.:– Claude du Bosc. 1736-37. 2 vols. Fo. Some plts. with marginal dampstains. Panel. cf., worn, rebkd. (C. Nov.5; 25) *Davidson.* £240
– A Political Survey of Britain. 1774. 1st. Edn. 2 vols. 4to. Cont. mott. cf. gt. (SBA. Jul.23; 369) *Frognal Bookshop.* £70
– – Anr. Copy. 2 vols. 4to. Cont. hf. cf. (C. Nov.20; 235) *Thorp.* £55

CAMPBELL, John Lord 1779-1861
– The Lives of the Lord Chancellors.–The Lives of the Chief Justices of England. 1846-48; 1849. 7 vols.; 2 vols. Unif. tree cf. gt. (SKC. Feb.26; 1422) £120

CAMPBELL, Rev. John
– Travels in South Africa. 1822. 1st. Edn. Cont. hf. cf. (C. May 20; 111) *Maggs.* £240
– – Anr. Copy. 2 vols. Some ll. spotted. Cont. diced cf. gt. (SD. Feb.4; 239) £170

CAMPBELL, Rev. John – Travels in South Africa.
-contd.
– – Anr. Copy. 2 vols. in 1. Slight foxing, fly-lf. &
1st. few ll. loose. Hf. cf., ex-liby. (CE. Jun.4; 45)
£90
– – Anr. Copy. 2 vols. Folding map torn at folds.
Cf., upr. cover off. (SSA. Jun.18; 76)   R. 270

CAMPBELL, Roy
– Adamastor. 1930. 1st. Edn., (90) numbered
copies. Orig. cl., s.-c. Sigd., this copy 'Out of
Series'. (SH. Dec.18; 70)   *Maggs.* £50

CAMPBELL, Thomas
– The Pleasures of Hope. Edinb., 1810. 16mo.
Some foxing. Cont. str.-grd. mor., gt. dentelles,
satin doubls. 2 fore-e. pntgs.; from the liby. of
Zola E. Harvey. (SG. Mar.19; 124) $400

CAMPBELL, W.S.
See–MAIDEN, Joseph Henry & Campbell, W.S.

CAMPBELL, Capt. Walter
– The Old Forest Ranger. 1845. 2nd. Edn. Hf.
mor., gt. by Rivière. (CE. Nov.20; 122)   £62

CAMPE, Joachim Heinrich
– Allgemeine Revision des Gesammten Schul-und
Unterrichtswens von einer Gesellschaft
Praktischer Erzieher. Hamburg, Wolfenbüttel
(from vol. 5), Braunschweig & Wien, 1785-92. 16
vols. Stpd. Cont. hf. leath. (R. Mar.31-Apr.4; 261)
DM 4,100
[–] Le Nouveau Robinson, pour servir à
l'Amusement et à l'Instruction des Enfans. Paris,
1792. 12mo. Cont. hf. cf. (SH. Mar.19; 37)
Rota. £70

CAMPER, Pierre
– Discours Prononcés Par Feu Mr Pierre Camper
. . . sur le Beau Physique. Utrecht, 1792. 4to. A
few ll. slightly spotted. Orig. bds., worn. (SBA.
Mar.4; 90)   *Marlborough Rare Books.* £65

CAMPIGLIA, Alessandro
– Delle Turbulenze della Francia in Vita del Re
Henrico il Grande. Libri X. Venice, 1617. 4to.
Cont. red mor., 2 fillets, cipher of Peiresc in centre,
decor. spine. (HD. Mar.18; 33)   Frs. 2,800

CAMPO, Antonio
– Cremona Fedelissima Citta, et Nobilissima
Colonia de Romani . . . Cremona, 1585. 1st. Edn.
Fo. Engraved title with port. on verso, 3 plts., 1
folding, torn & reprd. 34 medallion ports., 2
folding engraved maps, 1 reprd. & loosely
inserted, 3-sheet folding plt., torn. reprd. &
cropped, 19th. C. diced russ., blind-stpd. &
gt.-ruled. (CNY. May 22; 51) $2,200
– – Anr. Copy. Some pp. slightly stained, some
reprd. tears. 19th C. hf. vell. (SI. Dec.3; 114)
Lire 1,800,000
– Cremona Fedelissima Citta [– Historia delle Vite
de Duchi et Duchesse di Milano]. Milan,
1645-1642. 2 pts. in 1 vol. 4to. 1 plt. neatly reprd.,
1 mntd., very slightly soiled or spotted in places.
Cont. mor., gt. (S. Apr.7; 327)   *Facchinotti.* £280
See–GIOVIO, Paeolo–CAMPO, Antonio

CAMPOS, Mariano
– Catecismo de la Doctrina Cristiana en el idioma
Quechua. Cuzco, 1848. Stained. Mod. wraps.
(SPB. May 5; 129) $100

CAMUS, A.G.
– Memoire sur la Collection des Grands et Petits
Voyages, et sur la Collection des Voyages de
Melchisedech Thevenot. Paris, 1802. 4to. Hf. mor.,
gt., by Bedford. [Sabin 10328] (SPB. May 5; 130)
$225

CAMUS, Albert
– L'Etranger. Paris, [1942]. 1st. Edn. 12mo.
Sewed, wrap. Inscr., sigd. (HD. Dec.5; 32)
Frs. 3,900
– Le Malentendu.–Caligula. Paris, 1944. Stage
copy with many pencil entries, notes, text
alterations, etc. Orig. sewed, some signature or ll.
lose, worn, s.-c. Initialled & dated inscr. to Maria
Casares. (D. Dec.11-13; 867)   DM 1,500

CANADA
– Department of Crown Lands. Quebec, 1863. 4
works in 7 vols. (2 + 3 + 1 + 1). Fo. Errata slips
in each vol. Unif. cont. leath. (CB. Nov.12; 72)
Can. $550
– Enterprising Elmira. [Elmira], [1903]. Ob. fo.
Orig. wraps., metal spine, lacks corner on upr.
wrap., slightly soiled. (CB. Dec.9; 43)   Can. $120

CANADA Temperance Advocate, The
Montreal, Jan.1, 1852-Dec.15, 1853, & Mar.
1854. Vols. 18 & 19, & extra no. vol. 20, in 1 vol.
4to. 1 lf. with piece cut out, some ll. cropped, some
ll. soiled. Hf. leath. (CB. Feb.18; 9)   Can. $100

CANADIAN HANDBOOK & Tourist's Guide . . .
Ed.:– Henry Beaumont Small. Montreal, 1867.
Gt.-decor. cl. (SG. Oct.16; 431) $100

CANADIAN PACIFIC RAILWAY
– Descriptive Timeable of the Tour of Their Royal
Highnesses the Duke & Duchess of Connaught
across Canada. N.p., 1912. Padded mor. with
arms on cover, gt. dentelles with moire satin
end-papers. (SG. Mar.5; 105) $150
– Moeurs et Paysages. D'après les Clichés
Photographiques de M. Armstrong. Paris, n.d. Pt.
14. of a series entitled 'Autour du Monde,
aquarelles-souvenirs de voyage'. Ob. 8vo. Orig.
wraps. (CB. May 27; 289)   Can. $120

CANAYE, Sgr. de Frensne, Ph.
– Lettres et Ambassade. Paris, 1645. 1st. Edn. 3
vols. Fo. Some browning. Cont. parch. bds.,
slightly worn, bkplt. of Lord Sinclair. (S.
Apr.7; 328)   *Hyde Park.* £70

CANBY, Henry Seidel
See–THOREAU, Henry David–CANBY, Henry
Seidel

CANCELLARIA Apostolica
– Proulciale omnium Ecclesiarum Cathedraliû
vniuersi Orbis. Paris, 1518. Sm. 4to. Sm. repair to
b2 & 14, liby. stp. removed from title, inscrs. in
text in cont. hands. Cont. cf. over pasteboard (by
Jan Ryckaert of Ghent) with stps. of a shepherd &
a floral bouquet arranged in a diaper pattern in
double fillets, bee & fleur-de-lys stpds. at margins,
rebkd., new fly-ll., lacks ties, covers stpd. Inscr.
'Sum Bibliotheca P. P. Birgittanoru Coloniensium'
on title margin. (S. Jun.23; 225)   *Quaritch.* £200

CANDOLLE, Augstin Pyramus de
– Astragalogia. Ill.:– P.J. Redouté. Paris, 1802.
L.P. Fo. Orig. bds., unc. (C. Mar.18; 28)
Wheldon & Wesley. £550
– Théorie Elementaire de la Botanique, ou
Exposition des Principes de la Classification
Naturelle. Paris, 1813. 1st. Edn. Cont. cf.-bkd. bds.
(S. Dec.3; 928)   *Quaritch.* £110

CANEUON Ceiriog Detholiad
Gregy. Pr., 1925. Ltd. Edn. 4to. Cl.-bkd. bds. (P.
Oct.2; 14)   *Freeman.* £55

CANINE World & Sports & Sportsmen
L., May 23-Dec.26, 1890. Vol. I, nos. 1-32. Fo.
Occasional foxing. Publisher's gt.-lettered cl.,
covers worn. (SG. Dec.11; 294) $250

CANINI, G.A.
– Images des Héros et des Grands Hommes de
l'Antiquité. Ill.:– Picart. Amst., 1731. 4to. Lightly
spotted. Mod. hf. mor. (SH. Jun.25; 162)
Duran. £60

CANIS, Johannes Jacobus
– De Modo Studendi in Utroque Jure. Brunn,
[Conrad Stahel & Mathias Preunlein]. 1488. 4to.
Spaces for initial capitals, with guides,
unrubricated, sm. tear to extreme fore-margin of
1st. lf., lacks final blank, light browning. Old vell.
From the collection of Eric Sexton. [BMC III,
815, Goff C99, H 4325*] (CNY. Apr.8; 31)
$6,500

CANISIUS, Peter, Doctour in Theologie
– Ane Cathechisme of Schort Instruction of
Christian Religion. Paris, 1588. 1st. Edn. 12mo.
Old vell., soiled. [STC 4658] (TA. Feb.19; 443)
£110
– Institutiones Christianae, seu Parvus
Catechismus Catholicorum. Antw., 1589. Old
engrs. pasted onto end-ll., engraved bkplt. 'C.P.',
inscr. with purchase date 1817 in Heber's hand,
bkplt. of Edward Arnold & stp. of Henry Alfred
White. 17th. C. red mor. in Jansenist style with
cipher HD & 4 S fermés, gt., on covers. (SM.
Oct.7; 1625)   Frs. 3,200

CANNIFF, William
– History of the Province of Ontario. Toronto,
1872. 2nd. iss. with cancel title-p., etc. Orig.
buckram, lacks rear free end-paper. Sig. of Allan
Duncan on front free end-paper. (CB. Dec.9; 163)
Can. $160
– The Medical Profession in Upper Canada.
Toronto, 1894. Liby. stp. on title-p. Orig. cl. (CB.
Sep.24; 245)   Can. $160

**CANNON MISSAE ad usum Episcoporum, ac
Praelatorum**
Rome, 1725. Fo. Musical scores, a few pp. torn &
reprd. without loss of letters, soiling. Cont. mor.,
gt., with a cardinal's arms on covers. (CSK.
Nov.21; 248)   £55

CANTERBURY MARRIAGE LICENCES
1892-1906. 1st.-6th. Series. 6 vols. 4to. Cont. mor.
(SH. Nov.6; 6)   *Heraldry Today* £55

CANTICUM CANTICORUM
Berlin, 1922. Facs. of Holland ca. 1465 Edn.,
(400). 4to. Orig. vell. (HK. Nov.18-21; 3130)
DM 620
– – Anr. Edn. Ill.:– Eric Gill. Weimar, Cran. Pr.,
1930. (268). Without the 2-lf. prospectus laid in
most copies. Orig. qtr. vell. gt., partly unc., d.-w.
& s.-c., jacket slightly soiled, box. (CNY.
Oct.1; 155) $1,200

CANTILLON, Philippe de
– Délices du Brabant et de ses Campagnes. Amst.,
1757. 4 vols. Lacks 9 plts. Cont. marb. cf. (H.
Dec.9/10; 551)   DM 2,100

CANTIQUE DES CANTIQUES de Salomon
Ill.:– Eric Gill. Weimar, 1930. (100) numbered on
papier de Monval. 2-lf. prospectus laid in.
Un-bnd., unc. & unopened in orig. wraps. as iss.,
s.-c. (CNY. Oct.1; 156) $850
– – Anr. Edn. Trans.:– André Chouraqui. Ill.:–
Marianne Clouzot. Paris, 1951. (150) numbered
on vel. d'arches. Ll. in bd. covers & s.-c., slightly
defect. (HK. Nov.18-21; 2481)   DM 500

CANTIQUES et Pots-Pourris
Ill.:– Borel, engraved Elluin. L., 1789. 6 pts. in 2
vols. 12mo. Mor., spines decor., 3 fillets, inner
dentelles, unc., by Pagnant. (HD. Apr.8; 226)
Frs. 1,700

CANTU, Cesare
– Grande Illustrazione del Lombardo-Veneto.
Milan, 1858-61. 6 vols. Cont. hf. mor. (SI.
Dec.3; 115)   Lire 600,000
– Storia Universale. Torin, 1884-89. 17 vols. Hf.
vell., unc. (SI. Dec.3; 116)   Lire 180,000

CAP D'ENCRE 1964
Ed.:– Philippe Roberts Jones (preface). Ill.:– Pierre
Alechinsky, René Carcan, Francis de Bolle & oth-
ers. N.p., 1964. (89) on Rives BFK, format raisin
(80) numbered. Japan vegetable fibre, by Camille
Lejeune. (LM. Nov.8; 36)   B.Frs. 11,000

CAP, P.A.
See–LE MAOUT, Jean Emmanuel Marie & Cap,
P.A.

CAPACCIO, Giulio Cesare
– Delle Imprese . . . Naples, 1592. 3 pts. in 1 vol.
4to. A few pen-trials on title, a few ll. with
marginal staining, occasional spotting. Limp
vell.-bkd. bds. (S. May 5; 50)   *Pozzi.* £160

CAPE of Good Hope
– Papers . . . Great Namagualand & Damaraland.
Cape Town, 1885. Fo. Wraps. (VA. Oct.31; 146)
R. 110

CAPEFIGUE, Jean Baptiste Honoré Raymond
– Récit des Opérations de l'Armée Française en
Espagne. 1823. Mor., gt. & blind frame, arms, by
Simier. (HD. Oct.10; 226)   Frs. 1,500

CAPELL, Edward
[–] Prolusions. L., 1760. 1st. Edn. Foxed. Old cf.,
worn, covers detchd. (SG. Sep.25; 76) $110

CAPELLA, Martianus
– De Nuptiis Philologiae et Mercurii. Modena,
Dionysius Bertochus, 15 May, 1500. 2nd. Edn. Fo.
Spaces for initial capitals with guide letters, title-p.
stained with edges slightly frayed, blank verso of
final lf. soiled, sm. hole in upr. margin of last few
ll., some marginal annots. Limp vell. [BMC VII,
1068, Goff C118, Hain 4371*] (CNY. Oct.1; 98)
$2,400

CAPPARONI, Giuseppe
– Raccolta Degli Ordini Religiosi. Rome, 1828-29.
Fo. Some plts. slightly dis-cold. Cont. hf. vell.
(TA. Sep.18; 341)   £70

CAPPER, Benjamin Pitts
– A Topographical Dictionary of the United
Kingdom. 1808. Occasional light dampstains.
Cont. russ. (CSK. Nov.14; 16)   £55
– – Anr. Edn. L., 1813. Mott. cf. gt. (P.
Jun.11; 207)   *Map House.* £140

- – **Anr. Edn.** L., 1825. Some foxing. Hf. cf. (SG. May 21; 150) $100

CARACCIOLUS, Robertus, de Licio
- **Quadragesimale de Poenitentia.** [Venice], Vindelinus de Spira, 20 Jul. 1472. Pt. I only. 4to. 267 ll. (of 290, including blank f. 268 but lacks 1st. blank & pt. II, ff. 269-290, the last blank), f. 2 defect. & reprd. mainly in margin, slightly affecting text on verso, sm. cut in f. 151 slightly affecting 3 letters, slightly soiled or spotted in places. Mod. antique-style sheep spine, wooden covers, 2 clasps. [BMC V, 159; Goff C165; HC 4424] (S. Jun.23; 206) *Ponder.* £280
- **Sermones de Laudibus Sanctorum.** Naples, Mathias Moravus, 31 Jan. 1489. 1st. Edn., 4to. Lacks final blank, 1st. & last ll. preserved, tears in 1st. lf. affecting several letters of text, lacks blank portion of lr. margin, staining in margins & text at beginning & end. 19th. C. Spanish mott. cf. [Hain 4480; BMC VI p. 864; Goff C 143] (C. Apr.1; 19) *Mediolanum.* £400

CARADOC, of Llancarfan
- **Historie of Cambria, now called Wales.** Trans.:– H. Lloyd. 1584. 1st. Edn. Some dampstaining. 18th. C. cf. [STC 4606] (CSK. Mar.13; 12) £210
- – **Anr. Copy.** Some tears affecting title border, minor dampstaining thro.-out. Cont. limp vell., strips of 14th. C. MS. used in bdg., worn, upr. hinge brkn., stitching partly loose. (C. Nov.,20; 237) *Vine.* £130
[–] – **Anr. Edn.** Ed.:– David Powel. Trans.:– H. Lloyd. [1584]. 1st. Edn. 4to. Lacking ¶2-4 & blank B4 & final blank, title defect., cut down & mntd., some browning & soiling. 19th. C. mott. cf., gt. W.a.f. [STC 4604] (S. Oct.21; 523) *Elliot.* £110

CARADOC, of Llancarfan–PRICE, Sir John
- **The Historie of Cambria.–Historiae Brytannicae Defensio.** Trans:– H. Lloyd. 1584; 1573. 1st. Edns. 2 works in 1 vol. Sm. 4to. 1st. work: lacks final blank, title in pen facs., 3F2-4 & 2G1-3 of 'Table' in facs., tear in A1, several ll. with single wormhole cutting some letters, some ll. stained, some annots. & owner's inscrs.; 2nd. work: some ll. stained. 19th. C. blind-stpd. cf., rebkd, preserving orig., spine. W.a.f. [STC 4606; STC 20309] (S. Jul.27; 62) *Airth.* £200

CARAFFA, Livia Doria
- **Prose, e Versi per Onorare la Memoria . . . di Alcuni Rinomati Autori.** Ill.:– Morghen & Others. Parma, 1784. 1st. Edn. 4to. Inscr. on rear end-paper 'Tighe' & possibly pr. mark, inscr. on fly-lf. in Heber's hand. Cont. red mor., gt., by Derome le Jeune with his 1785 ticket, concentric roll borders including fillets, interlaced dots & stems, fleurs de lis, fillets entwined with branch & double spiral, spine gt. in compartments with sm. scroll ornament with lozenge & 4-pointed star in pointille, inner gt. dentelles, silk liners. (SM. Oct.7; 1628) *Frs. 11,000*

CARAN D'ACHE
- **Nos Soldats du Siècle.** Paris, n.d. Ob. 4to. Cl. (SG. Oct.30; 79) $100

CARBONI, Raffaello
- **Eureka Stockade.** [Sydney], Sunnybrook Pr., 1942. (150) numbered. Papered bds., qtr., canvas, with the card case, in slightly worn d.-w. (KH. Nov.18; 142) *Aus.* $450

CARCANO, Michael de
- **Sermoniarum de Poenitentia per Adventum et Quadragesimam.** Venice, Nicolaus de Frankfordia, 11 Dec., 1487. 4to. Spaces for initial capitals, with guide letters, capitals supplied in red, some with penwork flourishes, light worming at beginning & end, scattered minor dampstains to margins. Cont. blind-stpd. cf. over wood bds., upr. cover with central panel filled with 3 lattice rolls, borders with roll depicting stags in an enclosure, worn, rebkd., lacks clasp & bosses. Bkplts. of Robert Procter & F.S. Ferguson, lately in the collection of Eric Sexton. [BMC V, 336, Goff C196, HC 4506*] (CNY. Apr.8; 187) $1,300

CARCO, Francis
- **Dignimont.** Monte Carlo, 1946. (140) on Rives, with orig. litho. frontis. sigd. by artist. Fo. In sheets, publisher's s.-c. (HD. Dec.5; 33) *Frs. 1,000*
- **Trente Poèms de la Bohème et mon Coeur.** Ill.:– Dignimont. Paris, 1950. (225). Ll., in box. Francis Carco's copy sigd. by him & artist, A.L.s.'s by author, artist & wives & others. (HD. Apr.24; 125) *Frs. 2,200*
- **Rue Pigalle.** Ill.:– Vertes. Paris, 1927. 4to. Minor defects. Reverse cf. by Mirabelle, mor. onlays. (SPB. Jul.28; 31) $125
- **Vertes.** N.Y., [1946]. De Luxe Edn., (1,200) unnumbered. Fo. Ptd. wraps. (SG. Oct.23; 333) $150

CARCOPINO-TUSOLI, François 'Francis Carco'
- **L'Amour Vénal.** Ill.:– Vertès. Paris, 1926. (95); on Holland. 4to. 2 sets of ills., 1 with comments, some rejected plts. In sheets, str.-grd. hf. mor. folder, s.-c. Sigd. (HD. Jun.24; 159) *Frs. 1,900*

CARDONA
- **Lo Studio di Giovanni Boldini.** Milan, 1937. 4to. Publisher's cl. (CR. Mar.19; 48) *Lire 260,000*

CARDONNEL, Adam de
- **Antiquities of Scotland.** Priv. Ptd., 1788. 4to. Slight spotting. Cont. red str.-grd. mor., gt., possibly by Edwards of Halifax. (S. Feb.9; 115) *Welsh.* £60

CARELESS, John [Pseud.]
- **The Old English Squire . . .** L., 1821. 1st. Edn. 4to. Lacks lr. fly-lf. Cont. qtr. roan & marb. bds., mor. & cl. s.-c. Bkplt. & armorial stp. of A.E. Newton. (PNY. May 21; 120) $250

CARERI, Gemelli
- **Voyage de Tour du Monde.** Paris, 1727. 6 vols. Engraved plts., some folding & reprd., a few stains. Cont. cf. [Sabin 10821] (SPB. May 5; 134) $275

CAREW, Richard
- **The Survey of Cornwall.** 1602. 1st. Edn. Sm. 4to. 17th. C. cf., later label. From the collection of Eric Sexton. [STC 4615] (C. Apr.15; 169) *Crowe.* £200
- – **Anr. Copy.** 2 pts. in 1 vol. Title & 1st. few ll. torn & reprd., most ll. cropped at head, with loss of headlines & page-numerals, lacks 1st. (? blank) lf., some soiling & dampstaining. Cont. spr. cf., rather worn, rebkd. (S. May 5; 214) *Rix.* £60
- – **Anr. Edn.** Ed.:– T. Tonkin. Ill.:– Buck. 1811. 4to. Extra-ill. with 4 A.L.s.'s from Lord de Dunstanville (publisher) & 1 from Joseph Polsue. Hf. mor. gt. (P. Mar.12; 233) *Crow.* £220

CAREW, Thomas
- **Poems.** L., 1640. 1st. Edn. 7-line errata on A2, G7 uncancelled. Pol. cf. gt., by F. Bedford, covers detchd. Henry & Alfred Henry Huth bk.-Label. [STC 4620] (CNY. May 22; 52) $880
- **The Poems & Masques.** Ed.:– J.W. Ebsworth. L., 1893. (105) numbered. Crushed lev., with design of 7 floral inlays on upr. cover & 5 on spine, gt. dentelles, by Rivière. (SG. Sep.4; 45) $140

CAREY, David
- **Life in Paris . . .** Ill.:– George Cruikshank. 1822. 1st. Edn. 2B 1-4 reprd., lacks binder's instructions, some slight spotting. Mod. hf. cf. (S. Apr.7; 455) *Elliott.* £70
- – **Anr. Copy.** 21 hand-cold. aquatint plts., 1 mntd., lacks lf. of directions to binder. Hf. mor. gt. (CNY. May 22; 53) $100
- – **Anr. Edn.** Ill.:– George Cruikshank. L., 1822. 1st. Edn., L.P. Without lf. 'To the binder'. Red mor. gt., silk linings, unc., orig. covers bnd. in. (SPB. Oct.1; 185) $1,300

CAREY, Henry Charles & Lea, I.
[–] **A Complete Historical, Chronological & Geographical American Atlas.** Phila., 1823. Fo. 19th. C. cl. As an atlas, w.a.f., from Chetham's Liby., Manchester. (C. Nov.26; 14) *Arader.* £700

CAREY, Mathew
[–] **American Atlas** Phila., 1795. Fo. 1 plt. worn through at plt. mark, title from a shorter copy. Later hf. leath. [Sabin 10855] (SPB. Nov.24; 10) $4,000

CARI, G. de
- **Musée Grotesque.** Ill.:– Maleuvre after G. de Cari. Paris, ca. 1820. 4to. Lacks title, 58 plts. (of 67, lacks nos. 6, 12, 17, 27 bis, 30, 46, 48, 50 & 63). Str.-grd. hf. mor., corners, decor. spine, unc. (HD. Dec.5; 34) *Frs. 4,500*

[CARICATURES]
N.d. 2 vols. Fo. Approximately 220 cold. caricatures & songsheets with cold. vigs., & approximately 30 uncold. caricatures, the caricatures mntd., many identified with the ref. to the British Museum cat. of caricatures. 19th. C. mor. gt. Said (in letter from Messrs. Dulau & Co., tipped in), to be from Gladstone Liby. at Court Hey, with MS. identification of personalities in W.E. Gladstone's hand, most of these, however, in very sm. ptd. hand. (SPB. Oct.1; 186) $6,000

[CARICATURES]
Ill.:– Rowlandson, Cruikshank & others. N.d. 4 vols. Various sizes. Approximately 155 caricatures, most cold., most mntd. or inlaid. Various bindings, worn. (SPB. Oct.1; 187) $1,800

CARICATURES FRANÇAISES
Paris, 1824-26 & n.d. 4to. 91 hand-cold. lithos. Late 19th. C. mor. by F. Bedford, gt. As a coll., w.a.f. (S. Nov.24; 49) *Fiduciary.* £1,000

CARION, Johannes
- **Bedeutnuss und Offenbarung Warer Hymlischer influenz.** [Augsburg], 1531. 2nd. Edn. 4to. Cont. annots. on blank verso of last lf. Disbnd. (S. Dec.8; 159) *Hyde.* £80
- **Chronica von Anfang der Wetl bis vff Keiser Carolum den Fünfften.** Ed.:– Ph. Melanthonus & Caspar Peuber. Ill.:– L. Cranach the younger. Wittenberg, 1578. Fo. Text soiled. Cont. stpd. pig-bkd. wd. bds., lacks 2 clasps. (HK. Nov.18-21; 138) *DM 1,300*
- **Chronicon.** Ed.:– Ph. Melanchthon & C. Peucerus. Frankfurt, 1581. 2 vols. Some old underlining, slightly browned. Cont. vell., owner's mark of 1595 inside covers. (R. Oct.14-18; 35) *DM 430*

CARITAT, Marie, Marquis de Condorcet
See–CONDORCET, Marie Caritat, Marquis de

CARL, Erzherzog von Osterreich
- **Ausgewählte Schriften.** Vienna & Leipzig, 1893-94. 6 text & 1 map vol. in 7 vols. Orig. hf. leath., gt. spine, orig hf. leath. box. (R. Oct.14-18; 1165) *DM 450*

CARL, Johann Samuel
- **Zeugnuss von Chymischer Storgerey, sonderlich in neuen Exempeln . . . samt einer Nachrede von Fatis Chymicis.** Frankfurt & Leipzig, 1733. New bds., roan spine. (S. Dec.1; 88) *Phelps.* £58

CARLETON, George
- **A Thankfull Remembrance of God's Mercie.** Ill.:– Fridericus Hulsius & others. L., 1627. 3rd. Edn. 4to. Cont. sheep. Clarence S. Bement bkplt. [STC 4642] (CNY. May 22; 54) $550

CARLETON, William
- **Traits & Stories of the Irish Peasantry.** Boston, 1911. 4 vols. Mor. gt., red mor. gt. floral inlays on spines. With A.L.s. from Carleton tipped in. (SPB. May 6; 294) £750

CARLEVARIS, Luca
- **Le Fabriche e Vedute di Venetia.** Venice, [1703]. 1st. Edn. Ob. fo. Light soiling in parts, especially at beginning, title, ded., & 1st. 2 plts., lacks 3 etchings. Cont. vell., slightly soiled, corners defect. (R. Oct.14-18; 1935) *DM 16,000*
- – **Anr. Edn.** [Venice], [1705?]. Ob. fo. 49 plts. only (of 103), lacks dedication lf. Cont. hf. cf. (SH. Nov.6; 195) *L'Aquaforte.* £1,900

CARLISLE, Frederick, Earl of
- **The Father's Revenge, with other Poems.** Ill.:– Westall. 1800. 4to. Slightly spotted thro.-out. Cont. mor., covers blind-stpd., gt. fillets & title on upr. cover, gt. spine, publisher's bdg? (C. Feb.4; 118) *Titles.* £50

CARLISLE, Robert J.
- **Bellevue Hospital: An Account.** N.Y., 1893. 1st. Edn. Cl. Sigd. by Irving W. Lyon. (SG. Jun.11; 310) $110

CARLONI, Marco
- **Nuova Raccolta de Statue, Busti, Bassirilevi, e Urne Antiche esistenti nel nuovo Museo Pio-Clementino nel Vaticano.** Rome, 1784. Lge. fo. Cont. hf. vell. bds., slightly worn. (S. Jun.22; 12) *Duran.* £80

CARLOWITZ, H.C.V.
- **Sylvicultura Oeconomica.** Leipzig, 1713. 1st. Edn. 2 pts. in 1 vol. Fo. Lightly browned, lacks 1 frontis & 1 blank lf. at end of pt. Cont. style hf. leath. (R. Mar.31-Apr.4; 1675) *DM 560*

CARLTON & Porter
- **Specimen Book of Engravings.** N.Y., ca. 1870? Fo. 2 engrs. cut-out. Old hf. mor., brkn. (SG. Jan.22; 96) $330

CARLYLE, Thomas
- French Revolution. 1837. 1st. Edn. 3 vols. Hf. cf. (SH. Jul.9; 40) *Joughin*. £50
- - Anr. Copy. Orig. paper bds., some jnts. reprd., mor. gt. solander cases, unc. Pres. Copy, inscr. twice, to Mrs. Welsh, & Mrs. Dr. Russell, lately in the Prescott Collection. (CNY. Feb.6; 45) $2,800
- On Heroes, Hero-Worship, & the Heroic in History. L., 1841. 1st. Edn. 12mo. Cl. Tipped in is A.L.s. to John Forster (n.d., 24mo., 2pp.). (SG. Nov.13; 46) $210
- - Anr. Edn. L., ca. 1900. Diced cf. gt., spine gt., Harrow prize bkplt. Fore-e. pntg. (SG. Mar.19; 125) $280
[-] Sartor Resartus. L., Priv. Ptd., 1834. (58). Spr. cf. gt. by Maclehose. (SG. May 14; 42) $1,000
[-] - Anr. Edn. 1838. Cl.-bkd. bds., soiled. Front. free end-paper with an apparently unpubld. poem in MS. (CSK. Apr.3; 89) £65
[-] - Anr. Edn. L., 1838. 1st. Publd. Engl. Edn. 12mo. 6 pp. of Testimonies, lf. of advts. Orig. hf. cl. (SG. Nov.13; 45) $120
- - Anr. Edn. L., ca. 1900. Diced cf. gt., Harrow prize bkplt. Fore-e. pntg. (SG. Mar.19; 126) $190
- - Anr. Edn. Hammersmith, Doves Pr., 1907. (15) on vell. Sm. 4to. Niger mor., covers with double gt.-ruled border enclosing inner border of gt.-ruled straps round gt.-ruled indented panel, spine in 6 compartments, 5 raised bands, gt.-panel., sigd. by Doves Bindery 1913, qtr.-mor. s.-c. Cortlandt Field Bishop bkplt. (CNY. 22; 384) $4,500
- - Anr. Edn. Doves Pr., 1907. (300). 4to. Orig. limp vell., unc. Pres. Copy from Emery Walker. (SH. Feb.19; 41) *Barrie Marks*. £80
- - Anr. Copy. (SH. Feb.19; 42) *Joseph*. £75
- Works. 1831-27. 18 vols. Hf. cf. gt. (P. Jul.30; 309) *Payne*. £75
- - Anr. Edn. 1857, 1869 (when dtd.). 20 vols. Unif. cont. cf., spines gt. (LC. Jun.18; 256) £50
- - Anr. Edn. 1901-1897-1902. Centenary Edn. 31 vols. Hf. cf. (CSK. Sep.26; 58) £90

CARLYON-BRITTON COLLECTION OF COINS
1913-18. 3 vols. in 1. 4to. Mod. cl. (SH. Mar.6; 332) *Dawson*. £120

CARMAN, Bliss
- At Michaelmas. [Wolfville], Priv. Ptd., [1895]. (100). Ptd. wraps., hf. mor. s.-c. Inscr., with orig. mailing envelope. (SG. Nov.13; 48) $240
- The Gate of Peace. N.Y., 1907. 1st. Edn., (112) numbered, & sigd. Orig. publisher's prospectus laid in (slightly soiled along unc. upr. edge), owner's sig. on front free end-paper. Orig. ptd. bds. & cl. spine, unc. (CB. Feb.18; 57) Can. $850
- The Green Book of the Bards. [Camb., Mass.], [1898]. (100). 12mo. Wraps., hf. mor. s.-c. Inscr. (SG. Nov.13; 51) $210
- Poems. N.Y. & L., 1904. (500) numbered. 2 vols. Fo. Hf. lev., boxed. Sigd. (SG. Nov.13; 52) $120

CARMICHAEL, Mrs. A.C.
- Domestic Manners & Social Condition of the White, Coloured, & Negro Population of the West Indies. 1833. 1st. Edn. 2 vols. Slight foxing thro.-out. Orig. bds. (TA. Feb.19; 49) £65

CARMINUM Poetarum Novem–PINDAR
- Lyricae Poeseos Principum Fragmenta–Olympia, Pythia, Namea, Isthmia. Antw., 1567. 2 works in 1 vol. 16mo. Cont. mor., fanfare decor., with leaves, scrolls & angelot heads, monog. in centre, ex-liby., some repairs. Bkplt. of President of Lamoignon. (HD. Mar.18; 34) Frs. 3,800

CARNE, John
- Syria, The Holy Land, Asia Minor, & c. Ill.:– Bartlett & Purser. 1836. 3 vols. in 2. 4to. Some ll. slightly spotted. Cont. mor. gt. (SBA. May 27; 282a) *Museum Bookshop*. £55
- - Anr. Edn. 1836-38. 3 vols. 4to. Hf. mor. gt. (P. May.14; 70) *Stavridis*. £70
- - Anr. Copy. 3 vols. in 2. Cont. cf. gt., spines worn. (TA. Nov.20; 437) £60
- - Anr. Edn. L., [1836-38]. 3 vols. 4to. Hf. cf. (GM. Apr.30; 722) £140
- - Anr. Copy. 3 vols. in 1. Cont. hf. cf., spine gt. (S. Nov.25; 507) *Chesterman*. £120
- - Anr. Copy. 3 vols. 3 additional engraved titles, 118 engraved plts., engraved titles of vols. 1 & 2 interchanged, vol. 1 with 2 pp. misbnd. Orig. cl. gt. W.a.f. (C. Mar.18; 166) *Jamieson*. £105
- - Anr. Copy. 3 vols. in 1. A few ll. spotted. Cont. red mor. gt. (SBA. Jul.14; 23) *Hamerton*. £80

- - Anr. Edn. 1836-39. 3 vols. 4to. Some ll. slightly spotted. Cont. cf., gt. (SH. Nov.7; 405) *Irani*. £60
- - Anr. Edn. L., [1837-41]. 4to. Slightly browned in parts. Cont. hf. leath. (R. Oct.14-18; 1747) DM 470
- - Anr. Edn. Ill.:– W.H. Bartlett & others. L., [1838]. 3 vols. 4to. Red three-qtr. mor. gt. (SG. Feb.26; 51) $200
- - Anr. Edn. L., ca. 1840. 3 vols. 4to. Cf. gt. (P. Jun.11; 259) *Kassis*. £90
- - Anr. Edn. Ill.:– W.H. Bartlett, Fisher & others. N.d. 3 vols. in 1. 4to. Cf. gt. (RBT. Jan.22; 9) £100
- - Anr. Copy. 3 vols. A few ll. slightly dampstained. Cont. mor., spine chipped, 1 cover detchd. (CSK. Jul.3; 129a) £60
- The Turkish Empire, Syria, The Holy Land & Asia Minor. Ill.:– after William Henry Bartlett & Thomas Allom. [1836-38]. In orig. pts., 2-90, some lacking, together 74 pts. 4to. Orig. pict. wraps. As a periodical, w.a.f. (SBA. Oct.21; 110) *Lazard*. £170

CARNET de Notes
N.d. 16mo. Cont. red mor., very lge. gt. plaque on covers, inner dentelles, watered silk fly-ll. & doubls. MS. notes on the births of a family from 1763-1835. (HD. Apr.8; 80) Frs. 2,000

CARNET de Notes, début XIXe Siècle
Early 19th. C. Thin 64mo. 4 ll. Cont. watered silk, gt. decor., watered silk end-ll. & doubls., red mor., s.-c. with title 'Souvenir'. (HD. Apr.8; 79) Frs. 1,150

CARNET de Notes du XVIIIe Siècle
N.d. 18mo. Cont. paper, decor. by hand with red & green border, pearled texture, decor., white silk doubls. (HD. Apr.8; 78) Frs. 1,600

CARNET de Poche
N.d. 18mo. Cont. silk, covers & spine decor. with gold embroidery, lge. central bouquet with the world 'Souvenir', wooden box covered with cf. (HD. Apr.8; 81) Frs. 2,700

CARNET DE LA SABRETACHE: Revue Militaire Retrospective
Paris, 1894-1902; 1903-07; 1920; 1923. Vols. 2, 3, 4, 6-10 plus Index, Deuxième Serie vols. 1-6, together 17 vols. Vols. for 1920 & 1923 without title-pages. Three-qtr. mor. (SG. Feb.26; 70) $170

CARNOT, Lazare Nicolas Marguerite
- De la Defense des Places Fortes. Paris, 1812. 3rd. Edn. 4to. Hf. cf., rebkd. (SG. Feb.26; 71) $110

CARO, Annibale
See–ERIZZO, Sebastiano – CARO, Annibale

CAROCCIUS, V.
- Tractatvs de Remediis contra Praeivdiciales Sententias, vel Damnosas Executiones. Genf, 1521. 4to. Slightly browned or soiled. Cont. vell., soiled. (H. Dec.9/10; 901) DM 420

CAROCHI, Horacio
- Compendio del Arte de la Lengua Mexicana. Ed.:– Ignacio de Paredes. Mexico, 1759. [1st. Edn.?]. Owner's inscr. of José Camilo Urzua. Cont. cf. (SPB. May 5; 135) $550
- - Anr. Copy. 4to. Minor stains & worming. Cont. vell., leath. ties, somewhat loose in casing. (SG. Jan.8; 77) $130

CAROLINO, Pedro
- English as She is Spoke. Ill.:– Edward Bawden. Lion & Unicorn Pr., 1960. (200). Ob. 4to. Orig. cl. (SH. Feb.20; 317) *Reynolds*. £75

CARON DE BEAUMARCHAIS, Pierre Auguste
See–BEAUMARCHAIS, Pierre Auguste Caron de

CARPANIUS, M.
- Alphabetum Barmanum seu Bomanum regni avae finitimarumque regionum. - Compendium doctrinae Christianae idiomate Barmano sive Bomano. Ed.:– G.C. Amaduzzi (1st work). Rome, 1776; 1776. 2 works in 1 vol. Slight spotting. Cont. vell., gt. borders, s.-c. (S. Apr.29; 371) *Ad Orientem*. £150

CARPENTIER, Jean-Baptiste
- La Véritable Origine de la Très-Illustre Maison de Sohier . . . Ill.:– P. Holsteyn after E. den Otter (title). Leyden, 1661. Lge fo. Several arms in text heightened with colours. Cont. vell. (HD. Jun.29; 95) Fr. 1,700

CARR, Sir John
- Caledonian Sketches. 1809. 1st. Edn. 4to. Extra-ill. with over 130 ports. & plts., MS. list of extra ills. inserted. Maroon str.-grd. mor. gt., by Hering, with his ticket. (S. Nov.24; 51) *P. & C*. £170
- Descriptive Travels in the Southern & Eastern Parts of Spain & the Balearic Isles. L., 1811. 1st. Edn. 4to. Cont. cf., rebkd. (SG. Feb.26; 73) $275
- A Northern Summer; or Travels round the Baltic. 1805. 1st. Edn. 4to. Some ll. browned. Cont. cf. (SH. Jun.11; 185) *Armstrong*. £85
- The Stranger in Ireland or, a Tour in the Southern & Western Parts of that Country, in . . . 1805. 1806. 1st. Edn. 4to. Neat repairs in 2 ll., slightly affecting text in 1, occasional light foxing. Mod. hf. mor., unc. (S. Nov.4; 553) *Traylen*. £350
- - Anr. Copy. Advt. lf. at end. Cf., rebkd. (GM. Apr.30; 430) £330

CARRASCO de Saavedra, Bernardo
- Synodo Diocesana. Lima, 1691. Sm. 4to. Cont. limp vell. (SPB. May 5; 136) $950

CARRE, Louis
- Les Poinçons de l'Orfèvrerie Française du XIVè Siècle jusqu'au debut du XIXè Siècle. Paris, Priv. ptd., 1928. 4to. Publisher's bds. (HD. Apr.9; 584) Frs. 1,200

CARRE, William H.
- Art Work on Hamilton Canada. Ill.:– from photographs by C.S. Cochrane. N.p., 1899. 12 pts. in 1 vol. Fo. Cl. (CB. May 27; 291) Can. $500

CARRE de Montgeron
- La Vérité des Miracles Opérés à l'intercession de M. de Pâris et Autres Appellans . . . N.p., 1737. 1st. 12mo Edn. 3 vols. 12mo. Cont. mor., fillet, fleuron in corners, decor. spines, inside dentelle. (HD. Mar.18; 35) Frs. 2,100

CARRENO, Alberto M.
- Jefes del Ejercito Mexicano en 1847: Biografias de Generales de Division y de Brigada y de Coroneles. Mexico, 1914. Ptd. wraps., torn, with tape repairs. (SG. Mar.5; 305) $230

CARRIAGES
Ca. 1775. Fo. Complete section from the Diderot & D'Alembert Encyclopedie, comprising 4 pp. text & 25 copper-plts. (most folding), slight marginal staining. Disbnd. (SG. Dec.11; 196) $200

CARRINGTON, John B. & Hughes, George W.
- Plate of the Worshipful Company of Goldsmiths. 1926. 4to. Orig. buckram. (SH. Apr.9; 64) *Reed & Sims*. £65
- - Anr. Copy. (CSK. May 29; 56) £55

CARRINGTON, Richard Christopher
- Observations of the Spots on the Sun from November 9, 1853, to March 24, 1861, made at Redhill. 1863. 1st. Edn. 4to. Name on title. Orig. cl., upr. cover dampstained. (S. Dec.2; 697) *Celestial*. £55

CARROL, F. & Leclerq, H.
- Dictionnaire d'Archéologie Chrétienne et de Liturgie. Paris, 1907-53. 30 vols. in 15. 4to. Lacks 3 title pp., some defects. In pts., vol.1 in 2 vols., hf. chagrin, some unbnd. (B. Dec.10/11; 1349) Fls. 1,500

CARROLL, Lewis (Pseud.)
See–DODGSON, Rev. Charles Lutwidge 'Lewis Carroll'

CARROLL, William
- The Angler's Vade Mecum. Edinb., 1818. Some ink marginalia. Cont. hf. cf. gt. (LC. Feb.12; 127) £70
- - Anr. Copy. With the hf.-title & 12 p. catalogue dtd. Apr. 1818. Orig. bds., brkn. & torn, unc. (SG. Dec.11; 24) $130

CARSON, James
- An Inquiry into the Causes of Respiration; of the Motion of the Blood; Animal heat, absorption & muscular motion. 1833. 2nd. Edn. Tear in 3L1 at end & hole in last lf. just affecting a few letters. New cl., unc. (S. Jun.15; 151) *Norman*. £100

CARTARI, Vincenzo
- Le Imagini de i Dei de gli Antichi. Ill.:– after Bolognino Zaltieri. Lyons, 1581. Sm. 4to. Lacks blank ****4?, slight browning. 19th. C. maroon mor. by Darlaud, upr. cover detchd., partly unc. From liby. of André L. Simon. (S. May 18; 53) *Duran*. £100

CARTAS de Indias
- Publicalas por primera Vez el Ministerio de Fomento. Madrid, 1877. 1 vol. in 2. Fo. Hf. cf. (SPB. May 5; 140) $1,000

CARTER, G.
- A Narrative of the Loss of the Grosvenor East Indiaman, which was Unfortunately Wrecked upon the Coast of Caffraria . . . L., 1791. Lacks folding frontis. Cf. (SSA. Jan.22; 188) R. 160

CARTER, Howard & Mace, A.C.
- The Tomb of Tutankhamen. 1923-33. 1st. Edn. 3 vols. Orig. cl. (SH. Mar.5; 37) Fletcher. £170
- - Anr. Edn. 1930. 3 vols. Cl. (PD. Nov.26; 98) £65
- - Anr. Edn. 1930-27-33. Vols. 2 & 3 1st. Edn. 3 vols. Cl. gt., d.-w.'s. (P. Sep.11; 312) Traylen. £60

CARTER, John, Architect 1748-1817
- Specimens of the Ancient Sculpture & Painting now Remaining in this Kingdom. 1780-87[94]. 2 vols. Fo. Cont. red mor., Horace Walpole's arms gt. on sides. Walpole-Beckford copy. (S. Nov.24; 52) Marlborough. £350

CARTER, John, Bibliographer
- Binding Variants in English Publishing, 1820-1900. L., 1932. (500). Vell.-bkd. marb. bds. Inscr. (SG. Mar.26; 123) $170

CARTER, John & Muir, Percy H.
- Printing & the Mind of Man. 1967. 4to. Orig. cl., d.-w. (SH. Jan.29; 12) Maggs. £115
- - Anr. Copy. Fo. Orig. cl. in d.-w., catalogue in orig. wraps. (TA. Sep.18; 105) £105
- - Anr. Copy. Orig. cl. in slightly soiled d.-w. (TA. Mar.19; 211) £85

CARTER, John & Pollard, Graham
- An Enquiry into the Nature of Certain Nineteenth Century Pamphlets. L. & N.Y., 1934. 1st. Edn. Cl. (SG. Jan.22; 99) $180

CARTER, Dr. N.
See-WEST, W. & others

CARTER, William
- England's Interest Asserted, in the Improvement of its Native Commodities. 1669. 1st. Edn. 4to. Inner margin of title strengthened. Later cf. Bnd. with an impft. work. [Wing C674] (C. Apr.1; 175) Mahler. £90

CARTERET, Leopold
- Le Trésor du Bibliophile. Epoque Romantique. Paris, 1927. 4to. Red mor., partly unc. (SI. Dec.3; 123) Lire 320,000

CARTIER, J.B.
- L'Art du Violon. Paris, [after 1800]. 3rd. Edn. Fo. Lightly soiled thro.-out, some pencil marginalia, title stpd. Hf. leath., lacks spine. (H. Dec.9/10; 1088) DM 650

CARTIER-BRESSON, Henri
- The Decisive Moment. N.Y., [1952]. Fo. Separate pamphlet of captions laid in. Pict. bds., pict. d.-w. by Matisse. (SG. Apr.23; 50) $550
- - Anr. Copy. 'Captions' booklet inserted. Cold. pict. bds. designed by Matisse, d.-w. (head & tail of spine slightly to somewhat worn), bds. slightly warped. (PNY. Mar.26; 64) $200
- The Europeans. N.Y., [1955]. [1st. Amer. Edn.?]. Pict. bds. by Joan Miro, chipped plastic d.-w. (SG. Apr.23; 51) $300
- - Anr. Copy. Sm. fo. With the caption brochure inserted. Cold. pict. bds., designed by Joan Miro. (PNY. May 21; 121) $160
- - Anr. Copy. Pamphlet of Engl. captions laid-in. Pict. bds., designed by Joan Miro, owner's sig. on front paste-down end-paper. (SG. Jul.9; 72) $130
- From One China to the Other. With text by Han Suyin. Ed.:- Robert Delphire. N.Y., [1956]. 4to. Coarse buckram, d.-w. (chipped). (SG. Jul.9; 74) $120
- - Anr. Copy. Coarse buckram. (SG. Apr.23; 53) $110
- The People of Moscow. N.Y., 1955. 4to. Buckram, d.-w., (chipped.) (SG. Apr.23; 52) $160

CARTOLI, Eustachio
- Pro Neo-Caesare . . . Sistrum. Flor., 1746 [Perhaps 1747 or 1748]. Fo. Cont. vell., corners & foot of spine slightly worn. (C. Apr.1; 20) Marlborough. £150

CARTON, William
- The Union Atlas, Containing New & Improved Maps of all the Empires, Kingdoms, & States, in the Known World. 1809-12. 4to. Engraved title-p., remntd. Orig. hf. mor. (TA. Feb.19; 113) £70

CARTWRIGHT, Edmund
See-DALLAWAY, James & Cartwright, Edmund

CARTWRIGHT, John
- The Preachers Travels . . . 1611. 1st. Edn. Sm. 4to. Burn-mark in 1 lf. affecting rule. Cf. gt. by Roger de Coverly. Bkplt. of Boies Penrose, lately in the collection of Eric Sexton. [STC 4705] (C. Apr.15; 30) Ad Orientem. £500

CARTWRIGHT, William
- Comedies, Tragi-comedies with Other Poems. 1651. 1st. Edn. 2 vols. in 1. MS. additions. Cont. cf., rebkd. [Wing C709] (SH. Jul.16; 9) Hannas. £60

CARVER, Capt. Jonathan
- New Universal Traveller. Ill.:- T. Bowen. 1779. Fo. Cf. (P. Sep.11; 43) Kidd. £80
- Travels Through the Interior Parts of North America in the Years 1766, 1767, & 1768. L., 1781. 3rd. Edn. Slight staining & browning to text. Mod. hf. mor., marb. bds. & endpapers, gt. spine & borders From liby. of William E. Wilson. [Sabin 11184] (SPB. Apr.29; 49) $800
- [-] - Anr. Edn. 1789. 2 vols. Cont. hf. cf. (SH. May 21; 20) Crete. £70
- - Anr. Edn. Walpole, 1813. 12mo. Text browned. Orig. leath. [Sabin 11185] (CB. Feb.18; 113) Can. $150
- Voyage dans les Parties Interieures de l'Amérique Septentrionale. Trans.:- M. de Chanla. Paris, 1784. Perforated liby. stps. Cont. mor. [Sabin 11188] (CB. Feb.18; 114) Can. $110

CARY, John, Topographer
- A Discourse Concerning the Trade of Ireland & Scotland.-A Discourse Concerning the East-India Trade, Shewing it to be Unprofitable to the Kingdom of England. 1696, Reprints. 2 vols. 4to. 1st. work with minor foxing. Both in mor. by Sangorski. [Wing C727; Wing C726] (C. Apr.1; 176) Lawson. £150
- New & Correct English Atlas. 1787. 4to. Occasional soiling, Cont. cf., rubbed, upr. cover detchd. (CSK. Oct 3; 115) £290
- - Anr. Copy. Engraved title, dedication, & 46 maps, hand-cold. in outl., occasional spotting. Hf. cf. (CSK. Apr.10; 30) £240
- - Anr. Copy. Maps cold. in outl., some spotting & offsetting. Cont. hf. cf., covers detchd. (S. Jan.27; 507) Kentish. £180
- [-] - Anr. Edn. [1787, or later]. 4to. 41 (of 47) engraved maps, hand-cold. in outl., lacks title, 1 map torn. Orig. hf. cf., covers detchd., very worn. W.a.f. (S. Mar.31; 247) Byrne. £220
- - Anr. Edn. 1793. 4to. Hf. cf. W.a.f. (C. Nov.6; 248) Hughes & Smeeth. £180
- - Anr. Edn. 1809. 4to. Some staining, a few pp. loose. Bdg. defect. (P. Jan.22; 188) Ayres. £240
- - Anr. Edn. 1818. 4to. Maps hand-cold. in outl. Cont. hf. cf., covers detchd. W.a.f. (S. Jun.29; 1) Burgess. £200
- - Anr. Copy. Engraved title, general map, 46 engraved maps hand-cold. in outl. with wash borders. Cont. hf. mor., worn. As an atlas, w.a.f. (C. Jul.15; 23) Burgess. £200
- New Map of England & Wales with part of Scotland. 1794. 4to. Maps cold. in outl., some dampstains. Cl., defect. (P. Mar.12; 170) Cambridge. £95
- - Anr. Copy. Hand-cold. key map, title, dedication, explanation lf. & map in 76 sections numbered to 81, hand-cold. in outl., liby. stp. on verso of 1 lf. Cont. reversed cf., with red mor. gt., inlay, slightly worn. (SBA. Mar.4; 3) Symonds. £80
- - Anr. Edn. 1832. 2nd. Edn. 4to. Engraved map hand-cold. in outl. Cont. hf. cf. (CSK. Feb.6; 24) £70
- New Universal Atlas. 1808. Fo. Lacks 6 hand-cold. maps, all on guards, a few slightly spotted. Mod. hf. cf. W.a.f. (S. Nov.3; 26) Jeffery. £350
- [-] [-] Anr. Copy. 52 hand-cold. engraved maps only on 57 sheets, lacks pt. of United States of North America, slightly spotted. Orig. bdg. (CSK. Mar.6; 39) £200
- The Road from the New Port of Milford . . . Gloucester. L., 1 Oct., 1792. Cont. mott. cf. (SG. May 14; 43) $175

- Traveller's Companion or, a delineation of the Turnpike Roads. 1791. 43 engraved maps, hand-cold. in outl., browned. Cont. cf., worn, spine reprd. (CSK. Apr.10; 29) £70
- - Anr. Edn. L., 1807. 16mo. Cont. mott. cf., worn. (SG. May 21; 22) $160
- Traveller's Companion.-New Itinerary. 1817. 2 pts. in 1 vol. Includes 2 maps in pocket, slight browning. Cont cf., with flap. (S. May 5; 256) Burgess. £160
- - Anr. Copy. 1st. vol. with advt. ll., 1 map torn in 2nd. vol. Old leath. worn. (SKC. May 19; 371) £70
- - Anr. Edn. L., 1828. 2 works in 1 vol. Lge. folding map in 2nd. work defect. Disbnd. (SG. Feb.26; 74) $140

CARYLL, John
- [-] The English Princess. 1667. 1st. Edn. 4to. Some catchwords & sigs. shaved or cropped. Mor.-bkd. cl. by Sangorski. [Wing C744] (C. Nov.19; 59) Brett-Smith. £260
- [-] Sir Salomon. 1671. 1st. Edn. 4to. Recent mor.-bkd. bds. [Wing C746] (C. Nov.19; 60) Pickering & Chatto. £90

CASA, Giovanni Della
- Rime, et Prose. Venice, 1558. 1st. Edn. 4to. Inner margins dampstained, inscr. 'Bibliotheca Colbertina' on title, Colbert Liby. copy. 18th. C. mott. cf., arms of Count Hoym, gt., on covers & his Polish eagle insignia in spine compartments, inner edges dentelles. (SM. Oct.7; 1629) Frs. 2,200

CASABON, M.J.
See-HARTMANN, A. & Casabon, M.J.

CASANOVA de Seingalt, Giacomo
- Mémoires. Ill.:- Auguste Leroux. Paris, 1931-32. On vell. 10 vols. 4to. Spr. hf. roan, corners, spines decor. with raised bands, wraps. & spines. (HD. Feb.27; 96) Frs. 1,200
- Memoirs. Trans.:- Arthur Machen. L., Priv. ptd., 1922. (1000). 12 vols. 4to. Minor defects. Hf. mor. gt., soiled. (SPB. Jul.28; 75) $100
- - Anr. Edn. N.p., n.d. (750). 12 vols. Some browning. Hf. mor. gt. (SPB. May 29; 69) $175

CASAS, Bartholomé de las, Bp. of Chiapa
- Istoria o breuissima Relatione della Distruttione dell'Indie Occidentali. Venice, 1626. Sm. 4to. Text in Italian & Spanish, errata/advt. lf. at end, light dampstains affecting 1st. ll., sm. liby. stp. on title. Later vell. bds. [Sabin 11242] (SPB. May 5; 142) $500
- Le Miroir de la Cruelle, & Horrible Tyrannie Espagnole perpetuée au Pays Bas.-Les Tyrannies commises aux Indes Occidentales. Amst., 1620. 2 pts. in 1 vol. 4to. Some browning & offsetting, minor defects. Old mor. gt. (SPB. Jul.28; 76) $600
- Narratio Regionum Indicarum per Hispanos quosdam devastatarum verissima. Ill.:- J.T. de Bry. Oppenheim, 1616, etc. 4 vols. in 1. Sm. 4to. Some outer margins cut into. Old vell. (BS. Jun.11; 145) £110
- Principia queda ex quibus procedentum est in Disputatione ad manifestandam et defendam Iustitiam.-Breuissima Relacion de la Destruycion de las Indias.-Lo que signe es un pedaço de una Carta y Relation.-Aqui se contiene una Disputa . . . entre el Obispo dõ fray Bartholomé de las Casas . . . y el doctor Gines de Sepulveda.-Aqui se contiené treynta Proposiciones muy Juridicas. -Este es un tratado . . . sobre la Materia de los Yndios que se han hecho . . . Esclavos.-Entre los Remedios . . . para Reformacio de las Indias.-Aqui se côtiené unos Auisos & Reglas para los Confessores. Seville, 3rd. tract [Seville], 1st. & 3rd. tracts [1552], rest 1552. 1st. Edns. 8 tracts in 1 vol. Sm. 4to. 2nd. & 3rd. tracts pt. of same collation, fore-margin of 1st. lf. defect., without loss, wormhole affecting a few letters, some light stains, a few ll. loose. Old limp vell. (SPB. May 5; 141) $17,000
- Regionum indiarum per Hispanos olim devastatarum accuratissime Descriptio. Ill.:- after de Bry. Heidelberg, 1664. Sm. 4to. Some discolouration. Later bds. [Sabin 11285] (SPB. May 5; 143) $550

CASATI, Major G.
- Ten Years in Equatoria. 1891. 2 vols. Orig. pict. cl. (P. Sep.11; 215) Sawyer. £55

CASATI, Paolo
- Fabrica, et use del Compasso di Proportione. Bologna, 1664. 1st. Edn. 4to. 2 plts. with sm.

CASATI, Paolo – Fabrica, et use del Compasso di Proportione. *-contd.*
tears, sm. hole in title (not affecting text) cont. owner's inscr. on title of Adriano Minucci & Antonio his son. Cont. limp vell. (C. Apr.1; 21) *Goldschmidt.* £220

CASAUBON, Meric
– A Treatise Proving Spirits, Witches, & Supernatural Operations, by Pregnant Instances & Evidences. 1672. Text browned. Later hf. cf., gt. decor. spine. (TA. Nov.20; 211) £90

CASAUS Y TORRES, R.F.
– Informe que el cabildo eclesiastico de la Catedral de Guatemala. Guatemala, 1827. Sm. wormhole affecting some ll. Disbnd. (SPB. May 5; 144) $175

CASH, J. & others
– The British Freshwater Rhizopoda & Heliozoa. 1905-21. Vols. 1-5. Orig. embossed cl., gt., ex-liby. (PL. Jul.11; 83) *Wheldon & Wesley.* £50

CASH, John
*See-*POOL, R. & Cash, John

CASLEY, David
– A Catalogue of the Manuscripts of the King's Library . . . L., Priv. Ptd., 1734. 4to. Old leath., needs rebdg. Early armorial bkplt. of Sir William Curtis. (SG. Mar.26; 126) $100

CASLON & Livermore
*See-*FRY, Edmund & Co-CASLON & Livermore

CASSAS, L.F.
– Voyage Pittoresque de la Syrie, de la Phénicie, de la Palestine, et de la Basse Egypte. Paris, 1799. Fo. 180 engraved plts. (before letter), including 28 double-p. folding, 7 p. prospectus bnd. in, 1 plt. stained, 1 folding plt. frayed at outer edge. 19th. C. hf. mor., 1r. cover detchd. From Chetham's Liby., Manchester. (C. Nov.26; 73) *Quaritch.* £1,300
– – Anr. Copy. 30 pts. (all publd.). 177 plts (of 192?). 19th. C. hf. chagrin, unc. (HD. Mar.18; 36) Frs. 28,500

CASSEDAY, Ben
– The History of Louisville From its Earliest Settlement . . . Louisville, Ky., 1852. 1st. Edn. 12mo. Folding map torn & crudely reprd., advts., slight foxing. Orig. blind-stpd. cl., bumped, gt. spine, worn at head & foot. From liby. of William E. Wilson. [Sabin 11362] (SPB. Apr.29; 50) $125

CASSEL, Daniel K.
– History of the Mennonites. Phila., 1888. Soiled. Orig. cl. (CB. Feb.18; 129) Can. $110

CASSELL, Petter & Galpin
– County Atlas. L., ca. 1863. Fo. Maps, plans, cold. in outl. Bds., spine reprd. (JN. Sep.9; 4279) £60

CASSERIUS, Julius
– De vocis auditusque organis historia anatomica. Ferrara, 1600-01. 1st.Edn. Fo. Lacks 1st. 6 ll. Vell., stained. (S. Jun.15; 152) *Bennett.* £260

CASSIN, John
– Illustrations of the Birds of California. Ill.:– G.G. White & W.B. Hitchcock. Phila., 1862. Orig. cl., spine reprd. (SG. May 14; 44) $750
– – Anr. Copy. Faint liby. stp. on verso of plts. Buckram. (SG. Sep.18; 78) $650

CASSINI, Giovanni
– Nuova Raccolta . . . di Roma. Rome, 1779. Ob. fo. 72 plts. only, including 1 extraneous plt. tipped in at back, some spotting. Cont. hf. mor., worn. (CSK. Oct.10; 188) £150

CASSINI, Giovanni Domenico & others
– Recueil d'Observations faites en plusieurs Voyages . . . pour perfectioner l'Astronomie et la Géographie. Paris, 1679-93. 8 pts.in 1 vol. Fo. 2nd. pt. mis-bnd. before the 1st. pt., the main title & contents lf. Cont. cf., spine worn. (S. Nov.4; 468) *Bozzolato.* £450

CASSINI, J.D., Mechain, P.F.A. & Le Gendre, A.M.
– Exposé des Operationes faites en France en 1787, pour la Jonction des Observatories de Paris et de Greenwich. Paris, n.d. 4to. Repairs to title. Cont. mott. cf., arms of Baron Stuart de Rothesay gt. on covers, worn. (S. Dec.8; 160) *Quaritch.* £180

CASSINI, Jacques
– Elemens d'Astronomie; Tables Astronomiques du Soleil. Paris, 1740. 1st. Edns. 2 vols. 4to. Title of 1st. work torn & reprd., not affecting text, slight browning. 1st. work: mod. cf., unc.; 2nd. work: cont. mott. cf. (S. Jul.27; 266) *Bozzolato.* £200

CASSIODORUS Senator, Flavius Magnus Aurelius –Historia Ecclesiastica Tripartita. Augsburg, Johann Schussler, 'circiter' Feb. 5, 1472. 1st. Edn. Fo. Spaces for initials, the 1st. 2 decor. in red & green, & red & blue, rest left blank, lacks the 3 blank ll., slight soiling to 1st. lf. & several ll. at end, occasional cont. marginal annots. Mod. hf. mor., unbleached linen covers. The copy of Archibald Acheson (3rd. Earl of Gosford) & James Toovey, lately in the Pierpont Morgan Liby. [BMC II, 329, Goff C237, HC 4573] (CNY. Apr.8; 13) $2,500

CASSUTO, Umberto
– Codices Vaticani Hebraici. Vatican, 1956. Nos. 1-115. 4to. Cl. (S. Nov.17; 62) *Quaritch.* £55
– I Manoscritti Palatini Ebraici della Biblioteca Apostolica Vaticana e la Loro Storia. Vatican, 1935. 4to. Cl. (S. Nov.17; 63) *Dawson.* £50

CASTEL, Thérèse
– Destin de Femme. Ill.:– Louis Icart. Paris, 1945. (325); (11) on Pannekoek Holland. 4to. Orig. drawing, lacks inked copper-engr. Red hf. mor. (SM. Feb.11; 199) Frs. 1,600

CASTELL, Robert
– The Villas of the Ancients Illustrated. 1728. Fo. Cont. mott. cf., spine gt., worn. (C. May 20; 15) *Taylor.* £240

CASTELLAN, Antoine Louis
– Moeurs, Usages, Costumes des Othomans, et Abrégé de leur Histoire. Paris, 1812. 6 vols. 16mo. Cont. str.-grd. mor., spines finely decor., covers decor., lge. floral roulette border, 2 gt. fillets, inner dentelle, by Chilliat, sigd. (HD. Apr.9; 430) Frs. 6,800
– – Anr. Copy. Cont. mor., gt. dentelle, decor. spines, by Bozerian. (HD. Jun.30; 12) Frs. 5,200

CASTELLANO, Ogniben da
– Opera de Principii, & Ordini Rationali. Venice, 1561. 1st. Edn. Sm. 4to. Some marginal stains, extreme inner margin of title strengthened. Mod. bds. From Honeyman Collection. (S. May 20; 3198) *Howell.* £100

CASTELLANUS, L.
*See-*CLAVIUS, Chris.-THEODOUS TRIPOLITA –CASTELLANUS, L.

CASTELLI, Benedetto
[–] Risposta alle Opposizioni del S. Lodovico delle Colombe, e del S. Vincenzio di Grazia, contro al Trattato del Sig. Galileo Galilei, delle cose che stanno su l'Acqua, a che in quella si muouno. Flor., 1615. 1st. Edn. 4to. Title-p. in proof state, 1st. s in Risposta inverted, 7 MS. corrections to individual letters, some spotting & browning, a few ll. stained. Mod. limp vell., unc. From Honeyman Collection. (S. May 20; 3199) *Zeitlin & Verbrugge.* £1,500

CASTELLI, Ignace Friedrich
– Memoiren meines Lebens. Ed.:– J. Bindtner. Munich, ca. 1913. (150) Privilege Edn. on Bütten. 2 vols. Orig. mor., gt. (H. May 21/22; 1389) DM 1,500

CASTELVETRO, Lodovico
[–] Giunta fatta al ragionamento degli Carticoli et Verbi di messer Pietro Bembo. Modena, 1563. 1st. Edn. 4to. Vell. bds. (C. Apr.1; 22) *Goldschmidt.* £60

CASTENBAUER, S.
– Ain Köstlicher, Gutter Notwendiger Sermon, von Sterben wie sich der Mensch dazu schicken soll mit etlichen Schlüssreden vom Leyden Christi. Augsburg, 1523. Only Edn. 4to. Some old MS. underlining, erased stp. on title. Bds. (R. Oct.14-18; 36) DM 585

CASTIGLIONE, Arturo
[–] Essays in the History of Medicine presented to Castiglione on his 70th Birthday. Balt., 1944. With contributions by J.F. Fulton, Ascoli, Edelstein, Neuburger, & others. Buckram, orig. wraps. bnd. in. From Brooklyn Academy of Medicine. (SG. Jan.29; 89) $110

CASTIGLIONE or Castilio, Conte Baldsar
– Il Cortegiano. Venice, 1549. 12mo. A little browning & soiling, title & a few other ll. slightly defect., reprd. 17th. C. vell. bds., soiled, bkplt. of Edward Gibbon. (S. Oct.21; 524) *Edwards.* £90
– The Courtyer. Trans.:– Thomas Hoby. Essex House Pr., 1900. (200) numbered. 4to. Niger mor., gt. border composed of linked line tooling, sm. gt. circles inside outer edge & floral tools in blind at inner corners, by Douglas Cockerell, with his monog. & date 1920, spotted & worn. (S. Jul.31; 55) *Sanders.* £70
– – Anr. Copy. Orig. limp vell., silk ties, unc. (CNY. May 22; 307) $100
– Il Libro del Cortegiano. Venice, Apr. 1528. 1st. Edn. Fo. Mor. by David, covers gt. with device of Aldus in centre, gt. spine. Hoe bookplt. (C. Apr.1; 126) *Hopper.* £1,900
– – Anr. Edn. Flor., 1529. 16mo. Publisher's hf. cf. (CR. Mar.19; 205) Lire 220,000
– – Anr. Edn. Venice, 1545. Fo. Aldine anchor device on title & last lf., bkplt. of Marquess of Hertford. 18th. C. cf., triple gt. fillet, spine gt. in compartments crest, gt., effaced with gt. fleurons, of Joseph Gulston. (SM. Oct.7; 1630) Frs. 2,000
– Le Parfait Courtizan. Lyons, 1580. A few ll. slightly soiled. 19th. C. hf. cf., rebkd. & reprd. (SH. Oct.10; 426) *Meyer.* £50

CASTLE, Egerton
– English Book-Plates. L., 1892. Some foxing, some marginal notes, extra-ill. with 38 orig. bkplts. Orig. cl., extremities of spine slightly worn. (CB. Feb.18; 241) Can. $110

CATALOGO HISTORICO de los Virreyes, Governadores, Presidentes, y Capitanes Generales de Peru
[Lima], [1764-68?]. Sm. loss of text from several ll. towards end, some stains, series of supps. with erratic sigs. Cont. limp vell. W.a.f. (SPB. May 5; 146) $225

CATALOGUE OF BOOKS now selling by Auction
Gloucester, 1778. Title reprd. in fore-margin. Folded as issued. (SBA. Oct.22; 344) *Kossow.* £75

CATALOGUE OF THE HARLEIAN MANUSCRIPTS
*See-*BRITISH MUSEUM

CATALOGUE of the Library at Knowsley Hall
Priv. Ptd., 1893. 4 vols. Sm. fo. Orig. mor.-bkd. cl. gt., slightly worn. (SBA. May 27; 235) *Lister.* £155

CATALOGUS LIBRORUM RARISSIMORUM, ab artis typographicae inventoribus aliisque ejusdem artis principibus, ante annum millesimum quingentesimum excusorum
[Paris], ca. 1750. Cont. mor. gt., covers with roll-tooled borders, gt. spine. (C. Apr.1; 23) *Quaritch.* £520

CATANEO, Girolamo
– Opera del Misurare . . . libri II. Brescia, 1572. 1st. Edn. Sm. 4to. Browned. Mod. vell. From Honeyman Collection. (S. May 20; 3202) *Pilo.* £150
*See-*MACCHIAVELLI, Niccolo-CATANEO, Girolamo

CATANEO, Pietro
– Le Pratiche delle due prime Mathematiche . . . Libro d'albaco e Geometria. Venice, 1546. 1st. Edn. Sm. 4to. Stained, slight worming affecting text towards end, owner's inscr. (as on cover) on title. Cont. limp bds., worn, owner's inscr. of Camillo Baldini on upr. cover. From Honeyman Collection. (S. May 20; 3203) *Riley-Smith.* £55

CATECHESES Religionis Christianae. Quae in Ecclesiis & Scholiis Palatinatus, sub Frederico III. Electore tradebatur
Leyden, 1587. 12mo. Palatinate: Antw., 1585. Cont. cf., lge. gt. ornament on both covers, slightly defect. (VG. Dec.17; 1243) Fls. 480

CATECHISMUS
*See-*NEW TESTAMENT [Dutch]

CATECHISMUS of Korte Onderwijzing in de Christelijcke Religie
Trans.:– J. Crellius Frankus & J. Schlichting van Bukowiec. Vrijburg, [Amst.], 1667. 4to. Cont. vell. (VG. Oct.13; 37) Fls. 650

CATESBY, Mark
- The Natural History of Carolina, Florida & the Bahama Islands . . . L., 1731. 1st. Edn. Vol. 1 only. Tall fo. 100 hand-cold. copperplts. Cont. cf., jnts. very worn. (SG. Oct.9; 53) $21,000
- - Anr. Edn. 1731-43. 1st. Edn. 2 vols., including appendix. Lge. fo. Cont. diced Russ., covers gt. with double imp. of a roll incorporating snails, snakes, beetles, birds, etc., slightly worn. (S. Jun.1; 92) *Arader.* £16,000
- - Anr. Edn. 1731-[43]. 1st. Edn. 2 vols. Fo. 90 hand-cold. etched plts. only (of 220), lacks map, vol. 1 list of subscribers, title & all prelims. in vol. 2. Cont. red mor., gt., sides with central gt. lozenge, vol. 2 rebkd. W.a.f. (C. Mar.18; 28a) *Arader.* £3,200
- - Anr. Edn. Ed.:- [George] Edwards. 1754. 2nd. Edn. 2 vols. Fo. Plts. hand-cold., 'Catalogue of Animals & Plants represented' for each vol. loosely inserted (from 1771 edn.), 1st. gathering loose, pp. 3/4 in vol. 2 loose & soiled, map soiled, some plts. slightly discold. Cont. diced russ., gt. borders on sides, covers detched. From Chetham's Liby., Manchester. (C. Nov.26; 74) *Arader.* £8,000
- - Anr. Edn. Ed.:- [George] Edwards. 1771 [wtrmkd. 1808-09]. 3rd. Edn. 2 vols. Fo. Minor foxing. Cont. hf. russ. (S. Dec.3; 930) *Marks.* £6,600
- Piscium Serpentum Insectorum. Ed.:- Nic. Friedr. Eisenberger. Nuremb., 1750. Pt. 1 (of 2). Lge. fo. Liby. stp. on title, 4 plts. slightly soiled. Cont. bds. (HK. Nov.18-21; 507) DM 5,500

CATHARINE of Siena, Saint
- Epistole Devotissime. Ed.:- [Bartolommeo da Alzano]. Venice, Aldus Manutius. Sept. 15 [19?], 1500. 1st. Compl. Edn. Fo. Title torn, reprd., & rehinged, some early ll. inserted, sm. stain to some inner blank margins at end. Old qtr. pig gt., vell. bds., blind-stp. on upr. cover of Hon. George M. Fortescue. From the collection of Eric Sexton. [BMC V, 562, Goff C281] (CNY. Apr.8; 199) $5,800
- - Anr. Copy. Some ll. at front remargined, some stains cleaned & wormholes filled. Mod. lev. mor. gt., gt. anchor on covers, s.-c, by Gozzi of Modena. Bkplt. of Giorgio di Veroli. [BMC V, 562, Goff C281] (CNY. Oct.1; 124) $3,000

CATHARINE of Siena Saint-OPHOVIUS, Michael
- Dialogo d la Seraphica Uergine.-D. Catharinae Senensis Virginis . . . Vita ac Miracula Selectora Formis Aeneis Expressa. Venice; Antw., 4 Nov. 1517; 1603. 2 works in 2 vols. 8vo.; sm. 4to. Some slight dampstaining to 1st. work. 1st. work: vell., spine gt.; 2nd. work: old hf. roan gt. (CNY. Oct.1; 130) $320

CATHER, Willa
- April Twilights. Boston, 1903. 1st. Edn. 12mo. Bds., worn, unc. (SG. Nov.13; 63) $350
- Not Under Forty. N.Y., 1936. 1st. Edn. Cl., d.-w. Sigd. pres. copy to 'Mrs. [Bobsy] Goodspeed'. (PNY. Mar.4; 115) $150
- Sapphira & the Slave Girl. N.Y., 1940. 1st. Edn., (520) L.P. Tall 8vo. Buckram-bkd. bds., d.-w., boxed, partly unc. Sigd. (SG. Nov.13; 88) $130
- Shadows on the Rock. N.Y., 1931. 1st. Edn. loosely inserted (comprising: note by A.A. Knopf, followed by notice of the edns. & an advt. list, followed by 7 ll. stitched together (1st. 5 with blanks), 1 blank lf., & the title-p. Cl., shabby. Advance Salesman's Copy. (SG. Nov.13; 84) $120
- Youth & the Bright Medusa. N.Y., [1925]. 16mo. Decor. cl. Inscr. (SG. Nov.13; 77) $160

CATHERINE I, Empress of Russia & Peter II
- Ukazy [Decrees]. St. Petersb., 1777 [before 1793]. 4to. Some ll. slightly dampstained or spotted, a few marginal tears. Cont. cf., worn. (SH. Feb.5; 203) *Rosenthal.* £60

CATHERINE II, Empress of Russia
- Instruction . . . à la Commission établie pour travailler à l'éxécution du Projet d'un Nouveau Code de Lois. St. Petersb., 1769. 12mo. Foxing. Early 19th. C. str.-grd. mor. gt., roll-tooled borders on covers, spine with floral device repeated in a trellis, worming. (SPB. Jul.28; 32) $100

CATLIN, George
- The Manners, Customs & Condition of the North American Indians. 1841. 2 vols. A few plts. loose. Orig. cl., slightly soiled. (SH. Nov.7; 369) *Lenton.* £135
- - Anr. Copy. Lacks frontis., folding map defect., soiled. Cont. hf. cf. (SH. Apr.9; 141) *Schuster.* £65
- - Anr. Copy. Cf. [Sabin 11536] (SPB. Jun.22; 27) $250
- - Anr. Copy. Gt.-pict. cl., loose. (SG. Jun.11; 76) $170
- - Anr. Edn. L., Priv. ptd., 1841. Reprint of orig. edn. 2 vols. Mod. hf. mor. (SG. Jan.8; 78) $150
- - Anr. Edn. L., 1848. 7th. Edn. 2 vols. 4to. Cont. hf. mor. gt. (PNY. May 21; 124) $200
- - Anr. Edn. Phila., 1857. 2 vols. Cont. hf. cf., worn. (SG. Mar.5; 119) $120
- - Anr. Copy. Foxed, stained. Mod. buckram. (SG. Jun.11; 75) $110
- - Anr. Edn. L., ca. 1900? 2 vols. Gt.-pict. cl., partly unc. (SG. Jan.8; 81) $250
- - Anr. Copy. Orig. gt.-stpd. cl. (CB. Apr.1; 45) *Can.* $320
- - Anr. Edn. Phila., 1913. 2 vols. Gt.-pict. cl. (SG. Jun.11; 77) $220
- - Anr. Copy. 4to. Gt.-pict. cl., unc. (PNY. Dec.3; 63) $110
- - Anr. Edn. Ill.:- after Catlin. Phila., 1913. (75) numbered on H.M.P. 2 vols. Orig. hf. cl. & buckram bds., partly unç. (CNY. Oct.1; 138) $420
- - Anr. Edn. Edinb., 1926. 2 vols. Orig. cl. (SH. Nov.7; 371) *Bowes.* £75
- North American Indian Portfolio. L., 1844. 1st. Edn., early iss. Lge. fo. 25 unmntd. full-p. tinted litho. plts., finished on col. by hand. Orig. hf. maroon mor. gt. [Sabin 11532] (CNY. May 22; 55) $16,000
- - Anr. Edn. Priv. ptd., 1844. 1st. Edn. Fo. Some ll. loose. Orig. hf. roan. [Sabin 11532] (C. Feb.25; 79) *Davidson.* £2,700
- - Anr. Edn. L., 1844. Fo. 31 cold. plts., lacks title-p. & text, plts. reguarded. Later cf.-bkd. bds., stained. (SG. Jun.22; 28) $8,000

CATO, Dionysius
- Disticha de Moribus. Ed.:- [Robertus de Euremodio] (commentary). Antw., Gerard Leeu, Mar. 1, 1485. 4to. Spaces for initial capitals, unrubricated, lacks final blank. Blind-tooled cf., sm. leath. defects, vell. end-papers. From the collection of Eric Sexton. [BMC IX, 186, Goff C296] (CNY. Apr.8; 6) $5,000

CATO, Marcus [Porcius] & others
- Libri de Re Rustica. Flor., Jul. 1515. Capital spaces with guide letters, slight browning & soiling, device defect., reprd. 18th. C. vell. bds., soiled, upr. cover with 1 corner defect. From liby. of André L. Simon. (S. May 18; 55) *Facchi.* £100
- - Anr. Edn. Flor., 28 Sep. 1521. Capital spaces with guide letters, some later MS. notes, slight browning & soiling. 17th. C. vell. bds., soiled. From liby. of André L. Simon. (S. May 18; 56) *Facchi.* £100
- - Anr. Edn. [Zurich], 1528. A little slight browning, short tear in Hl. Mod. pol. cf. by Rivière, spine gt., rubbed. From liby. of André L. Simon. (S. May 18; 57) *Weiss.* £120
- - Anr. Edn. Paris, Feb. 1533. Fo. A few cont. marginalia, slightly spotted & dampstained. 17th. C. cf., rebkd., corners worn. (S. May 5; 26) *Fachinetti.* £160
- - Anr. Copy. Capital spaces with guide letters, slight dampstaining, title & following lf. slightly defect., without loss of text, reprd., tears & sm. holes in a few other ll., lacks final blank. 18th. C. cf., worn. From liby. of André L. Simon. (S. May 18; 58) *Marlborough.* £80

CATO, Marcus Porcius & Varro, M.T.- PALLADIUS Rutilius Taurus Aemilianus -VICTORIUS, P.
- Libri de Re Rustica.- De Re Rustica Libr XIII. -Explicationes suarum in Catonem, Varronem, Columellam Castigationum. Paris, Aug. 1543; 1543; 1543. 3 works in 1 vol. Slight browning & soiling, some later MS. notes. Cont. blind-stpd. cf., head of spine defect. From liby. of André L. Simon. (S. May 18; 65) *Harper.* £90

CATS, Jakob
- Alle de Wercken. Ill.:- Sweelinck after Van der Venne (engrs.). Amst., 1655. 1st. Fo. Edn. 13 pts. in 1 vol. Fo. Slightly worn thro.-out & browned. Cont. cf. (VG. Oct. 13; 38) Fls. 1,600
- - Anr. Edn. Amst./The Hague, 1726. Latest Printing. 2 pts. in 1 vol. Fo. Corners to pp. 37/8 & 525/6 torn off with loss of text, several tears reprd., 1 plt. defect. Cont. cf., slightly defect., jnts. & corners reprd., worn, stained. (VG. Nov.18; 1106) Fls. 1,200
- Proteus ofte Minne Beelden. Rotterdam, 1627. 6 pts. in 1 vol. Sm. 4to. Staining on some end-ll. Mod. hf. cf. W.a.f. (BS. Jun.11; 39) £120
- Silenus Alcibiadis, sive Proteus, Vitae Humanae ideam, Emblemate trifariam variato, Oculis subijciens.-Maechden-Plicht ofte Ampt der Ionck-Vrouwen, in eerbaer Liefde, aen-ghwesen door Sinne-beelden. Ill.:- F. Schillemans & J. Swellinck after A. vande Venne (1st work); after A. vande Venne (2nd. work). Middelburg; Middelburg, 1618; 1618. 1st. Edns. 2 works in 1 vol., 1st. work 3 pts. in 1 vol. 4to. Some light, mainly marginal, stains in places, the plt. 'Kinderspel' somewhat short & torn in fold (repairable). Cont. cf., back gt., top of spine slightly defect. (VG. Dec.17; 1286) Fls. 2,300
- Spiegel van den Ouden en Nieuwen Tydt. Amst., 1690. Pp. 70-100 wormed, stained in places, copper engraved title frayed. Cont. vell. (HK. Nov.18-21; 1565) DM 800
- Zinne- en Minne-Beelden. Amst., 1729. 16mo. Some stains, etc. Cont. vell., worn. (SG. Feb.5; 71) $120

CATTAN, Christofe de
- La Geomance . . . Paris, 1571. 4to. 1st. 5 ll. damp-stained at lr. margin. Mod. qtr. cf. & marb. bds. (PNY. Oct.1; 406) $140
- The Geomancie of Maister Christopher Cattan Gentleman . . . Trans.:- Francis Sparry. 1591. 1st. Edn. in Engl. Sm. 4to. Lacks final blank, lr. fore-corner of P2 reprd. affecting a few letters of text, short tear reprd. in Q4. 19th. C. mor., gt., by Rivière. Bkplt. of Henry Cunliffe; from Honeyman Collection. [STC 4864] (S. May 20; 3205) *Quaritch.* £600

CATULLUS, Gaius Valerius
- The Complete Poetry. Trans.:- Jack Lindsay. Ill.:- Lionel Ellis. Fanfrolico Pr., [1929]. Ltd. Numbered Edn. Orig. mor. (SKC. Feb.26; 1269) £50

CATULLUS, Caius Valerius, Tibullus, Albius & Propertius Sextus
- [Opera]. Venice, Jan., 1502. Iss. with 'Propetivs' on title, corrected title at end, sm. repair to A1. Red. mor., gt., Aldine device gt.-stpd. on covers, by Cape. (S. Feb.10; 426) *Maggs.* £170
- - Anr. Copy. 19th. C. mor., gt. fillet bords. & cornerpieces, spine gt., by Wright. (SG. Sep.25; 10) $300
- - Anr. Edn. Paris, 1529. Lacks final blank, slight browning, sig. on title. 18th. C. red mor., gt., slight wear. (S. Feb.10; 219) *Thomas.* £55
- - Anr. Edn. Paris, 1753. 12mo. Cont. cf., rebkd., old spine preserved, gt. Gift from Laurence Sterne to John Wilkes, inscr. & notes by Wilkes, bkplt. of Wilkes, bk.-label of Burnham Abbey, Bucks. (James Toovey). (S. Nov.24; 266) *Quaritch.* £400

See—MARTIALIS - CATULLUS, Tibullus & Propertius

CATULLUS, Tibullus & Gallus
- [Oeuvres]. Traduction en Prose. Trans.:- [Marquis de Pezay]. Ill.:- De Longueil after Charles Dominique Joseph Eisen. Delalain, Amst.-Paris, 1771. On Holland Paper. 2 vols. 2 additonal engraved titles & 1 cul-de-lampe repeated in vol. II, each with anr. copy loosely inserted, that of title to vol. II before letter. Cont. mor., triple gt. fillet, spine gt. with spider's web in each compartment, inner gt. dentelles. (SH. Oct.7; 1631) Frs. 1,800

CAUCES, Revista Literaria de Inspiración Falangista-Nacionalista
Jerez de la Frontera, 1936-43. 30 issues. 4to. & fo. Wraps. (DS. Apr.24; 1037) Pts. 40,000

CAULFIELD, James
- Cromwelliana, Chronological Detail of Events. 1810. Mor. gt. (P. Oct.2; 97) *Wilson.* £50
- Portraits, Memoirs, & Characters of Remarkable Persons . . . L., Priv. ptd., 1794-95. 1st. Edn. 2 vols. in 1. 4to. 59 (of 60?) copperplt.

CAULFIELD, James -contd.
ports., Vol. 1 interleaved with blanks. Later gt. hf. mor. (PNY. Oct.1; 130) $120
- - **Anr. Edn.** 1819. 4 vols. Cf. gt. (P. Apr.9; 84) Ghaffer. £50
- - **Anr. Edn.** L., 1819-20. 1st. Edn., L.P. 4 vols. Lge. tall 4to. 153 (of 155) copper-plt. ports. Mod. hf. mor. & cl., gt. (PNY. May 21; 125) $100
- - **Anr. Edn.** 1819-20. 4 vols. Cont. red str.-grd. mor., spines gt., covers blind-stpd. with gt. borders. (C. May 20; 16) Blackwell. £90

CAULFIELD, S.F.A. & Saward, Blanche, C.
- **The Dictionary of Needlework.** N.d. 2nd. Edn. 6 vols. 4to. 1 plt. detchd. Orig. cl. (CSK Sep.12; 141) £50

CAUMONT de la Force, Charlotte
- **Histoire de Marguerite de Valois, Reine de Navarre.** Paris, 1783. 6 vols. 12mo. Cont. Engl. str.-grd. mor., gold fillet border & on spine, inside fillet, watered silk doubls. & end-papers. (HD. Mar.18; 37) Frs. 1,900

CAUNTER, R.H.
- **Tableaux Pittoresques de l'Inde.** Trans.:- Auguste Urbain. Ill.:- after William Daniell. Paris, 1835. L.P. Cont. hf. cf. (SG. Feb.26; 176) $100

CAUS, Salamon de
- **Les Raisons des Forces Mouvantes.** Paris, 1624. 3 pts. in 1 vol. Fo. Lacks folding plt., long tear in plt. 24 of pt. II, stained at head at beginning. (SPB. Oct.1; 220) $2,900

CAUSEUS, Michelangelo
See-BELLORI, Giovanni Pietro & Causeus, Michelangelo

CAUSSINUS, Nicolaus
- **De Symbolica Aegyptiorum Sapientia im qua Symbola, parabolae . . . quae ad . . . Emblematum Hieroglyphicorum . . . praestant.** Cologne, 1631. Vell. (S. Dec.1; 89) Ribi. £50

CAVAFY, C.P.
- **Fourteen Poems.** Trans.:- Nikos Stangos & Stephen Spender. Ill.:- David Hockney. 1967. (500) numbered, sigd. by artist, (250) with additional etching sigd. by artist. Fo. Orig. cl., s.-c. (S. Jul.31; 237) Sims & Reed. £420

CAVALERIUS, Bonaventura
- **Geometria Indivisibilibus Continuorum.** Bologna, 1653. 4to. Browned, stained. Bdg. defect. (SH. Jul.16; 186) Nador. £150
- **Trigonometria Plana, et Sphraica, Linearis & Logarithmica.** Bologna, 1643. 1st. Edn. 4to. Engraved plt. loose. last 4 ll. nearly detchd., a few sm. holes, 2 slightly affecting some numbers, slightly spotted. Cont. limp vell. (S. Oct.21; 376) Lockwood. £55

CAVALLO, Tiberius
- **An Essay on the Theory & Practice of Medical Electricity.** Dublin, 1781. 12mo. Old mott. cf., rebkd. (SG. Jan.29; 90) $110
- **Geschichte u. Praxis d. Aerostatik.** Leipzig. 1786. 1st. German Edn. Slightly soiled. Cont. marb. wraps., slightly worn. (HK. Nov.18-21; 348) DM 520

CAVANILLES, Antonio Jose
- **Icones et Descriptiones Plantarum quae aut sponte in Hispania crescunt aut in Hortis hospitantur.** Madrid, 1791-1801. 6 vols. Fo. Plt. 588 bnd. after 558, marginal ink stain in text portion of vol. 6. Marb. cf. From collection of Massachusetts Horticultural Society, stpd. on plts. (SPB. Oct.1; 110) $3,100

CAVAZZI Montecuccolo, Giovanni Antonio
- **Istorica Descrizione de tre Regni Congo, Matamba, et Angola.** Bologna, 1687. Fo. Some ll. detchd. 19th. C. hf. cf., brkn., covers detchd., lacks portion of spine. From Chetham's Liby., Manchester. [Sabin 11592] (C. Nov.26; 75) Broseghini. £400
- - **Anr. Copy.** 4to. Hf. cf. (LM. Jun.13; 2) B.Frs. 29,000

CAVE, Henry
- **Antiquities of York.** L., 1813. 4to. Hf. cf., upr. cover defect. (P. Jun.11; 52) Kidd. £60
- **Picturesque Buildings in York.** 1813. 4to. With 17 additional plts., most cut down, 2 mntd. on endpapers, some foxing & offsetting. Orig. bdg. (C. Nov.6; 292) K. Books. £80

CAVE, William
- **Antiquitates Apostolicae . . .** L., 1677. 3rd. Edn. Title & 2 plts. mntd., repairs in text & margins. Mor., gt.-tooled designs, spine gt. Sold as a bdg. (SG. Sep.25; 78) $150

CAVENDISH, George
- **The Life of Thomas Wolsey.** Kelms. Pr., 1893. (250). 4to. Minor defects. Orig. vell., slightly soiled. (SPB. Jul.28; 203) $275

CAVENDISH, Henry
- **Electrical Researches.** Ed.:- J. Clerk Maxwell. Camb., 1879. Cl. (PD. Feb. 18; 61) £85

CAVENDISH, Margaret, Duchess of Newcastle
See-NEWCASTLE, Margaret Cavendish, Duchess of

CAXTON, William
- **The History of Renard the Fox.** Ed.:- H. Haliday Sparling. Kelms. Pr., 1892. (310), (300) on paper. Lge. 4to. Orig. limp vell., slightly soiled, silk ties, unc. (S. Jul.31; 5) Foyles. £280
- - **Anr. Copy.** Lacks one silk tie from lr. cover, unc. (SH. Feb.19; 3a) Fermoy. £230

CAYLUS, Anne Claude Philippe, Comte de
[-] **Les Etrennes de la St. Jean.-Les Ecosseuses.** Troyes, 1742; 1745. 1st. work, 2nd. Edn., L.P., 2nd. work, L.P. 2 works in 1 vol. 12mo. Sig. of A.A. Renouard on 1st. title dtd. 1789, & his accession number on fly-lf., 'Renouard' stp. in gt. on front pastedown. Cont. mor., triple gt. fillets, Renouard's name stp. at foot of upr. cover, spine gt. in empty compartments, inner gt. dentelles. (SM. Oct.7; 1635) Frs. 2,200
- **Faceties.** Ill.:- Dubouchet (figures); Lalauze (port.). Paris, 1879. Ltd. Edn. Figures in 2 states. Mor. by Pagnan, decor. spine, inside dentelle. Bkplt. of Francis Kettaneh. (SM. Feb.11; 147) Frs. 2,500
[-] **Les Manteaux. Recueil.** Ill.:- Etienne Fessard after Charles Nicholas Cochin. The Hague, 1746. 1st. Edn., L.P. 2 pts. in 1 vol. Cont. red mor., triple gt. fillet, spines gt. in compartments, inner gt. dentelles. Bkplt. of Laurence Currie. (SM. Oct.7; 1632) Frs. 2,700
- **Recueil d'Antiquités Egyptiennes, Etrusques, Grecques et Romaines.** Paris, 1752-67. 1st. Edn. 7 vols. 4to. Lacks hf.-titles in vol. VI, bkplt. of M. Moseley & his sig. on title of vol. II. Cont. cf., spine gt. with charges from arms of Prince de Soubise & his pres. mark in vol. I. (SM. Oct.7; 1633) Frs. 2,200

CAYLUS, Marthe-Marguerite, Marquise de
- **Les Souvenirs.** Amst., 1770. 'si bonge foi' on p. 174, line 141. Mor. by Trautz-Bauzonnet, triple gt. fillet round covers, spine with raised bands decor. with repeated cypher, inside dentelle. From liby. of Montgermont, Lurde & Ruble. (HD. Jun.24; 15) Frs. 2,000
- - **Anr. Edn.** Ed.:- Charles Asselineau. Paris, 1860. On vell. With 5 orig. sepia pen & wash drawings (unsgd.). 19th. C. mor. gt., sides decor. with bird & floral tools, repeated on spine in raised bands, inner dentelles, arms of the 12th. Duke of Hamilton gt.-stpd. in centre on both covers, in silk-lined marble-paper cover. (C. Nov.20; 182) Klusmann. £400

CAZABON, M.J.
- **Views of Trinidad.** Paris, 1851. Ob. fo. Some stains, marginal tears, foxing. Mor.-bkd. bds., inner hinges strengthened. (SPB. May 5; 146a) $3,000

CAZOTTE, Jacques
- **Contes.** Ill.:- Gery-Bichard (figures); Lalauze (port.). Paris, 1880. Ltd. Edn. Figures in 2 states. Mor. by Pagnan, decor. spine, inside dentelle. Bkplt. of Francis Kettaneh. (SM. Feb.11; 148) Frs. 3,500
- **Le Diable Amoureux.** Ed.:- Gerard de Nerval. Ill.:- Edouard de Beaumont. Paris, 1845. Orig. Edn., 1st. Printing. Cont. hf. red chagrin, decor. spine. (HD. Jun.10; 129) Frs. 1,200
- - **Anr. Edn.** Ill.:- Jean-Emile Laboureur. Paris, 1921. (20) numbered, with extra suite of plts. on 18th. C. paper. Lacks 2 of the 6 plts. on regular paper, 4 specimen ll. (from the orig. prospectus?) bnd. in. Crushed hf. lev., orig. wraps. bnd. in, bkplt. (SG. Apr.2; 167) $190

CECCHINI, G.B., Pividor, G. & Viola, T.
- **Vedute dei Principali Monumenti di Venezia.** Venice, ca. 1830. Ob. fo. 1 lithograph slightly spotted. Orig. ill. bds., slightly soiled. (S. Apr.7; 249) King. £260

CECIL, William
- **Certaine Advertisements Out of Ireland.** 1588. 1st. Edn. Sm. 4to. Lacks final blank. Mor. by Sangorski. From the collection of Eric Sexton. [STC 15412] (C. Apr.15; 89) Gamble. £320

CEDERCRONA, Daniel Gustaf
- **Sweriges Rikes Ridderskaps och Adels Wapenbok.** Stockholm, 1746. Fo. Engraved frontis., remargined, several ll. remargined or reprd. 19th C. hf. cf., worn. (S. Oct.20; 43) Heraldry Today. £80

CELA, C.J.
- **Geschichte ohne Liebe.** Trans.:- R. Specht. Ill.:- Picasso. Berlin, 1968. (100). Fo. Orig. goat, s.-c. (R. Mar.31-Apr.4; 626) DM 470

CELAN, P. Edgar Jene
- **Der Traum vom Traume.** Vienna, 1948. (700). Orig. wraps. (H. Dec.9/10; 1989) DM 520

CELINE, Louis-Ferdinand (Pseud.)
See-DESTOUCHES, Dr. Louis-Ferdinand 'Louis-Ferdinand Céline'

CELLARIUS, Andreas
- **Harmonia Macrocosmica seu Atlas Universalis et Novus, Totius Universi Creati Cosmographiam Generalem, et Novam Exhibens.** Amst., 1660. 1st. Edn. Lge. fo. Sm. worming at end, partly reprd. Cont. vell., gt. spine reprd. (R. Oct.14-18; 1535) DM 19,000

CELLARIUS, Christopher
- **Geographia Antiqua et Nova: Or, A System of Ancient & Modern Geography.** Trans.:- Mr. l'Abbé du Fresnoy. 1742. 4to. Orig. cf., worn. (TA. Feb.19; 125) £75
- - **Anr. Edn.** 1755. Engraved plt. of a Globe, 26 folding maps. Old cf. (P. Mar.12; 353) Duran. £60
- **Notitia Orbis Antiqui, sive Geographia Plenior . . .** Leipzig, 1731. 4to. Cont. vell., some soiling. (PNY. Mar.26; 67) $300
- - **Anr. Edn.:** [J.L.C. Schwarz]. Leipzig, 1731-32. 2 vols. 4to. Browned or soiled thro.-out. Cont. vell., slightly soiled, end-papers renewed. [Sabin 11655] (H. May 21/22; 643) DM 420

CELLINI, Benvenuto
- **Due Trattati.** Flor., 1568. 1st. Edn. 4to. Occasional slight foxing. 18th. C. cf., rebkd. (C. Nov.20; 183) Marques. £520
- **Treatises.** Essex House Pr. 1898. Ltd. Edn. 4to. Orig. cl. (SH. Jul.23; 263) Baker. £60

CENT Nouvelles Nouvelles, Les
Ill.:- G. Van der Gowen (frontis.); Romain de Hooghe (figures). Cologne, 1783. 1st. Printing. 2 vols. Sm. 8vo. Figures in best proofs. Red mor. by Hardy, fillet, decor. spines, inside dentelle. Bkplt. of Jules Lemaître. (HD. Mar.18; 38) Frs. 4,200

CENTAURE (Le)
Ed.:- H. Albert, A. Gide, A.-F. Herold, A. Lebey, P. Louÿs, H. de Régnier, J. de Tinan & P. Valéry. Ill.:- A. Besnard, J.E. Blanche, Fantin-Latour & others. Paris, 1896. (50) on imperial Jap. 2 vols. Lacks proofs with lge. margins separately publd. Publisher's s.-c. (HD. Dec.5; 36) Frs. 2,100

CENTENO, Amaro
- **Historia de Cosas del Oriente.** Cordoba, 1595. 1st. Edn. 1st. & 2nd. pts. 4to. Badly stained at beginning, title defect. & reprd. at head with some letters inked in, some headlines, sidenotes, rule-borders, etc., cut into. 19th. C. cf., gt. W.a.f. (S. Jan.27; 393) Diba. £140

CENTORIO, Ascanio
- **I Cinque Libri de gli Avvertimenti, Ordini, Gride, et Editti: fatti . . . in Malano, ne'tempi sospetosi della Peste.** Milan, 1631. 4to. Sm. hole in title & next lf. & inner margins in centre of book without text loss. Mod. bds. (SI. Dec.3; 130) Lire 220,000

CENTURY GUILD HOBBY HORSE, The
Ill.:- Selwyn Image & A.K. Mackmurdo. 1884. 1st. Iss. No. 1. 4to. Orig. wraps. (SH. Mar.26; 131) Tate Gallery. £60
- - **Anr. Run.** 1884-94. No. 1 & 2-28, new series No. 1-3. 4to. No. 21-24 orig. parch.-bkd. bds., rest orig. wraps., some stained, unc. (SH. Mar.26; 131a) Reed & Sims. £620

CENTURY ILLUSTRATED MONTHLY MAGAZINE
1881-1908. New Series, vols. 1-53 (lacks vols. 10

& 45). Cont. hf. mor. (SH. Jan.30; 416)
Jeffrey. £55

CEREMONIBOEK van de Regeering der Stad Amsteldam
[Amst.], ca. 1740. Fo. Cont. marb. cf., lge. gt. arms on covers in wide gt. borders & corner fleurons, spine gt., raised in compartments, inside dentelles (VG. Oct.13; 39) Fls. 900

CEREMONIES observed at the Royal Coronation of Her Most Sacred Majesty Queen Victoria
1838. Fo. Cont. mor., gt., Royal Arms on covers, watered silk doubls., slightly affected by damp. With 2 tickets to the Coronation mntd. on front free end-paper. (CSK. Jul.31; 8) £55

CERNUDA, Luis
– La Realidad y el Deseo. Madrid, 1936. 1st. Edn. Orig. wraps. (DS. Apr.24; 966) Pts. 26,000

CERVANTES Saavedra, Miguel de
– Don Quixote [Danish]. Trans.:– Charlotta D. Biehl. Ill.:– Georg Haus. Copen., 1776-77. 1st. Edn. 4 vols. Cont. panel. cf., 1st. vol. plain cf. (SG. Feb.5; 73) $120
– De voornaamste Gevallen van den Wonderlyken Don Quichot. [Dutch]. Ill.:– Tanjé & J. van Schley, B. Picart, S. Fokke & others after Charles Coypel. The Hague, 1746. 4to. Occasional foxing. Cont. vell., spine slightly defect., loose. (VG. Nov.18; 1118) Fls. 460
– Don Quixote [English]. 1687. Fo. Mod. leath. (HY. Jan.14; 58) £95
[–] – Anr. Copy. Cont. cf. with old reback, hinges brkn. (TA. Nov.20; 106) £66
– – Anr. Edn. Trans.:– Charles Jarvis. Ill.:– G. van der Gucht after Johann van der Bank. 1742. 1st. Edn. of this Trans. 2 vols. 4to. Cont. mott. cf. gt., 1 cover detchd. (S. Sep 29; 126) *Traylen.* £140
– – Anr. Copy. Some offsetting in text. Cont. mott. cf., gt., worn, bkplt. of Emo Park Liby. (S. Jan.26; 123) *Rhys.* £60
– – Anr. Copy. Slightly soiled. Cont. leath., spine renewed in cont. style. (R. Oct.14-18; 853) DM 800
– – Anr. Edn. Trans.:– Tobias Smollett. Ill.:– Picart, Vertue & others after Coypel, Vander Gucht & others. 1755. 4to. Extra ill., 127 engraved plts. Red mor. gt. by Ramage. (S. Nov.24; 53) *Bickersteth.* £320
– – Anr. Copy. Slightly spotted or soiled & offset in places. Cont. cf., rebkd., corners worn. (S. Dec.8; 83) *Mistrali.* £110
– – Anr. Edn. Trans.:– Charles Jarvis. Ill.:– J.H. Clark. 1819. 4 vols. Cont. str.-grd. mor. gt. (S. Jan.27; 448) *Duran.* £200
– – Anr. Edn. Trans.:– Thomas Shelton. Ill.:– after Louise Power. Ash. Pr., 1927. (225) on paper. 2 vols. Fo. Orig. vell., unc. (SBA. Dec.16; 121) *Chesters.* £380
– – Anr. Edn. Ill.:– E. McKnight Kauffer. Nones. Pr., 1930. (1,475). 2 vols. Orig. niger mor. (SH. Feb.19; 128) *Sherlock.* £80
– – Anr. Copy. (SKC. Feb.26; 1293) £55
– Don Quixotte [French]. [Amst.?], 1681. 4 vols. 12mo. Cont. vell., covers blind-panel. (CNY. May 22; 57) $450
– – Anr. Edn. Ill.:– Fokke, B. Picart, Tanjé & Van Schley after Coypel, Cochin, Boucher, Le Bas, Trémolières & B. Picart. The Hague, 1746. 1st. Printing. 4to. Cont. marb. cf., decor. spine, jnts. reprd. (HD. Dec.5; 37) Frs. 3,500
– – Anr. Edn. Ill.:– Coypel, Cochin, Picart & others. The Hague, 1746. L.P. Edn. Fo. Cont. cf., decor. spine. (HD. Feb.18; 16) Frs. 3,300
– – Anr. Edn. Ill.:– Coypel, Picart le Romain & others. Liège, 1776. Fo. 2nd. printing of plts. of The Hague edn., 1746. Early 19th. C. hf. roan, spine decor. with raised bands. (HD. Feb.27; 22) Frs. 2,500
– – Anr. Edn. Paris, An VII [1799]. 6 vols. Cont. hf. mor. (HD. Oct.10; 227) Frs. 1,200
– – Anr. Edn. Ill.:– Deveria. Paris, 1821. 4 vols. 16mo. Cont. cf., gt. & blind decor. spines, blind roulette border & gt. fillet, lge. centre blind lozenge motif, inner dentelle. (HD. Apr.9; 433) Frs. 1,050
– – Anr. Edn. Paris, 1825. 6 vols. Hf. cf. by Thouvenin. (HD. Oct.10; 228) Frs. 1,200
– – Anr. Edn. Ed.:– Louis Viardot. Ill.:– Tony Johannot. 1836-1837. 1st. Edn. 2 vols. Hf. cf., corners. decor. spines with crowned initials, by Bibolet, unc. (HD. Feb.18; 1076) Frs. 2,300
– – Anr. Copy. Lge. 8vo. 1st. Printing, 2 figures on China. Str.-grd. red hf. mor. by Canape, smooth decor. spines. (HD. Feb.27; 98) Frs. 2,000

– – Anr. Edn. Ill.:– after Grandville & Giradet. Tours, 1848. 1st. Printing. 2 vols. Some foxing. Cont. paper publisher's decor. bds. (HD. Apr.9; 586) Frs. 1,600
– – Anr. Edn. Trans.:– Louis Viardot. Ill.:– Gustave Doré engraved by H. Pisan. 1863. 1st. Printing. 2 vols. Fo. Some light browning. Three-qtr. red mor., spine raised bands, by David. (HD. Apr.24; 127) Frs. 1,350
– – Anr. Copy. Some stains. Mod. hf. red mor. (SI. Dec.3; 131) Lire 320,000
– – Anr. Edn. Trans.:– F. de Miomandre. Ill.:– L. Jou. Geneva, 1948. (30) on Arches vell. 4 vols. 4to. With extra set of engrs., engraved woodcut & orig. drawing. In sheets, s.-c. (HD. Feb.27; 99) Frs. 2,800
– – Anr. Edn. Ill.:– Salvador Dali. Paris, 1957. (50) on Rives with suite on Japon Imperial. Fo. Orig. wraps., folder & s.-c. (SPB. Nov.25; 247) $2,600
– – Anr. Edn. Ill.:– H. Lemarié. 1960. On Rives vell. 4 vols. In sheets, s.-c. (HD. Jun.25; 316) Frs. 2,100
– Don Quixote de la Mancha [German]. Ill.:– Walter Klemm. Weimar, 1923. (100) numbered. 4to. Orig. hand-bnd. hf. vell. Lithos. hand-sigd. (D. Dec.11-13; 1018) DM 500
– Le Luminose Geste Don Chisciotte [Italian]. Ill.:– Francesco Novelli. Venice, 1819. L.P. Some ll. spotted, occasional finger-soiling to margins. Qtr. vell., worn, buckram s.-c. From the collection of John A. Saks. (C. Jun.10; 36) *Quaritch.* £90
– Don Quixote [Spanish]. Brussels, 1607. 7th. Edn., 1st. Brussels Edn. Liby. stp. on title, slight browning, occasional staining, mostly in margins. 19th. C. russ. (C. Apr.1; 127) *Quaritch.* £900
– – Anr. Edn. Madrid, 1638. 7th. Edn., 1st. Brussels Edn. Segunda Parte. 4to. Browned thro.-out, occasionally severely. Cont. limp vell., lacks ties. (C. Apr.1; 128) *Quaritch.* £240
– – Anr. Edn. Antw., 1697. 2 vols. Slight browning. Cont. limp vell., slightly soiled. Bkplt. of Basset Down House. (S. May 5; 70) *Duran.* £500
– – Anr. Edn. Madrid, 1733. 2 vols. 4to. Vol. 1 lacks 2 ll. prelims. Vell. (DS. May 22; 811) Pts. 20,000
– – Anr. Edn. 1738. 4 vols. 4to. Some spotting. Cont. cf., worn, a few covers detchd. (S. Apr.7; 352) *Quaritch.* £220
– – Anr. Edn. Ed.:– Mayans [Vida]. Ill.:– Monfort. Madrid, 1777. 4 vols. Vol. IV title torn with loss of half. Cf (DS. May 22; 944) Pts. 26,000
– – Anr. Edn. Ill.:– Mostly after Antonio Carnicero. Madrid, 1780. 1st. Ibarra Edn. 4 vols. 4to. Endpapers lightly foxed. Cont. Spanish spr. cf. gt., flat spines gt. Neat early ownership stencils of H.U. Addington on titles. (CNY. Oct.1; 81) $1,600
– – Anr. Edn. Madrid, 1780. New Edn. 2 pts. in 4 vols. 4to. Slight spotting, marginal staining at beginning of vol. III & IV. Mod. red mor., gt., by Macdonald, 1 spine chipped at head. (S. Jun.23; 258) £800
– – Anr. Copy. Some light foxing. Cont. marb. sheep., gt. panel. spines, spines, hinges & corners worn, some worming. (SPB. May 6; 170) $1,800
– – Anr. Copy. 29 (of 31) plts. Cont. Spanish cf., covers partly renewed. W.a.f. (CR. Mar.19; 295) Lire 650,000
– – Anr. Edn. Paris, 1832. 2nd. Miniature Edn. 2 vols. 32mo. Cf. with imp. design, raised portions enamelled in col., spines gt. & enamelled, by Simier. (SG. Oct.9; 33) $425
– Novelas Exemplares. Pamplona, 1615. 5th. Edn. Tears in H2 & I1, rust-hole in 3A4, several ll. loose, some ll. stained from lr. inner margin, occasional browning, inscr. on title. Cont. limp vell. bds., some wear, lacks ties. Bkplt. of F. Carter. (S. Feb.10; 427) *Perela.* £450
– Die Novellen. Trans.:– K. Thorer. Ill.:– C. Czeschka. (book. decor.). Leipzig, 1907. (100) Privilege Edn. on Bütten. 2 vols. Hand-bnd. orig. mor. gt. (H. May 21/22; 1391) DM 540
– Los Trabaios de Persiles y Sigismunda. Brussels, 1618. Title slightly soiled. Early 19th. C. hf. cf. (CSK. Apr.24; 83) £400

CESCINSKY, Herbert
– Chinese Furniture. 1922. 4to. Cl. (C. Feb.4; 231) *Rosewood.* £70
– English Furniture from Gothic to Sheraton. Michigan, 1929. 1st. Edn. 4to. Orig. cl. gt., in orig. ptd. s.-c., reprd. (TA. Mar.19; 128) £50

– English Furniture of the Eighteenth Century. [1909-11] & n.d. 3 vols. 4to. Hf. mor. (SH. Jul.16; 46) *Blundell.* £80
– – Anr. Edn. L., ca. 1910. 3 vols. 4to. Three-qtr. leath., worn. (SG. Mar.12; 83) $140
– – Anr. Edn. N.d. 3 vols. 4to. Hf. mor. gt. (P. Mar.12; 364) *Sims & Reed.* £100
– – Anr. Copy. Orig. hf. mor., 3 covers detchd. (LC. Jun.18; 65) £65
– The Old English Clockmakers. 1938. Sm. 4to. Orig. cl. (SH. Oct.9; 115) *Quaritch.* £60
– – Anr. Copy. (SH. Jul.16; 163) *Walford.* £50

CESCINSKY, Herbert & Gribble, Ernest R.
– Early English Furniture & Woodwork. 1922. 2 vols. Fo. Orig. cl. gt. (SBA. Mar.4; 245) *Quaritch.* £90
– – Anr. Copy. 2 vols. in 1. 4to. Orig. cl., d.-w. (SH. Oct.9; 117) *Chesters.* £50
– – Anr. Copy. 2 vols. Gt.-lettered leatherette. (SG. Mar.12; 84) $220
– – Anr. Copy. 2 vols. in 1. Some sections loose, end-papers foxed. Orig. bdg. (JL. Dec.15; 766) *Aus.* $110
– – Anr. Edn. [1922]. 2 vols. in 1. 4to. Buckram-bkd. cl. (SKC. Feb.26; 1425) £110

CESCINSKY, Herbert & Webster, M.R.
– English Domestic Clocks. 1913. 4to. Hf. mor. (C. Feb.4; 236) *Morris.* £60
– – Anr. Copy. (C. Feb.4; 235) *Morris.* £50
– – Anr. Edn. 1914. 2nd. Edn. 4to. Orig. hf. mor. (SH. Mar.6; 504) *Thorp.* £550
– – Anr. Copy. Orig. hf. mor. gt. (PL. Nov.27; 184) *Smith.* £75

CESKOSLOVENSKA FOTOGRAFIE
Prague, 1932, 1934-1938. 6 vols., numbered 2, 4-8. 4to. Cl., soiled. (SG. Apr.23; 13) $325

CHABERT, J.
– Galérie des Peintres. Paris, [1822-34]. 3 vols. Lge. fo. Slightly soiled in parts. Cont. hf. leath., cover loose. (R. Mar.31-Apr.4; 1508) DM 650
– – Anr. Edn. Paris, n.d. 2 vols. Fo. Cont. mor. (SH. Jan.29; 86) *Nolan.* £100

CHABERT, Joseph Bernard, Marquis de
– Voyage fait par Ordre du Roi en 1750 et 1751, dans l'Amérique Septentrionale, pour Rectifier les Cartes des Côtes de l'Acadie, de l'Isle Royale & de l'Isle de Terre-neuve; et pour en fixer les Principaux Points par des Observations Astronomiques. Paris, 1753. 1st. Edn. 4to. Some browning, stain on 1st. map, owner's inscr. of Ant. Shepherd. Cont. cf., very worn, jnts. reprd. Bkplt. of Stuart W. Jackson; from Honeyman Collection. [Sabin 11723] (S. May 20; 3207) *Somma.* £100

CHABIB, Moshe Ibn
– Darchei Noam Nivchar Me'osher Rav Marpe Lashon. Venice, 1546. 2nd. Edn. 12mo. Sigd. by censors in 1610 & 1620, stained, reprd. Bds., soiled. (SPB. May 11; 165) $325

CHABRAEUS, Dominicus
– Stirpium Icones et Sciagraphia. Geneva, 1666. Fo. Title reprd. Old. cf., covers detchd. (P. Jan.22; 123) *Cambridge.* £400
– – Anr. Edn. Geneva, 1677. 1st. Edn. Additional engraved title dtd. 1666. Cont. gt. vell., upr. jnt. brkn. From Chetham's Liby., Manchester, bkplt. of Lord Halifax on title verso. (C. Nov.26; 76) *Wagner.* £300
– – Anr. Copy. Spotted, lacks Fr. table after Hypercoum. Cont. cf., worn, rebkd. W.a.f. (S. Feb.23; 25) *Leinweber.* £200

CHADWICK, Edwin
[–] Report . . . from the Poor Law Commissioners . . . Sanitary Condition of the Labouring Population of Great Britain. 1842. Orig. cl. (S. Mar.17; 325) *E. Mathews.* £90

CHAFFERS, William
– Marks & Monograms on European & Oriental Pottery & Porcelain.–Hall Marks on Gold & Silver Plate. Ed.:– F. Litchfield. (1st. work). 1912. 2 works in 2 vols. Both orig. cl. (LC. Feb.12; 77) £55

CHAGALL, Bella
– Burning Lights. Ill.:– Marc Chagall. 1st. Edn. in Engl. Cl., d.-w. Contains orig. india-ink & watercolour drawing, inscr. & sigd. 'A Bobsy Goodspeed, Marc Chagall, 1947'. (PNY. Mar.4; 118) $11,000

CHAGALL, Marc
- **La Bible.** Paris, 1956. Verve No. 33/34. 4to. Publisher's bds. (HD. Jun.24; 161) Frs. 12,000
- – **Anr. Copy.** Orig. cold. pict. bds. (D. Dec.11-13; 1024) DM 7,200
- **Dessins pour la Bible.** Ed.:– Fernand Mourlot. Paris, 1960. Verve Vol. X, No. 37/38. Lge. 4to. Orig. bds. (D. Dec.11-13; 1025) DM 5,000
- – **Anr. Edn.** Ed.:– G. Bachelard (intro.). & Fernand Mourlot. Paris, [1960]. Verve Vol. X, no. 37/38. Sm. fo. Orig. pict. bds. (H. May 21/22; 1528) DM 5,700
- – **Anr. Copy.** Orig. bds. (HK. May 12-14; 1805) DM 5,100
- **Drawings for the Bible.** Trans.:– Jean Wahl & Samuel Beckett. N.Y., [1956]. 4to. Orig. bds., slight soiling, chipping, end-papers slightly browned. (SPB. May 6; 171) $2,300
- – **Anr. Edn.** Ed.:– Gaston Bachelard (text). N.Y., 1960. Fo. Orig. bds., d.w. (SG. Oct.9; 55) $1,700
- – **Anr. Copy.** Cold.-pict. bds., d.-w.'s. (PNY. Mar.26; 68) $1,200
- – **Anr. Copy.** 22 (of 25) cold. lithos. only, 2 other plts. loose. Orig. bds. W.a.f. (SG. Apr.2; 51) $750
- **Drawings & Watercolours for the Ballet.** Jacques Lassaigne (text). N.Y., [1969]. Tall 4to. Cl., d.-w., boxed. (SG. Apr.2; 55) $150
- – **Anr. Copy.** Fo. Cl., cold. pict. d.-w., boxed. (SG. Oct.23; 55) $110
- **Illustrations for the Bible.** Ed.:– Meyer Schapiro. N.Y., [1956]. Fo. Text by Jean Wahl, front fly-lf. & margins of last 3 ll. (including final reproduction) reprd. Pict. bds., rebkd. preserving most of orig. spine, new endpapers, boxed. (SG. Apr.2; 49) $1,300
- – **Anr. Copy.** (SG. May 14; 45) $1,100
- **The Lithographs. 1962-1968.** Boston, 1969. 4to. Orig. cl., d.-w. (SPB. Jul.28; 83) $175
- **Vitraux pour Jérusalem ... Musée des Arts Decoratifs, Paris, 16 juin-30 septembre 1961.** Paris, 1961. Sm. 4to. Cold. pict. wraps. Sigd. pres. copy. (PNY. Mar.4; 120) $500
- – **Anr. Copy.** (SG. Apr.2; 52) $280
- – **Anr. Edn.** Ed.:– I. Leymarie (Intro.). [Monte Carlo], [1962]. 4to. Orig. linen. (H. Dec.9/10; 1992) DM 560

CHAGALL, Marc (Ill.)
See–ARLAND, Marcel
See–CHAGALL, Bella
See–DERRIERE LE MIROIR
See–LASSAIGNE, Jacques
See–LEYMARIE, Jean
See–MEYER, Franz
See–MOURLOT, Fernand
See–MOURLOT Press
See–PREVERT, Jacques
See–PREVERT, Jacques & Calot, F.
See–VERVE

CHAGIZ, Moshe
- **Or Kadmon.** Venice, 1703. 12mo. Slightly stained. Wraps. (SPB. May 11; 66) $275

CHAILAN, F.
- **Lou Gangui ...** Ill.:– C. Maurou (port.). Marsiho, 1882. (500). Lge. 4to. Some slight foxing. Cont. hf. chagrin, spine with raised bands. (HD. Jun.24; 162) Frs. 1,400

CHAIM, OF KAMINSK
- **Zichron Chaim.** Warsaw, 1883. 1st. Edn. Cl. (S. Nov.17; 230) Goldberg. £100

CHAIM, OF MOHILEV
- **Eretz Ja'chaim.** Czernowitz, 1861. Varied Edns. 2 pts. in 1 vol. 4to. Orig. bdg. (S. Nov.17; 235) Valmadonna. £50
- **Sha'ar Ha'tephila.** [Sudzilkow], [1825]. 1st. Edn., on blue paper. 4to. Lacks title, margin of 1st. lf. reprd., without loss of text. Leath. (S. Nov.17; 236) Low. £130
See–YAKOV YITZHAK Ha'levi of Lublin ['The Seer']-CHAIM, of Mohilev

CHAIM Ben Abraham Cohen, of Aleppo
- **Tur Bareket Hilchot Pessah ...** Amst., 1654. 1st. Edn. 4to. Lacks 1st. lf., title reprd. affecting arch border, stained, cropped. Mod. leath. (SPB. May 11; 67) $350

CHALCOCONDYLAS, Laonicus
- **L'Histoire de la Decadence de l'Empire Grec, et l'Establissement de Celuy des Turcs.** Trans.:– Blaise de Vigenere. Paris, 1584. 4to. Inscr. on title 'Canonicus(?) Bellecampens adscrip 1738.3' ', wormhole in title, some margins dampstained, 17th. C. bkplt. of Nicolas Paschal Marco

Ladvocat. Cont. mor., double gt. fillet, flat spine gt. with swirling branches, title within oval, 1 corner worn. (SM. Oct.7; 1637) Frs. 3,800

CHALLAMEL, Augustin
- **The History of Fashion in France.** Trans.:– Mrs. Cashel Hoey & John Lillie. 1882. 4to. Orig. decor. cl.-bkd. bds., slightly soiled. (SBA. May 27; 237) Jones. £55

CHALLIER, Jacques
- **La Véritable Arithmétique des Marchands ...** Lyons, 1671. 7 pts. in 1 vol. 4to. 1st. 50 ll. stained. Cont. mor., 3 fillets, arms of Lyons, decor. spine. (HD. Mar.18; 39) Frs. 1,700

CHALMERS, Alexander
- **A History of the College, Halls & Public Buildings, attached to the University of Oxford.** Oxford, 1810. 2 vols. Some spotting. Cont. str.-grd. cf. (CSK. Mar.20; 123) £70
See–BRITISH Essayists, The

CHALMERS, T.
- **The Works.** 1850. 25 vols. Cont. cf. (SH. May 28; 22) Landry. £70

CHALON, John James
- **Twenty Four Subjects Exhibiting the Costume of Paris.** 1822. Fo. Litho. plts. dtd. 1820-22. Cont. red hf. mor. (C. Jul.15; 142) Zanzotto. £800

CHAM (Pseud.)
See–NOE, Count Amedée 'Cham'

CHAMBERLAIN, Henry
- **A New & Compleat History & Survey of the Cities of London & Westminster ...** [1769]. Fo. Cont. cf., rebkd. Bkplt. of Nathan of Churt, lately in the collection of Eric Sexton. (C. Apr.16; 229) Howard. £140
- **Views & Costumes of the City & Neighbourhood of Rio de Janeiro.** 1822. 4to. 1 plt. stained, 2 slightly stained, 4 strong offsets, slight offset of letterpress onto 1 plt., slightly soiled, a few pencil notes. Cont. hf. cf., loose & worn. (SKC. Jul.28; 2527) £12,200

CHAMBERLAIN, R.
- [-] **The Gentleman's Compleat Jockey.** 1696. 12mo. Soiled. Cont. cf. [Wing S4] (SH. Jun.25; 205) Quaritch. £200

CHAMBERLAINE, John
- **Imitations of Original Drawings by Hans Holbein in the Collection of his Majesty, for the Portraits of Illustrious Persons of the Court of Henry VIII.** L., 1792. 1st. Edn. Vol. II. Fo. Guards slightly soiled, plts. less soiled. Cont. red mor., decor. spine, gt. cover, inner & outer dentelle, worn. (HK. Nov.18-21; 1577) DM 2,500
- **Original Designs of the Most Celebrated Masters of the Bolognese, Roman, Florentine & Venetian Schools ... in his Majesty's Collections.** Ill.:– Francesco Bartolozzi, Tomkins, Lewis & others after Da Vinci, the Caracci, Lorraine & others. 1812. Fo. A few imprints cropped, occasional spotting. Cont. hf. maroon mor., spine gt. (S. Sep.29; 219) Litman. £420

CHAMBERLAYNE, Edward
- [-] **England's Wants, or several Proposals Probably Beneficial for England.** 1667. 1st. Edn. 4to. Mod. hf. mor. [Wing C1839] (C. Apr.1; 177) Mahler. £90

CHAMBERLAYNE, John
- [-] **The Natural History of Coffee, Thee, Chocolate, Tobacco ...** 1682. Sm. 4to. Disbnd. [Wing C1859] (C. Jul.16; 375) Lawson. £300
- **Oratio Dominica in Diversas Omnium fere Gentium Linguas Versa.–Dissertationes ex Occasione Sylloges Orationum Dominicarum.** Amst., 1715; 1715. 2 works in 1 vol. 4to. Slight foxing. Bds., soiled, s.-c. (S. Apr.29; 372) Brill. £130

CHAMBERLAYNE, Thomas
- **The Complete Midwife's Practice Enlarged ...** Ed.:– [R.C. & others]. 1680. 4th. Edn. 14½ pp. advts. of Obadiah Blagrave, tiny rust-hole in R5. Cont. cf., rebkd. [Wing 1817f] (S. Jun.15; 157) Studd. £750

CHAMBERS, David
- **Le Recherche des Singularitez plus remarquables concernant l'estat d'Escosse.–Discours de la Succession des Femmes aux Possessions de leurs Parens.** Paris, 1579. 2 works in 1 vol. Slightly dampstained or soiled. 19th. C. cf., arms of Duke

of Sutherland on upr. cover, rebkd. (S. Dec.8; 134) Bart. £65

CHAMBERS, Ephraim
- **Cyclopaedia or an Universal Dictionary of Arts & Sciences.** N.d. Vol. 5 only. Fo. Cf. gt. (P. May 14; 250) £100
- **Encyclopaedia or a Dictionary of Useful Knowledge.** L., 1895. 10 vols. 4to. Hf. mor., gt. lettering & raised bands to spines, marb. end-pp. (JL. Mar.2; 526) Aus. $120

CHAMBERS, Ephraim–LEWIS, George
- **Dizionario Universale delle Arte e delle Scienze. –Supplemento ... Al Dizionario Universale delle Arte e Scienze.** Venice, 1748-65. Together 16 vols. 4to. Plts. & explanatory text bnd. separately, some browning thro.-out, occasionally affecting plt. vol., minor worming at beginning of plt. vol. Cont. vell. From the collection of John A. Saks. (C. Jun.10; 37) Weinreb. £140

CHAMBERS, Robert
- [-] **Vestiges of the Natural History of Creation.** 1844. 1st. Edn. 1st. & last ll. slightly spotted. Cont. hf. cf. (S. Dec.3; 931) Quaritch. £120

CHAMBERS, Sir William
- **Designs of Chinese Buildings, Furniture, Dresses, Machines, & Utensils.** 1757. 1st. Edn. Fo. 1 sm. marginal tear, some ll. slightly soiled. 18th. C. hf. cl. (S. Apr.7; 250) Foster. £320
- – **Anr. Copy.** Some spotting. Later hf. mor. (CSK. Sep.26; 45) £240
- – **Anr. Copy.** Title & 3 plts. foxed. Cont. hf. cf., upr. cover detchd., worn, contents loose. bkplt. of Baptist College Liby., Bristol. Ex dono plt. of Thomas Llewyn. (S. Sep.29; 245) Harris. £180
- **Plans, Elevations, Sections, & Perspective Views of the Gardens & Buildings at Kew in Surrey.** Ill.:– Rooker & others. 1763. 1st. Edn. Fo. Orig. hf. cf., worn. (BS. Sep.17; 12) £460
- – **Anr. Edn.** L., Priv. ptd., 1763. Lge. fo. Dampstain across head of text & plts. only in margin, 2 plts. with sm. marginal tears, sm. tear in fold of folding plt. Cont. cf. & marb. bds. Bkplt. of George A.F. Fitzclarence, 1st. Earl of Munster. (CB. May 27; 61) Can. $1,500

CHAMELEON, The
Trans.:– Lord Alfred Douglas. Ill.:– after Aubrey Beardsley. L., Dec. 1894. (100). Vol. I, no. 1. 4to. With contribution from Oscar Wilde. Orig. paper wraps., slightly torn, qtr. mor. gt. s.-c., unc. From the Prescott Collection. (CNY. Feb.6; 382) $250
- – **Anr. Copy.** Mor. folding case (slightly worn), unc. The Jerome Kern copy, lately in the Prescott Collection. (CNY. Feb.6; 383) $200

CHAMFORT, Sébastien Roch Nicolas, dit de
- **Oeuvres Complètes.** 1824-25. 1st. Compl. Edn. 5 vols. Ornam. hf.-cf. by Brigandat. (HD. Oct.10; 229) Frs. 1,700
See–FAUCHET, C., Chamfort, S.R.N., Ginguene, P.L. & Pagès, F.X.

CHAMISHA CHUMSHEI TORAH
Berlin, 1930-33. (850) on Van Gelder paper. Fo. Hf. leath. (S. Nov.17; 45) Green. £360

CHAMISSO, Adalbert von
- **Gedichte.** Leipzig, 1831. 1st. Coll. Edn. Soiled, owner's mark on end-lf. Cont. hf. leath. gt. (HK. May 15; 4153) DM 700
- **L'Homme qui a perdu son Ombre.** Ill.:– Bernard Naudin. 1913. Sewed. On Van Gelder. (HD. Oct.10; 181) Frs. 1,050
- **Merveilleuse Histoire de Pierre Schlémihl.** Ill.:– Cruikshank & Geissler. Leipzig, [1860]. Lightly browned. Cont. bds., browned. (H. May 21/22; 1036) DM 420
- **Peter Schlemihl's Wundersame Geschichte.** Ed.:– Fr. Baron de la Motte Fouqué. Nuremb., 1814. 1st. Edn. Soiled & partly stained in upr. margin. Cont. hf. leath. gt. (HK. May 15; 4157) DM 3,000
- [-] – **Anr. Edn.** Ed.:– F.H.K. La Motte Fouque. Trans.:– J. Bowring. Ill.:– George Cruikshank. 1824. 1st. Edn. in Engl. Undated Nuremberg edn. with woodcut ills. inserted at end. Cont. str.-grd. mor. by Leighton, Brewer Street. Bkplt. of Thomas Gaisford. (S. Nov.24; 68) Bickersteth. £65

CHAMOUIN, J.B.
- **Collection de Vues de Paris, prises au Dageurreotype.** N.p., ca. 1840. Ob. fo. Cont. hf. leath., lacks spine. (R. Oct.14-18; 1869) DM 450

– – Anr. Edn. Ca. 1870. Ob. fo. Some slight foxing, 1 plt. soiled. Cl., cf. spine. (BS. Jun.11; 146) £50
– – Anr. Edn. Paris, n.d. Ob. fo. Orig. cf.-bkd. cl. (SH. Nov.6; 196) *Loeb.* £80

CHAMPAGNAC & Olivier
– Le Voyageur de la Jeunesse . . . Ill.:– Rouargue. Paris, ca. 1850. Lge. 8vo. Publisher's decor. buckram. (HD. Feb.27; 100) Frs. 1,000

CHAMPFLEURY, Jules François 'Felix Husson'
– Le Violon de Faïence. Ill.:– Jules Adeline. Paris, 1885. (500); (150) on imperial Jap., numbered. Orig. watercolour on hf.-title, etchings in 3 states. Mor. by Chambolle-Duru, mosaic spine & covers, mor. doubls., mosaic & gt., wrap. preserved, s.-c. (SM. Feb.11; 149) Frs. 9,000

CHAMPIER, Victor
– Les Anciens Almanachs Illustrés. Paris, 1886. Fo. Cl. portfo., slightly defect. (SI. Dec.3; 134) Lire 100,000

CHAMPLAIN, Samuel de
– Oeuvres de Champlain Publiées sous le Patronage de l'Université Laval. Quebec, 1870. 2nd. Edn. 6 vols. in 3. 4to. Cont. hf. mor. (CB. Apr.1; 47) Can. $220
– Les Voyages . . . Paris, 1613. 2 pts. in 1 vol. 4to. 4 engraved maps (of 8) 1 plt. (of 3), lacks lge. folding map, A2-3, [M1], R2-3. S2-3 in facs., 3 ll. & 1 map defect. & reprd., both titles mntd., a few ll. holed affecting ills., several ll. marginally wormed, some browning & marginal staining. Cont. cf., worn. W.a.f. [Sabin 11835] (S. Jun.22; 167) *Crossley.* £700
– – Anr. Edn. Paris, 1632. 4 pts. in 1 vol. 4to. 2 engraved ills. in text (of 6), lacks folding engraved map, 2H3, 2L1, 2O2 & 2P4 (with text engrs.), & A1-B4 the 'Doctrine Chrestienne' & 'L'Orasion Dominicale' together 12 ll., engr. at 2K2 defect., piece torn from 2K3 with loss, some ll. stained, title reprd. Cont. sheep, spine gt., worn. [Sabin 11839] (S. Jun.22; 168) *Tzakas.* £160

CHAMPLAIN Society
– Alexander Begg's Red River Journal . . . (Vol. XXXIV). Toronto, 1956. (600) numbered. Orig. cl., unopened. (CB. Dec.9; 87) Can. $120
– The Canadian Journal of Lady Aberdeen. (Vol. XXXVII). Ed.:– John T. Saywell. Toronto, 1960. (600) numbered. Orig. cl. (CB. Dec.9; 90) Can. $120
– Customs of the American Indians . . . By Father Joseph Francois Lafitau. (Vols. XXXXVIII & IL). Toronto, 1974-77. (1750) numbered. 2 vols. Orig. cl. (CB. Dec.9; 97) Can. $160
– David Thompson's Narrative. (Vol. XXXX). Ed.:– Richard Glover. Toronto, 1962. (1025). Orig. cl. (CB. Dec.9; 91) Can. $120
– David Thomson's Narrative of his Explorations in Western Africa, 1784-1812. (Vol. XII). Ed.:– J.B. Tyrrell. Toronto, 1916. (550) numbered. Buckram, 4-sheet map in pocket in rear cover. (SG. Jan.8; 431) $375
– – Anr. Copy. Liby. stp. on title-p. Orig. cl. (CB. Dec.9; 69) Can. $450
– The Description & Natural History of the Coasts of North America. By Nicolas Denys. (Vol. II). Toronto, 1908. (520) numbered. Liby. stp. on title-p. Orig. cl. (CB. Dec.9; 63) Can. $110
– The Diary of Simeon Perkins. (Vols. XXIX, XXXVI, XXXIX, XXXXIII, & L). Toronto, 1948-78. Ltd. Edns. 5 vols. Orig. cl. (CB. Dec.9; 83) Can. $300
– Documents Relating to the Early History of Hudson's Bay. (Vol. XVIII). Ed.:– J.B. Tyrrell. Toronto, 1931. (500) numbered. Orig. cl., bkplt. (CB. Dec.9; 72) Can. $110
– Documents relating to the North-West Company. (Vol. XXII). Ed.:– W.S. Wallace. Toronto, 1934. (550) numbered. Orig. cl. (CB. Dec.9; 76) Can. $220
– Dufferin-Carnarvon Correspondence. (Vol. XXXIII). Ed.:– C.W. de Kiewiet & F.H. Underhill. Toronto, 1955. (575) numbered. Orig. cl. (CB. Dec.9; 86) Can. $100
– The Hargrave Correspondence. (Vol. XXIV). Ed.:– G.P. de Glazebrook. Toronto, 1938. (550) numbered. Orig. cl. (CB. Dec.9; 78) Can. $100
– An Historical Journal of the Campaigns in North America for the Years 1757, 1758, 1759 & 1760. By Capt. John Knox. (Vols. VIII-X). Toronto, 1914-16. (520) numbered. 3 vols. Orig. cl. Bkplt. of R.W. Reford. (CB. Dec.9; 68) Can. $220

– The History of New France. By Marc Lescarbot. (Vols. I, VII, & XI). Toronto, 1907. (520) numbered. 3 vols. Liby. stp. on titles. Orig. cl. (CB. Dec.9; 62) Can. $220
– Hudson's Bay Company Series: The Letters of John McLoughlin . . . (Vols. IV, VI, & VII). Toronto, 1941-44. 1st.-3rd. Series, 3 vols. Orig. cl. Bkplt. of R.H. Tupper. (CB. Dec.9; 102) Can. $220
– – Anr. Copy. (CB. Apr.1; 51) Can. $110
– Hudson's Bay Company Series: Minutes of the Hudson's Bay Company. (Vols. VIII & IX). Ed.:– E.E. Rich. Toronto, 1945-46. (550). 2 vols. Vol. 1 unnumbered. Orig. cl. Bkplt. of R.H. Tupper in vol. 2. (CB. Dec.9; 104) Can. $140
– John McLean's Notes of a Twenty-Five Year's Service in the Hudson's Bay Territory. (Vol. XIX). Ed.:– W.S. Wallace. Toronto, 1932. (550) numbered. Orig. cl. (CB. Dec.9; 73) Can. $130
– The Journal of Captain James Colnett aboard the Argonaut . . . (Vol. XXVI). Toronto, 1940. (550) numbered. Orig. cl. (CB. Dec.9; 80) Can. $220
– Journals & Letters of Pierre Gaultier de Varennes de la Verendrye & his sons. (Vol. XVI). Toronto, 1927. (550) numbered. Liby. stp. on title-p. Orig. cl. (CB. Dec.9; 71) Can. $140
– Journals of Samuel Hearne & Philip Turnor. (Vol. XXI). Ed.:– J.B. Tyrrell. Toronto. 1934. (550) numbered. Orig. cl., lr. cover stained, ex-liby. (CB. Dec.9; 75) Can. $120
– A Journey from Prince of Wales' Fort in Hudson's Bay . . . by Samuel Hearne. (Vol. VI). Toronto, 1911. (520) numbered. Liby. stp. on title-p. Orig. cl. (CB. Dec.9; 67) Can. $160
– The Letters of Lititia Hargrave. (Vol. XXVIII). Ed.:– M. A. MacLeod. Toronto, 1947. (550) numbered. Orig. cl., unopened. (CB. Dec.9; 82) Can. $120
– Lord Selkirk's Diary. (Vol. XXXV). Ed.:– Patrick C.T. White. Toronto, 1958. (600) numbered. Orig. cl., mostly unopened. (CB. Sep.24; 202) Can. $110
– Ontario Series. Toronto. 1957-77. Ltd. Edns. Vols. I-X. Orig. cl. (CB. Dec.9; 108) Can. $150
– The Papers of the Palliser Expedition. (Vol. XXXXIV). Ed.:– Irene M. Spry. Toronto, 1968. (825) numbered. Orig. cl. (CB. Dec.9; 93) Can. $110
– Records of the Nile Voyageurs . . . (Vol. XXXVII). Ed.:– C.P. Stacey. Toronto, 1959. (600) numbered. Orig. cl. (CB. Dec.9; 89) Can. $130
– Relation of the Voyage to Port Royal in Acadia . . . by the Sieur de Diereville. (Vol. XX). Toronto, 1933. (550) numbered. Orig. cl., bkplt. (CB. Dec.9; 74) Can. $110
– Select British Documents of the Canadian War of 1812. (Vols. XIII-XV, & XVII). Ed.:– William Wood. Toronto, 1920-28. Ltd. Edns. 4 vols. Orig. cl., jnts. reprd. in vol. 13. (CB. Dec.9; 70) Can. $650
– Telegrams of the North-West Campaign. (Vol. XXXX-VII). Ed.:– D. Morton & R.H. Roy. Toronto, 1972. (1000) numbered. Orig. cl. (CB. Dec.9; 96) Can. $100
– The Works of Samuel de Champlain. Ed.:– H.P. Biggar. Toronto, 1922-36. (550) numbered. 7 vols., including portfo. Orig. cl. (CB. Dec.9; 98) Can. $320

CHAMPOLLION, Jean François, le jeune
– Monuments de L'Egypt et de La Nubie. Ed.:– J.J. Champollion-Figeac. Paris, 1835-45. 4 vols. Lge. fo. Vol. I with 2 titles, 1 torn & defect. Cont. cl.-bkd. bds., worn, a few covers detchd. (SH. Mar.5; 38) *Cucchi.* £700
– Précis du Système Hiéroglyphique des Anciens Egyptiens. Paris, 1824. 1st. Edn. 2 vols. Slight spotting & browning. Orig. wraps., some wear on spines, unc., s.-c.'s. (S. Apr.29; 373) *Goldschmidt.* £200

CHANDLER, Alfred & Booth, William Beattie
– Illustrations & Descriptions of . . . the Natural Order of Camellieae . . . 1831-[37]. Vol. 1 (all publd.). Fo. 44 hand-cold. engraved plts., without additional letterpress. Lev. mor., gt., by Zaehnsdorf. (C. Mar.18; 30) *Quaritch.* £7,500

CHANDLER, Alfred & Buckingham, E.B., of Vauxhall
– Camellia Britannica. 1825. 4to. Orig. ptd. wraps., unc., spine & corners defect. (C. Mar.18; 29) *Wheldon & Wesley.* £420

CHANDLER, Richard
– Travels in Asia Minor. Oxford, 1775. 1st. Edn. 4to. Folding engraved map torn along fold. Mod. hf. cf., spine gt. (S. Mar.31; 453) *Troy.* £80

– Travels in Asia Minor.–Travels in Greece. 1776. 2nd. Edn.; 1st. Edn. 2 vols. 4to. 1st. work spotted. Cont. cf., worn. (SH. Jun.18; 63) *Makiya.* £130
– – Anr. Edn. 1817. 3rd. Edns. 2 vols. 4to. A few minor defects. Cont. spr. cf. gt., Earl of Wicklow's bkplts. (SBA. Dec.16; 72) *Martens.* £60
– Travels in Greece. Oxford, 1776. 1st. Edn. 4to. Some offsetting. Cont. hf. cf., slightly worn. (S. Sep.29; 195) *Finopolous.* £90

CHANDLER, Richard & others
– Ionian Antiquities. 1769. Vol. 1 only. Most margins dampstained. Cont. hf. cf. (CSK. Jul.17; 21) £85
– – Anr. Copy. Fo. (SH. Jul.16; 101) *Hawkins.* £75

CHANLAIRE, Pierre Gregoire
– Atlas National de la France, en Departemens. Paris, 1806. Fo. Some light spotting & soiling, mainly marginal. 19th. C. hf. cf., worn, upr. cover detchd. (S. Nov.4; 589) *Loeb.* £300

CHANNELL, Leonard S.
– History of Compton County . . . Ed.:– C.H. Mackintosh. Cookshire, Quebec, Priv. Ptd., 1896. 4to. Orig. cl. (CB. Sep.24; 204) Can. $150

CHANNING, Edward
– A History of the United States. N.Y., 1928-1930. 6 vols. Three qtr. mor. (SG. Sep.4; 97) $160

CHANNING, Walter
– A Treatise on Etherisation in Childbirth. Boston, 1848. 1st. Edn. Orig. cl. Pres. copy to Dr. J.G. Crosse. (S. Jun.15; 158) *Studd.* £220

CHANTREAU, Pierre Nicolas
– Philosophical, Political, & Literary Travels in Russia. Perth, 1794. 2 vols. Cf. gt. (P. Oct.23; 11) *Brooke-Hitching.* £85

CHANTS et Chansons Populaires de la France
Ed.:– M. du Mersam. 1843. 1st. Edn. 3 vols. Hf. mor. gt. (BS. Jun.11; 40) £75
– – Anr. Copy. Lge. 8vo. Foxed. Cont. hf. chagrin, square gt. fillets on spines. (HD. Dec.5; 38) Frs. 1,900
– – Anr. Copy. 4to. Slightly soiled or browned. Cont. hf. leath. gt. (HK. Nov.18-21; 2321) DM 950
– – Anr. Edn. Ed.:– H.L. Delloye. Ill.:– E. de Beaumont, Daubigny, Pascal, Staal & others. Paris, 1843-48. 3 vols. 4to. Slightly spotted. Cf.-bkd. bds., orig. wraps. bnd. in. (SH. Nov.20; 197) *Schwing.* £220
– – Anr. Edn. Ed.:– Dumersan. H. Colet (piano accompaniment). Paris, n.d. 4 vols. Many stains, most light. Cont. hf. mor., gt. spines, partly unc. (SI. Dec.3; 135) Lire 400,000

CHANVALON, Jean Baptiste Thibault de
– Voyage à la Martinique. Paris, 1763. 4to. 19th. C. hf. mor. From Chetham's Liby., Manchester. [Sabin 11936] (C. Nov.26; 77) *Baskett & Day.* £580

CHAP-BOOK, The
Chic., 1895-96. Vols. 3, 4, 5 & 6 (nos. 1-4) bnd. in 3 vols. 16mo. Vols. 3, 4 & 5 with indexes bnd. in. Buckram, partly unc. (SG. Nov.13; 93) $100
– – Anr. Run. Ed.:– Harold Munro. Jul. 1919-May 1923. Nos. 1-37 (of 40). 4to. Orig. decor. cold. ptd. wraps., wraps. to no. 9 detchd., cl. s.-c.'s. (C. Feb.4; 274) *Edrich.* £50

CHAPBOOKS
– An Abridgement of the New Testament.–Fun Upon Fun.–Divine Songs in Easy Language. Glasgow, ca. 1815. 3 works in vols. 32mo. Sm. hole to 1 plt. in 1st. work. All orig. wraps., publisher's MS. titles on upr. covers. (S. Feb.9; 11) *Reisler.* £90

The Cheerful Warbler.–A Collection of Birds & Riddles–Comic Adventures of Old Mother Hubbard . . . etc. York, ca. 1830. 14 vols. 32mo. Unbnd., 1st. & last pp. cold. yellow to form covers. (SH. Dec.10; 67) *Schierenberg.* £165

– Fairy Tales of Past Times.–The History of Little King Pippin.–Tommy Thumb's Song-Book. Glasgow, 1814. 3 works in 3 vols. 32mo. All orig. ptd. wraps. (S. Feb.9; 8) *Temperley.* £55
– Fun Upon Fun.–Nurse Dandlem's Little Repository of Great Instruction. Glasgow, ca. 1815. 2 works in 2 vols. 32mo. Both orig. wraps. (S. Feb.9; 10) *Reisler.* £70

CHAPELAIN & Conrart
– Les Sentimens de l'Académie Françoise sur la Tragi-Comédie du Cid. Paris, 1638. 1st. Edn.

CHAPELAIN & Conrart du Cid. -contd.
Cont. cf., decor. spine. (HD. Mar.18; 40)
Frs. 1,800

CHAPERON Rouge, Le
Paris, ca. 1900. 4to. Orig. cl.-bkd. pict. bds.
Moving Picture Book. (SH. Dec.12; 581)
Arts Anciens. £60

CHAPIN, James B.
- Birds of the Belgian Congo. N.Y., 1932-39-54. 3
vols., pts. 1, 2 & 4 only. Buckram, ex liby. (SG.
Sep.18; 46) $130
- - Anr. Edn. N.Y., 1932-54. 4 vols. Hf. cl. (CB.
Sep.24; 18)   Can. $400

CHAPIN, J.R.
- Advertising Annual: The Historical Picture
Gallery. Boston, 1856. Vol. V only. 4to. Gt.-decor.
cl., mod. cl. spine. (SG. Nov.20; 287) $130

CHAPMAN, Abel
- Savage Sudan. 1921. Cl. gt. (P. Jan.22; 295)
Cavendish. £50

CHAPMAN, Fredrik Henrik
- Architectura Navalis Mercatoria Navium.
Stockholm, 1768. 1st. Edn. Lge. fo. Lacks 7 text ll.
Late 19th. C. qtr., mor., spine gt. (CNY. May
22; 157) $6,500

CHAPMAN, George
See–MARLOWE, Christopher & Chapman,
George

CHAPMAN, Guy & Hodgkin, J.
- A Bibliography of William Beckford. 1930.
(500). Orig. vell.-bkd. bds. (SH. Mar.5; 192)
Johnson. £100

CHAPMAN, R.W.
- Cancels. L. & N.Y., 1930. (500). Vell.-bkd.
marb. bds., unopened. (SG. Mar.26; 133) $170

CHAPPE D'AUTEROCHE, Jean
- A Journey into Siberia. L., 1770. 1st. Edn. in
Engl. Lge. 4to. Liby. stps. on title. Cont. cf.,
rehinged. (SG. Oct.30; 85) $260
- Voyage en Siberie. Paris, 1768. 4 vols. including
atlas. Fo. Tree cf., rebkd. From liby. of Baron
Dimsdale. (MMB. Oct.8; 2)   Gooch. £1,100
- - Anr. Copy. 2 vols. in 3 of text, & 1 vol. atlas.
4to. & lge. fo. 56 plts. (only?), some dampstaining
& last lf. soiled in vol. 1, some soiling to atlas.
Text in 19th. C. hf. mor., & atlas in cont. hf. cf.
(covers detchd.). W.a.f., from Chetham's Liby.,
Manchester. (C. Nov.26; 78)   Remington. £130
- - Anr. Copy. 2 vols. in 3, plus Atlas, together 4
vols. Lge. 4to. Cont. mott. cf., spines gt., wormed.
(SG. Oct.30; 84) $1,000
- A Voyage to California to Observe the transit of
Venus . . . Also, A Voyage to Newfoundland &
Sallee, to make Experiments on Mr. Le Roy's
Time Keepers. By Monsieur de Cassini. 1778. 1st.
Engl. Edn. Spotted, lacks hf.-title. Mod. mor., gt.
[Sabin 12004] (S. Nov.4; 654)   Lawford. £150

CHAPPEL, Lieut. Edward
- Narrative of a Voyage to Hudson's Bay. 1817.
[1st. Edn.?]. Orig. bds., covers detchd. (SH. May
21; 21)   Brooke-Hitching. £120
- - Anr. Copy. Lightly browned. Cont. style hf.
leath. gt., unc. [Sabin 12005] (R.
Mar.31-Apr.4; 2428)   DM 470

CHAPPUIS, Adrien
- The Drawings of Paul Cezanne. Greenwich
[N.Y.], [1973]. 4to. Orig. linen. (H.
Dec.9/10; 1990)   DM 460

CHAPTAL, Jean Antoine
- Chemistry Applied to Arts & Manufactures.
Trans.:– [William Nicholson]. 1807. 1st. Edn. in
Engl. 4 vols. Lacks lf. before title in vol. IV
(blank?). Cont. diced cf., spine defect. (S.
Dec.1; 90)   Maggs. £80

CHAPUIS, Alfred
- Histoire de la Pendulerie Neuchâteloise. Paris &
Neuchâtel, 1917. 4to. Orig. linen. (HK. May
12-14; 2334)   DM 650

CHAPUIS, Alfred & Gelis, E.
- Le Monde des Automates. Paris, 1928. 2 vols.
4to. Sewed, wraps. (HD. Dec.5; 39)   Frs. 4,500

CHAPPUIS, Gabriel
- L'Histoire de Primaleon de Grèce continuant celle
de Palmerin d'Olive . . . Trans.:– François de
Vernassal. Lyon, 1608-12. 2 vols. 18mo. 17th. C.
mor., covers gt. with central shield dtd. 'Aoust
1695' ascribed to Leriche, triple gt. fillet, spine

compartments gt. with fleuron in pointillé in leafy
sprays, red mor. doubls., gt. Jérôme Pichon copy.
(SM. Oct.7; 1638)   Frs. 2,000

CHAR, René
- A La Santé du Serpent. Ill.:– Joan Miro. Paris,
1954. (54) numbered on vel. d'Arches, for René
Char. Black hf. mor., orig. wraps. preserved.
Full-p. sigd. & dtd. orig. litho. (D.
Dec.11-13; 1027)   DM 2,500
- Dent Prompte. Ill.:– Max Ernst. Paris & N.Y.,
1969. (5) 'numerotes en chiffres Romains reservés
à l'Auteur à l'Artiste et aux Collaborateurs' sigd.
by author & artist. Lacks added suite of plts.
Loose in pict. wraps. as issued, folding cl. box
worn. (SG. Oct.23; 108) $400

**CHARACKTERISTISCHE   DARSTELLUNG
DER   VORZUEGLICHSTEN** Europaeischen
Militärs
Augsburg, 1800-10. 15 Pts. in 1. 4to. 15 engraved
titles, 75 (of 97) hand-cold. plts., margins of last 4
pts. stained, some ll. loose. Cont. hf. cf., worn.
W.a.f. (C. Jul.15; 24)   Taylor. £1,300
- - Anr. Edn. Augsburg, [1800-10]. 4to. Engraved
title & 75 (of 97) hand-cold. plts., a few cut round
& mntd. Cont. rose mor., sides panel. in gt., spine
gt. W.a.f. (C. Mar.18; 32)   Map House. £2,800
- - Anr. Copy. 15 Pts. in 1 vol. 15 engraved titles
& 75 hand-cold. plts. loose, last 4 pts. stained.
Cont. hf. cf., worn. W.a.f. (C. Mar.18; 31)
Taylor. £1,800

**CHARACTERS in the Grand Fancy Ball given by
the British Ambassador Sir Henry Wellesley, at
Vienna**
1828. 4to. Very slightly spotted. Cont. hf. cf., a
few defects. (SBA. Dec.16; 10)   Laywood. £76

CHARAS, Moise
- Nouvelles Experiences sur La Vipère. Paris, 1669.
Cont. cf., rebkd. (SH. Jul.16; 39)   Ayres. £90
- The Royal Pharmacopoea. 1678. Fo. Title soiled.
Cont. cf., later end-papers. [Wing C2040] (CSK.
May 1; 144)   £75

CHARCOT, Dr. Jean
- The Voyage of the 'Why Not' in the Antarctic.
[1911]. Orig. cl. gt. (P. Sep.11; 228)   Arnold. £50

CHARCOT, Jean Martin
[-] Iconographie Photographique de la Salpétrière,
par Bourneville et P. Regnard. Paris, 1876-1877.
21 (of 40) mntd. photographs, rubber stp. on verso
of each mount. Completely unbnd., orig. bd.
covers retained. (SG. Apr.23; 129) $325
- Leçons sur les Localisations dans les Maladies du
Cerveau (et de moelle epinière) faites à la Faculté
de Médécine de Paris. Ed.:– Bourneville & E.
Brissaud. Paris, 1876-80. 2 pts. in 1 vol. Orig.
wraps. bnd. in. (S. Jun.15; 160)   Rota. £90
- Leçons sur les Maladies du Système Nerveux
faites à la Salpétrière. Ed.:– Bournville. Paris,
1875. 2nd. Edn. 3 pts. in 1 vol. 16 plts.
(?irregularly numbered). Cl. (S. Jun.15; 159)
Bickersteth. £60
- Oeuvres Complètes. Ed.:– Bourneville & Guinon.
Paris, 1886-93. 11 vols. Hf. mor. (SG. Jan.29; 91)
$400

CHARDIN, Sir John
- Persian-und Ost-Indische Reise-Beschreibung.
Leipzig, 1687. 1st. German Edn. 4to. A few plts.
slightly torn, 1 partly missing, 2 ll. loose, browned.
Cont. cf., worn. (S. Jan.27; 319)   Diba. £110
- Travels into Persia & the East-Indies. 1686. 1st.
Edn. Vol. 1 (all publd.). Fo. Map discold., 1 plt.
torn & reprd. Cont. cf., worn, rebkd. From
Chetham's Liby., Manchester. [Wing C2043] (C.
Nov.26; 79)   Taylor. £90
- Voyages en Perse et autres lieux de l'Orient.
Amst., 1711. 1st. Compl. Edn. 3 vols. 4to. Plts.
slightly discold., 3 slightly torn. Non-unif. cont. cf.
& 19th. C. hf. mor., worn, 2 covers detchd. From
Chetham's Liby., Manchester. (C. Nov.26; 80)
Kossow. £350
- - Anr. Copy. Cont. cf., rebkd. (P. Apr.30; 4)
Elliott. £220
- - Anr. Copy. 10 vols. 12mo. Some tears &
repairs, some staining & browning. Hf. cf. W.a.f.
(SM. Oct.8; 2171)   Frs. 1,300
- - Anr. Edn. Paris, 1811. Atlas vol. (only). Fo.
Bds., brkn. As an atlas, w.a.f. (BS. Jun.11; 147)
£130

CHARLES I, King of England
- Basilike, The Works. 1687. 2nd. Edn. Fo. Cont.
panel. cf., rebkd. (TA. Dec.18; 113)   £90

- Eikon Basilike. Ill.:– W. Marshall. 1648. Disbnd.
[Wing E287] (SG. Feb.5; 75) $110

CHARLES VII, Emperor
- Vollständiges Diarium von den . . . Wahl und
Crönung des . . . Carls des VII. Frankfurt, 1742.
Fo. Cont. cf. (S. Jun.23; 252)   Goldschmidt. £200

CHARLES, R.H.
- A Roundabout Turn. Ill.:– L. Leslie Brooke. L.,
[1930]. (65) numbered, sigd. by artist. Cl. (SG.
Oct.23; 46) $110

CHARLET, Nicolas Toussaint
- Collection of uncoloured Lithographs. Ca. 1835.
4to. Some minor spotting. Cont. hf. mor. (TA.
May 21; 282)   £115

CHARLETON, Walter
- Chorea Gigantum. 1663. 1st. Edn. 4to. Cont.
sheep, worn, lr. cover detchd. From the collection
of Eric Sexton. [Wing C3665] (C. Apr.15; 170)
Traylen. £110
- Onomasticon Zoicon . . . cui accedunt Mantissa
Anatomica. 1668. 1st. Edn. 4to. 1 folding engraved
plt. torn, hf.-title with license on verso torn in
blank margin. Cont. cf., worn & rebkd., stitching
brkn. [Wing C3688] (C. Apr.1; 100)   Rota. £100
- - Anr. Copy. From Chetham's Liby.,
Manchester. [Wing C3688] (C. Nov.26; 81)
Taylor. £90
- Two Discourses: I. Concerning the Different
Wits of Men; II. Of the Mysterie of Vintners. 1675.
2nd. Edn. Slight browning & soiling, tear in I2,
reprd., with slight loss of text, corner torn from I3,
reprd., with some loss of text, lacks 1st. & final
blanks. Mod. pol. cf. by Rivière, gt., upr. cover
detchd. From liby. of André L. Simon. [Wing
C3695] (S. May 18; 68)   Zeitlin. £65

CHARLEVOIX, Pierre François Xavier de
- Histoire et Description Générale de la Nouvelle
France. Paris, 1744. 1st. Edn. 3 vols. Lge. 4to.
Cont. mott. cf., spines gt. (SG. Oct.9; 56) $1,600
- Histoire de l'Isle Espagnole ou de S. Domingue.
Ill.:– B. Picart (fronts.), d'Anville (maps & plans).
Amst., 1733. 2nd. Edn. (4 vols.?). 1 map with
slight tear. Cont. marb. cf., gt. lines round sides,
gt. spines, foot of vol. 1 spine slightly defect.
[Sabin 12128] (VG. Oct.13; 41)   Fls. 1,400
- Histoire du Paraguay. Paris, 1756. 1st. Edn. 3
vols. 4to. Sm. tear to 1st. map. 19th. C. hf. mor.
From Chetham's Liby., Manchester. [Sabin 1229]
(C. Nov.26; 82)   Traylen. £200
- Journal of a Voyage to North America. L., 1761.
1st. Edn. in Engl. 2 vols. Cont. cf., rebkd., upr.
covers detchd. [Sabin 12139] (SPB. Jun.22 32)
$425

CHARLTON, Lionel–YOUNG, George
- The History of Whitby.–A History of Whitby.
York; Whitby, 1779; 1817. 2 works in 3 vols. (1 +
2). 4to; 8vo. 2nd. work extra ill. with 13 etched
plts. & 2 maps. Both in orig. bds., spine of 1st.
work defect., both unc. (C. Nov.6; 293)
Chesters. £130

**CHARMILLY, Col. Venault de & Williamson,
Gen. Adam**
- Lettre à M. Bryan Edwards . . . Refutation de son
Ouvrage, initulé Vues Historiques sur la Colonie
Française de Saint-Domingue. L., 1797. 4to. Hf. cf.
(PD. May 20; 209)   £60

CHARNIZAY, Rene Marou de
See–PLUVINEL, Antoine de & Charnizay, Rene
Marou de

CHARNOCK, John
- Biographia Navalis. 1794-98. 6 vols. Hf. cf. gt.
(P. May 14; 240)   Green. £120
- An History of Marine Architecture. 1800-02.
[1st. Edn.?]. 3 vols. 4to. Extra engd. title in vol. 1,
98 plts. (of 99). Cont. cf. gt. (C. Jul.15; 143)
Weinreb. £700
- - Anr. Copy. Orig. cl.-bkd. bds., unc., recased,
most of orig. spines preserved, lacks labels. (CNY.
May 22; 158) $1,700
- - Anr. Edn. 1801. 1st. Edn. 3 vols. 4to. Orig.
bds., unc. (C. Nov.6; 294)   Maggs. £1,200

CHARPENTIER, H.
- Costumes de la Bretagne . . . Nantes, [1829-31].
2 vols. in 1. Lge. 4to. 119 cold. litho. plts. (of 120),
lacks table & title of vol. 2. Cont. hf. cf., corners,
worn. (HD. Dec.5; 40)   Frs. 16,000

CHARRON, J. de
- Histoire Universelle de Toutes Nations . . . Ill.:–
L. Gaultier (title-frontis.). Paris, 1621. Fo. Errata

lf. reprd. Cont. mor., du Seuil fillets, fleurs-de-lys in corners, arms of Louis XIV, spine decor. with raised bands & fleurs-de-lys. (HD. Feb.27; 23) Frs. 3,500

CHARRON, Pierre
- **De la Sagesse Trois Livres.** Leiden, 1656. 2nd. Elr. Edn. 12mo. Str.-grd. mor., gt., by Bozerian jeune. (SM. Oct.8; 2393) Frs. 1,000

CHARTARIUS, or Cartari Vincentius
- **Imagines Deorum.** Ed.:– Paul Hachenberg. Frankfurt, 1687. 4to. Some plts. with MS. titles. Cont. vell. bds., soiled, corner worn. (S. Feb.23; 26) Goldschmidt. £70
- – **Anr. Copy.** Engraved title lr. corner defect., plt. 46 defect., 1st. few ll. torn in margin. 18th. C. marb. paper bds. (S. Jan.27; 320) Pearson. £55

CHARTIER, Alain
- **Oeuvres.** Paris, 1617. 4to. Several ll. stained. Chagrin by Capé, blind-tooled fillets, inside dentelle, spotted. (HD. Dec.5; 41) Frs. 1,100
- **Theatrum Ethnico Idolatricum Politico Historicum.** Mainz, 1699. 4to. Recent cf. (TA. Jul.16; 221) £75

CHASE, Owen & others
- **Narratives of the Wreck of the Whale-ship Essex.** Ill.:– Robert Gibbings. Gold. Cock. Pr., 1935. (275). Sm. fo. Orig. cl. (SH. Feb.19; 168) John. £170

CHASTELLUX, François, Marquis de
- **Travels in North-America, in the Years 1780, 1781, & 1782 . . .** L., 1782. 1st. L. Edn., 2nd. L. Edn. 2 vols. Orig. vell.-bkd. bds., unc. From liby. of William E. Wilson. (SPB. Apr.29; 52) $375
- – **Anr. Edn.** L., 1787. 1st. Edn. in Engl. of vol. I; 2nd. edn., unrevised. 2 vols. of vol. II. Maps reprd. & linen-mntd. Mod. hf. buckram, ex-liby. (SG. Mar.5; 123) $120

CHASTENET DE PUYSEGUR, J. Fr. de
- **Art de Guerre par Principes et par Regles.** Paris, 1749. 2 vols. 4to. Slightly soiled in parts. Cont. leath. (D. Dec.11-13; 2777) DM 800

CHATEAUBRIAND, Alphonse
- **La Brière.** Ill.:– Méheut. Paris, 1924. (1000); 912 on Rives. Sm. 4to. Orig. watercolour. Mor. by Vitoz, wrap. preserved. A.L.s. by author loosely inserted, bkplt. of Noël Gordon. (SM. Feb.11; 201) Frs. 2,000

CHATEAUBRIAND, François Auguste René, Vicomte de
- **Les Aventures du Dernier Abencerage.** Ill.:– Gaston Vuillier. Paris, 1912. (1) on imperial Jap. Sm. 4to. Plts. in 4 states, orig. watercolours. Mor. by Aussourd, mosaic doubls., wrap. preserved, s.-c. A.L.s. by artist. (SM. Feb.11; 200) Frs. 35,000
- **Itinéraire de Paris à Jérusalem . . .** 1811. 3 vols. Cont. grd. cf. (HD. Oct.10; 30) Frs. 1,500
- **Mémoires d'Outre–Tombe.** Brussels, 1848-50. 6 vols. Cont. hf. chagrin, decor. (HD. Jun.30; 13) Frs. 3,600
- **Oeuvres Complètes.** Paris, 1826-31. 28 vols. in 31. Cont. hf. cf., gt. (S. Oct.20; 48) Lyon. £260
- – **Anr. Edn.** Paris, 1835. 22 vols. Cont. hf. cf. (HD. Jun.29; 56) Frs. 1,800
- – **Anr. Edn.** 1836-39. 36 vols. Steel-engrd. plts. Hf. cf., ornam. spines, by Lanne. (HD. Oct.10; 230) Frs. 6,500
- **Oeuvres Complètes.–Mémoires d'Outretombe.** Ed.:– Sainte-Beuve (1st. work). Ill.:– J. Staal, Racinet & others (1st. work). Paris, [1859-61]; n.d. New Edn. (1st. work). 2 works in 18 vols. Str.-grd. hf. mor. by Pouillet, corners, smooth decor. spines, unif. bdg. (HD. Jun.24; 168) Frs. 2,750

CHATELAIN, Henri A.
- [-] **Atlas Historique.** Amst., 1714-20. 1st. Edn. vols. IV-VII. 7 vols. Fo. 10 copper engrs. with tears, lightly browned & soiled in parts. Cont. cf., very defect. & worn in parts. (H. Dec.9/10; 444) DM 6,500

CHATELAIN, M.
See–SANDBY, Paul & Chatelain, M.

CHATER Collection, The
- **Pictures relating to China, Hong Kong, Macao, 1655-1860.** Ed.:– James Orange. 1924. Ltd. Edn. 4to. Orig. cl., d.-w. (C. Feb.4; 237) Lyons. £140

CHATTERTON, Edward Keble
- **Old Sea Paintings.** 1928. 1st. Edn., (100) rag paper. 4to. The 3 extra ills. hand-ptd. in col. Buckram, gt., partly unc. (LC. Feb.12; 78) £65
- **Old Ship Prints.** L., 1927. Ills. from the Macpherson collection. Decor. cl., buckled. (JL. Mar.2; 615) Aus. $115

CHAUCER, Geoffrey
- **The Canterbury Tales.** Westminster, William Caxton, 1484? Fo. Single lf. ('lj') from 'The Reeve's Tale', margins reprd. not affecting text. Transparent case & buckram folder. (C. Apr.1; 199) O'Hern. £350
- – **Anr. Edn.** Ill.:– Sir William Russell Flint. Riccardi Pr., 1913. (512) numbered. 3 vols. 4to. Orig. limp vell., ties, d.-w's., s.-c's. (SH. Mar.26; 201) Marks. £270
- – **Anr. Copy.** Mntd. cold. plts. Orig. vell., lacks some ties. (CSK. Aug.29; 2) £130
- – **Anr. Copy.** Holland-bkd. bds., partly unc. (C. Feb.4; 205) Howard. £95
- – **Anr. Edn.** Ill.:– William Russell Flint. L., Ricc. Pr., 1913. (500) on H.M.P. 3 vols. 4to. Orig. vell., lin. ties, ptly. unc., d.w's. (SG. Oct.9; 57) $550
- – **Anr. Edn.** Ill.:– Eric Gill. Waltham Saint Lawrence, Gold. Cock. Pr., 1929. (485) on paper. 4 vols. Fo. Partly unc., bds., qtr. mor., gt. (KH. Nov.18; 150) Aus. $1,600
- – **Anr. Edn.** Ill.:– William Russell Flint. L., [1929]. 4to. Tissue guards. Crushed mor., inlaid at upr. cover with bedroom scene of knight & maiden, gt.-stpd. at corners with rosettes & at cover, with other gt. fillets, inner dentelles gt., by Rivière. (PNY. Dec.3; 43) $425
- – **Anr. Edn.** Ill.:– Eric Gill. Waltham St. Lawrence, Berks., Gold. Cock. Pr., 1929-31. (15) numbered, on vell. 4 vols. Fo. Orig. niger mor., upr. covers stpd. with symbols after Gill, metal clasps, by Sangorski & Sutcliffe, orig. buckram boxes. (CNY. May 22; 412) $24,000
- – **Anr. Edn.** Ill.:– Eric Gill. Gold. Cock. Pr., 1929-31. (485) numbered. 4 vols. Sm. fo. Niger-bkd. patterned bds. (SG. May 14; 85) $1,900
- – **Anr. Edn.** Ed.:– Frank Hill. Ill.:– Arthur Szyk. N.Y., Ltd. Edns. Cl., 1946. (1,500) numbered, sigd. by artist. 4to. Sheep back. (SG. Oct.23; 322) $100
- – **Anr. Edn.** Ill.:– Elizabeth Frink. Waddington, 1972. (175) boxed & unbnd., sigd. by artist, numbered. Fo. Unsewn in orig. cl. box., ties. (SH. Nov.21; 327) Bugler. £140
- **The Flower & the Leaf.** Ill.:– Edith Harwood. L. & N.Y., Essex House Pr., 1902. Priv. Edn., (165) numbered, on vell. This copy unnumbered. Hand-bnd. vell., gold-stpd. title & blind-tooled Pr. mark on upr. cover. (D. Dec.11-13; 1028) DM 1,625
- **The Prologue from the Canterbury Tales.** Ill.:– Ronald King. 1967. (125), numbered. Fo. Unsewn in orig. buckram folder, s.-c. Each ill. captioned & initialled in pencil. (SH. Nov.21; 354) Monk Bretton. £460
- **Troilus & Criseyde.** Ed.:– Arundel del Re. Ill.:– Eric Gill. St. Dominic's Pr., 1927. (225) numbered. Sm. fo. Orig. mor.-bkd. bds. (S. Jul.31; 80) Marks. £800
- – **Anr. Copy.** Orig. mor.-bkd. bds. (SH. Feb.19; 151) Marks. £640
- [-] **[Works].** [1542]. [2nd. Collected Edn.]. Fo. Some dampstaining. 19th. C. panel. cf. Impft. copy, w.a.f. (TA. Feb.19; 369) £475
- – **Anr. Edn.** [1545?]. Fo. 2 titles in woodcut border, woodcut at start of Knight's tale, a few ll. from smaller copy. 17th. C. cf., worn. Near cont. inscr. from Rog. Hughes to H. Jones, w.a.f. [STC 5072] (S. Mar.16; 25) Fletcher. £300
- – **Anr. Edn.** Ca. 1550. 3rd. Edn. 2 pts. in 1 vol. Fo. Lacks final blank, tear in 3E4, hole in 3I4, sm. rust-hole in 2H3, occasional light spotting, slight staining, inscrs. in margins of 1st. title, sig. on 2nd. title. 18th. C. mott cf., gt., slight wear, upr. cover detchd. [STC 5073] (S. Feb.10; 428) Traylen. £800
- – **Anr. Edn.** 1598. 6th. Edn. Fo. Sm. rust-hole in main title & a few other ll., several ll. stained from outer edges, some browning. Cont. cf., covers detchd, spine defect., worn, several ll. near end detchd. Sig. of Thomas Baker (1656-1740), author & antiquary) on title-margin, a few inscr. in his hand in text. [STC 5077] (S. Jun.23; 368) Bennett. £260

- – **Anr. Copy.** Slight staining on some pp. Old hf. cf., brkn. [STC 5077] (BS. Nov.26; 194) £140
- – **Anr. Copy.** Lacks 1st. & last blanks, title mntd., browning, slight stains, tears, slight staining. Old cf., rebkd. [STC 5077] (SPB. Nov.25; 73) $650
- – **Anr. Edn.** 1602. 7th. Edn. Fo. Lacks port., slight browning & sailing, a few rust holes & tears, slightly affecting text. 17th. C. cf., rebkd., slightly worn. [STC 5080] (S. Sep.29; 110) Hargreaves. £100
- – **Anr. Copy.** Slight browning & soiling, a few rust holes & short tears, slightly affecting text, lacks port. [STC 5080] (S. Jan.26; 9) Thorp. £80
- – **Anr. Edn.** 1687. Fo. Cont. cf., rebkd. [Wing C3736] (CSK. May 1; 157) £120
- – **Anr. Copy.** Some stains & tears. Old panel. cf., rebkd. (SPB. May 29; 73) $130
- – **Anr. Edn.** Ed.:– John Urry. 1721. Fo. Some ll. marginally stained in outer edges, some browning & spotting. Cont. panel. cf., spine gt., worn. (S. Jan.26; 92) Bickersteth. £90
- – **Anr. Copy.** Cont. panel. cf., rebkd. (CSK. May 1; 158) £70
- – **Anr. Copy.** Old cf., worn. Sm. early bkplt. of Robert Bristow. (SG. Feb.5; 86) $180
- – **Anr. Edn.** Ill.:– After Sir Edward Burne-Jones, William Morris. Hammersmith, Kelms. Pr., 1896. (425) on paper. Fo. Red mor., gt. crest centred on upr. cover, silk endpapers, inner hinge strengthened, mor.-bkd. folding box, worn. (SPB. Nov.25; 319) $8,250
- – **Anr. Copy.** Orig. holland-bkd. bds., unc. Cuthbert Castle Sloane bkplt. (CNY. May 22; 326) $7,000
- – **Anr. Edn.** Ed.:– W.W. Skeat. Oxford, 1897. Stiff vell. gt. Fore-e. pntg. (SG. Apr.9; 177) $425
- – **Anr. Copy.** (SG. Sep.4; 186) $300
- **Complete Works.** Ed.:– W.W. Skeat. Oxford, ca. 1910. 16mo. Mott. cf., gt. arms on upr. cover, spine gt., prize bkplt. Fore-e. pntg. (SG. Mar.19; 128) $300
- **The Ellesmere Chaucer.** Manchester, 1911. Ltd. Facs. Edn. 2 vols. Fo. Orig. mor. gt. (SBA. May 27; 237a) Quaritch. £230
- **Works.** Stratford-upon-Avon, Shakes. Hd. Pr., 1928-29. (375) numbered. 8 vols. 4to. Orig. holland-bkd. bds., unc. (SKC. Feb.26; 1311) £380
- – **Anr. Copy.** Cl. bkd. bds. (CE. Nov.20; 164) £360
- – **Anr. Copy.** 4to. Mor., spines gt.-lettered, partly unc., by MacDonald. The John A. Saks copy. (CNY. Oct.1; 205) $900
- – **Anr. Edn.** Ill.:– Burne-Jones, initials by Morris. 1975. Facs. reprint of Kelmscott Chaucer, (515) numbered. 2 vols. (companion vol. by Duncan Robinson). Fo. Orig. patterned cl., paper covered wooden s.-c. (S. Jul.31; 171) Forster. £210
See–SHERIDAN, Richard Brinsley–CHAUCER, Geoffrey

CHAUCER, Geoffrey (Trans.)
See–LORRIS, Guillaume de & Meung. Jean de

CHAUCHARD, Capt. J.H.B.
- **General Map of the Empire of Germany, Holland, the Netherlands, Switzerland . . .** 1800. Fo. Hf. cf., upr. cover loose, worn. (PD. Oct.22; 181) £110
- – **Anr. Copy.** Imp. fo. Cont. hf. leath. (HK. Nov.18-21; 1047) DM 800

CHAULLIAC, Guy de
- **Inventario, over Collectorio Universalissimo de tutte le Cose Notabele delli Antiquissimi Medici . . . Spectante alla Arte Cyrugical.** Venice, Jul. 1521. Fo. A few cont. marginal MS. notes, minor staining & other slight discolouration. Cont. cf. (C. Apr.1; 40) Lawson. £130

CHAULNES, [M.F. d'Albert d'Ailly, duc de]
- **Catalogue des Livres Manusrits et Imprimés, et des Estampes.** Paris, 1770. Priced thro-out, bkplt. of Bibliophile Jacob. Cont. cf., spine gt. in compartments. (SM. Oct.7; 1343) Frs. 4,000

CHAUMETON, Pierre François & others
- **Flore Medicale.** Paris, 1814-20. 7 vols. in 8. Lacks plts. L-LIII of 2nd. Series. Hf. roan, unc., worn. W.a.f., from collection of Massachusetts Horticultural Society, plts. unstpd. (SPB. Oct.1; 111) $1,500
- – **Anr. Edn.** Ill.:– after E. Panckoucke & P.J.F. Turpin. Paris, 1815-20. 1st. Edn. 8 vols. Vols. 5 & 6 slightly soiled in parts, vols. 7 & 8 slightly

CHAUMETON, Pierre François & others – Flore Medicale. *-contd.*
stained mainly in text. Cont. leath., gt., spine slightly defect. in parts. (R. Oct.14-18; 2921)
DM 3,800
– – **Anr. Edn.** Ill.:– E. Panckoucke & J. Turpin. Paris, 1841-45. 7 vols. 4to. Vols. 1-6 with 60 plts. each, lacks plt. 49, dupl. of plt. 222 in its place, 61 plts. in vol. 7. Hf. leath. (SG. May 14; 76) $1,700

CHAUNCY, Sir Henry
– **The Historical Antiquities of Hertfordshire.** 1700. Fo. 19th. C. russ., gt. & blind borders on sides, gt. panel. spine, jnts. brkn. [Wing C3741] (C. Feb.25; 26) *Crowe.* £400
– – **Anr. Copy.** Frontis. port. mntd., minor dampstain in lr. outer margin. 18th. C. cf., rebkd. preserving orig. spine. From the collection of Eric Sexton. [Wing C3741] (C. Apr.16; 230)
Weaver. £220
– – **Anr. Edn.** Bishops Stortford, 1826. [2nd. Edn.]. 2 vols. Spotting thro.-out. Later hf. mor. (CSK. Feb.13; 201) £55

CHAUVELIN, Germain-Louis
– **Catalogues des Livres.** Paris, 1762. 4 Catalogues in 1 vol. 2nd. Catalogue, 'Ordre des Vacations' misbnd. at end, 3rd. Catalogue, lacks last lf. (blank?), priced thro.-out., 4th. Catalogue, lacks title & 'Table des Divisions'. Cont. mott. cf., spine gt. in compartments. Bkplt. of A.N.L. Munby. (SM. Oct.7; 1344) Frs. 1,100

CHAUVIN, Jean
– **Ateliers, Etudes sur Vingt-Deux Peintres et Sculpteurs Canadiens . . .** Montreal & N.Y., 1928. (1000) numbered. Cl., orig. wraps. preserved. (CB. Apr.1; 105) Can. $110

CHAYON, Nechemya
– **Divrei Nechemya.** Berlin, [1713]. 4to. Stained, repairs. Mod. hf. leath. (SPB. May 11; 69) $950
– **Oz Le'elohim.** Berlin, [1713]. 4to. Repairs, some discolouration, cropped, browning. Mod. hf. leath., in case. (SPB. May 11; 70) $950

CHAZAN, David
– **Kohelet Ben David.–David Ba'mezudah.** Saloniki, 1748. 2 works in 1 vol. 4to. Stained, 1st. work: stp. of former owner on title. Hf. leath. (S. Nov.18; 740) *Low.* £65

CHECK List of Wisconsin Imprints
Madison, 1942-53. 5 vols. 4to. Ptd. wraps. (SG. Jan.22; 405) $220

CHEEK, John
[–] **Young Angler's Guide.** L., 1839. 2nd. Edn. Three-qtr. cf., cl. rebkd. (SG. Oct.16; 18) $110

CHEESEMAN, T.F.
– **Illustrations of the New Zealand Flora.** Ill.:– Matilda Smith. Wellington, 1914. 2 vols. 4to. Some minor spotting. Orig. cl. (TA. Jun.18; 117) £95

CHEETHAM, James
– **Annals of the Corporation, relative to the late Contested Elections. By Lysander.** N.Y., 1802. Heavily foxed. Later hf. roan. (SG. Jan.8; 327) $100

CHEF D'OEUVRE (Le) de la Nature ou le Modèle de la Perfection, Etrennes Lyrique
Paris, ca. 1820. 64mm × 43mm. Title reprd. & tipped in. Orig. roan gt., spine soiled, bkplt. of Wilbur Macey Stone, s.-c., new endpapers. (SH. Mar.19; 178) *Fletcher.* £85

CHEFFONTAINES, Christophle, Archbp. of Caesarea
– **Response familière a une Epistre Escrite contre le Liberal Arbitre.** Paris, 1571. Cont. sig. on title of Chr. Preudhôme, bkplts. of Girardot de Préfond & Hans Fürstenberg. 18th. C. red mor., gt. border of birds with outstretched wings on covers, flat spine gt. à la grotesque, inner gt. dentelles. (SM. Oct.7; 1639) Frs. 1,200
– **Varii Tractatus et Disputationes.** Paris, 1586. Sig. E inserted from anr. edn., with disruption of the sense, lacks R2 (blank), R1a a cancel, mntd. in margins of the cancellandum, browned, a few ll. spotted, paper bkplt. of Girardot de Prefond, the arms cut out of the mantle, ptd. name-ticket &

?accession number 'CIV'. 18th. C. mor. (by Derome le Jeune), triple gt. fillet spine in compartments (3 with title & date), inner gt. dentelles, 1 corner very slightly worn. (S. Apr.7; 314) *Foyles.* £70

CHEKE, Sir John
See–L., R.–EDWARD VI of England, King
–CHEKE, Sir John

CHEKHOV, Anton
– **Vishnevy Sad [Cherry Orchard].–Svad'ba. Yubilei. Tri Sestry [The Wedding. The Jubilee; Three Sisters].** St. Petersb., 1904-02. 1st. Edns. 2 works in 1 vol. Later hf. cl., orig. upr. wraps. preserved. (SH. Feb.5; 1) *Quaritch.* £150

CHELU BEY, A.
– **Le Nil et son Bassin.** Paris, 1910. (110). 2 vols. 4to. Red mor., arms, watered silk doubls. & endpapers. (HD. Dec.5; 42) Frs. 1,350

CHEMNITZ, J.H.
See–MARTINI, F.H.W. & Chemnitz, J.H.

CHENEY, A. Nelson
See–ORVIS, Charles F. & Cheney, A. Nelson

CHENU, Jean Charles
– **Manuel de Conchyliologie et de Paléontologie Conchyliologique.** Paris, 1859-62. 2 pts. in 1 vol. Name cut from hf.-title of vol. I. Cont. hf. roan, worn. (S. May 5; 152) *Duran.* £85

CHERBURY, Baron Edward Herbert
See–HERBERT, Edward, Baron of Cherbury

CHERRY-GARRARD, Apsley
– **The Worst Journey in the World.** 1922. 1st. Edn., later Iss. 2 vols. only, lacks supp. Orig. cl. (SH. Nov.7; 472) *Walcot.* £62

CHERUBIN d'Orléans, Père
– **La Vision Parfaite.** Paris, 1677-81. 1st. Edn. 2 vols. 4to. 19th. C. hf. mor. From Chetham's Liby., Manchester. (C. Nov.26; 83) *Rota.* £450

CHERUBINI, Francesco
– **Vocabulario Milanese-Italiano.** Milan, 1839-56. 1st. Edn. 5 vols. including supp. Hf.-titles. Cont. hf. cf., unc. (SI. Dec.3; 136) Lire 380,000

CHESELDEN, William
– **The Anatomy of the Human Body.** 1741. 6th. Edn. Cont. cf. (S. Dec.2; 799) *Haussman.* £50
– **Osteographia, or the Anatomy of the Bones.** Ill.:– after Van der Gucht. 1733. 1st. Edn. Some slight discolouration. Cont. sheep., rebkd. (C. Apr.1; 101) *Quaritch.* £880
– – **Anr. Copy.** Without explanatory text to plts., pp. very slightly brittle at some extreme outer blank margins mainly towards end. New hf. cf., unc. (S. Jun.15; 165) *Bennett.* £600
– – **Anr. Edn.** L., 1733. 1st. Edn., on L.P. Lge. fo. 56 copperplts. each in 2 states. Cont. mor., gt. borders, very worn, 7 extra engrs., the last inscr. to Martin Folkes, Syston Park bkplt. (SG. Oct.9; 58) $3,400
– – **Anr. Edn.** Ill.:– after Van der Gucht. 1733. Lge. fo. Title & some ll. stained. Cont. diced cf., gt.-tooled spray cornerpieces, worn, covers loose. From Chetham's Liby., Manchester. (C. Nov.26; 84) *King.* £650

CHESHIRE LINES Committee Survey of Railways & Estate
– **Book 1, Liverpool Central Station to Manchester Central Station, Throstlenest Junction to Chorlton, & Halewood to Huskisson, & Southport.** 1892-3. 4to. Orig. hf. mor. W.a.f. (TA. Aug.21; 205) £700

CHESNEAU, Ernest
– **Ecole Français, les Estampes en couleurs du XVIIIe Siècle.** Ill.:– reproductions after Delucourt, Lavreince, Fragonard, Janinet etc. Paris, 1885-89. (100) numbered. 2 vols. in 1. Fo. Plts. in 2 states, cold. & bistre, occasional very minor spotting. Red mor., gt., by Zaehnsdorf. (C. Feb.25; 214) *Wheeler.* £1,200

CHESNEY, F.R.
– **Reports on the Navigation of the Euphrates.** 1823. Fo. A few ll. marginally dampstained. Cont. mor., gt. (SH. Mar.5; 39) *Weinreb.* £95

CHESTERFIELD, Philip Dormer Stanhope, Earl of
– **Letters to his Son.** L., 1774. 1st. Edn. 2 vols. Lge. 4to. Early marb. bds., rebkd., orig. spine preserved. Armor. bkplt. of Elizabeth Sophia Lawrence. (SG. May 14; 46) $200

– – **Anr. Edn.** L., 1774. 4 vols. Foxing. Cf. gt. (SPB. May 29; 74) $150
– **The Letters [& Works].** Ed.:– Lord Mahon. 1847. New Edn. 5 vols. Slight offsetting to titles, some spots. Cf., gt., by Rivière. (S. Feb.10; 429) *Traylen.* £55
– **Maxims.** L., 1774. 1st. Edn. of the condensed version. 18mo. Lacks frontis., heavily foxed, with 5 pp. of advts. Marb. bds., new leath. back. (SG. Apr.30; 81) $200
– **Miscellaneous Works.** 1777. 2 vols. 4to. Cont. cf. (P. Dec.11; 279) *Georges.* £55

CHESTERTON, Gilbert Keith
– **Chaucer.** 1932. 1st. Edn., with corrections for new edn. (1959). Orig. cl., inscr. on d.-w., worn. Autograph revisions & other alterations, title verso with revised text pasted over. (SH. Dec.18; 75) *Lincoln.* £50
– **The Future of Religion [A Lecture delivered to the Cambridge 'Heretics'].** Late 1911. 1st. Edn., (400). 1 gathering of 12 ll. with no title. Orig. stapled wraps. With orig. cheque paid to Chesterton for the lecture, endorsed by his wife Frances, & A.L.s. from her to Ogden acknowledging it & conveying his feeling that he had 'not in the least earned it.'. (LC. Oct.2; 230) £50
– **The Turkey & the Turk.** Ill.:– Thomas Derrick. St. Dominic's Pr., 1930. (100) sigd. by author & artist. 4to. 24 ll. only. Unbnd., unc. (SH. Feb.19; 93) *Sherlock.* £55
– **The Way of the Cross.** Ill.:– Frank Brangwyn. [1935]. (250) sigd. by author & artist. Fo. Orig. vell. gt., s.-c. defect. (SH. Mar.26; 117) *Quaritch.* £80

CHESTON, Richard Browne
– **Pathological Inquiries & Observations in Surgery from the Dissections of Morbid Bodies.** Gloucester, 1766. 4to. Liby. stp. & name on title. Qtr. cf. (S. Dec.2; 800) *Gurney.* £55

CHEVALIERS FRANCAIS (Les)
Paris, ca. 1820. Sm. 16mo. Cont. bdg., gt. borders, engrs. cold. & painted on glass. (HD. Apr.8; 87) Frs. 3,100

CHEVIGNY, Sieur de
– **La Scienze delle Persone di Corte, di Spada, e di Toga.** Ill.:– Isabella Piccini (frontis.). Venice, 1720. 4 vols. 12mo. Scattered light foxing. Cont. vell. From the collection of John A. Saks. (C. Jun.10; 39) *Taylor.* £60

CHEVREUL, Michel Eugène
– **Des Couleurs et de Leurs Applications aux Arts Industriels . . .** Paris, 1864. Fo. Orig. cl. (S. Nov.25; 401) *Henderson* £380
– **Histoire des Connaissances Chimiques.–De la Baguette Divinatoire ou Pendule dit Explorateur et des Tables Tournantes.–The Laws of Contrast of Colour & their Application to the Arts.–Oeuvres Scientifiques . . . 1806-1886.–Examen Critique . . . d'un ecrit Alchimique Artefici: Clavis Majoris Sapientiae.** Ed.:– Godefroy Malloizel (4th. work). Trans.:– John Spanton (3rd. work). Paris; Paris; n.p.; Paris; Paris, 1866; 1854; 1857; 1886; 1867. 3rd. work 1st. Engl. Edn. 1st. work: Vol I (all publd.) together 5 vols. 8vo & 4to. 1st work with no advts. Bds., cl. spine; bds., mor. spine; cl.; cl.; cl. (S. Dec.1; 103) *Whitehart.* £100

CHEVRILLON, André
– **Les Puritains du Désert Sud-Algérien.** Ill.:– Paul Elie Dubois engraved by Pierre Bouchet. Paris, 1944. (130). 4to. Loose ll., Wrap. & publisher's bds. Proofs of L'Arabe & of un Menu, proof on japon nacré, lacking from suite, proof of a plt., complete cold. suite on Japon. (LM. Nov.8; 40) B.Frs. 8,000

CHEYNE, George
– **The English Malady.** 1733. 1st. Edn. Cont. cf., worn. (S. Dec.2; 699) *Blackwell.* £65

CHEYNE, Lieut. J.P.
– **A Series of Stereoscopic views of the Franklin Relics . . . with Original Descriptive Catalogue.** [L.], [1860]. 14 stereoviews on flat, beige cards., & 1 additional cont. card. Orig. bd. case, torn & reprd. (CB. Dec.9; 1) Can. $1,400

CHEYNE, John
– **Cases of Apoplexy & Lethargy with Observations upon the Comatose Diseases.** 1812. 1st. Edn. Orig. bds., spine defect. at top & bottom, unc. (S. Jun.15; 168) *Maggs.* £200

CHIARI, Giovanni
- Statue di Firenze Flor., ca. 1800-20. 3 pts. in 1 vol. Orig. marb. bds., spine worn, unc. (PNY. Oct.1; 491) $125

CHICHERIN, Aleksei
- Plaf'. Moscow, 1922. (1000). 4to. Orig. wraps., torn. V. Bryusov's copy. (SH. Feb.6; 417) *Quaritch.* £90
- Shlepnuvshiesya aeroplany [Falling Aeroplanes]. Kharkov, 1914. Ob. 8vo. Orig. wraps. (SH. Feb.6; 418) *Quaritch.* £85

CHIEREGATUS, Leonellus
- Oratio in Funere Innocentii VIII. [Rome], [after 28 Jul. 1492]. 4to. Disbnd. [Hain 4965*; BMC IV 113; Goff C453] (C. Apr.1; 24) *Maggs.* £90

CHILD, Sir Josiah
- A New Discourse of Trade. 1698. 3rd. Edn. 12mo. Title browned. Cont. sheep, worn, upr. cover detchd. [Wing C3862] (C. Feb.25; 151) *Frognal.* £60
- - Anr. Edn. Ca. 1740? 4th. Edn. 12mo. Advt. lf. at end, ex-liby. copy with stp. on title. Cont. cf. gt., very worn, rebkd. (SBA. Mar.4; 28) *Subunso.* £60

CHILDREN'S EMPLOYMENT COMMISSION
- First [Second] Report of Commissioners. 1842-45. 6 vols. only. Fo. Cont. cl.-bkd. bds., worn. (SH. Mar.5; 208) *Weiner.* £105

CHILD'S GUIDE (The), to Spelling & Reading, or an Attempt to Facilitate the Progress of Small Children when First Sent to School
Phila., 1810. 4th. Edn. 12mo. Orig. wraps., backstrip slightly worn. (SH. Mar.19; 51) *Maggs.* £100

CHILD'S PICTORIAL GEOMETRY
Hartford, Ohio, 1842. 4to. Orig. cl.-bkd. pict. wraps. with 2 additional ills., backstrip worn, loose. (SH. Mar.19; 52) *Maggs.* £100

CHILD'S PICTORIAL MUSIC BOOK
Hartford, Ohio, 1842. 4to. Some ll. dampstained at foot. Orig. cl.-bkd. pict. wraps., lacks backstrip, loose. (SH. Mar.19; 53) *Maggs.* £130

CHILD'S Rosary Book, A
Ill.:– David Jones. St. Dominic's Pr., 1924. Orig. wraps., unc. (SH. Feb.19; 92) *East Sussex County Liby.* £100

CHILE
- Constitucion de la Republica de Chile jurada y promulgada el 25 de Mayo de 1833. [Santiago de Chile], [1833]. 1st. Edn. Sm. 4to. Mod. hf. roan. (SPB. May 5; 150) $600

CHILONE, V.
- Album di Venezia. Ill.:– Aliprandi after author. Mailand & Venedig, ca. 1830. Ob. fo. Cont. bds., part of orig. wraps. pasted on. (R. Oct.14-18; 1936) DM 650

CHINESE ART
- The 'Hikko-En.' Album. [Tokyo], Aug., 1912. Fo. Cold. patterned wraps., in folding bd. case with ivory clasps, case worn. (SG. Dec.4; 94) $550

CHING, Raymond
- The Bird Paintings. [L.], [1978]. (350) numbered, & sigd. Fo. Mor., cl. s.-c. (KH. Mar.24; 95) Aus. $500

CHIODI, Pasquale
- Torantella Bello Napolitano. 1834. Disbnd. (P. Feb.19; 188) *Maggs.* £260

CHIPPENDALE, Thomas
- The Gentleman & Cabinet-Maker's Director. Priv. Ptd., 1754. Fo. Occasional minor spotting. Cont. cf., rebkd. Armorial bkplt. of the Duke of Beaufort, lately in the collection of Eric Sexton. (C. Apr.15; 64) *Traylen.* £750
- - Anr. Copy. Plts. numbered in roman & arabic type & MS., some browning, minor tears. Hf. cf. (SPB. May 6; 173) $3,500
- - Anr. Edn. 1762. 3rd. Edn. Fo. Red mor. gt., by Bedford. (S. Nov.24; 54) *Traylen.* £1,000
- - Anr. Copy. Browning & spotting. Cont. reversed cf., upr. cover detchd. (CSK. May 22; 86) £320
- - Anr. Copy. Engraved dedication lf. & 195 plts. (of 200), 6 plts. from anr. edn. loosely inserted, few plts. with 19th. C. press cuttings pasted to versos. Cont. cf., worn, brkn. (S. Mar.17; 404) *Woodruff.* £260

- - Anr. Copy. 201 engraved plts., lacks 6 plts., but with 7 bis numbers, first few ll. detchd., some browning & staining. Early 20th. C. buckram, worn, brkn. W.a.f. (S. Mar.17; 405)
- Le Guide du Tapissier, de l'Ebeniste, et de Tous Ceux qui Travaillent en Meubles. L., 1762. 3rd. Edn. Fo. Liby. stp. of Herzoglicher S. Meiningischer Bibliothek on title-p. verso. Unbnd. in cont. bds., remains of ties, worn. (S. Mar.17; 406) *Weinreb.* £700

CHIQUET, J.
- [Le Nouveau et Curieux Atlas Géographique et Historique]. [Paris], [1719]. Ob. 4to. 30 ll. engraved. text, 56 engraved. ll., including 23 outl. cold. copper maps. Cont. vell. (R. Oct.14-18; 1529) DM 800

CHISHOLM, C.R., & Bros.
- Chisholm's All Round Route & Panoramic Guide of the St. Lawrence. Montreal, 1875. Orig. cl., spine slightly faded, bkplt. (CB. Feb.18; 16) Can. $160
- Chisholm's Stranger's Illustrated Guide to the City of Montreal. Montreal, 1870. Orig. ptd. wraps., tattered & loose. (CB. Feb.18; 17) Can. $120

CHISHULL, Edmund
See–PERRY, Charles–CHISHULL, Edmund

CHISKIA Ben Abraham
- Malkiel. Thiengen, 1560. 1st. Edn. 4to. Some discolouration, lightly stained. Bds., worn, worming. Sig. of Meir Anschel. (SPB. May 11; 73) $2,900

CHITTY, Edward 'Theophilus South'
- The Fly Fisher's Text Book. L., 1841. 1st. Edn. Cl., unc. (SG. Oct.16; 19) $170

CHIVER, Philip
- Introducto in Universam Geograpniam tam verteram quam novam. 1711. 4to. 1 map slightly torn, some plts. lightly browned. Cont. panel. cf., worn. W.a.f. (CSK. Dec.12; 212) £180

CHLADNI, Ernst Florens Friedrich
- Beyträge zur Praktischen Akustik und zur Lehre vom Instrumentbau ... Leipzig, 1821. 1st. Edn. Slightly soiled, some underlinings. Cont. hf. leath. (R. Oct.14-18; 1293) DM 1,000

CHOCTAW NATION
- The Constitution of Laws of the Choctaw Nation. Doaksville, 1852. 12mo. Ex liby. Disbnd. (SG. Jun.11; 89) $190

CHODERLOS de Laclos, Pierre Ambroise François
- Les Liasions Dangereuses. Geneva, 1782. 4 vols. 18mo. Title reproduced. Cf. by Cazin. (HD. Apr.8; 234) Frs. 1,800
- - Anr. Edn. Paris, 1908. (200) on papier à la forme. Red mor. by Valmar, gt. fleuron semi in gt. panels of spine & covers, floral silk doublais., orig. wraps. bnd. in, s.-c. (SM. Oct.8; 2324) Frs. 7,500
- - Anr. Edn. Ill.:– G. Jeanniot. Paris, 1914. (200) numbered on Marais vell. 2 vols. 4to. Etchings in 2 states (black-&-white with comments & cold.). Red hf. mor., decor. spines, wraps. preserved. (SM. Feb.11; 202) Frs. 2,800

CHODZKO, Leonard
- La Pologne, Scènes Historiques, Monumens etc. Paris, ca. 1835. 3 vols. 4to. Frontis. in vol. II with blue stain in fore-margin, occasional light foxing, staining & offsetting. Cont. hf. cf. (S. Jun.29; 266) *Saphiena.* £180

CHOICE Collection of Riddles, Charades ... by Peter Puzzlewell Esq.
1800. 12mo. Orig. bds., worn, rebkd. (SH. Dec.10; 19a) *Vincent.* £52

CHOISEUL, Etienne François, Duc de
- Memoire Historique sur la Négociation de la France & de l'Angleterre. [Paris], 1761. 12mo. Last 8 ll. stained in margin, pp. 169-174 misnumbered as 187-192. Orig. marb. wraps. (CB. Dec.9; 39) Can. $120

CHOISEUL-GOUFFIER, M.G.F.A. de
[-] Voyage Pittoresque de la Grèce. Paris, 1782. Vol. I only. Lge. fo. 1 double-p. map inverted, slight foxing & marginal discolouration. Red hf. mor., very worn, covers detchd. (S. Jun.22; 169) *Dimakarakos.* £440
- - Anr. Edn. Paris, 1782-1809-1822. 1st. Edn. 2 vols. in 3 (vol. II in 2 pts.). Fo. With the double

plt. '76 bis' in vol. 2, engraved port. detchd., 1st. title detchd., stained & frayed, some margins spotted or discold. 19th. C. hf. cf., covers detchd., spines defect. From Chetham's Liby., Manchester. (C. Nov.26; 85) *Dimakarakos.* £1,000
- - Anr. Copy. Occasional minor foxing. Vol. I mor., gt., by Derôme with his ticket at foot of title-p., Comte de Ludolph arms on sides, his black-stp. at foot of hf.-title, head of spine chipped, vols. II & III mor., similar tooled, vol. I a little rubbed, vol. II lr. cover a little scuffed. (SM. Oct.8; 2394) Frs. 70,000

CHOIX DE GRAVURES a l'Eau d'après Les Peintures Originales et Les Marbres de la Galerie de Lucien Bonaparte
L., 1812. 4to. Decor. mor. (JL. Jul.20; 856) Aus. $200

CHOIX DE NOUVELLES VIGNETTES DE LA FONDERIE DE GILLE fils
Paris, ca. 1808. Fo. Mod. mor.-bkd. bds. (C. Apr.1; 38) *Goldschmidt.* £160

CHOMEL, A.F.
- Elémens de Pathologie Générale. Paris, 1841. 3rd. Edn. Slight spotting. Cont. cf.-bkd. marb. bds., head of spine defect. (S. Apr.6; 30) *Frich.* £100

CHOMEL, Noël
- Dictionnaire Oeconomique, contenant divers Moyens d'augmenter son Bien et de conserver sa Santé. Commercy, 1741. 4th. Edn. 2 vols. & 2 vols. supp. Fo. Old cf., 6 decor. spine raised bands. (LM. Jun.13; 49) B.Frs. 18,000
- Huishoudelyk Woordboek. Trans.:– J.L. Schuer & A.H. Wester. Leyden/Amst., 1743. 1st. Dutch translation. 2 vols. 4to. Cont. hf. roan. (VG. Nov.18; 1123) Fls. 550

CHOMPRET, Dr. J.
- Répertoire de la Majolique Italienne. Paris, 1949. 2 vols. 4to. Publisher's bds. (HD. Feb.27; 103) Frs. 3,300

CHOPPIN, Capt. Henri
- La Cavalerie Française. Paris, 1893. 1st. Edn. Three-qtr. mor., spine gt. with lge. fleurons. (SG. Feb.26; 84) $160

CHORIER, Nicolas
- Aloisiae Sigeae Toletanae Satyra Sotadica. De Arcanis Amoris et Veneris. Amst., n.d. 2nd. Edn. 3 pts. in 1 vol. 16mo. Early 18th. C. mor., decor. spine, inside dentelle, cipher of Louis-César de Cremeaux repeated on spine. Bkplts. of Talleyrand & Furstenburg. (HD. Mar.18; 42) Frs. 1,600
- Le Meursius François, ou Entretiens galans d'Aloisia. Ill.:– Borel, engraved by Elluin. Cythère [Paris], 1782. 1st. Printing. 2 vols. 16mo. Foxed. Cont. grained cf., spines decor. (HD. Apr.10; 327) Frs. 2,600

CHORON, A.
- Principes de Composition des Ecoles d'Italie. Paris, [1808]. 1st. Edn. 3 vols. Fo. Slightly soiled thro.-out. Cont. hf. leath., spine slightly defect. (H. Dec.9/10; 1094) DM 500

CHOULANT, Ludwig
- Geschichte und Bibliographie der Anatomischen Abbildung ... Leipzig, 1852. 1st. Edn. 4to. Foxed. Gt. cl., ex liby. (SG. Sep.18; 81) $120

CHRISTIAN, Friedrich Albrecht
- Der Juden-Glaube und Aberglaube. Ed.:– D.J.C. Wagenseil. Leipzig, 1705. 1st. Edn. Slight discolouration. Vell. (S. Nov.18; 650) *Gimesh.* £350
- - Anr. Copy. 12mo. Some worming. Orig. wraps. (S. Nov.18; 651) *Gimesh.* £190

CHRISTISON, Sir Robert
- A Treatise on Poisons. Edinb., 1829. 1st. Edn. Slight spotting, owner's inscr. on title. Orig. bds., worn, unc., bkplt. of William Ellis Wall. From liby. of Dr. E. Ashworth Underwood. (S. Feb.23; 178) *Jenner.* £80

CHRISTL. vnd Cathol. Gegen Berichtung, eyns Erwirdigen Dhomcapittels zu Cöllen, wider d. Buch gnanter Reformation ...
Cologne, 1544. Fo. Cont. limp vell., browned, spine torn. (HK. Nov.18-21; 221) DM 900

CHRISTMAS with the Poets
Ill.:– Birket Foster. L., 1862. 4th. Edn. Tall 8vo. Orig. crimson mor., gt.-lettered title & floral

CHRISTMAS with the Poets -contd.
sprays enclosing countersunk device in gold & red. (SG. Mar.19; 198) $160

CHRISTOPHE
- **La Famille Fenouillard.** [1895]. Ob. 4to. Publisher's decor. buckram. (HD. Jun.24; 200) Frs. 1,800

CHRISTYN, Jean Baptiste
- **Brabandts Recht ... Limborgh ... Mechelen.** Antw., 1682. 2 vols. Fo. Old cf., 6 decor. spine raised bands, worn. (LM. Nov.8; 162) B.Frs. 13,000
[-] **Histoire Générale des Pais-Bas.** Brussels, 1743. 4 vols. Later mott. cf. gt., gt. monog. of Earl of Rosebery on covers. (SBA. Jul.23; 466) Fairburn. £520

CHRISTYN, Jean Baptiste & Foppens
- **Les Délices des Pays-Bas.** Liège, 1769. 6th. Edn. 5 vols. 12mo. Cont. cf.-bkd. bds. (SG. Oct.30; 87) $325
- - **Anr. Edn.** Paris & Antw., 1786, 1785. Vols. 1, 3-4 (of ?5). Cont. bds., spines defect., unc. W.a.f. (VG. Nov.18; 124) Fls. 550

CHRONICLES of England
L., William de Machlinia, ca. 1486. Fo. 125 ll. only (of 238), comprising C2-8, D2-8, E-M8, N1 & 2, O3-8, Q2-7, R1-3, R6-8, S1-3, S5-8, X8, Y1-7, & 4 ll. of sig. Z, also 22 defect. ll. or fragments, the incompl. or fragmentary ll. margined to size. Mor., spine gt.-lettered. W.a.f. The copy of Henry Percy & Boies Penrose, lately in the collection of Eric Sexton. [Goff C480, HC 4999] (CNY. Apr.8; 81) $5,200

CHRONICON MANNIAE, or a Chronicle of the Kings of Man ... Supposed to be written by the Monks of the Abbey of Russin
Perth, 1784. Foolscap 8vo. in 4's. Cont. cf. (PD. Feb.18; 133) £50

CHRONIK DER ZEIT, Illustrirte
Stuttgart, 1872-1900. 5 vols. Lge. 4to. Slightly browned in parts. Cont. hf. linen, worn. W.a.f. (HK. Nov.18-21; 1533) DM 850

CHRONIQUE SCANDALEUSE, ou Histoire des Estrange Faicts arriuez soubs le Regne de Louys XI
[Paris], 1620. 4to. Lr. margins wormed. Cont. cf. (CSK. Jan.30; 99) £50

CHRYSOSTUM, Bp. Saint John
- **De Providentia Dei; De Dignitate Humanae Originis.** Alost, Thierry Martens, Mar. 22, 1487/88. 1st. Edn. 4to. Spaces for initial capitals, unrubricated, 2 clean tears across fo. 37 reprd. without loss, occasional light dampstaining to some ll., erased liby. stp. on 1st. p. Later ptd. vell. bds. From the collection of Eric Sexton. [BMC IX, 127, Goff J293, HC 5053] (CNY. Apr.8; 4) $3,500
- **Homiliae super Matthaeum.** Trans.:— [Georgius Trapezuntius]. [Strassburg], [Johann Mentelin]. [not after 1466]. 1st. Edn. Fo. Spaces for initial capitals, supplied in red & blue, 7-line capital L at fo. lr. illuminated in red, green & gold with foliage sprays extending into upr. margin (a portion of the illumination at fore-margin added later in unif. style), lr. & fore-margins of fo. 1 renewed with loss of some letters of text, inner margin renewed at fo. 13, 3 other ll. with portions of margins renewed, portion of inner margin of fo. 239 reinforced, 8 other ll. with sm. repairs, light dampstaining at end, light worming at front & back, catching some text, inscr. at fo. 2 recto. Mott. cf. gt., heavily rubbed & scuffed. From the collection of Eric Sexton. [BMC I, 51, Goff J288, HC 5034*] (CNY. Apr.8; 160) $7,500
- **The Homilies.** Oxford, 1840-77. 15 vols. Cont. cf. (SH. May 28; 59) Wade Gallery. £50
- **Sermo Super Psalmum L: Miserere mei Deus.** -**De Reparatione Lapsi.** [Cologne], [Ulrich Zel], ca. 1486; [1467-72]. 2 works in 1 vol. 4to. Both works with spaces for capitals, two 4-line capitals at folios 1r & 15r blue penwork decor., other capitals in 1st. work in red or blue, & initial strokes in yellow, scattered light foxing, mostly marginal. Recent cf., cover with gt. arms, orig. gt. spine preserved. From the collection of Eric Sexton. [Goff J298 & J294, HC 5031* & 5051] (CNY. Apr.8; 45) $6,500
- [**Tou en Agiois Patros Emon ... Archiepiskopou Konstantinoupoleos, apanta ta Ipiskomena**]. Antwerp, 1723. 12 vols. in 6. Fo. Orig. vell., spine soiled. (CB. Apr.1; 238) Can. $200

- **Works.** Eton, 1612-13. 8 vols. Fo. Some ll. slightly browned or spotted, lacks some blanks (?). Cont. spr. cf., worn. [STC 14629] (SBA. Oct.22; 280) Crete. £60

CHUBB, Charles
- **The Birds of British Guiana.** L., 1916-21. 2 vols. Title-p. to vol. 1 slightly foxed. Hf. leath., orig. wraps. bnd. at end of each vol. (CB. Sep.24; 20) Can. $350

CHUBB, Ralph
- **Songs Pastoral & Paradisal.** Ill.:— Vincent Stuart. Tintern Pr., 1935. (100) sigd. 4to. Orig. hf. mor., unc. Inscr. by artist. (SH. Feb.20; 262) Zinn. £150

CHURCH, Thomas
See-MORTON, Nathaniel-CHURCH, Thomas

CHURCH Windows: A Series of Designs
Ed.:— Sebastian Evans. Near Bg'ham, 1872. Fo. Orig. mor., gt., disbnd. (CSK. Oct.10; 121) £150

CHURCHILL, Awnsham & John
- **A Collection of Voyages & Travels.** 1704. 1st. Edn. 4 vols. Fo. A few plts. torn or soiled, slight browning & staining, hole in B1 vol. I, B3-4 soiled in vol. III. Cont. panel. cf., very worn. [Sabin 13015] (S. Apr.6; 175) Maggs. £360
- - **Anr. Edn.** L., 1732. 2nd. Edn. 6 vols. Fo. Cont. panel. cf., rebkd., spines gt. (CNY. May 22; 58) $700
- - **Anr. Edn.** 1732. [Vol. 5] Barbot. Slight dampstaining to 1st. few pp. Old panel. cf., rebkd. (BS. Jun.11; 148) £50
[-] - **Anr. Edn.** L., 1732 & 1744-46. 2nd. Edn. (vols. 1 & 2), 3rd. Edn. (vols. 3-6). 6 vols. Title-p. extended in vols. 4 & 6 & with minor repairs in vol. 5, some ll. inlaid or remargined in various vols., paper browned in vols. 3-5, liby. stps. on plts. of vols. 3-6. Unif. recent buckram. (CB. Feb.18; 70a) Can. $700
- - **Anr. Edn.** 1745-46. Vols. 3, 4, & 6 only. Fo. Old cf. W.a.f. (P. Mar.12; 45) Waterloo. £100

CHURCHILL, C.
- **Prophecy of Famine; A Scots Pastoral.-A Monody on the Decease of H.R.H. ... Duke of Cumberland.-The Conference.-The Fleece.-The Soldier.** 1763; 1765; 1763; 1757; 1764, 4th. Edn.; 2nd. Edn.; 1st. Edn. (5th work). 6 pts. in 1 vol. 4to. Cont. hf. cf. (TA. Oct.16; 328) £125

CHURCHILL, Charles
- **Poems.** 1766. 3rd. Edn. 2 vols. Cont. Engl. red mor., gt., spines tooled in compartments, covers elab. decor. (S. Nov.24; 54a) Fletcher. £380

CHURCHILL, James Morss
- **A Treatise on Acupuncturation being a description of a Surgical Operation originally peculiar to the Japanese & Chinese.** [1821]. Errata slip, advt. lf. Orig. bds., spine worn, unc. (S. Jun.15; 171) Norman £90
See-STEPHENSON, John & Churchill, James Morss

CHURCHILL, William Algernon
- **Watermarks in Paper, in Holland, England, France, etc.** Amst., 1965. 4to. Orig. cl. (S. Oct.21; 492) Dawson. £120

CHURCHILL, Sir Winston Leonard Spencer
- **Arms & the Covenant.** [1938]. 1st. Edn. Orig. cl. Pres. copy. (CSK. Aug.22; 235) £50
- **Divi Britannici: being a Remark upon the Lives of all the Kings of this Isle, from ... 2855 (B.C.) unto ... 1660 (A.D.).** 1675. 1st. Edn. Fo. Slight browning & soiling, 1 or 2 sm. holes, slightly affecting text. Cont. cf., worn. Title with cont. sig. & bkplt. of Thomas Arundell, (4th.) Lord Arundell of Wardour. [Wing C4275] (S. Sep.29; 14) Mansell Davies. £90
- **First Journey.** Ill.:— after Churchill, Arnold von Bohlen, & others. L., 1964. (260) numbered. Cf., boxed. Sigd. (SG. Dec.18; 104) $350
- **Great Contemporaries.-While England Slept.** -**Blood, Sweat, & Tears.** N.Y., 1937-41. 1st. Amer. Edns. 3 works in 3 vols. Cl. (SG. Dec.18; 106) $100
- **A History of the English-Speaking Peoples.** [1956-58]. 1st. Edn. 4 vols. Orig. buckram, d.-w.'s. Pres. copies. (CSK. Aug.22; 232) £100
- **Liberalism & the Social Problem.** 1909. 1st. Edn. Orig. cl., worn. (SH. Dec.19; 443) Maggs. £60
- **Lord Randolph Churchill.** L., 1906. 1st. Edn. 2 vols. Minor foxing. Gt.-armorial cl., unopened. (PNY. Mar.26; 74) $110

- **Man Overboard** L., [1899]. Compl., from Harmsworth Monthly Pictorial Magazine (Vol. I, 1898-99, pp. 662-664). Three-qtr. leath. (SG. Dec.18; 87) $170
- **Marlborough & his Times** 1933-38. 1st. Edn. 4 vols. Orig. buckram gt., vols. 3 & 4 with d.-w.'s. With an A.L.s. from the author to Lord Justice Vaughan Williams thanking him for dealing with the Welsh Church Commission dtd. Jul. 27 [19]10. (SKC. May 19; 294) £80
- - **Anr. Edn.** 1933-38. 1st. Edn. (155) numbered, sigd. 4 vols. Orig. red mor. gt. (S. Jul.22; 48) Sotheran. £350
- - **Anr. Edn.** L., 1947. 2 vols. Cl. (SG. Dec.18; 100) $110
- **Mr. Broderick's Army.** 1903. 2nd. Edn. Cancelled stp. of National Unionist Association on verso of title & 1 other p., title soiled. Cl. (SH. Dec.19; 438) Fine Art Society. £650
- **My African Journey.** L., 1908. 1st. Edn. With 16 p. catalogue at end; slightly foxed. Orig. pict. cl. (SG. Dec.18; 93) $95
- **My Early Life.** [1930]. 1st. Edn., 2nd. Iss. cl. Pres. copy. (CSK. Aug.22; 234) £55
- **The People's Rights.** [1910]. 1st. Edn. Sm. holes in 1st. 30 pp. Orig. wraps., lacks foot of spine, slight tear, holes. (SKC. Jul.28; 2343) £60
- **The River War.** 1899. 1st. Edn. 2 vols. Orig. cl. gt. worn. (SH. Dec.19; 437) Stanley. £100
- - **Anr. Copy.** Orig. cl. (SH. Jun.25; 18) Hosains. £85
- - **Anr. Copy.** Orig. pict. cl., spines discold. (SG. Dec.18; 88) $250
- - **Anr. Edn.** 1900. 2nd. Imp. 2 vols. Cont. hf. cf. by Sotheran, spines gt. (CSK. Jan.16; 174) £55
- - **Anr. Edn.** Ed.:— F. Rhodes. L., 1902. New & Revised Edn. (VA. Aug.29; 41) R. 110
- **Savrola.** N.Y., 1900. 1st. Edn. 24 pp of advts. at end. Orig. cl., bkplt. (SG. Dec.18; 89) $550
- **Step by Step.** 1939. 1st. Edn. Orig. cl. (SH. Dec.19; 448) Stanley. £55
- **The Story of the Malakand Field Force.** 1898. 1st. Edn. Errata slip before p.1. Orig. cl., gt. (C. Feb.4; 316) Maggs. £180
- - **Anr. Edn.** 1901. Orig. cl. Sigd. (SKC. May 19; 291) £85
- **The Story of My Early Life.-Secret Session Speeches.-The Sinews of Peace.-Maxims & Reflections.** Ed.:— Charles Eade (2nd. work); Randolph S. Churchill (3rd. work); Coote & Batchelor (4th. work). Boston & N.Y., 1945-49. 1st. Amer. Edns. 4 works in 4 vols. Cl. (SG. Dec.18; 108) $100
- **Thoughts & Adventures.** 1932. 1st. Edn. Orig. cl. Sigd. (SH. Dec.19; 447) Sotheran. £95
- **The War Speeches.** 1951-52. Definitive Edn. Sigd. 3 vols. 4to. Orig. cl., d.-w.'s. Envelope containing T.L.s. by Lady Churchill, sigd. photograph of Churchill, funeral instructions, compliments slip from Earl Marshall. (SH. Dec.19; 451) Sawyer. £330
- - **Anr. Edn.** [1951-52]. 1st. Edn. 3 vols. Orig. buckram, d.-w.'s. Pres. copies. (CSK. Aug.22; 233) £140
- **The World Crisis.** 1923-29. All but vol. 2 1st. Edns. 5 vols. only. Orig. cl., slightly soiled. Vol. 1 pres. copy. (SKC. May 19; 293) £70
- - **Anr. Edn.** N.Y., 1923-32. Orig. Amer. Edns. Vols. I, II, IV, & V. Cl. (SG. Dec.18; 94). $100

CHURRERIUS, Caspar
See-HUTTICH, Johannes-CHURRERIUS, Caspar

CHURTON, E.
See-RICHARDSON, William & Churton, E.

CIACONNO, Alphonso
- **Vitae, et Res Gestae Pontificum Romanorum et S.R.E. Cardinalium.** Rome, 1677. 4 vols. Fo. Sig. of Stephanus Baluzius Tutelensis on 1st. & last titles, bkplts. of abbé de Rothelin & Archibald Philip, Earl of Rosebery. Cont. red mor., triple gt. fillet, spines gt. in compartments, upr. cover worn. (SM. Oct.7; 1643) Frs. 6,000

CIBBER, Colley
- **An Apology for the Life of.** Priv. ptd., 1740. [1st. Edn.?]. 4to. Extra-ill. with numerous engraved & mezzotint ports., etc. Old russ. gt., brkn. (BS. Jun.11; 236) £90
- - **Anr. Copy.** Slight browning. Cont. cf., gt., rebkd. preserving orig. spine. (S. Jun.23; 401) Armstrong. £80
- **Love's Last Shift.** 1696. 1st. Edn. 4to. Foxing towards end. Recent mor.-bkd. bds. [Wing C4281] (C. Nov.19; 61) Pickering & Chatto. £90

CIBBER, Colley–BURDETT, William–FARLEY, J.–ANON
– The Egotist; or, Colley upon Cibber.–Life & Exploits of Three-Finger'd Jack, the Terror of Jamaica.–The Corsair; or the History of Tomar, the Pirate of Tunis.–Memoirs of the Bedford Coffee-House by a Genius. Sommers Town (2nd. & 3rd. works), 1743; 1801; 1801; 1763. 2nd. Edn. (last work). 4 works in 1 vol. Spotted or soiled in places, some ll. slightly defect. in margin, added description of the Ballet incompl. at end of 3rd work. 19th. C. hf. cf., worn, covers detchd. (S. Apr.7; 268) *Maggs.* £130

CICERI, Eugène
– Les Pyrenées. N.d. Ob. Cl. gt., marked. (CE. Feb.19; 191) £180

CICERO, Marcus Tullius
– Ad M. Fillium de Officiis, Libri Tres. Paris, 1562. 4to. Mor., sides & spine diapered with gt. fleurs-de-lys, gt. arms of Bouthillier de Chavigny, Bp. of Troyes in centre of both covers. (SG. Sep.25; 43) $380
– Büchlein vo dem Alter. Ed.:– Ulrich von Hutten. Trans.:– J. Neuber. Ill.:– Petrarcameister. Augsburg, 1522. 1st. Edn. Wormed, especially last lf., sm. browning at end. Bds. ca. 1800. W.a.f. (HK. Nov.18-21; 144) DM 5,500
– Cato Major. Phila., Benjamin Franklin, 1744. 1st. Edn., 1st. Iss. Liby. stps. Sheep-bkd. bds., corners & spine reprd., upr. cover detchd. [Sabin 13040] (SPB. Jun.22; 62) $1,300
– – Anr. Edn. Phila., 1744. 1st. Edn. Cont. panel. cf. (CSK. Mar.20; 93) *Quaritch.* £1,100
– – Anr. Edn. Ed.:– Benjamin Franklin. L., 1778. 1st. Engl. Edn. Old cf., rebkd. MS. ex-libris of George Griffith, 1782. (SG. Sep.25; 143) $120
– – Anr. Copy. Some ll. chewed at margins, some foxing. Later hf. leath., worn. (SG. Feb.5; 91) $100
– De Amicitia, sive Laelius de Amicitia [with other texts]. [Cologne], [Ulrich Zel], ca. 1467. 4to. Space for initial capital at p. 1, supplied in red, unrubricated, lacks final blank, minor foxing to some margins. Cf.-bkd. paper bds., gt. spine. From the collection of Eric Sexton. [Goff C559, H. 5302] (CNY. Apr.8; 42) $10,500
– De Officiis Amicitia & Senectute. Paradoxa eiusdem. Venice, 20 Feb. 1506. Fo. Lacks last blank lf., a few wormholes, some slightly affecting text, some ll. slightly spotted. Mod. antique-style cf. (S. Oct.21; 315) *Forsyth.* £170
– De Oratore. Rome, Ulrich Hans [Udalricus Gallus], Dec. 5, 1468. 2nd. Edn. Fo. 4 illuminated capital initials, lacks final blank, some ll. misbnd., extensively restored as a result of damp, several margins partly renewed with intermittent text loss, particularly at upr. portions from fo. 18 to end (final lf. severely defect.), the loss supplied in facs. Recent vell. W.a.f. From the collection of Eric Sexton. [BMC IV, 18, Goff 0655, HC 5099] (CNY. Apr.8; 141) $4,800
– De Deutsch Cicero. Trans.:– J. von Schwartzenburg. Ill.:– Schäuffelein, Burgkmaier, Weiditz after Dürer, Petrarcameister & others. Augsburg, 1540. Fo. Some sigs. slightly browned or stained in margin. Old cont. style leath., 4 bands, decor., sm. blind-tooled stp. (D. Dec.11-13; 16) DM 6,500
– Epistolae ad Atticum. Venice, 1544. Lacks colophon lf., slight browning. 18th. C. parch. bds., soiled. (S. Oct.1; 536) £85
– – Anr. Edn. Ed.:– P. Manutius. Venice, 1554 [1555]. Ruled thro.-out in red, some headlines & p. numbers trimmed or slightly cropped, occasional light soiling & browning. 19th. C. hf. mor., gt. (S. Feb.10; 250) *Ponder.* £60
– Gerpürlicher Werck. Ill.:– H. Weiditz. Augsburg, 1540. Sm. fo. Title badly defect. Hf. cf., worn. W.a.f. (BS. Jun.11; 101) £220
– In orationem . . . pro P. Sextio Commentarius. Ed.:– P. Manutius. Venice, 1559. Vell. (P. Dec.11; 116) *Balbi.* £60
– Opera. Leiden, 1642. 1st. Elzevir Edn. 10 vols. 12mo. Mor. gt. by Walters, Newcastle. (S. Nov.25; 376) *Lemos.* £150
– Rhetorica Vetus et Nova [with the commentary of Victorinus]. Venice, Marinus Saracensus, 18 Sep. 1487. Fo. Spaces for initial capitals with guide letters, initial capitals supplied thro.-out in red & blue, most ll. browned & spotted, slight worming reprd. in lr. margin of a number of ll. Old cf., rebkd., worn. [BMC V, 414, Goff C651, HC 5079*] (CNY. Oct.1; 117) $900

– Sämmtl. Briefe. Ed.:– F.D. Gräter. Trans.:– C.M. Wieland. Zürich, 1808-21. 1st. Edn. trans. Wieland. 7 vols. Lightly soiled in parts. Cont. hf. leath. gt. (HK. May 15; 5021) DM 500
– Der Teütsch Cicero.–Officia. Trans.:– Johann von Schwarsenberg. Ill.:– Schäufelein, Petrarcameister & others. J. von Schwarzenberg after Dürer (port). [Augsburg], 1534; 1 Oct. 1533. 1st. Edn. (1st. work). 2 works in 1 vol. Fo. Slightly browned, soiled in parts, vol. 1 title more heavily. Cont. vell., lacks 4 ties. (HK. Nov.18-21; 145) DM 11,000
– Those Five Questions . . . Manor of Tusculanum. Trans.:– John Dolman. 1561. 1st. Edn. in Engl. Cont. owner's inscr. & marginalia. Cont. Engl. cf., blindstpd. shield in centre covers, rebkd., spine worn. [STC 5317] (S. Mar.16; 120) *Thorp.* £160

CICERO, Marcus Tullius–GELLIUS, Aulus –VALERIUS Maximus
– Tres de Oratore ad Quintum Fratrem Libri. –Noctium Atticarum Libri XIX.–De Factis ac Dict. Memorabilib. Exemplorum Novem. Ed.:– Hans Franck. Leipzig; Basel; Leipzig, Apr. 1515; Sep. 1519; 1516. 3 works in 1 vol. Fo. Old MS. marginalia & notes. Cont. blind-stpd. pig-bkd. wood bds., clasps. brkn. (R. Oct.14-18; 38) DM 1,500

CICOGNARA, Leopoldo
– Storia della Scultura dal suo Risorgimento in Italia sino al secolo di Napoleone. Venice, 1813-18. 1st. Edn. 3 vols. Fo. Occasional slight spotting. Hf. roan, stained & worn, unc. (S. Apr.7; 369) *Weinreb.* £85

CICOGNINI, Jacopo
– In Lode Famoso Signor Galileo Galilei . . . Canzone. Flor., 1631. 4to. Disbnd. (C. Apr.1; 33) *Corby.* £700

CIEL BLEU (Le)
Ill.:– Robert Willems & others. Paris, 1945. Nos. 1-9, complete set. Fo. Loose as iss., folded, fitted case. (SH. Nov.21; 279) *Tate Gallery.* £60

CIEZA DE LEON, Pedro de
– La Prima Parte dell'Historie del Peru . . .–La Seconda Parte delle Historie dell'India. Venice, 1560; 1565. 2 works in 1 vol. 16mo. 1st. work with register lf. Later vell. (SG. Jun.11; 210) $190

CIEZA DE LEON, Pedro–LOPEZ DE GOMARA, Francesco
– Crónica del Gran Reyno del Perú.–Historia delle Nouve Indie Occidentali. Venice, 1560. 2 pts. in 1 vol. Cont. limp vell., soiled. [Sabin 13050] (SPB. May 5; 153) $300

CIGRAND, B.J.
– The Rise, Fall & Revival of Dental Prosthesis. Chic., 1892. 12mo. With advts. Disbnd. From Brooklyn Academy of Medicine. (SG. Jan.29; 127) $140

CILLE, F. & Rockstuhl, A.
– Musée de Tzarskoe-Selo ou Collection d'Armes de Sa Majesté l'Empereur de toutes les Russies. St. Petersb. & Carlsruhe, 1835-53. 3 vols. Fo. Lacks plts. but with 12 additional plts., some ptd. on India paper, some 2nd. states. Loose as Iss., orig. folders, lacks spines, covers detchd. (S. Jan.27; 490) *Nagel.* £90

CIM, Albert
– Amateurs et Voleurs de Livres . . . Paris, 1903. 1st. Edn. 12mo. Hf. mor. by David, corners, raised bands on spine, wrap. & spine preserved. Many autograph letters by author & publisher, publisher's copy. (HD. Jun.24; 170) *Frs.* 1,500

CIMARELLI, Vincenco Maria
– Risolutioni Filosofiche . . . Tratta da piu Occulti Secreti della Natura . . . Preposteli nel Viaggio, ch'ei fece per l'Italia, Grecia, Sicilia e Malta. Ed.:– Silvio Cimarelli. Brescia, 1655. 2 pts. in 1 vol. 4to. Cont. cf. (S. Dec.1; 104) *Quaritch.* £75

CIMAROSA, D.
– Il Matrimonio Segreto. Paris, ca. 1801. 1st. Edn. with Italian & Fr. text. Fo. Slightly browned. Cont. vell. (H. Dec.9/10; 1095) DM 600

CIMPINI, Joannis
– Vetera Monumenta. Rome, 1690-99. 2 vols. Fo. Some plts. browned. Cont. vell., soiled, bkplt. of 'Marchionis Salsae'. (CSK. Jan.9; 190) £150

CINCINNATI
– The Cincinnati Directory . . .; [Cinc.], Oct. 1819. 1st. Edn. 12mo. Foxed & soiled., owner's notation

on front free endpaper & blank. Cont. cf., worn, lr. cover loose, boxed. From liby. of William E. Wilson. (SPB. Apr.29; 53) $450

CINDERELLA
– Cinderella. L., 1814. Square 16mo. With the 8 hand-cold. cut-outs loosely laid in, also with a folding view of the carriage, heavily foxed thro.-out. Ptd. wraps. (SG. Apr.30; 88) $400
– La Petite Cendrillon. Ill.:– F. Janet. Paris, [1810]. 48mo. Bds., s.-c. (SG. Oct.9; 189) $400

CINGRIA, Charles Albert
– Les Limbes. Ill.:– Jean Lurçat. Paris, 1930. (10) on Japanese paper, numbered, sigd. by author & artist. Orig. wraps. (SH. Nov.21; 399) *Faure.* £130

CIPPICO, Coriolano
See–INGRESSO del Procuratore di San Marco Antonio Cappello

CIPRIANI, Giovanni B.
– Rudiments of Drawings. Ill.:– Francesco Bartolozzi. 1796. Ob. fo. 1st. few ll. slightly stained. Cont. wraps., stained. (CSK. Sep.5; 193) £90

CISTERNAY DU FAY, Charles Jeróme de
– Bibliotheca Fayana, seu Catalogus Librorum Bibliothecae. Paris, 1725. 2 folded ll. of 'Ordre des Vacations', priced in MS. thro.-out., many notes including buyer's names, note on fly-lf. in Heber's hand. Cont. cf., upr.-cover detchd., bkplt. of Bibliotheca Lindesiana. (SM. Oct.7; 1345) *Frs.* 1,800

CIVIALE, Jean
– De la Lithotritie, ou Broiement de la Pierre dans la Vessie. Paris, 1827. 1st. Edn. Some spotting, 1 plt. detchd. Orig. bds., slightly worn, unc. From liby. of E. Ashworth Underwood. (S. Feb.23; 179) *Rota.* £50
– Lettre sur la Lithotritie Uretrale . . . Paris, 1831. 1st. Edn. Ptd. wraps., unc. (SG. Sep.18; 83) $120

CIVIL ARTICLES (The) of Lymerick –MILITARY ARTICLES (The) of Lymerick
Dublin, 1692. 2 works in 1 vol. 4to. Disbnd. [Wing C4363; Wing M2050] (GM. Apr.30; 340) £100

CIVIL WAR
– Atlas to Accompany The Official Records of the Union & Confederate Armies. N.d. Vol. II only. Atlas fo. Disbnd. (SG. May 21; 26) $160

CIVILOGIE PORTATIVE (La) ou Le Manuel des Citoyens
Ill.:– Dorgez. Paris, [1792]. Sm. 32mo. Foxed. Cont. red. mor., covers gt. decor. fleurons. (HD. Apr.8; 88) *Frs.* 1,610

CLAIRAUT, Alexis Claude
– Théorie de la Lune, déduite du Seul Principe de l'Attraction. Paris, 1765. 2nd. Edn. 4to. Prize bdg. of 19th. C. cf., gt. & blind-tooled borders, ornamental stp. of Academie de Paris Prix du Concours Général on covers, by Bradel, with his ticket. (S. Jun.29; 325) *Porton.* £80

CLANCY, P.A.
– The Birds of Natal & Zululand. L., 1964. 4to. Cl., d.-w. (SSA. Jun.18; 81) R. 90
– – Anr. Edn. Edinb., 1964. 4to. Cl., d.-w. Pres. Copy. SSA. Nov.5; 124) R. 130

CLANRICARDE, Ulick Bourke, Marquis of
See–BOURKE, Ulicke, Marquis of Clanricarde

CLANVOWE, Sir Thomas
[–] The Floure & the Leafe. Ed.:– F.S. Ellis. Kelms. Pr., 1896. (300). 4to. Orig. holland-bkd. bds., unc. (SH. Feb.19; 10) *Quaritch.* £130

CLAPPERTON, Capt. Hugh
See–DENHAM, Maj. Dixon & Clapperton, Capt. Hugh

CLARE, John
– Village Minstrel & other Poems. 1821. 1st. Edn. 2 vols. in 1. 12mo. Frontis., hf.-title of 'The Shepherd's Calendar' sigd. by author (1849). Orig. cl. gt., remainder bdg.?, spine worn. Account sigd. by John Labram tipped in, sigd. by Labram on verso of frontis. (SH. Apr.9; 208) *Bayley.* £120

CLARENDON, Edward Hyde, Earl of
– Histoire de la Rebellion et des Guerres Civiles d'Angleterre. The Hague, 1709. 6 vols. 12mo. Early inscr. of bookseller in vol. 1, armorial bkplt. of Marquis de Coislin, some trimming. 18th. C. mor., gt., arms of Madame Sophie de France,

CLARENDON, Edward Hyde, Earl of – Histoire de la Rebellion et des Guerres Civiles d'Angleterre. -contd.
triple gt. fillet, spine gt. in compartments, inner gt. dentelles. (SM. Oct.7; 1645) Frs. 10,000
– The History of the Rebellion & Civil Wars in England. 1702-04. 1st. Edn. 3 vols. Fo. Cont. panel. cf., some covers detchd. (TA. Jun.18; 452) £55
– – Anr. Edn. [1707-59]. 4 vols. in 8. Fo. Extra-ill. with ca. 550 engraved portraits & views, 19th. C. ptd. titles, occasional interleaving with blanks. 19th. C. russ., gt. & blind borders on sides, gt. spines, jnts. brkn. W.a.f. (C. Feb.25; 27) *Potter.* £340
– – Anr. Edn. Oxford, 1826. 8 vols. Elab. mor. gt. by Mackenzie, arms in medallions on all covers of Sir W. Heathcote., end-papers foxed. Prize copy to Sir William Heathcote from Winchester College (7 Dec. 1832) (LC. Oct. 2; 304) £65
– The History of the Rebellion & Civil Wars in England.–Life of ... 1704; 1759. 1st. Edns. 3 vols.; 1 vol. Fo. 2nd. work, title browned. Unif. orig. diced cf. gt. (TA. Mar.19; 324) £210

CLARK, Bracy
– A Series of Original Experiments on the Foot of the Living Horse. Ill.:– Milton & Sydenham Edwards. L., Priv. ptd., 1809. 1st. Edn. 4to. Cont. bds., crudely rebkd., unc. (SG. Aug.7; 293) $100

CLARK, Daniel
– Proofs of the Corruption of Gen. James Wilkinson, & of His Connexion with Aaron Burr ... Phila., 1809. 1st. Edn. Foxed & discold., ink stain on title. Later wraps. From liby. of William E. Wilson. (SPB. Apr.29; 54) $600
– – Anr. Copy. Memorial notice of J. Watts de Peyster pasted to first blank. Orig. bds., rebkd. with mod. cl., worn, partly unopened, lacks free end-papers. [Sabin 13265] (SPB. Jun.22; 25) $250

CLARK, Daniel Kinnear & Colburn, Zerah
– Railway Machinery. 1855. 2 vols. 4to. Hf. mor., worn. (P. Apr.9; 236) £60
– – Anr. Edn. 1860-62. 3 vols. including supp. Fo. Vol. III dampstained. Cont. hf. mor. (SH. Jan.30; 419) *Walford.* £80

CLARK, D.W.
– Home Views of the Picturesque & Beautiful. Ill.:– Wellstood, Smillie, F.E. Jones & others. Cinc., [1863]. 4to. Orig. mor., emb. & with gt.-tooled ornaments. (SG. Oct.30; 88) $160

CLARK, Edwin
– The Britannia & Conway Tubular Bridges. Ed.:– Robert Stephenson. Ill.:– George Hawkins. Priv. ptd., 1850. 3 vols. including fo. vol. of plts. 8vo. & fo. Vol. 1 with errata slip, vol. 2: most plts. with slight stain in margin, owner's stp. on front free end-paper. Cl. & mor.-bkd. cl. (C. Feb.4; 167) *Ilford.* £280
– – Anr. Edn. N.d. 3 vols. including atlas of plts. 8vo. & fo. Spotted, loose. Orig. cl., text vol. rebkd., plt. vol. worn. (SH. Jun.18; 101) *Weinreb.* £390

CLARK, F. Ambrose
– The Collection of Sporting Paintings. N.Y., Priv. Ptd., 1958. 1st. Edn. (250). Lge. tall 4to. Orig. gt.-panel. mor., boxed (lacks tail panel). (PNY. May 21; 388) $150

CLARK, Hugh
– A Concise History of Knighthood. 1784. 1st. Edn. 2 vols. Cont. red mor. gt. (S. Nov.24; 60) *Traylen.* £65

CLARK, J.
– The Amateur's Assistant. 1826. 1st. Edn. 4to. Lacks 1 advt. lf. Mod. bds. (SH. Jun.11; 67) *Sims & Reed.* £80

CLARK, J.H.
– A Practical Illustration of Gilpin's Day ... with Instructions in ... the Improved Method of Colouring. 1824. 1st. Edn., 2nd. iss. Fo. Cont. cf.-bkd. bds., worn, covers detchd. (S. Apr.7; 457) *Sims & Reed.* £350

CLARK, John
[–] The Panorama of the Thames from London to Richmond. Ca. 1824. 1 vol. without the text vol. Ob. 4to. Containing a general view & 2 folding cold. aquatint panoramas. Fixed in orig. cl. portfo. with ties, orig. ptd. paper label on upr. cover, spine reprd. W.a.f. From the collection of Eric Sexton. (C. Apr.16; 231) *Burgess.* £480

– A Series of Practical Instructions in Landscape Painting in Watercolours. 1827. In 4 orig. pts. 4to. 55 aquatint plts. (only, of 56, lacks plt. 2), most cold. Text bnd. in orig. paper wraps., plts. loose & contained with text in orig. hf. roan portfo. (lacks ties, head & foot of spine torn) with view pasted in upr. cover. W.a.f. From the collection of Eric Sexton. (C. Apr.15; 65) *Henderson.* £450

CLARK, Larry
– Tulsa. N.Y., [1971]. 1st. Edn. 4to. Stiff pict. wraps. (SG. Apr.23; 60) $325

CLARK, R. & R.
– Golf: A Royal & Ancient Game. 1875. No bdg. stated. (CSK. Jul.20; 103) £170

CLARK, Roland
– Gunner's Dawn. 1937. (950) numbered. 4to. Leatherette, glassine wrap. With orig. sigd. etching. (SG. Dec.11; 226) $700
– – Anr. Edn. N.Y., Derry. Pr., 1937. De Luxe Edn., (50) numbered. 4to. Hf. mor. gt., partly unc., publisher's box. With a sigd. hand-cold. etching by author & his sig. on hf.-title. (CNY. Oct.1; 167) $4,500
– Roland Clark's Etchings. N.Y., Derry Pr., [1938]. De Luxe Edn., (50) numbered with an orig. sigd. etching. Fo. Hf. mor. gt., publisher's box. (CNY. Oct.1; 169) $5,200

CLARK, Samuel
[–] Reuben Rambles in the Eastern Counties.-... in the Southern Counties of England. [1845]. 2 booklets. 4to. Orig. semi-stiff ptd. wraps., inside covers forming integral pts. of the booklets. spines strengthened with cl. (TW. Sep.19; 162) £150

CLARK, Capt. William
– Ten Views in the Island of Antigua. L., 1823. 1st. Edn. Ob. fo. Offsetting, slight soiling. Orig. ptd. wraps., sewn, spotted, spine worn. (SPB. May 5; 154) $17,000
See–LEWIS, Capt. Meriwether & Clark, Capt. William

CLARKE, Edward Daniel
– Travels in Various Countries of Europe, Asia & Africa. 1810-23. 6 vols. 4to. Cont. marb. cf. (CSK. May 1; 104) £150
– – Anr. Edn. 1816-24. 4th. Edn. 11 vols. Hf. cf., worn. (PD. Feb.18; 168) £80

CLARKE, Rev. J.S. & McArthur, John
– The Life of Admiral Lord Nelson. 1809. 2 vols. 4to. Cont. cf., jnts. worn. (CSK. May 1; 167) £65

CLARKE, John
– A Demonstration of some of the Principal Sections of Sir Isaac Newton's Principles of Natural Philosophy. 1730. 1st. Edn. Cont. Engl. red mor. gt., spine tooled in compartments, covers elab. decor. (S. Nov.24; 61) *Quaritch.* £140

CLARKE, Joseph Clayton 'Kyd'
– Eleven Watercolour Drawings of Characters from Dickens. Wtrmkd. 1886. 4to. Mntd. in folder. (SH. Apr.10; 624) *Drummond.* £200
– A Series of Fifty-Five Original Designs for a Pickwick Pack of Playing Cards. [L.], ca. 1920. 56 orig. drawings in pen & ink & cols. Loose in silk-lined mor. gt. book-box. Purchased from Charles J. Sawyer Ltd., with their typed leaflet & A.L.s. from Clarke to Sawyer (May 18, 1931); from the Prescott Collection. (CNY. Feb.6; 88) $2,200
– Series of 72 Original Studies Illustrating Pickwick Papers. Ca. 1900. Pts. I & II. 4to. Each watercol. sigd., MS. title-pp. Loose in 2 cl. s.-c.'s. (SG. Mar.19; 84) $550

CLARKE, McDonald
– The Gossip, or a Laugh with the Ladies, a Grin at the Gentlemen, & Burlesques on Byron ... No. One. N.Y., Oct. 22, 1823. 1st. Edn. 18mo. Title heavily liby.-stpd., foxed. Later three-qtr. linen. (SG. Mar.5; 133) $100

CLARKSON, Thomas
– An Essay on the Impolicy of the African Slave Trade.–An Essay on the Comparative Efficiency of Regulation or Abolition, as Applied to the Slave Trade. L., 1788; 1789. 1st. Edns. 2 pts. in 1 vol.; 1 vol., together 2 vols. Some browning. Unif. mor.-bkd. cl. [Sabin 13480; 13478] (SPB. May 5; 155) $225
[–] Essay on the Slavery & Commerce of the Human Species, particularly the African, translated from a Latin Disertation. 1786. 1st. Edn. in Engl. Slightly spotted, title mntd. Cont.

cf., rebkd. [Sabin 13483] (S. Nov.4; 631) *Rota.* £80
– History of the rise, progress & accomplishment of the abolition of the African Slave Trade by the British Parliament. 1808. 1st. Edn. 2 vols. Some spotting & foxing. Cont. tree cf., rebkd. with orig. spines preserved, Lord Belper's bkplt. (S. Nov.4; 628) *Howell-Williams.* £140
– – Anr. Copy. Orig. bds., unc. (BS. Nov.26; 144) £110
– – Anr. Copy. Folding map slightly torn, a few ll. spotted. 19th. C. cl., upr. jnts. torn. (SBA. Jul.14; 111) *Awes.* £75
– – Anr. Edn. 1809. 1st. Edn. 2 vols. 1 plt. torn & mntd. on linen, other with sm. tear in fold. Recent qtr. cf. [Sabin 13486] (S. Dec.8; 271) *Scott.* £65

CLASSICAL LETTERS, OR ALPHABET OF MEMORY, intended for the Instruction of Young Gentlemen
1817. 16mo. Slight offsetting from plts. onto text, advts. Mod. wraps. (SH. Mar.19; 57) *Rota.* £75

CLAUDE le Lorraine
– Liber Studiorum. Ill.:– F.C. Lewis. L., 1840. 1st. Edn. 4 pts. in 1 vol. Lge. fo. Content loose in bdg. Bdg. not stated. W.a.f. (PNY. May 21; 253) $300
– Liber Veritatis. Ill.:– Richard Earlom. L., 1777-1819. 3 vols. Fo. Old russ. gt., most covers detchd, worn. The William Beckford copy, his sig. in vols 1 & 2. (SPB. Oct.1; 221) $6,750
– – Anr. Edn. Rome, 1815. Vol. 1 (of 3). Fo. 50 engraved plts. only, upr. margins slightly dampstained. Cont. hf. mor., worn, upr. cover detchd. W.a.f. (SBA. Mar.4; 247) *Kent Neilson.* £340

CLAUDEL, Paul
– Connaissance de l'Est. Paris, 1900. Orig. Ltd. Edn. on Alfa Vergé. 12mo. Bordeaux mor., unc., wrap., by Moscovitz. A.L.s. & dtd. 12 Mar. 1891, 3pp. (HD. Jun.10; 135) Frs. 1,600
– Livre de Christophe Colomb. Ill.:– Decaris. Paris, 1956. (275); (19) on mother-of-pearl Jap. with 2 separate sets of ills., 1 orig. drawing & 1 copper-engr. 4to. In sheets, publisher's s.-c. (HD. Dec.5; 44) Frs. 1,400

CLAUDIANUS, Claudius
– Opera. Ed.:– Thaddaeus Ugoletus. Venice, May 23, 1500. Sm. hole in title, some worming. Old decor. wraps. Richard Heber liby. stp. [BMC V, 473] (C. Jul.16; 254) *Rodgers.* £150

CLAVIGERO, Francisco Saverio
– Historia Antigua de Megico. L., 1826. 2 vols. Offsetting from engraved plts., advt. lf. Orig. hf. roan. [Sabin 13520] (SPB. May 5; 156) $950
– The History of Mexico, collected from Spanish & Mexican Historians ... Trans.:– Charles Cullen. L., 1787. 1st. Edn. in Engl. 2 vols. 4to. Cont. mott. cf., jnts. reprd. (SG. Jan.8; 96) $425

CLAVIUS, Chris
See–EUCLID–CLAVIUS, Chris

CLAVIUS, Chris.–THEODOSIUS TRIPOLITA –CASTELLANU S, L.
– Horologiorvm; Tabvla Altitvdinvm Solio pro Horis Astronomicis.–Sphaericorvm, Libri tres. –Responsio ad Expostvlationem F. Vietae adversus C. Clavius. Trans.:– I. Penam. (3rd. work). Rome; Rome; Paris; Rome, 1599; 1603; 1558; 1603. 1st. Edn. (1st. work) 1st Edn; 1st. Greek Edn.; 1st. Edn. 3 works in 1 vol. 4to. 1st. & 2nd. works old notes, all slightly stained. Cont. blind-stpd. pig-bkd. wood bds, 2 clasps, lacks lr. tie, slightly soiled, spine painted over. (HK. Nov.18-21; 146) DM 1,800

CLEAVER, Arthur
See–HATTON, Thomas & Cleaver, Arthur B.

CLELAND, John
– Memoirs of a Coxcomb. L., 1751. 1st. Edn. 12mo. Minor spotting & browning. Old cf., worn, rebkd. (SPB. Jul.28; 86) $175
– Woman of Pleasure, ou Fille de Joie.–Memoires de Mademoiselle Fanny Hill écrites par elle-même. Ill.:– Borel. L. [Paris], 1776. 2 vols. in 1. 16mo. Imitation old red mor., spine decor., 3 fillets, inner dentelle. (HD. Apr.10; 328) Frs. 8,500

CLEMENCEAU, Georges-Eugène-Benjamin
– Au Pied du Sinaï. Ill.:– H. de Toulouse-Lautrec. 1898. On vel. d'Arches. 4to. Sewed, wrap., spine unstuck. (HD. Jun.30; 14) Frs. 16,500

CLEMENS, Samuel Langhorne 'Mark Twain'
[-] **The Celebrated Jumping Frog of Calaveras County.** N.Y., 1867. 1st. Edn., 1st. Printing. 12mo. Orig. cl., with gt. frog in centre of upr. cover. (CNY. May 22; 60) $700
-- **Anr. Copy.** Some ll. dampstained, some foxing; together with a copy of the 2nd. printing. From the Prescott Collection. (CNY. Feb.6; 49) $450
-- **Anr. Copy.** 2 pp. of advts., no battered type, owners' sig. on title-p. Cl. over bevelled bds., covers soiled, spines & corners very worn. (SG. Nov.13; 693) $110
- **A Connecticut Yankee in King Arthur's Court.** N.Y., 1889. 1st. Edn. 1st. state with 'Sking' reading on p. 59. Gt.-pict. cl. (SG. Dec.18; 406) $150
-- **Anr. Edn.** N.Y., 1889. 1st. Edn. 4to. Later state of the plt. at p. [59], with p. [i] blank. Cont. sheep, partly unc., mostly unopened. Inlaid & bnd. in at front is a lf. (pp. 501-502) from anr. copy, with at the bottom of p. 502 the words 'Don't turn' in author's hand (beside the crossed-out words 'Go to'), p. 501 is a Dan Beard ill. on which he has written 'It was fun to make this.', sigd. pencil note by Merle Johnson on front end-paper; from the Prescott Collection. (CNY. Feb.6; 53) $3,000
[-] **A Connecticut Yankee in King Arthur's Court.** **-The American Claimant.** Ill.:- Dan Beard. N.Y., 1889; 1892. 1st. Edns. Together 2 vols. Orig. cl. Both inscr. by ill. (CNY. May 22; 67) $280
- **Huckleberry Finn.** N.Y., 1885. 1st. Amer. Edn. With 'was' on p. 57, uncorrected list of ills. Orig. cl. gt., mor.bkd. s.-c. (C. Feb.4; 314) *Basket & Day.* £160
-- **Anr. Copy.** Sq. 8vo. Frontis. in 1st. state, with the reading 'was' for 'saw' on p. 57, the 'him & another man' plt. listed at p. 88, lacks final 5 on fo. 155, title a cancel, p. 283 on a stub. Orig. pict. cl., qtr. mor. gt. s.-c. Pres. Copy, to H.M. Alexander, lately in the Prescott Collection. (CNY. Feb.6; 52) $3,000
-- **Anr. Copy.** 'Was' for 'saw' on p. 57, 'him & another man' ill. listed at p. 88, state 3 of fo. 155, title a cancel, frontis. in 1st. state, state 3 of p. 283. Orig. pict. cl. (CNY. May 22; 64) $300
-- **Anr. Copy.** Title & lf. (pp. 283-4) on stubs, 'was' for 'saw' p. 57), port. frontis. in 1st. state, later state of ills. at p. 283. Gt.-pict. cl. (PNY. Oct.1; 150) $225
-- **Anr. Copy.** Lf. (pp. 283-4) on stub, word 'was' for 'saw' on p. 57, line 23, final '5' on p. 155 from anr. font, & with mistake in list of ills, some foxing last lf. of text & rear blanks loose. Orig. gt.-pict. cl., loose in bdg., corners very worn. (PNY. Mar.26; 80) $150
- **The Innocents Abroad.** Hartford, 1869. 1st. Edn. 1st. iss., without p. references on last lf. of Table of Contents, & no ill. on p. 129. Orig. sheep, crudely rehinged, buckram folding case. (SG. Mar.19; 301) $280
[-] **Life on the Mississippi.** Boston, 1883. 1st. Amer. Edn. Hf. mor. (S. Jul.22; 55) *Zimmerman.* £60
[-] **Mark Twain's Sketches, New & Old.** Hartford & Chic., 1875. 1st. Edn., 1st. state. Orig. cl. (CNY. May 22; 61) $120
- **The Prince & the Pauper.** Montreal, 1881. 12mo. Wraps. (with imprint Toronto: Albert Britnell, Bookseller). (SG. Nov.13; 703) $3,000
-- **Anr. Edn.** Boston, 1882. 1st. Amer. Edn. Orig. cl., mixed bdg. states A & B. Pres. copy to Edmund C. Stedman. (CNY. May 22; 63) $1,600
-- **Anr. Copy.** 4to. Gt.-pict. cl. (SG. Mar.19; 303) $100
- **Punch, Brothers, Punch & other Sketches.** N.Y., [1878]. 1st. Edn., 1st. Iss. Pict. cl. (with ill. on rear paste-down end-paper). (SG. Nov.13; 701) $110
-- **Anr. Copy.** Gutter tear to 1st. few ll. Pict. wraps. (with ill. on lr. cover), hf. mor. s.-c. (SG. Nov.13; 700) $100
- **Roughing It.** Hartford, Conn., 1872. 1st. Edn. Later state of p. 242. Cl., very worn & dampstained. Inscr., w.a.f. (SG. Nov.13; 695) $350
- **Tom Sawyer.** Hartford, 1876. 1st. Amer. Edn. 1st. Printing (200). Sq. 8vo. 4 pp. of advts. at end. Orig. hf. mor. (publisher's de luxe bdg.), mor. folding case. Inscr. by Clara Clemens, to Mrs. Getz, on recto of frontis., lately in the Prescott Collection. (CNY. Feb.6; 51) $6,000
-- **Anr. Edn.** Hartford, Conn., 1876. 1st. Edn., 1st. Iss. Versos of hf.-title & preface blank. Crimson three-qtr. mor., spine gt. (SG. Nov.13; 698) $350

- **Tom Sawyer.-Huckleberry Finn.** Hartford; N.Y., 1876; 1885. 1st. American Edns. (1st is Blanck's 2nd Printing Iss. A. 2 vols. 4to. Slightly shaken, soiling, 2nd. title with title & p. 283 cancelled, p. 13 in 1st. state, p. 57 with misprint 'was' for 'saw', & frontis in Blanck's 2nd. state. Orig. decor. cl., s.-c.'s. (SPB. Nov.25; 175) $500
- **Tom Sawyer.-The Innocents Abroad.** Ill.:- T.H. Benton (1st. work); & F. Kredel. Ltd. Edns. Cl., 1939; 1962. Both (1500) numbered, & sigd. by artist. 2 works in 2 vols. Monthly letter laid in 2nd. work. Cl. (1st work); & cl.-bkd. bds.; both in orig. boxes. (SG. Jan.15; 277) $100
- **The Tragedy of Pudd'nhead Wilson** ... Hartford, 1894. 1st. Edn., 1st. state. Orig. gt. decor. cl. (CNY. May 22; 66) $170
-- **Anr. Copy.** Decor cl. Bkplt. of E. Hubert Litchfield. (SG. Mar.19; 306) $120
- **A Tramp Abroad.** Hartford, 1880. 1st. Edn. 1st. iss., with frontis. titled 'Moses'. Gt.-pict. cl. One p. of the orig. MS. tipped in, corresponding to pp. 388-389 in the book. (SG. Mar.19; 302) $1,100
- **Works.** L., 1899-1922. Unif. Liby. Edn. 22 vols. Cl., gt. title to upr. cover & spines. (JL. Mar.2; 528A) *Aus.* $110
-- **Anr. Edn.** L., 1906-08. Unif. Liby. Edn. 21 vols. Three-qtr. cf. (SG. Dec.18; 413) $230
- **Writings.** Hartford, 1899. Edn. De Luxe, (1000). 25 vols. Mor. gt., elab. gt. borders enclosing tulip design. Contains 2 MS. ll. from 'The Gilded Age'. (SPB. Nov.25; 439) $2,600
-- **Anr. Edn.** N.Y., 1922. Definitive Edn., (1024). 37 vols. Orig. cl., labels browned, stained. Sigd. by Clemens, also as Mark Twain. (SPB. Nov.25; 440) $750

CLEMENS, Samuel Langhorne 'Mark Twain' (Contrib.)
See-BEADLE & Co.

CLEMENS, Samuel Langhorne & Warner, Charles Dudley
- **The Gilded Age.** Hartford, 1873. 1st. Edn. Advance Copy 'for review', with the corrected state of pp. 351-353. Stitched without covers as iss., cl. case. From the Prescott Collection. (CNY. Feb.6; 50) $2,800

CLEMENS, Venceslaus
See-NARSIUS, Joannes-Clemens, Venceslaus

CLEMENT, Dom Francois
[-] **Art de Vérifier les Dates des Faits Historiques** (L') ... Paris, 1783-87. 3 vols. Fo. Cont. cf., triple gt. fillet around covers, spines decor. with raised bands, bdgs. slightly defect. (HD. Feb.27; 24) Frs. 1,200

CLEMENT, Nicolas
- **Austrasiae Reges et Duces Epigrammatis.** Ill.:- P. Woeirot. Cologne, 1591. 4to. Title mntd. & a little stained, sm. tear in margin of 1st. few ll., reprd. 19th. C. hf. mor. (C. Apr. 1; 129) *Ridge.* £220

CLEMENT-JANIN, Noel
- **Essai sur la Bibliophile Contemporaine de 1900 à 1928.** Ill.:- Henri Matisse & Others. Paris, 1931; 1932. (500) numbered copies on Velin à la Forme. 2 vols. Fo. Three qtr. lev., spine gt., orig. wraps. bnd. in. (SG. Oct.2; 82) $400

CLEO & EUTERPE, or British Harmony
L., n.d. 4 vols. Lacks folding engraved advts., some light foxing, some pp. washed. Tree cf. gt., richly gt. spines. (SPB. Oct.1; 222) $1,500

CLERCK, Carl
- **Svenska Spindlar ... Aranei Svecici.** Stockholm, 1757. 1st. Edn. Plts. hand-cold. Cont. cf., worn, covers detchd. From Chetham's Liby., Manchester. (C. Nov.26; 86) *Wheldon & Wesley.* £350

CLERCK, N. de
- **Tooneel der Keyseren en Coningen van Christenryck sedert den Onderganck van het Griecks Keyserdom ...-Tooneel der beroemder Hertogen, Princen, Graven ende Krygs-Helden ... binnen dese drij laeste Eeuwen.-Princelyck Cabinet** ... Arnhem; Delft; Delft, 1615; 1617; 1625. 2nd. work: the author; 3rd. work: his heirs. 3 works in 1 vol. Fo. A few light marginal stains, browned in places, lr. margin of 1st. engraved title short, inner margin of same reprd. Cont. vell., gt. central ornament on both covers, a bit Warped & soiled, lacks ties. (VG. Dec.17; 1250) Fls. 950

CLERISSEAU, Charles Louis
- **Antiquités de la France.-Monuments de Nismes.** Ed.:- J.G. Legrand. Paris, 1804. 2nd. Edn.; on vell. 2 vols. in 1. Lge. fo. Str.-grd. mor. by Simier, double border, gt. & blind-tooled, gt. fillets, inside border of several fillets, gt. motifs with fleur-de-lys in corners, motifs of 1 fleur-de-lys in middle of sides, arms of Duchesse de Berry on covers, & spine, mosaic bands, inside dentelle. (HD. Mar.18; 44) Frs. 29,000

CLERJON de Champagny
- **Album d'un Soldat pendant la Campagne d'Espagne en 1823.** Paris, 1829. Mod. marb. roan, decor. spine, 3 fillets, wrap. (HD. Dec.5; 45) Frs. 1,100

CLERK, John of Eldin
- **Series of Etchings; Views in Scotland.** Bannat. Cl., 1855. Fo. Cl., worn. (CE. Nov.20; 24) £100

CLERKE, Charles
[-] **A Voyage Round the World.** L., 1767. 1st. Edn. Cont. cf., disbnd. (SG. Oct.30; 91) $300

CLEVEDON, H.
- **Le Mirror des Dames.** Paris, n.d. Fo. Some marginal soiling. Cont. hf. cf., worn. (CSK. Oct.10; 158) £95

CLEVELAND (Contrib.)
See-CAMBRIDGE UNIVERSITY

CLEVELAND, P.
- **Elementary Treatise on Mineralogy & Geology.** Boston, 1822. 2 vols., Orig. bds., spines defect. (BS. Sep.17; 30) £50

CLEYER, Andreas
- **Specimen Medecinae Sinicae.** Frankfurt, 1682. 1st. Edn. 4to. Some plts. cropped (usually not affecting ill. or caption), engraved title vig. partly affected by liby. stp. 18th. C. paper bds., upr. cover gt.-stpd. 'Academ: Imper: German: Natur: Curios:', spine worn. Inscr. recording the book as a gift of Eugenianus II in 1735. (C. Nov.20; 185) *Dawson.* £980

CLINTON-BAKER, Henry William & Jackson A. Bruce
- **Illustrations of Conifers.** 1909-10. 3 vols. 4to. Hf. mor. gt. (P. May 14; 252) *Park.* £95
- **Illustrations of Conifers.-Illustrations of New Conifers.** Hereford, Priv. ptd., 1913-35. 4 vols. 4to. Orig. paper bds., slightly worn. (TA. Jun.18; 70) £110

CLIO: or, a Secret History of the Life & Amours of ... Mrs. S-n-m ...
L., 1752. 12mo. Disbnd. (SG. Sep.25; 87) $140

CLIO & EUTERPE or British Harmony
Ill.:- Arne & others. 1758-59. 2 vols. in 1 (without 3rd. of Supp. vols.). 19th. C. russ., slightly worn. (SBA. Jul.14; 112) *Cumming.* £190
-- **Anr. Edn.** L., 1762. 3 vols. Mod. three-qtr. cf. (SG. May 14; 47) $1,000

CLIVE, Robert
- **A Series of Lithographic Drawings from Sketches ... comprising the undermentioned subjects, lying principally between the Persian Gulf & the Black Sea.** Priv. ptd., [1852]. 3 pts. in 2 vols. Fo. Publisher's slip concerning the iss. of the frontis. bnd. in, frontis. & anr. plt. mntd. with the frontis. fore-edge strengthened, a few margins affected by light staining & spotting. Recent buckram with 2 orig. wraps. mntd. on upr. covers. (S. Nov.4; 635) *Hawker.* £280

CLOQUET, Hippolyte
- **Traité d'Anatomie Descriptive ...** Paris, 1835. 5 vols. 4to. Orig. cl.-bkd. ptd. bds., accompanying text pamphlets in wraps., worn. (SG. Sep.18; 84) $400

CLOQUET, Jules
- **Atlas du Manuel d'Anatomie Déscriptive.** [Paris], [1831]. 4to. Slight spotting. Mod. hf. mor., spine gt. (S. Apr.6; 32) *Schuster.* £70

CLOSE, Francis
- **The Book of Genesis Considered & Illustrated.** L., 1826. Cont. str.-grd. mor. Fore-e. pntg. (SG. Mar.19; 129) $220

CLOUET, J.B.L.
- **Geographie Moderne avec une Introduction.** Paris, 1793. 4th. Edn. Fo. Lacks 1 double-p. outl. cold. copper engraved map & 1 cold. plt., engraved dedication, index & plts. 2-4 enlarged from a 1780 Edn. & loose, engraved title lf., 1

CLOUET, J.B.L. – Geographie Moderne avec une Introduction. -contd.
astronomical table & 2 Africa maps with sm. faults at fold, pasted behind. Cont. hf. leath. (R. Oct.14-18; 1530) DM 650

CLOUGH, Arthur Hugh
– Poems; with a Memoir. L., 1877. 16mo. Mor. gt. Fore-e. pntg. (after Rowlandson?). (SG. Mar.19; 130) $400

CLOUZOT, H.
– La Ferronnerie Moderne. Paris, [1925-27]. 2 vols. Fo. Loose, orig. hf. linen portfo.'s. (R. Mar.31-Apr.4; 868) DM 600

CLOWES, William Laird
– The Royal Navy. 1897-1903. 7 vols. 4to. Orig. cl. (SH. Mar.5; 210) Fletcher. £340

CLUSIUS, Carolus
– Exoticorum Libri Decem ... item Petri Bellonii Observationes. Antw., 1605. Fo. Engraved title-p. (rebkd.), worming & some repairs. Later cl. (TA. Dec.18; 115) £170
– Rariorum Plantarum Historia.–Exoticorum Plantarum libri decem. Antw.; Leiden, 1601; 1605. 2 works in 2 vols. Fo. Engraved title to 2nd. work rubbed & loose. 19th. C. hf. mor., lettered I & II, 1 upr. cover detchd. From Chetham's Liby., Manchester, both inscr. on title 'Don de l'auteur à son neveu Jan de Maes'. (C. Nov.26; 87) Wagner. £850

CLUTTERBUCK, Robert
– The History of the Antiquities of the County of Hertford. 1813-27. 3 vols. Fo. 2 ll. torn & reprd. Hf. mor., spines gt. in compartments. (LC. Jun.18; 145) £240
– – Anr. Edn. 1815-27. 1st. Edn. 3 vols. Fo. Later crushed mor., gt. panel. spines, slightly soiled. (C. Feb.25; 28) Crowe. £360
– – Anr. Copy. Lr. margin of each vol. affected by damp. Cerise mor. gt. by Hayday. From the collection of Eric Sexton. (C. Apr.16; 232) Weaver. £220
– – Anr. Copy. Hf. mor. gt. (P. Oct.2; 299) Burden. £120

CLUVERIUS, Philippus
[–] Atlas. 1680? 4to. 44 engraved maps, mostly double-p. or folding, histor. vig. title cartouches, mostly defect., a few partly hand-cold. by an amateur hand. 19th. C. hf. cf., worn. W.a.f. (TA. Oct.16; 157) £120
– Germaniae Antiquae Libri Tres. Adj. sunt Vindelica et Noricum Ejusdem Auctoris. Leiden, 1631. Fo. Slightly browned in parts. Cont. vell. (HK. May 12-14; 601) DM 700
– – Anr. Copy. (D. Dec.11-13; 1614) DM 670
– – Anr. Edn. Ill.:– N. Geelkercken (maps). Leiden, 1631. 2nd. Edn. Fo. Stained, mainly at beginning & end, slightly foxed in places. Cont. cf., rebkd., new end-papers. (VG. Dec.17; 1252) Fls. 450
– Huic ed. acc. P. Bertii Breviarum Orbis Terrarum & D. Heinsii Oratio. Ill.:– J.V. Avel (frontis.). Amst., 1683. Lacks 1 folding copper engraved map, title & preface slightly stained. Cont. leath., spine reprd. (HK. Nov.18-21; 1141) DM 1,200
– Introductionis in Universam Geographiam tam veterem quae novem, Libn VI. Amst., 1659. 24mo. Soiling, several tears, 1 lf. of text torn with loss. Cont. vell. W.a.f. (CSK. May 8; 15) £130
– – Anr. Edn. Amst., 1672. 12mo. 1 table torn. Cf. (CSK. Apr.10; 7) £130
– – Anr. Copy. 12mo. Plts. & maps (some tipped in from another source?), lacks 2 ll. of text, not collated. Old cf., rebkd., worn. (KH. Nov.18; 163) Aus. $160
– – Anr. Edn. [Amst.], [1682, or later]. 4to. Lacks 2 engraved maps, on guards thro-out, all hand-cold. in outl., MS. index at end. Later panel. cf. As an atlas, w.a.f. (SBA. Dec.16; 50a) Holliday. £300
– – Anr. Edn. 1711. 4to. Some marginal tears. Cont. cf., worn. (CSK. Apr.10; 32) £180
– – Anr. Edn. Amst., 1729. 4to. Old vell., spine torn. (SG. Sep.25; 88) $230
– Sicilia Antiqua. Ill.:– N. Geilkerck (maps). Leiden, 1619. 1st. Edn. Fo. Short tear in 2E4. Cont. vell. bds., soiled, lacks ties. (S. Feb.10; 284) Erlini. £70

COAST SURVEY
– Report of the Superintendent [A.D. Bache], showing the Progress of the Survey during 1852-1853-1854. Wash., 1853; 1854; 1855. 3 vols. 4to. Some foxing. Orig. sheep. (SG. Jan.8; 98) $110

COATES, Charles
– The History & Antiquities of Reading. 1802. 4to. Folding town plan. Hf. cf. (P. Feb.19; 183) Hollingsworth. £70
– – Anr. Edn. L. & Reading, 1802; 1809. 1st. Edn. 2 vols. in 1, including supp. 4to. 8 plts., 1 folding, 1 double-p. & inserted, folding plan. Cont. diced russ. gt., upr. cover detchd. (S. Nov.24; 55) Thorp. £55

COBBETT, William 'Peter Porcupine'
– Rural Rides ... with Tours of Scotland ... & Letters from Ireland. Ed.:– G.D.H. & Margaret Cole. Ill.:– John Nash. 1930. Ltd. Edn. 3 vols. Cl.-bkd. bds., partly unc. (C. Jul.22; 9) Maggs. £60
– – Anr. Copy. (1,000) numbered. Hf. cl. & marb. bds., s.-c. (PJ. Jun.6 (80); 45) £52
– – Anr. Copy. This copy unnumbered. Cl.-bkd. bds., slightly warped, foxing to end-papers. (SPB. May 29; 78) $100
– The Rush-Light. N.Y., 15th. Feb., 1800. Marginal tears, stains, etc. Ptd. wraps., unc. (SG. Jan.29; 366) $100
– – Anr. Edn. [Phila.], 15th. & 31st. Mar., & 30th Apr., 1800. Comprising pp. 113-258 of vol. I, foxed, etc. Disbnd. (SG. Jan.29; 367) $160

COBDEN-SANDERSON, Thomas James
– Amantium Irae. Doves Pr., 1914. (153). 4to. Mor., sides with triple gt. fillet panels & tulip cornerpieces, spine gt. in compartments, by the Doves bindery after a design by Cobden-Sanderson. (C. Jul.22; 56) Fletcher. £150
– – Anr. Copy. (150). Lev. mor., gt.-ruled border, spine in 6 compartments, 5 raised bands, gt.-panel., sigd. by Doves Bindery, 1914, qtr. mor. s.-c. Willis Vickery, & Cortlandt Field Bishop bkplts. (CNY. May 22; 401) $400
– The Arts & Crafts Movement. Hammersmith, Chiswick Pr. 1905. 1st. Edn. Vell., by Doves Bindery. Pres. copy to his wife. (CNY. May 22; 370) $480
– – Anr. Copy. Orig. vell.-bkd. bds. Pres. copy to Sir Sydney Cockerell. (CNY. May 22; 371) $200
– Catalogue Raisonné of Books Printed & Published at the Doves Press. Hammersmith, Doves Pr., 1916. (10) on vell. Sm. 4to. Gt.-decor. niger mor., spine in 6 compartments, 5 raised bands, gt.-panel., sigd. by Doves Bindery, 1918, qtr. mor. s.-c. (CNY. May 22; 408) $10,000
– Credo: Pleni sunt Coeli et Terra Gloria Tua. Hammersmith, Doves Pr., 1909. (12) on vell. 12mo. Niger mor., upr. cover with central gt. ornament, spine in 6 compartments, 5 raised bands, sigd. by Doves Bindery, qtr. mor. s.-c. Cortlandt Field Bishop bkplt. (CNY. May 22; 386) $900
– Ecce Mundus. Hammersmith, Chis. Pr. 1902. Crushed lev. mor., single gt. rule on covers, spine in 6 compartments, 5 raised bands, all gt.-panel., sigd. 'The Doves Bindery 19 C-S 12', qtr. red mor. gt. s.-c. (CNY. May 22; 369) $300
– – Anr. Copy. Orig. vell.-bkd. bds. Pres. copy to S.C. Cockerell, lf. announcing the book laid in. (CNY. May 22; 368) $200
– The Ideal Book or Book Beautiful. Hammersmith, Doves Pr., 1900. (10) on vell. Sm. 4to. Orig. vell., unc., qtr. mor. s.-c. (CNY. May 22; 373) $1,800
– – Anr. Copy. (300). Orig. vell., soiled. (SPB. May 29; 125) $200
– Paper Read at a Meeting of the Art Workers Guild [London]. [Hammersmith], [Doves Pr.]. 1906. Mor. gt.-tooled with interlocking panels, sigd. by Cobden-Sanderson, Doves Bindery, 19 C-S 19. (P. Jan.22; 322) Maggs. £190
– – Anr. Edn. Hammersmith, Doves Pr. 1906. (5) on vell. Sm. 4to. Lev. mor., gt.-ruled border on covers, spine in 6 compartments, 5 raised bands, gt.-panel., sigd. 'Doves Bindery 19 C-S 21', qtr. mor. s.-c. (CNY. May 22; 378) $1,500
– – Anr. Copy. (200). Vell., slightly discoloured. (PNY. Dec.3; 117) $110

COBURG, Simon Jacob von
– Rechenbuch auff den Linien und mit Ziffern. Frankfurt a. M., 1559. [2nd. Edn.?]. Some light underscoring in red ink, a few marginal stains.

Mod. hf. vell. From Honeyman Collection. (S. May 20; 3209) Dr. Martin. £350

COBURN, Alvin Langdon
– London. Ed.:– Hilaire Belloc (intro.). L. & N.Y., [1909]. Fo. Title loose. Hf. leath., lacks spine, worn & stained. (SG. Jul.9; 86) $1,100
– Men of Mark. L., 1913. 4to. Two-toned cl. (SG. Apr.23; 63) $550
– Moor Park, Rickmansworth. Ed.:– Lady Edbury [introduction]. L., 1915. 4to. Bds., corners chipped. (SG. Apr.23; 64) $170
– More Men of Mark. L., [1922]. 1st. Edn. Tall 4to. Cl.-bkd. bds., inner hinge crudely retaped, covers worn. (SG. Apr.23; 65) $170

COCAIUS, Merlinus (Pseud.)
See–FOLENGO, Teofilo 'Merlinus Cocaius'

COCCHI, Antonio
– Dei Bagni di Pisa: Trattato. Firenze, 1750. L.P. 1st. Edn. 4to. Disbnd. (SG. Jan.29; 99) $130

COCHRAN-PATRICK, R.W.
– Catalogue of the Medals of Scotland. Edinb., 1884. (350) numbered. 4to. Cont. hf. mor. (SH. Mar.6; 335) Spink. £75
– Records of the Coinage of Scotland. Edinb., 1876. 2 vols. 4to. Cont. hf. mor. (SH. Mar.6; 336) Seaby. £80

COCHRANE, Archibald, 10th. Earl of Dundonald
See–DUNDONALD, Archibald Cochrane, 10th. Earl of

COCHRANE, John Dundas
– Narrative of a Pedestrian Journey through Russia & Siberian Tartary. 1824. 2nd. Edn. 2 vols. Mod. hf. cf., spines gt. (S. Mar.31; 454) Foyles. £75

COCKBURN, Sir George
– A Voyage to Cadiz & Gibraltar. [1815]. 1st. Edn. 2 vols. Vol. II lacks engraved title, lacks plan of Murat's camp. Cont. hf. cf. (SBA. Jul.22; 86) Shapero. £130
– – Anr. Edn. 1815. 2 vols. 3 folding maps & plans, 1 loose, 2 pp. of text loose. Hf. cf. (P. Apr.9; 121) Dupont. £90

COCKBURN, Major James
– Swiss Scenery. L., 1820. 1st. Edn. 4to. Cont. cf., spine gt., covers loose. Mary Rose Fitzgibbon bkplt. (S. Nov.25; 509) Chaponniere. £420
– – Anr. Copy. Lacks 2 plts., marginal dampstains, slight spotting. Hf. cf. (CSK. Feb.6; 29) £340
– – Anr. Copy. Slightly soiled. Cont. hf. leath., detchd., worn. (HK. Nov.18-21; 1391) DM 1,700
– – Anr. Copy. Lacks 11 plts. Cont. linen, worn. (HK. Nov.18-21; 1392) DM 600

COCKBURN, John
– A Journey over Land, from the Gulf of Honduras to the Great South-Sea, ... L., 1735. 1st. Edn. Advts., lacks ¾ of map, foxing & staining. Mod. hf. linen, ex-liby. (SG. Mar.5; 134) $160

COCKBURN, W.B. & Donaldson, T.L.
– Pompeii. Ill.:– after Cockburn. 1827. 2 vols. in 1. Fo. Last plt. slightly soiled & torn, vol. 1: title & contents lf. detchd., lacks index. Covers detchd., spine lacking. (CSK. Nov.28; 32) £55

COCKER, Edward
– Cockers Arithmetick ... 1678. 2nd. Edn. 12mo. Advt. lf., sm. tear at head of D6, rusthole in M2, some stains & browning. 19th. C. mor., gt. From Honeyman Collection. [Wing C4819] (S. May 20; 3210) Bennett. £60

COCKERELL, Sir Sydney Carlyle
– The Gorleston Psalter. 1907. Fo. Orig. hf. vell., unc. Inscr. 'To S.C. Cockerell ... from C.W. Dyson Perrins'. (C. Jul.22; 36) Traylen. £150
– The Work of W. de Brailes Camb., Roxb. Cl., 1930. Fo. Orig. mor.-bkd. cl. Author's copy, sigd., dtd. & inscr. by him 'This is a special copy, with extra illustrations', together with 30 A.L.s. from the Roxburghe Club & others. (C. Jul.22; 37) Quaritch. £450

COCLES, Bartholomaeus
– Physiognomiae & Chiromatiae Compendium. Strassburg, 1536. Title slightly soiled. Cont. vell. bds., lr. hinge nearly brkn. (S. Oct.21; 448) Broseghini. £310

COCTEAU, Jean
– L'Ange Heurtebise. Paris, 1925. 1st. Edn.; on Arches vell., numbered. Fo. Sewed, wrap. (HD. Dec.5; 46) Frs. 1,600

– – Anr. Edn. Ill.:– H. Mohr. Paris, 1925. (250) numbered, on velin d'Arches à la cuve. Tall fo. Lev., decor. onlay, lev. dentelles, by Myria, s.-c. 12 orig. water-cols., mntd., inscr. by artist, Comtesse Barbey de Jumilhac bkplt. & inscr. (SG. Oct.9; 59) $550
– **Aux confins de la Chine.** Ill.:– Lou Albert-Lassard. Paris, n.d. (200) on Chiffon Montval with lithos. on China. Fo. Loose ll. in orig. hf. linen & wood bds. portfo. Printer's mark sigd. by artist. (H. Dec.9/10; 2007) DM 460
– **Les Chevaliers de la Table Ronde.** Paris, 1937, Cl.-bkd. bds., orig. wraps. bnd. in., fitted case. Pres. copy to Leclair, with pen & ink sketch on hf.-title. (SH. Nov.20; 96) Fauré. £55
– **Dessins.** Paris, 1923. Ltd. Edn. sigd. 4to. Cont. cl. (SH. Apr.9; 21) Duran. £120
– **Le Grand Ecart.** Paris, [1926]. (419) numbered on Lafuma paper. Sm. 4to. Ptd. wraps., tissue guard. (PNY. Mar.4; 126) $240
– **Le Livre Blanc.** Paris, 1930. 1st. Edn. (380), numbered on Velin d'Arches. 4to. Ptd. wraps., cl. & bds. s.-c. (PNY. Mar.4; 127) $300
– **Morceaux Choisis: Poems.** [Paris], [1932]. 12mo. Hf. leath., lacks spine, orig. wraps. bnd. in. Orig. pen & ink drawing & some 50 words at various angles on hf.-title, sigd. 'Votre ami JeanC*'. (SG. Apr.2; 75) $400
– **Le Mystere Laic: Essai d'Etude Indirecte.** Ill.:– Giorgio de Chirico. Paris, [1928]. Ltd. numbered Edn. Ptd. wraps., unc. (SG. Apr.2; 74) $100
– **Les Ombres Heureuses de Monte-Carlo.** Ill.:– Claude Lepape. 1947. (110) on velin d'Arches. 3 vols. 4to. Ll. in s.-c., 1 cover for preservation. A.L.s. decor. by Cocteau. (HD. Feb.18; 209) Frs. 4,000
– **Picasso de 1916 à 1961.** Monaco, 1962. (255) numbered, sigd. by Cocteau & Picasso. Loose as iss. in orig. decor. wraps., unc., mor.-bkd. bd. folder, bd. s.-c. (C. Jul.22; 93) Taylor. £220
– **Soignez la Gloire de votre Firme et l'excellence de vos Marchandises** . . . Ill.:– Charles Martin. [Paris], [1925]. Fo. Booklet laid in with Engl. translation. Plts. loose as issued in orig. wraps. (SG. May 14; 140) $300
– **Twenty-Four Color Lithographs for J.M. Magnan's 'Taureaux'.** Paris, [1965]. (200) numbered on grand Velin d'Arches. Fo. Loose as iss. in ptd. folder. (SG. Dec.18; 117) $110
– **La Voix Humaine.** Ill.:– Bernard Buffet. Paris, 1957. (150) numbered on Auvergne H.M.P. specially produced by Richard de Bas & sigd. by author & artist. Tall fo. Loose in wraps., buckram folder & s.-c. (SG. Oct.9; 60) $1,200
See–ALEXANDRE, Arsène & Cocteau, Jean
See–BRAQUE, Georges, Cocteau, Jean & others

CODE d'Instruction Criminelle
Paris, 1810. 1st. Edn. 4to. Cont. str.-grd. red mor., smooth decor. spine, watered silk end-papers. (HD. Feb.27; 106) Frs. 52,000

CODE Napoléon
Paris, 1810. 1st. Edn. 4to. Cont. red mor., gt. roll-stp. around covers, smooth decor. spine, watered silk end-papers, inside dentelle. (HD. Feb.27; 104) Frs. 52,000
– – **Anr. Edn.** Trans:– Robert Samuel Richards. L., late 19th. C. Red mor. gt., gt. inner dentelle, by Hatchards. (D. Dec.11-13; 2695) DM 580

CODE PENAL
Paris, 1810. 1st. Edn. 4to. Cont. str.-grd. red mor., smooth decor. spine, watered silk end-papers. (HD. Feb.27; 105) Frs. 52,000

CODEX BARBERINI
– **Badianus Manuscript: an Aztec Herbal of 1552.** Ed.:– Henry E. Sigerist. Trans.:– Emily Walcott Emmart. Balt., 1940. 4to. Buckram, d.-w. (SG. Sep.18; 26) $175

CODEX DURMACHENSIS: THE BOOK OF DURROW
– **Evangeliorum Quattuor, Codex Durmachensis.** Ed.:– A.A. Luce. Olten, 1960. (650) numbered. 2 vols. Fo. Vol. 1 stpd. leath., vol. 2 matching qtr. leath., boxed. (SG. May 14; 48) $300

CODEX JUNG (F. I-LXX)
Ed.:– M. Malinine, H.C. Peuch & others. Zürich, 1956-75. 5 vols. Fo. Coptic text, Fr., Engl. & German trans., facs. of MS. etc. Hf. leath. (B. Dec.10/11; 675) Fls. 580

CODMAN, Ogden
See–WHARTON, Edith & Codman, Ogden

COE, Thomas–TISSOT, S.A.D.
– **A Treatise on Biliary Concretions . . .–An Essay on Bilious Fever.** 1757; 1760. Cf. (P. Sep.11; 9) Traylen. £50

COELHO, Simão
– **Compendio das Chronicas da orde de Nossa Senhora do Carmo.** Lisbon, 1572. 2 pts. in 1 vol. Fo. 3 sm. holes in title affecting 1 letter, a few ll. with marginal wormholes or light stains. Mott. cf. 17th. C. armorial stp. of Leneastre e Souza on verso of title, the Casa Lafoes copy, with stp. on A1. (SPB. Oct.1; 223) $800

COFFEE & Chocolate
– **Carta que Escrivio un Medico Christiano, que estava curando en Antiberi, à un Cardenal de Roma, sobre la Bebida del Cahuè, o Cafè.** N.p., 17th. C. Fo. Slight spotting. Disbnd., unc., cl. case. (S. May 5; 71) Simms. £110

COFFRET du Bibliophile, Le
– **Les Romains Libertins.** Paris, 1910-14. Ltd. Edns. 35 vols. 18mo. Red hf. mor., border of 3 fillets in compartments of spines, wraps. preserved. (SM. Feb.11; 22) Frs. 4,000

COGAN, Rev. A.
– **The Ecclesiastical History of the Dioceses of Meath.** Dublin, 1874. 3 vols. Cl. (GM. Apr.30; 241) £60

COGNIET, Leon & Raffet
– **Illustrations de l'Armée Française** . . . Ill.:– Llanta & A. Midy. Paris, ca. 1837. Fo. 18 hand-cold. litho. plts., 1 torn & reprd. Cont. hf. mor., rebkd. & recorned, orig. litho. wrap. bnd. in. (C. Jul.15; 25) Taylor. £350

COHEN, Henry
– **Guide de l'Amateur de Livres à Vignettes (et à Figures) du XVIIIe Siècle.** Paris, 1880. 4th. Edn. Simulated snake, orig. wraps. bnd. in. (SG. Mar.26; 142) $170
– – **Anr. Edn.** Paris, 1912. 6th. Edn. (50) on Bütten. Hf. leath. (H. Dec.9/10; 6) DM 620

COHEN, Tuvia
– **Maase Tuvia.** Venice, 1707-08. 1st. Edn. 3 pts. in 1 vol. 4to. Last p. in Italian, slight staining, some worming, without affecting text. Mod. cl. (S. Nov.18; 703) £750
– – **Anr. Copy.** 4to. Tear in lr. margin of 2nd. lf. without loss, lightly stained, cropped. Hf. leath., spine defect., cover & end-paper detchd. (SPB. May 11; 74) $1,600

COHEN, Yitzhak
– **Zivchei Cohen.** Livorno, 1832. 4to. In Hebrew & Italian, short tear in 1 plt. Hf. leath. (S. Nov.18; 526) Dingsgate. £190

COHN, Albert
– **George Cruikshank. A Catalogue Raisonné.** 1924. (500) numbered. 4to. Orig. cl. (SH. Mar.6; 506) Dawson's. £110
– – **Anr. Copy.** (TA. Mar.19; 169) £80

COIGNET, Jean Roch
– **Les Cahiers du Capitaine Coignet.** Ill.:– J. Le Blant. Paris, 1888. Fo. Crimson three-qtr. mor., spine gt., by Champs. (SG. Oct.30; 93) $160

COINS OF ANTIQUITY
Ca. 1840. 1 vol. of off-prints. Some ll. soiled. Cont. hf. cf. (SH. Mar.6; 339) Spink. £65

COKAYNE, George Edward
[–] **The Complete Peerage by G.E.C.** Ed.:– Hon. Vicary Gibbs. 1910-40. Vols. 1-10 & 13. Orig. cl., slightly soiled. W.a.f. (CSK. Sep.26; 130) £220
– – **Anr. Edn.** Ed.:– Vicary Gibbs & others. 1910-59. 13 vols. in 14. 4to. Orig. buckram gt., partly unc. (S. Nov.25; 390) Roberts. £850
– – **Anr. Copy.** Orig. cl. (SH. Jul.16; 212) Heraldry Today. £710

COKE, Sir Edward
– **A Book of Entries** . . . L., 1614. 1st. Edn. Fo. Title-p. worn. Cont. cf., rebkd. in mor. & sides reprd. W.a.f. (PNY. Oct.1; 153) $275
– **The First Part of the Institutes of the Lawes of England, or, a commentarie upon Littleton.** 1628. 1st. Edn. Fo. Later cf., upr. cover slightly stained. [STC 15784] (C. Feb.25; 153) Riley Smith. £1,100

COKE, Henry J.
– **A Ride Over the Rocky Mountains to Oregon & California.** L., 1852. 1st. Edn. Port. preserved. Later hf. mor. & marb. bds. [Sabin 14240] (SPB. Jun.22; 36) $110

COKE, Thomas
– **A History of the West Indies.** L'pool., 1808-11. 1st. Edn. 3 vols. Some spotting. New hf. mor. gt., unc. [Sabin 14244] (SPB. May 5; 157) $1,100

COKER, John
– **A Survey of Dorsetshire.** 1732. Sm. fo. Cont. cf. gt. From the collection of Eric Sexton. (C. Apr.16; 233) Crowe. £130
– – **Anr. Edn.** 1732. L.P. Fo. Borders red ruled thro.-out. Old spr. cf., spine gt. (C. Mar.18; 170) Traylen. £110

COLANGE, Leo de
– **Voyages & Travels.** Boston, 1887. 2 vols. in 4. Lge. 4to. Orig. linen. (R. Oct.14-18; 1465) DM 430

COLAS, Louis
– **La Mode . . . Pendant Quarante Ans de 1830-70.** Ca. 1900. Loose in orig. wraps. & cl. folder. (TA. Mar.19; 511) £100

COLAS, René
– **Bibliographie Générale du Costume et de la Mode.** Paris, 1933. (1000) numbered. 2 pts. Crude buckram. (SG. Jan.22; 126) $190

COLBATCH, John
– **A Collection of Tracts Chirurgical & Medical viz. A New Light of Chirurgery . . . essay concerning alkaly & acid . . . of gout, etc.** 1704. 2nd. Edn. Advt. lf. Cont. panel. cf. (S. Jun.15; 173) Joslen. £60

COLBERT, Jean Baptiste, Comte de Torcy
[–] **Mémoires . . . pour servir à l'Histoire des Negociations depuis le Traité de Riswick jusqu'à la Paix d'Utrecht.** The Hague, 1757-56. 3 vols. 12mo. Cont. red mor., gt. arms of Louis XV on covers, triple gt. fillet, spines gt. in compartments, inner gt. dentelles. Signet liby. stp. on covers. (SM. Oct.7; 1647) Frs. 1,800

COLBORNE, John & Brine, Frederic
– **The Last of the Brave or resting places . . . the Crimea & at Scutari.** 1857. 4to. Cl. gt. (P. Jul.30; 4) Trigg. £55

COLBURN, Zerah
See–CLARK, D.K. & Colburn, Zerah

COLDEN, Cadwallader
– **The History of the Five Indian Nations of Canada.** 1747. 1st. Engl. Edn. Cont. cf. [Sabin 14273] (C. May 20; 18) Quaritch. £130
– – **Anr. Copy.** 3 pts. in 1 vol. Map mntd., lf. K4 torn at corner, with loss of a few words in the bottom 13 lines. Rebkd., orig. spine label preserved. (SG. Jan.8; 100) $375
– – **Anr. Copy.** Lacks map, but with the 2 ll. between pp. 90 & 91. Crude hf. cl., ex-liby. (SG. Mar.5; 57) $130
– – **Anr. Copy.** Lacks the map. Cont. cf., neatly rebkd. (SG. Mar.5; 138) $110
– **Memoir . . . Presented to the Mayor of the City at the Celebration of the Completion of the New York Canals.** N.Y., 1825. 1st. Edn. 4to. 40 (of 47) maps & plts., 8 facs., some foxing, browning, some tears, staining. Hf. mor., worn, covers loose, spine torn. [Sabin 14279] (SPB. Jun.22; 37) $375
– – **Anr. Copy.** 4to. Hf. mor., marb. bds., worn, loose. [Sabin 14279] (SPB. Nov.24; 11) $350

COLE, Alan S.
– **Catalogue of the collection of Antique Lace (16-19 centuries)** formed by the renowned collector Samuel Chick. L., n.d. Ptd. on H.M.P. with red borders. Cont. hf. leath. & cl. by Buffery, Oxford Street, L. (JN. Apr.6; 357) £2,000

COLE, Timothy
– **Old Spanish Masters.** Ed.:– C.H. Caffin (historical notes). N.Y., 1907. (100) numbered on H.M.P. & sigd. by J.C. Bauer. Fo. Qtr. vell., soiled, unc., bkplt. (SG. Mar.12; 107) $120

COLECCION DE APLICACIONES que se continuan haciendo de los Bienes Casas y Colegios que fueron de los Regulares de la Compañia de Jesús, Expatriados de estos Reales Dominios
Lima, 1772-73. 2 vols. Sm. 4to. Limp vell. (SPB. May 5; 158) $300

COLENSO, F.E. & Durnford, E.
– **The Ruin of Zululand.** L., 1884. 2 vols. Cl., slight foxing. (SSA. Jun.18; 87) R. 140

[COLEOPTERA Injurious to Agriculture]
Ca. 1880. Fo. 38 lge. ll. sheets of watercolour drawings mntd. on mill bd. Unbound. According to Dulau & Co., cat. clipping sold with this lot,

[COLEOPTERA Injurious to Agriculture] -contd.
these are copies of orig. set of drawings made by Andrew Murray. (SPB. Oct.1; 189) $150

COLERIDGE, Samuel Taylor
- Biographia Literaria. 1817. 1st. Edn. 2 vols. 3 pp. of advts. in vol. II. Hf. cf., spines blind-stpd. & gt. (LC. Feb.12; 442) £55
- Christabel; Kubla Khan; Fancy in Nubibus; & Song from Zapolya. Ill.:– L. & E. Pissarro. Eragny Pr., 1904. (226). 12mo. Some foxing. Flowered bd. covers, bd. spine, end-papers discold., unc. & unopened. (SG. Jan.15; 24) $180
- Christabel; Kubla Khan; The Pains of Sleep. L., 1816. 1st. Edn. Some staining, 4 pp. of inserted advts. at end dtd. Mar., 1816. Orig. wraps., rebkd., mor. gt. solander case, unc. From the Prescott Collection. (CNY. Feb.6; 59) $600
- Poems Chosen out of the Works. Kelms. Pr., 1896. (300). 4to. Minor defects. Orig. vell., slight soiling. (SPB. Jul.28; 204) $475
- Poems ... To which are now added Poems by Charles Lamb, & Charles Lloyd. Bristol, 1797. 2nd. Edn. Without inserted errata slip. Cont. mott. cf., upr. cover loose, hf. mor. case. (S. Dec.8; 67) Cox. £100
- – Anr. Copy. Browned. Cont. cf. (SH. Jun.25; 213) Hill. £60
- Poems on Various Occasions. 1796. 1st. Edn. Later hf. cf. (SH. May 21; 22) Hannas. £210
- The Poetical Works. L., 1828. 1st. Coll. Edn., (12) L.P. 3 vols. Square 8vo. Orig. cl., spines faded & worn at extremities, some quires in vol. I sprung, qtr. mor. gt. folding case, unc. 20 line note of author on pp. 236-237 in vol. I, & publisher's note on fly-lf. of vol. I, owner's inscrs. of Mrs. Gillman in vols. I & III, & her notes & text corrections, with A.L.s to Mrs. Gillman from Coleridge (with integral address lf., torn at folds); lately in the Prescott Collection. (CNY. Feb.6; 61) $2,800
- The Rime of the Ancient Mariner. Ill.:– after Gustave Dore. N.Y., 1886. Tall fo. Gt.-pict. cl., orig. 2-pt. card box. (SG. Mar.19; 87) $400
- – Anr. Copy. Liby. label in upr. cover. (SG. Aug.21; 89) $150
- – Anr. Edn. Ill.:– W.W. Denslow. East Aurora, The Roycrofters, 1899. (400) numbered. sigd. by Elbert Hubbard. Pict. suede. (SG. Oct.23; 78) $110
- – Anr. Edn. Ill.:– W. Strang (frontis.), Florence Kingsford (initials). Essex House Pr., 1903. (150) numbered. 1 initial gt., others supplied in red & blue by Florence Kingsford. Orig. blind-stpd. vell., slightly worn, cl. wraps. (S. Jul.31; 57) Sanders. £70
- – Anr. Edn. Ill.:– Willy Pogany. 1910. Ltd. Edn. sigd. 4to. Vell. (CE. Nov.20; 155) £150
- – Anr. Copy. Orig. cl. gt. (SH. Dec.11; 391) Joseph. £60
- – Anr. Edn. Ill.:– David Jones. Bristol, 1929. (400) numbered. Fo. Buckram-bkd. bds., unc. (SG. May 14; 49) $400
- – Anr. Edn. Ill.:– David Jones. Bristol, 1929. (460) numbered. Fo. Cl.-bkd. bds., unc. (SG. Apr.2; 142) $400
- [-] [-] Anr. Edn. [Corvinus Pr.], [1944]. (16) proof copies on Japanese paper. 4to. Without title & colophon as issued. Orig. mor.-bkd. bds., gt. monog. of Lord Carlow on upr. cover, unc. (SH. Feb.20; 360) Slawson. £85
- – Anr. Edn. Ed.:– David Jones. N.Y., 1964. (115) Roman-numbered copies sigd. by Jones. 4to. Extra set of 10 engrs. & 5 discarded in folder, prospectus & 4 p. essay laid in. Linen, vell. spine, s.-c. (SG. Sep.4; 109) $350
- – Anr. Edn. Ill.:– Errol Le Cain. Arcadia Pr., 1972. (110) sigd. by artist, calligrapher & paper-maker. Fo. Orig. hf. parch., s.-c. (SH. Feb.20; 350) Ralph. £70
- Sibylline Leaves. 1817. 1st. Edn. Some ll. spotted. Cont. (orig. ?) bds., slightly worn, unc. (S. Apr.7; 424) Quaritch. £95
- – Anr. Copy. Hf.-title in fac. Crushed lev. mor., elab. gt. tooled, slightly hollowed spine in 6 compartments with gt. ornaments, 5 raised bands, sigd. & dtd. by T.J. Cobden-Sanderson, 1888, pig gt. solander case. Samuel Putnam Avery bkplt., Charles C. Kalbfleisch booklabel. (CNY. May 22; 357) $17,000
- – Anr. Copy. Some slight spotting. Orig. bds., edges worn, backstrip defect., jnts. brkn., cl. case. From the Prescott Collection. (CNY. Feb.6; 60) $320

- [Works]. 1847-53. 23 vols. Cont. cf. (SH. May 28; 25) Howes Books. £150
See–WORDSWORTH, William & Coleridge, Samuel Taylor

COLERUS, Johannes
- Oeconomia Ruralis et Domestic, darin das gantze Ampt aller trewer Hauss-Vatter, Hauss-Mutter ... Hauss-Buch ... begriffen ... sampt ... Hauss-Apotecken und kurtzer Wundartzney-Kunst. Mainz & Frankfurt, 1645. 3 pts. in 1 vol. Fo. Last lf. of pt. II & III blank. Cont. blind-stpd. vell. (S. Feb.23; 29) Baer. £600

COLETTE, Sidonie Gabrielle
- Chéri. Ill.:– Lobel-Riche. Paris, 1925. (275), numbered. 4to. Mor. by Buer, decor. spine, wrap. preserved, s.-c. (SM. Feb.11; 204) Frs. 3,800
- Claudine à l'Ecole.–Claudine à Paris.–Claudine en Ménage.–Claudine s'en Va. Ill.:– Charles Laborde. Paris, 1925. On Rives paper, numbered. 4 vols. Hf. mor., corners, decor. spines, unc., wraps. & spines. (HD. Dec.5; 49) Frs. 1,800
- Claudine s'en va. 1903. Numbered 1 on hollande. Sewed. (HD. Oct.10; 32) Frs. 1,000
- L'Ingenue Libertine. Ill.:– Dignimont. Paris, 1928. (16) on japon imperial, with extra suite of plts., numbered. 4to. Unsewn in orig. wraps., unc., unopened, folder, s.-c. (SH. Nov.21; 302) Lutrin. £80
- La Paix chez les Bêtes.–Le Voyage Egoiste, suivi de Quatre Saisons. Ill.:– Steinlen (frontis. of 1st. work). Paris, 1916; 1928. 1st. Edn.; (300) Priv. Ptd., reserved for the press, numbered. 2 vols. in 1 Hf. mor., orig. wraps. bnd. in. Both pres. copies, 1st. inscr. to Victor Snell, 2nd. to Jeanne Landre. (SH. Nov.20; 29) Jamieson. £50
- 'Regarde ...' Ill.:– Mathurin Méheut. Paris, 1929. (750). Fo. Sewed, ill. wrap. (HD. Dec.5; 50) Frs. 1,400

COLIFICHETS Lyrico-Galants, ou La Folie Amoureuse d'un Peintre
Ill.:– Dorgez. Paris, [1789]. Sm. 18mo. Cont. silk, spine & covers decor. with embroidery in gold & different cols. with spangles, watered silk fly-ll. & doubls. (HD. Apr.8; 89) Frs. 3,200

COLIN, Sébastien
- L'Ordre et Régime qu'on doit garder et tenir en la Cure des Fièvres ... Poitiers, 1568. 1st. Edn. Sm. 4to. Mod. vell. with bands. (HD. Jun.24; 18) Frs. 3,900

COLLAERT, Adrian
- Diversa Genera Animalium Quadripedum. Ill.:– Adrian Collaert. [Amst.], 1650. Mod. bds. (LM. Jun.13; 91) B.Frs. 18,000
- Vita Iesu Salvatoris variis iconibus ... expressa; Passio et Resurectio D.N. Iesu Christi. [Antw.?], ca. 1600. 2 works in 1 vol. 12mo. Very slightly soiled. 17th. C. black mor. gt. (S. Dec.8; 129) Haverbeeke. £110

COLLECTION ACADEMIQUE, composée des Mémoirs ... des plus Célèbres Académies ... étrangeres l'Histoire Naturelle ... la Physique Experimental ... la Médecine et l'Anatomie.
Dijon, 1755. Vols. I & II. 4to. Title of vol. II slightly soiled, a few ll. slightly spotted. Cont. cf., gt., arms of Louis-Antoine Crozat on covers, spines gt., slightly soiled. (S. Feb.23; 30) Riddett. £50

COLLECTION COMPLETE des Tableaux Historiques de la Révolution Française
Paris, [1804]. Lge. fo. Lacks 6 port. copperplts., soiled. Cont. leath., spine reprd. (R. Mar.31-Apr.4; 1509) DM 620

COLLECTION de Paris-Théatre
Ill.:– after Nadar & others. 1873-80. 2 vols., lacks some nos. Fo. No bdgs. stated. (BS. Jun.11; 237) £130

COLLECTION DE TRAGEDIES. Comédies et Drames
Livourne, 1774-75. 12 vols. Cont. cf. (P. Jan.22; 50) £65

COLLECTION des Jardins Anglais
Paris, 1776. Vols. 1-4. Ob. fo. 102 (of 105) engraved plans & views, occasional minor dampstaining or fraying. Wraps. (SG. Dec.4; 223) $600
- – Anr. Edn. Paris, ca. 1776. Vols. 6-8. Ob. fo. 84 (of 85) engraved plans & views. Wraps. (SG. Dec.4; 224) $450

COLLECTION des Moralistes Anciens
Paris, 1782-83. 10 vols. 12mo. Bkplt. of G. Montefiore. Cont. mor. in Jansenist style by Derome le Jeune with his ticket for Prince Radziwill, with title & his name, gt., on spines, inner gt. dentelles, pink & gt. end-papers, bkplt. of. G. Montefiore. (SM. Oct.7; 1649) Frs. 2,500
- – Anr. Edn. Paris, 1782-95. 17 vols. (of 18). 18mo. Perreau liby. stp., lacks the 'Sentences de Theognis'. Cont. red mor., decor. spines, Greek gt. on covers, inside dentelle. (HD. Dec.5; 51) Frs. 1,350

COLLECTION DES VUES DE PARIS AU DAGUERREOTYPE
Ill.:– Chamouin after daguerreotypes. Paris, ca. 1849. Ob. 4to. Lacks hf. of fly-lf. Embossed bds., covers loose, lacks spine. (SG. Apr.23; 157) $110

COLLECTION OF BULLFIGHT Hand-Coloured Engravings
Ca. 1800. Ob. fo. 12 engrs., 1 remntd., margins soiled. Later cl., worn. (TA. Oct.16; 200) £105

COLLECTION (A) of Certain Horrid Murthers in Several Counties of Ireland Committed since the 23. of Octob. 1641.
L., 1679. Sm. 4to. Contents list at end misbnd., as is anr. p. 'An Estimate'. Disbnd. [Wing C5118] (GM. Apr.30; 320) £80

COLLECTION OF 96 MACARONI & other engraved Cartoons & Charactures
L., 1870-72. Ob. 4to. A few slight marginal tears. Cont. hf. cf. with raised bands on spine, Hugh Cecil's bkplt. (SSA. Apr.22; 51) R. 180

COLLECTION of 12 HAND-COLOURED Drawings
Ca. 1830. Approximately 27cm. × 17cm. On rice paper. Cont. hand-ptd. folder, some wear. (TA. Oct.16; 198) £85

COLLECTION OF VOYAGES & TRAVELS ... Library of the Late Earl of Oxford
1745. Fo. Cf. W.a.f. (CE. Nov.20; 31) £280

COLLESSON, Jean
- L'Idée Parfaicte de la Philosophie Hermetique ou l'abregé de la Théorie & Pratique de la Pierre des Philosophes ... Paris, 1631. 2nd. Edn. 2 pts. in 1 vol. Limp vell. (S. Dec.1; 111) Quaritch. £100

COLLET, Pierre
[-] Traité des Dispenses en Général et en Particulier. Paris, 1742. 1st. Edn. 2 vols. 12mo. Old sig. of J. Menard & press mark on flylf. Cont. red mor., gt., arms of H.F. d'Agusseau, chancelier de France, wide dentelle border with tassels & sm. bird facing right in foliage, spine gt. in compartments with pomegranate tool, inner gt. dentelles. (SM. Oct.7; 1651) Frs. 3,500
- Vie de St. Vincent de Paul. Ill.:– Herissait (port.). Nancy, 1748. 1st. Edn. 2 vols. 4to. Slight foxing. Cont. red mor., fillet, fleuron in corners, decor. spine. (HD. Mar.18; 45) Frs. 2,100

COLLEZIONE DELLE MIGLIORI OPERE SCRITTE IN DIALETTO MILANESE
Milan, 1816-17. 12 vols. 12mo. Hf. mor. by Gruel, orig. wraps. (SI. Dec.3; 141) Lire 900,000

COLLIER, Jane
[-] An Essay on the Art of Ingeniously Tormenting. Ill.:– Wm. Hogarth. 1753. 1st. Edn. Cont. Engl. red mor. gt., covers with 3-line roll border. Bkplt. of Joshua Smith, Stoke Park. (S. Nov.24; 62) Howes. £130

COLLIER, Jeremy
- The Great Historical, Geographical, Genealogical & Poetical Dictionary ... (with) a Supplement to the Great Dictionary ... L., 1688 & 1727. 2nd. Edn. 3 vols. Fo. Cont. panel. cf. (CB. Apr.1; 220) Can. $280

COLLIER, Bp. Jeremy–[CONGREVE, William] –[VANBRUGH, Sir John]
- A Short View of the Immortality & Profaneness of the English Stage: A Defence of the Short View ... Being a Reply to Mr. Congreve's Amendments, & c.–Amendments of Mr. Collier's False & Imperfect Citations, & c.–A Short Vindication of the Relapse & the Provok'd Wife. 1699; 1699; 1698; 1698. 1st. work 4th. Edn., rest 1st. Edns. 3rd. work 2nd. Iss. 4 works in 1 vol. Some spotting, 1st. work with advt. lf., hole in title, 3rd. work with cancel D6 reprd. Cont. panel. cf., upr. cover detchd. [Wing C5266; C5248; C5844; V59] (S. Jun.23; 396) Maggs. £160

COLLIER, John
[-] **The Passions humourously delineated by Timothy Bobbin.** 1810. 4to. 1 text lf. with marginal tear. Orig. mor.-bkd. bds., unc., worn, stitching breaking. (C. Feb.4; 121) *Davidson.* £180

COLLIER, John Payne
- **A Catalogue ... of Early English Literature ... of the Library at Bridgewater House.** L., Priv. Ptd., 1837. (50?) L.P. 4to. Hf. leath., very worn. (SG. Mar.26; 143) $150
- **Punch & Judy.** Ed.:– Paul McPharlin. Ill.:– George Cruikshank. 1828. [1st. Edn.?]. 24 plts. by Cruikshank, each in 2 states, 1 hand-cold., the other plain. Later cf., spine gt., with orig. spine label tipped in at end. (CSK. Sep.12; 152) £140
- - **Anr. Copy.** Cont. hf. mor., spine gt. Bkplt. of Thomas Gaisford. (S. Nov.24; 70) *Quaritch.* £90

COLLINGRIDGE, George
- **Discovery of Australia.** Sydney, 1895. 4to. Title-p. foxed, occasional foxing thro.-out. Orig. cl., soiled. (KH. Nov.18; 169) Aus. $140

COLLINI, C.A.
- **Journal d'un Voyage, qui contient Differentes Observations Mineralogiques.** Mannheim, 1776. 1st. Edn. Slightly browned. Cont. bds. (HK. Nov.18-21; 653) DM 1,200

COLLINS, Anthony
[-] **Discours sur la Liberté de Penser.** Trans.:– [H. Scheuleer & Jean Rousset]. L., 1714-13. 2 pts. in 1 vol. 18th. C. red mor. by Derome le Jeune with his letterpr. ticket, triple gt. fillet, flat spine gt. in compartments, inner gt. dentelles. (SM. Oct.7; 1652) Frs. 2,200

COLLINS, Arthur
- **The Peerage of England.** 1768. 4th. Edn. 7 vols. Cont. cf., decor. spine gt. (CE. Jul.9; 134) £80
See–LODGE, John–COLLINS, Arthur–BURKE, John

COLLINS, David
- **An Account of the English Colony in New South Wales.** 1798. 1st. Edn. Vol. 1 only. 4to. Lge. folding chart with a short split at fold., very sm. hole in B2 affecting 1 letter of text, slight browning. Cont. diced cf., gt., Darlton Hall bkplt. (S. Nov.4; 623) *Quaritch.* £350
- - **Anr. Edn.** 1798-1802. 1st. Edn. 2 vols. 4to. Cf. gt. (P. Oct.23; 14) *Quaritch.* £2,900
- - **Anr. Copy.** Hf.-titles, 1 loose, 3 charts, 31 plts., 3 cold., some text browned, postscript loose at end of vol. 1. Cont. cf., covers detchd. (P. Jun.11; 281a) *Maggs.* £1,750

COLLINS, Capt. Grenville
- **Great Britains Coasting Pilot being an exact survey of the Sea Coast of England & Scotland.** 1763. Lge. fo. Charts & coastal profiles, mntd. on guards thro.-out, chart of Carlingford torn with loss, 2 charts soiled. Orig. cf., worn, spine worn. (CSK. Feb.6; 22) £1,800
- - **Anr. Edn.** 1764. Fo. Engraved frontis. & 47 maps, title, frontis. & following text ll. badly stained, 3 of folding charts stained, defect. & reprd., last 4 plts. torn & stained, 1 chart defect., another very soiled. 19th. C. hf. cf., worn. W.a.f. (S. Mar.31; 250) *Burgess.* £1,100
- - **Anr. Edn.** L., 1771. Lge. fo. Engraved frontis., 49 engraved charts mntd. on guards, frontis. title & prelims. reprd., some worming. Red lev. mor. gt., buckram box, by Sangorski & Sutcliffe. (C. Jul.15; 26) *Wilson.* £2,400
- - **Anr. Copy.** Frontis., title & prelims. reprd., minor worming affecting guards & some charts in latter hf. W.a.f., on 2 blank ll. before frontis. is MS. list of vessels on which this book was used between 1779 & 1788 (including Capt. Cook's ship Adventure). (C. Nov.6; 249) *Allen.* £2,000
- - **Anr. Edn.** 1792. Fo. Antique-style spr. cf. As an atlas, w.a.f. bkplt. of John Jarrett, lately in the collection of Eric Sexton. (C. Apr.15; 31) *Burgess.* £1,500

COLLINS, John
- **Salt & Fishery.** 1682. 1st. Edn., 2nd. Iss.? Sm. 4to. Cont. cf., gt. spine, arms of Stuart de Rothesay gt. on covers. [Wing C5380B] (C. Jul.16; 372) *Dawson.* £360

COLLINS, Lewis
- **Historical Sketches of Kentucky ...** Maysville, Ky., & Cinc., 1847. 1st. Edn., 2nd. Iss. 4to. Some browning & staining, 1 gathering loose. Mor. gt., foliate panel designs, gt. spine. Author's inscr. on

upr. blank, from liby. of William E. Wilson. [Sabin 1446] (SPB. Apr.29; 56) $175

COLLINS, Wilkie
- **The Moonstone.** L., 1868. 1st. Edn. 3 vols. Lacks hf.-titles & advts. Hf. cf. (P. Nov.13; 276) *Jarndyce.* £100
- **Mr. Wray's Cash-Box.** L., 1852. 1st. Edn. Cf., gt., by Zaehnsdorf. Tipped in before hf.-title is A.L.s by author, 4-pp., Gloucester Place, 1 Jan. 1883 to an unnamed lady. (SPB. Nov.25; 178) $300

COLLINSON, J.W.
- **Early Days of Cairns.–More About Cairns, The Second Decade.–Recollections of a Varied Life. –Tropical Coasts & Tablelands.–Echoes of the past.** Brisbane, 1939; 1942; 1946; 1941; 1945. All (500) numbered. 5 vols. all sigd. by author. 12mo. (1st. vol.). Orig. bdgs. (JL. Mar.2; 746) Aus. $120

COLLINSON, Rev. John
- **History of Somersetshire.** 1766. 4to. Plts. only. Cf. gt. (P. Dec.11; 23) *Leebe.* £60
- **The History & Antiquities of the County of Somerset.** Bath, 1791. 3 vols. Minor spotting to some plts. Cont. pol. cf., gt. (C. Feb.25; 29) *Thorp.* £160
- - **Anr. Copy.** Some foxing. Cont. cf. W.a.f. (TA. Aug.21; 291) £120

COLLINSON, John–WEAVER, F.W. & Bates, E.H.–WARD, Madeline
- **The History & Antiquities of the County of Somerset.–Index to Collinson's History of Somerset.–Supplement to Collinson's History of Somerset.** Bath; Taunton; Taunton, 1791; 1898; 1939. 3 vols.; 1 vol.; 1 vol. 4to. Occasional minor, mostly marginal, spotting to 1st. work. 1st. work: cont. cf., gt. panel. covers with gt.-tooled borders, rebkd. with mor.; 2nd. work: orig. cl., unc. & unopened; 3rd. work: orig. cl., unc. & unopened. From the collection of Eric Sexton. (C. Apr.16; 234) *Burgess.* £400

COLLIS, Maurice
- **Maps of the Estate of the Rt. Hon. Lord Fitzgerald & Vesey in the Counties of Clare & Galway.** Dublin, 1852. Ob. atlas fo. MS. title reference & hf. titles. Orig. bdg. (GM. Apr.30; 198) £130

COLLYER, J.N. & Pocock, J.I.
- **An Historical Record of the Light Horse Volunteers of London & Westminster.** 1843. Orig. cl., spine chipped. (CSK. Jun.26; 107) £50

COLMENAR, Juan Alvarez de
- **Les Délices de l'Espagne et du Portugal.** Leiden, 1740. 6 vols. in 3. Later mott. cf. gt., with Rosebery monogs. on covers. (SBA. Jul.23; 469) *Baer.* £380

COLMENARES Fernandez de Cordoba, Felipe –LAURNAGA, Pablo de
- **El Dia deseado.–Oracion Panegirica que en el Dia deseado de la Dedicacion y Estreno del Nuevo Temple del Santo Christo.** Lima, 1771. 2 pts. in 1 vol. Sm. 4to. Folding engraved plt. torn. Cont. limp vell., soiled. (SPB. May 5; 160) $175

COLNAGHI & CO., P. & D., Agnew, Thomas & Sons
- **Ancient & Modern Gems of the Art Treasures Exhibition.** 1857. 2 vols. Fo. Some foxing. Orig. gt. decor. mor. (TA. Oct.16; 156) £160

COLNETT, Capt. James
See–CHAMPLAIN Society

COLOGNE, Council of
- **Canones Concilii Provincialis Coloniensis. –[Formula ad quam Visitatio intra Diocoesim Coloniensis].** Cologne; [Cologne], Peter Quentell; [Peter Quentell], 1538; [1536]. 2 works in 1 vol. Fo. Full-p. woodcut on K2v with additional figures added in ink by early hand, worming at end, cont. marginal notes & underlining, early monastic inscr. on title, liby. stp. on verso of title. Cont. bevelled oak bds., blind-tooled pig spine, lacks 1 clasp, head of spine torn, lacks front end-paper. (CNY. Oct.1; 84) $300

COLOM, J.A.
- **De Vyerighe Colom. Klaer vertoonende in vyftich onderscheydene Curieuse Caarten de XVII. Nederlandse Provincien, alsmede de Hartogen, Houtvesters en Graven van Vlaenderen, Hollandt ende Zelandt.** Amst., [1660]. Maps, originally in ob. 8vo. size, folded in middle to plain 8vo. Cont.

limp vell. This copy published without text. (VG. Dec.17; 1177) Fls. 2,800

COLONIA, Père Dominique de
[-] **Dictionnaire des Livres Jansenistes.** Antw. 1755. 4 vols. 12mo. Cont. red mor., gt. arms of Choiseul-Stainville, on covers & spine, triple gt. fillet, spines gt. in compartments, inner gt. dentelles. (SM. Oct.7; 1347) Frs. 1,600
- **Histoire Litteraire de la Ville de Lyon, avec une Bibliothèque des Auteurs Lyonnais.** Lyon, 1728-30. 2 vols. 4to. Slight dampstaining. Cont. hf. cf. (CSK. Apr.24; 73) £50

COLONIAL Office of Great Britain–HIND, Henry Youle
- **Papers relative to the Exploration of the Country between Lake Superior & the Red River Settlement.–British North America, Reports of Progress.** L., 1859; Aug., 1860. 2 works in 1 vol. Fo. Sm. liby. stp. in 1st. work. Hf. leath. (CB. Sep.24; 225) Can. $200

COLONNA or Columna, Fabio, Naturalist
- **Lyncei Phytobasanos ...** 1744. 2nd. Edn. 4to. Later bds. (TA. Jun.18; 158) £200
- **Minus cognitarum rariorumque nostro Colo orintium Stipium Ekphrasis [Purpura, etc.].** Rome, 1616. 1st. Compl. Edn. 4 pts. in 2 vols. Sm. 4to. 152 etched plts. (2 with cancels pasted over). 18th. C. Fr. red mor., gt., the 2 vols. bnd. in reverse order & the last lf. of prelims. in the 'Pars altera' slightly short & ?from anr. copy, with single note in Beckford's hand & 2 bkplts. (S. Jun.1; 93) *Quaritch.* £800
- - **Anr. Copy.** Sig. of 'J. Cottin' on engraved title to purpura, Bernard Quaritch-Hamilton bkplt. & bkplt. of Edward Arnold. 18th. C. red mor., triple gt. fillet, spine gt. in compartments, inner gt. dentelles. (SM. Oct.7; 1654) Frs. 25,000
- **Minus Cognitarum Stirpium Aliquot ac etiem Rariorum Nostro Coelo Stirpium ...** Rome, 1606. 4to. 1 plt. dupl. at pp. 276 & 280, 3 ll. supplied in early MS., plts. at pp. 273, 276 & 277 ptd. on thin paper & mntd., with printer's error & later correction, indication of other corrections including plt. at p. 276 which may originally have had anr. engr. beneath it, slight worming to some initial (mostly blank) ll. & several ll. towards end. Pres. copy, inscr. on title (in Latin) to the very famous & learned ... master Carolo Clusio Atrebati, the gift of the author. (LC. Oct.2; 74) £380
- **Phytobasnos cui Accessit vita Fabi ...** Flor., 1744. 4to. Some plts. dampstained in upr. margin. 19th. C. buckram, stitching breaking. From Chetham's Liby., Manchester. (C. Nov.26; 88) *Taylor.* £50

COLONNA, Francesco, Dominican
See–COLUMNA, Franciscus, Dominican

COLONNE, Guido delle
[-] **The Auncient Historie & Onely Trewe & Syncere Cronicle of the Wars betwixte the Grecians & the Troyans.** Trans.:– John Lydgate. 1555. Fo. Sm. holes in some ll. affecting some text letters, G4 torn & reprd. affecting 5 lines of text, offsetting on some ll. Antique-style mor. by Mounteney, in mor. case. [STC 5580] (C. Nov.19; 15) *Engel.* £1,100

COLOPHON, The: A Book Collector's Quarterly. N.Y., Feb. 1930-Dec. 1931. Pts. 1-8, 8 vols. 4to. Decor. bds., unc. (SG. Oct.2; 87) $200
- - **Anr. Run.** N.Y., 1930-40. Pt. 1, 3-16; New Series vol. 1-3 in 12; New Graphic Series, nos. 1-4, together 31 vols. 4to. & 8vo. Orig. bds. & cl. (SH. Mar.6; 508) *Lenton.* £170
- - **Anr. Run.** N.Y., 1930-50. 46 vols. 4to. & 8vo. Orig. Series in 20 numbers, New Series, 12 vols., New Graphic Series, 4 vols., New Colophon, Numbers 1-8, Annual of Bookmaking, 1938, Index to Orig. Series, lacks vol. 3 'New Colophon'. Pict. bds. & cl. (SG. Oct.9; 61) $750
- - **Anr. Copy.** Orig. Series, 20 nos., New Series, 12 vols., New Graphic Series 4 vols., New Colophon, 8 numbers, together 44 vols., with Index to Orig. Series, 1967, & Index to New Series, New Graphic Series & New Colophon, 1968. 4to. & 8vo. Pict. bds. & cl. (SG. May 14; 50) $425
- - **Anr. Run.** N.Y., 1933-1935. Numbers 13-20, 8 vols. 4to. Pict. bds. (SG. Oct.2; 88) $120

COLOR PHOTOGRAPHY: a List of References in the New York Public Library
Ed.:– W.B. Gamble; E.J. Wall (Intro.). N.Y.,

COLOR PHOTOGRAPHY: a List of References in the New York -contd.
1924. Many entries annotated. Ptd. wraps., spine chipped. (SG. Apr.23; 67) $110

COLORADO MINING DIRECTORY: Containing an Accurate Description of the Mines, Mining Properties & Mills . . .
Ed.:– Robert A. Corregan & David F. Lingane. Denver, 1883. 1st. Edn. Orig. gt.-pict. cl. (PNY. Apr.23; 85) $170

COLORED AMERICAN, The
Ed.:– Samuel E. Cornish. N.Y., 4 Mar.1837-3 Mar. 1838. Whole nos. 9-59. Fo. Foxed. Cont. bds., leath. spine. Bnd. in is the Carrier's Address of the Colored American, 1838. (SH. Mar.5; 141) $360

COLPANI, Giuseppe
– Poemetti e Lettere in Versi Sciolti. Ill.:– Domenico Cagnoni. Brescia, 1769. Inscr. on title 'Dono dell' Autore'. Cont. mott. cf. gt., head of spine & upr. jnt. reprd. From the collection of John A. Saks. (C. Jun.10; 43) Lyon. £95

COLQUHOUN, Patrick
– A Treatise on the Commerce & Police of the River Thames. 1800. Hf. cf., worn. (S. Dec.9; 411) Crowe. £75
– A Treatise on the Police of the Metropolis. 1800. Cont. cf. gt. (P. Dec.11; 284) Traylen. £90
– A Treatise on the Wealth, Power & Resources, of the British Empire . . . 1815. 2nd. Edn. 4to. Slight browning. Cont. spr. cf., gt. (S. Apr.7; 423) Hyde Park. £110

COLSTON, Marianne
– Plates Illustrative of a Journal of a Tour in France . . . L., 1823. 1 vol. only, lacks 2 text vols. Fo. 50 cold. lithos. dtd. 1820-21, title laid down. Mod. hf. mor. (C. Jul.15; 27) Shaw. £300

COLTON, Calvin
– Tour of the American Lakes & Among the Indians of the North-West Territory in 1830 . . . L., 1833. 1st. Edn. 2 vols. Orig. bds., unc. From liby. of William E. Wilson. [Sabin 14783] (SPB. Apr.29; 57) $125

COLTON, George Woolworth
– Atlas of America, Illustrating the Physical & Political Geography of North & South America & the West India Islands. Ed.:– Richard Swainson Fisher. N.Y., 1857. 4to. Publisher's advt. lf. bnd. in at rear. Orig. cl. gt. with mor. backstrip. (TA. Feb.19; 106) £140
– Atlas of the World. N.Y., 1856. 2 vols. Fo. Orig. qtr. roan, gt., worn, vol. 1 disbnd. (S. Jan.27; 511) Franks. £90
– – Anr. Edn. N.Y., 1865. Some maps stpd. on versos. Cl., brkn., some foxing. (SG. Aug.21; 254) $250
– General Atlas. N.Y., 1857. Lge. fo. Hf. leath., needs re-bdg. (SG. Nov.20; 39) $400
– – Anr. Edn. N.Y., 1859. Fo. 1 map torn in fold. Orig. mor., gt., very worn. (S. Jan.27; 510) Franks. £110
– – Anr. Copy. Cont. hf. leath., defect. & loose. (R. Mar.31-Apr.4; 2294) DM 1,250
– – Anr. Edn. N.Y., 1861. Sm. fo. (JN. Apr.2; 824) £160
– – Anr. Copy. Orig. hf. mor. upr cover detchd. (TA. Oct.16; 180) £140
– – Anr. Edn. Ed.:– R.S. Fisher (text). N.Y. & L., 1865. Square fo. 1 map with route lightly pencilled in, extra map of England & Wales by Bartholomew tipped in. Crudely reinforced with tape on spine & all edges. (SG. May 21; 28) $225

COLTON, Joseph H.
– Atlas of the World. N.Y., 1865. Tall 8vo. Cl., worn, ex-liby. (SG. May 21; 29) $100
– The State of Indiana Delineated . . . N.Y., 1838. 1st. Edn. 16mo. Folding map worn at folds, owner's notation on upr. free endpaper, foxed. Orig. roan-bkd. bds. From liby. of William E. Wilson. (SPB. Apr.29; 58) $125

COLUMBIAN CENTINEL
Boston, 2 Jan.–7 Oct. 1793; 1805; 1809; 1812; 1816 & 1817. 6 vols. Lge. fo. Some repairs affecting text, a few articles cut out & paper reprd. Hf. cl., some hinges brkn. As a collection, w.a.f. (S. Jun.29; 205) Hughes. £190

COLUMBUS, Christopher
– His Own Book of Privileges. Ed.:– Henry Harrisse & B.F. Stevens. Trans.:– G.F. Barwick. L., Chiswick Pr., 1893. H.M.P. specially wtrmkd. Fo. Orig. pig.-bkd. wood, anchor-&-chain clasps, unc., worn, shaken. (SG. Feb.26; 88) $160

COLUMBUS, Matthaeus Realdus
– De Re Anatomica Libri XV. Venice, 1559. 1st. Edn. Fo. Inner & outer blank margins of last lf. reprd. Old limp vell. (S. Jun.15; 175) Jenner Books. £1,400

COLUMELLA, Lucius Iunius Moderatus
See–CATO, Marcus Poroius & others

COLUMNA, Franciscus, Dominican
– Hipnerotomachia ou Discours du Songe de Poliphile . . . Ill.:– Jean Goujon or Jean Cousin? Paris, 1554. 2nd. Fr. Edn. Fo. Mod. limp vell. (HD. Mar.18; 47) Frs. 23,000
[–] Hypnerotomachia Poliphili . . . Venice, Aldus Manutius, Dec., 1499. 1st. Edn. Fo. 170 woodcut ills., some full.-p. Mor. gt., strapwork design on sides & spine, mor. doubls., vell. endpapers, by Marius Michel, mor.-bkd. s.-c. [Goff C767] (C. Jul.16; 317) Beck. £11,00
– – Anr. Copy. Iss. with Senequam on a1r & no catchword at foot of a8v, other points mostly conform with Hofer's regular iss., n1 & 8 supplied from anr. copy, some slight worming, mostly to last 12 ll., some repairs to extreme lr. blank margins. 19th. C. red mor. gt., ruled in blind with gt. arms of Sir William Stirling Maxwell on upr. cover & his monog. gt. on lr. cover, by J. & J. Leighton, qtr. mor. s.-c. Lge. bkplt. of Maxwell at front, & the Keir Arts & Design bkplt. at end, bkplt. of John A. Saks. [BMC V, 561/562, Goff C767, HC 5501] (CNY. Oct.1; 123) $24,000
– – Anr. Edn. L., 1904. Facs. of 1499 Edn., (350). Fo. Orig. pig., partly unc. (SI. Dec.31; 143) Lire 300,000
– La Hypnerotomachia di Poliphilo . . . Vinegia, 1545. 2nd. Edn. Sm. fo. Jansenist red mor. by Huser, mor. doubls., watered silk end-papers, s.-c. (HD. Mar.18; 46) Frs. 31,000
[–] Hypnerotomachie, ou discours du Songe de Poliphile, deduisant comme Amour le combat à l'occasion de Polia. Paris, 11 Jul. 1566. Fo. Some dampstaining & at end. Cont. blind-stpd. cf., worn, plane defect. From liby. of André L. Simon. (S. May 18; 72) Hill. £450
– Le Tableau des Riches Inventions . . . Paris, 1600. 1st. Edn. of the trans., 1st. Iss. 4to. Some minor rust stains & slight discolouration of the paper. Mod. old-style blind-stpd. cf. (S. Jul.27; 128) Quaritch. £650

COLUZZI, Niccolo
– Poesie Varie. Ill.:– after Bartolozzi, Piazzetta & others. Venice, 1777. L.P. 4to. Cont. paper bds. gt. From the collection of John A. Saks. (C. Jun.10; 44) King. £50

COLVILLE, Eden
See–HUDSON'S Bay Record Society

COMANDUCCI, A.M.
– I Pittori Italiani dell'Ottocento. Dizionario Critico e Documentario. Milan, 1934. 4to. Hf. cf. (CR. Mar.19; 56) Lire 500,000

COMBE, George
– Notes on the United States of North America, During a Phrenological Visit in 1838-39-40. Edinb., 1841. 1st. Edn. 3 vols. Advts., map foxed. Orig. cl., soiled, spines & labels slightly worn. From liby. of William E. Wilson. [Sabin 14924] (SPB. Apr.29; 60) $125

COMBE, William
– The Dance of Life. Ill.:– after Rowlandson. 1817. Last advt. lf., browned. Later cf., upr. cover loose. (SH. Jun.25; 132) Duran. £150
– – Anr. Copy. Orig. blind-stpd. cl., gt.-pict. spine, partly unc. (SG. Oct.9; 62) $300
– Doctor Syntax in Paris. Ill.:– T. Rowlandson. L., 1820. Red str.-grd. mor., gt., by Bayntun. (SM. Oct.8; 2173) Frs. 2,200
– English Dance of Death. Ill.:– Thomas Rowlandson. 1815-16. 1st. Edn. 2 vols. Mod. hf. mor. (SH. Apr.9; 2) Salber. £260
– – Anr. Copy. Plts. without wtrmks., slight spotting, a few short tears. Cont. hf. cf., rebkd. preserving old spines. Bkplt. of Albert Julian Lell. (S. Jun.23; 313) Maggs. £220
– – Anr. Copy. A number of plts. & ll. with repairs, mostly marginal, some probably inserted from anr. copy, without wtrmks. Red mor., gt. (S. Jun.23; 314) Shapiro. £150
– – Anr. Copy. 73 cold. aqua. plts., lacks frontis., worn, some ll. loose, foxed. Cont. mor., gt. borders & spines. (SG. Oct.30; 94) $450

– The English Dance of Death.–The Dance of Life. Ill.:– Thomas Rowlandson. [Johann Mentelin], 1815-16; 1817. 2 works in 3 vols. 1st. work: offsets; 2nd. work: lacks 1st. advt. with 7-line capital L at fo. 1r illuminated in red, green Unif. mor., gt., by Rivière. (SKC. Jul.28; 2335) £580
– – Anr. Copy. Some offsetting & spotting. S.-c. (SPB. Oct.1; 190) $800
– – Anr. Copy. Rebkd., orig. spines preserved. (CNY. May 22; 74) $520
– – Anr. Edn. Ill.:– T. Rowlandson. 1815; 1817. 1st. Edns. Vol. I only; 1 vol.; together 2 vols. 1st. work: 35 hand-cold. aquatint plts. (of 38, lacks frontis., additional engraved title & plt. 18), tears in plts. 2 & 29, several ll. loose, 1st. plt. detchd., some soiling & browning; 2nd. work: 22 cold. plts. (of 24, lacks plts. 20 & 23), lacks 2M1, hole in 2G4, slight offsetting to text, flaw in plt. 19, several ll. & plts. detchd., advt. lf. at end. 1st. work: cont. hf. cf., spine gt., worn; 2nd. work: orig. cl., spine gt., slight wear. (S. Feb.10; 350) Nador. £90
– – Anr. Edn. L., ca. 1820. 2 vols. 70 hand-cold. plts., lacks titles, plts. & text loose. Hf. mor. gt. As a collection of plts., w.a.f. (P. Jul.2; 32) Phillips. £140
[–] The Grand Master of Adventures of Qui Hiæ in Hindostan . . . by Quiz. Ill.:– Thomas Rowlandson. L., 1816. Lacks C8 (a cancel) & errata slip as usual, offsetting. Hf. mor., s.-c. (SPB. Jul.28; 414) $300
– – Anr. Copy. L.P. With the pp. 31/2 (lf. C8) & errata slip, often missing. Mod. hf.-mor. (VG. Nov.18; 956) Fls. 500
– The History of Johnny Quae Genus. Ill.:– T. Rowlandson. 1822. [1st. Edn.?]. Orig. blind-stpd. cl. (P. Sep.11; 280) Chelsea. £230
– – Anr. Copy. Mod. mor., soiled. (SH. Jun.25; 133) Allsop. £190
– – Anr. Copy. 1 text lf. with sm. marginal tear, slightly discold. thro.-out. Lev. mor., gt., by Rivière, A. Edward Newton's orig. bkplt. (C. Feb.4; 123) Titles. £100
– – Anr. Copy. Orig. cl., gt. spine. (CNY. May 22; 78) $320
– A History of Madeira. 1821. 1st. Edn. 4to. Slight browning. Early 20th. C. mor. by Rivière, gt., spine tooled in compartments with floral ornaments, covers with arms. From liby. of André L. Simon. (S. May 18; 73) Crete. £350
– – Anr. Copy. 24 (of 27) plts. Cont. roan-bkd. bds., spine brkn., covers loose, worn, unc. (SKC. May 19; 482) $100
– The Journal of Sentimental Travels. Ill.:– T. Rowlandson. 1821. [1st. Edn.?]. Orig. blind-stpd. cl. (P. Sep.11; 280a) Magda. £200
– – Anr. Copy. Orig. bds., unc., hf. mor. case. (S. Mar.16; 205) Traylen. £160
– – Anr. Copy. 120 inserted advts. at end. Orig. cl., rather worn, covers & spine detchd. (S. May 5; 257) Blundell. £85
– – Anr. Copy. 18 hand-cold. aquatint plts., wtrmkd. 1820. Orig. cl., spine gt. (CNY. May 22; 77) $550
– – Anr. Copy. Lacks 2 advt. ll. sometimes present, browned, slight offsetting. Cf. gt., s.-c. (SPB. Jul.28; 415) $300
– The Life of Napoleon, a Hudibrastic Poem. Ill.:– George Cruikshank. L., 1815. 1st. Edn. Mor. gt., spine gt., by Zaehnsdorf. (CNY. May 22; 73) $400

– The Philosopher in Bristol. Bristol, 1775. 1st. Edn. 2 pts. in 1 vol. Title to 1st. pt. soiled, some foxing, 4 pp. of MS. notes bnd. in at front written by previous owner about the author & the work. Later hf. mor. (TA. May 21; 490) £60
– Tour of Doctor Prosody. 1821. Red mor. gt. (CE. Nov.20; 172) £130
– The Tour of Dr. Syntax [1st.]. Ill.:– after Thomas Rowlandson. 1812. 2nd. Edn. Cont. cf., hinges brkn. (TA. Feb.19; 572) £50
– – Anr. Edn. 1813. 3rd. Edn. Hf. mor., defect. (P. Feb.19; 29) Schapiro. £55
– – Anr. Edn. Ill.:– Thomas Rowlandson. [1813]. 5th. Edn. Cont. hf. cf., worn. (SH. Jul.9; 50) Burnand. £100
– – Anr. Copy. Some repairs, spotting & tears. Purple str.-grd. mor., gt., worn. (SPB. May 29; 377) $200
– – Anr. Edn. L., 1817. 7th. Edn. Slight soiling & browning in parts, some plts. dtd. 1816 for 1817. Cont. leath., lacks lr. cover, upr. cover loose. (R. Oct.14-18; 2533) DM 420
– – Anr. Edn. 1819. Hf. cf. gt. (P. Feb.19; 30) Turl. £55

– – **Anr. Edn.** Ill.:– after Thomas Rowlandson. N.d. 3rd. Edn. Occasional slight spotting, ll. soiled. Cont. hf. cf. (CSK. Oct.31; 185)   £50
– – **Anr. Edn.** N.d. 5th. Edn. A few pp. slightly shaken. Tree cf. gt. (PL. Nov.27; 75a)
Wrigley. £50
– **The Tours of Dr. Syntax [1st. & 2nd.].** Ill.:– Thomas Rowlandson. [1819]-20. 8th. Edn; 2nd. Edn. 2 vols. Lacks binder's ll. & plt. list to vol. 1, some browning. Cont. mott. cf., spines gt., vol. II rebkd., old spine preserved, worn. (S. Sep.29; 234)   *Sekuler*. £80
[–] – **Anr. Edn.** Ill.:– after Thomas Rowlandson. 1820. 5th. Edn.; 2nd. Edn. 2 vols. (2nd. work: vol. II only). Soiled. Not. unif. later hf. mor. or cf. (TA. Oct.16; 352)   £60
– – **Anr. Edn.** Ill.:– Thomas Rowlandson. [1855]. Vols. I-II only (of 3). 1 plt. loose. Orig. cl., spines gt., slightly worn. (S. Sep.29; 239) *Schuster*. £70
– – **Anr. Edn.** N.d.; 1820. 9th. Edn.; 3rd. Edn. Together 2 vols. Mod. hf. mor. (SH. Oct.10; 366)
Fairburn. £50
– – **Anr. Edn.** Ill.:– Thomas Rowlandson. N.d. 9th. Edn. 2 vols. Hf. mor. (SKC. May 19; 60)   £50
– **Tour of Dr. Syntax [1st. 2nd. & 3rd.].** Ill.:– Thomas Rowlandson. 1812-20-21. 2nd. Edn. vol. 1, 1st. Edn. vols. 2-3. 3 vols. 2 engraved titles with cold. vigs., 77 (of 78) hand-cold. plts., lacks C2 in vol. 1, tears in plts. 21 & 23 in vol. 1. Mod. hf. red mor., vol. 1 not unif. (S. Nov.25; 427)
Omniphil. £110
[–] – **Anr. Edn.** Ill.:– Thomas Rowlandson L., 1812-21. 1st. Edn. (Vol. 3), 2nd. edn. (vols. 1 & 2). 3 vols. 4 plts. mntd., some pp. vol. 3 browned. Marb. cf., gt. spine, cover, inner & outer dentelle. (HK. Nov.18-21; 2324)   DM 900
[–] – **Anr. Edn.** Ill.:– Thomas Rowlandson. [1813-21]. 4th. Edn. of vol. I. 3 vols. 2 plts. torn, some offsetting, soiled, a few imprints cropped on plts. Cont. hf. cf., rebkd., worn. (S. Jan.27; 499)
Pain. £150
– – **Anr. Edn.** 1815-21. 3 vols. 76 plts. only (of 78), some sm. tears, soiled. Cont. cf. & hf. cf., worn, some covers detchd. (SH. Jan.30; 323)
Ainsworth. £170
– – **Anr. Edn.** Ill.:– Thomas Rowlandson. [1819] 1820; 1821. 8th. Edn.; 1st Edn; 1st. Edn. 3 vols. Later hf. cf. (SH. Apr.9; 3)   *Kemp*. £220
– – **Anr. Edn.** Ill.:– Thomas Rowlandson. L., [1819]; 1820; [1821]. 1st. work: 3rd. Edn. 3 vols. Some foxing, offsetting. Mor. by Rivière, upr. covers detchd. (SPB. Nov.25; 121) $200
– – **Anr. Edn.** Ill.:– Thomas Rowlandson. [1819]; n.d.; n.d. 3 vols. Publisher's catalogue inserted at end of 3rd. tour. Orig. cl., gt. (C. Nov.6; 296)
Cumming. £130
– – **Anr. Edn.** L., ca. 1819-21. Vol. I 9th. Edn.; Vol. III 1st. Edn.; edn of vol. II unknown. 3 vols. 79 (of 80) plts. (lacks 1 extra hand-cold. title). Cont. hf. cf. & marb. bds. (PNY. Mar.26; 283)
$500
[–] – **Anr. Edn.** Ill.:– after Thomas Rowlandson. 1821. 3 vols., 2nd. tour: Vol. 2 only. Soiled. Cont. cf., or hf. cf., some wear. (TA. Oct.16; 351) £105
– – **Anr. Edn.** Ill.:– after Thomas Rowlandson. 1823. 3 vols. 12mo. Some slight spotting. Cont. cf., covers detchd., lacks spines. (CSK. Feb.13; 116)
£70
– – **Anr. Edn.** Ill.:– after Thomas Rowlandson. Ca. 1850. 3 vols. Orig. cl., spines worn. (TA. Dec.18; 63)   £150
– – **Anr. Edn.** Ill.:– after Thomas Rowlandson. 1855. 3 vols. Lacks additional title to vol. II? Mod. hf. cf., spines gt. (C. Feb.4; 122)
Titles. £170
– – **Anr. Copy.** Orig. blind-stpd. cl. gt. (P. Sep.11; 276)   *Robert*. £140
– – **Anr. Edn.** L., ca. 1860. Orig. linen gt., unc. (D. Dec.11-13; 719)   DM 530
– – **Anr. Edn.** Ill.:– after Rowlandson. N.d. 9th. Edn. 3 vols. Occasional soiling, margins of 1 plt. holed without loss. Orig. cl., soiled. (CSK. Oct.10; 36)   £100
– – **Anr. Copy.** 1 plt. torn, some ll. loose, soiled. (SH. Mar.5; 212)   *Capes*. £55
– **Tours of Doctor Syntax [1st. & 3rd.].** 1819-21. Various Edns. Vols. 1 & 3 only. Orig. cl. (SBA. Oct.31; 33)   *Jermy & Westerman*. £95
– **Tour of Dr. Syntax [2nd.].** Ill.:– Thomas Rowlandson. L., 1820. Frontis., 23 hand-cold. plts. Hf. mor. gt., covers loose. (P. Jul.2; 31)
Phillips. £55
– **The Tour[s] of Dr. Syntax [2nd. & 3rd.].** Ill.:– Thomas Rowlandson. 1820-[1821]. 2nd. Edn; 1st. Edn. 2 vols. only (lacks 1st. Tour). Engraved title

& 48 engraved plts., all hand-cold. Orig. bds. or mor.-bkd. bds., unc. (SBA. Jul.22; 87)
Reynolds. £130
– – **Anr. Edn.** 1820-[21]. 2 vols. Some plts. browned, a few ll. loose. Cont. hf. cf., 1 cover detchd. (SH. Jun.11; 151)   *Fairburn*. £65
– **The Tour of Doctor Syntax through London.** Ill.:– Robert Cruikshank & Thomas Rowlandson. L., 1820. 1st. Edn. Cont. hf. mor., spine gt. (CNY. May 22; 76) $280
[–] – **Anr. Edn.** 1820. 3rd. Edn. Text wtrmkd. 1818-19. Cont. hf. cf., spine gt. (S. Nov.25; 426)
Smith. £100
– – **Anr. Copy.** Orig. bds., rebkd., unc. (SKC. Feb.26; 1307)   £50
– **The Tour . . . through Scotland, the Hebrides, the Orkney & Shetland Isles.** Ill.:– C. Williams & W. Read. 1821. Some offsetting. Cont. str.-grd. mor., gt. borders on sides, gt. panel. spine. (C. Nov.5; 26)
Marshall. £70
See–PAPWORTH, John B. & others

COMBEFIS, F. Francisci
– **Bibliotheca Patrum Concionatoria.** Venice, 1749. 7 vols. Fo. Orig. cf., rebkd. (TA. Apr.16; 284)
£80

COMBRUNE, Michael
– **The Theory & Practice of Brewing.** L., 1767. 4to. Title verso stpd. Cont. bds. Title verso sigd. (HK. May 12-14, 975)   DM 600

COMENIUS or KOMENSKY, John Amos
– **Historia Fratrum Bohemorum . . .** Ed.:– J. Fr. Buddeus. 1702. 4to. Cont. vell. (HD. Feb.18; 17)
Frs 1,600
– **Janua Linguarum cum Versione Anglicana . . .** 1670. Text in Latin & Engl., slightly soiled in pts. Cont. sheep, worn. [Wing C5509] (S. Jan.26; 46)
Subunso. £50
– **The Labyrinth of the World & the Paradise of the Heart.** Ill.:– Dorothea Braby. Gold. Cock. Pr., 1950. (370), this 1 of (70) numbered specially bnd. Orig. mor., slightly dis-cold., s.-c., by Sangorski & Sutcliffe. (CSK. Apr.3; 62)   £85
– – **Anr. Copy.** Mor., lev. inlays on covers with gt. design, buckram s.-c., by Sangorski & Sutcliffe. (SG. Apr.9; 445) $200

COMERIO, A.
– **Opere dei Grandi Corrcorsi premiati dell I.R. Accademia delle Belle Arti in Milano.** Milan, 1825. 2 vols. in 1. Fo. Hf. cf. & hf. cl. (CR. Jun.11; 460)
Lire 210,000

COMICUS, Dr.
– **The Adventures of . . . or the Frolicks of Fortune.** [1815]. Cont. mott. cf., with old reback, gt. decor. spine. (TA. Jun.18; 217)   £60
– – **Anr. Edn.** L., ca. 1815. Orig. cl.-bkd. bds., disbnd., cl. & mor. gt. s.-c., unopened. Armorial bkplt. of Herman Le Roy Edgar. (PNY. May 21; 16) $170

COMMANDINUS, Federicus
– **L'Italia nei Cento Anni del Secolo XIX.** Milan, 1901-42. 5 vols. Lge. 16mo. Hf. red mor., some covers loose, orig. wraps. bnd. in, partly unc., ex-lib. (SI. Dec.3; 144)   Lire 200,000

COMMELIN, Caspar
– **Beschryvinge van Amsterdam. Oorspronk, Oudheyt, Vergrootingen, Gebouwen. Ben. een historisch Verhaal tot den Jare 1691.** Amst., 1693. 1st. Edn. 2 vols. Cont. cf., backs gt., worn, spines slightly defect. (VG. Dec.17; 1254)   Fls. 2,200
– – **Anr. Edn.** Amst., 1694. [1693]. 2 vols. Fo. Stains, mainly marginal, especially in vol. 1, some tears reprd., pp. 509-518 with lge. tear. Cont. blind-stpd. vell. (VG. Oct.13; 43)   Fls. 3,600

COMMELYN, Jan
– **Frederick Hendrick von Nassauw, Prince von Orangien.** Amst., 1651. 1st. Edn. 2 pts. in 1 vol. Fo. Lacks 1 plt., some wear in places, some short tears & some plts. a little short and frayed. Cont. blind-stpd. vell., worn, soiled & slightly defect. (VG. Oct.13; 64)   Fls. 2,200

COMMELIN, Jan & Caspar
– **Horti Medici Amstelodamensis Rariorum . . .** Amst., 1697-1701. 1st. Edn. 2 vols. Fo. Cii in vol. 2 with plt. on both recto & verso, vol. 1 spotted thro.-out., some sections becoming detchd from bdg. Old panel cf., rebkd. From Chetham's Liby., Manchester. (C. Nov.26; 89)   *Schrire*. £1,300
– – **Anr. Copy.** Lacks both frontis. Cont. style hand-bnd. leath. (R. Oct.14-18; 2923)
DM 30,000

– – **Anr. Edn.** Leiden, 1706. 1st. Edn. 4to. Lacks plts. 25 & 41, a few ll. & plts. spotted. Disbnd. (S. Dec.3; 932)   *Schrire*. £190

COMMERCIAL ART & INDUSTRY
1929-36. Vols. 7-9, 12, 13-18, 20. Fo. Ex-liby. copy, some stps. thro.-out text. Later unif. cl. (TA. Oct.16; 125)   £90

COMMERCIUM LITTERARIUM ad Rei Medicae et Scientiae . . .
Nuremb., 1731-45. 15 vols., all publd. 4to. Some stains. Cont. leath., worn. (D. Dec.11-13; 193)
DM 1,200

COMMINES, Philippe de
– **Cronicques et Histoires . . . contenant les Choses advenues durant le Règne du Roys Loys Unzieème . . .** 1539. 2 pts. in 1 vol. Old roan. (HD. Jun.30; 16)   Frs. 2,000
– **The Historie of Philip de Commines.** 1601. Fo. Faintly rubricated, dampstained. 18th. C. cf., rebkd., owners inscr. of Edward Hovell, Lord Thurlow. [STC 5603] (CSK. Feb.6; 162)   £65
– **The Historie;–An Historicall Collection of the Most Memorable Accidents . . . vntill . . . 1598.** Ill.:– [Thomas Danett] 1601; 1598. 1st. Edn. in Engl. (2nd. work). 2 works in 1 vol. Fo. 1st. work: some worming, 2nd. work: 2 pts., some ll. stained. 19th. C. red mor., lr. cover stained, some wear, bkplt. of Sir Francis Freeling. [STC 11275; STC 5603] (S. Sep.29; 113)   *Fletcher*. £65
– **Memoires.** Leiden, 1648. Latest Edn. (1st. Elzevier Edn.)., copy with lge. margins. 16mo. 18th C. mor., decor. spine, 3 fillets, inside dentelle. (HD. Dec.5; 52)   Frs. 1,100
– **The Memoirs . . .** Trans.:– Mr. Uvedale. 1712. 2 vols. Cont. Engl. mor. gt., spines tooled in compartments, covers with elab. border & arms of Lady Margaret Beaufort. Bkplt. of Lady Elisabeth Germain. (S. Nov.24; 63)
Maggs. £320

COMMON CAROL BOOK (The)
Ill.:– Eric Gill, David Jones & others. Gold. Cock. Pr. 1926. (225). Some pencil markings, some ll. poorly opened. Orig. linen-bkd. bds., worn, unc. (S. Jul.31; 73) *East Sussex County Library*. £70

COMMONS, John R. (Ed.)
See–AMERICAN INDUSTRIAL SOCIETY . . .

COMMUNICANTS Assistant
L., 1753. 2nd. Edn. 12mo. Cont. cf., gt. borders & centre panels, spine gt., cl. s.-c. Fore-e. pntg.; from the liby. of Zola E. Harvey. (SG. Mar.19; 131)
$250

COMPANION (A) to the Royal Kalendar
See–ROYAL KALENDAR (The) or . . . Annual Register for England, Scotland, Ireland & America, for . . . 1799–HERALDRY in Miniature –COMPANION (A) to the Royal Kalendar–EAST INDIA Kalendar (The)

COMPARETTI, Andrea
– **Observationes Anatomicae de Aure Interna Comparata.** Passau, 1789. 4to. Ex-liby., with sm. stp. on each plt. (SG. Sep.18; 94) $240

COMPENDIUM (A) of Authentic & Entertaining Voyages . . . exhibiting a clear View of the Customs, Manners, Religion, Government, Commerce, & Natural History of most Nations of the Known World
L., 1756. 7 vols. Marginal wormholes affecting letters in 2 vols. Cont. cf., worn, bkplt. & sigs. of William Forbes Leith. [Sabin 20518] (SPB. May 5; 162) $325

COMPLEAT COOK (The). Wayes, Whether Italian, Spanish or French, for Dressing . . .
1656. 12mo. Advts., some slight discolouration of text. Later diced cf. (TA. Apr.16; 367)   £95

COMPLEAT Florist, The
See–CURTIS, William–ANON

COMPLEAT GEOGRAPHER, The
Ill.:– Herman Moll. 1723. 4th. Edn. 2 pts. in 1 vol. Fo. Engraved frontis. loose. Cf., very defect., upr. cover detchd. W.a.f. (S. Jan.27; 512)
Franks. £130
– – **Anr. Edn.** [1723]. 4th. Edn. 2 pts. in 1 vol. Fo. Engraved frontis. reprd., folding map creased, lge. portion missing from title, some dampstains & soiling. Cont. cf., very worn. W.a.f. (S. Apr.7; 470)
Kentish. £180

COMPLEAT IRISH TRAVELLER (The)
1788. 2 vols. in 1. Cf. gt. (P. Jul.30; 117)
Crowe. £120

COMPLEAT Servant Maid's Guide
Derby, ca. 1789. Cont. wraps. (SH. Jun.4; 160)
Targett. £110

COMPLEETE ZAK-ATLAS van de Zeventien Nederlandsche Provincien
Amst., 1786. Cont. hf. cf. (SH. May 21; 23)
Forum. £190

COMPTES Rendus Hebdomadaires des Séances de l'Academie des Sciences
Paris, 1861-70. 4to. 13 issues, each with article or letter by Louis Pasteur. Ptd. wraps., spines torn, unc. (SG. Sep.18; 291) $110

COMPTON, Thomas
- The Northern Cambrian Mountains. 1817. Ob. fo. Orig. wraps., preserved in cl. box. (SH. Mar.5; 41) *Williams*. £620

COMTE, P. Le
- Afbeeldingen van Schepen en Vaartuigen, in Verschillende Bewegingen. Amst., 1831. Lge. ob. 8vo. Some very slight foxing in places. Orig. hf. cf., gt. spine. Each plt. warranted with author's personal blind stp. in lower margin, his autog. sig. at end of preface. (VG. Oct.13; 45) Fls. 3,800

COMUS
See—BALLANTYNE, Robert Michael 'Comus'

CONABERE, Betty & Garnet, J. Ros
- Wildflowers of South-Eastern Australia. Melbourne, 1974. (775) numbered, sigd. by author & artist. 2 vols. Fo. Cl., s.-c. (JL. Mar.2; 583) Aus. $220
- – Anr. Edn. [Melbourne] [1974]. (750) (this set unnumbered). 2 vols. Fo. Cl., cl. s.-c. (KH. Mar.24; 103) Aus. $150

CONANT, Thomas
- Upper Canada Sketches. Toronto, 1898. Orig. gt.-decor. cl. (CB. Sep.24; 207) Can. $260

CONARDZ DE ROUEN
- La Première Leçon des Matines Ordinaires du Grand Abbé des Conardzs de Rouen ... Paris, 1848. (2) on papier jonquille. Mor., double fillet decor., s.-c., by Trautz-Bauzonnet. N. to Trautz. (HD. Oct.10; 232) Frs. 3,800

CONCILIATORE [II]
- Foglio Scientifico-Letterario. Milan, 1818-19. On blue paper. Nos. 1-118. Fo. Later hf. mor., unc. (SI. Dec.3; 148) Lire 1,200,000

CONCILIUM LIMENSUM. Celebratum Anno 1583
Madrid, 1591. Sm. 4to. A few stains, wormholes affecting text, some reprd., lacks final lf with colophon. Later cf. (SPB. May 5; 322) $100

CONCILIUM Mexico
See—LORENZANA, F.A.—CONCILIUM Mexico.

CONCILIUM MEXICANUM Provinciale III. celebratum Mexici Anno MDLXXXV. Praeside D. D. Ptero Moya, et Contreras Archiepiscopo ejusdem Urbis
Mexico, 1770. Fo. Sm. piece torn from outer margin, sm. liby. stp., inner margin of final lf. torn. Cont. vell. bds., loose. (SPB. May 5; 163) $250

CONCORDIA Christliche Widerholete Einmeitige Bekentnues Nachbenanter Churfuersten/Fuersten und Stende Augspurgischer Confession
Tuebingen, 1580. Fo. Bnd. in at end single lf. broadside of first 4 lines of Psalm 9 in German, followed by 48-p. 'Vorzeichnues der Zeugnissen heiliger Schifft . . .' Tuebingen, 1580, Blind-stpd. vell. dtd. 1581. (SG. Oct.9; 154) $200

CONDAMINE, Charles Marie de la
- Journal du Voyage fait par Ordre du Roi à l'Equateur, servant d'Introduction Historique à la Mesure des Trois Premièrs Degrés du Meridien. Paris, 1751. 1st. Edn. 4to. With the 2nd. supp. Cont. mott. cf., spine gt. with flowers. (SG. Mar.5; 261) $375

CONDE, J. de (Ed.)
See—COSTUYMEN ENDE RECHTEN DER STADT BRUSSEL

CONDE, Louis I de Bourbon, Prince de
- Mémoires. Paris-L., [The Hague], 1743. 1st. Edn., L.P. 6 vols. 4to. Bkplt. of Languet de Gergy in vol. 1, Soubise pr. mark on free endpapers. Cont. cf., spines gt. with charges from Soubise

arms each surmntd. by couronne fermée, Soubise copy. (SM. Oct.7; 1658) Frs. 1,500

CONDER, Josiah
- Landscape Gardening in Japan, with Supplement. Ill.:– K. Ogawa. Tokyo, 1893. 1st. Edns. 2 vols. Fo. Sm. liby. stps. on titles. Gt.-pict. cl. (SG. Dec.4; 105) $150
- Paintings & Studies by Kawanabe Kyosa. Ill.:– T. Tamura. Tokyo, [1911]. Fo. Gt.-decor. cl., covers detchd. (SG. Dec.4; 106) $140

CONDER, Jospah
- The Modern Traveller. 1830. 29 vols. (of 30, lacks vol. 17). 12mo. Maps & plts. spotted. Cont. hf. mor., spines gt. (SKC. Jul.28; 2529) £65

CONDORCET, Jean Antoine Nicolas de Caritat, Marquis de
[-] Vie de Monsieur Turgot. L., 1786. 1st. Edn. Some ports. & other plts. added. Red mor. in Jansenist style, by Morrell. (S. Nov.24; 50) *Wilson*. £50
[-] – Anr. Copy. L.P. Inscr. on front flylf. Cont. red mor., by Derome le Jeune, with his ticket dtd. 1785, triple gt. fillet, flat spine gt. with sm. fountain in compartments, inner gt. dentelles. (SM. Oct.7; 1660) Frs. 5,500

CONDY, Nicholas & Arundell, Francis V.J.
- Cothele, on the Banks of the Tamar. ca. 1850. Fo. some ll. foxed. Cont. maroon mor.-bkd. bds., Edgcumbe arms, gt., on upr. cover, contents disbnd., worn. Bkplt. of Thomas Gaisford. (S. Sep.29; 145) *Frank*. £110

CONESTAGGIO, I.
- Historien der KönigKreich Hispannien, Portugal u. Aphrica. Trans.:– Albrecht Fürst. [Munich], 1589. 1st. German Edn. Fo. Text slightly soiled or stained in parts. Hf. leath. (HK. May 12-14; 88) DM 1,000

CONEY, John
- Ecclesiastical Edifices of the Olden Time. 1842. 2 vols. Fo. Cont. hf. mor. (SH. Nov.6; 83) *Weinreb*. £60

CONFESSIO Doctrinae Saxonicarum Ecclesiarum, . . .
See—MELANCHTHON, Philip–NIGRUS, A. –CAMERARIUS, J.–CONFESSIO Doctrinae Saxonicarum Ecclesiarum, . . .

CONFIDENCES (Les) d'une Jolie Femme
Amst. & Paris, 1775. 4 pts. in 2 vols. 12mo. Red mor., gt., by Belz-Niedrée. (SM. Oct.8; 2234) Frs. 1,800

CONFORTE, David
- Kore Hadorot. Venice, 1746. 4to. Leath. (S. Nov.18; 594) *Waters*. £55

CONFUCIUS
- Sinarum Philosophus sive Scientia Sinensis. Ed.:– Prosp. Intorcetta, Chr. Herdtrich, Fr. Rougement, Phil. Couplet. Paris, 1687. 1st. Edn. publd. in Europe. Fo. Lacks port., a few pp. at beginning thumbmarked. Vell. (S. Dec.1; 112) *Phelps*. £60

CO-GR-SS of Asses, The
ca. 1715? Fo. Title, woodcut ill, & 3 pp. of text, stained. (S. Oct.17; 3) £110

CONGRESS OF PARIS
- Galerie des Plénipotentiaires. Paris, 1856. Mor. gt. with bronze arms of double eagle laid on upr. cover, s.-c. (P. Apr.9; 17) *Horesh*. £150

CONGREVE, William, Dramatist
- Love for Love. 1695. 1st. Edn. 4to. Some stains. Mor. by Sangorski. [Wing C5851] (C. Nov.19; 62) *Brett-Smith*. £480
- The Old Batchelour. 1693. 1st. Edn. 4to. Some foxing. Mor. by Sangorski. [Wing C5863] (C. Nov.19; 63) *Brett-Smith*. £550
- Poems upon Several Occasions. Glasgow, Foulis Pr., 1752. 16mo. Mod. hf. mor. (SG. Sep.25; 89) £110
- Works. 1710. 1st. collected Edn. 3 vols. in 2. Recently rebnd. in qtr. cf. (TA. Feb.19; 237) £95
- – Anr. Edn. Bg'ham., 1756. 3 vols. Extra port. preserved, prelims. spotted. Cf. (TA. Mar.19; 255) £95
- – Anr. Edn. Bg'ham., 1761. 3 vols. Several ll. at beginning of vol. I spotted, some marginally wormed at foot in vol. II. Cont. cf., some wear. (S. Jun.9; 51A) *Pickering & Chatto*. £75
See—COLLIER, Bp. Jeremy–CONGREVE, William–VANBRUGH, Sir John

CONGREVE, Col. W., Inventor.
- The Details of the Rocket System. 1814. Ob. fo. 12 hand-cold. plts. only, lacks plain plt., soiled, title torn. Cont. cf., lacks spine, worn. (SH. Jan.30; 420) *Rostron*. £600

CONLIN, Albert Joseph
- Der Christliche Welt-Weise Beweinet Die Thorheit Derer in diesem Buch Beschriebener Narrinnen. Augsburg, 1710-11. Sm. 4to. Old hf. cf. (BS. Jun.11; 43) £280

CONNAISSANCE DES ARTS
Paris, 1954-67. Numbers 33-190 in 12 vols. 4to. Lacks advertisements. Mod. hf. mor., gt. ornaments on spines. (SH. Oct.9; 5) *Sanders*. £90

CONNECTICUT
[-] Acts & Laws of His Majesty's English Colony of Connecticut. New L., 1750. Fo. Soiled & browned thro.-out, occasional tears or holes, minor worming, paper loss at head of A3, newspaper clipping preserved on verso of title & on A2. Old sheep, very worn, s.-c. From liby. of William E. Wilson. (SPB. Apr.29; 61) $225
[-] Telephone Directory. New Haven, Conn., Nov. 1878. Vol. 1, no. 1. Sq. 8vo. Orig. ptd. wraps., slightly spotted, qtr. mor. case. From Honeyman Collection. (S. May 19; 2970) *'Percy'*. £2,800

CONNECTICUT NUTMEG
Ed.:– Heywood Broun. New Canaan, etc., May 26, 1938-Dec.9, 1939. Vol. 1, No. 1-Vol. 3, No. 26, in 1 vol. 4to. & fo. Buckram. (SG. Jun.4; 77) $140

CONNETT, Eugene V.
- American Big Game Fishing. N.Y., Derry. Pr., [1935]. De Luxe Edn., (56) (numbered). 4to. Mor. gt., partly unc. & unopened. With orig. sigd. drawing by Lynn Bogue Hunt. (CNY. Oct.1; 164) $3,200
- Magic Hours. Priv. Ptd., 1927. (100) numbered. 16mo. Cl.-bkd. bds., unc. (SG. Dec.11; 227) $7,400
- Upland Game Bird Shooting in America. N.Y., Derry. Pr., 1930. De Luxe Edn., (75). 4to. Mor. gt. Orig. drypoint sigd. by W. J. Schaldach. (CNY. Oct.1; 161) $3,200

CONNOISSEUR
1901-17. 49 vols. various, including some dupls. 4to. Some vols. affected by damp. Various bdgs. (CSK. Jan.16; 93) £75
- – Anr. Edn. 1901-18. Vols. 1-50 in 42. 4to. Orig. cl. or cont. hf. mor. (SBA. Oct.21; 178) *R. de Kessel*. £110
- – Anr. Edn. Sep. 1901-Apr. 1920. Vols. 1-LVI in 28 vols. 4to. Cont. buckram, slightly soiled. (SD. Feb.4; 162) £75
- – Anr. Edn. 1901-38. Vols. 1-102 in 65 vols. 4to. Bnd. for the Reform Club in cont. unif. hf. mor. gt. (TA. Apr.16; 353) £180

CONNOLLY, Cyril
- Enemies of Promise. 1938. 1st. Edn. Orig. cl., worn. Inscr. to Cecil Beaton. (SH. Dec.19; 346) *Quaritch*. £110
- The Evening Colonnade. 1973. 1st. Edn. Orig. cl., d.-w. Inscr. to Cecil Beaton. (SH. Dec.19; 350) *Elliott*. £75
- The Modern Movement. 1965. 1st. Edn. Orig. cl. Inscr. to Cecil Beaton. (SH. Dec.19; 348) *Quaritch*. £310
[-] The Unquiet Grave. 1944. 1st. Edn., (1000), unnumbered. Orig. wraps., worn. Inscr. to Cecil Beaton, some MS. corrections. (SH. Dec.19; 347) *Heywood Hill*. £210

CONNOLLY, Cyril & Zerbe, Jerome
- Les Pavillons. N.Y., 1962. 1st. Edn. 4to. Orig. cl. Inscr. to Cecil Beaton, some MS. corrections in text. (SH. Dec.19; 349) *Barry Scott*. £80

CONNOLLY, Arthur
- Journey to the North of India. 1834. 2 vols. Folding map mntd. on linen. Mod. cf.-bkd. cl. (SH. Nov.7; 339) *Cookey*. £50

CONOLLY, John
- The Construction & Government of Lunatic Asylums & Hospitals for the Insane. 1847. 1st. Edn. in book form. Orig. cl., gt. title on upr. cover. (S. Jun.15; 179) *Sargeant*. £170
- An Inquiry concerning the Indications of Insanity with Suggestions for the better Protection & Care of the Insane. 1830. 1st Edn. Cf. (S. Jun.15; 178) *Sargeant*. £130

CON

– The Treatment of the Insane without Mechanical Restraints. 1856. 1st. Edn. 16 pp. advts. dtd. Jun. 1856. Orig. cl., top of spine slightly torn. Copy of E. H. Chapin & Dr. S. E. Lawton. (S. Jun.15; 180) *Phillips.* £150

CONRAD, Joseph
– Conrad's Manifesto: Preface to a Career. Ed.:– David R. Smith. Ill.:– Leonard Baskin. Phila., Gehenna Pr., 1966. (100) numbered, with extra proof of port. ptd. on Shizuoka vell. sigd. by artist. 4to. Marb. bds., unc., bd. folder, s.-c. (SG. Jun.4; 81) $110
– Lord Jim. Edinb., 1900. 1st. Edn. Slight browning, spotting, inner hinges torn. Orig. cl., worn, cl. case. (SPB. Jul.28; 91) $150
– John Galsworthy. An Appreciation. Canterbury, Priv. ptd., 1922. 1st. Edn., (75), sigd. Orig. wraps., slightly worn, mor.-bkd. s.-c., unopened. (SPB. Jul.28; 90) $475
– The Mirror of the Sea. L., [1906]. 1st. Edn. 40 p. publisher's catalogue of advts. at end dtd. Aug., 1906. Orig. cl., fore-edges of covers slightly stained, qtr. mor. gt. s.-c., mostly unopened. Pres. Copy, to Elsie Hueffer, lately in the Prescott Collection. (CNY. Feb.6; 64) $1,400
– The Nigger of the Narcissus. L., 1898. 1st. Edn. 18 ll. of advts. Cl., folding case. Bkplt. of Jean Hersholt. (SG. Nov.13; 99) $160
– The Point of Honor. N.Y., 1908. 1st. Separate Edn. Orig. cl., qtr. mor. gt. s.-c. Pres. Copy, to Elsie Hueffer, lately in the Prescott Collection. (CNY. Feb.6; 67) $900
[–] Preface to the Nigger of the 'Narcissus'. Hythe, [1902]. 1st. Edn., (100). 8 pp., stain & tear from staple, slight soiling, lacks stitching. (SPB. May 6; 173A) $900
– The Secret Agent. L., [1907]. 1st. Edn. 40 p. publisher's catalogue at end dtd. Sep., 1907. Orig. cl., spine faded, qtr. mor. gt. s.-c. Pres. Copy, to Elsie Hueffer, lately in the Prescott Collection. (CNY. Feb.6; 65) $4,200
– – Anr. Edn. L., 1923. (1000) numbered, sigd. This copy unnumbered. Orig. bdg., d.-w., soiled. (SPB. May 29; 81) $200
– – Anr. Copy. Bds., unc., unopened. S.G. Williams bkplt. (SG. Jun.4; 79) $140
– A Set of Six. L., [1908]. 1st. Edn. 2nd. state, with hf.-title & title-p. cancelled & pasted on a stub, 40 p. publisher's catalogue at end dtd. Jun., 1908. Orig. cl., lr. cover slightly soiled, qtr. mor. gt. s.-c. Pres. Copy, to Elsie Hueffer, lately in the Prescott Collection. (CNY. Feb.6; 66) $900
– Some Reminiscences. L., 1912. 1st. Edn. Orig. cl., upr. cover soiled, qtr. mor. gt. s.-c. Pres. Copy, to Elsie Hueffer, lately in the Prescott Collection. (CNY. Feb.6; 69) $1,000
– Typhoon & other Stories. L., 1902. 1st. Edn. Orig. cl., qtr. mor. gt. s.-c. Pres. Copy, to Elsie Hueffer, lately in the Prescott Collection. (CNY. Feb.6; 63) $1,500
– Under Western Eyes. L., [1911]. 1st. Edn. 32 p. publisher's catalogue at end dtd. Sep., 1911. Orig. cl., covers slightly spotted, spines faded, qtr. mor. gt. s.-c. Pres. Copy, to Elsie Hueffer, lately in the Prescott Collection. (CNY. Feb.6; 68) $2,200
– Youth . . . & Two Other Stories. L., 1902. 1st. Edn. With 32 p. publisher's catalogue dtd. 10/02. Orig. cl., qtr. mor. gt. s.-c. Inscr. (in response to a typed question which is laid in, ob. 8vo., 1 p.); from the Prescott Collection. (CNY. Feb.6; 62) $3,000
– The Works. Garden City, 1920-1928. (735). Sun-dial Edn. 24 vols. Three qtr. crushed lev., worn. Vol. 1 sigd. (SG. Sep.4; 116) $300
– Works. 1921. (780). 18 vols. Orig. cl.-bkd. bds., soiled. (SD. Feb. 4; 103) £60
– – Anr. Copy. 20 vols. Mor. gt., gt. border surrounding ship design. (SPB. Nov. 25; 442) $2,300
– – Anr. Edn. L., 1921-27. (780) numbered, & sigd. 20 vols. Linen-bkd. bds., soiled, unc. & unopened. (SG. Feb.12; 150) $450
– – Anr. Edn. [1921-27]. (780) numbered sigd. by author. 20 vols. Orig. cl.-bkd. bds., slightly soiled, some d.-w.'s. (CSK. Jan. 16; 122) £240
– [–] Anr. Edn. N.Y., 1924. 24 vols. Uniform hf. maroon mor. gt. by Sangorski & Sutcliffe. (SPB. Nov. 25; 443) $750
– – Anr. Edn. 1925. 20 vols. Orig. cl. (SBA. Jul.22; 202) *Scott-Manderson.* £70
– – Anr. Edn. Garden City. 1925-26. Memorial Edn. (499) numbered (this copy 1 of only 99 with Conrad's sig. inlaid). 23 vols. Gt. cl. (PNY. Oct.1; 159) $500

CONRART
See–CHAPELAIN & Conrart

CONSETT, Matthew
– A Tour through Sweden, Swedish-Lapland, Finland & Denmark. Ill.:– Thomas Bewick, & Beilby. L., 1789. 1st. Edn., 2nd. Iss. 4to. Cont. hf. roan gt. (C. Nov.5; 27) *Franks.* £280
– – Anr. Edn. Ill.:– Thomas Bewick. 1789. 1st. Edn. 4to. Some defects, mostly marginal, facs. of Bewick's ills. bnd. in at end. Later hf. cf., worn, liby. labels on front pastedown. (SBA. May 27; 285) *Fletcher.* $130

CONSTABLE, John
– English Landscape Scenery. Ill.:– David Lucas. 1855. Fo. Cont. hf. mor. (SH. Nov.6; 84) *Sanders.* £210
– – Anr. Copy. A few ll. slightly spotted. Cont. cf.-bkd. bds. (SH. Oct.9; 67) *Ayres.* £155
– – Anr. Copy. Cont. hf. cf., worn. (SH. Nov.6; 85) *Walford.* £140
– – Anr. Copy. Light spotting on some engrs. Hf. mor. (P. Apr.30; 71) *Elliott.* £120
– – Anr. Copy. Cont. red hf. mor., spine gt. (LC. Jun.18; 146) £100
– Various Subjects of Landscape, Characteristic of English Scenery. Ill.:– David Lucas. 1833. 1st. Edn., L.P. Lge. ob. fo. 25 unlettered mezzotint plts., 22 only called for in plt. list. Mor. gt. by F. Bedford, orig. ptd. wrap., reprd., bnd. in at end. (S. Nov.24; 56) *L. & G.* £3,200

CONSTABLE, W. G.
– Canaletto. Oxford, 1962. 2 vols. 4to. Orig. bdg. (SH. Jun.11; 91) *Grassi.* £70

CONSTABLE'S Miscellany
1826-34. 80 vols. Cont. hf. cf., some spines worn. (SH. May 28; 26) *Harrington.* £60

CONSTANT, Benjamin
– Adolphe. Paris & L., 1816. 1st Edn. 12mo. Str.-grd. mor. by Vermorel, decor. spine, border of 4 fillets on covers. (SM. Feb.11; 111) Frs. 2,200
– Discours à la Chambre des Deputés. 1827. 2 vols. Cont. red hf. mor., gt. tooled crowned cypher on covers of Empress Marie-Louise. From L. Barthou liby. (HD. Jun.30; 17) Frs. 2,100

CONSTANTIUS I, Emperor of Rome
See–COUSTANS

CONSTITUCIONES Y ORDENANZAS del Hospital Real de Santa Ana de Lima
Lima, 1735. Fo. 2 sm. wormholes affecting text. Cont. limp vell. (SPB. May 5; 165) $425

CONSTITUTIO Criminalis Theresiana
Wien, 1769. Fo. Cont. cf., brkn. (SG. Feb.5; 95) $750

CONSTITUTION DE LA REPUBLIQUE FRANCAISE
Paris & Strasbourg, An VII [1798/99]. French German parallel, sm. stp. on title. Cont. wraps. (R. Oct.14-18; 1337) DM 650

CONSTITUTION FRANCAISE (La), decretée par l'Assemblée Nationale Constituante aux années 1789, 1790 et 1791
Paris, 1791. 32mo. cont. red mor., decor. spine, gt. decor. covers, fillets border. (HD. Apr.9; 440) Frs. 1,100

CONSTITUTIONS OF the Several Independent States of America
Phila., 1781. 1st. Edn., (200). 12mo. Tipped in at upr. blank is a partly ptd. Document, sigd. by John Kay, ob. 4to., 1 p., Boston, Dec. 24, 1779, countersigd. by John Avery & Charles Thomason, Secretaries. Cont. cf., bdg. defect. (PNY. Dec.3; 94) $1,800

CONTES A MES PETITS AMIS
Paris, ca. 1830. 41mm. × 56mm. Orig. decor. bds. & s.-c. (SH. Mar.19; 180) *Reisler.* £110

CONTES DU TEMPS JADIS
Ill.:– U. Brunelleschi. Paris, 1912. 4to. Hf. mor., covers loose, backstrip defect., orig. wraps. bnd. in (SH. Nov.20; 16) *Jones.* £50

CONTINENTAL TOUR BELGIUM & Nassau
Ca. 1846. Cl. gt., covers detchd. (P. Jan.22; 78) *Kestel.* £150

CONTINENTAL TOURIST, The
L., ca. 1835. Slightly soiled. Orig. linen, defect. & loose. (R. Oct.14-18; 2275) DM 850

– – Anr. Edn. [1840?]. A few ll. slightly spotted. Orig. cl. gt. (SBA. Jul.14; 24) *Wragg.* £130
– – Anr. Edn. N.d. Slightly spotted. Orig. cl. gt., lacks spine. (SBA. Dec.16; 51) *Nicholson.* £145

CONTULO, Joannes Baptista
– De Lapidibus Podagra, et Chiragra in Humano Corpore Productis. Rome, 1699 [1702]. 2 pts. in 1 vol. 4to. Auctoris epistolae ad amicos, dtd. 1702 & 1701 at end. Old. bds. (S. Feb.23; 32) *Dawson.* £50

CONVERSATIONS on the Art of Glassblowing
N.Y., 1836. 16mo. Pict. wraps., worn & soiled. (SG. Dec.4; 109) $275

CONWAY, Sir Martin
– Great Masters 1400-1800. 1903. Fo. Titles slightly soiled. Cont. cf. (CSK. May 8; 143) £70

CONYBEARE, Rev. William Daniel & Dawson, William
– Ten Plates . . . on the Coast of East Devon, between Axmouth & Lyme Regis. Ill.:– Hullmandel after Mary Buckland, W. Dawson & others. 1840. Ob. fo. Additional cold. frontis. plt. laid down. Orig. linen-bkd. card. wraps. (LC. Feb.12; 176) £180

COOK, Alexander
See–BANKES, Rev. Thomas, Blake, E.W. & Cook, Alexander
See–BANKES, Rev. Thomas & others

COOK, Capt. James
– A New Authentic, & Complete Collection of Voyages Round the World (1st., 2nd., 3rd. & Last). Ed.:– George William Anderson. Ca. 1780. Fo. 1 plt. torn. Cont. reversed cf., worn. (TA. Feb.19; 55) £190
[–] – Anr. Edn. 1790. 6 vols. Several maps torn in folds, lacks 7i4 in vol. III, some foxing & marginal tears. Cont. russ. W.a.f. (S. May 5; 231) *Duran.* £160
[–] – Anr. Copy Some maps torn in folds, lacks 714 in vol. III, some foxing & marginal tears. W.a.f. (S. Jan.27; 536) *Dorbrecht.* £130
– A Full Set of the Official Accounts of the Three Voyages. L., 1773-84. 1st. Voyage: 2nd. Edn.; 2nd. Voyage: 4th. Edn.; 3rd. Voyage: 1st. Edn. 8 vols. & atlas to 3rd. Voyage. 8 vols. 4to, 1 vol. fo. Slight foxing or offsetting, 1st. Voyage lacks Streight of Magellan chart & Directions for Placing Cuts & Chart of Part of the South Sea, 2nd. Voyage lacks Chart of Southern Hemisphere. Text in early tree cf., rebkd., atlas old bds., hf. mor., slightly worn. (KH. Nov.18; 175) Aus. $3,500
– Journal during his First Voyage Round the World. Ed.:– W. Wharton. 1893. (50) specially bnd., numbered. 4to. Mor.-bkd. wooden bds. 'from Cook's Tree on Clapham Common'. (SH. Mar.5; 43) *Remington.* £190
– Journal of Captain Cook's Last Voyage. N.d. 3 vols. Folding map defect. Hf. cf. gt., worn. (P. Nov. 13; 30) *Towers.* £65
– The Journals. Ed.:– J.C. Beaglehole & R.A. Skelton. Camb., 1955; 1961. Vols. 1 & 2, plus portfolio, together 3 vols. 4to. & fo. Buckram, d.-w.'s. (SG. Oct.30; 96) $130
– – Anr. Edn. Ed.:– J. C. Beaglehole. Camb., 1967. 5 pts. Orig. bdgs., d.-w.'s. (JL. Mar.2; 538) Aus. $200
– Relation des Voyages [–Voyage dans l'Hemisphere Austral], [1st. & 2nd. Voyages]. Paris, 1774-78. Together 17 vols. including 3 atlas vols. 8vo & 4to. Vol. I of text in 1st. voyage stained & 1 map in atlas with lr. section torn away, a few holes in folds, slight offsetting. Cont. hf. cf., spines gt. (S. Jun.22; 170) *Nixon.* £400
– Troisième Voyage de Cook, ou Voyage à l'Océan Pacifique . . . Ed.:– J. Hawkesworth. Paris, 1785. 1st. Fr. Hawkesworth. Edn. 4 vols. 4to. Cont. cf. gt. (PNY. May 21; 145) $300
– – Anr. Edn. Ed.:– Capt. J. King. Trans.:– M.D. [Emeunier]. Ill.:– after H. Roberts & M. Webber. Paris, 1785. 2nd. Fr. Edn. 4 vols. 4to. Few corners in vol 1 slightly stained. Cont. marb. cf., gt. spines. [Sabin 16261] (VG. Oct.13; 46) Fls. 1,300
– – Anr. Edn. Paris, 1819. 4 vols., no atlas. 19th. C. cf.-bkd. bds., slightly worn. (SPB. May 5; 169) $125
– Voyage dans l'Hemisphère Austral et autour du Monde, faits sur les Vaisseaux L'Aventure & La Resolution en 1772-75. Trans.:– Suard. Ill.:– after Hodges. Paris, 1778. 1st. Fr. trans. 5 vols. 4to. Cont. marb. cf., gt. spines raised in compartments. [Sabin 16249] (VG. Oct.13; 47) Fls. 1,700

COOK, Capt. James *-contd.*
– – **Anr. Copy.** 6 vols. A few liby. stps., stains affecting 2 text vols. Cont. cf., worn, several stains slightly defect. [Sabin 16429] (SPB. May 5; 168) £450
– – **Anr. Edn.** Paris, 1792. 7 vols. 8vo. & 4to. 19th. C. cf.-bkd. bds., worn. (SPB. May 5; 167) $300
– **Voyage to the Pacific Ocean [3rd. Voyage].** Ed.:– Capt. James King. 1784. 1st. Edn. 3 vols. only (lacks atlas vol.). 4to. With 83 (of 87) engraved charts & plans from atlas bnd. in, port. slightly foxed. Cont. tree cf., worn, jnts. brkn. W.a.f. (C. Nov.6; 299) *Maggs.* £380
– – **Anr. Copy.** Cont. russ. (CSK. May 1; 122) £220
– – **Anr. Copy.** Title to vol. 1 detchd., & with lower hf. lacking, slight dampstaining (affecting text & plts.) thro-out, plt. directions with 2 errors in vol. 1. Cont. diced russ., worn, lacks upr. cover to vol. 1 with lr. cover detchd., defect. spines to vols. 1 & 3. (C. Nov.5; 29) *Larnark Jones.* £150
– – **Anr. Copy.** 4 vols. Slight foxing, vol. 1 lacks general map, light stains to endpapers; Vol. 2; stained end-pp.; Vol. 3: lacks 'Death of Cook' plt., slight stain to front free endpaper, inscr. of Emma Marsh, advts. & instructions to binder. Tree cf., gt. fillets & decor. borders to upr. cover, spines reprd. & decor. with gt. anchor motif & embossed cartouche, marb. endpapers. (JL. Dec.15; 728) Aus. $550
– – **Anr. Edn.** Ed.:– Capt. James King. Ill.:– after Henry Roberts & J. Webber. [1784?]. Atlas vol. only. Fo. Lacks 2 (of 62) engraved plts., some foxing & slight soiling. Hf. cf., worn. As an atlas, w.a.f. (C. Nov.6; 300) *Bowes.* £600
– – **Anr. Copy.** Atlas vol. only. Lacks 1 plt., anr. plt. detchd. & torn, some soiling & foxing, several plts. torn (mostly marginal). Cont. hf. cf., defect. (C. Nov.6; 301) *Hinchcliffe.* £550
– – **Anr. Edn.** 1785. [3rd. Edn.?] 4 vols. including atlas of plts. 4to. & fo. Atlas of plts. lacks title, some dampstains, but mainly marginal, 1 lf. torn & reprd. Cont. russ. or hf. russ., atlas lacks upr. cover, others with covers detchd. W.a.f. (SBA. Oct.21; 112) *Lawton.* £850
– – **Anr. Edn.** 1785. 3rd. Edn. 3 Vols. (lacks atlas). 24 charts. Cf. (P. Oct.2; 69) *Femfert.* £110
[–] – **Anr. Edn.** [1786]. Atlas vol. only. Fo. Mod. cl.-bkd. bds. W.a.f. [Sabin 16250] (S. Mar.31; 456) *Hinchcliffe.* £750
[–] – **Anr. Copy.** 61 engd. plts., maps & charts (of 88) 9 damaged, (2 badly). Mod. hf. cf., old spine preserved. W.a.f. [Sabin 16250] (S. Mar.31; 458) *Hinchcliffe.* £550
– – **Anr. Edn.** Ed.:– Capt. James King. 1793. 4 vols. Cont. tree cf., lacks 1 label, bkplts. of the Earl of Wicklow. (SBA. Mar.4; 104) *Erlini.* £70
– **Voyage towards the South Pole & Round the World [2nd Voyage].** 1777. [1st. Edn.?]. 2 vols. 4to. Cont. cf. gt., worn. From liby. of Baron Dimsdale. (MMB. Oct.8; 1) £580
– – **Anr. Copy.** 1st. chart creased at fold, imprints of plts. at pp. 34, 120, 153 & 183 cropped. Cont. mott. cf., worn. (C. Nov.6; 298) *Egton.* £400
– – **Anr. Copy.** Lacks plt. 27 in vol. II, offset on title. Cont. cf., worn & rebkd., all covers detchd. (S. May 5; 230) *Traylen.* £260
– – **Anr. Copy.** Most maps & plts. dampstained. Cont. cf., upr. cover of vol. II detchd., bkplts. [Sabin 16245] (CB. Nov.12; 240) Can. $900
– **Anr. Edn.** 1784. 4th. Edn. 2 vols. 4to. Engraved port., 60 engraved plts., maps & charts, lacks 3 plts. in vol. 1 & one view in vol. 2. Cont. hf. cf., spines gt. Capt. A. Hood's copy with sig. in both vols. & note on title to vol. 1 stating 'present from Mr. Cook . . .', as an association copy, w.a.f. (C. May 20; 112) *Remington.* £320
– **Voyages [1st, 2nd & 3rd]** L., 1773-84. 1st. Edns. 9 vols. including atlas vol. to 3rd voyage. Lge. 4to. & atlas fo. Lacks 1 plt. & 1 map. Old hf. cf., needs rebinding. (SG. Oct.9; 63) $3,700
– – **Anr. Edn.** Ed.:– J. King & J. Hawkesworth. 1773; 1777; 1785. 1st. Edn.; 1st. Edn.; 2nd. Edn. 3 works, together 10 vols (3 vols. & plt. vol.; 2 vols.; 3 vols. & atlas vol.) 4to. & fo. The 9 4to. vols. unif. bound in cf., sides with gt. borders, spines gt., fo. atlas bound in hf. roan, gt. spine. (C. Nov.5; 28) *Gibbs.* £2,800
– – **Anr. Copy.** 3 vols.; 2 vols.; 3 vols. & atlas vol., together 9 vols. 4to & fo. Some ll. slightly spotted, 1 map torn & reprd. Cont. hf. cf., a few spines neatly reprd. or rebkd. using old spine. [Sabin 30934; 16245; 16250] (S. Nov.4; 471) *Slader.* £1,900

– – **Anr. Copy.** 3 vols.; 2 vols.; 3 vols. & Atlas vol., together 4 vols., 9 vols. in all. Lge. 4to. 3 vols. of 3rd. voyage with cont. sig. of Earl of Portsmouth, Eggesford House. Cont. cf., rebkd., unif. with text vols., 2 vols. of 2nd. voyage with armorial bkplt. of Theodore Henry Broadhead. (PNY. Mar.4; 130) $5,500
– **Voyages Round the World . . . for making Discoveries in the Northern & Southern Hemispheres.** Newcastle, 1790. 2 vols. in 4. Folding map lin.-bkd., port. in fac., lacks 2 plts. Mod. three-qtr. mor. (SG. Feb.26; 90) $250
See–ANDERSON, George William
See–HAWKESWORTH, J.

COOK, Capt. James & Lane, Michael
– **A Collection of Charts of the Coasts of Newfoundland & Labrador.** 1965. 2 vols. Fo. Charts loose as iss. Wraps., in buckram box. (C. Feb.4; 182) *Basket & Day.* £75

COOK, G.D., & Co.
– **Carriage Catalogue.** ca. 1860? Ob. 12mo. Some stains, etc. Sewed. (SG. Dec.11; 194) $130
– **Illustrated Catalogue of Carriages & Special Business Advertiser.** New Haven, Conn., 1860. Orig. embossed cl., casing detchd. (C. Nov 20; 20) *Taylor.* £220

COOK, Sir Theodore Andrea
– **History of the English Turf.** N.d. 3 vols. Orig. cl. (SH. Apr.9; 212) *Elkin Mathews.* £70

COOKE, Capt. Edward
– **A Voyage to the South Sea & round the World.** 1712. 2nd. Edn., 1st. Edn. 2 vols. Some short tears, occasional browning & soiling. Mod. spr. cf. [Sabin 16303] (S. Feb.10; 430) *Maggs.* £280

COOKE, Edward William
– **Fifty Plates of Shipping & Craft.** L., 1829. 1st. Edn. Fo. Foxed. Old hf. mor., worn. (SPB. May 29; 85) $600
– – **Anr. Copy.** 4to. Slightly soiled, mostly only in margins, title stained. Cont. hf. leath., spine renewed in cont. style, end-papers renewed. (R. Mar.31-Apr.4; 1787) DM 3,000
– **Leaves from my Sketch-Book.** 1876. Ob. fo. A few plts. detchd., slightly soiled. Orig. cl., slightly soiled. (CSK. Nov.28; 150) £50
– **Sixty-five Plates of Shipping & Craft.** 1829. 4to. Orig. cl., a little worn & stained. (S. May 5; 196) *Dallai.* £600
– – **Anr. Copy.** Some very slight foxing. Orig. blind-tooled cl. (S. Jun.23; 317) *Studio Books.* £380

COOKE, George
– **Views in London & its Vicinity.** [1834]. Fo. 48 engraved proof plts. on. lge. India Paper. Hf. mor. gt. (P. Sep.11; 251) *Way.* £130

COOKE, George Alexander
– **Modern & Authentic . . . Geography.** ca. 1800. 2 vols. 4to. Cf., upr. covers detchd. (P. Sep.11; 105) *Nicholas.* £110

COOKE, James
– **Mellificium Chirurgiae or the Marrow of Chirurgery with the Anatomy of the Human Bodies . . .** ca. 1685. 5th. Edn. 4to. Sm. hole in R1, extreme corner of plt. 1 reprd., tear in plt. 2 reprd. Cf., rebkd. (S. Jun.15; 181) *Busby.* £240
– – **Anr. Edn.** Ed.:– Thomas Gibson. L., ca. 1700. 5th. Edn. 4to. Port., title, & last lf. reprd., some other defects. Mod. buckram. (SG. Jan.29; 102) $160

COOKE, John
– **A Treatise on Nervous Diseases. I. On apoplexy including Apoplexia Hydrocephalica or Water in the Head . . . II. On Palsy & Epilepsy.** 1820-23. 2 vols. Hf. cf., spine gt. (S. Jun.15; 182) *Norman.* £260

COOKE, Mordecai Cubitt
– **Illustrations of British Fungi.** L., 1881-91. 8 vols. Hf. mor. From collection of Massachusetts Horticultural Society, stps on plts. (SPB. Oct.1; 112) $2,800

COOKE, William
See–STANFIELD, Clarkson–COOKE, William

COOKE, William Bernard
– **Rome & its Surrounding Scenery.** Ed.:– H. Noel Humphreys. Ill.:– after Roberts, Creswick, Leitch etc. L., 1845. 4to. Cl. gt. & blind-stpd. (CR. Mar.19; 207) Lire 380,000
– **Views of the Coloseum.** 1841. Fo. Spotted. Cont. mor.-bkd. cl. (SH. Nov.6; 197) *Strufaldi.* £85

See–DUNCUMB, John–COOKE, William Henry

COOKE, William Bernard & George
– **Thames Scenery.** 1818 [plts. dtd. 1814-33]. 1 vol. & plt. vol. 4to. & 8vo. Plt. vol. L.P. (lacks title, 1st. plt. foxed), occasional light foxing. Unif. bnd. cont. hf. mor., gt. spines. (C. Nov.6; 302) *Stanley-Gibbons.* £260
– **Views on the Thames.** L., 1812 & 1822. 2 vols. 8vo. & fo. Foxing, some browning. Hf. red mor. gt. (SPB. May 29; 86) $250
– – **Anr. Edn.** 1822; [text dtd. 1818; plts. dtd. 1814-22]. 2 vols. Fo. & 8vo. Engd. title, 74 engd. plts. on India paper. Cont. hf. mor. gt. (C. Jul.15; 28) *Edistar.* £150
– – **Anr. Edn.** 1822. 4to. Without the text. Cont. hf. cf. W.a.f. (CSK. Sep.5; 83) £210

COOKE, William Bernard & Owen, Samuel
– **The Thames.** 1811. 2 vols. in 1. Sm. 4to. Some offsetting onto text. 19th. C. hf. mor., gt., spine emblematically tooled, reprd., slightly soiled. (S. Jun.22; 19) *Crowe.* £150
– – **Anr. Copy.** 2 vols. Occasional light foxing. Cont. diced russ., gt. borders on sides, gt. panel. spines. (C. Nov.6; 303) *Walford.* £130
– – **Anr. Copy.** 78 engraved plts (of 84, lacks 6 plts. in vol. 1), liby. cancel stp. on verso of titles. Mod. mor.-bkd. bds., unc. (S. May 5; 197) *Elliot.* £90

COOMARASWAMY, Anada K.
– **Medieval Sinhalese Art.** [Broad Campden], [Essex House Pr.] [1908]. (425) numbered. 4to. Several related sheets loosely inserted, & separate 8-p. extract with stated limitation of 25 copies. Bds., qtr. canvas, loose, some wear & soiling. (KH. Nov.18; 176) Aus. $150

COOPER, Anice Page
– **Rudyard Kipling.** Ill.:– Arthur Rackham & others. Garden City, 1926. 1st. Edn. 12mo. Pict. wraps. Raymond M. Sutton, Jr. copy. (SG. May 7; 59) $220

COOPER, Sir Astley
– **The Anatomy of the Breast.** 1840. 1 vol. text & atlas with 27 plts. 4to. & sm. fo. Cl. (S. Jun.15; 186) *Pratt.* £160
– **The Anatomy of the Thymus Gland.** 1832. 1st. Edn. 4to. Plt. I only has an imprint intact, no appendix slip. Orig. bds., rebkd. Pres. copy inscr. 'Mr. Taylor, surgeon, with the author's best compliments & thanks'. (S. Jun.15; 185) *Norman.* £190
– – **Anr. Copy.** 5 litho. plts. dampstained, liby. ink-stp. on title & dedication lf. Cl.-bkd. bds. Pres. copy, inscr. to Joseph Swan. (SG. Sep.18; 96) $350
– **The Anatomy & Surgical Treatment of Inguinal & Congenial Hernia.** 1804. 1st. Edn. Lge. fo. Title dust-soiled & mntd. with lr. blank margin renewed, dedication lf. remargined, upr. blank corner of C1 & plt. 10 reprd., upr. section of plt. 11 & following lf. rebkd. Hf. cf. (S. Jun.15; 183) *Canale.* £50
– **Illustrations of the Diseases of the Breast.** 1829. Pt. I (all publd.). 4to. Cont. bds., rebkd. (S. Jun.15; 184) *Norman.* £160
– **Observations on the Structure & Diseases of the Testis . . .** Ed.:– Bransby B. Cooper. 1841. 2nd. Edn. 4to. Slight browning. Orig. cl. (S. Apr.6; 35) *Phelps.* £55

COOPER, C.H.
– **Memorials of Cambridge.** Camb., 1860. 3 vols. 4to. 29 (of 31) photos. by Frith., engrd. plts. Cont. hf. mor. (SH. Apr.9; 144) *Nolan.* £200

COOPER, Douglas
– **The Work of Graham Sutherland.** 1961. 1st. Edn. 4to. Orig. decor. bds. Pres. copy from artist. (SH. Mar.27; 505) *Marks.* £65

COOPER, James Fenimore
– **The American Democrat.–The Pathfinder.** Cooperstown; Phila., 1838; 1840. 1st. Edn.; 1st. Amer. Edn. 2 vols. 12mo. Foxing. Orig. cl. (SPB. Jul.28; 92) $200
– **The Bravo.–The Heidenmauer.** Phila., 1831; 1832. Both 1st. Amer. Edns., 2nd. work 2nd. printing. 2 vols.; 2 vols., together 4 vols. 12mo. Foxing. Orig. bds., worn. (SPB. Jul.28; 93) $175
– **The Deerslayer.** Phila., 1841. 1st. Edn. 2 vols. 12mo. Foxing, minor defects. Orig. cl., labels chipped. (SPB. Jul.28; 94) $225
– **Last of the Mohicans.** Phila., 1826. 1st. Edn. 2 vols. 12mo. Copyright notice in Vol. II in state B, some foxing, paper repairs, slight staining, owner's

inscr. of Eliza E. Ridgley, dtd. N.Y., Feb.25, 1826 on free endpaper Orig. bds., unc., rebkd., worn, mor.-bkd. s.-c. Whitman Bennett copy. (SPB. Nov.25; 179) $550
- **Lederstrumpf-Erzählungen.** Trans.:– K. Federn. Ill.:– M. Slevogt. Berlin, 1909. Priviledge Edn., (60) on Strathmore Japan. Fo. Lacks supp. series. of 52 full-p. lithos. Orig. mor. gt., spine with sm. faults. (H. Dec.9/10; 2348) DM 3,800
- – **Anr. Edn.** Trans.:– K. Federn. Ill.:– M. Slevogt. Berlin, 1909. (250) on Bütten. Fo. Orig. leath. (H. May 21/22; 1802) DM 3,000
- – **Anr. Edn.** Trans.:– K. Federn. Ill.:– M. Slevogt. Berlin, 1922. 5 vols. 4to. Orig. hf. leath. gt. (HK. Nov.18-21; 2934) DM 520
- – **Anr. Edn.** Trans.:– K. Feder. Ill.:– M. Slevogt. Berlin, 1922. (150) numbered Priv. Edn. on Van Gelder. 4 (of 5) vols. 32 (of 40) plts. & 129 (of 145) initials. Orig. vell. (D. Dec.11-13; 1031) DM 1,350
- **The Novels.** N.Y., 1859-1863. 32 vols. 12mo. Red three-qtr. mor., some foxing. (SG. Sep.4; 128) $100
- – **Anr. Edn.** N.Y., 1883. 32 vols. Hf. cf., gt. spines. (SPB. Nov.25; 444) $650
- **Oeuvres.** Paris, 1830-33. 12 vols. Cont. hf. cf., blind & gt. ornam. spines. (HD. Oct.10; 233) Frs. 1,700
- **Precaution.-The Deerslayer.-The Pathfinder.** Phila., 1820; 1841; 1840. 1st. Edn.; 1st. Edn.; 1st. Amer. Edn. 2 vols; 2 vols.; 2 vols.; together 6 vols. 12mo. 1st. work: without the inserted errata lf., text foxed in places; 2nd. work: with the Fagan-Ashmead imprints on copyright pp. of both vols., & on pp 6 & 4; 3rd. work: 2nd. (1st?) state of vol. 1. 1st. work: mor., orig. ptd. upr. wrap. of vol. 1 bnd. in; 2nd. work: orig. cl., covers slightly spotted, spines faded, qtr. mor. gt. case; 3rd. work: orig. cl., covers of vol. 1 stained, spines faded, qtr. mor. gt. case. From the Prescott Collection. (CNY. Feb.6; 71) $600

COOPER, Capt. T.H.
- **A Practical Guide for the Light Infantry Officers.** L., 1806. 1st. Edn. Cont. str.-grd. red mor. gt. Pres. copy to H.R.H. the Duke of York & Albany, armor. bkplt. of Lord Cheylesmore. (SG. Oct.30; 98) $160

COOPER, T.S.
- **Groups of Cattle drawn from Nature.** 1839. Fo. Tinted litho. title & 25 plts. only, upr. margin stained, spotted, 1 plt. rubbed with some loss. Orig. russ.-bkd. cl., worn. W.a.f. (CSK. Nov.28; 113) £220

COOPER, Thomas
- **Thesaurus Linguae Romanae & Britannicae ... accessit Dictionarium Historicum & Poeticum.** 1578. 3rd. Edn. 2 pts. in 1 vol. Fo. Some browning & soiling, a few short tears. 17th. C. cf., worn, rebkd., covers detchd. From liby. of André L. Simon. [STC 5688] (S. May 18; 74) *Quaritch.* £55

COOPER, Thomas
- **A Discourse of the Connexion between Chemistry & Medecine Delivered at the University of Philadelphia.** Phila., 1818. New qtr. cf., unc. (S. Dec.1; 113) *Quaritch.* £65

COOPER, William T. & Forshaw, Joseph M.
- **Birds of Paradise & Bower Birds.** 1977. Fo. Cl., d.-w., s.-c. (P. Mar.12; 283) *Hill.* £65
- **Parrots of the World.** [Melbourne], [1973]. De Luxe Iss. Leath. (KH. Mar.24; 155) Aus. $480
- – **Anr. Copy.** Fo. 1 lf. slightly creased. Cl., d.-w. (KH. Mar.24; 154) Aus. $320

COOTE, Sir Charles
- **Statistical Survey of the County of Armagh.** Dublin, 1804. Orig. bds., unc. (GM. Apr.30; 247) £95

COPELAND, Henry
See–COPLAND, Henry

COPERNICUS, Nicolaus
- **De Revolutionibus Orbium Coelestium.** Nuremb., 1543. 1st. Edn. 4to. Without errata lf, sm. hole in title affecting date & just touching letters on verso, a few stains (in sig. c with several letters partly obscured & made good in MS.), title with 18th. C. ownership inscr. of the Jesuit College of Clermont in Paris, label of the G.W. Cook bequest to the Franklin Institute, Philadelphia. 16th. C. sheep, sewing guard at end from a 14th C. scholastic MS., gt. in centre of covers, binding reprd. (S. Oct.21; 377) *Beres.* £13,50

- – **Anr. Edn.** Basle, 1566. 2nd. Edn. Fo. Lacks last lf., some neat marginalia, 2 ll. reprd. in upr. margin, just affecting a few letters, lr. blank corner dampstained at beginning. Mod. cf. (S. May 5; 100) *Bozzolato.* £900
- – **Anr. Copy.** 3 old owner's marks, erased stp., some cont., pen diagrams. in wide margin. Cont. vell. of antiphonar 15th. C., sm. initial 0 with ill. [Sabin 16662] (HK. May 12-14; 238) DM 19,000

COPIA EINES SENDTBRIEFFS VOM KONIG AUSS PERSIA Gen Constantinopel den Ersten Aprilis
Nuremb., 1560. Sm. 4to. 4 ll. 19th. C. hf. leath. (D. Dec.11-13; 50) DM 1,500

COPINGER, Walter Arthur
- **County of Suffolk.** 1904-07. 6 vols., including Index. Orig. cl. (SH. Nov.6; 43) *Somerville.* £90
- **Manors of Suffolk.** 1905-11. 8 vols., including a typescript Index. 4to. Orig. cl., soiled. Inscr. (SH. Nov.6; 42) *Doncaster.* £250
- **The Manors of Suffolk.-County of Suffolk.** 1905-11; 1904-07. 7 vols.; 6 vols. Fo.; 8vo. Both orig. cl. From the collection of Eric Sexton. (C. Apr.16; 235) *Castle.* £220

COPLAND, Henry
See–LOCK, Matthew & Copland, Henry

COPLEY, John
- **The Fall & Rise of His Imperial Majesty Jacques Demode, Emperor of the Sahura.** N.d. (25) numbered. Fo. 21 mntd. plts., each sigd. in pencil by Copley. Orig. cl. (CSK. May 29; 57) £50

COPPARD, Alfred Edgar
- **The Hundredth Story.** Ill.:– Robert Gibbings. Waltham St. Lawrence, Gold. Cock. Pr., 1931. (1,000). Qtr. mor. (P. Jul.2; 81) *Stevens.* £65

COPPEE, François
- **Le Passant ... Reproduction en Fac-simile du Manuscrit de l'Auteur.** Ill.:– Boisson (etchings); Louis Edouard Fournier (compositions). Paris, 1897. (300); (47) on vell. 4to. Mor. by Ruban, mosaic fuchsia on upr. cover, silk doubls., wrap. preserved, s.-c. (SM. Feb.11; 150) Frs. 13,000

COPPER PLATE MAGAZINE, or Monthly Treasure, for the Admirers of the Imitative Arts
Ill.:– Paul Sandby, Monnet & others. L., 1778. Lge. 4to. Mod. hf. cf. (SG. Sep.25; 95) $130
- – **Anr. Edn.** [1778]. 4to. Cf. gt. (P. May.14; 201) *Shapero.* £190
- – **Anr. Edn.** Ill.:– J. Walker after Turner, Girtin, Dayes & others. 1792-1802. 5 vols. in 2. Ob. 4to. Plt. 88 'Bridgenorth' in 2 states, plain & cold. Antique-style mott. cf. by Rivière. From the collection of Eric Sexton. (C. Apr.16; 236) *Burden.* £520
- – **Anr. Edn.** L., 1795-1800. 4 vols. Ob. 4to. Foxed. Disbnd. (SG. Oct.30; 99) $360

COPPOCK, Thomas
- **The Genuine Dying Speech of the Reverend Parson Coppock, Pretended Bishop of Carlisle, who was drawn, Hanged & quartered there, Oct.18, 1746 for High Treason & Rebellion.** Carlisle, [1746]. 12mo. Later roan-bkd. cl. (SBA. Oct.22; 319) *Quaritch.* £75

COQUIOT, Gustave
- **Poupées de Paris, Bibelots de Luxe.** Ill.:– Lobel-Riche. Paris, 1912. (300); on Arches vell. 4to. Final state of all ills. with the letter. Mor., sm. stain on upr. cover, wrap. preserved. (SM. Feb.11; 206) Frs. 3,400
- **La Terre Frotté d'ail.** Ill.:– Raoul Dufy. 1925. Priviledge Edn., (15) with ills on pink paper. No bdg. stated. (HD. Oct.10; 184) Frs. 1,700
- – **Anr. Copy.** 4to. Orange mor. sigd. by Creuzevault, decor., suede doublrs. & end-ll., orig. wraps. bnd. in., s.-c. MS. ded. from author to Fernand Fleuret dtd. Aug. 1926, Fleuret's name erased but visible. (D. Dec.11-13; 1053) DM 4,500

CORBETT, William
- **A Years Residence in the United States of America ...** N.Y., 1818-1819. 1st. Edn. 3 vols. 16mo. Foxed, vol. III stained. Later hf. cf., rebkd., worn, some staining. From liby. of William E. Wilson. [Sabin 14021] (SPB. Apr.29; 55) $175

CORBIERE, Tristan
- **Les Amours Jaunes.** Paris, 1873. 1st. Edn., on Holland. 12mo. Hf. mor. by Huser, corners, spine

decor. with raised bands, wrap., upr. cover of wrap. remntd. Bkplts. of P. Eluard & H. Thuile. (HD. Jun.24; 172) Frs. 2,700
- – **Anr. Copy.** Three qtr mor., mosaic spine, wrap. reprd., by Louis Guetant. (HD. Oct.10; 40) Frs. 1,600

CORDIER, François-Simon
- **Champignons de la France (Les).** Paris, 1870. Orig. Edn. Cont. hf. chagrin, decor. spine. (HD. Jun.10; 139) Frs. 1,150

CORDIER, Henri
- **Bibliotheca Sinica.** Paris & N.Y. 1904-24 & 1953. 6 pts. in 5 vols. 4to. Orig. linen. (HK. Nov.18-21; 3110) DM 440

CORDOVERO, Moshe
- **Pardes Rimonim.** Cracow, 1591-92. 1st. Edn. Fo. Kabbalistic woodcuts, sigd. by censors in 1602. Orig. blind-tooled leath. (S. Nov.18; 413) *Rock.* £1,300
- **Peirush Seder Avodat Yom Ha'kipurim.** Ed.:– Gedaliah Cordovero. Venice, 1587. 1st. Edn. Outer margins of last 9 ll. partly reprd. with facs., stained. Cl. (SPB. May 11; 93) $350

COREAL, François
- **Voyages ... aux Indes Occidentales ... pendant son Sejour depuis 1666 jusqu'en 1697.** Paris, 1722. 2 vols. 1 or 2 short tears. Cont. cf., worn. [Sabin 167681] (SPB. May 5; 172) $275

CORINTH, Lovis
- **Zeichnungen.** Ed.:– E. Waldmann [pref.] N.p., n.d. Lge. fo. 12 photos. under guards after originals, with separ. facs., hand-drawn title under guard. Orig. linen portfolio. (D. Dec.11-13; 1032) DM 700

CORINTHIAN
- **History of Yachting in the South of Ireland, 1720-1908.** Cork, 1909. 1st. Edn. Lge. 4to. 1 table loose. Hf. mor. gt. (GM. Apr.30; 104) £60

CORIO, Bernardino
- **Patria Historia.** Milan, 1503. 1st. Edn., 1st. Iss. Fo. Lacks 1st. 6 ll. including 'Legnano' title, inner margin of title reprd., some worming at beginning & end, some old Latin & Italian marginalia, some dampstaining. 18th. C. mor., triple gt. fillet, spine gt. with sm. repeated 'drawer-handle' tool, inner gt. dentelles. (SM. Oct.7; 1664) Frs. 4,000

CORNARO, Flaminio
- **Creta Sacra.** Venice, 1755. 1st. Edn. 2 vols. in 1. 4to. A few marginal tears & repairs. Cont. vell. bds. (S. Jun.23; 253) *Crete.* £320

CORNEILLE, Pierre
- **Oeuvres.** Paris, 1801. 12 vols. Cf. by Courteval (with his ticket), decor. spines, dentelle border on covers, inside dentelle, some minor defects. (SM. Feb.11; 123) Frs. 5,000
- **Le Théâtre.** Paris, 1663. 2 vols. Fo. Copy without engraved title port. & frontis., title reprd., 2 ll. reprd., 7 ll. wormed, 2 ll. with sm. ink stain, lightly browned in parts. Newer vell. (H. Dec.9/10; 1422) DM 650
- – **Anr. Edn.** Ed.:– Voltaire. Ill.:– Pierre & Gravelot. [Geneva], 1764. 1st. Printing. 12 vols. Cont. red mor., triple fillet, decor. spines, inner dentelle, by Derome. (HD. Jun.10; 20) Frs. 52,000
- – **Anr. Copy.** Some browning. Cont. marb. cf., limp decor. spines, sm. faults. (HD. Apr.24; 37) Frs. 3,000
- – **Anr. Edn.** Ill.:– Elizabeth Thiebaut (frontis.) & Gravelot (figures). N.p., 1776. New Edn. 10 vols. Cont. Porphyre roan, 3 fillets on covers, some defects. (HD. Apr.9; 587) Frs. 2,200
- **Le Théâtre.-Oeuvres Diverses.** Paris, 1738. 1st. work 5 vols., Cont. red mor. gt., gt. arms, 1 spine lightly wormed. (SM. Oct.8; 2111) Frs. 7,000
- **Théâtre avec les Commentaires de Voltaire.** Paris, 1795-96. (250), on L.P. 10 vols. 4to. Mod. hf. mor., corners, spines with raised bands. With extra ills. by Moreau le Jeune publd. in 1817 edn. (HD. Feb.27; 26) Frs. 2,500
- **Théâtre Choisi.** Paris, 1783. (200)., L.P. 2 vols. 4to. Cont. red mor. by Delorme with his red mor. ticket, spine gt. in compartments, single fleuron within lozenge of daisies, dots & stars, fleuron corner-pieces, inner gt. dentelles. (SM. Oct.7; 1666) Frs. 15,000
- – **Anr. Copy.** Cont. cf., gt. fillet around covers, spines decor. with raised bands, inside roll-stp. (HD. Feb.27; 25) Frs. 1,800

CORNEILLE, Pierre -contd.
- **Tragedie.** Trans.:- [Giuseppe Baretti]. Ill.:- G. Cattini (port.). Venice, 1747-48. 4 vols. 4to. Port. remargined. Cont. vell. From the collection of John A. Saks, (C. Jun.10; 45) *Maggs*. £50

CORNEILLE, Pierre & Thomas
- **Chefs d'Oeuvres Dramatiques.** Trans.:- port. after Le Brun, & Thomas after Mignard, both engraved by Delvaux. L., 1783. 5 vols. Red mor. by Cazin. (HD. Apr.8; 235) Frs. 2,200

CORNEILLE, Thomas
[-] **The Amorous Gallant.** 1675. 1st. Edn. 4to. Advt. lf. at end. Mor. by Sangorski. [Wing C6321] (C. Nov.19; 64) *Brett-Smith*. £320

CORNELIUS, W.
See-KOBBE, Th. von & Cornelius, W.

CORNELIUS AURELIUS
[-] **Die Cronycke van Hollant, Zeelant ende Vrieslant, beghinnende van Adams Tijden tot den Jare 1517.** Byghevoecht een cort Verhael totten Jare 1584. Ill.:- after W. Thibaut. Delft, 1585. 2 pts. in 1 vol. Sm. fo. Sm. lr. corner of title reprd., 2 missing letters supplied in MS., browned. 17th. C. vell. (VG. Dec.17; 1259) Fls. 950
- **D'oude Chronijcke ende Historien van Holland** [met WestVriesland] van Zeeland ende van Utrecht. ... Beginnende vanden Jare 449. tot 1636. Ed.:- W. van Gouthoeven. The Hague, 1636. 2 pts. in 1 vol. Fo. Cont. blind-stpd. vell. (VG. Dec.17; 1260) Fls. 750

CORNELL, F.C.
- **The Glamour of Prospecting** ... L., 1920. Orig. bdg. (VA. Oct.31; 295) R. 320
- - **Anr. Copy.** Cl. (SSA. Jan.22; 198) R. 280
- **A Rip van Winkle of the Kalahari & Other Tales of South-West Africa.** Cape Town, n.d. Orig. bdg. Inscr. (VA. Oct.31; 296) R. 120

CORNFORD, Francis
- **Autumn Midnight.** Ill.:- Eric Gill. 1923. 1st. Edn. Orig. wrap., unc. Inscr. to Walter de la Mare. (SH. Dec.18; 79) *Sawyer*. £60
- - **Anr. Copy.** Ptd. wraps., unc. (SG. Jan.15; 93) $120

CORNHILL MAGAZINE
1860-93. Vols. 1-47, & new series vols. 1-21. Cont. hf. cf., worn. (CSK. Aug.1; 149) £85
- - **Anr. Edn.** 1860-83; 1883-96; 1896-1909. Vols. 1-47; New Series vols. 1-26; 2nd. New Series vols. 1-27. together 100 vols. Unif. hf. roan. (CE. Apr.23; 300) £340

CORNUT, Jacques Philippe
- **Canadensium Plantarum.** Paris, 1635. 1st. Edn. 2 pts. in 1 vol. 4to. Cont. interleaving in pt. 2, with MS. notes & marginalia, slight staining to upr. corner of 1st. few ll., owner's inscr. in ink & sm. liby. stp. on title. 18th. C. hf. cf., covers detchd. From Chetham's Liby., Manchester (C. Nov.26; 91) *Junk*. £900

CORNWALLIS, Sir William
[-] **Essays of Certaine Paradoxes.** 1616. 1st. Edn. 4to. Unc. & disbnd. [STC 5779] (C. Apr.1; 200) *Quaritch*. £480

CORONATION ALBUM
Ed.:- Marquess of Aberdeen. 1953. (235) with U.K. coins & stamps. Ob. 4to. Orig. mor. (SH. Oct.10; 432) *Seaby Rare Books*. £75

CORONELLI, Vicenzo Maria
- **Isole Brittaniche: Inghilterra, Scozia, Irlanda.** -Oxoniae Atque Cantabrigiae Universitates Celeberrimae a Patre Cosmographo Coronelli ... Imaginibus Illustrata. [Venice], ca. 1705. 3 pts.; 2 pts; 5 pts. in 1 vol. Ob. sm. fo. (200mm.×280mm.). 1st. title: Great Britain plt. of arms dtd. 1681, short tears in a few folding plts.; 2nd. title: Oxford tear in 1 fold of folding plts.; Camb: lacks costume plts.(?). Cont. parch, spine lettered in MS. W.a.f. (S. Jun.29; 12) *Tooley*. £1,500
- **Memoires historiques & géographiques du Royaume de la Moree, Negrepont & de places maritimes jusques à Thessalonique.** Amst., 1686. 12mo. Cont. cf., gt. spine. (C. Feb.25; 84) *Quaritch*. £320
- - **Anr. Copy.** Occasional minor tears & foxing, sm. holes in last lf. Later bds. (SPB. May 29; 88) $275
- **Regatta nel Canale Grande di Venezia.** -**Regatta nel Canal Grande di Venezia di IV Marzo MDCCIX.** N.d., 2 works in 1 vol. Ob. 4to. 1st.

work: 1st. few ll. washed with margins reprd.; 2nd. work: last plt. laid down, some stains towards end. As a coll. of plts., w.a.f. (C. Nov.20; 186) *Parikian*. £650
- **Viaggio d'Italia in Inghilterra.** Venice, 1697. 2 vols. 1 plt. holed with loss, a few dampstains. Cont. cf. W.a.f. (CSK. Jun.5; 47) £320
- - **Anr. Copy.** Some plts. dampstained, 1 torn. Later cf. (CSK. May.8; 25) £220

CORONET
Chic., 1937-39. 34 iss., lacks iss. for Dec. 1937 & Mar. 1938. Pict. wraps., slight wear. (SG. Jul.9; 94) $110

CORPUS Vasorum Antiquorum. Italy, 11 vols; Great Britain, 9 vols. only; USA, 2 vols. only; Belgium, 1 vol. only
N.d. Tog. 23 vols. only. 4to. Liby. stps. Orig. portfos. & later cl. (SH. Apr.9; 66) *Falkener*. £260

CORREA, João de Medeiros-VAZ, Thomé
- **Perfeito Soldado, e Politica militar.** -Auqustissimo Ioanni IV. Lisbon; Coimbra, 1659; 1677. 2 works in 1 vol. Stained & soiled. Cf., rebkd. (SPB. May 5; 173) $400

CORRER-PISANI
- **Numismata.** Ill.:- Gian Antonio Faldoni (frontis.). Venice, ca. 1726. Fo. Sm. owner's stp. on frontis. Cont. vell. From the collection of John A. Saks. (C. June.10; 46) *Bartoli*. £120

CORREVON, Henry
- **Album des Orchidées de l'Europe centrale et Septentrionale.** Ill.:- after W. Muller & others. Geneva & Paris, 1899. 1st. Edn. All but 1 plt. cold., sm. tear to blank margin of dedication lf., contents loose in bdg., 4 pp. of inserted advts. at end. Orig. gt.-lettered cl., qtr. mor. gt. drop box. From the Prescott Collection. (CNY. Feb.6; 74) $140

CORRIERE DELLE DAME
Milan, 1834-43. 11 vols., inclg. 2 duplicate vols. Some sm. tears & other sm. faults. Cont. bds., not unif., some vols. lightly worn. W.a.f. (SI. Dec.3; 155) Lire 4,000,000

CORRIO, Bernardino
- [Historia continente da Lorigine di Milano tutti le Gesti, Fatti, e Detti Preclari ...] Milan, 13 Jul. 1503. 1st. Edn. Fo. Lacks 7 prelim ll. as often, many cont. margin notes Unbnd. with old parch covers, much reprd. (SI. Dec.3; 151) Lire 1,400,000

CORROZET, Gilles & Champier, Claude
[-] **Le Cathalogue des Villes et Citez assises et Troys Gaulles** ... Paris, 1539. 32mo. Mor., gt. dentelles, by Duru. Sm. gt. mor. bkplt. of Ambroise Firmin Didot. (SG. Sep.25; 96) $750

CORTES, Hernando
- **De Insulis Nuper Inventis** ... -**Etropius: Romana Historia Universa.** Ed.:- Sigismund Gelenius (2nd. work). Cologne; Basle, Sep. 1532; 1532. 2nd. Latin Edns. 2 works in 1 vol. Fo. 2 sm. wormholes at end of 1st. work. Cont. blind-stpd. cf. over wood bds., ornam. roll sigd. R.W., lacks clasps & sm. portions of leath. on sides, spine reprd. [Sabin 16949] (C. Nov.20; 187) *Kraus*. £600
- **Die Eroberung Mexikos.** Trans.:- M. Spiro. Ill.:- M. Slevogt. Berlin, 1918. (250) not sigd. by artist. 4to. Orig. raw silk. (R. Oct.14-18; 1076) DM 650

CORTESAO, Armando
- **Cartografia e Cartógrafos Portugueses de Sécolos XV e XVI.** Lissabon, 1935. 2 vols. 4to. Last few ll. & plts. slightly stained in lower blank border. Hf. leath. gt., orig. wraps. bnd. in. (R. Mar.31-Apr.4; 773) DM 480
- **History of Portugese Cartography.** Coimbra, 1969-71. 2 vols. Orig. bds. (CSK. Sep.19; 150) £65
- - **Anr. Copy.** 4to. Cl. (SG. Oct.2; 92) $110

CORVISART, Jean Nicolas
- **A Treatise on the Diseases & Organic Lesions of the Heart & Great Vessels.** Trans.:- C. H. Hebb. 1813. 1st. Engl. Edn. Sm. paper flaw in 2XI, liby. stps. on title & elsewhere. Hf. cf. (S. Jun.15; 189) *Phillips*. £150

CORVO, Baron (Pseud.)
See-ROLFE, Frederick W.S. 'Baron Corvo'

CORY, Charles B.
- **Birds of the Bahama Islands.** Boston. Priv. Ptd., 1880. 1st. Edn. 4to. Some plts. with liby. stps. on versos. Gt.-pict. cl. (SG. Jan.29; 107) $220
- **The Birds of Haiti & San Domingo.** Boston, 1885. 1st. Edn. Bnd. from pts. Lge. 4to. Hf. mor., unc., ptly. unopnd. (SG. Oct.9; 66) $475
- - **Anr. Edn.** Boston, 1885. 4to. Cl. (P. Nov.13; 193) *Dartmoor*. £220

CORY, G.E.
- **The Rise of South Africa.** L., 1910-30. 5 vols. Some foxing. Orig. bdg. (VA. Oct.31; 297) R. 210

COSSON, Baron de
- **Le Cabinet d'Armes de Maurice de Talleyrand-Perigord, Duc de Dino.** Paris, 1901. (200) numbered. Fo. Cont. bds. (SI. Dec.3; 156) Lire 220,000

COSTE, M.
See-CAILLAU, J.M.-CULLEN, William-HALLER, Albrecht-COSTE, M.

COSTELLO, Dudley
- **Piedmont & Italy ... Illustrated in a series of Views.** Ill.:- After William Henry Bartlett & others. 1861. 2 vols. 4to. Some spotting & soiling. Cont. mor., gt., worn, 1 cover detchd. (CSK. Oct.24; 181) £180
- - **Anr. Copy.** Vol. II only (of 2). Some plts. slightly stained at foot, occasional spotting. Cont. hf. roan, spine gt., slightly worn. (S. Jan.27; 585) *Mistrali*. £140
- - **Anr. Edn.** Ill.:- after Brockendon, Bartlett, Vacker, etc. L., [1861]. 2 vols. 4to. Cont. hf. leath. (VG. Dec.16; 905) Fls. 900

COSTELLO, Louisa Stuart
- **Specimens from the Early Poetry of France.** 1835. 1st. Edn. Each plt. in 2 states, slight spotting. Early 20th. C. pol. cf. by Rivière. (S. Feb.9; 36) *Traylen*. £85

COSTER, Charles de
- **Herr Halewijn. Eine Vlämische Märe.** Ill.:- Wilhelm Kohlhoff. Berlin, 1920. (60) A Edn., together (250) numbered & sigd. on H.M.P. 4to. Orig. pig., blind-tooled. (D. Dec.11-13; 1034) DM 650

COSTUME
- **Abbildungen der Uniformen.** Ill.:- Onfray de Breville 'Job' after Le Bourgois de Hambourg. France, ca. 1900. Ob. 4to. 158 watercolours. Leath.-bkd. marb. bds. (SG. May 14; 1) $950
- **Abito dei Rappresentanti del Popolo Francese.** Ill.:- Grasset de Saint-Sauveur. Nice, 1796. Cont. hf. cf. (SI. Dec.3; 2) Lire 440,000
- **Antique Costumes.** Ca. 1833-36. 50 (45 hand-cold.) plts., from Lady Magazine. Hf. mor. gt. (P. Sep.11; 173) *Kestel*. £100
- **Blätter für Kostümkunde.** Ed.:- A. v. Heyden. Berlin, 1876-81. Vols. 1-2. 4to. A few plts, in vol. 1 soiled. Hf.-leath. (R. Mar.31-Apr.4; 1532) DM 1,300
- **Collection des Costumes de la Suisse et de ses pays limitrophes.** Zurich, [1820?]. 12mo. Cont. red mor.-bkd. bds., sides panel. in gt. & blind. (C. Feb.4; 168A) *Walford*. £480
- **Collection des Costumes de tous les Ordres Monastiques supprimés à Differentes Epoques dans la ci-devant Belgique.** Bruxelles, Late 18th. C. Bds., spine detchd. (LM. Mar.21; 91) B.Frs. 33,000
- **Collection of the Dresses of Different Nations.** 1757. 2 vols. in 1. 4to. Text in Fr. & Engl. Hf. cf. (P. Jan.22; 286) *Cambridge*. £320
- - **Anr. Edn.** Ca. 1770. 4to. 32 hand-cold. plts., lacks text. Cf.-bkd. bds. W.a.f. (C. May 20; 137) *Walford*. £140
- **Collection of well-executed water-colour costume studies, mainly religious.** Ca. 1790-1810. Fo. Later qtr. cl. (TA. Feb.19; 480) £62
- **Costume of Malta.[?]** Ca. 1810? Sm. fo. (drawings ca. 195 × 16mm.). Collection of 19 orig. watercolour drawings unsigd. & undtd., mntd. in pairs on stubs in an album, interleaved. Cont. red hf. mor. (C. Feb.25; 216) *Henderson*. £280
- [Costume of Religious & Military Orders]. Ill.:- B. Jollivet, some after A. Henry. N.p., ca. 1850. 4to. 172 lithos. from 8 vol. work, 84 ll. cut in smaller format, some sm. tears, approx. 30 ll. with hole, partly albumen heightened. Loose, in mod. linen portfolio. (H. Dec.9/10; 752) DM 800

– Costume of Turkey. Ill.:– Dadley after Dalvimart. L., 1802 [1804]. Fo. Whatman wtrmks. dtd. 1819 & 1820. Cont. str.-grd. mor. gt., very worn. Rudolph Valentino's elab. pict. bkplt. (SG. Feb.26; 98) $375
– – Anr. Edn. 1804. Fo. Text wtrmkd. 1818, plts. 1823. 19th. C. str.-grd. mor., gt. (S. Oct. 21; 510) *Artico.* £280
– Costume Popolari Italiani. Milan. n.d. 2 vols. Fo. 164 hand-cold. plts. Unbound as issued in orig. pict. wraps., s.-c.'s. (CSK. Aug.29; 62) £75
– Costume Through the Ages. Ill.:– Arthur Rackham. L., [1938]. Brochure. Raymond M. Sutton, Jr. copy. (SG. May 7; 60) $160
– Costumes de Belgique, Anciens et Modernes, Militaires, Civils et Religieux. Brussels, 1830. 4to. Hf. red chagrin, corners, 4 lge. spine raised bands, decor. (LM. Jun.13; 55) B.Frs. 90,000
– Costumes de l'Empire de Russie. Ill.:– J. Dadley after Georgi. L., 1803. Sm. fo. Mod. Engl. hf. chagrin, unc. (HD. Dec.5; 54) Frs. 2,400
– – Anr. Edn. [1803]. Fo. 70 hand-cold. plts. only (of 73), 2 torn, liby. stp. on rectos, text in Engl. & Fr., lacks prelims. & a few ll. of text, browned, some tears. Mod. cl. (SH. Feb.5; 205) *Subunso.* £60
– Costumes du Puy-de-Dome ... Ill.:– Bour & Bertrand. N.d. Ob. 4to. Publisher's bds. (HD. Jun.24; 81) Frs. 4,300
– Costumes du Royaume des Pays-Bas. Ill.:– J. Madou. 1827. 4to. Bds. (P. Apr.9; 189) *Frankel.* £280
– Costumes Espagnols. N.p., end of 19th. C. 4to. 46 orig. drawings, on silk paper, glued on thick pastebd. Hf. chagrin, corners. (HD. Dec.5; 55) Frs. 3,200
– Costumes Européens du XVIIe au XIXe Siècle. Ill.:– Job & Herouard. Paris, n.d. Fo. 60 cold. mntd. plts. Mod. hf. cf. (SI. Dec.3; 158) Lire 250,000
– Costumes Françaises, de 1200 à 1715. Ill.:– G. Sharf. Ca. 1830. 4to. Red mor., elab. gt., by Bayntun. (S. Feb.10; 431) *Maggs.* £220
– Costumes Mexicains. N.p., mid 19th. C. 4to. 69 orig. cold. drawings, mntd. on thick pastebd. Hf. chagrin. corners. (HD. Dec.5; 56) Frs. 19,500
– Costumes of British Ladies from the Time of William I to the Reign of Victoria. Ca. 1860. Lge. fo. Cont. mor. elaborately tooled in gt. (S. May 5; 422) *Blundell.* £90
– Costumes of the Vatican. N.d. Accordian fold-out, 6 × 126½ inches. Orig. bds., backstrip worn, s.-c. (SG. Aug.29; 36) $60
– Costumes Suédois. Ill.:– Camino & Regamey engraved by Ch. Geoffroy. Paris, ca. 1860. 4to. Slightly browned in margins in parts. Mod. hf. leath. with orig. wraps. bnd. in, defect. & bkd. (H. May 21/22; 686) DM 420
– Les Costumes Théâtrales, ou Scènes Secrettes des Foyers. Helio-Foutropolis, 1793. 16mo. 2nd. state of engrs. bnd. in. Mod. red mor., decor. spine, 3 fillets, inner dentelles. (HD. Apr.10; 329) Frs. 5,000
– Dresses of the French. Ca. 1760. 4to. Recent qtr. cf. (TA. Sep.18; 342) £65
– Dutch Costumes. Tableaux de l'Habillement, des Moeurs et des Coutumes dans la Republique Batave. Amst., 1803. 4to. Orig. bds. (SH. May 21; 241) *Crete.* £230
– Etrennes Géographiques, ou Costumes des Principaux Peuples de l'Europe. Paris, 1815. New Edn. 12mo. Title & 1st. ll. slightly stained, last text signature stained. Red hf. mor., gt., sm. stps., gold fillets. (D. Dec.11-13; 566) DM 700
– Habillements de Plusieurs Nations. Leiden, ca. 1710. Ob. 4to. Slight staining on title & 1st. plt. Cf. (BS. Jun.11; 348) £320
– Italian Costume Plates. Ill.:– Pistolesi & others. Italy, ca. 1820-30. Fo. 71 hand-cold. copperplates of ecclesiastical, military & peasant figures. Cont. gt. hf. mor., upr. hinge brkn. (PNY. Dec.3; 193) $180
– Military Costume of Turkey. 1818. L.P. Fo. Extra hand-cold. aquatint vig.-title, 30 hand-cold. plts., hf.-title, advt. lf., text wtrmkd. 1813, plts. 1816, stained in lower margins thro.-out. Orig. str.-grd. mor., spine gt. & defect. Bkplt. of Duke of St. Albans. (S. Nov.25; 532) *Willow.* £280
– – Anr. Copy. Plts., some wtrmkd. 1822, some offsetting. 19th. C. str.-grd. mor., gt. (S. Oct.21; 507) *Walford.* £170
– – Anr. Copy. Plts. wtrmarked 1835-36, some plts. & text ll. detchd. Cont. maroon mor., gt., spine gt., contents loose. (S. Sep.29; 267) *Doran.* £140

– – Anr. Copy. Cont. hf. roan, worn, upr. cover detchd., unc. (C. Feb.25; 221) *McMamnon.* £100
– – Anr. Copy. Red chagrin. (DS. May 22; 871) Pts. 36,000
– – Anr. Edn. [1822 or later]. Fo. Wtrmkd. 1822, slight offsetting onto text. Cont. str.-grd. red mor., tooled in gt. & blind, slightly stained, bkplt. of Sidney Hill. (S. Apr.7; 458) *Foyles.* £150
– Modes. 1803-90. N.d 2 vols. Mod. cl. W.a.f. (SM. Feb.11; 93) £190
– Les Modes Parisiennes. Ill.:– Carache & others after Calix. Ca. 1855-1860. Cl., mor. spine. (HSS. Apr.24; 265) £190
– Munchener Bilderbogen. 1903. Fo. Slight browning. Orig. cl., spine slightly torn at head & foot. (CSK. Dec.10; 6) £90
– Picturesque Representations of the Dress & Manners of the English. Ill.:– After Pyne. 1814. 1st. Edn. Text wtrmarked 1809, plts. 1809-11, 1 lf. defect., sm. tear in plt. 14, some offsetting & spotting. Cont. str.-grd. mor., spine gt., slightly worn. (S. Sep.29; 268) *Elliot.* £100
– – Anr. Copy. 50 hand-cold. costume plts. Later hf. cf. (TA. Feb.19; 230) £68
– Picturesque Representations of the Dress & Manners of the Russians. Ca. 1820. 4to. 63 hand-cold. litho. costume plts. (of 64, lacks plt. 22), minor spotting. Cont. red mor., gt. (TA. Jun.18; 473) £75
– – Anr. Edn. Ca. 1823. 4to. Lacks plt. & text 22. Red mor., rebkd. (S. Jan.27; 497) *Russell.* £70
– Pyrenees–25 lithographed illustrations of Pyrenean costumes. [France], ca. 1880? Ca. 15.4 × 10.5mm. Partly hand-cold., on 3 joined sheets, some slightly spotted. Orig. cl. folder gt. (SBA. Mar.4; 123) *Crete.* £64
– [Swiss Costumes]. Ill.:– G. Scharf. Ca. 1828. Sm. 4to. Some lithos. soiled. Bds., worn. (SH. Jun.4; 162) *Russell.* £130
– Swiss & Tyrolean Costume. Ill.:– H. Lecomte. [Paris], [plts. dtd. 1817]. 4to. Occasional light spotting. Cont. hf. cf., scuffed. W.a.f. (CSK. Jul.3; 119) £280
– Uniformen, die, der Preussischen Garden, von Ihrem Entstehen bis auf die Neueste Zeit ... Berlin, 1828. Pt. 2. 4to. Cont. wraps. (D. Dec.11-13; 2791) DM 1,200
– Uniformes de l'Armée Française sous Louis-Phillipe. Ca. 1820-30. Fo. 12 military hand-cold. litho. plts. tipped in, captions in German & Fr. Later hf. cl. (TA. Nov.20; 302) £290
– Uniformi Militari Italiane. Ill.:– Crosio. Torino, 1863. Ob. 4to. Mod. cl., orig. wraps. bnd. in. (SI. Dec.4; 579) Lire 900,000
– Victorian Fashion Plates. 1864-90. 4to. 96 hand-cold. plts., mainly from the Englishwoman's Domestic Magazine. 19th. C. cl. (LC. Feb.12; 18) £140
– Vollstaendiges Voelkergallerie in Getreuen Abbildungen aller Nationen ... Meissen, ca. 1835-40. 3 Pts. in 4 vols. 4to. Hf. cf. (SG. Feb.26; 330) $325
– Zur Geschichte der Kostueme. Ill.:– Braun, Diez & others. Munich, 1912. 4to. Pict. cl. (SG. Oct.30; 102) $190

COSTUME–BERTRAND DE MOLEVILLE, Antoine François
– The Military Costume of Turkey.–The Costume of the Hereditary States of the House of Austria. 1818; 1804. 2 works in 1 vol. Fo. Cont. str.-grd. mor., gt. & blind tooled borders & central ornament, rebkd. (C. Jul.15; 29) *Zanzotto.* £420

COSTUYMEN ENDE RECHTEN DER STADT BRUSSEL
Ed.:– J. de Conde. Brussels, 1757. Fo. With 3 added ordonnances dated 21 Jan. 1817, n.d. & 29 Apr. 1777, old damp-staining at end. Old cf., 6 ornam. spine raised bands, worn. (LM. Nov.8; 30) B.Frs. 9,000

COSWAY, Richard
– Catalogue of a Collection of Miniatures in the Possession of Edward Joseph. 1883. Fo. Cont. hf. mor. Pres. copy. (SH. Jun.18; 35) *Magnanis.* £50
– The Life of Richard Cosway, R.A. illustrated with Engravings from his Works. Ill.:– after Cosway. Late 19th. C. Lge. fo. Made-up work from Smith's Life of Nollebens & Cunningham's Lives of the Painters, inlaid with 58 late 18th. & early 19th. C. engraved plts., some col. tinted, hand-cold. engraved caricature, dtd. 1782 & orig.

pencil sketch by him, dtd. 1815. Late 19th. C. mor. by Rivière, gt. (S. Nov.24; 64) *Grosvenor.* £850

COTERIE
1919-20. Nos. 1-6/7. 4to. Orig. wraps., cover designs by David Bomberg, William Roberts & others. (S. Jul.22; 98) *Thomson.* £120

COTMAN, John Sell
– Architectural Antiquities of Normandy. 1822. 1st. Edn. 2 vols. in 1. Fo. 95 (of 96) views of Rouen, lacks West Front, some plts. foxed. 19th. C. hf. maroon mor., spine gt. (S. Sep.29; 204) *Vine.* £100
– Engravings of Sepulchral Brasses in Norfolk –Suffolk. 1838. 2nd. Edn. 2 vols. Fo. Cont. hf. mor., gt. (SH. Oct.10; 328) *Traylen.* £180

COTTAFAVI, Gaetano
– Nuova Raccolta delle Principali Vedute di Roma. N.p., [1837 or later]. Ob. fo. Title & some plts. dust-soiled. Orig. wraps. worn. (S. Oct.21; 335) *Walford.* £110
– – Anr. Edn. Rome, ca. 1840. Sm. ob. fo. Lacks title, marginal staining thro.-out. 19th. C. red mor. (S. Oct.21; 333) *Walford.* £90
– – Anr. Edn. Rome, 1843. Ob. fo. Slightly spotted. Cont. hf. mor. (SH. Nov.6; 198) *L'Acquaforte.* £90
– – Anr. Copy. Cont. hf. mor. cf. (CSK. Mar.13; 9) £75

COTTAGE of Content or the Blessing of Cheerfulness & Good Temper
Ed.:– W. Sallis. N.d. 3¾ × 2½ inches. Occasional soiling. Orig. s.-c., with hand-cold. vig. (CSK. Sep.19; 136) £90

COTTER, Richard
– Sketches of Bermuda. L., 1828. 1st. Edn. Ex liby. Disbnd. [Sabin 17032] (SG. Oct.30; 52) $130

COTTON, Charles
See–WALTON, Isaac & Cotton, Charles
See–WALTON, Izaak, Cotton Charles & Venables, Col. Robert

COTTON, John
– The Bloody Tenent, Washed & Made White in the Blood of the Lamb. L., 1647. 1st. Edn. Sm. 4to. Lacks A1 (?blank). Cf. [Wing C 6409] (SPB. Jun.22; 43) $375
– A Brief Exposition upon the Whole Book of Canticles.–A Briefe Exposition upon the Whole Book of Ecclesiastes. L., 1655; 1657. Tog. 2 vols. 12mo. 1st title lacks 11. A2 & A3. Old cf., mod. red hf. mor. s.-c., worn. [Wing C6412; 6414] (SG. Sep.25; 97) $190
– An Exposition upon the Thirteenth Chapter of the Revelation. L., 1655. 1st. Edn. 4to. Lacks Mm4 (?blank), some browning, staining. Later hf. mor. [Wing C 6431] (SPB. Jun.22; 45) $275

COTTON, Sir Robert
– Cottoni Posthuma: Divers choice pieces. Ed.:– J. H[owell]. 1672. Engraved armorial bkplt. on verso of title. Old mott. cf. [Wing C 6486] (CSK. Mar.27; 52) £55

COUAILHAC, L.
See–BERNARD, P.P. & Couailhac, L.

COUCH, Jonathan
– History of Fishes of the British Islands. L., 1862. 4 vols. A few plts. slightly soiled. Orig. linen, 1 spine brkn. (R. Oct.14-18; 2956) DM 1,900
– – Anr. Edn. L., 1862-63. Vols. 1-2 (of 4). Some plts. soiled. Orig. linen. (HK. Nov.18-21; 509) DM 750
– – Anr. Edn. 1862-65. 4 vols. Cl. (S. Mar.17; 327) *Duran.* £240
– – Anr. Copy. Some slight spotting. Orig. cl. (CSK. Sep.19; 50) £200
– – Anr. Copy. A few ll. slightly spotted. Orig. cl. gt. (SBA. Jul.14; 223) *Way.* £180
– – Anr. Edn. 1864. 2 vols. only (of 4). Plts. hand-cold. or partly hand-cold., some ll. slightly spotted. Cont. mor. gt. (SBA. May 27; 172) *Vitale.* £100
– – Anr. Edn. Groombridge, 1864-65. 4 vols. 4to. Slightly spotted, inscr. erased from title of vol. I, sm. liby. stp. on titles. Orig. embossed cl., qt. (S. Jun.1; 94) *Vitale.* £180
– – Anr. Edn. 1866-67. 4 vols. Orig. cl. gt. (P. Apr.30; 289) £250
– – Anr. Copy. 4to. Few quires of vols. 1 & 4 shaken, contents lf. of vol. 4 loose, a few marks. Orig. embossed cl. pict. gt., ex-liby. (PL. Jul.11; 63) *Miles.* £160

COUCH, Jonathan – History of Fishes of the British Islands. -contd.
– – **Anr. Copy.** Slightly soiled in parts. Orig. linen. (R. Mar.31-Apr.4; 1354) DM 1,500
– – **Anr. Edn.** 1867. 4 vols. Orig. blind-stpd. & gt. decor. cl. (TA. Jun.18; 136) £190
– – **Anr. Copy.** Lge. 8vo. Orig. cl. gt. (TA. Apr.16; 100) £145
– – **Anr. Edn.** L., 1867-68. 4 vols. 4to. Cont. hf. leath., gt. spine, spine slightly defect. (HK. Nov.18-21; 508) DM 1,200
– – **Anr. Edn.** 1868-69. 4 vols. Some ll. loose or torn in margins. Orig. cl., gt., lacks spine of vol. 4, worn. (S. Jul.27; 282)
Dekker & Nordemann. £200
– – **Anr. Copy.** (C. Jul.15; 173) *Taylor.* £160
– – **Anr. Copy.** Slight offsetting, foxing of endpapers. Cf. (SPB. Oct.1; 191) £700
– – **Anr. Edn.** 1877. Some plts. foxed. Orig. cl., worn. (CE. Apr.23; 323) £210
– – **Anr. Edn.** 1877-78. 4 vols. 252 chromolitho. plts., lacks plt. LXXIX, with dupl. plt. LXXVII. Red mor. gt. (C. Mar.18; 171) *Duran.* £380
– – **Anr. Copy.** Orig. cl., 3 vols. slightly dampstained. (SKC. Feb.26; 1576) £170
– – **Anr. Copy.** Some spines worn. Bkplt. of G. Bickerton Evans, dtd. 1880. (JL. Jul.20; 804) Aus. $300

COUCHE, Jacques & Fontenai, Abbé de
– **Galerie du Palais Royal.** Paris, 1786-1808. 3 vols. Lge. fo. Many ll. bnd. in with MS. index slightly soiled. Cont. cf. (R. Oct.14-18; 2655) DM 3,600
– – **Anr. Copy.** Vols. 1 & 3 (of 3) Slightly soiled in parts. Cont. hf. leath. (R. Mar.31-Apr.4; 1579) DM 1,400

COULLERY, M.T. & Newstead, M.S.
– **Netsuke. [Baur Collection].** Geneva, 1977. 4to. Cl., d.-w., s.-c. (P. Jul.2; 154) *Mills Owen.* £55

COULON, Louise
– **Histoire des Israélites.** Paris, 1665. 3 vols. Leath. (S. Nov.18; 595) *Selig.* £120

COUNSEL FOR EMIGRANTS, & Interesting Information from Numerous Sources; with Original Letters from Canada & the United States–Sequel to the Counsel for Emigrants
Aberdeen, 1840; 1834. 1st. Edn. 12mo. Foxed. Orig. cl.-bkd. bds., loose in bdg.; orig. ptd. wraps., unc. & unopened. (SG. Mar.5; 158) $400

COUNSELL, G.
– **The Art of Midwifery: or the Midwife's Sure Guide.** 1752. 1st. Edn. Cf., 1 jnt. brkn. (BS. Sep.17; 42) £55

COUNTRY GENTLEMAN, The: a Journal for the Farm, the Garden & the Fireside
Ed.:– Luther Tucker & Son & J.J. Thomas. 1861-1862. Vols. 17-20 in 2 vols. Hf. leath. (SG. Mar. 5; 159) $100

COUNTRY GENTLEMAN'S COMPANION
Dublin, 1755. 2nd. Edn. 12mo. Cont. cf., rebkd. (SG. Apr.9; 343) $140

COUNTRY LIFE
1929-37. Vols. 65-82, together 18 vols. 4to. Orig. cl. (SH. Oct.10; 433) *Weinreb.* £230

COUPERUS, Louis
– **Verzamelde Werken.** Antw., Amst., 1953-57. India Paper. 12 vols. Orig. gt. cl. (VG. Nov.17; 66) Fls. 500

COURBIN, L.
– **Couronnement de S.M. l'Empereur Nicolas.** [Paris], [1825?] Fo. Lacks at least 3 ll. (including title), 11 folding plts. only (of 14, lacks nos. 11, 12, & 14), several plts. india mntd. proofs, text ll. heavily reprd. Orig. leath.-bkd. cl. W.a.f. (SG. Nov.20; 407) $275

COURBOIN, François & Roux, Marcel
– **La Gravure Française.** Paris, 1927-28. (525). 3 vols. 4to. Orig. wraps. (SH. Mar.6; 510) *Duran.* £110
– – **Anr. Copy.** (SH. Jun.4; 16) *Monk Breton.* £75

COURS Complet d'Agriculture . . .
Ed.:– Abbé Rozier. Paris, 1791-1805. 12 vols. 4to. Some foxing & damp-staining. Cont. diced cf., decor. spines. (SM. Feb.11; 51) Frs. 3,000

COURT DE GEBELIN, Antoine
– **Histoire Naturelle de la Parole, ou Précis de l'Origine du Langage . . . extrait du monde Primitif.** Ill.:– A Romanet after C.P. Marillier (frontis.).

Paris, 1776. 1st. Separate Edn. Folding plt. of organs of voice printed in colours by Gautier Dagoty Père dtd. 1775. Cont. cf. (S. Dec.2; 466) *Dr. Pike.* £170
– **Monde Primitif, Analysé et Comparé avec le Monde Moderne.** Ill.:– After Marillier & Barnet. Paris, 1773-82. 9 vols. 4to. Lamoignon pr. mark on hf.-titles or flylf. Cont. mor., triple gt. fillet, flat spines, inner gt. dentelles, lacks Lamoignon shelf labels. (SM. Oct.7; 1667) Frs. 3,500

COURT Magazine, The
1833-34. Vols. 2, 3, 4 & 5. Hf. cf. gt. (P. Sep.11; 247) *Smith.* £60

COURT OF SESSION
– **Cases.** 1821-1960. 139 vols. Cf. & hf. cf., many vols. worn, some rebnd. (CE. Feb.19; 21) £1,000
– – **Anr. Edn.** 1821-1968; 1930; 1931-68. 88 pts.; 20 pts. plus pts. from 1969 to 1973 pt. I. Cf.; Rebnd. cl.; cl., unbnd. pts., bdgs. to 1900 worn. (CSK. Feb.19; 14) £2,500
– – **Anr. Edn.** 1821-22-1972. 150 vols. Cf., some vols. rebkd. (PD. Apr.1; 45) £3,100
– – **Anr. Edn.** 1821-1978. 149 vols. & 21 pts. Cf., bdgs. of vols. 1915-32 worn, 1972-78 in unbound pts. (CE. Aug.28; 53) £3,100

COURTAULD, S.A. & Jones, A.E.
– **Some Silver Wrought by the Courtauld Family.** Shakes. Hd. Pr. 1940. Ltd. Edn. Fo. Orig. cl.-bkd. bds., s.-c. (SH. Jul.23; 265) *Sims & Reed.* £150

COURTELINE, Georges (ie. Georges-Victor-Marcel Moineaux)
– **Le Train de 8h. 47.** Ill.:– Dignimont. Paris, ca. 1927. (25) on holland. 4to. Cold.-pict. wraps, unopened, boxed. (PNY, Oct.1; 163) $120

COURTIERS & FAVOURITES OF ROYALTY
Paris, n.d. Edn. des Aquarelles, (26). 20 vols. Spanish gt. (SPB. May 6; 296) $550

COURTNEY, William Prideaux & Smith, David Nichol
– **Samuel Johnson: A Bibliography.** Oxford, 1923. Facs. Reprint, (350). Cl., d.-w. (SG. Oct. 2; 200) $100

COURTOIS, Edme Bonaventure
– **Rapport fait au Nom de la Commission chargée de l'examen des Papiers trouvés chez Robespierre.** 1795-96. 3 vols. Cont. hf. russ., corners. Lord Seymour arms on spines. (HD. Oct.10; 281) Frs. 1,300

COUSIN, Jean
– **Livre de Portraiture.** Paris, 1612. Lightly soiled thro.-out, some ll. stained slightly, Italian entry on verso of last lf. 1668. Sewed, s.-c. (D. Dec.11-13; 323) DM 3,200

COUSTANS
– **The Tale of Emperor Coustans & of Over Sea.** Trans.:– William Morris. Kelms. Pr. 1894. (525). 16mo. Orig. holland-bkd. bds., unc. (SH. Feb.19; 7) *Fletcher.* £120
– – **Anr. Copy.** 4to. Orig. cl.-bkd. bds., some soiling. (SPB. May 29; 240) $250

COUTEPOFF, Nicolas
– **La Chasse Gran-Ducale et Tsarienne en Russie. Période du Xe au [XVIII] Siècle.** St. Petersb., 1896-1902. 3 vols. 4to. Vol. I & II in Fr., vol. III in Russian. Orig. decor. cf., metal corners on covers, d.-w.'s, boxes worn. (SH. Feb. 5; 206) *Lyons.* £280

COVENS, Jean & Mortier, Corneille
– **Atlas.** 1735? Fo. 18 engraved double-p. maps, hand-cold. in outl. Old bds., upr. cover detchd. (TA. Nov.20; 294) £300
– – **Anr. Copy.** (TA. Sep.18; 4) £180

COVENY, Christopher
– **Twenty Scenes from the Works of Dickens.** Sydney, 1883. Some foxing, each etching in early state & has orig. description from Dickens on preceding p. Hf. cf., gt., J. Steele's bkplt. (JL. Dec.15; 724) Aus. $150

COWARD, Noel
– **Quadrille.** 1952. 1st. Edn. Orig. cl. gt. Pres. copy to Cecil Beaton. (S. Jul.22; 100) *Blackwell.* £95

COWLEY (contrib.)
See–CAMBRIDGE UNIVERSITY

COWLEY, Abraham
– **Works.** 1678. 4to. Cont. mor., richly gt. with flowers & leafy sprays, rolled tool border, gt. panel spine. (P. Feb.19; 217) *King.* £320

COWLEY, Sir Arthur Ernest
– **Concise Catalogue of the Hebrew Printed Books in the Bodleian Library.** Oxford, 1929. 1st. Edn. 4to. Cl. (S. Nov.17; 66) *Drachler.* £75

COWPER, William, Poet
– **The Diverting History of John Gilpin.** Ill.:– After Charles Brock, hand-cold. by Gloria Cardew. 1898. (10) on vell. for Guild of Women Binders. Orig. buckram, soiled. Sigd. by Gloria Cardew. (CSK. Oct.17; 95) £110
– **Poems.** L., 1835. 24mo. (5 × 2¾ inches). Early maroon mor., gt. floral design on covers & spine. Fore-e. pntg. (SG. Sep.4; 187) $160
– – **Anr. Edn.** 1872. 1st. Edn. Lacks cancelled preface as usual, E6 & 16 cancels, sigs. of A.M. & J.A. Thompson & pres. inscrs. of 1886 & 1893 on flylf. Cont. Fr. red mor., triple gt. fillet, flat spine gt. in compartments, title 'Poems by William', gt., in 2nd. (SMC. Oct.7; 1668) Frs. 2,000
– **Poetical Works.** Boston, 1853-54. 3 vols. 16mo. Cont. hf. cf., spines gt. 3 double fore-e. pntgs. (SG. Oct. 9; 100) $800
– – **Anr. Edn.** L., 1854. 12mo. Old gt.-tooled mor. Fore-e. pntg. (SG. Dec.18; 185) $170

COWPER, William, Surgeon
– **The Anatomy of Human Bodies . . .** Oxford, 1698. 1st. Edn. Fo. Mezzotint port. cut out & mntd. Hf. cf., worn. (S. Dec.2; 701) *Blackwell.* £520
– – **Anr. Copy.** Lacks port. & ptd. title, plt. 1 misbnd. at beginning of appendix, plts. 2 & 3 misbnd. at plt. 85, upper outer corner of last 4 plts. & the accompanying text & index ll. reprd. affecting some text, folding plt. 10 reprd., no plt. surface, missing except for numbers of plts., inner margins of plts. 2 & 3 reprd. affecting some engraved surface, repair to upr. blank margin of title. Cf., reprd. [Wing C6698] (S. Jun.15; 190) *Hudebrandt.* £200
– – **Anr. Edn.** Leyden, 1737. 2nd. Edn. Atlas fo. 112 (of 114) copperplts. Mod. buck., ex liby. (SG. Sep.18; 100) $1,200
– **Glandularum Quarundam, nuper Detectarum, Doctuumque Earum Excretoriorum, Descriptio.** 1702. 1st. Edn. 2 pts. in 1 vol. 4to. Margins browned. New cl. (S. Dec.2; 467) *Rota.* £70
– **Myotomia Reformata or an Anatomical Treatise on the Muscles of the Human Body . . . to which is prefixed an introduction concerning muscular motion.** Ed.:– [Richard Mead]. 1724. Fo. New hf. cf. (S. Jun.15; 191) *Norman.* £650
– – **Anr. Copy.** With plt. 13 in 2 states & 2 ll. engraved 'Syllabus Musculorum', 1 gathering detchd. from stitching, marginal browning thro.-out. 19th. C. hf. mor., upr. cover detchd. From Chetham's Liby., Manchester (C. Nov.26; 92) *Lester.* £520
– – **Anr. Copy.** Dampstained. Cont. (orig.?) bds., defect., lacks spine. (S. Apr.6; 215) *Preidel.* £320
– – **Anr. Copy.** Old cf., needs rebinding. (SG. Oct.9; 68) $2,400

COX, David
– **A Series of Progressive Lessons, Intended to Elucidate the Art of Landscape Painting in Water Colours.** L., 1812. 2nd. Edn. Ob. 8vo. Orig. red hf. mor. (CNY. May 22; 79) $100
[–] – **Anr. Copy.** Cont. cf. & bds. (CB. May 27; 73) Can. $450
[–] – **Anr. Copy.** 1st. 3 ll. loose. (CB. May 27; 236) Can. $380
– **Six Views of the City of Bath.** 1820. Ob. fo. Without title or text, aquatint views cold. Red hf. mor., by Rivière, orig. ptd. wraps bnd. in. From the collection of Eric Sexton. (C. Apr.16; 237) *Wood.* £1,000
– **A Treatise on Landscape Paintings in Water Colours.** Ed.:– Geoffrey Holme. 1922. (250) numbered. 4to. Orig. parch. gt. (SBA. Jul.22; 171A) *Jones.* £42

COX, Edward Godfrey
– **Reference Guide to the Literature of Travel.** N.Y., 1969. 3 vols. Orig. linen. (R. Mar.31-Apr.4; 776) DM 550
– – **Anr. Copy.** (R. Oct.14-18; 512) DM 450

COX, Joseph Mason
– **Practical Observations on Insanity in which some Suggestions are offered towards an Improved Mode of Treating Diseases of the Mind . . .** 1806. 2nd. Edn. Cont. cf. (S. Jun.15; 192) *Dawson.* £90

COX, Nicholas & Blome, Richard
- **The Gentleman's Recreation.** L., 1686. Fo. Text badly dampstained at end, 1 plt. defect. Old hf. russ., very worn. W.a.f. (SPB. Oct.1; 88) $1,300
- - **Anr. Edn.** 1721. 6th. Edn. Mod. spr. cf. gt., by Wallis. (S. Nov. 24: 58) *Old Hall.* £80

COX, Sir Richard
- **Hibernia Anglicana: or, the History of Ireland.** Ill.:– White. 1689-90. 2 vols. Fo. Engraved folding map detchd., a few minor defects. Later hf. cf., slightly worn. [Wing C6722] (SBA. Jul.14; 310) *Lyon.* £150
- - **Anr. Copy.** Some liby. stps., licence lf. torn in vol. 1. Old cf., 2 covers loose. (P. Mar.12; 218) *Gamble.* £65

COX, Ross
- **Adventures of Six Years on the Western Side of the Rocky Mountains, among Various Tribes of Indian.** 1831. 2 vols. Cont. hf. cf., gt. decor. spines. (TA. Mar.19; 233) £95
- **Adventures on the Columbia River, including the Narrative of a Residence of Six Years on the Western Side of the Rocky Mountains, among Various Tribes of Indian.** 1831. 2 vols. Cont. hf. cf., gt. decor. spines. (TA. Feb.19; 47) £105
- - **Anr. Copy.** Foxing & soiling, old liby. rubberstp. on titles & on a number of other pp., some badly erased, including 1 on 1st. title, several ll. reprd., 1 resulting in text loss. Orig. cl., newly rebkd. (SG. Jan.8; 115) $100
- - **Anr. Edn.** L., 1832. 2nd. Edn. 2 vols. Liby. stps. Later cl. Pres. copy [Sabin 17267] (SPB. Jun.22; 46) $120
- - **Anr. Edn.** N.Y., 1832. 1st. Amer. Edn. Orig. cl., unc. (SG. Oct.9; 69) $375
- - **Anr. Copy.** Advts., browned & foxed. Mod. hf. cf., gt. spine. From liby. of William E. Wilson. (SPB. Apr.29; 63) $175

COX, Sandford C.
- **Recollections of the Early Settlement of the Wabash Valley.** Lafayette, Ind., 1860. 1st. Edn. 4to. A little foxing. Orig. blind-stpd. cl., gt., cover loose, owner's inscr. on upr. free endpaper. From liby. of William E. Wilson. (SPB. Apr.29; 64) $150

COX, Thomas
- **The Compleat History of Berkshire.** Ill.:– John Speed, Morden, Moll & others (maps). 1730. 4to. Orig. bdg. (DWB. May 15; 94) £175
- [-] **Magna Britannia et Hibernia, Antiqua & Nova.** Ill.:– mostly by Robert Morden. 1720. Vols. 1 & 2 only. 4to. Some dampstaining. Orig. panel. cf., brkn. (TA. Apr.16; 472) £170
- [-] - **Anr. Edn.** Ill.:– Robert Morden. 1738. 6 vols. 4to. Some defects (mostly in text ll.). Cont cf., gt., some covers detchd. As atlas. W.a.f. (SBA. Jul.22; 48aa) *Nicholson.* £480
- [-] - **Anr. Copy.** A few plts. reinforced, 1 title defect. Cont. cf., a few bds. detchd. (SH. Oct.9; 8) *Traylen.* £360

COXE, Daniel
- **Description of the English Province of the Carolana, by the Spaniards call'd Florida, & by the French La Louisiane ... also of the Great & Famous River Meschacebe or Mississippi ...** L., 1722. 1st. Edn. Lacks map, blank head of title clipped. Cont. panel. cf., upr. cover detchd., armorial bkplt. of Henry Smith of Ellingham. Sigd. 'Dan'l. Coxe' at title, inscr. at upr. paste-down by Coxe's grandson, followed by wax seal, at lr. blank is Coxe's family tree in MS. in same hand to ca. 1780. (PNY. Mar.26; 91) $425

COXE, Daniel W. & Turner, Henry
- **Remarks on John Francis Girod's Exposition of the Title of the Marquis de Maison Rouge.** Natchez, 1820. Loose. (SPB. Jun.22; 48) $225

COXE, William Archibald
- **Account of the Russian Discoveries between Asia & America.** 1780. 2nd. Edn. 4to. Advt. lf. at end, Ragley hall bkplt. Cont. mor., by Derome le Jeune with his 1785 ticket, 'ED', gt., on upr. cover, triple gt. fillet, spine gt. with urn in each compartment, inner gt. dentelles. (SM. Oct.7; 1669) *Frs. 3,500*
- - **Anr. Edn.** 1787. 3rd. Edn. Plts./maps, 1 slightly torn, a few ll. slightly spotted. Mod. cf.-bkd. bds. (SH. Nov.7; 340) *Bowes.* £80
- - **Anr. Edn.** 1804; 1803. 4th. Edn.; 6th. Edn. 1 vol.; 3 vols.; 4to. Plts. spotted in 1st. work. Cont. cf. gt. (C. Feb.25; 85) *Hannas.* £220

- **An Historical Tour in Monmouthshire.** 1801. 2 vols. 4to. Some ll. spotted. Cont. hf. cf., worn & soiled. (SD. Feb.4; 224) £120
- - **Anr. Copy.** Cont. cf., rebkd. (SH. Nov.6; 87) *Beynon.* £80
- - **Anr. Edn.** 1801. (60) on royal paper. 2 vols. in 1. 4to. Occasional spotting. Cont. russ., rebkd., old spine preserved. (CSK. May 22; 106) £180
- **Travels in Switzerland.** 1789. 3 vols. Cont. diced cf. (CSK. May 1; 106) £55
- - **Anr. Edn.** 1791. 2nd. Edn. 3 vols. 1 folding engraved map torn. Cont. mott. cf., spines gt. (LC. Jun.18; 147) £70
- - **Anr. Copy.** Cont. cf., spines gt. (SG. Oct.30; 106) $190
- - **Anr. Edn.** 1794. 3rd. Edn. 2 vols. 4to. 1 partly hand-cold. folding map with sm. tear, some plts. discold., especially in vol. II. Cont. diced cf. (C. Feb.25; 86) *Burgess.* £170
- **Travels into Poland, Russia, Sweden & Denmark.** 1784. 2 vols. 4to. Some ll. soiled. Cont. cf. gt., worn. (SD. Feb. 4; 225) £60
- - **Anr. Edn.** L., 1787. 3rd. Edn., vol. 5 1st. Edn. 5 vols. Cont. cf., spines gt. (SG. Oct.30; 105) $200

COYKENDALL, Frederick
- **Arthur Rackham: a List of Books Illustrated by Him.** Ed.:– Martin Birnbaum. Ill.:– Arthur Rackham. Mount Vernon, 1922. (175) designed by Bruce Rogers. Vell.-style bds., unc., partly unopened. Pres. copy from Ed. to Mrs. George Laurence Nelson, Raymond M. Sutton, Jr. copy. (SG. May 7; 61) $500

COYNE, Joseph Stirling
See–WILLIS, Nathaniel Parker & Coyne, Joseph Stirling

COZIO, Conte Carlo
- **Il Giuoco degli Scacchi, o sia Nuova Idea d'Attacchi ...** Turin, 1766. 1st. Edn. 2 vols. Early mott. cf. (SG. Apr.9; 129) $1,200

CRAANDIJK, J. & Schipperius, P.A.
- **Wandelingen door Nederland.** Haarl, 1875-84. 6 (of 8) vols., lacks 1 vol. & atlas. Ex-liby. stps. on titles, a few plts. with some foxing, 98 (of 128) tinted plts. Orig. cl. gt. (VG. Dec.16; 907) *Fls. 1,100*

CRABB, George
- **Universal Technological Dictionary.** 1823. 2 vols. 4to. Cont. cf., worn. (CE. Jul.9; 221) £50

CRABBE, Rev. George
- **Tales.** Ill.:– Walter Sneyd. 1812. Mor. gt. (P. Jul.30; 110) *Rosbron.* £180

CRADDOCK, Harry
- **The Savoy Cocktail Book.** Ill.:– Gilbert Rumbold. N.Y., 1930. 1st. Edn. Silver & cold.-pict. bds., cl. back, outer corners worn. (PNY. May 21; 376) $110
- - **Anr. Edn.** Ill.:– Gilbert Rumbold. L. & N.Y., [1936]. 12mo. Cl., pict. d.-w. Inscr. (SG. Oct.23; 5) $100

CRAIG, Edith N.
See–ROBERTSON, Edward Graeme & Craig, Edith N.

CRAIG, Edward Gordon
- **Ellen Terry & her secret self.** [1931]. (256) on L.P., sigd. by the author. 4to. 8 plts., with 'A plea for G.B.S.' loosely inserted in wallet at end. Orig. cl., slightly soiled. (CSK. Sep.5; 222) £50
- **Nothing, or the Bookplate.** 1924. 1st. Edn., (280) L.P. Orig. buckram gt., unc. 1 wood-engr. sigd. by artist. (C. Jul.22; 53) *Fletcher.* £100
- - **Anr. Edn.** Ed.:– E. Carrick (handlist). L., 1925. Hf. cl. (SG. Mar.26; 69) $170

CRAIG, Gordon
- **Gordon Craig's Book of Penny Toys.** L., 1899. (550). Lge. 4to. Slightly worn. Orig. decor. bds., rebkd., corners reinforced with worn. Pres. copy with T.L.s. from the author. (SPB. May 6; 174) $1,100

CRAIG, John Roderick
- **Ranching with Lords & Commons, or Twenty Years on the Range. Being a Record of Actual Facts & Conditions Relating to the Cattle Industry of the North-West Territories of Canada.** Toronto, 1903. 4to. Pict. covers. (PWP. Apr.9; 201) *Can. $100*

CRAIG, Maurice
- **Irish Bookbindings, 1600-1800.** 1954. 4to. Orig. cl. (P. May 14; 91) *Forster.* £75

CRAIG-BROWN, T.
- **The History of Selkirkshire.** Edinb., 1886. (250) numbered. 2 vols. 4to. Plts. loose. Orig. cl. (SH. May 21; 252) *Pharos.* £75

CRAIK, nee Murloch, Mrs. Dinah Maria
- [-] **The Adventures of a Brownie.** N.Y., 1872. 1st. Amer. Edn. Sm. sq. 8vo. With the 2 p. list of the author's works before frontis., owner's sig. on fly-lf. Gt.-lettered cl., slightly worn. (SG. Apr.30; 100) $110
- **John Halifax, Gentleman.** L., 1856. 1st. Edn. 3 vols. With 2 pp. of inset advts. at end of vol. 3, but without the 24 p. inserted publisher's catalogue. Orig. blind-stpd. cl., spines gt.-lettered, qtr. mor. gt. s.-c. A.L.s. to Mr. Hall laid in (n.d., 16mo., 3 pp.), bkplts. of George B. McCutcheon, lately in the Prescott Collection. (CNY. Feb.6; 265) $220

CRAJENSCHOT, T.
See–VAN HUISTEEN, A. & G., Crajenschot, T., Van Esveldt, S. & other publishers

CRAMER, D. & Bachmano, C.
- **Emblemata Sacra.** Frankfurt, 1624. 1st. & only Edn. 2 vols. in 1. Lightly browned. Cont. vell., old paper pasted over, torn at spine. (R. Oct.14-18; 875) *DM 1,500*

CRAMER, G. & others
- **Henry Moore, Catalogue of Graphic Work 1931-72 & 1973-75.** 1973-76. 2 vols. 4to. Cl., d.-w.'s, s.-c.'s. (P. Jul.30; 21) *Thorp.* £60

CRAMER, John Andrew
- **Elements of the Art of Assaying Metals ... with notes ... by Cromwell Mortimer.** 1764. 2nd. Edn. Owner's inscr. of James Yonge 1771. Cont. cf. (S. Dec.1; 115) *Goldsmiths.* £50

CRAMER, Pieter
- **De Uitlandsce Kapellen.** Amst./Utrecht, 1775. Pt. 1 only 4to. 48 hand-cold. plts. (of 400), lacks title. 19th. C. hf. mor. As a vol. of plts., w.a.f. from Chetham's Liby., Manchester. (C. Nov.26; 93) *Gilbert.* £320

CRAMER, Zadok
- [-] **The Navigator.** Pittsb., 1818. 10th. Edn. 12mo. Heavily foxed & stained, ex liby. Old bds., rebkd. (SG. Jun.11; 128) $110

CRANACH, Lucas, the Elder
See–SUNDER, called Cranach, Lucas, the Elder

CRANACH, W. Lucas von
- **Stammbuch.** Ed.:– Christien von Mechel. Berlin, 1814. Tall fo. Lacks the cold. allegorical woodcut. Old wraps., loose. (SG. Mar.12; 114) $170

CRANE, Hart
- **The Bridge: A Poem.** Paris, Black Sun Pr., 1930. 1st. Edn., (200) numbered on Holland Paper. 4to. Ptd. wraps., edges browned, slightly soiled, backstrip cracked, slightly shaken. (PNY. Dec.3; 96) $180
- - **Anr. Edn.** N.Y., [1930]. 1st. Amer. Edn. Cl., with part of d.-w. Inscr. to Samuel Loveman. (SG. Jun.4; 84) $2,600
- - **Anr. Copy.** 4to. Orig. cl. Pres. copy 'For Matty & Hannah [Josephson] from Hart'. (SPB. Nov.25; 237) $650

CRANE, Stephen 'Johnston Smith'
- **The Lanthorn Book.** N.Y., [1896]. (125). Fo. Orig. bds., unopened. John Langdon Heaton's copy inscr. for his wife, each contribution sigd. by author, autograph correction by Heaton, note on rear end-paper by Heaton's daughter regarding limitation. (SPB. Nov.25; 240) $250
- **Maggie, a Girl of the Streets.** [N.Y.], [Priv. Ptd.], [1893]. 1st. Edn. 12mo. Orig. wraps., lacks sm. piece from foot of spine, fore-edge of upr. cover chipped, upr. cover rehinged, qtr. mor. s.-c. Pres. Copy, to Lucius Button with long inscr. (8 words affected by chipping to upr. cover), Button's sig. on upr. cover; sold by Mrs. Button to A.S.W. Rosenbach (purchased for Mrs. Prescott). (CNY. Feb.6; 75) $7,500
- **The Red Badge of Courage.** N.Y., 1895. 1st. Edn., 1st. Printing. Margins on some pp. cut away, slight browning. Orig. cl., s.-c. (SPB. May 29; 90) $350
- **War is Kind.** Ill.:– Will Bradley. N.Y., 1899. Pict. bds., unc., bkplt. (SG. Nov.13; 111) $260
- **Work.** Ed.:– Wilson Follett. N.Y., [1925-26]. (750) numbered. 12mo. Cl., soiled, unc. (SG. Nov.13; 112) $160

CRANE, Walter
- The Baby's Opera.–The Baby's Bouquet. Routledge, [1877-78]. 2 vols. 4to. Orig. cl-bkd. decor. bds., worn & soiled. (SH. Dec.10; 137)
Sherlock £50
- The Blue Beard Picture Book, containing Blue Beard, Little Red Riding Hood, Jack & the Bean-Stalk, Baby's Own A B C. [1875]. 4 separately iss. works in 1 vol. 4to. Orig. pict. cl. gt. (SH. Mar.19; 67) *Black.* £140
- Columbia's Courtship, a Picture History of the United States. Boston, [1893]. 1st. Edn. 4to. Orig. cl. (SH. Mar.19; 71) *Fletcher.* £85
- Eight Illustrations to Shakespeare's Tempest. Ill.:– Duncan C. Dallas after Crane. Priv. ptd., 1893. (650) numbered, sigd. by artist & printer. Fo. 8 mntd. india paper plts., 1 slightly torn. Contained in orig. box, worn. (CSK. Nov. 28; 179) £85
- The First of May, a fairy masque. 1881. (200) India Proof copies sigd. by artist. Fo. Loose in portfo., lacks ties. (C. Feb.4; 157) *Erlini* £80
- A Floral Fantasy, in an Old English Garden. 1899. 1st. Edn. 4to. Orig. pict. cl., d.-w. (SH. Mar.19; 74) *Fletcher.* £100
- Flora's Feast. 1895. 4to. Advt. dtd. 12.95. Orig. cl.-bkd. bds. (SH. Mar.19; 72) *Fletcher.* £60
- A Flower Wedding, Described by Two Wallflowers. 1905. 1st. Edn. 4to. Orig. cl.-bkd. decor. bds. (SH. Mar.19; 75) *Fletcher.* £60
- Flowers from Shakespeare's Garden. 1909. 4to. Orig. cl.-bkd. bds. (SH. Mar.19; 76) *Baldur.* £65
- Pan Pipes, a Book of Old Songs, with accompaniments by Theo Marzials. 1883. 1st. Edn. Ob. 4to. Orig. cl.-bkd. decor. bds. (SH. Mar.19; 68) *Fletcher.* £60
- Queen Summer or the Tourney of the Lily & the Rose. 1891. 1st. Edn. 4to. Publisher's advts. dtd. 10.91. Orig. cl.-bkd. decor. bds. (SH. Mar.19; 70) *Fletcher.* £60
- - Anr. Copy. Cold. pict. bds., worn. (SG. Mar.19; 55) $110
- Renascence. 1891. (65) numbered on L.P. 4to. Orig. vell.-bkd. bds., unc. Pres. Copy, to Mary F. Crane; 5 orig. pen sketches by Crane loosely inserted. (C. Jul.22; 53a) *Wood.* £400
- - Anr. Copy. 5 orig. pen sketches by Crane loosely inserted. Pres. copy to author's wife. (C. Feb.4; 45) *Long.* £120
- Slate & Pencil-vania, being the Adventures of Dick on a Desert Island. 1885. 1st Edn. Ob. 4to. Orig. cl.-bkd. decor. bds. (SH. Mar.19; 69) *Fletcher.* £60
- Triplets, Comprising the Baby's Opera, The Baby's Bouquet, & the Baby's Own Aesop. 1899. (500) numbered. 4to. Orig. vell.-bkd. cl. (SH. Mar.19; 73) *Baldur.* £160
- - Anr. Edn. Ill.:– Edmund Evans after Crane. 1899. (750), this a 'Review Copy'. Lge. ob. 4to. Occasional slight spotting. Orig. parch.-bkd. bds., slightly soiled. (CSK. Feb.20; 145) £55
See–GREENAWAY, Kate & Crane, Walter
See–HENLEY, William Ernest
See–QUIVER OF LOVE
See–WILDE, Oscar

CRANTZ, David
- Historie von Grönland. Leipzig, 1770. 2 vols. Cont. hf. leath. (D. Dec. 11-13; 1472) DM 650
- The History of Greenland, containing a description of the country & its inhabitants. 1767. 1st. Edn. in Engl. 2 vols. Cont. cf., lacks 1 lable. (C. Feb.25; 87) *Smith.* £150

CRANTZ, Heinrich Johann Nepomuk
- Stirpium Austriacarum ... Vienna, 1769. 6 fascicules in 1 vol. 4to. Folding plts. slightly spotted. 19th. C. hf. mor. From Chetham's Liby., Manchester. (C. Nov.26; 94) *Israel.* £150

CRASHAW, Richard (Contrib.)
See–CAMBRIDGE UNIVERSITY

CRASSO, L.
- Elogii di Capitani Illustri. Venice, 1683. Slightly soiled. Late 19th. C. hf. leath. (R. Oct.14-18; 2865) DM 610

CRAVEN, The Hon. Richard Keppel
- A Tour Through the Southern Provinces of the Kingdom of Naples. 1821. 4to. Some ll. spotted. Cont. hf. cf., gt. (SD. Feb.4; 189) £85

CRAWFURD, George
- Description of the Shire of Renfrew. Paisley, 1818. 4to. Mor. gt. (CE. Nov.20; 11) £55

CRAWFURD, George & Robertson, George
- History of the Shire of Renfrew. Paisley, 1818. 4to. Hf. cf. (CE. Nov.20; 57) £70

CRAWFURD, John
- History of the Indian Archipelago. Edinb., 1820. 1st. Edn. 3 vols. Some foxing & offsetting, sm. tear in fold of folding map. Cl., worn. (S. Jan.27; 545) *Remington.* £110
- Journal of an Embassy from the Governor-General of India to the Courts of Siam & Cochin China. 1830. 2nd. Edn. 2 vols. Cont. pol. cf., gt. & blind borders on sides, gt. panel. spines. (C. Nov.5; 30) *Bracken.* £120

CRAWHALL, Joseph
- Chap-Book Chaplets. Ill.:– Crawhall. 1883. 4to. Orig. bds., soiled, orig. wraps. of each of the 8 pts. bnd. in. (CSK. Mar.27; 59) £90
- - Anr. Copy. Cl.-bkd. pict. bds., unc. (SG. Oct.16; 24) $250
- - Anr. Copy. Orig. two-tone bds., pict. stpd. in colour at upr. cover, soiled. (PNY. Mar.26; 72) $150
- Chaplets from Coquet-side. [Newcastle], 1873. (100). New cl., gt.-vell. spine. Pres. Copy, sigd. & inscr. (SG. Oct.16; 23) $130
[-] Chorographia, or a Survey of Newcastle upon Tyne. Ill.:– Crawhall. Newcastle, 1884. L.P. 4to. Orig. vell., soiled. (CSK. Mar.27; 58) £75
- A Collection of Right Merrie Garlands for North Country Anglers. Newcastle, 1864. 1st. Edn., (50) numbered on L.P. 4to. Mor.-bkd. cl. (SG. Oct.16; 22) $400
- 'Impress Quaint'. Ill.:– Crawhall. Newcastle, 1889. [300]. 4to. Orig. cl.-bkd. bds., soiled. (CSK. Mar.27; 60) £70
- - Anr. Copy. Cl.-bkd. pict. bds. (SG. Oct.16; 25) $120
- Izaak Walton: his Wallet Booke. 1885. (100) sigd. by publishers. Orig. parch.-bkd. vell. gt., unc., ties, 1 defect. (SH. Mar.26; 146) *Henderson.* £125
- Olde Ffrendes wyth newe Faces. Leadenhall Pr., 1883. 4to. Orig. bds., unc., lacks backstrip, worn. (SH. Mar.26; 145) *Ayres.* £55
[-] Olde Tayles Newlye Relayted. [1883]. 4to. Orig. cl., soiled. (CSK. Mar.27; 61) £70

CREALOCK, J.N.
- Deer-Stalking in the Highlands of Scotland. 1892. Ltd. Edn. Fo. Decor. cl. (CE. Nov.20; 160) £210

CREASE, Francis
- Thirty-four Decorative Designs. Ed.:– Evelyn Waugh. Priv. Ptd., [1927]. 1st. Edn. (60) numbered, sigd. by artist. Fo. Orig. bds., spine worn. (S. Jul.22; 318) *Horowitz.* £320
- - Anr. Copy. This copy unnumbered & unsigd. (SH. Mar.26; 147) *Vaughan.* £300

CREATION DE PARIS
- Quarante Modèles Originaux. Paris, 1926; n.d.; n.d. 3 vols. 1st. vol.: slight foxing, plts. good; 2nd. vol.: stained, lacks title-p., slight foxing, plts. good; 3rd. vol.: lacks title-p., slight foxing, plts. good. 1st. vol.: spine worn; 2nd. vol.: upr. cover detchd.; 3rd. vol.: lacks upr. cover. (JL. Dec.15; 749) Aus. $260

CREBILLON, Claude Prosper Jolyot de, Fils
- Les Amours de Zeokinizul, Roi des Kofirans. Trans.:– Krinendon. Amst., 1757. Square 16mo. Cont. red mor., spine decor. in grotesque style, 3 gt. fillets, inner dentelle. (HD. Apr.9; 446) Frs. 1,200
- Contes. Ill.:– Milius (figures); Lalauze (port.). Paris, 1879. Ltd. Edn. Figures in 2 states. Mor. by Pagnan, decor. spine, inside dentelle. Bkplt. of Francis Kettaneh. (SM. Feb.11; 151) Frs. 2,500
- Egaremens du Coeur et de l'Esprit (Les). Paris, 1739-41. 2nd. Edn. 3 pts. in 1 vol. 12mo. Light browning in 3rd. pt. Cont. red mor., fillet, arms, decor. spine. (HD. Jun.10; 21) Frs. 2,000

CREBILLON, Prosper Jolyot de, Père
- Oeuvres. Ill.:– after Boucher. Paris, 1750. 2 vols. 4to. Extra-ill., with engraved ills. from a later edn. mntd. & bnd. in with 84 pp. Triumvirat on la Mort de Ciceron at end of vol. II. Mott. cf. gt., worn. (SBA. May 27; 146) *Duran.* £60
- - Anr. Copy. ? lacks port. Cont. cf., gt. (S. Oct.21; 293) *J. Booth.* £50
- Oeuvres Complètes. Ill.:– after Marillier. Paris, 1785. Engrs. in 2nd. state, stp. on title-lf. removed. Cont. cf., decor. gt. stpd., gt. outer dentelle, marb. end-papers. (D. Dec.11-13; 650) DM 700

CREDO
- Pleni Sunt Coeli et Terra Gloria Tua. Doves Pr., 1909. (250). Orig. mor. by the Doves bindery, extremities of spine worn. (C. Jul.22; 57) *Schrire.* £80

CREIGHTON, Charles
- A History of Epidemics in Britain from 664 to the Extinction of the Plague. Camb., 1891. 1st. Edn. 2 vols. Orig. cl. (S. Jun.15; 195) £50
- - Anr. Edn. Camb., 1891-94. 1st. Edn. 2 vols. Orig. cl., slightly marked. From liby. of E. Ashworth Underwood. (S. Feb.23; 186) *Dawson.* £60
- - Anr. Copy. Press cuttings mntd. on endpapers, unc. & mostly unopened. (KH. Mar.24; 111) Aus. $110

CREIGHTON, Mandell
See–SKELTON, John–CREIGHTON, Mandell

CRESCENTIIS, Petrus de
- Comodorum Ruralium. Augsburg, Johann Schüssler., ca. 16 Feb. 1471. 1st. Edn. Fo. 209 ll. (of 212), lacks 3 blanks at end, 2 initials, one in red & blue, the other in red, f.209 GKW variant printing, Ms. notes. Mod. vell. bds. Bkplts. of Rev. Francis Hopkins & William, 7th. Earl Beauchamp. [BMC II, 328] (S. Nov.25; 330)
Riley Smith. £4,100
See–ESTIENNE, Charles & Liebault, Jean –CRESCENTIUS, Petrus

CRESCENZIO, Bartolomeo
- Proteo Militare. Naples, 1595. 1st. Edn. 4to. Some worming, mostly marginal, stained. Old bds., spine defect. The Horblit copy. (S. Jul.27; 268) *Mursia.* £320

CRESSWELL, Samuel Gurney
- A Series of Eight Sketches in Colour ... of the Voyage of H.M.S. Investigator ... Jul.25, 1854. 1st. Edn. Fo. Several plts. spotted, slight soiling to title, slight staining in upr. blank margins, touching surface of 1st. plt. Cont. hf. russ., upr. cover detchd., spine defect. Pres. Copy, to Thomas Masters (?)Grendon. [Sabin 17490] (S. Feb.10; 357) *Maggs.* £700

CRESWELL, K.A.C. & others
[-] The Mosques of Egypt. Giza, 1949. 2 vols. Fo. 2 maps & index in pocket at end of Vol. 1. Orig. cl. (SH. Nov.7; 407) *Hosain.* £310

CREUTZBERGER, H.
- Eigentliche, Wolgerissene Contrafactur vnd Formen der Gebiss ... Vienna, 1591. Early Edn. Fo. Probably lacks 1 lf. with woodcuts I & II, 1st. 9 ll. restored, some sm. tears, some ll. with sm. holes, some stains in parts, 2 engraved exlibris in cover. Cont. vell., very defect., 1 corner reprd. (H. Dec.9/10; 364) DM 3,800

CREVECOEUR, J.H. St. J.
- Voyage dans la Haute Pennsylvanie. 1801. 1st. Edn. 3 vols. Cont. cf., worn. [Sabin 17501] (SH. Jun.18; 202) *Walford.* £120

CREVECOEUR, Michel Guillaume St. Jean de
- Letters from an American Farmer. 1783. Cf. gt., reprd. (P. Apr.30; 296) *Bickersteth.* £130
- Lettres d'un Cultivateur Americain, écrites à W.S., Ecuyer, 1770-1781. Paris, 1784. 1st. Edn. in Fr. 2 vols. This iss. with text of vol. II ending on p. 400. Cont. cf. gt., with binder's label, 'Courteval, Rue des Carmes'. (SG. Mar.5; 161) $220
- - Anr. Edn. 1786. 3 vols. Cont. cf. [Sabin 17495] (CB. Feb.18; 116) Can. $150

CREVEL, René
- Dali ou l'anti-obscurantisme. Ill.:– after Dali. Paris, 1931. (10) Priv. Edn. on Jap. Nacre. Orig. sewed. Sigd. orig. pen ill. (D. Dec.11-13; 1040) DM 2,700
- Feuilles Eparses. Ill.:– Hans Arp, Max Ernst & others. Paris, [1965]. (150) numbered, sigd. by artists. 4to. Loose sheets as issd. in wraps., unc., orig. vell.-bkd. bd. folder & s.-c. (SG. Oct.9; 71) $1,100

CREVENNA, afterwards BOLONGARO-CREVENNA, Pierre Antoine
- Catalogue des Livres de la Bibliothèque. Amst., 1789. 2nd. Edn., (50) L.P. 6 pts. in 5 vols. 4to. Lacks final blanks in vols. I, IV & V, & blank at end of 1st. pt. in vol. III, prices entered in cont. hand in margins. Cont. spr. cf., rebkd., slight wear, orig. labels preserved. Thomas Frognall Dibdin's copy, with his bkplt. in vol. I, & bkplt. of A.N.L. Munby. (S. Jun.9; 12) *Ximenes.* £400

- - Anr. Edn. Amst., 1789. 5 vols. Ptd. price-list in vol. V. Cont. wraps., unc. Bkplt. of F.H.M. Ouwerling. (SM. Oct.7; 1350) Frs. 1,600

CREVIER
See-ROLLIN, Charles & Crevier

CRICHTON, Sir Alexander
- An Inquiry into the Nature & Origin of Mental Derangement comprehending a Concise System of the Physiology & Pathology of the Human Mind. 1798. 1st. Edn. 2 vols. Blank portion of errata lf. reprd. Hf. cf. (S. Jun.15; 196) *Mollon.* £160

CRICKETER, The
Ed.:- P.F. Warner. 1922-27. Vols. 1-2, 4-7 only. 4to. Cont. cl. (SH. Oct.9; 214) *Hindley.* £55

CRIES of London, The
1794. 32mo. Lacks 1 ill. & last lf. of advts. Orig. Dutch floral bds., soiled, rebkd. (SH. Dec.10; 21) *Temperley.* £115

CRINESIUS, Christophorus–PAUL, Saint
- Lexicon Syriacum, e Novo Testamento et Rituali Severi.-Epistola . . . ad Rom. Lingua Syriaca. Ed.:- C. Crinesius (2nd. work). Wittenberg; 1612; 1612. 2 works in 1 vol. 4to. Some browning. Cont. blind-stpd. pig., arms on covers, some wear, soiled, s.-c. (S. Apr.29; 377) *Brill.* £100

CRISP, Frederick Arthur
- Armorial China, a catalogue of Chinese Porcelain with coats-of-arms in the possession of F.A. Crisp. 1907. (150). 4to. Hf. vell. (C. Feb.4; 239) *Marks.* £65
- Lowestoft China Factory & the Moulds Found There. Priv. ptd., 1907. (150) numbered. 4to. Hf. vell. (RBT. Jan.22; 26) £58

CROALL, Alexander
See-JOHNSTONE, William Grosart & Croall, Alexander

CROCE, Giovanni Andrea Della
- Chirurgiae . . . Libri Septem. Venice, 1573. 1st. Edn. Fo. Title reprd. not affecting text, a few later MS. notes in ink, sm. wormhole in 1st. few ll., affecting a few letters, a few other ll. reprd. not affecting text. Recent mor. (C. Apr.1; 102) *Schweitzer.* £1,300

CROCE, Guilio Cesare
[-] Bertoldo con Bertoldino e Cacasenno. Bologna, 1736. 4to. Title & 1st. plt. reprd. with slight text loss. Mod. cf., gt. spine. (SI. Dec.3; 160) Lire 550,000

CROCKER, H. Radcliffe
- Atlas of the Diseases of the Skin in a Series of Illustrations from Original Drawings & Descriptive Letterpress. 1903. Fo. Ptd. bds. (S. Jun.15; 198) *Jenner Books.* £55

CROKER, Rev. Temple Henry & others
- The Complete Dictionary of Arts & Sciences. L., Priv. ptd., 1764-66. 1st. Edn. 3 vols. separately issued. Fo. Cont. blind suede. (PNY. Oct.1; 177) $325
- - Anr. Copy. 3 vols. Cont. hf. leath., spine defect. (R. Mar.31-Apr.4; 1542) DM 1,000

CROLLIUS, Oswald
- Basilica Chymica . . . aucta a loan. Hartmanno . . . Ed.:- Johannes Michaelis & G. Everard Hartmann. [Geneva], 1635. 3 pts. in 1 vol. Place of printing supplied in ink, paper discold. Limp vell. The Liechtenstein copy. (S. Dec.1; 117) *Musch.* £80
- - Anr. Copy. Cont. cf. gt., hinges reprd., spine worn, the Andrew Fletcher copy. (S. Dec.1; 118) *Mediolanum.* £70
- - Anr. Edn. Geneva, 1643. Some browning. Cont. limp vell., soiled. (S. Apr.6; 40) *Morton-Smith.* £100

CROMBIE, Benjamin W.
- Modern Athenians. L., 1882. 4to. Qtr. mor. gt. (P. Jun.11; 334) *Cambridge.* £100

CROMBIE, Charles
- The Rules of Golf Illustrated. 1905. No bdg. stated. (CSK. Jul.20; 118) £200

CROMWELL, Thomas Kitson
- Excursions in the County of Essex. 1818-19. 2 vols. Occasional slight spotting. Cont. mor., gt. (CSK. May.1; 25) £50
[-] Excursions in the County of Suffolk. 1818-19. 2 vols. Qtr. leath. (O. Jun.3; 118) £100
- - Anr. Copy. Cont. hf. cf. (SH. Nov.6; 47) *Hayward.* £95
[-] - Anr. Copy. (O. Jun.3; 117) £84
[-] - Anr. Copy. Occasional light spotting. Cont. mor., gt. (CSK. Jun.26; 8) £55

[-] Excursions in the County of Sussex. 1822. Qtr. leath. (O. Jun.3; 120) £52
- Excursions through Ireland. 1820. 2 vols. Qtr. leath. (O. Jun.3; 116) £64

CRONE, G.C.E.
- Nederlandsche Jachten, Binnenschepen, Visschersvaartuigen en Daarmee Verwante Kleine Zeeschepen, 1650-1900. Met eene Korte vert. i.h. Engelsch. Amst., 1926. De Luxe Edn. Sm. fo. A few plts. slightly foxed, summary in Engl. inserted. at end of book. Leath. gt. (VG. Dec.15; 61) Fls. 500

CRONICA Cronicarum Abbregé et mis par Figures Descentes et Rondeaulx
Paris, [1532]. 3 pts. in 1 vol. 4to. 1st. gathering with inner marginal repairs, reprd. tears to F2, L1 & HH2. Mor., spine gt.-lettered, red mor. gt. doubls., marb. fly-ll., by Chambolle-Duru, cl. s.-c. Bkplts. of Robert Hoe, Silvain S. Brunschwig, C.N. Radoulesco & John A. Saks. (CNY. Oct.1; 105) $1,900

CRONICA van der Hilliger stat van Coellen
Cologne, Johann Koelhoff, the younger, 23 Aug. 1499. 1st. Edn. Fo. Most ills. cold. or partly cold., extensively reprd. thro.-out with restorations & facs. work, some ll. inlaid, many reprd. tears. Late 19th. C. mor gt. W.a.f. The copy of Thomas Brooke F.S.A., lately in the collection of Eric Sexton. [BMC I, 299, Goff C476, HC 4989*] (CNY. Apr.8; 48) $7,000

CRONIN, William Vine
See-GRAVES, Algernon & Cronin, William Vine

CRONSTEDT, Axel Frederic
- Essay towards a System of Mineralogy. 1772. 2nd. Edn. Cont. cf. (SH. Jan.30; 421) *Walford.* £60

CROOKE, Helkiah
- Mikrokosmographia, a Description of the Body of Man. 1651. Fo. Title remargined, sm. holes or tears in 4 ll. slightly affecting text, sm. rust-holes in anr. 3, lacks corner of 1 lf., affecting text, minor discolouration thro.-out, slight worming in blank upr. inside corner. Mod. vell. bds. [Wing C7231] (C. Apr.1; 103) *Hahn.* £120
- - Anr. Edn. [1651]. Fo. Lacks engraved title, short tears in K3, S6, X2-3, some stains in lr. margin, sig. L & tear & inner margin of L2-3 reprd. Cf., rebkd. [Wing C7230] (S. Jun.15; 199) *Phillips.* £120

CROOKES, Sir William
- A Practical Handbook of Dyeing & Calico-Printing. 1874. Orig. cl., worn at top & bottom of spine. (S. Dec.1; 119) *Gordon.* £80

CROOKSHANK, Edgar M.
- History & Pathology of Vaccination. 1889. 2 vols. Cl. (S. Dec.2; 468) *Whitehart.* £85
- - Anr. Copy. (S. Jun.15; 200) *Whitehart.* £60

CROONE, William
See-WILLIS, Thomas–CROONE, William

CROPPER, Percy James
- The Nottinghamshire Printed Chap-Books. Nottingham, 1892. (85) numbered, & sigd. 4to. Slight spotting, ptd. Nottinghamshire chapbook 'Rhyming Dick & the Strolling Player' bnd. in. Hf. cf. Sigd. by author. (SBA. Oct.22; 467) *Chesters.* £70

CROSBY, Harry
- Shadows of the Sun. Paris, Black Sun Pr., 1928. 1st. Edn., (44). 1st. vol. Multi-cold. drawing of abstract pyramid with black sun sinking behind it, annotated Black Sun, laid in, this copy unnumbered. Orig. ptd. wraps., slight soiling. (SPB. Nov.25; 228) $375
- The Sun. Paris, Black Sun Pr., 1929. 1st. Edn., (100) numbered. Miniature book 15/16 × 11/16 inches. This copy unnumbered. Orig. mor. gt., ptd. wraps. bnd. in, leath. case, upr. cover detchd. Goodwin copy. (SPB. Nov.25; 229) $700

CROSBY, Sylvester S.
- The Early Coins of America, & the Laws Governing their Issue. Boston, Priv. Ptd., 1875. 1st. Edn. 4to. Cl., ex-liby. (SG. Feb.12; 295) $375

CROSS, D.W.
- Fifty Years with the Gun & Rod. Cleveland, 1880. 1st. Edn. Gt.-decor. cl. Bkplt. of Eugene V. Connett. (SG. Oct.16; 26) $120

CROTCH, W.D.
- The Birds of Somersetshire. Taunton, 1851. 6 hand-cold. litho. plts. Lev. mor. by Zaehnsdorf,

orig. upr. wrap. bound in. (C. Jul.15; 174) *Weldon & Wesley.* £350

CROUCH, Edmund A.
- An Illustrated Introduction to Lamarck's Conchology. 1827. 4to. Some spotting & general browning of text. Recent cl. (TA. Sep.18; 92) £58

CROUSAZ, A. von
- Geschichte des Königlich Preussischen Kadetten-Corps. Berlin, 1857. Lge. 4to. Lacks hf.-title, slightly browned, MS. note on endpaper. Cont. hf. leath., worn. (H. Dec.9/10; 831) DM 420

CROW, Captain Hugh
- Memoirs . . . together descriptive sketches of the western coast of Africa; particularly of Bonny. 1830. 1st. Edn. Occasional foxing. Orig. cl.-bkd. bds., rebkd. with most of orig. spine preserved, unc. (S. Nov.4; 627) *Maggs.* £140

CROWLEY, Aleister
- Confessions. Mandrake Pr., 1929. Ltd. Edn. on Japanese vell. Vols. 1 & 2 (all publd.). Decor. buckram gt. (BS. Nov.26; 243) £96

CROWNE, John
- The English Frier. 1690. 1st. Edn. 4to. Advt. lf. at end, some stains. Mor.-bkd. bds. [Wing C7387] (C. Nov.19; 65) *Pickering & Chatto.* £150
- Henry the Sixth, the First Part.–Henry the Sixth, the Second Part. 1681. 1st. Edns. 2 pts. in 1 vol. 4to. 1st. work: title stained & with sm. wormhole; 2nd. work: 1 lf. stained. Recent mor.-bkd. bds. [Wing C7388; C7389] (C. Nov.19; 66) *Quaritch.* £320
- Juliana. 1671. 1st. Edn. 4to. With orig. initial blank. Recent mor.-bkd. bds. [Wing C7393] (C. Nov.19; 67) *Pickering & Chatto.* £140
- Thyestes. 1681. 1st. Edn. 4to. Title mntd. with sm. blank portions lacking, sm. hole affecting 1 letter, natural paper fault affecting 1 line, foxing thro.-out, inner margins strengthened. Recent mor. [Wing C7408] (C. Nov.19; 68) *Arnold.* £60

CROWQUILL, A. (Pseud.)
See-FORRESTER, Alfred Henry 'A. Crowquill'

CROZAT, Joseph Antoine, Marquis de Tugny
- Recueil d'estampes D'Après Les Plus Beaux Tableaux . . . qui sont en France. 1729-42. 2 vols. Fo. Some ll. slightly soiled. Cont. cf., worn, rebkd. (SD. Feb.4; 161) £370
[-] - Anr. Edn. Ill.:- Aubert, Cochin, Desplaces, Thomassin & others. Paris, 1763. 2nd. Edn. 2 vols. Fo. Light waterstaining to lower edges of several ll. in vol. II. Cont. Fr. mott. cf., spines defect., worn. (S. Oct.21; 300) *Broseghini.* £700
- - Anr. Copy. Some marginal staining, sm. tears, foxing, 3 plts. preserved. Cf.-bkd. bds., very worn. (SPB. May 6; 176) $300

CRUCK, Eugene
- Promenades dans Oran. Ill.:- Ligeron. Oran, 1938. (526); (1) on old tinted Jap., numbered. 2 vols. 4to. Orig. watercolours & drawings, both states of plts. Orig. wrap., folders & card s.-c., slightly defect. (SM. Feb.11; 152) Frs. 4,500

CRUIKSHANK, Capt. Ernest Alexander
- The Documentary History of the Campaign on the Niagara Frontier. Welland, Ontario, [1896]-1908. 9 vols. in 3. Cont. cl., bkplt. (CB. Apr.1; 62) Can. $100

CRUIKSHANK, George
- The Artist & the Author. [L.], [Jun., 1872]. 2nd. Edn. Extra-ill. with compl. suite of ills. for Ainsworth's 'The Miser's Daughter' & 'The Tower of London', Dicken's 'Oliver Twist', & 5 other plts. Hf. mor. gt. Pres. Copy, to Edwin Canton, 3 A.L.'s laid in: Ainsworth to Cruikshank (n.p., n.d., 1½ pp., 8vo., with drawing by Cruikshank on conjugate lf.); Ainsworth to [Peter Cunningham] (Kensal Manor House, Jul. 22, 1844, 8vo., 1½ pp.); Cruikshank to T.J. Pettigrew (Pentonville, Jul. 5, 1824); the William Glyde Williams-Jerome Kern copy with bkplt., lately in the Prescott Collection. (CNY. Feb.6; 77) $600
- The Bachelors Own Book. 1844. Orig. cl.-bkd. pict. wraps., worn, soiled. Inscr. to cousin Mrs. T.A. Southwood. (SH. Dec.10; 147) *Henderson.* £52
- - Anr. Edn. L., Aug. 1, 1844. 1st. Edn., 2nd. state. Crimson crushed lev. gt., gt. spines & dentelles by Wood. Inscr. to Joseph Sleap. (SG. Oct.9; 73) $300
[-] [Caricatures]. N.d. 3 vols. Fo. Approximately 320 caricatures of Engl. political & social life,

_RUIKSHANK, George -contd.
etc., during Regency Period, most cold., some from 1835 reprint of Cruikshank's works, most mntd. or inlaid. Red hf. mor. From David Solomon's Collection. (SPB. Oct.1; 188) $5,500
- **The Comic Almanack.** [1834-52]. 19 vols. in 5. Cont. str.-grd. mor. by Leighton, Brewer Street, orig. wraps. preserved. Bkplt. of Thomas Gaisford. (S. Nov.24; 71) _Klaussner._ £500
- - **Anr. Copy.** 19 iss. in 5 vols. 16mo., 2 iss. 24mo. Three-qtr. lev. by Bayntun, orig. pict. wraps. bnd. in. (SG. Oct.9; 72) $500
- - **Anr. Edn.** 1835-53. 5 vols. Hf. pold. cf., soiled. (CE. Nov.20; 184) £60
[-] [-] **Anr. Edn.** [1837]. 129 × 2019 mm. Folding strip with 24 etched hand-cold. ills., slightly stained. Marb. bds. Panorama. (SH. Dec.12; 589) _Glendale._ £100
- - **Anr. Edn.** L., ca. 1871. 2 vols. 16mo. Cf., double gt. fillet borders, spines gt., gt. dentelles, by Rivière. (SG. Dec.18; 146) $150
- - **Anr. Edn.** L., ca. 1873. 2 vols. 16mo. Each vol. with Hotten's 'Special List for 1873'. Cf., double gt. fillet borders, spines gt. with floral designs, gt. dentelles, by Zaehnsdorf, orig. gt.-pict. upr. covers bnd. in, bkplt. (SG. Mar.19; 59) $110
- **Cruikshankiana, An Assemblage of the Most Celebrated Works.** [1836?]. Fo. Title spotted, a few other ll. slightly so. Orig. cl.-bkd. bds., slightly worn & soiled. (SBA. Jul.14; 400) _Nolan._ £100
- - **Anr. Edn.** N.d. Fo. Outer margin of title & a few other ll. slightly stained, some ll. detchd. Orig. cl. gt., slightly stained. (SBA. Jul.14; 401) _Cumming._ £60
- **Derby-Day shown Six Reliefs.** ca. 1890. 86 × 320mm. The compl. set of panoramic cold. embossed scraps. Orig. ptd. wraps. (S. Oct.17; 215) £65
- **Fairy Library.** [1853-54]. Fo. 18 etched plts. from the set inlaid, with another plt. in proofs. Late 19th. C. maroon hf. mor. (S. Nov.24; 73) _Quaritch._ £75
- - **Anr. Edn.** [1853-64]. 1st. Edn. 4 vols. in 1. Sm. 4to. Late 19th. C. red lev. hf. mor. gt., orig. wraps. preserved. (S. Nov.24; 72) _Niedhart._ £240
- - **Anr. Edn.** L., n.d. Various Edns. 4 vols. Sq. 8vo. Unif. crushed lev., gt. fillet borders with floral cornerpieces, spines gt., gt. dentelles, by Worsfold, orig. pict. wraps. bnd. in. (SG. Mar.19; 56) $350
- **Fairy Library, I-III.-Hop-O'-My-Thumb & the Seven-League Boots.-Jack & the Bean-Stalk. -Cinderella ... Slipper.** [1853-1854]. 1st. Edns., 1st. Iss's. 3 vols. in 1. Cont. hf.-mor., worn. (SH. Dec.10; 148) _Schierenberg._ £80
- **Greenwich Hospital.** 1826. 4to. Text slightly discold. Later hf. mor. gt. (TA. Nov.20; 451) £130
- **The Humourist.** Ill.:- George Cruikshank. 1819-20. 4 vols. in 2. Hf. mor. by F. Bedford, spines gt. Bkplt. of Thomas Gaisford. _Klaussner._ £380
- - **Anr. Edn.** L., 1822; 1819-19-20. 1st. Edns. of all but vol. 1. 4 vols. 18mo. Each vol. with plt. list with advts. on verso. Old str.-grd. mor., some foxing. (SG. Sep.4; 262) $160
- - **Anr. Edn.** L., 1892. (260) numbered. 4 vols. 4to. Cl., partly untrimmed. (SG. Nov.20; 311) $120
- **The Life of Napoleon.** 1817. 2nd. Edn. Spotted. Mod. mor. (SH. Jun.25; 134) _Thorp._ £140
- **London Characters.** Ill.:- G. & R. Cruikshank. L., 1829. L.P. 4to. Orig. cl., spine gt.-lettered, backstrip slightly torn. From the Prescott Collection. (CNY. Feb.6; 76) $1,600
- - **Anr. Copy.** Mod. crushed lev. (SG. May 14; 52) $1,200
- **Phrenological Illustrations.** L., 1827. Ob. fo. Some browning, staining. Red hf. mor., wraps. (from 1826 edn.?) bnd. in. (SPB. May 29; 94) $150
- **The Pigeons ...** L., 1817. 9th. Edn. 12mo. Recent wraps., scarlet hf. mor. s.-c. William H. Woodin copy. (SG. Sep.4; 141) $150
- **Points of Humour.** 1823-24. 1st. Edn. Pts. 1 & 2 in 1 vol. 20 etched plts., text wdct. ills., plts. & wdcts. in Pt. 2 India proofs. 19th. C. hf. mor., spine gt. (S. Nov.24; 76) _Klaussner._ £95
[-] **The Sailor's Progress.** L., 1835. 1st. Edn. Tall fo. (10¾ × 16¾ inches including full margins). Plts. loose as iss., matted, apparently lacks orig. container. (PNY. Mar.26; 92) $300
- **Six Illustrations to Cowper's Diverting History of John Gilpin.** Ill.:- Thompson, Branston & others after Cruikshank. L., 1828. 2 short tears in blank margins. Ptd. wraps., cover detchd., unc. A sheet

inscr. 'M.H. Barker Esq. with the regards of Geo. Cruikshank' laid in. (SG. Apr.30; 106) $160
- **My Sketch Book.** 1834-36. Vol. 1 (all publd.). Ob. 4to. Cont. hf. mor. Bkplt. of Thomas Gaisford. (S. Nov.24; 75) _Klaussner._ £85
- **Table-Book.** 1845. Orig. wraps. & advts. preserved. Mod. mor. (SH. Jun.25; 135) _Allsop._ £150
- **Watercolours.** Ed.:- Joseph Grego. L., 1903. 1st. Edn. Rebnd. in cl. (SG. Dec.4; 115) $130

CRUIKSHANK, George (Ill.)
See-A'BECKETT, Gilbert Abbot
See-AINSWORTH, William Harrison
See-ANNALS OF SPORTING & Fancy Gazette
See-APEL, Johann August
See-BARHAM, Rev. Richard H. 'Thomas Ingoldsby'
See-BARKER, Matthew Henry
See-BERENGER, Baron de
See-CAREY, David
See CHAMISSO, Adelbert von
See-COLLIER, John Payne
See-COMBE, William
See-DICKENS, Charles
See-EGAN, Pierce
See-EVERITT, Graham
See-[GIFFORD, Lord Robert]
See-GRIMM, Jacob Ludwig Karl & Wilhelm Carl
See-IRELAND, Samuel William Henry
See-JERROLD, Blanchard
See-KOSEWITZ, W.F. von
See-LEVER, Charles
See-MAXWELL, William Hamilton
See-MAYHEW, Horace
See-MOGRIDGE, George
See-MUDFORD, William
See-PETTIGREW, Thomas Joseph
See-RASPE, Rudolph Erich
See-ROSCOE, Thomas
See-SCOTT, Sir Walter
See-SMEDLEY, Frank E.
See-WHITTY, M.J.
See-WIGHT, John

CRUIKSHANK, Isaac Robert or Robert
[-] **Lessons of Thrift.** 1820. Soiling. Cont. hf. cf. (SH. Jun.25; 72) _Questor._ £55
[-] - **Anr. Copy.** Lacks advt. lf. as usual, light foxing & offsetting. Hf. mor., s.-c. (SPB. Jul.28; 103) $150

CRUIKSHANK, Isaac Robert & George
- **The Cruikshankian Momus.** L., 1892. 1st. Edn., (520) on Bütten. 4to. Orig. linen. (H. Dec.9/10; 1431) DM 500

CRUISE, Richard A.
- **Journal of a Ten Months' Residence in New Zealand.** 1823. 1st. Edn. Stp. of the Royal Institution cancelled. Mod. hf. cf., spine gt. (S. Mar.31; 460) _Foyles._ £75

CRUNDEN, John
- **Convenient & Ornamental Architecture, consisting of original designs for plans, elevations & sections ...** Ill.:- Isaac Taylor. L., Priv. Ptd., 1767. 1st. Edn. Tears in folds of the 2 folding plts., occasional light dampstaining in margins. Cont. suede, worn. (CB. May 27; 77) _Can._ $400
- - **Anr. Edn.** 1791. Old cf., 1 jnt. brkn. (BS. Sep.17; 10) £50
- - **Anr. Edn.** 1797. New Edn. 4to. torn & reprd., one plt. cut & reprd. Cont. cf., worn. (PD. May 20; 110) £95

CRUSII, Martini
See-MEGISER, Heronymus-CRUSII, Martini

CRUSO, John
- **Militarie Instructions for the Cavallrie.** Camb., 1632. 1st. Edn. Fo. Engd. title & 14 plts. including lge. folding plt., shaved, torn & reprd. Mod. spr. cf. [STC 6099] (C. Jul.16; 347) _Taylor._ £240

CRUVEILHIER, J(ean)
- **Anatomie Descriptive.** Paris, 1834-36. 1st. Edn. 4 vols. Slight spotting. Cont. cf.-bkd. marb. bds. (S. Apr.6; 41) _Lang & Springer._ £50
- **Anatomie Pathologique du Corps Humain, ou Descriptions avec figures ... des diverses alterations morbides dont le corps humain est suceptible.** Ill.:- after A. Chazal. Paris, 1829-42. 1st. & only Edn. 2 vols. Fo. Lr. outer blank corners of 1st. 5 ll. in vol. I reprd., also extreme outer blank margin of last lf., title of vol. II dust-soiled & mntd. with lr. blank corner of title & following 2 ll. reprd., only a few letters affected

by repairs in 1 case. Hf. cf. Inscr. 'Presented to the Medical Institute of Women, 144 Euston Road, N.W. by Doctor Elizabeth Blackwell, January 1891'; afterwards in liby. of Sir Geoffrey Jefferson, neurologist (1886-1961), with his bkplt. (S. Jun.15; 202) _Quaritch._ £1,800

CRUZ, Juana Ines de la
- **Fama, y Obras Posthumas. Tomo Tercero del Fenix de Mexico, y Dezima Musa, Poetisa de la America ...** Ed.:- Juan Ignacio de Castorena y Ursua. Barcelona, 1701. 4to. Browning. Old vell. (SG. Jan.8; 117) $250

CRYSTAL PALACE
- **The Illustrated Exhibitor ... of the Principal Objects in the Great Exhibition of the Industry of all Nations.** L., [1851]. 29 weekly iss., & extensive introductory material. Hf. cf. (SG. Mar.12; 116) $240

CUBA
- **Album Pintoresco de la Isla de Cuba.** [Havana], ca. 1850. Fo. Cl., disbnd. (SG. Oct.30; 117) $360

CUCINIELLO, Domenico & Bianchi, L.
- **Programma e Figure della Mascherata de Quattro Principali Poeti d'Italia ...** [Naples], [1827]. Fo. Cont. hf. roan. (C. May 20; 23) _D'Arcy._ £90

CUDWORTH (Contrib.)
See-CAMBRIDGE UNIVERSITY

CUDWORTH, Ralph
- **A Treatise concerning Eternal & Immutable Morality.** 1731. 1st. Edn. Cont. Engl. red mor., gt., spine tooled in compartments, covers with elab. decor. (S. Nov.24; 94) _Waterfield._ £130

CUEUR DE PHILOSOPHIE ... (Le)
Paris, [Feb.12, 1534]. Fo. Title extensively but neatly restored with grotesque initial L in facs., several other ll. reprd. in margins, slightly dampstained at foot. Mod. reversed cf. From Honeyman Collection. (S. May 20; 3213) _Maggs._ £360

CUETO, Roderico de
- **Primus tractatus summularum.** Alcala, 1524. Fo. Wormed & reprd. affecting text, dampstained in lr. margins at end, cont. inscr. of Jacobus Breton on title & extensively closely written annots. in margins of some ll. Mod. blind-stpd. cf., Luis Bardon's bkplt. (S. Jan,27; 366) _Duran._ £50

CUFFY'S DESCRIPTION OF THE PROGRESS ON COTTON
Ca. 1830. Orig. ptd. wraps., last ill. repeated on upr. cover. (SH. Mar.19; 80) _Temperley._ £85

CUISINIER Gascon, Le
Amst. [Paris], 1740. 1st. Edn. Occasional light spotting, some ll. slightly stained in outer edges. Cont. red mor., gt. slight staining & wear. (S. Feb.10; 432) _Quaritch._ £350

CUITT, George
- **Etchings of Ancient Buildings in the City of Chester, Castles in North Wales & other Miscellaneous subjects.** Chester, 1813. 3 vols. Fo. A few very minor defects. Loose as Iss. in orig. wraps., orig. hf. gt. folder. W.a.f. (SBA. Dec.16; 255) _Chester._ £100
- **Six Etchings of ... Fountains Abbey, Yorkshire. -Rivealux Abbey, Yorkshire.-Castles in North Wales.-Eight Etchings of old buildings in the city of Chester.** Ill.:- Cuitt. Plts. dtd. 1809-25. Together 4 pts. Fo. Minor foxing to a few plts. Loose as Iss. in orig. ptd. wraps., soiled, torn. (C. Feb.25; 30) _Laywood._ £110
- **Wanderings & Pencillings amongst Ruins of the Olden Time.** 1848. Fo. Cont. hf. mor. (CSK. May 29; 8) £75
- - **Anr. Edn.** 1855. Fo. Cont. hf. mor., spine gt. (SKC. Feb.26; 1640) £120
- - **Anr. Copy.** Cont. hf. mor., gt. (SH. Nov.6; 88) _Weinreb._ £80
- - **Anr. Copy.** Qtr. mor., brkn. (SG. Dec.4; 116) $160

CUJACIUS, J.
- **Opera, quae de Iure fecit et edi volvit.** Hanau, 1602. 2nd. Edn. 4 pts. in 1 vol. Fo. 2 repeated printers marks, light worming in last index ll. Cont. blind-tooled pig. (R. Oct.14-18; 1396) DM 500

CULLEN, William
- **Lectures on the Materia Medica.** 1772. 4to. Cont. cf., upr. cover detchd. (TA. Jan.22; 205) £52
- - **Anr. Edn.** 1773. 1st. Edn., 2nd. iss. 4to. 19-p. emendanda slightly browned. Cont. cf., rebkd., covers rather worn. From liby. of E. Ashworth Underwood. (S. Feb.23; 187) *Quaritch.* £140
- **A Treatise of the Materia Medica.** Edinb., 1789. 1st. Edn. 2 vols. 4to. Advt. lf. in vol. II. Cont. tree cf., spines gt. (S. Dec.2; 803) *Silver.* £85
See–CAILLAU, J.M.–CULLEN, William –HALLER, Albrecht–COSTE, M.

CULPEPER, Nicholas
- **The British Herbal.** Halifax, ca. 1820. Cont. cf. (SG. Sep.18; 104) $120
- **Complete Herbal.** 1814. 4to. Browned. Cont. hf. roan, spine loose. (SH. Jun.18; 157) *Frick.* £60
- - **Anr. Edn.** 1824. 4to. Last plt. defect., some stains. Mod. hf. cf. (SH. Jun.25; 166) *Frick.* £60
- - **Anr. Edn.** 1828. 4to. Spotted. Mod. hf. cf. Inscr. by the Earl of Essex. (CSK. Nov.14; 243) £55
- - **Anr. Copy.** Lacks pp. 125-88, plt. 35 torn & restored, plt. 15 torn, rear end-paper stained. Hf. cf., marb. bds., worn. (JL. Jul.20; 805) Aus. $180
- - **Anr. Edn.** 1869. 4to. Some spotting of text. (P. Sep.11; 265) *Harris.* £60
- **Complete Herbal, & English Physician.–The British Florist; or Flower Garden Displayed.** Manchester; Manchester, 1826; 1825. 2 works in 1 vol. 4to. Slightly spotted. Cont. hf. cf., worn. (SBA. Oct.22; 392) *Wilson.* £65
- - **Anr. Copy.** 1 plt. torn, 1 reprd. Cont. hf. cf. with mod. marb. bds. (TA. Nov.20; 60) £55
- **English Physician; & Complete Herbal** . . . Ed.:– E. Sibley. 1805-07. 2 vols. 4to. Cont. diced cf., rebkd., old spines preserved. W.a.f. (CSK. Aug.22; 113) £110
- **Culpeper's Last Legacy** . . . 1655. 1st. Edn. 2 pts. in 1 vol. Publisher's advts. marginal tear affecting printed lines in title, tear in lr. margin 13 pt. I & Hl pt. II just affecting letters, some stains. Cont. cf., spine reprd. [Wing C7517] (S. Dec.1; 120) *Quaritch.* £100
- **Works.** Ed.:– A. Hogg. N.d. 3 vols. Cf. As a collection of plts., w.a.f. (BS. Sep.17; 56) £160

CULPEPER, Sir Thomas, the Younger
[-] **Essayes or Moral Discourses on Several Subjects.** 1671. 2nd. Edn. With licence-lf. before title & penultimate errata lf., some browning & soiling. Cont. sheep, worn, 1 cover detchd. [Wing C7556] (S. Oct.1; 543) £75

CULVER, Henry B.
- **Contemporary Scale Models of Vessels of the Seventeenth Century.** N.Y., 1926. Ltd. Edn. Fo. 1 lf. torn. Hf. vell., slightly worn. (SH. Jul.23; 127) *Heneage.* £70

CUMBERLAND, Richard, Bp. of Peterborough
- **De Legibus Naturae Disquisitio Philosophica.** 1672. 1st. Edn. 4to. Some corners stained., bkplt. of Henry J.B. Clements Early 18th. C. mor. by Padeloup le Jeune with his ticket, single pointillé border & corner sprays, spine gt. in compartments, inner gt. dentelles, 2 corners worn. [Wing C7580] (SM. Oct.7; 1672) Frs. 5,000

CUMBERLAND, Richard, Dramatist
- **John de Lancaster.** 1809. 1st. Edn. 3 vols. Cf. gt. (P. Dec.11; 292) *Jarndyce.* £90

CUMING, F[ortescue]
- **Sketches of a Tour to the Western Country, Through the States of Ohio & Kentucky** . . . Pittsburgh, 1810. 1st. Edn. 12mo. Some soiling & browning, MS. notations on end-papers & upr. blank. Cont. cf., scarred, gt. blind-stpd. spine. From liby. of William E. Wilson. (SPB. Apr.29; 69) $400
- - **Anr. Copy.** (SG. Mar.5; 164) $260

CUMINGS, Samuel
[-] **James' River Guide . . . Rivers of the Mississippi Valley with Forty-Four Maps.** Cincinnati, 1863. Mod. buckram, orig. wraps. bnd. in, slightly soiled. From liby. of William E. Wilson. (SPB. Apr.29; 70) $300

CUMMING, Roualeyn George Gordon
- **A Hunter's Life in South Africa.** 1850, 2 vols. Decor. cl., gt., soiled. (CE. Nov.20; 109) £52

CUMMINGS, Edward Estlin
- **No Thanks.** N.Y., [1935]. Holograph Edn. Sm. 4to. Lev. mor., red mor.-bkd. s.-c. Autograph correction on Poem 69, sigd. on endpaper & following the holograph poem 44. (SPB. May 6; 178) $1,700

CUMMINGS, M.F.
- **Architectural Details.** N.Y., 1873. 1st. Edn. Fo. Cl., ends of spine torn. (SG. Mar.12; 117) $140

CUMMINGS, M.F. & Miller, C.C.
- **Modern American architecture. Designs & plans for villas, farm-houses, cottages, city residences, churches** . . . Ill.:– Julius Bien. Troy, N.Y., Priv. ptd., 1868. 1st. Edn. 4to. 1 plt. loose. Orig. cl. (CB. May 27; 78) Can. $240

CUMMINGS, Samuel
- **The Western Pilot** . . . Ed.:– Capts. Charles Ross & John Klinefelter. Cinc., 1845. Ptd. bds, roan spine, some shelf wear. (SG. Jan.8; 118) $150

CUMMINS, John
See–BULKELY, John & Cummins, John

CUNAEUS, Petrus
- **De Republica Hebraeorum Libri Tres.** Ed.:– Johannes Nicolai. Leiden, 1732. 4to. Bds. (S. Nov.18; 652) *Rock.* £70

CUNARD, Nancy
- **Black Man & White Ladyship.** Toulon, Priv. Ptd., 1931. 1st. Edn. Orig. wraps. (SH. Dec.19; 455) *Rota.* £50

CUNARD, Nancy & others
- **Salvo for Russia.** [L.], [1942]. 9 (of 10) etchings, each ltd. to 100 numbered imps., all sigd. by etchers. Loose in cl.-bkd. bds., linen ties. (SG. Jun.4; 94) $260

CUNDALL, Herbert Minton
- **Birket Foster.** 1906. (500) de Luxe. Orig. cl. gt. Orig. etchings by Foster at front. (SBA. Jul.14; 351) *Mead.* £72

CUNHA MATTOS, Raimundo J.
- **Memorias de Campanha do Senhor D. Pedro S'Alcantara, ex Imperador do Brasil no Reino de Portugal.** Rio de Janeiro, 1833. 2 vols. Some stains. Mod. hf. cf., orig. ptd. wraps. bnd. in, worn. (SPB. May 5; 174) $150

CUNITIA, Maria
- **Urania Propitia sive Tabulae Astronomicae mire faciles.** 1650. Fo. Text browned, a few cont. annots. to margins. Old bds., spine worn. (TA. Nov.20; 453) £70

CUNNINGHAM, A.
- **The Stupa of Bharhut.** 1879. 4to. Orig. cl. (SH. Mar.5; 44) *Kossow.* £105

CUNNINGHAM, Peter Miller, Surgeon
- **Two Years in New South Wales.** L., 1827. [1st. Edn.]. 2 vols. 12mo. Vol. 2 with 6 prelims., numbered to viii, some ll. offset, without final advt. lf. Armorial cf. (KH. Mar.24; 114) Aus. $230
- - **Anr. Copy.** 2 ll. detchd., 1 bnd. out of order. Early pold. cf., several defects. (KH. Nov.18; 185) Aus. $150

CUOQ, Jean Andre
[-] **Etudes Philologiques sur quelques Langues Sauvages de l'Amérique, par N.O.** Montreal, 1866. 1st. Edn. Mor. gt., upr. cover gt.-lettered 'Offert à son Altesse Royale le Prince Arthur par la Province de Quebec.' [Sabin 17980] (SG. Mar.5; 107) $200

CURIE, Madame Marie Sklodowska
- **Traité de Radioactivité.** Paris, 1910. 1st. Edn. 2 vols. Numeral on plt. 2 cut away. Hf. cf., orig. upr. wraps. bnd. in. (S. Dec.1; 122) *Matthews.* £140

CURIE, Pierre
- **Oeuvres.** Paris, 1908. 1st. Coll. Edn. Hf. cf. (S. Dec.1; 123) *Matthews.* £70

[CURIEUSER NACHRICHTEN AUS dem Reich der Beschnittenen]
[Kana in Galilaea] Frankfurt am Main, 1737. 1st. Edn. 4 pts. in 1 vol. 4to. Slight tear at bottom of woodcut, affecting 2 words, slight staining. Mod. leath. (S. Nov.18; 637) *Rock.* £1,300
[-] – **Anr. Edn.** [Kana in Galilaea] Frankfurt am Main, 1738. 1st. Edn. except for pt. I (2nd. Edn.). 4 pts. in 1 vol. 4to. Slight discolouration. Orig. vell. (S. Nov.18; 636) *Valmadonna.* £900

CURIO, Caelius Secundus
[-] **Pasquillorum Tomi Duo.** 'Eleutheropoli' [Basle?], 1544. Old repairs to inner blank corner of 3 ll., including title, lacks blank R8. 18th. C. Fr. red mor., triple gt. fillet, flat spine gt. in compartments, inner gt. dentelles. (S. Apr.7; 304) *Hyde Park Books.* £70

CURL, Edmund 'William Egerton'
- **Faithful Memoirs of the Life** . . . **Mrs. Anne Oldfield.** 1731. Folding frontis. stained. Cf., brkn. (BS. Jun.11; 249) £80

CURLING, Bill
See–GRAHAM, Clive & Curling, Bill

CURR, Edward M.
- **The Australian Race; Its Origin, Languages, Customs, Place of Landing in Australia.** Melbourne & L., 1886. 1st. Edn. 3 vols., with fo. atlas of language tables. Binder's cl., gt. (KH. Nov.18; 186) Aus. $250

CURTAIN Drawn Up
L., 1818. 2 pts. in 1 vol. 17 engraved erotic scenes inserted. Cl. (P. Feb.19; 14) *Bibn.* £250

CURTIS, Benedictus
- **Hortorum Libri Triginta.** Lyons, 1560. 1st. Edn. Fo. Cont. vell. gt. From Chetham's Liby., Manchester, bkplt. of Lord Halifax. (C. Nov.26; 96) *Wheldon & Wesley.* £280

CURTIS, George Ticknor
- **A Treatise on the Law of Copyright in Books** . . . Boston, 1847. 1st. Edn. Some marginal stains. Later hf. cl., ex-liby. (SG. Mar.26; 148) $100

CURTIS, John
- **British Entomology.** 1823-40. 8 vols. A few pp. of text reprd. Hf. cf., defect. (P. Apr.30; 206) *Dillon.* £1,600
- - **Anr. Edn.** 1824. Vol. 1 only. Titles spotted, occasional spotting elsewhere. Cont. cf., jnts. worn. (CSK. Jan.30; 90) £110
- - **Anr. Copy.** Later cl. (SG. Jan.29; 111) $160
- - **Anr. Edn.** L., 1824-32. Vols. 1-9 in 9 vols. Cont. hf. leath. (R. Oct.14-18; 3056) DM 4,200
- - **Anr. Edn.** 1826-31. Vols. III-VIII only in 3 vols. Disbnd. W.a.f. (S. Jun.1; 95) *Schmieder.* £320
- **Farm Insects.** Glasgow, [1859]-60. 1st. Edn. Cont. hf. cf. (SH. Jun.18; 36) *Abacus.* £50
- **The Genera of British Lepidoptera.** 1858. 4to. Qtr. mor. (P. Apr.30; 207) *Park.* £70

CURTIS, William
- **The Botanical Magazine.** 1787. Vol. I only. Dedication & preface lf. torn. Cont. tree cf., gt. spine, covers detchd. W.a.f. (C. Nov.5; 33) *Nagel.* £160
- - **Anr. Copy.** Occasional browning or staining. Cont. cf., worn. (CSK. May 15; 35) £95
- - **Anr. Run.** 1787-88. Vols. 1-2 in 1 vol. Hf. mor. lettered in error 'Flora Londinensis'. W.a.f. (S. Jun.1; 100) *Tomes.* £220
- - **Anr. Run.** L., 1787-90. Vols. 1-3 only in 2 vols. Some soiling, foxing & marginal wear. Olf hf. cf., very worn. W.a.f. (SPB. Jul.28; 106) $450
- - **Anr. Run.** 1787-94. Vols. I-VIII. Cont. tree cf. some covers detchd. (C. Nov.5; 32) *Cumming.* £850
- - **Anr. Run.** 1787-96. Pts. I-X in 5 vols. 358 (of 360) engraved plts., lacks plts. 112 & 205, some slight browning. Cont. hf. cf., worn. (S. Jun.23; 295) *Koch.* £600
- - **Anr. Run.** 1787-1805. Vols. 1-21 in 9 vols. 784 (of 840) hand-cold. engraved plts., lacks 2 titles, 2 indices & some ll. of text, a few offsets. Hf. leath., worn. W.a.f. (SKC. May 19; 400) £1,000
- - **Anr. Run.** 1787-1808. Vols. 1-28 in 14. Cont. cf. (P. Jan.22; 65a) *Cambridge.* £2,500
- - **Anr. Run.** 1787-1815. Vols. 1-42 in 21 vols. Cont. cf. As a periodical, w.a.f. (S. Dec.3; 934) *Quaritch.* £2,800
- - **Anr. Run.** Ed.:– John Sims. 1787-1828. 56 vols. Vol. I title-p. incorrectly dtd. 1790, separate hand-written index for year 1828. Qtr. cf., marb. bds. W.a.f. (WW. May 20; 80) £3,200
- - **Anr. Run.** L., [1787]-1965. Vols. 83 (1857)–105 (1879) on L.P. 4to. Vols. 1-175; 3 Index vols. & 1 vol. 'Dedications & Portraits', together 151 vols. & 28 pts. Lge. 8vo. & 4to. Lacks some plts., a few plts. with tears bkd., text not collated. Vols. 1-82 in 61, unif. 19th. C. hf. linen, vols. 83-168 in 86, unif. red. hf. leath., vols. 169-175 in 28 pts., index vols. & 'dedication' vol. different. (R. Mar.31-Apr.4; 1330) DM 80,000
- - **Anr. Run.** 1788-1805. Vols. I-XIX in 13 vols. & General Index to the Plants, together 14 vols. 735 engraved plts. (of 739, lacks plts. 313-316 in vol. IX), lacks titles to vols. XV, VII & XIX &

CURTIS, William – The Botanical Magazine. *-contd.*
text to 313-315, text to 174 & 249 cropped at fore-e., a few plts. & text ll. loose. Vols. I-X in 9 vols. cont. hf. cf., vols. XI-XIX in 4 vols. cont. cf., index vol. cont. bds., many spines slightly worn, some covers detchd., corners worn. (S. Jun.1; 99) *Cristiani.* £1,500
– – **Anr. Run.** L., 1790; 1788-94. Vols. 1-8 in 4. Three-qtr. cf. (SG. Sep.18; 106) $2,000
– – **Anr. Run.** 1792. 1 vol. only. Some lr. corners dampstained, some ll. soiled, a few torn with loss of a few letters. Later cf.-bkd. bds. W.a.f. (CSK. Sep.26; 127) £130
– – **Anr. Copy.** Vol. 5 only. Cont. leath., upr. cover loose. (D. Dec.11-13; 124) DM 1,800
– – **Anr. Run.** L., 1792-94. Vols. 5 & 8. Slightly browned in places & lightly soiled. Cont. bds., worn, vol. 5 lacks cover. (HK. Nov.18-21; 440) DM 1,300
– – **Anr. Run.** 1793-1800. Vols. 1-14 in 7. Cont. tree cf., some labels lacking. As a periodical, w.a.f. (SBA. Oct.21; 148) *Dallai.* £1,500
– – **Anr. Run.** 1793-96-1808. 6 vols. in 3, vols V-VI, IX-X, XXVII-XXVIII only. Some offsetting & spotting to plts. Cont. hf. cf., lacks spines, covers loose or detchd., very worn. As a periodical, w.a.f. (S. Dec.3; 935) *Wagner.* £300
– – **Anr. Run.** 1794. Vols. 7 & 8 in 1 vol. Hf. cf., worn. (SKC. May 19; 401) £120
– – **Anr. Copy.** Vol. 10 only. Cont. leath., worn. (D. Dec.11-13; 125) DM 1,250
– – **Anr. Run.** 1794-1871. Vols. 7-97 (lacks vol. 63), & general index to vols. 1-53 in 71 vols. Vol. 34 lacks 1 plt. Cont. tree cf. As a periodical, w.a.f. (C. May 20; 195) *Fletcher.* £5,000
– – **Anr. Run.** L., 1799. Vol. 13. Cont. leath., upr. cover loose. (D. Dec.11-13; 126) DM 1,300
– – **Anr. Run.** 1799-1800. Vols. 13 & 14 only in 1 vol. Hf. cf., extremities of spine worn. (S. Jul.27; 283) *Gilbert's.* £260
– – **Anr. Run.** 1800. 1 vol. only. Slight spotting Cl.-bkd. bds., worn. W.a.f. (CSK. Aug.15; 107) £270
– – **Anr. Run.** 1804-05. Pts. 19-21 in 1 vol. Plts. no. 693-832, lacks plts. no. 780. Bdg. slightly defect. (HK. Nov.18-21, 443) DM 2,000
– – **Anr. Run.** 1805-07. Vols. 22-25. Hf. leath., worn. W.a.f., (S. Dec.3; 937) *Walford.* £210
– – **Anr. Run.** Ed.:– John Sims. 1809-15. Vols. 29-41 only, Some margins of plts. slightly stained, Cont. hf. cf., worn. (CSK. Sep.19; 54) £1,000
– – **Anr. Run.** 1823. Vol. 50. Cont. hf. leath., worn. (HK. Nov.18-21; 445) DM 1,000
– – **Anr. Run.** 1824. Cont. hf. leath., cover loose, spine defect. (HK. Nov.18-21; 446) DM 1,000
– – **Anr. Run.** L., 1827. Vol. 54. (= New Series Vol. 1). Cont. hf. leath. (HK. May12-14; 240) DM 1,400
– – **Anr. Run.** 1829. Vol. 56. (=New Series Vol. 3). Cont. hf. leath., (HK. Nov.18-21; 447) DM 1,400
– – **Anr. Run.** 1832. Vol. 59 (= New Series Vol. 6). Cont. hf. leath. (HK. Nov.18-21; 448) DM 1,400
– – **Anr. Run.** 1835. Vol. 62 (= New Series Vol. 9) Cont. hf. leath. (HK. Nov.18-21; 449) DM 1,400
– – **Anr. Copy.** Cont. leath., lacks upr. part of spine. (HK. May 12-14; 244) DM 800
– – **Anr. Run.** 1836. Vol. X of 3rd. series (vol. LXIII) in orig. 12 pts. (no. CIX-CXX). Advts., a few ll. slightly spotted or soiled. Orig. ptd wraps., some slightly worn. (S. Dec.3; 938) *Varekamp.* £130
– – **Anr. Copy.** Plt. 3458 with sm. tear at foot. Cont. leath., gt. spine, spine defect. (HK. Nov.18-21; 450) DM 650
– – **Anr. Run.** 1845-55. Vols. I, IV-VII, X & XI (3rd. Series), & vol. XVI (New Series). Cont. cl., worn, spines defect., some covers detchd. W.a.f. (C. Nov.5; 31) *Studio.* £400
– – **Anr. Run.** Ed.:– Sir William Jackson Hooker & J.D. Hooker. 1856-66. 3rd. series, 11 vols. (vols. 12-22). Cont. cl., worn, defect., some covers detchd. As a periodical, w.a.f. (C. May 20; 196) *Taylor.* £450
– – **Anr. Run.** 1859-63. 4 vols. only. Some spotting Cont. hf. mor. W.a.f. (CSK. Apr.10; 136) £300
– Flora Londinensis. Ill.:– after Edwards, Sowerby, Kilburn (& others?). Priv. Ptd., 1777-98. 1st. Edn. 2 vols. in 6. Fo. Plts. hand-cold. With MS. note in upr. cover 'This copy . . . was coloured purposely for me under Curtis's directions . . .', sigd. 'J.L.P.'), 1st. iss. of the 1st. title, 1st. title & dedication creased, titles, indexes, etc., & all plts. with sm. liby. stps., most blind. 19th. C. hf. mor., many covers detchd. From Chetham's

Liby., Manchester. (C. Nov.26; 95) *Taylor.* £2,700
– – **Anr. Edn.** 1777-98. 3 vols. Fo. Cont. diced russ., reprd. & Vol. 3 rebkd. & with a type facs. title Vol. 3 (but orig. never existed). Bkplts. of Lord Carrington & Earl Beauchamp. (S. Jun.1; 96) *Schierenberg.* £2,800
– – **Anr. Copy.** 2 titles only, 1 bnd. in at end, 420 (of 432) hand-cold. engraved plts. Cont. hf. cf., rebkd. W.a.f. (SKC. Feb.26; 1580) £2,500
– – **Anr. Copy.** 377 (of 432) cold. plts. Cont. hf. cf., covers detchd. W.a.f. (S. Jun.1; 97) *Carr.* £1,500
– – **Anr. Edn.** L., ca. 1800. Atlas fo. Comprising 94 hand-cold. copper-plts., most with accompanying text lf., loose. (SG. May 21; 347) $1,550
– – **Anr. Edn.** Ed.:– George Graves & Sir William Jackson Hooker. L., 1835. 5 vols. Fo. Some plts. browned, 1 shaved. Cont. mor. richly gt. by Mackenzie, vol. 1, jnts. worn. From collection of Massachusetts Horticultural Society, stps. on plts. (SPB. Oct.1; 113) $9,000
– Lectures on Botany. Ed.:– Samuel Curtis 1803. Vol. 1 only. Cont. cf., worn. (CSK. Nov.7; 42) £65
– – **Anr. Edn.** 1803-04. 3 vols. A few stains. Cont. cf., worn, covers loose. (SKC. May 19; 403) £50
– – **Anr. Edn.** 1805. 3 vols. in 1. Thornton's sketch of Life of Curtis bnd. at end. Cf., reprd., brkn. (S. Dec.3; 939) *Walford.* £150
– A Volume of Hand Coloured Engravings of Flowers. Ill.:– after J. Sowerby, Sydenham Edwards & others. Late 18th. & 19th. C. Probably taken from the Botanical Magazine. 19th. C. hf. cf. & cl. (HSS. Apr.24; 330) £110

CURTIS, William–ANON
– The Botanical Magazine–The Compleat Florist. 1747; 1787. 2 works in 1 vol.; vols. 1 & 2 of 2nd. work. 1st. work: engraved decor. title & 96 (of 100) plts., slightly soiled, 2nd. work: some offsets. Hf. mor., worn. W.a.f. (SKC. May 19; 398) £320

CURTIS, Winifred & Stones, Margaret
– The Endemic Flora of Tasmania. L., 1967-69. Pts. 1 & 2 only (of 6). Fo. Cl., d.-w.'s. (KH. Mar.24; 115) *Aus.* $160

CURTIUS, Rufus Quintus
– De Rebus Gestis Alexandri Magni Regis Macedonum. Ed.:– Henricus Snakenburg. 1724. 2 vols. 4to. Cont. mor., gt. decor. spine. (TA. Dec.18; 415) £56
– The Historie Conteyning the Actes of the Great Alexander. Trans.:– John Brende. 1592. Wormed. Cont. vell., gt., lacks ties, folding red mor. box. [STC 6146] (S. Mar.16; 127) *Maggs.* £180

CURWEN, J.C.
– Observations on the State of Ireland . . . Agriculture & Rural Population. L., 1818. 2 vols. Sm. piece cut from top of title-p. of vol. 1, some dampstains, 10pp. advts. at end, liby. stp. Crimson mor. (GM. Apr.30; 295) £60

CURWEN PRESS
– A Specimen Book of Pattern Papers . . . in Use at . . . Ill.:– Paul Nash & others. The Fleuron 1928. Lge. 4to. Orig. cl. John Carter's copy, with his label. (SH. Mar.27; 364) *Henderson.* £240

CURZON, Hon. Robert
– Visits to the Monasteries of the Levant. 1851. 4th. Edn. Orig. cl., spine slightly torn. A.L.s. inserted before title. (SBA. Jul.23; 314) *Morris.* £55

CUSHING, Harvey
– Andreas Vesalius: a Bio-Bibliography. N.Y., 1943. (800). 4to. Hf. leath., spine gt. (SG. Jan.22; 387) $325
– – **Anr. Copy.** Mor.-bkd. bds. (S. Feb.23; 335) *Way.* £120
– Intracranial Tumours, notes upon a Series of Two Thousand Verified Cases. [Springfield] L., [1932]. 1st. Edn., L. Iss., (180). Orig. cl. T.L.s. inserted. (S. Jun.15; 207) *Canale.* £110
– Meningiomas, their Classification, Regional Behavior, Life History & Surgical End Results. Springfield, Illinois, 1938. 1st. Edn. Orig. cl. (S. Jun.15; 209) *Jenner Books.* £110
– Papers Relating to the Pituitary Body, Hypothalamus & Parasympathetic Nervous System. Springfield, Illinois, etc., 1932. 1st. Edn. Orig. cl., d.w.'s. (S. Jun.15; 208) *Levy.* £80
– The Pituitary Body & its Disorders. Phila. & L., 1912. 1st. Edn. Orig. cl. (S. Jun.15; 204) *Studd.* £120

– – **Anr. Edn.** Phila., [1912]. 1st. Edn. Stp. of College of Physicians on title. From liby. of Dr. E. Ashworth Underwood. (S. Feb.23; 188) *Jenner.* £50
– Tumors of the Nervus Acusticus & the Syndrome of the Cerebellopontile Angle. Phila. & L., 1917. 1st. Edn. Orig. cl. (S. Jun.15; 205) *Levy.* £100

CUSHING, Harvey & Bailey, Percival
– A Classification of the Tumours of the Glioma Group on a Histogenetic Basis. Phila., L. & Montreal, 1926. 1st. Edn. Orig. cl. (S. Jun.15; 206) *Levy.* £80

CUSSANS, John Edwin
– History of Hertfordshire. 1870-81. 3 vols. Fo. Hf. mor., gt. (C. Nov.5; 36) *Traylen.* £250
– – **Anr. Copy.** Mod. red hf. mor. gt. (C. Jul.15; 30) *Taylor.* £220
– – **Anr. Edn.** 1879 & 1881. 2 vols. only (comprising the Hundreds of Cassio & Dacorum). Hf. mor., spines gt. (LC. Jun.18; 148) £65

CUST, Lionel
– The Bridgewater Gallery. 1903. (115). 4to. Canvas-bkd. bds., worn. (C. Feb.4; 212) *Doll.* £50
– Royal Collection of Paintings. 1905-06. 2 vols. Lge. fo. Some dampstains. Orig. mor., affected by damp. (CSK. Jan.30; 64) £50

CUSTINE, Astolphe Louis Leonard, Marquis de
– Mémoires et Voyages. Paris, 1830. 1st. Edn. 2 vols. Cont. hf. cf., smooth decor. spines. A.L. by author, bkplt. of Vanderem. (HD. Jun.24; 176) *Frs.* 3,700
– Russie – 1839. Paris, 1843. 1st. Edn. 4 vols. Cont. hf. cf., smooth decor. spines, 1 spine detchd., other bdgs. defect. (HD. Feb.27; 111) *Frs.* 1,600

CUTLER, Jervis
[–] Topographical Description of the State of Ohio, Indiana Territory, & Louisiana . . . Boston, 1812. 1st. Edn. 12mo. Lacks errata slip, owner's inscr. on title & p. 8, foxed & browned. Cont. mott. sheep, folding cl. s.-c. From liby. of William E. Wilson. [Sabin 18170] (SPB. Apr.29; 71) $600
[–] – Anr. Copy. Some foxing, plts. worn, lacks errata lf. Cont. cf. (SPB. Jun.22; 49) $300

CUTLER, Thomas W.
– A Grammar of Japanese Ornament & Design. 1880. 4to. Some plts. slightly soiled. Orig. cl., dampstained. (CSK. Oct.31; 152) £80
– – **Anr. Copy.** (P. Mar.12; 29) *Sims & Reed.* £75

CUVIER, Baron Georges Leopold Chretien
– The Animal Kingdom. 1827-35. 16 vols. Some engraved plts. hand-cold. Mor., spines gt. (SKC. Feb.26; 1581) £280
– – **Anr. Copy.** 4to. 5 vols. in orig. hf. mor., brkn., rest mod. buckram. (SG. Sep.18; 108) $240
– – **Anr. Edn.** 1834. 4 vols. Cl.-bkd. bds. (P. Apr.30; 250) *Schapiro.* £75
– – **Anr. Edn.** Trans.:– Henry McMurtie. 1834-37. 4 vols. text, & 4 vols. plts. Orig. embossed cl., cf. spines, gt., vols. III & IV loose, stitching brkn. W.a.f. (C. Nov.5; 37) *Wheldon & Wesley.* £160
– Animal Kingdom: Class Aves. 1829. 3 vols. Cl. (BS. Nov.26; 157) £190
[–] Histoire Naturelle des Poissons. Sammelband mit 211 Kupfern. Ill.:– after Werner & Costello. [Paris], ca. 1835. 198 copper-engrs. cold., slightly stained or soiled. Hf. leath. (D. Dec.11-13; 290) DM 5,000
– La Menagerie du Museum National d'Histoire Naturelle. Ill.:– after Marechal von Miger. Paris, 1801. Fo. Lacks 6 copperplts. Cont. hf. leath. (D. Dec.11-13; 296) DM 2,200
– Le Règne Animal distribué d'après son Organisation. Paris, 1817. 1st. Edn. 4 vols. End-ll. stpd. Mid. 19th. C. hf. leath. (HK. Nov.18-21; 453) DM 850
– – **Anr. Edn.** 1836-49. 22 vols. in 20. Margins slightly browned, slight foxing. Recent cl. by Kurt Gaebel & Sons, Holland. (TA. Sep.18; 86) £1,000
– – **Anr. Edn.** Paris, 1840-49. 20 vols. 4to. Vols. 1 & 10 dampstained, others with a few ll. slightly spotted. Cont. red mor. gt., vols. 1 & 6 defect., 4 others stained. W.a.f. (SBA. Jul.14; 224) *Shapiro.* £200

See–**GEOFFROY SAINT-HILAIRE, Isidor & Cuvier, Georges L.C.**

CUVILLIER, A.
- Souvenirs de la Suisse. Genf, ca. 1860. Ob. 8vo. Slightly soiled. Cont. leath., gt. stpd. (R. Oct.14-18; 1998)   DM 6,000

CUYPERS, Pieter & Guilliam
- Tractaet van Grond-Proceduren ofte van de Uyt-Werckinghe van de Actie Hypothecaire. Mechelen, 1679. 8 pts. 4to. Old cf., 4 spine raised bands, gt. (LM. Nov.8; 50)   DM 12,000

CYPRIAN, Saint Caecilius
- Genuine Works. Trans.:– Nath. Marshall. 1717. Fo. Cont. cf., gt. panel., decor. mor. centrepieces, spine torn. (S. Mar.16; 177)   Thomas. £60
- Opera. [Stuttgart], [Printer of the Erwahlung Maximilians], ca. 1486. Fo. Spaces for initial capitals, some with guide letters, portion of lr. corner of L5 torn away, light worming to lr. & inner margins, heavily wormed at end, affecting some text, last lf. reprd. & patched. Cont. blind-stpd. cf. over wood bds., a remboitage, covers with central panels of floral tools, roll-stpd. borders, brass clasps, rebkd. preserving orig. spine. From the collection of Eric Sexton. [BMC III, 675, Goff C1014, HC 5895*] (CNY. Apr.8; 172) $2,800
- Operum. Ed.:– D. Erasmus. Colonia, [1522]. 1st. Edn. 1 corner of title torn off, old stains. Old vell. (LM. Mar.21; 287)   B. Frs. 14,000
- A Sermon made on the Lord's Prayer. 1539. Last blank lf. defect., some tears. Cont. limp vell. [STC 6158] (SH. Jun.4; 156)   Poole. £55

CYRANUS, King of Persia
- The Magick of Kirani King of Persia, & of Harpocration; Containing the Magical & Medicinal Vertues of Stones, Herbs, Fishes, Beasts & Birds ... [L.], 1685. Some ll. wormed in lr. inner margins, slightly browned & soiled, stain in upr. margin of 1st. 3 ll., owner's inscrs. of Ambrose Pimlowe, Rector of Gt. Dunham, Norfolk. Cont. cf., spine defect. at head. Bkplt. of Scott Chad; from Honeyman Collection. [Wing M249] (S. May 20; 3214)   Quaritch. £480

CYRILLUS, Alexandrinus, Saint
- In XII Prophetas. Ingolstadt, 1607. Fo. Greek & Latin text. Cont. vell., metal clasps, worn. (SH. Jun.25; 74)   Dimakarakos. £65
- Opus Insigne in Evagelium Ioannis. Trans.:– Georgio Trapezzotio. [Paris], [1508]. Fo. Some initials in red, rubricated thro.-out, title-p. torn, stained, owner's inscr. of Carthusians at Dülmen dtd. 1529. Cont. German blind-stpd. cf. on wooden bds., lacks spine & clasps. (S. Mar.17; 268)   Maggs. £220

CZECH, Fr. H.
- Versinnlichte Denk-und Sprachlehre, mit Anwendung auf die Religions-und Sittenlehre und auf das Leben. Wien, 1836. 4to. 1 plt. duplicated. Cont. hf. cf., spine gt. (VG. Dec.16; 908) Fls. 850

CZERMANSKIEGO, Zdzislawa
- Jozef Pilsudski W 13 Planszach. Ed.:– General Smigly Rydz (intro.) Warsaw, 1935. Orig. cl.-bkd. folder. (LC. Feb.12; 258)   £50

CZERNICHEW, Comte G. de
- Théâtre de l'Arsenal de Gatchina. St. Petersb., 1821. 1st. Edn. Cont. mor., gt.-tooled covers & spine, gt. dentelles, moire satin end-ll. Pencilled notat identifies this as dedication copy for the Czarina Maria Feodorowna. (SG. Sep.4; 46) $200

CZWIKLITZER, Chr.
- Le Sculpteur-graveur de 1919 a 1967. Ill.:– O. Zadkine. [Paris], 1967. (375) privilege Edn. 4to. Orig. linen. Sigd. etchg. by Zadkine, printer's mark sigd. by artist & publishers. (H. Dec.9/10; 2401)   DM 620

DA BERG, F.H. von
- Untersuchungen über den Ursprung der Harmonie. Erfurt, 1800. 1st. Edn. Browned. Wraps. (H. Dec.9/10; 1103)   DM 560

D'ABRANTES, Mme. la Duchesse
- Mémoires ou Souvenirs Historiques sur Napoléon. Paris, 1831-35. 1st. Edn. 18 vols. Cont. cl. (SBA. Jul.23; 476)   Count de Salis. £100

D'ACHIARDI, P.
- I quadri Primitivi della Pinacoteca Vaticana. Rome, 1929. Fo. Cl. (CR. Jun.11; 152)   Lire 300,000

DACIER, Émile
- Catalogues de Ventes de Livrets de Salons illustrés par Gabriel de Saint-Aubin. Paris, 1909. (125). Tipped in collotype facs. of Saint-Aubin's drawings. Hf. mor. gt., mostly unc., orig. wraps. preserved. (CNY. Oct.1; 85) $140

DADIN de Hauteserre, Antoine
- De Ducibus, et Comitibus Prvincialibus Galliae Libri Tres ... De Origine et Statu Feudorum ... Toulouse, 1643. 1st. Edn. 4to. Cont. cf., 3 fillets, arms of Fouquet, spine decor. with alternate arms & ciphers of Paris Jesuits. (HD. Mar.18; 51)   Frs. 1,400

DADSON, W.
- Sketches of the Picturesque in Rochester & its Vicinity. [1825?]. Ob. 4to. Title & dedication bnd. after plt. 20, 1 plt. spotted. Cont. hf. cf. (C. Nov.5; 38)   Crowe. £110

DAFFORNE, James
- Modern Art. Ca. 1880? L.P. Fo. Orig. red hf. mor. gt. (SBA. May 27; 461)   Barker. £70

DAGUERRE, Louis Jacques Mande
- Historique et Description des Procédés du Daguerreotype et du Diorama. Paris, 1839. New Edn. Soiled & 1st. ll. stained. Orig. wraps., loose, slightly soiled & stpd. (H. Dec.9/10; 390)   DM 1,800

DAGUERREOTYPES
- Representant Les Vues et Les Monuments Le Plus Remarquables du Globe ... Ill.:– Salathe, Martens & Himely. Paris, 1840. Pt. 1 only. Ob. fo. Orig. ptd. wraps. (LC. Oct.2; 47)   £110

DAHLBERG, C. Th. v.
- Grundsätze der Aesthetik. ...–Versuch einiger Beyträge über die Baukunst. 1791, 1792. Cont. hf. leath. (R. Mar.31-Apr.4; 263)   DM 1,300

DAHLBERG, Edward
- Bottom Dogs. Ed.:– D.H. Lawrence [Introduction]. L., [1929]. 1st. Edn., (520). Orig. cl., d.-w. (discold.). (SPB. Nov.25; 245) $150

DAHLBERGH or Dalberg, Count Eric Johnsson
- Seucia Antiqua et Hondierna. Stockholm, [plts. dtd. 1690-1709]. 4to. 149 plts., mntd. on guards thro.-out. Diced russ., worn, upr. cover detchd. W.a.f. (C. Jul.15; 32)   Marshall. £800
[-] - Anr. Copy. 4to. Mntd. on guards thro.-out. Diced russ., worn, upr. cover detchd. W.a.f. (C. Nov.5; 39)   Taylor. £500
[-] - Anr. Edn. [Stockholm], [plts. dtd. 1690-1714]. 3 vols. in 1. Ob. fo. 3 engd. titles, engraved dedication, 328 engraved plts., all cut close to line border, unif. inlaid in early 18th. C. paper. 18th. C. tree cf., sides with gt. borders, red mor. gt. spine in compartments. As a collection of prints, w.a.f. (C. Jul.15; 31)   Taylor. £650
- - Anr. Edn. [Stockholm], [1690-1715]. 3 pts. in 1 vol. Ob. fo. 2 sm. added copper engrs., index with MS. additions, pt. 1 lf. 35 with lge. tear, a few other sm. tears & some stains, last copper engrs. slightly browned. Cont. cf., gt. spine. (H. Dec.9/10; 621)   DM 13,500
[-] - Anr. Edn. [Stockholm], 1691-1714]. 1st. Edn. 3 pts. in 1 vol. Ob. fo. 346 (of 352) engraved plts., 2 plts. slightly torn, some neatly reprd., many margins extended. Cont. cf., gt., name of J.H. Lefebure on upr. cover, worn. As a collection, w.a.f. (S. Oct.21; 275)   Chalmont. £350
- - Anr. Edn. Ill.:– J.V.D. Aveleen or Joachim von Sandrart. Stockholm, [1693-1713]. 1st. Edn. 3 vols. in 1. Ob. fo. 1 map torn, the other defect., some clean splits along the plt. marks & folds a some outer margins frayed with a few tears. Cont. cf., worn. Armorial bkplt. of Charlotta Joh. Gerner. (S. Jun.22; 119)   Hammond. £1,100
- - Anr. Copy. 2 maps, 1 torn, the other defect. Armorial bkplt. of Charlotta Joh. Gerner. (S. Oct.20; 55)   Brookfield. £800
[-] - Anr. Edn. Trans.:– Adam, N. Perelle, J. Marot & others. [Stockholm], [1693-1715]. 3 pts. in 1 vol. Ob. fo. 354 copperplts. (1 folding) 3 engraved titles (of 4), 13 p. index, a few ll. slightly soiled. Later leath., gt. (D. Dec.11-13; 1338)   DM 15,000
- - Anr. Edn. Stockholm, 1899. 1st. facs. Edn. 3 vols. in 1. Ob. fo. Orig. gt. two-tone mott. cf., very worn. (PNY. Oct.1; 169) $140

DAILY ADVERTISER (The)
N.Y., May 2, 1794-Apr.30, 1795. Fo. Stained. Sheep.-bkd. bds., stained. As a periodical, w.a.f. (SPB. Jun.22; 104) $800

DAISENBERGER, J.M. & others
- Sammelband mit sieben Kleinen Medizinischen Schriften. 1788-1816 & nd. Cont. paper bds. (H. Dec.9/10; 339)   DM 440

DALBERG, Count Erik Johnsson
See–DAHLBERG or DALBERG, Count Erik Johnsson

DALECHAMPS, Jacques
- Histoire Générale des Plantes. Lyon, 1615. 1st. Edn. 2 vols. Fo. 2nd. title defect. in margins, some browning & staining, a few edges strengthened. 18th. C. hf. cf., worn. (S. Jun.1; 259)   Van Haverbeke. £800

D'ALEMBERT, Jean Le Rond
See–ALEMBERT, Jean le Rond d'

DALI, Salvador
- La Conquête de L'Irrationel. Paris, [1935]. 1st. Trade Edn. Tall 16mo. Orig. photo-pict. wraps. Inscr. & sigd. (PNY. Mar.4; 132) $170
- The Secret Life of Salvador Dali. Trans.:– Haakon M. Chevalier. N.Y., 1942. Special 1st. Edn., (119) numbered. 4to. Qtr. cl. & bds., pict. paper cover., d.-w., boxed. Contains orig. pen & ink drawing by Dali, sigd. (PNY. Mar.4; 133) $5,000

DALL, William H.
See–HARRIMAN Alaska Expedition

DALLA TORRE, K.W.v.
- Atlas der Alpenflora. Ill.:– after A. Hartinger. Vienna, 1882-84. 1st. Edn. 5 vols. (text & 4 plt. vols.) Cont. hf. leath., spine slightly worn. (HK. Nov.18-21; 454)   DM 780
See–HARTINGER, A. & Dalla Torre, K.W.V.

DALLAS, Robert Charles
- History of the Maroons. 1803. [1st. Edn.?]. 2 vols. Orig. bds. (P. Oct.23; 16)   Burton-Garbutt. £210
- - Anr. Copy. Cont. pol. cf., rebkd., spines gt., partly unc. [Sabin 18322] (S. Feb.9; 38)   Thorp. £120
- - Anr. Copy. Very browned, some stains, tears. Cont. cf., rebkd., new endpapers. [Sabin 18322] (SPB. May 5; 176) $100

DALLAWAY, James
- Constantinople Ancient & Modern. 1797. 1st. Edn. 4to. Occasional light foxing & spotting in the text. Cont. cf., spine reprd. (S. Nov.4; 641)   O'Neill. £130
- Enquiries into the Origin & Progress of the Science of Heraldry in England. Gloucester, 1793. 4to. Later hand-colouring. Cont. cf. gt. (TA. Jan.22; 144)   £70

DALLAWAY, James & Cartwright, Edmund
- A History of the Western Division of the County of Sussex. 1815-30. 2 vols. in 3. 4to. Extra-ill. with 10 plts. & maps, including 2 cold. aquatints. Cont. mor. gt. by Clarke. Pres. Copy? to William Hamper, lately in the collection of Eric Sexton. (C. Apr.16; 238)   Hordern. £400

D'ALLEMAGNE, Henri René
- Récréations et Passe-Temps. Paris, 1905. 4to. Publisher's bds. (HD. Jun.10; 142)   Frs. 1,700
- Sports et Jeux d'Adresse. Paris, ca. 1903. 4to. Publisher's bds. (HD. Jun.10; 143)   Frs. 1,800
See–ALLEMAGNE, Henry-René d'

DALLINGTON, Sir Robert
[-] Aphorismes Ciuill & Militarie. 1613. 1st. Edn. 2 pts. in 1 vol. Fo. Title with inscr., cont. MS. notes, some ll. loose, some browning & soiling, lacks final blank. Cont. limp vell., worn. [STC 6197] (S. Sep.29; 17)   Armstrong. £100
- - Anr. Copy. 1st. title stained. Cont. cf., gt. centrepieces with initials 'S D MK' on covers. [STC 6197] (C. Jul.16; 348)   Taylor. £60

DALLY, N.
- Usi e Costumi Sociali, Politici e Religiosi di tutti i Popoli del Mundo. Torino, 1844-47. 4 vols. 4to. Some ll. at beginning of Vol. IV browned & the 1st. 3 reprd. Later hf. mor., partly unc. (SI. Dec.3; 162)   Lire 750,000
- - Anr. Edn. Torino, 1852. 4 vols. only. Slight foxing thro.-out. Cf.-bkd. bds., worn. (BS. Jun.11; 329)   £140

DALRYMPLE, Alexander
- A Collection of Voyages chiefly in the Southern Atlantic Ocean. Priv. Ptd., 1775. 1st. Edn. 4to. Some slight spotting. Mod. cf.-bkd. marb. bds.,

DALRYMPLE Alexander-contd.
spine gt. [Sabin 18366] (S. Feb.9; 39)
Quaritch. £600
- **An Historical Collection of the several Voyages & Discoveries in the South Pacific Ocean.** Priv. Ptd., 1770-71. 2 vols. in 1. 4to. 12 engraved plts. (8 double-p.), 3 folding engraved charts, 2 errata ll. at end of vol. 1, some slight spotting. Cont. spr. cf., spine reprd. [Sabin 18388] (S. Feb.9; 40)
Traylen. £600

DALRYMPLE, Sir John
- **Memoirs of Great Britain & Ireland.** Edinb., 1771. 4to. Cf., worn. (CE. Nov.20; 47)   £50

DALTON, John
- **A New System of Chemical Philosophy.** Manchester, 1808-10. 1st. Edn. Vols. I & II (of 3). Some browning & slight soiling, piece torn from foremargin of 2D2 vol. I. Vol. I rebnd. hf. cf. retaining old marb. bds., vol. II cl., stained, both unc., latter unopened, hf. red mor. cases. From Honeyman Collection. (S. May 20; 3215)
Zeitlin & Verbrugge. £550

DALTON, John Call
- **Topographical Anatomy of the Brain.** Phila., 1885. 1st. Edn. (250). 3 vols. Sm. fo. Ex-liby., stpd. on versos of all plts. Cl., 2 spines with tears. (SG. Apr. 23; 130) $400
- - **Anr. Edn.** Phila., 1885. 3 vols. 4to. Cl. (S. Jun.15; 217)   *Norman.* £170

DALTON, Michael
- **The Countrey Justice, containing the Practise of the Iustices of the Peace out of their Sessions.** 1626. 3rd. Edn. Fo. Cont. marginal notes in ink, MS. index at end, cont. inscr. at end of 'George Winn'. Cont. cf. [STC 6208] (C. Feb.25; 154)
Bennett. £70

DALTON, Richard
- **Antiquities & Views in Greece & Egypt.** [1751]. Fo. Cont. cf. gt. (P. Feb.19; 151)   *Kay.* £360
- [-] **Anr. Copy.** Cont. cf.-bkd. bds. bdg. & stitching brkn. W.a.f. (C. Feb.25; 88)
Maggs. £100

D'ALTON, Rt. Rev. Mons.
- **History of the Archdiocese of Tuam.** Dublin, 1928. 1st. Edn. 2 vols. 4to. Cl., d.-w.'s. (GM. Apr.30; 153)   £60

DALVIMART, Octavien
[-] **The Costume of Turkey.** 1802. Fo. Hand-cold. engraved vig.-title, 60 hand-cold. plts., text wtrmkd. 1796, plts. 1796-1801. Cont. str.-grd. mor. gt. Bkplt. of Capt. T. Gordon Caufeild, Royal Navy. (S. Nov.24; 96)   *Finopoulos.* £210
[-] - **Anr. Copy.** Hand-cold. title & 58 plts. only, lacks 'A Greek Woman' & 'A Dervise', titles & text in Engl. & Fr. Cont. russ. (CSK. Sep.26; 200)   £160
[-] - **Anr. Copy.** 4to. Title slightly soiled. Cont. cf., covers detchd. (C. Nov.5; 40)   *Elliott.* £100
- - **Anr. Edn.** 1804. Fo. Text in Engl. & Fr., 1 plt. crudely reprd. with sellotape, offsetting of plts. on text. Cl. (BS. Jun.11; 330)   £110
- **Dress & Manners of the Turks.** L., 1814? Cont. Engl. str.-grd. garnet mor., decor. spine, gt. blind-tooled roll-stps. on covers, inside dentelle. (HD. Dec.5; 59)   Frs. 3,500

DALY, Cesar
- **L'Architecture Privée au XIXe Siècle Troisième Serie Decorations Interieures Peintes.** Paris, 1877. 2 vols. in 1. Fo. Some spotting. Cont. hf. mor. (CSK. Jan.30; 16)   £100

DALYELL, Sir John G.
- **Musical Memoirs of Scotland.** 1849. 4to. Cl. (CE. Jul.9; 230)   £52

DALZEL, Archibald
- **The History of Dahomy.** 1793. 1st. Edn. 4to. c3 torn & reprd. Mod. qtr. cf., unc. (S. Jun.29; 218)
Villiers. £180
- - **Anr. Edn.** Priv. Ptd., 1793. 1st. Edn., L.P. 4to. Some tears slightly affecting text, reprd., some spotting. Mod. cf.-bkd. marb. bds., spine gt., unc. (S. Feb.9; 41)   *Gross.* £150
*See-*NORRIS, R. & others

DALZIEL, George & Edward
- **Bible Gallery** Ill.:– after Edward Burne-Jones & others. 1880. Fo. India page proofs of title, prelims. & 62 wood-engraved plts. Loose as issued in orig. vell.-bkd. folder. (SH. Mar.26; 151)
Fogg. £200

DAME WIGGINS OF Lee, & her Seven Wonderful Cats
Ed.:– John Ruskin. Ill.:– Kate Greenaway. Orpington, 1885. L.P. 1st. Edn. Gt.-pict. cl. (SG. Sep.4; 237) $175

DAMHOUDER, Jos de
- **Patrocinium Pupillorum.** Trans.:– Johannes Burckhard. Frankfurt, 1580. Fo. On p. 111 title: De Subhastatione … 1580, title remounted & partly backed, some short margins, some worming in some pp. & some restoration. Three quarter mor., mod. spine raised bands. (LM. Mar.21; 173)
B.Frs. 14,000
- **Practique Judiciaire es Causes Criminelles.** Antw., 1564. 4to. Mod. cf., 5 decor. spine raised bands, double border, gt. fillets, angle fleuron, inner dentelle. (LM. Mar.21; 171) B.Frs. 36,000
- - **Anr. Edn.** Antw., 1572. Fo. Cont. limp vells., old staining. (LM. Mar.21; 172)   B.Frs. 22,000
- **Practycke in Civile Saecken.** The Hague, 1626. 1st. Dutch Edn. 4to. Old name on title & a sm. liby. stp. on verso, light stains in places. Cont. vell. (VG. Oct. 13; 52)   Fls. 850

DAMPIER, William
- **A Collection of Voyages.** 1729. 1st. Coll. Edn. 4 vols. Some rust-holes, several ll. stained in outer edges, occasional browning & soiling. Cont. spr. cf., gt., some wear, 1 cover detchd., anr. loose. [Sabin 18373] (S. Feb.10; 433)   *Quaritch.* £580
- - **Anr. Copy.** 65 engraved maps & plts., 22 folding, ?includes 2 extra plts. Cont. cf. gt., rebkd. (S. Mar.31; 461)   *Ryman.* £380
- - **Anr. Copy.** 63 (of 64) engraved maps & plts., text edges cropped, some foxing. Cont. panel. cf., rebkd in cf. (PNY. Mar.4; 135) $325
- - **Anr. Edn.** Ed.:– John Masefield. L., 1906. (1000). 2 vols. Orig. cl., upr. cover & spine gt. (JL. Jul.20; 875)   Aus. $180
- **A New Voyage Round the World.** 1697. 2nd. Edn. Vol. I only, lacks 5 supp. vols. Advt. ll., a few spots. Cont. panel. cf., spine reprd. at head & foot. Parham bkplt. (S. Jun.9; 43)   *Quaritch.* £50
- - **Anr. Edn.** L., Argonaut Pr., 1927. (975) numbered on Japon vell. Buckram, qtr. vell., slight soiling, unc. & unopened. Dennis Wheatley's bkplt. (KH. Nov.18; 188)   Aus. $120
- **A New Voyage Round the World Describing … the Isthmus of America … -A Collection of Voyages.** L., 1703; 1729. 5th. Edn. (1st. work). 1 vol., 3 pts. in 1 vol.; together 2 vols. 1st. work: lacks 1 (of 5) engraved maps, some maps reprd.; 2nd. work: 1 map later cold., some repairs. Unif. cf., rebkd., some foxing. (VA. Oct.31; 305) R.280
- **A New Voyage Round the World.-Voyages & Descriptions.** L., 1697; 1699. 2nd. Edn.; [1st. Edn.]. 1 vol.; vol. II in 3 pts. Orig. bdgs. (CB. Sep.24; 175)   Can. $500

DAMPIER, William & Wafer, Lionel
- **Nieuwe Reistogt rondon de Wereld.** Nijmegen, 1771. Qtr. cf., spine worn. (JL. Mar.2; 542)
Aus. $110

DANA, E[dmund]
- **Geographical Sketches on the Western Country** … Cinc., 1819. 1st. Edn. 12mo. Some discolouration, slight foxing. Cont. mott. cf. From liby. of William E. Wilson. (SPB. Apr.29; 73) $375

DANA, James Freeman & Samuel Luther
- **Outlines of the Mineralogy & Geology of Boston & its Vicinity.** Boston, 1818. 1st. Edn. Old bds., needs rebdg., ex liby. (SG. Sep.18; 110) $230

DANA, Richard Henry, Jnr.
- **Two Years Before the Mast.** N.Y., 1840. 1st. Edn., 1st. Iss. Tears, some foxing, sig. on title. Orig. cl., reprd. (SPB. May 29; 99) $325
*See-*POE, Edgar Allan-DANA, Richard Henry, Jnr.-DOUGLAS, George Norman

DANCKWERTH, C.
- **Newe Landesbeschreibung der Zwey Herzogthümer Schleswich und Holstein.** Ill.:– J. Mejer. [Husum], 1652. Fo. Lacks engraved title & index as often, sm. owner's mark on ptd. title, text browned, soiled & stained, 1 lf. with tear bkd. without text loss, some ll. bkd., 1 map loose, added bnd. in after p. 52 Ducatus Sleswicensis, Nova Descriptio, cold. copper engraved map from Blaeu ca. 1650. Cont. vell., soiled, spine very defect., lr. cover reprd. (H. Dec.9/10; 445)   DM 13,000

D'ANCONA, P. & AESCLIMANN, E.
- **Dictionnaire des Miniaturistes du Moyen Age et de la Renaissance.** Milan, 1949. 2nd. Edn. 4to. Sewed. (CR. Jun.11; 154)   Lire 200,000

DANIEL, G.
- **The Modern Dunciad.** 1835. Later mor., gt. Inscr. with 2-p. poem 'To Stella' by author. (SH. Mar.5; 217)   *Sanders.* £60

DANIEL, Gabriel
- **Histoire de la Milice Françoise.** Paris, 1721. 1st. Edn. 2 vols. 4to. A few minor defects, barely affecting text. Cont. spr. cf., slightly worn, lacks labels. (SBA. Dec.16; 73)   *Shapiro.* £160
- - **Anr. Edn.** 1st. Edn.; on L.P. 2 vols. 4to. Cont. red mor., fillet, spines decor. with gt. cross-bars, inside dentelle. (HD. Mar.18; 52)   Frs. 5,900

DANIEL, Samuel
- **The Civile Wares betweene the Howses of Lancaster & Yorke.** Ill.:– Cockson (engraved title). 1609. 1st. Compl. Edn. 4to. Engraved title mntd., with the cancelled lf. E4, lacks blank A4. Red str.-grd. mor. by Hering for Richard Heber. Heber's copy, with fly-lf. inscr. by him, & his bibliographical note inserted. [STC 6245] (C. Nov.19; 4)   *Wisbech.* £240

DANIEL, Rev. William Barker
- **Rural Sports.** 1801. 2 vols. 4to. Hf. mor. gt. (P. Nov. 13; 250)   *Leete.* £70
- - **Anr. Edn.** [1801-02]. 2 vols. 4to. Cont. mott. cf. gt., worn. (CE. Jul.9; 217)   £75
- - **Anr. Copy.** 2 vols. in 3. 1 engraved plt. reprd., some soiled, a few ll. loose. Bds., worn. (SH. Jun.4; 216)   *Armstrong.* £60
- - **Anr. Edn.** 1801-13. 3 vols. including supp. 4to. Orig. bds., unc., vols. 1 & 2 spines worn. (C. Jul.15; 175)   *Taylor.* £140
- - **Anr. Copy.** 2 vols. & supp. (SBA. Jul.22; 91)   *Schuster.* £120
- - **Anr. Copy.** 2 vols. in 3, & supp. Some text & tissues foxed. Cont. hf. cf., gt. (C. Nov.5; 42)   *Turner.* £100
- - **Anr. Copy.** 3 vols. including Supp. Lge. 4to. Some foxing. Cont. russ., gt. borders & spines. (SG. Apr.9; 346) $220
- - **Anr. Edn.** 1802. 2 vols. 4to. No bdg. stated lacks covers. (P. Jan.22; 347)   *Lee.* £110
- - **Anr. Edn.** 1805-13. 4 vols. (including Supp. 1 vol.). 4to. Cont. str.-grd. mor. gt. Bkplt. of Eliza Gulston. (S. Nov.24; 97)   *Way.* £190
[-] - **Anr. Edn.** 1807. 4to. Atlas of plts. only, slightly spotted, mainly marginal. Cont. hf. cf. W.a.f. (SBA. Jul.22; 89)   *Temperley.* £100
- - **Anr. Edn.** 1807-13. 4 vols. including Supp. Engraved port., titles & plts., 1 cut down. Cont. russ., 2 vols. rebkd. preserving old spines. (CSK. May 1; 140)   £110
- - **Anr. Copy.** 4 vols. Royal 8vo. Some ll. loose in bdg. Hf. cf. (BS. Sep.17; 109)   £100
- - **Anr. Edn.** 1812-13. 4 vols. including Supp. 4to. A few ll. slightly dampstained, mainly marginal, a few other minor defects. Cont. russ. gt., lacks some labels. (SBA. Jul.14; 116)   *Beavan.* £110
- - **Anr. Copy.** 3 vols. & supp. Lacks 2? engraved plts. Cont. cf. gt. (SBA. Jul.22; 90)
Zentral Bibliothek. £80
- - **Anr. Edn.** N.d.-1813. 4 vols. (including supp.). Title to vol. 2, pt. 2, rubbed with loss of 1 letter, some browning & spotting. Cont. hf. cf. (CSK. Jan.16; 133)   £160

DANIELL, Samuel
- **African Scenery & Animals.** [L.], [1804-05]. 1st. & 2nd. Series. 10 vols. Ob. fo. Lacks engraved title to 2nd. Series & plts. 28, 29 & 30, also dupl. plts. 22, 23 & 24. Orig. wraps. in 10 sections each with 3 plts., stitched as iss. (CE. Jul.9; 236)   £9,500
- - **Anr. Edn.** Ed.:– Frank R. Bradlow. Cape Town, 1976. Facs. Reprint of 1804-05 Edn. (550) sigd. by Ed. Fo. Hf. leath. (VA. Oct.31; 306)   R. 320
- - **Anr. Copy.** Fo. Hf. leath. & marb. bds. (VA. Aug.29; 263)   R. 210

DANIELL, Thomas & William
- **Oriental Scenery.** 1795-1801. 4 (of 6) pts. in 2 vols., lacks 5 & 6. Elephant fo. 84 hand-cold. litho. plts. only, lacks text booklets & hf.-titles, final plts. to pts. 2 & 4 foxed, bnd. without the 2nd. section of plts. for pt. 3. Cont. hf. mor., gt. panel. spines, tears to covers. From Chetham's

Liby., Manchester. (C. Nov.26; 97) *Hobhouse & Eyre.* £10,500
– **A Picturesque Voyage to India.** 1810. Fo. Occasional light foxing. Cont. hf. russ., rebkd. (C. Nov.5; 41) *Quaritch.* £1,100

DANIELL, William
– **Illustrations of the Island of Staffa.** 1818. Ob. 4to. Plts. guarded, slightly spotted, offsetting onto text. Cont. maroon hf. mor., worn. (S. Nov.4; 543) *Quaritch.* £350
– – **Anr. Copy.** Aquatint plts. cold. & on thick paper with wash borders, some margins slightly soiled. Orig. roan-bkd. bds., worn. From the collection of Eric Sexton. (C. Apr.16; 240) *Aberdeen.* £180
– **Six Views of the Metropolis of the British Empire.** 1805. Lge. ob. fo. Plts. cold. & hand-finished, title & plts. slightly soiled, minor marginal foxing, some plts. with frayed corners, not affecting engr. 19th. C. cl. From Chetham's Liby., Manchester. (C. Nov.26; 98) *Quaritch.* £3,600
– **Views of Scotland.** L., n.d. 4to. 37 (of 42) hand-cold. plts., some loose. n.d. (SSA. Jan.22; 34) R. 400
See–**BLAGDON, Francis William, Daniell, William & others.**

DANIELL, William & Ayton, Richard
– **A Voyage Round Great Britain.** 1814-25. 8 vols. 4to. 1 engraved plt. & 308 hand-cold. plts., orig. pencil drawing pasted in. Cont. diced panel. cf., rebkd., preserving orig. gt. spines. (C. Mar.18; 34) *Traylen.* £7,500
– – **Anr. Copy.** 8 vols. in 4. Some foxing on end papers & text. Hf. cf., gt. & marb. bds. (CE. Nov.20; 68) £7,000
– – **Anr. Edn.** 1814-25. (25) on card. 8 vols. in 4. 4to. Aquatint plts. hand-cold., the 30 plts. in vol. II on paper, slight spotting to dedication lf. 19th. C. hf. mor. Bkplt. of the Earl of Cromer, lately in the collection of Eric Sexton. (C. Apr.16; 239) *Burgess.* £7,500

DANIELL, William & Samuel
– **Sketches Representing the Native Tribes . . . of Southern Africa.** L., [1820]. Bdg. not stated. (P. Jul.2; 216) *Cummings.* £400

DANISH NATIONAL MUSEUM
– **Sylloge Nummorum Graecorum.** Copen., 1942-77. 8 vols & pts 39-42 of Collection, with another, together 13 vols. Fo. Liby. stps. Later cl. & orig. wraps. (SH. Apr.9; 124) *Seaby.* £1,600

D'ANNUNZIO, Gabriele
See–**ANNUNZIO, Gabriele de**

DANSE des Morts
– **Chorea ab Erimio Macabro Versibus Alemanicis Edita.** Paris, G. de Marnef [Pilinsky], 1490 [1883]. Ltd. Edn.; on old paper; reprint. 4to. Stained, reprd., lacks third of title-p. 19th C. vell., cover. (HD. Mar.18; 53) Frs. 1,100

DANTE Alighieri
– **L'Amorosa Convivio.** Venice, 1531. Mor. [BM (Italian) STC p. 208] (CNY. Oct.1; 86) $120
– **La Comedia.** Ed.:– Alessandro Vellutello. Venice, 1544. Sm. 4to. Lacks last lf. (?blank), some worming. 19th. C. mor. (S. Nov.25; 356) *Boyl.* £450
– – **Anr. Copy.** 3 lines of Canto II omitted on lf. V7 recto stpd. in place, sig. AN misbnd., lacks final blank, early ecclesiastical liby. stp. on title & Register lf. Mod. crushed lev. (SG. May 14; 53) $850
– **La Commedia [Commentary by Jacopo della Lana, corrected by Christofal Berardi].** Venice, Vindelinus de Spira, 1477. Fo. 374 ll. (of 376), lacks first & last blanks, lge. histor. initial with decor. borders in pen & yellow wash on blue ground, enclosing vigs., other initials in red & blue, stained & wormed. 17th. C. red mor., gt. panel. [BMC V, 248] (S. Nov.25; 391) *Boyl.* £2,400
– **Convivio.** Flor., 1490. 1st. Edn. Later vell. [BMC VI, 673] (SG. Oct.9; 75) $3,400
Dante col Sito, et Forma dell'Inferno tratto dalla istessa Descrittione del Poeta. Venice, Aug. 1515. Stain on title & last p., upr. margins torn with slight text loss. 18th. C. vell. (SI. Dec. 3; 182) Lire 300,000
– **Dante con l'Espositione di Christoforo Landino et di Alessandro Velutello.** Venice, 1564. Fo. Ff. K4 & 5 from a smaller Edn. 19th. C. hf. cf. (SI. Dec. 3; 183) Lire 420,000
– – **Anr. Copy.** 28 unnumbered pp. & 4 unnumbered pp. between pp. 163 & 164, 90 xylographs, 4 larger from 1544 Marcolini Edn., map 62 lacks corners, frontis. port. restored, last map from 1578 Edn. Cf., tooled spine decor. (CR. Mar.19; 248) Lire 400,000
– – **Anr. Edn.** Venice, 1596. Fo. Lr. blank margin of some ll. wormed. Early 19th. C. hf. cf. (CSK. Apr.24; 62) £160
– **La Divina Commedia [Italian & Engl.].** Ill.:– after Sandro Botticelli. Nones. Pr., 1928. (1,475) numbered. Fo. Orig. parch. (CSK. Apr.3; 65) £150
– – **Anr. Copy.** Orig. vell. gt., partly unopened. (SH. Feb.20; 388) *C.P. Smith.* £130
– – **Anr. Copy.** (TA. Nov.20; 114) £110
– – **Anr. Copy.** Vell., warped. (SG. May 14; 156) $250
– – **Anr. Copy.** (SG. Apr.9; 536) $200
– – **Anr. Copy.** Fo. Partly unc., in orig. tinted buckram. (KH. Nov.18; 189) Aus. $240
– **[Divina Commedia] . . . con l'espositioni di Christoforo Landino, et d'Alessandro Vellutello. [Italian].** Ed.:– Francesco Sansovino. Venice, 1578. Fo. Dampstained & with some worming at end. 18th. C. vell., spine gt.-lettered. (CNY. Oct.1; 87) $650
– – **Anr. Edn.** Ed.:– Fr. Sansovino. Venice, 1596. Fo. Slightly browned, soiled & stained, early ll. wormed. 17th. C. vell., spine slightly wormed, lr. cover defect. (HK. Nov.18-21; 154) DM 800
– **Divina Commedia. Codex Altonensis. [German].** Ed.:– H. Haupt. Berlin, 1965. (600) numbered. 4to. Facs. & commentary vol. with 86 ills. Orig. linen. (D. Dec.11-13; 870) DM 1,000
– **La Divine Comédie [L'Enfer, Le Purgatoire, Le Paradis].** Trans.:– J. Briseux. Ill.:– Salvador Dali. Ca. 1959-65. (50) on vell. pur chiffon de Rives. 12 vols. 4to. Ll., in box. (HD. Apr.24; 136) Frs. 7,500
– – **Anr. Edn.** Ill.:– Dali. Paris, n.d. 6 vols. 4to. Loose in orig. wraps., folders & s.-c.'s. (SM. Oct.8; 2291) Frs. 2,600
– **The Divine Comedy.** Trans.:– Melville Best Anderson. Ltd. Edns. Cl., 1932. (1,500) sigd. by printer. Lge. 4to. Orig. cl., unc. (SH. Feb.20; 228) *Maggs.* £60
– **La Divina Commedia [Italian].** Ed.:– [Cristoforo Landino & Piero da Figino]. Venice, Bernardinus Benalius & Matteo Capcasa, Mar.3, 1491. 1st. Venice Ill. Edn. Fo. Some staining thro.-out, 4th. lf. & g1 rehinged, some repairs to a few other inner blank margins, some early marginal ink notes. Old vell., qtr. mor. gt. s.-c. 18th. C. bkplt. of Valperga di Masino e di Caluso, bkplt. of John A. Saks. [BMC V, 373, Goff D32, H. 5949] (CNY. Oct.1; 118) $8,500
– – **Anr. Copy.** Stain on last p., wormhole with slight text loss. 19th. C. antique style pig. [BMC V, 373; Goff D32] (SI. Dec.3; 181) Lire 3,400,000
– – **Anr. Edn.** Ill.:– M. Heylbroek after M.A. Cornale (frontis. port.). Padua, 1726-27. 3 vols. Cont. vell. bds. From the collection of John A. Saks. (C. Jun.10; 49) *Greindl.* £90
– – **Anr. Edn.** Ill.:– Giampiccolo, Magnini, Rizzi, & others. Venice, 1757-58. 4 vols. 4to. Some foxing in vol. IV. Cont. vell. From the collection of John A. Saks, (C. Jun.10; 50) *Greindl.* £480
– – **Anr. Edn.** Parma, 1795. 1st. Edn. ptd. by Bodoni, L.P. 3 vols. Fo. Cont. cf., panel on covers of entwined wide drawer-handle tool roll, floral spray cornerpieces, spines gt. in compartments, hinges worn. (C. Feb.25; 8) *Mediolanum.* £800
– – **Anr. Edn.** Milan, 1868-69. 3 vols. Fo. Hf. red mor. (SI. Dec.3; 185) Lire 200,000
– – **Anr. Edn.** Milan, 1878. 2¾ × 1⅜ inches. Pink mor. gt., gt. dentelles, marb. paper end-ll. (SG. Sep.4; 328) $450
– – **Anr. Edn.** Ill.:– Franz von Bayros. Zurich, 1921. (250) numbered, & sigd. by artist. 4to. Some ll. stained, a few badly, end ll. reinserted with sellotape. Orig. parch.-bkd. bds., slightly soiled. (SH. Nov.20; 221) *Kaufmann.* £65
– – **Anr. Edn.** Ill.:– F. v. Bayros. Vienna, [1921]. (250) numbered, & sigd by artist. 4to. Orig. hf. vell. (R. Mar.31-Apr.4; 403) DM 850
– – **Anr. Edn.** [Bremen], 1921. (300) numbered. Fo. Orig. vell, bosses, unc. (SI. Dec.3; 189) Lire 550,000
– – **Anr. Edn.** Ed.:– Dino Provenzal. Milan, 1958. Fo. Mor., gt. spine, partly unc. (SI. Dec.3; 190) Lire 220,000
– **L'Enfer.** Trans.:– Pier-Angelo Fiorentino. Ill.:– Gustave Doré. Paris, 1867. Fo. Red three-qtr. mor., bkplt. (SG. Dec.18; 166) $150
– – **Anr. Edn.** Ill.:– Edouard Georg. 1947. (250) Priv. ptd., on tinted vell. No bdg. stated. Note from ill. with orig. ill. (HD. Oct.10; 185) Frs. 1,800
– **Die Hölle.** Ill.:– W. Jaeckel. Berlin, 1923. (100) C Edn. on Bütten. Fo. Hand-bnd. orig. hf. leath. End sig. of artist. (H. May 21/22; 1645) DM 520
– **The Inferno.** Trans.:– Henry Francis Cary. Ill.:– William Blake. N.Y., 1931. (1,200) numbered. Fo. Tooled leath., partly unc. (SG. Sep.4; 69) $200
– **Inferno[-Purgatorio; Paradiso.–The Florence of Dante Alighieri].** Trans.:– Melville Best Anderson. San Franc., 1929. (250) numbered. 4 vols. Fo. Orig. vell. gt., partly unc., mor.-tipped cl. s.-c.'s. The Florence sigd. on upr. paste-down by Anderson & Nash & dtd. 3 & 8 Jun. 1932 respectively. Included is a propsectus for the work, San Franc. 1929, fo., orig. marb. bds., John A. Saks' copy. (CNY. Oct.1; 195) $750
– **Le Purgatoire et le Paradis.** Trans.:– Pier-Angelo Fiorentino. Ill.:– Gustave Doré. Paris, 1868. Fo. Red three-qtr. mor., bkplt. (SG, Dec.18; 167) $110
– **Le Terze Rime.** Venice, 1502. 1st. Aldine Edn. Slight worming reprd. in inner margins at end catching a few letters. Mor., vell. doubls., watered silk end-ll., by De Cuzin, chemise & s.-c., bkplt. of Maurice Baring. (S. Dec.8; 108) *Duran.* £300
– – **Anr. Copy.** 2nd. iss., with the woodcut device on verso of last lf., title reprd. & slightly soiled. Mor., elab. gt., by Bedford. (S. Feb.10; 434) *Thomas.* £260
– – **Anr. Edn.** Venice, Aug., 1502. 1st. Aldine Edn., 1st. Iss. Without the anchor device on final p., lf. 11 blank, spaces for initials with guide letters, 1st. ll. slightly spotted, blank upr. margins of a1 & a2 patched. Old velvet, silk linings. Bkplts. of John Ruskin & F. Haywood Joyce, later the copy of John A. Saks. (CNY. Oct.1; 125) $1,900
– **La Vita Nouva.** Ash. Pr., 1895. (45) numbered, on japan vell. 4to. Lev. mor. gt., decor. cover, silk linings by Zaehnsdorf, orig. ptd. wraps. preserved. (CNY. Oct. 1; 146) $1,500
– – **Anr. Edn.** Paris, 1933. (130). Fo. Mor. sigd. by Gruel, orig. wraps. bnd. in, partly unc., box. (SI. Dec. 3; 191) Lire 480,000

DANTE ALIGHIERI–ANDERSON, Melville B.
– **Divine Comedy.–The Florence of Dante.** Trans.:– Melville B. Anderson. San Franc., John Nash 1929. (250) numbered sets on specially wtrmkd. Van Gelder H.M.P. Together 4 vols. Fo. Orig. vell. (SG. Oct. 9; 76) $700

DANTY D'ISNARD
– **Catalogue des Livres.** Paris, 1744. 12mo. 2-lf. bookseller's advt. at end, priced in MS. Cont. cf., spine gt. (SM. Oct.7; 1354) Frs. 1,000

D'ANVILLE, Jean Baptist Bourguignon
– **[Atlas Générale. Cartes Géographiques].** Paris, 1743-60. Lge. fo. Occasional light soiling, 1 map creased at fold, all maps with sm. liby. stps. 19th. C. hf. mor. As an atlas, w.a.f., from Chetham's Liby., Manchester. (C. Nov.26; 17) *Aiden.* £240
– [–] **Anr. Edn.** [Paris], 1743-71. Lge. fo. 23 mostly outl. cold. double-p. engraved maps, soiled in parts, margin tears bkd., 1 outl. cold. map 'Le Royaume de France', Paris, 1793, fo. bnd. in. Hf. vell., defect. (H. May 21/22; 298) DM 460
– – **Anr. Edn.** Paris, 1743-80. 2 pts. in 1 vol. Lge. fo. Preliminary contents lf. & 'Avis' pasted in upr. cover, no title or text, some soiling & creasing at folds, all maps with sm. liby. stps. Cont. hf. cf., vell. corners, covers detchd. As an atlas, w.a.f. From Chetham's Liby., Manchester. (C. Nov.26; 16) *Aiden.* £550
– [–] **Anr. Edn.** Paris, ca. 1760. Fo. Publisher's list of maps & a 3-p. ptd. notice pasted to inside of upr. cover, lacks 3 maps, 1st. 2 slightly stained. Cont. marb. bds., rebkd. & with new corners in vell. (S. Nov.4; 480) *Slade.* £420
– **A Complete Body of Ancient Geography.** 1801. Fo. 13 hand-cold. engraved double-p. maps in wash borders, some titles in cartouches, 3 maps shaved, piece torn from prelim. blank. Cont. gt.-panel. cf., covers detchd., corners worn, upr. cover with abrasions, piece lacking from head & foot of spine. (C. Jul.15; 3) *Cash.* £60
– – **Anr. Edn.** 1812 [maps dtd. 1760-94]. Fo. Cont. hf. cf., worn, upr. cover detchd. (C. Nov.5; 3) *Tom.* £75

DAPPER, Olfert

- **Asia oder: Ausführliche Beschreibung des Reichs des Grossen Mogols und eines grossen Theils von Indien . . . nebst einer Vollkommenen Vorstellung des Königreichs Persien.** Nuremb., 1681. 1st. German Edn. 2 pts. in 1 vol. Fo. Engraved title-p. slightly torn & mntd. Cont. hf. cf., corners & spine worn. W.a.f. (S. Jun.22; 172) *Crete.* £300
- **– Anr. Copy.** (S. Nov.4; 605) *Slade.* £280
- **Description de l'Afrique.** Amst., 1686. 1st. Edn. in Fr. Fo. 41 (of 42) engraved double-p. plts., margins discold. thro.-out. 19th. C. hf. mor. From Chetham's Liby., Manchester. (C. Nov.26; 99) *Schrire.* £280
- **– Anr. Copy.** Ptd. title stpd., some sm. soilings & brownings. Cont. cf., defect. & soiled. (H. May 21/22; 336) DM 4,000
- **– Anr. Copy.** Lacks 1 plt. Hf. cf., 5 spine raised bands. (LM. Jun.13; 4) B.Frs. 30,000
- **Description Exacte des Isles de l'Archipel . . .** Amst., 1703. Fo. Occasional light foxing & browning. 19th. C. hf. mor. From Chetham's Liby., Manchester. (C. Nov.26; 100) *Nickalas.* £700
- **Gedenkweurgige Berrichtung der Niederlaendischen Ost-Indischen Gesellschaft in . . . Taising oder Sina.** Amst., 1676. 3 pts. in 1 vol. Fo. Frontis. loose & rehinged, 2 plts. reprd. affecting image, other defects. Cont. vell. bds., worn, upr. cover detchd. W.a.f. (CNY. Oct.1; 40) $650
- **Historische Beschryving der Stadt Amsterdam.** Amst., 1663. Fo. Some light staining in places, folding view loose & badly reprd., some other reprd. Cont. blind-stpd. vell., lacks ties. (VG. Oct.13; 53) Fls. 2,600
- **– Anr. Copy.** 71 (of 72) plans, views & plts., plts. pasted in in later period, partly resulting in glue stains in the folds, slight damage in a few folds, stains in places, some marginal wormholes, loosening. Mod. hf. leath. W.a.f. (VG. Dec.17; 1272) Fls. 1,500
- **Naukeurige Beschrijvinge der Afrikaensche Gewesten van Egypten . . .–Naukeurige Beschrijvinge der Afrikaensche Eylanden.** Amst., 1668. L.P. 2 works in 1 vol. Fo. Some mis-pagination, slight staining at end of vol. Old cf. (LM. Jun.13; 3) B.Frs. 65,000
- **Naukeurige Beschryving van Asie.** Amst., 1680. 13 double-p. maps & plts. (of 16), sm. wormholes in some ll. Old vell., defect. (BS. Jun.11; 150) £150
- **– Anr. Copy.** 2 pts. in 1 vol. Fo. 13 (1 extra) engraved plts. Cont. blind-stpd. vell., a little soiled. (VG. Oct.13; 54) Fls. 2,000
- **Naukeurige Beschryving van Gantsch Syrie, en Palestyn of Heilige Lant.** Amst., 1677. 1st. Edn. 2 pts. in 1 vol. Fo. Approx. 60 pp. Pt. 2 with worming, 3 plts with hole. Cont. leath., spine defect. (R. Oct.14-18; 1762) DM 2,300
- **Naukeurige Beschryving van Morea . . . Golf van Venetein.** Amst., 1688. Fo. Occasional marginal soiling. Cl.-bkd. bds., worn. (CSK. Apr.10; 39) £420
- **– Anr. Copy.** 15 (of 17) maps & plts. (lacks maps of Morea & Adriatic). Cont. blind-stpd. vell. (VG. Dec.17; 1273) Fls. 950
- **Umbstandliche und Eigentliche Beschreibung von Africa.** Amst., 1670-71. 1st. Edn. in German. 2 pts. in 1 vol. Fo. Cont. German blind-stpd. pig over wooden bds., arms of Franciscus Honorius Count Trauttmansdorff in centre of covers, 2 brass clasps, bkplt. of Frantz Ehrenreich Graf zu Trauttmansdorff. W.a.f. (S. Nov.3; 9) *Arader.* £1,500
- **– Anr. Copy.** Pagination from 376-379, lacks last lf. & 3 maps, 2 views heavily browned, 1 bkd. & with 2 holes, 1 map torn, 1st. ll. lightly soiled, some other staining & browning. Mod. vell. (H. May 21/22; 337) DM 3,000
- **Umbständliche und Eigentliche Beschreibung von Asia.** Trans.:– Johann Christoff Beern. Nuremb., 1681. Fo. Tear in fold of 1 plt., a few marginal tears, text browned, rust-hole in 3Q2. Cont. vell. bds. (S. Dec.8; 238) *Traylen.* £500

D'APRES de Mannevillette, Jean Baptiste N.D.

- **Le Neptune Oriental.** Ill.:– Tilliard after Boucher (frontis.). Paris, 1775. Lge. fo. Frontis. soiled at edge. 19th. C. hf. mor. As an atlas, w.a.f., from Chetham's Liby., Manchester. (C. Nov.26; 18) *Fisher.* £380

DARAN, Jacques

- **Observations Chirurgicales sur les Maladies de l'Urethre . . .** Ill.:– J. Gautier (folding engraved plt.). Paris, 1748. New Edn. 12mo. Short tear in fold of cold. ptd. engraved plt., text dampstained in lr. margins causing slight adhesion. Cont. cf., worn. (SH. Jul.27; 327) *Henderson.* £65

D'ARBLAY nee Burney, Frances 'Fanny Burney'

- **[–] Brief Reflections relative to the Emigrant French Clergy.** L., 1793. 1st. Edn. Blank portions of 2 final ll. with sm. stain, title slightly frayed at extreme blank margins. Unbnd., stitched as iss., qtr. mor. gt. s.-c. Cont. pres. inscr. of the Grenville family on title; from the Prescott Collection. (CNY. Feb.6; 37) $450
- **Camilla, or a Picture of Youth.** 1796. 1st. Edn. 5 vols. 12mo. Cont. cf. (C. Feb.4; 4) *Bennet.* £50
- **[–] Cecilia.** 1782. 1st. Edn. 5 vols. 12mo. Cont. cf., gt. spines. (C. Nov.20; 232) *Thorpe.* £75
- **[–] Cecilia.–Camilla.** L., 1782; 1796. 1st. Edns. 5 vols.; 5 vols.; together 10 vols. 12mo. Q10 & 11 in vol. V of 2nd. work stained. Old hf. russ. gt., badly worn (1st. work); & cont. qtr. cf. gt., bd. edges slightly worn; in qtr. mor. gt. s.-c.'s. From the Prescott Collection. (CNY. Feb.6; 38) $380
- **The Diary & Letters of Madame D'Arblay.** L., 1842-46. 7 vols. Foxed, extra-ill. Tree cf., worn. (SPB. May 29; 59) $125
- **Evelina.** 1778. 1st. Edn. 3 vols. 12mo. Some ll. browned. Cont. cf., spine gt., 1 cover detchd., some wear. (S. Feb.10; 423) *Traylen.* £1,100
- **– Anr. Edn.** Ed.:– Austin Dobson. Ill.:– Hugh Thomson. L., 1903. Mauve mor. gt., cold. mor. onlays on covers & doubls., mor. doubls. & free endpages, silk flyll. gt., mor. velvet-lined box, by Sangorski & Sutcliffe, sigd. with ticket 1942. (CNY. May 22; 352) $1,000
- **[–] The Wanderer or Female Difficulties.** 1814. 5 vols. Cf. gt. (P. Dec.11; 299) *Quaritch.* £80

DARBY, William

- **A Tour from the City of New York, to Detroit, in the Michegan Territory . . .** N.Y., 1819. 1st. Edn. 3 maps, frontis. map reprd. at folds, text foxed & stained. Mod. buckram, gt. spine. From liby. of William E. Wilson. (SPB. Apr. 29; 74) $150

DAREMBERG, Charles Victor, Saglio & Pottier

- **Dictionnaire des Antiquités Grecques et Romaines.** Ill.:– P. Sellier. Paris, 1877. 9 vols. 4to. Hf. chagrin, corners, spines with raised bands, wraps. & spines preserved. (HD. Feb.27; 112) Frs. 5,000

D'ARGENVILLE, Antoine Joseph

See–DEZALLIER D'ARGENVILLE, Antoine Joseph

DARIS, Joseph

- **Histoire du Diocèse et de la Principauté de Liège pendant le XVII Siècle.** Liège, 1884, 1877. Together 3 vols. Hf. chagrin. (LM. Jun.13; 123) B.Frs. 10,000
- **Notices sur les Eglises du Diocèse de Liège.** Liège, 1867-99. Vols. 1-17 bnd. in 10 vols. Hf. chagrin, last vol. slightly stained. (LM. Jun.13; 121) B.Frs. 13,000

DARLES DE LINIERE

- **Pompes sans Cuirs . . ., qui les a primitivement presentées pour la Service de la Marine.** Paris, 1768. 4to. Dupl. of plt. 6, contents slightly soiled. Cont wraps. (TA. Oct.16; 28) £65

DARLEY, J.

- **The Glory of the Chelsey Colledge Revived.** 1662. 1st. Edn. 4to. Last advt. lf., browned. 18th. C. cf.-bkd. bds. [Wing D259] (SH. Jun.18; 125) *Thorp.* £70

DARLY, Matthias

- **The Ornamental Architect.** [1770]. 1st. Edn. Fo. Mod. old-style panel. cf., gt., s.-c. (S. Mar.17; 408) *Traylen.* £380

DARNALL, Elias

- **A Journal Containing An Accurate & Interesting Account of the Hardships, Sufferings . . . of Those Heroic Kentucky Volunteers & Regulars . . .** Phila., 1834. 4th. Edn. 16mo. Foxed & stained, paper loss at top of lf. A1. Orig. ptd. bds., advts. on lr. cover, worn. From liby. of William E. Wilson. (SPB. Apr.29; 75) $100

DART, John

- **The History & Antiquities of the Cathedral Church of Canterbury.** 1726. L.P. Fo. Cont. mott. cf. gt., red mor. gt. spine. From the collection of Eric Sexton. (C. Apr.16; 242) *Foster.* £70

DARTON, F.J. Harvey

See–SAWYER, C.W. & Darton, F.J. Harvey

DARU, Pierre

- **Histoire de la République de Venise.** 1853. 4th. Edn. 9 vols. Cont. red hf. chagrin, decor. spines. unc. (HD. Feb.18; 111) Frs. 1,000

D'ARUSMONT, Frances Wright

- **[–] Views of society & manners in America.** 1821. 1st. Edn. Cont. hf. cf., gt. spine. William Beckford's copy with 1½ pp. of pencilled notes in his hand at the beginning. (S. Nov.4; 651) *Crete.* £95

DARWIN, Bernard

- **The Golf Courses of the British Isles.** 1910. No bdg. stated. (CSK. Jul.20; 104) £80
- **A Golfer's Gallery by Old Masters.** N.d. No bdg. stated. (CSK. Jul.20; 117) £100

DARWIN, Charles

- **The Descent of Man.** 1871. 1st. Edn., 1st. Iss. 2 vols. 16 pp. publisher's advts. dtd. Jan. 1871 in each vol. Orig. cl., top of spine of vol. 1 slightly torn. (CSK. Oct.24; 118) £170
- **– Anr. Copy.** End.-ll. foxed, occasional soiling, 16 pp. of advts. dtd. Jan. 1871 in each vol. Orig. cl., spine gt., worn, spine extremities & corners chipped. Inscr. by Frederick Engels to Karl Marx's wife Jenny on verso of each hf.-title: 'To Jenny Marx as an antidote against the ennui of the sick-room' (sigd.) 'The General', 1st. inscr. dtd. 5 March 1871, other undated. (CNY. Oct.1; 6) $900
- **– Anr. Copy.** Slight soiling, 16 pp. of publisher's advts. Orig. cl., cl. s.-c. (SPB. May 29;101) $250
- **– Anr. Copy.** L. 1871. 2 vols. With often lacking lf 'Postcript' in vol. 2, lightly soiled in places. Orig. linen. (R. Mar.31-Apr.4; 1101) DM 2,000
- **The Expression of the Emotions in Man & Animals.** 1872. Ownership inscription on title. Orig. cl. (SH. Oct.9; 215) *Prada.* £70
- **– Anr. Copy.** 2 ll. of advts. dtd. Nov. 1872. From liby. of Dr. E. Ashworth Underwood. (S. Feb.23; 190) *Meyer.* £50
- **Journal of Researches into the Geology & Natural History of the Various Countries visited by H.M.S. Beagle.** 1840. With cancel title, 1 folding engraved map torn, both slightly spotted or offset, advts. Orig. cl., spine worn at head & tail. From liby. of Dr. E. Ashworth Underwood. (S. Feb. 23; 191) *Woodall.* £200
- **– Anr. Edn.** 1845. 2nd. Edn. Cont. tree cf., worn, upr. cover held on with sellotape. Pres. copy inscr. to J.D. Hooker. (S. Dec.3; 942) *McBride.* £500
- **– Anr. Edn.** Ill.:– Robert Gibbings. N.Y., Ltd. Edns. Cl., 1956. (1,500) sigd. by artist. 4to. Orig. cl., s.-c. (SH. Feb.20; 233) *Maggs.* £120
- **– Anr. Edn.** [Surrey & c.], 1979. Facs. Autograph Edn., (500) numbered. Buckram, hf. cf. gt., cl. s.-c. (KH. Mar.24; 119) Aus. $350
- **On the Origin of Species.** 1859. 1st. Edn. Folding diagram torn, advts., slight spotting, sig. of James French on title-p. Orig. cl., slightly worn. (S. Dec.3; 943) *Hitchin.* £1,100
- **– Anr. Copy.** Publisher's advts., hf.-title & front free end-paper loose, some spotting, bkplt. removed. Upr. inner hinge brkn., cl. s.-c. Stockhausen copy. (SPB. Nov.25; 99) $3,700
- **– Anr. Copy.** 32 pp. publisher's advts. dtd. Jun. 1859. Orig. cl., recased, new endpapers, slight soiling, imprint 3mms. high on spine, cl. s.-c. (SPB. May 6; 180) $3,000
- **– Anr. Edn.** 1860. 2nd. Edn., 2nd. Iss. Advts., dtd. Jan. 1860. Orig. cl. gt. (variant a of bdg.), unc., bkplt. of A.C. Fitz-Gibbon. (S. Dec.1; 129) *Quaritch.* £80
- **– Anr. Edn.** 1860. 5th. thousand. Orig. cl. gt. (SH. Jun.25; 149) *Davies.* £100
- **– Anr. Edn.** Ltd. Edns. Cl., 1963. Ltd. Edn. Orig. bdg., box, slightly worn. (SPB. Jul.28; 246) $125
- **The Variation of Animals & Plants under Domestication.** 1868. 1st. Edn., 1st. Iss.(?). 2 vols. Errata at end of Contents, 2 pp. of advts. in 2nd vol. Orig. cl., slight loosening of 1 gathering in Vol. I. (TW. Sep.19; 155) £60
- **– Anr. Copy.** Lacks inserted advts. Late 19th. C. cf., spine gt. (S. Dec.3; 944) *Korn.* £55
- **[The Works].** 1889-1901. 17 vols. Hf. mor. spines, gt., by Sotheran, slightly faded. (SKC. Dec.4; 1562) £180

See–FITZROY, Capt. Robert & others

DARWIN, Erasmus
- **The Botanic Garden.** Ill.:– Blake after Fuseli, & others. 1791. 1st. Edn. of vol. I, 3rd. Edn. of vol. II. 2 pts. in 1 vol. 4to. Slip with directions to binder, hf.-title in vol. II only. Cont. qtr. cf., worn, unc. (S. Dec.1; 134) *Dr. Pike.* £55
[–] – **Anr. Copy.** (P. Apr.9; 98) *Walford.* £50
– – **Anr. Edn.** Ill.:– Blake after Fuseli, & others. L., 1791; 1789. 1st. Edn. 2 vols. 4to. Lacks hf.-titles, imprint on 1st. plt. vol. II cut into, some offset on title-pp. Cf., worn, covers loose. (S. Dec.1; 133) *Gurney.* £85
– – **Anr. Edn.** 1795-94. Pt. I 3rd., pt. II 4th. Edn. 2 pts. in 1 vol. 4to. Cont. tree cf., spine gt. (S. Dec.2; 805) *Marlborough.* £90
– – **Anr. Edn.** Ill.:– Tanner. N.Y., 1798. 1st. Amer. Edn. Liby. stps. on versos of plts. Later hf. linen. (SG. Jan.29; 116) $110
- **The Temple of Nature or the Origin of Society, a Poem with Philosophical Notes.** Ill.:– Fuseli. 1803. 1st. Edn. 4to. No hf.-title (? not called for), paper discold. in places. Cf., rebkd. (S. Jun.15; 226) *Phillips.* £65
- **Zoonomia.** 1792-94. 2 vols. 4to. Spotted. Cont. cf. (SH. May 21; 205) *Winer.* £60
– – **Anr. Edn.** 1794-96. 1st. Edn. 2 vols. 4to. Sm. hole in 1st. 8 ll. of vol. II, slight browning. Cont. cf., gt., some wear. From liby. of Dr. E. Ashworth Underwood. (S. Feb.23; 193) *Bickersteth.* £80

DASYPODIUS, or Hasenfuss, Conrad
- **Heron Mechanicus ... – Wahrhafftige Ausslegung ... Astronomischen Uhrwercks.** Strassburg, 1580. 2 works in 1 vol. 4to. Slightly browned & stained at beginning, vol. 1 title torn, slightly soiled. Cont. limp vell., cockled, lacks ties. (HK. Nov.18-21; 155) DM 1,700

DAUBENTON, L.J.M.
See–BUFFON, George Louis Leclerc de & Daubenton, L.J.M.

DAUBERVILLE, J. & H.
- **Bonnard ... Catalogue Raisonné de l'Oeuvre Peint.** Paris, 1966-74. 4to. Orig. cl., d.-w.'s. (S. Jul.27; 187) *Ursus Books.* £320

DAUDET, Alphonse
- **L'Arlésienne.** Ill.:– Lesueur after Guillonet. Paris, 1911. (50) on Jap. Imp. 4to. 2 states of etchings. Hf. mor., orig. wraps. bnd in. (SM. Oct.8; 2325) Frs. 2,400
- **Lettres de Mon Moulin.** Ill.:– Sylvain Sauvage. Paris, N.d. (2750); (2500) on Navarre vell., numbered. 4to. Orig. drawing. Mor. by Fourrieux, mill, goat & lamb in relief on spine & covers, silk doubls. decor. with sm. mills, wrap. preserved, s.-c. (SM. Feb.11; 207) Frs. 3,500
- **Oeuvres Complètes.** Paris, 1930-31. 20 vols. 4to. Hf. mor., orig. wraps. bnd. in. (SM. Oct.8; 2215) Frs. 1,800
- **Oeuvres Complètes Illustrées.** Ill.:– Marcel Roche. Paris, 1930-31. Definitive Edn., (1250); (800) on Lafuma, numbered. 20 vols. 4to. Hf. mor., some vols. slightly spotted, wraps. preserved. (SM. Feb.11; 25) Frs. 1,500
- **Petit Chose (Le) ...** 1868. 1st. Edn. 12mo. Cont. hf. roan, smooth spine. (HD. Feb.27; 113) Frs. 1,200
- **Sapho.** 1884. (175) on Hollande. Jansenist mor., mor. doubls., wrap., lacks spine, by Marius Michel. (HD. Oct.10; 42) Frs. 2,800
- **Tartarin sur les Alpes.** Ill.:– Aranda, de Beaumont, Rossi, & others. Paris, 1885. Edn. du Figaro. Lev. gt., orig. wraps. bnd. in, by Stikeman. Inscr. to Emile Zola, mor. bkplt. of Arthur M. Brown. (SG. Feb.12; 7) $170
- **Works.** Boston, 1898-1900. (1,000). 24 vols. Slight browning. Hf. red cf. gt. by Sangorski & Sutcliffe. (SPB. Nov.25; 446) $125
– – **Anr. Edn.** Boston, 1906. (1,000). 24 vols. Mor., mor. doubls. gt. with inlays, slightly worn. (SPB. Nov.25; 447) $425

DAUDET, Leon
- **Un Sauvetage.** Ill.:– Charles Fouqueray. Paris, 1907. (20) on Jap. Long royal 8vo. 2 states of ills. (black-&-white & cold.). Hf. mor. by Kieffer, mosaic spine, wrap. preserved. (SM. Feb.11; 55) Frs. 1,000

DAUMIER, Honoré
- **Les Cent et un Robert-Macaire.–Musée pour Rire.** Paris, 1839. 1st. Printing. 2 vols. in 1. 4to. Lacks titles & hf.-titles of both pts., lacks ladne, foxed. Mod. str.-grd. red hf. mor., decor. spine. (HD. Dec.5; 60) Frs. 2,400

- **Croquis d'Expressions.** Paris, n.d. Ob. 4to. Lacks plts. 21, 34, 39, 41, 45, 46 & 52, plt. 50 in double state (black-&-white & cold.). Violin hf. mor., unc. (HD. Dec.5; 63) Frs. 12,000
- **Les Gens de Justice.** Paris, [1845-47]. Sm. fo. Plts. 31-33 unnumbered, slightly browned & soiled in parts. Orig. wraps., spine defect. (H. Dec.9/10; 1435) DM 17,000
- **Monomanes.–La Journée du Celibataire.** Paris, ca. 1840. 2 works in 1 vol. Lge. 4to Str.-grd. red hf. mor., corners, decor. spine. (HD. Dec.5; 61) Frs. 6,500
- **Professeurs et Moutards.** Paris, [1845-46.] Lge. 4to. Str.-grd. red hf. mor., corners, decor. spine, unc. (HD. Dec.5; 62) Frs. 10,500

DAUXION LAVAYSSE, J. J.
- **Voyage aux Iles de Trinidad et dans divers Parties de Vénézuela.** Paris, 1813. 1st. Edn. 2 vols. Cont. cf.-bkd. bds., lacks 1 label. [Sabin 18673] (SPB. May 5; 178) $1,100

DAVANZATI, Bernardo
- **A Discourse upon Coins.** Trans.:– John Toland. 1696. 1st. Edn. 4to. Recent cf. [Wing D301] (C. Apr.1; 178) *Boyle.* £120

DAVENANT, Charles
- **Circe.** 1677. 1st. Edn. 4to. Hf. mor. by the Atelier Bindery. Bkplt. of John L. Clawson; from the Bridgewater Liby. [Wing D302] (C. Nov.19; 69) *Pickering & Chatto.* £130
[–] **An Essay upon the Probable Methods of making a People Gainers in the Ballance of Trade.** –**Discourse upon Grants & Resumptions.** 1700; 1704. 2nd. Edn.; 3rd. Edn. 2 works in 1 vol. Some browning, tear in title of the 1st. vol., reprd. 18th. C. vell. bds., soiled. [Wing D310] (1st. work) (S. Jan.26; 235) *Subunso.* £80

DAVENANT, William
- **The Witts.** 1636. 1st. Edn. 4to. Lacks initial blank or licence-lf?, last lf. mntd. with sm. portions of upr. blank margin lacking, catchwords or sigs. occasionally shaved or cropped. 19th. C. cf., Bridgewater arms blind-stpd. on covers. Bridgewater Liby. bkplt., bkplt. of John L. Clawson. [STC 6309] (C. Nov.19; 70) *Arnold.* £120
- **The [Works.** Ill.:– William Faithorne after Grenhill. 1673. 1st. Edn. Fo. 2 ll. advts. inserted at end, some browning. Cont. mott. cf., worn. [Wing D320] (S. Sep.29; 19) *Fletcher.* £140

D'AVENNES, Prisse
- **L'Art Arabe.** Beirut, n.d. Reprint of 1877 Edn. 1 vol. text, 3 vols, plts. Fo. Hf. mor. gt. (P. Feb.19; 2) *Abington.* £75

DAVENPORT, Cyril
- **English Embroidered Bookbindings.** Ed.:– Alfred Pollard, 1899. 4to. Lacks endpaper. Cl., unc., bkplts., worn. (SG. Oct.2; 100) $150
- **Samuel Mearne.** Chic., Caxton Cl., 1906. (252) on Amer. H.M.P. Fo. Cl-bkd. bds., unc., unopened. Fore-e. pntgs., orig. prospectus laid in. (SG. Oct.2; 238) $450
– – **Anr. Copy.** Fore-e. pntgs., 3-p. A.L.s. tipped in. (SG. Oct.2; 101) $325
- **Thomas Berthelet: Royal Printer & Bookbinder to Henry VIII.** Chic., Caxton Cl., 1901. (252). Fo. Cl-bkd. bds., unc., unopened. (SG. Oct.2; 30) $280
See–FLETCHER, William Younger–DAVEN-PORT, Cyril

DAVENPORT, R.
- **The Amateur's Perspective.** 1828-29. 2 vols (including supp.). 4to. Orig. bds., unc. & partly unopened. (S. Dec.9; 501) *Talerman.* £95

DAVENPORT, Robert
- **King Iohn & Matilda.** 1655. 1st. Edn. 4to. Mor. by Sangorski, partly unc. [Wing D370] (C. Nov.19; 71) *Quaritch.* £360
[–] **A Pleasant & Witty Comedy called A New Tricke to Cheat the Divell.** 1639. 1st. Edn., 1st. Iss. 4to. The ll. H2, H3, I2, & I3 misbnd., some sigs. & catchwords cropped, some browning. Mod. red lev. mor., gt. [STC 6315] (S. Feb.9; 45) *Quaritch.* £280

DAVEY, Henry
- **A Set of Etchings Illustrative of Beccles Church & other Suffolk Antiquities.** Norwich, 1818. Fo. Title soiled. Stitched. (CSK. Oct.17; 152) £60

DAVID, François Anne
- **Histoire d'Angleterre ...** Ill.:– David. Paris, 1786. In sanguine. 2 vols. 4to. Some margins

reinforced. Cont. red mor., guarland border, decor. spines. (HD. Feb.18; 18) Frs. 1,600

DAVID, J.B.F.C.
[–] **Anacreon Vengé.** Criticopolis: [Paris], 1755. 1st. Edn., Holland Paper. 12mo. 'Ex dono Authoris' written on title & initials ?J.D. Cont. red mor., gt., with arms of F.A.A. de Rohan, Cardinal de Soubise, lozenge & ermine from arms, gt., in alternate corners & spine panels, triple gt. fillet, inner gt. dentelles, Augsburg white & gt. starred endpapers. Pres. Copy to Cardinal de Soubise bkplt. of Laurence Currie. (SM. Oct.7; 1677) Frs. 3,500

DAVID, M.
- **Histoire de France.** Ill.:– M. David. Paris, 1787-1796. 5 vols. Cont. cf. (CR. Jun.11; 566) Lire 550,000

DAVID, P. J.
- **Veridicus Christianus.** Antw., 1601. 4to. 100 plts. (of 101), title defect. Old vell., spine defect. (BS. Jun.11; 102) £95

DAVID Ibn Yahya
- **Hilchot Treifot.** Constantinople, 1515-18. 1st. Edn. Sm. 4to. Slight worming, not affecting text, inner margins reprd. Mod. bds. (SPB. May 11; 80) $1,900

DAVIDSON, Major Hugh
- **History & Services of the 78th Highlanders.** Edinb. & L., 1901. 2 vols. 4to. Cont. hf. cf. gt., spines slightly torn. (SBA. May 27; 400) *Sutcliffe.* £80

DAVIDSON, Israel
- **Thesaurus of Medieval Hebrew Poetry.** Ed.:– A. Freimann (notes) & D. Sasson (review). N.Y., ca. 1929. 4 vols. Fo. Cl., slight tears. (SPB. May 11; 95) $150
– – **Anr. Edn.** Ed.:– J. Schirmann. N.Y., 1970. 4 vols. 4to. Cl. (S. Nov.17; 67) *Waters.* £70

DAVIDSON, William A.
[–] **Picturesque Dundas.** [Dundas], [1896]. Ob. sm. 8vo. Penned inscr. Orig. cl., slightly shaken. (CB. May 27; 294) Can. $120

DAVIES, Arthur B.
- **Essay on the Man & his Art.** Wash., [1924]. 1st. Edn., (50) numbered, on L.P., sigd. by Davies. Fo. Pastel landscape drawing by Davies, matted, inserted in rear folding sleeve, as iss. Gt.-ruled mor., panel. spine by MacDonald Binders. (PNY. Dec.3; 102) $850

DAVIES, Christopher
- **The Scenery of the Broads & Rivers of Norfolk & Suffolk.** Ill.:– T. & R. Annan (photo-engravings.). L., ca. 1890. (Special Printing?) with broad margins). Fo. Minor dampstaining in corners of margins. Loose as iss. in orig. ptd. portfo. (SG. Apr.23; 73) $700

DAVIES, Hugh W.
- **Catalogue of a Collection of Early French Books in the Library of C. Fairfax Murray.–Catalogue of a Collection of Early German Books in the Library of C. Fairfax Murray.** L., 1961; 1962. Both (250) (reprints of orig. edns.). 4 vols. 4to. Orig. bds. & cl. The John A. Saks copies. (CNY. Oct.1; 157) $420

DAVIES, Rhys
- **The Skull.** Ill.:– Sylvia Marshall. Tintern Pr., 1936. 1st. Edn., (15) specially bnd., sigd. Sm. 4to. Orig. pig., unc. Inscr. by Vincent Stuart. (SH. Feb.20; 264) *Nolan.* £65

DAVILA, Enrico Caterino
- **Historia delle Guerre Civili di Francia.** Ill.:– F. Zucchi, G. Cattini, & others. Venice, 1733. Fo. Cont. vell. bds., slightly worn. From the collection of John A. Saks. (C. Jun.10; 51) *Taylor.* £80

DAVILA Y PADILLA, Agustin
- **Historia de la Fundación y Discurso de la Provincia de Santiago de Mexico, de la Orden de Predicadores, por las Vidas de sus Varones Insignes, y Casos Notables de Nueva España.** Madrid, 1596. 1st. Edn. Fo. Lr. corners in careful pen-facs., woodcut following prelims. & 2 ll. at end almost certainly in facs., some discolouration. Mod. cf. (SPB. May 5; 179) $1,200

DAVILER, Augustin Charles
- **Ausführliche Anleitung, zu der gantzen Civil Baukunst.** Trans.:– L. Chr. Sturm. Amst., 1699. 4to. Browned or stained in parts. Cont. cf., worn, spine reprd. (H. Dec.9/10; 933) DM 720

D'AVILER, C.A.
See–AVILER, C.A. d'

DAVILLIER, Baron Jean Charles
– **Recherches sur l'Orfevrerie en Espagne.** Paris, 1879. (500) numbered. 4to. Cont. cf.-bkd. bds. (SH. Jul.23; 267) *Rosenberg.* £160
– **Spain.** Ill.:– Gustave Doré. 1876. 4to. Orig. cl. (CSK. Nov.14; 92) £65
– – **Anr. Copy.** 4to. Orig. cl. (CSK. Aug.1; 155) £60

DAVIS, David D.
– **Elements of Operative Midwifery comprising a Description of Certain New & Improved Powers for assisting Difficult & Dangerous Labour.** 1825. 4to. Cf., rebkd. (S. Jun.15; 228) *Quaritch.* £130
– **The Principles & Practice of Obstetric Medicine in a Series of Systematic Dissertations on Midwifery.** 1836. 2 vols. 4to. Hf. cf. worn. (S. Jun.15; 229) *Jenner Books.* £120

DAVIS, Edmund W.
– **Salmon-Fishing on the Grand Cascapedia.** [N.Y.], De Vinne Pr., 1904. 1st. Edn., (100) numbered. Vell.-bkd. bds., unc., boxed. (SG. Oct.16; 27) £800
– – **Anr. Copy.** Vell.-bkd. bds., unc. Bkplt. of Van Santvoord Merle-Smith. (SG. Dec.11; 29) £700

DAVIS, John
– **Travels ... in the United States of America.** Bristol, 1803. 1st. Edn. Mod. hf. mor. [Sabin 18851] (C. Nov.6; 206) *Moneypenny.* £65
– – **Anr. Copy.** Slight foxing, sm. stain on title. Cont. spr. cf., rebkd. From liby. of William E. Wilson; bkplt. of Carl R. Bogardus. [Sabin 18851] (SPB. Apr.29; 76) $125

DAVIS, Richard
– **A New Map of the County of Oxford.** 1797. Fo. Hf. cf. Sigd. (P. Jun.11; 203) *Kentish.* £260

DAVIS, Richard Harding
– **Novels & Stories.** N.Y., 1916. Crossroads Edn., (256) with MS. lf. 12 vols. Mor. elab. gt., watered silk endpapers. (SPB. May 6; 297) $550
See–IN MANY WARS

DAVY, Henry
– **A Series of Etchings Illustrative of the Architectural Antiquities of Suffolk.** Southwold, Priv. Ptd., 1827. Fo. Cont. hf. mor. From the collection of Eric Sexton. (C. Apr.16; 243) *Traylen.* £110
– – **Anr. Copy.** 69 engraved plts. only (lacks no 67), a few slightly dampstained. Cont. hf. cf. (CSK. Jun.26; 14) £70

DAVY, Sir Humphrey
– **Elements of Agricultural Chemistry.** 1813. 1st. Edn. 4to. Some spotting. Orig. bds., new paper spine & label., unc. (C. Apr.1; 104) *Cavendish.* £85
– – **Anr. Copy.** A few ll. slightly dampstained. Neatly rebkd. with cf., unc. (S. Dec.2; 703) *Dawson.* £55
– **Elements of Chemical Philosophy.** 1812. 1st. Edn. 12 plts., foxed. Hf. cl. (C. May 20; 24) *Taylor.* £160
– **Six Discourses Delivered before the Royal Society at their Anniversary Meetings on the Award of the Royal & Copley Medals preceded by an Address ... on the Progress & Prospects of Science.** 1827. 4to. Cl., cf. spine. (S. Dec.1; 140) *Phelps.* £55

DAVY, Sir Humphrey–WISSET, Robert
– **Elements of Agricultural Chemistry.–A Treatise on Hemp.** L., 1813; 1808. 2 works in 1 vol. 4to. Hf. cf. (P. Jun.11; 285) *Brooke-Hitchin.* £270

DAVY, John
– **An Account of the Interior of Ceylon.** 1821. 1st. Edn. 4to. 2 plts. cold., with errata slip, map slightly torn at fold. 19th. C. hf. mor. From Chetham's Liby., Manchester. (C. Nov.26; 101) *Taylor.* £90

DAWES, Richard
– **Miscellanea Critica.** Ed.:– Thomas Burgess. Oxford, 1781. Vell., spines gt. Fore-e. pntg. (SG. Oct.9; 99) $1,500

DAWKS, T.
– [–] **The Complete English-Man.** 1685. Frontis. & title cut-down & mntd. on blanks, some corners & tears reprd., stained, MS. exercises by a former owner. Cont. sheep, rebkd. preserving most of spine. (S. Feb.9; 15) *Quaritch.* £300

DAWSON, James
– **Australian Aborigines.** Melbourne, etc., 1881. 4to. Orig. cl. gt., slightly worn & marked. (S. Jul.27; 13) *P. Arnold.* £90

DAWSON, Moses
– **A Historical Narrative of the Civil & Military Services of Major-General William H. Harrison, & a Vindication of His Character.** Cincinnati, 1824. 1st. Edn. Some offsetting & foxing. Mod. hf. cf. From liby. of William E. Wilson. (SPB. Apr.29; 77) $450

DAWSON, Thomas Fulton & Skiff, F.J.V.
– **The Ute War.** Denver, 1879. 1st. Edn. Lacks 8-pp. advts., accession number in ink on title-p. verso. Mod. hf. mor. (CNY. May 22; 80) $550

DAWSON, William
See–CONYBEARE, Rev. William Daniel & Dawson, William

DAWSON, William Leon
– **The Birds of California.** San Diego, etc., 1923. (1,000). 4 vols. 4to. Unbnd. (SH. Jul.16; 152) *Book Room, Cambridge.* £110

DAY, Francis
– **The Fishes of India.** 1958. Reprint of 1878 Edn. 2 vols. 4to. Buckram. (C. Mar.18; 36) *Duran.* £55
– **The Fishes of Malabar.** 1865. 4to. Hf. leath., backstrip missing, covers detchd. (S. Dec.3; 947) *W. & W.* £85

DAY, Kenneth
See–MORISON, Stanley & Day, Kenneth

DAY, Lewis F.
– **Windows.** L., 1909. 3rd. Edn. Cl., worn. From the liby. of Clement Heaton. (SG. Mar.12; 339) $130

DAY, Richard
– **Christian Prayers & Meditations in English.** 1590. 4to. Lacks title, a few ll. slightly damaged in margin, some slightly dampstained or soiled. 19th. C. cf., gt., arms of Viscount Courtnay on upr. cover, this nearly detchd. [STC 6431] (S. Dec.9; 287) *Booth.* £65

DAYOT, Armand
– **Les Peintres Militaires: Charlet et Raffet.** Paris, ca. 1900. Red mor. (SG. Oct.30; 122) $110

DAYS OF THE DANDIES
L., Grolier Society, n.d. Connoisseur Edn., (150). 15 vols. Plts. in 2 states. Hf. mor. (SPB. May 6; 299) $425
See–JACKSON, Lady Catherine–ANON

DEAD SEA SCROLLS
Trans.:– Geza Vermes. Ill.:– Shraga Weil. Ltd. Edns., Cl. 1966. (1500) numbered. 2 vols. 4to. Monthly letter laid in. Leath.-bkd. linen, glassine wrap., orig. box. (SG. Jan.15; 155) $110
– – **Anr. Copy.** Orig. bdg., box, slight soiling. (SPB. Jul.28; 247) $100

DEAKIN, Richard, M.D.
– **Florigraphia Britannica.** L., 1857. 4 vols. Orig. cl. (SG. Sep.18; 112) $190

DEAN, Bashford
– **Catalogue of European Court Swords & Hunting Swords ...** N.Y., 1929. (900). Lge. 4to. Hf. cl. (SG. Oct.30; 123) $150
– **Catalogue of European Daggers.** N.Y., 1929. Ltd. Edn. Cont. cl. (SH. Oct.9; 167) *Fogg.* £125
See–GRANCSAY, Stephen V.

DEANS New Scenic Books
– **Number Two: Robinson Crusoe.** L., ca. 1880. Tall 8vo. 1 pop-up defect. Cl.-bkd. cold. pict. bds. (SG. Apr.30; 249) $110

DEARN, T.D.W.
– **Design for Lodges & Entrances to Parks, Paddocks & Pleasure-Grounds.** 1811. 1st. Edn. Orig. bds., 1 int. brkn. (BS. Sep.17; 150) £220

DE BELLECHAUME, Grenan
– **Recueil de Poesies Latines et Françoises sur les Vins de Champagne et de Bourgogne.** Paris, 1712. 1st. Edn. Slight browning, bnd. up with other Latin poems. 19th. C. cf.-bkd. bds. From liby. of André L. Simon. (S. May 18; 79) *Quaritch.* £80

DE BIE, Cornelius
– **Het Gulden Cabinet van de Edele Vry Schilder-Const.** Antw., 1662. 4to. Old vell. (LM. Mar.21; 35) B.Frs. 16,000

DEBRET, Jean B.
– **Voyage Pittoresque et Historique au Bresil.** Rio de Janeiro, 1965. Facs. of Pan's 1834-39 Edn., (900). 3 vols. Lge. fo. MS. ded. on 1 endpaper. Ll., orig. wraps, orig. linen portfolio. (HK. May 12-14; 506) DM 900
See–BRY, Johann Theodor de

DE BURE, Guillaume Françoise, le Jeune
– **Bibliographie Instructive.** Paris, 1763-69. 1st. Edn., (50) on Papier de Hollande. 9 vols. (of 10). 4to. Lacks title & 8 ll. from 'Ordre des Facultés', lacks flylf. & endpaper from 'Théologie', sig. of author on flylf. of each vol., under stpd. arms & inscr. in red ink on verso of title or hf.-title, priced thro.-out in red ink in same hand. Cont. red mor., triple gt. fillet, spine gt. in compartments with sunflower, inner gt. dentelles, stained. 1 ptd. sheet of verse loosely inserted. (SM. Oct.7; 1358) Frs. 4,200
– **Notices faites ... Années 1789-1797.** Paris, v.d. 13 catalogues in 1 vol. Priced thro.-out, some MS. additions to ptd. lots. Cont. spr. cf., spine gt. in compartments, inner gt. dentelles. (SM. Oct.7; 1359) Frs. 6,700

DE BUS, Bernard
– **Esquisses Ornithologiques; Descriptions et Figures d'Oiseaux Nouveaux ou peu Connus.** Brussels, 1845. 4 orig. pts. 4to. Orig. paper wraps., detchd., in mod. purpose-made cl. box. (TA. Jun.18; 111) £250

DE COMETIS
[Venice], Hans Aurl, 1474. Sm. 4to. A few marginal stains, 2 blanks soiled on recto & verso respectively. Bnd. in 2 vell. MS. fragments (1 12th. C. liturgical, other 14th. C. legal), stitching brkn., hf. red mor. case. From Honeyman Collection. [BMC V, 237; HC 15513; Goff C785] (S. May 20; 3212) *Lyon.* £1,100

DEBUSSY, Claude
– **Deux Arabesques pour le Piano.** Paris, 1904. 4to. Some staining. Orig. bdg. Inscr. on cover. (C. Oct.22; 260) *Rosen.* £80
– **Prélude à l'Apres–Midi d'un Faune; Nocturnes; 1er Quatuor pour 2 Violons, Alto et Violoncelle. op 10.** Paris, [1895; 1901; 1894]. 1st. Edn. 3 titles in 1 coll. vol. Linen, orig. wraps bnd. in. (H. Dec.9/10; 1110) DM 540

DECAEN, J.
– **Mexico y sus Alrededores.** Ill.:– C. Castro, G. Rodriguez, J. Campillo & L. Auda. N.p., n.d. 2nd. Edn. Fo. Hf. mor. gt. & marb. paper. Evrard de Rouvre ex-lib. [Sabin 48590] (D. Dec.11-13; 1344) DM 16,500

DE CANTILLON
– **Délices du Brabant et de ses Campagnes.** Amst., 1757. 4 vols. 4to. Wormed at end of vol. 1 Marb. cf., 5 spine raised bands, decor. (LM. Nov.8; 24) B.Frs. 41,000

DE CESENA, A.
– **Campagne de Piemont et de Lombardie en 1859.** Paris, 1860. Publisher's romantic bdg. (CR. Mar.19; 401) Lire 220,000

DE CHAIR, Somerset (Trans.)
See–FIRST Crusade

DE CHAULLIAC, Guy
See–CHAULLIAC, Guy de

DECKER, Ezechiel de
– **Eerste Deel vande Nieuwe Telkonst.** Gouda, 1626. 1st. Edn. 4to. Some browning & marginal staining. Cont. vell., soiled, lacks ties. Baron Napier's copy, with inscr. on fly-lf.; from Honeyman Collection. (S. May 20; 3216) *Quaritch.* £550

DECKER, J.M. & Weber, F.A.
– [–] **Naturgeschichte aus dem Schriftstellern.** Ill.:– M. Merian jun. Heilbronn, 1772-74. Fo. Lightly soiled in parts. Cont. cf., very worn. (H. Dec.9/10; 405) DM 1,600

DECKER, Paul
– [–] **Ausführliche Anleitung zur Civil Bau-Kunst.** Nuremb., ca. 1720. 2 pts. (of 3) in 1 vol. Fo. Some plts. soiled mainly in margins. Cont. hf. vell., worn. (S. Jan.27; 322) *Nester.* £130
– **Dess Furstlichen Baumeisters Erster Theil; (Anderer Theil, Anhang zum Ersten Theil).** Augsburg, [1711], 1713-16. 3 pts. in 1 vol. Ob. lge. fo. 130 engraved plts. (of 131, lacks plt. 25 in

pt. 2), lacks engraved & ptd. titles to pt. 1, 1 extension to plt. torn away & loosely inserted, pt. 2 plt. 21 & Anhang to pt. 1 plt. 40 partly lacking, some plts. slightly torn or damaged, 9 slightly affecting engr., last few plts. crumpled & frayed. Cont. cf., head of spine worn. (S. Feb.10; 200) *Mistrali.* £1,100

DECKER, Peter
- A Descriptive Check List. N.Y., 1960. De Luxe Reprint, (100) sigd. Buckram. (SG. Oct.2; 104) $100

DECLARATION de Droits de l'homme et du Citoyen
Ill.:– Jacques Touchet. Paris, 1928. (50) numbered, with orig. sigd. watercolour, & uncold. suite of ills. 4to. Crushed hf. lev., orig. wraps. bnd. in, bkplt. (SG. Apr.2; 293) $220

DECORATIVE Art
1930-1940 & 1943-51. 14 vols., 4to. Orig. cl., a few slightly worn, 5 with d.w.'s. (SKC. Oct.8; 1442) £120

DE COSTER, Charles
- La Légende et les Aventures Héroïques, Joyeuses et Glorieuses d'Ulenspiegel et de Lamme Goedzak ... Ill.:– Amédée Lynen. Brussels, 1914. 4to. Sewed. (LM. Mar.21; 92) B.Frs. 12,000

DE COURCY, M. & B.
- The Lady's Cabinet of Fashion, Music & Romance. L., Jan.–Jun. 1833; Jan.–Dec. 1834. Vol. 3; Vols. 5 & 6. Cf. (HSS. Apr.24; 61) £55

DECREE OF STAR CHAMBER concerning Printing
[N.Y.], [Grol. Cl.], [1884]. (2) on vell., Reprnt. of 1637 Edn. Lev. mor., silver & gt.-stpd. seal of Grol. Cl., blind roll-tooled border, gt. borders, spine gt. in 6 compartments, 5 raised bands, red mor. gt. doubls., watered silk endpp., orig. vell. wraps. bnd. in, by Lortic, sigd., s.-c. M.C.D. Borden & Cortlandt F. Bishop bkplts. (CNY. May 22; 413) $3,500

DECREMPS, Henri
- La Magie Blanche Dévoilée. Paris, 1784. Lacks final lf. with application form. Cl.-bkd. bds., with liby.-stp. (SH. Oct.23; 18) *Huber.* £60
[–] Les Petites Aventures de Jerome Sharp. Brussels, 1789. Cont. cf., worn. (SH. Oct.23; 126) *Masters.* £90

DEDALO Rassegna d'Arte
Ed.:– Ugo Ojetti. 1920-33. Year I–XIII, 41 vols. (Index in vol. 41) 4to. Partly publisher's bdg. & partly worn orig. bds., some orig. wraps. preserved. W.a.f. (CR. Mar.19; 62) Lire 2,600,000

DEDENON, A.
- Histoire du Blamontois ... Nancy, 1931. Lge. 8vo. Hf. chagrin. (HD. Jun.29; 188) Frs. 1,300

DEE, Arthur
[–] Fasciculus Chemicus: or Chymical Collections ... Trans.:– James Hasolle (i.e. Elias Ashmole). 1650. 1st. Engl. Edn. Some staining & soiling, cont. marginal annots. Cf., rebkd. From Honeyman Collection. [Wing D810] (S. May 20; 3217) *Ritman.* £4,200

DEE, John
[–] General & Rare Memorials pertayning to the Perfect Arte of Navigation: Annexed to the Paradoxal Cumpas. 1577. 1st. Edn. Fo. Title very slightly soiled. Cont. limp vell., spine slightly defect., buckram case, Boies Penrose bkplt. [STC 4659] (S. Nov.4; 477) *Quaritch.* £4,600

DEERING, Charles
- Catalogus Stirpium ... Plants naturally growing & commonly cultivated in divers Parts of England, more especially about Nottingham. Nottingham, Priv. ptd., 1738. 1st. Edn. Lacks additional dedication, a few minor defects. Hf. cf., worn. (S. Jun.1; 260) *Quaritch.* £80
- Nottinghamia Vetus et Nova or an Historical Account of ... Nottingham. Nottingham, 1751. 4to. Frontis. with short tear. Cont. cf. (SBA. Oct.22; 468) *Chesters.* £85

DE FER, N.
- Des Forces de l'Europe. Paris, 1723. Ob. fo. Old cf., worn. (BS. Sep.17; 24) £700

DE FLOU, Karel
- Woordenboek de Toponymie van Westelijk Vlaanderen ...–De Indices op het Woordenboek. Ed.:– D. Floribertus Rommel (2nd. work). Gent, Steenbrugge, 1914-28., 1935. 18 pts.; 19 pts. Full leath. with red mor. (LM. Nov.8; 140) B.Frs. 48,000

DEFOE, Daniel
- The Anatomy of Exchange-Alley.–Exchange Alley.–A Letter to a Conscientious Man. 1719; 1720; 1720. 1st. work 1st. Edn. 3 works in 1 vol. 1st. work; title reprd. Roan-bkd. bds. (C. Jul.16; 373) *Kamph.* £480
[–] A Brief Account of the Present State of the African Trade. 1713. 1st. Edn. Slight browning. Mod. pol. cf., spine gt., unc. (S. Feb.9; 48) *Rota.* £450
- The Consolidator; or, Memoirs of Sundry Transactions from the World in the Moon. 1705. Cont. tooled & panel. cf. bdg., cont. bkplt., worn. (PWP. Apr.9; 89) Can $180
[–] Giving Alms no Charity, & Employing the Poor a Grievance to the Nation. 1704. 1st. Edn. Sm. 4to. Disbnd. (C. Jul.16; 377) *Lawson.* £140
- Das Leben und die ganz Ungemeinen Begebenheiten des Weltberühmten Engelländers Robinson Crusoe. Leipzig, 1922. 1st. Edn. (800), Priv. Edn. 4to. Hand-made vell., cover vig., by R. Janthur. (D. Dec.11-13; 1042) DM 440
[–] Memoirs of a Cavalier, or A Military Journal ... Leeds, n.d. 2nd. Edn. Sm. piece cut from top of title, lacks front blank. Cf. (GM. Apr.30; 569) £60
- A New Voyage round the World. 1725. 1st. Edn. Late 19th C. lev. mor. by F. Bedford, gt. (S. Nov.24; 99) *Howes.* £220
[–] – Anr. Copy. 2 pts. in 1 vol. Some slight browning. Cont. spr. cf. [Sabin 19291] (S. Feb.9; 50) *Traylen.* £150
- The Novels & Miscellaneous Works. 1840-41. 20 vols. 12mo. Hf. mor. gt., decor. gt. spine. (CE. Mar.19; 229) £220
- Novels & Selected Writings. Shakes. Hd. Pr., 1927-28. (750). 14 vols. Orig. cl. (S. Jul.31; 126) *Joseph.* £90
– – Anr. Copy. (CSK. Jan.9; 165) £55
- Robinson Crusoe [English]. 1719. 4th. Edn.; 1st. Edn. 2 vols. Hand-cold. frontis. to vol. 1 remntd., newspaper cuttings pasted in at front, folding linen-bkd. maps to each & advt. ll. bnd. in at rear, text browned. Cont. spr. cf. gt., vol. 1 upr. cover detchd. (TA. Apr.16; 208) £110
– – Anr. Edn. Ill.:– Medland after Stothard. L., 1790. 1st. Edn. with these plts. 2 vols. With advts., some foxing. Cont. mott. cf., worn & brkn. (SG. Feb.5; 112) £150
[–] – Anr. Edn. Ill.:– after Stothard. 1820. 2 vols. Occasional spotting. Cont. str.-grd. mor., gt. (S. Feb.10; 435) *Traylen.* £75
– – Anr. Edn. Ill.:– Gerard. L., 1840. Slightly soiled and stained in parts. Blind-tooled orig. linen, gold-stpd. vig. on upr. cover & gt. spine, reprd. with orig. material. (D. Dec.11-13; 654) DM 500
Dec.11-13; 654) DM 500
– – Anr. Edn. Ill.:– E. McKnight Kauffer. 1929. (35) numbered, on Mould-made paper, sigd. by artist. 4to. Orig. mor.-bkd. cl., unc. (SH. Mar.26; 308) *Sherlock.* £105
[–] Robinson Crusoe [English & French]. Dampierre, 1797. 2 vols. 4to. Browned. Cont. bds. (SH. Jun.11; 203) *Rota.* £70
[–] Robinson Crusoe [German]. Nuremb., 1782-83. 2 vols. Title stpd., lightly soiled in parts. Cont. hf. leath., endpapers renewed. (HK. May 15; 5203) DM 700
– – Anr. Edn. Ill.:– [Richard] Seewald. Munich, 1919. (500) numbered & sigd. on Bütten. 4to. Orig. hf. leath. by E.A. Enders, cover vig. (D. Dec.11-13; 1043) DM 580
– – Anr. Edn. Ill.:– F. Heubner. Munich, 1922. (100) numbered with 20 full-p. sigd. orig. etchgs. & 1 sigd. frontis & etched vigs. at ends. 4to. Hf. mor., floral gt. spine, cold. paper over covers, sigd. by Gerber. (D. Dec.11-13; 1044) DM 640
[–] A System of Magick. 1727. 1st. Edn. 19th. C. hf. mor. (SH. Jul.16; 2) *Walford.* £100
[–] A Tour Thro' the Whole Island of Great Britain. 1724-27. 1st. Edn. 3 vols. Frontis. to vols. I & II misbnd., sm. tear in l, 2 inch tear in map to vol. III, lacks index to 'Scotland' in vol. III. Cont. cf. (C. Apr.1; 201) *Sawyer.* £160
[–] A Treatise concerning the Use & Abuse of the Marriage Bed. 1727. 1st. Edn. 2nd. iss., with the cancel title replacing that of 'Conjugal Lewdness', some slight browning. 19th. C. cf. (S. Feb.9; 53) *Waterfield.* £110
- La Vie et les Avantures Surprenantes de Robinson Crusoe. Trans.:– H. Cordonnier & J. van Effen. Amst., 1720-21. 1st. Fr. Edn. 3 vols. 12mo.

Red mor. gt. by Reymann. (S. Nov.24; 98) *Quaritch.* £180
– – Anr. Edn. Ill.:– Chapelain after Picart (frontis.). L., 1784. 4 vols. 18mo. Str.-grd. mor., gt. pointillé spine decor., roulette border, inner dentelles, by Bozerian, ca. 1800, some defects. to vol. III. 1st. vol. inscr. in gold letters 'A ma chère Malvina'. (HD. Apr.8; 246) Frs. 3,600
– – Anr. Edn. Ill.:– Delignon, Delvaux, Dupréel after Stothart. Paris, ca. 1800. 3 vols. Cont. grd. cf., gt. roulette border, limp decor. spines. (HD. Apr.24; 137) Frs. 1,700
– – Anr. Edn. Ill.:– Lassalle. Paris, ca. 1835. 2 vols. Square 12mo. Some foxing. Cont. roan, spine decor. in gt. & blind, gt. fillet border on covers, lge. centre motif in blind, inner dentelle. (HD. Apr.9; 477) Frs. 3,900

DEFOE, Daniel, attrib. to
[–] The Trade with France, Italy, Spain, & Portugal. 1713. 1st. Edn. Slight browning & soiling. Mod. cf. (S. Feb.9; 52) *Laywood.* £70

DEFOE, Daniel–ANON
[–] An Essay on the Treaty of Commerce with France; A letter from a Member of the House of Commons to his Friend in the Country, Relating to the Bill of Commerce.–The Consequences of a Law for Reducing the Duties upon French Wines, Brandy, Silks & Linen, to those of Other Nations. 1713; 1713; 1713. 1st. Edns. 3 works in 1 vol. Bnd. with anr. pamphlet, some browning, 1st. title with advts., 2nd. title with comma after 'Printed' on title, ornament instead of parallel lines at top of p., lr. case initial letter in 'Impartial', line 19, p. 23. Mod. pol. hf. cf. by Rivière, spine gt., slightly marked. From liby. of André L. Simon. (S. May 18; 82) *Quaritch.* £170

DEGAS, Edgar
- Catalogue des Tableaux, Pastels et Dessins [Sale Catalogue]. Paris, 1918-19. 4 pts. in 3 vols. (1st.–4th. Sales). MS. list of the prices realized in the 1st. sale loosely inserted. Red hf. mor. (C. Jul.22; 138) *Phillips.* £320
– – Anr. Copy. 4 vols. in 2. Some prices marked in pencil. Mod. cl. (SH. Oct.9; 68) *Scandecor.* £300

DEGAS, Edgar & Rouart, Denis
- Monotypes. Paris, [1948]. (1,000) numbered. 4to. Wraps., disbnd., boxed. (SG. Oct.23; 76) $110

DE GEER, Charles
- Memoires pour servir à l'histoire des Insectes. Stockholm, 1752-78. 1st. Edn. 7 vols. in 8. 4to. Cont. mott. cf., gt. spines. (S. Oct.20; 59) *Bjorck & Borjesson.* £950

DE GOUY, Louis
- The Derrydale Cook Book of Fish & Game. N.Y., 1937. (1250). 2 vols. Slight browning. Orig. cl. (SPB. May 29; 106) $175
– – Anr. Edn. [1937]. (950) numbered. 2 vols. Spotted. Cl., gt. medallion on covers, inscrs. & fragments of old brown paper on endpapers. (SG. Dec.11; 231) $120

DE GRAVE, Charles-Joseph
- République des Champs Elysées ou Monde Ancien. Gand, 1806. 3 vols. Hf. buckram, slightly browned. (LM. Nov.8; 43) B.Frs. 9,000

DE GRAY, Thomas
- The Compleat Horseman & expert Farrier. 1639. Fo. Title & port. reprd., soiled, stained. Old cf., worn, lacks upr. cover. [STC 12205] (CSK. Jan.16; 27) £80

DEGREVAUNT
- The Romance of Sire Degrevaunt. Ed.:– F.S. Ellis. Ill.:– Sir Edward Burne-Jones. Hammersmith, Kelms. Pr., 1896-97. (350). Orig. holland-bkd. bds., unc. (CNY. May 22; 330) $380

DEIDIER, Abbé
- Le Parfait Ingenieur François, ou la Fortification Offensive et Défensive. Paris, 1742. New Edn. 4to. Marginal offsetting to some plts, some browned, sm. tear in 1 folding plan, some soiling. Cont. Fr. mott. sheep, upr. cover detchd, 1st. gathering loose. (S. Oct.21; 299) *Licini.* £150

DE KANTER, J.
*See–*HAAS, H. de–DE KANTER, J. –SCHILPEROORT, T.O.

DE KAY, James E.
- Zoology of New York ... Pt. II: Birds. Albany, 1844. 1st. Edn. 4to. Orig. gt.-pict. cl., shaken, backstrip loose. (PNY. Dec.3; 46) $300
- - Anr. Copy. 5 plts. loose, 1 plt. browned, text soiled in parts, a few plts. soiled, lacks pp.355-56. Cont. linen, loose, lacks spine, defect. [Sabin 53784] (H. May 21/22; 252) DM 1,000

DEKKER, Thomas
[-] The Double PP. 1606. 1st. Edn. 4to. Mor. by Mattby. [STC 6498] (C. Nov.20; 240) *Dunbar.* £1,200
- The Magnificent Entertainment. 1604. 1st. Edn. 4to. 1st. word of title cropped. Mor. by Mattby. [STC 6510] (C. Nov.20; 241) *Bell.* £700

DE LA BOISSIERE, M. P. B.
See-NASH, Frederick & others

DE LA CHAPELLE, Jean Baptiste
See-LA CHAPELLE, Jean Baptiste de

DELACOUR, Jean
- The Pheasants of the World. Ill.:– J.C. Harrison. 1951. [1st. Edn.?]. 4to. Orig. buckram gt., transparent d.-w. (PL. Sep.18; 178) *Chilton.* £60
- - Anr. Copy. Orig. cl. (TA. Jun.18; 62) £52
- The Waterfowl of the World. Ill.:– Peter Scott. 1954-59. Vols. 1-3 only. 4to. Orig. cl., d.-w.'s. (CSK. May 22; 5) £50
- - Anr. Edn. Ill.:– Peter Scott. 1954-64. 1st. Edns. 4 vols. 4to. Orig. cl., slightly torn d.-w.'s. (TA. Sep.18; 32) £60

DELACOUR, Jean & Jabouille, P.
- Les Oiseaux de l'Indochine Française. N.p., [1931]. 4 vols. Cl. (CB. Sep.24; 22) Can. $550

DELACROIX, Eugène
- Correspondance Générale. Paris, [1935-38]. 5 vols. Buckram, orig. ptd. wraps. bnd. in. (SG. Dec.4; 121) $100
- Le Voyage d'Eugène Delacroix au Maroc. Ed.:– J. Guiffrey. Paris, 1913. (200). 2 vols. Publisher's hf. cl. s.-c. (HD. Dec.5; 64) Frs. 2,600

DELAFIELD, Col. Richard
- Report on the Art of War in Europe. Wash., 1861. Lge. 4to. Cl. (SG. Feb.26; 104) $100

DE LA FOLIE, Louis Guillaume
- Le Philosophe sans Pretention ou l'Homme Rare. Ill.:– C. Boissel after L.S. Paris, 1775. With frontis. showing flying machine, a few stains. Cont. cf. (S. Dec.2; 474) *Westwood.* £95

DELAMARCHE
- Atlas de Géographie Ancienne et Moderne. Paris, 1822. 4to. 33 plts., some folding, cold. boundaries. Hf. cf., worn. (LM. Nov.8; 8) B.Frs. 9,000

DELAMARE, Nicolas
- Traité de la Police. Amst., 1729. 2nd. Edn. 4 vols. Lge. fo. Old cf., 7 decor. spine raised bands, restored. (LM. Jun.13; 242) B.Frs. 20,000
- Traité de la Police ...–Description Historique et Topographique de Paris ... Ill.:– Lagrive. Paris, 1705-10. 2 works in 2 vols. Fo. Cont. cf., spines with raised bands. (HD. Jun.29; 182) Frs. 5,500

DE LA MARE, Walter 'Walter Ramal'
- On the Edge. Ill.:– Elizabeth Rivers. 1930. 1st. Edn. Lacks prelim. pp.i-viii. Loose in paper wrap. P. Proofs for 1st. Edn., autograph revisions by author. (SH. Dec.18; 90) *Barry Scott.* £55
- - Anr. Copy. Orig. cl. gt., d.-w., worn. Inscr. to Walter Sutton. (SH. Dec.18; 91) *Scott.* £50
- Poems. L., 1910. 1st. Edn. 12mo. Cl. gt., d.-w., hf. mor. s.-c. (SG. Nov.13; 118) $200
- - Anr. Edn. Corvinus Pr., Dec. 1937. 1st. Edn., (52) numbered, sigd. Orig. mor.-bkd. linen, s.-c. (S. Jul.31; 144) *Libris.* £180
- Poems for Children. 1930. 1st. Edn. Orig. cl., d.-w. Inscr. to Walter Sutton. (SH. Dec.18; 92) *Whiteson.* £50
- Songs of Childhood. L., 1902. 1st. Edn. 12mo. Vell.-bkd. gt. cl., endpapers foxed, hf. mor. s.-c., owners' sig. & dealer's note on front endpaper. Tipped in are: A.L.s. (Sep., 1903, 12mo., 2 pp.), & autograph of 2 stanzas of 'The Phantom'. (SG. Nov.13; 114) $400

DELAMOTHE, G.
[-] 'G.D.L.M.N.'. The French Alphabet, teaching in a very short tyme ... together with the treasure of the French-toung. 1592. Title, last lf. & a few corners frayed with loss of letters, some dampstaining. Cont. vell., worn. W.a.f. (CSK. Jan.9; 226) £380

DE LA MOTTE, A. Houdart
- Fables nouvelles dédiées au Roy ... Ill.:– Coypel, Gillot, B. Picart & others. Paris, 1719. 1st. L.P. Edn. 4to. Cont. cf. blind fillet, inner dentelles, decor. spine, reprd. Coat-of-arms of Duc de Penthièvre. (HD. Feb.18; 34) Frs. 2,100

DELAMOTTE, William Alfred & Ollier, C.
- Original Views of Oxford. 1843. Fo. Partly cold. title. Cont. mor.-bkd. cl. (SH. Mar.5; 45) *Remington.* £260

DELANGLEZ, Jean
- El Rio del Espiritu Santo. N.Y., £1945]. Ownership stp. on title. Cl. (SG. Aug.21; 60) $100

DELANO, Amasa
- A Narrative of Voyages & Travels in the Northern & Southern Hemisphere. Boston, 1817. 1st. Edn. Foxed. Cont. mott. cf., worn. (SG. Feb.26; 105) $300

DELAPORTE, L.
See-GARNIER, M.J.F. & Delaporte, L.

[DE L'ART Militaire]
16th. C. Fo. G1 to D6 only, some ll. torn with loss. Stitched. W.a.f. (CSK. Sep.12; 69) £140

DELASSAUX, V. & Elliott, John
- Street Architecture, a Series of Shop Fronts & Facades. 1855. Fo. Orig. bds. (BS. Sep.17; 14) £200

DELAUNAY, L.A.
- Etudes sur les Anciennes Compagnies d'Archers, d'Arbalétriers, et d'Arquebusiers. Paris, 1879. 4to. Red hf. mor. by Lesort, corners, spine decor. with raised bands. (HD. Jun.24; 179) Frs. 1,350

DELAUNAY, Sonia
See-ARP, Jean, Delaunay, Sonia & others

DE LAUNE, Thomas
- The Present State of London. 1681. 1st. Edn. 12mo. Frontis. & 12 plts. (Lowndes calls for 10 plts. only), sm. paper fault in title not affecting text, frontis. & anr. plt. laid down, some foxing. Cont. gt.-panel.cf., rebkd. From the collection of Eric Sexton. [Wing D894] (C. Apr.16; 244) *Hammond.* £120

DELBENE, B.
- Civitas Veri sive Morum ... Ill.:– Th. de Leu (title frontis.). Paris, 1609. Fo. Cont. vell., gt. fillet borders, centre floral motif, limp decor. spine. (HD. Apr.24; 40) Frs. 4,200

DELESSERT, Benjamin
- Icones selectae plantarum. Paris, 1820-46. 5 vols. Fo. Cl. From collection of Massachusetts Horticultural Society, stps. on plts. (SPB. Oct.1; 114) $1,600

DELESSERT, Eugène
- Voyages dans les deux Océans, Atlantique et Pacifique, 1844 à 1847. Paris, 1848. Light foxing, mainly to plts. Qtr. cl., papered bds. (KH. Nov.18; 202) Aus. $220

DE LETANG, Antoine
- The Practice of Farriery Calculated for the East Indies, with an Appendix containing the Names of Drugs. Pondichery, 1795. Appendix hand-written in Hindustani & Malabar. Cf., decor. spine gt. (CE. Jul.9; 197) £270

DELFINO, Domenico
- Sommario di tutte le Scientie. Venice, 1556. 1st. Edn. 4to. A few ll. discold. Cont. limp vell., a little stained, lacks ties. (C. Apr.1; 106) *Telford.* £240

DELFINO, Federico
- De Fluxu et Refluxu Aquae Maris ... Eiusdem De Motu Octavae Sphaerae. Venice, 1559. 1st. Edn. Fo. Vell., stained. From Honeyman Collection. (S. May 20; 3218) *Goldschmidt.* £420

DELGADO, Josef
- Tauromaquia O Arte de Torear A Caballo y a Pie. Madrid, 1804. A few clean tears, ll. soiled. Cont. mor. (CSK. Apr.24; 36) £160

DE L'HOPITAL, Winefride
- Westminster Cathedral & its Architect. N.Y., [1919]. 2 vols. 4to. Orig. cl. (CB. May 27; 85) Can. $110

DELICES de la Hollande (Les)
1697. 2 vols. in 1. Cont. cf. gt., spine defect. (P. Jul.30; 145) *Schapiro.* £85

- - Anr. Edn. Amst., 1728. 2 vols. 12mo. Cont. cf., gt. spines. (S. Apr.7; 491) *Symonds.* £140

DELICES de la Mode et du Bon Goût (Les)
Paris, n.d. (almanac for 13th. year). Sm. 18mo. Cont. red mor., covers decor. motifs. (HD. Apr.8; 91) Frs. 1,600

DELICES de Paris (Les)
Paris [1803]. Sm. 18mo. Traces of burning on some pp. Cont. red mor., fillets, central medallion. (HD. Apr.8; 92) Frs. 1,500

DELILLE
- Journal de la Vie de S.A.S. Madame la Duchesse d'Orléans. 1822. Red mor., Alexander I arms, by Zissio, with his ticket. (HD. Oct.10; 236) Frs. 2,800

DELILLE, Jacques
- L'Imagination, Poème.–Les Trois Regnes de la Nature. Ed.:– Cuvier & Lefevre-Gineau (2nd. work). Ill.:– after Le Barbier, St. Myris & Monsiau (1st. work); after Moreau Le Jeune (2nd work). Paris; Strassburg, 1806; 1809. On vell. 2 works in 4 vols. Lge. 4to. 2nd. work: slight foxing. Cont. red str.-grd. hf. mor., sm. corners, decor. spines, unc. (HD. Mar.18; 56b) Frs. 1,400

DELISLE, Guillaume
- Atlante Novissimo. Ill.:– Cattini (vig.), Giampicoli (cartouche), both after Piazzetta. Venice, 1740-50. 2 vols. Fo. Cont. cf.-bkd. bds. From the collection of John A. Saks. (C. Jun.10; 54) *Burgess.* £1,500
- Atlas Nouveau. Amst., ca. 1745. Fo., 527 × 345mm. Title-pp. detchd., lacking 70 maps & list of plts., letter press general title, separate title for geographical introduction. Cont. panel. cf., worn, covers detchd. W.a.f. (CNY. Oct.1; 30) $4,000

DELISLE de Sales, J.
- Ma République. N.p., 1800 [1791]. 12 vols. 16mo. Cont. marb. roan, decor. spines, 3 fillets. (HD. Apr.9; 450) Frs. 1,300
- Théâtre d'un Poète de Sybaris. Sybaris & Paris, 1788. 3 vols. 18mo. Mor., decor. spines, 3 gt. fillets, inner dentelle. (HD. Apr.9; 449) Frs. 1,450

DELKESKAMP, F.W.
- Malerisches Relief der Schweizer und angränzenden Alpen. Frankfurt, ca. 1840. Ob. 4to. Loose, ptd. orig. bd. covers, schematical map pasted in. (R. Oct.14-18; 1999) DM 420
- Panorama des Rheins u.s. Nächsten Umgebungen von Mainz bis Köln. Frankfurt, 1825. Sm. 4to. Hf. leath., orig. s.-c. (D. Dec.11-13; 1617) DM 800

DELLA CASA, Guido
- Rome, et Prose. Milan, Vinegia, 1559, 1558. Orig. Edn. 4to. Hf. vell. (CR. Mar.19; 208) Lire 500,000

DELLA CHIESA, A.O.
- Bernardo Luini. Novara, 1956. 4to. Publisher's cl. (CR. Mar.19; 63) Lire 200,000

DELLA TORRE, G.M.
- Storia e Fenomeni del Vesuvio. Naples, 1755. With supp. 1761. 4to. Cont. vell. (CR. Mar.19; 209) Lire 350,000

DELLON, Charles
[-] Relation de l'Inquisition de Goa. Paris, 1688. 12mo. Slight browning. Cf.-bkd. bds., defect. (SPB. May 5; 180) $175

DELLOYE, H. L.
- Chants et Chansons populaires de la France. Paris, 1843. Mixed Edns. 3 vols. 4to. Browned. Mod. hf. mor., gt. (SH. Jun.11; 92) *Baron.* £120

DE LOBEL, Matthieu
See-PENA, Pierre & De Lobel, Matthieu

DELORD, Taxile
[-] Un Autre Monde. Ill.:– after Grandville. Paris, 1844. 1st. Edn. 4to. Slightly soiled. Cont. roan gt. (SH. Nov.20; 154) *Droller.* £175
- Les Fleurs Animées. Ill.:– J.J. Grandville. Paris, 1867. 2 vols. Some spotting in text. Cont. hf. vell. (SH. Nov.20; 194) *Droller.* £150

DE L'ORME, Philibert
- Architecture. Rouen, 1648. Fo. Mispaginated in parts, title lf. & 2 ll. with sm. tears & holes, 1 sm. margin tear, 2 light stps. Later cf., restored, spine torn, worn. (H. May 21/22; 265) DM 1,700
- L'Oeuvre. Paris, 1894. Reprint. Fo. Orig. wraps. (SH. Mar.6; 540) *Duran.* £100

DELPHICK Oracle, The
1722 [Sep., 1719-Mar., 1720]. Pts. I–VII (compl.) in 1 vol. General title slightly defect., & reprd., some dampstaining. Cont. mott. cf., rebkd., spine gt. (S. Feb.9; 57) *Quaritch.* £150

DELREE, Pierre (Ed.)
See–ARMORIAL D'ABRY–TABLE DES MEUBLES HERALDIQUES

DEL RIO, Martin
- **Disquisitionum Magicarum Libri Sex.** Lyons, 1608. Fo. Some browning. Rough cf., worn. (S. May 5; 291) *Smith.* £110

DELTEIL, Loys
- **Francisco Goya.** Paris, 1922. (40/50) priv. Edn. on Jap., orig etchg. 2 pts. in 1 vol. Lge. 4to. Hf. leath., orig. wraps. bnd. in. (HK. Nov.18-21; 3359) DM 650
- **Le Peintre-Graveur Illustré.** N.Y., 1969. Collectors Edn. Vols. 4, 7, 8, 13, 16, 18, 20-29, (16 vols. only). 4to. Orig. cl. (SH. Oct.9; 69) *Phillips.* £190
- **H. de Toulouse-Lautrec.** Ill.:– Toulouse-Lautrec (1 etchg.). Paris, 1920. 2 pts. in 1 vol. Lge. 4to. Linen, orig. wraps. bnd. in. (HK. Nov.18-21; 2979) DM 1,700
- – **Anr. Copy.** 2 vols. in 1. Lge. 4to. Slightly worn. Linen, orig. wraps. bnd. in. (H. Dec.9/10; 2374) DM 1,250

DE MEAN, Corolo
- **Ad Jus Civile Leodiensium.** Liège,, 1654. 1st. Edn. 4 vols. Fo. Cont. vell., 5 spine raised bands, blind stpd. (LM. Nov.8; 52) B.Frs. 8,500

DEMIDOFF, Prince Anatole de
- **Album du Voyage dans la Russie Meridionale.** Ca. 1850. 1 vol. only (lacks text vol.). Fo. Occasional light foxing. Cont. mor.-bkd. bds. (C. Nov.6; 183) *Walford.* £180
- **Travels in Southern Russia & the Crimea.** 1853. 2 vols. 2 folding maps, slightly torn & reprd. Orig. cl. Pres. copy. (SH. Nov.7; 341) *Scott.* £105
- **Voyage Pittoresque et Archaeologique en Russie.** Ill.:– A. Durand & Raffet. Paris, [1840]. Atlas vol. only. Lge. fo. Lacks plts. 3-12 & 97-100, a little soiled. Orig. pictor. hf. linen. (R. Oct.14-18; 1978) DM 1,000
- **Voyages dans la Russie Méridionale et La Crimaée.** Paris, ca. 1850. Lge. fo. Some foxing thro.-out. Old russ. gt., arms on covers, worn. (BS. Jun.11; 153) £240

DEMOCRITUS JUNIOR (Pseud.)
See–BURTON, Robert 'Democritus Junior'

DE MOIVRE, Abraham
[–] **Miscellanea Analytica de Seriebus Et Quadraturis.** 1730. 4to. Margins browned. Cont. cf., rebkd. & recornered. (CSK. May 1; 7) £55

DEMOSTHENES
- **Oratione . . . Contra la Legge de Lettine.** Venice, 1555. Spanish marb. mor., probably by Bisiaux, gt., with his monog. at ft. of spine, inner gt. dentelles, silk liners. Syston Park & Henry J.B. Clements bkplts. A.A. Renouard's copy. (SM. Oct.7; 1679) Frs. 1,200
- **Orationum.** Ed.:– Paulus Manutius. Venice, 1554. 3 vols. Vell. bds. Sig. of Fletcher of Saltoun on each title. (C. Jul.16; 258) *Maggs.* £70
See–ASCHAM, Roger–DEMOSTHENES

DEMOUSTIER, Charles Albert
- **Lettres à Emilie . . .** Trans.:– Monnet. Paris, 1801. 6 pts. in 2 vols. 29 (of 36) figures. Str.-grd. red mor. by Bozérian, gt. roll-stp. around covers, spines decor. with raised bands, inside dentelle. (HD. Feb.27; 115) Frs. 1,900
- – **Anr. Edn.** Ill.:– Tardieu after Pajou fils (port.); Moreau (figures). Paris, 1809. 1st. Printing. 6 pts. in 2 vols. Mor. by Thivet, decor. spines, 3 fillets, inside dentelle. (HD. Dec.5; 65) Frs. 1,250

DEMPSEY, G. Drysdale
- **The Practical Railway Engineer.** L., 1847. 4to. Some foxing on plts. Hf. leath. (CB. Sep.24; 120) Can. $180

DE MUSSET, Paul
- **Voyage Pittoresque en Italie et en Sicile.** Paris, 1856. Publisher's romantic cl. (CR. Mar.19; 279e) Lire 300,000

DENHAM, Dixon & Clapperton, Hugh
- **Narrative of Travels & Discoveries in Northern & Central Africa.** L., 1826. 1st. Edn. 2 Pts. in 1 vol. 4to. Mod. hf. mor. (C. Jul.15; 34) *Taylor.* £70

- – **Anr. Copy.** Mod. three-qtr. cf. (SG. May 14; 54) $275
- – **Anr. Copy.** 4to. Liby. stps. on plt. versos. Disbnd. (SG. Feb.26; 6) $130
- – **Anr. Edn.** 1826. 2nd. Edn. 2 vols. Hf. cf. (P. Oct.23; 17) *Holmes.* £95
- – **Anr. Copy.** Orig. bds., rebkd. with cl., unc. (S. Jun.29; 215) *Adelson.* £60
- – **Anr. Edn.** 1828. 3rd. Edn. 2 vols. Some slight browning, 16 pp. of advts. inserted at beginning of vol. 1. Mod. maroon hf. mor., spines gt., partly unc. (S. Feb.9; 58) *Chambers.* £65
- – **Anr. Copy.** Early binder's cl. (SG. Oct.30; 10) $120
- – **Anr. Edn.** L., 1831. 4 vols. Slightly browned & stained. Cont. hf. leath. (R. Oct.14-18; 1590) DM 450

DENIS, Ferdinand
- **Brésil, Colombie et Guyanes par C. Famin.** Paris, 1837. 1st. Edn. 2 pts. in 1 vol. Cont. hf. mor. [Sabin 19541] (S. Jan.27; 564) *Faupel.* £55

DENIS, Maurice
- **Carnets de Voyage en Italie. 1921-22.** 1925. (175) on Arches . Orig. Edn. Sewed. With autog. notes by M. Denis. (HD. Jun.30; 19) Frs. 1,100

DENISOV, Vladimier
- **Voina i lubok [War & the Lubok].** Petrograd, 1916. 4to. Orig. wraps. by D.I. Mitrokhin, rebkd., loose. (SH. Feb.5; 208) *Landry.* £55

DENNIS, John
- **A Plot & No Plot.** [1697]. 1st. Edn. 4to. Staining thro.-out, lacks portion of 1 blank margin, reprd. Recent mor.-bkd. cl. [Wing D1038] (C. Nov.19; 72) *Arnold.* £80

DENNY, Arthur A.
- **Pioneer Days on Puget Sound.** Seattle, 1888. 1st. Edn. 12mo. Orig. cl. Pres. copy. (SPB. Jun.22; 50) $80

DENON, Baron Dominique Vivant
- **Eine Einzige Nacht.** Trans.:– Fr. Blei. Ill.:– K. Walser. Berlin, 1911. (400). Lightly soiled. Orig. wraps. in box, unc., 1 wrap. torn. (H. Dec.9/10; 1796) DM 820
- **Travels in Sicily & Malta.** 1789. Cf. gt. (P. Oct.23; 18) *Brooke-Hitching.* £55
- **Travels in Upper & Lower Egypt.** 1803. 1st. Engl. Edn. 2 vols. 4to. Occasional light spotting & offsetting. Cont. spr. cf., gt., rebkd. with orig. spines preserved. (S. Nov.4; 638) *Hosains.* £90
- **Viaggio Nel Basso ed Alto Egitto.** Flor., 1808. L.P. 2 vols. Lge. fo. Hf. cf., defect., unc. (GM. Apr.30; 732) £525
- **Voyage dans la Basse et la Haute Egypte.** Ill.:– after Denon, Rigo & others. Paris, 1802. 1 vol. Elephant fo. 1 double-p. plt. with crease, some plts. slightly browned, mainly marginal. 19th. C. hf. mor., corners scuffed. From Chetham's Liby., Manchester. (C. Nov.26; 105) *Spowers.* £450

DEN'SHIN, Al.
- **Vyatskaya Glinyannaya Igrushki v Risunkakh [Vyatka Earthenware Toys in Pictures].** Moscow, 1917. (300). 4to. Orig. wraps., lacks spine, slightly soiled, s.-c. (SH. Feb.5; 209) *Reed & Sims.* £70

DENSLOW, William Wallace
- **Mother Goose.** Phila., 1901. 1st. Edn., variant with 4pp. ills. before 'Humpty Dumpty'. 4to. Some ills. damaged. Pict. bds., rebkd. in buckram. (SG. Apr.9; 74) $110

DENTON, M.
See–PRATTENT, T. & Denton, M.

DENTON, Sherman F.
- **As Nature Shows them. Moths & Butterflies of the United States: East of the Rocky Mountains.** Boston, 1900. 1st. Edn., (500) numbered. 2 vols. 4to. Lacks 1 plt. but has dupl. of 1 plt., 2 plts. with species lacking, ex-liby. set, each plt. with embossed stp. not affecting mntd. species. Cont. hf. mor. (PNY. Dec.3; 265) $150
- – **Anr. Edn.** Boston, [1900]. 3 vols. Plts. guarded, slight stains, minor soiling. Mor. gt., gt. panel. spines. (SPB. May 6; 181) $700

DENVER & RIO GRANDE RAILWAY
- **First Annual Report of the Board of Directors . . . to the Stockholders, April 1st, 1873.** Phila., 1873. Marb. bds., leath. spine. (SG. Jan.8; 375) $100

DENYS, Nicolas
See–CHAMPLAIN Society

DE POMIS, David
- **Tsemach David.** Venice, 1587. 1st. Edn., with emblems of Pope Julius VI & the author. Fo. Slight staining. Mod. hf. vell. (S. Nov.18; 543) *Selig.* £500

DEPPING
- **La Suisse, ou Esquisse d'un Tableau Historique, Pittoresque et Moral des Cantons Helvétiques.** Paris, 1824. 4 vols. 16mo. Foxing. Cont. hf. cf., spines decor. in gt. & blind, worn. (HD. Apr.9; 451) Frs. 2,800
- – **Anr. Copy.** Cont. roan, spines decor., covers decor. in blind. & gt. fillet. (HD. Apr.9; 452) Frs. 1,350

DEPREAUX, Albert
- **Les Affiches de Recrutement du XVIIe Siècle . . .** Ed.:– Gabriel Cottreau. Paris, 1911. (300). 4to. Cont. hf. mor., orig. wraps. preserved. (S. Mar.16; 206) *Nat. Art Inst.* £70

DE PUY, Pierre & Jacques & Others
- **Catalogus Bibliothecae Thuanae.** Paris, 1679. Title partly detchd. Cont. cf., spine gt. Bkplt. of Charles Thoreau. (SM. Oct.7; 1365) Frs. 2,300

DE QUINCEY, Thomas
[–] **Confessions of an English Opium-Eater.** 1822. 1st. Edn. 12mo. Some spots, advt. lf. at end. 20th. C. maroon lev. mor. by Rivière, gt. (S. Feb.9; 59) *Forum.* £280
[–] – **Anr. Copy.** Lacks advt. lf., B2-11 loose. Orig. bds., rebkd., unc., s.-c. (S. Nov.25; 490) *Ohern.* £180
[–] – **Anr. Copy.** Slightly spotted, ex-liby. copy with labels of Northwich Reading Soc. on fly-lf. & pastedown. Spine slightly torn, unc. (SBA. Dec.16; 12) *Editions Claude Sivaudan.* £120

DE RAADT, J. Th.
- **Sceaux Armoiriés des Pays-Bas et des Pays Avoisinants.** Brussels, 1898. 4 vols. 4to. Sewed. (LM. Nov.8; 276) B.Frs. 11,000

DERAIN, André
- **Dessins.** Paris, 1947. (270). Fo. In sheets, publisher's portfo. (HD. Dec.5; 66) Frs. 1,300

DE RENNE, Wymberley Jones
- **Catalogue of Georgia Library.** Wormsloe, Priv. Ptd. 1931. (300) numbered on Rives H.M.P. 3 vols. 4to. Rebnd. in buckram. (SG. Jan.22; 148) $425

DERHAM, William
[–] **Artificial Clockmaker . . .** 1696. 1st. Edn. Slight browning. Cont. mott. cf. [Wing D1099] (S. May 5; 167) *Symonds.* £520
- – **Anr. Edn.** 1714. 3rd. Edn. 12mo. Some plts. torn, spotted. Cont. cf., worn. (SH. Jun.25; 200) *Gardner.* £130
[–] – **Anr. Edn.** 1734. 4th. Edn. 12mo. Slight dampstaining, some ll. frayed. Cont. cf., rebkd. (S. May 5; 168) *Bopp.* £140

DERHAM, William–SMITH, John, Chronologist
- **The Artificial Clock-Maker.–The Art of Painting in Oyl.** 1700; 1701. 1st. work 2 pts., 2 works in 1 vol. 1st. work, most ll. stained. Cf. (BS. May 13; 267) £160

DE RICCI, Seymour
- **French signed Bindings in the Mortimer L. Schiff Collection.** N.Y., 1935. 1st. Edn. 4 vols. Orig. cl. (SM. Oct.7; 1362) Frs. 4,200

DEROME, Léopold
- **La Reliure de Luxe. Le Livre et l'Amateur.** Paris, 1886. Ltd. Edn. 4to. Hf. mod. mor., orig. wraps. bnd. in, partly unc. (SI. Dec.3; 193) Lire 320,000
- – **Anr. Edn.** Paris, 1888. Ltd. Edn. Cont. mor.-bkd. bds. (SH. Jan.29; 16) *Duran.* £85

DERRIERE LE MIROIR
Ill.:– Chagall, Miro, Giacometti, Calder, Braque & others. Paris, 1946-79. Nos. 1-236 in 184. 4to. Unsewn in orig. wraps., in 12 folders. (SH. Nov.21; 296) *Nat. Art Inst.* £2,700
- – **Anr. Edn.** Ill.:– Chagall, Miro & others. Paris, 1952, 1958, & 1961. Nos. 46, 44/45, 107/108/109, & 123. 4to. Orig. wraps., slight wear. As a periodical, w.a.f. (SPB. May 29; 105) $275
- – **Anr. Edn.** Ill.:– Bazaine, Chagall, Giacometti & Miro. [Paris], 1956. Special issue. 4to. Orig. wraps. (H. Dec.9/10; 2020) DM 420
- – **Anr. Edn.** Ill.:– M. Chagall. Paris, 1969 & 1972. Nos. 182 & 198. Fo. Orig. bds. (HK. May 12-14; 1806) DM 450

DERRIEY, C.
- Gravure et Fonderie. Spécimen-Album. Paris, 1862. Fo. Orig. mor.-bkd. cl., gt. spine. (SH. Oct.9; 46) *Marlborough.* £220

DERRYDALE PRESS
- A Decade of American Sporting Books & Prints. Ed.:- Eugene V. Connett, III. N.Y., 1937. (950) numbered. Cl., gt. medallion on cover, unopened. (SG. Apr.9; 354) $170

DE RUYTER-BRANDT, Gerard
See-BRANDT, Gerard

DE RYCKEL, Joseph Gedolf
- Vita S. Beggae Ducissae Brabantiae Andetennensium Begginarum et Beggadorum Fundatricis . . .-Historia Begginasiorum Belgie . . . Louvain, 1631. 2 works in 1 vol. Sm. 4to. Old vell. (LM. Mar.21; 6) B.Frs. 7,000
- Vitae S. Gertrudis, Abbatissae Nivellensis, Brabantaie Tutelaris. Louvain, 1632. Mod. vell. (LM. Mar.21; 208) B.Frs. 9,000

DESAGULIERS, John Theophilus
- A Course of Experimental Philosophy. 1734-44. 1st. Edn. 2 vols. 4to. Advts. in each vol., one plt. slightly torn. Cont. cf., worn. (SBA. Jul.23; 378) *Prof. Maud.* £110
- - Anr. Edn. 1763. 3rd. Edn. 2 vols. Slight browning. Cont. cf., rebkd., spines gt. (S. Feb.9; 60) *Forum.* £100

DESAINLIENS, Claude
[-] The French Schoole-Maister. Ed.:- P. Erondelle. 1619. 7th. Edn. Initial & final blanks used as endpapers. Cont. limp vell. [STC 6754] (S. Feb.9; 61) *Quaritch.* £150

DESARCES, Henri
- Grande Encyclopédie pratique de Mécanique et d'Electricité. Paris, ca. 1913. 5 vols. 4to. Publisher's cl., special tool decor. (HD. Jun.10; 145) Frs. 2,200

DESAULT, Pierre Joseph
- Parisian Chirurgical Journal. Trans.:- Robert Gosling. 1794. 1st. Edn. in Engl. 2 vols. Lacks final blank in vol. 2, liby. inscrs. on title, some liby. stps. in text. Cont. tree cf., worn. Bkplt. of Sir W.T. Robertson (pasted over). (S. Feb.10; 373) *Jackson.* £60

DES AUTELS, Guillaume
- Encomium Galliae Belgicae. G. Altario Carolate authore. Accesserunt & alii aliquot eiusdem versiculi. Antw., 1559. 1st. Edn. Sm. 4to. Slight browning. Mod. pol. hf. cf., spine gt., slightly marked. From liby. of André L. Simon. (S. May 18; 83) *Maggs.* £280

DESBORDES-VALMORE, Marceline
- Elégies, Marie, et Romances. Ill.:- Chasselat & Desenne. Paris, 1819. Cont. bds., liby plts. Ex-libris. (HD. Oct.10; 43) Frs. 4,500

DESCARTES, Rene
- Discours de la Méthode pour Bien Conduire sa Raison & Chercher la Verité dans les Sciences. Leiden, 1637. 1st. Edn. 4to. Slightly wormed thro.-out, especially in inner margin sometimes affecting text, browned, most inner margins strengthened & some inner worming reprd., owner's inscr. on title. Mod. leath.-bkd. bds., spine with 1 or 2 wormholes. (S. Dec.2; 708) *Krenzer.* £1,500
- - Anr. Edn. Paris, 1668. 4to. Cont. spr. cf., decor. spine. (HD. Dec.5; 67) Frs. 1,700
- Epistolae. Amst., 1668. 1st. Edn. in Latin. 2 vols. in 1. 4to. Some slight browning. Cont. cf., rebkd. (S. Feb.9; 62) *Waterfield.* £55
- Epistolae.-Tractatus de Homine, et de Formatione Foetus.-Explicatio Machinarum vel Instrumentorum.-Magni Caresii Manes ab ipsomet defensi. Ed.:- D. Joh. Danielis Maioris (2nd. work). Amst., Kiel, Freistadt. 1668; 1677; 1672; 1656. 4 works in 1 vol. 4to. Cont. vell. (S. Oct.20; 61) *Goldschmidt.* £240
- L'Homme et un Traité de la Formation du Foetus. Ed.:- Louys de la Forge. Paris, 1664. 1st. Edn. in Fr. 4to. Some discolouration. Cont. cf. Presented to liby. of the Capucin monastery in Treviso in 1665 & from the liby. of Dr. Charles Singer. (S. Jun.15; 234) *Lawson.* £200
- L'Homme et la Formation du Foetus . . .-Le Monde . . . Ed.:- Louis de La Forge (1st. work). Paris, 1677. 2nd. Edns, 2 works in 1 vol. 4to. Cont. cf., decor. spine, sm. repairs. (HD. Mar.18; 57) Frs. 2,000

- Lettres où son Traitées les Plus Belles Questions de la Morale, Physique, Médécine et des Mathématiques. Paris, 1657. 4to. Cont. vell. (S. Jun.15; 236) *Duran.* £80
- Meditationes de Prima Philosophia. Amst., 1670. 4to. Slight dampstaining. Cf., rebkd., spine brkn. (S. Apr.6; 45) *Elliot.* £70
- Musicae Compendium. Utrecht, 1650. 1st. Edn. Sm. 4to. Wraps. (S. Jun.23; 242) *Quaritch.* £580
- Oeuvres Publiées par Victor Cousin. Paris, 1824-26. 11 vols. Foxed. Cont. hf. roan, smooth decor. spines. (HD. Jun.24; 180) Frs. 1,050
- Opera Philosophica. Amst., 1663-64. 4th. Edn. 4 pts. in 1 vol. 4to. Cont. vell. (VG. Oct.13; 56) DM 600
- - Anr. Edn. Frankfurt, 1692-97. 1st. Frankfurt Coll. Edn. 9 pts. in 7 vols. 4to. 2 repeated ports. copper engraved, 2 repeated engraved. title vigs. heavily browned in parts, some staining, especially Vol. IV. Cont. leath., gt. spine, vol. 1 later in same style. (R. Oct.14-18; 1308) DM 700
- Opera philosophica. Edition ultima (-Tractatus de homine et de formatione foetus). Amst., 1685-86. Together 7 pts. in 1 vol. 4to. Cont. cf., head & foot of spine worn. (S. Feb.23; 36) *Pythagoras.* £80
- Opuscula Posthuma, Physica et Mathematica. Amst., 1704. 6 pts. in 1 vol. Cont. vell. (VG. Oct.13; 57) Fls. 550
- Principia Philosophiae. Amst., 1650. 4to. Bnd. with Specimina Philosophiae, 1 lf. reprd. Old vell., defect. (TA. Sep.18; 213) £80
- Principia Philosophiae.-Dissertatio de Methodo, Dioptrice et Meteora.-Passiones animae. Amst., 1672. 3 pts. in 1 vol. 4to. Cont. panel. cf., rebkd. (S. Jun.15; 237) *Subunso.* £70
- Principia Philosophia, of Beginselen der Wysbegeerte.-Proeven der wijsbegeerte, or Predenering van de Middelen om de Reden wel to beleiden, en de Waarheit in de Wetenschappen te zoeken; de verregezichtkunde, verhevelingen, en Meetkunst. Ed.:- J.H. Glasemaker. Amst.; Amst., 1657; 1659. 2 works in 1 vol. 4to. 1st. work lacks port., slightly stained. Cont. vell., slightly soiled, a few minor defects. (VG. Dec.17; 1278) Fls. 1,200
- Principia Philosophiae.-Specimina Philosophiae. Amst., 1650. 2 works in 1 vol. 4to. 1st. work: I4 torn & reprd. with loss of letters; 2nd. work: lacks bbl. Cont. vell. (CSK. Apr.3; 114) £50
- Tractatus de Homine et de Formatione Foetus. Ed.:- Louys de la Forge. Amst., 1677. 4to. Marginal note on E2, some dampstains. New cl. (S. Jun.15; 235) *Shaftel.* £60

DES COURIERES, Edouard
- Van Dongen. Paris, 1925. (200) on japon. 4to. Engrs. in 2 states, some browning. Orig. wraps., soiled, tears. (SPB. Jul.28; 109) $150

DESCOURTILZ, Dr. Jean Theodore
- Ornitologia Brasiliera ou Historia Natural das aves do Brasil. Rio de Janeiro & Sao Paulo, 1944. Ltd. Edn. 4to. Cf. gt., s.-c. (P. Jun.11; 327) *Wilson.* £50
- - Anr. Edn. Rio de Janeiro, [1944]. Ltd. Edn. 4to. Hf. cf., orig. ptd. wrap. bnd. in. (C. Mar.18; 36) *Hill.* £70

DESCRIPCION DE LA PROVINCIA de los Quixos
Madrid, 1608. No title-p., very slight spotting. Cont. limp vell., gt., lacks ties. (S. Oct.21; 516) *Quevedo.* £350

DESCRIPCION SUMARIA de la Inclyta Milicia de Jesu-Christo, V.O.T. de Pentitentia del Cherubin San Francisco Nro. Glorioso P. y Patriarca Sto. Domingo de Guzman . . .
Lima, 1783. Franciscan liby. stp. on title. Cont. vell. (SPB. May 5; 181) $250

DESCRIPTION de l'Egypte
Ill.:- after H.J. Redouté, Duhamel, Prudhon & others. Paris, 1820-26. 2nd. Edn. 12 vols., including atlases. Elephant fo. Unif. cont. mor., all except atlases unc. From Chetham's Liby., Manchester. (C. Nov.26; 123) *Hollander.* £1,500

DESCRIPTION des Arts et Metier
- L'Art du Distillateur Liquoriste.-L'Art du Distillateur d'Eaux-Fortes. 1775; 1773. 2 works in 2 vols. Orig. bdgs. From Chetham's Liby., Manchester. (C. Nov.26; 122a) *Money.* £200

DESCRIPTION des Festes . . . à l'occasion du Mariage de Mme. Louise-Elisabeth de France, et de Dom Philippe . . . Grand Amiral d'Espagne
Ill.:- Blondel, Pierre Soubeyran & Rigaud. Paris, 1740. 1st. Edn. Fo. Cont. red mor., gt., arms of

Paris on covers, gt. border of acanthus & fleurs-de-lis, lge. fleur-de-lis in each corner & in spine compartments, inner gt. fleur-de-lis border. (SM. Oct.7; 1680) Frs. 5,000
- - Anr. Copy. Cont. spr. cf., arms of Paris, dentelle on covers, fleurs-de-lys in corners, raised bands & fleurs-de-lys on spine. (HD. Jun.29; 40) Frs. 2,300

DESCRIPTION EXACTE DE TOUT CE QUI S'EST PASSE DANS LES GUERRES ENTRE LE ROY D'ANGLETERRE, le Roy de France, les Estats des Provinces Unies du Pays-Bas . . . commençant de l'An 1664
Amst., 1668. 1st. Edn. in Fr. 4to. Sm. repair on title, last p. (verso blank) mntd., some stains. Old cf., reprd. (SG. Mar.5; 338) $450
- - Anr. Copy. Mod. bds. (SG. May 14; 155) $350

DESCRIPTION OF ENGLAND & WALES
1770-75. 10 vols. 232 plts. Cont. cf. gt. (P. Jul.2; 202) *Weston.* £125

DESCRIZIONE DELLE FESTE CELEVRATE IN PARMA L'Anno MDCCLXIX per le Auguste Nozze di . . .-Don Fernando Colla Reale Arciduchessa Maria Amalia
Parma, 1769. Fo. Hf.-title, sm. stain in outer margins near end. 19th. C. cl. (SI. Dec.3; 195) Lire 1,500,000
- - Anr. Edn. Parma, [1769]. Lge. fo. 34 engraved plts. (of 36). No bdg. stated, but brkn. (BS. Jun.11; 213) £200

DESCRIZIONE della Feste Fatte nelle Reali Nozze de Cosimo de' Medici e Maria Maddalena
Firenze, 1608. 8 in 1 vol. Sm. 4to. Old limp vell. (BS. Jun.11; 212) £2,500

DESCRIZIONE e Disegni della Mascherata . . . 1827
Naples, 1827. Sm. fo. Folding plt. torn & slightly defect., foxed thro.-out, Liby. stp. on title. Cl., mor. spine, worn. (BS. Jun.11; 214) £160

DESERET NEWS
Great Salt Lake City, U.T., Nov.15, 1851-Dec.22, 1853. Vols. 2 & 3, each in 26 numbers, plus Index for each vol., bnd. in 1 vol. Tall fo. Mod. buck.-bkd. bds. (SG. Oct.9; 78) $800
- - Anr. Edn. Salt Lake City, Mar. 11 1857-Mar. 3 1858. Vol. VII, in 52 numbers. Fo. Fly ll. torn., 1 with inscr. Qtr. mor., worn. (SG. Jan.8; 127) $450

DESFONTAINES, Abbé & others
- Histoire Particulière de la Ligue en Bretagne . . . Paris, 1739. 6 vols. 12mo. Cont. marb. roan, spines decor. with raised bands. (HD. Jun.24; 86) Frs. 1,900

DESFONTAINES, Rene Louiche
- Les Bains de Diane, ou le Triomphe de l'Amour, Poème. Ill.:- after Marillier. Paris, 1770. 1st. Edn. Mod. str.-grd. mor. gt., partly unc. (C. Apr.1; 130) *Sellars.* £60

DESGODETZ, Antoine
- Les Edifices Antiques de Rome. Paris, 1682. Fo. A few ills. mntd. & reprd. Cont. spr. cf., spine gt. (SH. Nov.6; 201) *Weinreb.* £280
- - Anr. Copy. A few pp. slightly browned. Cont. leath., gt. spine, head of spine defect. (R. Oct.14-18; 619) DM 1,700

DE SHANE, Brian
- De Sade. Ill.:- Beresford Egan. Fortune Pr., 1929. (1,600) sigd. by artist. 4to. Orig. cl. gt., d.-w. Egan's copy, with 3 A.N.'s. (SH. Mar.26; 181) *Illustrated Antiques.* £70

DESLAURIERS 'Bruscambille', Comedian
[-] Oeuvres de Bruscambille. Rouen, 1635. 12mo. Mor. by Trautz-Bauzonnet, triple fillet around covers. spine decor. with raised bands, inside dentelle. (HD. Jun.24; 26) Frs. 1,300

DESMAREST, N. & Bory de Saint Vincent, J.B.G.M.
- Atlas Encyclopédique, contenant les Cartes et les Planches Relatives à la Géographie Physique. Paris, 1827. 1st. Edn. 4to. Mod. buckram, unc. (SG. Nov.20; 42) $110

DESMOULINS, A.
See-MAGENDIE, François & Desmoulins, A.

DESNOS, Louis Charles
- Almanach Géographique, ou Petit Atlas Elémentaire Paris, Priv. ptd., [1770]. 1st. Year of this Almanach. 18mo. Coat of arms on frontis.,

date of title defect. Cont. red mor., decor. spine, 3 fillets, inner dentelles. (HD. Apr.8; 93) Frs. 2,000
- Atlas Général Méthodique et Elementaire. Paris, 1768. 4to. Maps neatly cold. or cold. in outl. with text pasted in on either side. Cont. vell.-bkd. bds., sides slightly worn. (S. Nov.4; 463) *Nagle.* £240
- - Anr. Edn. Paris, 1772. 3rd. Edn. 4to. 1 map detchd. Cont. hf. cf., decor. spine, slightly worn. (HD. Jun.10; 26) Frs. 2,600
- L'Indicateur Fidéle ou Guide des Voyagers ... dressé par la Sieur Michel. Paris, 1765. 4to. Light spotting. Cont. wraps., backstrip torn with loss. (CSK. Nov.7; 188) £130
- - Anr. Edn. 1785. 4to. Cl. (P. Apr.9; 148a) *Tabor.* £130
- Nouvel Atlas d'Angleterre ... avec toutes les Routes levées Topographiquement par ordre de S.M. Britannique et les Plans des Villes et Ports de ce Royaume. Paris, 1767. 4to. Slight browning & soiling. Cont. roan-bkd. bds., worn. As an atlas, w.a.f.; from liby. of André L. Simon. (S. May 18; 84) *Israel.* £420

DES OMBIAUX, Maurice
- Les Belles à Table, suivi du Coup du Milieu. Ill.:- Marie Laurencin. Paris, 1926. (400) numbered. Orig. wraps., unc., unopened. (SH. Nov.21; 374) *Subunso.* £70

DESPAUTERIUS, Johannes
- Prima pars Grammatice ... e diversis exemplaribus invicem collatis emendatissime recognita. Paris, 1542. Title a little soiled, owners' inscrs. of Carmelite monastery at Dijon on title & 2nd. lf. Mod. vell. (C. Apr.1; 26) *Telford.* £60

DESROCHES, Abbé
- Histoire du Mont Saint-Michel et de l'Ancien Diocèse d'Avranches ... Caen, 1838. 3 vols (including atlas). 8vo & fo. Publisher's Italian bds. (HD. Jun.29; 177) Frs. 1,050

DESROSCHES-NOBLECOURT, Christine
- Tutenkhamen. Arcadia Pr., 1969. (265) sigd. 4to. Orig. mor., centrepiece on upr. cover of gt.-tooled mor. onlays, cl. box. (SH. Feb.20; 336) *De Velasco.* £50

DESSAU, Shlomo Ben Yehuda Leib
- Oz Miv Tacha. Amst., 1734. Slight worming affecting some letters, browning, some staining, liby. stps. Cl.-bkd. bds. (SPB. May 11; 196) $800

DESSEINE, François-KENNET, Basilius
- Deschryving van Oud (en Nieuw) Rome.–De Aloudheden van Rome. Trans.:- W. Sewel (2nd. work). Ill.:- P. Sanctus Bartolus & J. Petrus Bellorius (1st.) Amst., 1704. 2 works in 1 vol. Lge. fo. Old cf., 7 decor. spine raised bands. (LM. Nov.8; 139) B.Frs. 36,000

DESSIOU, J.F.
- Petit Neptune Français. 1805. Qtr. cf., worn. (P. Apr.9; 306) *Fairburn.* £90

DESTOUCHES, A.C.
- Semiramis, Tragedie en Musique. Paris, [1718]. 1st. Edn. Ob. 4to. Slightly browned & soiled in parts. Cont. cf., defect. On p.391 MS. sigs. of composer & printer. (H. Dec.9/10; 1111) DM 1,000

DESTOUCHES, J.A. von
- Die Haupt-u, Residenz-Stadt München. Munich, [1827]. Orig. bds. (HK. Nov.18-21; 893) DM 580

DESTOUCHES, Dr. Louis-Ferdinand 'Louis-Ferdinand Celine'
- Les Beaux Draps. [1941]. (220) on Lafuma, orig. Edn. 12mo. Stitched, wrap. (HD. Apr.9; 585) Frs. 2,200
- Voyage au Bout de la Nuit. Paris, Priv. ptd., 1932. 1st. Edn., 1st. Iss.; on alfa. 12mo. Sewed, wrap. Inscr., sigd. by Louis Destouches. (HD. Dec.5; 35) Frs. 16,200

D'ESTOURMEL, Comte J.
- Journal d'un Voyage en Orient. 1844. 2 vols. Some spotting. Orig. bds. (P. Jan.22; 261) *Nicholas.* £170

DE STRZELECKI, P.E.
- Physical Description of New South Wales & Van Diemen's Land. L., 1845. 1st. Edn. Sig. of William Robertson. Unc., partly unopened, recased in orig. bds., new artificial cl. backstrip. (KH. Nov.18; 205) Aus. $350

DETMOLD, Maurice & Edward
- Sixteen Illustrations of Subjects from Kipling's Jungle Book. 1903. Fo. Loose as issued in orig. cl. gt. folder, stained & worn. (SH. Mar.26; 154) *Glendale.* £320

DETOUCHE, Henry
- Les Péchés Capitaux. Ill.:- Eugene Delatre, Henry Detouche. Paris, 1900. (125) numbered on papier Velin du Marais. Fo. Lev. with lge. floral inlay on upr. cover, gt. dentelles, by Rivière, orig. cold. pict. wraps. bnd. in, worn. (SG. Sep.4; 150) $425
- Sous la Dictée de la Vie.–Les Grains du Sablier. Paris, 1906; 1908. 1st. work: (175), (20) on laid paper, numbered; 2nd. work: (175), (5) on Jap. 2 works in 2 vols. Inlaid, covers decor. with 3 butterflies in a wheat field & a fruit with leaves. Letters by Jean Dolent, H. de Regnier, Gabriel d'Annuzio, Léon Benedicte & others. (SM. Feb.11; 153) Frs. 2,200

DEUCHAR, David
- Collection of 362 engraved prints after Flemish & Dutch Masters. N.d. Fo. Mntd. in an album. Early 19th. C. str.-grd. mor. gt., leath. on upr. cover badly abrased. (C. Feb.25; 180) *King.* £420
- A Collection of Etchings ... Edinb., 1803. Lge. fo. Tear in 1 lf., not affecting etchings, reprd., some slight spotting. Cont. str.-grd. mor., spine gt.-tooled in compartments, with arabesque decors., covers with diamond lozenge & arabesque border & lge. oval arabesque centrepiece round a sceptred figure framed in gothic church entrance, rubbed. (S. Feb.9; 63) *King.* £850

DEUTSCHLAND, das Malerische u. Romantische
Leipzig, 1846-47. Vols. 3-6 in 2 vols. 19 steel engraved plts. bnd. in 2 vols., plts. new cold. & soiled. Cont. hf. linen, spine pasted. (HK. Nov.18-21; 1144) DM 1,250

DEUX JUMEAUX VOYAGEURS (Les): de l'Engin Artificiel, et Usage Voluptueux d'une Rodingotte à l'Anglaise
Palais Royal, 1791. 12mo. Mor. gt., by Niedrée. (SM. Oct.8; 2240) Frs. 2,200

DE VEGIANO, Sr. D'HOVEL
- Nobiliaire des Pays-Bas et du Comté de Bourgogne. Ed.:- Baron J.F.S.F.J.L. de Herckenrode. Gand, 1865-76. 4 vols. & 2 vols. supp. & armorial. Hf. chagrin, 5 decor spine raised bands, arms. (LM. Nov.8; 204) B.Frs. 20,000

DEVENTER, Hendrik van
- The Art of Midwifery Improved ... laying down whatever instructions are requisite to make a compleat Midwife. 1716. 1st. Engl. Edn. Tear in last plt. reprd. Cont. cf. rebkd. (S. Jun.15; 239) *Phillips.* £250

DEVEREUX, W.B.
- Views on the Shores of the Mediterranean. 1847. 1st. Edn. Lge. fo. Slight spotting. Orig. hf. roan gt. (S. Feb.9; 64) *Robinson.* £400

DEVERIA, Achille
- Le Goût Nouveau. Ill.:- Lemercier after Devéria. Paris & L., ca. 1830. 4to. In sheets, with a pt. wrap. (HD. Dec.5; 68) Frs. 7,500

DE VINNE, Theodore Low
- Title-Pages as Seen by a Printer. N.Y., Grol. Cl., 1901. (352) on Italian H.M.P. Orig. three-qtr. mor., scuffed, unc. & unopened. (SG. Mar.26; 154) $190

DE VITA ET BENESICIUS Saluatore Jesu Cristi Deuotissime Meditationes cu Gratiaruactione
[Cologne], [U. Zell], [1478]. Approximately 12cm × 9cm. 79 ll., Slight spotting. Later pol. cf. by L. Petit. (TA. Oct.16; 185) £150

DETVOTI, Fabio
- Epistola. Ill.:- F. Zucchi (plts.) & C. Orsolini (port.). Brescia(?), ca. 1752. Cont. decor. paper wraps., end-papers renewed. From the collection of John A. Saks. (C. Jun.10; 55) *Taylor.* £90

DEVRYER, Abraham
- Histori van François Eugenius. Amst., 1737. 3 vols. Cont. hf. cf. (CSK. Jan.9; 63) £50

DEVYATY VAL [Ninth Wave]
Ed.:- [A.I. Yargin]. St. Petersb., 1906. Nos. 1-2. Fo. Mod. cl.-bkd. bds. (SH. Feb.5; 59) *Landry.* £160

DEWAR, George A.B.
- Wild Life in Hampshire Highlands. Ill.:- Arthur Rackham & R.W.A. Rouse. L., 1899. 1st. Edn. Deluxe, (150) numbered on H.M.P. Haddon Hall Liby. series. Extra copy of plt. by Rouse mntd. on India-proof paper laid in. Gt.-pict. vell., spine buckled, orig. wraps. bnd. in. Raymond M. Sutton Jr. copy. (SG. May 7; 65) $260

DEWEES, William P.
- A Treatise on the Physical & Medical Treatment of Children. Phila., 1825. 1st. Edn. Some foxing & stains. New leatherette. (SG. Sep.18; 115) $180

DEWEY, D.M.
- The Specimen Book of Fruits, Flowers & Ornamental Trees. Rochester, N.Y., [1867]. 4to. Title & 90 litho. plts., browned, foxed. Orig. sheep.-bkd. decor. gt. cl., worn. As a collection of plts., w.a.f. (SPB. Jun.22; 51) $900

DE WITTE, Alphonse
- Histoire Monétaire des Comtes de Louvain, Ducs de Brabant et Marquis du Saint Empire Romain. Antw., 1894. 3 vols. in 2. Three qtr. cl. (LM. Mar.21; 224) B.Frs. 11,000

DE WOLF, Gordon
- Flora Exotica. Ill.:- Jacques Hnizdovsky. Boston, 1972. (50) De Luxe, sigd. by artist, with complete suite of hand-cold. prints, each sigd. Fo. Vell.-bkd. buck., cl. folding case. (SG. Oct.23; 161) $130

DEZALLIER D'ARGENVILLE, Antoine Joseph
[-] Abrégé de la Vie des plus Fameux Peintres ... Paris, 1745. 2 vols. 4to. Cont. marb. cf., decor. spine raised bands. (HD. Apr.24; 41) Frs. 1,150
- Conchyliogie oder Abhandlung von den Schnecken, Muscheln und andern Schaaltjieren welche in der See, in Süssen Wassern und auf dem Lande gefunden werden, nebst der Zoomorphose oder Abbildung und Beschreibung der Thiere welche die Gehäuse bewohnen. Vienna, 1772. 7o. Cont. hf. cf., gt. spine, few minor defects. (VG. Oct.13; 58) Fls. 900
- L'Histoire Naturelle Eclaircie dans deux de ses parties principales, la Lithogie et la Conchyliologie ... Paris, 1742. 1st. Edn. 4to. Cont. mott. cf. (PNY. Oct.1; 174) $375
- L'Histoire Naturelle eclaircie dans une de ses Parties Principales, la Conchyliologie ... augmentée de la Zoomorphose. Ill.:- Chedel after Boucher. Paris, 1757. New Edn. 2 pts. in 1 vol. 4to. Cont. leath., gt. (D. Dec.11-13; 288) DM 2,200
- La Théorie, et la Pratique du Jardinage. The Hague, 1739. 3rd. Edn. 4to. Edges of text ll. darkened, plt. El with sm. paper flaw. Hf. mor., upr. jnt. cracked. (CNY. Oct.1; 5) $420
- - Anr. Edn. Paris, 1747. 4th. Edn. 4to. 1 plt. slightly torn in fold, a few ll. slightly spotted, title slightly soiled. Cont. cf., slightly worn. (S. Apr.7; 252) *Weinreb.* £180
[-] The Theory & Practice of Gardening. Trans.:- John James. 1712. 4to. Licence lf. before title loosening. Cont. cf., central panels with fleurons, worn, both covers detchd. (LC. Feb.12; 621) £150

DIABLE a Paris (Le)
Ill.:- Grandville, Bertall, Cham, Gavarni. Paris, 1868-69. 4 vols. Cont. hf. chagrin, decor. spines, fillets on covers, gt. heads, unc. (HD. Apr.9; 590) Frs. 1,800
- Paris et les Parisiens. Ill.:- Gavarni, Bertall, etc. Paris, 1845-46. 2 vols. Publisher's cl. bds., tooled. (HD. Apr.9; 589) Frs. 2,200

DIALOGUE between an Old Prodigal new sworn Constable & his young Noisy Wife
Ca. 1710. Fo. 2 pp., woodcut ill., stained. (S. Oct.17; 4) £130

DIALOGUE CONCERNING THE STRIFE OF OUR CHURCHE (A)
1584. Margins & corners of 1st. & last 3 ll. reprd., tear in corner of K3 affecting a few letters, reprd. Mor. gt. by C. Lewis. [STC 6801] (C. Apr.1; 202) *Lawson.* £150

DIALOGUS Creaturarum Moralisatus
Antw., Gerard Leeu, Apr.11, 1491. 4to. The woodcut of Dialogus CXX omitted with blank on fo. 87r, final lf. remargined with sm. portion of 5 lines in facs., some staining thro.-out, early pen &

DIALOGUS Creaturarum Moralisatus -contd.
ink inscr. on title-p., ink annots. & sketches on some pp., some cut away by binder, others affecting mostly blank portions, but 11 touching woodcuts. Mod. mor., spine gt.-lettered. British Liby. dupl. with stps. on fo. 2, the copy of Boies Penrose, lately in the collection of Eric Sexton. [BMC IX, 195, Goff N156, HC 6130] (CNY. Apr.8; 9) $9,500

DIARIVM, VOLLSTANDIGES, Von der Höchst-erfreuliches Crönung des . . . Herrn Franciscus etc.
Frankfurt, 1746. Pt. II. Sm. fo. Lacks 2 folding copperplts., & 1 lf. at end, 1 copper engr. browned, engraved ex libris inside cover. Cont. hf. leath., spine lightly defect., worn. (H. Dec.9/10; 758) DM 1,300

DIAZ, José Domingo
[–] **Recuerdos sobre la Rebelion de Caracas.** Madrid, 1829. Sm. 4to. Some discolouration, several ll. with text underlined in red. Later mor., slightly worn. (SPB. May 5; 182) $2,200

DIAZ, Sebastian
– **Noticia General de las Cosas del Mundo por el Orden de su Colocacion.** Lima, [1783]. Sm. 4to. Final lf. of errata with hole affecting letters. Cont. limp vell. (SPB. May 5; 183) $125

DIAZ del Castillo, Bernal
– **The Discovery & Conquest of America.** Ed.:– Harry Block. Trans.:– A.P. Maudsley. Ill.:– Miguel Covarrubias. N.Y., Ltd. Edns. Cl., 1942. (1500) numbered, & sigd. by Ed., artist & printer. Fo. Mott. cf. (SG. Apr.2; 80) $160
– **The Discovery & Conquest of Mexico.** Ed.:– Benaro Garcia. Trans.:– A.P. Maudslay. Ill.:– Miguel Covarrubias. Ltd. Edns. Cl., 1942. (1500) numbered, & sigd. by ed., artist, & printer. Fo. Mott. cf., orig. box (worn). (SG. Jan.15; 158) $160
– **Historia Verdadera de la Conquista de la Nueva España.** Madrid, 1632. Fo. Marginal wormholes affecting some letters, dampstain at end, sm. holes & repairs to title. Later cf. (SPB. May 5; 184) $2,200
– – **Anr. Edn.** Ill.:– I. de Courbes (engraved title). Madrid, ca. 1632. Fo. Browned & stained, final lf. badly stained & fragile, previous lf. with corners reprd. 18th. C. cf. (SPB. May 5; 185) $3,000

DIBDIN, Charles
– **Observations on a Tour through . . . England.** [1801-02]. 1st. Edn. 2 vols. Mod. hf. cf. (SG. Feb.26; 109) $110

DIBDIN, Rev. Thomas Frognall
– **Aedes Althorpianae.** 1822. 1st. Edn. 2 vols. (including Supp. to the Bibliotheca Spenceriana). Some offsetting onto text, slight spotting. Cont. pol. cf., gt., arms of Francis Darby on covers, by Lewis. (S. Feb.9; 65) Traylen. £160
– – **Anr. Copy.** Some offsetting onto text. Cont. russ., rebkd. (S. Oct.21; 498) Archdale. £95
– – **Anr. Copy.** 4to. Lacks list of ills., heavy offsetting from plts. onto text. Russ., gt. floral borders & spines. (SG. Mar.26; 158) $300
– **A Bibliographical, Antiquarian & Picturesque Tour in France & Germany.** 1821. 1st. Edn. 3 vols. in 4. Engraved plts., text ills., some additional plts. inserted, lacks hf.-titles. Cont. mor., gt. L.P. (S. Nov.24; 102) Dawson. £280
– – **Anr. Copy.** 3 vols. Some foxing & browning. Mod. qtr. leath., unc. (S. Jul.27; 169) Schuster. £230
– – **Anr. Copy.** Engraved plts. spotted & offset. Cont. cf., recased, spines preserved. (SKC. May 19; 486) £130
– – **Anr. Copy.** Panel. cf. gt. (BS. Jun.11; 154) £90
– – **Anr. Copy.** 3 pts. & supp. in 3 vols. Slightly soiled in parts. Cont. leath., gt. spine, cover inner & outer dentelle. W.a.f. (HK. Nov.18-21; 1145) DM 1,100
– – **Anr. Copy.** 3 vols. Mostly soiled in vol. 1 pt. 1, some wormholes. Cont. hf. linen. (R. Mar.31-Apr.4; 1830) DM 900
– **A Bibliographical, Antiquarian & Picturesque Tour in the Northern Counties of England.** 1837. 1st. Edn. 2 vols. Later hf. mor. (C. Jul.22; 113) Forster. £100
– **A Bibliographical, Antiquarian & Picturesque Tour in the Northern Counties of England & in Scotland.** 1838. 1st. Edn., L.P. 2 vols. 44 plts., 1 unlisted, text ills. Late 19th. C. mor., gt. (S. Nov.24; 105) Dawson. £220

– – **Anr. Edn.** 1838. 2 vols. 1 additional plt. of Glasgow cemetry, slight spotting. Cont. cf. (CSK. Feb.6; 41) £75
– **The Bibliographical Decameron.** 1817. 1st. Edn. 3 vols. Late 19th. C. mor., by F. Bedford, gt. (S. Nov.24; 101) Porter. £420
– – **Anr. Copy.** Cont. catspaw cf., rebkd. with gt. spines. (C. Jul.22; 114) Traylen. £220
– – **Anr. Copy.** Errata ll. at end of vol. II & III, some spotting. Late 19th. C. russ., jnts. a little worn. (S. Oct.21; 497) Quaritch. £130
– – **Anr. Copy.** Some spotting & discolouration. Cont. russ., Signet arms on sides, rebkd. (S. Jul.27; 168) Thorp. £70
– **The Bibliomania: or Book-Madness.** L., 1809. 1st. Edn. Orig. bds., lacks spine, unc. (PNY. Oct.1; 175) $180
– – **Anr. Edn.** 1811. 2 vols. in 1. 1 engraved plt. spotted & offset. Cf., spine gt., by Clarke & Bedford. With an A.L.s. loosely inserted. (SKC. May 19; 484) $95
– – **Anr. Edn.** 1842. 3rd. Edn., L.P. 2 pts. in 1 vol. Late 19th. C. mor. by F. Bedford, gt. (S. Nov.24; 106) Dawson. £180
– – **Anr. Copy.** Wide margins. Maroon three-qtr. mor. by Sotheran. (SG. Mar.26; 161) $250
– **Bibliomania.–The Library Companion, for Harding, Triphook, & Lepard.–Reminiscences of a Literary Life.** L., Priv. Ptd. [1st work], 1811; 1824; 1836. 1st. Edns. 1 vol.; 1 vol.; 2 vols. With ll. browned & 2 detchd. in 2nd. work. Hf. mor. gt., partly unc., by Hersant (1st. work); hf. cf., inner jnt. brkn. (2nd. work); & hf. mor. gt. From the Prescott Collection. (CNY. Feb.6; 344) $160
– **Bibliotheca Spenceriana.** 1814-15. 4 vols. 4to. Woodcut facs. ills. in text, slight spotting. Orig. bds., spine of vol. I very worn, unc. L.P. (S. Oct.21; 499) Kew Books. £200
– – **Anr. Copy.** Orig. bds., unc., vol. 1 spine very worn, vol. 2 upr. jnt. split, worn. (S. Mar.16; 190) Fletcher. £160
– – **Anr. Edn.** Shakespeare Pr., 1814/15, Supps. 1822/23. 4 vols., 3 vols. Supps. Dampstaining. Mor. gt., by Edmund Worrall, Birmingham. (TA. Sep.18; 31) £340
– – **Anr. Edn.** L., Priv. Ptd., 1814-18. 4 vols. 4to. Some browning & offsetting, owner's sig. on hf.-title. Later three-qtr. mor., slightly worn. Bkplts. of Ketterlinus, J.C. de Rosshall, & C.W. Burr. (SG. Mar.26; 157) $700
– – **Anr. Edn.** 1814-32. 1st. Edn. 7 vols. in 6. 4to. Some foxing & offsetting, no hf.-titles. 19th. C. purple hf. mor., gt., partly unc. (S. Nov.24; 100) Maggs. £270
– **An Introduction to the Knowledge of Rare & Valuable Editions of the Greek & Latin Classics.** 1827. 4th. Edn. 2 vols. Late 19th. C. mor. by F. Bedford, gt. L.P. (S. Nov.24; 104) Crete. £400
– – **Anr. Copy.** Cont. cf., gt. decor. spines. (TA. Sep.18; 35) £52
– – **Anr. Copy.** Old cf. gt. The John A. Saks copy. (CNY. Oct.1; 172) $140
– **The Library Companion.** 1824. 1st. Edn. Cont. cf., rebkd. (SH. Jun.11; 53) Thorp. £55
– – **Anr. Edn.** 1825. 2nd. Edn., L.P. 2 vols. in 1. Late 19th. C. mor., by F. Bedford, gt. (S. Nov.24; 103) Traylen. £110
– **Reminiscences of a Literary Life.** 1836. 2 vols. Mor. gt. by Rivière. (C. Jul.22; 115) Chelsea Rare Books. £130
– – **Anr. Copy.** Cont. cf., gt. (SH. Oct.10; 437) Forster. £85
– – **Anr. Copy.** Maroon three-qtr. mor., spines gt. (SG. Mar.26; 159) $240
– **The Sunday Library.** L., 1831. 1st. Edn. 6 vols. 16mo. Some foxing. Orig. cl., slightly worn, unc. & unopened. (SG. Dec.18; 156) $210
– **Venetian Printers.** [N.Y.], [1924]. (223). Fo. Orig. bdg. (SG. Mar.26; 162) $150

DICCIONARIO Castellano-Quichua
See–MOSSI, Honorio–ANON

DICCIONARIO Quichua-Castllano y Castellano-Quichua
See–MOSSI, Honorio–ANON

DICKENS, Charles
– **American Notes . . .** 1842. 1st. Edn., 1st. Iss. 2 vols. With verso of contents list numbered xvi, advt. lf. at beginning of vol., & 3 ll. of advts. at end of vol. 2. Orig. cl. by Leighton & Eeles, with their ticket, slightly rubbed & faded. [Sabin 19996] (S. Feb.9; 67) Jarndyce. £100

– – **Anr. Copy.** 12mo. 6 pp. of advts. at end of vol. 2. Publisher's blind-stpd. cl., unc., shelf worn. (SG. Aug.21; 87) $140
– **American Notes.–David Copperfield.–Little Dorrit.** L., 1842; 1850; 1857. 1st. Edns. 2 vols.; 1 vol.; 2 vols. 1st. work: minor browning; 2nd. work: spotting, browning; 3rd. work: bnd. from the pts., lacks 'white slip', foxing. 1st. work: orig. cl., spine faded; 2nd. work: hf. cf.; 3rd. work: hf. cf. (SPB. May 29; 115) $225
– **Bleak House.** Ill.:– Phiz. 1852-53. 1st. Edn., 1st. Iss. 20 orig. monthly pts. in 19. Most plts. slightly stained, advts., slips, including 'The Village Pastor' in pt. 15. Orig. ptd. wraps., 3 detchd., 1 lacks 1 sm. pt. As a periodical, w.a.f. (C. Feb.4; 126) Woolley. £260
– – **Anr. Copy.** Plts. spotted & browned, some dampstained, advts. & slips. Torn & soiled, some rebkd., 1 loose. (SH. Jan.30; 325) Wrigley. £100
– – **Anr. Edn.** Ill.:– H.K. Browne. L., Mar. 1852-Sep. 1853. 1st. Edn. Orig. 20 pts. in 19. Many plts. foxed. Pict. wraps., unc., hf. lev. solander s.-c. worn. (SG. May 14; 57) $650
– – **Anr. Copy.** 'Bleak House Advertiser' in each pt. & other inserted advts., no. 9 with inserted plt. cancellation slip. Orig. pict. wraps., cl. case, mor. spine gt. W.a.f. (CNY. May 22; 86) $500
– – **Anr. Copy.** Bleak House Advertiser in each pt., & other inserted advts. Orig. pict. ptd. wraps., covers slightly reprd., spines reprd., cl. case. From the Prescott Collection. (CNY. Feb.6; 82) $300
– – **Anr. Edn.** Ill.:– H.K. Browne. L., 1853. 1st. Edn. Bnd. from the pts. Pol. cf., triple gt. fillet borders, spine gt., gt. dentelles, wraps. of pt. 17 bnd. in, by Sangorski & Sutcliffe. (SG. Nov.13; 132) $210
– **Bleak House.–The Mystery of Edwin Drood.** L., 1852-53; 1870. 1st. Edn. in pts. 2 works in orig. 19/20 pts. & 6 pts. Foxing & spotting, some tears, many of inserted advts., with ptd. slip in Pt. IX of 1st. work, lacks 'cork' slip from 2nd. Orig. ptd. wraps., many covers detchd., a few lacking, soiling, tears. (SPB. Nov.25; 193) $375
– **The Chimes.** Ed.:– Edward Wagenknecht. Ill.:– Arthur Rackham. N.Y., Ltd. Edns. Cl., 1931. (1,500) numbered, sigd. by artist. 4to. Pict. cl., gt. stpd., pict. box. Raymond M. Sutton Jr. copy. (SG. May 7; 67) $425
– – **Anr. Copy.** Pict. buckram, boxed. (SG. Apr.2; 252) $200
– **[Christmas Books].** L., 1843-48. 1st. Edns., vol. 2 1st. Iss., vol. 4 2nd. Iss. 5 vols. 12mo. With advts. in 1st., 3rd., & 5th. works. Orig. cl. gt., 1st. vol. loose, slight loss of gt. on upr. cover of vol. 3, covers of vols. 4 & 5 slightly soiled, qtr. mor. gt. s.-c. From the Prescott Collection. (CNY. Feb.6; 80) $1,700
– – **Anr. Edn.** L., 1843-48. 1st. Edns., various issues. 5 vols. Unif. bnd. in str.-grd. red mor., spines gt., gt. dentelles, by Rivière. (SG. May 14; 58) $850
– **A Christmas Carol.** Ill.:– John Leech. 1843. 1st. Edn. 1st. Iss. Blue hf.-title 'Stave I', uncorrected text. Orig. cl., gt., slightly stained, green end-papers. (C. Feb.4; 127) Basket/Day. £200
– – **Anr. Copy.** Some slight foxing & soiling. (CE. Jul.9; 98) £160
– – **Anr. Copy.** 12mo. Red mor. gt. folding case, silk lining, for C.J. Sawyer. Ltd. Pres. Copy, to Burdett Coutts, & her sig. on front endpaper, lately in the Prescott Collection. (CNY. Feb.6; 79) $9,500
– – **Anr. Copy.** Orig. gt.-floral cl., green endpapers. (PNY. Mar.26; 94) $1,600
– – **Anr. Edn.** Ill.:– John Leech. 1843. 1st. Edn., 3rd. Iss. With 'Stave One' & appropriate iss.-points by Eckel, slight offsetting in text, some spots, advt. lf. Orig. cl., gt. design on upr. cover & spine, slightly faded. (S. Feb.10; 436) Jarndyce. £320
– – **Anr. Edn.** Ill.:– John Leech. Phila. 1844. 1st. Amer. Edn. 12mo. Early Hudson family inscrs. Plattsburgh, N.Y. at upr. blanks. Orig. gt.-floral & blind-decor. cl., slightly warped & spotted. (PNY. Dec.3; 105) $160
– – **Anr. Edn.** Ill.:– Arthur Rackham. 1915. (525) numbered, sigd. by artist. 4to. Orig. vell., gt., soiled, lacks ties. (SH. Jun.4; 147) Mirdan. £190
– – **Anr. Copy.** Pres. copy. (CSK. Sep.12; 85) £115
– – **Anr. Copy.** Gt.-decor. vell., orig. silk ties. Raymond M. Sutton Jr. copy. (SG. May 7; 68) $1,050
– – **Anr. Edn.** Ill.:– Arthur Rackham. Phila., [1915]. 1st. Amer. Trade Edn. Sm. 4to. Owner's

writing on end-paper, Xmas card inserted into hf.-title. Gt.-pict. cl., d.-w. Raymond M. Sutton Jr. copy. (SG. May 7; 69) $120

– **A Christmas Carol.–The Haunted Man.–The Battle of Life.–Cricket on the Hearth.** L., 1843; 1846; 1846; 1848. 1st. Edns. 4 works in 4 vols. 1st. work with the reading 'Stave I' on p. 1, foxing & staining to 1st. work, slight browning to last 3 works. 1st. work in orig. cl. (recased & reprd.), rest in unif. red mor., gt., end-paper & following blank cracked or detchd. in 2 vols. (SPB. May 29; 116) $350

– **Christmas Carol.–Haunted Man.–Battle of Life. –Cricket on the Hearth.–The Chimes.** L., 1843; 1848; 1846; 1846; 1845. 1st. Edns., 3rd. work: 2nd. Iss. 5 vols. Advts. present only in 1st. vol., 1st. work with 'Stave One', 3rd. work with 'A Love Story' in banner. Cf. gt. by Bayntun, orig. cl. of 1st. title bnd. in. (SPB. Nov.25; 198) $750

– – **Anr. Edn.** All L., 1843; 1848; 1846; 1846; 1845. 1st. Edns.; 3rd. work: 4th. Iss. 5 vols. Advts., some foxing, 5th work with publisher's imprint on vig. ptd. below ill., 1st. work with 'Stave I', 3rd. work with 'A Love Story'. Orig. cl., slightly worn, stains. (SPB. Nov.25; 196) $700

– **A Christmas Carol in Prose.** Leipzig, 1843. 1st. Continental Edn. Square 16mo. Old hf. leath. (SG. Apr.30; 110) $250

– **The Cricket on the Hearth.** L., 1846. 1st. Edn. 12mo. 1 lf. with sm. stain at inner margin, slightly affecting preceding lf. Orig. gt.-pict. cl. Sig. of Helen Fawcit, & a later MS. note concerning her. (PNY. May 21; 171) $150

– – **Anr. Edn.** Ill.:– Hugh Thomson. Ltd. Edns. Cl., 1933. (1,500) numbered. Lge. 4to. Orig. cl., unc., s.-c. (SH. Mar.27; 519) *Vincent.* £50

– **A Curious Dance Round a Curious Tree.** [1860]. 1st. Edn., 2nd. Iss. Sm. wormhole slightly affecting text. Orig. wraps., cl. folder. (S. Feb.9; 71) *Rota.* £140

– **David Copperfield.** Ill.:– H.K. Browne. L., 1849-50. 1st. Edn. 19/20 orig. pts. With most advts. & slips as listed by Hatton & Cleaver. Orig. wraps., rebkd., fore-edges of 2 pts. slightly reprd., mor.-bkd. s.-c. Stockhausen copy. (SPB. Nov.25; 185) $3,700

– – **Anr. Copy.** 40 etched plts., some foxed, with all inserted advts., but 'Lett's Diaries' in pt. 8 incompl. Orig. pict. wraps., 6 pts. rebkd., month erased from pts. 8 & 9 upr. covers, some pts. with ruled border & few letters in the month supplied by hand, cl. folding case. W.a.f. (CNY. May 22; 85) $1,000

– – **Anr. Edn.** Ill.:– H.K. Browne. L., 1850. 1st. Edn. Some foxing. Mod. hf. cf. (SG. Mar.19; 75) $110

– **David Copperfield.–Nicholas Nickleby. –Pickwick Papers.** All L., 1850; 1839; 1837. 1st. Edns. in book form. 3 vols. Foxed, some stains, 3rd. work without 'Buss' plts. Various bdgs., worn. (SPB. Nov.25; 199) $275

– **Dombey & Son.** Ill.:– H.K. Browne. L., Oct. 1846-Apr. 1848. 1st. Edn. 20 orig. pts. in 19. Last line on p. 324, no. 11 with the reading 'Capatin', line 9 on p. 426, no. 14 with the 1st. word 'if', errata slip in no. 5, some staining in pt. 6, light soiling elsewhere, Dombey & Son Advertiser in each pt., & other inserted advts. Orig. pict. ptd. wraps., rebkd., cl. case. Bkplt. of Jerome Kern, lately in the Prescott Collection. (CNY. Feb.6; 81) $750

– – **Anr. Copy.** 'Dombey & Son Advertiser' in each pt., & other advts. Orig. pict. wraps., unc., 1st. & last numbers rebkd., some other spines reprd., cl. s.-c. (SG. May 14; 60) $500

– – **Anr. Copy.** Pt. 11, p. 324 with 'Capatin', pt. 14, p. 426 line 9 without 'if'. Rebkd., lr. wrap. pt. 12 detchd., long tear to pt. 2 upr. wrap. W.a.f. (CNY. May 22; 84) $250

– **Great Expectations.** 1861. 1st. Edn. 3 vols. Orig. cl., worn. (SH. Jul.16; 53) *Taylor.* £140

– – **Anr. Copy.** Some slight spotting, without inserted advts. at end of vol. 3. (S. Feb.9; 72) *Thorp.* £100

– – **Anr. Copy.** 1st. free endpaper, title & dedication lf. loose, 32 pp. of inserted advts. (dtd. May, 1861) at end of vol. 3. Orig. blind-stpd. cl., spines gt.-lettered, corners slightly worn, mor. gt. solander case. From the Prescott Collection. (CNY. Feb.6; 84) $3,200

– – **Anr. Copy.** Publisher's advts. dtd. May 1861 at end of Vol. II, slight soiling. Orig. cl., shaken, some spotting. Pres. slip laid in 'To John Scott Russell from Charles Dickens' dtd. Thursday 4th. Sep. 1861. (SPB. Nov.25; 189) $750

– **Hard Times.** 1854. 1st. Edn. Orig. cl. (SH. Mar.5; 220) *Jarndyce.* £50

– – **Anr. Copy.** Mor., spine gt., by Zaehnsdorf. Autograph inscr. written at top of a 4 p. sheet of stationary tipped in. (SG. Mar.19; 77) $325

– **Little Dorrit.** Ill.:– Phiz. 1855-57. 1st. Edn., 1st. Iss. Orig. 20 monthly pts. in 19. Advts., slips, pt. 15 with 'Rigaud'. Orig. ptd. wraps., in cl. boxes. As a periodical, w.a.f. (C. Feb.4; 275) *Wooley.* £200

– – **Anr. Copy.** Author's correction slip at p. 481, spotted. Rebkd., some soiled. (CSK. Jun.26; 78) £70

– – **Anr. Copy.** Pt. 15 with 'Rigaud', pt. 16 with errata slip, 'Little Dorrit Advertiser' in each pt. & all but one of other inserted advts. Orig. pict. wraps., pts. 15-19/20 unopened, mor. gt. W.a.f. (CNY. May 22; 88) $1,100

– – **Anr. Copy.** With most of inserted advts. & correction slip at p. 481. Covers of 1st. pt. detchd., few stains on wraps. (SPB. Nov.25; 187) $375

– – **Anr. Edn.** Ill.:– H.K. Browne. L., Dec. 1855-Jun. 1857. 1st. Edn. 20 orig. pts. in 19. Errata slip in pt. 16, all plts. heavily browned, the 'Little Dorrit Advertiser' & other advertising material in each pt. Pict. wraps., some spines frayed, cl. folding case. (SG. Mar.19; 78) $240

– – **Anr. Copy.** Some browning, with most of the advts. called for by Hatton & Cleaver. Orig. wraps., some stains & repairs, soiled, mor.-bkd. s.-c. (SPB. May 29; 112) $275

– **Martin Chuzzlewit.** Ill.:– H.K. Browne. L., Jan. 1843-Jul. 1844. 1st. Edn., Early Iss. Orig. 20 Pts. in 19. 100£ reading on title, 'Chuzzlewit Advertiser' in each pt. & other advts. Pict. wraps., unc., worn, spines reprd., solander s.-c. brkn. (SG. May 14; 59) $475

– **Martin Chuzzlewit.–Edwin Drood.** Ill.:– H.K. Browne; S.L. Fildes. L., 1844; 1870. 1st. Edns. 1st. work: hf.-title & errata lf., engraved title in 2nd. iss., '£' mark properly placed; 2nd. work: 34 pp. of advts. at end. Orig. cl., recased. (SG. Nov.13; 136) $125

– **Master Humphrey's Clock.** 1840-41. 1st. Edn. 88 Orig. Pts. Orig. wraps., some torn, cl. case. (SH. Jul.16; 55) *Sotheran.* £280

– – **Anr. Edn.** Ill.:– George Cattermole & Hablot K. Browne. L., 1840-41. 1st. Edn. 20 orig. pts. Lacks 2 inserted advts. & with one not called for. Orig. pict. wraps., upr. cover pt. 1 detchd., cl. s.-c. W.a.f. (CNY. May 22; 83) $350

– – **Anr. Edn.** L., 1840-41. 1st. Edn. 3 vols., bnd. from the pts. Slight foxing. Mor. gt., orig. wraps. bnd. at end of each vol. A.L.s. by Lord George Gordon laid in vol. III. (SPB. May 29; 111) $200

– **Master Humphrey's Clock.–American Notes. –Martin Chuzzlewit.–Dombey & Son.–David Copperfield.–Little Dorrit.–Our Mutual Friends.** 1840-41; 1842; 1844; 1848; 1850; 1857; 1865. All 1st. Edns. 2nd. work later iss., ditto 3rd. 1st. work 3 vols. in 2; 2nd. work 2 vols.; last work 2 vols. in 1. 3rd. & 6th. works spotted. Mod. hf. mor.; mod. hf. cf.; cont. hf. cf., rebkd. cont. hf. cf., rebkd.; cont. hf. cf., rebkd.; cont. hf. cf.; cont. hf. cf., rebkd. (SH. Mar.5; 221) *Aiken.* £105

– **Master Humphrey's Clock.–Hard Times. –American Notes.–The Pic Nic Papers.** All L., 1840; 1854; 1842; 1841. 1st. & 1st. Edns. in book form, 3rd. work; 1st. Iss. 1st. work: 3 vols., bnd. from pts., 3rd. work: 2 vols., 4th. work: 3 vols. Various sizes. Some foxing & browning, frontis. & title of 1st. work marred with partially erased crayon marks. Orig. cl., slight shaking. (SPB. Nov.25; 195) $500

[–] **Memoirs of Joseph Grimaldi.** Ill.:– Cruikshank. 1838. 1st. Edn., 1st. Iss. 2 vols. Lacks hf.-title & advts. at end, occasional browning. 19th. C. mor. gt., spines slightly faded. (S. Jul.27; 96) *Scott.* £140

[–] – **Anr. Edn.** Ill.– George Cruikshank. 1838. 1st. Edn. 2 vols. 1 frontis. detchd., plts. slightly spotted. Orig. embossed cl. (C. Feb.4; 128) *Midgley.* £120

[–] – **Anr. Copy.** 2 vols. Engraved port.-frontis., 12 etched plts., last plt. in vol. 2 in 1st. state, without grotesque border, vol. 1 lacks plt. list. Cont. str.-grd. mor. by Rivière, spines gt. Bkplt. of Thomas Faisford. (S. Nov.24; 79) *Traylen.* £95

– **Mystery of Edwin Drood.** 1870. 1st. Edn., 1st. iss. In 6 orig. pts. Some ll. spotted, advts. Orig. wraps., rebkd., soiled & torn, 1 wrap. reprd., in cl. box. (SH. Jan.30; 327) *Wrigley.* £70

– – **Anr. Edn.** L., 1870. 1st. Edn. Orig. 6 pts. With most of inserted advts. & 'Cork Hat' slip in pt. II. Orig. ptd. wraps., some covers detchd., spines worn, some soiling. (SPB. Nov.25; 191) $250

– – **Anr. Copy.** 'Edwin Drood Advertiser' in each pt. & other advts., lacks 1st. lf. of 'Advertiser' in Pt. 3. Pict. wraps., unc. (SG. May 14; 62) $225

– – **Anr. Copy.** The 'Edwin Drood Advertiser' in pts. 4 & 5. Worn, last wrap. torn & loose, unc. & unopened. (SG. Mar.19; 80) $150

– **Nicholas Nickleby.** Ill.:– H.K. Browne. L., Apr. 1838-Oct. 1839. 1st. Edn. Orig. 20 pts. in 19. 'Nickleby Advertiser' in each pt. & other advts., 'visiter' on p. 123, some foxing. Pict. wraps., unc., 2 red lev. solander s.-c.'s. (SG. May 14; 61) $850

– – **Anr. Copy.** Pt. 5, p. 160 with 'latter', 'Nicholas Nickleby Advertiser' in each pt. & other inserted advts., many plts. browned. Orig. pict. wraps., few spines worn, hf. mor. solander case. W.a.f. (CNY. May 22; 82) $400

– **Nicholas Nickleby.–Martin Chuzzlewit. –Dombey & Son.–Bleak House.** Ill.:– H.K. Browne. L., 1839; 1844; 1848; 1853. 1st. Edns. in Book Form. 4 works in 4 vols. Orig. cl., worn & loose. (SG. Nov.13; 135) $190

– **Nicholas Nickleby.–Our Mutual Friend.** L., 1838-39, 1864-65. 1st. Edns. 2 works in orig. 19/20 pts. Some foxing, spotting, many inserted advts., 2 copies of Pt. I of 1st. work, the 1st. without advts., 2nd. with advts., but lacks wraps., 'latter' in Pt. V of Nicholas in orig. state, 'visiter' in Pt. IV in corrected state, lacks 'Foreign Banknotes' slip in 2nd. work. Orig. ptd. wraps., lacks several covers, some detchd., some staining, some repairs. (SPB. Nov.25; 192) $300

– **Oliver Twist.** 1838. 1st. Edn., 1st. Iss. 3 vols. Lacks hf.-titles. Cont. hf. cf., rebkd. (SH. Jul.16; 57) *Scott.* £120

– – **Anr. Edn.** Ill.:– George Cruikshank. L., 1838. 1st. Edn., 2nd. Iss. 3 vols. With the 'Rose Maylie & Oliver' plt. in vol. 3, & the plt.-list after the title-p. in vol. 1, 4 pp. of advts. at end of vol. 1. Orig. maroon blind-stpd. cl., spines gt.-lettered, red mor. gt.-lettered s.-c.'s. From the Prescott Collection. (CNY. Feb.6; 78) $1,100

– – **Anr. Copy.** Some foxing & spotting. Orig. cl., spines worn. (SPB. Nov.25; 184) $275

– – **Anr. Edn.** Ill.:– George Cruikshank. 1838. 1st. Edn., 3rd. Iss. 3 vols. Some dampstaining & spotting, 6 pp. advts. Orig. cl., unc. (SKC. Jul.28; 2348) £70

– – **Anr. Edn.** Ill.:– George Cruikshank. 1838. 1st. Edn. 3 vols. Iss. with shortened title, with author's real name & 'Fireside' plt. cancelled, lacks hf.-titles in vols. 1 & 2 & advts. in vols. 1 & 3. Cont. hf. mor., spines gt. Bkplt. of Thomas Gaisford. (S. Nov.24; 80) *Vassilopoulos.* £240

– – **Anr. Edn.** L., 1838. 3 vols. Foxed. Red mod. hf. mor. (SPB May 29; 110) $175

– – **Anr. Edn.** Ill.:– George Cruikshank. L., Priv. Ptd., 1846. New Edn. Each plt. with hand-cold. dupl. Cf., triple gt. fillet borders, spine gt., by Morrell. (SG. Mar.19; 62) $190

– **Our Mutual Friend.** Ill.:– Marcus Stone. 1864-65. [1st. Edn.?]. 20 orig. pts. Advts. to pts. 1-10, some spotting. 1st. 10 pts. in orig. ptd. wraps., rest in plain wraps. (TA. Mar.19; 482) £75

– – **Anr. Copy.** 20 orig. pts. in 19. Each pt. with 'Our Mutual Friend Advertiser' & many other advts., but without the 'Economic Life Assurance' advts., title slip tipped-in. Pict. wraps., buckram folding case, unc. & mostly unopened. (SG. Dec.18; 159) $750

– – **Anr. Copy.** 20 pts. in 19. 'Our Mutual Friend Advertiser' in each pt. & other advts. Orig. pict. wraps., rebkd., some worn or reprd., folding cl. case. W.a.f. (CNY. May 22; 90) $450

– – **Anr. Copy.** Some foxing, tears, with most inserted advts. & slip 'Foreign Banknotes' in Pt. 19/20, & the slip to Reader in Pt. 1. Orig. ptd. wraps., a few covers detchd., soiling, tears. (SPB. Nov.25; 190) $300

– – **Anr. Edn.** L., 1865. 1st. Edn. in book form. 2 vols. Foxed, minor defects. Orig. cl. (SPB. Jul.31; 112) $125

– **The Posthumous Papers of the Pickwick Club.** 1836-37. 1st. Edn. 20 in 19 orig. pts., & variant of pt. 1. Lacks advts. Orig. wraps., torn & soiled, a few reprd., in mor.-bkd. cl. box. (SH. Jan.30; 332) *Subunso.* £260

– – **Anr. Copy.** 20 in 19 orig. pts. Advts. Last pt. loose, in cl. s.-c. (SH. Jan.30; 331) *Quaritch.* £200

– – **Anr. Copy.** Foxing, browning, lacks most advts. Repairs. (SPB. May 29; 107) $550

DICKENS, Charles -*contd.*

– – **Anr. Edn.** L., 1837. 1st. Edn. in Book Form. Iss. with 'Veller' title, slight discolouration. Elab. lev. mor. gt. with miniature port. of a young Dickens inlaid in upr. mor. doubl. (SPB. Nov.25; 138) $1,500

– – **Anr. Copy.** Lev. gt., gt. dentelles, red lev. doubls., upr. doubl. enclosing port. painted on ivory, under glass, rehinged, worn. (SG. Oct.9; 79) $150

– – **Anr. Copy.** Early iss., with the 'Veller' reading on engraved title & the 2 Buss plts. (other plts. in various states), some foxing & staining. Mod. hf. cf. (SG. Mar.19; 71) $100

– – **Anr. Edn.** L., 1838. 2 vols. With the 'Veller' title, foxing, tears, extra-ill. with plts. Mor. gt. Envelope sigd. by Dickens tipped in. (SPB. May 29; 109) $350

– – **Anr. Edn.** Ed.:– J.H. Stonehouse. L., 1931-32. 20 pts. Orig. wraps. in box, unc., some tears in wraps. (H. Dec.9/10; 1797) DM 450

– – **Anr. Edn.** N.d. (8) on vell., numbered. 2 vols. Cont. mor., gt., mor. doubles. (SH. Mar.5; 223) *Jarndyce.* £165

– **Pickwick Papers.–David Copperfield.–Bleak House.–Little Dorrit.–Our Mutual Friend.** 1837; 1850; 1853; 1857; 1876. 1st. work later iss., all but last 1st. Edns. Spotted, 4th. work lacks hf.-title. Orig. cl., cont. hf. cf., gt. spine; cont. hf. cf.; cont. hf. mor.; cont. hf. cf. (SH. Jan.30; 333) *Jarndyce.* £140

– **Pickwick Papers.–Nicholas Nickleby.–David Copperfield.–Bleak House.–Little Dorrit.** Ill.:– H.K. Browne & others. L., 1837-57. 1st. Edns. 5 works in 5 vols. Plts. to 1st. work heavily discold. 1st. work cl., rest hf. leath., all bdgs. brkn. (SG. Nov.13; 134) $150

– **Pictures from Italy.–David Copperfield.–Little Dorrit.–Bleak House.–Nicholas Nickleby. –Pickwick Papers.–Dombey & Son.–Martin Chuzzlewit.** L., 1850; 1846; 1857; 1853; 1838; 1837; 1848; 1844. 1st. Edns. & 1st. Edns. in book form. 8 vols. Foxing, some stains, 3rd. work: lacks errata slip, 6th. work: bnd. from pts. with 2 suppressed Buss Plts., 8th. work: with vig. plt. corrected, hf.-titles lacking in 6th. & 3rd. works. Orig. cl., shaken. (SPB. Nov.25; 201) $1,400

– **The Short Stories.** Ed.:– Walter Allen. Ill.:– Edward Ardizone. 1971. (1,500) numbered. 4to. Orig. paper bds., s.-c. Sigd. by artist & printer. (P. Dec.1; 50) £65

– **Sketches by Boz.** Ill.:– George Cruikshank. L., 1836-37. 1st. & 2nd. Series, 2nd. Edn., 1st. Edn. 3 vols. Gt.-panel mor., unc., by Zaehnsdorf. (PNY. May 21; 170) $110

– **A Tale of Two Cities.** 1859. 1st. Edn., 1st. Iss. 8 in 7 orig. pts. Advts., orig. wraps., slightly soiled. (SH. Oct.10; 370) *Quaritch.* £920

– – **Anr. Edn.** Ill.:– H.K. Browne. L., 1859. 1st. Edn., 1st. iss. of Pt. 7/8. 8 orig. pts. in 7. Pt. 7/8 with p. 213 misptd. '113', list of plts. sigd. 'b'. 'Tale of Two Cities Advertiser' in each pt., & all but 2 of other inserted advts. Orig. pict. wraps., pts. 1-6 rebkd., pts. 7/8 spines reprd., cl. s.-c. W.a.f. (CNY. May 22; 89) $1,200

– – **Anr. Edn.** L., 1859. 1st. Edn. Bnd. from pts. Some foxing & spotting, mis-numbering of p. 213. Orig. cl., some tears along jnts. (SPB. Nov.25; 188) $400

– – **Anr. Edn.** 1859. 1st. Edn., 1st. state. 1st. state, with p. 213 numbered 113, some slight spotting. Orig. cl., slightly soiled, cl. book-box. (S. Feb.9; 73) *Jarndyce.* £170

– – **Anr. Copy.** With the engraved title & frontis., but bnd. without the other plts., p. 213 misnumbered 113. Orig. hf. red mor. & marb. bds., mor. solander case. Pres. Copy, to George Eliot; Mrs. Edward Hanson's & Gabriel Wells' copy, lately in the Prescott Collection. (CNY. Feb.6; 83) $16,000

– **Works (including Life of Dickens).** Ill.:– Phiz, H.K. Browne, & others. 1837-76. Some 1st. Edns. 22 vols. Unif. pol. cf. gt., spines worn. (TA. Feb.19; 272) £55

– **Works.** L., 1861-74. Liby. Edn. 30 vols. Hf. cf. gt. panel. spines, by Sangorski & Sutcliffe, slight stain on upr. panel of a few spines, slightly worn. (SPB. Nov.25; 448) $700

– – **Anr. Edn.** 1861-ca. 1885. 30 vols. Cont. hf. cf., spines gt. (SBA. Jul.23; 239) *Chesters.* £190

– – **Anr. Edn.** 1874-76 & n.d. Ill. Liby. Edn. 30 vols. Hf. mor., spines gt. (SKC. May 19; 313) £340

– [-] **Anr. Edn.** 1879-82. 29 vols. Cont. hf. cf., spines gt. (CSK. Jul.31; 60) £120

– – **Anr. Edn.** 1881. De Luxe Edn., (1,000) numbered. 30 vols. Mntd. india paper plts. & ills. Cont. hf. cf. (CSK. Mar.27) £110

– – **Anr. Copy.** 30 vols. in 60. Hf. mor. gt. (SPB. May 6; 301) $1,600

– – **Anr. Edn.** 1889. Ill. Liby. Edn. 30 vols. Cont. hf. cf. gt. (SBA. Jul.22; 50) *Scott-Manderson.* £260

– – **Anr. Copy.** Cont. hf. cf., spines gt., slightly worn, some jnts. torn & restored. (SBA. Jul.14; 124) *Shapiro.* £100

– – **Anr. Edn.** Boston, 1892. Roxburgh Edn. on L.P., 1000 numbered. 48 vols. Maroon three-qtr. lev., spines gt. (SG. Sep.4; 151) $150

– [-] **Anr. Edn.** 1892-94. 16 vols. Cont. hf. mor., spines gt., very slightly scuffed & faded. (SKC. Dec.4; 1543) £65

– **Die Illustrirten Werke.** Ed.:– K.M. Schiller, P. Hermann & others. Trans.:– C. Kolb, M. Färber, & others. Ill.:– H.K. Brown, G. Cruikshank, R. Seymour & others. Leipzig, [1927-33]. Monumental Coll. Edn. 12 vols. 4to. Orig. linen gt. (HK. May 15; 4177) DM 650

– – **Anr. Copy.** 11 (1 of 12) vols. Orig. sewed. (D. Dec.11-13; 1048) DM 600

– **The Nonesuch Dickens.** Ed.:– Arthur Waugh & others. Nones. Pr., 1937-38. (877) with orig. steel-plt. 24 vols. Orig. buckram, steel-plt. in case. (SH. Feb.19; 135) *Kenyusha.* £1,200

– – **Anr. Copy.** Orig. buckram gt., steel-plt. in case. Accompanied by Retrospectus & Prospectus (Nones. Pr., 1937). (SD. Feb.4; 169) £720

– – **Anr. Edn.** N.d. 30 vols. Cont. hf. mor. (SH. May 28; 29) *Harrington.* £110

– – **Anr. Copy.** 19 vols. Hf. cf. gt. (SPB. May 29; 118) $275

– **Works.–Sketches by Boz.** Ill.:– Hablot K. Browne & George Cruikshank. 1837-57; 1867. 1st. Edns.; New Edn. 7 vols.; 1 vol. 8vo & fo. Unif. blind-stpd. cl., slight wear to spines. (TA. Nov.20; 378) £155

DICKES, William Frederick

– **The Norwich School of Painting.** L. & Norwich, [1905]. (100). 4to. Orig. cl. gt. (P. Mar.12; 14) *Sims & Reed.* £120

DICKEY, James

– **Poems 1957-1967.–Drowning with Others.** Middletown, [1967]; 1962. 1st. Edns. 2 vols. 1st. work: with 5 T.L.s. tipped in, to Louis Untermeyer; 2nd. work: with 1p. T.L.s.tipped in. Orig. bdgs., d.-w.'s. (SPB. Nov.25; 252) $200

DICKINSON

– **Comprehensive Pictures of the Great Exhibition.** 1854. 2 pts. in 1 vol. Lge. fo. Without title to pt. 2. Loose as iss. in orig. roan folder, slightly worn. (S. Jul.27; 202) *Henderson.* £1,000

– – **Anr. Copy.** 2 vols. Fo. 1 plt. torn & reprd., a few slightly soiled, vol. II slightly dampstained. Cont. hf. mor., loose. (SH. Nov.6; 89) *Fogg.* £760

– – **Anr. Copy.** 53 plts. only (of 54), 1 torn & reprd., a few soiled, vol. II slightly dampstained. (SH. Mar.5; 47) *Weinreb.* £440

– [-] **Anr. Copy.** Vol. II only (of 2). 28 hand-cold. proof plts., 1 loose & marginally torn, lacks title, slightly soiled. (SH. Nov.6; 90) *Henderson.* £400

– – **Anr. Edn.** Ill.:– John Nash, Louis Haghe & Roberts. [1854]. Lge. fo. 50 hand-finished chromolitho. plts. (of 55), lacks title, all prelims. & 5 plts. Hf. cf. W.a.f. (C. Jul.15; 39) *Weinreb.* £500

DICKINSON, Emily

– **Poems.** Boston, 1891. 1st. Edn., 2nd. Series. Orig. cl. gt., slight soiling. (SPB. Jul.28; 113) $225

– **Riddle Poems.** [Northampton, Mass.], Gehenna Pr., 1957. (200) numbered. 12mo. Mor.-bkd. vell. bds. Sigd. by Esther & Leonard Baskin. (SG. Sep.4; 203) $380

DICKINSON, H.W. & Jenkins, Rhys

– **James Watt & the Steam Engine.** 1927. 4to. Orig. cl. (SH. Jun.18; 103) *Weinreb.* £110

DICKINSON, John

– [-] **An Essay on the Constitutional Power of Great-Britain over the Colonies in America; with the Resolves of the Committee for the Province of Pennsylvania; & their Instructions to their Representatives in Assembly.** Phila., 1774. 1st. Edn. Some stains. Completely disbnd. (SG. Mar.5; 176) $130

– [-] **The Maybe, or some Observations Occasion'd by Reading a Speech Deliver'd in the House of Assembly, the 24th of May last, by a Certain Eminent Patriot.** Phila., [1764]. 1st. Edn. 12mo. Unbnd. [Sabin 20050] (SG. Mar.5; 175) $350

DICKINSON, P.L.
See-SADLEIR, Thomas O. & Dickinson, P.L.

DICKINSON, Thomas

– **A Narrative of the Operations of for the Recovery of the Public Stores & Treasure sunk in H.M.S. Thetis.** 1836. 1st. Edn. Some spotting. Orig. cl. [Sabin 20076] (S. Feb.9; 74) *Maggs.* £90

DICKSON, Adam

– **Husbandry of the Ancients.** Edinb., 1788. 2 vols. Hf. cf. (PD. Oct.22; 106) £60

– **Treatise of Agriculture.** Edinb. & L., 1785. New Edn. 2 vols. Slight browning. Cont. cf., spines gt. (S. May 5; 423) *Hitching.* £85

DICKSON, R.W. 'Alex McDonald'

– **Complete Dictionary of Practical Gardening . . .** Ill.:– after Sydenham Edwards. 1807. [1st. Edn.?]. 2 vols. 4to. Some plts. stained, some ll. of text browned or stained. Cont. cf., gt., lacks head of 1 spine, lacks 2 labels. (S. May 5; 102) *Schuster.* £480

– – **Anr. Copy.** Slight browning. Covers detchd. Bkplt. of George Chetwynd. (S. Jun.1; 262) *Shapero.* £460

– – **Anr. Copy.** Some browning & spotting. 19th. C. hf. russ., gt. (S. Jun.22; 24) *Frick.* £200

– – **Anr. Copy.** 3 vols. in 2. 73 engrs., 60 (of 61) hand-cold. Str.-grd. mor., gt. fillet borders, inner dentelles. Inscr. 'Given me by The Queen. 1808. H. Chesterfield', armorial Bradby-Hall plts. (SG. Sep.18; 116) $1,250

– **Practical Agriculture.** 1805. 1st. Edn. 2 vols. 4to. Slight browning & soiling. Mod. hf. cf., spines gt. (S. Feb.9; 75) *Jacobs.* £220

– – **Anr. Copy.** 27 plts. hand-cold., some plts. slightly offset. Cont. hf.-cf. (SBA. Jul.23; 241) *Temperley.* £110

DICTIONARY OF NATIONAL BIOGRAPHY

1885-1904. 68 vols., including 3 vol. Suppl. Index & Errata. Orig. cl., some spines torn. (CSK. Oct.10; 113) £160

– – **Anr. Run.** 1885-1912. 68 vols. with 4 vols Supps. & Errata vol. Orig. cl., 1 vol. in cont. hf. cf. (SH. Jun.4; 35) *Powney.* £75

– – **Anr. Run.** 1885-1971. 63 vols. & 12 supps. & index. Most cont. hf. mor., worn. W.a.f. (SH. Jul.23; 108) *Baker.* £120

– – **Anr. Run.** 1900; 1901-21. 68 vols. & 5 vols. Supps. Fo. Unif. cl., except last 2 vols. (TA. Oct.16; 147) £170

– – **Anr. Run.** Ed.:– Leslie Stephen & Sidney Lee. L., 1908-49. 21 vols., & supps. to 1931-40, together 28 vols. Cl. (SG. Mar.26; 165) $600

– – **Anr. Run.** Ed.:– Leslie Stephen & Sidney Lee. [1920-22]-59. 28 vols., including supps. & Epitome. Cl. (C. Jul.22; 116) *Manson.* £180

– – **Anr. Run.** Ed.:– Sir L. Stephen & Sir S. Lee. 1921-22. 22 vols. Orig. cl. gt. (PL. Nov.27; 270) *Smith.* £100

– – **Anr. Run.** 1921-27. Vols. 1-24. Orig. cl. (SH. Mar.6; 514) *Fairburn.* £130

– – **Anr. Run.** Oxford, [1921]-49. 27 vols. (including the Concise Edn. & 20th. C. from 1901-1940). Orig. cl. (CSK. Sep.26; 124) £300

– – **Anr. Run.** Ed.:– Sir L. Stephen & S. Lee. 1937-38. 22 vols. including Supp., 4 vols. Twentieth Century including Index, together 26 vols. Cl. gt. (P. Jul.30; 48) *Aspin.* £160

DICTIONNAIRE DE CHIRURGIE. Recueil des Planches

Paris, [1799]. Atlas vol. only. Fo. 111 plts. (of 113, lacks plts. 13 & 52). 19th. C. vell.-bkd. bds. (S. Feb.23; 37) *Crossley.* £180

DICTIONNAIRE DE LA CONVERSATION et de la Lecture

Paris, 1832-51. 68 vols. including the supps. Cont. hf. cf. gt. (S. Oct.20; 64) *Lyon.* £240

DICTIONNAIRE DES MEDICINS, Chirurgiens et Pharmaciens Français Légalement reçu, avant et depuis la Fondation de la République Française, publié sous les Auspices du Gouvernement

Paris, 1802. Advts. Qtr. mor. (S. Dec.2; 475) *Phelps.* £55

DICTIONNAIRE MILITAIRE Portatif
Paris, 1759. 4th. Edn. 3 vols. 16mo. Later hf. mor., torn. (SG. Oct.30; 127) $170

DICTIONNAIRE PITTORESQUE D'HISTOIRE Naturelle et des Phenomènes de la Nature
Paris, 1833-39. 11 vols. Fo. Engraved plts. (709 of 720) in last 2 vols. Unif. tree cf. effect bds., some defect. (TA. Mar.19; 343) £260

DIDEROT, Denis
– **Les Bijoux Indescrets.** [Paris], [1771]. 2 vols. 18mo. Cont. marb. cf., 3 fillets, inner dentelle, slightly worn. (HD. Apr.9; 454) Frs. 1,100
– – **Anr. Edn.** Ill.:– Guirons de Scévola. Paris, 1928. (50) on imperial Japon, numbered. 2 vols. 4to. Ills. in 6 states. Mor. by Bruel (vol. with states of plts. bnd. in hf. mor.), silk doubls., wrap. preserved, s.-c.'s. (SM. Feb.11; 210) Frs. 15,000
– – **Anr. Edn.** Ill.:– Jean Dulac. Paris, 1947. (318), this 1 of 10 reserved for artist. 2 vols. Unbnd. as iss. in orig. wraps., in orig. s.-c. Pres. copy, inscr. twice by the artist. (CSK. Jan.30; 176) £100
– **Memoires sur Differens Sujets de Mathématiques.** Paris, 1748. 1st. Edn. Cont. cf., gt. decor. spine. (TA. Nov.20; 53) £90
– **Le Neveu de Rameau.** Ill.:– B. Naudin. 1924. (55) on Japon. Plts. in 2 states, 2 tone etchings. Vell., ornamental ill au fusain & à la sanguine on upr.-cover. (HD. Oct.10; 1856) Frs. 2,200
– **Oeuvres Complètes . . .** Ed.:– J. Assezat. Paris, 1875-77. 20 vols. Cont. hf. mor., corners, spine with raised bands. (HD. Jun.24; 181) Frs. 3,400
– **Pensées Philosophiques.** L., 1757. Sq. sm. 8vo. Cont. red mor., spine decor. in grotesque style, 3 gt. fillets, inner dentelle. (HD. Apr.9; 453) Frs. 1,200
– **Principes de la Philosophie Morale; ou Essai de M. S*** sur le Mérite et la Vertu.** Amst., 1745. Cont. cf., spine gt. Inscr. to Madame de Ste Croix. (S. Jun.9; 48) *Quaritch.* £2,800

DIDEROT, Denis & Alembert, Jean d'
– **Encyclopédie . . .** Livorno, 1770. 2 vols. Fo. 344 engraved plts. only (of 350), many plts. & text ll. stained in vol. 2. Mod. qtr. vell., 1 spine torn. As a collection of plts., w.a.f. (CNY. May 22; 160) $800
– – **Anr. Edn.** Livorno, 1770-79. 32 vols.: 21 vols. text including 4 vols. supp. & 11 vols (of 12) plts. Fo. Cont. vell. W.a.f. (CR. Jun.11; 568a) Lire 6,000,000
– – **Anr. Edn.** Genf, [Vol. 30: Neufchatel], 1777-79. New Edn. 36 text & 3 plt. vols. in 39 vols. 4to. Plt. vol. 1 lacks 5 plts. & 1 text lf., text vol. not collated. Cont. hf. leath., gt. spine. (R. Oct.14-18; 2561) DM 3,700
– – **Anr. Edn.** Genf, 1778-79. New Edn. 3 plt. vols. only. 4to. Lacks 10 copperplts. (America). Cont. leath. or hf. leath., defect. (R. Mar.31-Apr.4; 1547) DM 2,700
– **Encyclopédie: Architecture.** Ca. 1770. Fo. Disbnd. (P. Jul.2; 19) *Goddard.* £90
– **Architecture.** Ca. 1775. Fo. Disbnd. (P. May 14; 343) *Edistar.* £55
– **Encyclopédie: Carpentry, including Shipping.** Ca. 1775. Fo. Disbnd. (P. May 14; 339) *Kundlatsch.* £90
– **Encyclopédie: Drawing.** Ca. 1775. Fo. Disbnd. (P. May 14; 342) *Edistar.* £75
– **Encyclopédie: Machines de Théâtre.** Ca. 1770. Fo. Disbnd. (P. Jul.2; 22) *McKenzie.* £65
– **Encyclopédie: Military.** Ca. 1775. Fo. Disbnd. (P. May 14; 341) *Edistar.* £95
– **Encyclopédie, ou Dictionnaire Raisonné des Sciences, des Arts et des Métiers.–Receuil de Planches.** Paris & Neuchatel; Paris, 1751-65; 1762-72. 1st. Edn. 17 vols.; 11 vols., together 28 vols. (of 35, without supp., supp. of pts. & Analytical Tables publd. later in 1st. vol. of plts. Lacks engraved frontis. Cont. Fr. mott. cf., spines gt. W.a.f. (CNY. Oct.1; 7) $6,200
[–] –**Anr. Edn.** [Paris], [1772]. Vol. 10 only. Fo. Imprint excised from foot of title-page. Cont. mott. cf., gt. spine. W.a.f. (C. Nov.5; 45) *Quaritch.* £280
– – **Anr. Edn.** 1773. Vol. 9. Fo. 206 engraved plts. on Locksmiths, Blacksmiths, Tailors, Weavers etc. Hf. cf. (P. Mar.12; 41) *Davies.* £180
– – **Anr. Edn.** Paris, 1783-90. 7 vols. (of 8), lacks vol. 5. 4to. Lacks 1 single plt. (of lingerie) in vol. 6, 12 plts. in vol. 7 loosely inserted from anr. copy, slight worming in 2 vols., some staining & occasional tears. Cont. sheep, worn, vol. 7 in bds., disbnd., unc. As a collection of plts., w.a.f. (SPB. May 6; 189) $3,000
[–] – **Anr. Edn.** Paris, 1786. Vol. 6. Early 19th. C. hf. leath. (HK. May 12-14; 953) DM 750
[–] **[Encyclopédie Recueil de Planches,] Musique. –Lutherie.** [Paris], [1751]. 2 pts. Fo. Slightly soiled in parts, music slightly browned in parts. Old wraps. & paper bds., browned. (H. Dec.9/10; 1112) DM 600
– **[Encyclopédie]. Recueil de Planches: Planches des Pêches.** Paris, 1793. Lge. 4to. Text & some plts. lightly browned. 19th. C. hf. linen, spine defect., unc. (R. Oct.14-18; 2619) DM 900
– **Encyclopédie, Recueil de Planches sur la Science.** Paris, 1762-72. Vols. of plts. only, some lacking. Fo. Cf., not unif. As a collection of prints, w.a.f. (BS. Jun.11; 422) £1,800
– – **Anr. Edn.** Paris, 1772. Vol. II, Weaving. Fo. Cl.-bkd. bds. (P. May 14; 337) *Walford.* £190
– – **Anr. Edn.** 1776. Vol. 10, Méchaniques. Fo. Cf. (P. May 14; 338) *Walford.* £210
– **Encyclopédie.–Supplement à l'Encyclopedie. –Table Analytique et Raisonnée.–Recueil de Planches . . .–Suite de Recueil de Planches.** Paris, Neufchatel & Amst., 1751-77. 1st. Edns. Together 34 vols. (only, lacks livraison IV or vol. V in 4th work). Fo. 2555 engraved plts. (of 2556, lacks plt. 30 in last vol.), some ll. & plts. loose, 1 plt. slightly torn & reprd. Cont. mott. cf. (not quite unif.), spines gt., some slightly worn, 1 spine defect. & jnt. brkn., lacks 3 lettering pieces, some plt. vols. misnumbered. (S. Feb.10; 320) *Lester* £3,500

DIDOT, Firmin
– **Catalogue des Livres Rares, Précieux, et très-bien conditionnés.** Paris, 1810. Priced. Later cl.-bkd. bds., by Durvand, unc. (SM. Oct.7; 1367) Frs. 3,000

DIEDO, Giacomo
– **Storia della Repubblica de Venezia.** Ill.:– C. Orsolini after Jacopo Nazari (port.). Venice, 1751. 4 vols. 4to. Light dampstain to some ll. in vol. IV. Cont. vell. bds. From the collection of John A. Saks. (C. Jun.10; 56) *Lyon.* £160

DIEFENBACH, Ernest
– **Travels in New Zealand.** 1843. 2 vols. Browned, 2 advt. ll. in vol. II. Mod. cf. (SH. Nov.7; 456) *White.* £90

DIEFFENBACH, Johann Friedrich
– **Surgical Observations on the Restoration of the Nose . . .** Trans.:– John Stevenson Bushman. L., 1833. 1st. Engl. Edn. Old bds., brkn., ex liby. (SG. Sep.18; 117) $850
See–**HOFMANN, A.–DIEFFENBACH, Johann Friedrich**

DIEGO de Santistevan
See–**ERCILLA Y ZUNIGA, Alonso de & Diego de Santistevan**

DIEHL, Edith
– **Bookbindings.** N.Y., 1946. 2 vols. Orig. cl., some wear, publisher's box. (SPB. May 29; 120) $100

DIEHL, Katharine Smith
– **Early Indian Imprints.** N.Y., 1964. Cl. (SG. Jan.22; 218) $100

DIELHELM, Johann Hermann
[–] **Denkwürdiger u. Nützlicher Rheinischer Antiquarius.** Frankfurt, 1739. Lacks 5 plts., title with owner's mark cut out, pp. 207/8 defect. bkd., slightly browned in parts. Cont. leath., gt. spine & outer dentelle, rubbed, defect, corners. (HK. Nov.18-21; 1333) DM 800

DIELMANN, J. & Wegelin, D.
– **Album von Kissingen, Bocklet und Brückenau.** Frankfurt, ca. 1840. Orig. hf. leath., defect. & loose. (R. Oct.14-18; 2190) DM 4,400

DIEMONT, J. & M.
– **The Brenthurst Baines.** Johannesburg, 1975. (125) in hf. mor. Vol. 1 of Brenthurst Press Series. 4to. Hf. mor., orig. s.-c. (VA. May 8; 284) R. 720
– – **Anr. Edn.** Johannesburg, 1975. (850). 4to. Cl., d.-w. (VA. May 8; 285) R. 370
– – **Anr. Copy.** (VA. May 8; 408) R. 320
– – **Anr. Copy.** (SSA. Nov.5; 206) R. 210
– – **Anr. Edn.** Johannesburg, 1975. (1000). 4to. Cl., d.-w. (SSA. Jan.22; 216) R. 285
– – **Anr. Copy.** (SSA. Jan.22; 215) R. 240

DIEREVILLE, Sieur de
See–**CHAMPLAIN Society**

DIETRICH, Dr.
– **The German Emigrants, or Frederick Wohlgemuth's Voyage to California.** Trans.:– Leopold Wray. Guben, ca. 1855. 12mo. Inner margins stained at head thro.-out. Orig. decor. bds., slightly stained. (SH. Mar.19; 81) *Nador.* £50

DIETRICH, David Nathaniel Friedrich
– **Deutschlands Flora.** Jena, 1839. Some plts. lightly soiled, title with fault, corrected, MS addition. Cont. linen. (HK. Nov.18-21; 464) DM 650

DIETRICHS, J.G.
See–**WIENMANN, J.W., Dietrichs, J.G. & others**

DIETTERLEIN, Wendel
– **Architectura von Ausstheilung, Symmetria und Proportion der Funff Seulen.** Nuremb., 1655. 5 pts. in 1 vol. Fo. Folio 23 in 2 sections pasted together, (orig. ill. cancelled?), folios 58 & 59 preserved, occasional minor tears & repairs, lightly soiled thro.-out, some staining. Old sheep, worn. (SPB. May 6; 182) $750

DIETZ, August
– **The Postal Service of the Confederate States of America.–Catalog & Hand-Book . . . of the Confederate States.** Richmond, 1929; 1937. 2 works in 2 vols. Cl., leatherette spine, d.-w. (1st. work); & cl., d.-w. 1st. work sigd. by author. (SG. Feb.12; 312) $250

DIEU, Ludovico de
– **Grammatica Linguarum Orientalium, Hebraeorum, Chaldaeorum, & Syrorum, inter se Collatarum.** Leiden, 1628. 4to. Title reprd., some browning & spotting, marginal staining at end. Cl.-bkd. bds., worn, s.-c. (S. Apr.29; 378) *Brill.* £110

DIGBY, Sir Kenelm
– **A Late Discourse made in a Solemne Assembly . . . at Montpellier . . . Touching the Cure of Wounds by the Powder of Sympathy . . .** Trans.:– R. White, 1660. 3rd. Edn. 12mo. Cont. cf., spine reprd. [Wing D1437] (S. Dec.1; 145) *Gurney.* £50
– **Of Bodies, & of Mans soul to discover the Immortality of Reasonable Souls with two Discourses of the Powder of Sympathy & of the Vegetation of Plants.** 1669. 4 pts. in 1 vol. 4to. Without Ii 2 & 3A blank. Cont. panel. cf. Bkplt. of the Duke of Portland. [Wing D1445] (S. Jun.15; 240) *Maggs.* £90
– – **Anr. Copy.** Later gt. hf. mor. & marb. bds. Cont. sig. at verso of title. (PNY. Oct.1; 178) $180
– **Theatrum Sympateticum.** Ed.:– N. Papinus & A. Kircherus. Ill.:– [Luyken?] (frontis.). Leeuw. & Amst., 1692. Cont. vell., slightly loose. (VG. Nov.18; 1148) Fls. 550

DIGGES, Leonard
– **A Booke named Tectonicon.** 1592. 7th.(?) Extant Edn. Sm. 4to. Mod. mor. [STC 6851] (S. Mar.17; 333) *Phelps.* £240

DIGHTON, B.L.
See–**LAWRENCE, H.W. & Dighton, B.L.**

DIKENMANN, J.R.
– **Souvenir de la Suisse.** Zürich, ca. 1840. Ob. 4to. Some plts. soiled. Cont. linen, reprd. (R. Oct.14-18; 2000) DM 12,500

DILKE, Thomas
– **The Lover's Luck.** 1696. 1st. Edn. 4to. Some staining thro.-out. Mor. by Sangorski. [Wing D1476] (C. Nov.19; 73) *Pickering & Chatto.* £90

DILLENIUS, John Jacob
– **Historia Muscorum.** 1768. 1st. Edn. in Engl., 2nd. Iss. 4to. 19th. C. hf. mor. From Chetham's Liby., Manchester. (C. Nov.26; 124) *Junk.* £70
– – **Anr. Edn.** L., 1768. 1st. Edn. in Engl. Tall 4to. Each plt. identified in ink at margins in early hand. Cont. gt.-stpd. red. mor., minor wear. (PNY. May 21; 174) $220
– **Hortus Elthamensis.** 1732. 1st. Edn., (250). 2 vols. Fo. 19th. C. hf. mor. From Chetham's Liby., Manchester. (C. Nov.26; 125) *Fletcher.* £950

D'ILLESCAS, Yakov
– **Imrei Noam-Chidushim Al-Ha'Torah.** Cremona, 1566. 2nd. Edn. Sm. 4to. Title reprd. with loss of portion of border. Vell., spine & cover defect., torn, stained. (SPB. May 11; 133) $600

DILLON, Edward
– **Glass.** L., [1907]. Cl., worn. From the liby. of Clement Heaton. (SG. Mar.12; 340) $100

DILLON, Col. Henry Augustus
- A Commentary on the Military Establishments & Defence of the British Empire. L., 1811-12. 1st. Edn. 2 vols. Cont. mor., wide gt. borders. Inscr. to Duke of Kent. (SG. Feb.26; 110) $100

DILLON, John Talbot
- Travels through Spain. L., 1782. 2nd. Edn. Lge. 4to. Cont. tree cf., gt. borders & spines. Early armorial bkplt. of Thomas Hutton. (SG. Feb.26; 111) $100

DILLON, Capt. Peter
- Narrative ... of a Voyage in the South Seas. 1829. 1st. Edn. 2 vols. 1 folding plt. hand-cold., some slight spotting. Mod. hf. cf., spines gt. [Sabin 20175] (S. Feb.9; 77) *Maggs.* £300

DILLWYN, Lewis Weston
- British Confervae. 1809. 1st. Edn. 4to. 19th. C. hf. cf., spine defect. From Chetham's Liby., Manchester. (C. Nov.26; 126) *Junk.* £150

DINCOURT D'HANGARD
- Catalogue des Livres. 1789. L.P. Priced thro.-out. in MS., ptd. price-list bnd. at end, with supp. & table of authors, 1 lf. of MS. notes bnd. in after title. Cont. cf., triple gt. fillet, spine gt. with semicircles & stars, inner gt. dentelles, later marb. end-papers. (SM. Oct.7; 1368) Frs. 1,400

DINE, Jim
- Complete Graphics. Berlin, Hanover, L., 1970. Pict. bds., s.-c. Folder with 3 orig. cold. prints laid in, each sigd. in pencil. (SG. Oct.23; 87) $260
- Welcome Home Lovebirds. L., 1969. Sig. Edn., (100) specially bnd, with orig. screenprint on celluloid, initialled & dtd. Buckram, d.-w. (SG. Oct.23; 88) $120

DINET, Etienne & Ibrahim, Sliman Ben
- Vie de Mohammed, Prophète d'Allah, La. Ill.:- E. Dinet. Paris, 1918. (925) numbered. 4to. 12 decor. titles etc. by Mohammed Racim, ptd. in colours & gold. Cont. mor. gt., unc., orig. wraps. bnd. in. (SH. Apr.9; 223) *Hosain.* £120

DINGELDEIN, W.H., Singraven
See-DOEHMANN, K. & Dingeldein, W.H., Singraven

DINGELSTEDT, Franz
- Jean Gutenburg: Premier Maître Imprimeur. Trans.:- Gustave Revilliod. Ill.:- A. Gandon. Geneva, 1858. 4to. Bds., rebkd. in cl. (SG. Mar.26; 229) $120

DINKEL, M. & Locher, N.
- Recueil de Portraits et Costumes suisses les plus Elegants, Usités dans les 22 Cantons. [Berne], ca. 1817. Sq. 12mo. Port. medallions cut down & mntd. on card together with name of canton, the whole mntd. in a blank book, lacks title & text. 19th. C. red mor., gt. As a collection, w.a.f. (S. Apr.7; 253) *Champonniere.* £320

DIODORUS SICULUS
- Bibliothecae Historicae. Hanau, 1604. Grk. Latin parallel Edn. 2 vols. in 1. Fo. Lightly browned & slightly soiled in parts, some old marginalia. Cont. pig. (R. Mar.31-Apr.4; 16) DM 420
See-OROSIUS, Paulus-DIODORUS SICULUS -[TORRENTINUS, Hermann]

DIOGENES Laertius
- The Lives, Opinions, & Remarkable Sayings of the Most Famous Ancient Philosophers ... Made English by Several Hands. 1688-96. 1st. Engl. Edn. 2 vols. Cont. cf. (TA. Dec.18; 50) £50
- Vitae et Sententiae Philosphorum. Trans.:- Ambrosius Traversarius. Brescia, Jacobus Britannicus, 23 Nov. 1485. Fo. 123 ll. of 124, lacks final lf. with Register, supplied in facs., marginal stains & repairs affecting some letters, annots. in an early hand, later inscr. at end, a few wormholes. Mod. vell. bds. (SPB. May 6; 183) $600

DION Cassius, Nicaeus
- Historiarum Romanarum Fragmenta. Bassano, 1798. On vell. Margins of 4 ll. reprd. Cont. marb. cf., gt. spine (torn at head). (C. Nov.20; 188) *Leather.* £250

DIONIGE, Marianna
- Viaggi in Alcune Citta del Lazio che diconsi fondate dal Pre Saturno. Ill.:- After Dionigi. Rome, 1809. Ob. fo. Later mor.-bkd. bds., worn. (CSK. Nov.28; 25) £55

DIONIS, [Pierre]
- L'Anatomie de l'Homme, suivant la Circulation du Sang, & les derniers Decouvertes ... Paris, 1696. 3rd. Edn. Owners' inscrs. on title, slightly spotted. Cont. cf., spine gt., head & foot of spine worn. (S. Feb.23; 38) *Brienx.* £60
- The Anatomy of Humane Bodies improved according to the Circulation of the Blood. 1703. 1st. Edn. in Engl. Tear in last plt. reprd. New cl. (S. Jun.15; 241) *Norman.* £110
- Chirurgie, oder Chirurgische Operationes. Ed.:- L. Heister. Augsburg, 1722. 2nd. Edn. 1 plt. defect with some loss, most plts. loose. Cont. vell. (R. Mar.31-Apr.4; 981) DM 1,700
- Cours d'Operations de Chirurgie, Demontrées au Jardin Royal. Brussels, 1708. 1st. Edn. Cont. cf., worn. From liby. of Dr. E. Ashworth Underwood. (S. Feb.23; 197) *Rademaker.* £80
- - Anr. Edn. Paris, 1714. 2nd. Edn. Some liby. stps. Cont. cf., rebkd., covers not unif. (S. Jun.15; 242) *Rhys-Jones.* £70
- - Anr. Edn. Paris, 1740. 4th. Edn. Slightly spotted. Cont. mott. cf., worn. From liby. of Dr. E. Ashworth Underwood. (S. Feb.23; 198) *Brienx.* £60
- - Anr. Edn. Paris, 1750. 4th. Edn. 12 engraved plts. only, without the folding view, port. & all plts. facing in opposite direction, some ll. browned. Cont. cf., head & foot of spine slightly worn. (S. Feb.23; 40) *Clay.* £65
- - Anr. Edn. Ed.:- G. de la Faye. Paris, 1751. 4th. Edn. Some ll. slightly spotted. Cont. cf., spine & corners slightly worn. (S. Feb.23; 39) *Brienx.* £60

DIONYSIUS DE RICKEL, Carthusianus
[-] Alchoran.-Türckischer Keysser Ankunfft, Kreyg und Händlung, gegen und wider die Christen, bitz uff den yetzt Reygerenden Solymannum. Strassburg, 1540. 1st. German Edn. 2 works in 1 vol. Fo. Slightly stained, lacks pp. 101/102, wormed near end. Bds., loose. (R. Oct.14-18; 46) DM 520
- Enarrationes Piae ac Eruditae in Libros Iosue. Iudicum. Ruth. Regum ...-Piae ac Eruditae Enarrations in Lib. Iob. Tobiae ... Ed.:- Th. Loer; Fr. Taleman. Ill.:- A. Woensam v. Worms & others. Cologne, Jan. 1535; Mar. 1534. 1st. Edns. 2 works in 1 vol. Fo. Slightly soiled in parts, 1 p. slightly defect. Cont. blind-tooled pig-bkd. wd. bds., 2 clasps, spine & clasps renewed. (HK. Nov.18-21; 173) DM 420
- Summae Fidei Orthodoxae Libri Duo. Cologne, 1535. 4to. Slightly soiled thro.-out, some worming at beginning. Mod. hf. vell. (R. Mar.31-Apr.4; 18) DM 620

DIONYSIUS HALICARNASSENSIS
- Antiquitates Romanae. Trans.:- Lapus Biragus. Reggio Emilia, Franciscus de Mazalibus. 12 Nov., 1498. 2nd. Edn. Fo. 217 ll. (of 226) lacks first blank & 8 ll. of sig. k., 18th. C. owners. inscr. of Jesuit College Liby., Brescia. 19th. C. hf. cf., spine defect. W.a.f. [BMC VII, 1089] (S. Mar.17; 267) *Thomas.* £120

DIONYSIUS PERIEGETES
- Geographia Emendata & Locupletata. Oxford, 1709. Notes on end-papers in cont. hand. Cont. cf. (S. Mar.31; 462) *Crete.* £65

DIOSCORIDES, Anazarbei Pedacius -BARBARO, Ermolao
- De Medica Materia.-In Dioscoridem Corollarorum ... Trans.:- Marcello Vergilia (1st. work). Cologne, 1529; 1530. 2 works in 1 vol. Fo. Cont. blind-stpd. pig. on wood bds., 2 metal clasps. (SG. May 14; 63) $800

DIRECTORIUM Salisburgense
See-LEONARDUS, Deacon of Salzburg & others

DI RIETI, Chananya
- Meikiz Redumin. Mantua, 1648. 12mo. Stained, reprd., worming & browning. Bds. (SPB. May 11; 68) $250

DIROM, Maj. Alexander
- A Narrative of the Campaign in India. L., 1794. 2nd. Edn. Lge. 4to. Foxed. Disbnd. (SG. Feb.26; 112) $100

DIRUF, O.
- Kissingen. Its Baths & Mineral Springs. Würzburg, 1887. Slightly soiled in parts. Orig. linen. (R. Mar.31-Apr.4; 1949) DM 550

DISNEY, Walt
- Mickey Chercheur d'Or. Paris, 1931. 4to. Orig. cl.-bkd. pict. bds. (SH. Dec.10; 155) *Sotheran.* £65
- A Mickey Mouse Alphabet. Racine, 1938. Fo. Loose in orig. pict. wraps., backstrip worn. (SH. Mar.19; 83) *Fletcher.* £70

DISRAELI, Benjamin, Earl of Beaconsfield
- Lord George Bentinck. 1852. 1st. Edn. Lacks advts. Diced cf. gt. by Massey, gt. monog. of Earl of Rosebery on upr. cover. (SBA. Jul.23; 486) *Taylor.* £50
- Lothair. L., 1870. 1st. Edn. 3 vols. Cf., triple gt. fillet borders, spines gt. with flower design, by Hatchards, bkplt. in each vol. (SG. Mar.19; 85) $120
- Lothair.-Endymion. 1870; 1880. 1st. Edns. 3 vols.; 3 vols. 1st. work: a few spots, owner's inscr. of Hannah de Rothschild; 2nd. work: advt. ll. in vol. 3. Orig. cl., 1st. slightly worn. (SBA. Jul.23; 487) *Kingsdale Fine Arts.* £85
- Novels & Tales. 1881. Hughenden Edn. 11 vols. Rosebery liby. stp. on vig. titles. Orig. cl., unc. (SBA. Jul.23; 485) *Count de Salis.* £85
- - Anr. Copy. (SH. May 28; 30) *Walford.* £50
- - Anr. Edn. 1926-27. Bradenham Edn. 12 vols. Orig. cl. (SH. Mar.5; 224) *Wolfson.* £85
- Revolutionary Epic. 1834. 1st. Edn. 3 pts. in 2 vols. 4to. Orig. bds., spines torn. Hf.-title in both vols. inscr. by Disraeli. (SH. Apr.9; 224) *Jarndyce.* £80
- The Young Duke. 1831. 1st. Edn. 3 vols. 12mo. Hf.-title in vols. 2 & 3. Orig. cl. (SBA. Jul.23; 315) *Frost.* £120
- Works. L., n.d. 10 vols. Minor defects. Hf. cf. (SPB. Jul.28; 114) $125

DISTANT, W.L.
- Insecta Transvaaliensia. L., 1924. 4to. Cl. (SSA. Nov.5; 162) R. 260
- A Naturalist in the Transvaal. L., 1892. Pict. cl. (VA. Oct.31; 329) R. 150

DISTELI, Martin
- Die Wahrhaftige Geschichte vom Deutschen Michel und seinen Schwestern. Zürich & Wintherthur, 1845. Worn. Sewed, orig. wraps. (D. Dec.11-13; 655) DM 460

DIVISIONES DECEM NATIONUM TOTIUS CHRISTIANITATIS
[Rome], [Johann Besicken & Sigismund Mayer], ca. 1493-4. 4to. Paper bds. [Goff D 290] (C. Apr.1; 27) *Goldschmidt.* £160

DIX, John H.
- Treatise upon the Nature & Treatment of Morbid Sensibility of the Retina. Boston, 1849. 1st. Edn. 12mo. Orig. cl. From Brooklyn Academy of Medicine. (SG. Jan.29; 138) $130

DIXON, Charles
- Game Birds & Wild-Fowl of the British Islands. 1900. 2nd. Edn. 4to. Orig. parch.-bkd. pict. bds., slightly worn. Inscr. by publisher. (PL. Sep.18; 180) *Smith.* £180
- - Anr. Copy. Fo. Title slightly stained. Orig. parch.-bkd. cl., soiled, spine torn. (CSK. Jan.23; 108) £140
- - Anr. Copy. 4to. Cl. (BS. Nov.26; 167) £65

DIXON, George
- A Voyage Round the World. 1789. 1st. Edn., 2nd. Iss. 4to. Mod. hf. cf., spine gt. [Sabin 20364] (S. Mar.31; 463) *Quaritch.* £320
- - Anr. Copy. 2 pts. in 1 vol. Some slight browning. Cont. mott. cf. L.P. [Sabin 20364] (S. Feb.9; 79) *Maggs.* £300
- - Anr. Edn. L., 1789. 2nd. Edn. 4to. Folding maps & plts. with longish tears, some pasted, slightly soiled. Mod. linen. [Sabin 20364] (R. Mar.31-Apr.4; 2403) DM 1,500
- - Anr. Edn. 1789. Cf. spine, marb. bds. (HSS. Apr.24; 201) £95

DIXON, William Hepworth
- New America. 1867. 5th. Edn. 2 vols. Early 20th. C. hf. cf. gt. (S. Mar.31; 464) *Finabest.* £50

DOBEL, H.W.
- Neueröffriete Jäger-Practica. Leipzig, 1754. 2nd. Edn. 4 pts. in 1 vol. Fo. Lacks 8 copper engrs. & pt. 2 lacks pp. 19-22, lightly browned & slightly soiled. Later hf. linen. (H. May 21/22; 170) DM 1,050

DOBIE, J.
See-PONT, Timothy & Dobie, J.

DOBIE, J. Frank
- **Apache Gold & Yaqui Silver.** Ill.:– Tom Lea. Boston, 1939. (265) sigd. by author & artist. With extra suite of 5 cold. ills. loose in envelope. Orig. buckram-bkd. bds., s.-c., spine dampstained. (CNY. Oct.1; 88) $320
- – **Anr. Copy.** Qtr. cl. (PNY. Mar.26; 98) $240

DOBRIZHOFFER, Martin
- **An Account of the Abipones . . . of Paraguay.** 1822. 3 vols. Mod. cf.-bkd. bds. (SH. Nov.7; 373) *Rudge.* £60

DOBSON, Austin
- **The Ballad of Beau Brocade.** Ill.:– Hugh Thomson. 1892. (450) on L.P. Hf. mor. (SH. Mar.27; 511) *Donnithorne.* £70
- – **Anr. Copy.** 4to. Plts. on Jap. vell. & text ills. in mntd. india-proof state. Crushed lev., double gt. fillet borders with sm. floral cornerpieces, spine gt., gt. dentelles, by Bennett. Lge. H.M.P. (SG. Dec.18; 397) $120

DOBSON, Matthew
- **A Medical Commentary on Fixed Air . . . with an Appendix . . . by William Falconer.** 1787. 3rd. Edn. 2 pts. in 1 vol. Orig. bds., unc. From liby. of Dr. E. Ashworth Underwood. (S. Feb.23; 199) *Gurney.* £50

DOCKER, Alfred
- **Colour Prints of William Dickes.** [1924]. Ltd. sigd. Edn. 4to. Cl. (P. Nov.13; 52) *Sims.* £50

DOCTEUR en Medecine (Pseud.)
See–DUBE, Paul 'Docteur en Medecine'

DOCTRINALE CLERICORUM UNA CUM SANCTORUM MARTYROLOGIO PER ANNI CIRCULUM
Lubeck, (The Poppy Printer [Matthaeus Brandis? or Hans von Ghetelen?], 1490. 4to. Rubricated, some marginal pencil markings, title slightly soiled, 1 or 2 wormholes at beginning & end. 19th. C. blind-stpd. cf. in cont. style, worn, rebkd., bkplt. of Edward Parry, Bp. Suffragan of Dover. [BMC II, 558; HC 6318; Goff M332] (S. Dec.9; 102) *Quaritch.* £1,000

DODART, Denis
- **Mémoires pour servir à l'Histoire des Plantes.** Paris, 1679. 2nd. Edn. 12mo. Cont. cf., spine gt., slightly worn. Pres. copy. (S. Dec.3; 950) *Blackwell.* £110

DODDRIDGE, Sir John
- **A Compleat Parson.** 1630. 1st. Edn. Sm. 4to. Some staining, mostly to upr. margin, some cont. MS. notes. Cf. gt. by Sangorski. From the collection of Eric Sexton. [STC 6980] (C. Apr.15; 172) *Crowe.* £70
- **The History of . . . the Principality of Wales, Dutchy of Cornewalle, & Earledome of Chester.** 1630. 1st. Edn. Sm. 4to. Some staining on title & elsewhere, 1 gathering foxed. 19th. C. hf. cf. From the collection of Eric Sexton. [STC 6982] (C. Apr.15; 173) *Thorp.* £70

DODDRIDGE, Joseph
- **Notes on the Settlement & Indian Wars of the Western Parts of Virginia & Pennsylvania . . . 1763-1783 . . .** Wellsburgh, Va., 1824. 1st. Edn. Browned, stp. removed from title. Cont. cf., gt. spine, upr. cover loose. From liby. of William E. Wilson. (SPB. Apr.29; 79) $225

DODECATON, ou Le Livre des Douze
Paris, 1837. 2 vols. Noilly liby. stp. Hf. mor. by Allô, corners, unc., wraps. (HD. Dec.5; 69) Frs. 1,150

DODGE, Mary Mapes
- **Hans Brinker.** N.Y., 1866. 1st. Edn. 12mo. BAL's state 'A' of advts. Orig. cl., cl. case. With autograph MS. p. from the orig. MS., written in ink with some revisions & printer's markings, & inscr. 'For MFC from MMD . . .'; from the Prescott Collection. (CNY. Feb.6; 89) $750

DODGSON, Campbell
- **A Catalogue of Etchings by Augustus John.** 1920. (325) numbered. 4to. Orig. cl.-bkd. bds. (SH. Jun.25; 158) *Henderson.* £90
- **The Etchings of Charles Meryon.** L., 1921. 4to. Qtr. buckram gt. (P. Mar.12; 11) *Ayres.* £55
- – **Anr. Copy.** Orig. qtr. vell. (SG. Mar.12; 253) $110
- **The Etchings of James McNeill Whistler.** Ed.:– Geoffrey Holme. 1922. (200). Fo. Partly untrimmed. Orig. vell. gt., slightly soiled. (TA. Dec.18; 122) £60

- – **Anr. Copy.** (TA. Mar.19; 49) £50
- – **Anr. Copy.** Vell.-bkd. bds. (SG. Oct.23; 349) £130
- **An Iconography of the Engravings of Stephen Gooden.** L., 1944. (160) numbered with orig. frontis. proof engr. sigd. by artist. 4to. Orig. qtr. vell. gt., cl. s.-c. The John A. Saks copy. (CNY. Oct.1; 178) $220
- **Muirhead Bone Etchings & Dry Points.** 1898-1907; 1909. (275) numbered. 2 vols. Qtr. suede. (WW. May 20; 50) £64
- **Old French Colour Prints.** 1924. Ltd. Edn. 4to. Qtr. vell. gt., d.-w. (P. Mar.12; 5) *Fenton.* £70

DODGSON, Campbell–HARDIE, Martin
- **Etchings & dry Points by Muirhead Bone.** –**Etchings & Dry Points . . . 1902-1924 by James McBey.** N.p.; L., 1909; 1925. (275); (500). 2 works in 2 vols. 4to. Both orig. suede. Both with orig. etching as frontis. (that in 2nd. work sigd.); from the Prescott Collection. (CNY. Feb.6; 343) $200

DODGSON, Charles Lutwidge 'Lewis Carroll'
- **Alice's Adventures in Wonderland.** Ill.:– Sir John Tenniel. N.Y., 1866. 1st. Edn., 2nd. Iss. 1 p. defect., some ll. reinserted. Orig. cl. gt., rebkd. preserving spine, new end-papers, s.-c. (SH. Dec.10; 156) *Hatchards.* £520
- – **Anr. Copy.** Slight spotting, minor tears. Shaken. (SPB. Nov.25; 203) $700
- [–] – **Anr. Edn.** Ill.:– Sir John Tenniel. 1866. 1st. Publd. Edn. Orig. cl., spine loose, stitching defect. (SH. Dec.10; 155a) *Demetzy.* £170
- – **Anr. Edn.** Ill.:– Sir John Tenniel. L., 1866. 1st. Publd. Engl. Edn., 1st. Iss. Some staining to text. Orig. cl. gt., spine & corners worn, 1st. gathering loose, red mor. gt. solander case. From the Prescott Collection. (CNY. Feb.6; 90) $600
- – **Anr. Edn.** Ill.:– John Tenniel. L., 1866. 1st. Publd. Engl. Edn. Orig. gt.-decor. cl., some slight bdg. defects, hf. lev. s.-c. (SG. Apr.30; 54) $450
- – **Anr. Edn.** Ill.:– John Tenniel. N.Y., 1866. 1st. Amer. Edn. 3 brown pen & ink drawings for ills. in book inserted, each measuring about 3 × 2¼ ins. & mntd. on blank paper. Lev., with inlaid vari-cold. leath. design, spine gt. with sm. devices, gt. dentelles, by Baytun-Rivière, orig. gt.-decor. cl. covers & spine laid in. (SG. Apr.30; 53) $1,200
- – **Anr. Copy.** Title-lf. loose from conjugate hf.-title, & frayed at extreme fore-edge. Mor., gt.-decor. sides & spine, gt. dentelles. (SG. Apr.30; 52) $350
- – **Anr. Edn.** Ill.:– Arthur Rackham. L., [1907]. 1st. Trade Edn. Sm. 4to. Very worn. Gt.-pict. cl. Orig. ink drawing, sigd. & dtd. 7-12-09 by artist, Raymond M. Sutton Jr. copy. (SG. May 7; 45) $375
- – **Anr. Edn.** Ill.:– Arthur Rackham. L., [1907]. (1130) numbered. Lge. 4to. Gt.-decor. cl. Raymond M. Sutton Jr. copy, James Mann bkplt. (SG. May 7; 43) $475
- – **Anr. Copy.** Inscr. by Gabriel d'Annunzio to Victor de Goloubeff. (SG. Oct.9; 203) $425
- – **Anr. Edn.** Ill.:– Arthur Rackham. N.Y., [1907]. 1st. Amer. Trade Edn. Sm. 4to. Cl. Raymond M. Sutton Jr. copy. (SG. May 7; 46) $130
- – **Anr. Edn.** Ill.:– Arthur Rackham. L. & N.Y., [1907]. (550) numbered for U.S.A. sigd. by Publisher. Lge. 4to. Cl.-bkd. bds. Raymond M. Sutton Jr. copy. (SG. May 7; 44) $750
- – **Anr. Edn.** Ill.:– Arthur Rackham. [1907]. Ltd. Edn. 4to. Orig. cl. gt. (P. Oct.23; 134) *Gerrard.* £170
- [–] – **Anr. Edn.** Ill.:– Arthur Rackham. [1907]. Orig. pict. cl. gt., worn. (SH. Dec.11; 420) *Mundy.* £52
- – **Anr. Edn.** Ill.:– Marie Laurencin. Paris, Black Sun Pr., 1930. (790) numbered, this 1 of the American edn. Ob. 4to. Red hf. mor. with gt. rules & rabbit in black mor. onlaid on upr. cover, by Bennet, N.Y., orig. wraps. bnd. in. (SH. Nov.21; 377) *Kawamatsu.* £330
- – **Anr. Copy.** Orig. wraps., folder & s.-c., worn. (SH. Nov.21; 376) *Kawamatsu.* £250
- – **Anr. Copy.** Slight soiling. (SPB. Nov.25; 230) $800
- – **Anr. Edn.** Ill.:– Marie Laurencin. Paris, Black Sun Pr., 1930. (20) on Van Gelder, with extra suite in sanguine, each sigd. by artist. Ob. 4to. 6 orig. cold. lithos. Ptd. wraps., glassine d.-w. (SG. May 14; 127) $2,650
- – **Anr. Edn.** Ill.:– John Tenniel. Ltd. Edns. Cl. 1932. (1500) numbered, & sigd. by Alice Hargreaves & F. Warde. Red mor., wide & elab.

gt.-tooled borders, spine gt., in orig. cl. s.-c. (SG. Jan.15; 141) $425
- – **Anr. Copy.** (SG. Apr.30; 58) $350
- – **Anr. Edn.** Ill.:– Salvador Dali. N.Y., 1969. (2500) sigd. by artist, numbered. Fo. Unsewn in orig. cl. wraps., unc., fitted case. (SH. Nov.21; 288) *Limmer.* £500
- – **Anr. Copy.** Orig. wraps., unsewn as Iss., unc., mor.-bkd. box. (SPB. Nov.25; 248) $1,000
- – **Anr. Edn.** Ill.:– S. Dali. N.Y., 1969. (200) roman-numbered on Rives paper, & sigd. by artist, with additional suite of plts. on Japon nacré. Lge. fo. Loose sheets as iss. in folders & mor. folding case with clasps, additional plts. in separate portfo. (SG. Apr.30; 59) $1,200
- – **Anr. Copy.** (SG. Oct.23; 74) $800
- – **Anr. Edn.** Ill.:– Arthur Rackham. N.d. Ltd. Edn. 4to. Cl. gt. (P. Jul.30; 282) *Brook.* £170
- **Alice's Adventures in Wonderland.–Through the Looking Glass.** Ill.:– Sir J. Tenniel. L. (1st. vol.), Ltd. Edns. Cl. (2nd. vol.). 1866 [1865]; 1935. 2nd. Publd. Edn.; (1500) numbered. 2 vols. 1st. vol.: gt.-pict. cl., shaken; 2nd. vol.: cf. gt., spine defect. (PNY. Dec.3; 108) $140
- – **Anr. Edn.** Ill.:– Sir John Tenniel. N.Y., Ltd. Edns. Cl., 1932; 1935. Tog. 2 vols. Mor. gt., boxed. 1st work sigd. by typographer, Frederic Warde, both sigd. by Alice Hargreaves. (SG. Oct.9; 52) $700
- – **Anr. Copy.** Gt.-decor. crushed mor. & gt.-decor. cf., boxed. Sigd. at upr. blank by Alice Hargreaves & at colophon by type-designer, Frederic Ward; Glenn Davis Mathew's bkplt. (PNY. Dec.3; 215) $500
- – **Anr. Copy.** Leath. gt., covers spotted, boxed. Each work sigd. by Alice Hargreaves, 1st. work sigd. by the designer Frederic Warde. (SG. Jan.15; 140) $450
- [–] **Alice's Adventures under Ground.** 1886. 1st. Edn. Facs. of author's MS. & drawings. Orig. cl. gt., folder, mor.-bkd. s.-c. Pres. Copy to Lilian Janet Henderson. (SH. Dec.10; 157) *Subunso.* £260
- – **Anr. Copy.** (SH. Dec.10; 158) *Waggett.* £70
- – **Anr. Copy.** D.-w., qtr. mor. gt. s.-c. Pres. Copy, to E.F. Sampson, lately in the Prescott Collection. (CNY. Feb.6; 94) $1,100
- – **Anr. Edn.** [Vienna], Priv. Ptd., [1930's]. Eldridge Johnson Facs. Edn. 12mo. Last p. with sm. mntd. oval photograph of Alice, & laid in is facs. of last line & 'The End' as it appeared in the 1886 facs., also laid in is Vail's pamphlet on the orig. MS. Orig. gt.-lettered mor., cl. s.-c. Bkplt. of Francis Kettaneh. (SG. Apr.30; 57) $120
- **Aventures d'Alice au Pays des Merveilles.** Ill.:– Sir John Tenniel. L., 1869. 1st. Edn. in Fr. Lev. mor. gt., medallions on covers of the white rabbit & the Cheshire cat, orig. cl. covers preserved, by Noulhac. With A.L.s to Mrs. Richards (n.p., n.d., 12mo., 3 pp., in Fr.); from the Prescott Collection. (CNY. Feb.6; 91) $400
- – **Anr. Edn.** ill.:– Arthur Rackham. Paris, [1907]. 1st. Fr. Edn. Deluxe, (20) numbered on papier du Japon, sigd. by artist. Lge 4to. Gt.-decor. vell., warped. Raymond M. Sutton Jr. copy. (SG. May 7; 47) $4,000
- **Eight or Nine Wise Words About Letter-Writing.** –**The Wonderful Postage-Stamp Case.** Oxford, 1890; 1889. 1st. work Edn.; 2nd. Edn. of envelope; 3rd. Edn. of stamp case. 2 vols. 16mo. Orig. wraps., 2nd. title in pict. s.-c. with orig. ptd. envelope. (PNY. Mar.26; 99) $160
- **The Hunting of the Snark.** Ill.:– Henry Holiday. L., 1876. 1st. Edn. 12mo. Cf., covers gt.-ruled, gt.-panel. back, orig. pict. wraps. bnd. in at end. (PNY. May 21; 175) $110
- – **Anr. Edn.** L., 1876. 1st. Edn. in special bdg. variant. Orig. gt.-pict. cl., corners slightly worn. (PNY. Mar.26; 100) $260
- **The Nursery Alice.** Ill.:– Edmund Evans after Tenniel. L., 1890. 4to. Title & frontis. slightly foxed. Orig. pict. bds. by E.G. Thomson, sm. ink stains on lr. cover, corners slightly worn, red mor. gt. s.-c. Pres. Copy, to Mrs. Boyes, lately in the Prescott Collection. (CNY. Feb.6; 95) $750
- **Phantasmagoria & other Poems.** L., 1869. 1st. Edn. Gt. pict. cl. Bkplt. of A.C. Twentyman, sm. label of printer W. Parke. (SG. Apr.30; 60) $120
- **Rhyme? & Reason?** Ill.:– A.B. Frost & Henry Holiday. L., 1883. 1st. Edn. Gt.-decor. cl. (SG. Mar.19; 47) $140
- **A Tangled Tale.** Ill.:– A.B. Frost. L., 1885. Gt.-pict. cl. Inscr. on hf.-title to F.J. Dodgson, pencilled inscr. of L.F. Dodgson. (SG. Apr.30; 63) $240

DODGSON, Charles Lutwidge 'Lewis Carroll' *-contd.*
– Through the Looking Glass. Ill.:– John Tenniel. L., 1872. 1st. Edn., 1st. Iss. With the 'Wade' reading on p. 21. Lev., gt.-stpd. picture of the Red Queen on upr. cover, spine gt. with sm. emblems, gt. dentelles by Bayntun-Rivière, orig. gt.-pict. cl. covers & spine bnd. in. Inscr. on hf.-title, to Blanche H. Davys, & A.L.s. from author to Mrs. Davys. (SG. Apr.30; 61) $1,150
– – Anr. Edn. Ill.:– Sir John Tenniel. L., 1872. 1st. Edn. Orig. cl. gt., qtr. red mor. gt. s.-c. From the Prescott Collection. (CNY. Feb.6; 92) $550
– – Anr. Copy. With 'To all Child-Readers of Alice's Adventures in Wonderland' (Dec. 1871, 16mo., 4pp.) tipped in. Red mor. gt., with cold. mor. inlays on upr. cover, orig. cl. preserved, by Rivière. From the Prescott Collection. (CNY. Feb.6; 93) $180
– – Anr. Edn. Ill.:– John Tenniel. Ltd. Edns. Cl., 1935. (1500) numbered, & sigd. by Alice Hargreaves. Cf., elab. gt. border, orig. box. (SG. Jan.15; 142) $400
– – Anr. Copy. Cf., elab. gt. border, back gt., orig. cl. s.-c. (SG. Apr.30; 67) $250
– Sylvie & Bruno.–Sylvie & Bruno Concluded. Ill.:– Harry Furniss. L., 1889; 1893. 2 works in 2 vols. Lev., multiple gt. fillet borders enclosing, on upr. covers, the Professor & the camel in various cold. inlays, gt. panel. spines, gt. dentelles, orig. cl. covers bnd. in, by Bayntun, jnts. worn. (SG. Feb.12; 95) $150
– Wunderhorn. Stuttgart, 1970. (1000). 4to. Orig. linen. (R. Mar.31-Apr.4; 433) DM 800

DODONAEUS or Dodoens, Rembertus
– Cruydt-Boeck, volgens sijne laetste Verbeteringe . . . Leyden, 1608. Fo. Prelims. & headings of woodcuts printed in fine civilité type, corner of hf.-title stained & reprd. title & 1st. ll. a little stained, some marginal stains & worming, especially at end. Mod. hf. leath. (VG. Oct.13; 59) Fls. 7,000
– – Anr. Edn. Leyden, 1618. Fo. Some stains & browning. Mod. hf. cf. (LM. Mar.21; 95) B.Frs. 52,000
– A Neiwe Herball. Trans.:– Henry Lyte. 1578. 1st. Lyte Edn. Fo. Lacks 6 ll. of index, supplied in MS., occasional marginal staining, title slightly soiled & creased, to upr. blank margin of latter hf. Old cf., rebkd. W.a.f., from Chetham's Liby., Manchester. (C. Nov.26; 127) *Sotheran.* £650
– – Anr. Copy. Lacks 212, title & last few ll. detchd., some marginal worming, staining. Old rough cf., covers detchd. W.a.f. [STC 6984] (S. Jun.1; 263) *Finney.* £420
– A New Herbal. Trans.:– Henry Lyte. 1619. Fo. Slight paper fault on B4, occasional spotting. 19th. C. hf. mor. From Chetham's Liby., Manchester. [STC 6987] (C. Nov.26; 128) *Forum.* £260
– Stirpium Historiae. Antw., 1616. 2nd. Edn. Fo. Edge of title dust-soiled, fore-edge frayed. Old cf., rebkd. From Chetham's Liby., Manchester. (C. Nov.26; 129) *Van Loock.* £700
– Trium Priorum de Stirpium Historia. [Posteriorum Trium de Stirpium]. Antw., 1553-54. 1st. Edn. 2 vols. in 1. Sm. paper fault in 1 lf. of index, cont. Engl. marginal Ms. annot. 19th. C. vell. From Chetham's Liby., Manchester. (C. Nov.26; 130) *Junk.* £700

DODRIDGE, Sir John
– History of the Ancient & Moderne Estate of the Principality of Wales, Duchy of Cornewall, & Earldome of Chester. 1630. 4to. Some ll. heavily browned. Old spr. cf., rebkd. (TA. Nov.20; 18) £52

DODSLEY, Robert
[–] The Oeconomy of Human Life. L., 1795. 12mo. Some foxing. Old str.-grd. mor., worn. Fore-e. pntg.; from the liby. of Zola E. Harvey. (SG. Mar.19; 132) $200
– – Anr. Copy. 4to. Cont. gt.-ornamental tree cf., unc. Gt. mor. bkplts. of Robert Hoe, & of Mrs. Poyntz Ricketts. (PNY. Oct.1; 180) $160
[–] The Preceptor. 1748. 1st. Edn. 2 vols. Some ll. stained. Cont. cf., rebkd. (S. Feb.9; 17) *Traylen.* £100
[–] – Anr. Edn. L., 1769. 5th. Edn. 2 vols. Cont. cf., worn. (SG. Feb.5; 119) $275

DODSWORTH, Roger
See–**DUGDALE, Sir William & Dodsworth, Roger**

DODSWORTH, William
– Historical Account of Salisbury. 1814. L.P. Fo. Proof plts. of views. Hf. cf., jnts. worn. From liby. of Baron Dimsdale. (MMB. Oct.8; 10) *Bess.* £50

DODWELL, Edward
– A Classical & Topographical Tour through Greece. 1819. 1st. Edn. 2 vols. 4to. Some dampstaining. Mod. mor.-bkd. bds., unc. (S. Jun.22; 173) *Simmermader.* £420
– – Anr. Copy. Diced cf. gt. (P. Sep.11; 282) *Hughes.* £290
– – Anr. Copy. Minor offsetting. Cont. russ., gt. borders. (C. Feb.25; 89) *Wood.* £280
– – Anr. Copy. Slightly soiled in parts. Cont. hf. leath., defect. (R. Oct.14-18; 1914) DM 1,000
– Views in Greece. 1821. 1st. Edn. Lge. fo. Title with vig., 30 hand-cold. plts. mntd. on card, ptd. title slips pasted on verso of cards. Cont. mor., elab. gt. borders, spine gt. (C. Jul.15; 144) *Maggs.* £6,000
– – Anr. Copy. Some plts. offset, 5 lack title slips, occasional minor marginal spotting. Cont. hf. russ., covers detchd. (C. Nov.5; 46) *Wood.* £3,200

DOEHMANN, K. & Dingeldein, W.H., Singraven
– De Geschiedenis van een Twentsche Havezate. Brussels, 1934. (165) on H.M.P. 4 vols. Lge. 4to. Orig. wraps., orig. bd. s.-c.'s., 1 spine defect. & partly loose. (VG. Dec.15; 408) Fls. 550

DOES, J. Vander–HUYGENS, C.
– 's Graven-Hage, met de voornaemste Plaetsen en Vermaecklijckheden.–De Zee-straet van 's-Graven-Hage op Schevening. Door den Heer van Zuylichem. Ill.:– R. de Hooghe (2nd. work). The Hague; The Hague, 1668; 1668. 4to. 1st. work: the plan slightly defect. & pasted on stiff old paper. Cont. vell. 1st. work with lge. engraved folding plan loosely inserted, sigd. in MS. by C. Elandts. (VG. Dec.17; 1279) Fls. 675

DOESBURG, Theo van
– Klassiek, Barok, Modern. Antw., 1920. Spotted. Orig. wraps., slightly worn. (SH. Nov.21; 307) *Tate Gallery.* £75

DOGLIONI, G.N.
See–**FRANCO, Giacomo–DOGLIONI, G.N.**

DOHERTY, William James
– Inis-Owen & Tirconnel, Notes, Antiquarian & Topographical.–Account of Antiquities & Writers of the County of Donegal. Dublin, 1891; 1895. 1st. & 2nd. Series. 2 vols. Cl. Pres. copy sigd. (GM. Apr.30; 214) £70

DOLAEUS, Johannes
– Encyclopaedia Chirurgica rationalis [–Tractatus Varii . . . accessit vita a Christiano Francisco Paullini]. Venice, 1695. 2 pts. in 1 vol. Fo. Slightly spotted & dampstained, wormholes in margin, slightly affecting a few side-notes. Cont. vell. bds. worn & soiled, upr. hinge brkn. (S. Oct.21; 378) *King.* £60

DOLCE, Lodovico
– Le Trasformazioni di M. Ludovico Dolce con Privilegi. Venice, 1553. 1st. Edn. 4to. 6 unnumbered pp., 1 errata p., 1 with printer's mark & index, 94 xylographs. Mod. hf. cf. (CR. Mar.19; 250) Lire 360,000

DOLCE, Lodovico–DONI, Anton Francesco –ALBERTI, Leon Battista
– Dialogo della Pittura.–Disegno . . . partito in piu Ragionamente ne quali si tratta della Scoltura et Pittura.–La Pittura. Trans.:– L. Domenichi (3rd. work). Venice, 1557; 1549; 1547. 1st. 2 works 1st. Edns., 3rd. work 1st. Edn. in Italian. 3 works in 1 vol. 1st. work: some ll. stained; 2nd. work: some annots. in text; 3rd. work: some inscrs. in text. Old limp vell. bds., lacks titles, some wear & soiling. (S. Jun.23; 227) *Goldschmidt.* £320

DOLET, Etienne
– Commentariorum Linguae Latinae Tomus Primus [Secundus]. Lyon, 1536-38. 1st. Edn. 2 vols. Fo. Title of vol. 1 reprd., some old annots., MS. additions in index, MS. lf. tipped in vol. 1, 16th. or 17th. C. red stp. of Bibl[iotheca] Univer[sitatis] Par[isiensis] on titles, bkplt. of Girardot de Préfond, arms pasted to free end paper in vol. 1. 18th. C. cf., triple gt. fillet, spines gt. in compartments, some stains. (SM. Oct.7; 1683) Frs. 2,500
– Francisci Valesii Gallorum Regis Fata.–Les Gestes de Francoys de Valois, Roy de France. –Genethliacum Claudii Doleti . . . Lyon, 1539; 1540; 1540; 1539. 2nd. work 1st. Edn. in Fr., 4th. work [1st. Edn. in Fr.]. 2nd. work 3 pts. in 1 vol. 4to. Bibliotheca Heberiana stp. on flylf. 18th. C. mor., triple gt. fillet, flat spine, gt. à la grotesque, inner gt. dentelles, some worming. Bkplts. of Charles Nodier & La Roche Lacarelle. (SM. Oct.7; 1684) Frs. 17,000

DOLFIN, E.
– Acta seren. Principis Eugenij Francisci Sabaudiae, et Pedemontij Ducis. Vienna, 1735. Fo. Wormed at lr. corner. Cont. leath. gt., reprd. (HK. Nov.18-21; 1155) DM 550

DOLL, Anton
– Iconologie für Dichter, Künstler und Kunstliebhaber. Wien, 1801. Ob. 4to. Orig. bds. (P. Nov.13; 302) *Schapiro.* £75

DOLLFUS, Charles & Bouche, Henri
– Histoire de l'Aeronautique. Paris, 1932. 1st. Edn. Fo. Pict. leatherette. (SG. Oct.30; 130) $100

DOLMETSCH, H.
– Anthologie de l'Ornement. Paris, [late 19th. C.]. Fo. Orig. cl.-bkd. bds. (S. Feb.9; 81) *Marlborough.* £65

DOLPHIN, The
– A Journal of the Making of Books. N.Y., Ltd. Edns. Cl., 1933; 1935. (1200); (2000). 2 vols. 4to. Cl. (SG. Oct.2; 114) $120
– – Anr. Edn. N.Y., Ltd. Edns. Cl., 1933-41. 6 vols., numbers 1-4. Fo. Cl. The John A. Saks copy. (CNY. Oct.1; 174) $300
– – Anr. Edn. N.Y., Ltd. Edns. Cl., 1938. (1800). 3rd. number. 4to. This no. devoted entirely to Wroth's 'History of the Printed Book'. Buckram. (SG. Mar.28; 169) $150
– – Anr. Copy. (SG. Mar.16; 479) $130

DOMAT, J.
[–] Les Loix Civiles dans leur Ordre Naturel. Paris, 1695-97. 2nd. Edn. 3 vols. 4to. Lightly browned & soiled, II stained, engraved ex-libris. on inner cover. Cont. cf., spine reprd. & renewed. (H. Dec.9/10; 902) DM 420

DOMBRAIN, H. Honywood
See–**FLORAL Magazine**

DOMCKE, G.P.
– Philosophiae Mathematicae Newtonianae . . . 1730. 1st. Edn. 2 vols. in 1. Cont. spr. cf., spine gt. Bkplt. of Thomas Brand. (S. Feb.9; 83) *Quaritch.* £90

DOMENECH, Abbé Emmanuel
– Seven Years Residence in the Great Deserts of North America. 1860. [1st. Edn.?]. 2 vols. Orig. cl., unopened. (SH. Nov.7; 375) *Porruas.* £140
– – Anr. Copy. 1 plt. detchd., occasional spotting. Slightly soiled. [Sabin 20554] (CSK. Oct.31; 28) £50
– – Anr. Copy. All plts. stpd. on versos, Longman's 24 p. catalogue dtd. Sept. 1859, folding map linen-bkd. & laid in loose. Hf. linen, ex-liby. (SG. Mar.5; 178) $160

DOMENICA DEL CORRIERE
Milan, 1899-1945. 46 vols., lacks 1942 vol. Fo. Cold. wraps., hf. leath., not unif. W.a.f. (SI. Dec.3; 200) Lire 650,000

DOMENICHI, Lodovico
– Facetie, Motti, & Burle, di Diversi Signori. Venice, 1581. Some dampstains, bkplt. on flylf., & name stp. in gt. on doubl. of Girardot de Prefond, written press mark & crowned cipher on p. 3 of Lamoignon Liby., sig. of John Mildmay. 18th. C. red mor., triple gt. fillet, spine compartments gt. à la grotesque. (SM. Oct.7; 1685) Frs. 1,000

DOMESDAY BOOK, or the Great Survey of England of William the Conquerer, 1086
Ill.:– Col. Sir Henry James. [L.], 1860's. 22 vols. Tall fo. Gt.-lettered cl., most bdgs. brokn., ex-liby. (SG. Apr.23; 75) $180

DOMESDAY BOOK, seu Liber Censualis Willelmi Primi Regis Angliae
[L.], 1783-1816. 1st. Facs. Edn. 4 vols. Fo. Liby. buckram, worn. (SG. Sep.25; 113) $140

DOMINICUS Germanus
– Fabrica Linguae Arabicae cum Interpretatione Latina, & Italica. Rome, 1639. 1st. Edn. Fo. Some browning. Cont. vell. bds., soiled, s.-c. (S. Apr.29; 380) *Riley Smith.* £640

DOMINION Illustrated, The
Montreal, 7 Jul.-29 Dec. 1888. Vol. I, nos. 1-26.

Fo. Some ll. loose. Orig. buckram. (CB. Nov.12; 95) Can. $130

DOMINIS, Marco Antonio de
– **De Republica Ecclesiastica.** 1617-20. 2 vols. Fo. Cont. cf., not unif. [STC 6994] (S. Mar.16; 77) *Lord Dacre.* £80

DOMSELAER, Tobie van
[–] **Beschryvinge van Amsterdam.** Amst., 1665. 4to. Engraved title slightly defect., stained at beginning. Cont. vell., slightly soiled. (VG. Oct.13; 60) Fls. 3,000

DONALDSON, T.L.
See–**COCKBURN, W.B. & Donaldson, T.L.**

DONATI, Vitaliano
See–**OLIVI, Giuseppe–PLANCIUS, Janus–DONATI, Vitaliano**

DONATUS, Alexander
– **Roma Vetus ac recens utriusque aedificiis.** Rome, 1725. 4to. Slight spotting. Cont. vell. (CSK. May 8; 23) £85

DONAU-STROHM oder: Eigentl. Darstellung derer an ober and unter der Donau gelegenen Konigreiche
Nuremb., 1686. 12mo. Some ll. slightly browned, a few minor defects. Cont. hf. vell., worn, spine torn. (SBA. Dec.16; 52) *Hyde Park Bookshop.* £250

DONCK, Adriaen van der
– **Beschryvinge van Nieuw-Nederlant.** Ill.:– after N.J. Vischer (map). Amst., 1656. 2nd. Edn. 4to. Sm. tear & repair in map, hole in H3, cutting some letters, slight spotting. Mod. mor., covers slightly stained. [Sabin 20594] (S. Feb.10; 438) *Partington.* £1,300

DONCKER, Hendrick
[–] **[De Zee-Atlas, Ofter Water-Waerelt . . .]** Amst., [1644 or later]. Fo., (460mm × 290mm). 19 double-p. engraved charts (of 29?) hand-cold. in outl., a few charts dtd. 1656, 1661, or 1664, wanting title, text & possibly 10 charts, 1 corner of map of Greenland & anr. slightly defect., piece torn from bottom of 1st. with loss, staining of margins, sometimes affecting surface. Inserted into 18th. C. parch. covers, stained. W.a.f. (S. Nov.2; 8) *Yarrell.* £550

DONDE, Fr. Antoine
– **Les Figures et l'Abbrégé de la Vie, de la Mort, et des Miracles de Saint François de Paule [Les Portraits de quelques Personnes signalées en Pieté de l'Ordre des Minimes].** Paris, 1671 [1668]. 2 vols. in 1. Fo. Front endpaper partly detchd., some lr. margins dampstained, bkplt. of Henry J.B. Clements. Cont. red mor., gt. panel with corner sprays in pointillé, triple gt. fillet, spine gt. in compartments with double V, inner gt. dentelles. Beckford-Hamilton Palace copy. (SM. Oct.7; 1686) Frs. 6,000
See–**BARBIANI, Marcello Vestrio–DONDE, Antoine**

DONI, Antonio Francesco
[–] **La Libreria del Doni.–La Seconda Libreria del Doni.** Venice, 1550-51. 1st. Edns. 2 vols. 12mo. Antique cf. (BS. Jun.11; 103) £240
– **La Zucca.** Venice, 1551. 3 pts. in 1 vol. Hf. cf. (S. Jan.27; 376) *Broseghini.* £120
See–**DOLCE, Lodovico–DONI, Anton Francesco –ALBERTI, Leon Battista**

DONKIN, Maj. Robert
– **Military Collection & Remarks.** N.Y., 1777. 1st. Edn. Sm. pt. of pp. 189-90 excised as usual. Early 19th. C. hf. cf., worn. [Sabin 20598] (SPB. Jun.22; 52) $200

DONLEVY, Andrew
[–] **The Catechism, or Christian Doctrine by way of Question & Answer.** Paris, 1742. Cont. cf., gt. spine. (C. Apr.1; 204) *Lyon.* £160

DONNE, John
– **Deuotions upon Emergent Occasions.** 1624. 2nd. Edn. 12mo. Lacks 1st. blank, sm. holes to some ll., with slight text loss, some browning. 19th. C. mott. cf. gt. Bkplt. of Edmund Philips. [STC 7034] (S. Feb.9; 84) *Quaritch.* £220
– **The Holy Sonnets.** Ill.:– Eric Gill. Hague & Gill Pr., 1938. (550) sigd. by artist. Orig. cl. gt., unc. (SH. Mar.26; 247) *Donnithorne.* £100
– – **Anr. Edn.** Ed.:– Hugh I'A. Fausset. Ill.:– Eric Gill. L., [1938]. (500) numbered, ptd. by Hague & Gill, & sigd. by Gill. Gt.-decor. cl. (SG. Oct.23; 138) $110
[–] **Poems . . . by J.D., with Elegies on the Author's Death.** 1633. 1st. Edn. 4to. Lacks 1st. & last blanks, & the 2 ll. of 'The Printer to the Understanders', title & 3F2 & 3 washed, reprd. & inserted from anr. copy, some headlines & catchwords, etc. cropped. Early 20th. C. maroon lev. mor. by Zaehnsdorf, gt. [STC 7045] (S. Oct.1; 550) £460
[–] – **Anr. Edn.** 1639. 3rd. Edn. Cf. gt. by Pratt, rebkd. preserving orig. spine. Bkplt. of Edmund Gosse. [STC 7047] (C. Nov.19; 5) *Maggs.* £320
– – **Anr. Edn.** 1669. 7th. Edn. Lacks 1st. & final blank ll., A3 torn & reprd. without loss of text, some headlines cropped. Antique-style cf. [Wing D1871] (C. Apr.1; 204a) *Hannas.* £120
– – **Anr. Copy.** Browned, 1 lf. torn. Cont. cf., worn. [Wing D1871] (SH. Jun.25; 14) *Frost.* £60
– – **Anr. Copy.** Disbnd. (SG. Sep.25; 114) $180
– **Polydoron, or a Miscellania of Morall, Philosophicall, & Theologicall Sentences.** 1631. 1st. Edn., iss. with extra lf. of dedication. 12mo. Some stains, a few gatherings becoming loose in bdg. Cont. cf., very worn. [STC 7020] (C. Apr.1; 203) *Quaritch.* £120
– **Sermon Upon the xv verse of the viii Chapter of John.** 1634. 4to. Light soiling. Mod. mor. gt., worn. [STC 7056] (SPB. Nov.25; 74) $175
– **Sermons.** 1640. 1st. Edn. Fo. Engraved frontis. port. laid down & reprd., outer blank margin of title slightly frayed. Cont. cf., rebkd., corners reprd. From the collection of Eric Sexton. [STC 7038] (C. Apr.15; 94) *Tann.* £450
– – **Anr. Copy.** Additional engraved title in 1st. state, slight browning & soiling, few tears & sm. holes, slightly affecting text & additional title. Head & foot of spine defect. (S. Sep.29; 20) *Swales.* £160
– – **Anr. Copy.** Lacks initial blank, fore-corner of engraved & printed titles torn away with relevant portions supplied in pen & ink facs. [STC 7038] (S. Dec.9; 305) *Ohern.* £110

DONNEAU de Vize, Jean
[–] **The Husband Forc'd to be Jealous.** Trans.:– N.H. 1668. 1st. Edn. in Engl. Rust-hole in G8, just affecting text, slight browning. Mod. cf.-bkd. marb. bds., spine gt. [Wing H3805] (S. Feb.9; 85) *Thorp.* £100

DONOVAN, Edward
– **An Epitome of the Natural History of the Insects of China.** 1798. 1st. Edn. 4to. 50 hand-cold. engraved plts. Hf. mor. (C. May 20; 199) *Moffat.* £1,300
– – **Anr. Edn.** Ed.:– J.O. Westwood. 1842. New Edn. 4to. Some ll. slightly browned, a few slightly dampstained, mainly text. Orig. cl. gt., spine torn. (SBA. Dec.16; 136a) *Dekker & Nordeman.* £420
– **An Epitome of the Natural History of the Insects of New Holland, New Zealand, New Guinea . . .** 1805. 4to. Without 2nd. ptd. title. Pol. cf., gt., key-pattern borders on sides, spine gt. Bkplt. of Alexander Mackenzie. (C. Mar.18; 37) *Quaritch.* £3,800
– **The Natural History of British Birds.** 1794-98. 5 vols. Str.-grd. crimson mor. gt. (P. Nov.13; 194) *Smith.* £1,300
– – **Anr. Copy.** Vols. 1-5 (of 10). Hf. russ., worn. W.a.f. (S. Dec.3; 952) *Wagner.* £800
– – **Anr. Edn.** 1794-99. 5 vols. only (of 10) in 2. Lacks Index to vol. 1 & title to vol. 3, 1 title misbnd., a few minor defects. Cont. cf., very worn. W.a.f. (SBA. Jul.14; 226) *Schrire.* £440
– – **Anr. Edn.** 1794-1819. 10 vols. in 5. 244 hand-cold. engraved plts., lacks hf.-titles. Cont. hf. russ., lacks 1 cover, anr. detchd., 2 spines defect. (C. May 20; 198) *Quaritch.* £1,900
– – **Anr. Edn.** 1815-20. New Edn. Vols. 3 & 5 only. Orig. bds., worn & disbnd. W.a.f. (CSK. Jan.30; 87) £220
– **The Natural History of British Fishes.** 1802-08. 5 vols. in 3. A few ll. slightly spotted, mainly text. Cont. hf. cf., 1 hinge torn. (SBA. Mar.4; 145) *Schrire.* £800
– – **Anr. Edn.** L., 1808. Vol. 5. Slightly soiled. Cont. leath. (R. Oct.14-18; 2957) DM 700
– **The Natural History of British Insects.** 1792-97. Vols. 1-6 (of 16). Hf. cf., very worn. W.a.f. (S. Dec.3; 951) *Wagner.* £260
– – **Anr. Edn.** 1802-11. 16 vols. in 8. Lacks 1 plt., no hf.-titles, lacks 2nd. title-p. to each vol. Cont. tree cf., spines worn, 2 upr. covers detchd. (TA. Dec.18; 374) £840
– **The Natural History of British Quadrupeds.** 1820. 1st. Edn. 3 vols. Maroon lev. mor., gt., by Zaehnsdorf. (C. Mar.18; 38) *Schierenberg.* £750
– – **Anr. Copy.** Vols. 1 & 2 (of 3). Orig. bds. (BS. Nov.26; 149) £200
– **The Natural History of British Shells.** 1801-04. 5 vols. in 3. Lacks 2 ll. of text (supplied in photostat). Hf. mor., emblematically gt. spines, slightly worn. (S. Jun.1; 104) *Wheldon & Wesley.* £280
– **Natural History of the Insects of India.** Ed.:– J.D. Westwood. 1842. New Edn. 4to. A few plts. with liby. stp. on verso, lightly browned, some spotting, mostly affecting text, margins of title reprd., a few other margins torn. Mod. red mor. (CSK. May 8; 64) £500
– **The Naturalists's Repository of Exotic Natural History.** [1834?]. 2 vols. 72 hand-cold. engraved plts. Cont. hf. mor. gt., partly unc. (C. Jul.15; 176) *Taylor.* £450

DOOLITEL, Tho.
– **[Hebrew] or a Serious Enquiry for a Suitable Return for Continued Life in & after a Time of Great Mortality by a Wasting Plague [anno 1665].** 1666. Cont. gt. panel. cf., rebkd., worn. [Wing D1895] (S. Dec.2, 480) *Dawson.* £90

DOOLITTLE, Hilda
– **Kora & Ka.–The Usual Star.–Nights.** Vaud; L.; Dijon, 1930; 1928; 1935. Each (100). 3 vols. 4to. Slight browning, partly unopened. Orig. ptd. wraps., slight soiling. (SPB. Nov.25; 253) $400
– **Sea Garden.** 1916. 1st. Edn. Port. inserted. Orig. bds., unc. (S. Jul.22; 108) *Gidal.* £170
– **Tribute to the Angels.** 1945. 1st. Edn. Orig. limp bds. Inscr. to Walter de la Mare. (SH. Dec.18; 118) *Barry Scott.* £75
– **The Walls do not Fall.** 1944. 1st. Edn. Orig. limp bds. Inscr. to Walter de la Mare. (SH. Dec.18; 117) *Barry Scott.* £85

DOPPELMAIER, Johannes Gabriel
– **Atlas Novus Coelestis.** Nuremb., 1742. Lge. fo. Maps hand-cold. & mntd. on guards, slight soiling at edges. Cont. hf. cf., covers detchd. From Chetham's Liby., Manchester. (C. Nov.26; 131) *Nicholson.* £1,200
– – **Anr. Copy.** Lacks 1 double-p. copper engraved map, 1 map loose, slightly browned & soiled in parts., last map with fault & some loss, reprd. with Jap. Later marb. bds. (D. Dec.11-13; 1231) DM 7,500
– – **Anr. Copy.** Light soiling. Newer hf. leath. (R. Oct.14-18; 1536) DM 5,500
– **Historische Nachricht von den Nürnbergischen Mathematicis und Künstlern.** Nuremb., 1730. 1st. Edn. Fo. Double-p. map with short tear in centre fold, some browning, a few stains. Hf. vell., spine defect. (S. Jan.26; 279) *Quaritch.* £420

DORAN BOOKS FOR CHILDREN: a Selected List of Children's Books . . .
Ill.:– Arthur Rackham & others. N.Y., 1923. Pict. wraps. Raymond M. Sutton, Jr. copy. (SG. May 7; 70) $100

DORAT, Claude-Joseph
– **Les Baisers Précédés du Mois de Mai.** Ill.:– Ponce, De Longeuil & others after Eisen. The Hague, 1770. 1st. Edn., on papier de Hollande. Mor. gt. by Trautz-Bauzonnet. (S. Jul.27; 147) *Maggs.* £750
– **Le Célibataire, Comédie.** ill.:– Delaunay after Marillier. Paris, 1776. 1st. Edn. Occasional light spotting. Cont. red mor., gt. (SM. Oct.8; 2395) Frs. 3,000
– **Fables Nouvelles.** Ill.:– Marillier. 1773. 1st. printing. 2 pts. in 1 vol. Cont. cf. (HD. Jun.30; 21) Frs. 1,650
– – **Anr. Copy.** 2 vols. Sm. 8vo. Lacks 1 figure (not repeated at beginning of pt. 2, as often), margins rather narrow. Cont. marb. cf., spines grotesquely decor., 3 fillets, inside dentelle. (HD. Dec.5; 70) Frs. 1,250
– **Poésies.** Ill.:– De Launay after Denon. Geneva, 1777. 4 vols. 18mo. Red mor. by Cazin. (HD. Apr.8; 240) Frs. 1,700

D'ORBIGNY, Alcide Dessalines
See–**ORBIGNY, Alcide Dessalines d'**

DORE, Gustave
– **Gallery.** Ed.:– Edmund Ollier. L., [1870]. 2 vols. Lge. 4to. Orig. mor., worn & scuffed. (SG. Nov.20; 319) $100
– **Illustrations to Enid.** Priv. ptd., 1868. Plts. on India proof paper, slight spotting, loose. Orig.

DORE, Gustave -contd.
cl.-bkd. bds., worn. Plts. sigd. by artist. (SBA. Dec.16; 193) *Hamilton*. £75
See–ARIOSTO, Ludovico
See–BIBLES [Italian]
See–COLERIDGE, Samuel Taylor
See–DANTE Alighieri
See–D'AVILLER, Baron J. Charles
See–GAUTIER, Théophile
See–JERROLD, Blanchard
See–LA FONTAINE, Jean de
See–MILTON, John
See–RABELAIS, François.
See–TAYLOR, Samuel Coleridge
See–TENNYSON, Alfred Lord

DORE, Gustave & Blanchard, Jerrold
– London, a Pilgrimage. Ill.:– after Doré. 1872. Fo. Hf. mor., spine gt. (SKC. May 19; 442) £100
– – Anr. Copy. 4to. Orig. cl. gt., spine & corners slightly torn. (SBA. Dec.16; 191) *Petersfield Bookshop*. £85
– – Anr. Copy. Fo. Cl., rebkd., orig. spine intact. With the 'Malacrida' bkplt. (SG. Mar.19; 89) $170

DORE, Henry
– Recherches sur les Superstitions en Chine. Shanghai, 1911-19. Vols. 1-11 & 13-14 only. Orig. cl.-bkd. bd. folders. (SH. Jul.23; 74) *Bunsei*. £80

DOREY, Jacques
– Three & the Moon. Ill.:– Boris Artzybasheff. N.Y., 1929. 1st. Edn., (260) numbered, sigd. by artist. Fo. Bds., buckram spine. (SG. Oct.23; 7) $170

DORGELES, Roland
– Les Croix de Bois. Ill.:– Maurice Toussaint. Paris, Priv. Ptd., 1928. (25) on vell. Lge. 4to. Sewed, wrap. detchd., bds., box. Added A.L. by author. (LM. Nov.8; 46) B.Frs. 7,500
– Les Croix de Bois.–La Boule de Gui.–Le Cabaret de la Belle Femme. Ill.:– A. Dunoyer de Segonzac (1st. work). 1921-24. 1st. Ill. Edn. (1st. work); 1st. Edn. on Lafuma (2nd. work); 3rd. work on Rives laid paper. 3 works in 3 vols. 4to. 1st. work: orig. etchings. Sewed. (HD. Jun.24; 183) Frs. 3,000
– Synthèses Littéraires et Extralittéraires. Ill.:– Guy Bofa. Paris, 1923. (1,161) on vergé blanc. 4to. Maroon niger mor. with central onlay of mor., using alternative title from 'Advertissement' in letters blind-stpd., gt., or onlaid in red, green or black mor. & silver, orig. wraps. bnd. in., s.-c., by Marie J. Maudot. (SH. Nov.20; 231) *Sawyer*. £200

DORIGNY, Nicolas
– Pinacotheca Hamptoniana. [L.], ca. 1720. Lge. fo. Cont. Engl. red mor. gt., spine tooled in compartments, covers with border & arms of George II when Prince of Wales, elab. gold-blocked end-papers. (S. Nov.24; 107) *Marlborough*. £260

DORIGNY, Nicolaus–BERETTINI, Petro –ALBANI, F.–BERETTINI, Petro–BARTOLUS, P.S.
– Psyches et Amoris Nuptiae.–Barberinae Aulae Fornix Romae.–Picturae ... in Aede Verospia. –Heroicae Virtutis Imagines.–Sigismundi Augusti Mantuam Adventis, Profectio Ac Triumphus. All Rome except 2nd. work, 1693; n.d. 1704; n.d.; [1680]. 5 works in 1 vol. Lge. fo. 4th. work: 2 plts. torn. Cont. vell. As a collection, w.a.f. (GM. Apr.30; 733) £200

DORN, Gerhard
– Trevisanus de Chymico Miraculo quod Lapidem Philosophiae appellant. Dionys. Zecharius Gallus de eodem. Basle, 1600. 2nd. Edn. Paper browned. Cont. cf., rebkd. The Hopetoun copy. (S. Dec.1; 146) *Weiner*. £130

DORTU, Mme. G.
– Toulouse-Lautrec et son Oeuvre. N.Y., 1971. Collectors Edns., (1,500) numbered. 6 vols. 4to. Orig. cl. (CSK. Jan.9; 106) £150
– – Anr. Copy. (SH. Mar.6; 517) *Phillips*. £120
– – Anr. Copy. Orig. cl. in cellophane d.-w.'s. (TA. Mar.19; 33) £95
– – Anr. Copy. Fo. Orig. linen. (H. Dec.9/10; 2375) DM 1,200

DOS PASSOS, John
– U.S.A.: Nineteen Nineteen. Ill.:– Reginald Marsh. Boston, 1946. Cl. Orig. drawing on upr.

free end-paper & hf.-title., sigd. & inscr. by artist. (SG. May 14; 138) $800
– – Anr. Edn. Ill.:– Reginald Marsh. Boston, 1946. (365) numbered, specially bnd., sigd. by author & artist. 3 vols. Buckram, partly unc. & unopened. (SG. Jun.4; 107) £130

DOSSIE, Robert
[–] The Elaboratory Laid Open or the Secrets of Modern Chemistry & Pharmacy Reveal'd. 1758. 1st. Edn. A few dampstains. Cont. cf., rebkd. (S. Dec.1; 147) *Kurzer*. £55
[–] The Handmaid to the Arts. 1758. 1st. Edn. 2 vols. Cont. cf., vol. 1 upr. cover detchd. (S. Mar.17; 409) *Weinreb*. £110
– – Anr. Edn. 1764. 2nd. Edn. 2 vols. Cont. mott. cf., gt. (S. Mar.17; 410) *Weinreb*. £100

DOSTOEVSKY, Fyodor Mikhailovich
– Brat'ya Karamazovy [Brothers Karamazov]. St. Petersb., 1881. 1st. Edn. 2 vols. Some ll. slightly spotted. Cont. hf. cf. (SH. Feb.5; 2) *Bjorck*. £920
– Dnevnik Pisatelya [The Diary of a Writer for Jan.-Dec. 1877, Aug. 1880 & Jan. 1881]. St. Petersb., 1878-81. 11 pts. only in 1 vol. Lacks pt. 1876, dampstained thro-out., stp. of Lenin liby. Cont. mor.-bkd. cl. (SH. Feb.5; 3) *Bjorck*. £150
– Der Doppelgänger. Ill.:– A. Kubin. [Munich], [1913]. Privilege Edn., 4to. Orig. cf. gt., stained at foot. Printer's mark sigd. by artist. (H. May 21/22; 1694) DM 1,100
– Das Junge Weib. Ill.:– W. Geiger. Leipzig, n.d. (200). Fo. Orig. bds., lacks spine. (HK. May 12-14; 1853) DM 500

DOUAT, Dominique
– Méthode pour faire une Infinité de Desseins differens avec Carreaux mi-parties de deux Couleurs. Paris, 1722. 1st. Edn. 4to. Scattered soiling. Cont. cf., gt. spine, slightly worn. (CNY. Oct.1; 8) $280

DOUGAL, J.
See–HODSON, T. & Dougall, J.

DOUGHTY, Arthur George
– The Fortress of Quebec. Quebec, 1904. (75). Initials hand-illuminated by author, many plts. hand-tinted. Orig. mor. (CB. Sep.24; 226) Can. $240
– Under the Lily & the Rose. Toronto & L., [1931]. (250) numbered. 2 vols. Gt.-stpd. mor., cl. s.-c. (CB. Feb.18; 20) Can. $350
See–SHORTT, Adam & Doughty, Arthur George

DOUGHTY, Charles Montrose
– Travels in Arabia Deserta. 1888. 1st. Edn. Folding map in pocket at end of vol. II. Orig. cl., unopened. (SH. Mar.5; 48) *Shipley*. £500
– – Anr. Copy. 2 vols. Folding map in pocket at end of vol. I. Orig. cl., gt., unc. (S. Apr.7; 487) *Quaritch*. £320

DOUGHTY, Dorothy
– American Birds. Ed.:– George Savage. Worcester, 1962. (1,500) sigd. (ptd. sig.). 4to. Maroon mor. gt., lge. painted design on upr. cover, gt.-ruled, repeated flower tool, maroon mor. silk-lined box, by Max Grollimund, Basel. (CNY. May 22; 93) $500

DOUGLAS, David
See–PEREGRINUS, Petrus, Maricurtensis –DOUGLAS, David

DOUGLAS, George Norman 'Normyx'
– Capri. Flor., 1930. 1st. Edn., De Luxe Iss. (103). 4to. Orig. cl., unopened. Sigd. (SH. Dec.19; 467) *Scott*. £85
– – Anr. Edn. Flor., 1930. 1st. Edn., (525) sigd. by author. 4to. Slight browning. Orig. cl.-bkd. bds., faded, unopened & unc. (S. May 5; 242) *Fachinetti*. £85
– – Anr. Edn. Flor., 1930. [1st. Edn.], 500 numbered, & sigd. Slight early foxing. Bds., qtr. canvas, slightly marked, unc. (KH. Mar.24; 123) Aus. $210
– Looking Back. 1933. (535) sigd. 2 vols. Orig. cl.-bkd. bds., d.-w.'s, partly unc. (S. May 5; 398) *Scott*. £85
– Unprofessional Tales. L., 1901. 1st. Edn. Occasional heavy foxing. Cold. pict. cl., discold. & spotted. (SG. Nov.13; 141) $130
See–POE, Edgar Allan–DANA, Richard Henry, Jnr.–DOUGLAS, George Norman

DOUGLAS, Dr. James
– Bibliographiae Anatomicae Specimen sive Catalogue omnium pene autorum qui ab Hippocrate ad Harvaeum Rem anatomicam ... illustrarunt. Leiden, 1734. 2nd. Edn. New cl. (S. Jun.15; 247) *Dawson*. £150
– The History of the Lateral Operation or an account of a Method of extracting a Stone ...–An Appendix to the History of the Lateral Operation for the stone ... 1726-31. 2 pts. in 1 vol. Sm. 4to. Some stains, 'William Horsburgh' inscr. on title-pp. New hf. cf. (S. Jun.15; 246) *Zeitlin & Verbrugge*. £120

DOUGLAS, James, Antiquary
– Nenia Britannica: or, a Sepulchral History of Great Britain. Ill.:– Douglas & H. Rooke, & Stothard. 1793. 1st. Edn. Fo. Short tear in plt. 23, pieces torn from fore-e. margins of plts. 3 & 24, additional title creased & with sm. repair, a few plts. & text ll. slightly stained, mainly in upr. margins, slight browning. Cont. mott. cf., rebkd. & reprd., worn, contents loose, unc. (S. Dec.9; 377) *Crowe*. £90

DOUGLAS, Sir Robert
– Baronage of Scotland. Edinb., 1798. Fo. Cont. red mor., gt., head & foot of spine & corners worn. (S. Apr.7; 406) *Thorp*. £55

DOUGLAS, Thomas, Earl of Selkirk
See–SELKIRK, Thomas Douglas, Earl of

DOV BER Shneurch of Lubavitch
See–SHNEUR SALMAN of Laidi & Dov Ber Shneurch of Lubavitch

DOVE, H. Percy
– Plans of Sydney at a scale of Forty Feet to an inch. Sydney, 1880. Atlas fo. Index Map & 47 double-p. cold. sheets, many businesses & property owners named. Rebnd. cl., gt. (JL. Mar.1; 168) Aus. $1,000

DOVES PRESS
– Catalogue Raisonné of Books Printed & Published at the Doves Press, 1900-11. 1911. Orig. bds. (P. Jan.22; 328) *Cox*. £60
– – Anr. Edn. Hammersmith, Apr., 1913. Tall 8vo. Together with Cobden-Sanderson's 'Propice'. Unbnd. (SG. Mar.26; 172) $200
– – Anr. Edn. Ill:– A. Legros. Doves Pr., 1916. (150). 4to. Orig. vell.-bkd. bds., unc., s.-c. (SH. Feb.19; 50) *Dawson*. £110

DOW, Alexander
– The History of Hindostan. 1770-72. 2nd. Edn. 3 vols. 4to. 19th. C. hf. mor. From Chetham's Liby., Manchester. (C. Nov.26; 132) *Taylor*. £50

DOWER, John
– New General Atlas of the World. 1831. 4to. Hand-cold. engraved maps, lr. margins slightly soiled. Orig. wallet-style cl. folder with unmarked silver clasp. (TA. Oct.16; 174) £90
– – Anr. Copy. 4to. Bottom margins slightly soiled. (TA. Feb.19; 121) £70

DOWLING, Daniel
– Mercantile Arithmetic. Dublin, 1768. 2nd. Edn. Slight browning & soiling. Cont. mott. cf., rebkd. (S. Feb.9; 88) *Quaritch*. £80

DOWNEY, Edward
– Killarney's Lakes & Fells. Ill:– Francis I. Walker. L., 1902. Ob. fo. Cl. (GM. Apr.30; 396) £60

DOWNING, Andrew Jackson
– Cottage Residences; or, a series of designs for Rural Cottages & Cottage villas, & their Gardens & Grounds, adapted to North America. N.Y. & L., 1847. 3rd. Edn. Pt. 1 (only). Lacks free endpaper & hf.-title(?). Orig. decor. cl. (CB. May 27; 91) Can. $130
– A Treatise on the Theory & Practice of Landscape Gardening. N.Y. & L., 1841. 1st. Edn. Some foxing. Orig. cl., end-papers discold. (SG. Dec.4; 125) $180

DOWSON, Ernest
– Verses. L., 1896. (30) numbered on Japan vell. Square 4to. Mishandled & shabby. Gt.-decor. vell. 3-line autograph epigram in hand of author in upr. cover. (SG. Nov.13; 144) $130
– – Anr. Edn. 1896. (330). Orig. parch. gt., upr. cover design by Aubrey Beardsley, 'Leonard Smithers & Co.' on spine, unc. (S. Jul.22; 110) *Booth*. £190

DOYLE, Sir Arthur Conan
- The Adventures of Sherlock Holmes. Ill.:–
Sidney Paget. L., 1892. 1st. Edn. Three-qtr. lev.,
partly faded, orig. cl. covers & spine bnd. in.
A.N.s. & complimentary close & sig. (clipped
from letter) loosely taped on front fly-lf. (SG.
Mar.19; 90) $300
- The Adventures of Sherlock Holmes.–The
Memoirs of Sherlock Holmes. Ill:– Sidney Paget.
1892; 1894. 1st. Edns. 2 vols. Orig. cl. gt., cl.
folders & s.-c's. John Roland Abbey bkplt. (S.
Jul.22; 309) Sotheran. £260
- - Anr. Copy. Both orig. pict. cl. gt., covers
slightly soiled, qtr. mor. gt. s.-c. From the Prescott
Collection. (CNY. Feb.6; 97) $500
- - Anr. Edn. Ill.:– Sidney Paget. 1893; 1894. 2nd.
Edn., 1st. Edn. 2 vols. Orig. gt. decor. cl. (TA.
Jun.18; 420) £60
- - Anr. Copy. Tall 8vo. Orig. decor. cl. (TA.
Apr.16; 483) £52
- The Great Shadow. Bristol & L., [1892]. 1st.
Edn. With the lf. of advts. before hf.-title, & all
the advts. at end. Cl. Sigd., & dtd. 1891. (SG.
Mar.19; 92) $220
- His Last Bow. L., 1917. 1st. Edn. Gt.-ptd. cl.
(PNY. Oct.1; 185) $110
- The Hound of the Baskervilles. Ill.:– Sidney
Paget. 1902. 1st. Edn. Orig. pict. cl. gt. (S.
Jul.22; 114) Foley. £130
- The Lost World. [1914]. Re-Iss. of De Luxe Edn.
Orig. cl. gt. (SH. Dec.19; 470) Harris. £55
- The Memoirs of Sherlock Holmes. 1894. 1st.
Edn. in book form. Orig. cl. (CSK. Sep.5; 124)
£55
- - Anr. Copy. (S. Jul.22; 112) Duschnes. £50
- The Stark Munro Letters. 1895. 1st. Edn. Orig.
cl. Inscr. (S. Jul.22; 113) Green. £80
- A Study in Scarlet. Ill.:– Charles Doyle. 1888.
2nd. (1st. Ill.) Edn. Lacks advts. Hf. mor. (SH.
Dec.19; 469) Quaritch. £1,400

DOYLE, James William E.
- A Chronicle of England. Ill.:– Edmund Evans &
Doyle. L., 1864. 4to. Crimson str.grd. mor., gt.
borders & dentelles, by Rivière, slightly worn.
(SG. Mar.19; 93) $130

DOYLE, John, Caricaturist
[-] Political Sketches by H. B. 1830-34. Lge. fo.
Cont. hf. mor. gt. (TA. Apr.16; 275) £90
[-] Political Sketches.–Key to Political Sketches ..
[1829-]47. Together 21 vols. (19 + 2). Ob. fo. &
8vo. Litho. titles & ptd. index in each plt. vol.,
some titles & some indexes laid down, 894 lithos.,
3 extra lithos. bnd. in vol. 11. Cont. hf. mor., text
in orig. ribbed cl. W.a.f. (C. May 20; 26)
Rowland. £220

DOYLE, Richard
- In Fairyland, Pictures from the Elf-World. 1875.
2nd. Edn. Fo. Margin of 1 plt. slightly frayed.
Loose, orig. cl. gt. (SBA. Oct.21; 235)
Koike. £160

D'OYLY, Sir Charles
- Sketches of the New Road in a Journey from
Calcutta to Gyah. Calcutta, 1830. 1st. Edn. Ob.
4to. Occasional spotting & foxing. Orig. litho.
wraps. (S. Jun.29; 228) Ad Orientem. £650
[-] Tom Raw, The Griffin. 1828. Orig. blind-stpd.
cl. gt. (P. Sep.11; 278) Quaritch. £200

DOYLY, Sir Charles & Williamson, Capt. Thomas
- The Costume & Customs of Modern India. N.d.
[plts. dtd. 1813]. Fo. 20 hand-cold. aquatint plts.,
lacks hf.-title. Cont. str.-grd. mor., gt. &
blind-tooled border on sides, spine gt. (C. May
20; 114) Fielden. £250

DOYON, Réne-Louis–EBERHARDT, Isabelle
- La Vie Tragique de la Bonne Nomade.–Mes
Journaliers. Paris, 1923. On L.P.; numbered. 2
works in 1 vol. Mor., s.-c. Autograph dedication
from Isabelle Eberhardt to Duc de Clermont
Tonnerre. (HD. Jun.29; 46g) Frs. 1,100

DRABBLE, G.C.
- Catalogue of British Coins. 1939-43. 2 vols. 4to.
Orig. wraps. (SH. Mar.6; 348) Campbell. £70

DRAKE, Benjamin
- Tales & Sketches of the Queen City. Cinc., 1838.
1st. Edn. 12mo. Some owners' inscrs., 1
paperburned, slightly affecting title, slight foxing
& staining. Orig. cl., chipped at head & foot of
spine, lacks ptd. label, boxed. From liby. of
William E. Wilson; the Littell copy. (SPB.
Apr.29; 80) $350

DRAKE, B[enjamin] & Mansfield, E.D.
- Cincinnati in 1826. Cinc., 1827. 1st. Edn. 12mo.
Foxed & stained, sig. & blind-stp. of James
McBride & John Erwin on title. Orig. mor. gt.,
worn. From liby. of William E. Wilson; bkplt. of
John Erwin. (SPB. Apr.29; 81) $175

DRAKE, C.F.T.
See–BURTON, Sir Richard F. & Drake, C.F.T.

DRAKE, Daniel
- Discourse on the History, Character, &
Prospects of the West: Delivered to the Union
Literary Society ... Cinc., 1834. 1st. Edn. Top of
pp. stained, a few ll. browned, some foxing. Orig.
ptd. wraps., covers partially detchd., slightly foxed
& soiled, lr. cover stained, folding cl. case. From
liby. of William E. Wilson. (SPB. Apr.29; 86)
$250
- Discourses ... Before the Cincinnati Medical
Library Association ... Cinc., 1852. 1st. Edn.
12mo. Text soiled & stained. Orig. blind-stpd.
wraps., gt. title on upr. cover, spine worn, in
folding cl. case. From liby. of William E. Wilson.
(SPB. Apr.29; 89) $200
- - Anr. Copy. Some wear & soiling, p.20 torn &
reprd., not affecting text, perforated liby. stp. on
title. Mod. cl., ex-liby., bkplt. From liby. of
William E. Wilson. (SPB. Apr.29; 88) $175
- An Introductory Lecture on the Necessity &
Value of Professional Industry. Lexington, Ky.,
1823. 1st. Edn. 12mo. Foxed, blind-stpd. on title
& last lf. of text. Orig. wraps., stitched as iss., MS.
notation on upr. wrap., apparent inscr. on front
free end-paper. From liby. of William E. Wilson,
ex-liby. (SPB. Apr.29; 83) $325
- Natural & Statistical View, or Picture of
Cincinnati, & the Miami Country ... Cinc., 1815.
1st. Edn. 12mo. Staining & foxing. Orig. ptd. bds.,
unc., shabby. Pres. copy. (SG. Jan.8; 131) $650
- - Anr. Copy. Text foxed & stained, 2 folding
maps, browned & rebkd. Orig. cf., worn. From
liby. of William E. Wilson. (SPB. Apr.29; 82)
$300
[-] The People's Doctors. Cinc., 1830. 1st. Edn.
Foxed. Hf. cl., orig. ptd. wraps. bnd. in., ex liby.
Inscr. (SG. Sep.18; 121) $325
- A Practical Treatise on the ... Treatment of
Epidemic Cholera ... Cincinnati, 1832. 1st. Edn.
Foxed. Orig. cl., owners' notations on upr.
pastedown & blank. From liby. of William E.
Wilson. (SPB. Apr.29; 84) $225
- Remarks on the Importance of Promoting
Literary & Social Concert in the Valley of the
Mississippi as a Means of Elevating its Character
& Perpetuating the Union ... Louisville, 1833.
1st. Edn. Slight foxing & soiling, last lf. heavily
foxed. Disbnd., folding cl. case. From liby. of
William E. Wilson. (SPB. Apr.29; 85) $475
- A Systematic Treatise, Historical, Etiological,
& Practical, on the Principal Diseases of the
Interior Valley of North America ... Cinc., 1850.
1st. Edn. 4to. Plts. browned & foxed, text foxed.
Later cf., gt. spine. From liby. of William E.
Wilson. [Sabin 20825] (SPB. Apr.29; 87) $500
- - Anr. Copy. Foxed. Orig. sheep, crudely
rehinged, worn. Slip pasted in upr. cover inscr 'To
Mr. Hiram Powers ...', Powers' bkplt. (SG.
Sep.18; 120) $350

DRAKE, Edward Cavendish
- A New Universal Collection of Authentic &
Entertaining Voyages & Travels. 1768. Fo. Orig.
cf., worn. (TA. Apr.16; 281) $200
- - Anr. Edn. 1769. Fo. Frontis., title &
dedication stained, some marginal worming. Cont.
rough cf., rather worn, recased. (SKC.
Jul.28; 2446) £180

DRAKE, Francis, Surgeon
- Eboracum. 1736. 2 vols. in 1, L.P. Fo. Mezzotint
port. mntd. as frontis., 2 double-p. engraved plts.
crudely hand-cold., several MS. annots. (possibly
by the author). Cont. diced cf., covers with
blind-stpd. drawer-handle tool panel enclosing
inner panel with gt. floral cornerpieces, by
Benedict, rebkd. preserving orig. spine with some
flaking. From the collection of Eric Sexton. (C.
Apr.16; 246) Kelsall. £150
- - Anr. Copy. Some double-p. plts. mntd. on
guards, title & last 2 ll. detchd., 2 ll. cleanly torn,
1 affecting ill. Old cf., covers detchd. (CSK.
Mar.20; 94) £70

DRAKE, Francis S.
- The Indian Tribes of the United States ... Phila.,
1884. 2 vols. 4to. 'Buffalo Chase' plt. not present.
Hf. mor., worn, ex-liby. (SG. Mar.5; 179) $190

DRAKE, James
- Anthropologia nova; or a System of Anatomy
describing the Animal Oeconomy, & a Short
Rationale of Many Distempers incident to the
human body. Ill.:– Van der Gucht after Thomas
Forster. 1707. 1st. Edn. 2 vols. Cont. panel. cf.
rebkd. with mor. (S. Jun.15; 248) Phillips. £160
- - Anr. Copy. Some plts. torn & reprd., without
loss, some spotting. Cont. panel. cf., rebkd. (CSK.
Oct.24; 208) £65

DRAKE, Maurice
- A History of English Glass-Painting. L., 1912.
1st. Edn. Fo. Sm. marginal tear in title-p.
Parch.-bkd. bds. From the liby. of Clement
Heaton. (SG. Mar.12; 341) $120

**DRAMATIC CHARACTERS or different
portraits of the English stage**
1770. 1st. Edn. 4to. Cont. cf., lacks upr. cover. (S.
Dec.9; 451) Quaritch. £320

DRAYTON, John
- Letters During a Tour Through the Northern &
Eastern States of America. Charleston, S.C., 1794.
1st. Edn. Owner's inscr. cut from top of title,
slight foxing. Cont. cf.-bkd. bds. From liby. of
William E. Wilson. (SPB. Apr.29; 91) $600

DRAYTON, Michael
- Nimphidia & the Muses Elizium. Ed.:– John
Gray. Ill.:– Charles Ricketts. Vale Pr., 1896.
(210). Orig. bds., slightly soiled & worn, unc.,
unopened. (S. Jul.31; 38) Morten. £60
- Poems. 1613. 5th. Edn. Cont. cf., gt. lozenge on
covers, rebkd. [STC 7221] (S. Mar.16; 138)
Dawson. £240
- Poly-Olbion. [1612]. 1st. Edn., 1st. Iss. Sm. fo.
Without printed title, engraved title with sm. hole,
port., 2 double-p. maps torn, 2 with sm. holes,
some staining thro.-out. Cont. cf., spine gt.,
rebkd., orig. spine preserved. [STC 7226] (C.
Jul.16; 349) Taylor. £1,200
- - Anr. Copy. Double-p. maps in 1st. state, lacks
ptd. title, port., dedication & 2 ll. table, quire A
bnd. at end. Cont. cf., rebkd. Bkplt. of Sir Alfred
Mond. [STC 7226] (S. Nov.25; 411A)
Srossley. £900
- - Anr. Edn. 1613. 1st. Edn., 2nd. iss. Sm. fo. 2
double-p. folding engd. maps with sm. tears, sm.
hole in 1, lacks port. 19th. C. cf. [STC 7227] (C.
Jul.16; 322) Taylor. £160
- [-] Anr. Edn. 1622. 1st. Edn., 3rd. Iss. Fo. 1 map
reprd. in blank margin, another with slight paper
fault, some maps slightly browned, some liby. stps.
(1 on port.). 19th. C. hf. mor. From Chetham's
Liby., Manchester. [STC 7228] (C. Nov.26; 133)
Denman. £2,000
- Works. L., 1748. 1st. Coll. Edn. Fo. Cont. cf.,
worn, jnts. brkn. (SG. Sep.25; 115) $100

DREADNOUGHT, Deborah, (Pseud.)
- Beauties of Bloomerism. Ill.:– after W.S. Reed.
1852. Hf. cf. (SBA. Jul.14; 126) Fletcher. £130

DREISER, Theodore
- The 'Genius'. N.Y., 1915. 1st. Edn. With p. 497
numbered, slight spotting. Orig. cl., mor.-bkd. s.-c.
The Arthur Swann copy. (SPB. May 29; 130)
$125
- Sister Carrie. Ed.:– Burton Rascoe. Ill.:–
Reginald Marsh. N.Y., Ltd. Edns. Cl., 1939.
(1500) numbered, sigd. by artist. Buckram bkd.
cl., boxed. (SG. Oct.23; 209) $120

DRESDEN ROYAL GALLERY
- Recueil d'Estampes d'après les plus célèbres
Tableaux de la Galerie Royale de Dresde. Dresden
& Leipzig. 1753. 3 vols. Fo. A few minor defects.
Later hf. mor. gt., slightly worn. (SBA. Jul.22; 65)
King. £1,050
- - Anr. Edn. Dresden, 1753-57. 2 vols. Lge. fo.
Later hf. mor., jnts. split. (SG. Oct.9; 80) $2,200

DRESSER, Christopher
- Studies in Design. [1874-76]. Fo. Orig. cl. with 4
orig. wraps. bnd. in, 1 detchd. (CSK. May 1; 87)
£320
- - Anr. Edn. N.d. 20 orig. pts. Fo. Occasional
slight soiling. Loose as iss. in orig. wraps., soiled.
W.a.f. (CSK. Nov.28; 131) £550

DRESSER, Henry Eeles
- Eggs of the Birds of Europe. 1910. 2 vols. Fo.
Hf. mor. gt. by Rivière. (CE. Nov.20; 152) £190

DRESSER, Henry Eeles -contd.
A History of the Birds of Europe. Ill.:– Keulemans & others. 1871-81; 1895-96. 9 vols. including Supp. Lge. 4to. Cont. red hf. mor. Duncan R. Mackintosh bkplt. (C. Jul.15; 177) *Taylor.* £4,800
– – **Anr. Copy.** 9 vols. in 8. Common Kite plt. & 1 text-lf. with long tears, some ll. & plts. with short tears from outer edges, a few plts. with faint dust-lines, slight spotting. Mod. buckram, slight soiling. (S. Jun.1; 105) *Junk.* £3,200
– – **Anr. Copy.** 9 vols. including Supp. Occasional spotting, mainly of text. Cl. (S. Jun.23; 291) *Burgess.* £3,000
– **A Monograph of the Meropidae, or Family of the Bee-Eaters.** Ill.:– J.G. Keulemans. 1884-86. Lge. 4to. Maroon hf. mor. gt. (C. Mar.18; 125) *Pillar.* £2,700

DREUX DU RADIER, J.F.
[–] **Tablettes Historiques et Anecdotes des Rois de France.** L.-Paris, 1766. 2nd. Edn. 3 vols. 12mo. Lacks last lf. (blank?), 2 ll. & margin torn, 2 ll. partly. detchd. in vol. 1. Cont. mott. cf., flat spines gt. in compartments with cat of Madame de Deffand, spines rubbed. (SM. Oct.7; 1689) Frs. 1,600

DREW, William
See–HERNANDEZ, Francisco–KLAPROTH, Martin H.–DREW, William

DREXELIUS, Hieremias
– **The Christians Zodiake.** 1647. 12mo. Some short tears & sm. holes, slightly affecting text, some headlines cropped. 19th. C. pol. cf. Owner's stp. of Alexander Gardyne, bkplt. of Joseph Tasker, Middleton Hall. [Wing D2168] (S. Feb.9; 91) *Bicker.* £150

DREYFUS, Carle
See–NOCQ, Henry & Dreyfus, Carle

DRIESCH, G.C. v.d.
– **Historische Nachricht von der Röm. Kayserl. Gross-Botschafft nach Constantinopel ...** Nuremb., 1723. Slightly soiled in places. Cont. leath., gt. spine. (R. Oct.14-18; 1818) DM 900

DRINKWATER, John
– **History of the late Siege of Gibraltar.** Ill.:– Roberts. 1786. 3rd. Edn. 4to. A few tears, a few ll. slightly spotted. Cont. hf. russ. gt., recornered. Author's own copy(?) with his bkplt. (SBA. Dec.16; 16) *Duran.* £80
– **Loyalties.** Ill.:– Paul Nash. Beaumont Pr., 1918. 1st. Edn., (50) on cartridge paper, hand-cold. Orig. buckram-bkd. bds., unc. (SH. Mar.27; 352) *Brook.* £65

DRINKWATER, John & Rutherston, Albert
– **Claud Lovat Fraser.** 1923. 1st. Edn. (450) numbered, sigd by authors. Lge. 4to. Prospectus loosely inserted. Orig. cl., d.-w. worn. (SH. Mar.26; 225) *Greer.* £85
– – **Anr. Copy.** (S. Jul.31; 226) *McKenzie.* £50

DRONSFIELD, J.
– **Non-Europeans Only.** Cape Town, 1942. (350) sigd. by artist. 4to. 36 drawings. Ring binder. (SSA. Jan.22; 221) R. 190

DROSTE-HULSHOFF, Anette Elisabeth von
[–] **Gedichte.** Münster, 1838. 1st. Edn. Later bds., worn, orig. wraps. bnd. in, slightly soiled & reprd. (H. May 21/22; 1046) DM 3,200
– **Die Judenbuche.** Ill.:– H. Nauen. Frankfurt, 1923. (250) numbered Orig. bds. 9 etchgs. & printer's mark sigd. (HK. Nov.18-21; 2832) DM 600

DROUVILLE, Gaspard
– **Voyage en Perse.** Ill.:– Motte. Paris, 1825. 2nd. Edn. 2 vols. in 1. Cont. hf. cf., in bad condition. (HD. Dec.5; 71) Frs. 3,000

DRUCE, Herbert & Walsingham, Lord
– **Biologia Centrali-Americana.** Lepidoptera-Heterocera. L. 1881-1915. 4 vols. 4to. Red mor. gt. (SPB. Oct.1; 184) $1,800

DRUJON, Fernand
– **Les Livres à Clef.** Paris, 1888. (650). 2 vols. Later cl., unc., partly unopened, orig. wraps. preserved. (SM. Oct.7; 1369) Frs. 1,000

DRUMMOND, Alexander
– **Travels through different cities of Germany, Italy, Greece & several parts of Asia ...** 1754. 1st. Edn. Fo. Plts. & maps, 1 torn along folds, slight browning. Cont. spr. cf. (S. Jun.22; 174) *Dimakrakos.* £210
– – **Anr. Copy.** Cont. cf. gt. (P. Jul.30; 40) *Georges.* £130

DRUMMOND, Henry
– **Histories of Noble British Families.** 1842. 2 vols. Fo. Some spotting. Cont. hf. mor. (SH. Oct.10; 440) *Piesse.* £210
– – **Anr. Edn.** 1846. 2 vols. Fo. Hf. roan, dampstained. (CE. Nov.20; 29) £340
– – **Anr. Copy.** Cont. mor. (SH. Jan.30; 425) *Jubilee.* £115
[–] – **Anr. Edn.** 1846-52. 1st. Edn. 2 vols. Fo. Occasional light spotting, a few ll. loose. Cont. hf. roan, some wear. (S. Jan.26; 221) *Crowe.* £110

DRUMMOND, James
– **Ancient Scottish Weapons.** 1881. Fo. Dampstained. Cl. & mor. (CE. Nov.20; 17) £150
– – **Anr. Edn.** Ed.:– Joseph Anderson. Edinb., 1881. (500) numbered. Fo. Orig. mor.-bkd. cl. (CE. Jul.9; 202) £130
– – **Anr. Copy.** Cl., mor. spine, worn. (PD. May 20; 43) £110
– **Archaeologia Scotica.** Edinb., 1881. Fo. Cont. mor.-bkd. bds. (S. Nov.24; 109) *Tegner.* £80
– **Old Edinburgh.** 1879. (500). Fo. Orig. mor.-bkd. cl. (S. Apr.7; 499) *Aberdeen Rare Books.* £55
– **Sculptured Monuments.** 1881. Fo. Cold. mor.-bkd. bds. (CE. Apr.23; 325) £55

DRUMMOND, Rt. Hon. Sir W.
– **The Oedipus Judaicae.** L., 1811. (50). Ex-liby. copy with stps. to fly lf. & title-p. only, slight spotting. Cont. bds., detchd. Author's pres. copy. (TA. Oct.16; 356) £50

DRUMMOND DE MELFORT, Comte Louis Hector
– **Traité de Cavalerie.** Paris, 1776. 2 vols. in 3. Fo. 30 (of 32) lge. plts., some 20 folding plts., 2nd. title-p. reprd. Later mott. cf., worn. (SG. Feb.26; 116) $120
– – **Anr. Copy.** 2 vols. With atlas vol. Cont. style leath. gt., s.-c. (R. Oct.14-18; 2774) DM 10,500
– – **Anr. Edn.** Dresden, 1786. 2 vols. 4to. Nearly all pp. & plts. loose. Cont. hf. leath., very defect. (D. Dec.11-13; 2262) DM 650

DRURY, Dru
– **Illustrations of Natural History.** 1770. Vol. 1 only. 4to. Text in Engl. & Fr. Hf. cf. gt. (P. May 14; 16) *Trevors.* £130
– – **Anr. Copy.** Cont. cf. gt., rebkd., orig. spine preserved. (SBA. Dec.16; 137a) *Hyde Park Bookshop.* £64
– – **Anr. Edn.** Priv. Ptd., 1770-73. 2 vols. only (of 3). 4to. Plts. hand-cold., minor tears to margins of 2 ll. Cont. cf., very worn, rebkd. From Chetham's Liby., Manchester. (C. Nov.26; 134) *Wagner.* £300
– – **Anr. Copy.** Occasional light browning. Cf., worn, upr. covers detchd. & taped. (SPB. May 6; 185) $1,200

DRURY, Robert
– **The Pleasant & Surprising Adventures of ...** 1743. 3rd.(?) Edn. Cont. cf., rebkd. Westport House Bkplt. (S. Mar.31; 465) *Maggs.* £85

DRURY, Maj. W.P.
– **The Peradventures of Private Pagett.** Ill.:– Arthur Rackham. L., 1904. 1st. Edn. Foxed. Pict. stpd. cl. Raymond M. Sutton Jr. copy. (SG. May 7; 74) $100

DRYDEN, John
– **All for Love.** 1678. 1st. Edn. 4to. Spotted. Mod. mor.-bkd. buckram bds. [Wing D2229] (S. Jul.27; 78) *Pickering & Chatto.* £180
– **Amboyna.** 1673. 1st. Edn. 4to. Citron mor., centre & cornerpieces of mor. inlays, by Zaehnsdorf. [Wing D2232] (C. Nov.19; 74) *Brett-Smith.* £170
– **The Assignation.** 1673. 1st. Edn. 4to. Running-title sometimes cropped. Mor. by Sangorski. [Wing D2241] (C. Nov.19; 75) *Brett-Smith.* £160
– **Cleomenes, The Spartan Heroe.** 1692. 1st. Edn. 4to. Natural paper fault in 2 ll. affecting text. Mor. by Sangorski. [Wing D2254] (C. Nov.19; 76) *Arnold.* £60
– **The Conquest of Granada by the Spaniards.** 1672. 1st. Edn. 4to. Slight foxing, cont. owner's inscr. on title. Mor. by Wallis. [Wing D2256] (C. Nov.19; 77) *Brett-Smith.* £180
– **Eleonora.** 1692. 1st. Edn. 4to. 19th. C. hf. cf. [Wing D2270] (C. Nov.19; 6) *Courtland.* £70

– **An Evening's Love.** 1671. 1st. Edn., 1st. Iss. 4to. Slightly spotted in places, some marginal tears reprd. 19th. C. spr. cf., rebkd. [Wing D2273] (S. Jul.27; 77) *Pickering & Chatto.* £120
– – **Anr. Copy.** Slight staining thro.-out. 19th. C. hf. mor. (C. Nov.19; 78) *Longman.* £80
– **Fables Ancient & Modern.** 1700. 1st. Edn. Fo. Some staining. Cont. cf., rebkd. [Wing D2278] (SH. Jun.4; 94) *Pickering & Chatto.* £60
– **King Arthur.** 1691. 1st. Edn. 4to. Minor foxing, running-title sometimes cropped. Mor. by Sangorski. [Wing D2299] (C. Nov.19; 79) *Brett-Smith.* £90
– **Love Triumphant.** 1694. 1st. Edn. 4to. Last lf. torn & reprd. affecting some letters of text. Mor. by Sangorski. [Wing D2302] (C. Nov.19; 29) *Terry.* £110
– – **Anr. Copy.** Lacks hf.-title. Cont. spr. cf., rebkd. (C. Nov.19; 80) *Monash.* £60
– **Marriage-à-la-Mode.** 1673. 1st. Edn. 4to. Mor. by Sangorski. [Wing D2306] (C. Nov.19; 81) *Brett-Smith.* £150
[–] **The Medall.** 1682. 1st. Edn., 2nd. iss. 4to. With the 2 Latin lines at end, slight browning. Early 20th. C. hf. cf. [Wing D2311] (S. Feb.9; 96) *Waterfield.* £70
– **Of Dramatick Poesie, an Essay.** 1668. 1st. Edn. Sm. 4to. Last lf. restored with loss of some letters at inner margins, title sideld & reprd. in inner margin, sm. hole in B4. Spr. cf., by Sangorski & Sutcliffe. [Wing D2327] (S. Jun.23; 387) *Maggs.* £80
[–] **The Revolter.** 1687. 1st. Edn. 4to. Title & some other ll. with margins strengthened, sm. hole in 1 lf. affecting running-title. Recent mor.-bkd. bds. [Wing R1206] (C. Nov.19; 87) *Longman.* £60
– **The Rival Ladies.** 1664. 1st. Edn. 4to. Mod. mor. gt. Bkplt. of Robert Hoe. [Wing D2346] (C. Nov.19; 82) *Brett-Smith.* £380
– **Songs & Poems.** Ed.:– Gwyn Jones. Ill.:– Lavinia L. Blythe. Gold. Cock. Pr., 1957. (100) specially bnd. with dupl. set of 16 designs. Folio no. 9. Orig. Mor., gt. designs, s.-c., by Sangorski & Sutcliffe. (WW. May 20; 86) $200
– **The State of Innocence, & Fall of Man.** 1677. 1st. Edn. 4to. Recent mor. [Wing D2372] (C. Nov.19; 83) *Brett-Smith.* £220
– **Troilus & Cressida.** 1679. 1st. Edn. 4to. Lf. of advts. at end, several margins & corners frayed, sometimes affecting text, lf. of verses by Duke from anr. copy. Mor. by Sangorski. [Wing D2388] (C. Nov.19; 84) *Blackwell.* £170
– **The Comedies, Tragedies, & Operas [The Works].** Ill.:– Gerard Edelinck, Kneller. L., 1701. 3 vols. Fo. Cont. cf. worn, some foxing. (SG. Sep.4; 159) $140
– **The Dramatic Works.** Ed.:– William Congreve. 1735. 6 vols. 12mo. Cont. mott. cf., spines worn, lacks labels. (SBA. Jul.22; 13) *Duran.* £50
– **Works.** Edinb., 1882. 18 vols. Hf. mor. gt., gt. panel. spines, by Morrell, slight spotting on spines, slightly worn. (SPB. Nov.25; 450) $325
– **Dramatic Works.** L., [Nones. Pr.], 1931-32. (750), (50) on Van Gelder paper. 6 vols. Fo. Slight discolouration. Orig. hf. vell., some spotting. (SPB. Nov.25; 371) $200

DRYDEN, John & Lee, Nathaniel
– **The Duke of Guise.** 1683. 1st. Edn. 4to. Natural paper fault in 1 lf. affecting text, crudely reprd. Cont. spr. cf., rebkd. [Wing D2264] (C. Nov.19; 85) *Courtland.* £70
– **Oedipus.** 1679. 1st. Edn. 4to. Mor. cf. by Pratt. [Wing D2322] (C. Nov.19; 86) *Brett-Smith.* £180

DRYDEN, John & others.
[–] **Sylvae.** 1685. 1st. Edn. Lacks errata lf., slight browning. Cont. mott. cf., worn, reprd. [Wing D2379] (S. Feb.9; 100) *Waterfield.* £90

DUANE, William
– **Mississippi Question. Report of a Debate in the Senate of the United States ... on Certain Resolutions Concerning the Violation of the Right of Deposit in the Island of New Orleans.** Phila., 1803. 1st. Edn. Slight foxing, offsetting & discolouration. Orig. bds., worn. From liby. of William E. Wilson. [Sabin 20990] (SPB. Apr.29; 92) $100

DU BARTAS, Guillaume de Salluste, Seigneur de
– **La Sepmaine ou Creation du Monde.** Paris, 1601. 12mo. Red mor. by Capé, fillet, decor. spine, inside dentelle. (HD. Mar.18; 59) Frs. 1,200

DUBE, Paul 'Docteur en Medecine'
- Le Medecin des Pauvres.-Les Chirurgien des Pauvres. Paris, 1674. 4th. Edn. (1st. work). 2 works in 1 vol. 12mo. Cont. cf. (CB. Nov.12; 155)
Can. $110

DUBLIN MAGAZINE (The)
Dublin, 1762. 12 nos., complete with index Jan.-Dec. 1762. Hf. cf., unc. (GM. Apr.30; 18)
£65

DUBLIN UNIVERSITY MAGAZINE
1833-55. Vols. 1-46. Cont. hf. cf. (SH. Apr.9; 229)
Landry. £210

DU BOIS, J.P.I.-GUILLAUME, Gustave, Baron d'Imhoff
- Vies des Gouverneurs Généraux avec l'Abrégé de l'Histoire des Etablissemens Hollandais aux Indes Orientales . . .-Considérations sur l'Etat Présent de la Compagnie Hollandaise . . . The Hague; Amst., 1763; 1741. 2 works in 1 vol. 4to. Mod. covers. (HD. Jun.24; 29)
Frs. 2,300

DUBOIS, U.
- Cuisine Artistique. Paris, 1872-1874. Soiled. Mod. hf. leath. (R. Mar.31-Apr.4; 1613) DM 900
- Cuisine de tous les Pays. Paris, 1872. 3rd. Edn. Slightly soiled in parts. Mod. hf-leath. (R. Mar.31-Apr.4; 1614)
DM 400

DUBOS
- Les Fleurs, Idylles, suivies de Poésies diverses. Paris, 1817. 18mo. Foxed. Cont. str.-grd. mor., spine decor., lge. gt. motif covering nearly all of covers, inner dentelles. (HD. Apr.8; 96)
Frs. 1,400
- - Anr. Copy. 16mo. Cont. bds., watered silk, spine decor., lge. gt. fillet on covers. (HD. Apr.8; 97)
Frs. 1,100

DUBOURDIEU, Rev. J.
- Statistical Survey of the County of Down. Dublin, 1802. Errata slip. Hf. cf. (GM. Apr.30; 275) £90
- - Anr. Edn. Dublin, 1812. Orig. hf. cf. (GM. Apr.30; 274)
£100

DUBOURG, M.
- Views of . . . Rome, & its Vicinity. 1844. 4to. Orig. cl., upr. cover loose. (P. Jan.22; 248)
Cambridge. £250
- - Anr. Copy. Fo. Title spotted. Cont. mor.-bkd. cl. (CSK. Apr.24; 123)
£220

DUBRE, August
See-THUDICHUM, J.L.W. & Dubré, August

DUBREUIL, Jean
[-] Perspective Practical . . . Trans.:- Robert Pricke. 1672. 1st. Edn. in Engl. 4to. Some short tears & sm. holes, slightly affecting text, slight browning, 2 pp. of advts. at end. Mod. pol. cf. Title inscr. 'Ralph Pickstock's Book'. [Wing D2411] (S. Feb.9; 103) Marlborough. £100
- - Anr. Copy. Some staining, piece torn from A2 affecting diagram. Cont. panel. cf. gt., worn & reprd. [Wing D2411] (S. Jul.27; 205)
Marlborough. £50

DUBUISSON, A.
- Richard Parkes Bonington. 1924. Ltd. Edn. 4to. Buckram-bkd. bds., d.-w. (S. Jul.27; 184)
Zwemmer. £80
- - Anr. Copy. Orig. cl.-bkd. bds. (SH. Jan.29; 93)
Phillips. £70

DUBY, Tobieson
- Recueil General des Pièces Obsidionales et de Necessité, Gravées dans l'ordre Chronologique des Evenemens . . . Recreations Numismatiques. Paris, 1786. L.P. 4to. Rebnd. in mod. hf. cf., spine wrongly numbered Tome III. (PD. Apr.1; 123)
£70

DUCA, Lo.
- Bayard. Paris, 1943. (1400) numbered. 4to. Ptd. bds., worn. (SG. Apr.23; 27)
$110

DU CHAILLU, Paul
- Explorations & Adventures in Equitorial Africa. 1861. Hf. lev. mor., spine gt., orig. gt. wrap. bnd. at end, by Bayntun-Rivière. (C. Nov.6; 207)
Heywood Hill. £80

DUCHAMP, Marcel
- La Mariée Mise à Nu Par ses Celibataires Même. Paris, [1934]. (320) sigd., dtd., numbered. 4to. Loose as iss. in orig. box. (SH. Nov.21; 308)
Wilder. £1,600
- - Anr. Edn. [Paris], [Sep. 1934] De Luxe 1st. Edn., (20) numbered. Sm. fo. (13 × 11 inches). Facs. loose as iss., in green suede-bkd. heavy

folding box, edged in tan paper, with title hole-punched in reverse at recto of upr. cover, lined with felt (with title reading correctly at verso of upr. cover in embossed fashion), upr. & lr. covers with 6 thin copper strips mntd., forming initials 'MD', (copper strips at upr. cover also hole-punched to fit over hole-punched title design, name of subscriber (Bobsy Goodspeed) has been hole-punched in felt lining at verso of lr. folding cover, publisher's s.-c. (top & bottom panels separated, repairable). Sigd. (PNY. Mar.4; 142)
$16,000
- Notes & Projects for the Large Glass. Ed.:- Arturo Schwarz. Trans.:- George Heard Hamilton, Schwarz & Gray. L., [1969]. Fo. Cl., pict. glassine d.-w. s.-c. (SG. Oct.23; 93) $100

DUCHAMP, Marcel
See-SURREALISME EN 1947

DUCHARTRE, Pierre Louis & Saulnier, René
- L'Imagerie Populaire. Paris, [1925]. 4to. Red hf. mor., corners, unc., wrap. & spine. (HD. Dec.5; 73)
Frs. 1,900
- - Anr. Copy. Publisher's bds. (HD. Apr.9; 591)
Frs. 1,400

DUCHENNE de Boulogne, Guillaume Benjamin Armand
- De l'Electrisation Localisée et de son Application à la Physiologie, la Pathologie et à la Thérapeutique. Paris, 1855. 1st. Edn. New qtr. mor. (S. Jun.15; 250) Pratt. £90
- Physiologie des Mouvements demontrée à l'aide de l'expérimentation éléctrique . . . applicable à l'étude des paralysies et des Deformations. Paris, 1867. 1st. Edn. Qtr. mor. (S. Jun.15; 251)
Quaritch. £170

DU CHESNE, André
- Histoire des Papes et Souverains Chefs de l'Eglise. Ill.:- Nantueil. Paris, 1653. 2 vols. in 1. Fo. Cont. blind-stpd. vell. (SG. Sep.25; 118) $140

DUCHESNE, J.B. Philippoteau
- Histoire du Baianisme ou de l'Hérésie de Michel Baius. Douai, 1731. 1st. Edn. 4to. Cont. marb. cf., arms of Chancelier d'Aguesseau in centre. Père Duchesne's copy. (HD. Mar.18; 60) Frs. 2,100

DU CHOUL, Guillaume
- Discorso . . . [Padua], 1559. Sm. wormhole in 1st. 3 ll. slightly affecting text, some light stains. Later vell. (S. Jul.27; 113) Duran. £80

DUCIS, Jean François
- Oeuvres. Ill.:- after Gérard (port.); Colin, Desenne & Girodet (figures). Paris, 1827. Figures on China, some ll. yellowed, slight foxing. Glazed cf. by Thouvenin, blind-tooled plaques surrounded by gt. fillets on covers, spines decor. with raised bands, inside dentelle. Bkplt. of Henri Béraldi. (HD. Feb.27; 119) Frs. 2,200

DUCLOS, Ad.
- Bruges. Histoire et Souvenirs. Bruges, 1910. 4to. Sewed, spine brkn. (LM. Mar.21; 65)
B.Frs. 7,500

DUCLOS, Charles Pinot
- Contes. Ill.:- R. de los Rios (figures); Lalauze (port.). Paris, 1880. Ltd. Edn. Figures in 2 states. Mor. by Pagnan, decor. spine, inside dentelle. Bkplt. of Francis Kettaneh. (SM. Feb.11; 154)
Frs. 3,000
- Oeuvres Complètes. 1820-21. 9 vols. Cf., by Bibolet. (HD. Oct.10; 237) Frs. 1,300

DU COSTER, Charles
- La Légende d'Ulenspiegel et de Lamme Goedzak. Paris, Brussels, Leipzig & Livorno, 1869. 2nd. Edn. 4to. Pol. cf., 5 spine raised bands, by J. Massard of Liège. (LM. Jun.13; 58)
B.Frs. 15,000

DUCRET, Siegfried
- German Porcelain & Faience. N.d. Orig. bdg. (DWB. Mar.31; 230) £50

DUDLEY, Howard
[-] The History & Antiquities of Horsham. L. (colophon Milbank Street, Horsham), Priv. ptd., 1836. 12mo. Orig. cl., rebkd. preserving orig. spine, new end-papers. (SBA. Oct.22; 537)
Chambers. £70

DUDLEY, [Robert]
[-] Dell'Arcano del Mare. [Flor.], ca. 1661. Fo. 19th. C. hf. leath., spine defect. (H. Dec.9/10; 478) DM 1,400

See-RUSSEL, Sir William Howard & Dudley, Robert

DUERER, Albrecht-AUDRAN, J.
- Beschyvinghe . . . van de Menschelijcke Proportion.-Proportien der Menschelyke Lichamen. Arnhem (1st. work), 1622; n.d. Fo. Slight tear in lf. Z11 (1st. work). Hf. cf. (P. Mar.12; 250) Bishop. £620

DU FAY DE CHISTERNSL, Ch.-J.
- Anmerkungen über Verschiedene mit dem Magnet angestellte Versuche. Erfurt, 1748. Lightly browned & soiled thro.-out, lacks 1 plt. Mod. hf. linen. (H. Dec.9/10; 392) DM 450

DUFF, E. Gordon
- William Caxton. Chic., Caxton Cl., 1905. (252) on Amer. H.M.P. Fo. Cl-bkd. bds., unc., unopened. (SG. Oct. 2; 76) $300

DUFFET, Thomas
- The Spanish Rogue. 1674. 1st. Edn. 4to. Recent mor.-bkd. bds. [Wing D2453] (C. Nov.19; 88)
Pickering & Chatto. £170

DUFLOS Le Jeune
- Recueil d'Estampes, representant les Grades, les Rangs & les Dignités, suivant le Costume de toutes les Nations existants. Paris, 1780. 1 vol. only. Fo. 120 hand-cold. copperplts. Old cf., brkn. (SG. Oct.9; 81) $800

DUFOUR DE LA CRESPALIERE, C.
[-] Contes Facétieux tirez de Bocace, & autres Autheurs Divertissans, en Faveur des Melancholiques, et Fables Moralisées. Paris, 1670. 1st. Edn. 12mo. Some light staining. 18th. C. red mor., gt. Nodier & Bernard copy. (SM. Oct.8; 2244) Frs. 5,000

DUFOUR, H.
- Atlas Universel Physique, Historique et Politique de Géographie Ancienne et Moderne. Paris, 1860[-61]. Lacks 1 map of 42 double-p. outl. cold. steel engraved maps. Cont hf. leath., defect. (R. Oct.14-18; 1532) DM 600

DUFRENOY, Mme.
- Oeuvres. 1826. 2 vols. Long-grd. mor., gt. fillet frame, lge. blind panel, blind & gt. ornam. spines, by Thouvenin. (HD. Oct.10; 238) Frs. 1,800

DU FRESNE, Raphael T.
- Trattato della Pittura di Leonardo da Vinci . . . Trans.:- Leon Battista Alberti. Paris, 1651. Fo. Old mott. cf., worn. (SPB. May 6; 186) $850

DU FRESNOY, Charles Alphonse
- The Art of Painting. Ed.:- Sir Joshua Reynolds (annots.). Trans.:- William Mason. York, 1783. 1st. Edn. 4to. With lf. of advts. at end. Mod. qtr. cl. Pres. Copy, to Mr. Sykes. (SG. Mar.12; 132)
$120

DUGAY-TROUIN
- Memoires Augmentées de son Eloge par Monsieur Thomas. Rouen, 1788. 12mo. Cont. marb. roan, smooth decor. spine. (HD. Jun.24; 30)
Frs. 1,300

DUGDALE, James
- The British Traveller. 1819. 4 vols. 4to. Some foxing. Hf. cf., crudely rebkd. (P. Jul.30; 296)
Map House. £130

DUGDALE, Thomas
- England & Wales Delineated [Curiosities of Great Britain]. 1845. 3 vols. Plts. & folding maps hand-cold. in outl., some spotted. Hf. cf., spines & jnts. worn. (SKC. Feb.26; 1643) £80
- - Anr. Edn. [1845?]. 10 vols. only (of 11). 58 engraved double-p. maps on guards. Orig. cl., vol. 10 not unif., slightly worn. W.a.f. (SBA. Jul.14; 25) Hughes & Smeeth. £105
- - Anr. Edn. Ca. 1850. 11 vols. Cl., worn. (P. Apr.9; 35) Martin. £140
- - Anr. Edn. N.d. 2 vols. in 3. Plts. soiled & marked. Cont. cf. (SKC. Feb.26; 1644) £160
- - Anr. Edn. N.d. 10 vols. Spotted. Orig. cl., worn. (SH. Jun.11; 7) Walford. £130
- - Anr. Copy. Vols. 1-9 (of 11). (SH. May 21; 290) Kidd. £90

DUGDALE, Sir William
- The Antiquities of Warwickshire Illustrated. 1656. 1st. Edn. Fo. Engraved port. frontis. with tear in margin. Late 18th. C. red mor., spine gt. in 6 compartments. [Wing D2479] (C. Apr.1; 205)
Carson. £380

DUGDALE, Sir William - The Antiquities of Warwickshire Illustrated. *-contd.*
-- **Anr. Copy.** Slight stains & sm. wormhole in 1 map. 19th. C. russ., head of spine defect. [Wing D2479] (C. Feb.25; 31) *Crowe.* £200
-- **Anr. Copy.** 10 engraved plts. (of 11). Early 19th. C. russ., gt., rebkd. [Wing D2479] (S. Nov.24; 112) *Thomas.* £130
-- **Anr. Edn.** 1730. 2nd. Edn. 2 vols. Fo. A lge. copy. Cont. cf., worn. (S. Dec.9; 420) *Traylen.* £270
-- **Anr. Copy.** 4R2 reprd., flaw in 12L1, lacks final blank in vol. II. Rebkd., worn. Bkplt. of Francis Canning of Foxcote. (S. Sep.29; 158) *Fyer.* £130
- The Baronage of England. 1675-76. 1st. Edn. 2 vols. Fo. Early 19th. C. russ., gt., rebkd. [Wing D2480] (S. Nov.24; 113) *Smith.* £120
-- **Anr. Copy.** 3 vols. in 1. Last 2 ll. slightly defect., reprd., slight browning. Early 19th. C. maroon mor. gt. Bkplt. of the Earl of Orford. (S. Feb.9; 105) *Fletcher.* £95
- History of Imbanking & Drayning of Divers Fenns & Marshes, both in Foreign Parts & in this Kingdom. 1662. 1st. Edn. Fo. Margins slightly browned. Old cf., rebkd. (TA. Jan.22; 86) £230
-- **Anr. Edn.** 1772. 2nd. Edn. Fo. Early 19th. C. russ. gt., rebkd. (S. Nov.24; 118) *Quaritch.* £200
-- **Anr. Copy.** Cont. russ., gt., by I. Wilson, with his ticket, arms on covers, rebkd., bkplt. of Earl of Gosford. (S. Dec.9; 429) *Robertshaw.* £150
- The History of St. Pauls Cathedral in London. Ill.:- W. Hollar. 1658. 1st. Edn. Fo. Q2 inlaid, 1 folding plt. slightly defect., a few others with minor repairs, quires 2L, 2U, 3D & 3T inserted from a slightly smaller copy. 19th. C. russ., gt., monog. of the Earl of Essex on sides, slightly worn. [Wing D2482] (S. Jun.22; 26) *Maggs.* £50
-- **Anr. Copy.** Some ll. misbnd. at end, folding plt. reprd., some text ll. & plts. torn. Cont. cf. gt., rebkd. preserving orig. backstrip, qtr. cf. gt. drop-box. W.a.f.; Christopher Wren's sig. on title-p., initials of William Holder(?) above & on upr. paste-down (twice), bkplts. of B. Barrett & the Earl of Roseberry, lately in the Prescott Collection. (CNY. Feb.6; 99) $7,000
-- **Anr. Edn.** Ill.:- after Hollar & others. 1716. 2nd. Edn., L.P. Fo. Cont. cf., gt. arms & initials of Sir M. Masterman Sykes on covers, rebkd. Bkplts. of George Chetwynd & Nathan of Churt, lately in the collection of Eric Sexton. (C. Apr.16; 247) *Weinreb.* £75
-- **Anr. Edn.** 1716-15. 2nd. Edn. 3 Pts. in 1 vol. Early 19th. C. russ., gt., rebkd. (S. Nov.24; 117) *Scott.* £85
Origines Juridiciales. 1680. 3rd. Edn. 2 Pts. in 1 vol. Fo. Early 19th. C. russ., gt., rebkd. [Wing D2490] (S. Nov.24; 114) *Thorp.* £140

DUGDALE, Sir William & Dodsworth, Roger
- Monasticon Anglicanum. 1655-83. 1st. Edn. 3 vols. Fo. Early 19th. C. russ. gt., rebkd. [Wing D2483] (S. Nov.24; 110) *Maggs.* £240
-- **Anr. Edn.** L., 1682, 1661, & 1673. 2nd. Edn. (vol. I), 1st. Edn. (vols. II & III). 3 vols. Fo. Heavily foxed in parts. Old cf. (SG. Feb.5; 120) $280
-- **Anr. Edn.** 1718. Fo. List of plts. supplied in MS. Cont. panel. cf. with old reback. (TA. Jan.22; 87) £90
-- **Anr. Edn.** Ed:- John Stevens. 1718-23. 3 vols. Early 19th. C. russ. gt., rebkd. (S. Nov.24; 111) *Armstrong.* £210
-- **Anr. Copy.** 3 vols. including appendix. Fo. 18th. C. red mor., triple gt. fillet, spine gt. in compartments, inner floral gt. dentelles. L.P.; Bkplts. of Duc de Noailles, Gerald Gascoigne Lynde & Lord Roseberry. (SM. Oct.7; 1691) Frs. 4,000
-- **Anr. Edn.** 1817-30. 6 vols. in 8. Fo. Cont. mor., some covers detchd. (SH. Nov.6; 91) *Talbot.* £180
-- **Anr. Edn.** 1849. 6 vols. in 8. Fo. A few ll. slightly spotted. Cont. hf. mor. (SH. Nov.6; 92) *Jeffery.* £140

DUGDALE, Sir William & Dodsworth, Roger -DUGDALE, Sir William
- Monasticon Anglicanum.-History of St. Paul's Cathedral in London. Ed.:- Henry Ellis & others. L., 1817-30; 1818. 1st. work 6 vols. in 8, together 9 vols. Fo. Crimson mor., gt. borders, gt. spines & dentelles, by J. Mackenzie. (SG. May 14; 68) $1,200

DU GUAY-TROUIN, René
- Mémoires. Amst., 1730. 12mo. Early wraps., mod. s.-c., worn. (SG. Sep.25; 119) $130

DU HALDE, Jean Baptiste
- A Description of the Empire of China. 1738-41. 2 vols. Fo. 1 or 2 sm. areas of worming, slightly affecting text, occasional spotting. Cont. cf., defect. (C. Nov.5; 44) *Remington.* £400
-- **Anr. Copy.** 1 map detchd., 24 engraved plts. (wormed), slight spotting. Worn. W.a.f. (CSK. Jan.23; 136) £170
-- **Anr. Copy.** Lacks 4 maps & 1 plt., title-p. of vol. 1 rehinged, title-p. of vol. 2 detchd., some browning to a few plts. & ll. Non-unif. 19th. C. hf. mor., upr. cover of vol. 2 detchd. W.a.f., from Chetham's Liby., Manchester. (C. Nov.26; 135) *Quaritch.* £140
- Description Géographique, Historique, . . . et Physique de l'Empire de la Chine et de la Tartarie Chinoise. The Hague, 1736. 4 vols. 4to. A few ll. at end of vol. I slightly dampstained. Cont. vell. bds. (S. Jan.27; 323) *Veiss.* £600
-- **Anr. Copy.** (P. Jul.30; 298) *Walford.* £320
- The General History of China. 1736. 1st. Edn. in Engl. 18 engraved plts., 4 folding maps, 1 reprd. Cont. cf., rebkd., spines gt. Bkplt. of Thomas Fowler, Pendeford. (S. Mar.31; 466) *Ladensohn.* £160
-- **Anr. Edn.** Trans.:- R. Brooke. L., 1741. 3rd. Edn. 4 vols. Hf. linen, ex-liby. (SG. Feb.26; 121) $325

DUHAMEL, Georges
- Hollande. Ill.:- Jean Frelaut. 1949. (135). Leaves in s.-c. (HD. Feb.18; 213) Frs. 3,600

DUHAMEL du Monceau, Henri Louis
- Art de la Draperie.-L'Art de la Lingerie.-L'Art du Fabricant d'Etoffes en Laines.-L'Art du Fabricant de Velours de Coton.-Art de Faire les Tapis. Paris, 1765-80. 6 pts. in 1 vol., 2nd. work 2 pts. Fo. Margins spotted in pt. 6. Leath. From Chetham's Liby., Manchester. (C. Nov.26; 109) *Angus.* £300
- L'Art de Facteur d'Orgues. Paris, 1766-70. 2 vols. Fo. 2 lge folding plts. slightly torn, titles browned, some margins spotted. Leath. From Chetham's Liby., Manchester. (C. Nov.26; 119) *Angus.* £400
- Art de Faire le Papier.-Art du Cartier.-L'Art du Relieur Doreur de Livres.-L'Art de l'Indigothier. -L'Art du Plombier et Fontainier. Paris, 1762-73. 6 pts. in 1 vol. Fo. 1st. few ll. spotted in pt. 1, final plt. dust-soiled in pt. 6. Leath. From Chetham's Liby., Manchester. (C. Nov.26; 106) *Angus.* £2,300
- Art de Faire le Parchemin.-Art de Travailler les Cuirs.-Art du Chamoiseur.-Art du Tanneur.-Art du Megissier.-L'Art de Faire le Maroquin.-L'Art de l'Hongoyeur. Paris, 1762-65. 7 pts. in 1 vol. Fo. Title browned in pt. 1, plts. dampstained in pt. 5. Leath. From Chetham's Liby., Manchester. (C. Nov.26; 112) *Angus.* £200
- L'Art de la Peinture sur Verre et de la Vitrerie. -Art de la Teinture en Soie.-L'Art de Convertir le Cuivre Rouge.-Art de Rafiner le Sucre.-Art de Friser ou Ratiner les Etoffes de Laine. Paris, 1763-74. 5 pts. in 1 vol. Fo. Title to pt. 1 stained. Leath. From Chetham's Liby., Manchester. (C. Nov.26; 115) *Angus.* £300
- Art de Tirer les Carières la Pierre d'Ardoise. -L'Art de la Maconnerie.-L'Art du Tulier et du Briquetier.-Art du Couvreur.-Art du Chaufournier. -L'art du Potier de Terre.-L'Art de Faire les Pipes à Fumer le Tabac.-L'Art de la Porcelaine. Paris, 1763-83. 8 pts. in 1 vol. Fo. 1st. few ll. spotted in pt. 1. Leath. From Chetham's Liby., Manchester. (C. Nov.26; 107) *Angus.* £500
- L'Art d'Exploiter les Mines de Charbon de Terre. -L'Art du Tourneur Mecanicien.-Art du Paumier-Raquetier.-L'Art du Layetier.-Art du Tonnelier.-Art du Charbonnier. Paris, 1763-82. 1st. section in 2 vols., rest in 1 vol. Fo. Pt. 1: introduction bnd. before title, 3 plts. misbnd. in pt 6.; pt. 6: no separate pt. title, 13 pp. of 'additions & corrections'. Leath. From Chetham's Liby., Manchester. (C. Nov.26; 116) *Angus.* £550
- L'Art du Coutelier, Premiere-[Seconde] Partie. -L'Art du Coutelier en Ouvrages Communs. Paris, 1766-70. 4 pts. in 1 vol., pt. 1 in 3 sections. Fo. Title spotted in pt. 1. Leath. From Chetham's Liby., Manchester. (C. Nov.26; 118) *Angus.* £450
- Art du Curroyeur.-L'Art de Faire des Chapeaux. -Art du Cordonnier.-L'Art du Bourrelier et du Sellier. Paris, 1765-67. 4 pts. in 1 vol. Fo. Without separate pt. title to pt. 6. Leath. From Chetham's Liby., Manchester. (C. Nov.26; 110) *Angus.* £150
- L'Art du Fabriquant d'Etoffes de Soie. Paris, 1773-78. 2 vols. Fo. 1st. title spotted, some plts. slightly discold. Leath., 1 cover detchd. From Chetham's Liby., Manchester. (C. Nov.26; 120) *Angus.* £600
- L'Art du Menuisier [Menuisier-Carrossier, Menuisier en Meubles, Menuisier Eboniste, Menuiserie des Jardins]. Paris, 1769-1775. 6 pts. in 3 vols. Fo. Plt. 277 torn in margin affecting frame, some plts. dust-soiled or slightly discold. Leath. From Chetham's Liby., Manchester. (C. Nov.26; 117) *Angus.* £850
- Art du Tailleur.-L'Art du Brodeur.-Art du Perruquier.-Art de l'Epinglier.-Fabrique de l'Amidon.-Art du Cirier.-Art du Chandelier.-L'Art du Savonnier. Paris, 1762-74. 8 pts. in 1 vol. Fo. 1 plt. discold. in pt. 3, lacks separate title to pts. 4 & 7, margins discold. in pt. 8. Leath. From Chetham's Liby., Manchester. (C. Nov.26; 111) *Angus.* £250
- Arts des Forges et Forneux à Fer.-Nouvel Art d'Adoucir le Fer Fondu.-De la Forge des Enclumes. Paris, 1762. 6 pts. in 1 vol., 1st. work 4 pts. Fo. 1st. few ll. spotted in pt. 1., plt. discold. in pt. 6. Leath. From Chetham's Liby., Manchester. (C. Nov.26; 108) *Angus.* £200
- Description et Details des Arts du Meunier, du Vermicelier et du Boulanger. Paris, 1767. Fo. Title spotted. Leath. From Chetham's Liby., Manchester. (C. Nov.26; 113) *Angus.* £70
- De l'Exploitation des Bois. Paris, 1764. 1st. Edn. 2 vols. 4to. 19th. C. hf. mor., worn. From Chetham's Liby., Manchester. (C. Nov.26; 136) *Vien.* £50
- Fabrique des Ancres.-Art de Reduire le Fer en Fil.-Art du Serrurier. Paris, 1764-68. 3 pts. in 1 vol. Fo. Plts. dampstained in pt. 2, some margins discold. in pt. 3. Leath. From Chetham's Liby., Manchester. (C. Nov.26; 114) *Angus.* £150
- Del Governo dei Boschi. Venice, 1772. 2 vols. 4to. Sm. wormhole to upr. margin of vol. II title & 2 next ll. Orig. paper bds., unc. & unopened. From the collection of John A. Saks. (C. Jun.10; 57) *Pompelmo.* £140
- Nouvelle Methode pour Diviser les Instruments de Mathématique et d'Astronomie.-Description d'un Microscope.-Description et Usage des Principaux Instruments d'Astronomie.-Traité de la Construction des Vaisseaux.-Description de l'Art de la Nature.-L'Art de la Voilure. Paris, 1768-81. 6 pts. in 1 vol. Fo. Title spotted in pt. 1, some margins discold. in pt. 6. Leath. From Chetham's Liby., Manchester. (C. Nov.26; 121) *Angus.* £350
- Le Physique des Arbres. Paris, 1758. 1st. Edn. 2 vols. 4to. Lf. d3 defect. with serious text loss. 19th. C. hf. mor. From Chetham's Liby., Manchester. (C. Nov.26; 139) *Taylor.* £90
-- **Anr. Copy.** Cont. cf., spines gt., jnts. worn. (SG. Sep.18; 122) $450
- Des Semis et Plantations des Arbres. Paris, 1760. 1st. Edn. 4to. 19th. C. hf. mor. From Chetham's Liby., Manchester. (C. Nov.26; 137) *Baskett & Day.* £80
-- **Anr. Copy.** Cont. cf., triple gt. fillet border, decor. spine raised bands, sm. faults. (HD. Apr.24; 45) Frs. 1,300
- Des Semis et des Plantations des Arbres et de Leurs Cultures.-Les Additions pour le Traité des Arbres et Arbustes. Paris, 1760 (1st work). 1st Edn. (1st work). 2 works in 1 vol. 4to. Cont. marb. cf., spine decor. with raised bands, bdg. defect. (HD. Jun.24; 31) Frs. 1,400
- Traité des Arbres et Arbustes. Paris, 1755. 1st. Edn. 2 vols. 4to. 248 woodcut plts. (of 249, lacks the 1st. plt. in vol. II). 19th. C. hf. mor., worn. From Chetham's Liby., Manchester. (C. Nov.26; 140) *Quaritch.* £250
-- **Anr. Edn.** Ill.:- After P.J. Redoute & P. Bissa. Paris, [1800]-12. 2nd. Edn. (L.P.) Vols. I-V (of 7). Fo. Lacks 3 plts. in vol. II, 1 in vol. IV & 7 in vol. V), all but 2 ptd in colours, some finished by hand, plt. 32 in vol. I in dupl., pp. 77-80 bis & pp. 77-78 ter in vol. 1, & pp. 9-14 bis. & the 3 bis. plts. in vol. IV, lacks 1 index lf. in vol. II, occasional spotting & browning. Hf. maroon mor., spines gt., by Sizer, slight wear, slightly rubbed, partly unc., bkplt. of Ernest Ridley Debenham. (S. Dec.3; 953) *Arader.* £2,600

– – Anr. Edn. Ill.:– After Pierre-Joseph Redoute & Pancrace Bessa. Paris, [1800-] 1804-19 16 7 vols. Fo. Dupl. of plt. 5, vol. 7, some spotting & offsetting. Cont. hf. cf. gt., unc., worn. From collection of Massachusetts Horticultural Society, unstpd. (SPB. Oct.1; 115) $18,000
– Traité des Arbres Fruitiers. Ill.:– After Aubriet, M. Basseport & Le Berriays. Paris, 1768. 1st. Edn., L.P. 2 vols. Some margins dust-soiled or slightly spotted. 19th. C. hf. mor. From Chetham's Liby., Manchester. (C. Nov.26; 141) *Marshall.* £900
– Traité Général des Pesches. Paris, 1769-72. 2 vols. Fo. Leath. From Chetham's Liby., Manchester. (C. Nov.26; 122) *Junk.* £600
– Du Transport, de la Conservation et de la Force des Bois. Paris, 1767. 1st. Edn. 4to. 19th. C. hf. mor., cover detchd. From Chetham's Liby., Manchester. (C. Nov.26; 138) *Baskett & Day.* £60

DUILLIER, N. Facio
See–SALUSBURY, N. Facio

DUJARDIN, Felix
Histoire Naturelle des Zoophytes. Infusoires. Paris, 1841. 2 vols. (including Atlas). 8vo. & sm. 4to. A little dampstaining in text vol. Cont. cf.-bkd. marb. bds. (S. Apr.6; 48) *Wheldon & Wesley.* £50

DU JON, Francois
See–JUNIUS, Franciscus or Du Jon, François, the Younger

DULAC, Edmund
– Fairy-Book, Fairy Tales of the Allied Nations L., [1916.] 1st Edn. 4to. Publisher's decor. cl. Orig. watercolour & autograph dedication sigd. by artist to Princess of Monaco. (HD. Jun.24; 185) Frs. 2,450
– – Anr. Edn. [1916]. [1st. Edn.?] (350) numbered, sigd. by artist. 4to. Orig. cl., gt. (SBA. Mar.4; 212a) *Fletcher.* £250
– – Anr. Copy. Partly unc. (C. Feb.4; 53) *Baskett & Day.* £220
– – Anr. Copy. Slightly soiled, unc. (SKC. Sep.9; 1427) £75
– A Fairy Garland. 1928. (1000) sigd. by artist. 4to. Orig. vell.-bkd. bds., partly unc. (C. Feb.4; 55) *Baskett & Day.* £160
– – Anr. Edn. Copy. Orig. vell.-bkd. cl., slightly soiled. (SKC. Feb.26; 1266) £70
– Lyrics Pathetic & Humorous from A to Z. L. & N.Y., 1908. 4to. Orig. cl.-bkd. pict. bds. (S. Jul.31; 210) *Joseph.* £95
– – Anr. Copy. Loose as iss. in cl. folding case. (SG. Apr.2; 95) $700
– La Princesse Badourah. Paris, 1914. 4to. Cont. hf. mor., spine decor. with onlays & gt. tooling, slightly worn, orig. wraps. bnd. in, by Samblanx. (S. Jul.31; 207) *Hadfield.* £90

DULAC, Edmund (Ill.)
See–ANDERSEN, Hans Christian
See–APULEIUS, Lucius
See–ARABIAN NIGHTS
See–BELLE (La) au Bois Dormant, et quelques autres Contes de Jadis
See–BOOKMAN SPECIAL CHRISTMAS NUMBERS
See–BRONTE, Charlotte, Emily & Anne
See–HOUSMAN, Laurence
See–ILE ENCHANTEE (L'), conte d'après Shakespeare
See–MILTON, John
See–OMAR Khayyam
See–PERRAULT, Charles
See–POE, Edgar Allan
See–PUSHKIN, Alexandre Sergeevich
See–QUILLER-COUCH, Sir Arthur
See–ROSENTHAL, Leonard
See–SHAKESPEARE, William

DULAURE, Jacques Antoine
– Histoire de Paris . . . Environs de Paris. Ill.:– Rouargue & Tardieu. Paris, 1837-38. 15 vols. 8vo & ob. atlas fo. Cont. str.-grd. hf. chagrin, smooth decor. spines. (HD. Feb.27; 120) Frs. 2,400

DU LAURENS, André
– Historia Anatomica Humani Corporis et singularum ejus Partium multis controversis et Observationibus Illustrata. Ill.:– after Vesalius, Coiter, Valverde etc. Frankfurt, [1600]. Fo. Early purchase entry by Samuel Marchant 1686. Cont. vell., loose. (S. Jun.15; 252) *Maggs.* £460

– – Anr. Copy. Approx. 5 plts. with genital area inked out. Cont. cf., peeled from sides. (PNY. Oct.1; 187) $700

DULLER, Edouard
– Das Deutsche Volk in tseinen Mundarten, Siten, Gebräuchen, Festen und Trachten. Leipzig, 1847. 1 plt. slightly soiled. Cont. linen, upr. cover loose. (R. Mar.31-Apr.4; 1832) DM 3,700
– Die Donauländer. Leipzig, 1849. Slightly soiled. Orig. wraps. (HK. Nov.18-21; 1149) DM 1,700
– Topographical Panorama of the Rhine from Schaffhausen to the North Sea. Trans.:– [H. Howe]. L., [1845]. Soiled, lge. map bkd. at fold. Orig. linen. (R. Mar.31-Apr.4; 2160) DM 1,300

DUL'SKY, P.M.
– Grafika Satiricheskikh Zhurnalov 1905-1906 [Illustrations of the Satirical Journals of 1905-06. Kazan, 1922. (2000). 4to. Orig. wraps., slightly soiled and torn. (SH. Feb.6; 305) *De la Casa.* £100

DUMAS, Alexander, Père
– Celebrated Crimes. 1895. 8 vols. 1 vol. extra-ill. Cont. red hf. mor. (CSK. May.15; 24) £55
– – Anr. Edn. Phila., [1895]. De Luxe Edn. on Imperial Japan, (500). 8 vols. Plts. in 2 states. Mor. gt., watered silk end-papers & doubls. (SPB. May 6; 302) $650
– Georges. Paris, 1843. Orig. Edn. 3 vols. Hf. roan. (HD. Jun.30; 216) Frs. 1,650
– Herminie, l'Amazone. Ill.:– Deville after Robaudi. Paris, 1888. (225) numbered on papier de Velin Marais. 12 etched head & tail-pieces, in 3 states. Str.-grd. mor., by Bretault. (SG. Sep.4; 162) $140
– Napoleon Bonaparte . . . Paris, 1831. 1st. Edn. Hf. lev. Inscr., Robert Hoe bkplt. (SG. Sep.4; 161) $100
– The Romances. N.Y., 1893. Ill. Liby. Edn. 60 vols. Hf. crimson mor. gt. (SPB. Nov.25; 451) $1,000
– Les Trois Mousquetaires.–Vingt Ans Après.–Le Vicomte de Bragelonne.–La Reine Margot.–Les Quarante-Cinq.–La Dame de Monsoreau.–Le Comte de Monte-Cristo. Paris, n.d. 23 vols. 12mo. Red mor. by Bumpus, Oxford, double gt. fillet around covers, spines decor. with raised bands. (HD. Jun.24; 186) Frs. 3,100
– Works. Boston, n.d. Artist's Edn., (100). 47 vols. Plts., some in 2 states, 2 A.N.s. inserted. Crimson mor. gt., gt. fleur-de-lys decors. on spines. (SPB. May 6; 303) $1,500

DUMAS, Alexandre, Père & others
– Paris et les Parisiens. Ill.:– Lami, Gavarni & Rouargue. Paris, 1856. Mod. hf. mor., partly unc. (SI. Dec.3; 206) Lire 300,000

DUMAS, Alexandre, Fils
– Camille. Trans.:– Edmund Gosse. Ill.:– Marie Laurencin. N.Y., Ltd. Edns. Cl., 1937. (1500) numbered, sigd. by artist. 4to. Buckram. (SG. Oct.23; 196) $240
– – Anr. Copy. Orig. box. (SG. Jan.15; 176) $220
– – Anr. Copy. Sigd. by artist. (SG. Apr.9; 487) $130
– La Dame aux Camellias. Ill.:– Goujean after Lynch (frontis.); Champollion & Masse after Lynch (plts.). Paris, [1886]. 4to. Mor. by H. Jean, decor. spine, border of 3 fillets on covers, wrap. preserved. (SM. Feb.11; 212) Frs. 4,200
– Pechés de Jeunesse. Paris, 1847. 1st. Edn. Crimson lev., triple gt. fillet borders, spine gt., gt. dentelles, by Lortic, red hf. lev. s.c. Robert Hoe bkplt. (SG. Apr.9; 103) $275
– – Anr. Copy. Robert Hoe bkplt. (SG. Sep.4; 48) $225

DUMAS, Matthieu
[–] **Precis des Evements Militaires.** Paris & Hambourg, n.d. 1st. Edn. 19 vols. Lge. Red mor., gt., Napoleon monog. & symbols, spine raised bands, gt. spine, inner & outer dentelle, by Hatchards. (D. Dec.11-13; 2757) DM 8,000

DU MAURIER, George
– Trilby. L., 1894. 1st. Edn. 3 vols. 44 p. publisher's catalogue at end of vol. 3. Orig. pict. canvas, some staining to covers, spines discold. & soiled, cl. case. The W.K. D'Arcy & Jerome Kern copy, with bkplts., lately in the Prescott Collection. (CNY. Feb.6; 100) $140

DU MOLINET, Claude
– Le Cabinet de la Bibliothèque de Sainte Geneviève. Paris, 1692. 2 pts. in 1 vol. Fo. Some spotting, slight soiling & staining. Mor.-bkd. cl.

From the Liby. of Thomas Astle, with stp. of the Royal Institution at foot of spine. (S. Jun.22; 27) *Weinreb.* £200

DUMONT, Jean
– Batailles gagnées par le Prince Eugène de Savoye. Den Haag, 1720. Fo. Lacks ports. & 10 copper engrs. Cont. leath., gt. (R. Oct.14-18; 2835) DM 550

DUMONT, Jean & Rousset de Missey, Jean
– The Military History of . . . Prince Eugene of Savoy . . . Ill.:– Claude d. Bosc. L., 1735-37. 2 vols. Fo. Cont. panel. cf. (SG. Feb.26; 122) $600
[–] **– Anr. Edn.** 1736-37. 2 vols. Fo. A few ll. loose, slight dust-spotting. Cont. spr. cf., worn. (S. Jan.26; 118) *Broseghini.* £320

DUMONT DE MONTIGNY, Lieut.
– Mémoirs Historiques sur la Louisiane . . . depuis l'année 1687 jusqu'à présent. Paris, 1753. 1st. Edn. 2 vols. 12mo. Publisher's catalogue in cont. cf., worn, rebkd. [Sabin 9605] (CNY. Oct.1; 42) $1,100

DUMONT D'URVILLE, Jules Sebastien Cesar
– Voyage Pittoresque Autour du Monde. Paris, 1834-35. 1st. Edn. 2 vols. 4to. Cont. hf. leath. [Sabin 21211] (HK. May 12-14; 558) DM 420
– – Anr. Copy. Cont. cf.-bkd. bds., worn. (SPB. May 5; 187) $175

DUMONT D'Urville, Jules Sebastien César & others
– Histoire Générale des Voyages.–Voyage autour du Monde. Voyage dans les 2 Amériques.–Voyages en Afrique et en Asie. Paris, 1859. 4 vols. Lge. 8vo. Cont. hf. chagrin, corners, spines decor. with raised bands. (HD. Jun.24; 187) Frs. 3,900

DUMSKY Al'manakh [Duma Almanach]
Ed.:– [D.F. Chepikov]. St. Petersb., 1906. Orig. wraps. (SH. Feb.5; 62) *Lempert.* £70

DUNBAR, Seymour
– A History of Travel in America . . . Indianapolis, [1915]. L.P. Edn. (250) numbered. 4 vols. Bds., cl. spines, partly unc. (SG. Jan.8; 132) $150

DUNCAN, David Douglas
– The Private World of Pablo Picasso. N.Y., 1958. 4to. Ill. wraps., slightly soiled & creased. Inscr. to Douglas Glass, sigd. & dtd. by Picasso, with a port. sketch on title-p. in cold. crayons. (C. Jul.22; 94) *Quaritch.* £550

DUNCAN, George Sang
– Bibliography of Glass. Ed.:– Violet Dimbleby. [L.], 1960. 4to. Buckram. (SG. Jan.22; 184) $120

DUNCAN, J.
– Naturalist's Library. Edinb., 1835-41. 7 vols. 219 plts., cold. except background, vol. IV 1 plt. & vol. VI some ll. loose, some staining & light browning in parts. Orig. linen, heavily defect., spine & part of cover loose. (H. May 21-22; 167) DM 1,300
– – Anr. Copy. Slightly soiled in parts. Mod. hf. leath. (H. Dec.9-10; 290) DM 1,200

DUNCAN, Ronald
– Tale of Tails, ten fables. Ill.:– John Bratby. 1975. (200) sigd. by author & artist. Fo. Orig. mor. gt. to a design by Bratby. (C. Feb.4; 175) *MacDonald.* £55

DUNCKER, A.
– Die Ländlichen Wohnsitze, Schlösser und Residenzen der Ritterschaftlichen Grundbesitze in der Preussischen Monarchie. Berlin, 1875-77. Vols. 12 & 14. Ob. fo. Orig. linen, loose, vol. 12 defect. & slightly stained. (R. Oct.14-18; 2073) DM 7,500

DUNCUMB, John–COOKE, William Henry
– Collections towards the History & Antiquities of the County of Hereford.–Collections . . . in Continuation of Duncumb's History. Hereford; L., 1804-12; 1882. 2 vols.; 1 vol. Both in 19th. C. cf. gt. From the collection of Eric Sexton. (C. Apr.16; 249) *Chesters.* £200

DUNDONALD, Archibald Cochrane, 10th. Earl of
– A Treatise Shewing the Intimate Connection . . . between Agriculture & Chemistry. 1795. 1st. Edn. 4to. Slight worming, some spotting. Cont. spr. cf., spine gt. (S. Feb.9; 107) *Laywood.* £70

DUNDONALD, Thomas (Cochrane) Earl of
– Narrative of Services in the Liberation of Chili, Peru, & Brazil, from Spanish & Portuguese Domination. L., 1859. 1st. Edn. 2 vols. Rubberstp.

DUNDONALD, Thomas (Cochrane), & Brazil, from Spanish & Portuguese Domination. -contd.
exlibris & release stp. of Institution of Engineers in Scotland on title. Orig. cl. Pres. copy. (SG. Jan.8; 133) $220

DUNKARTON, R.
See–EARLOM, R., Turner, C. & Dunkarton, R.

DUNLAP, William
– History of the Rise & Progress of the Arts of Design in the United States. N.Y., 1834. 1st. Edn. 2 vols. Orig. bds., cl. spine, gt.-lettered. (SG. Dec.4; 126) $360

DUNLOP, John
– Mooltan. Ill.:– Andrew Maclure. 1849. Fo. Orig. cl. (C. May 20; 116) *Hosain.* £80

DUNLOP, William
– A History of the American Theatre. N.Y., 1832. 1st. Edn. Hf. mor. (GM. Apr.30; 681) £65

DUNN, Samuel
– A New Atlas of the Mundane System. 1788. 2nd. Edn. Fo. Cont. hf. cf., worn. W.a.f. (C. Nov.6; 252) *Traylen.* £240
– – Anr. Edn. 1796. 4th. Edn. Fo. 38 doubl-p. engraved maps cold. in outl., 6 plts., some maps soiled or torn in folds, title stained. Cont. hf. cf., cl. rebkd., very worn. W.a.f. (S. Mar.31; 251) *G. Terry.* £120

DUNNING, R.
– Views in Yorkshire. Ill.:– R. & D. Havell. N.d. Ob. fo. 8 cold. aquatint views (dtd. Ripon, 1813), no title or text. Cont. red hf. mor., lettered in gt., with oval gt. mor. label on side lettered 'Miss Augusta Ingilby Harrington Hall', mor.-bkd. cl. case. From the collection of Eric Sexton. (C. Apr.16; 250) *Maggs.* £4,800

DUNRAVEN, Caroline, Countess of
– Memorials of Adare. Oxford, Priv. ptd., 1865. Fo. Cl. Pres. copy. (GM. Apr.30; 405) £65
– – Anr. Copy. Inscr. (GM. Oct.30; 174) £55

DUNRAVEN, Edwin, 3rd Earl of
– Notes on Irish Architecture. L., 1875-77. 2 vols. 4to. Errata slip, text & plts. loosening. Orig. cl., gt. (GM. Apr.30; 426) £420
– – Anr. Copy. Actual photographs mntd., slightly spotted, some ll. loose. Precased. (SH. Nov.6; 94) *Weinreb.* £220

DUNS SCOTUS, Erigena, Joannes–MAURITIUS HIBERNICUS (O'Fihely)
– Universalia; Questiones Utiles super Libros Priorum [et] Posteriorum [Analyticorum Aristotelis].–Lectura in Q[uaestiones] Doc. Subtilis Scoti. Venice, 1520; 1520; 1504. 3 works in 1 vol., Fo. Slightly soiled, especially titles 1 & 2, 2nd. wormed in last 8 ll. Cont. vell., slightly stained. (R. Oct.14-18; 47) DM 1,400

DUNSANY, Lord E.J.M.D. Plunkett
– The Blessings of Pan.–My Talks with Dean Spanley. Ill.:– Sidney H. Sime. 1927; 1936. 1st. Edns. 2 vols. Orig. cl., 2nd. with d.-w. Loosely inserted in 2nd. work are 2 A.L.s from the author, 1st. to Sidney Sime, 2nd. to Mrs. Tovey. (S. Jul.31; 321) *Ferret Fantasy.* £50
– Chronicles of Rodriguez. Ill.:– Sidney H. Sime. 1922. 1st. Ed., (500). 4to. Orig. vell.-bkd. buckram, d.-w. Sigd. by author & artist. (SH. Dec.18; 120) *Wilson.* £85
– The Gods of Pegana. Ill.:– after Sidney H. Sime. 1905. 1st. Edn., sigd. Frontis. loose. Orig. linen-bkd. bds., worn, unc. Owner's inscr. of the artist's friend Duncan Tovey. (S. Jul.31; 313) *Ferret Fantasy.* £55
– The King of Elfland's Daughter. Ill.:– Sidney H. Sime. 1924. 1st. Edn., (250) numbered, sigd. by author & artist. 4to. Orig. vell.-bkd. cl., slightly stained. (S. Jul.31; 317) *Mirdan.* £55
– – Anr. Copy. Hf. vell., d.-w. (SG. Nov.13; 154) $190
– Time & the Gods. Ill.:– Sidney H. Sime. 1921. (250) numbered, sigd. by author & artist. 4to. Orig. vell.-bkd. cl., d.-w. (S. Jul.31; 315) *Jones.* £130

DUNTHORNE, Gordon
– Flower & Fruit Prints of the Eighteenth & Early Nineteenth Centuries. Their Histories, Makers & Uses, with a Catalogue Raisonné of the Works in Which They are Found. Wash., 1938. 1st. Edn. Fo. Orig. glazed buckram. (TA. Mar.19; 117) £150

– – Anr. Copy. Orig. cl., slight wear. (SPB. May 29; 132) $175
– – Anr. Edn. Wash., Priv. Ptd. 1938. (2500). 4to. Cl., box. (SG. Oct.2; 115) $200

DUOMO di Milano
Milan, 1863. Fo. Some light foxing. Cl., disbnd. (SG. Dec.4; 127) $100

DUPAIN DE MONTESSON
– La Science des Ombres, par rapport au Dessein. Paris, 1760. Sm. hole in plt. 3 from paper flaw. Cont. spr. cf., spine gt., & gt. lettered. (CNY. Oct.1; 9) $300

DU PERAC, Etienne
– Topographical Study in Rome in 1581. Ed.:– Thomas Ashby. Roxb. Cl., 1916. 4to. Orig. mor.-bkd. bds. The copy of Sydney Cockerell, sigd. & dtd. (C. Jul.22; 38) *Traylen.* £220

DUPERREY, L.I.
– Voyage autour du Monde Paris, ca. 1830. Fragment from Atlas vol. Fo. 45 col. ptd. & cold. copperplts., some ll. lightly soiled, most in margin. Cont. hf. linen, worn, defect., orig. wraps. bnd. in. (HK. Nov.18-21; 514) DM 900

DUPIN, Amandine Aurore Lucie, Baronne Dudevant 'George Sand'
– Les Beaux Messieurs de Bois Doré. Ill.:– Adrien Moreau. Paris, 1892. (110); (75) on imperial Jap., numbered. 2 vols. 4to. Engrs. in 2 states, etchings in 4 states (3 before the letter & 2 with comments). Mor. by Chambolle-Duru, spines & covers decor., wraps. preserved. (SM. Feb.11; 170) Frs. 14,000
– Le Diable à Paris. Ill.:– after Gavarni, vigs. after Bertall & others. Paris, 1845-46. 2 vols. Mor.-bkd. cl. (SH. Nov.20; 149) *Stevens.* £50
– Lettres d'un Voyageur. 1837. Orig. Edn. 2 vols. Cont. hf.-roan. Stps. & bdg. of lending liby. (HD. Feb.18; 185) Frs. 2,000
– La Marquise. Ill.:– Courboin after Baugnies. Paris, 1888. (225) numbered, with engrs. in 2 states. Lev., triple gt. fillet borders, spine & dentelles gt., by Marius Michel, ptd. wraps. bnd. in. (SG. Apr.9; 244) $375
– – Anr. Copy. Port., full-p. & vig. engrs., all in 2 states. (SG. Sep.4; 412) $275
– The Masterpieces. Phila., n.d. 20 vols. Hf. mor. gt., gt. panel. spines, slightly worn. (SPB. Nov.25; 485) $375
– Maurat. Ill.:– Toussaint & Leblant (plts.), gt. orig. aqua by G. Fraipont. Paris, 1886. (100) numbered on Jap. with 2 printings of plts. Mor., sigd. by Lortic, inner dentelle, box. (SI. Dec.4; 519) Lire 1,200,000
– Le Monde des Papillons, Promenades à travers Champs. Paris, 1867. 4to. Plts. soiled in parts, text more heavy. Mod. hf. leath. (R. Mar.31-Apr.4; 1443) DM 500
See–BALZAC, Honoré de & others.

DUPIN, Jacques
– Fits & Starts. Trans.:– Paul Auster. Ill.:– Alexander Calder. [Weston, Conn.], [1974]. (24) numbered, marked 'NC', sigd. by Calder, Dupin & Auster. 4to. Cl., boxed. (SG. Oct.23; 48) $225

DUPLESSIS-BERTAUX, Jean
– Recueil de Cent Sujets de Divers Genres. Paris, 1814. Ob. 4to. Some engrs. in dupl., some foxing on 1st. few pp. Hf. mor. gt. (BS. Jun.11; 333) £170

DUPPA, Richard
[–] The Classes & Orders of the Linnaean System of Botany. 1816. 3 vols. Cont. str.-grd. mor. gt., rubbed. (H. Jul.27; 285) *Crete.* £650
– Heads from Michael Angelo.–Heads from Raffaello. 1801; 1802. 2 works in 1 vol. Lge. fo. Str.-grd. hf. mor., gt. Bkplt. of Sir John Swinburne, Capheaton. (S. Jun.22; 28) *Traylen.* £220
– The Life of Michel Angelo Buonarroti, with his Poetry & Letters. 1807. 2nd. Edn. 4to. Very slight spotting. 'Cottonian' bdg. with cold. chintz over orig. bds., slightly soiled, unc. Robert Southey's copy, with A.L.s from John Murray. (S. Jun.9; 59) *Blackwell.* £320

DU PRAISSAC, Sieur
– Les Discours et Questions Militaires. Paris, 1638. Latest Edn. Outer margin of title reprd., slightly browned. Cont. limp vell., new endpapers. (C. Apr.1; 133) *Laughton.* £70

DUPRAT-DUVERGER, L.
– Nouvel Atlas du Royaume de France. Paris, 1827. Fo. Cl. covered bds., worn. (CSK. Sep.12; 104) £120

DUPUY DEMPORTES, J.B.
[–] Traité Historique et Moral du Blason. Paris, 1754. On Holland paper. 12mo. Cont. red mor., gt., arms of Paris de Meyzieu, gt. dentelle border with sm. bird, facing right & sunflower, flat spine gt. in compartments with apple from arms, inner gt. dentelles. (SM. Oct.7; 1693) Frs. 8,500

DUPUYTREN, Guillaume, Baron
– Clinical Lectures on Surgery, delivered at the Hotel Dieu, in 1832. Trans.:– A. Sidney Doane. N.Y., 1833. 1st. Edn. in Engl. & all publd. Cl. (S. Jun.15; 253) *Phillips.* £90
– Memoire . . . Operation de la Pierre. Paris, 1836. Fo. Creased. Bds., brkn. (SH. Jul.9; 131) *Wilson.* £55

DURAN, Diego
– Historia de las Indias de Nueva España y Islas de Tierra Firma. Mexico, 1867-80. 2 vols. Lge. 8vo. & 4to. atlas. 1 plt. stained. Qtr. cf. (SPB. May 5; 189) $1,600

DURAND, H.
– Le Rhin Allemand et l'Allemagne du Nord. Ill.:– H. Durand. Tours, 1865. Hf. leath. (D. Dec.11-13; 1284) DM 500

DURAND, Jean Nicolas Louis
– Receuil et Parallèle des Edifices de Tout Genre . . . Paris, an IX [1801]. Fo. Engraved double-p. title with ills., engraved double-p. table, 90 engraved double-p. plts., 2 folding plts. loosely inserted. Cont. cf.-bkd. bds., spine partly detchd. (S. Nov.25; 402) *Weinreb.* £260
– – Anr. Edn. Venice, 1833. 1st. Italian Edn. 2 vols. Fo. Old bds., roan spine, worn. (SG. Dec.4; 128) $170

DURAND, Sophie
– Napoleon & Marie-Louise. L., 1886. Cosway bdg. of mor. gt., covers set with 2 lge. port. miniatures on ivory (by C.B. Currie), watered silk linings, by Rivière, buckram s.-c. From the Prescott Collection. (CNY. Feb.6; 102) $1,000

DURANDUS, Gulielmus I, Bp. of Mende
– Rationale Diuinorum Offio[rum]. Venice, 1519. Fo. Some dampstaining, a few wormholes, scarcely affecting text. Cont. blind-stpd. Venetian goatskin. Bkplt. of Colonel K.H.M. Connal, Monktonhead, Monkton, Ayrshire; from liby. of André L. Simon. (S. May 18; 86) *Hammond.* £70

[DURANDUS, W.]
See–BRANT, Sebastian–[DURANDUS, W.]

DURANT de la Bergerie, Gilles
[–] Imitations du Latin de Jean Bonnefons . . . Paris, 1610. Sm. 8vo. Marginal dampstaining. Cont. red mor., 3 fillets, fleurs-de-lys in corners, decor. spine, inside dentelle. Bkplt. of Savalette de Buchelet. (HD. Mar.18; 63) Frs. 2,900

DURANTI, Durante
– Virginia. Ill.:– Domenico Cagnoni Brescia, 1768. Scattered foxing, mostly marginal. Cont. Italian red mor., gt. dentelle borders. From the collection of John A. Saks. (C. Jun.10; 59) *Mediolanum.* £90

DURANTY, Louis Edmond
– Théâtre des Marionnettes du Jardin des Tuileries. Paris, 1863. Lge. 8vo. Later hf. mor., wrap. preserved. (SM. Feb.11; 59) Frs. 1,500

DURAS, Desse de
– Ourika. 1826. 3rd. Edn. Cont. mor., cathédrale decor. (HD. Oct.10; 46) Frs. 2,500

DURER, Albrecht
– The Complete Woodcuts. Ed.:– W. Kurth. 1927. 1st. Edn., (500). Buckram. (HSS. Apr.24; 439) £72
– Della Simmetria de i Corpi Humani. [1591]. Fo. Lacks title-p., some dampstaining. Later bds. with linen backstrip. (TA. Feb.19; 431) £150
– Designs of the Prayer Book [of Maximilian I, Emperor of Germany]. 1817. Fo. Cont. hf. roan, worn. (S. Sep.29; 243) *Traylen.* £160
– – Anr. Copy. Orig. hf. roan. (C. Feb.4; 105) *Marks.* £130
– – Anr. Copy. 1st. & last few ll. spotted, some other discolouration, with litho. advt. slip. Mod. cl.-bkd. bds. (C. Jul.22; 65) *Taylor.* £70

– De Urbibus, Arcibus, Castellisque Condensis. Paris, 1535. 1st. Edn. in Latin. Fo. Some short tears & sm. holes, slightly affecting text & ills., slight browning & soiling, inscrs. on title & last lf. Mod. cf. (S. Feb.10; 226) *Subaldo.* £500
[–] Figurae Passionis Domini Nostri Jesu Christi. N.d. 4to. Some early MS. inscrs. Cont. limp vell., worn. w.a.f. (CSK. Aug.22; 136) £550
– Die Kleine Passion. Ed.:– G. Mardersteig. Ill.:– L. Farina after Dürer. Verona, 1971. (115). Orig. hf. leath., bd. s.-c. (HK. May 12-14; 2001) DM 700
– – Anr. Copy. With 1st. Edn. poems (1511) by Benedictus Chelidonius Musophilus. (HK. Nov.18-21; 2833) DM 650
[–] [Opera]. [Arnheim], [1603]. 1st. Coll. Edn. 3 pts. in 1 vol. Fo. (1) 5 blank ll. at end (signature Q) & 1 additional copperplt. after J6, (2) lacks hf. of double lf. E1, 2 blank ll. at end, (3) title without printer's mark, lacks hf. of double lf. Siiii, browned, stained in places, several ll. loose, torn or bkd., in vol. 1 old MS. notes. Cont. old MS. vell., soiled & wormed. (H. May 21/22; 1050) DM 1,700
– – Anr. Edn. Arnhem, 1604. Coll. Edn. Fo. Browned thro.-out, sig. U in pt. 3 appears to lack 6th. lf. Loose in old vell. covers. w.a.f. (SG. May 14; 67) $900
– Quatuor his Suarum Institutionum Geometricarum. Paris, Christian Wechel. 1535. Fo. Lacks 2 extension slips, few ll. loose. Cont. blind-stpd. cf., rebkd. (S. Nov.25; 352) *Broseghini.* £600
– Sym[m]etria Partium in Rectis Formis Hu[m]anorum Corporum. Trans.:– [J. Camerarius]. Nuremb., 1532. 2nd. Lat. Edn. Fo. With ills. of German 1528 Edn., lacks last blank lf., title-lf. very browned, with name & engraved ex-libris on verso, lightly soiled. Mor. (H. Dec.9/10; 1341) DM 3,600
– Underweysung der Messung mit dem Zirchel. [Nuremb.], 1538. 2nd. Edn. Fo. Old vell.-bkd. wraps., spine worn. (S. Nov.25; 353) *Duran.* £800

DURET, Theodore
– Edouard Manet sein leben und seine kunst. Berlin, 1910. 4to. Orig. cl. (CSK. Jan.9; 131) £90
– Die Impressionisten. Ill.:– Cézanne, Guillaumin, Morisot, Renoir & others. Berlin, 1909. (1000) numbered. 4to. Orig. leath., slightly defect. (HK. Nov.18-21; 2523) DM 1,300
– – Anr. Edn. Ill.:– A. Renoir (2 etchgs.), Beltrand after P. Cézanne (1 woodcut). Berlin, 1914. 4to. Orig. hf. vell. (HK. Nov.18-21; 2524) DM 420
– Lautrec. Paris, 1920. (200); (100) on Jap. 4to. Sewed, ill. wrap. (HD. Dec.5; 75) Frs. 1,300
– Manet & the French Impressionists. Pissarro, C. Monet, etc. Trans.:– J.E. Crawford Flitch. Ill.:– Manet, B. Morisot & Renoir (etchings) L., 1910. 4to. Cl. (VG. Dec.15; 136) Fls. 480
See–**MIRBEAU, Octave & others**

D'URFEY, Thomas
– The Banditti. 1686. 1st. Edn. 4to. Owners' inscr. 'Stamford 1693' on title. 19th. C. hf. cf., upr. cover almost detchd. [Wing D2700] (C. Nov.19; 89) *Pickering & Chatto.* £90
– The Comical History of Don Quixote . . . Part 1. – . . . Part the Second.–The Third Part. 1694; 1694; 1696. 1st. Edn. 3 works in 1 vol. 4to. Running title once affected by natural paper fault. Mor. by Sangorski. [Wing D2712; 2713; 2714] (C. Nov.19; 90) *Arnold.* £240
– A Fool's Preferment, or, The Dukes of Dunstable. 1688. 4to. Browning thro.-out, 1 lf. torn. Hf. vell. (BS. Jun.11; 247) £70
– Love for Money. 1691. 1st. Edn., 2nd. Iss. 4to. Slight staining, pagination of 1 lf. cropped. Recent mor. [Wing D2741] (C. Nov.19; 91) *Brett-Smith.* £90
– The Richmond Heiress. 1693. 1st. Edn. 4to. Sm. holes in 1 lf. affecting a few words. Mor. by Sangorski. [Wing D2769] (C. Nov.19; 92) *McKenzie.* £100
– The Siege of Memphis. 1676. 1st. Edn. 4to. Recent mor.-bkd. bds. [Wing D2777] (C. Nov.19; 93) *Pickering & Chatto.* £150

DURNFORD, E.
See–**COLENSO, F.E. & Durnford, E.**

DURNOVA, Sofiya
– Mat' [Mother]. Ill.:– N. Lyubavina. Petrograd, n.d. (125) numbered. Orig. wraps. by N. Lyubavina. (SH. Feb.6; 419) *Quaritch.* £75

DU ROSOI, B. de
– Les Sens. Ill.:– after Eisen & Wille. Londres [Paris], 1766. 1st. Edn. Red mor. gt. by Amand. (S. Jul.27; 150) *Hook.* £110

DUROV, Aleksandr
See–**MARKOV, Lev & Durov, Aleksandr**

DURRELL, Lawrence
– The Alexandria Quartet. 1962. 1st. Coll. Edn., (500). Orig. buckram, s.-c. Sigd. (SH. Dec.19; 472) *Fitton.* £90
– On Seeming to Presume. L., [1948]. Cl., d.-w. Inscr. to Mr. & Mrs. George Reavey. (SG. Jun.4; 116) $100
– The Parthenon. Rhodes, 1946. 1st. Edn. Orig. decor. wraps. Pres. Copy. (SH. Dec.18; 122) *Joseph the Provider.* £190
– Ten Poems. 1932. 1st. Edn. Orig. wraps., upr. cover defect. Inscr. to Walter de la Mare. (SH. Dec.18; 121) *Lincoln.* £920

DURRELL, Lawrence & Miller, Henry
– A Private Correspondence. Ed.:– George Wickes. N.Y., 1963. 1st. Edn. Cl., d.-w. Inscr. by Durrell to George Reavey. (SG. Jun.4; 120) $170

DURRET, M.
[–] Voyage de Marseille à Lima. Paris, 1720. 2 pts. in 1 vol. 1 or 2 short tears in plts., slight discolouration. Cont. cf., rebkd. [Sabin 21437] (SPB. May 5; 190) $125

DURUY, Victor
– History of Greece. 1892. (250). 4 vols. in 8. 4to. Later mor.-bkd. cl. (SH. Oct.10; 441) *Antico.* £50

DURY, Andrew
– A Collection of Plans of the Principal Cities of Great Britain & Ireland. [1764]. Ob. 8vo. Cont. mott. cf., numbered '2' on spine. W.a.f. (C. Nov.6; 253) *Sellars.* £300
– – Anr. Copy. Cont. red mor. (S. Nov.24; 120) *Traylen.* £240
– A New General & Universal Atlas. Ill.:– T. Kitchen & others. 1761. Ob. 8vo. Cont. cf. As an atlas, w.a.f. From the collection of Eric Sexton. (C. Apr.15; 33) *Traylen.* £150
– – Anr. Copy. Maps & plts. hand-cold. in outl., 1 slightly torn, a few other very minor defects. Cont. spr. cf. gt., slightly worn, rebkd. As an atlas, w.a.f. (SBA. Mar.4; 105) *Angle Books.* £100
– – Anr. Copy. Maps hand-cold. in outl., slight foxing. Cont. cf., covers detchd. (S. Jan.27; 515) *Pain.* £55
[–] [–] Anr. Edn. [1763?]. Ob. sm. 8vo. 39 engraved maps, hand-cold. in outl., 6 folding, numbered 1-45, lacks title. Cont. sheep, lacks upr. cover. (S. Jan.27; 516) *Kentish.* £80
See–**ANDREWS, John & Dury, Andrew**

DUSART, Cornelius
[–] Les Heros de la Ligue. Paris, 1691. Thick paper. Old name on title, sm. blank corner of 1 lf. torn away. Cont. cf., gt. spine, gt. borders. (VG. Oct.13; 61) Fls. 1,500

DU SOMMERARD, Alexandre
– Les Arts au Moyen Age. Paris, 1838-46. 5 text vols. & 6 plt. vols., together 11 vols. 8 vo. & tall fo. Three-qtr. mor. (SG. Oct.9; 82) $1,800

DUSSELDORF MONATSHEFTE
Ed.:– Clasen. Düsseldorf, 1854-55. Vols. 7 & 8 in 1 vol. 4to. Vol. 7 lacks plts. 4132 & 34, plt. 1 numbered double, vol. 8 lacks plts. 9 & 42, plt. 32 numbered double, text not collated. Cont. hf. leath., spine slightly defect. (R. Mar.31-Apr.4; 1487) DM 1,500

DUSSELDORFER KUNSTLER-ALBUM
Ed.:– W. Müller, Schauenburg & others. Düsseldorf, 1851-66. 1st. Edn. Yrs. I-VIII & XV-XVI in 11 vols. 4to. 6 plts. loose. 7 orig. bdgs., 3 hf. leath. & 1 cont. bds., worn, 3 spines defect. (H. May 21/22; 1052) DM 2,600

D'USSIEUX, Louis
– Le Décameron François. Ill.:– Masquelier, Godefroy & others, after Eisen & others. Paris, 1772-74. 1st. Edn. 2 vols. Cont. mor. gt., new end-papers. (SM. Oct.8; 2179) Frs. 3,000

DUTCH NEW GUINEA
– Reports on Collections made by British Ornithologists' Union Expedition & the Wollaston Expedition in 1910-13. L., 1916. 1st. Edn., (150) numbered. 2 vols. 4to. Cl. (SG. Sep.18; 126) $425

DU TERTRE, Jean Baptiste
– Histoire Générale des Antilles. Paris, 1667. 1st. Edn. 2 vols. only (of 4). 4to. Armorial plt. bnd. as frontis. in vol. II, corner of engraved title torn, marginal stains at beginning & end of each vol. 19th. C. hf. mor. From Chetham's Liby., Manchester. (Sabin 21458) (C. Nov.26; 142) *Cucchi.* £200
– – Anr. Edn. Paris, 1667-71. 4 vols. in 3. Sm. 4to. Engraved frontis., 2 armorial plts. (of 3), 4 engraved folding maps (of 5), & 18 plts., 2 folding views laid down. Later cf., Duke of Rutland's gt. crest on sides. [Sabin 21458] (C. May 20; 117) *Tzakas.* £600

DUTTON, Francis
– South Australia & its Mines, with an Historical Sketch of the Colony. L., 1846. Without advts., with folding map in end-pocket. Early hf. cf., marb. bds. (KH. Nov.18; 225) Aus. $320

DUTTON, Geoffrey
– Russell Drysdale. L., 1964. 4to. No bdg. stated, d.-w. Sigd. by Drysdale. (JL. Dec.15; 634) Aus. $130

DUTTON, Hely
– A Statistical & Agricultural Survey of the County of Galway. Dublin, 1824. Some cont. annots. in text. Cl. (GM. Apr.30; 258) £80

DUVAL, Nicolas
– Nouvelles Heures gravées au Burin, dediées au Roi. Paris, ca. 1660. 16mo. 18th. C. red mor., decor. spine, dentelles on covers, inner dentelle, mosaic angle decor. & centre motif. (HD. Apr. 9; 462) Frs. 1,200

DUVAL, Pierre
– Diverses Cartes et Tables, pour la Géographie Ancienne, pour la Chronologie, et pour les Itineraires, et Voyages Modernes. Paris, 1677. 3 pts. in 1 vol. 4to. Ptd. index, liby. stp. on title. Cont. red mor., gt., arms of Scaglia de Verrue, gt. panel with corner sprays, triple gt. fillet, spine gt. in compartments, inner gt. dentelles, lr. cover slightly worn. (SM. Oct.7; 1695) Frs. 6,500

DUVEEN, Denis I.
– Bibliotheca Alchemica et Chemica. L., 1949. (200). 4to. Orig. cl. (S. Feb.23; 337) *H.&G.* £160
– – Anr. Copy. Cl. (SG. Jan.22; 156) $450

DU VERDIER, Antoine
– Les Images des Dieux des Anciens, Contenans les Idoles, Coustumes, Ceremonies . . . Lyon, 1581. 4to. Title soiled, some dampstaining. Later bds. (TA. Feb.19; 449) £50

DU VERNEY, Joseph Guichard
– Traité de l'Organe de l'Ouie . . . Paris, 1683. 1st. Edn. Sm. 12mo. Cont. cf., worn. (SG. Oct.9; 83) $900
– – Anr. Copy. Without the 2 final blank ll. (SG. Jan.29; 140) $650

DUVERNEY, L.
See–**GAUTIER D'AGOTY, Jacques Fabien & Duverney, L.**

DUVOTENAY, C.
– Atlas et Itineraire de la Suisse. Paris, 1837. 4to. 43 engraved plts. & maps only. Orig. cf.-bkd. bds. (SH. Jul.16; 50) *Fairburn.* £160

DWELLY'S PARISH RECORDS
Herne Bay (etc.), 1913-26. Vols. 1-15 (vol. XIV never publd.). Orig. cl., slightly soiled. (SH. Nov.6; 17) *Ambra.* £80

DWIGGINS, W.A.
– Towards a Reform of the Paper Currency. N.Y., Ltd. Edns. Cl., 1932. (452) numbered, & sigd. Tall 8vo. Cf.-bkd. patterned bds. Sig. of Douglas C. McMurtrie on fly-lf. (SG. Mar.26; 177) $250

DYATEL [Woodpecker]
Ed.:– [E.E. Sno]. St. Petersb., 1905. No. 1 Trial (all publd.). Fo. A few sm. tears. Unbnd. (SH. Feb.5; 173) *Lempert.* £60
– – Anr. Edn. Ed.:– [A. Schastlivets]. St. Petersb., 1906. No. 1 (?all publd.). 4to. Unbnd. (SH. Feb.5; 64) *Quaritch.* £75

DYEING–GRUNDLICHER UNTERRICHT DER FARBEN, auff Wullen und Leinen Garn
N.p., 1677. Disbnd., hf. red mor. case. From Honeyman Collection. (S. May 20; 3221) *Goldschmidt.* £85

DYER, George
- History of the University & Colleges of Cambridge. Ill.:– after J. Greig. 1814. 2 vols. Cont. mor. gt. (TA. Mar.19; 249) £82
– – Anr. Copy. Plts. foxed. Red gt.-stpd. panel. mor. (CB. Sep.24; 122) Can. $200

DYER, R.A.
See–WHITE, A. & others

DYKES, William Rickatson
- Genus Iris. 1913. [1st. Edn.?]. Fo. Cl. (CE. Nov.20; 34) £360
– – Anr. Copy. Qtr. mor. gt. (P. Nov.13; 239) *Traylen.* £300
– – Anr. Copy. Orig. cl., partly unc. (CNY. May 22; 197) $300
- Notes on Tulip Species. 1930. [1st. Edn.?]. 4to. Cl. gt., unc. (P. Jan.22; 275) *Thorp.* £75
– – Anr. Copy. Cl. (CE. Nov.20; 35) £65
– – Anr. Edn. Ed. & Ill.:– E. Katherine Dykes. [1930]. Fo. Orig. cl., d.-w. (CSK. Aug.29; 111) £100

DYMENT, Elmer
[–] A Record of One Pioneer Family for Six Generations. [Hamilton], [1945]. Minor ink stain on 1 lf. Orig. cl. (CB. Dec.9; 174) Can. $120

EAGLE, W.
- Clans of Scotland. N.d. Fo. Tartan with gt. coat of arms, worn. (CE. Nov.20; 145) £340

EARDLEY-Wilmot, Sir John E.
- Reminiscences of the Late Thomas Assheton Smith, Esq. 1860. 1st. Edn. Extra-ill. with 47 additional plts. inserted. Early 20th. C. maroon mor. gt. by Root & Son. (S. Feb.9; 109) *Russell.* £120

EARLE, Bishop
[–] The World Displayed. 1767-68. 20 vols. in 10. Cont. cf., some covers detchd. (P. Apr.9; 246) *Shapiro.* £50

EARLE, Maj. Cyril
- The Earle Collection of Early Staffordshire Pottery. N.d. (250) numbered. 4to. Orig. cl. (SH. Jan.29; 172) *Talerman.* £100
– – Anr. Edn. N.d. 4to. Orig. cl., rebkd. (SH. Oct.9; 144) *Nebenzahl.* £110

EARLE, [Sir] James
- An Essay on the Means of lessening the Effects of Fire on the Human Body. 1799. Last advt. lf., a few ll. slightly spotted. Mod. mor.-bkd. cl. (SH. Oct.10; 295) *Drury.* £55

EARLOM, R., Turner, C. & Dunkarton, R.
- Fifteen Splendid Portraits of Royal Personages. 1816. Fo. Sm. flaw to 4th. plt. 19th. C. str.-grd. hf. mor., spine gt., 1 jnt. split, covers stained, slight wear. (S. Oct.21; 504) *Fogg.* £100

EARLY, Lt.-Gen. Jubal A.
- A Memoir of the Last Year of the War for Independence . . . Toronto, 1866. 1st. Edn. Orig. mor. Inscr. to Col. G.T. Denison, Jr. (SG. Jun.11; 108) $280

EARLY ENGLISH POTTERY
Ed.:– [Samuel Weller Singer]. 1817-23. 8 vols. (of 9) in 7, lacks vol. of Joseph Hall's Satires. 12mo. Some offsetting. Cont. red hf. mor., gt. (S. Dec.8; 48) *Bennett.* £60

EAST ANGLIAN
Ipswich & Norwich, 1864-1910. Vols. 1-4, New Series vols. 1-13, together 17 vols. Orig. cl. (SH. Nov.6; 45) *Cox.* £190

EAST INDIA Kalendar (The)
See–ROYAL KALENDAR (The) or . . . Annual Register for England, Scotland, Ireland & America, for . . . 1799-HERALDRY in Miniature –COMPANION (A) to the Royal Kalendar–EAST INDIA Kalendar (The)

EAST-INDIA Register & Directory
1803-38. 32 vols. Various, some earlier vols. bnd. with 'The Present Peerage of the United Kingdom' & 'Arms of the Peers, Peeresses & C. of the United Kingdom'. Cont. red mor. (CSK. Oct.10; 90) £400

EAST INDIES–LA HARPE, Jean François de
- Recueil des Voyages qui ont servi à l'établissement et aux Progres de la Compagnie des Indes Orientales; Voyage de Gautier Schouten aux Indes Orientales.–Abrégé de l'Histoire Generale des Voyages. Rouen; Rouen; Paris, 1725; 1715; 1820. 10 vols.; 2 vols.; 2 vols. Old cf. (LM. Nov.8; 147) B.Frs. 14,000

EASTLAKE, Charles L.
- A History of the Gothic Revival, an attempt to show how the Taste for Mediaeval architecture which lingered in England during the last two Centuries has been encouraged & developed. L., 1872. Orig. cl. (CB. May 27; 92) Can. $120

EASTMAN, Mary H.
- The American Aboriginal Portfolio. Ill.:– S. Eastman. Phila., [1853]. 4to. Orig. gt.-decor. cl. [Sabin 21682] (CB. Dec.9; 298) Can. $280
- Dahcotah. Ed.:– Mrs. C.M. Kirkland. Ill.:– Capt. Eastman. N.Y., 1849. 1st. Edn. 12mo. Ex liby. Gt.-pict. cl. (SG. Jun.11; 145) $140

EASTON, James
- Human Longevity recording the Name, Age, Place of Residence, & Year of the Decease of 1712 persons who attained a Century & upwards from A.D.66 to 1799. Salisbury & L., 1799. Orig. bds., rebkd., unc. (S. Jun.15; 254) *Heath.* £50

EASY WAY of Breeding Canary Birds
1747. Cont. mott. cf., gt. borders, rebkd. (C. Nov.6; 280) *Goodwin.* £90

EBATS Rustiques (Les)
- Almanach gaillard par le Citoyen Allegro. Paris, ca. 1780. Sm. 18mo. Cont. kid, gt. decor., 5 medallions, floral decor. & centre motif. (HD. Apr.8; 98) Frs. 1,400

EBERHARDT, Isabelle
See–DOYON, Rene-Louis–EBERHARDT, Isabelle

EBERS, G. & Guthe, H.
- Palestina in Bild und Wort. Stuttgart, 1883-84. 2 vols. Fo. Orig. hf. leath., gold stpd. (R. Oct.14-18; 1791) DM 700

EBSER, Johannes, Bp. of Chiemsee
- Onus Ecclesiae. Cologne, 1531. Fo. Blank head of margin reprd. erasing inscr., bkplt. of Paul Schmidt. 18th. C. mor., triple gt. fillet, spine gt. in compartments, inner gt. dentelles. (SM. Oct.7; 1696) Frs. 7,500

ECCLESIASTES oder der Prediger Salomo
Ill.:– M. Behmer. [Berlin], [1920]. (250) on Zandersbütten numbered. 4to. Vell. gt., cover fillets, bd. s.-c. Sigd. (HK. Nov.18-21; 2429) DM 480

ECCLESIASTICUS
- The Wisdom of Jesus the Son of Sirach. Ill.:– Graily Hewitt. Ash. Pr., 1932. (353), (328) on paper. Sm. fo. Orig. limp vell., ties, unc. (S. Jul.31; 66) *Jonathan.* £620
– – Anr. Copy. Hand-cold. initials in green & blue. (SH. Feb.19; 20) *John.* £420

ECHO des Bardes (L')
Paris, 1819. 16mo. Cont. painted silk bds., s.-c. (HD. Apr.8; 99) Frs. 1,000

ECHOS des Bocages (Les), Etrennes pastorales et chantantes
Paris, [1804]. 64mo. Cont. mor., gt. fillet, s.-c. (HD. Apr.8; 100) Frs. 1,000

ECKARTSHAUSEN, Karl von
- Aufschüsse z. Magie aus geprüften Erfahrungen. Munich, 1788-91. Vols. 1-3 (of 4). Pt. 3 probably lacks 1 plt., soiled in parts, lightly worn. Cont. leath. W.a.f. (HK. Nov.18-21; 1913) DM 420
- Ideen üb. das Affirmative Princip d. Lebens u. das Negative Princip d. Todes, zur Bestätigung d. Brownischen Systems. Trans.:– J.G.L. Blumenhof. Leipzig, 1798. 1st. Edn. Cont. hf. leath. (HK. Nov.18-21; 466) DM 760

ECKEL, John C.
- The First Editions of the Writings of Charles Dickens. 1913. (250) on L.P., sigd. by author & publishers. 4to. Some pencil notes by a former owner. Orig. vell.-bkd. cl. (SKC. May 19; 163) £75
– – Anr. Edn. L., 1913. (750) numbered copies. Cl., d.-w., partly untrimmed. (SG. Oct.2; 110) $160
– – Anr. Edn. 1932. Revised Edn., (750). Orig. publisher's bdg. in d.-w. (C. Feb.4; 59) *Davidson.* £70
– – Anr. Copy. Leatherette, d.-w., glassine wrap., partly untrimmed. (SG. Oct.2; 111) $170

ECKERT, H.A. & Monten, D.
- Les Armées d'Europe Représentées en Groupes Characteristiques. Wuerzbourg, 1838. Fo. Russian section only, pict. litho. title, 79 cold. plts. (of 144). Mod. three-qtr. crushed lev., gt.-panel. spine, by Jul. Hager, Leipzig. (SG. Oct.30; 143) $850

ECKERT, R.P.
- These Things the Poet Said. Pear Tree Pr., 1935. (150). Orig. cl.-bkd. bds., unopened, d.-w. (P. Jul.2; 130) *Stevens.* £60

ECKHEL, Joseph H.
- Choix des Pierres Gravées du Cabinet Imperial des Antiques. Vienna, 1788. Fo. Tears in L2 & M1 (reprd. with sellotape), slightly dampstained. Cont. mott. cf., gt., slightly worn. (S. Apr.7; 460) *Mistrali.* £60

ECLETIC REPERTORY & ANALYTICAL REVIEW
Phila. Jan. 1817-Oct. 1819. Vols. 7, 8 & 9 only. Some foxing. Cont. hf. roan., worn. (SG. Jan.29; 145) $500

ECOLE de la Bienfaisance (L')
Paris, n.d. Sm. 18mo. Dampstained. Cont. red mor., gt. decor. covers, centre medallion. (HD. Apr.10; 101) Frs. 6,150

ECOLE Polytechnique
- Livre du Centenaire, 1794-1894. Paris, 1895. 3 vols. Lge. 8vo. Chagrin, gt. roll-stps. around covers, medallion in centre, smooth decor. spines, wraps. & spines. (HD. Feb.27; 123) Frs. 1,100

EDDIS, William
- Letters from America. Priv. Ptd., 1792. 1st. Edn. Mod. hf. cf. [Sabin 21801] (C. Nov.6; 208) *Bond.* £65

EDDISON, E.R.
- Mistress of Mistresses, a Vision of Zimiamvia. Ill.:– Keith Henderson. 1935. 1st. Edn., (12). Orig. parch. gt. Pres. Copy to Richard de la Mare., autograph limitation statement by author. (SH. Dec.18; 127) *Temple.* £250

EDEN, [Emily]
- Portraits of the Princes & People of India. 1844. Fo. All plts. mntd., slightly soiled. Cont. mor.-bkd. cl., lacks spine, loose. (SH. Nov.7; 342) *Glazebrook.* £600
– – Anr. Copy. Orig. hf. mor. (C. May 20; 118) *Hosain.* £420
– – Anr. Copy. Some spotting & soiling. Worn & disbnd. (CSK. Sep.26; 33) £100
– – Anr. Edn. N.d. Fo. All plts. mntd., soiled. Cont. hf. mor., loose. (SH. Nov.7; 343) *Anderson.* £400

EDER, Josef Maria
- Ausfuehrliches Handbuch der Photographie. Halle, 1906-1932. Various edns. Vol. I, pts. 1-4 (in 5 vols.); Vol. III, pts. 1-4; Vol. IV, pt. 2; together 10 vols. 1 vol. cl.-bkd. bds., rest cl., worn, ex-liby. (SG. Apr.23; 82) $100
- Quellenschriften zu den Frühesten Anfängen der Photographie bis zum XVIII. Jahrhundert. Halle, 1913. Orig. wraps. (R. Oct.14-18; 472) DM 450

EDER, Josef Maria & Valenta, E.
- Versuche über Photographie mittelst der Röntgen'zchen Strahlen. Vienna & Halle, 1896. Lge. fo. Orig. hf. linen. (R. Mar.31-Apr.4; 1287) DM 1,350

EDGE-PARTINGTON, James & Heape, Charles
- An Album of the Weapons, Tools, Ornaments . . . of the Native of the Pacific Islands . . . Manchester, 1895. 2nd. Series. (150). Ob. fo. Liby. stp. on title. Orig. hf. mor. Sigd., from Chetham's Liby., Manchester. (C. Nov.26; 143) *Maggs.* £150
– – Anr. Edn. Manchester, 1895-98. 1st. Edn. 2nd. (& 3rd.) Series. Ob. 4to. Slight spotting. Orig. hf. mor. (KH. Nov.18; 226) Aus. $350

EDGEWORTH, Maria
- Castle Rackrent. 1800. 1st. Edn. Cont. tree cf. (C. Jul.22; 12) *Magee.* £160
- Tales & Novels. L., 1832. 18 vols. Some spotting. Cf. gt. Accompanied by 2-p. A.L.s. (Edgeworth Town, 28 Sep., 1836). (SPB. May 29; 133) $200
– – Anr. Edn. 1832-33. 18 vols. Cont. diced cf., spines gt. (SKC. May 19; 316) £140
– – Anr. Copy. Cont. hf. mor. (SH. May 28; 33) *Howes Books.* £100
– – Anr. Copy. Diced cf., slightly scuffed, spines gt. (SKC. Sep.9; 1466) £85

EDGEWORTH, Maria & Barbauld, Anna Letitia
- Letters. Ed.:– Walter Sidney Scott. Ill.:– Lettice Sandford. Gold. Cock. Pr., 1953. (300) numbered, (60) specially bnd., sigd. by editor & artist. Orig. mor.-bkd. cl. (S. Jul.31; 106) *Maggs Brothers.* £60

EDGEWORTH, Maria & Lovell, Richard
- Practical Education. 1798. 2 vols. 4to. Slight spotting. Cont. cf. (P. Apr.9; 133) *Walford.* £50

EDINBURGH
- Picturesque Views of Edinburgh . . . Ed.:– James Browne (historical sketch). Edinb., 1825. 4to. Foxing. Mor. gt. (SPB. May 29; 134) $200

EDINBURGH Imperial Atlas (The)
Ca. 1830. Fo. Hf. cf. (CE. Jun.4; 160) £75
- – Anr. Edn. 1850. Fo. Some dampstaining. Orig. hf. mor. (TA. Feb.19; 107) £60
- – Anr. Edn. Edinb., [1850]. Fo. Some browning. Cont. hf. mor., worn. (CSK. Jul.3; 14) £50

EDINBURGH UNIVERSITY LIBRARY
- Catalogue of the Printed Books. Edinb., 1918-23. 3 vols. 4to. Orig. buckram gt. (S. Apr.6; 181) *Steiner.* £50

EDMONDS, Harfield H. & Lee, Norman N.
- Brook & River Trouting. [1916]. (50) numbered, sigd. 4to. Orig. cl. (SH. May 21; 237) *Way.* £700

EDMONDS, Brigadier-General Sir James E.
- History of the Great War based on Official Documents. 1923-47. 32 vols. only. Orig. cl. some vols. worn. (CSK. Aug.1; 78) £210

EDMONDSON, Joseph
- A Complete Body of Heraldry. 1780. 2 vols. Fo. Cont. cf. rebkd., 1 cover loose. (SH. May 21; 207) *Miles.* £60
See–SEGAR, Sir William & Edmondson, Joseph

EDSCHMID, Kurt
- Die Fürstin. Ill.:– M. Beckmann. Weimar, 1918. (370) on Bütten. 4to. Orig. raw silk. (H. May 21/22; 1505) DM 2,300
- – Anr. Copy. (HK. May 12-14; 1779) DM 2,000
- – Anr. Copy. Orig. silk, slightly stained & cockled. (H. Dec.9/10; 1961) DM 1,500
- Kean. Ill.:– E. Schlotter. Darmstadt, Bläschke Pr., [1965]. (105). 4to. Orig. hf. vell. Printer's mark sigd. by author & artist, all 9 etchgs., including 2 cold., sigd. by artist. (H. Dec.9/10; 1786a) DM 520

EDWARD VI of England, King
See–[L., R.]-EDWARD VI of England, King –CHEKE, Sir John

EDWARD, Duke of Windsor
- A King's Story. N.Y., [1951]. (385) numbered, & sigd. Gt. red mor., inner dentelles, silk endpapers, s.-c., unc. (SG. Feb.12; 8) $190

EDWARD, P.J.
See–WHITEHEAD, P.J.P. & Edward, P.J.

EDWARDS, B.
See–RENNELL, James–EDWARDS, B.–FADEN, William

EDWARDS, Bryan
- An Historical Survey of the French Colony in the Island of St. Domingo. L., 1797. 1st. Edn. 4to. Map foxed. Cont. cf., spine gt. [Sabin 21894] (CNY. Oct.1; 43) $320
- The History . . . of the British Colonies in the West Indies. L., 1793. 2 vols. 4to. Lge. folding map strengthened at folds, blanks preceding titles in each vol. pasted together, some tears & browning, lacks R4 vol. 1 (final blank?). Cont. tree cf. gt., rebkd., orig. spine preserved, some wear. [Sabin 21901] (SPB. May 5; 194) $300
- – Anr. Edn. Ill.:– Bartolozzi & others. 1794. 2nd. Edn. 2 vols. but without additional appendix sometimes present. 4to. Some tears to engraved folding maps, a few ll. slightly soiled or spotted. Cont. tree cf. gt., worn. [Sabin 21901] (SBA. Jul.14; 26) *Shapiro.* £65
- – Anr. Copy. 2 vols. 15 (of 16) maps & plts. Mod. three-qtr. cf. (SG. Oct.30; 144) $240
- – Anr. Copy. 2 vols. Lge. tall 4to. 1 folding map in 2 sheets has 1 sheet separated but present. Orig. two-tone bds., spines worn, sigd. inscr. & armorial bkplts. of Thomas Best, Park House, Boxley, Kent. (PNY. Mar.26; 108) $180
- – Anr. Edn. 1794-1801. 3 vols. 4to. Cf. gt. (P. Oct.23; 21) *Brooke-Hitching.* £250
- Proceedings of the Governor & Assembly of Jamaica in regard to the Maroon Negroes. L., 1796. Cf. (P. Jun.11; 105) £70

EDWARDS, Edward
- The Napoleon Medals, engraved by the process of Achilles Collas. 1837. Fo. Red mor., multiple gt. fillets on sides with Napoleonic emblems of wreathed initial 'N', a bee & Imperial Eagle in shaped corners, spine similarly tooled in 6 compartments. (C. Feb.4; 214) *Morris.* £200

EDWARDS, Edwin
- Old Inns. 1880. 1st. Edn. (150). Pt. II only (of 3). Lge. fo. Slight browning. Cont. parch. bds., soiled. From liby. of André L. Simon. (S. May 18; 88) *Kopling.* £90

EDWARDS, George, Naturalist
- Gleanings of Natural History. L., 1758-64. 1st. Edn. 3 Pts. in 2 vols. Lge. 4to. Subscribers' lists in Pts. 2 & 3. Cont. red. mor., rebkd., very worn. (SG. May 14; 70) $5,200
- – Anr. Copy. 3 vols. Liby. stp. on verso of each plt. Mod. buckram. 9-pp. MS. index in last vol. (SG. Sep.18; 130) $4,200
- – Anr. Edn. 1760. Pt. 2 only. 4to. 49 hand-cold. plts. only, the majority depicting birds, 2 torn cleanly, some light offsetting. Cf. spine only. W.a.f. (CSK. Aug.15; 140) £400
- A Natural History of Birds. 1743. Pt. 1 only. Sm. fo. Hand-cold. engd. front., 52 hand-cold. engd plts, with plt 249 from another work loosely inserted, plt. 11 torn. Bds., very worn, lacks spine, contents loose. w.a.f. (S. Mar.17; 334) *Robinson.* £520
- – Anr. Edn. 1750. Vol. 3 only. 4to. 48 (of 52) plts., some tears, soiled, wormed. Mod. hf. cf. (SH. Jul.23; 27) *Loveday.* £450
- A Natural History of Birds.–Gleanings of Natural History. 1739-51; 1758-64. 4 vols.; 3 vols. 4to. 1st. work: 208 hand-cold. engraved plts. (of 210, lacks nos. 67 & 86), slight foxing on plts. & text in vol. I; 2nd. work: Fr. & Engl. titles. Unif. 18th. C. cf., decor. spine gt. (CE. Jul.9; 235) £4,000
- – Anr. Edn. 1743-64. 1st. work 4 pts., 2nd. work 3 pts., together 7 vols. 4to. Engl. & Fr. text, extra ptd. title with engd. vig. to Pt. 1 of each work, 363 hand-cold. engd. plts. including frontis., port. in 2nd. work, port. in dupl. in Pt. 2 of first work. Cont. tree cf., gt., rebkd., old spines preserved. (S. Nov.25; 392) *Hyde Park.* £4,000
- A Natural History of Uncommon Birds. –Gleanings of Natural History. Priv. Ptd., 1739-64. 1st. Edns. 4 vols. in 3; 3 vols., together 6 vols. 4to. 1st. work: 203 hand-cold. plts. only (of 210), margins finger-marked, 1 prelim. torn across; 2nd. work: 149 hand-cold. plts. (only, of 152) numbered 211-362, minor tear to plt. 269. Unif. 19th. C. hf. mor. W.a.f., from Chetham's Liby., Manchester. (C. Nov.26; 144) *Schuster.* £2,600
- – Anr. Edn. L., 1743-64. 1st. Edn. 3 pts. in 7 vols. 4to. Gleanings with parallel Engl. Fr. text, light browning & soiling in parts. 19th. C. red hf. mor., leath. corners, gt. (R. Oct.14-18; 2953) DM 18,000
- – Anr. Edn. 1745-51; 1743-64. Tgoether 7 vols. (4 & 3). 4to. 1st. work: 4 dupl. Fr. titles dtd. 1745-51, vol. 1 lacks subscribers list, 2nd. work: hf.-title only in vol. 1, lacks Engl. & Fr. titles & engd. port. Unif. late 18th. C. mor. gt. by Benedict. (C. Jul.15; 145) *Quaritch.* £4,500

EDWARDS, George–BROWN, Peter
- A Natural History of Birds; Gleanings of Natural History.–New Illustrations of Zoology. 1743-64 (1st. 2 works); 1776. 4 vols.; 3 vols.; 1 vol., together 8 vols. in 4. 4to. Slight browning & soiling. Early 19th. C. str.-grd. hf. mor., unc. (S. Jun.1; 264) *Traylen.* £4,000

EDWARDS, J.
- Companion from London to Brighthelmston in Sussex. 1801. 4to. Double-p. plan of Brighton. Hf. cf. (P. Dec.11; 158) *Crowe.* £240

EDWARDS, John
- The British Herbal . . . Priv. Ptd., 1770. 1st. Edn. Fo. Plts. hand-cold., 1 text lf. with sm. marginal tear reprd. 19th. C. red mor., gt., worn, covers detchd. From Chetham's Liby., Manchester. (C. Nov.26; 145) *Fletcher.* £4,800

EDWARDS, Jonathan
- A Careful & Strict Enquiry into . . . Freedom of Will . . . Boston, 1754. 1st. Edn. Cont. panel. cf., jnts. brkn. (SG. Oct.9; 84) $400

EDWARDS, Lionel
- A Leicestershire Sketch Book. 1935. (75) numbered copies sigd. by the author. 4to. Orig. vell.-bkd. cl., upr. cover slightly soiled. (SH. Oct.9; 217) *Hatchards.* £90

- The Passing Seasons. L., [1927]. (250) numbered. Fo. Plt. list loose. Cl., d.-w., head of spine torn. Each plt. sigd. on mount by Edwards. (SG. Dec.11; 298) $275
- – Anr. Copy. Each plt. sigd. in pencil in margin, some pp. loose. Orig. cl. (SPB. May 29; 135) $100
- – Anr. Edn. N.d. Ob. fo. Orig. bds. (SH. Oct.9; 218) *Hatchards.* £95
- A Sportsman's Bag. N.d. (650) numbered. Fo. Orig. cl., slightly soiled, spine slightly torn, d.-w. (SH. Oct.9; 219) *Hatchards.* £105

EDWARDS, Owen
- Clych Atgof. Gregy. Pr., 1933. Ltd. Edn. numbered. Orig. decor. mor., 1 corner slightly stained. (SBA. Oct.22; 728) *Ramage.* £52

EDWARDS, P.I.
See–WHITEHEAD, P.J.P. & Edwards, P.I.

EDWARDS, Ralph
See–MACQUOID, Percy & Edwards, Ralph

EDWARDS, Sutherland
- The Polish Captivity. 1863. 2 vols. Orig. cl. (P. Feb.19; 166) *Scott.* £60

EDWARDS, Sydenham Teak
- The New Botanic Garden. Ill.:– Sanson after Edwards. 1812. 2 vols. 4to. Some ll. loosening. Orig. bds., lacks spines, unc. (LC. Jun.18; 100) £650
- – Anr. Copy. Dupl. list of contents in vol. II, a few marginal stains. Cont. cf., jnts. worn & reprd. (S. Dec.3; 954) *Walford.* £580
- [-] The Ornamental Flower Garden & Shrubbery. L., 1854. 1st. Edn. 4 vols. Hf. leath., disbnd., ex liby. (SG. Sep.18; 131) $1,000

EDWARDS, Sydenham Teak & Lindley, John
- The Botanical Register. L., 1816. Vol. 2. Cont. leath., gold & blind-tooled. (HD. Nov.18-21; 467) DM 1,600
- – Anr. Edn. L., 1820. Vol. 6. Cont. leath. (R. Oct.14-18; 2954) DM 1,200
- – Anr. Edn. [1825-41]. 71 hand-cold. engd. plts., no title or text. Disbnd., loose in buckram bdg. w.a.f. (C. May 20; 201) *Schuster.* £75
- – Anr. Edn. 1836-37. 5 orig. pts. Orig. paper wraps. (TA. Jan.22; 76) £80
- – Anr. Edn. 1842-43. 14 pts. only. Orig. wraps. (CSK. Nov.7; 189) £230

EDWARDS, William H.
- The Butterflies of North America. Phila. & other places, 1868-[97]. 1st. Edn? (3 pts.). 4to. 90 (of 154) cold. litho. plts. loose. (HK. Nov.18-21; 733) DM 850
- – Anr. Edn. Boston, 1888-1897. 1st. Edn. of vols. 2-3. 3 vols. 4to. 152 plts (of 154), ex-liby. with blindstp. on title, slight foxing. Hf. mor. gt., sm. paper liby. labels on spine. (SPB. Oct.1; 193) $900

EDWARDS, William P.
- [-] Narrative of the Capture & Providential Escape of Misses Frances & Almira Hall . . . [St. Louis?], 1832. 1st. Edn. 1st. sig. loose, title torn & reprd. on verso, some foxing & staining. Pict. wraps., in protective cl. case. (SG. Jan.8; 209) $410

EFFENDI, Kara Mustapha Bashaw Reis
- The Mock Senator. ca. 1720. Fo. 4 pp., pict. vig., soiled. (S. Oct.17; 11) £180

EFROS, Abraham
- Kamerny Teatr [Kamerny Theatre & its Artists 1914-24]. Ill.:– after Ekster, Goncharora, Lentulov, Sudeikin & others. Moscow, 1934. (3,500). 4to. Orig. cl. (SH. Feb.5; 210) *Motley Books.* £360

EFROS, Abram & Ya.
- Tugendkhol'd. Iskusstvo Marka Shagala [The Art of Marc Chagall]. Moscow, 1918. (850) numbered. 4to. Orig. wraps. (SH. Feb.5; 211) *Quaritch.* £250

EGAN, Beresford
- The Sink of Solitude. Ed.:– P.R. Stephenson. Hermes Pr., 1928. (250) numbered. 4to. Orig. bds. Pres. copy to his mother. (SH. Mar.26; 180) *Jones.* £85

EGAN, Pierce
- Anecdotes. the Stage . . . 1827. [1st. Edn.?]. Orig. bds. (P. Sep.11; 273) *Traylen.* £220
- – Anr. Copy. 19th. C. hf. roan. (S. Jun.23; 320) *Harley Mason.* £140

EGAN, Pierce -*contd.*
- **Boxiana; Or, Sketches of Ancient & Modern Pugilism.** 1823-24. 4 vols. Cont. pold. cf. (TA. Nov.20; 407) £100
[-] **Diorama Anglais ou Promenades pittoresque à Londres.** Ill.:– After I.R. & George Cruikshank. Paris, 1823. Spotting. Cont. hf. mor. (CSK. Nov.7; 190) £80
[-] – **Anr. Copy.** Margins browned, title lacks top right hand corner. (TA. Nov.20; 39) £78
- **Finish to the Adventures of Tom, Jerry, & Logic, in their pursuits through Life in & out of London.** Ill.:– Robert Cruikshank. 1829-30. 1st. Edn., 1st Iss. Some minor offsetting on to text, 1 plt. with sm. marginal tear, very occasional minor spotting. Red str.-grd. mor., gt., by Bayntun. (C. Feb.4; 131) *Wolf.* £200
– – **Anr. Edn.** Ill.:– After Robert Cruikshank. 1889. Crimson hf. mor. (CSK. Sep.15; 221) £80
- **Life in London.** Ill.:– George & Robert Cruikshank. L., 1821. 1st. Edn., 1st. Iss. Without footnote at p. 9 & spelling 'good-bies' at p. 376, 36 hand-cold. plts., 3 folding plts. engraved music, lacks hf.-title, advts. & subscribers' lf. Red lev. mor. gt., spine gt., by Bayntun, cl. box. (CNY. May 22; 94) $220
– – **Anr. Copy.** Lacks lf. 'To the Subscribers' as usual, browning. Hf. mor., s.-c., brkn. (SPB. Jul.28; 120) $200
– – **Anr. Edn.** Ill.:– I.R. & George Cruikshank. 1821. 1st. Edn., 2nd. Iss. Some foxing & offsetting. Hf. cf. rebkd. preserving old spine, worn. (S. Jun.23; 318) *Shapiro.* £75
– – **Anr. Copy.** Lacks hf.-title. Hf. mor. (SH. Jul.9; 174) *Jacobs.* £55
– – **Anr. Copy.** Without the footnote on p. 9, first lf. of music unnumbered, lacks hf.-title. Maroon mor. gt., upr.-cover detchd. (SG. Oct.30; 145) $275
– – **Anr. Edn.** Ill.:– I.R. & George Cruikshank. 1822. '2nd. Edn.' [1st. Edn., 3rd. Iss.]. 4 pp. advts., slight browning & offsetting of plts. onto text. Cont. hf. cf. (S. Jun.23; 319) *Quaritch.* £110
– – **Anr. Copy.** With 'Second Edition' note on p. 9, & 1st. p. of music numbered, additional plt. inserted at p. 336, some heavy offsetting from plts. onto text. Diced cf., rebkd. (SG. Mar.19; 98) $200
– – **Anr. Edn.** Ill.:– I.R. & George Cruikshank. 1822. Some offsetting. Later cf. (CSK. Sep.12; 153) £85
– – **Anr. Copy.** Advt. lf., lacks Subscribers lf. Mod. cf. (SH. Jun.11; 201) *Armstrong.* £70
– – **Anr. Edn.** Ill.:– I.R. & George Cruikshank. 1823. Title mntd. on stub, lacks hf.-title & advts.?, occasional marginal spotting. Red str.-grd. mor., gt., by Bayntun. (C. Feb.4; 130) *Chelsea Rare Books.* £150
– – **Anr. Copy.** 4 ll. of advts., lacks hf.-title & lf. 'To the Subscribers', slightly spotted & offset. 19th. C. pol. cf., gt. (S. Dec.9; 508) *Hyde.* £70
- **Life in London.–Finish to Life in London.** L., 1821; 1830. Both 1st. Edn. 2nd. Iss. 2 vols. Minor repairs, browning. Red mor. gt. by Wood. (SPB. May 6; 187) $550
- **Life in London.–The Life of an Actor.** L., 1821; [1825]. Together 2 vols. 1st. work mor. gt., spine gt., rebkd., orig. spine preserved, 2nd. work, red mor. gt., spine gt., by Gregory. (CNY. May 22; 95) $240
- **The Life of an Actor.** 1825. 1st. Edn. Hf. cf., worn. (SH. Jul.9; 175) *McKenzie.* £60
- **Real Life in Ireland.** 1822. Cf., rebkd. (BS. Feb.25; 360) £80
[-] – **Anr. Edn.** 1824. 16 (of 18) hand-cold. plts. Orig. bds. (P. Sep.11; 274) *Davis.* £90
- **Real Life in London.** L., 1821-22. 1st. Edn. 2 vols. Red lev. mor. gt. (CNY. May 22; 96) $240
[-] – **Anr. Edn.** 1821-22. 1st. Edn., 2nd. Iss. Orig. bds., rebkd., unc., s.-c. (S. Nov.25; 431) *Adams.* £110
– – **Anr. Edn.** Ill.:– Thomas Alken, Thomas Rowlandson, & others. 1821-22. 2 vols. Pol. cf., spines gt., by Rivière. (C. Nov.5; 48) *Lanark Jones.* £130
– – **Anr. Edn.** 1821-31. 2 vols. Soiled, some slight foxing. Cl. (BS. Sep.17; 115) £50
- **Sporting Anecdotes.** 1825. Lacks advts. Cont. cf. gt. (S. Mar.16; 207) *Laughton.* £60
- **Walks through Bath . . .** Bath, 1819. 1st. Edn. 1 lf. & 1 plt. misbnd. Cont. hf. cf. (PNY. May 21; 181) $100

EGBERT, Donald Drew
- **The Tickhill Psalter & Related Manuscripts.** N.Y. & Princeton, 1940. 1st. Edn. Fo. Orig. cl., d.-w. The John A. Saks copy. (CNY. Oct.1; 175) $250

EGEDE, Hans Paulson
- **A Description of Greenland.** 1745. 1st. Engl. Edn. Sm. tear in fold of map. 19th. C. hf. mor., worn. From Chetham's Liby., Manchester. (C. Nov.26; 146) *Cash.* £100
– – **Anr. Copy.** Map torn, slight discolouration. Mod. hf. mor., gt. spine & borders. From liby. of William E. Wilson. [Sabin 22028] (SPB. Apr.29; 93) $400
- **Nachrichten von Grönland. Aus einem Tagebuch, geführt von 1721 bis 1788.** Kopenhagen, 1790. Browned & slightly soiled in parts. Cont. hf. leath., gt. spine. (R. Oct.14-18; 2035) DM 650

EGERTON, M.
[-] **Here & There Over the Water.** 1825. 4to. Frontis. pasted onto front free endpaper, some slight offsetting onto text. Cont. cl., rebkd. (S. Jun.23; 321) *Temperley.* £260

EGERTON, William
See–CURL, Edmund 'William Egerton'

EGINHART
See–FURER, C.-EGINHART

EGK, W.
- **Irische Legende.** Ill.:– O. Kokoschba. Freiburg, [1955]. (500). Lge. 4to. Orig. bds. (HK. May 12-14; 1925) DM 500

EGLINGTON, John
- **The Tournament.** Ed.:– Rev. J. Richardson. 1843. Fo. Roan & cl., worn. (CE. Nov.20; 28) £220

EGNATIUS, Joannes Baptista
- **De Exemplis Illustrium Virorum Venetae Civitatis atque Aliarum Gentium.** Venice, 1554. 4to. 2 wormholes at end slightly affecting a few letters. Cont. limp vell., lacks ties. (S. Jan.27; 324) *Pearson.* £55

EHRET, Georg Dionysius
- **Plantae et Papiliones rariores depictae et aeri incisae.** Ill.:– After Ehret. L., 1748-59. Fo. Hf. cf. From collection of Massachusetts Horticultural Society, stps. on plts. (SPB. Oct.1; 116) $5,750

EHRLICH, Paul
- **Farbenanalytische Untersuchungen zur Histologie und Klinik des Blutes.** Berlin, 1891. 1st. Edn. Pt. 1, (All published). New cl., unc. (S. Dec.2; 483) *Dawson.* £85
- **Das Sauerstoff-Beduerfniss des Organismus.** Berlin, 1885. 1st. Edn. Cl. gt. Inscr. (SG. Sep.18; 132) $230

EHRLICH, Paul & Sahachiro, Hata
- **The Experimental Chemotherapy of Spirilloses [syphilis, relapsing fever, etc.].** Ed.:– R.W. Felkin. Trans.:– A. Newbold. 1911. 1st. Engl. Edn. Orig. cl. (S. Jun.15; 259) *Stanley.* £90

EHRMANN, Th. F.
- **Neueste Kunde der Schweiz und Italiens.** Prag, 1809. Cont. bds. (R. Oct.14-18; 2001) DM 460

EHRMANN, T.F. & Lindner, F.L.
- **Neueste Kunde von Asien.** Prag, 1811-12. Cont. bds. (R. Oct.14-18; 1763) DM 450

EICHENDORFF, Joseph von
- **Lieder.** [Munich], Ernst Ludwig Pr. [1921]. (350). Orig. mor., gold fillets. (H. Dec.9/10; 1803) DM 1,200
- **Werke.** Berlin, 1842. Lightly soiled in parts & minimal browning of outer margins. Romantic cont. hf. leath. gt. & blind-tooled, marb. endpapers. MS. ded. on endpaper. (HK. May 15; 4186) DM 4,500
– – **Anr. Copy.** 4 vols. Slightly browned & soiled, stp. on title verso. New hf. leath. (H. Dec.9/10; 1448) DM 740

EINSTEIN, Albert
- **Die Grundlage der Allgemeinen Relativitätstheorie.** Leipzig, 1916. 1st. Separate Edn. Orig. ptd. wraps., in cl. folder. Inscr. 'To A.S. Eddington with kind regards from W. de Sitter' on title. (S. Jun.23; 274) *Simmonds.* £410

– – **Anr. Copy.** From Honeyman Collection. (S. May 20; 3222) *Norman.* £380
– – **Anr. Copy.** Orig. wraps., slightly spotted. (S. Jun.29; 329) *Heuer.* £160

See–LORENTZ, Hendrik Antoon, Einstein, A., & Minkowski, H.

EINSTEIN, Albert & Grossman, Marcel
- **Entwurf einer verallgemeinerten Relativitätstheorie und einer Theorie der Gravitation.** Leipzig/Berlin, 1913. 1st. Separate Edn. Orig. ptd. wraps. in buckram case. (C. Feb.4; 131a) *Quaritch.* £90

EINSTEIN, Lewis
- **The Humanist's Library.** Boston, 1906-13. (303) on H.M.P. 6 vols. Hf. cl., unc. & partly unopened. (SG. Jan.15; 23) $170

EISEN, Gustavus A. & Kouchakji, Fahim
- **Glass. Its Origin, History, Chronology, Technic & Classification to the Sixteenth Century.** N.Y., 1927. (525) numbered. 2 vols. 4to. Orig. bds. with linen backstrips & s.-c. (TA. Mar.19; 131) £190
– – **Anr. Copy.** Orig. parch.-bkd. bds., s.-c. (SH. Mar.6; 520) *Rosenberg.* £180

EISENBERG, Le Baron d'
- **Description du Manège Moderne dans sa Perfection.** Ill.:– B. Picart. N.p., 1727. Ob. 4to. Old cf. (LM. Jun.13; 64) B.Frs. 44,000
- **La Perfezione e i Difetti del Cavallo.** Flor., 1753. Fo. Slightly stained. 19th. C. hf. vell. (HK. May 12-14; 1247) DM 520

EISENLOHR, L. (Ed.)
See–ARCHITEKTONISCHE RUNDSCHAU

EISENMENGER, Johann Andreas
- **Entdecktes Judenthum, Oder Gruendlicher und Wahrhaffter Bericht, Welchergestalt die Verflockte Juden.** [Koenigsberg?], 1700. 1st. Edn. 2 vols. 4to. In German & Hebrew. Hf. leath. (S. Nov.18; 653) *Rock.* £700
– – **Anr. Edn.** Koenigsberg, 1711. [2nd. Edn.?]. 2 vols. 4to. Title & register in xerox, loosely inserted, slight discolouration. Buckram. (S. Nov.18; 654) *Valmadonna.* £200
– – **Anr. Copy.** Cont. vell. (R. Mar.31-Apr.4; 196) DM 1,650

EISLER, Max
- **Gustav Klimt.–eine Nachlese.** Vienna, 1931. (30) numbered, German Privilege Edn. Lge. fo. Cold. ills. partly printed with gold & silver. Orig. leath., silk doubls. & end-papers. (R. Oct.14-18; 695) DM 1,900

EKHO [Echo]
Ed.:– [N. Poshekhonsky]. St. Petersb., 1905. Fo. Unbnd. (SH. Feb.5; 65) *Quaritch.* £65

EKINS, C.
- **Naval Battles.** 1824. 4to. Hf. cf. (SH. Jul.23; 192) *Dallai.* £100

ELEGANT EXTRACTS
N.d. 14 vols. of 18. 12mo. Cont. str.-grd. mor. gt. (SKC. Sep.9; 1467) £50

ELEGANTE WELT
N.p., ca. 1840. 4to. 49 (of 52) hand-cold. litho. plts., all creased, few reprd., no text. Mod. hf. mor. (S. Mar.17; 411) *Symonds.* £220

ELEMENTI per Apprendere Facilmente l'Arte del Disegno
Venice, n.d. Ob. 8vo. Plts. ptd. in sepia. Cont. decor. paper wraps., unc. From the collection of John A. Saks. (C. Jun.10; 60) *Breslauer.* £320

ELEONORA MARIA ROSALIA, Herzogin zu Troppau u. Jägerndorff
- **Freywillig-aufgesprungener Granat-Apfel, des Christlichen Samaritans.** Vienna, 1752. 19th. Edn. 2 pts. in 1 vol. 4to. Slightly browned, wormed. Cont. leath. gt., clasps brkn., spine worn lightly at top. (R. Oct.14-18; 2701) DM 1,400

ELEONORE, ou l'Heureuse Personne–JOUJOU des Demoiselles (Le)
Paris, An VIII [1800]. 2 vols. in 1. 18mo. Cont. grained paper bds. (HD. Apr.10; 330) Frs. 1,400

ELGAR, F.
[-] **The Royal Navy.** 1873. 2nd. Edn. 4to. 1 plt. torn, some ll. soiled. Orig. cl., worn, loose. (SH. Mar.5; 228) *Walford.* £185

ELGIAS, T.E. & others
- **British Sports & Sportsmen.** N.d. (1000) numbered. No bdg. stated. (CSK. Jul.20; 132) £60

ELIANA. A New Romance formed by an English Hond
1661. 1st. Edn. Fo. Slight browning. Cont. sheep. Bkplt. of Knightly Rainald, Fawsely. [Wing E499] (S. Sep.29; 25) *Maggs.* £420

ELIESER, Ben Judah, of Pinczow
- **Damesek Elieser.** Jesnitz, 1723. 4to. Outer margin reprd. with loss to border, worming, repairs, stained, foxing. Vell.-bkd. bds. (SPB. May 11; 96) £150

ELIESER Ben Nathan
- **Maaamar Ha'sechel.** Ed.:- Wolf Heidenheim. Roedelheim, 1804. 2nd. Edn. Stained, repairs, browned & foxed. Cl. (SPB. May 11; 97) $125

ELIEZER BEN ELIJAH ASHKENAZI
- **Yoseph Lekah [commentary on Esther].** Cremona, 1576. Sm. 4to. Mor.-bkd. bds. (C. Jul.16; 305) *Stern.* £220

ELIMELECH OF LIZHENSK
- **Noam Elimelech-Iggeret Ha'kodesh.** [before 1850]. 4to. On blue paper. Cl. (S. Nov.17; 244) *Zysblat.* £105

ELIMELECH OF LIZHENSK–[Anonymous]
- **Noam Elimelech-Iggeret Ha'kodesh.–Likutim Yekarim.** [Lvov]; [Zolkiev], [before 1860?]; [1800]. 5th. Edn. [2nd. work]. 2 works in 1 vol. 4to. Hf. leath. (S. Nov.17; 245) *Goldberg.* £60

ELIOT, George (Pseud.)
*See–*EVANS, Marian 'George Eliot'

ELIOT, Thomas Stearns
- **Ash Wednesday.** N.Y., & L., 1930. 1st. Edn., (600). Orig. cl., s.-c. Sigd., but unnumbered. (SH. Dec.18; 140) *Chelsea.* £130
- - **Anr. Edn.** 1930. New Edn. 4to. Orig. cl., upr. cover with title & decors. as on 1st. Edn., unc. Proof Copy of Abandoned 4to. Edn., 3 gatherings including prelims. inscr. 'marked proof'. (SH. Dec.18; 138) *Lincoln.* £220
- - **Anr. Copy.** In 3 gatherings, including prelims. Unbnd., unc. Proof copy. (S. Jul.22; 8) *Clodd.* £160
- - **Anr. Edn.** 1933. Unbnd., stapled. P. Proofs for new reset Edn., some autograph corrections, inscr. on 1st. blank. (SH. Dec.18; 141) *Waterfield.* £200
- **The Builders.** Music by Martin Shaw. 1934. 1st. Edn. 4to. Orig. wraps. Inscr. to R.H.L. de la Mare. (SH. Dec.18; 148) *House of Books.* £220
- **The Confidential Clerk.** [1954]. 1st. Edn. Variant with 'Ihad' on p. 7. Orig. cl., d.-w., slight wear. Pres. copy to Isabel Jeans. (S. Jun.9; 71) *Sawyer.* £75
- **Excerpt.** Ill.:- Frederick Prokosch. New Haven, 1933. (5) numbered. 12mo. Orig. drawing frontis. Hand-sewn wraps. Extra drawing laid in, both drawings initialled & dtd. by artist, Prokosch bkplt., sigd. inscr. by him on 1st. blank lf. (SG. Jun.4; 131) $375
- **Four Quartets.** N.Y., [1943]. 1st. Edn., 1st. Iss. 'First American Edition [sic]' on copyright p. Cl., d.-w. (SG. Jun.4; 133) $200
- - **Anr. Edn.** N.Y., [1943]. Cl., d.-w. Pres. copy 'for Mrs. Charles Goodspeed', with correction by Eliot of word 'hermit' line 19, in 1st. stanza of 'The Dry Salvages', crossing it out & inserting the word 'horseshoe' in blue ink in margin, & initialling the correction 'T.S.E.', annots. on several pp. in pencil by Mrs. Goodspeed. (PNY. Mar.4; 143) $475
- **Fragment.** Ill.:- Frederic Prokosch (illuminated frontis.). New Haven, [after 1932]. (5). With inserted prelim. sketch & model ill., each sigd. by Prokosch. Marb. wraps. Prokosch's copy, with bkplt. (SPB. May 29; 139) $250
- **Gedenkschrift zur Verleihung des Hansischen Goethe-Preises 1954 der gemeinnützigen Stiftung F.V.S. zu Hamburg . . . an Thomas Stearns Eliot.** Hamburg, [1955]. 1st. Edn., [(1200), not for sale]. Engl. & German text. Orig. wraps. Inscr. to Richard de la Mare. (SH. Dec.18; 149) *Waterfield.* £60

- **Journey of the Magi.** Ill.:- Edward McKnight Kauffer. [1927]. 1st. Edn. Ariel Poem No. 8. Orig. wraps. Inscr. to Walter de la Mare. (SH. Dec.18; 133) *Barry Scott.* £210
- - **Anr. Copy.** Ariel Poem No. 8. Rough Proof Copy of 1st. Edn., inscr., 2 autograph corrections in text. (SH. Dec.18; 131) *Waterfield.* £100
- - **Anr. Copy.** 12mo. Orig. pict. wraps., cl. folding case. Pres. copy to his wife. (CNY. May 22; 98) $600
- **Marina.** Ill.:- Edward McKnight Kauffer. [1930]. 1st. Edn. Ariel Poem No. 29. Orig. wraps. Inscr. to Walter de la Mare. (SH. Dec.18; 144) *Abbott.* £120
- **Old Possum's Book of Practical Cats.** L., [1939]. 1st. Edn. Orig. cl., d.-w., cl. s.-c. Pres. copy to John Betjeman. (CNY. May 22; 99) $700
- **Poems 1909-1925.** 1932. Orig. plain paper wraps., with inscr. Proof Copy of new reset Edn., with autograph corrections & Greek quotation. (SH. Dec.18; 130) *Abbott.* £480
- **Prufrock & other Observations.** L., 1917. 1st. Edn., (500). 12mo. Orig. ptd. wraps., worn, cl. folding box. (SPB. Nov.25; 261) $500
- **Selected Essays 1917-32.** 1932. 1st. Edn., (115) sigd. Orig. vell. (SH. Dec.18; 146) *Quaritch.* £160
- - **Anr. Copy.** (SH. Dec.18; 145) *Rota.* £140
- **A Song for Simeon.** Ill.:- Edward McKnight Kauffer. [1928]. 1st. Edn. Orig. wraps. Inscr. to Walter de la Mare. (SH. Dec.18; 134) *Barry Scott.* £120
- **The Use of Poetry & the Use of Criticism.** 1933. Unbnd. P. Proofs for the 1st. Edn., autog. corrections. (SH. Dec.18; 147) *Quaritch.* £540
- **Waste Land.** N.Y., 1922. 1st. Edn. 'Mountain' spelled correctly, pp. 39-40 discold. Orig. cl. Pres. copy from publisher Horace Liveright to Glenway Westcott, sigd. by Westcott. (SPB. Nov.25; 262) $400
- - **Anr. Edn.** N.Y., 1922. 1st. Edn., (1,000) numbered, later state. 12mo. P. 41 lacks 'a' in 'Mountain'. Cl., unc. (SG. Jun.4; 127) $200
- - **Anr. Edn.** Hogarth Pr., 1923. 1st. Ltd. Engl. Edn. Orig. bds., unc., unopened. (SH. Jul.22; 118) *D.K.R. Thomson.* £420

ELIOT, W.
[-] **Some Account of Kentish Town.** 1821. Extra ill. Cf. gt. (P. Sep.11; 255) *Crowe.* £95

ELISOFON, Eliot
- **The Sculpture of Africa.** Ed.:- William Fagg & Ralph Linton. L., [1958]. Fo. Cl., d.-w. (SG. Aug.21; 8) $170

ELISSEEFF, S.
*See–*IACOVLEFF, Alexandre & Elisseeff, S.

ELIZABETH of Russia
- **Coronation of . . .** Ill.:- Stenglin after Caravaca. St. Petersb., 1744. Lge. fo. Engd. title, port. & 49 copperplts., many folding. Cont. cf., worn. (SG. May 14; 72) $650

ELLEN, OR THE NAUGHTY GIRL RECLAIMED
1811. 3rd. Edn. 16mo. 9 aquatinted cut-out figures, 5 hats & interchangeable head, all hand-cold. Orig. ptd. wraps., s.-c. soiled & reprd., fitted case. (SH. Mar.19; 62) *Gregory.* £160

ELLIOT, Daniel Giraud
- **A Monograph of the Bucerotidae.** Ill.:- J.G. Keulemans. [1877]-1882. 4to. 3 plts. foxed. 19th. C. maroon hf. mor., end-papers foxed, orig. wraps. bnd. in at end. (C. Nov.5; 50) *Taylor.* £2,500
- - **Anr. Copy.** Cont. hf. mor., wraps. to orig. 10 pts. bnd. at end. (C. Mar.18; 126) *Needham.* £1,500
- - **Anr. Edn.** Ill.:- J.G. Keulemans. [L.], 1882. 1st. Edn. Lge. fo. 57 hand-cold. litho. plts., bkplt. of American Museum of Natural History with stp. on title verso. Hf. mor. (SG. Oct.9; 86) $4,600
- **A Monograph of the Felidae or Family of Cats.** Ill.:- M. & N. Hanhart after Joseph Smit & Joseph Wolf. [L.], Priv. ptd., [1878-] 1883. Fo. Slight foxing to 3 plts., bkplt. of Boies Penrose. Old hf. mor. gt., orig. ll ptd. upr. wraps. preserved at end, bdg. worn & brkn. (CNY. Oct.1; 139) $8,000
- **A Monograph of the Paradiseidae or Birds of Paradise.** Ill.:- Smit after Wolf. L., Priv. ptd., 1873. Fo. Slight foxing. Cont. Engl. mor., gt., slightly worn. The Dearden family copy with sig. of A.J. Dearden dtd. 1924 & an inscr. to him from J.W. D[earden]. (S. Jun.1; 111) *Quaritch.* £5,800

- **A Monograph of the Pittidae.** N.Y., 1867. Atlas fo. 31 cold. plts. Mod. buck., liby. label inside cover, orig. wraps. of 7 pts. bnd. in. (SG. Oct.9; 86) $4,400
- - **Anr. Edn.** 1893-95. Lge. fo. Cont. hf. mor., upr. wraps. to orig. 5 pts. bnd. at end. (C. Mar.18; 127) *Ortlepp.* £4,000
- **A Monograph of the Tetraoninae or Family of the Grouse.** Ill.:- C.F. Tholey after the author. N.Y., Priv. ptd., 1865. Fo. Mod. hf. cf., orig. backstrip preserved. (S. Jun.1; 109) *Marks.* £3,300
- **The New & heretofore Unfigured Species of the Birds of North America.** Ill.:- Bowen & Co. after Elliott, Edwin Sheppard, et al. N.Y., [1866]-1869. 2 vols. in 1. Lge. fo. Cl. (C. Nov.5; 49) *Arader.* £2,900
- - **Anr. Copy.** 72 hand-finished cold. litho. plts., plts. guarded, text puckered, 1 text lf. torn. Hf. lev. mor., spine gt. (CNY. May 22; 198) $8,000
- - **Anr. Edn.** Ill.:- W.J. Linton & after Wolf & others. N.Y., Priv. ptd., 1869. 2 vols. in 1. Fo. 1 additional cold. plt. (P. occidentalis, a cancelland tipped in), text figures by Linton ptd. on India paper & pasted in, text slightly browned & with a few sm. tears. Cont. red mor., gt., slightly worn & stained, spine reprd. (S. Jun.1; 110) *Marks.* £4,000

ELLIOTT, Grace Dalrymple
- **Journal of My Life during the French Revolution.** L., 1859. Port., extra-ill. with approx. 70 engd. plts. Lev., spine gt., gt. dentelles, moire satin doubls. & end-ll. (SG. Apr.9; 169) $175
[-] - **Anr. Copy.** Extra ill. with about 70 engraved plts. (many of early origin) inlaid to size. Lev., spine diapered with fleurs-de-lys, gt. dentelles with doubls. & end-ll. of moire satin. (SG. Sep.4; 167) $160

ELLIOTT, Hugh
*See–*HANCOCK, James & Elliott, Hugh

ELLIOTT, John
*See–*DELASSAUX, V. & Elliott, John

ELLIOTT, Mary
- **The Children in the Wood, a Tale for the Nursery.** 1822. 12mo. Engraved folding frontis. cropped affecting caption, 1 p. advts. at end. Orig. ptd. wraps., worn. (SH. Mar.19; 89) *Quaritch.* £80
- **Grateful Tributes, or Recollections of Infancy.** N.Y., ca. 1820. 1st. Amer. Edn.? 16mo. Slightly spotted. Orig. pict. wraps. (SH. Mar.19; 88) *Ashton.* £55

ELLIOTT, Capt. Robert & Roberts, Emma
- **Views in the East; comprising India, Canton, & the Shores of the Red Sea.** 1833. [1st. Edn.?]. 2 vols. in 1. 4to. On india paper, some slight foxing. Cont. hf. cf., some wear. (TA. Dec.18; 108) £100
- - **Anr. Copy.** 2 vols. Plts. before title removed, minor tears, some foxing. Mor.-bkd. cl. bds., cl. faded. (SPB. May 29; 140) $120
- **Views in India, China, & on the Shores of the Red Sea.** Ill.:- after Prout, Stanfield & others, frontis. by G. Baxter. 1835. 2 vols. in 1. 4to. Some dampstaining. Cont. hf. mor., upr. cover detchd. (TA. Oct.16; 265) £80
- - **Anr. Copy.** A few ll. slightly spotted or browned. Cont. hf. cf. gt., worn, lacks spine. (SBA. Oct.21; 245) *Hyde Park Bookshop.* £55
- - **Anr. Edn.** N.d. Vol. 1. Orig. bdg. (DWB. May 15; 349) £60
- - **Anr. Copy.** 2 vols. in 1. 4to. Spotting. Cont. mor. (CSK. Jul.10; 6) £50

ELLIS, Frederick S. (Ed.)
*See–*DEGREVAUNT, Romance of . . .
*See–*PERECYVELLE, Syr of Gales
*See–*VORAGINE, Jacobus de
*See–*YSAMBRACE, Sir

ELLIS, G.
- **General Atlas of the World.** [1823]. 4to. Title-p. soiled & with 2 marginal defects reprd. Mod. hf. cf. (S. Apr.7; 473) *Hyde Park Books.* £70

ELLIS, H.D.
- **Catalogue of a Remarkable Collection of 16th & 17th Century Provincial Silver Spoons.** 1935. Orig. wraps., worn. (C. Jul.22; 140) *Taylor.* £55

ELLIS, Sir Henry, Diplomat
- **Journal of the Proceedings of the Late Embassy to China.** 1817. 1st. Edn. 4to. Prelims spotted. Cont. cf., gt. decor. spine. (TA. Dec.18; 383) £200

ELLIS, Sir Henry, Diplomat – Journal of the Proceedings of the Late Embassy to China. -*contd.*
– – **Anr. Copy.** Port. lightly foxed. Orig. bds., rebkd. with orig. paper label laid down, unc. (C. Nov.5; 52) *Quaritch.* £150
– – **Anr. Copy.** Folding map reprd. on recto, foxed & with tear, 1 plt. wtrmkd. 1813, some ll. foxed. Cont. paper-bkd. bds., unc. (S. Sep.29; 178) *Remington.* £100

ELLIS, Capt. Henry, Gov. of Georgia
– A Voyage to Hudson's Bay. 1748. 1st. Edn. Cont. cf., rebkd. (C. Nov.5; 51) *Arader.* £240

ELLIS, John
– English Atlas. 1766. Ob. 4to. 46 engraved maps only, map of South Wales very torn, some routes outl. in red, slightly spotted. Disbnd. W.a.f. (SBA. Mar.4; 105a) *Birch Books.* £300
– – **Anr. Edn.** Ca. 1780. 4to. Cont. mott. cf. (S. Apr.7; 255) *Kidd.* £380

ELLIS, John, Naturalist
– A Description of the Mangostan & the Bread-Fruit. Priv. Ptd., 1775. 1st. Edn. 4to. 19th. C. hf. mor. From Chetham's Liby., Manchester. (C. Nov.26; 147) *Quaritch.* £300
– – **Anr. Edn.** L., 1775. 4to. Browning, wormholes in lr. margin, tear on title reprd., offsetting. Hf. mor. (SPB. May 5; 195) $550
– An Essay Towards a Natural History of the Corallines . . . to which is added the Description of a Large Marine Polype taken near the North Pole . . . 1755. 1st. Edn. 4to. Some spotting. Cont. cf., rebkd. (TA. Jun.18; 133) £65

ELLIS, M.H.
– Francis Greenway; His Life & Times. Sydney, Shepherd Pr., 1949. (350) numbered, sigd. Mor., gt., worn, with s.-c. (KH. Nov.18; 231) Aus. $180

ELLIS, William, Farmer
– The Practical Farmer. 1732. 2 pts. (separately paginated) in 1 vol. Some woodcut head & tail pieces, plt. of the Hertfordshire wheel double plough. Cf. gt., front hinge loosening. (LC. Oct.2; 76) £65

ELLIS, Rev. William, Missionary
– Narrative of a Tour through Hawaii . . . 1826. 1st. Edn. Mod. hf. cf. (S. Jun.29; 197) *Crete.* £150
– – **Anr. Copy.** Some slight offsetting onto text. Mod. pol. hf. cf. by Root. (S. Feb.9; 120) *Gross.* £140
– Polynesian Researches. 1829. 1st. Edn. 2 vols. Spotted. Cont. hf. mor. (SH. May 21; 208) *Stuart.* £100
– – **Anr. Edn.** L., 1831-32. 2nd. Edn. 4 vols. Cl., gt., unopened (except vol. III). (JL. Dec.15; 861) Aus. $130

ELLIS, Sir William Charles
– A Treatise on the Nature, Causes & Treatment of Insanity with Practical Observations on Lunatic Asylums. 1838. 1st. Edn. Orig. cl. (S. Jun.15; 262) *Jenner Books.* £150

ELLSWORTH, Henry W.
– Valley of the Upper Wabash, Indiana, with Hints On Its Agricultural Advantages . . . N.Y., 1838. 1st. Edn. 1 plt. torn, not affecting image, text foxed, slightly soiled. Later wraps., worn. From liby. of William E. Wilson. (SPB. Apr.29; 94) $150

ELMER, Ebenezer
– An Address to the Citizens of New-Jersey. Elizabeth-Town, 1807. 1st. Edn. Somewhat browned. Disbnd. (SG. Jan.8; 137) $180

ELMES, James
See–SHEPHERD, Thomas Hosmer & Elmes, James

ELPHINSTONE, Mounstuart
– An Account of the Kingdom of Caubul. 1815. 1st. Edn. 4to. 1 map hand-cold. in outl., some margins lightly stained. Mod. hf. leath. (S. Jun.29; 221) *Hossain.* £120
– – **Anr. Copy.** 4to. Cont. diced cf., head of spine chipped, upr. cover detchd. (S. May 5; 243) *Bygone.* £70

ELSAM, Richard
– The Practical Builder's Perpetual Price-Book . . . L., 1826. Crude hf. leath., without fly-ll. (SG. Dec.4; 134) $110

ELSHOLTZ, Johann Sigismund
– Anthropometria sive de Mutua Membrorum Corporis Humani Proportione & Naevorum Harmonia Libellus. Frankfurt an Oder, 1663. Paper browned. Vell. (S. Dec.2; 484) *Rota.* £65

ELUARD, Paul
– Capitale de la Douleur. Paris, 1926. Orig. Edn., (109). Sm. 4to. Stitched, wrap. (HD. Apr.9; 592) Frs. 1,150
– Chanson Complète. Paris, [1939]. 1st. Edn. 4to. Orig. wraps. Inscr. to George Reavey. (SG. Jun.4; 143) $120
– Facile Poèmes. Ill.:– Man Ray. Paris, 1935. 1st. Edn., (1200). Loose in orig. pict. wraps. (HK. May 12-14; 2022) DM 650
– Poésie et Verité. Trans.:– Roland Penrose & E.L.T. Mesens. Ill.:– Man Ray. L., 1942. (500) sigd. by trans. Wraps., d.-w. reprd. (SG. Jun.4; 145) $110
– Sommmes-nous deux ou suis-je solitaire. Ill.:– Hans Erni. Paris, 1959. (125). Orig. vell., folding box. (SPB. May 6; 190) $650
– Un Soupçon. Poème. Ill.:– Guino. N.p.n., (1965). (25) on old Jap. Fo. Cf., sigd. & dtd. Paul Bonet 1968, decor. cold. leath. mosaic, suede-lined hf. cf. chemise & s.-c., leath. (D. Dec.11-13; 1055) DM 18,500
– Thorns of Thunder. Paris, Europa Pr., [1936]. 1st. sig. only, 8 ll. Unc., unopened. Sigd. by Eluard, Picasso, Man Ray, Beckett, Reavey & Max Ernst. (SG. Jun.4; 139) $425
– – **Anr. Edn.** Ed.:– George Reavey. Ill.:– Pablo Picasso. L., Europa Pr. & Stanley Nott, [1936]. (25) for Author & Publishers. Cl., d.-w. Sigd. by Eluard, Beckett, Reavey, Todd & Gascoyne. (SG. Jun.4; 138) $700
– – **Anr. Edn.** L., Europa Pr., [1936]. (50) numbered, sigd. Cl., d.-w. (SG. Jun.4; 141) $130
– Voir: Poemes, Peintures, Dessins. Ill.:– Picasso & others. Genève-Paris, [1948]. Ltd. Numbered Edn. 4to. Decor. wraps. (SG. Oct.23; 107) $130
See–ERNST, Max & Eluard, Paul
See–VALERY, Paul & others

ELUCIDARIUS, Eyn Newer
– Von allerhandt Geschöpffern Gottes, den Engeln . . . Gestirns, Planeten, und wie all Creaturen geschaffen seint. Strassburg, ca. 1540. 4to. Slightly spotted. Disbnd. (S. Oct.21; 380) *Simons.* £150

ELWE, I.B.
– Atlas. (Beknopte Beschrijving van de Gehele Wereld). Amst., ca. 1792. Fo. Old bdg., worn. (LM. Mar.21; 18) B.Frs. 14,000

ELWES, Henry John & Fitch, W.H.
– A Monograph of the Genus Lilium. 1880-1940. 1st. Edns. 2 vols. Fo. Lacks photographic plt. & 2 final pts. of supp. Mod. red hf. mor. (S. Jun.1; 113) *Mayers.* £1,400

ELWES, Henry John & Henry, Augustine
– The Trees of Great Britain & Ireland. Edinb., 1906-13. 7 vols. & Index in 15 orig. pts. 4to. Orig. wraps., soiled, 1 upr. wrap. detchd. (CSK. Feb.13; 29) £190
– – **Anr. Copy.** (CSK. Nov.21; 88) £100
– – **Anr. Edn.** 1969-72. 7 vols. Cl., d.-w.'s. (CE. Dec.4; 249) £50

ELWES, Robert
– A Sketcher's Tour round the World. 1854. 1st. Edn. Orig. cl. gt., new end-ll. (SKC. Feb.26; 1645) £75

ELWOOD, Anne Katherine
– Narrative of a Journey Overland from England . . . to India. 1830. 2 vols. Slight soiling, title of vol. 1 cleanly torn. Mod. cf.-bkd. cl. (CSK. Jan.9; 20) £60

ELZEVIR PRESS
– De Imperio Magni Mogolis sive India Vera Commentarius. Leiden, 1631. 16mo. Margins slightly browned. Later vell. (TA. Jun.18; 343) £74
– 'Republics'. Leiden, 1627-41. 28 vols., including 2 dupls. 16mo. Contents loose in some vols., some vols. with worming, occasional browning. Most vols. cont. cf. (not entirely unif.), some wear. W.a.f. (S. Feb.10; 288) *Chamberlain.* £260

EMANUEL, Cedric
– The Etchings . . . [Sydney], [1980]. (300) numbered, & sigd. 4to. Mor., cl. s.-c. (KH. Mar.24; 136) Aus. $240

EMBLEM Books
– Fasti Mariana cum Illustrium Diviorum Elogiis in Singulos Anni Mensis Diesque SS Natales a Sodalitate B.V. Munich, 1667. 24mo. Cont. stpd. pig, lacks clasps. (SG. Feb.5; 132) $180

EMBLEMATA cum aliquot nummis antiqui opera –EPISTOLIA Dialogi Breves
Ill.:– Jean Croissant (1st. work). Antw. (1st. work), 1564; 1577. 2 works in 1 vol. Pig. armorial bdg. in blindstp. with name of Ioachim von Alvenschleve & date 1579, cont. ink titles on spine, raised bands, brass clasps. [BMC STC 182] (1st. work). (PWP. Apr.9; 128) Can. $1,100

EMDEN, A.B.
– A Biographical Register of the University of Oxford to A.D. 1500. Oxford, 1957-59. 3 vols. Orig. cl., d.-w.'s. (SH. Oct.10; 342) *Eur. Univ. Inst.* £55

EMDEN, Yakov
– Akitzat Akrav. Altona [Amst.], Priv. Ptd., 1753. 4to. Browning, soiled, repairs. Cl. (SPB. May 11; 99) $1,900
– Bet El & Shaarei Shamaim. Altona [Amst.], Priv. Ptd., 1744-47. 1st. Edn. Cropped, lightly stained. Cf., worn. Bkplt. of Samuel Dresner. (SPB. May 11; 100) $850
– Etz Avot. Altona [Amst.], Priv. Ptd., 1751. 1st. Edn. 4to. Lr. margin of title reprd. without text loss, browning. Bds. (SPB. May 11; 101) $700
– Sefat Emet Ve'lashon. [Altona], Priv. Ptd., 1752-53. 4to. Some staining. Cl.-bkd. bds. (SPB. May 11; 102) $800
– Sefer Shimush. Altona [Amst.], Priv. Ptd., 1758. Sm. 4to. Last lf. in facs., staining, repairs, worming. Mod. hf. vell. (SPB. May 11; 103) $2,100

EMERSON, Caroline D.
– School Days in Disneyville. Ill.:– Walt Disney Studio. Boston, 1939. Orig. pict. cl. (SH. Mar.19; 84) *Fletcher.* £50

EMERSON, Peter Henry
– On English Lagoons: Being an Account of the Voyage of Two Amateur Wherrymen on the Norfolk & Suffolk Rivers & Broads. L., 1893. Pict. cl., wrinkled, unopened. (SG. Apr.23; 85) $100

EMERSON, Ralph Waldo
– Essays. Ed.:– Thomas Carlyle. Hammersmith, Doves Pr., 1906. (25) on vell. Sm. 4to. Orig. vell., unc., qtr. mor. s.-c. Thomas B. Lockwood bkplt. (CNY. May 22; 379) $3,000
– – **Anr. Edn.** Ed.:– Thomas Carlyle (preface). Hammersmith, Doves Pr., 1906. (300). 4to. Vell., slightly dis-cold., pin hole at upr. jnt. (PNY. Dec.3; 118) $220
– Essays.–Poems. Boston, 1841; 1847. 1st. Edn.; 1st. Amer. Edn. 2 works in 2 vols. 12mo. 1st. work: orig. cl., bkplt. removed from endpaper, qtr. mor. case; 2nd. work: orig. glazed bds., covers slightly stained, cl. folding case. From the Prescott Collection. (CNY. Feb.6; 105) $400
– Nature. Boston, 1836. 1st. Edn. 12mo. 1st. iss. with p. 94 misnumbered 92, heavily foxed, contents almost entirely loose in bdg., early owner's name on title. Orig. cl., covers with Blanck's 'B' frame, crudely rebkd., some repairs on covers. (SG. Mar.19; 101) $175
[–] – **Anr. Copy.** 2nd. state, with p. 94 correctly numbered. Blind-stpd., gt.-lettered cl., hf. mor. s.-c. Inscr. by Lidian Emerson, bkplt. of H.A. Igraham partly covering that of Henry Baldwin. (SG. Nov.13; 165) $170
– – **Anr. Edn.** [Munich], [1924]. (280) numbered. 4to. Orig. vell., orig. bd. s.-c. (HK. Nov.18-21; 2456) DM 610
– – **Anr. Edn.** [Muenchen], Bremer Pr., [1929]. (250) numbered. 4to. Patterned bds., vell.-bkd. (SG. Sep.4; 78) $140
– Society & Solitude. Boston, 1870. 1st. Edn. 12mo. Cf., triple gt. fillet borders, gt. panel. spine, gt. dentelles, by Root, orig. cl. covers & spine bnd. in, bkplt., cl. s.-c. (SG. Mar.19; 105) $100

EMERSON, William
[–] The Principles of Mechanics. Explaining & demonstrating the general Laws of Motion . . . Gravity . . . Projectiles, . . . Hydrostatica, & Construction of Machines. 1758. 2nd. Edn. 4to. Cont. cf., worn. (S. Oct.21; 343) *Walford.* £65

EMET VE'EMUNAH
Ed.:– Yitzhak Ben Chananiah Arubas. Venice, 1672. 12mo. Mod. cl. (SPB. May 11; 33) $375

EMMART, Emily Walcott (Trans.)
See-CODEX BARBERINI

EMMETT, John
- A Choice Collection of Excellent Receipts in Confectionary. York, 1737. A1-E4, a few stains. Cont. cf.-bkd. bds., worn. (SBA. Oct.22; 588)
Quaritch. £230

EMORY, Lieut. Col. William H.
- Report on the United States & Mexican Boundary Survey. Ill.:- Sarony & others. Wash., 1857-59. Vols. I & II in 3. 4to. Completely disbnd. (SG. Nov.20; 325) $350

EMPESE, Baron Emile de l'
- L'Art de Mettre sa Cravate . . .-L'Art de ne jamais Dejeuner chex soi et de Diner toujours chex les Autres. Honoré de Balzac, 1827. 2 vols. 16mo. Hf. mor. by Petit-Simier, spines decor. with raised bands. (HD. Jun.24; 132) Frs. 2,650

EMPIRE de la Beauté (L')
[1793]. Sm. 18mo. Cont. red mor., gt. decor. covers, lge. border, centre motif. (HD. Apr.10; 103) Frs. 1,300
- - **Anr. Edn.** Paris, [1796]. 18mo. Cont. silk, decor. gt. covers, lge. border, centre miniat., in copper under glass. (HD. Apr.10; 102) Frs. 3,300

EMPIRE des Légumes, L'
- Mémoires de Cucurbitus 1er. Ed.:- E. Nus & Antony Méray. Ill.:- A. Varin. Paris & Leipzig, [1851]. 1st. Printing. Cont. bds., smooth decor. spine. (HD. Jun.24; 189) Frs. 4,700
- - **Anr. Edn.** Ed.:- Eugène Nus & Antony Meray. Ill.:- Amédée Varin. Paris, [1861]. Hf. chagrin, corners, smooth decor. spine, unc., wrap. (HD. Jun.24; 190) Frs. 1,700

ENCICLOPEDIA Dello Spettacolo
Rome, [1954-66]. 10 vols. including Supp. Orig. cl. (CSK. Jul.10; 33) £160

ENCYCLOPAEDIA: or a Dictionary of Arts, Sciences, & Miscellaneous Literature
Phila., 1793-1803. 1st. Amer. Edn. 18 vols. & 3 supp. vols. 4to. Some light foxing. Old tree cf., worn, some covers detchd. W.a.f. (SG. Nov.20; 326) $300

ENCYCLOPAEDIA BRITANNICA
Edinb., 1778-1783. 2nd. Edn. 10 vols. 4to. Cont. cf. (SBA. Jul.23; 243) *Riley Smith.* £1,100
- - **Anr. Edn.** Edinb., 1778-84. 2nd. Edn. 10 vols. 4to. 4 titles detchd. (2 torn), occasional spotting. Later hf. russ., covers detchd., spines defect., worn. W.a.f. (S. May 5; 366) *Subunso.* £220
- - **Anr. Edn.** Edinb., 1797. 3rd. Edn. 18 vols. 4to. Lacks 1 plt., 2 ll. torn with no loss of text, a few ll. slightly spotted, a few other minor defects. Cont. spr. cf., slightly worn. (SBA. Mar.4; 37) *Carruthers.* £180
- - **Anr. Copy.** 22 vols. Lacks some plts. Cont. hf. cf., worn, some covers detchd. (SH. Jul.23; 215) *Dr. Molloin.* £70
- - **Anr. Edn.** Edinb., 1815. 5th. Edn. 20 vols. 4to. Slight foxing & offsetting. Cont. diced cf., gt., 2 spines torn at head. (S. Jan.26; 210) *Traylen.* £190
- - **Anr. Edn.** 1875. 24 vols. & index. Hf. mor. (MMB. Oct.8; 85g) £58
- - **Anr. Edn.** 1875-1903. 9th. Edn. 35 vols. including new vol. & index. 4to. Cont. mor. gt., gt. arms on upr. covers. (SBA. Jul.23; 244) £110
- - **Anr. Copy.** No bdg. stated but gt. decor. spines, worn. (TA. Jun.18; 385) £70
- - **Anr. Edn.** Camb., 1910. 11th. Edn. 29 vols. Orig. limp mor. (CSK. Aug.15; 69) £55
- - **Anr. Edn.** Camb., 1910-11. [11th. Edn.?]. 29 vols. 4to. Orig. cf. & cl., worn. (SBA. Jul.22; 14) *Gandy.* £150
- - **Anr. Copy.** Orig. hf. mor. (SH. May 28; 34) £75
- - **Anr. Copy.** Orig. roan & cl., worn. (SH. Jan.30; 426) *Henderson.* £60
- - **Anr. Edn.** Camb., 1910-22. 11th. Edn., India paper. 32 vols. Tall 4to. Orig. flexible maroon mor., spines faded. (SG. Mar.26; 181) $220
- - **Anr. Edn.** 1910-22. 11th. Edn., handy vol. iss. 32 vols. Orig. mor. (SH. Mar.5; 229) *Dawson's.* £90
- - **Anr. Edn.** N.Y., 1910-26. 11th. & 13th. Edns. Vols. 1-35 in 19. Orig. hf. mor. (SH. Apr.9; 233) *Fletcher.* £110
- - **Anr. Edn.** L. & N.Y., 1929. 14th. Edn. 24 vols. 4to. Orig. hf. leath., decor. spines, some sm. stains. (SM. Feb.11; 26) Frs. 1,100

ENCYCLOPAEDIA BRITANNICA-BRITAN-NICA BOOK of the Year 1953-62
1951; 1953-62. 25 vols. including atlas; 10 vols. 4to. Unif. cl. (SKC. Feb.26; 1432) £55

ENCYCLOPAEDIA JUDAICA
Ed.:- Jacob Klatzkin. Berlin, 1928-32. 10 vols. Hf. leath. (S. Nov.18; 531) *Kingsgate.* £240

ENCYCLOPAEDIA of the Laws of Scotland
Edinb., 1949-51. 16 vols. plus 2 Supp. vols. Cl. (PD. Apr.1; 48) £85

ENCYCLOPAEDIA OF SCOTTISH Legal Styles
N.d. 10 vols. including Index. Cl., soiled. (CE. Feb.19; 24) £65

ENCYCLOPAEDIA PERTHENSIS: or Universal Dictionary of Knowledge
Perth, [1796-1806]. 23 vols. Cont. diced russ. gt., a few spines chipped. (SBA. Oct.22; 681) *Quaritch.* £100

ENCYLOPEDIA of World Art
N.Y., [1959-68]. 15 vols. 4to. Buckram. (SG. Dec.4; 135) $550

ENCYCLOPEDIE METHODIQUE, Marine
Paris & Lüttich, 1783-87. 3 vols. in 6 & plt. vol. 4to. Last 20 plts. stained & Vol. 1 pt. 2 of text vol. Interim bdg. (R. Oct.14-18; 2878) DM 1,500

ENCYCLOPEDIE METHODIQUE Chirurgie
Paris, An VII [1798-99]. Plt. vol. only. Sm. fo. Plts. numbered 1-113, without 13 & 52, not publd., some plts. with sm. stain in outer margin. Hf. leath. gt. (R. Mar.31-Apr.4; 976) DM 2,500

ENCYCLOPEDIE METHODIQUE, ou par Ordre des Matières
Paris, Liège, 1782-91. 8 text & 8 plt. vols. 4to. & lge. 4to. 1085 copperplts., inclg. 219 dbl.-p. Cont. leath. (text) & hf. leath. (plts.) gt., 1 spine slightly defect. (R. Mar.31-Apr.4; 1548) DM 6,800

ENCYCLOPEDIE OECONOMIQUE, ou système Général
- I. D'Oeconomie Rustique . . . -II. D'Oeconomie Domestique . . . -III. D'Oeconomie Politique . . . Yverdon, 1770-71. 16 vols. Cont. hf. cf., spines gt., partly unc. (VG. Nov.18; 1154) Fls. 1,100

ENEMY, The; a Review of Art & Literature
Ed.:- Wyndham Lewis. 1927-29. Nos. 1-3 (all publd.) Sm. fo. Orig. pict. wraps. (S. Jul.22; 205) *Sims & Reed.* £90

ENGEL, Arthur & Serrure, Raymond
- Traité de Numismatique du Moyen Age. Paris, 1891-1905. 3 vols. Mod. buckram. (SG. Dec.18; 317) $100

ENGEL, Johann Jakob
- Practical Illustrations of Rhetorical Gesture and Action. Trans.:- Henry Siddons. 1822. 2nd. Engl. Edn. Cont. hf. cf. Sigd. on fly lf. by R.W. Mallison. (SH. Apr.10; 394) *Bayley.* £60

E[NGEL, Samuel, Bailli] d'E[chalens]
- Essai sur cette Question: Quand et comment l'Amerique a-t-elle été peuplé d'hommes et d'animaux. Amst., 1767. 4to. Cont. cf [Sabin 22568] (SPB. May 5; 197) $400

ENGELBACH, Lewis
[-] Naples & the Campagna Felice in a series of letters addressed to a friend in England in 1802. Ill.:- after Rowlandson. 1815. [1st. Edn.?] Mod. hf. mor. by C. J. Sawyer Ltd., spine gt. (CSK. May 15; 26) £180
[-] - **Anr. Copy.** Plt. at p.4 guarded & with imprint cropped, 1st. map reprd. in fold. Mott. cf., gt., by Rivière. (S. Jun.23; 324) *Primrose Hill Books.* £120
[-[- **Anr. Copy.** Text wtrmkd. 1814-15, plts. 1814, plt. 9 defect. & reprd., a few stains to frontis., additional title & plts. 12 & 14, some browning & spotting. Cont. cf., some wear. (S. Dec.8; 220) *Scott.* £60
- - **Anr. Copy.** Pp. 125-126 reprd. Worn, rebkd., spine gt. (CNY. May 22; 100) $150

ENGELMANN, E.
See-SAZERAC, J. M. H. & Engelmann, E. & others

ENGELMANN, Godefroy
- Manuel du Dessinateur Lithographe. Paris, 1822. 1st. Edn. Cont. hf. leath. (R. Oct.14-18; 562) DM 780

ENGELS, Frederick
- Socialism-Utopian & Scientific. L., 1892. 1st. Edn. Hf.-title browned. Orig. cl., soiled. Author's pres. copy inscr. on hf.-title by Engels to the Danish Socialist Ferdinand Wolf, dtd. 28 Sep., 1892, sigd. 'F.Engels'. (CNY. Oct.1; 90) $600

ENGLAND
- Maps of the English Counties. 1791. Marb. bds. W.a.f. (CE. Aug.28; 272) £100

ENGLAND, Customs
- The Rates of Merchandizes. 1635. Lacks last (?blank) lf., browned. Mod. mor. [STC 7695] (SH. Jun.11; 35) *Thorp.* £150

ENGLAND, Year Books (Edward III. 1-50)
- Liber Assisarum & Placitorum Coronne. [L.], [1514?]. Fo. Fr. text, wormed at beginning & end affecting text, some stains & soiling, cont. owner's inscr. of Thomas Maryet, extensive annots. & underlinings in his hand thro.-out. Near cont. L. bdg., blind-stpd. cf. over wooden bds., panel roll on sides incorporating medallion heads, birds & conventional foliage, very worn, lacks clasps & catches. [STC 9599] (S. Jan.26; 1) *Thorp.* £280

ENGLAND Displayed
See-RUSSELL, P. & Price, Owen

ENGLAND ILLUSTRATED, or, a Compendium of the Natural History, Geography, Topography . . . of England & Wales
Ill.:- Thomas Kitchen. 1764. 2 vols. 4to. Cont. spr. cf. As an atlas, w.a.f. (SBA. Oct.21; 98) *Nicholson.* £400
- - **Anr. Copy.** Plts. & maps stained. Cf., worn. (SH. May 21; 35) *Kidd.* £370

ENGLEFIELD, Sir Henry C.
- A Description of the Principal Picturesque Beauties, Antiquities, & Geological Phoenomena, of the Isle of Wight. 1816. 1st. Edn. Lge. 4to. Slight spotting. Cont. russ., gt. foliate borders & panel, rebkd. preserving old spine. The Coole Liby. copy. (S. Jun.22; 31) *Crowe.* £280
- - **Anr. Copy.** Orig. cl., worn, covers loose, spine brkn. (C. May 20; 120) *Traylen.* £120

ENGLEHEART, H.L.D.
See-WILLIAMSON, George C. & Engleheart, H.L.D.

ENGLER, A. & Prantl, K.
- Die Naturlichen Pflanzenfamilien nebst ihren Gattungen und Wichtigeren Arten. Leipzig, 1887-1915. 39 pts. in 23 vols. Orig. hf. mor. (VG. Dec.16; 845) Fls. 1,150

ENGLISH ARCHITECTURE, or the Publick Buildings of London & Westminster
[1756?]. Fo. 123 engraved plts., long tear in 1, sm. tear in anr. Cont. hf. cf., spine worn, unc. (C. Feb.25; 181) *Weinreb.* £520

ENGLISH DIALECT DIARY
1898-1905. 6 vols. 4to. Cont. hf. cf., 1 cover detchd. (SH. May 28; 35) *Howes Books.* £65

ENGLISH DIALECT SOCIETY
- Publications. 1873-96. Vols. 1-32 in 33 vols. Cont. hf. mor. (SH. May 28; 36) *Royal.* £160

ENGLISH MEN OF LETTERS
39 vols. Three-qtr. leath. (HY. Jan.14; 17) £105

ENGLISH PILOT, for the Southern Navigation: describing the Sea-Coasts, Capes, Headlands, Bays, Roads, Harbours, Rivers & Ports
L., 1771. Fo. Title-p. & first 7 maps severely stained at upr. margin & crudely reprd., anr. badly soiled & defect., others soiled, text also defect. Mod. cl.-covered bds., disbnd. As a collection of maps, w.a.f. (SPB. Nov.25; 116) $550
- - **Anr. Edn.** L., 1788. Fo. 21 (of 22?) double-p. or folding copperplts. maps, 1 defect., 1st. text ll. defect. Loose, no bdg. (R. Oct.14-18; 1563) DM 4,000

ENGLISH PORCELAIN (CERAMIC) CIRCLE -EXHIBITION CATALOGUE
1928-78; 1948. Vols. 1-10 in 20, together 21 vols. 8vo. & 4to. Orig. cl. & wraps. (SH. Jan.29; 173) *Cresswell.* £250

ENGLISH SCENERY
1889. Orig. cl. gt., worn. (SKC. May 19; 444) £50

ENGRAMELLE, Marie Dominique Joseph & Ernst, J.J.
- **Papillons d'Europe.** Paris, 1779-92. 8 vols. in 4. 4to. Cont. red mor.-bkd. bds., gt. borders on sides. (C. Mar.18; 39) *Quaritch.* £2,800
- - **Anr. Copy.** 8 vols. Lacks 1 cold. frontis. & 16 old cold. copperplts. New hf. vell. (R. Oct.14-18; 3057) DM 6,100

ENGRAVING & Maps
Ca. 1820. 1 vol. 4to. 60 engrd. views & 29 hand-cold. maps, 2 folding, torn, soiled. Cont. hf. cf., worn, 1 cover detchd. (SH. Apr.9; 147) *Fairburn.* £400

ENS, Gaspar
[-] **Indiae Occidentalis Historia.** Cologne, 1612. Browned. Later cf. [Sabin 22656] (SPB. May 5; 199) $200

ENSAYO ... del Idioma llamado Comunmente Quichua.
See–MOSSI, Honorio–ANON

ENSCHEDE, Charles
- **Fonderies de Caractères et leur Materiel dans les Pays-Bas du XVe au XIXe Siècle.** Haarl., 1908. H.M.P. Fo. Orig. cl. gt. (VG. Dec.16; 548) Fls. 800
- **Typefoundries in the Netherlands from the 15th. to the 19th. Centuries.** Trans.:– Henry Carter. Haarlem, 1978. 1st. Edn. in Engl. (1500). Fo. Cont. vell., mor. spine with 8 labels incorporating, between raised bands, the name 'Enschede', covers with free design in gold tooling & cold. inks based on Enschede founts, bds. lined in full vell. with mor. jnts., matching suede doubls., hand-made Fabriano end-papers, perspex s.-c., by Gemma O'Connor of Oxford, Jan., 1981. (S. Jun.9; 15a) *Forster.* £700

ENSLIE, John
- **Large Folding Chart Illustrating the Electric Telegraph.** 1851. 4to. Mntd. on linen. Orig. embossed cl. folder. Loosely inserted pamphlet on Allan's Electric Telegraph with 12 engraved ills. torn in fold. (S. Dec.2; 710) *Quaritch.* £70

ENSOR, James
- **Scènes de la Vie du Christ.** [Brussels], 1921. (275) numbered. & sigd. Ob. 4to. 21 cold. litho. plts. only (of 31, lacks nos. 4, 15, 16, 19, 21, & 23-27), all plts. on Hollande van Gelder paper & mntd., all but 1 with orig. lettered tissue guards. Loose as iss. in wraps. (SG. Apr.2; 106) $500

ENTICK, John
- **The General History of the Late War.** 1765-63. Vol. 1 2nd. Edn., others 1st. Edns. 5 vols. Cont. cf., upr. cover vol. 1 detchd. [Sabin 22667] (C. Nov.5; 53) *Rota.* £55
- **New & Accurate History & Survey of London, Westminster, Southwark.** 1766. 4 vols. Cf. gt. (P. Nov.13; 18) *Scott.* £75

ENTRECASTEAUX, Bruni d'
- **Voyage ... Envoyé à la Recherché de la Perouse.** Paris, 1808. 2 vols. 4to. Liby. stps. cut from both titles & reprd. Later hf. mor., slightly worn. [Sabin 22671] (SPB. May 5; 200) $150
See–LA PEROUSE, Jean Francoise Galaup de
–LABILLARDIERE, Jacques J. Houton de
–ENTRECASTEAUX, Bruni d'

EPEE, Abbé de L'
- **L'Art d'enseigner et Parler aux Sourds–Muets de Naissance.** Ed.:– L'Abbé Sicard. 1820. Cont. cf., border, crowned cypher on upr. cover. A.L.S. dtd. 14 Apr. 1791, 2pp. 4to., added port. (HD. Oct.10; 239) Frs. 2,100

EPHEMERIDES de la Généralité de La Rochelle
La Rochelle, 1783. Sm. 12mo. Cont. red mor., lge. gt. plaque on covers. (HD. Apr.10; 105) Frs. 1,250

EPHREM Syrus
- **Sermones.** Trans.:– Ambrosius Traversarius. Flor., Antonio di Bartolommeo Miscomini, 23 Aug. 1481. Fo. 89 ll. (of 90, lacks initial blank), cont. ms. foliation, blank corner of 1st. lf. missing, reprd. Mod. vell. bds. [HC 6599*; BMC VI p.636; Goff E 45] (C. Apr.1; 29) *Walton.* £340

EPICEDIUM Pro Immaturo Funere Mariae Clementinae Magnae Britanniae & Reginae ...
Rome, 1738. Sm. 4to. Parch. (PD. May 20; 117) £50

EPICTETUS
- **Manuall.** 1616. 2 pts. in 1 vol. 12mo. Browned. Cont. vell. [STC 10426] (SH. Jun.11; 36) *Poole.* £100
- **Nouveau Manuel, Extrait des Commentaires d'Arrien ...** Paris, 1784. 2 vols. 18mo. Red mor. by Derome, pointillé & gt. fillets repeated on spine, inside dentelle. (HD. Mar.18; 65) Frs. 2,500

EPINAY, Louise Florence Petronille Tardieu d'Esclavelles, marquise d'
- **Mémoirs et Correspondance.** Paris, 1818. Orig. Edn. 3 vols. Spotted in pts., liby. stp. on verso of titles. Cont. hf. cf. (S. Jan.27; 447) *Booth.* £60

EPISTLE FROM Lady Traffick to Sir John (Adultery à la Mode). The Fireside: A Pastoral Soliloquy by Isaac Hawkins Browne (& other works)
1745-n.d. 11 works in 1 vol. Fo. Some soiling. Cont. sheep-bkd. marb. bds., worn, armorial bkplt. of the Laird of Altyr. (CSK. Jan.30: 181) £650

EPISTOLAE Illustrium Virorum
Ed.:– [Jodocus Badius Ascensius]. Lyon, Feb.13, 1499. Fo. BM Liby. & dupl. sale stps. 18th. C. spr. cf., worn. [BMC VIII, 330.] (S. Mar.16; 112) *Thorp.* £320

EPISTOLAE INDICAE, de Stupendis et praeclaris Rebus, quas divina Bonitas in India ...
See–LISITANO, J.P.–EPISTOLAE INDICAE, de stupendis et praeclaris Rebus, quas divina Bonitas in India ...

EPISTOLIA Dialogi Breves
See–EMBLEMATA cum aliquot nummis antiqui opera.–EPISTOLIA Dialogi Breves.

EPOQUES les Plus Intéressantes des Révolutions de Paris, ou Le Triomphe de la Liberté
Paris, [1789]. Sm. 18mo. Cont. red mor., decor., lge. border. (HD. Apr.10; 106) Frs. 7,500
- - **Anr. Copy.** Cont. mor., decor., wide border & lge. centre motif, watered silk fly.-ll. & doubls. (HD. Apr.10; 107) Frs. 3,500

EPSTEIN, Aryeh Ben Mordecal
- **Sidur Ha'ari.** Koenigsberg, 1756. 1 section only (ll. 12-55), cropped, severely browned & soiled, reprd. Mod. cl. (SPB. May 11; 104) $350

EPSTEIN, Yitzhak Isaac Ha'levi, of Homel
- **Chana Ariel.** Berditchev, 1912. 1st. Edn. 7 pts. in 4 vols. 4to. Varied bdgs., Gerschom Scholem's bkplt. (S. Nov.17; 199) *Quaritch.* £130
- **Ma'amar Hashiflut Ve'hasimcha (Chasidut –Chabad).** [Wilno?], 1868. 1st. Edn. Bds. (S. Nov.17; 200) *Valmadonna.* £80

EQUICOLA, Mario
- **Libro di Natura d'Amore ...** Venice, 1531, 2nd. Edn. Lacks last lf. (blank?), sig. of Jean de Rièux, Comte de Largouët, bkplt. of Ginori-Conti. Early 17th. C. mor., gt., arms of de Rieux on covers, double gt. fillet, spine gt. in compartments. (SM. Oct.7; 1697) Frs. 1,200

ERARD, Pierre
- **The Harp.** L., 1821. 1st. Edn. Fo. Orig. decor. & ptd. wraps. (GM. Apr.30; 736) £85

ERASMUS, Desiderius
[-] [**Adagiorum Chiliadis**]. Ed.:– Johannes Frobenius. Basle, Oct. 1520. Fo. Title slightly defect. at corner, just affecting border, cont. marginalia, a few wormholes, 1 slightly affecting some letters, slightly spotted or soiled in pts. Cont. German blind-stpd. vell., worn, pulled from wooden bds. (S. Jan.27; 362) *Lister.* £55
- **Catalogus omnium ... lucubrationum.** Basle, Apr. 1523. Slight browning, lacks fo. 8 (?blank). Mod. buckram. (S. Jan.27; 363) *Quaritch.* £200
- **Colloquia Familiaria of Gemeensame t'samenspraken.–De onversochte Krijghsman of Verklaringe van 't oude Latijnsche Spreeck-woord Dulce Bellum inexpertis.** Haarl., 1634; 1633. 4to. Annot. dtd 1657 on last fly-lf. Cont. vell., soiled & worn, inner hinges brkn. (VG. Dec.17; 1311) Fls. 500
- **The Colloquies.** 1671. 1st. Engl. Edn. Cont. cf., worn. [Wing E3190] (SH. Jul.23; 91) *Murray-Hill.* £80
- **Eloge de la Folie.** Ill.:– after Holbein. Amst., 1745. 12mo. Cont. marb. cf., decor. spines. (HD. Apr.9; 593) Frs. 1,300
- **Epistola ad Diversos.** Ill.:– Urs Graf & Ambr. Holbein. Basel, 1521. 1st. Coll. Edn. Fo. Old MS. marginalia, worming at foot, title loss, 1st. p.

wormed in ill. Old MS. notes on lower title, stained in parts in margin or text. Later 18th. C. hf. leath., defect. at head & foot of spine. [BMC (German Books) S. 276; STC 276] (D. Dec.11-13; 21) DM 12,050
- **In Evangelium Marci Paraphrasis.** Basel, 1524. Slightly soiled in parts, some old MS. marginalia, 11 ll. MS. notes bnd. at front & end. Cont. gold-stpd. leath.-bkd. wd. bds., 2 clasps. (HK. Nov.18-21; 178) DM 1,100
- **Moriae Encomium.** Ill.– Holbein (ports.). Basle 1676. Slightly dampstained. Red mor., gt., rebkd., worn. (S. Dec.8; 75) *Armstrong.* £75
- **Moriae Encomium.–The Colloquies, or Familiar Discourses ...** Ed.:– G. Listrius (1st. work). Trans.:– H.M. (2nd. work). 1st. work. n.p., 1544; 1671. 2 vols. 1st. work: owner's inscrs. on title, 1 deleted; 2nd. work: a few sm. stains. Sheep, rebkd.; cont. sheep, worn. [Wing E3190] (2nd. work) (S. Dec.8; 80) *Quaritch.* £85
[-] **Pacis Querela ...** Venice, Sep. 1518. Some staining. Old vell. (HD. Apr.24; 19) Frs. 4,500
- **Paraphrase of Erasmus upon the newe Testament ... [only].** 1549. Vol. II only. Fo. Title preserved, some ll. stained. Early 19th. C. cf. W.a.f. [STC 2854] (CSK. May 15; 115) £100
- - **Anr. Edn.** 1551. Vol. I only. Fo. Port. & title mntd., some ll. soiled. 19th. C. cf. [STC 2866] (SH. May 28; 37) *Booth.* £120
- **Paraphrasin in Evangelium Matthaei ... Paraphrases in omneis Epistolicas.–In Evangelium Marci Paraphrasis.–In Evangelium Lucae Paraphrasis.–Paraphrasis in Evangelium secundum Ioannem.** Basle, 1522; 1524; 1524; 1523. 4 works in 1 vol. Fo. 1st. & 2nd. works wormed with some loss of text, dampstained. Early 19th. C. hf. cf. (CSK. Apr.24; 154) £260
- **The Praise of Folie.** Trans.:– Sir Thomas C. Knight. Ill.:– William Strang. [L.], [Essex House Pr.]. [1901]. (250) numbered on L.P. 4to. Cold. & patterned vell., wallet-edged. (PNY. Dec.3; 134) $140

ERASTUS, Thomas & Others
- **De Cometis Dissertationes Novae.** [Basel], 1580. 4to. Browned & stained. Cont. limp vell., lacks ties. From Honeyman Collection. (S. May 20; 3224) *Hill.* £160

ERCILLA Y ZUNIGA, Alonso de
- **Primera y Segunda Parte de la Araucana.** Madrid, 1578. 1st. Edn. of 2nd. pt. 2 pts. in 1 vol. Slightly defect. at beginning & end, light stains. Mod. vell. bds. [Sabin 22720] (SPB. May 5; 201) $2,200
- - **Anr. Edn.** 1733-35. 2 vols. in 1 (5 pts.). Fo. Inner margin of 1st. title soiled, marginal wormholes affecting 1st. ll., no port. 19th. C. hf. mor., soiled. (SPB. May 5; 202) $150
- - **Anr. Edn.** Madrid, 1776. 2 vols. A few ll. with short textual tears. Cont. cf. (SPB. May 5; 203) $300

ERCKER, Lazarus
- **Aula Subterranea.** Frankfurt, 1736. Latest Edn. Fo. Slightly browned or soiled, sm. paper faults. Cont. leath., worn. (HK. Nov.18-21; 395) DM 1,200
- **Beschreibung, Allerfurnemisten Mineralischen Ertzt unnd Bergwercks Arten.** Frankfurt a. M., 1580. 2nd. Edn. Fo. All but 1 woodcut hand-cold., lacks last blank lf., title very browned & spotted, some staining & discolouration, sm. hole in F4, old marginal annots. & underlinings. Vell. bds., warped & soiled. Mod. bkplt. of Louis Edwards Bryant; from Honeyman Collection. (S. May 20; 3225) *Zeitlin & Verbrugge.* £1,700
- - **Anr. Copy.** Slightly soiled & browned in parts, many ll. with old notes, prelims. & inner cover with 1616 notes. Cont. vell., soiled. (H. Dec.9/10; 267) DM 3,800

ERGAS, Joseph
- **Tochachat Megulah.** L., 1715. Soiled. Blind-stpd. mor. (SPB. May 11; 72) $900

ERHARD, Johann C.
See–TOUCHEMOLIN, Aegidius & Erhard, Johann C.

ERHART, B.
- **Nöthige Zugabe zu Adami Loniceri Kräuter-Buch.** Augsburg, 1783. Fo. Slightly soiled. Cont. leath. (D. Dec.11-13; 141) DM 3,600

ERICH, Adelarius
- **Gulichsche Chronik ...** Leipzig, 1611. 1st. Edn. Fo. Folding map reprd., some ll. reprd., 1 slightly

affecting text. 19th. C. cf.-bkd. embossed bds. (S. Feb.10; 201) *Quaritch*. £380

ERINNERUNG AN HANNOVER
Ill.:– after W. Kretschmer. Hannover, ca. 1840. Sm. ob. 4to. Added photo plt. dated Hannover, ca. 1840. Loose in orig. hf. linen portfolio, worn. (H. Dec.9/10; 693) DM 2,600

ERIZZO, Sebastiano–CARO, Annibale
– Le Sei Giornate.–Rime. Ed.:– Lodovico Dolce. Venice, 1568; 1572. 1st. Edn. 2 works in 1 vol. 18th. C. cf., spine gt. (C. Jul.16; 261) *Maggs*. £75

ERKLARUNG der Zwolf Artikel des Christlichen Glaubens
Ulm, Conrad Dinckmut, Aug. 21, 1485. 1st. Edn. Fo. 2 woodcuts with faint touches of hand-colouring, folios 1-4 with portion of inner margin renewed, 12 ll. with slight repairs at lr. margin, i2 with lr. margin renewed, slight repairs to last lf. Blind-stpd. pig over wood bds., a remboitage, very worn, rebkd. From the collection of Eric Sexton. [BMC II, 534, Goff E102, H 6668*=6667] (CNY. Apr.8; 179) $10,000

ERLUSTIERENDE Augen-Weyde ... Churfurstliche Residenz in Munchen als ... Pollatia und Garten ... Maximilian Emanuel ... erbanun lassen, Zweite Fortsetzung
Ill.:– after Matthias Disel. Augsburg, n.d. Engraved title & margins slightly soiled. Cont. bds. W.a.f. (CSK. Jul.17; 22) £400

ERNESTI, Johann Heinrich Godefroy
[–] Die Wol-eingerichtete Buchdruckerey. Nuremb., 1721. 1st. Edn. Ob. 4to. Cont. vell. (R. Oct.14-18; 524) DM 1,200

ERNST, J.J.
See–ENGRAMELLE, Marie Dominique Joseph & Ernst, J.J.

ERNST, Max
– La Femme 100 Tetes. Ed.:– André Breton. Ill.:– after Ernst. Paris, 1929. (1,000) numbered. 4to. Orig. wraps., disbnd., lacks backstrip. (CSK. Jul.31; 84) £140
– Lewis Carrolls Wunderhorn. Ed.:– W. Spies. [Stuttgart], 1970. (1,000) Normal-Ausgabe. Lge. 4to. Engl. & German text. Orig. pict. linen. (H. Dec.9/10; 2054) DM 520
– Microbes vus à travers un Tempérament. [Paris], 1953. (100). Orig. wraps. (D. Dec.11-13; 1057) DM 600
– Le Musée de l'Homme. [Paris], [1966]. (99) privilege Edn. Orig. pict. wraps. in orig. linen covers & s.-c. 2 sigd. etchgs. (1 cold.) (H. Dec.9/10; 2053) DM 1,400
– Une Semaine de Bonté. Ill.:– after Ernst. Paris, 1934. (800) numbered. 5 pts. 4to. Orig. wraps., s.-c. (CSK. May 15; 27) £450

ERNST, Max & Eluard, Paul
– Misfortunes of the Immortals. Trans.:– Hugh Chisholm. [N.Y.], [Black Sun Pr.] 1943. 1st. Edn. in Engl., (610). 4to. Pict. bds., d.-w. (PNY. Mar.4; 146) $260

ERNST, Max & Prevert, Jacques
– Les Chiens ont Soif. Paris, [1964]. (250) numbered. Fo. 25 cold. lithos., 2 sigd. orig. cold. etchings. Loose as issued in cold. pict. wraps., buck. folding case. (SG. Oct.23; 112) $1,100

EROS Parisian Girls
See–PARIS GIRLS–EROS Parisian Girls

ERRARD de Bar-le-Duc, J.
See–UFANO, Diego–BASTA, G.–ERRARD de Bar-le-Duc, J.

ERSH, [Ruff]
Tomsk, 1907. 2nd. Year, no. 1-2 only. Unbnd. (SH. Feb.5; 66) *De la Casa*. £100

ERSTAUNENSWUERDIGE Historie, des Jesuiten Pater Johann Baptista Girard
Coelln, 1732. Disbnd. (SG. Feb.5; 187) $190

ERSTE VERVOLG VAN DE ZEGEPRAAL DER MODE OF DE TRIOMPH-EERENDE KAPSELDRAGT DER JONGE DAMES EN HEEREN
Ill.:– H. Numan. [Holland], ca. 1780. 32mo. Disbnd. (SH. Mar.19; 91) *Schierenberg*. £100

ESCALONA AGUERO, Gaspar de
– Gazophilatium Regium Perubicum. Madrid, 1675. 2 pts. in 1 vol. Fo. Marginal stains at

beginning & end. Later cf. (SPB. May 5; 205) $200

ESCAPES, Wanderings, & Preservation of a Hare.
L., ca. 1825. 16mo. Frontis. & text woodcuts hand-cold. Pict. stiff wraps. (SG. Apr.30; 122) $100

ESCHKE, Ernest Adolf
– Galvanische Versuche. Berlin, 1803. 1st. Edn. 16mo. Bds., ex-liby. (SG. Jan.29; 154) $220

ESCHOLIER, Raymond
– Delacroix. Paris, 1926-29. De Luxe Edn., (200) on papier d'arches. 3 vols. 4to. Red hf. mor., orig. ptd. wraps. bnd. in, partly unc. (C. Jul.22; 141) *Zwemmer*. £90

ESCOBAR, Andreas de
– Canones Poenitentiales. [Rome], [Stephan Plannck], ca. 1490. Some cont. MS. notes, blank pt. of a8 missing. Wraps. [Goff A657.] (C. Jul.16; 262) *Wilkins*. £55

ESENIN, Sergei
– Isus Mladenets [Child Jesus]. Ill.:– E. Turova. Petrograd, n.d. Orig. wraps. by E. Turova. (SH. Feb.6; 424) *Quaritch*. £260
See–BLOK, Alexander & others

ESENIN, Sergei & others
– Plavil'nya Slov [Foundry of Words]. Moscow, 1920. Dupl. typescript. Orig. wraps. (SH. Feb.6; 427) *Flegon*. £50

ESMARCH, Friedrich von
– Handbuch der Kriegschirurgischen Technik. Hannover, 1877. 1st. Edn. Cont. hf. cf. (S. Feb.23; 42) *Dawson*. £70

ESMERIAN, Raphael
– Bibliothèque. Paris, 1972-3. 6 vols. 4to. Estimates & prices recorded by Major McLaughlin thro.-out. Orig. cl. (SM. Oct.7; 1371) Frs. 2,500

ESPAGNAC, Baron d'
– Histoire de Maurice, Comte de Saxe ... Paris, 1775. 3 vols. 4to. Romantic glazed cf., blind-stpd., limp decor. spines. (HD. Apr.24; 64) Frs. 2,200

ESPER, E.J.-Ch. & TOUSSAINT de Charpentier
– Die Schmetterlinge in Abbildungen nach der Natur. Erlangen, 1777-[1839]. 1st. Edn. 5 pts. & supp. in 7 vols. 4to. Text slightly soiled, lacks 1 cold. copperplt. Mod. hf. leath. (H. Dec.9/10; 288) DM 8,200

ESPER, Johann Friedrich
– Description des Zoolithes. Trans.:– J.F. Isenflamm. Nuremb., 1774. Fo. Plts. hand-cold., title lightly soiled & foxed, plts. lightly browned at edges. Cont. cf., covers detchd. From Chetham's Liby., Manchester. (C. Nov.26; 149) *Dawson*. £200

ESPEZEL, Pierre d'
– Paris Relief. Paris, [1945]. (500). 4to. Compl. with collapsible metal stereo viewer. Bds., hinges brkn. (SG. Jul.9; 304) $250

ESPINOSA, Isidoro Felix de
– El Peregrino Septentrional Atlante: delineado en la Exemplarissima Vida del ... Fr. Antonio Margil de Jesus ... Valencia, 1742. 1st. Edn. Sm. 4to. Owner's inscr. & stp. of the Franciscans at Tarija, Bolivia, on title, a few stains. Cont. vell., loose. [Sabin 22898] (SPB. May 5; 208) $700

ESQUIE, Pierre
– Traité élémentaire d'architecture comprenant l'étude complète des Cing Ordres le Tracé des Ombres et les premiers Principes de Construction. Paris, ca. 1920's. 4to. 2 ll. & 76 plts. Loose in bd. portfo., upr. bd. slightly defaced by light pen markings. (CB. May 27; 98) Can. $100

ESQUIROL, Jean Etienne Dominique
– Des Maladies Mentales considerées sous les Rapports Medical, Hygienique et Medico-Legal. Paris, 1838. 1st. Edn. 2 vols. Atlas of 27 plts. bnd. at end of vol. II, liby. stps. Hf. cf. (S. Jun.15; 265) *Rota*. £220
– Mental Maladies. Trans.:– E.K. Hunt. Phila., 1845. 1st. Edn. in Engl. 30 pp. advts. at end (of 32 pp, lacks pp. 1-2). Bds., cl. spine. (S. Jun.15; 266) *Gurney*. £180

ESSAY (AN) CONCERNING THE INFINITE WISDOM OF GOD, manifested in the Contrivance & Structure of the Skin of Human Bodies ... by a Lover of Physick & Surgery
1724. 1st. Edn.?. Some browning & soiling. Mod. wraps., bkplt. of Frederic Wood Jones. From liby. of Dr. E. Ashworth Underwood. (S. Feb.23; 202) *P. & C.* £110

ESSAYS ON SHOOTING
1789. 1st. Edn. Later cl. (SH. Jun.18; 158) *Graham*. £50

ESSEX, John
See–FEUILLET, Raoul Auger & Essex, John

ESSWEIN, H.
– Alfred Kubin. Kassel, 1928. Lge. 4to. Orig. wraps. 5 line MS. ded. Kubin. (HK. May 12-14; 1940) DM 520

ESTAMPE MODERNE, L': Publication Mensuelle
Ed.:– Leonce Benedite. Paris, 1897-98. Vol. 1. Tall fo. Pict. cl. (SG. May 14; 73) $3,100

ESTAMPES du Catalogue Raisonné et Figure des Tableaux de la Galerie Electorale de Dusseldorf
Basle, 1778. Ob. fo. Some ll. spotted. Stitched. (CSK. Jun.26; 134) £75

ESTEYNEFFER, Juan de
– Florelegio Medicinal de Todas las Enfermedades ... Provincas remotas ... Madrid, 1715-16. 1st. Edn. 4to. Cont. limp. vell., covers loosening. (PNY. Oct.1; 357) $170

ESTIENNE, Charles
– Abbregé de l'Histoire des Vicontes et Ducz de Milan. Ill.:– Geofroy Tory. Paris, 1552. 1st. Edn. 4to. Some slight browning, inscr. 'ex Lib' josephi Arnoult', some MS. notes in text in anr. hand. Mod. cf.-bkd. marb. bds., spine gt. (S. Feb.9; 122) *Ponder*. £75
– La Dissection des Parties du Corps. Ill.:– after Jean Jollat & others. Paris, 1546. 1st. Edn. in Fr. Fo. 19th. C. hf. mor. From Chetham's Liby., Manchester, 18th. C. sig. of Will: Godolphin on A1. (C. Nov.26; 150) *Quaritch*. £2,800
– O. et M., Roman. Ill.:– Charles Lapique. Paris, 1966. (80) on vélin d'Arches, numbered, with suite of 15 lithographs sigd. & numbered by artist, lithographed text sigd. by artist. 4to. Orig. vell., silk-screened cover design by artist, unc., unopened, text in mor. folder. vol. & folder in fitted s.-c. (SH. Nov.21; 367) *Landau*. £125

ESTIENNE [Stephanus], Charles & Liebault, Jean
– L'Agriculture et Maison Rustique ... auec vn Bref Recueil des Chasses du Cerf (etc.). Rouen, 1620. 2 pts. in 1 vol. A little slight dampstaining, 1 or 2 short tears. Cont. vell. bds., soiled. Bkplt. of Thomas Foley, Great Witley Court, Worcestershire; from liby. of André L. Simon. (S. May 18; 89) *Elliott*. £120
– XV. Bücher Von dem Feldbaw und ... Wolbestellung eines ... Landsitzes. Trans.:– Melchior Sebizio. Strassburg, 1588. Fo. Spotted & brown in places. Cont. German blind-stpd. pig over wooden bds., possibly by Wilhelm Funck of Stuttgart, arms of Wurttemberg with initials WF & 'Von Gottes Gnade Ludwig z. Wirtemb. v.z.Teck g.z.Mompe' in centre of covers, top of spine slightly worn, lacks clasps. (S. Jun.1; 22) *Koch*. £520

ESTIENNE, [Stephanus], Charles & Liebault, Jean–CRESCENTIUS, Petrus
– XV Bücher v.d. Feldbaw.–New Feldt vnd Ackerbaw. Trans.:– M. Sebizius, G. Marius, J. Fischart. Ill.:– After J. Amman, T. Stimmer & others. Strassburg; Frankfurt, 1588 or 1592; 1583. 2 works in 1 vol. Fo. 1st. work lacks title, some pp. defect., loose, soiled or browned in parts; 2nd. work lacks pp. 155-158 & last lf., folding plt. & last ll. slightly defect., slightly soiled or stained. Cont. blind-stpd. pig-bkd. wd. bds., 2 clasps, worn. (HK. Nov.18-21; 179) DM 2,800

ESTIENNE, Henri 'Henricus Stephanus'
– Thesaurus Gracae Linguae. [Geneva], 1572. 1st. Edn. 5 vols. bound in 4 divisional vols. Fo. 17th. C. cf, gt. spines, worn, with the lge. gt. arms of Louis-Charles Voisin de Saint-Paul. (S. Oct.20; 76) *Quaritch*. £650

ESTIENNE, Henri 'Henricus Stephanus' (Ed.)
See–POETAE GRAECI Principes ...

ESTIENNE, Robert
- Les Mots François Selon Lordre des Lettres, ainsi que les fault escrire, tournez en latin, pour les enfans. Paris, Robert Estienne, 1547. 2nd. Edn. 4to. Blank upr. outside corner of many ll. reprd. Cont. cf., gt. device in centre of covers, with initials 'B' & 'Q', slight stains, corners & extremities of spine reprd. (C. Apr.1; 30)   *Goldschmidt*. £480

ESTREES, le Marechal, duc de
- Catalogue des Livres de la Bibliothéque. Paris, 1740. 3 vols. Priced in MS. thro.-out, signs of removal of lf. after title in vol. 1. Cont. mott. cf., stained. (SM. Oct.7; 1372)   Frs. 1,600

ETAT du Régiment des Gardes Françaises du Roi
Paris, 1782. Square 18mo. Cont. mor., spine decor. with 6 repeated fleur-de-lys, 3 fillets on covers. (HD. Apr.9; 464)   Frs. 1,600
- - **Anr. Edn.** Paris, 1785. Sm. square 18mo. Cont. red mor., spine decor. with fleur-de-lys, 3 fillets. (HD. Apr.9; 465)   Frs. 1,600

ETAT ET DELICES DE LA SUISSE . . .
Neuchatel, 1778. New Edn. 2 vols. 4to. Slight browning. Cont. mott. cf., spines gt. (S. Apr.7; 284)   *Chaponniere.* £2,200

ETAT PRESENT DE LA NOBLESSE BELGE
Brussels, 1971-79. 17 vols., compl. Sm. 4to. (LM. Nov.8; 253)   B.Frs. 14,000

ETAT PRESENT DE LA NOBLESSE DU ROYAUME DE BELGIQUE
Brussels, 1960-79. 22 vols. Sm. 4to. Orig. bdg. (LM. Nov.8; 252)   B.Frs. 21,000

ETHEREGE, Sir George
- The Man of Mode. 1676. 1st. Edn. 4to. Sm. holes in 2 ll. slightly affecting text. Recent mor. gt. [Wing E3374] (C. Nov.19; 94)   *Quaritch.* £180

ETHERIDGE, Robert, Jnr.
- Contributions to a Catalogue of Works, Reports, & Papers on the ... Australian & Tasmanian Aborigines. Sydney, 1890-95. 3 pts. 4to. Wraps. as issued (defect.), lacks l. (KH. Nov.18; 236)   *Aus.* £130
See–JACK, Robert L. & Etheridge, Robert

ETLICH Christliche Lyeder Lobgesang und Psalm
Wittemberg [Augsburg], 1524. Sm. 4to. Outer title border torn with loss of 4cm of print area, minor worming, particularly to 1st. lf., staining on A1v & B1r. Mod. buckram, 18th. C. wraps. bnd. in. From the collection of Eric Sexton. (C. Apr.15; 12)   *Burgess.* £650

ETMULLE, Michel
- Nouvelle Chymie Raisonnée. Lyons, 1693. 12mo. Cont. cf., worn, hinges reprd. (S. Dec.1; 153)   *Quaritch.* £65

ETRANGER plainement instruit des choses les plus rares et curieuses, Anciennes & Modernes de la Ville de Venise
Venice, 1806. 12mo. Cont. limp parch., soiled, jnts. worn. (CSK. Feb.6; 129)   £50

ETRENNES aux Alsaciennes
1826. 16mo. Without figure of the Grand-Corteret. Cont. paper bds., title on upr. cover, s.-c. (HD. Apr.10; 109)   Frs. 1,400

ETRENNES aux Amateurs de Vénus
Paphos or Cythère [Paris], [1790]. 18mo. Cont. porphyre cf., spine decor., 3 fillets, inner dentelle. From the Liby. of Col. Sickles. (HD. Apr.10; 331)   Frs. 1,800

ETRENNES aux Fouteurs, ou Le Calendrier des Trois Sexes
Sodome & Cythere, 1793. 18mo. Jansenist roan, inner dentelle, ca. 1860 (HD. Apr.10; 333)   Frs. 1,200

ETRENNES aux Fouteurs Démocrates, Aristocrates, Impartiaux, etc. . . .
Sodome & Cythère, 1790. 16mo. 8 figures (9 called for). Mod. hf. cf., decor. spine, head gt., unc. (HD. Apr.10; 332)   Frs. 2,500

ETRENNES Géographiques
Paris, 1760. Square 16mo. Cont. red mor., decor. spine, lge. gt. fillet on covers, inner dentelles. (HD. Apr.10; 112)   Frs. 1,950

ETRENNES MIGNONNES Curieuses et Utiles
Paris, 1761. Sm. 18mo. Cont. bds., decor., lge. gt. borders, sm. figure on each cover. (HD. Apr.10; 118)   Frs. 3,800

- - **Anr. Edn.** Paris, 1766. Sm. 18mo. Cont. red mor., lge. plaque fan on covers. (HD. Apr.10; 122)   Frs. 1,400
- - **Anr. Copy.** 32mo. Later white pearled tissue, covers with different motifs, cold. floral centre decor. (HD. Apr.10; 120)   Frs. 1,150
- - **Anr. Copy.** Sm. 18mo. Cont. mor., gt. decor. motif covers, doubls. & fly.-ll. watered silk. (HD. Apr.10; 121)   Frs. 1,000
- - **Anr. Edn.** Paris, 1773. 32mo. Cont. red mor., lge. gt. decor. covers, centre figure in lozenge. (HD. Apr.10; 123)   Frs. 2,200
- - **Anr. Edn.** Paris, 1779. 18mo. Cont. mor., covers decor. gt., silver & pewter, centre painted medallion. (HD. Apr.10; 125)   Frs. 4,600
- - **Anr. Edn.** Paris, [1792]. Sm. 18mo. Cont. red mor., covers decor., centre figure. (HD. Apr.10; 128)   Frs. 1,150

ETRENNES MIGNONES pour l'Année 1777
Strassbourg, [1776]. Ob. 64mo. Cont. white watered silk with gold & other col. embroidery watered silk doubls. & end-ll., mor. s.-c. with title. (HD. Apr.10; 124)   Frs. 1,400

ETRENNES MUSICALES ou Recueil General de Chansons . . .
Paris, [1790]. 24mo. Cont. pol. cf., spine gt. (SG. May 14; 154) $400

ETRENNES NANTAISES, Ecclésiastiques, Civiles et Nauriques pour l'année bissextile 1776
[1775]. 16mo. Cont. red mor., lge. gt. plaque by Dubuisson on covers with motif in centre. (HD. Apr.10; 116)   Frs. 2,100

ETRENNES TOULOUSAINES, ou Calendrier très interessant pour l'année 1793
Toulouse, [1792]. Sm. 18mo. Cont. mor., covers decor., 2 medallion gouaches in centres. (HD. Apr.10; 129)   Frs. 1,200

ETRENNES Utiles et Nécessaires aux Commerçans et Voyageurs, ou Indicateur fidèle indiquant toutes les Routes Royales et particulières de la France
Paris, 1774. 18mo. Cont. red mor., spine decor., 3 fillets, inner dentelles. (HD. Apr.10; 130)   Frs. 2,700

ETRURIA PITTRICE (L'), ovvero Storia della Pittura Toscana . . . dal Secolo X. Fino al Presente
Ed.:– Lastri. Flor., 1791-95. 1st. Edn. 2 vols. in 1. Fo. Italian & Fr. text, ?lacks hf.-titles, slight browning, a few spots. Red mor., gt., by Cape, crest of the Earl of Lathom on upr. cover. (S. Jan.27; 461)   *Mistrali.* £300

ETTINGSHAUSEN, C. von & Pokorny, A.
- Physiotypia Plantarum Austriacarum. Vienna, [1855]-1856. 1st. Edn. Text & 5 plt. vols. 4to. & lge. fo. Vol. 1 title reprd., last plt. defect., some plts. slightly soiled. Mod. hf. leath. (H. May 21-22; 215)   DM 5,200

ETTMULLER, Michael
- Kurtzer Begriff der Gantzen Artzney-Kunst. Leipzig, 1717. 4to. Slightly browned & soiled, pp. 727/8 lacking. Cont. vell. (R. Oct.14-18; 326)   DM 530

ETUDES BIBLIQUES
Paris, 1921-69. 18 vols. 1 vol. cl. (B. Dec.10/11; 849)   Fls. 450

EUBERWEG, F.
- Grundriss der Geschichte der Philosophie. Berlin, 1923-28. 5 vols. Orig. hf. mor. gt. (VG. Dec.15; 21)   Fls. 600

EUBESCHUTZ, David Shlomo
- Levushei Srad. Safed, 1863. 4to. Slightly soiled. Cl.-bkd. bds. (SPB. May 11; 105) $150

EUBESCHUTZ, Jonathan
- Ahavat Jonathan. Ed.:– David Ben Joseph, of Magdeburg. Hamburg, 1766. 1st. Edn. 4to. Discolouration. Mor.-bkd. bds., lightly stained. (SPB. May 11; 106) $300
- Luchot Eidut. Altona, 1755. 1st. Edn. 4to. Inner margin of title & 1st. lf. reprd., without loss of text, 5 ll. loose, some discolouration. Hf. cf. (S. Nov.18; 422)   *James.* £95

EUBULUS OXONIENSIS DISCIPULIS SUIS.
- Being an Imitation of the Celebrated Qui mihi. In Praise of Drunkenness
1720 [1719]. 1st. Edn. Slight browning. Mod. pol. cf. by Rivière, slightly rubbed. From liby. of André L. Simon. (S. May 18; 90)   *Intercol.* £85

EUCLID
- Elementa. Ed.:– Campanus Noviensis. Vicenza, Leonardius de Basilea & Gulielmus de Papia. Jun. 1491. Fo. Lacks 1st. lf., woodcut border of 1st. lf. of text defect. at lr. outer corner, a few wormholes at beginning affecting some letters, worming in last 20 ll., sm. hole in 1st. lf. with slight damage to border & diagram on verso, a few light stains. Mod. cf.-bkd. bds. [HC 6694; BMC VII p. 1033; Goff E114] (C. Apr.1; 120)   *White.* £750
- Elementorum Geometricorum Lib. XV. Basle, Hervagius, 1537. Fo. Cont. cf. gt. (S. Nov.25; 354)   *Marriott.* £150
- - **Anr. Copy.** 1st. 4 ll., including title, loose, with sm. holes affecting woodcut device & a few letters, lower margin & stp. cut from title, 1st. ll. slightly dampstained, some old marginalia & long inscr. by same hand on blank verso of f.4. Cont. blind-stpd. cf., very worn, pt. of spine missing. This copy contains the preferatory letter by Philipp Melancthon which is often missing. (S. Oct.21; 381)   *Artico.* £100
- - **Anr. Edn.** Leipzig, 1549. Slight browning & soiling. Cont. mott. cf., rebkd., spine gt. (S. Feb.9; 123)   *Quaritch.* £130
- Elementorum Libri Tredecim. Ed.:– F. Commandinus. L., 1620. Fo. Parallel Grk. & Latin text, lightly stained at head, slightly wormed at beginning, cont. MS. notes on end-papers, inner joints strengthened. Cont. vell., soiled. (HK. Nov.18-21; 501)   DM 460
- Elements, the whole fifteen Books Compendiously Demonstrated ... Trans.:– Isaac Barrow. 1686. 2nd. Edn. 12mo. Title mntd., inner margin reprd. in 1st. few ll., slight staining, a few marginal tears not affecting text, some minor stains. Cont. cf., rebkd. & reprd., in cl. box. John Flamsteed's copy, with inscr. on title. (C. Apr.1; 105)   *Shaw.* £540
- - **Anr. Edn.** Ed.:– Robert Simpson. Edinb., 1772. 4th. Edn. Cont. cf., slightly worn. (S. Oct.21; 344)   *Artico.* £70
- - **Anr. Edn.** Ed.:– O. Byrne. 1847. 4to. Some spotting. Vell.-bkd. bds. (P. Oct.2; 298)   *Quaritch.* £75
- The First Six Books of the Elements in Which Coloured Diagrams & Symbols are Used Instead of Letters for the Greater Ease of Learners. Ed.:– Oliver Byrne. L., 1847. 4to. Orig. red cl., rebkd., orig. spine preserved. (CNY. Oct.1; 10) $800
- [Opera a Campano Interprete]. Ed.:– [Luca Pacioli]. Venice, May 22, 1509. Fo. Iss. with the 1st. lf. blank, some light & minor stains, owner's inscr. on a1r & a later inscr. on verso. Mod. hf. mor. (S. Jul.27; 110)   *Duran.* £800
- Quae Supersunt Omnia. Ed.:– David Gregory. Oxford, 1703. Fo. Cont. cf. (S. Mar.16; 113)   *P. Smith.* £55
- Quinto libro degli Elemnti d'Euclide, ovvero Scienza Universale delle Proporzioni Spiegata colla Dottrina del Galileo ... pubblicata da Vincenzio Viviani. Flor., 1674. 4to. Some spots & stains, a little marginal worming. Cont. vell., soiled. Pres. copy from ed.; from Honeyman Collection. (S. May 20; 3226)   *Zeitlin & Verbrugge.* £110
- Das Sibend, Achtynd Neünt Buch ... Operationen vnnd Regulen aller Germainer Rechnung ... Trans.:– J. Scheybl. Augsburg, 10 Apr. 1555. 1st. Edn. 4to. Cont. mor., gt., upr. jnt burst, lacks ties. (HK. Nov.18-21; 183)   DM 460
- [Works, in Hebrew]. Trans.:– Baruch Schick [Shklower]. The Hague, 1780. 1st. Edn. 4to. Leath. (S. Nov.18; 704)   *Israel.* £100
See–NICOMACHUS, of Gerasa–EUCLID

EUCLID–CLAVIUS, Chris
- Elementorum Lib. XV.-XVI de Solidorum Regularium Comparatione. Rome, 1574. 2 pts. in 1 vol. Cont. blind-stpd. pig-bkd. wood bds., dtd. 1580, lacks clasps. (HK. Nov.18-21; 182)   DM 460

EUCLID–FINE, Oronce
- In Sex Priores libros Geometricorum Elementorum Euclidis Megarensis Demonstrationes ...–De Rectis in Circuli Quadrante Subtentis ... Tabula Sinuum Rectorum; De Universali Quadrante, sinuumue organo; Sphaera Mundi, sive Cosmographia; Canonum Astronomicorum libri II; De Duodecim Caeli Domiciliis, & Horis Inaequalibus. Paris, 1551; 1550; 1550; 1552; 1553; 1553. 1st. work 3rd. Fine Edn. 6 works in 1 vol. 4to. 1st. work with some upr. margins wormed, browned. Cf., orig.

gt.-tooled covers preserved. From Honeyman Collection. (S. May 20; 3235) *Simonin.* £160

EUCLID–GLAREANUS, Henricus
– **Elementorum Libri XV.–De VI Arithmeticae Practicae Speciebus Epitome.** Cologne; Freiburg, 1564; 1555. 2 works in 1 vol. Slightly browned & stained in parts. Cont. limp vell., lacks ties, slightly cockled. (HK. Nov.18-21; 180) DM 500

EUDEL, Paul
– **L'Orfevrerie Algerienne et Tunisienne.** Algiers, 1902. 4to. Later hf. mor. (SH. Jul.23; 268) *Sims & Reed.* £190

EUDEL, Paul–GAUSSERON, B.H.–RETTE, A.
– **Balades dans Paris.** Ill.:– Alexandre Lunois. Paris, 1894. (160). 4to. Lithos. in 2 states. Hf. mor. by Carayon, corners, smooth mosaic spine, wrap. turned in. (HD. Jun.25; 240) Frs. 2,700

EULENSPIEGEL
– **Les Aventures de Til Ulenspiegel.** Ill.:– Lauters. Brussels, 1840. 1st. Edn. Lightly browned in parts, lacks last lf. blank. Hand-bnd. hf. leath., gt. spine, orig. pictor. wraps. bnd. in. (H. Dec.9/10; 1468) DM 720

EULENSPIEGEL, Der Widerstandene
N.p., ca. 1800. Hf. vell. (HK. May 15; 4197) DM 700

EULER, Leonhard
– **Dioptricae . . .** Petersburg, 1769-71. 1st. Edn. 3 vols. 4to. Slight browning & dust-soiling. 19th. C. hf. mor. From Chetham's Liby., Manchester. (C. Nov.26; 151) *Rota.* £270
– **Elements of Algebra . . .** Ed.:– M. de La Grange & others. Trans.:– (Francis Horner). 1797. 1st. Edn. in Engl. 2 vols. Some slight browning. Cont. russ. (S. Feb.9; 124) *Bicker.* £60
– **Institutiones Calculi Differentials.** Petersburg, 1755. 1st. Edn. 4to. Some browning thro.-out. 19th. C. hf. mor. From Chetham's Liby., Manchester. (C. Nov.26; 152) *Taylor.* £180
– – **Anr. Edn.** Petersburg, 1768-70. 1st. Edn. 3 vols. 4to. Minor dust-soiling, some spotting. 19th. C. hf. mor., spines misnumbered. From Chetham's Liby., Manchester. (C. Nov.26; 153) *Taylor.* £240
– **Mechanica.** Petersburg, 1736. 1st. Edn. 2 vols. 4to. Some browning. 19th. C. hf. mor. From Chetham's Liby., Manchester. (C. Nov.26; 155) *Rota.* £300
– **Methodus Inveniendi Lineas Curvas.** Lausanne & Geneva, 1744. 1st. Edn. 4to. Later cl., worn. (SH. Jan.30; 428) *Nador.* £130
– **Opuscula varii Argumenti.** Berlin, 1746. 1st. Edn. 4to. Some browning. 19th. C. hf. mor. From Chetham's Liby., Manchester. (C. Nov.26; 154) *Taylor.* £55
– **Scientia Navalis.** Petersburg, 1749. 1st. Edn. 2 vols. 4to. Some browning & dust-staining. 19th. C. hf. mor. From Chetham's Liby., Manchester. (C. Nov.26; 156) *Rota.* £300
– **Theoria Motuum Planetarium et Cometarium.** Berlin, [1744]. 1st. Edn. 4to. Stained & otherwise discold. thro.-out. Disbnd. (C. Apr.1; 31) *Maggs.* £150
– **Vollständige Anleitung zur Differential-Rechnung.** Trans.:– J.A.C. Michelsen. Berlin, 1790-93 & 1798. 1st. German Edn. 3 pts. & supp. in 2 vols. 2 old liby. stps to pts. 1 & 3. Cont. leath. (R. Oct.14-18; 274) DM 700

EUMORFOPOULOS, George, Collection: Cat. of Chinese, Corean & Persian Pottery . . .
See–**HOBSON, Robert Lockhart**

EURIPEDES
– **[Oeuvres].** Trans.:– Leconte de Lisle. Paris, 1884. (40) on Hollande numbered, L.-P. Red mor. by Zaehnsdorf, mor. doubls. decor. mor. onlay in centre, orig wraps. bnd. in, unc. (SM. Oct.8; 2328) Frs. 4,200
– **Tragoediae duae.** Trans.:– Erasmus Roterodamo. Basle, Feb., 1524. Slight dampstaining, owner's inscr. deleted from head of title. Early 19th. C. cf. Bkplt. of Osman Ricardo. (S. Feb.9; 125) *Maggs.* £55
– **Werke.** Trans.:– Fr. H. Bothe. Berlin & Stettin, 1800-03. 1st. Edn. Slightly soiled. Cont. hf. leath. gt. Erzherzogin Sophie v. Osterreich stpd. on ex-liby. (crowned initials) on all title versos. (HK. May 15; 4108) DM 950

EUROPEAN Magazine, The
Ca. 1789-1821. Vol. containing about 169 engraved plts. Hf. mor., lacks pt. of spine (worn). (SKC. Dec.4; 1645) £55

EUSEBIUS PAMPHILIUS, Bp. of Caesarea
– **Chronicon.** Ed.:– Matthias Palmerius. Paris, 1518. 4to. Cont. Camb. bdg. of blindstpd. cf. on wooden bds. by Garrett Godfrey, rebkd., recent clasps. (C. Jul.16; 221) *Quaritch.* £220
– **Ecclesia Historia . . . et Ecclesiastica Historia Gentis Anglorum Venerabilis Bede.** Strassburg, [George Husner]. 14 Mar. 1500. Fo. 14th. C. Engl. MS. lf. of cannon law on vell. pasted onto title p., old marginalia, soiled & slightly dampstained in places, some marginal tears, owner's inscr. 'Liber Collegii Sancti Johannis baptiste in Oxon ex dono d. doctoris Henrici Cole decani ecclesie Sancti Pauli' on 2nd. lf. Cont. Engl. blind-stpd. cf. over wooden bds., by the Half-Stamp Binder, with fillets & single stps. on side, upr. cover detchd. & lacks all leath., spine partly missing, lacks clasps. [BMC I, 162; HC 6714*; Goff E129] (S. Apr.7; 294) *Filsell.* £420
– – **Anr. Edn.** Paris, 1544. 1st. Edn. in Greek. Fo. Some ll. browned. Early 19th. C. Fr. red hf. str.-grd. mor. gt. Bkplt. of M.N. Yemeniz, later the copy of John A. Saks. (CNY. Oct.1; 106) $950
– **Historia Ecclesiastica.** Trans.:– [Rufinus]. Mantua, Johannes Schallus, [not before 15] Jul., 1479. Fo. Spaces for capital initials, with guide letters, initials supplied in red, rubricated, lacks final blank, gutter margins dampstained thro.-out & some torn with repairs causing loss of some marginal decoration. 19th. C. vell., spine gt.-lettered. From the collection of Eric Sexton. [BMC VII, 933, Goff E127, HC 6711*] (CNY. Apr.8; 98) $1,300

EUSEBIUS PAMPHILIUS & others –JOSEPHUS, Flavius
– **Chronica der Alten Christlichen Kirchen. –Juedische Chronic.** Trans.:– Caspar Hedion. [Strassburg]; Frankfurt. 1545; 1552 2 works in 1 vol. Fo. Cont. blind-stpd. pig on wood bds., metal clasps. (SG. Oct.9; 93) $400

EUSEBIUS PHILADELPHUS
See–**BARNAUD, Nicolaus**

EUSTACHIUS, Bartolomaeus
– **Explicatio Tabularum Anatomicarum.** Leiden, 1744. Fo. Engraved title vig. & 47 plts., most with dupls. in outl. Cont. cf., rebkd., worn. (SG. Sep. 18; 141) $700
– **Tabulae Anatomicae.** Rome, 1714. 1st. Edn. Fo. Slight browning. 19th. C. hf. mor. From Chetham's Liby., Manchester. (C. Nov.26; 157) *Rota.* £850
– – **Anr. Copy.** Errata lf. loosely inserted. Vell., soiled. (S. Jun.15; 267) *Rota.* £750
– – **Anr. Edn.** Ed.:– Joseph Maria Lancisi. Amst., 1722. 2nd. Edn. Fo. A few stains mainly at beginning. Hf. cf. G. Metivier's copy with his 18th. C. sig. on title-p. & descriptive notes to plts. 9-17, 25-28, 32-39, 41 & 42 on inserted ll., also some anatomical drawings in red on ll. inserted at plts. 2, 6, 8 & 22, some sigd. (S. Jun.15; 268) *Maggs.* £240
– – **Anr. Copy.** Old cf., worn, upr. cover detchd. (SG. Sep.18; 140) $850
– – **Anr. Edn.** Ed.:– Joh. Maria Lancisius. Ill.:– Gregori after Ricciolini (dedication lf.). Rome, 1728. Fo. Plt. 42 bnd. upside down, damp stain in inner upr. corners. Cont. cf. (S. Dec.2; 486) *Nador.* £220
– – **Anr. Copy.** Stained nearly thro.-out, last ll. soiled at upper corner, plt. 7 torn. Cont. leath., gt. spine, worn, 2 sm. holes in upr. cover. (HK. Nov.18-21; 503) DM 1,000
– – **Anr. Edn.** Ed.:– [Giovanni Maria Lancisi (preface & text).] Ill.:– Petrus Monaco. Venice, 1769. Fo. Minor spotting to some plts. Cont. cf.-bkd. bds., worn. From the collection of John A. Saks. (C. Jun.10; 64) *Burgess.* £150

EUSTRATIUS
– **Commentaria in Libros Decem Aristotelis de Moribus ad Nicomachum.** Venice, 1536. 1st. Edn. Fo. Lge. margins, lacks final lf. with printer's device. Old cf., covers detchd. (SG. Feb.5; 11) $120

EVANGELISCHE GEZANGEN
See–**NEW TESTAMENT [Dutch]**

EVANGELISTARION . . .
See–**THEION kai Ieron Evangelion –EVANGELISTARION . . .**

EVANS, Lieut.
[–] Account of the Conquest of Mauritius. 1811. 1st. Edn. Orig. cl.-bkd. bds., soiled. (SH. May 21; 37) *Maggs.* £140

EVANS, Sir Arthur J.
– **Cretan Pictographs & Prae-Phoenician Script. –Further Discoveries of Cretan & Aegean Script.** L., 1895; 1898. 2 works in 2 vols. Gt.-pict. cl., ex-liby.; bds., orig. wraps. preserved 1st. work inscr. to Dr. Felix von Luschan. (SG. Dec.18; 175) $100
– **The Palace of Minos.** 1921-28. Vols. 1-2 (of 5) in 3. 4to. Orig. cl. (SH. Jun.18; 85) *Troy.* £50
– – **Anr. Edn.** L./N.Y., 1921-64. 1st. Edns. (excepting index). 4 vols. & index vol., in 7. 4to. Some spots & stains, many pencil MS. notes. Orig. cl., gt. (S. Feb.9; 126) *Traylen.* £160
– **Through Bosnia & the Herzegovenia.** 1877. 2nd. Edn. Orig. cl. (SH. Nov.6; 203) *Sanders.* £50

EVANS, Charles Seddon
– **Cinderella.** Ill.:– Arthur Rackham. 1919. (850) numbered, sigd. 4to. Cold. frontis. tipped in. Orig. bds. with linen backstrip. (TA. Jan.22; 225) £105
– – **Anr. Edn.** Ill.:– Arthur Rackham. [1919]. (850) numbered, sigd. by artist. 4to. A little light offsetting. Orig. cl.-bkd. bds., d.-w. (CSK. Nov.7; 178) £300
– – **Anr. Copy.** Slight spotting. Slightly torn. (CSK. Apr.24; 47) £140
– – **Anr. Edn.** Ill.:– Arthur Rackham. L., [1919]. 1st. Trade Edn. 4to. Cl.-bkd. pict. bds., d.-w. Raymond M. Sutton Jr. copy. (SG. May 7; 77) $220
– – **Anr. Edn.** Ill.:– Arthur Rackham. L., [1919]. 1st. Edn. Deluxe, (325) numbered on Japanese vell., sigd. by artist. Lge. 4to. Vell.-bkd. vell.-style bds. Raymond M. Sutton Jr. copy. (SG. May 7; 76) $700
– – **Anr. Edn.** Ill.:– Arthur Rackham. [1919]. (325) on Jap. Vell. 4to. Orig. parch. bkd. bds., soiled. Sigd. by artist. (CSK. Aug.15; 125) £100
– – **Anr. Edn.** Ill.:– Arthur Rackham. L., [1919]. 1st. Edn. Deluxe, (525) numbered on H.M.P., sigd. by artist. Stained. Linen-bkd. pict. bds., d.-w. Raymond M. Sutton Jr. copy. (SG. May 7; 77) $450
– **Sleeping Beauty.** Ill.:– Arthur Rackham. [1920]. [1st. Edn.?] (625) numbered, sigd. by artist & with an additional plt. 4to. 1 mntd. cold plt. by Rackham, a little light offsetting. Mor.-bkd. bds. (CSK. Nov.21; 47) £75
– – **Anr. Copy.** Lge. 4to. Vell.-bkd. vell.-style bds., gt.-decor., stained. Raymond M. Sutton Jr. copy. (SG. May 7; 79) $425
– – **Anr. Edn.** Ill.:– Arthur Rackham. L., [1920]. (620) numbered, sigd. by Rackham. Lge. 4to. Vell.-bkd. bds. (SG. Oct.9; 204) $475

EVANS, David
See–**HARRISON, J.C. & Evans, David**

EVANS, Estwick
– **A Pedestrious Tour of Four Thousand Miles Through the Western States & Territories During the Winter & Spring of 1818.** Concord, New Hampshire, 1819. 1st. Edn. 12mo. Lacks frontis., offsetting & staining, a few pp. torn. Orig. ptd. bds., spine worn, cl. folding case, ex-liby., unc. From liby. of William E. Wilson. (SPB. Apr.29; 95) $175

EVANS, George William
– **A Geographical, Historical & Topographical Description of Van Diemen's Land.** L., 1822. 1st. Edn. Disbnd. (SG. Feb.26; 38) $260
– – **Anr. Copy.** Slight foxing. Cont. hf. cf. (KH. Mar.24; 139) Aus. $600
– – **Anr. Edn.** 1824. 2nd. Edn. Orig. bds., worn. (SH. May 21; 36) *Maggs.* £230

EVANS, J. Gwenogvryn
See–**RHYS, John & Evans, J. Gwenogvryn**

EVANS, Lewis
– **Geographical, Historical, Political, Philosophical & Mechanical Essays.** Phila., Benjamin Franklin, 1756. 1st. Edn. 4to. Disbnd. [Sabin 23176] (CNY. May 22; 115) $650

EVANS, Marian 'George Eliot'
– **Adam Bede.** 1859. 1st. Edn. 3 vols. Lacks hf.-titles. Cont. hf. cf. (SH. May 28; 119) *Vincent.* £50
– **Daniel Deronda.** 1876. 1st. Edn. 4 vols. Lacks hf.-titles & advt. Cont. cf., faded. (SH. Jul.23; 57) *Whiteson.* £50

EVANS, Marian 'George Eliot' -contd.

– – Anr. Copy. Orig. 8 pts. in 4 vols. Pts. 3 & 5 with tipped in errata slip, advts. in each pt. Ptd. wraps., unc. (SG. Mar.19; 99) $700

– Felix Holt. 1866. 1st. Edn. 3 vols. Lacks end-ll., 4 pp. advts. Orig. cl., unc. (SKC. May 19; 318) £60

– – Anr. Copy. 3 vols. 4 pp. of advts. in vol. III. Blind-stpd. cl., gt.-decor. spines (Carter's B variant). Bkplt. of Carleton Noyes. (SG. Nov.13; 158) $130

– The Mill on the Floss. 1860. 1st. Edn. 3 vols. Last 8 advt. ll. in vol. III, slightly browned & spotted. Orig. cl., hinges reprd. (SH. Oct.10; 373) *O'Hern.* £100

– – Anr. Copy. Spotted. (SH. Jul.23; 58) *Thorp.* £70

– Romola. L., 1863. 1st. Edn. 3 vols. Orig. blind-stpd. cl., spines gt.-lettered, qtr. maroon mor. gt. s.-c. From the Prescott Collection. (CNY. Feb.6; 103) $650

– Scenes of Clerical Life. 1858. 1st. Edn. 2 vols. Cont. hf. cf. (SH. May 28; 123) *Jarndyce.* £85

– – Anr. Copy. Slight spotting, stitching loose in a few places. Orig. cl. (SPB. May 6; 188) $250

– – Anr. Copy. Orig. blind-stpd. cl. by Edmonds & Remnants, with ticket in vol. I, worn & shaken. (SG. Nov.13; 157) $210

– Silas Marner. Edinb. & L., 1861. 1st. Edn. 16-p. publisher's catalogue at end. Orig. cl., unopened. (CNY. May 22; 97) $150

– Works. Edinb., ca. 1880. Standard Edn. 21 vols. Some browning thro.-out. Three-qtr. mor. by Lefort. (SG. Dec.18; 173) $110

– – Anr. Edn. Boston, 1887. Handy Vol. Edn. 12 vols. Slight browning. Hf. cf. (SPB. Nov.25; 452) $150

– – Anr. Edn. N.Y., ca. 1895. Illustrated Cabinet Edn. 24 vols. Cont. red hf. mor., spines gt. with mor. floral inlays. (CSK. Nov.7; 69) £140

– Works, with Life. Ed.– J.W. Cross. N.d. Cabinet Edn. 24 vols. Hf. cf. gt. (MMB. Oct.8; 74) *Cumming.* £115

EVANS, Oliver

– The Abortion of the Young Steam Engineer's Guide. Phila., 1805. (1st. Edn.?). Mathematical notations on endpapers, foxed & stained. Orig. cf. From liby. of William E. Wilson. (SPB. Apr.29; 96) $650

EVANS, Walker

– American Photographs. Ed.:– Lincoln Kirstein (essay). N.Y., [1938]. 1st. Edn. Square 8vo. Errata lf. tipped-in. Cl., d.-w. (SG. Jul.9; 127) $160

– – Anr. Copy. Torn. (SG. Apr.23; 87) $150

EVELYN, John

– Diary, 1624-55. Ed.:– William Bray; Life by Henry B. Wheatley. L., 1879. L.P. Edn. 4 vols. Tall 4to. Cont. gt. three-qtr. mor., occasional nicks. (PNY. Mar.26; 111) $100

– Memoirs . . . Ed.:– William Bray. L., 1818. 1st. Edn. 2 vols. 4to. Some foxing. Cont. drab bds., rebkd. preserving orig backstrips & labels, qtr. mor. gt. s.-c.'s, unc. From the Prescott Collection. (CNY. Feb.6; 106) $220

– – Anr. Copy. Mod. three-qtr. mor., spines gt. with lge. fleurons. (SG. Dec.18; 176) $100

– Numismata. A Discourse of Medals. 1697. Fo. Cont. cf., spine worn. [Wing E3505] (CSK. Feb.20; 80) £80

– – Anr. Copy. Worn, upr. cover loose. (PD. Apr.1; 118) £50

– – Anr. Copy. Cont. mott. cf., rebkd. in panel. cf. (PNY. Mar.26; 112) $240

– – Anr. Copy. Cont. cf. (SG. Feb.5; 256) $140

– Sculptura; or, the History & Art of Chalcography, & Engraving in copper. 1755. 2nd. Edn. Cont. cf., lr. cover almost detchd. (S. Dec.9; 484) *Quaritch.* £95

– – Anr. Copy. Later mor., covers decor. in gt. with mor. onlays depicting 2 figures. (CSK. May 29; 105) £65

– Sylva. 1664. 1st. Edn. 3 pts. in 1 vol. Fo. Cont. cf., rebkd. [Wing E3526] (S. Dec.1; 154) *Claridge.* £60

– – Anr. Edn. 1670 [but 1669]. 2nd. Edn. Fo. Sm. hole in D2, 18th. C. MS. owner's inscrs. on title & Latin verse on d2 verso. 18th. C. reversed cf., inner hinges reprd. [Wing E3517] (CSK. Feb.13; 1) £50

– – Anr. Edn. 1706. 4th. Edn. Fo. Panel. cf. (CE. Dec.4; 248) £130

– – Anr. Copy. Cont. cf. The Evelyn copy. (SH. Jan.30; 377) *George's.* £90

– – Anr. Edn. Ed.:– A. Hunter. Ill.:– Port. by Bartolozzi, plts. by J. Miller, A. Rooker & T. Nivares. York, 1776. 4to. Sm. hole in 1 plt., some spotting, front free end-paper inscr., annots., a few shaved. Late 19th. C. hf. cf. (CSK. Dec.12; 112) £110

– – Anr. Copy. Cont. mott. cf. gt. (SG. Sep.18; 142) $190

– – Anr. Edn. Ed.:– A. Hunter. York, 1801. 3rd. Edn. 2 vols. 4to. Lacks 1 engraved plt., various newspaper cuttings etc. preserved in margins. Cont. cf. (SBA. Oct.22; 590) *Smart.* £60

– – Anr. Edn. Ed.:– A. Hunter. York, 1812. 4th Edn. by Hunter. 2 vols. 4to. Lacks final blanks, port. detchd., offsetting to 1 title & some text-ll., occasional spotting. Later hf. roan, spines worn, contents loose, unc. (S. May 5; 373) *Canale.* £65

– Silva.–Prospectus for the Publication of 'Silva of Mr. Evelyn'. York, 1776; Mar.14, 1774. 4to. Cont. cf., spine gt. (1st. work); & old paper bds. From the collection of Eric Sexton. (C. Apr.15; 7) *Hever.* £150

– Silva.–Terra. Ed.:– A. Hunter (1st. work). Ill.:– Bartolozzi (frontis.) (1st. work). York, 1776; 1787. Thick paper Iss. 2 vols. in 1. 4to. 2nd. vol. some offsetting to text thro.-out & spotting of prelims. Cont. diced russ. gt. (TA. Jun.18; 93) £160

– – Anr. Edn. L., 1786. 3 vols. in 1. 4to. Cont. cf. (P. Jun.11; 322) *North.* £190

EVENTFUL HISTORY (THE) OF KING ARTHUR, or the British Worthy

Gainsborough, [watermkd. 1797]. 32mo. Orig. Dutch floral bds. (SH. Mar.19; 92) *Ashton.* £290

EVERARD, Anne

– Flowers from Nature, with the Botanical Name, Class & Order. 1835. Slim fo. Some foxing, margins slightly soiled. Mod. rexine. (TA. Jun.18; 174) £170

EVERGREEN Tales

Ed.:– Jean Hersholt. Ill.:– F. Kredel, E. Shenton, & others. Ltd. Edns. Cl. 1949-52. (2500) or (2000). Groups I-V (compl.), in 15 vols. Fo. Cl., boxed in groups of 3 vols. Some sets sigd. by artist and/or ed. (SG. Jan.15; 179) $220

EVERITT, Graham

–English Caricaturists & Graphic Humourists of the Nineteenth Century. Ill.:– George Cruikshank, John Leech & others. 1886. 4to. Extra ill., approx. 55 plts., most etched, some hand-cold., 1 lf. torn. Red mor. gt. by Ramage. (SH. Apr.9; 4) *Neale.* £190

EVERTH, E.

–Das Wesen der Zeitung. Leipzig, 1928-33. 8 pts. in 2 vols. Linden. (R. Oct.14-18; 1340) DM 600

EVREINOV, N.

– Teatr dlya debya [Theatre for itself]. Trans.:– N.I. Kul'bin & Yu. Annenkov. St. Petersb., 1915-17. 3 vols. 4to. Pres. inscr. on title of vol. III to A. Kruchenykh from V. Kamensky, owner's stp. on a few ll. Mod. cl., orig. wraps. by N.I. Kul'bin & Yu. Annenkov, (SH. Feb.5; 216) *Reed & Sims.* £150

EVREISKAYA ENTSIKLOPEDIYA [Jewish Encyclopaedia]

St. Petersb., [1910-14]. 16 vols. Slightly browned, liby. stps. on some pp. Orig. cl., worn, a few vols. loose. (SH. Feb.5; 217) *Flegon.* £250

EWALD, Mrs.

– Jerusalem & the Holy Land. Ill.:– Wm. Simpson. 1854. Ob. fo. Orig. cl. gt. (C. Jul.15; 137) *Cohen.* £100

– – Anr. Copy. Decor. cl. (PJ. Jun.6 (80); 18) £62

EXEMPLARY MOTHER (Mrs. Villars)

1769. 2 vols. Cont. cf. gt., worn. (CE. Feb.19; 185) £120

EX-LIBRIS SOCIETY

– Journals. 1892-6. Vols. 1-6 only. 4to. Orig. cl., orig. wraps. bnd. in. (CSK. Aug.1; 162) £55

EXQUEMLIN, Alexandre Olivier or John

– Histoire des Avanturiers Flibustiers. Paris, 1699. New Edn. 2 vols. 12mo. Slight clean tears. Cont. cf., spines gt. (CSK. Jan.9; 222) £70

– History of the Bucaniers of America. L., 1684. 12mo. Frontis. & 1 folding plt. apparently inserted from anr. Edn. Red mor. gt. spine & panels, by Bedford. [Sabin 23480] (SPB. Nov.24; 14) $350

[–] – Anr. Edn. 1684-85. 2nd. Edn. in Engl. 2 vols. in 1. 4to. Soiled, a few sm. holes & tears, some reprd. Later cf., upr. cover detchd. [Wing E 3896; 3897; Sabin 23479] (SH. Nov.7; 377) *Porruas.* £150

– – Anr. Copy. 1 folding map reprd., some browning, slight tears. Cf., slightly stained. [Sabin 23481] (SPB. May 5; 209) $200

– – Anr. Edn. L., 1698-99. 4 pts. in 1 vol. Cont. panel. cf., spine worn. [Sabin 23484] (CNY. May 22; 161) $250

[–] – Anr. Edn. 1771. '5th.' Edn. 2 vols. 12mo. Sig. on titles, some ll. marginally wormed. Cont. cf., rebkd., worn, ?bkplt. of Viscount Gage. [Sabin 23489] (S. Jan.27; 556) *Subunso.* £85

EXQUEMELIN, John–RAVENAU DE LUSSAN

[–] History of the Bucaniers of America.–Journal of a Voyage made into the South Sea by the Bucaniers or Freebooters of America . . . L., 1699; 1698. 1st. Edn. 2 works in 1 vol. 2nd. work in main title & with own title & pagination. Leath., gold-stpd., triple gold fillet, corner fleurons, inner dentelle border & marb. paper end-ll. [Sabin 23483 & 67986] (D. Dec.11-13; 1437) DM 2,150

– – Anr. Edn. 1704. 3rd. Edn.; 2nd. Edn. 2 works in 1 vol. Browned, 1st. work: 1 map torn & reprd. Cont. panel. cf., rebkd. Bkplt. of F.W. Dahlgren. [Sabin 23484] (S. May 5; 244) *Mursia.* £200

EXSTEENS, Maurice

– Felicien Rops: L'Oeuvre Gravé et Lithographié. Paris, 1928. (50) numbered on Japan vell. 4 vols., & portfo. of plt. reproductions. Fo. Wraps., unc. & unopened. (SG. Mar.12; 316) $2,000

EYMERICO, N.

– Manual de Inquisidores. Trans.:– J. Marchena. Montpellier, 1819. Sewed. (DS. Apr.24; 849) Pts. 26,000

EYRE, Edward John

– Journals of Expeditions of Discovery into Central Australia. 1845. [1st. Edn.?]. 2 vols. Slight spotting. Cont. cf., rebkd., spines gt., ex-liby. (CSK. Nov.28; 3) £190

– – Anr. Copy. Foxing & soiling. Orig. cl., unc., worn, backstrips defect., hinges weak or brkn. (KH. Nov.18; 238) Aus. $1,450

EYRE, H.

– A Brief Account of the Holt Waters [near Bath]. 1731. 1st. Edn. 12mo. Cont. mor., gt. (SH. Jun.4; 122) *Rota.* £50

EYRIES, Jean Baptiste Benoit

– La Suisse. Ill.:– after Lory & Moritz. Paris, [1825]. 4to. Text slightly soiled. Cont. hf. leath. (HK. May 12-14; 1150) DM 5,400

EYTON, Rev. Robert William

– Antiquities of Shropshire. 1854-60. 12 vols. in 6. Cont. mor. (SH. Apr.9; 148) *Thornhill.* £210

– – Anr. Edn. 1854-60. (300). 12 vols. Hf. mor., by Ramage. From the collection of Eric Sexton. (C. Apr.16; 252) *Traylen.* £480

EYTON, Thomas Campbell

– A Monograph on the Anatidae. Ill.:– Edward Lear & others. 1838. 4to. Orig. cl. (SBA. Jul.23; 318) *Quaritch.* £320

– – Anr. Copy. 6 hand-cold. plts., 18 uncold. plts., text engrs., 1 uncold. plt. & 1 text lf. torn. Mod. hf. leath. (SG. Oct.9; 94) $900

EYZAGUIRRE, José Ignacio

– Historia Eclesiastica, Politica y Literaria de Chile. Valparaiso, 1850. 3 vols. in 1. Some spotting at beginning & end. Cont. mor., gt., upr. cover gt.-stpd. 'A S.E. El Sr Almiraute Blanco', & detchd. (SPB. May 5; 210) $200

EZH [Hedgehog Collection]

Ed.:– [Yu. V. Gol'dberg]. St. Petersb., 1906. No. 1. 4to. Unbnd. (SH. Feb.5; 67) *De La Casa.* £55

– – Anr. Edn. Ed.:– [Yu. V. Gol'dberg]. St. Petersb., 1907. Nos. 1-7. 4to. Unbnd. (SH. Feb.5; 68) *Quaritch.* £310

F., W.
– Warme Be[ere] or a Treatise where[in] is Declared by Many Reasons, that Beere so Qualified is Farre more Wholesome than that which is Drunke Cold. 1641. 1st. Edn.? 12mo. Lacks 1st. lf. (blank?) & Ell (supplied in photofacs.), a little worming, scarcely affecting text, title slightly defect., reprd. Cont. sheep, rebkd. [Wing F27] (S. Jun.29; 383) *Quaritch.* £150

FABER, A.
– Codex Fabrianus Definitionum Forensium, et Rerum in Sacro Sabaudiae Senatu Tractarum ... accesserunt ultra Centum Senatus Consulta ... Lyon, 1649. Later Edn. Fo. Cont. vell. (D. Dec.11-13; 2159) DM 700

FABER, A.W.
– The Manufactories & Business Houses of the Firm of A.W. Faber. N.p., 1896. 4to. Orig. linen. (R. Oct.14-18; 411) DM 650

FABER du Faur, Curt von
– German Baroque Literature. New Haven, 1958. 4to. Cl., d.-w. (SG. Jan.22; 163) $110

FABLE of the Widow & her Cat
1712. Fo. 2 pp., slightly stained. (S. Oct.17; 6) £200

FABLES, Original & Selected
1839. 4to. Wood engraved frontis. mntd. on india paper. Later mor. by Henry Sotheran, spine gt., orig. cl. covers bnd. in. (CSK. Feb.6; 189) £50

FABRE, François
– Nemesis Medical Illustrée. Ill.:– Honoré Daumier (wood-engrs.). Paris, 1840. 2 vols. in 1. Lacks title & 1 prelim. of vol. II, some foxing. Hf. mor. (SG. May 21; 350) $360

FABRE, Jean Henri Casimir
– Book of Insects. Ill.:– E.J. Detmold. [1921]. 4to. Mor. (SH. Mar.26; 157) *Joseph.* £50
– Le Monde Merveilleux des Insectes. Ill.:– Jean Lurçat. Paris, 1950. (145), sigd. by president of Société des Femmes Bibliophiles, & vice-president, numbered. 4to. Spotted. Unsewn in orig. wraps., decor. folder & s.-c. (SH. Nov.20; 63) *Nat. Art Inst.* £130

FABRE, Pierre Jean
– Chirurgia Spagyrica, in qua de morbis cutaneis omnibus spagyrice & methodice agitur. Toulouse, 1626. 1st. Edn. Lr. margin of title reprd. affecting imprint, some ll. browned. Limp vell. (S. Dec.1; 157) *Quaritch.* £130

FABRICIUS, G.
See–REUSNER, Nicolaus–REUSNER, Elias –FABRICIUS, G.

FABRICIUS, Hieronymus, ab Aquapendente
– Opera Chirurgica. Leiden, 1723. Fo. Hf.-title soiled. Cont. cf., worn, rebkd. (S. Jul.27; 331) *Cleator.* £90
– Opera Omnia Anatomica et Physiologica. Leiden, 1738. 2nd. Edn. A few slight stains, marginal tear in 314. Cont. red mor., gt., worn. Bkplt. of Prince of Lichtenstein; from liby. of Dr. E. Ashworth Underwood. (S. Feb.23; 203) *Dawson.* £240

FABRICIUS [FABRY] HILDANUS, Wilhelm
– De Lithotomia Vesicae.–De Conservanda Valetudine, item, de Thermis Vallesianis, et Acidulis Griesbachcensibus.–De Gangraena et Sphacelo. Basle; Frankfurt; Oppenheim, 1628; 1629; 1617. 3 works in 1 Vol. Sm. 4to. Some ll. spotted or browned, mainly marginal barely affecting text. Later hf. reversed cf., slightly worn, upr. cover detchd. (SBA. Oct.21; 133) *Priedel.* £180
– Opera quae extant omnia, ... ad authore recognita ... additus ... Marci Aurelii Severini Liber de efficaci medicina. Frankfurt, 1682. 2 pts. in 1 vol. Fo. Lacks hf.-title & additional engraved title, spotted in places. Cont. cf., rebkd. using old spine, corners reprd. (S. Feb.23; 44) *Kerkove.* £110

FABRICIUS [FABRY] HILDANUS, Wilhelm –SENNERT, D.
– Observationum e Curationum Cheirurgicarum Centuria Secunda; De Dysenteria Liber Unus; De Vulnere Quodam Gravissimo & Periculoso, ictu Sclopeti Inflicto.–De Dysenteria Tractatus. Genf; Oppenheim; Oppenheim; Wittenberg, 1611; 1616; 1614; 1616. 1st. Edns. of 1st. 3 works. 4 works in 1 vol. Slightly browned in parts. Cont. limp vell. (R. Mar.31-Apr.4; 986) DM 950

FABRICIUS Hildanus, Wilhelm–SEVERINUS, Marcus Aurelius
– Opera quae extant Omnia ...–De Efficaci Medicinae. Frankfurt, 1646. 2 pts. in 1 vol. Thick fo. Owner's inscr. 'Robert Travers M.B. & John Knott M.D.'. Cont. vell., hinges torn. (S. Jun.15; 270) *Preidel.* £210

FABRICUS, Otto
– Fauna Groenlandica. Copen. & Leipzig, 1780. Foxed. Recent wraps., orig. wraps. preserved, unopened. (CB. Sep.24; 2) Can. $150

FABYAN, Robert
– Chronicle. 1559. 2 Pts. in 1 vol. Fo. 18th. C. cf., rebkd. [STC 10664] (S. Nov.25; 446) *Fletcher.* £150
[–] Anr. Copy Title of vol. 1 detchd., first 25 ll. supplied in MS. facs. Late 18th. C. diced russ, spine worn. W.a.f. [STC 10664] (CSK. Nov.28; 108) £100

FACCIOLI, Emilio
– Arte della Cucina ... Milan, [1966]. (300) numbered. 2 vols. 4to. Hf. mor., box. (SG. Sep.4; 179) $100

FADEN, William
See–RENNELL, James–EDWARDS, B.–FADEN, William

FADEN, William & others
– Atlas. N.d. Lge. fo. 52 engraved maps, 50 cold. in outl., many areas fully cold., holes in chart, 1 map torn, without title or text, MS. contents list, fly-lf. & 2 maps detchd., litho. chart inserted. Early 19th. C. hf. cf., covers detchd., worn. W.a.f. (S. Mar.31; 252) *Burgess.* £850

FAERNUS, Gabrielus
– Cent Fables en Latin et en François. Trans.:– Perrault. 1744. New Edn. 4to. Frontis. bkd., some ll. marginally stained, pieces torn from lr. outer corner of last 2 ll., occasional offsetting. Cont. hf. cf., rebkd., worn. (S. Jan.26; 125) *Broseghini.* £50
– Centum Fabulae ex Antiquis Scriptoribus Delectae. Brussels, 1682. Soiled. Cont. cf. (SH. Jun.4; 108) *Ayres.* £50
– Fabulae Centum ... Parma, 1793. 4to. 49 plts. (of 50?) before letters, occasional light offsetting. Red hf. mor. by Cape, gt. spine, partly unc. (S. Jul.27; 158) *Quaritch.* £160

FAGOT DE MYERRE
– Cy commence le livre intitule le Presché en Liglise de Saincte Croix en la Cite Dangiers. Paris, [1525?]. Notations in cont. hand at foot of title, some marginal wormholes reprd. 19th. C. mor., rebkd., by C. Smith, with his ticket. (SPB. Nov.25; 54) $1,300

FAHRT AUF DEM RHEIN (Die) von Mainz bis Köln
Wiesbaden, [1842]. Slightly soiled in places. Cont. hf. leath. (R. Oct.14-18; 2407) DM 1,300

FAILLE, Jean Baptiste de la
– L'Oeuvre de Vincent Van Gogh.–Les Faux Van Gogh. Paris & Brussels, 1928; 1930. 1st. work (633) numbered; 2nd. work (853) numbered. Tog. 4 vols. 4to. Orig. wraps., unc. 1st. work with 2-pp. supp. loosely inserted. (SH. Apr.9; 70) *Duran.* £160

FAIRBAIRN, James
– Crests of the Families of Great Britain & Ireland. Ed.:– Laurence Butters & Joseph Maclaren. Edinb. & L., [1860]. 2 vols. 4to. Red hf. mor. gt. by F. Bedford. (S. Nov.24; 123) *Howes.* £90

FAIRBAIRN, Thomas
– Relics of Ancient Architecture & other Picturesque Scenes in Glasgow. Glasgow, 1849. Fo. Cont. hf. mor. gt., lr. cover defect. (S. Nov.24; 124) *Marlborough.* £260

FAIRBRIDGE, Dorothea
– Historic Houses of South Africa. 1922. 4to. Orig. cl. (SH. Oct.9; 119) *Meyer.* £80
– – Anr. Copy. (SH. Apr.9; 71) *Sawyer.* £60
– – Anr. Copy. Hf. lev. mor. (VA. May 8; 312) R. 120

FAIRBURN, W.
– An Account of the Construction of the Britannia & Conway Tubular Bridges. 1849. 1st. Edn. Cont. mor.-bkd. cl. (SH. Jun.18; 106) *Weinreb.* £120
– Treatise on Iron Ship Building.–Iron Manufacture.–The Life ...–Treatise on Mills & Millworks. 1865; 1869; 1877; 1878. 2nd. work 3rd.

Edn.; 4th. work 4th. Edn. 4 vols. Liby stps. Orig. cl. (SH. Jun.18; 105) *Weinreb.* £130

FAIRHOLT, Frederick W.
– Miscellanea Graphica: Representations of Ancient, Mediaeval, & Renaissance Remains in the Possession of Lord Londesborough. Ed.:– Thomas Wright. 1857. Fo. Some foxing. Cont. gt. decor. cl. (TA. Feb.19; 396) £50

FAIRY ABC
N.Y., ca. 1880. 4to. Orig. pict. wraps. (SH. Mar.19; 93) *Maggs.* £55

FAIRY GARLAND: Being Fairy Tales from the Old French
Ill.:– Edmund Dulac. L., [1928]. 1st. Dulac Edn. (1,000) numbered, sigd. by Dulac. Lge. tall 4to. Qtr. vell. & cl. (some spotting). (PNY. Mar.26; 106) $120

FAKELY [Torches]
St. Petersb., 1906-08. Pts. 1-3 [all publd.]. 4to. & 8vo. Pts. 1 & 2 in orig. wraps., slightly torn, pt. 3 in mod. hf. mor., orig. wraps. preserved. (SH. Feb.6; 428) *Landry.* £75

FALASCHI, V.
– La Gerarchia Ecclesiastica e la Famiglia Pontificia. Ill.:– F. Ferrari. Macerata, 1828. Italian & Fr. text, last & 1st. ll. slightly stained. Mod. hf. leath., orig. wraps. bnd. in, unc. (H. Dec.9/10; 763) DM 850

FALBALAS ET FANFRELUCHES
– Almanach des Modes Presentes, Passées et futures pour 1924. Ill.:– George Barbier. Paris, [1923]. Unsewn in orig. wraps., unc., cover design by ill. (SH. Nov.20; 211) *Monk Bretton.* £160
– – Anr. Copy. (SH. Nov.20; 212) *Monk Bretton.* £150
– Almanach des Modes Présentes, Passées et futures pour 1925 Ill.:– George Barbier. Paris, [1924]. Unsewn in orig. wraps., cover design by Barbier. (SH. Nov.20; 214) *Pruskin.* £170

FALCONER, Capt. Richard
– The Voyage, Dangerous Adventures, & Imminent Escapes ... 1720. 1st. Edn. 3 pts. in 1 vol. Lacks blank A3. Mod. panel. cf., spine gt. [Sabin 23735] (C. Nov.6; 209) *Rota.* £170

FALCONER, William
– The Shipwreck. L., 1808. Early maroon str.-grd. mor., gt. floral border. Fore-e. pntg. (SG. Mar.19; 133) $350
– An Universal Dictionary of the Marine. L., 1776. 4to. Cont. cf. gt. (CNY. May 22; 162) $120
– – Anr. Edn. 1789. 4th. Edn. 4to. Cont. spr. cf. (S. Feb.9; 128) *Maggs.* £120
See–MOORE, John Hamilton–FALCONER, William

FALCONET, [Camille]
– Catalogue de la Bibliothèque. Paris, 1763. 2 vols. Table of authors, priced in MS. thro.-out. Cont. cf., spine gt. in compartments. (SM. Oct.7; 1373) Frs. 2,200

FALDA, Giovanni Batistta
– Novo Teatro delle Chiese di Roma. [1665-99]. Pt. 3 only. Ob. fo. Cf. gt. (P. Oct.2; 114) *Cucchio.* £95

FALDA, Giovanni Battista– SADELER, Marco
– Il Nuovo Teatro delle Fabriche et Edificii in Prospettiva di Roma Moderna ...–Le Fontane di Roma ...–Le Fontane delle Ville di Frascati ... –Le Fontane ne Palazzi e ne Giardini de Roma ... –Le Chiese di Roma.–Vestigi delle Antichitta di Roma. Rome, 1665-99. 6 works in 1 vol. Ob. fo. Old hf. roan, smooth decor. spine. (HD. Jun.24; 34) Frs. 13,000
See–ROSSI, Giovanni Giacomo & Falda, Giovanni Battista

FALKENSTEIN, K.
– Geschichte der Buchdruckerkunst. Leipzig, 1840. 4to. Cont. mor.-bkd. cl. (SH. Mar.6; 521) *Fairburn.* £95

FALKERA, Shem Tov Ibn
– Sepher Ha'mevakesh (philosophy). The Hague, 1772-79. 1st. Edn. Hf. cl. (S. Nov.18; 426) *Stern.* £55

FALKNER, Frank
– The Wood Family of Burslem. L., 1912. (450). 4to. Orig. cl. (SPB. Jul.28; 124) $150

FALLETTI, Girolamo
See–MANUTIUS, Paulus–FALLETTI, Girolamo
–HUTTICHIUS, Johannes

FALLO DEFINITIVO DEL SUPREMO TRIBUNAL DE LA GUERRA, al Examinar la Conducta Militar del Exmo. Sr. General D. Mariano Arista, en las Acciones de Guerra que sostuvo al Principio de la Invasion Americana
Mexico, 1850. Plain wraps., slight wear. (SG. Jan.8; 282) $160

FALLOU, L.
– Album de l'Armée Française. Ill.:– Aubry, Bellange & others. Paris, 1902. Fo. Cl. (SG. Oct.30; 148) $100

FAMIGLIA MENEGHINA
– I Libri della Famiglia Meneghina. Ed.:– Severo Cappellini. Milan, 1926-49. Ltd. Edn. numbered. 33 vols. together. 4to. 1st. 23 vols. mor. gt., sigd. by Torriani, rest hf. mor., orig. wraps bnd. in, partly unc. (SI. Dec.3; 212)   Lire 800,000

FAMIGLIE CELEBRI ITALIANE
Milan, 1843. Pt. 46 only. Fo. Cont. hf. cf. (SH. Jan.30; 429)   Strufeldi. £110

FAMILY MAGAZINE
– Part I . . . House-Keeping & Cookery; Part II . . . A Compendious Body of Physick. 1741. Old style spr. cf. (CSK. Sep.26; 196)   £85

FAMIN, A.
See–GRANDJEAN DE MONTIGHY, A. & Famin, A.

FARADAY, Michael
– Faraday's Diary. Ed.:– T. Martin. 1932-36. 8 vols. Orig. cl., gt. (P. Mar.12; 366)   Lenton. £55

FAREY, John, Civil Engineer
– Treatise on the Steam Engine. 1827. 4to. Mod. hf. cf. gt. (P. Oct.2; 75)   Manchester. £50

FARGUE, Léon, Paul
– Cotes Roties. Textes Pretextes. [Paris], 1928-38, 1949. Lge. 4to. (195) numbered on Arches with 2 orig. etchings. Loose ll., wrap. & publisher's box. (LM. Nov.8; 71)   B.Frs. 9,000
– Illuminations Nouvelles. Ill.:– Raoul Dufy. Paris, 1953. (250) on Arches. 4to. Loose ll. . . . publisher's wrap. & box. (LM. Nov.8; 70)   B.Frs. 8,000

FARIA, Francisco Xavier de
– Vida y Heroycas Virtudes del Vble. Padre Pedro de Velasco . . . Compañia de Jesus de Nueva-Espana. Mexico, 1753. 1st. Edn. Cont. vell., loose, lr. free end-paper lacking. (SPB. Jun.22; 55) $600

FARIA y Sousa, Manuel de
– Africa Portuguesa. Lisbon, 1681. 1st. Edn. Fo. Cont. mott. cf., worn. From Chetham's Liby., Manchester. (C. Nov.26; 158)   Taylor. £140
– – Anr. Copy. (C. Apr.1; 134)   Lawson. £110

FARISSOL, Abrahamo
See–PERITSOL or FARISSOL, Abrahamo

FARLEY, John
– The London Art of Cookery. 1789. Cf., worn & loose. (CE. Jul.9; 110)   £75
– – Anr. Edn. L., [1796]. 8th. Edn. New leatherette. (SG. Sep.25; 92) $180

FARLEY, J.
See–CIBBER, Colley–BURDETT, William–FARLEY, J.–ANON

FARMER, J.
– History of . . . Abbey, of Waltham. 1735. Some repairs. Cf. gt., worn, lr. cover detchd. (P. Jul.30; 54)   Thorp. £65
– – Anr. Copy. 1 plt. cleanly torn. Cont. cf., spine reprd. at head & foot. (CSK. May 22; 138)   £55

FARMER'S MAGAZINE
1843-70. 2nd. Series, vols. 7-12, 3rd. Series, vols. 23, 24, 29, 30, 37, & 38, 12 vols. in 9. Some staining. Cont. hf. leath., 3 worn. (SKC. Feb.26; 1722)   £180

FARNHAM, Thomas J.
– Travels in the Great Western Prairies . . . Poughkeepsie, 1841. 1st. Edn. Mod. cl. [Sabin 23872] (SPB. Jun.22; 53) $175

FARQUHAR, George
See–KENRICK, William–FARQUHAR, George–MASON, William–LEE, Nathaniel

FARRE, John Richard
– Pathological Researches. 1814. Essay I on Malformations of the Human Heart . . . (all publd.). Liby. stps. in text & on all plts. Cl. (S. Jun.15; 272)   Jenner Books. £110

FARRERE, Claude (Pseud.)
See–BARGONE, Frédéric Charles Pierre Edouard 'Claude Farrère'

FASHION Drawings. An Album of 27 Pencil and Watercolour Drawings of Fashion Designs
Wtrmkd. 1794. Sm. 4to. Cont. cf., rebkd. With book label of Jane de Courcy Russell. (SH. Apr.10; 629)   Drummond. £250

FASSAM, Thomas
– An Herbarium for the Fair. Ill.:– Betty Shaw-Lawrence. L., Hand & Flower Pr., 1949. (260), numbered. 4to. Orig. hf. mor. by Sangorski & Sutcliffe. (S. May 5; 106)   Elliot. £55

FAUCHARD, Pierre
– Le Chirurgien Dentiste. Paris, 1786. 3rd. Edn. 2 vols. Cont. hf. leath. gt. (R. Mar.31-Apr.4; 1057)   DM 4,600

FAUCHET, C, Chamfort, S.R.N., Ginguene, P.L. & Pages, F.X.
– Collection Complète des Tableaux Historiques de la Révolution Française. Paris, 1801. 3 vols. in 2. Fo. Lacks titles for vols. II-III, occasional spotting mainly round margins, some ll. browned. 19th. C. hf. russ, 1 cover detchd., worn. (S. Apr.7; 367)   Duran. £400

[FAUCHET, Claude]
See–SIMEONI, Gabriele–[FAUCHET, Claude]

FAUJAS de Saint-Fond, Barthélémi
– Description des Expériences de la Machine Aérostatique de MM. de Montgolfier. Paris, 1783-84. 1st. Edn. 2 vols. 6 engraved plts. (of 9). Cont. hf. cf., slightly worn. (SM. Feb.11; 4)   Frs. 1,400
– – Anr. Edn. Paris, 1784. 2nd. Edn. 1 vol. only. 2 plts. cut slightly short at sides, 1st. & last ll. lightly soiled, 3 further copperplts. (1 folding) from European Magazine bnd. in at end. Late 19th. C. hf. leath. (HK. Nov.18-21; 351)   DM 1,000
– Recherches sur les Volcans. Grenoble & Paris, 1778. Fo. 19th. C. hf. mor. From Chetham's Liby., Manchester. (C. Nov.26; 159)   Junk. £240

FAULKNER, Thomas
– An Historical & Topographical Description of Chelsea & its Environs. 1829. 2 vols. Folding map torn, occasional spotting. Hf. mor. (CSK. Jul.3; 27)   £70
– – Anr. Copy. Plts. & map spotted or offset. Cont. hf. mor., spines gt. (SKC. Feb.26; 1648)   £50
– An Historical & Topographical Description of Chelsea.–History & Antiquities of Kensington.–An Historical & Topographical Account of Fulham. 1829; 1820; 1813. 2 vols.; 1 vol.; 1 vol. Map reprd. at fold in 1st. work, occasional browning in 1st. & 3rd. works. 1st. work: cont. hf. cf.; 2nd. work: orig. paper-bkd. bds., worn, upr. cover detchd.; 3rd. work: cont. cf., rebkd. Sig. of William Wilberforce on upr. cover & title of 2nd. work, all lately in the collection of E. Sexton. (C. Apr.16; 253)   Grosvenor. £100

FAULKNER, William
– Absalom, Absalom N.Y., 1936. 1st. Edn. Orig. cl., d.-w. (CNY. May 22; 102) $450
– – Anr. Edn. N.Y., 1936. (300) numbered. Cl.-bkd. patt. bds., staining on front free end-paper, bkplt. Sigd. (SG. Nov.13; 183) $320
– As I Lay Dying. N.Y., [1930]. 1st. Edn. 12mo. Cl., bkplt. (SG. Nov.13; 174) $375
– – Anr. Copy. 2nd. Iss., cl., d.-w. (SG. Jun.4; 156) $120
– A Fable. N.Y., [1954]. (1,000) numbered, sigd. Cl., boxed. (SG. Jun.4; 171) $225
– – Anr. Copy. Cl., glassine wrap. (defect.), boxed, bkplt. (SG. Nov.13; 195) $190
– A Green Bough. N.Y., 1933. 1st. Edn. Sm. 4to. Cl., d.-w. reprd. (SG. Jun.4; 165) $120
– – Anr. Edn. N.Y., 1933. (350) sigd. by author. 4to. Slight browning around the edges. Orig. cl., slight soiling. (SPB. Nov.25; 270) $225
– The Hamlet. N.Y., 1940. 1st. Edn. Cl., d.-w. (SG. Jun.4; 168) $350
– – Anr. Edn. N.Y., 1940. (250) numbered, sigd. Hf. cl., staining on covers & end-papers, bkplt. (SG. Nov.13; 186) $375

– – Anr. Edn. N.Y., 1940. (250) sigd. Slight spotting. Orig. hf. cl., spine slightly faded, slight soiling. (SPB. May 29; 148) $800
– Idyll in the Desert. N.Y., 1931. 1st. Edn., (400) numbered, sigd. Marb. bds. (SG. Jun.4; 160) $425
– – Anr. Copy. Slightly worn, bkplt. removed from in upr. cover. (SG. Nov.13; 176) $300
– – Anr. Edn. N.Y., 1931. 1st. Edn. (400) sigd., this copy 'Out of Series'. Marb. bds. (SG. Jun.4; 159) $475
– Intruder in the Dust.–Collected Stories.–Requiem of a Nun.–The Mansion.–The Reivers. N.Y., [1948-62]. 1st. Edns. 5 works in 5 vols. Cl., all in d.-w.'s. (SG. Nov.13; 201) $130
– Knight's Gambit. N.Y., [1949]. 1st. Edn. Cl., d.-w. (SG. Nov.13; 189) $110
– Light in August. [N.Y.], [1932]. 1st. Edn., 1st. Iss. With 'Jefferson' for 'Mottstown' on p.340. Buckram, d.-w. (SG. Nov.13; 178) $280
– – Anr. Copy. Cl., d.-w., bkplt. (SG. Nov.13; 179) $220
– – Anr. Edn. [N.Y.], [1932]. 1st. Edn. Cl., d.-w. (SG. Jun.4; 162) $425
– The Mansion. N.Y., [1959]. 1st. Edn., (500) numbered, sigd. 12mo. Buckram. (SG. Jun.4; 174) $375
– – Anr. Copy. Cl., glassine d.-w., bkplt. (SG. Nov.13; 198) $180
– Miss Zilphia Gant. [Dallas], 1932. 1st. Edn., (300). 12mo. Slight browning, spotting. Orig. cl. (SPB. Nov.25; 268) $425
– Notes on a Horsethief. Ill.:– Elizabeth Calvert. Greenville, Levee Pr., 1950. (975) numbered, sigd. Pict. cl. (SG. Jun.4; 170) $325
– – Anr. Copy. Buckram, bkplt. (SG. Nov.13; 190) $170
– Pylon. N.Y., 1935. 1st. Edn. Cl., d.-w. (SG. Jun.4; 166) $160
– – Anr. Edn. N.Y., 1935. (310) numbered, sigd. Cl. back & tips, covers worn, staining on front free end-paper, box (defect.), bkplt. (SG. Nov.13; 182) $270
– The Reivers. N.Y., [1962]. 1st. Edn. (500) numbered, sigd. Cl., acetate d.-w. (SG. Nov.13; 199) $220
– Requiem for a Nun. N.Y., [1951]. 1st. Edn. (750) numbered. Cl.-bkd. marb. bds., acetate d.-w., bkplt. & owners' inscr. Sigd. (SG. Nov.13; 193) $180
– Salmagundi . . . Milwaukee, Casanova Pr., 1932. 1st. Edn., (525) numbered. Wraps., 2nd. state, publisher's box. (SG. Jun.4; 164) $425
– – Anr. Copy. 2nd. state of end-papers. Orig. wraps., box (worn). (SPB. Nov.25; 269) $350
– Sanctuary. N.Y., [1931]. 1st. Edn., 1st. Iss. 12mo. Cl.-bkd. bds., patt. end-papers, d.-w., bkplt. (SG. Nov.13; 175) $300
– Sartoris. N.Y., [1929]. 1st. Edn. 12mo. Cl., d.-w. (defect.), bkplt. (SG. Nov.13; 172) $100
– Soldier's Pay. N.Y., 1926. 1st. Edn. Cl., d.-w. (from a later edn.). (SG. Nov.13; 170) $110
– The Sound & the Fury. N.Y., [1929]. 1st. Edn. Cl.-bkd. patt. bds., spine faded, d.-w. wrinkled, bkplt. (SG. Nov.13; 173) $230
– Tandis Que J'Agonise. Trans.:– M.E. Coindreau. Ill.:– Courtin. Paris, 1946. (175) on pur fil de Lana. Sm. fo. Loose, as iss., in ptd. wraps., folding box, tissue guards (short crack at 2 seams). (PNY. Mar.26; 113) $160
– These 13. N.Y., [1931]. 1st. Edn. Orig. cl., d.-w. (CNY. May 22; 101) $500
– – Anr. Copy. Cl., d.-w. (SG. Jun.4; 161) $300
– This Earth. Ill.:– Albert Heckman. N.Y., 1932. 1st. Edn. Ptd. wraps. (SG. Nov.13; 180) $110
– The Town. N.Y., [1957]. 1st. Edn. (450) numbered, sigd. Cl., glassine wrap. (SG. Jun.4; 173) $375
– – Anr. Copy. Cl., acetate d.-w., bkplt. (SG. Nov.13; 197) $300
– The Unvanquished. N.Y., [1938]. 1st. Edn. (250) numbered & sigd. Orig. cl.-bkd. bds. (CNY. May 22; 103) $650
– – Anr. Copy. Cl.-bkd. patt. bds., staining on front free end-paper, bkplt. (SG. Nov.13; 188) $380
– The Wild Palms. N.Y., [1939]. 1st. Edn. Cl., d.-w. (SG. Jun.4; 167) $425
– – Anr. Copy. (250) sigd. Minor discolouration. Orig. cl.-bkd. bds., spine faded, slight soiling. (SPB. May 29; 147) $850
– – Anr. Copy. 1st. Edn. (250) numbered & sigd., L.P. Cl.-bkd. simulated wood bds., staining on front free end-paper, bkplt. (SG. Nov.13; 185) $250

FAUX, W[illiam]

- Memorable Days in America: Being a Journal of a Tour to the United States . . . to Ascertain . . . the Condition & Probable Prospects of British Emigrants; Including Accounts of Mr. Birkbeck's Settlement in the Illinois. L., 1823. 1st. Edn. Advts., slight soiling & foxing. Orig. bds., soiled. From liby. of William E. Wilson. (SPB. Apr.29; 97) $225

FAWCKNER, James

- Narrative . . . Travels on the Coast of Benin. 1837. 1st. Edn. Orig. cl., slightly marked. (S. Feb.9; 131) Remington. £90

FAY, H[eman] A.

- Collection of the Official Accounts . . . of the Battles Between the Navy & Army of the United States, & . . . Great Britain, During the Years 1812, 13, 14, & 15. N.Y., 1817. 1st. Edn. Slight foxing. Orig. bds., rebkd., unc., rear end-paper torn. From liby. of William E. Wilson. [Sabin 23940] (SPB. Apr.29; 98) $100

FAY D'HERBE, H.

See-THEUILLIER, J. & Fay d'Herbe, H. -SCHADTKISTE, de, der Philosophen ende Poeten . . . Porphyre en Cyprine Treurspel . . .

FAYSER VON ARNSTAIN, Johann

- Hippiatria. Grundlicher Bericht vnd Beschreibung der bewerten Rossartzney. Augsburg, 1576. 1st. Edn. Fo. Title very defect. in inner margin, with partial loss of border, & mntd., folding woodcut diagram of horse also defect. & mntd., inner margins at beginning rotted away through damp, spotting & staining elsewhere. 19th C. paper wraps. (S. Dec.8; 101) Way. £140

See-GRISONE, Federico-FAYSER VON ARNSTAIN, Johann-HORWART VON HOHENBURG, Hans Friedrich

FEA, Carlo

See-WINCELMANN, Johann Joachim-FEA, Carlo

FEARING, Daniel B.

- Check List of Books on Angling. N.Y., 1901. (25) priv. ptd. Wraps., spine labelled by previous owner. Numbered, & inscr. to George D. Smith. (SG. Jan.22; 28) $170

FEARNSIDE, William Gray

- Eighty Picturesque Views of the Thames & Medway. N.d. 4to. Some plts. loose, some ll. soiled & dampstained. Orig. cl. gt., worn, loose, lacks spine. (SD. Feb.4; 212) £200

- History of London: illustrated by views.-Select Illustrated Topography of Thirty Miles around London. Ed.:- Thomas Harral. N.d. 2 works in 1 vol. 4to. Browned, 1st. work: engraved title & 34 plts. only. Orig. cl., gt., worn. (SH. Nov.6; 97) Shapero. £80

- Picturesque Beauties of the Rhine. N.d. 39 plts. only (of 40), some spotted, a few marginally dampstained, 1 loose. Orig. cl. (SH. Mar.5; 54) Walford. £130

See-TOMBLESON, William & Fearnside, William Gray

FEBRES, Andrès

- Arte de la Lengua General del Reyno de Chile, con un Dialogo Chileno-hispano muy curioso . . . y por fin un Vocabulario Hispano-chileno y un Calepino Chileno-hispano más Copioso. Lima, 1765. 1st. Edn. Foremargins of 4P7-8 restored touching a few letters, title & a few other ll. with light stains. Later vell. bds. (SPB. May 5; 211) $650

FEDERALIST

- Collection of Essays, Written in Favour of the New Constitution, as agreed upon by the Federal Convention, September 17, 1787. N.Y., 1788. 1st. Coll. Edn. 2 vols. 12mo. Cont. tree cf., some wear, cl. s.-c. On thick paper owner's inscr. of Richard Hatfield on title of vol. II & front free end-paper of vol. II with note 'price of this other volume 15' the Stockhausen copy. [Sabin 23979] (SPB. Nov.24; 15) $8,500
- - Anr. Copy. Age-browned thro.-out, sm. tear in pp. 61-72, without loss of text. Disbnd, with orig. stitching, & rear bd. cover preserved, unc. (SG. Mar.5; 197) $600
- - Anr. Copy. Browned. Orig. bds. unc. (SPB. Jun.22; 56) $350

FELDBORG, A. Andersen

- Denmark Delineated. Edinb., 1824. 1st. Edn. Cont. str.-grd. mor. gt., upr. cover almost detchd. (C. Jul.15; 35) Traylen. £100

FELIBIEN, Andre

[-] Tapisseries du Roi, ou sont representez les Quatre Elemens et les Quatre Saisons. Paris, 1670. Imp. fo. Slightly soiled. Cont. red mor., gt., upr. cover loose. (R. Oct.14-18; 2514) DM 3,500
- - Anr. Edn. Paris, 1679. Fo. Slightly soiled & lightly browned in parts. Cont. leath. (R. Mar.31-Apr.4; 1501) DM 2,700
See-BOCKLER, Georg Andreas-FELIBIEN, Andre-WALLHAUSEN, Johann Jacob von

FELIBIEN, Jean François

[-] Entretiens sur les Vies et sur les ouvrages des plus excellens Peintres anciens et modernes. -Recueil historique de la Vie et des Ouvrages des plus célèbres Architectes. Paris, 1685-88. 2nd. Edn. (1st. work). 2 works in 2 vols., 2nd. work at end of 2nd. vol. 4to. Cont. mott. cf., worn. (S. Dec.8; 136) Weinreb. £55

FELICIANO, Felice

- Alphabetum Romanum. Bod. Pr. 1960. (400). Orig. mor.-bkd. bds. partly unc., s.-c. (CNY. Oct.1; 200) $380

FELKIN, W.

- History of the Machine-Wrought Hosiery & Lace Manufactures. 1867. Cl. gt. (P. Oct.2; 79) Powell. £65

FELLIG, Arthur 'Weegee'

- Weegee by Weegee: An Autobiography. N.Y., 1961. Cl., d.-w. Inscr. on fly-lf. 'To Sid, the Mayor of Hell's Kitchen, Weegee, 1962'. (SG. Apr.23; 208) $110

FELLOWES, William Dorsett

- A Visit to the Monastery of La Trappe in 1817. 1818. 1st. Edn. Cont. hf. cf., rebkd., orig. spine preserved, worn. (S. Jan.27; 501) Needham. £65
- - Anr. Edn. 1823. 4th. Edn. Cont. str.-grd. mor., gt. (SH. Nov.6; 204) Ferrow. £85
- - Anr. Copy. Cont. hf. cf. L.P. (S. Nov.4; 590) Elliot. £70
See-SCORESBY, William-FELLOWES, William Dorset

FELLOWS, Charles

- Journal Written during an Excursion in Asia Minor. 1839. 1st. Edn. 4to. Mod. hf. cf., spine gt. (S. Mar.31; 469) Crete. £110
- - Anr. Copy. Slight foxing. Orig. cl. gt. (TA. Nov.20; 413) £95

FELTON, William

- A Treatise on Carriages & Harness. 1805. 3rd. Edn. 3 vols. 52 engraved plts. (of 60) some folding. Mod. hf. cf. (C. May 20; 28) Cross. £250

FENDI, Peter

- Vierzig Erotische Aquarelle. Ed.:- Karl Merker. (Intro.) Ill.:- Josef Danhauser. Leipzig, Priv. ptd., ca. 1910. (600) numbered for Subscribers only. Tall fo. Text & plts. loose, as issued, each mnt. bears embossed publisher's stp. Gt. vell. & dyed bd. folder, inner folding panels separated, unc., ties. (PNY. Oct.1; 203) $950

FENELON, Apb. François de Salignac de la Mothe

- Les Aventures de Télémaque. Ill.:- Folkema after Picart (frontis.); Drevets after Vivien (port.); ills. after Picart, Debris & Dubourg. Amst., 1734. 4to. Some spotting & staining at heads of pages & plts. Cont. tree roan, gt. borders on covers, spine decor. with sm. interlaced roses, amphoras & suns, worn. (SM. Feb.11; 5) Frs. 1,200
- - Anr. Edn. Paris, 1781. 4 vols. 16mo. Cont. red mor., decor. spine, 3 fillets on covers, inner dentelle. From the 'Collection of works printed by the order of Monseigneur, Comte d'Artois'. (HD. Apr.9; 466) Frs. 1,900
- - Anr. Edn. Paris, 1783. (200) on Vélin paper. 2 vols. 4to. Cont. red mor by Gaudreau, triple gt. fillet, spine gt. in compartments, inner gt. dentelles, sigd. at foot of upr. inner cover 'Gaudreau relieur de la Reine'. (SM. Oct.7; 1704) Frs. 5,600
- - Anr. Edn. Paris, 1784. (350); on Vélin paper. 2 vols. Inscr. on flylf. 'M. Bain donné par son Frère' & 'Mary A. Hewitt, Gosford Castle, 1863'. Cont. mor. by Derome le Jeune with his ticket, narrow gt. borders of fleurs-de-lis, flat spine gt. in compartments with single fleuron, inner gt. dentelles. (SM. Oct.7; 1705) Frs. 1,600

- - Anr. Edn. Ill.:- Tilliard after Monet. Paris, 1785. 2 vols. 4to. Slight spotting. Cont. Fr. red mor., gt., watered silk linings. (S. Oct.21; 304) Quaritch. £390
- - Anr. Copy. 2 engraved frontis., 1 with insert port. Red mor., gt., by Simier On vell., lge. ex-liby. of F.R.H.B., 1905. (SM. Oct.8; 2396) Frs. 7,500
- - Anr. Edn. [Paris], 1785. On papier velin, Edn. without plts. 2 vols. in 1. Fo. Port. in 2 states inserted. Cont. red str.-grd. mor., inlaid borders gt., gt. dentelles. Fore-e. pntg. (SG. Oct.9; 96) $1,000
- - Anr. Copy. Cont. mor., concentric narrow roll borders, gt., spine gt. in compartments with intersecting zig-zag lines, inner gt. dentelles & pink silk liners. Malmesbury copy with written pr. mark. (SM. Oct.7; 1706) Frs. 3,300
- - Anr. Edn. L., 1791. 3 vols. Red mor., 'Cazin' on spine in gold letters. (HD. Apr.8; 242) Frs. 2,800
- - Anr. Edn. Ill.:- Trière after Vivien (port). Paris, 3rd. Year [1795]. 4 vols. Sm. 12mo. Some light foxing & dampstaining. Cont. red mor., decor. spines & roulette on covers, inner dentelle. (HD. Apr.9; 467) Frs. 1,000
- - Anr. Edn. 1820. 2 vols. Long-grd. mor., gt. & blind frame, ornamental spines, by Simier. (HD. Oct.10; 240) Frs. 2,200
- - Anr. Edn. Paris, 1824. 2 vols. Cont. cf., blind-stpd. borders enclosing gt. arms of Comte d'Artois, by Brigandat, red mor. s.-c.'s. Mortimer Schiff bkplt. (SG. Oct.9; 97) $200
- Oeuvres. Paris, 1787. 5 vols. 4to. Cont. cf. gt. (P. Jan.22; 64) Balham. £50

FENN, Lady Eleanor

[-] Rational Sports. L., ca. 1785. 2nd. Edn. 16mo. With 3 pp. of advts. Cont. sheep-bkd. marb. bds., spine worn. (SG. Apr.30; 126) $150

FENTON, Sir Geoffrey

- Golden Epistles. Oct.15, 1582. 3rd. Edn. 4to. Slight worming & dampstaining. 17th. C. cf., rebkd. Sig. of Edmond Tudor. (S. Feb.9; 133) Thorp. £170

FER, Nicolas de

- L'Atlas Curieux. Paris, priv. ptd., 1700. 2 pts. in 1 vol. Sm. ob. fo. Old cf., reprd., decor. spine, blind-tooled roll-stp. on covers. (HD. Dec.5; 78) Frs. 6,000

- Introduction à la Géographie. Paris, 1717. 2nd. Edn. Short tears in maps, some dampstaining. Cont. cf., rather worn. (S. Apr.7; 469) Hyde Park Books. £50

FERBER, Edna

- Giant.-Ice Palace-A King of Magic. Garden City, 1958-63. 1st. Edns. 3 vols. Cl., d.-w's on last 2 vols. 1st. 2 titles are sigd. pres. copies, 3rd. title has inserted A.L.s., & T.L.s., both 1 p., from author to Mrs Gilbert Chapman, orig. envelopes. (PNY. Mar.4; 147) $220

FERGUSON, Adam

- Essay on the History of Civil Society. Edinb., 1767. 4to. Cf. (P. Dec.11; 313) Picherstowe. £210

FERGUSON, G.

- Illustrated Series of Rare & Prize Poultry. 1854. 1 plt. loose, 1 torn, a few ll. marked. Orig. cl., worn, lacks spine. Pres. copy, inscr. by author to Vice-Admiral Currie. (SKC. Jul.28; 2408) £120

FERGUSON, James

- Astronomy Explained upon Sir Isaac Newton's Principles. 1756. 1st. Edn. 4to. Browned, a few tears. Cont. cf. (SH. Jun.18; 131) Walford. £75
- - Anr. Edn. L., 1764. 3rd. Edn. 4to. Later qtr. cf. & marb. bds. Cont. sig. of George Baillie at title. (PNY. Oct.1; 214) $200
- An Easy Introduction to Astronomy.-Astronomy Explained upon Sir Isaac Newton's Principles. 1769; 1772. 2nd. Edn.; 5th Edn. 2 vols. Vol.: 1 plt. torn: 2nd. vol.: a few prelim. margins wormed, slight loss. Cont. spr. cf. (SBA. Mar.4; 91) Campbell. £60
- Lectures on select Subjects in Mechanics . . . with the Use of the Globes, the Art of Dialing. Ill.:- J. Mynde after Ferguson. L., 1764. 4to. 1 plt. slightly spotted. Cont. cf., rebkd. (CNY. Oct.1; 11) $250
- - Anr. Edn. Edinb., 1806. 2nd. Edn. 3 vols. Spotted Orig. bds., worn. (SH. Jun.11; 223) Armstrong. £55

FERGUSON, James -contd.
- Lectures on Select Subjects ... with the Supplement. 1773. 2 pts. in 1 vol. 4to. Cont. cf., jnts. worn. (S. Oct.21; 347) *Quaritch.* £75

FERGUSON, John
- Bibliographical Notes on Histories of Inventions & Books of Secrets. L., [1959]. (350). 2 vols. Cl., boxed. (SG. Jan.22; 170) $130
- Bibliotheca Chemica: a Catalogue of the Alchemical. Chemical & Pharmaceutical Books in the Collection of the Late James Young. Glasgow, 1906. [1st Edn.?]. 2 vols. 4to. Orig. mor.-bkd. cl., slightly stained, unc. From Honeyman Collection. (S. May 20; 3231) *Goldschmidt.* £90
- - Anr. Copy. Orig. cl., unc., partly unopened, bkplt. (S. Oct.21; 489) *Ribi.* £70
- - Anr. Edn. 1954. Reprint of 1906 edn. 2 vols. Cl. (S. Feb.23; 338) *Dawson.* £75
- Chemisch-Pharmazeutisches Bio- und Bibliographikon. Glasgow, 1906. Orig. Edn. 2 vols. 4to. Buckram, unc. (SG. Jan.22; 169) $375

FERGUSON, John Alexander
- Bibliography of Australia. Sydney &c. 1951-69. Vols. 1 & 2 reprinted, Vols. 3-7 in orig. edn. 7 vols. Cl. or buckram, d.-w.'s., some bds. slightly damp-spotted. (KH. Nov.18; 242) *Aus.* £230
- - Anr. Edn. Canberra. 1975-77. Facs. Edn. 7 vols. Orig. bdg., d.-w. (JL. Jul.20; 761) *Aus.* $170

FERGUSON, Robert
[-] A Just & Modest Vindication of the Scots Design. [Edinb.], 1699. 1st. Edn. Some browning. Cont. sheep. [Wing F742] (S. Feb.9; 136) *Campbell.* £70

FERGUSSON, James
- Illustrations of the Rock-Cut Temples of India. Ill.:- T.C. Dibdin. 1845. Atlas fo. Loose in orig. hf. mor. cover, ex-liby. (SG. Oct.30; 151) $140

FERGUSSON, Robert
- Poems. Edinb., 1773. Slim rebnd. panel. cf. gt. (CE. Nov.20; 182) £90

FERMIN, Philippe
- Reise durch Surinam aus dem Franzosischen ubersetzt. Potsdam, 1782. 2 vols. in 1. Cont. hf. cf., sm. tear in head of spine. [Sabin 21420] (S. Jun.29; 180) *Lange & Springer.* £60

FERNANDEZ DE NAVARRETE, Domingo
- Tratados Historicos, Politicos, Ethicos, y Religiosos de la Monarchia de la China. Madrid, 1676, 1st. Edn. Fo. Title cropped, slightly defect. & mnt., spotted, soiled & in places dampstained, cut very short affecting headlines, side-notes, sigs. & a few last lines, last 20 ll. & 2 others defect. affecting text. Old limp vell. (S. Jan.27; 403) *Pereza.* £55

FERNANDEZ DE OVIEDO Y VALDES, Captain Gonzalo
- Historia General y natural de las Indias, Islas y Tierra-Firme del Mar Océano. Madrid, 1851-55. 1st. Compl. Edn. 4 vols. 4to. Wanting pp. 169-176 in vol. IV, pp. 161-168 present in dupl. Some orig. wraps. preserved, 19th. C. hf. cf., unc. W.a.f. [Sabin 57990] (S. Nov.4; 649) *Fleming.* £240

FERNANDEZ DE PALENCIA, Diego
- La Segunda Parte de la Historia del Peru. Seville, 1571. Fo. Woodcut initials, title, errata lf. & several ll. of text supplied from a shorter copy, 1 lf. with censored portion replaced from anr. copy, a few tears affecting text, errata lf. cropped, some stains. Limp vell. [Sabin 24133] (SPB. May 5; 213) $250

FERNANDEZ DE URIBE, Jose Patricio
- Sermon de Nuestra Senora de Guadalupe de Mexico, predicado en su Santuario el ano de 1777. Mexico, [1801]. Spanish cf. (SG. Jan.8; 288) $100

FERNE, John
- The Blazon of Gentrie ... 1586. 1st. Edn. Sm. 4to. The 2 ll. of genealogical tree slightly stained & reprd. Cont. vell., restored in the 19th. C. Owner's inscr. of Francis Doyle, later Thornhill armorial stp., lately in the collection of Eric Sexton. [STC 10824] (C. Apr.15; 176) *Heraldry Today.* £110

FERNELIUS or Fernel, Joannes or Jean
- De Naturali Parte Medicinae Libri Septem. Paris, 1542. 1st. Edn. Fo. Some stains, upr. outer corners of title & following ll. wormed & torn, last 4 ll. supplied from anr. copy, sm. hole in E3, many early MS. notes. Limp vell. 2 MS. ll. on vell., of

Lives of the Saints England, 14th. C., as end-ll. (S. Jun.15; 274) *Norman.* £700

FERRANDIS, Jose
- Marfiles Arabes de Occidente. Madrid, 1935-40. 2 vols. 4to. Orig. paper wraps. (TA. Mar.19; 132) £85

FERRARI, Giovanni Battista
- De Florvm Cvltvra Libri IV. Rome, 1633. 1st. Edn. 4to. Slightly browned in parts & soiled. Cont. vell. (H. Dec.9/10; 376) DM 600
- Flora, Overo Cultura di Fiori. Trans.:- L.A. Perugino. Rome, 1638. 1st. Edn. in Italian. 4to. Lr. margin of engraved title reprd., some plts, slightly stained. Cont. vell. From Chetham's Liby., Manchester. (C. Nov.26; 160) *Broseghini.* £350
- Flora, seu de Florum Cultura. Amst., 1646. New Edn. Vol. IV. 4to. A few sigs. wormed at inner edge slightly affecting text & plts. 18th. C. tree cf., gt. (S. Jun.1; 114) *Goldschmidt.* £260
- Hesperides. Ill.:- C. Bloemaerts after N. Poussin & others. Rome, 1646. Fo. Frontis. slightly soiled, very occasional sm. marginal tears. 19th. C. hf. mor. From Chetham's Liby., Manchester. (C. Nov.26; 161) *Antiqua Libri.* £950

FERRARI, Oreste & Scavizzi, G.
- Luca Giordano. Naples, 1966. 3 vols. Publisher's bdg. in box. (CR. Mar.19; 71) Lire 380,000

FERRARI, Filippo
- Raccolta di Costume della Stato Romano. 1826. 4to. Hf.cf. gt. (P. Jul.2; 54) £150

FERRARIO, Guilo
- Il Costume Antico e Moderne. Milan, 1817-27. 1st. Italian Edn., No. 329 of Subscription Edn. Together 12 vols. Fo. 7 vols. in orig. bds. (1 spine detchd. & loosely inserted), 1 vol. in cont. bds. (lacks spine), 1 vol. in cont. hf. cf. (worn), 3 vols. disbnd., all except 1 vol. unc. As a collection, w.a.f.; sigd. on each hf.-title (except America vol. II which is from the Fr. edn.). (S. Oct.21; 512) *Lockwood.* £1,350
- - Anr. Copy. (S. Jun.23; 323) *Faurre.* £1,000
- - Anr. Edn. Flor., 1823-37. 34 vols. Hf.-title. Cont. hf. cf. cf. (SI. Dec.3; 215) Lire 2,200,000
- - Anr. Edn. Ed.:- A. Levati & L. Bossi. Mailand, 1824. Orig. Edn. Fo. Lacks 2 aquatint plts. Cont. interim bds., lacks spine, unc. (R. Oct.14-18; 2074) DM 3,400
- Monumenti Sacri e Profani dell 'Imperiale e Reale Basilica di Sant' Ambrogio in Milano. Milan, 1825. 4to. Cont. hf. cf. (SI. Dec.3; 216) Lire 550,000
- Storia ed Analisi degli Antichi Romanzi di Cavalleria e dei Poemi Romanzeschi d'Italia. Milan, 1828-29. 4 vols. Cont. hf. mor., unc. (SI. Dec.3; 217) Lire 260,000

FERRARIS, Lieut. Gen., Comte de
- Carte Chorographique des Pays-Bas Autrichiens. N.p., n.d. 25 ll. mntd. on cl. 5 boxes, old hf. roan. (LM. Mar.21; 108) B.Frs. 85,000

FERRERAS, Jean de
See-BARRE, P.-FERRERAS, Jean de

FERRERIO, Pietro
- Palazzi di Roma di piu celebri Architetti. [Rome], [1655]. 2 vols. in 1. Ob. fo. 103 engraved plts. (of 105), including titles. Cont. cf., worn. (S. Jun.22; 121) *Gal 539.* £380

FERRETTUS, Nicolaus
- De Elegantiae Linguae Latinae Servanda in Epistolis. Forli, Hieronymus Medesanus, May 25, 1495. 4to. Reprd. tear to lr. margin of fo. 1, sm. portion at upr. corner of last lf. renewed, some slight marginal repairs. Red mor. gt., arms of Victor Massena, Prince d'Essling on covers, spine gt. with monogs., by Lortic. From the collection of Eric Sexton. [BMC VII, 1121, Goff G99, H 6974*=6975] (CNY. Apr.8; 67) $4,000

FERREY, Benjamin
- Recollections of A.N. Welby Pugin & his father, Augustus Pugin; with notices of their works. L., 1861. Plts. slightly soiled. Orig. cl. (CB. May 27; 172) Can. $110

FERRIAR, John
- Medical Histories & Reflections. 1810-13. 2nd. Edn. 4 vols. Hf. cf. (S. Jun.15; 277) *Zeitlin & Verbrugge.* £80

FERRIER, Sir David
- The Croonian Lectures on Cerebral Localisation. 1890. 1st. Edn. Orig. cl. (S. Jun.15; 279) *Whitehart.* £110

- The Functions of the Brain. 1876. 1st. Edn. Liby. stp. of Girton College. Orig. cl. (S. Jun.15; 278) *Rota.* £280
- The Localisation of Cerebral Disease being the Gulstonian Lectures.-On Tabes Dorsalis, the Lumleian Lectures.-The Functions of the Brain. 1878; 1906; 1886. Vols. 1 & 2 1st. Edns., 3rd. vol. 2nd. Edn. 3 vols. Orig. cl., 1st. vol. ex-liby. (S. Jun.15; 281) *Canale.* £140

FERRIER, J.P.
- Caravan Journeys & Wanderings in Persia, Afghanistan, Turkistan & Beloochistan. 1856. Folding map mntd. on linen. Mod. cf.-bkd. cl. (SH. Nov.7; 346) *Hosain.* £110
- - Anr. Edn. 1857; 1858. 2nd. Edn.; 1st. Edn. 2 vols. Cont. cf.; cont. hf. cf. (SH. Mar.5; 55) *Ad Orientem.* £140

FERRIS, Hugh
- The Metropolis of Tomorrow. N.Y., 1929. 1st. Edn. 4to. Buckram, slightly worn. (SG. Dec.4; 140) $150

FERUS, Johann
See-WILD or Ferus, Johann

FESTEGGIAMENTO per S.I. Maesta Francesco ... nella Basilica di S. Antonio
Ill.:- A. Buttafoco (vig.) & S. Manire (port.). Padua, 1798. Thick paper. 4to. Orig. ptd. paper bds. From the collection of John A. Saks. (C. Jun.10; 70) *King.* £120

FETES Publiques données par la Ville de Paris à l'Occasion du Mariage de Monseigneur le Dauphin ...
Ill.:- Eisen (frontis.); Charles Hutin, Cochin Père & Fils. Paris, 1745. Lge. fo. Cont. hf. cf., corners, spine with plain raised bands & roses. (HD. Jun.29; 42) Frs. 1,750

FEUERBACH, L.
- Geschichte der neuern Philosophie von Bacon bis Benedict Spinoza. Ansbach, 1833. 1st. Edn. Slightly soiled in parts. Cont. linen. (HK. May 15; 4208) DM 600

FEUILLEE, Louis
- Beschreibung zur Arzney Dienlicher Pflanzen ... in Peru und Chili. Ill.:- J.M. Seligmann. Nuremb., 1766. 2 vols. 4to. 100 hand-cold. engraved plts., & 2 plain plts. 19th. C. hf. roan, worn. From Chetham's Liby., Manchester. (C. Nov.26; 162) *Marshall.* £1,000

FEUILLET, Octave
- Julia de Trécoeur. Ill.:- after Henriot. Paris, 1878. (50) on Papier du Japon. Three-qtr. Bradel mor., limp mosaic spine, unc., wrap. preserved by Bretault. (HD. Apr.24; 141) Frs. 1,700
- - Anr. Edn. Ill.:- F. Clapes after Emile Henriot. Paris, 1885. (225) numbered on Marais Velin à la Cuve, with etchings in 2 states. Etchings in 2 states. Crushed lev., triple. fillet borders, spine gt., with fleurons, gt. dentelles, by Chambolle-Duru, orig. wraps bnd. in. (SG. Sep.4; 182) $275
- - Anr. Copy. (SG. Apr.9; 174) $120
- Le Village. [Paris], 1901. (43). Ills. in 2 states. Crushed mor., crimson mor. doubls. stpd. in gt. & black, silk & marb. end-papers, orig. wraps. bnd. in, s.-c. (SPB. Jul.28; 33) $100

FEUILLET, [Raoul Auger] & Essex, John
- For the Further Improvement of Dancing, a Treatise of Chorography or ye Art of Dancing Country Dances after a New Character ... 1710. 16mo. Light dampstain in some inner margins. Slightly later hf. cf. (S. Dec.9; 448) *Quaritch.* £450

FEULNER, Adolf
- Frankfurter Fayencen. Berlin, 1935. Fo. Orig. linen; soiled. (HK. May 12-14; 2379) DM 1,200

FEYDEAU, Ernest
- Fanny. Ill.:- Paul Avril. Paris, 1858. (100) numbered. 30 orig. watercolours in margins. Mor. by Noulhac, silk doubls., wrap. preserved, s.-c. Bkplt. of H. de Grandjean. (SM. Feb.11; 215) Frs. 50,000

FEYJOO Y MONTENEGRO, B. G.
- Theatro Critico Universal. 1751-60. 15 vols. Cont. limp vell. (P. Apr.9; 13) *De Metzy.* £110

FIALA, Eduard
- Muenzen und Medaillen der Welfischen Lande. Prag, 1904-17. 9 vols., & 3 dupls. 4to. Gt.-decor. cl., 2 vols. in ptd. wraps. (SG. Dec.18; 318) $450

FIALETTI, Odoardo
- **Habiti delle Religioni.** Venice, 1626. 4to. Some plts. soiled. 18th. C. vell. (SH. Jun.11; 135)
Duran. £60
- - **Anr. Edn.** Paris, 1658. Sm. 4to. Slightly soiled in parts. 19th. C. cf., worn & soiled. (H. Dec.9/10; 765)
DM 600

FIASCHI, Cesare
- **Trottato dell'Imbrigliare, Maneggiare, et Ferrare Cavalli.** Bologna, 1556. 4to. Stain on title, fo. A4 & fo. A2 misbnd. Mod. leath. (SI. Dec.3; 221)
Lire 440,000

FICHTE, Johann Gottlieb
- **Grundlage des Naturrechts nach Principien der Wissenschaftslehre.** Jena & Leipzig, 1796-97. 1st. Edn. 2 pts. in 1 vol. Later hf. leath. (D. Dec.11-13; 2555)
DM 450
- **Reden an die Deutsche Nation.** Berlin, 1808. 1st. Edn. Title & a few ll. slightly spotted. Cont. hf. cf., spine slightly worn. (S. Jun.29; 351)
Quaritch. £160
- - **Anr. Copy.** Cont. style old hf. vell. (HK. May 15; 4213)
DM 1,200
- - **Anr. Copy.** Some light browning. Cont. hf. leath. (H. Dec.9/10; 1473)
DM 840
- **Sämmtliche Werke.** J.H. Fichte. Berlin, 1845-46. 1st. Coll. Edn. 8 vols. Lightly browned, soiled in parts. Cont. hf. leath., worn, 2 covers defect. (H. Dec.9/10; 1472)
DM 1,100

FICINO or Ficinus, Marsilio
- **De Triplici Vita.** 16 Sep. 1506. Sm. 4to. A little dampstaining. 19th. C. bds., soiled. From liby. of André L. Simon. (S. May 18; 94) *Facchi.* £110
- **Tomo Primo [& Tomo Secundo] delle Divine Lettere.** Trans.:– M. Felice Figlivccii Senese. Venice, 1549 & 1548. 2 vols. in 1. 16mo. Some worming affecting 1st. 20 ll. & last 4 ll., a few other wormholes but in preliminary margins, some yellowing on prelims. Cont. vell. (VA. Aug.29; 63)
R. 120

FICKE, Arthur Davison
- **The Happy Princess.** Boston, 1907. 1st. Edn. 12mo. Cl. Inscr. to Witter Bynner, with Bynner's bkplt. & 2-pp. criticism written by Bynner. (SG. Jun.4; 176)
$200
- **Sonnets of a Portrait-Painter.** N.Y., 1922. 1st. Edn. 12mo. Cl. Inscr. to Witter Bynner, & 10-line MS. poem on fly-lf., Bynner's bkplt. (SG. Jun.4; 177)
$150

FICKE, Arthur & Metcalf, Tom
- **Their Book.** [1901]. (50). Pict. cl. Sigd. by Metcalf, Witter Bynner's bkplt. (SG. Jun.4; 179)
$170

FIELD, C. & Blumberg, H. D.
- **Britain's Sea-Soldiers. A History of the Royal Marines.** 1924-27. 3 vols. 4to. Orig. cl. (SH. Jun.4; 78)
Maggs. £75

FIELD, Eugene
- **Works.–Florence Bardsley's Story.** N.Y.; Chic., 1900-01; 1897. (175) (2nd. work). 17 vols.; 1 vol. Extra-ill. with plts. & letters, includes the sigd. pamphlet 'Dibdin's Ghost' by Field. Lev. mor. gt., orig. watercolour doubls. by Nicht, Matthews & Raymond. (SPB. May 6; 304)
$4,250
- **Writings in Prose & Verse.** N.Y., 1896. 10 vols. Hf. mor. (SPB. Nov.25; 453)
$150

FIELD of Mars
1781. 2 vols. 4to. Engraved plts. slightly browned. Cont. cf., rebkd. (SH. Jun.4; 116) *Shapero.* £130
- - **Anr. Edn.** 1810. 2 vols. 4to. Cont. hf. cf., worn. (TA. Feb.19; 545)
£60

FIELD, W.B. Osgood
- **Edward Lear on my Shelves.** N.Y., 1933. (155). Fo. Orig. linen-bkd. bds., unc., s.-c. (SH. Dec. 10; 173)
Joseph. £280

FIELDING, Henry
- **Amelia.** 1752. 1st. Edn. 4 vols. Advt. lf. in vol. 2, lacks blank ll. Cont. cf., new labels. (S. Nov.25; 477)
Quaritch. £160
- - **Anr. Copy.** 12mo. Occasional slight soiling. (CSK. Sep.26; 107)
£130
- **An Enquiry into the Causes of the Late Increase of Robbers, & c.** 1751. 1st. Edn. Mod. mott. hf. cf., spine gt., by Sangorski & Sutcliffe. (S. Feb.9; 137)
Traylen. £150
[–] **Joseph Andrews.** 1742. 1st. Edn. 2 vols. 12mo. Slight browning, publisher's advts. at beginning of vol. 2 & at end of each vol. Mod. mott. cf., gt., by Rivière? (S. Feb.10; 440)
Maggs. £130

- **Joseph Andrews.–Tom Jones.–Amelia.** L., 1742; 1749; 1752. 1st. Edns. 2 vols.; 6 vols.; 4 vols. 12mo. Some ll. browned. All cont. cf. gt., upr. cover of vol. 1 of 1st. work detchd., unif. qtr. mor. gt. s.-c.'s. Cont. bkplts. of Ambrose Isted, lately in the Prescott Collection. (CNY. Feb.6; 110)
$2,800
- **The Journal of a Voyage to Lisbon.** 1755. 1st. Edn. 12mo. Some slight browning. Cont. cf. Bkplt. of John Harvey. (S. Feb.9; 138)
Waterfield. £120
- - **Anr. Copy.** Later cf., rebkd. (SH. Mar.5; 56)
Scott. £55
- **Miscellanies.** 1743. 1st. Edn., L.P. 3 vols. Cont. cf., gt., rebkd., orig. spines preserved. (S. Jun.23; 402)
Quaritch. £200
- - **Anr. Edn.** 1743. 3 vols. Lacks the 2nd. title, A2 in vol. I. Cont. cf., rebkd. preserving orig. spine, upr. jnt. in 1st. vol. brkn., in buckram s.-c. From the collection of Eric Sexton. (C. Apr.15; 96)
O'Hern. £120
- **Oeuvres Diverses.** Reims, 1784. 16 vols. 18mo. Red mor., spines decor., 3 gt. fillets on covers, inner dentelle, by Cazin. From the Werlé liby. (HD. Apr.8; 243)
Frs. 5,600
- - **Anr. Copy.** 18 vols. Cont. marb. roan, spines decor. with gt. fillets, by Cazin, some defects. (HD. Apr.8; 244)
Frs. 1,200
[–] **Tom Jones.** 1749. 1st. Edn. 6 vols. 12mo. Cancels as listed by Rothschild. Cont. cf., worn, rebkd. preserving orig. spine, vol. IV not unif., in mor.-bkd. s.-c.'s. (C. Nov.20; 242)
Jamieson. £380
- - **Anr. Copy.** A few ll. soiled or stained. Cont. mott. cf., rebkd. & reprd. (S. Jan.26; 129)
Swales. £280
- - **Anr. Copy.** Cancels as listed by Rothschild, with the addition of N12 in vol. 2 & B1 in vol. 4, title & some following ll. in vol. 3 wormed near outer edges, several ll. in vol. 1 stained from upr. outer corners, vol. 5 stained thro.-out from upr. edges. Cont. spr. cf., gt., some wear. (S. Feb.10; 441)
Waterfield. £150
- - **Anr. Copy.** Some browning, in vol. III the cancels, H8, H9, & H10 have been correctly inserted, lr. free end-paper on vols. I & III loose. Cont. cf. Stockhausen copy, bkplts. of Herbert L. Carlebach & Hannah D. Rabinowitz. (SPB. Nov.25; 160)
$2,600
- - **Anr. Copy.** (SG. May 14; 74)
$550
- - **Anr. Edn.** L., 1749. 1st. Edn., 2nd. Iss. 6 vols. 12mo. Old pol. cf., gt., rebkd., worn, 2 hinges brkn. (SG. Sep.25; 135)
$220
- **Works.** 1783. New Edn. 12 vols. Cont. marb. cf., rebkd. (CSK. Oct.24; 2)
£55
- - **Anr. Edn.** 1806. 10 vols. Cont. cf. (SH. Mar.5; 232)
Booth. £55
- - **Anr. Edn.** Ed.:– Arthur Murphy. L., 1821. 10 vols. Mor. (SSA. Apr.22; 25)
R. 170
- - **Anr. Edn.** 1871-72. 11 vols. Hf. mor. gt. by Morrell. (C. Jul.22; 13)
Taylor. £180
- - **Anr. Edn.** L., 1882. (1,250). 20 vols. Some spotting, stains. Cranberry mor. gt. by the Monastery Hill Bindery. (SPB. May 6; 305)
$750
- - **Anr. Edn.** 1903. 12 vols. Cont. hf. mor. (CSK. Jan.14; 144)
£55
- - **Anr. Edn.** Oxford, Shakes. Head Pr., 1926. (1030). 10 vols. Orig. cl. (PG. Sep.3; 131)
£75
See–BROMHALL, Thomas–FIELDING, Henry

FIELDING, Henry–GODDEN, G.M.
- **Works.–A Memoir.** N.Y.; L., [1902]; 1910. 1st. work Drury Lane Edn., (285). 16 vols; 2 vols. Extra-ill. with plts. Unif. mor. gt., watered silk end-papers. (SPB. May 6; 306)
$950

FIELDING, Mantle
See–MORGAN, John Hill & Fielding, Mantle

FIELDING, Sarah
- **Familiar Letters.** 1747. 2 vols. Cf. gt. (P. Dec.11; 316)
Georges. £180

FIELDING, Theodore Henry
- **British Castles.** 1825. Ob. 4to. Plts. cold., some slight foxing, mainly affecting title & text. Cont. hf. mor. Bkplt. of Boies Penrose, lately in the collection of Eric Sexton. (C. Apr.16; 256)
Hollander. £220
- **Cumberland, Westmoreland & Lancashire Illustrated.** 1822. L.P. Fo. Cont. red mor. on wooden bds., sides gt. panel., elab. tooled, mor. doubls., central panel elab. gt. in gt. borders. (C. Mar.18; 40)
Spencer. £850
- - **Anr. Copy.** Mod. hf. str.-grd. mor., unc. (S. Sep.29; 154)
Franks. £400

- - **Anr. Copy.** 34 plts. (of 44), some loosely inserted. Cont. cf., worn. W.a.f. (TA. Aug.21; 297)
£200
- **English Landscape Scenery.** Ill.:– after Benjamin Barker. Bath, 1843. Ob. fo. 47 (of 48) aquatint plts. Cont. maroon hf. mor. gt. (S. Mar.17; 380)
Broseghini. £200
- - **Anr. Copy.** Cont. hf. mor., covers affected by damp. (S. Sep.29; 135)
Marsden. £160
- **Paintings in Oil & Water Colours.** 1839. 4to. Some spotting. Bds. (P. Apr.9; 262)
Fogg. £50
- **A Picturesque Description of the River Wye.** 1841. 4to. Aquatint views hand-cold. Orig. gt.-lettered ribbed cl. From the collection of Eric Sexton. (C. Apr.16; 257)
Crowe. £380
- - **Anr. Copy.** Orig. cl., title in gt. on upr. cover. (S. Nov.4; 538)
Hines. £240

FIELDING, Theodore Henry & Walton, J.
- **A Picturesque Tour of the English Lakes.** 1821. 4to. Title ill. & all plts. hand-cold. Cont. str.-grd. red mor., covers with double fillet diamond-shaped ornamentation. From the collection of Eric Sexton. (C. Apr.16; 255)
Traylen. £380
- - **Anr. Copy.** Some minor defects. Cont. hf. cf. (SBA. May 27; 362) *Hyde Park Bookshop.* £200
- - **Anr. Edn.** 1821. L.P. 4to. Slight stain on title, a few other minor defects. Cont. bds., rebkd., slightly soiled & worn, unc. (SBA. Mar.4; 106)
Dauncey. £440

FIELDS, Annie
See–STOWE, Harriet Beecher–FIELDS, Annie

FIFE
See–ALDIN, Cecil–FIFE

FIFTY PICTURESQUE VIEWS of the Seats of the Nobility & Gentry
Ill.:– Heath, Walker, etc. Ca. 1810. 4to. Cont. mor., worn. (TA. Jan.22; 405)
£55

FIGDOR, Alfred
- **Die Sammlung Figdor Wien.** Vienna & Berlin, 1930. Lge. 4to. Orig. bdg. (HK. Nov.18-21; 3390)
DM 440

FIGGES, John
See–KOYAMA, Fujio & Figges, John

FIGGIS, Darrell
- **The Paintings of William Blake.** 1925. (1150). 4to. Orig. buckram-bkd. bds., d.-w., worn. (SH. Mar.26; 93)
Fogg. £50

FIGUEIRA, Luiz
- **Arte de Grammatica da Lingua do Brasil.** Lisbon, 1795. Cf.-bkd. bds. (SPB. May 5; 215)
$350

FILHEUL
- **Catalogue des Livres Rares et Singuliers.** Paris, 1779. Priced in ink, some prices supplied by F. Lachèvre. Cont. red hf. mor., spine gt. in compartments with lyre & corner sprays. (SM. Oct.7; 1376)
Frs. 1,800

FILHOL, Antoine Michel
- **Galérie du Musée Napoléon.** Ed.:– Joseph Lavallée. 1804-1815. 10 vols. Lge. 8vo. Some foxing. Cont. tree roan, roll-stp. & gt. garland around covers, smooth decor. spines. (HD. Feb.27; 129)
Frs. 2,650
- - **Anr. Copy.** Cont. leath. gt. (R. Oct.14-18; 2657)
DM 4,000
- - **Anr. Edn.** Ed.:– Joseph Lavallée. Paris, 1820-1810. 10 vols. Cont. red str.-grd. mor. gt., alternate foliate gt. & blind-tooled borders, lge. Imperial Eagle & arms on both covers & in compartments on spines. (C. Feb.4; 61)
Elstein. £850

FILIPOWSKI, Herschel Zvi
- **Sefer He'asif.** L., 1847. 12mo. Some sigs. sprung. Wraps. (SPB. May 11; 108)
$150

FILIPPI, Filippo de
- **Karakoram & Western Himalaya.** 1912. 2 vols. 4to. 17 (of 18) panoramas. Orig. vell.-bkd. cl. gt., slightly soiled. (SBA. May 27; 289) *Jones.* £145
- - **Anr. Copy.** Parch-bkd. cl. (LC. Oct.2; 135)
£58

FILISOLA, Vincente
- **Memorias para la Historia de la Guerra de Tejas.** Mexico City, 1849. 2 vols. Orig. gt. cf.-bkd. bds., upr. hinge of vol. I neatly reprd. The Streeter copy, with many annots. in his hand. (PNY. Mar.26; 120)
$425

FILLINGERUS, C.
See–WOLFIUS, H. & Fillingerus, C.

FILMER, Sir Robert
- The Free-Holders Grand Inquest.–Patriarcha. 1680. 2 works in 1 vol. Perforation to 1st. title, some other minor defects. Cont. panel. cf., worn. [Wing F915 & F922] (SBA. May 27; 44a) *Stewart*. £80

FILSON, John
- The Discovery, Settlement & Present State of Kentucke: & an Essay Towards the Topography, & Natural History of That Important Country . . . Wilmington, 1784. 1st. Edn. Port. of Daniel Boone inserted, slight browning, stp. of Newberry liby. on title, also their bkplt. on upr. pastedown. Mod. mor., gt. blind-stpd. panels & spines. From liby. of William E. Wilson. (SPB. Apr.29; 100) $3,500

FINAEUS
*See–*FINE or FINÉ, Oronce

FINAUGHTY, W.
- The Recollections of William Finaughty, Elephant Hunter 1864-75. Phila., 1916. (250). Orig. cl. (SSA. Jan.22; 236) R. 330

FINBERG, Alexander J.
- The History of Turner's Liber Studiorum. L., 1924. (650) numbered, & sigd. 4to. Buckram, d.-w. (worn). (SG. Mar.12; 371) $130

FINCHAM, John
- A History of Naval Architecture. 1851. Lge. 8vo. Occasional slight spotting. Orig. cl. (CSK. Oct.17; 25) £60

FINCHAM, Henry W.
- Artists & Engravers of British & American Bookplates. 1897. (50) numbered., sigd. 4to. Orig. vell.-bkd. bds., worn. (SH. Jun.4; 158) *Forster*. £55

FINDEN, Edward Francis
- Illustrations of the Life & Works of Lord Byron. L., 1833. Lge. 8vo. Plts. only, lacks title-p. & 4 (?) plts. Cont. hf. leath., gt. (R. Oct.14-18; 1915) DM 650
– – **Anr. Edn.** 1833-34. [1st. Edn?]. 4to. A few ll. slightly spotted. Cont. cf., slightly soiled. L.P. (SBA. Jul.14; 134) *Dimakarkos*. £130
– – **Anr. Copy.** Occasional spotting. Cont. str.-grd. cf., gt. (CSK. Jan.30; 79) £100
– – **Anr. Copy.** Slight spotting. Cont. hf. mor. (SBA. Oct.21; 39) *Stavridus*. £70
– – **Anr. Copy.** 4to. Foxed. Cont. mor. gt. (SPB. May 29; 152) $150
– – **Anr. Edn.** Ed.:– W. Brockedon. [1837]. New Edn. 2 vols. 4to. Cont. hf. mor., spines gt. (S. Nov.25; 514) *Erlini*. £65

FINDEN, Edward Francis & William
- The Ports & Harbours of Great Britain. 1836-38. 2 vols. in 1. 4to. Cont. cl. (SH. May 21; 39) *Kidd*. £180
– – **Anr. Edn.** L., 1838. Vol. 1 only. Vig. title, 49 engraved plts. Qtr. mor. gt. (P. Jul.2; 49) *Kidd*. £80
– – **Anr. Edn.** Ca. 1840. 2 vols. 4to. Hf. mor. gt. (P. May 14; 352) *Donovan*. £230
– – **Anr. Edn.** Ill.:– After William Henry Bartlett. 1842. 2 vols. 4to. 123 plts. of 124, spotting. Cont. hf. cf., worn. (CSK. Oct.24; 71) £240
– – **Anr. Copy.** Some ll. spotted. Cont. hf. cf. gt. (SBA. May 27; 291) *Salinas*. £220
– – **Anr. Copy.** In 6 orig. pts. 120 (of 123) plts., some ll. spotted, loose. Orig. mor.-bkd. bds., slightly soiled. (SBA. May 27; 290) *Hulme*. £190
– – **Anr. Copy.** Lacks 1 plt., some ll. slightly spotted. Cont. hf. cf. (SH. Nov.6; 69) *Kidd*. £140
– – **Anr. Copy.** 4to. Some foxing. Hf. mor. gt. (SPB. May 29; 153) $300
– – **Anr. Edn.** Ill.:– after W.H. Bartlett. Ca. 1850. 2 vols. 4to. Slight dampstaining. Cont. hf. cf. Bkplt. of Rev. G. Williams. (S. Jun.22; 175) *Burden*. £180
– – **Anr. Edn.** Ill.:– after W.H. Bartlett. 1862. 2 vols. Mor. (HSS. Apr.24; 278) £190
– – **Anr. Edn.** Ill.:– After W.H. Bartlett. [1884]. 2 vols. in 1. 4to. 122 (of 124?) plts., slight spotting, lacks final text lf? Orig. cl. gt. (SBA. Oct.22; 267) *Hulse*. £300
– – **Anr. Edn.** N.d. 2 vols. in 1. Slight spotting. Hf. mor. gt. (P. Apr.30; 276) *Kentish*. £230
– – **Anr. Copy.** 2 vols. Some ll. spotted. Orig. cl., worn, vol. I loose. (SH. Nov.6; 72) *Wallis-Clark*. £110
- Views of the Ports & Harbours . . . & other Picturesque Objects on the English Coast. Ill.:– After J.D. Harding, G. Balmer & others, E. & W. Cooke. 1838. 1st. Edn. 4to. Extra-ill. with 2

engraved naval plts. by E. & W. Cooke, 10 sm. ills. tipped in, a few detchd., additional title & 1st. 4 plts. stained, several plts. stained in fore-edges, occasional spotting. Cont. hf. roan, worn. (S. Nov.4; 495) *Kidd*. £100
– – **Anr. Edn.** 1839. 2 vols. in 1. 4to. 84 plts. (of 123), some staining. Hf. cf. qt. (P. Feb.19; 50) *MacDonnell*. £250
- Royal Gallery of British Art 1839-51. Elephant 4to. Some engrs. heavily stained. Orig. mor. gt. (TA. Sep.18; 131) £115
– – **Anr. Edn.** Ca. 1850. Eelephant fo. Subscribers sigs. Hf. mor., worn. (CE. Apr.23; 131) £70

FINDEN, Edward & William & Horne, T.H.
- Landscape Illustrations of the Bible. 1836. 2 vols. 4to. A few ll. slightly spotted. Cont. hf. mor. (SH. Nov.7; 410) *Nador*. £105
– – **Anr. Copy.** (CSK. Sep.12; 214) £50
– – **Anr. Copy.** Staining, cont. gt. decor. mor., head of spine defect. (PNY. Mar.26; 149) $100
– – **Anr. Copy.** (R. Mar.31–Apr.4; 2529) DM 480

FINE or FINÉ, Oronce
- De Arithmetica Practica libri quatuor. Paris, 1555. 4to. Light foxing. Paper wraps. (C. Apr.1; 32) *Vernon*. £50
- Arithmetica Practica.–De Mundi Sphaera, sive Cosmographia.–Quadratura Circuli, tandem Inventa & Clarissime Demonstrata.–In Sex Priores libros Geometricorum Elementorum Euclidis Megarensis Demonstrationes . . . Trans.:– Bartholomaei Zamberti (4th work). Paris, 1542; 1542; 1544; 1544. 1st. work 3rd. Edn.; 3rd. work 1st. Edn. of this collection; 4th. work 2nd. Fine Edn. 4 works in 1 vol. Fo. 2nd. work lacks *6 (with woodcut of Urania); some worming thro.-out whole vol. (slight but for 1st. few ll.), owners' inscrs. of Joannes Baptista Tettelbarhius & Joh. Knoblock(?). Cont. wooden bds., blind-stpd. pig spine, clasps & catches. Bkplt. of Michael Chasles; from Honeyman Collection. (S. May 20; 3234) *Israel*. £650
- De Rebus Mathematicis, Hactenus Desideratis, libri IIII.–Arithmetica Practica. Ed.:– A. Mizauld (1st. work). Paris, 1556; 1542. 1st. Edn.; 3rd. Edn. 2 works in 1 vol. Fo. Slightly wormed thro.-out affecting text, badly stained at beginning & end, 1st. work with marginal repairs to n3 & t2, 2nd. work with I3 reprd. Cont. limp vell., lacks ties. From Honeyman Collection. (S. May 20; 3236) *Simonin*. £70
- In Sex priores Libros Geometricorum Elementorum Euclidis Megare[n]sis. Trans.:– B. Zamberti. Paris, 1544. 2nd. Edn. Fo. Slightly soiled or stained. Cont. limp vell., loose. (HK. Nov.18-21; 189) DM 700
[–] The Rules & Righte Ample Documentes Touching the Use & Practise of the Common Almanackes which are named Ephemerides . . . Trans.:– Humfrey Baker. [1558]. 1st. Engl. Edn. Title soiled & with 17th. C. owner's inscrs., quire F marginally frayed, marginal repairs to last 2 ll. Mod. panel. cf., gt. [NSTC 10878.5, formerly 21449] (S. Dec.9; 278) *Maggs*. £320
*See–*EUCLID–FINE, Oronce
*See–*REGIOMONTANUS, Joahannes–FINE, Oronce

FINE or Finé, Oronce–APIANUS, Petrus
- De Re & Praxis Geometrica, Libri tres. –Cosmographia, per Gemmam Frisium. Paris; Antw., 1556; 1564. 1st. Edn. 2 works in 1 vol. 4to. Cont. blind-tooled pig. dtd. 1568, 1 (of 2) clasps, this defect., slightly soiled. (HK. Nov.18-21; 190) DM 4,400

FINGESTEN, M.
- 12 Gelegenheitsblätter. [Berlin], [1932]. (50). 4to. Loose in orig. wraps. with cover litho., collector's stp. Dr. Heinrich Stinnes. All ll. sigd. by artist & numbered, artist's sig. & note 'Exemplar No. 1' inside wrap. (H. Dec.9/10; 2061) DM 620

FINLAISON, John
- An Account of some Remarkable Applications of the Electric Fluid. 1843. 1st. Edn. Slightly soiled. Cont. roan-bkd. cl. (SH. Jun.11; 146) *Quaritch*. £50

FINLAYSON, George
- The Mission to Siam & Hue . . . 1826. 1st. Edn. Cont. hf. cf. Bkplt. of Thomas Philip, Earl de Grey. (S. Mar.31; 470) *Foyles*. £70

FINN, Frank
- Indian Sporting Birds. Ill.:– E. Neale & others. 1915. 1st. Edn. Cl. (C. May 20; 205) *Hill*. £65

FINSCH, Otto
- On a collection of Birds from North-Eastern Abyssinia & the Bogos Country. Ca. 1869. Orig. bdg. (P. Nov.13; 196) *Bookroom*. £50

FIORAVANTI, Leonhardus
- Three Exact Pieces. 1652. 4 pts. in 1 vol. Sm. 4to. Some stains. Cont. cf., worn. [Wing F593] (SH. Jun.11; 18) *Fairburn*. £110

FIRBANK, Arthur Ronald
- Odette D'Antrevernes. L., 1905. 1st. Edn. 4to. Gt.-lettered wraps., unc. & unopened. (SG. Nov.13; 205) $130

FIRENZUOLA, Agnolo
- Le Rime. Ed.:– [Lorenzo Scala]. Flor., 1549. 1st. Edn. Red mor., gt., [by Binda, Milano]. [BM, Italian Books 254] (R. Oct.14-18; 60) DM 420

FIRMICIUS MATERNUS, Julius
- Astronomicon [Mathesis] Lib. VIII. per N. Prvckenrvm . . . Uindicati . . . [u.a. Schriften versch. Autoren]. Basel, Mar. 1533. Fo. Lacks pp. 85/86 of 2nd. pt., old MS. notes thro.-out, slightly stained at end. Cont. blind-stpd. leath., lacks ties. (HK. Nov.18-21; 191) DM 1,200

FIRST CRUSADE, The
Trans.:– Somerset De Chair. Ill.:– Clifford Webb. Gold. Cock. Pr., 1945. (500) numbered. Fo. Orig. hf. vell. (CSK. Apr.3; 60) £55
– – **Anr. Copy.** Orig. hf. vell. gt. (SH. Feb.19; 180) *Maggs*. £52

FISCHART, Joachim
- Geschichtklitterung. Ill.:– Br. Goldschmitt. Munich, 1914-15. 2 vols. 4to. With 2nd. series of woodcuts in orig. hf. linen portfo., defect. Orig. pig. [K. Ebert]. (H. Dec.9/10; 1842) DM 800

FISCHBACH, Friedrich
- Ornament of Textile Fabric. N.d. Fo. 158 cold. plts. only (of 160), no text, soiled. Orig. hf. cf., portfo., worn. (SH. Jan.29; 233) *A la Mode*. £105

FISCHER, Johann Leonhard
- Descriptio Anatomica Nervorum Lumbalium Sacralium et Extremitatum Inferiorum. Leipzig, 1791. Fo. 4 plts. by the author in 2 states with descriptive text, short marginal tear in title & following lf. Orig. ptd. wraps., hinges slightly torn. (S. Jun.15; 282) *Maggs*. £140

FISCHER VON ERLACH, Johann Bernard
- Entwurff einer historischer Architectur. Vienna, Priv. ptd., 1721. 5 pts. in 1 vol. Ob. fo. Sm. fo. lf. of directions to binder, some dampstaining, mostly confined to lr. blank margin, plt. III of Book IV extensively reinforced at fold, reprd. & reinforced. Later hf. vell. (SPB. Oct.1; 225) $2,500
– – **Anr. Edn.** Leipzig, Priv. ptd. 1725. 2nd. Edn. 5 pts. in 1 vol. Ob. fo. Title very soiled & defect. & bkd., 2 folding plts. soiled in parts. Cont. leath., defect., upr. cover loose. (R. Mar.31-Apr.4; 857) DM 4,000
*See–*BLUME, K.L. & Fischer von Erlach, Johann B.

FISHER, J.
*See–*BARING-GOULD, Sabine & Fisher, J.

FISHER, James
*See–*SITWELL, Sacheverell & others

FISHER, John, Bp. of Rochester
- Assertiones Lutheranae Confutatio. Venice, 1526. Fo. Lacks final blank, full-p. woodcut on a8 misbnd. with sm. paper fault affecting woodcut, e2 & 5 misbnd. in sig. c, erasure & repair to title. Mor. gt. by Wright, bkplt. (C. Nov.20; 243) *Thomas*. £250
– – **Anr. Copy.** Title ptd. in border of woodcut ornaments, latter slightly defect., inner margins reprd., early owners' inscrs. & a few wormholes, some penmarks & stains, a few ll. at end stained, 1 or 2 ll. discold., lr. fore-corner torn from A3, touching 1 letter. Old vell. (S. May 5; 24) *Thomas*. £85
[–] Episcopi De Veritate Corporis & Sanguinis Christi in Eucharistia . . . Cologne, 1527. 16mo. Early annot. on title. Cont. stpd. pig on bds., 2 metal clasps, very worn, lacks fly-ll., ex-liby. (SG. Sep.25; 136) $260

FISHER, Payne
[–] Marston Moore. 1650. 1st. Edn. Sm. 4to. Title & 1 lf. reprd. in outer corners, stabbed thro.-out in inner margins, some ll. stained in outer corners.

Mod. hf. mor. [Wing F1029] (S. May 5; 310)
K Bks. £50

FISHER, Son & Co.
- County Atlas. 1842-45. Lacks title, some ll. detchd. Hf. mor., covers detchd. (CSK. Nov.7; 214) £55

FISKAL (Sneak)
Ed.:- [G.P. Narusbek]. St. Petersb., 1906. Nos. 1-5. 4to. Unbnd. (SH. Feb.5; 69)
De la Casa. £70

FISKE, John (Ed.)
See-APPLETON'S CYCLOPAEDIA . . .

FISON, Lorimer & Howitt, Alfred William
- Kamilaroi & Kurnai; Group-Marriage & vols. Fo. Hf. mor. (KH. Mar.24; 148a) Melbourne &c., 1880. Unc. in orig. cl., slightly worn. Loosely inserted is W. Baldwin Spencer's copy of pamphlet by J.G. Frazer, with A.L.s. from Frazer to Spencer. (KH. Nov.18; 251) Aus. $200

FISTIANA: or, The Oracle of the Ring
L., 1868. 1st. Edn. 12mo. Orig. gt.-ptd. cl., corners worn. (PNY. May 21; 109) $180

FITCH, W.H.
See-ELWES, Henry John & Fitch, W.H.

FITE, Emerson D. & Freeman, Archibald
- A Book of Old Maps. Camb., 1926. Fo. Gt.-lettered cl., ex liby. (SG. Oct.2; 124) $110

FITTLER, James
- Scotia depicta; or, the antiquities, castles, public buildings . . . of Scotland. Ill.:- After Nattes. 1804. 1st. Edn. Ob. 4to. Stained thro.-out, usually only affecting margins, a few short tears. Cont. red str.-grd. mor., gt. (S. Nov.4; 577) *Green.* £90

FITTON, Elizabeth & Sarah Mary
- Conversations on Botany. 1818. 2nd. Edn. Publisher's catalogue at beginning. Mod. cl.-bkd. bds., unc. (S. Dec.3; 958) *Gregory.* £55

FITZCLARENCE, George Augustus Frederick
- Journal of a Route Across India, Through Egypt, to England. 1819. 1st. Edn. 4to. Some maps & plans with partial colouring, a few margins lightly foxed, tear in fore-margin of 3Q3. Orig. bds., unc. (S. Jun.29; 227) *Scott.* £150
- - Anr. Copy. Occasional foxing, liby. stps. on title, lacks hf.-title. Mod. cf.-bkd. bds. (S. Nov.4; 612) *Reid.* £140

FITZGERALD, Edward
[-] Agamemnon. [Priv. ptd.], [1865]. 1st. Edn. Orig. wraps., folder, s.-c. Autograph corrections by author, Pres. copy. (SH. Dec.18; 159)
Lincoln. £180
- The Downfall & Death of King Oedipus. N.p., [1880]. Ltd. 1st. Edn. for Private Circulation. 2 pts. in 1 vol. Orig. wraps., spine defect., hf. mor. s.-c. Bkplt. of Willis Vickery. (SG. Nov.13; 210) $220
[-] - Anr. Edn. [Guildford], [1880-81]. 1st. Edn. (50). 2 pts. in 1 vol. Mod. hf. mor. (S. Feb.9; 140) *Quaritch.* £60
- Euphranor. [Guildford], [1882]. (50) for Private Circulation. Several passages underlined. Cl.-bkd. bds., hf. mor. s.-c. Bkplt. of Willis Vickery. (SG. Nov.13; 211) $170
- Euphranor.-Agamemnon. L.; n.p., 1855; [1865]. 2nd. Edn. (1st. work). 2 works in 1 vol. 12mo. Special Pres. bdg? of cl.-bkd. marb. bds. Corrections in author's hand, Pres. Copy? from Loder (a bookseller) to DeWitt Miller, with his notes on front paste-down & owner's sig. on rear end-paper. (SG. Nov.13; 209) $500
- Letters & Literary Remains. 1902-03. 7 vols. Cont. hf. cf. (SH. May 28; 40) *Walford.* £70
- Readings in Crabbe: 'Tales of the Hall'. L., 1882. 12mo. With introduction. Cl., worn. Laid in are: postcard in Fr. from author to Aldis Wright (dtd. Mar.14, 1878), letter from Wright, & an A.L.s. from Crabbe to N. Clarke. (SG. Nov.13; 212) $280

FITZGERALD, F.
- Surveys of Nature. 1787. 2 vols. Sm. 4to. Cf. (P. Jul.30; 204) *Weston.* £60

FITZGERALD, Francis Scott
- All the Sad Young Men. N.Y., 1926. 1st. Edn., 1st. Iss. Copyright seal at verso of title. Cl. (PNY. Mar.26; 121) $100
- - Anr. Edn. N.Y., 1926. 1st. Edn. Orig. cl. (C. Feb.4; 278) *Brook.* £50

- - Anr. Copy. D.-w., qtr. mor. s.-c. Pres. copy to J. Stuart Groves. (CNY. May 22; 111) $3,400
- - Anr. Copy. Lacks battered text on pp. 38 & 248. Cl. Sig. of John Jay Johns. (PNY. Oct.1; 218) $140
- The Beautiful & Damned. N.Y., 1922. 1st. Edn. Slight browning, variant title in white with black outlines. Orig. cl., d.-w., repairs with tape to d.-w. (SPB. Nov.25; 273) $400
- The Great Gatsby. N.Y., 1925. 1st. Edn., 1st. Iss. Cl., d.-w., bkplt. (SG. Nov.13; 216) $2,600
- - Anr. Copy. With 'sick in tired' reading on p. 205. Sm. handstp. of John Jay Johns at blank. (PNY. Oct.1; 219) $325
- - Anr. Edn. N.Y., 1934. Light browning. Orig. cl. Pres. copy. (SPB. Nov.25; 275) $2,100
- The Last Tycoon; The Great Gatsby; & Selected Stories. N.Y., 1941. 1st. Edn. With the 'A' on copyright p. Cl., d.-w. (SG. Nov.13; 220) $100
- Safety First. Cincinnati, N.Y. & L., [1916]. 1st. Edn. 4to. Orig. cl.-bkd. pict. bds., qtr. mor. folding case. (CNY. May 22; 106) $2,400
- Taps at Reveille. N.Y., 1935. 1st. Edn., 1st. Iss., with unrevised reading. 12mo. Cl., pict. d.-w. (SG. Jun.4; 182) $170
- Tender Is the Night. N.Y., 1934. 1st. Edn. Orig. cl., qtr. mor. s.-c. Pres. copy to Malcolm Cowley, many pencilled annots. in Cowley's hand. (CNY. May 22; 112) $4,200
- - Anr. Copy. Ptd. wraps., 50×25mm section lacking from upr. cover. Advance or Review Copy. (SG. Nov.13; 218) $1,350
- This Side of Paradise. N.Y., 1920. 1st. Edn. Orig. cl., d.-w., qtr. mor. s.-c. Pres. copy to Harold Davis. (CNY. May 22; 107) $2,400
- - Anr. Copy. 1st. Iss. 12mo. Cl. Inscr. to Kenneth Brightbill. (SG. Jun.4; 181) $1,700
- - Anr. Copy. 1st. Iss. Tear along inner edge of 2 lr. blank ll., slight tear at lr. edge of upr. fly-lf. & next 8 ll. Orig. cl., head of spine slightly frayed. Pres. Copy, to John Jay Johns, & inscr. & sigd. by Johns, with his sm. hand-stp. (PNY. May 21; 189) $825
- - Anr. Edn. L., [1921]. 1st. Engl. Edn., 1st. Printing. Orig. cl., endpapers foxed, qtr. mor. s.-c. (CNY. May 22; 109) $550
- The Vegetable, or from President to Postman. N.Y., 1923. 1st. Edn. Orig. cl., pict. d.-w. designed by John Held, Jr., qtr. mor. s.-c. Inscr. beneath sig. of Ernest Truex. (CNY. May 22; 110) $1,800
- - Anr. Copy. Light browning. Pres. copy. (SPB. Nov.25; 274) $650
- - Anr. Copy. Cl., spine faded. Inscr. by Zelda & F. Scott Fitzgerald(?). (SG. Nov.13; 215) $425

FITZGERALD, Robert D., F.L.S.
- Australian Orchids. Sydney, 1882. [1st. Edn.]. Compl. in 12 orig. pts. Fo. 1 plt. in pt 5, & all plts. in pts. 2 & 3 are uncold., remnants of a sheet of tin-foil adhering to blank verso of 1 plt., some minor foxing & sm. defects. Wraps. (KH. Mar.24; 148) Aus. $2,000
- - Anr. Edn. 1977-79. Lansdowne Edn., (350) numbered, & sigd. by Fitzgerald's Grandson. 2 vols. Fo. Hf. mor. (KH. Mar.24; 148a) Aus. $320

FITZGERALD, S.J. Adair
- The Zankiwank & the Bletherwitch. Ill.:- Arthur Rackham. N.Y., [1896]. 1st. Amer. Edn. Sm. 4to. Cl. gt. Raymond M. Sutton Jr. copy. (SG. May 7; 83) $220

FITZHERBERT, Sir Anthony
- Loffice et Auctority de Iustices de Peace. 1606. Sm. 4to. Piece torn from foot of title, first few ll. stained. Cont. cf., spine worn. [STC 10982] (S. Mar.16; 34) *Thorp.* £55
- The New Natura Brevium. 1652. 1st. Edn. in Engl. Hole in 2R6, with some text loss, slight dampstaining. Early 19th. C. hf. cf. [Wing F1096] (S. Feb.9; 142) *Thorp.* £55

FITZINGER, Leopold Joseph
- Bilder-Atlas zur Wissenschaftlichen-Populären Naturgeschichte d. Amphibien. Vienna, 1860-64. 4 pts. in 3 vols. Fo. Plts. partly browned or slightly soiled. Cont. hf. leath. (HK. Nov.18-21; 517)
DM 4,900

FITZPATRICK, J.P.
- Through Mashonaland with Pick & Pen. Johannesburg, 1892. Cont. mor., title-p. & front end-paper loose. (SSA. Jun.18; 121) R. 120

FITZPATRICK, T.J.
- C.S. Rafinesque: a Sketch of his Life, with Bibliography. 1911. Qtr. buckram. (SG. Jan.22; 336) $110

FITZROY, Capt. Robert & others
- Narrative of the Surveying Voyages of His Majesty's Ships Adventure & Beagle. L., 1839. 1st. Edn. 4 vols. & matching box with maps. Cont. cf., jnts. worn, 1 cover detchd. Sir Robert Peel's bkplt., inscr. on 1st. title 'William Peel [1824-58] from his friend R[obert] F[itzroy] 1839'. (SPB. May 5; 177) $2,300
- - Anr. Copy. Vols. I-III, plus Appendix to vol. II, together 4 vols. Mod. gt. hf. mor. & cl. (PNY. Mar.4; 141) $1,500

FITZSIMONS, V.F.M.
- Snakes of Southern Africa. Cape Town, 1962. 4to. Cl., d.-w., s.-c. (SSA. Nov.5; 163) R. 110

FLACCHIO, Engelbert
- Genealogie de la Très-Illustre, très-ancienne et autrefois Souveraine Maison de la Tour. Brussels, 1709. 1st. Edn. 3 vols. Fo. Cont. vell., very worn & partly loose, ex-liby. (SG. Feb.5; 137) $240

FLACCUS, Aulus
See-JUVENALIS, Decimus Junius & Flaccus, Aulus

FLACCUS, Valerius
- Argonauticon Libri Octo. Ed.:- Aegidius Maserus (commentary). Paris, 1519. Fo. 8 unnumbered pp. Cont. vell. (CR. Mar.19; 279)
Lire 1,100,000

FLACIUS ILLYRICUS, Mathias
- Breves Summae Religionis Iesu Christi, et Antichristi. Magdeburg, 1550. 1st. Edn. 18th. C. red mor., triple gt. fillet, flat spine, longitudinal title, gt., inner gt. dentelles, bkplt. of Girardot de Préford. MacCarthy-Reagh copy. (SM. Oct.7; 1710) Frs. 2,000
- De Sectis, Dissensionibus, Contradictionibus et Confusionibus Doctrinae, Religionis, Scriptorum et Doctorum Pontificiorum. Basle, 1565. 4to. Some old marginalia on 1 lf., 2 liby. stps. on title, 1 repeated on blank verso of last lf., label of Girardot de Préfond, bkplt. of Edward Cane. 18th. C. red mor., triple gt. fillet, spine gt. in compartments, inner gt. dentelles, label of Girardot de Préford, bkplt. of Edward Cone. (SM. Oct.7; 1711)
Frs. 2,500
- Varia Doctorū Piorumque Virorum, de Corrupto Ecclesiae Statu, Poemata. Basle, 1557. Some staining. 18th. C. mor., triple gt. fillet, flat spine gt. in compartments with arabesque, inner gt. dentelles, bkplt. of James Whatman. (SM. Oct.7; 1712) Frs. 2,600

FLACOURT, Etienne de
- Histoire de la Grande Isle Madagascar . . . Paris, 1661. 4to. 1 or 2 short tears & a sig. cut from margin of title. Cont. spr. cf., gt. spine. (S. Oct.20; 87) *Rota.* £180

FLAGS OF THE ARMY OF THE UNITED STATES Carried during the War of the Rebellion, 1861-1865 . . . Compiled by the Quartermaster General U.S. Army
Phila., 1887. 1st. Edn. Sm. fo. Stain at top outer corner tips of tut. 30 plts. Orig. gt. cl., soiled. (PNY. Mar.26; 76) $240

FLAHERTY, Robert J. & Frances Hubbard
- My Eskimo Friends: 'Nanook of the North'. N.Y., 1924. 1st. Edn. 4to. Cl.-bkd. bds., bkplt. (SG. Apr.23; 90) $100

FLAMSTEED, John
- Atlas Coelestis. Ill.:- G. Vertue (port.), du Gernier (ill.). 1729. 1st. Edn. Lge. fo. 23 engraved charts only (of 27), 1 or 2 charts creased, some light foxing & soiling at edges. Cont. hf. cf., covers detchd. As an atlas, w.a.f., from Chetham's Liby., Manchester. (C. Nov.26; 163)
Nicholson. £750

FLATMAN, Thomas
[-] Heraclitus Ridens. 1 Feb. 1681-22 Aug. 1682. 1st. Edn. (except no. 2, 2nd iss.). Nos. 1-82 (all publd.). Fo. Sm. tear in no. 51, 52 holed with loss of a few letters, some nos. marginally stained, a few sm. marginal repairs. Cont. cf., rebkd., worn. W.a.f. (S. May 5; 328) *Heron.* £240

FLAUBERT, Gustave
- L'Education Sentimentale. 1870. Orig. Edn. 2 vols. Sewed. Vol. 2 with catalogue (publishers). (HD. Feb.18; 121) Frs. 2,100

FLAUBERT, Gustave -contd.
- **Herodias.** Ill.:– Rochegrosse (compositions). Paris, 1892. (500); (200) on Arches vell., numbered. Etchings in 2 states (1 with comments). Mor. by Ruban, gt. mosaic doubls., wrap. preserved. (SM. Feb.11; 157) Frs. 11,500
- – **Anr. Edn.** Ill.:– Lucien Pissarro. Eragny Pr., 1901. (226). Orig. cl.-bkd. bds., unc. (S. Jul.31; 20) *Quaritch.* £70
- **La Legende de Saint Julien l'Hospitalier.** Ill.:– Lucien Pissarro. Eragny Pr., 1900. (226). Orig. linen-bkd. bds. Pres. Copy from artist to Georges Lecomte. (SH. Feb.19; 34) *Libris.* £80
- **Madame Bovary.** 1857. [1st. Edn?]. 2 vols. Three-quarter red mor., ornam. spines, wrap. by Canape. (HD. Oct.10; 52) Frs. 3,900
- – **Anr. Copy.** 12mo. Hf. chagrin by David, unc., wraps. & spines. (HD. Dec.5; 80) Frs. 3,100
- – **Anr. Copy.** Sm. hole in 1 lf. Cont. hf. chagrin. (HD. Jun.30; 23) Frs. 2,000
- – **Anr. Edn.** Ill.:– William Fel. Paris, 1927. (100) numbered on Japan. 2 vols. Red hf. mor. by Klein, decor. spines, wrap. preserved. (SM. Feb.11; 216) Frs. 2,800
- – **Anr. Edn.** Ill.:– Huard. Paris, 1930. (50) on Japon Impérial. 4to. 4 states of ills. Hf. mor., by Breuzevault, orig. wraps. bnd. in, s.-c. Duc de Massa ex-libris. (SM. Oct.8; 2331) Frs. 1,500
- – **Anr. Edn.** Ill.:– Michel Cinj. Priv. ptd., 1951. Sewed. On vell. (HD. Oct.10; 186) Frs. 1,400
- – **Anr. Edn.** Paris, n.d. 2 vols. Mor., ornate gt., by Levitsky, orig. wraps. bnd. in, s.-c. (SM. Oct.8; 2330) Frs. 4,000
- **Oeuvres Complètes.** Ill.:– Dunoyer de Segonzac & others. Paris, 1921-29. 10 vols. 4to. Hf. mor., orig. wraps. bnd. in. (SM. Oct.8; 2216) Frs. 1,400
- **Die Sage von Sankt Julian dem Gastfreien.** Trans.:– Else von Hollander. Ill.:– Max Kaus. Weimar, 1918. (100) numbered, each plt. sigd. & dtd. by artist. 4to. Suede-bkd. cl. (SG. Oct.23; 172) $600
- **Salammbo.** Paris, 1863. Mor. by Aussourd, orig. wraps. bnd. in, s.-c. (SM. Oct.8; 2248) Frs. 5,000
- – **Anr. Copy.** Hf. mor. by Kieffer, corners, spine decor. with raised bands, wrap. & spine. (HD. Jun.25; 243) Frs. 1,700
- – **Anr. Edn.** Ill.:– Rochegrosse. Paris, 1900. (400) numbered on Arches vell. 2 vols. in 1. 4to. Mor. by Charles Meunier, mosaic borders on covers & in compartments of spine, wrap. preserved, s.-c. (SM. Feb.11; 217) Frs. 10,000
- – **Anr. Edn.** Ill.:– Gaston Bussière. Paris, 1921. Ltd. Edn., (30) on Jap. 2 vols. Sm. 8vo. Jansenist red mor. by Desnaux, 3 gt. inside fillets, unc., wraps. & spines. Sigs. by artist. (HD. Dec.5; 82) Frs. 1,600
- – **Anr. Edn.** Ill.:– Fritz Heubner. Munchen, 1924. (35) numbered. 2 vols. 4to. Vell. gt., s.-c. 30 orig. sigd. etchings by artist. (BS. Jun.11; 250) £180
- – **Anr. Edn.** Trans.:– Edward Powys Mathers. Ill.:– Robert Gibbings. Gold. Cock. Pr., [1931]. (500) numbered. 4to. Patterned bds., buckram spine. (SG. Sep.4; 207) $110
- **La Tentation de Saint Antoine.** Paris, 1874. 1st. Edn. Sewed, wrap. Sigd. dedication to Guy de Maupassant. (HD. Dec.5; 81) Frs. 13,500
- **The Works.** N.Y., [1904]. 1st. Edn., (26). 10 vols. Rose mor. gt., gt. border with inlaid diamond pieces, gt. fleur de lys inlays in each corner, gt. fleur de lys centered on each inlay, slight soiling. (SPB. May 6; 307) $2,900

FLAVIUS, Josephus
- **Histoire des Juifs.** Trans.:– Arnauld D'Andilly. Amst., 1681. 4to. Cf., worn. (JL. Mar.2; 838) Aus. $130
- **Hooghberomede Joodsche Historien, ende Boecken. Noch Egesippus vande ellendighe Verstoringe der Stadt Ierusalem.** Ill.:– Christoffel van Sichem. Amst., 1626. 2 pts. in 1 vol. Title slightly defect. & mntd., a few marginal repairs, marginal staining towards end. 19th. C. hf. cf. (VG. Dec.17; 1322) Fls. 650
- **Josippon.** Amst., 1742. 2 vols. In old Yiddish, slight discolouration. Mod. hf. cf. (S. Nov.18; 613) *Waechter.* £160

FLECKER, James Elroy
- **The Golden Journey to Samarkand.** 1913. 1st. Edn. (50) sigd. Orig. parch.-bkd. bds. (S. Jul.22; 125) *Johnson.* £130
- **The Letters of J.E. Flecker to Frank Savery.** Ill.:– Randolph Schwabe. Beaumont Pr., 1926. (390) numbered. Orig. parch.-bkd. bds., cover design by Claudia Guercio, unc., partly unopened. (S. Jul.22; 126) *Johnson.* £50

FLECHIER, Abbé Esprit
- **Oraison Funèbre de ... Henri de la Tour-Auvergne ...-Oraison Funèbre de Monsieur le Premier Président de Lamoignan.** Paris, 1676 [1679]. 1st. Edns. 2 works in 1 vol. 4to. Slight marginal worming. Cont. spr. cf., arms of François Dugué, decor. spine. (HD. Mar.18; 68) Frs. 3,200

FLEISCHMAN, Puntzelwitz, P.
- **Description: Des aller durchleuchtigsten ... Herrn Rudolfen d. andern, Erwölten Röm. Kaisero ... erstgehaltenem Reichstag zu Augspurg ...** Augsburg, 1582. 1st. Edn. 4to. Cont. limp 15th. C. MS. vell., lacks ties. (HK. Nov.18-21; 193) DM 520

FLEMING, Hans Friedrich von
- **Des Vollkommenen Teutschen Jägers ... Jagd und Forst Sachen ... Teutsche Fischer ...** Leipzig, 1724. 1st. Edn. Vol. 2. Fo. Stained or soiled in parts, 1 plt. slightly torn, 44 (of 50) copperplts. Cont. vell., spine renewed. (D. Dec.11-13; 2132) DM 1,660

FLEMING, Ian
- **Doctor No.** 1958. Orig. wraps., soiled & worn. Proof Copy of 1st. Edn., with autograph revisions & corrections by author, others by proof reader. (SH. Dec.19; 498) *Quaritch.* £1,150
- **You Only Live Twice.** [L.], [1964]. 1st. Edn. Cl., d.-w. Inscr. (SG. Jun.4; 183) $500
- **[Works] Novels.** 1953-66. 1st. Edns. 14 vols. Orig. cl., 13 in d.-w.'s, 1st. d.-w. from later iss. (S. Jul.22; 128) *Ginsberg.* £210

FLEMING, Sir Sandford, Newfoundland Railway Engineer
- **Report of Preliminary Survey & Explorations for 1875.** St. John's, 1876. Title-p. reprd. Orig. ptd. wraps., rebkd. with tape. (CB. Dec.9; 177) Can. $100

FLENDERUS, Johannes
- **Phosphorus Philosophicus seu Logica contracta Glaubergiana illustrata Commentario logico-metaphysico.** Amst., 1696. Vell. (S. Dec.1; 164) *Phelps.* £85

FLERS, Robert de
- **Ilsee, Princesse de Tripoli.** Ill.:– after Alphonse Mucha. Paris, 1897. (252) numbered. 4to. A few light stains. Orig. wraps., stitching almost brkn. (CSK. Jul.31; 85) £950
- – **Anr. Edn.** Ill.:– A. Mucha. Prague, 1901. 1st. Edn. in German, (800) numbered. Liby. stp. on recto of each p. Hf. mor., brkn. (SG. Apr.2; 211) $900
- – **Anr. Copy.** 4to. Slightly soiled. Orig. bds. (HK. May 12-14; 1993) DM 2,800

FLESSELLES, Mme. de
- **Les Jeunes Voyageurs en France.** Paris, 1822. 4 vols. 16mo. Cont. grd. roan, decor. spines & covers, roulette. (HD. Apr.9, 471) Frs. 1,000

FLETCHER, Banister F.
- **Andrea Palladio, his life & works.** L., 1902. Orig. cl. (CB. May 27; 102) Can. $160

FLETCHER, Giles, the Younger
- [-] **Christs Victorie & Triumph in Heaven & Earth, Over & After Death.** 1632. 2nd. Edn. 2 pts. in 1 vol. Sm. 4to. Slight browning, 1 or 2 short tears, reprd. Early 20th. C. str.-grd. mor. by Stikeman, gt. Bkplt. of Beverly Chew. [STC 11060] (S. Jun.29; 384) *Hannas.* £150
- – **Anr. Edn.** Camb., 1640. All plts. offset onto facing text pp. Mod. vell., gt., slightly soiled. [STC 11061] (S. Apr.7; 375) *Stuart Bennett.* £80
- **The History of Russia.** [L.], [1656]. 12mo. Lacks a prelim. lf. (? blank), slight worming affecting text, tear in G3. Cont. cf., worn. [Wing F1331] (S. Jan.27; 577) *Anderson.* £80

FLETCHER, John
- **The Elder Brother.** 1637. 1st. Edn. 4to. Title torn & reprd. affecting imprint, lacks portion of blank margin, reprd., 1st. word of title shaved, margins of a few other ll. reprd., slightly soiled thro.-out. Mott. cf., by Zaehnsdorf., gt. spine. [STC 11066] (C. Nov.19; 95) *Dyson.* £170
- **The Faithfull Shepheardesse.** Ca. 1610. 1st. Edn. 4to. Lacks 1st. lf. (blank except for sig.) & last blank, some ll. cropped at head or foot, with loss of headlines, catchwords, sigs., etc., slight browning. Mod. mor. [STC 11068] (S. Feb.9; 143) *Quaritch.* £220

[-] **Valentinian.** 1685. 1st. Edn. 4to. Title creased, slight foxing. Recent mor.-bkd. bds. [Wing F1354] (C. Nov.19; 96) *Blackwell.* £140
See–BEAUMONT, Francis & Fletcher, John
See–JONSON, Ben & others

FLETCHER, Phineas
- **Locustae, vel Pietas Iesuitca. (The Locusts, or Apollyonists).** 1627. 1st. Edn. 2 pts. in 1 vol. Sm. 4to. Late 19th. C. maroon lev. mor. by Wallis, gt. [STC 11081] (S. Jun.29; 385) *Hannas.* £200
- **The Purple Island.** Camb., 1633. 1st. Edn. 4to. 19th. C. mor. Bkplt. of Sir Henry Cunliffe, lately in the collection of Eric Sexton. [STC 11082] (C. Apr.15; 97) *Foyle.* £140
- [-] **Sicelides.** 1631. 1st. Edn. Sm. 4to. Title slightly stained, some stains to last few ll. 19th. C. hf. mor. Bkplts. of William Holgate & Henry W. Sherwin, lately in the collection of Eric Sexton. [STC 11083] (C. Apr.15; 98) *Foyle.* £150

FLETCHER, William Younger
- **English Bookbindings in the British Museum.** 1895. 1st. Edn. (500). Fo. Orig. cl., partly unc. (S. Nov.24; 127) *Way.* £220
- – **Anr. Copy.** 4to. Slightly marked. (S. Feb.9; 144) *Marlborough.* £190
- **Foreign Bookbindings in the British Museum.** 1896. 1st. Edn. (500). Fo. 63 chromo-litho. plts., tissue guard adhering to one plt. Orig. cl., partly unc. (S. Nov.24; 128) *Way.* £200
- – **Anr. Copy.** 4to. Slightly faded. (S. Feb.9; 145) *Marlborough.* £180
- – **Anr. Copy.** Fo. Cl., unc. & worn. (SG. Oct.2; 128) $375

FLETCHER, William Younger–DAVENPORT, Cyril
- **Bookbinding in France.–Royal English Bookbindings.** L., 1894; 1896. 2 works in 1 vol. 4to. Crimson three-qtr. mor., spine gt., raised bands, by Fazakerley. (SG. Mar.26; 42) $120

FLEURON (The): a Journal of Typography
Ed.:– O. Simon & S. Morison. 1923-30. Nos. 1-7 (all publd.). 4to. Orig. cl. (SH. May 28; 206) *Walford.* £200
- – **Anr. Copy.** Vols. 1, 4 & 7 only. Orig. cl.-bkd. bds. & cl. (SH. Mar.6; 523) *Forster.* £90
- – **Anr. Copy.** Vols. 1-7. Cl. (SG. May 14; 75) $600

[**FLEURY, Claude**]
See–GHUS, D. & [Fleury, Claude]

FLIEGENDE BLATTER
Munich, [1845-ca. 1854]. Vols. I-XVIII in 8 vols. 4to. Spotted. 1st. 3 in orig. pict. bds., worn, others in cont. cl. (SH. Jan.30; 432) *Lindenberg.* £95

FLINDERS, Matthew
- **Narrative of His Voyage in the Schooner Francis.** Ill.:– John Buckland Wright. Gold. Cock. Pr., 1946. (750) numbered. Fo. Orig. cl. (CSK. Apr.3; 56) £130
- **A Voyage to Terra Australia.** 1814. 1st. Edn. 1 vol. & Atlas. 4to. & fo. Some plts. foxed & offset on text, lacks hf.-titles. Mod. hf. cf. (S. Nov.6; 210) *Redford.* £2,400
- – **Anr. Copy.** 3 vols. (2 vols. text & atlas). Text with 9 engraved plts., some foxed & offset, lacks hf.-titles, atlas with 16 engraved charts & 12 plts. Mod. hf. cf. by Berkelouw, Sydney. (C. Jul.15; 36) *Taylor.* £2,200
- – **Anr. Edn.** Adelaide, 1966. Facs. Edn. 2 vols., with portfo. of charts & plts. 4to. Orig. freighting box. (KH. Nov.18; 257) Aus. $400
- – **Anr. Copy.** Orig. bdg. & box of charts & plans. (KH. Mar.24; 151) Aus. $380

FLINT, James
- **Letters from America Containing Observations on the Climate & Agriculture of the Western States ...** Edinb., 1822. 1st. Edn. Advts., erasure on title, slight browning. Orig. bds., rebkd., new end-papers. From liby. of William E. Wilson. (SPB. Apr.29; 103) $125
- – **Anr. Copy.** Advts., some foxing & offsetting. Orig. cl.-bkd. bds., spine worn, bds. soiled, folding cl. s.-c. From liby. of William E. Wilson. (SPB. Apr.29; 101) $100

FLINT, Timothy
- **A Condensed Geography & History of the Western States of the Mississippi Valley.** Cinc., 1828. 1st. Edn. 2 vols. Lacks errata lf. in vol. I, ink notations on 1st. 2 ll. of vol. I, paper burn on title affecting 1 word, owner's inscr. on title, anr. removed from 2nd. lf. affecting text on verso. 5th.

lf. torn at lr. corner, browning & foxing. Cont. cf., scarred. From liby. of William E. Wilson. (SPB. Apr.29; 106) $200
- **Indian Wars of the West** ... Cinc., 1835. 1st. Edn. 12mo. Slight browning & foxing. Cont. cf., rebkd., spine scarred. From liby. of William E. Wilson. [Sabin 24790] (SPB. Apr.29; 107) $150
- **Recollections of the Last Ten Years, Passed ... in the Valley of the Mississippi, from Pittsburgh & the Missouri to the Gulf of Mexico, & from Florida to the Spanish Frontier.** Boston, 1826. 1st. Edn. Slight discolouration to portions of text. Orig. tree cf., rebkd., folding cl. s.-c. From liby. of William E. Wilson. (SPB. Apr.29; 104) $200

FLINT, Sir William Russell
- **Drawings.** L., 1950. (500), sigd. Fo. Plts., lacks sigd. plt. Cl.-bkd. bds., box. (P. Jun.11; 297) *Porter.* £95
- - **Anr. Edn.** 1950. (125) numbered, sigd. Fo. Orig. qtr. mor., slightly faded. Ex. liby. copy, (stp. on title page verso & label pasted on inside upr. cover only), orig. drawing loosely inserted. (TA. Aug.21; 154) £150
- - **Anr. Copy.** 4to. Slightly soiled. Pres. copy. (SD. Feb.4; 152) £120
- - **Anr. Edn.** 1950. Cl. d.-w.'s. (WW. May 20; 46) £66
- - **Anr. Copy.** 4to. Artist's sig. on hf.-title. (BS. May 13; 278) £50
- **Minxes Admonished.** Gold. Cock. Pr., 1955. (550). 4to. Orig. mor.-bkd. bds., s.-c. (SH. Feb.19; 199) *Brook.* £65
- - **Anr. Copy.** Orig. qtr. mor., slightly soiled, s.-c. Pres. copy sigd. (SD. Feb.4; 153) £50
- **Models of Propriety.** L., [1951]. 1st. Edn., (500) numbered, sigd. 4to. Cl. 2 A.L.s. laid in, both in orig. envelopes. (SG. Oct.23; 129) $100
- **Shadows in Arcady.** 1965. (500) sigd. Fo. Orig. cl. gt., s.-c. (BS. May 13; 276) £50

FLINT, William Russell (Ill.)
See-ANTONINUS, Marcus Aurelius, Emperor
See-BRADSHAW, Percy V.
See-CHAUCER, Geoffrey
See-HOMER
See-MALORY, Sir Thomas
See-THEOCRITUS, Bion & Moschus

FLORA BATAVA, of Afbeelding en Beschrijving van de Nederlandsche Gewassen
Ed.:- J. Kops & others. Amst., [1800]-49. Pts. 1-10 & Algemeen Register 1-8, together 11 vols. Cont. hf. cf., gt. spines. (VG. Oct.13; 62) Fls. 10,000

FLORA DANICA
Ed.:- George Christian Oeder & others. Copen., 1761-[66]-1843[-49]; 1852-53. Vols. 1-14 & 2 fascicules. Fo. 2,630 hand-cold. engraved plts., some folding. Unif. 19th. C. cf. gt., last 2 fascicules ptd. wraps. (C. Mar.18; 41) *Quaritch.* £18,00
[-] - **Anr. Edn.** Ed.:- Georg Christian Oeoder & others. Copen., 1761-1883. 19 vols. including Index. 18 vols. fo., 1 vol. 4to. Vols. 1-6 cont. cf., rest bnd. to match in old cf., worn, some bds. of later vols. detchd. W.a.f. as a periodical, from collection as Massachusetts Horticultural Society, stp. on plts. (SPB. Oct.1; 117) $46,000
- - **Anr. Edn.** Ed.:- G.C. Oeder & O.F. Muller. Copen., 1766-82. 1st. Edn. 5 vols. Fo. 240 plts. hand-cold., some margins discold. 19th. C. hf. mor. (not entirely unis.), worn. From Chetham's Liby., Manchester. (C. Nov.26; 164) *Harris.* £1,900
- - **Anr. Edn.** Ed.:- W. Robinson. 1903-5. 3 vols. 4to. Orig. cl. (CSK. Sep.19; 48) £75
- - **Anr. Copy.** Some plts. very slightly spotted. Orig. hf. vell., unc. (S. Dec.3; 1118) *W. & W.* £55

FLORAL Magazine
Ed.:- H. Honywood Dombrain. Ill.:- J. Andrews. L., 1861-68. 7 vols. 400 (of 416) cold. lithos., each with text lf. Disbnd. W.a.f. (SG. Sep.18; 119) $1,200
- - **Anr. Run.** Ed.:- Thomas Moore & H.H. Dombrain. 1861-71. Vols. I-X. Some imprints cropped or trimmed, 1 text lf. detchd., occasional slight spotting. Cont. cf., spines gt. W.a.f. (S. Dec.3; 959) *Schuster.* £620
- - **Anr. Edn.** Ed.:- H.H. Dombrain. Ill.:- J. Andrews. 1862-[63]. 2 vols. only. 116 cold. litho. plts. Hf. mor. As a periodical, w.a.f. (C. May 20; 207) *Schuster.* £200
- - **Anr. Edn.** Aug. 1872-Dec. 1881. New Series. Numbers 8-120, 9 vols. in 3. 4to. Slight

---

dust-soiling to upr. edges of a few plts. Cont.hf. cf., very worn, 1 spine defect., 3 covers detchd., gt. crest of Campbell of Blythswood on upr. cover. W.a.f. (S. Dec.3; 960) *Cumming.* £620

FLORAL OFFERING (The)
Ill.:- P. Jerrard (Golddruck). L., ca. 1880. 4to. Slightly soiled, ex-lib. Orig. linen. (HK. Nov.18-21; 519) DM 460

FLORAVANTI, F.
- **L'Abitatore del Sole ovvero Discorsi Fisici.** L., 1743. Cont. red mor., sides gt. with thistle roll & 4-pointed centre piece, spine gt., slight wear. (S. May 5; 269) *Burgess.* £75

FLORE de la Botanique des Dames ...
Paris, 1821. Margins slightly soiled. Cont. cf. (TA. Jun.18; 77) £70

FLORE DES SERRES et des Jardins de l'Europe
Ed.:- L. Van Houtte. Gent, 1852-53. Vol. VIII, 1-11. Foxed, not affecting plts. Loose as iss., covers badly soiled & defect. Text not collated, w.a.f. (VG. Dec.16; 922) Fls. 600
- - **Anr. Edn.** Ghent, 1853-54. Vol. 9 only. Cont. hf. mor. gt., slightly worn. (SBA. Mar.4; 147) *Erlini.* £135

FLORENCE
- **Descrizione dell-Imp. e R. Palazzo Pitti de Firenze.** Flor., 1819. Vell., 2 early paintings on covers. (SG. Apr.9; 225) $180
- **Galerie de Florence, et du Palais Pitti.** Paris, 1789. On vell. d'Annonay. 2 vols. Fo. 1 plt. slightly frayed, 1 with sm. tear at lr. margin, some plts. lightly soiled. Cont. leath., gt. spine, cover, inner & outer dentelle, arms. (HK. Nov.18-21; 1590) DM 1,500
- **Nouvo Raccolta delle piu interessanti Vedute delle Citta di Firenze con alcune altre della Toscana.** Flor., early 19th. C. Ob. 4to. Cont. hf. mor. (CSK. Dec.12; 100) £240

FLORES LEGUM
[Paris], [Etienne Jehannot (?) for Denis Roce]. Ca. 1499. 19th. C. vell.-bkd. bds., soiled. [Goff F211] (S. Dec.8; 132) *Fletcher.* £420

FLORIAN, Jean Pierre Claris de
[-] [Fables]. Ill.:- Jean Michel Moreau le jeune. 1811-12. 12 Ink & wash drawings only, sigd. with initials & dtd. 1811-12. Mntd. in red mor. album, mor. doubls., by Chambolle-Duru, upr. jnt. brkn. (SM. Oct.8; 2397) Frs. 48,000
- - **Anr. Edn.** Paris, 1824. New Edn. 16mo. Cont. cf., spine decor., covers with blind stp., gt. fillet, inner dentelle. (HD. Apr. 9; 474) Frs. 1,350
- - **Anr. Edn.** Ill.:- Jean Dufy. Paris, 1938. (15) numbered, sigd. by artist. 4to. On japon paper, with additional 12 proof plts. of the ills. in earlier states. Loose in ptd. paper wrap. & pig folder. (C. Feb.4; 184) *Klausmann.* £200
- **Oeuvres Diverses.** Ill.:- Queverdo & Flouest. Paris, 1784-97. 14 vols. 18mo. Cont. red mor., decor. spines, 2 gt. fillets on covers, inside dentelle. (HD. Dec.5; 83) Frs. 1,900
- - **Anr. Edn.** Ill.:- Queverdo. Paris, 1786-99. 20 vols. 18mo. Cont. marb. cf., decor. spines, 3 fillets, inner dentelle. (HD. Apr.9; 475) Frs. 2,000
- [-] **Anr. Edn.** Paris, 1786-1807. Mixed Edns. 24 vols. 18mo. Early 19th. C. red mor., gt. (SM. Oct.8; 2398) Frs. 3,000

FLORICULTURAL CABINET, [The] & Florist's Magazine.
Ed.:- Joseph Harrison. 1833-35. Vols. 1-3. 2 engraved titles foxed, 40 hand-cold. engraved plts. Cont. hf. cf. As a periodical, w.a.f. (C. Jul.15; 179) *Map House.* £200
- - **Anr. Run.** Ed.:- Joseph Harrison. 1833-58. Vols. 1, 2, 17, 19, 21, 24-26, together 8 vols. Cont. hf. cf., slightly worn. (TA. Sep.18; 25) £175
- - **Anr. Run.** Ed.:- Joseph Harrison. 1834-37. Vols. 2, 3, & 5. Hf. cf., bdgs. defect. (PD. May 20; 181) £50
- - **Anr. Run.** Ed.:- Joseph Harrison. 1835-57. Vols. 3, 7, 9, 12-15, 22-25, together 11 vols. Cont. cl. (TA. Sep.18; 24) £210
- - **Anr. Run.** Ed.:- Joseph Harrison. 1837-49. Vols. 5-12, 15-17. Cont. non-unif. hf. cf., some wear. (TA. Jan.22; 75) £240

FLORIDA
- **Memorial of Inhabitants of Florida attached to Louisiana.-Inhabitants East Florida.**

- **Correspondence Sec. of War & Commanding Officer in Florida.-Actual Settlements in Florida, under the Armed Occupation Law.** Wash., 1818; 1825; 1834; 1842; 1844. Disbnd. (SG. Jan.8; 160) $100

FLORINUS, Franciscus Philippus
[-] [Oeconomus Prudens et Legalis.] [Nuremb., Frankfurt & Leipzig], [1705]. Pts. 5-9 (of 9) in 1 vol. Fo. Many ll. loose, frayed, soiled. Cont. vell., loose & soiled. (HK. Nov.18-21; 1680) DM 640
- **Oeconomus Prudens et Legalis. [-Oeconomus Prudens et leagalis continuatus].** Nuremb., Frankfurt & Leipzig, 1719-22. 4 vols. Fo. Engr. on f. (H) 3 pasted over different engr., ff. 3T4 & (A)3 torn slightly affecting text, corner torn from f. (X)2 with loss, slightly spotted in places. Cont. cf. (S. Jun.1; 23) *Koch.* £750

FLORIO, John
- **A World of Wordes, or ... Dictionarie in Italian & English.** 1598. 1st. Edn. Fo. Lacks 1st. & last ll., both probably blank, title dust-soiled & mntd., lightly browned. Mod. sheep, slightly worn. [STC 11098] (S. Jun.23; 369) *Quaritch.* £220

FLORIST, FRUITIST, & GARDEN MISCELLANY, The
1848-61. Vols. I-XIV. Tear in 1 plt., some plts. cropped, several imprints trimmed, occasional spotting. 19th. C. hf. cf., not unif. W.a.f. (S. Dec.3; 963) *Litman.* £240
- - **Anr. Edn.** 1854 & 1856-61. 7 vols. Some plts. cropped. Cont. hf. mor., almost unif., worn. (SKC. May 19; 408) £140

FLORIST & POMOLOGIST, The
Ed.:- R. Hogg, J. Spencer & T. Moore (& afterwards W. Paul). 1862-82. 20 vols. Several plts. & imprints lightly trimmed or cropped, offsetting to some plts. & text-ll., a few short tears, occasional spotting, some browning. Cont. hf. cf., not entirely unif., slight wear. W.a.f. (S. Dec.3; 962) *Litman.* £380
- - **Anr. Run.** Ed.:- R. Hogg, J. Spencer & T. Moore (& afterwards W. Paul). 1862-84. 23 vols. Some plts. or imprints lightly trimmed or cropped, offsetting to some plts. & text ll. a few short tears, occasional spotting & browning, cancel stp. of Lindley liby., Royal Horticultural Society. Cont. hf. cf., spines gt., not entirely unif., some wear. W.a.f. (S. Dec.3; 961) *W. & W.* £580
- - **Anr. Run.** L., 1868-77. 10 vols. Red hf. mor. (SG. May 14; 77) $650

FLORIST'S JOURNAL
1845-47. 3 vols. only. Slight spotting & offsetting, 1 plt. & 1 lf. torn in 1846 vol. Cont. hf. cf., worn. W.a.f. (S. Jan.26; 281) *Wooll.* £120
- - **Anr. Edn.** N.d. 3 vols. 1 ptd. title only. Cont. hf. mor., spines gt. (SKC. May 19; 409) £60

FLORUS, Lucius Annaeus
- **Epitomae Rerum Romanorum.** Ed.:- [Philippus Beroaldus]. Siena, Sigismundus Rodt, for Henricus de Colonia. [1486-87]. 4to. Spaces for capital initials, most with guide letters, extreme blank margins slightly browned. Mor., spine gt.-lettered, by Sangorski & Sutcliffe. From the collection of Eric Sexton. [BMC VII, 1102, Goff F236, H 7201*] (CNY. Apr.8; 156) $2,200
See-SALLUSTIUS CRISPUS, Caius & Florus, Lucius Annaeus

FLOSCULI SENTENTIARUM: Printers Flowers Moralised
[Northampton, Mass], [Gehenna Pr.]. [1967]. (50) specially handbound, & sigd. by Leonard Baskin. Sm. fo. Mor., mor.-bkd. folding box, by Arno Werner of Pittsfield Mass. Marked 'Printer's Copy'. (SG. Apr.9; 440) $450

FLOURE & the Leafe (The)
Kelms. Pr., 1896. (300). Minor defects. Orig. cl.-bkd. bds., soiled. (SPB. Jul.28; 205) $225

FLOURENS, Marie Jean Pierre
- **Recherches Expérimentales sur les Propriétés et les Fonctions du Systeme Nerveux dans les Animaux Vertébrés.** Paris, 1824. 1st. Edn. Probably lacks hf.-title, liby. stps. on title & at end. Qtr. cf. (S. Jun.15; 285) *Quaritch.* £160

FLOUTRIERES, Pierre de
See-HENRION, Denis-FLOUTRIERES, Pierre de

FLOWER, John
- Views of Ancient Buildings in the Town & County of Leicester. [1826?]. Fo. Orig. hf. roan. (S. May 5; 216) *Traylen.* £180
- - Anr. Edn. N.d. Fo. Some spotting. Cont. cl. (CSK. Jan.23; 148) £120

FLOWERDEN, Joseph
- [-] A Compendium of Physic & Surgery for the Use of Young Practitioners. 1769. 1st. p. of title slightly soiled, stp. 'T. Goldwyer 1773' on hf.-title. Cf., rebkd. (S. Jun.15; 287) *Joslen.* £80

FLOYER, Sir John
- The Ancient Psukhrologsia Revived or an Essay to Prove Cold Bathing both Safe & Useful, in Four Letters. 1702. 1st. Edn. Errata lf. bnd. at beginning. Bds., vell. spine., unc. (S. Dec.2; 487) *Rota.* £70
- Pharmaco-Basanos. 1687-91. 1st. Edn. 2 vols. in 1. 1 or 2 short tears, slightly affecting text, some dampstaining, advt. lf. at end of vol. 2. Cont. cf., rebkd., preserving old spine. [Wing F1388] (S. Feb.9; 146) *Bicker.* £100
- The Physician's Pulse-Watch or an Essay to Explain the Old Art of Feeling the Pulse & to Improve it by the Use of the Pulse-Watch. 1707. 1st. Edn. Advt. lf., title slightly dust-soiled, sm. rust-hole in Eel. New marb. bds., cf. spine. (S. Jun.15; 288) *Rota.* £240

FOCARD, Jacques
- Paraphrase de l'Astrolabe . . . revue & corrigée . . . avec une Amplification de l'Usage de l'Astrolabe. Ed.:- Iaques Bassentin Escossois. Lyon, 1555. 2nd. Edn. Lacks volvelle on k8. 19th. C. hf. mor. (C. Apr.1; 107) *Quaritch.* £160

[FOKKE, J.]
See-WAGENAAR, Jan & others

FOKKE, Simon, engraver
- Convoi-Funèbre de . . . Anne, Princesse Royale de la Grande Bretagne . . . executé le 23. Fevrier 1759. . . .-Description de la Chambre et Lit de Parade sur lequel le Corps de . . . Anne . . . Ill.:- P.C. La Fargue; M. de Swart. The Hague, 1761; 1759. 1st. Edns. 2 works in 1 vol. Fo. Splashed stain on titles of 1st. work. Cont. blind-stpd. panel. cf., spine gt., tooled in compartments, sm. hole near head. Bkplts. of Sir H.W.W. Wynn & A.M. Broadley: 2nd. work with preface sigd. with note of authenticity by publisher. (S. Jun.9; 52) *Quaritch.* £380

FOLARD, Jean Charles de
- Abregé des Commentaires sur l'Histoire de Polybe. Paris, 1754. 1st. Edn. 3 vols. Lge. 4to. Cont. mott. cf., spines gt. (SG. Oct.30; 155) $160

FOLENGO, Teofilo 'Merlinus Cocaius'
- [-] Chaos del Tri per Uno. Venice, 1527. 3 pts. in 1 vol. Bkplts. of Girardot de Préfond, Gomez de la Cortina & Marchetti. 18th. C. red mor., triple gt. fillet, spine gt. with single lge. fleuron in compartments, inner gt. dentelles. (SM. Oct.7; 1714) Frs. 3,600
- [-] Histoire Macaronique de Merlin Coccaie Prototype de Rabelais. Paris, 1606. 12mo. 18th. C. red mor., gt., arms of Count Hoym on covers, triple gt. fillet, spine compartments gt. à la grotesque, inner gt. dentelles with 'tulip' border. (SM. Oct.7; 1715) Frs. 5,500
- - Anr. Copy. 2 vols. Cf., gt. triple fillet border, decor. spine raised bands, inner dentelles, by Bausonnet-Trautz. (HD. Apr.24; 67) Frs. 1,750
- Merlini Covaii opus Macaronicum. Ill.:- F. Zuchhi & others. Amst. (i.e. Mantua), 1768. 4to. Some ll. very lightly browned. Cont. vell. bds. From the collection of John A. Saks. (C. Jun.10; 71) *Burgess.* £140
- Opus Macaronicum. Amst., 1768-71. 2 vols. 4to. 19th. C. hf. cf. (SI. Dec.3; 224) Lire 200,000
- [-] Opus Merlini Cocaii. 1521. 1st. Coll. Edn. 16mo. 18th. C. Fr. mor., triple gt. fillet, spine gt. in compartments, inner gt. dentelles, gt. & white end-papers. Bkplt. of George Rose. (SM. Oct.7; 1716) Frs. 2,800
- - Anr. Edn. Venice, 1581. 12mo. 1 blank, 5 unnumbered pp., last blank, 27 xylographs. Old vell. (CR. Mar.19; 251) Lire 350,000
- [-] Orlandino di Limerno Pitocco . . . Ill.:- Jean Michel Moreau le Jeune. L., Molini, 1773. On vell. Cont. mor., gt., with wide rococo dentelle border, spine gt. in compartments, inner gt. dentelles. (SM. Oct.7; 1717) Frs. 42,000

FOLEY, Edwin
- The Book of Decorative Furniture. 1910-11. 2 vols. 4to. Orig. decor. cl. & d.-w. (GM. Apr.30; 458) £60

FOLEY, P.K.
- American Authors, 1795-1895. Ed.:- W.L. Sawyer. Boston, 1897. (5) on L.P. & interleaved. 4to. Buckram, worn. Limitation handwritten & initialled by Foley. (SG. Jan.22; 173) $100

FOLK-LORE Journal
Cape Town, 1879-80. Vol. I pt. 1-vol. II pt. 6. Mod. cl., all orig. wraps. bnd. in. (SSA. Nov.5; 278) R. 420

FOLLETT, Frederick
- History of the Press of Western New-York. Rochester, 1847. 1st. Edn. Some foxing. Later three-qtr. cf. (SG. Jan.22; 174) $100

FOLMSBEE, Beulah
See-MAHONY, Bertha E. & others

FOLON, Jean Michel
- The Death of a Tree. Ill.:- Max Ernst. [1974]. Ltd. numbered Edn., with orig. litho. Ob. fo. Wraps., cold. pict. d.-w., bd. s.-c. (SG. Oct.23; 110) $130

FOLTZ, F.
- Rhein-Album. Frankfurt, ca. 1880. Sm. ob. fo. Orig. linen, gold-stpd. (R. Oct.14-18; 2408) DM 900

FOLTZ, F. (Ill.)
See-HALENZA'S RHEINISCHES ALBUM

FONAR' [Lantern]
Ed.:- [A.V. Zaikin]. St. Petersb., 1905-06. Nos. 1-3 (New Year no. 1-2; & a varient of the last). 4to. Unbnd. (SH. Feb.5; 70) *De la Casa.* £70

FONTAINE, Charles
See-PARADIN, Cl.-FONTAINE, Charles

FONTAINE, Mlle. G.
- Collection de cent Espèces ou Varieties du Genre Camellia. Brussels, 1845. 4to. Occasional minor foxing, some plts. slightly discold. Cont. red hf. mor., spine gt. with the Belgian royal monog. (C. Nov.5; 56) *Chatsworth.* £8,200

FONTAINE, Nicolas, Sieur de Royaumont
- History of the Old & New Testament . . . Ed.:- Anthony Horneck & others. Trans.:- John Coughen. Ill.:- Bouche, Kip & others after G. Fremont. L., 1690; 1688. 2 vols. in 1. Fo. 235 (of 238) copperplts., some text ll. torn. Disbnd. W.a.f. (SG. Sep.25; 42) $210
- [-] - Anr. Edn. 1705. Fo. Some tears, stained. Cont. sheep, worn, rebkd. (SH. Jul.16; 197) *Cohen.* £100

FONTAINE, Pierre-François-Léonard
- Choix des Plus Célèbres Maisons de Plaisance de Rome et de ses Environs. Paris, 1809. Lge. fo. Cont. hf. cf. (CR. Jun.11; 596a) Lire 1,500,000
See-PERCIER, Charles & Fontaine, Pierre François Leonard

FONTAINES
- Histoire des Ducs de Bretagne . . . Paris, 1739. 6 vols. 12mo. Glazed hf. cf., spine decor. with blind-tools & gt. fillets. (HD. Jun.29; 150) Frs. 1,000

FONTANA, Felix
- Traité sur le Velin de la Vipère sur les Poisons Americains. Flor., 1781. 1st. Edn. 2 vols. Some margins spotted. 19th. C. hf. mor. From Chetham's Liby., Manchester. (C. Nov.26; 165) *Cucchi.* £110
- Treatise on the Venom of the Viper, on the American Poisons & on the Cherry Laurel & some other Vegetable Poisons . . . Ed.:- Joseph Skinner. 1787. 1st. Edn. in Engl. 2 vols. Liby. stps. Marb. bds., rebkd. (S. Jun.15; 289) *Gurney.* £110

FONTANA, Fulvio
- I Pregi della Toscana nell'Impresse piu Segnalate de' Cavalieri di Santo Stefano. Firenze, 1701. 1st. Edn. Fo. Disbnd. (SG. Oct.30; 156) $800

FONTANA, Giacomo
- Chiese di Roma. Rome, 1833-55. 3 vols. Fo. Hf. cf., well worn. (CE. Oct.24; 198) £50
- Raccolta delle Miglion Chiese di Roma & Suburbane. Milan, 1825. 4 vols. bnd. in 2. Fo. Hf. cf. (CR. Jun.11; 463) Lire 300,000
See-COTTAFAVI, Gaetano, Fontana, Gaecomo & others

FONTANA, Giacomo & Crilanovich-Leopold
- [-] Palazzi di Venetia. Ill.:- M. Moro. Venice, ca. 1840. Ob. fo. Lacks title & plts. 52 & 53 including explanations, slightly soiled. Cont. hf. leath. (R. Oct.14-18; 1937) DM 1,500

FONTANE, Theodor
- Effi Briest. Ed.:- F. Behrend. Ill.:- Max Liebermann. [Berlin], [1927]. (325) numbered. Orig. vell., gt. spine & cover, orig. bd. s.-c. Hand-printed, 1 litho. sigd. (HK. Nov.18-21; 2772) DM 3,400
- - Anr. Copy. 4to. Orig. vell. gt. (Hübel & Denck). 1 sigd. litho. (H. Dec.9/10; 1861) DM 3,200
- Gesammelte Werke. Berlin, [1905-10]. 1st. Coll. Edn. Series 1, vols. 2, 3, 5-10 & series II, 11 vols., together 19 vols. Orig. linen gt., 1 spine slightly defect. (H. Dec.9/10; 1477) DM 1,000
- Jenseits des Tweed. Berlin, 1860. 1st. Edn. Slightly soiled. Cont. hf. leath. gt. (HK. May 15; 4227) DM 620
- Unterm Birnbaum. Berlin, 1855. 1st. Edn. Orig. linen, loose. (HK. May 15; 4231) DM 500
- - Anr. Edn. Berlin, 1885. 1st. Edn. Cont. hf. leath. (H. Dec.9/10; 1478) DM 520

FONTANI, Francesco
- [-] Viaggio Pittorico della Toscana. Flor., 1801-03. Lge. fo. Cont. red str.-grd. mor., sides with gt. & blind-tooled borders, spines gt. (C. Jul.15; 146) *Zanzotto.* £2,700

FONTANINI, J.
- De Antiquitatibus Hortae Coloniae Etruscorum. Leiden, n.d. 2nd. Edn. Fo. Spotted & dampstained. Cont. cf., worn. (CSK. Jan.30; 38) £75

FONTENAI, Abbé de
See-COUCHE, Jacques & Fontenai, Abbé de

FONTENELLE, Bernard le Bovier de
- Dialogues. Trans.:- Ezra Pound. 1917. 1st. Edn., 1st. Iss. Orig. wraps. (SH. Dec.18; 235) *Clodd.* £50
- [-] Entretiens sur la Pluralité des Mondes. Paris, 1686. 1st. Edn. 12mo. Engraved folding plt., slightly torn. Cont. cf., spine gt., reprd. (S. Oct.21; 383) *Thomas.* £180
- Oeuvres diverses . . . Ill.:- Bernard Picart. Amst., 1743. New Edn. 3 vols. Fo. Cont. mott. cf., spines gt. (S. Oct.21; 460) *Duran.* £100
- Ouvres, Précédées d'une Notice sur sa Vie et ses Ouvrages. Ill.:- Couché fils. 1825. 5 vols. Cont. veined cf., border, decor. spines, minimal faults. (HD. Feb.18; 124) Frs. 1,000
- Poésies Choisies. Ill.:- De Launay after Voiriot. Geneva. 1777. 2 vols. 18mo. Red mor. by Cazin. (HD. Apr.8; 247) Frs. 1,300

FONTES AMBROSIANA in Lucem . . . Cento Tavole del Codice Resta (17th Century).
Milan, 1955. (2030). Fo. Introductions in Fr., German, Italian, & Engl., slight browning. Photographic reproduction of bdg. of orig. vol., leath. spine, box. (SPB. Nov.25; 140) $300

FOORD, J.
- Decorative Flower Studies for Use of Artists, Designers, Students & others. L., 1901. Fo. Orig. linen, end-paper loose. (D. Dec.11-13; 325) DM 700

FOPPENS, J.F.
- Bibliotheca Belgica. Brussels, 1739. 2 vols. Sm. 4to. Old grd. bdg., decor. spines restored. (LM. Jun.13; 29) B.Frs. 36,000

FOPPENS, Pierre
See-CHRISTYN, Jean Baptiste & Foppens

FORBERG, Frederick Karl
- Manuel d'Erotologie Classique. Paris, 1906. (500); (340) on tub vell. Ob. 4to. Hf. mor. (SM. Feb.11; 218) Frs. 2,200

FORBES, Alexander
- California: A History. L., 1839. 1st. Edn. 10 plts., 1 folding map, cold. in outl., sm. tears at folds, lacks errata slip. Hf. red mor. gt. [Sabin 25035] (SPB. Jun.22; 57) $175

FORBES, Edwin
- Life Studies of the Great Army. N.Y., [1876]. Ob. fo. Orig. cl. loose. (SG. Feb.26; 131) $190

FORBES, Frederick E.
- Dahomey & the Dahomans. 1851. 1st. Edn. Cont. red hf. mor. (S. Mar.31; 471) *Foyles.* £80

– – Anr. Copy. 2 vols. Some spotting, 1 section detchd. Orig. cl. by Remnant & Edmonds. (CSK. Jan.30; 18) £70

FORBES, Henry O.
– **The Natural History of Sokotra & Abd-el-Kuri.** 1903. Buckram, soiled. (P. Sep.11; 223) *Ad Orientem.* £95
– **A Naturalist's Wanderings in the Eastern Archipelago.** 1885. Slight browning. Orig. cl. (CSK. Oct.10; 32) £55

FORBES, Sir James
– **Oriental Memoirs.** 1813. 1st. Edn. 4 vols. 4to. Cont. russ., elab. stpd. & ruled in gt. & blind, vols. 1 & 2 rebkd., old spine preserved. (CSK. May 1; 110) £450
– – **Anr. Copy.** Lacks plts. 5 & 82. Cont. hf. cf., upr. cover of vol. 1 detchd. (S. Sep.29; 162) *Faber.* £300
– – **Anr. Copy.** Cont. cf. gt., rebkd. (SPB. Oct.1; 194) $950
– – **Anr. Edn.** 1835. Plt. vol. only. 4to. 83 plts., 24 hand-cold., 1 torn. Mod. cl. (SH. Jun.18; 119) *Questor.* £150
– **Salicitum Woburnese: or, a Catalogue of the Willows, Indigenous & Foreign, in the Collection of the Duke of Bedford, at Woburn Abbey.** [L.], [Priv. ptd.]. 1829. (50). Hf. mor. gt., unc. From collection of Massachusetts Horticultural Society, stp. on plts., orig. ptd. slip stating number of copies ptd. on orig. preserved end-paper, above this is pres. inscr. to Sir Richard Cold Hoare. (SPB. Oct.1; 118) $2,500

FORBES, James David
– **Norway and its Glaciers Visited in 1851.** Edinb., 1853. Cont. hf. mor. (S. Jun.29; 285) *Crete.* £110
– – **Anr. Copy.** Orig. cl., spine chipped. (SBA. Jul.14; 58) *Astill.* £70

FORBES, Sir John
– **Original Cases with Dissections & Observations Illustrating the Use of the Stethoscope & Percussion in the Diagnosis of the Chest ... selected & translated from Auenbrugger, Corvisart, Laennec & others.** 1824. 1st. Edn. Orig. bds., paper label & spine worn, unc., in red hf. mor. case. Pres. copy inscr. 'To Gibbons, Esq. with the author's compliments'. (S. Jun.15; 21) *Norman.* £600

FORBIN, Louis N.P.A., Comte
– **Voyages dans le Levant.** Paris, 1819. Elephant fo. 2 engraved plans, 78 plts., 1 torn. Cont. hf. mor. (C. Jul.15; 37) *Rodgers.* £1,000

FORCADEL, Étienne
– **Penus Iuris Ciulis.** Lyons, 1542. 1st. Edn. Sm. 4to. Slight browning. Mod. pol. hf. cf. by Wood, spine gt., slightly rubbed. From liby. of André L. Simon. (S. May 18; 96) *Lyle.* £320

FORD, Charles Henri
– **Garden of Disorder.** Ed.:– William Carlos Williams. Ill.:– Pavel Tchelitchew. L., Europa Pr., 1938. (11) Hors-Commerce. Vell.-bkd. marb. bds., d.-w. Inscr. to George Reavey, sigd. by him, author & illustrator, with wood-mntd. orig. zinc block for d.-w. ill. (SG. Jun.4; 184) $425

FORD, Ford Madox (Pseud.)
See–HUEFFER, Ford Madox

FORD, Julia Ellsworth & Bynner, Witter
– **Snickerty Nick.** Ill:– Arthur Rackham. N.Y., 1919. 1st. Edn. 4to. Several MS. stage directions in pencil, typed transcription loosely glued on top. Cl., pict. d.-w. worn. Inscr. to Clifton Joseph Furness, Raymond M. Sutton Jr. copy. (SG. May 7; 85) $280

FORD, Richard
– **A Hand-Book for Travellers in Spain.** 1845. 1st. Edn. 2 vols. Cont. hf. mor. (SKC. Jul.28; 2536) £65

FORD, W. & F.
– **Australian Almanac for the Year 1852.** Sydney, ca. 1852. Occasional light soiling. Cont. (colonial?) mor. gt. (KH. Mar.24; 152) *Aus.* $170

FORDYCE, William
– **The History & Antiquities of the County Palatine of Durham.** Ill.:– after T. Allom & others. Newcastle & Edinb., 1857. 2 vols. 4to. Some very minor defects. Cont. russ. gt. (SBA. May 27; 363) *Chesters.* £100

FOREIGN FIELD SPORTS
N.d., some plts. wtrmkd. 1833. Lge. 4to. 45 hand-cold. aquatint plts. only, 1 cleanly torn, 1 defaced with pencil, title & some ll. torn with loss. Cont. hf. mor. W.a.f. (CSK. Jul.10; 62) £110

FOREIGN FIELD SPORTS ... with a supplement of New South Wales
Ill.:– Samuel Howitt & others. L., 1814. 4to. Diced cf., worn, rebkd. (SG. Oct.9; 101) $1,300
– – **Anr. Edn.** Ill.:– Samuel Howitt. L., Edward Orme, [1819]. 4to. Lacks title & hf.-title, few tears & repairs to text. Mor. gt., reprd. As a collection of plts., w.a.f. (P. Jun.11; 273) *Schrire.* £480
– – **Anr. Edn.** Ill.:– Howitt, Atkinson, Clark, Manskirch &c. N.d. (wtrmkd. 1817-23). Fo. Offsetting onto text, some stains & spots, F1 holed with loss of letters. Cont. cf., rebkd., old spine preserved. (CSK. Feb.20; 151) £600
– – **Anr. Copy.** 4to. 109 hand-cold. plts. (dtd. 1813) only (of 110), title defect., laid down, without 2nd. title to Supp. Mod. cl. W.a.f. (C. May 20; 122) *Reid.* £380
– – **Anr. Copy.** Wtrmkd. 1823, no hf.-title, also (in Supp.) without title, dedication & 'sketch' (4 ll.) which may not be called for in this iss. Cont. red mor. gt., spine emblematically tooled. W.a.f. (SPB. Oct.1; 89) $2,100

FORESTER, Thomas
– **Rambles in the Islands of Corsica & Sardinia.** 1858. 1st. Edn. Orig. cl. (SH. Nov.6; 206) *Walford.* £55

FORESTIER, A. de
– **Alpes Pittoresques.** Paris, 1838. Vol. 1. 4to. Some tears in folding plts. & maps bkd. in parts, some text & plts. lightly soiled, 1 lf. loose. Later hf. linen, worn, loose. (H. Dec.9/10; 625) DM 1,400

FORESTIERE Illuminato ... della Citta di Venezia
Ill.:– Zucchi. Venice, 1740. Early iss. Cont. tree cf. (SBA. Oct.21; 252) *O'Keefe.* £160

FORESTUS Bergomensis, Jacobus Philippus
See–BERGOMENSIS Forestus, Jacobus Philippus

FORGUES, Paul Emile Daurand 'Old Nick'
– **La Chine Ouverte ... Ill.:–** Auguste Borget. Paris, 1845. 1 facs. plt. Publisher's decor. bds. (HD. Jun.25; 360) Frs. 3,000

FORM, a Quarterly of the Arts
Ed.:– Austin O. Spare & Francis Marsden. Ill.:– Frank Brangwyn & others. 1916-17. Vol. 1, nos. 1 & 2. Fo. Subscription form with specimen p. on verso, loosely inserted. Orig. wraps. (SH. Mar.26; 208) *Talerman.* £55

FORMAN, Harry Buxton
– **Books of William Morris.** Chic., 1897. Buckram, partly unc. & unopened. (SG. Mar.26; 331) $110

FORNEY, Eugene
See–JAMAIN, Hippolyte & Forney, Eugene

FOROIULIENSIS, Paulus Diaconus
See–IORNANDES–FOROIULIENSIS, Paulus Diaconus

FORREST, Lieut. Col. Charles Ramus
– **A Picturesque Tour along the Rivers Ganges & Jumna, in India.** Ill.:– Hunt & Sutherland. 1824. 1st. Edn. 4to. Occasional light offsetting & spotting. Mod. hf. mor. (S. Nov.4; 611) *Hossains.* £700
– – **Anr. Copy.** Text slightly discold. Cont. hf. mor., partly untrimmed, some wear. (TA. Nov.20; 394) £525
– – **Anr. Copy.** Liby. stp. on title, plt. list & 1st. text lf. Hf. mor. (C. May 20; 123) *Taylor.* £380
– – **Anr. Copy.** 20 (of 24) cold. plts., some foxing, 2 ll. reprd., sm. nailhole through final 50 pp. Mod. three-qtr. mor., worn. (SG. Oct.30; 157) $480
– – **Anr. Edn.** 1842. L.P. 4to. Orig. wtr.-col. drawing pasted in. Red lev. mor., gt., by Zaehnsdorf. (C. Mar.18; 42) *Traylen.* £1,600

FORREST, Capt. Thomas
– **Voyage aux Moluques et à La Nouvelle Guinee ...** Paris, 1780. 1st. Fr. Edn. 4to. Lacks 1 plt? Cont. mott. cf., gt.-panel. back. (PNY. May 21; 193) $300
– **A Voyage to New Guinea & the Moluccas ...** Dublin, 1779. 1st. Irish Edn. Disbnd., ex-liby. (SG. Feb.26; 132) $110

FORRESTER, Alfred Henry 'A. Crowquill'
– **Absurdities: in Prose & Verse.** L., 1827. 12mo. Gt. cf. by Robson & Kerslake, worn. (SG. Sep.4; 135) $130

FORSHAW, J.M.
– **Parrots of the World.** Ill.:– W.T. Cooper. Melbourne, 1973. Fo. Orig. silk bds., d.-w. (S. Jun.1; 115) *Quaritch.* £130
– – **Anr. Copy.** 4to. Orig. cl., d.-w. (P. Nov.13; 197) *Hill.* £100
See–COOPER, W.T. & Forshaw, J.M.

FORSKAL, Petrus
– **Descriptiones Animalium, Avium, Amphibiorum, Piscium, Insectorum, Verminum; quae in itinere orientali ... Materia Medica Kahirina atque Tabula Maris Rubri Geographica.–Flora Aegypticao-Arabica ... Tabula Arabiae Felicis Geographico-Botanica.** Ed.:– Carsten Niebuhr. Copen., 1775. Both 1st. Edns. 2 works in 1 vol. 4to. Cont. hf. cf., gt. (S. Oct.20; 89) *Burrell.* £800
– **Icones Rerum Naturalium quas in Itinere Orientali.** Ed.:– Carsten Niebuhr. Copen., 1776. 1st. Edn. 19th. C. hf. mor. From Chetham's Liby., Manchester. (C. Nov.26; 166) *Riley-Smith.* £480

FORSSELL, C.
– **Une Année en Suede.** Ill.:– Sandberg. Stockholm, 1829. 4to. Title browned. Cl. (BS. Jun.11; 336) £240

FORSTER, C.
– **Sinai Photographed or Records of Israel in the Wilderness.** 1862. 4to. Cl. (RBT. Jan.22; 94) £55

FORSTER, Edward
– **British Gallery of Engravings.** L., 1807. Lge. fo. Slightly soiled. Cont. hf. leath. gt. (R. Mar.31-Apr.4; 1584) DM 1,300

FORSTER, Edward Morgan
– **A Passage to India.** 1924. 1st. Edn., (200) on L.P., sigd. by author. Orig. cl.-bkd. bds., partly unc. (C. Feb.4; 279) *Minerva Books.* £100
– **Pharos & Pharillon.** L., Hogarth Pr., 1923. 1st. Edn. Cl.-bkd. patterned bds. Inscr., Percy Whichelo sig. (SG. Jun.4; 186) $170

FORSTER, Fr.
– **Leben und Thaten Friedrich's des Grossen, Königs von Preussem.** Meissen, 1840. 1st. Edn. 5 vols. in 2. Other owner's mark on end-papers. Cont. hf. leath., worn. (H. May 21/22; 570) DM 680

FORSTER, Johann Georg Adam
– **A Journey from Bengal to England ...** L., 1808. 2 vols. Foxed. Three-qtr. leath. (SG. Feb.26; 134) $110
– **A Voyage Round the World in His Britannic Majesty's Sloop, Resolution.** L., 1777. 1st. Edn. 2 vols. Lge. 4to. Disbnd. (SG. Feb.26; 133) $650
– **Sämmtliche Schriften.** Leipzig, 1843. 1st. Coll. Edn. 9 vols. Title multi stpd. Hf. leath. (HK. May 15; 4239) DM 1,900

FORSTER, Johann Reinhold
– **History of the Voyages & Discoveries made in the North.** 1786. 4to. Tree cf. (P. Oct.23; 24) *Maggs.* £180

FORSTER, Johann Reinhold & Georg
– **Characteres Generum Plantarum quas in Itinere ad Insulas Maris Australis ...** 1776. 1st. Edn., L.P. 4to. 78 plts., numbered 1-75. 19th. C. hf. mor. From Chetham's Liby., Manchester. (C. Nov.26; 167) *Maggs.* £650

FORSTER, John
– **The Life of Charles Dickens.** L., 1872-74. 1st. Edn. 3 vols. in 10. 8vo. Extra-ill. with 2060 engrs., drawings, ports., autographs (including 2 A.L.s. by Dickens), theatre posters, wraps. of serial pts., & other material, orig. text inlaid to fo. sheets. Red lev. mor. gt., broad borders of interlaced geometric strapwork with stylized floral sprays, spines gt., partly unc., by Bayntun. From the Prescott Collection. (CNY. Feb.6; 87) $14,000
– – **Anr. Edn.** L., 1874. 3 vols. in 9. Extra-ill. with the insertion of many A.L.s., ports., scenes, caricatures & other ephemera, each item inlaid. Lev. mor., gt. letters on spines, gt. ports. & facs. sigs. of Dickens on covers, mor. gt. doubls., watered silk end-ll. (SPB. May 6; 308) $3,750

FORSYTH, Robert
– **Beauties of Scotland.** 1805-8. 5 vols. Cf. gt. (P. Sep.11; 53) *Bailey.* £60

FORSYTH, William, Gardener
– Treatise on the Culture & Management of Fruit-trees ... 1802. 1st. Edn. 4to. Slight browning. Cont. spr. cf. (S. May 5; 107)
Simms. £70

FORT, Paul
– Les Ballades Françaises. Ill.:– F.L. Schmied. 1927. (165) on Arches. 4to. In sheets, publisher's s.-c. 2 A.L.s. by author. (HD. Dec.5; 85)
Frs. 2,800

FORTESCUE, Sir John
– A Learned Commendation of the Politique Lawes of England. 1573. 2nd. Edn. in Engl. Slight dampstaining, some early owners' sigs. on title scribbled over. Mod. pol. cf. [STC 11195] (S. Feb.9; 148)
Tunkel. £240

FORTESQUE, Sir John–FORTESQUE, Thomas
– Works.–Lord Clermont, The Family of Fortesque. 1869; 1880. 2 vols. Lge. 4to. 1st. vol. text in Engl. & Latin; 2nd. vol. engraved plts. & ports., some foxed. Cf.-bkd. bds. (CE. Jul.9; 225)
£60

FORTESQUE, John William
– A History of the British Army. 1899-1930. 13 vols. in 20 with atlases. Orig. cl. (SH. Jun.4; 80)
Maggs. £250
– – Anr. Edn. 1910-30. 19 vols. Maps to vols. 4, 7, 8, 10, 12 & 13. Cl. (CE. Aug.28; 180) £150
– – Anr. Edn. 1935-30. 13 vols. in 20 including 6 vols. of Maps. Orig. cl. (SH. Oct.10; 450)
Sanders. £250

FORTIGUERRI, Niccolo
[–] Ricciardetto di Niccolo Carteromaco. Ill.:– F. Zucchi & others after G.A. Ghedini. Paris [i.e. Venice], 1738. 1st. Edn. 2 vols. 4to. Title slightly soiled. Cont. mott. Fr. cf., gt. spines. From the collection of John A. Saks. (C. Jun.10; 76)
Pompelmo. £100
[–] – Anr. Edn. Ill.:– A. Baratti after P.A. Novelli. Venice, 1766. 2 vols. Occasional foxing. Citron str.-grd. mor. gt., by [C. Lewis?]. The Beckford copy, bkplt. of Henry J.B. Clements, lately in the collection of John A. Saks. (C. Jun.10; 77)
Taylor. £60

FORTIN, Frère François de Grandmont
[–] Les Ruses Innocentes. Paris, 1688. 3rd. Edn. 4to. At end 'Traité très Utile de la Chasse' by Charles Strosse, 12 pp., added series of copper engrs. Old cf., 5 decor. spine raised bands. (LM. Jun.13; 46)
B.Frs. 20,000

FORTSAS, Comte J.N.A. de
– Catalogue d'une Tres-Riche mais Peu Nombreuse Collection des Livres ... Mons, [1840]. Together with the 'Avis' broadside (on coated white paper) announcing that the collection had been acquired by the Binche Liby. Later marb. wraps. (SG. Mar.26; 196)
$450

FOSCOLO, Ugo
– Poesie. Paris, 1938. Esemplare Unico on Jap. Loose in orig. wraps. & box. (SI. Dec.3; 227)
Lire 580,000

FOSKETT, Daphne
– A Dictionary of British Miniature Painters. 1972. 2 vols. 4to. Orig. cl., d.-w. (S. Sep.30; 393) £50

FOSSATI, Carlo Giuseppe
– Le Temple de Malateste de Rimini de Leon Baptiste Alberti. Ill.:– Giorgio Fossati. Foligno, 1794. Pt. 1 (all publd.). Fo. Light browning. Mod. cf.-bkd. paper bds. From the collection of John A. Saks. (C. Jun.10; 80) *Marlborough.* £190

FOSSATI, Giorgio
– Memorie della Vita del Glorioso Patriarcha San Giuseppe. Venice, 1750. Fo. Old vell.-bkd. bds., hf. mor. s.-c. From the collection of John A. Saks. (C. Jun.10; 81) *Lyon.* £380
[–] Storia dell' Architettura ... Venice, 1747. Pt. 1 (all publd.). Several plts. with reprd. tears, erasure to title. Cont. vell. bds., slight wear. From the collection of John A. Saks. (C. Jun.10; 82)
Breslauer. £600
– Vita del Glorioso San Rocco. Ill.:– after Giovanni Marchiori. Venice, 1751. Sm. fo. Portion of 1 plt. browned, occasional minor foxing to margins. Cont. vell. bds., slight tear at spine. From the collection of John A. Saks. (C. Jun.10; 83)
Lyon. £85

FOSSE, Charles Louis François
– Idées d'un Militaire pour la Disposition des Troupes ... Paris, 1783. 4to. 1 plt. detchd., some soiling & staining, mainly marginal, lacks hf.-title. Cont. mor., worn, ex-liby. (CSK. Sep.5; 240)
£140
– – Anr. Copy. Cont. Fr. red hf. mor. gt. Pierpont Morgan Liby. copy. (CNY. May 22; 113) $650

FOSTER, Birket
– Brittany ... Surrey, 1878. Fo. Some foxing. Orig. decor. cl., worn & wormed. (JL. Jul.20; 854)
Aus. $160

FOSTER, Joshua J.
– Miniature Painters, British & Foreign. L. & N.Y., 1903. 'Edition Royale', (45) sigd. by author. 2 vols. Fo. Lev. by Hatchards. (CSK. May 15; 138)
£120
– – Anr. Copy. Orig. cl.-bkd. bds. (SH. Jan.29; 95)
Lincolnshire Co. Library. £80
– – Anr. Edn. 1903. De Luxe Edn., (175). 2 vols. 4to. Orig. vell., soiled. (P. May 14; 3)
Leicester. £55

FOSTER, Myles Birket & others
– Gems of Scenery from Picturesque Europe. Ill.:– after Birket Foster & others. N.d. (300) numbered. 5 orig. pts. Fo. Plts. mntd. on India paper, a few detchd., outer margin of 1 soiled & worn. Orig. cl.-bkd. bds., soiled. (CSK. Jan.30; 179)
£250

FOSTER, Samuel
– Posthuma Fosteri.–Elliptical or Azimuthal Horologiography. 1652; 1654. 1st. Edns. 2 works in 1 vol. Sm. 4to. 1st. work: title partly detchd. & torn, several ll. stained from margins, a few cont. inscrs. in text; 2nd. work: advt. lf., lacks (?blank) lf. at beginning, a few marginal stains, 2 ll. in a cont. hand at end; bnd. with an incompl. section of Edmund Gunter's 'Workes' (1662). Cont. cf., 1 cover detchd., worn. [Wing F1635; Wing F1632] (S. May 5; 311)
Elliot. £55

FOTO-AUGE
Ed.:– Franz Roh & Jan Tschichold. Ill.:– After Max Ernst & L. Moholy-Nagy. Stuttgart, 1929. No bdg. stated. (VG. Nov.17; 343) Fls. 475

FOUCHET, Max-Pol
– Femme de Nuit et d'Aube. Ill.:– Corneille. Paris, 1966. (100) sigd. by author & artist, numbered. Ob. fo. Unsewn in orig. cl. portfo., with ties. Lithos. & cover design by Corneille sigd. & dtd. by artist. (SH. Nov.21; 285) *Haarlem.* £80

FOUCQUET, Jean
– L'Oeuvre de Jehan Foucquet. Paris, 1866-67. (500). 2 vols. 4to. 1st. vol.: red Jansenist mor.; 2nd. vol.: red hf. mor., corners (both by Pierson). (HD. Dec.5; 86)
Frs. 1,500

FOUILLOUX, Jacques du
[–] Adeliche Weydwerke. Prag, 1699. 2nd. German Edn. 4to. Lightly soiled & browned, slightly wormed. Bds. (HK. Nov.18-21; 1734) DM 1,900
– La Caccia. Milan, 1615. 1st. Edn. in Italian. Cont. vell. (P. Oct.23; 288) *Maggs.* £160
– La Venerie.–Le Miroir de Fauconnerie. Rouen, 1650. 2 works in 1 vol. 4to. 1st. work with minor staining at beginning & in middle of text, some gatherings loose, 2nd. work with some marginal staining. Cont. limp vell. (C. Apr.1; 135)
Goldschmidt. £250

FOUJITA
– A Book of Cats. N.Y., 1930. 1st. Edn., (500) numbered on Arches. Sm. fo. Cl., orig. box separated at seams. Sigd., extra set of plts. on Japan vell., loose in envelope. (PNY. Mar.4; 149)
$1,000

FOUQUIER, Marcel
– De l'Art des Jardins du XVe au XXe Siècle. Paris, 1911. Fo. Buckram, orig. upr. wrap. bnd. in. (SG. Mar.12; 153)
$220
– – Anr. Copy. Hf. chagrin, corners, unc., wrap. (HD. Dec.5; 87)
Frs. 1,100

FOURCROY, [Antoine Francois, Comte de]
– Elemens d'Histoire Naturelle et de Chimie. 1791. 4th. Edn. 5 vols. Slight browning, liby. stp. on title, owner's inscr. Cont. mott. cf. (S. Apr.6; 51)
Morton-Smith. £50

FOUREST, Georges
– Le Négresse Blonde, préface de Willy. Ill.:– Frank Kupka. Paris, 1913. (513). Mor. gt., inner borders decor. with cold. onlays, orig. wraps. bnd. in, s.-c. by Vermorel. Inscr. by artist to his wife &

subsequently to their 'chers amis Puc'. (SH. Nov.21; 361) *Bisson-Millet.* £150

FOURNIER, Edouard
– Le Theatre Français au XVIe et au XVIIe Siècle. Paris, [1872?]. 2 vols. Hf.-title. Cont. hf. mor., unc. (SI. Dec.3; 229) Lire 420,000

FOURNIER, Simon Pierre
– Manuel Typographique. Paris, 1764-66. 1st. Edn. 2 vols. Vol. 1 lacks hf.-title. Mor. gt., sides blind-stpd. with ornaments in triple fillet & gt.-tooled border. (C. Jul.16; 329)
Quaritch. £900

FOURREAU, Jules
See–JORDAN, Alexis & Fourreau, Jules

FOWLER, William
– Coloured Engravings of Mosaic Pavements, Stained Glass Windows ... in Great Britain ... [Winterton, Lincs.], [1804-09]. 2 vols. Elephant fo. Dedications & most plts. trimmed & mntd. on paper, ink ruled, publisher's advt. pasted in upr. cover of each vol., lacks titles? Cont. hf. russ., worn, covers detchd. W.a.f. (C. Jul.15; 38)
Woodruff. £950
[–] – Anr. Edn. [Winterton, near Brigg, Lincs.], [1804-13]. 2 vols. Fo. A few tipped in letterpress prospectuses, etc., with imprints variously in Oxford & Hull, a few ll. loose. Hf. russ., worn & brkn. (S. Dec.9; 468) *Quaritch.* £1,250

FOWLES, John
– The Collector. Boston, [1963]. 1st. Amer. Edn. Advance copy. Orig. pict. wraps. (PNY. May 21; 194)
$140

FOWLES, Joseph
– Sydney in 1848 ... Sydney, [1878]. 4to. Rebnd. hf. cf., marb. bds., gt. title on spine. (JL. Jul.20; 724) Aus. $140
– – Anr. Edn. Sydney, ca. 1882. 4to. Cl. gt., front free endpaper removed. From the Hobill Cole Liby. (KH. Mar.24; 157) Aus. $220

FOX, Augustus Henry Lane, afterwards Rivers, A.H.L. Fox Pitt
– Antique Works of Art from Benin. Priv. Ptd., 1900. 4to. Orig. cl. gt. (SKC. Feb.26; 1471) £110

FOX, Charles James–ROSE, Rt. Hon. George
– A History of the Early Part of the Reign of James II.–Observations on the Historical Work of the Late Rt. Hon. Charles James Fox. 1808; 1809. 4to. Matching cont. pol. cf., rebkd. (TA. May 21; 516)
£56

FOX, Edward & others
See–HENRY VIII, King of England–FOX, Edward & others

FOX, George
– Gospel-Truth Demonstrated. 1706. 1st. Edn., L.P. Fo. Cont. mor., gt. panel. (S. Nov.24; 130)
Thomas. £160

FOX, Rev. John
– Time & the End of Time. 1679. 5th. Edn.? 12mo. Browned, a few tears. Cont. sheep, rebkd., worn. (SH. Jun.18; 133) *Thorp.* £55

FOX, John, Jnr.
– The Little Shepherd of Kingdom Come. Ill.:– Newell Convers Wyeth. N.Y., 1931. L.P. 1st. Wyeth Edn., (512) numbered, sigd. by artist. 4to. Qtr. vell. gt. & plaid cl., glassine wrap. (worn). (PNY. Dec.3; 384)
$280
– – Anr. Copy. Cl., boxed. (SG. Oct.23; 352)
$150

FOX, Joseph
– The Natural History & Diseases of the Human Teeth. 1814. 2nd. Edn. 2 pts. in 1 vol. 4to. Lacks lf. before title (? blank or hf.-title), 1st. title-p. dust-soiled & repair to inner blank margin, some stains, plts. browned & discold. Hf. cf. (S. Jun.15; 231) *Facchinotti.* £200

FOX, Tilbury
– Atlas of Skin Diseases. L., 1877. 1st. Edn. Fo. Cont. three-qtr. mor. (SG. Sep.18; 151) $140

FOX-DAVIES, Arthur Charles
– The Art of Heraldry. 1904. Fo. Orig. cl., soiled. (SH. Jan.30; 434) *George's.* £70
– – Anr. Copy. Cl. gt. (P. Jan.22; 81)
Heraldry. £50
– The Book of Public Arms. 1915. 4to. Orig. letters & draft heraldic drawings, crests boxed. Author's revision copy with MS. annots. (P. Apr.9; 293) *Henderson.* £100

FOX-TALBOT, H.
- **The Talbotype-Sun-Pictures.** 1846. 4to. Cont. hf. mor., worn. W.a.f. (SBA. Jul.14; 358) *Fletcher.* £110
- - **Anr. Copy.** Cont. hf. cf., very worn. W.a.f. (SBA. Mar.4; 252) *Potterton Books.* £100

FOXE, John
- **Actes & Monumentes.** 1570. 2nd. Edn. 2 vols. Fo. Vol. II lacks title, 311, 5B5, 5H1, 5H3 & last 2 ll., 1st. lf. of vol. II & several other ll. defect. with pieces torn off, last lf. of vol. I creased & reprd., other imperfections. Cont. blind-stpd. cf. over wooden bds., very worn, lacks clasps. W.a.f. [STC 11223] (S. Dec.9; 281) *Booth.* £190
- - **Anr. Edn.** [1576]. 3rd. Edn. 2 vols. in 1. Fo. Folding woodcut at p. 1193 defect., lacks both titles & colophon lf. at end, margins of prelims. & last ll. reprd., several ll. defect. or with pieces torn off affecting text, some worming, browned & stained. Inscr. of Cardinal Henry Manning on fly lf. Cont. blind-stpd. cf., rebkd., worn, covers wormed. W.a.f. [STC 11224] (S. Dec.9; 282) *Quaritch.* £120
- [-] - **Anr. Edn.** [1583]. 4th. Edn. 2 vols. in 1. Fo. Lacks all before *3 & 2 ll. of Calendar, a few ll. defect. 18th. C. mott. cf., worn, 1 cover detchd. W.a.f. [STC 11225] (S. Sep.29; 102) *Quaritch.* £100
- - **Anr. Edn.** 1596-97. 5th. Edn. 2 vols. Fo. Lacks the 2 folding woodcuts, some browning & slight staining. 18th. C. panel. cf., worn. [STC 11226] (S. Dec.9; 283) *Quaritch.* £130
- - **Anr. Edn.** 1632-31. 7th. Edn. 3 vols. Fo. Lacks a folding cut at p. 44 vol. I, somewhat browned & dampstained, a few ll. torn, other imperfections. Cont. cf., very worn, 3 covers detchd., vol. II rebkd. W.a.f. (S. Dec.9; 284) *Quaritch.* £110
- - **Anr. Edn.** L., 1684. 9th. Edn. 3 vols. Fo. Early cf., worn, rebkd. (SG. Feb.5; 140) $120

FOY, Abbé de
- **Notice des Diplomes, des Chartes et des Actes Relatifs à l'Histoire de France.** Paris, 1765. Vol. 1 (all publd.). Fo. Malmesbury pr. mark on fly-lf. Cont. red mor., gt., arms of Louis XV, triple gt. fillet, spine gt. in compartments with Royal cipher, fleur de lis in each corner, sm. sun, gt., above & below vol. number, inner gt. dentelles. (SM. Oct.7; 1718) *Frs.* 4,500

FOY, Gen. Maximilien Sebastien
- **Histoire de la Guerre de la Peninsule sous Napoleon.** Paris, 1827. 1st. Edn. 4 vols. Cont. hf. leath., foxed. (SG. Oct.30; 159) $100

FRACASTORIUS, Hieronymus
- **Opera Omnia.** Venice, 1555. 1st. Edn. 4to. Slightly browned & soiled in parts & very stained, some ll. wormed, 3 ll. reprd. at fold, sm. stp. on title. 18th. C. cf., very defect. (H. Dec.9/10; 328) *DM* 1,200
- - **Anr. Edn.** Venice, 1584 [date at end: 1574]. 3rd. Edn. 4to. Hf. vell. (S. Dec.2; 814) *Dix.* £100

FRAIPONT, G.
- **Application de la Forme à L'Espace à Décorer.** Paris, n.d. Fo. Unbnd. as iss. in orig. cl.-bkd. portfo. (CSK. Oct.10; 119) £65

FRANCAIS peints par Eux-Mêmes
Paris, 1840-42. Vols. 1-4. Lacks 2 frontis. & 6 cold. wood engraved plts. Cont. hf. leath., gt. spine. (R. Oct.14-18; 2620) *DM* 1,820
- - **Anr. Edn.** Paris, 1840-42; 1841-42. Together 8 vols. Many hand-cold. plts. Cont. hf. cf., gt. spines (SI. Dec.3; 233) *Lire* 1,300,000

FRANCE
- **Collection Universelle des Memoires Particuliers Relatifs à l'Histoire de France.** L., 1785. 64 vols. Spr. cf., decor. spines, with raised bands. (HD. Jun.29; 206) *Frs.* 3,150
- **Pièces Politiques de 1814/15: A Collection of 239 Works by various authors ... the French Revolution & Napoleonic Wars.** Paris, 1814-15. 58 vols. Cont. MS. indexes in each vol. Unif. cont. bds., gt. Some ll. with Earl of Rosebery liby. stp., w.a.f. (SBA. Jul.23; 615) *Brian.* £300

FRANCE, Anatole
- **At the Sign of the Reine Pedauque.** Ill.:– Frank C. Pape. L., 1922. Gt.-pict. cl., bkplt., lev. s.-c. Inscr. by Pape to Miss Sybil Tietjens, & with pen & ink sketch on fly-lf. by him. (SG. Apr.2; 220) $170
Clio. Ill.:– Alphonse Mucha. Paris, 1900. [1st. Edn.?] Cont. hf. cf., orig. upr. cover bnd. in. (SH. Nov.21; 433) *Ayres.* £125

- - **Anr. Copy.** (SH. Nov.21; 434) *Ayres.* £80
- - **Anr. Copy.** Ill. title slightly soiled, last 4 ll. slightly cockled. Cont. snake, slightly soiled. (HK. Nov.18-21; 2825) *DM* 460
Clio.-La Révolte des Anges. Ill.:– Mucha (1st. work) Simeon (2nd. work). Paris [2nd. work], 1900; 1921. 1st. Edn., 1st Printing (1st. work). 2 works in 2 vols. Sm. 8vo. Jansenist red mor. by Lavaux, spines with raised bands, wraps., unif. bdg. (HD. Jun.25; 246) *Frs.* 1,250
- **Les Contes de Jacques Tournebroche.** Ill.:– Sylvain Sauvage. Paris, 1924. (50) on laid paper. Lge. 8vo. 3 states of etchings, unpubld. watercolour. Mor. by Kieffer, gt., wrap. preserved, s.-c. (SM. Feb.11; 219) *Frs.* 5,000
- **Les Désirs de Jean Servien.-Thais.-La Rotisserie de la Reine Pédauque.-Le Lys Rouge. -Le Puits de Sainte Claire.-Pierre Nozière.-L'Ile des Pingouins.-Les Dieux ont Soif.-Génie Latin. -Le Petit Pierre.-La Vie en Fleurs.-Les Contes de Jacques Tournebroche.-L'Invocation de Clio.** 1882; 1891; 1893; 1894; 1895; 1899; 1903; 1912; 1913; 1918; 1922; 1921. 1st. Edns. (1st. ll. works); on Holland. 13 works in 12 vols. 12mo. Red hf. mor. by Lavaux, corners, spines with raised bands, some wraps. defect., uniformly bnd. Autograph visiting card from author to Catulle Mendes. (HD. Jun.25; 245) *Frs.* 1,950
- **Histoire Contemporaine.-L'Orme du Mail.-Le Mannequin d'Osier.-L'Anneau d'Améthyste. -Monsieur Bergeret à Paris.** Paris, 1897-[1901]. 1st. Edns. 4 vols. 12mo. Hf. mor. by Kra, corners, decor. spines, unc., wraps. (HD. Dec.5; 88) *Frs.* 1,600
- **L'Ile des Pingouins.** Ill.:– Louis Jou. Paris, 1926. (410) numbered, on Hollande pur chiffon à la forme. 2 vols. Fo. Ptd. parch. wraps., unc., unopened, card. s.-c.'s. (SG. Oct.23; 169) $170
- - **Anr. Edn.** Ill.:– Louis Jou. Paris, Priv. ptd., 1926. (535); on Jap., with separate sets of ills. 2 vols. 4to. In sheets, wraps. (HD. Dec.5; 90) *Frs.* 1,300
- **Jeanne d'Arc.** [1909]. Definitive Edn.; (300) on Holland. 4 vols. 4to. Hf. vell., corners, smooth decor. spines, wraps. Sigd. autograph dedication by Léopold Kahn. (HD. Feb.27; 135) *Frs.* 1,150
- **Le Lys Rouge.** Ill.:– Omer Bouchery. Paris, [1925]. (83) numbered on Japon imperial, with additional suite of 2 orig. watercolours, & 35 etchings on China paper. 4to. Wraps., some wear. (SG. Apr.2; 29) $240
- **Mémoires d'un Volontaire.** Ill.:– Lesueur after Moreau. Paris, 1902. On lge. Arches vell. 2 states of etchings (including etching with comment). Hf. mor., wrap. preserved. (SM. Feb.11; 63) *Frs.* 1,000
- **Les Noces Corinthiennes.** 1876. Mor., mor. doubl., decor., wrap., s.-c., by Blanchetière, slightly soiled. (HD. Oct.10; 55) *Frs.* 1,000
- **Oeuvres Complètes.** Paris, 1925. (1500). 25 vols. 4to. Plts. in 2 states. Hf. mor. gt. (SPB. Nov.25; 454) $1,100
- - **Anr. Edn.** Ill.:– Chahine & Dethomas. Paris, 1925-35. Ltd. Definitive Edn. 25 vols. 4to. Vols. I-XV & XVII red mor. by Baruch, orig. wraps. bnd. in, rest orig. wraps., unc. Extra suite of ills. on papier de chine, lacking for Vol. XVI, bnd. in Vols. I-XV & XVII, in 8 folders for other vol. (SM. Oct.8; 2120) *Frs.*2,300
- - **Anr. Copy.** 2nd. series of ills. on China. Unc., orig. wraps. slightly browned & soiled, 25 orig. wraps. (H. May 21/22; 1563) *DM* 750
- **Le Puits de Sainte Clair.** Ill.:– G. Rochegrosse. Paris, 1925. (100) on lge. Jap. Lge. 8vo. 2 states, 1 with comments, separate printing in colour of tail-pieces. Hf. mor. by Valmar, corners, spine with mosaic raised bands, wrap. & spine preserved, bdg. slightly defect. (HD. Jun.25; 247) *Frs.* 1,150
- **Le Rôtisserie de la Reine Pédauque.** Ill.:– Auguste Leroux. Paris, 1911. (333) on vélin à la cuve. Mor., by Bernasconi & Goix, red mor. doubls., orig. wraps. bnd. in, s.-c. (SM. Oct.8; 2334) *Frs.* 3,800
- - **Anr. Edn.** Ill.:– Guy de Montabel. Paris, 1925. On Rives vell., numbered. Jansenist mor. by Blanchetière, unc., wrap. & spine. (HD. Dec.5; 89) *Frs.* 1,100
- **Selected Stories.** [L.], [1927]. 12mo. Hf. cf. gt. by Sangorski & Sutcliffe, s.-c. Fore-e. pntg., sigd. by F.R. Cross. (PNY. Dec.3; 153) $170

FRANCE, Anatole (Contrib.)
See–GIL BLAS: Illustre Hebdomadaire

FRANCESCO III, Duke of Modena
- **Per la Solenne Dedicazione della Statua Equestre Innalzata dal Pubblico di Modena ...** Ill.:– Antonio Baratti after Michel Angelo Borghi. Modena, 1774. L.P. Fo. Folding plt. with reprd. tear, minor worming to inner margins toward end, a broadside 'Per la Corsa de Barberi al Palio Scopredosi la Statua Equestre', Modena, 1774, inserted at front. Cont. gt. flowered wraps., buckram s.-c. From the collection of John A. Saks. (C. Jun.10; 84) *Marlborough.* £90

FRANCHIMONT A FRANCKENFELD, Nicolaus
-FRISCHMAN DE EHRENCRON, Matthaeus Johannes
- **Lithotomia Medica seu Tractatus Lithontripticus, de Calculo Renum & Vesicae** [resp. Frischman de Ehrencron]. Prague, 1683. New cl. (S. Dec.2; 489) *Gurney.* £55

FRANCI, Adriano
See–TOLOMEI, Claudio 'Adriano Franci'

FRANCIA, François L.T.
- **Progressive Lessons Tending to Elucidate the Character of Trees, with the Process of Sketching, & Painting Them in Water Colours.** 1813. 1st. Edn. Fo. Text wtrmkd. 1809-11, 1 plt. 1808, 1 orig. watercolour of Oak plt., sigd. 'Anna Baker' on verso, loosely inserted, inscr. by her & Lucy Baker on front pastedown. Orig. hf. roan, slightly worn. (S. Dec.3; 969) *Marks.* £190
- - **Anr. Copy.** 4to. Cont. hf. cf., loose. (SH. Jun.25; 152) *Hollander.* £80

FRANCIS, Saint, of Assisi
- **Laudes Creaturarum.** Hammersmith, Doves Pr., 1910. (12) on vell. 12mo. Niger mor., upr. with central gt. ornament, spine in 6 compartments, 5 raised bands, sigd. by Doves Bindery, qtr. mor. s.-c. John Quinn & Cortlandt Field Bishop bkplts. (CNY. May 22; 392) $950
- **The Little Flowers.** Trans.:– T.W. Arnold. 1909. (2) Pres. Copies on vell. 4to. Orig. limp vell., silk ties, partly unc. (C. Jul.22; 69) *Joseph.* £210

FRANCIS, Charles Richard
- **Sketches of Native Life in India.** 1848. Fo. 20 hand-cold. & finished litho. plts. (of 22). Cont. hf. mor. by Kelly, with his ticket, cl. box. Bkplt. of A.H. Paget. (S. Jun.29; 224) *Hossain.* £75

FRANCIS, Grant R.
- **Old English Drinking Glasses.** 1926. 4to. Orig. buckram, d.-w. (CSK. Sep.26; 203) £85
- - **Anr. Copy.** Cl. gt. (P. Jul.2; 50) £50

FRANCIS, Sir Philip 'Junius'
- **[Letters of Junius].** L., 1772. 1st. Authorized Edn., 1st. Iss. 2 vols. Orig. stiff wraps., old owner's sig. on covers, qtr. mor. gt. s.-c., unc. From the Prescott Collection. (CNY. Feb.6; 183) $320
- - **Anr. Edn.** 1796. 2 vols. Cf., decor. spine gt. (CE. Jul.9; 129) £58
- **Stat Nominis Umbra.** Edinb., 1807. New Edn. Cont. crimson str.-grd. mor., gt. Fore-e. pntg.; from the liby. of Zola E. Harvey. (SG. Mar.19; 142) $240

FRANCISCI, Erasmus
- **Guineischer und Americanischer Blumen-Pusches.** Nuremb., 1669. Sm. hole in S4. Cont. cf., stpd. 'B.P.B.F. 1681' on upr. cover, 18th. C. German ducal bkplt. (SPB. May 5; 216) $600
- **Neu-polirter Geschicht Kunst und Sitten-Spiegel Auslandischer Volcker.** Nuremb., 1670. Fo. 50 full-p. plts. (of 51), a few slightly defect., some browning thro.-out. Old cf. (BS. Jun.11; 104) £90
- **Ost- und West-Indischer wie auch Sinesischer Lust-und Stats-Garten ...** Nuremb., 1668. 1st. Edn. Fo. Cont. vell. bds. [Sabin 25463] (S. Mar.31; 472) *Bruckner.* £650

FRANCISCUS, Torrensis
See–POLACCO, Giorgio-FRANCISCUS, Torrensis

FRANCK, Richard
- **Northern Memoirs.** 1694. Rebnd. mor. gt. by Rivière. (CE. Nov.20; 180) £140
- - **Anr. Edn.** Edinb., 1821. Hf. roan, worn. (CE. Nov.20; 148) £55

FRANCK, Sebastian
- **Chronica.** Strassburg, 1531. 1st. Edn., 3rd Printing Fo. Slightly browned in parts, a few old MS. marginalia, 1 prelim. defect. with text loss, reprd., text replaced in MS, lack 1st. 6 ll. (title & index). Cont. style cf. (R. Mar.31-Apr.4; 44) *DM* 650

FRANCK, Sebastian – Chronica. -contd.
– – **Anr. Edn.** Leiden, 1583. 3rd. Dutch Edn. Fo. Slightly soiled or browned in parts, stp. on main title, lacks ll. 75 & 78. Cont. vell., heavily browned. (R. Mar.31-Apr.4; 45) DM 800
[–] **Sprichwörter.** Frankfurt, 1548. 3rd. Edn. 4to. Lightly browned, lightly soiled in parts, lf. 88 corner torn with slight text loss, light stp. on title, marginalia, old MS. notes on cover & end-ll. Cont. blind-tooled pig-bkd. wood bds., clasps. (R. Mar.31-Apr.4; 47) DM 2,000
– **Weltbuch.** Tübingen, 1534. 1st. Edn., 1st. Printing. Fo. Some cont. notes. Cont. blind-tooled leath.-bkd. wood bds., spine renewed, clasps brkn. (R. Oct.14-18; 66) DM 3,200
– – **Anr. Copy.** 227 (of 237) ll., lightly, 3 ll. torn at corners with loss of foliation, some cont. notes, unc. Bdg. worn. [Sabin 25468] (R. Mar.31-Apr.4; 48) DM 750

FRANCK V. FRANCKENAU, G.
– **Flora Francica Rediviva.** Ed.:– J.G. Thilo. Leipzig, 1736. 4th. Edn. Browned thro.-out & slightly soiled. Cont. blind-tooled pig-bkd. wood bds., 2 clasps. (HK. Nov.18-21; 520) DM 460

FRANCKENBERG, A.
– **Gemma Magica.** Amst., 1688. 1st. Edn. Hf. vell. (R. Oct.14-18; 191) DM 1,300

FRANCKLIN, William
– **Inquiry Concerning the Site of Ancient Palibothra.** L., 1815-17. 2 pts. in 1, pts. I & II only (of 4). 4to. Plts. with light browning & offsetting, sm. tear to 1 map. Cont. Engl. str.-grd. red mor., covers gt. & blind-tooled, gt. spine. (CNY. Oct.1; 44) $200

FRANCO, Giacomo
– **Habiti d'Huomeni et Donne Venetiane Con La Processione della Serma** . . . Venice, [1610]. Sm. fo. Folding view of Venice & 1 other plt. bnd. in at end. Vell. Owing to uncertainty of collation w.a.f. (BS. Jun.11; 337) £720

FRANCO, Giacomo–DOGLIONI, G.N.
– **Habiti d'Huomeni et Donne Venetiane Con La Processione della Serma** . . .**-La Citta di Venetia.** Venice; Ongania, [1623]; [1877]. Facs. Edns. 2 works in 1 vol. 4to. 1st. work: with title & 12 orig. plts. bnd. in; 2nd. work: with title & 15 orig. plts. in dupl. mntd. & bnd. in. Mor.-bkd. cl. Stirling-Maxwell copy. (BS. Jun.11; 338) £110

FRANÇOIS, Jean
– **La Science des Eaux** . . . **avec les Arts de Conduire les Eaux, et Mésurer la Grandeur tant des Eaux que des Terres.** Rennes, 1653. 1st. Edn. 7 pts. in 1 vol. Sm. 4to. Some ll. chewed in upr. outer corners, occasional browning, sm. inscr. on title. Mod. vell. bds. by the Studio Bindery. (S. Jun.29; 326) Porton. £70

FRANÇOIS-FRANCK, Charles Emile
– **Leçons sur les Fonctions Motrices du Cerveau** . . . **et sur l'épilepsie Cérébrale.** Ed.:– Professor Charcot (preface). Paris, 1887. 1st. Edn. Hf. mor. (S. Jun.15; 297) Quaritch. £90

FRANCQUART, J.
– **Pompa Fuenbris Optimi Potentissimique Principis Alberti Pii.** Brussels, 1623. Ob. fo. 2 folding plts. defect. & reprd. No bdg. stated. (BS. Jun.11; 216) £250
– – **Anr. Copy.** 2 plts. defect. & preserved, 1 torn. Bds. (BS. Jun.11; 217) £240
– – **Anr. Copy.** Plts. 3 & 47 folding, engraved title reprd. with sm. tears, 2 folding plts. defect. & partly reprd., 1 plt. torn, text (Latin, Fr., Flemish & Spanish) lightly browned & slightly soiled in parts. Cont. vell., soiled. (H. Dec.9/10; 766) DM 1,300

FRANEAU, J.
– **Jardin d'Hyver.** Dovay, 1616. 19th. C. hand-bnd. cf., 2 gold-stpd. fillets with 8 corner fleurons, gt. outer & wide inner dentelle, gt. spine. (D. Dec.11-13; 131) DM 9,000

FRANK, J.B.
– **Praxis Geometrica Universalis.** Augsburg, 1710. 4to. Lightly soiled in parts. Cont. leath. (HK. May 12-14; 316) DM 420

FRANK, Johann Peter
– **System einer Vollständigen Medicinischen Polizey.** Frankenthal, 1791-93. Cont. hf. leath. (D. Dec.11-13; 199) DM 1,000

FRANKAU, Julia
– **John Raphael Smith.** 1902. Fo. In portfo., worn. (BS. Sep.17; 170) £55
– **John Raphael Smith.-William Ward, James Ward.** 1902; 1904. 2 vols; 2 vols. Fo. & 8vo. Cont. hf. mor. (SH. Jan.29; 97) York. £240
– **The Story of Emma, Lady Hamilton.** 1911. (250) numbered. 2 vols. Fo. MS. note on verso of hf.-title by author. Orig. lev. by Hatchards, gt. (CSK. May 15; 137) £120

FRANKFURTER, Moshe
– **Shaar Shimon.** Amst., 1714. 16mo. Lightly stained, soiled, cropped. Cf.-bkd. bds., worn. (SPB. May 11; 164) $175

FRANKLAND, Capt. Charles Colville
– **Travels to & from Constantinople.** 1829. 2 vols. Some ll. spotted. Cont. hf. cf. (SH. May 21; 42) Dimakarakos. £75

FRANKLIN, Benjamin
– **Briefe von der Elektricität.** Trans.:– J.C. Wilcke. Leipzig, 1758. 1st. German Edn. MS. owner's mark on title, partly covered with ink, browned. Cont. bds. (HK. Nov.18-21; 479) DM 1,600
– **The Life of . . . Written by Himself.** Phila., 1794. 2nd. Amer. Edn. 12mo. Offset on title, browning & staining. Later buckram. (SPB. Jul.28; 134) $125
– **Oeuvres.** Trans.:– Barbeu Dubourg. Paris, 1773. 1st. Fr. Edn. 2 vols. 4to. Occasional spotting & browning. Cont. mott. cf., spines gt., some wear. [Sabin 25607] (S. May 5; 363) Quaritch. £120
– – **Anr. Copy.** Cont. hf. leath., gt. spine. [Sabin 25607] (HK. Nov.18-21; 521) DM 440
– **Opere politiche.** Trans.:– Pietro Antoniutti. Padua, 1783. 1st. Italian Edn. Cont. cf.-bkd. bds., gt. spine. (CNY. Oct.1; 94) $320
– **Political, Miscellaneous & Political Pieces.** 1779. 1st. Coll. Edn. 4to. A few ll. slightly spotted, pin-hole in 1st. 2 ll. & port. Cont. cf., neatly rebkd. (S. Dec.9; 378) Traylen. £100
– – **Anr. Copy.** Some slight browning. Cont. spr. cf., rebkd. preserving old spine. Inscr. in cont. hand to Edward Barry, bkplt. of Sir Windham Dalling. [Sabin 25565] (S. Feb.9; 152) Coquillette. £80
– – **Anr. Copy.** Cont. mott. cf. (SG. Oct.9; 102) $500
– **Private Life of.** 1793. Cf. gt. (P. Dec.11; 319) Georges. £90
– **Some Account of the Success of Inoculation for the Small-Pox** . . .**– Plain Instructions for Inoculation in the Small-Pox.** L., 1759. 2 works in 1 vol. 4to. Ex-liby., heavily restored & remargined. Mod. buckram folder. [Sabin 25589 (1st. work)] (SPB. Jun.22; 58) $650
– **The Way to Wealth.** Paris, 1795. L.P. 16mo. (in 4's). 31 p. 'Catalogue des Livres Imprimés par J.B. Bodoni . . .' at end. Orig. bds., unc. (SG. Feb.5; 141) $190
See–**WALPOLE, Thomas, Franklin, Benjamin & others**

FRANKLIN, Benjamin (Ed.)
See–**CICERO, Marcus Tullius**

FRANKLIN, Benjamin & Jackson, Richard
– **The Interest of Great Britain Considered, with regard to her Colonies.** L., 1763. Recent wraps. [Sabin 35450] (CB. Nov.12; 258) Can. $300

FRANKLIN, Sir John
– **Narrative of a Journey to the Shores of the Polar Sea.** 1823. 1st. Edn. 4to. Maps slightly creased, end-ll. & plts. stained in outer margins. Cont. hf. cf. Pres. Copy, to Mrs. Bright. [Sabin 25624] (S. Feb.10; 358) Maggs. £320
– – **Anr. Copy.** Errata slip, stitching brkn., some foxing & offsetting. Hf. cf., worn, lr. cover detchd. (S. Jun.22; 176) Jonkers. £220
– – **Anr. Copy.** Later three-qtr. mor., unc. (SG. Oct.30; 162) $550
– – **Anr. Copy.** Cont. blind-stpd. cf., disbnd. (SG. Feb.26; 137) $400
– – **Anr. Copy.** With errata slip. Cont. cf., bds. loose. Inscr. to Sir John Hayford Thorold from Thomas Wilson, M.D. (CB. Sep.24; 176) Can. $550
– – **Anr. Copy.** Hf.-title extended, lacks errata slip. New hf. mor. & marb. bds. (CB. Nov.12; 242) Can. $450
– – **Anr. Edn.** 1824. 2nd. Edn. 2 vols. Mod. pol. hf. cf., spines gt., partly unc. [Sabin 25625] (S. Feb.9; 153) Gross. £90
– – **Anr. Copy.** Mod. hf. cf., gt., partly unc. (S. Jun.29; 282) Bowes. £50

– – **Anr. Edn.** 1824. 3rd. Edn. 2 vols. Tears to 1 chart, reprd., slight browning. Mod. hf. cf., spines gt., unc. [Sabin 25625] (S. Feb.9; 154) Harris. £55
– **Narrative of a Journey to the Shores of the Polar Sea.–Narrative of a Second Expedition to the Shores of the Polar Sea.** 1823-28. 1st. Edns. Together 2 vols. 4to. With the inserted port. & plt. 10. Cont. cf. gt., jnts. split. [Sabin 25624; 25628] (S. Nov.24; 131) Bowes. £400
– – **Anr. Copy.** Diced cf., & cl., worn. (MMB. Oct.8; 28) Traylen. £290
– – **Anr. Copy.** 1st. work: occasional spotting & soiling; 2nd. work: occasional spotting, margins of some plts. discold. Unif. old cf., rebkd., covers detchd. From Chetham's Liby., Manchester. (C. Nov.26; 169) Bowes. £240
– **Narrative of a Second Expedition to the Shores of the Polar Sea.** 1828. 4to. Cont. cl., covers loose. (SH. May 21; 43) Bowes. £60

FRANSCHE (DE) MODE-KRAMERY, in Amstels Waereldstad aan't Y
Ill.:– H. Numan. [Holland], ca. 1780. 32mo. Disbnd. (SH. Mar.19; 99) Schierenberg. £75

FRANZETTI, Agapito
[–] **[Raccolta di 320 Veduti di Roma, si Antiche che Moderne].** [Rome], ca. 1800. Ob. 4to. Lacks title, slight marginal spotting. Hf. cf., very worn, covers loose. W.a.f. (S. Jan.27; 587) Mistrali. £110

FRASER, James
– **The History of Nadir Shah** . . . **the present Emperor of Persia.** 1742. 1st. Edn. Cont. cf. (S. Nov.4; 614) Billy. £60

FRASER, James Baillie
– **Journal of a Tour through part of the snowy range of the Himala Mountains & to the Sources of the Rivers Juma & Ganges.** 1820. 1st. Edn. 4to. Lge. engraved folding map spotted, 2 sm. tears. Cont. hf. russ., spine defect. (C. Feb.25; 95) McMamnon. £100

FRASER, R.
– **General View of the Agriculture & Mineralogy** . . . **of the County Wicklow.** Dublin, 1801. (150). Hf. vell. (GM. Apr.30; 284) £130

FRASER, William
– **The Lennox.** Edinb., 1874. 2 vols. Red cl. gt., worn. (CE. Nov.20; 62) £65
– **Memoirs of the Maxwells of Pollok & Illustrations.** Edinb., 1863. 3 vols. Grained cl. gt., soiled. (CE. Nov.20; 45) £50
– **Red Book of Menteith.** Edinb., 1880. 2 vols. Red cl. gt., soiled. (CE. Nov.20; 61) £50

FRAUBERGER, Heinrich
– **Mittheilungen der Gesellschaft zur Erforschung Juedischer Denkmaeler.** Frankfurt am Main, 1900-15. Nos. I-VIII in 5 vols. 4to. Orig. bds. (S. Nov.17; 13) Lanson. £350

FRAZER, James George
– **The Golden Bough.** 1936-37. 3rd. Edn. 13 vols. including index. Orig. cl. (SH. Jul.9; 98) Subunso. £70

FRAZER, Mrs.
– **The Practice of Cookery, Pastry, Pickling, Preserving, & c.** Edinb., 1791. 1st. Edn. 12mo. Lacks final blank, some soiling & browning. Cont. sheep, worn. (S. Jan.26; 173) Thorp. £55

FREART, Roland
– **A Parallel of the Ancient Architecture with the Modern** . . . Trans.:– John Evelyn. L., 1733. 4th. Edn. Fo. Old liby. stp. on title. Disbnd. (SG. Mar.12; 154) $170

FRECHETTE, Louis-Honoré
– **Mes Loisirs: Poésies.** Quebec, 1863. 1st. Edn. 12mo. Mor. gt., upr. cover gt.-lettered 'Presented to H.R.H. Prince Arthur by the Province of Quebec'. (SG. Mar.5; 108) $120

FREDERICK II, the Great, King of Prussia
– **Oeuvres.** Ed.:– [J.O. Preuss]. Ill.:– A. Mensel. Berlin, 1846-57. (200) on vell., Fürsten Edn. 30 pts. (pt. 27 in 3 vols.). Lge. fo. & imp. fo. Hf. linen, orig. wraps. (HK. May 12-14; 1584) DM 3,800
– **Oeuvres.–Oeuvres Posthumes.** Berlin & Cologne [Strassburg] (Supp.), 1789 & 1788-89 (Supp.). 4to. 15 vols. & 6 supp. vols. Cont. hf. leath. gt., 4 spines slightly defect., slight wear, monog. GTB on spine. (H. May 21/22; 1073) DM 1,400

– Oeuvres Postumes. Berlin, 1788. 1st. Edn. 15 vols. Cont. mott. cf., spines gt. (CSK. Sep.12; 93) £100
– – Anr. Copy. Engraved port. offset on title of vol. I. Cont. spr. bds. (S. Jan.27; 452) *Wenner.* £55

FREDERIKS, J.W.
– Dutch Silver. The Hague, 1952-61. 4 vols. 4to. Orig. cl. (S. Jul.23; 271) *Sims & Reed.* £230
– – Anr. Copy. 4 vols. (all publd.). Fo. Cl. gt. (VG. Dec.15; 144) Fls. 600

FREE CUSTOMES (The), Benefits & Priviledges of the Copyhold Tennants, of the Mannors of Stepny & Hackny . . .
1617. Sm. 4to. Some early marginalia. Later mor. [STC 23254] (CSK. Jul.24; 93) £120

FREEDMAN, Harold
– The Book of Canberra. Adelaide, [1966]. (250) numbered, & sigd. Ob. fo. Mor. over bds., recessed enamelled emblem on upr. cover. (KH. Mar.24; 160) Aus. $110

FREEMAN, Archibald
See-FITE, Emerson D. & Freeman, Archibald

FREER Gallery of Art
– Oriental Studies. Wash., 1933-63. Vols. 1-6. Fo. Liby. stps. Cont. & orig. cl. (SH. Apr.9; 73) *Fogg.* £65

FREIBERG, Heinrich von
– Tristan u. Isolde. Ill.:– A. Kubin. Reichenberg, 1935. (600) numbered, C Edn. Orig. linen. (HK. Nov.18-21; 2748) DM 540

FREILIGRATH, Ferdinand & Schücking, Christoph B. Levin
– Dss Malerische und Romantische Westphalen. Barmen & Leipzig, [1842]. Most plts. soiled; bnd. in L. Wiese: Westphalische Volkssagen in Liedern, Barmen, ca. 1842. Cont. leath., gold fillets on spine & covers. (R. Oct.14-18; 2412) DM 3,800

FREIND, Dr. John
– Chymical Lectures . . . to which is added an appendix. Trans.:– J.M. 1712. 1st. Edn. in Engl. Cont. panel. cf. (S. Dec.1; 170) *Bickesteth.* £100
– The History of Physick from the Time of Galen to the Beginning of the Sixteenth-Century. 1725-26. 1st. Edn. 2 vols. Cont. cf., not. unif. (S. Jun.15; 301) *Tait.* £80

FREITAG, Adam
– Architectura Militaris Nova et Aucta. Amst., 1665. Fo. Engraved title cut down & mntd., slightly spotted, ?lacks last blank. Cont. hf. vell., bds., worn, lr. corner torn away. (S. Jan.27; 327) *Hendricks.* £130
– L'Architecture Militaire ou la Fortification Nouvelle. Paris, 1640. Fo. 'La Table du Profil' plt. misbnd. at p. 77 (called for at p. 37), some marginal dampstains. Cont. cf. (CSK. Mar.13; 142) £220

FREKE, William
– Select Essays Tending to the Universal Reformation of Learning, concluded with The Art of War. 1693. 1st. Edn. Cont. cf. [Wing F2165] (C. Apr.1; 209) *Moore.* £120

FREMONT, John C.
– Report of the Exploring Expedition to the Rocky Mountains in 1842, & to Oregon & North California in 1843-'44. Wash., 1845. House iss. Map separated at some folds, but compl. Orig. cl., brkn. (SG. Jan.8; 165) $150

FRENCH, B.F.
– Historical Collections of Louisiana. N.Y.; Phila.; N.Y., 1846; 1850; 1851, 53. Pts. 1, 2, 3, & 5. in 4 vols. Foxed. Cl., worn. (SG. Jan.8; 166) $140
– Historical Collections of Louisiana & Florida. New Series.–Ditto, Second Series: Historical Memoirs & Narratives, 1527-1702. N.Y., 1869; 1875. 2 vols. Cl., 1st. vol. needs rebdg., 2nd. vol. unc. & unopened. (SG. Jan.8; 167) $120

FRENCH Colored Caricatures
Paris, Early 19th. C. 1 vol. Fo. (12½ × 10 inches). 26 hand-cold. lithos., plus other ills. Old qtr. mor., worn. (SG. Sep.4; 195) $700

FRENCH, George
– The History of Col. Parke's Administration . . . Leeward Islands; with an Account of the Rebellion in Antegoa. 1717. Some stains. Mod. cf. (S. Dec.8; 255) *Remington.* £90

FRENCH, John
– The Art of Distillation . . . to which is added the London Distiller. 1653. 2nd. Edn. (1st. pt.) 1st. Edn. (London Distiller). 2 pts. in 1 vol. 4to. Paper browned & discold., some edges fragile, upr. corners of title & following ll. torn & reprd., a few sm. marginal tears. Cont. cf., worn, spines reprd. [Wing F2170] (S. Dec.1; 172) *Music Mart.* £100
– – Anr. Edn. 1664. 3rd. Edn. 4to. Browned, sm. tears to some pp., separate pagination to 'The London Distiller'. Cont. cf. gt. decor. spine, upr. cover detchd. (TA. Jan.22; 192) £70
– The Yorkshire Spaw. 1652. 1st. Edn. 12mo. Lacks last lf. R4 (blank?), upr. margin shaved affecting p. numerals. 19th. C. mor. Owners' mark on B1 of Rev. Philip Bliss. [Wing F2175] (C. Nov.20; 244) *Quaritch.* £90

FRENCH REPUBLICAN FLAGS
Paris, ca. 1789. 4to. 60 full-p. engraved plts., all hand-cold. & heightened with gold. mntd. view detchd., frontis. foxed. Cont. mott. cf. gt., rebkd. Hf.-p. A.N.s. by Jean Sylvain Bailly tipped-in. (CNY. May 22; 163) $2,200

FRENCH REVOLUTION
– Collection Complete des Tableaux Historiques de la Revolution Française. Ill.:– Duplessix-Bertaux. Paris, An XIII-1804. 3 vols. Tall fo. Later hf. cf. (SG. May 14; 79) $600

FRENICLE DE BESSY, Bernard
– Traité des Triangles, Rectangles en Nombres. Paris, 1676. 1st. Edn. Cont. cf., upr. cover loose. Henry Cavendish's copy with his stp. on verso of title. (S. Oct.21; 384) *Phelps.* £60

FRENZEL, J.G.A.
– Die Vorzüglichsten Gemälde der Königlichen Galerie in Dresden. Dresden, 1836. 2 vols. Fo. 2 litho. ports. & 151 plts. only, all on india paper, text in Fr. & German, some spotting, soiling & damp staining. Cont. cf., worn. W.a.f. (CSK. Apr.10; 115) £2,200

FRERE, Walter Howard
– Graduale Sarisburiense. 1894. (300) numbered. Fo. Cont. mor. gt., ex-liby. copy with stps. to front end-paper & title. (TA. Jun.18; 318) £75

FRERET, Nicolas (attributed to)
[–] **Lettre de Thrasibule à Leucippe . . .** L., ca. 1768. Sm. 8vo. Cont. red mor., fillet, fleuron in corners, decor. spine, inside dentelle. (HD. Mar.18; 69) Frs. 1,500

FRESENIUS, J. Ph.
– Kirchen-Geschichte von denen Reformirten in Franckfurt am Mayn. Ed.:– J. Ph. Fresenius. Frankfurt & Leipzig, 1751. Lacks 1 copperplt. Cont. bds. (R. Oct.14-18; 2282) DM 420

FREUD, Sigismund
– Das Ich und das Es; Die Frage der Laienanalyse. Vienna, 1923-26. 1st. Edns. 2 vols. Orig. bds. & orig. wraps. (S. Mar.17; 336) *Traylen.* £50
– Die Traumdeutung. Leipzig & Vienna, 1900. 1st. Edn. Some ll. near end with slight paper defects. Red hf. leath. (HK. May 12-14; 318) DM 5,000
– – Anr. Copy. Misbnd, title & last ll. lightly soiled, title with owner's mark. Mod. hf. linen. (H. Dec.9/10; 400) DM 3,800
– – Anr. Edn. Leipzig & Vienna, 1909. 2nd. Edn. Hf. cf. (C. May 20; 31) *Taylor.* £140
– Uber den Ursprung der hinteren Nervenwurzeln im Ruckenmarke von Amnocoetes. [Vienna], [1877]. Offprint from 'Sitzungsberichte der K. Akademie de Wissenschaften, vol. 75. Disbnd., cl. folder. (S. Jun.15; 302) *Maggs.* £100

FREUD, Sigmund & Breuer, Joseph
– Studies in Hysteria. Trans.:– A.A. Brill. N.Y. & Wash., 1936. 1st. Separate & Compl. Engl. Edn. Cl. (S. Jun.15; 303) *Jenner Books.* £55

FREY, J.
[–] **Der Hof Ludwigs XIV.** Mainz, ca. 1850. Ob. fo. Plts. have descriptive MS. text in Engl. written in borders on sheets of thin paper bnd. in as guards. Orig. bds. gt., upr. cover loose. (SH. Mar.19; 100) *Crete.* £85

FREY, J.B.
– Historiae ab Orbe Condito Sacrae Profanaeque Viridarium etc. Feldkirch, 1678. Slightly browned in parts. Cont. cf., metal clasps. (H. Dec.9/10; 1480) DM 420

FREY, Johann Michael
See-GIGNOUX, Antoin Christoph & Frey, Johann Michael

FREYCINET, Louis
See-PERON, François & Freycinet, Louis

FREZIER, Amedé François
– Allerneuste Reise nach der Süd-See und denen Cüsten von Chili und Brasilien. Hamburg, 1718. Some discolouration to text, sm. liby. stp. on title. Cont. cf., sm. owner's cipher on sides (German). [Sabin 25928] (SPB. May 5; 220) $450
– Relation du Voyage de la Mer du Sud aux Côtes du Chily et du Perou. Paris, 1716. 1st. Edn. 4to. Some staining in upr. inner corner. Cont. cf. [Sabin 25924] (C. Feb.25; 97) *Maggs.* £220
– – Anr. Copy. Sm. marginal repairs. Worn. (SPB. May 5; 219) $500
– A Voyage to the South-Sea. 1717. 4to. Lacks frontis., title dust-soiled, occasional spotting thro.-out. 19th. C. hf. mor., vell. corners. From Chetham's Liby., Manchester. (C. Nov.26; 170) *Femfert.* £100

FRICX, Eugène Henry
– Table des Cartes des Pays Bas et des Frontières de France . . . Ill.:– Jean Harrewijn. Brussels, 1712. Fo. Disbnd. As an atlas, w.a.f. (C. May 20; 124) *Forum.* £450

FRIEDERICHS, Hulda
[–] **In the Evening of his Days: a Study of Mr. Gladstone . . .** Ill.:– Arthur Rackham & others. L., 1896. 1st. Edn. Cl., worn. Raymond M. Sutton, Jr. copy. (SG. May 7; 86) $160

FRIEDLANDER, Max J.
– Die Altniederländische Malerei. Berlin, 1924-37. 14 vols. 4to. Unif. hf. cl. (TA. Mar.19; 141) £120
– – Anr. Copy. Orig. hf. linen. (H. Dec.9/10; 213) DM 1,200
– – Anr. Copy. Fo. Hf.-cl. (VG. Nov.17; 465) Fls. 950
– – Anr. Edn. Berlin; Leyden, 1924-38. 10 vols. (of 14). Fo. Dupl. of vol. 1 added. Hf.-cl. (VG. Nov.17; 466) Fls. 500
– – Anr. Edn. Leiden, 1937. 14 vols. 4to. Publisher's bdg. (LM. Nov.8; 11) B.Frs. 13,000

FRIEDMAN, David Moshe, of Tchortkow
– Tiferet Adam. Lvov, ca. 1925. 1st. Edn. With notes by Joseph Weiss. Hf. cl. (S. Nov.18; 254) *Kornbluth.* £50

FRIEDMAN, Israel, of Ruzhin
– Bet Israel (pt. 11 of Knesset Israel). Pietrikow, 1912. 1st. Edn. Cl. (S. Nov.17; 250) *Zysblat.* £110

FRIEDRICH, André
– Emblèmes Nouveaux. Ill.:– Jacques de Zetter. Frankfurt, 1617. 1st Printing. 4to. Lacks 2 ll. with figures 33 & 47, 2 ll. reprd., title remntd., upr. margin very cropped, interfoliated. 18th. C. red mor., fillet, decor. spine. (HD. Mar.18; 70) Frs. 1,500

FRIEDRICH, Caspar David
– Paysage Marin avec un Capucin; Seelandschaft mit Kapuziner. Ill.:– Max Ernst. Zurich, 1972. (77) numbered with orig. litho. in 2 states sigd. by artist. Fo. Sm. prospectus in German & Fr. with text by Werner Spies laid in. Loose in ptd. wraps., unc., s.-c. (SG. Oct.23; 111) $950

FRIEND, The
Bloemfontein, Mar.15-Apr.17, 1900. 30 nos. Fo. With dupl. of the Mar.17 iss. (a variant, misnumbered & misdtd. Mar.16), folded as iss., 5 nos. defect. at folds with word loss, some marginal fraying & chipping, accompanied by a copy of Julian Ralph's 'War's Brighter Side' (L., 1901, 1st. Engl. Edn.). Mor.-bkd. s.-c.; accompanying work in orig. cl., with qtr. mor. s.-c. Holographic note by Kipling in the 1st. no., & with ptd. menu of 'The Dinner of the 28th. of March 1900 at Bloemfontein' (4 pp.), sigd. by Kipling & the other 23 guests; from the Prescott Collection. (CNY. Feb.6; 202) $1,900

FRIEND, Donald
– Birds from the Magic Mountain. Sanur, Bali, 1977. (400) numbered & sigd. Fo. Orig. decor. cl. with a Friend design. Orig. pen study by Friend, initialled, set to the verso of title-p. (KH. Nov.18; 265) Aus. $130

FRIGERIO, Ambrogio
– La Gloriosa Vita et gli Eccelsi Miracoli dell'almo Confessore Santo Nicola de Tolentino. Camerino,

FRIGERIO, Ambrogio Confessore Santo Nicola de Tolentino. -*contd.*
1578. 1st. Edn. 4to. 6 unnumbered pp., last map stained. Old cf. (CR. Mar.19; 252)   Lire 260,000

FRISCH, J.
[–] **Schau-Platz Barbarischer Sclaverey.** Hamburg, 1694. Lacks pp. 119-122, copper engraved title with sm. tears & loose, also 1 plt. (D. Dec.11-13; 660) upr. cover lacks paper. (D. Dec.11-13; 660)   DM 440

FRISCH, Joh. L.
– **Vorstellung der Vögel Deutschands und beyläufig auch einiger Fremden.** Berlin, [1733-] 1743-63 & 1817. 12 pts. & supp. in 3 vols. Fo. Liby. stp. on some plts., plt. 4 slightly soiled, text slightly browned. Cont. bds., gold-stpd. upr. cover. (HK. Nov.18-21; 802)   DM 28,000

FRISCHLIN, N.
– **Hebraeis.** Ed.:– M. Aichmannus & U. Bollingerus. Strassburg, 1499. 1st. Edn. Mod. hf. leath. (R. Oct.14-18; 67)   DM 950

FRISCHMAN DE EHRENCRON, Matthaeus Johannes
See–FRANCHIMONT A FRANCKENFELD, Nicolaus–FRISCHMAN DE EHRENCRON, Matthaeus Johannes

FRISIUS, Gemma
See–STRIGELUS, Victor & Frisius, Gemma

FRITH, Francis
– **Egypt & Palestine Photographed & Described.** 1857. 2 vols. Fo. Some internal spotting, affecting mounts only. Orig. qtr. mor., vol. 1 upr. cover defect. W.a.f. (TA. Aug.21; 8)   £310
– **Sinai & Palestine.** Ca. 1860. 2 vols. Fo. Lacks 1 plt., 1 torn in inner margin. Red mor.-bkd. cl., worn. (S. Jan.27; 568)   *Trotter.* £100
– – **Anr. Edn.** Ca. 1860-70. Fo. Cf.-bkd. cl., worn. (CE. Jun.4; 123)   £200
– – **Anr. Edn.** [After 1862]. Fo. 37 mntd. albumen prints, some of the mounts spotted, 1 detchd. Orig. mor.-bkd. cl. (CSK. Sep.26; 42)   £220
– **Upper Egypt & Ethiopia.** [1857]. Fo. Some dampstaining to outer margins slightly affecting some plts. Loose in orig. cl. with leath. backstrip. (TA. Mar.19; 331)   £210

FRITSCH, G.
– **Drei Jahre in Sud-Afrika.** Breslau, 1868. Some pencil notes in margins. Rexine, rebnd. (SSA. Jun.18; 130)   R. 130

FRIZZI, Antonio
[–] **La Salameide, Poemetto Giocoso con le Note.** Venice, 1772. Orig. paper wraps., unc. From the collection of John A. Saks. (C. Jun.10; 85)   *King.* £50

FROBEL, J.
– **Seven Year's Travel in Central America, Northern Mexico & the Far West of the United States.** L., 1859. 1st. Engl. Edn. Orig. linen. [Sabin 25992] (R. Oct.14-18; 1666)   DM 580

FROHAWK, Frederick William
– **Natural History of British Butterflies.** [1914]. 2 vols. Fo. Orig. cl., d.-w. (C. May 20; 208)   *Goodwin.* £140
– – **Anr. Copy.** Cl., d.-w.'s. (P. Apr.30; 208)   *Quaritch.* £80
– – **Anr. Edn.** [1925]. 2 vols. Fo. Orig. cl., sm. stain on 1 cover, slight wear. (S. May 5; 108)   *Wesley.* £85
– – **Anr. Edn.** [1926]. 1st. Edn. 2 vols. Fo. Orig. cl., slight soiling. (S. Dec.3; 970)   *W. & W.* £95
– – **Anr. Edn.** N.d. 2 vols. Fo. Orig. cl., d.-w.'s. (SH. Oct.9; 220)   *Head.* £115

FROISSART, Sir John
– **The Cronycles of England.** Trans.:– John Bourchier, Lord Berners. L., 28 Jan. 1523 & [31], Aug. 1525. 1st. Edn. in Engl. 2 vols. Fo. Variant iss. with Pynson's name spelt with a y in both colophons, vol. I with some worming filled thro.-out, severely towards front, inner margins of 1st. 10 ll. renewed, upr. margin of A2 renewed with slight facs. to headline, other blank marginal repairs to A3, ddd3, hhh3 & ooo3, slight tears reprd. at B2 & i3, vol. II with 8 ll. resized, inner margin of final lf. renewed, & a sm. reprd. tear, lr. outer blank corner of C2 reprd. Late 19th. C. crimson mor. gt., spines gt., qtr. red mor. s.-c.'s. The copy of William Randolph Hearst & John A. Saks. [STC 11396 (anr. iss.)] (CNY. Oct.1; 91) $8,000

[–] **Cronycles of England; the First [Thirde & Fourthe] Volum . . .** 1525-45. 2 vols. in 1. Fo. Both vols. mixed with most ll. from Pynson edn., some from Myddleton's reprint, lacks title, A2 & A6 in vol. 1 & last lf. in vol. 2 (last 2 in fac.) title of vol. 2 loosely inserted, lr. corner of A3 in vol. 1 & f. 301 in vol. 2 very defect., other ll. torn & defect., worming at end. Cont. L. blind-stpd. cf., metal bosses & centrepieces, rebkd. lacks clasps. W.a.f. [STC 11396-98] (S. Mar.16; 116)   *D.A. Rix.* £300
– **Chronicles of England, France, Spain & the Adjoining Countries . . .** Trans.:– Thomas Johnnes. Hafod Pr., 1803-10. 5 vols. 4to. Later hf. mor. (SBA. Oct.22; 732)   *College of Librarianship.* £90
– – **Anr. Edn.** 1839. 2 vols. Cont. mor. (SH. Jan.30; 338)   *Baer.* £70
– – **Anr. Copy.** Slightly foxed. Vell. (SSA. Jun.18; 12)   R. 100
– – **Anr. Edn.** Trans.:– Thomas Johnes. Ill.:– Henry Noel Humphries after MS. in British Museum. 1848. 2 vols. Occasional spotting. Cont. crimson mor., gt., jnts. reprd. (CSK. Jan.16; 2)   £55
– – **Anr. Edn.** Trans.:– Thomas Johnes. 1849. 2 vols. 4to. Frontis, title-p., plts., hand-cold. & heightened in gold. Mor.',gt., by J. Wright. (SBA. Jul.23; 503)   *Hendrecks.* £120
– – **Anr. Copy.** Extra illuminated titles, over 100 text wood-engrs., extra ill. with facs. in col. Crimson three-qtr. lev., spines gt. with fleurons. (SG. Apr.9; 179) $120
– – **Anr. Edn.** 1857. 2 vols. Mor. gt., gt. panels with corner fleurons, spines in compartments with fleur-de-lys device, by Holloway. (LC. Feb.12; 462) $50
– – **Anr. Edn.** L., 1868. 2 vols. Red hf. mor., 1 cover detchd. (SG. Feb.12; 192) $175
– – **Anr. Edn.** Ed.:– Kelms. Pr., 1896. (32). Lge. fo. Trial setting of 16 pp., lge. armorial woodcut border, ornamental initials, spaces left for others. Unbnd. as issued, cl. folder, s.-c. (SH. Feb.19; 12)   *J.P. Foster.* £550
– – **Anr. Edn.** Ed.:– W.P. Ker. Trans.:– J. Bourchier, Lord Berners. L., 1901-03. 6 vols. Sm. 4to. Crimson lev., multiple gt. fillet borders, spines gt., gt. dentelles, moire satin end-papers, by Zaehnsdorf. Armorial bkplt. of Fleming Crooks. (SG. Apr.9; 180) $200
– – **Anr. Edn.** Trans.:– Sir John Bourchier, Lord Berners. Stratford-upon-Avon, Shakes. Hd. Pr., 1927-28. (7) numbered, on vell. 8 vols. Sm. 4to. Heraldic devices & other decoration illuminated, some heightened with burnished gold, line endings in blue. Orig. limp vell., silk ties, unc. (CNY. May 22, 416) $11,000
– – **Anr. Edn.** Trans.:– Sir John Bourchier. Stratford-upon-Avon, Shakes. Hd. Pr., 1927-28. (350) numbered. 8 vols. 4to. Orig. linen-bkd. bds., unc. (SKC. Feb.26; 1310)   £250
– – **Anr. Copy.** S.-c.'s, worn. (SH. Feb.19; 56)   *Maggs.* £230
– – **Anr. Copy.** Hand-cold. coats of arms. Unc. (TA. Feb.19; 288)   £130
– **Histoire et Chronique Memorable.** Paris, 1574. 4 vols. in 1. Fo. Tear to d2 in vol. 3, several ll. in vols 1 & 4 stained, occasional browning & spotting. Cont. cf., covers detchd., spine defect., worn. (S. Feb.10; 262)   *Morton.* £60

FROMAGET, Nicolas
– **Contes.** Ill.:– Paul Avril (figures); de las Rias (port.). Paris, 1882. Ltd. Edn. Figures in 2 states. Mor. by Pagnan, decor. spine, inside dentelle. Bkplt. of Francis Kettaneh. (SM. Feb.11; 158)   Frs. 2,500

FROMENTIN, Eugène
– **Dominique.** Ill.:– Michel Cenj. 1943. Sewed. On vell. d'Arches, with suite, 1 orig. ill. (HD. Oct.10; 189)   Frs. 2,200
– **Les Maîtres d'Autrefois Belgique-Hollande.** Ill.:– Henri Manesse. Paris, 1914. (200) on Marais vell., numbered. 4to. Etchings in 3 states. Red mor. by Canape, decor. spine, border of 3 fillets on covers, wrap. preserved. (SM. Feb.11; 220)   Frs. 4,800

FROMMEL, C.
– **Ansichten von dem Schloss und der Stadt Heidelberg.** Ill.:– K. Lindemann & F. Würhtle after Frommel. Heidelberg, ca. 1850. Lightly soiled thro.-out, mainly in margin. Orig. bds., gold cover ill. (D. Dec.11-13; 1289)   DM 680

– **Pittoreskes Italien.** Leipzig, 1840. Text by W.v. Lüdemann & C. Witte. Cont. hf.-leath. (HK. Nov.18-21; 1224)   DM 700
– **Tyrol und seine Nächste Umgebungen.** Ed.:– A. Lewald. Karlsruhe, ca. 1840. Lightly soiled. Loose, upr. cover of orig. wraps. preserved. (R. Oct.14-18; 1970)   DM 2,500
– – **Anr. Edn.** Ed.:– A. Lewald. Karlsruhe, 1842. Imp. fo. Slightly soiled in parts. Cont. hf. mor. gt., crowned initials. (HK. May 12-14; 689)   DM 3,000
– – **Anr. Copy.** Cont. hf. leath., spine defect. (R. Mar.31-Apr.4; 2694)   DM 2,600
– **Tyrol Scenery.** N.d. Fo. Engraved title frontis. detchd., some light spotting. Orig. cl., spine torn. (CSK. Jun.12; 10)   £380

FRONSPERGER, Leonhart
– **Kriegssbuch.** Ill.:– J. Amman. Frankfurt, 1596. Latest Edn. 3 pts. in 1 vol. 20 (of 22) double-p. etched plts., approx. 600 text woodcuts, 3 double-p. woodcut plts. Cont. blind-stpd. pig, stained. (R. Oct.14-18; 68)   DM 8,500
See–[REISNER, Adam]–REINHARD, Count of Solms-Lich-[FRONSPERGER, Leonhard]

FRONT
Dec. 1930-Apr. 1931. Numbers 1-4. (All publd.) 4to. Wraps. (SG. Jun.4; 188) $140

FRONTINUS, Sextus Julius
– **De Aquaeductibus Urbis Romae Commentarius.** Ed.:– Joannis Poleni. Padua, 1722. 4to. Cont. hf. cf. (TA. May 21; 303)   £68
See–VEGETIUS, Flavius Renatus; Aelianus Tacticus; Frontinus, Sextus Julius–MODESTUS
See–VITRUVIUS Pollo, Marcus–FRONTINUS, Sextus Julius

FROSSARD, Edward & Jordan, J.
– **Vues, Prises dans les Pyrénées Françaises.** Ill.:– Engelmann. Paris, 1829. Fo. Many top margins slightly affected by damp. Cont. hf. roan, corners worn. (S. Nov.4; 591)   *Loeb.* £140

FROST, Robert
– **A Boy's Will.** L., 1913. 1st. Edn., 1st. Iss. Orig. cl., ink inscr. on front free end-paper mostly eradicated, qtr. mor. gt. s.-c. Inscr. to George M. Adams, lately in the Prescott Collection. (CNY. Feb.6; 118) $1,600
– – **Anr. Copy.** Slight spotting, front free end-paper pasted down. Cl. (Crane's A bdg.). (SPB. Nov.25; 277) $425
– – **Anr. Edn.** L., 1913. 1st. Edn., 2nd. Iss. Ptd. wraps. (bdg. variant 'D'). Inscr. (SG. Nov.13; 227) $150
– – **Anr. Copy.** 12mo. Wraps. (SG. Jun.4; 189) $100
– – **Anr. Edn.** N.Y., 1914. 1st. American Edn. Orig. cl. Sigd. & dtd. on front end-paper. (SPB. Nov.25; 278) $200
– **Collected Poems.** N.Y., 1930. (1000) Linen. (SG. Jun.4; 193) $105
– **Come In.**–**Selected Poems.** Ed.:– 1st. work: Louis Untermeyer. [N.Y.]; N.Y., [1942]; 1923. 2 vols. Slight browning. Orig. bdgs., 1st. with d.-w., worn. 1st. work: Untermeyer's copy, 2nd. work: sigd. & dtd. Amherst 1925 by author. (SPB. Nov.25; 281) $275
– **Complete Poems.** N.Y., Ltd. Edns. Cl. 1950. (1500). 2 vols. Fo. Orig. bdg. & publisher's box, slight wear on box. Sigd. by author, Bruce Rogers & Thomas Nason. (SPB. Nov.25; 333) $225
– – **Anr. Copy.** Cl., orig. box. (SG. Jan.15; 189) $220
– **The Cow's in the Corn.** Gaylordsville, 1929. 1st. Separate Edn., (91) numbered, & sigd. 12mo. Without the errata slip. Orig. decor. bds., qtr. mor. gt. s.-c. From the Prescott Collection. (CNY. Feb.6; 122) $300
– **A Further Range.** N.Y., [1936]. 1st. Edn. Cl., d.-w. Inscr., & with 24 line MS. poem in author's hand. (SG. Nov.13; 239) $350
– **Letters to Louis Untermeyer.** N.Y., [1963]. Hf. mor. Untermeyer's bkplt. (SPB. Nov.25; 282) $275
– **Mountain Interval.** N.Y., [1916]. 1st. Edn., 1st. State. Orig. cl., qtr. mor. gt. s.-c. Inscr. to George M. Adams, & A.N.s. to Adams laid in (May 1, 1947, 18mo., 1 p.); lately in the Prescott Collection. (CNY. Feb.6; 121) $1,200
– **North of Boston.** N.Y., 1914. 1st. Edn., 2nd. (1st. Amer.) Iss., (150). Sq. 8vo. Orig. cl.-bkd. bds., corners & edges worn, cl. s.-c. Inscr. to George M. Adams, lately in the Prescott Collection. (CNY. Feb.6; 120) $220

– – Anr. Edn. L., [1914]. 1st. Edn., 1st. Iss., (350). Sq. 8vo. Orig. buckram, mor.-bkd. folding case. Inscr. to George M. Adams, lately in the Prescott Collection. (CNY. Feb.6; 119) $1,800
– The Road Not Taken. Ed.:– Louis Untermeyer. N.Y., [1951]. Hf. red mor. Untermeyer's bkplt. (SPB. Nov.25; 284) $250
– A Way Out. N.Y., 1929. 1st. Edn. in book form, (485). Orig. cl.-bkd. bds. Pres. copy to Louis Untermeyer. (SPB. Nov.25; 285) $1,300
– Witness Tree.–Aforesaid.–Steeple Bush.–Masque of Reason. All N.Y., 1942; [1951]; 1947 [1945]. Ltd. sigd. Edns. 4 vols. Clippings, related materials, tipped in, some spotting. Orig. bdgs., boxes, worn. (SPB. Nov.25; 286) $250

FROUDE, James Anthony
– A History of England from the Fall of Wolsey to the Death of Elizabeth. L., 1858. 2nd. Edn. 12 vols. Slight browning. Cf. gt. (SPB. Nov.25; 455) $300
– – Anr. Edn. 1862-70. 12 vols. Hf. mor. (C. Jul.22; 187) *Traylen.* £80
– Works. 1858-96. Various Edns. 27 vols. Unif. mott. panel. cf. gt. by Hopkins. (CE. Mar.19; 230) £190

FRUGONI
– Opere Poetiche . . . Ill.:– Bassi (frontis.). Parma, 1779. 8 vols. in 9. Cont. red mor., triple gt. fillet around covers, arms of Ferdinand I, Duke of Parma, spines decor. with raised bands, 1 cover detchd., bdgs. defect. (HD. Feb.27; 31) Frs. 2,500
[–] Versi Sciolti. Ill.:– after P.A. Novelli & B. Nazari. Venice, 1758. 1st. Edn. 4to. Scattered foxing. Orig. paper bds., worn, buckram s.-c., unc. From the collection of John A. Saks. (C. Jun.10; 86) *Thomas.* £90
– – Anr. Edn. Ill.:– after P.A. Novelli & B. Nazari. Venice, 1766. 2nd. Edn. 4to. Fore-edges & some ll. foxed. Cont. paper bds., unc. From the collection of John A. Saks. (C. Jun.10; 87) *Witt.* £60

FRY, Edmund
– Pantographia; containing accurate copies of all the known alphabets in the world . . . 1799. [1st. Edn.?]. Mod. qtr. cf., unopened. (S. Jun.23; 201) *Quaritch.* £120
– – Anr. Copy. Rebnd. cf. gt. (P. Oct.2; 266) *Forster.* £60
– – Anr. Copy. L.P. 4to. Mod. three-qtr. cf., unc. (SG. May 14; 80) $275
– Specimen of Modern Printing Types. 1824 (with MS. deletion & '1827' added). Slight browning. Cl., rebkd. (S. Apr.7; 426) *Temperley.* £420

FRY, Edmund & Steele, Isaac
– A Specimen of Printing-Types. 1802. Lacks ornaments between specimens 10 & 18, & 69 & 78, a few ll. spotted or detchd. Cont. paper-bkd. bds., spines defect., 1 cover detchd., unc., worn. (S. Jun.9; 14) *Barker.* £320

FRY, Edmund & Co.–CASLON & Livermore
– A Specimen of Modern Printing Types.–Specimen of Printing Types. L.; n.p., 1788; n.d. 2 items bnd. in 1 vol. All ll. in both books ptd. on 1 side only between which many interleaved tissues have survived, lf. bnd. in at front dtd. Chiswell St., L., Sep.1, 1831, giving 'Prices of Printing Types Etc.' Cf., blind decor. fillet on bds., raised bands on spine, slightly worn. (TW. Sep.19; 84) £310

FRY, Sir Frederick Morris & Tewson, Roland Stuart
– An Illustrated Catalogue of Silver Plate of the Worshipful Company of Merchant Taylors. Priv. ptd. 1929. [(100)]. 4to. Orig. mor. With a related letter from R.S. Tewson to N.M. Penzer loosely inserted. (CSK. Jun.12; 93) £270

FRY, John Hemming
– Greek Myths & Other Symbols. Ed.:– Lilian Whiting. N.p., Priv. Ptd. [1927]. Lge. fo. Orig. pig, blind-tooled & gt.-lettered, in cl. folding case. Port. inscr. to Mrs. M.W. Harriman, dtd. Feb.20, 1928, & sigd. (SG. Dec.4; 150) $130

FRY, Joseph & Sons
– A Specimen of Printing Types. 1786. Cf-bkd. marb. bds., some foxing, ex-liby. (SG. Oct.2; 135) $1,000

FRY, W. Ellerton
– Occupation of Mashonoland. L., 1891. Fo. 140 of 155 photographs, some pp. worn & loose, some plts. stained & marked. Cont. hf. cf., cover soiled. (SSA. Apr.22; 169) R. 480

FRYER, John
– A New Account of East India & Persia . . . 1698. 1st. Edn. Fo. Cont. cf., rebkd. [Wing F2257] (C. Nov.5; 57) *Ad Orientem.* £320

FRYKE, Christopher & Schewitzer, Christopher
– A Relation of 2 several Voyages made into the East-Indies . . . Trans.:– S.L. 1700. 1st. Edn. in Engl. Advt. lf., later marginalia in pen & pencil & a p. of notes in an 18th. C. hand at the end, a few rust-holes. Early 20th. C. mor.-bkd. cl. [Wing F2230A] (S. Nov.4; 617) *Vangghjt.* £200

FUCHS, Eduard
– Illustrierte Sittengeschichte. Munich, [1909-12]. (200), main vol. numbered 15, 3 Supps. numbered 17. 6 vols. 4to. 1 plt. detchd. Hf. mor. by E.A. Enders, Leipzig. (CSK. Jul.17; 79) £130
– – Anr. Edn. Munich, 1909-12. 3 vols., each with Supp. together 6 vols. Cl., 1 bdg. defect. (BS. Jun.11; 49) £70
– – Anr. Edn. Munich, 1909-11-12. 6 vols., including Ergaenzungsband to each vol. Tall 4to. Cl. gt., spines faded. (PNY. May 21; 184) $160

FUCHS, Ernst
– Architectura Caelestis. Salzburg, [1970]. (200) numbered, with 2 numbered etchings sigd. by Fuchs. Ob. 4to. Gt.-pict. cl., d.-w., boxed. (SG. Apr.2; 118) $170

FUCHS, Leonhard
– De Historia Stirpium. Basle, 1542. 1st. Edn. Fo. Author's port. with ink stain & pieces torn from upr. & lr. margins, not affecting ptd. area, reprd., stained thro.-out in upr. margin, 2 sm. wormholes in lr. hf. of about 150 ll. at end. Cont. blind-stpd. cf.-bkd. wood bds., rebkd., lacks clasps. From Chetham's Liby., Manchester. (C. Nov.26; 171) *Fletcher.* £2,600
– – Anr. Copy. q4 & q6 reprd. at foot. Cont. cf. rebkd., lr. corners worn. From collection of Massachusetts Horticultural Society, stp. on plts. (SPB. Oct.1; 119) $1,400
– New Kreüterbuch. Ill.:– H. Füllmauer, A. Meyer & V.R. Speckle. Basle, 1543. 1st. German Edn. Fo. Lacks final lf. with 3 ports. of artists, full-page port. of author torn, lr. portion missing, many pp. torn, soiled & stained, some crudely reprd, BB2 loose, some worming. Cont. blind-stpd. pigskin over wooden bds., worn. (SPB. Oct.1; 195) $7,750
– Den Nieuwen Herbarius, dat is d boeck van den Cruyden. Basle, ca. 1545. Fo. Last lf. with device in facs., 2 ll. preface defect., with loss of text, partly reprd., some sm. tears, some slightly affecting text, slight spotting & soiling in places. Mod. antique-style cf. W.a.f. (S. Dec.3; 971) *Broseghini.* £1,300
– Primi de Stirpium Historia. Basle, 1549. Lacks the 1st. 8 ll. & the last 2, some worming, slightly affecting some woodcuts, some dampstaining. Cont. limp vell., worn. W.a.f. (S. Jul.27; 286) *Robinson.* £260

See–SCHONER, Johann–HEYLL, Christophorus –FUCHS, Leonhard–RICIUS, Paulus

FUELOP-MILLER, Rene & Gregor, Joseph
– The Russian Theatre: Its Character & History. Trans.:– Paul England. Phila., [1930]. Ltd. 1st. Edn. in Engl., (1000) numbered. Lge. 4to. Cl., boxed. (PNY. Mar.4; 225) $180

FUENTES, Francisco
– Consultum pro Veritate Super Validitate Electionis in Provincialem. Rome, 1757. Fo. Marginal annots. & some MS. corrections in text. Mod. cf. (SPB. May 5; 221) $1,000

FUESSLI, R.-H.
– Les Costumes Suisses les plus origineaux et les plus intéressants. Zurich, [1830]. 4to. Lacks 1 plt. & descriptive text, 1st. 3 plts. with sm. liby. stp. in upr. blank margin. Cont. red mor.-bkd. gt. panel. bds. W.a.f. (C. Feb.4; 168) *Basket & Day.* £1,000

FUESSLIN, Johann Caspar
– Raisonirendes Verzeichniss der Vornehmsten Kupferstecher und ihrer Werke. Zurich, 1771. 1st. Edn. Later marb. bds., unc. & unopened. (SG. Dec.4; 152) $100

FUGAS [Landmine]
Ed.:– [M.M. Brodovsky]. St. Petersb., 1906. Nos. 1-4. 4to. Unbnd. (SH. Feb.5; 71) *Quaritch.* £210

FUKS, L. & Fuks-Mansfeld, R.F.
– Hebrew & Judaic Manuscripts in Amsterdam Public Collection; Bibliotheca Rosenthaliana & Ets Haim/Livraria Montezinos. Leiden, 1973-75. 2 vols. 4to. Cl. (S. Nov.17; 73) *Kingsgate.* £55

FUKS-MANSFELD, R.F.
See–FUKS, L. & Fuks-Mansfeld, R.F.

FULCHER, G.W.
– Album. Miscellaneous Scraps, Autographs, Prints & Drawings collected from Oct. 1831 to Oct. 1847. 1831-47. Fo. MS. Calligraphic title & indices, many mntd. on cold. paper, some with ornam. or embossed borders imposed. Cont. cf. gt., covers loose. (SH. Apr.10; 591) *Doncaster.* £440

FULGOSUS, Baptista
– De Dictis Factisque Memorabilibus Collectanea . . . Milan, 1509. 1st. Edn. Fo. Old sig. on title of Robt. Tulle, sig. on fly-lf. of Mr. Wodhull, 1792, with his bibliographical notes, sig. of 'Alb. Muller, 16.1.86' on rear fly-lf. 18th. C. red mor., triple gt. fillet, spine gt. with urn in each compartment, inner gt. dentelles, lr. cover reprd. [Sabin 26140] (SM. Oct.7; 1721) Frs. 5,000

FULHAME, Mrs.
– An Essay on Combustion with a View to a New Art of Dying & Painting wherein the Phlogistic & Anti-Phlogistic Hypotheses are Proved Erroneous. Priv. ptd. 1794. 1st. Edn. Errata slip pasted on contents lf., liby. stps. Cl. (S. Dec.1; 174) *Maggs.* £170

FULKE, William
– A Most Pleasant Prospect into the Garden of Naturall Contemplation, to Behold the Naturall Causes of all Kinde of Meteors . . . 1640. Lacks blank before title, title cut close at head & slightly browned. 19th. C. cf., gt. crest on covers of dragon's head between 2 wings surmounting initial 'D', (Dalton?), rebkd. From Honeyman Collection. [STC 11441] (S. May 20; 3238) *Zeitlin & Verbrugge.* £75

FULLARTON, A.
– Royal Illustrated Atlas of Modern Geography. Ca. 1865. Fo., (475mm×315mm). Many full-p. plts. & some others with vig. views & other features, title soiled, last lf. of index torn, some plts. discoloured in centre fold or at inner margin, 1 or 2 maps loose. Orig. red mor. gt., 1 cover detchd., worn. W.a.f. (SPB. Nov.25; 34) *Jeffery.* £170

FULLARTON & Co.
– A Gazetteer of the World. 1856. 7 vols. Orig. leath.-bkd. cl. gt., 2 vols. reprd. at head. Bkplt. of W. Rosher. (LC. Feb.12; 183) £95
– The Royal Illustrated Atlas, of Modern Geography. Ed.:– Dr. N. Shaw. Ca. 1860. Fo. Orig. cf. gt., spine slightly worn. (TA. Feb.19; 104) £190

FULLER, George W. & Grimm, Verna B.
– A Bibliography of Bookplate Literature. 1926. (500) numbered, & sigd. Tall 8vo. Buckram, partly unc. & unopened. (SG. Mar.26; 71) $140

FULLER, Ronald
See–WHISTLER, Laurence & Fuller, Ronald

FULLER, Dr. Thomas
[–] Anthologia . . .–[Ornitho-logie]. 1655. 1st. Edn. 2 pts. in 1 vol. Lacks ptd. title & lf. between A2 & B1 of 1st. pt., some browning & soiling, a few ll. cropped at head or foot. 19th. C. cf., worn. [Wing F2409] (S. May 5; 109) *Cristani.* £85
– The Historie of the Holy Warre. Camb., 1640. 2nd. Edn. Fo. Later pol. cf. gt. with old reback. (TA. Feb.19; 552) £60
– History of the Worthies of England. L., 1662. 1st. Edn. Fo. Lacks 1st. blank & 18th. C. index, title stained, some wear of inner margins of last gathering. Cont. cf., rebkd., worn. [Wing F2440] (SPB. Nov.25; 76) $150
– A Pisgah-sight of Palestine & the Confines thereof . . . 1601. 1st. Edn., compl. with all plts. Fo. 18th. C. gt.-ornamental mott. cf., jnts. worn. (PNY. Oct.1; 231) $2,600
– – Anr. Edn. 1650. 1st. Edn. Fo. Lge. folding map with 2 sm. tears, 2 plts. with tears at folds, 4 with minor tears, mostly at folds. Cont. cf., worn, lr. cover loose. [Wing F2455] (C. Feb.25; 98) *Cohen.* £580
– – Anr. Copy. Lacks 2 double-p. copperplts., much mispagination. Cont. leath., upr. cover loose. (R. Mar.31-Apr.4; 2528) DM 1,500

FULLER, Dr. Thomas -contd.
- - **Anr. Edn.** 1662. [3rd Edn?]. Fo. Engraved additional title soiled, some plts. preserved, browned, 1 reprd. with slight loss. Later cf., covers almost detchd. W.a.f. (CSK. Sep.26; 49) £340
- - **Anr. Copy.** Some plts. & maps defect., some browning & soiling. Cont. cf., worn, covers detchd. [Wing F2457] (S. Sep.29; 30)
Primrose Hill Bks. £170

See–CAMBRIDGE UNIVERSITY

FULOP-MILLER, Rene & Gregor, Joseph
- The Russian Theatre. Its Character & History. Trans.:– Paul England. 1930. 1st. Edn., (650) numbered. 4to. Inner hinges reprd. Orig. cl., gt. decor. spine. (TA. Mar.19; 307) £100

FULTON, Robert
- The Illustrated Book of Pigeons. Ed.:– Lewis Wright. Ill.:– after J.W. Ludlow. Ca. 1860. 4to. Cont. hf. mor., upr. cover detchd., backstrip defect., unc. (TA. Jan.22; 79) £65
- - **Anr. Edn.** Ca. 1885. 4to. Cl., worn. (S. Dec.3; 972) *W. & W.* £60
- - **Anr. Copy.** Gt.-pict. cl. (SG. Jan.29; 177) $180
- - **Anr. Edn.** Ca. 1886. 4to. Cl. gt. (P. Sep.11; 171) *Hughes.* £75
- - **Anr. Edn.** Ed.:– Lewis Wright. Ill.:– after J.W. Ludlow. L., [1893]. 4to. Pict. cl., jnts. worn. (SG. Nov.20; 394) $140
- - **Anr. Edn.** [1895]. 4to. Orig. decor. cl., loose. (CE. Jun.4; 15) £56
- - **Anr. Edn.** N.d. 4to. Cl., worn. (P. Nov.13; 249) *Erlini.* £65
- - **Anr. Copy.** Mor. (SSA. Apr.22; 30) R. 110
- Treatise on the Improvement of Canal Navigation. 1796. 1st. Edn. 4to. Advt. lf. at end, slightly spotted, sm. marginal tear in title. Cont. bds., neatly rebkd., corners slightly worn. (S. Dec.2; 715) *Baldwin.* £230

F[ULWOOD], W.
- The Enemie of Idleness. 1598. 7th. Edn. Dampstains. 17th. C. cf., rebkd. [STC 11482] (SH. Jun.11; 37) *Quaritch.* £120

FUMEL, Jean Felix Henri de
[–] La Dévotion au Coeur de Jésus, pour l'Association chez les Religieuses de la Visitation de Strasbourg. Strasbourg, 1767. 4th. Edn. Cont. red mor. by La Ferté with his ticket, triple gt. fillet, sm. flower in each corner, spine gt. in compartments with same flower, inner gt. dentelles, bkplt. of Mortimer Schiff. (SM. Oct.7; 1722) Frs. 1,000

FUN UPON FUN, or the Humours of a Fair–An Abridgement of the New Testament.–The Pretty & Entertaining History of Tom Thumb
Glasgow, Glasgow, Otley, ca. 1820; ca. 1820; ca. 1820. 3 vols. in 1. 32mo. 1st. work: 1 plt. reprd. Orig. wraps. bnd. in, mor.-bkd. bds. (SH. Mar.19; 104) *Vincent.* £55

FUNCK, M.
- Le Livre Belge à Gravures. Paris & Brussels, 1925. Orig. cl. (CSK. Nov.14; 117) £60

FUNDAMENTU[M] ETERNE FELICITATIS. Cum Libro de Miseria Co[n]ditionis humane
Cologne, 30 Sep. 1506. Some early (cont.?) MS. notes, slight browning & soiling, tear at head of Bl, just affecting text. 19th. C. marb. wraps. From liby. of André L. Simon. (S. May 18; 99) *Kesel.* £70

FUNDAMENTUM ETERNE FELICITATIS ... Signa Electoru[m] vel Damnoru[m]
Cologne, [Retro Minores [Martin von Werden?] for] Heinrich Quentell, [between 16 May & Sep.] 1498. 1st Edn. 30 ll. only (of 32, lacks title & last lf., supplied in facs.], initials, paragraph-marks, etc., supplied in red, some browning & soiling. Cont. oak bds., rebkd. with cf., metal clasp. From liby. of André L. Simon. [BMC I, 312; Goff F331] (S. May 18; 98) *Kesel.* £160

FUNKE, Jaromir
- [Twelve Photographs]. Ed.:– Antonin Dufek [introduction]. Prague, [1979]. (2,500). Sm. portfo. Loose as iss. in pict. folder. (SG. Apr.23; 92) $160

FUNKE, V.V.
See–BARKHATOV, M.E. & Funke, V.V.

FUNNELL, William
- A Voyage Round the World containing an Account of Captain Dampier's Expedition into the South-Seas. 1707. Cf., rebkd. [Sabin 26213] (BS. Sep.17; 23) £410

FUR, FEATHER & FIN Series
L., 1893-1903. (157) numbered, on L.P. 10 (of 12) vols. Parch.-bkd. cl. (SG. Apr.9; 358) $375

FURER, C.-EGINHART
- Itinerarium Aegypti, Arabiae, Palastinae ... -Vita & Gesta Karoli Magni Imperatoris Invictissimi. Trans.:– G. Richter (1st. work). Nuremb.; Leipzig, 1621; 1616. 2 works in 1 vol. 4to. 1st. work, port., arms, 6 engrs., 4 folding; 2nd. work, 2 ports., printer's device, browning. Vell. (P. Jul.2; 170) *Timmons.* £230

FURBER, Robert & Bradley, Richard
- The Flower-Garden Display'd. 1732. 1st. Edn. 4to. Lacks 1 plt., margins of prelims. & 1st. plt. strengthened, slight marginal worming of titles. Cont. cf. worn, neatly rebkd. (SBA. Oct.21; 44) *Conradt.* £380

FURETIERE, Antoine
- Dictionnaire Universel. The Hague & Rotterdam, 1690. 1st Edn. 3 vols. Fo. Cont. cf., spines decor. with raised bands, worn. (HD. Jun.24; 36) *Frs.* 1,300
- - **Anr. Edn.** Ed.:– Basnage de Bauval. The Hague & Rotterdam, 1701. 2nd Edn. 3 vols. Fo. Cont. red mor., gt. fillet, decor. spine, inside dentelle. Bkplt. of Roger Peyrefitte. (HD. Mar.18; 71) *Frs.* 17,500

FURNITURE (Le) Magasin de Meubles
[–] A Collection of plates from a furniture pattern book. Paris, ca. 1850. Ob. fo. 91 hand-cold. plts. finished with varnish, a sm. number of ills. from the same publication loosely inserted, margins browned, occasional slight foxing. Bds., disbnd. As a collection of plts., w.a.f. (SPB. May 6; 193) $600

FURNIVAL BOOKS, The
Ill.:– Alan Odle & others. 1930-32. 1st. Edns. (550), sigd. Nos. 1-12. Orig. buckram. (S. Jul.22; 61) *Bow Windows.* £90

FURST, Hermann
- Illustriertes Forst- und Jagd- Lexikon. Berlin, 1888. Orig. hf. leath. (R. Oct.14-18; 2780) DM 480

FURST, Hermann (Ed.)
See–WOODCUT, The

FURSTENBERG, Jean
- Le Grand Siècle en France et ses Bibliophiles. Hamburg, 1972. 1st. Edn. (600). 4to. The 60 cold. slides in sleeves at beginning. Cl. (S. Jun.9; 16) *Quaritch.* £110
- La Gravure Originale dans l'Illustration du Livre Français au Dixhuitième Siècle. Hamburg, 1975. 1st. Edn. (600). 4to. Cl. (S. Jun.9; 17) *Quaritch.* £80

FURTTENBACH, J., the older
- Mannhafter Kunst-Spiegel. Augsburg, 1663. 1st. Edn. Sm. fo. Some copper engrs. very defect., torn, lacks part of frontis., 4 copper engrs. loose, 2 copper engrs. with old owner's mark on verso. Cont. vell., very defect. & loose. (H. Dec.9/10; 934) DM 750

FUSTEL de Coulanges, Numa Denis
- La Cité Antique ... Paris, 1864. 1st Edn. Cont. roan, blind-tooled plaque on covers, arms in centre, smooth decor. spine, bdg. slightly defect. (HD. Jun.25; 249) *Frs.* 2,100

FUTURISTY [First Journal of Russian Futurists]
Ill.:– Burlyuks & A. Ekster. Moscow, 1914. Nos. 1-2 in 1 vol. Wraps. supplied in facs. (SH. Feb.6; 429) *Kazinikas.* £95

FUX, Johann Joseph
- Gradus ad Parnassum. Vienna, 1725. 1st. Edn. Fo. Owner's mark on frontis., slightly soiled & browned thro.-out. Paper bds., defect., spine pasted. (H. Dec.9/10; 1118) DM 860
- Salita al Parnasso. Trans.:– A. Manfredi. 1761. 1st. Italian Edn. Fo. Some ll. slightly browned, 1 hf.-p. copper engr. cold. 19th. C. hf. leath. (H. Dec.9/10; 1119) DM 920

G., A.P.D.
- Sketches of Portuguese Life, Manners, Costume & Character. L., 1826. 1st Edn. Ex liby. Early hf. vell., worn. (SG. Oct.30; 331) $400

GABIROL, Shlomo Ibn
- Goren Nachon (& other works). Riva Di Trento, 1562. 1st Edn. Sm. 4to. Tears, cropped, worming, stained. Vell., warped, stained. (SPB. May 11; 109) $700
See–BECHAYE Ben Joseph Ibn Paduka
–GABIROL, Shlomo Ibn

GABRIEL, Peter–ROLL, Timotheus von –MONTIF, Lucian–M[ÜLLER], M.J.G.
- Der Reichs-Gärtner.–Neues Blumen-Büchlein. –Newe Garten-Lust.–Compendium triplicis horticulturae ... Entwurf eines dreyfachen Garten-Haus; Ungezieffer-Todt. Stuttgart; n.p.; Ulm; Stuttgart; n.p., 1682; 1687; 1698; 1675; 1683. 5 works in 1 vol. 12mo. 1 lf. reprd. affecting a few letters. 18th. C. cf., cypher FK on covers, upr. cover brkn. & wormed, foot of spine worn. (S. Jan.27; 328) *Quaritch.* £380

GABRIELSON, Ira N. & Lincoln, Frederick
See–BRANDT, Herbert–GABRIELSON, Ira N. & Lincoln, Frederick

GADBURY, John
- London's Deliverance Predicted in a Short Discourse Shewing the Cause of Plagues in General & the Probable Time ... when this Present Pest may Abate. 1665. 4to. Title & last p. soiled, some stains. Hf. cf. [Wing G86] (S. Dec.2; 491) *Dawson.* £95

GAEBELKHOVER, Oswald
- The Boock of Physicke. [Dordrecht], 1599. 1st. Edn. in Engl. Fo. Cont. owner's inscr. of Thomas Brown on blank verso of last lf., sig. of Andrew Fletcher of Saltoun on title. Cont. limp vell. [STC 11513] (S. Dec.2; 716) *Maggs.* £1,300

GAETANI, Pietro Antonio
- Museum Mazzuchellianum, seu Numismata. Ill.:– Antonio Zaballi after Giacomo Banazzi (port.). Venice, 1761-63. 2 vols. Fo. Scattered foxing & light dampstains. Cont. vell. bds., slight wear. From the collection of John A. Saks. (C. Jun.10; 88) *Bartoli.* £110

GAFFAREL, James
- Unheard-of Curiosities: Concerning the Talismanical Sculpture of the Persians, The Horoscope of the Patriarkes; & the Reading of the Stars. Trans.:– Edmund Chilmead. L., 1650. 1 folding plt. (of 2), reprd. Later cf., upr. cover detchd. (TA. Dec.18; 192) £66

GAFFKY, Dr.
See–KOCH, Robert–KOCH, Robert & others –KOCH, Robert & Wolffhugel, Gustav

GAGE D'AMITIE
- Itinéraire Pittoresque au Nord de l'Angleterre. 1832-38. 2 vols. 4to. Spotted. Orig. cl., gt. spines. (SH. Nov.6; 100) *Fairburn.* £55

GAGE, John
- History & Antiquities of Suffolk. Thingoe Hundred. 1838. Fo. Cont. hf. mor., gt. (SH. Nov.6; 48) *Doncaster.* £60

GAGE, Matilda Joslyn
See–STANTON, Elizabeth Cady, Anthony, Susan B. & Gage, Matilda Joslyn

GAGE, Michael Alexander, Surveyor
- The Trigonometrical Plan of the Town & Port of Liverpool. 1835. Features mntd. on linen, edges bnd. Folded into cont. mor. gt. pull-off case. (SBA. Oct.22; 407) *Temperley.* £75

GAGE, Thomas
- The English-American, his Travail ... or, A New Survey of the West-Indias. L., 1648. 1st. Edn. Fo. Some discolouration, mainly at end. 18th. C. russ. [Sabin 26298; Wing G109] (SPB. May 5; 223) $1,000
- Nouvelle Relation, contenant les Voyages ... dans la Nouvelle Espagne ... la Province de Nicaragua, jusques à la Havane. Amst., 1720. 2 vols. Cont. cf. [Sabin 26306] (SPB. May 5; 224) $275

GAGNAEUS, Joannes
[–] Doctissimorum nostra aetate Italorum Epigramata. Paris, [1546?]. 19th. C. red mor., gt., spine faded. (S. Oct.21; 281) *Quaritch.* £55

GAGUINUS, Robertus
- Compendium de Origine et Gestis Francorum. Paris, Thielman Kerver, for Durand Gerlier & Jean Petit, Jan.13, 1500. 4th. Edn. Fo. Spaces for 2 capital initials with guide letters, other initials ptd. in black, some lr. blank margins with light

dampstaining, some ll. darkened. Cont. Fr. blind-stpd. sheep, outer border of interlaced dotted circles, inner border of lattice work enclosing flower tool, central panel of opposing repeated hf. ovals, on either side a narrower panel of facing repeated hf. circles, all with saw-tooth edges, lacks ties, rebkd. with cont. blind-stpd. pig, upr. cover scuffed, corners worn. From the collection of Eric Sexton. [BMC VIII, 217, Goff G15, HC 7413*] (CNY. Apr.8; 125) $4,000

GAILER, J.E.
– Neuer Orbis Pictus für die Jugend nach der Anlage des Comenius bearbeitet. Reutlingen, 1833. 2nd. Edn. German, Latin & Fr. text, 2nd. title-lf. in Fr., lacks plts. 221/222, lightly soiled in places. Bds., orig. litho.-wraps. bkd. (R. Mar.31-Apr.4; 1539) DM 1,600
– – **Anr. Copy.** Cont. hf. linen. (D. Dec.11-13; 569) DM 1,000
– – **Anr. Copy.** 2 ills. double, minimal soiling. Orig. pict. bds., slightly soiled. (HK. May 15; 5085) DM 450

GAILLIARD, J.
– Bruges et le Franc. Bruges, 1857-[1864]. Hf. chagrin, 4 decor. spine raised bands, slightly worn. (LM. Nov.8; 167) B.Frs. 27,000

GAINSBOROUGH, Thomas
– A Collection of Prints Illustrative of English Scenery. Ill.:– Wells & Laporte. Ca. 1804. Fo. 60 soft-ground etchings, 37 hand-cold. Cont. red str.-grd. mor., covers with elaborate gt. & blind-tooled borders. From the collection of Eric Sexton. (C. Apr.16; 258) Maggs. £360
– – **Anr. Edn.** Ill.:– after Gainsborough. 1819. Fo. Slight spotting & soiling. Mod. hf. mor. (CSK. Feb.6; 157) £240

GALE, Norman
– Orchard Songs. 1893. Hand-cold. title & hf.-title. Cont. mor. by Guild of Women-Binders, inlaid with red, green & brown mor., elab. stpd. & tooled in gt. & black, vell. doubls. (CSK. Oct.17; 96) £120

GALE, Thomas
– Certaine Works in Chirurgerie. 1563. 4 pts. in 1 vol. Lacks A8 & C1 in pt. I, Aa2 in pt. 3, 3A1-2 & 8 ll. of general index in pt. 4, all replaced in photostat facs. New cf. with panels of Tudor Rose. W.a.f. [STC 11529] (S. Jun.16; 319) Vanderkerckhove. £120

GALENUS, Claudius
See–HIPPOCRATES & Galenus, Claudius

GALERIE de Florence
See–MONGEZ, Antoine

GALERIE DER ZEITGENOSSEN
Hildburghausen, ca. 1850. 2 vols. 4to. Lacks title. Orig. hf. leath. (D. Dec.11-13; 1249) DM 500

GALERIE des Femmes de Shakespeare
Paris, n.d. 1 plt. loose, text spotted. Orig. mor. (SKC. Jul.28; 2590) £50

GALERIE DU PALAIS PITTI
Ed.:– Louis Bardi. Flor., 1842-45. 4 vols. Fo. Cont. hf. mor. (SI. Dec.3; 242) Lire 1,200,000

GALERIE FRANCAISE de Femmes Célèbres par le Talens
Ill.:– Gatine after Lante. Paris, 1827. Fo. 54 (of 70) hand-cold. plts. Cont. bds., cf. back, brkn. (SG. May 21; 362) $300
– – **Anr. Copy.** Some spotting. Hf. mor., decor. spines, unc. (SM. Feb.11; 64) Frs. 3,100

GALERIE HISTORIQUE DE VERSAILLES
Paris, ca. 1840. Fo. Cont. hf. leath. gt. (R. Mar.31-Apr.4; 1511) DM 630

GALERIE INDUSTRIELLE, avec 150 Tableaux d'Art et Metiers. Par Mme H*
Paris, 1822. Ob. lge. 8vo. Wormed. Orig. pict. bds. (R. Oct.14-18; 2622) DM 2,800

GALERIE PITTORESKER ANSICHTEN DES Deutschen Vaterlandes
Leipzig, ca. 1850. Vols. 3-5 in 1 vol. Lge. 8vo. Slightly soiled. Cont. hf. leath., defect, cover loose. (R. Oct.14-18; 2071) DM 7,500

GALERIE ROYALE DE COSTUMES
– Italia. Ill.:– Pingret. Paris, ca. 1840. 1 vol. only. Fo. Without title. Cont. hf. red mor. (SI. Dec.3; 243) Lire 2,200,000

GALERIE THEATRALE ou Collection Gravée et Imprimée en Couleur . . .
Ill.:– A. Godfrey, Prud'hon & others. Paris, 1812-33. 3 vols. in 36 livraisons. Fo. 2 engraved titles, 143 (of 144) engraved plts., plt. no. 6 bis & engraved title to vol. 2, 3 plts. mntd. Orig. wraps., unc., no. 17 lacks upr. wrap. W.a.f. (CNY. May 22; 117) $850

GALERIES HISTORIQUES de Versailles
Paris, ca. 1840. 4 vols. Fo. Slightly soiled in parts. Cont. hf. leath. gt. (R. Oct.14-18; 2869) DM 750

GALET, J.
See–DESFONTAINES, Abbé & others

GALIANI, Ferdinando, Abbé
– Dialogues sur le Commerce des Blés. Berlin, 1795. New Edn. 2 vols. 12mo. Slight browning, stp. of the Mecklenburg Liby. on verso of titles. Mod. mor., cl. s.-c.'s. (S. Jan.26; 236) Rota. £110

GALIBERT, L.
– Storia d'Algeri dal Primo Stabilimento de' Cartaginesi fino alle Ultime Guerre combattutevi ai Giorni nostri dalle Armi di Francia. Trans.:– A. Bonucci. Flor., 1846-47. 2 vols. Cont. hf. cf. (CR. Mar.19; 214) Lire 300,000

GALILEI, Galileo
– Dialogo . . . sopra i Due Massimi Sistemi del Mondo . . . Ill.:– Stefano della Bella. (Frontis.). Flor., 1632. 1st Edn. 4to. Ptd. slip pasted into margin of p. 92, 2 ll. in quire Bb misbnd., brown or spotted in places. Cont. limp vell., hf. mor. case. Bkplt. of Franklin Institute Liby., owner's inscr. of Petrus Pieri. (S. May 5; 114) Bozzolato. £2,400
– – **Anr. Copy.** Ptd. slip on p. 92, lacks final blank, some browning, title reprd. where liby. stps. have been removed, sm. hole in dedication lf. 18th. C. vell. bds. (S. Jun.23; 275) Norton. £1,600
– – **Anr. Copy.** Ptd. slip on p. 92, lacks final blank, some browning, B4-5 detchd., tear in G4, partly deleted inscr. on title-p. Old limp bds., worn. From Honeyman Collection. (S. May 20; 3239) Thomas. £1,400
– Discorso Al . . . Gran duca di Toscana Intorno alle cose, che stanno in sù l'acqua, ò che in quella si muouono. Flor., 1612. 2nd. Edn. 4to. Interleaved thro-out., neat repair in title necessitating pt. of device to be supplied by hand, last lf. reprd. in top fore-corner, light foxing & spotting thro-out. Cont. vell. (S. Oct.21; 387) Thomas. £200
– Discorso al Serenissimo Don Cosimo II. Flor., 1612. 1st. Edn. 4to. Cont. hf. leath., hf. linen box. Andrew Fletcher of Saltoun copy. (HK. Nov.18-21; 525) DM 5,200
– Lettera a Cristina di Lorena nel 1615. Padova, 1897. Ltd. Edn. 1.6 × 1 cm. Cf., box. Miniature book. (CR. Jun.11; 598) Lire 700,000
– Opere. Ed.:– Giuseppe Toaldo. Ill.:– F. Zucchi (frontis.). Padua, 1744. 3rd. Compl. Edn. 4 vols. 4to. Minor foxing to fore-e., Orig. paper bds., unc. & unopened. From the collection of John A. Saks. (C. Jun.10; 89) Bozzolato. £150
– Systema Cosmicum. 1663. A few very minor defects, barely affecting text. Mod. cf. [Wing G168] (SBA. Mar.4; 107) Morton. £75
– – **Anr. Edn.** Leiden, 1699. 2 pts. in 1 vol. Lge. 4to. Unc., leath. (HK. May 12-14; 321) DM 1,000
– Systema Cosmicum.-Nova-Antiqua Sanctissimorum Patrum, & Probatorum Theologorum Doctrina, De Sacrae Scripturae Testimoniis, in Conclusionibus Mere Naturalibus.-Tractatus de Proportionum Instrumento. Strassburg, 1635; 1636; 1635. 1st. Latin Edn. of the Dialogo; 1st. Edn.; 2nd. Latin Edn. 3 works in 1 vol. Sm. 4to. Last 2 works badly browned, 1st. slightly so, 1st. work with inkblot in margin of p. 246, 2nd. work lacks plt. 18th. C. red mor., gt., hf. red mor. case, Italian note of purchase at Libreria Pisani, Venice, sale on fly-lf. Bkplt. 'Ex Libris Joannis de Bizzarro'; from Honeyman Collection. (S. May 20; 3240) Zeitlin & Verbrugge. £850

GALL, Franz Joseph & Spurzheim, Johannes Caspar
– Anatomie et Physiologie du Système Nerveux . . . Paris, 1810-19. 1st. Edn. 4 vols. & atlas. 4to. & fo. Some spotting & browning thro-out. Later roan-bkd. bds., spine of atlas very worn. (C. Nov.20; 189) Quaritch. £950
– – **Anr. Copy.** 5 vols. in 3, including atlas vol. Fo. Wide margins. Mod. mott. hf. cf., spines gt. (S. Apr.6; 218) Brieux. £800

GALLACINI, Teofilo–VISENTINI, Antonio
– Trattato . . . sopra gli Errori degli Architetti. –Osservazioni . . . de Continuazione al Trattato di Teofilo Gallaccini. Ill.:– Visentini (both works). Venice, 1767; 1771. 1st. Edn. (1st. work). 2 works in 1 vol. Sm. fo. Cont. hf. cf., qtr. mor. s.-c. From the collection of John A. Saks. (C. Jun.10; 90) Breslauer. £270

GALLANDIUS, Pierre
– Petri Castellani magni Franciae Eleemosynarii Vita . . . Ed.:– Stephanus Baluzius. Paris, 1674. 1st. Edn. Inscr. on fly.-lf. 'Pour Monsieur l'Abbé de Sainct Romain Ambassadeur du Roy en Suisse'. Cont. red mor., triple gt. fillet, spine compartments gt. en pointillé, inner gt. dentelles. Sigd. by Baluze. (SM. Oct.7; 1724) Frs. 2,000

GALLATIN, Albert Eugène
– Charles Demuth. N.Y., 1927. (450). Cl.-bkd. bds. (SG. Dec.4; 123) $140
– Whistler's Pastels & other Modern Profiles. –American Water-Colourist's. N.Y., 1912; 1922. (250); (950). 2 works in 2 vols. 8vo. & 4to. Cl.-bkd. bds., worn. (SG. Dec.4; 153) $160

GALLE, Thomas
– Illustrium Imagines, ex Antiquis Marmoribus, Nomismatibus et Gemmis Expressae. Antw., 1606. 2 pts. in 1 vol. Sm. 4to. Some stains. Later cf. (SH. Jun.11; 190) Fairburn. £130
– – **Anr. Copy.** Mod. mor. gt. (BS. Jun.11; 339) £60

GALLENSIS, Johannis
See–GILBERTUS–GALLENSIS, Johannis

GALLERIE DER MENSCHEN. Ein Bilderbuch für die Jugend
Leipzig, 1805-10. 3 vols. Sm. 4to. No bdg. (R. Oct.14-18; 2623) DM 1,400

GALLERIE du Palais du Luxembourg peinte par Rubens (La)
Ill.:– S. de Nattier. Paris, 1710. Lge. fo. Cont. marb. hf. cf., spine with plain raised bands. (HD. Jun.29; 44) Frs. 1,100

GALLERY OF THE CELEBRATED LANDSCAPES OF SWITZERLAND
Zürich & Leeds, 1884. Slightly soiled. Orig. vell. (D. Dec.11-13; 1581) DM 750

GALLERY OF ENGRAVINGS
N.d. 3 vols. 4to. 189 (of 190) plts. only, 2 detchd., occasional spotting. Cont. hf. cf. (CSK. Sep.12; 215) £65

GALLI, F.M.
– Miscellaneo Matematico Opera. Parma, 1694. 4to. Lacks plt. no. 74. Cont. pig. (D. Dec.11-13; 177) DM 1,600

GALLIARD, Johann Ernst
– The Hymn of Adam & Eve. Ill.:– J. Pine (engraved title). 1728. 1st. Edn. Ob. 4to. 15 folios of ruled blank MS. score bnd. at end. Cont. cf. From the collection of Eric Sexton. (C. Apr.15; 99) Morton-Smith. £95

GALLICO, Paul
– The Revealing Eye. Ill.:– Nicklas Muray. N.Y., 1967. 1st. Edn. Fo. Cl., d.-w., bkplt. (SG. Jul.9; 227) $100
– The Snow Goose. Ill.:– Peter Scott. 1946. Ltd. Edn. sigd. by Artist & Author. 4to. Buckram. (MMB. Oct.8; 143) Traylen. £60

GALLO, Agostino
– Le Vinti Giornate dell'Agricoltura et de' Piaceri della Villa. Venice, 1569. 1st. Ill. Edn. 4to. 15 full-p. woodcuts at end (of 19, lacks Ee2 & 7), fairly severe worming in upr. margin towards beginning & in the middle, some staining. Cont. limp vell., slightly worn. (S. Jul.27; 287) Marinoni. £60
– – **Anr. Edn.** Venice, 1572. Hole in title page, not affecting text, some stains. Hf. vell. (P. Sep.11; 188) Henderson. £250
– – **Anr. Edn.** Venice, 1615. Sm. 4to. Slight browning, ill. at end defect. & a few others slightly affected by tears at head of ll. Early 19th. C. vell. bds., slightly soiled. From liby. of André L. Simon. (S. May 18; 100) Howell. £85
– – **Anr. Edn.** Venice, 1629. Sm. 4to. A little dampstaining, a few ll. loose. Cont. limp vell., soiled. From liby. of André L. Simon. (S. May 18; 101) Facchi. £95

GALLONIO, Antonio
- **De SS. Martyrum Cruciatibus.** Rome, 1594. 1st. Edn. 4to. 6 unnumbered pp., 15 unnumbered pp., lacks last blank, 25 xylographs, last 20 pp. reprd. at corner. Vell. (CR. Mar.19; 253)   Lire 300,000
- - **Anr. Edn.** Ill.:– Antonio Tempesta. Paris, 1660. 4to. Old cf., rebkd., worn. (SG. Sep.25; 146) $225
- **Trattato de gli Instrumenti di Martirio.** Ill.:– Antonio Tempesta. Rome, 1591. 1st. Edn. 4to. ?Lacks 1st. lf. (?blank). Old vell. bds., restored. (S. Mar.17; 301)   Duran. £170
- - **Anr. Copy.** Cont. vell. (CR. Mar.19; 254)   Lire 820,000
- - **Anr. Copy.** (D. Dec.11-13; 24)   DM 1,800

GALLOWAY, Joseph
- [–] **A Letter to the Right Honourable Lord Viscount H-E, on his Naval Conduct in the American War.** L., 1779. 1st. Edn. Advt. lf. Mod. buckram. [Sabin 26435] (SG. Jan.8; 168) $110

GALLUCCI, Giovanni Paolo
- **Speculum Uranicum.** Venice, 1593. 1st Edn. Fo. Engraved title border slightly defect., many woodcut diagrams loose, a few lacking, with folding table 'Canon Sexagenarius' & rare 4 ll. in 4to. 'De harum paginarum usu' inserted, some foxing & soiling, C2 reprd. Cont. vell. bds., very worn. W.a.f; from Honeyman Collection. (S. May 20; 3241)   Rogers Turner. £280
- **Theatrum Mundi et Temporis.** Venice, 1588. 1st. Edn. 4to. 143 woodcuts, 44 with volvelles, errata, folding table, lacks front fly.-lf. Elab. blind-stpd. vell. dtd. 1589, lacks clasps. (SG. May 14; 81) $2,600

GALSWORTHY, John 'John Sinjohn'
- **The Country House.** L., 1907. Cl. Inscr. (SG. Nov.13; 248) $160
- **The Dark Flower.** L., 1913 [1923]. Manaton Edn. Loose in hf. mor. s.-c. Printer's Copy of sheets from the 1st. Edn. with changes in author's hand. (SG. Nov.13; 249($850
- **The Forsyte Saga.** L., 1922. Ltd. 1st. Edn., sigd. Orig. limp leath., folding box. (SPB. Jul.28; 140) $150
- - **Anr. Edn.** L., 1922. 1st. Edn., 1st. Iss. Orig. cl., d.-w., folding box. (SPB. Jul.28; 139) $125
- **The Freelands.** L., 1915 [1923]. Manaton Edn. Loose in hf. mor. s.-c. Copy-Text of 1st. Edn. with many holographic alterations. (SG. Nov.13; 250) $700
- [–] **From the Four Winds.** 1897. 1st. Edn. (500). Orig. cl. (S. Jul.22; 131)   Sotheran. £100
- - **Anr. Edn.** L., 1897. 1st. Edn. Gt.-decor. buckram, lacks front free endpaper, unopened. (SG. Nov.13; 247) $130
- **Justice.-The Little Dream.-The Pigeon.-The Fugitive.** L., [1919-20]. Manaton Edn. Loose in hf. mor. s.-c. Copy-Text with many corrections in author's hand, & some editorial markings by anr. (SG. Nov.13; 252) $800
- **A Man of Devon.** L., 1901. 1st. Edn. Slight spotting. Orig. cl., slightly worn, s.-c. (SPB. Jul.28; 146) $125
- **The Silver Spoon.** L., [1926]. 1st. Edn., inscr., sigd. Orig. cl., d.-w. in 3 states including the orig. suppressed version, folding box. (SPB. Jul.28; 153) $100
- **Works.** 1923. (530 sets), Manaton Edn. 30 vols. Orig. vell.-bkd. bds. (C. Feb.4; 62)   Traylen. £300
- - **Anr. Edn.** L., 1923-36. Manaton Edn. (350) numbered. 30 vols. Hf. vell., untrimmed. Sigd. (SG. Nov.13; 265) $200
- - **Anr. Edn.** L., 1933. Grove Edn. 26 vols. in 13. Hf. cf. gt., by Sangorski & Sutcliffe. (SPB. Nov.25; 456) $225

GALT, John
- **The Autobiography.** L., 1833. 2 vols. Some foxing on port. & title-pp. Orig. cl. [Sabin 26455] (CB. Sep.24; 224)   Can. $110

GALTON, D.
- **Report [Supplement] on the Railways of the United States.** 1857-58. 2 vols. Fo. Some ll. soiled. Disbnd. (SH. Mar.5; 237)   Weinreb. £160

GALTON, Sir Francis
- **Finger Prints.** 1892. 1st. Edn. Orig. cl. (S. Jun.16; 323)   Brooke-Hitching. £120
- - **Anr. Copy.** (C. May 20; 32)   Foreman. £90
- **Hereditary Genius: An Inquiry into Its Laws & Consequences.** 1869. [1st. Edn.?] Recently rebnd. in hf. cf. (TA. Mar.19; 396)   £70
- - **Anr. Copy.** 57 pp. advts. dtd. Nov. 1869. Orig. cl., soiled. (S. Jun.16; 322)   Decklin. £60

- **Inquiries into Human Faculty & its Development.** 1883. 1st. Edn. Actual photograph mntd. Orig. cl. (SH. Jan.30; 438)   Lehmann. £110

GALVANI, Luigi
- **Memorie Sulla Elettricita animale al Celebre Abate Lazzaro Spallanzani, agiunte alcune Elettriche Esperienze di Gio Aldini.** Bologna, 1797. 4to. New fancy bds. (S. Oct.21; 388)   Walford. £220
- **Opere edite ed inedite . . .** Bologna, 1841. 4to. Fac. plt. Hf. cf. (S. Jun.16; 324)   Gurney. £110

GAMBADO, Geoffrey (Pseud.)
See–BUNBURY, Henry William 'Geoffrey Gambado'

GAMBRILL, R.V.N. & Mackenzie, J.C.
- **Sporting Stables & Kennels.** Ed.:– James W. Appleton. [1935]. (950) numbered. Fo. Outer ll. slightly foxed. Gt.-decor. cl., owner's blind-stp. on endpaper. (SG. Dec.11; 234) $200

GAME, The, a Monthly Magazine
Ill.:– David Jones, Eric Gill & others. St. Dominic's Pr., 1921-23. Vol. 4 no. 9-12, vol. 5 no. 1, vol. 6 no. 34, together 6 issues. Unbnd. as issued. (SH. Feb.19; 91)   Quaritch. £115

GAMGEE, Joseph Sampson
- **History of A Successful Case of Amputation at the Hip-Joint (the limb 48 inches in circumference, 99 pounds weight).** Ill.:– Sarony & Pierre-Petit. 1865. 4to. Orig. cl., slightly soiled on upr. cover. Pres. copy. (S. Jun.16; 325)   Londry. £75

GAN, Aleksei
- **Konstruktivizm.** Moscow, 1922. (2,000). 4to. A few ll. slightly spotted. Orig. wraps., slightly soiled. (SH. Feb.5; 219)   Weinreb. £100

GANAY, Ernest de
- **Chateaux et Manoirs de France.** Paris, 1939. 5 vols. 4to. Cl., orig. wraps. bnd. in, bkplts. (SG. Mar.12; 90) $170

GANDEE, B.F.
- **The Artist.** L., 1835. 16mo. Orig. gt.-lettered mor. (SG. Mar.12; 165) $300

GANDELLINI, Giovanni Gori
- **Notizie Istoriche degl' Intagliatori.** Sienna, 1771. 3 vols. Cont. velvet, gt. brocade ribbon borders on covers, gt. metal arms (possibly cont.) on vol. 1 covers. (C. Jul.16; 330)   Marlborough. £350

GANDY, John Peter
See–GELL, Sir William & Gandy, John Peter

GANF, R.W.
See–SMITH, M.J. & Ganf, R.W.

GANILH, Anthony
- [–] **Ambrosio de Letinez: or the First Texian Novel, embracing a description of the Countries Bordering on the Rio Bravo . . . By A.T. Myrthe.** N.Y., 1842. 2nd. Edn. 2 vols. Somewhat foxed, vol. II upr. fly. Orig. cl.-bkd. bds., shelf labels removed. (PNY. Mar.26; 313) $100

GANIN, Aleksei
- **Raskovany mir [Unchained Peace].** [Kronshino], [1920]. A few ll. slightly soiled. Orig. wraps. (SH. Feb.6; 431)   Quaritch. £110

GANS, David
- **Nechmad Ve'naim.** Ed.:– D. Hebenstreit. Jessnitz, 1743. 1st. Edn. 4to. Slight discolouration. Leath. (S. Nov.18; 705)   Yadem. £90

GANYMED, Jahrbuch f.d. Kunst
Ed.:– J. Meier-Graefe & W. Hausenstein. Ill.:– Max Beckmann, R. Grossman & Adolf Schinnerer. Munich, 1921. Vol. 3. 4to. Orig. cl.-bkd. bds. (SH. Nov.21; 329)   Schwing. £85
- - **Anr. Copy.** Orig. linen. (H. Nov.18-21; 2571)   DM 750
- - **Anr. Edn.** Ill.:– Beckmann, Campendonck, Hecht & Seewald (woodcuts), F. Meseck (etchg.). Munich, 1922. 4to. Orig. linen. (HK. Nov.18-21; 2572)   DM 440

GARCELON, A.
- **Inspirations.** Paris, n.d. Fo. Unsewn as iss. in cl.-bkd. portfo., slightly worn, ties. (SH. Nov.20; 228)   Monk Bretton. £210

GARCIA, Gregorio
- **Historia Eclesiástica y Seglar, de la India Oriental y Occidental.** Baeza, 1626. Several letters inked in on A1, title & final lf. slightly defect. & preserved, light stains, a few headlines affected by

owner's brand on upr. edge. Limp vell. (SPB. May 5; 226) $400
- **Origen de los Indios, de el Nuevo Mundo e Indias Occidentales** Madrid, 1729. Fo. Title soiled & stained, 1 margin reinforced, a few wormholes & stains. Vell., soiled. [Sabin 26567] (SPB. May 5; 227) $500

GARCIA DE CESPEDES, Andres
- **Regimento de Navegacion.–Segunda parte:– en que se pone una Hydrographia.** Ed.:– Real Consejo de las Indias. Madrid, 1606. 1st. & only Edn. 2 pts. in 1 vol. Fo. Engraved map, slightly cropped, lacks blank lf. f.6 at end of prelims., a few ll. slightly spotted. 18th C. cf., spine gt. [Sabin 11718] (S. Nov.4; 473)   Raymond. £1,000

GARCIA LORCA, Federico
- **Bodas de Sangre.** Madrid, 1936. 1st. Edn. Mor., orig. wraps. (DS. Apr.24; 992)   Pts. 30,000

GARCILASSO de la Vega
- **La Florida del' Inca [with Appendix: Ensayo Cronologia para la Historia General de la Florida . . . por Andreas Gonzales Barcia].** Madrid, 1723. 1st. Edn. of the Appendix. 2 vols. Fo. 19th. C. hf. mor., spines misnumbered. From Chetham's Liby., Manchester. [Sabin 98745 & 3349] (C. Nov.27; 404)   Tzakas. £200
- **Histoire des Guerres Civiles des Espagnols dans les Indes.** Paris, 1658. 2 vols. 4to. Additional engraved title slightly defect. in margin, some marginal annots., spotting & sm. stains. Cont. cf., worn. (SPB. May 5; 309) $225
- **Histoire des Yncas Rois du Perou . . . on a joint à cette edition l'Histoire de la Conquête de la Floride.** Amst., 1737. 2 vols. 4to. A few short tears affecting plts. Cont. cf., spines defect., worn. (SPB. May 5; 313) $325
- **Historia General del Peru.** Cordoba, 1617. Fo. Sm. wormhole affecting 1 or 2 ll., some spotting, inscr. at foot of title relating to ownership by a Brigittine house. Cont. limp vell., slightly soiled. [Sabin 98755] (SPB. May 5; 308) $1,850
- **Historie de la Conquête de la Floride.** Leiden, 1731. 2 vols. Some discolouration. Qtr. cf., worn. [Sabin 98748] (SPB. May 5; 312) $225
- **Primera Parte de los Commentarios Reales, que tratan, de la Origen de los Incas . . . de su Idolatria, Leies, y Govierno, en Paz, y en Guerra . . .** Madrid, 1723. Enlarged Edn. Fo. Corners of index ll. dampstained, 1 lf. with marginal tear, & loss of a few words. Old. mott. cf., worn. (SG. Mar. 5; 363) $210
- **Primera parte de los Comentarios Reales [–Historia general del Peru, La Florida].** Madrid, 1722-23. 3 vols. Fo. Titles slightly defect., 2 with repairs, a few stains, a few wormholes affecting letters, no Supp. Mod. cf. (SPB. May 5; 310) $250
- **The Royal Commentaries of Peru.** Trans.:– Sir Paul Rycaut. 1688. 1st. Edn. in Engl. Fo. 19th. C. hf. mor. From Chetham's Liby., Manchester. [Sabin 98760; Wing G216] (C. Nov.27; 403)   Allen. £160
- - **Anr. Copy.** Cont. cf., covers detchd. John Hort's bkplt., Dublin 1757. [Wing G217] (SPB. May 5; 314) $350

GARCILASSO DE LA VEGA–[BARCIA, Andres Garcia de]
- **La Florida del Inca. Historia del Adelantado Hernando de Soto.–Ensayo Cronologico . . . de la Florida.** Madrid, 1723. 2 works in 1 vol. Fo. Light stains at beginning & end. Cont. cf., slightly worn. [Sabin 3349, 98745] (SPB. May 5; 311) $750

GARDEN, The
1878-83. Vols. 14-24. 4to. Cont. cl. (SH. Oct.10; 451)   K. Books. £110

GARDEN, Alexander
- **Anecdotes of the American Revolution, illustrative of the Talents & Virtues of the Heroes of the Revolution.** Ed.:– Thomas W. Field. Brooklyn, 1865. (150) numbered. L.P. reprint. 3 vols. in 1. 4to. Later buckram. (SG. Jan.8; 169) $110

GARDEN OF CARESSES
Ill.:– Gertrude Hermes. Waltham Saint Lawrence, Gold. Cock. Pr., 1934. Vell. gt. Accompanied by suite of 6 engrs. by artist, 5 sigd. in pencil by artist. (SPB. Nov. 25; 291) $225

GARDENS OLD & NEW: The Country House & its Garden Environment
Ill.:– Gertrude Hermes. Waltham Saint Lawrence, Pict. stpd. cl. Inscr. by Brander Matthews,

Raymond M. Sutton, Jr. copy. (SG. May 7; 87) $160

GARDINER, Samuel Rawson
- Oliver Cromwell. Goupil, 1899. (350) numbered on Japanese paper with dupl. set of parts. except frontis. 4to. Red mor. ornately gt. with coat of arms on both covers in geometrical design, watered silk doubls., in velvet case, slightly faded. Bookplt. of Sir William Bass Bt. (SBA. Oct.21; 180) *Anthony.* £105
- – Anr. Copy. Fo. Lacking dupl. set of plts. Silk end papers, mor. gt. by Zaehnsdorf. (P. Oct.2; 98) *Rees-Jones.* £60

GARDINER, Bp. Stephen
- An Admonition to the Bishoppes of Winchester, London & others & c. Rouen [L.], 1 Oct., 1553. Side-notes slightly cropped. Recent mor. [STC 11583] (C. Nov.20; 246) *Hart.* £240
- – Anr. Copy. (C. Apr.1; 34) *Field.* £200
- De Vera Obediencia, an oration made in Latine, ... with the preface of Edmunde Boner ... touchinge true Obedience. Rouen [L.], 26 Oct. 1553. Occasional slight staining. Recent mor. [STC 11585] (C. Apr.1; 35) *Telford.* £140
- – Anr. Copy. (C. Nov.20; 247) *Hart.* £130

GARDNER, G.A.
- Rock-Paintings of North-West Cordoba. Oxford, 1931. Fo. Orig. cl. (SH. Jan.29; 98) *Ars Artis.* £60

GARDNER, P.
See–HEAD, B.V. & Gardner, P.

GARDNER, Thomas
- Historical Account of Dunwich ... Blithburgh ... Southwold. 1754. 4to. Folding map linen-bkd. Cf. gt., worn. (P. Nov.13; 262) *Cox.* £190
- A Pocket-Guide to the English Traveller: Being a Compleat Survey & Admeasurement of all the Principle Roads & Most Considerable Cross-Roads in England & Wales. 1719. 4to. 1 map reprd., margins slightly discoloured. Cont. panel. cf. rebkd. W.a.f. (TA. Aug.21; 188) £825
- – Anr. Copy. Ob. fo. A few lr. margins just cropped without loss. Cont. cf.-bkd. bds., slightly worn, upr. cover detchd. As an atlas, w.a.f. (SBA. Jul.14; 29) *Angle Books.* £600

GARDNOR, John
See–WILLIAMS, David & Gardnor, John

GARENGEOT, Rene Jacques Croissant de
- Traité des Operations de Chirurgie fondés sur la Mechanique des Organes de l'Homme ... Paris, 1731. 2nd. Edn. 3 vols. 12mo. Some ll. slightly spotted or soiled, no hf.-titles. Cont. cf., slightly worn. (S. Feb.23; 48) *Rota.* £85

GARIDEL, Pierre Joseph
- Histoire des Plantes qui Naissent en Provence. Ill.:– H. Blanc. Paris, 1719. Fo. Lacks the plts. as in Nissen, & plts. 45 & 107, but excepting plts. 43, 95 & 105 which are present. Cont. cf., worn, rebkd. From Chetham's Liby., Manchester. (C. Nov.26; 173) *Wagner.* £400
- – Anr. Copy. Plts. erratically numbered, but all present?, extensive marginal annots. by early German owner, & German trans. of the Latin plt. captions. Brkn. (SG. Jan.29; 181) $400

GARLAND of British Poetry
Ill.:– Finden after William Westall. L., 1832. 18mo. (5¾ × 3½ inches) 4 engraved plts. Cont. mor. Fore-e. gt. (SG. Sep.4; 188) $170

GARNER, Thomas & Stratton, Arthur
- The Domestic Architecture of England during the Tudor period Illustrated in a series of Photographs & measured Drawings of Country Mansions, Manor Houses ... L., 1911. 2 vols. Fo. Orig. cl. (CB. May 27; 105) Can. $150

GARNET, J. Ros
See–CONABERE, Betty & Garnet, J. Ros

GARNIER, Edward
- La Porcelaine tendre de Sèvres. Paris, n.d. Fo. Orig. cl. (SH. Jan.29; 177) *Edwards.* £80
- – Anr. Copy. Mod. hf. cf. (SI. Dec.3; 246) Lire 200,000
- The Soft Porcelain of Sèvres. 1892. Fo. Orig. cl. (SH. Jan.29; 175) *Edwards.* £90
- – Anr. Copy. (C. Feb.4; 243) *Basket & Day.* £70

GARNIER, M.J.F. & Delaporte, L.
- Atlas du Voyage d'Exploration en Indo-Chine. Paris, 1873. 2 pts. in 1 vol. (lacks the 2 text vols.).

Fo. Cont. mor-bkd. cl., slightly worn. W.a.f. (C. Nov.6; 254) *F.A.M.* £400

GARRAN, Hon. Andrew
- Australasia Illustrated. Sydney, Melbourne; L. & N.Y., 1892. 3 vols. Fo. Cl., brkn., ex-liby. (SG. Aug.7; 237) $125
- Picturesque Atlas of Australasia. 1886. Vols. 1 & 2 only (of 3). Fo. A few ll. spotted. Orig. hf. mor. (SH. Mar.5; 58) *Lamm.* £150
- – Anr. Copy. 2 vols. 4to. With 7 separately issued cold. maps detailing railway, postal & telegraph routes, 1886-89, some margins defect. Orig. mor. gt., some wear. (TA. Nov.20; 292) £100
- – Anr. Copy. 3 vols. Slight spotting. Orig. leath., worn. (S. Dec.8; 273) *Elliott.* £70
- – Anr. Edn. N.d. 3 vols. Bdg. not stated. (JL. Jul.20; 840) Aus. $420

GARRARD, George
- A Description of the Different Varieties of Oxen Common in the British Isles. 1800-15. Ob. fo. 52 hand-cold. engraved plts., 'order of bdg.' slip, advt. lf. Lev. mor., gt., by Zaehnsdorf. (C. Mar.18; 43) *Michaelis.* £5,500

GARRETT, John
See–AUDEN, Wystan Hugh & Garrett, John

GARRICK, David
- A Catalogue of the Library. [L.], [1823]. 1st. Edn., 2nd Iss. With the 92 p. ptd. price-list interleaved, & the lf. of addenda. Mod. mott. hf. cf., partly unc. Bkplt. of R.H. Isham, lately in the Prescott Collection. (CNY. Feb.6; 128) $500
- The Farmer's Return from London. Ill.:– James Basire after W. Hogarth (port.). L., 1762. 1st. Edn. 4to. Fore-margins slightly frayed, slight wear from horizontal fold. Stitched as iss. in orig. wraps., unc. From the Prescott Collection. (CNY. Feb.6; 127) $500

GARSAULT, François Alexandre Pierre de
- Le Nouveau Parfait Marechal, ou la connoissance générale ... du cheval. Ill.:– after Tardieu. Paris, 1746. 2nd. Edn. 4to. Cont. mott. cf. (C. Feb.25; 11) *Anciens.* £100

[GART der Gesundheit]
Mainz, Peter Schoeffer., 1485. Fo. Lacks final blank lf., corner torn from f. (75) affecting 2 words on verso, woodcuts cold. by cont. hand, full-page woodcut cut down & mntd. 16th. C. blind-stpd. pig over wooden bds., clasps & catches. From collection of Massachusetts Horticultural Society, stps on plts. [H. 8948; BMC I, 35; Goff G97] (SPB. Oct.1; 120) $72,000

GARTH, Sir Samuel
[-] The Dispensary. L., 1706. 6th. Edn. Crimson str.-grd. mor., buckram folding case. 2 fore-e. pntgs. side-by-side; from the liby. of Zola E. Harvey. (SG. Mar.19; 135) $600

GARZONI, Tommaso
- Piazza Universale ... Ill.:– M. Merian (engraved title border). Frankfurt a. M., 1619. 1st. Edn. in German. Fo. Some extreme upr. margins slightly defect., a few ll. with marginal repairs (that on D6 touching a few letters). Cont. vell. bds., panel. in blind, soiled, clasps & catches, hf. red mor. case. Armorial bkplt. of J.J. Zur-Muhlen on verso of title & sm. stp. on recto; from Honeyman Collection. (S. May 20; 3243) *Riley-Smith.* £350
- – Anr. Edn. Ill.:– J. Amman. Frankfurt, 1659. 4to. Lightly soiled. Vell. (R. Mar.31-Apr.29; 1531) DM 4,000

GASKELL, Elizabeth Cleghorn
- Cranford. Ill.:– Hugh Thomson. 1888. Orig. cl. gt. (SH. Mar.27; 514) *Illustrated Antiques.* £200
- – Anr. Edn. Ill.:– Hugh Thomson. L., 1891. Red mor. gt. covers with cold. mor. onlays, mor. doubls. & free end-pp. with designs gt.-tooled in outl., flower onlays, silk fly-ll.; orig. cl. preserved, mor. velvet-lined, case, by Sangorski & Sutcliffe. (CNY. May 22; 353) $1,100
- Sylvia's Lovers. 1863. 1st. Edn. 3 vols. Some ll. spotted. Orig. cl., 2 vols. rebkd. (SH. May 28; 127) *Howes Books.* £50
- Wives & Daughters. 1866. 1st. Edn. 2 vols. A few ll. spotted. Mod. hf. mor. (SH. May 28; 128) *Howes Books.* £60
- The Works. 1906. Knutford Edn. 8 vols. Cont. hf. cf., gt. spines. (SH. Mar.5; 239) *Elkin Mathew.* £145

- – Anr. Copy. Orig. cl. (SH. May 28; 43) *Walford.* £120

GASPEY, Th.
- Bubbles from the Brunnen of Homburg. Darmstadt, 1866. Slightly soiled. Cont. linen. (R. Oct.14-18; 2272) DM 1,700
See–WILLIAMS, Lt. Col. & Gaspey, Thomas

GASPEY, W.
- Tallis's Illustrated London. N.d. 2 vols. (1 vol. text, other plts.). Some spotting. Cont. hf. mor. (CSK. Oct.24; 59) £75

GASS, Patrick
- A Journal of the Voyages & Travels ... Under the Command of Capt. Lewis & Capt. Clarke (sic) ... Pittsb., 1807. 1st. Edn. 12mo. Owners' inscrs. (1 on title), 1 reprd., browned, slight foxing. Mod. hf. mor., new marb. endpapers. From liby. of William E. Wilson. (SPB. Apr.29; 113) $375

GASSENDI, Pierre
- Institutio Astronomica ... 1653. 2nd. Edn., anr. Iss. 3 pts. in 1 vol. Short tear in general title, just affecting text, reprd. Cont. cf. [Wing 291A] (S. Feb.9; 164) *Bicker.* £50
- – Anr. Edn. 1683. 3rd. Edn. 3 pts. in 1 vol. Later cf., spine renewed. (CSK. May 8; 30) £65
- – Anr. Edn. 1685. 2nd. Edn. 3 pts. in 1 vol. Some browning. Mod. cf.-bkd. marb. bds. [Wing G291A] (S. Feb.9; 163) *Bicker.* £65
- Tychonis Brahei, Equitis Dani, Astronomorum Coryphaei. Hague, 1655. 2nd. Edn. 4to. Browned. Cont. cf., rebkd. (SH. Jun.18; 39) *Hannas.* £80

GASTINEAU, Henry
- Wales Illustrated. 1830. 4to. Proofs on India Paper, without text, a few plts. slightly spotted or soiled. Loose in cont. red mor. case, gt. (SBA. Oct.22; 726) *Teachers Charity.* £220
- – Anr. Copy. Some internal foxing. Cont. hf. cf. W.a.f. (TA. Aug.21; 244) £120
- – Anr. Copy. On india paper, some foxing. (TA. Sep.18; 108) £85
- – Anr. Copy. A very few stains, 86 views (only) on 43 plts. Cont. hf. mor., slightly worn. (SBA. Dec.16; 256) *Hulme.* £50
- Wales Illustrated.–South Wales Illustrated. L., ca. 1830. 2 vols. in 1. 4to. Pt. 1, 30 plts. only, lacks plt.-list, Pt. 2, 60 plts. Cont. str.-grd. mor., gt. borders & spine. (SG. Feb.26; 331) $150

GATINE, M.
See–LANTE, Louis Marie & Gatine, M.

GATTY, Mrs. Alfred
See–GATTY, Margaret

GATTY, Margaret
- British Sea-Weeds. L., 1872. 2 vols. 4to. Gt.-pict. cl. (SG. Sep.18; 155) $120

GAU, F.C.
- Antiquités de la Nubie.–Inscriptions Copiées en Nubie et en Egypte. Ed.:– B.G. Neibuhr (2nd. work). Stuttgart/Paris, 1822-23. 2 works in 1 vol. Fo. Title & margins of 1st. work rather spotted. 19th. C. hf. mor. From Chetham's Liby., Manchester. (C. Nov.26; 174) *Cucchi.* £150

GAUDEN, John
[-] A Discourse of Artificial Beauty, in point of Conscience between Two Ladies. 1662. 1st. Edn. Owner's inscr. on title & frontis. of George Burrard dtd. 1686. Cont. sheep. [Wing G353] (C. Apr.1; 211) *Laughton.* £120

GAUFRIDI, Jean Francois de
- Histoire de Provence. Aix, 1694. 2 vols. in 1. Fo. Wormed. Cont. cf., worn. (HD. Jun.29; 198) Frs. 2,000

GAUGUIN, Paul
- Letters to Ambroise Vollard & André Fontainas. Ed.:– John Rewald. San Franc., Grabhorn Pr. 1943. Fo. Linen-bkd. pict. bds., unc. (SG. Oct.23; 136) $190
- Noa Noa. Voyage de Tahiti. Ed.:– J. Meier-Graefe. Munich, 1926. Facs. Edn. of MS. Lge. 4to. Without note by Marees-Ges. Orig. linen, orig. pict. wraps. (HK. Nov.18-21; 2573) DM 850

GAUNT, William
- The Etchings of Frank Brangwyn. 1926. 4to. Orig. vell.-bkd. bds., slightly soiled. (CSK. Mar.20; 129) £65

GAUSS, Karl Friedrich
- Untersuchungen über Gegenstände der Höhern Geodaesie. Göttingen, 1844-47. 1st. book Edn. 2

GAUSS, Karl Friedrich – Untersuchungen über Gegenstände der Höhern Geodaesie. -contd.
vols. in 1. 4to. Slightly soiled in parts. Old wraps., spine reprd. (H. Dec.9/10; 358) DM 450

GAUSSERON, B.H.
See–EUDEL, Paul–GAUSSERON, B.H.–RETTE, A.

GAUSSON, Eugene
– The Island of Navassa. [Balt.], [1866]. Ob. fo. Foxing, marginal stains, ex-liby. with labels on endpapers, endpapers torn, inner hinges strengthened. Hf. mor., rebkd. with mor., worn. [Sabin 26768] (SPB. May 5; 229) $325

GAUTIER, Henri
– Architettura delle Strade Antiche e Moderne. Ill.:– C. dall' Acqua (port.) & Ignazio Avesani (plts.). Vicenza, 1769. 4to. Tear to lr. margin of title. Cont. vell. bds. gt. From the collection of John A. Saks. (C. Jun.10; 91) Maggs. £190

GAUTIER, Théophile
– Capitaine Fracasse (Le). Ill.:– Gustave Doré. Paris, 1866. 1st. Printing. In pts., hf. mor. wrap., decor., s.-c. (HD. Jun.10; 151) Frs. 5,000
– Celle-ci et Celle-là ou La Jeune France Passionnée. Ill.:– François Courboin. Paris, 1900. (125). 3 states of ills. Mor. by Aussourd, decor. spine, borders on covers, including 1 in mosaic, silk doubls., wrap. preserved. (SM. Feb.11; 221) Frs. 5,000
– Fortunio. Ill.:– A. Lunois. Paris, 1898. (50) on Japon. 4to. Each plt. in 3 states, slight spotting. Cont. Fr. lev. mor., gt., orig. wraps. preserved, partly unc. (S. Feb.9; 166) Klusman. £70
– Jean et Jeannette. Ed.:– Léo Claretie (preface). Ill.:– Lalauze. Paris, 1894. On Jap. Lge. 8vo. Ills. in 4 states. Mor. by Bernasconi, spine decor. with 3 compartments, 2 with border of 8 gt. fillets, border of 5 gt. fillets & corner decors. on covers, mor. doubls., wrap. preserved, s.-c. De luxe copy reserved for Léo Claretie. (SM. Feb.11; 223) Frs. 10,000
– – Anr. Edn. Ill.:– Lalauze. Paris, 1904. On lge. Arches vell. 2 states of plts. (1 with comments). Hf. mor. by Pougetoux, wrap. preserved. (SM. Feb.11; 65) Frs. 1,300
– Mademoiselle de Maupin. Double Amour. Paris, 1835-36. Orig. Edn. 2 vols. Title-pages & some prelim. ll. reprd. Long-grd. bordeaux hf. mor., blind & gt. decor. spines, unc., by Durrand. Stps. effaced on titles & hf.-titles. (HD. Feb.18; 127) Frs. 3,100
– – Anr. Edn. Ill.:– Champollion & others after Toudouze. Paris, 1883. (150) numbered on Japon extra. 2 vols. 22 engraved plts. in 2 states, extra ill. with 54 watercolour gouache ills. & decor by Alcide T. Robaudi & others, some full-p. & tipped in, most sigd. Mor. gt. extra, spine in compartments, inner dentelles, by A. Cuzin, s.-c.'s, ex-liby. with bkplt. (LC. Oct.2; 30) £200
– – Anr. Copy. Engraved plts. in 2 states. Red mor., by Rottier, interlacing thick mor., geometric onlays, orig. wraps. bnd. in s.-c. (SM. Oct.8; 2336) Frs. 8,000
– – Anr. Edn. Ill.:– Toudouze. Paris, 1883. Reprint of 1st. Edn., (500); on vell., numbered. 2 vols. German mor. by Tout, gt. plaques on covers, spines decor. with raised bands, unc. (HD. Feb.27; 138) Frs. 1,300
– – Anr. Edn. Ill.:– Serge de Solomko. Paris, 1914. On Jap. 2 vols. 3 states of engrs. Jansenist mor. by Flammarion, spines with raised bands, silk doubls. & end-papers, wraps. & spines preserved, unc., s.-c. (HD. Feb.27; 139) Frs. 1,400
– La Morte Amoureuse. Ill.:– Decisy after Laurens. Paris, 1904. (90) on Jap. 3 states of plts. (black-&-white, final cold. state, & with the letter). Hf. mor. by Bretault, wrap. preserved. MS. poem by author (in 3 verses, entitled 'De Goethe') loosely inserted. (SM. Feb.11; 66) Frs. 2,100
– Nature at Home. Ill.:– Karl Bodmer. L., 1883. 4to. Pict. cl. (SG. Mar.19; 26) $120
– Le Roman de la Momie. 1858. Sewed, box. (HD. Oct.10; 56) Frs. 1,150
– – Anr. Edn. Ill.:– A. Lunois & L. Boisson. 1901. (30) on vell. with triple state of ills. Mor., mosaic border decor., mor. doubls., mor. decor., silk end-ll., wrap. & spine, hf. mor. s.-c. & wrap, by Chambolle-Duru. (HD. Jun.30; 24) Frs. 7,600
– – Anr. Edn. Ill.:– Gasperini after George Barbier. Paris, 1929. (1,091) numbered. 4to. 2 supp. plts. loose. Cont. red hf. mor., orig. wraps. bnd. in.

Extra suite of ills. on chine. (SH. Nov.20; 216) Monk Bretton. £210
– Une Nuit de Cléopatre. Ill.:– P. Avril. 1894. Ltd. Edn. Crimson mor. covers tooled in gt. with border of shells & Greek geometric pattern, spine divided into 6 matching panels, by C. & C. McLeish. (P. Jan.22; 321) Maggs. £170
– The Works. Jenson Society. 1906. 24 vols. Cont. mor., gt. (SH. May 28; 44) Heald. £300
– – Anr. Copy. Cont. red hf. mor. by William Brown of Edinb., spines slightly soiled. (CSK. May 8; 128) £110
– – Anr. Copy. (1000), 24 vols. Hf. cf. gt., gt. decor. spines, by Sangorski & Sutcliffe. (SPB. Nov.25; 457) $400

GAUTIER [D'AGOTY, Jacques Fabien]
– Chroa-Génésie ou Generation des Couleurs, contre le Système de Newton. Paris, 1750-1. 2 vols., 2 pts. in vol. II. 12mo. 2 ll. in vol. II, pt. 2 misbnd., bkplt., sigd., of Moseley of Buildwas, Shropshire. Cont. red mor., gt., arms of Antoine-Louis Rouillé, Comte de Jouy, surrounded by triple gt. fillet, spine gt. in compartments, inner gt. dentelles, vol. 1 slightly worn. (SM. Oct.7; 1725) Frs. 4,500

GAUTIER D'AGOTY, Jacques Fabien & Duverney, L.
– Anatomie de la Tête en Tableaux Imprimés . . . Paris, Priv. ptd., 1748. Fo. Advt. lf., 7 mezzotint plts. (of 8, lacks plt. 2). New hf. cf., marb. paper covers. (S. Jun.16; 328) Quaritch. £500
– Myologie Complette en Couleur et Grandeur Naturelle . . . Ed.:– [M. Duvernoy]. Paris, Priv. ptd. 1746[-1748]. 2 vols. Fo. Each pt. with 'Advt.' lf., 18 mezzotint plts. (of 20, lacks plts. 17 & 20). New hf. cf., marb. paper covers. (S. Jun.16; 327) Quaritch. £1,900

GAUTRUCHE, Pierre
– L'Histoire Poëtique, pour l'Intelligence des Poëtes et des Autheurs Anciens. Paris, 1681. 10th. Edn. 12mo. Sig. on title of Lyonell Tollemache, 4th. Earl of Dysart, inscr. on flyf. in same hand. Cont. red mor., gt., arms of Elisabeth Charlotte de Bavière, Duchesse d'Orleans, gt. fillet, spine gt. in compartments, inner gt. dentelles, upr. cover worn. (SM. Oct.7; 1726) Frs. 1,200

GAVARD, Charles
– Galeries Historiques de Versailles. Paris, 1838. Vol. I only. Lge. fo. Hf. mor. (LC. Jun.18; 75) £58
– – Anr. Edn. Paris, 1838-41. 14 vols. in 12, 3 vols. text & 9 vols. plts. Fo. & 4to. Cont. hf. mor., partly unc. (SI. Dec.3; 248) Lire 2,400,000

GAVARNI, Charles
– La Correctionelle . . . 1840. 1st Printing. 4to. Cont. hf. chagrin, smooth decor. spine. (HD. Jun.25; 252) Frs. 3,100

GAVARNI, Paul, Guillaume-Sulpice-Chevalier 'dit'
[–] Le Diable à Paris: Paris et les Parisiens. Ill.:– Paul Gavarni & others. Paris, 1845-1846. 2 vols. Red hf. cf., needs rebdg. (SG. Sep.4; 201) $100
– – Anr. Copy. Cont. hf. mor. (SI. Dec.3; 249) Lire 320,000
– Gavarni in London. Ed.:– Albert Smith. Ill.:– Vizetelly after Gavarni. L., 1849. 1st Edn. 4to. Orig. cl., very faded & shaken. (SG. Nov.20; 336) $110
– Masques et Visages. Paris, 1857. Orig. Edn., 1st. Printing. Hf. mor., corners, fillet, decor. spine, unc., wrap., worn. (HD. Jun.10; 152) Frs. 1,200
– – Anr. Edn. Ed.:– C.A. Saint-Beuve (notice). Paris, ca. 1860. Fo. Slightly soiled in parts. Orig. hf. linen, gt. (R. Oct.14-18; 2505a) DM 650
– Oeuvres Choisies. Paris, 1846-48. 4 pts. in 2 vols. 4to. Cont. linen. (HK. Nov.18-21; 2340) DM 620
– – Anr. Edn. Paris, 1847. Cont. hf. mor. (SH. Apr.9; 245) King. £65
– Revues. Paris, 1846. Cf. (CR. Jun.11; 574) Lire 200,000

GAVARNI, Paul & Mery, J.
– Les Parures.–Les Joyaux. Paris, ca. 1850. 2 vols. in 1. 4to. 31 engraved plts., all mntd., India Proofs, each vol. with 'Perles et Parures' hf.-title & plt-list, bnd. in engd. title for 1st. 2 series & wdct. wrap. for both. Later three-qtr. mor., spine gt., occasional foxing. (SG. Sep.4; 199) $180

GAVARNI, Paul & others
[–] Les Français Peints par Eux-Mêmes. Paris, 1840. 2 vols. 4to. Hf. mor. (SG. Sep.4; 200) $100

GAVIN, Antonio
– Le Passe-par-tout de l'Eglise Romain. Cologne, 1730. 1st. German Edn. 5 vols. Cont. hf. vell. (D. Dec.11-13; 25) DM 850

GAY, Claudio
– Historica Fisica y Politica de Chile. Paris, 1843-65. 26 vols. & 2 atlas vols. 26 vols. 8vo & 2 vols. 4to. Some botanical plts. slightly foxed, none severely affected, slight foxing to text, several discreet liby. stps. & liby. discard stps., mostly on blank versos of plts., slight paper discolouration on about 20 plts. Uniform old mor. Author's sigd. inscr. in Vol. 1 of the Agricultura. (KH. Nov.18; 274) Aus. $3,000
– – Anr. Edn. Paris, 1844-72. 30 vols. 28 vols. 8vo, 2 vols. 4to. Some foxing, 1 map reprd., margins of hf.-title & title reprd. in vol. 1 of Atlas, some spotting in text vols. Text in cont. hf. mor., 1 vol. not unif., atlas in mod. cf. [Sabin 26779] (SPB. May 5; 230) $11,000

GAY, John
– The Beggar's Opera.–Polly. Priv. Ptd. (2nd. work). 1729. 3rd. L. Edn.; 1st. Edn. 2 works in 1 vol. 4to. Lacks 1st. blank in 2nd. vol., some slight dampstaining. Cont. vell.-bkd. marb. bds., soiled. (S. Feb.9; 167) Quaritch. £130
– Fables. 1727-38. 1st. Edn. 2 vols. in 1. 4to. Cont. cf., rebkd., upr. cover detchd. Bkplt. of Arthur Haughton. (CSK. Oct.10; 204) £75
– – Anr. Edn. Ill.:– William Blake & others. Stockdale, 1793. 2 vols. in 1. Cf. gt. (P. Dec.11; 3) Chelsea. £110
– – Anr. Copy. 2 vols. Cont. cf. (SH. Mar.26; 86) Bayley. £95
– – Anr. Copy. Titles slightly cropped, some spotting & offsetting. Worn, 1 jnt. reprd. (SKC. May 19; 6) £50
– – Anr. Edn. Ill.:– William Blake. 1793 [but 1811 or later]. [2nd. Edn.]. 2 vols. Engraved titles shaved with slight loss. Cont. marb. cf., vol. 1 rebkd., old spine preserved. (CSK. Jun.26; 149) £60
– Fables. With a Life. Ill.:– W. Blake, Skelton, Wilson & others. L., 1793. 1st. Blake Edn. 2 pts. in 1 vol. 4to. 1 copper engr. with sm. tear, slightly scratched & defect. Cont. leath., spine renewed in cont. style. (D. Dec.11-13; 663) DM 440
– L'Opera du Gueux. Ill.:– Louise Ibels. 1934. (115), numbered. 4to. 15 orig. drawings, 1 folding & 2 watercold. Mor. by G. Cretté, orig. copper-eng. in centre of both covers, wrap. preserved, folder & s.-c. (SM. Feb.11; 224) Frs. 13,500
– Rural Sports. Ill.:– Gordon Ross. N.Y., 1930. De Luxe Edn., (225) with hand-cold. plts. Fo. Mor., blind-tooled geometric design, spine gt. (SG. Dec.11; 318) $110
– Trivia. [1716]. 1st. Edn. Mod. cf. (S. Nov.25; 471) Quaritch. £95
– – Anr. Copy. L.P. crimson lev., triple gt. fillet borders, spines gt. with fleurons, gt. dentelles, by Rivière. (SG. Oct.9; 105) $600
– The Wife of Bath. 1713. 1st. Edn. 4to. Running-title on 2 ll. cropped, sm. tear in hf.-title reprd. Mor. by Rivière. (C. Nov.19; 97) Courtland. £120

GAY, John, Pope, Alexander & Arbuthnot, John –PARKER, E.
– Three Hours after Marriage.–A Complete Key to . . . Three Hours after Marriage. 1717. 1st. Edns. 2 works in 1 vol. 1st. work: lacks hf.-title & advt. lf. at end, 1 or 2 tears; 2 headlines cropped, some browning; 2nd. work: some dampstaining. 19th. C. hf. roan. Bkplt. of George Chetwynd. (S. Feb.9; 168) Quaritch. £55

GAY, Jules 'D'J, C.' le Comte d'Imry
[–] Bibliographie des Ouvrages relatifs à l'Amour, aux Femmes, au Mariâge . . . Turin, L., 1871-73. 3rd. Edn. 6 vols. Cont. hf. red mor., gt. (D. Dec.11-13; 508) DM 600
– – Anr. Edn. Ed.:– [J. Lemonnyer]. Lille, 1894-1900. 4th. Edn. 4 vols. Cl-bkd. bds with device from bkplt., gt. Bkplt. of L. Froissart. (SM. Oct.7; 1383) Frs. 1,300

GAY DE VERNON, François
– Traité Elementairé d'Art Militaire et de Fortification . . . Paris, XIII [1805]. 1st. Edn. 2 vols. 4to. Cont. leath.-bkd. marb. bds., worn. (D. Feb.25; 146) $110

GAZETTE des Sept Arts
Ill.:– after Goncharova, Larionov, Zadkine,

Picasso & others. Paris, 1923. Nos. 4/5 only. Fo. Orig. wraps. (SH. Feb.5; 220) *Tate Gallery.* £50

GAZETTEER (A) of the World
L., ca. 1850. 14 vols. Orig. decor. cl. (GM. Apr.30; 818) £65
– – **Anr. Edn.** N.d. 14 vols. Cl. gt., worn. (P. Oct.2; 258) *Whatley.* £80
– – **Anr. Copy.** 6 vols. Cont. diced cf. (CSK. Jun.19; 119) £60

GEBER, J.
– Chimiae . . . Chimia . . . accessit medulla alchimiae Gebrici . . . Ed.:– Georgius Horne. Leiden, 1668. 12mo. Old red mor. gt., flat spine gt. (S. Dec.1; 177) *Rota.* £100
– – **Anr. Copy.** New hf. mor. (S. Dec.1; 176) *Quaritch.* £55

GEBHART, Emile
– Les Trois Rois. Ill.:– Serge de Solomko. Paris, 1919. (25) on Japon or velin d'Arches. 4to. In 3 states. Mor., ornate gt., by de Samblanx, ornate onlaid mor. centre & cornerpieces, orig. wraps. bnd. in, s.-c. P. Brunet ex-libris. (SM. Oct.8; 2338) Frs. 7,000
– – **Anr. Edn.** Ill.:– Serge de Solomko. Paris, 1919. (820) numbered on Arches vell. Sm. 4to. Red hf. mor. by Ysieux, decor. spine, wrap. preserved. (SM. Feb.11; 225) Frs. 1,200

GEE, Ernest Richard
– Early American Sporting Books. 1928. (500). Cl.-bkd. bds., inscr. on front free endpaper. (SG. Dec.11; 235) $130
– – **Anr. Copy.** Cl.-bkd. bds. (SG. Jan.22; 179) $120
– The Sportsman's Library. Ed.:– Maclay, Paters, & Wagstaff. [1933]. Fo. Reprinted from Sportsman Magazine in the orig. format, & with 7 pp. of advts. Red hf. mor., spine gt., by MacDonald. (SG. Dec.11; 320) $130
– – **Anr. Edn.** N.Y., 1940. (600). Buckram. (SG. Apr.9; 405) $130

GEER, Charles de
– Memoires pour Servir à l'Histoire des Insectes. Stockholm, 1752-76. 1st. Edn. 7 vols. in 6 (only). 4to. Slightly foxed & dust-soiled. 19th. C. hf. mor., worn, 1 cover detchd. From Chetham's Liby., Manchester. (C. Nov.26; 175) *Wheldon & Wesley.* £300

GEFFROY, Gustave
– Claude Monet. Paris, 1922. Sm. 4to. Hf. chagrin. 3 A.N.'s by author, A.L. by Claude Monet. (HD. Dec.5; 91) Frs. 2,300

GEHLER, Johann Samuel Traugott
– Physikalisches Wörterbuch. Ed.:– Brandes, Gmelin & others. Leipzig, 1825-45. 11 pts. in 19 vols. Lacks copper engr. Cont. hf. leath. (D. Dec.11-13; 163) DM 600

GEIB, K.
– Maler. Wanderungen am Rhein von Konstanz b. Köln. Karlsruhe, 1838. 3 pts. in 1 vol. Text browned, lightly soiled. Cont. hf. leath. gt. (HK. May 12-14; 730) DM 2,800

GEIGER, Benno
– Magnasco. Bergamo, 1949. 4to. Hf. cf. (CR. Mar.19; 79) Lire 700,000

GEIGER, John Lewis
– A Peep at Mexico. Ill.:– after photographs by author, Spencer, Bird & Co. & Sawyer. L., 1874. Gt.-pict. cl., spotted. (SG. Jul.9; 216) $160

GEIGER, Ph.L.
– Handbuch der Pharmacie. Ed.:– J. Liebig & T.F.L. Nees v. Esenbeck, J.H. Dierbach & C. Marquart. Heidelberg, 1838-43. Vol. 1 in 2 pts., Vol. 2 in 5 pts. Lightly soiled in parts, all title ll. stpd. on recto & plts. stpd. on verso. Unif. hf. leath. (R. Mar.31-Apr.4; 1185) DM 650

GEIGER, W.
– Tauromachie. Leipzig, ca. 1925. (100) numbered. Lge. ob. 4to. 31 sigd. etchgs. Orig. pict. hf. vell. (HK. Nov.18-21; 2577) DM 1,700

GEIKIE, Walter
– Etchings Illustrative of Scottish Character & Scenery. Edinb., n.d. 4to. Some plts. mntd. on India paper, some spotting. Cont. mor., gt. (CSK. Nov.21; 76) £50

GEILER v. KAISERSBERG, Johann
– Christenlich Bilgerschafft zurn Ewige[n] Vatterla[n]d . . .–Das Buch Granatapfel. Ill.:–

Hans Baldung Grien. Basel; Strassb., 1512; 1516. 2 works in 1 vol. Fo. 1st. title slightly soiled, 1st. 30 ll. wormed at bottom corner & soiled. Cont. blind-stpd. cf.-bkd. wood bds., some faults & worming, spine renewed, 2 clasps. (HK. Nov.18-21; 198) DM 10,000
– Fragmenta Passionis Domini Nostri Jesu Christi. Strassburg, 1508. 1st. Edn. Sm. 4to. Cont. owner's mark & much old MS., light worming. Cont. wood bds., new leath. back. (R. Mar.31-Apr.4; 50) DM 1,600

GEILING, F.W.
– Bilder aus dem Deutschen Studentenleben in 16 Darstellungen. Jena, [1865]. Ob. 4to. Slightly soiled. Loose. (R. Mar.31–Apr.4; 1522) DM 1,500

GEISBERG, Max
– Die Kupferstiche des Meisters E.S. Berlin, 1924. (300). Fo. Hf. pig, worn. (SG. Dec.4; 155) $325

GEISER, Bernhard
– Picasso Peintre-Graveur: Catalogue Illustré de l'Oeuvre Gravé et Lithographié. Berne, 1955; 1968. Vol. 1 (900), vol. 2 (2,000). 2 vols. Fo. Three-qtr. mor. by Sangorski & Sutcliffe, orig. wraps. bound in. (SG. Oct.23; 269) $800

GEISLER, Maria, Publisher
– Collection de Vues Principaux, Palais, Eglises, Batimens, publiques. Vienna, n.d. Ob. fo. Hf. red mor. over marb. bds., by Zaehnsdorf. (LC. Oct.2; 177) £560
See–SHOBERG & Geisler

GEISSLER, R.
– Album von Coburg. Coburg, ca. 1860. Loose in orig. wraps. (R. Mar.31–Apr.4; 1954) DM 850

GEISTERGESCHICHTEN
Ed.:– Martha De Haas. Ill.:– Arthur Rackham. Zurich, 1923. 1st. Edn., (1,000) numbered. 4to. Gt. decor. cl. Raymond M. Sutton, Jr. copy. (SG. May 7; 89) $200

GEISTLICH MAY, Der
Munich, 28 Aug. 1550. Worming in 1st. 3 ll., slightly affecting text, reprd. tear in A8. Disbnd. (S. May 5; 34) *Goldschmidt.* £90

GEKKO
– 36 Coloured Prints of Japanese Women. [Japan], [Late 19th. C.]. Approx. 325 × 225 mm. A very few spots, hinged at margins. Folded in orig. patterned silk covers. (SBA. May 27; 472) *Kruml.* £400

GELATO, Ascoso (Pseud.)
See–MALVASIA, Count Carlo Cesare 'Ascoso Gelato'

GELENIUS, Ae.
– De Admiranda, Sacra, et Civili Magnitvdine Coloniae Clavdiae Agrippensis Avgvstae. Cologne, 1645. 1st. Edn. 4to. Slightly browned & wormed, owner's mark on title. Cont. blind-tooled pig-bkd. wood bds., 2 clasps. (HK. Nov.18-21; 1336) DM 900

GELIS, E.
See–CHAPUIS, Alfred & Gelis, E.

GELIS-DIDOT, P. & Laffilée, H.
– La Peinture Decorative en France du XIe au XVie Siècle. Paris, n.d. Spotting. Cont. hf. mor., worn. Sir Edward Burne-Jones copy with his sig. (CSK. Jul.3; 117) £120
– – **Anr. Copy.** Fo. Slight browning. (CSK. Jan.9; 47) £55

GELL, Sir William
– The Itinerary of Greece. 1810. 4to. Cont. hf. cf. (C. Nov.5; 58) *Weinreb.* £90
– Narrative of a Journey in the Morea. 1823. Orig. bds., unc. (P. Oct.23; 25) *BH.* £240

GELL, Sir William & Gandy, John Peter
– Pompeiana: the Topography Edifices & Ornaments of Pompeii. 1832. L.P. 2 vols. Vigs. in text on India proof paper, some margins slightly dampstained. Cont. diced russ. gt., rebkd. preserving orig. spine. (SBA. Dec.16; 53) *Quaritch.* £250

GELLERT, Chr.
– Fabeln. Ill.:– R. Seewald. Berlin, 1920. (125) Fo. Orig. hf. linen. 1st. woodcut sigd. by artist, MS. ded. of artist on endpaper. (HK. May 12-14; 2060) DM 800

GELLI, Giovanni Battista
– Circes of John Baptista Gello, Florentine. Trans.:– Henry Iden. 1557. 1st. Edn. in Engl. Mor. gt. by Bedford, slightly rubbed. [STC 11708] (C. Nov.19; 30) *Mann.* £190

GELLI, Jacopo–GELLI, Jacopo & Moretti, G.
– Gli Archiburgiari Milanesi.–Gli Armaroli Milanesi. I Missaglia e la loro Casa. Milan, 1905; 1903. [200]; [300]. 2 vols. 4to. Both in unif. hf. mor., gt. spines, 1 cover loose, orig. wraps bnd. in, partly unc. (SI. Dec.3; 252) Lire 350,000

GELLIUS, Aulus
– Noctes Atticae. Trans.:– Jacobus Prouse. Paris, 1681. 4to. Some browning. Cont. Fr. red mor., gt., spine tooled in compartments with arabesque ornaments, covers with three-line roll border, panel with arabesque corner compartments, & the arms of Pierre-Daniel Huet, slightly rubbed. Bkplt. of Huet, 1692, with book label of Bernard Edward (12th) Duke of Norfolk, pasted over head of it; from liby. of André L. Simon. (S. May 18; 103) *Thompson.* £280
– Noctium Atticarum Commentari. Venice, Nicolaus Jenson, 1472. [2nd. or 3rd. Edn.]. Fo. Gold & illuminated 8-line initial P on green background with a drawing of a rabbit & trees & an illuminated three-qtr. border of intertwined vine-scroll on a blue ground filled in with green, gold & red, the medallion for the coat-of-arms left blank, on fo. 16, 18 other lge. gold & illuminated initials intertwined with vine-scroll on cold. grounds, smaller initials supplied in alternating red & blue, lacks 1st. & last blank ll., extreme blank fore-margins of 1st. 17 ll. strengthened, minor tears to 4 or 5 upr. blank margins, some early marginal MS. notes washed out. Early 19th. C. Fr. diced russ. gt., broad wavy gt.-dotted border with blind tools, spine gt., jnts. brkn. & reprd., corners worn, upr. mor. gt. s.-c. Bkplts. of William Christmas, Charles Butler, Cortlandt F. Bishop & John A. Saks. [BMC V, 171, Goff G120] (CNY. Oct.1; 113) $8,500
– – **Anr. Edn.** Paris, 22 Mar. 1508. Sm. 4to. Slight browning & soiling. Early 19th. C. hf. cf., covers detchd., spine defect. From liby. of André. L. Simon. (S. May 18; 102) *Thompson.* £100
– – **Anr. Edn.** Venice, 1515. 2nd. Aldine Edn. Later cf.-bkd. marb. bds. (SG. Feb.5; 10) $120
See–CICERO, Marcus Tulluis–GELLIUS, Aulus –VALERIUS, Maximus

GEMS from the Poets
Ill.:– after F.A. Lydon. L., ca. 1860. 4to. Contents loose in bdg., several ll. removed & loosely replaced. Cont. mor., elab. gt. Double fore-e. pntg.; from the liby. of Zola E. Harvey. (SG. Mar.19; 136) $350

GEMS OF ANCIENT ART
L., 1827. 4to. Slightly soiled. Later hf. leath., gt. (R. Oct.14-18; 2659) DM 400

GENEALOGISTS' MAGAZINE
1925-79. Vols. 1-19 pt. 11, & an envelope of other publications, together in 26 vols. Mod. cl. & orig. wraps. (SH. Oct.10; 331) *Bunsei.* £90

GENERAL ORDERS
– Spain & Portugal. 1811-14. Vols. 1-5 (?only). Cont. diced Russ. (CSK. Jul.17; 11) £55

GENERAL P.E. Sunday School Union
– Wreath from the Woods of Carolina. Ill.:– Sarony, Major & Knapp. N.Y., 1859. 1st. Edn. 4to. Gt.-pict. cl., worn. (SG. May 21; 450) $100

GENERAL STUD BOOK
1858-55-61. Various Edns. Vols. 1-34. Cont. cf. & hf. cf. (CSK. Feb.27; 101) £120
– – **Anr. Edn.** L., 1891-1929. Vols. 1-26, lacks last vol. Spanish leath., covers off 2 vols. (SG. Apr.9; 360) $475

GENET, Edmond Charles
– Memorial on the Upward Forces of Fluids, & their Applicability to Several Arts, Sciences, & Public Improvements. Albany, 1825. 1st. Edn. Browned. Cl., spine defect, upr. cover detchd. From Honeyman Collection. (S. May 20; 3244) *Percy.* £240

GENGA, Bernardino
– Anatomia per Uso et Intelligenza del Disegno. Ill.:– Gio. Maria Lancisi. Rome, 1691. 1st. Edn. Book 1 (all publd.). Fo. Vell., slightly soiled. (S. Jun.16; 331) *Rootenberg.* £480

GENLIS, Stephanie Felicité, Contesse de
- Arabesques Mythologiques. Paris, 1810. Vol. 1 (of 2). Cont. hf. cf., cypher on upr. cover. (S. Mar.17; 243) *Norton.* £55

GENNETE, C.L.
- Nouvelle Construction de Cheminées. Liège, 1760. Advts. Cont. mott. sheep, worn. (S. Dec.9; 475) *Quaritch.* £95

GENOA
- Collection of 20 Engraved Views. Ill.:– after Giolfi, Torricelli & Riviera. [?Genoa], ca. 1760. Fo. Wtrmkd. 'SP/P', tear in 1st. plt., several plts. stained from upr. edge, a few plts. dust-soiled at edges, occasional browning & spotting. Cont. hf. cf., spine gt., worn. 1st. plt. with dedication to Giuseppi D'Oria, as a collection, w.a.f. (S. Nov.4; 580) *Loeb.* £2,900

GENT, Thomas
- Ancient & Modern History of the Famous City of York. 1730. 1st. Edn. 1 woodcut ill. mntd. to preserve, advt. lf. tipped in before title, a few slight tears (reprd.). Cont. spr. cf., neatly rebkd. (SBA. Oct.22; 596) *Spelman.* £62
- Ancient & Modern History of the Loyal Town of Rippon. York, 1733. Lge. folding woodcut map, slightly torn & reprd., advt. ll., stp. on title. Mod. bds. (SBA. Oct.22; 597) *Kelsall.* £62
- Annales Regioduni Hullini: or, the History of the Royal & Beautiful Town of Kingston-upon-Hull. York, 1735. Later hf. russ., neatly rebkd. preserving orig. spine. (SBA. Oct.22; 598) *Chambers.* £60

GENTHE, Arnold
- The Book of the Dance. N.Y., [1916]. 1st. Edn. Tall 8vo. Cl., owner's sig. on front free endpaper. (SG. Apr.23; 94) $110
- Impressions of Old New Orleans. Ed.:– Grace King (foreword). N.Y., [1926]. (200) numbered, in special bdg., with tipped-in card, sigd. by Genthe. 4to. Gt.-pict. bds. (SG. Apr.23; 95) $150
- – Anr. Copy. Cl.-bkd. bds., d.-w. (chipped). (SG. Apr.23; 96) $140

GENTIL, François
- Le Jardinier Solitaire ... Also the Compleat Florist ... 1706. Some browning, owner's inscr. on title. Cf., gt., rebkd. & reprd. (S. Jun.1; 265) *Marlborough Rare Books.* £100
- – Anr. Copy. Old panel. cf., cover detchd. (SG. Jan.29; 183) $150

GENTILIS Becchius Urbinas
- Florentinorum Oratio coram summo Pontiface Alexandro VI. [Rome], [Eucharius Silber], [After 28 Nov. 1492]. 4to. Paper bds., covers loose. [HC [Add] 7559*; BMC IV p. 114; Goff G 130] (C. Apr.1; 36) *Webber.* £120

GENTLEMAN Angler, The
L., 1736. 2nd. Edn. 12mo. With advts. & index. Old cf., needs rebdg. (SG. Dec.11; 38) $100

GENTLEMAN, David
- Bridges on the Backs. Ed.:– Peter Eden. Camb., 1961. (500). Ob. 8vo. Orig. wallet-type bdg., s.-c. (CSK. Apr.24; 104) £60

GENTLEMAN'S Library Containing Rules of Conduct in all Parts of Life
1715. Cf. gt. (P. Sep.11; 76) *Shaw.* £75

GENTLEMAN'S MAGAZINE
1731[-1845]. 160 vols. including index vols. to vols. 1-20 & 1-56. Lacks vols. for 1798-1806, vol. for 1830 pt. 2 & 1845 pt. 2. Cf., gt. spines to 1797, worn, many jnts. worn & spines defect. As a periodical, w.a.f. (C. Feb.4; 133) *Burden.* £1,200
- – Anr. Run. 1731-1876. 182 vols. Cf., worn, some covers detchd. & spines lacking. W.a.f. (SBA. Jul.23; 509) *Konuma.* £1,800
- – Anr. Run. 1793-1818. 52 vols., a broken run. Orig. hf. or full cf., unif. design gt. decor. spines, some wear. (TA. Oct.16; 21) £310

GENTRY, Thomas G.
- Nests & Eggs of Birds of the United States. Phila., n.d. 4to. Lacks port. Hf. mor. (CSK. Mar.20; 75) £50

GENTY, Louis
- L'Influence de la Découverte de l'Amérique sur le Bonheur du Genre-Humain. Paris, 1788. Marginal wormholes affecting a few ll., stains. Cont. cf., slightly worn. [Sabin 26598] (SPB. May 5; 231) $100

GEOFFROY, Etienne-Louis
[–] Histoire Abrégée des Insectes que se trouvent aux Environs de Paris. Paris, 1762. 2 vols. 4to. Some plts. slightly dampstained, soiling. Cont. cf. (CSK. Nov.28; 61) £65

GEOFFROY SAINT-HILAIRE, Isidore
- Histoire Générale et Particulière des Anomalies de l'Organisation chez l'Homme et les Animaux. Brussels, 1837-38. 3 vols. plus Atlas, tog. 4 vols. in 1. Mod. buck., ptd. wraps. bnd. in. (SG Sep.18; 156) $100

GEOFFROY SAINT-HILAIRE, Isidor & Cuvier, Georges L.C.
- Histoire Naturelle des Mammifères. Paris, 1819-22. 3 vols. Lge. fo. Livraisons 1-36 only (of 72), 239 hand-cold. plts., lacks hf.-titles & introduction. Cont. hf. roan, unc. W.a.f. (C. Jul.15; 147) *Elstein.* £900

GEOFFROY VILLENEUX, R.
[–] L'Afrique, ou Histoire, Moeurs, Usages et Coutumes des Africains. Le Sénégal, par R.G.V. Paris, 1814. 4 vols. 16mo. Cont. red str.-grd. mor., decor. spines, covers with floral roulette border, gt. fillets, inner dentelle, in the Bozerian style. (HD. Apr.9; 480) *Frs. 4,000*

GEOGRAPHIA ANTIQUA
1789. 4to. Qtr. cf. (P. Jan.22; 185) *Cambridge.* £55

GEOGRAPHICAL Handbook Series. Naval Intelligence Division
[1943-46]. 20 vols. Orig. cl. (CSK. Oct.10; 89) £110

GEOGRAPHIE EN ESTAMPES OU MOEURS ET COSTUMES
Paris, ca. 1830. Ob. 8vo. Minor stains, corner torn from 1 lf. with slight loss. Hf. leath., worn. (S. Dec.9; 516) *Hyde.* £90

GEOGRAPHISCHES REISE-, POST-UND ZEITUNGS-LEXICON VON TEUTSCHLAND
Jena, 1756. 1st. Edn. 2 vols. Lightly browned in places, title-lf. multi stpd. Cont. leath. (R. Mar.31-Apr.4; 1842) DM 2,600

GEORGE, Ernest
- Etchings in Belgium. 1878. 4to. Plts. & text loose. Cl. gt., covers defect. (P. Apr.9; 53) *Schapiro.* £70
- – Anr. Copy. Fo. Liby. linen. (R. Oct.14-18; 1894) DM 420
- – Anr. Edn. 1883. 2nd. Edn. Fo. Some plts. soiled. Orig. cl., loose. (SH. Apr.9; 149) *Schuster.* £85
- Etchings on the Mosel. 1873. Fo. Plts. loose in bdg. Cl., worn. W.a.f. (BS. Feb.25; 291) £190
- – Anr. Edn. 1878. Fo. A few ll. loose. Orig. cl. (SH. Apr.9; 150) *Gallery Christoph.* £240

GEORGE, Stefan
- Gesamt-Ausgabe der Werke. Endgültige Fassung. Berlin, 1927-34. 1st. Coll. Edn. Orig. linen. (H. Dec.9/10; 2076) DM 1,400

GEORGE, Waldemar
- Chirico avec des Fragments Litteraires de l'Artiste. Ill.:– Chirico. Paris, 1928. (560) numbered. Tall. 4to. Ptd. wraps., backstrip worn, tissue guard. (PNY. Mar.4; 125) $120

GEORGI, Johann Gottlieb
- Beschreibung aller Nationen des Russischen Reichs ... St. Petersb., 1776-80. 1st. Edn. 4 pts. in 2 vols. 4to. 94 (of 95) hand-cold. plts., pt. 3 lacks title, lacks third of one text lf., worn, foxed. Qtr. leath., needs rebdg. (SG. Oct.9; 216) $650
- – Anr. Edn. [1776-80]. 4to. Titles in Russian, German & Fr., lacks title. Vell. As a collection of prints, w.a.f. (BS. Jun.11; 341) £190
[–] Description de toutes les Nations de l'Empire de Russie. St. Petersb., 1776-77. Vols. 1-3 only (of 4) in 2 vols. 4to. A few ll. slightly soiled. Cont. cf., rebkd., 1 cover detchd. (SH. Feb.5; 221) *Bjorck.* £540
[–] – Anr. Edn. Ill.:– C.M. Roth. St. Petersb., 1776-80. Text vols. I-III & 1 plt. Lge. 4to. Vol. 3 stained. Later hf. leath., old wraps., unc. text vols. (H. Dec.9/10; 768) DM 3,000

GEORGIA HISTORICAL QUARTERLY
Savannah, 1917-71. Vols. 1-55. Lacks vol. 25, nos. 3 & 4, vol. 27, nos. 1 & 2, vol. 28, no. 1, ex liby. Wraps. (SG. Jun.11; 161) $1,700

GEORGIAN SOCIETY
Dublin, 1911-13. Ltd. Edn. Vols. III, IV, & V. Fo. Pict. buckram. (GM. Oct.30; 65) £90

- Records. Dublin, 1909-11. (300); (400); (550). 3 vols. (?only). 4to. Some spotting. Orig. cl., soiled. (CSK. Nov.14; 225) £55
- – Anr. Edn. Dublin, 1909-1913. Ltd. Edns. 5 vols. Lge. 4to. Buckram, a few spines defect. (GM. Apr.30; 90) £270

GEORGIUS de Hungaria
- De Ritu et Moribus Turcorum. [Urach], [Conrad Fyner], [1481]. 4to. Lacks 1st. blank, some wormholes to early ll., catching some text letters, 1 sm. wormhole extending through the vol., slight marginal repairs to 3 ll. at front & to penultimate lf., fo. 49 with paper defect affecting some letters in 2 lines, sm. monastic stp. at foot of 1st. text p. Mor., covers with gt. arms of W.H. Christie-Miller, by W. Pratt. From the collection of Eric Sexton. [BMC II, 611, Goff G151, HC 15672*] (CNY. Apr.8; 180) $3,500

GERALDINUS, Antonius
- Oratio in Obsequio Nomine Ferdinandi et Elisabeth Innocentio VIII exhibito. [Rome], [Stephan Plannck], ca. 1488-91. 4to. Paper wraps., stitching loose, lr. & outer edges unc. [HC. 7613*; BMC IV p. 93; Goff G 161] (C. Apr.1; 37) *Maggs.* £80

GERARD, A.
- Account of Koonawur, in the Himalaya. 1841. Folding map slightly torn. Orig. cl., recased. (SH. Nov.7; 348) *Remington.* £115

GERARD, Jean Ignace Isidor 'Jean Jacques Grandville'
- Un Autre Monde. Paris, 1844. 1st. Edn. 4to. Some foxing. Gt.-decor. mor. (SG. Mar.19; 204) $550
- – Anr. Copy. 1st. Printing. Lge. 8vo. Washed, some ll. reprd. Cont. hf. chagrin, spine with raised bands. (HD. Jun.25; 269) Frs.2,500
- – Anr. Copy. Some pp. stained. Cont. cl., gt. decor. (SI. Dec.3; 270) Lire 900,000
- Cent Proverbes. Paris, 1845. Hf.-title. Cont. red hf. mor., partly unc., inner covers reprd. (SI. Dec.3; 271) Lire 380,000
- – Anr. Edn. Ed.:– M. Quitard. Paris, n.d. Lge. 8vo. Cont. hf. chagrin, spine decor. with raised bands. (HD. Feb.27; 142) Frs. 1,700
- Les Etoiles. Dernière Féerie. Paris, [1845?]. 2 pts. in 1 vol. Hf. vell. (CR. Jun.11; 578) Lire 500,000
- – Anr. Edn. Paris, n.d. 2 pts. in 1 vol. Some stains. Orig. gt. decor. cl., lr. cover reprd. (SI. Dec.3; 272) Lire 500,000
- Les Fleurs Animées. Paris, 1847. 1st. Edn. Vol. 1 only (of 2). Dampstained. Orig. cl., gt. (GM. Apr.30; 531) £75
- – Anr. Edn. Paris, [1847]. 1st. Edn. 2 vols. Orig. decor. cl., covers & spines elab. blocked in gt. (CNY. May 22; 119) $400
- – Anr. Edn. Paris, 1867. 3 pts. in 1 vol. 4to. 50 plts., all hand-cold., 2 plts. not cold. Cont. hf. red mor. (SI. Dec.3; 273) Lire 720,000
- – Anr. Copy. 2 vols. Hf. red mor. (CR. Mar.19; 279h) Lire 600,000
- Flowers Personnified. Trans.:– N. Cleaveland. N.Y., 1847-49. 2 vols. Fo. Discoloured. Cont. hf. mor., vol. 1 rebkd. (TA. Oct.16; 312) £75
- Les Métamorphoses du Jour. Paris, 1854. Mod. red mor. (SI. Dec.3; 274) Lire 1,100,000
- – Anr. Copy. 4to. Wide margin. Cont hf. leath., fillets. (HK. Nov.18-21; 2348) DM 950
- – Anr. Edn. 1869. Reprint of 1854 Edn. 4to. Cont. red hf.-shagreen, decor. spine, 1 cover. (HD. Feb.18; 131) Frs. 1,800
- Scènes de la Vie privée et publique des Animaux. 1842. 1st. Edn. 2 vols. Cont. hf.-chagrin decor. spines. (HD. Feb.18; 132) Frs. 1,000
- – Anr. Copy. 4to. Vol. 2 probably lacks 1 plt., slightly soiled in parts. Cont. hf. leath. gt. (HK. Nov.18-21; 2349) DM 520
- – Anr. Copy. Publisher's blind-stpd. cl., gt. leath. spines. (SG. Sep.4; 232) $275
- – Anr. Copy. Disbnd. Lge. Copy, inscr. on hf. title from Mary A. Durell, dtd. Jan.1, 1842. (SG. Mar.19; 203) $150
- – Anr. Copy. 2 vols. Hf.-title. Cont. hf. mor. (SI. Dec.3; 275) Lire 520,000
- – Anr. Edn. Ed.:– P.J. Stahl. Paris, 1842-44. 1st. Edn., 3rd. printing vol. I, 2nd. Edn. vol. II. 2 vols. 4to. Lacks hf.-title, slightly soiled in parts, title-ll. stpd. Later hf. leath., slightly worn. (H. Dec.9/10; 1513) DM 480

GERARDE, John
– **The Herball or Generall Historie of Plantes.**
1597. 1st. Edn. Fo. Title-p. torn & reprd. with
some loss, some slight spotting & soiling, a few
rust-holes. Early 20th. C. mott. cf. by Rivière, gt.
[STC 11750] (S. Jun.1; 117)   *Tomes.* £1,100
– – **Anr. Copy.** Engraved title reprd., last lf. laid
down, ball-point marks on title & last lf. Cont. cf.,
rebkd., recornered. (C. Jul.15; 180)   £750
– – **Anr. Copy.** Engraved title guarded in inner
margin, cropped & with sm. repair, title & 3 ll. of
the 'Catalogus Arborum' (1599) bnd. after main
title, some fore-edges reprd. with occasional loss of
text, piece torn from foot of 401 affecting text,
5B4 reprd., a few rust holes, tears in 3 ll., last lf.
bkd., some spotting & soiling. 18th. C. cf., reprd.
(S. Dec.3; 974)   *Freeman.* £340
– – **Anr. Edn.** Ed.:– Thomas Johnson. 1633. 2nd.
Edn. Fo. Lacks lf. before title (blank?), title
dust-soiled, final index ll. soiled & frayed. 19th. C.
hf. mor., worn. From Chetham's Liby.,
Manchester. [STC 11751] (C. Nov.26; 176)
          Traylen. £580
– – **Anr. Copy.** Engraved title, preserved & soiled,
lacks 6 ll. Later cf., worn. W.a.f. (CSK
Nov.28; 112)   £540
– – **Anr. Copy.** Engraved title slightly defect. &
mntd., woodcut text ills., 3 cut out & mntd., some
index ll. defect. & reprd. Late 18th. C. russ.,
rebkd., orig spine preserved. [STC 11751] (S.
Mar.16; 115)   *M. Brass.* £440
– – **Anr. Copy.** Some light soiling in parts, index
slightly soiled, 3 ll. torn at margin or corner, 2
with slight text loss, engraved title, dedication & 8
ll. at end facs. on old paper, lacks pp. 1255/56 &
1261/62. Vell. (R. Mar.31-Apr.4; 1366)
          DM 2,300
– – **Anr. Copy.** Fo. Engraved title defect. Old cf.,
covers detchd. W.a.f. [STC 11752] (S.
Mar.16; 24)   *Maggs.* £400
– – **Anr. Copy.** Lacks pp. 101/102, 467/472 &
1343-1449 (presumably defect. pagination as
listed). Orig. leath. with holders for metal clasps,
leath. split, lacks most of spine but orig. stitching
& raised bands still intact, Table of Vertues
disbnd. W.a.f. [BMC 724K24] (JL. Dec.15; 735)
          Aus. $280

GERARDI, Filippo
– **Intorno alla Statua di Bolivar.** Ed.:– Pietro
Cavalier Tenerani. Livorno, 1845. Fo. Hf.-title.
Cont. hf. leath. (SI. Dec.3; 253)   Lire 70,000

GERARDIN, R.L.
– **Essay on the Landscape; or, on the means of
Improving & Embellishing the Country round our
Habitations.** 1783. Cf. (PD. Oct.22; 55)   £85

GERARDUS de Zutphania
– **Tractatus de Spiritualibus Ascensionibus.**
Montserrat, Johann Luschner, 16 May, 1499.
5-line white on black woodcut initials, some spaces
for other initials with guide letters, early ink
foliation cropped, some ll. dampstained, some ink
notes. Mor. gt. by Rivière. The copy of John
Francis Neylan, lately in the collection of Eric
Sexton. [BMC X, 78, Goff G179, H 1627] (CNY.
Apr.8; 107) $6,000

GERASCH, Franz
– **Das Oesterreichische Heer von Ferdinand II . . .**
Vienna, ca. 1854. 4to. 151 (of 153) hand-cold.
lithos., some plts. reprd., ex-liby. Loose as issued
in ptd. portfo. crudely reprd. (SG. Oct.30; 171)
          $800

GERBER, Adolf
– **Niccolo Machiavelli, die Handschriften,
Ausgaben und Ubersetzungen . . .** Turin, 1962.
Facs. reprint. Fo. Mor.-bkd. bds. (C. Jul.16; 281)
          Marlborough. £65

GERBIER, Balthazar
– **The First & Second Part of Counsel & Advice
to all Builders [A Brief discourse concerning the
three chief principles of magnificent building].**
1664 [title of 1st. 'Brief Discourse' dtd. 1662]. 2
pts. in 1 vol. Engraved frontis. port. laid down.
19th. C. cf. gt. Bnd. in is sm. fo. broadside, n.d.
[Wing G554; 540; 551] (C. Feb.25; 155)
          Marlborough. £380

GERHARD, Charles
– **Beiträge zur Chymie u. Geschichte d.
Mineralreichs.** Berlin, 1773-76. 2 vols. Cont. leath.
gt. (HK. May 12-14; 328)   DM 850

– **Traité de Chimie Organique.** Paris, 1853-56. 1st.
Edn. 4 vols. Some ll. very slightly spotted. Cont.
hf. cf. (S. Oct.21; 389)   *Kurzer.* £70

GERLACH, M.
– **Blumen und Pflanzen zur Verwendung für
kunstgewerbliche Dekorationsmotive und den
Zeichenunterricht.** Vienna, ca. 1895. 2nd. Edn. Fo.
Orig. hf. linen portfo. (D. Dec.11-13; 477)
          DM 610

GERLI, Agostino
– **Opuscoli.** Parma, 1785. Fo. 19th. C. hf. cf.,
wraps. preserved. (SI. Dec.3; 254)   Lire 1,400,000

GERM (THE)
– **Thoughts towards Nature in Poetry, Literature
& Art.** Jan.-Apr. 1850. 1st. Edn. Nos. 1-4 (all
publd.) in 1 vol. Date overlaid. Orig. wraps. bnd.
in, mor. gt. by Rivière. (P. Apr.30; 19)
          Sims & Reed. £400
– – **Anr. Copy.** Nos. 1-4 (all publd.). Crushed lev.
mor., elab. gt. tooled, spine in 6 compartments, 5
raised bands, sigd. by Thomas James
Cobden-Sanderson, dtd. 1886, qtr. gt. mor. s.-c.
(CNY. May 22; 355) $12,000
– – **Anr. Edn.** L., Jan.-Apr., 1850. Nos. 1-4 (all
publd.) in 1 vol. The 4 etched plts. (1 double-p.)
bnd in. Mod. buckram, all orig. wraps. bnd. in.
(SG. Mar.19; 202) $425
– – **Anr. Edn.** Portland, Maine, Mosher Pr., 1898.
(450). Lev. mor. gt., gt.-tooled panels on covers,
spine in 6 compartments gt.-tooled & lettered, 5
bands, silk linings, partly unc., by Zaehnsdorf.
Carolyn Wells bkplt. (CNY. May 22; 366) $300

GERMANO, G.
– **Vita, Gesti, e Predittioni circa i Sommi Pontefici
Romani, del Glorioso Padre S. Malachia.** Naples,
1670. 4to. Hf. vell. (CR. Mar.19; 215)
          Lire 200,000

GERMANY
– **Souvenirs Pittoresques du Rhin.** Frankfurt, 1826.
Ob. fo. 12 mntd. lithos. on India proof Paper. Hf.
mor., worn. (SBA. Jul.23; 658)   *Schuster.* £160

GERNING, Baron Johann Isaac von
– **A Picturesque Tour Along the Rhine.** Trans.:–
John Black. 1820. 4to. Red lev. mor., gt., by
Zaehnsdorf. L.P. (C. Mar.18; 45)
          Maggs. £3,500
– – **Anr. Copy.** Plts. unnumbered. Diced cf. with
triple gt. fillet border, spine gt. in raised band
compartments, marb. end-papers. (LC. Oct.2; 178)
          £2,500
– – **Anr. Copy.** Cont. cf. gt., spine defect. (C.
Jul.15; 148)   *Maggs.* £1,400
– – **Anr. Copy.** Lge. 4to. Text lightly browned in
parts. Cont. leath. (R. Oct.14-18; 2413)
          DM 14,500
– – **Anr. Copy.** Mod. mor., sigd. by Bayntun, gt.,
gt. cover and inner dentelle. Robert Bignold &
Bourlon de Rouvre ex-lib. (D. Dec.11-13; 1303)
          DM 11,000

GERONDI, Jonah Ben Abraham
– **Sha'arei Teshuva.** Constantinople, 1511. 2nd.
Edn. Sm. 4to. 33 ll. only (of 40, lacks ll. 2, 4, 5-8
& last lf.), without title, outer & inner margins
reprd. with loss of some letters, discolouration &
staining, worming. Mod. bds. (SPB. May 11; 82)
          $1,700

GERSHWIN, George
– **Song-book.** Ill.:– Alajalov. N.Y., 1932. (350)
numbered, sigd. by author & artist. Fo. Extra
score laid into lr.-cover pocket. Mor., 1 cover
detchd. (SG. May 14; 83) $600

GERSON, Johannes
– **Collectorium super Magnificat.** [Esslingen],
[Conrad Fyner], 1473. 1st. Edn. Fo. Spaces for
initial capitals, unrubricated thro.-out, the reading
'ope' on fo. 72r (i.e. 70r), lacks a1-2 with rubrics
& register, marginal worming to 1st. & last few
ll., wormhole at upr. inner of 1st. 10 ll., partly
effaced monastic inscr. at head of 1 p. Cont.
German blind-tooled pig over wood bds., covers
divided by parallel fillets into central panel & 2
frames, panel with floral diaper with lg. rosette
tools, broad inner frame with alternating imp. of a
palmette & a 'maria' scroll, narrow outer frame
with lattice roll, spine with 2 raised bands &
repeated imp. of the palmette tool, orig. clasps &
catches, lr. cover spotted. Ink stps. of the Allan
Liby. & the London Liby. (the latter cancelled),
lately in the collection of Eric Sexton. [BMC II,

512, Goff G199, H 7717*] (CNY. Apr.8; 56)
          $5,800
– **De Modo Vivendi Omnium Fidelium; De
Remedius contra Pusillanimitatem; De
Tentationibus Diaboli.** [Antw?], [Printer of Mensa
Philosophica], ca. 1487. 4to. 30 ll., spaces for
initials, rubricated, 1st. blank lf. stained, slight
staining to upr. edge of several other ll., not
affecting text. Vell. From the Pierpont Morgan
Liby. [BMC IX, 210, C 2682, Goff G234] (CNY.
Apr.8; 7) $4,800
– **De Pollutione Nocturna cum Forma Absolutionis
Sacramentalis.** [Cologne], [Ulrich Zel], ca. 1466.
1st. Edn. 4to. Spaces for initial capitals, these &
initial strokes supplied in red. Cf.-bkd. paper bds.,
spine gt. From the collection of Eric Sexton.
[BMC I, 179, Goff G254, HC 7694*] (CNY.
Apr.8; 39) $6,000
– **Imitatio Christi.** Paris, Philippe Pigouchet, 15
July, 1492. Rubricated thro.-out, decor. initial,
title-p. mntd, most of first text line in MS. fac.
19th. C. vell., gt. fillet borders. [HC 9104] (SG.
May 14; 109) $600
– **Monotessaron, sive Concordantiae
Evangelistarum.** [Cologne], [Printer of 'Dialogus
Salomonis et Marcolfi'], ca. 1478-80. Fo. Spaces
for capitals, 1st. capital space rubricated, rest left
blank, lacks 1st. & final blanks, 1st. & last ll.
soiled, sm. marginal repairs on folios 53 & 54, not
affecting text. Mod. qtr. mor., unbleached linen
covers. The copy of William Morris & Richard
Bennett, lately in the Pierpont Morgan Liby.
[BMC I, 260, Goff G236, HC 7719] (CNY.
Apr.8; 46) $2,600
– **Opus Tripartitum de Praeceptis Decalogi de
Confessione, et de Arte Moriendi.** [Cologne],
[Ulrich Zel], ca. 1467. 4to. Spaces for initial
capitals, supplied in red & touched with silver,
paragraph marks, underlines & initial strokes in
red & yellow, lacks 1st. & final blanks, fo. 9v
unptd. with text supplied in cont. hand, 8 ll.
guarded, sm. repairs to lr. inner margins of some
10 ll., scattered foxing, light dampstaining &
soiling, inscr. at foot of 1st. p. Mott. cf. gt., spine
gt.-lettered, rebkd. From the collection of Eric
Sexton. [BMC I, 180, Goff G238, HC 7653]
(CNY. Apr.8; 43) $2,600
– – **Anr. Edn.** [Marienthal], [Fratres Vitae
Communis], ca. 1474. 4to. Spaces for initial
capitals, 4-line capital C at fo. 2r supplied in red
with penwork ornamentation in purple, other
capitals, paragraph marks, & some initial strokes
in red or blue, slight foxing, mostly marginal.
Vell., bds. slightly warped. From the collection of
Eric Sexton. [BMC II, 547, C 2673, Goff G240]
(CNY. Apr.8; 99) $4,500

GERSON, Johannes or Nider, Johannes, Attrib. to
– **Alphabetum Divini Amoris.** [Cologne], [Ulrich
Zel], ca. 1466-67. 4to. Spaces for initial capitals,
supplied in red, as are some paragraph marks &
initial strokes, paper defect at lr. corner of fo. 26,
sm. rust-hole at fore-margin of last lf., cont. ink
marginalia. 19th. C. hf. mor., gt. spine. The copy
of Ross Winans, lately in the collection of Eric
Sexton. [BMC I, 179, Goff A524, H 7631*]
(CNY. Apr.8; 40) $5,200

**GERSON, Johannes–PETRARCA, Francesco &
others**
– **De Contemptu Omnium Vanitatum Mundi.**
–**Carmen in Laudem Hieronymie . . .** Venice; Fano,
1 Dec. 1501; 15 Sep. 1504. 2 works in 1 vol. Some
slight spotting (2nd work). 18th. C. mott. cf. (S.
May 5; 13)   *Quaritch.* £160

GERSTINGER, Hans
– **Die Griechische Buchmalerei.** Vienna, 1926.
Lge. fo. Orig. hf. linen, orig bd. s.-c. (R.
Oct.14-18; 505)   DM 850

GERVAIS, M. Paul
– **Histoire Naturelle des Mammifères.** Paris,
1854-55. 2 vols. Fo. Lacks 2 plts. Cont. qtr. mor.,
gt. decor. spines. (TA. Oct.16; 311)   £65

GERVAISE de la Touche, J. Charles
– **The Life & Adventures of Silas Showevenn.** Ill.:–
after Borel. L., Priv. ptd. 1801. 2 vols. Sm. 12mo.
Cont. red mor., decor spines, gt. fillet decor. covers,
inner dentelle. (HD. Apr.10; 316)   Frs. 2,200
– **Mémoires de Saturnin.** Ill.:– Borel, engraved by
Elluin. L., [Paris], 1787. 2 vols. Some foxing.
Mor., decor. spines, 3 fillets on covers, inner
dentelle, ca. 1810. (HD. Apr.10; 335)   Frs. 4,200
– **Le Portier des Chartreux.** Brussels, 1784. New
Edn. 2 vols. Sm. 12mo. Some defects. Porphyre

GERVAISE de la Touche, J. Charles -contd.
cf., decor. spines, 3 fillets, inner dentelle. (HD. Apr.10; 334) Frs. 2,800

GESCHIEDENIS, Algemene der Nederlanden
Ed.:– Jan Romein & Others. Zeist-Utrecht, 1949-58. 12 vols. With separate index. Cl. gt. (VG. Nov.18; 728) Fls. 550
– – **Anr. Edn.** Ed.:– J.A. van Houtte, J.F. Niermeyer, J. Presser, J. Romein & others. Zeist/Utrecht, 1959-68. 12 vols.; without the separate index. Cl. gt. (VG. Dec.15; 413) Fls. 600

GESNER, Conrad 'Euonymous Philiater'
– Bibliotheca Vniversalis . . . in Tribus Linguis, Latine, Graeca, & Hebraica . . . Zürich, Sep. 1545. Fo. Cont. blind-stpd. pig-bkd. wood bds., slightly worn, 2 clasps, lacks ties. (HK. Nov.18-21; 199) DM 5,500
– – **Anr. Edn.** Ed.:– Josias Simler & Jacob Fries. Tiguri [Zurich], 1583. 3rd Edn. Fo. Cont. blind-stpd. pig. over wooden bds., roll-stps. with Biblical characters in border, rectangle with sm. corner-pieces & central lozenge of various roll-stps., double band on spine, 2 clasps. (HD. Mar.18; 73) Frs. 10,500
– Fischbuch.–Thierbuch.–Schlangenbuch.
Frankfurt; Heidelberg; Zürich, 1598; 1606; 1589. 1st. German Edn. of 3rd. work. 3 works in 1 vol., Thierbuch bnd. 1st. Fo. 1st. work lacks lf. 166, 4 ll. prelims. & content defect. with text loss, browning; 2nd. work very defect., lacks 9 (of 172) numbered ll., half of 7 ll.; 3rd. work very defect., XLVIII (of LXXII) numbered ll., soiled throughout. Cont. blind-tooled pig-bkd. wood bds., defect. (H. Dec.9/10; 274) DM 1,200
– Historiae Animalium. [Tiguri], [1558]. 1st. Edn. Fo. Lacks title-p. & pt. of the lf. containing Latin & Fr. privileges (this lf. with liby. stp.). Old. vell., brkn. (SG. Dec.11; 39) $700
– Historiae Animalium Liber III. qui este de Auium Natura. Frankfurt, 1617. Fo. Lacks 2D1, slightly torn, a few ink-marks, some waterstaining & offsetting onto text. Cont. vell., stained, bkplt. of Baron Rolle. From liby. of Dr. E. Ashworth Underwood. (S. Feb.23; 209) Nagel. £180
– Opera Botanica.–Historiae Plantarum. Ed.:– Schmidel (2nd. work). Nuremb., 1751; 1759. 2 works in 1 vol. Fo. 1st. work: 43 engraved plts., 1 hand-cold., occasional light soiling to text edges; 2nd. work: some soiling at edges. 19th. C. hf. mor., covers detchd. From Chetham's Liby., Manchester. (C. Nov.26; 177) Wagner. £150
– Schlangenbuch.–De Scorpione. Zürich, 1589. 1st. German Edn. 2 works in 1 vol. 2mo. Later hf. vell., lacks spine. (D. Dec.11-13; 291) DM 2,000
– Vogelbuch.–Thierbuch. Trans.:– R. Heusslin; C. Forer. Zürich, 1557. 1st. German Edn. 2 works in 1 vol. Fo. Stained at beginning, lf. 164 defect. with text loss, lacks 5 prelim. ll. & ll. 7, 8, 12, 14 & 179; last part stained, some ll. defect. & reprd., some with loss, lacks title & 2 prelim. ll. & ll. 117-119, 157 & 161-172. 17th. C. leath., very worn, spine brkn. (R. Oct.14-18; 2972) DM 1,400

GESSNER, Salomon
– Gedichte. Zürich, 1762. 1st. Edn. Slightly soiled & stained in parts. Cont. hf. leath. gt., spine slightly torn. (HK. May 15; 4263) DM 520
– Mort D'Abel . . . Trans.:– M. Hubert. Ill.:– After Monsiau. Paris, 1793. Lge. 4to. Occasional spotting. Cont. mott. cf., spine worn. (CSK. Oct.17; 38) £140
– – **Anr. Copy.** Lge. 4to. On vell., Ills. engraved in colour. Cont. mor., smooth decor. spine, border of 3 fillets & gt. fleurons in angles, inside dentelle. Calligraphic poem by the husband at beginning of vol., sigd. L. Rolandin & dedicated to 'Mademoiselle Rosette Cailhol'. (SM. Feb.11; 126) Frs. 7,000
– Oeuvres. Zurich, 1777. 2 vols. 4to Cont. mott. cf., spines gt. (S. Mar.17; 244) Rota. £120
– – **Anr. Edn.** Ill.:– Marillier. N.p., [1778]. 3 vols. Red mor. by Cazin. (HD. Apr.8; 250) Frs. 1,800
– – **Anr. Copy.** 18mo. (HD. Apr.8; 251) Frs. 1,600
– – **Anr. Edn.** Ill.:– Le Barbier. Paris, [1780-93]. De Luxe Edn. 3 pts. in 1 vol. 4to. Ex-lib. Cont. mor., gt. spine, inner & outer dentelle, slightly grazed & soiled. (HK. Nov.18-21; 2347) DM 2,600
– – **Anr. Edn.** Ill.:– Lebarbier. Paris, [1786-93]. L.P. 3 vols. Lge. fo. Extra ill., engraved frontis. to vol. 1, 3 engraved titles, 4 headpieces, 64 culs-de-lamps, 73 plts., each with orig. pen &

wash drawing, 9 cold., 19 plts. also in etched state before letters, pen & wash port. of artist, (lacks engraved version). Fr. red str.-grd. mor., elab. gt. borders, spines gt. in 7 compartments, watered silk end-papers by Bozerian, sigd. (C. Jul.16; 323) Franklin. £9,000
– – **Anr. Edn.** Paris, 1795. 4 vols. Minor repairs & stains, some spotting. Cf.-bkd. bds., some corners brkn., lacks front free end-paper or blank in each vol. (SPB. May 29; 175) $100
– Schriften. Zürich, 1777-78. 1st. German 4to. Edn., on vell. 4to. Sm.˙stp. on title verso. Cont. hf. leath. gt. (HK. May 15; 4261) DM 4,400

GETREUE REISS–GEFERT Durch Ober und Nieder Teutschland (Der)
Nuremb., 1686. 12mo. Mor. gt. (P. Nov.13; 11) Koch. £4,200

GETTY, Edmund
– Notices of Chinese Seals found in Ireland. Dublin, 1850. Square 4to. Gt.-pict. cl., worn, ex-liby. Inscr. (SG. Mar.26; 206) $140

GETZ, John
– Chinese Art Objects collected by Edward R. Bacon. Ill.:– Zorn. N.Y., Priv. ptd. for Virginia P. Bacon, 1919. 4to. Gift bdg. of multiple gt.-ruled maroon crushed mor., inner dentelles gt., moire silk doubls., in soft-lined cl. folding-c. Pres. Copy (no. 7), frontis. by Bacon. (PNY. Oct.1; 141) $425

GEVARTIUS, Casp.
– Pompa introitus Serenissimi Principis Fernandi Austriaci Hispianarum Infantis. Ill.:– Pierre Paul Rubens. Antw., 1642. Fo. Cont. vell., light tears. (LM. Mar.21; 117) B.Frs. 140,000

GEZELLE, Guido
– Verzen.–De Nederlandsche Boekhandel. Amst.; Antw., 1902. (100) numbered on Holland. 2 vols. 4to. Mor., smooth spine with 4 raised bands, gt., unc., decor. (LM. Nov.8; 80) B.Frs. 75,000

GHEGA, Charles de
[-] Atlas Pittoresque du Chemin de Fer du Semmering en Autriche. Vienna, 1854. Ob. 4to. Old wraps., spine split. (C. Jul.15; 86) Taylor. £350

GHERARDI, E.
– Le Théâtre Italien. Paris, 1700. 6 vols. Cont. cf. gt. (P. Mar.12; 96) Duran. £105
– – **Anr. Copy.** 52 (of 56) engraved plts., 109 pp. of engraved music only?, 1 text lf. torn, some ll. slightly browned or spotted. Slightly worn. (SBA. Jul.14; 76) Shapiro. £60

GHEYN, Jacques de
– Wapenhandelinghe van Roers Musquetten ende Spiessen, Maniement d'Armes. The Hague, 1607. 3 pts. in 1 vol. Fo. Last plt. mntd., some neatly reprd. in margins, lacks title & 8 ll. of text, 1st. few plts. slightly soiled in margins, some plts. in pt. III slightly dampstained in margins, sm. stp. in margin of some plts., bkplt. 19th. C. vell. bds. (S. Apr.7; 319) Church. £2,200

GHIKA, Tiggie
– La Soife du Jonc: Poème. Trans.:– Jacques Dupin. Ill.:– Jacques Villon. Paris, [1955]. (200) numbered on velin de Rives, sigd. by artist. Fo. Loose in ptd. wraps., unc. (SG. Oct.23; 341) $300

GHIRARDACCI
– Della Historia di Bologna. Parte Prima. Bologna, 1596. 1 vol. only (of 2). Fo. Errata-lf. defect. Cont. red mor., 2 fillets, cipher of Peiresc in centre, later arms on upr. cover, decor. spine, ex-liby. Bkplt. of Cortlandt Bishop. (HD. Mar.18; 74) Frs. 3,800

GHUS, D. & [Fleury, Claude]
– De Zeeden der Israeliten ten Voorbeelde Eener Volkmaakte Republyk Ontworpen. Amst., 1702. Vell. (S. Nov.18; 657) Valmadonna. £100

GIAFFERRI, Paul Louis de
– L'Histoire du Costume Feminin Mondial. Paris, 1926. 20 pts. in 2 vols. Fo. Orig. wraps. & portfo. in box. (SI. Dec.3; 257) Lire 280,000
– The History of French Masculine Costume. N.Y., ca. 1927. Fo. Loose in cold. pict. wraps., cl. folder with ties. (SG. Oct.30; 174) $100

GIAMBULLARI, Pier Francesco
– De'l Sito, Forma, & Misure, déllo Inférno di Dánte. Flor., 1544. 1st. Edn. Sm. puncture thro. title & some following ll., a few marginal inscrs.

on title. Mod. blind-stpd. cf. [Sabin 27265] (S. Jun.9; 30) Thomas. £110

GIARDINI, Johannes
– Promptuarium Artis Argentariae. Rome, 1750. 2nd. Edn. 2 vols. in 1. Fo. Title-p. to 1st. vol. reprd. Mott. hf. cf., chipped. (SPB. May 6; 194) $1,100

GIBB, William
– The Royal House of Stuart. Ed.:– John Skelton & W.H. St. John Hope. L., 1890. Fo. Orig. three-qtr. mor., ex-liby. (SG. Oct.30; 175) $250

GIBBINGS, Robert
– Fourteen Wood Engravings . . . Gold. Cock. Pr., 1932. Fo. Orig. wraps., unc. (SH. Feb.19; 162) Marks. £70
– A True Tale of Love in Tonga. 1935. 1st. Edn. Orig. cl.-bkd. bds., d.-w. With series of 20 proofs & 2 dupls. of the 23 wood-engrs. used to ill. the book. (SH. Mar.26; 7) Blond. £155
– The Wood Engravings of . . . L., 1959. 1st. Edn. 4to. Orig. prospectus loosely inserted. Buckram, d.-w., in orig. box. (GM. Apr.30; 460) £75

GIBBON, Edward
– The Decline & Fall of the Roman Empire. 1776-88. 1st. Edn. 6 vols. 4to. Lacks hf.-titles, slight browning. Early 19th. C. pol. cf., spines gt. Bkplt. of [Sir John Thorald], Syston Park. (S. Sep.29; 32) Davies. £340
– – **Anr. Copy.** Lacks port. & hf.-titles to vols. 1-3. Cont. cf. (SH. Jan.30; 439) Burrows. £85
– – **Anr. Edn.** Trans.:– Leclerc de Septchênes. Paris, 1777. 1st. Edn. 3 vols. Cont. mor., fillet, arms of Duchesse de Gramont, spines grotesquely decor. (HD. Mar.18; 75) Frs. 4,600
– – **Anr. Edn.** 1782-88. 6 vols. 4to. Folding map slightly torn. Cont cf. (SD. Feb.4; 53) £65
– – **Anr. Edn.** 1788-90. 12 vols. Cont. cf. (SH. Mar.5; 240) Womersley. £60
– – **Anr. Edn.** 1789-81-88. Vol. 1: New Edn; Vols. 2 & 3: 2nd. Edn.; Vols. 4-6: 1st. Edn. 6 vols. 4to. Cont. cf. (CSK. Nov.28; 189) £70
– – **Anr. Edn.** 1789-91. New Edn. 12 vols. Cont. cf., spines gt., lacks some labels. (SBA. Jul.22; 94) Frognal Bookshop. £55
– – **Anr. Edn.** 1807. New Edn. 12 vols. Hf. cf. (PG. Dec.12; 17) £60
– – **Anr. Edn.** 1820. 12 vols. Some ll. slightly soiled. Cont. cf. (SD. Feb.4; 42) £65
– – **Anr. Edn.** L., 1828. 8 vols. Browning, tears. Cf., rebkd. (SPB. May 29; 176) $150
– – **Anr. Edn.** L., 1840. 4to. Cf., gt. decor. on upr. cover & spine, raised bands, marb. end-papers. (JL. Jul.20; 549) Aus. $100
– – **Anr. Edn.** L., 1854. 8 vols. Tissue cut away from port., spotted. Hf. mor. gt. (SPB. May 29; 177) $150
– – **Anr. Edn.** Ed.:– William Smith. L., 1862. 8 vols. Pol. cf. gt., slightly worn. (SG. Dec.18; 204) $160
– – **Anr. Edn.** Ed.:– J.B. Bury. L., 1896-1900. 7 vols. Orig. linen. (R. Mar.31-Apr.4; 102) DM 420
– – **Anr. Edn.** Ill.:– after G.B. Piranesi. Ltd. Edns. Cl., 1946. (1500) numbered. 7 vols. 4to. Leath-bkd. marb. bds., 5 spines eroded, boxed. (SG. Jan.15; 190) $110
– An Essay on the Study of Literature. L., 1764. 1st. Edn. in Engl. Publisher's advts., minor defects. Tree cf., worn. (SPB. Jul.28; 157) $150
– Miscellaneous Works. 1796-1815. 1st. Edn. 3 vols. 4to. Some ll. slightly spotted. Cont. spr. cf., worn. (SBA. May 27; 50) Museum Bookshop. £65
– – **Anr. Copy.** Mod. cf., spines gt. (SG. Dec.18; 220) $110
– A Vindication of some Passages in the Fifteenth & Sixteenth Chapters of the . . . Decline & Fall . . . L., 1779. 1st. Edn. Slight foxing at beginning & end. Cf.-bkd. marb. bds., worn. (SPB. Jul.28; 158) $150

GIBBS, James
– Bibliotheca Radcliviana. 1747. Fo. Cont. mott. cf. Bkplt. of Lord Polwarth, lately in the collection of Eric Sexton. (C. Apr.15; 67) Weinreb. £250
– – **Anr. Copy.** Some very minor defects. Orig. wraps., worn. (SBA. May 27; 51) Marlborough Rare Books. £180
– A Book of Architecture containing Designs of Buildings & Ornaments. L., 1728. Fo. 149 (of 150) plts., 2 folding plts. cropped to frame lines all round, 1 other cropped to 1 margin, some marginal dampstains on a few plts., dedication lf. with piece

torn away with loss of a few words. Cont. qtr. cf. & bds. (CB. May 27; 108) Can. $1,300
- **Rules for Drawing the Several Parts of Architecture.** 1732. Fo. Spr. cf. gt. by Sangorski & Sutcliffe. From the collection of Eric Sexton. (C. Apr.15; 68) *Weinreb.* £80
- – **Anr. Edn.** Priv. ptd. 1736. 2nd. Edn. Fo. Cont. mott. cf., gt. (C. Feb.25; 182) *Weinreb.* £180
- – **Anr. Edn.** 1753. 3rd. Edn. Fo. Bds., defect. (GM. Apr.30; 555) £65

GIBBS, James–MORRIS, Corbyn
- **Bibliotheca Radcliviana.–Observations on the Past Growth & Present State of the City of London.** 1747; 1751. 2 works in 1 vol. Fo. Bnd. in reverse order. Cont. cf. (S. Nov.25; 475) *Weinreb.* £220

GIBBS, Philip
- **An Historical Account of Compendious & Swift Writing.–An Essay towards a further Improvement of Short-Hand.** 1736. 2 pts. in 1 vol. Cont. cf., rebkd. From the collection of Eric Sexton. (C. Apr.15; 101) *Thorp.* £50

GIBSON, Charles Dana
- **London.–Sketches & Cartoons.–The Education of Mr. Pipp.–Pictures of People.–Americans.–A Widow & her Friends.–The Social Ladder.–Eighty Drawings.–Everyday People.–Our Neighbours.** N.Y. & L., 1898-1905. The 1st. 10 series in 2 vols. Ob. fo. Hf. mor., leath. lettering-pieces on covers. (SG. Nov.20; 337) $160
- **Works.** 1897-1905. 11 vols. Ob. fo. All orig. pict. bds. with linen backstrip, 5 vols. contained in orig. brkn. boxes, some slightly soiled. (TA. Nov.20; 311) £95

GIBSON, Frank
- **Charles Conder, his Life & Work.** 1914. 4to. Orig. cl. gt. (SH. Mar.26; 139) *Barkes.* £150
- – **Anr. Copy.** (P. Mar.12; 10) *Arnold.* £120

GIBSON, John, R. A.
- **Imitations of Drawings.** Ill.:– G. Wenzel & L. Prosseda. Rome, 1851-52. Ob. fo. Plt. on india paper, some spotting of prelims. Orig. cl. gt., crudely rebkd., some wear. (TA. Oct.16; 158) £60
- – **Anr. Copy.** (TA. Sep.18; 133) £55

GIBSON, R.W.
- **Francis Bacon: A Bibliography.** Oxford, 1950. 4to. Orig. buckram-bkd. bds. (LC. Feb.12; 83) £50
- – **Anr. Copy.** Hf. cl. (SG. Jan.22; 45) £140

GIBSON, Strickland
- **Early Oxford Bindings.** 1903. Bibliographical Society No. 10. 4to. Pict. cl.-bkd. bds. (P. Jan.22; 315) *Maggs.* £55

GIBSON, Thomas
- **The Anatomy of Human Bodies Epitomiz'd.** L., 1688. 3rd. Edn. Mod. buckram. (SG. Sep.18; 158) $160

GIBSON, William
- **A New Treatise on the Diseases of Horses.** L., 1751. 1st. Edn. 4to. 1 index lf. misbnd. Old cf., worn. (SG. Dec.11; 323) $110

GIBSON, William Sidney
- **The History of the Monastery Founded at Tynemouth, in the Diocese of Durham.** 1846-47. 2 vols. 4to. Ex-liby. stp. to front end-paper & hf.-title only, mainly unopened. Cont. qtr. mor., some wear. (TA. Jan.22; 399) £90
- – **Anr. Copy.** Mod. hf. mor. (SH. Nov.6; 101) *Crowe.* £65

GIDE, André
- **Les Caves du Vatican.** 1914. (559) on Paper à Chandelle d'Arches. 2 vols. (HD. Oct.10; 69) Frs. 1,400
- – **Anr. Edn.** Ill.:– J.E. Laboureur. Paris, priv. ptd., 1929-30. 1st. Ill. Edn., (377); on Jap. (vol. V on Holland). 5 vols. Sewed, wraps., s.-c. (HD. Dec.5; 93) Frs. 1,500
- **L'Immoraliste.** 1902. (300) on vergé d'Arches. Mor., doubl., wrap., by Marius Michel. (HD. Oct.10; 65) Frs. 3,300
- **Les Nourritures Terrestres.** 1917. (300) on Rives. Mor., fillet on spine, wrap. (HD. Oct.10; 70) Frs. 1,300
- – **Anr. Edn.** Ill.:– Galanio. Paris, 1930. (260) on vergé crème de Hollande. 4to. Mor. by Creuzevault, orig. wraps. (SM. Oct.8; 2339) Frs. 1,400

- **Paludes.** 1895. (388) on Old Hollande. Sewed. Double Letter. (HD. Oct.10; 61) Frs. 4,600
- **La Porte étroite.** 1909. (300) on vergé d'Arches Mor. doubl., wrap., by Marius Michel. Note. (HD. Oct.10; 67) Frs. 3,400
- **Le Prométhée mal Enchainé.** 1809. Sewed. Note. (HD. Oct.10; 64) Frs. 1,300
- **Thesées.** Trans.:– John Russell. Ill.:– Massimo Campigli. Bod. Pr., [1949]. (190) numbered on Pescia H.M.P. Fo. Plt. 3 bnd. in at page 33, plt. 4 bnd. in at page 25. Patterned bds., linen spine. (SG. Sep.4; 369) $425
- **Le Voyage d'Urien.** Paris, 1893. 1st. Edn. 4to. Later mor. gt., orig. wraps. bnd. in. (SM. Oct.8; 2255) Frs. 7,500
- – **Anr. Copy.** Cont. limp marb. cf., wrap. (HD. Oct.10; 62) Frs. 7,200

GIFFARD, William
- **Cases in Midwifery.** Ed.:– Edward Hody. 1734. 1st. (& only) Edn. Hf. cf. (S. Jun.16; 335) *Korn.* £85

GIFFORD, Lord Robert
[–] **Attorney-General's Charges against the Late Queen.** Ill.:– George & Robert Cruikshank & Theodore Lane. Ca. 1824. Fo. Lacks few interll. Cont. hf. mor., rebkd. (SH. Apr.9; 6) *Reid.* £570

GIGAULT, Louis, Comte de La Bedollière
- **Le Monde et seo Travers.** 1839. 2 vols. Cf., rococo tools, arms. A.L.s. dtd. 7 apr. 1840, 3pp. 8vo. to Duc de Chambord, from his liby., Maggs ticket. (HD. Oct.10; 243) Frs. 1,000

GIGNOUX, Antoin Christoph & Frey, Johann Michael
- **Voyage Pittoresque sur le Danube depuis Augsbourg jusqu'à Vienne.** Vienna, ca. 1782. Ob. fo. Tree cf. with gt. fillet. (LC. Oct.2; 179) £950

GIKATILA, Joseph Ibn
- **Sha'arei Orah.** Rive Di Trento, 1561. 2nd. Edn. Sm. 4to. Title reprd. with loss of 2 words, inner margins of 2 ll. reprd. without text loss, cropped, some staining. Mod. vell., in case. (SPB. May 11; 112) $600

GIL BLAS: Illustre Hebdomadaire
Ill.:– Forain, Van Dongen, & others. Paris, 2 Jan.-21 Aug. 1903. Vol. 12, nos. 1-34. Fo. With contributions of Prevost, Maupassant, Anatole France, Bernard, & others, some dampstains. Hf. mor. (SG. Nov.20; 339) $110

GILBERT, Charles Sandoe
- **An Historical Survey of the County of Cornwall, to which is added a complete Heraldry of the same.** Plymouth-Dock, 1817-20. 3 vols. 4to. Cont. cf., lacks pt. of spine to vol. III. (C. Feb.25; 32) *Pillar.* £260
- – **Anr. Copy.** 2 vols. Some ll. loose. Cont. hf. cf., worn. (SD. Feb.4; 214) £90

GILBERT, John T. & Lady Gilbert
- **Calendar of Ancient Records of Dublin.** Dublin, 1889-1944. Vols. 1-19. Hf. mor. Councillor Joseph Clarke's Copy. (GM. Oct.30; 302) £180

GILBERT, Louis
- **Collection de Differentes Pièces d'Ecriture . . .** Paris, ca. 1760. Fo. Mod. bds. (SG. Oct.9; 107) $475

GILBERT, Samuel
- **The Florists Vade-Mecum (The Gardeners Almanack for Five Years).** 1682. 1st. Edn. 2 pts. iss. as 1. 12mo. Title & a few other ll. a little stained. 19th. C. hf. cf., spine gt. [Wing G712 & G717] (C. Apr.1; 212) *Quaritch.* £200

GILBERT, William
- **De Magnete.** L., 1600. 1st. Edn. Fo. Tear affecting ptd. area of folding woodcut diagram, 2 sm. wormholes in lr. margin thro-out, sm. holes in *5 & C6 affecting some letters of text, some margins stained. Cont. limp vell., later end-papers. Bkplt. of Sylvanus P. Thompson. [STC 11883] (C. Nov.20; 248) *Thomas.* £2,500
- – **Anr. Copy.** Lacks folding diagram, sm. blank portion excised from title, some staining in margins. 19th. C. paper bds. (C. Nov.20; 249) *Thomas.* £400
- **De Mundo Sublunari Philosophia Nove.** Amst., 1651. 1st. Edn. 4to. Old owner's inscr. 'Ex Bibliotheca PP. Carmelitarum Cabilonensiu[m]' on title, bkplts. Cont. vell. bds. (S. Oct.21; 390) *Barrington.* £600

- **On the Magnet, Magnetick Bodies also, & on the Great Magnet the Earth.** Chis. Pr., 1900. Orig. limp vell., soiled. (CSK. Oct.31; 150) £50
- **On the Magnet, Magnetick Bodies also, & on the Great Magnet the Earth, a New Physiology.** –**Notes on De Magnete.** Trans.:– Silvanus P. Thompson & others (2nd. work). 1900-01. 2nd. work (250). 2 vols. in 1. Fo. Limp vell., unc. (S. Jun.16; 337) *Westwood.* £55

GILBERT de VOISINS, Auguste, comte
- **Le Bar de la Fourche.** 1928. (115) on Arches. Mor., gt. & blind decor., by Cretté. With orig. aqua. & suite & Note. (HD. Oct.10; 190) Frs. 4,200

GILBERTUS–Gallensis, Johannis
- **Sermonum Super Cantica Canticorum.–Summa Collantionum.** N.p.; Strassburg, [N. Laurentius] (1st. work), 1485; 1489. 2 works in 1 vol. 4to. Old limp vell., (loose in bdg.). (BS. Sep.17; 51) £500

GILCHRIST, Alexander
- **Life of William Blake.** 1863. 1st. Edn. 2 vols. Very slightly spotted. Orig. cl. gt., unc. (SBA. Oct.21; 211) *Koike.* £70
- – **Anr. Copy.** Orig. pict. cl. gt., 2nd. vol. rebkd. preserving spine, unc. (SH. Mar.26; 88) *Ayres.* £50
- – **Anr. Edn.** 1880. 2nd. Edn. 2 vols. Orig. cl. gt., unc. (SH. Mar. 26; 90) *Marsden.* £95

GILDON, C.
See–LANGBAINE, Gerard, the Younger & Gildon, C.

GILDON, Charles
[–] **The Post-Man Robb'd of his Mail.** 1719. 1st. Edn. 12mo. Some slight browning, lacks advt. lf. at beginning. Mod. mott. cf., spine gt. (S. Feb.9; 169) *Quaritch.* £110

GILES, Ernest
- **Geographic Travels in Central Australia, from 1872-74.** Melbourne, 1875. 1st. Edn. Orig. cl. (KH. Nov.18; 278) Aus. $720

GILES, Herbert A.
- **Chinese Biographical Dictionary.** L. & Shanghai, 1898. 1st. Edn. Three-qtr. mor., gt. panel. spine. (SG. Dec.18; 84) $110

GILFILLAN, George
- **The Gilfillan Poets.** L., 1853-60. 31 vols. Extra-ill. with ports. Cf. gt., inlays. (SPB. May 6; 310) $1,800

GILL, Eric
- **Art & Love.** Gold. Cock. Pr., 1927. (260). Orig. buckram, unc. (SH. Feb.19; 150a) *Appleton.* £130
- **Art & Prudence.** Gold. Cock. Pr., 1928. (500) Orig. buckram, unc., unopened, d.-w. (SH. Feb.19; 154) *Old Hall.* £80
- – **Anr. Copy.** Pres. Copy to Elizabeth Angela Gill. (SH. Feb.19; 98) *Ayres.* £60
- **Christianity & Art.** Ill.:– David Jones. Shakes. Hd. Pr., 1927. (200) numbered, sigd. by author & artist. Orig. buckram, unc. (SH. Mar.26; 243) *Marks.* £115
- **Engravings.** Hague & Gill Pr., 1934. [1st Edn.?]. 4to. Orig. buckram, unc., d.-w., s.-c. (SH. Mar.26; 11) *Tate Gallery.* £380
- – **Anr. Copy.** Fo. Foxed. Orig. cl., unc., unopened. (CNY. May 22; 313) $280
- **Engravings: a Selection of Engravings on Wood & Metal.** Bristol, Fanfare Pr., 1929. (400) numbered, on specially made paper. Fo. Gt.-decor. cl. (SG. Oct.23; 140) $325
- **An Essay on Typography.** Hague & Gill Pr., 1931. (500) sigd. by author & Rene Hague. Orig. cl., d.-w., linen cover. Pres. Copy, prospectus loosely inserted. (SH. Feb.19; 99) *Dawson.* £110
- – **Anr. Copy.** (CSK. Jun.12; 48) £85
- – **Anr. Copy.** (SH. Mar.26; 9) *Forster.* £75
- **Id Quod Visum Placet.** Gold. Cock. Pr., 1928. (150) sigd. Orig. linen-bkd. bds., unc. (SH. Feb.19; 148) *White.* £115
- **Sculpture.** St. Dominic's Pr., 1918. Orig. wraps., unc., unopened. (S. Jul.31; 69) *Sawyer.* £50
- **Twenty-Five Nudes.–Letters.** Ed.:– 2nd work: Walter Shewing. L., [1938; 1947]. Cl., d.-w.'s. (SG. Oct.23; 141) $170

GILL, Eric (Ed.)
See–BEEDHAM, R. John

GILL, Eric (Ill.)
See–CALENDARS
See–CHAUCER, Geoffrey
See–COMMON CAROL BOOK (The)
See–CORNFORD, Frances
See–DONNE, John
See–GAME, The . . .
See–GREEN, A. Romney
See–HORAE B.V.M.
See–HUXLEY, Aldous
See–JOHN OF THE CROSS, Saint
See–LECTIONES ad Matutinum Officii
Defunctorum . . .
See–MATHERS, Edward Powys
See–MORE, Sir Thomas
See–NEW TESTAMENTIANA [English]
See–PASSIO Domini Nostri Jesu Christi
See–PEPLER, Hilary Douglas Clerk
See–RILKE, Rainer Maria
See–SHAKESPEARE, William
See–SONG of Songs
See–VALERY, Paul
See–WOODCUT, The

GILL, Samuel Thomas
[–] [Sketches of the Victoria Gold Diggings &
Diggers, as they are]. L., [1853]. Pt. 1. 4to. 24
tinted litho. plts. only. Orig. wraps., slightly soiled,
backstrip torn. W.a.f. (CSK. May 22; 64)   £350
[–] Victoria Illustrated. 1857. Ob. 4to. Orig. cl. gt.
(P. Jul.30; 118)   Crowe. £520
– – Anr. Edn. 1862. Ob. 4to. Text & plts. loose.
Orig. cl. (P. Mar.12; 243)   Arnold. £350

GILLE, Fils, Printer
– Epreuves des Vignettes et Fleurons Gravée sur
Bois et Polytypes des Fondière et Imprimerie de
Gille. Paris, 1808. Fo. Paper over bds., worn. (LC.
Oct.2; 31)   £70

GILLE, Paris
– Corona Gratulatoria . . . Salzburg, 1681. 5 (of 6)
pts. in 1 vol. Fo. Title & a few ll. slightly spotted
or soiled. Old bds. (S. May 5; 66)   Hyde. £85

GILLELAND, J.C.
– The Ohio & Mississippi Pilot . . . Pittsb., 1820.
1st. Edn. Foxed. Old sheep, upr. cover detchd.
From liby. of William E. Wilson. (SPB.
Apr.29; 115) $425

GILLEN, F.J.
See–SPENCER, Sir Baldwin & Gillen, F.J.

GILLES, Nicolas
– Les Très Elégantes, très Veridiques et Copieuses
Annalles des très preux . . . moderateurs des
belliqueses Gaules. Paris, 1525. 2 vols. in 1. Fo. 3
woodcut ills., 1 full-p. woodcut & 6 ptd.
genealogical tables crudely cold. in a cont. hand,
paper fault in 1 lf. affecting text, lacks sm. portion
in last lf., affecting foliation only. 16th. C. mott. cf.
(C. Feb.25; 12)   Cucci. £140

GILLESPIE, Major Alexander
– Gleanings & Remarks collected during many
Months of Residence at Buenos Ayres. Leeds, 1818.
Slightly spotted. Cont. hf. cf. (SBA. Oct. 22; 600)
                                          Coffin. £50

GILLETT, Charles R.
– Catalogue of the McAlpine Collection of British
History & Theology. N.Y., 1927-30. 5 vols.
Buckram. (SG. Mar.26; 208) $110

GILLIES, John
– Memoires of the Life of the Reverend George
Whitefield, M.A. Late Chaplain to the Right
Honourable The Countess of Huntington. Ill.:–
Elisha Gallaudet [engraved port.]. 1774. 1st.
Amer. Edn. 12mo. Cont. cf., worn. (SG.
Jan.8; 174) $140

GILLINGWATER, Edmund
– An Historical Account of the Ancient Town of
Lowestoft. [1790]. 4to. Cont. hf. cf. (SH.
Nov.6; 50)   Ferrow. £85

GILLISS, James Melville
– The U.S. Naval Astronomical Expedition to the
Southern Hemisphere . . . Wash., 1855. Vol. II
only. 4to. Bird plts. clean, but others stained,
foxing at beginning & end. Hf. leath. Inscr. by
Capt. N. Darling. (CB. Sep.24; 54)   Can. $120

GILLRAY, James
– The Genuine Works. 1830. 2 vols. plts., 2 vols.
text., together 4 vols. Lge. fo. & 8vo. Plts.
hand-cold. & dtd. 1779-1810. Cont. hf. mor. gt.
As a collection of plts., w.a.f. (C. Nov.20; 250)
                                          Bell. £2,200

– – Anr. Copy. 1 vol. in 2. Lge. 4to. & fo. Cont.
red hf. mor. (S. Nov.24; 134)   Traylen. £1,600
[–] [Suppressed Plates]. [1779-1805]. Lge. fo. 45
numbered engravings on 23 plts. Cont. hf. mor.,
spine gt. (S. May 5; 200)   Schuster. £110
– Works. L., ca. 1849. 2 vols. Fo. 584 plts. & 45
suppressed plts., lacks plts. 33-35 & 238. Hf. leath.
(SG. May 14; 84) $700
– – Anr. Edn. Ca. 1850; n.d. Plt. vol. only. Fo.
With the 45 engraved suppressed ills. on 23 sheets,
slight soiling, marginal tear in 1 sheet. Cont.
hf. mor., gt. (S. Dec.9; 495)   Traylen. £300
– – Anr. Edn. N.d. 2 vols. Fo. Including the 'Suppressed Plates', 1 lf. cleanly torn & reprd. along
verso. Cont. hf. mor., spines gt. (CSK. Sep.26; 40)
                                              £480
– – Anr. Copy. 2 vols. Foxed. Cont. red hf. mor.,
corners, spines decor. with raised bands. (HD.
Jun.25; 255)   Frs. 2,000

GILLRAY, James (Ill.)
See–WRIGHT, Thomas

GILPIN, Rev. William
– The Last Work Representing the Effect of a
Morning, a Noon Tide, & an Evening Sun. 1810.
4to. Cont. hf. cf. (SH. Jun.25; 169)   Elliott. £95
– Observations relative chiefly to Picturesque
Beauty . . . Mountains & Lakes of Cumberland &
Westmorland. 1788. 2nd. Edn. 2 vols. Occasional
spotting. Cont. hf. cf. (CSK. Jun.26; 15)   £55
– – Anr. Edn. 1792. 3rd. Edn. 2 vols. Slight
offsetting. Cont. hf. russ. (SBA. Oct.22; 322)
                                        Marshall. £50
– Observations on the River Wye . . . & South
Wales.–An Essay on Prints.–Two Essays. 1789;
1802; 1804. 1st. vol. 2nd. Edn. 3 vols. in 1. Cf. (P.
Jul.30; 205)   Bickersteth. £80

GILPIN, William & Alken, Samuel
See–HEARNE,   Samuel–POUNCY,   B.T.
–BYRNE, Letitia–GILPIN, William & Alken,
Samuel

GILPIN, William Sawrey
– Practical Hints upon Landscape Gardening. 1835.
Cl., worn. (P. Oct.2; 305)   Marlborough. £65

GILRAY, James
– Works. L., n.d. Fo. Hf. maroon mor. As a
collection of plts., w.a.f. (SPB. Nov.25; 123a)
                                              $400

GIMBERNAT, Antonio de
– Nuevo Metodo de Operar en la Hernia Crural.
Madrid, 1793. 4to. Licence lf. misbnd. at end.
New cl., unc. (S. Dec.2; 495)   Rota. £210

GIMMA, Giacinto
– Della Storia Naturale delle Gemme, delle Pietre,
a di tutti Minerali, ovvero della Fisica Soterranea.
Ill.:– Ant. Baldi (frontis.). Naples, 1730. 2 vols.
4to. New qtr. cf. (S. Dec.1; 180)   Maggs. £85

GIMSON, Ernest
– His Life & Work. Ill.:– F.L. Griggs. Shakes.
Hd. Pr., 1924. (500). 4to. Orig. linen-bkd. bds.,
unc. (SH. Feb.19; 54)   Henderson. £210

GINANNI, Giuseppe
– Della Uova e Dei Nidi degle Uccelli. Venice,
1737. 1st. Edn. Book 1 (all publd.). 4to. Cont. vell.
bds., slightly worn & soiled. From the collection of
John A. Saks. (C. Jun.10; 93)   Burgess. £170
– Opere Postume. Ill.:– Giorgio Fossati? Venice,
1755 & 1757. L.P. 2 vols. Lge. 4to. Some sm.
wormholes to inner margins of last ll. in vol. 2.
Orig. paper bds., unc. From the collection of John
A. Saks. (C. Jun.10; 94)   Pompelmo. £140

GINANNI, Marc Antonio
– L'Arte del Blasone. Ill.:– Pietro Monaco after
Andrea Barbiani (frontis.). Venice, 1756. 4to.
Cont. vell., corners scuffed. From the collection of
John A. Saks. (C. Jun.10; 95)   Burgess. £140

GINGUENE, P.L.
See–FAUCHET, C., Chamfort, S.R.N., Ginguene,
P.L. & Pagés, F.X.

GINSBERG, Allen
– The Moments Return. San Franc., 1970. (200).
Ob. 4to. Cl.-bkd. bds., cl. s.-c. Inscr. to Paul Getty
Jr., sigd., with drawings in ink, by the author. (C.
Jul.22; 73)   Monk Bretton. £50

GIORNALE DE LETTERATI d'Italia
Venice, 1710-27-6. 41 vols. (?only), including 3
Supp. vols. 12mo. Cont. mott. cf., 2 vols. rebkd.,
lacks 2 labels. W.a.f. (CSK. Apr.24; 69)   £100

GIOVANNI della Croce, San
– Opere . . . di Alcuni Trattati Inediti Accrescuite.
Ill.:– F. Zucchi. Venice, 1748. 2 vols. Fo. Some
offsetting onto 2 frontis., liby. stp. on titles. Cont.
hf. cf., rebkd. From the collection of John A. Saks.
(C. Jun.10; 96)   Somers. £90

GIOVIO, Paolo
– Dialogo dell'Imprese Militari et Amorose. Lyon,
1559. 1st. Ill. Edn. 4to. Title reprd., 1 device with
a few ink stains, occasional browning & spotting.
Old limp vell. bds., sm. repairs, soiled. (S. May
5; 36)   Hyde. £160

GIOVIO, Paolo–CAMPO, Antonio
– Le Vite de i Dodeci Visconti che signoreggiarono
Milano.–Cremona   Fedelissima   Citta   et
Nobilissima Colonia de Romani. Milan, 1645;
1645, 1642. 2 works in 1 vol. 4to. 19th. C. hf. cf.
(SI. Dec.3; 259)   Lire 850,000

GIRALDUS, Cambrensis
– The Itinerary of Archbishop Baldwin through
Wales. Ed.:– Sir R.C. Hoare. 1806. 2 vols. 4to.
Some very minor defects. Cont. russ. gt. (SBA.
May 27; 52)   Hoare. £160
– – Anr. Copy. A few minor defects. Cont. russ.
gt., rebkd., slightly worn. (SBA. Jul.14; 324)
                                        Vitkovitch. £60

GIRARD, Guillaume
– Histoire de la Vie du Duc d'Epernon. Ill.:–
Scottin. Paris, 1730. 4to. Cont. red mor., fillet,
spine decor. with grenades. (HD. Mar.18; 76)
                                         Frs. 1,600

GIRARD, Le Sr. Pierre Jacques François
– Nouveau Traité de la Perfection sur le Fait des
Armes. Paris, 1736. Ob. 4to. Old cf., 5 decor. spine
raised bands. (LM. Jun.13; 19)   B.Frs. 33,000
– Traités des Armes. The Hague, 1740. Ob. 4to.
Later red mor. by Bedford, gt. borders, spine &
dentelles. (SG. Oct.9; 108) $1,000

GIRARDON, Francois
– Vue de Plusiers Morceaux des Ouvrages faites
par le Sr. Girardon plazez dans le milieu de sa
Gallerie aus quels il a fait adjouter les
Architectures dessinées par le Sr. Oppenort.–Suite
du Cabinet de Sr. Girardon. Ill.:– 1st. work: N.
Chevallier & R. Charpentier, 2nd. work: F.
Ertinger & N. Chevallier. Paris, ca. 1720. Fo.
2nd. work ptd. on 1 side of the paper only. Cont.
cf.-bkd. bds. (C. Feb.25; 183)   Weinreb. £320

GIRAUD, Jane Elizabeth
– The Flowers of Milton. Faversham, 1846. 4to.
Cont. hf. mor., worn. (SH. Mar.26; 255)
                                        Henderson. £55
– The Flowers of Shakespeare. [1845]. 4to. Some
spotting. Orig. cl., worn. (S. Jun.1; 121)
                                          Marks. £55
[–] – Anr. Edn. 1846. 4to. Cont. red mor. gt.,
slightly worn. (SBA. Dec.16; 139)   Marryat. £100
[–] – Anr. Edn. [1846]. Slight foxing. Mor. gt. (P.
Apr.9; 109)   Trevers. £85
[–] – Anr. Edn. N.d. 4to. Slight spotting &
marginal soiling. Orig. cl., worn & disbnd. (CSK.
Sep.5; 249)   £55

GIRAUD, Jane Elizabeth–THOMPSON, Robert
– The Flowers of Milton.–The Gardener's
Assistant. Ill.:– Day & Haghe after Girauld; after
Mrs. Withers. Faversham; n.p., 1846; 1859. 2
works in 2 vols. 4to.; 8vo. Orig. embossed cl., gt.,
slightly stained; pol. hf. cf. (C. Nov.5; 59)
                                        Fairburn. £130

GIRAUDOUX, Jean
– Hélène et Touglas . . . Ill.:– Laboureur. 1925.
(50) on imperial Japon. Square 8vo. Double ser of
engrs. Sewed, s.-c. (HD. Jun.25; 256)   Frs. 1,550
– Judith. Ill.:– M. Ernst & D. Tanning.
[Stuttgart], 1972. (500). Fo. Orig. hf. linen & s.-c.
Printer's mark sigd. by both artists. (H.
Dec.9/10; 2056)   DM 800

GIRTANNER, Chr.
– Historischer Nachrichten und Politischer
Betrachtungen über die Französische Revolution.
Berlin, 1792-95. 1 plt. loose. Cont. bds. (D.
Dec.11-13; 2657)   DM 440

GIRTIN, Thomas
See–TURNER, Joseph Mallord William & Girtin,
Thomas

GISBORNE, Thomas
– Inquiry into the Duties of Men. 1794. 4to. Cf. gt.
(P. Dec.11; 323)   Traylen. £50

GISSING, George
- Born in Exile. 1892. 1st. Edn. 3 vols. Orig. cl. (SH. May 28; 129) *Jarndyce.* £50

GITZ-JOHANSEN
See–SALOMANSEN & Gitz-Johansen

GIULINI, Giorgio
- Memorie spettanti alla Storia, al Governo, ed Alla Descrizione della Citta, e della Campagna Di Milano ne'Secoli Bassi. Milan, 1760. 9 vols. in ll. 4to. Hf.-title. Cont. hf. cf., unc. (SI. Dec.3; 260) Lire 1,800,000
- - Anr. Edn. Milan, 1854-57. 7 vols. Orig. ptd. bds., rebkd. with cf., unc. (SI. Dec.3; 261) Lire 550,000

GIUSTIANI, Vincenzo
- Galleria . . . Rome, [1631]. 2 vols. 4to. Plts. 133, 135, 153 & 161 in vol. 2 shaved affecting engraved surface, some others cut to plt.-mark, hole in plt. 22 of vol. 1, 2 or 3 marginal tears reprd. Red mor., with panels of orig. 17th. C. bdg. (bearing gt. arms of Louis XIV in centre & crowned intertwined 'L' at corners) remntd. on covers. From Chetham's Liby., Manchester. (C. Nov.26; 178) *Weinreb.* £380

GIUSTINIANO, Pompeo
- Delle Guerre di Fiandria Libri VI. Antw., 1609. 1st. Edn. 4to. Lacks pp. 233/4 (Gg 1), 1 tear reprd., old owner's entry on title. Cont. overlapping vell. (VG. Oct.13; 66) Fls. 2,800
- - Anr. Copy. Slightly browned in parts, 9 plts. with mostly sm. tears in margins. Cont. leath. gt., spine slightly defect. (R. Mar.31-Apr.4; 2169) DM 2,500

GIUSTINIANUS, Abbé Bernadus, Bonannus, Philippus & others.
- Histoire des Ordres Militaires ou des Chevaliers . . . Et un Traité Historique de Mr. Basnage sur les Duels. Amst., 1721. 4 vols. Possibly lacks plt. (slight offset on fo. B8 in vol. I). Cont. cf.,some jnts. brkn. (S. May 5; 73) *Fachinetti.* £130

GLAISHER, James & others
- Voyages Aériens. Paris, 1870 1st. Edn. 4to. Title stpd. Mod. hf. leath. (R. Mar.31-Apr.4; 1268) DM 480

GLAMORGAN
- Cartae et Alia Munimenta quae ad Dominium de Glamorgan pertinent. Ed.:– Geo. T. Clark. Dowlais & Cardiff, 1885-93. 4 vols. 4to. Orig. cl., unc. Pres. Copy., A.L.s. from Ed. preserved in vol. 1. (SBA. Jul.23; 320) *Chesters.* £55

GLANVILL, Joseph
- Saducismus Triumphatus. [L.], 1682-81. 2nd. Edn.; 1st. Edn? 2 pts. in 1 vol. Title-p. loose, occasional marginal worming. Cont. cf., worn, upr. cover detchd. [STC G823] (CB. Nov.12; 184) Can. $240
- - Anr. Edn. L., 1689. 3rd. Edn. Extra engraved title mntd., some foxing. 19th. C. hf. cf., ex-liby. (SG. Feb.5; 150) $120
- Scepsis Scientifica: or Confest Ignorance . . . –Scirei tuum nihil est, or the author's defence against the Vanity of Dogmatizing. 1665. 2 pts. in 1 vol. 4to. Pt. 2 bnd. before pt. 1, d1-2 (imprimatur & errata) misbnd. between N1 & 2, tear in H1 with no loss. Cont. cf., spine gt., unpressed copy. [Wing G827-828] (S. Jun.16; 338) *Lawson.* £120

GLANVILLA, Ranulphus de
- Tractatus de Legibus et Consuetidinibus Regni Anglie. [1555]. 1st. Edn. Corner torn from C1, tear in C2, sm. wormhole, not affecting text. Cont. cf., rather worn. [STC 11905] (S. Apr.7; 371) *Thorp.* £500

GLANVILLE, Barth. de
- [-] Propriétaire des Choses tresutile et prouffitable aux Corps humains . . . Paris, 20 May 1525. Fo. Lacks title, 1st. & last ll. reprd., some staining. Cont. wood bds. recovered in crimson silk velvet, crimson silk doubls. & guards, by Philippe Le Noir, reprd. (HD. Feb.18; 22) Frs. 1,600

GLANVILLE, T.B.
- Guide to South Africa, or the Cape Colony . . . L., 1878. 5th. Edn. Orig. bdg. (VA. Oct.31; 405) R. 280

GLAPTHORNE, Henry
- The Ladies Priviledge. 1640. 1st. Edn. 4to. Title slightly soiled. 19th. C. mor.-bkd. bds. [STC 11910] (C. Nov.19; 98) *Courtland.* £130

GLAREANUS, Henricus
See–EUCLID–GLAREANUS, Henricus

GLASCOCK, Capt. William Nugent
- [-] Naval Sketch-Book. 1831. 2 vols. Cont. hf. cf. (SH. Oct.10; 376) *Drury.* £50

GLASER, Christopher
- Chimischer Wegweiser. Jena, 1684. 2nd. German Edn. Frontis. & title loose, title torn. Cont. cf., spine defect. (H. Dec.9/10; 329) DM 480
- Traité de la Chymie. Paris, 1663. 1st. Edn. Engraved title slightly defect. dampstained at beginning, slightly soiled in places. Cont. limp vell., slightly worn. (S. Oct.21; 391) *Barnett.* £110
- - Anr. Edn. Lyon, 1676. New Edn. 12mo. Tear in outer blank margin C5. Cont. cf. (S. Dec.1; 182) *Rota.* £160
- - Anr. Copy. Title-p. scribbled on. (S. Dec.1; 181) *Walford.* £60

GLASER, Curt
- Edvard Munch. Ill.:– Munch. Berlin, 1918. Orig. hf. linen (HK. May 12-14; 1996) DM 420

GLASSE, Hannah
- [-] The Art of Cookery Made Plain & Easy . . . 1747. 1st. Edn. Fo. A few very minor stains at beginning, natural paper fault in 1 lf. touching 1 letter. Cont. spr. cf., rebkd. (C. Apr.1; 213) *Lyon.* £1,100
- [-] - Anr. Edn. 1751. 4th. Edn. Orig. bds. Sigd. (S. Mar.16; 180) *Bale.* £50
- [-] - Anr. Edn. 1767. New Edn. Slightly soiled. Cont. cf. (TA. Mar.19; 658) £50
- [-] - Anr. Edn. L., 1778. Mott. cf. gt., by Morrell. (SG. Dec.18; 123) $140
- - Anr. Edn. 1788. Folding list torn. Cont. cf. (SKC. Feb.26; 1725) £55
- - Anr. Copy. Last 3 ll. of index with sm. reprd. wormholes. Recased. (TA. Sep.18; 70) £50
- - Anr. Edn. L., 1796. New Edn. Old cf., rehinged. (SG. Sep.4; 124) $100
- The Compleat Confectioner. L., ca. 1770. [1st. Edn.] Some ll. dampstained, title reprd. Mod. hf. cf. (SG. Sep.4; 123) $160

GLAUBER, Johann Rudolph
- De Auri Tinctura sive Auri Potabili.–Consolatio Navigantium, in qua docetur . . . quomodo per Maria Peregrinantes a fame a ac siti etiam Morbis . . . suppetiare liceat.–Miraculum Mundi oder aussfuhrliche Beschreibung der Wunderbaren Natur . . . von den Alten Menstruum Universale oder Mercurius Philosophorum Genant.–Explicatio Tractatuli, qui Miraculum Mundi Inscribitur. Amst., 1651; 1657; n.d.; 1656. 2nd. work 1st. Edn. 3rd. work 2 pts. in 1 vol., together 4 vols. 3rd. work with insignificant worming in some inner upr. margins in pt. I. New leath., unc.; vell.; vell.; mor. (S. Dec.1; 183) *Rota.* £160
- A Description of New Philosophical Furnaces . . . Trans.:– J. F[rench]. 1651-52. 1st. Edn. in Engl. 7 pts. in 1 vol. 4to. Errata/advt. lf. at end, browned, considerable worming, affecting text. Mod. mor. [Wing G846]. (S. Sep.29; 93) *Van Haverberger.* £100
- Furni novi Philosophici, sive Descriptio Artis Destillatoriae novae.–Pharmacopoea Spagyricae.–Operis Mineralis. Amst., 1651; 1654-57; 1657-52. 3 works in 1 vol.; 1st. work 6 pts.; 2nd. work 3 pts.; 3rd. work 3 pts. Browned thro.-out, 1st. work with 1 folding plt. torn, 3rd. work with short tear in A2 & a few ll. slightly wormed affecting text in pt. 1, underscoring in pen in pt. 3. Cont. vell., soiled. red hf. mor. case. From Honeyman Collection. (S. May 20; 3246) *Rota.* £170
- Prosperitatis Germaniae pars prime . . . de Vini, Frumenti, & ligni Concentratione . . . [pars quarta]. –Consolatio Navigantium.–Tractatus de Natura Salium. Amst., 1656; 1659; 1659. 3 works in 1 vol., 1st. work 4 pts, 3rd. work 2 pts. Slight browning, title of 1st. work inscr. 'Bibliotheca Slacoveriensis Scholarum Piarum'. Early 18th. C. mott. cf. From liby. of André L. Simon. (S. May 18; 107) *Rota.* £110
- The Works . . . Trans.:– Christopher Packe. Priv. ptd., 1689. 1st. Coll. Edn. in Engl. 3 pts. in 1 vol. Fo. 10 plts. only (of 11), title & a few other ll. soiled, rusthole in 5l2 pt. 1, paper flaw in Y1 pt. 2 affecting text. 19th. C. hf. cf., by Lubbock of Newcastle, with his ticket, spine reprd., worn, hf. mor. case. From Honeyman Collection. [Wing G845] (S. May 20; 3247) *Quaritch.* £260

- - Anr. Copy. Some dampstaining. Cont. spr. cf., rebkd. (CSK. May 1; 155) £220

GLEADALL, Eliza Eve
- The Beauties of Flora. 1834. Vol. 1 only (of 2). 4to. Title loose, occasional light foxing (mostly textual). Orig. cl., gt., stitching brkn., spine worn. (C. Nov.5; 60) *Quaritch.* £360

GLEASON, E.P., & Co.
- Catalogue of Glassware . . . N.Y., 1892. Fo. Orig. cl. (SG. Dec.4; 160) $150

GLEICHEN, Wilhelm Friedrich, Baron von
- Decouvertes les plus Nouvelles dans le Regne Vetegal. Trans.:– J.F. Isenflamm. Ill.:– after J.C. Keller. [Nuremb. & Paris], 1770. 2 pts. in 1 vol., including supp. Fo. Plts. hand-cold. 19th. C. hf. mor.,covers detchd. From Chetham's Liby., Manchester. (C. Nov.26; 179) *Israel.* £480

GLEIG, George R.
- [-] A Narrative of the Campaign of the British Army at Washington & New Orleans . . . in the Years 1814 & 1815. L., 1826. 2nd. Edn. Crushed three-qtr. lev., spine gt. (SG. Jan.8; 175) $110

GLEIZES, Albert
- Kubismus. Bauhausbücher Bd. XIII. Munich, [1928]. 1st. Edn. Orig. linen. (H. Dec.9/10; 1952) DM 800

GLEIZES, Albert & Metzinger, Jean
- Du Cubisme. Ill.:– Duchamp, Laurencin, Picabia, Picasso, & Villon. Paris, 1947. (400) numbered on Lana wove paper. 4to. Loose as iss. in ptd. wraps., bd. folder, & s.-c. (SG. Apr.2; 124) $1,300

GLEN, Jan
See–TAYLOR, Alister & Glen, Jan

GLENDINING & CO.
- Priced Auction Catalogues. 1950-72. 9 vols. 4to. Mod. cl. (SH. Mar.6; 356) *Seaby.* £90

GLENNIE, I.D.
- Views on the Continent. L., 1849. Lge. fo. Slightly soiled, lacks plt. 10. Loose in orig. hf leath. (R. Mar.31-Apr.4; 2170) DM 5,600

GLOBUS, Septimus (Pseud.)
See–APEL, Johann August

GLOCERUS, G.
See–NEANDER, M.–BUSSIUS, I.–GLOCERUS, G.

GLUCK, Christoph Willibald
- Alceste. Vienna, 1769. 1st. Edn. Fo. Mostly slightly soiled, pagination incorrect in parts. Newer vell. (H. Dec.9/10; 1126) DM 4,600

GLUCK, Johann Christoph von
- [-] Orphée et Euridice.–Iphigenie en Aulide. Trans.:– [Moline] (1st. work). Paris, 1774; 1774. 1st. Edns. 2 works in 2 vols. 4to. Cl.-bkd. bds., old marb. wraps. bnd. in. (C. Oct.22; 261) *MacNutt.* £170

GLUECKEL von Hameln
- Memoiren. Ed.:– Bertha Pappenheim. Vienna, 1910. 4to. Vell., slightly soiled. (SPB. May 11; 113) $150

GMELIN, Johann Friedrich
- Göttingisches Journal der Naturwissenschaften. Göttingen, 1797-98. Vol. 1 in 4 pts., all publd. Orig. wraps., unc. (R. Mar.31-Apr.4; 1105) DM 500

GMELIN, Johann Georg
- Flora Sibirica. St. Petersb., 1747-69. 4 vols. 4to. 286 engraved folding plts. (correct, with some nos. omitted & others added), title spotted. 19th. C. mor.-bkd. bds. From Chetham's Liby., Manchester. (C. Nov.26; 180) *Baskett & Day.* £500
- - Anr. Copy. Cont. cf. rebkd. & restored. From collection of Massachusetts Horticultural Society, stps. on plts. (SPB. Oct.1; 121) $2,100
- Historia Fucorum. St. Petersb., 1768. 4to. Plts. numbered 1-33, & with 2 additional plts., some margins spotted. 19th. C. cl. From Chetham's Liby., Manchester. (C. Nov.26; 181) *Wheldon & Wesley.* £130

GNEDOV, Vasilisk
- Smert'iskusstvu [Death to Art]. St. Petersb., 1913. Sm. tears at top. Orig. upr. wrap., slightly torn. lr. lacking. (SH. Feb.6; 432) *Quaritch.* £340

GNEISENAU, August Nietthard, Count von
- The Life & Campaigns of Field-Marshal Prince Bluecher, of Wahlstatt. Trans.:– J.E. Marston. L., 1815. Cont. bds., unc., worn. (SG. Oct.30; 176) $160

GNOLI, U.
- Pittori e Miniatori nell'Umbria. Spoleto, 1923. (1000) numbered. 4to. Publisher's cl. (CR. Mar.19; 82) Lire 220,000

GOBET, N.
See–PICHON, T.J. & Gobet, N.

GOBINEAU, Comte Joseph Arthur
- La Chronique Rimée de Jean Chouan et de ses Compagnons.–Les Pleiades. Paris & Leipzig (1st. work), 1846; 1874. 1st. Edns. 2 works in 2 vols. 12mo. 1st. work: slightly later hf. chagrin, corners, spine with raised bands, wrap.; 2nd work: sewed, wrap. (HD. Jun.25; 258) Frs. 1,000
- Histoires des Perses. Paris, 1869. 2 vols. Cont. mor.-bkd. bds., vol. 1 upr. hinges brkn. (SH. Nov.7; 411) Diba. £50
- Savonarole. Ill.:– Frank Sepp. Munich, 1920. (250) numbered, & sigd. by artist. 4to. Vell. over wood bds. (SG. Apr.2; 115) $130

GOBLER, J.
See–LAETUS, Pomponius & Marlianus, Bartholomaeus–LESCUT, Nicolaus de –LERNSNER, J.–GOBLER, J.

GODARD d'Aucourt, Claude
- Contes. Ill.:– Jollain (figures); de las Rios (port.). Paris, 1883. Ltd. Edn. Figures in 2 states. Mor. by Pagnan, decor. spine, inside dentelle. Bkplt. of Francis Kettaneh. (SM. Feb.11; 160) Frs. 2,500

GODBY, J.
- Italian Scenery, representing the Manners, Customs & Amusements. 1806. 4to. Offsetting of plts. on text, foxing thro.-out. Cf., brkn. (BS. Jun.11; 158) £160

GODDARD, Robert H.
- Liquid-Propellant Rocket Development (Smithsonian Miscellaneous Collections, vol. 95, no. 3). Wash., D.C., 1936. 1st. Edn. Orig. ptd. wraps. From Honeyman Collection. (S. May 20; 3248) Norman. £800
- – Anr. Copy. Upr. cover stpd. 'The Royal Canadian Institute Mar. 27 1936'. From Honeyman Collection. (S. May 20; 3249) Zeitlin & Verbrugge. £350

GODDEN, G.M.
See–FIELDING, Henry–GODDEN, G.M.

GODDET, Maurice & Jacques
- Les Joies du Sport. Ed.:– Jules Rimet. Ill.:– Uzelac. Paris, [1932]. (115) numbered, on papier Madagascar. Fo. Loose as iss. in wraps. & linen folding case. (SG. Oct.9; 110) $350

GODEAU, Antoine
- Eloges des Evesques ... Paris, 1665. 1st. Edn. 4to. Lacks frontis. Cont. red mor., fleur-de-lys in corners, arms of Marseilles, decor. spine. (HD. Mar.18; 77) Frs. 1,850
- Histoire de l'Eglise. 1680. 6 vols. Cont. vell., dentelle. (HD. Jun.30; 25) DM 1,000

GODEFROY, Louis
- Jean-Emile Laboureur. Paris, 1929. (40) on Imperial Japan, with etching in 2 states. 4to. Cl.-bkd. bds., orig. wraps. bnd. in, bkplt. (SG. Apr.2; 169) $650
- L'Oeuvre Gravé de Adrian van Ostade. Paris, 1930. 4to. Orig. wraps. (H. Dec.9/10; 225) DM 520

GODELMANN, Johann Georg
- Tractatus de Magis, Veneficis et Lamiis. Frankfurt, 1591. 1st. Edn. 3 pts. in 1 vol. Sm. 4to. Several ll. at beginning & end slightly wormed, affecting some letters, pieces cut from lr. corners of title & K2 in pt. II, occasional spotting. Cont. limp vell. bds., lacks ties. Bkplt. of W.B.H.A. Heskes. (S. Jun.29; 343) Rhys-Jones. £65

GODELMANN, Johann Georg–SALCANTENTIUS, H.B.
- De Magis, Veneficis et Lamiis, recte Cognoscendis et Puniendis, libri III.–De Jure Pugnae, hoc est, Belli et Duelli, Tractatus Methodicus, (etc). Frankfurt; Tübingen, 1591; 1591. 1st. work 1st. Edn. 1st. work 3 pts. in 1 vol. 4to. Stp. on title, some underlinings. Cont. vell. (VG. Dec.17; 1335). Fls. 475

GODEY'S Lady's Book
Phila., 1854-62. 9 vols. Some browning. Hf. mor. gt. (SPB. May 29; 178) $200

GODFREY, Ambrose
- An Account of the New Method of Extinguishing Fires by Explosion & Suffocation. 1724. Mod. mor.-bkd. cl. (SH. Oct.10; 296) Fairburn. £65

GODFREY, Col. M.J.
- Monograph & Iconograph of Native British Orchidoceae. Ill.:– H.M. Godfery. Camb., 1933. 4to. Cl., d.-w. (P. Apr.9; 104) Park. £130
- – Anr. Copy. Orig. cl., d.-w. (SH. Oct.9; 221) Verdcourt. £105

GODLONTON, Robert
- Case of the Colonists of the Eastern Frontier of the Cape of Good Hope. Grahamstown, 1879. Orig. cl., new leath. spine, recased. Inscr. (VA. Oct.31; 411) R. 310

GODLONTON, Robert & Irving, E.
- A Narrative of the Kaffir War of 1850-51. L., 1851. All plts. mntd. on mod. wove paper, lacks table of Reciprocal Distances, 2 plts. & some ll. stained, plts. foxed, some browning. Mod. cf. (VA. Oct.31; 413) R. 170

GODMAN, Eva M.
See–ARCHER, Sir Geoffrey & Godman, Eva M.

GODMAN, Frederick du Cane
- A Monograph of the Petrels. Ill.:– J.G. Keulemans. 1907-10. (225) numbered. 4to. Mor., gt. inner dentelles, orig. wraps bnd. in at end. (C. Nov.5; 61) Ludgrove. £1,200
- – Anr. Copy. 4to. Emblematically gt. (R. Jun.1; 123) Milner. £1,100
See–SALVIN, Osbert & Godman, Frederick Ducane

GODONNESCHE, [Nicolaus]
- Medailles du Regne de Louis XV. Ill.:– Cars after le Moine (engraved frontis.). [Paris], ca. 1736. Sm. fo. Frontis. slightly browned, some inner & outer margins dampstained, stp. of Louis lier, duc d'Orleans on frontis., title & verso of last plt., bkplt. of William Wrixon Leycester. Cont. vell., gt. panel. with lge. fleur de lis at corners, triple gt. fillet, flat spine gt. with fleur-de-lis in compartments. (S. Apr.7; 350) Veulemans. £160
[-] Anr. Copy. Cont. mott. cf., gt. borders on covers with fleur-de-lys & fleur-de-lys cornerpieces, spine unif. gt., corners & spine slightly worn. (S. Feb.10; 328) Seaby. £80
- – Anr. Copy. Fo. Some margins dampstained, stp. of Louis lier, Duc d'Orléans, on frontis., title & verso of last plt. Cont. vell., gt. panel with lge. fleur de lis at corners, triple gt. fillet, flat spine gt. with fleur de lis in compartments, bkplt. of William Wrixon Leycester. (SM. Oct.7; 1734) Frs. 1,600

GODWIN, Bp. Francis
[-] The Man in the Moone. 1638. 1st. Edn. Lacks frontis., portions of title & A3-4 torn away, affecting text, rust-hole in B2 affecting 3 words, some staining, especially at beginning. Mod. cf. From the collection of Eric Sexton. [STC 11943] (C. Apr.15; 103) Burgess. £480

GODWIN, George & Britton, John
- The Churches of London: a History & Description of the Ecclesiastical Edifices of the Metropolis. L., 1839. 2nd. Edn. 2 vols. in 1. Extra-ill. with 4 18th. C. engrs. of churches, a few plts. towards end stained in margin. Cont. hf. leath. (CB. May 27; 110) Can. $160
- – Anr. Copy. Some pp. with clippings mtd. at blank portion, others mntd. & bnd. in. Mod. hf. cf. & marb. bds., unc. A.L.s. from Godwin to Herns & A.N.s from Godwin mntd. in text, sig. of Herns at title. (PNY. Oct.1; 145) $200

GODWIN, William
- Enquiry concerning political Justice & its influence on General Virtue & Happiness. Dublin, 1793. 1st. Dublin Edn. 2 vols. Specially bnd. Mod. mor.-bkd. bds. (S. Oct.21; 432) Quaritch. £260
- – Anr. Copy. Later hf. linen, ex-libry. (SG. Feb.5; 151) $150
- Fleetwood or the New Man of Feeling. 1805. 1st. Edn. 3 vols. Cf. gt. (P. Dec.11; 326) Murray-Hill. £200
- Manderville. Edinb., 1817. 1st. Edn. 3 vols. Pts. of text slightly browned. Cont. hf. roan. (TA. Dec.18; 15) £140
- Recherches sur la Population, et sur la Faculté d'accroissement de l'espèce Humaine ... Trans.:–

F.S. Constancio. Paris, 1821. 1st. Edn. in Fr. 2 vols. Staining to last ll. vol. I & pp. 17-40 vol. II. Orig. wraps., unc. & unopened, spines worn. (S. Oct.21; 431) Thomas. £60
- Thoughts on Man. 1831. 1st. Edn. Slight spotting. Mod. cf., spine gt. (S. Feb.9; 177) Subunso. £100

GOEBEL, Heinrich
- Wandteppiche.–1. Teil die Niederlande. Leipzig, 1923. 2 vols. 4to. Cl., worn. (P. Oct.23; 205) Ars Artis. £55

GOEDAERT, Joannes
- Metamorphosis et Historia Naturalis Insectorum. Middleburg, [1662-67-68]. 3 vols. 3 engraved titles, port. & 124 (of 125) hand-cold. plts., lacks plt. 26 in vol. 2. Vell., Rev. Sir John Cullum's bkplt. (P. Apr.30; 209) Quaritch. £300

GOEREE, Wilhelm
- Mosaize Historie der Hebreeuwse Kerke. Ill.:– Luyken. Amst., 1700. 4 vols. Sm. fo. 1 plt. torn. Cont. blind-stpd. vell., defect. in pts. & clumsily reprd. (VG. Nov.18; 1176) Fls. 750

GOESIUS, Wilelmi
- Rei Agrariae Auctores Legesque Variae. Amst. 1674. Sm. 4to. Some dampstaining. Cont. cf., rebkd. (TA. Jun.18; 21) £70

GOETHALS, Felix-Victor
- Archéologie des Familles Belges. Brussels, 1851-87. (95). 4to. Mod. bdg. (LM. Nov.8; 254) B.Frs. 8,000
- Dictionnaire Généalogique et Héraldique des Familles Nobles du Royaume de Belgique. Brussels, 1849. 4 vols. Lge. 4to. Hf. chagrin. (LM. Nov.8; 200) B.Frs. 17,000

GOETHE, Johann Wolfgang von
- Auserlesene Lieder, Gedichte und Balladen. Hammersmith, Doves Pr., 1916. (10) on vell. Sm. 4to. Gt.-decor. lev. mor., spine in 6 compartments, 5 raised bands, gt.-ruled panels, sigd. by Doves Bindery, 1918, qtr.mor. s.-c. (CNY. May 22; 407) $6,000
- – Anr. Edn. Hammersmith, Doves Pr., 1916. (185). 4to. Mor. gt. by the Doves bindery after a design by Cobden-Sanderson. (C. Jul.22; 58) Monk Bretton. £260
- – Anr. Copy. (185) Limp vell., unc. (C. Jul.22; 59) Maggs. £240
- – Anr. Copy. (175). Lev., 24 discs studded on each cover, suede end-papers, by René Kieffer, s.-c. (SG. May 14; 64) $800
- Balladen. [Darmstadt], [1924]. (500). Orig. bds. (MK. Nov.18-21; 2540) DM 720
- Erklärung der zu Goethes Farbenlehre Gehörigen Tafeln. [Tübingen], [1810]. 1st. Edn. Atlas vol. only; lacks 2 text vols. 4to. 15 engraved plts., a number cold. (of 17, lacks plts. 11 & 16). Cont. hf. cf., some wear. (S. Jun.9; 60) Barker. £75
- – Anr. Copy. I vol. MS. corrections on copperplts. XIV & XV, text slightly soiled, slightly browned in parts. Cont. cf., worn. (H. Dec.9/10; 1500) DM 2,200
- Faust. Hammersmith, Doves Pr., 1906; 1910. (25) & (22) on vell. 2 vols. 4to. Vol. 1 orig. vell., unc., vol. 2 lev. mor., covers gt.-ruled, spine in 6 compartments, 5 raised bands, gt. panel., sigd. 'Doves Bindery C-S 1917', qtr. mor. s.-c.'s. (CNY. May 22; 380) $2,000
- – Anr. Copy. 2 vols., separately Issued, (300). (250). Vell., cover of vol. 2 slightly warped. (PNY. Dec.3; 120) $400
- – Anr. Edn. Trans.:– Abraham Hayward. Ill.:– Willy Pogany. Boston, ca. 1910. (500) numbered, sigd. by publishers. 4to. Lev., multiple gt. fillet borders, with floral corner-pieces including rose inlays, spine unif. gt. (faded), wide floral gt. dentelles, lev. doubls., satin end-ll., bkplt. (SG. Apr.2; 243) $170
- – Anr. Edn. Ed.:– Max von Boehn. Berlin, 1924. (1000) numbered. 4to. Specially bnd. in vell., pict. stpd. in medieval style. (SG. Jan.15; 37) $100
- – Anr. Edn. Trans.:– John Anster. Ill.:– Harry Clarke. L., [1925]. (1,000) numbered, for England, sigd. by artist. 4to. Orig. hf. vell. partly unc. (SG. Oct.23; 65) $200
- – Anr. Edn. Trans.:– John Anster. Ill.:– Harry Clarke. N.Y., [1928]. (1000) numbered for the U.S., & sigd. by artist. 4to. Hf. vell., wrinkled, pict. end-papers, partly untrimmed. (SG. Apr.2; 72) $180
- Faust. Eine Tragödie. (Erster Teil). Tübingen, 1808. 1st. individual Edn. Lightly soiled, lacks

blank lf. Cont. hf. leath. gt. (R. Mar.31-Apr.4; 455) DM 1,050
- **Faust. Eine Tragödie,2. Teil.** Ill.:– Bruno Goldschmitt. Munich, 1923. (20), on Bütten. Lge. fo. Some browning. Hand-bnd. orig. vell. Etchings monogrammed, printer's mark sigd. by artist. (H. May 21/22; 1720) DM 480
– – **Anr. Edn.** Ill.:– O. Graf. Zürich & Leipzig, 1923. (150) C Edn. on Bütten. Fo. Hand-bnd. orig. hf. vell. 30 full-p. etchings sigd. by artist. (H. May 21/22; 1415) DM 520
– – **Anr. Edn.** Ill.:– Max Slevogt. Berlin, 1927. (250). Fo. Orig. vell. (H. Dec.9/10; 2350) DM 4,000
- **Gedichte.** Ill.:– H. Meid. Berlin, Hand-ptd., 1925. (100), on Zandersbütten. Fo. Orig. hf. vell. portfo. 2nd. series of 23 sigd. lithos. on thin Jap. (HK. May 12-14; 1982) DM 2,800
– – **Anr. Copy.** Red mor., gt. decor., spine gt., gold inner dentelle fillets (Holzhey & Sohn). (H. Dec.9/10; 1862) DM 2,200
- **Geschichte Gottfriedens von Berlichingen mit der Eisernen Hand.** Ill.:– L. Corinth. Berlin, 1921-22. (51) on Zanders-Velin, Lge. 4to. Red mor., gt., cover, spine, inner & outer dentelle, by B. Scheer, Berlin, bd. s.-c., ex-liby. Printer's mark sigd. by artist. (HK. May 12-14; 1811) DM 4,200
- **Goethes Lieder.** [Darmstadt], [1920]. (350). Orig. leath. (HK. May 12-14; 1835) DM 550
- **Hermann und Dorothea.** Ill.:– Chodowiecki [title]. Berlin, [1797]. 1st. Edn. 1st. ll. & copper engrs. loose & heavily soiled. Orig. red mor., worn, wormed. (H. Dec.9/10; 1503) DM 720
– – **Anr. Edn.** Ill.:– Esslinger after Kolb. Braunschweig, 1822. New Edn., 1st. Edn. ill. Esslinger, privilege Edn. on vell. Slightly soiled. Cont. red mor., gt. spine, covers, inner & outer dentelles. (H. May 21/22; 1093) DM 2,600
– – **Anr. Edn.** Braunschweig, 1822. New De Luxe Edn. Soiled, light staining. Cont. red mor., gt. spine, cover & outer dentelle, by J.J. Selencka, slightly loose. (HK. May 15; 4306) DM 550
- **Iphigenie Auf Tauris, ein Schauspiel.** Ill.:– Graily Hewitt (initials). Doves Pr., 1912. (12) on vell. with initials in gold. 4to. Mor., gt.-panel. sides, spine gt. in compartments, by the Doves bindery after a design by Cobden-Sanderson. (C. Jul.22; 60) *Scharcz.* £650
– – **Anr. Edn.** Ill.:– Graily Hewitt (initials). Hammersmith, Doves Pr., 1912. (20) on vell. Crushed lev., multiple gt. fillet borders, gt. dentelles, by Doves Bindery, sigd. C-S, 1921. Inscr. by T.J. Cobden-Sanderson. (SG. May 14; 65) $2,200
– – **Anr. Edn.** Ill.:– Graily Hewitt (initials). Hammersmith, Doves Pr. 1912. (32) on vell. Sm. 4to. Crushed lev. mor., gt.-ruled borders, spine in 6 compartments, 5 raised bands, gt.-panel., sigd. by Doves Bindery, 1912, qtr. mor. s.-c. Cortlandt Field Bishop bkplt. (CNY. May 22; 396) $1,500
– – **Anr. Edn.** Ill.:– Graily Hewitt (initials). Doves Pr., 1912. (200). Mor. gt., by the Doves bindery after a design by Cobden-Sanderson, head of spine worn. (C. Jul.22; 61) *Taylor.* £240
- **Die Leiden des Jungen Werther.** Hammersmith, Doves Pr. 1911. (20) on vell. Sm. 4to. Lev. mor., gt. borders & ornaments, spine in 6 compartments, 5 raised bands, gt.-tooled & panel., sigd. by Doves Bindery, 1912, qtr. mor. s.-c. (CNY. May 22; 393) $3,800
– – **Anr. Edn.** [Hammersmith], [Doves Pr.]. [1911]. (200). 4to. Vell., upr. cover slightly warped. (PNY. Dec.3; 121) $300
- **Der Mann v. fünfzig Jahren.** Ill.:– after Liebermann. Berlin, 1922. (600) numbered. Fo. 1 blank lf. with MS. entry. Orig. pict. vell. Printer's mark sigd. by artist, with 1 sigd. pen ill., torn without loss. (HK. Nov.18-21; 2773) DM 1,400
- **Marienbader Elegie.** Montagnola, Munich, Bod. Pr. 1923. (155). Lge. 4to. Orig. bds., spine defect. (HK. Nov.18-21; 2834) DM 1,800
– – **Anr. Copy.** (HK. May 12-14; 2002) DM 1,600
- **Die Natur. Ein Hymnus.** [Leipzig]. [1910]. (120). Orig. wraps. (HK. Nov.18-21; 2542) DM 460
- **Neue Schriften.** Berlin, 1792-1800. 1st. Edn. 7 vols. Lacks mus. supp. as usual in vol. VI, lightly soiled & browned in parts, vol. II on better paper. Cont. hf. leath., gt. spine, worn. (H. Dec.9/10; 1497) DM 1,400
– – **Anr. Edn.** Berlin, 1794-1800. 7 vols. 8 folding

mus. supps. Cont. hf. leath. gt., gold-stpd. decor., floral decor., slightly worn & soiled. (HK. May 4274) DM 3,400
– – **Anr. Copy.** Lacks mus. supps. in vol. VI & Vol. III, lightly soiled thro.-out & browned in parts. Cont. hf. leath. (H. Dec.9/10; 1498) DM 900
- **Reineke Fuchs.** Munich, 1846. 1st. Ill. Edn. Fo. Slightly soiled. Orig. leath., gt. cover, spine & outer dentelle, soiled. (HK. May 15; 4313) DM 470
– – **Anr. Edn.** 1846. Lge. 4to. Orig. cf., gt.-stpd., slightly affected by damp, boxed. (CSK. Jan.23; 36) £90
– – **Anr. Copy.** 1st. Iss. 4to. With plt. at page 43, 'Register der Stahlstiche' showing each plt. in miniature. Mor., gt. fillet borders, spine gt. in 6 compartments, rehinged, some foxing. (SG. Sep.4; 292) $300
– – **Anr. Edn.** Ill.:– Wilhelm von Kaulbach & others. Muenchen, 1846. Fo. Red three-qtr. mor., foxed. (SG. Aug.21; 214) $190
– – **Anr. Edn.** Ill:– Wilhelm von Kaulbach. Stuttgart, 1867. Fo. Extra-engraved title. Gt.-ornamental mor. (PNY. Oct.1; 240) $100
- **Sämtliche Werke.** Stuttgart, 1857-58. Compl. Edn. 30 pts. in 18 vols. Cont. hf. leath., gt. (D. Dec.11-13; 777) DM 500
– – **Anr. Edn.** Munich, 1909-13. (250) numbered on Bütten paper. Vols. 1-20 only. Orig. mor., s.-c.'s. (SH. Jan.30; 342) *Schwing.* £90
- **Schrifften der Goethe-Gesellschaft.** Weimar, 1885-1958. 44 vols., vols. 1-22, 25, 35 II, 37-45, 48, 49, 51, 53-55 & 57. 8vo., 4to. & fo. Orig. linen portfolios, bds. & orig. linen. (H. May 21/22; 1430) DM 500
- **Torquato Tasso.** [Leipzig], [1910]. (5) Privilege Edn. on vell. 4to. Lightly cockled. Hand-bnd. mor. écrasé, gt. bord. & corner fleurons, gt. spine & gold fillets on inner dentelles, by C. Sonntag jun. (H. May 21/22; 1398) DM 3,200
– – **Anr. Edn.** Hammersmith, Doves Pr., 1913. (27) on vell. Sm. 4to. Lev. mor., covers with gt.-ruled border & panel, spine in 6 compartments, 5 raised bands, gt.-panel., sigd. by Doves Bindery, 1913, qtr. mor. s.-c. (CNY. May 22; 399) $2,500
- **Versuch die Metamorphose der Pflanzen zu erklären.** Gotha, 1790. 1st. Edn., wide margin. Lightly soiled in parts. Hf. vell. (HK. May 15; 4323) DM 1,600
- **Die Wahlverwandtschaften.** Tübingen, 1809. [1st. Edn.?]. 2 pts. in 1 vol. Slightly soiled, some ll. more heavily, mostly in margins. Cont. hf. leath. gt. (HK. May 15; 4325) DM 2,400
– – **Anr. Copy.** 2 pts. 1st. title & 1 lf. with sm. hole, 3 ll. loose, 2nd. title with old owner's mark, slightly browned. Later hf. leath. (H. May 21/22; 1103) DM 2,000
- **Werke.** Tübingen, 1806-08. Vols. 1-12 (of 13) in 8 vols. Cont. hf. leath., gt. spines, 2 defect. (R. Oct.14-18; 986) DM 460
– – **Anr. Edn.** Stuttgart & Tübingen, 1827-30. Vollständige Ausgabe Letzter Hand. Vols. 1-40 (of 60) in 35 vols. Slightly soiled. Cont. hf. leath., gt. spine, 2 spines slightly defect. (H. Dec.9/10; 1499) DM 1,400
– – **Anr. Edn.** Stuttgart & Tübingen, 1827-33. Compl. Edn. Vols. 1-55 & index vol. Cont. hf. leath. (D. Dec.11-13; 775) DM 2,000
– – **Anr. Copy.** Vols. 1-55 & supp. Leben by H. Döring. Lacks 1 folding table. Cont. bds., supp. later hf. leath. (D. Dec.11-13; 774) DM 1,650
– – **Anr. Edn.** Stuttgart & Tübingen, 1827-35. Compl. definitive Edn. Vols. 1-55 & Index in 29 vols. 1st. & last ll. slightly browned at corners. Cont. hf. leath. gt., ex-lib. (HK. May 15; 4276) DM 4,200
– – **Anr. Edn.** Stuttgart & Tübingen, 1827-42. 60 pts. in 59 vols., 1 vol. Life & 1 vol. Index & 1 double vol. 19. Cont. marb. bds., gt., decor. (HK. May 15; 4277) DM 2,700
– – **Anr. Edn.** Stuttgart & Tübingen, 1828-33. Vols. 1-55 only (of 56) in 28. 12mo. Cont. bds. (SH. Jan.30; 341) *Schwing.* £140
– – **Anr. Edn.** Weimar, 1887-1918. 119 in 127 vols. Lacks Pt. I, vol. 5, II & 51-54, Pt. III: 14-15, Pt. IV: vols. 43-50. Orig. hf. leath. & 1 orig. hf. linen, very defect. in parts, several vols. loose. (H. May 21/22; 1409) DM 1,200
- **West-oestlicher Divan.** Stuttgart, 1819. 1st. Edn. Cont. hf. leath. (R. Oct.14-18; 903) DM 1,200
– – **Anr. Copy.** Slightly soiled. Cont. bds. (R. Mar.31-Apr.4; 466) DM 600
– – **Anr. Edn.** Ill.:– M. Behmer. Leipzig, 1910.

Ltd. Priv. Edn. numbered on Japan. Orig. vell., upr. cover gt. Etched ex-lib. Max von Steiger on upr. end-paper. (HK. Nov.18-21; 2431) DM 750
- **Wilhelm Meisters Lehrjahre.** Berlin, 1795. 1st. Edn., 1st. printing. 4 vols. With supp. ll. mus., II with Nachrichten an den Buchbinder, IV with advt. ll., 1 without 'Nachrichten', II-IV without hf.-title, II with corr. pagination, slightly browned in parts. Cont. hf. leath., lightly worn. (H. Dec.9/10; 1506) DM 1,350
- **Wilhelm Meisters Wanderjahre.** Stuttgart & Tübingen, 1821. 1st. Book Edn. Pt. 1, all publd. Slightly browned & soiled. Cont. bds. (R. Mar.31-Apr.4; 467) DM 530
– – **Anr. Copy.** Without last blank lf., MS. notes inside cover, light browning in parts. Cont. hf. leath., worn. (H. May 21/22; 1104) DM 500

GOETTINGER Taschen Calender
Ill.:– Chodowiecki, Hogarth, & Schubert. Goettingen, 1794; 1796; 1799; 1800. 4 iss. in 4 vols. 32mo. 2 text ll. defect. in 1st. iss. Orig. pict. bds., very worn. (SG. Feb.5; 154) $120

GOEUROT, Jehan
[-] **The Regiment of Life Whereunto is added a Treatise of the Pestilence.** Ed.:– Thomas Fayre. 1596. Sm. 4to. Sm. hole in B4. New vell. [STC 11976] (S. Jun.16; 340) *Chitton.* £750

GOEVERNEUR, J.J.A.
- **Nederlandsch Indie, of de Bewoners dezer Streken.** Leiden, ca. 1860. Cont. cl. gt. (VG. Dec.16; 881) Fls. 600

GOEZ, J.F.
- **Exercices d'Imagination de Differens Caractères et Formes Humaines.** [Augsburg], [1784]. Suite I. Fo. Some slight staining, etc., thro.-out. Old bds., cf. spine, worn. (BS. Jun.11; 415) £140

GOFFE, Thomas
- **The Raging Turke.** 1631. 1st. Edn. 4to. Mor. by Sangorski. [STC 11980] (C. Nov.19; 99) *Brett-Smith.* £300
- **Three Excellent Traoedies, viz. The Raging Turk ... The Couragous Turk ... & The Tragoedie of Orestes.** 1656. 2nd. Edn. General title bnd. at end, lacks sm. portion affecting text. Cont. sheep, spine defect. [Wing G1006] (C. Feb.25; 156) *Ad Orientem.* £110

GOGARTY, Oliver St. John
- **Wild Apples.** Cuala Pr. 1928. 1st. Edn. (50). Orig. linen-bkd. bds., unc. (S. Jul.22; 76) *Quaritch.* £130

GOGOL, Nicolas
- **Diary of a Madman.** Ill.:– A. Alexeieff. L., Cresset Pr. 1929. (30) with an additional suite of plts. Vell. bds., hf. reversed cf. (KH. Nov.18; 284) Aus. $140

GOLBERY, Ph. de
- **Histoire et Description de la Suisse et du Tyrol.** Paris, 1838. Browned. Cont. hf. leath. (R. Mar.31-Apr.4; 2742) DM 810
- **Schweiz und Tyrol.** Stuttgart, 1840. Lacks 1 port., 1 plt. cold. in, partly very soiled. Cont. hf. leath., loose. (R. Oct.14-18; 2004) DM 650

GOLBERY or Golbéry, Silvain L.X.
- **Storia e Descrizione della Svizzera e del Tirolo.** Trans.:– A.F. Falconetti. Venice, 1840. Plts. lightly browned in parts & soiled. Later hf. leath. (H. May 21/22; 439) DM 620

GOLD, Capt. Charles
- **Oriental Drawings.** 1806. 4to. Lacks 14 plts., 3 cut down & loosely inserted. Disbnd. W.a.f. (TA. Oct.16; 305) £170
– – **Anr. Edn.** [1806]. 4to. 35 (of 49) hand-cold. aqua plts. & 3 loose plts., lacks title-page. Cf., lacks upr. cover. W.a.f. (P. Sep.11; 269) *Bailey.* £160

GOLDAST V. HAIMINSFELD, M.
- **Rerum Alemannicarum Scriptores.** Ed.:– C. Ch. Senckenberg. Frankfurt & Leipzig, 1730. 3rd. Edn. 3 pts. in 1 vol. Fo. Cont. leath. gt. (R. Mar.31-Apr.4; 1905) DM 600

GOLDEN COCKEREL PRESS
- **Chanticleer.-Pertelote; A Sequel to Chanticleer.** Ill.:– John Buckland-Wright, Lettice Sandford & others (2nd. work). Gold. Cock. Pr. 1936; 1943. 1st. work: (300) numbered, sigd. by Christopher Sandford. 2 vols. Orig. mor.-bkd. cl. or cl. 1st. by Sangorski & Sutcliffe. (SBA. Dec.16; 123) *Emerald Isle Books.* £120
- **The First Crusade.** Trans.:– Somerset de Chair. Ill.:– Clifford Webb. 1945. (500) numbered. Slim fo. Orig. three-qtr. vell. (TA. Jun.18; 351) £54

GOLDEN COCKEREL PRESS -contd.
- **Pertelote; a Sequel to Chanticleer.** Ill.:– John Buckland-Wright, Helen Binyon, Lettice Sandford & others. Gold. Cock. Pr. 1943. (200) numbered, sigd. by Christopher Sandford & Owen Rutter. Orig. mor.-bkd. cl. by Sangorski & Sutcliffe. (SBA. Dec.16; 125) *Chesters.* £65

GOLDENER VLIES
See–ORDEN VOM GOLDENEN VLIES

GOLDFISH AT SCHOOL, or the Alphabet of Frank the Fisherman
1823. All but 1 of the ills. have been cut along 2 opposite sides, possibly so that each fish could be revealed within background by removing inserted strip of paper. Orig. wraps. (SH. Mar.19; 111) *Schiller.* £230

GOLDING, Louis
- **In the Steps of Moses the Lawgiver.** Corvinus Pr. Jun. 1938. (30) numbered, sigd. Orig. buckram-bkd. linen, s.-c. (S. Jul.31; 146) *Updike.*
- **Pale Blue Nightgown.** Corvinus Pr. Oct. 1936. 1st. Edn., (64) numbered, sigd. Orig. hf. vell., s.-c. (S. Jul.31; 137) *Ferret Fantasy.* £90
- **The Song of Songs.** Corvinus Pr. Apr. 1937. 1st. Edn., (178) numbered, sigd. 4to. Orig. limp vell., silk ties, s.-c. (S. Jul.31; 139) *Quaritch.* £90
- – **Anr. Copy.** (S. Jul.22; 69) *Sawyer.* £65

GOLDINI, Carlo
- **Le Bourrou bienfaisant.** Paris, 1771. Cont. Parisian red mor. gt., arms of Louis XVI in centre of covers, spine gt. in compartments. The Cortlandt F. Bishop copy. (SPB. Oct.1, 226) $900

GOLDMANN, C.J.
- **With General French & the Cavalry in South Africa.** 1902. Some spotting. Cont. red mor. by the Guild of Women Binders, central mor. inlays on upr. covers & C D tooled in gt., vell. doubls. Pres. copy to Sir Arthur Conan Doyle. (CSK. Jun.12; 83) £60

GOLDMANN, C.S.
- **The Financial, Statistical & General History of the Gold & other Companies of the Witwatersrand.** L., 1892. Orig. bdg. (VA. Oct.31; 415) R. 230

GOLDMANN, N.
- **Elementorum Architecturae Militaris Libri IV.** 1643. 3 pts. in 1 vol. Old vell. (HD. Apr.24; 50) Frs. 1,000

GOLDONI, Carlo
- **Delle Commedie.-Delle Componimente Diversi.** Ill.:– Baratti & others after P.A. Novelli (both works). Venice, 1761-[77]; 1764. 17 vols. in 9; 2 vols. Cont. vell. (1st. work); & cont. mott. cf., gt. spines. Bkplt. of Consul Joseph Smith in the 1st. vol. of the 1st. work, both works lately in the collection of John A. Saks. (C. Jun.10; 97) *Breslauer.* £3,000
- **Opere Teatrali.-Memorie . . .** Venice, 1788-95; 1788. 1st. Compl. Edn.; 1st. Edn. in Italian. 44 vols.; 3 vols. Without port. in vol. I of 1st. work called for by Morazzoni. Unif. mor.-bkd. bds., some spines darker than others. From the collection of John A. Saks. (C. Jun.10; 98) *King.* £500

GOLDSCHMID, Edgar
- **Entwicklung und Bibliographie der Pathologisch-Anatomischen Abbildung.** Leipzig, 1925. 1st. Edn. 4to. 44 plts. loose in folding case at end, some in proof state, a few with captions in author's hand, others by E.A. Underwood. Cont. red hf. mor. Author's interleaved copy, with his typed notes & bkplt., from liby. of Dr. E. Ashworth Underwood. (S. Feb.23; 210) *Goldschmidt.* £130
- – **Anr. Copy.** 4to. Orig. cl., soiled. From liby. of Dr. E. Ashworth Underwood. (S. Feb.23; 211) *Dawson.* £55

GOLDSCHMIDT, Adolph
- **Die Deutsche Buchmalerei.** Munich & Flor., 1928. Fo. Orig. hf. linen. (R. Oct.14-18; 506) DM 450

GOLDSCHMIDT, Lazarus
- **Der Babylonische Talmud.** Berlin, 1930-1936. 12 vols. Cl., some spines detchd. or crudely reprd. (SG. Aug.21; 167) $140

GOLDSCHMIDT, V.
See–VON FERSMANN, A. & Goldschmidt, V.

GOLDSMID, Sir F.J. & Blanford, W.T.
- **Journeys of the Persian Boundary Commission 1870-72, Eastern Persia.** 1876. 2 vols. Orig. cl. (P. Sep.11; 226) *Ad Orientem.* £160

GOLDSMITH, Oliver
[–] **The Bee.** 1759. 1st. Edn. Without blank at beginning & end (not called for?), slight browning, inscr. on title. Cont. cf. (S. Feb.9; 179) *Thorp.* £350
- **The Deserted Village.** 1770. 1st. Edn. 4to. Lacks hf.-title, slight browning, owner's stp. on title. Early 20th. C. lev. mor. by Rivière, slightly rubbed & faded. (S. Oct.1; 561) £150
- – **Anr. Copy.** Crimson mor. gt. by Rivière, lacks part of spine. (SG. Oct.9; 114) $200
- – **Anr. Edn.** Ill.:– C.R. Ashbee (frontis.). Essex House Pr. 1904. (150) numbered on vell. Orig. blind-stpd. vell., slightly soiled & warped. (CSK. May 15; 62) £85
- – **Anr. Copy.** (SH. Feb.19; 30) *Ayres.* £75
- **Dr. Goldsmith's Celebrated Elegy on that Glory of Her Sex, Mrs. Mary Blaize.** 1808. 16mo. Orig. wraps., Harris's cabinet label on upr. cover, backstrip & lr. cover crudely restitched, soiled. (SH. Mar.19; 112) *Schiller.* £250
[–] **An Enquiry into the Present State of Learning in Europe.** 1759. 1st. Edn. Slight browning. Cont. spr. cf., spine gt. (S. Feb.9; 180) *Waterfield.* £150
- **Essays.** 1765. 1st. Edn.(?). 12mo. With penultimate advt. lf. Cont. mott. cf., rebkd., spine gt. (S. Feb.9; 181) *Waterfield.* £60
- **The Good Natur'd Man.** L., 1768. 1st. Edn., 1st. Iss. Crimson lev. gt. (SG. Oct.9; 113) $475
- **The Haunch of Venison.** L., 1776. 1st. Edn., 1st. Iss. 4to. Lev., triple gt. fillet borders, gt. spine & dentelles, by Rivière. (SG. Oct.9; 117) $350
- **A History of the Earth & Animated Nature.** 1774. 8 vols. Cont. cf., spines elab. gt., some covers detchd. (C. Jul.22; 188) *Taylor.* £60
- – **Anr. Edn.** L., 1779. 8 vols. Cont. cf. (CR. Jun.11; 577) Lire 360,000
- – **Anr. Edn.** Glasgow, Edinb., & L., 1854. 2 vols. Some foxing. Cont. hf. leath. (CB. Nov.12; 157) Can. $130
- – **Anr. Edn.** N.d. 2 vols. Cont. cf., gt. (SH. Apr.9; 251) *Kauffman.* £55
- **The Life of Richard Nash, of Bath . . .** L., 1762. 1st. Edn. Frontis. port. tipped-in on a stub, tops of port. & title stained, approx. 2/3 of title replaced bearing MS. imprint, advts. Cont. gt.-ornamental mott. cf., rebkd. in cf. (PNY. Oct.1; 242) $110
[–] **The Mystery Revealed.** L., 1742 (1762). 1st. Edn., 2nd. iss. Hf. cf., lev. s.-c. by Stikeman. Austin Dobson bkplt., early owner indicated dating error. (SG. Oct.9; 112) $900
- **The Poetical & Dramatic Works.** Ed.:– T. Evans. 1780. 2 vols. The 2 prelims. usually found after main title in vol. II bnd. up between H5-6 in vol. I, H6 being cut-out, several ll. spotted. Cont. Fr. red mor., gt., flower design in 5 compartments. (S. Feb.10; 443) *Waterfield.* £150
- **Retaliation.** L., 1774. 1st. Edn. 4to. Iss. without the words 'Published as the Act directs 18th. April 1774' below the engraved port. on title-p., errata corrected by cont. hand, inner edges strengthened & reprd. thro.-out, some fore-margins reprd., sm. hole affecting 1 letter on p. 14. Mod. wraps., mor. gt. solander case. From the Prescott Collection. (CNY. Feb.6; 130) $220
- **She Stoops to Conquer.** L., 1773. 1st. Edn. Variant with the text ending on P2 (misnumbered p. 107 with P a 2 lf. gathering), the Craddock epilogue ptd. on (A4), & without the hf.-title as iss., title-p. conforms with Todd's 1st. imp. variant C, some edges & folds strengthened, some slight soiling to blank edges. Stitched as iss., folding cl. box, unc. The Frank L. Hogan copy, bkplt. in case, lately in the Prescott Collection. (CNY. Feb.6; 129) $950
- – **Anr. Copy.** Crimson lev. gt., gt. dentelles, by Rivière. (SG. Oct.9; 115) $475
- – **Anr. Edn.** Ill.:– Hugh Thomson. [1912]. (350) numbered, sigd. by artist. 4to. Orig. vell. gt., lacks ties, s.-c. (SH. Mar.27; 524) *Triggs.* £115
- – **Anr. Copy.** Orig. gt. ornamented vell., lacks ties, cl. folding case. Bkplt. of Adolph Zukor. (SG. Apr.2; 289) $185
- – **Anr. Edn.** Ill.:– Hugh Thomson. L., n.d. 4to. 24 tipped in cold. plts. Vell., gt. decor. (JL. Dec.15; 764) *Aus.* $120
- **The Vicar of Wakefield.** 1792. 2 vols. in 1. Cont. red str.-grd. mor. by C. Kalthoeber, with his ticket, gt., spine tooled in compartments, covers with 2-line roll border & panel. Book-labels of Madame De Bure & Comte H. de la Bedoyère, the de Bure copy with his collation note. (S. Nov.24; 135) *Klusmann.* £240
- – **Anr. Edn.** Ill.:– Thomas Rowlandson. L., 1817. Red mor. gt., by Rivière. (CNY. May 22; 258) $480
- – **Anr. Edn.** Ill.:– T. Rowlandson. 1823. Orig. blind-stpd. cl. gt. (P. Sep.11; 277) *Magda.* £240
- – **Anr. Edn.** Ill.:– Hugh Thomson. 1890. Orig. cl., unc. Pres. copy by artist to William Heighway. (SH. Mar.27; 509) *Illustrated Antiques.* £220
- – **Anr. Copy.** L.P. Red mor., by Rivière. (SH. Mar.27; 508) *Donnithorne.* £90
- – **Anr. Copy.** 12mo. Crushed mor., inlaid at upr. corner with figure by Kelliegram of the vicar in cold. mor., & stpd. with gt. rose & lf. strapwork inlaid in red mor., inner dentelles repeating strapwork design, silk doubls., silk place-marker. (PNY. Mar.4; 107) $300
- – **Anr. Edn.** Ill.:– H. George Webb. Bedford Park, Chiswick, Caradoc Pr. 1903. (14) numbered, on vell. Orig. vell., linen ties, unc. Port. sigd. by artist. (SG. May 14; 41) $850
- – **Anr. Edn.** Ill.:– Arthur Rackham. L., [1929]. 1st. Trade Edn. 4to. Publisher's cold. & gt.-pict. Persian mor. Raymond M. Sutton Jr. copy. (SG. May 7; 92) $275
- – **Anr. Edn.** Ill.:– Arthur Rackham. L., [1929]. 1st. Edn. Deluxe, (575) numbered, for England, sigd. by artist. 4to. Vell., gt. triple fillet border, warped. Raymond M. Sutton Jr. copy. (SG. May 7; 91) $400
- – **Anr. Copy.** Gt. vell., partly unopened, orig. publr's. box. (SG. Oct.9; 205) $375
- [**Works**] **Miscellaneous Works.** Phila., 1838. Cont. sheep. Inscr. by Abraham Lincoln to N.W. Edwards, Edwards' name inked over, opposite is a note written by Lincoln's partner W.H. Herndon, the Block copy. (SPB. Nov.24; 27a) $2,900
- **Works.** Ed.:– Peter Cunningham. N.Y. & L., 1900. Wakefield Edn., (500) numbered. 12 vols. Hf. lev., partly untrimmed. (SG. Dec.18; 212) $225

GOLDSMITH, Oliver & Parnell, Thomas
- **Poems.** Ill.:– Thomas & John Bewick. 1795. 4to. Cont. russ. gt., slightly worn. (SBA. Jul.23; 384) *Maggs.* £90
- – **Anr. Copy.** Cont. hf. cf., worn. (TA. Dec.18; 96) £56
- – **Anr. Edn.** Ill.:– Thomas & John Bewick. L., 1804. Tall 8vo. Early str.-grd. mor., very worn & loose. Three-panel fore-e. pntg.; from the liby. of Zola E. Harvey. (SG. Mar.19; 137) £550

GOLDSTEIN, Israel
- **A Century of Judaism in New York.** N.y., 1930. Gt.-decor. buckram. Sigd. (SG. Feb.12; 238) $100

GOLDSTON, Will
- **Exclusive Magical Secrets.** [1912]. 4to. Orig. maroon mor., lock & key. (SH. Oct.23; 36) *Quaritch.* £210
- – **Anr. Copy.** (SH. Oct.23; 213) *Masters.* £110
- – **Anr. Copy.** Dampstained, lock & key. (SH. Oct.24; 304) *Masters.* £50
- **Further Exclusive Magical Secrets.** [1927]. 4to. Orig. maroon mor., lock & key. (SH. Oct.23; 215) *Masters.* £130
- – **Anr. Copy.** Orig. lock replaced by padlock & 2 keys. (SH. Oct.23; 42) *Guenther.* £110
- **Great Magician's Tricks.** [1931]. 4to. Orig. cl., backstrip defective. (SH. Oct.23; 44) *Masters.* £110
- **More Exclusive Magical Secrets.** [1921]. 4to. Orig. maroon mor., orig. lock replaced by padlock & 2 keys. (SH. Oct.23; 40) *Masters.* £110
- – **Anr. Copy.** 4to. Cl., worn & stained. (SH. Oct.23; 41) *Linden.* £70

GOLDSTON, Will (Ed.)
See–MAGICIAN Annual, The

GOLGI, Camillo
- **Sulla Fina Anatomia degli Organi Centrali del Sistema Nervoso.** Milano, 1886. 1st. Edn. Disbnd. (SG. Aug.21; 317) $380

GOLIUS, Jacobus
- **Lexicon Arabico-Latinum . . . Index Latinus copiossimus.** Leyden, 1653. 1st. Edn. Fo. Cont. vell. (S. Oct.20; 92) *Riley-Smith.* £450

GOLL, Yvan
- **Bouquet de Rêves pour Neila.** Ill.:– Joan Miro. [Paris], [1967]. (150) sigd. by artist, from a total

Edn. of 200 copies. 4to. Quires un-bnd. as Iss. in wraps., canvas s.-c. (KH. Nov.18; 291) Aus. $240
- **Elegy of Ihpetonga, & Masks of Ashes.** Ill.:- Pablo Picasso. N.Y., 1954. (64) numbered. Fo. Orig. buckram, slightly soiled, unc. (SH. Nov.21; 450) *Quaritch.* £310

GOLOWNIN, Capt.
- **Narrative of Captivity in Japan.** 1818. 2 vols. Cf., worn. (CE. Nov.20; 83) £95

GOLTZ, Friedrich Leopold
- **Beiträge zur Lehre von den Functionen der Nervencentren des Frosches.** Berlin, 1869. 1st. Edn. Extreme lr. outer blank corners of title & following few ll. slightly stained. Mor.-bkd. cl. (S. Jun.16; 343) *Maggs.* £65

GOLTZIUS, Hubertus
- **Fastos Magistratum et triumphorum Romanorum.** Bruges, Mar. 1566. Fo. Liby. stp. on some ll., slight browning & soiling. 18th. C. vell. bds. (S. Sep.29; 94) *Van Haverberger.* £180
- **Icones Imperatorum Romanum.** Antw., [1558]. Fo. 133 ports., lacks title & end lf. Disbnd. William Michael Rossetti sig. on fly-lf. & note at end, w.a.f. (P. Jun.11; 344) *Dekesel.* £130

GOMBERVILLE, Marin le Roy, Sieur de
- [-] **La Doctrine des Moeurs Tirée de la Philosophia des Stoiques.** Paris, 1646. Fo. Title reprd. & preserved. Old cf., brkn. (BS. Jun.11; 342) £80

GOMES de Brito, Bernardo
- **Historia Tragico-Maritima.** Lisbon, 1735-36. 1st. Edn. 2 vols. Sm. 4to. 1 sub-title torn affecting vig., inside upr. cover & title of vol. II wormed, a few ll. slightly soiled, 1 slightly torn, cont. owner's inscr. on 1st. title. Cont. cf., spines s., not unif., corners & spines slightly worn. (S. Jun.23; 251) *Maggs.* £280

GOMES DE MORAIS, Silvestre
- [-] **Agricultura das Vinhas e Tudo o que Pertence a ellas ate Perfeito Recolhimento do Vinho, & Relacao das suas Virtudes, & da Cepa, Vides, Folhas, & Borras. Composto por Vicencio Alarte.** Lisbon, 1712. 1st. Edn. Some browning & soiling, lacks 1st. lf. (blank?), official stp. & some MS. notes & crossings out, probably in connection with new edn. of 1733. Cont. limp vell., soiled, corner cut from lr. cover. From liby. of André L. Simon. (S. May 18; 108) *Facchi.* £70

GOMEZ de la Serna, Ramon
- **Le Cirque.** Trans.:- Adolphe Falgairolle. Ill.:- Vertès. Paris, 1928. (103); (33) on Arches vell. with 2 separate sets of ills. Fo. In sheets, publisher's s.-c. (HD. Dec.5; 95) Frs. 1,950
- **Toda la Historia de la Puerta del Sol y otras Muchas Cosas.** Madrid, n.d. 1st. Edn. Ob. fo. Publisher's bds. (DS. Apr.24; 1029) Pts. 25,000

GONCHAROV, Ivan
- **Obryv [Precipice].** St. Petersb., 1870. 1st. Edn. 2 vols. Some ll. stained. Later roan-bkd. bds. (SH. Feb.5; 5) *Bjorck.* £120

GONCOURT, Edmond de
- **La Fille Elisa.** Ill.:- Georges Jeanniot. Paris, 1895. (300); (12) on imperial Jap. 4to. Red hf. mor. by Blanchetière, border of 5 gt. fillets in spine compartments, wrap. preserved. (SM. Feb.11; 227) Frs. 5,000

GONCOURT, Edmond & Jules de
- **L'Art de Dix-huitième Siécle.** Paris, 1883. (100) on Whatman paper, numbered. 4to. 2 states of plts. Red hf. mor. by Champs, decor. spines, wraps. preserved. (SM. Feb.11; 228) Frs. 5,200
- **Histoire de Marie Antoinette.** Paris, 1878. (15) on Papier de Chine. Sm. fo. Hf. lev. mor. gt., partly unc. (CNY. May 22; 314) $450
- **Histoire de la Société Française pendant la Révolution.** Paris, 1889. (25) on 'papier de Japon'. 4to. Cont. red hf. mor., gt. (SBA. Jul.23; 512) *Crete.* £55
- **Renée Mauperin.** Ill.:- James Tissot. Paris, 1884. (550); (450) on Holland. Lge. 8vo. Proofs of etchings with artist's stamp. Mor. by Whitman Bennett, decor. spine, border of 2 gt. fillets & vases in corners, sm. stain on lr. cover, lacks orig. wrap. (SM. Feb.11; 229) Frs. 1,400

GONCOURT, G. & Jules de
- **Sophie Arnould** ... Ill.:- Popelin; Flameng (port). Paris, 1877. On China paper. Sm. 4to. Mor. by Charles Meunier, mosaic covers with floral decor., inside dentelle, sewed silk doubls. & end-papers, wrap. preserved. MS. visiting card &

envelope from author to Charles Meunier. (HD. Jun.25; 262) Frs. 2,000

GONSE, Louis
- **L'Art Japonais.** Paris, 1883. 2 vols. 4to. Decor. silk bds., upr. cover detchd. (P. Feb.19; 46) £75

GONZALEA Laguna, Francisco
- **El Zelo Sacerdotal para los Ninos no-nacidos.** Lima, 1781. Sm. 4to. Wormholes affecting 1st. ll., a few sm. stains. Cont. mott. cf. (SPB. May 5; 235) $125

GONZALEZ BARCIA, Andres
- **Historiadores Primitivos de las Indias Occidentales** ... Madrid, 1749. 1st. Edn. 3 vols. Fo. Mod. three-qtr. mor. [Sabin 3350] (SG. May 14; 87) $2,000

GONZALEZ de Agueros, Pedro
- **Descripcion Historical de la Provincia y Archipieloga de Chilóe.-Clamores Apostólicos** ... **y un Estado de la Religion Sérafica en las dos Américas e Islas Filipinas.** [Madrid], 1791. 2 works in 1 vol. Sm. 4to. Inscr. on title 'De las Libreria del Colegio de Ntra. Sra. de los Angeles d. Tarija' (Bolivia), liby. stp. Cont. cf. (SPB. May 5; 232) $350

GONZALEZ de Mendoza, Juan
- **Historia de las Cosas mas Notables, Ritos y Costumbres, del Gran Reyno de la China, sabidas assi por los Libros de los mesmos Chinos** ... Antw., 1596. Some browning. Later hf. cf., defect. [Sabin 27777] (SPB. May 5; 233) $650

GONZALEZ de Rosende, Antonio
- **Vida del Ilmo i Excmo. Señor D. Iuan de Palafox i Mendoza** ... **Obispo de la Puebla de los Angeles, i Arzobispo Electo de Mexico.** Madrid, 1671. Fo. Corner of section-title defect. with loss of typographical border, some ll. browned or stained. 18th. C. cf., spine slightly wormed. (SPB. May 5; 234) $150

GOOCH, Benjamin
- **A Practical Treatise on Wounds** ... Norwich, 1767. 2 vols. Cont. cf., covers loose. (P. Nov.13; 297) *Traylen.* £75

GOOD, John Mason & Others
- **Pantologia.** L., 1813. 12 vols. Some foxing. Cont. cf., gt., rebkd. (VG. Nov.18; 927) Fls. 900

GOOD NEWES from Fraunce
Ca. 1595. 4to. Disbnd., loose in cf. bdg. (S. Mar.16; 219) *Frost.* £420

GOODEN, Stephen
- **12 proof engravings of vignettes & tailpieces for 'The Fables of Jean de la Fontaine'.** L., 1931. 4to., most ca. 255mm. × 185mm. 12 proof engravings. Loose in qtr. red mor. gt. s.-c. Sigd. & dtd. in pencil, John A. Saks' copy. (CNY. Oct.1; 179) $500

GOODENOUGH, Erwin R.
- **Jewish Symbols in the Greco-Roman Period.** N.Y., 1953-68. 13 vols. 4to. Cl. (S. Nov.17; 16) *Elberg.* £180

GOODLIFFE, C.G. Neale (Ed.)
See-ABRACADABRA

GOODRICH, Frank B.
- **Court of Napoleon.** Ill.:- Jules Champagne. N.Y., 1857. 1st. Edn. 4to. Orig. elab. blind & gt.-stpd. mor., rebkd., orig. spine laid down. (SG. Feb.26; 99) $130

GOODRICH, Lloyd
- **Thomas Eakins; His Life & Work.** N.Y., 1933. 1st. Edn. 4to. Cl. (SG. Oct.23; 106) $130

GOODWIN, Francis
- **Domestic Architecture.** 1833-34. 1st. & 2nd. series. 2 vols. 4to. Some foxing & offsetting. Cl.-bkd. bds., slightly worn & soiled. (S. Dec.9; 461) *Talerman.* £90

GOODY TWO SHOES
L., 1825. 1st. Edn. Square 16mo. With lf. of advts. Cont. Dutch bds., hf. lev. s.-c. (SG. Apr.30; 141) $160

GOOS, Pieter
- **The Sea-Atlas, or the Watter-World, wherein described all the Sea Coasts of the known World, very usefull & necessary for all Shipmasters, Pilots & Seamen.** Amst., Priv. ptd., 1675. Fo. Engraved histor. title, double-p. map of the World & 29 double-p. charts on guards, 8-p. introduction & index in Engl. Cont. cf., 18th. C. rebacking,

upr. cover partly detchd. (C. Feb.25; 217) *Burgess.* £5,500

GORCUM, Jan van
- **'t Bosch der Eremyten ende Eremitinnen, van Aegypten ende Palestinen** ... Ill.:- van Sichem after Blommaert. Antw., 1644. 4to. Slightly stained thro.-out, thin spot on title. Cont. cf., spine gt., defect., worn. (VG. Nov.18; 1388) Fls. 500

GORDEEV, Bogdan
- [-] **[Buben (Tambourine)].** Moscow, 1914. 1st. Edn. 4to. Orig. wraps. (SH. Feb.6; 435) *Quaritch.* £210
- [-] **Anr. Edn.** Ill.:- M. Sinyakova. Moscow, 1916. 4to. Orig. wraps. (SH. Feb.6; 436) *Quaritch.* £95

GORDON, Alexander
- **Itinerarium Septentrionale or A Journey through Scotland.** 1727. Fo. Cf. gt. (CE. Nov.20; 143) £100
- **Itinerarium Septentrionale.-Additions & Corrections, by Way of Supplement.** 1727-32. 2nd. work 1st. Edn. 2 vols. in 1. Fo. 1st. work; sm. repairs & tears to folding map, 2nd. work; 4 engraved plts. (of 5), ?lacks hf.-title. Mott. cf. gt., by Rivière, joints split. (S. Nov.24; 137) *Weinreb.* £65

GORDON, Patrick
- [-] **The History of the War in America, between Great Britain & Her Colonies.** Dublin, 1779. 1st. Edn. Vols. I & II (of 3). Contains both issues of pp. 349-352, 2 cont. sigs. on titles, 1 partly erased. Cont. cf., backstrips slightly to somewhat worn. (PNY. Mar.26; 12) $100

GORDON, Lt. Col. T.E.
- **Roof of the World.** 1876. 1st. Edn. Folding map detchd. Orig. cl. gt. (P. Mar.12; 277) *Way.* £50

GORDON, W.
- **The Universal Accountant.-The General Counting House.** Edinb., 1765-66. 2 vols.; 1 vol. Cont. cf., 2 covers detchd. (SH. May 21; 46) *Shaw.* £80

GORE, J.
- **Liverpool Directory, with its Environs.** L'pool, 1823. Some defects. Orig. bds., disbnd. (SBA. May 27; 339) *Curzon.* £50

GORER, Edgar & Blacker, J.F.
- **Chinese Porcelain & Hard Stones.** 1911. Ltd. Edn. 2 vols. 4to. Cl. (C. Feb.4; 244) *Basket & Day.* £230
- - **Anr. Copy.** Gt.-pict. buckram, soiled. (SG. Dec.4; 164) $450

GORI, Antonius Franciscus
- **Dactyliotheca Smithiana.** Ill.:- B. Brustolon & others. Venice, 1767. Thick paper. 2 vols. Lge. 4to. Cont. Venetian vell. gt., circular mor. inlay on each cover with gt. arms of Consul Joseph Smith, some sm. wormholes. From the collection of John A. Saks. (C. Jun.10; 99) *Lyon.* £480

GORIS, Gerard
- **Les Delices de la Campagne à l'entour de la Ville de Leide.** Leiden, 1752. 12mo. Old cf., 5 decor. spine raised bands. (LM. Mar.21; 309) B.Frs. 9,000

GORKY, M.
- **Ocherki i Razskazy [Sketches & Stories].** St. Petersb., 1899. 2nd. expanded Edn. 3 vols. in 1. Cont. hf. mor. by Schnell(?). (SH. Feb.5; 6) *Flegon.* £80

GÖRLING, A.
- **Deutschlands Kunstschätze.** Ed.:- A. Woltmann & B. Meyer. Leipzig, 1871-72. 4 vols. 4to. Cont. hf. leath. gt. (R. Oct.14-18; 2661) DM 1,300
- - **Anr. Copy.** Lacks 2 steel engraved plts. Orig. gold decor. linen. (R. Mar.31-Apr.4; 1585) DM 1,200
- - **Anr. Copy.** Lacks 1 plt. in vol. 3. Orig. linen gt. (HK. May 12-14; 1058) DM 800
- - **Anr. Edn.** Ed.:- A. Woltmann & B. Meyer. Leipzig, 1885. 4 vols. 4to. Orig. hf. leath. (D. Dec.11-13; 1250) DM 1,150
- **Die Dresdener Gallerie.** Leipzig & Dresden, ca. 1850. 2 vols. Some plts. soiled. Cont. linen, loose. (R. Mar.31-Apr.4; 1586) DM 1,250
- - **Anr. Copy.** 4to. Partly browned, slightly soiled in parts. Cont. mor., gt. spine cover & outer dentelle, loose. (HK. May 12-14; 1059) DM 650
- **Stahlstich-Sammlung der Vorzüglichsten Gemälde der Dresdener Gallerie.** Leipzig & Dresden, ca. 1850. 4 vols. 4to. Lacks 4 steel

GÖRLING, A. *-contd.*
engraved plts. Liby. linen. (R. Mar.31-Apr.4; 1587) DM 1,220
- - **Anr. Copy.** 2 vols. in 1. Cont. hf. leath., worn. (R. Oct.14-18; 2664) DM 900
- - **Anr. Edn.** Leipzig, ca. 1860. 2 vols. 4to. Some ll. & plts. in 1 vol. slightly defect. at margin. Orig. linen. (D. Dec.11-13; 1251) DM 600

GORLING, A. & others
- Art Treasures of Germany. The Galleries of Dresden, Cassel ... Boston, ca. 1870. Lge. 4to. Lacks 2 steel engraved plts. Linen. (R. Mar.31-Apr.4; 1590) DM 900

GORLITZ, Mattheus Friderich von
- Ein Sendbrieff an die Vollen Brüder in Teütschem lande Geschrieben. N.p., 1556. 1st. Edn. Sm. 4to. Slight browning. Mod. pol. hf. cf. by Rivière, spine gt., slightly marked. From liby. of André L. Simon. (S. May 18; 109) *Lyle.* £240

GORRINGE, Henry
- Egyptian Obelisks. Ill.:– Harroun & Bierstadt. N.Y., [1882]. Fo. Gt.-pict. cl., ex-liby. (SG. Apr.23; 101) $150

GORTON, Samuel
- Simplicities Defence against Seven-Headed Policy. L., 1646. 4to. Slight repairs to title & 1st. 3 ll. Red mor., gt. spine & panels. [Sabin 28044] (SPB. Nov.24; 16) $1,600

GOSSE, Edmund
- British Portrait Painters & Engravers of the 18th. Century. 1906. (100) on India paper. 2 vols. Fo. With dupl. set of plts. Orig. wraps., cl. s.-c. (SH. Jan.29; 101) *Skilton.* £95
- A Century of French Romance. N.Y., [1901]. (50). 20 vols. Mor. gt. with overall pattern of sm. gt. fleur de lys, laurel wreaths on spines, centre & corners of covers, suede doubls. (SPB. May 6; 311) $1,800

GOSSE, Edmund (Ed.)
See–ALLIES' FAIRY BOOK

GOSSE, Philip Henry
- Illustrations of the Birds of Jamaica. 1849. Fo. Mod. mor., gt., s.-c., by Gray of Cambridge. (S. Dec.3; 979) *Nielson.* £2,500
- Tenby: A Sea-Side Holiday. 1856. 1st. Edn. Publisher's advts. bnd. in at rear. Orig. cl., recased. (TA. Jun.18; 208) £52

GOTCH, J. Alfred
- The English Home from Charles I to George IV, its Architecture, Decoration & Garden Design. -The Growth of the English House.-Inigo Jones. -The Growth & work of the Royal Institute of British Architects, 1834-1934. L., [1919]; 1909; [1928]; [1934]. 1st. vol. 2nd. Imp. 4 vols. Orig. bdgs. (CB. May 27; 114) Can. $120

GOTHAISCHER [GENEALOGISCHER] HOF KALENDER auf das Jahr 1786, 1807 & 1817
Ill.:– after Chatelain by Riepenhausen; after Chodowiecki by Geyser. Gotha, 1786, 1807 & 1817. 3 vols. Slightly soiled in parts, lacks pp. 15-18 & 1 copper engr. Cont. vell. & 2 paper bds. (H. Dec.9/10; 1374) DM 420

GOTTFRIDUS, J.O.
- Historiche Chronica der Vier Monarchien von Erschaffung der Welt. Ill.:– M. Merion. Frankfurt, 1642. Sm. fo. Engraved & ptd. titles mntd. & slightly defect., some ll. loose. Old hf. cf., brkn. (BS. Jun.11; 106) £320

GOTTFRIED, Johann Ludwig (Pseud.)
See–ABELIN, Johann Philip

GOTTSCHALK, Fr. von
- Die Ritterburgen und Bergschlösser Deutschlands. Halle & Magdeburg, 1815-35 & 1840. 9 vols. & New Series Vol. 1, all publd., in 10 vols. Cont. hf. linen, 10 not quite uniform, unc. (R. Oct.14-18; 2083) DM 750

GOTTSCHED, Johann Christoph
[-] Der Biedermann. Leipzig, 1728-29. 2 pts. in 1 vol. 4to. Some light staining & soiling. Cont. bds., soiled, unc. (H. May 21/22; 1117) DM 4,000
- Versuch einer Kritischen Dichtkunst für die Deutschen. Leipzig, 1737. 2nd. Iss. Lightly browned. Cont. vell., darkened & soiled. (HK. May 15; 4364) DM 540

GOTZ, Th.
- Hunde-Gallerie. 1853. 2nd. Edn. Ob. fo. Text lightly soiled, plts. slightly browned. Cont. hf. leath. (HK. Nov.18-21; 1721) DM 1,600

GOUDEAU, Emile
- Parisienne Idylle. Ill.:– Pierre Vidal. Paris, 1903. (70) on China. Lge. 8vo. Separate set of all woodcuts on Jap. Publisher's Bradel marb. cf., mosaic cat on upr. cover, gt. bird, smooth decor. spine, wrap., s.-c. (HD. Jun.25; 265) Frs. 1,550

GOUFFE, Jules
- Die Feine Kuche. Leipzig, [1874]. 2nd. Edn. 2 vols. Cont. linen. (R. Mar.31-Apr.4; 1625) DM 700
- Le Livre de Patisserie. Paris, 1873. A few spots. Cont. hf. cf. (SBA. May 27; 54) *Clarke.* £90
- The Royal Book of Pastry & Confectionary. Trans.:– Alphonse Gouffe. 1874. Orig. cl., soiled, partly disbnd. (CSK. Jul.10; 79) £85
- - **Anr. Copy.** Some ll. detchd. Orig. cl. (CSK. Jul.10; 125) £60

GOUGH, Richard
[-] British Topography. 1780. 1st. Edn. 2 vols. 4to. 1 map slightly soiled at head, lacks 1st. ?blank ll. & final blank in vol. I. Cont. mott. cf., gt., some wear. (S. Jan.27; 603) *Leighfield.* £90
- A Catalogue of the Entire & Valuable Library of ... L., Apr. 1810. Priced thro.-out, without the section devoted to MSS. Disbnd. (SG. Mar.26; 214) $180
[-] Sepulchral Monuments in Great Britain. 1786-96. 2 pts. in 3 vols. Fo. Tree cf., covers detchd. (P. Apr.9; 134) £150

GOULD, John
- Asiatic Birds ... selected from 'The Birds of Asia'. 1890. Fo. Hf. mor., gt. (S. Dec.3; 983) *Symonds.* £2,300
- Birds of Asia. Ed.:– Richard Bowdler Sharpe. 1850-83. 7 vols. Lge. fo. 530 hand-finished cold. litho. plts. Cont. red hf. mor., spines gt. (C. Mar.18; 136) *Evans.* £24,000
- - **Anr. Copy.** Minor foxing. Cont. hf. mor., gt., slightly worn. The Harewood copy with bkplt. of Henry Charles, Viscount Lascelles. (S. Jun.1; 129) *Sbisa.* £20,000
- - **Anr. Copy.** Vol. 7 spine defect. (CNY. May 22; 199) $25,000
- - **Anr. Edn.** Apr. 2nd, 1855. Pt. 7 only. Fo. 17 cold. litho. plts., all plts. & text loose. Orig. bds., covers detchd., stitching brkn. W.a.f. (C. May 20; 210) *Burgess.* £450
- - **Anr. Edn.** Mar. 1st, 1871. Pt. 23 only. Fo. 15 cold. litho. plts. Orig. bds., covers detchd. W.a.f. (C. May 20; 211) *Lander.* £750
- The Birds of Australia & the adjacent Islands. L., Priv. ptd. 1837-38. 1st. Edn. Pts. I-II (all publd.). Fo. Plt. ll mntd. with tears in blank portion reprd. & slight damage by adhesion. Mod. hf. leath., orig. upr. wraps. & ptd. slip 'To Subscribers' bnd. in. Copy of John James Audubon; Maria Audubon (his grand-daughter) with her bkplt.; Leonard B. Audubon (his great-grandson), with xerox of a statement by him pasted inside upr. cover; from the Sir Edward & John E. Hallstrom Collection. (S. Jun.1; 125) *Maggs Brothers.* £7,500
- - **Anr. Copy.** Title & blank ll. at beginning & end foxed. Cont. hf. mor., spine gt. in compartments. (C. Nov.5; 61a) *Crozier.* £850
- - **Anr. Edn.** [1837-38]. 4to. Without title prelims. or index. Hf. leath., worn. (S. Dec.3; 980) *Old Hall.* £550
[-] - **Anr. Copy.** (S. Jun.1; 127) *McCormick.* £420
- - **Anr. Edn.** Ill.:– J. & J.E. Gould & H.C. Richter. 1840-48. 4 vols. only (of 7). Fo. Comprising 33 plts. from vol. 1, 53 from vol. 5, 31 from vol. 6, & 32 from vol. 7, irregularly bnd. in the 4 vols., no titles or text, 2 plts. with sm. reprd. tears, minor foxing to some plts., some slight soiling. Cont. hf. mor., vell. corners, slightly soiled. W.a.f., from Chetham's Liby., Manchester. (C. Nov.26; 182) *Rabbits.* £17,000
- - **Anr. Edn.** [1840]-48; [1851]-69. 8 vols. including supp. Lge. fo. 681 hand-finished cold. litho. plts. Cont. mor., sides with gt. tooled borders, spines gt. in compartments, raised bands, by J. Wright. (C. Mar.18; 132) *Burgess.* £46,000
- - **Anr. Edn.** Melbourne, 1979. Facs. Edn., (500) numbered. Fo. Canvas bds. (KH. Mar.24; 172) Aus. $240
- - **Anr. Copy.** (387) numbered. Hf. mor., card. s.-c. (KH. Mar.24; 176) Aus. $150
- - **Anr. Edn.** Melbourne, n.d. Facs. Edn. Vol. II only. Fo. Plastic cl. (KH. Mar.24; 170) Aus. $140

- The Birds of Europe. Ill.:– Elizabeth Gould & Edward Lear. [1832]-1827. 5 vols. Lge. fo. 448 hand-finished cold. litho. plts. Cont. hf. cf. (C. Mar.18; 130) *Burgess.* £13,000
- The Birds of Great Britain. [1862-]73. 5 vols. Lge. fo. 367 hand-finished cold. litho. plts. Cont. mor., covers with floral roll tool border, by Holloway. (C. Mar.18; 138) *Krausse.* £10,000
- - **Anr. Edn.** Ill.:– Walter & Cohn after Gould, H.C. Richter, W. Hart & Joseph Wolf. 1873. Ltd. Edn. 5 vols. Fo. Ribbed hf. mor. gt. Bkplt. of James Cowan Smith, Bothamsall Hall. (CE. Nov.20; 197) £9,200
- The Birds of Great Britain.-Introduction to the Birds of Great Britain. Ill.:– W. Hart after Gould, H.C. Richter, & Josef Wolf. 1862-73; 1873. 25 orig. pts.; 1 vol. Lge. fo. & 8vo. Orig. ptd. bds., cl. spines; orig. embossed cl. 2nd. work Pres. Copy. (C. Nov.5; 62) *Smith.* £11,000
- The Birds of New Guinea. 1875-88. 5 vols. Fo. Mod. hf. mor., gt. (S. Jun.1; 133) *Hammond.* £15,000
- - **Anr. Copy.** 1 lf. detchd. Cont. hf.-mor., spines gt. in compartments, by W.J. Mansell. (C. Mar.18; 139) *Krausse.* £14,000
- A Century of Birds from the Himalaya Mountains. Ill.:– C. Hullmandel. 1832. Lge. fo. 80 hand-finished cold. litho. plts., grounds uncold. Cont. maroon hf. mor. (C. Mar.18; 129) *Henniges.* £3,000
- Handbook to the Birds of Australia. L., 1865. Vols. 1 & 2. Some foxing. Decor. cl. (JL. Mar.2; 729) Aus. $130
- Icones Avium, or Figures & Descriptions of New & Interesting Birds ... L., Priv. ptd., 1837-38. 2 pts. (all publd.). Fo. Plts. 1 & 13 bkd., 1st. with long tear reprd., brown stain in upr. margin of 1st. few ll. in pt. 2. Mod. hf. leath. Copy of John James Audubon, with a sigd. pencil note in his hand; Maria Audubon (his grand-daughter), with her bkplt.; Leonard B. Audubon (his great-grandson) with Xerox of a statement by him pasted inside upr. cover; from the Sir Edward & John E. Hallstrom Collection. (S. Jun.1; 131) *Traylen.* £2,800
- The Mammals of Australia. [1845]-63. 3 vols. Lge. fo. Cont. hf. mor. (C. Mar.18; 134) *Quaritch.* £11,500
- A Monograph of the Odontophorinae, or Partridges of America. [1844]-50. Lge. fo. Cont. hf. mor. (C. Mar.18; 133) *Quaritch.* £3,500
- - **Anr. Edn.** L., 1850. Fo. Lacks plts. 5, 6, 11, 16 & 19, some spotting. Cont. mor. gt. The Markree Castle copy. (SPB. Oct.1; 197) $3,750
- Monograph of the Pittidae. 1880-81. Pts. 1 & 2 (all publd.) Lge. fo. Orig. cl.-bkd. bds., orig. wrap. to Pt. 2 bnd. in, mod. buckram s.-c. (C. Jul.15; 182) *Taylor.* £900
- A Monograph of the Ramphastidae, or Family of Toucans. [1852]-54. Lge. fo. 51 hand-finished cold. litho. plts., & 1 uncold. plt. Cont. mor., covers with broad gt. borders, spine gt., inner dentelles, by J. Andrews, Bloomsbury. (C. Mar.18; 137) *Krausse.* £3,800
- A Monograph of the Trochilidae or Humming Birds. L., 1849-61. Orig. 25 pts. Atlas fo. 356 (of 360) hand-cold. litho. plts., lacks 1 or 2 text ll. Loose, orig. ptd. bds. preserved. (SG. Oct.9; 119) $30,000
- - **Anr. Edn.** Ill.:– Hullmandel & Walton etc. after John Gould & H.C. Richter. L., Priv. ptd., [1849-] 1861. 5 vols., without the supp. Fo. Slight foxing to title-pp. Cont. hf. mor. gt. (CNY. Oct.1; 140) $35,000
- - **Anr. Edn.** Ed.:– Richard Bowdler Sharpe. [1849-]61; [1880]-87. 6 vols. including supp. Lge. fo. Cont. hf. mor., spines gt. in compartments, raised bands. (C. Mar.18; 135) *Elstein.* £19,500
- - **Anr. Edn.** 1861. 1st. Edn. 5 vols., lacks supp. Lge. fo. Cont. mor. by F. Bedford, gt., spines tooled in compartments, covers with elab. decor., gt. inside borders. (S. Nov.24; 140) *Quaritch.* £13,000
- - **Anr. Edn.** 1861-87. 6 vols., including supp. Fo. Slight foxing on a few ll. Cont. mor., gt., supp. bnd. to match in similar but not identical style (pastedowns of this vol. slightly cockled). (S. Jun.1; 130) *Arader.* £17,000
- - **Anr. Copy.** A little spotting. Spines tooled in compartments with arabesque ornaments, covers with elaborate border, supp. mod. mor. by Sangorski & Sutcliffe, in matching style, 1st. 5 vols. slightly rubbed, gt. inner borders. (S. Dec.3; 982) *Vischer.* £12,000

– **A Monograph of the Trogonidae or Family of Trogons.** Ill.:– C. Hullmandel. 1838. Lge. fo. Cont. hf. mor., spine gt. (C. Mar.18; 131) *Wheldon & Wesley.* £2,500
– **A Synopsis of the Birds of Australia.** 1837-38. Cont. hf. mor. gt. Sig. of W.H. Suttor & MS. index in his hand. (C. Jul.15; 181) *Quaritch.* £1,500

GOULD, Robert Freke
– **The History of Freemasonry.** Edinb., n.d. 2 vols. 4to. Orig. hf. mor. (CSK. May 22; 125) £50

GOUPIL Fesquet, F.A.A.
– **Voyage d'Horace Vernet en Orient.** Paris, [1843]. 1st. Printing. Lge. 8vo. Some slight foxing. Roan, arms in centre, smooth decor. spine. (HD. Jun.25; 266) Frs. 1,400

GOURDAULT, Jules
– **La Suisse ...** Paris, 1879. 2 vols. Lge. fo. Publisher's chagrin, upr. covers with arms of Switzerland, spines with raised bands. (HD. Jun.29; 274) Frs. 4,000

GOURLAY, Robert
– **General Introduction to Statistical Account of Upper Canada.–Statistical Account of Upper Canada.** L., 1822; [1822]. 2 works in 3 vols., 2nd. work 2 vols. 2nd. work: lacks frontis. to vol. 1, lacks title-p. in each vol., lge. folding map supplied in facs., vol. 1 slightly soiled. Both hf. leath. (CB. Sep.24; 82) Can. $500

GOURMONT, Remy de
– **Le Longe d'une Femme.** Ill.:– Jean-Emile Laboureur. Paris, 1925. (385) numbered. 4to. Crushed hf. lev., orig. wraps. bnd. in, bkplt. (SG. Apr.2; 168) $160

GOURVILLE, Jean Hérault de
– **Mémoires ... depuis 1642, jusqu'en 1698.** Paris, 1724. Orig. Edn. 2 vols. 12mo. Cont. cf., decor. spines. (HD. Feb.18; 23) Frs. 1,700

GOURY, Jules
See–JONES, Owen & Goury, Jules

GOUTHOEVEN, Valerius Van
– **D'Oude Chronijcke ende Historien van Holland [met West Vriesland] van Zeeland ende van Utrecht.** Dordrecht, 1620. 2 pts. in 1 vol. Fo. Some light traces of use, browned thro.-out, sm. corner of 1st. title torn. Cont. limp vell., defect. & soiled. (VG. Nov.18; 1181) Fls. 800

GOUTTARD
– **Catalogue des Livres Rares et Précieux.** Ed.:– Mérard de St. Just. Paris, 1780. L.P. Priced thro.-out. Cont. mor., triple gt. fillet, spine gt. in compartments, inner gt. dentelles. Bkplt. of Maurice Escoffier. (SM. Oct.7; 1391) Frs. 4,100

GOWER, Foote
See–BURNABY, Rev. Andrew–GOWER, Foote

GOWER, Lord Ronald Sutherland.
– **Sir Thomas Lawrence.** 1900. Ltd. Edn. 4to. Hf. mor., partly unc. (P. Feb.19; 262) *Cohen.* £60

GOWERS, Sir William Richard
– **The Border-Land of Epilepsy.** 1907. 1st. Edn. 8 ll. advts. dtd. Sep. 1908. Orig. cl. (S. Jun.16; 353) *Whitehart.* £110
– **A Manual of Diseases of the Nervous System.** 1886-88. 1st. Edn. 2 vols. Orig. cl. (S. Jun.16; 350) *Canale.* £80
– – **Anr. Copy.** Hf.-titles in vol. I not called for in vol. II, release stp. of Royal College of Surgeons, Edinb., on title & hf.-title. Orig. cl., vol. II with tears in spine, vol. I with stp. of liby. of Royal College of Surgeons, Edinb., on spine. From liby. of Dr. E. Ashworth Underwood. (S. Feb.23; 212) *Dawson.* £70
– – **Anr. Edn.** 1892-93. 2nd. Edn. 2 vols. Orig. cl. (S. Jun.16; 351) *Harding.* £85

GOYA y Lucientes, Francisco José de
– **Los Caprichos.** 1799. 1st Printing. Fo. Compl. set of 80 orig. aquatints in homogeneous proofs, with all margins, ll. 320 × 218mm, foxing in upr. right corner of 1st. 40 ll. & in margins, worming, sm. holes outside subject of plt. 1. Disbnd., preserved in 18th. C. bdg., red mor., dentelle. (HD. Mar.18; 78) Frs. 220,000
– – **Anr. Edn.** Madrid, 1868. 4to. Hf. leath. (H. Dec.9/10; 1510) DM 17,500
– – **Anr. Edn.** N.d. 6th. or 7th. Printing. Ob. 4to. Publisher's bds. (HD. Jun.25; 267) Frs. 18,500
– **Los Proverbios.** [Madrid], [1904]. Ob. fo. Hf. vell. (H. Dec.9/10; 1511) DM 6,900

GOZZI, Gaspare
– **Giudizio degli Antichi Poeti Sopre la Moderna Censura di Dante ...** Ill.:– Baratti, Magnini, Giampicoli & Scagiaro. Venice, 1758. 4to. Orig. paper bds., unc. From the collection of John A. Saks. (C. Jun.10; 100) *Witt.* £60

GOZZI, G. & others
– **Poesie per l'ingresso solenne di sua Eccellenza il Signor Gio. Girolami Zuccato.** Albrizzi, ca. 1770. Fo. Orig. Italian gt. decor. wraps. (BS. Jun.11; 218) £380

GRACE, Henry
– **The History of the Life & Sufferings of ...** Basingstoke, 1764. Ex-liby. 19th. C. three-qtr. mor. (SG. May 14; 89) $375

GRACE, William Gilbert
– **Cricket.** 1891. (662) numbered, sigd. by author. 4to. Orig. hf. mor. gt., worn, spine defect. (SD. Feb.4; 151) £85

GRACIA, B.
– **Uomo di Corte.** Altenburg, 1723. Cont. paper-bkd. wood bds., upr. cover defect. at corners. (HK. May 15; 4369) DM 500

GRAESSE, Jean George Theodor
– **Bibliotheca Magica et Pneumatica.** Leipzig, 1843. Some foxing. Hf. cl. (SG. Jan.22; 279) $140
– **Trésor de Livres Rares et Precieux.** Milan, 1950. 8 vols. 4to. Orig. cl. (SM. Oct.7; 1393) Frs. 1,900
– – **Anr. Copy.** 8 vols. including supp. (SI. Dec.3; 266) Lire 280,000

GRAFF, Regnerus de
– **Tractatus Anatomico-Medicus de Succi Pancreatici natura et usa.** Leyden, 1671. Sm. tear in 1 plt. Cont. cf., worn, upr. cover detchd. (C. Feb.25; 12a) *Phelps.* £120

GRAFTON, Richard
– [–] **A Chronicle.** 1569. Fo. Last lf. soiled. Cont. cf., blind-stpd., initials F.M. stpd. in gt., mod. rebacking & end-papers. [STC 12147] (CSK. May 1; 136) £280
– [–] – **Anr. Edn.** 1569-68. 2nd. Edn. 2 vols. in 1. Fo. Some dampstaining, title cropped, lacks 6B6? & last lf. (blank ?). Late 18th. C. spr. cf. [STC 12147] (S. Sep.29; 35) *Rix.* £150

GRAFTON, Duke of
– [–] **A Catalogue of a Most Elegant Collection of Books ... part of the Extensive Library of a Nobleman.** 1815. Cont. hf.-cf., spine gt. (SM. Oct.7; 1394) Frs. 1,200

GRAHAM, Clive & Curling, Bill
– **The Grand National.** Arcadia Pr., 1973. (105) numbered, sigd. by the authors. Fo. Orig. mor., gt. inner dentelles. (CSK. Sep.12; 111) £58

GRAHAM, Capt. G.A.
– **The Irish Wolfhound.** Dursley, 1885. Irish Wolfhound Club stp. on title. Cl.-bkd. bds., worn. (SG. Apr.9; 361) $150

GRAHAME, Maria
– [–] **Voyage of H.M.S. Blonde to the Sandwich Islands in the Years 1824-25 ... by Captain Byron.** 1826. [1st. Edn.?] 4to. Lacks rear end-paper. Orig. bds., spine worn. (TA. Jan.22; 375) £320
– – **Anr. Copy.** Maps & charts all cl.-bkd., 2 text ll. torn. Cont. hf. reversed cf., worn, upr. cover detchd. Ex-liby with Willan's British & Foreign Public Liby. plt. preserved on end-p. (SBA. Oct.21; 109) *Hinchcliffe.* £220

GRAHAME, Kenneth
– **The Golden Age.** Ill.:– Ernest Howard Shepard. 1928. (275) sigd. by author & artist. Orig. bds. (SH. Dec.10; 223) *Mirdan.* £50
– **The Wind in the Willows.** Ill.:– Arthur Rackham. N.Y., 1940. Orig. cl. gt., d.-w. torn. (SH. Dec.11; 445) *Mundy.* £75
– – **Anr. Edn.** Ed.:– A.A. Milne (intro.). Ill.:– Arthur Rackham. N.Y., Ltd. Edns. Cl., 1940. (2,020) numbered, designed & sigd. by Bruce Rogers. 4to. Cl.-bkd. patterned bds., partly unc. & unopened, orig s.-c. Raymond M. Sutton Jr. copy. (SG. May 7; 95) $900
– – **Anr. Copy.** Fo. Buckram-bkd. batik bds. (SG. Oct.23; 283) $550
– – **Anr. Copy.** (1,500) numbered, designed & sigd. by Bruce Rogers. 4to. Cl.-bkd. patterned bds., box split. (SG. Apr.9; 498) $450
– – **Anr. Copy.** (220) sigd. by Bruce Rogers. Fo. Orig. bdg. (SPB. Nov.25; 296) $425

– – **Anr. Copy.** (1500) numbered, & sigd. by Bruce Rogers. 4to. Cl.-bkd. patterned bds., stained, orig. box (recovered.). (SG. Jan.15; 193) $375
– – **Anr. Edn.** Ill.:– Arthur Rackham. L., [1950]. 4to. Cl., d.-w. Raymond M. Sutton Jr. copy. (SG. May 7; 97) $100
– – **Anr. Edn.** Ill.:– Arthur Rackham. 1951. Ltd. Edn. 4to. Pig. gt., unc. & unopened, s.-c. Out of series pres. copy. (P. Apr.9; 194) *Marks.* £280
– – **Anr. Copy.** Orig. pig., carton. (P. Dec.11; 210) *Thorp.* £200
– – **Anr. Edn.** Ill.:– Arthur Rackham. [1951]. (500) numbered. 4to. This copy unnumbered? Orig. vell., d.-w., s.-c. (CSK. Aug.22; 179) £220
– – **Anr. Copy.** Cf., partly unc. & unopened, orig. box worn. Raymond M. Sutton Jr. copy. (SG. May 7; 98) $500

GRAIMBERG, Charles de
– **Ansichten der Stadt, des Schlosses und der Umgebungen von Heidelberg.** Heidelberg, ca. 1840. Ob. fo. Slightly soiled in places. Orig. bds. (R. Oct.14-18; 2155) DM 2,800
– **Guide dans les Ruines du Château de Heidelberg.** Heidelberg, ca. 1860. Ob. fo. Soiled in parts, cold. lithos. torn. Mod. leath. (R. Mar.31-Apr.4; 1909) DM 3,800
– **Le Guide des Voyageurs dans la Ruine de Heidelberg.** Heidelberg, 1856. Slightly soiled in places. Cont. hf. linen. (R. Oct.14-18; 2156) DM 850
– **Guide to the Ruins of Heidelberg Castle.** Ill.:– after v. Graimberg. Heidelberg, ca. 1850. Clemens Perkes ... bnd. at front. Orig. bds., lacking spine with pasted paper. (HK. Nov.18-21; 1078) DM 650

GRAINGER, James
– **The Sugar-Cane. A Poem.** L., 1764. 1st. Edn. 4to. Slight offsetting. Mod. hf. mor., gt. (SPB. May 5; 237) $225

GRAMONT, Comte Ferdinand de
See–BALZAC, Honoré de & others.

GRANADA, Luis de [i.e. Ludovicus Granatensis]
– **Conciones quae de Praecipius Sanctorum Festis in Ecclesia habentur; Secondus Tomus concionum ... Tertius Tomus concionum.** Antw., 1584-88. Together 3 vols. Some browning. Cont. Spanish cf., blind-stpd., with arms of Franciscan Order on covers, slightly worn, arms possibly connected with owner's stp. on titles, which appears to be that of a Prince de Bauffremont. (S. Oct.21; 526) *Thomas.* £300
– **Ecclesiasticae Rhetoricae ...** Cologne, 1578. 1st. Edn. Owner's mark on title, 2 bkplts. Cont. blind-stpd. pig-bkd. wood bds., painted arms on upr. cover, 2 clasps, lacks 1 tie. (HK. Nov.18-21; 202) DM 420
– **A Memoriall of a Christian Life.** Rouen, 1586. 1st. Edn. in Engl. Some worming, occasionally affecting text, slight dampstaining, some MS. underlinings. Cont. limp vell., worn. [STC 16903] (S. Feb.9; 183) *Erasmus.* £120

GRANADOS Y GALVEZ, Joseph Joaquin
– **Tardes Americanas: Gobierno Gentil y Catolico: Breve y Particular Noticia de Toda la Historia Indiana.** Mexico, 1778. Sm. 4to. 1 plt. slightly cropped in outer edge. Cont. mott. cf., slightly warped. [Sabin 28255] (SPB. May 5; 238) $850

GRANCSAY, Stephen V.
– **The Bashford Dean Collection of Arms & Armour in the Metropolitan Museum of Art.** –**Catalogue of Armor.** Ed.:– C.O. v. Kienbusch. (1st. work). Portland, Southworth Pr., 1933; 1961. (250) 1st. work. Hf. buckram, partly unc. (SG. Feb.26; 34) $220

GRAND, Gordon
– **Colonel Weatherford & His Friends.–Old Man, & other Colonel Weatherford Stories.–The Southborough Fox.** 1933; 1934; 1939. Ltd. Edns. 3 works in 3 vols. Gt.-decor. cl. Each sigd. on hf.-title. (SG. Dec.11; 249) $100
– **Colonel Weatherford's Young Entry.** Ill.:– Paul Brown. 1935. (1350). Cl., owner's ticket & blind-stp. on endpaper. (SG. Dec.11; 244) $120
– **The Silver Horn, & other Sporting Tales.** Ill.:– J. Alden Twachtman. 1932. (950). Gt.-decor. bds. Inscr. to Bikie Ewing on hf.-title. (SG. Dec.11; 237) $100

GRAND JURIES (The) of the County of Westmeath from the year 1727 to the year 1853. Ledestown, 1853. 2 vols. in 1. Some MS. additions. Cl., reprd. (GM. Apr.30; 298) £160

GRAND LIVRE DE LA NATURE, ou l'Apocalypse Philosophique et Hermetique ... vu par une Societé de Ph. ... Inc. ... et Publié par D. [1790?]. New cl. (S. Dec.2; 498) *Quaritch.* £80

GRAND TOUR ON A COACH BOX (A) 1811. 12mo. MS. corrections & deletions (by the author?) on 52 pp., E1 reprd. 19th. C. red hf. mor. (S. Dec.8; 43) *Quaritch.* £65

GRAND-CARTERET, John
- **Les Almanachs Français, Bibliographie-Iconographie.** Paris, 1896. 1st. Edn., on Vell. Orig. wraps., mostly unopened. (SM. Oct.7; 1395) Frs. 2,000
- - **Anr. Edn.** Paris, 1896. Ltd. Edn. Lge. 8vo. Red hf. mor., wrap. preserved. (SM. Feb.11; 7) Frs. 1,100
- - **Anr. Edn.** Paris, 1896. (1200) numbered. Crude buckram. Bkplt. of Richard Wormser. (SG. Jan.22; 186) $180
- **L'Histoire, la Vie, les Moeurs et le Curiosité par l'Image, le Pamphlet et le Document [1450-1900].** Paris, 1927-28. (200) on Japon, numbered. 5 vols. 4to. Orig. hf. chagrin, covers & spines gt., some sm. stains. (SM. Feb.11; 27) Frs. 1,000

GRANDIDIER, Alfred & Milne-Edwards, Alphonse
- **Histoire Physique, Naturelle et Politique de Madagascar: Mammiferes.** Paris, 1875-90. Vols. VI, IX & X only. 4to. Mor.-bkd. bds., vol. X cl. bnd., non-unif. W.a.f. (C. Nov.5; 63) *Wheldon & Wesley.* £300

GRANDJEAN de Montigny, A. H. V.
- **Plan, Coupe, élévation et détails de la Restauration du Palais des Etats et de sa Nouvelle Salle.** [Paris], [1810]. Fo. Cont. marb. bds., orig. ptd. wraps. bnd. in. (S. Jun.22; 35) *Quaritch.* £180

GRANDJEAN de Montigny, A. & Famin, A.
- **Architecture Toscane, ou Palais, Maisons et Autres Edifices de la Toscane.** Paris, 1815. Fo. Lacks 1 engraved plt. Cont. mor.-bkd. bds. (SH. Nov.6; 209) *Cramer.* £50

GRANDPRE, Louis de
- **Voyage in the Indian Ocean & to Bengal.** 1803. 2 vols. Cf. gt. (P. Oct.23; 27) *Brooke-Hitching.* £210

GRANDVILLE, Jean Jacques (Pseud.)
See–GERARD, Jean Ignace Isidore 'Jean Jacques Grandville'

GRANET, J.J.
- **Histoire de l'Hotel Royal des Invalides ... Ill.:**– Cochin & Chauveau. Paris, 1736. Fo. Cont. red mor., gt. fillets & roulettes border round lge. dentelle, centre arms, decor. spine raised bands, inner dentelle. (HD. Apr.24; 68) Frs. 12,000

GRANGER, Rev. James
- **A Biographical History of England.** 1824. 10 vols. Fo. Extra-ill. with many mntd. engraved, mezzotint, aquatint & other port. plts. (including some in proof state) by P. Lely, W. Hollar, Van der Gucht, & others. Cont. hf. mor., spines gt. in compartments with floral centrepieces, partly unc., by Tout. W.a.f. From the collection of Eric Sexton. (C. Apr.16; 262) *Grosvenor.* £450

GRANNIS, Ruth S.
- **Descriptive Catalogue of the First Editions in Book form of Percy Bysshe Shelley.** N.Y., Grol. Cl., 1923. (350). Bds., unc., unopened. (SG. Oct.2; 331) $130

GRANT, Andrew
- **History of Brazil.** 1809. 1st. Edn. Slight browning. Hf. cf., spine gt. [Sabin 28291] (S. Feb.9; 184) *Maggs.* £160
See–CRAMER, G. & others.

GRANT, George Munro
- **Picturesque Canada; the Country as it Was & Is ... Illustrated under the Supervision of L.R. O'Brien, Pres. R.C.A.** Toronto, 1882. 2 vols. Fo. A few pp. shaken. Orig. ornate gt.-stpd. pict. cl. (PWP. Apr.9; 213) Can. $160
- - **Anr. Edn.** [1882]. 2 vols. 4to. Foxing, vol. 2 lacks free end-papers. Hf. cf. gt. (PL. Nov.27; 135) *Collins.* £75
- - **Anr. Copy.** Fo. Three-qtr. cf., spines gt. (SG. Mar.5; 79) $300

- - **Anr. Copy.** 4to. Occasional marginal staining. Orig. bdg., brkn. & worn. (CB. Dec.9; 187) Can. $150
- - **Anr. Edn.** L., ca. 1885. 2 vols. Sm. fo. Hf. roan, worn. (SG. May 21; 417) $120
- - **Anr. Edn.** Toronto, n.d. 4to. Orig. cl., rebkd. (CB. May 27; 297) Can. $150

GRANT, James
- **The Tartans of the Clans of Scotland.** 1886. 1st. Edn., (100). Lge. fo. Cont. cf., gt., by Curloss. (S. Apr.7; 502) *Maggs.* £110
- - **Anr. Copy.** 4to. Orig. cl., gt., slightly worn, loose. (SH. Oct.10; 456) *Bunsei.* £50

GRANT, James Augustus
- **A Walk Across Africa.** 1864. Folding map in pocket, some ll. spotted. Orig. cl., recased. (SH. Mar.5; 62) *Dawson's.* £100

GRANTLEY, Lord
- **Catalogue of Coins.** 1943-45. 11 vols. 4to. & 8vo. Orig. wraps. (SH. Mar.6; 358) *Sapori.* £190

GRANVILLE, Augustus Bozzi
- **Kissingen, its Sources & Resources.** L., 1846. Orig. linen. (R. Mar.31-Apr.4; 1950) DM 600

GRANVILLE, George, Lord Lansdowne
- **Genuine Works in Verse & Prose.** 1732. 4to. 1 lf. cleanly torn. Cont. cf., spine gt. (CSK. Jan.9; 82) £70
- [–] **The She-Gallants.** 1696. 1st. Edn. 4to. Tear in 1 lf. reprd., text on anr. cropped. Mor. by Sangorski. [Wing L423] (C. Nov.19; 107) *Blackwell.* £90

GRAPALDUS, Franciscus Marius
- **De Partibus Aedium.** [Parma], Angelus Ugoletus, [1494]. 1st. Edn. 4to. Unrubricated, sm. wormhole to last 13 ll., light dampstain to upr. portion of many ll., blank verso of last lf. soiled. Mor. gt., gt. dentelle borders, vell. doubls., by Gozzi, mor.-tipped s.-c. From the collection of Eric Sexton. [BMC VII, 945, Goff G349] (CNY. Apr.8; 130) $5,500

GRAPHIC Illustrations of Animals
Ill.:– William Hawkins. Ca. 1855. Fo. Lacks 1 plt. Orig. roan gt. (SH. Dec.10; 31) *Russell.* £60

GRAPHICS 70
Ed.:– Donald H. Karshan. Ill.:– Richard Anuskiewicz, Alexander Calder & others. N.Y., 1970. Tall fo. 6 sigd. prints. Bd. folder as iss. (SG. Oct.23; 6) $700

GRAPPE, George
- **H. Fragonard ...** Paris, 1913. On Japon, numbered. 2 vols. 4to. Hf. mor. by Stroobants, unc., wraps. & spines. (HD. Dec.5; 96) Frs. 1,100

GRASS, Guenter
- **Liebe Geprueft: Love Tested.** Trans.:– Michael Hamburger. N.Y., [1975]. (120) with each etching numbered & sigd. Lge. fo. Loose in linen folding case. (SG. Oct.23; 146) $275

GRASSET de Saint-Sauveur, André
- **Voyage Historique ...** Paris, An VIII [1800]. 3 vols. (lacks atlas). Cont. tree cf., garland in border, decor. spines. (HD. Mar.18; 79) Frs. 1,800

GRASSET de Saint-Sauveur, Jacques
- **Encyclopedie des Voyages: Afrique.** Paris, 1796. 1st. Edn. 4to. Lacks 1 copper engr., title & 1st. lf. stpd., 1 copper engr. torn slightly, some sm. stains in parts. Later hf. leath., slightly worn, unc. (H. Dec.9/10; 489) DM 1,600
- **Le Sérail, ou Histoire des Intrigues Secrètes et Amoureuses des Femmes du Grand Seigneur.–Les Amours de Fameux Comte de Bonneval, Pacha à deux Queues.** Paris (1st. work), 1796. 2 vols. in 1. 18mo. Hf. roan, decor. spine, ca. 1820. (HD. Apr.10; 337) Frs. 1,400

[GRASSHOFF, Johann]–RHENANUS, Johann
- **Harmoniae Inperscrutabilis Chymico-Philosophicae sive Philosophorum Antiquorum Consentientium ... Decas I ... collectae ab H.C. D.–Harmoniae Chymico-Philosophicae ... decas II.** Frankfurt, 1625. 2 pts. in 1 vol. Paper browned. Cont. cf. The Hopetoun copy. (S. Dec.1; 189) *Weiner.* £650

GRASSI, Giacomo di
- **Ragione di Addoprar Sicuramente l'Arme si da Offensa come a Difensa.** Venice, 1570. 1st. Edn. 4to. Title reprd. in margin, some ll. slightly soiled or spotted, 2 owners' inscrs. defaced, stp. 19th. C. mor. (S. Jul.27; 269) *Pilo.* £260

GRASTORF, Dennis J. & Marilyn
- **Wood Type of the Angelica Press.** [Brooklyn], Angelica Pr., [1975]. (220) numbered. Atlas fo. 4 monographs in loose sheet form. Folders with cover labels, unc., in wooden folding case, metal clasps. (SG. Apr.9; 418) $170

GRATIANUS
- **Decretum [with a commentary of Bartholomaei Brixiensis].** [Mainz], [Peter Schoeffer], [13 Aug. 1472]. 3rd. Edn. Fo. Spaces for capital initials, lacks final blank, 50 mm. blank marginal repair to 1st. lf. Ir. outer blank corner of fo. 317 cut-away, some slight soiling to a very few blank margins only, fo. 2v & some 6 other ll. with early ink deletions to some lines. Made-up bdg. of old mor. upr. cover & matching 18th. C. diced russ. Ir. cover, mor. spine gt., rebkd. & restored. [BMC I, 29, Goff G362, Hain 7885*] (CNY. Oct.1; 97) $14,000

GRATIOLET, Louis Pierre
See–LEURET, François & Gratiolet, Louis Pierre

GRATTAN, Thomas Colley
- **The Heiress of Bruges.** Paris & Brussels, 1830. 1st. Edn? 12mo. Some foxing. Early cf. (SG. Mar.19; 205) $110

GRATTELARD, Baron de
See–TABARIN, Grattelard, Baron de

GRATTENAUER, K.W.F.
- [–] **Wider die Juden. Ein Wort der Warnung an Alle Unsere Christliche Mitbuerger.** Berlin, 1803. 5th. Edn. Cl. (S. Nov.18; 660) *Valmadonna.* £100

GRATULATIO ACADEMIAE OXONIENSIS in nuptias auspicatissimas ... Principum Frederici Principis Walliae et Augustae Principissae de Saxo Gotha
Oxford, 1736. Fo. Old British Museum stp. on title verso & last lf. Cont. red mor. gt., rebkd., corners reprd. (C. Jul.16; 350a) *Waters.* £60

GRATULATORIA del Procurator di S. Marco Lodovico Manin ... della Citta di Udine
Ill.:– Pitteri after Angeli. Venice, 1764. Thick paper. Sm. fo. Orig. woodblock ptd. paper wraps., buckram s.-c. From the collection of John A. Saks. (C. Jun.10; 102) *Lyon.* £300

GRAUNT, John
- **Natural & Political Observations ... Made upon the Bills of Mortality.** 1665. 3rd Edn. 1 chart rebkd., lacks last (? blank) lf., slight browning. 18th C. cf., gt., rebkd. with mor. [Wing G1600] (S. May 5; 115) *Rota.* £120
- - **Anr. Edn.** Ed.:– Sir William Petty. 1676. 5th. Edn. Cont. sheep. [Wing G.1602] (S. Oct.20; 97) *Dawson.* £260
- - **Anr. Copy.** Licence lf. worn in fold, sm. tear in each of the lge. folding tables, slight staining thro.-out in lr. margin. Later cf.-bkd. cl. [Wing G1602] (C. Apr.1; 179) *Lawson.* £160

GRAVELOT, Hubert François Bourguignon
- **Almanach Iconologique, Année 1771.** Paris, [1770]. 1 vol. (of 17). 12mo. A few stains. Cont. Fr. red mor. (SH. Jun.4; 109) *Erlini.* £55

GRAVES, Algernon
- **Royal Academy of Arts: A Complete Dictionary of Contributors & their Work from its Foundation in 1769 to 1904.** 1905-06. 8 vols. 4to. Qtr. mor. (TA. Oct.16; 116) £180

GRAVES, Algernon & Cronin, William Vine
- **A History of the Works of Sir Joshua Reynolds.** 1899. (6) Extra-ill. on L.P. 13 vols., including Addenda. Lge. fo. Vol. I with 2 MS. ll. (a descriptive note of E.E. Leggatt & a list of unpubld. plts.), very occasional marginal spotting. Cont. gt.-lettered hf. mor. W.a.f. From the collection of Eric Sexton. (C. Apr.15; 69) *Saunders.* £500

GRAVES, George
- **British Ornithology.** 1811-13. Vols. 1-2 (of 3). Lacks hf.-title in vol. 1 (none called for in vol. 2?). Hf. russ., worn. (S. Dec.3; 984) *Wagner.* £170
- - **Anr. Edn.** 1821. [2nd. Edn.?]. 3 vols. in 1. Cont. hf. mor. (C. Mar.18; 46) *Taylor.* £1,200
- - **Anr. Edn.** 1821. 2nd. Edn. 144 hand-cold. engraved plts. (C. Jul.15; 184) *Hill.* £900

GRAVES, Rev. John
- **History of Cleveland in the North Riding of the County of York.** Carlisle, 1808. 4to. Slight

spotting. Cont. hf. cf. (SBA. Oct.22; 322a)
Kelsall. £55

GRAVES, Rev. John–HORNER, John
- **The History of Cleveland.–Buildings in the Town & Parish of Halifax.** Carlisle; Halifax, 1808; 1835. 2 works in 2 vols. 4to. & ob. fo. Foxing at beginning & end of 2nd. work. Cont. hf. vell., gt.; cont. red mor., gt. borders on side, worn, spine torn. (C. Nov.6; 308) *Weinreb.* £180

GRAVES, Robert
- **Country Sentiment.** 1920. 1st. Edn. Orig. decor. bds., d.-w. worn. Pres. copy to J. Isaacs, A.N.s., pencil autog. poem loosely inserted. (S. Jul.22; 140) *Blackwell.* £160
- **The Feather Bed.** Hogarth Pr., 1923. 1st. Edn., (250) sigd. 4to. Orig. decor. bds., designed by William Nicholson, unc., unopened. (SH. Dec.18; 173) *Sawyer.* £90
- – **Anr. Copy.** 3 Hogarth Pr. notices loosely inserted. (SH. Dec.18; 172) *Rota.* £80
- **Goliath & David.** [1916]. 1st. Edn. (200). Sm. 4to. Orig. wraps., unc. Pres. copy to J. Isaacs, 1920. (S. Jul.22; 138) *Horowitz.* £420
- – **Anr. Copy.** Inscr. to Walter de la Mare, A.N. on p.10. (SH. Dec.18; 169) *Barry Scott.* £370
- **Goodbye to All That.** L., [1929]. 1st. Edn. 1st. state, with the poem by Sassoon on pp.341-343. Orig. cl., d.-w., qtr. mor. gt. s.-c. From the Prescott Collection. (CNY. Feb.6; 132) $350
- **Over the Brazier.** 1916. 1st. Edn. Orig. pict. wraps., designed by C. Lovat Smith, unc. 'Pres. Copy' stpd. on title. (SH. Dec.18; 168) *Maggs.* £100
- **Ten Poems More.** Paris, Hours Pr., 1930. 1st. Edn. (200) numbered, sigd. Orig. mor.-bkd. pict. bds., unc. (S. Jul.22; 149) *Conway.* £120
- – **Anr. Edn.** Paris, Hours Pr., 1930. (200). Fo. Mor.-bkd. photographic bds. by Len Lye, slightly worn. (SPB. Jul.28; 161) $100
- **Treasure Box.** Ill.:– Nancy Nicholson. [1919]. 1st. Edn. (200). Sm. 4to. Orig. wraps. Inscr. by author & artist to F.A. Porter. (S. Jul.22; 139) *Scott-McCarthy.* £260
- **Whipperginny.** 1923. 1st. Edn. Orig. decor. bds., d.-w. (S. Jul.22; 141) *B. Marks.* £62

GRAVES, Robert & Hart, Liddell
- **T.E. Lawrence to his Biographer.** 1938. 1st. Edn., (1000) sigd., unnumbered. 2 vols. Orig. buckram. (SH. Dec.18; 174) *Chelsea.* £105

GRAVES, Robert James
- **A System of Clinical Medicine.** Dublin, 1843. 1st. Edn. Advt. lf., liby. stp. on title. Orig. cl. (S. Jun.16; 357) *Silver.* £50

GRAVESANDE, William Jacob S. van's
- **Mathematical Elements of Natural Philosophy ... or an Introduction to Sir Isaac Newton's Philosophy ...** Trans.:– J.T. Desaguliers. 1720. Some browning & spotting, some lr. margins wormed. Cont. cf. From liby. of Dr. E. Ashworth Underwood. (S. Feb.23; 214) *Rademaker.* £70
- – **Anr. Edn.** Trans.:– John Theophilus Desaguliers. 1747. 6th. Edn. 6 pts. in 2 vols. 4to. Advt. ll. Cont. cf. gt. (SBA. Jul.23; 385) *Minerva.* £150

Physica Elementa Mathematica.
- Leiden, 1748. 2 vols. 4to. Lightly browned in parts. cont. leath. gt., worn. (HK. Nov.18-21; 549) DM 440
- **Physices Elementa Mathematica, Experimentis Confirmata.** Leiden, 1725/1. Pt. 1 2nd. Edn.; pt. 2 1st. Edn. 2 vols. in 1. 4to. 71 (of 72) folding copperplt. engrs. Cont. cf. (TA. May 21; 425) £50

GRAVIER, Yves
- **Guide Pour le Voyage d'Italie en Poste.** Genoa, [1786]. New Edn. Mod. cf.-bkd. bds. (CSK. Jun.5; 153) £60

GRAVURES sur Bois Tirées des Livres Français du XVe Siècle
Paris, 1868. 4to. Mor. by Zaehnsdorf. (SH. Jun.25; 171) *Duran.* £60

GRAY, Andrew
- **The Plough-Wright's Assistant; or, a Practical Treatise on Various Implements employed in Agriculture.** Edinb., 1808. 1st. Edn. Some browning, inscr. on title. 19th. C. hf. cf. by J. Edmond, Aberdeen, with his ticket, spine gt. (S. Nov.4; 561) *Brook-Hitching.* £160

GRAY, Asa
- **Botany of the United States Expedition ... 1838-42.** Ill.:– Isaac Sprague. Phila., 1854. Atlas vol. XV only, Pt. 1 of the Wilkes Expedition. Fo. Without title or text. Mod. buckram. (SG. Sep.18; 394) $550
- **Report on the Forest Trees of America.** Ed.:– S.P. Langley. Wash., 1891. Fo. 23 plts. only, title-p. reprd. Mod. buckram. (SG. Nov.20; 345) $180

GRAY, David
- **Gallops I.–Gallops II.–Mr. Carteret.** Ill.:– Paul Brown. 1929. Hitchcock Edn., (750) numbered. 3 vols. Cl., sm. owner's label & blind-stp. on front free end-paper of each vol., unc. Sigd. (SG. Dec.11; 250) $110

GRAY, George Robert
- **A Fasciculus of the Birds of China.** Ill.:– W. Swainson. 1871. 4to. Orig. bds., covers stained, end-papers foxed. (C. Nov.5; 64) *Lestor.* £360
- – **Anr. Copy.** (P. Nov.13; 199) *Traylen.* £180
- **The Genera of Birds.** 1844-49. 3 vols. Lge. 4to. Cont. mor., gt. (C. Mar.18; 47) *Taylor.* £5,200
- – **Anr. Copy.** Fo. A few ll. loose. Cont. hf. mor. (S. June.1; 137) *Quaritch.* £3,200

GRAY, Henry
- **Anatomy Descriptive & Surgical.** Ill.:– H.V. Carter & author. 1858. 1st. Edn. 1 lf. advts. Orig. cl., in cl. box. (S. Jun.16; 359) *Whitehart.* £650
- – **Anr. Copy.** 1 lf. of advts., upr. blank margin of hf.-title with short tear. Upr. hinge torn at top. (S. Dec.2; 819) *Dawson.* £440
- – **Anr. Edn.** Phila., 1859. 1st. Amer. Edn. Considerable foxing, etc. Orig. sheep, worn & loose. (SG. Jan.29; 189) $160

GRAY, John
- **Silverpoints.** L., 1893. 1st. Edn., (250) numbered. Tall 8vo. Orig. gt.-decor. cl., water & willow lf. design by Ricketts, unc. From the Prescott Collection. (CNY. Feb.6; 408) $750
- – **Anr. Copy.** Gt.-decor. cl. Bkplt. of T.B. Mosher. (SG. Nov.13; 274) $500
- **Spiritual Poems.** Ill.:– Charles Ricketts. [L.], Vale Pr., [1897]. (210). Bds., soiled, unc. & unopened. (SG. Jan.15; 102) $160

GRAY, John Edward
- **Gleanings from the Menagerie & Aviary at Knowsley Hall.–Hoofed Quadrupeds.** Ill.:– J.W. Moore after Edward Lear (1st. work), by & after Waterhouse Hawkins (2nd. work). Knowsley, Priv. ptd., 1846; 1850. [1st. Series]; [2nd. Series]. 2 vols. in 1. Fo. 1st. title with cont. inscr. '... from the Earl of Derby', the name of recipient is erased, 2nd. vol. with a few captions cut into. Cont. inscr. gt. panel. russ. From the Powerscourt Liby., with inscr. by the 7th. Viscount. (S. Jun.1; 139) *Quaritch.* £2,300
- – **Anr. Edn.** Ill.:– after Edward Lear, & B.W. Hawkins. Knowsley, Priv. Ptd., 1846-50. 2 vols. in 1. Fo. Red hf. russ. Pres. Copy from the Earl of Derby & inscr. in both vols. on title. (C. Nov.5; 65) *Arader.* £1,900
- **Illustrations of Indian Zoology ... from the Collection of Major-General Hardwicke.** 1830-34. 2 vols. in 1. Fo. This copy without 2 listed plts. & has 2 others plain rather than cold., but with 5 plts. which are not mentioned in list of plts. & which are apparently unpublished. Hf. red mor., gt. by Sangorski & Sutcliffe. (S. Dec.3; 986) *Clarendon.* £2,400

GRAY, O.W.
*See–*WALLING, Henry F. & Gray, O.W.

GRAY, Prentiss N.
- **Records of North American Big Game.** 1932. (500). 4to. Buckram, ex-liby. (SG. Dec.11; 251) $850

GRAY, S.
*See–*SKOTNES, Cecil & Gray, S.

GRAY, Thomas
- **Designs by Mr. R. Bentley, for Six Poems by Mr. T. Gray.** 1753. Fo. Slight browning & spotting. Cont. cf., gt. spine. (S. Jun.22; 36) *Traylen.* £120
- **Elegia Inglese ... sopra un Cimitero Campestre.** Trans.:– Guiseppe Torelli. Parma, 1793. 1st. Bodoni Edn. 4to. Lacks port.?, several ll. stained. Cont. hf. red mor., spine gt., cipher 'EA' with crown gt.-stpd. on covers, unc., unopened. Eugene de Beauharnais' copy; bkplt. of Jean Furstenberg. (S. Jun.9; 57) *Quaritch.* £160
- [-] **An Elegy Wrote in a Country Church Yard.** 1751. 1st. Edn. 4to. Stabbed thro.-out in margins, 'Finis' punched through, with piece of the 'F' lacking, tear in title, marginal stains on title & 2 ll.

Disbnd., cl. box. (S. Feb.10; 444) *Quaritch.* £2,000
- [-] **Anr. Copy.** 4to. Letter 'F' in 'Finis' punched through (but intact), lacks final letters 'I' & 'S' (all due to faulty pr. work), old faded inscr. on title. Old wraps., added fly-ll., unc. Sir Walter Scott's copy, lately in the Prescott Collection. (CNY. Feb.6; 133) $14,000
- **Odes.** Straw. Hill Pr., 1757. 1st. Edn. 4to. Mor. gt. From the Prescott Collection. (CNY. Feb.6; 134) $450
- **Ode on the Pleasure Arising from Vicissitude.** Ed.:– Leonard Whibley. Ill.:– Thomas Rowlandson. San Franc., Nash Pr., 1933. (200) numbered, ptd. by John Henry Nash for W.A. Clark, Jnr. Fo. With facs. copy of orig. edn. in matching bdg. Hf. vell. (SG. Apr.9; 534) $100
- **Six Poems.** Ill.:– R. Bentley. 1789. 4to. Later hf. cf., rebkd. (TA. May 21; 285) £55

GRAY, Thomas de
- **The Complete Horseman & Expert Ferrier.** 1639. 4to. Title reprd., lacks port. Hf. cf., worn. (P. Dec.11; 21) *Comben.* £55

GRAZZINI, Anton Francesco
- **La Prima e la Seconda Cena, Novelle.** 1756. L.P. 4to. Lacks last lf. (blank?) some marginal dampstains at end, Ragley Hall bkplt. Cont. mor., triple gt. fillet, spine gt. in compartments with bird in foliage facing right, inner gt. floral dentelles, crest of Joseph Gulston, gt., & date in 5th. compartment, spine reprd. (SM. Oct.7; 1736) *Frs.* 1,000

GREAT EXHIBITION
- **Official Descriptive & Illustrated Catalogue of the Great Exhibition of the Works of Industry & all Nations.** 1851. 3 vols., & supp. 4to. Orig. cl. gt. (TA. Mar.19; 96) £68
- **'Wot is to be'. Or Probable Results of the Industry of All Nations in the Year '51 ... in short, How It's all Going to be Done.** L., 1850. Ob. 8vo. Recent cl. bds. (TA. Dec.18; 202) £55

GRECO, Gioachino
- **The Royall Game of Chesse-play ...** 1656. 1st. Edn. Some staining, few later MS. notes. Later cf. [Wing G.1810] (C. Jul.16; 351) *Taylor.* £250
- [-] **Anr. Copy.** Blank corner of A4 reprd., title stained with imprint & date cropped, some other stains. Hf. mor. by Birdsall. Owners' inscr. of Bulstrode Whitelocke on fly-lf. & title verso. (C. Nov.20; 251) *Ross.* £120

GRECOURT, Jean Baptiste Joseph Willart de
- **Oeuvres Choisies.** Geneva, 1777. 3 vols. 18mo. Red mor. by Cazin. (HD. Apr.8; 253) *Frs.* 1,400
- **Oeuvres Diverses.** Ed.:– Philotanus. L., 1780. New Edn. 4 vols. 18mo. Red mor. by Cazin. (HD. Apr.8; 254) *Frs.* 2,200
- – **Anr. Copy.** 4 vols. 18mo. Cf. by Cazin. (HD. Apr.8; 255) *Frs.* 1,000

GREDIAGA, I.G.
*See–*ALVAREZ, R. & Grediaga, I.G.

GREEN, A. Romney
- **Woodword in Principle & Practice.** Ill.:– Eric Gill & Ralph Beedham. St. Dominic's Pr., 1918. 1st. Edn., (240). Vol. 1 (all publd.). Orig. wraps., unc. From liby. of Guild of St. Joseph & St. Dominic. (SH. Feb.19; 72) *East Sussex County Liby.* £65

GREEN, James & Rowlandson, Thomas
- **Poetical Sketches of Scarborough.** 1813. 2nd. Edn. Lacks 'Spa Terrace' plt., text wtrmrkd. 1813., 1 plt. & some ll. loose. Cont. cf., covers detchd., worn, cropped. (S. Sep.29; 157) *Sekuler.* £50

GREEN, John
- [-] **A New General Collection of Voyages & Travels.** 1745-47. 4 vols. 4to. Some worming. Cont. sheep-bkd. bds. (SH. May 21; 213) *Vitale.* £260
- [-] – **Anr. Copy.** Hf. cf., worn. (P. Oct.23; 29) *Remington.* £200

GREEN, Prof. John Richard
*See–*MACAULAY, Lord Thomas Babington –GREEN, Prof. John Richard

GREEN, J[onathan] H.
- **An Exposure of the Arts & Miseries of Gambling ...** Cinc., 1843. 1st. Edn.? 12mo. Slight foxing. Later cf.-bkd. bds. From liby. of William E. Wilson. (SPB. Apr.29; 117) $550

GREEN, Mowbray A.
- The Eighteenth Century Architecture of Bath. Bath, 1904. (500) numbered. 4to. Errata slip. Orig. cl. (CB. May 27; 115) *Can.* $240

GREEN SHEAF, The
Ed.:- Pamela Coleman Smith. Ill.:- Gordon Craig & others. 1903-04. 13 issues. 4to. Orig. wraps., cl. case defect. (SH. Mar.26; 264) *Marks.* £200

GREEN, Thomas
- The Universal Herbal. L'pool, 1816-20. 2 vols. 4to. Cont. str.-grd. mor., gt., neatly rebkd. (S. Dec.3; 987) *Heur.* £400
- - Anr. Edn. 1824. [2nd. Edn?]. 2 vols. 4to. 2 frontis in vol. II cold., 4 plts. hand cold. Cf., spine defect. (P. Sep.11; 299) *Nicholas.* £210
- - Anr. Copy. 1 engraved plt. loose. Cont. tree cf. (SH. Jun.4; 7) *Nagel.* £190

GREEN, Valentine
- The History & Antiquities of the City & Suburbs of Worcester. 1796. 2 vols. 4to. Engraved titles, port. & 23 plts., extra-ill. with approx. 80 chromolithos., cold. aquatints, MS. documents & engrs., inlaid to size. 19th. C. mor. gt., rebkd. W.a.f. (C. Jul.15; 40) *Taylor.* £250
- - Anr. Copy. Some spotting & offsetting. Hf. cf., gt. spines, worn. (S. Jun.22; 37) *Quaritch.* £60

GREEN, William
- Seventy Eight Studies from Nature. L., & Ambleside, 1809. Ob. fo. 3 dupl. engrs. (cold. in india ink) are laid in, title & some margins stained. Hf. cf., stained on upr. cover, rebkd. (SG. Nov.20; 346) $160
- The Tourist's New Guide, containing a Description of the Lakes, Mountains, & Scenery, in Cumberland, Westmorland & Lancashire. Kendal, 1819. 2 vols. Later hf. mor. gt. (SBA. Dec.16; 176a) *Way.* £130

GREENAWAY, Kate
- A Apple Pie. L., [1886]. 1st. Edn. Ob. 4to. Cl.-bkd. cold. pict. bds., red hf. mor. s-c 3 pen & ink sketches on hf.-title, inscr. within the drawings 'Joan Ponsonby from Kate Greenaway'. (SG. Apr.30; 147) $500
- Almanachs. Paris; L., 1884, 1886, 1887, 1889-93; 1884, 1885, 1889. 11 vols. 16mo. Decor. bds. (HD. Jun.24; 205) *Frs.* 2,050
- Almanack.-Almanack & Diary. L., [1882-94]; [1896]. 1st. Edns. 13 vols., 1 vol. 24mo. & 12mo. Orig. bdgs., slight wear (mostly to corners); red mor. gt. box. Pres. inscr. in each vol. to Lady V. Herbert, with her bkplts., lately in the Prescott Collection. (CNY. Feb.6; 136) $4,500
- - Anr. Edn. L., N.Y., [1886]; [1896]. Ob. 32mo.; 16mo. Cold. pict. bds., loose; gt.-pict. leath. (SG. Dec.18; 220) $120
- Almanacks for 1883, & 1887-1894. [1882-1893]. 9 vols. in all. 24mo. Orig. cl.-bkd. pict. bds. (SH. Dec.10; 240) *Joseph* £390
- Almanacks for 1883-95, & 1897. L., [1882-94 & 1896]. 14 vols. 24mo. & 16mo. All in orig. pict. covers (that for 1884 present in 2 bdgs.), 3 vols. with orig. mailing covers present, in three-qtr. mor. folding case. (SG. Apr.30; 144) $1,550
- Almanacks for 1884 & 1891 . . . 1927. [1883-1926]. 3 vols. 12mo. 1st. in orig. wraps., 2nd. in orig. imitation mor., 3rd. in orig. cl.-bkd. bds. (SH. Dec.10; 242) *Drizen.* £70
- Almanack for 1888.-Almanack for 1895. [L.], [1887; 1894]. Tog. 2 vols. Cold. pict. cl.-bkd. bds. Both vols. inscr. (SG. Oct.9; 121) $450
- Kate Greenaway Pictures from originals presented by her to John Ruskin. 1921. 1st. Edn. 4to. Orig. cl., unc. (C. Feb.4; 65) *Dee.* £80
- Language of Flowers. L., [1884]. 1st. Edn. 12mo. Slight occasional spotting. Cl.-bkd. cold. pict. bds. (SG. Apr.30; 162) $140
- - Anr. Copy. Publisher's gt. imitation pig. (SG. Sep.4; 245) $120
- Marigold Garden. [1885]. 1st. Edn. 4to. Orig. pict. cl.-bkd. bds. (SBA. Dec.16; 197) *Subunso Books.* £65
- Mother Goose. [1881]. [1st.? Edn.]. Orig. cl., pict. d.-w. (SH. Dec.10; 236) *Joseph.* £105
- - Anr. Copy. 12mo. Cold. pict. wraps., loose. Inscr. on hf.-title 'Evelyn Goldsmith from Kate Greenaway, 1892'. (SG. Sep.4; 249) $220
- - Anr. Copy. Decor. cl., d.-w. (SG. Sep.4; 248) $125
- - Anr. Copy. 16mo. Decor. cl., Thomson's 3rd. variant of bdg., with only 'Mother Goose' on cover, & with the salmon d.-w. (slightly torn). (SG. Apr.30; 164) $100

- Under the Window. [1878]. 1st. Edns. 1st. Iss. 2 copies in 1 vol. 4to. Cl.-bkd. pict. bds., worn. (SH. Dec.10; 230) *Gamble.* £80
- - Anr. Copy. 4to. 1st. state, with the words 'End of Contents' at foot of p.14. Orig. glazed paper pict. bds., cl spine, qtr. red mor. gt. s.-c. Pres. Copy to Stuart M. Samuel, with pen & ink drawing below inscr., the E.H. Mills' copy, lately in the Prescott Collection. (CNY. Feb.6; 135) $650

GREENE, Graham
- Stamboul Train. [1932]. 1st. Edn. Title inscr. 'Affectionately Graham'. Orig. cl. (CSK. Jun.19; 6) £85

GREENE, Lt. Col. J. J.
- Pedigree of the Family Greene. Dublin, 1899. [150]. Vell.-bkd. buckram. (GM. Apr.30; 95) £85

GREENE, Robert
- Ciceronis Amor, Tullies Love. 1616. 4to. 2 sm. portions of last lf. lacking affecting 2 words, some slight staining. Mor. by Sangorski. (STC 12230) (C. Nov.19; 8) *Arnold.* £1,200
- Groatsworth of Wit. L., 1637. 4to. Lacks initial blank, lacks corner of 1 lf. affecting 3 words. Mor. by Sangorski. [STC 12250] (C. Nov.19; 10) *Quaritch.* £2,500
- Neuer Too Late. [1616 or 1631]. 4to. Title slightly stained & cropped with loss of date & some of imprint. 19th. C. cf., rebkd. [STC 12256 or 12258] (C. Nov.19; 11) *Arnold.* £1,500
- A Quip for an Upstart Courtier. 1635. 4to. With orig. initial blank. Mor. by Sangorski. [STC 12305] (C. Nov.19; 12) *Sharples.* £2,700
- Theeves Falling out, True-Men come by their Goods. 1637. 4to. Some staining in margins towards mid. end. Mor. by Sangorski. [STC 12238] (C. Nov.19; 9) *Day.* £1,600

GREENE, William Thomas
- Parrots in Captivity. 1884-87. 3 vols. Orig. cl. gt. (P. Sep.11; 12) *Hill.* £550
- - Anr. Copy. 81 cold. plts. Cont. cl. gt. (C. Jul.15; 185) *Taylor.* £350

GREENHILL, Thomas
- Nekrokedeia, or the Art of Embalming. 1705. 4to. Old cf., upr. cover detchd. (P. Apr.9; 85) *Fairburn.* £50

GREENHOW, Robert
- Memoir . . . on the North-West Coast of North America. Wash., 1840. Recent qtr. leath. & marb. bds. (CB. Nov.12; 15) *Can.* $120

GREENSLET, Ferris
See-ALDRICH, Thomas Bailey-GREENSLET, Ferris

GREENWOOD, Charles & John
- Map[s] of the Principality of Wales. 1831-34. Each 66cm×76cm. 5 engraved maps with vigs., cold. in outl., mntd. on linen & folded in sections. S.-c. (SH. Nov.6; 104) *Simon.* £65

GREENWOOD, Col. George
- Rain & Rivers. L., 1857. 1st. Edn. Contents loose in bdg., ex-liby. Cl. (SG. Jan.29; 190) $110

GREENWOOD, James
- The London Vocabulary, English & Latin. 1767. 15th. Edn. 12mo. Advts. Cont. sheep. (SH. Mar.19; 116) *Vincent.* £85

GREENWOOD, W.E.
- The Villa Madama Rome, a reconstruction. L., 1928. 4to. Orig. cl., d.-w. slightly tattered. (CB. May 27; 116) *Can.* $190

GREGO, Joseph
- Rowlandson the Caricaturist. 1880. 2 vols., 4to. Slight spotting. Cont. cl.-bkd. bds., soiled, spines worn. (CSK. Sep.12; 56) £55

GREGOIRE, Henri, Comte
- De la Litterature des Nègres. Paris, 1808. Cont. leath., very worn. (D. Dec.11-13; 780) *DM* 600

GREGOR, Joseph
- Masks of the World. 1936-37. 4to. Orig. buckram gt., pict. wrap. (LC. Feb.12; 86) £80
See-FULOP-MILLER, Rene & Gregor, Joseph

GREGORIUS IX, Pope
- Decretales. Venice, 22 XII 1486. 4to. Rubricated, sm. cold. initial at beginning, old MS. pagination in red ink, faulty in parts, browned in parts, lightly wormed at ends. Cont. blind-stpd. leath.-bkd. wood bds., lightly wormed, reprd.,

spine renewed, lacks ties. (HK. Nov.18-21; 204) *DM* 1,200
- - Anr. Edn. Venice, 20 May 1514. 4to. Worming thro.-out with occasional minor loss of text. Cont. Venetian blind-stpd. cf., a few restorations. (S. May 5; 18) *Panadero.* £150

GREGORIUS, G.
- Wanderings in Corsica: its Histories & its Heroes. Trans.:- Alex Muir. Edinb., 1855. 1st. Engl. Edn. 2 vols. Red mor., gt., decor., gt. spine, inner & outer dentelles, by Hatchards. (D. Dec.11-13; 2658) *DM* 900

GREGORIUS Magnus I, Pope
- Dialogorum liber Secundus de Vita et Miraculis S. Benedicti. Venice, Bernardinus Benalius. 17 Feb. 1490. 1st. Edn. 16mo. Spaces for initial capitals, supplied in red, as are paragraph marks, reprd. tear slightly affecting wood-cut at fo. lr, other slight marginal repairs to 1st. lf., some 8 ll. with sm. portions of corners renewed, scattered light soiling. Mor., gt.-lettered spine, mor.-tipped s.-c. Bkplt. of Carl J. Ulmann, lately in the collection of Eric Sexton. [Goff G398, H 7979*] (CNY. Apr.8; 189) $2,500
- [-] [Dialogorum Libri IV] [La Vita di Sancto Gregorio Papa]. Venice, Iohannis de Colonia: & Iohannis Manthen de Gherretzem. 1475. 2nd. Edn. in Italian?. 2 pts. in 1 vol. Fo. Lacks 1st. & last blanks, wide margins, initial spaces left blank for rubrication, with guide letters, inner margin of a2 strengthened, sm. repair to head margin of a2-6, slight worming of approximately 1st. 20 & last 30 ll., reprd. in o9 & last lf., some marginal dampstaining, 1 old MS. note & 1 or 2 words deleted in ink. 18th. C. red mor., triple gt. fillet, spine gt. in compartments, inner gt. dentelles, faint scratch on upr. & lr. covers. Valliere lot number & his ptd. sale ticket on fly-lf. Valliere lot number & his ptd. sale ticket on fly lf. at rear & front paste-down; bkplt. of Le Candele. [HC 7975; BMC V 231; Goff G-410] (S. Apr.7; 288) *Thorp.* £1,000
- In Nomine Sancte Trinitatis Amen. Venice, 1489. Fo. 4 unnumbered pp. plt. index, lacks 1st. & last lf. blank, text in red & black, all capitals red, blank margin repairs. MS. vell. (CR. Mar.19; 256) *Lire* 950,000
- Liber Dialogorum. [Augsburg], [Johann Wiener]. [1475-79]. Fo. Initials in red, rubricated, wormholes, some cont. marginalia, MS. note affecting some letters. Vell. bds., using old antiphonal lf. with initials. [BMC II, 358] (S. Nov.25; 317) *Fletcher.* £450
- Liber Moralium in Beatum Job. Basel, 31.1.1514. Fo. Some old MS. notes, owners mark on title, 1st. ll. soiled, wormed near end. Cont. blind-stpd. pig-bkd. wood bds., lr. cover wormed, lacks 2 clasps. (HK. Nov.18-21; 203) *DM* 440
- Moralia, sive Expositio in Job. [Basle], [Berthold Ruppel], ca. 1471. Fo. Spaces for initial capitals, larger capitals supplied in blue with red & green penwork elaboration extending into margins, paragraph marks, initial strokes & under-linings in red, 1st. 12 ll. with defect to upr. margins & portions of upr. outer corner renewed, affecting part of 9 lines text at fo. 1, 7 lines at fo. 2, & 4 lines at fo. 3, 1st. 3 ll. with all margins reinforced, following lf. with upr. & outer margins reinforced, folios 5-13 with upr. margin reinforced, some ll. marginal tears or slight dampstains, final 7 ll. with sm. rust-hole affecting some letters of text. 18th. C. mott. cf., worn, rebkd. in mor. preserving portions of orig. gt. spine. From the collection of Eric Sexton. [BMC III, 714, Goff G426, H. 7929*] (CNY. Apr.8; 19) $3,500
See-JOHANNES de Lapide-GREGORIUS I, Pope
-REGINALDETUS, Petrus

GREGORIUS Nyssenus
See-BERTHORIUS, Petrus-NAUSEA, Fredericus, Bp. of Vienna-GREGORIUS Nyssenus

GREGOROVIUS, Ferdinand
- Die Insel Capri. Ill.:- K. Lindemann-Frommel. Leipzig. 1868. Fo. Orig. hf. linen, worn, soiled. (H. May 21/22; 414) *DM* 500

GREGORY, David
- Astronomiae Physicae & Geometricae Elementa. Oxford, 1702. 1st. Edn. Fo. Tear in inner margin of 2Cl, 2 very sm. tears in title device. Mod. panel. cf., gt. sig. of G. Riggs, Queen's College, Oxford, on fly-lf. From Honeyman Collection (S. May 20; 3250) *Norton.* £50

GREGORY, Lady Isabella Augusta
- - **Anr. Edn.** Geneva, 1726. 2nd. Edn. 2 vols. 4to. Some slight browning. Cont. hf. cf., unc. (S. Feb.9; 188) *Thorp.* £100

GREGORY, Lady Isabella Augusta
- **The Full Moon.** Dublin, 1911. 1st. Edn. Orig. wraps., unc., unopened. Inscr. (SH. Dec.19; 527) *Quaritch.* £170
- **The White Cockade ... & the Travelling Man.** N.Y., 1905. 1st. Amer. Edn., (30). Orig. wraps. Sigd. (SH. Dec.19; 525) *Barry Scott.* £190

GREGORY, William
- **A Visible Display of Divine Providence; or, the Journal of a Captured Missionary,** designated to the Southern Pacific Ocean. L., [1800]. Mod. hf. mor. [Sabin 28746] (SPB. May 5; 239) $400

GREGSON, Matthew
- **Portfolio of Fragments relative to the History & Antiquities Topography & Genealogies of the County Palatine & Duchy of Lancashire.** Ed.:– John Harland. 1869. 3rd. Edn., (27) numbered. L.P. Fo. Some MS. entries on blank pp. Cont. cf. gt. Sigd. by publisher. (SBA. Oct.22; 396) *Kelsall.* £50

GREGYNOG PRESS–Llyfr y Pregeth-Wr
Gregy Pr. 1927. Ltd. Edn. 4to. Orig. cl. gt. (SBA. Jul.14; 412) *Herrick.* £90

GREIG, J.
See–STORER, James Sargent & Greig, J.

GRELOT, Guillaume Joseph
- **A Late Voyage to Constantinople.** 1683. Cont. cf., rebkd. (P. Oct.2; 4) £90

GRENIER, F.
- **Album de Chasses ...** Paris, ca. 1840. Ob. 4to. Publisher's decor. cl. s.-c. (HD. Dec.5; 97) *Frs.* 10,000

GRENVILLE, Robert Kaye
- **Scottish Cryptogamic Flora.** Edinb., 1823-28. 6 vols. Slight dampstaining. Cont. cf. (CSK. May 1; 147) £450
See–HOOKER, Sir William Jackson & GRENVILLE, Robert Kaye

GRESSET, Jean Baptiste Louis
- **Oeuvres.** Ill.:– Saint-Aubin (port.), Moreau & Simonet (engraver). Paris, 1811. 1st. Printing. 2 vols. Added port. of Gresset for 1780 Edn. Le Parrain Magnifique, title dtd. 1810, with separate pagination bnd. at end of vol. II. Jansenist mor., red mor. doubl., gt. dent, angle fleurons, s.-c., by Cusin. (HD. Jun.10; 35) *Frs.* 7,100

GRESTY, John
- **Illustrated Chester ... with a Useful Business Directory, & a Brief Sketch of Eaton Hall.** Ca. 1863. Ob. fo. Last 2 plts. with lr. margins slightly dampstained, advts. at end. Orig. cl., slightly worn. (SBA. Jul.14; 273) *Chesters.* £165

GREVILLE, Charles
- **Memoirs.** Ed.:– H. Reeve. 1875-87. 8 vols. Hf. mor. gt. (P. Apr.30; 17) *Quaritch.* £60
- - **Anr. Edn.** 1938. (630). 8 vols. including Index. Orig. cl. (SH. Oct. 10; 377) *Traylen.* £210
- - **Anr. Copy.** 8 vols. Slight spotting. (SBA. Oct.21; 48) *Borrom.* £100

GREVILLE, Fulke, Lord Brooke
See–BROOKE, Lord Fulke Greville

GREVILLE, Robert Kaye
- **Scottish Cryptogamic Flora, Or, Coloured Figures & Descriptions of Cryptogamic Plants, Belonging Chiefly to the Order Fungi; ...** Edinb., 1823-28. 6 vols. Some minor spotting. Cont. hf. mor. (TA. Jun.18; 18) £575

GREW, Nehemiah
- **The Anatomy of Plants.** Priv. ptd. 1682. 1st. Edn. Fo. Slight browning, short tears in N4, X4 & 2Q4 not affecting text, sm. wormhole marginally affecting a few plts. Mod. cf.-bkd. marb. bds. [Wing G1945] (S. Jun.1; 140) *Van Haverbeck.* £160
- **Cosmologia Sacra or a Discourse of the Universe as it is the Creature & Kingdom of God.** 1701. Fo. Cont panel. cf. rebkd. (S. Dec.1; 191) *Lindahall.* £50
- **Musaeum Regalis Societatis. Or a Catalogue & Description of the Natural & Artifical Rarities belonging to the Royal Society & Preserved at Gresham Colledge ... Whereunto is Subjoyned the Comparative Anatomy of Stomachs & Guts.** Priv. ptd., 1681. 1st. Edn. Fo. Slight discolouration & soiling, a few sm. holes in text, occasional MS.

deletions & additions to text. Cont. cf., rebkd., gt. arms on covers of Walter Chetwynd, F.R.S., covers very worn. From Honeyman Collection. [Wing G1952] (S. May 20; 3251) *Boston Museum.* £100
- - **Anr. Copy.** Additional port. of Johannes White pasted on verso of dedication lf., & 4 other engrs. pasted in at beginning & end, a few stains. [Wing G1952] (S. Dec.1; 190) *Jones.* £55
- - **Anr. Edn.** L., 1694. Fo. Some plts. bnd. out of sequence or inverted. Cont. cf., worn & reprd. (SG. Sep.18; 165) $170

GREY, Sir George
- **Journal of Two Expeditions of Discovery in North-West & Western Australia.** 1841. 1st. Edn. 2 vols. 2 frontis., 20 litho. plts., 6 hand-cold., 2 folding engraved maps in pocket reprd., advts., prospectus, some plts. browned & stained. Orig. cl. (C. Jul.15; 41) *Taylor.* £220
- - **Anr. Copy.** Folding map mntd. on cl. in a pocket in each vol., most plts. slightly foxed. Cont. hf. cf. (S. Nov.4; 626) *Cawthorn.* £200
- - **Anr. Copy.** Occasional foxing. Orig. cl., unc., 1 vol. recased with new end-papers. (KH. Nov.18; 302) *Aus.* $820
- **Poems, Traditions & Chaunts of the Maories.** New Zealand, 1853. Orig. cl. gt., unc. (CE. Jul.9; 182) £86
- **A Vocabulary of the Dialects of South Western Australia.** L., 1840. 2nd. Edn. Later hf. roan. (KH. Mar.24; 180) *Aus.* $240

GREY, Roch
- **Henri Rousseau.** Ill.:– Pablo Picasso. Rome, 1922. Orig. wraps., unc. Inscr. by Picasso to Sydney Schiff. (SH. Nov.21; 445) *Quaritch.* £135

GREY, Zane
- **Tales of the Angler's Eldorado, New Zealand. –Tales of Swordfish & Tuna.–Tales of Tahitian Waters.–Tales of Southern Rivers.** N.Y., 1926; 1927; 1931; [1924]. 1st. Edns. 4 works in 4 vols. 4to. & 8vo. Some foxing. Cl. (SG. Dec.11; 43) $330

GREYHOUND Stud Book, The
1882-1973. Vols. 1-92. Orig. cl. gt. As a periodical, w.a.f. (LC. Feb.12; 132) £100

GRIBBLE, Ernest R.
See–CESCINSKY, Herbert & Gribble, Ernest R.

GRIBELIN, Samuel
- **A New Book of Ornaments.** 1704. 4to. 12 engraved plts. including title, all cut out & mntd. Mod. bds. (S. Mar.17; 413) *Henderson.* £400

GRIBOEDOV, Aleksandr Sergeevich
- **Gore ot uma [Woe from Wit].** Moscow, 1833. 1st. Edn. 1 lf. torn, a few dampstained, browned. Cont. hf. cf. (SH. Feb.6; 316) *Lempert.* £150

GRIEBART, Hugo
- **A Study of the Stamps of Uruguay.–The Stamps of Spain, 1850-1854.** L., 1910; 1919. 2 works in 2 vols. 4to. Plts. in 1st. work in cover pocket, those in 2nd, laid in loose. Red three-qtr. mor. (SG. Feb.12; 314) $120

GRIECHENLAND oder Gallerie der Merkwurdigsten Ansichten und Ruinen
Ed.:– Iwan de la Croix. Riga, 1837. Ob. 4to. Orig. ptd. wraps. (C. Jul.22; 189) *Marlborough.* £50

GRIESHABER, Hap
- **Der Grosse Garten.** Hannover, 1965. (500) on Bütten. Sm. fo. Orig. hf. linen. 1 woodcut sigd. by artist. (H. May 21/22; 1585) *DM* 620
- **Totentanz von Basel.** Dresden, 1966. Fo. Orig. linen. (H. Dec.9/10; 2087) *DM* 2,000

GRIESINGER, T.
- **Württemberg Nachs. Vergangenheit u Gegenwart in Land u leuten.** Stuttgart, 1866. 4to. Cont. hf. leath. (HK. May 12-14; 563) *DM* 3,400

GRIEVE, Christopher Murray 'Hugh McDiarmid'
- **Complete Poems 1920-76.** Ed.:– Michael Grieve & W.R. Aitken. 1978. 1st. Edn. (50) sigd. Limitation slip loosely inserted. Orig. buckram, s.-c. (S. Jul.22; 213) *Quaritch.* £60
- **Drunk Man Looks at the Thistle.** 1926. 1st. Edn. sigd. Cl. gt. (P. Oct.23; 228) *Brown.* £60

GRIFFIN, William
- **An Essay on the Nature of Pain.** Edinb., 1826. Hf. cf., defect. Pres. copy to Sir A. de Vere Hunt. (GM. Apr.30; 607) £60

GRIFFITH, Samuel Young
- **New Historical Description of Cheltenham & its Vicinity.** 1826. L.P. 4to. 50 mntd. plts. on India paper, minor spotting to title & a few plts. Roan-bkd. orig. ptd. bds., unc. & unopened. (C. Feb.25; 33) *Maggs.* £200

GRIFFITHS, Arthur
- **Chronicles of Newgate.** L., 1884. 2 vols. in 4. Extra-ill. with over 100 old engrs. mntd. to size. Red mor. gt., worn. (SG. Feb.12; 145) $120

GRIGOREVICH, D.V.
- **Gutta. Perchevy mal'chik [Gutta Percha Boy].** St. Petersb., 1884. 1st. Edn. Slightly browned. Orig. wraps., spine torn, loose. (SH. Feb.5; 7) *Nijhoff.* £55

GRIGORIEV, Boris
- **Faces of Russia.** Ed.:– L. Reau, Cl. Sheridan & others (text). L., 1924. (500) numbered. 4to. Orig. hf. vell. (D. Dec.11-13; 1074) *DM* 500
- **Visages de Russie.** Paris, 1923. (450) (this copy unnumbered). Fo. Gt.-lettered bds., upr. cover marked 'Edition Speciale commandée par Morris Gest', vell. spine & tips. (SG. Apr.2; 127) $240

GRILLPARZER, Franz
- **Der Arme Spielmann.** Ill.:– J. Hoffmann (Bk. decor.). [Vienna], [1914]. (450). 4to. Orig. linen gt. (H. May 21/22; 1432) *DM* 500
- **Sämtliche Werke.** Ed.:– A. Sauer & R. Backman. Vienna, 1909-44. 38 vols. Lacks pt. 1: vol. 10, 16 & 17, pt. III: 7 & 8. Orig. hf. leath. (H. Dec.9/10; 1829) *DM* 800

GRIMALDI, Francesco Maria
- **Physico-Mathesis de Lumine, Colribus, et Iride.** Bologna, 1665. 1st. Edn. 4to. 1 title (of 2), with engraved arms of Cardinal Antonius de Sancte Petro, arms slightly defect. in 2 places, a few ll. slightly spotted or soiled. Cont. cf., gt., arms of Julie Lucile, Duchesse de Montausier on sides, decor. in corners & on spine, reprd. at corners & spine, bkplt. of the Museo Moutan-Fontenille. (S. Oct.21; 392) *Quaritch.* £620

GRIMALDI, Stacey
- [–] **A Suit of Armour for Youth.** Ill.:– Armstrong after W[alter] G[rimaldi], & Armstrong or R.I. Wright. 1824. 12mo. Cont. str.-grd. mor., wide gt. borders. (SH. Mar.19; 117) *Goldschmidt.* £180
- [–] **The Toilet.** 1823. 3rd. Edn. 16mo. Orig. bds., spine slightly worn. (S. Feb.9; 21) *Gross.* £65

GRIMBLE, Augustus
- **The Salmon Rivers of Ireland.** 1903. (250). [1st. Edn.?]. 2 vols. Vell.-bkd. bds., corners worn. (PD. May 20; 213) £75
- - **Anr. Copy.** 2 vols. Lge. 4to. L.P. Hf. vell. (SG. Apr.9; 285) $120
- **The Salmon Rivers of Scotland.** 1899-1900. 4 vols. 4to. Vell.-bkd. bds., worn. (PD. May 20; 164) £100

GRIME, J.
[–] **Here Begynnethe the Lanterne of Lyght.** Ca. 1535. D6 supplied in facs., some shaving slightly affecting a few side-notes, slight browning. Blind-stpd. cf. [NSTC 15225] (S. Jul.27; 57) *Quaritch.* £300

GRIMESTONE, Edward
- **A Generall Historie of the Netherlands.** Ill.:– C. von Sichem (engraved title border). 1608. 1st. Edn. Fo. Lacks 1st. blank, title with 2 sm. holes & erasures, mntd., hole in A3, sm. repairs to 3E1 & 3X1, a few rustholes, some underlinings in text, title & 1 lf. detchd. 19th C. tree cf., spine defect., upr. cover detchd. [STC 12374] (S. Dec.9; 318) *Armstrong.* £150
- - **Anr. Edn.** 1609. 1st. Edn., 2nd. Iss. Lacks 1st. & last lf. (blanks?), slight dampstaining, sig. 'P. Tyrwhitt' on title. Cont. cf., worn. [STC 12375] (S. Sep.29; 37) *Van Haverberge.* £110

GRIMM, Jacob Ludwig Carl & Wilhelm Carl
- **Fairy Tales.** Trans.:– Mrs. Edgar Lucas. Ill.:– Arthur Rackham. Phila., ca. 1900. 1st. Amer. Edn. Sm. 4to. Foxed. Cold. pict. cl. Raymond M. Sutton Jr. copy. (SG. May.7; 109) $110
- - **Anr. Edn.** Ill.:– Arthur Rackham. L., 1909. 4to. Orig. cl. gt., top of spine torn. (SH. Mar.27; 428) *Razzall.* £125
- - **Anr. Copy.** 1 plt. loose. Worn. (D. Dec.11; 426) *Rota.* £70
- - **Anr. Copy.** 40 mntd. cold. plts. Orig. cl. (CSK. Jan.9; 150) £55

GRIMM, Jacob Ludwig Carl & Wilhelm Carl – Fairy Tales. -contd.
– – **Anr. Edn.** Trans.:– Mrs. Edgar Lucas. Ill.:– Arthur Rackham. L., 1909. Deluxe Edn., (750) numbered, sigd. by artist. Lge. 4to. Gt.-pict. vell., lacks ties. Coker Court bkplt., Raymond M. Sutton Jr. copy. (SG. May 7; 111) $700
– – **Anr. Edn.** Trans.:– Mrs. Edgar Lucas. Ill.:– Arthur Rackham. N.Y., 1909. [1st.?] Amer. Edn. on L.P., sigd. by artist. Lge. 4to. Limp suede, gt. decor. spine. Raymond M. Sutton Jr. copy. (SG. May 7; 112) $550
– – **Anr. Copy.** Hf. suede & cork-style bds., gt. stpd. Raymond M. Sutton Jr. copy. (SG. May 7; 113) $350
– – **Anr. Edn.** N.Y., 1912. Title-p. with a sm. sigd. cartoon sketch by the artist dtd. 19.9.18. Buckram. (CE. Dec.4; 221) £110
– **Fleur-de-Neige et d'Autres Contes.** Ill.:– Kay Nielsen. Paris, 1929. (2400). 4to. Orig. pict. wraps., spine worn, unc. (SH. Dec.11; 375) Jones. £200
– **German Popular Stories.** Trans.:– Edgar Taylor. Ill.:– George Cruikshank. 1825-26. 3rd. Edn. 2 vols. Cont. mor. by Leighton, Brewer Street, gt. Bkplt. of Thomas Gaisford. (S. Nov.24; 83) Johns. £110
– **Hansel & Gretel.** Ill.:– Kay Nielsen. L., [1925]. (600) numbered, sigd. by artist. Lge. 4to. Cl.-bkd. batik bds. (SG. Oct.9; 178) $800
– – **Anr. Edn.** Ill.:– Kay Nielsen. N.Y., [1925]. Lge. 4to. Cl. (SG. Oct.23; 241) $240
– **Irische Elfenmärchen.** Leipzig., 1826. 1st. Edn. Some ll. minimum soiling. Cont. marb. hf. leath. gt. Johanna v Scharnhorst copy, ded. Christabend 1827 on end-paper & pasted in upr. cover. (HK. May 15; 5123) DM 480
– **Kinder- und Haus- Märchen.** Berlin, 1812 & 1815. 1st. Edn. Vols. 1 & II. Vol. I in 2nd. Fassung, heavily soiled thro.-out, 3 ll. with sm. tear, 1 lf. with margin tear. Cont. bds., worn, vol. I lacks spine. (H. May 21/22; 1124) DM 12,000
– **Little Brother & Little Sister.** Ill.:– Arthur Rackham. L., [1917]. 1st. Edn. Deluxe, (525) numbered, sigd. by artist. Lge. 4to. Pict. end-papers foxed. Cl. Extra mntd. plt. in envelope laid in, sigd. by artist, Raymond M. Sutton Jr. copy. (SG. May 7; 114) $1,250
– **Six Fairy Tales.** Ill.:– David Hockney. Petersburg Pr., 1970. Edn. D, (100) numbered, sigd. by artist, with s.-c. containing 6 etchings, each sigd. by artist. Fo. Mor., unc., s.-c. (SG. Oct.23; 162) $3,400

GRIMM, Wilhelm Carl
– **Die Deutsche Heldensage.** Göttingen, 1829. Slightly soiled in places, MS. poem in upr. end-paper. Cont. marb. bds. gt. (HK. May 15; 4384) DM 420
– **Deutsche Sagen.** Berlin, 1816-18. 1st. Edn. 2 vols. Both titles stpd. & soiled at beginning, vol. I slightly wormed in margin, tear in lr. margin reprd. Cont. hf. mor. gt. (HK. May 15; 4386) DM 800

GRIMMELSHAUSEN, H.J. Chr. von
– **Simplicius Simplicissimus.** Ed.:– W. Vesper. Leipzig, 1923. (25) Priviledge Edn. Orig. vell. (R. Oct.14-18; 914) DM 650

GRINDLAY, Capt. Robert Melville
– **Scenery, Costumes & Architecture chiefly on the Western Side of India.** 1826-30. 1st. Edn. 2 vols. in 1, pts. I, II & VI (of 6). Fo. Lacks 18 plts., text in vol. I wtrmkd. 1825, text & plts. in vol. II 1829, 1st. title browned, slight offsetting to a few plts., occasional light spotting. 19th. C. cl., spine defect., some wear. (S. Nov.4; 615) Symonds. £120
– – **Anr. Edn.** L., 1830. 2 vols. in 1. Fo. Minor browning, stitching loose. Hf. mor., loose. (SPB. May 6; 196) $1,000
– – **Anr. Copy.** Engraved title & 37 full-p. hand-cold. plts. Cont. hf. red mor. gt., spine gt., worn. (CNY. May 22; 121) $700
– – **Anr. Edn.** '1830' [late 19th. C.]. Lge. fo. Short tear in title, not affecting text, tear in Z1, slightly affecting text, 1 plt. loose & spotted. Cont. hf. mor., worn. (S. Apr.7; 482) Elliott. £60
– – **Anr. Edn.** 1892. Reprint. Fo. Orig. roan-bkd. cl., spine worn. (SH. Mar.5; 63) Hosain's Books. £85

GRINNELL, George Bird
See–HARRIMAN Alaska Expedition

GRISELINI, Francesco
– **Dizionario delle Arte e de Mestieri.** Venice, 1768-78. 18 vols. Cont. hf. cf. Owner's inscr. of Caietano Rangeri, lately in the collection of John A. Saks. (C. Jun.10; 104) Bozzolato. £280

GRISONE Federico–FAYSER VON ARNSTAIN, Johann–HORWART VON HOHENBURG, Hanns Friedrich
–**Hipoko Mike.–Hippiatria.–Von der Hochberhümpten, Adelichen und Ritterlichen Kunst der Reyterey.** Trans.:– Johann Fayser (1st work). Augsburg; Augsburg; Tegernsee, 1580; 1576; 1581. 3 works in 1 vol. Fo. Slightly spotted in places. 2nd. work lacks ff. A2 & 3. Cont. German blind-stpd. pig over wooden bds., 7 (of 8) brass, 2 clasps, title 'Rossz Buch' on upr. cover. (S. Jun.1; 25) Quaritch. £3,000

GRISWOLD, Frank Gray
– **The Cascapedia Club.** N.p., Priv. ptd., 1920. 1st. Edn. Cl. Pres. copy. (SG. Oct.16; 37) $160
– **Sport on Land & Water.** [N.Y.], Plimpton Pr., 1916-31. 1st. Edns. 7 vols. Roan. Each vol. sigd. (SG. Oct.16; 47) $170

GROHMANN, Adolf
See–ARNOLD, Sir Thomas W. & Grohmann, Adolf

GROHMANN, Johann G.
– **Moeurs et Coutumes des Chinois.** Ill.:– after Pu-Qua. Leipzig, [1810]. 4to. Text in Fr. & German, some slight foxing, etc. Hf. cf., worn. (BS. Jun.11; 344) $200

GROHMANN, Will
– **Karl Schmidt-Rottluf.** Stuttgart, [1956]. 4to. Orig. linen. (H. Dec.9/10; 2337) DM 540
– **Das Werk Ernst Ludwig Kirchners.** Munich, [1926]. Ltd. Edn. 4to. Loose, orig. hf. linen box, 1 corner torn. (H. May 21/22; 1664) DM 1,200

GROLIER CLUB
– **The Catalogue of Books from the Libraries . . . of Celebrated Bibliophiles . . .** N.Y., 1895. (350) on Holland Paper. Orig. cl. gt., unc. (CNY. May 22; 122) $130
– **A Description of the Early Printed Books owned by The Grolier Club . . .** N.Y., Grol. Cl., May, 1895. (400). Fo. Mor., broad borders of darker mor. interlaced strapwork, upr. cover with 7 painted ceramic plaques, lr. cover with centrepiece of cold. mor. onlays of seal of Grol. Cl., covers with Henry Walters blind-stpd. monog. repeated 10 times, spine in 6 compartments, 5 raised bands, maroon mor. doubls., lge. gt. dentelle panel & corner-pieces, sigd. by Charles Meunier, cl. box. (CNY. May 22; 363) $3,800
– **One Hundred Influential American Books printed before 1900.** N.Y., Grol. Cl., 1947. (600). Tall 8vo. Two-tone cl. (SG. Mar.26; 225) $220
– – **Anr. Copy.** (SG. Jan.22; 188) $160
– – **Anr. Copy.** Tall 8vo. (SG. Mar.26; 346) $130
– **Transactions.** 1885-1921. Pts. 1-4. 4to. Wraps., bds., some bdg. defects. (SG. Oct.2; 164) $110

GROLLIER DE SERVIERE, Nicolas
– **Recueil d'Ouvrages Curieux de Mathématique et de Mécanique, ou Description du Cabinet de Monsieur Grollier de Servière.** Lyon, 1719. 1st. Edn. 4to. Some browning, inscr. on title 'Ex Musao Joa. du Jilliot anno 1725'. Cont. mott. cf., gt. spine, worn. From Honeyman Collection. (S. May 20; 3252) Pilo. £600
– – **Anr. Copy.** 82 engraved plts. (of 85) (plts. numbered to 88 but plts. 39, 48 & 76 not issued), corner of 1 plt. torn away, some plts. cropped, some dampstaining. Cont. bds., worn & reprd. (S. May 5; 116) Diego. £220

GRONOVIUS, Joh. Friedrich
– **De Sestertiis, seu subsecivorum pecuniae veteris Graecae & Romanae.** Amst., 1656. Without inserted lf. of verse. 19th. C. red str.-grd. mor. (C. Apr.1; 136) Hoare. £55
– **Flora Virginica . . .** Leyden, 1762. Enlarged edn. of 1st. publd. flora of Virginia. 4to. Cont. hf. cf. [Sabin 28924] (S. Oct.20; 99) Baskett & Day. £450

GRONOVIUS, Laurentius Theodorous
– **Museum Ichthyologicum.** Ill.:– A. Delfos. Leyden, 1754. 2 vols. in 1. Fo. Plts. loose, 1 plt. creased, some foxing. Cont. cf.-bkd. bds., covers detchd. From Chetham's Liby., Manchester. (C. Nov.26; 184) Wheldon & Wesley. £110
– **Zoophylacium Gronovianum.** Leyden, 1763-64. 2 pts. only (of 3). Fo. 18 engraved plts. only (of 21)

title of pt. 2, foxed, edges of plts. lightly soiled. Cont. bds., later cl. spine, unc. From Chetham's Liby., Manchester. (C. Nov.26; 183) Taylor. £70

GRONOW, Capt. Rees Howell
– **The Reminiscences & Recollections.** 1889. (870). 2 vols. 4to. Plts. in 2 states, on plt. & Whatman paper, latter hand-cold. Orig. cl. gt., unc. Mentmore liby. stp. on title-p. (SBA. Jul.23; 518) Wilson. £85
– – **Anr. Copy.** (875) numbered. Fo. Dupl. plts. in black & white state. Orig. cl. gt., partly untrimmed. Mentmore copy. (TA. Nov.20; 98) £65

GROOT, A. de
– **Haga Comitis Illustrata.** The Hague, 1751. Lge. fo. Bds., slightly stained. (BS. Jun.11; 50) £50

GROOT, Constantin de
– **Joodse Oudheden, ofte Voor-Bereidsel Tot de Bybelsche Wysheid, en Gebruyk der Heilige en Kerklyke Historien.** Ill.:– J. van den Avelen, W. Swidde & others. Amst., 1690. 2 vols. Fo. 4 plts. torn along folds, slight discolouration. Orig. blind-tooled vell. (S. Nov.18; 661) Rock. £420

GROOTE TAFEREEL DER DWAASHEID
– **Vertoonende de opkomst, voortgang en ondergang der Actie, Bubbel en Windengotie, in Vrankryk, Engeland, en de Nederlanden.** Amst., 1720. 1st. Edn. Fo. 8 sm. plts. trimmed & mntd., frontis. & a few plts. with short tears, sm. hole in Laggende plt. Cont. Dutch cf., sides gt. with ornaments, rather worn, probably bnd. by Foot's 'Group IV' bindery. W.a.f. [Sabin 28932] (S. Oct.21; 466) Hendy. £320
– – **Anr. Copy.** Full-page & folding plts. Disbnd. Defect., very worn, loose in sheets, not collated, w.a.f. (SG. Sep.25; 287) $230

GROPIUS, Watther (Ed.)
See–STAATLICHES BAUHAUS WEIMAR

GROS DE BOZE, C. & others
[–] **Histoire de l'Academie Royale, des inscriptions et Belles Lettres . . . & Tableau Général, Raisonné et Méthodique . . .** Paris, 1717-1793. Vols. I-XVIII, XX, XXVII-XXXIII, XXXV-XLIV, 38 vols. 4to. Slight browning. Cont. mott. cf., worn, a few very worn. (S. Apr.7; 347) Weinreb. £170

GROSE, Francis
– **Antiquities of England & Wales.** 1773-76. 4 vols. 4to. Cf. (P. May 14; 96) £65
– – **Anr. Copy.** Lacks maps. Cont. tree cf. (SG. Sep.25; 157) $140
– – **Anr. Edn.** 1773-87. 6 vols. including 2 Supps. 4to. Cont. russ. cf. gt. (P. Nov.13; 19) Lee. £280
– – **Anr. Edn.** 1783-87. New Edn. 8 vols. 4to. Some spotting. Cont. tree cf., rebkd. (SH. Nov.6; 105) Burden. £250
– – **Anr. Copy.** Folding general map torn in vol. VII, lacks county maps, some browning & spotting. Cont. russ., gt., worn. W.a.f. (S. Jun.22; 38) Jeffries. £100
– – **Anr. Edn.** [1783]-97. New Edn. 8 vols. including 2 vol. supp. 4to. Some maps cold. or cold. in outl., some offsetting. Orig. bds., worn. W.a.f. (S. Sep.29; 140) Burden. £240
– – **Anr. Edn.** N.d. & 1785-87. 8 vols. 4to. Old mor., spines slightly worn. (SKC. Feb.26; 1652) £220
– **Antiquities of England & Wales.–Antiquities of Scotland.** [1783-97]; 1797. New Edns. 7 vols. (of 8, lacks vol. II), including Supp.; 2 vols. 4to. Occasional spotting & offsetting. Unif. cont. hf. russ., gt. W.a.f. (S. Jan.27; 473) Jeffrey. £140
– **Antiquities of England & Wales.–Scotland.–Ireland.** 1783-95. New Edn. 8 vols. (including 2 vols. supp.); 2 vols.; 2 vols., together 12 vols. 4to. 19th. C. red hf. mor., gt., unc., bkplt. of Viscount Birkenhead. (S. Nov.4; 547) Maggs. £420
– – **Anr. Edn.** [1783]-97; 1789-91; 1791-95. 1st. work New Edn. 8 vols. including Supp.; 2 vols.; 2 vols., together 12 vols. Fo. 1st. work minor foxing, end of 1st. vol. stained, 2nd. work, some plts. stained, foxing on end-papers & plts., 3rd. work minor foxing. Unif. cf. gt., decor. spine, slightly soiled. (CE. Jul.9; 233) £800
– **The Antiquities of England & Wales.–Antiquities of Scotland.–Antiquities of Ireland.–Military Antiquities.** 1773-87; 1789-91; 1791-95; 1812; 1791-95. 6 vols. in 4; 2 vols; 2 vols; 2 vols; together 10 vols. 4to. Cont. red str.-grd. mor., spines gt., Military Antiquities in mod. bdg. to match. (S. Nov.24; 143) Traylen. £650

- **The Antiquities of Ireland.** L., 1791. [1st. Edn.?]. 2 vols. 4to. 265 engraved plts. (of 266), lacks plt. 1 in Vol. II, a few sm. tears & stains. Cl. (GM. Apr.30; 431) £340
- - **Anr. Copy.** Mod. cl. (P. Oct.23; 260a) *Hollingsworth.* £130
- - **Anr. Copy.** Slight browning. 19th. C. hf. mor., soiled. (S. Dec.2; 501) *Nolan.* £75
- - **Anr. Copy.** Some spotting thro.-out. Cont. cf. gt., covers detchd. (TA. Jan.22; 265) £60
- - **Anr. Copy.** Slightly soiled in parts. Cont. linen, worn & defect. (HK. Nov.18-21; 1198) DM 600
- **The Antiquities of Scotland** 1789-91. 1st. Edn. 2 vols. Fo. Engraved folding map, hand-cold. in outl., 180 plts. washed? Later hf. mor. gt. (SBA. Mar.4; 108) *Spencer.* £86
- - **Anr. Copy.** Spotted. Cont. tree cf., rebkd. (SH. Jul.23; 13) *Greenwood.* £65
- - **Anr. Edn.** 1797. 2 vols. Fo. Cf., worn. (CE. Nov.20; 96) £130
- - **Anr. Copy.** 4to. Some foxing. Cont. diced cf., gt. decor. spines. Bkplt. of Richard Brinsley Sheridan. (TA. Jul.16; 390) £85
- - **Anr. Copy.** Occasional slight spotting. Cont. cf. (CSK. Oct.3; 198) £65
- - **Anr. Copy.** (SG. Feb.26; 149) $120
- **Lexicon Balatronicum.** 1811. Slight browning, interleaved with some MS. notes. Late 19th. C. mor., partly unc. (S. Feb.9; 191) *Quaritch.* £95
- **Military Antiquities Respecting a History of the English Army.** 1801. 2 vols. 4to. Some spotting thro.-out. Cont. cf. gt., vol. 1 rebkd., vol. 2 covers detchd. (TA. Jan.22; 267) £55
- - **Anr. Copy.** 139 (of 140) copper-plts. Cont. gt. & diced cf., cf. rebkd., edges & corners worn. Sig. of Basil Lubbock. (PNY. May 21; 205) $100
- **Rules for Drawing Caricatures: With an Essay on Comic Painting.** 1791. 2nd. Edn. Some foxing thro.-out. Cont. tree cf., recently rebkd. (TA. Sep.18; 159) £60
- **Supplement to the Antiquities of England & Wales.** L., ca. 1787. Vol. VIII. 4to. Tooled cf. (GM. Apr.30; 544) £65
- **A Treatise on Ancient Armour & Weapons.** 1786. 4to. Recent hf. cf. (TA. Jun.18; 300) £65

GROSE, Francis, Astle Thomas & others
[-] **The Antiquarian Repertory.** 1775-84. 4 vols. 4to. Cont. hf. cf., some covers detchd. (CSK. Aug.29; 250) £70
- - **Anr. Edn.** 1807-09. New Edn., L.P. 4 vols. 4to. Mott. cf. gt., by Bedford, 3 jnts. split, 1 jnt. renewed. (S. Nov.24; 144) *Traylen.* £90
- - **Anr. Edn.** 1807-09. 4 vols. Some plts. stained. Hf. cf. (SB. May 13; 222) £60

GROSS, A.J.
- **Quatre Sonates pour le Clavecin ou Piano-Forte . . . Oeuvre VII.** Paris, ca. 1780. (Opus I-VII bnd. in 1 vol). Sigd. by publisher on title, sig. of 'F. Krumpholtz' on 1st. title, & inscr. on flylf. in later hand. Cont. red mor., gt., arms of Mademoiselle d'Orleans, Princese de Bourbon-Condé, lge. fleur de lis in each corner, concentric gt. roll borders including baskets entwined with garland, flat spine gt. in compartments with fleur de lis, inner gt. floral dentelles. Dedicated to Fanny Krumpholtz. (SM. Oct.7; 1739) *Frs.* 2,200

GROSS, Samuel D.
- **The Anatomy, Physiologie, & Diseases of the Bones & Joints.** Phila., 1830. 1st. Edn. Orig. sheep, worn & scuffed. From Brooklyn Academy of Medicine. (SG. Jan.29; 191) $110
- **Daniel Drake.** Louisville, 1853. 1st. Edn. Mod. bd. binder. From Brooklyn Academy of Medicine. (SG. Jan.29; 139) $100

GROSSI, Pier Luigi
[-] **Poesie Oneste del Padre Pier-Luige da Gesu Maria.** Venice, 1766. 1st. Edn. 4to. Cont. marb. bds., unc. From the collection of John A. Saks. (C. Jun.10; 105) *Ford.* £60

GROSSMAN, Marcel
See-EINSTEIN, Albert & Grossman, Marcel

GROSSMAN, Mary Louise & Hamlet, John -MEINERTZHAGEN, R.
- **Birds of Prey of the World.-Pirates & Predators.** N.Y.; Edinb. & L., [1964]; [1959]. 2 works in 2 vols. 4to.; 8vo. Both orig. cl. (CB. Sep.24; 26) *Can.* $240

GROSSMITH, George & Weedon
- **The Diary of a Nobody.** Bristol & L., [1892]. 1st. Edn. Advts. Cl., some foxing. (SG. Nov.13; 278) $110

GROSZ, George
- **Ecce Homo.** Berlin, 1923. 1st. Edn., C Edn. Fo. Pict. wraps., folding cl. box. (SG. Oct.23; 149) $475
- - **Anr. Copy.** Title & 2 text ll. slightly soiled. Orig. pict. bds. (R. Mar.31-Apr.4; 478) DM 1,500
- - **Anr. Copy.** Fo. Slightly soiled. Orig. bds. (R. Oct.14-18; 915) DM 1,100
- - **Anr. Edn.** Berlin, 1923. Ltd. Edn., D. Edn. Fo. Orig. wraps, rather worn. (SH. Nov.21; 337) *Platemark.* £155.
- - **Anr. Edn.** Berlin, 1923. D. Edn. Fo. Orig. bds., spine defect. (HK. May 12-14; 1869) DM 800
- **Interregnum.** Ed.:– John Dos Passos. N.Y., Black Sun Pr., 1936. (280) numbered, designed by Caresse Crosby, with orig. cold. sigd. litho. Fo. Cl.-bkd. simulated wood. (SG. Oct.23; 152) $1,300

GROTIUS, Hugo
- **Annotationes in Libros Evangeliorum.** Amst., 1641. 1st. Edn. Fo. Browned. Cont. cf. (SG. Jun.25; 81) *Frognal.* £80
- **Le Droit de la Guerre et de la Paix.** Amst., 1724. 2 vols. in 1. 4to. Cont. cf. (SII. Jul.9; 46) *Frognal.* £75
- **De Jure Belli ac Pacis Libri Tres.** Amst., 1735. 2 vols. 18th. C. mor., gt. spine, sm. decor. stpd., triple fillet, corner fleurons, gt. outer dentelle. (D. Dec.11-13; 2160) DM 800
- **Of Warre & Peace . . .'III parts & Memorials of the Author's Life & Death.** Ill.:– Thomas Cross. 1654. 1st. Edn. in Engl. 4 ll. of publisher's advts. Cont. cf., spine & jnts. slightly worn. [Wing G2119] (S. Oct.21; 433) *Brooke-Hitchings.* £310
- - **Anr. Copy.** Minor tears, browned, 4 ll. of publisher's advts. Old cf., very worn. (SPB. May 29; 187) $150

GROVE, A. & others
- **A Supplement to Elwes' Monograph of the Genus Lilium.** 1933-40; 1950-62. 9 orig. pts. Lge. fo. 40 cold. plts. Stitched as issued in orig. wraps., 2 pts. not unif., cl. portfo. (C. Jul.15; 178) *Quaritch.* £560

GROVE, Sir George
- **Dictionary of Music & Musicians.** Ed.:– Eric Blom. 1954. 9 vols. Cl., gt. (CE. Aug.28; 97) £60

GROVE WHITE, Col. James
- **Historical & Topographical Notes, etc. on Buttevant, Castletownroche, Doneraile, Mallow & Places in their Vicinity.** Cork, 1911-25. Vols. II-IV only. Cl. (GM. Apr.30; 168) £130

GROVES, Lt. Col. Percy
See-ATKINSON, C.T.–GROVES, Lt. Col. Percy

G[RUBER], J.S.
- **Der Wol-unterwiesene Ingenieur.** Nuremb., 1726. 1st. Edn. 6 pts. in 1 vol. Hf.-title before p. 251 or 589, 2 old liby. stps. on title lf. Cont. leath., gt. spine. (R. Oct.14-18; 426) DM 2,100

GRUEBER, B.
- **Regensburg und seine Umgebungen.** Regensburg, 1844. Fo. Liby. bds. (R. Mar.31-Apr.4; 1981) DM 420

GRUEBER, H.A.
See-KEARY, C.F. & Grueber, H.A.

GRUEL, Leon
- **Manuel Historique et Bibliographique de l'Amateur de Reliures.** Paris, 1887. (50) numbered copies on Japan vell., & specially bnd. Lge. 4to. Maroon crushed lev. gt. with strapwork design round title, spine gt., gt. dentelles with red satin doubls. & end-papers. (SG. Oct.2; 168) $850
- - **Anr. Edn.** Paris, 1887. (700) numbered on Rives velin. 4to. Crimson three-qtr. mor., raised bands, orig. decor. wraps. bnd. in. Inscr. to Charles Fairfax Murray, with his bkplt. (SG. Mar.26; 228) $350
- - **Anr. Edn.** Paris, 1887; 1905. Vol. 1 (250) numbered on beau papier des Vosges; Vol. 2 (650) numbered on beau papier Vélin de Rives. 2 vols. Sm. fo. Three-qtr. lev., raised bands, orig. pict. wraps. & spines bnd. in, boxed. (SG. May 14; 90) $600
- - **Anr. Edn.** Paris, 1887-1905. 1st. vol.: (1000); 2nd. vol.: (700); on Vosges paper, numbered. 2 vols. 4to. Sewed, wraps. (HD. Dec.5; 98) *Frs.* 3,300
- - **Anr. Edn.** Paris, 1897-1905. Ltd. Edn. on Vélin Rives Paper. 2 pts. in 1 vol. 4to. Mod. cl.

---

orig. wraps. bnd. in. Pres. inscr. to Paul Champoudry. (SM. Oct.7; 1396) *Frs.* 3,000
- - **Anr. Edn.** Paris, 1905. (50) on papier des Vosges. 2nd. pt. only (lacks pt. 1). 4to. Buckram, orig. wraps. preserved. The John A. Saks copy. (CNY. Oct.1; 180) $100

GRUNDY, C. Reginald & Roe, F.G.
- **Catalogue of the Pictures & Drawings in the Collection of Frederick John Nettleford.** 1933-38. 4 vols. 4to. Mntd. cold. plts. Orig. cl. (CSK. Feb.6; 160) £380

GRUNER, Elioth
- **Twenty Four Reproductions in Colour from Original Oil Paintings.** Ed.:– N. Lindsay (foreword). Sydney, 1947. (2000) numbered. 4to. No bdg. stated. (JL. Jul.20; 643) *Aus.* $150
- - **Anr. Edn.** Sydney, n.d. (2000) numbered. 4to. Cl. (KH. Mar.24; 183) *Aus.* $120

GRUNER, Gottlieb Sigmund
- **Histoire Naturelle des Glacieres de Suisse.** Trans.:– M. de Keralio. Paris, 1770. 1st. Fr. Edn. 4to. 19th. C. hf. mor. From Chetham's Liby., Manchester. (C. Nov.26; 184a) *King.* £320

GRUNER, Lewis
- **Fresco Decorations & Stuccoes of Churches & Palaces in Italy.** 1848. 2 vols. in 1. Fo. Plts., loose, text mntd. Cont. hf. mor. (SH. Nov.6; 210) *Weinreb.* £80
- - **Anr. Edn.** 1854. 2 vols. in 1. Fo. Text mntd. Cont. mor., gt. (SH. Nov.6; 211) *Russell.* £80
- - **Anr. Copy.** 2 vols., including text. Fo. & 4to. Cont. hf. mor. (SH. Nov.6; 212) *Elliott.* £55
- **Specimens of Ornamental Art.** 1850. Fo. Occasional light spotting, without the text. Cont. hf. mor. (CSK. Sep.26; 47) £200
- **The Terracotta Architecture of North Italy.** 1867. 4to. 2 plts. loose. Qtr. mor. gt. (P. Feb.19; 199) *Fogg.* £85

GRUNPECK, Joseph
- **Speculum Naturalis Coelestis & Propheticae Visionis.** Nuremb., Nov.7, 1508. 1st. Edn. Fo. 1st. lf. rehinged, b1 torn & reprd. single sm. wormhole thro.-out, other very slight worming at end, some spotting. Recent vell. over bds., cl. s.-c. Bkplt. of John A. Saks. (CNY. Oct.1; 100) $1,400

GRUNSTEIN, Leo
- **Moritz Michael Daffinger u. s. Kreis.** Vienna, 1923. (1225). 4to. Orig. hf. leath. (HK. May 12-14; 2324) DM 600

GRUZINOV, Ivan
- **Imazhinizma Osnovnoe [Fundamental Imagism].** Moscow, 1921. Browned. Upr. wrap. torn, lacks lr. wrap., loose. (SH. Feb.6; 317) *Quaritch.* £65

GRYNAEUS, Simon
- **Novus Orbis refionum ac Insularum Veteribus Incognitarum.** Basle, 1555. Fo. Lacks world map, MS. notes in early hand in margins. Hf. mor. (BS. Jun.11; 159) £170
See-HUTTICH, Johannes

GSELL-FELS, Dr. Th.
- **Die Schweiz.** Munich & Berlin, [1876-77]. 2 vols. Fo. Slightly soiled in parts. Orig. hf. leath., gt. spine & upr. cover, vol. 2 spine torn at head. (HK. Nov.18-21; 1398) DM 1,300
- - **Anr. Edn.** Munich & Berlin, ca. 1880. 2 vols. Sm. fo. Frontis. soiled. Orig. hf. leath., gt. (R. Oct.14-18; 2005) DM 1,900
- - **Anr. Edn.** Zürich, 1883. 2nd. Edn., Volks Edn. Sm. fo. Orig. hf. leath. (R. Mar.31-Apr.4; 2743) DM 800
- **Switzerland.** L., ca. 1880. Sm. fo. Frontis. soiled. Orig. linen. (R. Oct.14-18; 2006) DM 1,900
- - **Anr. Edn.** 1881. Fo. Orig. cl. (SH. May 21; 286) *Crete.* £310
- - **Anr. Copy.** Fo. Some ll. soiled & loose. Orig. cl. (SH. Jul.9; 220) *Wazzau.* £220

GUADAGNOLUS, Philippus
- **Breves Arabicae Linguae Institutiones.** Rome, 1642. 1st. Edn. Fo. Some browning. Cont. limp vell., soiled, head of spine torn, s.-c. (S. Apr.29; 390) *Brill.* £200

GUAGNINUS, Alexander
- **Europeae Descriptio, quae Regnum Poloniae, Lituaniam . . . complectitur.** Speyer, 1581. Fo. Lacks A4 & all after O5 including general table, slightly spotted in some margins. 19th. C. hf. cf. (S. Jun.29; 267) *Saphiena.* £75

GUARANA, Jacopo
- Oracoli, Auguri, Auspici, Sibelle ... della Religione Pagana. Ill.:– A. Povelati, I. Alessandri & others after author. Venice, 1792. Fo. Cont. marb. paper bds. From the collection of John A. Saks. (C. Jun.10; 106) *Lyon.* £170

GUARINI, Giovanni Battista
- Il Pastor Fido, Tragicomedia Pastorale. Venice, 1590. 1st. Edn. 4to. 1st. & last ll. a little stained. Cont. vell. bds. (C. Apr.1; 39) *Penny.* £160
– – Anr. Edn. Venice, 1602. 4to. Light foxing. Later vell. gt., buckram s.-c. From the collection of John A. Saks. (C. Jun.10; 107) *Libri.* £70
– – Anr. Copy. 2 pts. in 1 vol. MS. note on fly-lf. 'a servare per le osservazione che sono buonissime'. 18th. C. red mor., triple gt. fillet, spine gt. in compartments, inner gt. dentelles. Paris d'Illens copy. (SM. Oct.7; 1741) Frs. 2,200
– – Anr. Edn. 1718. 4to. Cont. cf., worn. (SH. Jul.9; 75) *King* £55
[-] – Anr. Edn. 1732. Fr. & Italian text. Cont. Fr. red mor., gt., spine tooled in compartments, covers with roll-border & arms of Pierre Adolphe du Cambout, Marquis de Coislin. (S. Nov.24; 146) *Watchman.* £60
– – Anr. Edn. Didot; Paris, 1782. On vell. 2 vols. Sig. of Jos. Copley, 1809, on fly-lf. Cont. mor., gt., by Derome le Jeune with his ticket, arms of Paris d'Illens on covers, narrow gt. borders with interlaced dots & stems, fleurs de lis, tiny circles in gt. squares alternating with 3 vertical lines & fillets, flat spines gt. in compartments with leafy cross in panel of dots, inner gt. dentelles, pink silk liners, each vol. in s.-c., flat spine gt. in compartments with sm. bird in foliage & lozenge of stars. (SM. Oct.7; 1743) Frs. 78,000
– – Anr. Copy. L.P. Red mor. by Derome le Jeune with his ticket, triple gt. fillet, spine compartments with double gt. fillet, empty except for title & date, inner gt. dentelles. Vernon-Holford copy. (SM. Oct.7; 1744) Frs. 1,800

- Il Pastor Fido.–Aminta.–Filli di Sciro. Paris, 1656. 3 works in 1 vol. 4to. Inscr. on end-lf. 'Constantinople 1791', name erased. 18th. C. red mor., gt. arms of Duchesse de Lévis-Mirepoix, triple gt. fillet, flat spine gt. in compartments, inner gt. dentelles. (SM. Oct.7; 1742) Frs. 1,600
[-] Der Treue Schäffer. Trans.:– J.G. Scheffner. Mietau & Hasenporth, 1773. Cont. style hf. vell. (HK. May 15; 4814) DM 650
See–BONARELLI Della Rovere, G.–GUARINI, G.B.

GUDGEON, Thomas W.
- Reminiscences of the War in New Zealand. L.; 1879. 1st. Edn. Pict. cl. (SG. Feb.26; 150) $120

GUEDEVILLE, Nicolas
[-] Le Grand Théâtre Historique. Ill.:– I. Baptist (frontis.) & R. de Hooghe? (folding plts.). Leiden, 1703. 5 vols. in 3. Fo. Cont. cf. Lord Minto's copy, with bkplt. (S. Jul.27; 122) *De Jonge.* £240

GUELDENSTAEDT, Johann Anton
- Reisen durch Russland und im Caucasischen Gebuerge. Ed.:– P.S. Pallas. St. Petersb., 1787; 1791. L.P. 2 vols. Lge. 4to. Cont. mor. (SG Oct.9; 122) $1,900

G[UENEBAULD], I.
- Le Reveil de Chyndonax Prince des Vacies Druydes Celtiques Diionois. Dijon, 1621. 1st. Edn. 4to. Old sig. of Jacob Joye on title. 18th. C. red mor., in Padeloup style, broad gt. border, spine compartments gt. in pointillé, inner gt. dentelles, Dutch gt. flowered end-papers. (SM. Oct.7; 1745) Frs. 3,500

GUERCINI, G.F. (Pseud.)
See–BARBIER, Giovanni F.

GUERIN, E.
[-] Dictionnaire d'Histoire Naturelle. N.p., ca. 1855. 2 atlas vols. only. 4to. Cont. hf. roan. (SM. Feb.11; 70) Frs. 3,200

GUERIN, Marcel
- Catalogue Raisonné de l'Oeuvre Gravé et Lithographié de Aristide Maillol. Geneva, 1965. (600) numbered. Vol. I: Le Bois. Orig. wraps. (SH. Nov.21; 405) *Schwing.* £55
- L'Oeuvre Gravé de Gauguin. Paris, 1927. (600) numbered. 4to. Marginal browning. Orig. wraps., soiled, stitching shaken. (CSK. Apr.24; 15) £220
– – Anr. Copy. (550) numbered, 2 vols. (HK. Nov.18-21; 2574) DM 850

GUERIN, Maurice de
- Poèmes en Prose, Précédés d'un Petite Lettre sur les Mythes par P. Valéry. Ill.:– George Barbier. Paris, 1928. (150). Sm. 4to. 2 separate sets of ills. In sheets, ill. wrap. (HD. Dec.5; 99) Frs. 3,600

GUERINIERE, Monsieur de la
- Ecole de Cavalrie. Paris, 1769. 2 vols. Some browning. Later hf. cf., worn. (CSK. Nov.21; 164) £55

GUEST, Lady Charlotte
- The Mabinogion, from the Llyfr Coch o Hergest & Other Ancient Welsh Manuscripts. 1838-49. L.P. 6 pts. in 3 vols. Fo. Facs. MS.'s (including 2 ptd. on vell.), text in Welsh & Engl. Cont. crimson mor. gt. by Bedford, bkplts. partially removed. (TA. Sep.18; 367) £180

GUEST, Moses
- Poems ... To Which are Annexed Extracts from a Journal Kept by the Author ... Cinc., 1823. 1st. Edn. 12mo. Lacks plt. called for by Sabin & Thomson, text foxed, offset on title. Orig. cf.-bkd. bds., worn, upr. cover loose, folding cl. s.-c., endpapers stained & ink burned, sigs. on front free endpaper. From liby. of William E. Wilson. [Sabin 291369] (SPB. Apr.29; 118) $325
– – Anr. Copy. Foxing, spotting & staining, lacks plt. as above. Sheep. From liby. of William E. Wilson. (SPB. Apr.29; 119) $175

GUETERSLOH, P.
- Kain und Abel. Vienna, [1924]. (250). Fo. Orig. hf. linen. (H. May 21/22; 1597) DM 520

GUETTARD, J.E.
- Mémoires sur Différentes Parties des Sciences et Arts. Paris, 1768-70. 3 vols. 4to. Vol. 1 & 11 lack last lf. (blank?), stp. of Bibliothèque du Roi à Neuilly on titles. Cont. mor., gt., arms of Louise Marie Adelaide de Bourbon-Penthièvre, Duchesse d'Orléans, on covers, wide rococo dentelle border, spines gt. with fleurons in compartments, inner gt. dentelles. Holland House copy. (SM. Oct.7; 1746) Frs. 28,000

GUEUDEVILLE, Pier
[-] Theatre Des Rois et des Souverains de La Famille Roiale de France. Amst., n.d. Ob. fo. 12 hand-cold. engraved genealogies only, 11 double-p. & mntd. on guards, 1 folding & torn with loss of some letters, marginal repairs to title & a few genealogies, some slight soiling. Old bds., worn. (CSK. May 1; 79) £150

GUEVARA, Bp. Antonio de
- A Booke of the Invention of the Art of Navigation. Trans.:– Edward Hollowes. 1578. 1st. Engl. Edn. 4to. Lacks blanks at beginning & end, slightly dampstained & soiled. 19th. C. hf. cf., bkplt. of Scott Liby. Collection of the Institution of Naval Architects. [STC 12425] (S. Nov.4; 472) *Quaritch.* £1,100
- A Chronicle, conteyning the Lives of Tenne Emperours of Rome. Trans.:– Edward Hellowes. 1577. 1st. Edn. in Engl. 4to. Lacks last lf. (blank?), slight worming & dampstaining. 18th. C. mott. cf., rebkd. Bkplt. of the Hon. George Baillie. [STC 12426] (S. Feb.9; 192) *Fletcher.* £150
- The Diall of Princes. Trans.:– Thomas North. 1557. 1st. Edn. in Engl. Fo. Inscrs. on title & a few other ll., dampstaining. 17th. C. cf., worn. Bkplt. of Sir John Wentworth. (S. Sep.29; 103) *Flower.* £350
- The Familiar Epistles. 1577. 3rd. Edn. in Engl. 4to. Some short tears & sm. holes, slightly affecting text, slight browning & soiling. 17th. C. cf., rebkd. Bkplt. of Algernon Capel, Earl of Essex. [STC 12434] (S. Feb.9; 193) *Fletcher.* £95
– – Anr. Edn. Trans.:– Edward Hellowes. 1584. 4to. Lacks 1st. text lf., some marginal wormholes, some ll. slightly soiled. Cont. limp vell., soiled & worn. Bkplt. of Newton Hall, Camb. [STC 12435] (S. Jul.27; 63) *Allen.* £80

GUEVARA, Bp. Antonio de (Trans.)
See–AURELIUS, Marcus Antoninus

GUGGENHEIM, M.
- Le Cornici Italiane dalla Meta del Secolo XV allo Scorcio del XVI. Milan, 1897. Fo. Publisher's bds. (CR. Mar.19; 216) Lire 350,000

GUIAND, J.
- The Ruins of Mandoo. Ill.:– after Claudius Harris. 1860. Fo. Some plts. foxed, some ll. with edges frayed. Orig. cl. gt., upr. cover detchd., spine

defect. From Chetham's Liby., Manchester. (C. Nov.26; 185) *Ludgrove.* £50

GUICCIARDINI, Francesco
- La Historia d'Italia. Venice, 1565. 4to. Lacks last blank. Cont. mor., gt., lge. scrollwork centrepiece on each cover, central oval semé with tiny fleurons, some compartments semé with dots, arabesque cornerpieces, triple gt. & blind fillets, flat spine gt. in compartments with single gt. ornament divided by narrow arabesque borders, arms of Charles de Castellan, stpd. lr. left of centrepiece, lacks ties. Bkplt. of the Earl of Ilchester. (SM. Oct.7; 1747) Frs. 6,000
– – Anr. Edn. Ill.:– A. Visentini & J.M. Liotard. Venice, 1738. 2 vols. Fo. Several ll. browned. Cont. vell. bds., slightly worn. From the collection of John A. Saks. (C. Jun.10; 108) *Bozzolato.* £190
– – Anr. Edn. Venice, 1738. L.P. 2 vols. Lge. fo. Cont. maroon hf. mor. gt. (S. Dec.8; 109) *Norman.* £50

- The Historie ... conteining the VVarres of Italie & other Parts ... Trans.:– Geffray Fenton. 1579. 1st. Edn. in Engl. Fo. Lacks 1st lf. (blank?), slight browning & soiling, a few rust-holes affecting text slightly, some worming. 17th. C. cf., worn, 1 cover detchd. [STC 12458] (S. Sep.29; 39) *Armstrong.* £140

GUICCARDINI, Ludovico
- Belgicae. Amst., 1660. Later Edn. 3 pts. in 2 vols. 12mo. Cont. vell. (LM. Mar.21; 269) B.Frs. 30,000
- Beschrijvinghe van alle de Nederlanden. Trans.:– Cornelius Kilianus. Amst., 1612. [1st. Edn. with Dutch text?]. Fo. Old cf., worn. (LM. Mar.21; 122) B.Frs. 100,000
– – Anr. Copy. Lacks plan of Gouda, plt. of Bourse of Amst. in its place not mentioned in index, extra map, 4 plts. with pen annots. partly in margins, some on engraved surface, partly in red, some other margin pencil annots., 1 plt. slightly torn, some plts. with short tear, part of upper inner parts of plts. & text with light stain, some other mainly marginal stains. Cont. gt. stpd. & panel vell., slightly worn & soiled, new ties. (VG. Oct.13; 70) Fls. 7,100
- Description de tout de Païs-Bas autrement dict la Germanie Inferieure. Antw., 1567. Fo. Folding engraved map with tear reprd. Cont. blind-stpd. cf., gt. ornaments in centre of sides, rebkd., 1 corner reprd. (S. Jun.22; 177) *Jonkers.* £500
– – Anr. Edn. Antw., 1568. Fo. Folding plt. with minor tears, owner's inscr. removed from title leaving hole affecting the arms on verso. Cont. blind-panel. cf., gt. ornaments at corners & centre of sides, rebkd., worn. (S. Jun.22; 178) *Jonkers.* £460
– – Anr. Edn. Antw., 1582. Fo. Lacks plts. at pp. 196 & 326, some staining, tear in s4. 18th. C. cf., worn. (S. Jun.22; 179) *Burgess.* £1,900
– – Anr. Edn. Amst., 1635. Fo. Lacks 1 plt., but contains 4 plts. not listed in index, corner map Holland reprd., some short tears, plan of Groningen loosely inserted, stains in 1st. part, browned in places, last ll. a little frayed. Cont. vell., gt. supra-libros, slightly warped & soiled, lacks ties, spine defect. (VG. Oct.13; 71) Fls. 7,000
- Descrittione di Tutti i Paesi Bassi. Antw., 1588. 3rd. Edn. Fo. Engraved title, port., frontis. & 76 engraved plts., hand-cold. thro'-out, rust-hole in C6, 1 plt. reprd., S3 stained. Cont. hf. cf. gt., spine & outer corners reprd. (S. Mar.31; 475) *Forum Books.* £1,400
- Omnium Belgii. Ed.:– Regnerus Vitellius Zirizaeus. Amst., 1613. Fo. Slight worming at foot of some ll. Cont. vell. Plt. not called for mntd. between pp. 220 & 221. (LM. Nov.8; 84) B.Frs. 211,000

GUICHARD, Claude
- Funerailles, & diuerses Manières d'enseuelir des Rommains, Grecs, & autres Nations, tant Anciennes que Modernes. Lyon, 1581. 1st. Edn. 4to. Cont. vell. (S. Oct.21; 282) *Artico.* £200

GUICHART, Etienne
- L'Harmonie Etymologique des Langues. Paris, 1610. Late 19th. C. mor., blind fillet, inner dentelle. (HD. Jun.10; 36) Frs. 2,100

GUIDI, Guido
- Chirurgia. 1544. 1st. Edn. Fo. Tear in title reprd., some light dampstains, early Latin MS. ex

libris on title. Early vell. (SG. Jan.29; 196)

GUIDICKIUS, F.W. $8,800
See–WALPOLE, Horace–G[UIDICKIUS], F.W.

GUIDOTT, Thomas
– **De Thermis Britannicis Tractatus Accesserunt Observationes.** L., 1691. 1st. Edn. 4to. Slightly dampstained. Old panel. cf., rebkd. TA. Dec.18; 56) £50
– **A Discourse of Bathe & the Hot Waters There.** 1676. 1st. Edn. 2 folding plts. mntd., 1 torn in fold & defect. in lr. blank margin, extreme outer margin of frontis. reprd. New mor. [Wing G2192] (S. Jun.16; 360) *Jenner Books.* £75
– – **Anr. Copy.** Occasional slight soiling. Old cf., rebkd. [Wing G2192] (CSK. May 15; 19) £60

GUIGARD, Joannis
– **Armorial du Bibliophile.** Paris, 1870-73. 1st. Edn. 2 vols. in 1. Cont. hf. mor. gt., partly unc. (S. Nov.24; 148) *Nat. Art.* £90

GUIGO I, Prior General of Carthusians
– **Statuta Ordinis Cartusiensis a domino Guigone priore Cartusie edita.** Bales, 1510. Fo. D6 of pt. 1 blank, pt. 4 misbnd. before pt. 1, 2 sm. wormholes in some ll. at end, old sig. on 1st. lf., bkplts. of John Arthur Brooke & Alfred Ehrman with latter's stp. at end. 18th. C. red mor., triple gt. fillet, flat spine gt. in compartments, inner gt. dentelles. (SM. Oct.7; 1748) Frs. 11,500

GUIGOU, P. & Vimar, A.
– **L'Arche e Noe.** Paris, ca. 1900. Ob. 8vo. Cl. Sigd. inscr. by Vimar to Nadar, & with orig. pen & ink sketch. (SG. Apr.30; 181) $140

GUILLAUME, Gustave, Baron d'Imhoff
See–DU BOIS, J.P.I.–GUILLAUME, Gustave, Baron d'Imhoff

GUILLAUME, Simon, Maitre de Dance
– **Positions et Attitudes de l'Allemande.** Ill.:– J. Chapoulaud. Paris, 1768. 1st. Edn. 4to. Sm. tears in blank margins of title reprd. 19th. C. hf mor. (C. Apr.1; 137) *Quaritch.* £280

GUILLAUMET, T[annequi]
– **Traicté de la Maladie Nouuellement appelé Crystaline.–Liure Xenodocal, c'est à dire, hospitalier.–Traicté des ouuertures, Trous et vlceres spontanées.** Lyons, 1611. 1st. Edns. 3 works (?pts.) in 1 vol. 12mo. Some browning. Cont. cf., spine gt., soiled. (S. Oct.21; 393) *Booth.* £80

GUILLEMIN, J.B.A.
– **Icones Lithographicae Plantarum Australasiae Rariorum.** Paris, 1827. 4to. Mod. cl. (S. Jun.1; 141) *McCormick.* £260

GUILLERMUS Avernus, Bp. of Paris
– **Dyalogus . . . De Septem Sacramentis.** [Paris], ca. 1500? Mod. paper bds. [C. 2875] (C. Apr.1; 41) *Metzdorf.* £70
– **Postilla Super Epistolas et Evangelia de Tempore et Sanctis et pro Defunctis.** [Hagenau], Heinrich Gran. 10 Dec., 1492. 4to. Spaces for initial capitals, capitals supplied in red or blue, as are paragraph marks & initial strokes, title-p. woodcut lightly cold., lacks blank fo. m8 & final blank, title & next 6 ll. with worming at lr. outer margin patched, not affecting text, light browning, 1st. few ll. soiled. Mor., spine gt.-lettered, by Sangorski & Sutcliffe. Bkplt. of W.A. Harding, Ruddoff ink inscr. on blank fly-lf., lately in the collection of Eric Sexton. [Goff Supp. G692a, H. 8280*] (CNY. Apr.8; 76) $1,500

GUILLIE, Sebastian G.
– **Essai sur l'Instruction des Aveugles.** Ill.:– Dubois (frontis), Hubert after Ribault & Dubois. Paris, 1817. Mor. gt. (D. Dec.11-13; 202) DM 500

GUILLIM, John
– **A Display of Heraldry.** 1638. 3rd. Edn. 4to. Later cf. (SH. May 21; 212) *Miles.* £60
– – **Anr. Edn.** 1660. 4th. Edn. Fo. B1 reprd. with loss of a few letters, lacking pp. 433/434? Later hf. mor. [Wing G2219] (CSK. Nov.7; 154) £60
– – **Anr. Edn.** 1679. 5th. Edn. Fo. 2 pp. index torn with slight loss of text. Recently rebnd. in hf. cf. (TA. Dec.18; 112) £80
– – **Anr. Edn.** 1724. 6th. Edn. Fo. Cont. cf., rebkd. (SKC. Dec.4; 1406) £100
– – **Anr. Copy.** Cf. gt. (LC. Jun.18; 283) £60

GUINOT, Eugène
– **Les Bords du Rhin.** [Paris], [1847]. Soiled. Orig. linen, gold stpd. (R. Oct.14-18; 2414) DM 700

– **L'Eté à Bade.** Paris, [1847]. 1st. Edn. Slightly soiled. Cont. hf. leath. gt. (R. Mar.31-Apr.4; 1906) DM 1,000
– – **Anr. Copy.** Cont. hf. leath. (R. Oct.14-18; 2152) DM 820
– – **Anr. Copy.** Lacks 1 steel engraved plt., soiled. Orig. pict. linen. (HK. May 12-14; 564) DM 800
– – **Anr. Edn.** Ill.:– T. Johannot, E. Lami, Français & Jacquemot; port. after Sandoz. Paris, [1847]. 3rd. Edn., 1st. Printing. Lge. 8vo. 3 additional cold. plts. Cont. bds., smooth decor. spine. (HD. Jun.25; 272) Frs. 1,700
– – **Anr. Edn.** Paris, ca. 1850. Some slight foxing. Cl., slightly worn, orig. cold. litho. wrap. bnd. in. (BS. Jun.11; 347) £170
– – **Anr. Edn.** Paris, after 1857. 4th. Edn. 4to. Orig. wrap. (HK. May 12-14; 564a) DM 700
– **A Summer at Baden-Baden.** Ca. 1853. Orig. cl., gt. arms. (P. Jun.11; 318) *Dupont.* £200
– – **Anr. Copy.** Some ll. slightly stained. Outer margin of upr. cover slightly stained. (SBA. Jul.14; 33) *Bailey.* £160
– – **Anr. Copy.** Multi-stpd. on some plts. Cont. linen, lacks spine. (R. Oct.14-18; 2154) DM 500
– – **Anr. Edn.** L., ca. 1855. New Edn. Orig. linen. (R. Mar.31-Apr.4; 1907) DM 1,050

GUIRLANDE des Mois, La
Ed.:– George Barbier. Paris, 1917-21. 5 vols. 18mo. Publisher's decor. silk s.-c. (HD. Dec.5; 100) Frs. 3,200

GUISE, Henri, Duc de
– **Les Mémoires.** Ed.:– Saint-Yvon. Cologne, 1668. 1st. Elzevir Edn. of this date. 2 vols. 12mo. Late 19th. C. mor., by Bradel or Bisiaux, garland in border, decor. spines, inside dentelle, watered silk doubls. & end-papers. Bkplts. of Renouard & Comte de Béarn. (HD. Mar.18; 80) Frs. 3,600

GULICH, L. von Edler zu Lilienburg
– **Erb-Huldigung . . . Josepho dem Ersten.** Wien, [1705]. Fo. Cf., spine slightly defect. (BS. Jun.11; 218a) £440

GULLMANN, F.K.
– **Geschichte der Stadt Augsburg seit Ihrer Entstehung bis zum Jahre 1806.** Augsburg, ca. 1810. 6 vols. Vol. 4 bnd. inverted. Cont. bds. (R. Oct.14-18; 2176) DM 850

GUMILLA, Jose
– **Historia Natural Civil y Geografica de las Naciones Situadas en las Riveras del Rio Orinoco.** Barcelona, 1791. 3rd. Edn., L.P. 2 vols. 4to. Cont. Spanish mott. cf., spines gt. [Sabin 29276] (S. Feb.9; 195) *Rosenburg.* £360
– **Historie Naturelle, Civile et Géographique de l'Orenoque et des Principalas Rivières qui s'y jettent.** Avignon, 1758. 3 vols. Light stain affecting 1 vol. Cont. cf., 1 vol. lacks labels. (SPB. May 5; 244) $1,200
– **El Orinoco Ilustrado y Defendido. Historia Natural, Civil y Geographica de este Gran Rio y de sus Caudalosas Vertientes; Govierno, Usos y Costumbres de los Indios.** Madrid, 1745. 2 vols. Sm. 4to. Some discolouration. Qtr. mor. (SPB. May 5; 243) $3,750

GUMUCHIAN & Cie
– **Catalogue de Reliures du XVe au XIXe Siècle.** Paris, [1929]. Ltd. Edn. 4to. Orig. cl., d.-w. (SM. Oct.7; 1397) Frs. 1,400
– – **Anr. Edn.** Paris, ca. 1930. (1000) on papier velin. Fo. Ptd. wraps. (SG. Jan.22; 192) $250
– – **Anr. Edn.** Paris, n.d. Fo. Cl. gt., d.-w. (P. Jan.22; 311) *King.* £85
– **Les Livres d'Enfance du XVe au XIX Siècle.** Paris, [1930]. (100) on Hollande. 2 vols. 4to. Mod. hf. mor. (SH. Dec.12; 529) *Lenton.* £210
– – **Anr. Edn.** Paris, ca. 1930. (1000). 2 vols. Lge. 4to. Wraps., torn & loose, unc. & unopened. (SG. Apr.30; 182) $400
– – **Anr. Copy.** Hf. mor., corners, unc., wraps. & spines. (HD. Dec.5; 101) Frs. 3,600

GUN at Home & Abroad
– **British Game Birds & Wild Fowl** 1912. (950) numbered. 4to. Orig. mor. gt. (TA. Dec.18; 78) £52
– – **Anr. Copy.** Orig. mor., soiled. (CSK. May 22; 72) £50
– – **Anr. Edn.** Ed.:– W.R. Ogilvie-Grant & others. Ill.:– Thorburn, Lodge & others. 1912-15. (500) numbered. 4to. Orig. mor. (S. Jun.1; 142) *Lord George.* £340

GUNDLING, N.H.
– **Gundlingiana, darinnen allerhand zur Jurisprudenz Philosophie, Historie, Critic, Litteratur, und übrigen Gelehrsamkeit gehörigen Sachen abgehandelt werden.** Halle, 1715-32. 45 pts. in 9 vols. Liby. stp. on title. Cont. hf. vell. (VG. Dec.17; 1348) Fls. 950

GUNN, John
– **An Historical Enquiry Respecting the Performance on the Harp in the Highlands of Scotland.** Edinb., 1807. 4to. Slight spotting. Cl.-bkd. bds., worn, unc. (S. Dec.9; 434) *Crowe.* £100

GUNN, Neil M.
– **A Collection of Novels.** 1931-56. All but 2 1st. Edns. 20 vols. Orig. cl., some with d.-w.'s. (SH. Dec.18; 176) *Green.* £60

GUNN, Thom
– **Mandrakes.** Ill.:– Leonard Baskin. Rainbow Pr., 1973. 1st. Edn. (150) numbered, sigd. 4to. Orig. vell.-bkd. buckram, s.-c. (S. Jul.22; 156) *Hawthorn Books.* £60

GUNNER, John Ernst
– **Flora Norvegica.** Trondhjem, 1766. 2 pts. in 1 vol. Fo. 1st. 3 plts. foxed, 1st. title torn in fore-margin, & with liby. stp. Cont. hf. cf., covers detchd. From Chetham's Liby., Manchester. (C. Nov.26; 186) *Quaritch.* £340
– – **Anr. Edn.** Tronghjem & Copen., 1766; 1772. 2 vols. in 1. Fo. Liby. stp. on 1st. title. Cont. hf. cf., covers detchd. (C. Mar.18; 48) *Junk.* £220

GUNTHER, F.C.
See–WIRSING, A.L. & Gunther, F.C.

GUNTHER, Johann Christian
– **Sammlung von bis anhero herausgebenen Gedichten.** Breslau & Leipzig, 1751. 1 pt. in 2 vols. 1 hf.-title stpd., vol. 2 with sm. defects. Cont. marb. leath. gt. (HL. May 15; 4397) DM 420
– **Sammlung von bis anhero herausgebenen Gedichten.–Nachlese zu J. Chr. Günthers Gedichten.** Breslau & Leipzig; Breslau, 1742; 1745. 2 works in 1 vol. Cont. vell. (D. Dec.11-13; 781) DM 600

GUNTHER, John
– **Inside Asia.–Inside U.S.A.–Inside Russia Today. –A Fragment of Autobiography.–The Lost City. –Inside South America.** N.Y., 1939-[67]. 1st. Edns. 6 vols. Cl., all but 1st. title in d.-w.'s. 1st. title sigd., others are sigd. pres. copies to Mr. & Mrs. Gilbert Chapman. (PNY. Mar.4; 153) $150

GUNTHER, Robert T.
– **Early Science in Oxford.** Oxford, 1923-39. Vols. I-XIII (of 14). Orig. cl., slightly marked. W.a.f.; from Honeyman Collection. (S. May 20; 3253) *Rogers Turner.* £170

GUNTHERIUS, Antonius
– **Observationum ac Paradoxorum Chymiatricorum libri duo.** Leiden, 1631. 4to. B1 is cancelled. Limp vell., ties, Glyndebourne bkplt. (S. Dec.1; 193) *Phelps.* £70

GUNZBURG, David & Stassof, Vladimir
– **L'Ornement Hebraique.** Leipzig, 1905. Fo. 19 plts. (of 27), some in col., some marginal browning. Folding cl. case, tears, some staining, browning. (SPB. May 11; 226) $275

GURDON, Thornhagh
– **The History of the High Court of Parliament.** L., 1731. 1st. Edn. 2 vols. Errata slip pasted down. Cont. panel. cf., rehinged. (SG. Feb.5; 158) $130

GURLT, E[ernst Julius]
– **Geschichte der Chirurgie.** Berlin, 1898. 1st. Edn. 3 vols. Cont. hf. roan, rebkd. (S. Apr.6; 63) *Vanderkerkhove.* £80

GURNEY, William Brodie
– **Trials of Jeremiah Brandreth, William Turner, Isaac Ludlum, George Weightman, & others, for High Treason, under a Special Commission at Derby.** L., 1817. 2 vols. Orig. bds., unc. & unopened. (KH. Nov.18; 310) Aus. $140

GUTENBERG, Johann
– **Single Leaf from the Gutenberg or Forty-two Line Bible.** [Mainz], [1450-55]. Tall fo. 1 lf of Gutenberg Bible, inserted in 'A Noble Fragment' by A. Edward Newton (N.Y. 1921). Black mor. gt.-lettered. (SG. Oct.9; 123) $4,000
– – **Anr. Edn.** [Mainz], [Johann Gutenberg & Peter Schoeffer?], ca. 1454-55; not after Aug. 1456. Fo. With chapters 3 & 4 & pt. of chapters 2 & 5 from Book of Isaiah, lge. capitals & chapter numberings supplied in red & blue, sm. capitals with red initial strokes, clear Bull's head tau wtrmk., some spotting, tear at 1 side of the lf.,

GUTENBERG, Johann–Single Leaf from the Gutenberg or Forty-two Line Bible.–*contd.*
clumsily reprd., obscuring a few letters of text, bnd.-up with a 'Bibliographical Essay' ('A Noble Fragment') by A. Edward Newton, title dtd. 1921, (N.Y.). Black mor. From liby. of André L. Simon; the lf. is from the Mannheim Liby.–Baroness Zouche copy. (S. May 18; 43) *Facchi.* £4,000
– – **Anr. Copy.** Fo. 1 lf. only, comprising part of 38th. & 39th. chapter of Ecclesiasticus (fo. 40 from vol. II), creased & slightly stained from use as a bdg. Mntd. in maroon mor. fo. album. Bkplts. of Charles Lemuel Nichols & John A. Saks. (CNY. Oct.1; 96) $25,000
[–] – **Anr. Edn.** [Mainz], [?1455]. Fo. 1 lf. from the 42-line Bible, comprising Jeremiah 6-8 in a copy of A.E. Newton's 'A Noble Fragment', N.Y., 1921, some foxing. Orig. mor., publisher's box, worn. (SPB. Oct.1; 228) $5,000

GUTHE, H.
See–EBERS, G. & Guthe, H.

GUTHRIE, James
– **The Elf, a Little Book, Summer Number.** 1900. (20). 4to. 18 ills. including 2 dupls. mntd. on 16 card sheets, sigd., many with MS. captions, hand-cold., loosely inserted. Orig. wraps. (SH. Mar.26; 268) *Henderson.* £55
– – **Anr. Edn.** Old Bourne Pr., 1902-04. (250) numbered. 4 vols. Orig. cl.-bkd. bds., d.-w.'s, unopened. (CSK. Dec.10; 9) £110
– **The Elf, a [second] Sequence of Seasons.** 1902. (250) numbered. 4 vols. Sm. 4to. Orig. linen-bkd. bds., unc., 3 unopened, linen folder & mor.-bkd. s.-c. (SH. Mar.26; 269) *Henderson.* £70
– **To the Memory of Edward Thomas.** Pear Tree Pr., 1937. (250). 4to. Cl., unopened, d.-w. (P. Jul.2; 133) *Lawrence.* £70

GUTHRIE, William
– **Atlas to the Geographical Grammar.** N.p., ca. 1800. Lacks maps of Germany, West Indies, & the World. Orig. bds., leath. spine, bdg. shabby (SG. Nov.20; 20) $100
– **A New System of Modern Geography.** 1792. 5th. Edn. 4to. Engraved frontis. & 24 folding maps only (of 25), tears reprd, hand-cold. in outl., soiled thro.-out. Mod. mor.-bkd. cl. (SH. Mar.5; 64) *Lamm.* £90

GUTIERREZ DE GUALBA, Juan
– **Arte breve y muy provechoso de cuèta Castellana y Arismetica dòde se muestran las Cinco Reglas de Guarismo.** Toledo, 1539. 1st. Edn. Sm. 4to. Lacks 3 blank ll. at end, slight soiling, title neatly restored with portion of arms & text on verso in pen facs., sm. tear at head of A6. Cont. cf., gt., worn, remains of arms on covers, 1 silk tie. From Honeyman Collection. (S. May 20; 3255) *Gurney.* £260

GUTIERREZ DE GUALBA, Juan– PEREZ DE MOYA, Juan
– **Arte brue, y muy provechosa, de cuèta Castellana, y de Guarismo.–Libro segundo de Arithmetica, que trata de Proporcion, y Regla de tres, Monedas, Pesos Antiguos, con otras Cosas.** Seville; Salamanca, 1573; 1557. 2 works in 1 vol. 1st. work with some dampstaining & discolouration, 2nd. work with some browning & staining & some headlines cropped. 19th. C. cf., gt., blind-stpd. monog. on covers. Bkplt. of William Stirling, stp. of W.B. Chorley; from Honeyman Collection. (S. May 20; 3256) *Quaritch.* £320

GUTIERREZ FLOREZ, Pedro
– **Sermon . . . en la Cuidad de los Reyes a 13 de Marco de 1605.** Lima, 1605. Sm. 4to. Owners' inscr. of the Jesuits at Tarija, stains, hole in B3 with loss of letters. Disbnd. (SPB. May 5; 245) $950

GUTLE, Joh. C.
– **Magische Belustigungen aus. d. Mathematik, Physik, Chemie, Technologie u. Oekonomie.** Nuremb., 1797. 2 vols. Lacks 1 hf.-title in vol. 1, slightly soiled. Cont. hf. leath., gt. spine, worn. (HK. Nov.18-21; 552) DM 420

GUTTMANN, Henri
– **Hebraica-Documents D'Art Juif.** Paris, 1937. Fo. Folder. (S. Nov.17; 19) *Elberg.* £80
See–BOSSERT, H. & Guttmann, Henri

GUTZKOW, K.
– **Briefe aus Paris.** Leipzig, 1842. 1st. Edn. 2 vols. Cont. hf. leath. gt. (HK. May 15; 4398) DM 600

GUYON DE LA SARDIERE, J.B. Denis
– **Catalogue des Livres de la Bibliothèque.** Paris, 1759. Table of authors at end. Cont. cf., spine gt. à la grotesque. Sir Thomas Phillips copy, bkplt. of A.N.L. Munby & letter from him loosely inserted. (SM. Oct.7; 1398) Frs. 4,400

GUYOT, Charles
– **Le Printemps sur la Neige . . .** Ill.:– Arthur Rackham. Paris, [1922]. 1st. Edn., (1,300) numbered. 4to. Decor. wraps., spine worn. Raymond M. Sutton Jr. copy. (SG. May 7; 115) $650

GUYOT, Edme Charles
– **Nouvelles Récréations Physiques et Mathematiques.** Paris, 1769-70. 1st. Edn. 4 vols. in 2. Cont. hf. leath. (H. Dec.9/10; 394) DM 520

GUY'S HOSPITAL
– **Reports, vol. 1.** Ed.:– George H. Barlow & James P. Babington. 1836. Cont. cl., unc. (SH. Apr.9; 255) *Cohen.* £80

GVOZD' [Nail]
Ed.:– [I.M. Muravkin]. St. Petersb., 1906. No. 2 only (of 3). 4to. Unbnd. (SH. Feb.5; 73) *Landry.* £90
– – **Anr. Copy.** 4to. Extra & last pt. Unbnd. (SH. Feb.5; 74) *Landry.* £75

GWYNN, John
[–] **An Essay on Design: Including Proposals for Erecting a Public Academy.** 1749. 1st. Edn. Slight spotting, sm. repair to frontis., cont. inscrs. in text. Mod. spr. cf. Note on front free end-paper indicates that the inscrs. were copied 'from those in the Hand-writing of Mr. George Vertue'. (S. Jun.23; 403) *Maggs.* £80

GWYNNE, John
– **Military Memoirs of the Great Civil War: Being the Military Memoirs of John Gwynne & an Account of the Earl of Glencairn's Expedition . . . 1653-54.** Ed.:– [Sir Walter Scott]. L., 1822. 1st.Edn., (500) on paper. 4to. Orig. qtr. cl., spine split, unopened. (PNY. Dec.3; 163) $150

GYFFORD, E.–ROBERTSON, W.
– **Designs for Elegant Cottages & Small Villas.** –**Designs in Architecture for Garden Chairs.** 1806; 1800. 2 works in 1 vol. 4to; Ob. 4to. 1st. work: lacks 1 plt., dampstained, without advts.; 2nd. work: lacks 2 plts., some slightly soiled, a few shaved with slight loss, lacks dedication & 4 ll. of text. Cont. hf. cf. (CSK. Nov.28; 193) £60

H., M.
– **Sketches with the Microscope. In a Letter to A Friend.** Ill.:– R. Hendrick. Parsonstown, 1857. 16mo. Orig. cl. (GM. Apr.30; 223) £60

H.[S.]
– **Twelve New Designs of Frames for Looking Glasses, Pictures, & c.** 1779. 4to. Stitched as issued in folding cl. portfo. (S. Mar.17; 414) *Quaritch.* £320

HAAS, Charles
– **Erinnerung an Frankfurt a.M., Malerisches Album.** Frankfurt, [after 1860]. Orig. pict. wraps., loose. (R. Oct.14-18; 2283) DM 1,050
– **Kaiserliche Königliche Bilder-Gallerie im Belvedere su Wien.** Vienna & Prague, 1821-28. 4 vols. Some text ll. in vol 1 soiled & defect. Red hf. leath. gt., unc. (R. Mar.31-Apr.4; 1591) DM 2,400

HAAS, H. de–DE KANTER, J.–SCHIL-PEROORT, T.O.
– **De Boekbinder.–De Meekrapteler en Bereider.** –**De Azijnmaaker.** Amst., 1806; 1802; 1802. 3 pts. in 1 vol. Cont. hf. cf. (VG. Dec.16; 917) Fls. 500

HAAS, Martha de (Ed.)
See–GEISTERGESCHICHTEN
See–SAGENBUCH

HA'BAVLI, Nathan
– **Avot De'rabbi Nathan.** Ed.:– Elijah Gaon, of Wilno (notes). Wilno, 1833. 4to. Leath.-bkd. bds., worn. (SPB. May 11; 35) $175

HABERLY, Loyd
– **Ann Boleyn & other Poems.** Ill.:– Graily Hewitt. Shakes. Hd. Pr., 1934. (300) numbered. Orig. mor. gt., a few slight scratches. (S. Jul.31; 130) *Foyles.* £180
– **The Crowning Year.** Stoney Down, Corfe Mullen, Dorset, 1937. (150). Sm. 4to. Orig. decor. bds., niger mor. gt. spine. (CNY. May 22; 315) $180

– **Cymberina: An Unnatural in Woodcuts & Verse.** Long Crendon, Buckinghamshire, Priv. ptd., 1926. (600) numbered sigd. by Haberly. 4to. Elab. decor. bds., cl. spine, unopened. (PNY. Oct.1; 259) $120
– **Daneway.** Long Crendon, Buckinghamshire, Seven Acres Pr., 1929. (60). Pig., gt. & blind-tooled, by Loyd Haberly. John Roland Abbey bkplt. (CNY. May 22; 345) $550
– **Midgetina & The Scapegoat.** St. Louis, Priv. ptd., ca. 1943. (48) sigd. Crushed mor., elab. gt.-stpd. at sides, with gt. initials 'HF' stpd. at upr. covers under sm. crown. Bkplt. of Virginia Haberly. (PNY. Oct.1; 262) $100

HABERT-DYS, J.
– **Fantaisies Décoratives.** Paris, n.d. Fo. Occasional spotting. Unbnd. as issued in mor. cl.-bkd. portfo., worn, lacks spine. (CSK. Oct.10; 125) £90

HABICHT, T.
– **Der Rhein.** Bonn, ca. 1845. Mostly soiled. Cont. leath., gt., upr. cover loose. (R. Oct.14-18; 2415) DM 3,100

HACHISUKA, Masauji
– **The Birds of the Philippine Islands . . .** L., [1931-35]. 2 vols. 4to. 7 extra cold. plts. inserted. Hf. leath. & cl. (CB. Sep.24; 28) Can. $450
– **The Dodo & Kindred Birds, Or the Extinct Birds of the Mascarene Islands.** 1953. 1st. Edn., (485) numbered. 4to. Orig. cl., d.-w. (TA. Jun.18; 89) £100
– – **Anr. Copy.** This copy unnumbered? Cl., bkplt. of J.R. Danson by Stephen Gooden. (S. Dec.3; 988) *W. & W.* £80

HACKENBROCH, Yvonne
– **Chelsea & other English Porcelain [English & other Silver] in the Irwin Untermyer Collection.** Camb., Massachussetts, 1957-69. 2 vols. 4to. Orig. cl.-bkd. bds. & cl. (SH. Jan.29; 238) *Talerman.* £70

HACKERT, Ph.
– **Uber den Gebrauch des Firnis in der Mahlerey.** Trans.:– F.L. R[eischel]. Dresden, 1800. Soiled & lightly browned thro.-out. Old wraps. (H. May 21/22, 126) DM 450

HACKLANDER, Friedrich Wilhelm
See–Stieler, Carl, Wachenhusen, K.S.H. & Hackländer, Friedrich Wilhelm

HACKLANDER, Friedrich Wilhelm (Ed.)
See–UBER LAND UND MEER

HACKSPAN, Theodoricus
– **Liber Nizachon Rabbi Lipmanni.** Altdorf, 1644. 4to. Hebrew title-page torn & reprd., minor foxing thro.-out. Cont. vell. (CNY. Oct.9; 3) $380

HA'COHEN, Shimshon, of Ostropolye–MOSHE BEN Isaiah of Trani
– **Likutei Shoshanim.–Nechmad.** Tarnopol; Warsaw, 1813; ca. 1840. 1st. Edn. (1st work). 2 works in 1 vol. 2nd. work on blue paper. Cl. (S. Nov.18; 458) *Stern.* £55

HADELN, Detlev von
– **The Drawings of G.B. Tiepolo.** Paris, 1928. 2 vols. 4to. Orig. hf. mor., worn. (SH. Oct.9; 73) *Reed & Sims.* £85

HAEBERLIN, E.J.
– **Sammlung. Die Gold- und Silbermünzen der Römischen Republik.** Frankfurt am Main, 1933. 4to. Mod. cl. (SH. Mar.6; 361) *Trade Art.* £115

HAEBLER, Konrad
– **The Study of Incunabula.** Trans.:– Lucy E. Osborne. N.Y., Grol. Cl., 1933. (350) numbered. Cl., d.-w. (SG. Oct.2; 172) $110

HAECKEL, Ernst
– **Kunstformen der Natur.** Leipzig & Vienna, [1899-]1904. Fo. Supp. iss. bnd. in 1st. Hf. linen. (HK. Nov.18-21; 554) DM 960

HAEDUS, Petrus
– **[Anterotica sive] De Amoris Generibus.** Treviso, 13 Oct. 1492. 1st. Edn. 4to. Lacks last blank, title soiled & dampstained, sigs. supplied in early hand, early marginalia. 18th. C. red mor., triple gt. fillet, spine gt. in compartments, inner gt. dentelles, bkplt. of John Broadley. [BMC V1,885; HC 8343; Goff H-2.] (SM. Oct.7; 1749) Frs. 5,200

HAEFTEN, Benedictus van
– **Schola Cordis sive Aversi a Deo Cordis.** Antw., 1635. 2nd. Edn. Lacks ptd. title(?), 3 gatherings

at beginning ink-stained in upr. qtr. Cont. cf., elab. gt.-tooled, bishop's coat-of-arms in centre of covers, flat spine, lacks ties, corners & spine slightly worn, upr. jnt. brkn. (S. Jul.27; 140) *Russell.* £100

HA'ENCYCLOPAEDIA HA'IVRIT
Ed.:– Simcha Assaf, Joshua Gutman, Yeshayahu Leibowitz & others. Tel-Aviv, 1949-74. 26 vols. Cl. (S. Nov.18; 534) *Kornbluth.* £95

HAESTENS, H. van
– **De Magnificentie ofte Lust-Hoff van gantsch Christenrijck, bestaende, in verscheyden Tempels, Paleysen . . .** Amst., 1619. 4to. Slightly loosening, text a little browned. Cont. vell. (VG. Dec.17; 1351) Fls. 450

HAFNER, G.
[–] **Onomatologia Curiosa Artificiosa et Magica.** Ulm, Frankfurt, Leipzig, 1759. 1st. Edn. Lacks hf.-title or frontis. probably. Cont. leath., slightly soiled. (R.Oct.14-18; 196) DM 530

HAGECIUS, W.
– **Kronyka Czeska.** [Prag], [1819] Reprint of 1541 Edn. Slightly soiled, browned in parts. Leath. (HK. Nov.18-21; 1119) DM 420

HAGEDORN, Friedrich von
– **Poetische Werke.** Ill.:– C. Fritzsch. (port. copper engr.). Hamburg, 1757. 1st. Coll. Edn. 3 vols. Cont. vell. (R. Mar.31-Apr.4; 484) DM 500

HAGELSTANGE, H.
– **Venezianisches Credo.** Verona, 1945. (155) on Bütten. 4to. Orig. paper bds. (H. Dec.9/10; 1885) DM 420

HAGER, Joseph
– **Description des Médailies Chinoises du Cabinet Impérial de France, précédée d'un essai de Numismatique Chinoise.** Paris, 1805. L.P. 4to. Sig. Y detchd., slight foxing. Cont. red hf. mor., spine gt., unc. & unopened, s.-c. (S. Apr.29; 393) *Maggs.* £140

HAGGADAH, The [*Chronologically*]
– **The Amsterdam Hagadah.** Ill.:– Abraham Bar Jacob (map, sigd. at foot). Amst., 1712. 2nd. Edn. Fo. Map probably supplied from anr. copy, scattered stains & spotting, light worming, map torn & reprd. at folds. Recent maroon mor., linen case. (CNY. Oct.9; 7) $3,400
– **Haggadah Shel Pessah.** Ed.:– Don Yitzhak Abarhanel (commentaries). Amst., 1712. Sm. fo. Browning, repairs, stains, slight soiling. Cl.-bkd. bds. (SPB. May 11; 229) $3,500
– – **Anr. Copy.** Map laid-down & detchd., staining, browning, loss to 1 lf., repairs, marginal tears. Cf.-bkd. bds. (SPB. May 11; 230) $3,000
– **The Venice Hagadah.** Venice, 1740. Fo. Browned, scattered stains. Recent mor., linen case. (CNY. Oct.9; 8) $1,100
– **Seder Ha'moed including Passover Haggada (according to the Kabbalah of Yitzhak Lurie Ari).** Zolkiev, [1781]. Bds. (S. Nov.18; 392) *Yardeni.* £70
– **Seder Haggadah Shel Pessah.** Sulzbach, 1792. 4to. Marginal tears, some staining, browning. Bds., tears. (SPB. May 11; 114) $150
– **Haggadah Shel Pessah.** Livorno, 1794. Sm. 4to. Some browning. Vell.-bkd. bds., spine wormed. (SPB. May 11; 231) $200
– **The Vienna Hagadah.–The Furth Hagadah.** Vienna; Furst, 1813; 1773. 2 works in 2 vols. 4to. & fo. Stained & browned thro.-out in 1st. work, some loss of text at margins of 2nd. work. Recent red mor.; recent mor., extensively restored. (CNY. Oct.9; 5) $600
– **Haggadah Shel Pessach.** Ill.:– C.M. Basle, 1816. 4to. Slight staining. Mod. cl. (S. Nov.18; 695) *Berg.* £320
– **Haggadah Shel Pessah** [with the commentary on the Scroll of Esther by Moshe Alsheikh[. Warsaw, 1837. Some staining. Cl. (SPB. May 11; 116) $250
– **Seder Ha'Haggadah Shel Pessah.** Trans.:– Solomon Blogg. Hannover, 1841. Some staining. Bds., cover detchd., tears. (SPB. May 11; 117) $110
– **Haggadah Shel Pessah im Ha'pitaron Bilshon Sepharadi.** Livorno, 1842. Sm. 4to. Staining & browning. Bds. (SPB. May 11; 232) $250
– **Seder Haggadah Shel Pessah.** N.Y., 1863. Staining. Bds., detchd. (SPB. May 11; 119) $250
– **Haggadah Shel Pessah.** Berlin, 1864. Some staining. Wraps. (SPB. May 11; 121) $225

– **The Trieste Hagadah.** Trieste, 1864. 4to. Repairs to several ll. with some text loss, scattered staining. Recent red mor. (CNY. Oct.9; 9) $850
– **Die Haggadah von Sarajewo-Eine Spanisch-Jüdische Bilderhandschrift des Mittelalters.** Ed.:– David H. Mueller, J. von Schlosser & D.Kaufmann. Vienna, 1898. 2 vols. 4to. Orig. leath. (S. Nov.17; 21) *Schwarcz.* £550
– **Haggadah Shel Pessah.** Ed.:– Yitzhak Salman Guensberger (commentary). Budapest, 1914. Browning. Wraps. (SPB. May 11; 125) $125
– **The Darmstadt Hagadah.** Ed.:– Bruno Italiener. Leipzig, 1927. Facs. Edn. (350) numbered, sigd. 2 vols. Fo. & 8vo. Hf. maroon mor. gt. (CNY. Oct.9; 6) $2,400
– **The Haggadah.** Trans.:– Cecil Roth. Ill.:– Albert Rutherston. Soncino Pr., 1930. (100) numbered. Mor. gt. by Wood. (C. Jul.22; 98) *Schwarcz.* £500
– – **Anr. Copy.** 4to. Text in Hebrew & Engl., prospectus loosely inserted. Orig. mor. gt., s.-c. (S. Jul.31; 309) *Joseph.* £370
– – **Anr. Edn.** Ed.:– Cecil Roth. Ill.:– Arthur Szyk. L., Beaconsfield Pr., [1939]. (125) on vell., sigd. by Szyk & Roth. 4to. Slight soiling. Mor. gt. extra by Sangorski & Sutcliffe, hf. mor. folding box. (SPB. Nov.25; 126) $5,500
– **Kaufmann Haggadah.** Ed.:– Alexander Scheiber. Budapest, 1957. Facs. Edn. 4to. Hf. vell. (S. Nov.17; 20) *Schwarcz.* £65
– **Sarajewo Haggadah.** Ed.:– Cecil Roth. Tel-Aviv, [1965]. Facs. Edn. 4to. Vell. (S. Nov.17; 22) *Schwarcz.* £55

HAGGER, Conrad
– **Neues Saltzburgisches Koch-Buch.** Augsburg, 1719. 1st. Edn. Vols. I, III & IV (of 4) in 3 vols. Sm. 4to. Lacks copper engrs., 4pp. mispaginated in Vol. IV. Cont. vell., soiled, spine slightly defect., ties torn or lacking. (H. Dec.9/10; 991) DM 900

HAGHE, Louis
– **Monuments Anciens Recueillis en Belgique et en Allemagne.** Brussels, 1842. Fo. 25 (of 27) litho. plts., lacks plts. 13 & 27, margins soiled & affected by damp. Cont. hf. mor., covers detchd. (TA. Jul.16; 261) £60
– **Sketches in Belgium & Germany.** 1840. 3 vols. Fo. Qtr. mor. gt., loose, (P. Oct.2; 262) *Walford.* £220
– – **Anr. Copy.** Orig. mor.-bkd. cl., disbnd. (CSK. Nov.28; 88) £50
– – **Anr. Edn.** 1840-45. 1st. & 2nd. Series only (of 3). 2 vols. Fo. Lacks 8 plts., spotted. Cont. mor.-bkd. cl. (SH. Nov.6; 213) *Kundletsch.* £60
– – **Anr. Edn.** 1840-50. 3 vols. Fo. Most ll. detchd., some slight spotting. Cont. mor.-bkd. cl., gt., slightly damp stained. (CSK. Aug.1; 134) £190
– – **Anr. Edn.** L., 1845. 1st. & 2nd. series. Bnd. (LM. Jun.13; 264) B.Frs. 25,000
– – **Anr. Edn.** L., 1850. Imp. fo. Plts. stpd. Hf. mor., upr. cover loose. (R. Oct.14-18; 2086) DM 520
[–] [–] **Anr. Edn.** L., [1850]. Fo. 21 cold. plts. (of 27), anr. plt. inserted, frayed & soiled. Orig. mor.-bkd. portfo., worn. (SH. Jun.18; 146) *Frick.* £50
– **Sketches in London & Germany.** L., 1845. 2nd. Series. Fo. Soiled, title & 1 plt. verso stpd. Cont. linen, spine renewed. (R. Oct.14-18; 2086) DM 1,000

HAHN, C.W. & Herrich-Schäffer, G.A.W.
– **Die Wanzenartigen Insecten.** Nuremb. & Lotzbeck (vols. 8 & 9). 1831-53. 9 pts. & index in 5 vols. Text slightly soiled. Cont. linen gt. (HK. May 12-14; 300) DM 3,400
– – **Anr. Copy.** 9 vols. & index vol. in 2 text & 2 plt. vols. Title with old liby stp. Mod. hf. leath. (R. Oct.14-18; 3083) DM 2,900

HAHN, L.
– **Friedrich der Grosse.** Berlin, 1855. 1st. Edn. 4to. Cont. mor., gt. spine, cover & inner dentelle, lightly worn. (H. Dec.9/10; 895) DM 500

HAHNEMANN, S.
See–SANDE, J.B. van & Hahnemann, S.

HAIDER, M. & others
[–] **Herrn. Petermanns Jagdbuch.** Munich, [1860]. 7 vols. 4to. Slightly soiled in parts, some ll. more heavily, hf.-title to pt. 5 & 6 reprd., 2 ll. in pt. 1 with bkd. or restored tears. Bds., orig. cold. pict. wraps. pasted on, s.-c. (R. Mar.31-Apr.4; 1685) DM 1,400

HAIG-BROWN, Roderick L.
– **Return to the River: a Story of the Chinook Run.** Ill.:– Charles De Feo. N.Y., 1941. 1st. Edn., (520) numbered, sigd. by author & ill. Gt. leatherette-bkd. cl., unc., unopened., s.-c. (SG. Oct.16; 49) $190

HAIN, Ludwig
– **Repertorium Bibliographicum.** Milan, 1948. 4 vols. Orig. cl. (S. Feb.23; 340) *Duran.* £50

HAKANUNE [On the Eve]
Ed.:– [Yu. V. Gol'dberg]. St. Petersb., 1907. Nos. 1 & 2. 4to. Unbnd. (SH. Feb. 5; 95) *Quaritch.* £95

HAKE, Henry M.
See–O'DONAGHUE, F. & Hake, Henry M.

HAKEWILL, James
[–] **Eight views in the Zoological Gardens.** N.d. Ob. 8vo. Mod. wraps., orig. wraps. preserved. (SH. Oct. 10; 297) *Primrose Hill Books.* £70
– **The History of Windsor & its Neighbourhood.** 1813. 4to. Some offsetting & spotting onto title & text. Cont. red str.-grd. mor., covers with gt. key-pattern borders, spine gt. From the collection of Eric Sexton. (C. Apr.16; 267) *Foyle.* £60
– – **Anr. Edn.** N.d. Lge. 4to. Margins soiled. Cont. hf. cf., worn, upr. cover detchd. (CSK. Jun.12; 62) £50
– **A Picturesque Tour of the Island of Jamaica.** Ill.:– Sutherland, Fielding & Cartwright after the author. 1825. Fo. Lacks dedication lf., 1 text lf. torn & reprd. Mod. hf. mor. [Sabin 29591] (SBA. Mar.4; 109) *Way.* £810
– **A Picturesque Tour of Italy.** 1820. L.P. Fo. Some plts. slightly foxed. Cont. cf., lacks spine, covers detchd. (C. Feb.25; 102) *Pillar.* £200
– – **Anr. Copy.** L.P. Cl., covers detchd. (S. Dec.8; 218) *Quaritch.* £150
– – **Anr. Copy.** Additional engraved title & 63 plts. on India paper, slight spotting & offsetting. Cont. hf. mor., partly unc. (S. Sep.29; 199) *Traylen.* £110
– – **Anr. Edn.** Ill.:– [J.M.W. Turner]. 1820 [but later?]. Mor. gt. (CSK. Jun.5; 154) £130

HAKLUYT, Richard
– **The Principall Navigations, Voiages & Discoveries of the English Nation . . .** L., 1589. 1st. Edn. Fo. 6 suppressed ll. describing Drake's voyage inserted between pp. 643-44, lacks map, some ll. with marginal repairs. Old cf. (SG. Oct.9; 125) $4,700
– – **Anr. Edn.** L., 1809-12. New Edn. 5 vols. Fo. Prelims. spotted. Cont. pol. cf. gt. by Philanthropic Society, with old reback. (TA. Feb.19; 54) £160
– – **Anr. Edn.** Edinb., 1884-90. 16 vols. Folding map in vol. IV torn. Hf. mor. (SSA. Apr.22; 36) R. 160
– – **Anr. Edn.** 1903. 12 vols. Unc. cl. gt. (P. Sep.11; 89) *Traylen.* £60
– – **Anr. Edn.** Glasgow, 1903-05. Ltd. Edn. 12 vols. Some ll. spotted. Orig. cl. (SH. Nov.7; 510) *House.* £90
– – **Anr. Edn.** L., 1927-28. 10 vols. Orig. cl. (SH. Nov.7; 511) *Weekend Gallery.* £60

HAKLUYT SOCIETY
– **[Publications].** L., 1919-32. Vols. 45-68., together 24 vols. Orig. cl. (SH. Nov.7; 513) *Cavendish.* £195

HALBERSTADT, A.
– **Kolonisatie van Europeanen te Suriname.** Ill.:– after P.J. Benoit. N.p., Priv. ptd., ca. 1870. Some slight stains & foxing. 20th. C. artificial hf. leath. (VG. Nov.18; 934) Fls. 1,800

HALE, Right Rev. Bishop
– **Aborigines of Australia; Being An Account of the Institution for their Education at Poonindie, in South Australia.** L., n.d. Cl., soiled. (KH. Nov.18; 31) Aus. $130

HALE, Edward Everett, Sr.
[–] **The Man Without a Country.** Boston, 1865. 1st. Edn. 12mo. Staining to some ll., without the yellow inserted advt. slip. Orig. ptd. wraps., early ink owner's inscr. on upr. cover, qtr. mor. s.-c. From the Prescott Collection. (CNY. Feb.6; 140) $300

HALE, Edward Everett, Jr.
– **The Life & Letters of Edward Everett Hale.** Boston, 1917. (295) on L.P. with A.L. 4 vols. Extra-ill. with plts., letters & clipped sigs., some

HALE, Edward Everett, Jr. – The Life & Letters of Edward Everett Hale. -contd.
browning. Mor. gt., gt. panels. (SPB. May 6; 313) $600

HALE, John P.
– Trans-Allegheny Pioneers ... Cinc., 1886. 1st. Edn. Orig. blind-stpd. cl., gt. title on upr. cover & spine. From liby. of William E. Wilson, sigd. inscr. to Col. B.W. Byrne. (SPB. Apr.29; 128) $150

HALE, Sarah Josepha
– Poems for our Children. Boston, 1830. 1st. Edn. Pt. 1 (all publd.). 12mo. Accompanied by a copy of the 2nd. (facs.) edn. (Boston, 1916, 12mo.). Orig. ptd. wraps., lacks spine, some sm. stains on cover, hf. mor. folding case. T.L.s. from J. Blanck to F.J. Hogan laid in, Hogan's bkplt., lately in the Prescott Collection. (CNY. Feb.6; 142) $2,000

HALE, Thomas
– A Compleat Body of Husbandry. L., 1756. 1st. Edn. Fo. New three-qtr. cf., unc. (SG. Feb.12; 204) $300

HALENZA'S RHEINISCHES ALBUM
Ill.:– F. Foltz. Mainz, ca. 1870. Ob. 4to. Lacks 1 steel engraved plt. Orig. linen, 2 sm. defects. (H. Dec.9/10; 706)   DM 1,200

HALES, Stephen
– Haemastatique ou la Statique des Animaux: Experiences Hydrauliques faites sur des Animaux Vivans ... Trans.:– M. de Sauvages. Geneva, 1749. 1st. Edn. in Fr. 4to. Pages 347-8 with advt. Cf., rebkd. (S. Dec.1; 197)   Maggs. £110
– Statical Essays Containing Vegetable Staticks or an Account of Some Statical Experiments on the Sap in Vegetables.–Haemostatics or an Account of some Hydraulic & Hydrostatical Experiments made on the Blood & Blood-Vessels of Animals. L., 1738-40. Vol. I 3rd. Edn., vol. II 2nd. Edn. 2 vols. Cont. cf., worn, rebkd. (S. Jun.16; 368)   Phelps. £75
– – Anr. Copy. Not unif., vol. II rebkd. & bkplt. of A. Bracebridge, Atherston Hall & inscr.: Atherstone Society. (S. Dec.1; 194)   Phelps. £50
– – Anr. Edn. L., 1738-33. Vol. I 3rd. Edn., Vol. II 1st. Edn. 2 vols. Z4-5 detchd. in vol. I, slight dampstaining. Cont. cf., gt., some wear, lacks 1 label. (S. Apr.6; 67)   Clements. £150
– Statistical Essays: containing Vegetable Staticks. L., 1731-33. 2nd. Edn., 1st. Edn. 2 vols. Some ll. discold. Cont. cf., slightly worn. (SPB. Nov.25; 100) $300

HALEVY, Ludovic
– Recits de Guerre: L'Invasion, 1870-1871. Ill.:– L. Marchetti & Alfred Paris. Paris, ca. 1873. 1st. Edn. fo. Orig. gt.-pict. cl., orig. cold. pict. upr. wrap. bnd. in. (PNY. Mar.26; 131) $100

HALFORD, Frederic M.
– Dry Fly Entomology. L., 1897. 1st. Edn. Orig. three-qtr. mor., very worn. (SG. Apr.9; 288) $130
– – Anr. Copy. Orig. hf. leath. (SG. Dec.11; 47) $120
– Dry-Fly Fishing in Theory & Practice.–Dry-Fly Entomology.–Making a Fishery.–An Angler's Autobiography. L., 1902-03. 4 vols. Cl. (SG. Oct.16; 50) $360
– The Dry-Fly Man's Handbook. L., [1913]. (100) numbered, sigd. 4to. Some light spotting. Cont. hf. cf. (CSK. Jul.31; 73)   £220
– Floating Flies & How to Dress Them. L., 1886. 1st. Edn. 32-p. catalogue dtd. 1885, & advt. lf. Cl., shaken. (SG. Apr.9; 287) $160
– – Anr. Edn. N.Y., 1886. 1st. Amer. Edn. Advt. lf. with the Sampson Low imprint. Three-qtr. mor., partly unc. (SG. Dec.11; 46) $140
– Modern Developement of the Dry Fly. L., 1910. (75) numbered de Luxe, sigd. 2 vols. 4to. Orig. hf. cf., gt. (SH. Oct.9; 223)   Angle Books. £620

HALFPENNY, Joseph
– Fragmenta Vetusta or the Remains of Ancient Buildings in York. 1807. Fo. Slightly spotted, mainly marginal. Cont. russ. gt., spine torn. (SBA. Oct.22; 605)   Chesters. £54
– Gothic Ornaments in the Cathedral Church of York. L., 1795. 4to. Spotted. Later hf. cf. (SH. Nov.6; 107)   Fogg. £65

HALFPENNY, Joseph–LEYLAND, John
– Fragmenta Vetusta.–Views of Ancient Buildings ... of Halifax. York: Halifax, 1807; 1879. 2 works in 2 vols. 4to. & ob. 4to. Title of 1st. work foxed. Cont. hf. russ., worn; orig. cl. gt. (C. Nov.6; 309)   Traylen. £130

HALFPENNY, William & John
– Rural Architecture in the Chinese Taste. L., ca. 1770? 3rd. Edn. 4 Pts. in 1 vol. Wraps., stitching brkn. (S. Nov.25; 408)   Quaritch. £180

HALIBURTON, Thomas Chandler
[–] The Clockmaker. Halifax, 1836. [1st. Series], 1st. Iss. 12mo. Orig. cl., spine slightly faded, owner's sig. on free end-paper. (CB. Apr.1; 1)   Can. $1,400
[–] The English in America. L., 1851. 2 vols. Recent qtr. mor. [Sabin 29685] (CB. Apr.1; 2)   Can. $120
– An Historical & Statistical Account of Nova-Scotia. Halifax, 1829. 1st. Edn. 2 vols. New three-qtr. mor., spines gt., by Sangorski & Sutcliffe. (SG. Mar.5; 60) $280

HALKETT, John
– Historical Notes respecting the Indians of North America. L., 1825. Sm. tear in title-p. reprd. Hf. mor. & marb. bds. (CB. Nov.12; 17)   Can. $160
[–] Statement respecting The Earl of Selkirk's Settlement upon the Red River. L., 1817. Stp. on title verso. Cont. hf. cf., rebkd. (PNY. May 21; 208) $160

HALKETT, Samuel & Laing, John
– A Dictionary of the Anonymous & Pseudonymous Literature of Great Britain. Edinb., 1882. (50) numbered. 4 vols. 4to. Cl. (GM. Apr.30; 465)   £75
– – Anr. Edn. 1882-88. 4 vols. Rebnd. in scarlet hf. mor. (TA. Sep.18; 51)   £85
– – Anr. Copy. Mod. cl. (SH. Jul.23; 110)   Matthews. £65
– – Anr. Edn. Ed.:– Dr. James Kennedy & others. Edinb. & L., 1926-1934. Vols. I-VII (including Index & 2nd. supp.) of 9 vols. Orig. buckram, d.-w.'s. (S. Apr.7; 466)   Way. £280
– – Anr. Edn. Ed.:– Dr. James Kennedy & others. N.Y., 1971. New Edn. 7 vols. Orig. cl. (TA. Jun.18; 329)   £70

HALL, Anna Maria
– Book of Royalty. Ill.:– after W. Perring & J. Brown. L., 1839. Lge. 4to. Orig. red. mor. gt. (SH. Apr.9; 256)   Rostron. £70

HALL, Capt. Basil
– Account of a Voyage of Discovery to the West Coast of Corea, & the Great Loo-Choo Island. 1818. [1st. Edn.?]. 4to. Cont. cf., recased. W.a.f. (TA. Aug.21; 66)   £210
– – Anr. Copy. Some offsetting of text. Cont. cf., gt. decor. spine. (TA. Feb.19; 28)   £150
– – Anr. Copy. Lacks hf.-title, title slightly dust-soiled, light spotting. Cont. roan-bkd. bds. with cl. corners. (S. Nov.4; 604)   Weiss. £130
– – Anr. Copy. With final advt. lf., sm. liby. stp. on title & all plts. Orig. bds., lacks spine, covers detchd. From Chetham's Liby., Manchester. (C. Nov.26; 187)   Vine. £70
– Forty Etchings from Sketches made with the Camera Lucida in North America. 1829. 4to. Lacks ills., with inserts. Hf. mor. & bds. torn. (WW. May 20; 68)   £60
– – Anr. Copy. 4to. Some spotting, margins soiled. Orig. bds., rebkd., soiled. (TA. Jan.22; 373)   £40
– Travels in North America. Edinb., 1829. 1st. Edn. 3 vols. 12mo. Mod. three-qtr. cf., spines gt. (SG. Oct.30; 188) $190
– – Anr. Copy. Slight offsetting & 1 repair. 19th. C. hf. cf., marb. bds. From liby. of William E. Wilson. [Sabin 29725] (SPB. Apr.29; 122) $150

HALL, Francis
– Travels in Canada, & the United States, in 1816 & 1817. L., 1818. 1st. Edn. Some offsetting. Cont. hf. cf., rebkd., end-papers foxed. From liby. of William E. Wilson. [Sabin 29769] (SPB. Apr.29; 121) $250
– – Anr. Edn. L., 1819. 2nd. Edn. Cont. hf. leath., bkplt. [Sabin 29769] (CB. Apr.1; 72) Can. $130

HALL, Henry
– The Tribune Book of Open-Air Sports. N.Y., 1887. 1st. Edn. Advts. Orig. cl., slightly worn. (S. Dec.8; 2)   Laughton. £50

HALL, James
– Legends of the West. Phila., 1832. 1st. Edn. Advts., slightly foxed. Orig. bds., rebkd. new end-papers. From liby. of William E. Wilson. (SPB. Apr.29; 126) $125
– Letters from the East & from the West. Wash., [1840]. 1st. Edn. Slight browning & offsetting, slight foxing. Orig. bds., rebkd. From liby. of William E. Wilson. (SPB. Apr.29; 123) $125

– Letters from the West ... L., 1828. 1st. Edn. Remains of owner's stp. on front free end-paper, inscr. at top of title, slight foxing. Cont. cf.-bkd. bds., gt. spine, top of spine loose. From liby. of William E. Wilson. (SPB. Apr.29; 125) $150
– Statistics of the West at the Close of the Year 1836. Cinc., 1837. 1st. Edn. 12mo. Advts., foxed. Orig. cl., gt. spine, slightly worn at head & foot. From liby. of William E. Wilson. (SPB. Apr.29; 127) $125
See–M'KENNEY, Thomas L. & Hall, James

HALL, Manly P.
– An Encyclopedic Outline of Masonic, Hermetic, Cabbalistic & Rosicrucian Symbolical Philosophy ... Ill.:– Augustus Knapp. San Franc., 1928. (100) numbered. Fo. Lacks 2 ll. & 2 cold. plts. Hf. vell., batik covers & end-papers, book design by John Henry Nash. (JL. Jul.20; 829)   Aus. $300

HALL, Marshall
– New Memoir of the Nervous System. L., 1843. 1st. Edn. 4to. Orig. bds., rebkd. Photograph of port. & an A.L.s. by author inserted dtd. 1848. (S. Jun.16; 372)   Dillon. £65
– On the Diseases & Derangements of the Nervous System. L., 1841. 1st. Edn. 4 pp. advts. Orig. cl., loose, unc., bdg. stained. Loosely inserted is extract from British Annals of medicine, 1837, containing Marshall's 'On Spasmodic tic'. (S. Jun.16; 371)   Pratt. £70
– On the Reflex Function of the Medulla Oblongata & Medulla Spinalis. L., 1833. Offprint from 'Phil. Trans.'. 4to. Cl., upr. cover loose, spine defect. (S. Jun.16; 370)   Norman. £75

HALL, Radclyffe
– The Well of Loneliness. N.Y., 1929. Victory Edn., (225) numbered on Van Gelder H.M.P., sigd. 2 vols. Cl., s.-c. (SG. Jun.4; 207) $130

HALL, Samuel Carter
– Baronial Halls ... of England. L., 1856. Fo. 1 plt. loose. Cont. hf. mor. (SH. Nov.6; 110)   Cavendish. £70
– – Anr. Edn. L., 1858. 2 vols. Fo. Some ll. slightly spotted, a few loose. Cont. hf. mor. (SH. Nov.6; 112)   Cavendish. £70
– – Anr. Edn. Ill.:– J.D. Harding, G. Cattermole, S. Prout, W. Muller, J. Holland & others. L., 1881. 2 vols. 4to. All text & plts. loose. Orig. pict. cl. (CB. May 27; 119)   Can. $180
– Selected Pictures from the Galleries & Private Collections of Great Britain. N.d. 4 vols. Fo. Cont. hf. mor. (SH. Jan.29; 107)   Edistar. £750

HALL, Mr. & Mrs. Samuel Carter
– Book of the Thames. 1869. 15 actual photographs mntd. Orig. decor. cl., recased. (SH. Nov.6; 114)   Primrose Hill Books. £65
– Ireland: Its Scenery, Character ... L., 1841-43. [1st. Edn.?[. 3 vols. Hf. mor. gt. (P. Jun.11; 67)   Magee. £75
– – Anr. Copy. 3 vols. Foxing to some plts. Hf. cf. & marb. bds., spines gt. in compartments. (LC. Jun.18; 152)   £50
– – Anr. Edn. Boston, 1911. (1,000) numbered. 6 vols. Cl. (GM. Oct.30; 232)   £85
– – Anr. Edn. L., n.d. 3 vols. Hf. cf. & cl. (HSS. Apr.24; 312)   £60

HALL, Sidney
[–] [New British Atlas]. Ca. 1834. 4to. Lacks title, 4 maps soiled. Cl. (CSK. Sep.26; 135)   £110
– A New General Atlas. 1830. 1st. Edn. Lge. fo. Maps, cold. in outl., some ll. torn & soiled in margins. Disbnd. W.a.f. (S. Mar.31; 254)   Tooley. £160
– – Anr. Edn. 1830. Some marginal soiling. Cont. hf. cf., worn, covers detchd. (CSK. Jul.3; 16)   £140
– – Anr. Edn. L., ca. 1830. Disbnd. (SG. Nov.20; 61) $400
– A Travelling County Atlas: with all the Coach & Rail Roads. Ca. 1845. Slight spotting, some maps slightly loose or with inner margins strengthened, a few sm. marginal tears. Orig. mor. gt., slightly worn, lacks ties. (SBA. Oct.22; 268)   Hughes & Smeeth. £55

HALL, T.
– The Queen's Royal Cookery. 1713. 2nd. Edn. 12mo. No end-ll. Cont. sheep, rebkd. (SKC. Sep.9; 1691)   £110

HALL, William Henry
– The New Encyclopaedia. Ed.:– Th. A. Lloyd. L., ca. 1790. Vol. III, plts. only. Fo. Some plts.

slightly browned. Cont. leath., defect. (R. Oct.14-18; 2506) DM 580

HALL & Moreau
See–BANNERMAN, David Armitage–HALL & Moreau–ROSEVEAR, D.S.

HALL-STEVENSON, John
– The Works. 1795. 1st. Edn. 3 vols. Cont. marb. cf., spines gt. (CSK. May 8; 127) £130

HALLAM, G.
– Narrative of a Voyage from Montego Bay . . . to England . . . thence . . . to New York. L., 1831. Cont. pol. cf. gt. (SG. May 14; 91) $1,100

HALLARAN, William Saunders
– An Enquiry into the Causes Producing the Extraordinary Addition to the Number of the Insane together with Extended Observations on the Cure of Insanity. Cork, L. & Dublin, 1810. 1st. Edn. Errata slip, liby. stp. on title, also erasure causing sm. hole. New bds. (S. Jun.16; 375) *Phillips*. £130

HALLE, Johann Samuel
– Die Deutsche Giftpflanzen, zur Verhütung der tragischen Vorfälle . . . nebst den Heilungsmitteln. Vienna, 1785. Cont. hf. cf. (S. Jan.27; 330) *Venner*. £240
– Magie, oder die Zauberkräfte der Natur. –Fortgesetzte Magie . . . Vienna, & Berlin, 1787 [1783]-1800 & 1801. Vols. 1-4 (all publd.); Vols. 1-12 (all publd.) together 16 vols. Stps. on all title ll. Cont. bds. & 2 cont. leath. (R. Oct.14-18; 428) DM 1,600
– Werkstäte der Heutigen Künste, oder Neue Kunst-Historie. Brandenburg & Leipzig, 1761-65. Vols. 1, 2 & 4 in 3 Vols. 4to. Vol. 4 wormed. Various cont. bdgs., some corners reprd. (R. Oct.14-18; 2627) DM 1,300
– – Anr. Edn. Leipzig, 1762. Vol. 2 (of 4). 4to. Slightly soiled in parts, plt. VI torn. Cont. cf., worn, upr. cover loose. (H. Dec.9/10; 281) DM 1,220
– – Anr. Edn. Brandenburg & Leipzig, 1765. Vol. 4 (of 4). 4to. Slightly soiled. Cont. cf., worn, spine torn. (H. Dec.9/10; 282) DM 1,250

HALLER, Albrecht von
– Bibliotheca Anatomica. Zürich, 1774-76. 1st. Edn. 2 vols. 4to. No last blank in vol. II, spotted, bkplt. & a few stamps of the Library of the Medical Society of the County of Kings. Cont. cf., spines gt. (S. Oct.21; 395) *Quaritch*. £190
– – Anr. Edn. Zürich, 1774-77. 1st. Edn. 2 vols. 4to. A few ll. browned. Late 19th. C. hf. mor. (S. Feb.23; 341) *Way*. £190
– Bibliotheca Botanica. Zürich, 1771-72. 1st. Edn. 2 vols. 4to. Slightly spotted, no last blanks, bkplt. of the Liby. of the Medical Society of the County of Kings. Cont. mott. vell., spines very worn, upr. cover of vol. I nearly detchd. (S. Oct.21; 396) *Quaritch*. £220
– Bibliotheca Medicinae Practicae. Basle & Berne, 1776-88. 1st. Edn. 4 vols. 4to. Cont. mott. cf., backs gt. (SG. Sep.18; 168) $625
– A Dissertation on the Motion of the Blood & on the Effects of Bleeding Verified by Experiments made on Living Animals to which are added Observations on the Heart. 1757. Cf.-bkd. bds. (S. Jun.16; 380) *Gurney*. £110
– Elementa Physiologiae Corporis Humani. Lausanne; Berne, 1757-63; 1764-66. 1st. Edn. 8 vols. 4to. 5 engraved plts. (of 6), some browning & soiling, liby. stps. on title-pp., etc. Cont. vell. bds., a few spines slightly defect. or wormed. (S. Apr.6; 69) *Whipple*. £150
– – Anr. Edn. Lausanne, 1757-78. 1st. Edn. of vols. I-V; 2nd. Edn. of vols. VI-VIII. 8 vols. 4to. Lacks port., some browning. Cont. cf., gt. spines, 1 spine defect. at foot. Bkplt. of Dr. M.E. Rigollot, Fellow of Academy of Amiens; from Honeyman Collection. (S. May 20; 3257) *Elstein*. £70
– – Anr. Edn. Naples, 1763-68. 10 pts. in 5 vols. 4to. Title & text stpd., lightly soiled thro.-out, some ll. with sm. tears in margin. Marb. leath. ca. 1820, gt. spine & outer dentelle. (HK. May 12-14; 334) DM 4,100
– Enumeratio Methodica Stirpium Helvetiae Indigenarum. Gottingen, 1742. 1st. Edn. 2 vols. in 1. Fo. 19th. C. hf. mor. From Chetham's Liby., Manchester. (C. Nov.26; 188) *Rota*. £380
– Historia Naturalis Ranarum Nostratium.–Die Natürliche Historie der Frösche hiesiges Landes. Ill.:– Tyroff (frontis.). Augustus Johannes Roesel von Rosenhof. Nuremb., 1758. 2 works in 1 vol. Lge. fo. Frontis. & some plts. col. heightened. Old

marb. cf., 7 decor. spine raised bands, gt. dentelle border, angle fleurons. (LM. Jun.13; 92) B.Frs. 85,000
– Historia Stirpium Indigenarum Helvetiae Inchoata. Ill.:– after C.J. Rollin & others. Berne, 1768. 3 vols, in 2. Fo. 47 engraved plts. only (of 48). Non-unif. 19th. C. hf. mor. From Chetham's Liby., Manchester. (C. Nov.26; 189) *Wheldon & Wesley*. £200
– Icones Anatomicae . . . Corporis Humani. Gottingen, 1743-56. 8 pts. in 1 vol. Fo. Occasional marginal foxing to text ll. Cont. cf., rebkd. From Chetham's Liby., Manchester. (C. Nov.26; 190) *Dawson*. £800
– – Anr. Edn. Göttingen, 1756 [but the pts. dtd. 1781-82]. 8 pts. in 1 vol. Fo. Slightly discold. at beginning. Cf., worn, rebkd. (S. Jun.16; 379) *Norman*. £320
– Medical, Chirigical & Anatomical Cases & Experiments. 1758. Old cf., worn, sm. burnhole in centre of upr. cover. (TA. Mar.19; 387) £56
– Opera Minora Emendata. Lausanne, 1763-68. 3 vols. 4to. Lacks port., stained. Cont. hf. cf. (SH. Jul.16; 219) *Tzakas*. £60
See–CAILLAU, J.M.–CULLEN, William–HALLER, Albrecht von–COSTE, M.
See–MARIVAUX, Pierre Carlet de Chamblain de –HALLER, Albrecht von
See–SCHEUCHZER, Jean [Jacques]

HALLETT, M.W.
See–SMITH, A.W. & Hallett, M.W.

HALLEWELL, Edmund Gilling
– Views of the Bermudas. 1848. Fo. Title, dedication & 9 (of 13) litho. plts., loose. No bdg. stated. W.a.f. (SKC. Jul.28; 2539) £640

HALLIWELL, or HALLIWELL-PHILLIPS, James Orchard (Ed.)
See–PERECYVELLE, Syr of Gales

HALMA, François & Brouerius van Nidek, Matthew
– Tooneel der Vereenigde Nederlanden. Leeuwarden, 1725. 1st. Edn. Pt. 1 only. Lge. fo. Some foxing, old liby. stp. on title. Disbnd. (SG. Feb.5; 160) $750
– – Anr. Copy. 2 vols. Lacks 4 ports. 19th. C. hf. chagrin, defect., stpd. on titles. (VG. Oct.13; 73) Fls. 1,900

HALSBURY, Hardinge Stanley Giffard, Earl of
– Laws of England. 1907-17. 31 vols. Orig. cl., some covers dampstained. (TA. Sep.18; 276) £54

HAMBURGER BEITRAGE ZUR NUMISMATIK
Hamburg, 1951-77. Pts. 5-16 & 24-26 only, in 11. vols. Orig. wraps., 1 rebkd. (SH. Mar.6; 363) *Tietjen*. £130

HAMBURGISCHES KOCHBUCH
Hamburg, 1788. Cont. vell., worn. (D. Dec.11-13; 2065) DM 490

HAMELMANN, H.
[–] [Oldenburgische Chronicon]. Oldenburg, 1599. 1st. Edn. Lge. 4to. Lacks engraved title, 1 double-p. view & map & 1 genealogical table, some notes, heavily browned at beginning 6 ll. with sm. tears or hole. Later cf., spine & cover slightly defect., worn. (H. Dec.9/10; 696) DM 1,300

HAMELSVELD, Ij. van
– De Gewichtigste Geschiedenissen des Bijbels. Ill.:– Tanjé & Folkema. Amst., 1806. 2 pts. in 1 vol. Fo. Some repairs, stains, tears, worn. Cf., new covers. (VG. Nov.18; 1045) Fls. 500

HAMER, S.H.
– The Little Folks Picture Album in Colour. Ill.:– Arthur Rackham. L., 1904. 1st. Edn. 4to. Cold. pict. cl. Raymond M. Sutton Jr. copy. (SG. May 7; 116) $210

HAMERTON, Philip Gilbert
– Etching & Etchers. Ill.:– Rembrandt, Callot & others. L., 1868. 1st. Edn. Mor.-bkd. gt.-decor. cl., very worn. (SG. May 14; 92) $950
– – Anr. Copy. 4to. Sm. liby. stp. on title. Liby. bkplt. (SG. Dec.4; 169) $750
– – Anr. Edn. 1880. 3rd. Edn. 4to. Orig. cl. (P. Mar.12; 16) *Craddock & Barnard*. £280
– – Anr. Copy. Cont. lev. mor. by F. Bedford, partly unc. (S. Nov.24; 150) *Sadler*. £240
– – Anr. Copy. (1000). 4to. Occasional spotting. Orig. mor.-bkd. cl. (CSK. Sep.12; 200) £210

– – Anr. Copy. Sm. fo. Orig. hf. mor., unc., worn. (SG. May 14; 93) $550
– Landscape. 1885. (525) numbered on L.P. Fo. Orig. parch., soiled. (CSK. Feb.13; 11) £55
– – Anr. Copy. Gt.-decor. vell., unc. & unopened. (SG. Mar.12; 183) $350
– The Portfolio: An Artistic Periodical. L., 1870-93. Vols. 1 to 24, lacks 2 vols., together 22 vols. Fo. Few plts. removed. Hf. leath. & cl. W.a.f. (PNY. Oct.1; 440) $400

HAMETAIRE, J.N.
[–] Observations sur L'Art du Comedien. 1774. Old cf. (BS. Jun.11; 253) £75

HAMILTON, Alexander, Statesman
– American Negotiator or the Various Currencies of the British Colonies in America. L., 1765. Cont. cf., rebkd., hf. mor. gt. box. Inscr. (SPB. Nov.24; 17) $900
– Observations on Certain Documents Contained in No. V & VI of 'The History of the United States for the Year 1796' . . . Phila., 1797. 1st. Edn. 3 cont. sigs. Mod. gt. qtr. mor. From William E. Barton Collection. (PNY. Mar.26; 133) $150

HAMILTON, Capt. Alexander
– A New Account of the East Indies. Edinb., 1727. 1st. Edn. 2 vols. 1 map slightly torn, slightly discold. thro.-out. 19th. C. hf. mor. From Chetham's Liby., Manchester. (C. Nov.26; 191) *Taylor*. £90

HAMILTON, Count Anthony
– Contes. Paris, 1781. 3 vols. 16mo. Cont. red mor., decor. spines, 3 fillets on covers, inner dentelle. From the 'Collection printed by order of Comte d'Artois'. (HD. Apr.9; 486) Frs. 1,600
– – Anr. Edn. L., [1792]. 4to. Some slight foxing. Cont. str-grd. mor., gt. roll.-stps. around covers, spine decor. with raised border. (HD. Feb.27; 32) Frs. 1,650
– Contes.–Mémoires du Comte de Grammont. Paris, 1815. On vell. 3 vols.; 3 vols., together 6 vols. 16mo. Cont. str.-grd. mor., spines decor. with gt. fillets, 5 gt. fillets on covers, inner dentelles, ca. 1840. From the 'Collection of better Works in the French Language dedicated to women'. (HD. Apr.9; 487) Frs. 2,150

HAMILTON, Elizabeth
– The Cottages of Glenburnie, A Scotch Novel. South Hanover, 1835. 1st. Amer. Edn. 16mo. Some staining, lightly foxed, free end-papers & 1 blank torn. Orig. cl.-bkd. bds., worn. From liby. of William E. Wilson. (SPB. Apr.29; 153) $350

HAMILTON, Francis, formerly Buchanan
– An Account of the Kingdom of Nepal & of the Territories Annexed to this Dominion by the House of Gorkha. Edinb., 1819. 4to. Some spotting. Recent cf. (TA. Mar.19; 346) £90

HAMILTON, Gavin
– Schola Italica Picturae. 1773. Fo. Lacks 1 plt., some margins stained but plts. barely affected. Cont. hf. cf., defect. (SBA. Mar.4; 46) *Evro Erlint*. £70

HAMILTON, Robert
– The Natural History of British Fishes. Edinb., 1843. 2 vols. Mod. hf. mor. (SH. Oct.9; 224) *Lamm*. £85

HAMILTON, Robert M.D., of Ipswich
See–BERKENHOUT, John–HAMILTON, Robert M.D., of Ipswich

HAMILTON, Sinclair
– Early American Book Illustrators & Wood Engravers. 1958; 1968. 1 vol., & supp., together 2 vols. 4to. Buckram. (SG. Jan.22; 195) $300

HAMILTON, William, of Bangour, 1704-54
– Poems on Several Occasions. Edinb., 1760. 3rd. Edn. Late 18th. C. red mor., gt. Bkplt. of Thomas Gaisford. (S. Nov.24; 152) *Fletcher*. £55

HAMILTON, William, M.D. of Plymouth
– History of Medicine, Surgery & Anatomy . . . L., 1831. 1st. Edn. 2 vols. 12mo. Disbnd. (SG. Sep.18; 170) $130

HAMILTON, Sir William, 1730-1803
– Antiquités Etrusques, Grecques et Romains. Naples, 1766-67. 1st. Edn. 4 vols. Lge. fo. Fr. & Engl. text, some slight browning. Cont. Fr. red mor., gt., spines tooled in compartments, floral decor., covers with 3-line roll-border, gt. inside borders. (S. Nov.24; 151) *Quaritch*. £7,500

HAMILTON, Sir William, 1730-1803 - Antiquités Etrusques, Grecques et Romains. *-contd.*
- - **Anr. Copy.** Vols. I, II & IV dampstained. Cont. cf., triple gt. fillet around covers, vases in corners, spines decor. with raised bands, inside dentelle, lr. cover of vol. II dampstained. (HD. Feb.27; 31b) Frs. 12,000
- **Campi Phlegraei.** Ill.:– after Pietro Fabris. Naples, 1776. 1st. Edn. 2 vols. Fo. Cont. Italian hf. cf. & ptd. paper bds. with Ducal arms stpd. in gt. on upr. covers. (C. Nov.5; 67a) *Taylor.* £4,500
- - **Anr. Copy.** 3 vols. in 2, including supp. 19th. C. hf. mor., & supp. in cont. bds. (worn). From Chetham's Liby., Manchester. (C. Nov.26; 192) *Taylor.* £4,200
- **Collection of Estruscan, Greek & Roman Antiquities.** Ed.:– Hughes d'Hancarville. Ill.:– after Pignatari, Nolli, Bracci & others. Naples, 1766-67. 1st. Edn. 4 vols. 4to. Engraved titles & 194 plts. hand-cold., 2 titles & some plts. creased, titles & plts. with sm. liby. blind-stpds., bkplt. on verso of 3 titles. Cont. diced russ., rebkd. From Chetham's Liby., Manchester. (C. Nov.26; 193) *Marcus.* £1,300
- **Observations on Mount Vesuvius, Mount Etna & other Volcanos.** 1772. 1st. Edn. Slight foxing & offsetting onto text, map torn. Cont. russ. (S. Nov.4; 581) *Walford.* £160
- - **Anr. Copy.** Cont. tree cf. (SBA. Oct.21; 247) *Knight.* £60
- **Outlines from the Figures & Compositions upon the Greek, Roman & Etruscan Vases.** 1804. 1st Edn. 4to. Slight spotting. Cont. bds., spine defect., unc. (S. May 5; 181) *Lyon.* £70
[-] - **Anr. Copy.** Red mor. gt. (BS. Jun.11; 51) £50

HAMILTON, William J.
- **Researches in Asia Minor, Pontus & Armenia.** 1842. 1st. Edn. 2 vols. Some foxing & staining. Cont. cf.-bkd. cl., gt. (C. Nov.5; 68) *Classic.* £100

HAMILTON, Sir William Rowan
- **Elements of Quaternions . . .** Ed.:– William Edwin Hamilton. 1866. 1st. Edn. Mod. cl.-bkd. bds. (S. Dec.2; 721) *Teachers.* £95

HAMILTON Spectator
- **Hamilton . . . a Carnival Souvenir.** [Hamilton], Aug., 1903. Fo. 1st. & last ll. trimmed & mntd., 1 other lf. with sm. tear. Recent wraps., with orig. pict. wrap. trimmed & mntd. on front. (CB. Dec.9; 41) Can. $120

HAMLET, John
See–GROSSMAN, Mary Louise & Hamlet, John

HAMMER-PURGSTALL, J.V.
- **Geschichte des Osmanischen Reiches.** Pest, 1827-35. 1st. Edn. 10 vols. All vols. lightly stained, vol. 5 heavily, slightly soiled in parts. Cont. hf. leath. gt. 3 spines torn, 1 very worn. (R. Mar.31-Apr.4; 162) DM 1,400

HAMMETT, Dashiell
- **The Thin Man.** N.Y., 1934. 1st. Edn. 12mo. Cl., covers slightly faded, d.-w. (SG. Nov.13; 281) $400

HANBURY, Barnard
See–WADDINGTON, George & Hanbury, Barnard

HANBURY, William
- **A Complete Body of Planting & Gardening.** Ill.:– T. Lodge. Priv. ptd., 1770-71. 2 vols. Fo. Plts. numbered I-VII, 8-20, erratically disposed, some browning & spotting. Cont. hf. cf., worn, jnts. reprd. Bkplt. of Augustus Keppel, Elden Hall (Suffolk), the Plesch copy. (S. Jun.22; 39) *Traylen.* £180

HANCARVILLE, Pierre François Hugues d'
[-] **Monumens de la Vie Privée des Douze Cesars. -Monumens du Culte Secret des Dames Romaines.** Capri, 1780. 1st. Edns. 2 vols. in 1. 4to. Early red qtr. mor., spine gt., unc. (SG. May 14; 94) $1,000
[-] **Monumens du Culte Secret des Dames Romains . . .** Capri [Nancy], 1784. 4to. Old str.-grd. hf. mor., corners, spine decor. with raised bands. (HD. Jun.24; 39) Frs. 1,200
See–HAMILTON, Sir William

HANCKE, Erich
- **Max Liebermann, Sein Leben und Seine Werke.** Berlin, 1914. 4to. Cont. hf. mor. (SH. Nov.21; 395) *Kaufmann.* £70

- - **Anr. Copy.** Orig. hf. leath., spine lightly worn. (H. Dec.9/10; 2188) DM 540
- - **Anr. Edn.** Ill.: M. Liebermann. Berlin, 1923. Privilege Edn., 4to. Orig. vell. 1 sigd. ill. (HK. Nov.18-21; 2775) DM 6,000

HANCOCK, James & Elliott, Hugh
- **The Herons of the World.** Ill.:– Robert Gilmor & Peter Hayman. 1978. (150) numbered. Fo. Orig. hf. mor., s.-c. (TA. Jun.18; 90) £85

HANCOCK, John, Senator
- **An Oration . . . to Commemorate the Bloody Tragedy of Fifth of March, 1770.** Boston, 1774. 1st. Edn. 4to. Foxed. Sewed, unc., red hf. mor. s.-c. (SG. May 14; 95) $425

HANCOCK, Thomas
- **Personal Narrative of the Origin & Progress of the Caoutchouc or India-Rubber Manufacture in England.** 1857. 1st. Edn. Orig. cl., spine slightly worn. (S. Dec.2; 722) *Cavendish.* £55

HANCOCK, Walter
- **Narrative of Twelve Years' Experiments demonstrative of the Practicability & Advantage of Employing Steam-Carriages on Common Roads.** 1838. Plts. spotted, errata. Orig. cl., worn. (SKC. Feb.26; 1761) £150

HANDBUCH DER GEOGRAPHISCHEN WISSENSCHAFTEN
Ed.:– F. Klute. Potsdam, 1929. 4to. Orig. hf. leath. (D. Dec.11-13; 1390) DM 700
- - **Anr. Edn.** F. Klute. Potsdam, 1930-38. 10 vols. 4to. Orig. linen. (R. Oct.14-18; 1468) DM 700

HANDBUCH der Pharmaceutischen Botanik
Nuremb., 1804. Fo. Cont. qtr. leath., brkn. (SG. Oct.9; 129) $1,200

HANDT, K.
- **Buchlin und Experiment Hiler Arzneyen.** Nuremb., 1551. 16mo. Cf., blind-tooled, metal clasps. (CR. Jun.11; 579) Lire 800,000

HANDVESTEN, Privilegien, Octroyen, Costumen en Willekeuren der Stad Amstelredam
Amst., 1662[-70]. Fo. Cont. blind-stpd. vell., lacks ties. (VG. Dec.17; 1356) Fls. 750

HANKSCHEL, M.
- **Modell eines Aeroplans der Brüder Wright.** Ca. 1908. Ob. fo. Orig. ptd. bds., rebkd. (SH. Mar.19; 210) *Glendale.* £70

HANLEY, James
- **Boy.** [1931]. (145) numbered, sigd. Orig. cl., slightly soiled. (CSK. Jun.26; 72) £55

HANNAY, Patrick
- **Poetical Works.** Priv. ptd., 1875. Hf. mor. gt., by Ramage. (CE. Nov.20; 150) £210

HANOTAUX, Gabriel
- **La Seine et les Quais.** Ill.:– A. Robida. Paris, 1901. 1st. Edn.; on Jap. 12mo. Orig. watercolour. Hf. mor. by Pouillet, corners, spine with raised bands, wrap. & spine preserved. Autograph dedication from author to publisher, many letters. (HD. Jun.25; 276) Frs. 1,800

HANSARD, Thomas C.
- **Typographia.** 1825. Cont. hf. cf. (SH. May 28; 175) *Talerman.* £85

HANSI (Pseud.)
See–WALTZ, Jean-Jacques 'Hansi'

HANSMANN, Margarete
- **Grob, Fein und Göttlich.** Ill.:– H.A.P. Grieshaber. Hamburg & Düsseldorf, 1971. Fo. Orig. bds. (SH. Nov.21; 335) *Schwing.* £55

HANWAY, Jonas
- **An Historical Account of the British Trade over the Caspian Sea.** 1753. 1st. Edn. 4 vols. 4to. Cf. gt. (P. Oct.23; 31) *Maggs.* £130
- - **Anr. Copy.** Cont. cf., worn, rebkd. From Chetham's Liby., Manchester. (C. Nov.26; 194) *Vine.* £100
- - **Anr. Edn.** 1754. 2nd. Edn. 2 vols. 4to. A few plts. torn, browned, 1 lf. torn. Cont. cf., worn. (SH. Jun.18; 66) *Makiya.* £65
[-] **Journal of Eight Days Journey from Portsmouth to Kingston Upon Thames . . . to which is added an Essay on Tea.** 1756. 1st. Edn. 4to. Some spotting. Cont. cf., corners & spine worn. (S. Apr.7; 258) *Foyles.* £80
[-] - **Anr. Copy.** Orig. bds., rebkd. (SH. Nov.6; 106) *Sanders.* £60

HARAEIUS, Franciscus
- **Annales Ducum seu Principum Brabantiae.** Antw., 1623. 3 vols. in 2. Fo. Vell. (BS. Jun.11; 108) £150

HARBOUR, Henry
- **Where Flies the Flag.** Ill.:– Arthur Rackham. L., [1904]. 1st. Edn. Gt. & cold. pict. cl. Raymond M. Sutton Jr. copy. (SG. May 7; 118) $190

HARCOURT, Susan Vernon
- **Sketches in Madeira.** 1851. Fo. Spotted. Orig. cl., worn, loose. (SH. Nov.7; 300) *Remington.* £230

HARDENBERG, Friedrich Leopold von 'Novalis'
- **Schriften.** Ed.:– Fr. Schlegel & L. Tieck. Berlin, 1802. 1st. Coll. Edn. 2 vols. Lightly soiled in places. Cont. paper bds., slightly soiled, unc. (H: Dec.9/10; 1616) DM 4,600
- - **Anr. Copy.** Lacks XII pp. preface in vol. 1, lightly soiled in parts. Unc., cont. bds., slightly soiled & torn. (H. May 21/22; 1221) DM 1,800

HARDIE, Martin
- **Etchings & Dry Points from 1902 to 1924 by James McBey.** 1925. (500) numbered, with orig. sigd. etching. 4to. Qtr. sheep. (P. Jul.30; 106) *Thompson.* £80
- **Water-Colour Painting in Britain.** 1967-68. 3 vols. 4to. Orig. cl. (SH. Jan.29; 108) *Waggert.* £140
- - **Anr. Edn.** [1969; 1967; 1968]. 3 vols. 4to. Orig. cl. (CSK. Nov.21; 72) £60
See–DODGSON, Campbell–HARDIE, Martin

HARDIMAN, James
- **The History of the Town & County of Galway.** Dublin, 1820. 1st. Edn. 4to. Hf. mor. (GM. Apr.30; 409) £290
- **Irish Minstrelsy, or Bardic Remains of Ireland.** L., 1831. 1st. Edn. 2 vols. Cl. (GM. Apr.30; 245) £75

HARDIN, John Wesley
- **The Life of, from the original Manuscript.** Seguin, Texas, 1896. 1st. Edn., 1st. iss. 12mo. Ptd. pict. wraps. (SG. Jan.8; 187) $100

HARDING, Edward
- **Costume of the Russian Empire.** 1803. Fo. Wtrmkd. 1802. Red hf. mor. gt. From liby. of Baron Dimsdale. (MMB. Oct.8; 5) *Bess.* £165
- - **Anr. Copy.** 73 hand-cold. engraved plts., text & plts. wtrmkd. 1796. Cont. russ., gt., upr. cover detchd. Bkplt. of Sir William Jenningham. (S. Nov.24; 57) *Symonds.* £120
- - **Anr. Copy.** 72 hand-cold. engravings, wtrmkd. 1802. Gt. str.-grd. mor., rebkd. (SG. Oct.9; 67) $500
- - **Anr. Copy.** Cont. mor., 6 decor. spine raised bands, 2 lge. dentelle & fillet borders, gt., fillet, blind roulette. (LM. Jun.13; 56) B.Frs. 14,000
- - **Anr. Edn.** 1804. Fo. Several plts. wtrmkd. 1823, sm. tear in 1 lf., some offsetting. 19th. C. str.-grd. mor., gt., slightly worn. (S. Oct.21; 511) *Walford.* £150
[-] - **Anr. Copy.** Text in Engl. & Fr. Mor., gt., worn. (BS. Jun.11; 349) £140
[-] - **Anr. Edn.** 1810. Fo. Sig. on title. Hf. diced russ. (BS. Jun.11; 250) £95
- - **Anr. Copy.** 71 (of 72) cold. plts. Cont. red mor. gt., rebkd. with orig. spine laid on. (SG. Oct.30; 103) $350
- - **Anr. Edn.** 1811. Fo. Text in Engl. & Fr. Cont. hf. cf. (TA. Sep.18; 321) £210
- - **Anr. Copy.** 4to. Some slight offsetting. Cont. str.-grd. mor. gt., recased. (TA. Mar.19; 308) £130
- - **Anr. Copy.** Fo. Text wtrmkd. 1807, 1809-10, plts. 1808, 1810, some foxing & soiling. Cont. str.-grd. red mor., rebkd., preserving orig. spine, slightly worn. (S. Sep.29; 269) *Doran.* £110
- - **Anr. Copy.** Text in Engl. & Fr. Cont. hf. cf., lr. cover detchd., worn. (TA. Jul.16; 127) £95
- - **Anr. Copy.** Red chagrin. (DS. May 22; 870) Pts. 40,000

HARDING, James Duffield
- **Drawing Book for the Year 1838.** L., [1838]. Ob. 4to. Some plts. slightly soiled. Cont. hf. leath. (R. Mar.31-Apr.4; 2173) DM 3,600
- **Harding's Drawing Book for the Year 1841.** 1841. Ob. 4to. Advt. lf., 1 plt. stained, a few with slight staining in outer edges. Orig. hf. roan, spine gt., contents loose or detchd., some wear. (S. Nov.4; 498) *Walford.* £55
- **The Park & the Forest.** 1841. Fo. Orig. mor.-bkd. cl. (C. May 20; 128) *Cumming.* £190

– – Anr. Copy. Marginal soiling, liby. stp. on verso of each plts. & on 'list of plts.'. Cont. hf. mor. (CSK. Jun.19; 140) £160

– Sketches at Home & Abroad. [1836]. Fo. Tinted litho. title & 50 plts., lacks dedication; title & 2 plts. detchd. Orig. hf. mor. W.a.f. (C. May 20; 127) *Walford.* £850

HARDINGE, Charles Stewart
– Recollections of India. 1847. 2 Pts. in 1 vol. Lge. fo. Cont. mor.-bkd. cl. (C. Jul.15; 42) *Taylor.* £320

HARDT, Hermann von der
– Magnum Oecumenicum Constantiense Concilia, de Universali Ecclesia Reformatione et Fide. Helmstedt; Berlin, 1697-1700; 1742. 7 vols. in 3 & Vol. 7. Fo. Only slightly browned in parts, some arms plts. & text ll. in vol. 6. lightly stained, index lf. slightly browned. Cont. bds. (R. Oct.14-18; 2162) DM 8,000

HARDY, Campbell
– Forest Life in Acadie. L., 1869. Frontis. & title-p. slightly foxed & stained. Recent hf. mor. (CB. Dec.9; 193) Can. $100

HARDY, Joseph
– A Picturesque & Descriptive Tour in the Mountains of the High Pyrenees. 1825. Engraved map & aquatints trimmed & mntd. Orig. cl., upr. jnts. brkn. (C. Jul.15; 43) *Reid.* £320

HARDY, Thomas
– The Convergence of the Twain. L., 1912. 1st. Separate Edn., (10). MS. corrections to 5 lines of poem, printer's rubber-stp. on blank before title. Unbnd., in cl. folding. case. (SG. Nov.13; 282) $800

– The Dynasts. 1904-06-08. Vol. 3 1st. Edn. 3 vols., Orig. cl. Tipped in at front vol. 1 is A.L.s. by Hardy, 2 pp., Max Gate, Dorchester, 12.10.1909 in reply to a review of The Dynasts by Maurice Lanoire, Engl. pencil annots. & underlining, copy of review loosely inserted. (CSK. Sep.5; 206) £200

– – Anr. Edn. Ill.:– Francis Dodd (frontis. port.). 1927. (525) on L.P., sigd. by author & artist. 3 vols. Orig. vell.-bkd. decor. bds., unc. (C. Jul.22; 14) *Sawyer.* £160

– – Anr. Copy. Mor. gt., cold. mor. gt. onlays, cold. silk linings, by Mounteney. (CNY. May 22; 127) $350

– – Anr. Copy. 4to. Stiff vell.-bkd. batik bds., paper on lr. cover of 1 vol. separating from vell. below, unc. & unopened. (SG. Nov.13; 283) $150

– The Dynasts.–The Oxen. Ill.:– Francis Dodd (engraved frontis. 1st. work). 1927; 1915. (525) on L.P., sigd. by author & artist. 1st. separate Edn. 3 vols.; 1 vol. Orig. vell-bkd. batik-paper bds., unc., vols. 2 & 3 in d.-w.'s; orig. ptd. wraps., mor.-bkd. s-c. (C. Feb.4; 280) *Traylen.* £130

– England to Germany; the Pity of it; I Met a Man; A New Year's Eve in War Time. Priv. Ptd., 1917. 1st. Edn., (25) numbered, & sigd. by Florence Emily Hardy. Sm. 4to. Orig. wraps., unc. Inscr. to J.F. Symons-Jeune on title. (SH. Dec.19; 543) *Rota.* £360

– Far from the Madding Crowd. Ill.:– Agnes Miller Parker. N.Y., Ltd. Edns. Cl., 1958. (1500) sigd. by artist. Orig. mor.-bkd. bds., s.-c. Imp. of first ill. sigd., loosely inserted. (SH. Feb.20; 235) *Libris.* £170

– The Fiddler's Story; A Jingle on the Times. Priv. Ptd., 1917. 1st. Edn., (25) numbered, & sigd. by Florence Emily Hardy. 4to. Orig. wraps., unc. (SH. Dec.19; 544) *Painting.* £90

– Jezreel; The Master & the Leaves. Priv. Ptd., 1919. 1st. Edn., (25) numbered, & sigd. by Florence Emily Hardy. 4to. Orig. wraps., unc. (SH. Dec.19; 545) *Sawyer.* £85

– Jude the Obscure. Ill.:– Agnes Miller Parker. N.Y., Ltd. Edns. Cl., 1969. (1500) sigd. by artist. Orig. mor.-bkd. bds., s.-c. Wood-engr. sigd. by artist loosely inserted. (SH. Feb.20; 250) £110

– The Mayor of Casterbridge. Ill.:– Agnes Miller Parker. N.Y., Ltd. Edns. Cl. 1964. (1500) sigd. by artist. Orig. mor.-bkd. bds., s.-c. (SH. Feb.20; 243) *Maggs.* £110

– The Return of the Native. Ill.:– Clare Leighton. 1929. (1500) sigd. by artist. Orig. vell.-bkd. bds., s.-c., box. (CSK. Jul.24; 36) £65

– Tess of the D'Urbervilles. [L.], [1891]. 1st. Edn. 3 vols. Orig. cl., gt. art-nouveau double linear design on upr. covers (after C. Ricketts), cl.

folding case. From the Prescott Collection. (CNY. Feb.6; 143) $4,500

– – Anr. Edn. Ill.:– Vivien Gribble. L., 1926. (300) on L.P. sigd. by Hardy. 4to. Gt. qtr. vell. & marb. bds., partly unopened. (PNY. Oct.1; 272) $150

– Tess of the D'Urbervilles.–Dynasts. L., 1926; 1927. Ltd. Edns., sigd. by author. 1 vol.; 3 vols. Orig. bdgs., worn. (SPB. Nov.25; 299) $275

– To Shakespeare After Three Hundred Years. Priv. Ptd., 1916. 1st. Edn. in bk. form, (50) numbered, & sigd. by Florence Emily Hardy. 4to. Orig. wraps., unc. Inscr. to F. Symons-Jeune on title. (SH. Dec.19; 541) *Rota.* £290

– 'When I Weekly Knew'. Priv. Ptd., 1916. 1st. Edn. in bk. form, (25) numbered, & sigd. by Florence Emily Hardy. 4to. Orig. wraps., unc. A.L.s. from Florence Emily Hardy loosely inserted, 2pp., Feb. 6 [1917]. (SH. Dec.19; 542) *Rota.* £150

– The Woodlanders. 1887. 1st. Edn. 3 vols. Orig. cl., slightly marked, unc. (SKC. Feb.26; 1504) £190

– – Anr. Copy. (CNY. May 22; 126) $480

– Works [Collection of] L., 1871-[98]. 1st. Edns. 19 works in 40 vols. Unif. three-qtr. lev., spines gt., by Zaehnsdorf. (SG. Oct.9; 126) $800

– Writings in Prose & Verse. N.Y., [1893-1904]. (153) numbered & sigd. by author & publishers. 20 vols. Crimson three-qtr. mor., spines gt., slightly worn. (SG. Nov.13; 284) $800

– Works. 1919-20. Mellstock Edn., (500) sigd. 37 vols. Cl. (S. Dec.8; 29) *Sotheran.* £800

– – Anr. Copy. Slight browning. Orig. cl., d.-w.'s, some tears. (SPB. May 6; 314) $1,400

HARE, James H.
– A Photographic Record of the Russo-Japanese War. N.Y., 1905. Ob. 4to. Cl.-bkd. bds., lge. photo. on cover. (SG. Feb.26; 284) $140

HARE NAYLOR, Frances
– History of Helvetia Switzerland to the Middle of the Fifteenth Century. L., 1801. 2 vols. Orig. publisher's advts. bnd. in. Cf., worn, inner dentelles gt., spines badly worn, marb. end-papers. (JL. Dec.15; 721) *Aus.* $100

HARGRAVE, Catherine Perry
– History of Playing Cards & a Bibliography of Cards & Gaming. N.p., Riverside Pr., 1930. Fo. Orig. cl. (TA. Sep.18; 178) £120

– – Anr. Edn. Boston & N.Y., 1930. 4to. Orig. cl. (CB. Feb.18; 191) Can. $220

HARGRAVE, Joseph James
– Red River. Montreal, 1871. Orig. cl. (SPB. Jun.22; 67) $100

HARGRAVE, Letitia
See–CHAMPLAIN Society

HARIOT, John
See–BRY, Theodore de & others

HARKNESS, William Hale
– Temples & Topees. N.Y., Derry. Pr., 1936. 1st. Edn., (200) numbered. Cl., gt. spine lettering rubbed. Sigd. Pres. Copy. (PNY. Oct.1; 172) $120

HARLEIAN SOCIETY
– Visitations.–Registers. 1869-1917. Vols. 1-69; Vols. 1-50, 119 vols. in 117, & a supp. vol. Cf., spines gt., supp. vol. in cl. As a periodical, w.a.f. From the collection of Eric Sexton. (C. Apr.16; 268) *Heraldry Today.* £900

HARLEQUINADE
– Bunyan's Pilgrim's Progress from this World to that which is to Come, Exhibited in a Metamorphosis, or a Transformation of Pictures. Ill.:– John W. Barber. New Haven, ca. 1850. 6th. Edn. 12mo. Unbnd. as iss. (SH. Mar.19; 121) *Schiller.* £80

HARLEY, Robert & Edward, Earls of Oxford
– A Collection of Voyages & Travels . . . compiled from the Curious & Valuable Library of . . . L., 1745. 2 vols. Fo. Lr. portion of 1 title-p. strengthened, some foxing & staining. Early cf., some sm. defects. (KH. Mar.24; 187) *Aus.* $700

– Harleian Miscellany. 1744-46. 8 vols., 4to. Cont. cf. Bkplt. of Richard Cox, Quarley, Hants. (S. Sep.29; 41) *Fletcher.* £80

– – Anr. Copy. Rebkd. (CSK. May 1; 159) £55

– – Anr. Edn. 1744-53. Vol. 1 2nd. Edn., rest 1st. Edns. 8 vols. 4to. Unif. cont. cf., gt. decor. spines, some wear. (TA. Mar.19; 339) £125

– Proposals for Printing, the Two First Volumes of Bibliotheca Harleiana. [L.],

Nov.1, 1742. 1st. Edn. Fo. Minor tears at extreme blank margins, sm. piece torn from extreme lr. part of central fold, light stain at lr. outer corner, some other sm. marginal stains, sold with a facs. edn. In folding portfo. & mor.-tipped s.-c. From the Prescott Collection. (CNY. Feb.6; 174) $11,000

HARMON, Daniel W.
– A Journal of Voyages & Travels in the Interior of North America . . . From Montreal Nearly to the Pacific . . . Andover, 1820. 1st. Edn. Offsetting, lacks errata lf., text foxed & soiled, some later ll. torn at margin. Cont. tree cf. From liby. of William E. Wilson. (SPB. Apr.29; 129) $200

HARMONIA RURALIS; or, An Essay towards a Natural History of British Song Birds
1824. Vol. 1 only. 4to. Some spotting. Orig. hf. mor., spine chipped. (CSK. Nov.7; 37) £125

HARMSWORTH, Cecil
– A Little Fishing Book. Cuala Pr., 1939. 1st. Edn., (80). Orig. linen-bkd. bds., unc. (SH. Jul.22; 86) *Quaritch.* £85

HARMSWORTH, Cecil & Desmond
– Holiday Verses . . . Cuala Pr., 1922. 1st. Edn., (75). Orig. linen-bkd. bds., unc. (SH. Jul.22; 75) *Figgis.* £80

HARMSWORTH, Desmond
[–] Desmond's Poems. Cuala Pr. 1930. 1st. Edn., (75). Orig. linen-bkd. bds., unc. 2 T.L.s. from George Yeats to Miss Gill loosely inserted. (SH. Jul.22; 79) *Quaritch.* £95

HARMSWORTH Monthly Pictorial Magazine
Ill.:– Arthur Rackham. L., 1898-99. 4to. Orig. gt. decor., cl. Raymond M. Sutton Jr. copy. (SG. May 7; 119) $120

HARPEL, Oscar H.
– Harpel's Typograph. Cinc., Priv. ptd., 1870. 1st. Edn. Gt.-pict. cl., partly sprung in bdg. Bkplts. of Edmund Gress, Geiger & Paul A. Bennett. (SG. Oct.2; 173) $425

HARPER, J. Russell
– The Early History of Haldimand County. [Caledonia, Ontario], 1950. Orig. ptd. wraps. (CB. Sep.24; 227) Can. $110

– Paul Kane's Frontier, including Wanderings of an Artist among the Indians of North America. [Toronto], [1971]. (300) numbered. Sq. 4to. Suede, paper covered s.-c. (CB. Sep.24; 292) Can. $130

HARPER, J. Russell & Triggs, Stanley
– Portrait of a Period. A Collection of Notman Photographs, 1856-1915. Ed.:– Edgar Andrew Collard. Montreal, 1967. Fo. Orig. d.-w. (PWP. Apr.9; 216) Can. $200

HARPER'S Weekly
Ill.:– Homer, Darley, Nevin & others. N.Y., 1859. Fo. Minor browning. Hf. mor. (SPB. May 29; 192) $200

– – Anr. Run. N.Y., 1859-61. Vols. 3 (Apr. 9-Dec.31 only), 4, & 5. Fo. Vol. 5 with heavy fraying, staining, & c. Various bdgs., vol. 5 completely loose. (SG. Nov.20; 350) $350

– – Anr. Run. Ill.:– Winslow Homer & others. 1861. Cl., disbnd. (SPB. Jul.28; 171) $175

– – Anr. Run. N.Y., 1861-65. 5 vols. Sm. fo. Later three-qtr. mor., spines gt. (SG. Oct.9; 128) $1,500

– – Anr. Run. N.Y., 1863-64. Vols. 7 & 8. Fo. Vol. 8 ex-liby., with extensive marginal fraying. Three-qtr. leath., & bds. with roan spine respectively, vol. 8 disbnd. W.a.f. (SG. Nov.20; 349) $275

– – Anr. Run. N.Y., 1863-66. Vols. 7, 8, 9, & 10. Fo. Various bdgs., worn. (SG. Nov.20; 351) $600

– – Anr. Copy. Lacks many ll. W.a.f. (SG. May 21; 386) $325

– – Anr. Run. N.Y., 1872. Vol. XVI. Fo. Numerous supps. bnd. together at end. Hf. roan. (SG. May 21; 369) $375

– – Anr. Run. N.Y., Jan.-Dec., 1879. Vol. 23. Fo. Loose in old bd. covers. (SG. Nov.20; 352) $150

HARRADEN, Richard B.
– Cantabrigia Depicta . . . Camb., 1809. 4to. Occasional minor marginal spotting. Cont. cf., covers with blind-tooled borders & gt. cornerpieces, rebkd. preserving orig. spine. From the collection of Eric Sexton. (C. Apr.16; 270) *Temperley.* £190

HARRADEN, Richard B. -contd.
- **Costume of the Various Orders in the University of Cambridge.** Ill.:– J. Whessel after Harraden. 1805. 4to. All but 1 plt. cold., some offsetting. Cont. hf. cf., worn. (C. Nov.6; 310) *Harley.* £140
– – **Anr. Copy.** Plts. in wash borders & hand-cold., lacks ptd. title. Cont. mott. cf. gt., covers with central pol. cf. panels & gt.-tooled borders. Bkplt. of Earl Ferrers, lately in the collection of Eric Sexton. (C. Apr.16; 269) *Taylor.* £100
– – **Anr. Copy.** Earl Ferrers bkplt. (C. Jul.15; 44) *Chesters.* £70

HARRAL, Thomas & Ireland, Samuel
- **Picturesque Views of the Severn.** 1824. 2 vols. in 1. Fo. Recent hf. cf., unc. (TA. Sep.18; 337) £75

HARRIMAN ALASKA EXPEDITION
Ed.:– John Burroughs, John Muir, G.B. Grinnell & others (text). N.Y., 1901. 1st. Edn. Vols. I & II. 4to. Gt.-decor. cl., sm. dampstains at corners of 2 covers & on cl. d.-w.'s. (SG. Apr.23; 102) $325
– – **Anr. Copy.** (SG. Jul.9; 159) $250
– – **Anr. Copy.** Vol. I only. (SG. Jul.9; 160) $100
– – **Anr. Copy.** Vols. I & II. Embossed liby. stp. on title-p. Both orig. cl. (CB. Feb.18; 290) Can. $350

HARRINGTON, James, the Elder
[–] **The Commonwealth of Oceana.** 1656. 1st. Edn. Fo. Folding plt. from later edns. loosely inserted, some browning. Cont. cf., rebkd. & reprd. Bkplt. of Charles Purton Cooper, Wadham College & Lincoln's Inn. [Wing H809] (S. Sep.29; 42) *Subunso.* £70
- **The Oceana.** 1737. Fo. Spr. cf. (P. Dec.11; 330) *Brook-Hitchin.* £90

HARRIOT
See–BRY, Theodor de & others

HARRIOT, Thomas
- **Artis Analyticae Praxis.** 1631. 1st. Edn. Fo. Lacks lf. A1 (blank). 19th. C. hf. mor. From Chetham's Liby., Manchester. [STC 12784, Sabin 30376] (C. Nov.26; 195) *Rota.* £500

HARRIOTT, Lieut. John
- **Struggles through life, exemplified in the various travels . . . in Europe, Asia, Africa & America.** 1807. 1st. Edn. 2 vols. 12mo. Engraved port. somewhat foxed & offset onto title-p. Cont. hf. mor., gt. ornaments in panels of spines, bkplt. of Lord Rosebery. William Beckford's copy with 2½ pp. of pencilled notes in his hand. (S. Nov.4; 484) *Maggs.* £120
– – **Anr. Edn.** 1815. 3 vols. Cf. gt. (P. Oct.23; 32) *Scott.* £55

HARRIS, E.C.
- **New Zealand Flowers.–New Zealand Berries. –New Zealand Ferns.** N.d. 2 vols. in 1. 4to. Cf. gt. (P. Jul.30; 257) *Thorp.* £65

HARRIS, Joel Chandler
- **Uncle Remus: His Songs & His Sayings.** Ill.:– F.S. Church & James H. Moser. N.Y., 1881. 1st. Edn., 1st. Iss. Orig. gt.-pict. cl., text tightened at inner margin at centre of book. (PNY. Mar.26; 134) $110
– – **Anr. Edn.** Ill.:– F.S. Church & J. H. Moser. N.Y., 1881. 1st. Edn., 2nd. Iss. Misprint on p.9 corrected, 4 ll. publisher's advts., 1 plt. & a lf. with short tear. Orig. pict. cl., gt. Loosely inserted a cheque sigd. by Harris to the Cole Book Company 18 Apr. 1907. (C. Feb.4; 281) *Basket & Day.* £60

HARRIS, John
- **The History of Kent.** Ill.:– G. Vertue (port.). 1719. 1st. Edn. Vol. I (all publd.). Fo. Cont. cf., rebkd. From the collection of Eric Sexton. (C. Apr.16; 271) *Quaritch.* £520
– – **Anr. Copy.** Worn, upr. jnt. brkn. (C. Nov.6; 311) *Gibbons.* £500
- **Lexicon Technicum.** 1704-10. 1st. Edn. 2 vols. Fo. Vol. 2 browned & spotted, lacks engraved port. by White. Mod. old-style panel., spines gt. (S. May 5; 344) *Bopp.* £300
– – **Anr. Copy.** 10 (of 14?) engraved plts., some spotting & staining in vol. II. 19th. C. hf. mor., upr. cover to vol. I detchd. From Chetham's Liby., Manchester. (C. Nov.26; 196) *Taylor.* £90
- **Navigantium Atque Itinerantium Bibliotheca: or, A Compleat Collection of Voyages & Travels . . . of the most Authentick Writers.** 1705. 1st. Edn. Vol. I (of 2). Fo. 1 engraved folding map slightly torn, fo. 3H3 misbnd., 7D1 loose, lacks (? last

blank), a few marginal tears, some ll. slightly soiled. Cont. panel cf., worn, some leath. missing at foot of spine & on covers. [Sabin 30482] (S. Apr.7; 259) *Burgess.* £220
– – **Anr. Edn.** Ed.:– John Campbell. 1744-48. 2 vols. Fo. 52 plts. & maps (of 59, lacks 6 plts. & India map in vol. I), frontis. & a1-2L2 of vol. II misbnd. in front of vol. I, slight offsetting & soiling, plt. 47 spotted. 19th. C. hf. russ., 3 covers detchd., worn. Bkplt. of Sir John Stewart Richardson of Pitfour. [Sabin 30483] (S. Sep.29; 167) *Waterloo Inustm.* £550
– – **Anr. Edn.** Ill.:– Emanuel Bowen & Thomas Kitchin (maps). L., 1764. 2 vols. Fo. Occasional light offsetting. Cont. cf. Bkplts. of Lord Sampson Eardley in each vol. [Sabin 30483] (CB. Sep.24; 177) Can. $1,200

HARRIS, Joseph
- **Description & Use of the Globes.** 1745. 6th. Edn. Cf., worn. (CE. Mar.19; 225) £55
– – **Anr. Edn.** 1751. 7th. Edn. Cont. cf. (P. Apr.9; 11) *Morrison.* £60
- **The Mistakes.** 1691. 1st. Edn. 4to. Natural paper faults in last lf. partly reprd., slight browning thro-out. Mor. by Sangorski. [Wing H865] (C. Nov.19; 100) *Pickering & Chatto.* £90

HARRIS, Moses
- **The Aurelian.** Ed.:– J.O. Westwood. 1766 [ca. 1840]. Fo. Cont. red mor., sides with gt. borders of 4 triple fillets & 3 roll tools, spine gt., by J. Wright. (C. Mar.18; 52) *Henderson.* £1,100
– – **Anr. Edn.** Ed.:– J.O. Westwood. 1840. Fo. Cont. red hf. mor., spine gt. (C. Mar.18; 51) *Wheldon & Wesley.* £1,100
- **The Aurelian.–An Essay Preceding a Supplement to the Aurelian.** Priv. Ptd., [1758-] 66; [1767-80]. 1st. Edn. (1st. work). 2 works in 2 vols. Fo.; 4to. 1st. work: engraved port. offset onto title, several text nos. altered in ink, plt. XX slightly stained; 2nd. work: with port. not called for by Nissen. 1st. work: 19th. C. hf. mor.; 2nd. work: buckram-bkd. bds., spines torn. From Chetham's Liby., Manchester. (C. Nov.26; 197) *Map House.* £3,200
- **An Exposition of English Insects.** 1782. 4to. Slight foxing. Later hf. mor., some wear to spine. (TA. Jan.22; 376) £340
– – **Anr. Copy.** Hf. cf. (DWB. Mar.31; 65) £310
– – **Anr. Copy.** 4to. Frontis. loose. Covers detchd. (P. Apr.9; 120) *Hill.* £270
– – **Anr. Copy.** Title & frontis. reprd. Qtr. mor. (P. Jul.30; 85) *Henderson.* £160
– – **Anr. Copy.** Lacks scheme of colours, some slight foxing. Later hf. leath. (VG. Dec.17; 1362) Fls. 550

HARRIS, R.
- **South Africa.** Port Elizabeth, 1888. 4to. Publisher's leath., lacks spine, lr. cover loose. (VA. Oct.31; 451) R. 170
– – **Anr. Copy.** No bdg. stated, but covers loose, lacks spine. (SSA. Jun.18; 355) R. 120

HARRIS, [Robert]
- **The Drunkards Cup.** 1630. 4th. Edn. Sm. 4to. Slight browning & soiling. 19th. C. mor.-bkd. cl. From liby. of André L. Simon. [STC 12830] (S. May 18; 111) *Gabler.* £50

HARRIS, Thaddeus Mason
- **The Journal of a Tour into the Territory North West of the Alleghany Mountains . . . with a Geographical & Historical Account of the State of Ohio.** Boston, 1805. 1st. Edn. Some foxing, offsetting & repairs, specks of soiling, owners' inscrs., 1 removed from title, not affecting text. Orig. marb. bds., worn. From liby. of William E. Wilson; bkplt. of Benjamin French. [Sabin 30515] (SPB. Apr.29; 131) $150
– – **Anr. Copy.** Foxing & offsetting, stp. on title. Later cl.-bkd. bds. From liby. of William E. Wilson. (SPB. Apr.29; 130) $100

HARRIS, Tomas
- **Goya, Engravings & Lithographs.** Oxford, 1964. 2 vols. Fo. Plts. mntd. Orig. cl., d.-w.'s. (S. Sep.30; 400) £120
– – **Anr. Edn.** Oxford, [1964]. 2 vols. Fo. Orig. linen. (H. Dec.9/10; 161) DM 420

HARRIS, Walter
- **Hibernica.** Dublin, 1747. Fo. Old cf. (P. Apr.9; 266) £65

HARRIS, William Cornwallis
- **The Fishes of North America that are Captured on Hook & Line.** N.Y., 1898. Vol. 1, all publd. Fo. Liby. stp. cancelled on verso of title, a few minor tears reprd. Recent hf.. mor. (S. Jun.1; 143) *White.* £380
- **The Highlands of Aethiopia.** 1844. 1st. Edn. 3 vols. Folding map torn, a few ll. slightly spotted. Orig. cl. (SH. Nov.7; 302) *Francis.* £130
- **Portraits of the Game & Wild Animals of Southern Africa.** 1840. [1st. Edn.?]. Fo. Some foxing, mainly of text. Cont. red hf. mor. (S. Jun.23; 296) *Smith.* £2,400
– – **Anr. Copy.** Ptd. title & some text ll. foxed. Mod. hf. mor., spine gt. with animal figures, boxed. (C. Nov.5; 70) *Gibbs.* £2,000
– – **Anr. Copy.** Some foxing in text. Hf. roan, box, worn, & soiled. (CE. Nov.20; 23) £1,600
– – **Anr. Edn.** Mazoe, 1976. (540). Fo. Qtr. mor. (SSA. Jan.22; 254) R. 480
– – **Anr. Copy.** Front endpapers eaten by fishmoth, covers lightly soiled & stained. (SSA. Apr.22; 181) R. 300
- **Wild Sports of Southern Africa.** 1841. 3rd. Edn. Hf. mor. gt. (CE. Nov.20; 176) £170
– – **Anr. Copy.** Orig. cl. gt., rebkd., preserving orig. spine. (LC. Feb.12; 134) £140
– – **Anr. Copy.** Prize mor. bdg. (SSA. Nov.5; 214) R. 540
– – **Anr. Edn.** 1844. 4th. Edn. A little spotting. Red hf. mor. (S. Dec.3; 992) *Lindner.* £200

HARRISON, Fairfax
- **The Belair Stud, 1747-1761.–The Roanoke Stud, 1795-1833.–The St. John's Island Stud, 1750-1788.** Richmond, 1929; 1930; 1931. 3 works in 3 vols. Cl. (SG. Dec.11; 332) $170

HARRISON, Godfrey
- **J. Whatman.** Ill.:– H. Brooks (copper-etchings). Romford, 1931. 1st. Edn. Paper-bkd. bds., unc. (C. Jul.22; 118) *Quaritch.* £100

HARRISON, J.C. & Evans, David
- **The Birds of Prey of the British Isles.** Ed.:– Hon. Aylmer Tyron (foreword). 1980. (250) numbered, sigd. Lge. 4to. Orig. three-qtr. mor. with s.-c. (TA. Jun.18; 72) £275

HARRISON James
- **Life of Horatio Nelson.** L., 1806. 2 vols. Extra-ill. with 100 steel-engraved plts. Mor., double gt. fillet borders, gt.-panel. spines, gt. dentelles, by Kelly & Sons. (SG. Feb.26; 257) $350

HARRISON, John
- **Maps of the English Counties.** 1791. Ob. fo. 8 pp. of text, 38 county maps, each with descriptive text. Hf. cf. (P. Mar.12; 169) *Schuster.* £240

HARRISON, Joseph
- **The Floricultural Cabinet, & Florist's Magazine.** 1833-50. Vols. 1-4, 8-18 in 8 vols. Lacks some titles. Cont. cf., worn. (TA. May 21; 535) £190
– – **Anr. Edn.** 1833/53. 7 vols. Some foxing, single uncold. folding plts. defect. Rebnd. in unif. hf. cf., gt. decor. spines. W.a.f. (TA. Aug.21; 223) £120
– – **Anr. Edn.** 1836/49. 5 vols. Slight foxing. Orig. cl./hf. cf. W.a.f. (TA. Aug.21; 224) £150

HARRISON, Walter
[–] **[A New & Universal History, Description & Survey of . . . London & Westminster].** [1775]. Fo. Lacks title & A2, piece cut from 7E1 with some loss of text, frontis. guarded in lr. margin, some browning & offsetting in text. 19th. C. hf. cf., some wear. W.a.f. (S. Nov.4; 499) *Primrose Hill Books.* £130
– – **Anr. Edn.** 1776. Fo. Some spotting & soiling. Cont. marb. cf., worn. W.a.f. (CSK. Apr.10; 125) £180

HARRISON, William Henry
- **British & Foreign Dogs.** Ill.:– W.R. Smith. L., 1835. 4to. Foxed thro-out. Qtr. leath., worn. (SG. Apr.9; 399) $200
– – **Anr. Edn.** N.d. Fo. Slightly spotted, loose as iss. Roan-bkd. cl. portfo., spine worn, slightly marked, ties. (SKC. Jul.28; 2592) £65

HARROD, William
- **The History of Mansfield & its Environs.** Mansfield, Priv. ptd., 1801. 4to. Later hf. mor. gt. (SBA. Oct.22; 473) *Temperley.* £50

HARROW School Song Book
1904. Orig. cl. gt., defect., worn. Self-port. by Cecil Beaton on recto of upr. end-lf. with ink notes. (SH. Dec.19; 360) *Scott.* £70

HARSDORFFER, Georg Philipp
- Deliciae Mathematicae et Physicae. Der Mathematischen und Philosophischen Erquickungsstunden [Erster-Dritter] Theil. Nuremb., 1677, 1653. 3 pts. in 1 vol. 4to. 2 (of 3) additional engraved titles, volvelle in pt. II in orig. state with instructions, lacks titles & last blank in pt. I, 1st. & last few ll. reprd., some slightly affecting text, 1st. few ll. detchd. 18th. C. hf. cf., worn, jnts. reprd., upr. cover detchd. (S. Jun.23; 276) *Fletcher.* £380
- [-] Der Grosse Schau-Platz Lust- und Lehrreicher Geschichte. Hamburg, 1653. 3rd. Iss. 2 pts. in 1 vol. Cont. vell., slightly soiled, 4 sm. tears. (H. Dec.9/10; 1523) DM 700

HART, James
- Klinike or the Diet of the Diseased. 1633. Fo. No blank lf. before title. dampstain on lr. section at end. Cont. cf., rebkd., spine reprd. [STC 12888] (S. Dec.2; 506) *Blackwell.* £190

HART, Liddell
See-GRAVES, Robert & Hart, Liddell

HART, Capt. Lockyer Willis
- Character & Costumes of Afghaunistan. 1843. Fo. Occasional slight spotting. Orig. mor.bkd. cl., worn. disbnd. (CSK. Nov.28; 31) £150

HARTE, Francis Bret
- The Lost Galleon & other Tales.-The Luck of Roaring Camp. San Franc.; Boston, 1867; 1870. 2 works in 2 vols. 12mo. Both orig. cl., upr. cover of 1st. work slightly dampstained, qtr. mor. s.-c.'s. From the Prescott Collection. (CNY. Feb.6; 148) $480
- Mliss. An Idyl of Red Mountain. N.Y., [1873]. 1st. Edn., 1st. Printing, 1st. Iss. With 12 pp. of publisher's advts. at end. Orig. ptd. wraps., spine worn & reprd., qtr. mor. s.-c. (with typed note inserted in cl. protective cover). The Morris L. Parrish/Frank J. Hogan copy, lately in the Prescott Collection. (CNY. Feb.6; 147) $1,200
- Writings. Boston, N.d. Riverside Edn. 20 vols. Hf. cf. gt., by Sangorski & Sutcliffe, slight wear. (SPB. Nov.25; 458) $325

HARTE, Francis Bret-MERWIN, H.C.
- Writings.-Life of Bret Harte. Boston, n.d.; 1911. Autograph Edn., (350) sigd. by Harte. 20 vols.; 1 vol. Many frontis. sigd. in pencil by artists. Maroon mor. gt. (SPB. May 6; 315) $2,400

HARTGERS, Joast
- [-] Tragicum Theatrum Actorum, & Casuum Tragicorum, Londini Publice celebratorum. Amst., 1649. 12mo. Some ll. browned, folding plt. slightly stained. Cont. vell., inside hinges brkn. (S. Dec.9; 443) *Laywood.* £60

HARTIG, G.L.
- Lehrbuch f. Jäger u. die es Werden wollen. Tübingen, 1811. 1st. Edn. 2 vols. Ex-libris in vol. 2. Cont. hf. leath. gt. (HK. Nov.18-21; 1736) DM 2,200
- Lexikon f. Jäger u. Jagdfreunde. Berlin, 1836. 1st. Edn. Slightly soiled. Cont. hf. leath. gt. (HK. Nov.18-21; 1737) DM 700
- - Anr. Edn. Berlin, 1861. 2nd. Edn. MS. owner's mark on title, slightly stained & soiled in parts. Orig. linen gold & blind tooled, slightly stained. (HK. Nov.18-21; 1738) DM 420

HARTIG, G.L. & Th.
- Forstliches und Forstnaturwissenschaftliches Conversations-Lexikon. Berlin, 1834. 1st. Edn. Cont. bds. (R. Mar.31-Apr.4; 1686) DM 550

HARTIG, Th.
- Vollst. Naturgesch. d. forstl. Culturpflanzen Deutschlands. Berlin, 1840-51. Text slightly soiled, plts. browned. Bdg. soiled & defect., spine loose. (HK. Nov.18-21; 562) DM 520

HARTINGER, A. & Dalla Torre, K.W.V.
- Atlas der Alpenflora. Wien, 1887. 4 vols. Mor. (BS. Feb.25; 274) £280

HARTKNOCH, Chr.
- Altes und Neues Preussen. Frankfurt & Leipzig, 1684. Fo. Title port. & engraved title reprd. at lr. corner. Cont. leath., gt. spine. (HK. Nov.18-21; 1211) DM 18,000
- - Anr. Copy. 8 (of 15) copperplts., 1 (of 2) engraved maps, 83 text copper engrs., lacks port. of author. Cont. leath., 2 metal clasps. (D. Dec.11-13; 1287) DM 10,000

HARTLEY, David
- An Address to the Committee of Association of the County of York. York, 1781. 2nd. Edn. Disbnd. [Sabin 30685] (SG. Jun.11; 170) $140

HARTMANN, A. & Casabon, M.J.
- Album of Demerara. Paris, ca. 1850. Ob. 4to. Foxed, inner hinges strengthened, end-papers browned, tears. Mor.-bkd. cl. (SPB. May 5; 248) $2,200

HARTMANN, J.E.
- [-] Das Römische Carneval. Weimar, 1789. 1st. Edn., on holland, (250). 4to. Lightly soiled, slightly browned at margins, title & some copper engrs. with sm. tears in margin, title verso stpd. Unc., cont. bds., orig wraps. bnd. in, soiled, spine defect. (HK. May 15; 4316) DM 22,500

HARTNOLL, Phyllis
- The Grecian Enchanted. Ill.:- John Buckland-Wright. Gold. Cock. Pr., 1952. (360). Fo. Orig. cl. gt. (SH. Feb.19; 196) *Chesters.* £60

HARTSHORNE, Albert
- Old English Glasses. 1897. 4to. Occasional spotting to text. Orig. hf., vell., soiled. (CSK. Sep.26; 201) £65
- - Anr. Copy. 4to. (CSK. Oct.10; 26) £50

HARTZENBUSCH, Juan Eugenio
- The Lovers of Teruel. Trans.:- Henry Thomas. Gregy. Pr., 1938. (175). Orig. red mor., tooled in blind. (SH. Feb.20; 216) *Quaritch.* £220

HARVARD COLLEGE
- Pietas et Gratulatio Collegii Cantabrigiensis apud Novanglos. Boston, 1761. 4to. Mod. str.-grd. mor. (SG. Oct.9; 127) $1,200

HARVARD, Henry
- La Hollande à vol d'Oiseau. Ill.:- Lalanne. Paris, 1881. 4to. Orig. linen. (R. Oct.14-18; 1895) DM 530

HARVEY, Gideon
- The Vanities of Philosophy & Physick Together with Directions & Medicines Easily Prepared by any of the Least Skill. 1699. 1st. Edn. Cont. cf., rebkd. [Wing H1079] (S. Dec.2; 507) *Phelps.* £70

HARVEY, M.
- Across Newfoundland with the Governor ... St. John's, 1879. 1st. Edn. Wraps., spine defect. (SG. Jun.11; 68) $110

HARVEY, Thomas
See-STURGE, Joseph & Harvey, Thomas

HARVEY, William
- Geographical Fun: being humourous outlines of various countries. [1868]. 4to. Slight spotting. Unbnd., orig. cl. (CSK. Feb.6; 99) £170

HARVEY, William
- The Anatomical Exercises concerning the Motion of the Heart & Blood ... Ed.:- Dr. James de Back. 1653. 1st. Edn. in Engl. Title bkd. & dust-soiled with some sm. stains, a few sm. wormholes sometimes affecting letters, closely cut affecting headlines, sigs., etc. 19th. C. panel. cf., rebkd. with mor. [Wing H1083] (S. Jun.16; 390) *Hammond.* £2,400
- - Anr. Edn. 1673. 2 pts. Hf. cf. gt. (P. Oct.2; 290) *Phelps.* £250
- The Anatomical Exercises: De Motu Cordis 1628; De Circulatione Sanguinis 1649. Ed.:- Geoffrey Keynes. Ill.:- Sigrist after [Stephen Gooden]. Nones. Pr., [1928]. (1,450) numbered. Niger mor., unc. (SG. Sep.4; 358) $110
- Anatomical Exercitations concerning the Generation of Living Creatures to which are added particular Discourses of Births & Conceptions, etc. Ill.:- W. Faithorne (port.). 1653. 1st. Edn. in Engl. Port. a late iss., short tear in upr. margin N1. New mor. [Wing H1084] (S. Jun.16; 391) *Studd.* £300
- - Anr. Copy. Lacks errata lf. & 1st. & last blanks, wormed in upr. corners towards end, a few ll. dampstained, sm. tear reprd. in title, cont. sig. of Chr. Vevile. 19th. C. cf., upr. jnt. reprd., hf. red mor. case From Honeyman Collection. [Wing H1085] (S. May 20; 348) *Zeitlin & Verbrugge.* £280
- De Motu Cordis et Sanguinis in Animalibus Anatomica exercitio ... Johannis Walaei ... Epistolae duae. Pavia, 1643. 12mo. Some browning, repair to lr. margin of 2nd. lf. Mod. vell. (S. Jun.23; 277) *Rota.* £220

- Exercitationes de Generatione Animalium quibus accedunt quaedam de Partu ... 1651. 1st. Edn. 4to. Lacks 1st. & last blank, paper slightly browned & discold. New hf. mor. Dupl. from Royal College of Physicians Liby. (S. Jun.16; 389) *Studd.* £550
- - Anr. Edn. 1662. 12mo. Cont. cf. (S. Jun.16; 392) *Rota.* £75
- Opera Omnia. Ed.:- Mark Akenside. Ill.:- I. Hall after Cornelius Jonson (frontis. port.). 1766. 4to. Orig. wraps. rebkd. with paper, unc., in cl. box. (S. Jun.16; 393) *Engle.* £170
- - Anr. Copy. Lacks port., slight spotting & browning. Mod. hf. cf. 9 pp. MS. copy of Diploma bnd. in at end, from liby. of Dr. E. Ashworth Underwood. (S. Feb.23; 223) *Jenner.* £110

HARVEY, William Henry
- Nereis Boreali-Americana: or, ... the Marine Algae of North America. Wash., 1852-53. Vols. 1-2 (of 3). 4to. Titles reprd. Orig. cl., damp stained, gt. stp. of Smithsonian Institution on upr. covers. (S. Dec.3; 993) *W. & W.* £50
- Phycologia Britannica: Or, A History of British Sea-Weeds. 1846-51. 4 vols. Cont. hf. cf., some wear. (TA. Oct.16; 24) £135
- - Anr. Copy. Orig. cl. From Collection of Massachusetts Horticultural Society, stps. on plts. (SPB. Oct.1; 122) $500

HARVEY'S SEA TORPEDO
- Instructions for the Management of. 1871. Orig. cl. gt. (TA. Mar.19; 501) £65

HARZER, C.A.F.
- Naturgetreue Abbildungen der Vorzüglichsten Essbaren, Giftigen und Verdächtigen Pilz. Ed.:- L. Reichenbach (preface). Dresden, 1842. 4to. Some plts. loose. Orig. bds., worn. (D. Dec.11-13; 156) DM 1,650

HASAN
See-ALHAZEN

HASE, Johann Matthias
- Regin Davidici et Salomonaei Descriptio Geographica et Historica, una cum Delineatione Syriae et Aegypti ... Nuremb., 1739. Sm. fo. Cont. cf.-bkd. marb. bds. (PNY. Mar.26; 135) $800

HASELER, H. & others
- [-] Scenery on the Southern Coast of Devonshire. Ill.:- D. Havell. Sidmouth. 1819. Ob. 4to. Aquatint views cold. Hf. cf. by Root, covers detchd. From the collection of Eric Sexton. (C. Apr.16; 274) *Maggs.* £580

HASENFUSS, Conrad
See-DASYPODIUS or HASENFUSS, Conrad

HASKELL, Daniel C.
See-STOKES, Isaac Newton Phelps & Haskell, Daniel C.

HASKELL, Grace Clark
See-LATIMORE, Sarah Briggs & Haskell, Grace Clark

HASLAM, John
- Observations on Madness & Melancholy ... together with Cases. 1809. 2nd. Edn. New qtr. cf. (S. Jun.16; 396) *Dillon.* £140
- Sound Mind or Contributions to the Natural History & Physiology of the Human Intellect. 1815. 1st. Edn. 4 advt. ll. dtd. Nov. 1819. Orig. bds., rebkd., unc. (S. Jun.16; 397) *Jenner Books.* £120

See-MONRO, Thomas & Haslam, John

HASLEM, John
- The Old Derby China Factory. 1876. 1st. Edn. Orig. cl. gt. (SBA. Jul.22; 180) *Shaw.* £85
- - Anr. Copy. Sm. fo. (SBA. May 27; 250) *Chesters.* £52

HASLUCK, Paul N.
- The Automobile. [1905]. Special Edn. 3 vols. Orig. cl. (SH. Oct.10; 462) *Barnett.* £50

HASSALL, Arthur Hill
- The Microscopic Anatomy of the Human Body in Health & Disease. [1846]-49. 2 vols. Hf. mor. (S. Jun.16; 398) *Rota.* £120

HASSELL, John
- The Camera, or Art of Drawing in Water Colours. L., 1823. 1st. Edn. 1 plt. in 3 states, lightly dampstained thro.-out, inside upr. cover & following blank lf. with notes in early hand. Orig. bds., rebkd. (SG. Dec.4; 171) $160

HASSELL, John *-contd.*
- **Excursions of Pleasure & Sports on the Thames.** 1823. [1st. Edn.?]. 12mo. Aquatint plts. cold. Pol. cf., gt., by Rivière. From the collection of Eric Sexton. (C. Apr.16; 277) *Maggs.* £400
- - **Anr. Copy.** 16mo. Lacks plt.-list. Hf. cf. (SG. Apr.9; 289) $275
- **Picturesque Rides & Walks ... Thirty Miles Round the British Metropolis.** 1817-18. L.P. 2 vols. Lev. mor. gt., by Sawyer. (C. Mar.18; 53) *Chelsea.* £550
- - **Anr. Copy.** Plts. hand-cold. Hf. mor. gt., unc., by Rivière. From the collection of Eric Sexton. (C. Apr.16; 275) *Maggs.* £500
- - **Anr. Copy.** 12mo. Lacks hf.-title. Cont. spr. cf., gt. Bkplt. of Henry Carrington Bowles. (C. Nov.5; 71a) *Walford.* £120
- **Tour of the Grand Junction ...** 1819. [1st. Edn.?]. Aquatint views cold. Orig. bds., unc. From the collection of Eric Sexton. (C. Apr.16; 276) *Maggs.* £320
- - **Anr. Copy.** 24 hand-cold. plts., text wtrmkd. 1818, plts. 1819. Worn, unc. (S. Nov.24; 153) *Quaritch.* £300
- - **Anr. Copy.** Cont. red str.-grd. mor. gt. (C. Jul.15; 45) *Walford.* £240
- - **Anr. Copy.** Crushed three-qtr. lev. (SG. May 14; 96) $500
- **Tour of the Isle of Wight.** 1791. 2 vols. in 1. Hf. bd. (GT. Oct.2; 169) £68
See–IBBETSON, Julius & others

HASSELQUIST, F.
- **Voyages & Travels in the Levant.** 1766. Cf. gt. (P. Oct.2; 8) *Ad Orientem.* £85

HASTED, Edward
- **The History & Topographical Survey of the County of Kent.** Canterbury, 1778-99. 1st. Edn. 4 vols. Fo. 5 orig. pencil & wash drawings bnd. in vol. 4. 19th. C. mott. cf., gt. William Drew Ingall's bkplt. & stp. on titles. (C. Mar.18; 54) *Cumming.* £600
- - **Anr. Copy.** Some short tears, slight browning, some slight marginal spotting, a few plts. loose. Cont. hf. cf., worn & reprd., unc. (S. May 5; 209) *Burgess.* £450
- - **Anr. Edn.** Canterbury, 1797-1801. 2nd. Edn. 12 vols. 66 engraved plts. & maps only (of 68), some torn, some browning & soiling. Cont. mott. cf., rebkd. (S. Sep.29; 149) *Russell.* £230

HASTIE, T.
- **The Only Method to Make Reading Easy, or Child's Best Instructor.** Newcastle, 1839. 1 ill. sigd. with Thomas Bewick's initials, short tears along folds. Orig. bdg. (SH. Mar.19; 122) *Maggs.* £60

HASTINGS, James
- **Encyclopaedia of Religion & Ethics.** Edinb., 1908-26. 13 vols. Orig. hf. mor. (SH. May 28; 49) *Mills.* £70

HASTINGS, T.
- **The British Archer.** 1831. 4to. Cf. gt. (P. Apr.9; 110) *Fairburn.* £70

HATTON, Edward
- **The Merchant's Magazine.** 1697. 2nd. Edn. Sm. 4to. Cont. spr. cf. [Wing H1148] (C. Jul.16; 352) *Quaritch.* £420

HATTON, Thomas & Cleaver, Arthur H.
- **A Bibliography of the Periodical Works of Charles Dickens.** 1933. Ltd. Edn. Cl., facs. wraps. bnd. in. (P. May 14; 90) *Tallerman.* £80
- - **Anr. Copy.** Slightly spotted. Orig. buckram. (SKC. May 19; 182) £75
- - **Anr. Copy.** Buckram, gt., partly untrimmed, d.-w., box. (SG. Oct.2; 108) $140

HATZFELD, Adolf von
- **Sommer.** Ill.:– Marie Laurencin., etched port. by Adolf Kaufmann. Düsseldorf, 1920. (35) with etched port., sigd. by author & artist, numbered. Fo. Loose as iss. in folder. Etched port. sigd. by Kaufmann. (SH. Nov.21; 368) *Subunso.* £500

HAUSENSTEIN, Wilhelm (Ed.)
See–GANYMED, Jahrbuch f.d. Kunst

HAUSWEDELL, Ernst & Co.
- **Jahrbuch der Auktionspreise.** Hamburg, [1972]. Cl., ex-liby. (SG. Mar.26; 236) $100

HAUTHAL, F.
- **Geschichte der Sächsischen Armee in Wort und Bild.** Leipzig, 1859. 2nd. Edn. Text & plts. vol. Fo.

Some of bnd. in plts. loose. Cont. linen. (R. Oct.14-18; 2840) DM 4,800

HAUY, René Just
- **Exposition raisonnée de la Théorie de l'Electricité et du Magnetisme.** Paris, 1787. 1st. Edn. Plts. slightly spotted. Cont. cf.-bkd. bds., jnts. worn. (S. Oct.21; 397) *Phelps.* £85
- **Traité de Mineralogie.** 1801. 1st. Edn. 5 vols., including Atlas. 8vo. & ob. 4to. Cont. mott. cf., spines gt. (C. Apr.1; 108) *Frazier.* £620
- **Traité des Caractères Physiques des Pierres Précieuses, pour Servir à leur Détermination Lorsqu'elles ont été Taillées.** Paris, 1817. 1st. Edn. Cont. tree cf., spine gt. (C. Apr.1; 109) *Murphy.* £180

HAVANA
- **Instrucción que observará cade uno de los Capitanes de Partido dela Jurisdiccion de la Havana.** [Havana], [1765?]. Fo. Disbnd. (SPB. May 5; 249) $550

HAVARD, Henry
- **L'Art et les Artistes Hollandais.** Paris, 1879-81. 4 vols. Mor. gt., orig. wraps. bnd. in. The Robert Hoe copy. (SPB. May 29; 198) $100
- **La Céramique Hollandaise.** Amst., 1909. 2 vols. Fo. Hf. cl. (VG. Nov.17; 495) Fls. 650
- **Dictionnaire de l'Ameublement et de la Décoration depuis le XIII siècle jusquà nos jours.** Paris, 1887-90. 4 vols. 4to. Gt.-ornamental hf. mor. & cl., upr. jnt. defect at 1 vol. (PNY. Oct.1; 274) $250
- - **Anr. Edn.** Paris, [1887-90]. 4 vols. 4to. Hf. mor. by Féchoz, corners, spine with raised bands. (HD. Jun.25; 277) Frs. 1,650
- - **Anr. Edn.** Paris, n.d. 4 vols. 4to. Orig. wraps., torn, 1 vol. loose. (SH. Jan.29; 241) *Lady Stewart.* £50
- - **Anr. Copy.** Hf. red mor., gt. spines, orig. wraps. bnd. in, partly unc. (SI. Dec.3; 282) Lire 320,000
- **La Flandre à Vol d'Oiseau.** Ill.:– Maxime Lalane. Paris, 1883. Three quarter chagrin, 5 spine raised bands, repeated decor. between. (LM. Mar.21; 126) B.Frs. 9,000

HAVELL, E.B.
- **Indian architecture, its Psychology, Structure, & History from the first Muhammadan invasion to the present day.** L., 1913. 1st. Edn. 4to. Orig. cl. (CB. May 27; 120) Can. $120

HAVELL, Robert
- **A Series of Picturesque Views of Noblemen's & Gentlemen's Seats.** 1823. Fo. Hand-cold. aquatint title, 20 hand-cold. aquatints, title & plts. with margins trimmed, mntd. on card, title with loss of imprint, plts. with loss of imprint & sigs., interleaved. Cont. hf. mor. (C. Jul.15; 149) *Marlborough.* £4,000
- **The Tour, or Select Views on the Southern Coast.** 1827. Ob. 8vo. Plts. cold., stitching breaking, some ll. loose, others crudely hinged-in. Orig. mor.-bkd. pict. bds. From the collection of Eric Sexton. (C. Apr.16; 279) *Maggs.* £400

HAVEN, Samuel
- **The Supreme Influence of the Son of God in ... the Reign of Princes. A Sermon Occasioned by the Death of King George the Second ...** Portsmouth, 1761. 1st. Edn. Disbnd. (SG. Mar.5; 221) $100

HAVERKAMP, Sigebertus & others
- **Sylloge Scriptorum, qui de Linguae Graecae vera & recta Pronuntiatione Commentarios reliquerunt.** Leiden, 1736-40. 2 vols. Slight browning. Cont. vell. bds., soiled, s.-c. (S. Apr.29; 395) *Goldschmidt.* £65

HAVERS, Clopton
- **Osteologia or some new Observations of the Bones & the Parts Belonging to them.** 1729. 2nd. Edn. 3 pp. advts., lr. blank corner of title torn off, title written on. Cont. panel. cf. (S. Jun.16; 399) *Quaritch.* £100

HAVERSCHMIDT, F.
- **Birds of Surinam.** Ill.:– P. Barruel. 1958. 4to. Cl. gt., d.-w. (P. Nov.13; 201) *Hill.* £90

HAWKER, Col. Peter
- **Instructions to Young Sportsmen.** 1816. 2nd. Edn. Additional plt. loosely inserted, a few ll. slightly spotted. Orig. bds., neatly rebkd., preserving label, hinges strengthened. (SBA. Oct.21; 148a) *Holland & Holland.* £55
- - **Anr. Edn.** 1824. 3rd. Edn. 10 engraved plts., 4 hand-cold., extra-ill. with 61 engraved plts.

inserted. Late 19th. C. red crushed mor., gt., 1 jnt. split. (S. Nov.24; 154) *P. & C.* £400
- - **Anr. Copy.** A few upper margins slightly stained. Cont. hf. cf. (CSK. Jan.23; 110) £50
- - **Anr. Copy.** 16-p. Longman catalogue dtd. Oct. 1824 tipped in. Orig. bds., unc., cl. s.-c. (SG. Apr.9; 367) $110
- **Shooting Diaries.** Ed.:– Eric Parker. [1931]. Light foxing. Cl., bkplt. (SG. Dec.11; 254) $160

HAWKESWORTH, J.
- **Account of the Voyages for making Discoveries in the Southern Hemisphere.** 1773. 3 vols. 4to. Some ll. browned. Cont. cf. (SH. Apr.9; 143) *Quaritch.* £600
- - **Anr. Copy.** 1 plt. slightly soiled. Cont. diced cf. (CSK. May 1; 121) £580
- - **Anr. Copy.** W.a.f. (CSK. Nov.28; 177) £260
- - **Anr. Edn.** 1773. 1st. Edn. 3 vols. 4to. Cont. cf., worn, a few covers detchd. Bkplt. of City Liberal Club. [Sabin 30934] (S. Mar.31; 476) *Schrire.* £420
- - **Anr. Copy.** Upr. cover to vol. I slightly torn. (C. Nov.6; 297) *Marshall.* £350
- - **Anr. Edn.** 1773. 2nd. Edn. 3 vols. 4to. 51 (of 52) engraved plts. & charts, 5 torn, lacks chart of South Seas at beginning of vol. I, a few ll. spotted. Cont. cf., very worn, 1 cover detchd. (S. Feb.23; 342) Thorp. £230
- **Relation de Voyages ... dans l'Hemisphère Meridional.** Ed.:– J. Hawkesworth. Paris, 1774. 1st. Fr. 4to. Edn. 4 vols. 4to. Cont. cf. gt. (PNY. May 21; 144) $300
- - **Anr. Copy.** 4 vols., lacks atlas. Few margins slightly stained. Cont. marb. cf., gt. spine. [Sabin 30940] (VG. Oct.13; 48) Fls. 1,100
- [-] **Relation des Voyages ... exécutés par le Commodore Byron, le Capitaine Carteret, le Capitaine Wallis & le Capitaine Cook.** Paris, 1789, 1774. 9 vols. 8vo. & 4to. 19th. C. cf.-bkd. bds., worn. [Sabin 69276] (SPB. May 5; 166) $300

HAWKESWORTH, John & others
- **The Adventurer.** L., 1753-54. 1st. Edn. 140 orig. pts. in 2 vols. Fo. Sm. defects to blank portions of 1st. title, sm. tear to border of vig. Old bds., slight wear to spines & edges, chemises, mor.-tipped s.-c., unc. From the Prescott Collection. (CNY. Feb.6; 175) $850

HAWKINS, F. Bisset
- **Elements of Medical Statistics.** 1829. 1st. Edn. 8 pp. advts. dtd. 1827 inserted at beginning, owner's inscr. cut away from head of title, without loss of text, a little spotting. Orig. bds., worn, spine defect., unc. From liby. of Dr. E. Ashworth Underwood. (S. Feb.23; 225) *Jenner.* £70

HAWKINS, Sir John
- **A General History of the Science & Practice of Music.** L., 1776. 1st. Edn. 5 vols. 4to. Browned & soiled in parts. Cont. cf., very defect., partly loose. (H. Dec.9/10; 1144) DM 1,400
See–JOHNSON, Dr. Samuel–HAWKINS, Sir John

HAWKINS, L.M.
- **Rosanne; or a Father's Labour Lost.** 1814. 1st. Edn. 3 vols. Slight browning. Cont. cf., tooled in gt. & blind, bkplt. 'Miss Anna Jones, Stamford Hill, 1825, The Gift of her Grandpapa'. (S. Apr.7; 420) *Traylen.* £190

HAWKS, Francis L.
- **Narrative of the Expedition of an American Squadron to the China Seas & Japan under the Command of Commodore M.C. Perry.** Wash., 1856. 1st. Edn. 4to. Orig. linen, 1 spine defect. [Sabin 30968] (R. Mar.31-Apr.4; 2507) DM 2,000
- - **Anr. Copy.** 3 vols. Some maps torn. Defects., worn. (HK. Nov.18-21; 1037) DM 1,000

HAWLEY, Walter A.
- **Oriental Rugs Antique & Modern.** 1913. 4to. Orig. decor. cl. (TA. Mar.19; 19) £56

HAWORTH-BOOTH, Digby
- **Kleinias: Poems.** Boar's Head Pr., 1932. (200). Black mor., vertical line tooling in cols., gt. & blind, vell. doubls., sigd. & dtd. 1978, fitted case, by James Bockman. (SH. Feb.20; 389) *Smith.* £400

HAWTHORNE, Julian
See–HAWTHORNE, Nathaniel–HAWTHORNE, Julian

HAWTHORNE, Nathaniel
- Complete Writings. Boston, Riverside Pr., [1900]. Old Manse Edn. 22 vols. Red three-qtr. mor., spines gt., mostly unopened. (SG. Feb.12; 206) $160
[-] Fanshawe. Boston, 1828. 1st. Edn. Orig. muslin-bkd. bds., slightly warped, 2 bkplts. removed, qtr. mor. gt. s.-c., unc. The Herschel V. Jones & Dr. George C.F. Williams copy, lately in the Prescott Collection. (CNY. Feb.6; 153) $12,000
- The Gentle Boy. Ill.:- Sophia A. Peabody (frontis.). Boston, 1839. 1st. Separate Edn. Ob. fo. 1st. state(?), with 'faccs' for 'faces' on p. 18, line 9, engraved frontis. in 3rd. state. Orig. ptd. wraps., upr. blank portion of upr. cover cut-away & supplied, rebkd., some other sm. wrap. repairs, cl. folding case. The J. Chester Chamberlain & Walter T. Wallace copy, with bkplts., lately in the Prescott Collection. (CNY. Feb.6; 155) $280
- Grandfather's Chair.-Famous Old People. -Liberty Tree. Boston, 1841. 1st. Edns. 3 works in 3 vols. 12mo. All orig. cl., fitted cl. case. From the Prescott Collection. (CNY. Feb.6; 156) $380
- Grandfather's Chair.-Famous Old People. -Liberty Tree.-Twice-Told Tales. Boston, 1841; 1841; 1841; 1842. 1st. Edn. of 1st. 3, 1st. coll. Edn. of last. 5 vols. Various sizes. Orig. bds. Pres. copy, inscr. by recipient on inside upr. cover of both vols. 'Maria Manning, from her cousin, the Author, 15 Jan. 1842'. (SPB. Nov.25; 207) $650
- The Scarlet Letter. Boston, 1850. 1st. Edn., 1st. Iss. 12mo. With 'reduplicate' on p. 21, line 20, lacks advts. Unbound red mor., inlaid at upr. cover with a scarlet 'A' on a black shield surrounded by a gt. wreath of laurel by Sangorski & Sutcliffe for Charles Sessler Co., Phila., unc., orig. cl. covers bnd. in. (PNY. Dec.3; 165) $260
- - Anr. Edn. Boston, 1850. 1st. Edn. Publisher's advt. at front. Orig. cl., stains, chipping, mor.-bkd. s.-c. (SPB. May 29; 199) $275
- - Anr. Copy. Publisher's advts. dtd. Mar. 1 1850, some foxing. Worn, spine strengthened, slightly shaken. (SPB. Nov.25; 206) $175
- - Anr. Edn. Ill.:- G.H. Boughton. N.Y., Grol. Cl., 1908. (300). Fo. Plts. in 2 states. Bds., embossed scarlet 'A', cl. spine, unc. & unopened. (SG. Mar.26; 224) $110
- Twice-Told Tales. Boston, 1837. 1st. Edn. Orig. cl., slightly soiled, spine faded, mor. solander case. Pres. Copy, to Mrs. S.J. Merritt, & with card bearing author's sig. pasted in upr. cover, lately in the Prescott Collection. (CNY. Feb.6; 154) $2,000
- A Wonder-Book for Girls & Boys. Boston, 1852. 1st. Edn., 1st. Iss. 12mo. No advts. Cl., gt.-decor. to top of spine, light wear & cover staining, hf. mor. s.-c. (SG. Nov.13; 289) $180
- - Anr. Edn. Ill.:- Arthur Rackham. [1922]. (600) sigd. by artist. 4to. Orig. cl. gt. (SH. Mar.27; 438) Black. £230
- - Anr. Copy. (S. Jul.31; 288) Hatchards. £200
- - Anr. Copy. Gt.-pict. cl. Raymond M. Sutton Jr. copy. (SG. May 7; 121) $550
- - Anr. Edn. Ill.:- Arthur Rackham. N.d. (600) sigd. by artist. 4to. Orig. cl. (C. Feb.4; 162) Waley. £140

HAWTHORNE, Nathaniel-HAWTHORNE, Julian
- Complete Works.-Nathaniel Hawthorne & his Wife. Boston, 1891. Wayside Edn. 25 vols.; 2 vols. Slight offsetting & browning. Hf. mor. gt., gt. panel. spine by Sangorski & Sutcliffe. 2nd. work: Pres. copy. (SPB. Nov.25; 459) $425

HAWTHORNE, Nathaniel-WOODBERRY, George E.
- Complete Writings.-Nathaniel Hawthorne. Boston, 1902. Autograph Edn., (500), sigd. by Rose Hawthorne Lathrop. Some of the frontis. sigd. in pencil by artists. Hf. mor. gt., unc. (SPB. Nov.25; 460) $650

HAY, Ian
- Writings. Boston, 1921. Argyll Edn. 10 vols. Hf. mor. (SPB. May 6; 316) $325

HAY, John
See-NICOLAY, John George & Hay, John

HAY, Robert
- Illustrations of Cairo. 1840. Fo. Slightly soiled, 1 plt. dampstained. Cont. mor.-bkd. cl., worn, loose. (SH. Nov.7; 412) Walford. £250

HAYDEN, Arthur
- Old English Porcelain, the Lady Ludlow Collection. 1932. (100). Fo. Hf. mor. (C. Feb.4; 245) Amos. £600

HAYDEN, Ferdinand V.
- Geological & Geographical Atlas of Colorado & Portions of Adjacent Territory. Wash., 1877. Atlas fo. Cl., ex-liby. (SG. Aug.21; 252) $180
- - Anr. Edn. Wash., 1881. Atlas fo. Cl., ex-liby. (SG. Aug.21; 253) $140
- Reports of the United States Geological Survey. Wash., 1875-90. Vol. II, Vol. III (bk. I) & Vols. VI-XIII; together 10 vols. 4to. Cl., several vols. brkn., ex-liby. (SG. Aug.21; 493) $120

HAYDN, Joseph
- Oratorium. Leipzig, [1801]. 1st. Edn. (of full orchestral & vocal score). Ob. fo. Mod. cl.-bkd. bds., orig. ptd. wraps. bnd. in. (C. Oct.22; 263) Simeone. £90
- VI Original Canzonettas. [L.], [1794]. 1st. Edn. Fo. Paper bds. Haydn's sig. on title-lf. (H. Dec.9/10; 1145) DM 1,800

HAYEM, Georges
- Leçons sur les Modifications du Sang.-Du Sang et de ses Alterations Anatomiques.-Leçons sur les Maladies du Sang. Paris, 1882; 1889; 1900. 1st. Edns. 3 vols. 2nd. work with slight browning, liby.-stp. of Royal Medical & Chirurgical Society on title, loose, 3rd. work loose. Orig. wraps., slight wear; orig. cl., worn; orig. wraps., worn. 3rd. work pres. copy. (S. Apr.6; 75) Pratt. £80

HAYES, J. Gordon
- Antarctica. 1928. No bdg. stated. Pres. copy. (TRL. Dec.10; 88) £54

HAYES, William, Ornithologist
- A Natural History of British Birds & c. [1771]-75. Lge. fo. Plts. hand-cold., occasional minor soiling. Cont. cf., covers detchd., stitching brkn. From Chetham's Liby., Manchester. (C. Nov.26; 198) Davidson. £2,700
- Portraits of Rare & Curious Birds ... from the Menagerie of Osterly Park. L., 1794-99. 2 vols. in 1. 4to. 100 hand-cold. engraved plts. wtrmkd. 1794. Cont. diced russ. gt., by J. Bohn with his ticket, rebkd., spine defect. (CNY. May 22; 200) $2,200
- - Anr. Edn. 1794[-99]. 2 vols. in 1. 4to. 97 hand-cold. engraved plts. (of 101), lacks title to vol. II, a few plts. marginally torn & dampstained, many ll. loose, slight browning. Cont. mor., worn, covers detchd., lacks spine. (S. May 5; 111) Cristani. £650

HAYEZ, F.
- Le Mie Memorie. Milan, 1890. 4to. Publisher's bds. (CR. Mar.19; 84) Lire 220,000

HAYLEY, William
- Ballads. Ill.:- William Blake. 1805. Orig. bds. (P. Jul.30; 289) Davis. £260
- Life of George Romney. 1809. 4to. Cont. red mor. gt., slightly worn. (BS. Nov.26; 229) £90
- The Life, & Posthumous Writings, of William Cowper. Ill.:- William Blake. Chichester, 1803-04. 2nd. Edn. (vols. 1 & 2). 3 vols. 4to. Cont. mott. cf., rebkd. (SG. Mar.19; 23) $130
- - Anr. Edn. Ill.:- W. Blake. Chichester, 1803-04. 3 vols. 4to. Cont. cf. gt. (P. Jul.30; 66) Hanas. £60
- - Anr. Copy. Lacks hf.-titles. Orig. bds., badly worn, unc. (BS. Nov.26; 228) £50

HAYNE, Friedrich Gottlob
- Getreue Darstellung und Beschreibung der in der Arzneykunde gebrauchlichen Gewächse. Berlin, 1805-37-[46]. 14 vols., all publd. 4to. Ending with 2 fascicules only of vol. 14 (without prelims), some foxing in last vol. Cont. German hf. cf. From collection of Massachusetts Horticultural Society, stps on plts. (SPB. Oct.1; 123) $7,250
- - Anr. Edn. Berlin, 1813-16. 1st. Edn. Pts. III & IV (of 14) in 1 vol. 19th. C. hf. vell. (S. Feb.23; 51) Frick. £280

See-WILLDENOW, Karl Ludwig & Hayne, Friedrich

HAYTEROPHILES (Atelier 17, Paris 1952-53)
Ill.:- Pierre Alchinsky. Paris, 1968. (36), numbered. Ob. fo. Unsewn in orig. cl. portfo., tie. Each plt. sigd. & numbered by artist. (SH. Nov.20; 204) Simons. £100

HAYWARD, I.A.
- Eromena of Love & Revenge. 1632. Cf. (DWB. May 15; 299) £92

HAYWARD, Sir John
- The First Part of the Life & Raigne of King Henrie the IIII.-The Life & Raigne of King Edward the Sixt. 1599; 1630. 2nd. work 1st. Edn. 2 works in 1 vol. 4to. Cont. cf. [STC 12997a] [STC 12998] (C. Feb.25; 157) Wall. £180

HAYWOOD, Eliza
- Frederick. Dublin, 1729. Cont. cf. (P. Dec.11; 335) Quaritch. £95
[-] The Invisible Spy by Exploralibus. 1755. 1st. Edn. 4 vols. 12mo. Near cont. cf. (CSK. May 8; 101) £220

HAZARD, Samuel
- The Register of Pennysylvania. Phila., Jan. 1828-Jan. 1836. Vols. 1-16, compl. & all publd. 4to. Orig. qtr. cl. & bds., vol. 1 with loose lr. cover, other vols. worn. [Sabin 31106] (PNY. Dec.3; 287a] $180

HAZEN, Edward
- The Panorama of Professions & Trades. Phila., 1836. Sm. 4to. Slightly browned. Cont. hf. leath., defect., & loose. (R. Oct.14-18; 2627) DM 1,000
- Popular Technology; or, Professions & Trades. N.Y., 1842. 2 vols. in 1. Soiled. Cont. hf. leath. (R. Oct.14-18; 2629) DM 650

HAZLITT, William
- The Life of Napoleon. L., Grolier Society., n.d. Edn. Connoisseur Astral, (75). 16 vols. Plts. in 2 states. Cf. gt., mor. inlays, elab. gt. spine with mor. inlays. (SPB. May 6; 317) $1,200
[-] A Reply to the Essay on Population. L., 1807. 1st. Edn. Title-p. reprd., some browning. New antique-style cf. (SG. Dec.18; 231) $325

HAZLITT, William Carew
- British Columbia & Vancouver Island: a Historical Sketch of the British Settlement in the North-West Coast of America. Ill.:- Francis Young (folding map). L., 1858. 1st. Edn. 16mo. Mod. leatherette, orig. pict. upr. wrap. mntd. on cover. (SG. Jan.8; 63) $120

HEAD, Barclay V. & Gardner, P.
- Catalogue of Greek Coins. The Tauric Cheronese, Sarmatia, Dacia, Moesia, Thrace etc. 1877. Orig. cl. (SH. Mar.6; 370) Laskaris. £60
- - Anr. Edn. 1884. Liby. stp. on some pp. Orig. cl. (SH. Mar.6; 367) Quedar. £75

HEAD, Capt. C.F.
- Eastern & Egyptian Scenery. 1833. Ob. fo. Some spotting, 1st. gathering loose. Orig. ptd. bds., roan spine, worn, defect. Pres. Copy to Sir George Murray. (C. Nov.6; 312) Quaritch. £350
- - Anr. Copy. 1 map torn, spotting. Orig. mor.-bkd. bds. (SH. Nov.7; 414) Nolan. £180

HEAD, Sir Henry
- Aphasia & Other Kindred Disorders of Speech. Camb., 1926. 1st. Edn. 2 vols. 4to. Orig. cl., d.-w.'s. (S. Jun.16; 402) Rovy. £140

HEAD, Sir Henry & others
- Studies in Neurology. 1920. 1st. Edn. 2 vols. 4to. Orig. cl. (S. Jun.16; 403) Tait. £90

HEADLAM, C.
- The Milner Papers ... L., 1931. 2 vols. Some light foxing. Orig. bdg., d.-w. torn. (VA. Oct.31; 461) R. 200

HEAGERTY, John J.
- Four Centuries of Medical History in Canada. Ed.:- A.G. Doughty (preface). Toronto, 1928. 1st. Edn. 2 vols. Cl. (SG. Jan.29; 207) $120

HEAL, Sir Ambrose
- London Tradesmen's Cards of the XVIII Century. L., 1925. 4to. Cl.-bkd. bds., d.-w. torn. (P. Jul.2; 33) Maggs. £55

HEALY, John
- History of the Diocese of Meath. Dublin, 1908. 2 vols. Cl. (GM. Apr.30; 64) £52

HEANEY, Seamus
- Bog Poems. Ill.:- Barrie Cooke. Rainbow Pr., 1975. 1st. Edn. (150) numbered, sigd. 4to. Orig. mor.-bkd. bds., s.-c. (SH. Jul.22; 161) Radmall. £85

HEAPE, Charles
See-EDGE-PARTINGTON, James & Heape, Charles

HEARN, Lafcadio
- Glimpses of Unfamiliar Japan. Boston, 1894. 1st. Edn. 2 vols. Silver-decor. cl. Inscr., photograph of author & his wife mntd. in upr. cover with note tipped in below, A.L.s. laid in (cropped at both sides with loss of many words). (SG. Nov.13; 292) $260
- Kwaidan; Stories & Studies of Strange Things. Ed.:– Oscar Lewis. Ill.:– Yasumasa Fujita. N.Y., Ltd. Edns. Cl., 1932. Laced silk brocade, folding case with ivory clasps. (SG. Oct.23; 134) $160
- Writings. Ill.:– after C.S. Olcott & Burton Holmes. Boston, Riverside Pr., 1922. (750) numbered sets on L.P. 16 vols. Cl.-bkd. bds., unc. & unopened. Sigd. (in Japanese script) by Mrs. Hearn, MS. fragment in author's hand bnd. in vol. I. (SG. Nov.13; 297) $400

HEARNE, Samuel
- A Journey from Prince of Wales's Fort in Hudson's Bay to the Northern Ocean. 1795. 1st. Edn., L.P. 4to. 4 plts. stained, sm. hole in 03 affecting 4 letters. Cf.-bkd. bds., cl. box, unc. (C. Nov.5; 72) Quaritch. £950
See–CHAMPLAIN Society

HEARNE, Samuel–POUNCY, B.T.–BYRNE, Letitia–GILPIN, William & Alken, Samuel
- Antiquities of Great Britain.–(Six Etched Views).–(Eight Etched Views).–(Six Landscapes). 1786-[1807]; [1798]; [1805]; 1794. 5 pts. in 1 vol. (1st work 2.) Ob. 4to. Lacks 2nd. title to 1st. work, occasional light foxing in 1st. work. Cf., gt., upr. jnt. brkn. (C. Nov.6; 313) Traylen. £160

HEARNE, Thomas & Byrne, William
- Antiquities of Great Britain. Ill.:– W. Byrne & others after author. L., 1786. Vol. 1. Ob. fo. Cont. leath., gt., spine & jnts. reprd. (R. Oct.14-18; 1884) DM 2,200
- - Anr. Edn. 1807. 2 vols. in 1. Ob. 4to. Cont. russ., gt. in cathedral style, worn, upr. cover detchd. (S. Dec.9; 428) Kidd. £160
- - Anr. Copy. Fo. Engraved title numbered 'Vol. I', occasional spotting, no text. Cont. hf. mor., soiled. W.a.f. (CSK. Oct.3; 224) £100
- Sporting Plates. 1810. Ob. 4to. Hf. crimson mor. gt. by Rivière, Schwerdt bkplt. (P. May.14; 128) Way. £130

HEARTMAN, Charles F.
- American Primers, Indian Primers, Royal Primers & thirty-seven other Types ... issued prior to 1830. Highland Park, 1935. (300). Cl. (SG. Oct.2; 174) $120

HEATH, Charles (Ed.)
See HEROINES of Shakespeare, The

HEATH, Charles
See–PUGIN, Augustus Welby & Heath, Charles

HEATH, Francis George
- The Fern Portfolio. 1885. Fo. Occasional slight spotting. Cont. cl., slightly soiled. (CSK. Jan.30; 21) £70

HEATH, Henry
- Caricature Scrap-Book. 1840. Ob. fo. Orig. cl., some wear to spine. (TA. Nov.20; 309) £58
- The Caricaturist's Scrap Book. 1834. Recently rebnd. in cl. (TA. Feb.19; 326) £54

HEATH, Laban
- Infallible Counterfeit Detector at Sight ... Boston, [1864]. 16mo. Gt.-lettered cl. (SG. Sep.4; 365) $170
- - Anr. Edn. Boston & Wash., 1917. 12th. Edn. 16mo. Ptd. on title: 'Revised Pocket Edition'. Gt.-decor. cl. (SG. Dec.18; 131) $170

HEATH, Robert
- A Natural & Historical Account of the Islands of Scilly. 1750. 1st. Edn. Title partly detchd. Old cf. From the collection of Eric Sexton. (C. Apr.16; 280) Crowe. £100
- - Anr. Copy. Cont. mott. cf., gt. (S. Dec.9; 423) Crowe. £95

HEATH, William
- The Life of a Soldier, a narrative & descriptive poem. 1823. [1st. Edn.?]. Occasional minor spotting & offsetting. Orig. ptd. bds., unc., rebkd. (C. Feb.4; 135) Traylen. £150
- - Anr. Copy. 4to. Lacks errata & advt. ll., short tears in 2 plts., several ll. reprd., some plts. & ll. soiled (mainly in margins), some rust-holes. Orig. bds., very worn. (S. Feb.10; 352) Primrose. £85

- - Anr. Copy. Lacks errata & advt. ll., some ll. reprd. Orig. bds., very worn. (S. Sep.29; 240) Mellin. £50

HEAVYSIDE, Mary 'Lady Love', Attrib. to
- A Peep at the Esquimaux. L., 1825. Lacks 2 last ll. (blank?), occasional foxing, loose. Orig. cl., lacks spine, covers loose, lacks front & rear end-papers. (CB. Nov.12; 1) Can. $950

HEBBEL, Fritz
- Die Nibelungen. Ill.:– A. Kolb. Leipzig, [1924]. (400), on Bütten. Lge. 4to. Orig. hf. vell. 16 full-p. etchings sigd. by artist. (H. May 21/22; 1681) DM 440

HEBEL, Johann Peter
- Allemanische Gedichte. Ill.:– L. Richter. Leipzig, 1851. 1st. Edn. Cont. leath. gt., rebkd. (SH. Jul.23; 151) Hinterhaus. £50
- Sämmtliche Werke. Karlsruhe, 1832-34. 1st. Coll. Edn. 8 vols. in 4. Inner cover with Exlibris, his name on spine, port. slightly soiled. Cont. paper bds., 1 sm. spine tear. (H. Dec.9/10; 1526) DM 4,600

HEBER, F.A.
- Böhmens Burgen. Prag, 1844-49. Ob. 4to. Slightly soiled in parts. Cont. hf. leath. gt. (HK. Nov.18-21; 1120) DM 4,400

HEBER, Reginald
- Historical List of Horse-Matches Run ... 1751-67. 1752-68. 17 vols. Cf. (P. Apr.9; 86) Cavendish. £55

HEBER, Bp. Reginald
- Narrative of a Journey through the Upper Provinces of India from Calcutta to Bombay, 1824-25.–The Life of. 1828; 1830. 1st. Edns. 2 vols.; 2 vols. 4to. Some minor spotting to all vols. Cont. str.-grd. mor. with gt. decor. spines. (TA. Mar.19; 344) £68

HECK, Johann Georg
- Bilder-Atlas zum Conversations-Lexikon. Leipzig, 1849. 10 pts. in 2 text & 2 plt. vols. Lge. 8vo. & ob. 4to. Romantic bdg., text hf. leath., plts. full leath., gt. (R. Oct.14-18; 503) DM 2,400
- Iconographic Encyclopaedia of Science, Literature & Art. Trans.:– F. Baird. N.Y., 1857. 4 text & 2 plt. vols. Ob. fo. Soiled, lacks 6 steel engraved plts. Mod. linen. (R. Oct.14-18; 2494) DM 1,000

HECKEL, J. Chr.
[–] Atlas für die Jugend u. alle Liebhaber d. Geographie. Augsb., 1791. Lightly soiled in parts. Cont. hf. leath. (HK. Nov.18-21; 1049) DM 420

HECKSCHER, John G.
- Catalogue of the Library of ... N.Y., Feb.-Mar., 1909. With typed list of prices realized, bnd. in are 4 early 20th. C. angling auctions, & J. Winsor's 'List of Books on Angling, Fishes ...', dtd. Camb., 1896. Crude buckram. (SG. Jan.22; 30) $230

HECQUET, Philippe
- Explication Physique et Mechanique des effets de la Saignée, & de la Boisson, dans la Cure des Maladies. Chambery, 1707. 2nd. Edn. 2 pts. in 1 vol. 12mo. Slight browning. Cont. mott. cf., spine gt. From liby. of André L. Simon. (S. May 18; 112) Facchi. £75

HEDELIN, Abbé François
- The Whole Art of the Stage. 1684. 1st. Engl. Edn. 4to. Title soiled, last lf. defect., wormholing & staining to some ll. not affecting text. Old cf., rebkd. (BS. Jun.11; 254) £80
- - Anr. Edn. Priv. ptd., 1684. 4to. Mod. hf. cf. MS. note from E. Gordon Craig inserted. (SH. Jun.4; 177) Hannas. £110

HEDERICH, B.
- Progymnasmata Architectonica. Leipzig, 1730. Cont. vell. (R. Mar.31-Apr.4; 858) DM 1,250

HEDIN, Sven
- Through Asia. 1899. 2 vols. Orig. cl. gt. (P. Mar.12; 275) Hosain. £60
- Trans-Himalaya. 1910-13. 3 vols. Orig. cl. (SH. Nov.7; 349) Hosain. £115
- - Anr. Copy. Liby. stps. (SH. Jul.9; 115) Ghani. £50

HEDIO, Caspar
- Ein Ausserlessne Chronick von Anfang der Welt. Ed.:– Ph. Melanchthon. Strassburg, 1539. 1st. Edn. Title slightly soiled. Cont. blind-tooled pig-bkd. wood bds., lr. cover reprd., 8 brass bosses,

2 clasps, lacks 1 tie. (HK. May 12-14; 106) DM 1,500

HEDWIG, Joannes
- Descriptio et Adumbratio Microscopico-analytica Muscorum Frondosorum. Leipzig, 1787-95. 1st. Edn. 4 vols. Fo. 150 (of 160) hand-cold. plts., lacks final pt. with 10 plts. & text, vol. 2 with general title misbnd. in the middle & facs. title at front. Hf. cf., vol. 4 stilted to match. (S. Jun.1; 144) Junk. £220
- - Anr. Edn. 1787-97. 4 vols. in 2. Fo. Plts. hand-cold., lacks to vol 1 & dedication with sm. tears, both laid down, 1st. plt. slightly dust-soiled. 19th. C. hf. mor. From Chetham's Liby., Manchester. (C. Nov.26; 199) Wheldon & Wesley. £650

HEDWIG die Heilige, Herzogin von Schlesien
- Alhy hebet sich an dy Grosse Lege(n) da der Hailigsten Frawen Sandt Hedwigis ... Breslau, 19 Jun. 1504. 1st. Edn. Fo. Ll. Ed21 & EE8 replaced by facs., 1st. ll. restored, minimal worming of some letters. Mod. mor., gt. fillets. (D. Dec.11-13; 27) DM 14,500

HEERINGEN, Gustav von
- Wanderungen durch Franken (Das Malerische und Romantische Deutchland, III). Leipzig, ca. 1840. 2 plts. loose, spotted. Cont. cf., spine slightly worn. (S. May 5; 245) Schuster. £350

HEFNER-ALTENECK, J.H. von
- Costume du Moyen Age Chretien. Mannheim, 1840[-54]. 3 vols. Lge. 4to. Plts. finely cold. & gold heightened, most on brownish heavy paper, Fr. text, captions German, 1 plt. loose, some tearing & soiling. Later hf. leath., slightly worn, vol. 3 loose. (H. May 21/22; 691) DM 3,600
- Trachten, Kunstwerke und Gerätschaften vom Frühen Mittelalter bis Ende des Achtezhnten Jahrhunderts. Frankfurt, 1879-89. 10 vols. 4to. Lacks plt. 703. Loose in orig. hf. linen portfo. (D. Dec.11-13; 2212) DM 800

HEGEL, Georg Wilhelm Friedrich
- Dissertatio Philosophica de Orbitis Planetarum. Jena, 1801. 1st. & only Edn. Mod. bds. (R. Oct.14-18; 1315) DM 7,500

HEGGE, Robert
[–] The Legend of St. Cuthbert ... 1663. 1st. Edn. Title reprd. Early 19th. C. str.-grd. mor. William Beckford's copy, bkplt. of Thomas Brooke. [Wing H1370] (S. Mar.16; 161) Laywood. £65

HEIDELBERG
- Malerische Ansichten von Heidelberg. Heidelberg, ca. 1840. Sm. ob. 4to. 2 plts. slightly soiled. Orig. wraps., slightly soiled, with tears. (H. Dec.9/10; 648) DM 620
- - Anr. Edn. Ill.:– after Frommel, Verhas & others by Würtle, Hurlimann & others. Heidelberg, ca. 1850. Ob. 4to. Plts. slightly soiled in parts. Orig. pict. wraps., lightly soiled. (HK. Nov.18-21; 1079) DM 680

HEIDELOFF, Nikolaus Wilhelm von
- Gallery of Fashion. L., Apr. 1794-Mar. 1800. 1st. Edn. 6 vols. in 3, (1-6) of 9, without vols. 7-9, lacks issues for Oct.-Mar. 1799. in vol. 5. 4to. Jun. 1799 iss. loosely inserted from anr. copy, engraved title to vol. 4 loose, a very few plts. lightly browned or spotted, subscribers' lists & advt. ll. as called for. Cont. unmatched mott. cf. gt., worn, 1 vol. rebkd., some covers detchd. (CNY. Oct.1; 95) $3,200
[–] - Anr. Edn. Apr. 1798-Mar. 1803. Vols. V-IX, 5 vols. (of 9) in 2. 4to. Late 19th. C. str.-grd. mor. by Rivière gt. (S. Nov.24; 156) Douwma. £2,800

HEIDEN, J. vander (Sr. & Jr.)
- Beschryving der nieuwlyks uitgevonden en geoctrojeerde Slang-Brand-Spuiten, ... Amst., 1735. 2nd. Edn. 2 pts. in 1 vol. Fo. Lge. margins. Cont. hf. cf., spine gt., top & foot of spine & corners slightly defect., unc. (VG. Dec.17; 1363) Fls. 5,400

HEILPERN, Yechiel
- Erkei Ha'kinuim. Dehrenfurt, 1806. 1st. Edn. Fo. Bds. (S. Nov.18; 249) Stern. £70

HEIMS KRINGLA, ella Snorre Sturlusons Nordlandske Konunga Sagor ...
Ill.:– Johann Peringkiold. Stockholm, 1697-1700. 2 vols. Fo. Cont. mott. cf., worn. Pres. copy with long Latin inscr. from Peringskiold to Johann

Cederkrantz on fly-leaf. (S. Oct.20; 104)
Bjorck & Borjesson. £800

HEINE, Heinrich
– **Buch der Lieder.** Hamburg, 1827. 1st. Edn.
Minor spotting thro-out, lacks preliminary
dedication & advt. lf. Cont. hf. roan gt., orig.
paper wraps. bnd. in. Pres. Copy to Moses
Moser(?), inscr. badly cropped in bdg. (C.
Nov.20; 190) *Quaritch. £900*
– – **Anr. Copy.** Slightly spotted, sm. stp. on
hf.-title & title. Mod. bds., incorporating covers of
orig. wraps. & fragments of orig. spine. (S.
Jun.29; 349) *Quaritch. £400*
– – **Anr. Copy.** Lacks advt. lf. at end, title slightly
browned. Hand-bnd. hf. leath. [A. Kyster]. (H.
Dec.9/10; 1530) DM 2,200
– – **Anr. Copy.** Lacks hf.-title. & advt. lf. at end,
some browning. Cont. hf. leath. (H. May
21/22; 1142) DM 1,800
– **Italien.** Ill.:– Paul Scheurich. Berlin, 1919. (50)
numbered. 4to. Cf. (SG. Apr.9; 246) $100
– **Prose & Poetical Works.** N.Y., n.d. 20 vols. Hf.
Spanish gt., floral inlays on spine. (SPB. May
6; 318) $650
– **Sämmtliche Werke.** Hamburg, 1861-66. 1st.
Compl. Edn. 21 vols. Cont. hf. cf. (S. Jan.27; 451)
Wenner. £170
– – **Anr. Edn.** Ed.:– F. Strich. Munich, 1925. 10
vols. Orig. hf. leath. gt. (D. Dec.11-13; 898)
DM 500
– **Shakspeare's Maedchen und Frauen.** Ill.:– Kenny
Meadows. Paris & Leipzig, 1839. 1st. Edn. 4to.
Some foxing. Cont. hf. cf., spine gt. A.N.s. tipped
in (Paris, 1847), bkplt. of Dujardin-Van der
Avoort. (SG. Feb.12; 17) $475

HEINE, Th. Th. (Ed.)
See–SIMPLICISSIMUS

HEINE, William
– **Die Expeditionen in die Seen von China, Japan
und Ochotsk unter Commodore C. Ringgold und J.
Rodgers.** Leipzig, 1858. Orig. German Edn. 3 vols.
in 1. Lacks plt. 13. Cont. hf. leath. (R.
Oct.14-18; 1789) DM 580

HEINECCIUS, J.G.
– **Opera Omnia.** Genf, 1766-71. Sm. 4to. Cont. cf.,
worn, sm. defects., slight browning. (H.
Dec.9/10; 906) DM 620

HEINECKEN, Carl Heinrich von
[–] **Idee Généerale d'une Collection Complette
d'Estampes.** Leipzig & Vienna, 1771. 1st. Edn.
Old cf., rebkd. Armorial bkplt. of Sir Henry
FitzHerbert. (SG. Mar.12; 187) $160

HEINICHEN, J.D.
– **Der General-Bass in der Composition.** Dresden,
1728. 4to. Browned thro-out. Cont. hf. leath.,
spine defect. (H. Dec.9/10; 1156) DM 1,800

HEINROTH, J.C.A.
– **System der Psychisch-gerichtlichen Medizin.**
Leipzig, 1825. 1st. Edn. Slightly soiled in parts,
title with old owner's mark, ex-libris in cover.
Cont. paper bds., worn. (H. Dec.9/10; 331)
DM 560

HEINSE, Wilhelm
– **Musikalische Dialogen.** Ed.:– F.K. Arnold.
Leipzig, 1805. 1st. Edn. Cont. bds., worn. (HK.
May 15; 4459) DM 500
– **Sämmtliche Schriften.** Ed.:– H. Laube. Leipzig,
1838. 1st. Coll. Edn. 10 vols. in 5. Slightly
browned in parts, vols. VII & VIII heavier. Cont.
hf. leath., worn, 2 spine tears. (H. Dec.9/10; 1534)
DM 3,000

HEINSIUS, Daniel
– **Rerum ad Sylvam-Ducis atque alibi in Belgio aut
a Belgis.** Leyden, 1631. 1 map slightly holed,
slight spotting. Cont. vell., worn. (CSK.
Jan.9; 143) £85
– – **Anr. Copy.** Fo. Stained in lr. part thro-out.
Cont. limp vell. (VG. Oct.13; 74) Fls. 650

HEINSIUS, Johann Samuel, Publisher
– **Genealogisch-Historische Nachrichten von den
Allerneuesten Begebenheiten.** Leipzig, 1739-40.
Pts. 1-12 (compl.). Old cf., spine very worn. (SG.
Feb.5; 163) $100

HEISTER, Dr. Laurentius
– **Chirurgie.** Nuremb., 1719. 1st. Edn. 4to. Preface
dtd. Oct. 1718. Orig. hf. leath., very worn. (D.
Dec.11-13; 205) DM 1,500
– – **Anr. Edn.** Nuremb., 1724. 2nd. Iss. 4to. Lacks
frontis., title with several old, partly struck out

entries, some plts. browned or soiled, 3 plts. with
sm. defects, holes or tears. Cont. leath., very worn.
(HK. May 12-14; 336) DM 2,200
– **A General System of Surgery.** 1750. 4th. Edn.
4to. 3 folding engraved plts. slightly torn, some
foxing & staining. Cont. cf., rebkd., covers worn.
From liby. of Dr. E. Ashworth Underwood. (S.
Feb.23; 227) *Quaritch. £110*
– – **Anr. Edn.** 1757. 6th. Edn. 4to. Tear in plt. 40,
some browning, title slightly soiled. Cont. cf.,
worn, covers loose. (S. Jul.27; 339) *Pratt. £55*
– – **Anr. Edn.** 1768. 8th. Edn. 2 vols. in 1. 4to.
Cont. cf. (S. Dec.2; 823) *Westwood. £100*
– – **Anr. Copy.** 2 vols. Lacks upr. hf. of vol. II pp.
407-410 (2 ll. of index), replaced by blank paper.
Cf., rebkd. (S. Jun.16; 409) *Engle. £50*
– **Institutiones Chirurgicae.** Amst., 1750. 2 vols.
4to. Titles slightly soiled. Cont. cf., gt. spines,
head & foot of spines slightly worn. (S. Feb.23; 52)
Primrose. £170
– – **Anr. Copy.** Cont. mott. cf., spines gt., head of
spines slightly worn. (S. Feb.23; 53)
Nador. £160
– – **Anr. Copy.** Vol. 1 (of 2). Cont. bds. (HK. May
12-14; 337) DM 420
– **Instituzioni Chirurgiche.** Venice, 1793. 2 vols.
Slightly spotted in places. Cont. cf.-bkd. bds. (S.
Feb.23; 54) *Preidel. £55*
– **Medicinische Chirurgische und Anatomische
Wahrnehmungen.** Rostock, 1753. 1st. Edn. 4to. 8
folding engraved plts. attached to fore-margins,
some slightly frayed & creased, 2 defect. slightly
affecting engr., lacks lf. Oo4, following 6 ll.
slightly defect. in lr. corner, sometimes just
affecting text. Cont. cf. (S. Feb.23; 55)
Nagel. £80
– **Practisches Medicinisches Handbuch.** Leipzig,
1744. 1st. Edn. Browned thro-out, 3 ll. with
owner's mark in ink, several ll. stpd., Cont. bds.
(H. May 21-22; 191) DM 800

HEKSCH, A.F.
– **Die Donau von Ihrem Ursprung bis an die
Mündung.** Vienna & other places, 1881. Slightly
browned. Orig. pict. linen. (R. Oct.14-18; 2196)
DM 420

HELBACH, F.
– **Oenographia, Weinkeller oder Kunstbuch,**
Frankfurt, 1604. Only Edn. 4to. Lightly browned,
old stp. on title. Mod. cont. style leath. (R.
Oct.14-18; 2745) DM 2,400

HELD, Julius S.
– **Rembrandt & the Book of Tobit.** [Northampton,
Mass.], Gehenna Pr., 1964. (25) specially bnd.
Niger mor.-bkd. bds., by Harcourt Bindery. (SG.
Apr.9; 441) $120

HELIODORUS
– **Aethiopicae Historiae libri decem, nunc primum
e Greco sermone in Latinum . . .** Trans.:– Stanislao
VViczki. Basle, 1552. Fo. Some margins
dampstained. 18th. C. cf., rebkd., bkplts. of Sir
Charles Frederick, & Syston Park. (S. Apr.7; 306)
Armstrong. £50

HELIOT, R.P.
– **Histoire du Clergé Régulier et Séculier.** Ill.:– B.
Picart & Schoonebeck. 1716. 4 vols. 12mo. Cont.
marb. cf. Argenson ex-lib. (HD. Jun.30; 28)
Frs. 2,000

HELLER, D.
– **A History of Cape Silver, 1700-1870.** Cape
Town, 1949. 4to. Orig. bdg., d.-w. Sigd. (VA. May
8; 31) R. 94
– – **Anr. Copy.** (VA. Oct.31; 463) R. 90

HELLER, Edmund
See–ROOSEVELT, Theodore & Heller, Edmund

HELLER, Joseph
– **Catch-22.** N.Y., 1961. 1st. Printing, Advance
copy. Wraps., worn. (SG. Jun.4; 209) $425

HELLMAN, Lillian
– **Watch on the Rhine.** Ill.:– Rockwell Kent,
Quintanilla, & others. N.Y., 1942. Ltd. Edn. sigd.
by author, Dorothy Parker, & Quintanilla. 4to.
2-tone cl., box (worn). (SG. Nov.13; 301) $240

HELLWIG, Christoph von
– **Nosce te ipsum Anatomicum Vivum, oder . . .
Anatomisches Werk . . . nebst Beschreibung
todtlicher Wunden.** Ed.:– Theodor Andreas von
Hellwig. Frankfurt & Leipzig, [1720]. 2nd. Edn.
Fo. Slightly soiled. 19th. C. hf. roan. (S.
Feb.23; 56) *Rota. £120*

– **Nosce te Ipsum, vel Anatomicum Vivum, oder,
. . . Anatomisches Werck . . . und eine
Beschreibung Todtlicher Wunden . . . mit
verschiedenen Anmerkungen und in Kupfer
vorgestellten Theilen vermehrt . . . durch Johann
Gottlob von Hellwig . . . vorrede . . . Johann
Hieron. Kniphoff.** Frankfurt & Leipzig, [1744].
3rd. enlarged Edn. Fo. Plt. X has 2 dissections
missing, plt. XII has cl. overlay replaced in pen &
ink facs. Cont. hf. vell., slightly worn. (S.
Feb.23; 57) *Rota. £130*

HELLWIG, L. Christoph von, the Younger
– **Lexicon Pharmaceuticum.–Neu Eingerichtetes
Lexicon Medico-Chymicum.** Frankfurt & Leipzig,
1710; 1711. 2 pts. in 1 vol. Soiled & browned.
Cont. vell., spine torn. (R. Oct.14-18; 333)
DM 900

HELMHOLTZ, Hermann Ludwig Ferdinand von
– **Handbuch der Physiolog. Optik.** Leipzig, 1867.
1st. Edn. Stp. on title, slightly soiled in parts.
Cont. hf. leath. (HK. Nov.18-21; 565) DM 1,600
– – **Anr. Edn.** Hamburg & Leipzig, 1896. 2nd.
Edn. 4to. Cont. hf. leath. (S. Jul.27; 244)
Mollen. £80
– **Vorlesungen uber Theoretische Physik.** Ed.:– A.
Konig, K. Runge & others. Leipzig, 1897-1907. 6
vols. Cont. hf. cl., 2 spines faded. (S. Jul.27; 242)
Weiner. £60

HELMONT, Johannes Baptista van
– **Deliramenta Catarrhi or the Incongruities,
Impossibilities & Absurdities couched under the
Vulgar Opinion of Defluxions.** Trans.:– Dr.
Charleton. 1650. Sm. 4to. A few stains. New cf.
[Wing H1398] (S. Jun.16; 411) *Phelps. £70*
– **Oriatrike or Physick Refined.–Opuscula medica
inaudita, that is unheard of little works of medicine.**
Trans.:– J[ohn] C[handler] (1st. work). 1662. 1st.
Edn. in Engl. 2 pts. in 1 vol. Fo. Engraved frontis.
mntd. & slightly defect. at lr. margin affecting a
name & extreme lr. end of 1 coat-of-arms,
pagination jumps from 334 to 345. Panel. cf.,
hinges reprd. J.W. Mellor's copy with bkplt. &
from the collection of Dr. George Mitchell, with
bkplt. [Wing H1400] (S. Jun.16; 412)
Quaritch. £350
– **Ortus Medicinae.** Ed.:– Franciscus Mercurious
van Helmont. Amst., 1648. 1st. Edn. 4to. Later hf.
vell., ex liby. (SG. Sep.18; 175) $700
– **A Ternary of Paradoxes.** 1650. 1st. Engl. Edn.
Old pen marks in margin, browned. Cont. cf. (P.
Jul.30; 7) *Lawson. £180*

HELMUTH, J.H.
– **Gemeinnüteige Naturgeschichte des In-und
Auslandes.** Leipzig, 1808. 2nd. Edn. Vols. 2-8 (of
9) in 7 vols. Text soiled, 2pp. defect. in vol. 2.
Cont. hf. linen. (R. Mar.31-Apr.4; 1371)
DM 620

HELPS, Sir Arthur
[–] **Friends in Council.** L., 1852. 2 vols. Cont.
maroon mor. 2 double fore-e. pntgs. (SG.
Sep.4; 189) $500

HELVETIUS, Claude Adrien
[–] **De l'Esprit.** Paris, 1758. 1st. Edn. 4to. Cont.
cf., spine gt. (S. Oct.21; 434) *Ellison. £150*
– – **Anr. Copy.** 1-p. approbation at end, without
cancels, title reprd. Cont. mott. cf., triple gt. fillet.
spine compartments gt. with charges from arms of
M.L. de Rohan-Soubise, Comtesse de
Lorraine-Marsan or L.J.C. de Rohan, Comtesse
de Lorraine-Brionne. (SM. Oct.7; 1750)
Frs. 2,200
[–] – **Anr. Copy.** Some pp. lightly browned or
slightly soiled. Cont. marb. leath., gt. spine. (HK.
Nov.18-21; 1710) DM 620
– **De l'ésprit or Essays on the Mind & its Seven
Faculties.** Priv. ptd., 1759. 1st. Edn. in Engl. 4to.
Cf., rebkd. (S. Jun.16; 413) *Quaritch. £85*

HELVETIUS, Claude Adrien–PARIS, Archbp. of
[–] **De l'Esprit.–Mandement de . . . l'Archevêque de
Paris, Portant Condamnation d'un Livre qui a pour
Titre, De l'Esprit.** Paris, 1758. 1st work; 1st Edn. 2
works in 1 vol. 4to. 2nd work: slight browning.
Cont. marb. cf., decor. spine, 3 gt. fillets framing
covers, slightly worn. (SM. Feb.11; 71) Frs. 1,300

HELWIG, C. von
– **Neue Lustige u. vollst. Jagdkunst.** Leipzig, 1762.
5 pts. in 1 vol. Loss of text on title, liby. mark.
Cont. leath. gt. (HK. Nov.18-21; 1739)
DM 1,100

HELWIG, Hellmuth
- Handbuch der Einbandkunde. Hamburg, 1953-55. (900) Priv. Ptd. 2 vols. & index vol. 4to. Orig. linen. (H. Dec.9/10; 75) DM 440

HELYOT, Pierre
- Album . . . des Costumes de la Cour de Rome . . . Paris, 1862. 2nd. Edn. 4to. Some ll. loose. Cont. limp mor. (S. May 5; 259) *Crete.* £160

HELYOT, Pierre & Bullot, M.
- Histoire des Ordes Monastiques. Paris, 1714-19. 7 vols. only (of 8, lacks vol. 4). 4to. Some foxing, browning, & c. Disbnd. (SG. Nov.20; 380) $300
- [-] - Anr. Edn. Douay & Paris, 1714-21. 2nd. Edn. Vols. I-VII (of 8). 4to. Browning & soiling in parts, title lf. vol. I with lengthy MS. note, others with names. Cont. cf., some spines defect., 1 heavily. (H. Dec.9/10; 770) DM 850
- [-] - Anr. Edn. Ed.:- [M. Bullot]. Paris, 1715-21. 1st. Edn. 8 vols. 4to. Vol. 5 lacks plt. 49. Late 19th. C. leath. (HK. May 12-14; 1098) DM 480
- [-] - Anr. Edn. Paris, 1721. 8 vols. 4to. Cont. cf., spine decor. with raised bands, bdg. defect. (HD. Jun.24; 42) Frs. 2,000

HEMINGE, Nicholas
- A Postill, or Exposition of the Gospels . . . Trans.:- Arthur Golding. L., [1578]. 4to. Worn, browned. 18th. C.(?) blind-stpd. cf., rebkd. [STC 13064] (SG. Sep.25; 163) $110

HEMINGWAY, Ernest
- Across the River & into the Trees. N.Y., 1950. 1st. Amer. Edn. Cl., d.-w. (slightly wrinkled). Inscr. (SG. Nov.13; 317) $375
- Death in the Afternoon. N.Y. & L., 1932. 1st. Edn. Orig. cl. (S. Jul.22; 167) *Ghani.* £60
- - Anr. Copy. Cl., d.-w. (SG. Nov.13; 308) $100
- A Farewell to Arms. N.Y., 1929. 1st. Edn., 1st. Iss. Orig. cl. (S. Jul.22; 166) *Ghani.* £60
- - Anr. Copy. Cl., d.-w. (SG. Jun.4; 213) $325
- - Anr. Copy. Without the disclaimer notice. Damp affected, d.-w. stained, stains on front free endpaper. (SG. Nov.13; 305) $175
- - Anr. Edn. N.Y., 1929. (510) sigd. by author. Orig. vell.-bkd. bds., unc., bd. s.-c. (defect). (C. Feb.4; 283) *Henderson.* £250
- The Fifth Column & the First Forty-Nine Stories. N.Y., 1938. 1st. Edn. Cl., staining on end-papers, d.-w. (SG. Nov.13; 313) $100
- For Whom the Bell Tolls. N.Y., 1940 1st. Edn., 1st. Iss. Cl., d.-w. (SG. Jun.4; 216) $160
- Green Hills of Africa. N.Y., 1935. 1st. Edn. Owner's sig. Cl., d.-w. Inscr. & sigd. (SG. Nov.13; 310) $500
- In Our Time. Paris, Three Mountains Pr., 1924. 1st. Edn., Orig. bds., spine worn. Pres. copy to Edward J. O'Brien. (S. Jul.22; 162) *House of Books.* £1,900
- - Anr. Copy. Orig. ptd. bds., endpapers browned. Pres. copy. (SPB. Nov.25; 300) $4,250
- Introduction to Kiki of Montparnasse. N.Y., 1929. 1st. Edn., Unbnd. as issued. (S. Jul.22; 164) *House of Books.* £260
- Kiki's Memoirs. Trans.:- Samuel Putnam. Ill.:- Man Ray, Foujita, Kisling, & others. Paris, Black Manikin Pr., 1930. 4to. Wraps., wrinkled. (SG. Nov.13; 307) $100
- Oeuvres Complètes. Ed.:- Jean Dutourd (intro.). Ill.:- Commère, Guiramand, Minaux, Carzon, & others. Paris, [1963-65]. (100) numbered on L.P., with extra plts. on Japon Nacré. 8 vols. Lge. tall fo. Loose as iss. in heavy ptd. wraps., vell.-bkd. linen s.-c.'s. (PNY. May 21; 213) $1,100
- The Old Man & the Sea. [N.Y.], [1952]. Fo. 1st. lf. bearing publisher's 'Advance galley proofs' stp., 2nd. stpd. 'Advance galley proofs for your personal reading only. Life publication date, Sept. 1'. Folded & stapled, as issued. Complete set of advance galley proofs. (CNY. Oct.1; 96) $480
- Soldier's Home. [In: Contact Collection of Contemporary Writers]. [Dijon], [1925]. 12mo. Wraps. (SG. Jun.4; 210) $275
- The Sun Also Rises. N.Y., 1926. 1st. Edn., 1st. iss., with spelling 'stoppped'. Orig. cl. (S. Jul.22; 165) *Ghani.* £90
- Today is Friday. New Jersey, 1926. 1st. Edn., (300) numbered. Orig. wraps., upr. cover design by Jean Cocteau. Edward J. O'Brien copy. (S. Jul.22; 163) *House of Books.* £190
- - Anr. Copy. This copy unnumbered, lacks envelope. Pict. wraps., with design by Jean Cocteau. (SG. Nov.13; 303) $130
- To Have & To Have Not. N.Y., 1937. 1st. Edn. Cl., staining on end-papers, d.-w. (SG. Nov.13; 311) $125

HEMINGWAY, Ernest-REGLER, Gustav
- Preface to the Great Crusade.-The Great Crusdade. N.Y., 1940. 1st. Edn. of Hemingway's preface. Leaflet & book, 2 separate vols. 16 pp. of prelims. & Hemingway's preface only issued as publisher's leaflet. Bnd. in d.-w. later Iss. with the book. Goodwin copy, with added letter from publisher (1p. 4to), 30 Jun. 1939 to Hemingway. (SPB. Nov.25; 301) $200

HEMINGWAY, Joseph
- History of the City of Chester. Chester, 1831. 2 vols. Some minor defects. Orig. cl., spines chipped. (SBA. Jul.14; 274) *Duran.* £70
- - Anr. Copy. Cont. cf. gt. (SBA. Oct.22; 295) *Chesters.* £65

HEMM, J.P.
- [Portraits of the Royal Family in Penmanship]. [Nottingham], [1831]. Fo. Orig. cl.-bkd. wraps. (CSK. Aug.22; 41) £50

HEMMERLIN, Felix
- Opuscula et Tractatus. [Strassburg], [after Aug. 13, 1497]. Fo. Capital spaces with guide letters, some ll. loose as far as d5, very slight lr. marginal dampstaining to 3 or 4 ll. 16th. C. cf. over wood bds., covers with double blind-ruled border, spine in 4 compartments blind-tooled & gt.-lettered, inner jnt. brkn. Bkplt. of the General Theological Seminary Liby. [BMC I, 172, Goff H17, HC 8424] (CNY. Oct.1; 62) $950

HEMON, Louis
- Maria Chapdelaine. Paris, [1916]. 1st. Edn. Stp. on title-p. Recent hf. cf., orig. wraps. coated with plastic & mntd. on front fly-lf. (CB. Sep.24; 300) *Can.* $400
- - Anr. Edn. Ill.:- Suzor-Coté. Montreal, 1921. Wraps., carelessly opened resulting in a few marginal tears. (PWP. Jun.4; 167) *Can.* $120
- - Anr. Edn. Ill.:- Clarence Gagnon. Paris, 1933. On Rives, numbered. Sm. Bradel 4to. Hf. russ. by Fonsèque, strips, unc., wrap. & spine, s.-c. (HD. Dec.5; 102) Frs. 4,000

HEMPEL, Frederic
- Tableaux Pittoresques des Moeurs . . . des Russes . . . Ill.:- after J.G.G. Geissler. Paris & Leipzig. [1804]. 4 pts. in 1 vol. 4to. Lacks titles of last 3 pts. Hf. cf., ca. 1850, corners, decor. spine. (HD. Dec.5; 92) Frs. 5,000

HENAULT, Charles Jean François
- Nouvel Abrégé Chronologique de l'Histoire de France. Ill.:- Cochin. Paris, 1749. 3rd. Edn. 4to. Lacks frontis. Cf. by Thouvenin, decor. spine, blind-tooled roll-stps. on covers, inside dentelle. (HD. Dec.5; 103) Frs. 1,600
- [ ] Anr. Edn. Paris, 1752. 4to. Cont. red mor., gt. triple fillet border, centre arms, spine raised bands, inner dentelle. (HD. Apr.24; 69) Frs. 4,800

HENCKEL, J.F.
- Introduction à la Mineralogie . . . traduit de l'Allemand. Paris, 1756. 2 vols. 12mo. Cont. cf., gt. spines. (S. Dec.8; 169) *Chelsea.* £65

HENDERSON, Alexander
- The History of Ancient & Modern Wines. 1824. 1st. Edn. 4to. Cf. gt. by F. Bedford, upr. cover detchd. (S. Nov.24; 157) *Beaumont.* £130

HENDERSON, Ebenezer
- Iceland. 1819. Hf. cf. gt. (P. Oct.23; 33) *Scott.* £65

HENDERSON, Edward, George & Andrew
- [-] The Illustrated Bouquet. 1957-59. Vol. ! only. Fo. Disbnd. W.a.f. (SKC. Feb.26; 1586) £260

HENDERSON, George
- An Account of the British Settlement of Hunduras. 1809. 1st. Edn. Several tears in map, occasional spotting & soiling, advt. ll. at end. Mod. spr. cf. [Sabin 31308] (S. Feb.10; 445) *Maggs.* £60

HENDRICKS, Gordon
- The Photographs of Thomas Eakins. N.Y., 1972. Ob. fo. Buckram, d.-w. (SG. Apr.23; 80) $120

HENDSCHEL, A.L.R.
- Skizzenbuch. Frankfurt-a.-M., [1886]. 4 vols. 4to. Orig. cl. (SH. Jun.18; 154) *Dallai.* £60

HENDSCHEL, U.
- Neuester Eisenbahn-Atlas von Deutschland, Belgien, Holland und dem Elsass. Frankfurt, 1846. 3rd. Edn. Old bds. (R. Mar.31-Apr.4; 1151) DM 2,400

HENLEY, William E.
- The Graphic Gallery of Shakespeare's Heroines. 1883. (100) numbered. Fo. Each plt. sigd. in pencil by its artist. Cont. mor. by Zaehnsdorf. (CSK. Jun.19; 106) £60
- London Garland. Ill.:- Arthur Rackham, L., 1895. 1st. Edn. Lge. 4to. Vell., d.-w., publisher's s.-c. Raymond M. Sutton Jr. copy. (SG. May 7; 183) $240
- [-] London Types. Ill.:- Sir William Nicholson. N.Y., 1898. 4to. Enf-lf. loose. Orig. cl.-bkd. pict. bds., slightly worn. (S. Jul.31; 260) *Lord's Gallery.* £65
- - Anr. Copy. Orig. cl.-bkd. bds., worn. (CSK. Jul.31; 47) £60
- - Anr. Copy. Fo. Advt. lf. at end. Cl.-bkd. cold. pict. bds., some wear. (SG. Mar.19; 253) $225

HENNEPIN, Louis
- A New Discovery of a Vast Country in America, Extending Above Four Thousand Miles Between New France & Mexico . . . L., 1698. 1st. Edn. in Engl., 1st. Iss. ('Bon' Iss.). Sig. order as stated in Howes H-416, Graff 1862, Streeter 1-106. Mod. red hf. mor., gt. spine & borders. From liby. of William E. Wilson. (SPB. Apr.29; 133) $1,300
- - Anr. Copy. Last lf. of contents & front map detchd., browned & foxed, sig. order as in Howes H-416, Graff 1862, Streeter 1-106. 19th. C. hf. cf. From liby. of William E. Wilson. (SPB. Apr.29; 134) $600
- - Anr. Edn. 1698. 1st Engl. Edn., the 'Tonson' iss. of the imprint. Several plts. torn at fold, some browning & staining. Cont. cf. [Wing H1451] (S. May 5; 270) *Faupel.* £600
- Nouvelle Découverte d'un Très Grand Pays situé dans l'Amérique. Utrecht, 1697. 1st. Edn. Sm. 12mo. Engraved title, 2 folding copperplts., 1 (of 2) lge. folding maps. Disbnd. (SG. Jun.11; 174) $250
- Voyage curieux . . . qui contient une nouvelle decouverte d'un très-grand pays situé dans l'Amerique . . . ajouté ici un Voyage qui contient une relation . . . des Caraibes . . . faite par le Sieur De La Borde. Ill.:- Pierre van der Aa. Leiden, 1704. 12mo. 6 folding plts., including a View of Niagra Falls, marginal worming in upr. inner blank margin. Cont. cf. (C. Feb.25; 103a) *Potter.* £400

HENNINGS, H.
- Genealogiae aligrot Familiarum Nobilivm in Saxonia. Hamburg, 1590. Fo. Browned thro.-out. Hf. vell. (HK. Nov.18-21; 1657) DM 2,300

HENRICUS DE HASSIA
- Secreta Sacerdotum . . . que sibi placent vel displiccnt in missa etc. [Nuremb.], [Georg Stuchs], ca. 1497. 4to. Capitals in red & green, sm. stains & holes in blank margins at end. Paper wraps. [H. 8377*; BMC II p. 471; Goff H 31] (C. Apr.1; 42) *Branners.* £160

HENRICUS DE HERPF
- Sermones de Tempore et de Sanctis. [Speier], Peter Drach, [after 17 Jan. 1484]. 1st. Edn. Fo. Capitals, paragraph-marks, etc., supplied in red, some dampstaining, a few tears, slightly affecting text. Cont. South German or Austrian blind-stpd. pig. over oak bds., covers with pattern of oak-ll. & rosettes & with scroll 'S. Marai (?)' rebkd., rather worn, lacks clasps. Bkplt. of Benedictine Monastery of St. Peter, Salzburg; from liby. of André L. Simon. [BMC II, 493; Goff H38; HC 8257*] (S. May 18; 113) *Harper.* £500

HENRION, Denis
- Cosmographie, ou Traicté General des choses tant Celestes qu'Elementaires. Paris, 1620. 1st. Edn. Title dust-soiled. Mod. vell. From Honeyman Collection. (S. May 20; 3259) *McKittrick.* £110

HENRION, Denis-FLOUTRIERES, Pierre de
- L'Usage du Compas de Proportion . . .-Traitté d'Horologeographie, auquel est enseigné a descrire et construire toutes sortes d'Horologes au Soleil. Paris, 1631; 1619. 4th. Edn.; 1st. Edn. 2 works in 1 vol. Slight browning. Cont. vell., soiled. From Honeyman Collection. (S. May 20; 3260) *Wynter.* £240

HENRY VIII, King of England
- Assertio Septem Sacramentorum Adversus Martin Lutheru. 1521. 1st. Edn. 4to. Several sm. marginal repairs, slightly wormed thro.-out, affecting title & some letters, all reprd. & filled in. Mor., gt., by Pratt. [STC 13078] (S. Feb.10; 446) *Dawson.* £420

– – Anr. Edn. Augsburg, 1524. Early Edn. Title border & printer's mark, end-lf. bd. at front, slightly wormed. 19th. C. hf. linen. (R. Oct.14-18; 77) DM 480
– Songs, Ballads & Instrumental Pieces . . . Ed.:– Lady Mary Trefusis. Oxford, Roxb. Cl., 1912. Fo. Hf. mor. (S. Dec.8; 30) *Traylen.* £90

HENRY VIII, King of England–FOX, Edward & others
– Assertio Septem Sacramentorum . . .–Libello huic Regio Haec Insunt.–Gravissime atque Exactissimae Illustrissimarum . . . Jul. 1521; [1521]; 1530. 1st. Edn. [1st. work]. 3 works in 1 vol. 4to. 1st. work: with errata lf. & 2 orig. blanks at end, paper fault in m1 affecting text, cont. notes in ink (some cropped); 2nd. work: 12 ll. only (of 20), sm. holes in 2 ll. affecting woodcut borders; 3rd. work: sm. hole on title affecting woodcut border, marginal staining at beginning. 17th. C. cf., rebkd. [STC 13078; 13083; 14286] (C. Nov.20; 252) *Thomas.* £1,200

HENRY, Alexander
– Travels & Adventures in Canada, & the Indian Territories, Between the Years 1760 & 1776 . . . N.Y., 1809. 1st. Edn. With frontis. & errata not in Howes or Graff, port. offset on title, front free end-paper, title, port. & errata slip apparently inserted from anr. copy, slight foxing & soiling. Cont. cross grain mor.-bkd. bds. From liby. of William E. Wilson. (SPB. Apr.29; 135) $275
– – Anr. Copy. Some foxing & staining, a few tape repairs, lacks port. Crude hf. linen, ex-liby. (SG. Mar.5; 63) $110

HENRY, Augustine
*See–*ELWES, Henry John & Henry, Augustine

HENRY, David
[–] An Historical Account of all the Voyages round the World performed by English Navigators. 1774-73. 1st. Edn. 4 vols. 39 (of 44) engraved plts., some offsetting, lacks hf.-titles (?). 19th. C. hf. cf., 1 spine defect. W.a.f. [Sabin 31389] (S. Sep.29; 163) *Quaritch.* £190

HENRY, G.M.
– Coloured Plates of the Birds of Ceylon. 1927. 4to. Qtr. mor. gt. (P. Nov.13; 202) *Way.* £120
– – Anr. Edn. 1927-35. Pts. I-IV. 4to. Orig. wraps., pts. I-III brkn. (S. Jan.26: 283) *Rimmer.* £95

HENRY, John J.
– An Accurate & Interesting Account of the Hardships & Sufferings of that Band of Heroes . . . in the Campaign Against Quebec in 1775. Lancaster, 1812. 1st. Edn. 12mo. Owner's inscrs., foxing, offsetting. Cont. tree cf., worn, upr. cover loose. From liby. of William E. Wilson. [Sabin 31400] (SPB. Apr.29; 136) $275

HENRY, O. (Pseud.)
*See–*PORTER, William Sydney 'O. Henry'

HENRY, Samuel
– A New & Complete American Medical Family Herbal. N.Y., 1814. 1st. Edn. Foxed. Orig. cf., ex liby. (SG. Sep.18; 176) $450

HENSCHEN, Salomon Eberhard
– Klinische und anatomische Beiträge zur Pathologie des Gehirns. Stockholm, 1890-1930. 8 pts. in 10 vols. 4to. Orig. ptd. wraps., unc., 1 or 2 spines brkn. (S. Jun.16; 414) *Norman.* £80

HENSHALL, James A.
– Bass, Pike, Perch & Others. N.Y., 1903. 1st. Edn., (100) numbered on L.P. Three-qtr. mor., unc. (SG. Oct.16; 55) $100

HENSLOW, Rev. John Stephen
*See–*MAUND, Benjamin & Henslow, Rev. John Stephen

HENTY, George Alfred
– St. George for England. Ill.:– Gordon Browne. 1885. 1st. Edn. Orig. pict. cl. gt. (SH. Dec.11; 285) *Falcon.* £55
– Under Drake's Flag. 1883. 1st. Edn. Orig. pict. cl. gt. (SH. Dec.11; 284) *Hillingdon.* £50

HENTZNER, Paul
– Itinerarium Germaniae, Galliae, Angliae, Italiae. Nuremb., 1612. 1st. Edn. Sm. 4to. Some ll. stained, a few underlinings in text. Cont. vell. bds., new ties, 'HHH/IVL/1620' stpd. on upr. cover. (S. May 5; 53) *Hyde.* £60
– – Anr. Edn. Breslau, 1617. ?2nd. Edn. 4to. Cont. limp vell., loose. (S. Mar.17; 274) *Edwards.* £80

– A Journey into England. Ed.:– Horace Walpole. Trans.:– Richard Bentley. Straw. Hill Pr., 1757. 1st. Engl. Edn. Some spotting, lacks final blank lf. Mor. gt. by Rivière. (CNY. Oct.1; 97) $280

HEPPE, J. Chr. W. von
– Die Jagdlust. Nuremb., 1783. Soiled thro.-out. Cont. bds. (HK. Nov.18-21; 1741) DM 550

HEPPLEWHITE, Alice & Co.
– The Cabinet-Maker & Upholsterer's Guide. 1788. 1st. Edn. Fo. 8pp. 8vo. 'Catalogue of Modern Books on Architecture' bnd. in at end. Cont. cf., cl. s.-c. (S. Mar.17; 415) *Hammond.* £750
– – Anr. Edn. 1794. 3rd. Edn. Fo. Cont. tree cf., rebkd., cl. s.-c. (S. Mar.17; 416) *Gordon.* £400
– – Anr. Copy. Stained, spotted. Later mor., worn. (CSK. Nov.14; 219) £120

HEPWORTH, Barbara
– The Complete Sculpture of. Ed.:– Alan Bowness. 1971. 1st. Edn., (150) numbered, with orig. screenprint, sigd. & numbered. 4to. Orig. pict. cl. gt., d.-w., s.-c. (SH. Mar.26; 274) *Ayres.* £50

HERACLIDES, Ponticus
*See–*KRAG, Niels–NICOLAUS, Damascenus –HERACLIDES, Ponticus

HERALDRY in Miniature
*See–*ROYAL KALENDAR (The), or . . . Annual Register for England, Scotland, Ireland & America, for . . . 1799–HERALDRY in Miniature –COMPANION (A) to the Royal Kalendar–EAST INDIA Kalendar (The)

HERBARIUM
[Late 17th C?]. Fo. Album of pressed & dried specimens of plants & flowers, 1st. lf. of index largely torn away, some ll. removed at end of vol. Cont. vell. with remains of ties. (S. Oct.20; 106) *Delmonte.* £150

HERBARIUS Patavie
Passau, [Johann Petri], [14]86. 4to. Hf.-p. botanical woodcuts cold. by cont. hand, tears to folios 14, 57, 62 & 64 reprd. without loss, lr. corner of fo. 108 renewed with portion of 4 lines supplied, lr. portion of fo. 132 renewed with all text on recto & 2 lines at verso supplied, minor marginal tears to some 10 ll., foliation cropped in several places, title-p. soiled, finger-soiling & traces of use, old. inscrs. partly erased from title. 19th. C. vell., worn. From the collection of Eric Sexton. [Goff H65, H 8446*] (CNY. Apr.8; 132) $10,500

HERBE, Ch. A.
– Costumes Français Civils, Militaires et Religieux. Paris, [1837]. 2nd. Edn. Lge. 4to. Some soiling in parts, several text ll. browned. Mod. linen. (H. Dec.9/10; 771) DM 800

HERBERSTEIN, Sigmund
– Comentari Della Moscovia. Ill.:– Jacopo Gastaldo (folding map). Venice, 1550. 1st. Italian Edn. 4to. Dampstained in lr. margins, marginal repairs to 2 prelims. Cont. limp vell., soiled. (S. Dec.8; 122) *Hannas.* £270
– Rerum Moscouiticarum Commentarii. Basle, 1551. Fo. Folding map dtd. 1549, title slightly defect. & reprd. affecting text on verso, some ll. dampstained, wormholes in I1-2, slightly affecting text, owner's inscrs. & stp. on title-p. Cont. vell., gt. decor. on sides & spine, slightly soiled. (S. Jan.27; 578) *Anderson.* £220

HERBERT, Edward, Lord Herbert of Cherbury
– De Veritate prout distinguitur a revalatione, a verismili, a possibili, et a falso. [Paris], 1603. 1st. Edn. 4to. Sm. tear at head of K2. Cont. stained vell., gt. ornaments at corners. The Hely-Hutchinson copy. (SPB. Oct.1; 229) $3,500
– – Anr. Edn. 1633. 1st. Engl. Edn. 4to. Lacks first (?blank) lf. Mod. limp vell. [STC 13180] (S. Mar.16; 141) *Dawson.* £220
– The Life & Raigne of King Henry the Eighth. L., 1649. 1st. Edn. Fo. Title-p. slightly browned & remargined. Recent leath., old cf. laid down on covers. [Wing H1504] (CB. Feb.18; 190) *Can.* $280
– – Anr. Edn. 1672. Fo. Tooled mor., mor. onlays, by Rivière. [Wing H 1505B] (S. Nov.25; 464) *Ponder.* £110

HERBERT, George
– Oratio qua Auspicatissimum Serenissimi Principis Caroli Reditum ex Hispanis Celebrauit Georgius Herbert Academiae Cantabrigiensis Orator. 1623. 1st. Edn. Sm. 4to. Slight browning,

sm. scrape-mark on ornamental initial. Early 20th. C. lev. mor. Bkplt. of J.P.R. Lyell. [STC 13181] (S. Jun.29; 396) *Quaritch.* £380
– Works. L., 1853. Cf., gt. fillet & pointillé borders, spine gt. Fore-e. pntg. (SG. Mar.19; 138) $160

HERBERT, George (contributor)
*See–*CAMBRIDGE UNIVERSITY

HERBERT, Henry William 'Frank Forester'
– My Shooting Box. Ill.:– Robert Ball. 1941. (250) numbered. Gt. leatherette, unopened. (SG. Dec.11; 256) $190
– Trouting along the Catasauqua. Ed.:– Harry W. Smith. Ill.:– Gordon Ross (frontis.). 1927. (423) numbered. 4to. Linen-bkd. decor. bds., unc. & unopened, bkplt. (SG. Dec.11; 233) $180
– The Warwick Woodlands.–My Shooting Box. –The Quorndon Hounds.–The Deerstalkers. 1930. Hitchcock Edn., (750) numbered. 4 vols. Cl., bkplt., partly untrimmed. (SG. Dec.11; 255) $150

HERBERT, Thomas
– A Relation of Some Yeares Travaile . . . into Afrique & the Greater Asia . . . & some parts of the Orientall Indies. 1634. 1st. Edn. Sm. fo. Cont. cf., reprd. Bkplt. of Boies Penrose, lately in the collection of Eric Sexton. [STC 13190] (C. Apr.15; 35) *Hofmann & Freeman.* £220
– – Anr. Copy. Lacks ll. C4 & D1, some offsetting of text. Cont. cf., some wear. (TA. Jul.16; 342) £55
[–] – Anr. Edn. 1638. 2nd. Edn. Some 17th. C. sigs. on blank, slight dampstaining. Cont. cf., covers with gt. initials 'PT'. [STC 13191; Sabin 31471] (S. Sep.29; 44) *Quaritch.* £170
– – Anr. Edn. 1677. 4th. Imp. Fo. Cont. cf., upr. cover detchd. [Wing H1536] (CSK. May 1; 103) £110
– – Anr. Copy. 1 plt. torn, longitudinal hf.-title bnd. at end, lacks engraved title, cut in B3, some marginal tears & soiling. Worn. (S. May 5; 247) *McNulty.* £70

HERBERT, William
– Antiquities of the Inns of Court & Chancery. 1804. L.P. 4to. Smaller plt. inserted, occasional foxing, some offsetting. Cont. russ., rebkd. & reprd. (C. Nov.6; 314) *Taylor.* £55
*See–*AMES, Joseph & Herbert, William

HERBERT, Rev. William, 1778-1847
– Amaryllidaceae. L., 1837. Orig. cl., unc., rejointed. From collection of Massachusetts Horticultural Society, stps. on plts. (SPB. Oct.1; 124) $1,200

HERBST, J.F.W.
*See–*BOROWSKI, G.H. & Herbst, J.F.W.

HERCULANEUM
– Le Antiche di Ercolano Eposte (Le Pitture Antiche d'Ercolano). Naples, 1757-65. 1st. Edn. Vols. I-IV (of 9). Fo. Several ll. marginally stained, occasional offsetting & spotting. Cont. mott. cf., spines gt., some wear. Bkplt. of Earl Fitzwilliam. (S. May 5; 182) *Duran.* £180

HERDER, Johann Gottfried von
– Ideen zur Philosophie der Geschichte der Menschheit. Ritg & Leipzig, 1789-91. 1st. Edn. 4 vols. 4to. Soiled except vol. 3, all titles with 2 cont. MS. owner's marks. Cont. hf. leath. gt. (HK. May 15; 4465) DM 450
– Sämmtliche Werke. Ed.:– J.G. Müller & others. Stuttgart & Weimar, 1827-30 & 1829. 2nd. Coll. Edn. 60 vols. in 30. Lightly browned. Cont. paper bds. (H. Dec.9/10; 1536) DM 1,000
– Volkslieder. Leipzig, 1778-79. 1st. Edn. 2 vols. Slightly soiled in parts, title of I with old owner's mark, title II with pasted over hole. Cont. paper bds., slightly worn. (H. Dec.9/10; 1537) DM 1,200
[–] – Anr. copy. (HK. May 15; 4466) DM 900
– Von Deutscher Art und Kunst. Hamburg, 1773. Cont. style hf. leath. gt. (HK. May 15; 4469) DM 2,400

HERDERS THEOLOGISCHER KOMMENTAR ZUM NEUEN TESTAMENT
Ed.:– A. Wirkenhauser & A. Vögtle. Freiburg, 1953-76. 13 vols. 7 vols. linen. (B. Dec.10/11; 648) Fls. 550

HERDMAN, William Gawin
– Pictorial Relics of Ancient Liverpool. 1857. Fo. A few ll. slightly spotted, folding plts. torn & reprd., a few other minor defects. Cont. mor.,

HERDMAN, William Gawin – Pictorial Relics of Ancient Liverpool. *-contd.*
rebkd., hinges strengthened. (SBA. Mar.4; 175)
Chesters. £240
– – **Anr. Edn.** L'pool., 1878. 2 vols. Fo. Some spotting. Cont. hf. mor., soiled. (CSK. Jan.9; 199)
£55

HERDMAN, William Gawin & Picton, J.A.
– **Views in Modern Liverpool.** L'pool., 1864. Fo. Cont. mor., covers with gt. panel enclosing roll tool, gt. arms vig. on upr. cover, inner dentelles, rebkd., orig. spine preserved. (C. Jul.15; 46)
Weinreb. £600

HERE AFTER Folowith the Boke callyd the Myrroure of oure Lady
1530. Fo. Lr. & outer margins reprd. with sm. portion in pen facs., sm. tears & stains in A2-3 affecting text, lacks blank lf. 2G4. 19th. C. cf. Bkplt. of Daniel Canon Rock. [STC 17542] (C. Nov.20; 269)
Denham. £2,500

HERE, E.
– **Receuil des Plans, Elevations et Coupes . . . en Lorraine.** Ill.:– J.C. François. Paris, ca. 1760. 2 vols. bnd. in 1. Fo. Cont. marb. cf., blind fillet border, decor. spine raised bands. (HD. Apr.24; 70)
Frs. 12,500

HERESBACH, Conrad
– **Whole Art of Husbandry.** Ed.:– Gervase Markham. Trans.:– Barnaby Googe. L., 1631. 4to. 18th. C. cf., rebkd., orig. spine preserved. (SG. Sep.18; 242)
$310

HERIOT, George
– **Travels Through the Canadas.** L., 1807. 4to. Browning, foxing, some staining, margins torn, folds of a few plts. torn, textual repairs. Mod. cl. From liby. of William E. Wilson. (SPB. Apr.29; 138)
$700
– – **Anr. Copy.** Lacks plt. of the view of the City of Quebec, frontis. creased & linen-bkd., poor impression on plts. due to use of thin, hard paper. Recent mor. [Sabin 31489] (CB. Nov.12; 243)
Can. $950
– – **Anr. Copy.** Plts. cold., 2 folding plts. with 1 hf. lacking, rest reinforced & reprd., some marginal repairs to text, text dust-soiled, all plts. with liby. stp. in margin, affecting image. Mod. buckram. (CB. Dec.9; 195)
Can. $350

HERMANNIDES, Rutgerus
– **Britannia Magna.** Amst., 1661. 12mo. Engraved pict. title & ptd. title, 31 folding engraved plans, engraved title & 1st. 8 plans hand-cold., lacks final blank, engraved title defect. & mntd. Cont. cf., rebkd., old spine preserved, worn. W.a.f. (S. Mar.31; 324)
Franck. £220
– – **Anr. Edn.** Amst., [1661]. 1st. Edn. 12mo. Folding general map slightly wormed & with sm. tear reprd. prelims. marginally wormed. Vell., reprd. with sellotape. (S. Jan.27; 606)
Crowe. £160

HERMANS, Felicia
– **Poems.** 1862. Cont. mor., gt. Fore-e. pntg. (CSK. Oct.24; 73)
£60

HERMANT, Abel
– **Phili.** Ill.:– U. Brunellischi. 1921. (275) numbered. 4to. Mod. hf. mor. (SH. Nov.20; 244)
Francis Smith. £310

HERMANT, Godefroy–ALLEMAND, Comte
– **Histoire des Religions ou Ordres Militaires de l'Eglise et des Ordres de Chevalerie.–Précis Historique de l'Ordre Royal Hospitalier Militaire du St. Sépulcre de Jérusalem.** Rouen; Paris, 1698; 1815. 2 works in 1 vol. 1st. work: MS. supp. 'Ordre de la Mouche . . .' Later hf. cf., decor. spine. (HD. Jun.29; 104)
Frs. 1,420

HERMBSTADT, Sigismund Friedrich
– **Chemische Grundsatze der Kunst Branntwein zu brennen . . . nebst einer Anweisung zur Fabrikation der wichtigsten Liqueure . . . als Anhang die zweite verbesserte Auflage des Hern A.S. Duportal's Anleitung zur Kenntniss . . . der Brantweinbrennerei in Frankreich.** Berlin, 1817. Old bds. (S. Dec.1; 206)
Quaritch. £70

HERMES, Johann Timotheus
[–] **Sophiens Reise von Memel nach Sachsen.** Ill.:– after Chodowiecki by Geyser. Leipzig, 1778. 2nd. Edn. ill. Chodowiecki. 6 vols. Lightly browned in parts. Cont. paper bds. (H. Dec.9/10; 1539)
DM 420

HERMES Trismegistus
– **His Divine Pymander in Seventeen Books Together with his Second Book called Ascelpius.** 1657. 2nd. Edn. of 1st. Engl. translation. 2 pts. in 1 vol. 12mo. Advts., no blanks, closely cut at bottom just affecting some sigs., etc. Cf. [Wing H1566] (S. Dec.1; 205)
Quaritch. £500
– **Pimandras utraque Lingua Restitutus ed. D. Franciscus Flussatis Candalla. Aesculapius ad Ammonem Pregem Definitiones.** Bordeaux, 1574. 4to. Greek & Latin text, a few stains. Limp vell. (S. Dec.1; 204)
Poole. £110

HERNANDEZ, Francisco
– **Nova Plantarum, Animalium et Mineralium Mexicanorum Historia.** Rome, 1651. 2nd. Edn. Fo. Title dust-soiled, some margins slightly stained, some with minor tears. 19th. C. hf. mor. From Chetham's Liby., Manchester. (C. Nov.26; 200)
Wheldon & Wesley. £1,300

HERNANDEZ, Francisco–KLAPROTH, Martin H.–DREW, William
– **A Philosophical & Practical Essay on the Gold & Silver Mines of Mexico & Peru.–Observations relative to the Mineralogical & Chemical History of the Fossils of Cornwall.–The Art of Making Coloured Crystals to Imitate Precious Stones.** 1755; 1787; 1787. Together 3 works in 1 vol. Some spotting, last lf. torn. Cont. tree cf., lr. cover. detchd. (SH. Oct.10; 463)
Drury. £90

HERNANDEZ, Miguel
– **El Rayo que no cesa.** Madrid, 1936. 1st. Edn. 4to. Mor., orig. wraps. (DS. Apr.24; 987) Pts. 70,000
– **Seis Poemas Inéditos y Nuevo Más.** Alicante, 1951. 1st. Edn. Fo. Linen, chagrin, orig. wraps. (DS. Apr.24; 922) Pts. 22,000
– **Viento del Pueblo.** Valencia, 1937. 1st. Edn. 4to. Chagrin, orig. wraps. (DS. Apr.28; 980) Pts. 55,000

HERO OF ALEXANDRIA
– **Gli Artificiosi e Curiosi Moti Spirituali.** Trans.:– Giovanni Battista Aleotti. Bologna, 1647. 4to. Spotted. Cl. (S. Oct.21; 350)
Artico. £190
– **De gli Automati, overo Machine se moventi . . .** Trans.:– Bernardino Baldi. Venice, 1601. 4to. Slightly spotted. Mod. hf. mor. (S. Oct.21; 398)
Artico. £270
– **Spiritali.** Trans.:– A. Giorgi. Urbino, 1592. Sm. 4to. Owner's inscr. removed from title causing holing, sm. marginal repair. Mod. vell. bds. Bkplt. of E.N. da C. Andrade. (S. Jun.29; 335)
Rhys-Jones. £75

HERODIANUS
– **Historia de Imperio Post Marcum.** Bologna, Franciscus (Plato) de Benedictis, 31 Aug. 1493. 2nd. Edn. Fo. Mor. by Zaehnsdorf. [Hain 8467*; BMC VI p. 827; Goff H 86] (C. Apr.1; 43)
Fletcher. £380

HERODOTUS
– **Historiae.** Ed.:– Stephanus. [Geneva], 1566. Fo. Lacks plates, wormed. Cont. German cf. on wooden bds., arms of Bodewitz of Erfurt gt. on upr. cover., large. gt. medallion port. on lr. cover, new clasps & end-papers. (S. Nov.25; 385)
Goldschmidt. £280
– **Historiarum Lib. IX . . .** Ed.:– Henricus Stephanus. [Geneva], 1592. 2nd. Edn. Greek & Latin text, title torn & mntd., ptd. label on title 'Ex Bibliotheca Do. Gabrielis Lalemant . . .', inscr. in old hand. 17th. C. mott. cf. (S. Dec.8; 86)
Armstrong. £90
– **History.** Trans.:– George Rawlinson. L., 1875. 3rd. Edn. 4 vols. Crushed three-qtr. lev. by Root, bkplts. (SG. Feb.12; 209)
$110
– – **Anr. Edn.** Ed.:– A.W. Lawrence. Trans.:– G. Rawlinson. Ill.:– V. Le Campion. Nones. Pr., 1935. (675) numbered. 4to. Orig. vell.-bkd. cl. gt. (S. Jul.31; 117)
Maggs Brothers. £130
– – **Anr. Copy.** Fo. (SH. Feb.19; 134)
Quaritch. £65
– – **Anr. Copy.** Hf. vell. gt., partly untrimmed. (SG. Jan.15; 61)
$180
– **Libri Novem Quibus Musarum Indita sunt Nomina.** Venice, Sep., 1502. 1st. Edn. in Greek. Fo. Spaces for initials with guide letters, 1st. 3 ll. reprd. at inner margin, some slight staining. 18th. C. mott. cf., covers worn, rebkd., qtr. mor. gt. s.-c. Bkplts. of the Liechtenstein Liby., Giorgio Uzielli & John A. Saks. (CNY. Oct.1; 126)
$2,400
– – **Anr. Copy.** 18th. C. panel. cf., spine gt. (SG. May 14; 99)
$1,300

HEROINES of Shakespeare, The
Ed.:– Charles Heath. 1848. 2 plts. detchd. Cont. mor., gt. (CSK. Aug.1; 138)
£110

HEROLD, A. Ferdinand
– **La Guirlande d'Aphrodite.** Ill.:– Gasperini after P. Regnard. Paris, 1919. (50) on Japon, with state on Camaïeu. Sm. 4to. Mor., gt., by Kieffer, orig. wraps. in, s.-c. (SM. Oct.8; 2342) Frs. 1,200
– **Nala et Damayanti.** Ill.:– P. Zencker. Paris, 1927. (150), (30) on Jap. with 1 cold suite & 1 orig. aqua. Sm. 4to. Mor., gt. fillet frame, decor. spine raised bands, mor. doubl., mosaic motifs, orange mor. in angles, gt. fillets, watered silk end-ll., wrap & spine preserved, s.-c., by Affolter. (HD. Apr.24; 144) Frs. 2,400

HEROLT, Johannes
– **Sermones de Tempore et Sanctis.** Strassburg, 1495. Fo. Title with old notes & soiled, in parts, some browning, lacks last lf. 410, 2 ll. torn at foot. MS. vell., worn. (HK. Nov.18-21; 206)
DM 1,000

HERON, Robert
– **Elements of Chemistry Comprehending all the most Important Facts & Principles in the Works of Fourcroy & Chaptal.** 1800. Tree cf., worn, rebkd. (S. Dec.1; 207)
Barnet. £70
– **New General History of Scotland** Perth, 1794. 6 vols. Cont. cf. (CE. Jun.4; 133)
£70

HERON de Villefosse
– **L'Epopée Bohemienne.** Ill.:– Modigliani (port.); plts. after Kisling. Paris, Priv. ptd., 1959. (230); on Arches vell. Lge. 4to. In sheets, publisher's s.-c. (HD. Dec.5; 104)
Frs. 1,100

HERONDAS
– **The Miniambs.** Trans.:– Jack Lindsay. Ill.:– Alan Odle. Fanfrolico Pr., [1926]. (375). 4to. Orig. cl.-bkd. bds., s.-c. (SH. Feb.20; 368)
Ambra. £50
– – **Anr. Copy.** Buckram-bkd. patterned bds. (SG. Jan.15; 28)
$120

HERRERA, Antonio de
– **Descripcion de las Indias Ocidentales.** Madrid, 1725. Fo. Last folding engraved map defect. 19th. C. bds., spine defect. [Sabin 31541] (SPB. May 5; 254)
$450
– **Descripcion de las Islas, y Tierra Firme del Mar Oceano, que llaman Indias Ocidentales.** Antw., 1728. 4 vols. Fo. 1 folding engraved map with sm. stains. Later vell. [Sabin 32545] (SPB. May 5; 255)
$950
– **Histoire Générale des Voyages et Conquestes . . . Second Decade.** Paris, 1660. 4to. Some spotting. Cont. limp vell. (SPB. May 5; 252)
$250
– **Histoire Générale des Voyages et Conquestes . . . [Troisième Decade].** Paris, 1671. 4to. Title spotted. Cont. cf., worn. (SPB. May 5; 253)
$250
– **Historia General de las Indias Occidentales.** Antw., 1728. 4 vols. Fo. Maps rather browned, marginal worming at end of vol. I. 19th. C. hf. mor. From Chetham's Liby., Manchester. (C. Nov.26; 201)
Allen. £480
– **Historia General de los Hechos de los Castellanos en las Islas y Tierra Firme del Mar Oceano . . .** Madrid, 1726-36. 9 pts. in 4 vols. Fo. 3 ll. defect. & partially restored in facs. Mod. buckram, mor. spines. (BS. Jun.11; 161) £280
– **Novus Orbis, sive Descriptio Indiae Occidentalis.** Trans.:– C. Barlaeus. Amst., 1622. 1st. Edn. in Latin. Fo. 19th. C. hf. mor. From Chetham's Liby., Manchester. [Sabin 31540] (C. Nov.26; 202)
Arader. £750
See–**BRY, Theodore de & others**

HERRICK, Robert
– **Hesperides.** Boston, 1856. 2 vols. 12mo. Three-qtr. cf., spines gt. Double fore-e. pntg. in each vol. (SG. Mar.19; 139)
$850
– **Poems Chosen out of the Works.** Ed.:– F.S. Ellis. Hammersmith, Kelms. Pr., 1895. (250). Orig. limp vell., silk ties, unc. (CNY. May 22; 325)
$420
– **Poetical Works.** Ed.:– Humbert Wolfe. Ill.:– Albert Rutherston. Cresset Pr., 1928. (750) numbered. Orig. parch. (SH. Mar.27; 478)
D. White. £65
– **The Works.** Edinb., 1823. (25) L.P. 2 vols. 4to. Cont. hf. mor., gt. arms of Haystoune family on covers. (S. Dec.8; 37)
Chelsea. £50

HERRING, Richard
– **Paper & Paper Making, Ancient & Modern.** 1855. 1st. Edn. Advts. Orig. cl. (S. Dec.1; 208)
Bickersteth. £110

HERSCHEL, Sir John F.W.
- A General Catalog of Nebulae & Clusters of Stars. 1864. Offprint from the Philosophical Transactions, pt. 1. 4to. A few ll. loose. Orig. bds., worn. Orig. A.L.s. by author loosely inserted. (S. Dec.2; 725) *Dix.* £90
- Results of Astronomical Observations made During the Years 1834, 5, 6, 7, 8, at the Cape of Good Hope. 1847. 1st. Edn. 4to. Plts., spotted, advt. lf., cold. map of Africa inserted. Orig. embossed cl., worn. Special dedication lf. inserted at beginning reading 'Presented by Algernon Duke of Northumberland to (in print) Wm. Lassell Esq. by the hands & with best regards of The Author (in MS.), on verso tipped in orig. A.L. by author. (S. Dec.2; 724) *Quaritch.* £250

HERSCHEL, Sir W., Sir J.E.W., & Caroline
- A Collection of 25 Papers from the Philosophical Transactions of the Royal Society of London. 1787-1824. 4to. Slight browning. Disbnd. As a collection, w.a.f. (S. Apr.6; 219) *Kisser.* £220

HERTZ, Heinrich
- Untersuchungen ueber die Ausbreitung der Elektrischen Kraft. Leipzig, 1892. 1st. Edn. Orig. ptd. wraps., worn, spine defect., unc., fore-edges slightly defect. Stps. of Samuel Jacobsohn; from Honeyman Collection. (S. May 20; 3261) *Gurney.* £150
- - Anr. Copy. Title & 5 text ll. stpd. Cont. hf. leath. (D. Dec. 11-13; 164) DM 1,500
- - Anr. Copy. Title stpd. Slightly worn. (HK. May 12-14; 297) DM 900
- - Anr. Copy. Orig. linen, unc., ex-lib. (HK. Nov.18-21; 568) DM 850

HERVAS Y PANDURO, Lorenzo
- Catalogo de las Lenguas de las Naciones Conocidas, y Numeracion, Division y Clases de Estas segun la Diversidad de sus Idiomas y Dialectos. Madrid, 1800-05. 6 vols. Sm. 4to. Cont. blind-stpd. cf. (SPB. May 5; 256) $600

HERVEY, Alpheus B.
- Flowers of the Field & Forest. Ill.:– after Isaac Sprague. Boston, 1882. 1st. Edn. 4to. Title-p. loose. Gt.-floral cl. (PNY. Oct.1; 225) $140

HERVEY, Mrs. Elizabeth
- [-] The Moutray Family. 1800. 1st. Edn. 4 vols. Orig. bds. (CSK. Sep.5; 178) £180

HERVEY, John
- Lady Suffolk Ed.:– Harry T. Peters. [1936]. (500) numbered. 2-tone bds., partly unopened. (SG. Dec.11; 257) $110

HERVEY, John & others
- Racing at Home & Abroad. Racing & Breeding in America & the Colonies. L., 1931. Ltd. Edn. 4to. Mor. gt., partly unc., spine slightly faded. (CNY. Oct.1; 113) $200

HERVIEU, Paul
- Flirt. Ill.:– Madeleine Lemaire (compositions). 1890. (150); (100) on Jap., numbered. Lge. 4to. 3 states of plts. (1 in cameo on Whatman paper & 1 in sepia on Jap.), name of collector gummed. Mosaic mor. by Meunier, spine & covers richly decor., wrap. preserved. (SM. Feb.11; 161) Frs. 18,000

HERZBERG, F.
- [-] Leben und Meynungen des Till Eulenspiegel. [Breslau], 1779. 1st. Edn. 2 vols. Lightly browned in parts. Cont. hf. leath. gt., decor., spines slightly wormed. (HK. May 15; 4198) DM 1,900
- [-] - Anr. Copy. 2 vols. in 1. Slightly browned in parts. Worn. (H. Dec.9/10; 1469) DM 820

HERZL, Th.
- Der Judenstaat. Leipzig & Vienna, 1896. 1st. Edn. Lacks last blank lf., upr. end-paper slightly soiled. Bds., orig. upr. wrap. bnd. in. (HK. May 12-14; 1123) DM 2,200

HERZOG-HAUCK
- Realencyklopädie für Protestanische Theologie und Kirche. Leipzig, 1896-1913. 24 pts. in 12 vols. Hf. mor. (B. Dec.10/11; 1357) Fls. 650

HESIOD
- Opera et dies. Theogonia. Scutum Herculis. Venice, Jun. 1537. Sm. 4to. A few later MS. notes, slight dampstaining, tear in 1 lf. 19th. C. mor. by Hall, Oxford, gt. From liby. of André L. Simon. (S. May 18; 115) *Maggs.* £70

HESIUS, Guillaume
- Antverpiensis, e Societate Jesu. Emblemata Sacra de Fide, Spe, Charitate. Antw., 1636. 12mo. Hf. cf., decor. spine. (LM. Mar.21; 99) B.Frs. 16,000
- Emblemata Sacra de Fide, Spe Charitate. Ill.:– J.C. Jegher after E. Quellinus. Antw., 1636. 1st. Edn. Old perforated liby. stp. on title verso. 19th. C. hf. leath., spine defect. (R. Oct.14-18; 878) DM 460

HESKYNS, Thomas
- The Parliament of Chryste ... Antw., 1566. 1st. Edn. Fo. 17th. C. cf., rebkd. [STC 13842] (S. Mar.16; 122) *Cresswell.* £80

HESPERIAN, The, or, Western Monthly Magazine.
Ed.:– William D. Gallagher & Otway Curry. Columbus & Cinc., 1838-39. 3 vols. Slight foxing. Cont. cf.-bkd. bds., worn, covers loose, end-papers foxed. From liby. of William E. Wilson. [Sabin 31615]. (SPB. Apr.29; 112) $300

HESRONITA, Johannes
See–SIONITA, Gabriele & Hesronita, Johannes

HESS, J.L.
- [-] Hamburg Topographisch, Politisch, Historisch. Hamburg, 1787. Title with bkd. tear. Cont. bds. (R. Mar.31-Apr.4; 2100) DM 450

HESSE, Hermann
- Gesammelte Dichtungen. Berlin & Frankfurt, 1952-57. 1st. Coll. Edn. 7 vols. Orig. linen. (H. Dec.9/10; 2108) DM 420
- Unterwegs. Gedichte. Munich, 1911. 1st. Edn., (500) numbered. Erased entry on frontis. verso, slightly soiled in parts. Orig. hf.-leath., slightly soiled. (HK. Nov.18-21; 2628) DM 620

HESSELIUS, P.
- Hertzfliessende Betrachtungen von dem Elbe-strom. Altona, 1675. Pt. I (all publd.). Sm. 4to. Some ll. torn, loose or soiled. Cont. vell., worn. (SH. Jun.25; 35) *Heald.* £400

HESSEN, H.
- Neue Garten-Lust. Leipzig, 1705-06. 2 pts. in 1 vol. 4to. Cont. vell. (D. Dec.11-13; 136) DM 1,700

HESYCHIUS
- Dictionarium. Venice, Aug., 1514. 1st. Edn. Fo. Spaces for capital initials with guide letters, some dampstaining & slight worming. Old red hf. mor., worn. Bkplt. of the General Theological Seminary Liby. (CNY. Oct.1; 74) $600

HETHERINGTON, Arthur Lonsdale
- The Early Ceramic Wares of China. 1922. Ltd. Edn. sigd. by author. 4to. Orig. pig. (SH. Jan.29; 180) *Ars Artis.* £60
- - Anr. Copy. 4to. Buckram, stained, ex-liby. (SG. Dec.4; 76) $150
- - Anr. Copy. (50) numbered, sigd. by author. 4to. Pig, gt. decor., unc. (JL. Mar.2; 726) Aus. $200
See–HOBSON, Robert Lockhart & Hetherington, Arthur Lonsdale

HETLEY, Mrs. Charles
- The Native Flowers of New Zealand. 1887-88. 3 orig. pts. Fo. Loose in orig. bds., worn. (TA. Jun.18; 119) £50

HEUCHLER, E.
- Glück Auf. Freiberg, [1852]. Ob. fo. Borders slightly soiled, title with pasted over stp. Cont. linen, gold-stpd. (HK. Nov.18-21; 397) DM 2,100

HEUDE, William
- Voyage up the Persian Gulf. 1819. 4to. 4 plts. Cf. Westport House bkplt. (P. Jul.2; 172) *Timmons.* £560

HEURCK, Emile H. van & Boekenoogen, G.J.
- Histoire de l'Imagerie Populaire Flamande. Brussels, 1910. (520). 4to. Hf. mor. (S. Jul.27; 165) *De Jonge.* £80

HEURES de Paphos
- Contes Moraux par un Sacrifateur de Venus. [Paris], 1787. Mor., gt., by Pagnant, s.-c. (SM. Oct.8; 2343) Frs. 12,000

HEUSER, E.
- Porzellan von Strassburg u. Frankenthal im 18 Jhott. Neustadt a.d. Haardt, 1922. Lge. 4to. Orig. hf. linen. (HK. May 12-14; 2382) DM 800

HEUSINGER v. WALDEGG, E.
- Die Schmiervorrichtungen und Schmiermittel der Eisenbahnwagen. Wiesbaden, 1864. 1st. Edn. 4to. Stp. on title, slightly soiled. Cont. hf. linen. (R. Oct.14-18; 251) DM 750

HEVELIUS, Joachim
- Epistolae II.–Dissertatio de Nativa Saturni Facie. Ed.:– Johannes Baptistus Ricciolus & Petrus Nucerius. Danzig, 1654; 1656. 1st. Edns. 2 works in 1 vol. Fo. 3 (of 4) copperplts., 2 plts. cut slightly short, dbl. lf. loose. Cont. leath., very worn. (HK. Nov. 18-21; 569) DM 2,400

HEVIA BOLANOS, Juan de
- Cura Philipica . . . donde se trata de la Mercania, y Contratacion de Tierra, y Mar. Madrid, 1783. Fo. Last gathering loose, light stain, slight marginal worming. Limp vell., soiled, covers detchd. (SPB. May 5; 258) $150
- Labyrintho de Comercio Terrestre y Naval. Lima, 1617. Sm. 4to. Stained at beginning & end. Cont. vell., shrunk & detchd. (SPB. May 5; 257) $2,500

HEWETSON, J.
- Architectural & Picturesque Views of Noble Mansions in Hampshire. N.d. Fo. 24 plts. only, with dampstaining affecting lower left corner. Later portfo., 1 set of orig. wraps. preserved. W.a.f. (CSK. Oct.17; 107) £130

HEWETT, Daniel
- The American Traveller, or National Directory, Containing an Account of all the Great Post Roads, & most Important Cross Roads, in the United States ... Wash., 1825. 1st. Edn. 12mo. With the extra 24 pp. between 372 & 373. Hf. linen, ex-liby. (SG. Mar.5; 227) $150

HEWITSON, William Chapman
- British Oology. Newcastle, [1831-38]. 3 vols. Plts. 84 & 85 misnumbered, but bnd. correctly, minor foxing. Cont. str.-grd. mor. (SG. Jan.29; 213) $275
- Coloured Illustrations of the Eggs of British Birds. 1846. 2 vols. Mod. rexine covers. (P. Mar.12; 284) *Cambridge.* £110
- - Anr. Copy. 19th. C. cf. gt., raised bands on spine. (LC. Feb.12; 136) £55
- - Anr. Edn. 1856. 2 vols. Mod. cl. (P. Mar.12; 285) *Cambridge.* £110

HEWITT, Graily
- Lettering. 1930. (390) numbered., sigd. 4to. Orig. cl., unc. (SH. Mar.26; 275) *Henderson.* £55
- The Pen & Type Design. 1928. (250). Cont. red mor., covers with line borders enclosing lge. gt. V design of graded rules upon a base of rules, partly unc. (C. Jul.22; 120) *Cobley.* £60

HEWITT, N.R.
See–WYLD, James & Hewitt, N.R.

HEWLETT, Maurice
- Madonna of the Peach-Tree. 1929. (120). Orig. decor. cl., cl. s.-c. This copy ptd. for George & Pearl Adam. (SH. Feb.20; 221) *Lyon.* £380
- Works. N.Y., 1905. De Luxe Edn., (500). 10 vols. Hf. mor. gt., gt. floral inlays on spine. (SPB. May 6; 319) $850

HEWSON, William
- Experimental Inquiries; part the first containing an Inquiry into the Properties of the Blood ... –Part the Second containing a Description of the Lymphatic System in the Human Subject & in Other Animals.–Part the Third containing the Description of the Red Particles of the Blood ... Ed.:– Magnus Falconar. 1780; 1774; 1777. 1st. work 3rd. Edn., rest 1st. Edns. 3 works in 1 vol. Strip cut from upr. blank margin of 1st. title removing name, 1st. work lacks hf.-title, 3rd. work with 16pp. advts. of J. Callow. Cont. bds., unc. (S. Jun.16; 415) *Phillips.* £600
- An Experimental Inquiry into the Properties of the Blood. 1771. 1st. Edn. Tear in 1st. lf. of text reprd., very sm. tear in K2 affecting letters, sm. strip cut from blank margin of hf.-title. Cont. cf. (S. Dec.2; 824) *Rota.* £150

HEY, Mrs. Rebecca
- [-] The Moral of Flowers. 1835. 2nd. Edn. Slight spotting. Orig. hf. roan, spine gt. (S. Jun.1; 267) *Head.* £70
- [-] - Anr. Edn. 1836. 3rd. Edn. Cont. hf. mor. (CSK. Nov.7; 10) £90
- Spirit of the Woods. 1837. Hf. mor. (P. Jan.22; 251) *Nagel.* £65

HEY, Mrs. Rebecca -contd.
[-] – **Anr. Edn.** 1841. 2nd. Edn. Owner's. inscr. on hf.-title. Orig. cl., spine slightly faded & torn. (SBA. Oct.21; 149) *Hyde Park Bookshop.* £65
– – **Anr. Edn.** 1849. New Edn. Cont. cf., gt. (CSK. Jul.10; 130) £75

HEY, William
– **Practical Observations in Surgery.** 1803. 1st. Edn. New hf. cf. (S. Dec.2; 825) *Rota.* £90

HEYDEN, L. von
See–SAALMULLER, Max & Heyden, L. von.

HEYDT, Johann Wolfgang
– **Allerneuester Geog.-u. Topogr. Schau-Platz, von Africa u. Ost.-Indien** ... Wilhelmsdorf, 1744. Ob. fo. 1 (of 2) engraved titles, 256 (of 345) pp., 86 (of 115) copperplts., 2 cold., title mntd., tears, slightly soiled & browned in parts. Hf. linen, ca. 1880, (HK. May 12-14; 651) DM 1,300

HEYLL, Christophorus
See–SCHONER, Johann–HEYLL, Christophorus –FUCHS, Leonhard–RICIUS, Pauls

HEYLSAME HAUSS-APOTHECKEN
Innsbruck, 1714. 4to. Cont. bds., spine defect. (R. Mar.31-Apr.4; 994) DM 500

HEYLYN, Peter
– **Cosmographie in four Books containing the Chorography & history of the whole world.** 1657. 2nd. Edn. Fo. 3 (of 4) maps only slight staining. Later hf. cf. W.a.f. [Wing H1690] (CSK. May 8; 27) £170
– – **Anr. Edn.** 1670. Fo. 4 folding engraved maps, 1 torn & reprd., 1 with short tears, few fust-holes. Cont. mott. cf., rebkd. at early date, old spine preserved. (S. Mar.31; 477) *Burgess.* £280

HEYSEN, Hans
– **The Art of Hans Heysen.** Sydney, 1920. (1,700). Orig. bdg., d.-w., end-pp. slightly foxed. (JL. Mar.2; 723) Aus. $160
– – **Anr. Copy.** 4to. Some foxing. No bdg. stated. (JL. Jul.20; 648) Aus. $140

HEYWOOD, John
– **The Spider & the Flie.** 1556. 1st. Edn. Sm. 4to. Title in facs., C4 with port. inlaid & slightly defect., first gatherings detchd. Mor. gt. by Rivière. [STC 13308] (S. Nov.25; 445) *Thomas.* £130

HEYWOOD, Thomas
[-] **A Chronographical History of all the Kings** ... with the Life & Predictions of Merlin. 1641. 4to. Engraved port., preserved, a few holes with loss of some letters. Old spr. cf., new end-papers. (CSK. Nov.14; 11) £50
– **Gunaikeion.** L., 1624. 1st. Edn. Sm. fo. Lacks frontis. port.(?), damp-soiling at upr. corner of most ll. Cont. blind-stpd. cf., worn, rebkd. in gt. Sigs. of William Herbert & George Burton, bkplts. of Bertram Lloyd & Mr. Kortlucke. [STC 13326] (PNY. May 21; 216) $300
– – **Anr. Copy.** Engraved title severely browned, lacks 1st. & last blanks as usual, browning, staining & minor tears. Later hf. cf., chipped, jnts. & corners worn. (SPB. Jul.28; 175) $175

HIBBEN, T.H., & Co.
– **Views of Victoria.** Victoria, ca. 1922-24. Ob. 4to. Orig. wraps. (CB. Feb.18; 255) Can. $150

HIBBERD, Shirley
– **New & Rare Beautiful-Leaved Plants.** 1870. 2nd. Edn. A few spots & stains, a few ll. & plts. loose. Orig. cl. (S. Jan.26; 285) *Durell.* £90
– – **Anr. Copy.** 4to. Orig. cl., gt. decor. spine, slightly worn. (TA. May 21; 248) £52
– – **Anr. Copy.** Hf. mor. gt. (CNY. May 22; 201) $150

See–HULME, F. Edward & Hibberd, Shirley

HIBERNIA, Thomas de–AEGIDIUS, Columna Romanus
– **Manipulus Florum, seu Sententiae Patrum. –Quodlibeta.** Ed.:– [Simon de Ungaria] (2nd. work). Piacenza; Bologna, Jacobus de Tyela; Dominicus de Lapis, 5 Sep. 1483; 22 May 1481. 1st. Edns. 2 works in 1 vol. Fo. Both works with spaces for initial capitals (1st. work with guide letters), dampstaining, mostly marginal but affecting some text, lr. outer corner of 1st. 2 ll. renewed, light worming at end. Cont. blind-stpd. qtr. cf. & wood bds., leath. sides with imps. of a rectangular lattice tool, spine compartments with intersecting fillets & scattered sm. crosses, brass clasps & catches, early hand-painted bkplt. Bkplt.

of Thomas Philip, Earl de Grey, Ruddoff inscr. at fly-lf., lately in the collection of Eric Sexton. [BMC VII, 1072 & VI, 814, Goff H149 & A85] (CNY. Apr.8; 136) $3,200

HIC-ET-HEC, ou l'Elève des P.R.P.P. Jésuites d'Avignon
Berlin, 1798. 2 vols. Sm. 12mo. Mod. hf. lavallière mor., corners, unc. (HD. Apr.10; 339) Frs. 2,300

HICKERINGILL, Edmund
– **Jamaica Viewed** ... 1661. 2nd. Edn. Lacks map. Cont. sheep. [Wing H1817] (S. Mar.17; 385) *Traylen.* £65

HICKOK, Lorena A.
See–ROOSEVELT, Eleanor & Hickok, Lorena A.

HIEROGLYPHIC PICTURES. An Aboriginal Romance
[U.S.A.], ca. 1910. Ob. 8vo. Some words replaced by sm. cold. ills., ptd. on 7 pieces of buffalo (?) hide in 'Red Indian' style. Wraps. with title & 2 further ills. Probably produced by hand, & may be the only copy made. (SH. Mar.19; 124) *Temperley.* £70

HIERONYMO DA FERRARA, Frate
– **Epistola de Contemptu Mundi.** Ed.:– Charles Fairfax Murray. Ill.:– W.H. Hooper. Kelms. Pr., 1894. (150). Orig. holland-bkd. bds., unc. (SH. Feb.19; 8) *Fletcher.* £200

HIERONYMUS, St. Eustebius.
– **De Essencia Diuinitatis.** [Augsburg], [Günther Zainer], before 5 June 1473. Fo. Initials & paragraph marks supplied in red, some staining & worming. Mod. cf. [H. 8589] (S. Nov.25; 331) *Hargreaves.* £240
– **Epistolae.** [Strassburg], [Johann Mentelin], [not after 1469]. Fo. Rubricated thro.-out, very minor worming in blank margins, a few slight stains. Cont. vell.-bkd. wooden bds., clasps (upr. pt. of 1 lacking). [H. 8549*; BMC I p.53; Goff H162] (C. Apr.1; 44) *Pierman.* £2,400
– – **Anr. Edn.** Venice, B. Benalius, 14 Jul. 1490. 2 pts. in 1 vol. Fo. Lacks 1st. blank lf., many margins wormed. Cf., bosses & clasps. [BMCV, 372, Goff H172, HC8560*] (CR. Jun.11; 501) Lire 1,000,000
– – **Anr. Edn.** Ill.:– A. Dürer. Basel, 8 Aug. 1492. 1st. Edn. 2 pts. in 1 vol. Fo. Lacks last blank lf., woodcuts slightly soiled, 3 sm. wormholes, 2 in margin, verso with sm. stp. lf. a, 2 with sm. oval engraved vig. 1681 pasted on lr. margin, last text lf. in 1 mispaginated, some sm. margin tears, 1 fault, several ll. cut short at upr. margin affecting fo. lacks 2, 1 decor. initial, some soiling. Old pig-bkd. wd. bds., blind-tooled arms, metal clasps, very worn. [H. 8561; Goff H173; BMC III, 722] (H. May 21/22; 924) DM 8,200
– – **Anr. Edn.** Venice, Johannes Rubeus Vercellensis, 7 Jan. & 12 Jul. 1496. Fo. 380 ll. (of 398, lacks ff. q8, N3 & 6 Y8, facs. for the latter 10 loosely inserted), some marginalia, title & a few ll. soiled, sm. holes in last 2 ll. slightly affecting text, in last lf. reprd., a few marginal tears. Old vell. bds., spine slightly worn. W.a.f. [BMC V, 419; HC 8563*; Goff H175] (S. Apr.7; 293) *Hendrickx.* £140
– **Solitudo sive vitae Partum Eremicolarum.** Ill.:– Johann & Raphael Sadelev after Martin de Vos & others. N.p., ca. 1621. 5 pts. in 1 vol. Ob. 4to. Title detchd., a few plts. soiled & torn. 18th. C. hf. cf., worn, upr. cover detchd. W.a.f. (S. Jan.27; 397) *De Jonghe.* £260
– **Vitae Sanctorum Patrum.** Nuremb., 7 May 1478. 3rd. Incunable Edn. Fo. Rubric thro.-out, 1 lge. red & blue initial on folio, many sm. initials, 1st. ll. slightly stained & wormed, lacks blank ll. 1, 7 & 246 & lf. 16. Cont. blind-tooled pig-bkd. wood bds., lacks clasps. [BMC II, 416] (R. Mar.31-Apr.4; 58) DM 2,500

HIERONYMUS HANGESTUS
– **Propugnaculum ad Illustrissimi adversus Antimarianos.–De Lebero Arbitrio in Lutherum. –De Possibili Praeceptorum Divinorum Impletione in Lutherum.** Paris, 1515; 1528. Mod. blind decor. cf. (LM. Mar.21; 285) B.Frs. 7,500

HIERONYMUS, Saint Jerome
– **Vita Epistole de Sancto Hieronymo Ulgare.** Ferrara, Laurentius de Rubeis, de Valentia, 12 Oct. 1497. 1st. Edn. in Italian. Fo. Some dampstaining, principally to inner & lr. blank margins but just affecting the ptd. surface of the 1st. 16 & some other ll., 1st. gathering a trifle wormed, some ll. darkened. Old. vell., qtr. red

mor. gt. s.-c. Note on fly-lf. of Count Giulo B. Tomitano, note of R.C. Fisher on front paste-down, later the copy of C.W. Dyson Perrins & John A. Saks. [BMC VI, 614, Goff H178, HC 8566] (CNY. Oct.1; 87) $12,500

HIERONYMUS PADUANUS–BEROALDUS, Philippus Bononiensis–ANSONIUS MATUTINA –AENIUS SILVIUS–LACTANTIUS, Lucius Caelius Firmianus
– **De Christi Passione.–Veterum de Gantiarum Utiliorumque Doctrinarum ...–Precatio de Nota ad Deum; Egloga Aurea de Ambignitato Vite Digende.–De Passioni Christi Endecasyllabum–De Dominicae Resurrectionis Die ... De Morte** ... Vienna, 1515. 4to. MS. commentary in margins. Blank wraps. (LM. Mar.21; 286) B.Frs. 10,000

HIGDEN, Ranulphus
– **Polycronicon.** William Caxton, after Jul. 1482. 1 lf. (P. Nov.13; 65) *Arnold.* £150
– – **Anr. Copy.** 1 lf. only, rubricated, wide margins. (P. Sep.11; 79) £130
– – **Anr. Copy.** Fo. 1 lf. only, rubricated, laid in a copy of George Parker Winship's 'William Caxton & the First English Press' (N.Y., 1938. Blind-stpd. mor., s.-c.). The copy of John A. Saks. (CNY. Oct.1; 136) $900
– – **Anr. Edn.** Southwark, 1527. 3rd. Edn. Fo. Lacks all before a1, X2 & X8, P4 & 5, U8 & X1 from anr. copy (or copies), the former 2 remargined with slight loss of side-notes, the other 2 with reprd. tears, worming thro.-out slightly affecting text, faked colophon inked onto foot of last p. Mod. leath., s.-c. [STC 13440] (S. Jul.27; 56) *Rix.* £130

HIGGINS, Bryan
– **Experiments & Observations Relating to Acetous Acid, Fixable Air, Dense Inflammable Air, Oils & Fuel, the Matter of Fire & Light ... & other subjects of Chemical Philosophy.** 1786. 1st. Edn. Lacks lf. before title (blank or hf.-title?), title written on. Cf., rebkd. (S. Dec.1; 209) *Quaritch.* £100

HIGGINS, John
[-] **The Mirour for Magistrates.** 1587. 1st. Coll. Edn. Sm. 4to. Lr. fore-corner torn away & crudely reprd. with slight loss of border, lacks the 1st. blank & 1 lf. of epistle, some staining. 18th. C. cf., rebkd. [STC 13445] (S. Jun.23; 366) *Claridge.* £200

HIGGINS, William
– **Experiments & Observations on the Atomic Theory & Electrical Phenomena.** 1814. 1st. Edn. Hf. mor. (S. Dec.1; 210) *Quaritch.* £90

HIGGINSON, A. Henry
– **British & American Sporting Authors.** Ed.:– Sydney R. Smith. Berryville, Virginia, 1949. 4to. Photograph (of Smith?) on front free end-paper. Orig. cl., spine slightly marked. Sigd. by Smith, bkplt. of Geoffrey Sparrow. (SKC. Jul.28; 2458) £95

HILARIUS, Episcopus Pict.
– **De Trinitate Contra Arianos; Augustinus: Liber de Trinitate.** Ed.:– G. Cribellus. Milan, Leonardus Pachel, 9 Jul. & 26 May 1480. 1st. Edn. 2 works iss. together. Fo. Lacks final blank lf., capital spaces with guide letters only, inner blank margins reprd. & cut close thro.-out, with loss of occasional letters. 18th. C. hf. cf. gt. [H. 8666; BMC VI 777; Goff H 269] (C. Apr.1; 45) *Corby.* £240

HILARIUS, Saint–BOETHIUS, Anicius Manilius Torquatus Severinus
– **De Trinitate Contra Arianos.–De Trinitate.** [Venice], [Paganinus de Paganinis], ca. 1489. 2 works in 1 vol. 4to. 17th. C. limp vell., spine partly defect. [Goff B830] (C. Jul.16; 270) *Taylor.* £80

HILDRETH, James
– **Dragoon Campaigns to the Rocky Mountains** ... N.Y., 1836. 1st. Edn. Minor foxing. Orig. gt.-pict. cl. [Sabin 31769] (PNY. Mar.26; 144) $190

HILDRETH, Samuel P.
– **Pioneer History ... First Examinations of the Ohio Valley & the Early Settlement of the Northwest Territory** ... Cinc., 1848. 1st. Edn. Sig. of J.B. Livingston on front end-paper & title, slight foxing. Orig. cl., blind-stpd. panels & spine, chipped at top of spine. From liby. of William E. Wilson; the Littell copy. (SPB. Apr.29; 139) $225

HILL, Aaron
- Account of the Present State of the Ottoman Empire. 1709. 1st. Edn. Fo. Foxed. Hf. cf., covers detchd. & worn. (CE. Jun.4; 30)   £140

HILL, Allan Massie
- Some Chapters on the History of Digby County. Halifax, 1901. Recent buckram. (CB. Dec.9; 197)   Can. $120

HILL, David Octavius & Buchanan, George
- Views of the Opening of the Glasgow & Garnkirk Railway ... Edinb., 1832. Lge. ob. fo. Engr. on title verso, 4 full-p. litho. plts., 7 ills. on india paper, some ll. reprd. Stitched as issued in orig. wraps., mod. buckram box. John Phillimore label in upr. wrap. (C. Jul.15; 47)   Quaritch. £1,800

HILL, George Francis
- A Corpus of Italian Medals of the Renaissance before Cellini. 1930. 2 vols. Fo. Orig. cl. (SH. Oct.9; 171)   Drury. £1,200

HILL, George Francis & Pollard, G.
- Renaissance Medals from the Samuel H. Kress Collection.-Catalogue des Monnaies Royales et Seigneuriales de France. Paris (2nd. work), 1967; 1900. 2 vols. 4to. & 8vo. Orig. cl.; orig. wraps, spine torn. (SH. Mar.6; 374)   Münzen & Medaillen. £60

HILL, George Nesse
- An Essay on the Prevention & Cure of Insanity with Observations on the Rules for the Detection of Pretenders to Madness. 1814. 1st. Edn. Slight browning at end. Hf. cf. (S. Jun.16; 417)   Jenner Books. £120

HILL, Sir John, M.D.
- Book of Nature or History of Insects. 1758. Fo. Cf. (DWB. May 15; 305)   £175
- The British Herbal ... 1756. Fo. All plts. hand-cold., spotted. Cont. red mor. (SKC. Jul.28; 2413)   £620
-- Anr. Copy. Frontis. offset to title, occasional light foxing. 19th. C. hf. mor. From Chetham's Liby., Manchester. (C. Nov.26; 204)   Sotheran. £350
-- Anr. Copy. Cont. cf., worn, upr. cover loose. (S. Jun.1; 268)   Van Haverbeke. £250
-- Anr. Copy. Defect. (CE. Jun.4; 183)   £140
-- Anr. Copy. Frontis. & 1 lf. detchd., some spotting & soiling on plts. Worn. (CSK. Aug.1; 104)   £120
-- Anr. Copy. Slight browning, minor tears, cont. MS. notes identifying plts. & plants. Old cf., worn. (SPB. Nov.25; 90) $450
- Eden: or, a Compleat Body of Gardening. 1757. 1st. Edn. Fo. Lacks frontis., slight spotting & discolouration, 2 or 3 plts. with sm. holes, title browned & torn in inner margin. Cont. cf., worn, upr. cover detchd. (S. Jun.1; 269)   Joseph. £800
[-] -- Anr. Copy. Cont. leath., spine defect, cover loose. (R. Oct.14-18; 2975)   DM 3,500
- Exotic Botany. L., Priv. ptd., 1759. Fo. Some plts. stained. Maroon hf. mor. From collection of Massachusetts Horticultural Society, stp. on plts. (SPB. Oct.1; 125) $4,250
-- Anr. Edn. Priv. Ptd., 1772. Fo. Occasional spotting, some minor stains in margin. 19th. C. buckram, upr. cover detchd. From Chetham's Liby., Manchester. (C. Nov.26; 203)   Davidson. £650
-- Anr. Copy. Cont. hf. leath., cover brkn. (R. Oct.14-18; 2976)   DM 8,000
- The Family Herbal. Bungay, 1812. Some browning & soiling, blank portions torn from head of title & following lf. Cont. hf. cf., worn, covers detchd. (S. Jan.26; 286)   Edistar. £70
-- Anr. Copy. Some light soiling. Rebkd. (CSK. May 15; 12)   £60
-- Anr. Edn. Bungay, [1812]. A few margins slightly dampstained. Cont. cf.-bkd. bds., recornered. (SBA. Oct.22; 530)   Stirling. £54
-- Anr. Edn. Bungay, n.d. Plts. slightly soiled, 2 ll. mntd. Mod. cf. (SH. Oct.10; 464)   Crete. £90
- A General Natural History: A History of Fossils. 1748. Vol. 1 only (of 3). Fo. 12 hand-cold. engraved plts. Cont. mott. cf. (C. May 20; 212)   Lloyd. £50

- A General, Natural History, or new & accurate Descriptions of the Animals, Vegetables, & Minerals. 1748-52. 1st Edn. 3 vols. Fo. Lacks plt. 19 in vol. III, 1 plt. stained, a few others with minor stains or discolouration. Cont. cf., gt. spines, lacks some labels. (C. Feb.25; 14)   Midmer. £120

- The Vegetable System. L., 1773 (vol. 1), 1772-74 (vols. 2-26). Vols. 1 & 2 2nd. Edn. 26 vols. in 13. Fo. 1544 plts. on 1542 sheets (1541 well hand-cold.), 2 bis plts. not called for in the text, some stains & spotting. Cont. cf., gt. arms of Sir Simon R.B. Taylor Bt. on covers, brkn., very worn, 1st. vol. reprd. W.a.f. from collection of Massachusetts Horticultural Society, stps. on plts. (SPB. Oct.1; 126) $29,000

HILL, Lewis Webb
See-PHILLIPS, John C. & Hill, Lewis Webb

HILL, Robert Gardiner
- Lunacy, its Past & its Present. 1870. 1st. Edn. 4 pp. postscript at end & slip referring to it at beginning. Orig. cl. Pres. copy to editor of Le Constitutionnel on hf.-title. (S. Jun.16; 418)   Sargeant. £95

HILL, Rowland
- Post Office Reform. Priv. Ptd., 1837. 1st. Edn. Unbnd. (P. Sep.11; 260a)   Rota. £100
-- Anr. Edn. 1837. 2nd. Edn. Slightly soiled. Cont. cl. (SH. Jun.11; 9)   Pritchard-Jones. £50

HILL, S.S.
[-] A Short Account of Prince Edward Island ... for the Information of Agriculturists & other Emigrants of Small Capital. L., 1839. 1st. Edn. 12mo. Red three-qtr. mor., ex-liby. (SG. Mar.5; 64) $200
See-RAMEL, Jean Pierre-HILL, S.S.

HILL, Thomas
- A Contemplation of Mysteries: Contayning the Rare Effects ... of Certayne Comets. [1571]. 1st. Edn. Title with woodcut border probably in ptd. facs., mntd. with port. pasted on verso, some ll. at beginning & end restored, mainly in margins, some slightly affecting text & some letters added by hand. 19th. C. cf., covers detchd. [STC 13484] (S. Jun.29; 323)   West. £80
- A Pleasant History: Declaring the Whole Art of Phisiognomy. 1613. 2nd. Edn. Sig. on recto of 1st. lf., slight browning & soiling, lacks A4, 3 ll. very defect. Cont. limp vell., soiled. [STC 13483] (S. Dec.2; 726)   Music Mart. £100

HILLARY, William
- Observations on the Changes of the Air & the Concomitant Epidemical Diseases. Ed.:- B. Rush. Phila., 1811. 1st. Amer. Edn. Considerably foxed. Old mott. cf., brkn. (SG. Jan.29; 214) $190

HILLE, K. Chr.
- Die Heilquellen Deutschlands und der Schweiz. Leipzig, 1837/38. Pts. 1-4. 12mo. Slightly soiled in parts. Grd. mor., gt. spine, gold-stpd. fillets, outer gt. dentelle, orig. wraps bnd. in. (D. Dec.11-13; 206)   DM 1,200

HILLEL Ha'levi of Paritch
- Pelach Ha'rimon (on Genesis). Wilno, 1887. 1st. Edn. 4to. Hf. leath. (S. Nov.17; 203)   Zysblat. £90

HILLIARD, John Northern
- Greater Magic, a Practical Treatise on Modern Magic. Ed.:- Carl W. Jones & Jean Hugard. Minneapolis, Priv. ptd., 1938. 1st. Edn. Orig. cl. (SH. Oct.23; 50)   Van der Linden. £140

HILLIER, Jack
- Japanese Prints & Drawings from the Vever Collection. 1976. 1st. Edn. 3 vols. 4to. Cl., d.-w., s.-c. (P. Oct.23; 172)   Landau. £65

HILLS, John Waller
- A Summer on the Test. Ill.:- Norman Wilkinson. 1925. (100) numbered, sigd. 4to. Cl., unc. (CE. Jul.9; 220)   £120

HILLS, Margaret T.
- The English Bible in America. N.Y., 1961. Buckram. (SG. Jan.22; 60) $130

HILLS, Robert
- Sketches in Flanders & Holland. 1816. L.P. 4to. Cont. hf. cf., worn. (SH. May 21; 55)   Forum. £210

HILSCHER, G.
- Der Sammler für Geschichte und Alterthum, Kunst und Natur im Elbthale. Dresden, 1837. Nos. 1-47 in 1 vol., all publd. 9 copper engrs. with sm. corrections, 1 with sm. hole, slightly browned or soiled in parts. Cont. hf. leath., spine slightly defect. (H. Dec.9/10; 720)   DM 700

HILTON, Harold H. & Smith, Garden G.
- The Royal & Ancient Game of Golf. 1912. (900) numbered. No bdg. stated. (CSK. Jul.20; 132b)   £320
-- Anr. Copy. No bdg. stated. (CSK. Jul.20; 132a)   £190

HILTON, Walter
- The Scale of Perfection ... 1659. Minor worming through text at end. 19th. C. mor. [Wing H2042] (C. Nov.20; 254)   Ritman. £240

HIND, Arthur Mayger
- Engravings in England in the 16th & 17th Centuries. 1952-55. Vols. 1 & 2 (of 3). Orig. cl. (SH. Jul.16; 165)   Sims & Reed. £90
- Etchings of D.Y. Cameron. 1924. (200) numbered. Fo. Orig. cl.-bkd. cl. gt. (SBA. Dec.16; 108)   Hyde Park Bookshop. £50
-- Anr. Copy. Cf.-bkd. cl., worn, bkplt. (SG. Dec.4; 67) $120
- An Introduction to a History of Woodcut with a detailed Survey of Work done in the Fifteenth Century. 1935. 1st. Edn. 2 vols. Cl., ex-liby. (SG. Oct.2; 180) $160
- Wenceslaus Hollar & his views of London. 1922. 4to. Cl., d.-w. (P. Sep.11; 192)   Potter. £70
-- Anr. Copy. Orig. cl., d.-w. (SH. Oct.9; 76)   Forster. £60
- Wenceslaus Hollar & His Views of London & Windsor in the Seventeenth Century.-The Art of the Book. Bodley Head (1st. work), 1922; 1951. 2 vols. 4to. Orig. cl. (TA. Mar.19; 71)   £78

HIND, Henry Youle
See-COLONIAL Office of Great Britain-HIND, Henry Youle

HINDEMITH, Paul
- Wir bauen eine Stadt. Ill.:- R.W. Heinisch. Mainz, 1930. (200) Privilege Edn. 4to. Orig. hf. linen, slightly browned. Sigd. by composer & artist. (H. Dec.9/10; 1159)   DM 500

HINTON, John Howard
- History & Topography of the United States of America ... Ill.:- J. Rogers. Ca. 1850. 2 vols. in 6. Sm. fo. 1 engraved title, 2 engraved ports., 7 double-p. maps, hand-cold. in outl., & 56 steel engraved plts., lf. of facs. Orig. embossed cl. gt. (C. May 20; 129)   Faupel. £180
-- Anr. Copy. 4to. Several plts. loose, light foxing thro.-out. Gt.-stpd. cl., very worn, lacks spine to vol. I. (SG. May 21; 375) $210
-- Anr. Edn. Ca. 1860. 6 orig. divisions. Fo. Maps cold. in outl. Orig. cl., gt. decor. spines, some defect. (TA. Oct.16; 171)   £185
-- Anr. Edn. Ed.:- W.A. Crafts. Boston, 1861. New Edn. 4to. Orig. hf. mor. (SG. Jan.8; 196) $140
-- Anr. Edn. N.d. 4th. Edn. 2 vols. Lacks 3 plts., some ll. slightly spotted. Cont. cf. (SH. Nov.7; 379)   Waters. £80
-- Anr. Copy. 6 vols. Lge. 8vo. Engraved plts. & maps slightly spotted. Orig. cl., gt. (SKC. Jul.28; 2459)   £65

HIORT, J.W.
- A Practical Treatise on the Construction of Chimneys. 1826. 3 pts. in 1 vol. Cl.-bkd. bds., spine defect., unc. Pres. copy, inscr. to William Tooke. (S. Jun.22; 40)   Traylen. £100

HIPPEL, Th. G. von
[-] Ueber die Ehe. Berlin, 1774. 1st. Edn. Slightly soiled or browned in parts, title verso with stp. pasted over. Cont. paper bds., unc. (H. Dec.9/10; 1540)   DM 440

HIPPOCRATES
- De Capitis Vulneribus Liber Latinitate donatus a Francisco Vertuniano ... textus Graecus a Josepho Scaligero ... castigatus. Paris, 1578. Greek & Latin text. Limp vell. Andrew Fletcher's copy with his sig. (S. Jun.16; 419)   Phillips. £55
- Hippocrate de'païsé: ou la versio paraphrasée de ses Aphorismes; en Vers François. Par M.L. de F[ontenette]. Paris, 1654. 1st. Edn. 4to. Some browning. Mod. bds. From liby. of André L. Simon. (S. May 18; 117)   Offenbacher. £65
- Oeuvres Complètes ... Ed.:- E. Littre. Paris, 1839-61. 10 vols. Some spotting. Cont. mor.-bkd. cl. (S. Apr.6; 79)   Brieux. £260
- [Opera] Coi Aphorismi Graece et Latine. Ed.:- I. Heurnius. Leiden, 1638. 12mo. Greek & Latin text. Cont. vell. (S. Dec.2; 826)   Krenzer. £50
- Opera ... Commentaria Ioan. Marinelli. Venice, 1575. 2 pts. in 1 vol. Fo. Title & some ll. stained or browned, slightly wormed at beginning & end,

HIPPOCRATES -contd.
some margins strengthened at beginning, tears in S6 & 2N2, some sm. holes. 18th. C. hf. vell. (S. Jul.27; 340)   *Subunso.* £65
– **Opera Omnia.** Ed.:– J.A. van der Linden. Leiden, 1665. 1st. Edn. 2 vols. in 1. Cont. vell. (SG. Jan.29; 216) $150
– **Opera omnia quae extant in VIII sectiones ... distributa.** Ed.:– Anutius Foesius. Geneva, 1657-62. 2 vols. Fo. Greek & Latin text. Cont. cf., rebkd. (S. Jun.16; 420)   *Jenner Books.* £110
– **Opera, quibus addidumus commentaris Ioan. Marinelli.** Venice, 1679. 2 pts. in 1 vol. Fo. Slightly spotted & dampstained in places, 2 wormholes at end. Cont. limp vell., soiled. (S. Oct.21; 400)   *Artico.* £60

HIPPOCRATES & GALEN
– **Opera.** Paris, 1679. 13 vols. in 9. Lge. fo. Some browning & soiling, a little worming & some tears & sm. holes, occasionally affecting text. 19th. C. hf. cf., worn or defect., a few covers detchd. (S. Apr.6; 80)   *Whipple.* £170

HIRSCH Ben Chaim
– **Darchei Noam.** Wilmersdorf, 1724. 1st. Edn. 16mo. Leaves detchd., cropped, slight worming, browning, tears. Hf. sheep, very worn, bds. brkn. (SPB. May 11; 128) $375

HIRSCHFELD, Ch. C.L.
– **Theorie der Gartenkunst.** Leipzig, 1779-85. 1st. Edn. 5 vols. in 3. 4to. Vols. 1 & 2 slightly wormed at foot. Cont. hf. leath., gt. spine. (R. Oct.14-18; 667)   DM 3,000

HIRSCHFELD, Ludovic & Leveillé, J.B.
– **Neurologie ou description et Iconographie du Système Nerveux et des Organes des Sens de l'Homme.** Paris, 1853. Cf., bnd. as a prize for King's College, L., arms on upr. cover, rebkd. (S. Jun.16; 422)   *Rota.* £100

HIRTZ, Lise
– **Il etait une petite Pie: 7 chansons et 3 chansons pour Hyacinthe.** Ill.:– Joan Miro. [Paris], 1928. 1st. Edn., (280) numbered on Arches. Sm. fo. Orig. cl.-bkd. bds., mntd. cover label, & juxtaposed cold. strips mntd. at lr. cover designed by artist, as iss. (PNY. Mar.4; 189) $325

HISTOIRE abregée des Provinces-Unies des Païs-Bas, òu l'on voit leurs Progrés, leurs Conquêtes, leur Gouvernement, et celui de leurs Compagnies en Orient & en Occident
Amst., 1701. Fo. Some foxing & browning. Cont. cf., arms on covers. (VG. Nov.18; 1206)   Fls. 550

HISTOIRE DE L'ART DU JAPON
Paris, [1900]. Fo. Gt.-pict. vell.-bkd. gt.-lettered cl. (SG. Mar.12; 213) $100

HISTOIRE DE GUILLAUME III, Roi d'Angleterre ...
Amst., 1703. 3 vols. 12mo. Old spr. cf., 5 decor. spine raised bands, worn. (LM. Mar.21; 7)   B.Frs. 14,000

HISTOIRE DE MARGUERITE, fille de Suzon, nièce de Dom B ... portier des Chartreux
A J'enconne, 1784. 2 pts. in 1 vol. Square 16mo. Cont. red mor., decor. spine, 3 fillets, angle fleurons, inner dentelle. (HD. Apr.10; 340)   Frs. 2,600

HISTOIRE DES ANIMAUX
Berlin, 1786. New Edn. 12mo. Cont. mott. cfs., spine gt. Bkplt. of Walter Schatzki. (SG. Apr.30; 189) $100

HISTOIRE et Iconographie des Moeurs, Usages et Costumes de tous les Peuples du Monde
Brussels, 1846. 4 vols. Occasional browning & light spotting. Cont. hf. mor., some wear. (SPB. May 5; 259) $150

HISTOIRE GENERALE DES VOYAGES, ou Nouvelle Collection
Paris, 1746. Vol. I only. 4to. Orig. cf. gt. (TA. Sep.18; 325)   £55

HISTOIRE NATURELLE en Miniature
Paris, ca. 1820. 16mo. Cont. red mor., decor. spine, lge. gt. fillet, inner dentelle with Greek key-pattern. (HD. Apr.10; 135)   Frs. 1,400

HISTOIRE PHILOSOPHIQUE ET POLITIQUE des Establissemens et du Commerce des Européens dans les deux Indes
The Hague, 1774. 7 vols. Cont. cf. (SH. May 21; 56)   *Baron.* £100

HISTORICAL & Commercial System of Geography
1812. Fo. Cf., upr. cover detchd. (P. Oct.2; 257)   *Whatley.* £100

HISTORICAL MANUSCRIPTS COMMISSION
– **Calendar of the Manuscripts of the Most Hon. The Marquis of Salisbury.** 1883-1915. (50) L.P. 13 vols., including Addenda & Appendix vols. Fo. Hf. mor. (LC. Feb.12; 497)   £180

HISTORICAL Publishing Company of Canada
– **Toronto. Our Dominion.** Toronto, 1887. Orig. ptd. wraps., upr. wrap. nearly detchd. (CB. Feb.18; 165)   Can. $160

HISTORICAL RECORDS OF AUSTRALIA
Sydney, 1914-22. Series I: Vols. I-XXVI, Series III: Vols. I-VI, Series IV: Vol. 1, together 33 vols. Hf. cf. (KH. Nov.18; 336)   Aus. $480
– – **Anr. Edn.** 1846. 2 vols. Fo. Hf. roan, dampstained. (CE. Nov.20; 29)   £340

HISTORY & Adventures of Little Henry
L., 1810. Sq. 16mo. With the set of 7 hand-cold. aquatint figures with movable heads laid in (of the 4 hats to the set, only 1 remains), slight foxing. Ptd. wraps., orig. bd. s.-c. (SG. Apr.30; 213) $140
– – **Anr. Copy.** Orig. wraps. & s.-c. (P. Mar.12; 206)   *Questor.* £70
– – **Anr. Edn.** 1811. 6th. Edn. 16mo. 7 aquatinted cut-out figures, 4 hats (? 1 not orig.) & interchangeable head, all hand-cold. Orig. ptd. wraps., s.-c. soiled & crudely reprd. (SH. Mar.19; 61)   *Schierenberg.* £90

HISTORY [AN] OF THE CONFESSIONS OF THE FAITH OF THE CHRISTIAN & REFORMED CHURCHES ... [with] the Confession of the Church of Scotland
1586. 2 pts. in 1 vol. Slight browning, 1 or 2 short tears, slightly affecting text. Cont. 17th. C. limp vell., soiled. [STC 5155] (S. Jun.29; 394)   *Booth.* £75

HISTORY OF ENGLAND During the Reigns of the Royal House of Stuart & Several Original Letters from King Charles II ...
L., 1730. Fo. Cf. with raised band, spine title, corners & upr. cover very worn. (JL. Mar.2; 749)   Aus. $110

HISTORY OF THE GOODVILLE FAMILY, or the Rewards of Virtue & Filial Duty
York, ca. 1800. 16mo. Advts. Orig. Dutch floral bds., rebkd. (SH. Mar.19; 130)   *Schiller.* £80

HISTORY OF THE HOUSE THAT JACK BUILT
Harrisburg, ca. 1833. 12mo. Slightly spotted. Orig. ptd. wraps. (SH. Mar.19; 132)   *Maggs.* £280

HISTORY OF INK
N.Y., ca. 1860. 12mo. Contents partly loose in bdg. Cl., ex-liby. (SG. Mar.26; 271) $130

HISTORY OF LITTLE FANNY (The)
1810. 1st. Edn. [1st. iss.?]. 16mo. 7 aquatinted cut-out figures, 2 (of 4) hats, & interchangeable head, all hand-cold. Orig. ptd. wraps. (SH. Mar.19; 59)   *Hampstead Book Corner.* £75

HISTORY OF LITTLE GOODY TWO SHOES
Burslem, 1802. 16mo. Advts. Orig. Dutch floral bds., fitted case. (SH. Mar.19; 127)   *Quaritch.* £290

HISTORY OF LITTLE RED RIDING HOOD
Balt., 1837. Orig. ptd. wraps., 1st. ill. repeated on upr. cover, slightly worn. (SH. Mar.19; 129)   *Moon.* £60

HISTORY OF MISS KITTY PRIDE
Harvard, 1803. 3¾ × 2½ ins. Cont. sig. of Sally Mead on last blank lf. Orig. cold. Dutch paper wraps. (SG. Dec.18; 265) $150

HISTORY OF THE SEVEN WISE MASTERS OF ROME, containing Many Excellent & Delightful Examples
Boston, 1794. 12mo. Orig. wraps. (SH. Mar.19; 131)   *Schiller.* £55

HISTORY OF THE TIMES
1935-52. Pres. Edn. 5 vols. Fo. Orig. mor.-bkd. bds., s.-c's. This copy presented to Sir Roderick Jones, sometime Chairman of Reuters. (CSK. Oct.16; 46)   £220

HITLER, Adolf
– **Mein Kampf.** Muenchen, 1925. 1st. Edn. Vol. I only. With 32 pp. of advts. Cl.-bkd. bds. (SG. Feb.12; 213) $160
– – **Anr. Edn.** Munich, 1925-27. 1st. Edns., (500). 2 vols. Orig. parch., soiling. (SPB. Oct.1; 230) $2,500

HITZIG, Eduard
– **Untersuchungen über das Gehirn.** Berlin, 1874. 1st. Edn. Cl.-bkd. bds. (S. Jun.16; 427)   *Phelps.* £130

HOARE, Sir Richard Colt
– **The Ancient History of North [South] Wiltshire.** 1812-19. 2 vols. Fo. Mor. gt., centre circular gt. ornament on covers, by W. Pratt. From the collection of Eric Sexton. (C. Apr.16; 281)   *Hatchwell.* £240
– – **Anr. Edn.** Ill.:– after P. Crocker & others. 1812-21. 2 vols. Fo. Slight dampstain to some plts. Cont. gt. & blind-panel. cf. (C. Feb.25; 36)   *Crowe.* £150
– – **Anr. Edn.** 1812-19-21. L.P. 3 Pts. in 2 vols. Cont. russ. & hf. russ. gt., vol. 1 rebkd., spines unif. (S. Nov.24; 158)   *Wimborne.* £350
– **The History of Modern Wiltshire.** 1822. Fo. 1 engraved map partly hand-cold., frontis. port. torn & reprd. Cf.-bkd. bds., spine gt., new end-papers. Stp. of State Historical Soc. of Wisconsin. (LC. Feb.12; 188)   £50
– – **Anr. Edn.** 1822-44. 12 pts. in 12 vols. Fo. Later crushed mor., gt. (C. Feb.25; 37)   *Thorp.* £480
– **The History of Modern Wiltshire.–Registrum Wiltunense, Saconicum et Latinum.–Chronicon Vilodunense.** 1822-44; 1827; 1830. 1st. work 1st. Edn., 2nd. work (100). 1st. work 6 vols.; 2nd. & 3rd. works in 1 vol., together 7 vols. Fo. Unif. 19th. C. hf. russ. gt. 2nd. work Pres. Copy to Sir John Buckler. (S. Nov.24; 159)   *Traylen.* £700

HOBBES, Thomas
– **Le Corps Politique.** Leyden, 1653. 12mo. Browned. Cont. vell., gt. arms on covers. (SPB. Jul.28; 121) $125
– **Decameron Physiologicum.–Considerations upon the Reputation. Loyalty ... of.–Tracts.–The Art of Rhetoric.** 1678; 1680; 1681; 1681. 1st. 3 works 1st. Edns. 1st. work: 7 pp. advts., stained; 2nd. work: advts.; 3rd. work: slightly reprd. at title; 4th. work: sm. hole in 1 lf., a few ink marks on title. Unif. mod. mor.-bkd. bds. (SKC. Feb.26; 1729)   £520
– **Leviathan.** 1651. 1st. Edn., 2nd. Iss. Fo. Some browning. Cont. spr. cf., worn, 1 cover detchd. [Wing H2246] (S. Sep.29; 45)   *Rota.* £350
– – **Anr. Copy.** Sm. hole in Aa4. Cont. panel. cf., rebkd. (S. Jun.16; 428)   *Bisson Millet.* £200
– – **Anr. Edn.** [?Amst.], 1651. 2nd. Edn. Fo. Port. bnd. in, fo. 3C3 reprd. Cont. cf., rebkd. [Wing H2247] (S. Mar.16; 155)   *Pythagoras.* £120
– – **Anr. Edn.** [Amst.], ca. 1780? 3rd. Edn. Fo. Some foxing, a few ll. browned or stained. Mod. mor., gt. [Wing H2248] (S. Jun.23; 391)   *Armstrong.* £120

HOBSON, Geoffrey D.
– **English Binding before 1500.** 1929. Fo. Orig. cl. (SH. Jan.29; 23)   *Forster.* £100
– – **Anr. Edn.** Camb., 1929. (500). Fo. Cl. (SG. Mar.26; 43) $180
– **Maioli, Canevari & others.** 1926. 4to. Orig. cl., spine slightly worn. (SH. Oct.9; 49)   *W. Forster.* £60
– **Les Reliures à la Fanfare.** 1935. Ltd. Edn. 4to. Orig. cl., d.-w., torn. Sigd. (CM. Oct.7; 1406)   Frs. 2,000
– **Thirty Bindings.** 1926. (600) numbered. 4to. Red mor. gt. imitating the Fr. bdg., ca. 1630, (ill. as plt. 18.). Pres. copy inscr. by A.J.A. Symons to W.A. Foyle. (S. Jul.31; 173)   *Morton.* £240

HOBSON, Robert Lockhart
– **Catalogue of the Chinese, Corean & Persian Pottery & Porcelain: George Eumorfopoulos Collection.** L., [1925]. (750). 6 vols. Fo. Orig. brocade cl., ex-liby. (SG. May 14; 101) $2,200
– – **Anr. Edn.** 1925-28. (725). 6 vols. Fo. Orig. cl., gt., unc. (C. Feb.4; 252)   *Lyons.* £1,200
– **A Catalogue of Chinese Pottery & Porcelain in the Collection of Sir Percival David.** 1934. (680) numbered. Fo. Orig Chinese silk bds. by Sangorski & Sutcliffe. (S. Sep.30; 405)   £680
– **Catalogue of the Leonard Gow Collection of Chinese Porcelain.** 1931. (300) sigd. by Leonard Gow. 4to. Mor. gt. by Sangorski & Sutcliffe, cl. box. (SBA. Jul.22; 181a)   *Quaritch.* £350

- - **Anr. Copy.** Niger mor. gt., cl. box. (P. Nov.13; 323) *Tallerman.* £260
- **Chinese Porcelain & Wedgwood Pottery . . . a record of the collection in the Lady Lever Art Gallery.** 1924. (350). 4to. Cl. (C. Feb.4; 249) *Hughes.* £60
- **Chinese Pottery & Porcelain.** 1915. Ltd. Edn. 2 vols. Orig. cl. (SH. Apr.9; 77) *Kauffman.* £140
- - **Anr. Copy.** (SH. Jan.29; 181) *Maggs.* £115
- - **Anr. Edn.** N.Y., 1915. (1,500) numbered. 2 vols. Orig. cl. (CSK. Mar.27; 128) £95
- **The Later Ceramic Wares of China.** 1925. 4to. Orig. cl. (S. Sep.30; 404) £65
- - **Anr. Copy.** Buckram gt. (P. Nov.13; 260) *Tallerman.* £60
- **The Later Ceramic Wares of China.–The Wares of the Ming Dynasty.** 1925; 1923. Ltd. Edns. 4to. 2nd. work badly affected by damp. Orig. pig, 1 worn. (SH. Jan.29; 182) *Tallerman.* £85
- **The Wares of the Ming Dynasty.** 1923. (256) numbered, sigd. by author. 4to. 1 extra colour plt. Orig. pig. (CSK. Jan.30; 62) £95
- - **Anr. Copy.** Orig. cl., slightly soiled. (S. Sep.30; 403) £65
- **Worcester Porcelain.** 1910. 4to. Cl. gt., unc., d.-w. (P. Oct.23; 170) *Tallerman.* £90
- - **Anr. Copy.** Fo. Orig. cl. (SH. Jan.29; 184) *Ars Artis.* £70

HOBSON, Robert Lockhart & Hetherington, A.L.
- **The Art of the Chinese Potter.** 1923. (1500). 4to. Cl. (C. Jul.22; 145) *Maggs.* £65
- - **Anr. Copy.** Spotted. Vell. spine & tips. (SG. Mar.12; 72) $130

HOBSON, Robert Lockhart & others
- **Chinese Ceramics in Private Collections.** 1931. (625) numbered. 4to. Orig. cl. (SH. Oct.9; 146) *Tallerman.* £150
- - **Anr. Copy.** Gt.-lettered buckram, bevelled edges, partly untrimmed. (SG. Mar.12; 96) $250
- - **Anr. Copy.** Defect. (SG. Mar.12; 70) $180
- **Chinese, Corean & Japanese Potteries.** N.Y., 1914. (1500) numbered. 4to. Cl.-bkd. bds., unc. (SG. Dec.4; 91) $100

HOCHSTETTER, Ferdinand von
- **Neu-Seeland.** Stuttgart, 1863. 4to. Orig. linen, gold & blind-stpd., sm. stain on upr. cover. (HK. May 12-14; 559) DM 440

HOCKING, W.J.
- **Catalogue of the Coins, Tokens, Medals etc. in the Museum of the Royal Mint.** 1906-10. 2 vols. Orig. cl., soiled. (SH. Mar.6; 376) *James.* £50

HODDER, Edward Mulberry
- **The Harbours & Ports of Lake Ontario.** Toronto, 1857. Orig. ptd. wraps., spine worn. (CB. Sep.24; 231) Can. $140

HODDER, Edwin
- **History of South Australia, from its Foundation to the Year of its Jubilee.** L., 1893. Cl., slightly spotted. (KH. Nov.18; 337) Aus. $120

HODGES, William
- **Choix de Vues de l'Inde . . .** L., 1785-88. 2 vols. Fo. Engraved map torn, occasional marginal foxing, sm. liby. label in corner of each plt. Cont. cf.-bkd. decor. bds. From Chetham's Liby., Manchester. (C. Nov.26; 205) *Marlborough.* £300
- **Select Views in India.** [1785-88]. 1st. Iss. 2 vols. Lge. fo. Engraved map torn, sm. liby. label on each plt. Cont. bds., vol. 2 covers detchd., spines & corners worn. (C. Jul.15; 49) *Taylor.* £600
- - **Anr. Edn.** [1786-88]. Lge. fo. 2 extra dupl. plts. before letters. Cont. red str.-grd. mor., elab. gt. borders on sides. (C. Jul.15; 50) *Taylor.* £1,000
- **Travels in India.** 1793. 1st. Edn., L.P. 4to. Red str.-grd. mor. gt. by C. Hering, with his ticket. Bkplt. & sig. of George Gostling. (S. Nov.24; 160) *Kosson.* £400
- **Voyage Pittoresque de l'Inde fait dans les Années 1780-83.** Trans.:– Langlès. Paris, 1805. 2 vols. in 1. 16mo. Cont. bradel paper bds. (HD. Apr.9; 488) Frs. 1,100

HODGINS, J. & Macpherson, Mary-Etta
- **Canadian Homes & Gardens; book of Houses.** Toronto, 1930. 4to. Orig. cl., covers slightly soiled, hand-stp. on front free end-paper. (CB. May 27; 299) Can. $170

HODGKIN, J.
See–CHAPMAN, Guy & Hodgkin, J.

HODGKIN, Thomas
- **Italy & Her Invaders.** Oxford, 1892. 2nd. Edn. 9 vols. Slight browning. Cf. gt., by Zaehnsdorf. (SPB. Nov.25; 461) $175

HODGSON, Adam
- **Remarks During a Journey Through North America in the Years 1819, 1820 & 1821, in a Series of Letters . . .** N.Y., 1823. 1st. Edn. Foxing, a few marginal tears. Orig. bds., spine stained, label worn, bkplts. From liby. of William E. Wilson [Sabin 32358]. (SPB. Apr.29; 140) $150

HODGSON, John E.
- **The History of Aeronautics in Great Britain.** 1924. (1000). 4to. Orig. cl. (SH. Oct.10; 465) *Forster.* £90

HODGSON, Joseph
- **A Treatise on the Diseases of the Arteries & Veins Containing the Pathology & Treatment of Aneurisms & Wounded Arteries.** 1815. 1st. Edn. 1 vol. text & atlas with 8 plts. & explanatory text. 8vo. & sm. fo. Lacks hf.-title in text vol., title of text with liby. stp. & scribbled on, last lf. torn affecting letters. Text hf. cf., atlas orig. bds. (S. Jun.16; 430) *Maggs.* £260

HODSON, T. & Dougall, J.
- **The Cabinet of the Arts; being a New Universal Drawing Book.** 1810. 4to. Some soiling, extra-ill. with ca. 40 hand-cold. plts. Cont. hf. mor., covers detchd. W.a.f. (CSK. Mar.20; 28) $200
- - **Anr. Edn.** [1821]. 2 vols. in 1. 4to. 122 plts. (of 128), occasional slight soiling & staining. Cont. hf. mor., spine gt. (S. Jun.23; 325) *Traylen.* £150

HOE, Robert
- **A Lecture on Bookbinding as a Fine Art.** Ill.:– Edward Bierstadt. N.Y., Grol. Cl., 1886. (200). 4to. Three qtr. cl., soiled & browned, partly unc. (SG. Oct.2; 181) $325
- **One Hundred & Seventy Six Historic & Artistic Book-Bindings . . . from the library of . . .** Ill.:– Raubicheck (etchings), Prang & Bien (lithos.). N.Y., 1895. (200) numbered on Japan vell. 2 vols. Fo. Three-qtr. mor., gt.-panel. spines, by MacDonald. Armorial bkplt. of Robert Walshingham Martin. (SG. Mar.26; 243) $900

HOEFER, E.
- **Küstenfahrten an der Nord- und Ostsee.** Stuttgart, ca. 1890. Fo. Orig. linen, spine slightly defect. (R. Oct.14-18; 2329) DM 2,000

HOEFER, J.C.F.
- **Nouvelle Bibliographie Générale.** Paris, 1855-70. 46 vols. in 23. Cont. russ.-bkd. bds. (C. Jul.22; 121) *Manson.* £200

HOEHNE, F.C.
- **Iconografia de Orchidaceas do Brasil.** S. Paulo, 1949. 4to. Publisher's hf. mor. (C. Mar.18; 55) *Taylor.* £55

HOFDIJK, W.J.
See–LENNEP, J. van & Hofdijk, W.J.

HOFFBAUER, M.F.
- **Paris à travers les Ages.** Paris, 1885. 2 vols. Fo. Cont. hf. chagrin, spines with raised bands, mntd. on guards. (HD. Jun.25; 280) Frs. 2,300

HOFFMANN, Ernst Theodor Amadeus
- **Ausgewählte Schriften.** Berlin, 1827-28. 1st. Coll. Edn. 10 vols. Title stpd., slightly soiled in parts. Cont. linen. W.a.f. (HK. May 15; 4482) DM 480
- **Don Juan.** Trans.:– V. Rakinta. Ill.:– M. Lagorio. Berlin, 1923. (300) numbered. 4to. In Russian. Orig. bds. (D. Dec.11-13; 1090) DM 430
- **Das Fräulein v. Scuderi.** Ed.:– C.G.V. Maassen. Ill.:– K.M. Schultheiss. Hellerau, 1923. (350) numbered. Orig. red mor., gt. spine & cover dentelle, inner fillet dentelle. (HK. Nov.18-21; 2913) DM 420
- **Gesammelte Schriften.** Ill.:– T. Hosemann. Berlin, 1844-45. 1st. Edn. ill. Hosemann. Cont. linen. (R. Oct.14-18; 938) DM 720
- **Sämmtliche Werke.** Ed.:– C.G. Maasen. Munich, 1908-28. Vols. I-IV & VI-X in 8 vols. (all publd.) Orig. hf. leath., spine I defect. (H. Dec.9/10; 1840) DM 680

HOFFMANN, Friedrich, the older
- **Clavis Pharmacevtica Schroederiana.** Halle, 1681. 2nd. Edn. 2 pts. in 1 vol. 4to. Cont. vell. (HK. Nov.18-21; 575) DM 460
- **Opera Omnia Physico-Medica.** Geneva, 1748-53. 6 pts. in 3 vols., supp. I in 2 pts., supp. II, 3 pts, in 2 vols., together 5 vols. Fo. Name on title. Cont. vell. bds., slightly soiled. (S. Feb.23; 60) *Maggs.* £150

HOFFMANN, Georg Franz
- **[Plantae Lichenosae:] Descriptio et Adaumbratio Plantarum e Classe Cryptogamica Linnaei quae Lichenes dicuntur.** Leipzig, [1789-]1790-1801. 3 vols. Fo. Cont. cf., gt. spines (vol. 3 slightly later, with wraps. bnd. in). Fascicule from collection of Massachusetts Horticultural Society, stps. on plts. (SPB. Oct.1; 127) $1,500

HOFFMANN, Heinrich
- **The English Struwwelpeter.** Leipzig, 1848. 1st. Edn. in Engl. 4to. Orig. ptd. bds., covers almost loose, buckram d.-w., attached to spine. (SH. Dec.11; 313) *Vincent.* £820

HOFFMAN, Julius
- **Das Wunderbare Bilderbuch.** Stuttgart, [inscr. 1812]. 3rd. Edn. 4to. 12 hand-cold. plts., each with movable overlay, a few crayon marks. Orig. pict. bds., detchd. (SBA. Dec.16; 198) *Petersfield Bookshop.* £60

HOFFMANN, Professor L. (Pseud.)
See–LEWIS, Angelo John

HOFFMANN von Fallersleben, A.H.
- **Das Lied der Deutschen.** Hamburg, Stuttgart, 1 Sep., 1841. Fo. Folding mark on verso of last p., title slightly soiled. Unc. as iss. (C. Nov.20; 191) *Breman.* £160

HOFFMANNSEGG, Johann Centurius, Graf von & Heinrich Link
- **Flore Portugaise, ou Description de toutes les Plantes qui croissent naturellement en Portugal.** Berlin, 1809-20[-40.] 2 vols. in 3, all publd. Fo. Hf. mor. From collection of Massachusetts Horticultural Society, stps. on plts. (SPB. Oct.1; 128) $20,000

HOFLAND, Barbara
- **[-] Patience & Perseverence; or, the Modern Griselda.** 1813. 4 vols. 12mo. 1 lf. torn without loss, slightly spotted. Later hf. cf., hinges strengthened. (SBA. Dec.16; 20) *Way.* £85

HOFLAND, Thomas Christopher–HOWITT, Samuel
- **The British Angler's Manuel.–The Angler's Manuel.** N.p.; L'pool., 1839; 1808. 2 works in 2 vols. 8vo.; ob. 4to. Frontis. & title of 2nd work slightly browned. Orig. cl. gt.; cont. hf. mor. gt. (C. Nov.6; 316) *Williams.* £150

HOFMANN, A.–DIEFFENBACH, Johann Friedrich
- **Theoretisch-Praktische Anweisung zur Radical-Heilung Stotternder.–Die Heilung des Stottens durch eine neue Chirurgische Operation.** Berlin, 1840; 1841. 2 works in 2 vols. Disbnd. From Brooklyn Academy of Medicine. (SG. Jan.29; 398) $100

HOFMANN, Prof. Ernst
- **Die Raupen der Gross-Schmetterlinge Europas.–Die Gross-Schmetterlinge Europas.** Stuttgart, 1893-94. 4 vols. (text/plts.). 4to. Margins slightly browned. Later cl. (TA. Jun.18; 145) £90

HOFMANN, Friedrich H.
- **Geschichte d. Bayer. Porsellan–Manufaktur Nymphenburg.** Leipzig, 1923. 3 vols. Lge. 4to. Orig. linen. (HK. Nov.18-21; 3407) DM 2,300

HOFMANNSTHAL, Hugo von
- **Ausgewaehlte Gedichte.** Berlin, 1903. 1st. Book Edn. (300). MS. owner's mark on end-lf. & stpd. Orig. bds., slightly worn. (HK. Nov.18-21; 2646) DM 460
- - **Anr. Copy.** Worn. MS. dedication of H. van de Velde, Weimar 1903 on end-paper. (H. May 21/22; 1627) DM 420
- **Die Wege und Begegnungen.** [Bremen], Bremer Pr., 1913. 1st. Edn., (200) numbered on Bütten. 5 vols. Orig. red mor., sigd. Bremer Binderei, sm. floral blind stp., blind fillets on spine & covers, gold-stpd. inner & outer gt. dentelles. MS. dedication of Ludwig Wolde. (D. Dec.11-13; 1092) DM 3,000
- - **Anr. Copy.** Gt. inner & outer dentelle, blind-tooled, Bremer Binderei. (HK. May12-14; 1797) DM 1,700
- **Der Weisse Fächer.** Ill.:– E.G. Craig. Leipzig, 1907. (50) numbered on Jap., 1st. Edn. Fo. Ex-liby. Orig. vell., defect., silk covered box. (HK. Nov.18-21; 2645) DM 420

HOFMEISTER, Theodor & Oskar & others
[–] **Stimmungsbilder aus der Heide.** Ill.:–
Hofmeisters, Ludwig Roemer, Hermann Ebel &
others. Munich, 1921. 4to. Title detchd. Cl.-bkd.
bds., loose. (SG. Apr.23; 106) $100

HOFSTEDE de Groot, Dr. C.
– **Catalogue Raisonné of the Works of the Most
Eminent Dutch Painters of the Seventeenth
Century.** 1908-27. 8 vols. Orig. cl. (SH. Apr.9; 78)
Clarendon Gallery. £390
– – **Anr. Copy.**   (SH.   Oct.9; 77)
Reed & Sims. £260

HOGAN, Edmund
[–] **The Pennsylvania State Trials, containing the
Impeachment, Trial, & Acquittal of Francis
Hopkinson & John Nicholson** ... Phila., 1794.
Vol. I, all publd. Dampstained in pt. Disbnd. (SG.
Mar.5; 229) $100

HOGARTH, Joseph
See–FINDEN, Edward & William & Hogarth,
Joseph

HOGARTH, William
– **The Analysis of Beauty.** L., 1753. 4to. With the
receipt form, but uncompleted, some spotting,
offsetting. Later hf. mor., cover detchd., end-paper
torn. (SPB. May 29; 203) $100
– **The Genuine Works** ... Ed.:– John Nichols &
George Steevens. 1808-10. 2 vols. 4to. Some
spotting. Cont. hf.-cf. (CSK. Oct.3; 233)   £50
– **Graphic Illustrations of Hogarth.** 1799. 2 vols.
Cont. diced russ., gt. Inscr. to Sir James Lake.
(SBA. Jul.23; 253)   *Quaritch.* £70
– **Hogarth Moralized** ... Ed.:– John Trusler. Ill.:–
Corboult & Dent after Hogarth. L., 1768. Old spr.
cf., decor. spine. (HD. Dec.5; 106)   Frs. 1,000
– **Hogarth Restored. The whole Works** ... Ill.:–
Thomas Cook. 1802-03. 2 vols. Lge. fo. & 8vo.
Slight marginal soiling & tears in plts. vol. Text
vol. hf. russ., plts. hf. roan, worn. (S. Jun.23; 326)
Simonds. £220
– – **Anr. Edn.** Ill.:– Thomas Cook. 1806. Atlas fo.
111 engrs. on 95 (of 96) plts., including frontis.
(detchd.), without text. Orig. crimson hf. mor.,
partly unc., bds. detchd. W.a.f. (S. May 5; 201)
Cristani. £350
– – **Anr. Copy.** 110 engraved plts. on 94, port. &
title mntd., some staining. Cont. hf. mor., worn.
(SH. Mar.26; 277)   *Seibu.* £320
– – **Anr. Copy.** Engraved port. & 106 (of 110) ills.,
lacks 'Before' & 'After', frontis. spotted some plts.
stained, some cut down. Cont. hf. roan. (SH.
Apr.9; 7)   *Barker.* £260
– **Industry & Idleness.** N.d. Ob. 4to. As iss. in
orig. wraps., backstrip worn. (CSK. Jun.19; 71)
£50
– **The Original & Genuine Works.** N.d. Lge. fo.
Some engrs. soiled. Cont. hf. cf., worn, covers
detchd. (SH. May 21; 58)   *Sephton.* £360
– **Works.** 1795-1801. Fo. 54 engraved plts. only,
without title, etc., some minor defects., mainly
marginal. Disbnd. (SBA.   Dec.16; 229)
Marten's Bookshop Ltd. £62
– – **Anr. Edn.** 1821. Fo. Hf. mor. gt. (P.
Oct.2; 271)   *Flisher.* £460
– – **Anr. Edn.** Ed.:– J. Nichols. 1822. Lge. fo. 116
plts. plus 1 loose in back pocket (pocket detchd.).
Hf. mor. gt. (P. Jan.22; 285)   *Cambridge.* £460
– – **Anr. Copy.** 2 vols. Titles in vol. 2 preserved.
Hf. cf., covers detchd. (P. Jul.30; 261)
Schapiro. £400
– – **Anr. Edn.** Ed.:– James Heath & John Nichols.
1822. Lge. fo. 1 engraved plt. preserved, some
spotting, mainly towards end. Cont. hf. cf., covers
detchd. (CSK. Jul.31; 102)   £220
– – **Anr. Copy.** 116 copperplts., 2 of the suppressed
plts. laid into lr. cover. Early hf. mor., spine gt.,
worn. (SG. Oct.9; 130) $1,300
– – **Anr. Copy.** 116 copperplts., 3 suppressed plts.
laid into lr. cover sleeve. Cont. red three-qtr. mor.,
brkn. (SG. May 14; 102) $950
– – **Anr. Copy.** Lacks plt. 1 of the Rake's Progress,
but with 2 of the 3 suppressed plts., plts. wtrmkd.
1820 & 1821, some later plts. foxed. Loose as iss.
in fold-down cl. case. (SG. May 21; 378) $800
– – **Anr. Copy.** Port. of Hogarth (dtd. 1795) mntd.
on fly-lf., occasional foxing, some plt.-marks on
versos reprd. Hf. mor. (SG. Nov.20; 357) $450
– – **Anr. Copy.** Slightly soiled. Cont. hf. leath., gt.
spine. (R. Oct.14-18; 2507)   DM 2,350
– – **Anr. Edn.** L., 1824. New Edn. Vol. I only (of
2). 4to. Plts. dampstained at head of margin,
foxed. Leath.-bkd. cl., upr. hinge brkn. & loose.
(CB. Feb.18; 211)   Can. $120

– – **Anr. Edn.** L., 1827. 2 vols. 4to. Cont. str.-grd.
mor., recased. (SG. Dec.4; 174) $100
– – **Anr. Edn.** Ed.:– John Trusler. Ill.:– after
Hogarth. 1833. 2 vols. 4to. Occasional slight
soiling. Cont. cf., 1 cover detchd. (CSK.
Mar.20; 58)   £50
– – **Anr. Edn.** Ca. 1835. Fo. 1 plt. loose, 2 stained.
Cont. hf. mor., gt., worn. W.a.f. (SH. Jun.11; 155)
Duran. £350
– – **Anr. Edn.** Ed.:– John Nichols. [1835-37]. Fo.
Title cropped & mntd., a few sm. tears, mainly
marginal, some spots. Later hf. mor. gt., slightly
stained. (SBA. Jul.14; 149)   *Schuster.* £280
[–] **The Complete Works.** Ed.:– James Hannay. L.,
ca. 1850. Fo. Tooled leath., worn. (PWP.
Apr.9; 112)   Can. $140
– – **Anr. Edn.** Ed.:– James Hannay. Ca. 1860.
New Edn. 6 vols. 4to. Orig. cl. gt. (SBA.
Jul.22; 59)   *Kenyusha Books.* £70
– **Works.** Ed.:– John Trusler & others. L., ca.
1870. 2 vols. Hf. mor., scuffed. (SG. May 21; 379)
$100
– – **Anr. Edn.** Ed.:– James Heath & John Nichols.
N.d. Lge. fo. (25 × 19½ inches). Slight spotting,
lr. corners of text lightly stained. Cont. hf. mor.
(CSK. May 29; 59)   £370
– – **Anr. Copy.** 3 vols. 116 plts. Leath. spine & cl.,
worn. (CE. Aug.28; 293)   £170
– – **Anr. Edn.** Ed.:– John Nichols. N.d. Fo. Text &
some plts. slightly dampstained, some marginal
spotting. Cont. hf. mor., worn, covers detchd.
(CSK. Jul.10; 44)   £310
– – **Anr. Copy.** Hf. mor. gt. (P. May 14; 329)
Schapiro. £260
– – **Anr. Edn.** L., n.d. Fo. Browning, tears,
staining & soiling, some ll. loose. Hf. mor., worn,
covers detchd. As a collection of plts., w.a.f. (SPB.
Nov.25; 125) $375
– – **Anr. Edn.** Ed.:– John Trusler. L. & N.Y., n.d.
2 vols. 4to. Orig. blind-stpd. cf. (CB. Apr.1; 230)
Can. $170
– **Complete Works.** Ed.:– Rev. J. Trusler & E.F.
Roberts. N.d. 6 vols. 4to. Orig. cl. gt. (SBA.
Dec.16; 110)   *Omniphil Ltd.* £420
– **The Works ... from the Original Plates
Restored by James Heath.** [1835-37]. Fo. 3
suppressed plts. in pocket in lr. cover, title creased.
Cont. red hf. mor., gt., stain on 1 cover. (S.
Dec.9; 498)   *Sephton.* £360

HOGG, James
– **The Shepherd's Guide.** Edinb., 1807. 1st. Edn.
Slight spotting, short tear in 1 lf., (reprd.), inscr.
on title. 19th. C. hf. cf. by J. Edmond, Aberdeen,
with   his   ticket.   (S.   Nov.4; 562)
Brook-Hitching. £90

HOGG, Robert & Johnson, Geo. W.
– **The Wild Flowers of Great Britain.** L., 1863-69.
Cont. hf. leath. (HK. Nov.18-21; 580)   DM 850
– – **Anr. Edn.** Ill.:– W.G. Smith & F. Waller. L.,
1869-80. Vols. 5-11. Hf. leath. gt. (D.
Dec.11-13; 139)   DM 1,200

HOHBERG, Wolff Helmhard von, Freiherr
[–] **Georgica Curiosa Aucta.** Nuremb., 1695. 3 pts.
in 1 vol. Fo. 2nd. title with overslip, engraved title
to pt. II not present for pt. I, ?lacks some blanks,
some ll. torn, including 1st. title, affecting text, a
few larger, including f. 5G2, 2 corners torn off &
loosely inserted, ff. 4L2 & 3 heavily reprd. with
slight loss, sm. hole in f. *4K1 with slight loss.
Cont. cf. over wooden bds., worn, lacks spine &
clasps. (S. Jun.; 26)   *Koch.* £400
– **Die Volkommene Pferdund Reit-Kunst samt
ausführlichem Unterricht der Edlen Stütery ...
beygefügt   Ein   Vorrath   bewährtister
Artzney-Mittel.** Nuremb., 1689. Fo. A few ll.
neatly reprd., 2 slightly affecting text, ?lacks last
blank.   Mod.   bds.   (S.   Jun.1; 27)
Hindersdorff. £130

HOHE LIED SALOMOS
Ill.:– Ludwig Hofmann. Berlin, 1921. (350)
numbered on Zandersbütten. 4to. Mor. gt., gt.
cover & inner & outer dentelle, hand-finished
end-ll., sigd. by Holzey & Sohn, Leipzig.
Dedication from Holzey. (D. Dec.11-13; 1093)
DM 1,600

HOHENDORF, George Guillaume, Baron d'
– **Bibliotheca Hohendorfiana.** The Hague, 1720. 3
pts. in 1 vol. Old cf., rebkd., worn. Bkplt. of John
Rowden Freme. (SM. Oct.7; 1408)   Frs. 1,800

HOLBACH, Paul Heinrich Dietrich von, Baron
[–] **La Politique Naturelle, ou Discours sur les Vrais
Principes du Gouvernement.** (L. [?Paris], 1773. 2

vols. Slight browning, owner's inscr. on titles.
Early 19th C. mott. cf., spines gt. (S. Jan.26; 237)
Pharos. £80
[–] **Système social ou Principes Naturels de la
Morale et de la Politique avec un examen de
l'influence du Gouvernement sur les Moeurs.** L.
[Amst.], 1773. 1st. Edn. 3 vols. 12mo. Slight
browning & soiling. Cont. cf., worn. (S.
Jan.26; 238)   *Pharos.* £150

HOLBEIN, Hans
– **The Celebrated Hans Holbein's Alphabet of
Death.** Ed.:– Edwin Tross. Ill.:– after Holbein.
Paris, Priv. ptd., 1856. Orig. cl., slightly affected
by damp. Pres. copy to Rodolph Weigel dtd. 21
Aug. 1856. (CSK. Feb.27; 58)   £50
– **The Dance of Death.** Ill.:– D. Deuchar. 1803. 4to.
Hf. cf., brkn. (BS. Feb.25; 249)   £65
– – **Anr. Copy.** Considerably foxed. Disbnd. (SG.
May 21; 380) $100
– – **Anr. Edn.** Ill.:– after W. Hollar. 1804. 4to.
Some ll. slightly browned, mainly marginal. Cont.
str.-grd.mor. gt. (SBA. Mar.4; 93)   *Duran.* £90
– – **Anr. Edn.** 1816. Cont. str.-grd. mor. gt. with
old reback. (TA. Jan.22; 310)   £78
– – **Anr. Copy.** Descriptions in Engl. & Fr., some
spotting. Cont. mor., rebkd. (CSK. Nov.14; 23)
£65
– – **Anr. Copy.** Red str.-grd. mor., upr. cover loose.
(SG. Sep.4; 258) $120
– **Facsimiles of Original Drawings.** Ed.:– Edmund
Lodge. Ill.:– Francis Bartolozzi. 1884. Fo. Cont.
hf. mor. (CSK. May 1; 169)   £120
– **Imitations of Original Drawings** ... Ill.:–
Bartolozzi. 1792. 1st. Edn. Lge. fo. 86 cold. ports.,
2 on 1 lf., many mntd., lacks List of Plts. &
Announcement. Old red hf. mor. (C. Jul.16; 331)
Taylor. £1,450
– – **Anr. Copy.** Vol. 1 only (of 2). 37 cold. plts.
Cont.   russ.,   gt.,   (S.   Nov.24; 163)
Broseghini. £500
– – **Anr. Edn.** Ed.:– John Chamberlaine & E.
Lodge. 1812. 4to. 1 port. with short tear in
margin, most ports. a little browned, part with
marginal stains. Cont. russ., rebkd. (S. May
5; 183)   *Duran.* £200

HOLBEIN, Hans–LYDGATE, D.J.
– **The Dance of Death.–The Daunce of Macaber.**
Ill.:– Hollar (1st. work). Ca. 1790. 2 works in 1 vol.
12mo. Spotted, some tears. Cont. cf., spine worn.
(SH. Jun.4; 128)   *Duran.* £60

HOLBERG, Ludvig 'Nicolas Klimius'
– **Journey to the World Under-Ground.** 1742.
Cont. cf. gt., spine defect. (P. Jul.3J; 6)
Thorp. £130
[–] **Nicolai Klimii Iter Subterraneum ... ac
Historiam Quintae Monarchiae adhuc nobis
incognitae.** Copen. & Leipzig, 1741. 1st. Edn. Sig.
of H. Drury. 18th. C. mor. triple gt. fillet, spine
gt., inner gt. dentelles. (SM. Oct.7; 1759)
Frs. 2,000

HOLCOMB, Wynn
– **Elphie et son Eléphant.** Paris, 1926. (500)
numbered. Fo. Loose as iss. in cold. pict. wraps. &
stiff paper covers. Pres. Copy, to Paskman, with
inscr. on outer cover. (SG. Apr.2; 136) $140

HOLCOTH, Robert
See–THOMAS A KEMPIS–HOLCOTH, Robert

HOLDERLIN, Friedrich
– **Hyperion.** [Leipzig], 1911. (100) on Bütten. 4to.
Mor., gold fillets. (R. Mar.31-Apr.4; 511)
DM 1,400
– **Sämmtliche Werke.** Ed.:– C. Th. Schwab.
Stuttgart & Tübingen, 1846. 1st. Coll. Edn. 2 vols.
End-papers with cont. MS. owner's mark. Cont.
linen, gt. & blind-tooled. (HK. May 15; 4475)
DM 2,800
– – **Anr. Copy.** With list of printing errors &
supp., title with restored tear & stp., vol. 2 title
bkd. at foot, slightly soiled. Cont. hf. linen. (D.
Dec.11-13; 785)   DM 1,250

HOLINSHED, Raphael
– **Chronicles.** [1587]. 2 vols. Fo. Lacks 2nd. title,
some worming & staining, a few marginal tears.
Old cf., rebkd. W.a.f. [STC 13569] (CSK.
Jan.23; 120)   £150
– **The Historie of Scotlande.** 1577. Extract from
1st. Edn. of the 'Chronicles'. Fo. 2E3 inserted
from anr. copy, N6 torn. 18th. C. cf., rebkd.
preserving old spine. W.a.f. (S. Dec.9; 285)
Thomas. £110

HOLITSCHER, A. & Zweig, Stefan
- Frans Masereel. Ill:– Masereel. Berlin, [1923].
1st. Edn. (150) numbered. Orig. red mor., cover
fillets, bd. s.-c. 1 woodcut sigd. (HK.
Nov.18-21; 2807) DM 550

HOLKOT, Robertus
- Super Quatuor Libros Sententiarum Questiones.
Paris, 15 July 1505. 4to. Cont. notes on last blank,
lacks fo. 08, some wormholes slightly affecting
text, slightly dampstained in places. Mod.
antique-style cf., gt. (S. May 5; 14) *Fhion.* £55

[HOLLAND]
[Amst.], [late 17th. & early 18th. C.] Fo. 13
engraved maps in 1 vol., a few minor stains, on
guards thro.-out., all hand-cold. in outl., with
historiated cartouches, sailing ships etc. 19th. C.
cf. bkd. paper bds. (SPB. Oct.1; 261) $2,200

HOLLAND, Henry, M.D.
- Travels in the Ionian Isles, Albania, Thessaly,
Macedonia. 1815. 4to. Cf. gt. (P. Oct.23; 34)
Rogers. £120

HOLLANDER, Eugen
- Die Karikatur und Satire in der Medizin; Die
Medizin in der klassischen Malerei; Plastik und
Medizin; Wunder Wundergeburt und
Wundergestalt in Einblattdrucken. Stuttgart,
1905-21. All 1st. Edns., except the 2nd. Together,
4 vols. 4to. Orig. hf. cl. (S. Feb.23; 61)
King. £160

HOLLAR, William
- Theatrum Mulierum [1643]. ca. 1780. 12mo.
Mor., worn. (BS. Jun.11; 351) £240

HOLLINGSWORTH, S.
[-] The Present State of Nova Scotia: with a Brief
Account of Canada, & the British Isles on the
Coast of North America. Edinb., 1787. 2nd. Edn.
Early 19th. C. hf. cf. [Sabin 32544] (S.
Jun.29; 194) *Arader.* £220

HOLLITSCHER, A.
- Amerika. Ill:– H. Struck. Berlin, [1922]. (100)
Privilege Edn. 4to. Orig. mor. Inscr. by artist, all
etchings sigd. by artist. (H. May 21/22; 1830)
DM 420

HOLLOWAY, E.
- The Celebrated Galleries of Munich. Leipzig, ca.
1850. 2 vols. in 1. 4to. Soiled. Cont. leath. (R.
Oct.14-18; 2666) DM 500
- The Munich Gallery. N.Y., ca. 1860. 2 vols. in 1.
4to. Soiled. Cont. leath., defect. (R. Mar
31-Apr.4; 1594) DM 500

HOLLSTEIN, F.W.H.
- German Engravings, Etchings & Woodcuts.
Amst., [1954-80]. Vols. 1-11, 16-23, 27 & 28, all
publd. 4to. Orig. linen. (H. Dec.9/10; 170)
DM 3,800

HOLLY, Henry Hudson
- Country Seats. N.Y., 1863. 1st. Edn. 4to. Cl.
(SG. Dec.4; 176) $180

HOLM, P.
- Sturmans Zee-Meeter.–Het Peyl Compas . . .
–Mond-Exame voor de Stierlieden . . . [Amst.],
5844, 5852 [1748, 1756]; 5855 [1759]. 2 vols. in 1.
Slightly browned or soiled. Cont. cf., slightly
worn, spine slightly defect. (H. Dec.9/10; 480)
DM 1,500

HOLM, S.
- Studier öfver Uppsala Universitets Anglosaxiska
Mynstamling. Uppsala, 1917. Orig. wraps. (SH.
Mar.6; 377) *Spink.* £75

HOLME, Charles
- Art in Photography; Colour Photography.
1905-08. 2 vols. 4to. Orig. wraps. (SH. Jul.9; 21)
Landry. £75

HOLME, Geoffrey
- Drawings in Pen & Pencil from Duerer's Day to
Ours. Ed:– George Sheringham. Ill:– Arthur
Rackham & others. L., 1922. 1st. Edn. Deluxe,
(250) numbered. Lge. 4to. Vell. Raymond M.
Sutton Jr. copy. (SG. May 7; 125) $170

HOLME, Randle
- The Academy of Armory, or, A Storehouse of
Armory & Blazon. Chester, 1688. Fo. Later
panel. cf. (SBA. Oct.22; 297) *Evans.* £260

HOLMES, Lewis
- The Arctic Whaleman, or Winter in the Arctic
Ocean. Boston, 1857. 1st. Edn. 12mo. Gt.-pict. cl.
(SG. Jan.8; 459) $130

HOLMES, Oliver Wendell
[-] The Autocrat of the Breakfast Table. Boston,
1859. L.P. Edn. Cl. (bdg. 'A'), many gatherings
sprung. Inscr., bkplt. of Gordon Abbot. (SG.
Nov.13; 326) $550
- Crime & Automatism. [1875]. (35). Offprinted
from the Atlantic Monthly for Apr. 1875. Sewed.
Inscr. (SG. Nov.13; 330) $400
- Songs & Poems of the Class of Eighteen
Hundred & Twenty-Nine. Boston, 1868. 3rd. Edn.
(30). Orig. Loose Sheets. Unc. & unopened. (SG.
Nov.13; 329) $130
- Soundings from the Atlantic. Boston, 1864. 1st.
Edn. 12mo. With advts. & 24-p. catalogue,
occasional marginal foxing. Cl., gt.-decor. spine,
red hf. mor. s.-c. Sigd. (SG. Nov.13; 328) $130
- Writings. Boston, n.d. Riverside Edn. 14 vols.
Hf. red mor., gt. panel. spines, by Sangorski &
Sutcliffe, slightly worn. (SPB. Nov.25; 462) $175

HOLMES, Oliver Wendell–MORSE, John
- Works.–Life & Letters of Oliver Wendell
Holmes. Boston, n.d. 14 vols.; 2 vols. Unif. hf. mor.
gt., slight wear. (SPB. May 29; 207) $225
- - Anr. Edn. Boston, n.d. Artists Edn., (750). 15
vols. IIf. crimson mor. gt., unc. (SPB.
Nov.25; 463) $500

HOLMES, Samuel
See–McCLELLAND, John–HOLMES, Samuel
–SHEPHARD, Charles

HOLMES, Thomas
- Great Metropolis. Ed.:– W.G. Fearnside &
Thomas Harrel. L., ca. 1851. Gt.-pict. cl. (SG.
Oct.30; 226) $100

HOLMES, Thomas James
- Cotton Mather: A Bibliography. Camb., 1940.
(500). 3 vols. 4to. Hf. lev. (SG. Jan.22; 287) $200
- Increase Mather: A Bibliography. Cleveland,
1931. (500). Sq. 8vo. Orig. hf. mor., spine worn.
(SG. Jan.22; 288) $140
- The Minor Mathers. Camb., 1940. (200). 4to.
Orig. hf. lev. (SG. Jan.22; 289) $225

HOLT, John
- General View of the Agriculture of the County of
Lancaster. 1794. L.P. 4to. MS. note in margins,
slightly spotted. Cont. hf. red mor. gt. (SBA.
Oct.22; 400) *Borron.* £80

HOMAN, Johann George
- Die Land- und Haus-Apotheke, oder Getreuer
und Gruendlicher Unterricht fuer den Bauer und
Stadtmann. Reading, Pa., 1818. 1st. Edn. 12mo.
Cont. leath.-bkd. bds. (SG. Sep.18; 186) $140

HOMANN, Johann Baptist, Heirs of
- Atlas Compendiarius . . . Nuremb., 1752 (but
after 1781). Fo., (530mm × 330mm). Engraved
title incorporating contents list in Latin &
German, 50 double-p. engraved maps, most
hand-cold. in outl., & principal areas fully cold.,
historiated & other title-cartouches, etc., variously
dtd., between 1741 & 1781, some un-dtd., repairs
to blank outer margins of title, astronomical plt. &
last 2 maps (Africa & America), some other
repairs, occasionally affecting engraved surface, a
few maps mis-bnd., 3 inverted, on later guards
thro.-out. Orig. limp leath., title in blind on cover.
(S. Nov.3; 20) *Nagle.* £1,400
- - Anr. Copy. 48 (of 50) double-p. hand-cold.
engraved maps, lacks Phaniglobium Terrestre &
Portug et Hispania, dampstained thro.-out, some
minor repairs, a sm. hole affecting top margin &
titles of some maps. Old cf., worn. (TA
Jun.18; 369) £1,100
- Atlas Geographicus Major. Nuremb., 1759;
1753. Thick Paper. 2 vols. Lge. fo. 2 vig. titles, 2
frontis., port., 253 engraved maps dtd. 1729-62,
some undtd., 91 plans, 2 plts. of tables, principal
areas thro.-out hand-cold., lacks 2 plans,
numbered thro.-out in MS. on plt. versos. Cont.
blind-panel. russ., spines gt. W.a.f. (S.
Mar.31; 267) *Grosser.* £25,00
- Städt-Atlas. Nuremb., 1762. Lge. fo. Some
browning on a few plts. especially in 2nd. hf. Vell.,
index tabs., cont. leath., oxydised gt. (R.
Oct.14-18; 1537) DM 70,000

HOMANN, [Johann Baptist]
- Atlas Minor. Nuremb., ca. 1729. Fo., 522mm ×
310mm. Maps hand-cold. in outl., principal areas
fully cold., wanting 15 maps, but including world
map & map of the Americas, wanting engraved
title, ptd. title reprd. & mntd. with slight loss, 8

maps reprd., with loss of surface, outer margins
thro.-out reinforced & guards renewed, some
staining. Cf.-bkd. paper bds., worn. W.a.f. (S.
Nov.3; 17) *Schuster.* £450
- Atlas Novus. Nuremb., ca. 1720, or later. Fo.
Hand-cold. engraved title, 46 (of 49) engraved
maps, hand-cold. in outl., principal areas fully
cold., 1 map separated in centre fold, some maps
torn & reprd., title & following lf. reprd., last lf.
of text M1 & contents table torn, some stains.
Cont. cf.-bkd. bds., worn. W.a.f. (S. Mar.31; 296)
Burgess. £1,900
- [Atlas] Sammelbd. mit 51 Kolor Kupferktn.
Nuremb., ca. 1720. Lge. fo. Some sm. tears &
margin repairs, plts. slightly soiled. Cont. leath.
(HK. Nov.18-21; 1050) DM 6,200
- Major Atlas Scholasticus. Nuremb., 1752. Lge.
fo. Sm. stain nearly thro.-out. Cont. limp leath.
(HK. May 12-14; 551) DM 7,400
- Neuer Atlas. Ed.:– J.G. Doppelmayr. Nuremb.,
1712-[1714]. Lge. fo. Lacks 3 maps, 2 supp. cold.
engraved maps bnd. in, title slightly soiled & hf.
bkd., text wormed & with some holes, 2 maps torn
at centre fold, 15 bkd. at lr., some sm. tears, some
bkd. & some soiling, 3 maps slightly browned.
Cont. cf., worn, wormed, spine very defect. (H.
Dec.9/10; 446) DM 25,200

HOME, Sir Everard
- Lectures on Comparative Anatomy, in which are
Explained the Preparations in the Hunterian
Collection. Ill.:– after W. Clift & Bauer. 1814-28.
4 vols. & 2 vols. Supp. 4to. Orig. bds., cl. spine,
unc. (S. Jun.16; 433) *Phillips.* £220

HOME, Henry, Lord Kames
See–KAMES, Henry Home, Lord

HOME, Robert
- Select Views in Mysore. 1794. 1st. Edn. 4to.
Occasional light marginal spotting. Cont. hf. cf.,
rebkd., corners worn. (S. Jun.29; 226)
Walter. £95
- - Anr. Copy. 4to. Cont. cf. gt. (P. Sep.11; 186)
Bilgrami. £90
See–ALEXANDER, William–HOME, Robert

**HOMENAJE DE DESPEDIDA A LAS
BRIGADAS INTERNACIONALES**
N.d. Mor. orig. wraps. (DS. Apr.24; 979)
Pts. 22,000

HOMER
- Gnomologia, Duplici Parallelismo illustrata.
Ed.:– James Duport. Camb., 1660. 1st. Edn. 4to.
Greek & Latin text, occasional browning. Cont.
spr. cf., spine gt., some wear. Edward Gibbons
bkplt. on front pastedown, John, Lord Sheffield's
beneath it. [Wing H2538] (S. Jan.26; 43)
Swales. £55
- Hymn to Aphrodite. Trans.:– F.L. Lucas. Ill.:–
Mark Severin. Gold. Cock. Pr., 1934. (750)
numbered, (100) specially bnd. 4to. Orig. red mor.
gt., s.-c. (S. Jul.31; 85) *Foyles.* £150
- The Iliad. Trans.:– A. Pope. L., 1715. 5 vols. in 3.
4to. Cont. cf., tooled gt. spines. Markee copy with
Liby. ticket, inscr. 'Ex Libris Rob. Synge'. (GM.
Apr.30; 552) £80
- - Anr. Edn. Trans.:– Alexander Pope. 1715-20.
1st. Edn. 6 vols. Fo. Tall copy. Cont. cf., gt. spines.
From the collection of Eric Sexton. (C.
Apr.15; 132) *Quaritch.* £470
- - Anr. Edn. Trans.:– Alexander Pope. Ill.:–
Rudolph Koch. Nones. Pr., 1931. (1450)
numbered. Orig. niger mor., unopened, s.-c. (S.
Jul.31; 114) *Appleton* £65
- - Anr. Copy. Text in Engl. & Greek. Red mor.
(SPB. Nov.25; 375) $175
- L'Iliade. [French]. Trans.:– M. de Rochefort.
Paris, 1772. 3 vols. 18th. C. pr. mark on fly-lf. in
each vol. 'Tabl. I. No 64'. Cont. red mor., triple gt.
fillet, spine gt. in compartments, inner gt. dentelles.
(SM. Oct.7; 1760) Frs. 4,000
- Ilias [Greek]. Munich, 1923 (615) on Bütten. Fo.
2 ll. publisher's advts. Orig. vell., fillets, lr. cover
slightly soiled, by Fr. Thiersch, s.-c. (HK. May
12-14; 1799) DM 800
- The Iliad.–The Odyssey. Trans.:– Alexander
Pope. L., 1771. Compl. in 9 vols. Old mott. cf.,
later gt. spines, some end-papers loose, bkplt. (SG.
Feb.5; 173) $160
- - Anr. Edn. Trans.:– Alexander Pope. Ca. 1870?
2 vols. 32mo. Slightly browned. Orig. cl.,
dampstained, limp roan case & lev. mor. book-box.
General Charles George Gordon's copies, with an
A.Ls. by him inserted. (S. Jun.23; 415)
Hosain Books. £150

HOMER -contd.

– – **Anr. Edn.** Trans.:– Alexander Pope. Nones. Pr., 1931. 2 vols. Orig. pig. unc., s.-c.'s., upr. cover of 1 vol. slightly stained. (C. Feb.4; 201) *Walford.* £85

– **L'Illiade–L'Odyssée. [French]** Trans:– Bitaubé. 1787-88. 12 vols. 18mo. Cont. long-grd. red mor., gt. fillet, watered silk doubls. & end-ll. (HD. Jun.30; 31) Frs. 3,300

– **Inno a Cerere.** Trans.:– L. Lamberti. Parma, 1805. Fo. Text in Italian & Greek. Cont. str.-grd. mor. gt., with wide gt. borders. (BS. Jun.11; 29) £280

– **Odyssey [English].** Trans.:– John Ogilby. Ill.:– Faithorne (port.), White (frontis.). Priv. ptd., 1669. Fo. 4 ll. dampstained. Cont. panel. cf. [Wing H2555] (C. Feb.25; 158) *O'Hern.* £120

– – **Anr. Edn.** Trans.:– S.H. Butcher & Andrew Lang. Ill.:– William R. Flint. L., 1924. (530) numbered. 4to. Buckram, partly unc. (SG. Apr.2; 112) $130

– – **Anr. Copy.** (SG. Oct.23; 123) $110

– – **Anr. Edn.** Trans.:– Alexander Pope. Ill.:– Rudolf Koch & Fritz Kredel. Nones. Pr., 1931. (1300). Orig. niger mor., s.-c. (SH. Feb.19; 131) *Lawson.* £65

– – **Anr. Edn.** Trans.:– T.E. Lawrence. 1932. (530). 4to. Orig. mor., partly unc., s.-c (S. Jun.9; 9) *Maggs.* £320

– – **Anr. Copy.** Mor., s.-c., partly unc. (LC. Feb.12; 30) £240

– – **Anr. Copy.** Orig. mor., s.-c., worn slightly. Inscr. by Sir Emery Walker to Harry Count Kessler. (SH. Dec.19; 482) *Barry Scott.* £210

– – **Anr. Copy.** Spine gt.-lettered, partly unc., s.-c. by W.H. Smith & Sons, gt. & black roundels by Bruce Rogers. (CNY. Oct.1; 104) $750

– **Odyssée. [French].** Trans.:– Leconte de Lisle. Ill.:– Rochegrosse. Paris, 1930. (40) on grand Japon Impérial, sigd. by artist. 4to. 2 states of etchings, 1 with remarque, 8 orig. wtrcolr. ills. at end. Red mor. by Septier, orig. wraps. bnd. in, s.-c. A.L.s. by artist loosely inserted. (SM. Oct.8; 2344) Frs. 6,500

– – **Anr. Edn.** Trans.:– Victor Bernard. Ill.:– Hans Erni. Lausanne, 1957-58. (186). 3 vols. Fo. Orig. wraps., folders, & boxes. Sigd. by artist & publisher. (SPB. Nov.25; 264) $500

– **Odüssee. [German].** Trans.:– J.H. Voss. Hamburg, 1781. 1st. Compl. Edn. Title slightly soiled or browned, 1 lf. torn. Cont. hf. leath. (H. Dec.9/10; 1694) DM 850

– – **Anr. Edn.** Tübingen, 1806. 3rd. Iss. 2 pts. in 1 vol. Cont. cf. gt., double gold fillet & narrow border, gt. cover, inner & outer dentelle. (HK. May 15; 5000) DM 850

– – **Anr. Edn.** Trans.:– R.A. Schröder. Leipzig, 1910. (425) numbered. 2 vols. 4to. Orig. hf. vell. gt. (HK. Nov.18-21, 2788) DM 2,100

– – **Anr. Edn.** Trans.:– J.H. Voss. Munich, 1926. (280) numbered. Orig. vell., spine & cover fillets, bd. s.-c. (HK. Nov.18-21; 2461) DM 850

– **Odyssee. [Greek].** Ed.:– E. Schwarz. Munich, 1924. (615) on Zanders-Bütten. Fo. Orig. vell., fillets, by F. Thiersch, s.-c. (HK. May 12-14; 1800) DM 800

– **Oeuvres.** Trans.:– Madame Dacier. Leyden, 1766. 7 vols. 12mo. Red hf. mor. by Dupré, decor. spines. (SM. Feb.11; 76) Frs. 2,100

– **Opera. [Greek].** Glasgow, 1756-58. 4 vols. Fo. Set lacks general title. Cont. red str.-grd. mor., gt., spines tooled in compartments, decor. covers. (S. Nov.24; 164) *Cumming.* £450

– **Opere.** Trans.:– Anton Maria Salvini. Padua, 1742. 2nd. Edn. 2 vols. Cont. mor. by Padeloup with his ticket, triple gt. fillet, spine compartments semé with 'drawer handle' & sm. triangular tools & dots, wide inner & floral dentelles with 'drawer handle' border, sm. wormhole in vol. 11. (SM. Oct.7; 1761) Frs. 1,500

– **The Whole Works ...** Trans.:– George Chapman. Ill.:– John Farleigh. Oxford, Shakes. Hd. Pr., 1930-31. (450). 5 vols. 4to. Hf. cf. gt., unc. & unopened. The John A. Saks copy. (CNY. Oct.1; 106) $300

– – **Anr. Copy.** Numbered. Fo. Buckram covers, leath. spines & tips, unc., unopened. (SG. Sep.4; 417) $130

– **Werke.** Trans.:– J.H. Voss. Ill.:– Rosmaester. Königsberg, 1802. 2nd. Iss. 4 pts. in 2 vols. Slightly soiled. Cont. red mor., blind-stpd., gt. spine, cover, inner & outer dentelle. (HK. May 15; 4998) DM 900

– **Works. [Greek].** Glasgow, 1756-58. L.P. 4 vols. Fo. Red ruled thro.-out. Cont. mor. gt., gt. tooled

borders on sides with gt. Royal arms, spines gt. in 7 compartments. Sigd. inscr. by E. Barnard, Master of Eton School, notes this bk. was pres. by H.M. George III to George Talbot Hatley Foote. (C. Jul.16; 341) *Quaritch.* £2,400

See—MORRIS, William

HOMILIAE et Postillae Doctorum super Evangeliis de Tempore et Sanctis
Ed.:– [Paulus Diaconus]. Speier, Peter Drach, 7 Sep., 1482. Fo. Spaces for initial capitals, which are supplied in red, 1st. lf. torn from conjugate at top & bottom, some slight marginal tears, wormhole to margin of 1st. lf., a cont. MS. table of contents bnd. in at rear. Cont. South German blind-stpd. pig over wood bds., central panels of covers with floral diapeter & repetitions of floral lozenge tool, brass clasps & catches. From the collection of Eric Sexton. [BMC II, 492, Goff H316, HC 8790*] (CNY. Apr.8; 159) $2,200

HOMMAGE aux Dames
Paris, [1834]. 16mo. Cont. cold. decor. bds., covers decor., matching s.-c. (HD. Apr.10; 138) Frs. 1,300

HOMMAIRE DE HELL, Xavier
– **Les Steppes de la Mer Caspienne, Le Caucase, La Crimée et la Russie Meridionale.** 1843-44. 4 vols. including atlas. Atlas fo. Orig. bdg. (P. Feb.19; 152) *Maggs.* £520

– – **Anr. Edn.** Paris & Strasbourg, 1843-45. 5 vols. in 4, including atlas of plts. 8vo. & fo. Lacks 3 maps. Cont. cf.-bkd. bds. (SH. Nov.7; 415) *Kossow.* £350

HOMO Apostolicus Instructus in sua Vocatione
See-THEODORO a Spiritu Sancto ... HOMO Apostolicus Instructus in sua Vocatione

HONDIUS, Henricus
– **Icones Virorum Nostra Patrumque Memoria Illustrium ...** [The Hague], 1599. Fo. Title-lf. soiled with old owner's mark, several ports. soiled at margin. Loose in old bds., very defect. (H. May 21/22; 724) DM 1,100

HONDIUS, Jodocus
See-MERCATOR, Gerard & Hondius, Jocodus

HONESTO ESSEMPIO (L')
Venice, 1551. 4to. 14 (of 16) ll., soiled & spotted. Mor. gt. (SPB. May 6; 205) $425

HONEY, William Bowyer
– **The Ceramic Art of China & other Countires of the Far East.** L., [1954]. Cl., d.-w. (SG. Mar.12; 73) $100

HOOD
See-VERNOR, Hood & Sharpe

HOOD, Thomas
– **Poems.** Ill.:– W. Miller after Birket Foster. L., 1872. 4to. Gt. & cold. cl. (SG. Mar.19; 199) $200
See-TENNYSON, Alfred & Charles–HOOD, Thomas

HOOD, Thomas & Reynolds, J.H.
[–] **Odes & Addresses to Great People.** L., 1825. 1st. Edn. 12mo. Later gt. cf., unc., bkplt. of William H. Dunwoody. (PNY. Mar.26; 151) $100

HOOFT, Peter Cornelis
– **Alle de Werken.** Amst., Leyden, Utrecht, 1703-04. Vols. I & II 4th. Printing. 4 vols. Some marginal foxing & minor stains in some upr. margins of vol 2, vols. I-II: Vol. IV. lacks plt. 'Ontzet van Leiden'. 19th. C. tree cf., lr. cover of vol. 1 loose. (VG. Nov.18; 1217) Fls. 2,000

– **Mengelwerken.** Ill.:– A. Blooteling after F. de Lairesse (title), Le Blon or Serwouters (emblems). Amst., Leyden (etc.), 1704. Fo. Cont. blind-stpd. vell. (VG. Nov.18; 1218) Fls. 490

– – **Anr. Copy.** Cont. cf., back gt. (VG. Dec.17; 1376) Fls. 475

– **Neederlandsche Historien, sedert de Ooverdraght der Heerschappye van Karel den Vyfden op Philips [tot her einde der Landtvooghyschap van Leicester].** Ill.:– C. Decker. Dordrecht & Amst., 1677. Fo. With the port of the author., upr. & lr. corners of last quires stained, 1 lf. torn & clumsily reprd., some short tears & a few marginal stains in places, ample margins. Cont. blind-stpd. vell., soiled & stained, lacks ties. (VG. Dec.17; 1374) Fls. 550

– – **Anr. Edn.** Ill.:– J. Luyken & others. Amst., 1703. 4th. Edn. 2 vols. Fo. Leath., covers detchd. (VG. Oct.13; 86) Fls. 1,300

HOOGEWERFF, G.J.
– **De Noord-Nederlansche Schilderkunst.** The Hague, 1936-47. 5 vols. Cl. gt. (VG. Nov.17; 506) Fls. 750

HOOKE, Robert
– **An Attempt to Prove the Motion of the Earth.** 1674. 1st. Edn. 4to. Mod. antique style cf. [Wing H2613] (S. Dec.2; 728) *Quaritch.* £320

– **Micrographia Restaurata or the Copper-plates of Dr. Hooke's Wonderful Discoveries by the Microscope.** Ed.:– [Henry Baker]. 1745. Fo. Cont. cf., rebkd. (S. Jun.16; 434) *Phelps.* £260

– **Posthumous Works ...** Ed.:– Richard Waller. 1705. Fo. A few ll. slightly spotted, f. 2V2 torn slightly affecting text. Cont. panel. cf. (S. Dec.2; 729) *Bopp.* £300

HOOKER, Sir Joseph Dalton
– **Himalayan Journals.** 1854. 1st. Edn. 2 vols. Cl., worn. (SH. Jul.9; 117) *Hosains.* £70

– – **Anr. Copy.** Orig. cl., worn, spines torn with loss. (CSK. Jun.5; 150) £50

– **Illustrations of Himalayan Plants.** Ill.:– W.H. Fitch. 1855. Lge. fo. Loose in gutta percha bdg. Orig. bds. (C. Jul.15; 150) *Quaritch.* £2,800

– **The Rhododendrons of Sikkim-Himalaya.** 1849. Fo. A few ll. slightly soiled, lacks list of plts & subscribers. Orig. cl., rebkd. (SH. Oct. 9; 226) *Marshall.* £850

– – **Anr. Copy.** Pt. 1 only (of 3). Orig. ptd. wraps., detchd. & defect. W.a.f. (C. Mar.18; 56) *Marshall.* £350

– – **Anr. Edn.** Ill.:– W.H. Fitch after Hooker. L., 1849-51. 3 pts. in 1 vol. Lge. fo. Lacks hf.-titles for pts. 2 & 3. Linen. (HK. May 12-14; 341) DM 5,800

HOOKER, Richard
– **Of the Lawes of Ecclesiastical Politie, Eight Books.** [1638]. 6 pts. in 1 vol. Fo. Old press marks on fly-ll., 19th. C. Harcourt bkplt. Cont. Fr. mor., lge. gt. lozenge in pointillé, decor. in panel with pointillé corner pieces & corner sprays, triple gt. fillet, spine compartments gt. in pointillé, slight stain. [STC 13720] (SM. Oct.7; 1762) Frs. 1,000

HOOKER, Sir William Jackson
– **Botanical Miscellany.** L., 1830-33. 1st. Edn. 3 vols. 103 (of 113) copper-plts., with the extra plt. 67, 40 (of 41) fully hand-cold. plts., sm. liby. stp. on face of each plt. Mod. hf. buckram. W.a.f. (SG. May 21; 386) $300

– **A Century of Ferns.** 1854. 4to. Cont. mor.-bkd. cl. (CSK. Aug.1; 133) £90

– **Exotic Flora.** Edinb., 1823-27. 3 vols. Some offsetting. Hf. mor. gt. From collection of Massachusetts Horticultural Society, stps. on titles. (SPB. Oct.1; 129) $1,800

– **Filices Exoticae.** L., [1857-]1859. 4to. Orig. cl., jnts. worn, liby. marks on spine. From collection of Massachusetts Horticultural Society, stps on plts. (SPB. Oct.1; 130) $600

– **Garden Ferns.** 1862. Some ll. loose. Orig. cl. (SKC. Dec.4; 1564) £65

– **Journal of a Tour in Iceland.** 1811. Diced cf. gt., worn. (P. Jan.22; 245a) *Hanas.* £75

– **Perthshire Illustrated.** Ill.:– Joseph Swan. 1843. Fo. Slight foxing. Mor.-bkd. bds. (CE. Jun.4; 62) £70

HOOKER, Sir William Jackson & Grenville, Robert Kaye
– **Icones Filicum.** L., [1827]-29-31[-32] 2 vols. Fo. Without list of subscribers. Hf. mor. gt. From collection of Massachusetts Horticultural Society, stps. on plts. (SPB. Oct.1; 131) $3,400

HOOLA VAN NOOTEN, Berthe
– **Fleurs, fruits et feuillages choisis de la flore et de la pomone de l'île de Java.** Ill.:– G. Severeyns. Brussels, 1863-64. 1st. Edn. Fo. Slight tears, soiling. Hf. mor., worn. (SPB. Oct.1; 198) $600

– – **Anr. Edn.** Ill.:– Depannemaeker. Brussels, [1885]. 3rd. Edn. Lge. fo. 40 chromolitho. plts., last 10 & accompanying text ll. with sm. hole. Orig. mor.-bkd. bds. (C. May 20; 213) *Walford.* £350

HOOPER, Johnson Jones
[–] **Some Adventures of Captain Simon Suggs ... together with 'Taking the Census', & other Alabama Sketches.** Ill.:– Darley. Phila., 1845. 1st. Edn. 12mo. Frontis. mntd., 5 pp. of Carey & Hart advts. dtd. May 1845. Old hf. cf. (SG. Jan.8; 198) $100

HOOPER, Robert
– **The Morbid Anatomy of the Human Brain.** Ill.:– plts. by J. Howship, J. Kirtland & others, engraved by J. Wedgewood & others. 1826. Lge. 4to. Orig. bds., rebkd. unc. (S. Jun.16; 435) *Norman.* £450
– **The Morbid Anatomy of the Human Uterus & its Appendages.** Ill.:– J. Howship, J. Kirtland & others. Priv. ptd., 1832. Lge. 4to. Orig. bds., spine & hinges worn, unc. (S. Jun.16; 436) *Korn.* £220

HOOTON, Charles
– **Colin Clink.** L., 1841. 1st. Edn. 3 vols. 12mo. Lacks hf.-titles. Three-qtr. mor. (SG. Oct.30; 195) $120

HOP, Egbert
– **Korte Beschryving van het Geheele Land van Cleve.** Ntmegen (sic), 1783. Bds., loose, ex-liby. (SG. Feb.5; 174) $450

HOPE, Anthony
– **The Dolly Dialogues.** Ill.:– Arthur Rackham. L., 1894. 1st. Edn., 1st. Iss. Sm. 4to. Orig. pict. wraps., foxed, folding cl. box. Raymond M. Sutton Jr. copy. (SG. May 7; 127) $280

HOPE, James
– **A Treatise on the Diseases of the Heart & Great Vessels.** 1832. 1st. Edn. Advt. lf. Orig. bds., unc. From liby. of Dr. E. Ashworth Underwood. (S. Feb.23; 230) *Gurney.* £190
– – **Anr. Edn.** 1839. 3rd. Edn. 16 pp. advts. dtd. Oct.1838, liby. stp. on title. Orig. cl., recased, unc. (S. Jun.16; 437) *Palinvrus.* £80

HOPE, Thomas
– **Costumes of the Ancients.** L., 1841. New Edn. 2 vols. Foxed. Cl., bdgs. brkn. & detchd. (CB. Feb.18; 193) Can. $110
– **Household Furniture & Interior Decoration.** 1807. Fo. Cont. red str.-grd. mor., rebkd. (S. Mar.17; 417) *Gordon.* £200
– – **Anr. Copy.** Fo. Spotted. Hf. mor. (SKC. Feb.26; 1444) £50
– – **Anr. Copy.** Foxed. Worn. (SG. Dec.4; 177) $400

HOPE, William
– **The Compleat Fencing Master.** 1691. 1st. Edn. Cancel title using sheets of 'The Scots Fencing Master' lacks A2, 2 plts. with sm. tears reprd., upr. hf. dampstained thro.-out, cont. MS. vocabulary of fencing terms in ink on end-paper. Cont. cf., worn, covers loose, in mor.-bkd s.-c. [Wing H2711 & H2714] (C. Nov.20; 255) *Quaritch.* £70

HOPE, Sir William H. St. John
– **The Stall Plates of the Knights of the Order of the Garter.** 1901. 1st. Edn. Fo. Orig. mor.-bkd. cl. (SH. Jun.4; 144) *Heraldry.* £80
– – **Anr. Copy.** 4to. Some ll. spotted. (CSK. Sep.26; 119) £60
See–**JEWITT, Llewellyn & Hope, W.H. St. John**

HOPKINS, Charles
– **Pyrrhus King of Epirus.** 1695. 1st. Edn. 4to. Recent hf. cf. [Wing H2726] (C. Nov.19; 101) *Sharples.* £60

HOPKINSON, J.
See–**CASH, J. & others**

HOPPE, David Heinrich
– **Ectypa Plantarum Ratisbonensium.** Regensburg, 1787-93. 1st. Edn. 8 vols. in 4. Fo. Plts. nature-ptd., with details of method in loosely inserted prospectus, some edges slightly discold. Cont. paper bds., worn, unc. From Chetham's Liby., Manchester. (C. Nov.26; 206) *Kistner.* £2,000
– – **Anr. Copy.** 8 vols. in 3. Cont. hf. cf. gt. From collection of Massachusetts Horticultural Society, plts. unstpd. (SPB. Oct.1; 132) $6,750

HOPPER, Thomas
– **Designs for the Houses of Parliament.** N.d. Ob. fo. Some spotting, margins of title & dedication torn. Orig. hf. mor., worn & disbnd. (CSK. Aug.1; 220) £110

HORACE
See–**HORATIUS FLACCUS, Quintus**

HORAE B.V.M.
(Chronologically irrespective of use)
– **Heures à l'Usaige de Rome.** Paris, Philippe Pigouchet for Simon Vostre, 22 Aug., 1498. On vell. 4to. Lge. initials & many other capitals illuminated in gt., blue & red, remaining capitals touched with yellow pigment, ruled in red, all woodcuts uncold. paper covers, s.-c. Mod. hf. mor., decor. The copy of John Thomas Simes & Richard Bennet, lately in the collection of Eric Sexton. [BMC VIII, 119, Goff H394, HC 8855] (CNY. Apr.8; 120) $10,000
– **Ces Presentes Heures à l'Usaige de Rome.** Paris, Philippe Pigouchet for Simon Vostre, 16 Sep., 1498. On vell. Histor. initials supplied in red, blue & gold, histor. borders fully cold., lacks E1, 4 & 5 with 2 woodcuts, some slight staining & soiling, mostly marginal. 16th. C. Fr. red mor. gt., lge. gt. central arabesque on covers against background some with sm. stars, lge. Inscr. of J. Whitluck, bkplt. of D.H. Van Dam, lately in the collection of Eric Sexton. [BMC VIII, 119, Goff H395] (CNY. Apr.8; 121) $8,500
– **Heures à l'Usage de Poitiers.** 1498. On vell. Red mor., fillet border, angle motifs, crowned cypher in mosaic oval, Charles Louis de Bourbon arms, decor. & mosaic spine, mor. doubl. decor. fleur de lis & crowned cypher, centre mosaic figure, mor. s.-c., by Lortie. Duc Robert de Parme liby. (HD. Jun.10; 37) Frs. 72,000
– **Hore Intemerate Virginis Marie Secu-du usum Romanu.** Paris, Thielman Kervcr, 16 Sep., 1499. On vell. Thirty-two 7-line histor. woodcut initials, histor. borders thro.-out, 2-line initials supplied in blue on red ground with gold & filled with flowers, other initials in red, blue & gold thro.-out, lacks i8 & h3, some slight staining, mostly marginal. Cont. blind-stpd. Parisian mor. over wood bds., covers with 3 ruled panels filled with quartrefoil ornaments, spine & edges defect., lacks 1 clasp, paste-downs renewed. The copy of Rowland Gibson Hazard, lately in the collection of Eric Sexton. [Goff H400, H.8859?] (CNY. Apr.8; 124) $1,300
– **Officium Beate Marie Virginis ad Usum Romanae Ecclesie.** Lyons, [Jacobinus Suigus & Nicolaus de Benedictis], 20 Mar., 1499/1500. On vell. Several woodcuts & borders cold. or partly cold. by an early hand & heightened in gold, lacks E1 & L4-6, sm. wormhole in 1st. lf., sm. reprd. tear to T1, some fore-e.'s cropped affecting borders, some staining at front & back. Pig. spine gt.-lettered with 7 raised bands, vell. linings & free end-ll., clasps, (by Katharine Adams). Bkplt. & sig. of C.H. St. John Hornby, later the copy of Major J.B. Abbey, recently in the collection of Eric Sexton. [BMC VIII. 324. Goff 048]. (CNY. Apr.8; 87) $2,800
– **Hore Intemerate Marie Virginis Secundum usum Bituricen[sem].** Paris, for Antoine Verard, 9 Feb., 1500. On vell. Forty-four 6- to 9-line histor. initials & 19 lge. woodcuts, all illuminated & heightened with gold, sm. initials & line-endings supplied thro.-out in red, blue & gold, pp. with lge. woodcuts with illuminated three-qtr. borders of flowers, fruit & leaves against patterned backgrounds of red, green, blue & gold in the Parisian style, lacks title a1 & f3 with blank vell. lf. tipped in, some blank margins darkened. Mor., spine gt.-lettered, vell. linings, by Eedy. Bkplt. & label of C.D. Dyson Perrins, lately in the collection of Eric Sexton. [Goff H341] (CNY. Apr.8; 126) $12,000
– **Heures à L'Uisage de . . .** Feb. 1500. On vell. Many ll. blackened, initials painted in red. Mod. mor., double fillet, blind-tooled with gt. corner fleurons, decor. spine, inside border, vell. doubls. & end-papers. (HD. Mar.18; 81) Frs. 7,500
– **Hore Intemerate Virginis Marie Secundu Usum Romanum cum Pluribus Oratio[n]ibus tam in Gallico q in Latino.** Paris, 5 Jan., 1503. On vell. Capital initials in red & blue heightened with gold, all woodcuts uncold. Mor. gt., gt.-ruled & blind-stpd. panel covers & cornerpieces, maroon mor. doubls. gt. with onlaid outl. design, maroon watered silk & marb. fly-ll., by Lortic Freres, qtr. red mor. gt. s.-c. 17th. C. inscr. of Pierre Danglade, bkplts. of Robert Hoe, Roderick Terry & John A. Saks. (CNY. Oct.1; 102) $8,500
– – **Anr. Edn.** 10 Jan. 1503. On vell. 4to. Title-p. reprd. with slight loss, sm. cut at head of 2nd. lf., initials painted in gold on red or blue background. Blind-tooled cf. covers, double border of roll-stps. between thick fillets, entirely remntd. (HD. Mar.18; 82) Frs. 13,000
– **Horae in Laudem Beatiss. Virginis Secundum Consuetudinem Romanae Curiae.** Venice, Jul., 1505. 32mo. 12 inner blank hinges reinforced with archival tape, perforated liby. stp. to lr. blank margin of 1st. & last ll. Old vell., fly-ll. at end renewed, folding cl. box. Bkplt. of the General Theological Seminary Liby. (CNY. Oct.1; 72) $8,000
– **Book of Hours, Use of Rome.** [Paris], [1507]. Ptd. on vell., some ll. with borders cropped, a number of ll. stained, text obscured in places, a few sm. holes. 18th C. Fr. mor., gt. (S. Jun.23; 220) *Duran.* £900
– **Hore Beate Marie Viginis scdm. usum Romanu sine Require.** Paris, 8 Oct., 1508. On vell., 17 miniatures, 28 sm. vigs., all hand-cold. & heightened in gold, rubricated, lacks 1 lf. Late cf., rebkd., solander case by Sangorski & Sutcliffe. Jacques-Charles Brunet copy, with MS. note. (SG. Oct.9; 131) $2,400
[–] **[Use of Rome].** Paris, [1509]. Ptd. on vell., lacks 1 lf., occasional light soiling, slight worming touching calendar & 1st. 2 woodcuts, 2 ll. slightly reprd., 2 others holed, not affecting text. 17th. C. stiff vell. (SPB. Oct.1; 231) $2,750
– **Hore Dive Vgis Marie . . . usum Romanu.** Paris, 24 Jul., 1511. On vell. 34 histor. initials, other initials supplied in red, blue & gold, some slight finger-soiling at edges, some natural vell. flaws at margins, old. liby. stp. partially removed from title. Mor., elab. blind-stpd., spine gt.-lettered, by F. Bedford, qtr. mor. gt. folding box. Bkplt. of the General Theological Seminary Liby. (CNY. Oct.1; 42) $6,000
– **Hore Beate Vginis Scdm Usum Romanu.** Paris, [1512]. On vell. 36 histor. initials (these & woodcuts illuminated & heightened with gold), other initials supplied in red blue & gold, title with slight traces of soiling. Mor., elab. blind-stpd., spine gt.-lettered, by F. Bedford, qtr. mor. gt. folding box. Bkplt. of the General Theological Seminary Liby. (CNY. Oct.1; 43) $9,000
– **Les Presentes Heures à L'Usaige de Tours.** Paris, ca. 1513. 17th. C. leath., gt. spine, double gold fillets, spine formerly renewed. (R. Oct.14-18; 100) DM 8,000
– **Heures à l'Usage de Poitiers.** Ca. 1514. On. vell. Mor., 2 double fillets, crowned angle cypher, Prince Charles-Louis de Bourbon arms, decor. spine with repeated cypher, red mor. doubl., fleurs de lis semé decor. & crowned centre cypher, mosaic, watered silk end-ll., mor. s.-c., by Lortic. Duc Robert de Parme liby. (HD. Jun.10; 38) Frs. 58,000
– **Heures à l'Usage de Rome.** Ill.:– Gillet Hardouyn. Paris, ca. 1515. On vell. 4to. 1st. ll. cockled, some decor. & miniatures with sm. faults. 18th. C. leath. (D. Dec.11-13; 34) DM 29,000
– **Heures de la Vierge.–Calendrier de 1515 à 1530.** Paris, ca. 1515. 16mo. Sm. restoration in margin of 1st. lf. 16th. C. black mor., dentelle. (HD. Jun.30, 30) Frs. 6,600
– **Ces Presentes Heures à l'Usaige de Rome.** Paris, 20 Sep., 1517. On vell. 11 pp. in woodcut borders, initials supplied in red, blue & gold, outer margins of 1st. 2 ll. with light soiling, sm. wormhole to margins of last 3 ll., old liby. stp. erased from title, some natural vell. flaws. Velvet, cl. folding box. Bkplt. of the General Theological Seminary Liby. (CNY. Oct.1; 44) $8,500
– **Hore deipare Virginis Marie secundu Usum Romanum.** 1520. On vell. 131 (of 132) ll., B8 supplied in facs., initials illuminated in red, blue & gold. 16th or 17th C. green velvet over paste-bd., reprd., worn, pastedowns from a Florentine MS. of Bruni's preface to & translation of Pseudo-Aristotle, Economics, ca. 1420-40 & by the same scribe as B.L. Add. MSS. 11931. W.a.f. (S. May 5; 22) *Symonds.* £420
– **Horae Beatae Mariae Virginis ad usum Romanum.** Paris, ca. 1520?. Lacks all ll. before calendar, as well as 3 other ll., most inner margins badly wormed. Cont. cf., blind-stpd., spine worn, covers defect., cl. box. W.a.f. (VG. Nov.18; 1222) Fls. 1,300
– **Hore Divine Virginis Marie secundum Usum Romanum.** Paris, ca. 1520. New Imp.; on vell. Sm. 8vo. Some miniatures soiled, sigd. 'A-M par 8. Repère Ro' on all quires. Old cf. (HD. Dec.5; 105) Frs. 19,000
– **Ces Presentes Heures à L'Uisage de Paris . . .** Paris, 19 Jun, 1525. Several ll. with marginal dampstaining, 3 ll. reprd., notably L8, MS. prayers in a cont. hand on end-papers. Cont. cf., gt. blind-tooled fillet border with corner fleurons, decor. spine, central plaque & oval, bdg. reprd. (HD. Mar.18; 83) Frs. 17,000
– **Hore dive v[ir]g[in]is Marie . . . usum Romanu[m].** Paris, 1527. 8vo. (6½ × 4½ inches). Hand-painted woodcut of anatomical man at verso of A1, text ptd. in hand-cold. & illuminated floriated borders,

HORAE B.V.M. *-contd.*
initials supplied thro.-out in red, blue, gold, ruled in red thro.-out, minor staining at top outer corner of some ll., a few ll. with minor marginal defects. Red mor., blind-tooled (rebkd.) the gt.-lettered backstrip preserved. On vell. (PNY. Mar.26; 44) $3,000
– Heures de Nostre Dame . .T. Trans.:– Pierre Gringoire. Ill.:– Gabriel Salmon. Paris, ca. 1527. 2nd. Edn., 1st. Printing. 1 pt. only (of 2, lacks the 'Chantes Royaux'). 4to. Cont. cf., roll-stps. in border, 2 roll-stps. forming central panel, spine remade. Bkplt. of A. Firmin-Didot. (HD. Mar.18; 84) Frs. 16,000
– Horae Beate Marie Virginis secundum usum Romanum. Paris, ca. 1527. Minor worming in title & a few other ll., vell in lr. portion of 8 ll. severely discold., sm. natural hole in border of F3. 18th. C. cf. gt. On vell. (C. Apr. 1; 140) *Wade.* £1,700
– Hore Beate Marie Secundu usum Romanum. Paris, 1527-38. On vell. Vell. reprd. slightly affecting text. 18th. C. Fr. mor., by [Derome le Jeune], monog. & coronet of Duke of Devonshire, gt., on covers, triple gt. fillet, flat spine gt. in compartments, inner gt. dentelles, later vell. end-ll., Chatsworth bkplt. (SM. Oct.7; 1763) Frs. 5,000
– Ces Presentes Heures à L'Usaige de Romme. Paris, ca. 1534. On vell. Some miniatures slightly rubbed or creased, some ll. slightly stained. Velvet over cf., vell. panel on upr. cover, in cl. box. (C. Nov.20; 192) *Roberts.* £1,400
– Horae, in Laudem Beatis, Virginis Mariae, ad Usum Romanum . . . Ill.:– Olivier Mallard. Paris, 1542. Additional folding plt., 'Triomphe de la Vierge', ruled copy. Cf., old covers, remntd., decor. with scrolls & mosaic in wax, spine similarly decor., mod. chagrin s.-c. (HD. Mar.18; 85) Frs. 51,000
– Heures à l'Usage de l'Abbaye de Fontevrault. Paris, 1546. Mor., sm. border & fillet, crowned semé cypher of Prince Charles-Louis de Bourbon, spine decor, inner dentelle, mor s.-c. Arms of Abbesse Louise de Bourbon on title, from Duc Robert de Parme liby. (HD. Jun.10; 39) Frs. 37,000
– Heures de Nostre Dame (Use of Rome). Paris, 1556. Early 17th. sig. on title-p. Mor. gt. by Trautz-Bauzonnet. (S. Jul.27; 127) *Bozzalato.* £650
– Horae Beatissimae Virginis Mariae, ad Usum Romanum Repurgatissimae. Antw., 1570. On vell. 1 full-p. miniature on c8 & 16 full-p. engrs. hand-cold. & illuminated with gold, 4 with painted three-qtr. borders of flowers, fruit & birds on gold ground, cold, & gold coat-of-arms, on title in similar border, 37 similar histor. initials & 11 similar lge. initials with fruit & flower ornament on gold grounds, many smaller initials thro.-out in blue & gold, the miniature & the 1st. 3 engrs. on vell., the other 13 engrs. on paper, cut-round & mntd., title-p. rubbed, slight abrasions to some ills., inserted blank lf. at front & 2 inserted ll. at end with MS. prayers in 16th. C. hand. Cont. Parisian mor. with red mor. strapwork & mor. onlays richly gt. à la fanfare with many sm. gt. tools of foliage, sprays, swirls, etc., flat spine similarly decor. & gt., restored in the early 19th. C. using the orig. covers & spine, jnts. worn, qtr. red mor. gt. folding box, early 19th. C. armorial bkplt. Previously in the Joseph Baer & Co. catalogue, later the copy of Fritz Kreisler & John A. Saks. (CNY. Oct.1; 77) $26,000
– L'Office de la Vierge Marie. Ill.:– J. Rabel. Paris, 1586. Cont. mor., fanfare style, gold-stpd., spiral decor., 4 monogs. in corners & 3 on spines, some stains. (D. Dec.11-13; 706) DM 1,200
– Office de la Semaine Sainte. Latin et françois à l'usage de Rome et de Paris. Paris, 1712. 12mo. Cont. mor., decor. spines, fleurs de lis & crowned cypher, coat-of-arms of Charlotte-Elisabeth de Bavière. (HD. Feb.18; 52) Frs. 2,500
– – Anr. Edn. Paris, 1726. New Edn. Cont. red mor., gt. spine cover, inner & outer dentelle, gold-stpd. arms. (HK. Nov.18-21; 1556) DM 460
– Officium B.M.V. Ill.:– Marco Pitteri after G.B. Piazzetta. Venice. 1740. 12mo. Light staining at head of 1st. 3 ll. Cont. Venetian red mor. gt., orig. mott. cf. gt. pull-off case, buckram s.-c. From the collection of John A. Saks. (C. Jun.10; 189) *Quaritch.* £550
– – Anr. Edn. Venice, 1758. Cont. Italian roan gt., covers with gt. borders, fan sprays at corners & central gt. onlays with the initials G.P. & A.P., gt. spine with 3 mor. gt. onlays. From the collection of John A.Saks. (C. Jun.10; 191) *Massey.* £50
– Heures presentées à Madame la Dauphine. Ill.:– Soubeyran after Sueur & others. Paris, [1764]. Cont. red mor., 5 decor. spine raised bands, lge. dentelle border, fillet & pointillé gt., inner dentelle, arms, restored. (LM. Mar.21; 296) B.Frs. 12,000
– Heures Nouvelles à l'Usage du Diocese d'Orléans. Orleans, 1774. 12mo. Cont. red mor. perhaps by Nicolas Padeloup with his ptd. ticket on end-paper, triple gt. fillet, spine gt. in compartments, inner gt. dentelles. (S. Apr.7; 360) *Duran.* £50
– Le Livre d'Heures de la Reine Anne de Bretagne. Paris, 1841. 2 vols. (Transcription & Reproduction). 4to. Facs. reproduction on vell. Red mor., clasps. (SM. Oct.8; 2194) Frs. 2,500
– Livre d'Heures, ou, Offices de l'Eglise. Ill.:– A. Guilbert after mediaeval MS.[s]. Paris, 1843. Ptd. in colours & gold, 1 lf. slightly spotted. Red mor. gt., gt. inner borders, by Sangorski & Sutcliffe, brown mor. s.-c., not en suite. (SH. Apr.9; 264) *De Beaumont.* £160
– Laudes Beatae Mariae Virginis. Ed.:– Sidney Carlyle Cockerell. Hammersmith, Kelms. Pr. 1896. (250). Fo. Orig. holland-bkd. bds., unc. (CNY. May 22; 327) $350
– Book of Hours. Ill.:– M. Kirkman & D. Hodgson. Late 19th. C. Ltd. Edn. 4to. Crimson mor. with ormolu onlays of religious figures, brass clasps. (P. Apr.9; 18) *De Metzy.* £190
– Libro de Horas. Bergamo, ca. 1900. 16mo. (5 × 2¾"). Ivory bdg., hinged at spine, with elab. floriated & strapwork sterling silver mounting at upr. cover, clasps, in soft cl.-lined diced red mor. folding-case, clasp. (PNY. Oct.1; 105) $225
– Horae Beatae Virginis Mariae. Ill.:– Eric Gill & Desmond Chute. St. Dominic's Pr., 1923. (220). 4to. Orig. linen, dampstained, unc. (S. Jul.31; 71) *Marks.* £120
– The Rohan Book of Hours . . . preface by the Duke of Rohan. Ed.:– M. Meiss & M. Thomas. Arcadia Pr., 1973. (55) numbered, sigd. by the Duke of Rohan. Fo. Orig. vell. by Zaehnsdorf. (CSK. Sep.12; 113) £70

HORAM, Son of Asmar 'Tales of the Genii'
See–**RIDLEY, James**

HORAPOLLO
– De Sacris Aegyptiorum Notis, Aegyptiace Expressis Libri Duo. Paris, 1574. Lacks final lf. o4 with printer's device, ll. *2-8 misbnd. at end, outer border of title-p. cropped. Purple mor. gt., mor.-tipped s.-c., by Noulhac. The copy of John A. Saks. (CNY. Oct.1; 108) $550
– Selecta Hieroglyphica. Rome, 1599. 32mo. Vell., soiled. (SH. Dec.10; 33) *Victoria Bookshop.* £125

HORATIUS Flaccus, Quintus
– Emblemata. Ed.:– Stefano Mulinari. Ill.:– after Otto van Veen. Flor., 1777. Pts. I-III (of 6). 4to. Cont. ptd. paper wraps., unc. (S. May 5; 80) *Parikian.* £160
– Horatius. [Colophon: Venice, May 1501]. Rubricated thro.-out, a few initials illuminated in gt. & cold ink, some early marginalia & underscoring. 18th. C. cf. Sir Shane Leslie's bkplt. (CSK. Nov.21; 14) £680
– Odes & Epodes. [Quotations]. Boston, 1901-04. (467) for the Bibliophile Society. 8 vols. in 10. Frontis. in 2 states, the proofs sigd. in pencil by the artists. Mor. gt., grape vine design with mor. gt. inlays. (SPB. May 6; 321) $650
– Oeuvres. Ed.:– Bentley, Cunningham & Sanadon. Hambourg, 1733. 5th. Edn. 4 vols. 4to. Cont. marb. cf., 5 spine raised bands, decor. (LM. Mar.21; 142) B.Frs. 7,500
– Opera. Ed.:– Christophorus Landinus. Flor., Antonio di Bartolommeo Miscomini, 5 Aug. 1482. Fo. 265 ll. (of 272), rubricated, 1st. & last ll. preserved, old liby. stp. on (*)2, a few marginal annots., stains. 18th. C. vell. bds. [HC 8881; BMC VI 637; Goff H447] (SPB. May 6; 198) $250
– – Anr. Edn. 1733. 2 vols. Cf.-bkd. bds. by Sangorski & Sutcliffe. (C. Jul.16; 332) *Taylor.* £60
– – Anr. Edn. 1733-37. Pine's Edn., 1st. Iss., with 'post est' on p. 108 of vol. 2. 2 vols. Cont. red str.-grd. mor. gt. (S. Nov.25; 473) *Duil.* £240
– – Anr. Copy. 4 ll. in vol. 1 with old tears & repairs, without the List of Antiques sheet sometimes present after the dedication in vol. 1, 10 watercolour drawings of Italian scenes bnd. in, inscrs. & sigs. of Revd. Joseph Parsons on title, Charles Price's sigs. on rectos of frontis.'s, later sig. on title of vol. 1 of W.H.D. Boyle. Late 18th. C. vell., diced & decor. gt. covers in painted borders gt. with tool, gt. lattice patterned spines, green lettering, rose silk linings, in style of Edwards of Halifax. 18th. C. bkplt. of C.J. Clarke, later the John A. Saks copy. (CNY. Oct.1; 182) $1,100
– – Anr. Copy. Mor., triple gt. fillet borders, spines gt., gt. dentelles, by Rivière. (SG. Oct.9; 190) $500
– – Anr. Copy. Cont. cf., gt. borders & spines, worn at jnts. Armorial bkplt. of Charles Hamilton of Hamwood. (SG. Sep.25; 251) $400
– – Anr. Edn. 1733-37. Pine's Edn., 2nd. Iss., with 'potes' on p. 108. of vol. 2 2 vols. Cont. Fr. (?) mor., gt., spines tooled in compartments, covers elab. decor., labels defect. (S. Nov.24; 166) *Niedhardt.* £300
– – Anr. Copy. 2 vols. Cont. Fr. red mor., gt. Bkplts. of W.G. Mack. (S. May 5; 430) *Lyon.* £220
– – Anr. Copy. 1 sm. liby. handstp. Cont. mott. cf., rebkd. in panel. cf., armorial bkplt. of Henry Beaumont, Whitley Hall, Yorkshire. (PNY. Mar.26; 154) $250
– – Anr. Copy. Minor tears. Cf. gt. by Tout. (SPB. May 29; 211) $125
– – Anr. Edn. Bg'ham., 1770. 4to. With the 4 other plts., slight browning, a little dampstaining to margin of frontis. & a few ll. Cont. Fr. red mor., spine gt., bkplt. of J. Buckle, Trinity College, Camb. (S. Apr.7; 397) *Murray Hill.* £90
– – Anr. Edn. 1773. 2 vols. Cf.-bkd. bds. by Sangorski & Sutcliffe. From the collection of Eric Sexton. (C. Apr.15; 9) *Harp.* £100
– – Anr. Edn. Parma, 1793. Lge. 4to. Cont. red str.-grd. mor., gt. border, gt. dentelles, satin doubls. & endll., spine gt., unc. (SG. May 14; 22) $750
– – Anr. Edn. Ill.:– Christ. Guil. Mitscherlich. Leipzig, 1800. 2 vols. in 4. Some browning., pencil inscr. on fly-lf. of vol. I. 'Payne & Foss, 1826 . . . fine paper'. Cont. red str.-grd. mor. by Bozerian, gt., spines tooled in compartments with ornaments, covers with border of ornaments, slightly rubbed. (S. Apr.7; 366) *Foyles.* £280
– Poemata Omnia. Venice, Sep., 1527. Initials, paragraph & headline marks supplied in blue & red (some of the red faded), slight offsetting & light spotting. Mor., elab. gt., by Charles Lewis, with his label, vell. end-papers, slightly spotted. (S. Feb.10; 447) *Maggs.* £240
– Poetae Venusini. Venice, 1549. Fo. Last lf. soiled, slightly stained. Later cf., jnts. worn. (CSK. Apr.24; 155) £60
– Satyra V. Parma, 1818. 4to. Cont. cf. Pres. copy, to Earl Cowper from Elizabeth, Duchess of Devonshire, Panshanger bkplt. (S. Jul.27; 160) *Marlborough Rare Books.* £60
– Zinnebeelden . . . met Bygedichten. Ill.:– Otto van Veen. Amst., 1683. 4to. Cont. vell. bds., soiled. (S. Feb.10; 310) *Haverbeke.* £95

HORATIUS, Flaccus Quintus–JUVENALIS, Decimus Junius
– Opera.–Satyrae. Ill.:– after N. Poussin (1st. engraved title). Paris, 1642; 1644. 2 works in 1 vol. Fo. 18th. C. mott. cf. (S. Dec.8; 145) *Quaritch.* £60

HORBLIT, Harrison D.
– One Hundred Books Famous in Science, based on an Exhibition held at the Grolier Club. N.Y., Grol. Cl., 1964. Ltd. Edn. 4to. Orig. buckram, s.-c. From Honeyman Collection. (S. May 20; 3262) *Simonin.* £180
– – Anr. Copy. Prospectus laid in. 2-tone buckram, boxed. Inscr. to Richard Wormser. (SG. Jan.22; 210) $300

HORBRECKER, K.
– Alte Vergessene Kinderbücher. Berlin, 1924. Orig. bds. (R. Oct.14-18; 553) DM 520

HORCHER, Phillipus
See–**STEMPEL, G. & Zelst, A.–ROMANO, A. –HORCHER, Phillipus**

HORE, P.H.
– History of the Town & County of Wexford. L., 1900-11. 1st. Edn. 6 vols. Orig. cl., gt. (GM. Apr.30; 414) £540

HORIZON: a Review of Literature & Art
Ed.:– Cyril Connolly. 1940-49. Nos. 1-121 in 119,

Index for nos.1-108. Orig. wraps. (S. Jul.22; 168)
Thomson. £115

HORMAN, William
- Vulgaria uiri Doctissimi Guil. L., 1519. 1st. Edn. 4to. Some ornamental woodcut initials, space for other initials with guide letters, lacks title & last lf., supplied in facs., 1st. 9 lines of 2nd. lf. in facs., lr. inner portions dampstained, more severely at end with dampstaining to upr. margins, minor worming at end, 16th. C. ink inscr. on t4r, later sig., some other early inscrs. Cont. blind-stpd. cf. over wood bds., the panels containing Tudor rose, crown & bird tools & the initials G.G., by Garrett Godfrey of Camb., brass clasps renewed, worn & carefully restored with portions of old backstrip by Riviere in 1926 & Gerlach in 1961, qtr. mor. gt. folding box. Bkplt. of Nathan C. Starr, bkplt. of John A. Saks, together with his 4to. cl. bnd. album of 48 ll. of typescript & inserted correspondence concerning this & other copies. [STC 13811] (CNY. Oct.1; 90)
$2,400

HORMANN, L.v. & others
- Wanderungen durch Tirol und Vorarlberg. Stuttgart, ca. 1890. Orig. linen. (R. Oct.14-18; 1971)
DM 450

HORN, or Hornius, Georg
- Accuratissima Orbis Delineatio. Den Haag, 1740. 7th. Latin Edn. Lge. fo. 53 (of 54) double-p. copper engraved maps. Cont. style hf. leath., gt. spine. (R. Oct.14-18; 1538)
DM 5,500
- A Compleat Body of Ancient Geography. Ill.:– Joannes Jansson. The Hague, 1741. 3rd. Edn. Fo. On guards thro.-out. Cont. hf. cf. & marb. bds. As an atlas, w.a.f. (C. May 20; 140)
Potter. £1,400

HORN, W.
- Moravian Costume: A Collection of 20 Coloured Plates. Ca. 1860. 2 plts. reprd., some slight soiling. In cl. portfo. As a collection of prints, w.a.f. (BS. Jun.11; 375)
£150

HORN, W.O. von
- Der Rhein. Geschichte und Sagen ... Wiesbaden, 1881. [3rd. Edn.?]. Hf. leath., blind-stpd., gt. (D. Dec.11-13; 1304)
DM 1,100
- - Anr. Copy. Orig. linen, gold-stpd., spine renewed. (R. Oct.14-18; 2419)
DM 900

HORN BOOK: Magazine of Books & Reading for Children & Young People
Ill.:– Arthur Rackham & others. Boston, May/Jun. 1940. Cold. pict. wraps. Raymond M. Sutton Jr. copy. (SG. May 7; 130)
$100

HORNBY, Joseph
- The Journal ... Ash. Pr., 1895. (33). Orig. paper-bkd. bds. (SH. Feb.19; 17) Maggs. £500

HORNE, H.P.
See–NICHOLSON, James B.–HORNE, H.P.

HORNE, Thomas Hartwell
- An Introduction to the Study of Bibliography. 1814. 1st. Edn. 2 vols. Some offsetting. Hf. cf. (S. Oct.21; 495)
Dawson. £65
- The Lakes of Lancashire, Westmoreland & Cumberland. 1816. [1st. Edn.?]. Fo. Spotted. Cont. cl., worn. (SH. Jun.18; 183) Tracchi. £95
- - Anr. Copy. 1st. plt. spotted. Hf. mor., worn. (P. Sep.11; 268)
Kidd. £90
See–FINDEN, Edward & William & Horne, T.H.

HORNEMANN, A.
- Ansichten der Adeligen Güter Holstein's, der Canzlei-Güter und der Adeligen Klöster. Hamburg, 1850. Ob. fo. Lacks 1 chiaroscuro, 1 added litho., lightly browned & soiled. Mod. pig. (H. Dec.9/10; 728)
DM 18,600

HORNER, John
- Views of buildings in the town & parish of Halifax. [1835]. Ob. fo. 1 plt. torn. Orig. wraps., soiled & torn. (CSK. Nov.7; 223)
£140
See–GRAVES, John–HORNER, John

HORNIGK, L.V.
See–SCHOTT, C.–HORNIGK, L.V.

HORNIUS, Georg
See–HORN, or Hornius, Georg

HOROWITZ, Isaiah
- Shnei Luchot Ha'brit. Amst., 1648-49. 1st. Edn. Fo. Lacks title, lr. margins of some ll. reprd. with loss of some words, lightly stained. Mod. hf. leath. (SPB. May 11; 129)
$450

HOROWITZ, Shabtai Scheftel
- Shefa Tal. Hanau, 1612. 1st. Edn. Fo. Title reprd. without loss, outer margins of 1st. 10 ll. reprd. with text loss, other repairs, cropped, some staining. Mod. hf. cf. (SPB. May 11; 131)
$375

HORR, Norton T.
- A Bibliography of Card-Games & of the History of Playing-Cards. Cleveland, 1892. 1st. Edn., (250) numbered & sigd. Cl., unc. (SG. Jan.22; 327)
$130

HORREBOW, Niels
- The Natural History of Iceland. 1758. 1st. Edn. in Engl. Fo. Mor.-bkd. cl. From Chetham's Liby., Manchester. (C. Nov.26; 207) Cash. £220
- - Anr. Copy. Some browning & soiling, a few short tears. Cont. hf. cf., worn, 1 cover detchd. Bkplt. & sig. of E.C. Chitty. (S. Dec.2; 515)
Hannas. £100

HORSBRUGH, Major Boyd
- The Game-Birds & Water-Fowl of South Africa. L., 1912. Qtr. mor. (SSA. Nov.5; 132) R. 650

HORSCHELT
- Etudes Militaires faites au Caucase. St. Petersb., 1896. 6 orig. pts. in 1 vol. Fo. Orig. wraps., orig. cl. portfo. (SH. Feb.5; 223) Lewinson. £60

HORSFIELD, Thomas Walker
- The History, Antiquities & Topography of the County of Sussex. 1835. 1st. Edn. 2 vols. 4to. Extra-ill. with some 350 plts., some tinted or cold. 19th. C. mor. gt., arms on covers. W.a.f. (C. May 20; 131)
Taylor £650
- - Anr. Copy. Slight foxing & spotting to prelims. Cont. pol. cf., rebkd. with old spine relaid. (TA. Nov.20; 83)
£150
- - Anr. Copy. Spotted. Cont. hf. cf. (SH. Nov.6; 116)
Wallis. £120
- - Anr. Copy. Spotting & browning, vol. 2 title preserved, clean tear in p.407, vol. 1 reprd. Cont. hf. mor., rebkd. (CSK. Sep.12; 212)
£60

HORSLEY, John
- Britannia Romana: or the Roman Antiquities of Britain. 1732. 1st. Edn. Fo. Slight staining at head of some ll. Cont. cf., gt., some wear. (S. Jan.27; 471)
Apthorp. £75

HORSLEY, Sir Victor
- The Structure & Functions of the Brain & Spinal Cord, being the Fullerian Lectures for 1891. 1892. 64 pp. advts. Orig. cl. (S. Jun.16; 438)
Levy. £90

HORSMANDEN, Daniel
[-] Journal of the Proceedings in the Detection of the Conspiracy ... for Burning the City of New-York. N.Y., 1744. 1st. Edn. 4to. No hf.-title (? if called for). Cont. wraps., unc., slightly worn. (S. May 5; 271)
Quaritch. £250

HORST, G.C.
- Dämonomagie. Frankfurt, 1818. Only Edn. 2 vols. Cont. bds. (R. Oct.14-18; 198) DM 980

HORST, Horst P.
- Photographs of a Decade. Ed.:– George Davis. N.Y., [1944]. 1st. Edn. 4to. Cl. (SG. Jul.9; 172)
$100

HORST, Tilman von der
- Bau-Kunst. Nuremb., 1763. 1st. German Edn. Slightly browned. Cont. leath., gt. spine, spine & lr. cover defect. (R. Oct.14-18; 434) DM 1,200
- Theatrum Machinarum Universale; of Nieuwe Algemeene Bouwkunde. Ill.:– Jan Schenk. Amst., 1739. 1st. Edn. Fo. Some spotting. Cont. russ., worn, covers detchd. From Chetham's Liby., Manchester. (C. Nov.26; 209) Taylor. £190
- - Anr. Copy. Plt. vol. only. Cont. hf. cf. (SH. Oct.9; 122)
Henderson. £140
- - Anr. Copy. Old russ. gt., covers detchd., worn. (C. May 20; 32A)
Taylor. £90

HORST, Tileman van der–ZYL, Jan van
- Theatrum Machinarum Universale.–Theatrum Machinarum Universale. Ill.:– Jan Schenk. Amst., 1736-34. 1st. Edns. 2 works in 2 vols. Fo. Cold. engraved map inserted at end of each vol., last pt. of each vol. in 8vo. & inlaid to size, plts. slightly spotted & discold. Cont. russ., worn, covers detchd. As a collection of plts., w.a.f. From Chetham's Liby., Manchester. (C. Nov.26; 208)
Weinreb. £500

HORT, Lieut. Col. John Josiah
[-] The Horse Guards, by the Two Mounted Sentries. 1850. Orig. pict. bds., soiled. (TA. Nov.20; 223)
£50

HORTENSE DE BEAUHARNAIS, Queen of Holland
- Reine Hortense en Italie, en France et en Angleterre pendant l'Année 1831. Fragmens de ses Mémoires ... 1834. Orig. Edn. Cont. pol. roan, fillet border., decor. spine, by Gouhbeau (HD. Feb.18; 139)
Frs. 1,400
- Romances Mises en Musique ... Ill.:– Normand, Richomme, Muller & Piringer. Paris, 1813. Ltd. 1st. Edn. Ob. 4to. Cont. red str.-grd. mor., smooth spine decor. with gt. fillets, palm-leaf border on covers, lyres in angles, crowned H cypher in centre, inside dentelle. (SM. Feb.11; 127)
Frs. 1,800
- - Anr. Edn. Ill.:– W. Read. [L.], [1824]. Ob. 4to. Extra-ill. with 56 engraved ports. & plts. (most cold., 3 on vell.), & 7 autographs (including A.L.s. from Hortense & D.s. from Napoleon I). Lev. mor. gt., covers tooled with 4 compartments of imperial olive-branches & Barberini bees, with the imperial Napoleonic monog. as cornerpieces, upr. cover set with circular port. in cols. on ivory, lr. cover with gt.-tooled imperial eagle, spine gt. in 6 compartments, 5 with bee & olive tools & 1 gt.-lettered, doubls. of ivory mor. seme with sm. onlaid cold. & gt.-tooled violet, floral brocade free end-papers, by Chambolle-Duru, mor. gt. silk-lined box (slightly worn) with Napoleonic emblems. From the Prescott Collection. (CNY. Feb.6; 162)
$5,200

HORTI Adonidis
See–THESAURUS Cornucopiae–HORTI Adonidis

HORTICULTURAL SOCIETY OF LONDON
- Transactions. 1812-30. 1st. Series. Vols. I-VII. 4to. Some imprints & plt. numbers cropped, occasional spotting & staining. 19th. C. russ., spines gt., not unif., 2 spines defect., 2 others worn, bkplt. of Baron Lynedoch. W.a.f. (S. Dec.3; 1163)
Walford. £580
- - Anr. Edn. 1820-30. Vols. I-VII. 4to. Some spotting. 19th. C. hf. mor. W.a.f. (S. Jun.1; 270)
Joseph. £420
- - Anr. Edn. 1820-42. 1st. Series vols. 4-7; 2nd. Series, vols. 1-3, in 37 pts. (includes 2 dupls.). 4to. Orig. ptd. wraps., some worn. W.a.f. (S. Dec.3; 1164)
Varekamp. £520

HORTINUS JULIUS ROSCIUS
- Icones Operum Misericordiae. Rome, 1585. 2 pts. in 1 vol. Fo. 14 unnumbered pp. Mod. hf. vell. (CR. Mar.19; 258)
Lire 460,000

HORTLEDER, Friedrich
- Der Romischen Keyser & Koniglichen Maiesteten. Gotha, 1645. [2nd. Edn.?] [1st. III. Edn.?]. Fo. Cont. vell. bds. (S. Oct.20; 112)
Fairburn. £480
- - Anr. Copy. 2 vols. Cont. blind-stpd. pig-bkd. wood bds., 2 brass clasps. (R. Oct.14-18; 2088)
DM 5,200

HORTON, Charles H.
- Photographs of Bristol Antiquities. 1908. Ob. fo. Orig. hf. mor., spine worn. From liby. of Reece Winstone. (TA. May 21; 401)
£90

HORTULUS ANIME
Ill.:– H. Springinsklee. Lyon, 9.xi.1517. 4 woodcuts & 2 initials cold & gold heightened, woodcut borders on each p., slightly soiled or stained in parts. Cont. cf.-bkd. wood bds., blind-tooled, slightly defect. & worn, lacks clasps. (H. May 21/22; 925)
DM 4,600
- - Anr. Edn. Dillingen, 1572. Scribbling & stp. on title, foxed & browned in places, tears in some pp., old annots. in places. Mod. blind-stpd. cf., brass clasps, antique style. (VG. Dec.17; 1381)
Fls. 500
- - Anr. Edn. Ed.:– Friedrich Doernhoeffer. Utrecht & The Hague, 1907. (50) numbered for the U.S. Sm. fo. Stpd. pig. (SG. May 14; 104)
$125

HORTUS SANITATIS
Ed.:– Joh. Wonnecke v. Cuba. Augsburg, 1485. 2nd. German Edn. Fo. 346 (of 370) ll., lacks full-p. title woodcut, some pp. bnd. on side, most plants in cont. MS. in ink, in German or Hebrew, also 19th. C. MS. in ink & pencil in German later numbers in MS., soiled thro.-out, 20 ll. approx. with faults, MS. notes on index ll. 19th. C. hf. linen, browned. (HK. Nov.18-21; 209) DM 8,500

HORTUS SANITATIS -contd.
– – **Anr. Edn.** Mainz, 23.VI.1491. 1st. Edn. Fo. Lacks 9 ll. including full-p. woodcuts, 1 full-p. woodcut present, slightly soiled in parts. especially at beginning & end, 2 ll. with tears reprd., 1 bkd., last lf. wormed, old MS. ills on pp. Mod. cf.-bkd. wood bds., spine torn. (H. Dec.9/10; 1347) DM 6,500
– – **Anr. Edn.** [Strassburg], [Johannes Pruess], [1497]. 2nd. or 3rd. Edn. 3 pts. in 1 vol. Fo. Lacks F1, G5 & 02 in pt. 2, some words on a2 erased & inserted in ink, all ills. crudely cold., 1st. & last quire detchd. from stitching, some cont. marginal notes in ink, sm. liby. stp. & owners' inscr. on title. 19th. C. hf. mor. From Chetham's Liby., *Way*. £160
Nov.20; 283) *Traylen*. £3,100

HORWART VON HOHENBURG, Hanns Friedrich
See–GRISONE, Federico–FAYSER, Johann –HORWART VON HOHENBURG, Hanns Friedrich

HORWOOD, Richard
– **Plan of the Cities of London & Westminster.** [1792-99]. Fo. With 32 sectional engraved maps (pasted together in 4's to form 8 sheets), with subscribers' list & index. Cont. hf. russ., worn, covers detchd. W.a.f. (C. Nov.6; 257) *Matthau*. £350
– – **Anr. Copy.** Iss. without engraved New Road view on A1, engraved plan on 32 double-p. sheets (A-H × 4), lacks index & subscribers' list. Mod. hf. mor. (S. Nov.25; 518) *Fletcher*. £120
– – **Anr. Edn.** 1799-1800. Fo. Lacks 2 engraved plans, index map. Loose as iss., slightly soiled. (SH. Nov.6; 117) *Fletcher*. £190

HOSHOUR, Samuel Klinefelter
[–] **Letters to Esq. Pedant, in the East, by Lorenzo Altisonant, an Emigrant to the West . . .** Camb. City, 1844. 1st. Edn. 12mo. Foxed. Cont. cross grain mor.-bkd. bds., worn. From liby. of William E. Wilson. (SPB. Apr.29; 142a) $325

HOSHU, Minamoto
– **Japanese Painting on Screens of the Momoyama Period.** [Kyoto], [1936]. Fo. Loose as iss. in brocade-covered bd. folding case with ivory clasps. (SG. Dec.4; 200) $300

HOSKINS, G.A.
– **Travels in Ethiopia.** 1835. 4to. Orig. cl. (C. Nov.5; 75) *Sawyer*. £380
– – **Anr. Copy.** Some slight foxing. Orig. cl. gt., worn. (BS. Jun.11; 163) £240

HOSMANN, Sigismund, the Younger
[–] **Fürtreffliches Denck-Mahl der Göttlichen Regierung . . .** Frankfurt & Leipzig, 1701. 2nd. Edn. 4to. Cont. cf., gt. arms of Danish family Helverskov on covers. (S. Mar.17; 248) *Norton*. £110
– – **Anr. Edn.** Leipzig, 1718. 4to. Short tear at bottom of 1st. plt., lacks 1 plt., 2 ll. & register, slight discolouration. Bds. (S. Nov.18; 662) *Valmadonna*. £130

HOTTEN, John Camden
[–] **Tracts on Flagellation Published from the Original Editions Collected by the Late Henry Thomas Buckle.** [1872]. Nos. 1-7. Orig. bds. with linen backstrip, s.-c. (TA. Nov.20; 465) £52

HOTTENROTH, Frederic
– **Deutsche Volkstrachten.** Frankfurt, 1898. Cont. hf. leath. (HK. May 12-14; 1153) DM 520
– – **Anr. Edn.** Frankfurt, 1898-1900. Vols. 1-2 (of 3). Sm. 4to. Orig. linen. (R. Mar.31-Apr.4; 1845) DM 2,400

HOTTINGER, Johann Henrico
– **Discursus Gemaricus de Incestu Creationis et Currus Opere.** Leiden, 1704. 4to. In Hebrew & Latin. Cl. (S. Nov.18; 663) *Rock*. £100
– **Etymologicum Orientale; sive Lexicon Harmonicum . . . Chaldaicae, Syriacae, Arabicae, Samaritanae, Aethiopicae, Talmudico-Rabbinicae Dialectorum.** Frankfurt, 1661. 1st. Edn. 4to. Some browning. Cont. cf., s.-c. (S. Apr.29; 399) *Brill*. £190

HOUBRAKEN, Arnold
– **De Groote Schouburgh der Nederlantsche Konstschilders en Schilderessen.** The Hague, 1753. 3 vols. Cont. mott. cf. (CSK. Oct.24; 188) £70

HOUDIN, Robert
– **Memoirs.** Ed.:– R. Shelton Mackenzie. Phila., 1859. 12mo. Cl. (SG. Apr.9; 209) $120

HOUGHTON FISHING Club
– **Chronicles.** Ed.:– Sir Herbert Maxwell. 1908. Ltd. Edn. Cl. (CE. Nov.20; 49) £50
– **Chronicles.–Further Chronicles.** Ed.:– Sir Herbert Maxwell; R.P. Page. L., 1908; 1932. 1st. work (350) numbered, on H.M.P. Together 2 vols. 4to. Cl., unc. (SG. Oct.16; 205) $180

HOUGHTON, John
– **England's Great Happiness, or a Dialogue between Content & Complaint . . .** 1677. 1st. Edn. 4to. Cl.-bkd. bds., lr. & outer edges unc. [Wing H2922] (C. Apr.1; 180) *Lawson*. £100

HOUGHTON LIBRARY, 1942-67
– **Selection of Books & Manuscripts in the Harvard Collections.** Camb., U.S.A., 1967. Fo. Many facs. ills. Orig. cl. (TA. Sep.18; 83) £54

HOUGHTON, Rev. William
– **British Fresh-Water Fishes.** Ill.:– after A.F. Lydon. 1879. Fo. Frontis. soiled, some foxing. Orig. hf. mor., spine worn. (TA. Oct.16; 314) £260
– – **Anr. Copy.** Orig. bdg. (DWB. May 15; 265) £200
– – **Anr. Copy.** 2 vols. Fo. Orig. cl., worn. (P. Jun.11; 266) *Graham*. £170
– – **Anr. Copy.** 1 vol. only (of 2). Some ll. slightly spotted. Orig. cl. gt. (SBA. May 27; 181) *Wilkinson*. £125

HOUPPELANDE, Guillermus
– **De Immortalitate Animae.** Paris, Denis Roce, 4 Apr. 1499. 4to. Vell. bds. [Goff H 495] (C. Apr.1; 47) *Fletcher*. £700

HOUSE of Commons
– **Report from the Select Commitee on the Hudson's Bay Company.** [L.], [1857]. Fo. Hf. leath. & cl. [Sabin 33549] (CB. Sep.24; 83) Can. $400
See–BODLEIAN Library–HOUSE of Commons

HOUSE of Commons of Canada
– **Official Reports of the Debates.** Ottawa, 1885. Vols. 17-20. 4to. Hf. leath. (CB. Sep.24; 191) Can. $160

HOUSE (THE) OF PEERESSES, or Female Oratory, Containing the Debates of Several Peeresses on the Bishop of Landaff's Bill for the more Effectual Discouragement of the Crime of Adultery.
1779. 4to. Slight browning. Late 19th. C. maroon mor. by W. Pratt, gt., Christie-Miller arms on covers. The Britwell copy. (S. Apr.7; 402) *Way*. £160

HOUSELL Brothers
– **Flags & Signals of all Nations.** L., ca. 1890[?]. Fo. New buckram. (SG. Oct.30; 154) $260

HOUSMAN, Alfred Edward
– **Poems.** L., Alcuin Pr., 1929. (325) sigd. Lev. mor. gt., gt. lf. trellis design, inlaid red mor. roses at each junction, round inlaid mor. centre ornament of initials of J.G., bnd. by Douglas Cockerell for Leippert, with his bkplt. With 1p. note by Housman. (SPB. Nov.25; 303) $500
– **A Shropshire Lad.** L., 1896. 1st. Edn., (350). 12mo. Orig. bds., with Carter & Sparrow's 'A' label, qtr. mor. s.-c., partly unopened. Pres. Copy, to Mrs. Sherburne Prescott, & with 2 A.L.s.'s to Prescott from Housman (26 Dec., 1930 & 3 Jan., 1931), & 2 other L.'s to Prescott from H.W. Auburn & John Carter. (CNY. Feb.6; 163) $9,500
– **Thirty Letters to Witter Bynner.** N.Y., 1957. (700). Cl.-bkd. patterned bds. Witter Bynner's copy with bkplt. (SG. Jun.4; 62) $110

HOUSMAN, Laurence (Ed.)
See–VENTURE . . .

HOUSSAYE, Abraham Nicolas Amelot de la
See–AMELOT de la Houssaye, Abraham Nicolas

HOUSSAYE, Arsène
– **Voyage à ma Fenêtre.** Ill.:– after Tony Johannot (frontis.), Celestin Nanteuil (title vig.). [1851]. Lge. 4to. Some foxing, mainly to 1st. pp.

Publisher's cold. cl. bds., tooled. (HD. Apr.9; 597) Frs. 1,000

HOUTTUYN, M.
[–] **Natuurlijke Historie of Uitvoerige Beschryving der Dieren . . .** Ed.:– Linnaeus. Amst., 1761-84. 1st. pt. nos. 1-7, 9 & 10; 2nd. pt. nos. 1-14; 3rd. pt. nos. 1-4, 3 vols. in 32 (of 37) pts. 1 plt. disbnd. & 2 loose. Cont. hf. cf., lacks 1 spine, 1 loose. W.a.f. (VG. Nov.18; 1257) Fls. 1,600
See–NOZEMAN, Cornelius & Houttuyn, Martinus
See–SELIGMANN, J.M. & Houttuyn, M.

HOUZEAU, J.C. & Lancaster, A.
– **Bibliographie Générale de l'Astronomie.** Brussels, 1887-89-82. 2 vols. in 4. 4to. A few ll. slightly defect. at fore-edges. Mor.-bkd. bds. From Honeyman Collection. (S. May 20; 3263) *Forster*. £85

HOW, George Evelyn Paget
– **English & Scottish Silver Spoons.** 1952-53. (550). 3 vols. Fo. Cl., d.-w. Pres. Copy. (C. Jul.22; 146) *Argentum*. £280

HOW TO DRESS A DOLL
Boston, ca. 1850. 16mo. Orig. ptd. wraps., pict. title repeated on upr. cover in red & blue. (SH. Mar.19; 137) *Clements Libr*. £70

HOWARD, Adolph Gislingham
– **Some Wild Flowers of South Africa.** Ca. 1910? 2 vols. 4to. Ll. loose, some browning & foxing. Spine defect. (VA. Aug.29; 301) R. 500

HOWARD, Brian
– **God Save the King.** Paris, Hours Pr., 1930. 1st. Edn. (150), sigd. Orig. mor.-bkd. pict. bds., unc. (S. Jul.22; 150) *Conway*. £80

HOWARD, David S.
– **Chinese Armorial Porcelain.** 1974. 4to. Orig. cl., d.-w. (S. Sep.30; 409) £65

HOWARD, Henry Eliot
– **The British Warblers.** Ill.:– H. Gronvold. 1907-14. 2 vols. Hf. mor. gt., by Sotheran. (C. May 20; 214) *Quaritch*. £420
– – **Anr. Copy.** Pts. 1-9 & supp. to pt. 9. Orig. bdgs. (DWB. Mar.31; 358) £260

HOWARD, J.E.
– **Illustrations of the Neuva Quinologia of Pavon.** L., 1862. Fo. Lightly soiled. Cont. hf. leath., upr. end-ll. loose. (HK. Nov.18-21; 584) DM 1,000

HOWARD, James
– **The English Mounsieur.** 1674. 1st. Edn. 4to. Mor. by Sangorski. [Wing H2980] (C. Nov.19; 102) *Quaritch*. £160

HOWARD, John
– **An Account of the Present State of the Prisons, Houses of Correction, & Hospitals in London & Westminster.** [1789]. Bnd. with 9 other pamphlets, all separately paginated. Cf. gt., spine in compartments. (LC. Oct.2; 302) £50
– **An Account of the Principal Lazerettos in Europe; with Various Papers Relative to the Plague: Together with Further Observations on Some Foreign Prisons & Hospitals.** 1791. 2nd. Edn. 4to. Margins soiled. Orig. bds., soiled, unc. & partly unopened. (TA. Apr.16; 453) £110
– – **Anr. Edn.** 1793. 2nd. Edn. 4to. Lacks table, slightly spotted. Later hf. cf. (SH. Nov.6; 220) *Ferrow*. £50
– **The State of the Prisons in England & Wales . . .** Warrington, 1784. 3rd. Edn. 4to. A few minor stains. Cont. diced russ., worn, bkplt. & monog. on covers of JD (John Disney D.D.?) with a note that the book was presented by author & 3 pieces of related ephemera loosely inserted including 4 pp. printed leaflet. (S. Dec.9; 395) *Weinreb*. £170
– – **Anr. Edn.** 1792. 4th. Edn. 4to. Margins soiled. Orig. bds., soiled, unc. & mainly unopened. (TA. Apr.16; 454) £95
– **The State of the Prisons in England & Wales. –Appendix to the State of the Prisons.** Warrington, 1777; 1784. 2 pts. in 1 vol. 4to. Most plts. folded & mntd. on linen, some soiling. Mod. hf. mor. (CSK. Jul.10; 87) £130

HOWARD, Sir Robert
– **Four New Plays.** 1665. 1st. Edn. Fo. Title mntd. with minor worming affecting imprint, tears in several ll., usually slightly affecting text, some staining. 19th. C. hf. cf. [Wing H2995] (C. Nov.19; 103) *Ludgrove*. £60

HOWARD, W.
See–LOWE, Edward Joseph & Howard W.

HOWAY, F.W.
See–SCHOLEFIELD, E.O.S. & Howay, F.W.

HOWE, E.R.J. Gambier
– Catalogue of British & American Bookplates Bequeathed by Sir W.A. Franks. 1903-04. 3 vols. Orig. cl. (SH. Jul.16; 98)   *Bentham.* £90
See–MELLOR, Meigs & Howe

HOWE, Henry
See–BARBER, John W. & Howe, Henry

HOWEL, J.
– Dendrologie ou la Forest de Dodonne. Paris, 1641. 4to. 19th. C. cf., triple blind-tooled fillets around covers, raised bands on spine, arms of Pavé de Vandoeuvre. (HD. Jun.24; 43)   *Frs.* 1,600

HOWEL, Laurence
[–] The Orthodox Communicant. 1721. Cont. Engl. mor., gt., spine tooled in compartments. Bkplt. of Shute Barrington, Bp. of Durham. (S. Nov.24; 168)   *Thorp.* £90

HOWEL, T.
– Journal of the Passage from India ... Asia Minor. [1789]. Cf. gt. (P. Oct.2; 7)   *Diba.* £75

HOWELL, James
[–] Dodona's Grove, or, the Vocall Forrest. Ill.:– Merian. 1640. 1st. Edn. Fo. Cont. cf., owner's inscr. on front end-paper of 'Jno. Scudamore 1685'. [STC 14872] (C. Feb.25; 159)
                                                      Laywood. £100
– Epistolae Ho-Elianae. L., 1737. 10th. Edn. Disbnd. Fore-e. pntg.; from the liby. of Zola E. Harvey. (SG. Mar.19; 140) $450
– Instructions for Forreine Travell. 1642. 1st. Edn. 12mo. Pp. 1/2 defect. Recent panel. cf. (TA. Jul.16; 226)   £70
– Londinopolis. 1657. Fo. Frontis. preserved. Old cf. (P. Nov.13; 42)   *Maggs.* £90
See–GIRAFFI, A.–HOWELL, James

HOWELL, Laurence
[–] The Orthodox Communicant. 1721. Cont. mor., gt. (S. Jun.9; 46)   *Thomas.* £60

HOWELLS, William Dean
– Venetian Life. Ill.:– Childe Hassam, Rhoda H. Nicholls & others. Boston, Riverside Pr., 1892. 2 vols. Gt.-decor. cl. (SG. Oct.23; 158) $130

HOWES, Clifton A.–JARRETT, Fred
– Canada: its Postage Stamps & Postal Stationary.–Stamps of British North America. Boston; Toronto, 1911; [1929]. 2 works in 2 vols. 4to.; 12mo. Ptd. wraps. (1st. work); & limp leatherette. (SG. Feb.12; 309) $130

HOWES, Wright
– U.S.-iana (1700-1950). N.Y., 1954. Cl. (SPB. Jul.28; 179) $225

HOWET, Marie
– A la Source d'ara. Ed.:– Stephen Gwyann (Preface). Paris, 1934. Orig. Edn., 1st. printing, (120) (30) priv. ptd. (15) numbered & sigd. on Montval. Ob. fo. In ll., ptd. wrap., publisher's s.-c. box. Orig. aquarelle & 41 metal reproduction stencils. (LM. Nov.8; 89)   *B.Frs.* 17,000
– Les Chansons d'Evangelia. Ed.:– Gustave Kahn (Preface). Paris, 1927. (155), (30) priv. ptd., (100) numbered & sigd. on Arches. 4to. Bds. (LM. Nov.8; 88)   *B.Frs.* 8,000

HOWIE, Charles
See–JEFFREY, John & Howie, Charles

HOWISON, John
– Sketches of Upper Canada. Edinb., 1821. 1st. Edn. Mod. cf.-bkd. bds. [Sabin 33366] (C. Nov.6; 213)   *O'Toole.* £55
– – Anr. Copy. Cont. bds., spine worn, orig. wraps. bnd. in. From liby. of William E. Wilson. (SPB. Apr.29; 143) $175
– Skizzen von Ober-Canada. Jena, 1822. Slightly soiled in parts. Cont. bds. (HK. May 12-14; 510)
                                                      DM 400

HOWITT, Alfred William
– The Native Tribes of South-East Australia. 1904. Orig. cl. (SH. Mar.5; 66)   *Dawson's.* £85
See–FISON, Lorimer & Howitt, Alfred William

HOWITT, Richard
– Impressions of Australia Felix ... L., 1845. 12mo. Rebnd. new marb. bds., qtr. mor., gt. title on spine. (JL. Jul.20; 732)   *Aus.* $150

HOWITT, Samuel
– British Preserve. 1824. 1st. Edn. 4to. Cl. spine reprd. (BS. Sep.17; 108)   £100
– The British Sportsman. L., 1 Mar. 1800. 1st. Bk. Edn. Ob. 4to. Slightly soiled, lacks 10 copperplts. Old hf. linen. (R. Oct.14-18; 2785)   DM 3,200
[–] – Anr. Edn. 1806. Ob. 4to. 1 plt. loose, 1 with tear. Hf. cf. (P. Jan.22; 249)   *Walford.* £620
– – Anr. Edn. 1812. New Edn. Ob. 4to. Extra hand-cold. engraved title & 71 hand-cold. etched plts. Lev. mor., gt., by Root. (C. Mar.18; 57)
                                                  Map House. £1,900
– – Anr. Copy. Hf. leath. (S. Mar.16; 209)
                                                      Dallai. £900
– – Anr. Copy. Title & frontis. foxed. Cont. str.-grd. mor., gt. & blind borders on sides, gt. spine. (C. Nov.5; 81)   *Marsden.* £650
– – Anr. Copy. Extra etched title & 71 etched plts. on india paper. Old style cf., gt. (C. Mar.18; 58)
                                                      Arader. £550
– – Anr. Copy. Etched frontis. & 70 plts., many with sm. ills. pasted over plt. imprints, some staining. Cont. hf. cf. gt. (C. May 20; 215)
                                                      Schuster. £180
– – Anr. Copy. Cont. diced russ. gt. (SPB. Oct.1; 90) $2,300
– – Anr. Copy. Lacks plts. 10, 21, 26 & 59. Red cont. long-grd. mor. gt., unif. newer hf. mor. s.-c. Cont. Fore-e.-pntg. (R. Mar.31-Apr.4; 1689)
                                                      DM 3,800
– – Anr. Edn. 1834. New Edn. 4to. Slight spotting. Later hf. mor. gt. (SBA. Dec.16; 130)
                                              Wienar Antiquariat. £630
– Etchings. Ca. 1830? New Edn. Ob. 8vo. A few margins slightly spotted. (SBA. Mar.4; 50a)
                                                  Angle Books. £100
– Groups of Animals. 1811. 4to. Some spotting. Cont. hf. cf. W.a.f. (TA. Aug.21; 232)   £180
– A New Work of Animals ... 1811. 4to. 98 (of 100) plts., 1 torn, anr. reprd. in upr. margin, text of smaller format, title mntd. 19th. C. red mor., gt., worn. (S. Apr.7; 415)   *Hyde Park.* £180
– – Anr. Copy. Hf. cf., spine gt., slight scuffing to bds. (LC. Feb.12; 27)   £120
– – Anr. Copy. Some margins slightly soiled or stained. Orig. cl., slightly worn, rebkd. new end-papers. (SBA. Mar.4; 51)   *Chesters.* £92
– – Anr. Copy. 4to. Some spotting. Cl., worn. (CSK. Aug.15; 104)   £85
– – Anr. Edn. L., 1818. [2nd. Edn.?] 4to. Slightly soiled, lacks plt. 20. Cont. leath. gt., worn. (R. Oct.14-18; 2788)   DM 920
See–HOFLAND, Thomas Christopher–HOWITT, Samuel
See–WILLIAMSON, Capt. Thomas & Howitt, Samuel

HOWITT, Samuel (Ill.)
See–FOREIGN Field Sports ...

HOWITT, W.
– The Student-Life of Germany. L., 1841. 4to. Cont. hf. leath. (D. Dec.11-13; 2330)   DM 450
– – Anr. Copy. Newer hf. leath. (H. Dec.9/10; 1030)   DM 420

HOWITT, William
– The Northern Heights of London, Highgate, Hampstead, Islington. 1871. 3 vols. Fo. A.L.s., ports., playbills etc. Hf. mor. gt., T.J. Barratt's bkplt. (P. Apr.9; 82)   *Walford.* £220

HOWLETT, Bartholomew
– A Selection of Views in the County of Lincoln. 1805. 4to. 1 or 2 plts. foxed, some browning of text. Cont. red str.-grd. mor., gt. borders & spine. (S. Jun.22; 44)   *Quaritch.* £130

HOWLETT, Bartholomew–TURNOR, Edmund
– A Selection of Views in the County of Lincoln. –Collections for the History of the Town & Soke of Grantham. 1805; 1806. L.P. 2 works in 1 vol. 4to. 1st. work: some browning of text; 2nd. work: 1 plt. spotted. Cont. russ., elab. gt. ornamental borders, rebkd., old gt. spine preserved, crest of an eagle at head. (S. Jun.22; 43)   *Traylen.* £160

HOWLETT, Robert
[–] The Anglers Sure Guide. 1706. 1st. Edn. Early 20th. C. lev. mor. by Roger de Coverly & Sons. (S. Nov.24; 170)   *Thorp.* £200
– School of Recreation. 1684. 1st. Edn. Browned thro.-out, lacks the 2 ll. of additional advts. called for by Schwerdt. Cf., rebkd., upr. cover detchd. [Wing H3194] (S. May 5; 272)   *Ockleton.* £60

HOWSON, John–TWYNE, Brian
– Uxore Dimissa Propter Fornicationem Aliam non Licet Superinducere.–Antiquitatis Academiae Oxoniensis Apologia. Oxford; Oxford, 1606; 1608. 2nd. Edn.; 1st. Edn. 2 works in 1 vol. 4to. Cont. cf. with central blind-stpd. medallion, lacks ties. (TA. Nov.20; 278)   £90

HOYER, Michael
– Flammulae Amoris. Ill.:– G. Collaert. Antw., 1708. 12mo. Lacks M12 blank. 19th. C. vell. bds. (S. Feb.10; 329)   *Hendricks.* £70

HOYLAND, John
– A Historical Survey of the ... Gypsies.–The Dangerous Voyage Performed by Captain Bligh. York; Dublin, 1816; 1824. 1st. Edn. (1st. work). 2 vols. Hf. cf.; sheep, worn. (S. Dec.8; 57)
                                                  Armstrong. £55

HOYM, Charles Henri, Comte d'
– Catalogus Librorum Bibliothecae. Paris, 1738. Priced in ink thro.-out., lacks 1st. lf (blank?), inscr. on fly-lf. Cont. cf., spine gt., worn. (SH. Oct.7; 1410)   *Frs.* 1,400

HOYNINGEN-HUELNE, George
– Hellas. N.Y., [1943]. 1st. Edn. Sm. fo. Cl., d.-w. (worn). Sigd. on hf.-title. (SG. Jul.9; 173) $100

HOYO, Jose del
– Relacion Completa, y exacta del Auto Publico de Fe, que se celebro en esta Ciudad de Lima a 20 Diziembre de 1694. Lima, 1695. Sm. 4to. Fly-ll. with owners' inscr. of the Franciscans at Buenos Aires, 1 dtd. 1732, some wormholes affecting text, a few ll. loose or soiled, sm. conventual stp. on title. Cont. limp vell., slightly defect. (SPB. May 5; 261)
                                                      $600

HOZIER, Capt. Henry Montague
– The Franco-Prussian War. With the Topography & History of the Rhine Valley by W.H. Davenport. Ill.:– After Birket Foster. [1870-72]. 3 pts. in 2 vols. 4to. Slight spotting. Cont. hf. cf. gt. (SBA. Oct.21; 53)   *Dupont et Fils.* £220
– – Anr. Copy. 3 pts. in 1 vol. 23 (of 27) engraved views, some maps partly cold. Cont. hf. mor., worn. (SBA. May 27; 295) *Hyde Park Bookshop.* £160
– – Anr. Edn. L., ca. 1875. 3 vols. in 2. 4to. 2 plans torn, title-lf. stpd., text & plts. slightly soiled in parts, some views with light stain at margin. Cont. hf. leath., worn. (H. May 21/22; 590)   DM 900
– – Anr. Edn. Ed.:– W.H. Davenport Adams. N.d. 2 vols. 4to. Some spotting. Cont. hf. cf. (CSK. Jan.30; 77)   £210
– – Anr. Copy. Mor., spines gt. (SKC. Dec.4; 1590)   £190
– – Anr. Copy. Divisions 1, 3-5 only. Orig. cl. gt. (P. Jul.30; 222)   *Schuster.* £50

HOZIER, Capt. H.M.–DAVENPORT-ADAMS, W.H.
– The Franco-Prussian War.–The Topography & History of the Rhine. N.d. Vol. 2 only. 4to. 3 folding maps torn, some spotting. Cont. hf. mor., jnts. worn. (CSK. Feb.13; 115)   £220

HOZIER, Louis Pierre de
[–] Armorial Général de la France. Ill.:– Jacob (port.). 1821, 1823. 2 vols. (all publd.). 4to. Cont. str.-grd. red mor., gt. roll-stps. & fillets around covers, arms of Comte d'Artois, smooth decor. spines, watered silk end-papers, inside dentelle, sm. stain on upr. cover of 2nd. vol. (HD. Feb.27; 147)   *Frs.* 3,500

HUART, L.
See–ALHOY, Maurice & Huart, L.
See–MUSEE POUR RIRE

HUARTE Navarro, Juan de Dios
– Essame de gl'Ingegni de gli Homini. Trans.:– C. Camilli. Venice, 1582. 1st. Edn. in Italian. Slight browning, owner's inscr. on title. Hf. cf., jnts. reprd. (S. Jul.27; 341)   *Allen.* £55

HUBBARD, Elbert
– A Little Journey to the Home of Thomas Alva Edison. East Aurora., [1913]. 12mo. Following text are 2 pp. of speech programmes at the Camp Co-operation, Sep.3-6, 1913, & 9 ll. of autograph sigs. (over 100). Specially bnd. in full crushed lev., gt.-lettered 'Camp Co-operation, Association Island, 1913. Do it electrically', lev. doubls. with gt. border round design, moire satin end-ll., by the Roycroft binders, in lev. solander s.-c. (SG. Aug.7; 308) $220

HUBBARD, Gurdon Saltonstall
- Incidents & Events in the Life of ... Ed.:–
Henry E. Hamilton. [Chic.], Priv. ptd., 1888. 1st.
Edn. Verso of port. soiled. Cl., bkplt. (SG.
Jan.8; 201) $100

HUBBARD, R.H.
- The National Gallery of Canada Catalogue of
Painting & Sculpture by ... Volume III:
Canadian School. Ottawa, 1910. 4to. Orig. card
covers. (PWP. Apr.9; 221) Can. $110

HUBBARD, William
- A Narrative of the Indian Wars in New-England,
from the First Planting, 1607, to 1677.
Stockbridge, May 1803. 1 lf. torn. Cont. mott. cf.
(SG. Jan.8; 203) $110
- A Narrative of the Troubles with the Indians in
New-England ... to which is added a Discourse
about the Warre with the Pequods in the year 1637.
Boston, 1677. [1st. Edn.]. 4to. Map & all prelims.
in photostat, headlines cropped, Table &
Postscript (7 ll.) followed by 88-p. 'Narrative of
the Troubles with Indians ... from Pascataqua to
Pemmaquid', light dampstaining, 10 line errata.
Old. cf., brkn. [Sabin 33445] (SG. Jan.8; 202)
$550

HUBER, Victor Aime
- The English Universities. Ed.:– Francis W.
Newman. L., 1843. 2 vols. in 3, as iss. Cont. cf. gt.,
rebkd. in gt.-panel. cf. (PNY. May 21; 220) $180

**HUBERT THE COTTAGE YOUTH, being a
Sequel to Phoebe, the Cottage Maid**
1812. 1st. Edn. 16mo. 7 aquatinted cut-out
figures, 2 hats & interchangeable head, all
hand-cold. Orig. ptd. wraps., s.-c. reprd., fitted
case. (SH. Mar.19; 65) *Schiller.* £210

HUBNER, Jacob
- Sammlung exotischer Schmetterlinge.–[Zütrage
zur Sammlung exotischer Schmetterlinge].
Augsburg; [Augsburg], 1806[-41]; [1808-37]. 3
vols.; 1 vol. 4to. Engraved titles in 1st. 2 vols. only,
Index Systematicus bnd. at end. of vol. III,
otherwise no text, some discolouration. 19th. C.
qtr. mor. (SPB. Nov.25; 91) $6,500

HUBNER, Jean
- Neu-vermehrtes und verbessertes Reales Staats-,
Zeitungs- und Conversations-Lexicon. Vienna,
1765. Slightly stained. Cont. leath., gt. spine. (R.
Oct.14-18; 550a) DM 420
- Reales Staats-, Zeitungs- und
Conversations-Lexicon. Leipzig, 1804. 2 pts. in 1
vol. Cont. hf. leath., reprd. (R. Mar.31-Apr.4; 128)
DM 580
- Schul-Atlas aus achtzehn Homannischen
Landkarten. [Nuremb.], 1754. Lge. fo. Later
maps heavily soiled & torn, many other maps
stained at margin. Cont. limp leath., cockled.
(HK. Nov.18-21; 1051) DM 2,800

HUC, le P.
- Souvenirs d'un Voyage dans la Tartarie ... 1844,
1845 et 1846. Paris, 1850. Orig. Edn. 2 vols. Some
browning. Cont. hf. mor., corners, decor. spines,
unc. (HD. Jun.10; 163) Frs. 2,200

HUCH, F.
- Neue Träume. Ill.:– A. Kubin. Munich, 1921.
(100) numbered Privilege Edn. Lge. 4to. Orig. hf.
vell. (HK. Nov.18-21; 2749) DM 850

HUDSON
See–BRY, Theodore de & others

HUDSON, William Henry
- Afoot in England. L., 1909. 1st. Edn. Cl. Inscr.
(SG. Nov.13; 342) $140
- Birds of La Plata. Ill.:– H. Gronvold. N.Y.,
1920. (1500). 2 vols. Fo. Orig. cl. (TA. Sep.18; 30)
£68
- The Book of a Naturalist. L., [1919]. 1st. Edn.
Cl., slightly worn. Inscr. (SG. Nov.13; 343) $120
- Collected Works. 1922-23. Ltd. Edn. 24 vols. A
few ll. crudely opened. Orig. cl. (CSK. Jun.26; 98)
£300
- - Anr. Copy. (CSK. Aug.15; 111) £280
- - Anr. Copy. Cl. gt., embossed port. medallion
on upr. covers, partly unc. (C. Jul.22; 15)
Joseph. £190
- Collected Works.–Biography of Men, Books &
Birds. 1923; 1924-25. 1st. work Ltd. Edn. 1st.
work: 24 vols., 2nd. work: 2 vols. Both cl. gt. (CE.
Oct.24; 16) £230

HUDSON'S BAY COMPANY
- Report of the Select Committee. 1857. Fo. Cont.
cl.-bkd. bds., worn. (SH. Mar.5; 69)
Remington. £130

HUDSON'S BAY RECORD SOCIETY
- London Correspondence inward from Eden
Colville ... [Vol. XIX]. Ed.:– E.E. Rich. L., 1956.
Ltd., numbered Edn. Orig. cl. (CB. Dec.9; 30)
Can. $120

HUE, J.
See–VERNET, Claude Joseph & Hue, J.

HUEFFER, Ford Madox
- Some do not.–No More Parades.–A Man could
Stand Up.–Last Post. L., [1924; 1925; 1926;
1928]. 1st. Edns. (except 1st. work). 4 works in 4
vols. 12mo. Cl., d.-w.'s. (SG. Nov.13; 225) $700
- Women & Men. Paris, Three Mountains Pr.,
1923. 1st. Edn. (300) numbered. Tall 8vo. Hf. cl.,
orig. wraps. bnd. in. (SG. Nov.13; 224) $110

HUET, N.
- Collection de Mammifères du Museum d'Historie
Naturelle de Paris. Paris, 1829. 2nd. Edn. 4to.
Title & 1 or 2 other ll. slightly dampstained. Later
mor.-bkd. bds. (S. May 5; 260) *Duran.* £170

HUETTE, Charles
See–BERNARD, Claude & Huette, Charles

HUFELAND, Christoph Wilhelm
- Enchiridion Medicum. Berlin, 1836. 1st. Edn.
Cont. blind-stpd. roan, ex liby. (SG. Sep.18; 190)
$220
- Die Homöopathie. Berlin, 1831. 1st. Book Edn.
Orig. bds. (R. Oct.14-18; 345) DM 420
- Praktische Uebersicht der Vorzüglichsten
Heilquellen Teutschlands nach eigenen
Erfahrungen. Berlin, 1815. 1st. Edn. Lightly
browned. Cont. hf. linen. (D. Dec.11-13; 209)
DM 460
- - Anr. Edn. Berlin, 1820. 2nd. Edn. Orig. hf.
leath. (D. Dec.11-13; 208) DM 560
- - Anr. Copy. 1 lf. torn. Cont. bds. (R.
Mar.31-Apr.4; 997) DM 550

HUGHES, George Ravensworth
See–CARRINGTON, John B. & Hughes, George
Ravensworth

HUGHES, Griffith
- The Natural History of Barbados. Priv. Ptd.,
1750. 1st. Edn., L.P. Fo. Lacks map, title loose,
tear in Hh1 reprd., some margins discold. 19th. C.
hf. mor. From Chetham's Liby., Manchester. (C.
Nov.27; 210) *Taylor.* £140
- - Anr. Edn. Ill.:– Ehret & others. 1750. 1st. Edn.
Fo. Cont. mott. cf., arms of Duke of Rutland gt.
stpd. on sides. [Sabin 33582] (C. May 20; 132)
Maggs. £450
- - Anr. Copy. Folding map reprd. & preserved,
repairs, severely browned, ex-liby. with stps. on
title & anr. p. Mod. hf. mor., some wear. (SPB.
May 5; 262) $250

HUGHES, John Arthur
- Garden Architecture & Landscape Gardening
illustrating the Architectural Embellishment of
Gardens. L., 1866. Orig. cl. (CB. May 27; 124)
Can. $200

HUGHES, John T.
- Doniphan's Expedition; Containing an Account
of the Conquest of New Mexico. Cinc., 1848. 2nd.
Edn., 2nd. Iss. Map slightly torn, some foxing &
soiling. Cont. cf., rebkd., scarred, new end-papers.
From liby. of William E. Wilson. (SPB.
Apr.29; 145) $200

HUGHES, Langston
- Scottsboro Limited. Ill.:– Prentiss Taylor. N.Y.,
1932. 1st. Edn., (30) sigd. by Hughes & Taylor.
Fo. Orig. cl.-bkd. ptd. bds., slight wear. Pres. copy
from Taylor to H. Bacon Collamore. (SPB.
Nov.25; 304) $450

HUGHES, Richard
[-] Lines written upon first Observing an Elephant
devoured by a Roc. Gold. Cock. Pr., [1922]. Ltd.
1st. Edn., numbered Orig. wraps., unc. Inscr. to
Walter de la Mare & family. (SH. Dec.18; 183)
Lincoln. £80

HUGHES, Ted
- Cave Birds, ten poems. Ill.:– Leonard Baskin.
1975. (100) sigd. by author & artist. Text
interspersed with facs. of MSS. Text in vell.-bkd.
portfo. with prints, all in canvas portfo. with ties.
(C. Feb.4; 189a) *Ayres.* £50

HUGHES, Thomas
- Ancient Chester. 1880. (300). Fo. Slight spotting.
Cont. hf. mor., slightly soiled. (CSK. Jan.9; 202)
£75
[-] The Scouring of the White Horse. Ill.:– after
Richard Doyle. 1859. 1st. Edn. Slightly spotted.
Orig. cl. gt., worn. Pres. Copy. (S. Oct.1; 571)
£80
[-] Tom Brown at Oxford. 1861. 1st. Edn. 3 vols.
Mntd. photograph port. as frontis. Mor. gt. Pres.
Copy from publisher to Mrs. Thomas Hughes. (S.
Oct.1; 572) £130

HUGHES, Rev. Thomas Smart
- Travels in Sicily, Greece & Albania. 1820. [1st.
Edn?]. 2 vols. 4to. Cont. panel. cf. (CSK. May
1; 100) £150
- - Anr. Copy. Cont. cf. (SG. Feb.26; 173) $220
- - Anr. Edn. 1830. 2nd. Edn. 2 vols. Cont. cf., gt.
(CSK. May 1; 101) £95
- - Anr. Copy. 13 (of 15) plts., some tears, a few
other very minor defects. Cont. hf. cf., slightly
worn. (SBA. Mar.4; 111) *O'Neil.* £90

HUGHES, William
- Compleat Vineyard: or A most excellent Way for
the Planting of Vines. 1665. 1st. Edn. 4to. Some ll.
stained. Wrap. (BS. Sep.17; 48) £85

HUGHSON, David
- Walks through London. L., 1817. 2 vols. Sm.
12mo. Old cf., spines gt. (SG. Feb.26; 174) $170

HUGNET, Georges
- La Chevre-feuille. Ill.:– Pablo Picasso. Paris,
1943. Ltd. Edn. on Lafuma. 4to. Orig. sewed. (D.
Dec.11-13; 456) DM 1,200
- Ombres Portées. Ill.:– Stanley William Hayter.
Paris, [1932]. (20) Hors de Commerce, sigd. by
author & artist. Wraps., unc., unopened. Inscr. to
George Reavey. (SG. Jun.4; 225) $300
See–PETITE ANTHOLOGIE ...

HUGO, Anatole
- France Militaire Histoire des Armées Françaises.
Paris, 1833-38. 5 vols. 4to. Soiled in parts, 4 plts.
torn. Cont. hf. leath. (R. Mar.31-Apr.4; 1846)
DM 2,700
- - Anr. Copy. Cont. hf. leath. (R.
Oct.14-18; 2090) DM 2,000

HUGO, Herman
- Pieux Desirs Imités. Antw., 1627. Mor. (P.
Jun.11; 347) *Weston.* £60
- The Siege of Breda. Trans.:– C.H. G[age].
[Ghent], 1627. 1st. Edn. in Engl. Fo. Slight
browning & soiling. Cont. sheep, worn. [STC
13926] (S. Sep.29; 46) *Trotman.* £85

HUGO, Hermann & Veen, Otto
- L'Ame Amante de son Dieu Representée dans les
Emblèmes. Ill.:– J. Smit. Cologne, 1717. 1st. Edn.
Cont. cf., rebkd. & reprd. (S. Mar.17; 303)
Broseghini. £130

HUGO, Victor
- L'Année Terrible. Ill.:– L. Flameng & D. Vierge.
Paris, 1874. On vell. 1st. printing of ills. by D.
Vierge. Cont. Bradel hf. cl., wrap., slightly detchd.
Autograph dedication from author to Theodore de
Banville, bkplt. of Banville. (HD. Jun.25; 286)
Frs. 2,250
- Châtiments. Geneva & N.Y., 1853. 1st. Edn.
12mo. Orig. wraps., slightly soiled, upr. cover
loose, unopened. Sig. of Georges Victor Hugo on
hf.-title. (SH. Oct.10; 379) *Traylen.* £170
- - Anr. Edn. L. & Brussels, 1854. Cont. red mor.
A.N. (HD. Oct.10; 88) Frs. 1,300
- Les Contemplations. Paris, 1856. 1st. Edn. 2 vols.
Str.-grd. hf. mor. by Lavaux, corners, wraps. &
spines preserved. Photograph of author by
Neurdem, dtd. 3 Apr. 1867. (HD. Jun.25; 284)
Frs. 1,700
- Eviradnus. Ill.:– P.M. Ruty & P. Gusman. 1900.
(5) on Japon. 4to. Mor., spine raised bands, gt.
inner roulette, embroidered silk guards, by
Wandling. (HD. Apr.24; 146) Frs. 1,000
- Hernani. Ill.:– after Déveria (port.); Michelena
(compositions). Paris, 1890. (150) on Japon.,

HUG

numbered. Lge. 8vo. Compositions in 2 states. Red mor. by Ruban, 5 fillets framing compartments of spine, 7 fillets framing covers, inside dentelle, wrap. preserved. (SM. Feb.11; 163)   Frs. 2,600
- **La Légende des Siècles** ... Paris, 1859, 1877, 1883. 1st. Edn. (4th vol. is '4th Edn.'). 5 vols. Some foxing. Cont. hf. chagrin, spines decor. with raised bands. Autograph dedication & note from author to Theodore de Banville, bkplt. of Theodore de Banville, autograph dedication from author to Fourquier. (HD. Jun.25; 285)
Frs. 1,350
- **Les Misérables.** Paris, 1890-91. (50) on Papier du Japon numbered. 5 vols. 4to. Eaux-fortes pures, many engrs. in 3 states. Red hf. mor., gt. (SM. Oct.8; 2345)   Frs. 6,000
- - **Anr. Edn.** Trans.:– Lascelles Wraxall. Ill:– Lynd Ward. Ltd. Edns. Cl., 1937. (1500) numbered, & sigd. by artist. 5 vols. Cl., orig. box (worn). (SG. Jan.15; 209) $110
- **Notre-Dame.** L., 1833. 1st. Edn. in Engl. 3 vols. Old hf. cf., s.-c. (CNY. May 22; 130) $300
- - **Anr. Edn.** Ill:– Luc-Olivier Merson. Paris, 1889. On laid paper. 2 vols. 4to. Double set of engrs Iansenist mor. by Blanchetière & Bretault, spines with raised bands, red mor. doubls. with gt. fillets, sewed silk end-papers, wrap. & spines preserved. (HD. Feb.27; 149)   Frs. 2,100
- - **Anr. Edn.** Trans.:– Jessie Haynes. Ill.:– Fr. Maserell. Paris, Priv. Ptd., 1930. 1st. Edn. 2 vols. 4to. Orig. wraps. Printer's mark sigd. by artist. (H. Dec.9/10; 2223)   DM 500
- **Novels in English.** 1895. (100) on Imperial Japan Paper. 28 vols. Plts., each with a mntd. dupl. Cont. hf. mor. (CSK. Oct.17; 47)   £95
- **Oeuvres.** Ill:– Merson, Bracquemond, Rodin, Giacomelli, Flameng & others. 1885-95. Edition Nationale: (50), on China. 43 vols. 4to. Double state of engrs., extra set of 31 engrs. on satin, bnd. in 4to. album. Hf. mor. by M. Magnin, corners, spines decor. with raised bands. (HD. Feb.27; 150)
Frs. 9,100
- - **Anr. Edn.** Ill.:– After Flameng. Paris, n.d. 48 vols. Hf. cf., gt. (SM. Oct.8; 2293)   Frs. 2,200
- **Oeuvres Complètes.** Ill.:– Flameng. ca. 1880-89. (15) on China paper. 48 vols. (in 25). Suite of ills. by Flameng added. Cont. hf.-chagrin, corners, decor. spines. (HD. Feb.18; 141)   Frs. 4,800
- - **Anr. Edn.** [Paris], n.d. 19 vols. Lge. 8vo. Most vols. spotted. Red hf. mor., decor. spines. (SM. Feb.11; 30)   Frs. 1,200
- **Ruy Blas.** Ill:– Champollion. Paris, 1889. (150) numbered on Japan vell. 4to. Port., 15 full-page & text etchings, each in 3 states. Maroon str-grd. mor. gt., gt. dentelles, by Champs, orig. wraps. bnd. in. Initialled by publisher. (SG. Sep.4; 261)
$275
- - **Anr. Copy.** Lge. 8vo. Ills. in 2 states. Red mor. by Ruban, 5 fillets framing compartments of spine, 7 fillets framing covers, inside dentelle, wrap. preserved. (SM. Feb.11; 162)   Frs. 2,600
- **Sämmtliche Werke.** Trans:– G. Büchner, F. Freiligrath, O.L.B. Wolff & others. Frankfurt, 1835-42. 1st. German Coll. Edn. 19 vols. Slightly soiled in parts. Cont. linen. W.a.f. (HK. May 15; 4493)   DM 700
- **Works.** Boston, 1889-90. Liby. Edn. 12 vols. Slight offsetting. Red hf. mor. gt., some bkplts. removed. (SPB. May 29; 214) $150
- - **Anr. Edn.** Boston, ca. 1900. Centenary Edn., (1000) numbered, on wtrmkd. paper. 30 vols. Crushed three-qtr. lev., gt. monog. on upr. covers. (SG. May 14; 105) $200
- - **Anr. Edn.** Trans:– A. Baillot. Boston. n.d. Ltd. Edn. 18 vols. only. Hf. red mor. gt. (P. Oct.2; 301)   Fleisher. £80
- - **Anr. Edn.** N.Y., n.d. Cabinet Edn., (1000). 28 vols. Minor offsetting from plts. Hf. crimson mor. gt., gt. panel. spine, worn. (SPB. Nov.25; 464)
$425

HUGO DE PRATO FLORIDO

- **Sermones de Sanctis.** [Bologna], [1486]. 4to. Soiled in parts, 1st. & last ll. very soiled & with sm. holes, slightly wormed, some old marginalia, lacks 1 lf. Cont. wood bds., hf. leath. spine, soiled & worn, lacks ties. (HK. Nov.18-21; 210)   DM 850
- **Sermones Dominicales Super Evangelia et Epistolas.** [Reutlingen], [Michel Greyff], ca. 1478. Fo. Capitals supplied in red, early (cont.?) MS. notes, some browning & soiling, slight worming, occasionally affecting text. Cont. blind-stpd. pig over oak bds., cont. title-label on upr. cover, rather wormed & worn, lacks clasps. From liby. of André

L. Simon. [Goff H505; Hain 8999*] (S. May 18; 121)   Harper. £580

HUGO DE SANTO CARO, Carol

- **Postilla super Evangelia.** Basel, [1482]. Lge. fo. Rubricated thro.-out, 1st. lf. defect. with loss, last 2 ll. very defect. & backed, slightly soiled at ends, lacks last lf. blank. 19th. C. leath., very worn, upr. jnt. brkn., spine torn. (HK. Nov.18-21; 211)
DM 2,400
- **Postilla Super Psalterium.** Venice, Johannes & Gregorius Gregoriis for S. & B. de Nallis, 12 Nov. 1496. 1st. Edn. A few cont. notes in ink, incipit in cont. hand in red, lacks 2 prelim. ll. & blank 2C6 & z8, lr. outer corner of 281 restored, 2C1 & y2 torn affecting a few letters, inner margins of sig. z reprd. (incorrectly joined, & whole sig. detchd. from bdg.), z1-3 occasionally laminated, z4-5 torn & reprd. affecting 1 initial & a few words of text, & laminated as 1 lf.), lacks much of z6-7 (the whole mntd. & laminated as 1 lf.), marginal staining, worming & a little in text, affecting a few words. Cont. panel. cf., rebkd. & recornered, mod. end-papers. [HC 8972; BMC VII p. 349; Goff H 530] (C. Apr.1; 121)   Bowyer. £240

HUGO SENENSIS

- **Expositio super Aphorismos Hypocratis & super Co[m]mentum Galieni eius interpretis.** Venice, 1498. 2nd. Edn. Fo. Lacks 1 lf. lf. 84 defect. with MS. filling, photo of lacking lf. 1002 loose, slightly wormed & stained in parts. Leath. ca. 1700, fillets, inner gt. dentelle. (HK. Nov.18-21; 212a)
DM 420

HUGO SPECHTSHART, of Reutlingen

- **Flores Musice Artis.** Strassburg, Johann Pruss., 1488. 4to. Spaces for initial capitals with blanks, lacks final blank, folding diagram reprd. at 2 folds with slight loss, minor repair to extreme fore-margin of 1st. lf., slight marginal repair to H5, 1st. lf. with lr. corner renewed, reprd. wormhole to lr. margin of 1st. 47 ll. Jansenite mor., spine gt.-lettered, by Chambolle-Duru. Bkplt. of Dr. Lucien Graux, lately in the collection of Eric Sexton. [BMC I, 121, Goff F217, HC 7174*] (CNY. Apr.8; 168) $12,000

HUHN, E.

- **Topographisch-Statistisch-Historisches Lexikon von Deutschland.** [Hildburghausen], 1845-47. Vols. 1-2 & 5-6 (of 6) in 4 vols. Slightly soiled in parts. Cont. hf. leath., gt. spine. (R. Oct.14-18; 2091)   DM 3,000

HUISH, Marcus B.

- **Samplers & Tapestry Embroideries.** L., 1900. (600) numbered. 4to. Pict. cl., recased. (SG. Dec.4; 309) $100
See–TURNER, Joseph Mallard William & Huish, M.B.

HUISTEEN, A. & G. van, Crajenschot, T., Van Esveldt, S. & other publishers

- **[Atlas of the World]** Amst., ca. 1747-70. 12mo, sheets 128mm × 148mm. 45 maps guarded & bnd. together, some mntd. Cont. cf. gt. W.a.f. (CNY. Oct.1; 35) $600

HUIZINGA, J.

- **Verzamelde Werken.** Harlem. 1948-53. 9 vols. Cl. (VG. Nov.17; 199)   Fls. 450

HULBERT, Charles

- **History & Antiquities of Shrewsbury.** 1837. 2 vols. in 1. 4to. Edges untrimmed. Recent hf. cf. (TA. Sep.18; 338)   £72
- - **Anr. Copy.** Some plts. spotted & offset. Cont. hf. cf., worn, covers detchd. (SH. Mar.5; 70)
Crowe. £55
- **Memoirs of Seventy Years of an Eventful Life.** Ill.:– Tolley & others. Providence Grove, near Shrewsbury, Priv. ptd., [1848]-52. (500). 4to. Orig. wraps. & 2 advts. bnd. in at end, later cl. (SBA. Oct.22; 509)
Rochdale Book Company. £170

HULL GENERAL (ROYAL) INFIRMARY

- **A collection of annual reports for Hull General Infirmary, & for the local Subscription & Servants Schools, also the State of the School at Kingston-upon-Hull, together with a report from the Hull Police.** Hull, 1782-1866. Approximately 95 items in 1 vol. Various sizes. Related A.L.s. & ptd. material bnd. in. Cont. spr. cf. gt., neatly rebkd. (SBA. Oct.22; 615)   Temperley. £340

HULL, Gen. William

- **Memoirs of the Campaign of the North Western Army of the United States, A.D. 1812.** Boston,

1824. 1st. Edn. Heavily foxed, last lf. reprd. Mod. hf. cl. (SG. Jan.8; 204) $120

HULLMANDELL, Charles

- **Continental Views.** 1823-25. Fo. Plts. on india paper, minor foxing. Old bds. (TA. Jan.22; 229)
£66

HULME, F. Edward

- **Familiar Wild Flowers.** L., n.d. 5 vols. Pict. cl. gt. (GM. Apr.30; 775)   £52

HULME, F. Edward & Hibberd, Shirley

- **Familiar Garden Flowers.– Familiar Wild Flowers.–Familiar Trees.** Ca. 1880. Together 12 vols. Unif. hf. mor. gt. (P. Mar.12; 32)
Davies. £100

HULSIUS, Levinus

- **Ausszug auss des Abr. Orteley Theatro Orbis Teutsch.** Frankfurt, 1604. Ob. 4to. Lacks 1st. folding map & pp. 45/46, 2 maps reprd. at lower corner, slightly browned or soiled. Late 19th. C. hf. leath., defect. (HK. Nov.18-21; 1052)
DM 3,100

HUMBERT, Aime

- **Japan & the Japanese Illustrated.** Ed.: H.W. Bates. Trans.:– Mrs. Cashel Hoey. N.Y., 1874. 4to. Three-qtr. mor., spines gt. (SG. Feb.26; 186)
$150
- **Le Japon Illustré.** Paris, 1870. 2 vols. 4to. Some spotting, 1 plan torn. Orig. roan-bkd. cl. (S. Dec.2; 516)   Maggs. £55
- - **Anr. Copy.** Cont. hf. leath. gt. (R. Oct.14-18; 1790)   DM 1,050

HUMBERT, Rev. Lewis Macnaughton

- **Memorials of the Hospital of St. Cross & Alms House of Noble Poverty.** Ill.:– William Savage. Winchester, 1868. 4to. Advt. Rebnd. in liby. buckram. Inscr. (SG. Apr.23; 175) $180

HUMBOLDT, Baron Friedrich Heinrich Alexander von

- **Atlas Geographique et Physique du Royaume de la Nouvelle-Espagne.** Paris, 1811. Lge. fo. 19 engraved maps & profiles of 21, 2 liby. stps. Disbnd. (SPB. May 5; 265) $4,750
- **Atlas zu Kosmos.** Stuttgart, [1851]. 1st. Edn. Ob. 4to. Cont. leath.-bkd. marb. bds., upr. cover nearly detchd. (SG. Sep.18; 192) $475
- - **Anr. Copy.** Ob. fo. Slightly soiled, 3 steel engrs., 40 cold. litho. plts. Cont. hf. leath., linen pasted on spine. (HK. Nov.18-21; 586)   DM 650
- **Historische Hieroglyphen der Azteken, im Jahr 1803.** [Berlin], [1893]. Lge. fo. Light stain affecting title & contents lf. Unbnd. (SBP. May 5; 266) $600
- **Kosmos. Entwurf einer physischen Weltveschreibung.** Stuttgart & Tubingen, 1845-62. 6 vols. 8vo., atlas 4to. Liby. stps. on titles. Cont. hf. mor., worn, 1 vol. in orig. cl., atlas rebkd. [Sabin 8201; 33726] (SPB. May 5; 267) $450
- **Reise in die Aequinoctial-Gegend des Neuen Continents.** Ed.:– W. Hauff. Stuttgart, 1859-60. 1st. Edn. 4 vols. Stp. on title. Cont. hf. linen. [Sabin 33738] (R. Oct.14-18; 1676)   DM 450
- **Researches Concerning the Institutions & Monuments of the Ancient Inhabitants of America.** Trans.:– H.M. Williams. 1814. 2 vols. in 1. Hf. mor. (C. May 20; 133)   Burton-Garbett. £100
- **Uber die Unterirdischen Gasarten.** Braunschweig, 1799. 1st. Edn. Slightly soiled, title heavily browned & old name pasted over. Cont. bds. (R. Oct.14-18; 229)   DM 950

HUMBOLDT, Baron Friedrich Heinrich Alexander von & Bonpland, Aime

- **Personal Narrative of Travels to the Equinoctial Regions of the New Continent.** Trans.:– Helen Maria Williams. 1822-29. 2nd. & 3rd. Edns. 7 vols. Later cl., unc. (TA. Jul.16; 291)   £120
- **Recueil d'observations de Zoologie et d'anatomie comparée.** Paris, 1805. 4to. Spotted. Cont. hf. cf., defect. (SPB. May 5; 268) $200
- **Vues des Cordillères et Monumens des Peuples Indigènes de l'Amérique.** Paris, 1810 [1st. Edn.?] 1 vol. in 2. Lge. fo. Cont. hf. mor. & marb. bds. [Sabin 33754]. (C. Jul.15; 151)
Quaritch. £1,800
- - **Anr. Copy.** Some foxing. Corners, spine decor. with fillet. (HD. Mar.18; 87)   Frs. 46,000

HUME, A.O. & Marshall, Chas. H.T.

- **The Game Birds of India, Burmah, & Ceylon.** Calcutta, [1879]-81. 1st. Edn. 3 vols. 'To the Reader' slip & 5 correction/addition slips tipped into vol. I, 4 plts. with short marginal tears,

HUME, A.O. & Marshall, Chas. H.T. – The Game Birds of India, Burmah, & Ceylon. -contd.
occasional light spotting. Orig. pict. cl. (S. Dec.3; 1001) *W. & W.* £85

HUME, David
– **An Enquiry Concerning the Principles of Morals.** L., 1751. 1st. Edn. Cont. cf., slight worming to extremities of spine, portion of free end-paper cut-away at head. (CB. Apr.1; 233) *Can.* $350
– **Essays, Moral & Political.** L. & Edinb., 1748. 3rd. Edn. Cont. cf., owner's sig. cut-away at head of free end-paper. Sig. of Thomas Cook the engraver. (CB. Apr.1; 231) *Can.* $220
– **Four Dissertations.** 1757. 1st. Edn. 12mo. Without the 4 folio dedication to 'The Reverende Mr. Hume', lacks M9 hf.-title & advt. lf., C12 a cancel, K5-8 are stubs. Cont. cf., upr. cover detchd. (C. Nov.20; 256) *Terry.* £65
– **The History of England.** Ed.:– T. Smollett. 1796. 11 vols. Cont. cf., decor. gt. spine. (CE. Jul.9; 160) £130
– – **Anr. Edn.** L., 1796-1802. 16 vols. Cont. cf. gt., worn. (SG. Mar.19; 215) $120
– – **Anr. Edn.** Ed.:– Tobias Smollett. 1803-5. 16 vols. Tree-cf., gt. (P. Sep.11; 100) *Snowdon.* £90
– – **Anr. Edn.** Ed.:– Tobias Smollett. 1805-10. 16 vols. Later cf. (SH. May 28; 54) *Makey.* £50
– – **Anr. Edn.** L., 1806. 10 vols., including Notes & Index. Fo. Some foxing. Cont. cf., rebkd. with orig. spine preserved (SPB. Nov.25; 161) $350
– – **Anr. Edn.** Ed.:– Tobias Smollett. 1808-11. 16 vols. Cont. cf. (SH. May 21; 60) *Cooley.* £50
– – **Anr. Edn.** Ed.:– T. Smollett. 1818. 16 vols. Slight foxing & offsetting. Cont. cf., gt., spines worn. (S. Jan.26; 211) *Subunso.* £100
– – **Anr. Copy.** 13 vols. Panel. cf. gt., worn, bkplt. (CE. Mar.19; 2) £52
– **The History of the Houses of Douglas & Angus.** Edinb., 1644. 4to. Lf. with poem 'On the Booke' inserted facing preface, 1st. few ll. tattered around edges. Cont. cf., rebkd., worn, bkplt. (CB. Sep.24; 128) *Can.* $200
[–] **Philosophical Essays Concerning Human Understanding.** 1748. 1st. Edn. Without publisher's advts. Cont. panel. cf. (S. Jun.16; 440) *Lawson.* £200
– – **Anr. Edn.** L., 1751. 2nd. Edn. Cont. cf., portion of free end-paper cut-away at head. (CB. Apr.1; 232) *Can.* $320

HUMOURIST (The)
See–CRUIKSHANK, George

HUMPHREY, Samuel Dwight
– **A Practical Manual of the Collodion Process.** N.Y., 1857. 3rd. Edn. 12mo. Errata slip tipped-in, 4 p. advt. Orig. embossed cl., worn, lacks rear free end-paper. (SG. Jul.9; 176) $120

HUMPHREYS, Alexander
– **Narrative of the Oppresive Law Proceedings . . . to Overpower the Earl of Stirling.** Edinb., 1836. 4to. Orig. bds., rebkd. (CB. Feb.18; 7) *Can.* $170

HUMPHREYS, Arthur L.
– **Old Decorative Maps.** 1926. Ltd. Edn. 4to. Orig. cl. (SH. Jan.29; 25) *Forster.* £50
– – **Anr. Copy.** Buckram, spine faded, ex-liby. (SG. Mar.26; 250) $120

HUMPHREYS, David
– **An Historical Account of the Incorporated Society for the Propagation of the Gospel in Foreign Parts.** 1730. 1st. Edn. Mod. cf.-bkd. bds. (C. Nov.5; 79) *Arader.* £150
– – **Anr. Copy.** 1 map & 1 quire detchd. Cont. blind-stpd. cf., rebkd. [Sabin 33801] (C. May 20; 134) *Quaritch.* £100

HUMPHREYS, Henry Noel
– **The Coinage of the British Empire.** 1863. 3rd. Edn. Orig. papier maché cover with emblems & arms of Great Britain, in relief. (SBA. Jul.14; 84) *Lawton.* £60
– **Genera of British Moths.** L., [1845]. 4to. Some foxing, plts. good. Orig. marb. bds. detchd. (JL. Dec.15; 790) *Aus.* $120
– – **Anr. Edn.** Ca. 1860. Hf. cf. gt. (P. Feb.19; 164) *Graham.* £80
– – **Anr. Edn.** N.d. 2 vols. in 1. 4to. Some ll. detchd. Orig. cl., spine faded. (CSK. Nov.7; 38) £120
– – **Anr. Copy.** Plts. & text loose. (P. Mar.12; 242) *Cambridge.* £60
– **The Genera & Species of British Butterflies.** N.d. Plts., a little loose. Orig. cl., gt. (SH. Oct.9; 229) *Edistar.* £90

– **History of the Art of Printing.** 1867. Fo. Spotting thro.-out. Orig. gt. decor. cl., recased. (TA. Sep.18; 81) £130
– – **Anr. Edn.** 1868. 1st. Edn., 2nd. Iss. Fo. Cont. red hf. mor., spine gt. (S. Nov.24; 171) *Talerman.* £160
– – **Anr. Copy.** Red three-qtr. mor., worn. (SG. Mar.26; 251) $100
– **Illuminated Illustrations of Froissart.** 1844-45. 2 vols. 4to. Cont. roan gt., cold. onlays, vol. 2 spine loose, cl. box. (SH. Mar.26; 290) *Talerman.* £80
[–] **Illuminations from the Manuscript Froissart.** Ca. 1850. 4to. Prelims. spotted. Cont. hf. mor. (TA. Mar.19; 247) £54
– **Masterpieces of the Early Printers & Engravers.** 1870. 1st. Edn. Fo. Cont. red hf. mor., spine gt. (S. Nov.24; 172) *Talerman.* £150
– – **Anr. Copy.** Many facs., spotting thro.-out. Slightly loose in orig. gt. decor. cl., slightly worn. (TA. Sep.18; 82) £105
– – **Anr. Copy.** Cont. hf. mor. (SH. Jan.29; 27) *Forster.* £60
– – **Anr. Edn.** L., 1822. Vols. 1-8, Diced cf., gt. decor. covers & spine. (JL. Mar.2; 528) *Aus.* $210
– – **Anr. Copy.** Vols. 1-5, (JL. Mar.2; 528) *Aus.* $140
– **Record of the Black Prince.** 1849. Publisher's advt. lf. bnd. in (slightly torn), some spotting. Orig. papier-maché bds. in high relief, mor. backstrip. (TA. Oct.16; 171) £62

HUMPHREYS, Henry Noel & Westwood, John Obadiah
– **British Butterflies & their Transformations.** 1841. 4to. Some foxing. Cont. hf. mor. (TA. Feb.19; 542) £110
– – **Anr. Edn.** 1843-45. 2 vols. 4to. Occasional light foxing. Cont. crushed mor., gt. borders on sides, gt. spines. (C. Nov.5; 78) *Hughes.* £220
– – **Anr. Edn.** 1849. 4to. Orig. embossed cl. gt., spine head torn. (C. Mar.18; 176) *Negro.* £230
– – **Anr. Edn.** 1849. 2 vols. 4to. Hf. cf. (P. Apr.30; 226) *Schapiro.* £110
– – **Anr. Edn.** 1851. Vol. 1 (of 2). 4to. Spotted. Orig. cl., spine worn. (SH. Jun.4; 127) *Nagel.* £130
– – **Anr. Edn.** 1857. New Edn. 2 vols. 4to. 4 plts. in vol. I detchd. & badly frayed, 1 plt. & several ll. in vol. II stained in upr. & lr. edges, occasional spotting, several ll. detchd. Orig. pict. cl., lacks 1 cover, very worn. (S. Dec.3; 1002) *Bailey.* £90

HUMPTY DUMPTY, THE GREAT TRICK BOOK, introducing Eight Changes
N.Y., 1869. 16mo. Place overstpd. with address of Judd's Magic C. Orig. decor. wraps., lacks lr. cover. (SH. Mar.19; 97) *Hackhofer.* £210

HUNGARIA, Michael de
– **Sermones Praedicabiles.** Strassburg, [Printer of the 1483 Jordanus de Quedlinburg (Georg Husner)]. Mar. 24, 1487. 4to. Spaces for initial capitals, some with guide letters, capitals, paragraph marks & initial strokes in red, 1st. p. soiled & spotted, h7-j2 stained, sm. hole affecting text on h8, reprd. marginal tears at k7 & m2, lr. corner of p1 renewed, browned thro.-out, finger-soiling, Jesuit college inscr. dtd. 1622, old ink inscrs. on 1st. p. Qtr. cf., gt. spine, worn. From the collection of Eric Sexton. [BMC I, 135, Goff M541, H 9046*] (CNY. Apr.8; 167) $750

HUNNIUS, Aeg
– **Postilla.** Spiess, 1592. 3 pts. in 1 vol. Fo. 5 woodcuts cold. with red ink, title & pt. 2 dtd. 1591, slightly soiled in parts, some old MS. marginalia, some worming at end. Cont. blind-tooled pig-bkd. wood bds., worn, lacks 2 ties. (HK. Nov.18-21; 213) *DM* 480

HUNT, A.W.
See–MASON, William I. & Hunt, A.W.

HUNT, James Henry Leigh
– **The Autobiography.** L., 1850. 1st. Edn. 3 vols. Pol. cf., double-fillet border, spines gt. with raised bands, by Zaehnsdorf. Bkplt. of Willis Vickery. each vol. (SG. Nov.13; 359) $120
– **Christianism: or Belief & Unbelief Reconciled.** [1832]. 1st. Edn., (75) for private circulation. Slight spotting. Orig. cl., label defect. Pres. copy to Vincent & Mary Novello. (S. Jun.9; 62) *Blackwell.* £280
– **Critical Essays on the Performers of the London Theatres.** L., 1807 [1808]. 1st. Edn. Lacks hf.-title & advt. lf. Pol. mor. cf., triple-fillet border, spine gt., by Rivière, bkplt. MS. pres. lf., inscr. 'To Mrs. Whiteing, the Gift of the Author.', sig. below (not in Hunt's hand?). (SG. Nov.13; 352) $110

– **Foliage.–Hero & Leander & Bacchus & Ariadne.** L., 1818; 1819. 1st. Edns. 2nd. work lacks A1 (the hf.-title?). Pol. cf., spine gt. with raised bands, by Rivière. Bkplt. of Willis Vickery. (SG. Nov.13; 353) $120
– **A Jar of Honey from Mount Hybla.** Ill.:– Richard Doyle. L., 1848. 1st. Edn. Gt.-pict. glazed bds. (designed by Owen Jones), cl. folding case. (SG. Nov.13; 358) $110
– **Juvenilia.** 1801. 1st. Edn. Some ll. detchd. from stitching, occasional slight browning. Orig. bds., lacks spine, buckram s.-c. Sig. of Charles Williams on hf.-title, bkplt. of E.P. Rich, lately in the collection of Eric Sexton. (C. Apr.15; 107) *Thorp.* £75
– **Lord Byron & some of His Contemporaries.** 1828. 1st. Edn. 4to. Bds. (P. May 14; 258) £70

HUNT, John
– **British Ornithology.** Norwich, 1815-22. 3 vols. Old hf. cl., slightly soiled. (S. Dec.3; 1003) *W. & W.* £620

HUNT, Lynn Brogue
– **An Artist's Game Bag.** N.Y., Derry. Pr., [1936]. De Luxe Edn., (25) numbered. 4to. Mor. gt. With a sigd. orig. watercolour by author. (CNY. Oct.1; 166) $4,200

HUNT, P. Francis
– **Orchidaceae.** Ill.:– Mary Grierson. [Berkshire], 1973. (600) numbered, & sigd. by author & artist. Vell. gt. by Zaehnsdorf, cl. s.-c. (KH. Mar.24; 203a) *Aus.* $270

HUNT, Rachel McMasters Miller
– **Catalogue of Botanical Books in the Collection of . . .** Ed.:– Allan Stevenson. Pittsb., 1961. (750). Vol. II only, in 2 pts. 4to. Buckram. (SG. Jan.22; 211) $275

HUNT, Robert
– **A Manual of Photography.** L., 1854. 4th. Edn. Publd. as Vol. 16 of the Encyclopaedia Metropolitana. 11 pp. of publisher's advts. & 32 p. catalogue. Orig. embossed cl., worn. (SG. Jul.9; 177) $140
– **Researches on Light & its Chemical Relations, Embracing a Consideration of all the Photographic Processes.** L., 1854. 2nd. Edn. Lacks covers. (VA. Aug.29; 87) *R.* 90

HUNT, Thomas Frederick
– **Designs for Parsonage Houses . . .–Exemplars of Tudor Architecture.–Half a Dozen Hints on Picturesque Domestic Architecture.** 1827; 1830; 1833. 3 vols. 4to. Unif. hf. cf., spines gt. Bkplt. of Heathcote of Hursley. (S. Mar.17; 418) *Simms & Reed.* £160

HUNTER, Dard
– **Chinese Ceremonial Paper: A Monograph Relating to the Fabrication of Paper & Tin Foil & the Use of Paper in Chinese Rites & Religious Ceremonies.** [Chillicothe, Ohio], [Mountain House Pr.], 1937. (110) numbered, sigd. Fo. 4-p. prospectus laid in. Qtr. lev. mor., pict. bds., unc., s.-c. The John A. Saks copy. (CNY. Oct.1; 185) $2,600
– **The Literature of Papermaking 1390-1800.** [Chillicothe, Ohio], [Mountain House Pr.], [1925]. (190) numbered, sigd. Fo. Loose in hf. linen folder, unc. The John A. Saks copy. (CNY. Oct.1; 183) $1,300
– **Papermaking: the History & Technique of an Ancient Craft.** N.Y., 1943. 1st. Edn. Cl., d.-w. (SG. Mar.26; 256) $200
– – **Anr. Edn.** N.Y., 1947. 2nd. Edn. Buckram, d.-w. (SG. Jan.22; 212) $120
– **Papermaking by Hand in India.** N.Y., 1939. (370) numbered, sigd. by author & Elmer Adler. Fo. 2 4-p. prospectuses laid in. Hf. cf. gt., hand-blocked India print cl., unc., s.-c., by Gerhard Gerlach. The John A. Saks copy. (CNY. Oct.1; 188) $800
– **Papermaking in Southern Siam.** [Chillicothe, Ohio], [Mountain House Pr.], 1936. (115) numbered, sigd. Fo. 6-p. prospectus for Papermaking Through 18 Centuries laid in. Qtr. lev. mor., pict. bds., unc. The John A. Saks copy. (CNY. Oct.1; 186) $1,900
– **A Papermaking Pilgrimage to Japan, Korea & China.** N.Y., 1936. (370) numbered, sigd. by author & Elmer Adler. Fo. Specimen sheet of shogun paper & photocopies of reviews in the N.Y. Herald Tribune & Times Literary Supplement laid in. Qtr. lev. mor., pict. bds., unc., s.-c., by Gerhard Gerlach. The John A. Saks copy. (CNY. Oct.1; 187) $1,100

- - **Anr. Copy.** Lge. 4to. Lev.-bkd. patterned bds., boxed, designed by Gerhard Gerlach. (SG. Oct.9; 132) $750
- - **Anr. Copy.** Some spotting to specimen papers. Orig. bdg., publisher's box (worn). (SPB. May 29; 215) $625
- **Papermaking through Eighteen Centuries.** N.Y., 1930. 1st. Edn. Buckram, d.-w., partly unc. & unopened. Bkplt. of Vincent Starrett. (SG. Mar.26; 254) $230
- - **Anr. Copy.** (SG. Mar.26; 255) $100
- **Papermaking through Eighteen Centuries.** –**Papermaking. The History & Technique of an Ancient Craft.** N.Y., 1930; 1947. 2 works in 2 vols. Some spotting. Both orig. cl. (SPB. May 29; 216) $150
- **Primitive Papermaking: An Account of a Mexican Sojourn & of a Voyage to the Pacific Islands in Search of Information . . . Relating to the Making & Decorating of Bark-Paper.** Chillicothe, Ohio, [Mountain House Pr.], 1927. (200) numbered, sigd. Fo. Loose in hf. linen folder, unc., s.-c. The John A. Saks copy. (CNY. Oct.1; 184) $1,800

HUNTER, F.R.
- **J.E.H. MacDonald. A Biography & Catalogue of His Work.** Ed.:– Thoreau MacDonald. Toronto, 1940. (500) on Rag Paper. 4to. Cl. with orig. pict. d.-w. (PWP. Apr.9; 224) Can. $360

HUNTER, Henry
- **The History of London, & its Environs.** 1811. 2 vols. 4to. Folding engraved map of the Thames hand-cold. in outl., some foxing to a few plts. Cont. cf., gt., hinges worn, upr. covers loose. (C. Feb.25; 38) Potter. £90

HUNTER, Capt. John
- **An Historical Journal of the Transactions at Port Jackson & Norfolk Island.** 1793. 1st. Edn. 4to. Most plts. slightly foxed, unsightly deletion of an owners' inscr. on title-p., & with facing port. offset onto it. Mod. cf.-bkd. bds. (S. Nov.4; 622) Maggs. £400
- - **Anr. Copy.** 15 plts. & maps, 1 map torn along folds. Mod. hf. mor. (S. Mar.31; 479) Schrire. £350
- - **Anr. Copy.** Title cropped with loss of date & 1 letter of text. Cont. hf. mor. gt. (C. Nov.6; 317) Rheckert. £180
- - **Anr. Copy.** Lge. folding map slightly torn. Cont. tree cf. (C. Feb.25; 104) Maggs. £80
- - **Anr. Copy.** 1 map strengthened along fold on blank verso, some ll. stained, with additional advt. lf. not called for by Ferguson, several inked sigs. Old qtr. cf., corners reinforced with vell. (KH. Mar.24; 204) Aus. $700
- - **Anr. Copy.** 4to. Some offsetting, slight foxing, 2 folding maps set down on coarse linen. Mod. cf. or mor. (KH. Nov.18; 348) Aus. $600
- - **Anr. Edn.** 1810. Orig. bdg. (KH. Mar.24; 205) Aus. $450

HUNTER, Dr. John
- **Essays & Observations on Natural History, Anatomy, Physiology, Psychology, & Geology.** Ed.:– Richard Owen. 1861. 1st. Edn. 2 vols. A little spotting. Orig. cl. (S. Dec.2; 831) Westwood. £90
- **Historia Naturalis Dentium Humanorum.** Trans.:– P. Boddaert. Dordrecht, 1773. 1st. Latin-Dutch parallel Edn. 4to. 1st. & last text ll. & some plts. slightly soiled. Cont. hf. leath., spine slightly defect. (R. Mar.31-Apr.4; 1059) DM 1,200
- **The Natural History of the Human Teeth.** 1771. 1st. Edn. 4to. Title & hf.-title loose. 19th. C. hf. roan, worn, covers detchd. From Chetham's Liby., Manchester. (C. Nov.27; 211) Riley-Smith. £480
- **The Natural History of the Human Teeth explaining their Structure, Use, Formation, Growth & Diseases; A Practical Treatise on the Diseases of the Teeth intended as a Supplement.** 1771-78. 1st. Edn. 2 pts. in 1 vol. No hf.-title to pt. II, ? not called for. Cf.-bkd. bds., unc. (S. Jun.15; 232) Norman. £1,200
- - **Anr. Edn.** 1778. 1st. work 2nd. Edn., 2nd. work 1st. Edn. 2 vols. in 1. 4to. 16 engraved plts., most reprd. Cont. cf., rebkd. (C. Jul.16; 354) Maggs. £450
- **Observations on Certain Parts of the Animal Oeconomy.** 1786. 1st. Edn. 4to. Marb. bds., gt. spine. (S. Dec.2; 828) Dawson. £170
- - **Anr. Edn.** 1792. 2nd Edn. 4to. A few stains. New panel. cf. (S. Jun.16; 444) Tait. £80

- **A Treatise on the Blood, Inflammation, & Gun-Shot Wounds.** 1794. 1st. Edn. 4to. A few ll. foxed. Orig. bds., lacks spine, upr. cover detchd., unc. (S. Apr.6; 87) Phillips. £320
- - **Anr. Copy.** Engraved port. reprd. in margin, some foxing. Cont. cf.-bkd. bds., worn. From liby of Dr. E. Ashworth Underwood. (S. Feb.23; 231) Canale. £240
- - **Anr. Edn.** 1812. [2nd. Edn.?] 2 vols. Offset from plts. onto text. New hf. cf., unc. (S. Jun.16; 445) Pratt. £90
- - **Anr. Copy.** Lacks hf.-titles, some foxing. Hf. cf. (S. Dec.2; 517) Jenner. £65
- **A Treatise on the Venereal Diseases.** 1786. 1st. Edn. 4to. Some marginal stains at end, outer margins of plts. browned. Cf., rebkd., upr. cover stained. (S. Jun.16; 442) Salah. £220

HUNTER, John Dunn
- **Memoirs of a Captivity among the Indians of North America.** 1823. 2nd. Edn. Slightly spotted. Cont. hf cf. [Sabin 33921]. (S. Sep.29; 175) Quaritch. £55
- - **Anr. Edn.** L., 1824. 3rd. Edn. Minor foxing to port. Hf. cf. [Sabin 33921] (CB. Dec.9; 284) Can. $140

HUNTER, Rev. Joseph
- **Hallamshire. The History & Topography of the Parish of Sheffield in the County of York.** Ed.:– Rev. Alfred Gatty. 1869. New Edn. Cl. (HSS. Apr.24; 1) £80
- - **Anr. Copy.** Fo. 1 lf. slightly torn & reprd. Cont. hf. cf., worn. (SBA. Oct.22; 616) Phelps. £54
- **South Yorkshire–The History & Topography of the Deanery of Doncaster.** L., 1828 & 1831. 2 vols. Tooled cf. (HSS. Apr.24; 112) £190

HUNTER, Rachel
- **Letitia.** Norwich, 1801. 1st. Edn. 4 vols. 12mo. No hf.-titles. Cont. hf. cf., worn. (S. Feb.10; 403) Hannas. £100

HUNTER, Dr. William
- **Anatomia Uteri Humani Gravidi . . . The Anatomy of the Human Gravid Uterus Exhibited in Figures.** Bg'ham., 1774. [1st. Edn.?] Lge. fo. Text in Latin & Engl., plts. 1, 2, 4, 6, etc. publd. 15 Nov., 1774 by Hunter, tear in plt. 20 reprd. without loss. Hf. cf. (S. Jun.16; 451) Studd. £900
- - **Anr. Copy.** Lacks plt. 1), tear reprd. in foot of plt. 6, sm. liby. label in corner of each plt. Cont. cf., worn, upr. cover loose. From Chetham's Liby., Manchester. (C. Nov.27; 212) Taylor. £170
- - **Anr. Edn.** 1851. Fo. Orig. cl., reprd. (S. Jun.16; 452) Phillipp. £110
- **The Anatomy of the Human Gravid Uterus.** 1851. Fo. Text in Latin & Engl., slip 'notice to members'. Orig. cl. (S. Dec.2; 833) Preidel. £85
- - **Anr. Copy.** Orig. limp cl., a little loose in bdg. (S. Dec.2; 518) Studd. £65

HUNTER, William S.
- **Hunter's Eastern Townships Scenery, Canada East.** Montreal, 1860. 4to. Lacks 1st. blank, a few plts. loose. Orig. cl., sm. tear in spine. [Sabin 33936] (S. Dec.8; 251) Remington. £560
- **Ottawa Scenery.** Ottawa City, 1855. 4to. Washed thro.-out. Orig. blind-stpd. cl., rebkd. & recased. (CB. Feb.18; 26) Can. $1,000

HURAULT, M. Iaques
- **Politicke, Moral, & Martial Discourses.** Trans.:– Arthur Golding. 1595. 1st. Edn. in Engl. 4to. Lacks corner of 1 lf. affecting 4 words. 17th. C. panel. mor., gt. spine. [STC 14000] (C. Nov.19; 7) Courtland. £120

HURLBUTT, Frank
- **Bristol Porcelain.** 1928. 4to. Orig. cl., slightly soiled. (SH. Oct.9; 147) Talerman. £80
- **Old Derby Porcelain & its Artist-Workmen.** 1925. 4to. Orig. vell.-bkd. bds., d.-w., torn. (SBA. Jul.22; 139) Shaw. £55

HURST, Col. G.T.
- **Short History of the Volunteer Regiments of Natal & East Griqualand, Past & Present.** Durban, 1945. Cl. (SSA. Jun.18; 160) R. 100

HURTADO de Mendoza, Antonio
See–MENDOZA, Antonio Hurtado de

HURWITZ, Isaiah–HURWITZ, Sheftel
- **Shnei Luchot Habrit (Shelah).– Vavei Ha'amudim.** Ill.:– Abram Bar Yakov (1st. work). Amst., 1698. 3rd. Edn. (1st. work). 2 works in 1 vol. Fo. Slight staining, 1st. work: sigs. of former owners on title

& fly-lf. Orig. leath. engraved with former owner's name. (S. Nov.18; 432) Israel. £350

HURWITZ, Sheftel Shabtai
- **Shefa Tal.** Frankfurt am Main, 1719. 2nd. Edn. 12mo. Slightly discoloured. Hf. cl. (S. Nov.18; 434) Waters. £70

HUSENBETH, F.C.
- **Vespers Book for the Use of the Laity.** L., 1847. 12mo. Red mor., sacred monog. in gt. Panoramic fore-e. pntg. on all edges. (SG. Mar.19; 189) $300

HUSS, Ioannes
- **De Anatomia Antichristi.– Locorum aliquot ex osee . . . Tommus Secundus.–Sermonum . . . ad Populum, Tomus Tertius.** Ed.:– [Otho Bruntels]. [Strassburg; Wittemburg], ca. 1530. 3 works in 2 vols. 4to. Last 2 ll. & some inner gt. dentelles. 18th. C. mott. cf., triple gt. fillets, spines gt. in compartments, inner gt. dentelles, bkplts. of Girardot de Préfond & Henry Drummond. (SM. Oct.7; 1767) Frs. 11,000

HUSSEY, Christopher
- **English Country Houses.** 1955-58. 3 vols. Fo. Orig. cl. (SH. Jul.16; 17) Grove. £200
See–JEKYLL, Gertrude & Hussey, Christopher

HUSSEY, Mrs. Thomas John
- **Illustration of British Mycology.** 1847-55. 2 vols. 4to. Some marginal stains. Mod. hf. mor. gt. (S. Jun.1; 146) Portmeirion. £75

HUSSON, Felix
See–CHAMPFLEURY, Jules Francois 'Felix Husson'

HUSUNG, Max Joseph
- **Bucheinbände aus der Preussischen Staatsbibliothek zu Berlin.** Leipzig, 1925. Lge. fo. Photocopy explanations bnd. in. Mod. hf. leath. (R. Oct.14-18; 522) DM 900

HUSWIRT, Johannes
[–] **Enchiridion artis Numerandi, paruo Admodum Negotio omne Calculi Praxim docens in Integris, Minutiis Vulgaribus, & Proiectilibus.** Cologne, 1525. Title cropped at fore-edge & soiled. 19th. C. hf. red mor., gt. From Honeyman Collection. (S. May 20; 3265) Dr. Martin. £90

HUTCHESON, Francis
- **A System of Moral Philosophy.** Glasgow & L., 1755. 1st. Edn. 2 vols. 4to. With the 6 p. subscribers' list, some foxing, staining, & minute worming. Cont. cf., worn. (SG. Feb.5; 176) $300

HUTCHINS, John
- **History & Antiquities of the County of Dorset.** 1774. 1st. Edn. 2 vols. Fo. Clean tear at foot of 1 plt. nearly reprd. Cont. russ. (CSK. Dec.12; 103) £280
- - **Anr. Copy.** Short tears to folds of some plts. Cont. hf. cf., rebkd., reprd., orig. spines preserved, vol. 1 covers detchd. (C. Mar.18; 173) Schrire. £220
- - **Anr. Copy.** Edges of some folding plts. cropped, 1 plan cropped. Hf. cf., orig. spine labels. Armorial bkplt. of Sir William Oglander. (LC. Jun.18; 153) £200
- - **Anr. Copy.** A few plts. stained. Cont. hf. cf., spines gt., rebkd. (C. Mar.18; 174) Shapiro. £180
- - **Anr. Edn.** 1796-1815. 2nd. Edn. 4 vols. including Appendix. Fo. Cont. mor., covers with gt. roll tool borders, spines gt. (C. Mar.18; 175) Harper. £380
- - **Anr. Edn.** Ed.:– William Shipp & James Whitworth Hodson. 1861-70. 3rd. Edn. 4 vols. Fo. Hf. title in vol. II only. Hf. mor., gt. panel. spines. (C. Feb.25; 39) Thorp. £380
- - **Anr. Edn.** 1861-70. Some plts. dampstained. Cont. mor., covers with gt. roll tool panel, spine gt. by Henry Ling, with his ticket, tooling on vol. IV not totally unif. From the collection of Eric Sexton. (C. Apr.16; 283) Gilbert. £320
- - **Anr. Copy.** Without the map. Cont. hf. mor. (C. Jul.15; 51) Taylor. £220

HUTCHINS, Thomas
- **A Topographical Description of Virginia, Pennsylvania, Maryland, & North Carolina . . .** L., 1778. 1st. Edn. 12mo. Slight browning & foxing. Mod. mor., gt. borders & spine. From liby. of William E. Wilson. (SPB. Apr.29; 146) $1,200

HUTCHINSON, Francis
- **Historical Essay concerning Witchcraft.** 1718. 1st. Edn. Occasional light spotting. Cont. cf., gt.

HUTCHINSON, Francis – Historical Essay concerning Witchcraft. *-contd.*
Signet arms on covers, rather worn. (S. May 5; 347) *Thorp.* £75
– – **Anr. Copy.** Cont. panel. cf. (SG. Sep.25; 331) $150
– – **Anr. Copy.** With advt. lf. (SG. Feb.5; 346) $120
– – **Anr. Edn.** 1720. 2nd. Edn. Advt. lf., occasional spotting & browning. Mod. hf. mor. (S. May 5; 348) *Quaritch.* £65

HUTCHINSON, Horace G.
– **Big Game Shooting.** L., 1905. 2 vols. Crushed three-qtr. lev., spines gt. (SG. Dec.11; 174) $130
– **British Golf Links.** 1897. No bdg. stated. (CSK. Jul.20; 131) £160

HUTCHINSON, Sir Jonathan
– **Archives of Surgery.** 1890-1900. 11 vols. (index in last vol.). Cl., tops of vols. 1 & 2 slightly defect., 1 or 2 vols. loose in bdg. As a periodical, w.a.f. (S. Jun.16; 453) *Levy.* £140
– **A Smaller Atlas of Illustrations of Clinical Surgery.** 1895. Orig. cl. Inscr. 'with the author's compliments'. (S. Jun.16; 454) *Phillips.* £80

HUTCHINSON, Thomas
– **Geographia Magnae Britanniae.** 1748. Cont. cf., upr. cover detchd., lacks lr. cover. (C. Nov.5; 80) *Gibbons.* £380

HUTCHINSON, Thomas J.
– **Two Years in Peru, with Exploration of Its Antiquities.** 1873. 2 vols. Cont. hf. cf. (TA. Jan.22; 23) £50

HUTCHINSON, Walter
– **Dog Encyclopaedia.** L., ca. 1935. 3 vols. 4to. Ex-liby. Cl. (SG. Apr.9; 375) $100

HUTCHINSON, William
– **The History of the County of Cumberland.** Carlisle, 1794. 2 vols. Sm. 4to. Minor dampstaining in vol. I. Cont. cf. From the collection of Eric Sexton. (C. Apr.16; 285) *Taylor.* £85
– – **Anr. Copy.** 2 vols. 4to. Cont. cf. (PG. Dec.12; 56) £70
– **A View of Northumberland.** Newcastle, 1778. 2 vols. 4to. Cont. cf., gt. spine. Bkplt. of Richard Hill, lately in the collection of Eric Sexton. (C. Apr.16; 284) *Heraldry Today.* £100

HUTH, Frederick H.
– **Works on Horses & Equitation.** L., 1887. Square 4to. Hf. vell. (SG. Jan.22; 213) $325

HUTH, Henry
– **Catalogue of Printed Books & Illuminated Manuscripts.** 1911-20. 8 pts. (of 9, lacks pt. 8), 1st. 5 pts. bnd. in 1 vol. 4to. With a dupl. of pt. 5, some pts. with prospectuses laid or bnd. in. 1st. 5 pts. in buckram (wraps. bnd. in), rest in wraps. (SG. Mar.26; 257) $100

HÜTTER, A.
– **Funffiz [und Andere Funffzig] Chirurgische Observationes.** Rostock, 1718-20. 2 pts. in 1 vol. Cont. hf. vell. (R. Oct.14-18; 347) DM 600

HUTTER, E.–OTTO, J.K.
– **Alphabetum, ein ABC Buchlein, daraus man die vier Hauptsprachen, als Ebraisch, Griechisch, Lateinisch, Deutsch & c.-Gali Razia Occultorum Detectio.** Nuremb., 1597; 1605. 2 works in 1 vol. 4to. Some browning, slight stains & marginal worming. Cont. vell., worn, arms & owner's inscr. 'Gotshaus Velden' on upr. cover, s.-c. (C. Apr.29; 400) *Goldschmidt.* £360

HUTTICH, Johann
– [-] **Imperatorum et Caesarum Vitae.** Ill.:– Hans. Weiditz. [Strassburg], 1534. 2 pts. in 1 vol. 4to. Slightly browned in parts, slightly stained, some old Ms notes in pt. 2. Cont. leath, spine renewed. (HK. Nov.18-21; 214) DM 420
– – **Anr. Edn.** Lyon, 1550. Slightly stained in parts, owner's mark on title. 19th. C. hf. leath., fillets. (HK. May 12-14; 112) DM 440
– **Imperatorum et Caesarum Vitae, cum Imaginibus ad Vivam Effigiem expressis.-Consulum Romanorum Elenchus.** 1534; 1537. 2 works iss. as 1. 4to. 1st. title slightly soiled, tear in margin of 1 lf., not affecting text, some old MS. notes, minor discolouration & staining. Cont. limp vell., a little worn. (C. Apr.1; 141) *Simpson.* £240
– [-] **Die New Welt, der Landschaften unnd Insulen.** Trans.:– [Michael Herr]. Strassburg, 1534. 1st. Edn. in German. Fo. Cont. marginalia in ink. Vell.

MS. lf. over bds. [Sabin 34106] (C. Nov.20; 194) *Goldschmidt.* £580

HUTTICH, Johannes–CHURRERIUS, Caspar
– **Imperatorum Romanorum Libellus una cum Imaginibus.-Quisquis es Gloriae Germanicae & Maiorum Studiosus.** Strassburg; Tubingen, 1525; 1525. 2 works in 1 vol. Some sections sprung from bdg. Old cf., spine worn. Early owners' inscr. on Ph. Ant. de Sestich. (C. Nov.20; 193) *Goldschmidt.* £170

HUTTICHIUS, Johannes
See-MANUTIUS, Paulus–FALLETTI, Girolamo –HUTTICHIUS, Johannes

HUTTON, Charles
– **Tables of the Products & Powers of Numbers. -A Mathematical & Philosophical Dictionary. -Mathematical Tables.-Tracts on Mathematical & Philosophical Subjects.** 1781; 1796-95; 1801; 1812. 3rd. work 3rd. edn. 1 vol.; 2 vols.; 1 vol.; 3 vols. Various sizes. All cont. cf., 2nd. & 4th. works rebkd. (SH. Jan.30; 449) *Weiner.* £70
– **A Treatise on Mensuration, both in theory and practice.** Ill.:– Thomas Bewick. Newcastle-upon-Tyne, Priv. Ptd., 1770. 1st. Edn., L.P. 4to. Owner's inscr. on title, MS. note in anr. hand on 1st. lf. of subscription list. Cont. cf., neatly rebkd., orig. spine preserved. (SBA. Oct.22; 447) *Spelman.* £130

HUTTON, Edward
– **The Children's Christmas Treasury of Things New & Old.** Ill.:– Arthur Rackham & others. L., [1905]. 1st. Edn. 4to. Cold. pict. cl., rebkd., orig. spine preserved, new end-papers. Raymond M. Sutton, Jr. copy. (SG. May 7; 131) $130

HUTTON, W.
– **A Journey from Birmingham to London.** B'gham., 1785. 1st. Edn. 12mo. A few quires spotted. Cont. pold. cf., gt., by Kalthoeber, with his ticket, William Beckford's copy with 5-line pencilled note on front free end-paper, Lord Rosebery's bkplt. (S. Nov.4; 531) *Maggs.* £110
– **A Tour to Scarborough in 1803; including a Particular Survey of the City of York.-A Description of Blackpool, in Lancashire; frequented for Sea Bathing.** 2nd. work: Kirkham, 1817; ca. 1800. 2nd. Edn.; 2nd. (pirated) Edn. 2 works in 1 vol. 1st. work: a few ll. slightly browned; 2nd. work: MS. note on verso of hf.-title, lacks final blank(?). Cont. hf. russ., slightly worn, new end-papers. (SBA. Oct.22; 617) *Spelman.* £56

HUTTON, William
– **Canada.** L., [1857]. [2nd. Edn.]. 12mo. Orig. ptd. wraps., upr. wrap. loose, slightly soiled. (CB. Sep.24; 89) Can. $140

HUTTON, William, Geologist
See-LINDLEY, John & Hutton, William

HUXHAM, John
– **An Essay on Fevers, & their Various Kinds.** 1750. 1st. Edn. Slight marginal worming to 1st. few ll. Cont. cf. gt. (LC. Jun.18; 105) £60

HUXLEY, Aldous
– **Brave New World.** L., 1932. Engl. Edn., (324), sigd. Orig. cl., soiled. (SPB. Jul.28; 182) $400
– – **Anr. Copy.** L.P. numbered. Buckram, partly unc, & unopened. (SG. Nov.13; 363) $325
– – **Anr. Copy.** Orig. cl., d.-w., chipped. (SPB. Jul.28; 183) $125
– **The Burning Wheel.** Oxford, 1916. 1st. Edn. Orig. wraps., slight soiling. (SPB. Jul.28; 185) $225
– **Chrome Yellow.** 1934. Orig. cl., d.-w. 2 sigd. photographs of author loosely inserted. (SH. Dec.19; 460) *Quaritch.* £55
– **Leda.** L., 1920. 1st. Edn., (160), sigd. 4to. Slight browning. Orig. cl.-bkd. bds., some soiling. (SPB. Jul.28; 188) $100
– – **Anr. Edn.** Ill.:– Eric Gill. Garden City, 1929. (361) numbered, sigd. Linen, boxed. (SG. Jun.4; 229) $110
– **Point Counter Point.** L., 1928. L.P. 1st. Edn. (256) numbered & sigd. Buckram, slightly worn, partly unc. (SG. Nov.13; 361) $110
– – **Anr. Edn.** L., 1928. 1st. Edn. Cl., d.-w. Sigd. (SG. Jun.4; 228) $150

HUYGENS, Christian
– **De la Pluralité des Mondes.** Trans.:– Du Four. The Hague, 1724. Cont. cf., spine gt. (VG. Nov.18; 1226) Fls. 600

– **Horologium Oscillatorium sive de Motu Pendulorum ad Horologia Aptato Demonstrationes Geometricae.** Paris, 1673. 1st. Edn. Fo. Some browning, owner's inscr. on title. 19th. C. hf. vell. (S. Apr.6; 220) *Brieux.* £1,300

HUYGENS, Constantin
– **Koren-Bloemen. Nederlandsche Gedichten.** Ill.:– Romeyn de Hooghe. Amst., 1672. 2nd. Edn. 2 pts. in 1 vol. 4to. Cont. blind-stpd. vell., slightly stained, top of spine defect., a bit warped, lacks ties. (VG. Dec.17; 1389) Fls. 550
– **Koren-Bloemen, Nederlandsche Gedichten. Tweede Druck.-Gedichten: Tweede Deel; Vervolg der Gedichten.** Amst.; Delft, 1672; 1728; 1735. 2 vols. in 1; 1 vol.; 1 vol.; together 3 vols. 4to. Old vell., spine of 1st. work loose. (SG. Feb.5; 177) $130

See-DOES, J. Vander–HUYGENS, C.

HUYSMANS, Joris Karl
– **La Cathédrale** Ill.:– Delattre & Roche. 1898. (300) on Hollande. Etching & frontis. on églomisé parch. as upr. doubl. Jans. mor., wrap. (HD. Oct.10; 89) Frs. 3,500
– **La Cathédrale.–L'Oblat.** Paris, 1898, 1903. 1st. Edns. 2 works in 2 vols. 12mo. Mor. by Lavaux, doublt gt. fillet round covers, spines decor. with raised bands, wraps. & spines. (HD. Jun.25; 290) Frs. 1,300
– **Un Dilemne.-Là-Bas.-Pages Catholiques.** Paris, 1887, 1891, 1899. 1st. Edns. 3 works in 3 vols. 18mo. Mor. by Lavaux, double gt. fillet round covers, spines decor. with raised bands, wraps. defect. & reprd. A.N.s. & dated by author. (HD. Jun.25; 289) Frs. 1,000
– **Le Drageoir aux Epices.** Ill.:– Auguste Brouet. [Paris], [1929]. (215); (40) on imperial Jap. 4to. Jansenist mor. by Paro, unc., wrap. (HD. Dec.5; 107) Frs. 2,200
– **Là-Bas.** Ill.:– Hertenberger. Paris, 1926. (40) on Japon Impérial. 4to. 2 states of etchings, separate ptd. outl. of wood engrs., orig. sketch. Mor. by Mabilde, red mor. doublrs., orig. wraps. bnd. in, chemise & s.-c. 2 orig. pen & pencil drawings. (SM. Oct.8; 2346) Frs. 7,000
– **Oeuvres Complètes.** Paris, 1928-34. Ltd. Edn. 18 vols. in 23. Sm. 4to. Hf. mor., orig. wraps. bnd. in. (SM. Oct.8; 2218) Frs. 1,400
– **A Rebours** Ill.:– Auguste Leroux. Paris, 1920. (70) on Jap. Imp. with 3 states. Mor., 4 spine raised bands, decor & mosaic, lge. gt. inner dentelle, watered silk doubl., pict. wraps. preserved, s.-c., by Flammanon Vaillant. (LM. Jun.13; 99) B.Frs. 22,000
– – **Anr. Edn.** Ill.:– Coussens. Paris, 1927. (160) numbered on imperial Arches vell. 4to. Mor. by Klein, red mor. doubls., wrap. preserved, s.-c. (SM. Feb.11; 236) Frs. 5,500
– **A Rebours.-En Route.** Paris, 1884; 1895. 1st. Edns. 2 works in 2 vols. 12mo. Port. on China (1st. work). 1st. work: mor. by Lavaux, double gt. fillet around covers, spine decor. with raised bands, wraps. preserved; 2nd. work: mor. by Lavaux, wrap. & spine preserved. (HD. Jun.25; 288) Frs. 1,600
– **Trois Eglises.** Ill.:– Ch. Jouas. 1920. (20) on vell, with orig. cold. ill. sigd. & 3 states of etchings. 4to. Sewed. (HD. Jun.30; 34) Frs. 1,700

HYDE, Edward, Earl of Clarendon
See-CLARENDON, Edward Hyde, Earl of

HYDE, J.A. Lloyd
– **Oriental Lowestoft.** N.Y., 1936. (1000) numbered. 4to. Orig. cl., slightly soiled. (CSK. Oct.31; 143) £55

HYDE, James
– **Emanuel Swedenborg: a Bibliography.** L., 1906. (500). 4to. Buckram. (SG. Jan.22; 370) $160

HYDE, Thomas
– **Historia Religionis Veterum Persarum.** Oxford. 1700. 1st. Edn. 4to. 2 proposals for publishing the work bnd. in, followed by a variant title-p. & a sample p. Later cf., spine gt. Sig. of Thomas Smith. (SG. Feb.5; 178) $1,100

HYGINUS, Caius Julius
– **Poeticon Astronomicon.** Ed.:– Jacobus Sentinus & Johannes Lucilius Santritter. Venice, 14 Oct. 1482. 1st. Ill. Edn. 4to. Slightly soiled in margin & a few ll. slightly wormed. Old limp vell. [HC 9062; BMC V, 286] (D. Dec.11-13; 28) DM 8,000
– – **Anr. Edn.** Ed.:– [Jacobus Sentinus & J.L. Santritter]. Venice, [Thomas de Blavis, de

Alexandria. Jun.7, 1488. Sm. 4to. Sm. hole runs thro.-out (reprd.), with affected letters in pen facs., 1st. few ll. slightly stained, a few wormholes in outer margins at end. Mod. hf. vell., covers from 2 rubricated ll. of early German religious text. Bkplt. of James Stokley; from Honeyman Collection. [BMC V, 318; Goff H562; HC 9065] (S. May 20; 3266) *Roberts.* £550

HYMANS, Henry
- Bruxelles à travers les Ages. Brussels, n.d. 3 vols. 4to. Hf. chagrin, corners, 5 decor. spine raised bands, arms. (LM. Nov.8; 31) B.Frs. 11,000

HYMANS, L.
- Le Rhin Monumental et Pittoresque. [Cologne à Mayence]. Ill.:– Fourmois, Lauters & Stroobant. Brussels, Gent & Leipzig, ca. 1860. 2nd. Edn. Fo. Cont. leath., gold & blind-tooled, gt. inner dentelles. (R. Oct.14-18; 2420) DM 7,600
- Le Rhin Monumental et Pittoresque. Francfort a Constance. Ill.:– F. Stroobant. Brussels, Gent & Leipzig, ca. 1860. Fo. Cont. leath., gt. & blind-stpd. inner. gt. dentelle. (R. Oct.14-18; 2158) DM 7,000

HYMNALS
- Ausbund, das ist etliche schöne christliche Lieder, wie sie in dem Gefängnüss zu Bassau in dem Schloss von den Schweitzer Brüdern ... gedichtet worden. Germantown, Penn., 1785. Cont. cf., 2 brass clasps. (C. Jul.15; 76) *Rodgers.* £80

HYMNORUM Expositio cum Notabili Commeto ...
Basle, M. Furter. 1497. 4to. Upr. margin of title reprd., dampstaining at end. Mod. hf. chagrin. [HC 6789] (HD. Jun.24; 44) Frs. 2,200

HYRTL, Josef
- Antiquitates Anatomicae Rariores ... Vienna, 1835. 1st. Edn. Later hf. cl., ex-liby. (SG. Aug.21; 328) $150
- Verleichend-anatom. Untersuchungen über das Innere Gehörorgan des Menschen u.d. Säugethiere. Prag, 1845. 1st. Edn. Fo. Lightly soiled in parts. Wraps. with typographic decor. upr. orig. wraps., unc. & lr. cover renewed, upr. cover worn. (HK. May 12-14; 346) DM 950

IACOVLEFF, Alexandre
- Dessins et Peintures d'Asie. Paris, ca. 1930. (500) numbered, on Lafuma paper. Fo. Loose in ptd. bd. folder, ties defect. Orig. pencil drawing on blank lf. preceding text title-p., sigd. & inscr. (SG. May 14; 106) $400

IACOVLEFF, Alexandre & Elisseeff, S.
- Le Théâtre Japonais (Kabuki). Paris, [1933]. (500) numbered. Tall fo. Ptd. wraps., unc. & unopened. (SG. May 14; 107) $325

IBBETSON, Julius & others.
- A Picturesque Guide to Bath, Bristol, Hot-Wells, the River Avon. 1793. [1st. Edn.?]. Extra-ill. with 9 cold. aquatint views. Str.-grd. maroon mor. gt. by Wallis. From the collection of Eric Sexton. (C. Apr.16; 286) *Hammond.* £300
- – Anr. Copy. 4to. Cont. tree cf., gt. (S. Jun.22; 46) *Harley-Mason.* £240
- – Anr. Copy. Partly untrimmed, ex-liby. copy but blind stps. removed & almost unnoticeable. Recently rebnd. in qtr. cf. (TA. Dec.18; 351) £85
- – Anr. Copy. Partly untrimmed. Ex-liby. but blind stps. removed & almost unnoticeable. (TA. Apr.16; 460) £75

IBBETSON, Julius & Tookey, James
- Selections from Animated Nature. 1799-1801. 4to. Cont. hf. mor., worn. (TA. Feb.19; 637) £55

IBIS: A Magazine of General Ornithology
Ed.:– P.L. Sclater & others. 1859-1912. Series 1-Series 14, continued as vols. 85-115, General Index to Series 1-6, 2 vols., Subject Index to Series 1-9, 2 vols., & List of British Birds, together 120 vols. Unif. hf. mor. As a periodical, w.a.f. (C. Jul.15; 187) *Taylor.* £2,400

IBN BAITHAR
- Grosse Zusammenstellung ueber die Kraefte der Bekannten Einfachen Heil- und Nahrungsmittel. Trans.:– Joseph von Sontheimer. Stuttgart, [1840]; 1842. 1st. Edn. in German. 2 vols. Lacks 1st. title page, foxed. Mod. buckram, ex-liby. (SG. Sep.18; 355) $110

IBRAHIM, Sliman Ben
See–DINET, Etienne & Ibrahim, Sliman Ben

IBSEN, Henrik
- Peer Gynt. Ill.:– Arthur Rackham. [1936]. 1st. Edn. Deluxe, (460) numbered, sigd. by artist. 4to. Vell., foxed, orig. box. Raymond M. Sutton, Jr. copy. (SG. May 7; 132) $550
- Works. N.Y., 1911. Viking Edn., (250). 16 vols. Hf. mor. gt., gt. decor. on spines of corn, by Stikeman. (SPB. May 6; 323) $800
- Collected Works. N.Y., 1923. Copyright Edn. 13 vols. Red mor. gt., gt. panel. spines, by Sangorski & Sutcliffe, slightly worn. (SPB. Nov.25; 465) $350

ICONES PLANTARUM rariorum ... des Konigl. botanischen Gartens zu Berlin ... Erster[-Zweiter] Johrgang.
Ed.:– Heinrich Friedrich Link & others. Berlin, 1841-44. 2 vols. (all publd.). 4to. Most plts. browned. Hf. cl. From collection of Massachusetts Horticultural Society, stpd. on plts. (SPB. Oct.1; 142) $1,100

ICONIBUS, Historia Deorum Fatidicorum, Vatum, Sibyllarum, Phoebadum ...
Geneva, 1675. Sm. 4to. 2 ll. reprd., browned. Hf. parch. (TA. Dec.18; 195) £55

IDES, Evot Ysambronts
- Driejaarige Reize naar China, te Lande gedaan. Amst., 1704. 1st. Edn. 4to. Outer margin frontis. slightly defect. & reprd., 1 blank margin reprd., some light wear, old owner's entry on title. Old hf. vell., worn & defect. (VG. Oct.13; 88) Fls. 1,050
- Three Years Travels from Moscow Overland to China ... 1706. 1st. Engl. Edn. 4to. Lacks lf. of directions to binder. Late 18th. C. str.-grd. mor., gt. (S. Nov.24; 173) *Kosson.* £550

IGNY, S.
- Elemens de Pourtraiture. Paris, ca. 1630. Later mott. cf. (TA. Feb.19; 451) £64

IJSVERMAAK, Het, op de Maas te Rotterdam in Februarij 1855
Ill.:– G.J. Bos. Rotterd./Leyden, 1855. Some foxing, some upper corners stained. Hf. leath., orig. litho. pict. upr. wrap. pasted on, defect. (VG. Oct.13; 172) Fls. 950

IL 22 MARZO, PRIMO GIORNO DELL'INDIPENDENZA LOMBARDA. Giornale Officiale
Milan, 1848. Nos. 1-128 in 1 vol. Fo. Some slight repairs, some pp. slightly browned. Later hf. mor. (SI. Dec.3; 291) Lire 620,000

ILBACHIO, O.
- Acta Sanctorum Christi Martyrum Vindicata. Rome, 1723. 2 vols. 4to. Cont. red mor., gt., arms of Innocenzo XIII in centre of covers. (SI. Dec.3; 289) Lire 600,000

ILE ENCHANTEE (L'), conte d'après Shakespeare
Ill.:– Edmund Dulac. Paris, n.d. (300) numbered, sigd. by artist. 4to. Cont. hf. mor., spine decor. with onlays, orig. wraps. bnd. in, by Samblanx. (S. Jul.31; 203) *Mirdan.* £240

ILIFFE & Sons
- Cartoons from 'Bicycling News'. Ill.:– after G. Moore. 1885-89. 4to. Collection of 128 lithos., some captions shaved. Hf. bnd., covers detchd. (MMB. Oct.8; 43) £82

ILLINOIS & OUABACHE LAND COMPANIES
- Memorial of the Ilinois (sic) & Ouabache Land Companies, to the Honourable Congress of the United States Intended as a Full Recapitulation ... of the Former, Addresses, Petitions, Memorials &c of the Company ... [Phila.?], [1802]. Slightly browned. Disbnd., cl. folding case. From liby. of William. E. Wilson. [Sabin 34295] (SPB. Apr.29; 147) $650

ILLUSTRATED LONDON NEWS
May-Dec. 1842, publd. 1843. Vol. 1. Fo. Folding linen-bkd. panorama of L. Orig. cl. gt. (TA. Feb.19; 375) £100
- – Anr. Run. 1844-99. 25 vols. Fo. Ills., some excised. Various bdgs., worn. W.a.f. (CSK. Nov.14; 70) £180
- – Anr. Run. 1845-98. 25 vols. Fo. Ills., some excised. Various bdgs., worn. W.a.f. (CSK. Nov.14; 71) £200
- – Anr. Run. 1847-69. 38 vols., various. Fo. Various bdgs., worn. W.a.f. (CSK. Jan.16; 100) £400
- – Anr. Run. 1847-86. 20 vols., various. Fo. Various bdgs., most worn. (CSK. Feb.6; 196) £180

- – Anr. Run. 1847-98. 10 vols., various. Fo. Various bdgs., worn. W.a.f. (CSK. Oct.17; 238) £110
- – Anr. Run. Jan.-Dec. 1848; Jul.-Dec. 1871; Jul.-Dec. 1872. Vols. 12 & 13, 59 & 61. Fo. Folding plts. in 1st. 2 vols. very defect. Orig. gt. decor. cl., some wear. (TA. Jan.22; 101) £70
- – Anr. Run. 1848-91. 20 vols., various. Fo. Various bdgs., most worn. (CSK. Feb.6; 197) £190
- – Anr. Run. 1848-92. 10 vols., various. Fo. Various bdgs., worn. W.a.f. (CSK. Oct.17; 237) £110
- – Anr. Run. 1848-99. 20 vols., various. Fo. Various bdgs., most worn. (CSK. Feb.6; 194) £135
- – Anr. Run. 1850-89. 20 vols., various. Fo. Various bdgs., most worn. (CSK. Feb.6; 195) £170
- – Anr. Run. 1852-84. Vols. 21-85. Fo. Cont. hf. cf., some worn. (CSK. Jan.23; 7) £1,200
- – Anr. Run. 1854 & 1856. Vols. 25, 26, 28 & 29 only. Fo. Cont. hf. cf. (CSK. Nov.14; 63) £70
- – Anr. Run. 1854-78. 4 vols. only. Fo. Various bdgs., worn. (CSK. Jan.30; 3) £200
- – Anr. Run. 1854-97. 25 vols. Various bdgs., worn. (CSK. Nov.21; 100) £180
- – Anr. Run. L., Jan.-Dec., 1856. Vols. 28 & 29. Fo. Occasional lf. torn or loose, etc. Hf. leath. (CB. Apr.1; 235) Can. $140
- – Anr. Run. L., Jan.-Dec., 1857. Vols. 30 & 31. Fo. Cold. front. in vol. 30 defect. Hf. leath. (CB. Apr.1; 236) Can. $140
- – Anr. Run. 1857-67. 15 vols., various. Fo. Unif. hf. mor. (CSK. Dec.12; 132) £250
- – Anr. Run. L., Jan.-Dec., 1858. Vols. 32 & 33. Fo. Title & first few ll. of both vols. tattered. Hf. leath., brkn. in hinge. (CB. Apr.1; 237) Can. $160
- – Anr. Run. L., Jul.-Dec., 1860. Vol. 37. Fo. Orig. cl., crudely rebkd., hinges reprd. (CB. Apr.1; 237A) Can. $170
- – Anr. Run. 1860-98. 10 vols., various. Fo. Various bdgs., worn. W.a.f. (CSK. Oct.17; 239) £130
- – Anr. Run. 1864-70. Vols. 44, 47-9, 53, 54, 56, 58-65. Fo. Backstrips defect., most covers detchd. W.a.f. (TA. Aug.21; 88) £240
- – Anr. Run. L., 1870. Vol. 57. Fo. Cont. hf. leath., defect., loose. (R. Oct.14-18; 2093) DM 950
- – Anr. Run. L., 1870-71. Fo. Not collated. Cont. hf. leath. (R. Mar.31-Apr.4; 1848) DM 1,500
- – Anr. Run. 1870-99. 37 vols., various. Fo. Various bdgs., worn. W.a.f. (CSK. Jan.16; 101) £350
- – Anr. Run. Jul.-Dec. 1878. Vol. 73. Fo. Orig. cl. gt. (TA. Dec.18; 84) £100
- – Anr. Run. Jul.-Dec./Jan.-Jun. 1878/9. vols. 73-4. Fo. Orig. cl. gt., dampstained. W.a.f. (TA. Aug.21; 85) £150
- – Anr. Run. 1897/98-1904. Vols. 111/112, 114/115, 118/121, 123/125, together 10 vols. 4to. Orig. gt. decor. cl. (TA. Dec.18; 85) £110
- – Anr. Run. 1935-49. 185 orig. weekly Iss.'s. Fo. Staples mostly rusted. Orig. wraps. (TA. Dec.18; 89) £58
- Her Majesty's Glorious Jubilee, 1897. [1897]. Fo. Orig. gt.-lettered cl., mor. spine & tips. (SG. Mar.19; 310) $180
- – Anr. Run. 1954-66. Vols. 224-249. Fo. Unif. cl. gt. (TA. Dec.18; 87) £65

ILLUSTRATED POCKET LIBRARY of Plain & Coloured Books
Ill.:– Rowlandson, Leech, Alken & others. 1903-05. 32 vols. Orig. cl. (SKC. Feb.26; 1286) £55

ILLUSTRATED RECORD of Important Events in Europe
1815. Fo. Decor. hf. roan & bds., marked. (CE. Nov.20; 161) £420

ILLUSTRATED SPORTING & DRAMATIC NEWS
1881-84. Vols. XIV-XX in 3 vols. Fo. Advts. Cont. hf. cf. (TA. Jun.18; 261) £64

ILLUSTRATION HORTICOLE (L')
Ed.:– Charles Lemaire. Ghent, 1860-81. Vols. VII-XVI (2nd. series), vols. XVII-XXVIII (3rd. series), together 22 vols. Several imprints trimmed or slightly cropped, tissue adhering to 3 plts., several plts. loose or detchd., occasional spotting. Cont. roan-bkd. bds., not unif., 2 spines defect., some others worn. (S. Dec.3; 1004) *Elliot.* £520

ILLUSTRATION HORTICOLE (L') -contd.
- **Journal Spécial des Serres et des Jardins.** Ghent, 1862-63. Vols. 9 & 10 only. First lacks titles, a few minor defects. Cont. hf. mor. gt. (SBA. Mar.4; 150)   *L'Acquaforte.* £110

ILLUSTRATIONS of Armorial China
1887. (100). Fo. Orig bds., worn & disbnd. (CSK. Sep.5; 242)   £65

ILLUSTRATIONS OF JAPANESE LIFE
Ed.:- S. Takashima. (captions). Ill.:- K. Ogawa, K. Tamamura, S. Kajima, W.K. Burton. Tokyo, 1896. 3 vols. Sm. 4to. Japanese style pict. wraps. with silk stitching, 2 vols. with brocaded silk spines, upr. & lr. covers of orig. pict. s.-c. present, with bkplt. (SG. Apr.23; 111) $400

ILLUSTRATIONS of Missionary Scenes in Western Africa, India, New Zealand, North-West America & China
Ca. 1855. Ob. fo. Linen-bkd. cold. litho. plts., index supplied in MS. Cont. hf. mor., upr. cover detchd. (TA. Jun.18; 494)   £75

ILLUSTRIERTE ZEITUNG [Leipziger]
Leipzig, 1843-44. Fo. Not collated. Cont. bds. W.a.f. (R. Mar.31-Apr.4; 1860)   DM 1,100
- - **Anr. Run.** Leipzig, 1876-80. Vols. 66-75 in 10 vols. Not collated. Orig. linen. (R. Mar.31-Apr.4; 1861)   DM 4,200

L'IMAGE
1896-97 (all publd.). 4to. Orig. wraps. bnd. in at end. Hf. cf. gt. (P. Feb.19; 56)   *Arts Anciens.* £150
- - **Anr. Copy.** Publisher's hf. cf. à la crocodile, corners, gt. fillet, special tool decor., 12 pict. wraps. (HD. Jun.10; 164)   Frs. 2,100
See-ALPHABET & Image-IMAGE

IMAZHINISTY SERGEI ESENIN, RYURIK, ANATOLY MARIENGOF
Moscow, 1921. (1500). Orig. wraps., spine torn. (SH. Feb.6; 441)   *McVay.* £80

IMBERT, Barthelemi
- **Le Jugement de Paris.** Ill.:- after Moreau & Choffard. Amst. [Paris], 1774. Late 19th. C. earlier style cf. gt., unc. (S. Jul.27; 152)   *Morton-Smith.* £55

IMITATION de Jésus-Christ
Trans.:- M. l'Abbé Valart. Ill.:- Dambrun after Marillier (frontis.). Paris, 1780. 18mo. Red mor. by Cazin. (HD. Apr.8; 257)   Frs. 1,000
- - **Anr. Edn.** 1856. Without Appendice vol. Mor., gt. fleurs de lys semis, centre crowned cypher, silk fleurs de lys doubls. & end-ll. (HD. Jun.30; 36)   Frs. 1,000

IMLAY, Gilbert
- **A Topographical Description of the Western Territory of North America . . .** L., 1793. 2nd. Edn. Advts. Mod. hf. mor., blind-stpd. floral pattern, gt. spine. From liby. of William E. Wilson. (SPB. Apr.29; 150) $425
- - **Anr. Edn.** L., 1797. 3rd. Edn. Advts. Orig. bds., spine worn, upr. cover loose, boxed. From liby. of William E. Wilson. (SPB. Apr.29; 151) $1,200

IMPARTIAL History (An) of Michael Servetus burnt Alive at Geneva for Heresie
1724. Cont. cf. (S. Jun.17; 762)   *Henry.* £85

IMPARTIAL INQUIRY (An), into the Advantages & Losses that England hath Received since the Beginning of this Present War with France
1693. 1st. Edn. 4to. Recent cf. [Wing I84] (C. Apr.1; 181)   *Lawson.* £80

IMPERATO, Ferrante
- **Historia Naturale.** Ed.:- Giovanni Maria Ferro. Venice, 1672. 2nd. Edn. Fo. A few ll. slightly soiled, sm. hole in outer margins. Cont. vell., bkplts. of Marchese Salsa & Viscount Dudley. From liby. of Dr. E. Ashworth Underwood. (S. Feb.23; 233)   *Robinson.* £280

IMPERIAL GALLERY OF BRITISH ART
Ca. 1875. Fo. Hf. mor., worn. (P. Feb.18; 214)   *Davies.* £170
- - **Anr. Edn.** N.d. Fo. Some plts. spotted. Cont. cl. (SH. Jun.4; 89)   *Heald.* £190
- - **Anr. Copy.** 4 vols. Marginal spotting. Orig. cl.-bkd. bds. (CSK. Oct.17; 225)   £170

IMPERIALE, Giovanni
- **Musaeum Historicum et Physicum.** Venice, 1640. 1st. Edn. 4to. 18th. C. hf. cf. (C. Apr.1; 142)   *Moroni.* £70

IMPRIMATUR. Ein Jahrbuch für Bücherfreunde
Ed.:- S. Buchenau, E.L. Hauswedell & R.J. Meyer. Hamburg, 1930-40. 4to. Orig. linen. (H. Dec.9/10; 102)   DM 1,200
- - **Anr. Copy.** Vols. 1-9. Orig. linen & 1 orig. hf. linen. (HK. May 12-14; 2243)   DM 900

IMPRINT. A Typographical Journal
Jan.-Nov. 1913. Nos. 1-9. 4to. Orig. wraps., boxed. (P. Jul.30; 134)   *Thorp.* £120
- - **Anr. Edn.** 1913. 2 vols. [all publd.]. 4to. Cont. hf. mor. (SH. Oct.9; 52)   *Marks.* £75
- - **Anr. Run.** 9 vols., all publd. Orig. wraps., some torn. (SH. Mar.6; 529)   *Thorp.* £60

IMREI NOAM
Ed.:- Joseph Shalom Galliago. Amst., 1628-30. Marginal repairs, some affecting text, some stains, browned. Vell., soiled, lacks ties, front free end-paper browned & defect., lacks lr. free end-paper. (SPB. May 11; 134) $600

IN EVANGELIUM secundum Matthaeum, Marcum et Lucam Commentarii . . .
Ed.:- Robertus Estienne (or Stephens). [Geneva], Jan. 1553. fo. Overslip on fo. AA1 reading 'Harmonia Evangelica', dampstained in places. 18th C. cf., slightly worn, jnts. brkn. Cont. sigs. of John Hunt & John Walpole on title, the 1st dated 1652. (S. May 5; 35)   *Cristani.* £70

IN MANY WARS
Ed.:- George Lynch & Frederick Palmer. Tokyo, [1904]. Tall 8vo. With autographs of the contributors (including Jack London & R.H. Davis) pasted under the articles. Pict. wraps., laced. (SG. Nov.13; 427) $320

IN PRINCIPIO
Hammersmith, Doves Pr., 1911. (12) on vell. 12mo. Niger mor., gt. ornament, spine gt. in 6 compartments, 5 raised bands, sigd. by Doves Bindery, qtr. mor. s.-c. Cortlandt Field Bishop bkplt. (CNY. May 22; 395) $950

INCE, William & Mayhew, John
- **The Universal System of Household Furniture.** Ill.:- A. Darly. [?1762]. 1st. Edn. Fo. Late 19th. C. old-style panel. cf., rebkd., cl. s.-c. (S. Mar.17; 419)   *Marlborough Rare Books.* £3,500

INCHBALD, Mrs Elizabeth
- **Simple Story.** 1791. 1st. Edn. 4 vols. Some pp. loose. Cf. gt., upr. cover detchd. on vol. 1. (P. Dec.11; 346)   *Sanders.* £110

INCHOFER, Melchior
- **Monarchie des Solipses (Les) . . .** Trans.:- Restaut. Amst., 1721. 12mo. Cont. cf. decor. spine, jnts. split. Liby. of Marquise de Pompadour (with her arms). (HD. Feb.18; 28)   Frs. 2,000

INDIA LOVE POEMS
Trans.:- Tambimuttu. Ill.:- John Piper. 1977. (200) sigd. by trans. & artist. Fo. 18 cold. plts. Qtr. niger mor. gt., sandalwood case. (P. Jul.2; 6)   *Hosain.* £140

INDIAN Antiquary
Bombay, 1872-1910. 38 vols. 4to. Various, including index (lacking vol. 13 & 16). Unif. hf. mor, 1 cover detchd. (CSK. Oct.10; 91)   £110

INDIANA
- **Illustrated Historical Atlas of the State of Indiana.** Chic., [1876]. 1st. Edn. Atlas fo. Orig. gt.-pict. qtr. mor., some wear. (PNY. Mar.26; 159) $240

INFANTS CABINET of Fishes
[1801]. 2 vols. 64mo. 1 title-page pasted in at end of vol. Text orig. bds., cards in orig. wooden box, with engraved pict. sliding cover. (SKC. Sep.9; 1435a)   £120

INFANT's GRAMMAR, or a Pic-Nic Party of the Parts of Speech
1822. 1st. Edn. 1 p. advts., slightly stained. Orig. ptd. wraps., further ill. on upr. cover, soiled & worn. (SH. Mar.19; 140)   *Maggs.* £55

INFANT'S LIBRARY, The
Ed.:- E. Marshall. N.d. 5 vols. only. 2¼ × 2 inches. Occasional slight soiling. Orig. bds., 4 rebkd. (CSK. Sep.19; 151)   £100

INFANT'S Path Strewed with Flowers, The
[wtrmkd. 1794]. 32mo. With 2 corrections by former owner. Orig. Dutch floral bds. (S. Feb.9; 23)   *Temperley.* £90

INFANT-TUTOR, The
1767. 32mo. Orig. dutch floral bds., lacks

backstrip & upr. end-lf. (SH. Dec.10; 33a)   *Quaritch.* £320

INGEN-HOUZ, Jan
- **Expériences sur les Végétaux . . .** Paris, 1787-89. 3rd. Edn. 2 vols. Some ll. slightly spotted, title to vol. II damaged in upr. margin. Cont. hf. cf., worn. The 1st. Fr. 2 vol. edn. (S. Oct.21; 401)   *Kcw Books.* £200

INGERSOLL-SMOUSE, Florence
- **Joseph Vernet . . .** Paris, 1926. 2 vols. 4to. Sewed. (HD. Jun.25; 291)   Frs. 1,200

INGHIRAMI, Francesco
- **Monumenti Etruschi o di Etrusco Nome disegnati.** 1821-26. 6 vols. plus Index. 4to. Hf. mor. gt. Signet liby. copy. (P. Oct.2; 113)   *Sims & Reed.* £250

INGOLDSBY, Thomas (Pseud.)
See-BARHAM, Rev. Richard H. 'Thomas Ingoldsby'

INGRAHAM, Henry Andrews
- **American Trout Streams.** N.Y., Priv. Ptd., 1926. (350) numbered. New 2-tone buckram, unopened. (SG. Dec.11; 59) $220

INGRAM, James
- **Memorials of Oxford.** Ill.:- John Le Keux after F. Mackenzie. Oxford, 1837. 3 vols., L.P. 4to. Cont. hf. mor. gt. Kirtlington Park bkplt. (C. May 20; 135)   *Swift.* £250
- - **Anr. Copy.** Slight stain to fore-margin of some plts., liby. stp. on verso of titles. Cont. hf. mor. From the collection of Eric Sexton. (C. Apr.16; 287)   *Kentish.* £170

INGRESSO del Procurator di San Marco Alessandro Albrizzi
- **Andrea Gritti Principis Venetiarum Vita (by) Nicolaus Barbadicus.** Venice, 1792. Thick paper. Sm. fo. Orig. ptd. paste-paper wraps., upr. cover with Albrizzi arms, buckram s.-c. From the collection of John A. Saks. (C. Jun.10; 111)   *Breslauer.* £220
- **Componimenti Poetici.** Venice, 1762. Thick paper. Sm. fo. Orig. paste-paper wraps., in bistre, upr. cover with arms of Rezzonico, slightly stained. From the collection of John A. Saks. (C. Jun.10; 131)   *Lyon.* £240
- - **Anr. Edn.** Venice, 1764. Thick paper. Sm. fo. Orig. 'Broccato d'Oro' paper wraps., buckram s.-c. From the collection of John A. Saks. (C. Jun.10; 123)   *Quaritch.* £820
- - **Anr. Edn.** Ill.:- T. Viero & others. Venice, 1780. Thick paper. Sm. fo. Orig. paste-paper wraps., ptd. in white, upr. cover with arms of Pisani, buckram s.-c. From the collection of John A. Saks. (C. Jun.10; 127)   *Barton.* £100
- - **Anr. Edn.** Ill.:- T. Viero after F. Bartolozzi (frontis.). Venice, 1792. 4to. Orig. paper bds., all-over wood-block decor., upr. cover with Albrizzi arms, lr. cover with Eviva initials, in wide ornamental border. From the collection of John A. Saks. (C. Jun.10; 112)   *Breslauer.* £260
- **De Angelo Contareno cum Divi Procurator Electus . . . Orationes.** Ill.:- [Fosati]. Venice, 1754. 4to. Cont. velvet, sides decor. with wide ornamental foliate border surrounding lge. Contarini arms with flourishes, executed in gold & silver needlework, silver of upr. cover oxydised & showing wear, silk paste-downs, velvet-lined leath. case. From the collection of John A. Saks. (C. Jun.10; 118)   *Lyon.* £150
- **Della Guerre de'Veneziana nell' Asia [by] Coriolano Cippico.** Ill.:- T. Viero (frontis.). Venice, 1796. 4to. Orig. paper bds., upr. cover with Capello arms in floral border, lr. cover with similar border & central cartouche with Eviva initials, soiled, buckram s.-c. From the collection of John A. Saks. (C. Jun.10; 114)   *Marston.* £80
- **Oratio Natalis Lastesi.** Venice, 1772. Thick paper. Sm. fo. Orig. ptd. paper wraps., upr. cover with arms of Zuccato. From the collection of John A. Saks. (C. Jun.10; 135)   *Lyon.* £60
- **Oranzione.** Venice, [1785]. Thick paper. Sm. fo. Orig. paper wraps., ptd. in red, upr. cover with Gabriel arms, buckram s.-c. From the collection of John A. Saks. (C. Jun.10; 120)   *Breslauer.* £160
- - **Anr. Edn.** Venice, 1796. 4to. Orig. paper bds., upr. cover with Cappello arms surrounded by floral border, lr. cover with similar border & central cartouche with Eviva initials, spine renewed, buckram s.-c. From the collection of John A. Saks. (C. Jun.10; 115)   *Marston.* £60

- Orazione dell'Ab. Pietro Berti. Ill.:– Baratti after Compagnoni (frontis. port.) & T. Viero (borders). Venice, [1780]. Thick paper. Sm. fo. Paste-paper wraps., buckram s.-c. From the collection of John A. Saks. (C. Jun.10; 124) *Quaritch.* £100
- Poesie. Venice, 1772. Thick paper. Orig. ptd. paper wraps., upr. cover with arms of Zuccato in gt., buckram s.-c. From the collection of John A. Saks. (C. Jun.10; 136) *Quaritch.* £480
– – Anr. Edn. Venice, 1779. Thick paper. Sm. fo. Orig. paper wraps., embossed with arms of Giovanelli, rebkd., buckram s.-c. From the collection of John A. Saks. (C. Jun.10; 122) *Barton.* £70
– – Anr. Edn. Ill.:– T. Viero after Novelli, Visentini & G. David. Venice, 1780. Thick paper. Sm. fo. Paste-paper bds., buckram s.-c. From the collection of John A. Saks. (C. Jun.10; 125) *Quaritch.* £140
– – Anr. Edn. Ill.:– P.A. Novelli (frontis.). Venice, 1785. Thick paper. Sm. fo. Mor. paper wraps., buckram s.-c. From the collection of John A. Saks. (C. Jun.10; 121) *Bernard.* £200
- Poesie nel Felice Ingresso. Venice, 1746. L.P. Bnd. with 2 similar ingressi. Cont. mott. cf. gt., foot of spine reprd. From the collection of John A. Saks. (C. Jun.10; 134) *Taylor.* £90
- Rime d'Autori Diversi. Ill.:– F. Bartolozzi. Venice, 1759. Thick paper. Sm. fo. Tear to margin of title, reprd., just affecting plt., slight staining. Cont. decor. paper bds., buckram s.-c. From the collection of John A. Saks. (C. Jun.10; 132) *King.* £190

INNES, Cosmo
- Campbells–The Black Book of Taymouth Edinb., 1855. 9 vols. 4to. Orig. cl., worn. (CE. Jul.9; 144) £140

INNOCENT VIII, Pope
- Bulla Canonizationis Sancti Leopoldi Marchionis. [Vienna], [Stephen Koblinger?] [after 6 Jan. 1485]. With 'homie' in line 2 on f. 2r. 4to. Sm. stain of 1st. lf. Unsewn & unc. [Copinger 3267; BMC III p.809, var. iss; Goff I 102] (C. Apr.1; 49) *Walton.* £350
- Regule Cancellarie Apostolice . . . nuper correcta et emendata. Strassburg, Johann Pruss, [not after 1492]. 4to. Cont. owner's inscr. on title & notes at end, ink-stains on a few ll., some marginal staining spreading to text. Recent cf. (Hain 9221*; BMC I p. 126; Goff I 153] (C. Apr.1; 48) *Goldschmidt.* £160

INSEL, Die
Ed.:– O.J. Bierbaum, A.W. Heymel & R.A. Schröder. Berlin & Leipzig, 1899-1900. Year 1 in 4 vols. 4to. Unc., orig. hf. vell., orig. wraps. bnd. in. (H. May 21/22; 1643) DM 520
– – Anr. Run. Ed.:– Otto Julius Bierbaum, Alfred Walter Heymel, Rudolf Alexander Schröder. 1899-1901. Years I & II in 8 vols. 4to. Orig. hf. vell., & orig. bds., orig. wraps. bnd. in. (D. Dec.11-13; 1097) DM 1,500

INSTITUTION OF LOCOMOTIVE ENGINEERS
- Proceedings. 1911-50. Vols. 1-40 in 30. Later cl. (SH. Oct.9; 270) *Haut.* £80

INSTRUCCION de Revistas o Matriculas formada por el Señor Don Jorge Excobedo y Alarcón
Lima, 1784. Fo. Cont. sig. of certification at end. Disbnd. (SPB. May 5; 270) $130

INSTRUCTIVE Picture Book
Edinb., 1867. 2nd. Edn. Fo. Orig. cl.-bkd. pict. bds. (CSK. Sep.12; 134) £50

INTERMEDIAIRE DES GENEALOGISTES–De Middlelaar Tussen de Genealogische Navorschers
Brussels, Jan. 1946-1980. No. 1-207, lacks no. 15 & 60. In pts. (LM. Nov.8; 235) B.Frs. 8,000

INTERNATIONAL CHESS MAGAZINE, The
Ed.:– W. Steinitz. N.Y., 1885-88. Vols. 1-4, in 2. 4to. Hf. mor. (SG. Apr.9; 130) $160

INTERNATIONAL Scientific Series
1872-1910. 39 vols. only. Plts. soiled. Orig. cl., a few spines torn. (SH. May 28; 56) *Pythagoras.* £100

INTERNATIONAL ZOO YEARBOOK (The)
Ed.:– D. Morris & C. Jarvis & others. 1959-74. Vols. 1-14, 4to. Vols. 2-14 in d-w.'s (VA. Aug.29; 91) R. 110

INTERNATIONALE ZEITSCHRIFTENSCHAU für Bibelwissenschaft und Grenzgebiete
Düsseldorf, 1951-71. 16 (of 17) vols., lacks vol. XII. (B. Dec.10/11; 1346) Fls. 1,200

INTRATIONUM Excellentissimus Liber
Feb., 1510. 1st. Known Edn. Fo. Some margins & corners reprd., lacks final blank. 18th. C. cf. [STC 14116] (C. Nov.19; 14) *Courtland.* £1,400

INTRIGUES de la Capital, accompagnées de plusieurs autres
Ill.:– Binet, engraved by Dorgez. Paris, [1787]. 18mo. Cont red mor., gt. covers mosaic decor., with device 'Jamais assez', watered silk fly-ll. & doubls. (HD. Apr.10; 139) Frs. 1,750

IONA, Giovanni Battista
- Dottrina Christiana breve. Rome, 1658. Liby. stps. on title, some spotting & browning. Cont. vell., soiled, lr. inside hinge brkn., s.-c. (S. Apr.29; 401) *Hirschler.* £70

IONIDES, Alexander C., Jnr.
- Ion. A Grandfather's Tale. Dublin, Cuala Pr., 1927. (200) numbered. Sm. 4to. Orig. cl.-bkd. bds. (S. Jun.9; 2) *Quaritch.* £55

IORNANDES–FOROIULIENSIS, Paulus Diaconus
- De Rebus Gothorum.–De Gestis Langobardorum. Ill.:– H. Burgkmair (title woodcut), Daniel Hopfer (Arms woodcut). Augsb., 1515. 1st. Edns. 2 works in 1 vol. Fo. Red mor., inner gt. dentelle. (HK. Nov.18-21; 216) DM 1,600

IRBY, C. L. & Mangles, J.
- Travels in Egypt & Nubia, Syria & Asia Minor. 1823. Cont. cf. (SH. Nov.7; 417) *House.* £70
– – Anr. Copy. 1 map mntd. on linen, a few ll. spotted. Later hf. mor., gt. (SH. Nov.7; 418) *Hosain.* £65

IRBY, Leonard Howard Lloyd
- The Ornithology of the Straits of Gibraltar. 1895. 2nd. Edn. Cont. cl. gt., rebkd., orig. spine preserved. (C. May 20; 216) *Hill.* £240

IREDALE, Tom
- Birds of New Guinea. Ill.:– Lilian Medland. Melbourne, 1956. 2 vols. 4to. Mor.-bkd. cl. gt., s.-c. (C. May 20; 217) *Hill.* £160
– – Anr. Edn. Ill.:– Lilian Medland. Melbourne, [1956]. 2 vols. 4to. Orig. bdg. & d.-w. (CB. Sep.24; 32) Can. $350

IRELAND
- The Over-throw of an Irish Rebell, in a Late Battaile, or the Death of Sir Carey Adoughertie, who Murdred Sir George Paulet in Ireland . . . L., 1608. 1st. Edn. Sm. 4to. Lev., triple gt. fillet borders, gt. spine & dentelles by Rivière. [STC 18785] (SG. Oct.9; 134) $600

IRELAND, Joseph N.
- Records of the New York Stage from 1750 to 1860. N.Y., 1866-1867. 1st. Edn.; (200). 2 vols. Extra ill. with many ports. (mostly sm. mntd. reproductions). Three qtr. mor., partly loose. (SG. Aug.7; 103) $175

IRELAND, Samuel
- Graphic Illustrations of Hogarth. L., 1794-99. 2 vols. Some plts. heavily soiled. Hf. leath. (D. Dec.11-13; 679) DM 500
- A Picturesque Tour through Holland, Brabant & Part of France. 1790. 1st. Edn. 2 vols. Mod. hf. cf. (SH. Jul.16; 166) *S. Roberts.* £200
– – Anr. Copy. 2 titles, 43 (of 46) aquatints, 1 engraving. Cont. spr. cf. gt. (C. May 20; 136) *Forum.* £140
– – Anr. Edn. 1796. 2nd. Edn. 2 vols. 2 engraved titles with cold. vigs., imprints cropped, & 49 plts., 45 cold., title of 1 plt. cropped. Lev. mor. by the Hampstead Bindery. (C. Jul.15; 56) *Taylor.* £450
- Picturesque Views . . . Inns of Court in London & Westminster. 1800. 21 cold. aquatint plts. Lev. mor. by the Hampstead Bindery. (C. Jul.15; 53) *Taylor.* £280
– – Anr. Copy. Plts. cold. Hf. mor. gt. by Bartlett & Co., Boston. From the collection of Eric Sexton. (C. Apr.16; 292) *Mason.* £200
- Picturesque Views on the River Medway. 1793. [1st. Edn.?] L.P. Fo. 28 plts. plus dupl. black & white plts., lacks plt. of Upnor Castle, untrimmed. Later hf. mor. gt. (TA. Dec.18; 362) £165
– – Anr. Copy. Early 19th. C. cl.-bkd. bds., title in gt. on spine, edges slightly defect. (S. Nov.4; 532) *Clark.* £130

– – Anr. Copy. 4to. Cont. diced cf., gt. decor. spine. (TA. Oct.16; 54) £100
– – Anr. Copy. Some dampstaining thro.-out. Cont. hf. mor. (SH. Nov.6; 119) *Greenaway.* £80
– – Anr. Edn. N.d. 4to. 1st. few pp. loose. Hf. mor. (CE. Jun.4; 46) £150
- Picturesque Views on the River Medway. –Picturesque Views on the River Thames. 1733; 1792. 2nd. work: vol. 2 only. 1st. work: some soiling, engraved map (not called for in list of plts), margins browned; 2nd. work: aquatint additional title & 24 plts. only, lacks plt. no. 3, some soiling, margins browned. Unif. mor. W.a.f. (CSK. Feb.13; 89) £100
- Picturesque Views on the River Medway. –Picturesque Views on the Upper, or Warwickshire Avon.–Picturesque Views on the River Wye. 1793; 1795; 1797. 3 works in 3 vols. Plts. cold. (excepting 2 in 2nd. work & 1 in 3rd. work). Unif. hf. mor. by Bartlett & Co., Boston. From the collection of Eric Sexton. (C. Apr.16; 291) *Wilson.* £380
- Picturesque Views on the River Thames. 1792. [1st. Edn.?]. 2 vols. Lev. mor., by the Hampstead Bindery. (C. Jul.15; 54) *Bailey.* £300
– – Anr. Copy. Plts. cold. Hf. mor. by Bartlett & Co., Boston. From the collection of Eric Sexton. (C. Apr.16; 290) *Traylen.* £220
– – Anr. Copy. 2 vols. 51 (of 52) plts. Cont. cf., spines gt. (SG. Feb.26; 180) $160
– – Anr. Edn. 1848. 2 vols. Occasional slight spotting. Orig. cl., slightly soiled, jnts. slightly torn. (CSK. Oct.24; 57) £95
- Picturesque Views on the River Wye. 1797. L.P. Fo. Lacks 4 plts. Cont. tree cf., gt., covers detchd. (TA. Nov.20; 429) £65
– – Anr. Copy. 4to. Fo. Lacks 4 plts. Cont. tree cf. gt., covers detchd. (TA. Sep.18; 336) £50
- Picturesque Views of the Severn. Ill.:– after Ireland. 1824. 2 vols. 4to. Orig. cl., soiled. (CSK. Nov.21; 242) £50
- Picturesque views on the Upper, or Warwickshire Avon. 1795. [1st Edn.?]. Cont. cf. gt. with old reback. (TA. Nov.20; 430) £75
– – Anr. Copy. Cf., rebkd. (P. Apr.30; 263) *Schapiro.* £70

See–HARRAL, Thomas & Ireland, Samuel

IRELAND, William Henry
- England's Topographer or a New & Complete History of . . . Kent. N.d.-1829-30. 4 vols. Vol. 1, 2 plts. detchd., vol. 1 lacks plt. 'St. Augustine's gate, Canterbury', called for in plt. list, while vol. 4 contains additional unlisted view of Gravesend. Cont. str.-grd.-cf., lr. jnts. of vol. 4 brkn. (CSK. Aug.1; 213) £130
- The Life of Napoleon Bonaparte. Ill.:– after George Cruikshank. 1823-27. Vols. I-III only (of IV). Cont. hf. cf. (TA. May 21; 235) £70
– – Anr. Edn. Ill.:– George Cruikshank. 1828. 4 vols. Mor. gt., arms on covers, by Rivière. (P. Sep.11; 14) *Traylen.* £320
– – Anr. Copy. Occasional foxing & spotting, affecting some plts. Red lev. mor. gt. by Rivière. (CNY. Oct.1; 99) $650

IRELAND ILLUSTRATED; Devonshire Illustrated; London Illustrated; London in the Nineteenth Century
1829-32. Extracts from 4 works in 1 vol. 4to. 4 engraved titles & 32 plts. only, spotted. Cf., worn, lacks pt. of spine. (CSK. Feb.6; 31) £50

IRELAND'S LAMENTATION; being A Short but Perfect, Full & True Account of the Scituation, Nature, Constitution & Product of Ireland . . .
L., 1689. 4to. Liby. stp. on title-p., top right corner reprd. Hf. mor. [Wing I1025] (GM. Apr.30; 330) £75

IRENICUS, F.
- Germaniae Exegeseos Volumina Duodecim. Hagenau, 1518. 1st. Edn. Fo. Slightly soiled or browned, stp. erased from title, some wormholing near end. Old hf. vell. (R. Oct.14-18; 85) DM 900

IRVING, E.
See–GODLONTON, Robert & Irving, E.

IRVING, Washington
- Astoria or Anecdotes of an Enterprise Beyond the Rocky Mountains. Phila., 1836. 1st. Edn. 2 vols. Advts., foxed. Orig. cl., slightly defect. thro. damp. From liby. of William E. Wilson. (SPB. Apr.29; 159) $200

IRVING, Washington -contd.

- **The Legend of Sleepy Hollow.** Ill.:– Will H. Bradley. N.Y., for Bradley. [1897]. 1st. Bradley Edn. Tall 12mo. Pict. bds., unopened, spine chipped at head. (PNY. Mar.26; 55) $160
- – **Anr. Edn.** Ill.:– Arthur Rackham. [1928]. (375) numbered, sigd. by artist. 4to. Orig. parch., orig. box. (CSK. Feb.13; 181) £280
- – **Anr. Copy.** Orig. vell. gt. (SBA. Oct.21; 230) *Jones.* £240
- – **Anr. Edn.** Ill.:– Arthur Rackham. L., [1928]. (250) numbered for England, sigd. by artist. Lge. 4to. Vell., cl. s.-c. Raymond M. Sutton Jr. copy. (SG. May 7; 136) $1,000
- – **Anr. Edn.** Ill.:– Arthur Rackham. Phila., [1928]. (125) numbered for U.S.A., sigd. by artist. Lge. 4to. Vell. Raymond M. Sutton Jr. copy. (SG. May 7; 139) $400
- – **Anr. Edn.** Ill.:– Arthur Rackham. L., [1928]. 1st. Trade Edn. 4to. Gt.-pict. cf. Raymond M. Sutton Jr. copy. (SG. May 7; 137) $275
- – **Anr. Copy.** Gt.-pict. cl., cold. pict. d.-w. Raymond M. Sutton Jr. copy. (SG. May 7; 138) $120
- – **Anr. Edn.** Ill.:– Arthur Rackham. Phila., [1928]. 1st. Amer. Trade Edn. 4to. Cl., cold. pict. d.-w. defect. Raymond M. Sutton Jr. copy. (SG. May 7; 140) *$160*
- **The Letters of Jonathan Oldstyle.** N.Y., 1824. 1st. (Pirated) Edn. Text foxed. Orig. ptd. drab wraps., spine partly rebkd., qtr. mor. gt. s.-c., unc. From the Prescott Collection. (CNY. Feb.6; 167) $180
- **Life of George Washington.** N.Y., 1855-59. 1st. Edn. 5 vols. BAL's 2nd. (?) printing of vol. I, 1st. printings or states of the other vols. Orig. cl., spines,& covers of vol. V faded, some soiling to covers, each in cl. jacket, open-face cl. Lf. from orig. MS. mntd. at front of vol. IV (comprising pp. 284-285 of vol. IV), some revisions; from the Prescott Collection. (CNY. Feb.6; 168) $140
- – **Anr. Copy.** Extra ill. with 100 ports. etc., liby. blind-stp on each title-p. Cf., spines gt., liby. bkplts. (SG. Sep.4; 268) $110
- **The Life & Voyages of Christopher Columbus, & … the Companions of Columbus.** N.Y., Oct.21, 1892. Quadri-Centennial Edn. 3 vols. 4to. Orig. vell., gt. (SG. Jan.8; 219) $200
- **Rip Van Winkle.** Ill.:– Arthur Rackham. 1905. 4to. 50 mntd. & guarded cold. plts. Rebnd., cl. pict. gt. spine, cover pasted on. (PL. Nov.27; 82) *Smith.* £50
- – **Anr. Edn.** Ill.:– Arthur Rackham. 1905. (250) sigd. by artist. 4to. Orig. vell. gt., lacks ties. (SH. Mar.27; 419) *Rosenblatt.* £460
- – **Anr. Copy.** Numbered. Gt.-pict. vell., orig. silk ribbon ties, window marb. s.-c., boxed. Raymond M. Sutton Jr. copy. (SG. May 7; 142) $1,800
- – **Anr. Edn.** Ill.:– Arthur Rackham. 1907. 4to. Orig. cl. gt. (SH. Dec.11; 419) *Mundy.* £60
- – **Anr. Copy.** Slight spotting. Orig. cl., slighly soiled. (CSK. Oct.17; 8) £50
- – **Anr. Edn.** Ill.:– Arthur Rackham. N.Y. & L., [1916]. 4to. Pict. gt.-stpd. cl., pict. d.-w. Raymond M. Sutton Jr. copy. (SG. May 7; 143) $425
- **Sketch Book.** N.Y., 1819-20. 1st. Edn. 7 pts. in 2 vols. Slight browning & tears. Red str.-grd. mor. gt. (SPB. Nov.25; 208a) $200
- – **Anr. Edn.** Ill.:– Arthur Rackham & others. N.Y., 1895. 1st. Edn. 2 vols. Cl. gt., cl. d.-w's, orig. ribbon bookmarks, 1 detchd. Raymond M. Sutton Jr. copy. (SG. May 7; 144) $110
- **Works.** N.Y., 1860. 28 vols. 4to. Slightly discold. Cf. gt. (SPB. Nov.25; 466) $300
- [–] **Anr. Edn.** 1871-74. Knickerbocker Edn. 27 vols. Orig. cl. (SH. May 28; 57) *Mellor.* £70
- – **Anr. Edn.** N.Y., n.d. Joseph Jefferson Edn., (250) with MS. fragment. 40 vols. Mor. ornately gt. in tulip pattern, dentelles, panel. spines decor. with heart & tulip design. (SPB. Nov.25; 467) $2,300

IRWIN & CO., W.H.

- **Eastern Townships Gazetteer & Directory …** 1875-76. Montreal, 1875. Many advts. inserted. Orig. leath.-bkd. papered bds. (CB. Nov.12; 103) *Can.* $300

IRWIN, Eyles

- **Series of Adventures … Voyage up the Red Sea.** 1787. 3rd. Edn. 5 maps (1 loose). Cf. (P. Oct.23; 36) *Hosain.* £75

ISAAC, Ledyard

- **An Essay on Matter, in Five Chapters.** Phila., Priv. ptd., 1784. 1st. Edn. Mod. bds., cf. spine, liby. bkplt. & release on upr. pastedown. (SG. Jan.8; 240) $100

ISAAC, Sciadrensis

- **Grammatica linguae Syriacae.** Rome, 1636. Sm. 4to. Some browning & staining. Cont. limp vell., very worn, s.-c. (S. Apr.29; 402) *Brill.* £90

ISABEY, J.

- **Voyage cn Italie.** [Paris?], 1822. Fo. Without title as Iss.?, slightly spotted. Orig. hf. mor., slightly worn. (SBA. Jul.14; 36) *Hamilton.* £160

ISABEY, Jean Baptiste

- **Caricatures.** Ill.:– Motte after Isabey. Paris, 1818. Ob. 4to. Str.-grd. hf. mor., ca. 1880. (HD. Dec.5; 108) *Frs.* 1,800

ISERT, Paul Erdman

- **Voyages en Guinée et dans les Îles Caraïbes en Amérique.** Paris, 1793. Some browning. Cont. mott. cf., gt., spine defect. at foot. [Sabin 35244] (S. Jun.22; 180) *Crete.* £130

ISHILL, Joseph

- **Free Vistas.** 1933; 1937. (290) numbered; (205) numbered. 2 vols. Qtr. cl. (PG. Dec.12; 220) £78

ISIDORUS HISPALENSIS

- **De Summo Bono.** [Nuremb.], [Johann Sensenschmidt], before Apr., 1470. 1st. Edn. Fo. 50 ll. (of 66), lacks ff.4, 15, 19 & 54-66. Old MS. vell. bds. [BMC II, 404] (S. Nov.25; 318) *Fletcher.* £120
- **Etymologiae.** Venice, Petrus Löslein, 1483. Fo. Lacks Register & blank 5th. lf., full-p. woodcut cropped at head, lacks portion of upr. margin of 1 lf., reprd., affecting foliation & a few letters on verso, sm. hole slightly affecting text, some early lr. blank margins stained & slightly torn, occasional minor stains, blank margin of last lf. reprd. 19th. C. cf. [H-C 9279*; BMC V p. 379; Goff I 184] (C. Apr.1; 46) *Penny.* £350

ISIDORUS, Hispaliensis–ANON

- **Synonma de Homine et Ratione.–Admonitio de Profectu Animae.** [Albi], [Printer of Aeneas Sylvius], ca. 1480; ca. 1478. 2 works in 1 vol. (possibly issued together). Fo. 1st. work: 1st. p. with illuminated hf. border of fruit & leaf in cols. & gold, a 4-line capital initial U in red on gold ground; 2nd. work: 1st. p. with 4-line capital Q in gold, with pen & ink & gold marginal ascender & descender; both works with spaces for capital initials, 3-line initials in alternating red & blue with penwork decor., & rubricated in red, blue & yellow; dampstaining (more so in 2nd. work), blank fore-margin of fo. 4 of 1st. work restored, last lf. of same work with parch to blank portion, sm. wormhole through central margin of last 10 ll. of 2nd. work, some old, faded ink inscrs. 18th. C. Fr. mor. gt., dampstained, corners worn. Bkplt. of Le Candelle, lately in the collection of Eric Sexton. [Goff I206 & A53] (CNY. Apr.8; 1) $5,800

ISLANDS Landnamabok

Copen., 1744. 2nd. Edn. 4to. Some foxing. Cont. qtr. cf. (CB. Dec.9; 2) *Can.* $350

ISOCRATES

- **Logoi [Orationes].** Ed.:– Demetrius Chalcondylas. Milan, Uldericus Scinzenzeler. 24 Jan. 1493. 1st. Edn. Fo. Lacks 2Bii, 2Bv & 3 blanks, slight worming affecting a few letters, last few ll. stained. Old bdgs. covered with vell. Stp. of the Grennadius Liby. [Goff I-210] (SPB. Nov.25; 67) $450
- **Oratio de Laudibus Helenae, Herodoti Historiae.** Trans.:– Johannes Petrus Lucensis; Laurentius Valla. [Venice], [Christophorus de Pensis], ca. 1498-1500. Fo. Lacks a3-4 of table, slight staining on title. 17th. C. sheep over wooden bds., worn, 2nd. work in vol. removed. [Hain 9314; BMC V p. 475; Goff I 212] (C. Apr.1; 50) *Laughton.* £160

ISOLA, Agostino

- **Pieces Selected from the Italian Poets.** Camb., 1784. 2nd. Edn. Cont. red. str.-grd. mor., gt., tooled in compartments. (S. Nov.24; 174) *Waterfield.* £95

ISON, Walter

- **The Georgian Buildings of Bath from 1700-1830. –The Georgian Buildings of Bristol.** L., [1948]; [1952]. 2 vols. Orig. cl. (CB. May 27; 128) *Can.* $140

ISRAEL TAUB OF MODZHITZ

- **Divrei Israel [on Genesis & Exodus].** Lublin, Warsaw, 1904; 1912. 1st. Edn. 2 vols. 4to. Leath. (S. Nov.18; 267) *Laurie.* £120

ISSACHAR BEN NAPHTALI KATZ

- **Mareh Kohen.** Cracow, 1589. 1st. Edn. Sm. 4to. Liby. stp. on title. Mod. mor. (C. Jul.16; 307) *Stein.* £400

ISSERLIS, Moses ben Israel

- **Zot Torath ha'Chatoth.** Cracow, 1591. 3rd. Edn. Sm. 4to. Some staining thro.-out, liby. stp. on 1st. text lf. Old hf. mor. (C. Jul.16; 308) *Joseph.* £260

ITALY

- **Atlante Geografico delli Stati Italiani.** Firenze, 1844. Vol. II. Fo. Old bds., brkn., some foxing, ex-liby. (SG. Aug.21; 260) $400
- **Descrizione dell'Imp. e R. Palazzo Pitti di Firenze.** Firenze, 1819. Vell., 2 early paintings on covers. (SG. Sep.4; 373) $160
- **L'Italie, Illustrée en CXXXV Figures …** Leyden, 1757. 2 pts. in 1 vol. Fo. Engraved frontis., pict. title, pt. titles & 135 double-p. plts., mntd. on guards, 2 with sm. tears. Cont. mott. cf. gt. with arms of Jean de Boullongue, Comte de Nogent, rebkd. (C. Jul.15; 152) *Carter.* £2,800

ITINERANT, The: a Coll. of Views in G.B. & Ireland

Ed.:– J. Walker. 1799. Fo. Cf. gt. (P. Sep.11; 289) *Traylen.* £460

IT IS: A Magazine for Abstract Art

N.Y., 1958-60. Numbers 1-5, all publd. Fo. Pict. wraps. (SG. Oct.23; 165) $140

IVANOV, Vsev.

- **Bronepoezd [Armoured Train no. 14, 69].** Ill.:– Yu. Annekov. Moscow, 1923. Browned. Later cl.-bkd. bds., orig. wraps. by ill. (SH. Feb.6; 442) *Flegon.* £50

IVNEV, Ryurik

- **Chetyre vystrela [Four Shots at Esenin, Kusikov, Mariengof, Shershenevich].** [Moscow], [1921]. Orig. wraps. (SH. Feb.6; 444) *Quaritch.* £170
- **Zoloto Smerti [Gold of Death].** Moscow, 1916. Orig. wraps., slightly browned, spine torn. (SH. Feb.6; 445) *Lempert.* £55

IZOBRAZITEL'NOE iskusstvo [Fine Arts]

Ill:– Chekhonin, Lebedev, & others. St. Petersb., 1919. No. 1 (all publd.). Fo. 3 ll. torn & reprd. Orig. wraps. by D. Sterenberg & N. Al'tman, torn & reprd. (SH. Feb.5; 224) *Nijhoff.* £130

IZQUIERDO, Sebastian P.

- **Practica de los Exercicios Espirituales de Nuestro Padre San Ignacio.** Mexico, 1709. Sm. 4to. Sm. hole with loss of letters in last lf., some stains. Cont. limp vell. (SPB. May 5; 271) $100

IZVESTIYA [News of the Committee of Unemployed Humourists]

St. Petersb., n.d. No 1. Fo. Slightly torn & soiled. Unbnd. (SH. Feb.5; 77) *Quaritch.* £50

JABOUILLE, P.

See–DELACOUR, Jean & Jabouille, P.

JACK, Robert L. & Etheridge, Robert

- **The Geology & Palaeontology of Queensland & New Guinea.** Brisbane & c., 1892. 2 vols. 1 lf. detchd. at end of vol. 1, long tear (without loss) in 1 folding map, without the 6 sheet geological map of Queensland (iss. separately). Orig. cl., slight wear, end-paper detchd. (KH. Mar.24; 209) *Aus.* $100

JACK, Thomas

- **Onomasticon Poeticum …** Edinb., 1592. 1st. Edn. 4to. Cont. mott. cf., gt. spine. [STC 14293] (S. Oct.20; 117) *Paul Grinke.* £180

JACKSON, A. Bruce

See–CLINTON-BAKER, Henry William & Jackson, A. Bruce

JACKSON, Abraham Valentine Williams

- **History of India.** L., Grolier Soc., [1906]. Connoisseur Edn., (200). 9 vols. Some plts. in 2 states. Hf. mor. gt., gt. lf. with inlays, unopened. (SPB. May 6; 324) $1,400
- – **Anr. Copy.** Plts. in 2 states. Three qtr. lev., spines gt. with lotus lf. inlays, unc., partly unopened. (SG. Sep.4; 267) $200
- – **Anr. Copy.** 4to. Some plts. on Japan vell. Orig. gt.-floral hf. mor. & gt.-marb. bds. (PNY. Oct.1; 299) $100

JACKSON, Lady Catherine Charlotte

- **Works.** Paris & Boston, Grolier Soc., n.d. De Luxe Edn., (1000). 14 vols. Hf. mor. by Bennett. (SPB. Nov.25; 468) $375

JACKSON, Lady Catherine–ANON–ANON
– Works.–Days of the Dandies.–Beaux & Belles of England. L., All Grol. Soc., n.d. Edn. des Amateurs, (1000); Edn. des Aquarelles, (26); Edn. des Amateurs, (100). 15 vols.; 14 vols.; 14 vols. Plts. in 2 states. Unif. cf. gt., ornately gt. spines. (SPB. May 6; 300) £1,000

JACKSON, Sir Charles James
– An Illustrated History of English Plate. 1911. 2 vols. 4to. Cont. hf. mor. (SH. Jan.29; 247) *Blundell.* £50
– – **Anr. Copy.** Two-tone cl. (SG. Mar.12; 201) $150

JACKSON, Mrs. E. Nevill
– Ancestors in Silhouette. L., 1921. 1st. Edn. 4to. 56 p. catalogue of silhouette ports. by Edouart laid in. Pict. buckram, discold. (SG. Mar.12; 323) $100
– A History of Hand-Made Lace. 1900. 4to. Examples of lace mntd. on card. Decor. mor., gt. (CE. Jul.9; 211) £120
– – **Anr. Copy.** With 10 specimens of lace mntd. on 5 card. ll. Orig. gt.-decor. mor., upr. cover loose. (SG Dec.4; 212) $200

JACKSON, Frederick John
– The Birds of Kenya Colony & the Uganda Protectorate. L. & Edinb., 1938. 3 vols. 4to. Orig. cl., bkplts. (CB. Sep.24; 33) *Can.* $800

JACKSON, Herbert J.
– European Hand Firearms. 1923. Ltd. Edn. Fo. Cl. (CE. Nov.20; 153) £52

JACKSON, Holbrook
– The Anatomy of Bibliomania. Soncino Pr. 1930-31. (1000), this 1 of (48) numbered on H.M.P. sigd. by author. 2 vols. Mor. by Wood, soiled. (CSK. May 29; 18) £90
– – **Anr. Copy.** Buckram, d.-w.'s. (SG. Sep.4; 269) $150
– The Fear of Books. Soncino Pr. 1932. (2000), this 1 of (48) numbered on H.M.P. sigd. by author. Mor. by Sangorski & Sutcliffe, soiled. (CSK. May 29; 19) £60

JACKSON, James Grey
– An Account of the Empire of Morocco . . . Ill.:– J.C. Stadler. L., 1811. Lge. 4to. Mod. buckram-bkd. old marb. bds. (SG. Feb.26; 182) $110
– – **Anr. Edn.** 1814. [3rd. Edn.?]. 4to. Tree cf. (P. Oct.23; 37) £110
– – **Anr. Copy.** Mod. hf. mor. (S. Mar.31; 480) *Foyles.* £80
– Account of the Empire of Morocco, & the Districts of Suse & Tafilelt . . . to Which is added an Account of Shipwrecks on the Western Coast of Africa . . . 1814. 3rd. Edn. 4to. Some plts. hand-cold., some folding & torn along creases, port. extra to list, dampstained, affecting some plts. Loose in cont. bds., backstrip defect. (TA. Nov.20; 402) £70

JACKSON, John
– A Treatise on Wood Engraving. L., 1839. 1st. Edn. With the 2 specimens of 'Knight's Patent Illuminated Prints', Baxter's 'Parsonage at Ovingham' & about 6 early engrs. tipped in. Cont. maroon str.-grd. mor. gt., rebkd. (SG. Mar.12; 202) $200
– – **Anr. Edn.** L., 1839. Hf. leath. (CB. Apr.1; 263) *Can.* $100

JACKSON, John, Dramatist
– The History of the Scottish Stage. Edinb., 1793. 1st. Edn. Old liby. stamp on title. Disbnd. (SG. Sep.4; 270) $110

JACKSON, John Hughlings
– Selected Writings. Ed.:– James Taylor & others. 1931-32; 1925. 2 vols.; 1 vol. Cl. (S. Jun.16; 459) *Jenner Books.* £75

JACKSON, K.A.
– Views in Afghanistaun. [1841]. Fo. Spotted. Cont. mor.-bkd. cl. (SH. Mar.5; 72) *Remington.* £150

JACKSON, Richard
[–] The Interest of Great Britain considered with regard to her Colonies. Boston, 1760. Orig. marb. wraps., reprd., tears, worn. [Sabin 35450] (SPB. Jun.22; 73) $150
See–FRANKLIN, Benjamin & Jackson, Richard

JACKSON, Stuart W.
– Egg Collecting & Bird Life in Australia. Sydney, 1907. 4to. Orig. bdg. (JL. Mar.2; 728) *Aus.* $300

JACKSON, William Henry
– Descriptive Catalogue of Photographs of North American Indians. Wash., 1877. Ptd. upr. wrap., lacks lr. wrap., disbnd. (SG. Apr.23; 110) $175

JACOB, Alexander
– A Complete English Peerage. L., Priv. Ptd., 1766-69-67. 2 vols. in 3. Fo. Some foxing, etc., sm. liby. stp. on title-pp. Disbnd. (SG. Feb.5; 186) $210

JACOB Ben Asher
– Arba Turim. Constantinople, David & Samuel aben Nahmias, Dec.13, 1493. Vol. III only (of 4). Fo. 60 ll. only (of 409), sm. repairs & restoration to inner margins of 1st. 4 ll., slight worming to extreme inner margins of 1st. 9 ll., minor worming to lr. outer corners of some 15 ll. Niger mor. gt., gt.-lettered spine, by Sangorski & Sutcliffe. Bkplt. of Boies Penrose II, lately in the collection of Eric Sexton. [Goff Heb 49] (CNY. Apr.8; 49) $13,000

JACOB, G.
– Lex Constitutionis. 1719. Cont. cf., worn. (SH. May 21; 62) *Skinner.* £70

JACOB, Max
– La Côte. Paris, 1927. (210), (200) numbered on vell. 4to. Mor., limp decor. & mosaic spine, inner border of 4 fillets, embroidered silk centre gt., mor. guards. with marb. paper doubls., wrap. preserved, s.-c., by Louis Gilbert. (LM. Nov.8; 91) *B.Frs.* 7,500
– Le Siège de Jérusalem . . . Ill.:– Pablo Picasso. Paris, 1914. (104); (85) on Holland by van Gelder, numbered, sigd. by author & artist. Some sm. stains. Orig. wrap., slightly loose, unc. (SM. Feb.11; 115) *Frs.* 16,000

JACOB, Nicolas Henri
– Storia Naturale delle Scimie [Naturgeschichte der Affen]. Ill.:– L. Rados. Mailand, 1812. 1st. Edn. Vol. I only (of 2). Fo. Some soiling & tearing, 2 sm. tears pasted, 1 plt. loose. Later hf. leath. (H. Dec.9/10; 254) DM 1,900
[–] – **Anr. Edn.** Milan, [1822]. 2 pts. in 1 vol. Fo. 22 ll. ptd. on recto only in woodcut border. Cont. hf. cf., rebkd., unc. (S. Dec.3; 1005) *Asher.* £420

JACOB, William
– Travels in the South of Spain in Letters Written A.D. 1809-1810. 1811. [1st. Edn.?]. 4to. Cont. cf. with old reback. (TA. Feb.19; 35) £105
– – **Anr. Copy.** Text wtrmkd. 1809. plts. 1808, some offsetting to text & a few plts. Cl., worn. (S. Sep.29; 213) *Rosenberg.* £100
– – **Anr. Copy.** Lacks hf.-title. Cont. mott. cf., rebkd., orig. spine laid down. (SG. Feb.26; 184) $180

JACOBAEUS, O.
– Museum Regium. Ed.:– J. Laurentzen. [Copen.], [1710]. Fo. Old erased MS. note on title. Cont. cf. gt., slightly worn. (H. May 21/22; 169) DM 1,000

JACOBI, Moritz Hermann von
– Die Galvanoplastik. St. Petersb., 1840. Orig. ptd. wraps., soiled, hf. red mor. case. From Honeyman Collection. (S. May 20; 3268) *Rota.* £50

JACOBS, A.
See–DUMONT D'Urville, Jules Sebastien César & others

JACOBS, Professor J. Bernards
– Vroedkundige Oeffenschool. Gend, 1784. 4to. Old cf. (LM. Mar.21; 197) *B.Frs.* 18,000

JACOBS, Rev. Peter
– Journal of . . . Toronto, 1853. 1st. Edn. Orig. ptd. wraps., sm. piece torn from upr. wrap. (CB. Apr.1; 76) *Can.* $200

JACOBS, W.W.
– [Works]. L., v.d. 18 vols. Unif. hf. cf. gt., gt. panel. spines with nautical designs, by Sangorski & Sutcliffe, slightly worn. (SPB. Nov.25; 469) $225

JACOBSEN, Jens Peter
– Die Pest in Bergamo. Ill.:– A. Kolb. Vienna & Leipzig, [1922]. (25) of privilege Edn. 4to. Orig. leath. (H. Sperling). 2nd. series of etchings on Japan all sigd. by artist. (H. Dec.9/10; 1775) DM 420

JACOBUS de Clusa
– De Animabus exutis a Corporibus, sive De Apparitionibus et Receptaculis Animarum. [Blaubeuren], [Conrad Mancz], ca. 1477. Fo. Spaces for initial capitals, initials in red, rubricated, some dampstaining, mostly to lr. outer portions, final lf. rehinged, marginal tear to fo. 16, some early ink annots. Old bds., spine worn. Bkplt. of Boies Penrose, lately in the collection of Eric Sexton. [BMC II, 565, Goff J22, HC 9346*] (CNY. Apr.8; 27) $2,200
– Sermones de Sanctis. [Speier], [Printer of the Gesta Christi], ca. 1472. Fo. Spaces for initial capitals, which are supplied in red or blue, on fo. 2r an illuminated capital A with floral sprays filling margins & incorporating 2 lge. flowers & 2 escutcheons, slight worming to 1st. 6 ll., sm. ink stp. on 1st.p. Cont. blind-stpd. cf. over wood bds., covers divided into central panel & 2 frames by multiple fillets extending to edges of covers, panel of upr. cover divided into lozenge & triangular compartments by triple fillets, middle compartments with lozenge tool of 3 acorns & oak leaves, others with double-headed eagle in lozenge or an open floral tool, outer frame with the double-headed eagle tool & a palmated leaf stp. at bottom, outermost panel with alternating imps. of a sm. palmated leaf tool & a scroll lettered 'maria hilf', 5 brass bosses on each cover, brass catches (lacks clasps), bnd. at Benedictine Monastery of Saint Goergenberg (with orig. paper label in cover, & a partly erased inscr., dtd. 1661, at fo. 1v), minor repairs to corners, rebkd. with plain spine, orig. spine preserved. Cancelled ink stp. of the London Liby., lately in the collection of Eric Sexton. [BMC II, 483, Goff J38, HC 9329*] (CNY. Apr.8; 158) $5,500

JACOBUS de Gruitroede
– Colloquium Peccatoris et Crucifixi Jesu Christi; Tractatulus de Vita Religiosa; Isidorus Hispalensis, Dialogus sive Synonyma de Homine et Ratione. Antw., Claes Leeu, 17 May, 1488. 4to. Lombards, woodcut initials, some slight soiling on 1st. & last pp. Qtr. mor., patterned paper covers. The copy of Cornelius Paine, William Morris, & Richard Bennett, lately in the Pierpont Morgan Liby. [BMC IX, 198, Goff J57, HC 9296] (CNY. Apr.8; 8) $3,800
– Lavacrum Conscientiae. [Augsburg], [Johann Froschauer], [not after 1498]. 4to. Ornamental 11-line capital initial on fo. 2, smaller capital initials elsewhere, wormed, mostly at front & back, some ll. dampstained, 2 monastic inscrs. Mod. parch.-bkd. bds. From the collection of Eric Sexton. [BMC II, 396, Goff L103, H 9955*] (CNY. Apr.8; 15) $500

JACOBUS de Voragine
See–VORAGINE, Jacobus de

JACOBUS di Bangio
– Settenario Magnificat. Aquila, [Adam de Rottweil], 1482. 4to. Capital space on 1st. pr., traces of old staining, some ink inscrs. Mod. blind-stpd. mor. The copy of John F. Neylan, lately in the collection of Eric Sexton. [BMC VII, 1098, Goff J17] (CNY. Apr.8; 10) $3,800

JACOBUS, Magdalius
– Passio Magistralia dni nri Iesu Christi. Cologne, 1506. 2nd. Edn. 4to. Some blank margins slightly dust-soiled & with smudges from early inscrs. Kelmscott-style limp vell., silk ties, unc. Bkplt. of William Morris, later the copy of Richard Bennett & John A. Saks. (CNY. Oct.1; 83) $550

JACOBUS Phillipus Foresti de Bergomensis
See–BERGOMENSIS Forestus, Phillipus Jacobus

JACQUEMART, Albert & Jules
– Histoire de la Céramique Paris, 1873. Publisher's cf., recent gt. stpd. (CR. Jun.11; 503) Lire 200,000
– History of the Ceramic Art . . . Trans.:– Mrs. Bury Palliser. N.Y., 1877. 2nd. Edn. Heavily foxed. Red three-qtr. mor., spine & top gt. (SG. Dec.4; 78) $110

JACQUEMART, Albert & Le Blant, Edmond
– Histoire Artistique, Industrielle et Commerciale de la Porcelaine. Paris, 1862. 4to. Cont. hf. mor. (SBA. Jul.23; 533) *Quaritch.* £50

JACQUEMENT, Victor
– Correspondance . . . pendant son Voyage dans l'Inde (1828-33). 1833. Orig. Edn. 2 vols. Lge. folding map of India. Cont. hf.-cf., decor. spines. (HD. Feb.18; 142) *Frs.* 1,200

JACQUEMIN, Raphael
– Iconographie Générale et Méthodoqie du Costume du IVe au XIXe Siècle. Paris, [1869]. Fo.

JACQUEMIN, Raphael–*contd.*
Cont. hf. mor., gt. spine, partly unc. (SI. Dec.3; 296) *Lire* 800,000

JACQUES, Henry
– **Sous le Signe de Rossignol.** Ill.:– Kay Nielsen. Paris, 1923. (150) with extra suite of plts. 4to. Orig. wraps. (SH. Mar.27; 381) *Illustrated Antiques.* £330
– – **Anr. Edn.** Ill.:– Kay Nielsen. Paris, 1923. (1500) numbered. 4to. Mor., orig. wraps. bnd. in, s.-c. (SH. Mar.27; 382) *Crete.* £150
– – **Anr. Edn.** Ill.:– Kay Neilsen. Paris, [1923]. Ltd. Edn. on Japan vell. 4to. With extra suite of cold. plts. Orig. ptd. wrap. with protective tissue. (BS. Sep.17; 158) £190

JACQUIN, Nicolaus Joseph von
– **Florae Austriacae.** Ill.:– J. Adam after Franz Scheidel & others. Vienna, 1773-78. 5 vols. in 3. Fo. Titles with hand-cold. vig. views, & all plts. hand-cold. (except no. 392*), title to vol. 3, hf.-titles to vols. 1 & 3, & plts. at end of vols. 2 & 4 all detchd., detchd. plts. slightly soiled, some marginal discolouration. 2 vols. in cont. russ., very worn, covers detchd., stitching of 1 vol. brkn., vol. 5 in 19th. C. hf. mor. From Chetham's Liby., Manchester. (C. Nov.27; 213) *Baskett & Day.* £6,500
– – **Anr. Copy.** 5 vols. With the uncold. plt., annot. on plts. in cont. hand. Cont. cf., richly gt. spines, vol. 5 with restorations to sides & head of spine, arms of German & Austrian Abbey on covers. From collection of Massachusetts Horticultural Society, stps. on plts. (SPB. Oct.1; 133) $31,000
– **Icones Plantarum Rariorum.** Ill.:– J. Adam after J. Hofbauer, J. Scharf & others. Vienna & L., 1781-93. 3 vols. Fo. Plts. hand-cold., unsigd. & unnumbered, 1 folding plt. slightly stained, 5 others with sm. tears, edges & some margins dust-stained. 19th. C. hf. mor., covers detchd., lacks cover to vol. 3, unc. From Chetham's Liby., Manchester. (C. Nov.27; 214) *Maggs.* £6,200
– – **Anr. Edn.** Ill.:– After Ferdinand Bauer & others. Vienna, 1781-93[-95]. 3 vols. Fo. Vol. 3 dampstained at foot, few tears reprd., some affecting engraved surface. Hf. mor., unc. From collection of Massachusetts Horticultural Society, stps. on plts. (SPB. Oct.1; 134) $10,500
– **Miscellanea Austriaca.** Vienna, 1778-81. 2 vols. in 1. 4to. Cont. Engl. hf. cf., gt. spine, slightly worn. (S. Jun.1; 147) *Schierenberg.* £400
– **Observationum Botanicarum Iconibus.** Ill.:– Wangner after author. Vienna, 1764-71. 4 pts. in 1 vol. Fo. Some plts. slightly discold. 19th. C. hf. mor. From Chetham's Liby., Manchester. (C. Nov.27; 215) *Heuer.* £300
– **Selectarum Stirpium Americanarum Historia.** Vienna, 1763. [1st. Edn.?]. Fo. 184 plts. numbered to 183. 19th. C. hf. mor. From Chetham's Liby., Manchester. [Sabin 35521] (C. Nov.27; 216) *Taylor.* £650
– – **Anr. Copy.** (SG. May 14; 112) $800
– – **Anr. Copy.** Text slightly wormed in parts, last text ll. more so, slightly soiled in parts. Cont. style red mor., gt. cover, spine & outer dentelle. (D. Dec.11-13; 1442) DM 7,500

JAEGER, Eduard von
– **Ophthalmoskopischer Hand-Atlas.** Vienna, 1869. Advt. lf. Cl. (S. Jun.16; 461) *Westwood.* £85
– – **Anr. Copy.** Hf. cf., worn, spine defect. (S. Jun.16; 460) *Levy.* £70

JAGER, J.G.A.
– **Grand Atlas d'Allemagne.** Frankfurt, 1789. Ob. fo. 1 extension map bnd. after the map, 1 engraved sub-title included in the map numbering. Cont. hf. cf., slightly worn. (S. Feb.10; 203) *Grosse.* £1,700

JAGER, W.
– **Geographisch-Historisch-Statistisches Zeitungs-Lexicon.** Nuremb., 1782-84. 1st. Edn. 2 vols. Slightly soiled. Cont. leath. (R. Oct.14-18; 1177) DM 650

JAGO, Richard
– **Edge-Hill, or, the Rural Prospect delineated & moralized. A Poem.** 1767. 1st. Edn. 4to. Cont. cf., spine chipped at foot. (S. Jun.22; 47) *Hannas.* £60

JAHN, C.F.
– **Illustr. Reisebuch ... durch Deutschland, die Schweiz, Tyrol ...** Leipzig, 1855. Orig. linen. (HK. Nov.18-21; 1216) DM 700

JAHNN, H.H.
– **Fluss ohne Ufer.** Munich & Frankfurt, 1949-61. 1st. Edn. 3 pts. in 4 vols. Owner's marks. Orig. linen. (H. May 21/22; 1648) DM 500

JAHRBUCH DER AUKTIONSPREISE
Hamburg, [1961]-76. Vols. XI-XXV. Orig. linen. (HK. Nov.18-21; 3168) DM 1,100

JAHRBUCH DER NEUESTEN und Wichtigsten Erfindungen und Entdeckungen
Ed.:– H. Leng. Ilmenau, 1824-33. Years 1-9 in 1 vol. Slightly stained, stps. on title. Cont. leath., gt. spine. (R. Oct.14-18; 435) DM 2,700

JAHRBUCH DER ORIGINAL-GRAPHIK
Ed.:– H.W. Singer. Ill.:– L. Corinth & others. Berlin, n.d. C Edn., 1st. year, (150) numbered. Fo. Orig. bd. portfo. (D. Dec.11-13; 1099) DM 550

JAILLOT, Hubert & Sanson, Nicolas
– **Atlas Nouveau.** Paris, 1684. Vol. 1 only (of 2). Lge. fo. 80 maps, partly hand-cold. in outl., 19 tables, some maps dtd. 1674-85, plts. numbered thro.-out in MS., similar numbering of contents lf., including some compl. MS. entries, some tears & stains. Cont. cf. gt., very worn. W.a.f. (S. Mar.31; 290) *Douwma.* £2,800
– – **Anr. Edn.** Amst., ca. 1695. 2 vols. Fo. Ptd. table pasted in, map of East Indies in vol. 2 added to contents table in MS.; clean slit in 1 map & tear in centre fold of 2 others, sm. stp. on subtitles. Orig. mott. cf. gt., roll tooled borders & inner panels, ornaments, spines similarly tooled but defect., worn. As an atlas, w.a.f. (SPB. Oct.1; 273) $31,000

JAIME, E.
– **Musée de la Caricature.** Paris, 1838. 2 vols. Lge. 4to. Minimal soiling. Cont. hf. leath. gt. (HK. Nov.18-21; 2352) DM 650

JAMAICA
– **Histoire de la Jamaique.** Londres, 1751. 2 vols. in 1. 12mo. 2nd. title reinforced at verso. Mod. qtr. cf., gt. (PNY. May 21; 227) $160
– **The Laws of Jamaica.–The Laws of Jamaica.** L., 1683; 1684. 2 works in 1 vol. Browning, spotting, some tears, publisher's advts. in 1st. work, lacks map in 2nd.? Old cf., worn, jnts. brkn., worming. [Wing J-124, Sabin 35622; Sabin 35623] (SPB. May 5; 279) $300
– **The Laws of Jamaica. Volume the Second [only].** –**An Abridgement of the Laws of Jamaica.** St. Jago de la Vega, 1792; 1793. 2 vols. 4to. Some stains, tears, some repairs to margins, browning, 1st. work 4D2 badly torn, 2nd. work marginal repairs to several pp. Cf., rebkd., inner hinges reprd. [Sabin 35625 (1st. work)] (SPB. May 5; 283) $150
– **A Narrative of Affairs Lately received from his Majesties Island of Jamaica.** L., 1683. Fo. Slight browning. New cf. gt. (SPB. May 5; 282) $400

JAMAIN, Hippolyte & Forney, Eugene
– **Les Roses. Histoire-Culture-Description.** Ed.:– Charles Naudin (preface). Paris, 1873. 2nd. Edn. Orig. qtr. mor. (TA. Jun.18; 159) £325
– – **Anr. Copy.** Some plts. loose. Hf. linen. (R. Oct.14-18; 3048) DM 1,400

JAMBLICHUS
– **De Mysteriis Aegyptorum. Chaldeorum. Assyriorum [& other Tracts].** Venice, Aldus Manutius, Sep., 1497. 1st. Edn. Fo. Gold & illuminated 7-line capital initial A on fo. 2, with cold. coat-of-arms in lr. margin, lacks final blank lf. Early 19th. C. str.-grd. mor. gt., smooth spine, silk doubls. gt., very slightly rubbed, qtr. mor. gt. s.-c. Bkplts. of Lieut.-Col. Sir George Holford & John A. Saks. [BMC V, 557, Goff J216, HC 9358] (CNY. Oct.1; 122) $3,800

JAMES I, King of England
[–] **His Majesties Speach in this last Session of Parliament.** 1605. 4to. Mod. mor. [STC 14392.5] (CSK. May 29; 101) £50
– **The Kings Maiesties Declaration to His Subjects, Concerning lawfull Sports to be used.** L., 1618. Sm. 4to. Hf. cf., by Zaehnsdorf, mor. s.-c. by Mounteney. Harold Greenhill bkplt. [STC 8566] (CNY. May 22; 202) $550
– **The Workes.** 1616. 1st. Coll. Edn. Fo. Liby. stp. on title-p. Cont. cf., gt., worn. [STC 14344] (S. Nov.25; 458) *Sotheran.* £50

JAMES, Edward
– **The Next Volume.** Ill.:– Rex Whistler. 1932 [colophon 1932]. (525) numbered. 4to. Orig. cl., slightly soiled. Pres. copy. (CSK. Jun.12; 146) £60
[–] **Opus Septimum.** Ill.:– Rex Whistler. 1933. (30). 4to. Orig. mor., 'Your Name is Lamia' in gt. on upr. cover. Inscr. to Peter Watson by author & to Cecil Beaton by Cyril [Connolly]. (SH. Dec.19; 363) *Lincoln.* £260

JAMES, Edwin
– **Account of an Expedition from Pittsburgh to the Rocky Mountains ... in the years 1819, 1820.** Ill.:– John Clark after S. Seymour. L., 1823. 1st. Engl. Edn. 3 vols. Folding map with reprd. tear, scattered foxing or spotting. Hf. lev. mor., gt. spines, partly unc. [Sabin 35683] (CNY. Oct.1; 46) $650

JAMES, H.A.
– **Hand-Book of Australian Horticulture.** Ill.:– Guglielmo Autoriello. Sydney, 1892. Lge. 8vo. Rebnd. mor., gt. decor. on upr. cover, raised bands on spine, inside dentelles. (JL. Jul.20; 812) *Aus.* $140

JAMES, Henry
– **The Diary of a Man of Fifty & a Bundle of Letters.** N.Y., 1880. 1st. Authorized Amer. Edn. 32mo. Orig. ptd. wraps., lacks portion of upr. corner from upr. cover, sm. sticker removed from spine, mor. & cl. gt. s.-c. (PNY. May 21; 229) $100
– **An International Episode.** N.Y., 1879. 1st. Edn. 32mo. 1st. iss., with the last line on p. 44 repeated at head of p. 45, 8 pp. of advts. at end. Wraps., cl. s.-c. (SG. Mar.19; 220) $220
– **A Little Tour in France.** Ill.:– Joseph Pennell. 1900. 1st. Engl. Edn., (150) on japanese vell. Cont. mor. gt. (S. Jul.22; 62) *Wardman.* £75
– **The Novels & Tales.** N.Y., 1907-17. (156) numbered, on Ruisdael H.M.P. 26 vols. Some top edges discold. Buckram-bkd. bds., spines soiled, unc. & partly unopened. (SG. Feb.12; 225) $1,400
– **Roderick Hudson.** Boston, 1876 [1875]. 1st. Edn. Orig. cl. (S. Jul.22; 182) *Sotheran.* £55
– **Roderick Hudson.–The Portrait of a Lady.** Boston, 1876; 1882. 1st. Edn.; 1st. Amer. Edn., 1st. Printing. 2 works in 2 vols. 12mo. Orig. cl., very worn (1st. work); & cl., some cont. reviews pasted to end-papers & fly-ll., qtr. mor. s.-c. 1st. work Pres. Copy to Lucien Biart, & with some notes by him(?), 2nd. work with owner's inscr. L.E. Opdycke & his note on fly-lf.; both lately in the Prescott Collection. (CNY. Feb.6; 172) $600
– **William Wetmore Story & his Friends.** Boston, 1904. 2 vols. Cl., worn. Tipped in are A.L.'s or notes of Story, James, Robert Browning Lowell & others, bkplt. of Evelyn Smalley. (SG. Nov.13; 368) $450

JAMES, Holman
– **Voyage Round the World.** Ill.:– mostly Louis Haghe. 1834-35. 4 vols. Some soiling, 4 plts. & title of vol. 2 mntd. on cl. Mod. cf.-bkd. bds. (CSK. Jan.9; 21) £75

JAMES, John
– **The Theory & Practice of Gardening.** 1712. 4to. 19th. C. mor.-bkd. bds., upr. cover detchd. From Chetham's Liby., Manchester. (C. Nov.27; 217) *Marlborough.* £150

JAMES, John Thomas
– **Journal of a Tour in Germany, Sweden, Russia & Poland.** 1816. [1st. Edn.?]. 4to. Cf. (P. Oct.23; 38) *Brooke-Hitching.* £75
– – **Anr. Copy.** Some plts. lightly browned & soiled. Mod. hf. leath. (H. May 21/22; 319) DM 450
– – **Anr. Edn.** 1817. 2nd. Edn. 2 vols. Lacks hf.-titles? Cont. diced cf. gt., 1 stained & lacking label. Earl of Wicklow's bkplt. (SBA. Mar.4; 113) *Chesters.* £55

JAMES, Dr. Montague Rhodes
– **Marvels of the East.** Oxford, Roxb. Cl., 1929. Fo. Orig. mor.-bkd. cl., partly unc. Sydney Cockerell's copy, sigd. & dtd. (C. Jul.22; 39) *Marlborough.* £200
– – **Anr. Copy.** 4to. (SH. Jun.18; 155) *Makiya.* £55

JAMES, Robert
– **Medicinal Dictionary.** L., 1743. 1st. Edn. Fo. Fragment only, comprising title-p., dedication & 99-p. preface from vol. 1. Mod. cl. Tipped-in typed note sigd. by Sir William Osler, R.B. Adam bkplt., bkplt. & handstp. of Rochester Academy of Medicine. (SG. Sep.18; 197) $180

– – Anr. Edn. Ed.:– Dr. Johnson (preface). 1743-45. [1st. Edn.?] 3 vols. Fo. Cont. cf., rebkd. (S. Jun.16; 462) *Norman.* £400
– – Anr. Copy. Cont. cf., upr. cover of 1st. vol. detchd. (C. Apr.1; 110) *Traylen.* £350

JAMES, T.
– The History of the Herculean Straits. 1771. L.P. 2 vols. 4to. A few tears, 1 lf. loose. Mod. mor.-bkd. bds. (SH. Jun.4; 164) *Browning.* £60

JAMES, Thomas
– Catalogus Universalis Liborum in Bibliotheca Bodleiana. Oxford, 1620. 2nd. Edn. 4to. With the 36 p. 'Appendix ad Catalogum'. 19th. C. hf. mor. Bkplts. of the Earl of Ilchester & J.R. Abbey, lately in the collection of Eric Sexton. [STC 14450] (C. Apr.15; 110) *Quaritch.* £800
[–] Ecloga Oxonio-Cantabrigiensis. 1600. 1st. Edn. Sm. 4to. Sm. paper fault to title not affecting text, some minor stains. Old limp vell., bkplt. The copy of J.R. Abbey, with bkplt., lately in the collection of Eric Sexton. [STC 14453] (C. Apr.15; 109) *Dawson.* £400

JAMES, William, Historian
– A Full & Correct Account of the Military Occurrences of the late War between Great Britain & the United States of America. L., Priv. ptd. 1818. 1st. Edn. 2 vols. Mod. hf. cf. (SG. Mar.5; 253) $150
– – Anr. Copy. Cont. marb. bds., cf. spines & tips, jnts. brkn. (SG. Jan.8; 223) $125
– – Anr. Copy. Some offsetting. Cont. cf., upr. bd. to vol. 1 loose. (CB. Sep.24; 90) Can. $240
– The Naval History of Great Britain. 1837. 6 vols. Cont. hf. cf. (SH. Jan.30; 450) *Franks.* £65
– – Anr. Copy. Panel. cf. (PG. Dec.12; 156) £55

JAMES FRANCIS Edward [Stuart], Prince of Wales
– Funerali de Giacomo III Re della Gran Brettagna celebrati per ordine de ... Papa Clemente XIII l'anno MDCCLXVI. Rome, [1766]. Fo. 1 folding plt. slightly torn & reprd., the other with sm. hole. 19th. C. cf., gt. (S. Jun.22; 48)
Goldschmidt. £130

JAMES' RIVER GUIDE
Cinc., 1856. Lacks blank end-paper, 4-p. time-table laid in. Elab. gt.-pict. roan, spine defect. (SG. Jun.11; 188) $100

JAMESON, Mrs. Anna Brownell
– Winter Studies & Summer Rambles in Canada. N.Y., 1839. 2 vols. Some foxing to both vols. Cont. cf., rebkd. (CB. Feb.18; 28) Can. $120

JAMESON, J. Franklin
– Original Narratives of Early American History. N.Y., 1907-1930. 18 vols. Three qtr. lev., gt.-panel. spines. (SG. Sep.4; 370) $325

JAMIESON, Alexander
– Celestial Atlas Comprising a Systematic Display of the Heavens. 1822. [1st. Edn.?]. Ob. 4to. Occasional slight spotting. Orig. hf. mor., worn. (CSK. Nov.21; 127) £120
– – Anr. Copy. Plt. 26 loose, plt. 27 partly detchd., slight foxing to several plts., most plts. cold. by cont. hand. Orig. brown paper bds., unc., rebkd. & corners renewed in cl. (CNY. Oct.1; 12) $420

JAMISON, D.F.
– The Life & Times of Bertrand Du Guesclin. L. & Charleston, 1864. 1st. Edn. 2 vols. Pol. cf., defect. [Sabin 35743] (SG. Jun.11; 116) $100

JAMMES, Francis
– Le Poète Rustique. Ill.:– Madeleine Luke. Paris, 1943. (10) numbered on vell de Rives. 4to. Orig. aquatint, cold. suite on japon nacré of all ills. & lettrines. Mor. by Lévèque, overall geometrical pattern gold & silver, soft pig doubls., semé of oval gt. drops, chemise & s.-c., orig. wraps. bnd. in. (SM. Oct.8; 2347) Frs. 7,500

JANIN, Jules
– Les petits Bonheurs. Ill.:– after Gavarni. Paris, 1857. Ill. Edn. 8 line MS dedication on end-paper, hf.-title stpd. twice, slightly soiled thro.-out. Red mor. by C. Niedrée, gt. spine, cover & inner dentelle. (HK. Nov.18-21, 2345) DM 540
– – Anr. Copy. Buckram, covers & spine decor. with special gt. mosaic stps. engraved by Damote, publisher's s.-c. A.L.s. by author. (HD. Dec.5; 109) Frs. 1,350
– Voyage en Italie. Paris, 1842. Romantic cl., gt. tooled decor. (CR. Mar.19; 425) Lire 260,000

JANIS, Harriet & Sidney
– Picasso: the Recent Years. Garden City, 1947. (350) numbered, sigd. by Picasso. 4to. Buckram. (SG. Oct.23; 267) $150

JAN KLEYKAMP Collection, The
N.Y., 1925. Ltd. numbered Edn. Fo. Rebnd., with orig. upr. wrap. bnd. in. (SG. Dec.4; 210) $130

JANSEN, W.
– Der Schwarzwald. Ill.:– Hasemann. Berlin, 1890. Cont. liby. linen, slightly soiled. (R. Oct.14-18; 2159) DM 610

JANSON, Charles William
– The Stranger in America. 1807. 1st. Edn. 4to. Cont. hf. cf. [Sabin 35770] (C. May 20; 139) *Allen.* £100
– – Anr. Copy. Light browning & staining. Mod. hf. mor. (S. Jun.29; 191) *Robinson.* £65

JANSSEN, H.
– Zeichnungen. Berlin, 1972. Sm. fo. Orig. linen. (D. Dec.11-13; 1101) DM 1,250

JANSSON, Jan or Johannes
– Le Nouvel Atlas ou Théâtre du Monde. Amst., 1646. 1st. Edn. in Fr. Vol. IV only (of 6). Fo. Lacks 4 (of 56) double-p. engraved maps, title & 1st. 20 (approx.) ll. with marginal worming & some damp-staining. Cont. mott. cf., gt., worn, spine & edges defect. W.a.f. (C. Nov.6; 259) *Kentish.* £2,800
– Novus Atlas ... Amst., 1646. Thick Paper. Vol. 4. Fo. Maps hand-cold. in outl., histor. & other cartouches, arms etc. fully cold., title cold. & heightened with gold, torn in top margin, 2 maps torn in centre fold, 2M1 & 3L1 perforated, G1-2, H1 very browned. Orig. vell., gt. panel., worn, wormed, lacks ties. W.a.f. (S. Mar.31; 280) *Schuster.* £2,600
– – Anr. Edn. Amst., 1647. Vol. 3, pts. in 1 vol. Fo. Maps hand-cold. in outl., histor. & other cartouches, etc. & titles fully cold., centre of 2nd. title partly detchd., 1 map defect., 3 torn, others separated in centre fold. Orig. vell., gt. panel., worn, lacks ties. W.a.f. (S. Mar.31; 278) *Mistrah.* £3,500
– – Anr. Copy. Vol. no. not stated, 2 Pts. in 1 vol. Pict. engraved title, 94 double-p. engraved maps, hand-cold. in outl., including inset maps & plans, histor. cartouches, coats of arms etc. & titles fully cold., 3 maps defect., some torn in centre fold. Orig. vell., gt. panel., later end-ll., lacks ties. W.a.f. (S. Mar.31; 279) *Schuster.* £2,600
– – Anr. Copy. Vol. 2, 2 pts. in 1 vol. Maps hand-cold. in outl., histor. & other cartouches, etc. & titles fully cold., some worming. Orig. vell., gt. panel., lacks ties. W.a.f. (S. Mar.31; 277) *Loose.* £2,200
– – Anr. Edn. Amst., ca. 1650. Vol. 4. Fo. With text from Camden's Britannia Illustrate, containing 22 (of 56) hand-cold. maps of British Counties, lacks title-p. & some text ll., some maps age-darkened. Embossed vell. over bds. W.a.f. (SG. May 21; 55) $1,800
– Theatrum Urbium. Amst., 1657. 8 vols. Fo. 490 engraved plts. (of 500, lacks 9 Italian & 1 Spanish plt.), sm. holes in most titles, some spotting & light discolouration, occasional minor dampstaining to margins, some sm. tears in blank margins, & to folds. Hf. mor., & vols. 3 & 4 in cl., 1 cover detchd. As an atlas, w.a.f. From Chetham's Liby., Manchester. (C. Nov.27; 218) *Burgess.* £49,00

JANSSON, Jan or Johannes & others
– Atlas. Amst., [1646 or later]. Lge. fo. 94 double-p. engraved maps (no text on verso), no title, some light foxing & discolouration, all maps with sm. liby. stp. 19th. C. hf. mor., covers detchd. As an atlas, w.a.f., from Chetham's Liby., Manchester. (C. Nov.27; 219) *Nicholson.* £5,000

JANSSON, Jan or Johannes & G.
– La Guerre d'Italie. Amst., 1702. Lge. fo. Slightly browned, slight worming. Cont. hf.leath., very defect. (HK. Nov.18-21; 1053) DM 2,200

JAPANESE ART
– Old Japanese Screens by Japanese Masters. N.d. Fo. Decor. wraps., laced. (SG. Dec.4; 201) $110

JAPANESE COLOURED PHOTOGRAPHS showing social & domestic scenes ...
Ca. 1870-80. Ob. fo. Preserved & double sided. Orig. lacquered bds. with gt. & ivory pict. panel., backstrip defect. (TA. Dec.18; 214) £62

JAPANESE FAIRY TALE SERIES
Tokyo, ca. 1900. Nos. 1-4 & 10, 5 vols. Text in German, on crêpe paper. Orig. pict. wraps. (SH. Mar.19; 144) £95
– – Anr. Edn. Tokyo, ca. 1900. 2nd. Edns. (2 nos. only). Nos. 1, 2, 3, 5, 6, 8, 10 & 13, 8 vols. Text in Engl., ptd. on paper. Orig. ptd. wraps. (SH. Mar.19; 142) *Baldur.* £85

JAPANESE TEMPLES & Their Treasures
Tokyo, 1910. 3 vols. Loose, in boxes. (PD. May 20; 182) £100

JAPANESE THEATRICAL DESIGNS
Ca. 1870. Vol. VII. Loosely contained in portfo. (TA. Nov.20; 161) £80

JARDINE, Sir William
– British Birds. N.d. 4 vols. Orig. bdg. (DWB. Mar.31; 218) £80
– British Salmonidae. [Edinb.], [1839-41]. Lge. fo. 12 partly hand-cold. engraved plts. & text ll., many with engraved vigs., 1 cold., lacks title, 1 plt. torn & reprd., other sm. marginal tears reprd. Mod. mor.-bkd. bds., orig. gt. label on upr. cover. W.a.f. (C. Mar.18; 59) *Taylor.* £2,200
– – Anr. Edn. L., 1979. (500) numbered. Elephant 4to. Orig. cl. with mor. backstrip, matching s.-c. (TA. Jun.18; 71) £100
– Humming Birds. Edinb., 1833. 2 vols. Cont. hf. cf. (SBA. Jul.22; 63) *Schuster.* £70
– – Anr. Copy. Orig. cl. (MMB. Oct.8; 33) £58
– – Anr. Edn. L., 1833. 2 vols. Orig. cl. (P. Jun.11; 267) *Wabeling.* £95
– – Anr. Edn. Edinb., 1833-34. 2 vols. Recently rebnd. in crimson mor. gt. (TA. Oct.16; 251) £105
– – Anr. Edn. 1834-33. 2 vols. 63 (of 64) cold. plts. (lacks no. 25 in vol. 2). Mod. hf. cf. not unif. W.a.f. (P. Oct.23; 213) *Bailey.* £95
– – Anr. Edn. Edinb., 1840. 2 vols. Hf. mor., raised spines. (SSA. Nov.5; 134) R. 380
– – Anr. Edn. Edinb., 1843. 2 vols. Hf. cf., damaged. (P. Oct.2; 40) *Walford.* £120
– – Anr. Copy. Orig. linen. (R. Mar.31-Apr.4; 1378) DM 455
– Ichthyologie. Edinb., 1835-43. 1st. Edn. Vols. I-VI: J.S. Bushnan's 'Fishes', & V.R.H. Schomburgh's 'Fishes of Guinea' (2 vols.); R. Hamilton's 'British Fishes' (2 vols.); & Jardine's 'Fishes of the Perch Family' (2 vols.). 191 cold., & 4 uncold. plts., slightly soiled in pts. Mod. hf. leath. [Sabin 77788] (H. Dec.9-10; 275) DM 800
– – Anr. Edn. Edinb. & L., 1854. Vols. I-VI. Hf. leath. (R. Oct.14-18; 3015) DM 950
– Leaves from the Book of Nature. Edinb., [1846]. Lge. fo. Cont. hf. mor. gt., rebkd., orig. gt. spine preserved. (C. Mar.18; 60) *Schuster.* £1,900
– Mammalia. Edinb., 1833-42. 1st. Edn. Vols. 1-13: Monkeys, Felinae, Ruminating Animals (2 vols.), Pschydermes, Hamilton: Cetacea, Macgillivray: British Quadrupeds, Hamilton: Amphibious Carnivora, Smith: Dogs (2 vols.), Waterhouse: Marsupialia, Smith: Horses, Introduction to the Mammals (2 vols.). If. stpd., lightly soiled in parts. Some plts. & ll. loose, 1 (last) Mod. hf. leath. (H. Dec.9/10; 406) DM 2,000
– – Anr. Edn. Edinb., 1843. Pts. 2-9 & 11-13 in 11 vols. Plts. mostly slightly browned. Cover loose, lacks spines. (HK. Nov.18-21; 590) DM 800
– – Anr. Edn. Edinb. & L., 1854. Vols. I-III. Hf. leath. (R. Oct.14-18; 3004) DM 420
– – Anr. Copy. Vol. VI. (R. Oct.14-18; 3008) DM 530
– – Anr. Copy. Vols. VII, VIII, & XIII. Lacks plt. 30 in vol. VIII. Cont. hf. leath. (R. Oct.14-18; 3010) DM 500
– – Anr. Copy. Vol. XII. Engraved title port. Hf. leath., sm. 4to. (R. Oct.14-18; 3012) DM 520
– The Naturalist's Library. Edinb., 1833-43. Vols. 1-40. Engraved titles & ports. lacking in vol. 1, some ll. spotted, a few ll. from vol. 9 misbnd. in vol. 25. Cont. hf. mor., a few covers detchd. (SH. Jan.30; 380) *Handler.* £620
– – Anr. Edn. Edinb., 1833-66. 33 vols. Various bdgs., soiled. W.a.f. (CSK. Nov.7; 1) £600
– – Anr. Edn. Edinb., 1843. [2nd. Edn.?]. 28 vols. various. Some ll. detchd., some torn, some lacking. Cont. hf. cf., worn, lacks most bdgs. W.a.f. (CSK. Jun.26; 127) £400
– – Anr. Copy. 40 vols. (without 2 vol. supp.) Some offsetting thro.-out. Cont. hf. cf. gt., pressed floral pattern cl. covers. W.a.f. (CNY. Oct.1; 142) $2,400
– – Anr. Copy. 40 vols. Bnd. in 1st. Edn. vol. order lacks 5 plts. birds & 3 insects, slightly soiled.

JARDINE, Sir William -contd.
Cont. hf. leath. (R. Mar.31-Apr.4; 1376) DM 5,000
– – **Anr. Edn.** Edinb., [1843]. 38 vols. (of 40). Cont. hf. cf., some labels missing. W.a.f. (S. Dec.3; 1006) *Schuster.* £500
– – **Anr. Edn.** Edinb., [1845-46]. 40 vols. Many plts. loose, some browning. Hf. mor. As a collection of plts., w.a.f. (SPB. Nov.25; 91a) $900
– – **Anr. Edn.** Edinb., 1846. 41 vols. Orig. cl. gt., a few spines slightly stained. W.a.f. (SBA. Dec.16; 142) *Dekker & Nordemann.* £800
– – **Anr. Edn.** Edinb., 1883-54. 40 vols. Orig. cl. (SSA. Nov.5; 166) R. 850
– – **Anr. Edn.** Edinb., n.d. 38 vols. (of 40). Tooled cl. (HSS. Apr.24; 101) £620
– – **Anr. Edn.** L., n.d. 40 vols., lacks vol. 16, but includes unnumbered, vol. of 'Hummingbirds'. 16mo. Liby. stps. Orig. cl., all bdgs. brkn. W.a.f. (SG. Sep.18; 199) $1,800
[–] **Naturgesch Cabinet d. Thierreiches. I. Ornithologie.** Trans.:– A. Diezmann. Budapest, 1836. 1st. Edn. in German. Pt.1. Cont. bds., worn. (HK. Nov.18-21; 805) DM 420
– **Ornithology** . . . Ill:– Lizars. Edinb., 1833-34. Vols. 1 & 2 only. Sm. 8vo. Lacks 1 cold. plt. Loose in bds., defect. (JL. Jul.20; 814) Aus. $120
– – **Anr. Edn.** Edinb., 1833-43. 1st. Edn. (all except 1st. vol.). Vols. I-XIV. Humming Birds (2 vols.), Gallinaceous Birds, Game birds, Selby: Pigeons, Selby: Parrots, Swainson: Birds of Western Africa (2 vols.), Birds of Great Britain & Ireland (4 vols.), Swainson: Flycatchers, Nectariniadae. Slightly soiled in parts. Mod. hf. leath. (H. Dec.9/10; 413) DM 2,000
– – **Anr. Edn.** L., 1834. 3 vols. (of Gallinaceous Birds). Orig. cl. (P. Jun.11; 268) *Finney.* £85
– – **Anr. Edn.** Edinb., 1834-42. Vols. I-XII. Hf. cf. gt. W.a.f. (S. Dec.3; 1008) *Wheldon & Wesley.* £300
[–] – **Anr. Edn.** Edinb., 1837. Vols. VII & VIII. Cont. hf. leath. (HK. Nov.18-21; 804) DM 820
– – **Anr. Edn.** Edinb. & L., 1854. Vol. X. Hf. leath. (R. Oct.14-18; 3000) DM 600
– – **Anr. Copy.** Vols. I-IV. Cont. hf. leath. (R. Oct.14-18; 2994) DM 550
– – **Anr. Copy.** Vols. VI & VII. Hf. leath. (R. Oct.14-18; 2997) DM 600

JARDINE, Sir William & Selby, Prideaux John
– **Illustrations of Ornithology.** Edinb., [1826-35]. 3 vols. Lge. 4to. Cont. diced cf., gt. fillet borders, spines gt. (C. Mar.18; 162) *Pillar.* £2,600

JARRELL, Randall
– **The Animal Family.–The Woman at the Washington Zoo.–Losses.–Pictures from an Institution.–The Bat Poet.–The Seven League Crutches.** N.Y., [1965]; 1960; [1948]; [1954]; 1964; [1951]. Most 1st. Edns. 6 vols. Many with clipping tipped in, some discolouration, 2nd. title with T.L.s., 3rd. with postcard. Orig. bdgs., d.-w.'s., bdg. on 1 vol. stained, worn. (SPB. Nov.25; 310) $375

JARRETT, Fred
See–HOWES, Clifton A.–JARRETT, Fred

JARRY, Alfred
– **Ubu Roi.** 1806. Sewed. (HD. Oct.10; 92) Frs. 2,000

JASMIN
– **Las Papillotas.** 1835. 1st. Edn. Some foxing. Cont. hf. roan, smooth decor. spine. (HD. Jun.25; 292) Frs. 1,000

JAUFFRET, Louis François
– **Histoire Impartiale du Procès de Louis XVI ci-devant Roi des Français** . . . Paris, 1792-93. 8 vols. Some foxing. Cont. hf. roan, smooth decor. spines, spines defect. (HD. Jun.24; 44b) Frs. 1,600
– **Petite Ecole des Arts et Metiers.** Paris, 1816. 4 vols. Slightly soiled. Cont. leath., gt. spine. (R. Oct.14-18; 2631) DM 720

JAUME SAINT-HILAIRE, Jean Henri
– **Traité des Arbrisseaux et des Arbustes.** Paris, 1825. 2 vols. 4to. Cont. three-qtr. mor., decor. spine raised bands, some browning. (HD. Apr.24; 147) Frs. 12,500

JAUNA, Dominique
– **Histoire Générale des Roiaumes de Chypre, de Jérusalem, D'Armenie, et d'Egypte, comprenant les Croisades** . . . **Egypte** . . . **Hieroglifiques** . . . Leiden, 1747. 1st. Edn. 4to. Cont. leath., gt. spine,

spine slightly wormed at head. 1 corner reprd. (R. Oct.14-18; 1760) DM 1,600

JAURGAIN, Jean de
– **La Maison de Caumont La-Force** . . . Paris, priv. ptd., 1912. (300), numbered. Lge. 4to. Red hf. mor., corners. (HD. Jun.29; 107) Frs. 1,600

JAY, A.
See–ARNAULT, Antoine Vincent, Jay, A. & others

JEANCON, J.A.
– **Pathological Anatomy, Pathology, & Physical Diagnosis.** Cinc., 1885. Fo. Stp. on verso of plts. Hf. mor., brkn. From Brooklyn Academy of Medicine. (SG. Jan.29; 237) $100

JEANNERET, Charles Edouard 'Le Corbusier'
– **La Ville Radieuse.** 1933. 1st. Edn. Ob. 4to. Orig. cl.-bkd. bds. (SH. Jul.16; 169) *Brennan.* £60

JEANNIN, Pierre
– **Les Negotiations.** Ed.:– [Abbé de Castille]. Ill.:– van Meurs. Paris [Amst.], 1659. 2 vols. 12mo. Some cont. MS. notes on hf.-title verso vol. II. Str.-grd. mor., gt. by Thouvenin. From collection of M. de Chateaugiron, Mr. Beaupré ex-liby. (SM. Oct.8; 2400) Frs. 1,800

JEAURAT, Edme-Sébastien
– **Traité de la Perspective à l'usage des Artistes.** Ill.:– Babel, Cochin & Marvye. Paris, 1750. 1st. Edn. 4to. Sm. dampstain at lower margins, just touching text or ills. in a few places, a few pp. lightly browned, with 29 full page engraved plts., of which 19 are dupls. not called for. Cont. spr. cf., gt. spine. (CNY. Oct.1; 13) $380

JEFFERIES, Richard
– **Hodge & His Masters.** 1880. 1st. Edn. 2 vols. Publisher's advts. bnd. in at end of vol. 2 (4pp.). Orig. cl. gt., tops & bottoms of spine slightly worn. (TA. Sep.18; 39) £80
– – **Anr. Copy.** (TA. Mar.19; 354) £50
– **A Memoir of the Goddards of North Wiltshire, Compiled by Ancient Records, Registers & Family Papers.** [1873]. 4to. Title-p. reinforced. Rebnd. in hf. vell. (TA. Mar.19; 485) £100

JEFFERS, Robinson
– **Californians.** N.Y., 1916. 1st. Edn. 12mo. Pict. cl. gt., d.-w. with some sm. tears. Bkplt. of Donald Friede. (SG. Nov.13; 372) $175
– **Hungerfield & Other Poems.** N.Y., [1954]. 1st. Edn. Cl., d.-w. Inscr. to Witter Bynner, with his bkplt. (SG. Jun.4; 235) $300
– **Roan Stallion, Tamar & Other Poems.** N.Y., 1925. (12) Hors de Commerce. Stained thro.-out. Hf. lev., marb. bds. Bkplt. of Donald Friede. (SG. Nov.13; 374) $120
– **Solstice, & Other Poems.** N.Y., Grabhorn Pr., 1935. 1st. Edn., (320) sigd. Buckram-bkd. patterned bds. (SG. Jun.4; 234) $100
– **Tamar & Other Poems.** N.Y., [1924]. 1st. Edn. Cl., soiled, lr. cover slightly wrinkled. (SG. Nov.13; 373) $100
– **The Women at Sur Point.** N.Y., [1927]. (265) numbered & sigd. 2-tone bds., box (worn). (SG. Nov.13; 375) $110

JEFFERSON, Samuel
– **History & Antiquities of Leath Ward in the County of Cumberland.** 1840. Hf. leath. (TRL. Dec.10; 125) £52

JEFFERSON, Thomas, President of the U.S.A.
– **Catalogue of the Library of** . . . Ed.:– E. Millicent Sowerby. 1952-59. 5 vols. 4to. Some ink markings on text. Cl., with gt. medallions. (SG. Jan.22; 224) $150
– **Message from the President of the United States, Transmitting Information Touching an Illegal Combination of Private Individuals Against the Peace & Safety of the Union** . . . Wash., 1807. Soiled, marginal tears & repairs, not affecting text. In folding cl. case. From liby. of William E. Wilson. [Sabin 9428] (SPB. Apr.29; 43) $650
– **Notes on the State of Virginia.** L., 1787. 1st. Engl. Edn. Folding map mntd. on linen, slight dust staining. Hf. red. mor. gt. by Sangorski & Sutcliffe. [Sabin 35896] (CNY. Oct.1; 100) $800
– – **Anr. Copy.** Lge. folding map, partly hand-cold. in outl. Cont. hf. cf. & marb. bds., hinges brkn., lacks spine label. Samuel Latham Mitchell Barlow & James F. Woodward's armorial bkplts. (PNY. Dec.3; 197) $360

– – **Anr. Edn.** L., 1787. Reprint of 1st. (Paris) Edn. Slight spotting. Hf. cf. [Sabin 35896] (SPB. Nov.24; 22) $650
– – **Anr. Edn.** Trenton, 1803. 1st. Trenton Edn. 1 lf. lacks bottom outer corner affecting a few words, blanks stained, title stained at edges, foxed & cropped. Mod. gt. qtr. cf. & cl. (PNY. Mar.26; 165) $100
– **The Papers** . . . Ed.:– Julian P. Boyd. Princeton, 1950-65. 19 vols., & 2 index vols. for vols. 7-18. Cl., d.-w.'s, index vols. in wraps. (SG. Feb.12; 227) $175

JEFFERYS, Thomas
– **The American Atlas.** 1776. [1st. Edn.?]. Fo. 23 engraved maps on 29 sheets, many double-p. & folding, hand-cold. in outl., pict. cartouches, inset maps & plans, on guards thro.-out. Cont. hf. cf. & marb. bds. As an atlas, w.a.f. (C. May 20; 143) *Quaritch.* £4,200
– – **Anr. Edn.** L., 1776. 1st. Edn., 2nd. Iss. Lge. fo. All maps with cont. outl. colouring, some creases near fold on a few maps. Cont. hf. cf., worn, jnts. brkn., slightly defect. (VG. Dec.17; 1179) Fls. 16,000
– **A Collection of the Dresses of the Different Nations, Ancient & Modern, particularly Old English Dresses.** 1757. 2 vols. in 1. Text in Engl. & Fr., 1 plt. reprd., upr. margins of titles cut into. Hf. cf. by Zaehnsdorf. (BS. Jun.11; 355) £100
[–] – **Anr. Edn.** 1799. 4 vols. 4to. 478 (of 480) engraved plts. Orig. bds. (SH. Oct.9; 4) *Fairburn.* £120
– **The County of York Surveyed.** 1771-72. 1st. Edn. Lge. fo. Double-p. title & dedication with views, plan & map on 18 doubl-p. sheets, partly hand-cold. in outl. with 5 inset plans, on guards, title detchd. Cont. hf. cf. & marb. bds., spine worn. (C. May 20; 141) *Burgess.* £200
– – **Anr. Edn.** 1775. Lge. fo. Double-p. title & dedication with views, map on 18 doubl-p. sheets with inset plans, mntd. on guards. Cont. mott. cf. (C. May 20; 142) *Singleton.* £200
– – **Anr. Copy.** Key map hand-cold. in outl., lge. inset town plans, title vigs., etc., lacks 1 hf. sheet, a few other slight tears in centrefolds, slightly soiled. Loose in vell. folder. As an atlas, w.a.f. (SBA. Mar.4; 190) *Waggett.* £175
– **Le Petit Neptune François.** 1761. 4to. 33 engraved plts. Old cf., upr. cover detchd. As an atlas, w.a.f. (C. Jul.15; 127) *Cash.* £160
– **The West-India Atlas.** L., 1775. Fo. Slight foxing, staining, soiling. Hf. cf. (SPB. May 5; 287) $6,000

JEFFREY, John & Howie, Charles
– **The Trees & Shrubs of Fife & Kinross.** Leith, priv. ptd., 1879. 4to. Hf. mor., worn. (PD. May 20; 131) £80

JEFFREYS, John Gwyn
– **British Conchology.** Ill.:– James Sowerby. 1862-69. 5 vols. 12mo. Orig. cl. gt., unc. (PL. Nov.27; 160) *Miles.* £180
– – **Anr. Edn.** 1904-1863-69. 1st. Edns., except vol. 1, 2nd. Edn. 5 vols. 12mo. Unif. cl. (SBA. Dec.16; 142a) *Petersfield Bookshop.* £100

JEFFRIES, David
– **A Treatise on Diamonds & Pearls** . . . Priv. Ptd., 1751. 2nd. Edn. Cont. cf. From the collection of Eric Sexton. (C. Apr.15; 11) *Snellenberg.* £180

JEFFS, W.
– **Recollections of Italy 1826-27.** 1829. Fo. Orig. bdg. (DWB. May 15; 374) £100

JEKUTHIEL BEN MOSHE
– **Kizzur Amudei Golah.** Cracow, 1579. 1st. Edn. Sm. 4to. Some staining thro.-out. 19th. C. cl.-bkd. bds. (C. Jul.16; 309) *Valmadonna.* £420

JEKYLL, Gertrude & Hussey, Christopher
– **Garden Ornament.** 1927. 2nd. Edn. Fo. Orig. cl. (SBA. Oct.21; 184) *Temperley.* £65

JELLICOE, G.A.
See–SHEPHERD, J.C. & Jellicoe, G.A.

JEMMAT, Mrs. Catherine
– **Miscellanies in Prose & Verse.** 1766. 1st. Edn. 4to. Orig. bds., unc. (C. May 20; 79) *Blackwell.* £90

JENINGS, Edmund, Attrib. to
– **The Late Occurences in North America & Policy of Great Britain Considered.** L. 1766. Mod. cl. by Sangorski & Sutcliffe. [Sabin 39156] (CB. Nov.12; 266) Can. $200

JENKINS, C. Francis
- Animated Pictures: an Exposition of the Historical Development of Chromophotography, its Present Scientific Applications & Future Possibilities. Wash., 1898. 1st. Edn. Cl. (SG. Apr.23; 113) $110
- - Anr. Copy. Ex-liby. (SG. Jul.9; 185) $100

JENKINS, James
[-] The Martial Achievements of Great Britain. [1814-15]. 4to. Minor browning, wtrmkd. 1812. Unif. near cont. str.-grd. mor. by J.B. Pharoah of Madras, with his ticket dtd. 1834. (S. Jun.23; 310) *Hammond.* £1,800
- - Anr. Copy. 52 hand-cold. plts. including frontis. wtrmkd. 1812. Cont. pol. cf., sides elab. panel. in gt. & blind, spine gt., inner gt. dentelles, by Hering with his ticket. (C. Mar.18; 61) *Rostrom.* £600
- - Anr. Copy. Lacks list of subscribers. Cont. red hf. mor. (C. Nov.5; 82) *Fawkes.* £580
- - Anr. Copy. Engraved title, hand-cold. dedication, 52 hand-cold. plts. wtrmkd. 1812. Mod. hf. cf. (C. Jul.15; 48) *Taylor.* £500
- - Anr. Edn. 1815. 4to. 1 plt. torn in corner & reprd. Orig. hf. mor. (TA. Feb.19; 327) £525
- - Anr. Edn. [1815]. 4to. Frontis. & vig. title-p. soiled. Cont. hf. mor., covers detchd. (TA. Jan.22; 100) £300
[-] - Anr. Edn. 1835 or later. Lge. 4to. 44 (of 54) hand-cold. plts. only, text wtrmkd. 1812, plts. 1835, 1 plt. torn, some spotting & soiling. Cont. red mor. Pres. copy to Count Jean Baptiste Metaxa from Lady Maclaine. (S. Mar.16; 210) *Schuster.* £300
- - Anr. Edn. Ill.:- after W. Heath. Priv. Ptd., N.d. 4to. Lacks subscriber's list. Mod. red hf. mor., gt., by Rivière, in cl. box. (C. Nov.6; 214) *Traylen.* £650
- - Anr. Copy. Fo. Plts. wtrmkd. 1829-35. Cont. red mor., spine gt., partly unc. (CNY. May 22; 164) $1,000
- - Anr. Copy. Plts. wtrmkd. 1829-35. Red lev. mor. gt., covers with gt. borders & crossed sword tooled in gt. at corners, spine unif. gt., by Morrell. From the Prescott Collection. (CNY. Feb.6; 173) $950

[-] The Naval Achievements of Great Britain. [1817]. 4to. Minor browning, wtrmkd. 1812-16. Near cont. str.-grd. mor., decor. in gt. & blind, corners raised & bevelled in a Gosden style, by J.B. Pharoah [of Madras], with his ticket dtd. 1834, spine slightly worn. (S. Jun.23; 310) *Hammond.* £1,800
- - Anr. Copy. Without apparently optional port. Cont. maroon str.-grd. mor. gt., slight wear, hf. mor. box. (SPB. Oct.1; 199) $5,000
- - Anr. Edn. L., [1817-31]. Lge. 4to. A little light soiling in margins. Later long-grd. red mor., gold fillets & inner dentelles, by Rivière, spine restored. (R. Mar.31-Apr.4; 1789) DM 12,000
- - Anr. Edn. [1835 or later]. 4to. Lacks the 2 ports. & subscribers list, but with 'Landing of the British Troops in Egypt' plt., not on plt.-list, sm. natural flaw in frontis. & Le Sparvière plt., slight spotting, offsetting in text, lacks final blank. 19th. C. roan, spine defect., covers detchd. (S. Jun.23; 327) *Marshall.* £800
- - Anr. Edn. N.d. 4to. Some plts. wtrmkd. 1827, some ll. stained, mainly marginal but some plts. affected, lacks ports. & subscription list, a few other defects. Loose in cont. hf. mor. gt., very worn. W.a.f. (SBA. Mar.4; 54) *Angle Books.* £760
- - Anr. Copy. Some plts. wtrmkd. 1831, title vig. cold., occasional light soiling. Str.-grd. mor. gt. by Rivière. (SPB. Oct.1; 200) $4,000

JENKINS, Rhys
*See-*DICKINSON, H.W. & Jenkins, Rhys

JENNER, Edward
- An Inquiry into the Causes & Effects of the Variolae Vaccinae. 1800. 2nd. Edn. 4to. Some MS. notes or marks, almost all pencil. Cl. (SKC. May 19; 267) £160

*See-*TRIALS: Trial of Mrs. Mary Reed ...

JENNER, Thomas
- A Book of the Names of all Parishes ... in England & Wales. 1657. Sm. 4to. Extra engraved title dtd. 1643, folding table, 38 engraved maps (of 39), table torn & stained. Cont. cf., worn. W.a.f. (C. May 20; 144) *Burden.* £280

JENNINGS' LANDSCAPE ANNUALS
[-] Ill.:- after David Roberts. 1835-38. 4 vols. A few ll. detchd. Orig. mor., 1 inner hinge brkn. W.a.f. (CSK. Sep.26; 216) £120
- Switzerland & Italy.-Italy.-France. 1830; 1832; 1834. Loose in orig. mor., worn. (TA. Feb.19; 511) £60

JENNINGS, Preston J.
- A Book of Trout Flies. Ill.:- Alma W. Froderstrom. N.Y., Derry Pr. [1935]. De Luxe Edn., (25) numbered with mntd. flies by author. 2 vols. Hf. mor. in cl. case. Sigd. by author & artist on hf.-title. (CNY. Oct.1; 165) $12,000

JERRARD, Paul
- Flowers from Stratford on Avon. L., n.d. Lge. 8vo. Quotations ptd. in gt. Orig. gt. decor. bds., new spine & end-papers. (JL. Jul.20; 815) *Aus.* $120
- The Hummingbird Offering. Ca. 1880. Sm. fo. 10 plts. in gt. borders. Orig. cl. gt., soiled. (TA. Dec.18; 82) £80

JERROLD, Blanchard
- Life, in Two Epochs. Ill.:- George Cruikshank. L., 1882. 2 vols. in 4. 12mo. Extra ill. with about 200 plts. (60 cold.). Lev.' with artist's autograph in gt., rehinged. (SG. Sep.4; 143) $210
- London, a Pilgrimage. Ill.:- after Gustave Doré. 1872. Fo. Frontis. slightly dampstained, not affecting ill., some spotting. Orig. cl. gt., slightly worn. (S. Jul.31; 201) *Salinas.* £80
*See-*DORE, Gustave & Jerrold, Blanchard

JERROLD, Walter
- Highways & Byways of Kent. Ill.:- Hugh Thomson. 1907. 1st. Edn. Orig. cl. gt. Pres. copy from artist to J.P. Collins. (SH. Mar.27; 517) *Vincent.* £180

JERUSALEM
- The Saga of the Holy City. Jerusalem, 1954. Ltd. Numbered Edn. 4to. Pict. linen-bkd. bds., d.-w. (SG. Aug.21; 180) $100

JESSE, George R.
- Researches into the History of the British Dog. 1866. 2 vols. Extra-ill. Cont. cf., gt., covers detchd. & crudely reprd. (CSK. Jan.16; 145) £60

JESSE, John Heneage
- London: its Celebrated Characters & Remarkable Places. L., 1871. 3 vols. in 6. Extra-ill. with hundreds of copperplts. Crushed lev., gt. dentelles, marb. endpapers, partly untrimmed. (SG. Dec.18; 248) $250
- Memoirs of the Court of England. Boston, n.d. Westminster Edn., (100). 30 vols. Hf. crimson mor. gt., inlays on spine, silk endpapers. With 3 A.L.s. (SPB. May 6; 325) $2,100

JESSEL, Frederic
- A Bibliography of Works in English on Playing Cards & Gaming. L., 1905. 1st. Edn. With sm. errata slip. Buckram, spine detchd., mostly unopened. Inscr. (SG. Jan.22; 328) $180

JESTER, The
Barberton, 23 Jul., 1887-17 Dec., 1887. Vol. I, nos. 1-21. 4to. Cl., some stains on cover. As a periodical, w.a.f., bkplt. of T.M. Horsefield. (VA. Oct.31; 518) R. 780

JÉSUITES (Les) de la Maison Professé de Paris, en belle Humeur
Cologne, 1725. 16mo. 18th. C. red mor., decor. spine, 3 gt. fillets, inner dentelle. (HD. Apr.10; 341) Frs. 3,100

JEU de Cartes
N.p., ca. 1820. Square 16mo. Cont. cl. bds., covers decor. roulette. (HD. Apr.10; 342) Frs. 6,100

JEW, The
N.Y., 1844. Hf. leath. (S. Nov.18; 638) *Rock.* £95

JEWEL, John
- A Replie unto M. Hardinges Answeare. 1565. Fo. 2A4 holed with loss of a few letters, outer blank margin of last few ll. holed, margins of some ll. affected by damp. Cont. blind-stpd. cf., rebkd., old spine preserved, lacks clasps. [STC 14606] (CSK. Mar.13; 6) £120

JEWISH AGENCY
- 36 Koepfe: Original Lithographien Von Gregor Rabinovitch. Zurich, 1929. (125) numbered. 4to. Loosely contained in folding wraps., soiled. (SPB. May 11; 239) $250

JEWISH ENCYCLOPAEDIA
1901-06. 12 vols. Orig. cl. (SH. May 28; 58) *Pilkington.* £50

JEWITT, Llewellyn & Hope, W.H. St. John
- The Corporation Plate & Insignia of Office of England & Wales. 1895. 2 vols. 4to. Orig. cl. (SH. Jul.23; 278) *Sims & Reed.* £75

JHESUS. The Floure of the Commaundmentes of God
Trans.:- Andrew Chertsey. 8 Oct., 1521. 2nd. Edn. Fo. Some wormholes towards end, some minor stains. 18th. C. mor. gt., covers inlaid with panels of early blindstpd. bdg. Bkplt. of James Brindley, dupl. stp. of Huntingdon Liby. [STC 23877] (C. Nov.19; 22) *Kyrle.* £3,500

JIMENEZ, Juan Ramón
- Elegías Intermedias. Madrid, 1909. 1st. Edn. Linen & mor., orig. wraps. (DS. Apr.24; 971) Pts. 20,000
- Estío. Madrid, 1916. 1st. Edn. Orig. wraps. (DS. Apr.24; 913) Pts. 26,000

JOANNES DE SANCTO GEMINIANO
- Summa de Exemplis ac Similitudinibus Rerum. [Deventer], [Richardus Pafraet]. Ca. 1477. 1st. Edn. Fo. Lacks ll. 259-524, capitals, paragraph-marks, etc., supplied in red, slight browning, 1 or 2 short tears. Cont. blind-stpd. cf. over oak bds., worn, reb kd. From liby. of André L. Simon [BMC IX, 45; C. 2469; Goff J427] (S. May 18; 123) *Harper.* £320
- - Anr. Edn. Venice, J. & G. de Gregoriis, Forlivio, for S. & B. de Nallis. 10 Apr. 1497. Sm. 4to. Some initials supplied in red, slight browning & soiling, corner torn from fo. 7, without loss of text, reprd. 18th. C. vell. bds., soiled. From liby. of André L. Simon. [BMC V, 350; Goff J429; HC 7545*] (S. May 18; 124) *Harper.* £580

JOBLIN, M.
- Cincinnati Past & Present or Its Industrial History. Ill.:- James Landy. 1872. Embossed gt. mor. (HSS. Apr.24; 15) £70

JODE, Gerard de
- Speculum Orbis Terrae. Antw., 1593. 2nd. Edn. 2 pts. in 1 vol. In pt. 1 1 map with bkd. fault & text loss, pt. 2 lacks map 47, plt. 1 with bkd. tear, 1 map with some text loss. Leath. (D. Dec.11-13; 1236) DM 68,000

JOHANNES Climax
- Scala Paradisi; Sermo ad Pastorem. Torrebelvicino, Giovanni Leonardo Longo. Sep.19, 1478. 4to. Spaces for initial capitals with guide letters, initials supplied in red, lst. 8 ll. sprung, inner marginal repairs from fo. 153 to end causing loss of portion of some letters, oil stain on fo. 5, final lf. mntd. & portion of a letter & punctuation in facs., some staining. Early 19th. C. qtr. russ. gt. & rose bds. From the collection of Eric Sexton. [BMC VII, 1080, Goff J308] (CNY. Apr.8; 173) $2,200

JOHANNES de Capua
- Directorium Vitae Humanae. [Strassburg], [Johann Pruss]. [not after 1489]. 1st. Edn. Fo. Fo. 81 (n9r) on lst. state, with an incorrect woodcut, paper tears reprd. in folios 1, 8, 31, 78 & 79, some marginal staining to other 11. Red jansenite mor. by Duru, upr. cover rehinged. Deleted inscr. of Jacob Weiner(?), bkplt. of F.X.J.G. Boorluut de Noortdonck, shelf-mark of James Ludovic Lindsay, recently in the Pierpont Morgan Liby. [Goff J268a, HC(+Add) C 4411] (CNY. Apr.8; 169) $14,000

JOHANNES de Lapide-GREGORIUS I, Pope -REGINALDETUS, Petrus
- Resolutorium Dubiorum circa Celebrationem Missarum Occurentium.-Dialogorum Libri Quattuor.-Speculum Finalis Retributionis. Perigueux; Basle; Lyons, Jean Carant; Michael Furter; Michel Topie. 1498; 1496; 1496/97. 3

JOHANNES de Lapide-GREGORIUS I, Pope -REGINALDETUS, Petrus-*contd.*
works in 1 vol. 4to. Each work with spaces for initial capitals (with guide letters in last 2 works); 1st. work: sm. blank portion of title-p. woodcut cut out & replaced; 2nd. work: 1st. 8 ll. defect. at fore-margins, 3 with loss of portion of text, soiled; 3rd. work: lacks a1-8, last lf. of text torn at inner margin, affecting 5 lines of text, wormhole in fore-margin of some 20 ll., staining. Recent vell. From the collection of Eric Sexton. [Goff (Supp.) J371a; Goff G407 & R87] (CNY. Apr.8; 134)
$12,000

JOHANNES de Sancto Dominico
- Tractatus de Universalibus. Zamora, Antonio de Centenera. Feb.27, 1484. 4to. Spaces for capital initials, with guide letters, sm. patch of abrasion at d1r with loss of some letters. Mor. gt., gt. arms on covers, gt. spine, by Sangorski & Sutcliffe, qtr. vell. s.-c. From the collection of Eric Sexton. [Goff J426] (CNY. Apr.8; 208)
$8,000

JOHANNES de Verdena
- Sermones. [Cologne], [Conrad Winters de Homborch]. Ca. 1480. Fo. 146 ll. (of 148), lacks first & last blanks, initials in red some with penwork extending into margin, rubricated thro.-out, donation inscr. dtd. 1486 at end, stained. 18th. C. cf.-bkd. bds. [Goff J446] (S. Nov.25; 319)
Erasmus. £190

JOHANNES Friburgensis
- Summa Confessorum. Magdeburg, Moritz Brandis. Sep.21, 1491. Fo. Lacks 1st. lf. of table at front & x1, 2nd. lf. of table torn at fore-margin & reprd. affecting some text, b2v & b3r soiled, n3 with clean tear to text, inner margin n8 torn, last 2 ll. with sm. patch of worming to lr. margin, scattered dampstains & soiling. Old MS. vell., worn. From the collection of Eric Sexton. [Goff J323, H 7375] (CNY. Apr.8; 88)
$4,500

JOHANNES VON BERIS [Parisiensis]
- Eyn New Wund Artznei. Strassburg, ca. 1540. Early Edn. 4to. Sm. worm thro.-out, many old MS. marginalia. Mod. vell. (R. Mar.31-Apr.4; 1000)
DM 3,500

JOHN, William David
- Nantgarw Porcelain. 1948. Plus supp. in slip. 4to. Cf. (P. Oct.23; 179)
Sims & Reed. £85

JOHN OF THE CROSS, Saint
- The Song of the Soul. Trans.:- John O'Connor. Ill.:- Eric Gill. Abergevenny, 1927. (150) numbered, sigd. by artist. Sm. 4to. Orig. cl.-bkd. bds., unc. (SH. Mar.26; 244)
Maggs. £190

JOHNSON, A.
- Dictionary of American Biography. N.Y., 1957-58. 11 vols. 4to. Orig. cl. (SH. Mar.6; 531)
George's. £100

JOHNSON, A.E., Writer on Art
- The Russian Ballet. Ill.:- René Bull. 1913. (100) numbered, sigd. by artist. 4to. Orig. vell. (SH. Jun.18; 120)
National Art Institute. £100

JOHNSON, A.J.
- New Illustrated Family Atlas. N.Y., 1864. Tall fo. With an unlisted double-p. map of the Peninsular Campaign. Gt.-pict. cl., leath. back & tips, worn. (SG. May 21; 58)
$300
- - Anr. Edn. Ed.:- Richard S. Fisher. N.Y., 1866. Lge. fo. 1 double-p. map defect. Orig. cl., leath. spine, bdg. shabby & brkn. W.a.f. (SG. Nov.20; 67)
$225
- - Anr. Copy. Tall fo. Many stains & c. Shabby. W.a.f. (SG. Nov.20; 66)
$200
- - Anr. Edn. N.Y., 1873. Imp fo. Orig. hf. leath. (R. Oct.14-18; 1540)
DM 500

JOHNSON, Benjamin F. (Pseud.)
See-RILEY, James Whitcombe 'Benjamin F. Johnson'

JOHNSON, Capt. Charles
- A General History of ... the Most Famous Highwaymen ... 1734. [1st. Edn.?]. Fo. Cont. cf., rebkd., orig. spine preserved. (S. Nov.25; 474)
Quaritch £280
- - Anr. Copy. Late 19th. C. panel. cf. gt., in s.-c. (BS. Jun.11; 54)
£130

JOHNSON or Johnstone, Charles
[-] Chrysal; Or the Ventures of a Guinea, by an Adept. 1821. 3 vols. Str.-grd. mor. gt. (TA. Oct.16; 353)
£95
- The Village Opera. 1729. 1st. Edn. Browning thro.-out. Cl. (BS. Jun.11; 258)
£70

JOHNSON, Charles Pierpont
See-SOWERBY, John Edward & Johnson, Charles Pierpont

JOHNSON, E.J.
- Journal of a trip to Paris. 1822. 4to. Folding menus, sm. engrs. stuck down, 5 full page plts. Str.-grd. cf. gt. (P. Nov.13; 173)
Shaw. £85

JOHNSON, Edwin F.
- Railroad to the Pacific: Northern Route, Its General Character, Relative Merits, etc. N.Y., 1854. 2nd. Edn. (1st. Edn. in Book Form). Light soiling. Orig. ptd. wraps., sewed, upr. wrap. detchd. (PNY. Mar.26; 244)
$220

JOHNSON, Frank M.
- Forest, Lake & River. Ill.:- after A.D. Turner. Boston, 1902. 17½ × 27¾ ins. Comprising the 12 chromolitho. plts. only. Mntd. on gt.-paper cover bds., in cl. portfo. (SG. May 21; 305)
$600

JOHNSON, George W.
See-HOGG, Robert & Johnson, George W.

JOHNSON, Henry Lewis
- Gutenburg & the Book of Books. N.Y., 1932. (750). Tall fo. With anr. copy of the facs. lf. in folder (with title-p. 'privately printed for the friends of Mr. & Mrs. Bernard Gimbel ...'). Cl., folding box. (SG. Mar.26; 230)
£160

JOHNSON, John
- A Journey from India to England through Persia, Georgia, Russia, Poland & Prussia. 1818. 4to. Cont. spr. cf. (SH. Nov.7; 419)
Diba. £125

JOHNSON, John, Printer & Smith
- Specimen of Printing Types & Ornaments. Phila., 1834. Woodcut folding plts. reprd. at folds or inner margin, 3 type plts. brittle or torn. Mod. cl. (PNY. Mar.26; 323)
$275
- Typographia. 1824. 1st. Edn. 2 vols. L.P. Mod. hf. mor., partly unc. (SH. Jul.27; 171)
Bickersteth. £180
- - Anr. Copy. 12mo. Orig. bds. with linen backstrip, soiled. (TA. Mar.19; 224)
£70
- - Anr. Copy. 24mo. Cf. gt. (S. Oct.21; 496)
Ponder. £60
- - Anr. Copy. 2 vols. in 4. 32mo. Cf., blind-stpd. arabesque design on all covers, spines & inner dentelles gt., by Bayntun. (SG. Mar.26; 280)
$170

JOHNSON, Merle
- American First Editions ... 199 American Authors. N.Y., 1936. 3rd. Edn. Buckram. (SG. Oct.2; 199)
$100
- High Spots of American Literature. N.Y., 1929. (50) in full bdg., sigd. Crushed lev. gt. partly. untrimmed, by Bennett. (SG. Oct.2; 196)
$110

JOHNSON, Richard
[-] The Adventures of a Bee. 1790. 1st. Edn. 32mo. Advts. Orig. Dutch floral bds. (SH. Dec.10; 1)
Temperley. £190
[-] The Drawing School for Little Masters & Misses ... To Which are added, The Whole Art of Kite Making. 1774. 4¼ × 3 inches. Engraved frontis. preserved & cleanly torn, slight soiling. Cont. bds., worn. (CSK. Feb.13; 148)
£60
[-] Juvenile Trials for robbing Orchards, Telling Fibs ... by Master Tommy Littleton, Secretary to the Court. 1781. An Edn. 12mo. Orig. ptd. bds., s-c. 2 ills. sigd. J. Bell on lr. cover. (SH. Dec.10; 4)
Quaritch. £150

JOHNSON, Robert
[-] The Paintings of Robert Johnson. Sydney, n.d. 4to. Decor. bds., cl. spine. (JL. Jul.20; 656a)
Aus. $130

JOHNSON, Rossiter
- Author's Digest. [N.Y. & Boston], Priv. ptd. N.d. Autograph Edn., (32) with sigd. article by Charles D. Warner. 20 vols. Hf. mor. gt., gt. panel. spines with mor. floral inlays. (SPB. May 6; 326)
$2,800

JOHNSON, Dr. Samuel
[-] A Catalogue of the Valuable Library of Books of ... [L.], 1785. 1st. Edn. 19th. C. hf. cf. (CNY. May 22; 137)
$8,000
- A Diary of a Journey into North Wales. Ed.:- R. Duppa. 1816. 1st. Edn. 2 facs., errata slip tipped in at beginning, slight offsetting. Cont. russ. gt. (SBA. Oct.22; 737)
Vitkovitch. £55
- A Dictionary of the English Language. 1755. 1st. Edn. 2 vols. Fo. Some spotting, marginal tear in 7R2 vol. I. Cont. cf., gt., worn. (S. Jun.23; 362)
Traylen. £1,100
- - Anr. Copy. Fo. Cont. hf. cf., worn. W.a.f. (SBA. Jul.23; 388)
Smith. £1,050
- - Anr. Copy. Rebnd. in hf. mor. (CE. Mar.19; 240)
£1,000
- - Anr. Copy. Both titles & C2 in vol. I reprd., occasional spotting. Cont. cf., rebkd., worn. (S. Jun.23; 418)
Simmonds. £550
- - Anr. Copy. 1st. 2 ll. in vol. 1 slightly sprung, light foxing to some ll. Orig. hf. sheep & marb. paper bds., spines gt.-lettered, covers of both vols. worn, qtr. red mor. gt. folding cases. From the Prescott Collection. (CNY. Feb.6; 176)
$8,500
- - Anr. Copy. Cont. cf., worn, buckram folding cases. Hopetoun bkplt. (SG. May 14; 115)
$4,800
- - Anr. Edn. 1755-73. 1st. Edn.; 4th. Edn. 2 vols. Fo. Inner margin of vol. 1 slightly torn, a few other margins slightly dampstained, some other minor defects. Cont. cf., very worn, 1 cover lacking. W.a.f. (SBA. Mar.4; 55)
Sterling Books. £240
- - Anr. Edn. Dublin, 1775. 4th. Edn. 2 vols. 4to. Cont. cf. (GM. Apr.30; 632)
£70
- - Anr. Edn. L., 1783. 7th. Edn. 2 vols. Early tree cf., spines gt., ex-liby. (SG. Feb.5; 189)
$120
- - Anr. Edn. 1784. 5th. Edn. 2 vols. Fo. Some discolouration. Recent cf. (TA. Mar.19; 597)
£160
- - Anr. Copy. Mntd. port. frontis. in vol. I dtd. 1786. Cont. cf., upr. cover of vol. I detchd., lacks upr. cover to l. II. With 19th. C. MS. copy of Johnson's famous letter to the Earl of Chesterfield (wtrmkd. 1839). (CB. Nov.12; 160)
Can. $350
- - Anr. Edn. 1785. 6th Edn. 2 vols. 4to. Title of vol. 2 spotted. Old cf., worn, lacks head of 1 spine. (SKC. Jul.28; 2466)
£55
- - Anr. Edn. Dublin, 1798. 8th. Edn. 2 vols. 4to. Some discolouration or spotting, a few repairs. Hf. cf., worn. (SKC. May 19; 195)
£70
- - Anr. Edn. 1799. 8th. Edn. 2 vols. 4to. Soiled. Later cl.-bkd. bds., worn. (SH. Jan.30; 452)
Subunso. £100
- - Anr. Edn. Ed.:- H.J. Todd. 1818. 5 vols. 4to. Slight offsetting to 1st. title, occasional spotting. 19th. C. hf. cf., spines gt., some wear. (S. Jan.26; 212)
Grant. £75
- - Anr. Edn. 1820. 2 vols. 4to. A few minor defects. Later hf. cf. (SBA. Dec.16; 25)
Ghani. £65

- The Idler. L., 1761. 1st. Coll. Edn. 2 vols. 12mo. Cont. cf., spines & corners worn, mor. solander case. Pres. Copy, to Mrs Margaret P. Strahan, lately in the Prescott Collection. (CNY. Feb.6; 178)
$3,800
- - Anr. Edn. L., 1767. 3rd. Edn. 2 vols. 12mo. Cont. cf. gt., rebkd., worn. (SG. Sep.25; 174)
$130

- Johnsoniana, or Supplement to Boswell. 1836. L.P. 1 vol. in 3. 4to. 45 engd. plts., extra-ill. with 240 additional plts., 11 items of poetry & prose inserted, some inlaid to size, with 2 examples of Johnson's autograph. Late 19th. C. red lev. mor. by Rivière, gt. W.a.f. (S. Nov.24; 178)
Quaritch. £5,500

[-] A Journey to the Western Islands of Scotland. 1775. 1st. Edn. 1st. Iss. 12-line errata lf. at end, title slightly spotted & stained. Cont. cf., rebkd. (SH. Jul.27; 48)
Argyl Etkin. £130
[-] - Anr. Copy. 12 line errata lf. at end, U4 (cancel, verso numbered correctly P.296) crudely tipped in, some marginal browning. Cont. cf. (CSK. Sep.12; 201)
£55
[-] - Anr. Copy. Light foxing. Qtr. leath. (CB. Feb.18; 194)
Can. $320

- The Lives of the Most Eminent Poets. 1781. 1st. separate L. Edn. 4 vols. Cont. cf. (SH. Oct.10; 470)
Barnett. £65
- - Anr. Edn. L., 1781. 1st. Authorized Edn. 4 vols. Orig. bds., rebkd., orig. spine labels mntd., unc. (SG. Oct.9; 135)
$450
- - Anr. Copy. Port. without imprint, with the integral advt. lf. at end of vol. IV. Cont. tree cf., 2 covers detchd. Sm. bkplt- of R.W. Chapman in vol. I. (SG. Feb.5; 188)
$120
- - Anr. Edn. Dublin, 1781. 3 vols. Occasional lf. foxed. Cont. tree cf., rebkd. (CB. Sep.24; 129)
Can. $150

- The Plan of a Dictionary of the English Language ... 1747. 1st. 8vo. Edn. Some cont. underlining in ink, slightly stained. Unc. & stitched. (S. Oct.20; 119)
Frost. £200
[-] Political Tracts. 1776. 1st. Edn. A few ll. slightly soiled, portion cut from title. Cont. bds., rebkd. (SH. Oct.10; 302)
Drury. £95

– – Anr. Edn. Dublin, 1777. Slight browning. Cf., lacks final free end-paper. (SPB. May 29; 227) $275

– Prayers & Meditations . . . L., 1785. 1st. Edn. Gatherings N & O spotted. Orig. bds., spine & upr. bd. edge worn, jnts. reprd., qtr. mor. gt. s.-c. Cont. owner's inscr. of Maria De Home Scott, lately in the Prescott Collection. (CNY. Feb.6; 179) $1,500

[–] [Rasselas] The Prince of Abissinia. 1759. 1st. Edn. 2 vols. 12mo. Later qtr. cf. (TA. Nov.20; 210) £500

[–] – Anr. Copy. Red mor., gt., by Bedford, slightly worn. (SKC. Jul.28; 2364) £480

– – Anr. Copy. A2 in vol. 1 holed with loss of pagination, blank inner margin of title of vol. 2 holed, slight borwning, lacks final blank M4 in vol. 2. Cont. cf., spines worn. (CSK. May 8; 100) £200

[–] – Anr. Copy. 16mo. Mott. cf., gt. borders & spines, gt. dentelles. (SG. May 14; 116) $650

[–] – Anr. Copy. 1st. Iss. With p. 45 in vol. 2 unpaginated, lacks final blank in vol. 2. Mor. gt., by Birdsall. The George B. McCutcheon copy, with bkplt., lately in the Prescott Collection. (CNY. Feb.6; 177) $420

– – Anr. Edn. L., 1828. 16mo. Cont. mor. gt. Double fore-e. pntg.; from the liby. of Zola E. Harvey. (SG. Mar.19; 141) $650

– The Vanity of Human Wishes. L., 1749. 1st. Edn. 4to. Title & last lf. of text soiled, some browning. Disbnd. (SPB. May 6; 199) $1,200

– The Works of the English Poets. 1790. 75 vols. Sm. grained mor., gt. (CE. Aug.28; 224) £270

– Works. 1796. 12 vols. Some spotting. Cont. tree cf., spines gt. Bkplt. of Maitland of Eccles. (S. May 5; 433) *Maggs.* £190

– – Anr. Edn. 1826. 12 vols. Cont. cf. (SH. May 28; 60) *Mills.* £65

– – Anr. Edn. Troy, N.Y., 1903. Literary Club Edn., (774). 16 vols. Mor. gt., gt. panel. spines with red inlays. (SPB. May 6; 327) $1,700

JOHNSON, Dr. Samuel–HAWKINS, Sir John
– Works.–His Life, & Notes on His Lives of the Poets. 1787-89. 17 vols. Complete with Piozzi's Letters, water colour port. bnd. in. Unif. 19th. C. hf. mor., gt. decor. spine. (TA. Sep.18; 375) £160

JOHNSON, Dr. Samuel–ANON
– Dictionary of the English Language. –Biographical Dictionary; Geographical Dictionary; Geographical Grammar. Ca. 1810. 4 vols. Red mor., mor. bnd. wood case, worn. (CE. Jul.9; 199) £105

JOHNSON, Theo
– Illustrations of British Hawk Moths & their Larvae . . . **with Thirty-six Drawings by the Author.** [Manchester?], 1888. New Edn. 4to. 35 watercolour plts., lacks 1, 6 & 21, dupls. of 4 &7. Orig. hf. roan by H. Rawson & Co. of Manchester with their ticket. (S. Jun.1; 148) *Rostron.* £180

JOHNSON, Thomas
– A Discourse Consisting of Motives for the Enlargement & Freedom of Trade, Especially that of Cloth. 1645. 1st. Edn. 4to. Stains on title, sm. hole in title reprd. Old sheep, rebkd. (C. Apr.1; 182) *Mahler.* £90

JOHNSON, Thomas
– One Hundred & Fifty New Designs . . . **Ceilings, Chimney-Pieces** . . . 1758. 1st. Edn. Fo. Later hf. cf., upr. cover detchd. (S. Mar.17; 420) *Quaritch.* £1,500

JOHNSON, Thomas B.
– The Sportsman's Cyclopaedia. Ill.:– after Landseer, Ward, Cooper, Hancock, & others. L., 1848. Some foxing & browning. Later three-qtr. mor. (SG. Dec.11; 345) $110

JOHNSON, William
– The Imperial Cyclopaedia of Machinery. N.d. Fo. Most plts. folding & mntd. on guards, a few slightly torn, most spotted, margins shaved with loss of a few letters. Cont. hf. mor., worn. (CSK. Nov.14; 135) £70

JOHNSON, Sir William
– The Papers. Ed.:– [James Sullivan & others]. Albany, 1921-65. 14 vols., including index. Orig. cl., ex-liby. (CB. Nov.12; 132) Can. $550

JOHNSTON, Alexander Keith
– Physical Atlas of Natural Phenomena. Edinb., 1856. 3rd. Edn. Fo. Orig. hf. cf., rebkd. using old spine. (S. Nov.4; 467) *Lockwood.* £90

– Royal Atlas. 1869. Fo. Maps cold. (JN. Apr.2; 825) £50

JOHNSTON, David Claypoole
– Scraps. Boston, 1832, 1835, 1837, 1840, & 1849. Nos. 3, 6-8, & New Series no. 1. Ob. fo. Orig. pict. & ptd. wraps., 1 cover detchd. (SG. May 21; 391) $140

JOHNSTON, Francis Benjamin & Waterman, Thomas Tileston
– The Early Architecture of North Carolina, a pictorial survey. Chapel Hill, 1941. Orig. cl., s.-c. (CB. May 27; 130) Can. $110

JOHNSTON, Sir Harry H.
– The Negro in the New World. L., [1910]. 1st. Edn. Rebnd. in mott. hf. cf. (SG. Feb.12; 290) $130

JOHNSTON, J.
– Historia Naturalis . . . **Quadrupeds; Serpents; Insects.** Ill.:– C. & M. Merian Jr. Amst., 1665 & 57. 3 pts. in 1 vol. (in total, 6 pts.). Fo. 1 engraved title, 80 engraved plts. with pt. 1; 12 plts. with pt. 2; 28 plts. with pt. 3, lacks title of 1st. pt., 2 plts. in same misbnd. Cont. cf., back gt. W.a.f. (VG. Dec.17; 1397) Fls. 900

JOHNSTON, Robert
– Travels through part of the Russian Empire & the Country of Poland. L., 1815. 4to. Cont. leath., upr. cover loose, spine pasted. (HK. Nov.18-21; 1361) DM 550

JOHNSTONE, Charles
See–JOHNSON or Johnstone, Charles

JOHNSTONE, George Horace
– Asiatic Magnolias in Cultivation. 1955. 4to. Orig. buckram, slightly marked. (SKC. May 19; 419) £70

– – Anr. Copy. (C. May 20; 218) *Joseph.* £55

– – Anr. Copy. Foreword by D. Bowes-Lyon. Cl. (SG. Sep.18; 203) $120

JOHNSTONE, James
– An Essay on the Use of the Ganglions of the Nerves.–An Historical Dissertation Concerning the Malignant Epidemical Fever of 1756 . . . **in Kidderminster.** Shrewsbury (1st. work), 1771; 1758. 2 works in 1 vol. Marb. bds., cf. spine. (S. Jun.16; 469) *Jenner Books.* £140

JOHNSTONE, John
– An Account of the most Approved Mode of Draining Land . . . 1797. 1st. Edn. 4to. Some browning. Cont. tree cf. (S. Apr.7; 404) *Morton-Smith.* £60

JOHNSTONE or Jonston, Dr. John, Naturalist
– Beschrijving van de Natuur der Viervootige Dieren. Vissen en Bloedloze Water-Dieren, Vogeln, Gekerfde of Kronkel-Dieren, Slangen en Drangen. Ill.:– C. & M. Merian Jr. Amst., 1660. 6 pts. in 1 vol. Fo. Cont. cf., top & bottom of spine slightly defect., frag. torn off 2 text ll., but present. (VG. Oct.13; 89) Fls. 4,200

– Historia Naturalis. Ill.:– Caspar & Matlhäus Merian. Frankfurt, 1650-53. 1st.Edn. 5 works with 11 pts. in 2 vols. Vol. 1 some plts. loose, 5 with tears or margin tears, vol. 2 lacks 5 copperplts., engd. title torn, some plts. slightly defect., vol. 3 engraved title slightly defect. Cont. leath. gt., spine defect. (R. Mar.31-Apr.4; 1381) DM 1,800

– Historia Naturalis de Piscibus et Celtis. Libri V. –Historiae Naturalis de Exanguibus Aquaticis Libri IV. Ill.:– C. & M. Merian. Frankfurt, 1650. 2 works in 1 vol. Fo. 1st. work lacks 2 copperplts., both works stained, browned & soiled down right. Cont. leath. (R. Oct.14-18) DM 430

– Theatrum Universale Omnium Animalium. Amst., 1718. 6 pts. in 2 vols. Fo. With 20 extra irregularly numbered plts. of insects at end of vol. 1, some discoloration & occasional light foxing of plts., last lf. soiled. 19th. C. hf. mor. From Chetham's Liby., Manchester. (C. Nov.27; 220) *Hoorn.* £420

JOHNSTONE, William Grosart & Croall, Alexander
– The Nature Printed British Seaweeds. Ill.:– Henry Bradbury. 1859-60. 4 vols. Occasional light foxing, loose in bdg. Orig. decor. cl. gt. (C. Nov.6; 319) *Grosart.* £100

– – Anr. Copy. Some ll. & plts. loose. Bdg. not stated. (S. Jul.27; 295) *Dekker & Nordemann.* £90

– – Anr. Copy. Slightly soiled in parts. 2 liby. hf. linen & 2 cont. hf. leath., slightly defect., orig. wraps. bnd. (R. Mar.31-Apr.4; 1410) DM 700

JOINVILLE, John, Lord
– Histoire de St Louis . . . Paris, 1874. (325) on H.M.P. 4to. Ills. in facs. Mor. by Hardy, gt. fillets & arabesques by M. Michel on covers, spine decor. with raised bands, inside dentelle. (HD. Feb.27; 152) Frs. 1,200

– The History of Saint Louis. Trans.:– Joan Evans. Ill.:– Reynolds Stone. Shakes. Hd. Pr., 1937. (200) numbered. Fo. Orig. mor. gt., s.-c. (S. Jul.31; 132) *Appleton.* £620

JOLIMONT, François Gabriel Théodore Blasset de
– Les Mausolées Français. Paris, 1821. Fo. Lightly browned & soiled in parts. Cont. hf. leath., unc. (H. Dec.9/10; 935) DM 640

JOLY, A.F.
[–] Mémoires de Feu M. Omer Talon, avocat Général en la Cour de Parlement de Paris. Ill.:– Baron. The Hague, 1732. 8 vols. 12mo. 18th. C. mor., arms of Mesdames de France, gt., on covers, triple gt. fillet, spines gt. in compartments, inner gt. dentelles. Wilmerding copy, with his bkplt., bkplt. of Madame Victoire de France. (SM. Oct.7; 1773) Frs. 6,500

JOLY, Adrien
[–] Les Petits Acteurs du Grand Théâtre ou Recueil de Divers Cris de Paris. Paris, ca. 1815. 4to. Lacks plts. 61 & 62 as usual. Cont. red mor.-bkd. bds., gt., unc., binders gt. monog. in top fore-corner of upr. cover. (SM. Oct.8; 2401) Frs. 25,000

JOLY, Henri L.
– Legend in Japanese Art. 1908. 4to. Orig. cl. gt. (P. Oct.23; 165) *Maggs.* £85

– – Anr. Copy. Orig. cl. (SH. Apr.9; 85) *Eskanazi.* £65

– W.L. Behrens Collection: Catalogue. L., 1913-14. (100) (this set unnumbered). 4 vols. 4to. Three-qtr. cf., scuffed, wraps. of orig. fascicules bnd. in, ex-liby. (SG. Mar.12; 218) $750

JOLY, Victor
– Les Ardennes. Ill.:– Martinus A. Kuytenbrouwer. Brussels, n.d. Lge. 4to. Publisher's bds. (LM. Jun.13; 16) B.Frs. 7,000

JONA
Trans.:– M. Luther. Ill.:– G. Marcks. [Hamburg], [1950]. (300) on Bütten. 4to. Loose in orig wraps. Printer's mark sigd. by artist. (H. Dec.9/10; 2208) DM 500

JONES, A.E.
See–COURTAULD, S.A. & Jones, A.E.

JONES, David, Artist
– An Introduction to the Rime of the Ancient Mariner. Clover Hill Edns., 1972. (115) sigd. 4to. Orig. parch.-bkd. cl., s.-c. (SH. Feb.20; 412) *Kaye.* £60

– In Parenthesis. Ed.:– Thomas Stearns Eliot. 1961. (70) sigd. by author & T.S. Eliot. Orig. buckram. (SH. Dec.18; 190) *Brook.* £200

JONES, E. Alfred
– Catalogue of the Collection of Old Plate of Leopold de Rothschild. 1907. 4to. Orig. cl. (SH. Jul.23; 279) *Sims & Reed.* £75

– Catalogue of the Gutman Collection of Plate. 1907. 4to. Orig. cl. (SH. Jul.23; 280) *Rosenberg.* £100

– – Anr. Copy. Cl., d.-w. (P. Oct.23; 156) *Sims & Reed.* £70

– Catalogue of the Objects in Gold & Silver in the Rothschild Collection. 1912. (175). Fo. Orig. cl.-bkd. bds., worn, loose. (SH. Apr.9; 86) *Reed & Sims.* £85

– Catalogue of Plate belonging to the Duke of Portland . . . 1935. Ltd. Edn. 4to. Orig. cl. (SH. Jul.23; 281) *Ars Artis.* £50

– Catalogue of the Plate of Queen's [Merton; Christ; Magdelen; Oriel] College. 1938-44. 5 vols. 4to. Orig. cl. (SH. Jul.23; 283) *Sims & Reed.* £60

– The Gold & Silver of Windsor Castle. 1911. (285) numbered. Fo. Orig. cl. (SH. Jan. 249) *Talerman.* £85

– – Anr. Copy. Cl., partly unc. (C. Jul.22; 147) *Maggs.* £85

– The Old English Plate of the Emperor of Russia. Priv. Ptd., 1909. 4to. Orig. hf. mor. (SH. Jul.23; 287) *Baker.* £55

JONES, Edward
– Musical & Poetical Relicks of the Welsh Bards. –The Bardic Museum . . . 1794; 1802. 2 works in 1 vol. Fo. Cont. hf. russ. From the collection of Eric Sexton. (C. Apr.15; 111) *Crowe.* £140
– – **Anr. Copy.** Lacks frontis. (2nd. work). (C. Jul.16; 368) *Hannas.* £110

JONES, H.A.
See–**RALEIGH, Walter & Jones, H.A.**

JONES, Herschel V.
– Adventures in Americana. Ed.:– Dr. Wilberforce Eames. N.Y., 1928. (200) numbered copies. 2 vols., 4to. Facs. title-pp. Gt-decor. cl., box. (SG. Oct.2; 203) $210

JONES, Inigo
– The Designs. Ed.:– William Kent. Ill.:– after Jones & A. Palladio. 1727. [2nd. Edn.?]. 2 vols. in 1. Fo. Cont. mott. cf. gt. Bkplt. of Sir William Beauchamp Proctor, lately in the collection of Eric Sexton. (C. Apr.15; 70) *Wood.* £350
– – **Anr. Copy.** 2 vols. Some spotting, dupl. from the Royal Institute of British Architects with its liby. stp. on verso of each plt. Cont. bds., worn & rebkd. (SPB. May 6; 200) $550
– The Most notable Antiquity of Great Britain, vulgarly called Stone-Heng. L., 1655. 1st. Edn. Fo. Lacks port., some spots. Old cf., worn. (SPB. Nov.25; 77) $150
– – **Anr. Edn.** 1725. Fo. 1 plt. torn, some discolouration. Cont. cf. (C. Feb.25; 40) *Quaritch.* £160

JONES, Inigo & Kent, William
– Some Designs . . . Ill.:– John Vardy. 1744. Fo. Cont. mott. cf., rebkd. (S. Mar.17; 421) *Traylen.* £320

JONES, Owen
– Grammar of Ornament. 1856. [1st. Edn.?]. Fo. Hf. cf., defect. (P. Oct.2; 282) *Rees-Jones.* £65
– – **Anr. Copy.** Cont. burgundy mor., spine gt. (SG. Oct.9; 136) $1,000
– – **Anr. Edn.** [1856]. Fo. Loose in orig. cl., jnts. split, worn. (SH. Mar.26; 303) *Hancock.* £50
– – **Anr. Edn.** 1868. Fo. Orig. cl. (SBA. Dec.16; 112) *McGill's Bookshop.* £125
– – **Anr. Copy.** Later mor. (SBA. May 27; 252) *Honeyfield Books.* £105
– – **Anr. Copy.** Orig. cl., rebkd. (SH. Jan.29; 250) *Reed & Sims.* £70
– – **Anr. Copy.** Mod. mor.-bkd. cl. (SH. Apr.9; 87) *Clarendon Gallery.* £65
– – **Anr. Edn.** L., 1910. Fo. Contents partly loose in bdg. Gt.-pict. cl. (SG. Dec.4; 208) $150
– – **Anr. Copy.** Orig. cl., spine brkn. & loose. (CB. May 27; 131) Can. $140
– – **Anr. Copy.** Decor. cl., hinges reprd. (JL. Mar.2; 727) Aus. $190
– – **Anr. Edn.** N.d. Fo. Some plts. soiled. Mod. cf.-bkd. cl. (SH. Jul.23; 122) *Browne.* £60
– The Preacher. 1849. 4to. Wooden carved bdg., decor., mor. spine, worn at head & foot. (C. Feb.4; 137) *Bickersteth.* £100
– The Psalms of David Illuminated. [L.], ca. 1840-60. Fo. Orig. gt.-fillet mor. (PNY. Dec.3; 175) $190
– – **Anr. Edn.** N.d. Fo. Orig repoussé cf., disbnd. (CSK. Aug.1; 128) £80
– The Words of the Preacher. 1849. 4to. Loose in orig. cl.-bkd. moulded wood bds., by Remnant, Edmonds & Remnants. Pres. copy to sister. (SH. Mar.26; 300) *Slade.* £100

JONES, Owen & Goury, Jules
– Plans, Elevations, Sections & Details of the Alhambra. 1842-45. 2 vols. Fo. Text in Engl. & Fr., occasional light spotting. Cont hf. mor., spines gt. (CSK. Sep.26; 41) £1,300
– – **Anr. Copy.** Some foxing. (C. Feb.4; 158) *Marlborough.* £1,100

JONES, Paul
– Flora Magnifica. Ed.:– Wilfrid Blunt & E.G. Waterhouse. L., [1976]. (500) for sale, sigd. by artist. Fo. Orig. buckram & hf. vell. bdg. by Zaehnsdorf, cl. s.-c. (KH. Nov.18; 357) Aus. $450
– Flora Superba: Selected & Painted by the Artist. Ed.:– Wilfrid Blunt & Sir George Taylor. L., [1971]. (400) numbered for sale, sigd. by artist. fo. Orig. bdg. of buckram, hf. vell. by Zaehnsdorf, cl. s.-c. (KH. Nov.18; 358) Aus. $500

JONES, Rev. Peter
– History of the Ojebway Indians. 1861. Plts, spotted. Orig. cl. (SH. Apr.9; 155) *Crete.* £65

JONES, Philip
– An Essay on Crookedness or Distortions of the Spine. Priv. ptd., 1788. New cl. (S. Dec.2; 519) *Maggs.* £50

JONES, Philippe Roberts (Preface)
See–**CAP D'ENCRE 1964**

JONES, Robert
– The Muses Gardin [sic] of Delights. Ed.:– William Barclay Squire. Oxford, Daniel Pr., 1901. (130). Sm. 4to. Cont. limp vell., ties. (SH. Feb.20; 371) *Sawyer.* £55

JONES, S.
See–**BAKER, David Erskine & others**

JONES, T.R.
– Cassell's Book of Birds. N.d. 4 vols. in 2. 4to. Mod. cl. (P. Mar.12; 325) *Duran.* £150
– – **Anr. Copy.** Hf. cf. (P. Apr.30; 290) *Gilbert.* £50

JONES, Theophilus
– A History of the County of Brecknock. 1805-09. 2 vols. in 3. 4to. 3 additional hand-cold. ll. of coats of arms in vol. 2, sm. hole in a few ll. vol. 2, slightly dampstained, mainly marginal. Cont. hf. russ., spines torn. (SBA. Oct.22; 742) *Morgan.* £160
– – **Anr. Copy.** 2 vols. 1 engraved plt. torn. Later cl. (SH. Jun.18; 223) *Chesters.* £60

JONES, William
– The Gentlemens or Builders Companion. 1739. 4to. Cont. cf., rebkd. (S. Mar.17; 422) *Marlborough Rare Books.* £420

JONES, William
– Poikilographia. Or Various Specimens of Ornamental Penmanship Comprising Twenty Two Different Alphabets. Ca. 1830. Fo. Recently rebnd. in qtr. cf. with orig. paper label laid on upr. cover. (TA. Jan.22; 236) £75
– – **Anr. Copy.** Fo. Recently rebnd. in qtr. cf. with orig. paper label laid on upr. cover. (TA. Mar.19; 145) £65
– Works. L., 1799. 6 vols. 4to. Mod. cl. (P. Jun.11; 46) *Hossain.* £65
– – **Anr. Edn.** Ed.:– Lord Teignmouth. 1799-1806. 7 vols. 4to. Cont. tree cf., gt. decor. spines. (TA. Mar.19; 340) £240

JONES & CO.
– Views of the Seats of Noblemen, & Gentlemen in England, Wales, Scotland, & Ireland. 1829. 2nd. Series. 4to. Occasional slight spotting. Cont. hf. cf. (CSK. May 1; 83) £60
– – **Anr. Edn.** 1829. 4to. Some offsetting. Cont. red hf. mor., gt., worn. (S. Nov.4; 552) *Strafaldi.* £70
– Views of Seats, Mansions, Castles etc. N.d. 2 vols. 4to. Spotted. Cont. cf. (SH. Mar.5; 73) *Strufaldi.* £105

JONGHE, Clemendt de
– [Icones Praecipuarum Urbium Totius Europae]. Ill.:– 5 views by H. Allard, rest by De Jonghe. Amst., [1675]. Fo. 39 engraved views of the major cities of Europe cold. by hand, no title or frontis., on guards thro.-out, plts. of L., Lisbon, Ghent, Geneva & Basle have tears reprd., repairs to a few other sm. holes & tears at the bottom of the central folds, some soiling & spotting. 19th. C. hf. mor., gt. Bkplt. of the Earl Beauchamp. (S. Jun.22; 156) *White.* £19,000

JONGHE d'Ardoye, T.A.J.H.G., Vicomte de & others
– Amorial Belge du Bibliophile. [Brussels], 1930. Ltd. Edn. 3 vols. 4to. Cont. cl., base of spines stained. (SBA. Mar.4; 291) *Randerla.* £75

JONSON, Ben
– Songs. Ill.:– Lucien Pissarro. Eragny Pr., 1906. (180). Orig. bds., top of spine torn, unc. (S. Jul.31; 34) *Heringa.* £60
– – **Anr. Edn.** Ill.:– L. Pissarro. L., Eragny Pr., [1906]. (175). Orig. bds. (D. Dec.11-13; 1102) DM 450
– The Workes. L., 1616 [-1640]. 1st. Coll. Edn. 2 vols. Fo. Without preliminary blank in vol. 1 as usual, some ll. lightly browned, engraved title in vol. 1 by William Hole in 2nd. state. Maroon lev. mor. gt. by Rivière. [STC 14751] (CNY. Oct.1; 101) $1,400
– – **Anr. Edn.** 1692. 3rd. fo. Edn. Fo. Cont. mott. cf., rebkd. & reprd. in mor. [Wing J1006] (SH. Oct.9; 11) *Duran.* £100
– – **Anr. Edn.** 1875. Gifford's Liby. Edn. 9 vols. Hf. mor. (CE. Dec.4; 239) £65
– The Workes.–[The Workes . . . Second Volume]. 1616-1640. 1st. Edns. 2 vols. Fo. Engraved title to vol. I with Greg's 1st. imprint, engraved port. by Vaughan inserted as frontis. in vol. I (in both states). Spr. cf. gt. by Bedford. Bkplts. of F.A. Marshall, Lefferts, Lewisohn, & Blairhame. [STC 14751; 14754] (C. Nov.19; 104) *Thomas.* £2,000

JONSON, Ben & others
– The Widdow. 1652. 1st. Edn. 4to. Upr. outer corners frayed, occasionally affecting text, running-title sometimes cropped, each lf. laminated on both sides with gauze. Recent mor. [Wing J1015] (C. Nov.19; 105) *Quaritch.* £80

JONSSON, Arngrimr
– Brevis Commentarius de Islandia . . . Copen., 1593. 1st. Edn. Light stains & some early marginal notes, early Latin inscr. on title. 17th. C. qtr. cf. gt. (S. Oct.20; 120) *Hannas.* £800

JONSTON, John
See–**BURCHIUS, Lambertus van der–ANDREAS –JONSTON, John**

JONSTON, John
See–**JOHNSTONE or JONSTON, Dr. John, Naturalist**

JORDAN, Alexis & Fourreau, Jules
– Icones ad Floram Europae novo fundamento instaurandam Spectantes. Paris, 1866-70. 2 vols. 4to. Hf. mor. From collection of Massachusetts Horticultural Society, stps. on plts. (SPB. Oct.1; 135) $2,100

JORDAN, J.
See–**FROSSARD, Edward & Jordan, J.**

JORDANUS, Nemorarius
– Opusculum de Ponderositate Nicolai Tartaleae studio correctum. Venice, 1565. Sm. 4to. Mod. bds. Bkplt. of Stillman Drake; from Honeyman Collection. (S. May 20; 3269) *Fletcher.* £260
See–**SACROBOSCO, Johannes de–FABER Stapulensis [Jacobus]–JORDANUS, Nemorarius**

JORDENS, K.H.
– Lexikon dt. Dichter u. Prosaisten. Leipzig, 1806-11. 5 pts. & supp. in 6 vols. Lightly browned thro.-out. Cont. hf. leath. gt., cold. end-papers. (HK. May 15; 4525) DM 500

JOSEPH BEN DAVID IBN YACHYAH
– Torah Or. Bologna, 1538. [1st. Edn.?]. Lacks title, worming in upr. outer corner, reprd. affecting text. Antique style mor. W.a.f. (C. Jul.16; 310) *Pizan.* £160
– – **Anr. Copy.** 4to. Repairs, worming, staining & browning. Mod. hf. leath. (SPB. May 11; 136) $950

JOSEPH Ben Gurion
– Josippon. Constantinople, Aug., 1510. 4to. Marginal glosses in Hebrew & German, worming affecting some letters, stained. Blind-tooled leath., raised bands & title in Fr. on spine, in cl. covered folding box, worming, torn. (SPB. May 11; 83) $27,000

JOSEPH DAVID OF SALONIKI
– Batei Avot. Saloniki, 1825. Slight discolouration & worming. Cl. (S. Nov.18; 743) *Rabinovitch.* £50

JOSEPH, Erzherzog von Osstereich
– Atlas der Heilpflanzen des Praelaten Kneipp. Ill.:– Margarete Furstin von Thurn und Taxis. [Regensburg], 1903. 1st. Edn. 4to. Port of Sebastian Knepp tipped in. Cont. mor., bkplt. (S. Feb.23; 64) *Quaritch.* £260

JOSEPH JOSKE BEN YITZHAK of Constantin
– Yesod Joseph.–Likutei Joseph. Minkowitch, 1803. 2nd. Edn. (1st. work). 2 works in 1 vol. 4to. 1st. work: 2 ll. on blue paper, last lf reprd. with loss of text, 2nd. work: wanting last 2 ll., some tears without loss of text. Hf. leath. (S. Nov.18; 438) *Freedman.* £70

JOSEPHUS, Flavius
– De Antiquitatibus ac de Bello Judaico. Venice, 23. x. 1499. Fo. Title stpd & with old MS. owner's mark, slightly soiled in parts, slightly wormed at end. Cont. wood bds., vell. pasted over spine, remains of old paper bdg., 19th. C. paper pasted on covers, 2 clasps. (HK. Nov.18-21; 217) DM 2,400
– De Bello Iudacio in Lingua Toscana. Flor., Jul. 1512. Fo. Sm. hole in i8, long tear in p7, holes in

last lf., all affecting text, last lf. with a few letters in facs., margin of r3 reprd., slightly affecting text, margins of 1st. & last gatherings strengthened, minor worming in text from q3 on. Antique-style mor. gt. (C. Apr.1; 144) *Nicholas.* £70
- **De Bello Judaico; De Antiquitate Judaeorum contra Apionem.** Ed.:– [Ludovicus Cendrata]. Trans.:– [Rufinus Aquileiensis]. Verona, Petrus Maufer, 25 Dec. 1480. Fo. Spaces for initial capitals, lacks blank fo. 3, 1st. 48 ll. supplied from anr. copy, lr. corner of fo. 1 renewed with loss of some letters in 3 lines, next 7 ll. with sm. repairs & restorations to margins, minor worming to last few ll., last 4 with sm. portions of lr. corners & fore-edge torn away. Hf. mor., gt.-lettered spine. From the collection of Eric Sexton. [BMC VII, 951, Goff J484, HC 9452*] (CNY. Apr.8; 201) $1,600
- **Historien und Bücher: Von Alten Jüdischen Krieg. Geschichten Zwentig ... [Nebst] Egesippi fünff Bücher vom Jüdischen Krieg.** Ill.:– T. Stimmer. Strassburg, 1587. Fo. Cont. blind-tooled pig-bkd. wood bds., clasps brkn., defect. (R. Oct.14-18; 88) DM 1,600
- **Opera.** Basle, 1544. 1st. Edn. of Greek text. Fo. Capital spaces with guide letters, sm. piece cut from lr. margin of title. Cont. blind-stpd. vell., upr. jnt. defect. (S. Jan.27; 373) *Symonds.* £300
- – **Anr. Copy.** Remains of a later paper slip near upr. edge of title, tears in outer edges of title & some following ll. caused by tie-nails, some short tears, some marginal stains & inscrs. Cont. blind-stpd. cf. on bds., figures in borders & compartments, very worn, spine defect., lacks ties. Bkplt. of the Convent at Woodchester. (S. Feb.10; 233) *Thomas.* £220
- **Opera Omnia Graece et Latine.** Ed.:– J. Hudson, E. Bernard, H. Reland, S. Havercamp & others. Amst., Leiden & Utrecht, 1726. 2 vols. Slightly browned. Cont. marb. cf., gt. (R. Oct.14-18; 1256) DM 650
- **Sämtliche Werke.** Tübingen, 1736. 2 vols. in 1. Fo. Cont. vell. (SG. Sep.25; 177) $170
- **Works.** Trans.:– Thomas Lodge. [L.], 1609. Fo. Disbnd. (SG. Sep.25; 176) $180
- – **Anr. Edn.** Trans.:– Sir Roger l'Estrange. 1702. L.P. Fo. Cont. mor., gt. panel., rebkd. preserving old spine. (S. Nov.24; 179) *Fletcher.* £160
- – **Anr. Edn.** 1716. 3rd. Edn. 3 vols. Cont. cf., spines worn. (CSK. Aug.22; 74) £75

JOSEPHUS, Flavius–EGESIPPUS
- **Des Hochberuhmten Judischen Geschichtschreibers und Bucher.–Funff Bücher.** [Colophon: Strassburg], [colophon: 1578]. 2 vols. in 1. Fo. Title of 1st. work torn & reprd., pt. of lr. margin excised, some ll. torn, spotted & dampstained. Cont. blind-stpd. pig over bevelled wooden bds., brass corner bosses, lacks clasps, lr. cover reprd. (CSK. Jan.30; 37) £160

JOSSELYN, John
- **New-Englands Rarities Discovered ...** L., 1672. 1st. Edn. 16mo. Lf. of advts., ex-liby. stp. on several pp., 2 ll. & folding woodcut in facs. & repairs with tape, without damage to text, dragon woodcut mntd., & appears after advts. Mod. cf. (SG. Jan.8; 227) $1,100

JOUBERT DE L'HIBERDERIE
- **Le Dessinateur, pour les Fabriques d'Etoffes d'Ore, d'Argent etc.** 1765. No bdg. stated. (P. Oct.23; 293) *Sims & Reed.* £120

JOUFFROY, Alain
- **Les Anagrammes du Corps.** Ill.:– Hans Bellmer. Paris, 1973. (125) sigd. Fo. 10 engraved plts. Orig. wraps., unsewn as iss. in cl. folder & s.-c., soiled. (SPB. May 6; 156) $1,200
- **L'Antechambre de la Nature.** Ill.:– Wilfredo Lam. Paris, 1966. (15) exemplaires de collaborateurs on Rives B.F.K., sigd. by author & artist, numbered. Fo. Unsewn in orig. wraps., unc., folder & s.-c. (SH. Nov.21; 362) *Landau.* £100

JOUGLA DE MORENAS, Henri
- **Grand Armorial de France.** Paris, 1934-74. 6 vols. & 1 vol. supp. 4to. Mod. bdg. (LM. Nov.8; 205) B.Frs. 13,000

JOUHANDEAU, Marcel
- **Petit Bestiare.** Ill.:– Marie Laurencin. Paris, 1944. (30) with extra set of ills. in 3 variant states. Slight offsetting. Unsewn in orig. wraps., folder & s.-c., unc. (SH. Nov.21; 382) *Henderson.* £360
- – **Anr. Edn.** Ill.:– Marie Laurencin. Paris, 1944. (358) numbered. (SH. Nov.21; 383) *Kawamatsu.* £270

JOUHANNEAUD, Abbé Paul
- **Album des Voyages Anciens et Modernes.** Limoges & Paris, 1854. Lge. 8vo. Cont. buckram, smooth decor. spine. (HD. Jun.25; 295) Frs. 1,200
- – **Anr. Edn.** Limoges & Paris, 1858. Lge. 8vo. Cont. buckram, smooth decor. spine. (HD. Jun.25; 296) Frs. 1,200

JOUJOU des Demoiselles (Le)
Ill.:– Le Mire after Eisen (frontis. & title). N.p., n.d. Cont. marb. cf., decor. spine with Arms of Duke of Orleans. (HD. Apr.10; 343) Frs. 1,700

JOURDAIN, Francis
See–MIRBEAU, Octave & others

JOURDAIN, Margaret & Lenygon, Francis
- **English Decoration & Furniture (1500-1820).** Batsford, [1914-22]. 4 vols. 4to. Orig. cl. (CSK. Nov.21; 38) £80
- – **Anr. Edn.** 1924-27. 4 vols. 4to. Cl., d.-w.'s. (P. Sep.11; 310) *Collins.* £100
- **Library of Decorative Art: English Decoration & Furniture of the Early Renaissance.–Decoration in England from 1640-1760.–Furniture in England from 1660-1760.–English Decoration & Furniture of the Later 18th. Century.** Batsford, 1924-27. 4 vols. Fo. Orig. cl. in slightly torn d.-w.'s. (TA. Oct.16; 115) £130

JOURNAL DES CHASSEURS
Paris, [Oct. 1836-Sep. 1850]. Yrs. 1-4. 14 vols. Lacks 5 plts., not collated, slightly soiled in parts. Unif. cont. hf. leath., vol. 2 cover renewed. (R. Oct. 14-18; 2791) DM 1,800

JOURNAL DES DAMES ET DES MODES
[Paris], 1809. Some plts. slightly soiled. Cont. bds., worn. (HK. Nov.18-21; 1799) DM 1,000
- – **Anr. Run.** Paris, 1817-18, 1820. 2 vols. Glazed hf. cf. (HD. Jun.29; 45) Frs. 2,050
- – **Anr. Run.** 1819-33. 15 vols. Approx. 1,066 hand-cold. engraved plts., lacks plt. 11 for 1824 & few others, liby. stp. on most titles. Cont. bds. As a periodical, w.a.f. (C. May 20; 145) *Hammond.* £2,400
- – **Anr. Run.** Ed.:– J.P. Lemaire. Frankfurt, Jul.-Dec. 1844. 47th. year. Plts. browned thro.-out. Cont. bds. (HK. May 12-14; 1154) DM 420
- – **Anr. Run.** Ill.:– Barbier. Paris, 1912-14. 4 vols. Orig. wraps., unc., in portfo. & boxes. (SI. Dec.3; 298) Lire 2,900,000

JOURNAL DES DEMOISELLES
Paris, 1855-87. Vols. 23-55 in 21. Cont. cf.-bkd. bds. (SH. Jan.29; 252) *Walford.* £580
- – **Anr. Edn.** L., 1867-73. Vols. 35 & 41. 4 folding & 96 hand-cold. plts. Qtr. cf. As a collection of plts., w.a.f. (P. Jun.11; 281) *Map House.* £180
- – **Anr. Edn.** Paris, 1871-95. Vols. 39-63. 4to. Cont. roan-bkd. cl., gt. (SH. Oct.9; 12) *Walford.* £720

JOURNAL des Modes–MODE, LA
1831-33; 1831. 2 works in 6 vols. Some dampstaining. Cont. roan, worn. (HD. Jun.25; 297) Frs. 2,100

JOURNAL-MANUEL de Peintures
Paris, 1855-69. Vols. 6-20 in 3. Lge. fo. Occasional marginal staining. Covers loose, cl. spines worn. (SG. Nov.20; 367) $220

JOURNAL OF AMERICAN HISTORY
[New Haven], 1907-08. 2 vols. 4to. Hf. leath. (SG. Jun.11; 194) $110

JOURNAL of Glass Studies
Corning, N.Y., 1959-76. Vols. I-XIV, & Special Bicentennial Iss. Vol. XVIII. 4to. Wraps. (SG. Mar.12; 219) $425

JOURNAL POUR RIRE
Ed.:– Ch. Philipon. Ill.:– Delaroche, Miderich, Belin, Morin, etc. Paris, 8 Feb. 1848-24 Jan. 1851. Nos.1-156. Hf. chagrin (LM. Jun.13; 41) B.Frs. 12,000

JOUTEL, Henri
- **Journal Historique du dernière Voyage que feu M. de la Sale fit dans la golfe de Mexique pour trouver l'embouchure & le Cours de la rivière de Missicipi ... la Louisiane.** Paris, 1713. 1st. Edn. 12mo. Cont. cf., lacks label. [Sabin 36760] (C. Feb.25; 104a) *Brooke-Hitching.* £700
- – **Anr. Copy.** Cont. cf., spine gt., hf. mor. s.-c. (SG. Oct.9; 138) $1,700

- **A Journal of the Last Voyage Perform'd by Monsr. de la Sale to the Gulph of Mexico, to Find out the Mouth of the Mississipi (sic) River ...** L., 1714. 1st. Edn. in Engl. Folding map torn & reprd., silked on verso, slight staining. Mod. mor., gt. spine & borders. From liby. of William E. Wilson. [Sabin 36762] (SPB. Apr.29; 163) $950

JOUVANCOURT, Hugues de
- **Clarence Gagnon.** Ill.:– Edwin Holgate (port.). Montreal, [1970]. (200) initialled & numbered. 4to. Orig. mor., raised bands, gt. marb. end-ll., felt-lined marb. s.-c. (CB. Feb.18; 146) Can. $1,200

JOUVIN, A.
- **Le Voyageur d'Europe où est le Voyage de Turquie.** Paris, 1676. 12mo. Ink stains on 1 lf., Franchetti bkplt. Cont. red mor., gt., arms of Simon Arnauld, Marquis de Pomponne, his cipher in corners, covers semé with palm fronds & mountains, charges from arms, spines gt. in compartments with fleurons, inner gt. dentelles. (SM. Oct.7; 1775) Frs. 7,000

JOVIUS or Giovio, Bp. Paulus
- **Elogie Virorum Bellica Virtute illustrium. Elogia Virorum Literis Illustrium.** Petri, 1575; 1577. 2 vols. Fo. Old vell. (BS. Jun.11; 109) £240
- – **Anr. Edn.** Basle, 1577 [1575]. 2 works in 1 vol. Fo. 2nd. work lacks last blank, 1 or 2 wormholes, 18th. C. ownership inscr. on 1st. title of Corberan de la Fosse, inscr. at foot 'Coepi volvere 3 November 1655' & on final lf. 'Absolvi 22 December 1655'. 18th. C. cf., triple gt. fillet, spine compartments gt. à la grotesque, inner gt. dentelles. (SM. Oct.7; 1776) Frs. 3,000

JOYANT, Maurice
- **Henri de Toulouse-Lautrec.** Paris, 1926-27. 2 vols. 4to. Cl., orig. wraps. bnd. in. (C. Jul.22; 148) *Sims & Reed.* £170
- – **Anr. Edn.** Ill.:– Henri de Toulouse Lautrec. Paris, 1927. 4to. Hf. cf., orig. upr. wrap. bnd. in. (SH. Nov.21; 488) *Toole Stott.* £70

JOYCE, James
- **Anna Livia Plurabelle.** Ed.:– Padraic Colum. N.Y., 1928. 1st. Edn., (800) sigd. Orig. cl. (SH. Dec.18; 192) *Garbor.* £190
- – **Anr. Copy.** 12mo. (C. Feb.4; 284) *Gekowski.* £170
- – **Anr. Copy.** (CSK. Sep.5; 200) £130
- – **Anr. Copy.** 12mo. Orig. bdg. (SPB. Nov.25; 312) $550
- – **Anr. Copy.** Cl. (SG. Jun.4; 246) $425
- – **Anr. Copy.** Gt.-decor. cl. (SG. Nov.13; 384) $320
- **Chamber Music.** 1907. 1st. Edn., 2nd. variant. Orig. cl. (SH. Dec.18; 191) *Barry Scott.* £160
- **Dubliners.** 1914. 1st. Edn. Lacks upr. end-lf. Orig. cl. (S. Jul.22; 185) *Treadwell.* £110
- **Finnegans Wake.** 1939. 1st. Edn. Orig. cl., d.-w. 'Corrections of Misprints' loosely inserted. (SH. Dec.18; 196) *Blackwell.* £95
- – **Anr. Copy.** (P. Jul.2; 180) *Roberts.* £85
- – **Anr. Edn.** L. & N.Y., 1939. 1st. Edn., (425) numbered, sigd. Many pencil marks. Orig. cl. Marked 'Out of Series', disbnd. & revised for new edn., revisions ptd. & pasted in, pp. 547-54 compl. reset on separate sheets. (SH. Dec.18; 197) *House of Books.* £420
- – **Anr. Copy.** This copy unnumbered & unsigd. Orig. buckram, s.-c. 'Corrections of Misprints' (1945) loosely inserted. (SH. Dec.18; 194) *Schrire.* £160
- – **Anr. Copy.** Unopened, cl. box. 'Corrections of Misprints in Finnegans Wake', L., 1945, laid in. (CNY. May 22; 139) $1,100
- – **Anr. Edn.** L., [1939]. 1st. Edn. Cl., d.-w. (CNY. Jun.4; 248) $500
- **The Mime of Mick Nick & the Maggies.** Ill.:– Lucia Joyce. The Hague, 1934. 1st. Edn., (1029), unnumbered. Orig. wraps., unc., unopened, s.-c. (SH. Dec.18; 193) *Gekoski.* £55
- – **Anr. Edn.** The Hague & c., 1934. [1st. Edn.]. Wraps., s.-c., unc. & unopened. (KH. Mar.24; 215) Aus. $230
- **A Portrait of the Artist as a Young Man.** N.Y., 1916. 1st. Edn. 12mo. Cl. (SG. Jun.4; 237) $75
- **Storiella as She is Syung.** L., 1937. 1st. Edn., (176). 4to. Orig. vell., box., worn. (SPB. Nov.25; 314) $950
- – **Anr. Edn.** Ill.:– Lucia Joyce. [Corvinus Pr.], [Oct. 1937]. 1st. Edn. (125) numbered. 4to. Orig. limp vell., unc., s.-c. Inscr. for L.A.G. Strong from

JOYCE, James-*contd.*
(Viscount) Carlow' (printer, Corvinus Pr.). (S. Jun.9; 70) *Blackwell.* £480
- **Tales Told of Shem & Shaun: Three Fragments from Work in Progress.** Paris, Black Sun Pr., priv. ptd. 1929. 1st. Edn. (100) numbered sigd. by Author. Ptd. wraps., tissue wrap., boxed, faded & separated at 1 seam. (PNY. Oct.1; 311) $1,000
- **Ulysse . . .** Trans.:– Valérie Larbaud. 1929. 1st. Edn. in Fr.; (25) on Holland. 4to. Old rose mor. by Semet & Plumelle, spine & covers decor. with mosaic & gt. fillets, buckskin doubls. & end-papers, wrap. & spine preserved, folder, s.-c. From liby. of Dr. Lucien Graux. (HD. Jun.25; 298) *Frs.* 8,500
- **Ulysses.** Paris, Egoist Pr. 1922. 1st. Edn. for England, (2000). 4to. Orig. wraps., unc. (C. Feb.4; 319) *Stewart.* £160
- – **Anr. Copy.** Minor browning, a few tears. Spine & corners reprd., soiled, chipped, mor.-bkd. folding box. (SPB. May 6; 201) $375
- – **Anr. Edn.** (2000) numbered on H.M.P. 4to. Lacks errata ll. Crude leath., orig. wraps. bnd. in (SG. Jun.4; 240) $250
- – **Anr. Edn.** (1000) numbered. Orig. wraps., backstrip torn. (CSK. Dec.12; 190) £240
- – **Anr. Edn.** (100) numbered & sigd. Colophon lf. creased, 2 final blank ll. reprd., some offsetting on verso of hf.-title. Oasis, cf. onlay lettering, silk end-papers, orig. wraps. mntd., oasis fold-down box, by Gerard Charrière. (SG. Nov.13; 383) $5,000
- – **Anr. Edn.** (750) numbered on H.M.P. Wraps., unc., partly unopened, hf. mor. s.-c. (SG. Jun.4; 238) $4,000
- – **Anr. Copy.** Browned. Disbnd., orig. wraps. bnd. in, soiled. (SPB. Jul.28; 200) $325
- – **Anr. Edn.** (750) numbered. Lacks spine & lr. wrap. (SG. Jun.4; 239) $275
- – **Anr. Edn.** N.Y., 1934. Publisher's dummy of 1st. authorized American Edn. Includes title, copyright p., Foreword, 1st. few pp. of text & text of letter from Joyce to Cerf. Orig. cl., d.-w. (SPB. Nov.25; 313) $1,500
- – **Anr. Edn.** Ed.:– Stuart Gilbert. Ill.:– Henri Matisse. N.Y., [Ltd. Edns. Cl.], 1935. (1500) numbered, & sigd. by artist. Gt. pict. buckram, in publisher's box. Sigd. at end by artist. (GM. Apr.30; 384) £1,400
- – **Anr. Copy.** 4to. Orig. buckram, gt., unc. (SH. Nov.21; 412) *Jamieson.* £460
- – **Anr. Copy.** This copy unnumbered. Orig. cl., publisher's box, box worn. 6 orig. etchings by Matisse, each with reproductions of the prelim. studies. (SPB. May 6; 216) $1,500
- – **Anr. Copy.** 4to. Gt.-pict. cl., boxed, some wear. (PNY. Mar.4; 179) $1,300
- – **Anr. Edn.** (PNY. Dec.3; 216) $1,000
- – **Anr. Copy.** (SG. Apr.2; 194) $800
- – **Anr. Edn.** 1936. 1st. Engl. Edn. (100) numbered on mould-made paper sigd. 4to. Orig. cf. vell. gt., designed by Eric Gill, partly unc., s.-c. (C. Jul.22; 16) *Joseph.* £750
- – **Anr. Copy.** (1000). Hf.-vell. On H.M.P. & sigd. (SH. Dec.19; 565) *Nolan.* £430

JOYCE, P.W.
- **The Origin & History of Irish Names of Places.** Dublin, 1910-13. 3 vols. Orig. cl., gt. (GM. Apr.30; 126) £60

JOYNER, William
- **The Roman Empress.** 1671. 1st. Edn. 4to. Sm. hole in 1 lf. slightly affecting text. Mor. by Sangorski. [Wing J1159] (C. Nov.19; 106) *Ludgrove.* £120

JUAN, Jorge
- **Compendio de Navegacion para el uso de los Cavalleros Guardias-marinas.** Cadiz, 1757. 1st. Edn. 4to. Lightly stained at beginning. Cont. mott. sheep, gt. spine. (S. Nov.4; 475) *Duran.* £130
See–ULLOA, Antonio de & Juan, Jorge

JUCH, Carl Wilhelm (Ed.)
See–PHARMACOPOEA BORUSSICA . . .

JUDISCHES LEXIKON
Ed.:– Georg Herlitz & Bruno Kirschner. Berlin, 1927-30. 5 vols. Hf. leath. (S. Nov.18; 536) *Bloch.* £130
- – **Anr. Copy.** Orig. hf. leath. (R. Mar.31-Apr.4; 205) DM 1,100

JUGEL, Ch.
- **Rheinisches Album.** Frankfort-a-Main, 1844. Ob. 4to. Orig. cf.-bkd. bds., worn. (S. Mar.31; 482) *Schuster.* £620

- **Souvenirs Pittoresques du Rhin.** Frankfurt, 1826. Ob. 4to. Soiled in parts. Orig. bds., soiled, loose. (R. Mar.31-Apr.4; 2177) DM 950

JUGEND
Ed.:– G. Hirth. Munich, 1891-97. 9 vols. 4to. Orig. linen, 2 spines defect., slightly soiled. (H. Dec.9/10; 2120) DM 760
- – **Anr. Run.** 1901-02. 4 vols. 4to. Orig. wraps. bnd. in Cl. (P. Feb.19; 57) £130
- – **Anr. Run.** Munich, For 1901-15. 29 vols. only, lacks pt. 2 for 1910. 4to. Orig. pict. cl. (SG. Apr.2; 145) $500

JULIE PHILOSOPHE, ou Le Bon Patriote
N.p., 1791. 2 vols. 18mo. 7 figures (only 6 called for). Cont. hf. chagrin, spines decor. in rocaille style, ca. 1830. (HD. Apr.10; 345) *Frs.* 2,000
- – **Anr. Copy.** Crude red three qtr. mor. (SG. Sep.4; 35) $200

JULIEN, R.J.
- **Atlas Topographique et Militaire.** Paris, 1758. 4to. Cont. cf. (CSK. Nov.7; 49) £100

JULIEN le Bibliophile (Pseud.)
See–LACROIX, Paul 'Julien le Bibliophile'

JULLIEN, Adolphe
- **Hector Berlioz.** Ill.:– Fantin-Latour. 1888. 4to. Cont. hf. mor. (C. Jul.22; 78) *Ortiz.* £260

JUNCKER, Chr.
- **Das Guldene und Silberne Ehren-Gedächtniss des . . . Martini Lvtheri.** Frankfurt & Leipzig, 1706. Cont. vell., slightly defect. (H. Dec.9/10; 1357a) DM 520

JUNG-STILLING, H.
- **Das Heimweh.–Der Schlüssel zum Heimwe.** 1794-96. 1st. Edn. 5 vols. Slightly soiled in parts, vol. IV wormed in lr. margin. Hf. leath. (HK. May 15; 4526) DM 950
- **Versuch eines Lehrbuchs d. Forstwirthschaft.** Mannheim & Lautern, 1781. 1st. Edn. Vol. 1 (of 2). Cont. leath., gt. spine. (HK. Nov.18-21; 594) DM 800

JÜNGKEN, J.H.–KRAUTERMANN, V. 'C.V. Hellwig'
- **Wohlunterrichtender Sorgfältige Medicus . . . –Curieuser u. Vernünfftiger Urin-Arzt.** Nuremb.; Arnstadt, 1729; 1748. 2 works in 1 vol. Slightly stained at beginning, slightly browned, 2nd. work lacks title & folding plt. Cont. leath., worn. (HK. Nov.18-21; 531) DM 650

JUNGMANN, R.
- **Costumes Moeurs et Usages des Algériens.** Strassburg, 1837. Ob. 4to. 36 plts. (of 39). Cont. hf. roan. (IID. Jun.25; 299) *Frs.* 1,400

JUNIOR, Democritus (Pseud.)
See–BURTON, Robert 'Democritus Junior'

JUNIUS (Pseud.)
See–FRANCIS, Sir Philip 'Junius'

JUNIUS, Franciscus or Du Jon, François, the Younger
- **De Pictura Veterum.** Amst., 1637. 1st. Edn. Sm. 4to. Cont. cf., worn. (SH. Jun.11; 69) *Thorp.* £50
- **Observationes in Willerami Abbatis Francicam Paraphrasin Cantici Canticorum.** Amst., Priv. ptd., 1655. Old name & sm. stp. on title. Cont. vell., soiled, annots. on front end-paper. (VG. Dec.17; 1401) Fls. 450
See–SOMNER, William–JUNIUS, Franciscus –LYE, Edward

JUNKER, Wilhelm
- **Reisen en Afrika 1875-86.** Ed.:– R. Buchta. Vienna & Olmütz, 1889-91. 3 vols. Orig. pict. linen, slightly soiled. (R. Mar.31-Apr.4; 2356) DM 720

JURGENS, A.A.
- **The Handstruck Letter Stamps of the Cape of Good Hope 1792-1853 & the Postmarks 1853-1910.** Cape Town, [1943]. Subscriber's Edn. (200) sigd. 4to. Orig. bdg. (VA. Oct.31; 553) R. 110

JUSTEL, Henri
- [-] **Recueil de divers Voyages faits en Afrique et en l'Amérique.** Paris, 1674. 1st. Edn. 4to. 4 folding maps, including the lge. map of the Nile on 4 sheets pasted together, slight staining on some ll., minor marginal repairs, slight tears, lacks F4 (probably blank). Vell., slightly soiled. [Sabin 36944] (SPB. May 5; 291) $600

JUSTI, F.
- **Hessisches Trachetenbuch.** Marburg, 1905. Fo. Cl. (BS. Jun.11; 355) £55

JUSTINIANUS I, Emperor
- **Institutiones, with the Glossa Ordinaria of Accursius Florentinus.** Nuremb., Anton Koberger, 27 Dec. 1486. Fo. Capital initial I on fo. 2, other spaces for initials left blank, most with guide letters, illuminated miniature of author, lacks final blank lf., some slight worming, cont. inscr. on fo. 1v, followed by a coat-of-arms, MS. contents list on verso. Cont. blind-stpd. & gt. cf. over wood bds., upr. & lr. covers elab. decor., spine with 4 raised bands, each compartment with 2 cartouches, orig. brass fixtures for clasps (lacking), probably bnd. by Jorg Schapf of Augsburg, covers & corners slightly worn, head & foot of spine & sm. piece at fore-edge of lr. cover patched, cl. s.-c. Bkplt. of John A. Saks. [BMC II, 430, Goff J529, HC 9519] (CNY. Oct.1; 99) $6,500
- – **Anr. Edn.** Venice, de Tortis. 1489. Fo. 8 ll. only, comprising folios 4, 5, 68 & 69 of the 1st. book, & folios 97, 104, 140, & 141 of the 2nd. book, heavily rubricated & many initials decor. [Goff 532] (SG. Feb.5; 182) $140
- **Institutiones Imperiales.** Paris, 5 Dec. 1505. 4to. Ownership inscrs. on title, some ll. soiled, tear in f. p2 reprd. affecting text. 18th. C. pol. cf. gt., rebkd. (S. Oct.21; 280) *Burns.* £150
- **Leges de Re Rustica . . .** Trans.:– Francois Badoin. Louvain, Feb. 1542. Sm. 4to. Some browning & soiling. Cont. Netherlandish cf., probably by Jacob Pandelaert, covers with good impression of the 'Spes' panel in blind, sigd. I.P., rebkd., slightly worn, lacks ties. From liby. of André L. Simon. (S. May 18; 125) *Maggs.* £280

JUSTINUS, [Marcus Junianus]
- **Warhafflige Hystorien, die auss Trogs Pompeio gezogé, vn inn Viertzig Vier Bücher aussgeteylt, darinn er v. vil Künigreychen d. Welt . . .** Ill.:– Petrarcameister, J. Breu the older & younger, & others, Augsburg, 1531. 1st. Edn. Fo. Slightly stained or browned in parts, some old notes, lacks last blank lf. Hf. leath. ca. 1800, slightly worn. (HK. Nov.18-21; 219) *Frs.* 3,000

JUVENALIS, Decimus Junius
- **Opus.** Ed.:– Joanne Britannico. Venice, 1548. Fo. 6 unnumbered pp., lacks blank lf. Old vell. (CR. Mar.19; 259) Lire 250,000
- **Satyrae.** Venice, Jannes Tacuinus, de Tridino, 2 Dec., 1492. Fo. Some worming & staining. Mod. cf.-bkd. buckram [BMC V, 527] (S. Nov.25; 343) *Schuster.* £220
- – **Anr. Copy.** Dampstained, mainly in lr. margin, slightly brown in places, some ll. badly affected, wormholes, some affecting a few letters. Mod. cf.-bkd. buckram bds. [BMC V, 527, Goff J662, HC 9709*] (S. Jul.27; 103) *Thorp.* £200
- [-] **Anr. Edn.** Ed.:– Domitii Calderini & Georgii Vallae. Venice, B. Locatellus for O. Scotus, 8 Mar. 1942. Fo. Interleaved copy with MS. verse translation and numerous notes in a 17th. C. hand, all up to 2A6 frayed, slightly affecting text, some dampstaining. 17th. C. panel. cf., head of spine defect. Bkplt. of David Garrick. [BMC V, 439; Goff J658] (S. Jun.23; 214) *Claridge.* £260
- **Satyrographi Opus.** Ed.:– Jodocus Badius Ascensius. Trans:– John Britain. Venice, 1539. Rare Edn. (reprint of 1523 Edn.). Fo. Lr. margin of title cut out. 17th. C. cf., decor. spine. (HD. Feb.18; 31) *Frs.* 1,100
See–HORATIUS Flaccus, Quintus–JUVENALIS, Decimus Junius

JUVENALIS, Decimus Junius & Persius Flaccus, Aulus
- **Satyrae.** Venice, 1501. 1st. Ald. Edn. Liby. stp. on title verso. Later cf., covers detchd. (SG. Sep.25; 11) $350
- [-] **Anr. Edn.** Venice, 1501. Title lightly stained. 19th. C. hf. cf. (SI. Dec.3; 299) Lire 250,000

JUVENILE Miscellany
Boston, 1830-31. New Series. Vol. V, nos. 1-3. 16mo. Containing the 1st. printing of 'Mary's Lamb' in pt. 1, with the inserted plt. for each pt., lacks pp. 5-8 in 1st. pt. Cont. hf. roan & marb. bds., qtr. mor. gt. s.-c. From the Prescott Collection. (CNY. Feb.6; 141) $200

JUVILLE, Jean
- Traité des Bandages Herniaires. Paris, 1786. 1st. Edn. All but 1 plt. hand-cold., occasional offsetting. Cont. sheep, spine gt. (S..Jun.29; 303) *Lange & Springer.* £70

KADEN, Woldemar
- Das Schweizerland. Ill.:– A. Closs. Stuttgart, ca. 1880. Fo. Orig. linen, gold-stpd. (R. Mar.31-Apr.4; 2747) DM 1,900
- – Anr. Copy. Orig. pict. linen. (R. Oct.14-18; 2007) DM 1,600
- – Anr. Edn. Stuttgart, ca. 1890. Fo. Orig. linen. (D. Dec.11-13; 1333) DM 950
- Switzerland, its Mountains & Valleys. 1878. 4to. Orig. cl. (CSK. Feb.27; 22) £280
- – Anr. Copy. Orig. cl. gt. (P. Oct.23; 258) *Dupont.* £260
- – Anr. Copy. Ill.:– A. Closs. L., 1878. Fo. Orig. pict. linen. (R. Mar.31-Apr.4; 2748) DM 1,700
- – Anr. Edn. Ill.:– A. Closs. N.Y., 1879. Fo. Cont. leath., gt. (R. Oct.14-18; 2009) DM 1,600

KADMAN, L.
- Corpus Nummorum Palaestinensium. Jerusalem, 1956-61. 4 vols. Orig. cl. (SH. Mar.6; 383) *Quedar.* £90

KAEMPFER, Englebert
- Amoenitatum Exoticarum Politico–Physico–Medicarum... Lemgo, 1712. 4to. Cont. hf. cf., very worn. (S. Oct.20; 122) *Bjorck & Borjesson.* £900
- – Anr. Copy. 5 pts. in 1 vol. 3 ll. stained, some plts. & ll. slightly browned. Cont. vell., soiled, 2 sm. chain-clasp holes in lr. cover. From Chetham's Liby., Manchester. (C. Nov.27; 223) *Israel.* £550
- – Anr. Copy. Lacks plt. to p. 170. Cont. hf. cf., very worn. W.a.f. (S. Feb.10; 316) *Maggs.* £240
- Histoire Naturelle, Civile et Ecclesiastique de l'empire du Japon ... Trans.:– Jean-Gaspar Scheuchzer. The Hague, 1729. 1st. Fr. Edn. 2 vols. Fo. Owners' inscrs. on title of vol. 1 deleted. Cont. mott. cf., gt. spine. (S. Nov.4; 603) *Nortan.* £900
- The History of Japan. 1727. 1st. Edn. 2 vols. in 1. Fo. 45 engraved plts. & maps, most folding, 1 map torn along fold. Cont. cf., worn, upr. cover detchd. (S. Mar.31; 483) *Maggs.* £800
- – Anr. Copy. 2 vols. Old panel. cf., worn, vol. 2 covers torn & defect. (C. Jul.15; 138) *Remington.* £450
- – Anr. Edn. Trans.:– J.G. Scheuchzer. Priv. Ptd. 1728. 1st. Edn. in Engl. 2 vols. Fo. 44 engraved plts. (of 45, lacks plt. 9). Cont. cf., rebkd. From Chetham's Liby., Manchester. (C. Nov.27; 224) *Remington.* £700
- The History of Japan.–The Second Appendix to ... History of Japan. 1728; 1728. 2 works in 1 vol. 1st. work vol. 2 only. Fo. Old cf. (CSK. Sep.12; 91) £160

KAFKA, Franz
- Betrachtung. Leipzig, 1913. 1st. Edn., (800) numbered. 2 sm. erased entries, some ll. with sm. scratches in upr. margin, lightly soiled in parts. Orig. wraps., unc., slightly defect. (HK. Nov.18-21; 2690) DM 950
- Der Prozess. Berlin, 1925. 1st. Edn. Bds., slight bdg. wear. (SG. Nov.13; 389) $375
- Das Schloss. Munich, 1926. 1st. Edn. Orig. wraps., slightly soiled, d.-w., slightly worn. (SH. Nov.20; 115) *Quaritch.* £70

KAHNWEILER, Daniel Henry
- Les Sculptures de Picasso. Ill.:– from photographs by Brassai. Paris, [1949]. 1st. Edn. Lge. 4to. Cl.-bkd. pict. bds. (SG. Apr.23; 39) $110

KAIN, Saul (Pseud.)
See–SASSOON, Siegfried 'Saul Kain'

KAISER, E.
- Die Diamantenwüste Südwest-Afrikas. Berlin, 1926. 2 vols. 4to. Orig. bdg., d.-w. (VA. Jan.30; 39) R. 340

KAISERSBERG, Geiler von
- Nauicula siue Speculum Fatururu [M]. Ill.:– A. Dürer. Strassburg, 1511. 7 ll. with 7 woodcuts. (HK. Nov.18-21; 330) DM 440

KALENDARIO Manual y Guia de Forasteros
Madrid, 1806. 18mo. Cont. mor., spine with repeated gt. motif, covers with gt. motifs in Greek key pattern border on mosaic ground, mosaic centre motif, inner dentelle, silk doubls. & fly-ll., border Greek key pattern in blind, red mor. s.-c. (HD. Apr.10; 144) Frs. 3,500

KALLIR, Otto
- Egon Schiele: The Graphic Work. N.Y., 1970. (80) with orig. etching. 4to. & fo. Orig. mor.-bkd. cl., etching in cl. folder. (SPB. May 29; 230) $300

KALM, Peter
- Travels into North America. Warrington, 1770. 1st. Edn. in Engl. 3 vols. Lacks folding map, 5 (of 6) plts., slight discolouration. Mod. buckram. From liby. of William E. Wilson. (SPB. Apr.29; 165) $250
- – Anr. Edn. Warrington & L., 1770-71. 1st. Engl. Edn. 3 vols. With dupls. of the 3 ornithological plts., but lacks folding map & title-p. to vol. 1. Disbnd. W.a.f. [Sabin 36989] (CB. Feb.18; 118) Can. $200

KALMYKOVA, Mariya
See–BAYAN, Vadim & others

KALONYMOS BEN KALONYMOS
- Eben Bohan. Cremona, 1558. 3rd. Edn. Sm. 4to. Roan-bkd. bds. (C. Jul.16; 311) *Kornaluth.* £220

KAMES, Henry Home, Lord
- Elements of Criticism. Edinb., 1769. 4th. Edn. 2 vols. Cont. red mor., spines gt. (S. Nov.24; 180) *Fletcher.* £85
[–] The Gentleman Farmer. Being an Attempt to improve Agriculture, by subjecting it to the test of Rational Principles. Edinb., 1788. 3rd. Edn. Advt. lf., slight browning. 19th. C. hf cf by J. Edmond, Aberdeen, with his ticket, spine gt. (S. Nov.4; 563) *Brook-Hitching.* £60

KAMPEN, Nicolaas G. Von
- The History & Topography of Holland & Belgium. Ill.:– W.H. Bartlett. 1837. Orig. cl., worn. (CE. Jul.9; 90) £95
- – Anr. Edn. Trans.:– W.G. Fearnside. Ill.:– after W.H. Bartlett. L., ca. 1840. Cont. hf. leath. (R. Oct.14-18; 1897) DM 650
- – Anr. Copy. Cont. linen, loose, lacks spine. (R. Mar.31-Apr.4; 2648) DM 560
- Holland und Belgien. Trans.:– J. von Horn. Ill.:– after W.H. Bartlett. L., ca. 1840. Plts. slightly soiled & browned. Cont. linen, slightly soiled. (H. Dec.9/10; 598) DM 510
- Vues de la Hollande et de la Belgique. Ill.:– after W.H. Bartlett. L., ca. 1840. Plts. stained at margins & slightly soiled. Cont. linen, bumped & soiled. (R. Mar.31-Apr.4; 2650) DM 560

KANDINSKY, Vasily V.
- Kandinsky 1901-1913. Berlin, [1913]. Ob. 4to. Orig. pict. wraps., worn. (SH. Nov.21; 352) *Reed & Sims.* £50
- Tekst Khudozhnika [Text of the Artist]. Moscow, 1918. Fo. Mod. cl. (SH. Feb.6; 322) *Kazinikas.* £160
- – Anr. Copy. Fo. Cold. plt. loose. Orig. wraps., torn, spine reprd. (SH. Feb.5; 226) *Reed & Sims.* £150
- Uber das Geistige in der Kunst. Munich, 1912. 1st. Edn. Orig. wraps. & tie. (HK. Nov.18-21; 2695) DM 1,400

KANDINSKY, Wassily (Ed.)
See–BLAUE REITER, Der
See–STAATLICHESBAUMAUS WEIMAR

KANDINSKY, Wassily & Marc, Franz
- Der Blaue Reiter. Munich, 1912. 1st. Edn. 4to. Linen with lr. wrap. with cold woodcut pasted on, lr. wrap loose. (R. Mar.31-Apr.4; 528) DM 3,600
- – Anr. Edn. Munich, 1914. 4to. Orig. bds., spine torn, browned & soiled. (H. May 21/22; 1661) DM 900

KANDLER, W.
See–KAPPER, S. & Kandler, W.

KANE, Elisha Kent
- Arctic Explorations ... in Search of Sir John Franklin. Phila., 1856. 2 vols. Occasional light foxing. Orig. cl., unc. [Sabin 37001] (S. Jul.27; 24) *Bickersteth.* £80

KANT, Immanuel
- Critick of Pure Reason. 1836. 1st. Engl. Edn. 2 ll. publisher's advts. at beginning, errata lf. at end. Orig. cl. rebkd. retaining orig. spine, unc., partly unopened. (S. Oct.21; 430) *Bennett-Gilbert.* £140
- Critik der Reinen Vernunft. Riga, 1751. 1st. Edn. Lightly soiled in places, at beginning 1 p. with 2 sm. pasted old marginalia, ink stain in margin near end. Cont. hf. leath. gt. (HK. May 15; 4532) DM 4,200

- Critik der Urtheilskraft. Berlin, & Libau, 1790. 1st. Edn. Some underlining & notes. Cont. marb. bds. gt. (HK. May 15; 4533) DM 1,400
- – Anr. Copy. 1st. ll. slightly soiled, underlining on p. 3. 19th. C. hf. leath., gt. spine, 3 sm. wormholes. (R. Oct.14-18; 1316) DM 1,300
- Die Religion innerhalb der Grenzen der blossen Vernunft. Königsberg, 1793. 1st. Edn. Lacks last blank. Cont. bds. (S. Oct.21; 429) *Lockwood.* £80
- Werke. Ed.:– E. Cassirer, H. Cohen, A. Buchenau & others. Berlin, 1912-18. (100) Privilege Edn. on van Geldern Bütten. Orig. marb. leath., gt. spine, cover & outer dentelle. W.a.f. (HK. May 15; 4529) DM 2,200

KANT, Imogen
- Zum Ewigen Frieden. Königsberg, 1795. 1st. Edn., 1st. printing. Some sm. stains in parts & browning, owner's mark on title. Cont. bds., very soiled. (H. May 21/22; 1173) DM 800

KAPLAN, E.I. & others
- Revizor Veatre Imeni Vs. Meierkhol'da [The Government Inspector at the Meyerhold Theatre]. Leningrad, 1927. (3100). Orig. wraps. by Kaplan, spotted. (SH. Feb.6; 323) *Kent University.* £55

KAPPER, S. & Kandler, W.
- Das Böhmerland. Prag, 1865. Slightly soiled in parts. Cont. hf. leath. (R. Oct.14-18; 1953) DM 600

KARL, of Braunschweig, Duke
- Serenissimi Gnaedigste Verordung die Zwischen den Messen Anherskommenden Juden Betreffend. 6 Aug. 1770. Fo. 4 ll. Unbnd. (S. Nov.18; 617) *Konig.* £220

KARLSON, W.
- Lundensiskt Silversmide. Lund, 1952. Light dampstains. Cont. cl. (SH. Jul.23; 288) *Sims & Reed.* £55

KARO, Joseph
- Shulchan Aruch. Ed.:– Moshe Isserles & Gur Aryeh (commentaries). Mantua, 1721-23. 1st. Edn. of Aryeh's commentary. 4 pts. in 3 vols. 4to. 1 title with pictures of Rashi & others in facs., some staining, cropped, tears & repairs, browning. Various bdgs. (SPB. May 11; 138) $275
- – Anr. Edn. Jerusalem, 1961. 10 vols. Fo. Cl. (S. Nov.18; 744) *Kornblutt.* £75
- Shulchan Aruch-Orach Chaim & Yore De'ah. Ed.:– Moshe Isserles (glosses). Berlin, 1693-1700. 12mo. Slight staining. Vell., worn, stained. (SPB. May 11; 137) $375

KARO, Yitzhak
- Toldot Yitzhak. Constantinople. 1518. 1st. Edn. Sm. fo. Margins reprd., last 2 ll. reprd. with loss of words, some staining, slight worming. Mod. cl. (SPB. May 11; 84) $3,500

KARPINSKI, Louis C.
- Bibliography of Mathematical Works Printed in America. 1940. 4to. Cl. (SG. Mar.26; 286) $210
- – Anr. Copy. Minor browning, slight stains. Stain on spine, MS. notes on end-papers. From liby. of William E. Wilson. (SPB. Apr.29; 166) $200

KARR, Alphonse
- Voyage autour de mon Jardin. Ill.:– Freeman, L. Marvy, Steinheil, Meissonier & others. Paris, 1851. 1st. Printing. Lge. 8vo. Buckram, covers & spine decor. with special gt. mosaic stps. engraved by Harhaus, publisher's s.-c. (HD. Dec.5; 110) Frs. 1,400

KARSAVINA, Tamara Platonovna
- Brodyachaya Sobaka [Stray Dog]. [St. Petersb.], [1914]. (200). 4to. Sm. dampstain at head. Orig. cl.-bkd. wraps. by S. Sudeikin, loose. (SH. Feb.6; 448) *Dance Books.* £190

KARSTEN, Karl Heinrich Gustav Hermann
- Florae Columbiae Terrarumque adiacentium specimina selecta. Berlin, 1858-69. 2 vols. Fo. Some plts. stained by colourist. Cont. hf. mor. gt., vol. 2 spine damaged. From collection of Massachusetts Horticultural Society, stps. on plts. (SPB. Oct.1; 136) $6,750

KASPAR, J.D.
- Der in der Wald- und Jagdwirtschaft, dann in der Rechnungslegung gesetzlich unterrichtete Forstbeamte und Revierjäger. Vienna, 1828. 1st. Edn. Cont. bds. (R. Mar.31-Apr.4; 1694) DM 500

KATZ, Elias & Narkiss, B.
- Machsor Lipsiae. Leipzig, 1964. Ltd. Edn. 2 vols. (1 of plts.). Fo. 68 facs. plts., with prefaces in German, Engl. & Hebrew. Case. (S. Nov.17; 28) *Kingsgate.* £500

KAUFMANN, R. von
- Die Eisenbahnpolitik Franbreichs. Stuttgart, 1896. 2 vols. Hf. leath. (R. Mar.31-Apr.4; 1153) DM 700

KAUSLER, F. von
- Atlas des plus memorables Batailles . . . Atlas der Wichtigsten schlacten. Carlsruhe & Freiberg, 1831-37. 5 vols. 152 plans, hand-cold. in outl. & mntd. on cl., some dampstained. In cl.-bkd. s.-c.'s. W.a.f. (CSK. Apr.10; 10) £120

KAVANAGH, Peter
- The Irish Theatre. Tralee, 1946. 1st. Edn. Cl. (GM. Apr.30; 188c) £50

KAY, Joannes
See–CAIUS or Kay, Joannes

KAY, John
- A Series of Original Portraits & Caricature Etchings. Edinb., 1837-38. [1st. Edn.?]. 2 vols. in 4. 4to. Orig. cl., rebkd. (SH. Oct.9; 33) *Gregory.* £200
- – Anr. Copy. 2 vols. Cont. red hf. mor., spines gt. in compartments. Northbrook bkplt., lately in the collection of Eric Sexton. (C. Apr.15; 71) *Dewar.* £120
- – Anr. Copy. Tear in folding plt. at p. 448 in vol. II, slight offsetting. Cont. mor. (S. Apr.7; 453) *Booker.* £65
- – Anr. Edn. Edinb., 1877. 2 vols. 4to. Cont. qtr. mor., partly unc. (TA. Aug.21; 72) £120
- – Anr. Copy. Mor. spine, worn. (CE. Oct.24; 104) £68
- – Anr. Copy. Publisher's qtr. mor., partly unc. (KH. Mar.24; 218) Aus. $180

KAYSER, J.C.
- Deutschlands Schmetterlinge . . . Leipzig, [1852-60]. Cont. hf. leath. (HK. Nov.18-21; 736) DM 1,700

KEARY, C.F. & Grueber, H.A.
- A Catalogue of English Coins in the British Museum; Anglo-Saxon Series. 1887-93. 2 vols. Orig. cl., worn. (SH. Mar.6; 384) *Tietjen.* £50

KEATE, George
- An Account of the Pelew Islands. 1788. 1st. Edn. 4to. Orig. bds., lacks spine, unc. (P. Jul.30; 41) *Chelsea.* £80
- – Anr. Copy. With the final errata lf. Cont. gt. & blind-stpd. cf., rebkd. in gt.-panel. cf (PNY. May 21; 232) £130
- – Anr. Edn. 1788. [2nd. Edn.?]. 4to. Some light spotting & offsetting, a few stains. Cont. cf., crudely rebkd. (CSK. Mar.13; 129) £120
- – Anr. Copy. Hf. mor., marb. bds. (JL. Mar.2; 617) Aus. $250
- – Anr. Edn. L., 1789. 3rd. Edn. Lge. 4to. Lge. folding map mntd., 16 plts., 1 mntd. & defect. Cont. cf., rebkd. (SG. Feb.26; 193) £120

KEATING, William H.
- Narrative of an Expedition to the Source of St. Peter's, Lake Winnepeek, Lake of the Wood's . . . Performed in the Year, 1823. Phila., 1824. 1st. Edn. 2 vols. Foxing & staining. Cont. tree cf., worn, covers loose, spine worn. From liby. of William E. Wilson. (SPB. Apr.29; 167) $150

KEATS, John
- Endymion. L., 1818. 1st. Edn. [2nd. Iss.]. With the 5 line errata slip tipped in, 4 pp. of publisher's advts. at end. Orig. bds., covers very slightly foxed, mor. solander case, unc. From the Prescott Collection. (CNY. Feb.6; 184) $4,500
- – Anr. Copy. Lacks advts., slight spotting, last gathering loose, inner margins slightly wormed. Mor., upr. cover rehinged, worm hole on spine. (SPB. Nov.25; 162) $375
- – Anr. Edn. Ill.:– John Buckland-Wright. Gold. Cock. Pr., 1947. (500). Sm. fo. Orig. parch.-bkd. cl. gt. (SH. Feb.19; 182) *Fermoy.* £175
- – Anr. Copy. (CSK. Apr.3; 61) £150
- Lamia, Isabella, The Eve of St. Agnes, & other Poems. L., 1820. 1st. Edn. Some slight foxing, 8 pp. of publisher's advts. at end. Orig. bds., qtr. mor. gt. s.-c. From the Prescott Collection. (CNY. Feb.6; 185) $2,000
- – Anr. Copy. Mor. gt., inlays, by Sangorski & Sutcliffe, inscr. on end-papers. (SPB. May 29; 234) $500

- Letters to Fanny Brawne written in the Years 1819 & 1820. Ed.:– H. Buxton Forman (introduction & notes). L., 1878. 1st. Edn. 12mo. With a broadside facs. poem on the Letters by Christopher Morley inserted. Orig. cl., rebkd., orig. backstrip preserved, cl. s.-c., unc. Autograph MS. poem on fly-lf. by Oscar Wilde, sigd., & then inscr. & initialled to Richard Le Gallienne. (PNY. May 21; 233) $2,600
- The Poems. Ed.:– F.S. Ellis. Kelms. Pr., 1894. Ltd. Edn. Orig. limp vell., ties. (P. Oct.2; 21) *Quaritch.* £210
- – Anr. Edn. Ill.:– Robert Anning Bell. 1901. Cont. mor., elab. tooled in gt. with red mor. inlays, red mor. doubls. floral decor., watered silk free end-papers. (CSK. Sep.19; 113 £110
- – Anr. Edn. Hammersmith, Doves Pr., 1914. (12) on vell. Mor. Gt.-decor. crushed lev. mor., spine in 6 compartments, 5 raised bands, gt.-panel., sigd. by Doves Bindery 1915, qtr. mor. s.-c. (CNY. May 22; 404) $3,500
- – Anr. Edn. Doves Pr., 1914 [1915]. (200). 4to. Orig. limp vell., unc. (SH. Feb.19; 49) *McKenna.* £120
- Poetical Works & other Writings. N.Y., 1938. Hampstead Edn., (1,050) numbered. 8 vols. This copy unnumbered. Hf. mor. gt. (SPB. May 6; 328) $1,800
- – Anr. Copy. Cl., boxed. Sigd. by M.B. Forman & Masefield. (PNY. Oct.1; 315) $300

KEELER, Charles
See–HARRIMAN Alaska Expedition

KEEN, William W.
See–MITCHELL, Silas Weir & others

KEENE, J. Harrington
- Fly-Fishing & Fly-Making for Trout, etc. N.Y., 1887. 1st. Edn. 12mo. Including 2 plts. of actual fly-making material, & 14 p. catalogue. Gt.-pict. cl. (SG. Dec.11; 62) $200
- – Anr. Edn. N.Y., 1891. 2nd. Edn. Including 2 plts. of actual fly-making material, & 11 p. catalogue. Gt.-pict. cl. (SG. Dec.11; 63) $190

KEEPSAKE, The
Ed.:– Countess of Blessington. Ill.:– Charles Heath. L., [1847 & 1848]. 2 vols. Orig. gt.-tooled cl. (SG. Dec.18; 255) $160

KEER, Peter
See–SPEED, John–[KEER, Peter]

KEILL, Joannis
- Introductionnes ad Veram Physicam et Veram Astronomiam. Quibus Accedunt Trigonometria de Viribus Centralibus. Leyden, 1725. 4to. Cont. spr. cf. (TA. Feb.19; 640) £58

KEIM, F.
See–NIBELUNGEN, Die

KELLER, D.
- Freulicher Unterricht im General-Bass. Hamburg, 1737. 2nd. Edn. 4to. Browned. Cont. cf. (SH. May 21; 64) *Shaw.* £55

KELLWAYE, Simon
- A Defensative Against the Plague contayning two partes or Treatises . . . whereunto is annexed a short Treatise of the Small Poxe. 1593. Sm. 4to. 2 ll. misbnd. New cf. From the collection of Dr. George Mitchell. [STC 14917] (S. Jun.16; 472) *Hammond.* £800

KELLY, Christopher
- A New & Complete System of Universal Geography. 1815-17. 2 vols. 4to. Cont. hf. cf. (TA. Jun.18; 470) £50

KELLY, Howard Atwood
- Operative Gynecology. Ill.:– Max Broedel & H. Becker. N.Y., 1898. 1st. Edn. 2 vols. 4to. Orig. hf. mor. (SG. Sep.18; 207) $130

KELLY, William
- Life in Victoria, or Victoria in 1853, & Victoria in 1858. L., 1859. 2 vols. 2 ll. marked, reprd. tear in folding map. Cl. (KH. Nov.18; 361) Aus. $200

KELSON, George M.
- The Salmon Fly. Priv. ptd., 1895. Orig. cl. (SH. Oct.9; 230) *Bookroom.* £150
- – Anr. Copy. 4to. Advts. Orig. cl. gt. (SBA. Mar.4; 13) *Rochdale Bookshop.* £135
- – Anr. Copy. Gt.-decor. cl. (SG. Apr.9; 291) $700
- The Salmon Fly.–Tips. 1895; 1901. 4to. 2nd. work slightly soiled. Orig. cl.; orig. cl., rebkd. (SH. Jan.30; 381) *Handerson.* £130

KELTIE, John S.
- A History of the Scottish Highlands . . . Edinb. & L., 1875. 1st. Edn. 2 vols. 4to. Hf. mor. (SG. Feb.26; 194) $130

KELVIN, William Thomson, Lord
- Popular Lectures & Addresses. 1891-94. Vol. I 2nd. Edn., vols. II & III 1st. Edns. 3 vols. Orig. cl. Pres. copy, 4 orig. A.L.s.'s by author loosely inserted. (S. Dec.2; 733) *Rota.* £110

KEMBLE, Frances Anne afterwards Butler
[–] Journal of Frances Anne Butler. L., 1835. 1st. Edn. 2 vols. 12mo. Cf., elab. gt. spine, gt. dentelles, marb. end-papers, liby. bkplts. (SG. Jan.8; 228) $110

KENDALL, George Wilkins
- Narrative of the Texan Santa Fe Expedition, comprising a Description of a Tour Through Texas . . . & Final Capture of the Texans. N.Y., 1844. 1st. Edn. 2 vols. 12mo. Some foxing, map torn but complete. Early cf., worn. (SG. Mar.5; 258) $120

KENDALL, George Wilkins & Nebel, Carl
- The War between the United States & Mexico Illustrated . . . N.Y. & Phila., 1851. Lge. fo. Text in ptd. wraps, plts. loose, all in cont. cl. portfo. [Sabin 37362] (CNY. May 22; 140) $1,600

KENDALL, Henry
- Songs from the Mountains. Sydney, 1880. [1st. Edn.]. The suppressed iss., with 'The Song of Ninian Melville' at p. 144. Orig. cl., slight wear, unc. (KH. Mar.24; 222) Aus. $210

KENDALL, Katherine
- The Interior Castle. Ill.:– Margaret Alexander. Worcester, Stanbrook Abbey Pr., 1968. (40) with 1 burnished gold initial & 2 col. Orig. silk gt., fitted case. Pres. copy, calligraphic inscr. by artist. (SH. Feb.20; 391) *Pickering.* £55

KENNEDY, Edward
- The Etched Work of Whistler. N.Y., Grolier Club, 1910. (404). 4 vols. 4to. Orig. bdgs., worn. (SPB. May 6; 270) $750

KENNEDY, John F. President of the U.S.A.
- Why England Slept. N.Y., 1940. [1st. Edn.?]. Cl., slightly worn, mor. box. Pres. copy. (SPB. Nov.24; 24) $500
- – Anr. Copy. Orig. cl., front end-paper slightly foxed, d.-w. Sigd.; from the Prescott Collection. (CNY. Feb.6; 186) $400

KENNEDY, R.F.
- Catalogue of Pictures in the Africana Museum. Johannesburg, 1966-72. 6 vols., & Supp. vols. H-Z & Index to Vols. 6 & 7, together 7 vols. 4to. Orig. bdg. (VA. Jan.30; 44) R. 120
- Shipwrecks On & Off the Coasts of Southern Africa, a Catalogue & Index. Johannesburg, 1955. Wraps. (SSA. Jun.18; 172) R. 100

KENNET, Basilius
See–DESSEINE, François–KENNET, Basilius

KENNETT, White–WATNEY, Vernon
- Parochial Antiquities . . .–Cornbury & the Forest of Wychwood. Oxford; L., Priv. Ptd. (2nd. work), 1695; 1910. 2 works in 2 vols. 4to.; lge. 4to. Cf., covers with gt.-tooled borders enclosing the seal of the Rt. Hon. Thomas Grenville, by Hering, rebkd. preserving orig. gt. spine (1st. work); & lev. mor. by Hatchards. From the collection of Eric Sexton. (C. Apr.16; 295) *Laughton.* £160

KENRICK, William–FARQUHAR, George –MASON, William–LEE, Nathaniel
Falstaff's Wedding.–Sir Harry Wildair.–The Lyrical Part of the Drama of Caractacus.–Lucius Junius Brutus. L., 1795-96. 4 works in 1 vol. Each work with port. of a cont. actor. Str.-grd. mor. Fore-e. pntg. (SG. Mar.19; 127) $325

KENT, James
- Commentaries on American Law. N.Y., 1826-30. 1st. Edn. 4 vols. Some sigs. partly sprung. Old sheep, very worn. (SG. Jan.8; 230) $190

KENT, Rockwell
- The Bookplates & Marks. N.Y., 1929. (1,250) numbered, sigd. On Japan. Orig. cl. gt., unc., d.-w. (SH. Mar.26; 309) *Music Sales.* £55
- – Anr. Copy. 16mo. Gt.-decor. cl., d.-w. Loosely inserted is announcement of exhibition of Kent's Beowulf lithos. (SG. Oct.2; 207) $120
- The Bookplates & Marks.– Later Bookplates & Marks. N.Y., 1929; 1937. Each (1250) numbered, & sigd. 2 works in 2 vols. Square 16mo.

Prospectuses laid in. Both gt.-decor. cl., d.-w.'s. (SG. Mar.26; 288) $160
– – **Anr. Copy.** Together 2 vols. 12mo. Cl. gt., 2nd. work with d.-w. (SG. Oct.23; 174) $150
– **N. by E.** N.Y., 1930. (900), sigd. 4to. Cl. with silver-stpd. compass on upr.-cover, boxed. (SG. Oct.23; 178) $120
– – **Anr. Copy.** Pict. cl., boxed. Sigd. (SG. Nov.13; 392) $100

KENT, William
– **The Designs of Inigo Jones.** L., 1770. 3rd. Edn. 2 vols. in 1. Lge. fo. 1 plt. with reprd. tear, some plts. lightly browned or soiled. Mod. hf. leath. (H. Dec.9/10; 936) DM 2,200
See–JONES, Inigo & Kent, William

KENTFIELD, E.
– **The Game of Billiards.** 1839. Fo. Orig. cl., worn. (SH. Jul.16; 106) Questor. £60

KENTON, Edna
– **The Indians of North America.** N.Y., [1927]. 2 vols. Orig. cl. (CB. Dec.9; 286) Can. $110

KENYON, C.R.
– **The Argonauts of the Amazon.** Ill.:– Arthur Rackham. L., 1901. 1st. Edn. Cold. pict. cl. Raymond M. Sutton Jr. copy. (SG. May 7; 147) $120

KEPLER, Joannes
– **Ad Vitellionem Paralipomena, quibus Astronomiae Pars Optica traditvr.** Frankfurt, 1604. 1st. Edn. 4to. Slightly browned & soiled thro.-out, penstrokes on errata lf. Cont. blind-tooled pig-bkd. wood bds., 2 clasps. (HK. Nov.18-21; 596) DM 2,200
– – **Anr. Copy.** Old vell., browning. (CR. Jun.11; 504) Lire 1,500,000
– **Astronomia Nova ... seu Physica Coelestis, tradita Commentariis de Motibus Stellae Martis, ex Observationibus G.V. Tychonis Brahe.** [Heidelberg], 1609. 1st. Edn. Fo. Folding table torn, lacks blank before title, very browned, title dust-soiled, owner's entry of Nathan Wright of Englefield. 18th. C. mott. cf., gt., jnts. & head & foot of spine reprd., hf. mor. case, note on front free end-paper 'Left by Revd. G. Powell to the Radcliffe Observatory. Feb. 1830'. Stps. & bkplt. of Radcliffe Observatory; from Honeyman Collection. (S. May 20; 3270) Quaritch. £3,000
– – **Anr. Copy.** Lacks final blank lf., folding table slightly torn, some browning & spotting thro.-out. Cont. cf., worn, rebkd. From Chetham's Liby., Manchester. (C. Nov.27; 226) Riley-Smith. £2,600
– **Ausszug auss der Vralten Messekunst Archimedis ... bestättigung der Osterreichischen Weinvisier Ruthen.** Linz, 1616. Fo. Ptd. slip at p. 73, lacks last lf., 05 torn & reprd. slightly affecting text, marginal repairs to 04, slight staining. Cont. vell. bds., stained, hf. mor. case. From Honeyman Collection. (S. May 20; 3272) Pichler. £480
– **Chilias Logarithmorum.** Marburg, 1624. 1st. Edn. 4to. 1 folding table before p. 5. Vell. (R. Oct.14-18; 276) DM 1,000
– **Ephemerides Novae Motuum Coelestium ... ex Observationibus Potissimum Tychonis Brahei, Hypothesibus Physicis et Tabulis Rudolphinis.** Linz, [1617 & 1619]. 1st. Edn. Vol. 1, pts. 1-3 in 1 vol., all publd. 4to. Lightly browned, 1st. & last ll. with sm. wormholes. Cont. vell., cover slightly wormed. (HK. Nov.18-21; 599) DM 7,000
– **Epitome Astronomiae Copernicae.** Linz, 1618. 1st. Edn. Pt. 1 (of 3) Lightly soiled. Cont. leath. gt. (HK. Nov.18-21; 601) DM 1,100
– – **Anr. Edn.** Linz & Frankfurt, 1618-20; 1621. 1st. Edn. 3 pts. in 1 vol. Soiled. Cont. vell. (HK. Nov.18-21; 600) DM 6,500
– **Epitome Astronomiae Copernicanae. I-III De Doctrina Sphaerica, IV Physica Coelestis, V-VII Doctrina Theorica.** Frankfurt, 1635. 7 pts. in 1 vol., forming 3 sections. Each under separate title-p., folding plt. in pt. 3 a little torn, some worming in middle of the book & in lower inner corners at beginning of pt. l, MS. annots. Cont. cf., spine gt., outer margin of lower bd. defect. (S. Oct.21; 403) Phelps. £170
– **Nova Sterometria Doliorum Vinariorum ... Accessit Stereometriae Archimedeae Supplementum.** Linz, 1615. 1st. Edn. Fo. With the sm. lf. of errata at end, ptd. liby. slip affixed to foot of title & inscr. at head. Cont. limp vell., upr. cover defect., hf. red mor. case. From Honeyman Collection. (S. May 20; 3271) Hill. £2,000

– – **Anr. Copy.** Some browning. Mod. panel. cf. (S. Jun.23; 278) Rota. £1,100
– **Tabulae Rudolphinae, Quibus Astronomicae Scientiae.** Ulm, 1627. 1st. Edn. Fo. 1st. gathering in 3rd. state, iss. with the 4 ll. of Sportula added, lacks lf. M1, titles dust-soiled. 19th. C. hf. mor. From Chetham's Liby., Manchester. (C. Nov.27; 227) Taylor. £400
– – **Anr. Edn.** 1675. 1st. Engl. Edn. Last few ll. satined affecting a few letters, final lf. with margin reprd. Paper wraps. [Wing K332] (C. Apr.1; 51) Quaritch. £200

KEPLER, Joannes–SCHEINER, C. & Locher, J.G.–SCHEINER, C.–SCHEINER, C.–PHILIPPI, H.–MARTILINGEN, J.
– **Phaenomenon Singvlare seu Mercvrivs in Sole.:–Disqvisitiones Mathematicae, de Controversis et Novitatibvs Astronomics.–Sol Elliptic[us] ...–Tres Epistolae de Macvlis Solarilovs.–Introductio Chronologica–Tri–horarivm Annvlare.** Leipzig; Ingolst., Augsberg, Augsberg; Cologne; Trier, 1609; 1614; 1615; 1612; 1621; 1621. 1st. Edns. 6 works in 1 vol. 4to. Lightly browned in parts. Cont. vell., upr. end-lf. with reprd. tears, lacks lower, spine defect., leath. bkd., lacks ties. (HK. Nov.18-21; 597) DM 9,500

KEPPEL, Maj. Hon. George
– **Narrative of a Journey Across the Balcan.** 1831. 2 vols. Hf. cf. gt. (P. Dec.11; 77) Georges. £85

KEPPEL, Capt. the Hon. Henry
– **Expedition to Borneo of H.M.S. Dido for the Suppression of Piracy: With Extracts from the Journal of James Brooke.** 1846. 1st. Edn. 2 vols. Foxing thro.-out, publisher's advts. bnd. in at end of vol. 1 (16pp.). Orig. blind-stpd. cl. (TA. Sep.18; 60) £60
– – **Anr. Copy.** Foxed. Hf. cf., worn. (SG. Feb.26; 195) $110
– – **Anr. Edn.** 1846. 2nd. Edn. 2 vols. Orig. cl., unc. Bkplt. of Admiral Archibald Duff. (S. Jun.29; 236) Maggs. £110

KER, Charles Henry Bellenden
– **Icones plantarum sponte China nascentium; e Bibliotheca Braamiana excerptae.** L., 1821. Fo. Some plts. with slip of paper with botanical notes tipped to upr. edge. 19th. C. hf. mor. From collection of Massachusetts Horticultural Society, stps. on plts. (SPB. Oct.1; 137) $4,000

KER, Henry
– **Travels through the Western Interior of the United States, from the year 1808 up to the year 1816.** Elizabethtown, Jew Jersey, 1816. 1st. Edn. Title & early ll. foxed, later ll. lightly foxed & offset. 19th. C. hf. cf., upr. cover detchd. From liby. of William E. Wilson. (SPB. Apr.29; 169) $200

KERCHEVAL, Samuel
– **A History of the Valley of Virginia.** Winchester, 1833. 1st. Edn. 12mo. Slight foxing, owner's inscr. on front free end-paper. Cont. spr. cf., gt. spine. From liby. of William E. Wilson; bkplt. of Bryan Edwards. (SPB. Apr.29; 170) $375

KERCKRINGIUS, Theodor
– **Commentarius in Currum Triumphalem Antimonii Basilii Valentini a se Latinitate Donatum.** Ill.:– Romain de Hooghe (frontis.). Amst., 1671. 12mo. Vell. (S. Dec.1; 220) Quaritch. £55

KERNER, J.
– **Figures des Plants Economiques.** 1792-3-4. Vols. 5, 6 & 7 only. 4to. Hf. cf. (P. Sep.11; 13) Walford. £920

KERNER, Justinus
– **Gedichte.** Stuttgart, 1826. 1st. Edn. Errata lf. at end. Cont. paper bds. (C. Nov.20; 196) Leather. £100
– **Die Seherin von Prevorst.** Stuttgart & Tübingen, 1829. 1st. Edn. 2 vols. Slightly soiled, 9 folding litho. plts. Cont. bds. (R. Oct.14-18; 201) DM 560

KEROUAC, Jack
– **Doctor Sax.** N.Y., [1959]. 1st. Paperback Edn. Wraps. Sigd. (SG. Jun.4; 253) $120
– **Visions of Cody.** [N.Y.], [Nov. 1972]. Tall 4to. Orig. wraps., backed with cl. tape. Page proofs, pulled from uncorrected galleys, ptd. on rectos only. (PNY. Mar.26; 173) $280

KERR, A.
– **Krämerspiegel.** Berlin, 1921. 1st. Edn. (30) Privilege Edn. on Imp. Jap. Fo. Hand-ptd. Orig. mor., spine slightly defect. Sig. by composer & artist. (H. Dec.9/10; 1290) DM 1,500

KERR, John
– **The Golf Book of East Lothian.** 1896. (500) numbered, sigd. No bdg. stated. (CSK. Jul.20; 106) £400

KERR, Admiral Lord Mark Robert
– **Coast Views taken on a Voyage to China 1792-94.** Ca. 1810. Sm. ob. fo. MS. in ink including 2 ports. of Macartney & Gower & a silhouette of Kerr in ink. Mor. gt. with clasp, mor. s.-c. (worn). (CE. Jul.9; 237) £8,000
– **A General History & Collection of Voyages & Travels.** Edinb., 1824. 18 vols. Mod. hf. mor., unc. [Sabin 37631] (S. Nov.4; 483) Arader. £270

KERR, W.M.
– **The Far Interior.** L., 1887. 2nd. Edn. 2 vols. Pict. cl. (SSA. Jun.18; 173) R. 110

KERRICH, Isabel Harriet
– **The Peacock at Home.** 1875-76. Cf. (DWB. Mar.31; 313) £340

KERSLAKE, John
– **Early Georgian Portraits.** [1977]. 2 vols. 4to. Orig. cl., d.-w.'s, s.-c. (CSK. Aug.29; 120) £50

KERSSENBROCH, Hermann von
– **Catalogus Episcoporum Padibornensium oerumque acta.** Lemgo, 1578. Soiled, 2 ll. torn affecting text, 1 reprd., lge. wormhole in last 5 ll. affecting 5 letters, owner's inscr. & annots. on title. Cont. limp vell., soiled & worn, wormhole in lr. cover. (S. Jan.27; 332) Wenner. £260

KERTESZ, Andre
– **Day of Paris.** N.Y., [1945]. 1st. Edn. Cl., d.-w. Inscr. (SG. Apr.23; 116) $250

KETHAM, Johannes de
– **The Fasciculus Medicinae.** Ed.:– Karl Sudhoff & Charles Singer. Milan, 1924. Facs. of 1st. (Venetian) Edn. of 1491. Fo. Hf. mor., soiled. (S. Jun.16; 473) Cooper. £60

KEULEMANS, John Gerrard
– **Onze Vogels in Huis en Tuin.** Leiden, 1869-76. 4to. Cont. linen. (HK. Nov.18-21; 806) DM 3,600

KEY, Axel & Retzius, Gustav
– **Studien in der Anatomie des Nervensystems und des Bindegewebes.** Stockholm, 1875-76. 2 vols. Fo. Hf. mor. (S. Jun.16; 474) Jenner Books. £190

KEYNES, Sir Geoffrey
– **A Bibliography of Sir Thomas Browne.–A Bibliography of the Writings of William Harvey. –A Bibliography of Dr. Robert Hooke.** 1st. 2 vols. Camb., 3rd. Oxford, 1924; 1953; 1960. 1st. Edn., (500); 2nd. Edn., (750); 1st. Edn. 3 vols. Orig. cl., last 2 with d.-w.'s. (S. Jun.16; 476) Jenner Books. £120
– **A Bibliography of William Blake.** N.Y., Grolier Club, 1921. Ltd. Edn. 4to. Orig. mor.-bkd. cl. (SH. Mar.6; 534) Henderson. £200
– **Bibliography of William Hazlitt.** Nones. Pr., 1931. Ltd. Edn. Orig. bds., d.-w. (S. Apr.6; 187) Talerman. £55
– **Engravings by William Blake ...** Dublin, 1956. (500). 4to. Orig. cl. (SH. Mar.26; 95) Forster. £85
– – **Anr. Copy.** (SH. Mar.26; 94) Forster. £75
– **Jane Austen: A Bibliography.** L., Nones. Pr., 1929. (875) numbered. 16mo. 2-tone bds., unc. (SG. Jan.22; 41) $110
– **A Study of the Illuminated Books of William Blake.** Trianon Pr., 1964. 1st. Edn., (525) sigd. Fo. Red mor.-bkd. bds., bd. s.-c. (C. Jul.22; 49) Wood. £100

KEYNES, John Maynard
– **The Means to Prosperity.–The General Theory of Employment Interest & Money.** 1933; 1936. 1st. Edns. Orig. wraps.; orig. cl. (SH. Jan.30; 453) Hill. £85

KEYS, John
– **The Antient Bee-Masters Farewell.** 1796. 1st. Edn. Browned. Orig. bds., worn. (SH. Jun.18; 43) Walford. £110

KEYS, Thomas E.
See–WILLIUS, Frederick A. & Keys, Thomas E.

KEYSER, Henrich
- Swerges Rijkes Ridderskavs och Adels Wavenbook. Stockholm, 1650. Ob. 4to. Engraved title mntd., some plts. mntd., many reprd., 1 with loss supplied in pencil, 1 index lf. reprd. with slight loss, slightly soiled. 19th. C. roan. W.a.f. (S. Apr.7; 331)   *Hannas.* £160

KEYSLER, Johann Georg
- Neueste Reise durch Teutschland, Böhmen, Ungarn, die Schweiz, Italien und Lothringen. Hannover, 1740-41. 2 vols. in 1. 4to. Slightly soiled & stained. Cont. vell. (R. Oct.14-18; 2095)   DM 900
- Travels through Germany, Bohemia, Hungary, Switzerland, Italy, & Lorrain. 1756-57. 2nd. Edn. 4 vols. 4to. Some minor spotting. Orig. spr. cf., rebkd. (TA. Feb.19; 43)   £65

KEYSTONE VIEW COMPANY
- Stereographic Library: Tour of the World. Meadville, Pa., etc., ca. 1910-15. Vols. I-XII. 594 (of 600) stereograms. Loose in orig. cl. folding cases; accompanied by Telebinocular viewer in its orig. unif. case. (PNY. Mar.26; 257) $275

KHABIAS-KOMAROVA, N.
- Stikhetty [Little Poems]. Petrograd, 1922. (100) numbered. Orig. wraps., loose. (SH. Feb.6; 449)   *Quaritch.* £85

KHISL DE KALTENPRUN, Georgius
- Herbardia Urspergy Baronis . . . Vita et Mors. Laibach, 1575. 4to. Owner's inscr. on title deleted. Disbnd. (S. Jan.27; 334)   *Goldschmidt.* £85

KHLEBNIKOV, V.
- Bitvy 1915-1917 [Battle of 1915-17]. Petrograd, 1915. Orig. wraps., rebkd. (SH. Feb.6; 450)   *Nijhoff.* £90
- Izbornik stitkov [Selection of Poems 1907-1914]. Ill.:- Malevich & Filonov. St. Petersb., 1914. 1st. Edn. Mod. cl.-bkd. bds., orig. wraps. by Burlyuk preserved. (SH. Feb.6; 451)   *Sackner.* £340
- Nastoyahschee [Today, a Poem. Al'vek Poems. Sillov Bibliography]. Moscow, 1926. (2000). 4to. Orig. wraps., spine torn. (SH. Feb.6; 452)   *Quaritch.* £160
- - Anr. Copy. Soiled, rebkd., loose. (SH. Feb.6; 453)   *Lempert.* £65
- Otryvok iz dosok sud'by [Fragment from the Boards of Fate]. St. Petersb., 1922. (500). Orig. wraps. by A. Borisov, spine reprd., frayed. (SH. Feb.6; 454)   *Quaritch.* £130
- Ryav [Roar. Gauntlets 1908-1914]. Ill.:- Malevich & Burlyuk. St. Petersb., 1914. 1st. Edn. Mod. cl.-bkd. bds., orig. wraps. (reprd.) preserved. (SH. Feb.6; 455)   *Nijhoff.* £290
- Zapisnaya knizhka [Notebook]. Ed.:- [A Kruchenykh]. Moscow, 1925. (2000). Orig. wraps. by V. Kulagina-Klyutsis, soiled. (SH. Feb.6; 456)   *Lempert.* £65
See-KRUCHENYKH, A. & Khlebnikov, V.

KHLEBNIKOV, V. & others
- Treonik Troikh [Service Book for a Trio]. Ill.:- D. Mayakovsky, Burlyuks & Tatlin. Moscow, 1913. 4to. Orig. wraps., slightly soiled. (SH. Feb.6; 457)   *Kazinikas.* £460

KHRESHCHATITSKY, B.P. & Bobrovsky, P.O.
- Istoriya Leib-Gvardy Kazach'yago Ego Velichestva Polka [History of His Highness' Household Cossack Regiment]. St. Petersb., 1913-03. Vol. I only (in 2 including Supp.). Fo. Dampstained. Orig. mor., worn, loose. (SH. Feb.5; 228)   *Lempert.* £110

KHRYPFFS, Nicolaus de Cusa
- Opera. Paris, 1514. 3 vols. in 2. Fo. Minor repairs to title of vol. 1, a few wormholes at beginning of vols. I & II slightly affecting text, some ll. wormed in margins, Innsbruck convent owner's inscr. on title to vol. II & some marginalia. Mod. vell., ties. From Honeyman Collection. (S. May 20; 3273)   *Barchas Library.* £4,000

KHUNRATH, Conrad
- Medulla Destillatoria et Medica Quintum Aucta et Renovata das ist Grundliches und Vielbewertes Destillier und Artzney Buch . . . wie des Spiritus Vini . . . Oliteten, Spiritus, Salie . . . destillirt . . . zur Hochsten Exaltation Gebracht. Hamburg, 1623. 4to. Paper browned. Vell. (S. Dec.1; 221)   *Grammers.* £110

KIDD, William
- [-] A Full Account of the Proceedings in Relation to Captain Kidd. In Two Letters Written by a Person of Quality to a Kinsman of the Earl of Bellmont in Ireland. L., 1701. 1st. Edn. 4to. Some browning, stains. New cf. [Sabin 37703] (SPB. May 5; 294) $400

KIDGELL, Rev. John
- [-] Original Fables/Fables Originales. Priv. ptd., 1764. 2 vols. in 1. 19th. C. red mor. gt. (C. Apr.1; 214)   *Quaritch.* £260

KIEPERT, H.
- Neuer Atlas von Hellas und den Hellenischen Colonien. Berlin, 1872. Maps measure 18×24 inches. Maps partly cold., some margins frayed. Ptd. wraps., torn. (SG. May 21; 61) $110

KIKI'S Memoirs
See-HEMINGWAY, Ernest

KIKKERT, P.
- Proeve van ets-Kundige Uitspanningen, of Verzameling van Plaatjens. Amst., 1798. 4to. Hf. cf. (BS. Jun.11; 356)   £220

KILBY, Rev. Thomas
- Scenery in the Vicinity of Wakefield. Wakefield, 1843. 1st. Edn. Fo. Ptd. title & dedication detchd. Orig. cl. gt., slightly worn, spine torn. (SBA. Oct.22; 620)   *Anthony.* £160
- Views in Wakefield. 1853. Lge. fo. Orig. embossed cl., gt., spine & corners worn. (C. Nov.6; 215)   *Burton.* £480

KILGOUR Collection of Russian Literature, 1750-1920
1959. 4to. Cl. (SG. Jan.22; 347) $110

KILIAN, Hermann Friedrich
- Schilderungen Neuer Beckenformen und ihres Verhaltens im Leben. Mannheim, 1854. 1st. Edn. Fo. Plts. stpd. in lr. left corners. Disbnd. From Brooklyn Academy of Medicine. (SG. Jan.29; 249) $160

KILMER, Joyce
- Trees & Other Poems. N.Y., 1914. 1st. Edn. Orig. cl., worn along upr. spine, boxed in suede & gt. case. Sigd. & inscr. by author. (SPB. Nov.25; 326) $175

KINBERG, J.G.H.
See-SUNDEVALL, C.J. & Kinberg, J.G.H.

KINDLERS LITERATUR LEXIKON
Ed.:- G. Woerner, R. Geisler & R. Radler. Zürich, 1974. Special Edn. 12 vols. Sm. 4to. Leath. (D. Dec.11-13; 915)   DM 800

KING, Adam P.P.
See-FITZROY, Capt. Robert & others

KING, Charles
- The Fifth Cavalry in the Sioux War of 1876. Milwaukee, 1880. 1st. Edn. Orig. wraps. loose in mor.-bkd. folding s.-c., liby. stp. on upr. cover. (SPB. Jun.22; 78) $300

KING, Clarence & others
- United States Geological Exploration of the Fortieth Parallel. Wash., 1870's & 80's. Vol. I-VII. 4to. Cl., several vols. brkn., ex-liby. (SG. Aug.21; 492) $180

KING, Daniel
- The Vale-Royall of England. 1656. 1st. Edn. 3 Pts. in 1 vol. Fo. Late 18th. C. red str.-grd. mor. gt., spine tooled in compartments. Bkplt. of John Peachey, book-label of Westdean Library. [Wing K488] (S. Nov.24; 182)   *Thorp.* £220
- - Anr. Copy. 4 pts. in 1 vol. Fo. Without plan of Chester. Cont. panel. cf., neatly rebkd., new end-papers. (SBA. Oct.22; 302)   *Chesters.* £120
- - Anr. Edn. Ed.:- William Smith & William Webb. 1656. Fo. Later mott. cf., rebkd., old spine preserved. [Wing S4286] (CSK. Mar.13; 4) £150
See-LEYCESTER, Sir Peter-KING, Daniel

KING, Edward
- Munimenta Antiqua; or, observations on Antient Castles. 1799-1805. 1st. Edn. 4 vols. Fo. Minor spotting to a few plts., dampstain to upr. margins. Cont. diced cf., gt. stylised 'Greek-key' panel to covers enclosing inner border of arabesques, gt. spines including ducal device, hinges worn. (C. Feb.25; 41)   *Maggs.* £100

KING, Edward (contributor)
See-CAMBRIDGE UNIVERSITY

KING, J.G.
- Die Gebraüche u. Ceremonies der Griechischen Kirche in Russland. Riga, 1773. 1st. German Edn. Lge. 4to. Lightly soiled in parts. Cont. hf. leath. gt., spine defect, engrd. Duchesse de Courlande arms ex-lib. (HK. May 12-14; 745)   DM 560

KING, Jessie M. & Arcambeau, Edme
- The Book of Bridges. 1911. Ltd. Edn. Cl. gt. (CE. Oct.24; 146)   £64

KING, Captain Philip Parker
- Narrative of a survey of the intertropical & Western Coasts of Australia. 1827. 1st. Edn. 2 vols. Occasional light foxing. Later hf. mor. (S. Nov.4; 625)   *Maggs.* £380

KING, Thomas
- Designs for Carving & Gilding. Ca. 1840. 4to. Later qtr. roan, worn, orig. upr. wrap. preserved. (S. Mar.17; 423)
                                Marlborough Rare Books. £190

KING, W.R.
- Campaigning in Kaffirland . . . The Kafir War of 1851-52. L., 1855. 2nd. Edn. Hf. cf. gt., some foxing. (VA. Jan.30; 52)   R. 110

KING, William, 1685-1763, of Oxford
- [-] The Toast. Ed.:- Peregrine O'Donald. L., 1747 [actually 1736]. 2nd. Edn. Lge. 4to. Cont. tree cf., spine gt. (SG. May 14; 119) $325

KING, William
See-HOBSON, Robert Lockhart & others

KINGSLEY, Charles
- The Works. 1878-80. 22 vols. Cont. hf. cf. (SH. May 28; 62)   *Wade Gallery.* £50

KINGSLEY, Henry
- Works. L., 1894-95. 12 vols. Hf. mor. gt. (SPB. May 6; 329) $400

KINLOCH, A.
- Large Game Shooting in Thibet & the North West. 1869. 4to. Hf. mor. gt. (P. Sep.11; 23)
                                Hessun. £55

KINO-FOT
Ill.:- Rodchenko & others. Moscow, 1922. No. 1 (4000), others (8000). Nos. 1, 2, & 5. 4to. Orig. wraps., by Rodchenko & others, the last slightly browned. (SH. Feb.5; 229)   *Tate Gallery.* £280

KINSEY, Rev. William Morgan
- Portugal Illustrated. 1828. 25 engraved plts., many on India proof paper, 9 hand-cold. Cont. diced russ., gt. Pres. copy. (SBA. Dec.16; 56)
                                Hyde Park Bookshop. £64

KINSKY, Georg
- Katalog des Musikhistorischen Museums von Wilhelm Heyer in Cöln. Cologne, 1912. 1st. Edn., (50) Privilege Edn. on Bütten. Vol. II. 4to. Mor., unc. Dedication copy. (H. May 21/22; 812)
                                                    DM 720

KIP, John
- [-] Britannia Illustrata. 1714 (Index dtd. 1722). 2 vols. Fo. Titles guarded in inner margins, some plts. defect., browning & soiling. Cont. cf., covers loose, worn. Bkplt. of Kirkleatham liby., as a coll., w.a.f. (S. Sep.29; 139)   *Sims & Reid.* £1,400
- Nouveau Théâtre de la Grande Bretagne. Ill.:- J. Kip. 1724. Fo. 69 plts. of 70, plt. 49 reprd. Disbnd. (P. Sep.11; 290)   *Street.* £650
- - Anr. Edn. Ill.:- L. Knyffe & others. 1724-28. 5 vols. including Supp. & Atlas Angloise. Lge. fo. Maps, plans & plts. mntd. on guards thro.-out, plt. list in each vol. Cont. mott. cf., gt. panel. sides, central gt. ornament, spines gt. (C. Jul.15; 153)
                                Quaritch. £12,00

KIPLING, Rudyard
- The Absent-minded Beggar. [1899]. Fo. On satin. Orig. bdg. 1 of the copies presented by Mrs. Langtry but lacks silk fringe. (C. Feb.4; 140)
                                Kleusman. £80
- - Anr. Copy. With the 'Absent-Minded Beggar Song . . .', with music by Arthur Sullivan [L.], [1899], 4to., folded as iss. Cl. s.-c. From the Prescott Collection. (CNY. Feb.6; 200) $550
- Brazilian Sketches. 29 Nov.-20 Dec. 1927. Compl. set of cuttings from 'The Morning Post' preserved in a blank vol. Hf. mor. (C. Feb.4; 75)
                                Pullen. £120
- - Anr. Copy. Compl. set of the orig. contributions to the 'Morning Post'. Mntd. in hf. mor. album. (C. Jul.22; 16a)   *Sawyer.* £60
- Brother Square-Toes. L., 1910. 1st. Edn., (8) for copyright. Orig. ptd. wraps., slightly wrinkled, qtr.

mor. s.-c. From the Prescott Collection. (CNY. Feb.6; 205) $500
- **Collected Verse.** Ill.:– W. Heath Robinson. N.Y., 1910. Gt.-pict. cl., worn. Sig. tipped in. (SG. Oct.23; 307) $100
- **Departmental Ditties & other Verses.** Lahore, [1886]. 1st. Edn., (350). Tall 8vo. Orig. ptd. wraps., flap designed to resemble an official envelope, ends of spine & folds of flap reprd., mor. solander case. From the Prescott Collection. (CNY. Feb.6; 191) $600
[-] **Echoes.** Lahore, [1884]. 1st. Edn. 12mo. Remnant of paper pasted to verso of title. Orig. ptd. wraps., recased with end-papers renewed, lacks backstrip, mor. solander case. Pres. Copy(?), to W. Lawrence, with his name on upr. cover, note by Kipling in index, lately in the Prescott Collection. (CNY. Feb.6; 189) $1,700
- **The Jungle Book.–The Second Jungle Book.** L., 1894-95. 1st. Edns. 2 vols. Orig. cl. gt. (P. Jun.11; 300) Young. £260
- - **Anr. Copy.** Slightly spotted. Orig. cl. (SH. Jun.18; 72) Questor. £110
- - **Anr. Copy.** 2nd. vol. with advt. lf., a few ll. slightly spotted. Orig. cl. gt. (SBA. Mar.4; 221) Fletcher. £70
- - **Anr. Copy.** Orig. cl. (S. Feb.9; 24) Traylen. £50
- - **Anr. Copy.** Orig. cl., cl. folding case. Bkplt. of Paul H. Bonner in 1st. work; both lately in the Prescott Collection. (CNY. Feb.6; 198) $300
- - **Anr. Copy.** Old owner's mark on end-paper vol. II, minimal browning. Spine vol. II slightly defect., mod. hand-bnd. s.-c. (H. Dec.9/10; 1567) DM 800
- **Just So Stories.** L., 1902. 1st. Edn. 4to. Advance copy, marginal tear to 1st. few ll. Orig. wraps., fore-edge of upr. cover torn, foot of spine reprd., qtr. mor. s.-c. With the bkplt. of George B. McCutcheon, lately in the Prescott Collection. (CNY. Feb.6; 203) $1,600
- **Kim.** Ill.:– Robin Jacques. N.Y., Ltd. Edns. Cl., 1962. (1500) sigd. by artist. Orig. mor.-bkd. cl. gt., s.-c. (SH. Feb.20; 242) Maggs. £65
- **Letters of Marque.** Allahabad, 1891. 1st. Edn. 8pp. advts., A.H. Wheeler & Co.'s rubber stp. & stp. 'Issued 11 Nov.91' on end-paper. Orig. cl., rebkd., old spine laid down, worn. (S. Jul.22; 352) Diamond. £120
- - **Anr. Edn.** L., 1891. 1st. Engl. Edn. Vol. I (all publd.). Orig. pict. wraps., spine & lr. cover supplied to approximate orig. bdg., mor.-bkd. folding case. From the Prescott Collection. (CNY. Feb.6; 196) $1,000
- **Le Livre de la Jungle.–Le Second Livre de la Jungle.** Ill.:– Maurice de Becque. Paris, 1924-26. 2 vols. 4to. Sewed, wraps., s.-c.'s. (HD. Dec.5; 111) Frs. 2,300
- **The Phanton Rickshaw . . .–The Jungle Book.** Allahabad; L., [1888]; 1894. Together 2 vols. 1st. work: orig. pict. wraps., worn, 2nd. work: orig. cl. gt. (S. Jul.22; 187) Sawyer. £65
- **Plain Tales from the Hills.** Calcutta, 1888. 1st. Edn. 12mo. With the p. no. on p. 192 misplaced, 24 pp. of advts. at end (dtd. Dec., 1887). Orig. plain olive cl., spine gt.-lettered, qtr. mor. gt. s.-c. Inscr. on hf.-title 'E.W. Buckeley/Pioneer Press/Allahabad/1892.', lately in the Prescott Collection. (CNY. Feb.6; 193) $1,100
- **Poems, 1886-1929.** 1929. (525) numbered, sigd. by author. 3 vols. 4to. Orig. cf., d.-w., in orig. box. (SD. Feb.4; 105) £85
- - **Anr. Copy.** This copy unnumbered. Red mor., gt., d.-w.'s. (SPB. May 29; 245) $500
- - **Anr. Copy.** Maroon mor., some soiling to lr. cover of vol. 1, spines slightly faded, unopened. From the Prescott Collection. (CNY. Feb.6; 209) $320
- **The Potted Princess.–Collah-Wallah & the Poison Stick.–A Tour of Inspection.** N.Y., Priv. Ptd., 1925; 1925; 1928. 1st. (Unauthorized) Edns. 3 works in 3 vols. Ltd. to (66), (66), & (93) copies respectively. Unif. bds., qtr. mor. s.-c. From the Prescott Collection. (CNY. Feb.6; 213) £250
- **A Priest in Spite of Himself.** L., 1910. 1st. Edn., (8) for copyright. Orig. ptd. wraps., slightly wrinkled, qtr. mor. s.-c. With the bkplt. of Raymond J. Schweizer, lately in the Prescott Collection. (CNY. Feb.6; 206) $650
- **Puck of Pook's Hill.** Ill.:– Arthur Rackham. N.Y., 1906. 1st. Edn. Gt. stpd. pict. cl. Raymond M. Sutton Jr. copy. (SG. May 7; 150) $100
- **Schoolboy Lyrics.** Lahore, Priv. Ptd., 1881. 1st. Edn., (50). 12mo. Orig. plain white wraps., spotted with fore-edges slightly frayed, mor.

solander case. Pen & ink design by Kipling on upr. wrap.; bkplt. of Frank Bemis on case, lately in the Prescott Collection. (CNY. Feb.6; 187) $10,000
- **Simple Simon.** L., 1910. 1st. Edn., (8) for copyright. Orig. ptd. wraps., slightly wrinkled, qtr. mor. s.-c. From the Prescott Collection. (CNY. Feb.6; 204) $600
- **Soldiers Three.–The Story of the Gadsbys.–In Black & White.–Under the Deodars.–Wee Willie Winkie & other Child Stories.** Allahabad, [1888]. 1st. Edns. Vols. 1-4, & 6, of the Indian Railway Liby. Series. Vol. 1 lacks advt. ll., remainder lack advt. lf. at front. Disbnd., lacks covers, cl. protective covers, mor. solander case. With some 800 corrections, etc. in Kipling's hand; the E.A. Ballard copy, lately in the Prescott Collection. (CNY. Feb.6; 195) $11,000
- **A Song of the English.** Ill.:– William Heath Robinson. [1909]. (500) numbered, sigd. by artist. 4to. Orig. vell. gt., lacks 1 tie, slightly soiled. (SBA. Mar.4; 228) Drollier. £130
- - **Anr. Copy.** Lacks ties. (SH. Mar.27; 461) Mirdan. £95
- **Songs of the Sea.** Ill.:– Donald Maxwell. L., 1927. (500) on L.P., & sigd. Tall 4to. Qtr. vell. gt., d.-w. (frayed), box (worn, & with portion of upr. panel lacking). (PNY. May 21; 238) $100
- **Under the Deodars.** Allahabad, [1888]. 1st. Edn. With the lf. of advts. at front & 4 at rear, title-p. reprd. Orig. pict. wraps., 1st. state of upr. cover, without shading round 'No. 4' & 'One Rupee', rebkd. & corners renewed, new end-papers, mor. solander case. Pres. Copy, to Mrs. Carmichael-Carr, Jerome Kern's copy with bkplt., lately in the Prescott Collection. (CNY. Feb.6; 194) $1,600
- **Verse.** 1919. Inclusive Edn., (100). 3 vols. Orig. vell. gt., in mor.-bkd. cl. s.-c.'s. Each vol. sigd. (SH. Dec.19; 568) Lewis. £140
- **White Horses.–The White Man's Burden.** L., 1897; 1899. 1st. Edn.; 1st. Engl. Edn.; both Wise Piracies. 2 works in 2 vols. 12mo. Unif. orig. ptd. wraps., each in qtr. mor. s.-c. From the Prescott Collection. (CNY. Feb.6; 199) $550
- **The Works.** 1899-1913. Unif. Edn. 20 vols. Unif. hf. cf., spines gt. (LC. Feb.12; 506) £120
- - **Anr. Edn.** 1908-32. Pocket Edn. 30 vols. Unif. orig. roan gt., with elephant head roundel, worn. (SH. Dec.19; 567) Fitton. £55
- - **Anr. Edn.** 1913-27. Bombay Edn. 26 vols. Orig. holland-bkd. bds., spotted. Vol. 1 sigd. (SH. Jan.30; 346) Old Hall Bookshop £110
- - **Anr. Edn.** L., 1913-n.d. Bombay Edn. 24 vols. of 25, lacks vol. VI. Orig. linen-bkd. bds., unc. Sigd. (GM. Apr.30; 735) £90
- - **Anr. Edn.** Garden City, 1914-26. Seven Seas Edn. on L.P., (1,050) on specially wtrmkd. paper, sigd. 27 vols. Linen-bkd. bds., unc., unopened. (SG. May 14; 120) $375
- - **Anr. Edn.** 1917-1937. 29 vols. Cf. gt. (P. Oct.2; 276) Shaw. £60
- **Writings in Prose & Verse.** Ill.:– Strang. L., 1900. De Luxe Edn. (1,050). 27 vols. Slight spotting. Mor. gt., gt. tooled panel design, unc., mor. doubls., silk end-papers. (SPB. Nov.25; 471) $1,100

See–**FRIEND, The**

KIPLING, Rudyard (Ed.)
See–**NICHOLSON, William**

KIRBY, James
- **Old Times in the Bush of Australia; Trials & Experiences.** Melbourne, n.d. Imprint varies from Ferguson's with rubber stp. 'New Issue'. Orig. cl. (KH. Nov.18; 364) Aus. $120

KIRBY, John
- **The Suffolk Traveller.** 1735. Mott. cf. (O. Jun.3; 110) £68
- - **Anr. Edn.** 1764. 2nd. Edn. Cf. (O. Jun.3; 111) £90

KIRBY, Joshua
- **The Perspective of Architecture.** 1761. 2 vols. Fo. Recent hf. cf. (TA. Mar.19; 42) £75

KIRBY, Mary & Elizabeth
- **Beautiful Birds in Far off Lands.** L., 1872. Some plts. hand-cold. in part. Orig. decor. cl. (JL. Jul.20; 817) Aus. $100

KIRBY, William Forsell
- **European Butterflies & Moths.** 1882. 4to. 1 plt. detchd., slight browning. Later buckram, slightly soiled. (CSK. Nov.7; 41) £140
- - **Anr. Copy.** 4to. A few plts. browned or spotted. Orig. cl., soiled. (CSK. Jun.5; 149) £90

- - **Anr. Copy.** 4to. Cont. hf. mor. (TA. Jun.18; 144) £60
- - **Anr. Edn.** 1889. 4to. Orig. cl., worn. (P. Nov.13; 14) Bailey. £85
- - **Anr. Copy.** Cont. hf. vell. (R. Oct.14-18; 3060) DM 430
- - **Anr. Edn.** 1898. 4to. Hf. cf. gt. (P. Feb.19; 82) McDonnel. £95
- - **Anr. Copy.** Hf. cf. (SH. Jul.9; 44) Bookroom. £95
- - **Anr. Copy.** Some minor defects. Orig. cl. gt. (SBA. May 27; 184) Barker. £54
See–**MORRIS, Rev. Francis Orpen & Kirby, William Forsell**

KIRCHER, Athanasius
- **China Monumentis.** Amst., 1667. [1st. Edn.?] Fo. A few minor defects, MS. note on end-paper 'Ex Bibliotheca Ducis Saxo Weidensis'. Cont. cf. gt., rebkd. & restored, preserving orig. spine. (SBA. Dec.16; 57) Ad Orientem. £360
- - **Anr. Copy.** Some wormholes in 1st. few pp., 1 plt. torn. Old vell. (BS. Jun.11; 167) £340
- - **Anr. Copy.** Lacks port. & one plt? Old cf., upr. cover detchd. W.a.f. (C. Jul.15; 128) Taylor. £140
- - **Anr. Copy.** Stained, browned in places. Mod. cf. (VG. Dec.17; 1410) Fls. 900
- **La Chine Illustrée.** Trans.:– F.S. Dalquie. Amst., 1670. [1st. Edn. in Fr.?]. Fo. Some ll. spotted. Cont. cf., rebkd. & cornered. (SBA. Dec.16; 58) Quaritch. £310
- - **Anr. Copy.** Old spr. cf., decor. spine. (HD. Dec.5; 112) Frs. 4,800
- **Historia Eustachio-Mariana.** Rome, 1665. 1st. Edn. 4to. Orig. vell. (GM. Apr.30; 702) £70
- **Iter Extaticum Coeleste . . . Accessit . . . Iter Exstaticum Terrestre, & Synopsis Mundi Subterranei.** Ed.:– G. Schott. Würzburg, 1660. 2nd. Edn. 4to. A few blank corners reprd., wormhole at beginning, slight defect on 3L2r, dupl. stp. of Hamburg Public Liby. on verso of title. Cont. vell. bds., soiled. (S. Jan.26; 288) Nador. £90
- - **Anr. Copy.** Slightly soiled in parts. Cont. vell., lack ties. (HK. Nov.18-21; 603) DM 1,000
- **Mundus Subterraneus.** Amst., 1665. 1st. Edn. 2 pts. in 1 vol. Lge. fo. Some ll. stpd. at head, owner's mark on end-paper. Cont. vell., worn & soiled. (HK. May 12-14; 350) DM 3,000
- **Mvsvrgia Vniversalis sive Ars Magna Consoni et Dissoni in X. Libros digesta.** Rome, 1650. 1st. Edn. 2 vols. in 1. Fo. Lacks plts. XI & XII as usual, plt. XX with lge. tear, pp. 575-576 paginated double, frontis. torn, some stains & lightly browned & soiled in parts. Cont. vell., slightly soiled & cockled. (H. Dec.9/10; 1173) DM 2,600
- - **Anr. Copy.** 2 pts. in 1 vol. Slightly soiled in parts, lacks 12 ll. index at end of pt. 2. Cont. style leath. (R. Mar.31-Apr.4; 243) DM 1,650
- **Obelisci Aegyptiaci Nuper inter Isaei Romani rudera effossi interpretation Hieroglyphica.** Rome, 1666. 1st. Edn. Fo. Cont. vell. (S. Oct.21; 324) Carroll. £620
- **Pantometrum Kircherianum.** Ed.:– G. Schotts. Würzburg, 1660. 1st. Edn. 4to. Slightly browned. Cont. leath. gt., lacks ties. (HK. Nov.18-21; 604) DM 430

KIRCHHAN, Elchanan
- **Simchat Ha'nefesh.** Fuerth, 1727. 6th. Edn. Pt. 2 only. 4to. Title mntd. & reprd., other repairs, discoloration. Mod. hf. cl. (SPB. May 11; 139) $500

KIRCHNER, Paul Christian
- **Juedisches Ceremoniel Oder Beschreibung Dererjenigen Gebrauche.** Nuremb., 1724. 2nd. Edn. 4to. Blind-tooled leath. (S. Nov.18; 665) Gimesh. £350
- - **Anr. Edn.** Nuremb., 1734. 4th. Edn. 4to. Slight discoloration. Hf. leath. (S. Nov.18; 666) Waechter. £480

KIRCHWEGER, Ant. Josephus
- **Microscopium Basilii Valentini sive Commentariolum et Cribrellum uber den Grossen Kreuzapfel der Welt, ein Euphoriston der Ganzen Medicin.** Berlin, 1790. New cl., unc. (S. Dec.2; 524) Quaritch. £100
- - **Anr. Copy.** Vell., unc. (S. Dec.1; 222) Quaritch. £55

KIRK, Thomas
- **The Forest Flora of New Zealand.** Wellington, 1889. 1st. Edn. Fo. Orig. cl. (C. May 20; 219) Quaritch. £65

KIRKCONNELL, Watson
- Victoria County Centennial History. Lindsay, 1921. Orig. wraps. (CB. Sep.24; 236) Can. $100

KIRKLAND, Thomas
- A Commentary on Apoplectic & Paralytic Affections & on Diseases Connected with the Subject. 1792. Advt. lf. of the author's works. Cont. cf., rcbkd. (S. Jun.16; 478) *Pratt.* £50

KIRKPATRICK, Col. William
- An Account of the Kingdom of Nepaul. 1811. 1st. Edn. 4to. Some spotting & offsetting onto text, sm. tear in fold of map. Cont. hf. cf., spine defect. (S. Dec.8; 250) *Plant.* £150
- - Anr. Copy. Lge. folding map torn at fold. Cf., slightly wormed. (S. Dec.8; 248) *Moore.* £80

KIRMES, Marguerite
- Dogs. Ed.:– R.T. Townsend. 1930. (750). 4to. Three-qtr. cl. Frontis. inscr. (SG. Dec.11; 265) $300

KIRNBERGER, Joh. Ph.
- Die Kunst des Reinen Satzes in der Musik.–Die Wahren Grundsätze zum Gebrauch der Harmonie. Berlin, 1774-79. 1st. Edn. (2nd. title). 2 vols. in 4. (2nd. title bnd. first). 4to. Browned. 3 vols. cont. hf. leath. & 1 new hf. leath. (H. Dec.9/10; 1174) DM 1,800

KIRSCH, A.Fr.
- Neu-verfertigtes u. in zwey Theil eingerichtetes Kunst-Hause-Arzney-u. Wunder-Buch. Nuremb., 1719. 4to. Slightly soiled in parts. Cont. leath. (HK. Nov.18-21; 1691) DM 1,200

KIRSCHBAUM, Johann Michael
- Neues Bild- und Muster-Buch. Heilbronn & Rothenburg, plts. dtd. 1793. Ob. 4to. Including the 32 pp. of text (with the title-p. dtd. 1771). Old leath.-bkd. bds. (SG. Dec.4; 209) $325

KIRSTEN, Peter
- Grammatices Arabicae. Breslau, [1608-10]. 1st. Edn. 3 pts. in 1 vol. Fo. Some browning, slight marginal worming thro.-out. Cont. blind-stpd. cf., letters I S G Z I stpd. on upr. cover with central ornament in conventional decoration, similar ornament on lr. cover, rebkd. & reprd., s.-c. (S. Apr.29; 406) *Riley Smith.* £550
- Vitae Evangelistarum Quatuor. Breslau, 1608. 1st. Edn. Fo. Some browning & spotting. Mod. cf., s.-c. (S. Apr.29; 405) *Burrell.* £360

KITCHEN, John
- Le Court Leete, et Court Baron . . . et les cases et matters necessarie pur Seneschals de ceux courts a scier. 1580. 1st. Edn. A few cont. MS. notes in ink in margins & at end, owner's inscr. at head of title. Cont. cf., worn, blind-stp. in centre of covers. [STC 15017] (C. Feb.25; 160) *Thorp.* £200

KITCHEN or KITCHIN, Thomas
- A General Atlas. 1777. Lge. fo. (560mm. × 400mm.). 21 engraved maps (of 23) in 32 sheets (of 35), hand-cold. in outl., pts. of India fully cold., title detchd. & torn, lacks maps numbers 5-7, some tears. Disbnd. W.a.f. (S. Jun.29; 13) *Burgess.* £350
- Geographia Scotiae. 1749. 12mo. 33 engraved maps, mntd. on guards. Old cf., worn. W.a.f. (C. Jul.15; 60) *Potter.* £220
- A New Universal Atlas. 1798. 2nd. Edn. Fo., (540mm. × 390mm.). Wanting index lf. & 2 maps, tears or repairs in some folds, 1 or 2 stains, some slight offsetting. 19th. C. pig panel. in blind, stain on lr. cover. W.a.f. (S. Nov.3; 24) *Jeffery.* £550
- - Anr. Edn. Ed.:– James Rennel. 1801. 5th. Edn. Fo. 75 engraved maps, hand-cold. in outl. with wash borders, many double-p. & folding, cartouches, inset plans, etc., on guards thro.-out. Cont. tree cf., rebkd., orig. spine preserved. As an atlas, w.a.f. (C. May 20; 146) *Burgess.* £2,000
- Pocket Atlas of the counties of South Britain, or England & Wales. 1769. Ob. 8vo. 10 maps with sm. reprd. tears, 7 folded, 3 soiled. Hf. cl. (CSK. Sep.12; 99) £250
See–BOWEN, Emmanuel & Kitchen, Thomas & others

KITE, Charles
- An Essay on the Recovery of the Apparently Dead. 1788. 1st. Edn. Cont. hf. cf., bkplt. of Sir John Smith, Bart. From liby. of Dr. E. Ashworth Underwood. (S. Feb.23; 237) *Bickersteth.* £130

KITTEL, G.
- Theologische Wörterbuch zum Neuen Testament. Stuttgart, 1933-78. Vols. I-X, pt. 17. 4to. 7 vols. orig. linen, 2 orig. portfolios, 1 in pts. (B. Dec.10/11; 892) Fls. 625

KITTLEBY, Mary
See–KETTILBY or Kittleby, Mary

KITTLIZ, F.H. von
- Denkwürdigkeiten einer Reise nach dem Russischen Amerika . . . Gotha, 1858. 2 vols. Slightly browned. Cont. hf. leath. [Sabin 38204] (R. Oct.14-18; 1686) DM 1,000

KITZUR Sefer Mitzvot Gadol–OVER Orach
Ed.:– Shimon Ben Meir. Carlsrube, 1763. 1st. Edn. of Abridgement. 2 works in 1 vol. 12mo. Lightly stained. Leath.-bkd. bds. (SPB. May 11; 28) $300

KJERSMEIER, Carl
- Centres de Style de la Sculpture Nègre Africaine. Paris & Copen., 1935-1938. Vols. I-IV. 4to. Ptd. bds., d.-w.'s Sigd. & inscr. in each vol. to the Guillaume Dehondts. (SG. Aug.21; 9) $450

KLAPROTH, Julius von
- Travels in the Caucasus & Georgia. Trans.:– Frederic Schoberl. L., 1814. 1st. Edn. in Engl. Lge. 4to. Old liby. stp. on title verso. Disbnd. (SG. Oct.30; 206) $160

KLAPROTH, Martin Henry
See–HERNANDEZ, Francisco–KLAPROTH, Martin H.–DREW, William

KLAPROTH, Martin Henry & Wolff, F.
- Chemisches Wörterbuch. Berlin, 1807. 5 vols. & 4 supp. vols. in 9 vols. Cont. leath., gt. spine. (R. Oct.14-18; 277) DM 1,700

KLAUSER, Th. & others
- Reallexikon für Antike und Christentum. Stuttgart, 1950-77. 10 vols. 6 hf. mor., 4 in pts., 3 with orig. wraps. (B. Dec.10/11; 35) Fls. 1,100

KLEBS, Arnold C.
- Incunabula Scientifica et Medica: Short Title List. Bruges, 1937. Cl., orig. wraps. preserved. (S. Apr.6; 189) *Talerman.* £55

KLEE, Paul
- Paintings, Watercolors, 1913 to 1939. Ed.:– Karl Nierendorf & J.J. Sweeney N.Y., [1941]. 4to. Flexible bds., spiral back. (SG. Oct.23; 188) $120

KLEE, Paul (Ed.)
See–STAATLICHES BAUHAUS WEIMAR

KLEEMAN, Christian Friedrich Carl
See–ROESEL von Rosenhof–KLEEMAN, Christian Friedrich Carl

KLEIN, J.A.
- Radirungen. Nuremb., [1844-48]. Lge. 4to. Slightly soiled in places, some margins stained. Mod. hf. leath. (H. May 21/22; 1175) DM 5,500
- Voyage du Rhin de Mayence à Cologne. Trans.:– J. Lendroy. Ill.:– J.A. Lasinsky. Koblenz, 1829. Cont. hf. leath. gt. (D. Dec.11-13; 1623) DM 820

KLEIN, Jacob Theodor
- Naturalis Dispositio Echinodermatum. Danzig, 1766. 4to. Plt. no. 23 repeated, nos. 35 & 36 on 1 plt. Buckram, stitching brkn. From Chetham's Liby., Manchester. (C. Nov.27; 229) *Weldon & Wesley.* £55
- Ova Avium . . . Leipzig/Konigsberg/Mitau, 1766. 1st. Edn. 4to. 19th. C. hf. mor., upr. cover detchd. From Chetham's Liby., Manchester. (C. Nov.27; 230) *Phelps.* £100
- Stemmata Avium . . . Leipzig, 1759. 4to. 19th. C. hf. mor. From Chetham's Liby., Manchester. (C. Nov.27; 231) *Weldon & Wesley.* £100
- Vorbereitung zu einer Vollständigen Vögelhistorie.–Classification und Kurz Geschichte der Vierfüssigen Thiere. Trans.:– D.H. Behn. Leipzig & Lübeck; Lübeck, 1760. 1st. German Edns. 2 works in 1 vol. Both works soiled in parts. Cont. leath. (R. Oct.14-18; 3018) DM 500

KLEIN, Jacob Theodor–VINCENT, Levinus –SELL, Godefried
- Descriptiones Tubulorum Marinorum.–Elenchus Tabularum Pinacothecarum.–Historia Naturalis Terendinus. Utrecht; Harlem, 1733; 1719. 1st. Edns. 3 works in 1 vol. 1st. work on thick paper, 2nd. work with the 2 folding plts. in 2 states (cold. & uncold.). Cont. cf., rebkd., covers detchd. From Chetham's Liby., Manchester. (C. Nov.27; 228) *Taylor.* £120

KLEIN, William
- Rome: the City & its People. N.Y., [1959]. 4to. Cl., d.-w. (reprd.). (SG. Apr.23; 118) $120

KLEINE UNIVERSUM
Stuttgart, 1840. Ob. 8vo. Lacks 1 steel engr. Cont. hf. linen. (R. Oct.14-18; 1469) DM 850

KLEIST, Heinrich von
- Gesammelte Schriften. Ed.:– Ludwig Tieck. Berlin, 1826. 1st. Coll. Edn. 3 vols. Vol. 2 hf.-title, MS. note in ink. Cont. linen, gt. spine. (R. Oct.14-18; 958) DM 2,500
- - Anr. Copy. Vols. 1 & 2 soiled, vol. 3 less. Linen. (HK. May 15; 4556) DM 900
- - Anr. Copy. Vol. I & II (of 3). Lightly browned in parts., end-papers Vol. II with pencil notes. Cont. paper bds., worn, spine torn. (H. Dec.9/10; 1568) DM 550
- Hinterlassene Schriften. Ed.:– L. Tieck. Berlin, 1821. 3 vols. Slightly soiled. Cont. bds., spine defect at head. (HK. May 15, 4557) DM 800
- Das Käthchen von Heilbronn. Berlin, 1810. 1st. Edn. Cont. hf. leath. gt. (HK. May 15; 4558) DM 2,900
- Kleine Schriften. Ill.:– M. Liebermann. Berlin, [1917]. Lge. 4to. Orig. vell. (HK. May 12-14; 1962) DM 1,500
- Penthesilea. Munich, 1917. (200). Lge. 4to. Cont. mor. gt. Printer's mark sigd., 5 cold. & sigd. lithos. (HK. May 12-14; 2058) DM 540
- Robert Guiskard. [Toelz], Bremer Pr., [1919]. (270) numbered copies on H.M.P. 4to. Crushed lev., elab. gt.-tooled borders, spines gt., gt. dentelles, by F.Th. at Bremer Bindery. (SG. Oct.9; 44) $750
- Der Zerbrochene Krug. Berlin, 1811. 1st. Edn. Stp. on title verso, lightly soiled in parts. Cont. wraps., soiled. (H. May 21/22; 1176) DM 1,800

KLENK, K. van
- Historische Verhael of Beschryving van de Voyagie . . . aan Zijne Zaarsche Majesteyt van Moscovien. Amst., 1677. 1st. Edn. Sm. 4to. Slightly soiled, title with erased owners mark, slight text loss on copper engraved title & printed title, pp. 85-90 numbered double. Cont. style hf. vell. (H. Dec.9/10; 615) DM 520

KLEPPISIUS, Gregorius–BESLER, Basilius
- Theatrum Emblematicum.–Fasciculus Rariorum et Aspectu Dignorum Varii Generis quae Collegit. [Leipzig]; [Nuremb.], [1623]; [1616]. 2 works in 1 vol. Ob. 4to. 1st. work: lacks lf. 61, some tears, 3 slightly affecting engr., title slightly spotted; 2nd. work: lacks 6 engraved text ll. at end. Cont. stained vell. bds. (S. Feb.10; 205) *Israel.* £350

KLETTENBERG, Susanne Katharina von
- Neue Lieder. [Frankfurt], [1809]. Slightly soiled. Red mor. ca. 1830, wide decor. border gold & blind-stpd., gold-stpd. monog. crowned on both covers. (HK. May 15; 4343) DM 2,200

KLEUKENS, Ch. H.
- Die Fabel vom Wind u. andere Fabeln. [Darmstadt], [1923]. (50) on Japon. Orig. leath., gt. spine, inner, & outer dentelle, by Kleukens. (HK. Nov.18-21; 2543) DM 950

KLICH [Call]
Ed.:– [I.A. Bunin]. Moscow, 1915. 4to. Cont. hf. mor., orig. upr. wrap. by G. Pashkov preserved. (SH. Feb.5; 230) *Harris.* £50

KLIMIUS, Nicolas (Pseud.)
See–HOLBERG, Ludvig 'Nicolas Klimius'

KLIMSCH, F.E.
- Die Etiquettir-Kunst. Frankfurt, [1873]. 4to. Orig. hf. leath. (D. Dec.11-13; 404) DM 500

KLIMT, Gustav
- Fünfundzwanzig Handzeichnungen. Vienna, 1919. (500). Lge. fo. Loose in orig. bd. portfo., spine reprd. (H. May 21/22; 1672) DM 1,900

KLINEFELTER, Walter
- The Fortsas Bibliohoax. Newark, 1941. (128) numbered. 12mo. Linen-bkd. bds. (SG. Mar.26; 197) $100

KLINGER, Friedrich Maximilian
- Orpheus. Genf, 1778-80. 1st. Edn. 5 pts. in 2 vols. Cont. style hf. leath. (HK. May 15; 4567) DM 3,600

KLINGER, Max
– Intermezzi. Op. IV. Ill.:– M. Klinger. [Munich], [1881]. Lge. fo. Lacks title lf. as usual. Orig. linen portfo. (HK. Nov.18-21; 2719)   DM 1,400

KLIPHAUSEN, H.A. von
See–ZIEGLER & Kliphausen, H.A. von

KLIPSTEIN, August
– The Graphic Work of Käthe Kollwitz. N.Y., 1955. (200) for U.S.A. 4to. In German. Orig. linen. (H. Dec.9/10; 2159)   DM 1,600

KLOPSTOCK, Friedrich Gottlob
– Der Messias. Halle, 1751-73. 1st. Edn., 1st. printing vols I & IV. 4 vols. Lightly browned. Cont. cf., gt. spine, blind-tooled, slightly worn, vols. III & IV not unif. (H. Dec.9/10; 1571)   DM 420
– Werke. Leipzig, 1798-1806. 1st. Coll. Edn. Vol. I-X (of 12). Slightly browned in parts. Cont. hf. leath., slightly soiled. (H. Dec.9/10; 1569)   DM 650

KLYUEVA, Vera
See–LANE, Ary & Klyueva, Vera

KLYUV [Beak]
Ed.:– [A.A. Gol'mstrem]. St. Petersb., 1905. No. 1 & 2 (all publd.). Fo. Unbnd. (SH. Feb.5; 176)   *Lempert.* £80

KNAPP, Andrew & Baldwin, William
– Criminal Chronology: or, The Newgate Calendar ... L., ca. 1826. 6 vols., separately issued, 3 vols. rehinged. Cont. tree cf., 1st. 3 vols. foxed. (PNY. Oct.1; 396) $130

KNAPP, F.
See–BODE, Dr. Wilhelm von & Knapp, F.

KNAPTON, Charles
See–POND, Arthur & Knapton, Charles

KNESCHKE, E.H.
– Neues Allgemeines Deutsches Adels-Lexicon. Leipzig, 1859-70. 9 vols. Orig. hf. leath., gt. spine. (R. Oct.14-18; 1222)   DM 600

KNEWSTUB, John
– A Confutation of monstrous & horrible Heresie, taught by H[endrik] N[iclas] & embraced of a number, who call themselves the Familie of Love. 1579. 1st. Edn. 2 pts. in 1 vol. 4to. Inscr. in outer margin of title, a few in text, short marginal tear in C2, 2 pieces torn from outer edge of K2, slight staining in lr. edges of some ll. Disbnd., contents loose. [NSTC 15040] (S. Jan.26; 5)   *Forum.* £100

KNICKERBOCKER, Dietrich (Pseud.)
See–IRVING, Washington 'Dietrich Knickerbocker'

KNIGGE, Adolph Freyherrn von
– Ueber den Umgang mit Menschen. Hannover, 1788. 1st. Edn. Partly lightly stained. Cont. bds. (R. Oct.14-18; 959)   DM 700
– – Anr. Edn. Leipzig, [1789]. 3rd. Edn. 3 pts. in 1 vol. Slight discoloration. Bds. (S. Nov.18; 667)   *Waechter.* £260
– Ueber Eigennutz und Undank. Leipzig, 1796. 1st. Edn. Slightly soiled in parts. Cont. hf. leath., gt. spine, slightly worn. (H. Dec.9/10; 1572)   DM 700

KNIGHT, Charles
– The Popular History of England. L., 1856-62. 8 vols. Extra-ill. with some 100 steel-engraved ports. Cf., triple gt. fillet borders, spines gt. with fleurons, gt. dentelles, by Kaufmann. (SG. Feb.12; 255) $140
See–SHAKESPEARE, William–KNIGHT, Charles

KNIGHT, Ch.R.
– Scenery on the Rhine. L., [1850]. Lge. fo. Lacks 2 lithos. Cont. hf. leath. (R. Mar.31-Apr.4; 2181)   DM 3,000

KNIGHT, Ellis Cornelia
– Dinarbas. 1790. Cf. (P. Apr.30; 26)   *Bickersteth.* £80
[–] Translations from the German in Prose & Verse. Frogmore Lodge, Windsor, 1812. (30). 12mo. Cont. tree cf. gt. Inscr. on fly-lf. 'M. Ilchester–the gift of the Queen'. (SBA. Oct.22; 279)   *Frost.* £50

KNIGHT, Henry Gally
– The Ecclesiastical Architecture of Italy. Ill.:– Owen Jones. 1842. 2 vols. Fo. 2nd. title altered to 1844. Cont. hf. mor. (C. May 20; 147)   *Marsden.* £350

– – Anr. Copy. Vol. 1 only (of 2), some ll. slightly spotted. Cont. mor., gt. (SH. Nov.6; 223)   *L'Acquaforte.* £250
– – Anr. Edn. 1842-43. 2 vols. Fo. Some ll. in vol. II spotted. Cont. hf. mor., worn, loose. (SH. Nov.6; 224)   *Rebecchi.* £460
– – Anr. Edn. 1842-44. 2 vols. Fo. Corners of last 2 ll. of vol. 2 stained, plt. not affected. Hf. mor., worn, most ll. loose (Gutta-Percha). (PD. May 20; 108)   £320
– Saracenic & Norman Remains ... in Sicily. N.d. Fo. Slightly soiled. Cont. hf. mor., worn. (SH. Nov.6; 225)   *Russell.* £60
– – Anr. Copy. Fo. Some spotting. (CSK. Feb.6; 147)   £55

KNIGHT, Richard Payne
– An Account of the Remains of the Worship of Priapus. L., 1786. 1st. Edn. 4to. Disbnd. (SG. Feb.5; 199) $425
See–SOCIETY of Dilettanti–KNIGHT, R.P.

KNIGHT, Thomas Andrew
– Pomona Herefordiensis. Ill.:– W. Hooker after Elizabeth Matthews & Frances Knight. 1811. 4to. 30 hand-cold. engraved plts. Cont. cf., diced panels on covers in 2 roll tooled & double gt. fillet borders, spine gt. Inscr. to Earl of Stamford from his daughter, dtd. 1825. (C. Mar.18; 62)   *Rostrom.* £1,600

KNIGHTLY TALE OF GLOGARUS & Gawane & Other Poems
1908. 4to. Tooled red mor. (CE. Nov.20; 72)   £180

KNIP, Antoinette Pauline Jacqueline & Temminck, Conrad Jacob
– Les Pigeons. Paris, 1808. Vol. 1 only (of 2). Fo. 87 engraved plts., col. ptd. & hand-finished, title reprd., lower pt. in facs. Cont. red hf. mor., spine reprd. (C. Mar.18; 140)   *Christopher.* £7,000

KNIPHOF, Johann Hieronymus
– Botanica in originali seu herbarium vivum. Halle, 1757-64. 12 vols. in 4. Fo. Offsetting caused by printing process, index lf. to vols. 3 & 4 & plt. 656 mntd. before binding, without index of 1767. Cont. German cf. gt., rebkd., orig. spines preserved. From collection of Massachusetts Horticultural Society, stps. on plts. (SPB. Oct.1; 138) $17,500

KNIPSCHILDT, Ph.
– Tractatus Politico-Historico-Juridicus de Juribus et Privilegiis Civitatum Imperialium. Ulm, 1657. Cont. vell., wormed. (R. Oct.14-18; 1411)   DM 450

KNOLLES, Richard
– General Historie of the Turkes ... together with the Lives & Conquests of the Ottoman Kings & Emperours, unto the yeare 1621. 1621. [but 1620]. 3rd. Edn. Fo. Engraved titles, 1 holed with a little loss, some soiling, a few ll. torn & reprd. without loss of letters. Old cf. [New STC 15053] (CSK. Jan.23; 139)   £70

KNOLLES, Richard & Rycart, Sir Paul
– The Turkish History. 1687-1700. 6th. Edn. 3 vols. Fo. Cf. (P. Apr.9; 97)   £100
– – Anr. Copy. 4 pts. in 3 vols. Frontis. & titles of vols. I & II reprd., vol. II lacks last lf. (blank?), Bibliotheca Lamoniana ptd. label & written press mark in each vol., & crowned cipher stpd. on p. 3. 18th. C. mor., triple gt. fillet, flat spine gt. with title, inner gt. & press mark, inner gt. floral dentelles. [Wing K702; R2407; R2414A] (SM. Oct.7; 1778)   Frs. 2,600

KNOOP, Jean Herman
– Beschrijving en Afbeeldingen van de beste Scoorten van Appelen en Peeren.–Beschryving van Vruchtboomen en Vruchten. Amst. & Dordrecht, 1790. 2 works in 1 vol. Fo. Mod. cf., gt. decor. covers, gt. lettering of author's name & book-title, with ties. (VG. Nov.18; 1243)   Fls. 950
– Fructologie, ou Description des Arbres Fruitiers. Amst., 1771. Fo. 3 plts. & several text ll. browned, sm. hole in 3B2. Cont. hf. cf., worn, unc. (S. Dec.3; 1017)   *Walford.* £150
– Pomologia. Trans.:– G.L. Huth. Ill.:– J.M. Seligmann. Nuremb., 1760-66. 2 vols. in 1. Fo. Plts. hand-cold., 2 index ll. detchd. at end. Cont. cf., worn, cover detchd. From Chetham's Liby., Manchester. (C. Nov.27; 232)   *Tzakas.* £500

KNORR, Georg Wolfgang
– Auserlesenes Blumen-Zeichen-Buch für Frauenzimmer. Ill.:– Knorr & Dietsch. Nuremb.,

ca. 1775. 2nd. Edn. 2 pts. in 1 vol. Fo. Lacks 1 copper engr. Cont. wraps. (R. Oct.14-18; 3019)   DM 1,200
– Les Délices des Yeux et de l'Esprit. Nuremb., 1760-73. 6 pts. in 3 vols. 4to. Plt. 22 in pt. IV slightly smaller, additional plt. in pt. VI. Cont. mott. cf., gt., spines slightly worn. (S. Jun.23; 300)   *Gilbert's.* £1,400
– – Anr. Copy. 6 pts. in 4 vols. 4to. 6 extra hand-cold. engraved plts. & 190 hand-cold. engraved plts. Cont. cf., spines gt. (S. Jul.15; 188)   *Taylor.* £1,200
– – Anr. Edn. Nuremb., 1764-65. 1st. Edn., 2nd. Iss. of pt. 1. 2 pts. only (of 6). 4to. 60 hand-cold. plts. (of 190). 19th. C. hf. mor. W.a.f., from Chetham's Liby., Manchester. (C. Nov.27; 234)   *Wagner.* £300
– Deliciae Naturae Selectae. Nuremb., [1751] 1766-67. L.P. 2 vols. in 1. Fo. Hand-cold. engraved general title dtd. 1754, 91 hand-cold. engraved plts. Cont. Engl. rococo bdg. in chinoiserie style, red mor., emblematic gt. borders, spine gt. in 8 compartments, by John Baumgarten? (C. Jul.15; 154)   *Quaritch.* £4,000
– – Anr. Copy. 2 vols. Plts. & engraved title hand-cold., upr. margins in vol. 2 lightly dampstained. 19th. C. hf. mor., covers detchd. From Chetham's Liby., Manchester. (C. Nov.27; 233)   *Pickering.* £1,500
– Recueil de Monumens des Catastrophes ... Nuremb., [1768]-78. 5 vols. in 4. Fo. Plts. hand-cold., some soiling. 19th. C. hf. mor. From Chetham's Liby., Manchester. (C. Nov.27; 235)   *Wheldon & Wesley.* £700

KNOW, John
– An Historical Journal of the Campaigns in North-America, for the Years 1757, 1758, 1759 & 1760. L., 1769. 1st. Edn. 2 vols. 4to. Offsetting, text foxed. Cont. cf., rebkd., worn. From liby. of William E. Wilson. (SPB. Apr.29; 172) $900

KNOWLES, G.B. & Westcott, Frederic
– The Floral Cabinet. 1837-40. 3 vols. 4to. Lacks the plt. of Sphenogyne Speciosa in vol. 2. Cont. mor. gt. by Thomas Pennell of Kidderminster, with his ticket, some slight scuffing. (LC. Feb.12; 139)   £460
– – Anr. Edn. 1838. Cf. (DWB. May 15; 301)   £130

KNOWLES, James Sheridan
– Various Dramatic Works ... Ed.:– Francis Harvey. L., Chiswick Pr., 1874. (25). 2 vols. Lge. 4to. Mor., borders & spines gt., gt. dentelles, by Rivière. (SG. May 14; 121) $275

KNOWLES, John
– The Life & Writings of Henry Fuseli. 1831. 1st. Edn. 3 vols. Hf. mor. (SBA. Jul.23; 542)   *Frost.* £55

KNOWLTON, Dr. C.
– Two Remarkable Lectures Delivered in Boston ... Boston, 1833. 1st. Edn. Wraps. (SG. Jun.11; 199) $220

KNOWLTON, Charles
– Fruits of Philosophy. An Essay on the Population Question. 28, Stonecutter St., EC, ca. 1880. 2nd. New Edn. Orig. printed wraps. (S. Dec.2; 837)   *Quaritch.* £90

KNOX, Hubert Thomas
– Notes on the Early History of the Dioceses of Tuam, Killala & Achonry. Dublin, 1904. 1st. Edn. Cl. (GM. Apr.30; 260)   £60

KNOX, John
– An Answer to a Great Number of Blasphemous Cavillations ... Geneva, 1560. 1st. Edn. Blank margins of title reprd., tears in A2 reprd. affecting a few letters, inner margin of A5 reprd., headline on Q1 cropped, some staining. 19th. C. mor. [STC 15069] (C. Apr.1; 215)   *Duffield.* £100

KNOX, John
– An Historical Journal of the Campaigns in North America. ... Geneva, 1769. 1st. Edn. 2 vols. 4to. Map torn. Cont. cf. (SH. Jul.16; 83)   *Roberts.* £330
– A New Collection of Voyages, Discoveries & Travels ... L., 1767. 7 vols. Cont. cf., rebkd. (SG. Oct.30; 208) $500
See–CHAMPLAIN Society

KNOX, Robert
– Ceylonische Reise-Beschreibung ... Leipzig, 1689. 4to. Old hf. cf., worn, spine defect. (S. Oct.20; 124)   *Goldschmidt.* £180

KNOX, Robert & Mitchell, E.
- Engravings of the Nerves Copied from the Works of Scarpa, Soemmering & other Distinguished Anatomists. 1829. 4to. No plt. numbered XII, but apparently complete, many MS. notes on fly.-ll. & elsewhere. Hf. roan, spine defect. (S. Jun.16; 480) *Canale.* £70

KOBBE, Th. von & Cornelius, W.
- [-] [Wanderungen an der Nord- und Ostsee]. Leipzig, ca. 1840. 2 vols. in 1. Slightly soiled & browned in parts. Cont. hf. leath., cover soiled, slightly defect. (H. Dec.9/10; 704) DM 1,900

KOBER, Jacques
- Le Vent des Epines. Ill.:– Bonnard, Braque, & Matisse. [Paris], [1947]. (300) numbered on Auvergne H.M.P. 4to. Orig. wraps., bd. folder with ties, spine titled in ink by previous owner. (SG. Apr.2; 162) $200

KOCH
- Tables Généalogiques des Maisons Souverains de l'Europe. Strassburg, 1782. Lge. 4to. Glazed hf. cf. (HD. Jun.29; 108) Frs. 1,100

KOCH, E.J.
- Die Mineral-Quellen Deutschlands und der Schweiz. Vienna, 1844. Slightly soiled. Cont. hf. leath. (R. Oct.14-18; 2096) DM 700

KOCH, Robert–KOCH, Robert & others–KOCH, Robert & Wolffhugel, Gustav
- Ueber Desinfection.–Versuche über die Verwerthbarkeit heisser Wasserdämpfe zu Desinfectionszwecken.–Untersuchungen über die Desinfection mit heisser Luft. [Berlin], [1881]. 3 offprints in 1 vol. 4to. 1 lf. of text in vol. 3 misbnd. Cl. (S. Jun.16; 481) *Rootenburg.* £80

KOCH, Rudolf
- Das Blumenbuch. Ill.:– F. Kredel. Leipzig, 1929-30. (1000). 3 vols., orig. bds., 2 spines lightly soiled. (R. Oct.14-18; 945) DM 1,100
- – Anr. Edn. [Darmstadt], Ernst Ludwig Pr., [1929-30]. (135). Lge. 4to. Mor., lightly worn. (H. Dec.9/10; 1806) DM 1,400
- – Anr. Edn. Ill.:– Fritz Kredel. Leipzig, 1942. 4to. Hf. vell. (H. Dec.9/10; 2153) DM 700
- Untersuchungen über die Aetiologie d. WundinfectionsKrankheiten. Leipzig, 1878. 1st. Edn. 1st. 3 ll. with light stain. Cont. hf. linen, bd. s.-c. (HK. Nov.18-21; 605) DM 3,000

KOCHEL, Ludwig Ritter von
- Chronologisch-thematisches Verzeichniss Sämmtlicher Tonwerke Wolfgang Amade Mozart's. Leipzig, 1862. 1st. Edn. 4to. Cont. hf. leath. (H. May 21/22; 825) DM 520

KOCHNO, Boris & Luz, Maria
- Le Ballet. Ill.:– P. Picasso. Paris, 1954. Lge. 4to. Orig. linen. (HK. Nov.18-21; 2855) DM 540

KOCK, Charles Paul de
- Works. Ill.:– John Sloan, William Glackens & others. Boston, [1903-04]. Author's Edn., (1,000) sigd. 25 vols. Cl., partly. unc. (SG. Oct.9; 139) $300

KOECHER, H.F.
- Nova Bibliotheca Hebraica Secundum Ordinem Bibliothecae Hebraicae B. Io. Christoph Wolfi. Ed.:– Io. Gottpr. Eichhorn. Jena, 1783. 2 pts. in 1 vol. 4to. Slightly browned. Orig. vell., Robert Mason's bkplt. (S. Nov.17; 83) *Dawson.* £60

KOEHLER, H.A. & others
- Medizinal–Pflanzen. N.d. 2 vols. 4to. Spotting. Cont. cl. (CSK. Feb.6; 64) £130

KOEHLER, Johan David
- Kurtzgefaste u. gründl. Teutach Reichs-Historie. Frankfurt & Leipzig, Nuremb., 1736. 4to. Slightly soiled in places, old owner's mark on title. Cont. leath. gt. (HK. Nov.18-21; 1243) DM 420

KOEHLER, Johann David & Weigel, Christoph
- Descriptio Orbis Antiqui. Nuremb., ca. 1720. Fo., (380mm. × 240mm.). 36 engraved double-p. maps (of 45), hand-cold. in outl., principal areas fully cold., all on guards, some stains. Cont. cf.-bkd. limp marb. bds., worn. W.a.f. (S. Nov.3; 16) *Schuster.* £150

KOEHLER, S.R. & others
- Twenty American Etchings. Ill:– Gilbert Stuart & others. Troy, N.Y., 1887. (250) on Holland. Fo. Orig. pict. cl. (SH. Mar.27; 504) *Davidson.* £65

KOHL, Johann Georg
- Die Donau von Ihrem Ursprunge bis Pesth. Triest, 1854. Fo. Cont. hf. leath., lr. cover defect. (R. Mar.31-Apr.4; 1960) DM 2,200

KOHLER, Christian
- Neu Eingerich Eisenachisches Gesangbuch, Eisenach.-Episteln und Evangelia auf alle Sonn-, Fest-, und Feiertage durchs ganze Jahr. Erfurt, 1825. 2 works in 1 vol. Cont. German str.-grd. mor. gt., covers with border & blocked centrepiece inlaid with red mor., gt. with gothic ornament, spine in 6 compartments, 5 raised bands, marb. cf. doubls., buckram box. Eric Sexton, Henri Beraldi & J.R. Abbey bkplts. (CNY. May 22; 346) $1,100

KOHLER, [H.A.]
- Medizinal-Pflanzen in Naturgetr. Abb mit erläut. Texte. Atlas sur Pharmacopoea Germanica ... Ed.:– G. Pabst. Gera-Untermhaus, 1887[-90]. 3 vols. 4to. Orig. hf. leath. (HK. Nov.18-21; 606) DM 1,700

KOHLER, J.D.
- Historische Muns-Belustigung. Nuremb., 1729-32. Vols. 1-4 in 2. Cont. leath., spine defect. (R. Mar.31-Apr.4; 176) DM 700

KOIZUMI, Bokujo
- The Scenery & Customs of Japan. Tokyo, n.d. 2 vols. Ob. fo. Orig. Japanese-style cl. binding, contained in orig. portfo.'s. (CSK. Oct.31; 205) £75

KOK, Jacobus
- Vaderlandsch Woordenboek. Amst., 1780-96, & 1797-99. 1st. Edn. 35 vols. in 18, & 3 vol. supp. Cont. bds., leath. spine (very worn), ex-liby. (SG. Feb.5; 200) $375
See–WAGENAAR, Jan & others

KOKOSCHKA, Oskar
- Die Träumenden Knaben. Vienna, 1908. Ob. 4to. Linen with mntd. litho. Dedication. (HK. May 12-14; 1923) DM 9,500
- Vier Dramen. Berlin, Pan Pr., 1919. 1st. Edn. (50) Privilege Edn. on Bütten. Orig. hf. leath. gt., marb. end-papers. Sigd. frontis. litho. on Japan. (D. Dec.11-13; 1113) DM 2,000

KOLBEN, J.C.
- Das Frolockende Augspurg. Augsburg, 1716. Fo. Hf. cf. (BS. Jun.11; 58) £380

KOLBEN, Peter
- The Present State of the Cape of Good Hope. 1731. 2 vols. Mod. leath. (S. Dec.8; 270) *Bart.* £130

KOLDEWEY, Capt.
- The German Arctic Expedition of 1869/70 & Narrative of the Wreck of the 'Hansa' in the ice. 1874. Orig. bdg. (TRL. Dec.10; 89) £54

KOLSTOI, Casimir Stephen
- International Gallery: A Collection of One Hundred Select Works by Ancient & Modern Masters. Ill:– Rajon, Peter Moran, Forberg, Boilvin, & others. Boston, [1886]. 2 vols. Fo. 110 plts. (1st. title-p. calls for 120, the 2nd. for 100). Orig. gt.-tooled mor., slightly worn. (SG. Mar.12; 197) $120

KOMENSKY, John Amos
See–COMENIUS or KOMENSKY, John Amos

KONIG, L.F.C.–SCHMIDLIN, Ed.
- Abb. u. Beschreibg. d. nützl. Getriedearten.–Abb. u. Beschreibg. d. Wichtigsten. Futter-u. Weisenbräuter; Abb. u. Beschreibg. d. wichtigsten Futtergräser. Esslingen, 1868. 3 vols. in 1. 4to. Old MS. marginalia on vol. I plts., slightly soiled in parts. Cont. hf. linen. (HK. Nov.18-21; 608) DM 420

KONIGREICH HANNOVER in Malerischen Ansichten
Darmstadt, 1852. Lacks 9 plts., Appell, Frankfurt, ca. 1850 bnd. in, heavily browned in parts. Cont. hf. leath., worn. (H. Dec.9/10; 697) DM 13,000

KONNITSA BUR' [The Horse's Bur]
[Moscow], 1920. 2 vols. Pt. 1 in orig. wraps. by V. Kamardenkov, pt. 2 unbnd. & unopened as Iss. (SH. Feb.6; 459) *Lempert.* £50

KOPP, Hermann
- Geschichte der Chemie. Braunschweig. 1843-47. 1st. Edn. 4 vols. Slightly spotted. Cont. cl.-bkd. bds. (S. Jul.27; 238) *Van Der Wijk.* £70

KOPPEN, F. von
- Bilder aus den Deutschen Alpen, dem Alpenvorlande und aus Oberbayern. Leipzig, 1878. Hf. leath., worn. (R. Oct.14-18; 2200) DM 14,500
- Bilder aus der Schwäb.-bayerischen Hochfläche, den Neckar- und Maingegenden. Leipzig, 1879. Hf. leath. (R. Oct.14-18; 2161) DM 800

KOPS, Jan
- Flora Batava. Amst., [1800]-07. Vols. I & II. 4to. Slight browning & soiling. Cont. mott. cf., spines gt., unc. (S. Jun.1; 272) *Junk.* £440

KORAN, The
Trans.:– George Sale. 1734. 1st. Edn. 4to. Mod. leath. (SKC. Sep.9; 1612) £60
- Al-Coranus S. Lex Islamitica Muhammedis, filii Abdallae Pseudoprophetae. Ed.:– A. Hinckelmann. Hamburg, 1694. Sm. fo. Later owner's inscrs. on title & annots. in text, a few marginal stains. Cont. vell. bds., slightly soiled & spotted. (S. Apr.29; 407) *Riley Smith.* £2,800
- The Alcoran of Mahomet. Trans.:– Sieur Du Ryer. 1649. 1st. Edn. in Engl. 4to. Cont. cf., covers slightly defect., bkplt. of John Evelyn. [Wing K747] (S. Dec.8; 326) *Hosains.* £210
- – Anr. Copy. Mor. gt. by Zaehnsdorf. [Wing K747] (C. Apr.1; 216) *O'Hern.* £150
- – Anr. Copy. Title backed. Old cf., reprd. (SG. Sep.25; 190) $270
- – Anr. Edn. Trans.:– Sieur Du Ryer. [1649]. 4to. In eights, title bkd. to preserve, some other defects. Cont. cf. gt., worn, lacks spine. [Wing K747] (SBA. Dec.16; 27) *Ghani.* £70
- – Anr. Edn. Trans.:– George Sale. 1734. 1st. Edn. 4to. Short tear in map, occasional browning. 19th. C. str.-grd. mor., gt. Bkplt. of Viscount Valentia. (S. May 5; 354) *Maggs.* £70
- – Anr. Copy. Later cf., spine gt. (SG. Feb.5; 201) $180
- – Anr. Edn. Trans.:– George Sale Bath, 1795. 2 vols. Cont. Engl. str.-grd. red mor., gt., spine tooled in compartments. (S. Nov.24; 183) *Riley Smith.* £380

KORNER, M.
- Skandinaviska Foglar. Lund, 1839-46. 4to. Title & text stained. Cont. hf. mor., worn, spine gt. (SKC. Jul.28; 2417) £95

KORNFELD, Eberhard W.
- Verziechnis des Graphischen Werkes von Paul Klee. Bern, 1963. Orig. linen. (H. Dec.9/10; 2143) DM 720

KOSA [Scythe]
Ed.:– [G. Ya. Kaizerman]. St. Petersb., 1906. Nos. 1-7. Fo. Unbnd. (SH. Feb.5; 80) *Landry.* £220

KOSCHATZKY. W.
- Die Kunst der Graphik. Ill.:– H. Antes (frontis.), E. Fekete (woodcut), E. Fuchs & others. [Offenbach], [1975]. 8vo. & fo. Orig. wraps. & loose ll. in orig. plastic box. All ills. sigd. by artist. (H. Dec.9/10; 2085) DM 1,200

KOSEWITZ, W.F. von
- Eccentric Tales. Ill.:– George Cruikshank after Crowquill (A.H. Forrester). 1827. 1st. Edn. Late 19th. C. red lev. mor. by Rivière, gt., spine tooled in compartments. (S. Nov.24; 81) *Millet.* £180
- – Anr. Copy. Cl., worn, s.-c. Orig. sketch by Cruikshank or Forrester tipped-in, Albert M. Cohn & William H. Woodin bkplts. (SG. Oct.9; 74) $500

KOSINSKI, Jerzy
- The Painted Bird.–The Art of the Self. N.Y. 1965; 1968. 2 vols. Wraps. Each inscr. to George Reavey. (SG. Jun.4; 256) $120

KOSMANN, J.W.A.
- Der Herrn Ritters Pinetti de Merci Physikalische Belustigungen oder Erklärung der Sämmtlichen in Berlin angestellten Künststücke. Berlin, 1797. 2nd. Iss. Pt. 1. 2 Pts. in 1 vol. 1 title lf. with old stp., slightly stained. Cont. bds. (R. Oct.14-18; 209) DM 1,200

KOSTER, Henry
- Travels in Brazil. 1817. 2nd. Edn. 2 vols. in 1. Occasional slight soiling, 1 folding map cleanly torn. Later hf. mor., rebkd. (CSK. Jan.9; 19) £100

KOTSCHY, [Carl Georg] Theodor
- Die Eichen Europa's und des Orients. Vienna & Olmütz, 1862. Fo. Cont. cl., gt. arms on upr. cover.

From collection of Massachusetts Horticultural Society, stps. on plts. (SPB. Oct.1; 139) $800
– – **Anr. Copy.** Slightly soiled in parts. Cont. red. hf. mor. gt. (HK. May 12-14; 358) DM 800

KOTTABOS
Dublin, 1876-79. Vol. II, nos. 10 & 11 & vol. III, nos. 2, 6 & 8. Containing many contributions by Oscar Wilde, ptd. errata slip at end of vol. III, no. 2, scattered light foxing. Orig. paper wraps. From the Prescott Collection. (CNY. Feb.6; 360) $300

KOTZEBUE, August von
– **Almanach Dramatischer Spiele …** Leipzig, 1814. Cont. hf. leath., worn. (S. Mar.17; 293)
Hyde Park Books. £80
– **Les Bijoux Dangereux. Imité de l'Allemand.** Ill.:– Canu. Paris, 1802. 2 vols. 16mo. 1st. pp. of vol. II spotted. Cont. str.-grd. mor., decor. spines & covers, roulette, inner dentelle. (HD. Apr.9; 492)
Frs. 1,000
– **Erinnerungen von einer Risen aus Leifland nach Rom. u. Neapel.** Berlin, 1805. 1st. Edn. 3 vols. Slightly soiled in places. Cont. hf. leath. gt., slightly torn. (HK. May 15; 4579) DM 580
– **Theater.** Leipzig & Vienna, 1840-41. Orig. Iss. 40 vols. in 13. Minimal browning. Later hf. leath., 4 spines slightly defect. (H. Dec.9/10; 1576a)
DM 540

KOTZEBUE, Otto von
– **A New Voyage Round the World.** 1830. [1st. Edn. in Engl.?]. 2 vols. in 1. Cont. hf. cf. (SH. May 21; 66) *Brooke-Hitching.* £200
– – **Anr. Copy.** 2 vols. 12mo. Mod. moire cl. (SG. May 14; 124) $1,400
– **Reise um die Welt in den Jahren 1823, 24, 25 und 26.** Weimar & St. Petersb., 1830. 1st. German Edn. 2 vols. Slightly soiled. Cont. bds. [Sabin 38286] (R. Oct.14-18; 1689) DM 1,900
– **A Voyage of Discovery into the South Sea & Beering's Straits, for the purpose of exploring a North-East Passage.** 1821. 1st. Edn. in Engl. 3 vols. Lacks hf.-titles, sm. liby.-stps. erased from title-pp., light offsetting. Mod. cf.-bkd. marb. bds. [Sabin 38291] (S. Nov.4; 597) *Holler.* £520

KOUCHAKJI, Fahim
*See–*EISEN, Gustavus A. & Kouchakji, Fahim

KOYAMA, Fujio & Figges, John
– **Two Thousand Years of Oriental Ceramics.** N.Y., [1960]. 4to. Cl., d.-w. (SG. Mar.12; 228) $130

KRACHENINNIKOW, S.P.
– **Histoire et Description du Kamtchatka.** Amst., 1770. 2 vols. Slightly soiled in parts. Cont. leath., gt. spine. (R. Oct.14-18; 1794) DM 500

KRAEMER, Hans
– **Der Mensch und die Erde. [Man & the World].** Berlin, 1905. 10 vols. Fo. Gold-stpd. & decor. cf. in the 'Art Deco' style. (PWP. Apr.9; 114)
Can. $150
– **L'Univers et l'Humanité.** Paris, n.d. 5 vols. 4to. Decor. hf. cf., gt. (SM. Oct.8; 2188) *Frs. 1,000*

KRAEVSKY, Aleksandr
*See–*ZEMENKOV, Boris & others

KRAFFT, George Wolffgang
– **Description et Representation exacte de la Maison de Glace constuite à St. Pétersbourg au Mois de Janvier 1740, et de tous les Meubles qui s'y trouvoient.** Trans.:– Pierre Louis le Roy. St. Petersb., 1741. 4to. Some worming & dampstaining of inner margin, Russ. bkplt. on rear end-paper. Cont. wrap., lacks spine & lr. cover. (SM. Oct.7; 1779) *Frs. 1,800*

KRAFFT, Jean Charles
– **Plans de plus beaux Jardins pittoresques de France, d'Angleterre et d'Allemagne.** Paris, 1809-10. 2 vols. Ob. 4to. Slight marginal staining in vol. I. Cont. bds., worn, 1 jnt. brkn. (S. Jun.22; 125) *Marlborough Rare Books.* £420

KRAG, Neils–NICOLAUS, Damascenus–HERA-CLIDES, Ponticus
– **De Republica Lacedaemoniarum Libri IIII.– Ex … Universali Historia seu De Moribus Gentium. –De Politiis Libellus.** Ed.:– Niels Krag (2nd. & 3rd. works). [?Lyon; Lyon; Heidelberg], 1593; 1593; 1593. 1st. work: 1st. Edn. 3 works in 1 vol. 4to. 1st. work: several ll. wormed in inner margins. Mod. limp vell. (S. May 5; 51) *Hannas.* £50

KRASNY SMEKH [Red Laughter]
Ed.:– [Ya. A. Gibyansky]. St. Petersb., 1906. Nos. 1-4. Fo. Unbnd. (SH. Feb.5; 82) *Landry.* £170

KRAUS, Karl
– **Die Chinesische Mauer.** Ill.:– Oskar Kokoschka. Leipzig, 1914. (200). Fo. Vell., gt., d.-w., s.-c. brkn. (SPB. Oct.1; 232) $1,500
– – **Anr. Copy.** Box. (DS. May 22; 813)
Pts. 170,000

KRAUSE, Fedor
– **Surgery of the Brain & Spinal Cord.** Trans.:– Herman A. Haubold (vol. 1); Dr. Max Thorek (vol. 2 & 3). 1910-[1911?]. 1st. Edn. in Engl. 3 vols. 4to. Liby. stp. on titles. Hf. mor. (S. Jun.16; 483) *Jenner Books.* £85

KRAUSS, Johann Ulrich
– **Historische Bilder Bibel.** Augsburg, 1702. 4to. Disbnd. (SG. Feb.5; 202) $550
– – **Anr. Copy.** 5 pts. in 1 vol. Copperplts. soiled, lacks 6, slightly soiled in parts, plts. numbered in col. on verso, lacks end-papers. Cont. leath. (HK. May 12-14; 963) DM 840
– – **Anr. Edn.** Augsburg, 1705. Fo. Lacks 1 engraved title, copper engraved title & plts. 1, 5, 134 & 135 bkd., some ll. with sm. tears & repairs, slightly soiled or worn thro.-out. 19th. C. hf. leath., worn, spine brkn. (IIK. Nov.18-21; 1510) DM 900
– – **Anr. Copy.** 5 pts. in 1 vol. Lacks copper engraved pt. 1 title & plt. 3 pt. 1, slightly soiled. Cont. hf. vell., worn. (HK. Nov.18-21; 1511) DM 800
– – **Anr. Copy.** Inkstains, slight staining, some pp. torn. Cont. vell., soiled. (VG. Dec.17; 1143)
Fls. 750

KRAUTERMANN, V. 'C.v. Hellwig'
*See–*JUNGKEN, J.H.–KRAUTERMANN, V.

KREBEL, Rudolph
– **Ueber die Erkenntniss und Heilung des Scorbuts.** Leipzig, 1838. 1st. Edn. 16mo. Old bds., lacks spine. From Brooklyn Academy of Medicine. (SG. Jan.29; 254) $130

KREBS, F.L.
– **Vollständige Beschreibung und Abbildung der Sämmtlichen Holzarten, welche im Mittleren und Nördlichen Deutschland wild wachsen.** Braunschweig, 1826. Text & plt. vol. 4to. Lacks 1 cold. litho., plts. lightly soiled, text more soiled. Cont. hf. leath. (R. Oct.14-18; 3022) DM 3,800

KREDEL, Friedrich
*See–*KOCH, Rudolf & Kredel, Friedrich

KREDEL, Fritz & Todd, Frederick P.
– **Soldiers of the American Army.** Ed.:– Brig.-Gen. O.L. Spaulding. N.Y., 1941. (20) numbered, on Chatham H.M.P., sigd. by Kredel & Todd. Fo. Gt.-decor. red mor., partly unc. (SG. Oct.30; 209)
$140
– – **Anr. Edn.** N.Y., [1941]. 1st. Edn. (500) numbered, sigd. Fo. Gt.-pict. cl., lacks sm. portion of bottom edge of box. (PNY. Mar.26; 299) $160

KREFFT, Gerard
– **The Mammals of Australia.** Melbourne, 1979. Facs. Edn., (350) numbered. Fo. Canvas bds. & qtr. leath. (KH. Mar.24; 231) Aus. $100

KRETSCHMER, Albert
– **Deutsche Volkstrachten.** Leipzig, 1870. 4to. 86 chromolitho. plts. (of 88). Hf. cf., brkn. As a collection of plts., w.a.f. (BS. Jun.11; 357) £620
– – **Anr. Edn.** Leipzig, [1887-90]. 2nd. Edn. Sm. fo. Priv. linen. (R. Oct.14-18; 2099) DM 5,400
– – **Anr. Copy.** 150 (of 166) pp. Orig. linen, loose, spine brkn. (R. Oct.14-18; 2100) DM 5,200

KRETSCHMER, Albert & Rohrbach, Carl
– **Die Trachten der Voelker …** Ill.:– J.G. Bach. Leipzig, 1882. 2nd. Edn. Lge. 4to. Gt.-pict. leath. (SG. Oct.30; 210) $140

KRETSCHMER, Konrad
– **Die Entdeckung Amerikas in Ihrer Beduutung f. d. Geschichte d. Weltbildes.** Berlin, 1892. 2 vols. Fo. & Lge. Fo. Orig. hf. leath. (HK. May 12-14; 513) DM 950

KRIGER, J.F.
– **Leben und Thaten Friedrichs des Einzigen Königs von Preussen in einer Reihe von Kupferstichen und Holzschnitten.** Halberstadt, 1817. Title browned, soiled. [N] No bdg. (R. Oct.14-18; 1179) DM 520

KRIVENKO, V.S.
– **Les Solennités du Saint Couronnement [of Nikolai II & Aleksandra].** St. Petersb., 1899. 2

vols. in 1 (including Supp.). Fo. A few ll. loose. Orig. decor. mor. (SH. Feb.5; 232) *Baldur.* £400

KROMBHOLZ, J. von
– **Naturgetreue Abbildungen und Beschreibungen der essbaren schädlichen und verdächtigen Schwämme.** Prague, 1831-46. Text in 10 orig. parts. Fo. & lge. fo. Plts. loose, lightly soiled in parts. Portfo. (R. Oct.14-18; 3044) DM 5,200

KROUGLY, Alexandre
– **La Cour de l'Imperatrice Catherine II.** St. Petersb., 1899. 2 vols. 4to. Text in Fr. & Russian, a few ll. slightly soiled. Cont. hf. mor., orig. wraps. preserved. (SH. Feb.5; 233) *Hall.* £60

KRUCHENYKH, A.
– **Apokalipsis v russkoi literature [Apocalypse in Russian Literature].** Ill.:– N. Nagorsky. Moscow, 1923. (2,000). Orig. wraps., slightly soiled & torn. (SH. Feb.6; 462) *Lempert.* £50
– **10 Ballads o Yade Kormorane [Ten Ballads of Poison to Kormoran etc.].** [Moscow], 1921. 4to. Orig. bdg. (SH. Feb.6; 464) *Quaritch.* £400
– **Chornaya taina Esenina [Dark Secret of Esenin].** Ill.: V. Kulagina. Moscow, priv. ptd., 1926. (5,000). Orig. wraps. by V. Kulagina, slightly torn. (SH. Feb.6; 463) *Lempert.* £65
– **Na Bor'bu s Khuliganstvom v Literature [On the Struggle with Hooliganism in Literature].** Moscow, 1926. (5,000). Slightly browned. Orig. wraps. by Gustav Klutsis, reprd. (SH. Feb.6; 325)
Nijhoff. £65
– **Pustynniki Pustynnisa [Hermits].** Ill.:– after N. Goncharova by S. Mukharsky. [Moscow], [1913]. [(100)]. Ptd. on recto only. Orig. bdg., lacks upr. wrap. (SH. Feb.6; 465) *Kazinikas.* £230
– **Razboinik Van'ka-Kain i Son'ka Manikyurshchitsa [The Robber Vanka-Cain & Sonka the Manicurist].** Ill.:– M. Sinyakova. Moscow, 1926. (1,000). Orig. wraps. by M. Sinyakova, slightly soiled. (SH. Feb.6; 467)
Quaritch. £150
– **Vozropshchem [Lets Grumble].** Ill.:– Malevich & Rozanova. St. Petersb., [1913]. Mod. cl.-bkd. bds., orig. wraps. preserved. (SH. Feb.6; 468)
Sackner. £520

KRUCHENYKH, A. & Khlebnikov, V.
– **Igra v adu [A Game in Hell].** Ill.:– K. Malevich & O. Rozanova. [St. Petersb.], Svet, [1913]. 2nd. Edn. Orig. wraps., soiled, spine worn. (SH. Feb.6; 472) *Dembeck.* £600

KRUGER, E.
– **Wild u. Wald.** Hamburg, ca. 1860. Ob. fo. All plts. mntd., lightly soiled. Cont. hf. leath., traces of wear. (HK. May 12-14; 1105) DM 1,600

KRUL, Jan H.
– **Pampiere Wereld ofte Wereldsche Oeffeninge.** Amst., 1644. Old cf. (BS. Jun.11; 60) £80
– – **Anr. Copy.** Fo. Old vell., worn. (BS. Jun.11; 59) £65
– – **Anr. Edn.** Amst., 1681. 2 pts. in 1 vol. 4to. Sm. wormhole through many ll., not affecting text. Old cf. (BS. Jun.11; 61) £65

KRUNITZ, Johann Georg
– **Okonom.–technologische Encyklopädie. Tl. 107. Papieradel bis Pasternak.** Berlin, 1807. Cont. bds. (R. Oct.14-18; 468) DM 440
– **Okonom.–technologische Encyklopädie. Tl. 115. Polypädie bis Post.** Berlin, 1810. Cont. bds. (R. Oct.14-18; 475) DM 530

KRUSENSTERN, Adam Johann von
– **Poutechestvie Vokroug … –Atlas.** St. Petersb., 1809-12; 1813. 1st. Edn. Together 4 vols. (3 + 1). Lge. 4to. & elephant fo. Lacks frontis., 47 plts. with German & Russian text, 1 map German only, 4 plts. badly stained. Red mor., gt. borders. (SG. May 14; 125) $17,000
– **Voyage Round the World.** Trans.:– R.B. Hoppner. 1813. 1st. Edn. in Engl. 2 vols. in 1. 4to. Folding map mntd. on linen. 19th. C. cl. From Chetham's Liby., Manchester. (C. Nov.27; 236)
Hammond. £750

KRUSINSKY, Judas Thaddeus, S.J.
– **Ta'rih-i seyyah [The History of the Traveler].** Istanbul, [1729]. 1st. Edn. Sm. 4to. In Turkish, dampstained thro.-out. Old roan-bkd. bds., brkn. (SG. Sep.25; 191) $425

K SVETU [Towards the Light]
Ed.–– [N.B. Teitel'baum]. St. Petersb., 1906. Nos. 1-3. 4to. Unbnd. (SH. Feb.5; 83) *Landry.* £170

KUBIN, Alfred
– **Kritiker.** Munich, 1920. 1st. Edn., (100) numbered, Privilege Edn. on Japan. Fo. All ll. guarded. Orig. linen portfo. Printer's mark sigd. by artist. (HK. Nov.18-21; 2737) DM 850
– – **Anr. Edn.** Munich, 1920. (1,000) numbered. Ob. 8vo. Orig. cl.-bkd. bds., worn. Pres. copy, with the wash & ink sketch for colophon ill., sigd., tipped in below reproduction. (SH. Nov.21; 359)
Schwing. £110
– **Von Verschiedenen Ebenen.** Berlin [1922]. (20) numbered Privilege Edn. on Bütten. Fo. 6 sigd. litho. plts. Orig. vell, upr. cover ill. by Kubin. (HK. Nov. 18-21; 2739) DM 1,400
– – **Anr. Copy.** (400). Orig. pict. linen, loose, soiled. 4 lithos. sigd. (H. Dec.9/10; 2162) DM 900

KUHNAU, J.Chr.
– **Vierstimmige Alte und Neue Choralgesänge.** Berlin, 1790. 1st. Edn. Pt. 2. 4to. Lightly browned in parts. Cont. cf., worn, 1 jnt. brkn. (H. Dec.9/10; 1178) DM 440

KUHNERT, Wilhelm
See–LYDEKKER, Richard & Kuhnert, Wilhelm

KULMUS, Johann Adam
– **Anatomische Tabellen nebst Anmerckungen.** Amst., 1732. 3rd. Edn. Cont. leath. (R. Oct.14-18; 353) DM 950
– – **Anr. Edn.** Ed.:– K.G. Kühn. Leipzig, 1814. New Edn. 4to. 1 plt. partly removed. Cont. hf. leath. (D. Dec.11-13; 214) DM 500
– **Tables anatomiques ... du Corps humain, et toutes ses Parties.** Amst., 1734. 1st. Fr. Edn. Stp. on title, 26 plts. numbered 1-28. Cont. cf., reprd. (S. Feb.23; 66) *Dawson.* £280
– **Tabulae anatomicae ... accesserunt ... Annotationes et tabulae aeneae.** Amst., 1744. 26 plts. numbered 1-28, slightly spotted. Bds. (S. Feb.23; 67) *Dawson.* £260

KUNHART, C.P.
– **Small Yachts, their Design & Construction.** 1887. 4to. Orig. cl. (SH. Oct.10; 474)
Abbey Books. £50

KUNSTGESCHICHTE, PROPYLAEN
Berlin, 1923-'29. Pts. 2-4; 6-9; 13-15; 10 (of 16) vols. Orig. hf. mor. gt. (VG. Dec.15; 203)
Fls. 475

KUNSTLICHE GOLD–UND SILBER–ARBEITER
Nuremb., 1726. 1st. & last ll. slightly stained. Cont. vell. (R. Oct.14-18; 229a) DM 1,200

KUNZ, George F.
– **Ivory & the Elephant in Art.** Garden City, 1916. 1st. Edn., L.P. Sm. 4to. 4 ll. loose. Cl., slightly shaken. (PNY. May 21; 240) $130

KURTH, Betty
– **Die Deutschen Bildteppiche d. Mittelatters.** Vienna, 1926. 3 vols. Fo. Orig. linen. (HK. Nov.18-21; 3516) DM 600

KURTH, Willi
– **The Complete Woodcuts of Albrecht Durer.** 1927. Ltd. Edn. Fo. Orig. cl. portfo. (SH. Jan.29; 117) *Talerman.* £50

KUSEL, Melchior
– **Icones Biblicae Veteris et Novi Testamenti.** Ill.:– Kusel. Nuremb., 1678. 2 vols. in 1. Sm. 4to. A few margins strengthened, some dampstains, mainly marginal, a few other minor defects. Cont. cf. gt., very worn, rebkd., lacks clasps. Fore-e. pntg. showing ships plying in Constantinople? harbour, sigd. by John T. Beer, w.a.f. (SBA. Jul.14; 75) *Hyde Park Bookshops.* £210

KUSSMAUL, Adolph
– **Die Farbenerscheinungen im Grunde des Menschlichen Auges.** Heidelberg, 1845. 1st. Edn. Foxed. Bds., covers loose, ex-liby. (SG. Jan.29; 256) $550
– **Die Störungen der Sprache.** Leipzig, 1877. 1st. Edn. Qtr. mor. (S. Jun.16; 484)
Jenner Books. £55
– **Untersuchungen ueber das Seelenleben des Neugeborenen Menschen.** Leipzig & Heidelberg, 1859. 1st. Edn. Mod. bds., orig. wraps. (torn) bnd. in., ex-liby. Inscr. to Dr. Ludwig, Wien. (SG. Aug.21; 331) $130

KUYPER, Jacques
See–SIEBOLD, M. & Kuyper, J.
See–STUART, Martinus & Kuyper, Jacques

KUZMIN, M.
– **Dvum [For a Pair].** Ill.:– E. Turova. Petrograd, n.d. (125) numbered. Orig. wraps. by E. Turova. (SH. Feb.6; 477) *Quaritch.* £170

KYD (Pseud.)
See–CLARKE, Joseph Clayton 'Kyd'

KYPSELER, Gottlieb
– **Les Delices de la Suisse.** Leiden, 1714. 4 vols. 12mo. Natural paper fault in 1 plt. Cont. cf., gt. spines. (C. Feb.25; 105) *Davidson.* £1,700
– – **Anr. Copy.** Extra engraved title, frontis. & 72 (of 74) plts. & maps, many folding. (C. May 20; 147A) *Schoeni.* £1,400

[L., R.]-EDWARD VI of·England, King–CHEKE, Sir John
– **Copye of a Letter Contayning Certayne Newes, & the Articles ...–Message sent ... to Certain of his People. Assembled in Deuonshire–Hurt of Sedition ...** 1549; Jul. 1549;·Dec. 1569. 3 works in 1 vol. 1st work: title frayed with a few sm. tears; slight soiling & browning. Cont. spr. cf., slight wear. Sig. of Humphrey Dyson on titles. [NSTC 15109.3; STC 7506; STC 5110] (S. May 5; 273) *Hill.* £2,500

LABACCO, A.
See–VIGNOLA, Giovanni Barozzi–LABACCO, A.

LABADIE, Dom.-SAINT-HYACINTHE, Themiseul de
– **Les Avantures de Pomponius ...–Histoire du Prince Titi.** Ed.:– Abbé Prevost (1st work). Rome; Paris, 1725; 1736. 2nd. Edn. (1st. work). 2 works in 1 vol. Cf. by Lortic, fillet, spine grotesquely decor., inside dentelle. (HD. Mar.18; 90)
Frs. 1,000

LA BARRE, Jean de
– **Les Antiquitez de la Ville, Comté et Chatellenie de Corbeil ...** Paris, 1647. 4to. Cont. vell. (HD. Jun.29; 184) Frs. 1,600

LA BARRE DE BEAUMARCHAIS, Anthony
[–] **Le Temple des Muses, orné de LX tableaux, où sont représentés les evenemens le plus remarquables de l'antiquité fabuleuse.** Ill.:– Bernard Picart. Amst., 1742. Fo. Additional title slightly cropped in outer margin. Cont. mott. cf., gt. spine. (C. Feb.25; 185) *Gilbert.* £80

LABAT, Jean Baptiste
[–] **Nouveau Voyage aux Isles de l'Amérique.** Paris, 1722. 1st. Edn. 6 vols. 12mo. Cont. cf., worn. [Sabin 38409] (C. Nov.5; 87) *Maggs.* £260
[–] – **Anr. Edn.** The Hague, 1724. [2nd. Edn.?]. 6 vols. Cf. gt. (P. Oct.23; 39) *Remington.* £200
– – **Anr. Copy.** 2 vols. 4to. 64 of 65 engraved plts. & maps, light stain affecting 1 vol. Cont. cf.-bkd. bds., worn, unc. [Sabin 38411] (SPB. May 5; 294) $300
[–] – **Anr. Copy.** Heavily browned in parts. Cont. vell. (R. Mar.31-Apr.4; 2432) DM 2,100
– **Nouvelle Relation de l'Afrique Occidentale.** Paris, 1728. 5 vols. 12mo. Old cf., 5 spine raised bands. (LM. Jun.13; 5) B.Frs. 20,000
– – **Anr. Edn.** Paris, [1728]. 5 vols. 12mo. Date clipped from all title-pp. Old panel. cf., very worn. (SG. Feb.26; 202) $160
– **Voyage du Chevalier de Marchais en Guinée, Isles Voisines et à Cayenne.** Paris, 1730. 4 vols. Several short tears reprd. Cont. cf., worn. [Sabin 38414] (SPB. May 5; 295) $150

L'ABBAT, Abbé
– **The Art of Fencing.** Ill.:– Lud. Du Dempsy. Dublin, 1734. 1st. Edn. in Engl. 11 (of 12) copperplts., foxed, ex-liby. Old cf., crudely rebkd. (SG. Oct.30; 150) $110

LABE, Louis
– **Oeuvres.** 1845. (200). Ornam. cf., by Simier. (HD. Oct.10; 244) Frs. 1,000

LABICHE, Eugène
– **Théatre Complet.** Paris, 1878-79. 10 vols. Red mor. by Baruch, partly unc., orig. wraps. bnd. in. (SM. Oct.8; 2130) Frs. 1,800

LABILLARDIÈRE, Jacques Julien Houton de
– **An Account of a Voyage in Search of La Perouse.** 1800. Atlas vol. only. 4to. 41 engraved plts. (of 43), folding map torn in folds, some foxing. Cont. hf. cf., worn. [Sabin 38423] (S. Mar.31; 484) *Gibbs.* £65
– – **Anr. Edn.** L., 1802. 2nd. Edn. 2 vols. & atlas vol. 8vo. & 4to. Several sm. repairs, 1 corner defect., some foxing & discoloration of text,

occasional staining, atlas index mntd. on stub, general chart loosely inserted. Text in mod. hf. mor. & marb. bds., atlas in mor. (KH. Mar.24; 232) Aus. $700
– **Atlas pour Servir à la Relation du Voyage à la Recherche de la Pérouse ...** Paris, An VIII de la Republique. Fo. Some browning. Cont. three quarter roan, limp decor. spines, defects. (HD. Apr.24; 71) Frs. 2,600
– **Relation du Voyage à la Recherche de la Perouse.** Ill.:– after Audebert, Redoute, Piron, & others. Paris, [1800]. 1st. Edn. 2 vols. & atlas. 4to. & fo. 19th. C. cl., & atlas in 19th. C. hf. mor. From Chetham's Liby., Manchester. (C. Nov.27; 237) *Cash.* £550
– – **Anr. Copy.** 2 vols. No atlas. Cont. mott. cf. [Sabin 38420] (SPB. May 5; 296) $275
– **Voyage in Search of La Perouse.** L., 1800. Atlas vol. only. Tall 4to. Very foxed. Cont. leath.-bkd. marb. bds. (SG. Feb.26; 206) $400
See–LA PEROUSE, Jean Françoise Galaup de
–LABILLARDIERE, Jacques J. Houton de
–ENTRECASTEAUX, A.R.J. de Bruni

LABORDE, Alexandre Louis Joseph, Comte de
– **Description des Nouveaux Jardins de France et de ses Anciens Châteaux.** Ill.:– G. Bourgeois. Paris, 1808. Lge. fo. Hf. chagrin. (LM. Jun.13; 104) B.Frs. 16,000
– **Les Monumens de la France Classée Chronologiquement ...** Paris, 1816, 1836. 2 vols. Lge. fo. Some browning of plts. Cont. hf. chagrin, decor. spine raised bands. (HD. Apr.24; 148) Frs. 11,000
– **Voyage pittoresque et historique de l'Espagne.** Paris, 1806-20. 2 vols. in 3. Fo. 253 (of 272) plts., also lacks 2 maps & text of vol. 2 pt. 4, & pt. 2 text to vol. 2 pt. 3. Hf. mor. gt. As a collection of plts., w.a.f. (SPB. Oct.1; 233) $2,000

LABORDE, Jean Benjamin de
– **Choix de Chansons** Rouen, 1881. (150) Privilege Edn. on vell., New Edn. 4 vols. 4to. With 2 ports., 2 plts., 2 ll. in II & 2 plts. & frontis. in III browned. Hand-bnd. hf. mor. with orig. wraps. bnd. in, spine of IV slightly defect. MS. inscr. on hf.-title vol. I. (H. Dec.9/10; 1179) DM 1,300
– **Essai sur l'Histoire Chronologique de plus de quatre-vingt Peuples de l'Antiquité, composé pour l'Education de Monseigneur le Dauphin.** Paris, 1788. 2 vols. (all publd.). 4to. Ptd. tables, some folding, in vol. 11, sig. of Sophia Potocka & Biblioteka Tulczynska stp. on titles. Cont. red mor., triple gt. fillets, spine gt. in compartments, inner gt. dentelles. (SM. Oct.7; 1780) Frs. 1,800

LABORDE, Jean Benjamin de & others
– **Description Générale et Particulière de la France ...** Ill.:– Masquelier & others. Paris, 1781-1800. 1st. printing. 12 vols. Fo. Vol. VI lacks hf.-title & plt. 13 bis. Cont. porphyr cf., gt. fillet borders, decor. spine raised bands, inner dentelles. (HD. Apr.24; 72) Frs. 82,000
[–] – **Anr. Edn.** Paris, 1781-92. Vols. I-X only (of 12). Lge. fo. In a few vols. the number of plts. & vol. numbers differ from that given by Cohen-De Ricci, slight browning & staining, occasional tears, mostly marginal, possibly lacks 3 plt.-lists in vol. X. Cont. hf. cf., unc., spines gt., label of R.M. Bitler, Bookseller, Dublin, in some vols. (S. Apr.7; 492) *Loeb Larocque.* £5,000

LABORDE, Jean Benjamin de & Zurlauben, Baron B.F.A. de
– **Tableaux Topographiques, Pittoresques, Physiques, Historiques, Moraux, Politiques, Litteraires de la Suisse.** Ill.:– Nee, de Longeuil, & others after Le Barbier & others. 1780-86. 2 vols. in 4 (Vol. 1, 3 pts., vol. 2, 2 pts.). Fo. Hf.-titles slightly soiled & creased, occasional light soiling & discoloration, title to vol. 2, pt. 2 bnd. at end of vol. 2. Non-unif. hf. mor., hf. cf., all cont. russ., all worn, most covers detchd. W.a.f., from Chetham's Liby., Manchester. (C. Nov.27; 415) *Wenner.* £10,50
– – **Anr. Edn.** Ill.:– Moreau, Masquelier, Zurlauben, Laborde, Marillier & others. Paris, 1780-88. 4 vols. Fo. Sm. worm-holes. Cont. marb. cf., gt. triple fillet border, decor. spine raised bands. (HD. Apr.24; 111) Frs. 100,000

LABOUREUR, Jean Emile
– **Chansons Made'casses.** Trans.:– Evariste Parny. 1920. On natural Jute paper. 12mo. Sewed. (HD. Jun.30; 37) Frs. 1,050

LA BRUYÈRE, Jean de
- **Les Caractères.** Paris, 1688. 2nd. Orig. Edn., 1st. printing, 2nd. state. 12mo. Errata & privilege ll. Jansenist mor., mor doubl., centre arms & crowned cypher at angles, by Thierry. From Escoffier liby. (HD. Jun.10; 46) Frs. 2,700
- – **Anr. Edn.** Paris, 1689. 4th. Orig. Edn. 12mo. Jansenist mor., mor. doubl., centre arms & crowned angle cypher, by Thierry. From Escoffier liby. (HD. Jun.10; 47) Frs. 2,800
- – **Anr. Edn.** Paris, 1690. 5th. Orig. Edn. 12mo. Sm. restoration to title-p. Jansenist mor., mor. doubl., centre arms & crowned cypher at angles, by Thierry. From Escoffier liby. (HD. Jun.10; 48) Frs. 2,000
- – **Anr. Edn.** Paris, 1691. 6th. Orig. Edn. 12mo. Jansenist mor., mor. doubl., centre arms & crowned cypher at angles, by Thierry. From Escoffier liby. (HD. Jun.10; 49) Frs. 2,000
- – **Anr. Edn.** Paris, 1694. 8th. orig. Edn., 2nd printing. 12mo. Jansenist mor., mor. doubl., centre arms & crowned cypher at angles, by Thierry. From Escoffier liby. (HD. Jun.10; 50) Frs. 2,800
- – **Anr. Edn.** Paris, 1699. 10th. Edn. 12mo. Mor., mor. doubl., centre arms, crowned cypher at angles, cypher at foot of spine, by Thierry. From Escoffier liby. (HD. Jun.10; 51) Frs. 2,000
- **Les Caractères, suivis des Caractères de Théophraste.** Ill.:– Pourvoyeur (port.). Paris, 1824. 3 vols. 18mo. Cont. cf., decor. spine & gt. fillet decor. covers, angle fleurons, inner dentelle. (HD. Apr.9; 495) Frs. 1,000

LABYRINTE DE VERSAILLES
Ill.:– Sebastien Le Clerc, the Elder. Paris, 1679. Cf., Royal arms of Louis XIV on covers, upr. cover detchd. Holland House bkplt. (P. Jul.2; 168) *Marlborough.* £190

LA CAILLE, Nicolas Louise
- **Journal Historique du Voyage fait au Cap de Bonne-Esperance.** Paris, 1763. Spr. cf. (SSA. Apr.22; 141) R. 140

LA CALPRENEDE, Gualtier de Coste, seigneur de
- **Hymen's Praeludia, or Loves Master-Piece, being the last parts of that so much admired Romance, intituled, Cleopatra.–Hymen's Praeludia-9th & 10th parts.–Hymen's Praeludia-11th, 12 & last parts.** 1663; 1659; 1659. 3 works in 1 vol. Fo. 1st. & 2nd. titles misbnd. Cont. cf., corners & head & foot of spine worn. 2nd. work [Wing L119]; 3rd. work [Wing L120] (C. Feb.25; 161) *Hannas.* £110

LACAUCHIE, A.
- **Galerie des Artistes Dramatiques de Paris.** Paris, 1841-44. 2 vols. 4to. Some slight stains. Cont. hf. mor. (SI. Dec.3; 302) *Lire 300,000*

LACE
[?France], ca. 1880-1900. Fo. A sample book containing some 3,000 pieces of lace, mntd. in 2 columns on glazed blue paper with gt. lines at edges. Cl. (SH. Apr.10; 551) *Demetzy.* £170

LACEPEDE, B.G.E. Delaville, Comte de
- **Oeuvres.** Ill.:– Massard (port.). Paris, 1832-33. 12 vols. Some spotting. Cont. hf. cf. (SM. Feb.11; 9) Frs. 1,600

LA CHAMBRE, Marin Cureau de
- **L'Art de Connoistre les Hommes.** Paris, 1659. 1st Edn. 2 pts. in 1 vol. 4to. Cont. red mor., 2 pointillé borders, lge. central rectangle, fleurs-de-lys in corners, 2 fillets, pointillé fleurons & scrolls around central oval containing arms of Barthélémy Hervart, decor. spine, inside dentelle. (HD. Mar.18; 91) Frs. 7,500
- **Nouvelles Observations et Coniectures sur l'Iris.** Paris, 1650. 1st. Edn. 4to. 1 engraved diagram now detchd., lacks 1st. lf. (blank?), some margins dampstained, old sigs. on title of L. Milton & John McLeod, Isle of Sky. Cont. red mor., gt.-tooled to fanfare design, arms of Cardinal Mazarin, pointillé ornams. in compartments, ground tooled in pointillé, spine compartments tooled to fanfare design, inner gt. dentelles. (SM. Oct.7; 1784) Frs. 28,000

LA CHAPELLE, Jean Baptiste de
- **Le Ventriolque.** 1772. 2 pts. in 1 vol. 12mo. Cont. mott. cf. (SH. Oct.23; 128) *Huber.* £160

LA CHAU, Abbé Géraud de
- **Dissertation sur les Attributs de Vénus.** Ill.:– after Titien engraved by Saint-Aubin. Paris, 1780.

4to. Cont. mor., dentelle border, decor. spine. (HD. Jun.10; 51a) Frs. 1,100

LA CHAU, Abbé Geraud de & Le Blond, Abbé de
- [–] **Description des Principales Pierres Gravées du Cabinet de S.A.S. Monseigneur le Duc d'Orléans.** Paris, 1780-84. 1st. Edn. 2 vols. Fo. 177 engraved plts. (of 179), some slight browning. Cont. Fr. red mor., gt. (S. May 5; 434) *Duran.* £260
- – **Anr. Copy.** Includes 7 erotic plts. Cont. str.-grd. mor., gt. (SM. Oct.8; 2407) Frs. 22,000
- – **Anr. Copy.** L.P., 2 vols. Fo. Cont. mor. by Derome le Jeune with his 1785 ticket, triple gt. fillet, spine gt. with fleurons in compartments, inner gt. dentelles. Northwick Park copy. (SM. Oct.7; 1785) Frs. 3,200
- – **Anr. Copy.** 3 vols. 1st. 2 vols.: mod. red hf. mor., corners; 3rd. vol.: red hf. mor. (HD. Dec.5; 113) Frs. 1,100

LA CHAUSSE, Michelange de
- **Romanum Museum.** Rome, 1746. 3rd. Edn. 2 vols. Fo. Cont. hf. cf., corners worn. (S. Jul.27; 214) *Drury.* £110

LACLOS, Pierre-Ambroise-François Choderlos de
- **Les Liaisons Dangereuses.** Ill.: Monnet & others. 1796 [1812]. 2nd. printing. 2 vols. Some browning. Cont. decor. cf. (HD. Jun.30; 38) Frs. 1,150
- – **Anr. Copy.** Red mor., 5 decor. spine raised bands, triple gt. fillet border round fleurons, angle fleurons. (LM. Mar.21; 86) B.Frs. 14,000
- – **Anr. Edn.** Ill.:– Sylvain Sauvage & D.A. Maillart. Paris, 1930. 2 vols. 4to. Mor., 5 decor. spine raised bands, double border, gt. fillets, pointillé & roulette, angle fleurons. gt. double fillet, mor. doubls. & paper guards, by Dubois d'Enghien. (LM. Nov.8; 41) B.Frs. 16,000

LACOMB DE PREZEL
- [–] **Dictionnaire du Citoyen ou Abrégé historique, théorique et practique du Commerce.** Paris, 1761. 2 vols. Cont. marb. cf., decor. spines. (HD. Feb.18; 32) Frs. 1,000

LA CONDAMINE, Charles-Marie de
- **Journal du Voyage.–Mesure des Trois Premiers Degrés du Meridien dans l'Hemisphere Austral.** Paris, 1751. 1st. Edns. 2 works in 2 vols. 4to. 19th. C. hf. mor. From Chetham's Liby., Manchester. [Sabin 38479, 38483] (C. Nov.27; 238) *Quaritch.* £380
- **Relation Abrégé d'un Voyage de l'Amérique Méridionale ... en descendant la Rivière des Amazones.** Paris, 1745; 1746; 1745. 3 pts. in 1 vol. Folding engraved map slightly soiled. Cont. cf., worn. [Sabin 38484] (SPB. May 5; 297) $275
- – **Anr. Edn.** Maastricht, 1778. Some discoloration. Cont. wraps., spine defect., unc. [Sabin 38485] (SPB. May 5; 298) $175

LACORDAIRE, H.D.
- **Vie de Saint Dominique.** Ill.:– Jacques Beltrand after Maurice Denis. Paris, 1919. (330). Lge. 4to. In sheets, publisher's portfo. (HD. Dec.5; 114) Frs. 1,000

LACOSTE
- [–] **[Bramadante].** [Paris], [1707]. 1st. Edn. Ob. 4to. Lacks title-lf., slightly browned. Cont. cf., spine defect. (H. Dec.9/10; 1180) DM 620

LACRETELLE, Jacques
- **Lettres Espagnoles.** Ill.:– Marie Laurencin. Paris, 1926. (325) numbered. Orig. wraps., unc. (SH. Nov.21; 371) *Kawamatsu.* £185
- **Luce, ou l'Enfance d'une Courtisane.** Ill.:– Marie Laurencin. Paris, 1931. (1000) numbered. 4to. Orig. wraps., unc. (SH. Nov.21; 378) *Subunso.* £50

LA CROIX, A.P. de
- **Geographia Universalis** Leipzig, 1697. 1st. German Edn. 4 pts. in 1 vol. Slightly browned thro.-out. Cont. vell.-bkd. wood bds., 2 metal clasps, spine torn. (R. Mar.31-Apr.4; 2317) DM 1,300

LACROIX. Gen. Baron François J. Pamphile de
- **Memoires pour servir à l'Histoire de la Revolution de Saint-Domingue.** Paris, 1820. 2nd. Edn. 2 vols. Cont. maroon pol. cf. gt., gt. borders, gt. panel & central medallion device. Pres. copy to Sir George Stratton. [Sabin 38496.] (CNY. May 22; 165) $100

LACROIX, Paul 'Julien le Bibliophile'
- **XVIIe Siècle.–XVIIIe Siècle.–Directoire etc.** Paris, 1875-84. 2 vols.; 2 vols.; 1 vol., together 5

vols. Cont. hf. mor. (SH. May 28; 63) *Duran.* £70
- **XVIIIme Siècle: Institutions, Usages et Costumes.** Paris, 1885. 4th. Edn. 4to. Gt.-decor. cl., gt. lettered on upr. cover, red mor. spine. Prize Copy. (SG. Dec.4; 214) $120
- **The Eighteenth Century.–Science & Literature in the Middle Ages.–Manners, Customs & Dress in the Middle Ages.–The Arts of the Middle Ages. –Military & Religious Life in the Middle Ages.** 1876; 1878; n.d.; n.d.; n.d. 5 vols. 4to. Cont. mor.-bkd. cl., gt. (SH. Jan.30; 458) *Skilton.* £55
- **Moeurs, Usages et Costumes au M.A. et à la Renaiss.–Les Arts au M.A. à la Renaiss.–Sciences et Lettres au M.A. et à la Renaiss.–Vie Militaire et Religieuse au M.A. et à la Renaiss ...** Paris, 1873-82. 4th. Edn; 5th. Edn. Together 8 vols. Hf.-chagrin, gt. (VG. Nov.17; 330) Fls. 450
- **Moyen Age, XVIIme Siècle, XVIIIme Siècle, Directoire, Consulat et Empire.** Paris, 1871-84. 4 vols.; 2 vols.; 2 vols.; 1 vol. 4to. A few ll. spotted. Cont. hf. mor., last not unif. (SH. Jan.30; 457) *Duran.* £110
- **Moyen Age et Renaissance.–XVIIme Siècle. –XVIIIme Siècle.–Directoire, Consulat et Empire.** Paris, 1877-80; 1880-82; 1875-78; 1884. 4 vols.; 2 vols.; 2 vols.; together 9 vols. 4to. Cont. hf. mor., gt. spines. (SI. Dec.3; 303) Lire 380,000

LACROIX, Paul & Seré, Ferdinand
- **Le Moyen Age et la Renaissance: Histoire et Description des Moeurs et Usages ... des Littératures et des Beaux-Arts en Europe.** Paris, 1848-51. 5 vols. 4to. Occasional foxing, not collated. Partly unc., marb. bds. & hf. mor. by Zaehnsdorf. (KH. Nov.18; 366) Aus. $250

LA CROIX DU MAINE, Sieur de
- **La Bibliothèque.** Paris, 1584. 1st. Edn., L.P. Fo. 18th. C. mor., triple gt. fillet, spine gt. in compartments with bird & flower tool, inner gt. dentelles, 1 corner worn. MacCarthy-Reagh copy, bkplt. of Brancas de Lauraguais. (SM. Oct.7; 1786) Frs. 6,400

LACTANTIUS, Lucius Coelius Firmianus
- **Opera.** [Venice], Adam de Ambergau. 1471. 4th. Edn. Fo. Lacks [b] 5 & 6, & initial & final blank, painted initial M on fo. [a] 1r & same p. in fairly crude painted border, several inner margins reprd., almost all fore-margins discold. to a certain degree, cont. marginalia almost completely washed out, a few wormholes at beginning & end slightly affecting text, 1st. lf. with minor tear. 18th. C. Italian vell. [BMC V, 188; Goff L4; H. 9809*] (S. Jun.9; 28) *Thomas.* £320
- – **Anr. Edn.** [Venice], Vindelinus de Spira, 1472. Fo. Without the Nephithomon, (8 ll. at end, which are found added in a few copies), 196 ll. (of 198, lacks only 1st. & last blank ll.), guide letters & capitals supplied in red thro.-out, upr. blank margin of 1st. 5 & last 2 ll. reprd. hardly affecting 1 or 2 letters on 1st. p. Early 19th. C. russ., intersecting diamond-shaped panels, gt. fillets, broad decor. gt. border of a pattern of leaves & trees, 2 sphinxes 4 times repeated at inner border, rebkd. Syston Park copy with bkplt. [Goff Census L5; Hain 9810; BMC V, 160] (S. Jun.16; 485) *Lyon.* £750
- – **Anr. Edn.** Venice, Simon Bevilaqua, 4 Apr., 1497. Fo. Spaces for capital initials, most with guide letters, & 7 ornamental woodcut initials, last 12 ll. wormed at lr. blank margins, light dampstaining to final third of book. Cont. Osnabruck (Hannover) blind-stpd. cf. over wood bds., borders with rosette, tongue & fleur-de-lys tools, a bird, & 'ihesus' & 'maria' tools, lge. central rectangular panel on upr. cover in 2 vertical strips with lge. round historiated tools, lr. cover with central panel of the same size but with double rules to a lattice design enclosing alternating fleur-de-lys & rose tools, the borders similar but with the addition of the W monog. tool appearing twice & a sq. tool of a crowned figure holding 2 fish, rebkd. & corners restored, lacks clasps & bosses, mor. gt.-lettered box. From the collection of Eric Sexton. [BMC V, 522, Goff L13, HC 9818*] (CNY. Apr.8; 193) $7,500
- – **Anr. Edn.** Basle, Mar. 1563. Fo. 1 or 2 tears & sm. holes, slightly affecting text, a little dampstaining. 17th. C. cf., rebkd. From liby. of André L. Simon. (S. May 18; 127) *Fredrikstad.* £55

LACTANTIUS, Lucius Coelius Firmianus -contd.
See-HIERONYMUS PADUANUS-BEROALDUS, Philippus Bononiensis-ANSONIUS MATUTINA-AENIUS SILVIUS-LACTANTIUS

LACUNZA, Manuel 'Juan Josafat Ben-Ezra'
- Venida del Mesias en Gloria y Magestad. [Cadiz], [1812]. 3 vols. Sm. 4to. Cont. marb. cf. (SPB. May 5; 299) $275

LADIES' CABINET (The)
1844-n.d. Vols. 1 & 2. Hf. cf. (BS. May 13; 291) £55
- - Anr. Edn. 1846. Vols. 5 & 6 bnd. together. Cont. hf. cf., upr. cover detchd., backstrip defect. (TA. Jan.22; 8) £60

LADIES CABINET OPENED
1639. 1st. Edn. 4to. Mor. by Rivière, gt. [NSTC 15119] (SH. Jun.18; 121) Hammond. £440

LADIES MAGAZINE (The)
1846. No bdg. stated. (DWB. Mar.31; 273) £55

LADIES MONTHLY MAGAZINE, The
1859. 4to. Hf. cf. (P. Mar.12; 236) Cambridge. £110

L'ADMIRAL, Jacob
- Naauwkeurige Waarrneemingen Omtrent de Veranderingen van veele Insekten of Gekorvene Diertjes. Amst., 1774. Fo. Plts. impressed in reverse, 2 plts. & 1 text lf. stained, 2 plts. smudged. Mod. mor.-bkd. bds., front free end-paper reprd. (C. Nov.5; 88) Taylor. £240

LADY GILBERT
See-GILBERT, John T. & Lady Gilbert

LADY LOVE (Pseud.)
See-HEAVYSIDE, Mary 'Lady Love', Attrib. to

LAENNEC, René-Théophile-Hyacinthe
- De L'Auscultation Médiate ou Traité du Diagnostic des Maladies des Poumons et du Coeur. 1819. Orig. Edn. 2 vols. Browning. Cont. marb. paper bds. (HD. Jun.30; 39) Frs. 6,000
- A Manual of Percussion & Auscultation ... Ed.:- Meriedec Laennac. Trans.:- James Birch Sharpe. 1832. 1st. Edn. of this translation. Lf. with notes at end. Cl. (S. Jun.17; 766) Jenner Books. £50
- Traité de l'Auscultation et des Maladies des poumons et du Coeur. Paris, 1826. 2nd. Edn. 2 vols. Hf.-title in vol. I misbnd., spotted in places. Orig. upr. wrap. of vol. II preserved, mod. hf. mor., unc. (S. Feb.23; 68) Jenner. £190
- - Anr. Copy. Some browning. Cont. hf. cf., worn, vol. I with covers & spine detchd. (S. Apr.6; 95) Blackwell. £160
- A Treatise on the Diseases of the Chest. Trans.:- John Forbes. Phila., 1823. 1st. Amer. Edn. Cont. mott. cf., rebkd. (SG. Sep.18; 212) $320
- - Anr. Edn. Trans.:- John Forbes. 1827. 2nd. Edn. Lacks hf.-title(?). Bds., mor. spine. (S. Dec.2; 838) Jenner. £60
- - Anr. Edn. Trans.:- John Forbes. 1834. 4th. Edn. Cl., spine torn at top. Owner's inscr. 'Thomas Carr, Guy's Hospital, 1882'. (S. Jun.16; 487) Gimesh. £50

LAET, Jean de
- L'Histoire du Nouveau Monde ou Description des Indes Occidentales. Leiden, 1640. Fo. Some restoration to device on title, stains, some ll. loose. Cont. vell., soiled. [Sabin 38558] (SPB. May 5; 300) $1,600

LAETUS, Pomponius
See-MODESTUS-LAETUS, Pomponius

LAETUS, Pomponius & Marlianus, Bartholomaeus-LESCUT, Nicolaus de -LERNSNER, J.-GOBLER, J.
- De Antiquitatibus Urbis Romae Libellus ... Topographiae veteris Romae ... Epitome.-De Testium Examinatione tractatus.-Oratio de Dignitate ... Iuris civilis.-Summa Othonis de ordine Iudicario. Basle; Strassburg; Cologne; Mainz, 1538; [1540]; 1542; 1536. 4 works in 1 vol. 1st. work: very unsightly ink scrawlings on c2v, light stains. Cont. blind-stpd. pig over wooden bds., soiled & a little wormed. (S. Oct.21; 450) Pearson. £50

LAFAILLE, Germain
- Annales de la Ville de Toulouse depuis la Réunion ... à la Couronne. Toulouse, 1687-1701. 1st. Edn. 2 vols. Fo. 18th. C. red mor., gt., stpd. Sicard Relieur at foot of spine, arms of Vignerot du

Plessis, Duc de Richelieu & stp. of Society of writers to Signet, wide regular gt. border, spine gt. in compartments with sm. tools including sun, lion, & fleur de lis, mor. doubls. with border & couronne fermée with triple fleur de lis in each corner, silk liners. (SM. Oct.7; 1787) Frs. 9,500

LA FARINA, G. da
- La Svizzera Storcca ed Artistica. Flor., 1842/43. 2 vols. 4to. Most plts. soiled. Cont. hf. leath. gt. (HK. Jun.12-14; 776) DM 1,200

LAFAURIE, J.
See-BABELON, J. & Lafaurie, J.

LA FAYETTE, Marie Madeleine Pioche de la Vergne, Comtesse de
- Histoire de Madame, Henriette d'Angleterre. Maestricht, 1779. 2 vols. Cont. mor. gt., arms of Comte Boutourlin on sides. Sold as bdgs., w.a.f. (SPB. Oct.1; 234) $300
- La Princesse de Clèves. L., 1782. 2 vols. 18mo. Red mor. by Cazin, slightly worn. (HD. Apr.81; 260) Frs. 2,100
- - Anr. Copy. Porphyre cf. by Cazin. (HD. Apr.8; 261) Frs. 1,650
- - Anr. Edn. Ill.:- Maurice Leloir. Paris, 1926. (200) numbered. 4to. Red hf. mor., decor. spine, wrap. preserved. Bkplt of Lucien Tissot Dupont. (SM. Feb.11; 237) Frs. 1,800
- - Anr. Edn. Ill.:- Marie Laurencin. Paris, 1947. (300) numbered. 4to. Unsewn in orig. wraps., folder & s.-c. (SH. Nov.21; 385) Kawamatsu. £310
- - Anr. Copy. Leaves in s.-c. (HD. Feb.18; 214) Frs. 4,700
[-] [-] Anr. Edn. Ill.:- Marie Laurencin. [Paris], [1947]. 4to. 7 (of 10) etched plts. sigd. by artist, mntd. in album. Album, gold & silver thread brocade, s.-c. (SH. Nov.21; 386) Kawamatsu. £280
[-] Zaïde-Histoire Espagnole. Paris, 1764. 2 vols. 12mo. Sig. of W. Grant on flylf. Cont. red. mor., gt., arms of Marie Thérèse de Savoie, Comtesse d'Artois, flat spine gt. in compartments, inner gt. dentelles. (SM. Oct.7; 1788) Frs. 11,200
- - Anr. Copy. Cont. grd. cf., decor. spines & covers, roulette, inner dentelles. (HD. Apr.9; 496) Frs. 1,000

LAFFILLEE, H.
See-GELIS-DIDOT, P. & Laffillée, H.

LAFFREI, A.
[-] Vie Privée de Louis XV. 1788. 4 vols. Red mor. gt., unc., s.-c. (SKC. Feb.26; 1450) £60

LAFITAU, Joseph François
- De Zeden der Wilden van Amerika. The Hague, 1731. 2 vols. in 1. 4to. Cont. spr. cf., decor. spine. (HD. Dec.5; 115) Frs. 1,500
See-CHAMPLAIN Society

LAFOLIE, Ch.-J.
- Mémoires Historique ... Pont-Neuf à Paris. Paris, 1819. Long-grd. mor., border, arms of Duc d'Angoulême, decor. spine, inner dentelle, by Simier. (HD. Jun.10; 168) Frs. 3,800

LA FOLLIE, Louis Guillaume de
[-] Le Philosophe sans Prétention. Ill.:- Boissel. Paris, 1775. Cont. red mor., gt., arms of C.G. de Lamoignon de Malesherbes, triple gt. fillet, spine gt. in compartments, inner gt. dentelles, single wormhole in upr. hinge. (SM. Oct.7; 1789) Frs. 3,200

LAFOND, G.
- Voyages autour du Monde et Naufrages Célèbres. Paris, 1844. 8 vols. in 4. Several titles & some ll. slightly defaced by ballpoint pen, some foxing & other discoloration. Cont. qtr. mor., slightly worn. [Sabin 38606] (SPB. May 5; 301) $275

LAFOND, Paul
- Degas. Ill.:- Edgar Degas. Paris, 1918-19. 2 vols. 4to. Mor.-bkd. cl., orig. wraps. bnd. in. (SH. Nov.20; 38) Symonds. £50

LA FONTAINE, Jean de
- Les Amours de Psyché et de Cupidon. Paris, 1782. 2 vols. sm. 12mo. Cont. red mor., decor. spines, 3 fillets on covers, inner dentelle. From the 'Collection of Works printed by order of Monseigneur, Comte d'Artois, for the Education of Dauphin'. (HD. Apr.9; 498) Frs. 1,750
- - Anr. Edn. Paris, [1795]. 4to. Slight browning. Early 20th. C. maroon mor., gt., by Sotheran,

bkplt. of Joshua Hutchinson. (S. Apr.7; 365) Duran £180
- - Anr. Copy. Mor., gt., by Belz-Niedrée. (SM. Oct.8; 2348) Frs. 14,000
- - Anr. Copy. Cont. red mor., gt. triple fillet border, limp decor. spine, inner dentelle. (HD. Apr.24; 75) Frs. 1,500
- Contes et Nouvelles en Vers. Ill.:- Romeyn de Hooghe. Amst., 1685. 1st. Coll. & Ill. Edn., 1st printing. 2 vols. in 1. 12mo. Engraved title detchd. 19th. C. hf. mor., worn. (SG. May 14; 126) $700
- - Anr. Copy. Cont. mor., 3 fillets, decor. spines. (HD. Mar.18; 92) Frs. 9,500
- - Anr. Copy. 2 vols. in 1. Red. mor., by Hardy-Mesnil. (HD. Jun.30; 40) Frs. 7,100
- - Anr. Edn. Ill.:- Romaine de Hooghe. Amst., 1685. 1st. Coll. & Ill. Edn., 2nd. Iss. 2 pts. in 1 vol. 12mo. Cont. mor., spine grotesquely decor., gt. fillet. (HD. Mar.18; 93) Frs. 8,500
- - Anr. Edn. Ill.:- after Romeyn de Hooghe. Amst., 1685. 1st. Coll. & Ill. Edn., 3rd. Iss? 2 vols. Some ll. slightly torn, barely affecting text, some other minor defects. Cont. mott. cf., cont. rebkd. (SBA. May 27; 152) National Library of Wales. £130
- - Anr. Edn. Ill.:- Romain de Hooghe. Amst., 1685. 2 pts. in 1 vol. Lge. 12mo. Slight spotting in places. 18th. C. cf., rebkd. (S. Apr.7; 261) Sheppard. £260
- - Anr. Edn. Ill.:- After Romain de Hooge. Amst., 1699. 2 vols. Cont. Fr. red mor., gt., Jean de la Vieuville arms on covers, arms in wreath, slightly marked. Roederer copy with label. (SM. Oct.8; 2403) Frs. 20,000
- - Anr. Edn. Amst. [Paris], 1762. Fermiers-Généraux Edn. 2 vols. Cont. Fr. red mor., elab. gt. borders, flat spines gt. (S. Nov.25; 395) Quaritch. £3,000
- - Anr. Copy. 2 engraved ports., 80 plts., & 19 of the Plats Refusées (including 'Le Cas de Conscience' in 2 states), very slight browning & light spotting. Cont. Fr. red mor., gt., 3 line borders, flat spines tooled in compartments, narrow gt. inside border, slight wear. Bkplt. of William Downes. (S. Feb.10; 448) Klusmann. £2,000
- - Anr. Copy. Cont. red mor., fillet border, dentelle, decor. spine raised bands, inner dentelle, mod. wraps. & s.-c.'s. (HD. Jun.10; 54) Frs. 56,000
- - Anr. Edn. Amst. [Paris], 1764. 2 vols. Cf., 1 spine defect. (BS. Nov.26; 123) £200
- - Anr. Copy. Cont. porphyre cf., decor. spines, 3 fillets on covers, angle motifs, inner dentelle. (HD. Apr.9; 598) Frs. 4,100
- - Anr. Edn. Ill.:- after Eisen. Amst., 1764. 1st. Pirated Edn. [Fermiers-Généraux]. 2 vols. Cont. diced cf., decor. spines. (HD. Feb.18; 33) Frs. 2,300
- - Anr. Edn. Ill.:- Vidal, & after Eisen. [Paris], 1777. 2 vols. A few ll. slightly soiled. Cont. red mor., name Racine Demonville on upr. covers, vol. I slightly worn & discold.. (S. Oct.21; 291) Favre. £140
- - Anr. Copy. Some rust spots, mostly marginal, some other very minor defects. Cont. spr. cf., slightly worn. (SBA. May 27; 154) Hyde Park Bookshop £125
- - Anr. Copy. 4to. Cont. mott. cf. gt., worn. (CNY. Oct.1; 102) $220
- - Anr. Copy. Rebkd. in cf., covers worn at edges & brittle. (PNY. Mar.26; 176) $150
- - Anr. Copy. Early 19th. C. str.-grd. mor., gt. (SM. Oct.8; 2189) Frs. 2,800
- - Anr. Copy. Cont. mor., triple fillet border gt. (LM. Mar.21; 157) B.Frs. 45,000
- - Anr. Copy. Slightly browned in parts. Later hf. leath, gt. spine. (H. Dec.9/10; 1579) DM 480
- - Anr. Edn. Ill.:- Launay after Rigaud (port.). 1778. 2 vols. 18mo. Red mor. by Cazin. (HD. Apr.8; 262) Frs. 1,600
- - Anr. Edn. Ill.:- Desrais. L., 1780. 2 vols. 18mo. Porphyre cf. by Cazin. (HD. Apr.8; 264) Frs. 1,800
- - Anr. Edn. Ill.:- Desrais (& others). L., 1790. 2 vols. 18mo. Some defects. Red mor. by Cazin. (HD. Apr.8; 265) Frs. 1,800
- - Anr. Edn. Ill.:- after Eisen, by Choffard, Baquoy & others. Paris, 1792. 2nd. Edn. 2 vols. Vol. 1 slightly soiled, vol. 1 hf-title & 2 prelims. reprd. Cont. style leath., gt. (R. Oct.14-18; 972) DM 1,010
- - Anr. Copy. Port. & ills. from the 1762 edn., smaller than text, spotting, slight browning.

Mor.-bkd. bds., chipped, unc. (SPB. May 29; 252)
$100
- - **Anr. Edn.** Paris, 1795. On vell. 2 vols. 12mo. Lacks hf.-titles & 4 folios 'Vie de la Fontaine', final ll. of each vol. slightly stained, vol. I with title probably partly in penwork. Early 19th C. vell. bds., gt. spines, in vell. double s.-c. (C. Nov.20; 197) *Klusmann.* £350
- - **Anr. Edn.** Paris, An XII[1804]. 2 vols. 32mo (3⅝ × 2¾ inches). Hf.-titles. Cont. cf. gt. (SG. Sep.4; 296) $120
- - **Anr. Edn.** Paris, 1874. Reprint of edn. of Fermiers Généraux. 2 vols. 3 rejected plts. Mor., gt. fillet around covers, spines decor. with raised bands, watered silk doubls. & end-papers, s.-c.'s. (HD. Feb.27; 155) Frs. 1,600
- - **Anr. Edn.** Ill.:– After Fragonard. Paris, 1883. (100) on Japon. 2 vols. 4to. Hf. mor. (SM. Oct.8; 2219) Frs. 1,200
- - **Anr. Edn.** Ed.:– A. de Montaiglon. Ill.:– Fragonard. Paris, 1883. Reprint of Didot edn., 1795, (250) on Van Gelder laid paper. 2 vols. 4to. Bordeaux hf. mor. by Vermorel, corners, spines decor. with raised bands. (HD. Feb.27; 157) Frs. 1,450
- - **Anr. Edn.** Ill.:– Maggy Monier. Paris, [1929]. Sig. orig. aquatint wraps, spine lightly browned. (H. Dec.9/10; 1854) DM 420
- - **Anr. Edn.** Ill.:– Fragonard. Paris, 1939-45. Ltd. Facs. Edn., (200). 2 vols. Lge. 4to. Red mor., lge. Louvre dentelle, decor. spines, watered silk doubls. & end-papers. (HD. Feb.18; 152) Frs. 5,800

- **Fables.** Ill.:– Simon & Coiny. 1796. 6 vols. Sm. 12mo. Cont. red mor., gt. dentelle border. (HD. Jun.30; 41) Frs. 8,000
- - **Anr. Edn.** Paris, An IV [1796]. 4 vols. Cont. cf., limp decor. spine, lge. gt. border, inner dentelle. (LM. Mar.21; 159) DM 16,000
- - **Anr. Edn.** Ill.:– Duplat. Paris, 1811. 2 vols. 12mo. Jansenist mor. by Pagnant, inside dentelle vol. I lightly spotted. (HD. Mar.18; 94) Frs. 2,000
- - **Anr. Edn.** Paris, 1813. 2 vols. Cont. mor. by Thouvenin. (SH. Jun.11; 174) *Tzakas.* £80
- - **Anr. Edn.** Ill.:– Ingouf (port.). Paris, 1823. 2 vols. 18mo. Some foxing. Cont. cf., spines decor. with gt. fillets, gt. fillet on covers with lge. plaque in blind, inner dentelle, by Bibolet. (HD. Apr.9; 499) Frs. 1,400
- - **Anr. Edn.** Ill.:– Cherrier, Brevière after J.J. Grandville. Paris, 1838. 1st. Edn. 2 vols. Orig. ptd. wraps. (VG. Nov.18; 931) Fls. 500
- - **Anr. Edn.** Ill.:– after J.J. Grandville. Paris, 1839. 2 vols. Spotted. Cont. mor. gt. (SH. Nov.20; 192) *Duill.* £80
- - **Anr. Edn.** Trans.:– Walter Thornbury. Ill.:– Gustave Dore. L. & N.Y., ca. 1860. 4to. Hf. mor., bkplt. (SG. Dec.18; 165) $160
- - **Anr. Edn.** Ill.:– Gustave Doré. Paris, 1868. Orig. Doré Edn. Fo. Mor., upr. cover with monog. & coronet inlaid in leath., raised bands, gt. dentelles with doubls. & end-ll. of moire Satin, by Gruel. (SG. Sep.4; 297) $350
- - **Anr. Edn.** Ed.:– M. Anatole de Montaiglon. Ill.:– Oudry. Paris, 1886-89. (175) numbered, re-imp. of 1755 Edn. 4 vols. 4to. Each plt. dupl., some spotting. Cont. hf. mor. (CSK. Jan.30; 76) £150
- - **Anr. Edn.** Trans.:– Edward March. Ill.:– Stephen Gooden. L., 1921. (525) numbered sets sigd. by artist & translator. 2 vols. Orig. vell., unc., unopened. Bernard Rota's catalogue of Gooden Copperplt. Engravings, 1933 laid in. (SG. Oct.23; 142) $425
- - **Anr. Edn.** Ill.:– Hans Erni. Lausanne, [1925]. (15) numbered, sigd. by Erni & Gonin, 30 added sheets of litho. studies for ills. & suite of lithos. on China Paper. Lge. 4to. Loose in pict. wraps. & pict. bd. covers & s.-c. (SG. Oct.9; 142) $750
- - **Anr. Edn.** Trans.:– Joseph Auslander & Jacques Le Clerq. Ill.:– Rudolph Ruzicka. Ltd. Edns. Cl., 1930. (1500) numbered, & sigd. by artist. 2 vols. Gt.-decor. cl., partly unc. & unopened. (SG. Apr.2; 269) $100
- - **Anr. Edn.** Trans.:– Edward Marsh. Ill.:– Stephen Gooden. 1931. (525) numbered, sigd. by trans. & artist. 2 vols. 4to. Orig. vell., unc. (SH. Mar.26; 259) *Mirdan.* £70
- - **Anr. Copy.** Sm. 12mo. Edges slightly soiled. Warping. (SPB. May 29; 180) $110

- **Fables Choisies.** Lyon, 1698. 6 pts. in 1 vol. Page 98 ptd. upside down. Traditional style recent cf. (TA. Mar.19; 493) £70

- - **Anr. Edn.** Ill.:– Henrick Cause. Antw., 1698-1703. 5 pts. in 2 vols. 1 lf. in vol. II neatly reprd., slightly affecting text. 18th. C. cf. (S. Apr.7; 260) *Shapero.* £110
- - **Anr. Edn.** Ill.:– Jean Baptiste Oudry. Paris, 1755-59. [1st. Edn. of the Oudry plts.?]. 4 vols. Fo. 'Le Singe et le Leopard' in 1st. state. Cont. diced cf., sides with gt. fillet & blind-tooled borders, gt. cornerpieces & spines. (C. Jul.16; 324) *Beck.* £2,200
- - **Anr. Copy.** A few ll. browned or slightly soiled. Cont. tree cf., gt. borders, inner dentelles, slightly wormed. (S. Jun.23; 254) *Duran.* £1,500
- - **Anr. Copy.** 273 (of 275) plts., inserted from a smaller copy, vol. II defect. affecting lr. portion of the front half of the vol., some tears, repairs, browning, foxing. Cf.-bkd. bds., some stains. (SPB. May 29; 251) $500
- - **Anr. Copy.** Wide margins, with inscription to Leopard. Cont. marb. cf., triple gt. fillet around covers, inside dentelle, bdgs. defect. (HD. Jun.24; 47) Frs. 15,000
- - **Anr. Copy.** With inscr. to Leopard. Cont. spr. cf., triple fillet around covers, spines decor. with raised bands, bdgs. slightly defect., reprd. (HD. Feb.27; 34) Frs. 13,500
- - **Anr. Copy.** Cont. marb. leath. gt., fillets & inner & outer dentelles, much restored using old material. (HK. Nov.18-21; 2356) DM 9,000
- - **Anr. Edn.** Paris, 1756-59. 1st. Edn. of the Oudry plts. Vols. III & IV only (of 4). Fo. 136 engraved plts. only (of 275, also lacks a plt. in vol. III), the 'singe et leopard' plt. in the less common state. Cont. cf., gt. spines. (SH. Jun.25; 176) *Tropper.* £250
- - **Anr. Edn.** Ill.:– Fessard. Paris, 1765-75. 6 vols. Mor., gt., by Pagnard. (SM. Oct.8; 2259) Frs. 4,000
- - **Anr. Edn.** Ill.:– after Oudry. Bouillon, 1776. 4 vols. Cont. marb. cf., decor. spines. (HD. Apr.9; 599) Frs. 3,100
- - **Anr. Copy.** Cf., limp decor. spine, gt. triple fillet. Sigd. by artist. (LM. Jun.13; 107) B.Frs. 10,000
- - **Anr. Edn.** Ill.:– De Launay after Marillier (frontis.). Geneva, 1777. 2 vols. 18mo. Mor. by Cazin. (HD. Apr.8; 266) Frs. 1,500
- - **Anr. Edn.** Paris, 1783. 2 vols. Fo. 260 plts. only, lacks 7, several marginal tears reprd. Cont. cf. W.a.f. (CSK. Jun.26; 3) £240
- - **Anr. Edn.** Ed.:– T.P. Bao. Ill.:– T.P. Bao. [Paris], [1934]. (18) on Japon. 4to. 2 additional orig. gouaches. In sheets, s.-c. (HD. Dec.5; 117) Frs. 1,500
- **La Fontaine en Estampes.** Paris, 1821. 4to. Later cf.-bkd. bds., upr. hinge brkn. (SH. Dec.10; 38) *Schierenberg.* £65
- **Oeuvres.** Paris, 1875-91. 7 vols. (complete). Partly untrimmed. Three-qtr. mor. (TA. Mar.19; 259) £72

LA FORCE, Mlle. Caumont de
- **Histoire de Marguerite de Valois, Reine de Navarre.** Paris, 1783. Fine Paper. 6 vols. 12mo. Folding ptd. table in vol. VI. Cont. red mor. by Derome le Jeune with his 1785 ticket, triple gt. fillet, flat spines gt. in compartments with single lozenge, inner gt. dentelles. (SM. Oct.7; 1790) Frs. 6,500
- **Histoire Secrète de Bourgogne.** Paris, 1782. 3 vols. 12mo. Advt. in vol. I. Cont. red mor., triple gt. fillet, flat spine gt. in compartments, inner gt. dentelles, old bookseller's ticket(?) partly erased from inner cover of vol. 1. (SM. Oct.7; 1791) Frs. 1,900

LAFORGUE, Jules
- **Les Complaintes.** 1885. Jansenite mor., wrap., by Cretté. (HD. Oct.10; 93) Frs. 1,700
- **Moralités Legendaires.** Ill.:– Lucien Pissarro. Eragny Pr., 1896. (220). 2 vols. Orig bds., unc. (S. Jul.31; 17) *Quaritch.* £110

LAFOSSE, Etienne Guilliaume
- **Cours d'Hippiatrique.** Ill.:– after De Lafosse, Harguinier & others. Paris, 1772. Lge. fo. Port. & some plts. browned. 19th. C. hf. mor. From Chetham's Liby., Manchester. (C. Nov.27; 239) *Way.* £850
- - **Anr. Copy.** Cont. red mor., fillet, angle fleurons, decor. spine, inner dentelle, slightly restored. (HD. Jun.10; 55) Frs. 27,000

LA FRESNAYE, Roger de
- **Dessins et Gouaches.** Paris, [1927]. (300) numbered. Fo. Three-qtr. leath., patterned bds. (SG. Apr.2; 170) $110

LAGARRIGUE
- **Nouvelle Suite de Costumes de Pyrenées par Ferogio.** Paris, [1841]. Fo. Title & margins of a few plts. spotted. Cont. cf.-bkd. bds. (C. Feb.4; 159) *Baird.* £140

LA GIRAUDIERE
- **Joyeuses Epigrammes (Les).** Paris, 1634. date 18th C mor fillet border, decor border, inner Greek key dentelle. MS. N. of Pierre Louys (HD. Jun.10; 56) Frs 1,800

LAGRANGE, Joseph Louis
- **Méchanique Analitique.** Paris, 1788. 1st. Edn. 4to. Slight spotting. Cont. mott. cf., worn. From Honeyman Collection. (S. May 20; 3274) *Quaritch.* £900

LA GUERINIERE, Françoise Robichon de
- **Ecole de Cavalerie.** Paris, 1723. 1st. Fo. Edn. Fo. Wide margins. Cont. leath. (D. Dec.11-13; 2265) DM 6,000
- - **Anr. Edn.** Ill.:– Parrocel (frontis.); Borde, Aveline, Audran, Tardieu & Dupuis after Coquart & Parrocel (plts.). Paris, 1751. Fo. Some dampstaining at end. Cont. diced cf., decor. spine. (SM. Feb.11; 128) Frs. 6,000

LA HARPE, Jean François de
- **Abregé de l'Histoire Générale des Voyages.** Ill.:– J.N. Bellin & others. Ca. 1780. Atlas vol. only. 4to. 52 engraved maps only & 1 table, maps dtd. 1738-74, on guards thro-out. Cont. hf. cf., worn, upr. cover detchd. W.a.f. (S. Mar.31; 485) *Libris.* £380
[-] [-] **Anr. Edn.** [Paris], [1780-1801]. Atlas only. 4to. Cont. cf. (CSK. Sep.26; 210) £310
- **Del Fanatismo en la Lengua Revolucionaria o de la Persecucion suscitada contra la Religion Christiana y sus Ministros por los Bararos del siglo 18.** Guatemala, 1797. Sm. 4to. Sm. marginal stains. Cf. (SPB. May 5; 302) $325
- **Oeuvres.** Paris, 1778. 6 vols. Cont. crimson mor. by Derome le Jeune with his ticket, in vol. 1, triple gt. fillet, flat spines gt., inner gt. dentelles, maroon mor.-bkd. chemises & s.-c.'s. Mortimer L. Schiff copy. (SM. Oct.7; 1792) Frs. 18,000
See–**EAST INDIES–LA HARPE, Jean François de**

LAHONTAN, Louis Armand de Lom d'Arce, Baron de
- **New Voyages to North America. Containing an Account the Several Nations of that Vast Continent . . .** L., 1703. 1st. Edn. in Engl. 2 vols. Lacks frontis. plt. in vol. II. Mod. cf.-bkd. bds., gt. spine. From liby. of William E. Wilson. (SPB. Apr.29; 174) $550
- - **Anr. Edn.** Ed.:– Reuben Gold Thwaites. Chic., 1905. (50) numbered on L.P. 2 vols. 4to. Orig. paper bds., vell. spines (soiled). (CB. Feb.18; 31) Can. $140
- **Nouveaux Voyages dans l'Amérique Septentrionale [Memoires de l'Amérique Septentrionale ou la suite des Voyages[.** The Hague, 1703. 1st. Edn. 3rd. Iss. 2 vols. 12mo. Cont. mott. cf., gt. spine. (C. Feb.25; 108) *Feldman.* £340
- - **Anr. Edn.** The Hague, 1703. 2 pts. in 1 vol. 12mo. 1 plt. torn. Cont. spr. cf., spine decor. with raised bands. (HD. Jun.24; 48) Frs. 3,100
- - **Anr. Edn.** The Hague, 1715. 2 vols. 12mo. 24 plts. & maps, 1 torn. Cont. wraps., unc. (SPB. May 5; 303) $250
- **Voyages dans l'Amérique septentrionale [mémoires de l'Amérique septentrionale . . . Suite du voyage].** Amst., 1705-04. 3 vols. in 1. 12mo. Engraved frontis. & 34 engraved maps & plts. (only 29 called for), 1 loose, a few tears, some spotting & staining. Old bds., worn. [Sabin 38641-3] (S. Jun.22; 181) *Robinson.* £360

LAINEZ, [Alexandre]
- **Poësies.** The Hague, 1753. 1st. Edn. Slight browning. Early 19th. C. cf.-bkd. marb. bds., spine gt. From liby. of André L. Simon. (S. May 18; 128) *Facchi.* £75

LAING, David
- **Poems & Fables of Robert Henryson.** Edinb., 1865. Mor. gt., by Ramage. (CE. Nov.20; 105) £180

LAING, Rev. John
See–**HALKETT, Samuel & Laing, Rev. John**

LAIRD, Macgregor & Oldfield, R.A.K.
- Narrative of an Expedition into the Interior of Africa by the River Niger. 1837. 2 vols. Mod. hf. cf. (SH. Nov.7; 309) *Enfield.* £80

LAIRESSE, Gerard de
- Le Grand Livre des Peintres ou l'Art de la Peinture. Paris, 1787. 2 vols. 4to. Some spotting. Cont. marb. cf., decor. spines. (SM. Feb.11; 32) Frs. 1,200
- Principles of Drawing. 1748. 2 pts. in 1 vol. 4to. 47 sheets of engrs., 1 reprd., stained. Hf. cf., defect. (P. Jan.22; 287) *Orssich.* £60

LAKIER, Aleksandr
- Travels through the United States, Canada & the Island of Cuba. [St. Petersb.], 1859. 2 vols. In Russian, some browning, offsetting. Hf. sheet. (?cont.). (SPB. Jun.22; 79) $200

LAKING, Sir Guy Francis
- The Armoury of Windsor Castle, European Section. 1904. 4to. Orig. pig-bkd. buckram. (C. Jul.22; 150) *Taylor.* £140
- - Anr. Copy. Orig. pig-bkd. cl. (SH. Jan.29; 255) *Edwards.* £70
- - Anr. Copy. Fo. Lev. mor.-bkd. bds., by Nils Lindes. (CNY. May 22; 166) $450
- - Anr. Edn. [1904]. 1st. Edn. 4to. Orig. mor.-bkd. bds., sm. stain, d.-w., partly unc. (S. Jun.9; 21) *Barra Books.* £240
- The Furniture of Windsor Castle N.d. 4to. With card loosely inserted 'Presented to the Lord Rothschild, G.C.V.O. By the King.' Orig. pig-bkd. buckram, slightly spotted. Pres. copy, bkplt of Tring Park. (CSK. Oct.31; 110) £70
- A Record of European Armour & Arms through Seven Centuries. 1920-22. 5 vols. 4to. Buckram, soiled. (S. Sep.29; 262) *Trotman.* £300

LALAISSE, Hippolyte
[-] Types Militaires du Troupier Français. Paris, ca. 1870. Fo. 48 plts. (of 59), lacks lithographed title, a few spots. Cont. roan-bkd. bds. from another Lalaisse work, slightly worn. (S. Oct.21; 503) *Broseghini.* £200
See-BENOIST, Felix & Lalaisse, Hippolyte

LALANDE, Joseph M. de
- The Art of Papermaking. Trans.:– R. Atkinson. Mountcashel Castle, Co. Clare, 1976. (405) numbered, & sigd. by Ian V. O'Casey. Fo. Cf.-bkd. buckram, cf. tips, unc. (SG. Mar.26; 353) $100

L'ALLEMAND, Fritz
[-] Die K.K. Oesterreichische Armee in Laufe Zweyer Jahrhunderte Ca. 1846. Ob. fo. 39 (of 40) hand-cold. litho. plts. Mod. cl. (C. Mar.18; 63) *Christopher.* £220

LALLEMENT, J.P.
[-] Le Veritable Esprit des Nouveaux Disciples de S. Augustin . . . Brussels, 1706-07. 3 vols (of 4?). 12mo. Cont. mor., fillet, arms of Louis-Charles Machault d'Arnouville, decor. spine, inside dentelle. Bkplt. of Van der Helle. (HD. Mar.18; 95) Frs. 2,200

LA LOUBERE, Simon de
- A New Historical Relation to the Kingdom of Siam. 1693. 1st. Edn. in Engl. 2 pts. in 1 vol. Fo. 19th. C. hf. roan, upr. cover detchd. From Chetham's Liby., Manchester. [Wing L201] (C. Nov.27; 240) *Maggs.* £200
- - Anr. Copy. 1 of the 11 engraved maps & plts. loose. Cont. panel. cf., spine gt. (S. Apr.7; 262) *Hammond.* £180

LALOUX, Victor & others
[-] Grecian Architecture & Ornament, including the principal Pompeian Subjects of Recent Discovery by Eminent French Artists. Boston & N.Y., n.d. Fo. Orig. bds. & buckram spine. (CB. May 27; 135) Can. $190

LALOY, Louis
See-BRAQUE, Georges, Cocteau, Jean & others

LA MAOUT, Emmanuel
- Histoire Naturelle des Oiseaux. Paris, 1853. 4to. Cont. hf. cf. (CSK. Sep.26; 128) £70

LA MARQUISE DE SILLERY
See-BUCHOLZ, Pierre Joseph & La Marquise de Sillery

LAMARTINE, Alphonse Marie Louis Prat de
- Jocelyn. Paris, 1882. Mor. gt., mor. inlays, crimson & purple tooled in gt., in floral pattern on upr. cover & spine, silk doubls. & free end-papers. (SPB. Jul.28; 35) $150
- Meditations Poetiques. Ill:– C. Motte after Mendoze. Paris, 1823. 9th Edn., on China paper. 5 litho. plts. only (of 6), some ll. slightly spotted. Str.-grd. mor., gt. & blind tooled, with gothic rosette in centre, spine unif. gt. & blind tooled, by Vogel, slightly rubbed, unc. (S. Feb.10; 317) *Rota.* £55
- Souvenirs, Impressions, Pensées et Paysages pendant un Voyage en Orient. 1835. Orig. Edn. 4 vols. Hf. mor., corners, wrap & spine, doubls., unc. by Canape. (HD. Jun.30; 43) Frs. 1,100

LAMB, Lady Caroline
[-] Glenarvon. 1816. 1st. Edn. 3 vols. Hf. cf. gt. (P. Dec.11; 351) *Harris.* £100
[-] - Anr. Edn. 1816. 2nd. Edn. 3 vols. 12mo. Orig. bds., unc. (C. Feb.4; 76) *Basket & Day.* £160

LAMB, Charles
- Album Verses. L., 1830. 1st. Edn. With advt. lf. at end. Orig. bds., buckram box, unc. From the Prescott Collection. (CNY. Feb.6; 225) $480
- Beauty & the Beast. L., ca. 1810. 1st. Edn. 16mo. The 'surprise' iss. with watermark 1810 on B2, without title-p. or engraved sheet of music, fore-edge of final lf. frayed & with some sm. reprd. tears, marginal tear reprd. in lf. B2, some staining. Orig. ptd. wraps., lr. fore-edge of cover cut short & slightly frayed, mor. gt. solander case. From the Prescott Collection. (CNY. Feb.6; 224) $900
[-] [-] Anr. Edn. Ca. 1811. 1st. Edn.?, 'Surprise' iss. 16mo. Short tear in folding sheet of engraved music, lacks title?, text wtr mkd. 1805, plts. 1810. Hf. roan. (SH. Mar.19; 152) *Vincent.* £280
- John Woodvil: a Tragedy. 1802. 1st. Edn. Cont. hf. cf., s.-c. Pres. Copy to William Dawson. (S. Nov.25; 485) *Dawson.* £350
[-] The King & Queen of Hearts. L., 18 Nov. 1805. 3rd. Iss. 16mo. Minor restoration to a few corners affecting some letters, slightly soiled thro.-out. Orig. ptd. wraps. (with the date 1806), stitched, covers creased with portions strengthened, mor. gt. s.-c. From the Prescott Collection (CNY. Feb.6; 222) $1,600
- The Last Essays of Elia. Ed:– Augustine Birrell. Ill.:– C.E. Brock. L., 1900. 12mo. Crimson lev., gt.-tooled, gt. dentelles, satin end-papers, by Zaehnsdorf. (SG. Apr.9; 105) $120
[-] Prince Dorus. 1811. 1st. Edn. 16mo. Spotted. Orig. ptd. wraps., slightly worn, cl. case. (S. Feb.9; 26) *Quaritch.* £320
- Specimens of the English Dramatic Poets. 1808. 1st. Edn. Mod. cf. by Rivière, gt. (SH. Jun.4; 209) *Bennett.* £60
- A Tale of Rosamund Gray. L., 1798. 1st. Edn. Orig. end-papers bnd. in, hf. cf., upr. cover detchd. (P. Apr.9; 215) *Hannas.* £250
- The Works. 1818. 1st. Edn. 2 vols. 12mo. Advt. lf. in vol. 2. Cl.-bkd. bds., unc. (S. Jan.26; 193) *Maggs.* £100

LAMB, Charles & Mary
- Tales from Shakespear. Ill.:– after William Mulready. L., 1807. 1st. Edn., 1st. Iss. 2 vols. 12mo. With printer's imprint on verso of p. 235 in vol. 1, some slight soiling, mostly to vol. 1. Pol. cf. gt. by F. Bedford. The George L. Craik copy, with bkplts., lately in the Prescott Collection. (CNY. Feb.6; 223) $450
- - Anr. Edn. Ill.:– William Blake after Mulready. L., 1810. 2 vols. 12mo. Foxed. Early binder's cl., brkn. Hugh Walpole's bkplt. in each vol. (SG. Dec.18; 271) $100
- - Anr. Edn. Ill.:– Arthur Rackham. 1909. (750) sigd. by artist. 4to. Orig. cl. gt., ties. (SH. Dec.11; 427) *Rosenblatt.* £200
- - Anr. Copy. Endpapers stained, soiled ties. (SH. Dec.11; 428) *Joseph.* £100
- - Anr. Copy. Foxed. Orig. ribbon ties. Raymond M. Sutton Jr. copy. (SG. May 7; 153) $450
- - Anr. Copy. L.P., with extra plt. Soiled, front free end-paper cut away. (SPB. May 29; 358) $200
- The Works. 1903. 12 vols. Cont. hf. cf. (SH. May 28; 64) *Howes Books.* £50

LAMB, Charles & White, James
- Original Letters & c. of Sir John Falstaffe & His Friends. L., 1796. 12mo. Lacks blank A1. Pol. cf., triple fillet gold borders, spine gt. floriated, by Rivière. (SG. Feb.12; 256) $120

LAMB, Dana S.
- On Trout Streams & Salmon Rivers. Barre, 1963. 1st. Edn. Cl. Pres. copy. (SG. Oct.16; 65) $150

LAMB, Patrick
- Royal-Cookery: or, the Compleat Court-Cook. 1716. 2nd. Edn. A few sm. tears, some browning. Cont. panel. cf., covers detchd., spine & stitching brkn. (S. Dec.2; 734) *Haussman.* £110
- - Anr. Edn. L., 1726. 3rd. Edn. 39 (of 40) folding plts. Rebkd. (SG. Sep.25; 93) $190

LAMBARDE, William
- Perambulation of Kent. 1576. 1st. Edn. 4to. Slight worming not affecting text, some staining. Cf. gt., worn. (P. Apr.9; 213) *Dartmoor.* £120
- - Anr. Edn. L., 1595. 4to. P7 holed with loss of a few characters, slight soiling. 19th. C. cf. [STC 15176] (CSK. Aug.1; 214) £150
- - Anr. Edn. 1596. 2nd. Edn. 4to. 1 map on a new guard, early ink marginalia. Red mor. gt. extra, central panels on each cover with acorn fleurons, spine in compartments, by F. Bedford. Bkplt. of Charles Edward H. Chadwyck-Healey. [STC 15176] (LC. Feb.12; 194) £300
- - Anr. Copy. Inner blank margin of title reprd., sm. hole in last lf. reprd., folding map with caption cropped. Mod. mor. From the collection of Eric Sexton. (C. Apr.15; 181) *Crowe.* £200

LAMBE, Robert, Vicar of Norham upon Tweed
- The History of Chess. L., 1704. 1st. Edn. (D. Dec.11-13; 2293) DM 1,300
- - Anr. Edn. L., 1764. Orig. sewed, in linen-bkd. box. (D. Dec.11-13; 2294) DM 1,200

LAMBECIUS, Petrus
- Commentariorum de Augustissima Bibliotheca Caesarea Vindobonensi. Vienna, 1665-90. 9 vols. including supp. Fo. 18th. C. mor., triple gt. fillet, spine gt. in compartments, inner gt. dentelles. J.R. Abbey copy, with his bkplt. (SM. Oct.7; 1794) Frs. 10,000

LAMBERT, Abbé
See-MEMOIRES de Martin et Guillaume du Bellai-Langei . . . auxquels on a joint les Mémoires du Marechal de Fleuranges . . . et le Journal de Louise de Savoye

LAMBERT, C.D.L.
- The Adventures of Cooroo. Norwich, n.d. Cf., decor. spine gt. (CE. Jul.9; 196) £140

LAMBERT, George W.
- The Art of George Lambert . . . Sydney, 1924. (750) numbered. Some foxing. No bdg. stated. (JL. Jul.20; 664) Aus. $150

LAMBERT, John
- Travels Through Canada & the United States of North America, in the Years 1806, 1807, & 1808 . . . L., 1810. 1st. Edn. 3 vols. 14 (of 18) maps & plts., offsetting, foxing & soiling. Orig. cf.-bkd. bds., rebkd., worn, upr. cover of vol. III detchd. From liby. of William E. Wilson. (SPB. Apr.29; 175) $225

LAMENAIS
- Oeuvres Complètes. 1836-37. 4 vols. orig. Edn. 12 vols. Cont. hf. cf. (HD. Oct.10; 247) Frs. 1,500

LAMENTATIONS of Jeremiah
Ill.:– Blair Hughes-Stanton. Gregy. Pr., 1934. (250). Fo. Orig. blind-stpd. mor. (SH. Feb.20; 211) *Simon.* £270

LA MESANGERE, Pierre
- Journal des Dames et des Modes. Paris, An V [Jun. 1797]-Jan. 1839. 20 vols. 3616 (of 3624) plts., plus 242 variants, lacks ptd. text, except for beginning of 1839. In sheets, hf. roan s.-c.'s. (HD. Dec.5; 118) Frs. 57,000

LAMI, Eugène
- Les Contretemps. Ill.:– Villain after Eugène Lami. [Paris], [1823-24]. Ob. 4to. Str.-grd. red hf. mor. by Pagnant, corners, decor. spine. (HD. Dec.5; 119) Frs. 2,000
- Souvenirs de Londres. Ill.:– Villain after Eugène Lami. N.p., [1826]. Ob. 4to. 1 additional plt.: 'Première idée de la première figure'. Str.-grd. red hf. mor., corners, decor. spine. (HD. Dec.5; 120) Frs. 2,800
- Souvenirs du Camp de Lunéville. Paris, 1829. Ob. 4to. Str.-grd. red hf. mor., corners, decor. spine, unc., wrap. (HD. Dec.5; 122) Frs. 2,000

- La Vie de Château. Paris, [1828-32]. Ob. 4to. 1 title-cover (of 2). Str.-grd. red hf. mor., corners, decor. spine, unc. (HD. Dec.5; 121)   Frs. 3,200
See–VERNET, Carl & Horace & Lami, Euguene

LA MODE
See–JOURNAL des Modes–LA MODE

LA MODE ILLUSTREE Journal de la Famille
Jan.–Dec. 1876. Fo. Cont. cl. (TA. Nov.20; 122)
£180

LAMOIGNON, Chrétien François de
- Catalogue des Livres de la Bibliothèque. Paris, 1791-92. 3 vols. Cont. tree cf., 2 covers detchd. Bkplt. of A.N.L. Munby. (SM. Oct.7; 1420)
Frs. 4,200

LA MORLIERE, Jacques Rochette, Chevalier de
- Contes. Ill.:– Lepec (figures); Lalauze (port.). Paris, 1879. Ltd. Edn. Figures in 2 states. Mor. by Pagnan, decor. spine, inside dentelle. Bkplt. of Francis Kettaneh. (SM. Feb.11; 164)   Frs. 2,500

LA MOTHE LE VAYER, François de, the Elder
[–] Quatre Dialogues faits à l'Imitation des Anciens, par Orasius Tubero, [Cinq autres Dialogues de mesme Autheur]. Frankfurt, '1506' [sic for 1606]. 1st. Edn. 2 pts. in 1 vol. 4to. 18th. C. red mor., triple gt. fillet, flat spine gt. with repeated sm. oval interspersed with dots, inner gt. dentelles, Roseberry bkplt. Beckford copy. (SM. Oct.7; 1796)   Frs. 3,200

LA MOTRAYE, Aubry de
- Voyages en Anglois et en François . . . Prusse . . . Russie . . . Pologne . . . 1732. Fo. Mod. cf., spine gt. (S. Mar.31; 486)   Foyles. £140

LAMOTTE, A.
- Voyage dans le Nord de l'Europe. 1813. 4to. Cf. (P. Oct.23; 40)   Brooke-Hitching. £130

LA MOTTE, Guillaume Mauquest de
- Traité Complet des Accouchemens Naturels . . . Paris, 1765. New Edn. 2 vols. Cont. mott. cf., spines gt. (SG. Sep.18; 246) $170

LA MOTTE FOUQUE, Baron Friedrich Heinrich Karl
- Ausgewählte Werke. Halle, 1841. 1st. Edn. 12 pts. in 4 vols. Owner's mark on end-paper, Der Pappenheimer Kürassier . . . Leipzig, 1842, bnd. in. Cont. hf. leath. gt., decor. (HK. May 15; 4236)   DM 2,100
- Undine. Trans.:– W.L. Courtney. Ill.:– Arthur Rackham. 1909. (1000) numbered, sigd. 4to. Orig. gt. decor. parch., soiled, partly untrimmed. (TA. May 21; 501)   £100
– – Anr. Copy. (100) sigd by artist. Some browning, minor spotting. Orig. vell. gt., warped, slight soiling, front free end-paper cut away. Orig. watercolour & ink drawing sigd. on limitation p. (SPB. May 6; 240) $1,500
– – Anr. Copy. Parch. gt. (SG. Oct.23; 285) $450
– – Anr. Copy. 1st. Edn. Deluxe sigd. by artist. Gt.-pict. vell., warped, lacks ties, hf. mor. box. Raymond M. Sutton, Jr. copy. (SG. May 7; 155)
$375

LAMPADIUS, Wilhelm August
- Neue Erfahrungen im Gebiete der Chemie und Hüttenkunde. Weimar, 1816-17. 1st. Edn. 2 vols. in 1. Sm. stp. on title lf. Cont. hf. leath. (R. Oct.14-18; 230)   DM 900

LAMPE, Louis
- Signatures et Monogrammes des Peintres. Brussels, 1895-98. 3 vols. Browning. Later cl., affected by damp. (CSK. May 29; 141)   £80
– – Anr. Copy. Hf. mor. (CR. Mar.19; 91)
Lire 420,000

LANCASTER, A.
See–HOUZEAU, J.C. & Lancaster, A.

LANCELOT, Claude, Grammarion
- Jardin des Racines Greques . . . Paris, 1657. 1st. Edn. 12mo. Jansenist red mor. by Thibaron-Joly, inside dentelle, ex-liby. (HD. Mar.18; 96)
Frs. 1,500
[–] Nouvelle Méthode pour apprendre facilement la Langue Latine. Paris, 1709. 10th. Edn. Cont. red mor., arms of Count Hoym, gt., on covers, spine compartments gt. in pointillé, inner gt. dentelles, sm. scratch on cover dulled with red. (SM. Oct.7; 1797)   Frs. 2,200

LANCELOT du Lac
Paris, 1533. 6th. Edn. 3 vols. in 1. Fo. 1st. gathering loose, several ll. stained, occasional browning & soiling, marginal inscrs. on final lf. &

on blank. 18th. C. cf., spine gt. & defect. (S. Feb.10; 449)   Bond. £750

LANCE'S UPPER RHINE
Ca. 1830. Some spotting. Hf. cf. (P. Nov.13; 271)
Rheinbrich. £140

LANCKORONSKA, Maria & Oehler, R.
- Die Buchillustration d. XVIII Jhdts. in Deutschland, Osterreich u.d. Schweiz. Frankfurt, 1932-4. (800) 4to. Orig. bds. (HK. May 12-14; 2251)   DM 600

LANCKORONSKA, Maria & Rümann, A.
- Geschichte der Deutschen Taschenbücher und Almanache. Munich, [1954]. (700). Orig. hf. leath. (H. Dec.9/10; 22)   DM 420

LAND OF ENCHANTMENT
Ill.:– Arthur Rackham. 1907. 1st. Edn., 1st. Iss. on Japan paper. Lge. 4to. Gt.-pict. cl. Raymond M. Sutton, Jr. copy. (SG. May 7; 157) $100

LANDA, Diego de
- Relation des Choses de Yucatan. Trans.:– E.G. Brasseur de Bourbourg. Paris, 1864. 1st. Edn. Ex liby. Mod. hf. leatherette. (SG. Jun.11; 215) $140

LANDAU, Yakov
- Sefer Agur. [Naples], [Azriel Ben Joseph Ashkenazi], ca. 1490-92. 1st. Edn. Sm. 4to. Lacks 1st. sig. & 1st. lf. of 14th. sig., replaced in MS., lacks all but fine of Thazon at end, partly replaced in the MS., tears in 1 lf. affecting some letters, other tears, staining, worming. Hf. mor., cased. (SPB. May 11; 16) $2,300

LANDE, Lawrence M.
- The Lawrence Lande Collection of Canadiana in the Redpath Library of McGill University. Ed.:– Edgar Andrew Collard. Montreal, 1965. (950) numbered, sigd. by author, 1 of the 1st. 75 being a De Luxe Edn. in Oasis Niger Goat. Fo. 186 reproduced title-pp. plus facs. of broadsides, proclamations & posters on special mould-made paper. Gt. decor. raised bands with matching qtr. leath. s.-c. (PWP. Apr.9; 228)   Can. $600
– – Anr. Edn. Montreal, 1965. (950) numbered, sigd. by author. Lge. 4to. Orig. mor.-bkd. cl., unc., s-c. (SH. Apr.9; 157)   Talerman. £100
– – Anr. Copy. Fo. Qtr. pig & canvas. (CB. Dec.9; 206)   Can. $170
– – Anr. Edn. Montreal, 1965-71. Ltd. Edn. sigd. 2 vols. Orig. cl. (SH. Jun.4; 176)   Milton. £110

LANDER, Richard & John
- Journal of an Expedition to Explore the Course & Termination of the Niger. L., 1832. 1st. Edn. 3 vols. 16mo. 2 ll. in vol. I with hole at outer margin, plts. browned. Cont. cf. gt. (PNY. May 21; 242)
$100

LANDER – und Völkerkunde
Ed.:– Th. Fr. Ehrmann [II], G. Hassel [VI]. Prag, 1808-09. Vols. II & VI. Slightly soiled in parts, sm-stp. on end-ll. Cont. hf. leath., worn, slightly wormed. (HK. Nov.18-21; 1246)   DM 560

LANDESIO, E. & Rosa, P.
- Vedute Principali della Villa Borghese. Rome, 1842. Ob. 4to. Cl. (P. Feb.19; 185)
Weinreb. £65

LANDMANN, George
- Historical, Military & Picturesque Observations of Portugal. Ill.:– J.C. Stadler & others. 1818. 1st. Edn. 2 vols. 4to. Occasional spotting. Cont. red mor., gt., rebkd. (C. Nov.5; 89)   Rostron. £1,100
– – Anr. Copy. 15 hand-cold. engraved maps, 2 double-p., including dupl., 62 plts., 4 folding with tears. Old hf. roan. (C. Jul.15; 140)
Harley. £1,000

LANDON, Charles Paul
- Annales du Musée et de l'École Moderne des Beaux Arts. Paris & L., 1815. Vols. 1-21. Occasional light browning. Cont. str.-grd. mor., covers with a stylized border of foliage, with a central motif of an imperial eagle surrounded by oak & laurel wreath, spine with a similar motif on 3 of the 5 panels, all gt. (CSK. May 15; 100)
£190

LANDSBOROUGH, William
- Journal of Landsborough's Expedition from Carpentaria . . . Melbourne, 1862. 1st. Edn. Litho. frontis. stained in margin, folding engd. map with short tear in fold. Hf. roan. (C. Jul.15; 61)
Quaritch. £150

LANDSCAPE ALPHABET
1830. Ob. 8vo. Some plts. spotted, lacks front

end-paper. Orig. decor. cl., slightly stained. (SH. Mar.19; 153)   Korn. £75
– – Anr. Edn. Ill.: L.E.M. Jones. Ca. 1830. Spotted. Cont. hf. cf. (SKC. May 19; 35)   £85
– – Anr. Edn. N.d. Sm. 4to. Browned & spotted. Cont. hf. cf. (CSK. Jun.26; 148)   £60

LANDSCAPE ANNUAL
[–] Jenning's Landscape Annual. 1830-33. 3 vols. only. Orig. mor. (SH. Nov.7; 515)
Allegretti. £105
– – Anr. Edn. Ed.:– Thomas Roscoe Ill.:– after Prout, Harding, Roberts & Holland. L., 1830-39. 10 vols. Some plts. lightly soiled. Cont. leath. gt., slightly rubbed. (HK. Nov.18-21; 1356)
DM 1,000
– – Anr. Edn. Ill.:– Samuel Prout, David Roberts & A.G. Vickers. L., 1831; 1836-37. 3 vols. 1st. vol. 25 (of 26) plts., 2nd. vol. 21 plts., 3rd. vol. 16 (of 17) plts. Orig. leath., very worn & foxed. (SG. Feb.26; 204) $375

LANDSEER, Sir Edwin
- The Works . . . with a history of his art life by William Cosmo Monkhouse. N.d. Fo. Cont. mor., gt. (CSK. Sep.12; 211)   £60
– – Anr. Copy. 2 vols. 4to. Hf. cf. (P. Mar.12; 228)
Cambridge. £50

LANDSEER, Thomas
- Works. N.d. 4 vols. Fo. Full-p. engrs. loose. Cl. gt. (P. Jan.22; 302)   Cambridge. £50

LANDSEER, Thomas & Barrow, John Henry
- Characteristic sketches of animals. Ill.:– Thomas Landseer. 1832. Fo. Additional engraved title, frontis. & many India proof plts., engraved title defect., ptd. title & some plts. foxed. Cont. hf. mor., gt. (C. Feb.25; 219)
Hermans. £60

LANE, Ary & Klyueva, Vera
- Krasochnye Pyatna [Colourful Blemishes]. Kazan, 1920. Slightly browned. Orig. wraps., torn, loose. (SH. Feb.6; 480)   Quaritch. £75

LANE, Ary & others
- Taranom Slov [With the Ram of Words]. Ill.:– G. Pleshcinsky. Kazan, 1921. (1000). Orig. wraps. by G. Pleschcinsky. Pres. inscr. from Polotsky (joint author) to Yu. V. Sobolev. (SH. Feb.6; 481)
Quaritch. £100

LANE, Michael
See–COOK, Capt. James & Lane, Michael

LANE, William Coolidge
- Catalogue [of Books] in the Washington Collection in the Boston Athenaeum. Boston, 1897. (55) numbered. Orig. cl. (SH. Apr.9; 91)
Talerman. £65

LANE, William Coolidge & Brown, Nina E.
- Library of Congress. A.L.A. Portrait Index. Wash., 1906. Orig. cl. (SH. Oct.9; 80)
Grosvenor Prints. £70

LANE-POOLE, Stanley
See–WILSON, Sir Charles William & Lane-Poole, Stanley

LA NEUVILLE (-de)
- An account of Muscovy, as it was in the year 1689. 1699. 1st. Edn. Some browning. Cont. sheep, rebkd., worn. (S. Jan.27; 579)
Anderson. £150

LANFRANCHI, G.
[–] In Diesern Bichlin find ma[n] gar ain Schöne Und'wysung un[d] heer wie sich die Cyrurgici . . . [Cologne], ca. 1515. 4to. Some sm. worming thro.-out. Mod. bds. (R. Mar.31-Apr.4; 1005)
DM 4,600

LANFRANCUS de Oriano
[–] [Repetitiones Disputationes] Incipit Defensorium Iuri compositum per Venerabilem Virum Dominum Gebhardum Iuris Canonici Doctorem. (Venice), [Wendelin de Spira for Johannes de Colonia), [1472]. Fo. 10 ll. (only, comprising ff. 61-70 of the above work), very slight foxing in margins Disbnd. [Hain 9884 [9887]; BMC V p. 161; Goff L 57] (C. Apr.1; 52)   Maggs. £70

LANFREY, M.
- History of Napoleon I. L. & N.Y., 1871-79. 4 vols. Cont. hf. leath., gt. (R. Mar.31-Apr.4; 319)
DM 2,200

LANG, Andrew
- Fairy Books. – The True Story Book. 1889-1908. 10 vols.; 1 vol. Some ll. slightly spotted. Orig. pict. cl. gt., some soiled. (SD. Feb.4; 165) £195
- Prince Charles Edward. 1900. Ltd. Edn. 4to. Red mor. gt. with initials by Sotheran & Co. (CE. Jun.4; 130) £55
- The Princess Nobody. Ill.:– Richard Doyle. [1884]. 4to. Orig. cl.-bkd. pict. bds., worn. (SH. Dec.10; 169) *Quaritch.* £100
- The Tercentenary of Isaac Walton. L., 1893. 4to. Bds., cl. folder, three-qtr. lev. s.-c. 3 p. A.L.s. from the printer T.J. Wise tipped-in, bkplt. of G.J. Platt, Llandudno. (SG. Dec.11; 149) $250

LANG, Henry C.
- Rhopalocera Europae ... Butterflies of Europe. 1884. 2 vols. 4to. Mor., spines gt. (S. Mar.17; 350) *Mrs. Gregory.* £160

LANG, John
- Too Clever by Half. Melbourne, n.d. Wraps., slightly worn & soiled. (KH. Mar.24; 234) Aus. $110

LANG, John Dunmore
- An Historical & Statistical Account of New South Wales. 1834. 1st. Edn. 2 vols. Folding engraved map hand-cold. in outl. Cl.-bkd. cont. bds., unc. (C. Jul.15; 62) *Walford.* £80
- – Anr. Edn. 1840. 2 vols. 1 folding map cold. in outl. torn. Orig. cl. (P. May 14; 105) *Bailey.* £50

LANG, Dr. W.H.
- Racehorses in Australia. Ill.:– Martin Stainforth. Sydney, 1922. 4to. Cold. plts. & clippings tipped in, advts. Orig. bdg., covers soiled. (JL. Dec.14; 484) Aus. $225

LANGBAINE, Gerard, the Younger
- An Account of the English Dramatick Poets. Oxford, 1691. 1st. Edn. Bds. (P. Mar.12; 267) *Bennett.* £95

LANGBAINE, Gerard, the Younger & Gildon, C.
- The Lives & Characters of the English Dramatick Poets. [1699]. Advt. lf., spotting. Cont. sheep, worn. [Wing L375] (SH. Jun.11; 57) *Hannas.* £75

LANGDALE, Charles
- Memoirs of Mrs. Fitzherbert. L., 1856. 1st. Edn. Extra ill., 56 engrs. including frontis. Red mor. gt., upr. doubl. blue mor., with orig. oval port. miniature of Mrs. Fitzherbert at centre, glazed, watered silk linings, orig. cl. bdg. preserved, for J.W. Robinson Co., mor. box, by Sangorski & Sutcliffe. (CNY. May 22; 354) $750

LANGDON, John Emerson
- Canadian Silversmiths & their Marks. Lunenburg, Priv. Ptd. [1960]. 1st. Edn., (500) numbered. Orig. cl. Pres. Copy, sigd. & inscr. (CB. Feb.18; 148) Can. $280
- – Anr. Edn. Toronto, 1966. Ltd. Edn. 4to. Orig. cl., d.-w. (SH. Jul.23; 291) *Rosenberg.* £95

LANGE, Dorothea
- An American Exodus: A Record of Human Erosion. Ed.:– Paul Schuster Taylor [text]. N.Y., [1939]. 1st. Edn. 4to. Cl. (SG. Apr.23; 119) $120

LANGE, Eduard
- Die Soldaten Friedrich's des Grossen. Ill.:– Albert Kretzschmer after Adolph Menzel. Leipzig, 1853. 1st. Edn. 4to. Foxed. Later cl. (SG. Oct.30; 212) $170

LANGE, Louis
- Original–Ansichten d. Historisch merkw. Städte in Deutschland. Darmstadt, 1840. Vol. 2. 4to. Lacks 1 plt. Cont. marb. bds. (HK. Nov.18-21; 1247) DM 3,300
- – Anr. Edn. Darmstadt, 1843. Vol. 4. 4to. Lacks 1 plt. Cont. marb. bds. (HK. Nov.18-21; 1248) DM 5,000
- – Anr. Edn. Darmstadt, 1846. Vol. 5. 4to. Lacks 2 plts., lightly soiled in parts, some plts. slightly browned. Cont. marb. bds. (HK. Nov.18-21; 1250) DM 2,000
- – Anr. Copy. Vol. 6. Slightly soiled in parts or lightly browned. Cont. marb. bds. (HK. Nov.18-21; 1250) DM 2,600
- Original–Ansichten der Historisch Merkwürdigsten Städte in Deutschland. Sammelmappe. Frankfurt, Ca. 1880. Sm. fo. Loose, 2 orig. linen portfos. (R. Oct.14-18; 2102) DM 11,500
- Original–Ansichten von Deutschand. Darmstadt, 1846. 4to. Lacks 2 steel engrs., slightly soiled in

places. Cont. bds. (R. Mar.31-Apr.4; 2183) DM 3,400
- Der Rhein und die Rheinlande von Mains bis Köln. Darmstadt, 1846. Slightly soiled in parts, some signatures loose, lacks 1 steel engr. Cont. linen. (R. Mar.31-Apr.4; 2184) DM 4,500
- – Anr. Edn. Ill.:– J. Poppel after Lange. Darmstadt, 1852. Lacks 1 plt. Romantic cont. mor., gt. spine, cover & outer dentelle, rubbed. (HK. Nov.18-21; 1340) DM 4,100
- The Upper Rhine. Ed.:– Gaspey. Ill.:– after Rohbock, L. & J. Lange & others. L., Darmstadt, N.Y., ca. 1850. 127 (of 134) steel engrs., including front. & engraved title. Cont. hf. leath., gt. spine. (R. Oct.14-18; 2164) DM 8,000

LANGE VAN WIJNGAERDEN, C.J. de
- Geschiedenis en Beschrijving der Stad van der Goude. Amst./The Hague, 1813-79. 3 vols. Pencil annots. on fly-ll. Cont. hf. cf., gt. spines (vols. 1-2), & orig. bds., spine defect. & brkn., lacks 1 spine label, slightly loose. (VG. Oct.13; 93) Fls. 650

LANGEN, A.
See–SIMPLICISSIMUS

LANGENBECK, Conrad Johann Martin
- Tractatus Anatomico-Chirurgicus de Nervis Cerebri in Dolore faciei Consideratis. Göttingen, 1805. 4to. New hf. cf. (S. Jun.16; 489) *Jenner Books.* £130

LANGEVIN, Hector L.
- Le Canada: ses Institutions, Ressources, Produits, Manufactures, etc., etc., etc. Quebec, 1855. 1st. Edn. Mor. gt., upr. cover gt.-lettered 'Presented to H.R.H. Prince Arthur by the Province of Quebec'. (SG. Mar.5; 109) $240

LANGFELD, William R. & Blackburn, Philip C.
- Washington Irving: A Bibliography. N.Y., 1933. (450). 4to. Gt. cl. (SG. Oct.2; 191) $120

LANGLAND, William
[–] The Vision of Pierce Plowman ... 1561. 4to. Some staining thro.-out. 18th. C. cf., rebkd., bkplt. of Gaddesden liby. (STC 19908) (C. Apr.1; 217) *Ridge.* £340

LANGLE, Victor
- Album de Fleurs, Fruits, Oiseaux, Insectes, et Coquilles. Paris, 1843. Ob. fo. Hand-cold. litho. title & 12 plts. with uncold. dupls., plain plts. of roses lightly cold. by a former owner, some slight foxing, mainly marginal. Orig. blind-stpd. & gt. decor. bds. with later linen backstrip. (TA. Jun.18; 175) £525

LANGLES, Louis Mathieu
- Monuments Anciens et Modernes de l'Hindoustan. Ill.:– after Lecerf, Daniell, & others. Paris, 1821. L.P. 2 vols. Fo. 148 plts., 12 hand-cold., some heightened in gold, 3 plts. in 2 states, & 1 dupl. plt. 19th. C. hf. mor., unc. From Chetham's Liby., Manchester. (C. Nov.27; 241) *Ludgrove.* £100

See–MELIK-SHAHNAZARIANTS, Tauit Dzadourian & Langlès, M.

LANGLEY, Batty
- The City & Country Builder's & Workman's Treasury of Designs. 1740. 1st. Edn. 4to. Cont. cf., rebkd., upr. cover defect. (S. Mar.17; 424) *Woodruff.* £260
- – Anr. Edn. 1750. 4to. Lacks hf.-title (?), 1st. few ll. wormed in margin touching 1 letter, plt. XCVIII slightly stained. 19th. C. hf. cf., worn. (S. Dec.9; 462) *Traylen.* £130

LANGLEY, Batty & Thomas
- The Builder's Jewel. 1757. Some stains. Cont. cf. (SH. Jun.11; 6) *Marlborough Rare Books.* £55
- Gothic Architecture, improved by Rules & Proportions. N.d. 4to. Cont. sheep. (S. Dec.9; 460) *Traylen.* £230

LANGLEY, Samuel Pierpont & Manley, Charles M.
- Memoir on Mechanical Flight. Wash., 1911. 1st. Edn. 4to. Orig. cl., spine worn. (SH. Jun.18; 211) *Tracchi.* £75

LANGLOIS, L.P.
- Prosper, ou Le Petit Peureux Corrigé par des Exemples Naturels et Frappans. Paris, 1822. Ob. 4to. Some ll. of text dampstained. Orig. pict. bds. with 2 further ills., rebkd., worn. Pict. title & cover dtd. 1823. (SH. Mar.19; 155) *Vincent.* £50

LANGUET, Hubert
[–] The Apologie or Defence, of the most noble Prince William ... of Orange. Delft, [L.], 1581 [1584]. Sm. 4to. Catchword cropped on A4r, title slightly soiled. 18th. C. cf., gt., gt. cipher surmounted by a baron's coronet on covers, slightly worn. [NSTC 15209] (S. Jun.23; 365) *Malkiewicz.* £130

LANGUET de Gergy, J.J.
- Vita della Venerabile Madre Margherita Maria Alacoque Religiosa ... Parma, 1801. 4to. Cont. Spanish veined roan, sm. dentelle with fleurons in corners, arms of Ferdinand I, decor. spine, inside dentelle, lr. cover slightly defect. (HD. Mar.18; 97) Frs. 1,200

LANIER, Henry William
- A.B. Frost. [1933]. (950). 4to. Cl. (SG. Dec.11; 260) $280

LA NOUE, [Francois de]
- Discours Politiques et Militaires ... nouvellement recueillis. Basle, 1588. 12mo. Some margins dampstained, sig., slightly trimmed, of Petrus Bonifans on title, Latin verses to author on verso of title in cont. hand. 17th. C. red mor., gt. panel with corner sprays, triple gt. fillet, gt. arms of Fauconnet de Vilde on covers, spine gt. in compartments. (SM. Oct.7; 1799) Frs. 2,800

LANQUET, Thomas
- An Epitome of Cronicles, conteining the whole Discourse of the Histories as well of this Realme of England. '1569' [i.e. 1549]. 1st. Edn. 4to. Cont. owner's. inscr. & marginal notes, title a little stained, minor worming in 1st. 6 ll., affecting only title border. 18th. C. cf., gt. spine, spine chipped at head & foot. [STC 15217] (C. Apr.1; 218) *Quaritch.* £300

LANSDOWNE, George Granville, Lord
See–GRANVILLE, George, Lord Lansdowne

LANSINSKY, J.A.
- Skizzenbuch. Fünf und fünfzig Ansichten des Rheins von Mainz bis Köln. Frankfurt, 1829. Ob. fo. Soiled. Cont. hf. leath., ptd orig. wraps., soiled. (R. Oct.14-18; 2429) DM 8,000

LANTE [Louis Marie & Gatine, M.
- [Les Femmes celebres de l'ancienne France]–[Haute et moyenne Classes]–[Costumes des Femmes de Hambourg, de la Hollande, du Tyrol, de la Hollande, de la Suisse (etc.)]. [Paris], ca. 1847-50; ca. 1828; ca. 1827. 3 works in 1 vol. Fo. 1st. work: 28 plts. only, 2nd. work: 10 (of 14) plts., 3rd. work: 76 (of 100) plts., together 122 cold. plts. by Lante, includes 8 from other works, a few other cold. plts. bnd. at end. Cont. cf., decor. in gt. & blind. W.a.f. (S. Dec.9; 520) *Schwarz.* £3,200
- Galerie Francaise de Femmes Celèbres. Paris, 1832. 4to. 68 hand-cold. engraved plts., title soiled, lacks text. Disbnd. (CSK. Jun.5; 82) £85

LANZ, Phillipe Louis & Bétancourt, Augustin de
- Analytical Essay on the Construction of Machines. ca. 1820. 1st. Edn. in Engl. 4to. Plt., slightly spotted. Cont. bds., mod. cl. back. (S. Oct.21; 352) *Quaritch.* £170

LANZI, Luigi
- Storia Pittorica dell'Italia dal Risorgimento delle Belle Arti fino presso al Fine del XVIII Sec. Bassano, 1809. 3rd. Edn. 6 vols. Hf. cf. (CR. Mar.19; 92) Lire 220,000

LAO TZU
- The White Cow & other Chinese Fairy Tales. Ill.:– Francis Rose. L., [1945]. Sm. 4to. Pict. cl., d.-w. Pres. copy from Gertrude Stein to 'Bobsie & Barney' (Chapman). (PNY. Mar.4; 163) $350

LAPAUZE, Henry
- Ingres. Paris, 1911. 4to. Hf. chagrin, unc., wrap. (HD. Dec.5; 123) Frs. 1,350

LA PEROUSE, Jean François de Galaup, Comte de
- Atlas du Voyage de La Pérouse. Ill.:– Moreau le Jeune [title-frontis.]. Paris, 1797. Lge. fo., Stps. of Ecole Royale d'Artillerie Navale de Toulon on plts. Glazed hf. cf. (HD. Jun.29; 276) Frs. 6,600
- Charts & Plates to Voyages. 1798. Fo. Bds. (DWB. May 15; 307) £350
- Voyage Autour du Monde. Ed.:– L.A. Milet-Mureau. Paris, 1797. 1st. Edn. 5 vols. & atlas fo. Cont. unif. cf.-bkd. marb. bds., text vols. worn at spine extremities, spine of atlas vol. very worn. (PNY. May 21; 273) $1,800
- – Anr. Copy. 4 vols. L.P. No atlas. Orig. bds., unc. [Sabin 38960] (SPB. May 5; 306) $950

– – **Anr. Edn.** Paris, [1797]. 1st. Edn. 5 vols. (4 vols. text & atlas vol.) 4to. & fo. 69 engraved charts & plts., 1 torn. Cont. hf. russ., spines defect., upr. cover of atlas detchd. (C. Jul.15; 61A)
Remington. £1,100

– – **Anr. Copy.** 4 vols. & atlas. 19th. C. cl., & atlas in cont. cf. (worn, covers detchd.). From Chetham's Liby., Manchester. [Sabin 38960] (C. Nov.27; 242) *Cash.* £650

[-] [-] **Anr. Copy.** Atlas only. Fo. Cont. glazed bds., roan spine gt. As a collection of plts., w.a.f. (SPB. Oct.1; 202) $1,200

– – **Anr. Edn.** Ed.:– De Lesseps. Paris, 1831. Mod. hf. cf., orig. wraps. bnd. in, unc. (P. Jul.31; 97)
Quaritch. £55

– **A Voyage Round the World.** 1798. 1st. Edn. in Engl. Atlas vol. only. Fo. 67 engraved plts., maps & charts (of 69). Mod. cf., spine gt., unc. [Sabin 38962]. (S. Mar.31; 487) *H. Lamm.* £450

– – **Anr. Edn.** 1798. 2 vols. 50 engraved maps & plts., 3 folding, lacks port., F3 torn. Mod. hf. cf., spines gt. [Sabin 38964] (S. Mar.31; 488)
Charles Harris. £380

LA PEROUSE, Jean François Galaup de
-LABILLARDIERE, Jacques J. Houton de
-ENTRECASTEAUX, Bruni d'
– **Voyage de la Perouse Autour du Monde.**
– **Relation du Voyage à la Recherche de la Perouse.**
– **Voyage d'Entre-casteaux Envoyé à la Recherche de la Perouse.** Ed.:– M.L.A. Milet-Mureau [1st. work]; M. de Rossel [3rd. work]. Ill.:– after Prevost & others [1st. work]; after Piron, Audebert, & Redouté [2nd. work]. Paris, [1797]; [1799-1800]; 1808-07]. 1st. Edns. 4 vols. in 2, & atlas; 2 vols., & atlas; 2 vols., & atlas; together 9 vols. 4to. & fo. Unif. cont. cat's-paw cf., spines gt., atlases bnd. in matching hf. cf. & marb. bds., covers of La Perouse atlas detchd. [Sabin 38960; 3842; 22671 & 22672] (C. Nov.6; 321)
Maggs. £6,200

LAPIDE, Johannes de 'Heynlin, Joann'
– **Resolutorium Dubiorù circa Celebrationè Missar[um] Occurentiù.** [Rome], ca. 1490. 4to. Title soiled. 16 ll. (HK. Nov.18-21; 215)
DM 1,000

– – **Anr. Edn.** Cologne, Heinrich Quentell, 1493. 4to. Rubricated thro-out, minor stain on title, heavy stain in last few ll., margin of 1 lf strengthened. 19th. C. hf. roan. [Hain 9906*; Goff J 359] (C. Apr.1; 53) *Warner.* £240

LAPIE, Pierre
– **Atlas Universel de Géographie Ancienne et Moderne.** Paris, 1829. Fo. Qtr. mor. W.a.f. (TA. Aug.21; 7) £120

LAPLACE, Pietre Simon, Marquis de
– **Mechanik des Himmels.** Trans.:– J.C. Burckhardtt. Berlin, 1800-02. 1st. German Edn. 2 vols. 4to. Cont. marb. leath. (HK. Nov.18-21; 612)
DM 500

LAPORTE, Julius
See–IBBETSON, Julius & others.

LA PRIMAUDAYE, Pierre de
– **The French Academie wherein is discoursed the Institution of Manners & whatsoever else concerneth the Good & Happie Life of all Estates & Callings.** 1589. 2nd. Edn. 4to. Title-p. soiled & with a few very sm. holes reprd., B2 soiled, sm. tear in upr. margin B1 & S2 affecting letters & ornaments, tiny rust-hole in Aa3, a few stains. New cf. antique style. [STC 15234] (S. Jun.23; 367) *Fletcher.* £75

– – **Anr. Copy.** Slight marginal staining, title soiled, marginal tear in 2C7, a few rust-spots & holes. Cont. cf., blind-stpd. ornament in centre of sides, worn. (S. Jan.26; 6) *Thorp.* £55

LA QUINTINYE, Jean de
– **The Compleat Gard'ner, or Directions for Cultivating & Right Ordering of Fruit-Gardens & Kitchen-Gardens . . .** Trans.:– John Evelyn. 1693. 1st. Edn. in Engl. 3 pts. in 1 vol. Fo. Mor. by Rivière. [Wing L431] (C. Apr.1; 218A)
Fredericks. £450

– – **Anr. Edn.** Ed.:– George London & Henry Wise. 1704. 2 vols. in 1. 2-lf. advt. of John Evelyn for anr. edn. bnd. in, lacks final blanks?, 9 engraved folding plts. only?, 1 torn, some other defects, mainly marginal. Cont. panel. cf., worn. (SBA. Dec.16; 29) *Carter.* £58

LARBAUD, Valéry
– **A.O. Barnabooth.** 1913. Mor., fillet & mosaic ornam. motif, wrap., by Anthorne Legrain. (HD. Oct.10; 95) Frs. 2,400

– **Beauté mon Beau Souci.** Ill.:– J.E. Laboureur. 1920. Orig. Edn. Mor. by Louise Levéque. On vell. Lafuma Navarra, orig aqua. ill. (HD. Oct.10; 193) Frs. 6,800

– – **Anr. Edn.** Ill.:– J.E. Laboureur. Paris, 1920. (412) on Lafuma vell. Sewed, wrap. (HD. Dec.5; 124) Frs. 3,000

LARCHEY, Lorédan
– **Ancien Armorial Equestre de la Toison d'or et de L'Europe au 15e Siècle.** Paris, 1890. Loose ll. in publisher's portfo. (LM. Nov.8; 287)

– – **Anr. Copy.** (500); on tinted vell., numbered. Lge. fo. Facs. of MS. 4790 of Bibliotheque de l'Arsenal, some damp-staining at beginning. Publisher's decor. cl., spine reprd. (HD. Jun.29; 110b) Frs. 1,200

LARIMER, Gen. William
– **Reminiscences of, & of his son William H. H. Larimer, Two of the Founders of Denver City.** Ed.:– Herman S. Davis. Lancaster, Pa., Priv. ptd. 1918. Flexible leath., spine gt. Sigd. inscr. by ed., 1919, to G.H. Taber. (SG. Jan.8; 235) $200

LAROCHE, L.A.H.
– **Neueste Conditorey-Buch oder Arbeiten eines wohlerfahrenen Conditors aus 40 Jähriger Erfahrung.** Weimar, 1800. Old MS. receipts on end-papers. Cont. bds. (R. Oct.14-18; 2712)
DM 480

LA ROCHE, Sophie v.
[-] **Journal einer Reise durch Frankreich.** Altenburg, 1787. 1st. Edn. Slightly soiled at beginning, ink stain in Vig., bkd. Cont. marb. leath., floral gt. (HK. May 15; 4587) DM 1,500

– **Schönes Bild der Resignation.** [Leipzig], 1795. 1st. Edn. Vol. 1. Slightly browned in parts. Cont. hf. leath., spine slightly torn. MS. dedication in inner cover. (H. Dec.9/10; 1581) DM 1,100

LA ROCHEFOUCAULD, François VI, Duc de, prince de Marcillac
– **Maximes et Réflexions Morales.** Ill.:– Delvaux after Saint Jean [port.]. Geneva, 1782. 18mo. Old red mor. by Cazin. (HD. Apr.8; 258) Frs. 1,200

– – **Anr. Edn.** Ill.:– Duponchel [port.]. L., 1784. 18mo. Red mor. by Cazin. (HD. Apr.8; 269)
Frs. 1,800

LA ROCHEFOUCAULD–LIANCOURT, François Alexandre F.
– **Voyage dans les Etats-Unis d'Amérique, fait en 1795, 1796 et 1797.** Paris, [1799]. 1st. Edn. 8 vols. in 4. 4th. vol. stained in bottom margin thro-out. Hf. cf. (SG. Mar.5; 262) $350

– – **Anr. Copy.** 8 vols. Occasional foxing & dampstaining, sm. liby. stps. Cont. hf. leath. & paper bds. (CB. Feb.18; 119) Can. $260

LA ROQUE, Jean de
[-] **Voyage de l'Arabie Heureuse.–Voyage . . . dans la Palestine–Voyage de Syrie et du Mont-Liban.** Amst.; Paris; Paris, 1716; 1717; 1722. 2nd. & 3rd. works: 1st. Edns. 1 vol.; 1 vol.; 2 vols. 12mo. 1st. work: title & frontis. slightly browned; 3rd. work: 1 plt. stained. Cont. cf. (C. Feb.25; 109)
Feldman. £250

LAROUSSE, Pierre
– **Grand Dictionnaire Universel Français.** Paris, n.d. 17 vols. Orig. hf. mor. (SM. Feb.11; 33)
Frs. 2,700

– **Grand Dictionnaire Universel du XIXe Siècle.** 1866-76. 17 vols. 4to. Publisher's red hf. chagrin. (HD. Apr.24; 149) Frs. 4,500

– – **Anr. Copy.** 15 vols. Red mor.-bkd. cl. (SM. Oct.8; 2260) Frs. 1,300

LARPENT, Francis Seymour
– **The Private Journal.** Ed.:– Sir George Larpent. L., 1853. 1st. Edn. 3 vols. 12mo. Orig. cl. (SG. Feb.26; 207) $100

LARREMORE, Thomas A. & Amy H.
– **The Marion Press.** Ed.:– J.W. Rogers. Jamaica, N.Y., 1943. (210) numbered on Strathmore all rag paper. Hand-bnd. in buckram. (SG. Jan.22; 281) $190

LARREY, Baron Dominique
– **Memoirs of Military Surgery & Campaigns of the French Armies.** Trans.:– Richard Willmott Hall. Balt., 1814. 1st. Amer. Edn. 2 vols. No hf.-title in vol. II (? not called for), some stains.

Cf., rebkd. Owners' inscrs. 'Thomas Moore M.D., C.H. von Jagen M.D., Dr. L. Lewis Cox 1858'. (S. Jun.16; 490) *Rovy.* £130

LARREY, Isaac de
– **Histoire d'Angleterre, d'Ecosse et d'Irlande . . .** Ill.:– after A. Van der Weiff. Rotterdam, 1697-1713. 1st. Edn. 4 vols. Fo. Slight foxing. Cont. red mor., covers decor. with gt. fillets & du Seuil motifs for 1st 3 vols., 4th vol. with triple gt. fillets around covers, spines decor. with raised bands, inside roll-stp., bdgs. slightly defect., reprd. (HD. Feb.27; 35) Frs. 3,800

LARROUY, Maurice
– **Le Révolté.** Ill.:– Charles Fouqueray. Paris, 1929. (300) numbered on vélin blanc de Cuve. 4to. Red mor. by Kieffer, gt. & decor. spine, impressed panel on covers, decor. gt. & mor. onlays, silk doubls., orig. wraps. bnd. in, s.-c. (SM. Oct.8; 2349) Frs. 3,000

LASCARIS, Constantinus
– **Compendium Octo Orationis . . .** Venice, Oct. 1512. 4to. Lacks title-p. Later vell.-bkd. bds. (SG. Sep.25; 12) $110

– **De Octo Partibus Oronis . . .** Venice, 1512. 3rd. Edn. 4to. Sm. repairs to title-p. & last ll. Mod. hf. vell. (HD. Apr.24; 1) Frs. 3,200

– – **Anr. Edn.** Ed.:– Bernardus Giunta. [Flor.] [P. Giunta], [1515?]. Title slightly stained, slight paperfault in nl, 4 ll. of Hebrew Alphabet & grammar at end. Mod. vell. (C. Apr.1; 54)
Root. £140

LASCARIS, Evadne
– **The Golden Bed of Kydno.** Ill.:– Lettice Sandford. Gold. Cock. Pr., 1935. (200) on Joynson's mould-made paper. 4to. Orig. pict. cl. gt. (SBA. Dec.16; 124) *Emerald Isle Books.* £130

LAS CASAS, Barolomé de
– **Istoria ò brevissima Relatione della Distruttione dell 'Indie Occidentali.** Venice, 1626. 1st. Edn. in Italian. 4to. 18th. C. hf. cf., rebkd. & corners reprd. [Sabin 11242] (S. Nov.4; 648)
Bence. £120

LAS CASES, Count Emmanuel de 'A. Le Sage'
– **Gil Blas [Adventures of].** Trans.:– Tobias Smollett. L., 1819. 3 vols. Three-qtr. mor., spines gt., by Tout. (SG. Dec.18; 279) $110

[-] – – **Anr. Edn.** L., n.d. Vol. 3 of 4. New end-papers. Cont. cf., rebkd., boxed. Sigd. by George Washington at top of title-p. (SPB. Nov.24; 61) $1,900

– **Histoire de Gil Blas de Santillane.** 1819. 3 vols. Hf. mor., cont decor. spines. (HD. Oct.10; 249)
Frs. 1,800

– – **Anr. Edn.** Ed.:– Victor Hugo. Ill.:– Roger. Paris, Orig. Edn. on L.P. vell., 1825. 3 vols. Hf.-mor., corners, decor. spines, by Meslant. (HD. Feb.18; 155) Frs. 1,150

– – **Anr. Edn.** Ill.:– Maurice Leloir. Paris, n.d. (50) numbered on Japon Impérial. 4to. Red hf. mor. by Carayon, orig. wraps. bnd. in. Maurice Quarré ex-libris. (SM. Oct.8; 2352) Frs. 1,000

– **Journal of the Private Life . . . of Emperor Napoleon at Saint Helena.** L., 1824. New Edn. 8 Pts. in 4 vols. Cont. cf. (SG. Oct.30; 216) $100

– **Mémorial de Saint-Hélène.** 1823. Orig. Edn. 8 vols. Cont. decor. hf. chagrin. (HD. Oct.10; 248)
Frs. 2,000

– – **Anr. Copy.** 9 vols. Cont. roan. (HD. Jun.30; 45) Frs. 1,100

LA SENA, Petrus
– **Cleombrotos, sive de Iis, qui in Aquis Pereunt, Philologica Dissertatio.** Rome, 1737. 1 old MS. note, Mazarine Liby. stp. on title & at end, bkplt. of J.B. Clements. 18th. C. mor., triple gt. fillet, spine gt. in compartments, inner gt. dentelles. William Beckford copy. (SM. Oct.7; 1801)
Frs. 1,000

LA SERRE, Abbé de
– **Livre d'Eucchariste.** Ill.:– M. Denis. 1920. (130) on vell. Sm. 4to. Salmon mor., lge. decor. of gt & blind cross, mor. doubl., silk end-ll., wrap., s.-c. & box, by Canape & Corriez. (HD. Jun.30; 46) Frs. 4,200

LASINIO, Carlo
– **Pitture A Fresco Del Campo Santo Di Pisa.** Firenze, 1812. Elephant fo. Hf. cf., rebkd. (GM. Apr.30; 723) £110

LASINSKY, J.A.
- Croquis Pittoresques, Cinquante-cinq Vues du Rhin. Frankfurt, 1829. Ob. 4to. Slightly spotted. Orig. mor.-bkd. bds. (CSK. Feb.6; 48) £850

LASOR A VAREA, Alphonsi
- Universus Terrarum Orbris Scriptorum Calamo Illustratus. Padua, 1713. 2 vols. Fo. Cont. vell. (R. Oct.14-18; 1470) DM 25,000

LASSAIGNE, Jacques
- Chagall. Ill.:– Marc Chagall. [Paris], [1957]. 4to. Cold. pict. wraps. (SG. Oct.23; 64) $200
- Le Plafond de l'Opera de Paris. Ill.:– Marc Chagall. 1965. 4to. Many ll. detchd. Orig. cl., d.-w. Pict. inscr. by artist in biro & crayon 'pour Doris'. (C. Feb.4; 179) Blakey. £110
See–CHAGALL, Marc

LASSALA, Emmanuel
- De Serifico Coorum Bononiensium Libellus Singularis ad Pium Sextum Pontificem ... Bologna, 1782. Fo. Cont. Bolognese crimson mor. gt., elaborate spiral & key-pattern border, corner ornaments, surrounding arms of Pius VI, silk end-papers, buckram s.-c. The Dedication Copy, with name of Pius VI ptd. in gold, lately in the collection of John A. Saks. (C. Jun.10; 140) Quaritch. £520

LASSALLE, Ferdinand
- Gesammelte Reden und Schriften. Ed.:– E. Bernstein. Berlin, 1919-20. Orig. hf. leath. (R. Oct.14-18; 1350) DM 430

LASSAR, O.
- Deutsche Kurorte Festschrift f.d. Mitglieder d.x. Internationalen Medicinischen Congresses. Berlin, 1890. Orig. linen. (R. Mar.31-Apr.4; 1856) DM 500

LASSELS, Richard
- The Voyage of Italy.-[The Voyage of Italy ... the Second Part]. Paris, 1670. 1st. Edn. 2 pts. in 1 vol. 12mo. Minor staining at end, cont. owner's inscr. of K. Rooper. Cont. cf. [Wing L464] (C. Feb.25; 162) Marlborough. £50

LASTARRIA, J.V. & others
- Historia Jeneral de la República de Chile desde su Independencia hasta nuestros Dias. Santiago, 1866-82. 5 vols. Some spotting & discolouration. Qtr. mor. [Sabin 39151] (SPB. May 5; 315) $100

LASTEYRIE, C.P. de
- Typographie Economique. Paris, 1837. 1st. Edn. Slightly soiled & browned in parts, copperplt. port misbnd. Orig. wraps., unc. (H. Dec.9/10; 172) DM 800

LATHAM, Charles
- The Gardens of Italy. 1905. 2 vols. Fo. Orig. cl. gt. (C. Feb.4; 160) Marlborough. £55

LATHAM, John
[-] Allgemeine Übersicht der Vögel. Trans.:– J.M. Bechstein. Ill.:– G. Vogel after Kühne, Reinecke & others. Nuremb., 1792-98. 1st. Edn. Vols. 1-3, lacks vol. 4 (1811-12) as usual. 4to. Lightly soiled in parts. 19th. C. hf. linen, worn, 1 cover reprd. (R. Mar.31-Apr.4; 1383) DM 3,400
- - Anr. Edn. Trans.:– J.M. Bechstein. Nuremb., 1793-98. 3 pts. in 6 vols. 4to. Cont. bds. (D. Dec.11-13; 308) DM 5,000
- General Synopsis of Birds. 1781-85. 3 vols. in 6. 4to. Rebnd. qtr. cf. gt. (P. Oct.2; 269) Smith. £650
[-] A General Synopsis of Birds.-Supplement to the General Synopsis.-Index Ornithologicus. 1781-85; 1787; 1790. 1st. Edn. 1st. work: 3 vols. in 6; 2nd. work: vol. 1 (of 2); 3rd. work: vols. 1-2 (of 3, lacks supp.). 4to. Directions ll. near end of 4 vols., occasional offsetting to text & several plts., slight spotting & browning. Cont. cf., rebkd. & reprd., worn. (S. Dec.3; 1019) W. & W. £420

LATHOM, F.
- Men & Manners. 1799. 1st. Edn. 4 vols. 12mo. Cf. gt. (P. Dec.11; 352) Quaritch. £290

LATIMER, Louise P.
See–MAHONY, Bertha E. & others

LATIMORE, Sarah Briggs & Haskell, Grace Clark
- Arthur Rackham: a Bibliography. Ill.:– Arthur Rackham. Los Angeles, Ward Ritchie Pr., 1936.

1st. Edn. (550) numbered. Pencil marked thro.-out. Cl.-bkd. decor. bds., box. Raymond M. Sutton, Jr. copy. (SG. May 7; 159) $300
- - Anr. Copy. (SG. Oct.2; 302) $250
- - Anr. Copy. Spine faded. (SG. Apr.30; 271) $170

LATREILLE, Pierre André
- Histoire Naturelle ... des Crustaces et des Insectes. Paris, [1801-02]. 4 vols. 37 plts. in 2 states. Bds. worn. (P. Apr.30; 215) Elliott. £55

LATROBE, Christian Ignatius
- Journal of a Visit to South Africa. 1818. [1st. Edn.?]. 4to. Cont. hf. cf., lacks upr. cover, worn. (SH. Nov.7; 311) Deacon. £440
- - Anr. Copy. Some spotting, marginal tear in R1. Worn. (S. Jun.22; 182) Simons. £400
- - Anr. Copy. Later hf. mor. by C. & J. Abbott. (S. Mar.31; 489) Yarrell. £380

LATTRE, Jean
- Atlas Moderne. Paris, ca. 1783. Fo. Cont. hf. leath., gt. spine. (R. Oct.14-18; 1542) DM 2,000

LAUCEVICIUS, E.
- Paper in Lithuania in XV-XVIII Centuries. Vilnius, 1967. 2 vols., including atlas. Fo. Gt.-pict. cl. (SG. Mar.26; 354) $180

LAUCKHARD, [C.F.]
- Die Welt in Bildern. Leipzig, ca. 1870. 3pts. in 1 vol. Text lightly browned, plts. slightly soiled. Orig. linen, orig renewed spine. (HK. May 15; 5154) DM 1,850

LAUDERDALE, James Maitland, Earl of
- An Inquiry into the Nature & Origin of Public Health. Edinb., 1804. 1st. Edn. Slightly spotted. Cont. hf. str.-grd. mor. (S. Apr.7; 263) Laywood. £260
- - Anr. Copy. Cf. (P. Dec.11; 353) Brook-Hitchin. £130

LAUGHLIN, Ledle Irwin
- Pewter in America. Boston, 1940. 2 vols. 4to. 2-tone cl., s.-c. (brkn.), unc. Pres. Copy. (SG. Dec.4; 279) $140

LAUGHTON, L.G. Carr
- Old Ship Figure-Heads & Sterns. 1925. [1st. Edn.?] (1500) numbered. 4to. Orig. cl., gt., d.-w. (SH. Oct.9; 172) Talerman. £120
- - Anr. Copy. Slightly spotted. (SKC. Feb.26; 1779) £100
- - Anr. Copy. Lev. mor. gt., spine with emblems in compartments, partly unc., by Bayntun. (CNY. May 22; 167) $160

LAUGIER DE BELLECOEUR, C.
- Fasti Militari, ossia Guerre dei Popoli Europei dal 1792 al 1815. Flor., 1843-47. 4 vols. 4to. Slightly soiled in parts. Cont. hf. leath. (R. Oct.14-18; 2104) DM 1,200

LAUNAY, C.L. de
- Der Geigen zu Erziehen Habenden jungen Cavalier. Augsburg, 1738. 4to. Slightly browned. Bds., worn. (SH. Jun.4; 138) Wohler. £90

LAURE
- Atlas Topographique des Environs de Paris, dédié et présenté au Roy. Ill.:– Choffard. Paris, Priv. ptd., ca. 1780. 18mo. Cont. red mor., decor. spine, 3 fillets on covers, angle motifs, inner dentelles. (HD. Apr.10; 145) Frs. 2,200

LAURENCE, Edward
- The Duty of a Steward to his Lord ... wherein may be seen the ... Practices tending to lessen & ... to Improve their Lords Estates. 1727. 4to. Cont. reversed cf., rebkd. (CSK. Jul.24; 108) £90
- - Anr. Copy. Cont. panel. cf. (S. Dec.3; 1020) Dr. Pike. £85

LAURENCE, John
- The Clergy-Man's Recreation: shewing the Pleasure & Profit of the Art of Gardening.-The Gentleman's Recreation: or the Second Part of the Art of Gardening. L., 1715; 1716. 2 works in 1 vol. Lacks initial blanks, some staining. Old sheep, rebkd. (SPB. Jul.28; 213) $100
- A New System of Agriculture. Being a complete body of Husbandry & Gardening. 1726. 1st. Edn. Fo. Cont. panel. cf., spine chipped at head. (S. Jun.22; 52) Quaritch. £100

LAURENCIN, Marie
- Petit Bestiare, poèmes inedits. Paris, 1926. (151) numbered. 4to. Unsewn in orig. wraps. (SH. Nov.21; 373) Scopazzi. £170

- Les Petites Filles. Paris, Ltd. Edn. numbered, n.d. 16mo. Orig. batik bds. & s.-c., backstrip & s.-c. slightly worn. (SH. Nov.21; 369) Kawamatsu. £75

LAURENT & Perrot
- Les Femmes de l'Asie, ou Description de leurs Physionomies, Moeurs, Usages et Costumes. Paris, n.d. 18mo. Cont cf., spine decor. in gt. & blind, gt. fillet on covers, angle motifs, lge. gt. centre lozenge. (HD. Apr.9; 508) Frs. 1,000

LAURENT DE L'ARDECHE, P.M.
- Histoire de l'Empereur Napoleon. Paris, 1840. Hf. cf., upr. cover detchd. (P. Dec.11; 5) Schapiro. £65

LAURI, Jacobus
- Antiquae Urbis Splendor. Rome, 1612. Ob. 4to. A few repairs. Cont. limp vell. (SH. Mar.5; 80) Roole Dhiero. £140
- - Anr. Copy. (LM. Jun.13; 251) B.Frs. 33,000

LAURIE, Richard Holmes
- New Traveller's Companion. 1813. 7th. Edn. 26 double-p engraved maps, hand-cold. in outl., some spotting. Cont. hf. mor., upr. cover detchd. (TA. Feb.19; 126) £120
- - Anr. Edn. 1828. Occasional soiling. Orig. mor. wallet, stitching worn. (CSK. Oct.3; 117) £55

LAURIE, Robert & Whittle, James
- A Complete Body of Ancient Geography. 1819. Fo. 13 engraved maps hand-cold. in outl. Cf.-bkd. bds. (CSK. Apr.10; 40) £55
- General Atlas. 1804. 4to. Slightly soiled. Cont. hf. mor., worn. (CSK. Nov.21; 218) £130

LAURNAGA, Pablo de
See–COLMENARES Fernandez de Cordoba, Felipe–LAURNAGA, Pablo de

LAURON, M.
See–TEMPEST, P. & Lauron, M.

LAURUS, Jacobus
- Antiquae Urbis Splendor ... Splendore Dell'Antica e Moderna Roma. Ed.:– Johannes Alt. Rome, 1641 [latin title 1612]. Ob. fo. A few marginal tears, 2 just affecting engraving, sm. hole in index 1f., Latin title cut down & mntd. 18th. C. cf., slightly worn. (S. Apr.7; 264) Mistrali. £380

LAUTENSACK, Heinrich
- Unpaar. Berlin, 1926. 1st. Edn. (300) Privilege Edn. Orig. suede, ill. on upr. cover by Kubin. Plts. sigd. (HK. Nov.18-21; 2750) DM 2,600

LAUTREAMONT, Comte de
- Les Chants de Maddror. Ill.:– Bernard Buffet Paris, [1952]. (125). 4to. Slight offsetting. Loose as iss. in wraps., orig. boxes, worn. (SPB. May 29; 262) $300

LAUTS, G.
- De Kaapsche Landverhuisers of Neerlands Afstammelingen in Zuid Afrika. Leyden, 1847. Cl., leath. spine, sigd. by D.F. du Toit. (VA. Aug.29; 316) R. 160

LAVALLE, Jean
- Plates from the Album to Histoire et Statistique de la Vigne et des Grands Vins de la Côte-d'Or. Paris, [1855]. Fo. Slightly spotted. Loose, in decorated bd. s.-c. From liby. of André L. Simon. (S. May 18; 129) Clark. £110

LAVALLEE, Joseph
- Voyage Pittoresque et Historique de l'Istrie et de la Dalmatie. Paris, 1802. 1st. Edn. Fo. Cont. diced russ., gt., worn, upr. cover detchd. From Chetham's Liby., Manchester. (C. Nov.27; 243) Simons. £630

LAVARD, Henry
- La Hollande à Vol d'Oiseal. Paris, 1881. 4to. Slightly soiled in parts. Orig. pict. linen. (D. Dec.11-13; 1537) DM 700

LA VARDIN, Jacques de
- The Historie of George Castriot ... Trans.:– Z. I[ones]. 1596. 1st. Edn. in Engl. Fo. Blank with inscr., slight browning & soiling, a few sm. holes affecting text. Cont. limp vell., gt., covers with initials 'FB', worn. [NSTC 15318] (S. Sep.29; 47) Quaritch. £130

LAVAT, Jean Baptiste
- Nouveau Voyage aux Isles de l'Amerique ... The Hague, 1724. 6 vols. 12mo. 82 (of 91) plts., some tears with losses to some plts., foxing, browning, soiling, some worming in vol. V affecting text & some plts. Cf., gt. spine, spines chipped & torn,

worn. From liby. of William E. Wilson. [Sabin 38410] (SPB. Apr.29; 173) $225

LAVATER, Jean Gaspard
- L'Art de Connaitre les Hommes par la Physionomie ... Paris, 1835. New Edn. 10 vols. Some foxing. Orig. bds., corners slightly worn. (CB. Feb.18; 196)   Can. $240
- Essays on Physiognomy Trans.:– Henry Hunter. Ill.:– Thomas Holloway & others. 1789-98. 1st. Engl. Edn. 3 vols. in 5. 4to. 19th. C. cf., gt., some covers loose. (S. Mar.17; 351)   Traylen. £170
-- **Anr. Copy.** 3 vols. Lacks hf-title to vol. 1 & title & index to vol. III. Cont. hf-vell. gt., unc. W.a.f. (SBA. Jul.22; 101)   Salinas. £110
-- **Anr. Copy.** 3 vols. in 5. Early cf., brkn., partly unc. (SG. May 14; 128) $425
-- **Anr. Edn.** Trans.:– H. Hunter. Ill.:– Th. Holloway. L., 1792 & 1810. On vell. Lge. 4to. Cont. leath., renewed in cont. style. (R. Mar.31-Apr.4; 549)   DM 1,250
-- **Anr. Edn.** Trans.:– Henry Hunter. 1810. 3 vols. in 5. 4to. Occasional offsetting to text. Cont. russ., gt., spine gt. (S. Sep.29; 220)   Heald. £120
- Le Lavater Portatif, ou Precis de l'Art de connaitre les Hommes par les Traits du Visage ... augmenté ... d'un Receuil d'anecdotes Physionomiques; Le Lavater des Dames ... suivi d'un essai sur les Moyens de procriéer des Enfans d'esprit ... Paris, 1815. 6th. Edn.; 5th. Edn. 2 works in 1 vol. 16mo. Some plt. numbers cropped, slightly soiled in places. Cont. hf. cf. (S. Feb.23; 69)   Hyde. £100
- Physiognomische Fragmente. 1775-78. 1st. Edn. 4 vols. 4to. Lacks 4 plts. Cf.-bkd. bds., worn. (BS. Jun.11; 62)   £110

LAVATER, Louis or Ludwig
- Trois Livres des Apparitions des Esprits, Fantosmes, Prodiges et Accidens Merveilleux. Zürich, 1581. 2nd. Edn. in Fr. 2 pts. in 1 vol. Bkplt. of Stuart of Dunnairn. 17th. C. mor., gt. panel with corner sprays of flower-vases, triple gt. fillet, flat spine gt. with vases in compartments, inner gt. dentelles. (SM. Oct.7; 1805)   Frs. 3,000

LAVEDAN, Antonio
- Tratado de los Usos, Abusos, Propiedades y Virtudes del Tabaco, Café, Te y Chocolate. Madrid, 1796. Some spotting. Cont. cf., worn. [Sabin 39290] (SPB. May 5; 316) $425

LAVER, James
- A Complete Catalogue of the Etchings & Dry-Points of Arthur Briscoe. 1930. 4to. Plts., 1 etched & sigd. Orig. cl. (SH. Jan.29; 118)   Lott. £100

See–OLIVER, Charles & Laver, James

LA VERANDE, Jean de
- Côtes de Normandie (Les). Ill.:– Aymar de Lézardière. 1954. (105) on velin du Marais. 4to. Ll. in s.-c. (HD. Feb.18; 215)   Frs. 4,500

LA VERENDRYE
- [–] Journals & Letters of Pierre Gaultier de Varennes de La Verendrye & his Sons ... Ed.:– Lawrence J. Burpee. Toronto, 1927. (550) numbered, for members of the Champlain soc. Buckram. (SG. Jan.8; 237) $200

LA VERITE
See–ROUSSEAU, Jean–Jacques–TRONCHIN, J.R.–LA VERITE

LAVISSE, Ernest
- Histoire de France ... 1900-10. 18 vols. in 9. Sm. 4to. Hf. chagrin by Falmmarion-Vaillant, spines with raised bands. (HD. Feb.27; 160)   Frs. 2,300

LAVOISIER, Antoine Laurent de
- Méthode de Nomenclature Chimique, proposée par MM. de Morveau, Lavoisier, Bertholet, & de Fourcroy. Paris, 1787. 1st. Edn., 1st. Iss. Lge. folding table with short tear, stab-holes in some inner margins. Cont. mott. cf., gt. spine, hf. red mor. case. From Honeyman Collection. (S. May 20; 3276)   Quaritch. £260
-- **Anr. Copy.** Some spotting at beginning. Qtr. cf., soiled. (S. Dec.1; 227)   Rota. £170
-- **Anr. Edn.** Paris, 1787. 3rd. printing. Slightly soiled, partly browned. Hf. leath. (HK. Nov.18-21; 613)   DM 1,100
- Traité Elementaire de Chimie Presenté dans un ordre Nouveau et d'après les Découvertes Modernes. Paris, 1793. 2nd. Edn., 1st. Iss. 2 vols. Qtr. cf. (S. Dec.1; 228)   Kurzer. £100

-- **Anr. Copy.** 1 plt. with ink spots, strip with name stuck on title-pp. Cont. cf. gt. (S. Dec.1; 229)   Phelps. £55
- Traité Elementaire de Chimie, & Nomenclature Chimique. Paris, 1789. 3 vols. Some browning thro.-out. Cf.-bkd. bds. (BS. Feb.25; 245)   £50

LAW, Judge John
- Address Delivered Before the Vincennes Historical & Antiquarian Society ... Louisville, 1839. 1st. Edn. Map in facs., foxing & soiling thro.-out text. Orig. ptd. wraps., spine worn, folding cl. case. From liby. of William E. Wilson; author's inscr. on title to Hon. Nathan F. Dixon. (SPB. Apr.29; 176) $150

LAW, [John], of Lauriston
- Considerations sur le Commerce et sur l'argent. The Hague, 1720. 1st. Edn. in Fr. 12mo. Advts., some browning & soiling. Cont. cf., slightly worn. (S. Jan.26; 240)   Martin. £160
- Money & Trade Considered: with a Proposal for Supplying the Nation with Money. Glasgow, 1760. Slight browning & soiling, tears in a few ll. Mod. cf. (S. Jan.26; 241)   Frognall. £130

LAWRANCE, Miss Mary
- A Collection of Roses from Nature. 1799. Fo. A little soiling. Cont. str.-grd. mor., gt., worn, spine reprd. (S. Dec.3; 1021)   Quaritch. £6,500

LAWRENCE, David Herbert
- Birds, Beasts & Flowers. Ill.:– B. Hughes-Stanton. Cresset Pr., 1930. 4to. Qtr. vell., unc. (P. Sep.11; 203)   Kent. £65
-- **Anr. Copy.** (500) Fo. Orig. vell.-bkd. bds. (C. Feb.4; 286)   Primrose Hill Books. £50
-- **Anr. Copy.** (500) numbered on Batchelor L.P. Qtr. vell. & marb. bds., gt. (PNY. May 21; 152) $130
- Collected Poems.–Last Poems. Ed.:– Richard Aldington & Giuseppe Ortoli (2nd work). Flor. (2nd work), 1928; 1932. (100) numbered, sigd. by author; Ltd. Edn. 2 vols.; 1 vol. Orig. bds., d.-w.'s (torn); orig. bds. (2 corners chipped). (C. Feb.4; 287)   Gekowski. £120
- The Escaped Cock. Black Sun Pr., 1929. 1st. Edn., (500). 4to. Orig. wraps., s.-c. (C. Feb.4; 288)   Cohen. £140
-- **Anr. Copy.** (450). Publisher's box, worn. (SPB. Nov.25; 329) $200
-- **Anr. Copy.** (SPB. May 29; 263) $150
- Lady Chatterley's Lover. [Flor.], Priv. ptd., 1928. 1st. Edn. (1000) sigd. by author. Orig. bds., slight wear, unc. (S. Jun.9; 74)   Sotheran. £240
-- **Anr. Copy.** (S. Jul.22; 191)   Hosain. £210
-- **Anr. Copy.** (SH. Dec.19; 575)   Forster. £190
-- **Anr. Copy.** Corners & backstrip defect. (S. Jul.22; 193)   J. Schrire. £75
-- **Anr. Copy.** Upr. cover & 1st. gathering almost detchd., lacks spine. (C. Feb.4; 290)   Morris. £60
-- **Anr. Copy.** Unc., spine & jnts. badly chipped. (SG. Jun.4; 262) $325
-- **Anr. Copy.** Variations to paper size, slight foxing to some pp. Upr. cover with phoenix motif, bds. handsewn, spine chipped & slightly split. (JL. Dec.15; 519)   Aus. $550
- Love Poems & others. 1913. 1st. Edn., 1st. Iss. Orig. cl. gt. (C. Jul.22; 17)   Forster. £55
-- **Anr. Copy.** (SH. Dec.19; 573)   Wimpole. £50
- An Original Poem. Ed.:– Catherine Carswell. 1934. 1st. Edn. (150). Orig. wraps. (S. Jul.22; 195)   Brueck. £65
-- **Anr. Copy.** (SH. Dec.19; 576)   Forster. £50
- Paintings of D.H. Lawrence. Mandrake Pr., [1929]. (510). Fo. Orig. hf. mor., s.-c., (worn). (C. Feb.4; 294)   Morris. £160
-- **Anr. Copy.** (C. Feb.4; 317)   Forster. £150
-- **Anr. Copy.** Numbered Subscriber's Edn. Fo. Mor.-bkd. buckram. (SG. Nov.13; 410) $160
- Pansies. Jun. 1929. (50) numbered, sigd. by author. Orig. pig., s.-c. (C. Feb.4; 295)   Gekowski. £130
-- **Anr. Edn.** Priv. ptd., Jun. 1929. (500) numbered, sigd. Orig. wraps. (CSK. Oct.31; 75)   £95
-- **Anr. Edn.** 1929. 1st. Edn., (250) sigd. decor. bds., unopened & unc., d.-w. slightly soiled with 2 sm. tears. (C. Jul.22; 18)   Wood. £160
-- **Anr. Copy.** Numbered. Parch.-bkd. patterned bds., d.-w. soiled & stained. (SG. Nov.13; 411) $160
- The Rainbow. 1915. 1st. Edn. 4pp. advts. Orig. cl. (S. Jul.22; 190)   Sotheran. £190
- Rawdon's Roof. 1928. (530) numbered, sigd. by Author. Orig. bds., d.-w., torn. (SD. Feb.4; 91)   £55

- Rawdon's Roof.–Psychoanalysis & the Unconscious. L.; N.Y., 1928; 1921. (530) numbered; 1st. Edn. 4to. & 8vo. Decor. bds., spine brittle, d.-w., unopened; bds. (SG. Nov.13; 409) $200
- Sons & Lovers. 1913. 1st. Edn., 1st. Iss. Orig. cl., worn. (SH. Dec.19; 479)   Brurck. £60
- Unpublished Foreword to 'Women in Love'. San Franc., Grabhorn Pr., 1936. 1st. Edn. 4to. Orig. bds. (C. Feb.4; 300)   Rota. £110
- The Virgin & the Gypsy. Flor., 1930. 1st. Edn., (810) numbered. Orig. bds., unc., in orig. d.-w. (LC. Jun.18; 26)   £50
- The White Peacock. 1911. 1st. Edn., Engl. Imp. Orig. cl. (S. Jul.22; 188)   Maggs. £90
-- **Anr. Copy.** (C. Feb.4; 302)   Gekowski. £70
- Women in Love. N.Y., 1920. 1st. Edn. (50) sigd. & numbered. Staining at lr. edges of 1st. 12 ll. Cl. (SG. Nov.13; 404) $1,400

LAWRENCE, Frieda
- Not I, but the Wind ... Santa Fe, 1934. 1st. Edn., Ltd. Edn., sigd. by author. Orig. cl., d.-w. (slightly torn). (C. Feb.4; 308)   Delancey. £50

LAWRENCE, H.W. & Dighton, B.L.
- French Line Engravings of the Late XVIII Century. 1910. 4to. Orig. cl. (TA. Mar.19; 31)   £72

LAWRENCE, John 'William Henry Scott'
[–] British Field Sports. 1818. [1st. Edn.?]. Some soiling. Cont. diced cf., rebkd., old spine preserved. (CSK. Oct.17; 12)   £110
-- **Anr. Copy.** 1st. sig. loose, some foxing & browning. Worn, upr. cover detchd. (SG. Dec.11; 350) $220
-- **Anr. Copy.** Some foxing & discolouration, a few ll. stained, additional plts. tipped in or laid on blank versos of plts., sewing opening before title-p. Old mor., lr. free end-paper defects. (KH. Nov.18; 531)   Aus. $150
-- **Anr. Copy.** Slightly soiled. Cont. style hf. leath. gt. (R. Mar.31-Apr.4; 1698)   DM 1,400
[–] -- **Anr. Edn.** Ill.:– Rudolph Ackermann, Thomas Alken & others (extra ills. only). [1818]. Fo. Section on racing extracted & mntd., MS. title, heavily extra ill. with engraved racing prints (some hand-cold.). Panel. mor. gt. by Watson. (SBA. Jul.22; 103)   Adamson. £900
-- **Anr. Edn.** 1820. 2nd. Edn. Advts., dtd. Jan. 1822, at end, some light offsetting, title & frontis. detchd. Orig. bds., worn & almost brkn. (CSK. May 15; 37)   £120
-- **Anr. Copy.** Lacks 1 copperplt., 1 plt. loose, 1 stained. Hf. cf., worn. (PD. Oct.22; 52)   £95
- New System of Agriculture. 1726. Cf., worn. (CE. Nov.20; 63)   £160

LAWRENCE, R.
- The Complete Farrier & British Sportsman. L., [1816]. 4to. Later leath. (D. Dec.11-13; 2140)   DM 860

LAWRENCE, Richard, Artist
- Elgin Marbles. 1818. 1st. Edn. Ob. 4to. Hf. cf. (LC. Jun.18; 80)   £75
-- **Anr. Copy.** Ob. fo. Mid-19th. C. cf. by Carss, Glasgow, with his ticket, upr. cover detchd. Bkplt. of John Tennant. (S. Nov.24; 188)   Lady Stewart. £55

LAWRENCE, Sir Thomas
- Engravings from the Choice Works of Sir Thomas Lawrence. Ill.:– after Lawrence. N.d. Fo. Spotted. Cont. hf. mor., bkplt. of James S. Virtue. (CSK. Feb.13; 85)   £50

LAWRENCE, Thomas Edward 'T.E. Shaw'
- Crusader Castles. Gold. Cock. Pr., 1936. 1st. Edn., (1000). 2 vols. 4to. 2 folding maps in loosely inserted envelope. Orig. hf.-mor., worn. (SH. Dec.19; 578)   Jones. £150
-- **Anr. Copy.** Niger three-qtr. mor. by Sangorski & Sutcliff . (SG. May 14; 86) $600
-- **Anr. Copy.** Orig. hf. mor., red mor.-bkd. c.'s. (SPB. Nov.25; 290) $375
- Crusader Castles: The Thesis. The Letters. Gold. Cock. Pr., 1936. 1st. Ltd. Edn. 2 vols. 4to. Cont. hf. mor., partly unc., by Sangorski, spines faded. From the collection of Eric Sexton. (C. Apr.15; 36)   Kassis. £150
-- **Anr. Copy.** Three qtr. mor., unc. Pres. copy to author's mother, A.l.s. from her to 'Hettie' loosely inserted. (SG. Sep.4; 208) $375
- The Diary. Corvinus Pr., Jun. 1937. 1st. Edn., (203) numbered, (40) on Medway paper. 4to.

LAWRENCE, Thomas Edward 'T.E. Shaw' -contd.
Orig. limp vell., silk ties, unc., s.-c. (S. Jul.31; 140)
Johnson. £540
– **An Essay on Flecker.** Corvinus Pr., May 1937.
1st. Edn., (30) numbered. 4to. Orig. limp vell., silk
ties. (S. Jul.31; 142) *Johnson.* £420
– **Revolt in the Desert.** 1927. 1st. Edn., (315). 4to.
Orig. mor.-bkd. cl. (SH. Dec.19; 577)
Von Bargen. £75
– **Secret Despatches from Arabia.** Gold. Cock. Pr.,
1939. (1000) numbered. Sm. 4to. Orig. mor.-bkd.
cl. by Sangorski & Sutcliffe, s.-c. (slightly torn).
(SBA. May 27; 474) *Maguire.* £180
– – **Anr. Copy.** (SKC. May 19; 31) £140
– – **Anr. Copy.** (SH. Dec.19; 579) *Jones.* £65
– **Seven Pillars of Wisdom.** Ill.:– Eric Kennington,
Blair-Hughes-Stanton & others. Priv. Ptd., 1926.
1st. Edn. 4to. 2 folding maps in dupl. Mor. by Best,
partly unc. Inscr. 'complete copy TES', & MS.
correction, orig. wood-engraving. sigd. by
Hughes-Stanton tipped in, 2 ll. 'Some notes on writ-
ing of Seven Pillars of Wisdom by T.E. Shaw'
loosely inserted. (S. Nov.25; 396) *Watt.* £1,400
– – **Anr. Copy.** Orig. mor., spine. gt.-lettered,
partly unc., by Best, s.-c. Inscr. on page xix
'Complete copy I.X-II.26 TES'. (CNY.
Oct.1; 103) $5,500
– – **Anr. Edn.** 1935. (750) numbered. 4to. Orig.
qtr. mor., partly untrimmed, partly unopened.
(TA. Jun.18; 272) £140
– – **Anr. Copy.** Orig. hf. pig. gt. (P. Nov.13; 259)
Hosain. £90

**LAWRENCE, Thomas Edward & Woolley,
Charles Leonard**
– **The Wilderness of Zin.** [1915]. 1st. Edn. Being
vol. III of the Palestine Exploration Fund. 4to.
Orig. cl.-bkd. bds. (SH. Jul.23; 191)
Johnson. £130
– – **Anr. Copy.** (SH. Mar.5; 159) *George's.* £110
– – **Anr. Copy.** 4to. Orig. cl.-bkd. bds., slight wear.
(SPB. Nov.25; 330) $300

LAWSON, John Parker
– **Scotland: Picturesque: Historical: Descriptive** . . .
N.d. 4to. Cl. (PD. Aug.20; 136) £65

LAWSON, William
[–] **A New Orchard & Garden.** 1668. 4to. Slight
stains on title & at end. Recent spr. cf. [Wing
L735] (C. Apr.1; 219) *Cavendish.* £110

LAXDAELA-SAGA
Copen., 1826. 1st. Edn. 4to. Later wrap., torn,
unopened. (SH. Oct.10; 380) *Solnes.* £70

LAXTON, Henry
– **Examples of Building Construction.** 1857-n.d. 4
vols. Fo. Orig. hf. mor. W.a.f. (CSK. Sep.26; 48)
£120

LAYARD, Sir Austen Henry
– **Early Adventures in Persia, Susiana &
Babylonia** . . . 1887. 1st. Edn. 2 vols. Orig. cl. (S.
Mar.31; 491) *Hosain Books.* £110

LAYARD, Edgar Leopold
– **The Birds of South Africa.** Cape Town, 1867.
Orig. cl. (SSA. Nov.5; 136) R. 100
– – **Anr. Edn.** 1874-84. Hf. mor. gt. (P.
Nov.13; 206) *Quaritch.* £120
– – **Anr. Edn.** Ed.:– R. Bowdler Sharpe. 1875-84.
New Edn. Plt. 5 detchd. & with tear,
discolouration in margin of plt. 11. Orig. hf. mor.,
covers slightly soiled, unc. (S. Jun.1; 151)
Schire. £240
– – **Anr. Copy.** Cl. (P. Oct.2; 34) £50

LAYARD, George Somes
See–SPIELMANN, Marion Harry & Layard,
George Somes

LAYCOCK, Thomas
– **Mind & Brain or the Correlations of
Consciousness & Organisation.** Edinb., 1860. 1st.
Edn. 2 vols. Orig. cl. (S. Jun.16; 494)
Palinvrus. £120

LAZIUS, Wolfgang
– **Commentarii: Rerum Grecarum Libri II.** [Vienna
or Frankfurt], 1558. 1st. Edn. Ded. copy. Fo. Sm.
tear in 1 map fold. Cont. limp vell., lacks ties.
Exlibris Bibliothek Oberherrlingen. (D.
Dec.11-13; 31) DM 4,500
– **De Gentium Aliquot Migrationibus, Sedibus
fixis, reliquijs, Linguarumq(ue)** . . . **Libri XII.** Basle,
Mar. 1557. 1st. Edn. Fo. Title & some ll. reprd.
mainly in margins, title slightly affected, sm. hole
in 2D2 slightly affecting 2 letters, 2G6 torn

affecting text, some wormholes at end, a few
slightly affecting text, some ll. slightly spotted, upr.
inner corner soiled at beginning, inscr. on title.
18th. C. bds., slightly worn. (S. Jan.27; 336)
Stewart. £150

LEA, I,
See–CAREY, Henry Charles & Lea, I.

LEA, Tom
– **Calendar of Twelve Travelers through the Pass of
the North.** At the Pass, Carl Hertzog, 1946. (365)
numbered. Fo. Cl., d.-w. (SG. Jun.11; 243) $325
– **The Wonderful Country.** Boston, [1952]. Ltd.
1st. Edn. (10), sigd. Pict. cl., d.-w., orig. cl. folding
box. Sigd. by Lea at mntd. print of his painting
'Recuerdo de Lagrimas', in folding box (designed
by Carl Hertzog), with publication broadside laid
in. (PNY. Mar.26; 178) $130

LEACOCK, Stephen
– **Further Foolishness.** N.Y., 1916. Publisher's
dummy copy, comprising 1st. 23 pp. & the title-p.,
the remaining ll. blank. Orig. cl., slightly spotted.
(CB. Dec.9; 23) Can. $120
– **Methuen's Library of Humour.** Ed.:– E.V. Knox.
L., [1934]. Orig. cl. (CB. Dec.9; 25) Can. $110

LEAF, Munro
– **The Story of Ferdinand.** Ill.:– Robert Lawson.
N.Y., 1936. 1st. Edn. Square 12mo. Cl.-bkd. pict.
bds., d.-w. (SG. Apr.30; 207) $325
– **Wee Gillis.** Ill.:– Robert Lawson. N.Y., 1938.
Thistle Edn., (525) numbered, & sigd. by author
& artist. Coarse-weave buckram, boxed. (SG.
Apr.30; 208) $120

LEAKE, William Martin
– **Travels in the Morea.–Peloponnesiaca: a
Supplement** . . . 1830-46. 1st. Edn. Together 4 vols.
Cont. cf., vol. 1 rebkd., vol. 3 cover detchd., vol. 3 mod.
cl., vol. 4 orig. cl., Signet arms on covers of vols.
1-3, vol. 4 unopened. (S. Nov.25; 525)
Crete. £300
– **Travels in Northern Greece.** 1835. 1st. Edn. 4
vols. Liby. stp. of the Royal Institution on titles.
Orig. cl., rebkd. (S. Nov.25; 526) *Karakos.* £240

LEANDER, Richard
– **Dreams by French Firesides.** Trans.:– J. Raleigh.
Ill.:– Louis Wain. Edinb., 1890. Orig. pict. cl.
(SH. Dec.11; 301) *Quaritch.* £65

LEANERD, John
[–] **The Counterfeits.** 1679. 1st. Edn. 4to. Advt. lf.
at end. Mor.-bkd. bds. [Wing L794] (C.
Nov.19; 108) *Quaritch.* £200

LEAR, Edward
– **Illustrated Excursions in Italy.** 1846. 1st. Edn. 2
vols. 4to. Occasional minor foxing. Orig. ribbed
cl., gt., rebkd. Pres. Copy to W. Holman Hunt,
with inscr. in both vols. (C. Nov.5; 90)
Quaritch. £580
– – **Anr. Edn.** 1846. 1st. & 2nd. Series. 2 vols. Fo.
Some ll. spotted or soiled, 1st. few ll. in vol. 1
marginally dampstained. Orig. cl., rebkd. (SH.
Nov.6; 227) *Walford.* £370
– **Illustrations of the Family of Psittacidae or
Parrots.** [1830-32]. Lge. fo. Litho. title on grey
paper (orig. wrap. to Pt.12), 42 hand-cold. litho.
plts., 1 torn, lacks general title, dedication, list of
subscribers & plt. list. Cont. hf. cf. (C.
Mar.18; 141) *Crawley.* £5,000
– – **Anr. Edn.** 1978. Pion-Johnson Facs. Edn.,
(500) numbered. Fo. Hf. mor. (KH.
Mar.24; 238A) Aus. $500
– **Journals of a Landscape Painter in Albania.**
1851. Some spotting. Cont. hf. mor. (SH.
Nov.6; 228) *Walford.* £150
– **Journal of a Landscape Painter in Corsica.** Ill.:–
after Lear. 1870. Recently rebnd. in hf. cf. (TA.
Mar.19; 82) £65
– – **Anr. Copy.** Orig. cl. (SH. Nov.6; 230)
Glazebrook. £50
– – **Anr. Edn.** L., 1870. 1st. Edn. 4to. Orig. gt. cl.
(PNY. Oct.1; 324) $100
– **Journals of a Landscape Painter in Southern
Calabria.** 1852. Cont. hf. mor. (SH. Nov.7; 233)
King. £150
– – **Anr. Copy.** Plts. stained. Orig. cl., worn. (SH.
May 28; 179) *Crete.* £55
– **Views in Rome & its Environs.** 1841. [1st.
Edn.?]. Some ll. spotted. Orig. cf.-bkd. cl. (SH.
Nov.6; 234) *Marsden.* £620
– – **Anr. Copy.** Some marginal stains, a few clean
tears. Orig. mor.-bkd. cl., worn & disbnd. (CSK.
Nov.28; 82) £300

– – **Anr. Copy.** Foxed. Mor.-bkd. cl., defect. Sig.
& armorial bkplt. of Sir John P. Boileau. (SG.
Oct.9; 143) $600
– – **Anr. Edn.** [1 Dec.] 1863. [1st. Edn.?]. Fo.
Text & plts. loose. Orig. cl. gt. (P. Sep.11; 281)
Hughes. £1,200
– – **Anr. Copy.** Minor spotting on title, plts. loose.
Orig. cl. (C. Feb.25; 111) *Smith.* £1,000
– – **Anr. Copy.** Some spotting, heavy in 1st. 2 plts.,
most ll. detchd. from bdg. (C. Feb.4; 161)
Davidson. £900
– – **Anr. Copy.** Loose in cl. covers. (SG.
Oct.9; 145) $2,400
See–SOWERBY, James de Carle & Lear, Edward

LEASIDE Town Council
– **The Story of Leaside.** [Leaside], [1931]. Orig.
ptd. wraps. (CB. Dec.9; 44) Can. $160

LEAUTAUD, Paul
– **Petit Ami (Le).** Paris, 1974. (310). 4to. Ll.,
Plexiglas box. Orig. aqua. & A.L.s. by artist on
hf.-title. (HD. Apr.24; 150) Frs. 2,950

LE BAS, Philippe
– **Allemagne.** Paris, 1838. 2 vols. Some browning,
lacks 4 steel engrs. Orig. paper bds., worn. (H.
Dec.9/19; 646) DM 1,500
– – **Anr. Edn.** Paris, 1839. Vol. 1. Qtr. vell. gt. (P.
Feb.19; 170) *Russell.* £90
– – **Anr. Edn.** Venice, 1853-55. 2 vols. Text
slightly soiled in parts. Later hf. leath. (H. May
21/22; 463) DM 1,300
– **Allemagne.–Etats de la Confederation
Germanique.** Paris, 1838-42. 2 vols. & 1 vol.
Slightly soiled. Cont. hf. leath. (R.
Oct.14-18; 2105) DM 3,800
– **Estados de la Confederacion de Alemania.**
Barcelona, 1843. 1 plt. defect., slightly soiled.
Cont. hf. leath., gt. spine. (R. Oct.14-18; 2106)
DM 1,250

LE BEAU, Claude
– **Avantures du Sr. C. Le Beau** . . . Amst., 1738. 2
vols. Sm. 8vo. Cont. spr. cf., decor. spines. (HD.
Dec.5; 125) Frs. 3,500
– **Fabulae, Narrationes et aliae Amplifications.**
Paris, 1782. Cont. Fr. red mor., gt. armorial stp. of
Louis Philippe I, Duc d'Orleans on covers in gt.
fillet border, spine gt. in 6 compartments. (C. May
20; 34) *Marsden.* £260

LEBEL, Robert
– **Marcel Duchamp.** Trans.:– G.H. Hamilton.
N.Y., [1959]. Fo. Cl., d.-w. (SG. Oct.23; 94)
$110

LE BERRYAIS, Pierre
[–] **Traité des Jardins.** Paris, 1789. 3rd. Edn. 4 vols.
Cont. old marb. cf., 5 decor. spine raised bands.
(LM. Jun.13; 103) B.Frs. 21,000

LEBERT, Hermann
– **Traité d'Anatomie Pathologique, Générale et
Spéciale ou Description et Iconographie
Pathologique des Altérations Morbides tant
Liquides que solides Observées dans le Corps
Humain.** Ill.:– P. Lackerbauer. Paris, 1857-61. 2
vols., 2 vols. atlas. Fo. Qtr. mor. (S. Jun.16; 496)
Norman. £110

LE BLANT, Edmond
See–JACQUEMART, Albert & Le Blant, Edmond

**LE BLON, Jacob Christoph & Gautier de
Montdorge, A.**
– **L'Art d'Imprimer les Tableaux.** Paris, 1756. 1st.
Edn. Cont. Fr. mott. cf., spine gt. (CNY. May
22; 141) $900

LE BLOND, Abbé de
See–LACHAU, Abbé Geraud & Le Blond, Abbé de

[**LE] BLOND, Alexandre [Jean Baptiste]**
– **Neueröffnete Gärtner-Akademie** . . . **Pracht- und
Lust-Gärten sammt dereselben Auszierungen und
Wasserwerken.** Trans.:– Franz Anton Danreitter.
Augsburg, 1764. Cont. hf. cf. (S. Jan.27; 337)
Wenner. £340

LE BOE, Fr. de
– **Opera Medica.** Ill.:– C.V. Dalen (port. front.)
Amst., 1679. 1st. Edn. Slightly soiled in parts.
Cont. vell. (HK. Nov.18-21; 614) DM 460

LE BON, G.
– **La Civilisation des Arabes.** Paris, 1884. 4to.
Publisher's cf., gt. stpd. (CR. Jun.11; 506)
Lire 200,000

LE BON GENRE
- Selection of fashion plates from the years 1920-22. Ill.:– Barbier, Benito, Bonfils, Lepape, Thayaht & others. Paris, ca. 1923. 4to. 3 additional plts. inserted. Orig. marb. bds., backstrip loose. (PNY. Dec.3; 27) $650

LE BOURSIER du Coudray, Angélique Marguerite
- Abrégé de l'Art des Accouchemens ... Ill.:– J. Robert after P. Chaparre. Paris, 1785. 6th. Edn. New limp vell., covers buckled. (S. Jun.16; 497) *Jenner Books.* £240

LE BRAZ, Anatole
- Au Pays des Pardons. Ill.:– Péters-Destéract. Paris, 1912. (50) with 3 extra suites of etchings. 4to. The 3 extra suites of the etchings include 2 with remarques, 1 with proof annots. by either artist or publisher, 7 etchings with 1 additional state, 6 with additional 2 states, 2 with 3 additional states, 2 with 4 additional states, proofs with remarques of 2 unused plts., 2 proofs with remarques of the design on lr. doublr. Maroon mor., with orig. copper plt. for 4th. ill. inlaid in upr. cover, inner borders gt., silk doubls., upr. printed with unused title design & lr. 1 with unused plt., orig. wraps. bnd. in, by Rene Kieffer. (SH. Nov.21; 444) *Klusmann.* £120

LE BRET, Comte Robert Cardin
- Maison Le Bret ... Le Mans, 1889. Fo. Glazed cf., fillets on covers, spine decor. with raised bands. (HD. Jun.29; 111) Frs. 2,000

LEBRUN, Charles
- Divers Desseins de Decorations de Pavillons. Ill.:– P. Decker, Jean Marot & others. Paris, ca. 1703. Fo. Title with sm. abrasion to imprint, 1 plt. with short tear in fold, a few plts. with minor repairs to edges, title & 1 plt. mntd. Cont. spr. cf., hinges worn. (C. Feb.25; 186) *Weinreb.* £320
- La Grande Galerie de Versailles ... Ill.:– J.B. Massé; Tocqué (port.). Paris, 1752. Fo. Cont. hf. roan, corners, spine with raised bands. (HD. Jun.24; 51) Frs. 1,700

LEBRUN, J.B.P.
- Galerie des Peintres Flamands, Hollandais et Allemands. Paris, 1792-96. 3 vols. in 2. Fo. 201 plts. avant la lettre. Cont. mor., gt., slightly marked. William Beckford's copy, Hamilton Palace Liby., 'Beckford Collection' ex-libris. (SM. Oct.8; 2404) Frs. 24,000

LE BRUYN, Cornelius
- Travels into Muscovy, Persia & Part of the East Indies ... 1737. 1st. Edn. in Engl. 2 vols. Fo. Cont. cf., rebkd., spines gt. (S. Mar.31; 490) *Guevedo.* £550
- – Anr. Copy. 1 engraved frontis. (of 2). Unif. cont. spr. blind-panel. cf. (C. Feb.25; 112) *Rasteghr.* £300
- Voyage to the Levant. 1702. Fo. Some plts. cleanly torn at folds, spotting. Later cf., rebkd., old slip. preserved. (CSK. Feb.6; 109) £700
- Voyages au Levant. The Hague, 1732. 5 vols. 4to. Titles lightly stained in vols. I & II, slight browning in vols. IV & V, a few ll. reinserted with tape, occasional liby. stps. of the Kings Inn Liby., Dublin. Cont. cf., rebkd., corners reprd., case. (S. Nov.4; 636) *Feldman.* £350

LEBWALD, A.
- Damographia. Salzburg, [1693]. Sm. 4to. Slightly soiled. Cont. leath., spine wormed. (R. Oct.14-18; 2793) DM 2,800

LE CAMUS DE LIMARRE
- [–] Catalogue des Livres Rares. Paris, 1786. Table of authors & ptd. price-list at end, priced in MS. thro.-out. Cont. mor., gt., sm. concentric dentelle borders, spine gt. in compartments, inner gt. dentelles, pink silk liners. The Renouard copy. (SM. Oct.7; 1426) Frs. 3,000

LE CAT, M. Claude Nicholas
- A Physical Essay on the Senses. 1750. Cont. cf. (TA. Mar.19; 388) £50

LECHTER, M.
- Tagebuch d. Indischen Reise. Berlin, 1912. (315) on old Bütten. Fo. Orig. vell., gt. inner dentelle, leath. inset on upr. cover gold-stpd., s.-c. defect. Printer's mark monogrammed & numbered. (HK. May 12-14; 1957) DM 500

LECKY, Halton Stirling
- King's Ships. 1913. Vols. 1-3 (of 6). Cl. (PG. Dec.12; 128) £52

LECKY, William Edward Hartpole
- [Works]. 1865-99. 17 vols. Unif. hf. mor. gt. (BS. Nov.26; 132) £85

LE CLERC, Daniel
- Histoire de la Médecine. Amst., 1723. 2 pts. in 1 vol. 4to. A few spots. Cont. cf., slightly worn. Engraved bookplt. of John Mitford. (SBA. Oct.21; 135) *Vanderkerckove.* £100
- – Anr. Copy. Cont. cf. The Hopetoun copy. (S. Jun.16; 499) *Levy.* £65
- – Anr. Copy. Disbnd. Ex-liby. (SG. Sep.18; 214) $130
See–MANGETUS, Johannes Jacobus & Le Clerc, Daniel

LE CLERC, Sebastian
- Practical Geometry. Trans.:– Nattes. 1805. Hf. cf. gt. (P. Nov.13; 292) *Strauss.* £90
- A Treatise of Architecture with Remarks & Observations ... Trans.:– Mr. Chambers. Ill.:– John Sturt. 1732. Slight soiling, short tear in plts. 95/96. Cont. cf., rebkd. (S. Jun.22; 53) *Marlborough Rare Books.* £90
- Veues de Plusiers Petis Endrois [sic] des Fauxbourgs. De Paris ... Paris, n.d. 2 pts. in 1 vol. Ob. 12mo. Lacks 2 plts. in part 2. Cont. marb. cf., spine decor. with raised bands, bdg. worn. (HD. Jun.24; 52) Frs. 2,100
See–PILES, Roger de–LECLERC, Sebastian

LECLERE, Paul
- Venise Seuil des Eaux. Ill.:– Van Dongen. 1925. (341). 4to. Sewed, case. (HD. Feb.18; 217) Frs. 1,400

LECLERCQ, Paul
- Autour de Toulouse Lautrec. 1921. (30) on Japon paper. 4to. Sewed, case. 2 verified sketches & visiting card of Toulouse-Lautrec added. (HD. Feb.18; 216) Frs. 3,500

LECLERQ, H.
See–CARROL, F. & Leclerq, H.

LECOMTE, Georges
- Chats et Autres Bêtes. Ill.:– Steinlen. Paris, 1933. (35) on Japon impérial numbered. 4to. Separate suite of ills. on Chine. Hf. mor., orig. wraps. bnd. in. (SM. Oct.8; 2375) Frs. 7,000

LECOMTE, Hippolyte
- Choix de Costumes des Differentes Peuples de l'Europe. Ill.:– Delpech & C. De Lasteyrie after Lecomte. Paris, [1817-19]. On vell. Fo. Slightly soiled or browned in parts. Hand-bnd. hf. leath., orig. wraps. bnd. in, spine slightly torn. (H. Dec.9/10; 778) DM 3,200
- Costumes de Théâtre de 1600 à 1820. Paris, [1820]. 4to. Litho. title & 103 plts., 7 hand-cold., probably from anr. copy. Mod. cl. (SI. Dec.3; 320) Lire 450,000

LECONTE de Lisle, Chas.-Marie-René
- Poèmes Barbares. Ill.:– Freida. Paris, 1914. (301); (78), on Jap. 2 vols. 4to. 3 states of plts. Hf. mor., corners, smooth mosaic spines, wraps., s.-c. (HD. Feb.27; 161) Frs. 1,350
- – Anr. Edn. Ill.:– Perrichon after Paul Jouve. 1929. (119). 4to. Ll. in s.-c., some worming on 1st & last ll. (HD. Feb.18; 218) Frs. 1,800
- – Anr. Copy. (119), (99) numbered. Red mor. by Creuzevault, wrap. preserved, s.-c. (SM. Feb.11; 239) Frs. 12,500

LE CORDEUR, B. & Saunders, C.
- The Kitchingham Papers ... Johannesburg, 1976. (125) in hf. mor. Vol. 2 of Brenthurst Press Series. Hf. mor., orig. s.-c. (VA. May 8; 286) R. 160

LECOUSTURIER l'Ainé
- Le Livre de Poste. Paris, 1826. Long-grd. mor., fleur de lis feston border, arms of Duc d'Angoulême, fleurs de lis, inner dentelle, by Bradel, with his ticket. (HD. Jun.10; 194) Frs. 4,600

LE COUTEUR, J.D.
- Ancient Glass in Winchester.–English Mediaeval Painted Glass. Winchester; L., 1920; [1926]. 2 works in 2 vols. Both cl. Both from the liby. of Clement Heaton. (SG. Mar.12; 344) $110

LECTIONES AD MATUTINUM Officii Defunctorum
Ill.:– Eric Gill. Ditchling, 1925. 4to. Orig. cl., slightly warped, d.-w. (CSK. Apr.24; 106) £150
- – Anr. Copy. (150). Fo. Cl.-bkd. bds., unc. (SG. Jan.15; 36) $320

LECUIRE, Pierre
- Cortège. Ill.:– Andre Lanskoy. Paris, Priv. ptd., 1959. 1st. Edn., (170). Fo. In sheets, s.-c. Sigd. by artist. (HD. Jun.25; 312) Frs. 3,000

LEDEBOUR, Carl Friedrich von
- Icones Plantarum Novarum vel imperfecte cognitarum Floram Rossicam, imprimis Altaicam, illustrantes. Ill.:– After Karl Scheffer & others. Riga (etc), 1829-34. 5 vols. Fo. Some spotting. Cont. diced cf. russ., unc., spines defect. From collection of Massachusetts Horticultural Society, stps. on plts. (SPB. Oct.1; 140) $19,000

LEDERMULLER, Martin Frobenius
- Phisicalisque Mikroskopische Vorstellung und Zergliederung einer angeblichen Rokenpflanze, das Staudten, Stekoder Gerstenkorn insgemein genannt. Nuremb., 1765. Fo. Cont. bds. (S. Feb.23; 70) *Frick.* £60

LEDESMA, Bartolomé de
- De septem nouae Legis Sacramentis Summarium. Mexico, 1566. Sm. 4to. Light stain affecting title & sm. repair with adhesive tape. Cont. limp vell. soiled, Franciscan owner's brand on upr. & lr. edges. (SPB. May 5; 317) $8,500

LEDIARD, P.M.
- Block Book of Twenty-Third Ward, New York City. N.Y., ca. 1900. Ob. atlas fo. Some linen-bkd. index maps reprd. Hf. mor., needs rebdg. (SG. May 21; 79) $120

LEDIEU, Alcius
- Les Reliures Artistiques et Armoriées de la Bibliothèque Communale d'Abbeville. Paris, 1891. (50). 4to. Cont. hf. mor. (SM. Oct.7; 1427) Frs. 1,800

LEDOUX, Louis V.
- Japanese Prints of the Primitive Period. N.Y., 1942. (1000). Fo. Buckram-bkd. bds. (SG. Dec.4; 199) $180

LE DRAN, Henri-François
- The Operations in Surgery ... with remarks, plates of the Operations, & a sett of instruments by William Cheselden. 1749. 1st. Engl. Edn. Slight foxing & offsetting. Cont. cf., worn. From liby. of Dr. E. Ashworth Underwood. (S. Feb.23; 242) *Dawson.* £100

LEE, Guy Charleton & Thorpe, Francis Newton
- The History of North America. Phila., 1903-07. Japan vell. Edn. 20 vols. Title-page of vol. 15 detchd., frontispieces & some ills. in 3 states. Lev. mor., covers decor. with mor. onlays & doubls., spines gt.-lettered, wtrd. silk free end-papers, cl. s.-c.'s. Bound for Mrs. Elizabeth A. Harter. (CNY. Oct.1; 105) $320

LEE, Henry
- Memoirs of a Manager. Taunton, 1830. 1st. Edn. 2 vols. Later three qtr. mor., 1 title-lf. loose. (SG. Sep.4; 300) $150

LEE, Nathaniel
- Caesar Borgia; Son of Alexander the Sixth. 1680. 1st. Edn. 4to. Mor.-bkd. bds. [Wing L846] (C. Nov.19; 109) *A. Thomas.* £110
- Constantine the Great. 1684. 1st. Edn. 4to. Recent cf. [Wing L848] (C. Nov.19; 110) *Arnold.* £80
- Lucius Junius Brutus. 1681. 1st. Edn. 4to. Mor.-bkd. bds. [Wing L852] (C. Nov.19; 111) *Arnold.* £60
- The Works. 1694. 2nd. Coll. Edn. 13 pts. in 1 vol. 4to. Title of 1694 edn. of Otway's Works inserted between 'Oedipus' & 'The Duke of Guise', advt.-lf. inserted at end, some browning. Cont. mott. cf., worn. [Wing L845A] (S. Sep.29; 48) *Pickering & Chatto.* £480
See–DRYDEN, John & Lee, Nathaniel
See–KENRICK, William–FARQUHAR, George –MASON, William–LEE, Nathaniel

LEE, Norman N.
See–EDMONDS, Harfield H. & Lee, Norman N.

LEE, Oswin A. J.
- Among British Birds in their Nesting Haunts. 1897-99. 4 vols. Fo. Cl. gt. (P. Mar.12; 288) *Cambridge.* £100

LEE, R.A.
- The Knibb Family. 1964. Ltd. Edn. 4to. Orig. cl. (SH. Jun.25; 7) *Hill.* £110

LEE, William
- The Plan of the Boxes at the King's Theatre, Haymarket. [London], [1797]. 18mo. Old mor., worn. (SG. Aug.7; 95) $100

LEECH, Sir Bosdin
- History of the Manchester Ship Canal. Manchester & L., 1907. 2 vols. 4to. 3 folding plans in end pocket. Orig. cl. gt., slightly stained. (SBA. Oct.22; 403)   *Hayden.* £60

LEECH, John
- Catalogue of an Exhibition of Works. Ed.:- Stanley K. Wilson. N.Y., Grol. Cl., 1914. (240). Bds., unc. (SG. Oct.2; 219) $110

LEECH, John (Ill.)
See-DICKENS, Charles
See-EVERITT, Graham
See-ILLUSTRATED POCKET LIBRARY of Plain & Coloured Books
See-LEIGH, Percival
See-MILLS, John
See-PUNCH
See-SURTEES, Robert Smith

LEENHEER, Joannes de
- Virto Maria Mystica . . . Ill.:- G. Boutats. N.p. [?Antw.]. 1681. 1st. Edn. Old wraps. (S. Nov.25; 378)   *Gilberts.* £100

LEEUWEN, Simon van
- Nederlandse Practyk ende Oeffening der Notarissen. Amst., 1680. 3rd. Printing. Slightly stained at beginning & end. Cont. vell., loose, a few other defects. (VG. Nov.18; 1249)   Fls. 500

LEEUWENHOEK, Antoni van
- [Brieven seu Werken]. Ill.:- A. de Blois after J. Verkolje (engraved ports. in vols. I & IV). Leiden, 1686-1718. 1st. Collected Dutch Edn. 4 vols. 4to. Additional engraved titles to vol. I, III & IV dtd. 1685, 1696 & 1718 respectively, Letter 37 in vol. I inserted from anr. copy, 1 plt. torn in vol. II, some worming in inner margins at beginning of vol. II, occasional slight staining, bnd. at end of vol. II is 'Register' ptd. by Boutesteyn, Leiden, 1695. Cont. vell. bds., hf. mor. cases. W.a.f.; from Honeyman Collection. (S. May 20; 3277)   *Israel.* £1,550
- Epistolae Physiologicae . . . Delphi, 1719. 1st. Latin Edn. 4to. Later hf. mor. (SG. Sep.18; 217) $450
- Ontdeckte Onsigtbaarheeden. Ill.:- Romeyn de Hooghe (1 front.). 1684-96. 11 pts. in 1 vol. 4to. 2 frontis., stained. Cont. hf. roan, traces of burning. W.a.f. (VG. Oct.13; 94)   Fls. 650

LEF [Journal of the Left Front for the Arts]
Ed.:- [V.V. Mayakovsky]. Ill.:- Stepanova, Rodchenko & Grosz. Moscow & Petrograd, 1923. (5,000). No. 2 only. Orig. wraps. by Rodchenko, unopened. (SH. Feb.6; 330)
                              National Art Centre. £70
- - Anr. Edn. Ed.:- [V.V. Mayakovsky]. Moscow & Petrograd, 1923-24. (5,000); (3,000). Nos. 1 & 5 only. No. 1 dampstained. Mod. cl. with wraps. mntd.; orig. wraps. by Rodchenko, rebkd. (SH. Feb.5; 236)   *Lemos.* £160

LE FEBURE
- Traité de la Chimie . . . Paris, 1669. 2 vols. in 1 12mo. Cont. vell. with bands. (HD. Feb.27; 37)
                                      Frs. 1,200

LEFEVRE, André
See-CAMMAS, Henry & Lefevre, André

LE FEVRE, G.
- Expédition Citroën Asie. Paris, 1933. 4to. 7pp. appendix (by Père Teilhard de Chardin) at end. Mor., spine with raised bands, wrap. & spine, s.-c. Sigd. autograph dedication from M.A. Citroën to the Ambassador Naggiar. (HD. Jun.25; 313)
                                      Frs. 1,250

LE FEVRE DE CAUMARTIN, Jean François Paul
- Catalogue des Livres de la Bibliothèque. Paris, 1734. 12mo. Lacks rear free endpaper. Cont. cf., spine gt. in compartments, defect. (SM. Oct.7; 1429)   Frs. 2,100

LE GALLOIS, Julien Jean César
- Experiments on the Principle of Life & Particularly on the Principle of the Motions of the Heart. Trans.:- N.C. & J.G. Nancrede. Phila., 1813. 1st. Amer. Edn. A few stains at beginning, paper slightly discold. in places. Cont. cf. (S. Jun.16; 503)   *Pratt.* £110

LEGEAR, Clara Egli
See-PHILLIPS, Philip Lee-LEGEAR, Clara Egli

LE GENDRE, A.M.
See-CASSINI, J.D., Mechain, P.F.A. & Le Gendre, A.M.

LEGER, Fernand
- [La Figure dans l'Oeuvre de Leger]. Mon Ami Leger par André Maurois. Comment je conçois la Figure par Leger. Paris, 1952. 1st. Edn. (1,000) on Arches. 4to. Orig. lithographic wraps. designed by Leger, glassine d.-w. Sigd. pres. copy. to Mr & Mrs Gilbert Chapman. (PNY. Mar.4; 165) $650
- - Anr. Copy. Pict. wraps. from a Leger lithograph, d.-w. (PNY. Mar.4; 166) $140

LEGER, Jean
- Algemeine Geschichte der Waldenser oder Evangelischen Kirchen in den Thälern von Piemont. Breslau, 1750. 1st. German Edn. 2 vols. in 1. Cont. bds. (R. Mar.31-Apr.4; 236)   DM 600
- Gedenck-Schrift aangaende de Voor-Vallen der Evangelischen-Kercken van de Valleyn van Piedmont; anders Waldensen. Trans.:- M. Oe. Leyden, 1670. Sm. fo. Cont. vell., soiled, foot of spine defect. (VG. Oct.13; 95)   Fls. 320

LEGGE, William Vincent
- A History of the Birds of Ceylon. 1878-80. 3 vols. 4to. Cont. hf. mor. (C. Jul.15; 189)   *Hill.* £750
- - Anr. Edn. Ill.:- Keulemans. Priv. ptd., 1880. 4to. With the list of subscribers & lf. 2226b (sometimes missing). Recent leath. (S. Jun.1; 153)
                                      Milner. £900

LEGISLATIVE Assembley of Canada
- Report of the Select Committee appointed to receive & collect Evidence & information as to the rights of the Hudson's Bay Company. [Toronto], 1857. Orig. ptd. wraps., slightly tattered. MS. family tree of George Gladman & his wife on verso of p. (26). (CB. Dec.9; 158)   Can. $240

LEGOUVE, Gabriel Marie Jean-Baptiste
- Le Merite des Femmes. Paris, 1813. 18mo. Heavily foxed. Disbnd. Fore-e. pntg.; from the liby of Zola E. Harvey. (SG. Mar.19; 143) $240
- - Anr. Edn. Ill.:- Bonvoisin, Lecomte & others after Devéria. Paris, 1830. 12mo. Cont. cf., smooth spine, borders on covers, inside dentelle. A.L.s. by author loosely inserted. (SM. Feb.11; 165)   Frs. 1,000

LEGRAND, A.
- Recueil de Fables d'Esope. Paris, 1801. Ob. 8vo. Slightly worn, some browning & foxing, 1 plt. margin reprd. Cont. hf. vell., slightly worn. (VG. Oct.13; 3)   Fls. 475

LE GRAND, F. Albert, de Morlaix
- La Vie, Gestes, Mort et Miracles des Saints de la Bretagne Armorique . . . Ed.:- Guy Autret. Rennes, 1659. 2nd. Edn. 4to. MS. title-p. & dedication letter. Later mor., spine with raised bands, decor. with blind-tools. (HD. Jun.29; 157)
                                      Frs. 1,200

LEGRAND, Gerard
See-BRETON, André & Legrand, Gerard

LEGRAND, Louis
- Le Livre d'Heures de Louis Legrand. Paris, 1898. (5) Priv. Ptd. on old Jap. 4to. Mor. sigd. by Cretté, doublrs. with 2 cold. etchgs. ptd. on satin, gold fillets, silk end-ll. & doubled marb. paper end-ll., s.-c. (D. Dec.11-13; 1129)   DM 7,000

LEGRAND D'Aussy, Pierre Jean Baptiste
[-] Fabliaux ou Contes de XIIe et du XIIIe Siècle . . . Paris, 1779. 1st. Edn. 4 vols. Str.-grd. red mor. by Bozérian, border of fillets, decor. spines, garland inside. (HD. Mar.18; 99)   Frs. 1,800

LE GRAS, Sieur de
- La Rethorique Française. Paris, 1671. 4to. 'Bibliotheca Colbertina' inscr. on title, Bibliotheca Lindesiana booklabel. Cont. red mor., gt., arms of Colbert on covers, triple gt. fillet, his cipher, gt., in spine compartments, inner gt. dentelles. Dedication copy to J.B. Colbert. (SM. Oct.7; 1808)   Frs. 3,500

LE GRAVEREND, J.M.
- Traité de la Legislation Criminelle en France . . . Paris, Priv. ptd., 1816. 1st. Edn. 2 vols. 4to. Cont. cf., multiple borders, arms of the chancellor Dambray, decor. spines, inside dentelle, bdg. slightly defect. (HD. Mar.18; 100)   Frs. 2,200

LE HARPE, J.F. de
- Abrégé de l'Histoire Générale des Voyages. Paris, 1780-81. 32 vols., without atlas. Cont. marb. leath., gt., gold-stpd. fillets. [Sabin 38632] (D. Dec.11-13; 1397)   DM 2,200

LE HAY, M.
- Explication des Cent Estampes qui représentent Différentes Nations du Levant. Paris, 1715. 2nd. Enlarged Edn. Fo. Cont. red mor., gt., arms of Marquise de Pompadour, with three towers tooled in silver, mantle gt., narrow gt. dentelle border with floral corner sprays, gt. fillet & 'drawer handle' border, spine gt. in compartments, inner gt. dentelles. (SM. Oct.7; 1809)   Frs. 7,200
- Receuil de Cent Estampes Representant Differentes Nations du Levant. Paris, 1714. Fo. Engd. title, 102 engd. plts., 3 double-p., lacks plt. of engd. music, 1 plt. reprd. Cont. hf. cf., worn. (C. May 20; 148)   *Placeglow Ltd.* £450
- - Anr. Copy. Title & last plt. reprd. & preserved. Disbnd. W.a.f. (BS. Jun.11; 361)   £220
- - Anr. Edn. Ill.:- J. Haussard, G. Scotin & others. Paris, 1714-15. Fo. 102 hand-cold. engraved plts., some heightened with gold, plt. of mus. notat. Cont. cf.-bkd. bds. (C. Mar.18; 153)
                                      Negro. £1,200

LEHRS, M.
- Geschichte und Kritischer Katalog des Kupferstichs. N.Y., n.d. 10 vols. 8vo. & fo. Orig. cl. (SH. Mar.6; 537)   *Haut.* £80

LE HUEN, Nicole
- Le Grant Voyage de Jherusalem. Paris, 1517. Fo. Lacks h1-2. the 2 lge. woodcuts & the map, heavy worming, affecting text. Early 19th. C. cf.-bkd. bds., worn, spine defect. W.a.f. (S. Nov.4; 645)
                                      Feldman. £140

LEIBNITZ, Gottfried Wilhelm
- Epistolae ad Diversos, Theologici, Iuridici, Medici, Historici et Philologici Argumenti. Ed.:- Ch. Kortholt. Leipzig, 1734-42. 1st. Edn. 4 vols. Slightly browned. Cont. vell. (R. Oct.14-18; 1319)
                                      DM 700

LEIBBRANDT, H.C.V.
- Precis of the Archives of the Cape of Good Hope. Cape Town, 1896-1905. 11 vols. only. Red hf. mor., gt. (SH. Jun.11; 124)   *Wade Gallery.* £70

LEICHHARDT, Ludwig
- Journal of an Overland Expedition in Australia. Ill.:- H. Melville & others. 1847. 1st. Edn. Orig. cl., rebkd., orig. spine preserved. (C. Jul.15; 63)
                                      Dawson. £200
- - Anr. Copy. Occasional foxing, lacks 2 advt. ll. but has an additional slip tipped in before p. 1. Unc., reprd. (KH. Nov.18; 373)   Aus. $520

LEIGH, Charles
- Natural History of Lancashire, Cheshire & the Peak in Derbyshire. Ill.:- Moll. 1700. [1st. Engl. Ed.]. Fo. Rebnd. in qtr. cf. (RBT. Jan.22; 18)
                                      £100
- - Anr. Copy. Orig. panel. cf., gt. decor. spine, worn. (TA. Apr.16; 279)   £60
- - Anr. Copy. 3 pts. in 1 vol. Slight browning in margins. Cf., slightly worn. [Wing L975] (SPB. Nov.25; 93) $350

LEIGH, M.A.
- New Atlas of England & Wales. 1837. 12mo. 1 folding map cold. in outl. slightly torn. Cf. (P. May 14; 135)   *Martin.* £60

LEIGH, Percival
- The Comic English Grammar. Ill.:- John Leech. L., 1840. 12mo. Some foxing & staining. Cf. gt. by Zaehnsdorf. (SG. Mar.19; 232) $200
- The Comic English Grammar.-The Comic Latin Grammar. Ill.:- John Leech. 1840. 1st. Edns. Together 2 vols. Late 19th. C. pol. cf. by F. Bedford, spines gt. (S. Nov.24; 190)   *Sawyer.* £65

LEIGH, Samuel
- New Picture of London; Or, A View of the . . . British Metropolis Presenting a Luminous Guide to the Stranger . . . 1822. 12mo. Lacks plan of L., margins browned. Recent cf. (TA. Jan.22; 429)
                                      £60

LEIGHTON, John M.
- The Lakes of Scotland. Ill.:- Joseph Swan after John Fleming. 1834. 2 vols. in 1. 4to. Some ll. slightly spotted. Cont. mor. gt., rebkd. (SD. Feb.4; 232)   £50
See-SWAN, Joseph, Engraver & Leighton, John M.

LEINER, Mordecai Joseph, of Izbitza
– Bet Yakov [on Leviticus]. Lublin-Warsaw, 1937. 1st. Edn. 4to. With notes by Joseph Weiss. Cl. (S. Nov.18; 276) *Goldberg.* £50

LEIRIS, Michel
See–**MASSON, Andrée & Leiris, Michel**

LEIRIS, Michel & Mourlot, Fernand
– Joan Miro, Lithographe. Paris, 1962-77. 4to. Orig. linen. (D. Dec.11-13; 454) DM 660
– – Anr. Edn. Paris, 1972-76. Vols. I-III. Lge. 4to. Orig. linen, cold. orig. pict. wraps. (H. May 21/22; 1728) DM 2,000

LEISCHING, Edward
– Der Wiener Congress. Culturgeschichte, die Bildende Künste und das Kunstgewerbe, Theater, Musik in der Zeit von 1800 bis 1825. Vienna, 1898. (500). Fo. Orig. red mor. gt. (R. Oct.14-18; 1976) DM 1,000

LE JEUNE, Paul
– Relation de ce qui s'est Passé en la Nouvelle France en l'année 1635. Paris, 1636. Lacks pp. 1-16 & approbation lf. at end, title & several other ll. remargined or reprd., closely cropped, occasionally affecting headlines. Recent vell. (CB. Feb.18; 29) Can. $320
– Relation de ce Qui s'est Passé en la Novvelle France en L'Année 1637. Rouen, 1638. 1st. Edn., 1st. Iss. Folding plt. torn away, marginal tears, stains & spotting, lacks upr. free endpaper. Vell., worn, tears, stained. (SPB. Jun.22; 83) $1,600

LE JEUNE, S. Adrian–ALCIATUS, Andreas
– Emblesmes . . .–Les Emblèmes . . . Antw.; Lyons, 1570; 1555. 2 works in 1 vol. 16mo. Some ll. defect. thro.-out. Old cf. (TA. Jan.22; 175) £50

LE KEUX, John
– Memorials of Cambridge. Ed.:– Thomas Wright & H. Longueville Jones. 1845. 2 vols. Slight spotting. Orig. cl., spines gt., slightly worn. (S. Jan.27; 607) *Pain.* £130

LE LABOUREUR, J.
– Les Mémoires de Messire Michel de Castelnau . . . Brussels, 1731. New Edn. 3 vols. Fo. Cont. cf. MS. bkplt. of Bigot de Préameneu. (HD. Jun.29; 211) Frs. 2,000

LELAND, John
– The Laboryouse Journey & Serche of . . . for England's Antiquities . . . Ed.:– John Bale. 1549. 1st. Edn. Title slightly dust-soiled, some cont. MS. notes (cropped). 17th. C. cf. Owner's inscr. of Robert Davies, Heber Liby. stp., bkplt. of Boies Penrose, lately in the collection of Eric Sexton. [STC 15445] (C. Apr.15; 182) *Murray-Hill.* £600

LELAND, Thomas
– The History of Ireland. L., 1773. 1st. Edn. 3 vols. 4to. Port. tipped in at end. Rebnd. cf.-bkd. cl. bds. (GM. Apr.30; 123) £90
– – Anr. Copy. Cont. red mor. gt. (S. Nov.25; 479) *G.R. Armstrong.* £65

LELOIR, Maurice
– Cinq Mois à Hollywood avec Douglas Fairbanks. Paris, Priv. ptd., 1929. Ltd. Edn., numbered. Sm. 4to. Orig. watercolour by Leloir, dedicated to Justin Peyronnet. Mor., silk doubls., s.-c. (SM. Feb.11; 166) Frs. 1,500

LE LONG, Isaak
– Boek-Zaal der Nederduitsche Bybels. Hoorn, 1764. 2nd. Edn. 4to. A few slight marginal stains. Cont. hf. cf., top & foot of spine slightly defect., unc. (VG. Dec.17; 1154) Fls. 800
– Historische Beschryvinge van de Reformatie der Stadt Amsterdam. Amst., 1729. Fo. Lacks ff. 301 & 4 of text. Cont. cf., corners & spine worn. (S. Mar.17; 387) *Faupel.* £160
– – Anr. Copy. Sm. hole in 1 folding plt. Cont. pold. cf., spine gt. (VG. Oct.13; 96) Fls. 850
See–**BROUERIUS VAN NIDEK, M. & Le Long, I.**

LE LORRAIN, Claude
– Liber Veritatis. Ill.:– R. Earlom. 1777. Vols. 1 & 2 only (of 3). Fo. Port. stained, some foxing, mostly marginal. Cont. diced russ., very worn. (S. Feb.10; 336) *Mistrali.* £1,700

LEMAIRE, Charles Antoine
– L'Illustration Horticole. Gand, 1854-68. 15 vols. Hf. mor. gt. (P. Jun.11; 1) *Cambridge.* £1,000

LEMAIRE, Charles & others
– Flore des Serres et des Jardins de l'Europe. Ghent, 1845-67. Vols. I-XVI (of 23). Cont. cf.-bkd. bds., bdg. of vol. VII detchd. & brkn. W.a.f. (S. Jun.1; 152) *Vitale.* £1,500

LE MAIRE, J.
– Dentiste des Dames (Le). Paris, 1818. 2nd. Edn. 12mo. Cont. hf. chagrin, corners, gt. fillet, cypher. (HD. Jun.10; 176) Frs. 1,150

LEMAITRE, Jules
– Contes Blancs, La Cloche, La Chapelle blanche, Le Mariage blanc. Ill.:– Blanche Odin. Paris, 1900. (210) numbered. Square 8vo. Suite of 71 orig. water-col. designs, MS. text, suite of proof un-cold. ills., suite of final col.-ptd. version on papier velin. Hf. lev. mor. gt., onlay floral design on spine, by Noulhac, partly unc. (C. Feb.4; 192) *Kleusman.* £500
– Sérénus. Histoire d'un Martyr. Paris, 1905. (115) numbered. Mor. by Canapé, gt., silk doubls., orig. wraps. bnd. in, s.-c. Louis Fricotelle ex-libris. (SM. Oct.8; 2350) Frs. 2,600

LE MAITRE de Claville
– Traité du Vrai Mérite de l'Homme . . . Paris, 1740. 4th Edn. 12mo. Cont. red mor., fillet, pointillé fleuron in corners, spine decor. with sm. tools, arms of Franquetot de Coigny. (HD. Mar.18; 101) Frs. 2,200

LE MAOUT, Jean Emmanuel Marie & Cap, P.A.
– Le Museum d'Histoire Naturelle.–Botanique. –Histoire Naturelle des Oiseaux. Ill.:– after Gavarni & others. Paris, 1853-54. 3 vols. Orig. publisher's cl. gt., elab. floral panel stp., gt. spines. (CNY. Oct.1; 143) $600

LE MASSON, Edmond
– Traité de la Chasse Souterraine du Blaireau et du Renard. Paris, 1865. (275) sigd. Cf. gt. (P. Feb.19; 91D) *Schapiro.* £70

LEMBERGER, Ernst
– Meisterminiaturen aus funf Jahrhunderten. Stuttgart, 1711. 4to. Plts. slightly foxed in mounts. Orig. pict. cl. (CB. Apr.1; 265) Can. $150
– – Anr. Copy. Orig. linen. (HK. May 12-14; 2325) DM 750

LEMERY, Nicolas
– Cours de Chimie Contenant la Manière de Faire les Operations qui sont en Usage dans la Medecine. Paris, 1683. 5th. Edn. Cont. cf., spine gt. (S. Dec.1; 236) *Walford.* £100
– – Anr. Edn. Leiden, 1716. 11th. Edn. Cont. cf., worn. (S. Dec.1; 237) *Verburg.* £50
– – Anr. Edn. Ed.:– [Hyacinthe Theodore]. Ill.:– B. Sudran (engraved vig.). Paris, 1757. New Edn. 4to. Inner & outer margin of hf.-title & outer blank margin of title strengthened & a little mended. Tree cf., spine gt. (S. Dec.1; 239) *Kurzer.* £60
– A Course of Chymistry Containing an Easie Method of Preparing those Chymical Medicines which are used in Physick . . . Trans.:– Walter Harris. 1686. 2nd. Edn. No advt. lf., a few ll. in middle with worming in inner lr. blank corners. Cont. cf. [Wing L1039] (S. Dec.1; 240) *Vine.* £55
– – Anr. Copy. Contents soiled, title-p. reprd., Imprimatur lf. preserved on inside upr. cover. Old cf., rebkd. (TA. Oct.16; 26) £50
– Dictionnaire. Rotterdam, 1727. 4th. Edn. 4to. Cont. cf., worn. (SG. Jan.29; 260) $300
– – Anr. Edn. Paris, 1759. New Edn. 4to. Plts. misbnd., but all present. Old cf., brkn. (SG. Jan.29; 261) $180
– – Anr. Edn. Paris, 1760. New Edn. 4to. Slightly soiled. Cont. leath. (D. Dec.11-13; 216) DM 1,200
– Traité Universel des Drogues Simples mises en order Alphabétique. Paris, 1699. 4to. Cont. cf., rebkd. (S. Jun.16; 505) *Walford.* £110
– Woordenboek of algemeene Verhandeling der enkele Droogeryen. Trans.:– C.V. Putten & Isaac de Witt. Rotterdam, 1743. 4to. Cont. cf.-bkd. bds., slightly worn. (S. Feb.23; 72) *Walford.* £160

LEMNIUS, Levinus
– De Miraculis Occultus Naturae, Libri IV. Jena, 1588. Slightly wormed at beginning, slightly soiled & browned. Cont. blind-stpd. pig-bkd. wood bds., 2 clasps, lacks ties. (HK. Nov.18-21; 223) DM 530
– Occulta Naturae Miracula, ac Varia Rerum Documenta . . . Antw., 1559. 1st. Edn. Slightly stained. Cont. vell., spine with old leath. pasted on, spine slightly defect., lacks ties. (HK. Nov.18-21; 222) DM 550
– Occulta Naturae miracula: das ist, Wunderbarliche Geheimnisse der Natur . . . auss dem Latein in Teutsche Sprach gebracht, sondern num zum viertten mal vermehret . . . Theils von neuem selbst geschreiben durch Jacobum Horstium. Frankfurt & Hamburg, 1672. 4to. Sm. liby. stp. & owner's inscr 'Collegij Wengensis' on title, spotted. 18th. C. vell. bds. (S. Feb.23; 73) *Quaritch.* £55

LEMOINE, Henry
– Modern Manhood. L., [1788]. 1st. Edn. Old cf., reprd. (SG. Dec.11; 183) $200

LEMOISNE, Paul André
– Degas et Son Oeuvre. Paris, [1946-49]. (980) numbered sets on specially wtrmkd. paper. 4 vols. 4to. Cl. (SG. Oct.9; 77) $1,000

LEMONNIER, Camille
– Felicien Rops, l'Homme et l'Artiste. Paris, 1908. (100) on japon with 2 extra cold. plts. & 2nd. suite of plts. & ills., numbered. 4to. Red hf. mor., orig. wraps. bnd. in. (SH. Nov.20; 79) *Klusmann.* £120
– – Anr. Edn. Paris, priv. ptd., 1908. 1st. Edn.; on Jap. 4to. 2 additional cold. plts. Garnet hf. mor. by Kieffer, corners, gt. fillets, unc., wrap. & spine. (HD. Dec.5; 126) Frs. 2,300
– Les Maris de Mlle Nounouche. Ill.:– A. Vimar. Paris, 1906. (400); (32) on imperial Jap. 4to. 2 orig. watercolours. Mor. by Kieffer, mosaic border on covers, wrap. preserved, s.-c. Bkplt. of Maurice Quarré. (SM. Feb.11; 240) Frs. 10,000

LE MOYNE, Jacques
– Brevis Narratio eorum quae in Florida Americae Provincia Gallis acciderunt . . . Ed.:– Theodore de Bry. Frankfurt, 1609. Fo. Engd. title dtd. 1591, some plts. in 2nd state. Disbnd. 4-lf. 'Historia Luctuosa Expeditionis Gallorum'. (SG. Oct.9; 147) $1,900
See–**BRY, Theodore de & others**

LE MOYNE, Pierre
– De l'Art des Devises avec Divers Recueils. Ill.:– Le Pautre. Paris, 1666. Orig. Edn. 4to. Light browning. Cont. cf., decor. spine, restored, end-ll. renewed. (HD. Jun.10; 57) Frs. 1,000
– La Galerie des Femmes Fortes. Leyden & Paris, 1660. 12mo. 18th. C. mor., 3 fillets, fleurons in corners, decor. spine, arms of J.J. de Bourguignon-Bussiere. Bkplts. of Baron Double & Marigues de Champ-Repus. (HD. Mar.18; 103) Frs. 2,000

LE MUET, Pierre
– Manière de bien Bastir pour Toutes Sortes de Personnes . . . Augmentation de Nouveaux Bastimens faits en France . . . 1663. 2 pts. in 1 vol. Fo. Title-frontis. dtd. 1664, dampstaining, plt. on p. 101 torn. Old spr. cf., smooth decor. spine. (HD. Jun.24; 53) Frs. 1,250

LENAU, N.
– Faust. Ill.:– H. Meid. Berlin, [1921]. (75) on Bütten. 4to. Hand-bnd. red mor., by H. Sperling, Berlin. All etchings sigd. by artist. (H. May 21/22; 1718) DM 1,600

LENCLOS, Ninon de or Anne
– Lettres au Marquis de Sévigné, avec sa Vie. L., 1782. 2 vols. 18mo. Red mor. by Cazin. (HD. Apr.8; 270) Frs. 1,350

LENFANT, Jacques
– Histoire de la Guerre des Hussites et du Concile de Basle. Utrecht, 1731. 2 vols. 4to. Cont. mott. cf. (S. Oct.1; 582) £50

LENG, H.
– Lehrbuch der Gewerbskunde. Ilmenau, 1834. 88 ills. on 22 partly folding litho. plts. Cont. bds. (R. Oct.14-18; 447) DM 470

LENGLET DU FRESNOY, Abbé Nicolas
– Méthode pour étudier l'Histoire. Paris, 1735-41. 12 vols. including 3 vols. of supp. 12mo. Bkplts. of Brahan Castle in vol. 1 & John Clerk Brodie. Cont. red mor., triple gt. fillet, spines gt. in compartments, tooling of 'Méthode' & Supp. not unif., inner gt. dentelles. (SM. Oct.7; 1811) Frs. 2,200

LENIN, Vladimir Ilyich Ulyanov
– Ekonomicheskie Etyudy i Stat'i [Economic Studies & Articles]. St. Petersb., 1899. 1st. Edn.

LENIN, Vladimir Ilyich Ulyanov Articles]. *-contd.*
Cont. cf.-bkd. bds. (SH. Feb.5; 28)
Maggs. £1,400
– **Materializm i Empiroktritisizm.** Moscow, 1909.
(2,000). Orig. cl. (SH. Feb.5; 29)
Dreesman. £600
– **Proletarskaya Revolyutsiya i Renegat Kautsky**
[The Proletarian Revolution & Renegade Kautsky].
[N.Y.], 1920. Orig. cl. (SH. Feb.5; 30)
Maggs. £100
– **Razvitie Kapitalisma v Rossii** [Development of
Capitalism in Russia]. St. Petersb., 1899. 1st. Edn.
Cont. cf.-bkd. bds. (SH. Feb.5; 31)
Maggs. £1,000

LENNEP, H.J. van
– **Oriental Album.** Ill.:– C. Parsons after author.
N.Y., 1862. 1st. Edn. Tall fo. Gt.-pict. cl., leath.
spine, bds. brkn. (SG. Nov.20; 387) $280

LENNEP, J. Van & Hofdijk, W.J.
– **Merkwaardige Kasteelen in Nederland.** Amst.,
1854-60. 6 vols. Some light foxing, a few plts. & ll.
loose. Orig. cl., richly gt., worn. (VG. Dec.16; 932)
Fls. 575

LENYGON, Francis
– **The Decoration & Furniture of English
Mansions during the Seventeenth & Eighteenth
Centuries.** L., 1909. 4to. Orig. cl. (CB. May
27; 138)   Can. £120
See–JOURDAIN, Margaret & Lenygon, Francis

LENZ, Jakob Michael Reinhold
– **Gesammelte Schriften.** Ed.:– L. Tieck. Berlin,
1828. 1st. Coll. Edn. 3 vols. Lightly browned
thro.-out, ex-libris in inner cover. Cont. paper bds.,
worn. (H. Dec.9/10; 1591)   DM 1,900
– – **Anr. Copy.** Lightly soiled thro.-out, some
pencil marks in margin. Later hf. linen. (D.
Dec.11-13; 797)   DM 1,350
– – **Anr. Copy.** Title lf. washed, text slightly soiled
& lightly browned. Cont. style marb. bds. (HK.
May 15; 4603)   DM 750

LEO VI, Der Weise, Emp. of Constantinople
– **Vaticinium Severi, et Leonis Imperatorum, in quo
videtur Finis Turcarum . . .** Brescia, 1596. 1st. Edn.
Latin & Italian text. Vell. (D. Dec.11-13; 33)
DM 1,500

LEO Africanus, Johannes
– **Africae Descriptio.** Leiden, 1632. 1st. Elzevir
Edn. 32mo. Cont. vell., spotted. (SG. Feb.5; 207)
$100
– **A Geographical Historie of Africa.** Trans.:– John
Pory. 1600. 1st. Edn. in Engl. Fo. Double-page
map mntd. on guard. 19th. C. str.-grd. mor., gt.
From Sutherland liby. with sig. of Robert
Gordone on title. [STC 15481; Sabin 40047] (C.
Nov.5; 91)   *Ludgrove.* £2,000
– **De Totius Africae Descriptione Libri IX. . . .
Hannonis Navigatio, qua Libycam oram ultra
Herculis Columnas lustravit.** Ed.:– J. Florianus.
Trans.:– C. Gesnerus. Zürich, 1559. 2nd. Latin
Edn. Cont. MS. vell, slight worming. (R.
Oct.14-18; 94)   DM 600

LEO BAECK Institute of Jews from Germany
– **Yearbook.** 1956-1973. 18 vols. Cl. (SG.
Aug.21; 187) $110

LÉON, Emp. d'Orient 'Le Sage, et le Philosophe'
– **Documenti e Avisi Natabili di Guerra.** Trans.:–
Filippo Pigafetta. Venice, 1602. 4to. Later cf.,
centre arms of Duc & Duchesse de Montausier,
crowned cyphers in angles & on spine. (HD.
Feb.18; 37)   Frs. 1,500

LEON FELIPE
– **Drop a Star.** Mexico, 1933. 1st. Edn. 4to. Cl. &
mor., wraps. Orig. A. ded. (DS. Apr.24; 942)
Pts. 24,000

LEONARD, Nic.-G.
– **Poesies Pastorales.–Le Temple de Gnide,
L'Amour Vengée.** Ill.:– Marillier & Eisen; Desrais.
Geneva/Paris, 1771. 2 works in 1 vol. Possibly
lacks ptd. title, no separate title (probably issued
together with 1st. work). Cont. Fr. red mor. gt.,
spine ornam. with drawer-handle tools, gt. arms of
Charles II de Joannis, Marquis de Chateauneuf on
covers, by Padeloup? As a bdg., w.a.f. (C.
Nov.20; 198)   *Klusmann.* £350

LEONARDO da Vinci
– **The Madrid Codices.** 1974. 5 vols. Facs. Orig. cl.
(SH. Jun.4; 46)   *Wogenstein.* £100
– **Quaderni d'Anatomia.** Christiania, 1911-16.
(248) numbered. 6 vols. Fo. Orig. bds. Inscr. by

editors to Professor Dr. S. Torup. (S. Jun.16; 506)
Norman. £260
– **Traité de la Peinture.** Paris, 1651. Fo. Some
soiling & browning, a few marginal stains,
rust-hole in A4. Cf., very worn. (S. Jun.23; 243)
£130
– **Trattato della Pittura di Leonardo da Vinci, & il
Trattato della Statua di Leon Battista Alberti.**
Paris, 1651. 1st. Edn. Fo. 1 blank margin reprd.,
occasional dampstaining. Old vell. bds. With the
Di Veroli bkplt. (SG. Dec.4; 220) $1,100
– – **Anr. Edn.** Ed.:– R. Du Fresne. Il.:– P.
Panfilius. Bologna, 1786. Lge. 4to. Cont. interim
paper bdg., spine defect, loose, unc. (R.
Oct.14-18; 696)   DM 700

LEONARDO, Manuel Ferreira
– **Noticia Verdadeyra do Terrivel contagio.** Lisbon,
1749. Sm. 4to. Mod.cf. (SPB. May 5; 319) $300

LEONARDUS, Camillus
– **The Mirror of Stones.** 1750. 1st. Engl. Edn.
Slightly damp stained, but seriously affecting title.
Cont. cf. (S. Dec.2; 738)   *Elliot.* £55

LEONARDUS, Deacon of Salzburg & others
– **Directorium Salisburgense.** Nuremb., Georg
Stuchs, [not before 1497]. 4to. 1st. p. soiled,
worming at beginning & end, catching some
letters of text. Mor., spine gt.-lettered, by
Sangorski & Sutcliffe. From the collection of Eric
Sexton. [BMC II, 472, Goff D265, H 6269*]
(CNY. Apr.8; 115) $1,300

LEONARDUS de Utino
– **Sermones de Sanctis.** Venice, Franciscus
Renner, de Heilbronn, with Nicolaus de
Frankfordia. 1473. 4to. Capital spaces, initials &
paragraph strokes & foliation supplied in red by
cont. hand, some dampstaining, mostly marginal
but affecting some ll. at front & back with blank
edges softened. Maroon mor. gt. by Sangorski &
Sutcliffe. Bkplts. of Dr. Georg Kloss & the
General Theological Seminary Liby. [BMC V,
192, Goff L152, HC 16129] (CNY. Oct.1; 65)
$1,200

LEONHARDI, Fr. G.
– **Bildliche Darstellung aller Bekannten Völker.**
Leipzig, 1798-1801. 1st. Edn.; 2nd. End. Pt. I. 32
pts. in 2 vols. 4to. Slightly browned in parts, 1
copper engraving reprd, liby. stp. Cont. hf. leath.,
slightly worn. (H. Dec.9/10; 781)   DM 2,200

LEONICENUS, Nicolaus
– **De Serpentibus Opus.** Bologna, 25 Nov. 1518.
4to. Red mor. label of Girardot de Préfond. 18th.
C. pol. cf., triple gt. fillet, flat spine gt. with
fleurons in compartments, inner gt. dentelles.
(SM. Oct.7; 1814)   Frs. 3,400

LEOPARDI, Giacomo
– **Canti.** Paris, 1934. (120) numbered. 2 vols. Fo.
Orig. wraps., unc. (SI. Dec.3; 321)   Lire 300,000
– – **Anr. Edn.** Paris, 1937. Esemplare Unico on
Jap. Unbnd., orig. wraps. (SI. Dec.3; 322)
Lire 380,000

LEOPOLD, R.
– **Egon Schiele.** Salzburg, 1972. Lge. 4to. Orig.
linen. (HK. May 12-14; 2045)   DM 420

LEOPOLD WILLIAM, Archduke of Austria
[–] '**Il Crescente**'. Diporti del Crescente divisi in
Rime Morali, Devote, Heroiche, Amorose. Brussels,
1656. 4to. Lf. inserted after **4 with blank recto,
rubrication, inscr. on flylf., later MS. note of
'Paris d'Illens' sale beneath, J.B. Clements bkplt.,
Beckford inventory number in upr.-cover. 18th. C.
red mor., triple gt. fillet, flat spine gt. with single
fleuron in compartments, inner gt. dentelles. 'Paris
d'Illens–Wilbraham–Beckford–Clements copy.
(SM. Oct.7; 1815)   Frs. 1,600

LEOVITIUS, Cyprianus
– **Eclipsium Omnium ab anno domini 1554 usque in
annum domini 1606 accurata descriptio & pictura,
a Meridianum Augustanum ita supputata.**
Augsburg, 1556. 1st. Edn. Fo. Cont. limp vell.,
creased, lacks ties. From Honeyman Collection.
(S. May 20; 3278)   *Hill.* £450

LE PAGE DU PRATZ, Antoine Simon
– **Histoire de la Louisiane.** Paris, 1758. 1st. Edn. 3
vols. Cont. leath., gt. [Sabin 40122] (R.
Mar.31-Apr.4; 2434)   DM 1,100

LEPAPE, Georges
– **Costumes de Théâtre, Ballets & Divertissements.**
Paris, 1920. Loose as iss. in orig. folder, ill. in

silver on upr. cover, silver ties. (SH. Nov.21; 391)
Reed & Sims. £105

LE PAUTRE, Antoine
– **Les Oeuvres d'Architecture.** Paris, [1652]. Fo.
Some foxing & soiling, lacks ptd. dedication.
Mod. hf. cf. (S. Jun.22; 126)   *Duran.* £120

LE PAUTRE, Jules & others
– **Sammelband mit 29 Ornamentstich-Folgen aus
der 2. Hälfte des 17. Jahrhunderts.** Paris, Amst.,
Augsburg & Nuremb., 1644-85 etc. Fo. 195
copper engrd. or etched plts., including 10 folding,
some lightly browned or soiled. Cont. leath., gt.
spine, spine defect. (R. Oct.14-18; 2521)
DM 5,000

LE PETIT, Jean Françoise
– **La Grande Chronique Ancienne et Moderne de
Hollande.** Dordrecht, 1601. 2 vols. Fo. Somewhat
browned thro.-out, stained at edges. Antique-style
cf. over wood bds. (C. Nov.20; 199)   *Kraus.* £160

LE POIS, Antoine
– **Discours sur les Médailles et Gravures Antiques,
primcipalement Romaines.** Paris, 1579. 1st. Edn.
4to. Lacks port., Soubise pr. mark on flylf.,
book-label of Wiston Old Rectory. Cont. limp
vell., gt., with batchelor arms of J.A. de Thou,
double gt. fillet, flat spine gt. in compartments
with his cipher. (SM. Oct.7; 1816)   Frs. 2,600

LE PRESTRE DE VAUBAN, Sebastien
See–VAUBAN, Sebastien le Prestre de

LE PRÉVOST, Auguste
– **Mémoires . . . pour servir à l'Histoire du
Département de l'Eure.** Ed.:– Leopold Delisle &
Louis Passy. Évreux, 1862-69. 3 vols. Lge. 8vo.
Hf. chagrin. (HD. Jun.29; 180)   Frs. 2,300

LE PRINCE, Jean Baptiste
– **An Album containing 71 Engraved Plates from
the 'Divers Ajustements et Usages de Russie' &
other works.** [1822 or later] (plts. wtrmkd. 1811
& 1822). 4to. Occasional spotting. Mod. hf. roan,
spine gt. (S. Oct.21; 480)   *Chester.* £150
– **Divers Ajustements et Usages de Russie.** Ca.
1765. Some foxing thro.-out, title crudely reprd.
Hf. russ., brkn. (BS. Jun.11; 362)   £75

LEPROHON, Mrs.
– **Antoinette de Mirecourt, or Secret Marrying &
Secret Sorrowing. A Canadian Tale.** Montreal,
1864. 1st. Edn. Mor., upr. cover gt.-lettered
'Presented to H.R.H. Prince Arthur by the
Province of Quebec'. (SG. Mar.5; 110) $100

LEPSIUS, Carl Richard
– **Denkmaeler aus Aegypten und Aethiopien.** Berlin,
[1849-58]. 12 vols. Elephant fo. Some spotting,
minor tears & repairs to 2 plts. Publisher's hf. mor.
From Chetham's Liby., Manchester. (C.
Nov.27; 244)   *Goodwin.* £850

LERMONTOV, [Mikhail Yurevich]
– **A Hero of our own Times.** 1854. 1st. Engl. End.
Lost 12 advt. ll., few ll. slightly soiled. Orig. cl.
(SH. Oct.9; 14)   *O'Hern.* £95
– **A Song about Tsar Vasilyevitch.** Trans.:– John
Cournos. Ill.:– Paul Nash. 1929. (750) numbered.
Orig. rust mor., geometric black & white onlays,
unc. (S. Jul.31; 252)   *Music Sales.* £60
– – **Anr. Copy.** Orig. mor. (SH. Mar.27; 365)
Ayres. £50
– **Stikhotvoreniya** [Poems]. St. Petersb., 1842. 1st.
Edn. Pt. 3 only (of 4). 12mo. Last lf. of Index torn
& reprd. with loss of text, slightly spotted. Cont.
bds. (SH. Feb.5; 8)   *Flegon.* £60

LERNSNER, J.
See–LAETUS, Pomponius & Marlianus,
Bartholomaeus–Lescut, Nicolaus de–Lernsner, J.
–Gobler, J.

LE ROUGE, George Louis
– **Détails des Nouveaux Jardins à la Mode.** Paris,
[1774-78 & n.d.]. Cah. 1-7 only (of 21). 4to.
Cont. marb. bds., some spines & jnts. just torn.
(SBA. Jul.23; 547)   *Temperley.* £750
– – **Anr. Copy.** Cahier 1-4, 6-8 only (of 21). A few
ll. slightly spotted, mainly marginal. Cont. bds.,
slightly worn. W.a.f. (SBA. Dec.16; 100)
Holliday. £320
– **Jardins Anglo-Chinois à la Mode.** Ill.:– M.
Chambers. Paris, 1776 & following. Pt. 1-Pt.
21(1) bnd. in 4 vols. Ob. 4to. Lacks. plt. 28 of pt. 3
& plt. 28 of pt. 8, 1 plt. & 1 plan not numbered
included, before pt. 5, ptd. 4to text: Traité des
Edifices, Meubles, Machines . . . des Chinois',
Paris 1786, 30 pp., plts. 26 & 27 of pt. 3 double,

plt. 27 slightly defect. Cont. hf. cf. (LM. Jun.13; 105) B.Frs. 270,000

LE ROUX DE LINCY, Adrien Jean Victor
- **Les Femmes Célèbres de l'Ancienne France.** Ill.:– Gatine after Lante. Paris, 1852. Fo. Some foxing thro.-out. Gt.-pict. cl., torn & brkn. (SG. Nov.20; 304) $400
- – **Anr. Edn.** Ill.:– Gatine after Lanté (plts.); frontis. after Sauvageot. Paris, 1858. 2 pts. in 1 vol. Lge. 4to. Cont. hf. chagrin. (HD. Dec.5; 127) Frs. 2,400
- **Researches Concerning Jean Grolier.** N.Y., Grol. Cl., 1907. (300). Fo. Minor defects. Hf. mor. (SPB. Jul.28; 164) $175

LEROY, Andre
- **Dictionnaire de Pomologie.** Paris, 1867-79. 6 vols. Many MS. notes. Hf. chagrin. (LM. Mar.21; 284) B.Frs. 40,000

LE ROY, Baron Jacques
- **Castella et Praetoria Nobilium Brabantiae.** Antw., 1696. Fo. All engravings heightened in col. Old jaspered cf., 6 decor. spine raised bands, worn. (LM. Nov.8; 92b) B.Frs. 215,000
- **Délices de la Noblesse.** Amst., 1706. Ob. 4to. Some stains. Old cf., 4 decor. spine raised bands. (R. Oct.14-18; 43b) B.Frs. 70,000
- **Le Grand Théâtre Sacré du Duché de Brabant.** The Hague, 1729. Fo. Old marb. cf., 6 decor. spine raised bands, gt. triple fillet border, arms. (LM. Nov.8; 26) B.Frs. 180,000
- **Groot Werreldlyk Tooneel des Hertogdoms van Brabant.** Haage, 1730. Fo. Marb. bds., bkplt. W.a.f. (CE. Oct.24; 202) £620
- – **Anr. Copy.** Old cf., 5 decor. spine raised bands. (LM. Mar.21; 57) B.Frs. 75,000
- **Notitia Marchionatus Sacri Romani Imperii, Hoc. est Urbis et Agri Antverpiensis Oppidorum, Dominiorum, Monasteriorum, Castellorumque ...** Amst., 1678. Fo. Lacks 2 maps & 1 plan, 3 plts & 12 lge. views, plts. remntd. Cf., 7 decor. spine raised bands, double fillet frame & gt. guarlands, inner dentelle. (LM. Jun.13; 12) B.Frs. 45,000

LE ROY, Jules David
- **Les Navires des Anciens.** Paris, 1783. 1st. Edn. Browned. Cont. cf., rebkd. (SH. Jun.18; 45) O'Neill. £55
- **Les Ruines des plus Beaux Monuments de la Grèce.** Paris, [& Amst.], 1758. 1st. Edn. Fo. Cont. mor., gt. (SH. Nov.6; 236) Weinreb. £1,300
- – **Anr. Copy.** 2 Pts. in 1 vol. Some plts. browned, 'Chenavard Arch.' stpd. on title. 19th. C. cf.-bkd. bds. (S. Nov.25; 528) Karakos. £1,050

LEROY, L. Archier
- **Wagner's Music Drama of the Ring.** Ill.:– Paul Nash. [1925]. 1st. Edn. Orig. buckram-bkd. bds. Prints of 3 of the wood-engrs. numbered 1, 2 & 4 of 12 copies, sigd. & dtd. by artist & set of the 4 unsigd. in card mounts loosely inserted. (SH. Mar.27; 360) Brook. £490

LE ROY, Pierre Louis
See–STAEHLIN von Storcksburg, Jacob–LE ROY, Pierre Louis

LÉRY, Jean de
- **Histoire d'un voyage fait en la terre de Brésil.** [Geneva], 1600. Light stain on title, marginal wormholes at end. Cf., rebkd. (SPB. May 5; 320) $1,600

LE SAGE, A. (Pseud.)
See–LAS CASES, Count Emmanuel de

LESCALLIER, Antoine
- **Vocabulaire des Termes de Marine Anglois-François et François-Anglais.** Paris, 1800. 2 pts. in 1 vol. Cont. mott. cf. gt., spine gt. (CNY. May 22; 168) $100

LESCARBOT, Marc
See–CHAMPLAIN Society

LESCUT, Nicolaus de
See–LAETUS, Pomponius & Marlianus, Bartholomaeus–Lescut, Nicolaus de–Lernsner, J. –Gobler, J.

LESHY [Wood Goblin]
Ed.:– [M.P. Miklashevsky]. St. Petersb., 1906. Nos. 1-4. 4to. Unbnd. (SH. Feb.5; 84) Landry. £290

LESLIE, Charles 'Philathes'
- **New & Exact Account of Jamaica.** 1739. Cf. gt. (P. Oct.23; 42) Brooke-Hitching. £170

LESLIE, John, Bp. of Ross
- **De Origine, Moribus, Et Rebus Gestis Scotorum Libri Decem.** Rome, 1578. 1st. Edn. 2 pts. in 1 vol. 4to. Late 17th. C. red mor., spine gt. (S. Jan.26; 4) Crowe. £160
- – **Anr. Copy.** (S. Sep.29; 101) Colbeck. £70

LESSER, F.C.
- **Typographia Ivbilans.** Leipzig, 1740. Lightly browned in parts, some ll. slightly soiled. 19th. C. hf. vell. (HK. May 12-14; 2252) DM 500

LESSING, Gotthold Ephraïm
- **Laokoon.** Berlin, 1766. 1st. Edn. Pt. 1, all publd. Some ll. slightly browned, slightly wormed endpapers. Cont. hf. leath., gt. spine. (HK. May 15; 4616) DM 1,000
- – **Anr. Copy.** Slightly browned & soiled. Later paper bds., slightly worn. (H. Dec.9/10; 1597) DM 950
- **Lustspiele.** Berlin, 1767. 1st. Edn. 2 vols. Lightly soiled in parts. Cont. hf. leath. (1) & bds. (1). (HK. May 15; 4618) DM 1,000
- **Nathan der Weise.** [Berlin], 1779. 1st. Edn., 1st. Printing., Subscribers' Edn. Lightly soiled, 1st 2 ll. more heavily. Cont. leath., gt. spine, covers & double fillets. (HK. May 15; 4620) DM 1,500
- – **Anr. Copy.** 'Introïte' on title, 'reichre' on p. 95Z. ll, heavily soiled & browned. Unc., cont. bds., defect., loose. (H. May 21/22; 1189) DM 640
- **Sämmtliche [vermischte] Schriften.** Berlin & Stettin, 1784-1809. 30 vols. Cont. hf. cf. gt., slightly soiled in parts. W.a.f. (HK. May 15; 4607) DM 2,100
- – **Anr. Edn.** Ed.:– K. Lachmann. Berlin, 1838-40. 1st Edn. 13 vols. Lightly browned in parts. Cont. hf. leath. (H. Dec.9/10; 1596) DM 820

LESSING, Gotthold Ephraim–LOTTICH, Karl
- **Nathan der Weiss.–Wer war wohl mehr Jude?** Berlin; Leipzig. 1779; 1783. 1st. Edn. (2nd. work). 2 works in 1 vol. 12mo. Cont. paper bds. (C. Nov.20; 200) Quaritch. £120

LESSON, Rene Primevère
- **Histoire Naturelle des Colibris.** Paris, [1830-32]. 1st. Edn. With added suite of uncold. proof plts. Bds., hinges brkn., unc. (C. Nov.5; 92) Quaritch. £850
- **Histoire Naturelle des Oiseaux-Mouches.** Ill.:– Constant after Bévalet, Prêtre & others. Paris, 1829. 4to. Lacks text, some ll. slightly soiled. Orig. portfolio in orig. bd. s.-c. (HK. Nov.18-21; 807) DM 2,000
- – **Anr. Edn.** Paris, [1829-30]. 1st. Edn. With added suite of uncold. proof plts. Bds., 1 hinge brkn., unc. (C. Nov.5; 93) Quaritch. £1,000
- **Voyage autour du Monde, entrepris par Ordre du Gouvernement sur la Corvette La Coquille.** Brussels, 1839. 4 vols. in 2. A few ll. foxed. Orig. patterned cl. (KH. Nov.18; 374) Aus. $200

L'ESTRANGE, Roger
- **The Observator in Dialogue.** Ill.:– after Kneller [frontis.]. 1684. Vol. I only, nos. 1-470. Fo. Cont. cf., worn, no. 214 loose. (LC. Feb.12; 521) £130

LESUEUR, Charles A.
- **Dessins Executés aux Etats-Unis.** Ed.:– Jean Guiffrey. [Paris], ca. 1930? (200) numbered. Ob. 4to. 50 plts., individually matted. Loose in gt.-decor. bd. folding-case. (SG. Jun.11; 244) $130

LE TELLIER, François César, Marquis de Courtanvaux
- **Catalogue des Livres de la Bibliothèque.** Paris, 1782. Ptd. price-list at end. Cont. mott. cf., spine gt. (SM. Oct.7; 1433) Frs. 2,200
- **Journal du Voyage ... sur la Fregate l'Aurore.** Ill.:– after Auvray & Haussard. Paris, 1768. 4to. 19th. C. hf. mor. From Chetham's Liby., Manchester. (C. Nov.27; 245) Tzakas. £100

LETI, Grégorio
- **Le Putanisme ...** Cologne, 1670. Attributed to Elzevir. 12mo. Red mor. by Joly, triple gt. fillet around covers, spine decor. with raised bands, inside dentelle. (HD. Jun.24; 55) Frs. 1,900
- **La Vie de l'Empereur Charles V.** Brussells, 1710. 4 vols. 12mo. Old cf., all bdgs. brkn. (SG. Sep.25; 80) $110

LETTER [A] to the Rt Hon. A. Earl of Essex, from Dublin declaring the Strange Obstinacy of Papists, [as here, so] in Ireland
L., 1679. Sm. 4to. Disbnd. [Wing L1747] (GM. Apr.30; 321) £50

LETTERA APOLOGETICA dell'Esercitato Accademico della Crusca continente la Difesa del libro intitolato Lettre d'una Peruana [by F.P. Huguet de Grafigny] per Rispetto alla Supposizone de' Quipu
Naples, 1750. 4to. Minor maginal wormholes at end. Cont. vell., worn. [Sabin 40560] (SPB. May 5; 321) $150

LETTRES d'Abaillard et d'Heloise
Trans.:– J.F. Bastien. Ill.:– Alexandre Moitte & Marillier. Paris, 1782. (5) on vell. Vols. 1 & 3-5 only. With the specially ptd. titles & hf.-titles for the extension of the work from 2 to 5 vols. Cont. Fr. red mor., gt., gt. arms of Paris d'Illens on sides, & emblazoned on titles, silk liners, card s.-c.'s. The Masterman Sykes, Robert Hoe, Cortlandt F. Bishop, & Lucius Wilmerding copy. (S. Feb.10; 321) Klusmann. £650

LETTSOM, John Coakley
- **History of the Origin of Medicine, an Oration delivered at the Anniversary Meeting of the Medical Society of London.** 1778. 4to. 1 folding plt. (black & white, without the same plt. cold. sometimes found also). New cf. Inscr. 'William Dawson, surgeon, & H. Hodgson, M.D.' on title-p. (S. Jun.16; 508) Jenner Books. £75
- **John Fothergill.** L., 1783. 3 pp. of advts. Orig. bds., loose, spine defect., unc. From Brooklyn Academy of Medicine. (SG. Jan.29; 169) $110
- **Natural History of the Tea-tree.** 1799. 2nd Edn. 4to. Sm. liby. stp. on plts., short tear in 1 plt., some browning. Mod. cf. (S. May 5; 121) Subunso. £70

LETTY, C.
- **Wild Flowers of the Transvaal.** Pretoria, 1962. Subscriber's Edn., (600) sigd. 4to. Hf. mor., covers slightly scarred. (VA. Aug.29; 321) R. 95

LETUCHAYA pochta [Airmail]
Ed.:– [P.I. Dubovitsky]. St. Petersb., 1907. Nos. 1-2. 4to. Unbnd. (SH. Feb.5; 85) De la Casa. £65

LE TURC
- **Description des Procedés Mechaniques en Usage en Flandre pour Construire des Fontaines; Barrière d'une Nouvelle Construction; Description du Camion Prysmatique de Mr de Perronet; Echelles pour les Bibliothèques; Description des Machines Employées en Hollande, pour Boucher les Chambres ... des Canons.** 1781. 1st. Edn. 6 works in 1 vol. 1 plt. misbnd. 19th. C. mott. cf., gt. (S. Apr.7; 265) Nolan. £360

LETZNER, J.
See–BUNTING, H. & Letzner, J.

LEUCHS, Johann Carl
- **Haus-u. Hülfsbuch.** Nuremb., 1822-23. 2 vols. Cont. hf. linen gt. (HK. Nov.18-21; 1697) DM 770
- **Zusammenstellung der in den Letzten 30 Jahren in der Gerberei und Lederfabrikation bemachten Beobachtungen und Verbesserungen.** Nuremb., 1828. Unc. (R. Oct.14-18; 446) DM 650

LEUPOLD, J. Chr.
- **Geistliche Herzens-Einbildungen, Inn Biblischen Figur-Sprüchen angedeutet.** Augsburg, ca. 1730 2 pts. in 1 vol. Ob. 4to. 19th. C. hf. leath., gt. spine. (R. Oct.14-18; 879) DM 2,000

LEUPOLD, Jacob
- **Theatrum Arithmetico-Geometricum.** Leipzig, 1727. Fo. Last 6 ll. slightly stained. Cont. hf. leath, spine & corners slightly defect. (R. Oct.14-18; 448) DM 1,600
- – **Anr. Copy.** Cont. vell. (R. Mar.31-Apr.4; 1258) DM 2,300
- **Theatrum Machinarum Générale.** Leipzig, 1724. Fo. Slightly browned, perforated liby. stp. on title. Cont. style hf. leath. (R. Oct.15-18; 450) DM 2,100
- – **Anr. Edn.** Leipzig, 1724-35. 9 pts. only (of 12) in 5 vols. Fo. Margins slightly spotted or dust-soiled. Cont. vell., soiled. From Chetham's Liby., Manchester. (C. Nov.27; 246) Marcus. £1,300
- **Theatrum Machinarum Hydrotechnicarum.** Leipzig, 1724. [1st. Edn.?]. Fo. Text & a few plts. slightly browned, lacks plt. 46. Cont. style hf. leath. (R. Oct.14-18; 452) DM 1,700
- – **Anr. Copy.** Slightly browned & soiled, some plts. slightly soiled. Late 18th. C. leath., wormed. (HK. Nov.18-21; 616) DM 900

LEUPOLD, Jacob -contd.
- **Theatrum Staticum.–Theatrum Pontificate.** Leipzig, 1726. Fo. Old Ms. owner's mark on title, marginalia on some ll., lightly browned in parts. Hf. leath., old bds. bnd. in. (HK. Nov.18-21; 617) DM 1,500

LEURET, François & Gratiolet, Louis Pierre
- **Anatomie Comparée du Système Nerveux considerée dans les Rapports avec l'Intelligence.** Paris, 1839-57. Orig. Edn. 2 vols. text, 1 atlas vol. in 3 orig. pts. 8vo. & fo. 48 pp. advts. dtd. May 1864 at end & 4 pp. at beginning of vol. II. Text vols. in orig. wraps., atlas vol. in 3 orig. pts. in wraps., loose in folder, vol. 1 brkn., lr. corner of upr. cover of atlas pt. 3 torn off, all unc. Bkplt. & stp. of Dr. Gaultry, Fontainebleau. (S. Jun.16; 509) *Norman.* £280

LEUSDEN, Johannes
- **Philologus Hebraeus Continens Quaestiones Hebraicas.** Basle, 1739. 5th. Edn. 4to. Vell. (S. Nov.18; 669) *Selig.* £170

LEUSSE de Syon, Robert de
- **Histoire Généalogique de la Famille de Leusse** ... Lyons, 1885. (50), numbered. Lge. 8vo. Hf. cl. (HD. Jun.29; 114) Frs. 3,050

LEUTHNER, Coelestin
- **Coelum Christianum, in quo Vita, Doctrina, Passio D.N. Jesu Christi ... Symbolicis Figuris Expressa** ... Ill.:– Klauber after Goez. Augsburg & Würzburg, 1749. 1st. Edn. Old cf. (SG. Sep.25; 125) $130

LE VACHER de Charnois, Jean Charles
- **Recherches sur les Costumes et sur les Théâtres de Toutes les Nations.** Ill.:– Chéry. Paris, 1790. 2 vols. in 1. 4to. Hf. chagrin, ca. 1850, corners. (HD. Dec.5; 128) Frs. 3,100

LEVAILLANT, François
- **Histoire Naturelle des Oiseaux d'Afrique.** Ill.:– Fissard & Peree after J. Lebrecht Reinold. Paris, [1799]-1805-98. 6 vols. Lge. fo. 300 engraved plts. in 2 states, one col.-ptd. & hand-finished, the other uncold., 1st. plt. & text lf. detchd. Cont. Fr. str.-grd. mor., sides with gt. & blind-tooled borders, spines gt. in compartments. (C. Mar.18; 143) *Quaritch.* £12,00
- **Histoire Naturelle des Oiseaux de Paradis et des Rolliers.** Ill.:– Boquet, Grémillier & Pérée after Barraband. Paris, [1801-] 1806. 1st. Edn. 2 vols. Lge. fo. All plts. on vell., unc., soiled in parts, some text ll. heavily, vol. 2 3 ll. prelims., last text ll. & plts. 50-57 slightly stained in margin, vol. 1 lacks plts. 40 & 41., some plts. retouched with gold., mispaginated. Unc. ll. loose in cont. red hf. mor. portfolios. gt. some ties defect. (R. Mar.31-Apr.4; 1385) DM 25,000
- – **Anr. Copy.** Vol. 1 lacks plts. 40-41, some text ll. including general title foxed, 1st. 2 ll. & last 4 ll. with marginal stain. Cont. red hf. mor. portfolios, unc. & loose as issued. (VG. Oct.13; 98) Fls. 34,000
- – **Anr. Edn.** Paris, 1806. 2 vols. Fo. 114 engd. plts., ptd. in col. & hand-finished, some heightened with gold. Cont. bds. (C. Jul.15; 155) *Chaponnière.* £9,000
- **Histoire Naturelle des Oiseaux de Paradis, des Toucans et des Barbus; Suivie de Celle des Promerops, Guepiers et des Couroucous.** Paris, 1806-07. 3 vols. Fo. 196 plts. (of 197), ptd. in col. & hand-finished. Cont. mor., gt., sides gt. roll tool & fillet borders enclosing gt. arms of J.B. Powis, spines gt. in compartments, sm. tears in upr. covers of vols. 2 & 3. Powis bkplt. (C. Mar.18; 145) *Junk.* £10,00
- **Histoire Naturelle des Perroquets.** Paris, 1801-05. L.P. 2 vols. in 1. Fo. 145 engraved plts., col. ptd. & hand-finished, plt. 131 inlaid. Cont. roan-bkd. bds., spine gt. (C. Mar.18; 142) *Quaritch.* £12,00
- **Histoire Naturelle des Promerops et des Guepiers ... faisant suite à celle des Oiseaux de Paradis.** Paris, 1807. Fo. Some foxing, severe on a few ll., plt. 9 in pt. 3 in earliest state with misptd. caption, 2 cancel plts. with misptd. captions (pt. 1, plt. 9 mislettered as 17; plt. 23 (or 22a) mislettered as 9). Cont. diced russ., gt., arms of Francis I, Emperor of Austria gt. on sides. Large copy. (S. Jun.1; 156) *Black.* £3,500
- **Histoire Naturelle d'Une Partie d'Oiseaux Nouveaux et rares de l'Amerique et des Indes.** Paris, 1801. Vol. 1, all publd., L.P. Fo. 49 plts. each in 2 states, 1 ptd. in colour & finished by hand, slightly

foxing. Cont. Fr. hf. leath., gt., unc. (S. Jun.1; 154) *Chaponnier.* £4,000
- – **Anr. Copy.** 4to. 49 engd. plts. ptd. in col. & hand-finished., 1 plt. reprd. Cont. cf. gt., lr. cover detchd. (C. Mar.18; 144) *Arader.* £1,400
- **New Travels into the Interior Parts of Africa.** 1796. 3 vols. Cf. (P. Oct.23; 40a) *Brooke-Hitching.* £270
- – **Anr. Copy.** Cont. cf., worn. (PD. Nov.26; 169) £70
- – **Anr. Copy.** Folding map slightly torn. Orig. bds. (SSA. Jan.22; 275) R. 300
- **Reize in de Bennenlanden van Afrika** ... Amst., 1791-98. 5 vols. Cont. hf. cf. & bds. (SSA. Jun.18; 190) R. 220
- **Second Voyage dans l'Interieur de l'Afrique par le Cap de Bonne-Espérance dans les Années 1783, 84 et 85.** Amst., 1797. 3 vols. Orig. bds., rebkd. (SSA. Jun.18; 189) R. 310
- – **Anr. Edn.** Cape Town, 1973. (2500) in Engl. 2 vols. 4to. Orig. bdg. (VA. May 8; 334) R. 130
- – **Anr. Copy.** Cl. (VA. May 8; 464) R. 110
- **Travels/New Travels into the Interior Parts of Africa.** 1796. Vols. 1 & 2: 2nd. Engl. Edn., Vols. 3-5; 1st. Engl. Edn. 5 vols. Vols. 1 & 2: 11 (of 12) folding engraved plts. Unif. cont. pold. cf. gt. (TA. Nov.20; 403) £100

LEVANTO, Leonardo
- **Catechismo de la Doctrina Christiana, en Lengua Zaapoteca.** Puebla, 1776. 4to. Cont. vell., covers spotted, lacks ties. (SG. Mar.5; 309) $400

LEVASSEUR, Victor
- **Atlas Classique Universel de Géographie Ancienne et Moderne** ... Paris, ca. 1840. 16mo. Some dampstaining. Cont. hf. leath. (SG. Nov.20; 71) $160
- **Atlas National Illustré ... des Departments et des Possessions de la France.** Paris, 1856. 4to. Orig. qtr. mor. W.a.f. (TA. Aug.21; 97) £170
- – **Anr. Edn.** Paris, 1859. Atlas fo. Bdg. detchd., corners worn. As an atlas, w.a.f. (S. Nov.25; 405) *Moxon.* £200
- – **Anr. Edn.** Paris, 1861. Fo. Cont. hf. chagrin, spine decor. with raised bands. (HD. Feb.27; 167) Frs. 1,600

LEVEILLE, Jean Baptiste François
See–HIRSCHFELD, Ludovic & Leveillé, Jean Baptiste François
See–SCARPA, Antonio & Leveille, Jean Baptiste François

LEVEL, Andre
- **Picasso.** [Paris], [1928]. 1st. Edn., (120). 4to. Ptd. wraps., stain at upr. wraps., affecting only slightly the lithograph at bottom margin. Orig. lithographic frontis., 1 of 200 impressions, sigd. & marked in pencil by Picasso. (PNY. Mar.4; 215) $2,600
- **Souvenirs d'un Collectionneur.** Ill.:– Pablo Picasso. Paris, 1959. (2,200) numbered. 4to. Orig. wraps., unc. (SH. Nov.21; 452) *Tate Gallery.* £50

LEVER, Charles James
- [–] **Arthur O'Leary.** Ill.:– George Cruikshank. 1844. 1st. Edn. 3 vols. Lacks errata lf. at end vol. 3. Late 19th C. hf. mor., spines gt. (S. Nov.24; 85) *Howes.* £75
- [–] **Confessions of Con Gregan.** Ill.:– H.K. Browne. L., [1849]. 1st. Edn. 14 orig. pts. in 13. Without advts. in pts. 3, 9, 11 & 12. Pict. wraps., some soiled, ends of 2 or 3 spines defect., cl. s.-c., unc. (SG. Mar.19; 239) $300
- **The Dodd Family Abroad.** 1853. 1st. Edn. 20 orig. pts. in 19. Orig. wraps., slightly torn & soiled, some spines torn, later s.-c. (SBA. May 27; 80a) *Dr. Schwarz.* £70
- **Luttrell of Arran.** Ill.:– H.K. Browne. L., Dec., 1863-Feb., 1865. 1st. Edn. 16 orig. pts. in 15. With the 'Luttrell of Arran Advertiser' & other advts. in each pt. Pict. wraps., slight wear, cl. folding case, unc. (SG. Mar.19; 240) $375
- [The Novels]. 1897-99. Copyright Edn., (1,000). 37 vols. Cont. mor., gt. W.a.f. (CSK. Apr.3; 29) £120
- [Works]. 1901. 7 vols. Hf. mor., spines gt. (SKC. Feb.26; 1506) £55
- [–] **Anr. Edn.** N.d. 31 vols. Cont. hf. cf. (SH. May 28; 66) *Wade Gallery.* £100
- – **Anr. Copy.** 34 vols. Occasional spotting. Hf. cf. (CSK. Sep.26; 60) £90

LEVER, Darcy
- **The Young Sea Officer's Sheet Anchor.** 1808. 1st. Edn. 4to. Slightly foxed, marginal staining,

title detchd., cont. owner's inscr. of George Blackman, H.M.S. Defiance. Hf. cf., worn, upr. cover detchd. (S. Jan.26; 194) *Lester.* £270

LEVER, Thomas
- **Sermon Preached ye Fourth Sūdaye in Lente** ... 1550. Title & some headlines cropped, slightly soiled & dampstained. 19th C. mor., gt. ·[NSTC 15548.5] (S. May 5; 281) *Booth.* £75

LEVERHULME ART COLLECTIONS
1928. (200). 3 vols. 4to. Orig. cl. (SH. Jan.29; 257) *Smith.* £190

LEVETT, John
- **The Ordering of Bees.** 1634. 4to. Lacks frontis., last lf. supplied in MS., margins of title reprd., cancelled Rothamsted liby. stp. on verso. Mod. hf. cf. [STC 15555] (CSK. Feb.6; 94) £55

LEVINE, Jack
See–MICHENER, James A. & Levine, Jack

LEVINSON, Andre
- **Bakst: the Story of the Artist's Life.** N.Y., [1922]. (250) numbered copies for America. Fo. Orig. vell. (SG. Oct.9; 24) $700
- – **Anr. Copy.** (SG. Oct.23; 11) $650
- **Histoire de Léon Bakst.** Paris, 1924. (345), on Arches vergé teinté. Lge. 4to. Three-qtr. roan, unc., wrap. (HD. Jun.10; 118) Frs. 4,100
- **Serge Lifar: Destin d'Un Danseur.** Ill.:– Picasso (frontis.), Man Ray & others. [Paris], [1934]. Ltd. 1st. Edn. on Arches, numbered. Lge. 4to. Orig. wraps., disbnd., text unopened. Pres. copy., sigd. (PNY. Mar.4; 139) $280

LEVIS, François-Gaston, Duc de
- [Collection des Manuscrits du ...]. Montreal & Quebec, 1889-96. 12 vols. Orig. ptd. wraps., tattered & loose on most vols., unc. & mostly unopened (CB. Apr.1; 79) Can. $310

LEVIS, Howard C.
- **A Descriptive Bibliography of the Most Important Books ... relating to the Art & History of Engraving.** L., 1912. (350) numbered. 4to. 141 p. supp. & index bnd. in (dtd. 1913). Qtr. cl., soiled, unc. (SG. Jan.22; 243) $180
- – **Anr. Edn.** L., 1912 & 1913. (350) numbered. 4to. Qtr. cl. (SG. Mar.12; 234) $300

LEVITA, Elijah
- **Meturgeman.** Isny, 1541. 1st. Edn. Fo. Lacks Latin title, title mntd. & reprd. without loss at outer margin, lightly stained. Mod. cf. (SPB. May 11; 144) $1,000
- **Sefer Harkavah.** Venice, 1546. 12mo. Title reprd. without loss, last lf. reprd., staining & browning. Cl. (SPB. May 11; 143) $143
- **Tuv Ta'am Sefer Ha'te'amin & Masoret Ha'masoret.** Trans.:– Sebastian Munster. Basle, 1539. 2nd. Edn. Some worming, browning & staining. Mod. hf. vell., worn, stained. (SPB. May 11; 145) $1,300

LEVITA, Leone [Judah Abarbanel]
- **Dialogi D'Amore.** Venice, 1546. 2nd. Edn. 12mo. Tears, loss to corner of 1 lf., stained, browning. Cl. (SPB. May 11; 142) $750

LEVRET, André
- **L'Art des Accouchemens demontrée par des Principes de Physique et de Méchanique.** Ill.:– L. Legrand after Chardin. Paris, 1766. 3rd. Edn. Cont. cf., rebkd. (S. Jun.16; 510) *Studd.* £95
- **Wahrnehmungen von den Ursachen u. Zufällen vieler Schweren Geburten.** Trans.:– J.J. Walbaum. Lübeck & Altona, 1758. 1st. German Edn. 2pts. in 1 vol. Slightly soiled., lacks 1 folding copperplt. Cont. hf. leath. (HK. May 12-14; 322) DM 600
- – **Anr. Edn.** Lübeck u. Altona, 1758-61. 1st. German Edn. 2 vols. Lightly soiled, owner's mark on vol. 1 title. Cont. hf. leath. (HK. Nov.18-21; 532) DM 490

LEVY, Julien
- **Surrealism.** N.Y., Black Sun Pr. 1936. 1st. Edn., (1,500). 4to. Pict. bds., d.-w. (PNY. Mar.4; 167) $160

LEVY, Mervyn
- **The Drawings of L.S. Lowry, Public & Private.** 1976. (50) numbered, sigd. by Lowry. 4to. Orig. mor. (SH. Apr.9; 97) *Makiya.* £55

LEWES, G.H.
- **The Life & Works of Goethe.** 1855. 2 vols. Extra-ill. with ports. & views, some German. Hf. mor. gt. by Rivière. (P. Apr.30; 321) *Fairburn.* £125

LEWIN, John William
- **The Birds of Great Britain, with their Eggs, Accurately Figured.** L., Priv. Ptd. 1789-1794. 1st. Edn. (60). 7 vols. 4to. Some staining to edges of plts. 77, 100 & 103 to 105. Cont. Engl. str.-grd. mor. gt., gt. arms on covers of John Ker, spines with red mor. onlays, gt. (CNY. Oct.1; 144)
$30,000
- - **Anr. Edn.** L., 1795-1800. 8 vols. in 4. 4to. Some sm. stains. Later diced hf. cf., spines decor. with gt. birds in compartments. (SM. Feb.11; 140)
Frs. 13,000
- - **Anr. Edn.** 1795-1801. 8 vols. 4to. Cont. hf. mor., spines gt. (C. Mar.18; 65)　　*Taylor.* £1,800
- - **Anr. Copy.** 8 vols. in 2. Titles & text in Engl. & Fr., 336 hand-cold. engd. plts., Engl. title & frontis. to vol. 1 detchd. Cont. diced cf., 3 covers detchd. (C. May 20; 221)　　*Hett.* £1,000
- - **Anr. Edn.** L., 1800/01. Vols. 7 & 8 (of 8) in 1 vol. Lge. 4to. Engl. & Fr. text. Cont. hf. leath. (HK. Nov.18-21; 808)　　DM 2,000
- **A Natural History of the Birds of New South Wales.** Melbourne, 1978. Facs. Edn. Fo. Additional plt. loosely inserted. Leath., cl. gt. box (slightly defect.). (KH. Mar.24; 241)　　Aus. $210

LEWIS, A.J., 'Professor Hoffmann'
[-] **Conjuror Dick.** Warne, 1885. Orig. pict. cl. gt., worn. (SH. Oct.24; 329)　　*Doerflinger.* £50
[-] - **Anr. Edn.** Warne, n.d. Orig. pict. cl. gt. (SH. Oct.23; 155)　　*Marks.* £60
[-] **Modern Magic.** 1876. 1st. Edn. Orig. pict. cl. gt., 1st. state. (SH. Oct.23; 149)　　*Marks.* £75
[-] **More Magic.** 1890. 1st. Edn. Pt. of endlf. cut. Orig. pict. cl. (SH. Oct.23; 152)　　*Rastorp.* £50

LEWIS, Charles Thomas Courtney
- **George Baxter: his Life & Works.** L., 1908. 1st. Edn. Cl., worn. (SG. Mar.26; 27)　　$130
- **The Story of Picture Printing in England during the XIXth Century.** N.d. 4to. Cl., d.-w. (P. Nov.13; 325)　　*Henderson.* £65

LEWIS, Frederick Christian
- **Imitations of Claud Lorraine . . . engraved from drawings in the British Museum.** 1837. Fo. A few light marginal stains. Cl., soiled, spine torn with loss. (CSK. Nov.28; 89)　　£200
- **Scenery of the River Dart.** 1821. 1st. Edn. Fo. Hf. cl., unc. (LC. Jun.18; 157)　　£170
- **Scenery of the River Dart . . .-Scenery of the Rivers Tamar & Tavy.** N.d.; 1823. 1 vol.; 2 pts. in 1 vol. Fo.; 4to. 1st. work: plts. dtd. 1820-21, occasional minor marginal spotting; 2nd. work: lacks plt. 1 in pt. 2. 1st. work: hf. cl. & marb. bds.; 2nd. work: orig. bds., spine defect., unc. From the collection of Eric Sexton. (C. Apr.16; 299)　　*Elliott.* £170
- **The Scenery of the River Tamar & Tavy.** 1823. Lge. 4to. All but 6 of the 47 engraved ills. mntd., a slip with plan of Breakwater. Orig. bds., unc. (LC. Jun.18; 156)　　£90
- - **Anr. Edn.** [1823]. 2 pts. 4to. No text, bnd. with 26 litho. views of Devon & Cornwall by T.H. Williams, dtd. 1821-22. Cont. blind-stpd. cf. W.a.f. (S. Jun.22; 55)　　*Crowe.* £150
- **Scenery of the Rivers of England & Wales.** N.d. 3 pts. in 1 vol. Fo. Some plts. spotted. Cont. hf. mor., rebkd. (SH. Mar.5; 83)　　*Quaritch.* £180

LEWIS, George
See-CHAMBERS, Ephraim-LEWIS, George

LEWIS, J.
- **The Life of Mayster Wyllyam Caxton.** 1737. 1st. Edn. Browned. Cf. by Rivière. (SH. Jun.25; 203)　　*Talerman.* £160

LEWIS, James
- **Original Designs in Architecture.** Priv. Ptd. 1780. Vol. 1 only (of 2). Fo. Cont. hf. cf., defect. (C. Nov.6; 185)　　*Kitz.* £180
- - **Anr. Edn.** 1780-97. 1st. Edn. 2 vols. in 1. Fo. Text to vol. I in Engl. & Italian, 1st. title & some margins soiled, a few marginal repairs. Recent red hf. mor., gt. spine, unc. (S. Dec.9; 459)
Weinreb. £390

LEWIS, John
- **The Church Catechism Explained . . .** Trans.:- John Richardson. L., 1712. 12mo. Early 18th. C. mor., gt. panel. sides with floral extensions, spine gt. (SG. Dec.18; 244)　　$150

LEWIS, John
See-AMSINCK, Paul-LEWIS, John

LEWIS, John Frederick
- **Illustrations of Constantinople.** N.d. Fo. Soiled. Cont. mor.-bkd. cl., lacks spine, loose. (SH. Nov.6; 237)　　*Dupont.* £300
- **Sketches & Drawings of the Alhambra.** [1835]. Lge. 4to. 26 tinted lithos., partly cold. & mntd. in ruled borders on card, without title. Loose in mor.-bkd. cl. portfo., cl. ties. (C. Mar.18; 154)
Marlborough Rare Books. £420
- - **Anr. Edn.** N.d. Fo. Spotted. Cont. hf. mor. (SH. Nov.6; 238)　　*Duran.* £250
- - **Anr. Copy.** Oxidised. Mor. (DS. May 22; 794)
Pts. 79,000
- **Sketches of Spain & Spanish Character.** N.d. Fo. Dedication lf. & frontis. detchd., spotting. Cont. cl., rebkd., worn. (CSK. Aug.1; 105)　　£110

LEWIS, Matthew Gregory
- **Journal of a West India Proprietor.** L., 1834. 1st. Edn. Early three-qtr. cf. (SG. Feb.26; 209)　　$110
- **Tales of Wonder.** 1801. 2 vols. Tall 8vo. Prelims. spotted. Recent hf. cf. (TA. Apr.16; 87)　　£80

LEWIS, Matthew Gregory-MONTULE, Edouard de
- **Journal of a West India Proprietor.-Voyage to North America & the West Indies.** 1834; 1821. 1st. Engl. Edn. (2nd. work). 2 works in 2 vols. Mod. hf. mor.; mod. cl., unc. (C. Nov.6; 221)
Newman. £55

LEWIS, Meriwether & Clark, William
- **History of the Expedition . . . to the Sources of the Missouri.** Ed.:- Paul Allen. Phila., 1814. 1st. [American] Edn. 2 vols. Cont. Engl.(?) hf. russ. gt., bds. worn. [Sabin 40828] (CNY. May 22; 143)　　$6,300
- - **Anr. Copy.** Map torn, tapestained, partially rebkd., lacks lr. right corner, title-p. tapestained with tape on verso, some foxing thro.-out. Cont. cf., worn. (SPB. Nov.24; 27)　　$7,600
- **Original Journals.** Ed.:- Reuben Gold Thwaites. N.Y., 1904-05. 1st. Complete Edn. 8 vols. including Atlas vol. Gt. cl. (PNY. Mar.26; 181)　　$500
- **The Travels of Capts. Lewis & Clarke, from St. Louis . . . to the Pacific Ocean . . . in the Years 1804-06.** L., 1809. 1st. Engl. Edn. Map foxed, browned. Cont. hf. cf., disbnd., worn. (PNY. Mar.26; 182)　　$260
- **Travels to the Source of the Misouri River & Across the American Continent to the Pacific Ocean.** L., 1814. 1st. Engl. Edn. 4to. Orig. bds., new backstrip & paper label, hf. mor. folding case. From liby. of William E. Wilson. (SPB. Apr.29; 177)　　$1,400

LEWIS, Samuel
- **Atlas Comprising the Counties of England.** L., ca. 1835. 4to. Lacks title-p. Cl. (GM. Apr.30; 478)　　£50
- **Atlas of England & Wales.** L., 1845. 4to. Cl. (P. Jun.11; 207b)　　*Campbell.* £85
- **Atlas to the Topographical Dictionary of England.** 1848. 4to. Cl. gt. (P. Jan.22; 187)　　*Kentish.* £80
- **Topographical Dictionaries of England, Ireland, Scotland & Wales, with maps of Scotland & Ireland & General Atlas.** 1846-47. 13 vols. 4to. Orig. cl., soiled & dampstained. (SD. Feb.4; 215)　　£70
- **A Topographical Dictionary of England.** 1831. 4 vols. 4to. Some foxing. Binder's cl., spines worn. (TA. Apr.16; 290)　　£60
- - **Anr. Edn.** 1835. Vol. V & atlas only. 4to. Unif. bnd. hf. mor., upr. cover of vol. 5 detchd. (P. Sep.11; 124)　　*Hughes.* £110
- - **Anr. Copy.** 5 vols. 4to. Cl. (GM. Apr.30; 479)　　£80
- - **Anr. Edn.** 1849-8. 7th. Edn. 5 vols. including plt. vol. Slight spotting. Orig. cl., soiled. (CSK. Nov.28; 100)　　£65
[-] [-] **Anr. Edn.** N.d. Atlas only. 4to. 1 folding general map, mntd. on cl. Orig. cl. (CSK. Sep.26; 211)　　£70
- **Topographical Dictionary of England.** -**Topographical Dictionary of Wales.** 1831-33. 4 vols.; 2 vols. 4to. Slightly spotted. Cont. hf. roan. (SH. Jul.23; 233)　　*Hammond.* £110
- **A Topographical Dictionary of Ireland.** L., 1837. 2 vols. 4to. Cl., spine strengthened. (GM. Apr.30; 422)　　£80
- **A Topographical Dictionary of Wales.** L., 1833. 2 vols. 4to. Cl., unc. (GM. Apr.30; 480)　　£65
- **View of Representative History of England.** Ca. 1850. Lacks lr. hf. of title-p., maps cold. in outl. on

116 sheets, sheet 116 lacks pt. of lr. margin. Cl. (P. Apr.9; 144)　　*Martin.* £95

LEWIS, Sinclair
- **Arrowsmith.** N.Y., [1925]. [1st. Edn.?], (500) numbered, sigd. by Lewis. Qtr. buckram, backstrip soiled. (PNY. Dec.3; 212)　　$160
- - **Anr. Copy.** Buckram-bkd. bds., partly unc. (SG. Jun.4; 278)　　$140
- **Main Street.** Ill.:- Grant Wood. N.Y., Ltd. Edns. Cl., 1937. (1,500) numbered, sigd. by artist. Sq. 4to. Flexible cl., boxed. (SG. Oct.23; 351)　　$150

LEWIS, Thomas
- **Antiquities of the Hebrew Republick.** Dublin, 1735. 2nd. Edn. 4 pts. in 1 vol. Blind-tooled cf. (S. Nov.18; 670)　　*Laurie.* £95

LEWIS, Sir Thomas
- **The Mechanism & Graphic Registration of the Heart Beat.** 1920. 1st. Edn. 4to. Orig. cl. (S. Jun.16; 511)　　*Jenner Books.* £65

LEWIS, William
- **Commercium Philosophico-Technicum of the Philosophical Commerce of Arts Designed as an Attempt to Improve Arts, Trades & Manufactures.** 1763. 4to. Some outer blank margins dampstained. Cont. cf. (S. Dec.1; 246)　　*Barnet.* £100
- **A Course of Practical Chemistry . . . all the Operations Described in Wilson's Complete Course of Chemistry.** 1746. 1st. Edn. 2 advt. ll., a few ll. at beginning with a brown stain. New cf. (S. Dec.1; 244)　　*Blackwell.* £55

LEWIS, Wyndham
- **The Apes of God.** 1930. Ltd. Sigd. Edn. Orig. cl. (P. Feb.19; 34)　　*Waldron.* £55
- **Doom of Youth.** 1932. 1st. Edn. Orig. cl., d.-w. (S. Jul.22; 206)　　*Thomson.* £200
- **Thirty Personalities & a Self-Portrait.** 1932. (200) numbered, & sigd. Fo. Loose as iss. in orig. cl.-bkd. bd. portfo., ties. Bkplt. of A.J.A. Symons. (C. Jul.22; 79a)　　*Radmell.* £450
- - **Anr. Copy.** (300) (S. Jul.31; 247)
Bell, Book & Radnall. £240

LEWIS, Wyndham (Ed.)
See-BLAST
See-ENEMY, The
See-TYRO, The

LEYARD, Austen Henry
- **Monuments of Nineveh.** 1849. Fo. 98 plts. only, lacks 16 & 23, slight spotting. Un-bnd. as iss. in orig. hf. mor. portfo., worn. (CSK. Nov.28; 35)　　£50

LEYBOURN, William
- **Cursus Mathematicus. Mathematical Sciences.** 1690. Fo. A few ll. cleanly torn, some blank margins holed without loss, dampstaining & spotting. Old cf., worn. [Wing L1911] (CSK. Feb.20; 50)　　£80
- **Dialling . . . Relating to the Course of the Sun.** Ill.:- R. White [engraved port.] 1700. 2nd. Edn. Fo. Engraved port. with sm. hole, cont. annots. on plts., some soiling & stains. Cont. hf. cf., rebkd., worn. [Wing L1913] (S. Apr.6; 223)　　*Rogers-Turner.* £120
- **Panarithmologia, being a Mirror for Merchants, Breviate for Bankers, Treasure for Tradesmen, Mate for Mechanicks.** 1693. 1st. Edn. With Dd4 in both orig. & cancel state (with value of lease corrected. Cont. mott. cf., rebkd. Sig. & bkplt. of Edward Monckton, Sumerford Hall, Staffordshire; the Kenney copy; from Honeyman Collection. [Wing L1926] (S. May 20; 3279)　　*Riley-Smith.* £160
- **Pleasure with Profit: consisting of Recreations of Divers Kinds.** 1694. 1st. Edn. Fo. Some ll. browned. Cont. mott. cf., worn. [Wing L1931] (S. Jun.23; 394)　　*Fletcher.* £170

LEYCESTER, Sir Peter
- **Historical Antiquities.** 1673. 1st. Edn. Fo. Folding engraved map of county laid-down, marginal wormhole affecting lst. 35 ll. Early hf. cf. (LC. Jun.18; 158) £60

LEYCESTER, Sir Peter (1st. work)-KING, Daniel
- **Some Antiquities touching Cheshire.-The Vale-Royall of England.-A Description Historicall & Geographicall of the County Palatine of Chester.** -**A Treatise of the Isle of Man.** 1672; 1656; 1656; 1656. Together in 7 vols. Extra-ill., MS. hf.-titles, additional hand-cold. MS. titles, 3 hand-cold. armorial frontis.'s, heightened with gold, dedications & many ll. of additional MS. text

LEYCESTER, Sir Peter (1st. work)–KING, Daniel – Some Antiquities touching Cheshire.–The Vale-Royall *-contd.*
including some in 17th. C. hand, all mntd. on guards, some interleaving with blanks, occasional light foxing, 1 or 2 minor tears. Cont. diced russ., gt. & blind borders on sides, partial clasps. (Assembled ca. 1813); owing to uncertainty of collation, w.a.f. (C. Feb.25; 42) *Allen.* £2,600

LEYLAND, John
See–**HALFPENNY, Joseph–LEYLAND, John**

LEYMARIE, Jean
– Vitraux pour Jerusalem. Ill.:– Marc Chagall. [Monte Carlo], [1962]. Fo. Cl. (SG. Oct.23; 61) $130

L'HERITIER DE BRUTELLE, CH. L.
– Stirpes Novae. Ill.:– P.J. Redouté, Hubert, Maleuvre & others. Paris, 1784. 6 pts. in 1 vol., all publd. Lge. fo. Cont. bds., worn. (D. Dec.11-13; 135) DM 7,500
– – Anr. Edn. Ill.:– After Pierre-Joseph Redouté & others. Paris (etc). 1784-[85-88.] 4 pts. (of 6). 4to. 45 dupl. plts., 4 others replaced by orig. watercolour drawings sigd. by Henri-Joseph Redouté, some marginal dampstaining. Cont. Fr. mor. gt. L.P., from collection of Massachusetts Horticultural Society, plt. XXX not stpd. (SPB. Oct.1; 141) $20,000
– – Anr. Edn. Ill.:– Redouté & others. Paris, 1784[-91]. Pts. 1-6 (all publd.) in 1 vol. Fo. A few plts. stained. Cont. cl.-bkd. bds., worn. (S. Dec.3; 994) *W. & W.* £600

L'HERITIER DE VILLANDON, Marie Jeanne
– L'Adroite Princesse, ou les Aventures de Finette. Ill:– Marie Laurencin. Paris, 1928. (480) numbered. Fo. Loose in orig. wraps., folder. (SH. Nov.21; 375) *Kawamatsu.* £260
– – Anr. Copy. In sheets, wrap., publisher's s.-c. (HD. Dec.5; 129) Frs. 2,000

LIANCOUR, Sieur de
– Le Maitre d'Armes ou l'Exercice de l'Epée seule dans sa Perfection. Paris, 1692. Ob. hf. 4to. Mod. bds., old stains. (LM. Mar.21; 104) B.Frs. 6,800

LIAUTARD, Abbé
– Eloge Funèbre de . . . Louis XVIII . . . Paris, Feb. 1825. 3rd. Edn. 4to. Cont. black mor., border, fleurs-de-lys in corners, beaten gold title on upr. cover. decor. spine, inside dentelle. (HD. Mar.18; 104) Frs. 1,300

LIBAUT, Ian
See–**STEVENS, Kaerle & Libaut, Ian**

LIBAVIUS, Andreas
– Syntagmatis Selectorum Undiquaque et perspicue traditorum Alchymiae Arcanorum. –Examen Philosophiae Novae.–Analysis Confessionis Fraternitatis de Rosea Cruce. Frankfurt, 1615. Fo. 1st. work: 3 plts. in 1 vol. with Appendix, some worming affecting text, 2nd. work: title wormed, 3rd. work: badly wormed. Cont. vell., soiled, short tears on spine. (S. Oct.20; 138) *Goldschmidt.* £350

LIBER QUOTIDIANUS CONTRAROTULATORIS GARDEROBAE. Anno Regni Regis Edwardi primi vicesimo octavo . . . 1299 & 1300.–A collection of Ordinances & Regulations for the Government of the Royal Household . . . from . . . Edward III to . . . William & . . . Mary. Also Receipts in Ancient Cookery
1788; 1790. 2 works in 1 vol. 4to. Some spotting. Cont. mott. cf., rebkd., old spine preserved. From liby. of André L. Simon. (S. May 18; 173) *Segal.* £50

LIBERMAN, Alexander
See–**AVEDON, Richard–LIBERMAN, Alexander**

LIBRARY, The
– Quarterly Review of Bibliography. Mar. 1963-Jun. 1980. 70 orig. issues. In bdg. cases. (TA. Sep.18; 94) £65
– Transactions of the Bibliographical Society. 1920-39. 4th. Series, last 2 vols. orig. iss. Vols. I-XIX, & index. Orig. canvas-bkd. bds., last 2 vols loose in bdg. case. (C. Jul.22; 122) *Quaritch.* £100

LIBRARY of Literary Criticism of English & American Authors
Ed.:– Charles W. Moulton. Buffalo, 1901-05. 8 vols. 4to. Cl., ex-liby. (SG. Mar.26; 333) $110

LIBRI, Guillaume
[–] Catalogue de la Bibliothèque de M. L**.** Paris, 1847. Later cl. Rubberstpd. sig. of Pierre Louys on hf-title. (SG. Oct.2; 223) $130
– Monuments Inedits . . . 1862-64. 1st. Edn. 2 vols. in 1, including Supp. Lge. fo. 65 plts., most chromolitho., some in gold & cols. or silver & cols., with alternative version of plt. 44 & Bedford's pencil note 'to be cancelled'. Cont. mor. by Francis Bedford, gt., spine tooled in compartments, covers with geometric design, based on early 16th. C. Italian bdg. ill. in the work, & with initials C[harles] T[ennant]. Pres. Copy, title inscr. by Francis Bedford in pencil 'pres. copy to FB by Count Libri'. (S. Nov.24; 191) *Breslauer.* £950

LIBRI de Rustica
Venice & Mense, May 1514. 4to. Sm. defects. Old cf., gt. roulette border, centre arms, gt. decor. spine raised bands. (HD. Apr.24; 2) Frs. 1,800

LICETUS, Fortunius
– De Monstries . . . (with appendix Monstra quaedam Nova & Prariora). Ed.:– G. Blasius. Amst., 1665. 4to. Lacks last lf. (blank?). Cont. tree cf., gt., corners slightly worn. (S. Feb.23; 74) *Goldschmidt.* £310
– – Anr. Copy. Slight marginal worming to a few ll. near end, lacks final blank, sm. liby. stp. on title. Cont. vell. bds. (S. Jun.29; 288) *Duran.* £260
– – Anr. Copy. Engraved title preserved, worming, a few ll. loose, staining, tears, lacks 2R1 (index lf.), & 2T4 (final blank). Vell.-bkd. bds., worn. With bkplt. & sig. of Georges-Frederic Hildebrandt. (SPB. Jul.28; 219) $200
– De Monstris . . . [with Appendix Monstra quaedam Nova & Rariora]. Ed.:– G. Blasius. Padua. 1668. 4to. Lacks last lf. (blank?). Cont. mott. cf. (S. Feb.23; 75) *Pilo.* £160
– Hieroglyphica sive Antiqua Schemata Gemmarum Anularium quaesita Moralia . . . Medica, Philosophica. Padua, 1653. [1st. Edn.?]. Fo. Slightly dampstained. Cont. cf. with arms of Benzoni family of Cremona on covers, worn & reprd. (S. Feb.23; 76) *Nador.* £100
– – Anr. Copy. Some browning, 1 or 2 tears. Cont. vell. bds., slightly worn. From liby. of André L. Simon. (S. May 18; 130) *Lyon.* £80

LICHTENBERG, Geo Christoph
– Vermischte Schriften. Ed.:– L. Chr. Lichtenberg & Fr. Kries. Göttingen, 1800-06. 1st. Coll. Edn. 9 vols. Pref. misbnd. pp. XVII-XXIV, vol. IX wormed. 7 cont. hf. leath. & 2 later hf. leath. (H. Dec.9/10; 1599) DM 900

LICHTENBERGER, Johannes
– Prognosticatio. Mainz, [Jacob Meydenbach], Jun. 8, 1492. 2nd. Edn. in Latin. Fo. Lacks 1st. lf., supplied in facs., sm. wormhole from A2 to B1, some light staining, some inner margins strengthened, some pencilled notes. Mod. mor., blind-stpd. & gt.-lettered. Bkplt. of Boies Penrose, lately in the collection of Eric Sexton. [Goff L205, H 10082] (CNY. Apr.8; 96) $3,600
– – Anr. Edn. [?Cologne], 4 Jun., 1526. 4to. Slightly soiled in places, tear in H2 slightly affecting text, title & 1st. & last few ll. reprd. in inner margin, lacks last blank lf. Limp vell. (S. Oct.21; 404) *Broseghini.* £860

LICHTENSTEIN, Henry
– Travels in Southern Africa. L., 1812 & 1815. 2 vols. Orig. paper bds. (HSS. Apr.24; 133) £190
– – Anr. Copy. 4to. Foxed & browned. Old hf. cf., rebkd. (SG. Feb.26; 9) $375
– – Anr. Copy. 4to. Some foxing. Spr. cf. (SSA. Nov.5; 225) R. 800

LICHTENSTEIN, Isaac
See–**WALKOWITZ, Abraham & Lichtenstein, Isaac**

LIEBAULT, Jean
– Secrets de Medecine, et de la Philosophie Chimique. Rouen, 1643. 18th. C. mor., triple gt. fillet, spine gt. in compartments, inner gt. dentelles. Mirabeau copy. (SM. Oct.7; 1819) Frs. 2,400
See–**ESTIENNE, Charles & Liebault, Jean**
See–**ESTIENNE, Charles & Liebault, Jean –CRESCENTIUS, Petrus**

LIEBE, Christian Sigismund
– Gotha Numaria. Ill.:– J.C. Philips. Amst., 1730. Fo. Cont. hf. cf., spine gt. (VG. Nov.18; 1256) Fls. 700

LIEBERMANN, Max
– Ein ABC in Bildern. Ed.:– R. Graul. Berlin, n.d. (100) on Jap. Orig. vell. With 2 sigd. pen ills. by M. Liebermann. (HK. May 12-14; 1961) DM 2,300
– Holländisches Skizzenbuch. Ed.:– O. Bie. (text). Berlin, 1911. (500) numbered. Lge. ob. 4to. Orig. linen, 2 ties. (HK. Nov.18-21; 2770) DM 580

LIEBIG, Justus
– Animal Chemistry, or Organic Chemistry in its Application to Physiology & Pathology. Ed.:– William Gregory. 1842. 1st. Edn. in Engl. Advts. Orig. embossed cl., slightly worn. (S. Dec.2; 740) *Routenberg.* £80
– – Anr. Copy. Orig. cl., upr. inner hinge brkn. From liby. of Dr. E. Ashworth Underwood. (S. Feb.23; 245) *Giordano.* £50
– Die Organische Chemie in Ihrer Anwendung auf Physiciologie und Pathologie. Braunschweig, 1842. 1st. Edn. Cont. hf. leath., gt. spine. (R. Oct.14-18; 280) DM 1,200

LIECHTENSTEIN, Gundaber Fürst von
– Von Zaumung d. Pferde. Vienna, 1625. Lge. 4to. 1 supp. plt. with 1 full-p. & 1 double-p. copper engr., margins very stained, 1st. 4 ll. with reprd. faults, title very soiled. Cont. leath., wormed. (HK. May 12-14; 1251) DM 1,100

LIECHTENSTEIN, Princess Marie
– Holland House. 1874. 2 vols. Extra-ill. with views & ports., some hand-cold. Later lev., gt., by Bayntun, spines slightly faded, with orig. bindings preserved at ends. (CSK. Oct.24; 212) £55

LIEDER DER DEUTSCHEN MYSTIK
Ed.:– Josef Bernhart. Ill.:– Anna Simons. Munich, Bremer Pr., 1922. (270). Orig. vell., gt. fillet, slightly soiled, end-ll. slightly soiled, sigd. Bremer Binderei. F. Th., orig. bd. s.-c. (D. Dec.11-13; 1009) DM 600
– – Anr. Copy. 4to. (HK. Nov.18-21; 2462) DM 420

LIEN-TEH, Wu
See–**WONG, K. Chimin & Lien-Teh, Wu**

LIEVRE, Edouard
– En Italie.–En Crimée. Paris, ca. 1860; ca. 1855. 1st. Printing (1st. work). Ob. 4to. Publisher's decor. s.-c. (HD. Dec.5; 130) Frs. 2,400

LIFE & Adventures of . . . Miss Ann Elliot
See–**MEMOIRS . . . of Charles Augustus Fitz-Roy . . . with Miss Parsons.–LIFE & Adventures of . . . Miss Ann Elliot**

LIFE OF JOSEPH, a Scripture Narrative
Harrisburg, 1833. 12mo. Slightly stained. Orig. ptd. wraps. (SH. Mar.19; 158) *Schiller.* £160

LIGER, Louis
– Le Jardinier Fleuriste. Paris, 1742. New Edn. Some slight dampstaining to upper portions just touching text, 2 slight tears to plts. Cont. mott. sheep, spine gt., heat & foot of spine chipped. (CNY. Oct.1; 14) $140
– Nouvelle Maison Rustique ou Economie General . . . de Campagne. Ed.:– [H. Besnier]. Paris, 1721. 3rd. Edn. 2 vols. 4to. A few ll. slightly spotted or dampstained, T4 in vol. I torn & slightly damaged, just affecting text. Mod. antique style hf. sheep. (S. Dec.3; 1024) *Maggs.* £80
– – Anr. Edn. Paris, 1775. 2 vols. 4to. Cont. roan, gt. spine. (CR. Jun.11; 507) Lire 400,000
– – Anr. Edn. Paris, 1790. 2 vols. 4to. Cont. cf. (SH. May 21; 70) *Nador.* £65

LIGHT, Maj. Henry
– Sicilian Scenery. 1823. Fo. With dupl. proof set of all but 1 plt., India paper, spotted. Cont. mor. (SH. Mar.5; 85) *Vitale.* £170
– – Anr. Copy. Hf. Mor. (P. May 14; 54) *Guest.* £110
– – Anr. Copy. Dampstained. Cont. hf. mor., gt. spine. (SH. Nov.6; 239) *Shapiro.* £60

LIGHTBODY, Fr. & others
– Working Drawings & Designs in Mechanical Engineering & Machine-Making. L., ca. 1870. Fo. Hf. leath. (D. Dec.11-13; 275) DM 600

LIGHTBODY, James
– Every Man his own Gauger . . . [with] the True Art of Brewing Beer . . . [&] the Vintner's Art of Fining . . . [&] the Compleat Cofee-Man. Ca. 1695. 1st. Edn.? 12mo. Browned & soiled, edges of ll. frayed, with very slight loss of text. Cont. sheep, rebkd. From liby. of André L. Simon. (S. May 18; 131) *Segal.* £80

- - **Anr. Edn.** Ca. 1700? 2nd. Edn.? 12mo. Slight browning & soiling. Mod. hf. cf. From liby. of André L. Simon. [Wing L2048] (S. May 18; 132)
Segal. £130

LIGHTFOOT, John
- Flora Scotica. 1777. 2 vols. Cont. cf. (SH. Apr.9; 289)   *Aberdeen Rare Books.* £60

LIGON, Richard
- A True & Exact History of the Island of Barbados. 1657. 1st. Edn. Fo. Map & diagrams & sheet of text torn with hardly any loss of text, slight soiling & thumbmarks in places. Old bds., soiled, rebkd. [Sabin 41057; Wing L2075] (S. Dec.1; 251)   *Rota.* £130
- - **Anr. Edn.** 1673. 2nd. Edn. Fo. Lacks A1 (blank?), 2 folding plts. with short tears, folding map with portion of inner border cropped & sm. tear reprd. Cont. sheep, spine restored, qtr. mor. case. From the liby. of Thomas Gray, with his sig. on title-p. & note of purchase (for 3s 3d) at end, stp. of T.U. Writtle. [Wing L2076, Sabin 41058] (S. Feb.10; 361)   *Maggs.* £300
- - **Anr. Copy.** 2 ll. publisher's catalogue, no hf.-title, title detchd., sm. hole in contents lf, just affecting surrounding line. Cont. hf. cf., worn, pt. of spine missing. [Wing L2076] (S. Nov.4; 655)
Sisnet. £260

LILFORD, Thomas Littleton Powys, Baron
- Coloured Figures of the Birds of the British Islands. Ill.:– A. Thorburn & others. 1885-97. 7 vols. Stp. of F.C. Peal on title-pp. Cont. maroon hf. mor. (C. Mar.18; 66)   *Bosworth.* £1,400
- - **Anr. Copy.** 8 vols. including Index. Port., 420 chromolitho. plts., extra ill. with 8 dupl. plts. in variant states. Cont. hf. mor. A.L.s. from publisher R.H. Porter to T.E. Buckley. (C. Jul.15; 190)   *Taylor.* £1,200
- - **Anr. Copy.** 7 vols. Hf. red mor. (P. Jul.30; 51)
Thorp. £700
- - **Anr. Copy.** Hf. mor., marb. bds. (SSA. Apr.22; 50)   *R.* 2,000
- - **Anr. Edn.** L., 1885-99. 7 vols. Port., 421 plts. Hf. mor. gt. (P. Jun.11; 287)   *Traylen.* £1,050
- - **Anr. Edn.** Ill.:– A. Thorburn. 1891-97. 7 vols. Hf. mor. gt. (P. Nov.13; 208)   *Quaritch.* £1,550
- - **Anr. Copy.** Hf. mor. gt., arms of Earl of Dartmouth on upr. cover, by Zaehnsdorf. (P. Mar.12; 289)   *Hill.* £1,400
- - **Anr. Copy.** 8 vols. Hf. red mor. gt. (CE. Nov.20; 173)   £1,250
- - **Anr. Copy.** 7 vols. (P. Oct.2; 86)
Hatchards. £1,100
- Notes on the Birds of Northamptonshire & Neighbourhood. Ill.:– A. Thorburn & G.E. Lodge. 1895. 2 vols. Folding map, 65 ills., extra ill. with 100 chromolitho. plts. Cont. red hf. mor. (C. Jul.15; 191)   *Taylor.* £420
- - **Anr. Copy.** Lacks map. Mod. hf. mor. (CSK. Mar.20; 2)   £55
[-] - **Anr. Copy.** 4to. Hf. red mor. & buckram. (CB. Sep.24; 42)   Can. $180

LILIENTHAL, M.
[-] Vollständiges Thaler-Cabinett. Königsberg & Leipzig, 1747. Cont. leath. gt., spine partly restored. (R. Mar.31-Apr.4; 178)   DM 1,200

LILIENTHAL, Otto
- Der Vogelflug als Grundlage der Fliegekunst. Berlin, 1889. 1st. Edn. Orig. linen. (HK. Nov.18-21; 356)   DM 2,300

LILLIE, John
See–NEWTON, James–LILLIE, John

LILLY, William Astrologer
- The Starry Messenger. 1645. 1st. Edn. 4to. Mod. cf.-bkd. bds. [Wing L2245] (SH. Jun.25; 216)
Hill. £100

LIMA GOZOSA Descripcion de las Festibas Demostraciones con que esta Ciudad, Capital de la America Meridonal
Lima, 1760. Sm. 4to. Sm. wormholes, conventual liby. stp. on 1st. lf. of text & elsewhere, some slight spotting & sm. wormholes affecting text. Orig. bdg. (SPB. May 5; 324) $125

LIMBOURG, H.
[-] Le Duc d'Aumale et ses Soeurs Louise d'Orléans ... Clementine d'Orléans ... Correspondance. Evreux, 1910. Ltd. Edn. Priv. Ptd. Red mor., crowned centre cyphr, decor. spine raised bands, inner dentelle, wrap & spine, by Noulhac. MS. note by author & ded. (HD. Apr.24; 151)   Frs. 1,400

- - **Anr. Copy.** Red mor. crowned centre cypher, decor. spine raised bands, inner dentelle, wrap & spine by Noulhac. A.L.s. (HD. Apr.24; 152)
Frs. 1,200

LIMIERS, Henri B. Philippe de
- Annales de la Monarchie Françoise. Amst., 1724. 1st. Edn. 3 pts. in 1 vol. Fo. Slightly browned in parts. Hf. leath. (HK. Nov.18-21; 1897) DM 600

LIMITED EDITIONS CLUB
- Quarto-Millenary; the First 250 Publications & the First 25 Years ... Ill.:– Arthur Rackham & others. N.Y., Ltd. Edns. Cl., 1959. (2,250) numbered. Sm. fo. Lev. bkd. cl., inlaid lev. medallion on sides, boxed. Raymond M. Sutton Jr. copy. (SG. May 7; 239) $220
- - **Anr. Edn.** N.Y., Ltd. Edns. Cl., 1959. (1,500) numbered. Sm. fo. Mor.-bkd. cl., leath. medallion on cover. orig. box. (SG. Apr.9; 519) $220

LINCOLN, Abraham
- Complete Works. N.Y., 1905. 24 vols. Exta-ill. with autographs, ports. & prints. Maroon hf. mor., many spines brkn. & covers detchd. (SPB. Jul.28; 323) $175

LINCOLN, Frederick
See–GABRIELSON, Ira N. & Lincoln, Frederick

LIND, James
[-] An Answer to the Declaration of the American Congress. L., 1776. 1st. Publd. Edn. With the hf.-title, (torn), some ll. loose. Disbnd. (SG. Mar.5; 270) $150

LINDBERGH, Charles A.
- The Spirit of St. Louis. N.Y., 1953. Orig. cl. Inscr. (SH. Jul.16; 184)   *Young.* £110
- 'We'. N.Y., 1927. Author's Autograph Edn. (1000) numbered. Vell. spine & tips, bkplt. Sigd. by author & publisher. (SG. Nov.13; 422) $275

LINDBERGH, Charles A.–RICKENBACKER, Capt. Edward V.
- 'We'.–Seven Came Through. N.Y.; Garden City, 1927; 1943. (1000) numbered, sigd. by author & publisher; 1st. Edn. 2 works in 2 vols. Tall 8vo.; 8vo. Orig. bds., cl. case (1st. work); & orig. cl., d.-w., qtr. mor. s.-c. 2nd. work inscr. to Mrs. Prescott, & with author's return ticket (carried by him while lost at sea) laid in. (CNY. Feb.6; 228)
$600

LINDE, Antonius van der
- Das Schachspiels des XVI Jahrhunderts nach unedirten Quellen bearbeitet. Berlin, 1874. Hf. leath. (D. Dec.11-13; 2298)   DM 620

LINDELBACH, Michael
- Praecepta Latinitatis. Heidelberg, [Eponymous Pr. (Johann & Conrad Hist?)], 15 Dec., 1486. 1st. Edn. 4to. Spaces for initial capitals, with guide letters, section of fore-margin of a3 torn away & renewed with loss of some letters, 1st. p. soiled, light browning, some early inscrs. on 1st. p., 1 erased. Vell. bds., soiled. From the collection of Eric Secton. [BMC III, 667, Goff L223, HC 10112*] (CNY. Apr.8; 77) $2,800

LINDEMANS, Ir. Paul
- Geschiedenis van de Landbouw in Belgie. Antw., 1952. 2 pts. 4to. Linen. (LM. Mar.21; 167)
DM 10,500

LINDEN, J.
- Lindenia. Iconographie des Orchidées. Gent, 1885-99. 125 pts. in 112. Fo. Slightly soiled in parts. Orig. pict. wraps., Pt. I/1 very defect. (HK. Nov.18-21; 619)   DM 6,000

LINDLEY, Dr. John
- The Genera & Species of Orchideous Plants. Ill.:– Francis Bauer. 1830-32. Pts. 1-2 (of 3). 4to. Orig. ptd. wraps. Pres. copy to Nees von Esenbeck. (S. Dec.3; 1026)   *W. & W?* £50
- Ladies Botany. N.d. 3rd. Edn. 2 vols. Hf. cf. (DWB. Mar.31; 266)   £62
- Rosarum Monographia. 1820. 1st. Edn. Cf. gt. rebkd. (Pr. Oct.23; 224)   *Ashwell.* £180
- Sertum Orchidaceum: A Wreath of the Most Beautiful Orchidaceous Flowers. Ill.:– M. Gauci after Miss Drake & others. [1837]-1838-[4]. Fo. Slight foxing. Cont. mor., gt. by J. Law of L'pool., covers decor. with intertwined columbine-like flowers surrounding lge. central oval. Bkplt. of Earl of Derby. (S. Jun.1; 157)   *Quaritch.* £3,400
- - **Anr. Edn.** Ill.:– M. Gauci after Miss Drake, W. Griffith, & others. 1838. Fo. Occasional minor foxing, mainly affecting tissues. 19th. C. hf. mor.,

worn, covers detchd. From Chetham's Liby., Manchester. (C. Nov.27; 247)   *Fletcher.* £2,500
See–EDWARDS, Sydenham Teak & Lindley, John
See–MOORE, Thomas & Lindley, John
See–PAXTON, Sir Joseph & Lindley, John

LINDLEY, John (Ed.)
See–POMOLOGICAL MAGAZINE

LINDLEY, Dr. John & Hutton, William
- The Fossil Flora of Great Britain. 1831-37. 3 vols. Hf. str.-grd. mor., defect., partly unc., ex-liby. (PL. Jul.11; 70)   *Wheldon & Wesley.* £60
- - **Anr. Copy.** Cont. leath., 1 cover loose. (SKC. Feb.26; 1593)   £50

LINDLEY, John, Sweet, Robert & others
- The Ornamental Flower Garden & Shrubbery. 1854. 4 vols. Cl., worn. (S. Dec.3; 1027)
Quaritch. £600

LINDLEY, Th.
- Narrative of a Voyage to Brasil. L., 1805. Without errata lf. Orig. interims bdg. [Sabin 41294] (R. Mar.31-Apr.4; 2388)   DM 550

LINDNER, C.
- Gründliche Anleitung zum Nützlichen Gebrauche der Erd- u. Himmels-Kugel. Nuremb., 1726. 1st. Edn. Cont. leath. (R. Oct.14-18; 281)   DM 580

LINDNER, F.L.
See–EHRMANN, T.F. & Lindner, F.L.

LINDSAY, Sir David
See–LYNDSAY or LINDSAY, Sir David

LINDSAY, Jack & Norman
- A Homage to Sappo. [L.], Fanfrolico Pr., 1928. (70) numbered, on Japan vell., sigd. by Jack Lindsay. 4to. Gt.-decor. stiff vell. (SG. Oct.9; 148) $1,700

LINDSAY, Lionel
- A Book of Woodcuts. Sydney & c., 1922. Cl., slightly worn. (KH. Mar.24; 247)   Aus. $140
- Conrad Martens ... Sydney, 1920. 4to Facs. letter to Charles Darwin tipped in. Orig. bds., cl. spine. (JL. Jul.20; 682)   Aus. $120

LINDSAY, Norman
- The Etchings. 1927. (31) sigd. Fo. 1 sigd. etched plt., 45 reproductions. Orig. vell.-bkd. cl. (SH. Mar.26; 326)   *Arnold.* £560
- - **Anr. Copy.** (129) numbered, sigd. Orig. cl. (SH. Mar.26; 327)   *Arnold.* £230
- Exhibition of Watercolours & Etchings. Adelaide, 1926. (250) numbered. 4to. Stapled in wraps. (KH. Mar.24; 249)   Aus. $350
- Micomicana. Melbourne, 1979. [1st. Edn.], (527) sigd. by Jane Lindsay. Fo. Leath. gt., lettered cl. box. (KH. Mar.24; 252)   Aus. $600
- Paintings in Oil. Sydney, 1945. (1000) numbered. L.-w., hinges reprd. (JL. Jul.20; 669)
Aus. $340
- Pen Drawings. Sydney, 1924. (500) numbered, sigd. Fo. Orig. parch.-bkd. bds., worn. Pres. copy. (SH. Mar.26; 325)   *Illustrated Antiques.* £125
- - **Anr. Copy.** Some foxing. No bdg. stated. (JL. Jul.20; 672)   Aus. $170
- Watercolours. Ed.:– Godfrey Blunden. Sydney, 1939. (1,850). Orig. cl. covers, very slight marks. (JL. Mar.2; 739)   Aus. $100

LINDSAY, Norman & Stewart, Douglas
- Paintings in Oil. N.d. (1,000) numbered. 4to. Orig. bdg., d.-w. (JL. Dec.15; 775)   Aus. $190

LINDSAY, Vachel
- Collected Poems. N.Y., 1923. 1 lf. excised. Orig. cl., slight wear. Pres. copy to Louis Untermeyer, MS. corrections in text, by author, T.L.s. tipped into back with MS. note added at foot. (SPB. Nov.25; 340) $325

LINDSAY, William Schaw
- History of Merchant Shipping & Ancient Commerce. L., 1874-76. 1st. Edn. 4 vols. Old liby. stp. on tiles. Gt.-decor. cl. (SG. Feb.26; 211) $170

LINDT, J.W.
- Picturesque New Guinea. L., 1887. Occasional slight foxing. Recased in orig. bdg., slightly marked. (KH. Mar.24; 254)   Aus. $380

LINEUS Buscimducis [Thomas]–S., Th. N.
- Oratio in Laudem Belli, habita ab ipso Marte in postremo Cameracensi concilio, ad conciliandam pacem convocato.–De Bello Germanico in Laudem Joannis Pedionaei. Paris, [Germany], 1531; ca. 1548. 1st. Edn. (1st. work). 2 works in 1 vol. 17th.

LINEUS Buscimducis [Thomas]–S., Th. N. Cameracensi concilio, ad conciliandam pacem convocato.–De -contd.
C. inscr. on title of 1st. work of 'Christophori Echstein ab Ebrenegg', marginal wormhole at end not affecting text, slight spotting in places. 19th. C. mor.-bkd. bds. (C. Apr.1; 55) *Corby.* £350

LINIERE, Raoul de
– Armorial de la Sarthe. Le Mans, 1942-48. 3 vols. Lge. 8vo. Hf. cf. (HD. Jun.29; 116) *Frs.* 1,000

LINNE or Linnaeus, Sir Charles or Carolus
– Amoenitates Academicae. Leiden or Amst., 1749-60. 1st. Edn. 5 vols. Vol. I is the Camper Edn., & vols. 2-5 are the Linnaeus Edn. with the 2nd. Iss. Wetstein cancel titles, plts. browned. 19th. C. hf. mor., 1 cover almost detchd. From Chetham's Liby., Manchester. (C. Nov.27; 248) *Taylor.* £300
– Critica Botanica ... Leiden, 1737. 1st. Edn. 2 pts. in 1 vol. 19th. C. hf. mor. From Chetham's Liby., Manchester, bkplt. of Earl of Bute on title verso, with his MS. annots. in ink. (C. Nov.27; 249) *Baskett & Day.* £300
– Decas Prima Plantarum Horti Upsalensis. Stockholm, 1762. Fo. 19th. C. hf. leath. (R. Oct.14-18; 3023) DM 1,600
– Fauna Svecica. Stockholm, 1761. 2nd. Edn. Folding plts. rather browned. 19th. C. hf. mor. From Chetham's Liby., Manchester. (C. Nov.27; 252) *Wheldon & Wesley.* £90
– Flora Lapponica. Amst., 1737. 1st. Edn. Lacks frontis. Cont. vell. From Chetham's Liby., Manchester. (C. Nov.27; 253) *Wheldon & Wesley.* £170
– Flora Svecica ... Stockholm, 1755. 2nd. Edn. Folding plt. browned, some spotting. 19th. C. hf. mor. From Chetham's Liby., Manchester. (C. Nov.27; 254) *Quaritch.* £150
– Flora Zeylanica. Amst., 1748. Some spotting. 19th. C. hf. mor. From Chetham's Liby., Manchester. (C. Nov.27; 255) *Quaritch.* £220
– Genera Plantarum ... Stockholm, 1754. 5th. Edn. Some spotting. 19th. C. hf. mor. From Chetham's Liby., Manchester. (C. Nov.27; 256) *Wheldon & Wesley.* £170
– Hortus Cliffortianus. Ill.:– Wandelaar after Ehret. Amst., 1737. 1st. Edn. Fo. Title slightly dust-soiled. 19th. C. hf. mor., upr. cover detchd. From Chetham's Liby., Manchester. (C. Nov.27; 250) *Wheldon & Wesley.* £1,200
– Hortus Upsaliensis. Amst., 1748. 1st. Amst. Edn. Some spotting. 19th. C. hf. mor. From Chetham's Liby., Manchester. (C. Nov.27; 251) *Quaritch.* £260
– Museum Ludovicae Ulricae Reginae. Stockholm, 1764. 1st. Edn. 2 pts. in 1 vol. Bdg. completely brkn. From Chetham's Liby., Manchester. (C. Nov.27; 257) *Wheldon & Wesley.* £320
[–] Museum Tessinianum ... Stockholm, 1753. 1st. Edn., L.P. Fo. Cont. spr. cf., worn, rebkd. From Chetham's Liby., Manchester. (C. Nov.27; 258) *Quaritch.* £300
– Oratio de Necessitate Peregrinationum. Ed.:– J. Browall & J. Gesner. Leiden, 1743. 1st. Publd. Edn. 2 pts. in 1 vol. Title nearly detchd. 19th. C. hf. mor. From Chetham's Liby., Manchester. (C. Nov.27; 259) *Taylor.* £190
– Philosophia Botanica in qua Explicantur Fundamenta Botanica. Ed.:– J.G. Gleditsch. Berlin, 1780. 2nd. Edn. Sm. wormholes in margins at end, name on title & upr. cover. Vell. (S. Dec.1; 254) *Quaritch.* £65
– Species Plantarum exhibentes Plantas Rite Cognitas, ad Genera relatas ... Secundum Systema Sexualis Digestas. Stockholm, 1753. 1st. Edn. 2 vols. Number of cont. annot.'s early in vol. 1, E6, F5 & R2 in vol. 1 cancels. Cont. hf. cf. gt. From collection of Massachusetts Horticultural Society, stps. on plts. (SPB. Oct.1; 143) $2,500
– – Anr. Copy. Slightly browned thro.-out & soiled, some ll. stained, some old MS. notes. Cont. cf., gt. spine, defect. (H. Dec.9/10; 380) DM 6,200

See–BRITISH MUSEUM

LINNIG, J.
– Historisch Album der Stad Antwerpen. Ed.:– F.H. Mertens. Antw., 1868. 4to. 113 pp. (of 126), 55 plts. (of 60). Lacks title, some end-pp. & etchgs. 56 to 60. Bdg. worn. (LM. Mar.21; 18) *B.Frs.* 14,000

LINSCHOTEN, Jan Huygen van
– Discours of Voyages into ye Easte & West Indies. [1598]. Fo. 1 folding engraved map only, reprd., lacks engraved general title, title to book 2 preserved, top section excised with loss. Mod. leatherette. W.a.f. [STC 15691] (CSK. Sep.5; 172) £140
– – Anr. Copy. 4 pts. in 1 vol. 8 (of 12) folding maps, 3rd. pt. lacks extra title, lower pt. of C2 torn away. Disbnd. (SG. Oct.30; 222) $1,200
– – Anr. Copy. Some marginal staining & browning. Later cf., covers detchd. W.a.f. [NSTC 15691; Sabin 41374] (SPB. May 5; 325) $600

See–BRY, Theodore de & others

LINTON, William James
– Masters of Wood Engraving. 1889. (600) numbered, sigd., subscribers Edn. Fo. On india paper. Orig. cl. (TA. Sep.18; 104) £180
– – Anr. Copy. (500) numbered. Liby. stps. thro.-out. Cont. mor.-bkd. cl., slightly soiled. (SH. Oct.9; 82) *Tate Gallery.* £70

LIPPE, E. Zur
– Musaren-Buch. Berlin, 1863. Cont. hf. leath. (HK. May 12-14; 1196) DM 750

LIPSCOMB, George
– The History & Antiquities of the County of Buckingham. 1831-47. 4 vols. 4to. Some ll. spotted. Mod. mor. (SH. Mar.5; 86) *Crowe.* £360
– – Anr. Copy. L.P., 8 vols. Some plts. foxed. Orig. ptd. bds., unopened, unc. (C. Feb.25; 43) *Maggs.* £130
– – Anr. Edn. L., 1847. 1st. Edn. on L.P. 4 vols. Fo. Maps & lithos., extra-ill. with 350 copperplts. etc. Three-qtr. mor., raised bands. (SG. Oct.9; 149) $1,700

LIPSIUS, Justus
– Opera Omnia. Antw., 1614. 11 vols. Sm. 4to. Old marb. cf., 4 spine raised bands. (LM. Jun.13; 161) *B.Frs.* 45,000
– – Anr. Edn. Wesel, 1675. 4 vols. Liby. stps. on end-papers. Cont. cf., gt. spines, gt. lines, liby tickets. (VG. Oct.13; 99) *Fls.* 1,300
– Poliorceticon, sive de Machinis, Tormentis, Telis, Libri quinque. Antw., 1596. 1st. Edn. 4to. Minor worming in blank margin of title & 1st. few ll. Cont. cf. (C. Apr.1; 146) £120
– Saturnalium Sermonum Libri Duo.–De Cruce Libri tres ab Sacram Profamque Historiam Utiles. Antw., 1598; 1599. 4th. Edn. 2 vols. in 1. Fo. 4 unnumbered pp. Hf. vell. (CR. Mar.19; 261) *Lire* 200,000

LIRON d'Airoles, Jules de
– Album de la Civelière. Brussels, 1855. (20). Slim 4to. Some discolouration. Later hf. cl. (TA. Jun.18; 173) £575

LISCOW, Christian Ludwig
[–] Sammlung Satyrischer und Ernsthafter Schriften. Frankfurt & Leipzig. 1739. 2nd. printing of 1st. Edn. Lacks copper to (2) 'Vitrea Fracta' (only publd. in 1st. printing?). Cont. bds. (R. Oct.14-18; 981) DM 520

L'ISLE, Guillaume de
– Atlas Nouveau. Amst., 1730. Fo., (550mm. × 340mm.). Maps hand-cold. in outl., armorial & other title cartouches, etc., apparently wanting a table of Departments of France & a map of the same, but with an additional map of Africa not called for by Koeman, last 3 maps detchd., & slightly worn, tears in some folds of maps of Brabant & Poland & the plan, titles & some prelims. detchd., short title of each map written on verso of top margin. Cont. hf. cf., marb. bds., lacks spine, covers detchd., worn. W.a.f. (S. Nov.3; 18) *Hamilton.* £1,500

LISLE, Maj. James George Semple
– The Life. 1799. 1st. Edn. Cont. bds., unc. (S. Jan.26; 15) *Bickersteth.* £55

LISLE, Joe
– Play Upon Words. Ca. 1830-40. Ob. 8vo. Lacks title. Cont. hf. mor. (TA. May 21; 523) £130

LISSITSKY, El.
– Russland. Die Rekonstruktion der Architektur in der Sowjetunion. Vienna, 1930. 4to. Orig. pict. wraps., torn, sm. faults, paper pasted on spine. (HK. Nov.18-21; 2779) DM 1,000
– – Anr. Copy. Orig. linen, lacks orig. wraps. (H. Dec.9/10; 2191) DM 440

LISSITZKY, El. & Arp, Hans
– Die Kunstismen.–Les Ismes de l'Art.–The Ismes of Art. Zürich, 1925. Orig. Edn. 3 works in 1 vol. 4to. Stp. on title verso. Orig. bds. (HK. Nov.18-21; 2780) DM 1,300

LISTER, Joseph, Baron
– The Collected Papers. Oxford, 1909. 1st. Edn. 2 vols. 4to. Orig. cl. From liby of Dr. E. Ashworth Underwood. (S. Feb.23; 248) *Canale.* £110
– – Anr. Copy. (S. Jun.16; 519) *Engle.* £70

LISTER, Dr. Martin
– Conchyliorum Bivalvium ... 1696. 1st. Edn. 2 pts. in 1 vol. 4to. Slight dampstaining in 1st. section, blank inner margin of 1st. ll. partly frayed & detchd. from bdg. 19th. C. hf. mor. Pres. Copy to 'Sr. John Frankland' with inscr. on blank lf. facing title & Frankland's note on earlier lf. 'Ex dono authoris 3 June' (the year torn off), from Chetham's Liby., Manchester. [Wing L2516] (C. Nov.27; 262) *Wheldon & Wesley.* £200
– A Journey to Paris ... 1698. 1699. 1st. Edn. Advt., lacks 1st. lf. (blank?), slight damp-staining. Cont. cf., rebkd., worn. (S. Oct.1; 584) £50

LITERARY EXAMINER, & WESTERN MONTHLY REVIEW, The
Ed.:– E. Burke Fisher. Pittsb., May-Dec. 1839. 1st. printing. Vol. I (all publd.?). 4to. Some foxing. Orig. blind cl. (PNY. Mar.26; 192) $140

LITERARY GARLAND, The
Montreal, Dec., 1838 to Dec. 1846. Vol. I, nos. 1-12, vol. III, nos. 1-12, & vol. IV (new series), nos. 1-12. Leath. & hf. leath., vol. IV disbnd. Inscr. by publisher in vol. 1 to Mrs. Moodie, bkplt. of J.W. Dunbar Moodie in vols. 1 & 3, vol. 4 with sig. of Catherine Mary Moodie. (CB. Sep.24; 239) *Can.* $.140

LITERARY & HISTORICAL SOCIETY OF QUEBEC
– Transactions, Sessions of 1867-8 & 1868-9. Quebec, 1869. New Series, pt. 6. Mor. gt., upr. cover gt.-lettered 'Presented to H.R.H. Prince Arthur by the Province of Quebec'. (SG. Mar.5; 111) $120

LITHGOW, William
– 19 Jaarige Lant-Reyse, uyt Schotlant nae de Vermaerde Deelen des Werelts Europa, Asia en Africa. Amst., 1653. 2 pts. in 1 vol. 4to. Most fore-margins slight wormed with very slight damage to text, some staining. Early 19th. C. bds., slightly worn. (S. Jul.27; 51) *Van Der Wijk.* £140
– The Totall Discourse of the Rare Adventures & Painefull Peregrinations of Long Nineteen Yeares Travayles. 1632. 4to. Cont. reversed cf., initials TW in gt. on centre of covers, new gt. fillets on covers, rebkd. Owner's inscr. of Thomas Wilbraham, bkplt. of Boies Penrose, lately in the collection of Eric Sexton. [STC 15713] (C. Apr.15; 37) *Dawson.* £220
– – Anr. Edn. 1640. Sm. 4to. Slight worming from 2E5 to end cutting headlines, sm. repair to 2H8, flaw in 2K4, sm. marginal tear in frontis., title slightly soiled with faint marginal inscr., occasional spotting. Mod. hf. cf. [NSTC 15714] (S. Jun.23; 381) *Armstrong.* £160

LITTA, Conte Pompeo
– Celebri Famiglie Italiane. Milan, 1819. 8 vols. Lge. fo. Some plts. hand-cold. & heightened with gold. Mor. gt. by J. Wright. (SBA. Jul.23; 550) *Watson.* £2,400
– – Anr. Edn. Milan, 1844. 9 vols. only (of 11). Fo. Hf. cf., gt. spines, unc. W.a.f. (SI. Dec.3; 335) *Lire* 3,000,000

LITTLE, Janet
– Poetical Works. 1792. Cl. gt. (CE. Nov.20; 85) £200

LITTLE FOLKS; a Magazine for the Young
Ill.:– Arthur Rackham & others. L., 1901-07. 7 vols. 4to. 1904, Pt. 2 lacks pp. 401-416. Various bdgs., 1907 vol. orig. gt. & cold. pict. publisher's cl. Raymond M. Sutton Jr. copy. (SG. May 7; 182) $275

LITTLE GOODY TWO-SHOES; otherwise called Mrs. Margery Two-Shoes
Ill.:– Thomas Bewick. York, 1803. 18mo. Slight browning. Mod. wraps. (SBA. Oct.22; 610) *Temperley.* £95

LITTLE RED RIDING HOOD
ca. 1865. Lacks upr. end-lf. Orig. cl.-bkd. pict. bds., worn. Moving Picture Book. (SH. Dec.12; 584) *Demetzy.* £60

LITTLE, Thomas (Pseud.)
See–MOORE, Thomas, Poet 'Thomas Little'

LITTLETON, A.
[-] Tragi-Comoedia Oxoniensis. 1603. Sm. 4to. Later hf. mor. [Wing L2574] (SH. Jul.16; 205) *Quaritch.* £65

LITURGIA Sacra seu Ritus Ministerii in Ecclesia Peregrinorum Profugorum Propter Evangelium Christi Argentinae
[Netherlands?], 1551. Cont. Engl. cf., panel. with blind & gt. fillets, gt. fleurons at corners, Royal arms surmounted by crown & flanked by initials ER in gt. at centre of covers, rebkd., in hf. mor. box. Bkplts. of John Temple & J.R. Abbey, lately in the collection of Eric Sexton. [STC 16566] (C. Apr.15; 115) *Quaritch.* £1,100

LITURGY & Ritual
– Theion kai Hieron Euangelion . . . Euangelistarion. [Greek]. [Venice], [1754]. 2 Pts. in 1 vol. Fo. Lacks general title. Cont. silver on velvet bdg., upr. cover with gt. embossed cornerpieces, centrepiece on both covers, 3 (of 5) bosses, lacks 1 clasp, worn. W.a.f. (S. Nov.25; 382) *Schwing.* £450

LIVING TALMUD (The)
Ltd. Edns. Cl., 1960. Ltd. Edn. Orig. bdg., box. (SPB. Jul.28; 274) $110

LIVINGSTON, John
– Portraits of Eminent Americans. N.Y., 1853-54. 4 vols. Gt.-decor. cl. (SG. Jun.11; 248) $100

LIVINGSTON, William
[-] America: or a Poem on the Settlement of the British Colonies, addressed to the Friends of Freedom, & their Country. By a Gentleman Educated at Yale-College. New-Haven, ca. 1770? 1st. Edn. 4to. Several tears, without serious loss of text. Stapled. (SG. Mar.5; 274) $220

LIVINGSTONE, David
– Missionary Travels & Researches in South Africa. 1857. 1st. Edn. Orig. cl., lr. jnt. torn. Pres. copy inscr. to Sir George Grey. (CSK. Apr.3; 87) £190
– – Anr. Copy. Orig. cl. gt. Pres. copy. (P. Oct.2; 94) *Sawyer.* £150

LIVIUS, Titus
– Dat is de Roemsche Historie . . . Ill.:– after Funck. Antw., 1541. 1st. Edn. in Dutch. Fo. Old cf., copper clasps, worn. (LM. Nov.8; 97b) B.Frs. 110,000
– Les Décades. Trans.:– Blaise de Vigenere (1st.). Jean Hamelin de Sarlac (3rd.), Antoine de la Faye (others). Paris, 1583. Lge. fo. Cont. vell., some old staining. (LM. Jun.13; 162) B.Frs. 8,000
– Duobus Libris Auctus cum L. Flori Epitome. Et Annotatis in Libros VII. Belli Maced. Mainz, Nov. 1518 [-19]. 1st. Edn. in Latin. Fo. Prefs. by Ulrich v. Hutten & Erasmus, 2 repeated woodcut title borders, 1 further woodcut border & many woodcut initials slightly browned & soiled, slight worming at end, last index ll. slightly stained. 17th. C. hf. leath., spine defect. (R. Oct.14-18; 98) DM 2,100
– Ex XIII Decadibus Prima, Tertia, Quarta. Venice, 1520-21. 2nd. Aldine Edn. 4 pts. in 1 vol. Fo. Stained at front & back. 18th. C. red mor. gt., spine gt., worn. (CNY. May 22; 145) $150
– Histoire Romaine . . . Trans.:– M. Guerin. Paris, 1741. 10 vols. 12mo. Cont. cf., centre arms, decor. spine raised bands with arms. (HD. Apr.24; 77) Frs. 1,950
– – Anr. Edn. 1810. 15 vols. Cf., fillet, blind border & panel, by Vogel. (HD. Oct.10; 290) Frs. 2,600
– Historiarum ab Urbe Condita. Ed.:– C. Sigonius. Venice, 1555. 1st. Sigonius Edn. 2 pts. in 1 vol. Fo. Some ll. marginally stained, sigs. on 1st. title, index bnd. in near beginning. 18th. C. panel. cf., some wear. (S. Feb.10; 251) *Chamberlain.* £90
– – Anr. Copy. A few marginal inscrs., several ll. browned, a few stained in margins. 18th. C. red mor., gt., upr. cover detchd., worn, from the Mead Liby. (S. Jan.27; 379) *Fentimore.* £65
– Historiarum Libri ex Recensione I.F. Gronovii. Leiden, 1644. 3 vols. 12mo. Engraved title vol. 1 (dtd. 1644) out & mntd., device on titles of other vol., vol. 1 lacks 11 prelims., without vol. of Gronovius' notes. Str.-grd. mor., gt., by Simier, Lord Stuart de Rothesay arms. (SM. Oct.8; 2406) Frs. 1,000
– Historicorum Romanorum. Frankfurt, 1588. 4 pts. in 3 vols. 16mo. Some worming affecting text. Cont. Fr. red mor. by Clovis Eve for Pietro Duodo, gt., spines & covers elab. decor., Duodo's arms on

upr. & motto on lr. covers. Bkplt. of George Gostling, bkplt. of Burnham Abbey, Bucks., (James Toovey). (S. Nov.24; 192) *Breslauer.* £4,500
– Romanae Historiae Principis, Libri Omnes. Frankfurt-a.-M, 1578. Fo. Slight browning, a few short tears & sm. holes, general title mntd., lacks last 5 ll. 18th. C. tree cf. (S. Apr.6; 191) *Hamilton.* £110
– Romane Historie. Trans.:– Philemon Holland. 1600. 1st. [Engl.] Edn. Fo. Sig. on title-margin, a few marginal inscrs. in text. Cont. mott. cf., spine gt. Bkplt. of Algernon Capell, Earl of Essex. [NSTC 16613] (S. May 5; 290) *Thorp.* £200
– – Anr. Copy. Lacks 1st. & final blanks, a little dampstaining, a few sm. holes & short tears slightly affecting text. Cont. cf., worn, reprd., front free end-paper with inscr. (S. Sep.29; 49) *Fletcher.* £150
– – Anr. Copy. Lacks first & last blanks, both loose fly-ll. torn. 18th. C. cf., rebkd. (S. Nov.25; 457) *Fletcher.* £90

LIVRE (Le) Revue Mensuelle: Bibliographie Ancienne
Paris, 1880-89. 10 vols. 4to. Cont. hf. mor., unc. (SI. Dec.3; 336) Lire 300,000

LIVRE (Le) & L'IMAGE
Paris, 1893-94. 3 vols. 4to. Cont. hf. mor., orig. wraps. bnd. in, partly unc. (SI. Dec.3; 338) Lire 350,000

LIVRE Curieux contenant la Naifue Representation des Habits des Femmes des diverses Parties du Monde
Paris, [1662]. Sm. 4to. Engraved title & 27 engraved plts. (of 28), title reprd., 3 plts. soiled, slight foxing. Vell. (BS. Jun.11; 364) £100

LIVRE des Sonnets (Le)
Paris, 1874. Bordeaux mor., gt. fillet border, blind tools, decor. spine, inner dentelle, by Auguste Petit. (HD. Jun.10; 178) Frs. 1,400

LIVRE MAGIQUE (Le), tombé de la Lune 1500 Ans avant la Création du Monde et Retrouvé en 1863
Metz, [1863]. All but 1 series of ills. cold. by hand. Orig. pict. wraps., rebkd., worn. (SH. Mar.19; 96) *Till.* £300

LIVSHITS, Benedikt
– Vol'che Solntse [Wolf's Sun]. Ill.:– Ekster. & Burlyuk. Moscow, 1914. Advt. ll. Mod. cl.-bkd. bds., orig. wraps. preserved. (SH. Feb.6; 482) *Quaritch.* £230

LIZARS, Daniel
– The Edinburgh Geographical & Historical Atlas. Edinb., [1831?]. Fo. 58 cold. engraved maps only (of 59), no title or text. Mod. maroon hf. mor. As an atlas, w.a.f. (C. Jul.15; 65) *Wilson.* £350
See–LIZARS, William Home & Daniel

LIZARS, John
– A System of Anatomical Plates of the Human Body Accompanied with Descriptions. Edinb., 1822-26. 12 pts. in 3 vols. & atlas with 101 litho. plts. 8vo. & fo. Text red hf. mor., atlas hf. cf. (S. Jun.16; 521) *Preidel.* £170
– – Anr. Edn. Edinb., [1823-27]. Fo. No text, 15 plts. on brain cold. Hf. cf. (S. Dec.2; 536) *Quaritch.* £200
– – Anr. Edn. Ca. 1825. Fo. Lacks engraved & ptd. title-pp., some minor repairs to margins. Cont. hf. mor., worn. (TA. Sep.18; 115) £110
– – Anr. Edn. Edinb., ca. 1840. Fo. Margins soiled. Orig. cl., unc., backstrip defect. (TA. Jun.18; 457) £75
– – Anr. Edn. Edinb., ca. 1850. Fo. Some plts. with cont. annots., some browning & soiling. Hf. cf., lacks spine, covers detchd. From liby of Dr. E. Ashworth Underwood. (S. Feb.23; 249) *Mistrali.* £200
– – Anr. Edn. Edinb., n.d. Fo. 101 hand-cold. plts. only (of 103). Later hf. cf., rebkd. (CSK. Aug.22; 22) £160

LIZARS, Kathleen MacFarlane
– The Valley of the Humber. Toronto, 1913. Orig. cl., spotted on fore-edge. (CB. Feb.18; 33) Can. $100

LIZARS, William Home & Daniel
– General Atlas. Edinb., ca. 1850. Fo. Occasional staining, 3 maps torn. Cont. hf. mor. (CSK. Oct.10; 199) £160
– New Edinburgh General Atlas. Edinb., ca. 1850. Lge. fo. Folding maps worn or torn in some folds,

others frayed. Orig. hf. cf. & bds., covers detchd., worn. W.a.f. (S. Mar.31; 246) *Quaritch.* £350

LLOYD, Edward
– Butterflies & Moths.-British Birds.-Game Birds. -Monkeys.-Cats., etc.-Mammals/Marsupials. 1896/97. 5 vols.; 4 vols.; 2 vols.; 2 vols., in 16 vols. Orig. cl. gt. (TA. Sep.18; 85) £140
– – Anr. Copy. Orig. cl., spines slightly worn. (TA. Mar.19; 352) £100
– Natural History. Ed.:– R. Bowdler Sharpe. 1896-97. 16 vols. Hf. leath. (S. Jun.1; 5) *Erlini.* £100
– – Anr. Copy. Orig. cl. (TA. Apr.16; 406) £90
– – Anr. Edn. 1896-98. 16 vols. Qtr. mor. gt. (P. Nov.13; 256) *Erlini.* £160
– – Anr. Copy. Orig. cl. gt., some stained. (SBA. Mar.4; 154) *L'Acquaforte.* £120
– – Anr. Copy. Orig. cl., 1 slightly torn. (SBA. Jul.14; 240) *Hyde Park Bookshops.* £85

LLOYD, G.
– Sketches of Ancient Egyptian Sculpture & Painting [Album]. Thebes, 1843. Fo. Orig. hf. roan, worn. Title sigd. by artist., & with pencil decors. (SH. Apr.9; 158a) *Nolan.* £400

LLOYD, George Thomas
– Thirty-three Years in Tasmania & Victoria. L., 1862. Repairs to clean tears in lge. folding map. Unc., orig. cl., (possibly varnished), lr. bd. slightly soiled. (KH. Nov.18; 382) Aus. $120

LLOYD, Gen. Henri
– Introduction à l'Histoire de la Guerre en Allemagne. L., 1784. 1st. Edn., L.P. Lge. 4to. Three-qtr. mor., unc. (SG. Oct.30; 223) $130

LLOYD, James T.
– Lloyd's Steamboat Directory, & Disasters on the Western Waters . . . Cinc., 1856. 1st. Edn., 1st. Iss. Newspaper clipping tipped-in on verso of title, advts., lightly foxed thro.-out. Orig. blind-stpd. cl., upr. cover & spine gt., crudely reinforced at jnts. From liby. of William E. Wilson. (SPB. Apr.29; 178) $275

LLOYD, Lewis
– Game Birds & Wild Fowl of Sweden & Norway. L., 1867. 1st. Edn. Cl. gt., spine reprd. (P. Nov.13; 209) *Falk.* £110
– – Anr. Copy. Considerable foxing. Later hf. mor. (SG. Dec.11; 351) $150

LLOYD, Lodowick
– The Stratagems of Jerusalem. L., 1602. 4to. Bnd. in at end is Thomas Newton's 'Notable History of the Saracens', 1st. Edn., L., 1575, lacking title & 1st. 4 ll. Old cf., rebkd. (SG. Sep.25; 198) $210

LLOYD, Nathaniel
– A History of English Brickwork . . . with an introduction by Sir Edwin L. Lutyens. 1925. 4to. Occasional spotting. Orig. cl., warped, d.-w. torn. (CSK. Sep.5; 243) £60

LLOYD'S Register of British & Foreign Shipping
1854. Covering 1st. Jul. 1854 to 30th Jun. 1855, subscriber copy. Mor. gt., 'William Henry Thompson' blocked on upr. cover. (LC. Oct.2; 212) £55

LLWYD, Humphrey
– The Breviary of Britayne, as this most noble & renowned (sic) Lland was of auncient times divided into three kingdomes . . . Trans.:– Thomas Twyne. L., 1573. 1st. Edn. in Engl. Title stained from glue of bkplt. on verso. Cont. limp vell., worn, cont. notes, drawings & copy of legal contract on end-papers & owner's note on cover. [STC 16636] (S. Apr.1; 221) *Hewitt.* £130

LLYFR Y PREGETH-WR
Gregy. Pr., 1927. Ltd. Edn. Orig. cl., slight wear. (P. Nov.13; 317) *Saunders.* £65
– – Anr. Copy. Cl. soiled. (P. Oct.2; 13) *Freeman.* £50

LOBECK, Tobias
See–LOTTER, Tobias Conrad & Lobeck, Tobias

LOBEL, Matthias de
[-] Icones Stirpium seu Plantarum . . . Antw., 1591. Ob. 4to. Minor dampstain affecting 1st. 50 pp., sm. liby. stp. on title, last lf., & some other ll. Old cf., worn, rebkd. From Chetham's Liby., Manchester. (C. Nov.27; 263) *Kistner.* £800
– – Anr. Copy. Sm. ob. 4to. Cont. vell. (HD. Jun.30; 35) Frs. 10,900
See–PENA, Petrus & Lobel, Matthias de

LOBINEAU, Gui Alexis
- Histoire de Bretagne ... Ill.:– Chaperon & Pitan. Paris, 1707. 2 vols. Fo. 1 port. remntd. Cont. pebbled cf., spines decor. with raised bands. (HD. Jun.24; 87) Frs. 2,900
- La Vie des Saints de Bretagne. Ed.:– Abbé Tresvaux. Paris, 1836-38. New Edn. 5 vols. Lge. 8vo. Glazed cf., seal of College de l'Immaculée Conception de Paris on upr. covers, decor. spines. (HD. Jun.29; 158) Frs. 1,500

LOBO, Jerome
- A Voyage to Abyssinia. Trans.:– Dr. Samuel Johnson. L., 1735. Cont. cf., brkn. (SG. May 14; 132) $325

LOBSTEIN, Jean Frederic
- De Nervi Sympathetici Human fabrica ... Paris, 1823. 4to. Some plts. stained. Orig. bds. soiled. (P. Nov.13; 23) Bickerstowe. £65
- - Anr. Copy. Lacks hf.-title. New cl. (S. Jun.16; 522) Gurney. £60

LOCHER, J.G.
See–KEPLER, J.–SCHEINER, C. & Locher, J.G. –SCHEINER, C.–PHILLIPPI, H.–MARTILINGEN, J.

LOCHER, Jacobus
- Spectaculum ... more tragico effigiatum ... Eiusdem iudiciũ Paridis. [Augsburg], [1502?]. 4to. Cont. marginalia & underlining, slightly soiled, marginal tear. 19th. C. hf. cl. (S. Jan.27; 339) Quaritch. £450

LOCHER, Jacobus–REMUS Favinus–UGUITON –WIMPHELING, Jacobus–VALLIBUS, Hieronymus de
- Panegyricus ad Maximilianum; Epitoma Rhetorices Graphicum.–De Ponderum Mensurarumque Vocabulis Carmen.–Tractatulus Intricationes Numeralium Vocabulorium.–Egantiarum Medulla Oratoriaque Praecepta; Isidonius Germanicus de Erudienda Iuventute. –Jesuida. Strassburg; [Freiburg im Breisgau]; [Leipzig]; [Leipzig?]; [Strassburg]; [Strassburg]; [Ingolstadt], Johann Gruninger; [Friedrich Riederer]; [Martin Landsberg]; [Martin Landsberg]; [Johann Gruninger]; [Johann Gruninger]; [Georg Wirffel & Marx Ayrer], 1497; [after Feb.24, 1496]; [1494]; ca. 1495; ca. 1500; [after Aug.22, 1497]; ca. 1497. 7 works in 1 vol. 4to. Spaces for initial capitals in 5th. work, woodcut calligraphic initial capitals in 2nd. work, several ll. with light marginal dampstains. Cont. German blind-stpd. cf. over wood bds., covers with narrow central panel & an outer frame filled with floral roll, spine compartments with repeated fleur-de-lys tools, lightly worn, recased, end-papers renewed. From the collection of Eric Sexton. (CNY. Apr.8; 171) $11,000

LOCHER, N.
See–DINKEL, M. & Locher, N.

LOCK, Matthew & Copland, Henry
- A New Book of Ornaments ... 1752. 1st. Edn. Fo. Engraved title & 11 plts. on thick paper, all torn & reprd. Mod. hf. mor., unc. (S. Mar.17; 429) Quaritch. £260
- - Anr. Edn. 1768. 2nd. Edn. Fo. Early 20th. C. red hf. mor., old wraps. preserved. (S. Mar.17; 430) Marlborough Rare Books. £350
- A New Book of Pier-Frame's, Oval's ... 1769. Sm. fo. Title stained. Unbnd. in folding cl. box. (S. Mar.17; 425) Quaritch. £300
- A New Drawing Book of Ornaments. Ca. 1768. 4to. Cont. hf. cf. (S. Mar.17; 426) Quaritch. £300
- The Principles of Ornament. [1770]. Disbnd. & loose in folding cl. box. (S. Mar.17; 427) Quaritch. £260
- Six Sconces. 1768. 2nd. Edn. 4to. Early 20th. C. qtr. cf. (S. Mar.17; 428) Quaritch. £300

LOCKE, John, Philosopher
[–] A Common-Place Book to the Holy Bible. 1697. 1st. Edn. 4to. Sm. paper fault in 1 lf., a few minor stains. Cont. cf., rebkd. & recornered. [Wing L2737] (C. Apr.1; 222) Jameson. £60
- An Essay Concerning Humane Understanding. 1694. 2nd. Edn. Fo. Recent hf. mor. [Wing L2737] (TA. Feb.19; 355) £120
- - Anr. Copy. 4 Books. Port. & title slightly soiled. Cont. cf., fly-ll. browned. (VG. Nov.18; 1262) Fls. 550
- - Anr. Edn. Ill.:– Vanderbanck after Sylvester Brounower (port.). 1700. 4th. Edn. Fo. Lacks last lf. (presumably blank), very sm. hole in T2, Bb3

& Dd4, a few inkstains on pp. 220-21. Panel. cf., reprd. & rebkd. [Wing L2742] (S. Jun.16; 523) Thoemmes. £60
- Mr. Locke's Reply to the ... Bishop of Worcester's Answer to his Letter ... relating to Mr Locke's Essay on Humane Understanding. 1697. 1st. Edn. Advts. Cont. panel. cf., rebkd. [Wing L2753] (SBA. Jul.23; 332) Frost. £65
[–] The Reasonableness of Christianity, as delivered in the Scriptures. 1695. 1st. Edn. N1 torn, short tear in B4, cont. MS. annots. Cf., spine worn at head. [Wing L2751] (S. Jan.26; 63) Pythagoras. £90
- Two Treatises of Government. 1690. 1st. Edn. Some browning. Cont. cf., spine worn. [Wing L2766] (S. Apr.7; 388) Maggs. £3,200
- Works. 1714. 3 vols. Fo. Cont. cf, (P. Dec.11; 357) Jarndyce. £60
- - Anr. Edn. Ill.:– Vertue. L., 1722. 1st. 2 vols. 2nd. Edn. 3 vols. Fo. Old panel. cf., all covers detchd. (SG. Sep.25; 199) $100
- Works.-An Essay concerning Humane Understanding in Four Books. 1751; 1700. 5th. Edn.; 4th. Edn. 3 vols.; 1 vols. Cf. (HSS. Apr.24; 389) £110
- The Works. Books. 1823. 10 vols. Cont. cf. (SH. May 28; 70) Boyle. £85

LOCKER, Edward Hawke
- Views in Spain. Ill.:– W. Westall, C. Hullmandel & others. 1824. Cont. hf. mor. (C. Mar.18; 177) Duran. £320

LOCKER, Frederick
- Poems. Priv Ptd., 1868. (20) L.P. Extra-ill., with 4 ports of Locker, an imp. of the etching (with Cruikshank's sig. mntd. on, & anr. sig. of Cruikshank mntd. on frontis.), & a pamphlet collection of press reviews. Red mor. gt., double fillet panel, spine with raised bands, cold. end-papers. Pres. Copy, to Francis Grant; with A.L.s (initials) to Cruikshank & 25 line note by Locker; ticket & sig. of Holbrook Jackson. (LC. Feb.12; 35) £100

LOCKETT, R.C.
- Catalogue of the Celebrated Collection of Coins. Glendining, 1955-61. 13 vols. 4to. Orig. wraps. (SH. Mar.6; 390) Spink. £230

LOCKHART, John
See–SCOTT, Sir Walter–LOCKHART, John

LOCKHART, Robert Bruce
- My Rod, My Comfort. Ill.:– J. Caastra. Dropmore Pr., 1949. (550) numbered, sigd. 4to. Orig. mor. gt. by Evans, Croydon, partly untrimmed, s.-c. (TA. May 21; 379) £90

LOCKMAN, John
- Travels of the Jesuits into Various parts of the World. 1743. 1st. Edn. 2 vols. Maps & plts., 1 torn in folds, 1 slightly defect., slight spotting. Mod. mor.-bkd. bds. [Sabin 40708] (S. Nov.4; 466) Gibbons. £80
- - Anr. Copy. Sm. liby. stp. on titles Disbnd. (SG. Oct.30; 224) $190
- - Anr. Copy. Lacks prelim. essay. Mod. mor. gt. (SG. Feb.26; 212) $110
- - Anr. Edn. L., 1762. 2nd. Edn. 2 vols. Old cf., early rebkd. (SG. Feb.26; 213) $275
See–MENASSEH, David–LOCHMAN–BENJAMIN, of Tudela

LOCKWOOD, Anthony
- A Brief Description of Nova Scotia. 1818. 4to. Some stains to text. Hf. cf., defect. (P. Nov.13; 336) Maggs. £190

LOCKWOOD, Luke Vincent
- Colonial Furniture in America. N.Y., 1913. New Edn. 2 vols. 4to. Gt.-decor. buckram. (SG. Dec.4; 100) $120
- The Pendleton Collection. Rhode Island, 1904. (150) on Japan vell. Fo. Crushed lev., gt. design on covers & spine, gt. dentelles enclosing lev. doubls., brocaded satin end-ll., by Adams. (SG. Dec.4; 226) $300

LOCKWOOD, Lt. Col. W.
- Aeronautical Prints & Drawings. 1924. 4to. Cold. plts. tipped in, margins slightly soiled. Orig. cl. gt., recased. (TA. Mar.19; 112) £60

LOCOMOTIVE Railway Carriage & Wagon Review (formerly Moore's Monthly Magazine)
1896-1959. Vols. 1-65 in 58. 6 vols: cont. hf. roan, rest orig. cl. (SH. Oct.9; 271) Humm. £310

LODDIGES, Conrad & Sons
- The Botanical Cabinet. 1817. Vol. 1 only. 4to. 60 hand-cold. plts. (lacks some?). Cont. mor. gt. (SKC. Dec.4; 1567) £150
- - Anr. Edn. 1817-24. Vols. 1-9. Engraved titles & plts. (898 of 900). Recent hf. mor., gt. decor. spines. (TA. Jun.18; 73) £400
- - Anr. Edn. L., 1817-33. 20 vols. 12mo. Red str.-grd. hf. mor., some vols. with spine renewed, the others worn, unc. (SM. Feb.11; 34) Frs. 13,000
- - Anr. Edn. 1818-28. Vols. 1-15 (of 20). Cont. str.-grd. cf., gt. spines. W.a.f. as a periodical. (S. Dec.3; 1031) Wagner. £600
- - Anr. Edn. Ill.:– G. Cooke. L., 1821-25. Vols. 6, 7 & 11. Linen. (HK. Nov.18-21; 626) DM 1,600

LODER, Justus Christian
- Anatomische Tafeln. Weimar, 1794-1803. 1st. Edn. 2 text & 2 plt. vols. Fo. Soiled. Cont. bds. (R. Oct.14-18; 359) DM 2,200

LODGE, Edmund
- Portraits of Illustrious Personages of the Court of Henry VIII. Ill.:– Holbein. L., 1828. Fo. Hf. mor., spine torn. (P. Jun.11; 101) A. Wilson. £170
- Portraits of Illustrious Personages of Great Britain. 1821-34. L.P. 4 vols. Fo. Engraved proof plts. on india paper. 19th. C. mor. gt. Bkplt. of Sir Charles Cockerell. (S. Nov.24; 193) Foster. £200
- - Anr. Edn. L., 1829-35. 1st. Quarto Edn. 1st. Quarto Edn. 13 vols., normally seen in 12 vols. 4to. 5 vols. with hf.-titles. Cont. gt. cf., lacks 8 (of 26) mor. spine labels. Sig. of Thomas Richardson, 1836 & armorial bkplt. of F.C. Tottie in each vol. (PNY. Oct.1; 331) $150
- - Anr. Edn. 1835. 12 vols. 4to. Cont. red hf. mor., gt., a few vols. a trifle worn. (S. Dec.9; 486) Mistrali. £70

LODGE, John–COLLINS, Arthur–BURKE, John
- The Peerage of Ireland.–The Peerage of England. –A Genealogical & Heraldic History of the Commoners of Great Britain & Ireland. Dublin; L.; L., 1789; 1741; 1833-38. 2nd. Edn. (2nd. work). 7 vols.; 4 vols.; 4 vols. Hf. cf., rebkd. (1st. work); antique-style spr. cf. (2nd. work); & cont. hf. roan, rebkd. preserving orig. gt. spines. From the collection of Eric Sexton. (C. Apr.16; 301) Rokeby-Johnson. £320

LODI, Giacinto
[–] Amore Prigioniero in Delo. Bologna, [1628]. Fo. Lacks first blank. Cont. limp vell., 1 corner & spine worn. (S. Nov.25; 374) Breslauer. £1,300

LOEFFLER, Dr.
See–KOCH, Robert–KOCH, Robert & others –KOCH, Robert & Wolffhugel, Gustav

LOEFLING, Petrus
- Iter Hispanicum. Ed.:– Charles Linne. Stockholm, 1758. 1st. Edn. Folding plts. browned. 19th. C. hf. mor. From Chetham's Liby., Manchester. [Sabin 41772] (C. Nov.27; 261) Junk. £190

LOFFLER, F.L.
[–] Neues Kochbuch. Stuttgart, 1791. Lacks pp. 127/28, slightly browned & soiled. Cont. hf. leath. (R. Oct.14-18;) DM 430

LOFFLER, Konrad
- Lexikon des Gesamten Bücherwesens. Leipzig, 1935-37. 3 vols. Orig. hf. leath. (R. Oct.14-18; 563) DM 750

LOGAN, James
- The Scottish Gael. 1831. L.P. 2 vols. Plt. in vol. 2 detchd. Orig. cl. (C. May 20; 149) Maggs. £100

LOGAN, James & McIan, Robert Ronald
- The Clans of the Scottish Highlands. 1845. 1st. Edn. 2 vols. Fo. Recased in orig. embossed cl. gt., cl. boxes. (C. Jul.15; 66) Taylor. £700
- - Anr. Edn. 1845-47. [1st. Edn.?]. 2 vols. Fo. Some spotting, some plts. loose. Decor. mor.-bkd. cl., gt., gutta percha bdg. (CE. Jul.9; 243) £700
- - Anr. Copy. A few plts. at end of vol. I slightly defect. at fore-margin. Orig. mor.-bkd. cl., loose. (S. Jun.23; 339) Gilbert's. £600
- - Anr. Copy. Some tears, front free end-paper & a few ll. following brkn. at hinge. Mor. gt., spine chipped. (SPB. May 6; 212) $1,500
- - Anr. Edn. L., 1857. 2 vols. Fo. Qtr. mor. gt. (P. Jun.11; 276) Baer. £520

LOGGAN, David
- Oxonia Illustrata. Oxford, 1675. Fo. Cont. mott. cf., spine gt. [Wing L2838]. (C. Jul.15; 67) *Taylor.* £500

LOHLEIN, G.S.
- Clavier-Schule. Leipzig & Züllichau, 1782-88. Early Edn. 2 vols. in 1. Lge. ob. 8vo. Browned thro.-out. Cont. paper bds., defect. (H. Dec.9/10; 1184) DM 600

LOIR, J.
- Théorie du Tissage des Etaffes do Soie. Lyon & Paris, 1923-29. 3 vols. Fo. Red hf. mor. (SM. Oct.8; 2195) Frs. 2,000

LOISIRS d'un Patriote Lillois (Les). Recueil de Chansons pour la présente Année
[1795]. Sm. 16mo. Cont. silk, spine & covers decor. with embroidery gt. with spangles in gold & other colours. (HD. Apr.10; 149) Frs. 2,100

LOLLIEE
- Catalogue des Livres Précieux. Paris, 1790. Vell. end-lf. inserted at beginning & end, priced thro.-out., supp. at end. Cont. mor. for Renouard, with his name, gt., concentric roll borders, gt., early rebacking, spine gt. with fountain in each compartment, inner gt. dentelles, pink silk liners. On vell. (SM. Oct.7; 1438) Frs. 1,300

LOLLIUS, Antonius
- Oratio habita in Funere Philiberti Cardinalis Matisconensis. [Rome], [Stephan Plannck], [not before 30 Sep. 1484]. 4to. Disbnd. [H. 10178*; BMC IV p. 84; Goff L 277] (C. Apr.1; 56) *Fane.* £90

LOMAZZI or LOMAZZO, Giovanni Paolo
- Rime . . . diviso in sette Libri. Milan, 1587. 4to. 18th. C. cf., ex-liby. gt. stpd. on upr. cover, gt. spine. (SI. Dec.3; 339) Lire 700,000
- Trattato dell 'Arte della Pittura, Scoltura, et Architettura. Milan, 1585. Sm. 4to. Inscrs. on title, several ll. slightly wormed in inner margins, a few sm. stains. 19th. C. hf. vell. bds. (S. Jun.23; 231) *Licini.* £220

LOMBARD, Achbp. Petrus
See-PETRUS LOMBARDUS

LOMONOSOV, Mikhail Vasilievich
- Collected Works [Russian]. St. Petersb., 1784-87. 6 vols. 4to. Cont. red mor., gt. arms on covers, spines gt. (SG. May 14; 133) $2,800

LONDINA ILLUSTRATA
L., 1819; 1825. 1st. Edn. 2 vols. Fo. Liby. bkplt. in each vol. Red hf. mor. (SG. Oct.30; 225) $375

LONDON
- Civitas Londinum Circiter Ano Domini MDLX. 1737. Ob. lge. fo. (380 × 550mm.). Engraved reproduction of woodcut map of L. & Westminster before Great Fire, 8 sheets, some slight discolouration, a few sm. stains. Orig qtr. cf., marb. bds., worn. W.a.f. (S. Jun.29; 18) *Burgess.* £320
- Select Views of London & its Environs. Ill.:- J. Storer & J. Greig. 1804-05. L.P. 2 vols. in 1. 4to. Cont. str-grd. mor., blind-tooled borders, gt. cornerpiece & central gt. panel, spine gt. with raised bands. (C. May 20; 170) *Maggs.* £280

LONDON CABINET MAKERS' Book of Prices, for the Most Improved Extensible Dining Tables
1846. 4to. Mod. cl. (S. Mar.17; 431) *Sims & Reed.* £60

LONDON CABINET MAKERS' Union Book of Prices-The London Cabinet Makers' Book of Prices; for Work not Provided in the Union Book -The London Cabinet Makers' Book of Prices for the Most Improved Extensible Dining Tables
1866; 1863; 1856. 3 works in 1 vol. 4to. Mod. hf. cf. (S. Mar.17; 433) *Sims & Reed.* £110

LONDON CHAIR-MAKERS' & Carvers' Book of Prices
1802. 4to. Slight staining in margins. Cont. cf. (C. Feb.4; 218) *Marlborough.* £170

LONDON & COUNTY BREWER
1759. 7th. Edn. Last advt. lf. Cont. cf., rather worn. (SH. Oct.10; 479) *Abacus.* £65

LONDON COUNTY COUNCIL
- Survey of London. Ed.:- Charles Robert Ashbee & others. 1900-1967. Vols. 1, 6, 8, 29-39, & plan pocket of maps. 4to. Orig. wraps., or buckram in d.-w.'s. (MMB. Oct.8; 110) £56

- - Anr. Edn. 1912-75. Vols. 3-38 & 1 vol. of plans for 29 & 30, together 37 vols. 4to. Vols. 3-11 in orig. wraps., the rest in orig. cl., 7 in d.-w.'s. (SKC. Feb.26; 1454) £370
- - Anr. Edn. 1949-77. Vols. 21, 22, 24, 29-34, 37 & 39; together ll vols. in 12. 4to. Orig. cl., mostly with d.-w.'s. (SH. Nov.6; 124) *Cooper.* £130

LONDON GAZETTE
The Savoy, 1666-68. 40 iss., various. Fo. Unbnd. (SG. Feb.5; 212) $700

LONDON, Jack
- Adventure. N.Y., 1911. 1st. Edn. Slightly browned. Orig. decor. cl. Pres. copy. (SPB. Nov.25; 308) $375
- The Call of the Wild. Ill.:- Philip R. Goodwin & Charles L. Bull. N.Y., 1903. 1st. Edn. With publisher's 4 p. leaflet laid in. Orig. pict. cl., qtr. mor. gt. s.-c., unc. From the Prescott Collection. (CNY. Feb.6; 229) $600

LONDON, Jack (Contrib.)
See-IN MANY WARS

LONDON MAGAZINE
L., 1751-82. 30 vols. only, lacks 1767 & 1778. Cont. hf. leath., worn or brkn. W.a.f. (SG. May 21; 400) $1,000

LONDON-SOCIETY of Antiquaries
- Collection of Various engraved Prints published on behalf of the Society. [1713-85]. Fo. 11 lge. folding double-p. plts. & 16 fo. plts., some with descriptive text bnd. in. Cont. mott. cf. (C. Feb.25; 44) *Burgess.* £400

LONDONDERRY, Lt. Gen. Charles William Vane, Marquis of
- Narrative of the War in Germany & France. L., 1830. 1st. Edn. 4to. Hf. cf. (SG. Feb.26; 215) $120

LONDONIO, Francesco
- Collezione Completa di Tutte le Stampe Originali. Parma, 1837. Ob. fo. 1 plt. with tear in margin. Hf. vell. (SI. Dec.3; 340) Lire 1,500,000

LONG, Edward
[-] The History of Jamaica. L., 1774. 1st. Edn. 3 vols. 4to. 12 engraved plts. only, repair to 1st. map, browning, 1st. gathering severely browned, lacks final blank in vol. II, minor worming, stain. Hf. cf. gt. (SPB. May 5; 326) $125

LONG, John
- Voyages & Travels of an Indian Interpreter & Trader. L., 1791. 1st. Edn. Lge. 4to. Cont. cf.-bkd. marb. bds. Armorial bkplt. of Lord Bradford, Weston Park. (SG. Oct.9; 150) £900
- - Anr. Copy. Folding map reprd. & offset, a few sm. paper losses, later ll. reprd. Red mor. gt. by Zaehnsdorf. From liby. of William E. Wilson. (SPB. Apr.29; 179) $650

LONG, Sydney
[-] The Etched Works of Sydney Long . . . Ed.:- Dorothy Ellsmore Paul. 1928. 4to. Orig. etching tipped in. D.-w. (JL. Jul.20; 674) Aus. $560

LONG, S.H.
- Birds of Handa. Norwich, 1908. Mor. gt. (P. Mar.12; 291) *Langmead.* £70

LONGEPIERRE
[-] Idylles Nouvelles. Paris, 1690. 1st. Edn. 12mo. Cont. red mor., decor. with Golden Fleece repeated on covers & spine, mor. doubls., decor. with dentelle & Golden Fleece. Author's copy, ruled & bnd. with his emblem, bkplts. of Whitney Hoff & Zierer. (HD. Mar. 18; 106) Frs. 5,000
[-] Medée, Tragédie. Paris, [1694]. 1st. Edn. 12mo. Cont. red mor., 3 fillets, decor. spine. (HD. Mar.18; 107) Frs. 1,200

LONGFELLOW, Henry Wadsworth
- Complete Writings. Boston, 1904. De Luxe Edns. (750). 11 vols. Hf. red mor. gt. (SPB. Nov.25; 472) $300
- The Courtship of Miles Standish, & other Poems. Boston, 1858. 1st. Amer. Edn. 12 pp. of advts. (dtd. Oct., 1858) bnd. in. Crushed lev., gt. double fillet borders & spine panels, by Bennett, orig. cl. covers bnd. in. (SG. Mar.19; 242) $110
- Evangeline. Boston, 1847. 1st. Amer. Edn. 12mo. With the misprint 'Lo' for 'Long' in the 1st. line of p. 61. Orig. drab bds., lacks spine, qtr. mor. gt. s.-c., unc. Pres. Copy, to Anne Stephenson, lately in the Prescott Collection. (CNY. Feb.6; 234) $1,300
- - Anr. Copy. With 'Lo', p. 61, line 1, publisher's advts. dtd. Oct.1, 1847, slight browning, foxing.

Bds., mor. solander case. A.L.s. from author tipped in, lf., dtd. from Camb., 6 Dec., 1876, to Rev. Jahu De Witt Miller. (SPB. Nov.25; 209) $400
[-] Outre-Mer. Boston, 1833 & 1834. 1st. Edns. Nos. I (& II) in 2 vols. Upr. margins dampstained thro.-out first hf. of vol. 1. Orig. ptd. marb. wraps. (BAL's wrap. B), lacks spine & front fly-lf. unc., & orig. bds., unc.; cl. folding case. 1st. vol. a pres. copy, however, the recipient's name cut from upr. wrap. & pres. inscr. in author's hand crossed through in ink; lately in the Prescott Collection. (CNY. Feb.6; 231) $600
- - Anr. Edn. L., 1835. 1st. Engl. Edn. 2 vols. 12mo. Slight discoloration. Orig. bds., cl. spines. Nathaniel Hawthorne's copy, with his autograph sig. on inside upr. cover of each vol. (SPB. Nov.24; 20a) $1,000
- Poems on Slavery. Camb., 1842. 1st. Edn. Orig. ptd. glazed wraps., lr. cover slightly discold., mor. solander case. From the Prescott Collection. (CNY. Feb.6; 232) $280
- Poetical Works. Ill.:- G. & E. Dalziel after John Gilbert. L., 1856. 4to. Cont. gt.-tooled mor., spine worn & scuffed, 2 bkplts. Fore-e. pntg.; from the liby. of Zola E. Harvey. (SG. Mar.19; 144) $500
- The Song of Hiawatha. Boston, 1855. 1st. Amer. Edn., 1st. Printing. 12mo. Orig. cl., covers stpd. in gt. & blind, gt. spine, ends of spine & corners slightly worn, cl. d.-w. Sigd. autograph quotation laid in; from the Prescott Collection. (CNY. Feb.6; 235) $450
- - Anr. Edn. Ill.:- Frederic Remington. Boston, 1891. Ltd. L.P. Edn. (250) numbered. Sm. 4to. Orig. gt.-pict. vell., backstrip loose & very worn, covers spotted. (PNY. Mar.26; 274) $140
- Tales of a Wayside Inn. Boston, 1863. 1st. Amer. Edn., 1st. Printing. 12mo. With 22 p. publisher's catalogue (1st. printing) at end, dtd. Nov., 1863. Orig. cl., mor.-bkd. s.-c. Pres. Copy, to Mrs Felto, lately in the Prescott Collection. (CNY. Feb.6; 236) $200
- The Works. Boston & N.Y., 1904. (750) Edn. de Luxe. 11 vols. Crushed red three-qtr. lev. (SG. Sep.4; 313) $260
- - Anr. Edn. Boston, n.d. Standard Liby. Edn. 14 vols. Hf. mor. gt. by Sangorski & Sutcliffe, slightly worn. (SPB. Nov.25; 473) $450

LONGHURST, Peter
- Hibiscus. Melbourne, [1978-79]. (350) numbered, & sigd. 2 vols. Fo. Leath. (KH. Mar.24; 257) Aus. $220

LONGUEVILLE JONES, H.
See-WRIGHT, Thomas & Longueville Jones, H.

LONGUS
- Les Amours Pastorales de Daphnis et Chloe. Trans.:- [Amyot]. Ill.:- Benoit Audran, after Coypel. [Paris], 1718. Lacks 'petits pieds' plt. Cont. mor., single gt. fillet, spine gt. in empty compartments, gt. & painted flowered end-papers. Colonel Stanley copy. (SM. Oct.7; 1821) Frs. 1,000
- - Anr. Edn. Ill.:- Scotin. [Paris], [1731]. 1st. Edn. 12mo. Cont. mor., decor. spines (grotesque), inner dentelle. (HD. Feb.18; 39) Frs. 1,800
[-] - Anr.Edn. Ill.:- B. Audran after A. Coypel & others. [Paris], 1745. 2nd. Edn. Cont. red mor., gt. spine & inner dentelle, outer dentelle fillet, decor. (HK. May 12-14; 1600) DM 1,300
- - Anr. Edn. Ill.:- Coypel (frontis.). L., 1779. Sm. 4to. Cont. red mor., decor. spine, 3 fillets, inside dentelle, worn. (HD. Dec.5; 131) Frs. 1,800
- - Anr. Edn. Versailles, 1784. 18mo. Cont. red str.-grd. mor., decor. spine & roulette covers, inner dentelle, ca. 1820. (HD. Apr.9; 514) Frs. 1,650
- - Anr. Edn. Ill.:- Champollion after Collin. Paris, 1890. Tirage de grand luxe, (50) numbered. Mor., spine & covers with elaborate borders & floral decor. of cold. mor. onlays outlined in gt., those covers enclosing sm. panels painted in oils by A. Giraldon, watered silk doubls., & end-ll., mor.-bkd. folder & s.-c., by Noulhac. (SH. Nov.21; 283) *Givaudon.* £490
- - Anr. Edn. Ill.:- Carlègle. Paris, 1919. (395) numbered. 4to. Mor. (SH. Nov.21; 256) *Klusmann.* £50
- - Anr. Edn. Trans.:- J. Amyot. Ill.:- Gwen Raverat & Graily Hewitt. Ash. Pr., 1933. (290). 4to. Orig. vell.-bkd. bds., unc., s.-c. (SH. Feb.19; 21) *Campus.* £210

LONGUS – Les Amours Pastorales de Daphnis et Chloe. -contd.
– – **Anr. Edn.** Ill.:– Aristide Maillol. [Paris], 1937. Slightly spotted. Unbnd. as iss. in orig. wraps., in orig. s.-c. (CSK. Jan.30; 177) £250
– – **Anr. Copy.** (500) numbered. Red mor., gt. cover, spine, inner & outer dentelle, silk end-ll., leath. wrap., lined bd. s.-c., by W. Ewert. Printer's mark sigd. by artist, 2nd. series of woodcuts, 3 woodcuts in 1st. state. (HK. Nov.18-21; 2789) DM 5,500
– – **Anr. Edn.** Ill.:– Pierre-Yves Trémois. 1948. (125) on vélin du Marais. 4to. Ll. in s.-c. Ill. menu added. (HD. Feb.18; 219) Frs. 2,100
– **Daphnis & Chloe.** Trans.:– George Thornley. Ill.:– Charles Shannon & Charles Ricketts. Vale Pr., 1893. (210). 4to. Cl., unc. (SG. Jan.15; 103) $350
– – **Anr. Edn.** Ill.:– Aristide Maillol. Corvinus Pr., 1937. (250), (10) ptd. for subscribers to Corvinus Pr., sigd. by artist. Orig. vell., Corvinus device on upr. cover, unc., s.-c. (S. Jul.31; 145) Joseph. £360
– – **Anr. Copy.** (250) sigd. by artist. Unc. (C. Feb.4; 196) Duval. £280
– – **Anr. Copy.** (10). Last blank ll. soiled. Vell. Printer's mark sigd. by artist. (H. May 21/22; 1705) DM 2,200

LONICERUS, Adam
– **Kreuterbuch.** Frankfurt, 1582. 8th. Edn. Fo. Soiled. 18th. C. hf. leath., defect. W.a.f. (R. Oct.14-18; 360) DM 2,800
– – **Anr. Edn.** Frankfurt, 1598. Sm. fo. Approx. 15 ll. with faults bkd., MS. marginalia. Cont blind-tooled pig-bkd. wood bds., 2 clasps. W.a.f. (HK. May 12-14; 364) DM 2,600
– **Vollständiges Kräuter-Buch; samt der Kunstzu destilliren, wie auch Bauung der Gärten ... Thieren, Vögeln, Fischen; Metallen ... Edelgesteinen, Gummi ...** Ed.:– P. Uffenbach. Ulm, 1713. Late Edn. Fo. Slightly soiled, lightly browned or soiled in margins, heavier at end, prelims., last text ll. & index with margin defects, index with some text loss, a little worming in fold. Cont. blind-tooled pig-bkd. wood bds., very defect. (R. Mar.31-Apr.4; 1386) DM 1,800

LONITZER, Adam
See–LONICERUS, Adam

LONNBERG, E.
See–WRIGHT, Magnus, W. & F. von & Lönnberg, E.

LONSDALE, John, Viscount Lonsdale
– **Memoir of the Reign of James II.** York, 1808. 4to. Hf.-title slightly spotted. Later red mor. gt., with elab. tooled Grolieuresque design enclosing cf. inlays at corners, by Hayday. Pres. Copy. (SBA. Oct.22; 625) Temperley. £85

LOOFT, Marcus
– **Niedersächsisches Koch-Buch.** Lübeck, 1781. Cont. hf. leath. (R. Oct.14-18; 2720) DM 550

LOON, Gerard van
– **Aloude Hollandsche Histori der Keyzeren, Koningen, Hertogen en Graaven, welken in Holland, tot de herstel Herstelling van Florents den Ferstens zoon, het Hooggebied hebben gehad.** Ed.:– Hooggebied hebben gehad. The Hague, 1734. L.P. 2 vols. Fo. A few stains, mainly marginal. Cont. mott. & panel. cf., gt., spines & corners defect. (VG. Dec.17; 1427) Fls. 500
– **Beschrijving der Nederlandsche Historipenningen, of beknopt Verhaal van 't Gene tot het Sluyten van den Uytrechtschen Vreede, in de 17 Nederlandsche Gewesten is voorgevallen.** Ill.:– J. Houbraken (port.). The Hague, 1723-31. 4 vols. Fo. slightly browned in places. Cont. vell., a few light stains. (VG. Oct.13; 100) Fls. 3,400
– – **Anr. Copy.** Engraved frontis. bnd. in vol. 2. Cont. blind-stpd. vell., spines of 2 vols. defect. (VG. Dec.15; 491) Fls. 2,000
– – **Anr. Edn.** The Hague, 1731. 4th. pt. only. Fo. Cont. cf., spine gt., worn. (SG. Feb.5; 261) $200
– **Beschryving der Nederlandsche Historipenningen. –Hedendaagsche Penningkunde.** The Hague, 1723-31 & 1734. 4 vols, 5 vols. Fo. Browned in parts, some MS. notes. 19th. C. hf. leath. (H. Dec.9/10; 1002) DM 2,150
– **Hedendaagsche Penningkunde.** The Hague, 1732. Fo. Some foxing, a few light marginal stains. Cont. vell. (VG. Nov.18; 1263) Fls. 500

LOON, Jan van
– **Klaer-Lichtende Noort-Star ofte Zee-Atlas.** Amst., 1666. Fo. Chart of Oost Zee torn & sm. portion of surface fragile, fore-margin of some charts stained, a few other stains. Cont. parch., inside upper hinges brkn., lacks ties. As an atlas, w.a.f. (SPB. Oct.1; 274) $8,500

LOOSJES, J.
See–BIE, J.P. de Loosjes, J.

LOPES DE CASTANEDA, Hernan
– **Historie of the Discoverie & Conquest of the East Indias ...** Trans.:– [Nicholas Lichfield]. L., 1582. 1st. Edn. in Engl. Sm. 4to. Lacks most of lf. F4, foxed, marginal annots. by early owner, writing dtd. 1591 on title. Disbnd. [STC 16806] (SG. Feb.26; 216) $1,000

LOPEZ, Bernard
See–MOORE, George & Lopez, Bernard

LOPEZ, Duarte
– **A Report of the Kingdome of Congo.** Ed.:– Philippo Pigafetta. Trans.:– Abraham Hartwell. 1597. 1st. Engl. Edn. Sm. 4to. 2 title-pp., 1 reprd., folding map, 10 woodcut ills., initials & head-pieces. 19th. C. cf., Signet Liby. arms stpd. in gt. on covers, rebkd., orig. spine preserved. [STC 16805] (C. Jul.15; 68) Quaritch. £600
– – **Anr. Copy.** 1 title-p. a variant, folding map made-up of 3 sections joined to form 1 sheet. (C. Nov.6; 218) Heston. £550

LOPEZ DE GOMARA, Francesco
– **La Historia Generale delle Indie Occidentali.** Rome, 1556. Sm. 4to. Inkstain affecting L2, lacks final lf. with printer's device. Later vell.-bkd. bds., worn. [Sabin 27736] (SPB. May 5; 328) $250
See–CIEZA DE LEON, Pedro–LOPEZ DE GOMARA, Francesco

LOPEZ de VARGAS Machucca, Tomas
– **Atlas Geografico de España.** Madrid, [1774, or later]. Ob. fo. 22 engraved maps, most hand-cold. in outl., dtd. 1761-73, some undtd. Loose in mod. wrap. W.a.f. (S. Mar.31; 255) Duran. £220
– – **Anr. Edn.** Madrid, n.d. [maps dtd. 1760-92]. Fo. Engraved title, 97 engraved maps, mostly hand-cold. in outl., & plan dtd. 1781, maps numbered in MS., cont. MS. index & fly-lf. mntd. Cont. spr. cf., rebkd. Sir John Moore's copy with inscr., bkplts. of George & George Fortescue Wilbraham, & Royal United Service Institution. (S. Mar.31; 300) Burgess. £1,000

LOPEZ PINCIANO, Alonso
– **Philosophia Antigua Poetica.** Madrid, 1596. 4to. Later marb. sheep, covers stpd. with crest & initials HT. (CSK. Apr.24; 82) £130

LORENTZ, Hendrik Antoon, Einstein, A. & Minkowski, H.
– **Das Relativitatsprinzip (Fortschritte der Math. Wiss. in Monographien, Heft 2).** Leipzig & Berlin, 1913. 1st. Edn. Orig. ptd. wraps., unc. From Honeyman Collection. (S. May 20; 3281) Hener. £100

LORENZANA, F.A.–CONCILIUM Mexico
– **Concilios Provinciales; Concilium Mexicanum Provinciale III [&] Statuta Ordinata a Sancto Concilio Provinciali Mexicano III.–Sanctum Provinciale Concilium Mexici Celebratum.** Mexico; Mexico; Mexico, 1769; 1770; [1622]. 3 works in 1 vol., 3rd. work in 2 pts. 4to. 3rd. work lacks title, & with sm. holes affecting 1st. & last ll. Qtr. cf. (SPB. May 5; 164) $700

L'ORME, Philibert de
– **Le Premier Tome de l'Architecture.** Paris, 1567. 1st. Edn., 1st. Iss. Fo. 18th. C. cf.-bkd. bds. (S. Nov.25; 406) Marlborough. £750

LORRAIN, Jean
– **Monsieur de Bougrelon.** Ill.:– Drian. Paris, 1927. (75) on Van Gelder Holland, numbered. 4to. Etchings in 2 states (black-&-white & definitive state). Red mor., richly gt. on spine & covers, wrap. preserved, s.-c. (SM. Feb.11; 242) Frs. 2,600

LORRAINE, Claude
See–CLAUDE le Lorraine

LORRIS, Guillaume de & Meung, Jean de
– **Cy est le Roumant de la Roze.** Paris, 1531. Fo. Lge. device at end, repair in margin, repair to title not affecting letters, a few other minor marginal repairs, washed. Mor. with elab. doubls. by R.

Petit, bkplt. of Henry Vane Millbank & with his arms on sides. (SPB. May 6; 206) $3,250
– **Le Rommant de la Rose ...** Ed.:– Clément Marot. Paris, 1538. Slight dampstaining at beginning, title lacks sm. corner piece. Cf. by Simier, decor. with lge. blind-stpd. Cathedral plaque, decor. spine. (HD. Mar.18; 108) Frs. 7,800
– – **Anr. Edn.** Paris, 1735. 3 vols. 12mo. Cont. cf., decor. spines. (HD. Dec.5; 132) Frs. 1,100
– – **Anr. Edn.** Paris & Dijon, 1735-37. 4 vols., including supp. 12mo. Later 18th. C. red mor. gt. (SM. Oct.8; 2133) Frs. 3,600
– – **Anr. Copy.** Cont. spr. cf., triple gt. fillet around covers, arms of Plélo Comte de Bréhant in centre & corners, raised bands & arms on spine. Bkplts. of Barons de Fleury & Werlé. (HD. Jun.24; 56) Frs. 2,400
– **The Romaunt of the Rose.** Trans.:– Geoffrey Chaucer. Ill.:– Keith Henderson & Norman Wilkinson. Florence Pr., 1908. (312). 4to. Niger mor., gt. tooled, inner borders gt., silk doubls. & end-ll., cl. folder & mor.-bkd. s.-c. by Sangorski & Sutcliffe. Markes 'presentation copy'. (SH. Feb.19; 59) Joseph. £85
– – **Anr. Edn.** Ill.:– Ann Brunskill. World's End Pr., 1974. (25) with 7 cold. plts. sigd. by artist. Fo. Orig. vell., unc., s.-c. (SH. Feb.20; 418) Smith. £150

LORY, Gabriel, the Younger
[–] **Picturesque Tour Through the Oberland in the Canton of Berne, in Switzerland.** 1823. Cont. cl., loose. (S. Jun.29; 264) Crete. £1,500
[–] **Voyage Pittoresque de Genève à Milan par le Simplon.** Paris, 1811. 2 vols. Fo. 35 hand-cold. aquatints, each cut round & mntd., plt. titles & sigs. engraved on mounts. Mod. red hf. mor., [Lonchamp 1858]. (C. Jul.15; 69) Maggs. £9,000
[–] – **Anr. Copy.** Hf. mor., spine with gt. raised bands. (LC. Oct.2; 180) £4,400

LOSA, Francisco
– **Vida que el Siervo de Dios Gregorio Lopez hizo en algunos Lugares de la Nueva Espana, principalmente en el Pueblo de Santa Fe.** Madrid, 1674. 6th. Edn. 4to. Cont. patterned cf., rebkd. [Sabin 42576] (SG. Mar.5; 310) $240

LOSER, R.
– **Salzburg und seine Umgebungen.** Ill.:– J. Poppel & M. Kurz. München, [1845]. Cont. linen. (R. Oct.14-18; 1961) DM 1,400
– – **Anr. Edn.** Ill.:– J. Poppel & M. Kurz. Munich, [1845/46]. 1st. Edn. Title verso stpd., plts. soiled in margin. Orig. linen, worn. (HK. May 12-14. 701) DM 650
– – **Anr. Edn.** Munich, ca. 1850. Lightly soiled. Orig. linen. (HK. Nov.18-21; 1303) DM 900

LOSSING, Benson J.
– **The Pictorial Field-Book of the War of 1812.** Ill.:– Lossing & Barritt. N.Y., 1869. Gt.-pict. cl. (SG. Jan.8; 249) $100

LOSSIUS, Lucas
– **Arithmetices Erotemata Puerilia.** Frankfurt a.d. Oder, [1557?]. Mod. bds. From Honeyman Collection. (S. May 20; 3282) Maggs. £90

LOTHROP, S.K. & others
– **Robert Woods Bliss Collection of Pre-Columbian Art.** N.Y., 1957. 1st. Edn. Sm. fo. Gt. pict. cl., glassine wrap., boxed. (PNY. Mar.4; 221) $170

LOTI, Pierre
– **Aziyade.** Ill.:– William Fel. Paris, 1925. (50) numbered on Hollande. Double state of ills., 1 cold. 4to. Mor., 5 spine raised bands, decor. & mosaic, gt. fillet decor., orange mor. doubls., lge. inner mosaic & gt. border, wrap. preserved, box, P. Affolter, 1925. (LM. Mar.21; 180) B.Frs. 10,000
– **Les Désenchantées.** Ill.:– Charles Fouqueray. Paris, 1934. (15) numbered on Japon. impérial. Sm. 4to. Cold. state on Hollande & black on Chine. Red hf. mor., orig. wraps. bnd. in s.-c. (SM. Oct.8; 2355) Frs. 1,800
– **Madame Chrysanthème.** Ill.:– Foujita. Paris, 1926. (400) on Arches. 4to. Hf. mor. by Flammarion, gt. & decor. spine, orig. wraps. bnd. in. (SM. Oct.8; 2356) Frs. 3,600
– **Pêcheur d'Islande.** 1886. Orig. Edn. Three qtr. mor., wrap. & spine. (HD. Jun.30; 48) Frs. 1,300
– **Vers Ispahan.** Ill.:– Henri Deluermoz. Paris, 1936. Cf., covers with panel. & floral mor. onlays, spine with floral mor. onlays, silk doubls. &

end-papers, partly unc., by Louis Forest, orig. wraps. bnd. in. (C. Jul.22; 190) *Sawyer.* £100

LOTTER, Tobias Conrad & Lobeck, Tobias
- Atlas Geographicus Portatilis. Augsburg, ca. 1760. Lacks contents list, some centre-folds browned. Cont. cf., blind-tooled, worn. (H. May 21/22; 300) DM 900
- - **Anr. Edn.** Augsburg, [1762?]. Sm. ob. 8vo. Partly soiled. Cont. style mod. leath. (R. Oct.14-18; 1544) DM 2,000
- - **Anr. Edn.** Augsburg, ca. 1775. Ca. 11½ × 14½ cm. Cont. cf. gt., worn. (TA. Feb.19; 135) £125

LOTTICH, Karl
See–LESSING, Gotthold Ephraim–LOTTICH, Karl

LOUBAT, G.
- Medallic History of the United States of America. Ill.:– J. Jacquemart. N.Y., 1878. Text & plt. vol. Fo. Linen. (R. Mar.31-Apr.4; 179) DM 500

LOUBAT, Joseph F.
- The Medallic History of the United States of America, 1776-1876. Ill.:– Jules Jacquemart. N.Y., Priv. ptd., 1878. L.P. on Rives H.M.P. 2 vols. Fo. Cl., partly unc. (SG. Sep.4; 314) $160
- - **Anr. Copy.** (SG. Sep.4; 366) $130

LOUDON, J.C.
- The Suburban Gardener. L., Priv. Ptd., 1838. 1st. Edn. With advts. Early cf., spine gt. (SG. Dec.4; 227) $100

LOUDON, Mrs. Jane W.
- British Wild Flowers. 1846. [1st. Edn.?]. 4to. Frontis. foxed, a few plts. spotted. Cont. mor. gt., recased. (TA. Oct.16; 310) £360
- - **Anr. Copy.** Occasional light foxing Cont. cf., gt. spine. (C. Nov.5; 94) *Harcourt-Williams.* £300
- - **Anr. Copy.** Slight spotting. Cont. red mor., gt. (S. Jun.1; 159) *Smith.* £240
- - **Anr. Copy.** Lacks covers & spine. (CSK. Mar.20; 69) £220
- - **Anr. Edn.** 1847. 4to. 60 cold. litho. plts., title detchd., lacks hf.-title. Cont. hf. mor. (C. Mar.18; 68) *Map House.* £230
- - **Anr. Edn.** 1849. 2nd. Edn. 4to. Some ll. dust-soiled at edges & frayed, a few short edge-tears, several plts. spotted, some dust-soiled at edges. Orig. pict. cl., gt., spine defect., contents disbnd. (S. Dec.3; 1039) *Litman.* £240
- - **Anr. Copy.** Cl., stained, spine torn. (PD. May 20; 137) £200
- - **Anr. Edn.** 1859. 3rd. Edn. 4to. Mod. leath. (S. Dec.3; 1040) *Nagel.* £200
- - **Anr. Edn.** N.d. 4to. Lacks plts. 21 & 23. Hf. mor. gt. (P. Nov.13; 7) *Edistar.* £300
- - **Anr. Copy.** 59 hand-cold. litho. plts. only, a few detchd., some spotting. Orig. cl. W.a.f. (CSK. May 1; 133) £200
- - **Anr. Copy.** Without ptd. ll. before the contents list, lacks title. 19th. C. cl. gt. W.a.f. (LC. Feb.12; 140) £140
- The Ladies' Flower Garden of Ornamental Annuals. 1840. 1st. Edn. 4to. A few plts. slightly spotted. Cont. vell. bds., gt. spine. (SH. Oct.9; 231) *Edistar.* £550
- - **Anr. Copy.** Some spotting, mainly to tissue guards. Cont. hf. cf. (TA. Jun.18; 160) £525
- - **Anr. Copy.** Mor. (SKC. Feb.26; 1594) £480
- - **Anr. Copy.** Cont. hf. mor. (SBA. Oct.21; 156) *Hyde Park Bookshop.* £450
- - **Anr. Copy.** Some ll. loose or detchd., occasional slight spotting. Cont. mor., gt., lacks spine, covers detchd., worn. (S. Dec.3; 1034) *Wagner.* £360
- - **Anr. Copy.** Cl., covers detchd. (S. Dec.8; 173) *Hollingsworth.* £340
- - **Anr. Copy.** 8 plts. with tears & some soiled. Disbnd. (P. Feb.19; 169) *Bailey.* £250
- - **Anr. Edn.** 1841. 1st. Edn. 4to. Cf., defect. (BS. May 13; 293) £380
- - **Anr. Edn.** 1844. 4to. 47 cold. plts. only (of 48), some marginal tears, slight soiling. Orig. cl., faded, spine defect. (S. Jul.27; 296) *Mohler.* £300
- - **Anr. Edn.** [1849]. 2nd. Edn. 4to. Orig. cl., contents loose. (S. Dec.3; 1038) *Litman.* £320
- The Ladies Flower Garden of Ornamental Bulbous Plants. Ill.:– Day & Haghe. 1841. Mor. gt. (HSS. Apr.24; 298) £360
- - **Anr. Edn.** 1849. 2nd. Edn. 4to. Some ll. frayed at edges & dust-soiled, several plts. lightly soiled

at edges. Orig. pict. cl., gt., spine defect., contents disbnd. (S. Dec.3; 1036) *Litman.* £360
- - **Anr. Copy.** Fo. Hf. cf., spine defect. (VG. Oct.13; 102) Fls. 2,000
- - **Anr. Edn.** Ca. 1850. 2nd. Edn. 4to. A few ll. & plts. detchd. Orig. cl., slightly worn. (S. Dec.3; 1037) *Demetzy.* £380
- The Ladies' Flower Garden of Ornamental Greenhouse Plants. 1848. 4to. 1 hand-cold. plt. detchd., some other minor defects. Orig. mor.-bkd. cl., slightly worn. (SBA. May 27; 185) *Omniphil.* £360
- [-] – **Anr. Edn.** N.d. 2nd. Edn. 1 plt. detchd., some spotting. Orig. cl. (CSK. May 1; 135) £280
- The Ladies' Flower-Garden of Ornamental Perenials. 1843. 2 vols. Cont. mor., gt., worn. (S. Dec.3; 1035) *Robinson.* £600
- - **Anr. Copy.** 4to. Cont. hf. leath. (HK. May 12-14; 365) DM 2,800
- - **Anr. Edn.** 1843-44. 2 vols. 4to. 95 hand-cold. plts. only, some margins soiled & torn. Orig. cl., worn & partly disbnd., covers detchd., lacks spines. W.a.f. (CSK. Mar.20; 68) £450
- - **Anr. Edn.** L., 1849,, 2nd. Edn. Fo. Hf. cf., covers & spine loose. (VG. Oct.13; 101) Fls. 2,600
- [-] [-] **Anr. Edn.** N.d. 2nd. Edn. 4to. 87 hand-cold. litho. plts. only, lacks title & 1st. few ll. Orig. cl. W.a.f. (CSK. May 1; 134) £420
- The Ladies' Flower-Garden of Ornamental Perennials.–The Ladies' Flower-Garden of Ornamental Bulbous Plants.–The Ladies' Flower-Garden of Ornamental Annuals.–British Wild Flowers.–The Ladies' Flower-Garden of Ornamental Greenhouse Plants. 1843-44; 1844; 1844; 1847; 1848. 5 works in 6 vols. 4to. All plts. hand-cold., many spotted. Unif. mor., spines soiled. (SKC. Jul.28; 2418) £1,850
- The Ladies' Magazine of Gardening. 1842. [All publd.]. Cont. cl. (TA. Jun.18; 161) £75

LOUDON, John Claudius
- Arboretum et Fruiticetum Britannicum. 1838. 8 vols. Cold. plts. Cont. cl., bkplts. of G. Croxton & F.E. Sotheby. (S. Dec.3; 1032) *W. & W.* £320
- - **Anr. Edn.** 1844. 8 vols including 4 vols. of plts. Orig. cl. (P. Feb.19; 91) *Smith.* £80
- - **Anr. Edn.** 1854. 2nd. Edn. 8 vols. Some spotting. Orig. cl., soiled. (CSK. Jun.26; 50) £60
- An Encyclopaedia of Gardening. 1825. 3rd. Edn. Publisher's advts. bnd. in at front, untrimmed. Orig. bds., soiled. (TA. May 21; 240) £50
- - **Anr. Edn.** L., [1834]. New Edn. Orig. cl. (CB. May 27; 145) Can. $320
- Hints on the Formation of Gardens & Pleasure Grounds. 1813. 4to. Minor soiling. Hf. mor., some wear. (S. Dec.8; 172) *Traylen.* £340

LOUIS XIV, King of France
- Arrest du Conseil d'Estat du Roy, par lequel sa Majeste Conserue les Ecclesiastiques de son Royaume en la Jouyssance du Priuilege qu'ils ont de Vendre en gros ou en Destail en leurs Maisons, les Vins, Sildres, & Autres Boissons Prouenans de leur Creu, sans payer aucun Droict d'aydes. Rouen, 1651. Slight browning. Mod. pol. hf. cf. by Rivière, spine gt. From liby. of André L. Simon. (S. May 18; 134) *Booth.* £55
- Cabinet du Roi. Ill.:– N. Cochin & G. Perelle after Portault de Beaulieu & others. ?Paris, ca. 1750. Fo. No title. Cont. mott. cf., gt., Fr. royal arms in centre of covers, upr. cover with inscr. 'Donné Par Le Roy [Louis XVI] à Mr Anisson en 1777', slightly worn. (S. Oct.21; 290) *Favre.* £2,600
- [-] L'Entrée Triomphante de Leurs Maiestez Louis XIV et Marie Thérèse d'Austriche. Ed.:– [Jean Troncon]. Paris, 1662. Fo. Some slight foxing thro-out, lacks port. of Louis XIV. Cf., arms on covers, worn. (BS. Jun.11; 227) £320

LOUIS XV, King of France
- Cours des principaux Fleuves et Rivières de l'Europe, composé et imprimé par Louis XV, Roy de France . . . en 1718. Ill.:– Benoit Audran. Paris, 1718. 1st. Edn. 18th. C. red mor., triple gt. fillet, flat spine gt., inner gt. dentelles, 1 fore-corner slightly worn, bkplt of Robert, Marquess of Crewe. (SM. Oct.7; 1825) Frs. 12,000
- Relation de l'Arrivée du Roi au Havre de Grace, le 9 Septembre 1749, et des fêtes que se sont données a cette occasion. Ill.:– J.P. Le Bas after Descamps & Le Bas after Sledtz. Paris, 1753. Elephant fo. (25 × 18¾ inches). Cont. Fr. bdg. of scarlet mor., gt.-stpd. on covers with royal arms at centre,

fleur-de-lys at corners, sprays of leaves & 3 different tools at borders, gt.-panel. back (tail of spine worn). (PNY. Mar.26; 193) $10,000
- Le Sacre de Louis XV . . . dans l'Eglise de Reims, Le Dimanche XXV Octobre MDCCXXII. N.p. [1722]. 1st. Edn. Atlas fo. Old red hf. mor. gt. & marb. bds., worn. (CNY. May 22; 105) $450

LOUKOMSKI, G.K.
See–LUKOMSKI, Geo. K.

LOUMYER, J.F.N. 'A. Wahlen'
- Moeurs, Usages et Costumes de tous les Peuples du Monde. Brussels, 1844. Vols. III & IV. 4to. Albumen heightened, a few soilings or brownings. Later hf. leath., orig. wraps. bnd. in. (H. Dec.9/10; 794) DM 420

LOUNGER, The
Edinb., 5 Feb. 1785-6 Jan. 1787. Nos. I-CI in 1 vol. Fo. Complete set of orig. iss. with added title-p. Mott. cf., gt., by F. Bedford. (S. Nov.24; 195) *Riley Smith.* £240

LOUREIRO, Jose Marques
- Jornal de Horticultura Pratica. Porto, 1870-92. 23 vols. Cont. cf.-bkd. bds., spincs gt. As a periodical, w.a.f. (C. Nov.5; 96) *Quaritch.* £350

LOUTHERBOURG, Philippe Jacques de
- The Romantic & Picturesque Scenery of England & Wales. 1805. 1st. Edn. Fo. 18 hand-cold. aquatints. Hf. cf. (C. Jul.15; 70) *Maggs.* £1,200
- - **Anr. Edn.** 1805 [but ca. 1824]. Fo. Cold. frontis. dtd. 1801, 18 cold. aquatints. Cont. hf. roan. (C. Jul.15; 71) *Taylor.* £550
- - **Anr. Copy.** 15 hand-cold. plts. only (of 19), all lack sig. & imprint, text wtrmkd. 1822, plts. 1824, repair to fore-e. of 1 plt., 3 plts. & several ll. near end stained, first title soiled. Orig. hf. roan, spine gt., worn. (S. Nov.4; 548) *Cumming.* £320

LOUVET, Pierre
- Histoire des Troubles de Provence . . . Aix, 1679. 1st. Edn. 2 vols. 12mo. Cont. red mor., Du Seuil decor., decor. spine. (HD. Mar.18; 109) Frs. 3,500

LOUVET DE COUVRAY, Jean Baptiste
- Vie du Chevalier de Faublas. Ill.:– Chaillou, engrs. by Lorieux. Paris, 1796. 1st. Ill. Edn. 13 vols. 12mo. Cont. hf. leath., star-form gold stps. (D. Dec.11-13; 696) DM 600

LOUYS, Pierre
- Aphrodite. Ill.:– Calbet. Paris, 1896. (25), on China. Red mor. by Blanchetière, gt. fillets on covers, spine decor. with raised bands, mor. doubls. with blind-tooled decor., sewed silk end-papers, wrap. & spine preserved, s.-c. (HD. Feb.27; 169) Frs. 1,300
- - **Anr. Edn.** Ill.:– Ernest Florian after Raphaël Collin. Paris, 1909. On lge. imperial Jap. 4to. 2 states. Hf. mor. by Blanchetière, spine decor. with multi-cold. mosaic mor., wrap. preserved. (SM. Feb.11; 84) Frs. 4,000
- Les Aventures du Roi Pausole. Ill.:– Pierre Vidal [head & tail pieces]. Paris, 1906. New Edn., (325) numbered on papier velin de Rives. 4to. Cont. mor., diamond-shaped centrepieces built up with massed tools with stylized peacocks perched amidst foliage & flowers, similar cornerpieces, spine gt., by Rene Kieffer, with his ticket, slightly worn at head, orig. wraps. bnd. in, partly unc., bkplt. of Walter Schick. (S. Jun.23; 267) *Ponder.* £160
- - **Anr. Copy.** Red mor. by Joly fils, spine compartments with blind-tooled decor., borders of 3 fillets on covers, wrap. preserved, s.-c. (SM. Feb.11; 243) Frs. 6,000
- - **Anr. Copy.** Mor. by Kieffer, incised multi-cold. leath. on upr. cover, spine with raised bands, wrap. & spine preserved, s.-c. (HD. Feb.27; 170) Frs. 3,500
- - **Anr. Edn.** Ill.:– Vèrtes. Paris, 1930. (99) on Arches. 2 vols. 4to. Set of copper-engrs. with comments, 15 rejected plts, orig. watercolour drawing dedicated to F. Kettaneh, 74 orig. dry-points. Jansenist mor. by Cretté, smooth decor. spines, buckskin end-papers & doubls., wrap. & spine preserved, folder, s.-c. From liby. of F. Kettaneh. (HD. Feb.27; 172) Frs. 7,000
- Byblis. Ill.:– Henri Caruchet. Paris, 1901. (300). Partially cold. thro-out, (?)proofs before letter inserted with each lf. Mor. gt., cold. mor. inlays, floral end-papers. (SPB. Jul.28; 36) $225

LOUYS, Pierre -contd.
- **Les Chansons de Bilitis.** 1898. Hf. mor., by Champs, wrap., lacks spine. On vell., A.N. (HD. Oct.10; 99)   Frs. 1,600
- - **Anr. Edn.** Ill.:– Chessa after Collin. Paris, 1909. (60) on lge. Arches vell. 4to. 2 states of etchings. Hf. mor. by Blanchetière-Bretault, spine decor. & mosaic in various colours, wrap. preserved. (SM. Feb.11; 85)   Frs. 2,500
- - **Anr. Edn.** Ill.:– Pierre Bouchet after Sylvain Sauvage. Paris, 1927. (285); (235) on Montval laid paper, numbered. 4to. Mor. by Semet & Plumelle, red mor. doubls., wrap. preserved, s.-c. (SM. Feb.11; 244)   Frs. 2,500
- - **Anr. Edn.** Ill.:– Georges Barbier. [Paris], 1929. 1st. compl. text Edn. (25) on vell., copy B (of 5). Gold fillet border on each page. Cont. mor. by Cretté, decor., gold fillets, blind-stpd. & gold-stpd. fillets, silk end-ll., doubled with hand-finished gold, silver & green cold. paper, hf.-leath. s.-c., suede lined, wrap. J. Brayat & Henri Bonasse ex-liby. (D. Dec.11; 1133)   DM 25,000
- - **Anr. Edn.** Ill.:– Mariette Lydis. Paris, 1948. (365) numbered. 4to. Unsewn in orig. wraps., unc., folder & s.-c. (SH. Nov.21; 401)   *Henderson.* £75
- **Dialogue sur la Danse.** Ed.:– Serge Lifar. Ill.:– Marie Laurencin. Paris, 1949. (190); (30) on lge. Arches vell. Fo. Publisher's s.-c. (HD. Dec.5; 134)   Frs. 14,000
- **La Femme et le Pantin.** Ill.:– after Goya. Paris, 1898. Ltd. Edn. Mor. gt., decor. mor. onlays, orig. wraps. bnd. in. (SM. Oct.8; 2265)   Frs. 1,600
- - **Anr. Copy.** (500) numbered on alfa. Red mor. by Baruck, partly unc., orig. wraps. bnd. in. Pres. Copy, 2 pp. A.L.s. (n.p., 11 Oct. 1916), & corrected proofs to p. 77, 1,4. (SM. Oct.8; 2134)   Frs. 1,000
- **Lucien de Samosate.** 1894. Red mor. by Creuzevault, wrap., reproduction on cover. Note. (HD. Oct.10; 98)   Frs. 4,800
- **Mimes des Courtisanes, de Lucien.** Ill.:– Maurice Potin after Edgar Degas. Paris, 1935. (20) lettered copies not for sale, in total Edn. of 325. 4to. Orig. wraps., some looseness in sewing, unc. (KH. Nov.18; 386)   Aus. $230
- **Les Poésies de Méléagre.** 1893. (5) numbered on chine. Jansenist old pink mor., mor. doubl., wrap., s.-c., by Noulhac. (HD. Oct.15; 97)   Frs. 1,800
- - **Anr. Edn.** Ill.:– Edouard Chimot. Paris, 1926. (50) on japon imperial, numbered. 4to. Plts. in 3 states, 1 with remarques, extra state of frontis., crayon drawing sigd. by artist. Mor., mor. onlay between gt. & blind tooling, round foot of covers in chevron form, & onto spine & mor. doubls., s.-c., by V. Ollivier. (SH. Nov.20; 26)   *Klusmann.* £400
- - **Anr. Copy.** (15) on japon ancien special, numbered. Plts. in 4 states, 1 with remarques, 2 extra states of frontis., extra state of each of 8 other plts., orig. crayon drawing. Unsewn in orig. wraps., folder, s.-c., slightly defect. Inscr. by artist. (SH. Nov.20; 25)   *Klusmann.* £260
- - **Anr. Copy.** (30) on Jap. 15 orig. etchings in 4 states, set of 6 loose engrs. in several states, 1 set on vell. Mosaic mor. by Gruel, spine with raised bands, mor. doubls. with mosaic border, silk end-papers, wrap., folder, s.-c. 3 orig. drawings, sigd. (HD. Feb.27; 171)   Frs. 7,000
- **Psyche.** Ill.:– Carlègle. Paris, 1935. (1,765), numbered. Mor. gt., cover design by ill., mor. onlays repeating cover design, inner borders gt., orig. wraps. bnd. in, s.-c. (SH. Nov.20; 21)   *Klusmann.* £50
- **The Songs of Bilitis.** Trans.:– Horace M. Brown. Ill.:– James Fagan. L. & N.Y., Aldus Soc., 1904. Edn. des Bibliophiles. (26) numbered on Japan vell., sigd. by Trans. Each etching in 3 states, 1 hand-cold., anr. sigd. by Fagan, 3rd. with remarque, few ll. loose. Crushed lev. with lge. floral inlays, lev. doubls. with floral mor. inlays, moire satin end-ll. (SG. Sep.4; 50) $190
- **The Twilight of the Nymphs.–Aphrodite.** Trans.:– Phillis Duveen (1st. work). Ill.:– Cecil Beaton (1st. work); & Beresford Egan. 1928. (1200); (1075). 2 works in 2 vols. Cl.-bkd. bds., d.-w. (1st. work); & cl.-bkd. bds., unc. (C. Jul.22; 69)   *Joseph.* £210

LOVELACE, Richard
- **Lucasta.** Ill.:– Faithorne after Lely. L., 1649. 1st. Edn. Earlier state of lf. B2 with 'Warres' in the heading, port. inserted from anr. copy, 5 headlines in sig. K just cropped. Early 19th. C. pol. cf. gt., mor. solander case. The James Perry,

George Daniel copy (with inscr. of former on fly-lf.), bkplts. of J. Haslewood, Jerome Kern, & the Huth Collection, lately in the Prescott Collection. [Wing L3240] (CNY. Feb.6; 239) $4,200

LOVELL, Richard
*See–*EDGEWORTH, Maria & Lovell, Richard

LOVELL, Robert
- **Panzoologicomineralogia.–Pammineralogicon.** Oxford, 1661; 1661. 1st. Edns. 2 works in 1 vol. Mor. [Wing L3245; L3246] (C. Nov.19; 31)   *Terry.* £120

LOVER, Samuel
- **Collected Writings.** Boston, 1903. Treasure Trove Edn., (900). 10 vols. Extra-ill. with plts. & A.L.s. Mor. gt., gt. panel. spines, red inlays. (SPB. May 6; 330) $350

LOVERA, Josephus Joachimus
- **Gestorum ab Episcopis Salutiensibus Anakephalaiosis . . .** Parma, 1783. 1st. Edn. (300). Lacks first & last blank. Roan-bkd. marb. bds., unc. Bkplt. of Robert Hoe. (S. Nov.24; 196)   *Lyon.* £90

LOVES OF MIRTIL, The, Son of Adonis
1770. 1st. Edn. in Engl. Cont. Engl. red mor., gt., spine tooled in compartments. Bkplt. of Stephen Payne Galwey. (S. Nov.24; 197)   *Bickersteth.* £75

LOW, Lieut. Charles Rathbone
- **Her Majesty's Navy.** L., Ca. 1892. 3 vols. 4to. 1 text p. slightly defect. Cont. hf. leath. (HK. Nov.18-21; 1828)   DM 650
- - **Anr. Edn.** Ca. 1895. 3 vols. 4to. Orig. decor. cl., spines worn. (TA. Dec.18; 376)   £105
- - **Anr. Copy.** Cont. hf. leath., 1 spine torn. (R. Mar.31-Apr.4; 1790)   DM 850
- - **Anr. Edn.** N.d. 6 vols. 4to. Orig. cl., slightly worn. (SKC. Feb.26; 1780)   £100

LOW, David
- **The Breeds of the Domestic Animals of the British Islands.** Ill.:– W. Nicholson after W. Shiels. 1842. 2 vols. in 1. Fo. Cont. red hf. mor. (C. Mar.18; 69)   Michaelis. £4,500
- - **Anr. Copy.** Tear affecting 1 plt. in vol. 2, some slight spotting. Hf. mor. (S. Jun.1; 160)   *Traylen.* £1,900

LOW, Hugh
- **Sarawak.** 1848. Orig. cl. gt. (P. Feb.19; 161)   *Dawsons.* £65

LOWE, Constance M.
- *See-Saw Pictures.* Nister, ca. 1890. 4to. 6 cold. ills., moving pts. worked by levers, a few sm. tears, margins strengthened. Orig. cl.-bkd. bds. (SBA. Dec.16; 201)   *Petersfield Bookshop.* £54

LOWE, Edward Joseph
- **Ferns: British & Exotic.** 1856-60. 1st. Edn. 8 vols. Some foxing. Cont. hf. mor. (TA. Jun.18; 15)   £80
- - **Anr. Copy.** Offsetting, foxing. Hf. cf., gt. (SPB. May 29; 271) $250
- - **Anr. Edn.** 1872. [2nd. Edn.?]. 8 vols. Some ll. slightly spotted. Orig. pict. cl. gt. (SD. Feb.4; 261)   £65
- - **Anr. Copy.** Orig. cl. gt., vols. 1-7 orig. d.-w.'s, vol. 1 defect., anr. torn. (CNY. May 22; 205) $280
- **A Natural History of New & Rare Ferns.–Ferns: British & Exotic.** 1871; 1872. 1 vol.; 8 vols. Unif. bnd. in orig. cl. gt., some minor defects. (SBA. May 27; 186)   *Hyde Park Bookshop.* £54

LOWE, Edward Joseph & Howard, W.
- **Beautiful Leaved Plants.** 1861. Some spotting, contents slightly loose. Orig. cl., gt. decor. spine. (TA. May 21; 247)   £52
- - **Anr. Copy.** Orig. cl., slightly soiled. (CSK. May 22; 115)   £50
- - **Anr. Edn.** 1866. Cont. hf. cf. (SD. Feb.4; 263)   £55
- - **Anr. Edn.** 1872. Orig. blind & gt.-stpd. cl. (GM. Apr.30; 621)   £80
- - **Anr. Copy.** Hf. mor. gt. (CNY. May 22; 204) $160

LOWE, F.
*See-*SMYTH, W. & Lowe, F.

LOWE, Peter
- **A Discourse of the Whole Art of Chyrugerie . . .** 1612. 2nd. Edn. 4to. Blank corners of first few ll. reprd. just affecting lr. border on title, sm.

rust-hole in R3, some cont. MS. recipe notes on fly-lf. Vell., new end-papers. Inscr. 'Robert Watson' on title. (S. Jun.16; 527)   *Vanderkerckove.* £400

LOWELL, Amy
- [-] **Dream Drops.** Boston, [1887]. 1st. Edn., (250). Elab. mor. gt., floral inlay design in corners of each cover surrounding sm. moonstone, by Sangorski & Sutcliffe. (SPB. May 6; 208) $1,500
- [-] - **Anr. Copy.** (99). 12mo. Orig. ptd. wraps., slightly soiled, qtr. mor. gt. s.-c. The Arthur Swann copy, with bkplt., lately in the Prescott Collection. (CNY. Feb.6; 240) $700
- **Sword Blades & Poppy Seed.** N.Y., 1914. 1st. Edn. Tall 12mo. Cl.-bkd. bds. Pres. copy; inserted is A.L.s. from Lowell to Mrs. Fuller, to whom the book is inscr., 2 pp., 12mo., Chic., Mar.23, 1916. (PNY. Mar.4; 168) $100

LOWELL, James Russell
- **Complete Writings.** Camb., 1904. De Luxe Edns. (100). 16 vols. Hf. mor. gt. (SPB. Nov.25; 474) $225

LOWENFELS, Walter
- **Apollinaire.** Paris, Hours Pr., 1930. 1st. Edn. (150) numbered, sigd. Orig. mor.-bkd. pict. bds., unc. (S. Jul.22; 151)   *Lady Couchman.* £80
- - **Anr. Copy.** 4to. (S. Jul.22; 212)   *Conway.* £60

LOWER, Richard
- **Tractatus de Corde.** Amst., 1669. 2nd. Edn. Browned. Cont. vell. bds. (S. Jul.16; 199)   *Walford.* £110
- - **Anr. Edn.** 1670. 2nd. Edn. Lr. margin of title renewed, some browning & slight staining, MS. additions & corrections. Hf. cf., very worn. [Wing L3311] (S. Jun.23; 280)   *Quaritch.* £100
- - **Anr. Edn.** Amst., 1671. 3rd. Edn. Cont. cf. Pres. copy inscr. 'ex dono authoris Januarii vicesimo sexto 1671' (S. Jun.16; 528)   *Engel.* £140
- - **Anr. Edn.** Ill.:– W. Faithorne. 1680. 4th. Edn. Cont. cf., spine reprd. with orig. spine preserved. Sir G.L. Keyne's copy. [Wing L3312] (S. Jun.16; 529)   *Gurney.* £58
- - **Anr. Edn.** Leiden, 1728. 6th. Edn. New bds., cf. spine. (S. Dec.2; 538)   *Demetzy.* £55

LOWER CANADA, House of Assembly
- **Standing Rules & Regulations.** Quebec, 1809. Cont. red gt.-tooled mor. (CB. Sep.24; 96)   Can. $400

LOWINSKY, Thomas
- **Modern Nymphs.** Ed.:– Raymond Mortimer [introductory essay]. L., 1930. (150) numbered. Tall 4to. Cl.-bkd. decor. bds., unc. & unopened. (SG. May 21; 402) $130

LOWNDES, William Thomas
- **The Bibliographer's Manual of English Literature.** L., 1857. New Edn. 6 vols. in ll. Cl. (GM. Apr.30; 572)   £62
- - **Anr. Edn.** 1857-64. 11 vols. Orig. cl. (SH. Jul.9; 23)   *Talerman.* £65
- - **Anr. Edn.** 1864. 4 vols. Lacks hf.-title to vol. 1. Cont. mor.-bkd. cl. (SBA. Oct.21; 185)   *Whittle.* £60
- - **Anr. Edn.** L., [1864]. 4 vols. Mor.-bkd. (GM. Apr.30; 648)   £60
- - **Anr. Edn.** Ed.:– Henry G. Bohn. 1871. New Edn. 4 vols. Cont. mor.-bkd. bds. (S. Feb.23; 344)   *Forster.* £65

LOWRY, Lawrence Stephen
- **The Paintings of.** 1975. (100) numbered, sigd. 4to. Orig. mor. (SH. Apr.9; 96)   *Harrison.* £60

LOYER, Godefroy
- **Relation du Voyage du Royaume d'Issny, Côte d'Or, Päis de Guinée, en Afrique.** Paris, 1714. 12mo. Rust-hole in H4. Cont. cf., gt. spine, worn. (S. Jun.22; 183)   *Thorp.* £180

LOYOLA, Saint Ignatius
- **Exercitia Spiritualia.** Ill.:– after Antoine Bouzonnet Stella. Paris, 1644. 4 pts. in 1 vol. Fo. Cont. red mor., gt., pres. bdg., arms of Louis XIII on covers, broad borders & inner gt. dentelles with fleurs-de-lis, spine gt. with lge. single fleur-de-lis in compartments surrounded by pointillé ornament, bkplts. of Dominicus Barnabus Turgot, de St.-Clair, 1716, Bp. of Seez & Lord Arundel of Wardour. (SM. Oct.7; 1826)   Frs. 31,000

LUACH
Prague, 1731; 1736. 16mo. Calendars for the years 1731 & 1736, repairs affecting text,

cropped, soiled, stained. Cl.-bkd. bds. (SPB. May 11; 146) $250

LUBBOCK, Basil
- Sail, The Romance of the Clipper Ships. Ill.:– J. Spurling. 1927-36. 3 vols. 4to. Decor. cl. (CE. Mar.19; 218) £150
- – Anr. Edn. N.d. 4to. Cl. gt. (P. Mar.12; 3) *Green.* £60

LUBBOCK, Sir John
- Pre-Historic Times. L., 1878. 4th. Edn. Lev., gt. borders enclosing gt. college arms, Winchester School prize bkplt. Fore-e. pntg. (SG. Mar.19; 145) $325

LUC, Jean André de
- Recherches sur les Modifications de l'Atmosphère . . . Geneva, 1772. 1st. Edn. 2 vols. Non-unif. mor.-bkd. cl. & cf. From Chetham's Liby., Manchester. (C. Nov.27; 264) *Taylor.* £70

LUCANUS, Marcus Annaeus
- Civilis Belli. Venice, 1502. 1st. Ald. Edn. Mor., elab. gt. borders, spine gt., gt. dentelles, by Renouard. (SG. Sep.25; 13) $500
- – Anr. Edn. Venice, 1515. 19th. C. mor., worn. (SG. Sep.25; 14) $160
- Pharsalia. Venice, Batholomaeus de Zaris pro Octavianus Scotus, 31 Mar. 1492. Fo. 144 ll. (of 156), missing text supplied in facs., first & a few other ll. soiled & reprd., some stains. Mod. vell. bds. [Variant of BMC V431 (1B 23706)] (SPB. May 6; 209) $400
- – Anr. Edn. Strawberry Hill, 1760. 4to. Later gt.-ruled & blind-tooled cf. Armorial bkplt. of James Remington. (PNY. Oct.1; 335) $170

LUCAS, Captain
- Pen & Pencil Reminiscences . . . L., 1861. 4to. Hf. roan, corners. (HD. Dec.5; 135) Frs. 1,800

LUCAS, Edward Verrall
- Edwin Austin Abbey. N.Y. & L., 1921. (50) numbered with orig. drawing. 2 vols. 4to. Hf. linen, unc. (SG. Dec.4; 1) $225

LUCAS, Fielding
- A General Atlas Containing Distinct Maps of All Known Countries in the World . . . Balt., [1823]. Fo. Slight browning, offsetting, initial ll. detchd. & 1 other plt. lf. Red cross grain mor. gt., spine chipped & torn, scarred. From liby. of William E. Wilson. (SPB. Apr.29; 180) $1,900

LUCAS, Frank Laurence
- Gilgamesh, King of Erech. Ill.:– Dorothea Braby. Gold. Cock. Pr., 1948. (500). Mor., blind-tooled design on covers enclosing mor. onlays, suede doubls., sigd. & dtd. 1978, fitted case, by Bryan Cantle. (S. Feb.20; 392) *Quaritch.* £170
- – Anr. Copy. Orig. hf. mor. gt. (S. Jul.31; 99) *Maggs Brothers.* £70

LUCAS, S.E.
- Catalogue of Sassoon Chinese Ivories. 1950. (250) numbered, sigd. by author & Sassoon. 3 vols. Fo. Orig. hf. vell. (S. Apr.9; 98) *Talerman.* £250

LUCAS, T.J.
- Camp Life & Sport in South Africa. L., 1878. Pict. cl. gt. (VA. Jan.30; 107) R. 90

LUCCOCK, John
- Notes on Rio de Janeiro, & the Southern parts of Brazil. 1820. 1st. Edn. 4to. Cont. pol. cf., covers becoming detchd. (C. Feb.25; 114) *Burton-Garbett.* £850

LUCIAN, of Samosata
- I Dialogi Piacevoli. Venice, 1541. Cont. limp vell., slightly soiled. (S. Jul.27; 112) *Pearson.* £90
- Gli dilettevoli Dialogi, le Vere Narrationi: le Facete Epistole . . . in volgare Novamente tradotte & historiate. Venice, 1543. Sig. of D. Crozat on verso of title. 18th. C. red mor., gt., arms of L.A.A. de Rohan-Chabot on covers, triple gt. fillet, spine gt. in compartments, inner gt. dentelles. Crozat-Firmin-Didot–Wilmerding copy. (SM. Oct.7; 1828) Frs. 1,000
- Opera. Flor., [Laurentius Francisci de Alopa], 1496. 1st. Edn. Fo. Additional later MS. title. Old cf. sides, red str.-grd. mor. spine gt., cypher of Duke of Devonshire on spine. Chatsworth bkplt. [BMC VI, 667] (S. Nov.25; 344) *Maggs.* £2,400
- Scènes de Courtisanes. Trans.:– H. Piazza & C. Chabault. Ill.:– Richard Ranft. Paris, 1901. (262); (220) on vell., numbered. Sm. 4to. Mor. by Kieffer, mosaic upr. cover, mor. doubls., orig. wrap., s.-c. (SM. Feb.11; 245) Frs. 4,000

- – Anr. Edn. Trans.:– H. Piazza & C. Chabault. Paris, 1901. (262), on vel. à la cuve. Chaudron mor., mosaic listel border in gt. fillets, mor. palmette angle motifs, spine decor., mor. doubls., mosaic decor. lge. border, wrap, s.-c., by Charles Lanoë. (HD. Jun.10; 180) Frs. 5,200
- True Historie. Ill.:– Robert Gibbings. [Waltham Saint Lawrence], Gold. Cock. Pr., 1927. (275) numbered. Fo. Buckram, qtr. mor. gt., partly unc. (KH. Nov.18; 388) Aus. $160

LUCIANI, Luigi
- Il cervelletto, nuovi studi di Fisioligia Normale e Patologica. Flor., 1891. 1st. Edn. Qtr. cf., orig. ptd. wraps. (S. Jun.16; 531) *Norman.* £300

LUCIOLLI, G.
See–RONZANI, Fr. & Luciolli, G.

LUCKIUS, Johannes Jacobus
- Sylloge Numismatum Elegantiorum. Ill.:– Aubry (engraved title). Strassburg, 1620. Fo. Browned & spotted. Cont. cf., gt. spine, worn. (S. Jul.27; 215) *Drury.* £65

LUCRETIUS, Carus Titus
- [De la Nature des Choses]. Trans.:– La Grange. Ill.:– Gravelot, engraved by Binet. Paris, 1768. Ist. Printing. 2 vols. Latin text parallel. Red mor., fillet, decor. spines, wtrd. silk end-ll., by Bozérian. (HD. Jun.10; 61) Frs. 8,500
- – Anr. Copy. 2 vols. Cont. porphyre cf., decor. (HD. Jun.30; 49) Frs. 1,300
- Della Natura delle Cose libri sei. Trans.:– Alessandro Marchetti. Ill.:– Eisen, Cochin, Vasse & Le Lorrain. Amst., 1754. 1st. Edn. on Holland P. 2 vols. Cont. decor. vell., sm. tools, inner dentelle, decor. spines, 1 jnt. brkn. (HD. Feb.18; 41) Frs. 2,500
- De Rerum Natura. Venice, Theodorus de Ragazonibus, 4 Sep. 1495. 4to. Very slightly spotted. 19th. C. red mor., jnts. brkn. [BMC V,478, HC 10283*, Goff L334] (S. May 5; 435) *Maggs.* £360
- – Anr. Edn. Ed.:– Thomas Creech. Oxford, 1695. Str.-grd. mor., gt. borders in fillets, spine gt. (SG. May 14; 135) $350
- De Rerum Natura Libri sex. Leiden, 1545. Lacks final blank?, corner cut from title. Cont. vell. Owner's inscr. of James Beattie (philosopher?) on title & his MS. annots. in text. (SBA. Oct.21; 60) *Ponder.* £50
- – Anr. Edn. Bg'ham, 1772. 4to. Some ll. slightly browned. Cf. gt. by Charles Hering, gold fillets on spine & covers in ornamental gold borders on inner & outer dentelles. Fürst Starhemberg liby. (H. May 21/22; 986) DM 660

LUDEMANN, Wm. von & Witte, C.
- Pittoresker Italien. Leipzig, 1840. 3 vols. in 1. Lacks 1 plt., slightly browned in parts. Cont. cf. gt., slightly worn. (H. Dec.9/10; 584) DM 600

LUDEWIG, J.H.
- Frankfurt am Main und seine Umgebung. Ein Wegweiser fur Einheimische und Fremde. Frankfurt a. M., 1843. 2nd. Iss. Some foxing. Orig. ptd. bds., worn, bookblock loose. (VG. Dec.16; 936) Fls. 550

LUDOLF, H.
- Vollständige und Gründliche Einleitung in die Chymie. Erfiert, 1752. 1st. Edn. Lacks port. frontis. Hf. linen. (R. Mar.31-Apr.4; 1121) DM 1,600

LUDOLF Hiob, The Elder
- [–] Allg. Schau-Bühne der Welt. Frankfurt, 1699-1718. 1st. Edn. Vols. 1-4 (of 5). Fo. Vol. 1 lacks copper engrs. 13 & 14 (on 1 plt.), copper engraved title & 2 next ll. frayed, lightly soiled. Cont. vell., 1 spine slightly defect. (HK. Nov.18-21; 1256) DM 750
- New History of Ethiopia. Trans.:– J.P. L., 1682. 1st. Engl. Edn. Fo. 6 (of 9?) engrs., lacks map. Recent cl. (TA. Nov.20; 104) £55

LUDOLPHUS de Saxonia
- Vita Christi. [Strassburg?], [Heinrich Eggestein?], 1474. 1st. Edn. Fo. Capital spaces, 2 lge. initials in blue & green respectively, the 1st. with green & white ornament in margin, 2nd. with lge. green descender incorporating flowers in lr. margin, other initials, underlinings & initial strokes supplied in red, all by cont. hand., lacks final blank lf., light dampstaining to some ll. from fo. 300 to end. Cont. blind-tooled German cf. over

wood bds., upr. cover with floral diaper pattern, lr. cover with lge. intersected double lozenge, later brass clasps, rebkd., edges & corners renewed. Bkplts. of J.B. Inglis & the General Theological Seminary Liby. [BMC I, 75, Goff L337, HC 10290] (CNY. Oct.1; 58) $4,600
- – Anr. Edn. Nuremb., Anton Koberger, 20 Dec. 1478. Fo. Rubricated thro.-out, blank corner of lf. reprd., last 2 ll. slightly stained with sm. wormholes affecting a few letters of text. Old. cf., rebkd. with buckram. [H. 10292*; BMC II p. 417; Goff L339] (C. Apr.1; 122) *Kleinwort.* £240
- – Anr. Edn. [Lyon], [1486]. 2 pts. in 1 vol. Fo. Lightly wormed thro.-out, more at beginning, some old marginalia, lacks lf. & blank end-lf. 16th. C. style leath.-bkd. wood bds. gt., 2 metal clasps. (R. Mar.31-Apr.4; 56) DM 5,200

LUDOVICUS GRANATENSIS
See–GRANADA, Luis de

LUDOVICUS OF PRUSSIA
- Trilogium Animae. Ed.:– Nic. Glasberg de Moravia. Ill.:– Albrecht Duerer. Nuremb., Anton Koberger, 6 Mar. 1498. 4to. Initials thro.-out painted in red, 2 ll. loose. Cont. blind-tooled cf. over wooden bds., vell. pastedowns, 2 metal clasps, leath. markers on fore-edges, back defect. & covers worn & weakened, mod. cl. folding case. [H. 10315; Goff L379] (PNY. Mar.26; 194) $2,000

LUDOVICUS RABUS von Memmingen
- Historien der Heyligen Ausserwoelten Gotten Zeuegen . . . Strassburg, 1554. 4to. Mod. gt. purple mor. Bkplt. (PNY. Oct.1; 336) $140

LUDWIG, Carl Friedrich Wilhelm
- Arbeiten aus der Physiologischen Anstalt zu Leipzig. Leipzig, 1867-77. Vols. 1-11 in 5 vols. Bds. As a periodical, w.a.f. (S. Jun.16; 533) *Jenner Books.* £420

LUFF, John N.
- The Postage Stamps of the United States. N.Y., 1902. 4to. Buckram. (SG. Feb.12; 319) $130

LUGAR, Robert
- Plans & Views of Buildings . . . in the Castellated & other Styles. 1823. New Edn. 4to. Slight offsetting. Cl.-bkd. bds., worn. (S. Jun.22; 57) *Marlborough Rare Books.* £160
- Villa Architecture. 1828. Fo. 2 additional cold. aquatint plts. (1 with overslip) pasted to front end-papers. Cont. hf. mor., worn, upr. jnt. brkn. (C. Nov.5; 97) *Cooper.* £550

LUGO, Bernardo de
- Gramatica en la Lengua General del Nouevo Reyno, llama da Mosca. Madrid, 1619. Inscr. on title 'Libreria de Augso Descs de Sta Fee'. Mod. pig. (SPB. May 5; 330) $850

LUGT, Frits
- Les Marques des Collections de Dessins et d'Estampes. Amst., 1921. Orig. cl. (CSK. Aug.29; 206) £85
- – Anr. Edn. Amst. & The Hague, 1921 & 1956. 4to. Orig. linen. (R. Mar.31-Apr.4; 895) DM 650
- – Anr. Copy. Sm. fo. Linen. (R. Oct.14-18; 698) DM 660
- – Anr. Edn. The Hague, 1956. 2 vols. 4to. Orig. buckram. (SM. Oct.7; 1441) Frs. 4,000
- – Anr. Edn. The Hague, 1956. Vol. 1 reprint of 1921 Edn. 4to. Orig. linen. (H. Dec.9/10; 23) DM 500
- – Anr. Edn. San Franc. & the Hague, 1956-75. 2 vols. including supp. 4to. Orig. cl. (SH. Mar. 6; 543) *Ward-Jackson.* £280
- – Anr. Copy. 2 vols. (SH. Jun.4; 21) *Pilkington.* £200
- – Anr. Copy. Orig. linen, not unif. (H. Dec.9/10; 24) DM 550
- – Anr. Copy. 2 vols. (H. May 21/22; 5) DM 500
- Les Marques des Collections de Dessins & D'Estampes.-Les Marques . . . Supplement. San Franc.; The Hague, 1975; 1956. 1 vol.; 2 vols. Orig. cl. (CSK. Jan.9; 103) £200

LUGT, Frits & Vallery-Radot, J.
- Bibliothèque National. Inventaire général des Dessins des Ecoles du Nord. Paris, 1936. 4to. Mod. cl. (SH. Mar.6; 545) *Sapori.* £50

LUHE, H.E.W.v.d.
- Militair–Conversations–Lexibon. Leipzig, 1833-41. Cont. bds. (R. Mar.31-Apr.4; 1772) DM 600

LUIKEN, Jan
- **Afbeeldingen der Merkwaardigste Geschiedenissen van het Oude en Nieuwe Testament.** Ed.:– P. Langendyk. Amst., 1729. Fo. Hf. roan, defect. (B. Dec.10/11; 1390) Fls. 1,200
- **Beschouwing der Wereld ...** Amst., 1708. 1st. Edn. Cont. vell. (HK. May 12-14; 1003) DM 640
- **Icones Biblicae ...** Amst., ca. 1729. Fo. 61 engraved double-p. plts. including title (of 62), 7 engraved double-p. maps. 19th. C. hf. roan, corners & spine worn. (S. Nov.25; 420)
Cohen. £160
- **Het Leerzaam Huisraad.** Ill.:– Jan Luykens. Amst., 1711. 1st. Edn. Cont. blind-tooled vell. (R. Mar.31-Apr.4; 1639) DM 500
- – **Anr. Edn.** Amst., 1756. 3rd. Edn. Cont. vell., soiled. (VG. Nov.18; 1269) Fls. 475
- **De Onwaardige Wereld, Vertoones in Vyftig Zinnebeelden met Godlyke Spreuken.** Ill.:– Jan Luiken. Amst., 1728. Cont. vell. bds., slightly soiled. (S. Apr.7; 266) *Temperley.* £100
- **De Schriftuurlyke Geschiedenissen en Gelykenissen van het Oude en Nieuwe Verbond. Met het Leven van den Dichter.** Ill.:– Jan Luiken. Amst., 1712. 2 pts. in 1 vol. 4to. Tear in 5 ll. reprd., stained. 19th. C. hf. roan, defect. & reprd. (VG. Dec.17; 1144) Fls. 500

LUITPOLD, Herzog in Bayern.
- **Die Fränkische Bildwirkerei.** Munich, 1926. Text & plt. vol. Lge. fo. Orig. hf. leath. (R. Oct.14-18; 775) DM 850

LUITPRANDUS Ticinensis, Bp. of Cremona
- **Rerum Gestarum per Europam ...** [Paris], 1514. Fo. Title & some ll. slightly soiled, some cont. marginalia. 18th. C. vell. bds., gt. border & fleur-de-lys corner-pieces on covers, spine unif. gt. (S. Feb.10; 330) *Thomas.* £65

LUKIAN
- **Die Hetärengespräche.** Trans.:– Fr. Blei. Ill.:– G. Klimt. Leipzig, 1907. (100) privilege Edn. 4to. Doe. (H. Dec.9/10; 2147) DM 2,600
- – **Anr. Copy.** (450). Orig. linen. (H. May 21/22; 1673) DM 1,100

LUKMAN called AL-HAKIM
- **Fabulae et selecta quaedam Arabum Adagia.** Trans.:– T. Erpenius. Leiden, 1615. Some soiling & staining. Mod. cf. (S. Apr.29; 415) *Hosain's Books.* £240

LUKOMSKI, Geo. K.
- **L'Architecture Religieuse Russe.–Le Kreml de Moscou.** Paris, 1929; n.d. 2 vols. 4to. Orig. wraps.; cont. hf. mor. (SH. Mar.6; 541) *Weinreb.* £50

LULLIUS, Raimundus
- **Codicillus seu Vade Mecum, in quo Fontes alchimicae Artis ac Philosophiae reconditioris uberrime traduntur.** Cologne, 1572. Sm. burn hole in lr. blank margin of pp. 63-66. Limp vell. (S. Dec.1; 258) *Rota.* £85
- **Künstliche Eröffnung aller Verborgenheyten und Geheymnussen der Natur, durch wölche die war Kunst der Artzney und Alchimey ...** Augsburg, 1532. 4to. Vell. (R. Oct.14-18; 203) DM 6,000

LULLY, J.B. de
- **Atys.** Paris, 1689. 1st. Edn. Fo. Cont. marb. cf., flor. spine gt. (H. Dec.9/10; 1185) DM 1,800

LUMEN ANIMAE
Ed.:– M. Farinator. [Strassburg], [1481]. Fo. Rubricated thro.-out, hundreds of red initials, upr. end-paper stpd., end-lf. & 1st. p. with MS. entry, some light staining, lacks ll. 2-8 & last. Cont. blind-tooled leath-bkd. wood bds., 2 clasps, lacks ties. [H. 10, 333; BMC 1, 97; Goff L 396] (D. Dec.11-13; 217) DM 2,400

LUMISDEN or LUMSDEN, Andrew
- **Remarks on the Antiquities of Rome & its Environs.** 1797. 1st. Edn. 4to. Extra-ill. with 48 orig. watercolour drawings by Martorana of Rome, some foxing & offsetting (not affecting the drawings). Cont. str.-grd. mor., gt. The John Dent copy, bkplt. of Rev. Sidney Mead, stp. of the Franleigh House Liby. on title. (S. Feb.10; 337) *Thomas.* £1,200
- – **Anr. Copy.** Port., 12 full-p. & folding engraved views & maps, extra-ill. with 24 orig. water-cols. on vell. Elab. gt.-tooled str.-grd. mor. (SG. Oct.9; 152) $1,500

LUNAN, John
- **Hortus Jamaicensis.** Jamaica, 1814. 1st. Edn. 2 vols. 4to. Browned, some stains, minor tears. New

mor.-bkd. marb. bds., unc. [Sabin 42683] (SPB. May 5; 331) $325

LUNARDI, Vincenzo
- **An Account of the First Aerial Voyage in England.** Ill.:– Bartolozzi after Cosway (engraved port.). 1784. 1st. Edn. Advts., lacks hf.-title, blank corner torn from f. E4. Mod. bds. (S. Dec.2; 743) *Cavendish.* £160

LUND (or Lundius), Johannes
- **Die Alten Juedischen Heiligthuemer Gottesdienste und Gewohnheiten Fuer Augen Gestellet in Einer Ausfuehrlichen Beschreibung des Ganzen Levitischen Priesterthums.** Hamburg, 1704. 5 books in 1 vol. Fo. Slight discoloration. Vell. (S. Nov.18; 672) *Valmadonna.* £170
- – **Anr. Edn.** Ed.:– H. Muhl & J.C. Wolf. Hamburg, 1738. Fo. Browned, some plts. slightly defect. Cont. hf. leath. (R. Oct.14-18; 1259) DM 1,100

LUNE, La
Ill.:– Andre Gill & others. Paris, 10 Dec. 1876-Jun. 1879. Weekly iss. & 3 special nos. in 2 vols. Tall fo. Many iss. of various papers (from 1869-1875) bnd. at end of 2nd. vol. Leath.-bkd. bds., 1 vol. disbnd. W.a.f. (SG. May 21; 365) $700

LUPSET, Thomas
- **Workes.** 1546. 1st. Edn. Slight marginal dampstaining, owner's inscr. on fly-lf. Cont. cf., rebkd. [NSTC 16932] (S. Jul.27; 60) *Sibu.* £180

LURCAT, Jean
- **Tapisseries, 1939-1957.** Dordogne, 1957. (100) numbered & sigd., with orig. cold. litho. (numbered & sigd.) laid in. 4to. Pict. cl., cold. pict. s.-c. (SG. Apr.2; 178) $350

LUSCINIUS, Ottomar
See–THEOPHRASTUS–Luscinius, Ottomar
–RINGELBERGIUS, Joachimus–Marulus, Marcus
–PLATINA, Bartholomaeus

LUSITANO, J.P.–EPISTOLAE INDICAE, de stupenddis et praeclaris Rebus, quas divina Bonitas in India et Variis Insulis per Societatem Nominis Jesu, operari dignata est, in tam copiosa Gentium ad Fidem conversione. (In lucem missae per J.R. Berg)
- **De Societatis Jesu Origine.** Leuven, 1566; 1566. 2 works in 1 vol. Upr. margin of 12 ll. defect. & reprd. with loss of some words, a few stains, browned in places, bnd. in reverse order. Cont. limp vell., loose. [Sabin 22704 (1st. work)] (VG. Dec.17; 1308) Fls. 500

LUSSAN, Mlle. de
- **Les Veillées de Thessalie.** Paris, 1741. 3rd. Edn. 4 vols. 12mo. Sigd. on titles by Guyon de Sardiére, bkplt. of Henry J.B. Clements. Cont. mor., gt. dentelle border, flat spines gt. in compartments, inner gt. dentelles, gt. & white starred end-papers. (SH. Oct.7; 1827) Frs. 1,200

LUSSAN, Ravenau de
See–[EXQUEMELIN, A.O.]-LUSSAN, Ravenau de

LUTH FRANCAISE, (Le): Almanach Lyrique, dedié aux Dames
Paris, [1820]. 32mo. Bds., gt. border, ornate gt. spine, gt. ornam. s.-c. Label of Susse, Papetier de S.A.R., le Duc de Berry. (SG. Oct.9; 153) $425

LUTHER, Martin
[–] **Aliquot Nomina Propria Germanorum ad Priscam Etymologiam restituta.** [Augsburg], ca. 1545. Title with sm. margin tears & bkd., slight staining in parts in margin & soiling. Bds. (D. Dec.11-13; 35) DM 450
- **Alle Bücher vnd Schrifften.** Ed.:– [N. von Amsdorff, J. Aurifaber & others.] Jena, 1558-62. 2nd., Jena Compl. Edn. in German. Lacks Vols. III & VIII, 6 vols. Fo. Vol. 1 with pasted woodcut port. of Bugenhagen pasted in lr. cover, old notes in upr. cover. browned thro.-out, stained or soiled in parts, some MS. notes, monog. on upr. cover, dated 1566. (H. Dec.9/10; 1350) DM 1,600
- **A Commentarie upon the Epistle of S. Paule to the Galathians.** [L.], 1580. 4to. Old cf., rebkd. [STC 16967] (SG. Feb.5; 217) $250
- **Enchiridion piarum precationum, cum Passionali, ut vocant, quibus accessit nouum Calendarium cum Cisio iano ietere & novo.** Wittenberg, 1543. Title soiled & cropped at fore-e., some headlines slightly cropped, a few cont. MS. marginal notes,

occasional minor stains. 19th. C. mott. bds., worn. (SPB. May 6; 210) $550
- **Der Erste [–Achte] Teil aller Bücher und Schrifften.** Jena, 1555-77. 1st. Iss. I-III, V-VII, 4th. Iss. IV; 3rd. Iss. VIII. 8 vols. Fo. Title & a few ll. with old MS. notes, some tears & faults, slightly wormed in parts with minimal text loss, slightly browned & soiled, sm. defects. Cont. blind-stpd. pig, lacks clasps. (HK. Nov.18-21; 227) DM 5,000
- **Der Erste Theil der Bücher über Etliche Epistle der Aposteln.** Ill.:– Lucas Cranach (title woodcut). Wittenburg, 1552. Fo. Lightly browned. Cont. blind-tooled pig-bkd. wood bds., 2 brass clasps, 1 renewed. (R. Mar.31-Apr.4; 66) DM 650
- **Hauspostil.** Ed.:– V. Dietrich. Wittenberg, 1552. Later Edn. Lightly browned, 1 lf. with sm. hole. Cont. cf.-bkd. wood bds., blind-tooled, spine & 1 corner torn, lacks clasps, dtd. 1555, decor. (H. Dec.9/10; 1355) DM 380
- **Eine Nutzliche Predigt.** Wittenberg, 1531. 1st. Edn., 1st. printing. 4to. Some sm. wormholes, sm. stain thro.-out at head. Paper bds., spine defect. (H. Dec.9/10; 1356) DM 800
- **In Esaiam Prophetam Scholia.** Wittenberg, 1534. 2nd. Edition. Some old MS. marginalia in parts. 18th. C. vell., spine defect. (R. Mar.31-Apr.4; 68) DM 530
- **Opera Omnia.** Jena, 1566 & 1579. Fo. Old MS. entries, lightly browned. Cont. blind-tooled pig-bkd. wood bds., 2 (of 4) clasps. (HK. May 12-14; 124) DM 600
- **Operationes in duas Psalmorum Decades.** Basle, 1521. Fo. Inscr. on fore-e. Old bds., corners worn. (S. Jan.27; 340) *Goldschmidt.* £320
[–] **Die Psalmen.** [Darmstadt], Ernst Ludwig Pr., [1911]. (500). Fo. Gt.-lettered & decor. vell., partly unc. (SG. Sep.4; 172) $140
- **Sämmtliche Schriften.** J.G. Walch. Halle, 1740-53. 4to. Lightly soiled in parts. Cont. leath. W.a.f. (HK. May 12-14; 1183) DM 520
- **Ein Sermö Vber den Herrlich Spruch, Joannis am v. Suchet in der Schrifft.** Wittenberg, 1546. 1st. Edn. 4to. Title slightly soiled. Bds. (HK. Nov.18-21; 229) DM 460
- **Ain Sermon von der Beraytung zum Sterben.** Ill.:– H. Schaufelein. [Augsburg], [1519]. 4to. Stained thro.-out. Wraps. (H. May 21/22; 929) DM 1,400
- **Eyn Sermon von Stercke und Zunemen des Glaubens und der Liebe. Aus der Epistel S. Pauli xum Ephesern.** Ill.:– L. Cranach. Wittenberg, 1526. 3rd. Wittenberg Edn. 4to. 12 ll. (R. Oct.14-18; 108) DM 520
- **Das Tauff Buchlin.** [Wittenberg], [1523]. 1st. Edn., 1st. Printing. 4to. Owner's mark on title, slightly soiled. Hf. leath. (H. May 21/22; 933) DM 2,700
- **Vom Abedmal Christi, Bekenntnis.** Ill.:– L. Cranach (title border). Wittenberg, 1534. 3rd. Edn. Wide margin. 4to. Owner's mark on title. Later 19th. C. vell., gt. inner & outer dentelle, by J. Baden. (HK. May 12-14; 138) DM 420
- **Von beyder Gestalt des Sacraments tzu nemen: vnd ander new rung.** [Wittenberg], [1522]. 2nd. Edn. Sm. 4to. 3 sm. tears in title bkd., title lightly browned, some old MS. notes. Wraps. (H. May 21/22; 931) DM 600
- **Von dem Bapstum zu Rome.** [Nüremb.], [1520]. 3rd. Edn. 4to. 24 ll. (R. Oct.14-18; 103) DM 550
- **Von Kauffshandlung und Wucher.** Wittenberg, 1524. 1st. Edn. 4to. Slightly stained. Leath. (R. Oct.14-18; 107) DM 2,100
- **Der Zehen Gebot Gotes ain Schöne Nutzliche Erklerung.** Ill.:– H. Schäufelein. Augsburg, 1520. 3rd. Printing. 4to. 1st. ll. with slight browning, title lf. with marginal stain. Wraps. (H. May 21/22; 928) DM 1,300
See–ETLICH Christliche Lyeder Lobgesang und Psalm

LUTHER, Martin–OECOLAMPADIUS, Joannes
- **Enarrationes Epistolarvm, qvas Postillas Vocant. –De non habendo Pavpervm Delectu.** Basel, 1521; 1523. 3rd. Edn.; 1st Edn. 2 works in 1 vol. 4to. Title slightly defect (1) & soiled (2). Cont. limp vell., slightly cockled, lacks ties. (HK. Nov.18-21; 228) DM 420

LUTTEROTTI, O.R. von
- **Joseph Anton Koch, 1768-1839.** Berlin, 1940. 4to. Orig. cl., stained. (S. Jul.27; 183) *Zwemmer.* £55
- – **Anr. Copy.** [With Index & letters]. Fo. Orig. linen. (HK. May 12-14; 2393) DM 650

LUTYENS, Sir Edwin Landseer
- Houses & Gardens. Ed.:– Lawrence Weaver. L., 1914. Reprinted from 1913 1st. Edn. Fo. Orig. hf. cl. & bds. (CB. May 27; 213)   Can. $200
– – **Anr. Edn.** Ed.:– Lawrence Weaver. L., 1921. Orig. bds. & cl. spine. (CB. May 27; 214)   Can. $110
– – **Anr. Edn.** Ed.:– Sir Lawrence Weaver. 1925. Fo. Cl. (CE. Apr.23; 68)   £55

LUTYENS, Robert
[–] Sir Edwin Lutyens, an Appreciation in Perspective By His Son. [1942]. Orig. cl., d.-w. (CB. May 27; 146)   Can. $110

LUTZOW, C.V.
- Die Vervielfältigende Kunst d. Gegenwart. Vienna, 1887-1903. 4 vols. Fo. Cont. hf. leath., worn. (HK. Nov.18-21; 2785)   DM 700

LUXAN, Mariano
- Relación Fúnebre de las Reales Exequias. Lima, 1760. Sm. 4to. Cont. cf. (SPB. May 5; 322) $150

LUYKEN, Jan
See–LUIKEN or LUYKEN, Jan

LUYS, Jules Bernard
- Iconographie Photographique des Centres Nerveux. Paris, 1873. 1 vol. text & atlas with 70 photographic plts. 8vo. & sm. fo. Orig. cl., stained. (S. Jun.16; 537)   Norman. £650
- Recherches sur le Système Nerveux Cerebro-Spinal. Paris, 1865. 1 vol. text & atlas with 40 cold. plts. Lacks hf.-title in text vol. Text hf. cf., worn, atlas orig. ptd. bds., very worn. (S. Jun.16; 536)   Rota. £130

LUZ, Diario de la República
[1932]. Yr. I, 5 vols., lacks May & Jun. Linen. (DS. Apr.24; 868)   Pts. 50,000

LUZ, Maria
See–KOCHNO, Boris & Luz, Maria

LUZERNE, Cardinal de la
- La Déclaration de l'Assemblée du Clergé de France en 1682. 1821. Long-grd. mor., palmette border ornamental spine. Comte d'Artois arms. (HD. Oct.10; 276)   Frs. 2,400

LUZURIAGA, Juan de
- Paranympho Celeste. Historia de la Mystica Zarza . . . y prodigioso Santuario de Aranzazu . . . en la Provincia Guypuzocoa. Mexico, 1686. 4to. Engraved frontis. reprd. with loss of engraved surface, title & last lf. with margins restored. Cont. limp vell., new end-papers. (SPB. May 5; 333) $550

LYALL, Robert
- The Character of the Russians & a Detailed History of Moscow. 1823. [1st. Edn.?]. 4to. Mod. hf. cf., earlier spine preserved. (SH. Nov.7; 351)   Walford. £170
– – **Anr. Copy.** Loose, disbnd. (SH. May 21; 72)   Moore. £120
– – **Anr. Copy.** Mod. hf. cf. (SG. Oct.30; 316) $600

LYDEKKER, Richard
- Animal Portraiture. 1912. 1st. Edn. 2 vols. Fo. Some marginal spotting. Loose in orig. cl. folder. (TA. Jun.18; 82)   £70
– – **Anr. Edn.** N.d. Fo. Decor. cl. gt. (CE. Nov.20; 7)   £50
- The Deer of all Lands. 1898. Ltd. Edn., sigd. by publisher. 4to. Cl. gt., slightly soiled. (P. Nov.13; 242)   Quaritch. £320
– – **Anr. Copy.** Cl. (SG. Dec.11; 354) $700
- The Great & Small Game of Europe, West & Northern Asia & America. 1901. 1st. Edn. 4to. Orig. cl. gt., slightly worn. (BS. Sep.17; 70)   £80
- Wild Oxen, Sheep & Goats of all Lands. 1898. [1st. Edn.?], (500) numbered, sigd. by publisher. 4to. Cl. gt., slightly soiled. (P. Nov.13; 243)   Quaritch. £380
– – **Anr. Copy.** Cl. (SG. Sep.18; 228) $600
– – **Anr. Copy.** With the corrigenda & errata ll. tipped-in. Gt.-lettered cl., liby. bkplt. (SG. Dec.11; 352) $275
– – **Anr. Copy.** With the corrigenda & errata slips, liby.-stps. on verso of all plts. Rebnd. in buckram. (SG. Dec.11; 353) $275

LYDGATE, D.J.
See–HOLBEIN, Hans–LYDGATE, D.J.

LYE, Edward
See–SOMNER, William–JUNIUS, Franciscus
–LYE, Edward

LYELL, Sir Charles
- Elements of Geology. 1838. 1st. Edn. 12mo. Orig. bds., unc. (S. Dec.2; 843)   Quaritch. £60
- Principles of Geology. L., 1830-33. 1st. Edn. 3 vols. Some staining along top section of prelims. of Vols. 1 & 3, some foxing & offsetting, with hf.-titles in vols. 1 & 3. Cont. hf. cf. & marb. bds. (VA. Jan.30; 658)   R. 480
– – **Anr. Edn.** 1832-33. 2nd. Edn. 3 vols. Some foxing & offsetting. Cont. hf. pig. (S. Dec.3; 1044)   Villiers. £160
- A Second Visit to the United States of North America. L., 1849. 1st. Edn. 2 vols. Slight foxing. Orig. blind-stpd. cl., gt. spine. From liby. of William E. Wilson. [Sabin 42763] (SPB. Apr.29; 181) $175
– – **Anr. Edn.** N.Y., 1849. 1st. Amer. Edn. 2 vols. 12mo. Cl. (SG. Mar. 5; 288) $110

LYELL, James P.R.
- Early Book Illustration in Spain. Ed.:– Dr. Konrad Haebler. 1926. (500) numbered, sigd. 4to. Orig. cl., partly unc. (TA. Sep.18; 1)   £95

LYNCH, George & Palmer, Frederick (Ed.)
See–IN MANY WARS

LYNDSAY or LINDSAY, Sir David
- Facsimile of an Ancient Heraldic Manuscript. 1822. Fo. Mor.-bkd. bds. (CE. Jul.9; 203)   £140
– – **Anr. Copy.** 4to. Orig. cl. (SH. Jan.29; 32)   Heraldry Today. £55
- Heraldry. 1822. Fo. Bds. & roan, worn. (CE. Nov.20; 144)   £80

LYON, Capt. George Francis
- A Brief Narrative of an Unsuccessful Attempt to reach Repulse Bay. 1825. Cont. hf. cf. gt., rebkd. preserving orig. spine. (C. Nov.6; 323)   Walford. £60

LYS (Les)
- Etrennes aux Dames. Ill.:– after Beranger, Bres, Madame de Genlis, Parmy, etc. Paris, 1815. 16mo. Cont. cf., decor. spine, gt. decor. covers, roulette border in gt. fillets, inner dentelles. (HD. Apr.10; 151)   Frs. 1,250

LYSONS, Daniel
- The Environs of London: being an historical account of the towns . . . within twelve miles of that capital. 1796 [1791]-1811. 1st. Edn. (L.P.). 6 vols. (including 2 supps.). 4to. Extra-ill. with 26 additional plts. of cont. or slightly later views, inscrs., etc. Cont. russ., 3 vols. rebkd., Sir Gore Ouseley's bkplt. (S. Nov.4; 530)   Reid. £400
– – **Anr. Edn.** 1800-11. 3 vols. in 7 including supp. Extra-ill. with views, plans, ports., etc. Hf. mor. worn. As an extra-ill. copy, w.a.f. (P. Jan.22; 118)   Hunter. £190
– – **Anr. Copy.** 4to. Extra ill. Cont. hf. mor., worn. W.a.f. (CSK. Oct.17; 108)   £120

LYSONS, Daniel & Samuel
- Magna Britannia. 1806-22. 7 vols. in 9, including the atlas of 'Additional Plates'. 4to. Some maps & c. hand-cold. Cont. crimson str.-grd. mor. gt., the seal of Lord Grenville gt-stpd. on covers, the atlas bnd. in crimson str.-grd. mor. gt. by Bumpus. From the collection of Eric Sexton. (C. Apr.16; 302)   Quaritch. £850
– – **Anr. Edn.** Ill.:– Neele. 1810. Vol. 2 only (of Cambridgeshire & Chester). 4to. Qtr. cl., covers & a few ll. at beginning & end detchd. (TA. Oct.16; 286)   £70
– – **Anr. Edn.** 1817. Vol. 5 only (of Derbyshire). Hf. cf. (DWB. Mar.31; 351)   £78
– – **Anr. Edn.** 1822. Vol. 6 only in 2 vols. 4to. 1 plt. cold., 1 folding plt. torn. Orig. embossed cl., lacks 1 cover, 2 others detchd., spines defect. (LC. Feb.12; 199)   £55
- Topographical & Historical Account of Bedfordshire. N.d. 4to. Spotted. Cont. hf. cf., rebkd. & reprd. (SH. Mar.5; 91)   Inskid. £70

LYSONS, Samuel
- An Account of Roman Antiquities descovered at Woodchester in the County of Gloucester. 1797. Lge. fo. Plts. wtrmkd. 1794, text & a few plts. foxed. Cont. str.-grd. mor., gt., by Kalthoeber, with his ticket, broad ornamental borders with Greek key-pattern, etc., spine gt. with urns in 6 compartments. Bkplt. of Thomas Lambert (nephew & heir of Sir Robert Smirke). (S. Jun.22; 59)   Maggs. £750
– – **Anr. Copy.** Cont. red hf. mor., rebkd. with orig. gt. spine preserved. (C. Nov.5; 99)   Temperley. £250

– – **Anr. Copy.** Some plts. slightly spotted. Cont. hf. mor., soiled. (SD. Feb.4; 240)   £140

LYTLE, Horace
- Point a Book about Bird Dogs. N.Y., Derrydale Pr., [1941]. (950) numbered. Orig. bdg. (SG. Apr.9; 350) $100

LYTTON, Edward George Lytton Bulwer, Baron
- Zanoni. Edinb., 1861. Vol. 1 (of 2). Cf. gt. Fore-e. pntg. on both upr. & lr. edges. (SG. Sep.4; 185) $375
- Works. 1873-75. Knebworth Edn. 40 vols. Prelims. slightly spotted. Cont. hf. mor. gt. (SBA. Dec.16; 235)   Mortens of Manchester. £55
– [–] **Anr. Edn.** 1887-89. 14 vols. Cont. hf. cf. (SH. May 28; 71)   Wade Gallery. £50
– – **Anr. Edn.** N.d. (500) numbered, De Luxe Edn. 32 vols. Hf. red mor., gt. (CE. Jul.9; 55)   £130
– – **Anr. Copy.** Hf. mor., unc. (SPB. Nov. 25; 475) $375

M., [A.D.]
- Gamiani. Paris, 1864. In 2 pts. Hf. mor. gt. (P. Feb.19; 13)   Bibn. £160

M, L.C.B.
- Noveau Traité des Oeillets. Paris, 1689. 12mo. A few tears, dampstains. Cont. vell. (SH. Jun.18; 47)   Shaw. £55

M., W.
- The Queens Closet Opened.–[A Queens Delight. –The Compleat Cook]. 1679. 3 pts. in 1 vol. 12mo. 1 gathering loose in bdg. Cont. sheep. [Wing M103] (C. Feb.25; 163)   Segal. £600

MAANDELYSKE Nederlandsche Mercurius
Amst., 1757-75. Vols. 1-39 in 10. 4to. Cont. hf. cf. (SH. May 21; 27)   Forum. £110

MAASKAMP, E.
- Representations of Dresses, Morals & Costumes in the Kingdom of Holland. Amst., 1808. 4to. 12 cold. plts. (of 20). Bds., worn. (BS. Jun.11; 367)   £60
[–] Tableaux de l'Habillement . . . Republique Batave. Amst., [1805]. 4to. Some slight foxing & staining, not affecting plts. Hf. cf., worn. (BS. Jun.11; 366)   £150
- Voyage dans l'Interieur de la Hollande, fait dans les Années 1807-12. Amst., ca. 1812. Vols. 1 & 2 (of 3). 23 plts. (of 24, lacks the plt. of 'Mausolée de M. de Ruiter') aquatint views & 13 hand-cold. costume plts. Cont. hf. leath. (VG. Dec.16; 937)   Fls. 1,400

MABILLON, Johann
- De Re Diplomatica libri IV. Paris, 1681. 1st. Edn. Fo. Slight spotting, both titles slightly damaged. Cont. cf., slightly worn, rebkd. (S. Oct.21; 284)   Quaritch. £250
– – **Anr. Edn.** Paris, 1681-1704. 1st. Edn. 2 vols, including supp. Fo. Some browning. Cont. spr. cf., spines gt., bkplts. of Biblioteca Turkheimiana & Dr. Maximilian Joseph Pfeiffer. (S. Apr.7; 339)   Quaritch. £240

MABINOGION
Trans.:– Gwyn & Thomas Jones. Ill.:– Dorothea Braby. Gold. Cock. Pr., 1948. (550) numbered. Fo. Orig. hf. mor. (CSK. Apr.3; 54)   £160
– – **Anr. Copy.** (S. Jul.31; 101)   Adams. £120
– – **Anr. Copy.** Cont. three-qtr. mor. gt. by Sangorski & Sutcliffe. (SBA. Oct.22; 727)   Chesters. £100
– – **Anr. Copy.** Buckram covers with lge. gt. emblematic device, lev. spine, by Sangorski & Sutcliffe. (SG. Sep.4; 209) $260

MacADAM, John Loudon
- Bemerkungen uber das Gegenwartige System des Chausseebau's. Darmstadt, 1825. 1st. German Edn.(?). Orig. ptd. wraps. (S. Dec.2; 744)   Quaritch. £55

McAFEE, Robert B.
[–] History of the Late War in the Western Country . . . Lexington, 1816. 1st. Edn. Browned & foxed. Mod. cf., gt. spine. From liby. of William E. Wilson. (SPB. Apr.29; 182) $500
– – **Anr. Copy.** Sig. of A. McNair on title, browned & foxed. Mod. hf. cf., marb. bds. & end-papers, gt. spine. From liby. of William E. Wilson. (SPB. Apr.29; 183) $300

McALMON, Robert
- A Companion Volume. Paris, n.d. Slight browning. Orig. wraps. bnd. in buckram, s.-c., bkplt. of Shakespeare & Co. Pres. copy. (SPB. Nov.25; 343) $150

MACARTHUR, James
– New South Wales. Ill.:– J. Gross. 1837. 1st. Edn.
Orig. cl. (C. Jul.15; 72) *Walford.* £60

MACARTHUR, John
– The Army & Navy Gentleman's Companion. L.,
1784. 4to. Cont. bds., unc., worn, lacks spine. MS.
dedication. (HK. Nov.18-21; 1582) DM 700
See–CLARKE, Rev. J.S. & MacArthur, John

MACARTNEY, George, Earl of
– Voyage en Chine et en Tartarie. Trans.:– J.B.
Breton. Paris, 1804. 7 vols. 16mo. Cont. cf., decor.
spines, gt. decor. on covers, inner dentelle. (HD.
Apr.9; 517) Frs. 1,700

MacASKILL, Wallace R.
– Out of Halifax. Ed.:– G.M. Adams. Ill.:– after
MacAskill. 1937. (450) numbered for Canada. 4to.
2-tone buckram, very worn. (SG. Dec.11; 262)
$160

MACAULAY, Lord Thomas Babington
– Works. Ed.:– Lady Trevelyan. L., 1875. 8 vols.
Crimson red three-qtr. lev., raised bands. (SG.
Sep.4; 316) $140

**MACAULAY, Lord Thomas Babington–GREEN,
Prof. John Richard**
– History of England.–A Short History of the
English People. L., 1861; 1892. 5 vols.; 4 vols. Cf.;
hf. leath. (SG. Dec.18; 46) $100

MacBEAN, Forbes
– Sketches of Character & Costume in
Constantinople. 1854. 5 orig. pts. Fo. Orig. wraps.
(SH. Nov.6; 241) *Placeglow Ltd.* £270

MACBETH, George
– The Night of Stones. 1968. (110) sigd. Mor.,
irregular designs of gt. line tooling, some
compartments enclosing raised crumpled onlays,
designs repeated in reverse with smooth onlays on
mor. doubls., sigd. with initials, fitted case, by
Sally Lou Smith. (SH. Feb.20; 406) *Maggs.* £200

McCALMONT, Rose E.
– Memoirs of the Binghams. L., 1915. 1st. Edn.
4to. Cl. (GM. Apr.30; 106) £65

MAC CARTHY, J.
– Choix de Voyages dans les Quatre Parties du
Monde . . . Paris, 1821-22. 10 vols. Glazed hf. cf.,
spines richly decor. (HD. Jun.29; 277) Frs. 1,250

MACCARTHY-REAGH, le Comte
– Catalogue des Livres . . . de la Bibliothèque.
Paris, 1815-16. 2 vols. 'Ordre des Vacations . . .
corrections et additions' at end of vol. II, lacks
hf.-title in vol. II, title reprd, at end of vol. 11, lacks
hf.-title in vol. 11, title reprd in vol. 1., 4 MS. ll.
tipped in vol. I, listing books bought by persons.
Cont. bds. rebkd. in cl., old paper spines laid down,
corners worn. (SM. Oct.7; 1443) Frs. 1,800
– – Anr. Edn. Paris, 1816. 2 vols. Ptd. prices bnd.
at end of Vol. 2, 16 pp. 'Ordre des Vacations . . .
Corrections (etc.)' loosely inserted, many annots.
Cont. marb. sheep, Stuart de Rothesay arms gt. on
covers. (SM. Oct.8; 2197) Frs. 1,300

**McCLELLAND, John–HOLMES, Samuel–SHEP-
HARD, Charles**
– Some Inquiries in the Province of Kemaon.–The
Journal . . . on Lord Macartney's Embassy to
China & Tar-Tary.–An Historical Account of the
Island of Saint Vincent. 1835; 1798; 1831. 3 works
in 3 vols. 1st. work: reprd. tear to folding map,
liby. stp. on title & some text ll.; 2nd. work:
subscriber's list detchd.; 3rd. work: frontis.
spotted, 2 text ll. with reprd. tears. 1st. work: cont.
cl., unc.; 2nd. work: orig. bds., unc.; 3rd. work:
cont. cl. From the collection of Eric Sexton. (C.
Apr.15; 38) *Farley.* £500

M'CLINTOCK, Sir Francis L.
– The Voyage of the 'Fox' in the Arctic Seas. 1859.
1st. Edn. Orig. cl. gt., rebkd. Inscr. by Lady
Franklin to Anna & Clara Waddington. (S.
Jul.27; 26) *Plant.* £60

McCOY, Frederick
– Natural History of Victoria. Melbourne,
1885-90. 2 vols. in orig. 20 pts. Orig. wraps.,
slightly worn. (S. Jun.1; 161) *White.* £100
– Prodromus of the Zoology of Victoria.
Melbourne, 1879. Decades 3-20 only (of 20). Ptd.
wraps. as iss., 4 or 5 wraps. detchd. & 2 lacking,
some backstrips & wraps. reprd. (KH.
Mar.24; 261) Aus. $130

McCOY, James C.
– Jesuit Relations of Canada, 1632-1673. Ed.:–
Lawrence C. Wroth. Paris, 1937. (325) numbered
on H.M.P. Buckram. (SG. Jan.22; 226) $150

McCRAE, Hugh
– Columbine. Ill.:– Norman Lindsay. Sydney,
1920. (25) numbered. 4to. Text pp. foxed, orig.
etching. Upr. cover slightly stained. (JL.
Jul.20; 675) Aus. $900
– Satyrs & Sunlight. Ed.:– Thomas Earp. Ill.:–
Norman Lindsay. Fanfrolico Pr., 1928. 4to. Orig.
mor. (SH. Mar.26; 328) *Quaritch.* £50

MACCULLOCH, Dr. John
[–] Remarks on the Art of making Wine. 1816. 1st.
Edn. 12mo. Lacks last (?blank) lf. Cont. hf. cf.
(SH. Oct.10; 309) *Abacus.* £95

McCULLOCH, John Ramsay
– Treatise on the Principles & Practical Influence
of Taxation & the Funding System.–Treatise on
the Succession to Property vacant by Death. 1845;
1848. 1st. Edns. 2 works in 1 vol. Cont. hf. cf.,
Lord Belper's bkplt. (S. Jan.26; 242)
Frognall. £80

McDIARMID, Hugh (Pseud.)
See–GRIEVE, Christopher Murray

McDONALD, Alexander (Pseud.)
See–DICKSON, R.W. 'Alexander McDonald'

**MACDONALD, Alexandre Charles, Duc de
Tarente**
See–TARENTE, Alexandre Charles Macdonald,
Duc de

McDONALD, Edward D.
– A Bibliography of D.H. Lawrence. Phila., 1925.
(100) numbered L.P. copies, sigd. by Lawrence &
McDonald. Linen-bkd. patterned bds. (SG.
Oct.2; 218) $100

MACDONALD, George
– Dealings with the Fairies. Ill.:– Arthur Hughes.
1867. 1st. Edn. 16mo. Orig. cl., worn. (SH.
Dec.11; 346) *Morton Wise.* £170
– A Threefold Cord. L., [1883]. 1st. Edn. 16mo.
Cl., unc. Sigd. & inscr., & with 3 p. A.L.s. (SG.
Mar.19; 244) $110

McDONALD, John
– Biographical Sketches of General Nathaniel
Massie, General Duncan McArthur, Captain
William Wells & General Simon Kenton . . . Cinc.,
1838. 1st. Edn. 12mo. Slight foxing & soiling, a
few gatherings loose. Cont. cf., soiled, gt. spine.
From liby. of William E. Wilson. [Sabin 43160]
(SPB. Apr.29; 186) $250

MacDONALD, Capt. R.J.
– History of the Dress of the Royal Regiment of
Artillery 1625-1897. 1899. (1500) numbered, sigd.
by author. 4to. Orig. cl.-bkd. bds., slightly soiled,
unc. (SKC. Feb.26; 1456) £55
– – Anr. Edn. L., 1899. (300) numbered & sigd.
Lge. 4to. Cl.-bkd. ptd. bds. (SG. Oct.30; 230)
$100

MACDOUGALL, Arthur R., Jnr.
– If it Returns with Scars: Dud Dean & Doc
Blakesley Stories. Bingham, Maine, Priv. ptd.,
[1942]. 1st. Edn. (750) numbered. Cl. (SG.
Oct.16; 169) $100

M'DOUGALL, George F.
– Voyage of H.M.S. 'Resolute'. 1857. Orig. cl.
(TRL. Dec.10; 85) £68

MACE, A.C.
See–CARTER, Howard & Mace, A.C.

MACE, Thomas
– Musick's Monument. 1676. 1st. Edn. Cont. cf.,
rebkd., spine worn. From the collection of Eric
Sexton. [Wing M120] (C. Apr.15; 116)
Fenyves. £700

MACERONI, Col. Francis
– Memoirs of the Life & Adventures of. L., 1838.
1st. Edn. 2 vols. Foxed. Hf. cf., needs rbdg. (SG.
Feb.26; 219) $100

M'EVOY, John
– Statistical Survey of the County of Tyrone.
Dublin, 1802. Orig. bdg., lacks covers. (GM.
Apr.30; 285) £100

MACEWEN, Sir William
– Atlas of Head Sections. Glasgow, 1893. 1st. Edn.
4to. Slight spotting. Orig. cl., slightly marked. (S.
Apr.6; 103) *Canale.* £150

– – Anr. Copy. Errata slip. Qtr. mor. (S.
Jun.16; 540) *Whitehart.* £120
– Pyogenic Infective Diseases of the Brain &
Spinal Cord. Glasgow, 1893. 1st. Edn. Orig. cl.,
unc. From liby. of Dr. F. Ashworth Underwood.
(S. Feb.23; 250) *Page.* £135
– – Anr. Copy. (S. Jun.16; 539)
Jenner Books. £110

MacFALL, Haldane
– The History of Painting. 1911. 8 vols. 4to. Cl. gt.
(P. Feb.19; 236) *Magda.* £55

MACFARLANE, Charles
– Constantinople in 1828. L., 1829. 1st. Edn. Lge.
4to. Mod. qtr. mor. (SG. Feb.26; 220) $325

MACGEORGE, Bernard Buchanan
– Catalogue of the Library of. Glasgow, 1892.
Orig. hf. parch. bds., partly unc. Pres. Copy to Sir
Charles Tennant. (S. Nov.24; 198)
Breslauer. £95

M'GHIE, J., Photographer
– Photographs of Lanarkshire Scenery. Edinb., ca.
1860-70. Ob. 4to. Orig. cl. gt. (S. Nov.24; 199)
Weinreb. £280
– Photographs of Tweeddale Scenery. Edinb., ca.
1860-70. Ob. 4to. Orig. cl. gt., spine split. (S.
Nov.24; 200) *Weinreb.* £300

McGIBBON, David & Ross, Thomas
– Castellated & Domestic Architecture of
Scotland. Edinb., 1887-92. 5 vols. Cl., soiled. (CE.
Nov.20; 162) £140
– – Anr. Copy. Cl. gt. (CE. Dec.4; 252) £120
– – Anr. Copy. Soiled. (CE. Mar.19; 198) £50
– Ecclesiastical Architecture of Scotland. Edinb.,
1896-97. 3 vols. Cl. gt. (CE. Nov.27; 74) £110
– – Anr. Copy. (CE. Mar.19; 199) £56

M'GILLIVRAY, Duncan
– The Journal of . . . Ed.:– Arthur S. Morton.
Toronto, 1929. (350) numbered. Orig. cl.,
unopened. (CB. Nov.12; 270) Can. $160
– – Anr. Copy. Bkplt. (CB. Sep.24; 241)
Can. $120

McGOWN, Thompson
– A Practical Treatise on the Most Common
Diseases of the South. Phila., 1849. 1st. Edn. Cl.
From Brooklyn Academy of Medicine. (SG.
Jan.29; 276) $100

McGRATH, Raymond H.
– The Seven Songs of Meadow Lane. Sydney, 1924.
(30) on Japanese vell. 6 full-p. woodcut ills.
numbered & sigd. Orig. parch.-bkd. bds. Pres.
copy to Walter de la Mare. (SH. Mar.26; 17)
Schrire. £145

MACGREGOR, C.M.
– Narrative of a Journey through the Province of
Khorassan. 1879. 1st. Edn. 2 vols. Orig. cl. (SH.
Mar.5; 93) *Ad Orientem.* £340

**MacGREGOR, John, Secretary to the Board of
Trade**
British America. 1832. [1st. Edn.?]. 2 vols. Cont.
hf. cf. (SH. May 21; 74) *Crete.* £50
– – Anr. Copy. Maps slightly foxed & offset, slight
foxing to text. Orig. bds. From liby. of William E.
Wilson. [Sabin 43280] (SPB. Apr.29; 187) $200
– – Anr. Edn. Edinb., 1833. 2nd. Edn. 2 vols. Cont.
hf. cf. [Sabin 43280] (S. Jun.29; 189)
Faupel. £65

MacGREGOR, John, Teacher of Mathematics
– Practical Mathematics. 1792. Cont. cf. gt.,
decor. spine gt. (CE. Jul.9; 111) £95

MACHEN, Arthur
– The Glorious Mystery.–The Shining Pyramid.
Chic., 1924; 1925. 1st. Edns., 1st. work (250) sigd.
Orig. cl., unc., d.-w.'s. 1st. work with A.L.s.
inserted. (S. Jul.22; 214) *Hale.* £60
– The Works. L., 1923. (1000) sigd. 9 vols. Slight
browning. Orig. cl., soiled. (SPB. May 29; 275)
$150

MACHIAVELLI, Niccolo
– Discorsi.–Il Principe.–Libro dell' Arte della
Guerra. Venice, 1540; 1546. Together 2 vols., 1st.
2 works in 1 vol. Cont. vell. & mod. hf. mor. Sig.
of Fletcher of Saltoun in lr. cover. (C. Jul.16; 275)
Quaritch. £800
– I Discorsi.–Il Principe.–I Sette Libri dell'Arte
della Guerra. Palermo [i.e. L.], 3rd. work n.p.,
1584; 1584; 1587. 3 works in 1 vol. 1st. work iss.
with 'cura' in imprint. Cont. limp vell. [STC
17159; 17167] (C. Jul.16; 277) *Griendl.* £300

– Discourses. Trans.:– E. D[acres]. 1636. 1st. Edn. in Engl. 12mo. Iss. without cancelled B1, some stains, tear in 1 lf. reprd. Cont. cf. [STC 17160] (C. Nov.19; 32) *Jamieson.* £110
– Historie. Rome, 1532. 1st. Edn. 4to. Leaves 58-64 with sm. burnhole, text replaced in MS., stained in parts. New vell. (H. Dec.9/10; 1358) DM 560
– La Mandragola. Ill.:– A. Bartoli. Verona, 1957. (120) hand-ptd. on Bütten. 4to. Printer's mark sigd. Orig. wraps., s.-c. (R. Mar.31-Apr.4; 586) DM 1,000
– Oeuvres Complètes. Paris, 1823-26. 12 vols. Cont. hf. chagrin. (HD. Oct.10; 250) Frs. 2,600
– Tutte le Opere ... [Rome], 1550. 4to. Early 18th. C. marb. mor., gt. fillets & line of dots, spine gt. in compartments, gt. crest of Joseph Gulston & publication date in 5th., 1 corner slightly worn. Ragley Hall bkplt. (SM. Oct.7; 1829) Frs. 3,200
– The Works. L., 1675. 1st. Engl. Edn. Fo. Lacks front blank. Cont. cf., reprd. (GM. Apr.30; 564) £80

MACHIAVELLI, Niccolo–CATANEO, Girolamo
– The Arte of Warre ...–Most Briefe Tables ... 1573; 1574. 2nd. Edn. in Engl.; 1st. Edn. in Engl. 2 works in 1 vol. 4to. Some minor staining. Cont. limp vell. [STC 17165; 4790] (C. Nov.20; 261) *Marcheson.* £550

McIAN, Robert Ronald
See–LOGAN, James & McIan, Robert Ronald

McINTOSH, Charles
– The Practical Gardener & Modern Horticulturist ... L., 1828. 2 vols. Hf. cf. (SG. Sep.18; 231) $210

McINTOSH, Dr. W.C.
– A Monograph of the British Annelids. 1873-1923. 4 vols. in 9 pts. 4to. 1 plt. loose. Orig. cl.-bkd. bds., ex-liby. (PL. Jul.11; 94) *Wheldon & Wesley.* £120

MACINTYRE, Maj.-Gen. Donald
– Hindu-Koh. Edinb., 1889. 1st. Edn. With 24 p. catalogue dtd. 6/89. Gt.-pict. cl. (SG. Dec.11; 355) $130

MACKAIL, John William
– Biblia Innocentium. Kelms. Pr., 1892. (200). Orig. vell., silk ties. Pres. Copy, A.L.s. loosely inserted. (SH. Feb.19; 2) *Sawyer.* £100
– – Anr. Copy. 1 tie defect., unc. (SH. Feb.19; 3) *Pickering.* £80
– William Morris, an Address ... Hammersmith, Doves Pr., 1901. (15) on vell. Sm. 4to. Orig. vell., unc., qtr. mor. s.-c. (CNY. May 22; 374) $1,800
– – Anr. Edn. Doves Pr., 1901. (325) on paper. Orig. limp vell. (SH. Jan.30; 463) *Quaritch.* £90

MacKAY, Alexander
– The Western World; or, Travels in the United States in 1846-47 ... including a Chapter on California. L., 1849. 1st. Edn. 3 vols. Slight discoloration. Cont. hf. cf., rebkd., marb. end-papers. From liby. of William E. Wilson. [Sabin 43351] (SPB. Apr.29; 188) $125

McKELVEY, Susan Delano
– Botanical Exploration of the Trans-Mississippi West. Jamaica Plain, 1955. Cl. (SG. Jan.22; 251) $110

MACKENNA, F. Severne
– Cookworthy's Plymouth & Bristol Porcelain. Leigh-on-Sea, 1946. (500) sigd. 4to. Orig. cl., d.-w. (SBA. Jul.14; 371) *Potterton Books.* £68
– Worcester Porcelain. 1950. Ltd. Edn. 4to. Orig. cl. (SH. Jan.29; 189) *Talerman.* £105

McKENNEY, Thomas L.
– Memoirs, Official & Personal; with Sketches of Travels Among the ... Indians ... N.Y., 1846. 2nd. Edn. Slight staining, lightly foxed. Orig. blind-stpd. cl., gt. spine, worn at head & foot. From liby. of William E. Wilson. [Sabin 43403] (SPB. Apr.29; 190) $125
– Sketches of a Tour to the Lakes ... Baltimore, 1827. 1st. Edn. Slight, mostly marginal, tears in text, 29 plts., foxing, offsetting, slight staining to later ll., hf.-title detchd. Mod. buckram, ex-liby. Inscr. to Joseph Lopez Dias; from liby. of William E. Wilson. [Sabin 43407] (SPB. Apr.29; 189) $150

M'KENNEY, Thomas L. & Hall, James
– History of the Indian Tribes of North America. Phila., 1836. 3 vols. Fo. 120 cold. plts. & ports., text reprd., some ll. loose or detchd. ex liby. Hf.

mor., covers detchd., spines torn & brkn., worn. [Sabin 431a] (SPB. Jun.22; 93) $5,500
– – Anr. Copy. 3 vols. Fo. Some ll. loose, offsetting, browning, ex liby. Old hf. roan, very worn, covers detchd., spines torn & brkn. (SPB. Jun.22; 94) $4,750
– – Anr. Edn. Phila., 1836-42-44. Vols. I & II 2nd. Edn., vol. III 3rd. Edn. 3 vols. Fo. Vol. I with 6 individual wraps. loosely inserted, slight staining & foxing. Cont. hf. mor. gt. [Sabin 43410A] (SPB. May 6; 213) $7,500
– – Anr. Edn. Phila., 1836-42-44. 1st. Iss. of vols. I & III. 3 vols. Fo. Some offsetting, dupl. plts. mntd. on inside covers. 19th. C. hf. roan, covers detchd., very worn, spines torn. W.a.f. [Sabin 4310a] (SPB. Jun.22; 95) $3,000
– – Anr. Edn. Phila., 1848-49-50. 1st. 8vo Edn. 3 vols. in 1. Hand-cold. plts., tissue guards. Later blind-decor. mor. (PNY. Dec.3; 225) $1,800
– – Anr. Edn. Phila., 1855. 3 vols. Red 19th. C. mor. gt. (SG. Oct.9; 155) $2,600
– – Anr. Edn. Phila., 1858. 3 vols. 117 (of 120) hand-cold. lithos., lacks frontispieces, foxed thro.-out, some stains. Orig. blind-stpd. mor. (SG. Jun.11; 255) $1,200
– – Anr. Edn. Phila., 1865. 3 vols. Cont. blind-stpd. mor. (SH. Nov.7; 385) *Skinner-Klee.* £1,000
– – Anr. Edn. Phila., ca. 1870. 2 vols., all publd. Tall 4to. Orig. gt. hf. mor. & marb. bds., some wear. (PNY. Mar.26; 195) $550
– – Anr. Edn. Edinb., 1933. 3 vols. Cl. (BS. Nov.26; 225) £65
– – Anr. Edn. 1933-34. 3 vols. Orig. cl. (SH. Jul.16; 170) *Trocchi.* £120
– – Anr. Copy. 4to. (SH. Nov.7; 386) *House.* £80
– – Anr. Copy. Cl. (SG. Jan.8; 255) $210
– – Anr. Copy. Blind-pict. cl. (PNY. May 21; 276) $180
– – Anr. Copy. Pict. cl. (PNY. Oct.1; 339) $150
– – Anr. Edn. Phila., n.d. 2 vols. Roan spine gt., worn. (CE. Nov.20; 76) $310

MACKENZIE, Sir Alex.
– Voyages from Montreal on the River St. Laurence ... North America. 1801. [1st. Edn.?]. 4to. Cf. gt. (P. Oct.23; 43) *Monk.* £440
– – Anr. Copy. 3 lge. folding maps, lacks port. Cont. tree cf., spine gt. Armorial bkplt. of Lord Bradford, Weston Park. (SG. Oct.30; 231) $850
– – Anr. Copy. Lacks folding map of America, sm. tear in each map at 1st. fold, maps & port. offset. sm. stains on hf.-title. light foxing on port. Recent buckram, ex-liby. [Sabin 43414] (CB. Sep.24; 178) Can. $320
– – Anr. Edn. L., 1802. 2nd. Edn. 2 vols. Lightly soiled; maps with sm. tears. Cont. leath., upr. cover vol. 1 loose. [Sabin 43415] (R. Mar.31-Apr.4; 2429) DM 1,350
– – Anr. Edn. Phila., 1802. 2nd. Amer. Edn. 2 pts. in 1 vol. 1 (of 3?) folding copper engraved maps. Cont. leath. gt. [Sabin 43415] (R. Mar.31-Apr.4, 2438) DM 900

MACKENZIE, Colin
– [–] Tavern Anecdotes, & Reminiscences of the Origin of Signs, Clubs, Coffee-Houses, Streets, City Companies, &c. By One of the Old School. L., [1825]. 1st. Edn. Later 19th. C. hf mor., unc. [H. & L., Vol. III, column 2547] (PNY. Mar.26; 196) $150

MACKENZIE, Eneas
– A Descriptive & Historical Account of the Town & County of Newcastle upon Tyne. Ill.:– J. Knox. 1827. 2 vols. 4to. Minor foxing. Cont. hf. mor., slightly soiled. From the collection of Eric Sexton. (C. Apr.16; 303) *Singleton.* £75
See–WALLIS, John–MACKENZIE, E.

MACKENZIE, Sir George Steuart
– Travels in the Island of Iceland. Edinb., 1811. 1st. Edn. 4to. 1 folding map only (of 7), 7 plts. mntd., sm. liby. stp. on title & plts. Cont. hf. russ. From Chetham's Liby., Manchester. (C. Nov.27; 265) *Cash.* £70
– – Anr. Edn. Edinb., 1812. Lge. 4to. Hf. leath. (D. Dec.11-13; 1340) DM 1,100

MACKENZIE, Helen
– [–] The Mission Camp & Zenana. 1847-51. Slim fo. Some foxing, mainly marginal. Cl., covers detchd. (TA. May 21; 233) £70

MACKENZIE, Henry
– [–] The Man of the World. 1773. 2 vols. 12mo. Cont. cf. (P. Jul.30; 127) *Nightingale.* £150

MACKENZIE, J.
– Austral Africa. L., 1887. 2 vols. Pict. cl. (SSA. Jun.18; 199) R. 130
– – Anr. Copy. Slightly foxed. (VA. Jan.30; 111) R. 90

MACKENZIE, J.C.
See–GAMBRILL, R.V.N. & Mackenzie, J.C.

MACKENZIE, Sir James
– The Study of the Pulse, Arterial, Venous & Hepatic & of the Movements of the Heart. Edinb. & L., 1902. 1st. Edn. 31 pp. advts., name written on title. Orig. cl. (S. Jun.16; 542) *Pratt.* £55

MACKENZIE, John
– A Narrative of the Siege of London-Derry ... L., Priv. ptd., 1690. Sm. 4to. Disbnd. [Wing M216] (GM. Apr.30; 335) £60

MACKENZIE, Kenneth
– Our Earth. Ill.:– Norman Lindsay. Sydney, 1937. Fo. Orig. cl.-bkd. bds., gt. Pres. Copy to Lady Stonehaven, with her MS. note, orig. etching by Lindsay, later sigd. by him. (SBA. Jul.23; 265) *Arnold.* £120

MacKENZIE, Murdoch
– Maritime Survey of Ireland & the West Coast of Great Britain. 1776. 2 vols. Fo. Hf. cf., worn. (PD. Oct.22; 180) £540
– Orcades: or a Geographic & Hydrographic Survey of the Orkney & Lewis Islands. 1750. Fo. Old cf., worn. (BS. Sep.17; 16) £100

MACKENZIE, Roderick
– A Sketch of the War with Tippoo Sultan. Calcutta, priv. ptd. 1793. 2 vols. 4to. Cont. cf.-bkd. bds., rebkd. (C. Nov.5; 100) *Ad Orientem.* £280

MACKENZIE-QUIN, Quin
– A Method to Multiply or Divide Any Number of Figures ... Priv. Ptd. 1750. Fo. Cont. wraps., cl. case. (S. Feb.9; 28) *Maggs.* £130

McKERROW, Ronald B. & others
– A Dictionary of Printers & Booksellers in England, 1557-[1775]. 1910-32. 4 vols. 4to. Orig. buckram-bkd. bds. (SH. Jan.29; 35) *Subunso.* £85

McKIM, Charles
– A Monograph of the Work of Mead & White. N.Y., [1915]. 4 vols. Fo. Some plts. stpd. on versos. Loose as iss. in portfo., ex-liby. W.a.f. (SG. Dec.4; 228) $700

MACKINTOSH, Alexander
– The Driffield Angler. Gainsborough, 1806. 1st. Edn. Mod. leath., unc. (SG. Oct.16; 177) $240
– – Anr. Edn. Gainsborough, [1806]. 2 pts. in 1 vol. 12mo. Engraved frontis. slightly torn, rebkd., spotted. Mod. hf. cf. (SBA. Mar.4; 16) *Fletcher.* £52

MACLAURIN, Colin
– An Account of Sir Isaac Newton's Philosophical Discoveries. Ed.:– Patrick Murdoch. Priv. Ptd. 1748. 1st. Edn. 4to. New cl. (S. Dec.2; 542) *Celestial.* £75
– – Anr. Copy. Cont. cf., worn. (S. Dec.1; 294) *Barnet.* £70
– Geometria Organica. L., 1720. 4to. L1. yellowed. Cont. Engl. cf., blind-tooled & acid decor. on covers, spine with raised bands, bdg. defect. (HD. Feb.27; 40) Frs. 1,500
– A Treatise of Fluxions. Edinb., 1742. 1st. Edn. 2 vols. 4to. Cont. cf., very worn, lacks 1 label. From Honeyman Collection. (S. May 20; 3283) *Pichler.* £130

MACLAURIN, Colin–PEMBERTON, Henry
– An Account of Sir Isaac Newton's Philosophical Discoveries.–A View of Sir Isaac Newton's Philosophy. 1748; 1728. 1st. Edns. 2 works in 2 vols. 4to. Cont. cf. (1st. work); & cf. by Sangorski & Sutcliffe. From the collection of Eric Sexton. (C. Apr.15; 13) *Traylen.* £70

McLEAN, John
See–CHAMPLAIN Society

M'LEAN, Thomas, publisher
- Historical Portraiture of Leading Events in the Life of Ali Pacha, Bizier of Epirus. Ill.:– G. Hunt after W. Davenport. 1823. Fo. Publisher's advt. lf. bnd. in at rear. Orig. bds., crudely rebkd. (TA. Jan.22; 228) £160
- Picturesque Representations of the Dress & Manners of the Russians. Ca. 1820. 4to. 63 (of 64) hand-cold. litho. plts., minor spotting. Cont. red mor. gt. (TA. Jul.16; 128) £80

McLEAN, Thomas
- A Picturesque Description of North Wales. 1823. Ob. 8vo. Cont. hf. cf. (C. Jul.15; 75)
Maggs. £450

MACLEAY, Kenneth
- Highlanders of Scotland. 1870. 2 vols. Elephant fo. 31 cold. litho. plts. mntd. on card. Mor., gt. decor. geometric & floral pattern, MacGregor tartan in cl. pasted on end-papers. Pres. copy to Miss A. Murray MacGregor from the publishers, 1st. Nov. 1869. (CE. Jul.9; 216) £430
– – Anr. Copy. 1 extra plt. of John Brown. Orig. red cl. gt. (CE. Nov.20; 27) £350
– – Anr. Copy. 2 vols. Text & plts. loose, some slight foxing. Cl., worn. (BS. Jun.11; 369) £180

MACLEHOSE, James
- The Picture of Sydney & Strangers' Guide in New South Wales . . . Ill.:– J. Carmichael. Sydney, 1838. Ills. on thin tinted paper, map of Sydney loose, some sm. stains. Covers detchd. (JL. Jul.20; 741) Aus. $800
– – Anr. Edn. Ill.:– J. Carmichael. Sydney, [1839]. Orig. cl., paper label torn. (C. Nov.6; 324)
Quaritch. £300

MacLEISH, Archibald
- Yale University Prize Poem. New Haven, 1915. 4to. Slight browning. Orig. ptd. wraps., glue marks on lr. wrap. Pres. copy, the H. Bacon Collamore copy. (SPB. Nov.25; 345) $400

M'LELLAN, A.
- Essay on the Cathedral Church of Glasgow. Glasgow, 1833. 4to. Cont. mor., covers with Edmond & Remnants plaque à la cathédrale, inner gt. borders, silk liners, by Carss of Glasgow, with their ticket. (S. Nov.24; 201)
Quaritch. £160

M'LEOD, John, Surgeon
- Narrative of a Voyage . . . Yellow Sea. 1817. Hf. cf. gt. (P. Oct.23; 46) *Brooke-Hitching.* £65

MACLISE, Joseph
- Surgical Anatomy. 1856. 2nd. Edn. Fo. Hf. mor., soiled, loose in bdg. (S. Jun.16; 547)
Hildenbrandt. £50

McLOUGHLIN, John
See–CHAMPLAIN Society

MacLURE, William
- Opinions on Various Subjects, Dedicated to the Industrious Producers. New Harmony, Indiana, 1831. 1st. Edn., 2nd. state. Slightly browned, slight soiling. Cont. cf., spine partially perished, covers detchd. From liby. of William E. Wilson. (SPB. Apr.29; 185) £650

McMICHAEL, William
- [–] The Gold-Headed Cane. 1827. 1st. Edn. Orig. cl., unc., in s.-c. Pres. copy to T.L. Freer (the author's father-in-law) & bkplt. of Richard Lane Freer. (S. Jun.16; 548) *Jenner Books.* £120
– [–] – Anr. Edn. 1828. 2nd. Edn. Some thumbmarking, tear in K4 reprd. Hf. cf. Pres. copy from Sir William Osler to G.A. Auden, dtd. Sep.21, 1903, & with A.L.s. to same inserted, also latter's bkplt. (S. Dec.2; 846) *Blackwell.* £100

McMURTRIE, Douglas C.
- Early Printing in Wisconsin. Seattle, 1931. (300). Fo. Buckram, unopened. (SG. Mar.26; 314) $110

McMURTRIE, Douglas C. & Allen, A.H.
- Early Printing in Colorado. Denver, 1935. (250) numbered. Buckram. (SG. Jan.22; 267) $100

McMURTRIE, Henry
- Sketches of Louisville & its Environs . . . Louisville, 1819. 1st. Edn. Slight tear to map, title foxed, light foxing thro.-out. Later hf. mor., marb. bds. & end-papers, gt. spine. From liby. of William E. Wilson. (SPB. Apr.29; 192) $325
– – Anr. Copy. Map torn at folds, sm. repairs at top of title, some soiling & foxing thro.-out. Orig.

bds., rebkd., worn. From liby. of William E. Wilson. (SPB. Apr.29; 191) $275

M'NAB, W.
- A Treatise on the Propagation, Cultivation & General Treatment of Cape Heaths in a Climate where they Require Protection during the Winter Months. Edinb., 1832. Orig. wraps. (SSA. Jan.22; 293) R. 330

McNALLY, M.J.
- [–] The Watercolours of M.J. McNally & Harold Herbert. Sydney, 1920. (600). Orig. wraps. (JL. Jul.20; 679) Aus. $120

McNAUGHTON, Arnold
- The Book of Kings . . . foreword by the Earl Mountbatten of Burma. Arcadia Press. 1973. (55) numbered sigd. by Lord Mountbatten. 3 vols. Fo. Orig. mor. by Zaehnsdorf, gt. inner dentelles. (CSK. Sep.12; 112) £75

MACNEICE, Louis
- The Burning Perch. 1963. 1st. Edn. Mor., gt. line tooling over panel of cold. onlays, suede doubls., sigd., fitted case, by Elizabeth Greenhill. (SH. Feb.20; 407) *Quaritch.* £290

MacNEILL, Eoin
See–BEST, R.I. & MacNeill, Eoin

MACOMB, Capt. John N. & Newberry, J.S.
- The Exploring Expedition from Santa Fe. Wash., 1876. 1st. Edn. 4to. Cl., ex-liby. (SG. Aug.21; 241) $150

MACORLAN, Pierre
- La Couronne de Paris. Ill.:–André Jacquemin. 1947. (200) on Lana. Ob. fo. In sheets, s.-c. (HD. Feb.27; 173) Frs. 1,750
- Vlaminck. Ill.:– Maurice de Vlaminck. Paris, 1958. (2000) numbered. 4to. Orig. wraps., s.-c. (SH. Nov.21; 506) *Duran.* £52

M'PARLAN, James
- Statistical Survey of the County of Sligo. Dublin, 1802. Bds., spine reprd., unc. (GM. Apr.30; 281) £110
– – Anr. Copy. Lge. folding map browned, some MS. annots. Hf. cf., upr. cover detchd. Pres. copy to Geological Society, sigd. (GM. Apr.30; 280) £85

MACPHERSON, James
- The Poems of Ossian. 1790. New Edn. 2 vols. Lf. of advts. in vol. II, occasional slight staining. Mod. panel. cf., gt., by Morrell. (S. Dec.9; 381)
Wilson. £55

MacPHERSON, James & others
- Fingal. 1762. 4to. Cf., decor. spine gt. (CE. Jul.9; 232) £80

MACPHERSON, Mary-Etta
See–HODGINS, J. & Macpherson, Mary-Etta

MACQUEEN, Kenneth
- Adventure in Watercolour. Sydney, n.d. (1100) numbered, & sigd. 4to. Cl., d.-w., protective cellophane. (KH. Mar.24; 268) Aus. $110

MACQUER, Pierre Joseph
- Chymisches Worterbuch oder allgemeine Begriffe der Chymie. Trans.:– Johann Gottfried Leohardi. Leipzig, 1788-91. 2nd. Edn. 7 vols. Bds., unc., some unopened, 1 backstrip detchd. (S. Dec.1; 264) *Bucherkabinett.* £100
- Elemens de Chymie Pratique . . . Paris, 1756. 2nd. Edn. 2 vols. 12mo. Pp. xxv-xxvi duplicated in numbering. Cont. Fr. cf. (S. Dec.1; 262)
Maggs. £65
- Elemens de Chymie Théorique. Paris, 1749. 1st. Edn. 12mo. Cont. Fr. cf. (S. Dec.1; 261)
Quaritch. £90
- Elements of the Theory & Practice of Chymistry. Trans.:– [Andrew Reid]. 1758. 1st. Edn. in Engl. 2 vols. cf. (S. Dec.1; 263) *Quaritch.* £110

MACQUOID, Percy
- History of English Furniture. 1904-08. 4 vols. Fo. Cont. mor., spines with raised bands terminating in blind-stpd. foliate finials on covers, by Hatchards. (C. Jul.22; 154) *Traylen.* £250
– – Anr. Copy. Cont. hf. mor. (C. Jul.22; 155)
Traylen. £200
– – Anr. Copy. Orig. cl. (CSK. Aug.29; 8) £130
– – Anr. Edn. 1919. 4 vols. Fo. Orig. cl. (SH. Jan.29; 260) *Reed & Sims.* £95
– – Anr. Copy. Orig. cl. gt., slightly soiled. (P. Jul.30; 262) *Sims & Reed.* £80
– – Anr. Edn. 1923. 3 vols. Fo. Buckram gt., covers stained. (LC. Feb.12; 100) £60

– – Anr. Edn. 1923-38. 4 vols. Fo. Orig. cl., slightly stained. (SBA. May 27; 256)
Davisson. £100
– – Anr. Edn. 1925-28. 4 vols. Fo. Orig. cl. gt. (LC. Feb.12; 99) £170
– – Anr. Copy. Cl., d.-w.'s torn. (C. Jul.22; 156)
Taylor. £135
– – Anr. Copy. Orig. linen. (R. Oct.14-18; 703)
DM 700
– – Anr. Edn. L., 1938. 4 vols. Fo. Orig. cl. gt., d.-w. torn. (P. Jun.11; 27) *Alan.* £140
– – Anr. Copy. Orig. cl. (SH. Jan.29; 261)
Primrose Hill. £90
– – Anr. Edn. N.d. 4 vols. Fo. Orig. cl., d.-w.'s. (SKC. Feb.26; 1458) £160

MACQUOID, Percy & Edwards, Ralph
- The Dictionary of English Furniture. 1924. 3 vols. Fo. A few final ll. in vol. 3 dampstained, mainly marginal. Orig. cl. gt. (SBA. Jul.14; 372)
Hyde Park Bookshops. £230
– – Anr. Edn. 1924-27. 3 vols. Fo. Orig. cl., d.-w.'s. (SH. Apr.9; 100) *Demetzy.* £270
– – Anr. Copy. Cl., gt. (C. Jul.22; 153)
Traylen. £240
– – Anr. Copy. Orig. cl. (P. Nov.13; 69)
Talerman. £220
– – Anr. Copy. Orig. cl. gt. (P. May 14; 92)
Elliott. £200
– – Anr. Copy. Some ll. in vol. III reprd. & soiled. Cont. cl., slightly soiled. (SH. Oct.9; 128)
Blundall. £90
– – Anr. Edn. [1953]. 3 vols. Fo. Orig. cl. (CSK. May 1; 37) £380
– – Anr. Edn. 1954. 2nd. Edn. 3 vols. Fo. Cl., in d.-w.'s, some torn. (C. Feb.4; 260)
Rosewood. £520
– – Anr. Copy. Orig. cl. (SH. Mar.6; 548)
Barra Books. £440
– – Anr. Copy. Orig. cl. (SH. Jan.29; 263)
Barra Books. £420
– – Anr. Copy. Cl., d.-w.'s. (P. Sep.11; 311)
Sims & Reed. £360
– – Anr. Copy. Orig. buckram, vols. I & II slightly soiled. (S. Apr.7; 450) *Sims & Reed.* £260
– – Anr. Copy. Lightly marked, d.-w. (SKC. Sep.9; 1585) £200
– – Anr. Edn. [1954]. 2nd. Edn. 3 vols. Orig. cl., d.-w. (CSK. Jun.12; 141) £420
– – Anr. Edn. N.d. 3 vols. Fo. Orig. cl. gt. (P. Jul.30; 131) *Sims & Reed.* £360

MACQUOID, Percy & others
- A Record of the Collections in the Lady Leverhulme Art Gallery. 1928. (350). 3 vols. Fo. Orig. buckram, dust-jackets. (CSK. Oct.24; 41) £75

McRAE, John (Contrib.)
See–PUNCH

MACROBIUS, Aurelius Theodosius
- In Somnium Scipionis Expositio. Saturnalia. Venice, Joannes Rubeus Vercellensis, 29 Jun., 1492. Fo. Capital spaces left blank, some later MS. notes, slight browning, some worming, affecting text. Mod. parch.-bkd. bds., slightly soiled. From liby. of André L. Simon. [BMC V, 417; Goff M12; HC 10429*] (S. May 18; 136)
Hoppen. £320
- Interpretatio in Somnium Scipionis (& other works). Flor., 1515. A little browning & staining, occasional marginal annots., owner's. inscr. of A.L. Politianus, with his note of purchase. 19th. C. vell., gt. (S. Dec.8; 117) *Hoppen.* £90
- Interpretatio in Somnium Scipionis a Cicerone confictum. Eiusdem Saturnaliorum libri VII. Ed.:– Nicolaus Angelius (etc.). Venice, 1521. Fo. Old inscr. on title, some stains, lacks last blank. Mod. vell. (VG. Nov.18; 1271) Fls. 650

MACSWINY, Eugene
- Tombeaux de Princes, Grands Capitaines et autres Hommes Illustres. L., 1741. Lge. fo. Slight marginal soiling, 3 folding or double-p. sheets of letterpress with engraved vigs., 1 with marginal tear. Cont. cf., rebkd., worn. (S. Jun.22; 127)
Weinreb. £1,800

MACTAGGART, John
- Three Years in Canada. L., 1829. 2 vols. Cont. hf. mor. (CB. Apr.1; 93) Can. $300

McURE, John
- A View of the City of Glasgow. 1736. Mor., by Henderson & Bisset. (CE. Apr.23; 236) £90

MADAN, Falconer
See–WILLIAMS, Sidney Herbert & Madan, Falconer

MADAN, Martin
[–] Thelyphthora; Or, A Treatise on Female Ruin. 1780. 2 vols. Cont. cf. (TA. Feb.19; 277) £50

MADDEN, Sir Frederic
– Illuminated Ornaments. Ill.:– Henry Shaw. 1833. 4to. Cont. hf. cf. (C. Nov.6; 186) Quaritch. £150
– – Anr. Copy. 2 plts. folding & mntd. on guards, 1 with portion of lr. margin torn away without loss, occasional slight soiling, a few ll. reprd. without loss. Mod. hf. mor. (CSK. Feb.27; 114) £70

See–SHAW, Henry & Madden, Sir Frederick

MADDEN, Dr. Samuel
[–] Memoirs of the Twentieth Century . . . Letters of State under George the Sixth. 1733. Vol.1, all publd. Red mor. by Rivière. (S. Nov.24; 202) Bickersteth. £320

MADDISON, Sir Ralph
– Great Britains Remembrancer, looking In & Out, tending to the Increase of the Monies of the Commonwealth. 1655. 1st. Edn. 4to. Title a little stained. Recent cf. [Wing M245] (C. Apr.1; 183) Lawson. £100

MADDOCK, James
– The Florist's Directory. Ed.:– Samuel Curtis. L., 1810. New Edn. Mod. three-qtr. cf. (SG. Sep.18; 233) $150

MADDOX, Willes
– View of Lansdown Tower, Bath. Ill.:– C.J. Richardson after Maddox. 1844. Fo. With the slip 'the tomb was reluctantly removed', loose, title slightly soiled. Cont. roan.-bkd. cl., gt., worn, brkn. (C. Nov.6; 325) Weinreb. £220
– – Anr. Copy. Qtr. mor. (P. Apr.30; 55) Fogg. £180

MADOL, Roger
See–SITWELL, Sacheverell & Madol, Roger

MADOU, [Jean Baptiste]
– Album. [1832]. Ob. 4to. 12 lithos. on Chine, collés. Cl. (LM. Nov.8; 99) B.Frs. 7,500
– Vie de Napoleon. Brussels, 1827. Ob. 4to. Soiled. Cont. hf. linen, defect. & loose. (R. Oct.14-18; 2519) DM 900

MADOX, J.
– Excursions in the Holy Land, Egypt, Nubia, Syria . . . 1834. 2 vols. Cf. (P. Jul.2; 169) Timmons. £75

MADOX, Thomas
– History & Antiquities of the Exchequer of the Kings of England. 1769. 2nd. Edn. 2 vols. 4to. Cont. cf. Sir Humphrey Mackworth of Gnole Castle's sig. on inside upr. cover. (TA. Jan.22; 82) £60

MADWEIS, F.
See–WEIGEL, Erhard–TUAST, J.G.–MADWEIS, F.–STRAUCH, Egidius

MAE DOS HOMENS, Francisco da
– Oraçao Funebre, que nas exequias da Serenissima Senhora Dona Maria Anna. Rio de Janeiro, 1813. Sm. 4to. Mod. cf. (SPB. May 5; 335) $150

MAEDER, Clara Fisher
– Autobiography. Ed.:– Douglas Taylor. N.Y., 1897. Ltd., L.P. 1st. Edn. (260). 2 extra title-pp. Gt.-ruled & gt.-panel. mor., unc. by Blackwell, orig. wraps. bnd. in. Extra-ill., with 37 A.L.s.'s, 3 A.N.s.'s, 8 clipped sigs., 5 other autograph items & 18 Engl. & Amer. Theatre Broadsides, 2 early programmes, over 200 port. plts. (most mntd. or inlaid & including 12 orig. photographs), 17 view plts., an orig. drawing of the Fisher cottage Jolin A. Fisher. (PNY. Mar.26; 14) $550

MAERCHENWALD
Trans.:– H.E. von Thewalt. Ill.:– Arthur Rackham. Zurich, 1919. 1st. Edn. 4to. Pict. cl. gt. Raymond M. Sutton Jr. copy. (SG. May 7; 187) $100

MAETERLINCK, Maurice
– The Blue Bird. Trans.:– A.T. de Mattos. Ill.:– F. Cayley Robinson. 1912. 4to. Orig. cl. gt., slightly worn. (S. Jul.31; 303) Ralph. £55
– Décors et Costumes pour L'Oiseau Bleu, préface de Gerard d'Houville. Ill.:– Georges Lepape. Paris, 1927. (230) numbered. 4to. Cont. hf. mor. gt. (SH. Nov.21; 392) Lutrin. £460

– Insectes et Fleurs. Ill.:– after Hans Erni. Paris, 1954. Ltd. numbered Edn. 4to. Cold. decor. leatherette. (SG. Apr.2; 107) $120
– The Life of the Bee. Ill.:– Edward J. Detmold. 1911. 4to. Orig. pict. parch. gt., unc. (SH. Mar.26; 155) Illustrated Antiques. £60
– – Anr. Edn. Ill.:– Edward J. Detmold. 1912. 4to. Orig. pict. cl., slightly soiled, unc. (SKC. May 19; 21) £50
– La Vie des Abeilles.–La Vie des Termites.–La Vie des Fourmis. Ill.:– J.E. Laboureur. Paris, 1930. Ltd. Edn.; on Rives, numbered. 3 vols. Sewed, wraps., s.-c. (HD. Dec.5; 136) Frs. 1,800

MAFEKING MAIL
1899-1900. Numbers 1-152 only (of 165) & preface, & Special Edn. of 8th. Mar. 1900 in 1 vol. Fo. A few tears. Cont. hf. cf. (SH. Nov.7; 315) Proud. £70

MAFFEI, Francesco Scipione
– Verona Illustrata. Ill.:– M. Heylbroek, F. Zucchi, & others. Verona, 1731-32. 4 pts. in 1 vol. Fo. Title lightly soiled & spotted, dampstain to upr. inner margin of some ll. Cont. vell., slightly soiled. From the collection of John A. Saks. (C. Jun.10; 150) Marlborough. £180
– [–] Verona Illustrata.–La Verona Illustrata. Verona, 1731-32; 1771. 4 vols.; vol. II only (of 2). Very minor tears in 2 plts. of 2nd. work. Unif. 19th. C. blind-stpd. cf. From the collection of John A. Saks. (C. Jun.10; 151) Romano. £80

MAFFEI, Giovanni Pietro
– L'Histoire des Indes Orientales et Occidentales. Paris, 1665. 4to. Owner's inscr. & faint liby. stp. on title, slight discolouration. Cont. red Fr. mor. From the liby. of F.-A. Rochechouart, marquise de Montespan with her cypher surmounted by a coronet on sides & spine. [Sabin 43783] (SPB. May 5; 337) $550
– Historiarum Indicarum Libri XVI. Flor., 1588. 1st. Edn. Fo. Some spotting, marginal stains affecting 1st. ll. Cont. vell. bds., covers detchd. (SPB. May 5; 336) $325

MAFFEI, Paolo Alessandro
– Gemme Antiche Figurate. Rome, 1707-09. 4 vols. 4to. Cont. vell., slightly soiled. (CSK. Apr.24; 64) £160

MAGALOTTI, Lorenzo
[–] Travels of Cosmo the Third, Grand Duke of Tuscany, through England, during . . . 1669. 1821. 1st. Edn. 4to. Some offsetting of text, minor dampstaining affecting lr. inner corner of frontis. & most plts. Cont. diced cf. with gt. decor. spine. (TA. May 21; 65) £200
– – Anr. Copy. Advt. lf., lacks hf.-title, title reprd., folding plt. bkd. with slight soiling. Mod. mor., gt. (S. Jun.29; 254) Elliott. £75
– Varie Operette con qiunta di Otto Lettere su le Terre Odorose d'Europa e d'America. Milan, 1825. (2) on L.P. Turchina. Cont. hf. cf., unopened. (SI. Dec.3; 346) Lire 240,000

MAGAZINE OF ART, The
1881-98. Vols. 4-21. 4to. Unif. hf. mor. (SKC. Dec.4; 1646) £70
– – Anr. Run. L., 1884-92. 4to. 9 vols. Hf. cf. (CR. Jun.11; 510) Lire 800,000

MAGENDIE, François & Desmoulins, A.
– Anatomie des Systèmes Nerveux des Animaux à Vertèbres Appliquée à la Physiologie et à la Zoologie. Paris, 1825. 2 vols. 8vo & 4to. New bds. (S. Jun.16; 550) Norman. £80

MAGENTA, Carlo
– I Visconti e gli Sforza nel Castello di Pavia. Milan, 1883. 2 vols. Fo. Cont. hf. cf. (SI. Dec.3; 347) Lire 350,000

MAGGI, Francesco Maria
– Syntagmaton Linguarum Orientalium quae in Georgiae Regionibus Audiuntur. Rome, 1670. 2 vols. in 1. Fo. Some foxing & staining. Cont. vell. bds., soiled, s.-c. (S. Apr.29; 416) Brill. £280

MAGGI, Giovanni Battista
– Uniformi Militari dell'Armata di S.M. Sarda. Torin, 1844. Fo. Lacks 2 plts., 1 reprd. tear, margins lightly soiled. Mod. hf. cl., orig. wraps. bnd. in. (SI. Dec.3; 349) Lire 2,200,000

MAGGI, Lucillo
– De Modo Recitandi Curas ad Eos, qui Lauream petunt nuper edi... us, una cum tomo secundo de Re Medica Consiliorum. Padua, 1565. 2 pts. in 1 vol. Wormhole in title & 1st. few ll. slightly affecting

text. Cont. limp vell., worn, loose in bdg., using vell. lf. from an incunable. (C. Apr.1; 57) Schreiber. £120

MAGGS Brothers
– Bibliotheca Brasiliensis. L., 1930. Pict. wraps. (SG. Mar.26; 109) $110

MAGICAL NOTE & its Consequences (The)
1809. Interleaved copy. Cont. cf. (CE. Jul.9; 194) £60

MAGICIAN Annual, The
Ed.:– Will Goldston. [1907]-12. Vols. 1-5. 4to. Vol. 1 lacks title & wraps., rest in orig. cl. gt., worn, vol. 2 with orig. wraps. bnd. in. (SH. Oct.23; 178) Van der Linden. £70
– – Anr. Edn. Ed.:– Will Goldston. 1908-12. Vols. 2-5. 4to. Orig. cl. gt. (SH. Oct.23; 72) Van der Linden. £55

MAGINUS, Joannes Antonius
– De Planis Triangvlis Liber Vnicus. Venice, 1592. 4to. Cont. limp vell., lacks ties. (HK. Nov.18-21; 634) DM 420
– Italia . . . Bologna, 1620. Fo. Hand-cold. engraved title heightened with gold, 61 engraved maps cold. by cont. hand, mntd. on guards, hand-cold. engraved head-pieces & decor. initials, lacks port. Cont. red mor., gt. fillet borders & cornerpieces, spine wormed, ties defect. W.a.f. (C. May 20; 150) Burgess. £2,400
– – Anr. Edn. Ed.:– Fabio Magini. Bologna, 1620. [1630 at end]. Fo. Slightly browned, all maps rehinged. some sm. wormholes, 1 full-p. map bnd. inverted, map 15 lightly soiled. Old vell., spine renewed, rehinged. (R. Oct.14-18; 1545) DM 10,000

MAGIRUS, Johann
– Physiologiae Peripateticae libri sex. Camb., 1642. Slight browning & soiling. Early 18th. C. cf. From liby. of Dr. E. Ashworth Underwood. [Wing M251] (S. Feb.23; 251) Whipple. £60

MAGNA CARTA
– [The Great Charter called i[n] Latyn Magna Carta with diuers Olde Statutes]. Trans.:– George Ferrers. [?1541]. Lacks title & 3 unsigd. prelims., piece torn from outer margin of F1, tear in F5, wormhole from R2 to end, affecting some letters, some ll. stained, some inscrs. & underlinings in text. 19th. C. cf. Owner's inscr. & sig. of Sir W. Fairfax, G. Eolliott & H. Marshall's bkplts. [STC 9275] (S. Jan.26; 2) Ferrers. £70
– Magna Charta, cum Statutis, tum Antiquis, tum Recentibus. 1576. Some cont. MS. notes. 19th. C. cf. Owners' inscrs. of G. Clifford & M. Hunte, lately in the collection of Eric Sexton. [STC 9280] (C. Apr.15; 183) Thorp. £180

MAGNAGUTI, A.
– Ex Nummis Historia. Rome, 1949-59. Pts. 2 & 5-12 only. Plts. loose as iss., orig. wraps. (SH. Mar.6; 392) Spink. £190

MAGNELLI, Alberto
See–ARP, Jean, Delaunay, Sonia & others

MAGNI, Pietro Paolo
– Discorsi . . . Sopra il Modo di Sanguinare, Attaccar le Sanguisughe & le Ventose far le Fregagioni & Vesicatorii a Corpi Humani. Rome, [1626]. 4to. Dampstained & margins frayed thro-out. Mod. bds. (S. Jul.27; 351) Faccinotti. £100

MAGNUS, Johannes
– Gothorum Sueonum que Historia. Rome, 1554. 1st. Edn. Fo. Lacks final blank, tear on LLL2. 17th. C. cf., 2 line gt. border, spine gt. in compartments, a little worn & torn at head & foot of spine. (S. Oct.20; 150) Bjorck & Borjesson. £500
– Historia de Omnibus Gothorum Sveonvmque Regibus quivnquam . . . Rome, 1554. 1st. Edn. Fo. Lacks pp. 469/470 & 479/480, title stpd., lightly soiled thro-out, some pp. more heavily browned. 17th. C. vell., some sm. wormholes in spine. (HK. Nov.18-21; 230) DM 1,200

MAGNUS, Olaus, Archbp. of Uppsala
– Historia de Gentibus Septentrionalibus. Rome, 1555. Fo. Lacks F1-2 index, 1 or 2 margins reprd., some dampstains, ownership inscr. of Order of Minims at Soissons, 1604. 18th. C. red mor., triple gt. fillet, spine gt. in compartments including border of 'drawer-handle' tools, inner gt. dentelles. Marquess of Hamilton's copy. [Sabin 4380] (SM. Oct.7; 1832) Frs. 9,000

MAGNUS, Olaus, Archbp. of Uppsala -contd.
- **Historish der Mittlenachtigen Länder.** Basle, 1567. Fo. Lacks map? Hf. vell. (BS. Jun.11; 170)
£260

MAGRIEL, P.D.
- **A Bibliography of Dancing.** N.Y., 1936-38. 3 vols. Orig. cl., Supps. in orig. wraps. (SH. Jun.4; 32) *Shapero* £75

MAHE DE LA BOURDONNAIS, [Bertrand François]
Mémoire pour le Sieur de la Bourdonnais, avec les Pièces Justificatices.– . . . Observations sur les deux Mémoires à consulter, Distribués par la Famille du Sieur Dupleix. Paris, 1750-51. 6 works in 1 vol. 4to. 1st. work title reprd., 1 lf. Dispositif at end. Cont. red mor., gt., arms on covers, gt. cornerpieces of standard, fasces, flag, helmet & bugle, triple gt. fillet, spine gt. in compartments with charges from arms in same cornerpieces, inner gt. floral dentelles, lr. hinge rubbed. Bkplt. of F.E. Lauber. (SM. Oct.7; 1833) Frs. 6,500

MAHLER, Gustav
- **Symphonie in C-moll No. 2.** Leipzig, 1897. 1st. Edn. Sm. fo. Title & wraps. stpd. Orig. wraps., spine defect., soiled & worn. (H. Dec.9/10; 1186)
DM 520

MAHONY, Bertha E. & others
- **Illustrators of Children's Books, 1744-1945.** Boston, 1947. 1st. Edn. 4to. Cl.-bkd. pict. bds. (SG. Jan.22; 113) $160
- - **Anr. Copy.** (SG. Oct.2; 233) $120

MAIDEN, Joseph Henry & Campbell, W.S.
- **The Flowering Plants & Ferns of New South Wales.** Sydney, 1895-98. 7 pts. (all publd.). Sm. 4to. Orig. wraps. (SKC. May 19; 420) £120
- - **Anr. Copy.** Wraps. (KH. Nov.18; 398)
Aus. $270

MAIDMENT, James
[-] **Roxburghe Revels.** Edinb., 1837. 1st. Edn. 4to. Late 19th. C. mor., gt. (S. Nov.24; 203)
Quaritch. £110

MAIER, Michael
- **Secretioris Naturae Secretorum Scrutinium Chymicum per Oculis et Intellectui Accurate Accomodata.** Frankfurt, 1687. Reprint of Atlanta Fugiens. 4to. Vell. Lichtenstein bkplt. (S. Dec.1; 269) *Maggs.* £400
- - **Anr. Copy.** Slightly soiled, wormed in fold. Cont. vell., slightly soiled. (H. Dec.9/10; 1463)
DM 3,400

MAILLARD, Leon
- **Les Menus & Programmes Illustrés.** Paris, 1898. Ltd. Edn. 4to. Mod. hf. mor., orig. wraps. laid in, partly unc. (SI. Dec.3; 350) Lire 420,000

MAILLARD, Olivier
- **Oliverii Maillardi Sermones de Adventu; Quadragesimales, et Dominicales.** Paris, 7 May 1500-14 Aug. 1500. 3 pts. in 1 vol. Mod. vell. (HD. Dec.5; 137) Frs. 2,000

MAIMBOURG, Louis
- **Histoire de la Cadence de l'Empire aprés Charlemagne.** Paris, 1679. L.P. 4to. Title inscr. 'Bibliotheca Colbertina'. Cont. red mor., arms of J.B. Colbert, gt., on covers, triple gt. fillet, spine gt. in compartments with his cipher & snake from arms, inner gt. dentelles, upr.-cover slightly rubbed. (SM. Oct.7; 1834)
- **Histoire de la Ligue.** Ill.:– S. Le Clerc; Licherie (frontis.). Paris, 1683. 4to. Cont. red mor., triple gt. fillet around covers, restruck arms of Marquis de Chateau-Gontier, spine decor. with raised bands. (HD. Feb.27; 41) Frs. 1,300
- **Histoire du Grand Schisme d'Occident.** Paris, 1678. 1st. Edn. 4to. Lge. burnholes in folios N2-4 affecting text. Cont. deep purple mor., gt., arms of Louis XIV on covers, triple gt. fillet, spine with his cipher, gt., in compartments, with fleur-de-lis in each corner, inner gt. dentelles, 2 sm. wormholes in upr.-cover & spine, bkplt. May be dedication copy to king. (SM. Oct.7; 1835) Frs. 4,800

MAIMONIDES, Moses
- **Mishne Torah-Yad Hachazakah.** Ed.:– Abraham Ben David, Joseph Karo & Levi Ibn Chabib. Venice, 1574-76. 7th. Edn. 4 vols. Fo. Sm. hole on title of vol. I, without loss of text, lacks ll. 188-189 in vol. III. some ll. from anr. copy, some repairs. Vell., 1 spine reprd. (S. Nov.18; 745)
James. £1,100

MAIMONIDES, Moshe
- **Sepher Ha'mitzvot.** Trans.:– Moshe Ben Shmuel Ibn Tibbon. [Constantinople], [1516-18]. 1st. Edn. 4to. Ptd. without title, slight staining & worming, tear in last lf. affecting 3 words, sig. of former owner on 1st. lf., sigd. by censor in 1629. Cl., bkplt. of Elkan Nathan Adler. (S. Nov.18; 747)
Rock. £6,000

MAINDRON, Ernest
- **Les Affiches Illustrées, 1886-1895.** Paris, 1896. 4to. Cont. bradel bds. hf. vell. bds., tail-piece on spine, unc. (HD. Apr.9; 602) Frs. 2,000
- **Les Programmes Illustrés des Théâtres et des Cafés-Concerts.** Paris, [1897]. 4to. Orig. cl., gt. decor., orig. wraps., a little soiled. (SI. Dec.3; 351)
Lire 270,000

MAINTENON, Françoise d'Aubigne de
- **Mémoires pour servir à l'Histoire de Madame de Maintenon et à celle du Siècle Passé.–Lettres Inédites de Mme de Maintenon et de Mme la Princesse des Ursins.** Amst.; Paris, 1755; 1826. 2 works in 19 vols. 8vo; lge 8vo. 1st. work: cont. cf.; 2nd. work: glazed hf. cf., spine with raised bands. (HD. Jun.29; 212) Frs. 1,200

MAIRAN, Jean Jacques Dortous de
- **Traité Physique et Historique de l'Aurore Boréale.** Paris, 1754. 2nd. Edn. 4to. New cl. (S. Dec.2; 544) *Celestial.* £65

MAIRN, Johann Baptist von, Edler von Mairsfield
- **Beschreibung was auf ableiben . . . Ihrer Keyserl. Majestät Josephi . . . sich Merkwürdiges Hat Augetragen.** Vienna, ca. 1712. Fo. 11 plts., including frontis. (of 12, lacks plt. no. 11), a few wormholes at beginning & end, slightly affecting frontis. Cont. cf., spine & lr. cover worn. (S. Oct.21; 471) *Wagner.* £160

MAISON, K.E.
- **Honoré Daumier, Catalogue Raisonné of the Paintings, Watercolours & Drawings.** L., 1968. (500). 2 vols. 4to. Cl., s.-c. (SSA. Jan.22; 84)
R. 140

MAISTRE, Joseph de
[-] **Oeuvres Diverses.** 1829-70. 16 vols. Hf. chagrin, spines faded. (HD. Oct.10; 252)
Frs. 1,300

MAISTRE, Xavier de
- **Les Prisonniers du Caucase.** Ill.:– Julien Le Blant. Paris, 1897. (150) on Japon, numbered. 9 compositions in 3 states, 2 with comments, 2 prospectus ll. at end. Mor., 4 gt. fillets bordering covers, s.-c. Bkplt. of Paul Gavault. (SM. Feb.11; 246) Frs. 4,500

MAITLAND, William
- **The History of Edinburgh.** Edinb., 1753. 1st. Edn. Fo. Lacks last lf. (?blank). Mott. cf., gt. by Rivière. (S. Nov.24; 204) *Thorp.* £80
- **History of London.** 1739. [1st. Edn.?]. Fo. 2 plts. with slight tears. Cf. (P. Apr.9; 80)
Lee. £200
- - **Anr. Copy.** Cont. cf. (C. Jul.15; 131)
Weinreb. £140
- - **Anr. Copy.** Slight tear in fold of 1st. plt., some text pp. spotted. From the collection of Eric Sexton. (C. Apr.16; 304) *Burgess.* £65
- - **Anr. Edn.** 1756. 2 vols. Fo. 118 (of 120) engraved plts. & plans. Cont. spr. cf. (SBA. Jul.22; 104) *Nicholson.* £220
- - **Anr. Copy.** Lacks 2 plts., vol. 1 title-pp. loose. Covers loose. (P. Jun.11; 298) *Jeffreys.* £190
- - **Anr. Copy.** Map of London torn. Reversed cf., worn. W.a.f. (BS. Sep.17; 59) £160
- - **Anr. Copy.** 2 vols. 102 engraved plts. only, some tears, some ll. soiled. 19th. C. cl. (SH. Mar.5; 94) *Primrose Hill.* £90
- - **Anr. Edn.** 1760. 3rd. Edn. 2 vols. Fo. 1st. title spotted, 2nd. title detchd. Cont. cf., worn. (C. Nov.5; 101) *Walford.* £220
- - **Anr. Edn.** 1775. 2 vols. Fo. Cont. cf., jnts. brkn. (C. Feb.25; 45) *Shapiro.* £200
- - **Anr. Copy.** Cf., worn. (S. Dec.9; 412)
Crowe. £160

MAITRE A DANSER, Le
1819. Slight offsetting onto text, price erased from title. Cont. red str.-grd. mor. (S. Feb.9; 42)
Maggs. £170

MAITRE-JAN, Antoine
- **Traité des Maladies de l'Oeil.** Troyes, 1707. 1st. Edn. 4to. May lack a lf. after privilege at beginning (sub-title?). Vell. (S. Dec.2; 545)
Verburg. £170

MAIUS, Junianus
- **De Priscorum Proprietate Verborum.** [Venice], Johannes Rubeus Vercellensis, [Feb.23] 1490. Fo. Cont. wooden bds., lacks backing & clasps, corners defect. [Hain 10545*; BMC V p. 416; Goff M100] (C. Apr.1; 58) *Schweitzer.* £280
- - **Anr. Copy.** Badly wormed. 17th. C. cf., arms of Charles, 3rd. Duke of Marlborough, on covers, worn, lr. cover detchd. (S. Mar.16; 37)
Fletcher. £200

MAJOR, Johannes
- **In quartum Sententiarum Quaestiones.** Paris, 14 Oct. 1521. Fo. Some dampstaining, worming or tears in a few ll., affecting text, lacks final blank. 17th. C. cf., worn. (S. Jan.27; 365)
Fentiman. £50

MAJOR, R.H.
- **Early Voyages to Terra Australis, now called Australia.** L., Hakluyt Soc., 1859. 1st. Edn. Pagination error before p. 177, clean tear in 1 lf. Orig. cl., worn, unc., head of backstrip defect. (KH. Nov.18; 401) Aus. $180

MAJOR, Thomas
- **The Ruins of Paestum.** 1768. Fo. Some staining & spotting. Later bds., rebkd., corners reprd., worn. (S. Jun.22; 128) *Duran.* £140

MAKOVSKY, Serge
See–ROERICH, N. & Makovsky, Serge

MALATESTA, A.M.
- **Tractatus de Modo Equos Fraenandi . . .** Venice, 1607. 1st. Edn. Lge. fo. Collation varies, 1st. & last ll. restored at lower corner, 3 wormholes without text loss, some light stains at margins. Cont. vell. (D. Dec.11-13; 2267) DM 3,100

MALCOLM, James Peller
- **Anecdotes of the Manners & Customs of London during the Eighteenth Century.** 1808. 1st. Edn. 4to. Cont. diced cf. gt. (TA. Nov.20; 433) £140
- - **Anr. Copy.** Cont. hf. russ., gt. spine. (S. Mar.16; 189) *Quaritch.* £90
- - **Anr. Edn.** L., 1811. 2nd. Edn. 4 vols. Three-qtr. mor. (SG. Oct.30; 235) $110
- - **Anr. Edn.** 1818. 4to. Margins untrimmed. Orig. bds., rebkd. (TA. Nov.20; 434) £120
- - **Anr. Copy.** 4to. (TA. Dec.18; 77) £85

MALCOLM, Sir John
- **History of Persia.** 1815. 2 vols. 4to. Cf. gt., covers detchd. (P. May 14; 208) *Hosain.* £75

MALCOLM Furniture Co. Ltd.
- **148 Display Plates of Furniture . . .** [Kincardine?], [1937]. Sq. 4to. With 8 price-lists & 5 T.L.s. of the company. Cl. covered portfo. (CB. Nov.12; 110) Can. $110

MALDONADO, Angel
- **Respuesta . . . a un Informe y Manifesto que ha hecho Fr. Antonio de Torres . . . En el Pleyto sobre la Division de Nuevos curatos en las Doctrinas . . .** [Mexico], ca. 1740? Fo. A few light stains, wormhole. Vell. bds., sprung. (SPB. May 5; 338)
$275

MALERISCHE Naturgeschichte der Drei Reiche, fur Schule und Haus
Braunschweig, 1848. Cont. cl.-bkd. bds. (SH. Jan.30; 466) *Henderson.* £65

MALES DE BEAULIEU, Mme.
- **La Poupée Bien Elevée.** Paris, ca. 1830. 5th. Edn. Ob. 4to. 10 (of 11) plts. cold. by hand, frontis. & 3 ll. neatly reinserted, text neatly edited by a former owner. Orig. pict. bds., rebkd. (SH. Mar.19; 165)
Golding. £80

MALET, Capt. Harold Esdaile
- **Annals of the Road.** 1876. Orig. cl., gt. (SH. Nov.6; 125) *Hindley.* £80

MALEVICH, K.
- **Ot Kubizma i Futurizma k Suprematizmu [From Cubism & Futurism to Suprematism].** Moscow, 1916. 3rd. Edn. Orig. wraps., slightly soiled. (SH. Feb.5; 244) *Dembeck.* £1,000
- **Ot Kubizma k Suprematizmu [From Cubism to Suprematism].** Petrograd, 1916. 1st. Edn. Orig. wraps., slightly spotted. (SH. Feb.5; 245) *Nijhoff.* £95
- **Ot Sezanna do Suprematisma [From Cezanne to Suprematism].** [Moscow], [1920]. Orig. wraps. (SH. Feb.6; 333) *Lempert.* £80
- - **Anr. Edn.** [Moscow], n.d. Orig. wraps. (SH. Feb.5; 246) *Nijhoff.* £70

MALFI, T.
- Neue Anleitung z. Barbier-u. Wund-Artzney-Kunst. Nuremb., 1676. Old MS. owner's mark on title, multi-stpd., slightly browned in parts, some ll. with sm. tears in margin. Cont. blind-tooled pig-bkd. wood bds., 2 clasps. (HK. May 12-14; 370) DM 2,200

MALGAIGNE, Joseph François
- Traité d'anatomie Chirurgicale et de Chirurgie Expérimentale. Paris, 1838. 1st. Edn. 2 vols. Sm. stp. in lr. blank margin of titles. Cont. bds. (S. Jun.16; 552) Quaritch. £110

MALKIN, Benjamin Heath
- The Scenery, Antiquities & Biography of South Wales. Ill.:– after J. Laporte. 1804. 4to. Recently rebnd. in hf. cf. (TA. Mar.19; 594) £55

MALLARME, Stéphane
- L'Après-midi d'un Faune. Trans.:– Aldous Huxley. Ill.:– John Buckland-Wright. Gold. Cock Pr., 1956. (200) numbered. Orig. mor.-bkd. cl. Inscr. to William Russell Flint. (CSK. Dec.10; 13) £80

MALLET, Allain Manesson
- Description de l'Univers. 1683. Vol. 3 only. Sm. 4to. 107 maps & plts. disbnd. Sold as collection of plts. (P. Oct.23; 242) Donovan. £80
- La Geometrie pratique. Paris, 1702. 1st. Edn. 4 vols. Finger-soiled. Cont. cf., gt. spines, worn. (CNY. Oct.1; 16) $550
- Les Travaux de Mars, ou l'Art de la Guerre. Amst., 1696. 3 vols. 19th. C. qtr. mor. gt. (CNY. Oct.1; 15) $900

MALO, Charles
- Guirlande de Flore. Paris, [1818]. 16mo. Cont. paper bds. (HD. Apr.10; 153) Frs. 1,250
- Histoire des Roses. Paris, [1818]. Cont. leath. (R. Oct.14-18; 3049) DM 900
- - Anr. Edn. Ill.:– Bessa. N.d. 12mo. Cont. cf., gt. fillet & blind cornerpieces, decor. gt. spines, inner garland. (HD. Feb.18; 158) Frs. 1,500
- Les Insectes. Paris, [1818]. 16mo. Publisher's paper bds., s.-c. (HD. Apr.10; 154) Frs. 1,050
- Les Papillons. Paris, [1816]. 16mo. Cont. paper bds., s.-c. (HD. Apr.10; 155) Frs. 1,300

MALON, M. de
- Essais sur neuf Maladies également dangéreuses. Paris, 1770. Cont. red mor., gt., arms of Lorraine, triple gt. fillet & corner sprays, spine gt. in compartments, inner gt. dentelles, Augsburg gt. & white starred end-papers. (SM. Oct.7; 1837) Frs. 1,800

MALONYAY, Deszo
- A Magyar Nep Muvezete. Budapest, 1909-22. Vols. 2-5. 4to. Mod. buckram, ex-liby. (SG. Dec.4; 179) $100

MALORY, Sir Thomas
- The Birth, Life & Acts of King Arthur. Ill.:– Aubrey Beardsley. 1893-94. Ltd. Edn. 2 vols. 4to. Orig. cl. gt., rubbed, partly unc. (S. Jul.27; 98) Sotheran. £200
- Morte D'Arthur. Ed.:– Robert Southey. L., 1817. 1st. Edn. 2 vols. 4to. Cf., gt. borders, spines & dentelles, by J. Clarke. (SG. Apr.9; 210) $210
- - Anr. Edn. Ill.:– Aubrey Beardsley. L., 1893. (1500). 2 vols. 4to. Browned, tears. Cl., slightly warped. (SPB. May 29; 25) $100
- - Anr. Edn. Ill.:– Aubrey Beardsley. 1893-94. Ltd. Edn. 2 vols. 4to. Orig. pict. cl. gt., cover design by artist. (SH. Mar.26; 50) Fletcher. £240
- - Anr. Copy. Orig. gt.-floral cl., covers spotted, some fraying at extremities of spine. (PNY. May 21; 76) $200
- - Anr. Edn. Ill.:– Aubrey Beardsley. 1909. (1500). 4to. Orig. cl. gt. (SH. Mar.26; 60) Wogenstein. £50
- - Anr. Edn. Ill.:– William Russell Flint. L., 1910-11. (50) numbered, on hand-made Riccardi paper. 4 vols. 4to. Crushed lev., gt. spines & dentelles, by Birdsall, design on each upr. cover of cold. mor. inlays, each reproducing a cold. plt. (SG. May 14; 137) $3,600
- - Anr. Edn. Ill.:– William Russell Flint. 1910-11. Ltd. Edn. 4 vols. 4to. Holland-bkd. bds., partly unc. (C. Feb.4; 207) Marks. £50
- - Anr. Edn. Ill.:– Aubrey Beardsley. L., 1924. (1600). 2 vols. 4to. Tears, some spotting, browning. Orig. gt.-decor. cl. (SPB. May 29; 27) $170
- - Anr. Edn. Ill.:– Aubrey Beardsley. L., 1927. (1600). 4to. Orig. cl. gt., head & tail of spine frayed. (LC. Feb.12; 38) £55
- - Anr. Copy. Gt.-pict. cl. (SG. Oct.9; 156) $275
- - Anr. Copy. Partly unc. (SG. Oct.23; 25) $160
- - Anr. Edn. Ill.:– Sir William Russell Flint. 1929. Red mor., cold. mor. onlays on upr. cover, wide gt. borders incorporating on laid mor. shields at corners, by Rivière. (SH. Mar.26; 204) Wood. £95
- - Anr. Edn. Oxford, Shakes. Hd. Pr., 1933. (350) 2 vols. 4to. Orig. mor. (CSK. Apr.3; 64) £160
- - Anr. Copy. Hf. mor. (PD. Feb.18; 20) £130
- - Anr. Edn. Ed.:– A.W. Pollard. Ill.:– Robert Gibbings. N.Y., Gold. Cock. Pr. for the Ltd. Edns. Cl., 1936. (1500) numbered, sigd. by artist. 3 vols. Slim fo. Orig. ptd. bds. with linen backstrips. (S. Jun.18; 352) £65
- - Anr. Copy. Cl.-bkd. patterned bds., orig. box. (SG. Jan.15; 222) £120
- - Anr. Copy. 3 vols. Tall 4to. Cl., tissue d.-w.'s, boxed. (PNY. Mar.26; 189) $100
- Le Morte D'Arthur.–Morte D'Arthur Portfolio. Ill.:– Aubrey Beardsley. L., 1893-94; 1927. (300) on H.M.P. Together 4 vols. 4to. Offsetting, some foxing, plts. browned. Orig. vell. gt., spotted, warped & soiling. (SPB. May 6; 154) $1,700
- The Romance of King Arthur. Ed.:– A.W. Pollard. Ill.:– Arthur Rackham. 1917. (500) sigd. by artist, numbered. 4to. Orig. vell., gt., slightly spotted & soiled. (SKC, Jul.28; 2333) £150
- - Anr. Copy. This copy unnumbered? (P. Apr.30; 187) £95
- - Anr. Copy. Vell., crushed hf. mor. folding box. Orig. watercolour sigd. by artist on limitation page. Raymond M. Sutton Jr. copy. (SG. May 7; 191) $6,200
- - Anr. Edn. Ed.:– Alfred W. Pollard. Ill.:– Arthur Rackham. N.Y., 1917. 1st. Amer. Trade Edn. Gt.-pict. cl., cold. pict. d.-w. foxed. Raymond M. Sutton Jr. copy. (SG. May 7; 193) $100
- - Anr. Edn. Ed.:– A.W. Pollard. Ill.:– Arthur Rackham. N.Y., 1917. (250). Lge. 4to. Gt.-pict. goat., remains of orig. d.-w., orig. folding box worn. Raymond M. Sutton Jr. copy. (SG. May 7; 192) $700

MALPIERRE, D. Bazin de
- La Chine et les Chinois. Ill.:– after Aubry-le-Comte, Devéria, Grévédon, Régnier, Schall, Schmit, Thévenot & Vidal. 1848. 2nd. Edn. 4 pts. in 2 vols. Lge. 4to. Cont. hf. chagrin, decor. spines. (HD. Dec.5; 138) Frs. 8,100

MALPIGHI, Marcel
- Discourse Anatomique sur la Structure des Viscères ... Trans.:– M. Sauvalle. Paris, 1683. Mor., 5 spine raised bands, decor. gt., triple gold fillet, gt. inner & outer dentelle. (D. Dec.11-13; 218) DM 1,700
- Dissertatio Epistolica de Bombyce. 1669. 1st. Edn. 4to. Licence lf., title & last lf. soiled. 19th. C. hf mor. 18th. C. bkplt. of Richard Middleton Massey, lately in Chetham's Liby., Manchester. [Wing M349] (C. Nov.27; 267) Junk. £400
- Dissertationes Epistolicae duae, una de Formatione Pulli in Ovo; Altera de Bombyce. 1673; [1669]. 1st. Edns. 2 works in 1 vol. 4to. Plts. slightly stained. Russ.-bkd. cl., corners worn. From Chetham's Liby., Manchester. (C. Nov.27; 266) Dawson. £400
- Opera Omnia.–De Structura Glandularum Conglobatarum Consimiliumque Partium Epistola. –Opera Posthuma. Leiden; Leiden; Amst., 1687; 1690; 1698. 3 works in 1 vol. 4to. Some ll. stained at head, 1st. work with sm. piece torn away from top of additional engraved title, worn. (S. Apr.6; 105) DeMetzy. £180

MALRAUX, André
- Psychologie de l'Art.–Le Musée Imaginaire de la Sculpture Mondiale. [Geneva]; [Paris], 1947-48-[50]; [1952]. 3 vols.; 1 vol. 4to. Pict. wraps.; cl. (SG. Dec.4; 231) £110

MALTE-BRUN, Conrad
- Géographie Universelle. Ed.:– J.-J.-N. Hout. Paris, 1841. 6 vols. Soiled, plts. slightly browned. Cont. hf. leath. (R. Mar.31-Apr.4; 2228) DM 700
- - Anr. Edn. Ed.:– E. Cortambert. Paris, 1860-62. 8 vols. Hf.-mor. (VG. Nov.18; 943) Fls. 550
- A New General Atlas ... Phila., 1828. 4to. Maps hand-cold. Orig. hf. mor., scuffed. (SG. May 21; 63) $180
- - Anr. Edn. Phila., 1830. Lge. 4to. Maps cold. Orig. hf. roan, worn. (SG. May 21; 64) $180
- - Anr. Edn. Phila., 1832. 4to. Maps hand-cold. Orig. hf. roan, worn. (SG. May 21; 65) $120
See–ANNALES des Voyages ...

MALTE-BRUN, Victor Adolphe
- L'Allemagne Illustré. Paris, 1885-88. 5 vols. 4to. 99 (of 100) double-p. cold. maps, slightly soiled. Cont. hf. leath., gt. spine. (R. Oct.14-18; 2110) DM 8,300
- - Anr. Copy. Lightly soiled in parts. (R. Mar.31-Apr.4; 1863) DM 8,000
- - Anr. Copy. Vols. 1, 2, 4, 5 in 4 vols. 80 (of 100) double-p. cold maps & plans, 75 (of 95) woodcut plts., approx. 150 text woodcuts, lightly browned. Slightly defect. (R. Oct.14-18; 2111) DM 6,000

MALTHUS, Rev. Thomas Robert
- Definitions in Political Economy. 1827. 1st. Edn. Cont. hf. cf., head of spine chipped, corners worn. (S. May 5; 383) Dawson. £200
- An Essay on the Principles of Population ... 1803. 4to. Cont. hf. cf., spine very worn, upr. cover almost detchd. (C. Nov.20; 262) Lawson. £180
- - Anr. Edn. 1806. 3rd. Edn. 2 vols. Mod. hf. cf. (PD. Oct.22; 210) £65
- - Anr. Copy. Disbnd. (SG. Sep.18; 236) $130
- - Anr. Edn. 1809. 4th. Edn. Cf., worn. (CE. Feb.19; 169) £80
- - Anr. Edn. 1817. 5th. Edn. 3 vols. Cont. cf., rebkd. (S. Oct.21; 439) Traylen. £60
- - Anr. Copy. Early mott. cf. (SG. Mar.19; 245) $170
- Observations on the Effects of the Corn Laws. 1814. 1st. Edn. Orig. wraps., slightly soiled & torn. (SH. Oct.10; 310) Drury. £220
- Principles of Political Economy Considered with a View to their Practical Application. 1820. 1st. Edn. Mod. hf. cf. (C. Apr.1; 184) O'Hern. £350
- - Anr. Copy. Cont. cf. (P. Jul.30; 300) Walford. £320
- - Anr. Edn. 1836. 2nd. Edn. Slight browning. Orig. cl., soiled. (S. Jan.26; 243) Marle. £50
- - Anr. Copy. Disbnd., ex-liby. (SG. Feb.12; 262) $100

MALTON, Thomas, the Elder
- A Complete Treatise on Perspective. 1775. 4to. Cont. cf., upr. cover detchd., worn. (CE. Jun.4; 73) £80
- - Anr. Edn. 1778. 2nd. Edn. Fo. Hf. mor. (BS. Jun.11; 126) £80
- - Anr. Copy. Lacks 1 plt. Old cf. (BS. Nov.26; 174) £55

MALVASIA, Count Carlo Cesare 'Ascoso Gelato'
- Felsina Pittrice. Bologna, 1678. 1st. Edn. 2 vols. 4to. Old vell., soiled. (SH. Jul.23; 213) Marlborough Rare Books. £130
[–] Le Pitture di Bologne. Bologna, 1686. 1st. Edn. 24mo. Some foxing, etc. Old bds. (SG. Mar.12; 242) $220

MALYAR [Painter]
Ed.:– [M.K. Mukalov]. St. Petersb., 1906. Nos. 1-5. 4to. Unbnd. (SH. Feb.5; 86) Quaritch. £160

MAN, Abraham
[–] An Amulet. [1617]. 12mo. Title dust-soiled & frayed affecting ptd. border & with partial loss of imprint, sm. wormhole through headline of first 10 ll. Recent antique-style cf. [STC 17238.5] (C. Nov.20; 263) Quaritch. £50

MAN RAY
- Alphabets for Adults. Beverly Hills, 1948. [500]. 4to. Cl.-bkd. bds. (SG. Oct.23; 201) $450
- Facile. [Poems by Paul Eluard]. Paris, [1935]. (1,200) numbered. Pict. wraps., pp. loose. Inscr. & sigd. by Man Ray & Eluard. (SG. Apr.23; 125) $550
- Photographs: Paris 1920-1934. Hartford, [1934]. 1st. Edn. Lge. 4to. Orig. cold. photographic stiff wraps., ringed. Sigd. pres. copy. (PNY. Mar.4; 170) $1,100
- Les Treize Cloches Vierges. Milan, 1968. (50) numbered, with added suite of 8 engrs. & photo., each numbered & initialled by artist, in folding cl. portfo. Cl., s.-c. (SG. Oct.23; 203) $1,100

MANCHESTER, Herbert
- Four Centuries of Sport in America. Ed.:– Harry W. Smith. 1931. (850). 4to. Cl. Sigd. (SG. Dec.11; 263) $130

MANDEL'SHTAM, O.
- Egipetskaya Marka [Egyptian Mark]. Leningrad, 1928. (4,000). Slightly soiled. Orig. wrap. by E. Belukha. (SH. Feb.6; 483) Bjorck. £90
- O Poezii [On Poetry]. Leningrad, 1928. (2,100). Orig. wraps., spine torn, loose. (SH. Feb.6; 334) Bjorck. £65
See–BAYAN, Vadim, Mandel'shtam, O. & others
See–BLOK, Alexander & others

MANDELSLO, J.A. von
See–OLEARIUS, Adam–MANDELSLO, J.A. von

MANDERSTOWN, William
– Moralia Magistri Guillermi Manderston Scoti Philosophi . . . Philosophia Bipartita . . . collecta cum Recentibus Additionibus . . . revisa. [Paris?], 23 Nov. 1535. Mor. gt. by Bedford, rebkd. Huth bkplt. (C. Apr.1; 149) *Stewart.* £280

MANDEVILLE, Bernard de
[–] Fable of the Bees. 1723. 2nd. Edn. Some browning. Old cf. (P. Dec.11; 363) *Georges.* £65
– A Treatise of the Hypochondriack & Hysterick Diseases in Three Dialogues.–An Enquiry into the Causes of the Recent Executions at Tyburn . . . to which is added a Discourse on Transportation. 1725-30. 2nd. Edn. 2 works in 1 vol. Cf., rebkd. (S. Jun.16; 553) *Lawson.* £85

MANDEVILLE, Sir John
– The Voiage & Travaile . . . 1727. L.P. Cont. panel. cfs., jnts. split, worn. Bkplt. of Thomas Anson of Shugborough. (S. Nov.24; 205) *Kosson.* £170
– – Anr. Edn. Ill.:– Valenti Angelo. Grabhorn Pr., 1928. (150) numbered. Fo. Wood, leath. spine, raised bands, worn. Laid in is fo. leaflet from Grabhorn Pr. (SG. Sep.4; 222) $600

MANE-KATZ
– Douze Lithographies pour 'Stempeniou' de Cholem Aleikhem. Ed.:– Pierre Mazars. Boston, [1966]. (300) numbered. Atlas fo. Loose as issued in linen folder with linen ties. (SG. Oct.23; 205) $300

MANESSON MALLET, Alain
– Den Arbeid van Mars, of Nieuwe Vestingbouw, soo wel Geregelde als Ongeregelde. Ill.:– R. de Hooghe. Amst., 1672. 1st. Edn. in Dutch. 3 vols. P1 in vol. 1 inserted (trimmed; probably from another copy). Cont. vell., slightly soiled, light scoring on upr. cover of vol. II. (S. Oct.21; 452) *Breman.* £260

MANGETUS, Johannes Jacobus
– Bibliotheca Medico-Practica. Geneva, 1695-98. 4 vols. Fo. Browned thro.-out. Old vell., spines torn & partly lacking. (SG. Sep.18; 237) $170
– Theatrum Anatomicum.–Tabulae Anatomicae. Ill.:– after Sellier, J.D. Hartman & others. Geneva & Cologne, 1717. 2 works in 2 vols. Fo. Sm. tear in corners of folded plts., title to vol. 2 & some plts. soiled, some ll. browned. 19th. C. hf. mor. From Chetham's Liby., Manchester. (C. Nov.27; 268) *King.* £350

MANGETUS, Johannes Jacobus & Le Clerc, Daniel
– Bibliotheca Anatomica. Geneva, 1685. 1st. Edn. 2 vols. Fo. Plt. no. 42 torn. Cont. cf. gt., spines defect. (P. May 14; 8) *Duran.* £220
– – Anr. Edn. Geneva, 1699. 2nd. Edn. 2 vols. Fo. Old panel. cf., newly rebkd. (SG. Sep.18; 215) $550

MANGIN, Arthur
– The Desert World. Ill.– W. Freeman, Foulquier & Yan'Dargent. L., 1872. Mor., gt.-tooled borders & spine. Fore-e. pntg. (SG. Mar.19; 146) $200
– The Mysteries of the Ocean. Trans.:– W.H. Davenport-Adams. Ill.:– W. Freeman & J. Noel. L., 1874. New Edn. Cont. mor., gt. borders & spines. Fore-e. pntg. (SG. Mar.19; 147) $275

MANGLES, J.
See–IRBY, C.L. & Mangles, J.

MANLEY, Charles M.
See–LANGLEY, Samuel Pierpont & Manley, Charles M.

MANLEY, Mrs. Mary de la Rivière
[–] Secret Memoirs & Manners of Several Persons of Quality, of Both Sexes. 1709. 2 vols. in 1. Cont. spr. cfs., gt. decor. spine. (TA. Jan.22; 296) £82
– – Anr. Copy. 2 vols. Orig. bdg. (P. Apr.30; 28) *Jarndyce.* £80

MANLIIS, Johannes Jacobus de
– Luminare Maius super Mesue Antidotarium et Practica. Venice, Bernardinus Staginus, de Tridino, 2 Jan., 1499. 3rd. Edn. Fo. 14-line ornamental woodcut capital initial E on a2r, other capital initials, lacks final blank, slight worming to lr. portion of text, occasionally filled & with slight loss, some inner margins reprd. Rose mor. gt., to a 16th. C. Italian design, vell. From the collection of Eric Sexton. [BMC V. 368, Goff M209, H. 10713*] (CNY. Apr.8; 197) $2,200

MANN, D.D.
– The Present Picture of New South Wales . . . L., 1811. 4to. Without the views in 4 lge. sheets, slight foxing. Early tree cf., recornered & rebkd. (KH. Mar.24; 270) Aus. $1,150

MANN, James
– Medical Sketches of the Campaigns of 1812-14. Dedham, Massachusetts, 1816. 1st. Edn. Foxed. Orig. ptd. bds., unc., cl. s.-c. (SG. Sep.18; 239) $300

MANN, Thomas
– The Beloved Returns: Lotta in Weimar. Trans.:– H.T. Lowe-Porter. N.d. Ltd. L.P. 1st. Amer. Edn., (395) numbered. Sm. 4to. Gt. buckram-bkd. bds., silk place-marker. Sigd. (PNY. Mar.4; 172) $120
– Die Betrogene. Ed.:– Ernst. Morgenthaler (orig. litho.). 1953. Facs. reproduction of MS., (400) numbered, on Pannekoek. 4to. Orig. bds. Orig. litho. with monog. dtd. (D. Dec.11-13; 925) DM 500
– Herr und Hund. Ill.:– E. Preetorius. Munich, 1919. 1st. Edn. (120) numbered on hand-made Zandersbütten sigd. by artist. Orig. bds., slightly worn, jnts. strengthened inside. (D. Dec.11-13; 1136) DM 1,200
– – Anr. Edn. Ill.:– E. Preetorius. Munich, 1919. 1st. Edn. Pict. orig. bds. Author's copy. printer's mark sigd., with later foreword. (HK. Nov.18-21; 2795) DM 750
– A Sketch of My Life. Trans.:– H.T. Lowe-Porter. Paris, [1830]. 1st. Edn. in Engl. (75) numbered on Imperial Japan paper, sigd. Qtr. vell., d.-w., boxed. (PNY. Mar.26; 199) $190
– Der Tod in Venedig. Novelle. Berlin, 1925. Cl. Sigd. pres. copy. to Bobsy Goodspeed. (PNY. Mar.4; 173) $240
– Tristan. Ill.:– E. Scharff. Munich, [1922]. (70) numbered Privilege Edn. on Zanders-Bütten. 4to. Orig. pict. vell., bd. s.-c., lightly worn. Printer's mark sigd. by artist. (HK. Nov.18-21; 2797) DM 1,000

MANN, William
– Six Years' Residence in the Australian Provinces. 1839. 12mo. Engraved map, hand-cold. in outl., a few minor defects. Orig. cl., slightly soiled, unc. (SBA. Jul.23; 394) *Roberts.* £60

MANNE, E.D. de–MANNE, E.D. de–MANNE, E.D. de & Menetrier, C.–MANNE, E.D. de & Menetrier, C.
– Galerie Historique des Comédiens de la Troupe de Talma.– . . . de la Troupe de Voltaire.– . . . de la Comédie Française . . .–des Acteurs Française . . . Lyon, 1866; 1877; 1876; 1877. Together 4 vols. Unif. hf. mor., orig. wraps bnd. in, partly unc. (SI. Dec.3; 354) Lire 200,000

MANNERS, Lady Catherine Rebecca
– Poems. L., 1793. 2nd. Edn. 4to. Cf., needs rebdg. Fore-e. pntg. (SG. Mar.19; 148) $220

MANNERS, Lord John
See–SCHETKY, John Christian & Manners, Lord John

MANNI, Domenico Maria
– Vita di Aldo Pio Manuzio . . . delle Lettere Greche, e Latine in Venezia. Ill.:– Antonio Baratti. Venice, 1759. 1st. Edn. Privilege lf. Old limp bds. (SG. Oct.2; 234) $180

MANNI, Giovanni Battista
– Varii et Veri Ritratti della Morte . . . Milan, 1671. Old bds. (S. Mar.17; 306) *Broseghini.* £150

MANNING, Owen & Bray, William
– The History & Antiquities of the County of Surrey. 1804-14. 3 vols. Fo. Red lev. mor. gt., partly unc. Bkplt. of Henry Cunliffe, lately in the collection of Eric Sexton. (C. Apr.16; 305) *Traylen.* £300

MANO, Count
See–ANDRASY, Emmanuel, Count Mano & others

MANSART, Jules Hardouin, Architect
– 'Eglise des Invalides'. (Fourteen Copperplate Plans). Paris, ca. 1706. Mostly lge. fo. & folding. Cont. gt.-ornamental gift bdg. of red mor., armorially stpd. at both covers for Louis XIV. (PNY. Oct.1; 182) $750

MANSBERG, Richard-Freiherr von
– Mittelalterliche Turnierzug zur 800 Jaehrigen Jubelfeier des erlauchten Hauses Wettin. Dresden, 1890. Lge. fo. Cold. pict. title, 62 cold.

chromolithos., plt. guards, extra-pict. title & 2 ll. music. Orig. dye-design bds., gt. vell. spine & corners. (PNY. Oct.1; 352) $200

MANSFIELD, Charles Blachford
– Aerial Navigation. Ed.:– Robert Blachford Mansfield. 1877. Orig. cl., slightly soiled, unc. (S. May 5; 125) *Crete.* £90

MANSFIELD, Edward D.
– Memoirs of the Life & Services of Daniel Drake . . . with Notices of the Early Settlement of Cincinnati. Cinc., 1855. 1st. Edn. Port. & title foxed, advts., text lightly foxed. Orig. blind-stpd. cl., gt. spine. From liby. of William E. Wilson. [Sabin 44369] (SPB. Apr.29; 90) $100
See–DRAKE, B[enjamin] & Mansfield, E.D.

MANSFIELD, Katherine
– The Garden Party. Ill.:– Marie Laurencin. 1939. (1,200). Orig. bds., d.-w. (SH. Feb.20; 222) *Hatchard.* £150
– – Anr. Copy. Orig. cl., d.-w. 'Press copy'. (SH. Nov.21; 381) *Kawamatsu.* £125
– – Anr. Copy. Orig. bds., unc. (SH. Nov.21; 380) *Kawamatsu.* £115
– – Anr. Copy. Decor. cl., unc. (C. Feb.4; 320) *Maggs.* £85
– Prelude. Richmond, Hogarth Pr., [1918]. 1st. Edn., 1st. Iss. (250). Loose. Orig. wraps., designs on upr. & lr. wraps. by J.D. Ferguson, cl. s.-c. (SG. Nov.13; 450) $190

MANSON, Sir Patrick
– The Filaria Sanguinis Hominis & Certain New Forms of Parasitic Disease in India, China, & Warm Countries. 1883. 1st. Edn. Orig. cl., ex-liby. A paper on the same subject by the author with additional MS. notes by him loosely inserted. (S. Jun.16; 554) *Rota.* £75

MANSOUR, J.
– Jules César. Ill.:– Hans Bellmer. Paris, 1955. (7) on Vél. de Rives. Orig. bds., s.-c. (R. Mar.31-Apr.4; 571) DM 450

MANSTEIN, Gen. Christoph Hermann de
– Memoires Historiques . . . sur la Russie. Lyon, 1772. New Edn. 2 vols. Cont. red mor., lge. gt. crowned arms on all covers. (SG. Oct.30; 317) $220
– – Anr. Copy. Cont. marb. cf., decor. spines. MS. ex-lib. of P.H. de Humbold. (HD. Jun.10; 62) Frs. 1,500

MANTELL, Gideon Algernon
– Pictorial Atlas of Fossil Remains. 1850. 1st. Edn. 4to. Slight offsetting in text. Cont. hf. cf. (S. May 5; 126) *Duran.* £80
– – Anr. Copy. 4to. Orig. cl., hinges & spine reprd. (S. Dec.2; 550) *Blackwell.* £75

MANTZ, Paul
– Les Chefs-D'Oeuvre de la Peinture Italienne. Ill.:– F. Kellerhoven Paris, 1870. Fo. Slightly spotted. Orig. cl. gt., restored. (SBA. Mar.4; 269) *Acquaforte.* £50

MANUCCI, Niccolao
– Storia do Mogor, or Mogul India. Trans.:– William Irving. L., 1906-08. 4 vols. Decor. cl., d.-w.'s (frayed). (SG. Feb.12; 218) $120

MANUEL, N.
– Todtentanz. La Danse des Morts. Bern, n.d. Ob. fo. Title & 1 litho. reprd. Orig. bds. (P. May 14; 14) *Duran.* £120

MANUTIUS, Paulus
– Adagia quaecunque ad hanc Diem exierunt. Flor., 1575. 1st. Edn. Fo. Worming in blank margin of title & 1st. few ll., sig. of Fletcher of Saltoun on title. Cont. limp vell. (C. Apr.1; 150) *Quaritch.* £130

MANUTIUS, Paulus–FALLETTI, Girolamo –[HUTTICHIUS, Johannes]
– Antiquitatum Romanarum.–Orationes xii. –Collectanea antiquitatum in Urbe, atque Agro Moguntino Repertarum. Venice; Venice; Mainz, 1557; 1558; 1520. 3 works in 1 vol. Fo. Slight dampstaining & sm. holes affecting prelims of 1st. work, other minor stains elsewhere. Later blind-stpd. vell. (S. Jun.23; 228) *Goldschmidt.* £80

MANWARING, Robert
– The Cabinet & Chair-Maker's Real Friend & Companion. 1765. Lacks 7 text ll. Mod. hf. mor. (S. Mar.17; 435) *Henderson.* £70

- **The Chair-Maker's Guide.** 1766. 19th. C. qtr. roan, folding cl. box. (S. Mar.17; 436)
Quaritch. £800

MANWAYRING, Sir Henry
- **The Sea-Man's Dictionary.** 1670. 2nd. Edn. Sm. 4to. Owner's sig. on title, sm. book-ticket on A3. Old cf., corners worn. (LC. Jun.18; 218) £300

MANWOOD, John
- **A Treatise of the Lawes of the Forest.** 1615. Sm. 4to. Slightly soiled & stained, MS. inscr. erased. Old cf., worn. (SKC. Jul.28; 2420) £60

MANZANEDA Y ENCINAS, Diego M.B. de
- **Sermon que en las Solemnes Honras celebradas en Obsequio de los Predicadores Apostolicos ...** Garces (et al). Madrid, 1819. Sm. 4to. Mod. gt. qtr. mor. & patterned bds., edges cropped. (PNY. Mar.26; 200) $220

MANZINI, C.
- **Angelo Dall'Oca Bianca nell'Arte e nella Vita.** Milan, 1939. 4to. Publisher's cl. (CR. Mar.19; 104) Lire 200,000

MANZOLLI, Pietro Angelo 'Marcellus Palingenius'
- **Zodiacus Vitae Pulcherrimum Opus atque Utilissimum.** Venice, [1531?]. 1st. Edn. Cont. limp vell., soiled, hf. red mor. case. From Honeyman Collection. (S. May 20; 3284)
Quaritch. £1,300

MANZONI, Alessandro
- **Il Conte di Carmagnola. Tragedia.** Milan, 1820. Orig. Edn. Orig. wraps., unc. (CR. Mar.19; 221) Lire 260,000
- - **Anr. Copy.** Hf.-title. Cont. hf. cf. (SI. Dec.3; 356) Lire 240,000
- **Opere Varie.** Milan, 1845. 4to. Orig. ptd. bds., unc., box. Ded. (SI. Dec.3; 373) Lire 540,000
- **I Promessi Sposi.** Milan, 1825-26. 1st. Edn. 3 vols. Hf.-title, uncorrected errors, some ll. near end Vol. III reprd. Maroon mor. sigd. by Gruel bnd. with his account, partly unc., box. (SI. Dec.3; 357) Lire 1,800,000
- - **Anr. Edn.** Torin, 1838-39. 2 vols. 12mo. Hf. mor. sigd. by Gruel, gt. spines, partly unc. (SI. Dec.3; 363) Lire 280,000
- - **Anr. Edn.** Milan, 1840. 4to. Many ill. lightly soiled. Orig. decor. bds., upr. cover slightly defect. box. Inscr. (SI. Dec.3; 364) Lire 920,000
- **Urania.** Milan, 1809. 1st. Edn. Mod. cf., orig. wraps. bnd. in. (SI. Dec.3; 376) Lire 200,000

MAO TSE-TUNG
- **Poèmes.** Ill:- Ill:- Dali. Paris, 1967. (20) on Japon nacré, sigd. by artist. Fo. One black & 1 sanguine engr. Linen folder & box. (SM. Oct.8; 2305) Frs. 3,600

MAOUT, E. le
- **Histoire Naturelle des Oiseaux.** Paris, 1855. 2nd. Edn. 4to. Some slight spotting. Orig. cl., spine holed & chipped at head & foot. (CSK. Nov.7; 19) £50
- - **Anr. Edn.** Edinb., n.d. Fo. Some foxing. Red mor. gt. (SPB. May 29; 282) $400
- - **Anr. Edn.** Glasgow, n.d. 4to. Minor tears, browning, some foxing. Mor. gt. (SPB. May 29; 283) $300

MAPEI, Camillo
- **Italy.** Ill:- Prout, Leitch & others. L., n.d. Fo. Margins browned thro.-out. Cont. mor., gt. (CSK. Oct.10; 43) £180

MAPLESON, T.W. Gwilt
- **Pearls of American Poetry.** Ill:- T. Sinclair & A. Brett. N.Y., [1853]. 1st. Edn. 4to. Some foxing. Bevelled mor., title in shield on upr. cover, rubbed. (SG. Nov.20; 376) $110

MAPP, Marcus
- **Historia Plantarum Alsaticarum.** Ed:- J.C. Ehrmann. Strassburg & Amst., 1742. 1st. Edn. 4to. 19th. C. cl. From Chetham's Liby., Manchester. (C. Nov.27; 269) *Quaritch.* £70

MAR, Susanna
- **Abem.** Moscow, 1922. (500) numbered. Orig. wraps. by G. Yakulov, slightly soiled, loose. (SH. Feb.6; 484) *Lempert.* £95

MARANHÁ
- **Esboco Historico sobre a Origem da Dizima.** Maranhaõ [sic], 1826. Sm. 4to. Some discoloration. Mod. cf. (SPB. May 5; 339) $550

MARBOT, Jean Baptiste A.M., Baron de
- **Memoires.** Paris, ca. 1880? 3 vols. Red hf. mor., spines gt. (SG. Oct.30; 237) $100

MARBURY, Mary Orvis
- **Favorite Flies & their Histories.** Boston & N.Y., 1892. 1st. Edn. 4to. Gt.-decor cl. (SG. Oct.16; 182) $325
- - **Anr. Copy.** Gt.-pict. 2-tone cl. (SG. Dec.11; 67) $240
- - **Anr. Copy.** Gt.-pict. cl. (SG. Apr.9; 293) $210

MARC, Franz
*See-*KANDINSKY, Wassily & Marc, Franz

MARC, Franz (Ed.)
*See-*BLAUE REITER, Der

MARCEL, Jean Jacques
- **Adlocutio et Encomia variis Linguis expressa.** Paris, 1805. Fo. Orig. bds., worn, unc., new s.-c. (S. Apr.29; 418) *Brill.* £160
- **Alphabet Irlandais, précédé d'une notice historique, litteraire et typographique.** Paris, 1804. 1st. Edn. Slight soiling. Orig. bds., worn, unc. (S. Apr.29; 419) *Maggs.* £220

MARCELLINUS, Ammianus
*See-*AMMIANUS Marcellinus

MARCELLO, Benedetto
- **Estro Poetico-Armonico. Parafrasi sopra li Primi Venticinque Salmi.** Ill:- G.A. Faldoni, S. Ricci & F. Zucchi. Venice, 1724-26. 8 vols. in 4. Fo. Fore-edge of vol. 7 frontis. stained, light foxing to vol. I title & frontis. Later hf. cf., very worn, 2 spines detchd., unc. From the collection of John A. Saks. (C. Jun.10; 156) *Haas.* £550

MARCELLUS, Petrus
*See-*TARAPHA, Franciscus–MARCELLUS, Petrus

MARCH, J.
- **The Jolly Angler.** L., [1833]. 1st. Edn. Mod. hf. mor. (SG. Oct.16; 183) $110

MARCHAIS, Chevalier Renaud des
- **Voyage ... en Guinée, Isles Voisines, et à Cayenne.** Paris, 1730. 1st. Edn. 4 vols. 12mo. 1 plt. with sm. tear, some minor stains. Cont. cf., lacks some labels. (C. Feb.25; 115) *Rota.* £190

MARCHANGY, Louis Antoine François
- **Gaule Poétique (La).** Paris, 1813-17. 1st. Edn., on multi-cold. tinted paper. 8 vols. Cont. str.-grd. red mor., gt. roll-stp. around covers, smooth decor. spines, watered silk end-papers, inside dentelles, bdgs. slightly defect. (HD. Feb.27; 174) Frs. 3,500

MARCHE, Olivier de la, Jaille, Hardouin de la & others
- **Traicte de la Forme et Devis comme on Faict Les Tournois.** Ed:- Aenard Prost. Paris, 1878. L.P. Edn. (258) numbered on Verge Fort. Tall 8vo. Cont. gt.-panel. hf. mor. (PNY. Mar.26; 73) $140

MARCHEN VOM GESTIEFELTEN KATER
Ed:- Straparola, Basile, Perrault & L. Tieck. Ill:- Otto Speckter. Leipzig, 1843. 1st. Edn. 4to. Slightly soiled in parts. Hf. linen, slightly soiled. (H. Dec.9/10; 1668) DM 3,600

MARCHESINUS, Joannes
[-] **Mammotrectus super Bibliam.** Venice, Franciscus Renner & Petrus de Bartua. 1478. 4to. 259 ll. (of 260), lacks 1st. blank, on f. 27 are 2 initials supplied in blue with red penwork, all other initials & chapter-marks supplied in red or blue, a few ll. slightly soiled or spotted, 1st. & last few ll. with wormhole slightly affecting a few letters, parts of gatherings s & t with old marginalia. Cont. Italian blind-stpd. cf. over wooden bds., lacks spine & pts. of leath. on both covers, 1 clasp (of 2). [BMC V, 194; Goff M238; H. 10558] (S. Jun.23; 208) *Emerald Isle Books.* £420
- - **Anr. Edn.** Venetia, N. Jenson. 1479. Sm. 4to. Lacks A1, some ll. stained. Mod. bds., mor. spine. [H 10559] (BS. Jun.11; 112) £170

[MARCHEVILLE COLLECTION] CATALOGUE DE MONNAIES FRANCAISES Paris, 1927-29. 3 vols. Orig. wraps. (SH. Mar.6; 393) *Spink.* £85

MARCILLETUS, Stephanus
- **Doctrinale Florum Artis Notariae.** Turin, Jacobinus Suigus & Nicolaus de Benedictis. Oct.16, 1492. Spaces for initial capitals with guide letters, 1st. 3 ll. of text defect. with hole causing loss of a total of 18 partial lines which

have been supplied in pen & ink facs., some ll. stained, some ll. with margins restored & some early ink notes cropped. Recent blind-stpd. cf., spine gt.-lettered, by V. Artas. From the collection of Eric Sexton. [BMC VII, 1057, C 1372, Goff M255, H 10750] (CNY. Apr.8; 177) $700

MARCOLINI, Francesco
- **Giardino dei Pensieri Composta.** Ill:- Giuseppe Daniotto. Venice, 1784. (36) numbered. Fo. Cont. vell., buckram s.-c. From the collection of John A. Saks. (C. Jun.10; 157) *Lyon.* £620

MARDRUS, Joseph Charles
- **L'Avenement de Salomon. [Livre des Rois].** Ill:- François Louis Schmied. Lausanne, ca. 1930. (20) numbered in Roman Numerals sigd. by Publisher. 4to. Contains 2 cold. woodcut plts. sigd. by Schmied. Loose, as issued, in wraps., s.-c. (PNY. Oct.1; 478) $800
- **Histoire Charmante de l'Adolescente Sucre d'Amour.** Ill:- F.L. Schmied. Paris, 1927. (170). 4to. In sheets, publisher's s.-c. (HD. Dec.5; 139) Frs. 1,800
- **Le Livre des Rois. l'avènement de Salomon.** Ill:- F.L. Schmied, Gonin after Schmied. Lausanne, 1930. (175) on vell., 4to. Loose in orig. wraps., bd. s.-c. Printer's mark sigd. by Gonin. (R. Mar.31-Apr.4; 594) DM 500
- **Paradis Musulman (Le).** Ill:- F.L. Schmied. 1930. (177) on Imperial Japan paper. 4to. Ll. in s.-c. (HD. Feb.18; 222) Frs. 5,100

MARDRUS, Dr. Joseph Charles (Ed.)
*See-*ARABIAN NIGHTS

MAREE, Valentin
- **Traicte des Conformités du Disciple avec son Maistre.** Liège, 1658-60. 1st. Edn. 4 pts. in 3 vols. 4to. Slightly browned thro.-out, binder's ticket at foot of title in vol. I, dtd. 1785. 18th. C. mor. by Derome Le Jeune, triple gt. fillet, spine compartments gt. with single sm. cruciform fleuron, inner gt. dentelles. The William Beckford-Harmsworth copy. (S. Apr.7; 332) *Maggs.* £160

MARESCHAL, Charles
[-] [**Artillerie**]. Ill:- Engelmann & others after author. [Paris], 1822-25. Lge. fo. With 1 dupl. plt. on tinted paper, & 2 slightly smaller litho. plts. in a different hand, some plts. slightly spotted or dampstained. 19th. C. bds. roan spine, corners & spine worn. As a collection of plts., w.a.f. (S. Feb.10; 353) *Paine.* £400

MAREY, Etienne Jules
- **Physiologie Experimentale, Travaux du Laboratoire de M. Marey 1875-1879.** Paris, 1866 [i.e. 1876]-1880. 4 vols. Cl., spines reprd. or rebkd., vol. 2 rebnd. Pres. copy inscr. to Carl Ludwig with an A.L.s. to him dtd. 19 Jan. 1902; afterwards in the collection of Sir Charles Sheerington with his sig., dtd. 1905 on hf.-title of vol. 1 & a note (presumably by the librarian) about the presentation of the work by Sir Charles Sherrington to Gonville & Caius College in 1915; bkplt. of the College with cancellation stp. (S. Jun.16; 555) *Norman.* £260
- **Physiologie Médicale de la Circulation du Sang.** Paris, 1863. 1st. Edn. Cl. (S. Apr.6; 108) *Rota.* £100

MARGARITHA, Antonius
- **Der Gantze Juedische Glaube Mit Samt Einer Gruendlichen und Wahrhaftigen Anzeigung Aller Satzungen, Ceremonien, Gebeten, Heimlich und Oeffentlichen Gebrauchen.** Ed:- Christian Reinec. Leipzig, 1705. 8th. Edn. Slight discoloration. Mod. vell. (S. Nov.18; 674) *Valmadonna.* £180

MARGRY, Pierre
- **Découvertes et Etablissements des Français dans l'Ouest et dans le Sud de l'Amérique Septentrionale (1614-1754).** Paris, 1875-86. 1st. Edn. 6 vols. Ptd. wraps., unc. & unopened, moderate wear, some vols. brkn. (SG. Jan.8; 261) $400

MARGUERITE d'Angoulême
- **Contes et Nouvelles ...** Ill:- J. Van Vianen after Goerée [frontis.]; Romain de Hooghe [figures]. Amst., 1698. 1st Printing. 2 vols. Outer margin of frontis. remade. Mor. by Trautz-Bauzonnet, fillet, decor. spines, inside dentelle. (HD. Mar.18; 115) Frs. 4,300

MARGUERITE de Valois, Queen of Navarre
- **Les Cent Nouvelles.** Ill:- Malassis. Paris, 1931. (550); (300) on vell., numbered. 4to. Plts. in

**MARGUERITE de Valois, Queen of Navarre –
Les Cent Nouvelles.** -contd.
definitive state (cold.). Cont. mor., inside dentelle,
wrap. preserved, unc. (SM. Feb.11; 248)
Frs. 1,800
– **Contes et Nouvelles.** Ill.:– Jourdan after
Freudeberg. L., 1784. 8 vols. 12mo. Cont. marb.
roan, gt. fillets on spines. Bnd. at end of Vol. 8 are
2 Nouvelles of Antoine-François Grazzini. (HD.
Apr.9; 518) Frs. 2,000
– **Heptaméron des Nouvelles (L').** Paris, 1879. 3
vols. 12mo. Mor., gt. fillet, red mor. listel, decor.
spines, inner dentelle, s.-c. (HD. Jun.10; 181)
Frs. 1,300
– **Heptaméron Français.** Ill.:– Dunber [frontis.],
Freudeberg. Berne, 1780-81. 1st. Printing. Large
margins. 3 vols. Cont. cf., triple fillet, angle
fleurons, decor. spines, inner dentelle (HD.
Jun.10; 65) Frs. 8,800
– **L'Heptameron ou Histoires des Amans Fortunez
des Novvelles de tresillustre & tresexcellente
Princesse Marguerite de Valois.** Paris, 1571. 16mo.
Mod. mor. by Pagnant, inner dentelles & gt.
arabesque on covers. (C. Apr.1; 151)
Posada. £150
– **Neuigkeiten.** Bern, 1791. 1st. German Edn. 2
vols. Late 19th. C. hf. leath. (R. Oct.14-18; 989)
DM 3,100
– **Les Nouvelles.** Ill.:– Halbou, de Longueil &
others, after Freudenberg. Berne, 1780. 3 vols.
Some staining & browning. Cont. str.-grd. mor.,
gt. (SM. Oct.8; 2137) Frs. 4,500
– – **Anr. Copy.** 1st. Printing. Mor., lge. dentelle
border. (HD. Jun.30; 51) Frs. 3,850
– – **Anr. Edn.** Ill.:– after Freudenberg & Dunker.
Berne, 1780-81. [1st. Edn.?]. 3 vols. Occasional
light spotting & browning. Lev. by Roger de
Coverley & Sons, gt., gt. inner dentelles. (CSK.
Jan.30; 48) £260
– – **Anr. Copy.** Mor., gt. back & inner dentellers,
gold fillets. (R. Mar.31-Apr.4; 595) DM 6,100
– – **Anr. Edn.** Berne, 1780-83. 3 vols. Red mor., gt.
(S. Oct.21; 306) Duran. £175

MARGUERITTE, Victor
– **La Garçonne.** Ill.:– Paul-Emile Becat. Paris,
1957. (1015). 4to. (58) with an extra set of the
plts. & 1 rejected plt. Unsewn as issued in orig.
wraps., folder & s.c., unc. (SKC. Sep.9; 1414)
£70

MARIA THERESIA
– **Constitutio Criminalis Theresiana oder der
Römisch-Kaiserl ... Majestät Maria Theresia
Erzherzogin zu Oesterreich ...** Vienna, 1769. L.P.
Fo. 30 engd. ills. & plts., some folding. Cont. red
mor., Austrian double eagle on sides in elab.
tooled gt. borders, spine gt. in compartments.
Bkplt. of Liechtenstein Liby. (C. Jul.16; 327)
Quaritch. £800

MARIANA, Juan de
– **The General History of Spain ... [with] Two
Supplements ...** Trans.:– Capt. John Stevens.
1699. 1st. Edn. in Eng. (L.P.). 2 pts. in 1 vol. Fo.
Some dampstaining. Cont. cf., worn. [Wing M599]
(S. Sep.29; 55) Quaritch. £70

MARIANA, Juan de–VIALART, Charles
– **The General History of Spain.–The History of
the Government of France under the
Administration of ... Richelieu.** Trans.:– Capt.
John Stevens (1st. work). 1699; 1657. Fo. Slightly
discold. thro.-out 1st. work. Cont. cf., 2nd. work
rebkd. [Wing V291] (C. Nov.20; 264)
Maggs. £110

MARIE, Adrien
– **Une Journée d'Enfant.** Paris, 1883. 4to.
Publisher's cl., tooled decor. (CR. Mar.19; 314)
Lire 200,000

MARIE-ANTOINETTE, Archiduchesse d'Autriche, Reine de France
Paris, [1815]. 16mo. Foxing. Cont. paper bds., s.-c.
(HD. Apr.10; 157) Frs. 1,050

MARIENGOF, Anatole
– **[The Candied Sun].** Moscow, 1919. 1st. Edn.
16mo. Orig. wraps., ptd. in gold, stapled, wraps.
with some minor defects. Inscr., possibly in
author's hand, at title, dtd. 1919. (PNY.
Mar.26; 203) $160
– **Ruki galstukom.** Ill.:– G. Yakulov. [Moscow],
[1920]. (150). Fo. Orig. wraps. (SH. Feb.6; 485)
Quaritch. £440
See–**ESENIN, Sergei & others**

MARIETTE, Pierre Jean
– **L'Architecture Françoise, ou receuil des plans,
elevations, coupes et profils des églises, palais,
hotels et maisons particulières de Paris.** Ill.:– Le
Pautre, Chevotet, Blondel & others. Paris, Priv.
ptd. 1727 2 vols. Fo. Some discoloration at end of
vol. I, border of 1 plt. cropped, incompl. cont. MS.
index loosely inserted. Cont. spr. cf., gt. spines.
W.a.f. (C. Feb.25; 187) Weinreb. £550
– – **Anr. Copy.** 3 vols. Fo. MS. table at end of each
vol. Cont. marb. cf., decor. spines. (HD.
Dec.5; 140) Frs. 29,000
[–] **Recueil des Plans, Elevations, Profils et
Decorations de l'Architecture Françoise.** Ca. 1760.
Fo. Cont. hf. cf. (C. Nov.6; 188) Weinreb. £150
– **Traité des Pierres Gravées.** Paris, 1750. [1st.
Edn?]. 2 vols. Fo. Cont. Fr. mor., gt. decor. border
on covers, arms of Comte Henri de Calenberg gt.
on covers, spines fully gt. in compartments with
tool, 6 raised bands, marb. end-ll., 19th. C. bkplt.
of Francis Hutchinson. As a bdg., w.a.f. (S.
Dec.8; 72) Bart. £460
– – **Anr. Copy.** 4to. Cont. red mor., decor. spines, 3
fillets, inside dentelle. (HD. Dec.5; 141)
Frs. 4,100
– – **Anr. Copy.** Loosely inserted pres. letter to Mrs.
Townshend from Dr. Mark Akenside, dtd. Jun.7
1770, bkplt. of Mrs. Mary Townshend, sig. on
titles of Lord Sydney. Cont. mor., triple gt. fillet,
spine gt. in compartments, inner gt. dentelles,
label of Joseph Gulston in spine compartment.
(SM. Oct.7; 1841) Frs. 4,000

MARILLIER, Clement Pierre
– **Figures de la Bible.** [Paris], ca. 1790. Hf. mor.,
spine gt. by Mercier. (SG. Oct.9; 157) $750
– **Suites de Figures pour les Oeuvres de Le Sage et
de l'Abbé Prévost.** Ill.:– Guélard & Schmidt
(ports.). 1783-84. Lge. 8vo. Str.-grd. red hf. mor.
by Champs, corners, decor. spine, unc. (HD.
Dec.5; 142) Frs. 8,500

MARILLIER, Clement-Pierre (Ill.)
See–**TRESSAN, Comte Louis Elisabeth de la
Vergne de Braussin**

MARILLIER, Henry Currie
– **Dante Gabriel Rossetti.** 1899. Ltd. Edn. specially
bnd. Fo. Niger mor., tooled in gt. & blind, elab.
centre-piece on upr. cover enclosing initials
'C.W.M.', the artist's monog. on lr. cover, by
Douglas Cockerell. (SH. Mar.27; 472)
Quaritch. £410

MARIN, John
– **Drawings & Water Colors.** N.Y., [1950]. (300)
sigd. 4to. Loose as iss. in linen folder. (SG.
Dec.4; 233) $130

MARINE RESEARCH SOCIETY
– **The Art of Rigging.–The Sea, The Ship & the
Sailor.–The Frigate Constitution & Other
Historical Ships.–The Built-Up Ship Models.**
Salem, Massachusetts, 1925; 1925; 1928; 1933. Fo.
Orig. cl. (TA. Feb.19; 641) £65

MARINETTI, F.T. & others
– **Manifesty Ital'yanskago Futurisma [Manifestos
of Italian Futurism].** Trans.:– [Vadim
Shershenevich]. Moscow, 1914. Orig. wraps.,
slightly soiled. (SH. Feb.6; 335)
National Art Gallery. £50

MARINIS, Tammaro de
[–] **Studi di Bibliografia e di Storia, in Onore di
Tammaro de Marinis.** Vatican City, Jun.-Dec.
1964. 4 vols. Orig. cl., partly unc., s.-c.'s. The John
A. Saks copy. (CNY. Oct.1; 191) $220

MARINO, Giambattista
– **L'Adone.** Paris, 1623. 1st. Edn. Sig. 3R misbnd.,
inkstain on 1 lf., old sig. of P. Guenaut on title &
initials F.S.L.A. Cont. red mor., gt. panel with
double λ at each corner, triple gt. fillet, spine gt. in
compartments with double λ single wormhole in
upr.-cover (SM. Oct.7; 1842) Frs. 3,000
– **La Sampogna.** Ill.:– I. Isaac. Paris, 1620. 1st.
Edn. 12mo. Bkplt. of Henry J.B. Clements. Cont.
mor., gt. panel. covers, flat spine gt. with
abbreviated title & longitudinal design.
Beckford-Hamilton Palace copy. (SM. Oct.7;
1843) Frs. 1,700

MARION, F.
– **Les Ballons et Les Voyages Aeriens.** Ill.:– P.
Sellier. Paris, 1867. Pict. cl. (GM. Apr.30; 485)
£62

MARIONETTE TONIGHT, the
Ed.:– Edward Gordon Craig. Flor., 1918. Nos.

1-12. Extra play with no ll. Orig. wraps. (P.
Jan.22; 327) McKenzie. £110

MARIOTTE, Edmond
– **Traité du Mouvement des eaux et des autres
Corps Fluides.** Ed.:– P. de La Hire. Paris, 1686.
1st. Edn. 12mo. Sm. hole in title just touching
date. 19th. C. hf. cf., corners worn. (C. Apr.1; 111)
Johns. £300

MARITAIN, Raissa
– **Chagall.–Chagall, ou l'Orage Enchanté.** N.Y.;
n.p., 1943; [1965]. (1500) numbered, & sigd. (1st.
work). 4to. Wraps. (1st. work); & cl., d.-w. (SG.
Apr.2; 69) $110

MARIUS, Michel
– **La Reliure Française.** Paris, 1880. 1st. Edn. Fo.
Red three qtr. mor., spine gt., jnts. worn. (SG.
Oct.2; 235) $260

MARIVAUX, Pierre Carlet de Chamblain de
– **Les Meilleures Oeuvres.** Ill.:– Paul-Émile Bécat.
Paris, 1952-53. (2,200), numbered. 6 vols. Unsewn
in orig. wraps., folders, s.-c.'s. (SH. Nov.20; 8)
Kaufman. £70
– **Oeuvres.** Paris, 1781. 12 vols. Cont. tree cf. gt.
(P. Jan.22; 57) Balham. £160
– **Oeuvres Complettes.** 1781. 1st. Coll. Edn. 12 vols.
Spr. cf. (HD. Jun.30; 52) Frs. 5,400
– **La Vie de Marianne, ou les Aventures de
Madame la Comtesse de ...** Ill.:– Chevaux,
engraved by Duponchel. L., 1782. 4 vols. 18mo.
Frontis. of vols. 1 & 2 are alike. Red mor. by
Cazin. (HD. Apr.8; 274) Frs. 4,000

**MARIVAUX, Pierre Carlet de Chamblain de
–HALLER, Albrecht von**
– **Le Paysan Parvenu.–Usong.** 1735; 1773. 1st.
Edn. in Engl. (1st. work). 2 works in 2 vols. Advts.
at end. Cont. cf.; 2nd. work with gt. spine. (C.
Nov.20; 210) Murray-Hill. £85

MARKHAM, Edward
– **The Man with the Hoe.** San Franc., 1899. Supp.
to the Sunday Examiner. Fo. Slight browning. Cl.
s.-c. (SPB. Nov.25; 346) $200

MARKHAM, Col. Frederick
– **Shooting in the Himalayas.** 1854. [1st. Edn.?].
Cont. hf. mor. (CSK. Oct.3; 164) £60
– – **Anr. Copy.** Three-qtr. mor., lacks blank
endpaper. (SG. Apr.9; 381) $180

MARKHAM, Gervase
– **Cheape & Good Husbandry for the
Well-Ordering of all Beasts & Fowles ...** L.,
1631. Sm. 4to. Mod. leath. (SG. Oct.16; 186)
$300
– **A Way to Get Wealth ...** [1656-] 1657. 5 (of 6)
pts. in 1 vol. 4to. Main title mntd., additional
engraved double-p. plt. tipped in at front, slightly
spotted, soiled, dampstained. 19th. C. cf., spine
worn, piece at head missing. [Wing M477] (S.
Apr.7; 267) Traylen. £130
– – **Anr. Edn.** 1660. 4to. Old leath., worn. (SKC.
Dec.4; 1410) £170

MARKHAM, Gervase & Venables, Robert
– **The Pleasures of Princes.** L., Cress. Pr., 1927.
(50) numbered on Arnold H.M.P. 4to. Limp vell.,
spine gt., linen ties, unc. (SG. Oct.16; 187) $220

MARKOV, Lev & Durov, Aleksandr
– **Kabluk Futurista [Heel of the Future].** Moscow,
1914. Orig. wraps. (SH. Feb.6; 486)
Quaritch. £110

MARLE R, Van
– **The Development of the Italian Schools of
Painting.** The Hague, 1923-38. Tog. 19 vols.
including index vol. Cl. (VG. Nov.17; 565)
Fls. 1,000

MARLIANUS, Bartholomaeus
See–**LAETUS, Pomponius & Marlianus,
Bartholomaeus–LESCUT, Nicolaus de–LERNS-
NER, J.–GOBLER, J.**

MARLOIS, Samuel
– **La Perspective.** Ill.:– J. Aelst, some by H.
Hondius after P. Stephanus. Amst., 1638. 1st. Edn.
Fo. Sm. dampstain to lower inner portion of title
& a few following ll., text & some plts. browned.
18th. C. Fr. cf., flat spine gt. & gt. lettered.
(CNY. Oct.1; 17) $350
– – **Anr. Copy.** Old vell., crudely rebkd., worn.
(SG. Dec.4; 234) $140

MARLOTH, [Hermann Wilhelm] Rudolf
– **The Flora of South Africa.** Capetown, 1913-15.
4 vols. in 6. 4to. Blind-stpd. on titles. Orig. cl.,

liby. marks on spine. From collection of Massachusetts Horticultural Society, stps. on plts. (SPB. Oct.1; 144) £800
- - **Anr. Edn.** 1913-32. 4 vols. in 6. Sm. fo. Vol. 4 lacks plt. 59, as often. Orig. cl., soiled, most vols. lack free end-paper. (TA. Jun. 18; 52) £325
- - **Anr. Copy.** 4 vols. in 6, & additional vol. IV. 4to. Additional vol. IV with 23 plts. only (but with fig. 59 at p. 186). Cl., vols. II & III, pts. 1 & 2 with d.-w.'s. (SSA. Nov.5; 57) R. 850

MARLOWE, Christopher
- **Edward the Second.** L., 1929. (500) numbered on H.M.P. Vell., gt. (GM. Apr.30; 801) £65

MARLOWE, Christopher & Chapman, George
- **Hero & Leander.** Ill.:- Charles Ricketts & Charles Shannon. Vale Pr. 1894. (220). Orig. vell., with gt. design by Ricketts, unc. & unopened. (SG. Jan.15; 104) $500
- - **Anr. Edn.** Ill.:- Lettice Sandford. Golden Hours Pr., 1933. (206) numbered. 4to. Hf. mor., partly unc. (S. Jun.9; 4) *Golden.* £52
- **The Rich Jew of Malta.** Ill.:- Eric Ravilious. Golden Hours Pr., 1933. 4to. Hf. mor., partly unc. (S. Jun.9; 5) *Golden.* £52

MARMADUKE MULTIPLY'S Merry Method of Making Minor Multiplications
[1816-17]. 16mo. 1 section loose. Mor.-bkd. bds. (CSK. Aug.15; 43) £80

MARMIER, Xavier
- **Voyage Pittoresque en Allemagne Partie Méridionale.** Ill.:- Rouargues brothers. Paris, 1859. Soiled. Cont. hf. leath. gt. (R. Mar.31-Apr.4; 1865) DM 1,150

MARMONTEL, Jean François
- **Contes Moraux.** Ill.:- Cochin (port.) & Gravelot. Paris, 1765. 1st. Edn., 1st Printing. 3 vols. Cont. marb. cfs., decor. spines, cold. pieces, 3 gt. fillets on covers, inside dentelle. (HD. Dec.5; 143) Frs. 2,900
- - **Anr. Edn.** Ill.:- Cochin (port.); Gravelot (figures). L. [Paris], 1780. 3 vols. 18mo. Cont. red mor., fillet, decor. spines, inside dentelle. (HD. Mar.18; 116) Frs. 1,700
- - **Anr. Edn.** Ill.:- Dupin after Cochin & Gravelot. Liège, 1780. 3 vols. 18mo. Red mor. by Cazin. (HD. Apr.8; 276) Frs. 2,000

MARMORA ARUNDELLIANA ... publicavit & commentariolos adiecit Ioannes Seldenus
1628. 1st. Edn. 4to. A few running-titles cropped, title a little stained. Cont. red mor. gt., spine gt. in 6 compartments, gt. borders on covers. (STC 823] (C. Apr.1; 189) *Quaritch.* £240

MARMORA OXONIENSIA
Ed.:- Richard Chandler. Oxford, 1763. L.P. Lge. fo. 1 folding plt. with sm. marginal tear, some browning. Cont. russ., gt., spine reprd. at head & foot. (S. Jun.22; 71) *Dimakrakos.* £50

MARNIX VAN SINT ALDEGONDE, Ph. van
[-] **De Byen-corf, der H. Roomscher Kercke.** Amst., 1611. 2 pts. in 1 vol. Sm. wormholes in several lr. margins. Cont. limp vell., soiled & a bit warped, outer parts of vell. on covers cut away. (VG. Oct.13; 104) Fls. 550

MAROLDUS, Marcus
- **Oratio de Epiphania.** [Rome], [Bartholomaeus Guldinbeck], ca. 1485. 2nd. Edn. 4to. Paper bds. [Copinger 3884; Goff M 278] (C. Apr.1; 59) *Goldschmidt.* £190

MAROLLES, Abbé Michel de Villeloin
- **Tableaux du Temple des Muses.** feu Mr. Favereau. Paris, 1655. [1st. Edn.?] Fo. Old cf., rebkd. (BS. Jun.11; 66) £200
- - **Anr. Copy.** Extra title defect., Dd4 torn & reprd. Cont. cf., rebkd., worn. (S. Mar.17; 275) *Duran.* £150
- - **Anr. Edn.** Ed.:- Abraham Van Diepenbeck. Paris, 1663. 1st. Diepenbeck Edn. Fo. 1st. Edn. 100 pp. damp-stained at edges of outer margins. Later tree cf., title stained, & blank lr. outer corner replaced. (PNY. Oct.1; 349) $180
*See-*VRIES, Jan Vredman de-MAROLOIS, Samuel

MAROT, Clement
- **Les Oeuvres.** Paris, 1548. 2 pts. in 1 vol. 16mo. Some sidenotes cropped, some ll. slightly stained in outer edges, inscr. on title. Cont. cfs., worn, spine defect. at head. (S. Feb.10; 240) *Leone.* £70
- - **Anr. Edn.** The Hague, 1700. 1st. Printing. 2 vols. 12mo. 19th. C. red mor., blind & gt. fillet

border, decor. spine raised bands, inner dentelles. (HD. Apr.24; 81) Frs. 2,600
- - **Anr. Edn.** Ill.:- de Brié (port.-frontis.); A. Van der Laan. The Hague, 1731. 4 vols. 4to. Slight foxing. Hf. mor. by Champs-Stroobants, spines decor. with raised bands. (HD. Feb.27; 42) Frs. 1,800
- - **Anr. Edn.** Ill.:- De Launay after Holbein (port.). Geneva, 1781. 2 vols. 18mo. Red mor. by Cazin. (HD. Apr.8; 277) Frs. 1,800

MARPERGER, P.J.
- **Nothwendig u. Nützl. Fragen über die Kaufmannschaft-Erster Fortsetzung.** Leipzig & Flensburg, 1714-15. 1st. Edn. Slightly browned, end-papers soiled. Cont. vell. gt. (HK. May 12-14, 1141) DM 1,300

MARPURG, Friedrich Wilhelm
- **Abhandlung von der Fuge.** Berlin, 1753. Orig. Edn. Pt. 1. 4to. Browned, 2 old owner's marks on title lf. Cont. paper bds., defect. (H. Dec.9/10; 1191) DM 420
- **Neue Methode Allerley Arten von Temperaturen dem Claviere aufs bequemste mitzutheilen.** Berlin, 1790. 1st. Edn. Sm. 4to. Heavily browned, soiled. Loose ll., no wraps. (H. Dec.9/10; 1195) DM 600
- **Storia della Musica.** Bologna, 1757-81. 1st. Edn. Vol. I-III, all publd. 4to. Lacks 2 maps, as usual, 3 copperplts., 1 text column engr. cold., slightly soiled in parts, some sm. stains, light browning. Mod. linen, unc. (H. Dec.9/10; 1197) DM 1,700

MARPURG, Friedrich Wilhelm-ALEMBERT, Jean le Rond d'
- **Anfangsgründe der Theoretischen Musik.** -**Systematische Einleitung in die Musicalische Setzkunst.** Trans.:- F.W. Marpurg (2nd. work). Leipzig, 1757. 1st. Edn. 2 works in 1 vols. 4to. Sm. stp. on 1st. title, browned. Cont. paper bds. (H. Dec.9/10; 1192) DM 490

MARQUIS, A.L.
- **Recueil d'Opuscules.** Ed.:- E. Carault. Rouen, 1830. Cont. qtr. cf. Ex-libris Arpad Plesch. (TA. Jun.18; 28) £62

MARR, James
[-] **The City & County of El Paso, Texas ...** El Paso, 1886. Ptd. wraps. Pres. copy. (SG. Jan.8; 426) $325

MARRA, James (?)
[-] **Journal of the Resolution's voyage ... on discovery to the Southern Hemisphere ... also, A Journal of the Adventure's Voyage ... with an account of the separation of the 2 ships.** Dublin, 1776. Occasional slight soiling, clean tears in folding map. Cont. cf. (KH. Nov.18; 409) Aus. $400

MARRAULT, Abbé J.A.
- **Histoire des Abenakis, depuis 1605 jusqu'a à nos Jours.** Sorel, 1866. 1st. Edn. Red mor. gt.-tooled, upr. cover gt.-lettered 'Presented to H.R.H. Prince Arthur by the Province of Quebec'. (SG. Mar.5; 113) $260

MARRYAT, Frank S.
- **Borneo & the Indian Archipelago.** 1848. 1st. Edn. Orig. cl., gt., by Westleys & Co., with their ticket, unc. (S. Jun.29; 235) *Crete.* £160
- - **Anr. Copy.** Fo. 1 plt. loose. (SBA. Oct.21; 116) *Grosvenor Prints.* £70
- **Mountains & Molehills.** Ill.:- after author. 1855. 1st. Edn. Cont. hf. cf., spine gt. (LC. Feb.12; 201) £80

MARRYAT, Capt. Frederick
- **Mr. Midshipman Easy.** 1836. 1st. Edn. 3 vols. Advt. lf. at end of vols. 2 & 3. Orig. bds., rebkd., unc. A.N. (reprd.) & sigd. autograph receipt (both by Marryat) loosely inserted; Sir Thomas Masterman Hardy's copy with his sig. in each vol., bkplt. of Oliver Brett. (LC. Feb.12; 251) £150
[-] **Peter Simple.** 1834. 1st. Engl. Edn. 3 vols. 12mo. Errata slip in vol. 3, lacks hf.-titles & advts. Cont. hf. cf. (S. Jul.27; 93) *Hollis.* £60
*See-*MOORE, Lieut. Joseph & Marryat, Capt. Frederick

MARSAN, Eugène
- **Les Cannes de M. Paul Bourget et le Bon Choix de Philinte.** Ill.:- Henri Farge. Paris, 1923. (1300); (60) on Jap., numbered. 20 pp. of orig. drawings & watercolours at end. Mor. sigd. by Marie-Louise H. Farge, spine & covers richly gt., wrap. preserved. (SM. Feb.11; 252) Frs. 5,000

MARSCIANO, F.O. de
- **Der Unterwiesene Anfänger in der Chemie.** Vienna, 1752. 2nd. (title) Edn. 9 sm. text woodcuts, partly repeated, some old Engl. marginalia, browned. Cont. style leath. (R. Oct.14-18; 204) DM 2,000

MARSDEN, William
- **The History of Sumatra.** Priv. Ptd. 1784. 2nd. Edn. 4to. Title dust-soiled. 19th. C. cl. Inscr. on endpaper 'From the Author', from Chetham's Liby., Manchester. (C. Nov.27; 270) *Armstrong.* £80
- - **Anr. Edn.** [1811]. Atlas vol. only. Lge. fo. 27 engd. ills. on 19 plts. Orig. bds. (C. Jul.15; 121) *Remington.* £220
- - **Anr. Edn.** 1811. 3rd. Edn. 4to. With maps & plts. usually found in separate atlas vol., occasional light foxing. Orig. bds., unc. (C. Nov.5; 102) *Ad Orientem.* £190
- - **Anr. Copy.** Errata slip, sm. tears in map, slightly spotted. Cont. cf., rebkd., worn. (S. Dec.8; 235) *Remington.* £130
- - **Anr. Copy.** Atlas vol. only. Fo. Hf. mor. (P. Jul.30; 213) *Walford.* £100
- - **Anr. Copy.** 2 vols. 4to. & atlas fo. 4to. vol. cont. diced cf., worn, atlas fo. vol. qtr. mor., brkn. (SG. Oct.30; 239) $350

MARSH, Lt. Col. W. Lockwood
- **Aeronautical Prints & Drawings.** 1924. (100) numbered. 4to. Orig. pig. (SH. Oct.9; 84) *Talerman.* £150
- - **Anr. Copy.** Browned. Orig. cl., worn. (SH. Jan.29; 122) *Talbot.* £60

MARSHALL, C.F. Dendy
- **Two Essays in Early Locomotive History.** -**Centenary History of the Liverpool & Manchester Railway.**-**A History of British Railways.** 1928; 1930; 1938. 4to. Orig. cl. (SKC. Feb.26; 1764) £80

MARSHALL, C.H.T.
*See-*HUME, A.O. & Marshall, C.H.T.

MARSHALL, George
- **Epistles in Verse between Cynthio & Leonora ...** Ill.:- after Thurston. Newcastle-on-Tyne, Priv. ptd. 1812. 1st. Edn. 4to. Orig. bds., worn, unc. (S. Apr.7; 417) *Tattersfield.* £80

MARSHALL, Henry Rissik
- **Coloured Worcester Porcelain.** Newport, 1954. Ltd. Edn. 4to. Orig. cl. (SH. Jan.29; 190) *Reed & Sims.* £85

MARSHALL, H[umphrey]
- **The History of Kentucky.** Frankfort, 1824. 2nd. Edn. 2 vols. Foxed. Cont. spr. cf., worn, covers loose. From liby. of William E. Wilson. [Sabin 44780] (SPB. Apr.29; 195) $300

MARSHALL, John
- **The Life of George Washington.** L., 1804-07. 5 vols. 12 folding maps. plts., extra ill. with plts., some hand-cold. Red mor. gt. by Bayntun. (SPB. Jun.22; 89) $300
- - **Anr. Copy.** Later hf. linen, ex-liby. (SG. Mar.5; 294) $130
- - **Anr. Copy.** 10 folding maps, plts.; maps & publisher's advts. at end vol. 1 lacking, advts. in vol. 5 lacking, some foxing & staining. Cf. gt., rebkd. new endpapers. (SPB. Jun.22; 90) $125

MARSHALL, William
- **Rural Economy of Gloucestershire.** 1789. 1st. Edn. 2 vols. in 1. Advts. in vol. I. Cont. tree cf. (S. May 5; 437) *Smith.* £75
- **Rural Economy of Yorkshire.** 1788. 1st. Edn. 2 vols. in 1. Cont. tree cf. (S. May 5; 436) *Smith.* £85

MARSIGLI, Luigi Ferdinando Marsilli
- **Danubius Pannonico-Mysicus.** The Hague & Amst., 1726. 1st. Edn. 6 bols. Lge. fo. Occasional foxing & soiling at edges. Cont. blind-stpd. vell., spines soiled. From Chetham's Liby., Manchester. (C. Nov.27; 271) *Junk.* £1,500

MARSTON, George
*See-*MURRAY, Sir James & Marston, George

MARSTON, John
- **The Metamorphosis of Pygmalion's Image.** Ill.:- Rene Ben Susan. Gold. Cock. Pr., 1926. (325). Orig. cl.-bkd. bds., unc., d.-w. (SH. Feb.19; 150) *Ayres.* £55

MARTELLI, Niccola
*See-*BONELLI, Georgio & Martelli, Niccola

MARTENS, Conrad
- Sketches in the Environs of Sydney. 1850. Bnd. in 1 vol. Ob. 4to. Consisting of 10 tinted litho. plts. (only, of 25). Hf. mor. gt. by Morrell, bnd. without wraps. The Edge-Partington copy, with bkplt. (KH. Mar.24; 447)   Aus. $2,800

MARTHOLD, Jules de
- Daniel Vierge. Paris, [1906]. (50) numbered on Japan vell. 4to. Plts. in 2 states, & with lettered tissue-guards. Lev., raised bands, wide gt. dentelles, by A. Destrees, orig. cold. pict. wraps. bnd. in, partly unc. (SG. Dec.4; 353) $200

MARTIALIS, Marcus Valerius
- Epigrammata. Ed.:– [Georgius Merula]. Milan, Philippus de Lavagnia, 1478. Fo. Initial on aii recto in gold on red & blue ground, with diamond-shaped ornament at inner margin, lacks last blank, some wormholes slightly affecting text towards end, cont. MS. headings, pagination & text markings. Early 19th. C. maroon str.-grd. mor. gt. Last lf. inscr. 'Hic liber est Micael Angeli Corazini', the Syston Park/C.S. Ascherson copy. [BMC IV, 706, Goff M302] (S. Jul.27; 105)   Lyon. £1,100
- [-] Anr. Edn. Venice, Dec. 1501. 1st. Aldine Edn. Mor., gt., by Cuzin. (S. Feb.10; 450)   Maggs. £160
- [-] Anr. Copy. Quire A loose, B1 detchd., a few wormholes at beginning & end slightly affecting text, light staining thro.-out, owner's inscr. on title-p. Late 16th. C. vell., spine wormed. (S. Dec.8; 119)   K Books. £70
- [-] Anr. Edn. Venice, 1517. Cont. mor., sides with panel of multiple gt. & blind fillets with gt. dolphins at corners, sewing guards from a 14th C. Flemish liturgical MS., spine labelled & part gt. in 18th. C. Cont. sig. of Claudius Rabottus on title, later in collections of Stephan Rous (inscr.) & C.F. Lamoignon (label & stp.). (S. May 5; 274)   Lyon. £350
- Martialis cum Duobus Commentis. Venice, Bartholomaeus de Zanis, 1493. Fo. Lacks final blank, mod. owner's sig. on title, earlier sig. eradicated, few ll. stained. Mod. hf. cf., gt. decor. spine. (SG. May 14; 139) $1,000

MARTIALIS, Marcus Valerius–CATULLUS, Tibullus & Propertius
- Epigrammaton Libri XIII.-Elegiarum Libri Quatuor. Venice, 151 [sic]; 1520. 2 vols. in 1 Fo. 2 unnumbered ll., 2nd. vol. 4 unnumbered ll. Cont. cf., blind-tooled decors., ties. (CR. Mar.19; 263)   Lire 650,000

MARTILINGEN, J.
See–KEPLER, J.–SCHEINER, C. & Locher, J.G. –SCHEINER, C.–PHILIPPI, II.–MARTI-LINGEN, J.

MARTIN, Benjamin
- Bibliotheca Technologica or a Philological Library of Literary Arts & Sciences. 1740. 2nd. Edn. Advt. ll. Cont. cf. (S. Dec.1; 273)   Music Mart. £50
- A New & Compendious System of Optics. 1740. Plt. 1 defect., some discolourations & dust-soiling. Cont. cf. (S. Dec.1; 274)   Quaritch. £75
- Sur les Dents. Paris, 1679. 12mo. Cont. cf. (S. Dec.2; 551)   Riley Smith. £500
- The Young Gentleman & Lady's Philosophy L., 1781. 3rd. Edn. 3 vols. Cont. hf. cf., jnts. brkn. & bds. loose in all 3 vols. (CB. Apr.1; 245)   Can. $200

MARTIN, Charles & Leopold
- The Civil Costume of England. 1842. 1st. Edn. 4to. Cont. hf. mor., lr. cover detchd. (C. May 20; 151)   Rostron. £50

MARTIN, Charles Wykeham
- The History & Description of Leeds Castle, Kent. 1869. Fo. Orig. cl., gt. (S. Dec.9; 424)   Crowe. £75

MARTIN, Corneille
See–BARLAND, Adrien–MARTIN, Corneille

MARTIN, Fredrik R.
- Miniature Paintings & Painters of Persia, India & Turkey. 1912 [1968]. (500). 2 pts. Fo. Orig. cl., d.-w. (SH. Oct.9; 85)   Ayres. £55
- - Anr. Copy. (HK. May 12-14; 2258)   DM 900
See–SARRE, Friedrich & Martin, F.R.

MARTIN, Gabriel
- Catalogus Librorum Bibliothecae ... Caroli Henrici Comitis de Hoym. Paris, 1738. 1st. Edn. Sale Catalogue priced in MS. thro-out, lacks final

blank lf. Cont. mott. cf., spine gt. Pres. copy 'A.M. Ch. Cottier' on ptd. label. (S. Jun.23; 250)   Dawson. £90

MARTIN, Gregory
- A Discoverie of the Manifold Corruptions of the Holy Scriptures, by the Heretikes of our Daies, specially the English Sectaries. Rheims, 1582. 1st. Edn. Corner torn from 1 lf., affecting text, slight worming in inner margin towards end, just affecting text, 17th. C. annots. on title & 8 pp. 18th. C. cf. [STC 17503] (C. Apr.1; 224)   Thor. £220

MARTIN, Henry
- La Miniature Française du XIIIe au XVe Siècle. Paris & Brussels, 1924. 2nd. Edn. Fo. Contents loose in bdg. Ptd. wraps. (SG. Mar.12; 257) $130

MARTIN, Rev. James
- [-] The Angler's Companion. L., ca. 1841. 12mo. Three-qtr. cf., orig. pict. wraps. bnd. in. (SG. Oct.16; 199) $170

MARTIN, John
- Illustrations of the Bible. 1838. Fo. A few ll. slightly spotted. Orig. cl. gt., slightly torn. (SBA. Jul.14; 415)   Salinas. £300

MARTIN, John, Bibliographer
- A Bibliographical Catalogue of Books Privately Printed. 1834. 1st. Edn. Slightly spotted. Hf. mor. (SBA. Jul.23; 563)   Dawson. £80
- - Anr. Edn. 1854. 2nd. Edn. Mod. hf. mor. (SBA. Jul.23; 564)   Dawson. £80

MARTIN, John, Meteorologist
- An Account of the Natives of the Tonga Islands ... with an Original Grammar & Vocabulary of their Language. Priv. ptd. 1817. 1st. Edn. 2 vols. Slight browning, ? vol. II lacks 1st. lf. (blank?) Cont. diced cf., spines gt., bkplt. of Hugh Percy. (S. Apr.7; 481)   Traylen. £100

MARTIN, Martin
- A description of the Western Islands of Scotland. 1703. 1st. Edn. Map with tear, some browning. Cont cf., worn, upr. cover detchd. (S. Nov.4; 578)   Quaritch. £85

MARTIN, Philip
- Earnest-Pennies. Ill.:– Margaret Adams. Stanbrook Abbey Pr., 1973. (5) on Eltham paper for special bdg. Mor. gt., blind-tooled designs, inscr. on fly-lf. 'Bound by Bede Stanbrook Abbey'. (SH. Feb.20; 364)   Quaritch. £90

MARTIN, Robert Montgomery
- Australia: Comprising New South Wales, Victoria or Port Philip, South Australia, & Western Australia. Ca. 1853. 4to. A few marks, 2 × 4 slightly torn without loss. Blind & gt.-tooled diced cf., worn. (PL. Jul.9; 129)   Ainsworth. £150
- - Anr. Edn. N.d. Pts. 1-3 only. 4to. 8 double-p. maps hand-cold. in outl., 1 loose, slightly soiled. Orig. cl. (SH. Mar.5; 95)   Campbell. £180
- The British Colonies. Ill.:– John Tallis. L., ca. 1850. 6 vols. in 2. Engd. titles, ports., 39 maps cold. in outl. Bdg. not stated. (P. Jul.2; 5)   Brown. £300
- History of the British Colonies. 1834-35. 5 vols. Ex-liby. copy with stps. on inside upr. covers only. Later cl. (TA. Dec.18; 35)   £60
- Hudson's Bay Territories & Vancouver's Island, with an Exposition of the Chartered Rights, Conduct & Policy. Ill.:– J. Wyld. 1849. Engraved folding map, cold. in outl., ex-liby. copy with blind stps. to title-p. & top of map only, 26pp. publisher's advts. bnd. in. Orig. blind-stpd. cl., recent mor. backstrip, untrimmed. (TA. Nov.20; 344)   £85
- - Anr. Copy. Three qtr. lev., unopened. Inscr. (SG. Mar.5; 295) $300
- Illustrated Atlas & Modern History of the World. Ed.:– John Tallis. 1851. Fo. Lf. directions to binder, maps hand-cold. in outl., & with vigs. & other features, blank fore-margin of frontis. wormed, engraved title slightly spotted. Orig. crimson cl. gt., 1 jnt. reprd. worn. (S. Nov.3; 33)   Gibbons. £600
- - Anr. Copy. Titles & frontis. stained, slight browning. Cont. hf. cf., contents detchd. from bdg. (S. Jan.27; 525)   Marshall. £550
- - Anr. Copy. 4to. Cf., covers loose. (P. Apr.30; 92)   Burgess. £460
- Illustrated Atlas & Modern History of the World.–Index-Gazetteer of the World. L., ca. 1850.

Together 2 vols. Fo. Cont. hf. mor. gt., worn. W.a.f. (S. Mar.31; 257)   Map House. £800
- - Anr. Edn. Ed.:– John Tallis (1st. work). Ca. 1851. 2 vols. Fo. 1st. work: all but 1 map hand-cold. in outl., 2 with marginal tears, 2nd. work: 1 plan folded & mntd. on linen. Unif. cont. hf. cf., worn. (S. Jan.27, 524)   Postaprint. £750
- The Indian Empire. L., ca. 1856-61. 1st. Edn. 8 vols. Tall 4to. Plts. foxed. Unif. gt.-pict. cl., some vols. unopened. (PNY. May 21; 224) $130

M[ARTIN], S[arah] C[atherine]
- The Comic Adventures of Old Mother Hubbard & Her Dog. 1806. 2nd. Edn. 16mo. Orig. ptd. wraps., worn & soiled. (SH. Mar.19; 166)   Schiller. £260
- [-] - Anr. Edn. N.Y., ca. 1825. Loose in orig. ptd. wraps., rebkd., upr. cover reprd. (SH. Mar.19; 167)   Ashton. £160

MARTIN, Thomas, Civil Engineer
- The Circle of the Mechanical Arts. 1813. 4to. Orig. cl.-bkd. bds., worn. (SH. May 21; 76)   Bennett. £50

MARTIN du Gard, Roger
- Vieille France. Ill.:– Théo van Elsen. 1935. (115), numbered. 4to. Mor. by G. Cretté, blind-tooled border on covers, wrap. preserved, s.-c. 2 A.L.s. by author & 1 by publisher, mntd. (SM. Feb.11; 253)   Frs. 4,500

MARTIN [LINIUS] von Cochem
- Das Dritte in zween Theil abgetheilte History -Buch, in Welchem ... Sechzig Lebens -Beschreibungen von den Lieben Gottes Heiligen. Ill.:– J.U. Kraus (frontis.). Augsb. & Dillingen, 1732. 4to. Pp. 449/450 with slight text loss in above corner, last 30 ll. soiled in upper corner, slightly soiled in places. Cont. blind-tooled pig-bkd. wood. bds., 2 clasps, renewed. (HK. Nov.18-21; 1455)   DM 420

MARTINEAU, H.
- English Lakes. ca. 1855. 4to. Orig. cl. gt. (P. Nov.13; 268)   Steedman. £50

MARTINEAU, Harriet
- Illustrations of Political Economy. 1834. 9 vols. in 4. 12mo. Some ll. spotted. Cont. hf. mor. (SH. May 28; 137)   Stevens. £70

MARTINET-HAUTCOEUR FRERES, publishers
- Caricatures par Divers Artistes. Paris, ca. 1840. 4to. Some minor foxing. Orig. paper bds., spine worn. (TA. Jan.22; 230)   £85

MARTINEZ DE LA PUENTE, Joseph.
- Epitome de La Crónica del Rey don Juan el Segundo de Castilla. Madrid, 1678. Fo. Vell. (DS. May 22; 828)   Pts. 45,000

MARTINI, F.H.W.
- Neues Systematisches Conchylien-Cabinet. Nuremb., 1768-69. Vol. I (of 11) in 2. 4to. Cont. cf., gt. spines. (SH. Jun.4; 185)   Erlini. £65

MARTINI, F.H.W. & Chemnitz, J.H.
- Systematisches Conchylien-Cabinet. Nuremb., 1841-78. Vols. III & V (2 pts. in each). 4to. Text incomplete at beginning of both vols. Cont. hf. roan. W.a.f. (S. Dec.3; 1045)   Gibbs. £280

MARTINI, Giambattista
- Storia della Musica. Bologna, 1757-81. 1st. Edn. 3 vols. Fo. Hf.-title vol. 3. 19th. C. hf. vell. (SI. Dec.3; 382)   Lire 1,700,000

MARTINI, J.
- Collection. Monnaies de la Republique Romaine. Lugano, 1930. Orig. wraps. (SH. Mar.6; 394)   Spink. £75

MARTINI, M.
- Der Geschickte Haushalter und Fertige Kauffmann. Berlin, 1730. 1st. Edn. Slightly soiled. Cont. hf. leath. (R. Oct.14-18; 1452)   DM 600

MARTINIUS, Martin
- De Bello Tartarico Historia. Antwerp, 1654. 2nd. Edn. Slightly soiled. Old bds., defect. (R. Oct.14-18; 1754)   DM 340

MARTINUS SILICEO, Joannes
- De Usu Astrolabi Compendium. Paris, 1546. Lr. margin of title renewed. Hf. cl. From Honeyman Collection. (S. May 20; 3285)   McKittrick. £220

MARTIUS, Karl Friedrich Phillip von
- Flora Brasiliensis. Leipzig, 1840-1906. 15 vols. in 40. Fo. Some offsetting. Hf. mor. gt. As a periodical, w.a.f., from collection of Massachusetts

Horticultural Society, stps. on plts. [BMC/NH page 1,256] (SPB. Oct.1; 147) $40,000
- **Historia Naturalis palmarum.** Leipzig, [1823-ca. 1850.]. 3 vols. in 2. 4to. Errata slip, title-pp. of vols. 2 & 3 transposed. Hf. mor. From collection of Massachusetts Horticultural Society, unstpd. (SPB. Oct.1; 145) $11,000
- **Icones Plantarum Cryptogamicarum quas in . . . Brasiliam . . . collegit et descripsit.** Munich, Priv. ptd., 1828-34. 4to. Dupl. of plts. XXVII & XXVIII (uncold. lithographic), 2 titles dtd. 1827. Cont. bds., unc. From collection of Massachusetts Horticultural Society, stps on plts. (SPB. Oct.1; 146) $2,200
See-SPIX, J.B. & Martius, C. Fr. Ph. von

MARTY, A., Architect
- **Architecture pittoresque et moderne à l'usage des Proprietaires des Architectes et Entrepreneurs.** Ill.:- Lallemand fils & Ch. Walter. Paris, ca. 1880. Fo. A few wormholes in blank margins. Cont. hf. cf., corners slightly worn. (S. Dec.9; 472)   *Marlborough.* £80

MARTYN, Benjamin
- [-] **Reasons for Establishing the Colony of Georgia . . .** 1733. 1st. Edn., 1st. Iss. 4to. Disbnd. [Sabin 45002] (C. Jul.16; 388)   *Kosser.* £220

MARTYN, Benjamin-SAVILLE, Sir George
- [-] **Reasons for Establishing the Colony of Georgia, with Regard to the Trade of Great Britain; The Whole Proceedings Upon the Tryal of Robert Marral.-An Argument Concerning the Militia.** Ill.:- T. Pine. L., 1733; 1733; [1762]. 1st. work: 1st. Edn., 1st. Iss, 3 works in 1 vol. 4to. 1st. work: engraved map (the 2nd. Iss. of the 1st. map bearing the name Georgia upon it), without Postscript. Old hf. cf., worn. [1st. work: Sabin 45002] (CNY. Oct.1; 48) $380

MARTYN, Thomas, Entomologist
- **The English Entomologist.** L., 1792. Hf. mor., spine gt., by Hering, spine reprd. (C. Mar.18; 70)   *Harding.* £300
- - **Anr. Copy.** 4to. Cont. hand-cold. plts. Recent hf. mor. (TA. Jan.22; 377)   £280
- **Thirty-Eight Plates with Explanations . . . to Illustrate Linnaeus's System of Vegetables.** 1788. MS. list of species on end-paper. Orig. bds., unc. (C. Nov.5; 103)   *Larnark Jones.* £60
- **The Universal Conchology.** 1784. 4 vols. Lge. fo. Cont. mott. cf. gt., rebkd. Bkplt. of Edward, 1st. Lord Harewood, MS. note by author. (S. Nov.24; 206)   *Quaritch.* £4,000
- - **Anr. Copy.** Priv. Ptd. 4to. 159 only (of 160) plts., frames & numbers partly ptd. & partly inserted in MS., all finely hand-cold. & mntd. on paper., titles foxed. Cont. hf. diced russ., covers detchd. Possibly the Author's Proof Copy, from Chetham's Liby., Manchester. (C. Nov.27; 272)   *Wheldon & Westley.* £2,500

MARTYN, William Frederick
- **New Dictionary of Natural History.** L., 1785. [1st. Edn.?]. 2 vols. Fo. Vol. 1 lacks title-p., 5K reprd. with loss of 2 words, some tears & repairs. Hf. cf., reprd. W.a.f. (P. Jun.11; 270)   *L. Hill.* £320
- - **Anr. Copy.** Piece torn from S2 with slight loss of text, sm. hole in plt. 29, stain at foot of plt. 54, occasional browning & light offsetting. Cont. mott. cf., spines gt., covers detchd., worn. (S. Dec.3; 1046)   *Litman.* £220
- - **Anr. Copy.** 2 vols. in 1. Slight soiling, last 2 ll. creased. Cf., upr. cover detchd. (S. Dec.3; 1047)   *Litman.* £210

MARTYR of Vermigli, Pietro
- **Common Places . . .** Trans.:- Anthonie Marten. 1584. 6 pts. in 1 vol. Fo. Tears in A6 & B1, a few sm. holes etc. Early 19th C. russ., slightly worn. [STC 24669] (S. May 5; 286)   *Lachman.* £100
- **De Rebus Oceanicis & Orbe novo decades tres . . . Eiusdem praeterea Legationis Babylonicae Libri tres.** Basle, 1533. Fo. 2 ll. browned at end, Jesuit owner's inscr. on title. Limp vell., soiled, preserved in fold-over cl. box. [Sabin 1557] (SPB. May 5; 346) $650
- - **Anr. Edn.** Cologne, 1574. Cont. blind-stpd. vell. over wooden bds., clasps. Liechtenstein bkplt. (SPB. May 5; 347) $950

MARULUS, Marcus
See-THEOPHRASTUS-LUSCINIUS, Ottomar -HINGELBERGIUS, Joachimus-MARULUS, Marcus-PLATINA, Bartholomaeus

MARVELL, Andrew
- [-] **Advice to a Painter, & c.** [1666?]. 1st. Edn. Fo. Hf. cf. by Sangorski. [Wing M863] (C. Nov.19; 33)   *Goad.* £120

MARX, K.F.H.
- **Herophilus.** Carlsruhe & Baden, 1838. 1st. Edn. 16mo. Rubber-stp. ex-libris on title. Liby. buckram. From Brooklyn Academy of Medicine. (SG. Jan.29; 285) $260

MARX, Karl
- **Le Capital.** Paris, [1872-75]. 1st. Fr. Edn. 4to. A few ll. slightly spotted, dampstained at foot, mainly marginal. Cont. cl., slightly worn & loose. (SH. Feb.5; 35)   *Subunso.* £460
- **Das Kapital, Kritik der politischen Oekonomie.** Hamburg, 1872. 2nd. Edn. Vol. 1. Spotted. Cont. hf. mor. (S. Oct.21; 435)   *Bjorck & Borjesson.* £120
- - **Anr. Edn.** Ed.:- Fr. Engels. Hamburg, 1890-94. 3 vols. Hf. leath. (D. Dec.11-13; 2747)   DM 1,050

MARY, Queen of Roumania
- **Kildine: Histoire d'une Mechante Petite Princess.** Ed.:- Robert de Flers (preface). Ill.:- Job. Tour, n.d. Fo. Three-qtr. cf., spine gt., cold. pict. wraps. bnd. in. (SG. Apr.2; 141) $110

MASCAGNI, Paolo
- **Vasorum Lymphaticorum Corporis Humani Historia et Ichnographia.** Siena, 1787. 1st. Edn. Lge. fo. Stain at lr. margin of last few plts. Hf. cf. (S. Jun.16; 557)   *Jenner Books.* £480
- - **Anr. Copy.** L.P. Atlas fo. Mod. buckram. (SG. Oct.9; 158) $1,100

MASCALL, Leonard
- **The First Booke of Cattell.** 1605. 3 pts. in 1 vol. Sm. hole in title & prelims., some pp. misnumbered, dampstains thro.-out. Cont. vell. [STC 17584] (P. Apr.9; 83)   *Contend.* £100

MASCARDI, Agostino
- **La Congiura del Conte Gio. Luigi de Fieschi.** Anvers, 1629. 2nd. Edn. 4to. 18th. C. red mor. by Padeloup with his ticket, triple gt. fillet, flat spine gt. in compartments with sm. bird in foliage facing right, inner gt. dentelles. Amherst & Wilmerding bkplts. (SM. Oct.7; 1845)   *Frs.* 4,000
See-ROSCIO, Guito, Mascardi, Agostino & others

MASCHA, Ottokar
- **Felicien Rops und sein Werk.** Munich, 1910. (500). Orig. linen, slightly defect. (D. Dec.11-13; 461)   DM 450

MASEFIELD, John
- **Reynard the Fox.** L., 1919. 1st. Edn. Cl. Sigd. drawing & poem on fly-lf., autograph postcard, sigd. with initials, tipped in. (SG. Jun.4; 290) $160
- **Salt Water Ballads.** 1902. 1st. Edn. Orig. cl. (S. Jul.22; 218)   *Vignoles.* £85
- - **Anr. Copy.** 1st. State. Cl., bkplt. (SG. Nov.13; 453) $140
- **The Taking of Helen.** L., 1926. (750) numbered & sigd. Tall 8vo. Vell.-bkd. bds., partly untrimmed, d.-w. Pres. Copy to Thomas Hardy (with his bkplt.). (SG. Nov.13; 461) $250

MASEN, J.
See-BROUWER, C. & Masen, J.

MASEREEL, Frans
- **Geschichte ohne Worte.** Ill.:- Fr. Masereel. Munich, 1922. (50) Priv. Edn. on Japon. 4 vols. Orig. leath., gt. spine, inner & outer gt. dentelle. (D. Dec.11-13; 1140)   DM 700
- **La Ville. Cent Bois Graves.** [Paris], [1925]. (50) numbered Priv. Edn. on Japon Imperial with 2nd. series of ills. on China, (together (275), sigd. by artist. 4to. Mor., decor. silk end-ll., sigd. on upr. cover P. Bonet, on lr. cover M. Bailly Dor & J. Trinckvel, suede lined wrap. (D. Dec.11-13; 1138)   DM 6,300

MASILLON
- **Oeuvres Complètes.** 1822-25. 13 vols. Cont. marb. cf. From Marquis de Lespine liby. (HD. Oct.10; 254)   *Frs.* 1,000

MASKELL, William
- **A Letter to the Rev. Dr. Pusey . . .** 1850. Ptd. on Vell. Cont. hf. mor., unc. Sigd. (S. Nov.25; 494)   *Porter.* £170

MASKI [Masks]
Ed.:- [S.V. Chekhonin]. St. Petersb., 1906. Nos. 1-6 only (of 9). 4to. 3 slightly dampstained. Unbnd. (SH. Feb.5; 87)   *De la Casa.* £60

MASON, George Henry
- **The Costume of China.** 1800. [1st. Edn.?]. Fo. Text in Engl. & Fr., browned. Cont. mor. (SH. Jul.16; 213)   *F.A. Miller.* £310
- - **Anr. Copy.** Text wtrmkd. 1794-97, plts. 1796. Cont. str.-grd. red mor. gt. Bkplt. of Sir William Jennington. (S. Nov.24; 207)   *Roberts.* £260
- - **Anr. Copy.** Last few ll. spotted. Cont. str.-grd. mor., gt. borders with cornerpieces on sides, gt. panel. spine. (C. Nov.5; 104)   *Quaritch.* £200
- - **Anr. Copy.** Fo. Frontis. chipped at fore-edge. Cont. striated cf., elab. gt.-decor. cl. rebkd., corners & edges worn. (PNY. May 21; 135) $500
- - **Anr. Copy.** Fo. Chagrin, gt. & blind roll stps. (DS. May 22; 868)   Pts. 65,000
- **The Punishments of China,.** 1801. Fo. Plts. wtrmkd. 1823, advt. lf. at end dtd. 1821, text in Engl. & Fr., some offsetting, slightly soiled. 19th. C. str.-grd. mor. gt., a little worn. (S. Oct.21; 508)   *Duran.* £90
- [-] - **Anr. Copy.** A few minor repairs to some margins. Cont. gt. decor. mor. (TA. Feb.19; 329)   £74
- [-] - **Anr. Copy.** Fo. Plts. slightly soiled. Cont. mor. gt. (P. Apr.9; 54)   *Horesh.* £65
- - **Anr. Edn.** 1801 [but later]. Fo. Offsetting on to text, titles & text in Engl. & Fr., advts. the only wtrmks. appear to be 'J. Whatman 1823' on plts. 2, 8 & 14. Cont. str.-grd. mor. (CSK. Dec.12; 114)   £85
- - **Anr. Edn.** 1804. Fo. Most plts. slightly offset onto facing text pp. Cont. red str.-grd. mor. (S. Jul.27; 209)   *Shapiro.* £80
- - **Anr. Edn.** 1808. Fo. Cont. str.-grd. mor., gt. & blind borders on sides, with central gt. cypher on upr. cover, lr. cover slightly torn. (C. Nov.5; 105)   *Bruckner.* £90
- **Les Punitions des Chinois . . .** Ill.:- Dadley. L., 1801. Lge. 4to. Sewed, roan back. (HD. Dec.5; 145)   *Frs.* 1,450

MASON, James
- **The Anatomie of Sorcerie.** 1612. 1st. Edn. 4to. Some sigs. discold. Cont. spr. cf., rebkd. [STC 17615] (C. Nov.20; 265)   *Shaw.* £380

MASON, John
- **More Papers Hand Made . . .** Ill.:- Blair Hughes-Stanton. Leicester, Twelve by Eight Pr., 1971. Ltd. Edn., variant 19, sigd. Fo. Orig. parch. gt., unc. (SH. Feb.20; 334)   *Basilisk.* £80

MASON, R. Hindry
- **The History of Norfolk.** 1884. 2 vols. Fo. Cont. hf. mor. (CSK. Apr.3; 22a)   £55

MASON, Stuart (Pseud.)
See-MILLARD, Christopher Sclater 'Stuart Mason'

MASON, William
See-KENRICK, William-FARQUHAR, George -MASON, William-LEE, Nathaniel

MASON, William I. & Hunt, A.W.
- **The History & Antiquities of Birkenhead Priory.** Oxford, L. & L'pool., 1854. Fo. Some ll. slightly spotted. Orig. mor.-bkd. cl. gt., disbnd. (SBA. May 27; 341)   *Howell-Williams.* £55

MASPERO, Gaston
- **The Dawn of Civilization Egypt & Chaldea.** Ed.:- A.H. Sayce. Trans.:- M.L. McClure. 1894. Orig. cl. worn, ex-liby. (SBA. Mar.4; 59)   *Pelizzi.* £60
- **History of Egypt.** L., Grol. Soc., [1903]. Connoisseur Edn., (200). 13 vols. Some plts. in 2 states. Hf. mor. gt., red gt. floral & crescent inlays on spines, unopened. (SPB. May 6; 331) $1,600

MASSACHUSETTS Horiticultural Society
- **Catalogue of the Library.** Camb., 1918; 1920. 2 pts. 4to. Later buckram. (SG. Jan.22; 286) $350

MASSACRE of Glenco
1703. 1st. Edn. 4to. Browned. Hf. cf., rebkd. (S. Feb.9; 173)   *Campbell.* £70

MASSE, Pierre
- **De l'Imposture et Tromperie des Diables.** Paris, 1579. Bkplt. of Lord Northwick. 18th. C. mor., title, gt., on flat spine, inner gt. dentelles. (SM. Oct.7; 1846)   *Frs.* 4,000

MASSENET, Jules
- **Manon.** Paris, [1884]. Hf. mor. gt., paper wraps. bnd. in. (C. Oct.22; 265)   *MacNutt.* £50

MASSILLON, [Jean Baptiste], Bp. of Clermont
- **Sermons.** Paris, 1745-49. 15 vols. 12mo. Lacks hf.-titles in vol XV. Cont. cf., double gt. fillet,

MASSILLON, [Jean Baptiste], Bp. of Clermont –
Sermons. -contd.
spines gt. à la grotesque, inner gt. dentelles, head
of spines slightly worn. Bkplt. of Thomas
Maitland. (SM. Oct.7; 1847)   Frs. 1,200

MASSINGER, Philip
– The City-Madam, a Comedie. 1659. 1st. Edn.,
2nd. iss. 4to. Title remargined & a little soiled,
running-title occasionally cropped, sm. hole in
blank margin of last lf. reprd. Paper bds. [Wing
M1047] (C. Apr.1; 225)   *Quaritch.* £110
– The Emperour of the East. L., 1632. 1st. Edn.
4to. Mor. by Sangorski. [STC 17636] (C.
Nov.19; 112)   *Brett-Smith.* £350
– The Great Duke of Florence. 1636. 1st. Edn. 4to.
Mor. gt. by Rivière, in cl. box. Huth bkplt. [STC
17637] (C. Nov.19; 113)   *Quaritch.* £350
– – Anr. Copy. Lacks final blank. 19th. C. cf., gt.
Bkplt. of Jerome Kern (1885-1945, composer). (S.
Jun.23; 379)   *Bennett.* £120
– The Maid of Honour. 1632. 1st. Edn., 1st, Iss.
4to. K4 sigd. K2. 19th. C. hf. cf. [STC 17638] (C.
Nov.20; 266)   *Winter.* £240
– A New Way to Pay Old Debts. 1633. 1st. Edn.
4to. 2 catchwords cropped. Mor. gt. by Bedford, in
mor.-bkd. s.-c. Huth & R.H. Taylor bkplts. [STC
17639] (C. Nov.19; 114)   *Arnold.* £480
– The Renegado. 1630. 1st. Edn. 4to. Recent hf.
mor. [STC 17641] (C. Nov.19; 115)
    Quaritch. £300
– The Unnatural Combat. 1639. 1st. Edn. 4to.
Catchword & 1 letter on L2 in facs. Mor. gt. by
Rivière. [STC 17643] (C. Nov.20; 267)
    Winter. £240
– – Anr. Copy. Sm. piece torn from upr. blank
margin of title, hole in K2 with loss of a few
letters, some browning. 19th. C. russ., worn.
Bridgewater bkplt. (S. Jun.23; 380)
    Maggs. £130
– – Anr. Copy. Later hf. mor. [STC 17643] (SG.
Oct.9; 159) $600

MASSMANN, H.F.
– Geschichte des Mittelalterlichen, vorzugsweise des
Deutschen Schachspiels. Quedlinburg & Leipzig,
1839. Hf. leath. (D. Dec.11-13; 2297)   DM 640

MASSON, Andre
– Feminaire. Paris, 1957. (59) sigd. by the artist.
Fo. Cold. etchings. Orig. wraps., folder & box.
(SPB. Oct.1; 235) $2,750
– Graphiks. Trans.:– Roger Passeron. [Stuttgart],
[1973]. (50) numbered & initialled. Fo. 3 orig.
cold. lithos. bnd. in, & extra suite of 4 orig. cold.
lithos. (sigd. by Masson), & orig. sigd. etching,
together in folding cl. portfo., extra loose suite of
dupls. of the 3 orig. lithos. in text. Cl., d.-w., s.-c.
(SG. Apr.2; 191) $500
– Mythology of Being. N.Y., 1942. (30)
numbered, sigd., orig. sigd. etching laid-in. Tall fo.
Wraps., s.-c. (SG. Oct.9; 160) $550

MASSON, André & Leiris, Michel
– Simulacre. Poèmes & Lithographiés. Paris, 1925.
(100). 4to. 5 of the lithos. sigd. in pencil by
Masson, slight browning. Orig. wraps. Sigd. by
Leiris & Masson. (SPB. Nov.25; 347) $400

MASSON, Charles
– Narrative of Various Journeys in Balochistan,
Afghanistan, & the Panjab. 1842. 3 vols. 2 frontis.
with sm. tears, 1 reprd., 1 plt. folding & mntd. on
guards. Later cf.-bkd. cl. (CSK. Oct.10; 77)   £50

MASSON, Frederic
– Cavaliers de Napoleon. Ill.:– Edouard Detaille.
Paris, 1895. (25) numbered. Fo. Frontis. & plts. in
3 states, 1 frontis. cold. Orig. mor. gt. (SH.
Nov.20; 147)   *Klusmann.* £60
– Impératrice Marie-Louise. Paris, 1902. 1st.
Edn., on Rives paper. 4to. Str.-grd. mor. by
Durvand, gt. roll-stp. around covers, olive
branches in corners, arms in centre, smooth decor.
spine, inside dentelle, wrap. & spine preserved.
(HD. Feb.27; 176)   Frs. 1,500
– – Anr. Edn. Paris, 1902. (150) on 'papier
Impériales du Japon'. 4to. Hand-cold. frontis. Hf.
red mor. by Rivière. (SBA. Jul.23; 566)
    Claveuil. £100
– Napoléon à Sainte-Helene. Paris, 1912. (300) on
Arches laid paper. 2 vols. 4to. Publisher's str.-grd.
mor., gt. fillets & roll-stps. around covers, arms of
Napoleon I, spines decor. with raised bands, inside
dentelles, watered silk end-papers, wraps. & spines
preserved. (HD. Feb.27; 177)   Frs. 1,800

MASSON, Jean Papire
– Descriptio Fluminium Galliae, qua Francia est
. . ., nunc primum in lucem edita. Ed.:– [Jean
Baptiste Masson]. Paris, 1618. 1st. Edn. Staining
in upr. outside corner thro.-out, worming in
middle affecting text, reprd. & with some letters
in pen facs. Cont. Fr. red mor., gt. arms on covers
(over smaller achievement), spine gt. in 6
compartments, head of spine reprd. (C.
Apr.1; 152)   *Nicholas.* £140

MASSUE DE RUVIGNY, M.
– The Plantagenet Roll of the Blood Royal.
1905-11. (520). 4 vols. Fo. Orig. cl. Several A.L.s.
inserted, E.H. Fellowes copy. (SH. Jul.16; 87)
    Heraldry Today. £120

MAST, BUFORD & BURWELL CO.
– Agricultural Implements. Minnesota, ca. 1887.
Cl. gt. (P. Apr.9; 252)   *Comben.* £75

MASTERPIECES of Japanese & Chinese
Paintings & Sculpture
[Tokyo], [1913]. 12 vols. Fo. Coarse linen with
ties. (SG. Dec.4; 236) $130

MASTERS, The
Ed.:– Sir John Rothenstein. L., 1963-67. 100 vols.
(nos. 1-100). Fo. No bdg. stated. (JL. Jul.20; 683)
    Aus. $140

MASTERS OF ETCHING
1924-32. Vols. 1-19, 21-28, 32 & 33 only. Ob. fo.
Some plts. spotted. Cl. (SH. Jan.29; 124)
    Bennett. £80

MATAL, Jean Natale
See–METELLUS or MATAL, Jean Natale

MATHER, Cotton
– The Christmas Behaviour under Bereavements.
–The Fatal Consequence of a People's Persisting in
Sin . . . Boston, [1714]. 2 works in 1 vol. 12mo.
Lacks 1st. (blank?) lf., slight browning, advts. lf. at
end. Mod. mott. cf., spine gt. (S. Jul.27; 33)
    J.C. Dann. £75
– Help for Distressed Parents. Boston, 1695. 1st.
Edn. of rare Mather imprint. 12mo. Advts.,
browned, worn, numerous marginal & textural
tears. Cont. cf., worn, upr. cover detchd. [Sabin
46358] (SPB. Nov.24; 38) $600
[–] Pietas in Patri[am] The Life of His Excellency
Sir William Phips. 1697. Upr. right hand corner of
title torn away & crudely reprd., with loss of 2
letters, worming with loss of a few letters. Cont.
cf., cover detchd. & crudely reprd. [Wing M1138]
(CSK. Oct.17; 222)   £80

MATHER, Increase
– A Brief History of the VVarr with the Indians in
Nevve-England. Boston. 1676. 1st. Edn. Sm. 4to.
Lacks 1st. 4 ll. & without 'Exhortation' mentioned
on title, some browning & soiling, some portions
torn from margins & some worming, with slight
loss of text, reprd. Pol. cf. by Pratt, 1871, gt.,
slightly marked. [Sabin 46640; Wing M1187] (S.
Apr.7; 381)   *Quaritch.* £160

MATHERS, Edward Powys
– Love Night. Ill.:– John Buckland-Wright. Gold.
Cock. Pr., 1936. (200). Orig. vell.-bkd. cl. (SH.
Feb.19; 170)   *Campus.* £65
– Procreant Hymn. Ill.:– Eric Gill. Gold. Cock. Pr.,
[1926]. (200) numbered. Orig. cl., d.-w., a little
soiled. (CSK. Oct.31; 62)   £130

MATHESIUS, J.
– Bergpostilla. Nuremb., 1587. Fo. 'Ein Christl.
Lied. für Gemeine Wolfart . . .' with music at end,
several ll. strengthened at part of margins. Leath.
(HK. May 12-14; 214)   DM 1,500

MATHEWS, Gregory McAllister
– The Birds of Australia. Ill.:– J.G. Keulemans, H.
Gronvold & others. 1910-27. (225). 13 vols.
including 5 Supps. 4to. Lev. mor., gt., by
Zaehnsdorf, wraps. to orig. pts. bnd. in. (C.
Mar.18; 71)   *Schrire.* £8,250
– – Anr. Edn. Ill.:– Lodge, Keulemans, Gronvold
& others. 1910-36. Early vols. (300), later (225).
16 vols. in 14. 4to. Cont. red hf. mor., orig. wraps.
bnd. in. (S. Jun.1; 162)   *Maggs.* £8,000
– Birds of Australia.–Birds of Norfolk & Lord
Howe Islands. L.; L., 1910-27; 1928-36. 12 vols. in
16 & 5 supps. in 1 vol; 2 vols. including supp. Fo.
Slight tear in Vol. X, page 272. Cl., orig. wraps.
bnd. in at back. (SPB. Oct.1; 203) $11,000

MATHEWS, Henry
– The Diary of an Invalid . . . in Portugal, Italy,
Switzerland, & France . . . 1817 [-19]. 1820. 1st.

Edn. Cont. pol. cf., spine gt. William Beckford's
copy, with 6 pp. of notes by him. (S. Apr.7; 409)
    Traylen. £170

MATHIAS, T.J.
– Poesie Liriche Toscane. Napoli, 1824. 8vo. (in
4's). Inscr. on title. Early str.-grd. gt.-panel. mor.
Double fore-e. pntg.; from the liby. of Zola E.
Harvey. (SG. Mar.19; 149) $400

MATIENSSEN, Heather
– Portfolio of Graphic Art in Honour of . . . Ed.:–
Maurice Kahn & F. Harmsen. N.d. (100). Lge.
4to. Loose in orig. box. (VA. May 8; 472)   R. 155

MATIENZO, J.
– Commentaria . . . in Librum quintum
Recollectionis Legum Hispaniae. Madrid, 1613.
Fo. Colophon lf. at end dtd. 1612, owners' inscrs.
erased from title, some discolouration & stains.
Vell. bds., 1 hinge brkn. (SPB. May 5; 348) $250

MATISSE, Henri
– Cinquante Dessins. [Paris], 1920. 1st. Edn.,
(1000) on Holland Van Gelder. 4to. Orig. frontis.
etching, sigd. by Matisse. Orig. ptd. wraps.,
shaken. (PNY. Mar.4; 176) $1,200
– Dessins, Thèmes et Variations. Paris, 1943. (10)
on imperial Japon, sigd. by artist. 4to. In sheets,
wrap. (HD. Dec.5; 146)   Frs. 2,300
– Pierre à Feu. Paris, 1947. (49) sigd. by artist of
(999). 4to. Orig. ptd. wraps., folder & box. (SPB.
Nov.25; 351) $600
– Portraits. Monte Carlo, 1954. Ltd. numbered
Edn. 4to. Orig. litho. frontis. loose. Cold. pict.
wraps., bd. box (labeled in ink by previous owner).
(SG. Apr.2; 192) $160
– – Anr. Edn. Monte Carlo, 1955. (2850), 4to.
Wraps., folder & box. (SPB. Nov.25; 352) $300
– – Anr. Copy. Slight fading. (SPB. May 29; 289)
    $225

MATTHAEUS de Cracovia
– De Modo Confitendi. Paris, [Printer of Ockham],
ca. 1476. 1st. capital initial Q supplied in red,
rubricated in red & yellow, lr. blank margin of
final lf. restored, early marginal ink annots.
cropped away. Early 18th. C. Fr. red mor. gt.
From the collection of Eric Sexton. [Goff M372,
HC 3507] (CNY. Apr.8; 117) $7,500
– Dialogis Rationis et Conscientiae de Frequenti
usu Communionis. [Mainz], [Johann Gutenburg?],
[1460]. 1st. Edn. 4to. 6-line initial M on 1st. p.
supplied in blue with purple & red penwork
ground with descender in inner margin, the words
'Ratio' & 'Conscientia' supplied thro.-out in red,
rubricated. Blind-stpd. mor., silver-lettered, vell.
linings & free end-ll., by Trautz Bauzonnet. Bkplt.
of Sir M. Masterman Sykes, bkplt. & sig. of E.
Paillet, lately in the collection of Eric Sexton.
[BMC I, 40, Goff M367, H 5803] (CNY.
Apr.8; 90) $38,000

MATTHESON, Johann
– Grosse General-Bass-Schule. Hamburg, 1731.
4to. Slightly stained in parts & lightly browned.
Cont. vell. (HK. Nov.18-21; 1869)   DM 1,200

MATTHEW, Patrick
– Emigration Fields. North America, the Cape,
Australia & New Zealand. 1839. 1st. Edn. 4 pp.
publisher's advts., slight offset on title. Orig. cl.,
spine slightly worn. (S. Nov.4; 620)   *Lawson.* £60

MATTHIAE, G.
– Conspectus Historiae Medicorum Chronologicus.
Göttingen, 1761. Cont. bds. (R. Oct.14-18; 366)
    DM 430

MATTHIEU, Pierre
– Histoire de France. Paris, 1605. 1st. Edn. 2 vols.
in 1. 4to. Port. of Henry IV tipped in, sig. h in vol.
11 misbnd. after 2k4. Mid 17th. C. mor., gt., panel
with corner sprays on covers, triple gt. fillet, flat
spine gt. with central title with squirrel
surmounted by couronne fermée in oval of 'drawer
handle' with leafy sprays, couronne fermée round
design, inner gt. dentelles. Bkplts. of Michael
Delacour & Mortimer L. Schiff. (SM.
Oct.7; 1848)   Frs. 2,200

MATTHIOLUS, Petrus Andreas
– Les Commentaires svr les Six Livres de Pedacivs
Dioscoride de la Matière Médecinale. Trans.:– A.
du Pinet. Lyon, 1655. Last Edn. Fo. Lightly
browned & slightly soiled in parts. Hf. leath., very
defect., soiled. (H. Dec.9/10; 381)   DM 680
– – Anr. Edn. Trans.:– Antoine du Pinet. Lyon,
1680. Fo. Old cf., brkn. (SG. Oct.9; 161) $650

– **Commentarii in Libros Sex Pedacii Dioscoridis Anasarbei, de Medica Materia.** Venice, 1554. 1st. Edn. in Latin. Fo. Some old MS. marginalia. 18th. C. hf. leath. (HK. May 12-14; 376) DM 2,000
– – **Anr. Edn.** Venice, 1558. Fo. 19th. C. hf. mor. From Chetham's Liby., Manchester. (C. Nov.27; 273) *Antiqua Libri.* £950
– – **Anr. Edn.** Venice, 1560. Fo. Lacks 46-p. 'Apologia Adversus Amathum Lusitanum', title-p. rebkd. Cf.-bkd. 18th. C. bds., worn. (SG. Sep.18; 245) $1,200
– – **Anr. Edn.** Venice, 1565. 2 vols. Fo. Calligraphic title-p. added to vol.2, lacks B2-5 preliminary index, supplied in MS. facs., p.339 reprd., browned, heavy in vol.2, final lf. reprd. & rehinged. 17th. C. vell. (CNY. May 22; 206) $3,000
– **Discorsi . . . ne i Sei Libri de Pedacio Diosori de . . . della Materia Medicinale.** Venice, 1559. Fo. Lacks title. 17th. C. cf., worn. (S. Jun.23; 204) *Francesco.* £200
– – **Anr. Edn.** Venice, 1597. Fo. Some tears & other defects, lightly stained. 19th. C. hf. vell. (SI. Dec.3; 385) Lire 1,100,000
– **Epiatolarum Medicinalium Libri Quinque.** Prag, 1561. 1st. Edn. Fo. Pages 375-378 mispaginated, slightly browned. old owner's mark on title. 19th. C. hf.-vell. (HK. Nov.18-21; 233) DM 600
– **Kreutterbuch.** Ed.:– J. Camerarius Frankfurt, [1590-1626]. Fo. Slightly browned, lacks title lf. at beginning, & end of index, 1st. 5 ll. of preface & last 6 ll. of index partly restored in margins. Cont. pig over pig bdg. with clasps. (R. Mar.31-Apr.4; 1394) DM 2,200
– **Opera que extant omnia.** Ed.:– G. Bahuin. Basle, 1674. 2nd. in Latin. Edn. Fo. Some ll. browned, inscr. on hf.-title. Cont. vell. bds., soiled. Sig. of Robert Travers, Trinity College, Dublin. (S. Jun.1; 277) *Cristiani.* £650
– – **Anr. Copy.** Liby. stp. on title, foxing thro.-out. Hf. vell., worn. (BS. Nov.26; 187) £550

MATTSON, Ofverste H.
– **Minnen.** Lund, [1890]. 20th. C. hf. mor. & marb. bds. (CB. Dec.9; 45) Can. $110

MATURIN, Charles Robert
[–] Melmoth, the Wanderer. 1820. 1st. Edn. 4 vols. Hf. cf. gt. (P. Dec.11; 364) *Stevens.* £250
– – **Anr. Edn.** Boston, 1821. 1st. Amer. Edn. 2 vols. 18mo. Mod. hf. linen, ex-liby. (SG. Mar.5; 300) $110

MAUCLAIR, Camille
– **Ames Bretonnes.** Ill.:– Wély. Paris, 1907. (10) numbered on Japon. Sm 4to. Orig. aquatints cold. state on Japan mince & black state. Mor. by Noulhac flor. mor. onlays in spine panels & a flor. border & 2 interlacing line borders, orig. wraps. bnd. in, chemise & s.-c. (SM. Oct.8; 2357) Frs. 8,000
– – **Anr. Edn.** Ill.:– J. Wély. 1907. (300) on vell à la Cuve. (300), on vell à la Luve o Sewed, s.-c. (HD. Apr.24; 154) Frs. 1,400
– **Henri le Sidonier.** Paris, 1928. 4to. Sewed, ill. wrap. (HD. Dec. 5; 148) Frs. 1,250
– **Jules Cheret.** Ill.:– Jules Cheret. Paris, 1930. (730) numbered. 4to. Some ll. discold. Hf. mor., orig. wraps. & prospectus bnd. in. (SH. Nov.20; 24) *Tate Gallery.* £60
– **Les Miniatures du XVIIIe. Siècle.** Paris. 1912. (350) on vell. 4to. Jansenist Bordeaux mor. by Lahaye, spine with raised bands, inside dentelle, wrap. (HD. Feb.27; 178) Frs. 1,200
– **Les Miniatures du XVIIIe Siècle.–Les Miniatures de l'Empire et de la Restauration.** Paris, 1912-13. 2 vols. 4to. Sewed, wraps. (HD. Dec.5; 147) Frs. 2,600

MAUCLERC, Julian
– **A New Treatise of Architecture, according to Vitruvius.** Trans.:– Robert Pricke. 1669. Fo. Lr. fore-corners stained at beginning & a wormhole in inner margins, tear in A2m Bl slit in inner margin. 18th. C. panel. cf., worn. [Wing M1326] (S. Jun.22; 131) *Weinreb.* £1,400

MAUDE, John
[–] Visit to the Falls of Niagara in 1800. L., 1826. (50) L.P. & ptd. with proof plts. Royal 8vo. With errata slip, extra ill. with 2 ports. & 1 hand-cold. litho., 2 p. critical review of the bk., & 16 p. section entitled 'Additional Notes' tipped in, the 2 extra ports. foxed, sm. liby. stp. on title-p. Recent leatherette. Pres. Copy to Rev. Godfrey Massey, dtd. 25th. Nov., 1850. (CB. Sep.24; 179) Can. $850

MAUGHAM, William Somerset
– **Ah King.** L., [1933]. 1st. Edn. Cl., d.-w. Inscr. to Lawrence Thomson. (SG. Jun.4; 347) $170
– – **Anr. Edn.** L., 1933. (175) numbered on L.P., sigd. Buckram, partly unc. & unopened. (SG. Jun.4; 348) $160
– **Ah King.–The Book-Bag.–Theatre.** L.; Flor.; L., 1933; 1932; 1937. (175) sigd. (1st. work); (725) sigd. (2nd. work). 3 works in 3 vols. 3rd. work is a proof copy, slight browning to all 3 works, 1st. work with some spotting. 1st. work: orig. cl., publisher's box; 2nd. work: orig. cf.-bkd. bds., d.-w., soiled; 3rd. work: ptd. wraps., spine faded, s.-c. (SPB. May 29; 292) $175
– **Ashenden, or the British Agent.** L., 1928. Cl. Inscr. (SG. Jun.4; 338) $425
– **The Book-Bag.** Flor., 1932. 1st. Separate Edn., (725) on H.M.P., sigd. Hf. cl., unc., d.-w. (SG. Jun.4; 344) $120
– **The Book-Bag.–The Hour Before the Dawn.** Flor.; Garden City, 1932; 1942. 1st. & 1st. Amer. Edns., (1st. work 725 numbered L.P.) 2 vols. Cl., d.-w.; cl., d.-w. 1st. work sigd., 2nd. work pres. copy. (PNY. Mar.4; 180) $170
– **Books & You.** L., [1940] 1st. Edn. 12mo. Cl., d.-w. Inscr. (SG. Jun.4; 356) $100
– **Cakes & Ale.** L., [1930]. [1st. Edn.?]. 12mo. Proof sheets. Wraps. Inscr., T.L.s. laid in, with orig. envelope to W.M. Stone. (SG. Jun.4; 339) $550
– – **Anr. Copy.** Cl., d.-w. Inscr. to Lawrence R. Thomson. (SG. Jun.4; 340) $180
– – **Anr. Edn.** Ill.:– Graham Sutherland. 1954. (1,000) numbered, sigd. by author & artist. Orig. cf., partly unopened., s.-c. (SH. Jul.22; 223) *Maggs.* £90
– – **Anr. Copy.** This copy unnumbered. Orig. hf.-mor., s.-c. (SH. Dec.19; 593) *Sawyer.* £65
– – **Anr. Copy.** Orig. leath. (SH. Jul.23; 14) *Nox.* £55
– – **Anr. Copy.** Vell.-bkd. mor., partly unc. & unopened, boxed. (SG. Jun.4; 367) $180
– – **Anr. Edn.** Ill.:– Graham Sutherland. N.d. Ltd. Edn. sigd. by author & artist. Qtr. pig gt., unopened. (P. May 14; 287) *Sims & Reed.* £60
– **The Casuarina Tree.** L., 1926. 1st. Edn. Cl., d.-w. Inscr. to Lawrence Thomson. (SG. Jun.4; 336) $160
– **Cosmopolitans: Very Short Stories.** L., [1936]. 1st. Engl. Edn., 1st. Iss., Proof copy. 12mo. Wraps. (SG. Jun.4; 350) $180
– **Don Fernando.** L., 1935. 1st. Edn., (175) numbered, sigd. Buckram, boxed. (SG. Jun.4; 349) $170
– **First Person Singular.** L., [1931]. 1st. Engl. Edn. Cl., d.-w. Inscr. to Lawrence Thomson. (SG. Jun.4; 342) $130
– **The Gentleman in the Parlour.** L., [1930]. 1st. Edn. Gt.-pict. cl., d.-w. Inscr. to Lawrence Thomson. (SG. Jun.4; 341) $160
– **The Land of the Blessed Virgin.** N.Y., 1920. Hf. cl. Inscr. (SG. Jun.4; 327) $280
– **Liza of Lambeth.** 1897. 1st. Edn. 6pp. advts. Orig. pict. cl. gt., s.-c. (S. Jul.22; 221) Blackwell. £120
– – **Anr. Copy.** Cl., worn & shaken, hf. mor. s.-c. Inscr. to Mrs. Suell (grandmother), 2.-p.A.L.s. laid in. (SG. Jun.4; 315) $800
– **The Making of a Saint.** L., 1898. 1st. Engl. Edn. Cl. Inscr. to Lawrence R. Thomson. (SG. Jun.4; 318) $250
– **The Mixture as Before.** L., [1940]. 1st. Edn. Cl., d.-w. Inscr. to Lawrence Thomson. (SG. Jun.4; 357) $150
– **Mrs. Craddock.** L., 1902. 1st. Edn. 32-pp. advts. Rebnd. in mor.-bkd. marb. bds. Inscr. to Fred Bason. (SG. Jun.4; 320) $100
– **The Moon & Sixpence.** L., 1919. 1st. Edn., 1st. Iss. 12mo. 4-pp. advts., lacks front free endpaper. Cl. Inscr. (SG. Jun.4; 326) $300
– **The Narrow Corner.** L., [1932]. 1st. Edn. Cl., d.-w. Inscr. to Lawrence Thomson. (SG. Jun.4; 345) $160
– **Of Human Bondage.** 1915. 1st. Engl. Edn. 16pp. advts. Orig. cl. gt. (S. Jul.22; 222) *Britton.* £65
– – **Anr. Copy.** Orig. cl., pict. d.-w., qtr. mor. gt. s.-c. Inscr. to Keith Baker, lately in the Prescott Collection. (CNY. Feb.6; 244) $1,400
– – **Anr. Edn.** N.Y., [1915]. 1st. Edn., 2nd. Iss. Cl., d.-w. torn. (SG. Jun.4; 325) $130
– – **Anr. Edn.** Ill.:– Randolph Schwabe. Garden City, 1936. (751) numbered, on L.P., sigd. by author & artist. Buckram gt. (SG. Jun.4; 352) $150
– – **Anr. Edn.** Ed.:– Theodore Dreiser (intro.). Ill.:– John Sloan. Ltd. Edns. Cl. 1938. (1500) numbered, & sigd. by artist. 2 vols. Cl., spines slightly discold., boxed. (SG. Apr.2; 277) $340
– – **Anr. Copy.** Orig. bds., boxed. (SPB. Jul.28; 282) $250
– – **Anr. Copy.** Cl., orig. box (reprd. with tape). (SG. Jan.15; 227) $225
– – **Anr. Copy.** (SG. Oct.23; 316) $200
– **Of Human Bondage; with a Digression on the Art of Fiction.** [Wash.], 1946. (500) sigd. 12mo. Bds. Laid in, programme for Maugham's address to the Liby. of Congress. (SG. Jun.4; 370) $100
– **Orientations.** L., 1899. 1st. Edn., 2nd. Iss. Loose in cl. Inscr. (SG. Jun.4; 319) $170
– **The Painted Veil.** L., 1925. 1st. Engl. Edn. Iss. with Author's Note tipped in; 'Tching-Yen' reading thro.-out, no sig. mark on p.17. Cl., d.-w. Inscr. to Lawrence Thomson. (SG. Jun.4; 333) $200
– **Princess September & the Nightingale.** Ill.:– Richard C. Jones. L., [1939]. 1st. Edn. Cl., pict. d.-w. Inscr., A.N. initialled laid in. (SG. Jun.4; 355) $260
– **The Razor's Edge.** Garden City, 1944. 1st. Edn. (750) numbered, sigd. Cl., boxed. (PNY. Mar.4; 181) $260
– – **Anr. Copy.** Buckram., partly unc., boxed. (SG. Jun.4; 361) $150
– – **Anr. Copy.** (SG. Nov.13; 474) $100
– **My South Sea Island.** Chic., Black Cat Pr. 1936. 1st. Edn., (50). With mis-spelling 'Sommerset' on title-p. Orig. ptd. wraps., unc. & unopened. (SPB. Nov.25; 353) $300
– **The Summing Up.** L., [1938]. 1st. Edn. Cl., d.-w. Inscr. to Lawrence R. Thomson. (SG. Jun.4; 354) $170
– – **Anr. Edn.** Garden City, 1954. (391) numbered, on L.P., sigd. Buckram, partly unc. & unopened, boxed. (SG. Jun.4; 366) $100
– **The Trembling of a Leaf.** L., 1921. 1st. Engl. Edn. Cl. Inscr. to Lawrence Thomson. (SG. Jun.4; 329) $150
– **The Unconquered.** N.Y., 1944. 1st. Edn., (300) numbered, sigd. 12mo. Cl., tissue d.-w. (PNY. Mar.4; 182) $110

MAUGHAM, W. Somerset (Ed.)
See–VENTURE

MAULNIER, Thierry
– **La Course des Rois.** Ill.:– Jean Cocteau. Paris, 1947. (1,200) numbered on Velin Pur Fil L.L.L.L. des Frères Lafuma P. 4to. Wraps, unopened. (PNY. Oct.1; 152) $110

MAUND, Benjamin
– **The Book of Hardy Flowers; or Gardener's Edition of the Botanic Garden.** N.d. 2 vols. Floral register bnd. at rear, some ll. slightly spotted. Cont. hf. cf., slightly worn. (SD. Feb.4; 264) $320
– **The Botanic Garden.** 1824-30. 4 vols. (1-4 only, of 13). Sm. 4to. Vols. 1-3 orig. bds., 1 spine defect., vol. 4 hf. cf. W.a.f. (C. May 20; 223) *Schuster.* £350
– – **Anr. Edn.** 1825-26. 8 vols. Sm. 4to. Over 760 hand-cold. plts. Lev. mor. gt., by Zaehnsdorf. W.a.f. (C. Mar.18; 72) *Quaritch.* £2,600
– – **Anr. Copy.** Vol. I only. Loose in orig. bds., spine worn. (TA. Mar.19; 607) £120
– – **Anr. Copy.** Vol. 1 only. (TA. Jun.18; 163) £90
– – **Anr. Edn.** 1825-28. Vol.s I-II (of 13). 4to. Slightly spotted. Cont. mor., gt. (SH. Jun.4; 143) *Maggs.* £210
– – **Anr. Edn.** 1825-32. Vols. 1-4 only. Occasional slight soiling, some ll. spotted. Cl. W.a.f. (CSK. Apr.3; 147) £420
– – **Anr. Edn.** 1825-36. Vols. 1-6 in 3. 4to. Many plts. loose, some dampstaining to text. Cl., worn. (P. Jul.30; 207) *Weston.* £440
– – **Anr. Edn.** 1825/26-1835/36-n.d. Vols. 1-9 only. 4to. Slight spotting, only occasionally affecting plts. Vols. 1-7 mor., vols. 8 & 9 hf. mor. (CSK. Mar.27; 73) £1,350
– – **Anr. Edn.** L., 1825-37. Vol. 1 pt. II-vol. 6 pt. 1, 'encadre' Iss., vol. 1, Ordinary Iss. 13 vols. 4to. Cont. hf. mor., brkn. As a periodical, w.a.f., from collection of Massachusetts Horticultural Society, stps. on plts. (SPB. Oct.1; 148) $2,600
– – **Anr. Edn.** 1825-40. L.P. Vols. 1-8. 4to. Some spotting of prelims. Cont. unif. hf. cf., gt. decor. spines. (TA. May 21; 524) £1,025
– – **Anr. Edn.** L., 1825-49. Vols. 1-12 (of 13) in 10 vols. Slightly soiled in parts. Cont. linen. (HK. Nov.18-21; 640) DM 5,500

MAUND, Benjamin -*contd.*
– – **Anr. Edn.** 1825-[50]. 13 vols. Vols. 6 & 7 dampstained. Hf. cf. gt. (P. Jan.22; 65C) *Litman.* £1,300
– – **Anr. Edn.** 1825-?1851. 12 vols. (vols. I-V & pts. XI-XIII, XV-XVIII). 4to. 202 hand-cold. engraved plts. (? of 205), slight browning, some ll. loose. Orig. bds, rather worn, a few spines crudely reprd. (S. May 5; 95) *Dallai.* £950
– – **Anr. Edn.** L., ca. 1825. Pts. 3 & 5 in 1 vol. No text. Cont. hf. leath., linen pasted on spine. (HK. Nov.18-21; 641) DM 1,550
– – **Anr. Edn.** 1827-28. Vol. II only (of 13). 4to. Cont. hf. cf., gt. spine. W.a.f. (C. Nov.5; 16) *Studio.* £120
– – **Anr. Edn.** 1831-33. Pts. 7-9 only. 4to. Engraved titles & 35 plts. only, some spr. Cont. hf. cf. (SH. Apr.9; 296) *Russell.* £140
– – **Anr. Edn.** 1832. Pt. 8 only. 4to. Orig. bds., 1 bd. detchd., the other loose, lacks spine paper. (LC. Oct.2; 91) £50
– – **Anr. Edn.** L., 1832-36. Cont. hf. leath. (R. Mar.31-Apr.4; 1396) DM 2,400
– – **Anr. Edn.** 1835-36. Vol. VI only (of 13). 4to. Cont. hf. cf., gt. spine. W.a.f. (C. Nov.5; 17) *Studio.* £120
– – **Anr. Edn.** L., [1837-41]. Vols. 7-9. Cont. hf. leath. (R. Mar.31-Apr.4; 1397) DM 2,600
– – **Anr. Edn.** Ca. 1840. Vol. 1 only. Hf. cf. (P. Sep.11; 245) *Welsh.* £120
– – **Anr. Copy.** Vols. 8 & 9. Cont. hf. leath., spine reprd. (R. Oct.14-18; 3025) DM 1,900
– – **Anr. Copy.** Vols. 9 & 10. Cont. hf. leath. (R. Mar.31-Apr.4; 1398) DM 1,800
– – **Anr. Edn.** Ed.:– James C. Niven. 1878. 2nd. Edn. 6 vols. Lacks 2 plts. Orig. cl. gt. (SBA. Oct.21; 158) *J. Cumming.* £360
– – **Anr. Edn.** L., n.d. & 1830. Vols. 1 & 3 only. 188 hand-cold. ills. on 47 sheets. Orig. cl. gt. (P. Jun.11; 302) *Schuster.* £180
– – **Anr. Edn.** N.d. & 1837. Vols. 7 & 8 only, 2 vols. in 1. 4to. Lacks some text ll. Cont. hf. cf. W.a.f. (SBA. Jul.22; 62) *Schuster.* £150
– – **Anr. Edn.** L., n.d. 13 vols. Mor.-bkd. cl. gt. (P. Jun.11; 2) *Bailey.* £1,100
– – **Anr. Copy.** Vols. 10, 11 & 12 only. Occasional spotting. Cont. hf. mor. (CSK. May 15; 32) £380
– **The Botanic Garden.–The Auctarium.–The Fruitist.–The Floral Register.** 1825-[42], 1st. work: 13 vols.; 2nd. work: 2 vols.; 3rd./4th. works: 2 vols., together 18 vols., complete set. 4to. Early cl. (S. Dec.3; 1049) *Traylen.* £1,500
– **The Botanic Garden.–Floral Register, etc.** 1825-[41?]. 1st. work: vols. 1-9 (of 13), 2nd. work: 2 vols. together 11 vols. in 13 (vols. 4 & 5 each in 2 pts.). 4to. Orig. bds., worn. W.a.f. (S. Dec.3; 1051) *Marks.* £1,000
– – **Anr. Copy.** 1st. work: vols. 1-9 (of 13), 2nd. work: 10 vols. Hf. leath. W.a.f. (S. Dec.3; 1052) *Robinson.* £950
– **Fruitist.** L., n.d. 4to. Cont. hf. cf., corners, decor. spine. (HD. Jun.10; 185) Frs. 1,000

MAUND, Benjamin & Henslow, Rev. John Stephen
– **The Botanist.** Ca. 1835-40. Vol. IV only. 4to. Orig. cl., covers detchd. (TA. Jun.18; 162) £95
– – **Anr. Edn.** 1837-42. L.P. Vols. 1-5 (all publd.), in 61 orig. pts. 4to. Lacks pts. 19, 58 & 60, but with supps. for 1837 & 1839-41. Orig. wraps., slightly soiled. As a periodical, w.a.f. (SBA. Oct.21; 143) *Dekker & Nordemann.* £450
– – **Anr. Edn.** [1837-42]. 1st. Edn. 5 vols. 4to. A few spots. Cont. hf. roan, spines gt. & defect., 5 covers detchd., very worn, memorial bkplt. to Thomas Agnew. W.a.f. (S. Dec.3; 1053) *Litman.* £460
– – **Anr. Copy.** Spotted, occasional light offsetting. Orig. cl.-bkd. bds., 3 spines defect., covers detchd. or loose, worn. W.a.f. (S. Dec.3; 1054) *Elliot.* £380
– – **Anr. Edn.** L., ca. 1840. Vol. 2. Cont. hf. leath., slightly soiled, joints reprd. (HK. Nov.18-21; 642) DM 500
– – **Anr. Edn.** n.d. 5 vols. in 3. 4to. 239 (of 244) hand-cold. engraved plts., lacks some ll of text. Hf. mor. W.a.f. (SKC. Feb.26; 1598) £400
– **The Floral Album.** n.d. 4to. 59 (of 60?) hand-cold. engraved plts. Orig. cl. gt., a few ll. loose, spine soiled. W.a.f. (SKC. Feb.26; 1599) £120

MAUNDEVILE, Sir John
See–MANDEVILLE, Sir John

MAUNDRELL, Henry
– **A Journey from Aleppo to Jerusalem, at Easter . . . 1697.** 1810. L.P. Most plts. with some foxing. Russ. gt., by Lewis. The Beckford-Rosebery copy. (S. Jun.29; 250) *Bonham.* £60

MAUPASSANT, Guy de
– **Bel Ami.** 1885. (200) on Hollande. Mor., fillet, wrap., lacks spine, by Farez. (HD. Oct.10; 107) Frs. 4,200
– – **Anr. Edn.** Ill.:– Grau-Sala. 1945. Sewed. On tinted paper, 4 orig. aquas., 2 suites, black & cold. & 4 unedited plts. in double state. (HD. Oct.10; 196) Frs. 3,400
– **Boule de Suif.** Ill.:– A. Romagnol after Francois Thevenot. Paris, 1897. (12) on Japan paper. 4to. Plts. in 3 states, all text engrs. in 2 states, proof of cold. upr. wrap. design & full p. of orig. pencil sketches. Lev., raised bands, wide gt. dentelles., cold. pict. wraps. bnd. in. (SG. Apr.9; 213) $250
– – **Anr. Copy.** Proof of cold. front wrap design, full-page of orig. pencil sketches by Thevenot. (SG. Sep.4; 320) $220
– – **Anr. Copy.** Royal 8vo. Separate printing of text ills., hand-drawn by engraver on Jap., orig. watercolour, prospectus in 4 ll. at end. Red mor. by Mercier, border of 6 gt. fillets on compartments of spine & covers, mor. doubls. with border of mosaic flowers, wrap. preserved, s.-c. (SM. Feb.11; 255) Frs. 16,000
– **Clair de Lune.** 1888. (20) on Hollande numbered. Mor., by Hepe & Farez, fillet wrap. (HD. Oct.10; 109) Frs. 1,900
– **Les Dimanches d'un Bourgeois de Paris.** Ill.:– Geo-Dupuis. Paris, 1901. 1st. Edn., (70) on China paper, numbered. Lge. 8vo. Maroon mor. by Parez, decor. spine, border of 3 fillets on covers, wrap. preserved. (SM. Feb.11; 256) Frs. 5,000
– **Dix Contes du Pays de Caux.** Ill.:– Charles Léandre. Rouen, 1929. (100); on Rives vell., numbered. Lge. 8vo. In sheets, publisher's s.-c. (HD. Dec.5; 149) Frs. 1,000
– **Le Horla.–Sur l'Eau.** 1887; 1888. 1st Edns. 2 works in 2 vols. 12mo. Hf. mor. corners, spines with raised bands, wraps. & spines. 2nd work: autograph dedication from author to Edouard de Goncourt. (HD. Jun.25; 329) Frs. 1,400
– **La Maison Tellier.** 1881. 12mo. Hf.-mor., wrap. N., A.L.s. (HD. Oct.10; 105) Frs. 2,300
– **Oeuvres Complètes Illustrées.** Ill.:– Falké, Dunoyer de Segonzac, Bonfils & others. 1934-38. (10) Priv. Ptd., on vell. d'Arches. 15 vols. Sm. 4to. Three quarter chagrin. (HD. Jun.30; 54) Frs. 5,000
– **Les Soeurs Rondoli.** 1884. (50) on hollande. Jansenist mor., wrap., by Marius Michel. (HD. Oct.10; 106) Frs. 3,500
– **Sur L'Eau.** Paris, [1888]. 1st. Edn. Red mor. gt., unc., slightly worn, orig. pict. wraps. bnd. in. Inscr. (SPB. Nov.25; 210) $250
– – **Anr. Edn.** Ill.: – Paul Baudier. Paris, 1951. (30) on Arches vell., numbered. 4to. Orig. watercolour, sigd. Mor. by Kieffer, design of sm. port in gold on both covers, wrap. preserved, s.-c. (SM. Feb.11; 257) Frs. 5,000
– **Des Vers.–Une Vie.–Bel Ami.** 1880; 1883; 1885. 1st Edns. 3 works in 3 vols. 12mo. 1st. work: orig. drawing by Faure-Dujarric. Hf. mor., corners, spines with raised bands, wraps., bdgs. defect. Autograph dedication from author to Faure-Dujarric, 2 letters, autograph poem (L'Oiseleur). (HD. Jun.25; 326) Frs. 1,300
– **Une Vie.** Ill.:– G. Lemoine after A. Leroux. Paris, 1901. (30) on Jap. 4to. Mor., gt. inner & outer dentelle, orig. wraps. Sigd. aqua by Leroux & compl. series of wdcts. on china bnd. in. (HK. May 12-14; 1980) DM 1,300

MAUPASSANT, Guy de (Contrib.)
See–GIL BLAS: Illustre Hebdomadaire

MAUPERTIUS, Pierre Louis Moreau de
– **La Figure de la Terre Determinée par les Observations.** Paris, 1738. 1st. Edn. 19th. C. hf. roan. From Chetham's Liby., Manchester. (C. Nov.27; 274) *Quaritch.* £150

MAUPOINT
[–] **Bibliothèque des Théâtres.** Paris, 1733. Bkplt. of Reiner Bachofen & note in his hand on flylf., dtd. Vienna, May 1908, with his liby. stp. Cont. red mor. by Etienne Boyet, triple gt. fillet, arms of Prince Eugène of Savoy, gt., on covers & his cipher & arms, gt., repeated in alternate spine compartments, inner gt. dentelles. (SM. Oct.7; 1850) Frs. 3,800

MAUQUEST DE LA MOTTE, Guillaume
See–LA MOTTE, Guillaume Mauquest de

MAURIAC, François
– **Genitrix.** Ill.:– Gernez. Paris, 1926. (25) on imperial Jap. 4to. Mor. by Leroy-Dor, title & name of author in gold on covers, folder & s.-c., wrap. preserved. (SM. Feb.11; 258) Frs. 7,500
– – **Anr. Edn.** Ill.:– Michel Ciry. 1968. (140) on vell. de Rives, nominative. (HD. Oct.10; 197) Frs. 1,100
– **Le Noeud de Vipères.** 1932. (25) on Montval paper. Sewed. (HD. Oct.10; 112) Frs. 1,400

MAURITIUS HIBERNICUS (O'Fihely)
See–DUNS SCOTUS Erigena, Joannes

MAURO, Lucio
– **Le Antichita de la Citta di Roma.** Venice, 1556. 19th. C. cf.-bkd. bds. (S. Mar.17; 272) *A.G. Thomas* £75

MAUROCENO, D. Petro
– **Thesaurus Numismatum . . . & Aere.** Venice, ca. 1683. 4to. Extra-engraved title. Cont. vell., upr. hinge split. (PNY. Oct.1; 404) $180

MAUROCENUS, Paulus
– **De Generatione Aeterna et Temporali Christi.** Padua, 'Bartholomaeus Campanus Ponticuruanus', Apr.28; 1473. Spaces for capital initials, lr. outer margin with wormhole from fo. 10 to end, touching a single letter on 2 pp., some ll. browned. Red. mor. gt., spine gt.-lettered, by Gruel. Bkplt. of Herschel V. Jones, lately in the collection of Eric Sexton. [BMC VII, 905, Goff M380, HC 10924] (CNY. Apr.8; 116) $1,400

MAUROIS, André
– **Climates.** Ill.:– Jean Hugo. Paris, 1929. Ltd. 1st. Edn., (240) numbered on d'Arches. 4to. Orig. wraps., in cl. folding case. Sigd. pres. copy to Mrs. (Gilbert) Chapman. (PNY. Mar.4; 183) $350
– **Les Erophages.** Ill.:– André Masson. Paris, 1960. (145) sigd. by artist, editor & author. Fo. Orig. wraps., folder & box. (SPB. Oct.1; 236) £700
– – **Anr. Copy.** Orig. bdg., box. (DS. May 22; 815) Pts. 75,000
– **Le Peseur d'Ames.** Ill.:– Francis Picabia. Paris, 1931. (8) numbered, on Japan vell., with extra suite of plts. laid in & orig. water-col. for one of them. Lge. 4to. Ptd. wraps., unc., box defect. (SG. Oct.23; 260) $3,100
– – **Anr. Copy.** (24) lettered. Unopened, tissue guard, bd. s.-c. Sigd. pres. copy 'Pour Bobsy . . .' (Goodspeed). (PNY. Mar.4; 184) $220

MAUROLYCO, Francesco
– **Cosmographia . . . in tres dialogos distincta.** Venice, 1543. 1st. Edn. 4to. Title browned, occasional slight foxing, minor tears. Vell., slightly warped. [Sabin 46957] (S. May 6; 218) $500

[MAURY, D.H.]
See–ROBERTS, Capt. Joseph–[MAURY, D.H.]

MAURY, Matthew Fontaine
– **The Physical Geography of the Sea.** N.Y., 1855. 1st. Edn. Very slightly spotted. Orig. cl., (S. Dec.2; 745) *Gurney.* £90
– – **Anr. Copy.** [Sabin 46969] (SH. Jun.18; 15) *Treleaven.* £80
– – **Anr. Copy.** Ian Fleming's copy, in folding s.-c. with his monog. (SG. Sep.18; 247) $250
– – **Anr. Copy.** Upr. blank margin occasionally dampstained. Cl., crudely rebkd. in buckram, ex-liby. (SG. Jan.29; 287) $110

MAVOR, William
– **The English Spelling Book.** Ill.:– Kate Greenaway. L., 1885. 1st. Edn. 12mo. Pict. bds. (SG. Apr.30; 155) $120

MAW & CO.
– **Patterns of Maw & Co's encaustic Tile, Geometric, Mosaic & Plain Tile paves, & Majolica & Enamelled Wall Tiles, . . .** Broseley, ca. early 20th. C. Fo. Orig. bds., lacks spine, bds. loose. (CB. May 27; 150) Can. $220
– – **Anr. Edn.** Ill.:– after Digby Wyatt & others. N.d. Fo. Orig. cl., lge. paper onlay on upr. cover, chromolitho. from a design by Owen Jones. W.a.f. (CSK. Jul.10; 71) £290

MAWE, John
– **Travels in the Interior of Brasil, Particularly in the Gold & Diamond Districts.** L., 1812. [1st. Edn.?]. Cont. hf. cf., worn, loose. (SH. Jul.16; 5) *Tzakas.* £85
– – **Anr. Copy.** 4to. 1 plt. slightly affected by adhesion, offsetting, from frontis. onto title. Cont.

russ., rebkd., with ticket of George Mullen, Dublin. (SPB. May 5; 349) £450
- **A Treatise on Diamonds & Precious Stones . . .** L., 1813. Hf. mor., marb. bds., raised spine. (SSA. Jan.22; 89) R. 100
- **- Anr. Edn.** L., 1815. 2nd. Edn. Hf. mor., unc. (SSA. Nov.5; 373) R. 140

MAWSON, Sir Douglas
- **Home of the Blizzard.** 1915. 2 vols. Orig. bdg. (TRL. Dec.10; 108) £120

MAWSON, Thomas Hayton
- **The Art & Craft of Garden Making.** L., [1912]. 4th. Edn. Fo. Orig. cl. (CB. May 27; 151) Can. $180

MAWSON, Thomas H. & Sons
- **Calgary, a preliminary scheme for controlling the economic Growth of the City.** L., 1914. Sm. fo. Orig. gt.-stpd. cl., slightly soiled & spotted. (CB. May 27; 303) Can. $500

MAXIMILIAN, I. Kaiser
- **Das Jagdbuch.** Ed.:- M. Mayr. Innsbruck, 1901. Fo. Orig. vell. (R. Oct.14-18; 2796) DM 650

MAXIMILIAN ZU WIED-NEUWIED, Prince
- **Abbildungen zur Naturgeschichte Brasiliens.** Weimar, 1822-31. Fo. Engl. & Fr. text, some plts. & text ll. lightly browned or soiled, owners note on prelim. lf. Hf. leath., very worn, spine loose, 2 orig. part wraps. bnd. in. [Sabin 47011] (H. Dec.9/10; 527) DM 10,000
- **- Anr. Edn.** Weimar, 1822-32. 12 (of 15) Pts. Fo. 72 plts., 71 hand-cold., announcement for subscriptions & advts. inserted. Orig. wraps., unc., pt. 12 cover badly eroded. (SG. May 14; 142) $1,400
- **Reise Nach Brasilien.** Frankfurt, 1820-21. 3 vols. including Atlas vol. 4to. & fo. 39 engd. plts., 3 hand-cold., 3 maps, atlas lacks 2 plts. Orig. bds., stitching partly brkn. (C. Jul.15; 118) Burgess. £400
- **Travels in the Interior of North America.** Trans.:- H. Evans Lloyd. L., 1843. 2 vols. Lge. 4to. & atlas fo. 81 hand-cold. plts., foldg. map creased. Three-qtr. mor. by Sangorski & Sutcliffe, hf. mor. foldg. cases. (SG. Oct.9; 162) $34,000

MAXIMILIEN
- **Souvenirs de ma Vie.** Trans.:- Jules Gaillard. Paris, 1868. 1st. Edn. in Fr. 2 vols. Mor. by Petit, triple gt. fillet around covers, spines decor. with raised bands, inside dentelle. (HD. Jun.25; 335) Frs. 1,100

MAXIMUS, Pacificus
- **De Componedo Hexametro et Pentametro.** Flor., [Antonio di Bartolommeo Miscomini], Jul.14, 1485. 1st. Edn. 4to. Spaces for initial capitals, with guides, rubricated in yellow. Mor., covers with gt. arms of Victor Massena, Prince d'Essling, spine gt. with monogs., by Lortic. From the collection of Eric Sexton. [BMC VI, 638, Goff M398, HC10935*] (CNY. Apr.8; 59) $7,500

MAXWELL, Sir Herbert
- **Fishing at Home & Abroad.** L., 1913. 1st. Edn., (750) numbered. Fo. Mor., unc. (SG. Oct.16; 206) $160
- **Memories of the Months.** 1907-22. 7 vols. Hf. mor. gt. (CE. Nov.20; 114) £72
- **Sixty Years a Queen.** L., [1897]. Fo. Three-qtr. lev., spine gt. (SG. Mar.19; 311) £120

MAXWELL, Sir Herbert (Ed.)
See-CHRONICLES of the Houghton Fishing Club

MAXWELL, James Clerk
- **A Treatise of Electricity & Magnetism.** L., 1873. 1st. Edn. 2 vols. Ex-liby copy from Amer. Telephone Historical Liby. Orig. cl. (PNY. Dec.3; 234) $275

MAXWELL, William Hamilton
- **History of the Irish Rebellion in 1798 with Memoirs of the Union & Emmett's Insurrection in 1803.** Ill.:- George Cruikshank. 1845. 1st. Edn. Red mor. gt. (SKC. Feb.26; 1258) £85
- **Wanderings in the Highlands & Islands.** 1852. 2 vols. in l. Mor. gt., soiled. (CE. Nov.20; 179) £50

MAYAKOVSKY, Vladimir
- **Dlya Golosa [For the Voice].** Ill.:- El Lissitsky. Berlin, 1923. Orig. wraps. (SH. Feb.6; 487) Bjorck. £820
- **Grozmy Smekh [Raucous Laughter].** Ill.:- V. Stepanova. Moscow & Leningrad, 1932. (3,000). 4to. Orig. bds., slightly torn & soiled. (SH. Feb.6; 488) Bjorck. £320

- **Kak delat' stikhi [How to write Poetry].** Moscow, 1931. (5,000). Orig. wraps., lacks spine. (SH. Feb.6; 489) Bjorck. £110
- **Mayakovskaya Gallereya [Mayakovsky's Gallery].** Moscow, 1923. Mod. wraps. with orig. upr. cover pasted down. (SH. Feb.6; 490) Kazinikas. £90
- **Mayakovsky izdevaetsya [Mayakovsky mocks. First Book of Satire].** Moscow, 1922. Title torn & reprd. Orig. wraps., torn. (SH. Feb.6; 491) Kazinikas. £130
- **Ni Znakhar', ni Bog, ni angely Boga -Kres'yanstvu ne Podmoga [Not Sorcerer, nor God, no Angels of God-no 'Help to the Peasantry].** Moscow, 1923. Wraps. by author, upr. wrap. torn & reprd. in facs. (SH. Feb.6; 492) Kazinikas. £150
- **Pesni Rabochim [Songs to the Workers].** Moscow, 1925. (3,000). Orig. wraps. by the author?. (SH. Feb.6; 493) Bjorck. £220
- **SSSR na stroike [U.S.S.R. in Construction, no. 7 devoted to V.V. Mayakovsky].** Moscow, 1940. 1 Fo. Some ll. slightly soiled or torn. Orig. wraps., torn. (SH. Feb.6; 337) Bjorck. £150
See-ASEEV, Nikolai
See-BLOK, Alexander & others
See-KHLEBNIKOV, V. & others

MAYAKOVSKY, Vladimir & others
- **Rasskaz pro to, kak uznal Fadei zakon, zashchish-chayushcht rabochikh lyudei [Tale of how Fadei learnt of the Law protecting Working People].** Moscow, 1924. Orig. wraps by Mayakovsky. (SH. Feb.6; 497) Nijhoff. £320

MAYER, Alfred M.
- **Sport with Gun & Rod in American Woods & Waters.** Edinb., 1884. 2 vols. Orig. mor.-bkd. bds. (CSK. Jun.26; 75) £50

MAYER, August L.
- **Dominico Theotocopuli, El Greco.** Muenchen, 1926. Fo. Buckram. (SG. Dec.4; 133) $150
- **Velazquez. A Catalogue Raisonné of the Pictures & Drawings.** 1936. 4to. Orig. cl. (SH. Oct.9; 86) Scandecor. £150
- **- Anr. Copy.** (S. Jul.27; 179) Nakajima. £120

MAYER, Brantz
- **Mexico; Aztec, Spanish & Republican.** Hartford, 1851-52. 2 vols. in 1. Ex liby. New buckram. (SG. Jun.11; 218) $110

MAYER, Karl
- **Wiener-Porzellan Sammlung.** Vienna, 1928. 4to. Sale Catalogue of Nov. 1928. Orig. bds. (C. Feb.4; 261) Reichest. £100
See-AINSLIE, Sir Robert & Mayer, Luigi

MAYES, C.
- **Victoria Contractors' & Builders Price-Book.** Melbourne, 1859. 1st. Edn. Orig. cl., slightly soiled & worn. (KH. Nov.18; 414) Aus. $190

MAYEUX
- **Les Bédouins, ou Arabes du Désert.** Ill.:- Massard. Paris, 1816. 3 vols. 16mo. Cont. marb. roan, decor. spines. (HD. Apr.9; 521) Frs. 1,100

MAYHEU, P.
- **Verschiedene Reitkünste, nach den Wahren Originalen dargestellt.** Agram, 1795. 4to. 1st. plt. stpd., title soiled. No. bdg. (R. Oct.14-18; 2795) DM 1,400

MAYHEW, Henry
- **London Labour & the London Poor.** 1861-62. 4 vols. Tall 8vo. Orig. blind-stpd. cl. gt., worn. (TA. Apr.16; 229) £80
- **- Anr. Copy.** Orig. cl. gt. (TA. Dec.18; 286) £65
- **- Anr. Edn.** N.d. 4 vols. Mod. cf.-bkd. bds. (SH. Apr.9; 298) Drury Hill. £120
- **The Rhine.** Ill.:- Birkett Foster. 1856. Orig. cl. gt. (P. Jul.30; 114) Schuster. £120

MAYHEW, Horace
- **1851: or the Adventures of Mr. & Mrs. Sandboys . . .** Ill.:- George Cruikshank. L., [1851]. Orig. 8 Pts. Pict. wraps., unc., hf. mor. s.-c. W.G. Woodin copy. (SG. May 14; 143) $350
- **The Tooth-ache.** Ill.:- George Cruikshank. [1845]. 12mo. Engraved bds., rebkd., worn & torn. (CE. Jun.4; 181) £50

MAYHEW, John
See-INCE, William & Mayhew, John

MAYNE, Jaspar
- [-] **The Amorous Warre.** 1648. 1st. Edn. 4to. Margin of title strengthened slightly affecting text.

Mod. mor. Bridgewater Liby. dupl. stp. on title verso. [Wing M1463] (C. Nov.19; 116) Brett-Smith. £150
- [-] **- Anr. Copy** Red mor. by Rivière. (SH. Jun.18; 73) Maggs. £90

MAYO, Herbert
- **Anatomical & Physiological Commentaries.** 1822. No. 1, Aug. 1822. Orig. ptd. wraps., rebkd., unc. From Sir Thomas Phillipps' collection. (S. Jun.16; 562) Norman. £220
- **A Series of Engravings Intended to Illustrate the Structure of the Brain & Spinal Cord in Man.** Ill.:- David Lucas after J. Lonsdale (port.). 1827. Fo. Some foxing & offset on title-p. Hf. cf. (S. Jun.16; 563) Norman. £130

MAYO, J.H.
- **Medals & Decorations of the British Army & Navy.** 1897. 2 vols. Orig. cl., soiled. (SH. Jun.4; 36) Maggs. £80

MAYOW, John
- **Tractatus Quinque Medico-Physici quorum primus agit de Sal-nitro et spiritu nitro-aero, secundus de Respiratione, tertius de Respiratione Foetus in Utero et Ovo, quartus de Motu Musculari, ultimus de Rachitide.** Ill.:- [Faithorne] (port.). Oxford, 1674. 1st. Edn. Short tear in Cl & sm. rust-hole in M4. New mor. [Wing M1537] (S. Jun.16; 564) Palinvrus. £65
- **- Anr. Copy.** Lightly browned & soiled. Hf. leath., spine & corners renewed. (HK. Nov.18-21; 647) DM 2,800

MAYUYAMA, J.
- **Japanese Art in the West.** Tokyo, 1976. 2 vols. 4to. Orig. cl., s.-c. (S. Sep.30; 420) £65

MAYUYAMA & Co. Ltd.
- **Mayuyama, Seventy Years.** Tokyo, 1976. 2 vols. 4to. Orig. cl. (CNY. Sep.30; 421) £150

MAZO, Bondi di
- **La Spada Maestra . . .** Venice, 1696. 1st. Edn. Ob. 4to. Folios X1 & 2 with text on overslips, some ll. slightly brown or dampstained, some wormholes, 1 slightly affecting engrs. Old wraps. (S. Jul.27; 270) Pilo. £320

MAZZE, Clemens
- **Vita di San Zenobio.** Flor., [Bartholommeo di Libri], Dec.8, 1487. 1st. Edn. 4to. Spaces for capital initials with guide letters, some ll. severely stained, mostly marginal, 11 pp. of notes in 17th. C. Italian hand (& sigd.) bnd. in at end. Early 19th. C. str.-grd. mor. gt., rebkd. preserving orig. backstrip. Bkplts. of Sir M. Masterman Sykes & Sir John H. Thorold, Syston Park, later the copy of F.K.G. Maitland, recently in the collection of Eric Sexton. [BMC VI, 648, Goff M417, HC(Add) R10981] (CNY. Apr.8; 60) $1,500

MEAD, Richard
- **Mechanical Account of Poisons in Several Essays.** L., 1702. 1st. Edn. Folding plt. worn, slight worming not touching the text, 3 ll. slightly soiled. Cont. panel. cf. (SPB. Nov.25; 103) $175
- **The Medical Works.** Ill.:- R. Houston after A. Ramsay (port.). 1762. 4to. Cont. cf. (S. Jun.16; 566) Silver. £90
- **- Anr. Edn.** Edinb., 1763. 3 vols. Inscr. 'E.S. Sitwell' on title-pp. Cont. cf., rebkd. (S. Jun.16; 567) Phelps. £50
- **A Treatise Concerning the Influance of the Sun & Moon upon Human Bodies & the Diseases Thereby Produced.** Trans.:- Thomas Stack. 1748. 1st. Edn. in Engl. Cont. cf. (S. Dec.2; 554) Maggs. £55

MEADON, Joseph
- **Graphic Arts & Crafts Year Book.** v.d. Tog. 3 vols. 4to. Orig. leath. & hf-leath., 1 bdg. brkn. (SG. Oct.2; 145) $100

MEARES, John
- **Collection de Cartes Géographiques, Vues . . . Relatifs aux Voyages.** Paris, 1795. Atlas vol. only. 4to. Cont. tree cf. gt., rebkd. preserving old spine. (S. Jul.27; 54) Remington. £100
- **- Anr. Edn.** Paris, ca. 1795. 4to. Some marginal browning. Cont. hf. roan. (HD. Jun.10; 66a) Frs. 1,900

MECANICIEN Moderne (Le)
Paris, n.d. 2 vols. in 4. Publisher's cl., decor. tools. (HD. Jun.10; 188) Frs. 45,000

MECHAIN, P.F.A.
See-CASSINI, J.D., Mechain, P.F.A. & Le Gendre, A.M.

MECHELEN
- **Prael-Treyn verrykt door Ry-benden, Prael-Wagens, Zinne-Beelden en andere Oppronkingen toogeschikt an het duyzend-jaerig Jubile van den Heyl. Rumoldus ... Apostel ende Patroon.** Mechelen, [1773]. 4to. 14 folding plts. all heightened with col. & gold. Mod. marb. cf., 5 decor. spine raised bands, triple border, gt. fillet, inner dentelle. (LM. Nov.8; 113) *B.Frs.* 12,000

MEDAILLES sur les Principaux Evénements du Règne de Louis le Grand, avec des Explications Historiques
Paris, 1702. Fo. Cont. red mor., Louis XIV arms, decor. spine fleur de lis & crowned cypher. (HD. Jun.10; 67) *Frs.* 7,000

MEDECINE PITTORESQUE [LA], Musée medico-chirurgical, ... principalement envisagés sous le Point de Vue pratique
Paris, 1834-37. Pt. I-IV in 2 vols. 4to. A few plt. headlines cropped, some ll. spotted. Mod. bds., unc. (S. Feb.23; 80) *Korn.* £80

MEDIAVILLA, Ricardus de, i.e. Richard Middleton
- **In Quartum Sententiaru (cum Expositiona Longe Utilissima).** Lyon, Oct., 1527. 4to. Tear & natural flaws in 2 ll. affecting side-notes, some ll. marginally wormed affecting some letters, some ll. stained from margins, occasional browning & soiling. Cont. limp vell. bds., spine defect., 1 hinge brkn. (S. Feb.10; 218) *Panadero.* £50

MEDICAE ARTIS PRINCIPLES POST HIPPOCRATEM & GALENUM
Geneva, 1567. 1st. Edn. 5 pts. in 2 vols. Fo. Some ll. stained or foxed, general title & divisional title to pt. 3 with marginal tears & old inscrs., 5A2 slightly wormed. Cont. cf., worn, rebkd. From liby. of Dr. E. Ashworth Underwood. (S. Feb.23; 253) *Gurney.* £110

MEDICI, Lorenzo de'
- **Poesie Volgari.** Venice, 1554. 19th. C. russ. gt. Firmin Didot booklabel. (C. Jul.16; 222) *Quaritch.* £440
- - **Anr. Copy.** Sig. 0 consists of only 4 ll. (105-108), numbers 109-112 not used. 18th. C. red mor., crowned & gartered arms gt.-stpd. on cover. B.M. dupl., sold in 1787. Earl of Cromer's bkplt. (SG. Oct.9; 13) $850
- - **Anr. Copy.** Sig. 0 lacks last 4 ll. as usual, text supplied in 18th. C. MS. on 3 ll. tipped in at end, bkplt. of Newton Hall, Camb. 18th. C. red mor., triple gt. fillet, spine gt. in compartments, inner gt. dentelles, 2 corners slightly worn. (SM. Oct.7; 1823) *Frs.* 5,000

MEDICI Antiqui Omnes qui Latinis Literis Diversorum Morborum Genera et Premedia persecuti sunt
Ed.:- Celso Grassi. Trans.:- Guinio Paolo Grassi. Venice, 1547. Fo. 2-star ll. after f.8, I4-5 & R1 & 6 discold. Cont. cf., arms (probably those of Odi or Oddi of Padua) in a central gt. ornament, gt. ornamental corners, rebkd. (S. Jun.16; 571) *Norman.* £300

MEDINA, Jose Toribio
- **Coleccion de Documentos Ineditos para la Historia de Chile, desde el Viaje de Magallanes hasta la Batalla de Maipo, 1518-1818.** Santiago de Chile, 1888-1902. 30 vols. 4to. Mod. buckram, liby. bkplt. (SG. Mar.5; 124) $750

MEDITATIONES De Vita Jesu Christi
[Cologne], ca. 1498. Without wdct. on title-p. 19th. C. str.-grd. mor. gt. John B. Inglis copy, with his engrs. on endpapers, rubricated. [Hain 10991] (SG. Oct.9; 133) $550

MEDWIN, Thomas
- **The Angler in Wales.** L., 1834. 1st. Edn. 2 vols. Cont. cf., spines gt. (SG. Oct.16; 210) $100

MEE, Arthur
- **The King's England.** 1937-59. Var. Edns. 41 vols. Orig. cl., some with d.w.'s. (SBA. Jul.22; 206) *Aspin.* £75

MEE, Margaret
- **Flowers of the Brazilian Forest.** 1968. (500) sigd. Fo. Qtr.-mor. gt., rubbed. (P. Sep.11; 200) *Ashwell.* £100

MEEHAN, Thomas
- **The Native Flowers & Ferns of the United States.** Boston, [1878-80]. 4 vols. Gt.-decor. cl. (SG. Sep.18; 253) $175

- **Wayside Flowers.** Ill.:- L. Prang & Co. Phila., 1881. 4to. Gt.-pict. cl., ex-liby. (SG. Jan.29; 290) $100

MEERBURGH, Nic.
- **Afbeeldingen van Zeldzaame Gewassen.** Leiden, 1775. 1st. Edn. Fo. 19th. C. hf. cf. (VG. Oct.13; 105) *Fls.* 3,200

MEERSCH, Mayence van der
- **La Maison dans la Dune.** Ill.:- H. Casseniers. Paris, 1937. (130) on Van Gelder Holland. Mor. by Jean, mosaic upr. cover, wrap. preserved, s.-c. (SM. Feb.11; 293) *Frs.* 4,200

MEERZA, H.R.H. Najaf Koolee
- **Journal of a Residence in England & of a Journey from & to Syria.** [1839]. 2 vols. Cl. gt. (P. Oct.23; 237) *Wood.* £50

MEFFRETH
- (Sermones de Temporae et de Sanctis) ... Estivales Sermonum. [Nuremb.], [Anton Koberger], [14 Feb. 1487]. Pt. II only [of 3]. Fo. 202 ll. (of 488 for the whole work), rubricated initials supplied in red, 2 ll. torn affecting text, old marginalia, slightly dampstained in places, some wormholes, slightly affecting some letters. Cont. blind-stpd. pig. over wooden bds., wormed, spine slightly worn, lacks clasps. [BMC II 431; HC 11004*; Goff M443] (S. Apr.7; 290) *Symonds.* £140

MEFISTOFEL'
Ed.:- [N.A. Sokolov]. Moscow, 1906-07. Nos. 1-3 & 5 only (of 8). Fo. Slightly soiled. Unbnd. (SH. Feb.5; 88) *Landry.* £170

MEGERLE, Johann Ulrick
See-SANTA CLARA, Abraham a

MEGGENDORFER, Lothar
- **Drehbilder ABC. Ein lehrreiches Bilderbuch. Zweite auflage.** Stuttgart, ca. 1900-05. 4to. Some foxing. Cl.-bkd. cold. pict. bds., worn, head of spine neatly replaced with cl. (PNY. Mar.26; 205) $300
- **Travels of Little Lord Thumb & his Man Damian: A Movable Toybook.** L., ca. 1885. Ob. sm. fo. Apparently lacks title-p. Orig. cold. pict. bds., cl. back (badly shaken). (PNY. Mar.26; 206) $180

MEGILLAH Esther
Nyitra, [1834]. Vig. ills. hand-cold., 1st. section bkd., with reprd. tears, on turned wood handle. (CNY. Oct.9; 24) $4,200

MEGISER, Heronymus-CRUSII, Martini
- **Septentrio Novantiquus, oder die newe Nort-Welt. Aethiopicae Helidori Historiae Epitome.** Ill.:- maps by Christopher Bogel (1st. work). Leipzig; Frankfurt, 1613; 1684. 2 works in 1 vol. 12mo. 1st. work title cont. rebkd.; 2nd. work, early ex-liby stp. on title-p. Cont. vell., cont. MS. ink titles on spine. [Sabin 47383] [1st. work] (PWP. Apr.9; 237) *Can.* $3,200

MEGNIN, P.
- **Notre Ami le Chat.** Ill.:- Grandville, F. Delacroix & others. Paris, 1899. Publisher's decor. bds. (HD. Apr.24; 155) *Frs.* 2,000

MEHLIS, C.
- **Bilder aus den Landschaften des Mittelrheins.** Leipzig, 1881. Hf. leath. (R. Oct.14-18; 2426) *DM* 600

MEHTA, Nanalal Chamanlal
- **Studies in Indian Painting ...** Bombay, 1926. 1st. Edn. Tall 4to. Cl. (SG. Mar.12; 250) $110

MEIER-GRAEFE, J. (Ed.)
See-GANYMED, Jahrbuch f.d. Kunst

MEIGS
See-MELLOR, Meigs & Howe

MEIKLE, James
- **Famous Clyde Yachts.** Ill.:- after Henry Shields. 1888. Fo. Cl. gt., worn. (CE. Oct.24; 153) £170
- - **Anr. Copy.** Lge. fo. 2 text ll. slightly torn. Orig. linen gt., spine slightly defect. (R. Mar.31-Apr.4; 1792) *DM* 2,500

MEIKLEJOHN, J.M.D.
- **The Golden Primer.** Ill.:- Walter Crane. [1910]. 2 pts. in 1 vol. Orig. pict. cl. (SH. Mar.19; 77) *Fletcher.* £50

MEILLEUR LIVRE [Le] ou Les Meilleures Etrennes que l'on puisse donner ou recevoir
Paris, 1775. Sm. 18mo. Cont. Kid, gt. decor.

covers, lge. red gt. mor., motif, gt., silver & copper motifs, centre painted medallion. (HD. Apr.10; 158) *Frs.* 3,500

MEINERTZHAGEN, Col. Richard
- **Birds of Arabia.** Edinb. & L., 1954. 1st. Edn. 4to. Orig. buckram, d.-w. (S. Jun.1; 163) *Hill.* £360
- - **Anr. Copy.** (SBA. May 27; 188) *Blackburn.* £140
- **Kenya Diary 1902-1906.** L., 1957. Cl. (SSA. Jun.18; 205) R. 100
See-GROSSMAN, Mary Louise & Hamlet, John
-MEINERTZHAGEN, R.

MEINERTZHAGEN, Richard (Ed.)
See-NICOLL, Michael John

MEINHOLD, William
- **Sidonia the Sorceress.** Trans.:- Francesca Speranza, Lady Wilde. Kelms. Pr. 1893. (300). 4to. Orig. limp vell., silk ties, unc. (C. Feb.4; 190) *Maggs.* £200

MEIR HA'LEVI STALEVITCH of Stobnitz & Apta
- **OrLa'shamaim.** [Lvov], [1850?]. 1st. Edn. 4to. Slight worming, without loss of text. Hf. cl. (S. Nov.18; 285) *Low.* £55

MEISS, M. & Kirsch, E.W.
- **The Visconti Hours.** Ed.:- Duca Uberto Visconti di Modrone [Pref]. Arcadia Pr. 1973. (55) sigd. by di Modrone. 4to. Orig. vell., gt. inner dentelles. (CSK. Sep.5; 41) £50

MEISSNER, Daniel
- **Thesaurus Philo-politicus.** Frankfurt, 1623-24. 1st. Edn. Vol. I, pts. 1-4 in 1 vol. Ob. 8vo. Some soiling or browning, lacks 1 engraved title & 6 copperplts. Cont. vell., monog. & date 1628, hinges brkn. (R. Oct.14-18; 1471) *DM* 46,000

MEISSNER PORZELLAN 1710-1810. Ausst. im Bayer. Nationalmuseum.
Ed.:- R. Rückert. Munich, 1966. 4to. Orig. wraps. (HK. Nov.18-21; 3414) *DM* 900

MEISTERWERKE DER HOLZSCHNEIDE-KUNST au dem Gebiete der Architektur, Skulptur und Malerei
Leipzig, 1882-85. Vols. IV & VII only. Fo. Orig. gt. decor. cl., some wear to spines. (TA. Oct.16; 108) £65

MELA, Pomponius
- **[Cosmographia sive de Situ Orbis].** Venice, 1482. 1st. Edn., with world map, wide margin. 4to. 18th. C. Engl. red mor., gold tooled borders, gt. spine & inner dentelles, mor. s.-c., sigd. by Riviére, From Earl of Pembroke liby. with his MS. notes to binder & sig., T.W. Streeter & Harrison D. Horblitt ex-lib. [Hain 11019; BMC V286; Goff 452] (D. Dec.11-13; 36) *DM* 13,500
- - **Anr. Copy.** [Venice], [Christophorus de Pensis], [after 1493?]. 4to. Cont. marginal notes. Later vell. bds. Liby. stp. of Richard Heber.]HC 11013*; BMC V p. 476; Goff M 453] (C. Apr.1; 60) *Johns.* £340
- [-] **Anr. Edn.** Paris, 1530. 2 pts. in 1 vol. Fo. Title stained at fore-edge margin & lr. margin. Late 19th. C. hf. mor. [Sabin 63957] (PNY. May 21; 267) $180
- **[De Situ Orbis Libri Tres].** Ed.:- Franc, Asulanus. [Venice], 1518. 17th. C. red mor., 4 raised bands, gt. spine, sm. decor. stps., corner fleurons, gold-stpd., centre-piece, inr. & outer gt. dentelle, marb. end-papers. (D. Dec.11-13; 37) *DM* 1,100
- **De Situ Orbis Libri III et C. Iulii Solini, Polyhistor.** Basle, Apr. 1576. 2 pts. in 1 vol. 31 woodcut maps only, lacks 3 from book 2. Later vell., slightly soiled. W.a.f. (CSK. Jun.5; 25) £220
- - **Anr. Edn.** Basel, 1595. 18th. C. hf. vell. (R. Oct.14-18; 1546) *DM* 1,500
- **[De Situ Orbis, & works by other authors].** Ed.:- F. Asulanus. Venice, 1518. Wormhole in inner margins almost thro.-out, a few marginal stains. Mod. vell. (S. Jun.23; 224) *Marlborough Rare Books.* £60

MELANCHTHON, Philip
- **Ain Schrifft wider die Artickel der Baurschaft.** [Augsburg], 1525. 4to. Mod. hf. vell. (R. Oct.14-18; 116) *DM* 3,000
- **Corpus Doctrinae Christianae.** Frankfurt, 1561. Fo. Cont. pig., defect., lacks clasps, some worming at margin. (D. Dec.11-13; 2607) *DM* 420

- **Loci Theologici Recens Recogniti.** Wittenberg, 1543, [1544 at end], Later Edn. Some old MS. marginalia, wormed & old staining at end. Cont. blind-tooled pig-bkd. wood bds., 1 (of 2) clasps. (R. Mar.31-Apr.4; 75)   DM 650

MELANCHTHON, Philip–NIGRUS, A.–CAMERARIUS, Jochim–CONFESSIO Doctrinae Saxonicarum Ecclesiarum, scripta A.D. 1551. ut Synod exhiberetur
- **Quaestiones aliquot Ethicae, de iuramentis, excommunicatione & aliis casibus obscuribus explicatae.–Psalmi aliquot Davidis Graecis versibus compositi.–Arithmologia ethike [in Greek]. Cum conversione Latina.** Cont. numeris comprehensae Indicationes variae, de quibus Animus instrui poterit Multiplici Cognitione, in primis Prudentiae & Honestatis Praeceptis. Wittenberg; Leipzig; Leipzig; Leipzig, 1552; 1552; 1552; 1553. 1st. Edn. of the so-called 'Repetitio August. Confessionis'. 4 works in 1 vol. Sm. 8vo. The Confessio bnd. before the 3 other works, with the title loose. Cont. blind-stpd. & panel. cf, central panel with ornaments, initials HVL & date 1553 on upr. cover, top of spine slightly defect., upr. jnt. brkn., lacks clasps. (VG. Dec.17; 1257)   Fls. 450

MELDOLA, Raphael
- **Shever Be'mitzraim.** Livorno, 1742. 12mo. In Hebrew. Bds. (S. Nov.18; 622)   *Yarden.* £75

MELIK-SHAHNAZARIANTS, Tauit Dzadourian & Langlès, M.M.
- **L'Etat actuel de la Perse, par Myr-Davoud-Zadour de Melik Schahnazar, envoyé de Perse en France.** Paris, 1817-18. L.P. on vell. 16mo. Plts. in 2 states (black & white & colour). Cont. str.-grd. mor., decor. spine & roulette covers, inner dentelle. (HD. Apr.9; 505)   Frs. 1,400

MELINE, James F.
- **Two Thousand Miles on Horseback. Sante Fe & Back.** N.Y., 1867. 1st. Edn. 12mo. Folding map torn. Orig. blind-stpd. cl., gt. spine. From liby. of William E. Wilson. (SPB. Apr.29; 196) $100

MELISH, John
- **A Geographical Description of the United States.** Phila., 1816. 2nd. Edn. Sig. on shortened title, foxing & offsetting. Orig. cf.-bkd. bds., gt. spine, worn. From liby. of William E. Wilson. (SPB. Apr.29; 197) $150
- – **Anr. Edn.** Phila., 1822. 4th. & New Edn. 12 maps (of 14 listed), advts., portions of text & 3 maps browned. Orig. cf.-bkd. bds., covers loose. From liby. of William E. Wilson. (SPB. Apr.29; 198) $200

MELLERIO, Andre
- **Odilon Redon.** Paris, 1913. (475) on velin d'arches. 4to. Liby. buckram. (SG. Oct.23; 299) $400
- – **Anr. Edn.** Paris, 1913. (75) privilege Edn. on Japan. 4to. Orig. wraps. (H. Dec.9/10; 2311)   DM 620

MELLI, Sebastiano
- **La Comare Levatrice Istruita nel suo Uffizio.** Venice, 1766. 4to. Scattered light spotting. Cont. vell. bds., minor wear. From the collection of John A. Saks. (C. Jun.10; 160)   *Goldschmidt.* £85

MELLIN, August Wilhelm von
- **Unterricht Eingefriedigte Wildbahnen oder Grosse Thiergärten ansulegen.** Berlin, 1800. 1st. Edn. 4to. Title stpd.-twice, slightly soiled & stained in places, lacks upr. end-paper. Mid. 19th. C. hf. linen. (HK. May 12-14; 1107)   DM 800

MELLOR, Meigs & Howe
- **An American Country House, the Property of Arthur E. Newbold, Jr. Esq., Laverock, Pa.** N.Y., 1925. Fo. Orig. qtr. cl. (CB. May 27; 152)   Can. $120
- **A Monograph of the work of Mellor, Meigs & Howe.** N.Y., 1923. Fo. Orig. cl. (CB. May 27; 153)   Can. $160

MELNICK
- **Kurtze doch Grundliche Vorstellung und Recommendation des Rothen Bohmischen Melnicker-weins. Als ein Bewehrtes Mittel wider das Podagra und den Stein-Schmertzen.** Nuremb. & Prague, 1736. 1st. Edn. Slight browning, tear at 1 fold in plt., neatly reprd. Mod. bds. From liby. of André L. Simon. (S. May 18; 138)   *Offenbacher.* £110

MELVILLE, A.G.
See–**STRICKLAND, Hugh Edwin & Melville, A.G.**

MELVILLE, Herman
- **Battle-Pieces & Aspects of War.** N.Y., 1866. 1st. Edn. Orig. cl., spine faded. From the Prescott Collection. (CNY. Feb.6; 252) $220
- **Clarel.** N.Y., 1876. 1st. Edn. 2 vols. 12mo. Orig. cl., ends of spines worn. From the Prescott Collection. (CNY. Feb.6; 253) $600
- **The Confidence-Man.** L., 1857. 1st. [Engl.] Edn. 12mo. With 24 p. publisher's catalogue (dtd. Sep., 1855) inserted at end. Orig. cl., advts. on endpaper (bnd. inverted). From the Prescott Collection. (CNY. Feb.6; 251) $800
- **Israel Potter.** N.Y., 1855. 1st. Edn., 1st. Iss. 12mo. Chapter XIV misnumbered XVI. Orig. cl. (SG. Dec.18; 296) $170
- **Mardi: & a Voyage Thither.–The Piazza Tales.** N.Y., 1849; 1856. 1st. Amer. Edn.; 1st. Edn. Together 3 vols. (2 & 1). 12mo. 1st. work foxed. Orig. blind-stpd. cl., gt.-stpd. spines, endpapers & last lf. of advts. in 2nd. work removed. (CNY. May 22; 179) $170
- **Mardi.–White Jacket.–The Refugee.** N.Y.; N.Y.; Phila., 1849; 1850; [1865]. 1st. Amer. Edn.; 1st. Amer. Edn., 1st. Printing. 2 vols.; 1 vol.; 1 vol. 12mo. All orig. cl., front fly.-lf. loose in 3rd. work. From the Prescott Collection. (CNY. Feb.6; 254) $280
- **Moby Dick.** N.Y., 1851. 1st. Amer. Edn. 12mo. 6 pp. advts. at end. Orig. cl., slightly worn, orange end-papers. (SBA. Jul.14; 175)   *Fletcher.* £380
- – **Anr. Copy.** Text foxed. Corners worn, 1st. bdg., with dark orange endpapers, qtr. mor. gt. s.-c. From the Prescott Collection. (CNY. Feb.6; 247) $2,200
- – **Anr. Edn.** Ill.:– Rockwell Kent. Chic., Lakeside Pr., 1930. (1,000). 3 vols. 4to. Cl., orig. aluminium s.-c. (SG. May 14; 144) $800
- – **Anr. Edn.** Ed.:– Clifton Fadiman. Ill:– Boardman Robinson. Ltd. Edns. Cl. 1943. (1500) numbered, & sigd. by artist. 2 vols. 4to. Cf., spines worn, orig. box (defect.). (SG. Jan.15; 229) $100
- – **Anr. Copy.** Orig. silver decor. cl., aluminium s.-c. (CNY. May 22; 332) $700
- – **Anr. Edn.** Ed.:– Jacques-Yves Costeau [preface]. Ill.:– LeRoy Neiman. 1975. De Luxe Edn., (1500) numbered, & sigd. by Neiman & Costeau. Fo. Mor., gt. design on cover, spine gt., by G. Wieck, linen s.-c. Sigd. pres. card from Clarke (the typographer) laid in. (SG. Apr.2; 212) $300
- **Omoo.** N.Y., 1847. 1st. Edn. Slight foxing. Orig. gt.-pict. cl., some fraying at head & tail of spine, sm. light stain on upr. cover. (PNY. May 21; 268) $150
- **The Piazza Tales.** N.Y., 1856. 1st. Edn. 1 sig. sprung, some stains, 7 pp. of publisher's advts. Orig. cl., some bubbling, minor stains, mor.-bkd. s.-c. (SPB. May 29; 295) $250
- – **Anr. Edn.** L. & N.Y., 1856. 1st. Edn., Engl. Iss. With 12 p. publisher's catalogue inserted at end. Orig. cl., worn & faded. From the Prescott Collection. (CNY. Feb.6; 250) $2,500
- **Pierre.** N.Y., 1852. 1st. Edn. Orig. cl., ends of spines & lr. fore corners worn. From the Prescott Collection. (CNY. Feb.6; 248) $380
- **Redburn: His First Voyage.** L., 1849. 1st. Edn. 2 vols. Slight foxing. Orig. blind-stpd. cl., spines gt.-lettered. From the Prescott Collection. (CNY. Feb.6; 245) $1,300
- **Typee.** Ed.:– Raymond Weaver (intro.). Ill.:– Miguel Covarrubias. Ltd. Edns. Cl. 1935. (1500) numbered, & sigd. by artist. Tapa bds. (SG. Apr.2; 81) $140
- **The Whale.** L., 1851. 1st. Edn. 3 vols. 2 slight marginal tears to hf.-title in vol. 1. Orig. cl. covers & contrasting spine, gt.-stpd. whale on spines, slight soiling & discoloration to covers. Joseph W. Wilson's copy, with his ink marginal additions (from the Amer. edn.), bkplts. of A.R. Pollock, S.A. Gimson, & A.H. Wiggin, lately in the Prescott Collection. (CNY. Feb.6; 246) $11,000
- **White-Jacket.** L., 1853. 1st. Edn. 2 vols. in 1. Remainder iss., consisting of the 1850 sheets with new title-p. Orig. cl., outer lr. jnt. partly torn, spine soiled, mostly unopened. From the Prescott Collection. (CNY. Feb.6; 249) $450

MELZI, G.
- [–] **Dizionario di Opere Anonime e Pseudonime di Scrittori Italiani.** Milan, 1848-1887. 4 vols. in 3, including supp. Cont. hf. cf., last vol. not unif. (SI. Dec.3; 3)   Lire 260,000

MELZO, Lodovico
- **Regole Militari Sopra il Governo e Servito Particolare della Cavalleria.** Antw., 1611. 1st. Edn. Fo. 18th. C. cf., spine & corners worn. (S. Nov.25; 366)   *Ross.* £400
- – **Anr. Copy.** Cont. vell. gt., single fillet border, central medallion on each cover. Inscr. 'Tosti Wright from Tim (A.N.L.) Munby'. (LC. Jun.18; 219)   £220

MEMOIRE Historique sur la Negociation de la France & de l'Angleterre.
L., 1761. 4to. 20th. C. bds. [Sabin 47516] (CB. Dec.9; 219)   Can. $120

MEMOIRES du XVIe au XVIIIe Siècles
Paris, 1840-73. 48 vols. Cont. hf. cf. (SH. May 28; 73)   *Linden.* £130

MEMOIRES pour l'Histoire des Sciences et des Beaux-Arts
Trévoux & Paris, 1709. 12mo. Cont. red mor., Royal arms of France, inner dentelle, some defects. (HD. Apr.9; 522)   Frs. 1,000

MENA, J. de
- **Copilacion d[e] todas las Obras.** Toledo, 1547. 2 vols. in 1. Fo. Title lf. & 1st. text lf. with old MS. notes, some corrections & bkd., lightly browned, 4 ll. more heavily, stained in parts. 18th. C cf., gt. spine, slightly defect. (H. Dec.9/10; 1359)   DM 520

MENACHEM Azaria de Fano
- **Pelach Ha'rimon.** Koretz, 1786. 4th. Edn. 4to. Losses to some corners, repairs, some staining. Mod. vell., in case. (SPB. May 11; 156) $200

MENACHEM MENDEL KROCHMAL of Nicolsburg
- **Zemach Zedek [responsa].** [Fuerth] [Amst.], 1766. 2nd. Edn. 4to. Outer margin reprd., without loss of text. Cl., spine defect. (S. Nov.18; 749)   *Israel.* £70

MENAGERIE IMPERIALE
Paris, 1812. 4 vols. 16mo. Hole in plt. 10 in vol. I, occasional browning. 19th. C. mott. cf., gt., spines gt. (S. Oct.21; 477)   *Studio Books.* £75

MENASSEH Ben Israel
- **De La Fragilidad Humana.** Amst., 1642. 1st. Edn. 4to. Port. of author by Salom Italia inserted after title, lacks ll. 3-6, outer & lr. margins of title reprd. without text loss, staining, foxing, cropped. Hf. cl. (SPB. May 11; 158) $3,750

MENASSEH Ben Israel–BENJAMIN, of Tudela
- **Mikveh Israel.–Ma'sa'ot Benjamin.** Trans.:– Eliakim Ben Yakov (1st. work). Amst., 1697. 1st. Edn.; 7th. Edn. 2 works in 1 vol. 24mo. Several gatherings loose, 1st. work lacks title & 1st. 2 ll. of register, browning, stains, some repairs at inner margins. Old sheep, wormholes. (SPB. May 11; 159) $650

MENASSEH Ben Israel–BENJAMIN, of Tudela –LOCMAN
- **De Creatione Problemata XXX; De Resurrectione Mortuorum Libri III-IX.–Fabulae et Selecta Quaedam Arabum Adagia cum Interpretatione Latina.–Masa'ot Shel Rabbi.** Amst.; Amst.: Leiden; Leiden, 1635; 1636; 1615; 1633. 1st. Edn.; 1st. Edn.; No Edn.; 4th. Edn. in Hebrew & 2nd. Edn. in Latin. 4 works in 1 vol. Slight browning. Vell., worn. (SPB. May 11; 157) $3,750

MENAVINO, Giovanni Antonio
- [–] **Türckische Chronica.** Trans.:– Heinrich Müller. Ill.:– Jost Amman. Frankfurt, 1577. 3 pts. in 1 vol. Fo. Bkplt. on verso of title, spotted, some ll. soiled, fo. M4 torn, slightly affecting text, owners' inscrs. on title, earliest dtd. 1578. Disbnd. (S. Jan.27; 342)   *Chester.* £300

MENDEL, P.H. & Reding, H.
- **Atlas van het Konigrijk der Nederlanden en de Overzeesche Bezittingen. Album voor Aardrijkskunde.** The Hague, 1841. Ob. 4to. Some plts. stained. Cont. hf. leath., slightly worn & reprd. (D. Dec.11-13; 1237)   DM 1,100

MENDEL of Lisko
See–**SCHNEUR Salman of Liadi–MENDEL of Lisko–AZULAI, Chaim Joseph David**

MENDEL of Vitebsk, Menachem
- **Pri Etz.** Zhitomir, 1874. 1st. Edn. Bds. (S. Nov.18; 296)   *Rock.* £55

MENDELSOHN, Erich
- Amerika: Bilderbuch eines Architekten. Berlin, 1928. 6th. Edn. Tall 4to. Cl.-bkd. ptd. bds., discold. & worn. (SG. Apr.23; 133) $130

MENDELSSOHN, Joanna
- The Life & Work of Sydney Long. [Cremorne], [1979]. (275) numbered, & sigd. Fo. Leath. gt. (KH. Mar.24; 275)   Aus. $220

MENDELSSOHN, Moses
- Jerusalem. Berlin, 1783. 1st. Edn. Upr. blank margin of 1st. section title trimmed, liby. blind-stp. on title. 19th. C. bds., crude cl. spine. (SG. Feb.12; 245) $150

MENDELSSOHN, Sidney
- South African Bibliography. L., 1910. (500). [2nd. Edn.?]. Cl. (SSA. Jun.18; 209)   R. 220
- - Anr. Copy. 2 vols. 4to. Orig. bdg., d.-w.'s. (VA. Jan.30; 146)   R. 160

MENDES, Catulle
- La Reine Flammette. Paris, [1898]. Ltd. Edn. numbered on Japan vell. 4to. Mott. cf., upr. cover with lge. floral vari-cold. inlay, spine worn, orig. wraps. bnd. in, by CH. Meunier, s.-c. untrimmed. Sigd. by publisher. (SG. Sep.4; 322) $180

MENDES PINTO, Ferdinando
- Historia Oriental de las Peregrinaciones. Madrid, 1620. 1st. Spanish Edn. Fo. Worming affecting text in title & 1st. 6 ll., filled in, some other worming in text & blank margins, severely in text of 2A1-2B3, foxing & staining. 19th. C. hf. cf. cf. (C. Apr.1; 153)   Barker. £230
- Peregrinacao e por ell escritta que consta de muytas, e muyto estranhas Cousas que vio & ouvio no Reyno da China, no da Tartaria ... e acrecentada com o Itenerario de Antonio Tenreyro. Lisbon, 1725. 4th. Edn. in Portuguese. Fo. 1 lf. from anr. copy, 1st. & last quires rather stained. Mod. cf., gt. spine. (S. Nov.4; 601)   Rawson. £170
- The Voyages & Adventures, of Ferdinand Mendez Pinto during his travels ... Trans.:- H.C. Gent. 1653. 1st. Edn. in Engl. Fo. Cont. cf. [Wing M1705] (C. Apr.1; 154)   Cavendish. £350
- Les Voyages Adventureux. Paris, 1628. 1st. Edn. in Fr. 1st. Edn. in Fr. 1 vol. in 2. 4to. Title reprd. affecting inscr., 1st. lf. in vol. II reprd. with some letters supplied in MS., inscr. on 1st. lf. of each vol. 'Je suis au duc de mortemart, stp. of Gabriel de Civray on title & at end of each vol. Cont. spr. cf., gt. arms of de Rochechouart, duc de Mortemart, & his cipher, gt., in alternate spine compartments. (SM. Oct.7; 1853)   Frs. 1,700

MENDOZA, Antonio Hurtado de
- Querer por Solo Querer: To Love Only for Love Sake. Trans.:- Sir Richard Fanshawe. 1671. 4to. Cont. mor., covers slightly wormed, rebkd. [Wing H3799] (C. Nov.19; 13)   Brett-Smith. £180

MENDOZA, Diego Hurtado de
- [-] Vie de Lazarille de Tormes. Ill.:- Maurice Leloir. Paris, 1886. (50) numbered on Jap. Lge 8vo. Orig. wrap., portfo. & folder of mor. with gold design on upr. cover. (SM. Feb.11; 235)   Frs. 2,000

MENESTRIER, Claude François, S.J.
- Traité des Tournois ... Lyons, 1669. 1st. Edn. 4to. Title-p. slightly worn & soiled, some browning, slight dampstaining. Cont. limp vell., slightly soiled. (S. May 5; 261)   Duran. £120

MENETRIER, C.
See-MANNE, E.D. de-MANNE, E.D. de & Menetrier C.

MENGHI, Girolamo
- Flagellum Daemonum, Exorcismos Terribles, Potentissimos, et Efficaces. Lyon, 1610. Without the 'Fustis Daemonum' & the 'Fuga Satanae'. Mor., triple gt. fillet borders, spine gt., gt. dentelles, by Auguste Petit. (SG. Feb.5; 347) $130
- Flagellum [et Fustis] Daemonum. [Milan?], 1727. Foxed. Old hf. mor. gt., red mor. gt. solander case, unc. W.M. Thackeray's copy, sigd. by him on fly.-lf. with his note below & his ink liby. stp., bkplt. of Jerome Kern, lately in the Prescott Collection. (CNY. Feb.6; 316) $400

MENGS, Antonio Raffaello
- Opere. Ed.:- Giuseppe Niccola d'Azara. Parma, Bod. Pr. 1780. 2 vols. 4to. Cont. red mor., gt. borders & spines. (SG. Sep.25; 57) $160

MENIN, L.
- Il Costume di Tutti i Tempi e di Tutte le Nazioni Descritto. N.p., n.d. Fo. Without atlas vol. Hf. cf., renewed. (CR. Mar.19; 279M)   Lire 260,000

MENNES, Sir John
- Recreation for Ingenious Head-Peeces. L., [1663]. 5th. Edn. Additional engraved title-p. with different imprint, cropped at head, occasionally affecting running titles. 19th. C. hf. leath. [STC W1715] (CB. Nov.12; 166)   Can. $300

MENNESSIER de la Lance, General
- Essai de Bibliographie Hippique. Paris, 1915; 1917. 1st. Edn. 2 vols. Ptd. wraps. (SG. Jan.22; 298) $325

MENNI, Ottaviano
- Amassis Munitoria continens Elementa et Vera Munitionis fundamenta divisa. Naples, 1702. Fo. 4 unnumbered pp., 2 unnumbered pp. 23 folding plts. with geometrical figure. Cont. cf., spine reprd. (CR. Mar.19; 264)   Lire 260,000

MENNIE, Donald
- The Grandeur of the Gorges. Shanghai, 1926. 1st. Edn., (1,000) numbered. 4to. Orig. silk bdg., boxed (TA. Mar.19; 572)   £90
- The Pageant of Peking. Ed.:- Putname Weale. Shanghai, 1920. 2nd. Edn. Fo. Orig. silk with gt. lettering, boxed. (TA. Mar.19; 573)   £60

MENON
[-] Cuisine et Office de Santé ... Paris, 1758. 12mo. Cont. spr. roan, spine decor. with raised bands. (HD. Feb.27; 43)   Frs. 1,000
[-] La Cuisinière Bourgeoise. Brussels, 1764. 12mo. Cont. mott. cf., spine gt. (SG. Feb.5; 96) $140

MENSI, A.
- Giovanni Migliara [1785-1837]. Bergamo, 1937. 4to. Publisher's cl. (CR. Mar.19; 110)   Lire 220,000

MENTELLE, Edme
- Atlas de la Monarchie Prussienne. L., 1788. Fo. 1 map defect., 92 (of 93) copperplts., 4 folding. Cont. leath. (R. Oct.14-18; 1547)   DM 1,000

MENTET DE SALMONET, Robert & Riordan de Muscry, D.
- Histoire des Troubles de la Grand' Bretagne. -Relation des veritables Causes ... du Roy de la Bretagne. Paris, 1661. 2 works in 1 vol. Fo. Dupl. stp. of Vienna Hofbibliothek on verso of title, bkplt. of Marquess of Bute. 18th. C. red mor., gt., by Etienne Boyet, arms of Prince Eugène of Savoy on covers triple gt. fillet, arms & cipher, gt. in alternate spine compartments, inner gt. dentelles. (SM. Oct.7; 1854)   Frs. 3,200

MENTMORE
Edinb., 1884. (20), this copy unnumbered. 2 vols. Fo. 1st. & last few ll. spotted. Orig. vell., slightly soiled. Bkplt. of Lord Battersea. (CSK. Jun.12; 142)   £270

MENTZEL, O.F.
- Life at the Cape in Mid Eighteenth Century, being the Biography of Rudolf Siegfried Allemann ... Cape Town, 1919. Orig. Iss. Van Riebeeck Society vol. 2. Cl. (SSA. Jun.18; 297)   R. 250
- - Anr. Edn. Cape Town, 1919. (82?), Darter Iss., with extra-plts., V.R.S. Format. Van Riebeck Soc., Vol. 2. Cl. (SSA. Jan.22; 381)   R. 700
- - Anr. Copy. Van Riebeck Soc., Vol. 2. Pres. copy from John X. Merriman. (SSA. Jan.22; 380)   R. 240

MENUSIER en Voitures
1775. Fo. 30 engraved plts., & 6 pp. of descriptive text (extract from Diderot's Encyclopedie). Mod. hf. cf. (C. Nov.6; 291)   Way. £90

MENZEL, Adolph
- Die Armee Friedrichs des Grossen in ihrer Uniformierung. Ed.:- F. Skarbin & C. Jany. Berlin, (1908). Fo. Three-qtr. mor., marb. bds. (SG. Oct.9; 164) $850

MENZIES, William
- History of Windsor Great Park & Windsor Forest. 1864. Fo. 20 actual photographs mntd., 2 folding maps torn, slightly soiled. Orig. hf. mor., worn, loose. (SH. Nov.6; 127)   Henderson. £160

MERCATOR, Gerard
- Atlas Minor. Ed.:- J. Hondius. Amst., 1634. Ob. 4to. Lacks 1 map, with Moskau map of 1628 Edn. on p. 123, browned & soiled in parts, title stpd. Cont. pig., decor. blind-tooled, rubbed. (H. Dec.9/10; 447)   DM 4,600

[-] - Anr. Edn. Amst., 1648. 2 pts. in 1 vol. Ob. 4to. Slightly browned & soiled, 1 map with light fault, pt. 1 lacks 1 map, part 2 lacks 2 maps, MS. owner's mark on title. Cont. vell., soiled, upr. cover loose. (HK. May 12-14; 553)   DM 8,500
- - Anr. Edn. Amst., 1651. 4th. Edn. Ob. 4to. 1 map cut out & pasted over an old map. Cont. vell., slightly soiled. (R. Oct.14-18; 1549)   DM 10,000
- Atlas, or a geographicke description ... of the World, through Europe, Asia, Africa & America ... Amst., 1638. 2nd. vol. Fo. 112 (of 113) double-p. engraved maps, lacks map of Holy land, a few maps reprd. or a little worn at bottom of centre fold, sometimes affecting engraved surface, 1 or 2 other repairs, a few tears, sm. stains on maps of Peru & Paraguay, old inscr. on foot of title. Orig. blind-panel. parch., lacks ties, soiled. As an atlas, w.a.f. (SPB. Oct.1; 276) $22,000
- [Atlas sive Cosmographicae Meditationes de Fabrica Mundi et fabricati figura]. Duisburg, [1589-95]. 4 pts. in 1 vol. Fo. Maps hand-cold., text on verso of all but 2 additional maps, wanting general title & Pars Altera, tear in lower left corner of map of Hanau slightly affecting engraved surface, few stains, a little discoloration. Cont. hf. cf. As an atlas, w.a.f. (SPB. Oct.1; 275) $13,000
- - Anr. Edn. Amst., 1619. 4th. Edn. Lge. fo. Partly stained, engd. main title heavily restored, text incomplete. Cont. style vell. (R. Oct.14-18; 1548)   DM 54,000
- Atlas-Section concernant la France de la Première Partielle de l'Atlas. Ill.:- J. Jolivet. [Duisburg], [1585]. 12 maps, lacks 1 of Aquitania, replaced by general map of France from cont. Ortelius. Mod. hf. vell. (LM. Nov.8; 9)   B. Frs. 76,000
- Belgii Inferioris Geographicae Tabulae. Duisburg, [1585]. Fo. Maps lightly browned & soiled, last 5 wormed, index stained & tear bkd. Mod. paper bds. (H. Dec.9/10; 448)   DM 1,600
- Galliae Tabulae Geographicae; Belgii Inferioris Geografacae Tabulae; Germaniae Tabulae Geographicae. Duisburg, [1585]. 1st. Edn. 3 pts. in 1 vol. Fo. Titles & maps cont. cold., lacks? port. from 1st. gathering, some text ll. & maps slightly torn (mostly marginal), cont. sig. partly erased from foot of 1st. title. 18th. C. mott. cf., gt. spine, sides worn & leath. peeling. W.a.f. (C. Nov.6; 263)   Traylen. £10,500

MERCATOR, Gerard & Hondius, Jocodus
- Atlas sive Cosmographicae. Amst., 1630. Fo., 470mm X 308mm. Lacks 47 maps & general title-p., 4 maps with tears at centre fold, port. plt. torn & reprd. with slight loss, plts. cold. by cont. hand Cf., worn, rebkd. in cl. W.a.f. (CNY. Oct.1; 31) $14,000
- Atlas Novus. Amst., 1633. German Text Edn. Fo. Engraved pict. title, partly hand-cold., labels in centre with ptd. title & imprint, ports., 161 double-p. engd. maps, histor. cartouches, plans, vigs. etc., some partly hand-cold., 2 text engrs., engraved. Title 'Italiae' from Fr. text edn. inserted, lacks dedication & all but last lf. of contents, port. plt. & few maps torn & reprd., some maps stained, many outl. in red crayon, similar underscoring of place names & some text 17th. C. qtr. cf., worn. W.a.f. (S. Mar.31; 274)   Burgess. £7,000
- Latin Atlas. [1607]. Fo. Vell. (CE. Nov.20; 58)   £3,000

MERCATOR, Nicolaus
- Institutionum Astronicarum Libri Duo. 1676. 1st. Edn. Recent cf. [Wing M1729] (TA. Sep.18; 211)   £120
- - Anr. Edn. Padua, 1685. 2nd. Edn. 4to. 1 folding engraved diagram a little stained, sm. holes in 2. Cont. paper bds., unc. & mostly unopened. (C. Apr.1; 61)   Goldschmidt. £130

MERCIER, L.S.
- Jenneval.-Le Déserteur.-Olinde et Sophronie. -L'Indigent.-Le Faux Ami. Paris, 1769; 1772; 1771; 1772; 1772; 5 works in 1 vol. A few ll. slightly dampstained. Cont. cf., rebkd. (SH. Oct.10; 382)   Quaritch. £85

MERCKWORDIGKEITEN DER WELT
Ill.:- G.R. Schindelmayer. Vienna, 1805-08. 8 vols. 4to. Cont. hf. leath., partly wormed. (R. Oct.14-18; 1472)   DM 2,400

MERCURI, Paolo
See-BONNARD, Camillo [& Mercuri, Paolo]

MERCURIALIS, Hieronymus
- De Arte Gymnastica Libri Sex. Venice, 1601. 4to. Some ll. dampstained, sm. marginal wormhole. Cont. cf. (SH. Mar.5; 197) *Schuster.* £105
- De Morbis Cutaneis et de Omnibus Corporis Humani Excrementis . . . Venice, 1585. 2nd. Edn. 2 pts. in 1 vol. 4to. Bds. Bkplt. of Denis I. Duveen. (S. Jun.16; 572) *Maggs.* £220

MERE GATEAUX (La), l'Amie Intime des Petits Enfans et l'Ennemie Jurée du trop Fameux Croque –Mitaine. Ill.:– Mellidor. Paris, 1819. 12mo. Concealed in centre of book is box with 2 cut-out figures on India paper, starched & hand-cold., lacking arms. Mor.-bkd. bds. (SH. Mar.19; 171) *Libris.* £150

MEREDITH, D.
- The Grasses & Pastures of South Africa. Parow, 1955. 4to. Cl., d.-w. (SSA. Nov.5; 65) R. 140

MEREDITH, George
- The Egoist. L., 1879. 1st. Edn. 3 vols. Vol. 1 lacks advt. lf. Crushed red lev., filleted borders, raised bands, by Sangorski & Sutcliffe, orig. spine & 1 cover bnd. into each vol. Receipt for Copyright sigd., tipped in. (SG. May 14; 145) $375
- Novels. 1894. 14 vols. Hf. cf., spine gt. (BS. Nov.26; 129) £80
- The Ordeal of Richard Feveral. L., 1859. 1st. Edn. 3 vols. Orig. ripple-grain cl., Carter's A bdg. William Marchbank bkplts. (CNY. May 22; 180) $800
- Works [Collection of] L., 1856-1912. 32 works in 57 vols. 12mo. & 8vo. Mor., unc., orig. bdgs. bnd. in. (SG. Oct.9; 165) $900
- – Anr. Edn. 1896-98. Ltd. Edn. 32 vols. Cl., unc. (P. May 14; 254) *Primrose.* £55
- [-] Anr. Edn. 1897-1903. 16 vols. Cont. hf. lev. by Bumpus. (CSK. Jul.10; 134) £60
- [-] Anr. Edn. 1912. Surrey Edn. 22 vols. Occasional slight spotting. Cont. hf. cf. by Rivière, spines gt. (CSK. Jan.16; 146) £70

MEREDITH, Louisa Anne Twamley
- Flora's Gems. [1830.]. Fo. Lacks 1 plt. Orig. cl. gt. (P. Oct.2; 307) *Wagner.* £200
- The Romance of Nature. 1836. 1st. Edn. Orig. Mor. (SH. Jun.18; 171) *Frick.* £100
- – Anr. Edn. 1836. [2nd. Edn.?]. Cont. mor. gt. (SBA. Jul.22; 106) *Fairburn.* £110
- – Anr. Copy. Orig. mor. (SH. Jun.18; 172) *Frick.* £100
- – Anr. Copy. Orig. mor., sides blind-stpd. with central-gt. bouquet, upr. cover stained. (C. May 20; 225) *Walford.* £60
- Some of My Bush Friends in Tasmania. 1860. Fo. Some slight soiling. Orig. cl., disbnd. (CSK. Apr.3; 106) £95
- – Anr. Copy. Cont. embossed cl. gt. (C. Mar.18; 74) *Schrire.* £65
- – Anr. Copy. Foxed. Cont. decor. suede, spine slightly defect. (SSA. Nov.5; 374) R. 95
- Tasmanian Friends & Foes . . . Hobart &c., 1880. 4to. Some inner margins strengthened, occasional foxing. Recased in orig. cl., new end-papers. (KH. Nov.18; 420) Aus. $130

MERGHELYNCK DE BEAUVOORDE
- Les Etrangers dans la Weste-Flandre . . . Tournai, 1910. (152) Vol. 1 only, all publd. Orig. bdg. (LM. Nov.8; 279) B.Frs. 7,000

MERIAN, Maria Sibylla
- Dissertatio de Generatione de Metamorphosibus Insectorum Surinamensium. Ill.:– J. Mulder & P. Sluyter after Merian. Amst., 1719. 2nd. Latin Edn., wide margin. Lge. fo. Lacks frontis., all copper engrs. with sm. repair in lower margin, slightly browned or stained, mostly in borders, heavier on last ll. & plts., last pp. mispaginated. Cont. vell., very defect. & soiled. (H. May 21/22; 166) DM 17,000
- Dissertation sur la Génération et les transformations des Insectes de Surinam.–Histoire des Insectes de l'Europe. The Hague; Amst., 1726; 1730. 2 works in 1 vol. Fo. 1st work: Fr. & Latin titlepages (1 letter of Fr. titlepage punched out). Cont. cf. extensively restored. From collection of Massachusetts Horticultural Society, stps. on title. (SPB. Oct.1; 149) $16,500
- Histoire des Insectes de l'Europe . . . Trans.:– Jean Marret. Ill.:– Picart [engraved vig.]. Amst., 1730. Fo. Plt. 101 cut out, plts. 56 & 87 upside down, stain on plt. 153, occasional spotting, dust-soiling in inner margin of title, inscr. on

hf.-title. Cont. mott. cf., worn. (S. Dec.3; 1056) *Kistner.* £2,200
- Histoire Générale des Insectes de Surinam et de Toute l'Europe. Ed.:– M. Buch'oz. Paris, 1771. 3 vols. Fo. Plts. hand-cold., some margins soiled in vol. 3. Cont. mott. cf., worn, covers detchd. From Chetham's Liby., Manchester. (C. Nov.27; 276) *Kistner.* £5,500
- Leningrad Watercolours. N.Y. & L., [1974]. (1750) numbered. Fo. Qtr. vell. gt. & bds., unif. portfo. (containing prints & accompanying text sheets), both in heavy card. s.-c. (KH. Mar.24; 277A) Aus. $500
- Metamorphosis Insectorum Surinamensium. Amst., 1705. 1st. Edn. Fo. 60 hand-cold. engd. plts., 2 bnd. out of order, Fr. Ms. ink notes at foot of each plt. 18th. C. (?Dutch) red mor., sides with gt. tooled borders, spine gt. (C. Jul.15; 157) *Quaritch.* £10,000
- – Anr. Copy. Spotted thro.-out. 19th. C. hf. mor. Chetham's Liby., Manchester. (C. Nov.27; 277) *Mohler.* £2,200
- – Anr. Edn. Ed.:– H. Decker. Leipzig, 1975. Facs. of Amst. 1705 Edn., (600). 2 vols. Lge. fo. & 4to. Orig. marb. leath., gt. spine, cover & inner & outer dentelle, s.c., orig linen. (HK. May 12-14; 377) DM 700
- – Anr. Edn. Amst. [Dresden/Utrecht], n.d., [1975]. Facs. Lge. fo. Hf. cf. gt. in cl. s.-c. (VG. Dec.16; 853) Fls. 650
- Der Raupen Wunderbare Verwandelung und Sonderbare Blumennahrung. Ill.:– J. Houbraken. 1679. (ca. 1717). 4to. Title slightly browned at lower margin, plts. 1-8 with light browning, plts. 46-50 with restored margin tear. 19th. C. bds. (R. Mar.31-Apr.4; 1401) DM 7,800

MERIAN, Matthew
- Theatrum Europaeum. Frankfurt, 1635-1738. 21 vols. Fo. Lacks view of Athlone in vol. 14, & view of Regensburg in vol. 16, 1 or 2 titles cropped at foot, title of vol. XI frayed, all titles & plts. with liby. stps. Unif. 18th. C. vell., oval gt. device on covers, last vol. in cont. cf. W.a.f., from Chetham's Liby., Manchester. (C. Nov.27; 278) *Maggs.* £18,00
- – Anr. Edn. Frankfurt, 1682. Vol. XI. Fo. Lightly browned. Cont. leath., spine very defect. (HK. Nov.18-21; 1266) DM 4,400
- Todten Tanz wie derselbe in der Stadt Basel zu sehen ist. Basel, 1756. 2nd. Edn. 4to. Copper title with dte. of 1st. Chovin-Edn. 1744, end lf. with revolving head ptd. as text copper eng. & Memento mori omitted. Some soiling. Hf. mor. (R. Mar.31-Apr.4; 1526) DM 660
See–ZEILLER, Martin & Merian, Matthew
See–ZEILLER, Martin–MERIAN, Matthew

MERIAN, Matthew (Ill.)
See–ZEILLER, Martin

MERIGOT, James
- A Select Collection of Views & Ruins in Rome . . . L., 1797-99. 2 Pts. in 1 vol. 4to. Cf., worn. (SG. May 14; 147) $175
[-] – Anr. Edn. [1826]. L.P. Fo. Text in Engl. & Fr., plts. wtrmkd. 1821-25, plt. 21 torn, slight spotting. Recent hf. cf., preserving orig. bds., worn, unc. (S. Nov.4; 582) *Reid.* £420
[-] – Anr. Edn. Ca. 1828. L.P. Fo. 57 cold. plts. (of 62), 2 detchd., preface loosely inserted from a smaller copy, slight soiling. Hf. cf., very defect., upr. cover detchd. W.a.f. (S. Jun.23; 328) *Wilson.* £200
- – Anr. Edn. L., n.d. [paper wtrmkd. 1827 & 1828]. On L.P. (Whatman). Tall fo. Lacks plt. no. 40 (Ponte Nomentano), but with extra plt. at end (The Cascatelle & Stables of Mecoenas). Crude hf. leath., bd. covers very defect. (SG. Nov.20; 377) $425

MERIMEE, Prosper
- Carmen. Ill.:– Barta. Paris, 1942. (23) numbered on Japon nacré. 4to. 5 orig. gouaches & bistre suite of ills. Red mor. gt. by A. Thiollière, orig. wraps. bnd. in, s.-c. (SM. Oct.8; 2358) Frs. 3,000
- – Anr. Edn. Ill.:– Clavé. 1946. (15) on Arches teinté,. Sewed. With orig. aqua. & 2 suites, black & cold. (HD. Oct.10; 198) Frs. 2,800
- – Anr. Edn. Ill.:– Clavé. [1946]. Sm. 4to. Ll., vell. (HD. Jun.30; 55) Frs. 1,400
- Colomba. Ill.:– Bouchery after Vuillier. Paris, 1913. On Jap. Engrs. in 2 states. Hf. mor. by Blanchetière, wrap. preservd. (SM. Feb.11; 91) Frs. 1,600

MERIWETHER, Lewis & Clark, William
- The Journals of the Expedition. Ltd. Edns. Cl., 1962. Ltd. Edn. 2 vols. Orig. bdg., box. (SPB. Jul.28; 273) $125

MERKUSHEV, M.
See–LANE, Ary & others

MERKWÜRDIGKEITEN, Annehmliche, derer an, ober und unter der Donau gelegenen Königreiche, Fürstenthümer, Länder, Städte etc. Nuremb., 1685. Slightly soiled in parts. Cont. leath. (R. Oct.14-18; 2112) DM 13,000

'MERLINUS COCAIUS' (Pseud.)
See–FOLENGO, Teofilo 'Merlinus Cocaius'

MERLO, Diego Joseph
See–SAINZ DE VALDIVIESO Y TORREJON –MERLO, Diego Joseph

MERRICK, Leonard
- Works.–The Little Dog Laughed. N.Y., n.d.; 1930. 15 vols.; 1 vol. 8vo, last vol. smaller than others. Cf. gt., gt. panel. spines. (SPB. Nov.25; 476) $225

MERRIMAN, Henry Seton
- The Grey Lady. Ill.:– Arthur Rackham. L., 1897. 1st Edn. Cl. Raymond M. Sutton, Jr. copy. (SG. May 7; 205) $100

MERSENNE, Merin
- Harmonicorum Libri (12) in quibus agitur de sonorum naturam causis, et effectibus . . . orbisque Harmonicis Instrumentis. Paris, 1636. 2 pts. in 1 vol. Fo. Title ruled in red, apparently lacks single lf. cancels intended to replace lacking sheets R & X in pt. I, several repairs to D3 in pt. II, woodcut on a4 slightly cropped at foot, title & several ll. neatly guarded in inner margins, several marginal repairs, a few ll. slightly stained at outer edges. 19th. C. vell. bds., upr. cover detchd., worn, & soiled. (S. Dec.9; 444) *Baron.* £440

MERTON, Thomas
- The Tower of Babel. Ill.:– Gerhard Marcks. [1957]. (250) numbered, sigd. by author & artist. Fo. Vell.-bkd. bds., s.-c. (SG. Jun.4; 372) $180

MERWIN, H.C.
See–HARTE, Bret-MERWIN, H.C.

MERY
See–BARTHELEMY & Mery

MÉRY, (F.J.P.A.)
- Constantinople et la Mer Noire. Paris, 1855. Spotted. Orig. mor.-bkd. cl. (SH. Jun.18; 89) *Makiya.* £55

MERY, J.
See–GAVARNI, P. & Mery, J.

MESHULAM FEIBUSH HA'LEVI Hurwitz of Krementz
- Mishnat Chachamim. Ostroho, 1796. 1st. Edn. 3 pts. in 1 vol. 4to. Pt. III ptd. without title, lacks last lf. in pt. III. Leath. (S. Nov.18; 301) *Landau.* £65

MESMER, F.A.
- Mémoire sur la Découverte du Magnétisme Animal. Geneva & Paris, 1779. 1st Edn. Cont. cf., bkplts. of F.G. Irwin, David P. Wheatland & the Westcott Hermetic Liby. (S. Apr.6; 226) *Phillips.* £650

MESSENIUS, Johannes
- Theatrum Nabilitatis Svecanae . . . Stockholm, 1616. 1st. Edn. Fo. Lacks front flyleaf, title-page slightly browned with an early ownership inscr. at foot. Cont. vell. bds., slightly cockled & stained on lr-cover. Pres. inscr. on back pastedown from J.G. Gronovius to Daniel Heinsius. (S. Oct.20; 157) *Bjorck & Borjesson.* £160

MESSISBURGO, Christoforo di
- Banchetti Compositioni di Vivande, et apparecchio Generale. Ferrara, 1549. 1st. Edn. 4to. Inscrs. on title, slight browning & soiling, a few ll. loose. 17th. C. limp vell., soiled. Bkplt. of Baron Landau liby.; from liby. of André L. Simon. (S. May18; 139) *Hoppen.* £6,000
- Libro Novo nel qual s'insegna il modo d'ordinar Banchetti . . . Venice, 1581. Old bds., worn. (S. Oct.20; 158) *Quaritch.* £360

METASTASIO, Pietro
- Opere. Ill.:– after P.A. Novelli, De Gobbis, & others. Venice, 1783-85. 7 vols. 4to. Occasional offsetting. Cont. mott. cf. gt., rebkd. From the

METASTASIO, Pietro – Opere. -contd.
collection of John A. Saks. (C. Jun.10; 162)
Greindl. £350
– – **Anr. Edn.** L., 1784. 12 vols. 18mo. Marb. cf. by Cazin. (HD. Apr.8; 278) Frs. 1,300
– **Opere Drammatiche.** Ill.:– G. Zucchi. Venice, 1758-66. (200). 7 vols. 4to. Cont. vell. Owner's inscr. of John Hussey, lately in the collection of John A. Saks. (C. Jun.10; 161) *Lyon.* £140

METCALF, Samuel L.
– **A Collection of Some of the Most Interesting Narratives of Indian Warfare in the West ...** Lexington, 1821. 1st. Edn. Errata preserved on verso of final lf., slight foxing. Red mor. by Bedford, head of spine worn, gt. spine & borders. From liby. of William E. Wilson. (SPB. Apr.29; 199) $1,000

METCALF, Tom
See–FICKE, Arthur & Metcalf, Tom

METCHNIKOFF, Elie
– **L'Immunité dans les Maladies Infectieuses.** Paris, 1901. 1st. Edn. Rebnd. in buckram, ex-lib. (SG. Jan.29; 291) $160
– **Lecons sur la Pathologie Comparée de l'Inflammation.** Paris, 1892. 1st. Edn. Crude hf. cl., ex-liby. (SG. Aug.21; 341) $140
– **Lectures on the Comparative Pathology of Inflammation delivered at the Pasteur Institute in 1891.** Trans.:– F.A. & E.H. Starling. 1893. 1st. Edn. in Engl. 56 pp. advts. Orig. cl. (S. Jun.16; 574) *Rootenberg.* £65

METELLUS or MATAL, Jean Natale
– **Germaniae Superior 38, Inferior quae etiam Belgium Dicitur 16 Tabulis Aeneis Descripta.** [Cologne], [1598]. Fo. 51 engd. double-p. maps (of 54?), lacks title, all ll. detchd. from guards. Cont. limp vell., sm. garter crest of Henry Percy, 9th. Earl of Northumberland gt.-stpd. on covers, upr. cover torn, lacks ties. W.a.f. (C. May 20; 153) *Rheinbuch.* £2,200

METEREN, Emanuel van
– **Historie der Neder-landscher ende haerder Na-buren Oorlogen ende Geschiedenissen ...** Ill.:– C. van Sichem. The Hague, 1614. Fo. Occasionally slightly browned & foxed. Cont. cf., top & lr. pt. of spine defect., ties worn. (VG. Nov.18; 1292) Fls. 900
– – **Anr. Copy.** Engraved frontis. soiled, with some marginal damage, mntd., map & last pp. of index defect. in margin, reprd., occasionally stained & browned. Mod. hf. cf. (VG. Dec.17; 1455) Fls. 500
– – **Anr. Edn.** Amst., 1663. Fo. Cont. panel russ.-bkd. wood, brass clasps & catches. (VG. Oct.13; 106) Fls. 1,800
– **Nederlantsche Historen.** 1612. 4to. Lacks ptd. title? Cont. vell. (SG. Feb.5; 238) $130

METEYARD, Eliza
– **The Life of Joshia Wedgewood.** L., 1865-66. 2 vols. Orig. decor. cl., gt. (GM. Apr.30; 529) £52

MÉTHODE AMUSANTE OU ABÉCÉDAIRE RÉCRÉATIF
Lyon, 1813. 'Dernière Édn.' 12mo. 1 lf. lacks corner slightly affecting text. Mor.-bkd. bds. (SH. Mar.19; 174) *Libris.* £50

MÉTHODE AMUSANTE POUR ENSEIGNER L'ABC
1801. 12mo. Orig. roan-bkd. bds. (SH. Mar.19; 173) *Schiller.* £190

METHODIUS, Saint
– **Gottliche Offenbarungen von der Heligen Engeln Geschehen.** Memmingen, [Albrecht Kunne], 1497. 4to. Unrubricated, lacks final blank, 1st. lf. restored & reprd. at inner & upr. margins, with 2 sm. patches & loss of some letters on verso, single wormhole thro.-out. Old hf. vell. From the collection of Eric Sexton. [BMC II, 606, Goff M526, HC 1123*] (CNY. Apr.8; 100) $2,400

METHODUS GEOMETRICA. Das ist: Kurtzer wolgegrundter unnd aussfuhrlicher Tractat von der Feldtrechnung und Messung
Nuremb., 1598. 1st. Edn. Fo. Some plts. with p. reference numbers cropped, sm. hole in plt. at p. XVI, title & a few ll. soiled or discold. in lr. margins, note in 19th. C. hand at foot of title-p. describes this work as being ascribed by Doppelmayr, Historische Nachricht von den Nurnbergischen Mathematicis und Kunstlern (Nuremb. 1730) to Paul Pfintzing. Bnd. in 2 ll. of 16th. C. missal over new bds. From Honeyman

Collection. (S. May 20; 3286) *Goldschmidt.* £2,600

METIUS, Adrianus
– **Primum Mobile, Astronomice, Sciographice, Geometrice, & Hydrographice.** Amst., 1633. 4 vols. in 1, as iss. Light dampstains to corners. 19th. C. heavy vell., metal clasps, edges stained red. (PNY. Mar.26; 209) $200

METZ, Conrad Martin
– **Imitations of Ancient & Modern Drawings.** 1798. Lge. fo. Upr. margin of frontis. dampstained, a few other minor defects. Cont. hf. mor. gt., worn. (SBA, Jul.14; 176) *Hamilton.* £140

METZGER, Johann
– **Europaeische Cerealien.** Ill.:– W. von Jenison. Heidelberg, 1824. 1st. Edn. Fo. Cont. bds., worn, lacks pt. of spine. (S. Jan.27; 344) *Wenner.* £110

METZINGER, Jean
See–GLEIZES, Albert & Metzinger, Jean

MEUNG, Jean de
See–LORRIS, Guillaume de & Meung, Jean de

MEURDRAC, Maria
– **Die Mitleidende und Leichte Chymie Dem Löblichen Frauen-Zimmer zu Sonderbahrem Gefallen.** Ed.:– J.L.M.C. Frankfurt, 1712. Frontis. with tear bkd. & loss, lightly browned, some soiling. Cont. vell., spine with sm. tear, soiled. (H. Dec.9/10; 920) DM 420

MEURSIUS
– **Elegantiae Latinis Sermonis.** Ill.:– Duponchel after Chevaux (frontis.). L., 1781. 2 vols. 18mo. Red mor. by Cazin. (HD. Apr.8; 279) Frs. 1,000

MEW, Egan
– **Old Bow China.–Old Chinese Porcelain.–Royal Sevres China.–Japanese Porcelain.–Old Dresden Meissen Porcelain.–Chelsea & Chelsea-Derby China.** N.d. 6 vols. Orig. decor. cl., some covers marked, unc. (JL. Mar.2; 765) Aus. $150

MEXICAN PICTURE-CHRONICLE OF CEMPOALLAN & other States of the Empire of Aculhuacan
L., 1890. 4to. Mod. marb. wraps. (SG. Jan.8; 277) $100

MEXICO
– **Manifiesto del Exmo.** Mexico, 1812. 4to. Disbnd. (SG. Feb.12; 266) $120

MEYENDORFF, Baron Georges de
– **Voyage d'Orenbourg à Boukhara ...** Ed.:– Amedée Jaubert. Paris, 1826. 1st. Edn. Mor., gt. borders, rebkd .(SG. Oct.30; 246) $375

MEYER, Dr. A.B.
– **Unser Auer Rackel-und Birkwild und seine Abarten.** Vienna, 1887. Atlas vol. only. Fo. Occasionally defect. & discold. edges. Un-bnd. in orig. portfo. case, very worn, folders detchd. (SPB. Nov.25; 95) $800

MEYER, F.
– **Collection de Costumes Suisses originaux.** Zürich, 1837. Square 8vo. A few plts. slightly soiled or with faint offsets from text, some ll. of text spotted. Orig. decor. bds., lacks spine, covers detchd. (S. Jun.23; 329) *Chaponnière.* £900

MEYER, F.A.
– **Vollständiger Unterricht wie Nachtigallen, Kanarienvögel, Finken, Lerchen ... und Tauben zu fangen, zu warten, vor Krankheiten zu bewahren, und ... heilen.** Vienna, 1803. Slightly soiled. Mod. bds. (R. Oct.14-18; 2822) DM 600

MEYER, Franz
– **Marc Chagall.** Trans.:– Philippe Jaccottet. Ill.:– Marc Chagall. [Paris], [1964]. 1st. Fr. Edn. Tall 4to. Cl., d.-w. Sigd. pres. copy from Chagall, with his orig. ink bust sketch, dtd. 1971. (PNY. Mar.26; 69) $900

MEYER, G.F.
See–MEYER, J.–MEYER, G.F.

MEYER, H.
– **[Ein Totentanz].** [Berlin], [1910]. Ltd. Edn. Lge. fo. 15 ll. with various dry stps. of Deutschen Kunstverleger Vereins, all under passepartouts. Loose in linen portfolio. All etchings on China, 16 (of 19) etchings sigd., most dtd. & monogrammed. (H. May 21/22; 1723) DM 480

MEYER, Henry Leonard
– **Game Birds & their Localities.** Ca. 1848. Ob. 4to. 6 hand-cold. litho. plts. Stitched as issued in

orig. ptd. paper wraps. (C. Jul.15; 192) *Weldon & Wesley.* £1,200
– **Illustrations of British Birds.** [1837]. Vol. 2 only (of 4). Fo. Cont. hf. mor. W.a.f. (C. Mar.18; 75) *Duran.* £420
– – **Anr. Edn.** [1837-44]. 4 vols. Lge. 4to. 313 cold. litho. plts. Cont. hf. mor., spines gt. (C. Mar.18; 146) *Israel.* £2,600
– – **Anr. Edn.** 1842. Vol. 1 only (of 7). Most plts. cold. & hand-finished, text ll. slightly spotted. Orig. cl., slightly worn. (SBA. May 27; 190) *Hindley.* £60
– – **Anr. Edn.** 1842-50. 1st. 8vo. Edn. 7 vols. Hf. mor. gt. by T. Bosworth, vol. I rebnd. in similar style. (LC. Jun.18; 121) £550
– – **Anr. Edn.** 1842-50. 7 vols. Cont. mor., gt., 1st. 2 vols. slightly stilted. (S. Jun.1; 164) *Milner.* £700
– – **Anr. Edn.** 1842-57. 7 vols. Occasional light spotting. 19th. C. hf. mor., gt. (S. Dec.3; 1058) *Freeman.* £540
– – **Anr. Edn.** 1853-57. 7 vols. Hf. mor., emblematically gt. spines. (S. Dec.3; 1057) *Freeman.* £500
– – **Anr. Edn.** 1857. 7 vols. Mor. gt. (C. Mar.18; 76) *Loose.* £800
– [-] / **Anr. Edn.** N.d., plts. dtd. 1837-38. Fo. 116 hand-cold. litho. plts. only, 1st. & last plts. heavily soiled, slight soiling elsewhere, several marginal tears crudely reprd., lacks title. Bdg. not stated. W.a.f. (CSK. Jun.19; 139) £480

MEYER, J.
– **Grosses Konversations-Lexikon.** Leipzig & Vienna, 1874-78. 16 vols. & 2 supp. vols. Orig. hf. leath. (D. Dec.11-13; 2202) DM 800
– – **Anr. Edn.** Leipzig & Vienna, 1904-13. 20 vols. & 4 supp. vols. Orig. hf. leath. (D. Dec.11-13; 2200) DM 700
– – **Anr. Edn.** Leipzig & Vienna, 1905-13. 24 vols. Orig. hf. leath. (D. Dec.11-13; 2203) DM 900
– **Konversations-Lexikon.** Hildburghausen, Ca. 1850. Slightly soiled in parts. Loose in 3 orig. hf. leath. boxes. (R. Oct.14-18; 2517) DM 1,500
– – **Anr. Edn.** [Hildburghausen], Ca. 1850. Slightly soiled in parts. Cont. hf. leath., spine defect. (R. Mar.31-Apr.4; 2230) DM 2,400
[-] **Pittoreskt Universum.** Stockholm, 1840 & 1841. Vols. 3 & 4. Vol. 3 lacks view of Berlin, together 1 engraved title & 94 steel engraved plts. Leath. gt. (D. Dec.11-13; 1266) DM 750
– **Universum.** Hildburgh., 1833-36. Vols. 1 & 3. Ob. 4to. Soiled. Cont. bds. (HK. Nov.18-21; 1270) DM 650
– – **Anr. Edn.** Hildburghausen, 1833-60. Vols. 1-21, lacks vol. 11. Engraved title & 943 steel engrs., slightly soiled in parts. Orig. linen. (D. Dec.11-13; 1265) DM 8,700
– – **Anr. Edn.** Hildburghausen, 1835. 6th. Edn. Vol. 2. Lge. ob. 8vo. Lacks Mont S. Michel steel engr. Cont. hf. leath. (R. Oct.14-18; 1478) DM 480
– – **Anr. Copy.** (R. Oct.14-18; 1477) DM 450
– – **Anr. Edn.** Hildburghausen, 1835-36. Vols. 2 & 3 Bnd. in 1 vol. Lge. ob. 8vo. 75 (of 79) steel engrs., Vol. 3 text in Danish Edn. Cont. hf. leath. (R. Oct.14-18; 1479) DM 700
– – **Anr. Edn.** Copen., 1835-42. Ob. 4to. A few stains, tears & light browning. Hf. leath. (H. May 21/22; 315) DM 3,200
– – **Anr. Edn.** Hildburghausen, 1836. Vol. 3. Lge. ob. 8vo. Cont. hf. leath. (R. Oct.14-18; 1481) DM 650
– – **Anr. Copy.** Cont. bds. (R. Oct.14-18; 1487) DM 600
– – **Anr. Edn.** Hildburghausen, 1839. Vol. 6. Lge. ob. 8vo. Cont. hf. leath. (R. Oct.14-18; 1485) DM 660
– – **Anr. Copy.** Cont. bds. (R. Oct.14-18; 1480) DM 500
– – **Anr. Edn.** Stockholm, 1839-41. Ob. 4to. Slightly stained. Cont. hf. leath. & hf. linen. (HK. Nov.18-21; 1278) DM 900
– – **Anr. Edn.** Hildburghausen, 1840. Vol. 7. Lge. ob. 8vo. Cont. hf. leath. (R. Oct.14-18; 1488) DM 500
– – **Anr. Copy.** Vol. VII. Ob. 4to. Lacks 5 steel engraved views, soiled & lightly browned in parts, title stpd. (H. Dec.9/10; 467) DM 580
– – **Anr. Edn.** Hildburgh., 1844. Vol. 11. Ob. 4to. Lacks 1 steel engraved plt., some plts. bnd. in extra, slightly browned & stained. Cont. hf. leath. (HK. Nov.18-21; 1272) DM 500
– – **Anr. Edn.** Hildburghausen, 1847. Vol. 12. Lge. ob. 8vo. Cont. hf. leath. (R. Oct.14-18; 1489) DM 800

– – Anr. Edn. Hildburghausen, [1847]. Vol. XII. Ob. 4to. Lacks ptd. title, some browning. Cont. paper bds., spine defect. (H. Dec.9/10; 468) DM 540

– – Anr. Edn. Hildburghausen, 1848. Vol. 13. Lge. ob. 8vo. Cont. hf. leath. (R. Oct.14-18; 1490) DM 460

– – Anr. Edn. N.Y., 1851. Vol. 1. Lge. ob. 8vo. Lacks 1 steel engr. Cont. linen, lacks spine. (R. Oct.14-18; 1496) DM 450

– – Anr. Edn. Hildburghausen, 1852. Vol. 15. Lge. ob. 8vo. Cont. hf. leath. (R. Oct.14-18; 1491) DM 650

– – Anr. Copy. Vol. 1. Cont. linen, spine defect., soiled. (R. Oct.14-18; 1495) DM 550

– – Anr. Edn. N.Y., 1852 & 1853. 2 vols. in 1. Ob. 4to. Sm. nailhole to lr. blank margin of some 15 ll. Cont. gt.-tooled mor. (SG. May 21; 408) $475

– – Anr. Edn. N.Y., 1853. Red cl. gt., worn, some foxing. Not collated, w.a.f. (SG. Aug.21; 397) $200

– – Anr. Edn. 1854. Vols. 6, 7 & 8 in 1. Ob. 4to. Slightly browned. Hf. mor. (P. Jul.30; 2) *Baumer.* £160

– – Anr. Copy. Vol. 16. Lge. ob. 8vo. Bds. (R. Oct.14-18; 1493) DM 600

– – Anr. Edn. Hildburghausen, 1855-56. Vols. 17 & 18. Lge. ob. 8vo. 92 (of 96) steel engrs., lacks vol. 17 pt. 7. Orig. pts. (R. Oct.14-18; 1494) DM 960

– – Anr. Edn. Hildburgh., 1858. Vol. 1. Slightly stained & browned in parts. Orig. linen, spine & corners with linen pasted over. (HK. Nov. 18-21; 1275) DM 480

– – Anr. Edn. Hildburgh., 1858-60. Octavo Edn. Vols. 1-5 (of 16). Vols. 3 & 4 slightly browned in parts. Cont. hf. leath. gt., vols. 1 & 2 spines worn. (HK. Nov.18-21; 1274) DM 2,400

– – Anr. Edn. Hildburgh., 1859. Vol. 2. 40 (of 41) steel engraved plts., 1 plt. caption with MS. correction. Orig. linen, spine & corners with linen pasted over. (HK. Nov.18-21; 1276) DM 950

– – Anr. Edn. Hildburghausen, 1859-60. Octavo Edn. Vols.3 & 5. 2 engraved titles & 77 (of 81) steel engrs. Orig. linen. (D. Dec.11-13; 1264) DM 900

– – Anr. Edn. Hildburgh., 1862. Pts. 11 & 12 in 1 vol. Many plts. soiled. Cont. hf. leath., spine defect., worn. (HK. Nov.18-21; 1277) DM 520

– – Anr. Edn. Hildburghausen, 1862-63. Vols. 11-16. Slightly soiled in parts. Orig. linen. (D. Dec.11-13; 1267) DM 3,200

– – Anr. Edn. N.Y., n.d. Vol. 1 only. Ob. 4to. Some ll. spotted & dampstained. Orig. cl. (SH. Mar.5; 99) *Strufaldi.* £110

– Zeitungs-Atlas [Hildburghausen] ca. 1852. Ob. 4to. Lacks engraved title, soiled. Cont. hf. leath., very worn. (H. Dec.9/10; 449) DM 800

MEYER, J.–MEYER, G.F.
– Geometria Theoretica; Compendium Geometriae Practicae, sive, Planimetria.–Stereometria sive Dimensio Solidorvm; Doctrina Triangvlorvm. Basel, [1676]; 1663; 1675; 1678. 3 works in 1 vol. Slightly soiled thro.-out. Cont. vell. (HK. Nov.18-21; 651) DM 480

MEYER, Jacob, of Bailleul
– Commentarii sive annales rerum Flandricarum. Antwerp, 1561. Fo. Woodcut device slightly torn & reprd, just affecting woodblock. 18th. C. cf., spine gt. (S. Oct.21; 445) *Pearson.* £160

MEYER, Johann Daniel
– Angenehmer und Nutzlicher Zeit-Vertreib, mit Betrachtung Curioser Vorstellungen . . . Nuremb., 1748-56. 3 vols. in 2. Plts. hand-cold., 1 plt. with sm. marginal tear reprd. Old cf., very worn, covers detchd. From Chetham's Liby., Manchester. (C. Nov.27; 298) *Smith.* £2,100

MEYER, Johann Jakob
– Vues de la Suisse. Zurich, 1826. Ob. fo. Title & 36 plts. laid down in border, extra ill. with 20 uncold. plts. by Louis Bleuler bnd in. Grained mor., gt. fillets with corner fleurons. (LC. Oct.2; 181) £2,500

MEYER, Maurits de
– De Volks- en Kinderprent in de Nederlanden van de 15e tot de 20e Eeuwe. Antw./Amst., 1962. 4to. Cl.-bkd. bds. boxed. (SG. Jan.22; 116) $160

MEYNELLIAN SCIENCE or Fox-Hunting upon System
1848. Crimson mor. gt. (CE. Nov.20; 118) £90

MEYNIER, Johann Heinrich
– Erzählungen für Kinder, zur Erweckung eines seineren moralischen Gefühls. Ill.:– J. Fluschmann after J. Voltz. Nuremb., 1812. Lacks upr. end-lf. Orig. bds., worn. (SH. Dec.10; 42) *Maggs.* £135

MEYRICK, Samuel Rush
– Critical Enquiry into Antient Armour. 1824. 3 vols. Fo. Hf. mor. gt. (CE. Nov.20; 157) £300

– – Anr. Copy. 4to. Additional engraved titles foxed. Red crushed mor., gt. borders & central lozenges on sides, gt. panel. spines, by J. Clarke. (C. Nov.5; 108) *Way.* £280

– – Anr. Copy. 3 vols. Fo. Some offsetting. Liby. cl., unc. (S. Sep.29; 263) *Gilbert.* £240

– – Anr. Edn. 1842. 2nd. Edn. 3 vols. 4to. Cont. hf. mor., spines gt. (SH. Oct.9; 173) *Traylen.* £400

– – Anr. Copy. Hf. mor. gt., slightly worn. (BS. Jun.11; 372) £200

– – Anr. Copy. Sm. fo. Cont. hf. mor. gt. (SPB. May 6; 221) $800

– – Anr. Edn. L., n.d. 3 vols. Fo. Red three-qtr. mor., reprd. Armor. bkplt. of E.H. Litchfield. (SG. Oct.9; 167) $950

MEYRICK, Sir Samuel Rush & Skelton, Joseph
– Engraved Illustrations of Ancient Arms & Armour . . . at Goodrich Court. Oxford, 1830. 2 vols. 4to. Slightly spotted. Cont. hf. cf., 1 cover detchd. (S. Sep.29; 261) *Mellin.* £70

– – Anr. Copy. Cont. hf. red mor., spine of vol. I defect., vol. II rebkd., liby.-stp. of Devon & Exeter Institution. (S. Sep.29; 260) *Gilbert.* £50

– – Anr. Edn. L., 1830. L.P. Edn. 2 vols. Lge. 4to. Red three-qtr. mor., 2 covers detchd. A.B. Maclay mor. bkplt. (SG. Oct.9; 229) $225

– – Anr. Edn. 1854. 2 vols. Fo. Hf. mor. gt. (CE. Nov.20; 156) £160

– – Anr. Copy. 4to. Cont. hf. mor. (SH. May 28; 216) *Elliot.* £50

MEYRICK, Samuel Rush & Smith, Charles Hamilton
– The Costume of the Original Inhabitants of the British Islands . . . & that of the Gothic Nations on the Western Coasts of the Baltic. 1815. Fo. Cont. hf. mor., some wear. W.a.f. (TA. Aug.21; 17) £210

– – Anr. Copy. Some offsetting of plts. on text. Russ. gt., brkn. (BS. Jun.11; 373) £50

– – Anr. Edn. 1821. [1st. Edn.?] Fo. Cont. red str.-grd. mor., sides panel. in gt. & blind. (C. Nov.5; 107) *Jones.* £120

– – Anr. Copy. 4to. Lacks 1 hand-cold. plt. Mor. gt., spine defect. (P. Feb.19; 186) *Vine.* £50

– – Anr. Copy. L.P. Fo. Cont. mor., elab. gt.-tooled. (PNY. May 21; 272) $300

– – Anr. Edn. N.d. [plts. dtd. 1815]. 4to. Title slightly spotted. Cont. hf. mor. (C. Feb.25; 220) *Midmer.* £80

MEYRICK, William
– The New Family Herbal; or, Domestic Physician. Bg'ham., 1790. Captions of 2 plts. shaved, errata/advt. lf., some spotting & browning. Cont. cf. (CSK. Dec.12; 129) £65

MEYSONNIER, Lazare
– La Belle Magic ou Science de l'esprit. Lyon, 1669. 1st. Edn. 12mo. Some browning, stain on Y9-10, title slightly soiled. Cont. cf., spine worn, new label. (S. Dec.8; 175) *Thorp.* £65

MEZONIN POEZII [Attic of Poetry]
Moscow, 1913. Nos. 2-4 in 2 vols. Orig. wraps. by L. Zak & B. Fridenson. (SH. Feb. 6; 498) *Flegon.* £65

MIARKO
– ABC D'Art: Croquis d'Animaux & Lettres Ornées, par Miarko. Paris, ca. 1920. Fo. Loose as iss. in orig. pig.-bkd. bds., lacks ties. (SH. Mar.19; 175) *Schiller.* £210

MIBES, Fr.
– Himmliches Jerusalem . . . oder Vollständiges Gebet-Buch . . . Sultzbach, 1796. Vell, blind-tooled, slightly defect., soiled, 'M.R.L. 1802' on cover. (H. Dec.9/10; 1609) DM 420

MICHAELIS, Johann David
– Mosaisches Recht. Kiehl, 1777. 3rd. Edn. 5 pts. in 3 vols. Slight browning on some ll. Vell.-bkd. bds. (SPB. May 11; 235) $130

MICHALLON, Achille Edna
– Vues d'Italie et de Sicile. Ill.:– Mme. Villeneuve, Devoi & Renoux. Paris, 1827. Fo. Plts. on india paper. Orig. bds., soiled, rebkd. (CSK. Feb.13; 7) £100

MICHAUD, Joseph François
– Histoire des Croisades. 1817-19 (I-III); 1822 (IV-VII). 7 vols. Cont. grd. cf., sm. border, by Blaise Jeune with his ticket. Marquis de Lespine liby. (HD. Oct.10; 255) Frs. 1,750

MICHAUD, Joseph François & Poujoulat, J.J.F.
– Correspondence d'Orient. Paris, 1833-35. 7 vols. Browned. Cont. cf. (SH. Jun.18; 90) *O'Neill.* £50

MICHAUX, François Andre, 1770-1855
– Histoire des Arbres Forestiers de l'Amérique Septentrionale. Ill.:– Redouté, A. Riche & P. Bessa. 1810-[13]. 1st. Edn. 3 vols. 133 engd. plts., col.-ptd. & hand finished, lacks final title, general index & 5 plts. Cont. str.-grd. mor., gt. (C. Mar.18; 77) *Wheldon & Wesley.* £800

– Travels to the Westward of the Alleghany Mountains, in the States of Ohio, Kentucky, & Tennessee . . . Undertaken in the Year 1802 . . . L., 1805. 1st. Edn. in Engl. Advts. Orig. bds., spine & label worn, mor.-bkd. s.-c. From liby. of William E. Wilson. (SPB. Apr. 29; 200) $200

– – Anr. Copy. Folding map, offset on title. Mod. cf-bkd. bds., head & foot of spine worn. From liby. of William E. Wilson. (SPB. Apr.29; 201) $150

MICHAUX, Francois André, 1770-1855 & Nuttall Thomas
– The North American Sylva. Phila., [1865]. 2 vols. 119 cold. litho. plts., plts. numbered 1-120, none numbered 30 & 31, but a 'bis' plt. 5. Cont. three-qtr. mor. (SG. Sep.18; 277) $110

– – Anr. Edn. Trans.:– J. Jay Smith. Phila., 1871. 5 vols. including Supp. (3 & 2). Port., 277 cold. plts. Unif. cont. hf. mor. (C. Jul.15; 193) *Taylor.* £450

MICHEL
See–DESNOS & MICHEL

MICHEL, Etienne
– Traité du Citronier. Ill.:– P. Bessa. Paris, 1816. L.P. Fo. Mod. mor.-bkd. bds. (C. Jul.15; 194) *Baskett & Day.* £1,200

MICHEL, Marius
– La Reliure Française. Ill.:– Hedouin (frontis.). Paris, 1880. Fo. Crushed three-qtr. lev., spine gt.-tooled with fleurons & sm. birds, by J.W. Menzies, orig. wraps. bnd. in. (SG. Mar.26; 44) $325

– – Anr. Edn. Paris; L., 1880. 1st. Edn. 4to. Cont. hf. red mor. Pres. inscr. & bkplt. of C. Wingfield. (SM. Oct.7; 1448) Frs. 1,100

MICHEL, Nicholas Leopold
– Recueil des Fondations et Establissemens faits par le Roi de Pologne . . . Luneville, 1762. New Edn. Fo. Old cf., very worn. (SG. Sep.25; 230) $110

MICHELE, Agostino
– Trattato della Grandezza dell' Acqua et della Terra. Venice, 1583. 1st. Edn. Sm. 4to. Some staining. New wraps. From Honeyman Collection. (S. May 20; 3287) *Howell.* £90

MICHELESSI, Domenico
See–ALGAROTTI, Francesco–MICHELESSI, Domenico

MICHELET, Jules
– The Bird. Ill.:– Giacomelli. L., 1872. New Edn. Mor., gt. borders & spine. Fore-e. pntg. (SG. Mar.19; 150) $350

– Histoire de France. Ill.:– Daniel Vierge. Paris, n.d. 19 vols. Cont. red chagrin, decor. spine raised bands. (HD. Apr.24; 156) Frs. 2,300

– The Mountain. Ill.:– Percival Skelton. L., 1872. Crimson mor. gt. Fore-e. pntg. (SG. Mar.19; 151) $240

MICHELI, Pier' Antonio
– Nova Plantarum Genera . . . Flor., 1729. 1st. Edn. Fo. 19th. C. cl., bdg. brkn. From Chetham's Liby., Manchester. (C. Nov.27; 299) *Mediolanum.* £200

MICHELSON, Albert A.
– Light Waves & their Uses. Chicago, 1903. 1st. Edn. Cl., ex-liby. (SG. Jan.29; 296) $100

MICHENER, James A. & Levine, Jack
– Facing East. N.Y., 1970. (2500) numbered & sigd. Fo. Loose as iss. in satin folding case with leath. strap. (SG. Dec.18; 297) $180

– – Anr. Copy. Water damage across upr. edge of book, causing some marginal wrinkling to lithos. (SG. Apr.2; 175) $100

MICHON, Louis Marie
- Les Reliures Mosaïqués du XVIIIe Siècle. Paris, 1956. 1st. Edn. 4to. Orig. wrap., s.-c. (SM. Oct.7; 1449) Frs. 1,200

MIDDIMAN, Samuel
- Select Views in Great Britain. 1784-92. Ob. 4to. Cont. russ. gt. (S. Nov. 24; 211) *Steedman.* £90
- - Anr. Edn. [Plts. dtd. 1784-92]. Ob. 4to. Cont. hf. cf. (C. Mar.18; 178) *Sommers.* £60
- - Anr. Edn. 1812. Ob. 4to. Mor. gt. (P. Sep.11; 286) *Traylen.* £100

MIDDLETON, Charles
- The Architect & Builder's Miscellany. 1799. A few ll. slightly soiled. Cont. cf. (SH. Oct.9; 130) *Weinreb.* £130
- - Anr. Copy. Some plts. have India-proof steel-engraved views mntd. at verso of appropriate plts. Dampstained at lr. jnt. (PNY. Mar.26; 18) $220

MIDDLETON, Charles Theodore
- A New & Complete System of Geography. Ill.:- Grignion, White, Le Roux, & others. [1777-78]. 2 vols. Fo. Some maps & plts. frayed & torn, some foxing & browning. Cont. mott. cf., worn, upr. cover of vol. 1 detchd. As an atlas, w.a.f. From the collection of Eric Sexton. (C. Apr.15; 39) *Burgess.* £170
- - Anr. Edn. L., 1778. 2 vols. Fo. 99 engraved plts. of 120 plts., maps, etc., some tears, browning, endpapers loose. Old cf., rebkd. [Sabin 48854] (SPB. May 5; 354) $125
- - Anr. Edn. 1778-79. 2 vols. in 1. Fo. Engraved frontis. detchd., slight browning & marginal tears. Cont. cf., covers detchd., worn. W.a.f. (S. Jun.22; 159) *Fairburn.* £150
- - Anr. Edn. Ill.:- Grignion, White, Le Roux, & others. 1779-? 2 vols. Fo. Lacks pp. 153-158 in vol. 1, some maps & plts. frayed & torn, some foxing. Cont. cf., worn, upr. cover of vol.1 detchd. As an atlas, w.a.f. From the collection of Eric Sexton. (C. Apr.15; 40) *Burgess.* £150

MIDDLETON, Erasmus & others
- The New Dictionary of Arts & Sciences. 1778. 2 vols. in 1. Fo. Engraved frontis., reprd. Cont. cf., rebkd. (SH. Oct.9; 176) *Fairburn.* £70

MIDDLETON, J.J.
- Grecian Remains in Italy. 1812 (wtrmkd. J. Whatman 1805-1818). 1st. Edn. Fo. Plts. 1 & 8 pasted together to form panorama (latter detchd. & slightly spotted with slight wear at folds). Cont. hf. roan, worn. (C. Nov.5; 109) *Quaritch.* £600

MIDDLETON, Richard
See–MEDIAVILLA, Ricardus de, i.e. Richard Middleton

MIDDLETON, Thomas
See–JONSON, Ben & others

MIDRASH Ha'mechilta
Venice, 1545. 2nd. Edn. Sm. fo. Lightly stained, owners' sigs. on title. Cf.-bkd. bds. (SPB. May 11; 161) $800

MIECHAELIS, Monsieur
See–NIEBU, Carsten–MIECHAELIS, Monsieur

MIEGE, Guy
[-] A Relation of Three Embassies from . . . Charles II to the Great Duke of Muscovie. 1669. 1st. Edn. Mod. hf. cf. [Wing M2025] (S. Dec.9; 333) *Remington.* £75

MIERIS, Frans van
- Histori der Nederlandsche Vorsten, uit de Huizen van Beijere, Borgonje en Oostenryk; Welken sedert Albert, Graaf van Holland, tot den dood van Karel den Vyf den, het hoogezag aldaar gevoerd hebben. Ill.:- B. Picart (vigs.). The Hague, 1732-35. 3 vols. Fo. Lacks port. of author, some marginal stains. Cont. hf. cf., backs gt., spines slightly defect. & worn, new chintz on covers. (VG. Dec.15; 504) Fls. 950
- - Anr. Edn. The Hague, 1735. 3 pts. Fo. Cf. (LM. Mar.21; 259) B.Frs. 20,000

MIES VAN DER ROHE, Ludwig
- Drawings in the Collection of the Museum of Modern Art. Ed.:- Ludwig Glaeser. N.Y., [1969]. (125) numbered. Ob. atlas fo. Loose in special linen folding case. (SG. Oct.23; 221) $140

MIGEON, Gaston
- 1900 L'Exposition Retrospective de l'Art Decoratif Français. Paris, n.d. (200) numbered. 10 orig. pts. Fo. Some slight spotting. Unbnd. as iss.

in orig. wraps., in 2 cont. mor. portfos. W.a.f. (CSK. Jan.30; 20) £160

MIKHA'IL AL-SABBAGH
- La Colombe, Messagère plus Rapide que l'Eclair. Trans.:- A.I. Silvestre de Sacy. Paris, 1805. Cont. mor.-bkd. bds., spine gt., unc., s.-c. Pres. copy. (S. Apr.29; 424) *Hourani.* £360

MILAN
- Les Curiosités de la Ville de Milan et de ses Environs. Mailand, 1820. Heavily soiled. Cont. hf. leath., gt. spine. (H. Dec.9/10; 582) DM 700
- Governo della ven. Fabrica del Duomo di Milano. Milan, 1662. Fo. Cont. limp vell. gt. (SI. Dec.3; 398) Lire 280,000
- Gridario Generale delle Gride, Bandi, Ordini, Editti [& c.]. Milan, 1688. 4 pts in 1 vol. Fo. Lacks antiporta & port., lightly stained & browned. 19th. C. vell. (SI. Dec.3; 399) Lire 220,000
- Milano e il Suo Territorio. Milan, 1844. 2 vols. Some light staining. Cont. cf., mor. arms on upr. cover. (SI. Dec.3; 395) Lire 480,000
- Milano. Sommario delli Ordini Pertinenti al Tribunale de Provisione della Citta e Ducato di Milano. Milan, [1657]. Fo. Cont. limp vell., gt. emblems on spine & covers. (SI. Dec.3; 401) Lire 350,000
- Milano. Le Vicende di Milano durante la Guerra con Federigo I Imperatore. Milan, 1778. 4to. Hf.-title. 19th. C. hf. vell., unc. (SI. Dec.3; 402) Lire 320,000

MILANO ILLUSTRATO. Album
[Milan], ca. 1855. 4to. Cont. hf. leath. (SI. Dec.3; 396) Lire 500,000

MILCHAMA La'shem-Cherev La'shem
Amst., 1714. Discolouration. Cl. (SPB. May 11; 71) $950

MILCHEMET Chova & Re'amim U're'ashim
Constantinople, 1710. 1st. Edn. Worming, staining. Vell., warped, worn, end-papers torn. (SPB. May 11; 86) $900

MILES, Edmund & L.
- An Epitome descriptive of the Royal Naval Service. L., 1841. [1st. Edn.]. Mor. gt., orig. wraps. bnd. in. (R. Oct.14-18; 2884) DM 1,500
- - Anr. Edn. 1844. Orig. cl. rebkd. worn, stitching brkn. (CSK. Aug.15; 2) £100
- - Anr. Copy. Disbnd., partly loose. (SG. Oct.30; 249) $300

MILES, Henry Downes
- The Book of Field Sports. N.d. 2 vols. 4to. 1 plt. torn & reprd. Cont. hf. cf. (CSK. Jul.31; 30) £230
- British Field Sports. N.d. Vol 1 only. 4to. Fingering thro.-out, 1 lf. torn. Hf. cf., worn., crudely rebkd. (PD. Apr.1; 40) £50
- Pugilistica, the History of British Boxing. Edinb., 1906. 3 vols. Slightly spotted. Orig. cl. gt. (SBA. Dec.16; 3?) *Subunso.* £50
- - Anr. Edn. N.d. & 1880. 3 vols. Orig. cl., gt. (SKC. Jul.28; 2514) £50

MILES, Henry H.
- The Child's History of Canada, for . . . the Elementary Schools & the Young Reader. Montreal, 1870. 1st. Edn. No. III of New Series of Histories of Canada. 16mo. Mor. gt., by Dawson Brothers, upr. cover gt.-lettered 'Presented to H.R.H. Prince Arthur by the Province of Quebec'. (SG. Mar.5; 115) $150
- A School History of Canada, for use in the Elementary & Model Schools. Quebec, 1870. 1st. Edn. 1st. vol. in New Series of Histories of Canada. 16mo. Mor. gt., by Dawson Brothers, upr. cover gt.-lettered 'Presented to H.R.H. Prince Arthur by the Province of Quebec'. (SG. Mar.5; 114) $180

MILES VAN DER ROHE, Ludwig
- Drawings in the Collection of the Museum of Modern Art. Ed.:- Ludwig Glaeser. N.Y., [1969]. 1st. Edn. Ob. tall fo. Ptd. gold bds., ringed, in publisher's box. (PNY. Mar.4; 187) $100

MILET-MUREAU, M.L.A.
- Voyage de la Pérouse autour du Monde. 1799. 2 vols., lacks Atlas. 4to. Cf. gt. (P. Oct.23; 41) *Maggs.* £120

MILITARY ARTICLES (The) of Lymerick
See–CIVIL ARTICLES (The) of Lymerick
–MILITARY ARTICLES (The) of Lymerick

MILL, James
- The History of British India. 1826. 6 vols. Cf. gt., worn (CE. Jun.4; 107) £65
- - Anr. Edn. Ed.:– Horace Hayman Wilson. 1858. 5th. Edn. 10 vols. in 9. Cont. hf. mor., spines gt. (CSK. Nov.21; 25) £65

MILL, John Stuart
- Autobiography. 1873. 1st. Edn. Orig. cl. Inscr. by Florence Nightingale. (SH. May 21; 270) *Sotheran.* £130
- Principles of Political Economy. 1848. 1st. Edn. 2 vols. Advt. lf. in vol. I, cont. marginal annots. Hf. cf., gt. arms of Christ Church, Oxford, on upr. covers. (S. Dec.8; 64) *Subunso.* £260
- - Anr. Copy. Lacks advts. Cont. hf. cf. (S. Dec.8; 65) *Subunso.* £230
- - Anr. Copy. Slight spotting & soiling. Orig. cl., labels chipped & soiled, cl. s.-c. The Litchfield copy. (SPB. May 6; 223) $850
- Principles of Political Economy.–Autobiography. 1852; 1873. 3rd. Edn.; 1st. Edn. 2 vols.; 1 vol. Orig. cl. (SH. May 28; 138) *Subunso.* £70
- The Subjection of Women. 1869. 1st. Edn. Orig. cl. Ownership inscr. of 'Jac. Rothschild' on hf.-title. (SBA. Jul.23; 571) *O'Hern.* £180
- - Anr. Copy. (SH. Apr.9; 301) *Monier-Williams.* £55
- Utilitarianism. 1863. 1st. Edn. 2 advt. ll. slight spotting. Orig. cl. Pres. copy. (S. Jan.26; 245) *Bickersteth.* £160

MILLAIS, John Guille
- Birds & Shooting Sketches. 1892. Fo. Hf. roan & red cl. gt. Pres. inscr. from Lady Millais. (CE. Nov.20; 25) £200
- A Breath from the Veldt. 1895. [1st. Edn.?]. Fo. Dampstained. Cl. (CE. Nov.20; 16) £70
- - Anr. Copy. Soiled, loose. (SH. Nov.7; 317) *Countryside Books.* £60
- - Anr. Copy. (60) numbered on L.P. sigd. Lge. fo. Mntd. India-proofs of all plts. & text ills. Mor.-bkd. pict. cl. Armorial bkplt. of Villiers Hatton. (SG. Apr.9; 383) $850
- - Anr. Edn. 1899. 4to. Orig. cl., gt., partly unc. (LC. Feb.12; 202) £50
- - Anr. Edn. Bulawayo, 1974. Collector's Edn., (50) in leath. Leath., s.-c. (VA. May 8; 342) R. 130
- British Deer & their Horns. 1897. Fo. Cl., gt. (CE. Nov.20; 21) £180
- - Anr. Copy. 4to. Decor. buckram, loose. (CE. Jun.4; 132) £105
- - Anr. Copy. Orig. buckram, soiled. (BS. Sep.17; 180) £50
- - Anr. Copy. Fo. Pict. cl., spine soiled. (SG. Dec.11; 360) $130
- British Diving Ducks. 1913. Ltd. Edn. 2 vols. Fo. Hf. crimson mor. gt. (P. Nov.13; 211) *Traylen.* £460
- - Anr. Copy. Orig. buckram gt. (C. May 20; 230) *Walford.* £380
- - Anr. Copy. Orig. cl. (S. Jun.1; 170) *Beynon.* £340
- - Anr. Copy. Red cl., gt. letters. (P. Nov.20; 59) £320
- Game Birds & Shooting-Sketches. 1892. 4to. Orig. hf. mor. (SH. Jul.9; 108) *Morten.* £170
- - Anr. Copy. (SH. Oct.9; 235) *Lindner.* £120
- - Anr. Copy. Cont. red hf. mor. (C. Mar.18; 78) *Tydeman.* £100
- - Anr. Copy. Orig. hf. str.-grd. red mor., bkplt. of E.M.S. Granville, Earl of Wharncliffe. (S. Dec.3; 1059) *Way.* £75
- The Mammals of Great Britain & Ireland. 1904-06. Ltd. Edn. 3 vols. Fo. Cl. gt., d.-w.'s. (P. Nov.13; 212) *Steedman.* £230
- - Anr. Copy. 4to. (CE. Jul.9; 67) £200
- - Anr. Copy. Orig. cl. (TA. Nov.20; 77) £180
- - Anr. Copy. Orig. buckram-bkd. cl. (SKC. Jul.28; 2634) £160
- - Anr. Copy. Occasional light spotting. Orig. cl.-bkd. bds. (S. Dec.3; 1065) *Old Hall.* £140
- - Anr. Copy. Cl. gt. (CE. Dec.4; 84) £110
- The Natural History of British Game Birds. 1909. Ltd. Edn. Fo. Cl. gt. (P. Nov.13; 213) *Smith.* £280
- - Anr. Copy. 4to. Slightly worn. (P. May 14; 318) *Graham.* £260
- The Natural History of the British Surface-Feeding Ducks. 1902. (600) numbered on L.P. Lge. 4to. This copy unnumbered? Cont. lev. mor., sides with 5 gt. fillets & corner-pieces & foliage sprays, spine gt. in 6 compartments, inner gt. dentelles. (C. Nov.5; 110) *Dawes.* £550

– – **Anr. Copy.** This copy unnumbered? Cl. gt. (CE. Nov.20; 22) £380
– – **Anr. Copy.** This copy unnumbered? Cl. (S. Dec.3; 1064) *Asher.* £240
– – **Anr. Copy.** Dampstained thro.-out, affecting lr. hf. of most pp. Orig. cl., dampstained. (TA. Oct.16; 212) £50
– **Newfoundland & its Untrodden Ways.** L., 1907. Orig. gt.-decor. cl. (CB. Sep.24; 250) Can. $100
– **Rhododendrons.** 1917-24. (550) numbered. Fo. Orig. cl. (CE. Nov.20; 36) £340
– – **Anr. Copy.** 1st. & 2nd. Series. Some marginal dampstaining to 2nd. vol. Cl. (TA. Mar.19; 295) £110
– – **Anr. Copy.** Vol. 1 only (of 2). Orig. cl., worn. (SH. Jan.30; 470) *Way.* £55
– **The Wildfowler in Scotland.** Ill.:– after Sir J.E. Millais. 1901. 4to. Cont. hf. cf. (SBA. Dec.16; 131a) *Petersfield Bookshop.* £80
– – **Anr. Copy.** Hf. parch. (CE. Nov.20; 33) £50

MILLAR, Alexander Hastie
– **Castles & Mansions of Renfrewshire & Buteshire.** Glasgow, 1889. Fo. Cl. (CE. Nov.20; 90) £130
– – **Anr. Copy.** Cl. gt., soiled. (CE. Dec.4; 103) £120

MILLAR, Eric George
– **English Illuminated Manuscripts from the Xth to the [XVth] Century.** Paris & Brussels, 1926-28. 2 vols. Fo. Orig. cl., soiled. (SH. Oct.9; 53) *Dawsons.* £170
– **The Library of A. Chester Beatty. A Descriptive Catalogue of the Western Manuscripts.** Oxford, 1927-30. 1st. Edn. 4 vols. Fo. Orig. cl., unc., spines faded. The John A. Saks copy. (CNY. Oct.1; 147) $600
– **The Luttrell Psalter.** 1932. Fo. Orig. cl. (SH. May 28; 217) *Talerman.* £100
– **A Thirteenth Century Bestiary in the Library of Alnwick Castle.** Oxford, Roxb. Cl., 1958. 4to. Orig. mor.-bkd. cl., partly unc. Sydney Cockerell's copy, inscr. & dtd. (C. Jul.22; 41) *Traylen.* £370

MILLAR, George Henry
– **The New & Universal System of Geography.** Ill.:– after T. Kitchin & others. [1782]. 2 vols. Fo. Some tears & other defects. Cont. cf., worn. As an atlas, w.a.f. (SBA. May 27; 302) *Hyde Park Bookshop.* £320

MILLAR, John
– **Observations concerning the distinction of Ranks in Society.** 1771. 4to. Cf. (P. Dec.11; 168) *Brook-Hitchin.* £150

MILLARD, Christopher Sclater 'Stuart Mason'
See–WILDE, Oscar–MILLARD, Christopher Sclater 'Stuart Mason'

MILLAY, Edna St. Vincent 'Nancy Boyd'
– **The Ballad of the Harp-Weaver.** N.Y., 1922. 1st. Edn. 4to. Orig. wraps., hf. mor. s.-c. (SG. Nov.13; 485) $120
– **Conversations at Midnight.** N.Y., 1937. 1st. Edn., on L.P., (579) numbered on Worthy Charta paper, sigd. 4to. Qtr. cl., unopened, glassine wrap., boxed. (PNY. Dec.3; 242) $100
– **Fatal Interview.** N.Y., 1931. 1st. Edn., (36) numbered on Japan vell., sigd. Bds., vell. back & tips, tissue wrap., boxed. (PNY. Dec.3; 243) $130
– **Invocation to the Muses.** N.Y., 1941. 1st. Edn., (60) numbered. 4to. Orig. ptd. wraps., sewed, mint in orig. 4-way cl. folding case. (PNY. Dec.3; 248) $120
– **The King's Henchman.** Ill.:– Harry Cimino. N.Y., 1927. (26) on Shidzuoka Imperial Japan vell., sigd. Sigd. artist's proof on Japanese tissue or orig. woodcut. Linen-bkd. patterned bds., boxed. (SG. Jun.4; 376) $260
– – **Anr. Edn.** N.Y., 1927. Artist's Edn. (500) numbered, & sigd. Tall 8vo. Linen-bkd. bds., linen tips, unc. & unopened. (SG. Nov.13; 486) $110
– **The Murder of Lidice.** N.Y., 1942. 1st. Edn. 12mo. Wraps. Sigd. (SG. Jun.4; 380) $100

MILLER, Alfred
[–] **Fishless Days.** Ill.:– Charles De Feo. N.Y., Priv. ptd., 1954. 1st. Edn., (591). Cl. Pres. copy. (SG. Oct.16; 218) $160

MILLER, C.C.
See–CUMMINGS, M.F. & Miller, C.C.

MILLER, Frances Trevelyn
– **The World in the Air: The Story of Flying in Pictures.** N.Y., 1930. 1st. Edn., (500) numbered on Ragleaf paper, sigd. by author, publisher & 7 aviation pioneers. 2 vols. 4to. Plain & dyed bds., slightly soiled. (PNY. Dec.3; 1) $150

MILLER, Henry
– **Aller Retour New York.** Paris, [1935]. 1st. Edn. (150) on thin paper, sigd. Orig. ptd. wraps. (SPB. Nov.25; 358) $550
– **Black Spring.** Paris, [1936]. 1st. Edn. 4to. Partly unopened. Orig. ptd. wraps., worn. Pres. copy. (SPB. Nov.25; 359) $500
– **Book of Friends.** Santa Barbara, Capra Pr., 1976. (250) specially bnd., sigd., with orig. sigd. pen & ink drawing on H.M. MBM. paper. Mor., boxed. (SG. Jun.4; 384) $140
– **Insomnia.** [Garden City], [1974]. (150) numbered, with orig. litho., ptd. on H.M. Japanese Paper, & sigd & dtd. 4to. 'Morrocan' leath., s.-c. (SG. Oct.23; 222) $160
– **Max & the White Phagocytes.** Paris, Obelisk Pr., 1938. 1st. Edn. Orig. wraps., worn. Pres. copy. (S. Jul.22; 227) *House of Books.* £120
– – **Anr. Edn.** Paris, [1938]. 1st. Edn. Slight browning. Orig. ptd. wraps., slight discolouration. Pres. copy. (SPB. Nov.25; 360) $300
– **Money & How It Gets that Way.** Paris, [1938]. 1st. Edn. Square 12mo. Browned slightly, slight stain. Orig. ptd. wraps. Pres. copy, inscr. by author. (SPB. Nov.25; 361) $225
– **Scenario.** Paris, Obelisk Pr., 1937. 1st. Edn., (200) numbered, sigd. Orig. wraps. (S. Jul.22; 226) *House of Books.* £230
– **Sunday After the War.** Norfolk, New Directions, 1944. 1st. Edn. Orig. cl. Pres. copy to George Woodcock. (S. Jul.22; 230) *House of Books.* £75
– **Tropic of Cancer.** Paris, [1934]. 1st. Edn. Orig. pict. wraps., slip attached to upr. cover. (SPB. Nov.25; 355) $4,100
– – **Anr. Edn.** Paris, Obelisk Pr., [1934]. Sm. 4to. Pict. wraps., upr. wrap. detchd. Inscr. to George Reavey. (SG. Jun.4; 382) $550
– **Tropic of Capricorn.** Paris, Obelisk Pr., 1939. 1st. Edn. Errata slip tipped on to title, name on title. Orig. wraps., unc. (S. Jul.22; 229) *Marks.* £155
– – **Anr. Copy.** Sq. 8vo. Yellow errata slip tipped-in. Pict. wraps., unc. & mostly unopened. (SG. Nov.13; 491) $425
– – **Anr. Copy.** Tipped-in errata list. (SG. Jun.4; 383) $160
– **Tropic of Capricorn.–Tropic of Cancer.** Paris, 1939. 1st. work 1st. Edn., 2nd. work 5th. printing. 2 vols. 1st. work with errata slip tipped-in. Loose in orig. wraps. (PNY. Mar.26; 212) $100
See–DURRELL, Lawrence & Miller, Henry

MILLER, Hugh
– **Miscellaneous Works.** Edinb., n.d. 12 vols. Hf. cf., worn. (PD. Feb.18; 162) £50

MILLER, John
– **Illustratio Systematis Sexualis Linnaei . . .** Priv. Ptd., 1777. 1st. Edn. Lge. fo. 212 engraved plts., including 4 hand-cold. plts. of leaves & 104 plts. in 2 states, 1 state hand-cold. before all letters, frontis. & 3 plts. dampstained. 19th. C. hf. mor. From Chetham's Liby., Manchester. (C. Nov.27; 300) *Fletcher.* £5,500
– **An Illustration of the Sexual System of Linnaeus.** L., Priv. Ptd., 1779-1789. 2 vols. Most plts. full or partly hand-cold., lacks final text lf?. Cont. hf. cf. W.a.f. (SBA. Jul.22; 107) *Libris.* £250
– – **Anr. Copy.** Cont. hf. cf., slightly worn, unc. (VG. Oct.13; 107) Fls. 1,300

MILLER, Philip
– **Catalogus Plantaru Officinalium quae in Horto Botanico Chelseyano aluntur.** 1730. 1st. Edn. Frontis. detchd., slight stains. Cont. cf., covers detchd. From Chetham's Liby., Manchester. (C. Nov.27; 301) *Wheldon & Wesley.* £150
– **Dictionnaire des Jardiniers . . .** Paris, 1787. 10 vols. 4to. Includes 2 vols. of supps. by M. de Chazelles. Cont. cf. (HD. Jun.29; 267) Frs. 4,300
– **Figures of the . . . Plants described in the Gardeners Dictionary.** 1760. Vol. 1 only. Fo. About 120 engraved plts. only, soiling, spotting. Disbnd. W.a.f. (CSK. Mar.6; 158) £120
– **Gardeners Dictionary . . .** 1733. 2nd. Edn. Fo. Some ll. slightly dampstained. Cont. diced cf., rebkd. using old spine. (S.May 5; 129) *Crete.* £80
– – **Anr. Copy.** 1 plt. detchd., some cont. MS. notats. & corrections. Cont. panel. cf., jnts. worn. (CSK. Nov.7; 22) £50
– – **Anr. Edn.** 1743-40. 2 vols. Fo. Sm. wormhole in vol. 1. Mod. cf. (SH. Jan.30; 382) *Jubilee Books.* £65

– – **Anr. Edn.** 1743. 2 vols. in 1. Fo. Mod. hf. cf. (P. Apr.30; 244) *Park.* £50
– **The Gardener's & Botanist's Dictionary . . .** Ed.:– Thomas Martyn. L., [1795]-1807. 1st. Edn. 2 vols. in 4. Fo. A few pp. lightly browned, plts. with slight foxing. Cont. reversed cf. (CNY. Oct.1; 145) $380
– – **Anr. Edn.** Ed.:– Thomas Martyn. 1807. 2 vols. in 4. Fo. Cont. cf., rebkd. with orig. spines preserved. (S. Oct.1; 593) £260

MILLER, Thomas
– **Common Wayside Flowers.** Ill.:– Edmund Evans after Birket Foster. L., 1860. 4to. Elab. gt.-pict. cl., cold. floral designs in corners of both covers, spine gt. (SG. Mar.19; 200) $180

MILLER, William
– **The Costume of Turkey.** 1802. Fo. Engl. & Fr. text, some foxing. Cont. mor., worn. Bkplt. of Countess of Macclesfield. (CE. Jul.9; 208) £240

MILLES, Thomas
[–] **Archaio-Ploytoe.** 1619. Fo. Engraved title preserved, contents lf. reprd. & tipped in. Panel. cf., rebkd. old spine preserved. [STC 17936.5] (CSK. Jan.9; 191) £55
– **The Catalogue of Honor.** 1610. L.P. Fo. Cancel slip removed from 3S4 leaving hole, cont. marginal MS. annots. Cont. panel. cf., gt. roll-tooled fillet surrounding gt. arms of Henry Prince of Wales with initials HP, plumes as cornerpieces surrounded by elaborate gt. flourishes, spine in 7 compartments, each tooled with a lion passant & stars, rebkd., orig. spine preserved. Bkplt. of J.R. Abbey, lately in the collection of Eric Sexton. [STC 17926] (C. Apr.15; 184) *Maggs.* £4,000

MILLIET DE CHALES, Claude Francois
– **Cursus seu Mundus Mathematicus.** Lyons, 1674. 1st. Edn. 3 vols. Fo. Browning & foxing, some ll. with minor worming & tears to margins, scattered light dampstaining. Cont. vell., old rebacking. (CNY. Oct.1; 18) $250

MILLIN de Grandmaison, Aubin Louis
– **Antiquités Nationales . . .** Ill.:– Aubry, Masquelier & others. Paris, 1790-98. L.P. 5 vols. Fo. Minimal browning. Old marb. cf., gt. Chaînette border, decor. spine raised bands, some sm. defects. (HD. Apr.24; 82) Frs. 5,000
[–] **La Mythologie mise à la Portée de tout le Monde.** Ill.:– Mixelle. Paris, 7th. Year [1799]. 12 vols. 16mo. Cont. colouring. Cont. marb. cf., decor. spines, gt. roulette inner dentelle. (HD. Apr.9; 525) Frs. 3,900
– **Peinturs de Vases Antiques.** Paris, 1808-10. Minor spotting to titles & a few ll. Cont. hf. mor., gt., partly unc. (C. Feb.25; 189) *Hamilton.* £1,200

MILLINGEN, James
– **Peintures antiques de Vases Grecs de la Collection de Sir John Goghill.** Rome, 1817. Lge. fo. Nail-hole partly reprd. through last few plts. 19th. C. red mor., by J. Clarke, gt. ornamental borders, partly unc. (S. Jun.22; 63) *Duran.* £160

MILLINGEN, John Gideon
– **The History of Duelling.** L., 1841. 1st. Edn. 2 vols. Extra-ill. with 80 ports. Maroon three-qtr. crushed lev., raised bands, by L. Broca. (SG. Feb.26; 230) $110

MILLOT, Claude François Xavier, Abbé
– **Tableaux de l'Histoire Romaine.** Ill.:– Tardieu, Gaucher & others after author. Paris, 1796. Fo. Cont. red str.-grd. mor., gt., gt. monog. in shield on sides. Château du Tremblay plt. (SM. Oct.8; 2412) Frs. 3,500

MILLOT
– **L'Ecole des Filles.** Liège, ca. 1680. 16mo. 36 figures of 37. Hf. roan, ca. 1820. (HD. Apr.10; 350) Frs. 5,000

MILLS, Alfred
– **Costumes of Different Nations, in Miniature.** 1811. 1st. Edn. 61 X 54 mm. Orig. red roan, new endpapers. (SH. Dec.12; 556) *Schierenberg.* £65
– **Pictures of English History in Miniature.**
– **Pictures of Grecian History in Miniature.** L., n.d. 3 vols. 2¾ X 2⁷⁄₁₆ inches. Blind-stpd. cl. (SG. Sep.4; 331) $250
– **Pictures of Grecian History in Miniature.** 1810. 1st. Edn. 60 X 55mm. Orig. red roan. Miniature Book. (SH. Dec.12; 554) *Gregory.* £55

MILLS, John
- The Flyers of the Hunt.–The Life of a Racehorse.
–Stable Secrets. Ill.:– John Leech (1st. work).
1859; 1861; 1863. 3 vols. 2nd. work: 1 margin
slightly torn; 3rd. work; slightly spotted. Unif. cf.
gt. by Rivière, orig. cl. upr. covers bnd. in. (SBA.
Dec.16; 132) *Hindley.* £80

MILMAN, Rev. H.H.
[–] History of the Jews. L., 1829. 3 vols. Cont. red
long-grd. mor., gt. 3 orig. fore-edge paintings: the
river at Bastow, Watton Bridge on the Thames,
Stoke-Poges. (VG. Oct.13; 63) *Fls.* 800

MILNE, Alan Alexander
- By Way of Introduction. N.Y., [1929]. (166)
numbered, sigd. Cl.-bkd. patterned bds.,
unopened, partly unc., box. (SG. Sep.4; 325)
$110
- A Gallery of Children. Ill.:– H. Willebeck le
Mair. [1925]. (500) numbered, on L.P., sigd. Fo.
Orig. cl. gt., dampstained. (SH. Dec.11; 355)
Joseph. £100
– – Anr. Copy. Fo. Gt. pict. buckram, hf. mor.
s.-c., partly unc. (SG. Apr.30; 221) $425
– – Anr. Edn. Ill.:– H. Willebeek Le Mair. L., n.d.
(500) sigd. 4to. Orig. cl. gt., slight wear. (SPB.
May 29; 303) $300
- The House at Pooh Corner. Ill.:– Ernest Howard
Shepard. 1928. 1st. Edn., (350) numbered, sigd.
by author & artist. 4to. Orig. buckram-bkd. bds.,
soiled & worn, unc. (SH. Dec.11; 357)
Mirdan. £80
- The Hums of Pooh. Ill.:– Ernest Howard
Shepard. 1929. 1st. Edn., (100). Fo. Orig. cl.-bkd.
bds., stained & worn. Sigd. by author, composer
& artist. (SH. Dec.11; 360) *Drizen.* £110
- The King's Breakfast [with] Music by H.
Fraser-Simson. Ill.:– E.H. Shepard. L., [1925].
(500) numbered, & sigd. by author, artist &
composer. Fo. Buckram-bkd. bds., hf. mor. s.-c.,
unc. (SG. Apr.30; 222) $210
- Toad of Toad Hall. L., 1929. (200) on H.M.P.,
sigd. by Milne & Kenneth Grahame. 4to. Cl.-bkd.
bds., unopened & unc., d.-w. (C. Jul.22; 24)
Maggs. £260
– – Anr. Copy. Orig. cl.-bkd. bds., spine slightly
faded, lr. portion of bds. soiled. (SPB. May
29; 302) $325
– – Anr. Edn. L., [1929]. (200) numbered on
H.M.P., & sigd. by Milne & Grahame. Sq. 8vo.
Buckram-bkd. bds. (with extra label tipped in at
end), d.-w., hf. mor. s.-c., unc. (SG. Apr.30; 223)
$375
- When We Were Very Young. Ill.:– E.H. Shepard
1924. 1st. Edn. Orig. cl., d.-w. (S. Mar.16; 221)
Cummins. £120
– – Anr. Edn. Ill.:– E.H. Shepard. N.Y., 1930.
(842) numbered, & sigd. Tall 8vo. Patt. cl. (SG.
Nov.13; 506) $100
- When We Were Very Young.–Winnie-the-Pooh.
–Now We Are Six.–The House at Pooh Corner.
Ill.:– Ernest Howard Shepard. 1924; 1926; 1927;
1928. 1st. Edns. 4 vols. Orig. cl. gt., last with
damp blister, d.-w.'s, worn. (SH. Dec.11; 354)
Gerrard. £250
– – Anr. Copy. Gt.-pict. cl., d.-w.'s., maroon hf.
mor. s.-c. (SG. May 14; 148) $1,600
– – Anr. Copy. 1st. work sigd. by Milne, & with
postcard photograph laid in (also sigd.), bkplt. of
Paul Hyde Bonner in 1st. work. (SG. Apr.30; 224)
$1,300
– – Anr. Copy. All orig. cl. gt., covers of 1st. works
slightly spotted, all but 3rd. work in pict. d.-w.,
qtr. rose mor. gt. s.-c. From the Prescott
Collection. (CNY. Feb.6; 255) $700
– – Anr. Copy. Gt.-pict. cl., all but last in d.-w.
(slightly frayed). Laid into last work in
photograph captioned 'A.A. Milne with
Christopher Robin & 'Tishy'.'. (SG. Nov.13; 503)
$500
- Winnie the Pooh. Ill.:– E.H. Shepard 1926. 1st.
Edn. Orig. decor. leath. (S. Mar.16; 222)
Fletcher. £80
- Winnie the Pooh.–The House at Pooh Corner.
Ill.:– E.H. Shepard. L., 1926; 1928. Each (200)
sigd. by author & artist. 2 works in 2 vols. 4to.
Both orig. cl.-bkd. bds., spines faded, slight
browning to end-papers, 2nd. work very crudely
opened. (SPB. May 29; 301) $450

MILNE, Samuel Milne
- The Standards & Colours of the Army. Leeds,
1893. (200) numbered inscr. by author. Orig. cl.
gt. (SKC. Feb.26; 1460) £65

MILNE-EDWARDS, Alphonse
See–GRANDIDIER, Alfred & Milne-Edwards,
Alphonse

MILNER, Henry Ernest
- The Art & Practice of Landscape Gardening.
1890. 4to. Orig. cl., partly untrimmed, recased.
(TA. Jun.18; 36) £50

MILNOR, William
[–] An Authentic Historical Memoir of the
Schuylkill Fishing Company of the State in
Schuylkill. Phila., 1830. 1st. Edn. Hf. mor. [Sabin
49133] (SPB. Jun.22; 103) $300

MILTON, John
- Areopagitica. Ill.:– Lucien Pissarro. Eragny Pr.,
1903. (200). 4to. Orig. bds., worn, unc. (SH.
Feb.19; 35) *Ayres.* £75
– – Anr. Edn. Ill.:– Lucien & Esther Pissarro. L.,
Eragny Pr., 1904. (160). 4to. Bds. (SG.
Apr.9; 435) $160
– – Anr. Edn. Hammersmith, Doves Pr., 1907.
(25) on vell. Sm. 4to. Orig. vell., unc., qtr. mor.
s.-c. (CNY. May 22; 383) $1,300
– – Anr. Edn. Doves Pr. 1907. (300). Orig. limp
vell., unc. Bkplt. of J.W.R. Brocklebank. (SH.
Feb.19; 40) *Thomas.* £110
- Comus. Ill.:– Arthur Rackham. [1921]. 1st.
Trade Edn. 4to. Orig. cl. gt. (SH. Mar.27; 437)
Razzall. £55
– – Anr. Edn. Ill.:– Arthur Rackham. L. & N.Y.,
[1921]. (550) numbered, sigd. by artist. 4to. Orig.
parch.-bkd. bds., a little soiled. (CSK. Nov.7; 177)
£140
– – Anr. Copy. Vell.-bkd. vell.-style bds. Raymond
M. Sutton Jr. copy. (SG. May 7; 209) $650
– – Anr. Copy. Partly unc. (SG. Oct.23; 287)
$450
– – Anr. Edn. Ill.:– Arthur Rackham. N.Y.,
[1921]. 1st. Amer. Trade Edn. 4to. Gt.-pict. cl.,
d.-w. reprd. Raymond M. Sutton Jr. copy. (SG.
May 7; 210) $100
– – Anr. Edn. Ill.:– Arthur Rackham. N.d. Ltd.
Edn. sigd. by artist. Orig. vell.-bkd. bds. Ink
drawing sigd. by artist dtd. 6.12.21. on hf.-title.
(P. Dec.11; 215) *Lawson.* £200
– – Anr. Edn. Ill.:– Edmund Dulac. Camb.,
Heritage Pr., n.d. Orig. buckram-bkd. bds., s.-c.
(SH. Mar.26; 174) *Palmer.* £55
- Early Poems. Ill.:– Charles Ricketts. [Vale Pr.],
[1896]. (310). 4to. Orig. buckram, covers slightly
stained. (CSK. May 15; 98) £85
– – Anr. Copy. Cl. (SG. Sep.4; 449) $175
[–] Eikonklastes. 1649. 1st. Edn. 4to. Printer's
MS. corrections, title detchd., 1 cont. note. Cont.
cf. [Wing M2112] (C. Nov.20; 212) *Terry.* £130
- Four Poems. Blair Hughes-Stanton. Gregy. Pr.
1933. (250) numbered. Orig. smooth mor. (TA.
May 21; 380) £130
- The History of Britain, that part especially called
England . . . 1670. 1st. Edn. 4to. Title-p. slightly
dust soiled, some fingering thro.-out. Cf., worn,
upr. cover loose. (PD. Apr.1; 72) £120
– – Anr. Copy. 1st. Iss. Slight browning &
spotting. Old cf., rebkd. (SPB. Jul.28; 369) $350
- Justa Edovardo King naufrago, ab Amicis
Moerentibus, Amoris. Camb., 1638. 1st. Edn. of
'Lycidas'. 4to. The mispaginations 31 & 32
corrected in early ink, slight spotting to some ll.
Disbnd., laid in velvet-lined mor. gt. case. From
the Prescott Collection. [STC 14964] (CNY.
Feb.6; 256) $33,000
- Lycidas. Ill.:– Philip Evergood. N.Y., 1929. 1st.
Edn. (60) numbered. Sm. fo. Gt.-stpd. two-tone
bds. (PNY. Mar.26; 215) $160
- Le Paradis Perdu. Ill.:– after M. Schall. Paris,
1792. 2 vols. Lge. 4to. Text in Engl. & Fr., some
staining. 19th. C. hf. red mor. (SPB. May 6; 227)
$325
– – Anr. Copy. Fo. Text in Engl. & Fr., 9 (of 12)
cold engrs., vol 1, pp. 179/180 sm. tear, vol. 2
endpaper lacks lower corner. Cont. red mor., gt.
spine, inner & outer dentelle, 2 sm. stains. (HK.
Nov.18-21; 2365) DM 1,600
- Paradise Lost. 1668. [1st. Edn.] [4th. Title].
Sm. 4to. Slight mark on title, a few ll. lightly
damp-stained. Old cf., mor. s.-c. by Rivière.
(SKC. Jul.28; 2360) £1,700
– – Anr. Edn. 1669. 1st. Edn. 4to. 6th. state of
title, fore-corners of title reprd. affecting rule
borders, several ll. with similar repairs, slight
browning. Mor., gt., by Rivière, upr. cover detchd.
[Wing M2143] (S. Feb.10; 398) *Swales.* £380
– – Anr. Copy. 18th. C. cf., Ralph Sneyd's emblem
on covers. (S. Nov.25; 455) *Thorp.* £360

– – Anr. Copy. 5th. state of title, paper repairs to
F4, 2C3, lacks 1st. blank. Cf., rebkd., worn. (SPB.
Nov.25; 78) $700
– – Anr. Edn. 1674. 2nd. Edn. Lacks last blank lf.
Later cf. [Wing M2144] (SH. Jan.30; 350)
Jarndyce. £190
– – Anr. Edn. 1688. 4th. (1st. Ill.) Edn. L.P. Fo.
With subscribers' list at end. Cont. panel. red
mor., gt. spine. [Wing M2146] (C. Nov.19; 16)
Maggs. £2,400
– – Anr. Copy. L.P. Sm. wormholes in outer blank
margins, dampstaining to upr. corner of frontis.,
title & several ll. Cont. blind-panel. mott. cf.,
rebkd. From the collection of Eric Sexton. [Wing
M2147] (C. Apr.15; 118) *Quaritch.* £190
– – Anr. Copy. Some soiling, 1 plt. cropped. Cont.
cf., head of spine defect. (S. Dec.9; 335)
Thorp. £130
– – Anr. Copy. Lacks plt. for book 9, considerably
soiled & stained thro.-out. Old cf., worn, rebkd.
(SG. Feb.5; 240) $425
– – Anr. Edn. 1794. 4to. Red str.-grd. mor. gt. by
C. Hering, with his ticket. Bkplt. of George
Gostling. (S. Nov.24; 212) *Quaritch.* £240
– – Anr. Edn. Ill.:– John Martin. 1827. 2 vols. 4to.
Spotted, 1st. gathering of vol. I loose. Cont.
blind-tooled red mor. (S. Jul.31; 250)
Joseph. £220
– – Anr. Copy. Some dampstains & soiling Cont.
mor. gt., worn, upr. hinge brkn. (CE. Jun.4; 187)
£90
– – Anr. Edn. Ill.:– John Martin. 1833. 4to.
Spotted. Cont. mor. (CSK. Feb.6; 149) £75
– – Anr. Edn. Ill.:– John Martin. 1838. Fo. Margins
browned. Orig. blind-stpd. cl., spine defect. (TA.
Nov.20; 99) £120
– – Anr. Edn. Ill.:– John Martin. 1846. Fo. 23 (of
24) plts., 20 marked 'proof'. Later hf. mor. (SH.
Mar.27; 335) *Joseph.* £210
– – Anr. Edn. Ill.:– John Martin. 1858. 4to. Sm.
tear to title. Orig. embossed cl., new end-papers.
(C. Jul.22; 82) *Fine Art Society.* £260
– – Anr. Edn. Ill.:– John Martin. 1866. Fo. Cont.
hf. mor. (SH. Mar.27; 336) *Joseph.* £240
– – Anr. Edn. Ed.:– Robert Vaughan. Ill.:–
Gustave Dore. L., ca. 1900. Fo. With 8 p.
catalogue at end. Red three-qtr. mor., bkplt. (SG.
Dec.18; 168) $190
– – Anr. Edn. Hammersmith, Doves Pr. 1902.
(300). Vell. (PNY. Dec.3; 122) $375
– – Anr. Edn. Ill.:– after William Blake. L'Pool.,
1906. 4to. Cl.-bkd. bds., unc. (SBA. Jul.23; 337)
Subun-so. £65
– – Anr. Copy. Slightly spotted. Orig. cl.-bkd.
bds., label slightly stained & torn. (SBA.
Oct.21; 201) *Kawamatsu.* £55
– – Anr. Edn. Ill.:– Mary Groom. Gold. Cock. Pr.
1937. (200) numbered. Fo. Orig. hf. pig. by
Zaehnsdorf, s.-c. rubbed. (CSK. Jan.30; 148)
£240
- Paradise Lost; Paradise Perdu. Trans.:– Jacques
Delille. Ill.:– after Monsiau (frontis.). Paris, 1805.
L.P. 3 vols. Cont. hf. cf., brkn., unc. (SG.
Dec.18; 301) $100
- Paradise Lost.–Paradise Regained. Ill.:– Edward
Johnston & Graily Hewitt (2nd. vol.). Doves Pr.,
1902-05. Each (300). 2 vols. 4to. Orig. limp vell.,
unc. (S. Jul.31; 58) *Foyles.* £330
– – Anr. Copy. Orig. vell. (SPB. Nov.25; 256)
$800
- Paradise Lost . . .–Paradise Regain'd . . . to
which is added Samson Agonistes. 1688; 1688. 4th.
Edn.; 3rd Edn. 2 works in 1. Fo. Later mor. gt.,
Cremorne bkplt. [Wing M2146; 2154] (SBA.
Oct.21; 67) *Quaritch.* £400
– – Anr. Copy. 1st. work: a few marginal stains;
2nd. work: slight browning. Modern hf. cf., 1 jnt.
brkn., spine worn. [Wing M2147; Wing M2154]
(S. May 5; 335) *Traylen.* £160
- Paradise Lost.–Paradise Regain'd to which is
added Samson Agonistes, & Poems upon Several
Occasions. Birmingham, 1758. 2 vols. Mor.,
gt. borders, spines & dentelles, by C. Wright. (SG.
May 14; 149) $450
– – Anr. Edn. Hammersmith, Doves Pr., 1902;
1905. (25) on vell. Together 2 vols. 1st. work with
some blue initials. 1st. work, lev. mor., double
gt.-ruled borders, spine in 6 compartments with 5
raised bands, gt. patterned, by Frieda Thiersch,
2nd. work, niger mor., gt.-ruled border, spine with
6 compartments, 5 raised bands, all gt. panel.,
sigd. 'Doves Bindery 19 C-S 19', qtr. mor. s.-c.'s.
(CNY. May 22; 376) $5,000
- Paradise Regained . . . to which is added Samson
Agonistes. 1671. 1st. Edn. Some minor rust-holes,

soiled & stained, early name on license lf. Cont. cf., brkn. [Wing M2152] (S. Jul.27; 86) *Sotheran.* £150

– Paradise Regain'd ... to which is added Samson Agonistes & Poems upon Several Occasions. Bg'ham., 1758. 4to. ?Lacks hf.-title, with cancel ll. Cont. cf., gt.-tooled with wide border on sides, lozenge-shaped centre-piece of sm. tools, spine similarly tooled. (S. Jan.26; 138) *Jones.* £50

– – **Anr. Edn.** Hammersmith, Doves Pr. 1905. (300). 4to. Vell. (PNY. Dec.3; 123) $375

– – **Anr. Copy.** Orig. limp vell., unc. (CNY. May 22; 301) $280

– Il Paradiso Perduto. Trans.:– Paolo Rolli. Ill.:– F. Zucci after Tiepolo, Piazzetta & others. Parigi [i.e. Verona], 1740. 2 vols. 12mo. Orig. spr. paper wraps., spine of vol. I slightly chipped. From the collection of John A. Saks. (C. Jun.10; 163) *Quaritch.* £550

– – **Anr. Edn.** Ill.:– after Piazzetta, Tieplolo, Cignaroli, & others. Parigi [i.e. Verona], 1742. Fo. Hf. cf. From the collection of John A. Saks. (C. Jun.10; 164) *Pompelmo.* £350

– Poems. 1673. 2nd. Edn. 5 pp. advts. at end. Mod. red mor. (SH. Oct.10; 383) *Bennett.* £170

– Poems, &c. upon Several Occasions ... with a Small Tractate of Education to Mr. Hartlib. 1673. 2nd. Edn., 2nd. state. Advt. ll., sm., neat repair to title & blank margin of Ll, sm. piece torn from lr. corner of section-title, Huntington dispersal stp. Red mor., gt., by Rivière. Bkplts. of Charles B. Foote & Beverly Chew (member of the Grolier Club). [Wing M2161] (S. May 5; 321) *Quaritch.* £150

– Poems in English. Ill.:– William Blake. Nones. Pr., 1926. (90) on india paper. 2 vols. in 1. Orig. parch., unc. (SH. Feb.19; 124) *Henderson.* £100

– – **Anr. Copy.** (1450) numbered. Vell., unc. Kenneth Rae's bkplt. by R. Whistler. (P. Jul.30; 202) *Thompson.* £75

– – **Anr. Copy.** 2 vols. Ptd. paper bds., vell. spine. (HSS. Apr.24; 24) £55

– – **Anr. Copy.** Vell.-bkd. patterned bds., unc. (SG. Jan.15; 63) $130

– The Shorter Poems. Ill.:– Samuel Palmer. 1889. (135) numbered on L.P. Fo. Orig. vell. gt., slightly soiled, unc. (SBA. May 27; 491) *Temperley.* £130

– – **Anr. Copy.** Orig. cl. gt., unopened & unc. (C. Jul.22; 91) *Joseph.* £100

– – **Anr. Copy.** Unc., partly unopened. (SH. Mar.27; 394) *Triggs.* £50

– – **Anr. Copy.** (135) numbered on L-P. Fo. Gt.-decor. vell., unc. (SG. May 14; 163) $425

– Works. 1697. 1st. Coll. Edn. Fo. Cont. cf., rebkd. [Wing M2086] (S. Nov.25; 466) *Armstrong.* £95

– The Works ... in Verse & Prose ... Ed.:– Rev. John Mitford. 1851. 8 vols. Cont. mor. gt. by G. Winstanley, Manchester. (TA. Jun.18; 221) £52

– The Poetical Works. 1854. Later mor., tooled in gt., by E.I.W. dated 1903. Fore.-e. pntg. (CSK. Sep.12; 128) £55

– Works. L., 1867. 8 vols. Slight staining. Cf. gt. by Sotheran, staining on lr. portion of a few vols. (SPB. Nov.25; 477) $125

– Poetical Works. Ill.:– William Hyde. Guildford, Astolat Pr., 1904. 4to. Mor. gt., wide border of linked line-tooling, cornerpieces of foliate tools, lge. centrepieces of similar tools & mor. onlays, spine compartments similarly decor., inr. borders gt., line-tooling on edges of covers. (SH. Feb.20; 372) *Quaritch.* £600

MILTON, Thomas & others
– The Chimney-Piece-Makers Daily Assistant ... 1766. 1st. Edn. 2 advt. ll. at end, some browning, soiled. Cont. cf., worn, upr. cover stained black. (S. Sep.29; 247) *Weinreb.* £300

– – **Anr. Copy.** 19th. C. hf. cf., rebkd. (S. Mar.17; 437) *W. Clements Liby.* £280

MINADOI, Giovanni Tommaso
– Historia della Guerra fra Turchi et Persiana. Venice, 1594. 4to. Single wormhole through title & some early ll. affecting some letters, several ll. stained at head. Cont. vell. bds., soiled, defect at head of spine. Dupl. stp. of the Folger Liby. at end. (S. Feb.10; 270) *Diba.* £150

MINARD VAN HOOREBEKE, I.
– Description de Méreaux et autres Objets Anciens des Gildes et Corps de Métiers, Eglises. Gand, 1877. 2 vols. 4to. Fr. & Dutch text parallel.

Sewed, spine brkn. (LM. Mar.21; 236) B.Frs. 12,000

MINER, Harriet Stewart
– Orchids. 1885. 4to. Orig. cl., soiled. (P. Oct.2; 304) *Hatchards.* £70

– – **Anr. Copy.** Fo. Plts. offset onto text. Orig. pict. cl., rebkd. & jnts. strengthened, with orig. backstrip preserved. From the Prescott Collection. (CNY. Feb.6; 257) $280

– The Royal Family of Plants. Boston, 1885. 1st. Amer. Edn. Fo. Loose in separated wraps., gt.-pict. cl. box, brkn. (PNY. Oct.1; 413) $180

MINERALOGISCHE BELUSTIGUNGEN zum Behuf der Chymie und Naturgeschichte des Mineralreichs
Ed.:– [Chr. Adelung]. Leipzig, 1768-71. Cont. hf. leath. (D. Dec.11-13; 247) DM 1,320

MINEROPHILUS [Pseud.]
– Neues und wohleingerichtetes Mineral-und Bergwercks-Lexicon. Chemnitz, 1743. 2nd. Edn. Slightly browned. Cont. hf. leath., gt. spine. (R. Oct.14-18; 233) DM 900

MINGAUD, Capt. M.
– The Noble Game of Billiards. Trans.:– J. Thurston. 1833. 4to. Engraved advt. for Thurston Billiards Tables bnd. in at end. Hf. roan. A.L.s. from translator inserted. (P. May 14; 226) *Nathan.* £60

MINHAGIM Buch
Amst., 1707. Sm. 4to. Hole to margin of 1 lf., browning, repairs, staining. Leath.-bkd. bds. (SPB. May 11; 236) $550

MINKOWSKI, H.
– Die Grundgleichungen für die Elektromagnetischen Vorgänge in bewegten Körpern. Göttingen, 1908. 1st. Edn. Orig. wraps. (HK. Nov.18-21; 657) DM 700
See–LORENTZ, Hendrik Antoon, Einstein, A. & Minkowski, H.

MINNTOLI, Alexander Freiherrn von
– Der Dom Zu Diontheim und die Mittelalterliche Christliche Baukunst der Scandinavischen Normannen. Berlin, 1853. Fo. Occasional slight spotting. Orig. cl.-bkd. bds., spine torn. (CSK. Nov.28; 34) £60

MINOTAURE
Ill.:– Breton, Dali, Eluard, Man Ray & others. Paris, 1933. Nos. 3/4. 4to. Hf. mor., orig. wraps. bnd. in, cover design by Andre Derain. (SH. Nov.21; 422) *Grob.* £50

– – **Anr. Edn.** Ill.:– Man Ray & others. [Paris], [1933-39]. Numbers 1-7 & 10-13, together 11 numbers in 9 vols. as iss., all publd. 4to. Orig. cold. pict. wraps. designed by Ernst, et al. (PNY. Mar.4; 190) $1,150

– – **Anr. Edn.** Paris, 1937-39. Nos. 10, 11, & 12/13, together 3 vols. 4to. Cold. pict. wraps., by Magritte, Ernst, Masson & Rivera. (SG. Apr.2; 197) $450

MINSHEU, John
– Ductor in Linguas, the Guide into Tongues ... 1617. 1st. Edn. Fo. Subscriber's list in 7th. state. Cont. reversed cf., arms of Charles I gt.-stpd. on covers, rebkd., corners reprd. From the collection of Eric Sexton. [STC 17944 & 17944a] (C. Apr.15; 120) *Lake.* £60

– Ductor in Linguas, the Guide into Tongues ... –Vocabularium Hispanico Lantinium ... 1617. 1st. Edn. 2 works in 1 vol. 1st. work with STC's variant 9 of subscriber's list. Cont. cf., rebkd., extremities of spine worn. From the collection of Eric Sexton. [STC 17944; 17944a & 17949] (C. Apr.15; 119) *Morton-Smith.* £75

– Hegemon eis tas Glossus. 1617. 1st. Edn. 2 pts. in 1 vol. Fo. 2 ll. remargined, not affecting text, some other minor repairs, slightly cropped, some browning, orig. price written on title. Mod. mor., new end-papers. Cont. sig. of Richard Wynne, later sig. of Edward Mompesson, woodcut bkplt. of Edward Monckton. (LC. Feb.12; 539) £100

MINTON, Hollins & Co ... Manufacturers of Encaustic, Venetian, & Plain Tiles
– Pattern Book. Ill.:– Leighton Brothers. N.d. Fo. Each plt. with stp. of 'William Hawley Tile Layer', some slightly soiled. Orig. mor.-bkd. wraps., soiled, backstrip torn with slight loss. W.a.f. (CSK. Jul.10; 70) £200

MIRABAUD
– Système de la Nature. [Amst.?], 1771. New Edn. 2 vols. Cont. vell., gt. spines. (VG. Nov.18; 1296) Fls. 480

MIRABEAU, Honoré Gabriel Riquetti, Comte de
[–] **Atlas de la Monarchie P.ussienne.** L., 1788. Fo. Cont. Leath., gt. spine, cover loose. (R. Oct.14-18; 2113) DM 500

– Catalogue des Livres de la Bibliothèque. Paris, 1791. Lacks last lf. (blank?), priced in MS. thro.-out. Cont. cf.-bkd. bds., worn. (SM. Oct.7; 1451) Frs. 1,100

– De la Monarchie Prussienne sous Frédéric le Grand. Ill.:– Mentelle. L., 1788. 1st. Edn. 8 vols. in 9 including atlas. 8vo. & fo. Cont. red mor., gt., arms of Marie Thérèse de Savoie, sm. gt. flower in each corner, triple gt. fillet, flat spines gt. in compartments with same fleuron & 'drawer handle' border at ft., inner gt. dentelles, Signet arms, de-gilded, on covers. Atlas in cf.-bkd. bds., spine gt., Signet arms, gt., in covers. (SM. Oct.7; 1859) Frs. 3,500

[–] **Histoire Secrète de la Cour de Berlin.** N.p., 1789. 1st. Edn. 2 vols. Cont. hf. cf., armorial bkplt. (SG. Feb.5; 243) $120

– Le Libertin de Qualité, ou Confidences d'un Prisonnier au Château de Vincennes, Ecrites par lui-même. Istanbul, 1784. Square 12mo. Cont. marb. cf., decor. spine, 3 fillets on covers, inner dentelle. (HD. Apr.10; 351) Frs. 3,900

– – **Anr. Edn.** Paris, 1796. 16mo. Frontis. & 4 figures (6 figures called for). Havanna mor., blind-stpd. fillets, inner dentelles, by Petit. (HD. Apr.10; 352) Frs. 2,200

– Ueber Moses Mendelssohn. Ueber die Buergerliche Verbesserung der Juden. Berlin, 1787. 1st. Edn. Slight discolouration. Hf. leath., spine defect. (S. Nov.18; 677) *Barber.* £100

MIRAEUS, Aubertus
– Opera Diplomatica et Historica. Ed.:– Joannes Franciscus Foppens. Brussels, 1723. 2nd. Edn. 4 vols. Fo. Cont. marb. cf., 6 decor. spine raised bands. (LM. Nov.8; 60) B.Frs. 15,000

– Opera Diplomatica et Historica.–et Diplomatum Belgicorum Nova Collectio ... Brussels, 1723; 1734-48. 2nd. Edn. 2 vols. & 2 vols. Fo. Lacks port. frontis. vol. 1. Old cf., 6 decor. spine raised bands, double gt. fillet. (LM. Jun.13; 203) B.Frs. 12,000

MIRBEAU, Octave
– Le Jardin des Supplices. Ill.:– Raphaël Freida. Paris, 1927. (538);(360) on Arches vell. 4to. Some spotting, 1 state. Red mor. by Trinckvel, wrap. preserved. (SM. Feb.11; 259) Frs. 3,000

– La 628-E-8. 1908. (200) on vell d'Arches. Sewed. (HD. Oct.10; 122) Frs. 1,400

MIRBEAU, Octave & others
– Cézanne. Ill.:– Cézanne (frontis.); Vuillard, Bonnard, Denis, Matisse, K.X. Roussel, Maillol (lithos.); Signac & Valotton after Cézanne (drawings). Paris, 1914. (400) on papier à grain. Lge. 4to. 6 orig. lithos., some foxing. Sewed. (HD. Jun.24; 160) Frs. 2,500

MIRE, Loys
[–] **La Concordances des Quatre Evangelistes au Discours de la Vie de Nostre Seigneur.** Paris, 1561. 2 pts. in 1 vol. 16mo. With the 12 lf. 'Repertoire ou inventoire des Evangiles' before pt. 2, lacks 1 lf. of the movable feasts at end of Calendar & the 108 lf. 'Description de la Terre sainte', reference to latter cut from title & name Guillaume Postel in MS. inserted, a few lr. blank margins of Calendar in pt. 1 reprd. 18th. C. mor. by Derome Le Jeune with his ticket, wide rococo dentelle border, spine gt. in compartments, inner gt. dentelles, pink silk liners. The MacCarthy-Reagh copy. (S. Apr.7; 307) *Fletcher.* £190

MIREUR, Hippolyte
– Dictionnaire des Ventes d'Art. Paris, 1911-12. 7 vols. Mor.-bkd. bds., orig. wraps. bnd. in. (CSK. Jan.30; 57) £110

MIRIBILIA Romae
[–] **In dem, Buechlein Steet Geschriben wie Rom Gepauet Ward und von dem Ersten Kunig.** Rome, Stephen Plannck, [before Aug.27], 1500. Full-p. woodcuts in decor. borders, lacks 1st. blank, H1 & H4 (both supplied in facs.), lr. corners of A2-8 renewed, not affecting text, 6 other ll. with lr. corners reinforced, soiling. Early vell., slightly worn. Bkplt. of Prince Liechtenstein, lately in the

MIRIBILIA Romae Ward und von dem Ersten Kunig. -contd.
collection of Eric Sexton. [BMC IV, 100, Goff M612, H 11215*] (CNY. Apr.8; 146) $2,500

MIRO, Joan
- **Constellations. Introduction et vingt-deux proses parallèles par Andre Breton.** N.Y., 1959. Ltd. 1st. Edn. (22) for collectors. Fo. Plt. 19 dupl. Loose, as iss. in orig. cold. lithographic heavy wraps. & laid in pict. linen folding case designed by artist. Contains orig. lithograph, untitled, numbered & sigd. in pencil, followed by orig. ink & gouache design of Miro's sig. sigd. by Miro & Breton at limitation lf. (PNY. Mar.4; 188) $2,200
- **Dibujos y Litografias Papeles de son Armadans.** N.Y., [1960]. (738) numbered, with orig. sigd. litho. Lge. 4to. Unsewed, pict. wraps., boxed. Sigd. & inscr. (SG. Oct.23; 225) $350
- **Der Lithograph.** Genf, [1972]. Privilege Edn., (140), on Velin-Rives. Lge. 4to. Orig. linen. (H. Dec.9/10; 2231) DM 2,200
- **Lithographs.** N.Y., 1972. Ltd., numbered Edn. Vol. I. 4to. Cl., pict. d.-w. (SG. Dec.18; 302) $180
- – **Anr. Copy.** Vol. I. 4to. Cl., cold. pict. d.-w. (SG. Apr.2; 198) $100
- – **Anr. Edn.** N.Y., [1972], [1975], [1977]. Ltd. numbered Edns. Vols. I-III. 4to. All linen, pict. d.-w.'s. (SG. Apr.2; 200) $400
- – **Anr. Edn.** Ed.:– Raymond Queneau (preface). N.Y., [1975]. (150) numbered. Vol. II. Fo. Lacks pp. 9-12. Loose as iss. in cold. litho. wraps., linen box. 2 lithos. numbered & sigd. by Miro. (SG. Apr.2; 199) $750
- – **Anr. Copy.** Vol. 2, (5,000) numbered in Engl. Cl., cold. pict. d.-w. (SG. Oct.23; 227) $110
- **Quelques Fleurs pour des Amis.** Paris, [1964]. (150) numbered, on Grand Velin, with orig. sigd. cold. litho. Lge. fo. Loose in cold. wraps & decor. bd. folder & orig. shipping box. (SG. Oct.23; 229) $850
- **Trace sur l'Eau ...** Paris, 1963. Ob. 4to. Watercolours ptd. on onion skin du Marais. Orig. litho. cover. (JL. Jul.20; 686) Aus. $240

MIROIR des Graces dédié aux Dames, ou Dictionnaire de Parures et de Toilettes
Paris, ca. 1820. Cont. paper bds., matching s.-c. (HD. Apr.10; 160) Frs. 1,000

MISKIN
- **Les Saint Lieux. Pélérinage à Jerusalem.** Paris, 1858. 3 vols. Leath., gt. covers, spine & inner & outer dentelles. (D. Dec.11-13; 1553) DM 780

MISS & HER DOLL
1821. 4th. Edn. 16mo. Orig. ptd. wraps., advts. on lr. cover, loose. (SH. Mar.19; 202) Temperley. £100

MISSA GOTHICA seu Mozarabica
Puebla de los Angeles, 1770. Fo. Some slight discolouration to margins at beginning & end. Cont. cf., reprd. (SPB. May 5; 355) $800

MISSALS
- **Missal (Use of Rome).** Nuremb., Georg Stuchs, 1484. 4to. 2-line capital initials ptd. in red, spaces for lge. initials at section heads, the 1st. crudely supplied in red, slight worming affecting few letters only of last 3 ll., single sm. wormholes to blank margins of some other ll., 16th. C. monastic ink inscr. at top of 1st. p. of calendar. Cont. German pig over wood bds., covers with central panel of repeated vine-like tools filled with a flower tool, with 2 outer borders of 2 different floral rolls, spine in 5 compartments with 4 raised bands, compartments with vine tool, brass cornerpieces & catches for clasps (lacking), later label on spine. Bkplts. of Rev. E.H. Wainwright & J. Leslie, sig. of Rev. William Maskell, blind-stp. of William Evans, recently in the collection of Eric Sexton. [BMC II, 467, Goff M697, HC 11384] (CNY. Apr.8; 113) $3,800
- – **Anr. Copy.** Lombard initial capitals ptd. red, spaces left for lge. capitals at section heads, which are supplied in red & yellow (probably at a later date), light dampstaining to margins, occasionally touching text, wormhole to last ll., catching some letters of text, last p. soiled. Mod. mor., preserving orig. cover panels of blind-stpd. cf., gt. spine, qtr. mor. gt. folding case. Bkplt. of the General Theological Seminary Liby. (CNY. Oct.1; 37) $1,600
- **Missale Romanum œ Eremitarum).** Venice, 1501. Old scribbling on title & in calendar. 16th. C. blind-stpd. cf.-bkd. wood bds., rebkd., worn. (VG. Oct.13; 108) Fls. 1,500

- **Missale Monasticum Secumdum Consuetudinem Ordinis Vallisumbrose.** Venice, Dec.13, 1503. On vell. Fo. 16 of the lge. capitals, the crucifixion woodcut & 11 of the 12 full architectural borders illuminated in cols. & gold, lacks last 5 ll. (1 blank), 1 or more margins renewed at 8th. lf., folios 289-296 & 299, affecting text or foliation at 8th. lf. & folios 293 & 299, some 12 other ll. with minor repairs or restoration to margins, last 3 ll. on guards, minor finger-soiling to Canon of Mass & some other ll. Fr. 19th. C. red mor. gt., covers with overall baroque design of lge. cornucopiae & leaf tools, gt. arms of Henry II of France stpd. on covers, worn, rebkd., red hf. mor. s.-c. Bkplt. of the General Theological Seminary Liby. (CNY. Oct.1; 71) $22,000
- **Missale Constantiense.** Ill.:– H. Burgkmair. Augsburg, 8th. Oct. 1505. Some old notes. Wood bds. ca. 1550, blind-tooled, 6 (of 8) bosses, 2 clasps, soiled. 8 ll. on vell. (HK. Nov.18-21; 234) DM 32,000
- **Missale Monasticum Secundum Morem et Ritum Casinensis.** Venice, Apr.18, 1506. 1st. Edn. Fo. Eleven ll. with corners or sm. portions of margins renewed, some 20 ll. with reprd. tears, 10 of these affecting text but reprd. without loss, light worming at beginning & end, catching some letters, 9 woodcut borders slightly cropped at bottom. Late 19th. C. red lev. mor. gt., covers with gt. panels & borders, gt. spine, mor. doubls., with lge. design in gt. & with onlays of mor., watered silk end-ll., by Bradstreet. Bkplt. of the General Theological Seminary Liby. (CNY. Oct.1; 73) $4,200
- **Missal [Use of Regensburg].** Bamberg, 1510. Fo. Canon of the Mass (12 ll.) on vell. with full-p. woodcut cold. by cont. hand, & a circular Agnus Dei woodcut, 8 ll. of additional text bnd. in after the Canon, lacks title-p., 9 ll. on guards, 27 ll. with portions of margins reinforced (with slight paper loss at fo. 239), some 18 ll. with marginal tears, 11 affecting text (reprd. without loss), cont. inscr. & some cont. marginal notes. Sig. & bkplt. of Rev. William Maskell, sig. of Rev. W. J. Blew, bkplt. of the General Theological Seminary Liby. (CNY. Oct.1; 4) $2,400
- **Missale ad Usum Ecclesie Cenomanasis.** -**Missale Parvum ad Usum Insignis Ecclesie Parisiensis.** Paris, Wolfgang Hopyl, 10 July, 1520; 1 Aug., 1505. Together 2 vols., each in 3 Pts. Second work lacks fo. a1. 18th C. cf., second work rebkd. & worn. (S. Nov.25; 348) Quaritch. £200
- **Missale S[ecundu]m Ritum Ecclesie Lugdun.** Lyons, 1530. 4to. Lr. blank margin of title-p. renewed, sm. rust-hole in E4 just touching ruled border. Mor. gt., gt. arms on sides of Charles Louis de Bourbon, Duc de Parme, & crowned gt. monog. cornerpieces joined by double blind-rule, spine gt. in 6 compartments with gt.-lettering & repeated monog., by Lortic. Bkplts. of C.L. de Bourbon & John A. Saks. (CNY. Oct.1; 93) $1,400
- **Missal [Use of Tournai].** Antw., 1540. Fo. 2 ll. of the Canon on vell. with full-p. woodcut cold. by cont. hand, 3 ll. with marginal tears affecting text, but without loss, other ll. with minor marginal tears or fraying, t1 & E2 with sm. replacements to outer margin, light worming to early ll., slight dampstaining to some ll. at end, soiling & traces of use. Cont. blind-panel. cf. over wood bds., worn, rebkd., lacks 1 clasp. Bkplt. of the General Theological Seminary Liby. (CNY. Oct.1; 2) $3,600
- **Missale Romanum.** Venice, 1549. 4to. Some ll. slightly browned & with light traces of damp-staining, convent inscr. on fly-lf. & ink stp. on title. Cont. mor. over wood bds., blind-tooled with central arabesque in lozenge & rectangular frame with leaf ornament. Bkplt. of the Carmelite Liby. in Turin, later the copy of John A. Saks. (CNY. Oct.1; 132) $1,100
- **Missale iuxta Morem Sanctissimi Doctoris & Pontificis Ambrosii.** Milan, 1560. Fo. Stain on last p. & outer margin reprd. Mod. cf. gt. (SI. Dec.3; 404) Lire 320,000
- **[Missale Romanum.]** Venice, 1575. 4to. Title rebkd. Old blind-stpd. cf., gt. ornaments, very worn. (SG. Sep.25; 232) $140
- **Missale Romanum.** Ill.:– Jacob Kerver. Paris, 1588. Fo. 10 lf. index. vell. frontis. inserted with unidentified arms, with motto Odore et patientia dtd. 1595, 2 of tailpieces incorporate monogs. ORSVE & RSVE, additions to calendar in old (16th. ?) hand. Cont. Fr. mor., gt., lge. medallion of Crucifixion on upr.-cover & Annunciation on lr.

in panel with lfy. cornerpieces, single marguerite in each corner, wide border of spiral ornams., spine compartments gt. with lfy. sprays springing from fleur-de-lis. (SM. Oct.7; 1863) Frs. 31,000
- **Missale Romanum ex Decreto Sacrosancti Concilij Tridetini Restitutum Pii V. Pont. Max. Iussu Editum. Cum Kalendario Gregoriano ...** Venice, 1597. 4to. Mor., blind fillet, gt. cyphers in angles & spine, centre arms of Duc Robert de Parme, inner dentelle, by S. Zini. (HD. Jun.10; 70) Frs. 3,000
- **Missale Romanum ex Decr. Sacrosancti Concilii Tridentini ...** Venice, 1694. Fo. Cont. velvet, with lge. intricate silver cornerpieces & lge centrepiece, lacks spine, edges of cover very frayed. (SG. Feb.12; 277) $190
- **Missale Romanum.** Antw., 1724. 4to. 1 lf. defect., wormhole. Cont. red mor. gt., rebkd., lacks 1 clasp. (P. Jun.11; 102) Fairburn. £60
- **Missale Sanctae Lugdunensis Ecclesiae.** Lyon, 1737. Fo. Cont. mor. gt. by 'Claude Devers fils Aîné maitre relieur à Lyon' (inscr. on rear fly-lf.), arms of Entraigues of Lyonnais on covers surrounded by gt. decorations, wide gt. border, spine gt. in compartments with central lozenge surmounted by fleur-de-lis & couronné fermée, inner gt. dentelles, silk liners & finger tabs on fore-e., spine with 1 or 2 sm. wormholes, slight worming on lr. cover. (S. Apr.7; 351) Braunschweig. £250
- **[Missale Armenum].** Venice, 1786. Fo. Some ornamented margins cropped, slight soiling & browning. Wraps., holed, s.-c. (S. Apr.29; 425) Maggs. £160
- **Missale Romanum.** Bremer Pr., 1931. Fo. Orig. holland-bkd. bds., slightly soiled. (SH. Oct.10; 486) Fairburn. £55

MISSELDEN, Edward
- **Free Trade. Or, the Meanes to Make Trade Florish.** 1662. 1st. Edn. Lacks blanks A1 & A2, title & last lf. soiled. 19th. C. mor., gt., stp. of Alexander Gardyne, 1883, on verso of title. [NSTC 17986] (S. Dec.9; 339) Rota. £800

MISSON, Henri, Sieur de Valbourg
- [–] **Memoires et Observations faites par un Voyageur en Angleterre.** The Hague, 1698. 12mo. Cont. cf. (C. Feb.25; 117) Cumming. £55

MISSON, Maximilian
- **Nouveau Voyage d'Italie.** The Hague, 1698. 3rd. Edn. 3 vols. 12mo. 1 ptd. folding table. Cont. mor., gt., arms of Jean de la Vieuville, dentelle border, spine gt. in compartments, inner gt. dentelles, pink & gt. floral patterned endpapers. (SM. Oct.7; 1865) Frs. 2,400
- – **Anr. Edn.** La Haye, 1702. 3 vols. Old cf. (BS. Jun.11; 171) £70

MISTRAL, Frederic
- **Mireille, Poème Provencal.** Ill.:– Eugène Burnand & others. Paris, 1884. (150) on Japon. Fo. Mor. gt., upr. cover with cold. mor. onlays, title in central cartouche, surrounded by ornaments, lr. cover with interlaced onlaid panel, spine in 6 compartments, ornaments in 4, 5 riased bands, silk doubls. & endpapers, by M. Ritter. Watercolour drawing by Paul de Langpie tipped in. (CNY. May 22; 349) $800

MITCHELL, Donald G.
- **The Lorgnette, or Studies of the Town, by an Opera Goer.** N.Y., Jan.20-Sept.25, 1850. 1st. Edn., no. 1 marked '2nd. Edn.' Nos. 1-11, 16-20, 22, & 23, together 18 iss. 12mo. Pict. wraps., unc., some wear. (SG. Mar.5; 323) $125

MITCHELL, E.
See–**KNOX, Robert & Mitchell, E.**

MITCHELL, Margaret
- **Gone with the Wind.** N.Y., 1936. 1st. Edn., 1st. Iss. With the May copyright. Cl., d.-w. torn. (SG. Nov.13; 508) $180
- – **Anr. Edn.** Ltd. Edns. Cl., 1968. Ltd. Edn. 2 vols. Orig. bdg., box. (SPB. Jul.28; 286) $100

MITCHELL, Samuel Augustus
- **New General Atlas.** Phila., 1866. Fo. Gt.-lettered cl., leath. spine. (SG. Nov.20; 77) $325
- – **Anr. Copy.** Lacks all the maps of Canada. Gt.-decor. cl., corners reprd., rebkd. (SG. Nov.20; 78) $120
- – **Anr. Edn.** Phila., 1869. Tall fo. Orig. leath. bkd. gt.-lettered cl., worn. (SG. May 21; 71) $200
- – **Anr. Edn.** Phila., 1882. Fo. Disbnd. (SG. May 21; 72) $150

- A New Universal Atlas. Phila., 1847. Tall fo. With the unnumbered extra map of Oregon & Upper California, browned thro.-out. New leatherette. (SG. May 21; 69) $650
- - **Anr. Edn.** Baltimore, 1859. Tall fo. Some soiling. Orig. cl., leath. back & tips, upr. cover gt.-stpd., worn. (SG. May 21; 70) $300

MITCHELL, Silas Weir
- **Injuries of Nerves & their Consequences.** Phila., 1872. 1st. Edn. Cl. (S. Jun.16; 583) *Phelps.* £130

MITCHELL, Silas Weir & others
- **Gunshot Wounds & Other Injuries of Nerves.** Phila., 1864. 1st. Edn. New hf. cf. (S. Jun.16; 582) *Jenner Books.* £220

MITCHELL, Lt. Col. Sir Thomas Livingston, Snr.
- **Journal of an Expedition into the Interior of Tropical Australia.** L., 1848. Slight foxing & offsetting. Unc., recased in orig. cl., new cl. backstrip with pt. of orig. mntd. (KH. Nov.18; 427) Aus. $480
- **Three Expeditions into the Interior of Eastern Australia.** 1838. 1st. Edn. 2 vols. Litho. titles & 51 plts., vol. 1 lacks folding map. Cont. tree cf., spines gt. (C. May 20; 154) *Titles.* £240
- - **Anr. Copy.** Vol. II only. Some staining thro.-out. Hf. mor. With the Ingleton bkplt. (JL. Mar.2; 142) Aus. $130
- - **Anr. Edn.** L., 1839. 2nd. Edn. Vol. 2 only. Hf. cf., marb. bds., worn. Bkplt. of George Bennet, M.D., holograph letter to Bennet tipped in to rear end-paper, dtd. 7 Mar. 1849. (JL. Jul.20; 745) Aus. $260
- - **Anr. Copy.** 2 vols. Some spotting & foxing of plts., lacks the General Map of the exploratory routes. Orig. cl., unc., repairs to backstrips & jnts. chiefly of 1 vol., probably recased. (KH. Nov.18; 428) Aus. $250

MITCHELL, W. Frederick
See-SYMONS, W. Christian & Mitchell, W. Frederick

MITCHELL & Co.
- **County of Carleton & Ottawa City Directory.** Toronto, 1864. Dampstained thro.-out. Orig. cl., rebkd. (CB. Feb.18; 35) Can. $600

MITCHELL-WITHERS, M.
- **Enter Clowns.** Ill.:- Henry Hoyland. Dulwich Village, College Pr., 1932. Mor., gt. lines enclosing mor. onlays on covers, linked on spine to form compartment, mor. doubls. with similar decor., sigd. & dtd. in lr. cover James Brockman 1978, in specially designed perspex & mor. display case. (SH. Feb.20; 394) *Maggs.* £410

MITCHINER, M.
- **Indo-Greek & Indo-Scythian Coinage.** 1975-76. 9 vols. 4to. Orig. wraps. (SH. Mar.6; 403) *Pardoe.* £65

MITCHINSON, D.
See-CRAMER, G. & others

MITE, The
1891. 21×17mm. Orig. cl. gt. Miniature Book. (SH. Dec.12; 562) *Fletcher.* £100

MITELLI, Giuseppe Maria
- **Proverbi Figurati Consecrati al Serenissimo Principe Francesco Maria di Toscana.** Bologna, 1678. 1st. Edn. Fo. Engraved title & 48 plts., extra engraved plt. inserted, 1st. 28 plts. stained. Old bds., covers stained. (CNY. May 22; 181) $2,400

MITFORD, John, Journalist 'A. Burton'
- **The Adventures of Johnny Newcome in the Navy.** Ill.:- Thomas Rowlandson. L., 1818. 1st. Edn. 16 hand-cold. plts., soiled & some trimmed, minor defects. Mott. cf. gt. by Rivière, slightly worn, folding box. (SPB. Jul.28; 412) £150
- - **Anr. Edn.** 1819. 2nd. Edn. Hf. mor., gt. spine, by Tout. (S. Dec.9; 512) *Hyde.* £70
- - **Anr. Copy.** Orig. bds., cl. case, unc. (C. Nov.6; 326) *Way.* £65
[-] **My Cousin in the Army.** 1822. 15 hand-cold. plts. (of 16). Mod. cf. (SH. Jun.25; 136) *Scott.* £55

MITFORD, Mary Russell
- **Our Village.** Ill.:- Hugh Thomson. 1893. (470) on L.P. Orig. cl. Pres. copy from artist to William Heighway. (SH. Mar.27; 513) *Illustrated Antiques.* £160

MITFORD, Nancy
- **The Sun King.** Arcadia Pr., 1969. (265) numbered. 4to. Orig. mor., box. (SH. Jul.23; 181) *Smith.* £60

MITHOBIUS, B.
- **Wie man sich für der Hefftigen und Tödtlichen Seuche der Pestilenz bewaren sol.** Erfurt, 1552. 4to. Slightly soiled & stained in margins, old MS. marginalia. Hf. vell. (R. Mar.31-Apr.4; 1015) DM 580

MITING [Meeting]
Ed.:- [A.I. Bol'kenau]. St. Petersb., 1905-06. Nos. 1-4. Fo. (SH. Feb.5; 89) *De la Casa.* £50
- - **Anr. Edn.** Ed.:- [P.M. Yuzhny]. St. Petersb., 1906. No. 1 only (of ?4). 4to. Unbnd. (SH. Feb.5; 90) *Quaritch.* £55

MODA (La) ELEGANTE Ilustrada Periodico de las Familias
Madrid, 1884-89 & 1903-05. 9 vols. Fo. Text in Spanish, some repairs, tears, chipping, some pp. loose. Hf. cf., gt. spines. As a periodical, w.a.f. (SPB. May 6; 204) $600
- - **Anr. Edn.** Madrid, [1893-1902]. 2 vols. 4to. Later cl.-bkd. bds., worn. (SH. Jan.29; 269) *Walford.* £280

MODE (La)
Paris, 1835-36. A few plts. lightly soiled, a few sm. margin tears. Cont. hf. leath., spine defect. & loose. (R. Mar.31-Apr.4; 1561) DM 800

MODE FEMININE de 1490 à 1920
[Paris], ca. 1925. 12 series in 3 vols. Orig. wraps., 3 pictor. orig. bd. portfolios. (R. Mar.31-Apr.4; 1558) DM 1,000

MODELLES DE MENUISERIE, choisis parmi ce que Paris offre de plus nouveau
Paris, 1825. Fo. Some spotting. Cont. hf. cf., worn. (S. Dec.9; 481) *Fogg.* £90

MODERN MASTERS OF ETCHING
L., 1924-30. 23 vols. No bdg. stated. (JL. Jul.20; 687) Aus. $260
- - **Anr. Edn.** 1924-32. 31 vols., various, including 2 duplicates. Ob. 4to. Lacks a few plts. in number 17. Most orig. bds., some soiling. (CSK. Oct.17; 115) £100

MODERN MASTERS OF PHOTOGRAPHY
- **Series I: Pictorialists.** Ed.:- Heyworth Campbell. N.Y., ca. 1930? Fo. Loose as iss. in orig. bd. box, worn. (SG. Jul.9; 218) $110

MODERN MINIATURE; A Novel
1792. 2 vols. No hf.-titles (not called for?). Cont. mott. cf. (CSK. Jan.30; 81) £140

MODERN PART OF A UNIVERSAL HISTORY
1759-66. 44 vols. Cont. mott. cf., gt. spines, some wear. W.a.f. (S. Feb.23; 359) *Wade.* £150

MODERN STYLE of Cabinet Work Exemplified, The
1829. 4to. 72 engraved plts., some reprd., 2 inlaid. Later qtr. cf. (S. Mar.17; 438) *Marlborough Rare Books.* £260

MODES, Les
Paris, 1901-28. Numbers 1-295 in 25 vols. 4to. Some ll. loose. Cont. cf.-bkd. bds., 2 spines worn. (SH. Oct.9; 15) *Reed & Sims.* £280

MODES et les Belles (Les)
- **Almanach nouveau rédigé par le Caprice.** Paris, [1821]. 16mo. Cont. silk bds., decor. spine, gt. roulette decor. on covers. (HD. Apr.10; 161) Frs. 1,250

MODESTUS
See-VEGETIUS, Flavius Renatus; Aelianus Tacticus; Frontinus, Sextus Julius-MODESTUS

MODESTUS-[LAETUS, Pomponius]
- **De Re Militari.-[De Magistratibus Urbis].** [Rome], [?Johannes Schurener de Bopardia], ca. 1474-5. Sm. 4to. 29 ll. (of 30), wormed, reprd. 18th. C. hf. cf. Bk.-label of Georg Kloss. [BMC IV, 59] (S. Nov.25; 320) *Quaritch.* £110

MODIUS, Franciscus
- **Cleri Totius Romanae Ecclesias Subjecti.-Liber Singularis . . .** Ill.:- after Jost Amman. Frankfurt, 1585. 1st. Edn. 2 pts. in 1 vol. Old vell. (HD. Dec.5; 3) Frs. 1,400
See-AMMAN, Jost & Modius, Fr.

MOE, Jorgen I.
See-ASBJORNSEN, Peter Christen & Moe, Jorgen I.

MOEDRATI, L. Iunii
See-VARRO, Marcus Terentius, Moedrati, L. Iunii & Rutilii, Paladii

MOEHSEN, J.C.W.
- **Beiträge zur Geschichte der Wissenschaften in der Mark Brandenburg bis zum Ende des 16. Jahrhunderts.** Berlin & Leipzig, 1783. 4to. Title & copperplt. lightly stained. Cont. leath., gt. spine. (R. Oct.14-18; 206) DM 500
- **Verzeichnis einer Sammlung von Bildnissen, grösstentheils berühmter Aerzte.** Berlin, 1771. 1st. Edn. 2 pts. (5 sections) in 1 vol. Old liby. stp. on title. Cont. leath., gt. spine. (R. Oct.14-18; 368) DM 700

MOELLHAUSEN, Baldwin
- **Diary of a Journey from the Mississippi to the Coasts of the Pacific . . .** Trans.:- Mrs. Percy Sinnett. L., 1858. 1st. Edn. in Engl. 2 vols. Three-qtr. mor., spines gt., by Bayntun. (SG. Oct.9; 169) $475
- **Resor i Norra Americas Klippberg till NY-Mexicos Hoegslaett . . .** [Stockholm], [1867]. 1st. Swedish Edn. 2 vols. in 1. Cont. hf. cf., orig. ptd. wraps. bnd. in. (PNY. Mar.26; 220) $130

MOERDER, Jean de
See-SIMONOFF, Leonid de & Moerder, Jean de

MOERENHOUT, J.A.
- **Voyages aux Iles du Grand Ocean.** Paris, 1837. 2 vols. Orig. ptd. wraps., unc. [Sabin 49829] (SPB. May 5; 356) $450

MOEURS ET COSTUMES DE DIFFERENS PEUPLES DE LA TERRE
Paris, [Wtrmkd. 1828]. 16mo. 1 plt. with a short tear, slightly stained. Hf. cl., slightly worn. (SH. Mar.19; 204) *Vincent.* £55

MOFFET, Thomas
- **Insectorum sive Minimorum Animalium Theatrum.** 1634. Fo. Some discolouration, lge. portion of title-p. torn away. Later reversed cf. (TA. Dec.18; 114) £60
See-TOPSELL, Edward-MOFFETT, Thomas

MOGG, Edward
- **Survey of the High Roads of England & Wales.** 1817. 1st. pt. (all publd.). Hand-cold. general map, & 233 hand-cold. road maps. Hf. cf., worn, D. Lloyd George's bkplt. (P. Dec.11; 157) *Tabor.* £580

MOGGRIDGE, John Traherne
- **Contributions to the Flora of Mentone.** L., 1871. 1st. Edn. (Subscribers). Mod. three-qtr. lev. gt., bnd. from the pts., orig. wraps. bnd. in at end. (SG. Sep.18; 259) $275

MOGRIDGE, George
- **Sergeant Bell & his Raree Show.** Ill.:- George Cruikshank, Thompson & others. L., 1839. 1st. Edn. Square 12mo. Slight foxing. Red mor. gt. by Rivière. Proof of title-vig. by Cruikshank tipped in, Cruikshank's pencilled instructions to engraver on proof. (SPB. Nov.25; 181) $125

MOHOLY-NAGY, Laszio
- **Malerei, Photographie, Film.** Munich, 1925. Sm. 4to. Orig. linen, orig. wraps., defect. (R. Oct.14-18; 704) DM 550

MOHOLY-NAGY, Laszlo (Ed.)
See-STAATLICHES BAUHAUS WEIMAR

MOHR, E.
- **To the Victoria Falls of the Zambesi.** Trans.:- N. d'Anvers. Ill.:- after Thomas Baines. L., 1876. Decor. cl. (VA. Jan.30; 168) R. 120

MOI PULEMET [My Machine-Gun]
Ed.:- [P.I. Shoshin]. St. Petersb., 1906. Nos. 1-5. 4to. No. 1 torn. Unbnd. (SH. Feb.5; 91) *De la Casa.* £190

MOIVRE, Abraham de
- **The Doctrine of Chances . . .** L., Priv. ptd., 1738. 2nd. Edn., corrected. 4to. Cont. mott. cf., upr. cover loose. (PNY. Oct.1; 377) $150

MOLESWORTH, Robert
[-] **An account of Denmark, as it was in the year 1692.** 1694. 1st. Edn. Cont. cf. [Wing M2382A] (C. Feb.25; 164) *Hammond.* £50

MOLIERE, Jean-Baptiste Poquelin dit
[-] **The Citizen turn'd Gentleman.** Trans.:- [Edward Ravenscroft.] 1672. 1st. Edn. 4to. Some staining. Mor. by Sangorski. [Wing M2383a] (C. Nov.19; 117) *Brett-Smith.* £170

MOLIERE, Jean-Baptiste Poquelin dit -contd.
- **Le Misanthrope Précédé d'un Dialogue aux Enfers par Anatole France et suivi de la Conversion d'Alcester par Georges Courteline.** Paris, 1907. (350). 4to. Lev. mor. by G.L.R.D., covers with cold. inlays forming ornament, s.-c. (CSK. Sep.5; 230) £120
- **Les Oeuvres.** Ill.:– F. Chauveau. Paris, 1666. 1st. Coll. Edn. 2 vols. 12mo. Continuous pagination, lge. margins, title restored & last lf vol. 1. Red mor., decor., jeux de fillet compartments & pointillé, sm. tool decor., decor. spines, red mor. doubls., gt. fillet borders, by Toly fils. (HD. Jun.10; 71) Frs. 5,900
- – **Anr. Edn.** Ed:– [Vinot & La Grange]. Paris, 1682. 1st. Ill. Edn.; 1st. Compl. Coll. Edn. 8 vols. Lacks 4 copper engrs. in vol. I & 1 copper engr. in vol. V, slightly soiled thro.-out & stained. Cont. cf., gt. spine, worn & wormed, some tears. (H. Dec.9/10; 1612) DM 1,000
- – **Anr. Edn.** Ill.:– Lépicié after Coypel (engraved ports), Cars after Boucher (copperplts.). Paris, 1734. New Edn., 1st. printing. 6 vols. 4to. Vol. 5 lacks 1 copperplt., vol. 4 with variant title & vig., some text vigs. soiled. Cont. cf., gt. spine & outer dentelle, cover fillets, spine & corners reprd., vol. 1 upr. cover loose, vol. 1 lr. cover slightly defect., soiled lightly. Duke of Northumberland, Stanwick ex lib. (HK. Nov.18-21; 2366) DM 4,000
- – **Anr. Edn.** Ill.:– Boucher. New Edn., 1734. 2nd. printing. 6 vols. 4to. Browning of last ll. vols V & VI. Cont. cf. (HD. Jun.30; 57) Frs. 8,800
- – **Anr. Edn.** Ill.:– after Boucher. Paris, 1734. New Edn. 6 vols. 4to. Cont. Fr. mott. cf. gt., rebkd. preserving orig. spines, worn. (BS. Jun.11; 268) £240
- – **Anr. Copy.** Cont. cf., decor. spine raised bands. (HD. Apr.24; 84) Frs. 9,600
- [-] [-] **Anr. Edn.** [1734]. Fo. Late 19th. C. red mor. gt. (SM. Oct.8; 2413) Frs. 3,500
- – **Anr. Edn.** Paris, 1739. 8 vols. 12mo. Cont. marb. cf., decor. spines, slightly worn. (HD. Apr.9; 603) Frs. 1,700
- – **Anr. Edn.** Ill.:– Boucher & Legrand. Paris, 1760. 8 vols. 12mo. Cont. marb. cf., gt. decor. spine. (HD. Feb.18; 46) Frs. 4,100
- – **Anr. Edn.** Paris, 1770. 8 vols. 12mo. Cont. marb. cf., decor. spines. (HD. Apr.9; 604) Frs. 1,900
- – **Anr. Edn.** Ill.:– after Moreau. Paris, 1773. 6 vols. Vols. 2 & 3 without hf.-titles. Cont. cf., very worn. (SBA. May 27; 135) Duran. £110
- – **Anr. Copy.** Cont. diced cf., triple fillet, decor. spines, bdg. defect. (HD. Feb.18; 47) Frs. 4,600
- – **Anr. Copy.** Old MS. entry in port. margin. Cont. marb. leath. gt. spine, cover, inner & outer dentelle, worn, ex-lib. (HK. May 12-14; 1605) DM 1,800
- – **Anr. Edn.** L., 1784. Vol. 3 only. 12mo. Cont. cf. gt., spine worn, folding box. Thomas Jefferson's copy with his initials on J1 & T1, sig. of M. Randolph/Monticello on verso of front free endpaper. (SPB. Nov.24; 23) £950
- – **Anr. Edn.** Paris, 1791-94. (250). Vélin paper. 6 vols. Without port. by St. Aubin. Cont. paper bds., unc., unopened, gt. (SM. Oct.7; 1866) Frs. 1,000
- – **Anr. Edn.** Ed.:– Bret. Ill.:– Mignard (port.), Moreau. Paris, 1804. 6 vols. Cont. cf., gt., triple fillet border, decor. spine raised bands, inner dentelle. (HD. Apr.24; 160) Frs. 3,400
- – **Anr. Copy.** Cont. cf., gt. (R. Oct.14-18; 1004) DM 820
- – **Anr. Edn.** Ed.:– M. Sainte-Beuve. Ill.:– Tony Johannot. 1844. 1st. 40 ll. lightly stained in upr. margin. Cont. chagrin, blind fillet & gt. border, blind centre motif, decor. spine. (HD. Feb.18; 160) Frs. 1,000
- – **Anr. Edn.** Ill.:– Leloir & Leman. Paris, 1882-96. (75) on China. 10 vols. 4to. 2 states of engrs., sepia & black-&-white. Hf. mor., corners, smooth decor. spines. (HD. Feb.27; 183) Frs. 2,000
- [-] **Anr. Edn.** Paris, 1888-94. 10 vols. 12mo. Mor. by Kieffer, orig. wraps. bnd. in. (SM. Oct.8; 2222) Frs. 1,500
- – **Anr. Edn.** Ill.:– M. Leloir & J. Leman. Paris, 1888, 1896. 10 vols. 4to. Hf. chagrin, corners, smooth decor. spines. (HD. Feb.27; 184) Frs. 1,200
- **Oeuvres Complètes.** Paris, 1868. Some spotting. Orig. mor.-bkd. cl., worn. (CSK. Sep.5; 199) £75
- – **Anr. Edn.** Ed.:– Adolphe Regnier. Ill.:– Hédouin, Flemeng & others. Paris, 1878. 5 vols. 4to. Red mor. by Marius Michel, decor. spines, covers with 2 borders of 3 gt. fillets, inner border

with motifs in corners. Most etchings sigd. by artists. (SM. Feb.11; 260) Frs. 20,000
- **Oeuvres avec des Remarques Grammaticales, des Observations ... par Bret (et Voltaire).** Ill.:– Simonet, Moreau & others. Paris, 1773. 6 vols. Some foxing, slight stain on initial ll. of Vol. V. Cont. mott. gt. (SPB. Nov.25; 58) $375
- **Sämmtliche Lustspiele.** Trans.:– [F.S. Bierling]. Hamburg, 1769. 2nd. Edn. 4 vols. Lightly browned thro.-out. Mod. hf. leath. (H. May 21/22; 1209) DM 460

MOLINA, John Ignatius
- **Essai sur l'Histoire Naturelle du Chili.** Trans.:– M. Gruvel. Paris, 1789. Cont. leath. gt. [Sabin 49820] (D. Dec.11-13; 1449) DM 1,200
- **Compendio de la Historia Geografica, Natural y Civil del Reyno de Chile.** Madrid, 1788-95. 2 vols. Sm. 4to. Liby. stps. Cont. cf. [Sabin 49889] (SPB. May 5; 358) $325

MOLINAEUS (Du Moulin), C.
- **Consuetudines sive Constitutiones Almae Parisiorum Urbis adeo Totius Regni Franciae Principales Commentariis.–Tractatus de Origine, Progressu et Excellentia Regni et Monarchiae Francorum, & Coronae Franciae.** Frankfurt, 1575. 2 works in 1 vol.; 1st. work: 2 pts. in 1 vol. Fo. Cont. blind-tooled pig. (R. Oct.14-18; 1421) DM 1,200

MOLL, Hermann
- **Atlas Geographus.** 1711-17. 5 vols. 4to. Approximately 94 folding engraved maps & plts. only, lacks approximately 8 maps & plts. in vols. I-III, map of Africa stained., many ll. foxed., a few plts. cropped Cont. panel. cf., lacks 1 cover, 1 detchd., others loose, W.a.f. [Sabin 49902]. (S. Sep.29; 168) Maphouse. £800
- – **Anr. Copy.** 86 maps only, some hand-cold. in outl., some spotting, slight worming affecting text in vol. 1. Cont. cf., worn, some covers detchd. W.a.f. (CSK. Feb.6; 21) £400
- – – **Anr. Copy.** Lightly browned in parts, slightly soiled, several MS. owner's marks & sm. stps. engraved exlib on title verso. New hf. leath. [Sabin 2308 & 49902] (H. Dec.9/10; 441) DM2,800
- – **Catalogue of A New & Compleat Set of Twenty-Five Two-Sheet Maps.** [L.], n.d. Fo. Some browning, slight staining, some margins & folds reprd. Cf., scarred, worn, spine torn. From liby. of William E. Wilson. (SPB. Apr.29; 206) $6,500
- – **The Compleat Geographer.** 1709. 3rd. Edn. Some maps browned, dampstains affecting title & frontis. Cont. cf., worn. W.a.f. (CSK. Feb.6; 38) £200
- **A New Description of England & Wales.** 1724. Fo. Some light staining & soiling, mainly marginal. Cont. cf., crudely rebkd. (CSK. Feb.13; 9) £580
- – **Anr. Copy.** All county maps trimmed to plt. line (& may be inserted from a smaller Moll atlas), county map of Cumberland lacks lr. right corner, folding map age-browned, some lr. text margins reprd. Old panel. cf., crudely rebkd. (SG. May 21; 73) $375
- **A Set of Fifty New & Correct Maps of England & Wales.** 1724. Ob. fo. Maps hand-cold. in outl., title slightly soiled, a few other defects., barely affecting plts. Cont. hf. cf., worn. As an atlas, w.a.f. (SBA. Mar.4; 116) Broadbent. £860
- – **Anr. Copy.** Ob. 4to. (folded as 8vo.). Lacks map of Cornwall. Cont. cf., rebkd. W.a.f. (C. Nov.6; 264) Gibbons. £420
- – – **Anr. Copy.** Ob. fo. Many maps reprd. in folds. Removed from cont. narrow 8vo. blind-panel. suede bdg. W.a.f. (S. Mar.31; 258) Marshall. £320
- **A Set of Thirty-Six New & Correct Maps of Scotland.** Ca. 1740. Sm. 4to. Maps numbered in MS. at upr. fore-corners, sm. perforation to 1 map. Orig. cf.-bkd. bds., spine defect., worn. (S. Jul.27; 47) Franks. £200
- – **Anr. Edn.** Ed.:– John Adair. N.d. Ob. fo. Hf. leath., bds. (SKC. May 19; 362) £170
- **A Set of Twenty New & Correct Maps of Ireland.** 1728. Ob. fo. Lacks general map at end, deleted from contents list on title, fore-margin of map 19 reprd. Cont. cf. W. Wilson's Map of the Roads of Ireland, n.d., & Plan of Dublin, 1794, inserted on guards at end; w.a.f. (S. Jun.29; 101) Emerald Isle. £480
- **A System of Geography.** 1701. 2 pts. in 1 vol. Fo. Marginal browning. Cont. cf., spine preserved. (CSK. Apr.10; 31) £300

[-] **The World Described.** Ca. 1720. Fo. 18 engraved double-p. folding maps only, lacks title, many maps torn on folds, etc., some defect. Orig. bdg. As an atlas, w.a.f. (BS. May 13; 242) £380

MOLL, Herman–TEMPLEMAN, Thomas
- **Atlas Minor.–New Survey of the Globe.** 1729. 2 pts. in 1 vol. Ob. fo. A few sm. tears, a few margins soiled, 1 just cropped, other minor defects., barely affecting plts. Cont. cf. gt., worn. As an atlas, w.a.f. (SBA. Mar.4; 115) Studio. £900

MOLLARD, J.
- **Art of Cookery made easy & refined.** 1807. Some spotting. Orig. bdg. (P. Nov.13; 265) Segal. £65

MOLLENBECKE, Petrus–CALDERINUS, Johannes
- **Tabula in Libros Veteris ac Novi Testamenti Nicolai de Lyra.–Concordantia, sive Ambidexterium.** Ed.:– [Thomas Dorniberg] (2nd. work). [Cologne]; Speier, [Johann Koelhoff, the Elder]; Peter Drach, [not before 1480]; 1481. 1st. Edns. 2 works in 1 vol. Fo. Spaces for initial capitals, supplied in red or blue in both works, underlines, paragraph marks & initial strokes of both works in red, dampstains to upr. margins of some quires, long tear to f5 of 2nd. work. Cont. blind-stpd. vell. over bds., covers divided by widely spaced double fillets into lozenge compartments, each filled with sm. rosette, circular eagle or double fleur-de-lis tool, borders with alternating imp. of the same tools, spine undecor., orig. cornerpieces, bosses & clasps (lacks 1), by Blasius Orger of Prague, fold-padded cl. case. Inscr. of Martinus Wroblicius, dtd. 1626, on fo. 2r, later belonging to Martin Breslauer, recently in the collection of Eric Sexton. [BMC I, 223 & II, 492, Goff M807 & C45] (CNY. Apr.8; 47) $8,500

MØLLER-Christensen, Vilhelm
- **The History of the Forceps ...** Copen. & L., 1938. Liby. buckram. From Brooklyn Academy of Medicine. (SG. Jan.29; 303) $130

MOLLHAUSEN, Baldwin
See–**MOELLHAUSEN, Baldwin**

MOLLIEN, Gaspard
- **Travels in the Interior of Africa, to the sources of the Senegal & Gambia.** 1820. 4to. Slight soiling, occasional spotting. Cl.-bkd. bds., soiled. (CSK. Apr.24; 88) £75
- **Travels in the Republic of Colombia.** L., 1824. Hf. cf. William Henry Harrison's copy, with autograph annots. on over 30 pp. (SPB. Jun.22; 197) $1,600
- **Voyages dans la République de Colombie, en 1823.** Paris, 1824. 1st. Edn. 2 vols. Some slight spotting. 19th. C. hf. cf. (SPB. May 5; 359) $425

MOLLO, Tranquillo
- **Abbildung der Neuen Adjustirung der K.K. Armee.** Ill.:– J.G. Mansfeld after V.G. Kininger. Vienna, [1796-98]. Fo. Cont. red str.-grd. mor., sides panel. gt. & blind. (C. Nov.6; 219) Fairburn. £3,800

MOLMENTI, Pompeo
- **La Storia di Venezia nella Vita Privata dalle Origini alla Caduta della Repubblic.** Bergamo, 1927. 7th. Edn. 3 vols. 4to. Publisher's cl. gt. (CR. Mar.19; 114) Lire 270,000

MOLT [Hammer]
Ed.:– [O.I. Dikson & N.N. Gerardov]. St. Petersb., 1905-06. Nos. 1-2. Fo. Unbnd. (SH. Feb.5; 92) De la Casa. £80
- – **Anr. Copy.** Nos. 1 & 2 (all publd.). 4to. (SH. Feb.5; 178) De la Casa. £55

MOMENT
Ed.:– [M.S. Kaufman & K.V. Khryapin]. St. Petersb., 1907. Nos. 1-4 (of 5?). Fo. Unbnd. (SH. Feb.5; 93) Quaritch. £190

MOMORO, Ant.-Fr.
- **Traité Elementaire de l'Imprimerie.** Paris, 1796. Slightly soiled. Cont. leath. gt., worn, ex-liby. (HK. May 12-14; 2260) DM 1,800

MONACAZIONE di Orsola e Cecilia Santonini
- **La Perfezione Religiosa Canti IX.** Ed.:– Giacomo Pappafava. Ill.:– C. Calcinotto & A. Baratti after Visentini & others. Venice, 1763. Fo. Pres. inscr. on prelim. blank. Mod. marb. paper bds., buckram s.-c. From the collection of John A. Saks. (C. Jun.10; 167) Lester. £280

MONARDES, Nicolo
See-ORTA, Garcia de & Monardes, Nicolo

MONATLICHE CORRESPONDENZ ZUR BEFORDERUNG DER ERD UND HIMMELSKUNDE
Ed.:- Fr. von Zach. Gotha, 1800-13. 22 vols., vols. 2-4, 6, 7, 9, 10, 12-22, 24-27. 11 engraved ports., 70 mostly folding copperplts. & many tables, slightly soiled in parts, title-lf. stpd. Cont. paper bds. (H. Dec.9/10; 260) DM 1,000

MONCEAU, Henri Louis Duhamel Du
See-DUHAMEL DU MONCEAU, Henri Louis

MONCRIEFF, A.R. Hope
- Bonnie Scotland, Painted by Sutton Palmer. L., 1904. (500) sigd. 4to. Citron mor. gt., covers with elab. mor. onlays forming arms of Scotland in thistle wreath, spine with thistle motif mor. onlays in compartments, doubls. with elab. floral designs in mor. onlays, mor. free end-pp., partly unc., spine & upr. cover folded. (CNY. Oct.1; 108) $350

MONCREIFF, F. & Moncreiffe, W.
- The Moncreiffs & The Moncreiffes. 1929. Ltd. Edn. 2 vols. 4to. No bdg. stated, but decor. gt. (CE. Jul.9; 222) £65

MONCRIF, François-Augustin Paradis de
- Contes. Ill.:- Paul Avril (figures); Lalauze (port.). Paris, 1879. Ltd. Edn. Figures in 2 states. Mor. by Pagnan, decor. spine, inside dentelle. Bkplt. of Francis Kettaneh. (SM. Feb.11; 167) Frs. 2,200

MONDRIAN, Piet
- Le Neo-Plasticisme. Paris, 1920. Orig. wraps, slight tears reprd., fitted case. (SH. Nov.21; 428) Rota. £90

MONETTE, John W.
- History of the Discovery & Settlement of the Mississippi. N.Y., 1846. 2 vols. Slight foxing, browning & staining. Cf. gt., stained, slightly chipped. From liby. of William E. Wilson. (SPB. Apr.29; 207) $125

MONGE, Gaspard
- Description de l'Art de Fabriquer les Canons. Paris, [1793]. 1st. Edn. 4to. Cont. interim wraps. (R. Oct.14-18; 2848) DM 920

MONGEZ, Antoine
- Tableaux, Statues, Bas-Reliefs et Camées de la Galerie de Florence ... Ill.:- Wicar. Paris, 1789 [1819]. 3 vols. (of 4). Fo. Plt. 39 of vol. 3 torn. Cont. str.-grd. red mor., unc. (HD. Mar.18; 72) Frs. 3,200
- - Anr. Edn. Paris, 1789-1807. 1st. Edn. 4 vols. Lge. fo. Slightly soiled. Cont. hf.-leath. gt. (R. Mar.31-Apr.4; 903) DM 2,200
- - Anr. Edn. Ill.:- C.L. Masquelier. Paris, 1789-1821. Wide margin. 4 pts. in 2 vols. Lge. fo. Late 19th. C. hf. leath. gt., marb. end-ll. (D. Dec.11-13; 1248) DM 650

MONICART, J.B. de
- Versailles Immortalisé. Paris, 1720. 2 vols. 4to. 95 plts. (of 100?). Cont. leath. gt. (R. Mar.31-Apr.4; 928) DM 1,250

MONITEUR de la Mode
Paris, 1892. Yr. 50, Nos. 1-53 in 1 vol. Slightly soiled in parts. Cont. hf. linen. (HK. May 12-14; 1162) DM 520

MONK, Sir James
[-] State of the Present Form of Government of the Province of Quebec. 1789. 1st. Edn. Qtr. mor. [Sabin 90622] (C. May 20; 40) St. Jean. £100

MONKHOUSE, William Cosmo
- Works of Sir Edwin Landseer. Ill.:- after Landseer. N.d. 2 vols. 4to. Cont. hf. mor., spines slightly torn. (SBA. Dec.16; 115) Monkhouse. £70
- - Anr. Copy. Fo. Slight spotting. Worn, inner hinges brkn. (CSK. Nov.21; 73) £50

MONNET, Charles (Ill.)
See-VOLTAIRE, François Marie Arouet de

MONOGRAPHIE DE NOTRE-DAME DE PARIS ET DE LA NOUVELLE SACRISTIE, de Mm. Lassus et Viollet-le-Duc
Ill.:- Hibon, Ribault, Normand, etc. (engrs.). Lemercier (chromolithos.), Louis & Auguste Bissori (photos.). Paris, ca. 1853. Fo. With albumen images, some foxing thro.-out. Hf. mor., lacks spine, covers loose. (SG. Apr.23; 32) $3,000

MONOGRAPHIEN ZUR DEUTSCHEN KULTUR GESCHICHTE
Ed.:- G. Steinhausen. Jena, 1899-1905. Pts. 1-4, 6-12. 4to. Orig. linen. (HK. Nov.18-21; 1860) DM 500

MONRO, Alexander, Primus
- Traité d'Osteologie. Trans.:- John Joseph Su. Paris, 1759. 1st. Ill. & 1st. Fr. Edn. 2 vols. Fo. Engraved anatomical plts. in 2 states, 1 fully engraved, other engraved in outl., except plt. 5 which is present only in outl. engr., a few ll. slightly soiled, a few ll. torn slightly affecting text, some ll. & plts. loose, bookblock of vol. I brkn. Cont. bds., worn, covers detchd., unc. (S. Feb.23; 81) Phelps. £500

MONRO, Alexander, Secundus
- A Description of all the Bursae Mucosae of the Human Body. Edinb., 1788. Fo. Hf. roan, marb. paper covers worn, mor. label preserved. (S. Jun.16; 585) Norman. £130
- Observations on the Structure & Functions of the Nervous System. Edinb., 1783. 1st. Edn. Fo. Some browning & foxing. Linen-bkd. bds., worn. From liby. of Dr. E. Ashworth Underwood. (S. Feb.23; 257) Jenner. £320
- - Anr. Copy. 19th. C. hf. mor. From Chetham's Liby., Manchester. (C. Nov.27; 302) Dawson. £280
- - Anr. Copy. Plt. 8 with dupl., title mntd. & defect. with lr. outer portion & most of imprint missing, blank corners of following 2 ll. reprd., some margins discold. or browned. New cl., unc. (S. Jun.16; 584) Rota. £120

MONRO, Alexander, Tertius
- The Morbid Anatomy of the Brain. Edinb., 1827. Vol. I, Hydrocephalus (all publd.). Errata slip, some off-set from plts. onto text, liby. stp. on title. Hf. cf. (S. Jun.16; 587) Phillips £85
- Observations on Hydrocephalus Chronicus. Edinb., 1803. Advt. lf., some stains. New bds. Pres. copy inscr. to Dr. Duncan Senr. (S. Jun.16; 586) Tait. £90

MONRO, Robert
- Monro His Expedition. 1637. 1st. Edn. Cont. Engl. mor., gt., arms of Charles I gt. on both covers surrounded by 2 double fillet saw-tooth panels, arabesque blocked cornerpieces, fleurons at outer corners, flat spine gt. in compartments (faded), bnd. for presentation to the King? lacks ties. Bkplts. of Edmund Poley & J.R. Abbey, lately in the collection of Eric Sexton. [STC 18022] (C. Apr.15; 122) Quaritch. £4,000

MONRO, Thomas & Haslam, John
[-] Observations of the Physicians & Apothecary of Bethlem Hospital upon the Evidence taken before the Committee of the Hon. House of Commons for regulating mad-houses. 1816. Owner's inscr. of Thomas Baker. Hf. cf. Bnd. at end is a list of the governors of the Royal hospitals of Bridewell & Bethlem, 4pp. fo., folded, slightly torn in fold, with pres. inscr. from Dr. Monro to J.R. Baker & has several additions in the recipient's(?) hand. (S. Jun.16; 589) Jenner Books. £110

MONROE, Harriet
- The Passing Show. N.Y., 1903. 1st. Edn. Cl.-bkd. bds. Pres. copy, to Dr. & Isabel Fuller, inserted is author's engraved card with long autograph inscr. to the Fullers. (PNY. Mar.4; 196) $100

MONSTRELET, Enguerran de
- Chronicles. 1809. 5 vols. in 4. Engraved titles browned. Cont. hf. cf., vol. 1 rebkd. (SH. Apr.9; 302) Blundell. £60
- - Anr. Copy. 5 vols. (including an atlas of plts.). 4to. Slight spotting. Cont. russ. gt. (SBA. Oct.22; 731) Davies. £50
- Chroniques. Paris, 1512. 2 vols. 4to. Worming & dampstaining, affecting text. Cont. cf., worn. (HD. Jun.29; 213) Frs. 1,700
- - Anr. Edn. Paris, 1572. 3 vols. Fo. Later hf. leath. (D. Dec.11-13; 38) DM 1,700

MONTAGU, Charles
See-PRIOR, Matthew & Montagu, Charles

MONTAGU, George
- Ornithological Dictionary. 1802. 1st. Edn. 2 vols. With errata slips at end of both vols. Cf. (LC. Oct.2; 94) £60

MONTAGU, John
See-SANDWICH, John Montagu, Earl of

MONTAGU, Lady Mary Wortley
- Briefe wahrend Ihrer Reisen in Europa, Asia und Afrika. Leipzig, 1764 & 1767. 2 pts. & supp. in 1 vol. Heavily browned, pencil notes. Cont. cf., gt. spine, worn. (H. Dec.9/10; 1613) DM 620
[-] Letters of the Right Honourable Lady M--y W ---y M----e: Written, during her Travels in Europe, Asia & Africa to Persons of Distinction, Men of Letters, etc. in different Parts of Europe. L., 1763; 1767. 1st. Edn. 3 vols.; 1 vol. to the letters. Unif. gt.-stpd. cf. (PWP. Apr.9; 117) Can. $130
[-] - Anr. Edn. L., 1763. 3rd. Edn. 3 vols. Cont. tree cf. Armorial bkplt. of Steuart of Allanton. (SG. Sep.25; 234) $100

MONTAGU COLLECTION OF ANGLO-SAXON & ENGLISH COINS
1896-97. Pts. 2-5 only. 4to. Plts., priced. 1 vol. mod. cl., orig. wraps., torn, loose. (SH. Mar.6; 404) Spink. £100

MONTAGU COLLECTION OF GREEK COINS
1896-97. 2 vols. 4to. Orig. wraps., pt. 1 torn & loose. (SH. Mar.6; 405) Spink. £230

MONTAIGNE, Michel Eyquem de
- Essais. Bordeaux. 1580. 1st. Edn. 2 vols. in 1. Mor., red mor. doubls. gt., by Trautz-Bauzonne, qtr. mor. box. J.P. Morgan booklabel. (CNY. May 22; 183) $18,000
- - Anr. Edn. Ed.:- Mlle. de Gournay. Paris, 1595. New Edn., 1st. Edn. of this version. 2 pts. in 1 vol. Fo. Dampstained at head, some ll. slightly spotted. Cont. vell., worn, rebkd. & reprd. (S. Jan.27; 394) Quaritch. £260
- - Anr. Edn. Paris, 1598. 2nd. Edn. Lightly browned thro.-out, slightly stained in parts. Cont. vell., lightly cockled. (D. Dec.11-13; 39) DM 1,400
- - Anr. Edn. Paris, 1649. 12mo. Engl. red mor., gt. dentelle on covers, arms in centre, spine decor. with raised bands. (HD. Feb.27; 45) Frs. 2,000
- - Anr. Edn. Brussels, 1659. New Edn. 3 vols. 12mo. Some spotting. Mor.-bkd. bds. (CSK. Feb.13; 153) £50
- - Anr. Edn. Ed.:- Amaury Duval. Ill.:- Audouin (port.). Paris, 1827. 6 vols. Cf. by Cassassus, decor. spines, fillet & lge. roll-stp. gt. on covers, blind-tooled rose in centre, inside dentelle, upr. cover of vol. IV slightly defect. Sigd. by binder. (HD. Dec.5; 151) Frs. 4,500
- - Anr. Edn. Ed.:- J.V. Le Clerc. Paris, 1865-6. New Edn. 4 vols. Sm. 4to. Cont. gt. hf. mor., gt.-panel. backs, 1 vol. spotted at lr. cover jnts. Sigd. by 'Henry James 1915' at upr. blank of vol. I. (PNY. Mar.26; 221) $160
- - Anr. Edn. Paris & Liège, n.d. 9 vols. 32mo. Str.-grd. mor., decor. spines with gt. fillets, 5 gt. fillets on covers, inner dentelles, ca. 1850. From the 'Bibliotheque du Voyageur'. (HD. Apr.9; 527) Frs. 3,800

- Essayes or Morall, Politike & Militarie Discourses. Trans.:- John Florio. L., 1603. 1st. Edn., early Iss. Fo. Correction slip pasted onto B1 & 2Q4 blank but lacks 2 final unsigned errata ll., spotting & browning thro.-out, later port. inserted, title washed with sm. repair at head. Mod. hf. cf., gt. spine. [New STC 18041] (SPB. Nov.25; 80) $1,100
- - Anr. Edn. Trans.:- Iohn Florio. 1613. 2nd. Edn. in Engl. 3 pts. in 1 vol. Fo. Title sigd. 'Jo: fermor 1614', slight browning & soiling. Cont. cf., rebkd. [NSTC 18042] (S. Sep.29; 56) Cranford. £150
- - Anr. Edn. Trans.:- John Florio. Boston, River. Pr., 1902-1904. (265) numbered. 3 vols. Fo. Mott. bd. sides, buckram spines, unc., liby. bkplt. & stp. on title of each vol., folding cases, unc. (SG. Sep.4; 339) $550

- Journal du Voyage. Ed.:- M. de Querlon. Paris & Rome, 1774. 4to. Cont. cf., 5 spine raised bands, gt. stpd. spine, defect. (CR. Mar.19; 404) Lire 500,000

MON 326 MON

MONTAIGNES, François de
[–] **The Plains: Being A Exploration the Year 1845, from the Western Settlements of Missouri to the Mexican Border, & from Bent's Fort on the Arkansas to Fort Gibson via South Fork of Canadian-North Mexico & Northwestern Texas.** St. Louis, 1852-3. In 'The Western Journal & Civilian, ed. by M. Tarver & H. Cobb, Vol. 9, nos. 1-6 & Vol. 10, nos. 1-6, Oct. 1851-Sep. 1853, 12 iss. together. Orig. ptd. wraps., mor.-bkd. s.-c. (PNY. Mar.26; 222) $350

MONTANARI, Gemignano
– **Manualetto de Bombisti . . .** Venice, 1680. 1st. Edn. Cont. cf., lge. gt. borders. (CR. Mar.19; 265) Lire 360,000

MONTANUS, Arnoldus
[–] **America: being the latest & most accurate Description of the New World . . .** Ed.:– J. Ogilby. L., 1671. 1st. Engl. Edn. Fo. 31 (of 32) double-p. or folding copperplts. Cont. style hf. leath. [Sabin 50089] (R. Oct.14-18; 1700) DM 6,400
– **Atlas Chinensis.** Trans.:– John Ogilby. 1671. [1st. Engl. Edn.?] Fo. Title-p. loose. Old cf., brkn. (BS. Jun.11; 172) £580
– – **Anr. Copy.** 2 maps & 37 plts. only, 1 preserved with marginal loss, soiling & browning. Old bds., crudely recovered, worn. W.a.f. [Wing M2484] (CSK. Feb.13; 10) £150
– **Gedenwaerdige Gesantschappen der Oost-Indische Maatschappy in 't Vereenigde Nederland aan de Kaisaren van Japan . . .** Amst., 1669. Fo. Wormholed thro.-out, partly with loss of text & damaging several plts. (neatly reprd.). Mod. hf. cl., loose, spine defect. (VG. Dec.17; 1459) Fls. 640
– **Die Unbekante Neue Welt, oder Beschreibung des Weltei Amerika, und des Sud-landes.** Trans.:– O. Dapper. Amst., 1673. Fo. Occasional browning, frequent ownership stp. of Verplanck Colvin, stp. on verso of most plts., plt. following p. 248 torn near fold. Vell. [Sabin 50087] (SPB. Nov.24; 39) $2,900

MONTANUS, Marcus
– **Oratio pro Rhodiorum Obedientia.** [Rome], [Francesco Minizio Calvo?] [after Mar. 1493]. [1525?] 4to. Paper bds. [Goff M 825]. (C. Apr.1; 62) Telford. £60

MONTAUDOUIN, J.G.
See–ABEILLE, L.P. & MONTAUDOUIN, J.G.

MONTCALM, Louis Joseph de Montcalm-Gozon, Marquis de
– **Journal du Marquis de Montcalm durant ses Campagnes en Canada de 1756 a 1759.** Quebec, 1895. L.P. 4to. Buckram. (CB. Sep.24; 99) Can. $140

MONTEATH, R.
– **The Forester's Guide & Profitable Planter . . .** Edinb., 1824. 2nd. Edn. Slight browning. Orig. bds., slightly worn, unc., bkplt. of W.A. Stables. (S. Apr.7; 427) Sims & Reed. £60

MONTECUCCOLI, Raimond von
– **Besondere u. Geheime Kriegs-Nachrichten** Leipzig, 1736. 1st. German Edn. 4to. Browned & soiled, 1st. ll. very stained at margin. Cont. leath., worn, spine, corners & sm. fault restored, end-ll. renewed. (HK. Nov.18-21; 1848) DM 700
– **Memoires.** Amst. & Leipzig, 1770. 3 vols. Mod. mott. three-qtr. cf., spines gt. with fleurons. (SG. Oct.30; 254) $250

MONTEN, D.
See–ECKERT, H.A. & Monten, D.

MONTESQUIEU, Charles-Louis de Secondat, Baron de la Brède et de
– **Oeuvres.** Amst. & Leipzig, 1758. 2nd. coll. Edn. 3 vols. 4to. Cont. marb. cf., decor. spines. (HD. Feb.18; 48) Frs. 2,300
– – **Anr. Edn.** 1822. 8 vols. Blind-ornam. cf. by Thorvenin. (HD. Oct.10; 259) Frs. 2,700
– **Lettres Persanes.** Ill.:– Pierre Rousseau. Paris, 1948. On Arches vell. 2 vols. Ills. in black-&-white with comments, orig. watercolour, inked copper-engr. Jansenist mor. by Barnicaud, spines with raised bands, watered silk doubls. & end-papers, leath. in front end-paper of vol. 1, wrap. & spine, s.-c. (HD. Feb.27; 185) Frs. 1,200
– **Persian Letters.** 1722. 1st. Engl. Edn. 2 vols. Cf. gt. (P. Apr.30; 29) Bickersteth. £120
– **Le Temple de Gnide.** Ill.:– Eisen. Paris, 1772. New Edn., 1st. Printing. Cont. marb. cf., decor. spine. (HD. Dec.5; 152) Frs. 2,100

– – **Anr. Edn.** Ill.:– Lavallée after Payron. Paris, 1796. (100). 4to. Cont. hf. cf., limp decor. spine. (LM. Mar.21; 204) B.Frs. 11,000

MONTESQUIOU, Comte Robert de
– **Les Chauves-Souris. Clairs-Obscurs.** Ill.:– after Laszlo (port.). 1907. Definitive Edn.; on Jap. Lge. 8vo. Mor. by Meunier, 1914, mosaic covers with fillets & fleurons in corners, raised bands & mosaic motif on spine, arms of Clermont-Tonnerre, double end-papers of silk & marb. paper, s.-c. Sigd. (HD. Jun.29; 68b) Frs. 1,420
– **Le Chef des Odeurs Suaves.** Ill.:– after Laszlo (port.). 1907. Definitive Edn.; on Jap. Lge. 8vo. Mor. by Meunier, 1914, mosaic covers with fillets & fleurons in corners, raised bands & mosaic motif on spine, arms of Clermont-Tonnerre, double end-papers of silk & marb. paper, s.-c. Sigd. (HD. Jun.29; 68c) Frs. 1,550
– **Les Hortensias Bleus.** Ill.:– after Laszlo (port.). 1906. Definitive Edn.; on Jap. Lge. 8vo. Mor. by Meunier, 1914, mosaic covers with fillets & fleurons in corners, spine with raised bands & mosaic motif, arms of Clermont-Tonnerre, double end-papers of silk & marb. paper, s.-c. Sigd. (HD. Jun.29; 68a) Frs. 1,700
– **Les Paons.** Ill.:– after Laszlo (port.). 1908. Definitive Edn.; on Jap. Lge. 8vo. Mor. by Meunier, 1914, mosaic covers with fillets & fleurons in corners, raised bands & mosaic motif on spine, arms of Clermont-Tonnerre, double end-papers of silk & marb. paper, s.-c. Sigd. (HD. Jun.29; 68e) Frs. 1,600
– **Le Parcours du Rêve au Souvenir.** Ill.:– after Laszlo (port.). 1908. Definitive Edn.; on Jap. Lge. 8vo. Mor. by Meunier, 1914, mosaic covers with fillets & fleurons in corners, raised bands & mosaic motif on spine, arms of Clermont-Tonnerre, double end-papers of silk & marb. paper, s.-c. Sigd. (HD. Jun.29; 68d) Frs. 1,500
– **Les Perles Rouges. Les Paroles Diaprées.** Ill.:– after Laszlo (port.). 1910. Definitive Edn.; on Jap. Lge. 8vo. Mor. by Meunier, 1914, mosaic covers with fillets & fleurons in corners, raised bands & mosaic motif on spine, arms of Clermont-Tonnerre, double end-papers of silk & marb. paper, s.-c. Sigd. (HD. Jun.29; 68f) Frs. 1,820
– **Prière de Tous.** Ill.:– Madelaine Lemaire. Paris, 1902. On China. Sm. 4to. Mor. by Meunier, 1908, mosaic decor. on upr. cover & spine, double end-papers of silk & marb. paper, arms of Clermont-Tonnere on spine. (HD. Jun.29; 67b) Frs. 4,000
– **Les Prières de Tous.–Passiflora.** Ill.:– after Laszlo (port.). 1912. Definitive Edn.; on Jap. 2 works in 1 vol. Lge. 8vo. Mor. by Meunier, 1914, mosaic covers with fillets & fleurons in corners, raised bands & mosaic motif on spine, arms of Clermont-Tonnerre, double end-papers of silk & marb. paper, s.-c. Sigd. (HD. Jun.29; 68g) Frs. 1,700
– **Professionnelles Beautés.** Paris, 1908. On L.P. Red mor. by Meunier, 1908, mosaic decor. on covers, raised bands & gt. figures on spine, double end-papers of silk & marb. paper, wrap. with raised bands & mosaic on spine, s.-c. Dedication copy to Philibert, Marquis de Clermont-Tonnerre, 16-verse autograph poem at beginning. (HD. Jun.29; 67a) Frs. 1,800

MONTESSON, Mme. de la Haie de Riou, Marquise de
[–] **Oeuvres Anonymes: Theatre (Mélanges).** Paris, 1782-85. 1st. Edn. 8 vols. Vols. I-V & Mélanges in red mor. by Derome le Jeune with his ticket, triple gt. fillet, flat spine gt. with sm. fleuron in compartments, inner gt. dentelles, vols. VI-VII in bright red mor., tooling not unif. (SM. Oct.7; 1869) Frs. 5,800

MONTFAUCON, Bernard de
– **L'Antiquité Expliquée et Representée en Figures.** Paris, 1719-24. Vol. 1, pt. 2; Vol. 2 pts. 1 & 2; vol. 3 pt. 1; vol. 5 pts. 1 & 2, supp., vol. 2 & 3., together 8 vols only (of 15). Fo. Cont. spr. cf. (SH. Jan.29; 270) Tropper. £150
– – **Anr. Edn.** Paris, 1722. 2nd. Edn. 5 vols. in 10. Fo. Lacks later supp., some marginal stains in vol. III pt. 2. Cont. cf., gt., arms of Prondre de Guermantes on covers, but without cipher, double gt. fillet, spines gt. in compartments with fleurons & couronnes fermées on pointillé ground, inner gt.

dentelle. Bkplt. of Admiral Duff. (SM Oct.7; 1870) Frs. 9,000
– – **Anr. Edn.** Paris, 1722-24. 2nd. Edn in 10 vols. plus Supp., together 15 vols. Lge. fo. Cont. cf., very worn. (SG. May 14; 151) $450
– – **Anr. Edn.** Paris, n.d. Vols. 1-10 2nd. Edn. 15 vols., including 5 Supp. vols. Fo. Later hf. cf., recovered. (CSK. Apr.24; 71) £550
– **L'Antiquité expliquée et représentée en Figures. –Supplement au Livre de l'Antiquité expliquée et Representée en Figures.** Paris, 1722. 2nd. Edn. 5 vols. bnd. in 10; 5 vols., together 15 vols. Fo. A few plts. loose. Unif. cont. marb. cf., gt. spines, raised in compartments, some corners & spines with minor imperfections. (VG. Oct.13; 109) Fls. 4,500
– **Antiquitiy Explained.** Trans.:– David Humphreys. 1721-25. 1st. Edn. in Engl. 7 vols., including 5 vols. Supp. in 2 vols. Fo. Lacks final blanks in vol. IV & 2nd. vol. of Supp., some staining in vol. IV-V, affecting some plts., vol. V wormed thro.-out in lr. margins, occasional browning & spotting. Cont. spr. cf., gt., some wear. W.a.f. (S. Jan.26; 94) Hendrick. £150
– – **Anr. Copy.** Cont. cf., worn. (SG. Sep.25; 236) $650
– **Bibliotheca Coisliniana [H.C. du Cambout], olim Segueriana.** Paris, 1715. 1st. Edn. Fo. Lacks final blank, occasional browning & spotting. Mod. hf. cf. (S. Jun.23; 249) Dawson. £120
– **Griechische und Römische Alterthümer.** Ed.:– J.S. Semier. Trans.:– J.J. Schatz. Nuremb., 1757. 1st. German, shortened Edn. Sm. Fo. Lacks pp. 373-74. Engraved title reprd., 2 ll. text restored tears, light browning in parts. Cont. vell., soiled. (H. Dec.9/10; 924) DM 420
– **Les Monuments de la Monarchie Françoise.** Paris, 1729-33. Vols. 1-5. Fo. Old cf. (BS. Feb.25; 250) £110
– – **Anr. Copy.** Old cf. gt., worn. (BS. Jun.11; 69) £90
– **Palaeographia Gracea . . .** Paris, 1708. 1st. Edn. Fo. 2XI damaged, slightly affecting engraving, 1 lf. slightly torn, just affecting text, some old marginalia. Mod. hf. cf. (S. Oct.21; 305) Artico. £270

MONTFORT, Eugène
– **La Belle Enfant.** Ill.:– Raoul Dufy. 1930. Mor., stylised decor., by Cretté. On vell. d'Arches. (SH. Oct.10; 199) Frs. 9,000

MONTGOMERY, Viscount Bernard Law of Alamein
– **El Alamein to the River Sangro, Normandy to the Baltic.** Arcadia Pr., 1971. (265) sigd. Orig. mor. gt., s.-c. (SH. Feb.20; 347) Downing. £55
– **History of Warfare.** 1969. Ltd. sigd. Edn. 4to. Mor. gt. with overlay on upr. cover, by Zaehnsdorf, buckram box. (P. Sep.11; 26) £60
– – **Anr. Copy.** (265) sigd. Orig. mor., centrepiece of mor. onlays & gt. tooling, cl. box. (SH. Feb.20; 339) Mrs J.F.E. Smith. £50

MONTHERLANT, Henry de
– **Cardinal d'Espagne.** Ill.:– Pierre-Yves Tremois. Paris, 1960. (250), sigd. by artist, author & publisher. Fo. Orig. wraps., folder & box. (SPB. Nov.25; 417) $275
– **Le Chant des Amazones.** Ill.:– Mariette Lydis. Paris, 1931. (165); (1) on tinted China, numbered. 4to. Orig. drawings & states of lithos. Mor. by Gozzi, profile of a girl in gold on upr. cover, silk doubls., wrap. preserved, s.-c. (SM. Feb.11; 261) Frs. 30,000
– **Les Jeunes Filles.** Ill.:– Marie Laurencin. Paris, 1937. Ltd. Edn. numbered. Orig. wraps., unc., unopened. (SH. Nov.21; 379) Fletcher. £80
– – **Anr. Edn.** Ill.:– Mariette Lydis. Paris, 1938. (350) numbered on Rives vell. 4to. Set of ills. at end in 5 or 6 states, 3 orig. drawings. Maroon mor. by Trinckvel, mosaic title in mor. on spine, silk doubls., wrap. preserved, s.-c. (SM. Feb.11; 262) Frs. 26,000
– **Les Lépreuses.** Ill.:– Van Dongen. Paris, 1946. (342) numbered on Rives vell. 4to. Hf. mor., wrap. preserved. (SM. Feb.11; 263) Frs. 1,000
– **La Relève du Matin.** Ill.:– Michel Ciry. Paris, 1949. (236); (50) on Montval. Sm. 4to. In sheets, publisher's s.-c. (HD. Dec.5; 153) Frs. 1,500
– **La Ville dont le Prince est un Enfant.** Ill.:– Raymond Carrance. Bourg-La-Reine, 1967. (17) on Jap. nacré. 4to. With suite on Japon nacré, 1 on Arches, 2 copper engrs. in portfo., 3 double plts., 2 plts. on wtrd-silk lined satin. Wraps & folding cl. box. Sigd. (SM. Oct.8; 2306) Frs. 1,400

MONTHLY CHAPBOOK, The
Ed.:– Harold Monro. 1919-25. Nos. 1-40, compl.
set & 3 dupls. Orig. wraps. or bds., some worn. (S.
Jul.22; 233) *Sherlock.* £130

MONTHOLON, Charles Jean François Tristan, Marquis de
– **Mémoires.** 1823-24. 5 vols. Cont. hf. cf. (HD.
Oct.10; 260) Frs. 1,050

MONTI, Antonio
*See–*BERTARELLI, Achille & Monti, Domenico

MONTIF, Lucian
*See–*GABRIEL, Peter–ROLL, Timotheus von
–MONTIF, Lucian–M[ULLER], M.F.G.

MONTIGNY
[–] **Les Stratagèmes des Echecs . . .** Paris &
Strassburg, An X [1802]. 1st. Edn. 2 vols. 32mo.
Cont. red str.-grd. mor. gt. W.A. Marsden
bk.-label. (SG. Apr.9; 132) $150
– **Stratagems of Chess.** L., 1818. 4th. Edn. 16mo.
Cont. mor., stpd. design in gt. borders, spine gt.
Armorial bkplt. of Derwent Coleridge. (SG.
Apr.9; 134) $110

MONTIGNY, Charles Claude de
– **Thérèse Philosophe.** Ill.:– Comte de Caylus.
Glasgow, 1773. 2 pts. in 1 vol. Sm. 18mo. Cont.
marb. cf., decor. spine. (HD. Apr.10; 354)
Frs. 3,600

MONTLUC, Blaise de
– **The Commentaries.** Trans.:– [Charles Cotton].
1674. 1st. Edn. in Engl. Fo. Title sigd. 'P.
Tyrwhitt', slight browning, 1 or 2 sm. holes
slightly affecting text. Cont. cf. [Wing M2506]
(S. Sep.29; 57) *Trotman.* £70

MONTORGUEIL, Georges
– **Joons à l'Histoire, La France mise en scène avec
les Joujoux de deux Petits François.** Ill.:– Job.
Paris, 1908. 4to. Ills. mntd. on stubs. Orig. pict.
cl., very slightly soiled. (SH. Mar.19; 145)
Schierenberg. £65
– **Paris Dansant.** Ill.:– Vigna Vigneron after A.
Willette. Paris, 1898. 1st Edn., (200). 4to.
Havanna hf. mor. by Marius Magnim, corners,
mosaic spine, unc., wrap. & spine. (HD.
Dec.5; 154) Frs. 2,700
– **La Parisienne peinte par Elle-Meme.** Ill.:– Henry
Somm. Paris, 1897. (150) numbered on Holland
paper with publisher's initials. Text foxed
thro.-out. Crushed lev., triple gt. fillet borders,
spine gt. with floral inlays, gt. dentelles, by
Canape, orig. wraps. bnd. in. (SG. Sep.4; 53)
$200
– – **Anr. Copy.** Crushed lev., triple gt. fillet
borders, spine gt. with inlays, wide gt. dentelles, by
Canapé, orig. wraps. bnd. in. (SG.
Apr.9; 107) $170
– – **Anr. Copy.** Mor. gt. by Rivière, orig. wraps.
bnd. in. (SM. Oct.8; 2359) Frs. 5,500
– **La Tour d'Auvergne, Premier Grenadier de
France.–Louis XI.–Napoléon.** Ill.:– Job. Paris,
1902; 1905; [1921]. 3 vols. Fo. All cold. pict. cl.,
ex-liby. (SG. Apr.2; 140) $200

MONTPENSIER, Anne Marie Louise d'Orléans, Duchesse de
– **Mémoires . . .** Amst., 1735-46. New Edn. 8 vols.
in 4. 12mo. Lacks some first & final blank ll., 1 lf.
strengthened. 18th. C. mor., triple gt. fillet, flat
spines gt., inner gt. dentelles, 2 perforations in lr.
cover of 2nd. vol. (SM. Oct.7; 1872) Frs. 3,200
– – **Anr. Edn.** Ed.:– M. Petitot. 1825. 3 vols. (nos.
41, 42, 43 & last pt. vol. 40). Lacks title-p. at head
of 1st. vol. Cont. cf., blind decor. borders, gt.
spine, inner dentelle, 1 jnt. brkn. Ex liby.,
coat-of-arms of Louis Philippe d'Orleans. (HD.
Feb.18; 161) Frs. 2,400

MONTUCLA, Jean Etienne
– **Histoire des Mathématiques.** Paris, 1758. 1st.
Edn. 2 vols. 4to. Some staining & browning. Cont.
mott. cf., worn. From Honeyman Collection. (S.
May 20; 3288) *Phelps.* £120
– – **Anr. Edn.** Paris, 1799-1802. New Edn. 4 vols.
4to. Some spotting. Cont. 'Spanish' cf., gt. spines.
Bkplt. of Bibliotheca Lindesiana; from Honeyman
Collection. (S. May 20; 3289) *Hill.* £140
– – **Anr. Copy.** Slight dampstaining, disposal stp.
of Lincoln's Inn liby. on verso of 1st. title. Mod. cl.
From Honeyman Collection. (S. May 20; 3290)
Rogers Turner. £90

MONTULE, Edouard de
– **Recueil des Cartes et des Vues du Voyage en
Amérique . . .** [Paris], [1821]. Ob. fo. 59 litho.

plts., without 2 text vols. Cont. hf. cf., worn. Sigd.
(S. Mar.31; 493) *Gal. San Giorgio.* £100
– **A Voyage to North America & the West Indies
in 1817.** L., 1821. Foxed, lacks 04 (blank?). Hf.
mor. From liby. of William E. Wilson. [Sabin
50230] (SPB. Apr.29; 208) $150
*See–*LEWIS, Matthew Gregory–MONTULE,
Edouard de

**MONUMENS DE LA VIE Privée des Douze
Césars**
Capri, 1782. Cont. mott. sheep, spine gt. & torn at
head & foot. (CSK. Mar.13; 11) £75

MONZO, Elias Tormo y
– **Fray Juan Ricci.** Ed.:– E. Lafuente Ferrati.
Madrid, 1930. 2 vols. 4to. Ptd. wraps., unc. (SG.
Mar.12; 310) $220

MOODIE, D.C.F.
– **The History of the Battles & Adventures of the
British, the Boers & the Zulus etc. in Southern
Africa.** Cape Town, 1888. 2 vols. Hf. mor. Hans
Sauers copy. (SSA. Jun.18; 217) R. 130

MOORCROFT, W. & Trebeck, G.
– **Travels in the Himalayan Provinces of Hindustan
& the Panjab.** Ed.:– H.H. Wilson. 1841. 2 vols.
Orig. cl. (SH. Mar.5; 101) *Quaritch.* £270

MOORE, Sir Alan
– **Sailing Ships of War, 1800-1860.** 1926. (100). 2
vols. including portfo. of plts. 4to. Hf. pig., s.-c.
(P. Mar.12; 1) *Green.* £110
– – **Anr. Edn.** 1926. 1st. Edn. (1,500) numbered.
4to. Orig. cl. (SKC. Feb.26; 1782) £65

MOORE, Clement Clarke
– **Night Before Christmas.** Ill.:– W.W. Denslow.
N.Y., 1902. 1st. Edn. 4to. Cl. (2nd. state of bdg.).
(SG. Apr.9; 75) $110
– – **Anr. Edn.** Ill.:– Arthur Rackham. L., [1931].
(275) numbered for England, sigd. by artist. Limp
vell., orig. s.-c. Raymond M. Sutton Jr. copy. (SG.
May 7; 211) $600
– – **Anr. Edn.** Ill.:– Arthur Rackham. L., [1931].
1st. Trade Edn. Cold. pict. wraps. & d.-w. Cold.
gift card & card advertising Deluxe Ltd. Edn. laid
in, Jeannette M. Hopkins bkplt., Raymond M.
Sutton Jr. copy. (SG. May 7; 212) $200
– – **Anr. Edn.** Ill.:– Arthur Rackham. Phila.,
[1931]. (275) numbered for America, sigd. by
artist. Limp vell., orig. s.-c. Jeannette M. Hopkins
bkplt., Raymond M. Sutton Jr. copy. (SG. May
7; 213) $600
– – **Anr. Copy.** Inscr. on hf.-title. Orig. vell. gt.,
box, slight wear. (SPB. May 29; 359) $450
– – **Anr. Edn.** L., [1939]. Cold. pict. wraps., unc.,
unopened, envelope. Raymond M. Sutton Jr. copy.
(SG. May 7; 215) $100

MOORE, Edward
– **Poems, Fables & Plays.** 1756. 1st. Coll. Edn.
4to. Cont. cf., gt. spine. (S. Nov.24; 214)
Traylen. £65

MOORE, Francis
– **Travels into the Inland Parts of Africa.** 1783. 1st.
Edn. Folding engraved map & 10 plts., 1 folding,
folding map & plt. rebkd., Birmingham Liby. stp.
on map, plts. & few ll. Mod. panel. cf., spine gt.
(S. Mar.31; 494) *Reddui.* £90

MOORE, George
– **The Brook Kerith.–Peronnik.** Ill.:– Stephen
Gooden (both works). 1929; 1933. (375); (525);
each sigd. by author & artist. 2 works in 2 vols.
Vell., unc. & unopened, s.-c. (1st. work); & vell.,
gt., partly unc., s.-c. (C. Jul.22; 84) *Wood.* £80
– **Flowers of Passion.** L., 1878. 1st. Edn. Square
8vo. Errata slip tipped-in, lf. of advts. at end. Cl.,
with lge. gt. design, rebkd. (SG. Nov.13; 509)
$190
– **Literature at Nurse or Circulating Morals.** L.,
1885. 1st. Edn. Wrinkled & slightly dampstained.
Sewed as iss., in mor. solander s.-c. Bkplt. of John
Quinn laid-in. (SG. Nov.13; 513) $550
– **Modern Painting.** L., 1893. 1st. Edn. Advts. Cl.,
unopened. Inscr. (SG. Nov.13; 515) $110
– **Pagan Poems.** L., 1881. 1st. Edn. Cl., shaken, in
lev. solander s.-c. by Rivière. Inscr. on title verso
& title recto. (SG. Nov.13; 512) $850
– **Peronnik the Fool.** Ill.:– Stephen Gooden. L.,
1933. (525) sigd. by author & artist. 4to. Vell.,
partly unc., boxed. (SG. Oct.23; 144) $200

MOORE, George H.
– **Washington as an Angler.** N.Y., [H] 1887. 1st.
Edn. Cl., unc. Pres. copy to Fred Mather. (SG.
Oct.16; 224) $240

– – **Anr. Copy.** 12mo. Bnd. without the ports.
Gt.-lettered limp cl. Inscr. to C.W. Fredrickson.
(SG. Dec.11; 77) $130
– – **Anr. Copy.** Sheet presenting this to Reynolds
from Woodward tipped in. (SG. Dec.11; 111)
$100

MOORE, George & Lopez, Bernard
– **Martin Luther.** L., 1879. 1st. Edn. Gt.-lettered cl.
Inscr. to Edmund Gosse (with his bkplt.), T.L.s.
from G. Russell with autograph postscript
tipped-in. (SG. Nov.13; 510) $600

MOORE, Henry
– **Heads, Figures & Ideas.** Ed.:– Geoffrey Grigson.
1958. Fo. Orig. cl.-bkd. bds., d.-w. (SH.
Mar.27; 340) *Duran.* £60

MOORE, John
[–] **A Treatise on Domestic Pigeons.** 1765. Slight
browning. Cont. mott. cf. (S. Jun.1; 174)
Quaritch. £180

MOORE, John Hamilton
– **A New & Complete Collection of Voyages &
Travels.** L., ca. 1780. 1st. Edn. 2 vols. Fo. Old cf.,
needs rebdg. (SG. Oct.30; 255) $375
– – **Anr. Edn.** [1788]. 2 vols. Fo. 1 map torn, slight
staining. Cont. tree cf., rebkd. Countess of
Sutherland bkplt. (S. Nov.4; 485) *Heines.* £180

MOORE, John Hamilton–FALCONER, William
– **The Practical Navigator.–A New Universal
Dictionary of the Marine.** Ed.:– William Burney
(2nd. work). 1791; 1815. 9th. Edn. (1st. work). 2
works in 2 vols. 8vo.; 4to. Sheep (1st. work); & cf.
(S. Jul.27; 7) *Remington.* £130

MOORE, Sir Jonas
– **A Mathematical Compendium, or, Useful
Practices in Arithmetick, Geometry, & Astronomy.**
Ed.:– Nicholas Stephenson. 1674. 1st. Edn. 12mo.
Some worming, mostly marginal. Cont. mor., gt.,
spine wormed. From Honeyman Collection.
[Wing M2572] (S. May 20; 3291)
McKittrick. £130

MOORE, Joseph
– **Eighteen Views Taken at And Near Rangoon.** L.,
ca. 1825-26. Fo. Aquatints & letter press tipped in.
Cont. hf. crimson mor. by Andrews, Waterford.
(GM. Apr.30; 725) £675

**MOORE, Lieut. Joseph & Marryat, Capt.
Frederick**
– **Rangoon Views & Combined Operations in the
Birman Empire.** Ill.:– T. Stothard & others.
1825-26. 2 series in 1 vol. Fo. Lacks map, last plt.
in 2nd. series & all text. Cont. cl. gt. W.a.f. (C.
May 20; 155) *Cumming.* £320

MOORE, Mrs. M.B.
– **The Dixie Speller.** Raleigh, 1864. 1st. Edn.
12mo. Sewed, laid in orig. cl.-bkd. ptd. bds. (SG.
Jun.11; 118) $120

MOORE, Marianne
– **Poems.** 1921. 1st. Edn. Orig. wraps. (SH.
Dec.18; 215) *Words. etc.* £100

MOORE, T. Sturge
– **A Brief Account of the Origin of the Eragny
Press.** Ill.:– Lucien Pissarro. Eragny Pr., 1903.
(241). Orig. bds., unc. (S. Jul.31; 26)
Warrack & Perkins. £260
– **The Little School, a Posy of Rhymes.** Eragny Pr.,
1905. (185). Orig. bds., unc. (S. Jul.31; 33)
Quaritch. £160

MOORE, Thomas, Botanist
– **The Ferns of Great Britain & Ireland.** Ill.:–
Henry Bradbury. 1855. [1st. Edn.?]. Fo. Spotting,
some browning & offsetting, title & hf.-title
cleanly torn, both with plts. Orig. hf. mor.,
worn & disbnd. (CSK. Mar.27; 68) £320
– – **Anr. Copy.** Slight browning & soiling. Cont.
hf. roan, worn. (S. Sep.29; 95) *Harris.* £260
– – **Anr. Copy.** Dampstained, loose. Hf. mor.,
worn & stained. (S. Jul.27; 300) *Morrow.* £190
– – **Anr. Copy.** Qtr. mor., gt. spine, unc., jnts.
reprd. From collection of Massachusetts
Horticultural Society, plts. unstpd. (SPB.
Oct.1; 150) $3,500
– – **Anr. Edn.** Ed.:– John Lindley. 1857. Fo.
Hf.-title detchd., loose. Cont. hf. mor. gt., slightly
worn. (SBA. Dec.16; 146a) *Harris.* £200
– **Illustrations of Orchidaceous Plants . . .** L., 1857.
100 hand-cold. engraved plts., some detchd. Cont.
qtr. mor., spine gt. (CNY. May 22; 208) $1,000

MOORE, Thomas, Botanist *-contd.*
– **Nature Printed British Ferns.** 1859. 2 vols. A few ll. slightly spotted or stained. ?Orig. cl.-bkd. bds., soiled. (SKC. May 19; 424) £65

MOORE, Thomas & Dombrain, Rev. H. Honeywood
– **The Floral Magazine.** 1861-67. Vols. 1-6. Some ll. slightly spotted. Orig. cl. (SKC. Feb.26; 1601) £580

MOORE, Thomas, Poet 'Thomas Little'
– **Irish Melodies.** Ill.:– D. Maclise. 1846. 4to. Proof impressions of ill. text after Maclise, slight browning. Orig. bds., boxed. (CSK. Jan.23; 37) £170
– **Lalla Rookh.** L., 1822. Early crimson str.-grd. mor. gt. Fore-e. pntg.; from the liby. of Zola E. Harvey. (SG. Mar.19; 152) $375
– **Memoirs of the Life of . . . Richard Brinsley Sheridan.** L., 1827. 2 vols. Early mor., worn. Fore-e. pntg. in each vol.; from the liby. of Zola E. Harvey. (SG. Mar.19; 153) $500

MOORE, William
– **The Story of Australian Art.** Sydney, 1934. 2 vols. 4to. Orig. cl., d.-w.'s. (SKC. May 19; 215) £100

MOOREHEAD, Alan
– **Darwin & the Beagle.** Arcadia Pr., 1970. (265) sigd. 4to. Orig. mor. gt., upr. cover centrepiece of mor. onlays & gt. tooling, cl. box. (SH. Feb.20; 342) *Smith.* £65
– – **Anr. Edn.** L., Arcadia Pr., 1970. (250) for sale, in Zaehnsdorf bdg. Mor. by Zaehnsdorf, with contrasting inlays, in fleece-lined s.-c. (KH. Nov.18; 429) Aus. $170

MOQUIN-TANDON, Alfred
– **Historie Naturelle des Mollusques.** Paris, 1855. 3 vols. Cont. hf. Fr. cf., gt. spines, slightly worn. (S. Jun.1; 175) *Verdcourt.* £120

MORAIS, C. de
– **Le Veritable Fauconnier.** Paris, 1683. 1st. Edn. 12mo. Some spots. Mor., gt., by Niedrée. (S. Feb.10; 451) *Maggs.* £220

MORALISTES ANCIENS (Collection des)
Paris, 1783. 20 vols. 16mo. Various bdgs., some in mor., the first 7 consecutive vols. in old cf. (HD. Apr.9; 530) Frs. 2,200

MORAND, Paul
– **Fermé la Nuit.** Ill.:– Jules Pascin. Paris, 1925. (407) numbered. 4to. Orig. wraps., spine worn. (SH. Nov.21; 438) *Graziani-Levy.* £95
– **Magie Noire.** Paris, 1928. Orig. Edn., (35) on Montval. 4to. Hf. mor., art africain decor. limp spine, gt. & mosaic fillets, by Paul Bonet. (LM. Mar.21; 205) B.Frs. 11,000
– **Ouvert la Nuit.–Fermé la Nuit.** 1922; 1923. Reprint, on vergé pur fil Lafuma, 4to. Ornamental hf. cf., by Anthoine Legrain. (HD. Oct.10; 127) Frs. 2,500

MORAND, S.F.
– **Opuscules de Chirurgie.** Paris, 1768-1772. 1st. Edn. 2 pts. in 1 vol. 4to. Slightly browned & spotted. Cont. mott. cf., worn. From liby. of Dr. E. Ashworth Underwood. (S. Feb.23; 258) *Dawson.* £110

MORANDI, Giambattista
– **Historia Botanica Pratica.** Milan, 1744. 1st. Edn. Fo. Sm. tear in additional etched title just touching plt.-mark. Cont. cf., worn, rebkd. From Chetham's Liby., Manchester. (C. Nov.27; 303) *Phelps.* £350
– – **Anr. Copy.** Slight browning. Very worn, covers detchd. (S. Apr.6; 112) *Frick.* £200

MORANT, Philip
– **The History & Antiquities of the County of Essex.** 1768. 1st. Edn. 2 vols. Fo. Cont. tree cf., gt. spines. (C. Feb.25; 46) *Hughes.* £320
– – **Anr. Copy.** Cf. (P. Jan.22; 308) *Roberts.* £300
– – **Anr. Copy.** 2 vols. in 4. Maps, some folding, inter-ll., extra-ill. with plts., maps, orig. sketches, including a pencil sketch attributed to Samuel Prout, lacks text relating to Colchester, some ll. detchd. Cont. hf. russ., worn. W.a.f. (CSK. May 15; 80) £220
– – **Anr. Copy.** 2 vols. Lr. margin of title & 1st. lf. in vol. II reprd. Bkplts. of R. Ruding & William Bree, lately in the collection of Eric Sexton. (C. Apr.16; 308) *Castle.* £180

MORAZZONI, Giuseppe
– **Il Libro Illustrato Veneziano del Settecento.** Milan, 1943. 1 vol. in 3. 4to. Buckram. From the collection of John A. Saks, with many MS. corrections & typed slips tipped in. (C. Jun.10; 278) *Weinreb.* £200
– **Il Mobile Veneziano del '700.** Milan, 1927. 4to. Limp publisher's cl. (CR. Mar.19; 225) Lire 380,000
– – **Anr. Copy.** Publisher's cl. (CR. Jun.11; 290) Lire 300,000
– **La Rilegatura Piemontese nel '700.** Milan, 1929. (300) numbered. 4to. Mod. hf. cf., orig. wraps. bnd. in. (SI. Dec.3; 411) Lire 220,000

MORDEN, R.
– **[New Description & State of England.]** [1701 or later]. 50 engraved maps only (Hertfordshire, Worcestershire, Somerset & England lacking), soiling, some margins torn, title & contents lf. lacking. Cont. cf., rebkd. (CSK. Oct.3; 116) £340

MORE, Cresacre
[–] Life & Death of Sir Thomas More. ?Douai, [1631]. 1st. Edn. Sm. 4to. Sm. hole in 3H4 cutting 1 letter. Mod. mor., gt., cont. mott. cf. panels with gt. centre ornaments bnd. in as doubls. Bkplts. of Walter Bagot, Gladys Robinson, W.T. Shirley II, Robert Hoe, John J. Phelan & R.B. Adam. [NSTC 18066] (S. May 5; 298) *Traylen.* £280
[–] – Anr. Copy. Title & 1st. lf. of dedication extended & reprd. at inner margin, soiling, stains, tears & foxing. Later cf. (S. May 6; 228) $375

MORE, Hannah
– **Sacred Dramas, Search after Happiness, & Essays on Various Subjects.** L., 1845. 16mo. Gt.-tooled mor., 1 cover detchd. Fore-e. pntg.; from the liby. of Zola E. Harvey. (SG. Mar.19; 154) $180
– **Strictures on the Modern System of Female Education.** 1799. 1st. Edn. 2 vols. Orig. bds., worn, unc. (SH. Dec.10; 42a) *Maggs.* £70

MORE, Henry
– **Enchiridon Ethicum.–Epistola H. Mori ad V.C.** L., 1669; n.d. 2nd. Edn.; 3rd. Edn. 2 works in 1 vol. Cont. cf., bkplt. (CB. Feb.18; 198) Can. $100
[–] Observations upon Anthrosophia Theomagica, & Anima Magica Abscondita. By Alazonomastix Philalethes.–The Second Lash of Alazonomastix . . . [L.]; Camb., 1650; 1651. 1st. Edns. 2 works in 1 vol. Some browning & soiling; 1st. work lacks 1st. lf. (blank?) & G8; 2nd. lacks last lf. (blank?). Cont. cf., worn. [Wing M2667; 2677] (S. Jun.29; 401) *Weiner.* £200
– **Philosophicall Poems.** 1647. 1st. Collected Edn. 4 pts. in 1 vol. Title sigd. 'Alex: Tytler, 1770', slight browning & soiling. Cont. cf., rebkd. [Wing M2670] (S. Jun.29; 402) *Pickering & Chatto.* £260

MORE, John
– **A Table from the Beginning of the World to this Day.** 1593. Cont. cf., rebkd. 17th. C. sigs. of W. & J. Bartlet on title, lately in the collection of Eric Sexton. [STC 18074] (C. Apr.15; 123) *Laywood.* £60

MORE, Sir Thomas
– **La Description de l'Isle d'Utopie.** Paris, 1550. 1st. Fr. Edn. Mor. gt., sigd. by Cuzin, decor. gt. fillets, stps. etc., triple gold fillets on covers inner & outer dentelles, marb. paper end-ll. (D. Dec.11-13; 2573) DM 11,000
– **De Optimo Reipublicae Statu, Deque Nova Insula Utopia Libellus Vere Aureus [Epigrammata . . . Epigrammata des Erasmi].** Ill.:– Hans Holbein & Urs Graf. Basle, J. Froben, Nov.-Dec., 1518. 3 pts. in 1 vol. 4to. 17th. C. cf., spine gt., upr. cover detchd. (S. Nov.25; 350) *Martin.* £850
– **Utopia.** Trans.:– R. Robinson. L., 1551. 1st. Edn. in Engl. Sm. tear reprd. in lr. margin of M1 touching sig., some slight staining. Red mor. gt., by Rivière, some wear to jnts. & corners, qtr. red mor. s.-c. From the Prescott Collection. (CNY. Feb.6; 259) $29,000
– – **Anr. Edn.** Trans.:– Ralphe Robynson. [1556]. 2nd. Edn., 1st. State. Title reprd., without textual loss, next 7 ll. washed & resized, repairs to corners of S5-6. 17th. C. spr. cf., gt., rebkd. [STC 18095] (S. Feb.10; 452) *Quaritch.* £850
– – **Anr. Edn.** Trans.:– Gilbert Burnet. 1684. 1st. Edn. of this trans. Lacks 1st. blank. Cont. red mor., panel. in gt. [Wing M2691] (S. Dec.9; 340) *Quaritch.* £130
– – **Anr. Copy.** Cont. cf., worn. (S. Jan.26; 60) *Traylen.* £50
– – **Anr. Edn.** Ed.:– T.F. Dibdin. 1808. L.P. 4to. Late 19th. C. red lev. mor. by F. Bedford, gt., partly unc. (S. Nov.24; 215) *Howes.* £240
– – **Anr. Edn.** Ed.:– T.F. Dibdin. 1808. (250) L.P. Some slight spotting, plt. shaved at lr. edge with some loss of imprint. Cont. mor., gt., bkplt. of Edward Bellamy. (S. Apr.7; 411) *Hyde Park.* £90
– – **Anr. Edn.** Ed.:– F.S. Ellis. Hammersmith, Kelms. Pr., 1893. (300). Orig. limp vell., silk ties, unc. (CNY. May 22; 317) $500
– – **Anr. Copy.** Vell., lacks ties. (SG. Jan.15; 47) $400
– – **Anr. Edn.** Ill.:– Eric Gill. Gold. Cock. Pr., 1929. (500). 4to. Orig. buckram gt. (SH. Feb.20; 395) *Greenhill.* £65
– **Workes.** 1557. 1st. Coll. Edn. Fo. With the unsigd. lf. after CC5 & the 8 unpaginated ll. of Juvenile poems, wormed thro.-out. Cont. cf., rebkd. [STC 18076] (C. Nov.19; 17) *Hartley.* £1,200

MOREAS, Jean
– **Les Stances.** Lyons, 1923. (20) on imperial Japon, numbered. Mosaic mor. by Marcel Day, mor. doubls., wrap. preserved. A.L.s. by author. (SM. Feb.11; 264) Frs. 2,600

MOREAU
See–**HALL & Moreau**

MOREAU, Hegesippe
– **Petits Contès à ma Soeur.** Ill.:– Dunki. Paris, 1896. (145) on vell. 4to. Ills. on China paper. Mor. by Canape, gt. red mor. doubls., wrap. preserved. (SM. Feb.11; 265) Frs. 5,000

MOREAU, Jean Michel le Jeune
– **Estampes destinées à orner les Editions de M. de Voltaire dediées à sons Altesse Royale Monseigneur le Prince de Prusse.** Ill.:– after Moreau le Jeune, engrs. by Baquoy & others. Paris, [1784-88]. Red brown mor. by Anker Kyster, gt., stpd. decor., triple gold fillets & blind-stpd. borders, gold borders on inner dentelles, s.-c. (D. Dec.11-13; 699) DM 2,200

MOREAU-NELATON, Etienne
– **Corot, Raconté par Lui-Même.** Paris, 1924. (600) on papier d'arches. 4to. Red hf. mor., orig. wraps. bnd. in, unc. (C. Jul.22; 85) *Sims & Reed.* £160
– **Jongkind Raconté par lui-même.** Paris, 1918. (600) numbered. 4to. Orig. wraps. (SH. Oct.9; 87) *D. Lindsay.* £155
– **Manet, Raconté par Lui-Même.** Paris, 1926. (700) on papier de arches. 2 vols. 4to. Red hf. mor., orig. wraps. bnd. in, partly unc. (C. Jul.22; 86) *Sims & Reed.* £190

MOREHOUSE, George R.
See–**MITCHELL, Silas Weir & others**

MORELL, Sir Charles (Pseud.)
See–**RIDLEY, James**

MORELLI, Jacopo
– **Bibliotheca Maphaei Pinelli Veneti.** Ill.:– Bartolozzi (frontis. port.). Venice, 1787. 6 vols. Cont. cf.-bkd. bds., slight worming to spines. From the collection of John A. Saks. (C. Jun.10; 279) *Forster.* £160
– **Notizia d'Opere de Disegno nello prima meta' del Secolo XVI.** Bassano, 1800. 1st. Edn. Later vell., gt., soiled. The Beckford copy. (SH. Jun.11; 77) *Barra Books.* £50

MORERI, Louys
– **Le Grand Dictionnaire Historique.** Amst. & The Hague, 1702 [1716]. 9th. Edn. 4 vols. & 2 vols. supp. Fo. Old cf., worn. (LM. Nov.8; 117) B.Frs. 10,000
– – **Anr. Edn.** Ed.:– Vaultier. Paris, 1707. Latest Edn. 4 vols. Fo. Cont. red mor., gt. Du Seuil fillets, fleurs de lis & centre arms, decor. spine raised bands. (HD. Apr.24; 85) Frs. 12,200
– – **Anr. Edn.** Paris, 1759. 10 vols. Fo. Old cf., worn. (BS. Nov.26; 147) £50
– – **Anr. Copy.** Cont. spr. cf., decor. spines. (HD. Jun.29; 123) Frs. 4,600
– – **Anr. Copy.** Old marb. cf., 5 decor. spine raised bands. (LM. Jun.13; 205) B.Frs. 25,000

MORETTI, Tomaso
– **A General Treatise of Artillery.** Trans.:– Sir Jonas Moore. 1683. 1st. Edn. in Engl. A few plts. torn, some browning, sm. wormholes not affecting text. Cont. mott. cf., worn. Bkplt. of J.W. Knightley. [Wing M2726] (S. Jun.23; 392) *Licini.* £220

MORGAGNI, Giovanni Battista
- Adversaria Anatomica Omnia. Ed.:– G.B. Vulpius. Ill.:– G. Fabri after J.N. Francia (frontis. port.). Padua, 1717-19. 1st. Edn. (except for pt. I). 6 pts. in 1 vol. 4to. No advt. lf. at end, plt. 5 cut into by binder. Hf. cf. (S. Jun.16; 590) *Clay*. £170
- – Anr. Edn. Ed.:– G.B. Vulpius. Passau, 1719. 1st. Coll. Edn. 6 pts. in 2 vols. Lge. 4to. Cont. vell. (SG. Sep.18; 264) $375
- – Anr. Edn. Leiden, 1740-41. 7 pts., in 1. 4to. Browned. Cont. qtr. mor. (TA. Dec.18; 426) £72
- De Sedibus et Causis Morborum per Anatomen indagatis Libri quinque. Ill.:– after Jean Renard (port.). Padua, 1765. 2nd. Edn. 2 vols. in 1. Fo. Mott. cf., spine gt. (S. Jun.16; 591) *Palinurus*. £120
- – Anr. Copy. 2 vols. Foxing thro.-out. Cont. hf. vell. (SPB. Nov.25; 104) $400
- Opera Omnia. Ill.:– Renard (frontis. ports.). Padua, 1765. 5 vols. Fo. Worming in blank margin of vol. I. Cont. vell. From the collection of John A. Saks. (C. Jun.10; 168) *Burgess*. £80
- The Seats & Causes of Diseases Investigated by Anatomy. Trans.:– Benjamin Alexander. L., 1769. 1st. Edn. in Engl. 3 vols. Lge. 4to. Disbnd., ex liby. (SG. Sep.18; 265) $450
- – Anr. Copy. Occasional light foxing, 3rd. vol. title soiled & reprd. Cont. cf., very worn, some covers detchd., upr. hinge of 3rd. vol. reprd. (SPB. Nov.25; 105) $375

MORGAN, John Hill & Fielding, Mantle
- The Life Portraits of Washington & their Replicas. Phila., [1931]. (100) numbered, sigd. & specially bnd. 4to. Errata slip tipped-in. Gt.-decor. red mor., rebkd., unc. (SG. Dec.4; 253) $110

MORGAN, Thomas
- Philosophical Principles of Medicine in three parts . . . a Demonstration of the General Laws of Gravity . . . Laws which Obtain in the Motion & Secretion of the Vital Fluids, etc. 1725. Cont. cf. (S. Jun.16; 593) *Phelps*. £90

MORGUES, Matthieu de, Sieur de Saint Germain
- Recueil de Pièces pour la Defense de la Reyne Mère du Roy Trèschrestien Louys XIII. Antw., 1643. 4to. Slight browning & soiling. 18th. C. limp vell., slightly soiled. (S. Jul.27; 142) *De Jonge*. £60

MORICE, Charles
- Paul Gauguin. Paris, 1919. 4to. Mor. by Stroobants, wrap. preserved. Bkplt. of Louis Barthou. (SM. Feb.11; 266) Frs. 1,200
See–ALEXANDRE, Arsène–MORICE, Charles

MORICE, Dom P.H.
- Histoire Ecclésiastique et Civile de Bretagne. Ill.:– Guélard (vigs.). Paris, 1710-56. 2 vols. Fo. Lacks title of vol. 2, 18 (of 24) plts. Cont. marb. cf., spines decor. with raised bands, bdgs. defect. (HD. Jun.24; 92) Frs. 1,200
- Mémoires pour Servir de Preuves à l'Histoire Ecclésiastique de Bretagne . . . Paris, 1742-46. 3 vols. Fo. Cont. marb. cf., spines decor. with raised bands, bdgs. defect. (HD. Jun.24; 91) Frs. 1,400

MORIER, Sir James J.
- The Adventures of Hajji Baba . . . L., 1828. 1st. Edn. 2 vols. 12mo. Orig. hf. linen, slightly worn, bkplts., unc. (SG. Nov.13; 528) $100
- A Journey through Persia, Armenia & Asia Minor to Constantinople. 1812. 4to. Outer border of 1st. map cropped. Cont. hf. russ. From Chetham's Liby., Manchester. (C. Nov.27; 304) *Crete*. £200
- – Anr. Copy. 2Y2 reprd., 2 maps torn, some offsetting, slightly spotted. Cont. hf. cf., worn. (S. Sep.29; 186) *Troy*. £100
- A Journey through Persia, Armenia, & Asia Minor, to Constantinople.–A Second Journey. 1812; 1818. 2 vols. 4to. Some foxing & offsetting. Cont. panel. cf., rebkd., old spine of vol. I preserved, worn. (S. Jun.22; 184) *Rastegar*. £360
- – Anr. Copy. 1st. work lacks hf. title, minor spotting to some plts. Unif. cont. diced cf., gt. (C. Feb.25; 118) *Rastegar*. £320

MORIKE, Edouard
- Gedichte. Stuttgart & Tübingen, 1838. 1st. Edn. Cont. lacquered-paper-bkd. bds., gt. fillets, orig. wraps bnd. in. (HK. May 15; 4675) DM 5,200
- Vier Erzählungen. Stuttgart, 1856. 1st. Edn. Minimal soiling in places. Orig. linen, gt. spine & upr. cover. (HK. May 15; 4674) DM 480

MORIN, Claude
- [–] La Platine, l'or Blanc ou le Huitième Metal, Recueil d'Experiences faites dans les Academies Royales de Londres, de Suède etc. Paris, 1758. 12mo. Tear in last 3 ll. Qtr. cf. (S. Dec.2; 561) *Quaritch*. £130

MORIN, Louis
- French Illustrators. Ed.:– Jules Claretie. N.Y., 1893. (1030) numbered. 5 pts. in 1 vol. Fo. Each pt. with cold. pict. wraps., loose in portfo., pict. bds. (SG. Oct.2; 134) $100
- La Revue des Quat' Saisons. Paris, 1900-01. (50) numbered. 4 vols. Each vol. with dupl. set of ills. in black & white bnd. at rear. Cont. three-qtr. mor. with gt. decor. spines, orig. cold. wraps. bnd. in. (TA. Mar.19; 579) £80

MORIN, M.
- Les Cousettes. Ill.:– Henry Somm. 1895. (100) on Japon. Three quarter mor., wrap., by Carayon. (HD. Jun.30; 58) Frs. 1,150

MORIN, Simon
- Pensées.–Factum contre Simon Morin. –Déclaration de Morin depuis peu delivré de la Bastille.–Déclaration de Morin, de sa Femme et de Mademoiselle Mal'herbe . . .–Arrest de la Cour de Parlement.–Les Proces Verbal de Execution de mort de Simon Morin. 1647; 1662; 1649; 1649; 1663; 1663. 6 works in 2 vols. 18th. C. red mor., triple gt. fillet, spine compartments gt. with single fleuron (not unif.), inner gt. dentelles. Girardot de Préfond-MacCarthy-Reagh-la Bedoyere-William Beckford copy. (SM. Oct.7; 1874) Frs. 7,000

MORIS, Giuseppe Giacinto
- Flora Sardoa, seu Historia plantarum in Sardinia et Adjacentibus Insulis. Ill.:– after Jean-Cristoph Heyland & others. Turin, 1837-59. 3 vols. 4to. Hf. cf. From collection of Massachusetts Horticultural Society, stps. on plts. (SPB. Oct.1; 151) $1,800

MORISON, Sir Alexander
- Outlines of Lectures on Mental Diseases. 1826. 2nd. Edn. Light dampstain in upr. margins of last few plts. New hf. cf. (S. Jun.16; 594) *Jenner Books*. £80
- The Physiognomy of Mental Diseases. Priv. ptd., 1840. 2nd. Edn. Orig. cl. (S. Jun.16; 595) *Cooper*. £120

MORISON, Douglas
- Views of the Ducal Palaces & Hunting Seats of Saxe Coburg & Gotha. 1846. Fo. Slightly soiled. Orig. cf.-bkd. cl., loose. (SH. Nov.6; 244) *Cumming*. £250
- – Anr. Copy. Slightly soiled in parts, 1 plt. & 2 text ll. stpd. Cont. liby. linen. (R. Oct.14-18; 2188) DM 2,000
- – Anr. Copy. 17 (of 20) views, slightly browned & soiled. Hf. leath., defect. & loose. (R. Oct.14-18; 2189) DM 1,100

MORISON, Robert
- Plantarum Historiae Universalis Oxoniensis. Ed.:– J. Bobart (pt. 3). Oxford, 1680-99. 1st. Edn. Pts. 2 & 3 (all publd.) in 2 vols. Fo. Lacks 7 plts. in pt. 2, & 6 in pt. 3, but with 12 plts. at end of pt. 2 not included in Hunt, title of pt. 2 detchd., many plts. browned. 19th. C. hf. mor., covers detchd. W.a.f., from Chetham's Liby., Manchester. (C. Nov.27; 305) *Wheldon & Wesley*. £200

MORISON, Sir Stanley
- The English Newspaper. Camb., 1932. 4to. Orig. cl. (SH. May 28; 186) *Talerman*. £110
- Four Centuries of Fine Printing. 1924. (503) numbered. Fo. Cont. cl., worn. (TA. Sep.18; 103) £110
- – Anr. Edn. L., [1949]. De Luxe Edn. Minor defects. Orig. cf. (SPB. Jul.28; 373) $150
- Fra Luca de Pacioli of Borgo S. Sepolcro. N.Y., Grol. Cl., 1933. (300) numbered on Batchelor's H.M.P. Fo. Vell.-bkd. patterned bds., partly unc. (SG. Oct.2; 247) $1,000
- – Anr. Edn. Ill.:– Bruce Rogers. N.Y., Grol. Cl., 1933. (397). Lge. 4to. Orig. vell.-bkd. bds., s.-c. (SH. Feb.20; 374) *Appleton*. £290
- – Anr. Copy. Fo. Orig. bds., vell. spine & partly unc., boxed. (CNY. May 22; 334) $500
- Meisterdrucke aus Vier Jahrhunderten. Trans.:– [Anna Simons]. Berlin, 1924. (100). Lge. fo. Orig. hf. linen. (R. Oct.14-18; 571) DM 820
- Meisterdrucke Der Natur. Berlin, 1925. (150). Lge. fo. Orig. hf. linen. (R. Oct.14-18; 572) DM 950
- Modern Fine Printing. 1925. Ltd. Edn. Fo. Hf. canvas. (SH. Jul.9; 103) *Morten*. £160

- – Anr. Copy. Hf. cl., corners worn, d.-w. soiled & torn. (C. Jul.22; 123) *Forster*. £70
- Splendour of Ornament. Lion & Unicorn Pr., 1968. (400). 4to. Orig. decor. silk. (SH. Feb.20; 324) *Van Otterloo*. £55

MORISON, Stanley (Ed.)
See–FLEURON, The

MORISON, Sir Stanley & Carter, Harry
- John Fell. Oxford, 1967. (1,000). Fo. Orig. cl. (SH. Jan.29; 42) *George's*. £95
- – Anr. Copy. D.-w. (CSK. May 29; 94) £65

MORISON, Sir Stanley & Day, Kenneth
- Study of Fine Typography through Five Centuries. 1963. 4to. Numerous facs. ills. Orig. cl., d.-w. (TA. Sep.18; 16) £50

MORITZ, K. Ph.
- Anthousa oder Roms Alterthümer. Berlin, 1791-96. 1st. Edn. 2 pts. in 1 vol. Slightly soiled in parts. Cont. bds., worn. (HK. May 15; 4681) DM 850

MORLAND, Sir Samuel
- The History of the Evangelical Churches of the Valleys of Piemont. 1658. 1st. Edn. Fo. Mor. gt. by Clarke & Bedford. Bk.-label of Lord Gosford. [Wing M2779] (S. Nov.24; 216) *Howes*. £110
- – Anr. Copy. 4to. Cf., worn. (P. Sep.11; 85) *Dupont*. £50

MORLEY, Christopher
- The Eighth Sin. Oxford, 1912. 1st. Edn., (250). 12mo. Orig. ptd. wraps., qtr. mor. gt. s.-c. From the Prescott Collection. (CNY. Feb.6; 260) $400
- – Anr. Copy. Ptd. wraps., slightly frayed at edges, unc. Sig. of H.F. Miles on hf.-title. (SG. Nov.13; 529) $350
- – Anr. Copy. Orig. wraps., lacks upr. & lr. wraps., unc. Double inscr. initialled pres. copy to A. McG. (the poet Andrew McGraw) & to D.W.B. (David W. Bone), with MS. correction by author at p. 40. (PNY. Mar.26; 224) $325
- The Haunted Bookshop. Garden City, 1919. 1st. Edn., 1st. Iss. 12mo. Cl. 12-line autograph poem & inscr. to Alfred F. Goldsmith, with Goldsmith's bkplt. (SG. Jun.4; 389) $160
- Where the Blue Begins. Ill.:– Arthur Rackham. L., 1925. 1st. Trade Edn. 4to. Cl. gt., Doubleday & Page d.-w. Inscr., Raymond M. Sutton Jr. copy. (SG. May 7; 217) $150
- – Anr. Edn. Ill.:– Arthur Rackham. L. & N.Y., [1925]. (100) numbered, sigd. by author & artist. Lge. 4to. Ex-liby. Cl.-bkd. mott. bds., orig. s.-c. worn. Raymond M. Sutton Jr. copy. (SG. May 7; 218) $750
- – Anr. Copy. (175) numbered, sigd. by artist. Lge. 4to. Cl.-bkd. vell.-style bds., unc., unopened. Raymond M. Sutton Jr. copy. (SG. May 7; 216) $700

MORLEY, Christophorus Love
- Collectanea Chymica Ledesnia, id est Maestsiana Margraviana, le Mortiana. Leiden, 1684. 1st. Edn. 4to. Henry Cavendish's stp. on verso of title. Cont. panel. cf., rebkd. (S. Dec.1; 280) *Asher*. £130

MORNAS, Claude de Buy
See–BUY de Mornas, Claude

MORNAY
- A Picture of St. Petersburgh . . . A Collection of . . . interesting Views of the City, the Sledges, & the People. [1815]. Fo. Text wtrmkd. 1825, plt. 1823-25, lacks un-cold. engraved frontis., slight offsetting on recto of a few plts. Cont. hf. str.-grd. red mor., spine gt., some wear, bkplt. of J.R. Austen. (S. Nov.4; 599) *Walford*. £350

MORNAY, Philippe de
- De la Verité de la Religion Chrestienne. Paris, 1585. Sm. burnhole in X5 affecting text, some stains. Cont. natural mor. covers, gt. with 2 interlaced initials Cs surrounded by 4 S fermés within wreath, surrounded by 4 interlaced Cs on ground semé with fleurs-de-lis, leafy corner sprays in border of fillets & repeated smaller interlaced Cs, flat spine gt. with interlaced Cs & 4 S fermés in oval in same border of interlaced Cs, ground semé with fleurs-de-lis. (SM. Oct.7; 1875) Frs. 5,200

MORO, Anton-Lazzaro
- De Crostacei e degli Altri Marini Corpi che si Truovano Su'monti. Venice, 1740. 1st. Edn. 4to. Cont. cf., slightly worn. (S. Dec.3; 1071) *Asher*. £160

MORO, Anton-Lazzaro Su'monti. -*contd.*
– – **Anr. Copy.** 19th. C. buckram. From Chetham's Liby., Manchester. (C. Nov.27; 306)
Junk. £65

MORO, Marco
– **Album delle Principali Vedute di Venezia.** Ill.:- A. Berselli & Moro. Venice, ca. 1850. Ob. fo. Browned & soiled thro.-out, old MS. note on upr. inner dentelle. Orig. hf. linen. (HK. Nov.18-21; 1237) DM 1,200

MORRELL, B.
– **Narrative of a Voyage to the South & West Coast of Africa ...** L., 1844. Orig. cl. (SSA. Jan.22; 308) R. 250

MORREN, C. & E.
– **La Belgique Horticole.** Liege, 1851-62. 12 vols. (of 35) nos. 1-12. Cont. red hf. mor. gt. W.a.f. (C. Jul.15; 195) *Taylor.* £350

MORRIS, Beverley Robinson
– **British Game Birds & Wildfowl.** 1855. [1st. Edn.?]. 4to. 1 plt. detchd. Cont. hf. red mor. gt., slightly worn. (SBA. Oct.21; 159) *King.* £600
– – **Anr. Copy.** Cont. cf., gt. panel. spine (torn at head). (C. Nov.5; 112) *Traylen.* £480
– – **Anr. Copy.** A few plts. detchd., margin soiled, some spotting. Cont. mor. W.a.f. (CSK. Dec.12; 101) £420
– – **Anr. Copy.** Foxing & browning, fly-lf. torn out. Hf. mor. (S. Dec.3; 1072) *Nagel.* £360
– – **Anr. Copy.** 55 cold. plts. (of 60), slightly soiled. Mor. gt. W.a.f. (P. May 14; 350) *Bailey.* £200
– – **Anr. Edn.** [1855]. 4to. Liby. stp. on title. Cont. cl. (C. May 20; 231) *Nagel.* £470
– – **Anr. Copy.** 1 plt. defect. at margins. Cont. hf. cf., worn, upr. cover detchd. (S. Jun.23; 305) *Koch.* £360
– – **Anr. Copy.** Orig. linen, lacks spine, cover loose. (R. Mar.31-Apr.4; 1403) DM 2,600
– – **Anr. Edn.** 1891. 4to. Orig. cl. gt. (P. Oct.23; 312) *Nagel.* £340
– – **Anr. Edn.** 1897. 5th. Edn. 2 vols. Orig. cl., gt (SH. Oct.9; 237) *Maggs.* £280
– – **Anr. Edn.** N.d. 4to. Prelims. spotted, occasional spotting elsewhere. Orig. cl. (CSK. Mar.20; 60) £600

MORRIS, Corbyn
See–GIBBS, James–MORRIS, Corbyn

MORRIS, Edward E.
– **Picturesque Australasia.** L., 1887-89. 4 vols. 4to. Cl., gt. (JL. Dec.14; 82) Aus. $130
– – **Anr. Edn.** L. etc., 1889-90. 4 vols. Square 8vo. Some staining. (KH. Nov.18; 434) Aus. $120

MORRIS, Rev. Francis Orpen
– **A History of British Birds.** 1851-55. Vols. 1-4. only. 241 hand-cold. plts. only. Cont. hf. cf. W.a.f. (CSK. Feb.20; 27) £190
– – **Anr. Edn.** 1851-56. 1st. Edn. 6 vols. Spotted. Cont. hf. cf. (SH. Jun.25; 128) *Frick.* £290
– – **Anr. Copy.** 5 vols. only (of 6). Plts. spotted, few loose. Orig. cl., worn. (SH. Apr.9; 305) *Elliott.* £230
– – **Anr. Edn.** 1851-57. 1st. Edn. 6 vols. Some margins strengthened. Orig. cl. gt., slightly worn, some rebkd. preserving orig. spine, hinges strengthened. W.a.f. (SBA. Oct.21; 160) *Dallai.* £400
– – **Anr. Copy.** A few ll. slightly spotted, barely affecting plts., a few other minor defects. (SBA. Mar.4; 159) *Spencer.* £330
– – **Anr. Copy.** Slightly worn. Thomas Coutts Morison's bkplt. (S. Jun.1; 178) *Cristiani.* £280
– – **Anr. Copy.** Some ll. loose. Hf. cf., very worn & shabby. W.a.f. (S. Jun.1; 177) *Cristiani.* £240
– – **Anr. Copy.** Lacks 12 text ll. in vol. VI, replaced with 4 ll. from anr. edn., & 8 ll. in MS., occasional spotting, name stpd. in upr. margins of titles, & on verso of 4 plts. Cont. hf. cf., spines gt., some labels lacking or defect., some wear. (S. Dec.3; 1075) *Primrose.* £220
– – **Anr. Edn.** L., 1851-62. 1st. Edn. vols. 1 & 2. 6 vols. 4 orig. linen & 2 cont. hf. leath. (R. Mar.31-Apr.4; 1405) DM 2,000
– – **Anr. Edn.** 1855. Vol. IV only. Some spotting. Cont. cf., upr. cover detchd. (TA. Dec.18; 375) £72
– – **Anr. Edn.** 1858-64. 6 vols. 5 plts. in vols. I-II detchd. & frayed, 1 with a few tears, occasional spotting, mainly marginal. Cont. hf. str.-grd. red mor., spines gt. (S. Dec.3; 1076) *Litman.* £280
– – **Anr. Edn.** 1860. 6 vols. 4to. Orig. cl. (P. May 14; 229) *Duran.* £340

– – **Anr. Edn.** L., 1860-57. 6 vols. 4to. 358 hand-cold. plts. Orig. cl. gt. (P. Jun.11; 286) *Cambridge.* £400
– – **Anr. Edn.** 1860-61. Vols. 1-4 (of 6). Some staining & soiling, tears. Hf. cf., ex-liby. (PL. Jul.11; 71) *Wrigley.* £80
– – **Anr. Edn.** 1860-67. 6 vols. Slight browning. Orig. cl. (CSK. Sep.19; 52) £420
– – **Anr. Edn.** 1863-64. 6 vols. Occasional light spotting. Cont. hf. mor., spines gt. (CSK. May 29; 66) £300
– – **Anr. Edn.** 1863-65. 6 vols. A few ll. slightly spotted. Orig. cl. gt., 1 spine torn, others slightly worn. (SBA. Jul.14; 247) *Roberts.* £280
– – **Anr. Edn.** 1865. 6 vols. 358 hand-cold. plts., some foxing. Pol. cf., spines gt. (C. Mar.18; 160) *Duran.* £250
– – **Anr. Edn.** 1866. 6 vols. Orig. pebble-grd. cl. decor. in blind & gt. (TW. Nov.26; 242) £375
– – **Anr. Copy.** Orig. cl. gt. (TA. May 21; 528) £340
– – **Anr. Edn.** 1868. 6 vols. A few ll. loose, 1 plt. soiled. Orig. cl., worn, inner hinges brkn. (S. Dec.3; 1077) *Nagel.* £300
– – **Anr. Copy.** 4to. Plts. soiled & stained, some ll. detchd. & tattered. Hf. cf. (CE. Mar.19; 160) £170
– – **Anr. Edn.** 1870. 2nd. Edn. 6 vols. 4to. Orig. cl., soiled. (PD. Oct.22; 87) £320
– – **Anr. Copy.** Cl. gt. (HSS. Apr.24; 45) £300
– – **Anr. Copy.** 6 plts. stained in vol. 4. Hf. roan, worn. (S. Jul.27; 301) *Midwest Galleries* £240
– – **Anr. Copy.** Vols. 2, 3, 4 & 6 only. Hf. mor., defect. As a collection of plts. (P. Mar.12; 241) *Cambridge.* £200
– – **Anr. Copy.** Vols. 1 & 4 only (of 6). Orig. cl., worn. (P. Jul.30; 244) *Schapiro.* £80
– – **Anr. Copy.** 6 vols. Orig. linen. (R. Oct.14-18; 3029) DM 1,700
– – **Anr. Copy.** Vols. 2, 4 & 6 in 3 vols. Vols. 2 & 4 2nd. Edn. 2 vols. spine defect. (R. Oct.14-18; 3030) DM 580
– – **Anr. Edn.** L., 1870-91. Various Edns. Vols. 2, 3, 4, & 6 only. Gt.-pict. cl., 1 vol. brkn. W.a.f. (SG. Nov.20; 381) $350
– – **Anr. Edn.** Ca. 1880. 8 vols. Some spotting, mostly to text, stitching loose. Orig. cl., spines worn. (S. Jun.1; 184) *Cristiani.* £260
– – **Anr. Copy.** Orig. cl., gt. (S. Jun.1; 183) *Cristiani.* £220
– – **Anr. Edn.** 1882. 6 vols. 4to. Hf. cf. gt. (P. May 14; 232) *Donovan.* £320
– – **Anr. Edn.** [1886?]. 8 vols. Lacks 1 hand-cold. plt. Orig. cl. gt. (LC. Oct.2; 97) £180
– – **Anr. Edn.** [1888]. 8 vols. Slight spotting, sm. edge-tear in 1 plt. Orig. cl., gt., worn at head & foot, contents a bit loose. (S. Dec.3; 1084) *Gibbs.* £260
– – **Anr. Copy.** Cl. (S. Dec.3; 1083) *Nagel.* £240
– – **Anr. Copy.** Some ll. & plts. loose in vols. I & VII. Orig. embossed cl., worn, partly unc. (LC. Oct.2; 96) £200
– – **Anr. Edn.** 1890. 2nd. Edn. 6 vols. 356 cold. plts. only, lacks one from vol. 2, slight marginal soiling. Orig. cl. W.a.f. (CSK. Jun.19; 49) £220
– – **Anr. Edn.** 1891. '3rd. Edn.' Short marginal tear in 1 plt. Orig. pict. cl., gt., slight wear. (S. Dec.3; 1080) *Gibbs.* £300
– – **Anr. Copy.** 6 vols. Orig. cl. gt. (S. Jun.1; 182) *Cristiani.* £280
– – **Anr. Edn.** L., 1893. 5th Edn. 6 vols. Orig. cl., decor. spines & upr. covers. Engraved bkplt. of W.M.G. Stocker. (JL. Jul.20; 819) Aus. $800
– – **Anr. Edn.** 1895. 6 vols. No bdg. stated. (SH. Jul.16; 72) *Duran.* £250
– – **Anr. Edn.** 1895-97. [4th. Edn.?] 36 orig. pts. making 6 vols. Each vol. in cl. gt. box. (P. Nov.13; 215) *Traylen.* £400
– – **Anr. Copy.** 6 vols. 4to. Partly unc., orig. hf. mor. with marb. bds., panel. & gt. decor. spine. (PL. Nov.27; 138) *Levi.* £370
– – **Anr. Copy.** Orig. pts. 1-12 (vols. 1 & 2) & 25-30 (vol. 5) only. Orig. wraps., some torn with loss. W.a.f. (CSK. May 29; 138) £120
– – **Anr. Edn.** 1903. 5th. Edn. 6 vols. Orig. cl., sm. clean tear in vol. 3 spine, some inner hinges split. (CSK. Oct.3; 78) £400
– – **Anr. Copy.** Orig. pict. cl., gt. (S. Dec.3; 1081) *Nagel.* £320
– – **Anr. Copy.** Orig. cl., spines discold. (SKC. May 19; 426) £240
– – **Anr. Edn.** 1903. 6 vols. Orig. cl., some stains. (P. Nov.13; 13) *Bailey.* £300
– – **Anr. Copy.** Orig. cl. gt., some dampstaining. (P. May 14; 87) *Bozz.* £280

– – **Anr. Copy.** Vols. 1, 4 & 5 (of 6) only. Few pp. loose. W.a.f. as a collection of plts. (P. Oct.2; 277) *Omniphil.* £170
– – **Anr. Copy.** Vols. 2 & 5 only (of 6). Cl. gt., soiled. As a collection, w.a.f. (P. Mar.12; 326) *Cambridge.* £100
– – **Anr. Edn.** N.d. 8 vols. 1 plt. almost detchd., occasional light spotting. Orig. cl. (CSK. Mar.6; 167) £280
– – **Anr. Copy.** At least 1 plt. lacking, page 85. (SH. Oct.9; 240) *Wilson.* £200
– – **Anr. Copy.** A few ll. loose. Cl. (PD. Oct.22; 9) £160

– **A History of British Birds.–A Natural History of the Nests & Eggs of British Birds.** 1851-57; 1864. 1st. work: Vols. 1, 3-6; 3 vols. Cl., worn. (S. Dec.3; 1086) *Rimmer.* £160
– – **Anr. Edn.** 1865; 1865-64. Together 9 vols. (6+3). Unif. cont. hf. mor. gt. (C. Mar.18; 179) *Negro.* £360
– – **Anr. Edn.** 1870-71. 2nd. Edn. 6 vols.; 3 vols., together 9 vols. Some spotting. Orig. cl., gt. (S. Jun.1; 180) *Joseph.* £300

– **A History of British Birds.–A Natural History of the Nests & Eggs of British Birds.–A History of British Butterflies.– A History of British Moths.** 1895-97; 1896; 1895; 1896. 4th. Edn.; 4th. Edn.; 8th. Edn.; 5th. Edn. 6 vols.; 3 vols.; 1 vol.; 4 vols., together 14 vols. Slight spotting. Unif. hf. mor. (S. Jun.1; 176) *Honeyfields.* £640

– **A History of British Butterflies.** 1853. 1st. Edn. Cont. hf. cf., gt. spine. (C. Nov.5; 113) *Quaritch.* £100
– – **Anr. Copy.** A few ll. slightly spotted. Orig. cl. gt. (SBA. Mar.4; 160) *Chambers.* £80
– – **Anr. Copy.** Some plts. detchd. & with margins slightly frayed. Orig. bdg. (SBA. May 27; 190a) *Hindley.* £65
– – **Anr. Edn.** 1857. 1 lf. torn & detchd., some other defects. Orig. cl. gt., worn. (SBA. Mar.4; 161) *Spencer.* £55
– – **Anr. Edn.** 1864. Hf. cf. (BS. Feb.25; 259) £65
– – **Anr. Edn.** 1865. Orig. bdg. (DWB. May 15; 345) £65
– – **Anr. Edn.** 1870. 3rd. Edn. Sm. fo. Some spotting. Orig. cl. (TA. Apr.16; 96) £52
– – **Anr. Edn.** 1870. 5th. Edn. 4to. Occasional slight spotting. Orig. cl. (CSK. Oct.24; 30) £55
– – **Anr. Edn.** 1876. Orig. embossed cl. gt., 2 corners worn. (LC. Feb.12; 148) £50
– – **Anr. Edn.** 1890. Cl. gt. (P. Feb.19; 80) *Duran.* £70
– – **Anr. Edn.** 1895. 8th. Edn. 4to. Some ll. detchd. Cont. hf. mor. (CSK. Jan.9; 35) £60
– **Natural History of British Moths.** 1871. 4 vols. A few ll. slightly spotted. Orig. cl. gt. (SBA. Dec.16; 147a) *Chambers.* £70
– – **Anr. Edn.** 1872. 4 vols. Cl. gt. (P. Nov.13; 95) *Bookroom.* £50
– – **Anr. Copy.** Cont. hf. leath. (R. Oct.14-18; 3064) DM 650
– – **Anr. Edn.** [1894?]. 4 vols. Cl. gt. (P. Feb.19; 81) *Duran.* £70
– – **Anr. Edn.** 1896. 4 vols. Cl. gt. (P. Apr.9; 329) *Duran.* £55

– **A Series of Picturesque Views of the Seats of the Noblemen & Gentlemen of Great Britain & Ireland.** Ca. 1880. 6 vols. 4to. Orig. cl. gt., 1 vol. soiled. (SBA. May 27; 305) *Barker.* £75
– – **Anr. Copy.** (SBA. Jul.14; 299) *Shapiro.* £56
– – **Anr. Copy.** Orig. gt.-armorial red mor., armorial bkplts. of M.G. Best. (PNY. Mar.26; 225) $425
– – **Anr. Copy.** 6 vols. Orig. crimson mor., elab. gt.-tooled borders enclosing royal arms & title in gt. on all covers. (SG. Dec.4; 254) $375
– – **Anr. Copy.** Orig. elab. gt.-decor. cl. (SG. Oct.30; 256) $220
– – **Anr. Copy.** Orig. armorial gt. stpd. red mor., gt. dentelles. (SG. Apr.9; 216) $150
– – **Anr. Copy.** Orig. linen. (R. Oct.14-18; 1886) DM 550
– – **Anr. Edn.** N.d. 6 vols. 4to. Orig. mor., gt. (SH. Apr.9; 303) *Harrison.* £170
– – **Anr. Copy.** 6 vols. Occasional spotting. Orig. mor.-bkd. cl. (CSK. Jul.10; 127) £60
– – **Anr. Edn.** Leeds, n.d. Tooled cf. (HSS. Apr.24; 86) £50

MORRIS, Frank T.
– **Birds of the Australian Swamps. Volume I: Grebes & Cormorants.** [Melbourne], [1978]. (500) numbered, & sigd. Fo. Buckram & hf. leath. gt. (KH. Mar.24; 288) Aus. $320

– – Anr. Copy. Orig. bdg. (KH. Mar.24; 289)
Aus. $210
– Birds of Prey of Australia. [Melbourne], [1973]. (500) numbered, & sigd. Fo. Orig. leath. (KH. Mar.24; 287) Aus. $550
– Pencil Drawings, 1969-78. [Melbourne], [1978]. (500) numbered, & sigd. Fo. Leath. (KH. Mar.24; 291) Aus. $210
– Pigeons & Doves of Australia. [Melbourne], [1976]. (500) numbered, & sigd. Fo. Leath. (KH. Mar.24; 292) Aus. $550
– Robins & Wrens of Australia. Melbourne & c., [1979]. (500) numbered, & sigd. Fo. Buckram & qtr. leath. (KH. Mar.24; 293) Aus. $270

MORRIS, Henry
– Roller Printed Paste Papers for Bookbinding. 1975. Vell.-bkd. patterned bds. On Hodgkinson B. & B. H.M.P. (SG. Oct.2; 36) $240

MORRIS, Ivan
– Tale of Genji Scroll. Ed.:– Yoshinobu Tokugawa. [Tokyo], [1971]. (1500) numbered. Ob. fo. Cl., with decor. bdg. ribbon, cl. folding case. (SG. Dec.18; 391) $180

MORRIS, Lewis
– Plans of the Principal Harbours, Bays & Roads, in St. George's & the Bristol Channels ... with Hints on Improvements necessary to be made for the Greater Security of the Navigation on the Coast of Wales. Ed.:– William Morris. Shrewsbury, 1801. New Edn. Fo. Later cl., orig. wraps. bnd. in. (SBA. Oct.22; 510)
Temperley. £360
– – Anr. Copy. Mod. cl. (SH. Nov.6; 136)
Simon. £200

MORRIS, Maurice O'Connor
– Rambles in the Rocky Mountains: With a Visit to the Gold Fields of Colorado. L., 1864. 1st. Edn. Orig. cl., blind-stpd. borders, gt. spine. From liby. of William E. Wilson. (SPB. Apr.29; 209) $150

MORRIS, Richard
– Essays on Landscape Gardening. 1825. 4to. 3 plts. cold. & 3 sepia, 2 plts. with overslips. Orig. bds., spine torn, ink stain on spine & upr. cover, unc. & unopened. From the collection of Eric Sexton. (C. Apr.15; 74) Sims & Reed. £290
– Flora Conspicua. Ill.:– W. Clark. 1826. 60 hand-cold. engraved plts., 5 with ink marks, 1 lf. reprd. Cont. str.-grd. mor. gt. (C. Jul.15; 196)
Henderson. £380

MORRIS, William
– An Address ...–Art & the Beauty of the Earth. –Some Hints on Pattern Designing.–Architecture & History & Westminster Abbey. L., Chis. Pr., 1898; 1899; 1899; 1900. 4 vols. in 1. Mor. gt., gt.-ruled borders, gt. device with sm. mor. onlays, by Annie Ricketts, sigd. 'AR 1901'. (CNY. May 22; 365) $420
– An Address delivered ... at the ... Birmingham Municipal School of Art.–Some Hints on Pattern Designing.–Architecture & History, & Westminster Abbey.–Art & Its Producers. 1898; 1899; 1900; 1901. Together 4 vols. Orig. cl.-bkd. bds. (SKC. Feb.26; 1257) £75
– Child Christopher & Goldilind the Fair. Hammersmith, Kelms. Pr., 1895. (600). 2 vols. 16mo. Orig. holland-bkd. bds., unc. (CNY. May 22; 324) $280
– – Anr. Copy. Worn. A.K. Coomaraswamy bkplt. in each vol. (SG. Apr.9; 459) $225
– The Defence of Guenevere. 1858. Orig. cl. Inscr. (SH. Jul.9; 125) Frognall. £80
– The Defence of Guenevere & Other Poems. Ill.:– Jessie M. King. 1904. Orig. cl. gt., slightly stained & worn. (S. Jul.31; 245) Ross. £60
– A Dream of John Ball & a King's Lesson. Ill.:– after Sir Edward Burne-Jones (frontis.). Kelms. Pr., 1892. (300) on paper. Orig. limp vell., silk ties. (S. Jul.31; 4) Foyles. £240
– The Earthly Paradise. [Kelms. Pr.], [1896-97]. [(231)]. 8 vols. 4to. Orig. limp vell., silk ties. (CSK. Apr.3; 78) £360
– Gothic Architecture. Kelms. Pr., 1893. (1500). 16mo. Orig. holland-bkd. bds., unc. (SH. Feb.19; 4) Fletcher. £130
– – Anr. Edn. [L.], [Kelms. Pr.], [1893]. Mor. by Sangorski & Sutcliffe, after a sketch by Morris. (KH. Nov.18; 435) Aus. $580
– The Hollow Land: A Romance. Ill.:– Walter J. Enright & Bror J. Olsson Nordfelt. [Hingham, Massachussetts], [Village Pr.], [1905]. (200) on L.P., designed by Frederic W. & Bertha M. Goudy from the Village Type. Mor., gt.-stpd., decor.,

design on panel. spine, inner dentelles gt., by Charles McLeish at the Doves Bindery. (PNY. Dec.3; 110) $300
– Hopes & Fears for Art. L., 1882. 1st. Edn., (25) on Whatman Paper. Crushed lev. mor., elab. gt. decor., slightly hollowed spine in 6 compartments with tooling, 5 raised bands, by T.J. Cobden-Sanderson, sigd. 'C 1886' and inscr., qtr. mor. gt. s.-c. M.C.D. Borden & A. Edward Newton bkplts. (CNY. May 22; 356) $13,000
– The Life & Death of Jason. Ill.:– Sir Edward Burne-Jones. Kelms. Pr., 1895. (200) on paper. 4to. Orig. limp vell., silk ties. (S. Jul.31; 9)
Sims & Reed. £340
– Love is Enough. Kelms. Pr., 1897. (300). 4to. Orig. limp vell., in box. (SH. Jul.23; 15)
Henderson. £370
– – Anr. Copy. Silk ties, unc. (CNY. May 22; 331) $750
– News from Nowhere, or an Epoch of Rest, being some Chapters from an Utopian Romance. Ill.:– after C.M. Gere (frontis.). Kelms. Pr., [1893]. (300) on paper. Orig. limp vell., lacks ties. (S. Jul.31; 6) Auuchin-Po Books. £240
– – Anr. Copy. Silk ties, unc. (CNY. May 22; 316) $400
– A Note on his Aims in Founding the Kelmscott Press. Ed.:– S.C. Cockerell. Ill.:– after Sir Edward Burne-Jones (frontis.). Kelms. Pr., 1898. (525) on paper. Red mor., upr. cover divided into 14 compartments by blind rules, each filled with vine ornament, gt. (S. Jul.31; 14) Seibu. £300
– Poems by the Way. L., Kelms. Pr., 1891. (13) on vell. 4to. Vell. Hugh G. McKinney bkplt. laid in. (SG. Oct.9; 171) $2,400
– – Anr. Edn. Hammersmith, Kelms. Pr., 1891. (300). Some staining on a few ll., 1 lf. torn affecting text. Orig. vell., soiling, stain on lr. cover. With a 3½-p. A.L.s. from Morris dtd. Hammersmith, 16 Jun. [1891], to unknown recipient discussing the publication of Poems by the Way. (SPB. May 6; 202) $500
– Sigurd the Volsung. Kelms. Pr., 1897. (32). Lge. fo. Trial setting of 2 pp., woodcut border, 2 initials, space left for anr. Unbnd. as iss. (SH. Feb.19; 13) Quaritch. £105
– Sir Galahad. Ill.:– H.M. O'Kane. [New Rochelle], [Elston Press], [1902]. (180). Fo. Laid in 4-page brochure listing 14 books, & description of present one. Bds., linen spine, d.-w. (SG. Sep.4; 169) $240
– The Story of Cupid & Psyche. Ill.:– after Burne-Jones. Douglas Cleverdon & Clover Hill Edns., 1974. (130) with portfo. of proofs of ills. 2 vols. & prospectus. Fo. Mor. gt., s.-c., mor.-bkd. box. (SH. Feb.20; 419) Dowd. £360
– – Anr. Copy. 4-p. prospectus & sample p. laid in. Mor. & hf. mor., s.-c.'s. covered with paper after a Morris design, by Sangorski & Sutcliffe. The John A. Saks copy. (CNY. Oct.1; 193) $700
– The Story of the Glittering Plain. L., Kelms. Pr., 1891. (200) on Bütten. Sm. 4to. Orig. vell., linen ties, 1 defect., unc. (SG. May 14; 117) $500
– – Anr. Copy. 4 ties. (HK. Nov.18-21; 2701) DM 950
– – Anr. Edn. Ill.:– after Walter Crane. Hammersmith, Kelms. Pr., 1894. (250) on paper. 4to. Orig. limp vell., silk ties, unc. (CNY. Oct.1; 189) $900
– A Tale of the House of the Wolfings.–The Roots of the Mountains.–Grettir the Strong.–The Volsunga Saga & 3 Northern Love Stories.–The Odyssey of Homer.–The Aenids of Virgil.–Hopes & Fears for Art & Signs of Change.–Architecture, Industry & Wealth.–Four Lectures. L., Chis. Pr., 1901-02; 1900 (last work). Each (315) (all but last). 9 vols. 4to. 3 prospectuses laid in 1st. vol., slight foxing. Orig. bds., linen spines, unc., qtr. mor., gt. s.-c.'s., upr. cover with floral designs, bkplt. of E.L. Turner, last vol. gt., circular floral decor. on upr. cover. As a collection, w.a.f., John A. Saks copy. (CNY. Oct.1; 192) $400
– The Tale of King Florus & the Fair Jehane. Kelms. Pr., 1893. (350) on paper. 16mo. Orig. holland-bkd. bds., unc. (S. Jul.16; 7)
Quaritch. £150
– The Well at the World's End. Ill.:– Sir Edward Burne-Jones. Kelms. Pr., 1896. (350) on paper. Lge. 4to. Orig. limp vell., slightly stained, silk ties, unc. (S. Jul.31; 13) Duchnes. £240
– – Anr. Copy. Fo. Minor defects. Orig. vell., slight soiling. (SPB. Jul.28; 206) $600
– The Wood beyond the World. Ill.:– Sir E. Burne-Jones (frontis.). Kelms. Pr., 1894. (350) on

paper. Orig. limp vell., silk ties, unc. (S. Jul.31; 8)
Sims & Reed. £300
[–] – Anr. Copy. 4to. Silk ties. (CSK. Apr.3; 77) £280
– – Anr. Copy. Vell., cl. ties. (PNY. Dec.3; 206) $500
– – Anr. Copy. 4to. Minor defects. Orig. vell., slight soiling. (SPB. Jul.28; 207) $425
– Collected Works. Ed.:– May Morris. L., 1910-15. 1st. Coll. Edn., (1050) numbered. 24 vols. 4to. Orig. linen-bkd. bds., spine discold. (PNY. Dec.3; 264) $350

MORRIS, William (Trans.)
See–AMIS
See–BEOWULF
See–COUSTANS

MORRIS, William (Ed.) *See*–MORRIS, Lewis

MORRISON, William Maxwell
– Dictionary of Decisions.–Synopsis. Edinb., 1801-04; 1814. 22 vols. together. Cf., worn. (CE. Aug.28; 26) £70

MORSE, Edward S.
See–HOBSON, Robert Lockhart & others

MORSE, Jedidiah
– The American Geography, or, a View of the Present Situation of the United States ... L., 1792. 2nd. Edn., 1st. L. printing. 2 folding maps, foxed, offset, possibly inserted from anr. copy, text slightly stained. Orig. bds., rebkd. From liby. of William E. Wilson. (SPB. Apr.29; 210) $225
– – Anr. Edn. Dublin, 1792. 3rd. Edn. One lge. folding map reprd., ex-liby. Old cf., needs rebdg. (SG. Jun.11; 272) $150
– Geography Made Easy. Boston, 1794. 4th. Edn. 12mo. Map of U.S.A. badly torn but compl. Cont. leath., very worn. (SG. Nov.20; 81) $110
– A Report to the Secretary of War of the United States, on Indian Affairs. New-Haven, 1822. 1st. Edn. Map torn at fold, corner torn from title, lacks errata lf., frontis. & title dampstained. Liby. buckram, crudely rebkd. (SG. Jan.8; 310) $100

MORSE, John T.
– American Statesmen.–... Second Series. Boston & N.Y., 1898-1906. (500) numbered on L.P. Together 40 vols. Three-qtr. mor., spines gt. in 6 compartments. (SG. Sep.4; 9) $450
See–HOLMES, Oliver Wendell–MORSE, John T. Jr.

MORTIER, Corneille
See–COVENS, Jean & Mortier, Corneille

MORTIER, Pieter
– Atlas Antiquus. Ill.:– after N. Sanson & others. Amst., Priv. Ptd., 1705. Fo. 42 engraved double-p. maps only (of 93), lacks title, 5 maps detchd., 1 map with hole at centre fold. Bdg. brkn., lacks covers. W.a.f. (C. Nov.6; 265) Schuster. £280
– Histoire des Ouden en Nieuwen Testamenten. Amst., 1700. 2 vols. in 3; vol. 1 in 2 pts. Lge. fo. Lacks 1 copperplt. Cont. leath., 1 spine defect at head. (R. Oct.14-18; 2491) DM 900

MORTIMER, R.
– French 16th. Century Books. Camb., 1964. 2 vols. Orig. linen. (R. Mar.31-Apr.4; 826) DM 450
– Italian 16th. Century Books. Camb., 1974. Orig. linen. (R. Mar.31-Apr.4; 827) DM 450

MORTON, Arthur Silver
– A History of the Canadian West. L., Edinb., Paris, Melbourne, Toronto & N.Y., [1939]. Occasional pencilled annots., owner's sig. on end-paper & title-p. obliterated with gum paper. Orig. cl. (CB. Feb.18; 169) Can. $120

MORTON, Hamilton
– The America Cup. N.Y., 1874. 1st. Edn. Gt.-pict. cl. (SG. Apr.9; 415) $120

MORTON, John
– The Natural History of Northampton-shire. Ill.:– John Speed & John Harris (maps). 1712. 2 pts. in 1 vol. Fo. Cont. cf., gt. (C. Feb.25; 47)
Old Hall. £160
– – Anr. Copy. Cont. panel. cf., jnts. brkn., spine slightly worn. (S. May 5; 218) Books Etc. £110

MORTON, Nathaniel
– New England's Memorial: Or ... Planters of New England, in America. Boston, 1772. 3rd. Edn. Some discolouration, owner's inscr. on front free end-paper. Mod. mor. gt. [Sabin 51014] (SPB. Nov.24; 40) $750

MORTON, Nathaniel–CHURCH, Thomas
- New England's Memorial.–The Entertaining History of King Philip's War. Newport, 1772. 2 works in 1 vol. Some browning, offsetting. Mod. mor. gt. [Sabin 12997] (SPB. Jun.22; 34) $600

MORTON, Richard
- Phthisiologia or, A Treatise of Consumption. Ill.:– R. White (port.). 1694. 1st. Engl. Edn. Some mod. ink markings in margins of pp. 168-9. Cont. panel. cf., rebkd. Inscr. of Richard Bryan on fly-lf., bkplt. of James Tobin. [Wing M2830] (S. Jun.16; 596) *Hammond.* £220

MORTON, Samuel George
- Illustrations of Pulmonary Consumption. Phila., 1834. Errata slip loosely inserted. Cont. cf. (C. Jul.16; 358) *Taylor.* £55

MORTON, Thomas, Bp. of Durham
- A Sermon Preached before the Kings most Excellent Majestie, in the Cathedrall Church of Durham, upon Sunday, being the 5th. day of May 1639. Newcastle-upon-Tyne, 1639. 4to. Lacks final blanks(?). Disbnd., preserved in mor.-bkd. case. [STC 18196] (SBA. Oct.22; 449) *Fletcher.* £50

MORYSON, Fynes
- An Itinerary. 1617. 1st. Edn. 3 pts. in 1 vol. Fo. 2nd. p. of title with 1st. variant of description (roman letter) of pts., a little browning, 1 or 2 rust holes slightly affecting text. 17th. C. rough cf., rebkd., old spine preserved. [NSTC 18205] (S. Sep.29; 58) *Cohen.* £280
- – Anr. Copy. Lr. blank margin of 1st. lf. reprd. Cont. cf., gt. arabesque ornament on covers, rebkd. preserving orig. spine. Early sig. of William Robinson on title, lately in the collection of Eric Sexton. (C. Apr.15; 41) *Figgess.* £160
- – Anr. Copy. Lacks 1st. & last blanks, 1 title cropped down & bkd., other title & approx. 12 ll. reprd. Later gt.-armorial cf., rebkd. in blind cf. The George Agar Ellis copy. (PNY. Oct.1; 382) $220
- – Anr. Edn. 1907-08. Reprint, (100) numbered. 4 vols. Orig. vell.-bkd. cl. (SH. Jun.11; 210) *O'Neill.* £95

MOSCH, C.F.
- Die Bäder und Heilbrunnen Deutschlands und der Schweiz. Leipzig, 1820. Pt. 1 (A-J) only. Orig. wraps., unc. (R. Mar.31-Apr.4; 1867) DM 1,400

MOSCHETTI, Andrea
- Principali Monumenti di Roma e sue Vicinanze. Rome, 1851. Ob. 4to. Orig. cl.-bkd. pict. wraps., soiled. (SH. Mar.5; 102) *Vitale.* £70

MOSCHUS
See–ANACREON & others–MUSAEUS
See–THEOCRITUS, Bion & Moschus

MOSELY, Martin E.
- The Dry-Fly Fisherman's Entomology. L., 1921. 1st. Edn. 12mo. Cl., with wallet flap. (SG. Oct.16; 227) $160

M[OSER], H.C.
- Allgemeine Praktische Forstnaturgeschichte Deutschlands. Leipzig, 1794. 2 pts. in 1 vol. Title pt. 1 reprd., pt. 2 heavily stained. Hf. linen. (D. Dec.11-13; 172) DM 500

MOSER, Joseph
- The Hermit of Caucasus, an Oriental Romance. Min. Pr., 1796. 1st. Edn. 2 vols. 12mo. Advt. lf. in vol. 2. Spr. bds. (S. Oct.20; 166) *Quaritch.* £280

MOSER, W.G.
- Grundsätze der Forst-Oeconomie. Frankfurt & Leipzig, 1757. 2 vols. Browned. Cont. leath. (R. Oct.14-18; 2799) DM 700

MOSES, Henry
- A Collection of Vases, Altars . . . 1814. L.P. 4to. Str.-grd. mor. gt., Hibbert-Beckford copy. (S. Nov.24; 218) *Marlborough.* £75
- The Gallery of Pictures Painted by West. [L.], ca. 1820. Fo. Orig. bds., rebkd. (SG. Mar.12; 381) $150
- Sketches of Shipping. 1824. Ob. 4to. Orig. pict. wraps., lacks lr. cover. (SH. Mar.27; 343) *Denistoun.* £100
- – Anr. Edn. 1837. 4to. Cl. gt., well worn. (CE. Oct.24; 47) £52
- Visit of William the Fourth . . . As Lord High Admiral, to Portsmouth. [1840]. Fo. 1 plt. dampstained in margin. Cont. cf. (S. Dec.8; 46) *Crossley.* £150

MOSES ALMOSNINO
- M'Ametz Koach. Venice, 1588. 2nd. Edn. Sm. 4to. Liby. stp. on title. Antique-style mor. (C. Jul.16; 312) *Joseph.* £180

MOSHE, of Coucy
- Sefer Mitzvot Gadol. Ed.:– Yitzhak Eisik Stein (notes). Venice, 1547. 4th. Edn. Fo. Title reprd., cropped, worming, browning, repairs, staining, soiled. Mott. cf. (SPB. May 11; 167) $650
- – Anr. Copy. Some sigs. loose & ll. detchd., stitching brkn. or loose, repairs, worming, staining, soiling. Cf. gt. (SPB. May 11; 166) $600

MOSHE BEN ISAIAH, of Trani
See–HA'COHEN, Shimshon, of Ostropolye
–MOSHE BEN Isaiah, of Trani

MOSHE BEN ISRAEL, of Wuerzburg
- Bet Avot. Wilmehrsdorf, 1712. 4to. Slight discolouration. Mod. cl. (S. Nov.18; 752) *James.* £50

MOSHE BEN MAIMON
- Milot Ha'higayon. Cremona, 1566. 2nd. Edn. 4to. Loss of corner of 1 lf., some staining. Vell., stained. Bkplt. of Dr. Samuel Dresner. (SPB. May 11; 152) $700
- More Nevuchim [in Hebrew & Latin]. Trans.:– Shmuel Ibn Tibbon & Johannes Buxtorf, the Younger. Basle, 1629. Discolouration. Vell., slightly warped, end-paper torn. (SPB. May 11; 153) $400

MOSHE BEN NACHMAN
- Beur Al Ha'Torah. Venice, 1545. 5th. Edn. Sm. fo. Text heavily censored by Yehuda Ben Yitzhak Cohen, slight staining, minor repairs. Hf. vell. (SPB. May 11; 162) $900
- Chidushei Baba Batra. Venice, 1523. 1st. Edn. Lge. 4to. Last 2 ll. & inner margins reprd. without text loss, worming, soiled. Mor.-bkd. bds. (SPB. May 11; 163) $1,600
- Dina De'garmei. Constantinople, [1515-20]. 1st. Edn. Sm. 4to. Without title, lacks last 6 ll., margins reprd. without loss, staining. Mod. bds. (SPB. May 11; 87) $1,200
- Mishpetei Ha'cherem Ve'hanidui Ve'hanzifah. Constantinople, [1515-18]. 1st. Edn. Sm. 4to. Margins reprd., slight worming, browning. Mod. bds. (SPB. May 11; 88) $2,900

MOSHE SHAHAM, of Dolino
- Divrei Moshe. [Polonnoye?], 1795. 1st. Edn., on blue paper. 4to. Bds. (S. Nov.18; 309) *James.* £190

MOSKOWITZ, Ira
- Great Drawings of all Time. N.Y., [1962]. 4 vols. 4to. Cl., box. (SG. Aug.21; 129) $110

MOSS, Fletcher
- Pilgrimages to Old Homes. Didsbury & Manchester, 1901-20. 7 vols. 1 vol. an ex-liby. copy. Orig. cl. gt., a few minor defects. (SBA. Dec.16; 261) *Morten's Bookshop Ltd.* £65

MOSS, William George
- The History & Antiquities of the Town & Port of Hastings. 1824. 14 hand-cold. views, 5 uncold. plts., & an additional hand-cold. view inserted, 4 pp. of publisher's advts. before title. Cont. bds., poorly rebkd., unc., by W.G. Moss. From the collection of Eric Sexton. (C. Apr.16; 309) *Hollander.* £150

MOSSI, Honorio–ANON
- Gramatica de la Lengua General del Peru. –Ensayo . . . del Idioma llamado Comunmente Quichua; Diccionario Castellano-Quichua; Diccionario Quicha-Castellano y Castellano-Quichua. Sucre, [1856]; 1857; 1860; [1860]. 4 works in 1 vol. Fo. Later hf. cf., spine defect. (SPB. May 5; 362) $100

MOTHER Goose
Ill.:– Arthur Rackham. L., 1913. Ltd. Edn., sigd. by artist. 4to. Orig. cl. gt., soiled. (SH. Dec.11; 436) *Hough.* £190
- – Anr. Copy. Gt.-pict. cl. Raymond M. Sutton Jr. copy. (SG. May 7; 219) $750
- – Anr. Edn. Ill.:– Arthur Rackham. N.Y., 1913. 1st. Amer. Trade Edn. 4to. Cl. Raymond M. Sutton Jr. copy. (SG. May 7; 220) $350

MOTIF
1958-67. Nos. 1-13, all publd. 4to. Orig. bds. & wraps. (SH. Mar.6; 549) *Bennett.* £70

MOTLEY, John
- Works. N.Y., 1900. Netherlands Edn., (500). 17 vols. Spanish mor. gt., gt. lily design on corners, mor. doubls. (SPB. May 6; 332) $800

MOTOGRAPH MOVING PICTURE BOOK
1898. 4to. Transparency inserted in pocket in lr. cover. Cl.-bkd. bds. with orig. pict. upr. cover prcserved. (SH. Mar.19, 211) *Fletcher.* £130

MOTT, J.L.
- Iron Works. N.Y., 1881. Tall 8vo. Gt.-lettered cl. (SG. Mar.12; 271) $110

MOTTE, Benjamin, Editor
- The Lords Prayer in above a Hundred Languages. 1700. 4to. Slight soiling & staining, H3 frayed & re-inserted. Cont. panel. cf., s.-c. (S. Apr.29; 428) *Brill.* £130

MOTTELAY, Paul Fleury
- Bibliographical History of Electricity & Magnetism. Ed.:– S.P. Thompson. L., 1922. Buckram, ex-liby. (SG. Jan.22; 302) $160

MOTTEUX, Peter
- Love's a Jest. 1696. 1st. Edn. 4to. Last lf. with outer margin reprd., title stained, & slight staining thro.-out. Mor. by Sangorski. [Wing M2953] (C. Nov.19; 118) *Ludgrove.* £80
See–RAVENSCROFT, Edward & Motteux, Peter

MOTTLEY, John
[-] Joe Miller's Jests. L., 1739. 1st. Edn. Many ll. browned, lr. portion of C4 with slight tear. 19th. C. stained cf. gt., gt. arms of Ralph Sneyd on covers. From the Prescott Collection. (CNY. Feb.6; 263) $3,500

MOUBACH, A.
- Naaukeurige Beschryving der Uitwendige Gotdienstplichten, Kerkzeden en Gewoontens aan alle Volkeren der Waereldt. Ill.:– B. Picart. 's-Grav., Rotterdam, Amst., 1727-38. 6 vols. in 7. Fo. Lacks 4 plts. Cont. hf. cf., gt. spines with floral decor. (VG. Oct.13; 110) Fls. 3,000

MOUCHON, Pierre
- La Chasse des Oiseaux d'Eau en France. Ill.:– Eugene Lelipevre. Paris, 1931. (500) numbered. Lge. 4to. Pict. wraps. (SG. Apr.9; 384) $130

MOULE, Thomas
- Englands Topographer or the English Counties Delineated. Ill.:– after Bartlett. 1838. 2 vols. 4to. 2 plts. (of 4?). Cont. tree cf. gt., worn, spines torn. As an atlas, w.a.f. (SBA. Oct.22; 270) *Cumming.* £550
- The English Counties Delineated. 1837. 2 vols. 4to. Maps & plans, some spotted, some soiling. Hf. cf., worn. (CSK. Mar.6; 44) £420
- – Anr. Copy. Occasional spotting. Cont. cf., worn. (CSK. Jul.3; 9) £400
- The English Counties in the Nineteenth Century. 1837. 2 vols. 4to. A few margins cropped, folding map slightly torn, a few other minor defects. Cont. hf. russ., slightly worn. (SBA. Jul.1; 301) *Hughes & Smeeth.* £420
See–WESTALL, William & Moule, Thomas

MOULIN, Gabriel du
- Histoire Générale de Normandie . . . Rouen, 1631. Fo. Cont. cf., worn. (HD. Jun.29; 181) Frs. 1,000

MOUNT, William & Page, Thomas
- The Sea-Coasts of France from Calais to Bayone. Priv. ptd. Ca. 1715. Fo. No text. Cont. cf.-bkd. bds. As an atlas, w.a.f. (C. Feb.25; 119) *Schwedt.* £280

MOUNTAGUE, W.H.
- History of England. N.d. 2 vols. Fo. Cf. gt. (P. Sep.11; 55) *Greenaway.* £440

MOUNTAIN, George Jehoshaphat, Bp. of Montreal
[-] The Journal of . . . L., 1845. 12mo. Orig. cl., faded & slightly soiled. Inscr. [Sabin 51186] (CB. Nov.12; 275) Can. $130

MOUNTFORT, William
- Greenwich-Park. 1691. 1st. Edn. 4to. Some foxing. Mor. by Sangorski. [Wing M2973] (C. Nov.19; 119) *Brett-Smith.* £150
- The Successfull Straingers. 1690. 1st. Edn. 4to. Some staining in 1st. few ll. Mor. by Sangorski. [Wing M2977] (C. Nov.19; 120) *Pickering & Chatto.* £90
- – Anr. Copy. Title mntd. with tears reprd., tear in anr. lf. reprd., some stains thro.-out. (C. Nov.19; 34) *Wisbech.* £70

MOURLOT, Fernand

- **Chagall Lithograph.** Trans.:– O. Baumgartner & E. Weiser. Monte-Carlo, 1960-74. German Edn. Vols. I-IV, all publd. Lge. 4to. Orig. linen, litho. orig. wraps. (D. Dec.11-13; 423) DM 4,000
- – **Anr. Edn.** Ed.:– Julien Cain. Monte-Carlo, 1960-63. German Edn. Vols. I-II (of 4). 4to. Orig. linen, cold. orig. pict. wraps. (H. May 21/22; 1529) DM 3,300
- – **Anr. Edn.** Ed.:– Julien Cain. Trans.:– O. Baumgartner. Monte Carlo, 1960-69. German Edn. 3 vols. Lge. 4to. Orig. linen, cold. litho. orig. wraps. (D. Dec.11-13; 424) DM 3,800
- – **Anr. Edn.** Ed.:– Julien Cain. Monte Carlo, [1960]. German Edn. Vol. I only. Orig. linen with cold. pict. orig. wraps. (H. Dec.9/10; 1996) DM 2,600
- – **Anr. Edn.** Monte Carlo, [1963]. German Edn. Vol. II only. 4to. Orig. linen, orig. wraps. (D. Dec.11-13; 425) DM 1,000
- **Chagall Lithographe.** Ed.:– Julien Cain & C. Sorlier. Monte Carlo, 1960-74. 4 vols. 4to. Publisher's cl. s.-c. (HD. Dec.5; 29) Frs. 9,000
- – **Anr. Edn.** Paris, 1963-74. 3 (of 4) vols. Fo. Lacks vol. 1. Cl. (VG. Nov.17; 422) Fls. 800
- – **Anr. Edn.** Ed.:– Julien Cain. Ill.:– M. Chagall. [Monte Carlo], [1969]. Vo. III only. 4to. Orig. linen. (HK. Nov.18-21; 2476) DM 420
- **Chagall Lithographs.** Ed.:– Julien Cain & C. Sorlier. Monte Carlo, [1960-74]. Vol. I & IV Engl., II-III Fr. Edns. Vols. I-IV. 4to. Orig. linen, cold. pict. orig. wraps. (H. Dec.9/10; 1994) DM 4,000
- **The Lithographs of Chagall.** Ill.:– Marc Chagall. Monte Carlo & Boston, [1963]. (Vol. 2, 1957-62). 4to. Cl., cold. pict. d.-w. (SG. Oct.23; 60) $525
- – **Anr. Copy.** Cold. pict. glassine covered d.-w. (SG. Apr.2; 45) $300
- – **Anr. Edn.** Ill.:– Marc Chagall. Boston, 1969. Vol. 3. (1962-68). 4to. Orig. cl., d.-w. (SH. Nov.21; 271) Whiteley. £60
- – **Anr. Edn.** Boston, [1969]. (Vol. 3, 1962-68). 4to. Cl., glassine covered d.-w. (SG. Apr.2; 46) $100
- – **Anr. Edn.** Ill.:– Marc Chagall. Boston; N.Y., 1969; 1974. (Vols. 3 & 4). 4to. Text in Engl. Orig. cl. & d.-w. (SH. Nov.21; 274) Reed & Sims. £80
- – **Anr. Edn.** N.Y., [1974]. (Vol. 4, 1969-73). 4to. Cl., cold. litho. glassine covered d.-w. (SG. Apr.2; 47) $200
- **Picasso: Lithographe.** Ed.:– Jaime Sabartès (preface). Monte Carlo, 1949-64. 4 vols. 4to. Sewed, wraps. (HD. Dec.5; 156) Frs. 6,100
- – **Anr. Edn.** Monte Carlo, [1949-64]. Vols. I-IV. 4to. Orig. wraps. (SG. Apr.2; 225) $1,100
- **Picasso Lithographe III. 1949-1956.** Monte Carlo, [1956]. 4to. Pict. wraps. (SG. Oct.23; 268) $170
- **Picasso Lithographe III, 1949-56.–Picasso Lithographe IV, 1956-63.** Monte-Carlo, 1956; 1964. 2 vols. 4to. Orig. wraps. (SPB. Nov.25; 383) $200
- **Picasso Lithographe III.– Picasso Lithographe IV.–The Lithographs of Chagall.** Monte Carlo; Monte Carlo; Boston, 1957; 1964; 1969. 3 works in 3 vols. 4to. Orig. litho. wraps. (1st. & 2nd. works); & cl., d.-w. (SPB. May 29; 338) $200
- See–CAINE, Jules & Mourlot, Fernand
- See–LEIRIS, M. & Mourlot, Fernand
- See–PONGE, Francis & Mourlot, Fernand

MOURLOT PRESS

- **Prints from the Mourlot Press.** Ill.:– Marc Chagall & others. [Paris], [1964]. (2000). 4to. Cold. pict. wraps. (SG. Mar.26; 334) $150
- – **Anr. Copy.** (SG. Apr.2; 210) $110

MOXON, Joseph

- **A Tutor to Astronomy & Geography ... the Use of both the Globes Caelestrial & Terrestrial ... added the Antient Poetical stories of the Stars.** 1774. 3rd. Edn. 4to. Cont. cf., slightly worn. [Wing M3024] (S. Oct.21; 409) Strauss. £80

MOZART, Leopold

- **Grondig Onderwys in het behandelen der Viool.** Haarlem, 1766. 1st. Edn. 4to. Slight browning. Cont. hf. leath. (H. Dec.9/10; 1207) DM 1,100
- – **Anr. Copy.** Lacks 1 copperplt., minimal browning. Defect. (H. May 21/22; 821) DM 580

MOZART, Wolfgang Amadeus

- **Aria, non piu Andrai Farfallone Amoroso, per il Clavicembalo ... dall Opera Le Nozze di Figaro.** Vienna, 1793. 1st. Edn. Ob. 4to. Mod. marb. bds. (C. Oct.22; 266) Simeone. £100
- **La Clemenza di Tito.** Leipzig, [1809]. 1st. printing. Fo. With German text supp., slightly browned & soiled thro.-out. Cont. hf. leath. defect. (H. Dec.9/10; 1208) DM 1,600
- **Cosi fan Tutte.** Leipzig. [end of 1810]. 1st. Edn. Fo. Lightly browned thro.-out. Linen. (H. Dec.9/10; 1209) DM 1,800
- **Die Entführung aus dem Serail.** Bonn, [Winter 1811-early 1812]. 1st. Edn. Fo. German & Fr. text, some ll. loose, some sm. stains, stp. on title. Hf. leath. (H. Dec.9/10; 1211) DM 1,800
- **Le Nozze di Figaro.** Bonn, [1819]. 1st. Edn. New hf. leath. (H. Dec.9/10; 1213) DM 1,300
- **Die Zauberfloete.** Bonn, [after 1816]. 1st. Edn. Fo. Cf. gt. by Kühn, linen box. F. Mendelssohn-Bertholdy copy with his MS. sig. in ink on end-paper & text corrections in pencil pp. 308-10 & 356-62. (H. Dec.9/10; 1218) DM 4,000
- **Don Juan.** Leipzig, [1801]. 1st. Edn. 2 vols. Ob. fo. Slightly soiled. Hf. leath., with orig. wraps. pasted over, very defect. (H. Dec.9/10; 1210) DM 3,000

MOZART des Dames (Le)

Paris, [1827]. 16mo. Some foxing. Cont. str.-grd. mor., decor. & mosaic spine, lge. gt. plaque & mosaic on covers. (HD. Apr.10; 164) Frs. 1,150

MRS. LOVECHILD'S Golden Present for all Good Little Boys & Girls–The History of Tommy & Harry ...

York, ca. 1820. 9 vols. 32mo. Orig. ptd. wraps., 5th. with ill. & verse on each cover, rest with titles in typographical borders, 19th. C. folder. (SH. Dec.10; 66) Gamble. £105

MUDFORD, William

- **An Historical Account of the Campaign in the Netherlands, in 1815.** Ill.:– George Cruikshank & others. L., 1817. 1st. Edn. Sm. fo. Folding plan with tear, 1 lf. worn at edges, occasional foxing to text. Cont. hf. mor., shaken. (PNY. May 21; 293) $200
- – **Anr. Edn.** Ill.:– J. Rouse after G. Cruikshank & others. L., 1817 [plts. wtrmkd. 1818]. 4to. 1 folding map aquatinted (with slight tears, some reprd.), text foxed, without Abbey's plt. 23. Red mor. gt., by Bennett. From the Prescott Collection. (CNY. Feb.6; 264) $550

MUDGE, Thomas

- **Narrative of Facts relating to some Time-Keepers ...** L., 1792. 1st. Edn. Old sewed, unc. (R. Mar.31-Apr.4; 1308) DM 450

MUDGE, Lieut.-Col. William

- **General Survey of England & Wales, pt. 2, Devon & Cornwall.** N.d. Cf. gt., s.-c. (P. Nov.13; 138) Crowe. £140

MUDIE, Robert

- **The Feathered Tribes of the British Isles.** 1835. 2nd. Edn. 2 vols. Orig. cl., spines gt., unc. (SKC. May 19; 427) £50
- [–] **The Picture of Australia.** 1829. 1st. Edn. Folding linen-bkd. engraved map, some foxing to title & map, lacks hf.-title & advt. lf. Cont. hf. mor. (C. Jul.15; 78) Taylor. £70

MUELLER, Baron Ferdinand von

- **Iconography of Australian Species of Acacia, & Cognate Genera.** Melbourne, 1887-88. 13 decades in 13 pts. as iss. 4 plts. stained at corners. Stiff ptd. wraps. (KH. Mar.24; 295) Aus. $210
- **The Plants Indigenous to the Colony of Victoria. [Volume II]: Lithograms.** Melbourne, 1864-65. 4to. Staining to blank margins of some plts. Cl. (KH. Mar.24; 298) Aus. $110

MUELLER, Jacob, Vicar of Ratisbon

- **Ornatus Ecclesiasticus. Hoc est: Compendium praecipuarum Rerum.** Munich, 1591. 1st. Edn. 2 pts. in 1 vol. 4to. 2 ills. slightly cropped, folding plt. reprd. on verso, slight spotting, a few marginal stains. Cont. limp vell. bds., lacks ties, soiled, letters 'M C P C' 'P F' stpd. on upr. cover. Stp. of the Princes of Ottingen-Wallerstein Maihingen. (S. Jun.23; 233) Quaritch. £280

MUHAMMAD IBN HUSAIN

- **The Khoolasat-ool-Hisab: A Compendium of Arithmetic & Geometry in the Arabic Language.** Calcutta, 1812. Some worming affecting text, marginal stains. Cont. hf. russ., worn. (S. Apr.29; 430) Loman. £65
- **The Oriental Geography.** Trans.:– Sir W. Ouseley. 1800. 4to. Slight browning. Cont.

russ.-bkd. bds., upr. cover detchd., s.-c. (S. Apr.29; 429) Hosain's Books. £90

MUHAMMED II (Sultan of the Turks)

- **Letters.** Trans.:– Lodovico Dolce. Venice, 1563. Slightly soiled. Cont. vell., soiled. (S. Oct.21; 309) Artico. £50

MUIR, John

- **Picturesque California.** N.Y. & San Franc., [1887-88]. Ltd. India-Proof Edn., with extra plts. on Satin. Orig. 10 pts. Fo. Pt. 9 lacks extra satin plt. Loose in orig. pict. wraps., unc., pict. cl. protective covers soiled, & lack linen ties. (SG. May 14; 152) $600
- **Writings.** Boston, 1916[-24]. MS. Edn., (750) with a lf. of MS. 10 vols. Burgandy mor. gt., floral design on covers. (SPB. May 6; 333) $1,700
- – **Anr. Copy.** Buckram, slightly worn, unc. (SG. Nov.13; 535) $260
- See–HARRIMAN Alaska Expedition

MUIR, Percy Horace

- **English Children's Books, 1600 to 1900.** L., [1954]. 1st. Edn. 4to. Cl., d.-w. (SG. Jan.22; 117) $130
- – **Anr. Copy.** (SG. Mar.26; 134) $120
- See–CARTER, John & Muir, Percy H.

MUIRHEAD, L.

- **Journals of Travels in Parts of ... France, The Pays de Vaud, & Tuscany.** 1803. Orig. bds. (P. Oct.23; 52) Brooke-Hitching. £65

MULHOLLAND, Rosa

- **Puck & Blossom.** Ill.:– Kate Greenaway. Ca. 1875. 4to. Orig. decor. cl. gt. (SH. Dec.10; 228) Joseph. £80

MULINARI, Stefano della Pittura ... Real Galleria di Firenze ...

- **Istoria Practica dell'Incominciamento, e Progressi.** Flor., 1778. Fo. 49 (of 50) plts. Hf. cf., defect. (CR. Mar.19; 316) Lire 800,000

MULLER, Adam

- **Von der Idee der Schönheit.** Berlin, 1809. Cont. hf. leath., gold decor. (D. Dec.11-13; 2574) DM 800

MULLER, Hermann Alexander & Singer, Hans Wolfgang

- **Allgemeines Künstler-Lexikon.** Frankfurt, 1920. 5 vols. Orig. hf. linen. (HK. May 12-14; 2264) DM 420
- – **Anr. Edn.** Frankfurt, 1920 & 1922. 4th. Edn. Orig. hf. linen. (R. Oct.14-18; 707) DM 650

MULLER, Johannes Peter, Physiologist

- **Handbuch der Physiologie des Menschen.** 1837-40. 1st. Edn. (Vol. 2), 3rd. Edn. (Vol. 1). 2 vols. in 3 pts., vol. 1 in 2 pts., vol. 2 in 3 pts. Cont. linen. (R. Mar.31-Apr.4; 1017) DM 510
- **Vergleichende Anatomie der Myxonoiden ...** Berlin, 1835-46. 1st. Edns. 3 works in 1 vol., 1st. work in 5 pts. Fo. 2nd. work slightly smaller on different paper. Cl.-bkd. bds. (S. Mar.17; 359) Bolden & Webb. £160

MULLER, Louis

- **Tableau des Guerres de Frédéric le Grand ... ou Combats essentiels donnés dans les trois Guerres de Silésie.** Berlin & Potsdam, 1786. 1st. Edn. in Fr. 4to. Maps trimmed & mntd. Cont. hf. cf., upr. cover detchd., very worn. (S. Oct.21; 472) Hyde Park Books. £50

M[ULLER], M.J.G.

See–GABRIEL, Peter–ROLL, Timotheus von –MONTIF, Lucian–M[ULLER], M.J.G.

MULLER, O.

See–PABST, G. & Muller, O.

MULLER, Otto Friderich

- **Von Wurmern des Süssen und Salzigen Wassers.** Copen., 1771. 1st. Edn. 4to. Slight dampstaining. Cont. hf. cf., spine gt., soiled, bkplts. of the Bibliotheca Honkeniana & the von Arnim Neuensundschen Bibliothek. From liby. of Dr. E. Ashworth Underwood. (S. Feb.23; 260) Hyde. £55

MULLER, Philippus

- **Miracula Chymica et Mysteria Medica.** Paris, 1644. 12mo. Cont. cf. (S. Dec.1; 281) Asher. £50

MULTUM IN PARVO: Fashionable Tours from London ...

[L.], 1802. 2 vols. in 1. Cont. cf., blistered, rebkd. (SG. May 14; 153) $750

MUMEY, Nolie
- A Study of Rare Books with Special Reference to Colophons, Press Devices & Title-pages ... Denver, 1930. (1000) numbered, & sigd. 4to. Orig. hf. cl. & paper bds. (CB. Feb.18; 247) Can. $220

MUN, Thomas
- England's Treasure by Forraign Trade. 1669. 2nd. Edn. Cont. sheep. [Wing M3074] (S. Dec.9; 341) *Boyle.* £480

MUNCHHAUSEN, Baron
See–RASPE, Rudolph Erich

MUNCHENER Bilderbogen
- Costumes of all Nations. 1901. 4to. Orig. cl. (P. Apr.9; 249) *Schapiro.* £130
- Zur Geschichte der Kostüme. Ill.:– after W. Diez, E. Fröhlich & others. Munich, n.d. Cold. Edn. Fo. 125 dbl-p. cold. costume plts. Orig. linen, spine defect. (R. Mar.31-Apr.4; 1562) DM 800
[–] - Anr. Copy. Some plts. stpd., 79 (of 125) double-p. cold. plts. Orig. hf. linen, defect. (R. Oct.14-18; 2642) DM 550

MUNDAY, Anthony & others (attributed to Shakespeare)
[–] The First Part of the True & Honourable History, of the Life of Sir John Old-Castle, the Good Lord Cobham ... L., 1600 [1619]. 2nd. Edn. 4to. (176 × 134mm). 2 ll. reprd., affecting a few letters. Red lev. mor., gt., Louis H. Silver bkplt. (S. Sep.29; 107) *Rappaport.* £500

MUNDY, Lt. Godfrey Charles
- Our Antipodes; or, Residence & Rambles in the Australian Colonies, with a Glimpse of the Gold Fields. L., 1852. 2nd. Edn. 3 vols. Occasional light foxing. Old hf. cf., title labels defect. (KH. Nov.18; 440) Aus. $140

MUNICIPAL CORPORATION BOUNDARIES
- Reports of the Commissioners. 1837. 3 vols. only. Fo. Cont. cl.-bkd. bds., worn. (SH. Mar.5; 71) *Fairburn.* £190

MUNK, Hermann
- Ueber die Funcionen der Grosshirnrinde. Berlin, 1881. 1st. Edn. Cl. (S. Jun.16; 598) *Maggs.* £75

MUNKACSI, Martin
[–] Nudes. N.Y., 1951. 1st. Edn. 4to. Cl., d.-w., a few minor chips. (SG. Apr.23; 143) $110

MUNNICKS, Johannes
- Cheirurgia, ad praxin hodiernam adornata. Amst., 1735. 4to. Spotted. Cont. limp vell., soiled & slightly worn. (S. Oct.21; 410) *Phelps.* £55

MUNNINGS, Sir Alfred
- An Artist's Life.-The Second Burst.-The Finish. 1950; 1951; 1952. 1st. Edns. 3 works in 3 vols. All orig. cl., in d.-w's. (SKC. Dec.4; 1683) £50
- Ballads & Poems. 1957. 1st. Edn. (250) numbered, sigd. Orig. cl., d.-w. (SH. Mar.27; 344) *Brinker.* £55

MUNOZ, Juan Bautista
- Historia del Nuevo-Mondo. Madrid, 1793. Vol. 1 (all publd.). Wide margins. Later hf. mor., worn & detchd. [Sabin 51342] (SPB. May 5; 364) $350

MUNSTER, Sebastian
- Das Achte Buch der Weltbeschreibung. [Basel], [1550-1628]. Fo. Pp. 1628-1686, woodcut map of Africa & other ills. Mod. wraps. (VA. Jan.30; 178) R. 190
- Aruch-Dictionarium Chaldaicum. Basle, 1527. 1st. Edn. 4to. Slight staining. Vell. with blind-tooled medallions, 2 metal clasps, dtd. 1573, slight worming, stained, worn. (SPB. May 11; 168) $1,100
[–] Cosmographei: od. Beschreibung aller Länder. [Basel], ca. 1555. Fo. Lacks 1st. 10 ll. (title & pref.) & maps I-III, maps IV & XI with sm. tears, lacks pp. 103/04, 465/66, 587/88, 755/56, 987/88, 1165/66 & 1229-1233, pp. 753-56 806, 826, 987/88, 1057-60, defect., tears pp. 185, 189, 225, 397, 811, 895, 983, 1023, 1025, 1125, 1167, 1199, 1201, 1221, lacks end pp. 1229-33. Cont. blind-tooled pig-bkd. wood bds., lacks clasps, wormed, especially lr. cover. (HK. May 12-14; 684) DM 8,200
- - Anr. Edn. [Basel], [1561 or 1564]. Fo. 8 (of 14) double-p. woodcut maps, approx. 900 variously old cold. text woodcuts, including 37 double-p. views & parts of 3 folding woodcut views, 3 (of 6) prelim. ll, 1400 (of 1475) pp., 5 (of 10) ll. Cont. leath.,

defect., loose. W.a.f. (R. Oct.14-18; 1511) DM 6,500
- Cosmographia. Basel, 1544. 1st. Edn. Fo. 6 (of 24) double-p. woodcut maps, slightly soiled & stained in parts, owner's mark on title. Cont. blind-tooled pig-bkd. wood bds., lacks clasps, slightly loose. (HK. May 12-14; 152) DM 2,600
- - Anr. Edn. Basel, ca. 1550. 10 ll., 1 doubl-p., with cold. woodcuts, slightly browned & soiled. (HK. Nov.18-21; 333) DM 420
- Cosmographiae Universalis. Lib. VI. Basel, Mar. 1550. 1st. Latin Edn. Fo. Cold. thro.-out, 8 (of 14) maps, 3 foldg., 38 (of 39) double-p. plts., 950 text ills., all cold. woodcuts, 1154 (of 1162) pp., sm. hole in title, slightly soiled, some ink notes. Cont. leath., restored heavily probably in 19th. C. (R. Oct.14-18; 1509) DM 22,000
- - Anr. Edn. 1552. Fo. Some repairs, mis-paginated. Cont. cf., blind fillets & gt. centre fleurons & in angles, decor. spine raised bands. (HD. Apr.24; 86) Frs. 12,000
- Cosmography. Basle, 1564. Fo. 5 (of 14) double-p. maps, defect., 1314 (of 1475) pp., mostly browned or soiled, at least third of ll. with Jap. paper on both sides, some text ll. & views with text loss. Vell. W.a.f. (R. Mar.31-Apr.4; 2271) DM 1,300
- - Anr. Edn. Basle, 1567. Fo. 3 × 1 slightly torn, affecting text & woodcut on verso, a few ll. very slightly soiled. Cont. blind-stpd. pig. over wooden bds., scratched corners worn, brass clasps, 1 detchd. (S. Apr.7; 309) *Traylen.* £4,200
- - Anr. Edn. Basel, 1578. Fo. Lightly browned or soiled, some old MS. underlining. Cont. pig-bkd. wood bds., blind-stpd., lacks clasps. (R. Oct.14-18; 1510) DM 18,000
- - Anr. Edn. Basel, 1614. Fo. Lacks 1st. 6 ll. & 23 maps & last blank lf., many pp. misbnd., pp. 249-270 bnd. in at beginning, some views with MS. repairs, from p.1471 on increasing text & plt. loss, reprd. with old paper, partly soiled, some worming, very worn & defect. Cont. paper-bkd. wood bds., spine defect. (HK. Nov.18-21; 1280) DM 9,500
- - Anr. Edn. Basel, [1614?] Fragment. Fo. Many wdcts, lacks nearly all woodcut plts., many ll. defect., some with corrections. Wood bds., defect & loose. Not collated, w.a.f. (R. Mar.31-Apr.4; 2272) DM 800
- Dictionarium Hebraicvm. Basel, Aug. 1539. Cont. Hebrew note in red ink inside cover. Cont. blind-tooled pig-bkd. wood bds., 2 clasps, lacks ties, slightly wormed. (HK. Nov.18-21; 236) DM 500
- Dictionarium Trilingue in quo scilicet Latinis Vocabulis in Ordinem Alphabeticum digestis respondent Graeca & Hebraica. Basel, 1530. Sm. fo. 1st. Edn. Cont. limp vell., soiled, lr. cover defect. (R. Oct.14-18; 120) DM 650
- Institutiones Grammaticae in Hebraeam Linguam. Basel, 1524. Only Edn. Cont. cf., blind-tooled decor., worn, spine brkn. (HK. Nov.18-21; 235) DM 1,100

MUNTER, B.
- Erste Sammlung Geistliche Lieder. Leipzig, 1773. Ob. fo. Title-lf. heavily browned with stp., stp. on 1st. lf. Unbnd., unc. (H. Dec.9/10; 1221) DM 860

MUNTING, Abraham
- Naauwkeurige Beschrijving der Aardgewassen, waar in de Veelerley Aart en Bijzondere Eigenschappen der Boomen, Heesters, Bloemen ... Leiden & Utrecht, 1696. Fo. Minimal soiling & browning. Mod. hf. leath. (R. Mar.31-Apr.4; 1407) DM 9,000
- - Anr. Copy. Cont. cf., upr. & lr. parts of spine slightly defect. (VG. Oct.13; 111) Fls. 7,000
- Phytographia Curiosa ... Leiden & Amst., 1702. 2 pts. in 1 vol. Fo. Some plts. slightly discold., text ll. browned. 19th. C. hf. mor., upr. cover detchd. From Chetham's Liby., Manchester. (C. Nov.27; 308) *Schmidt.* £1,000

MUNTZER VON BABENBERG, W.
- Reyssbeschreibung von Venedig auss nach Jerusalem, Damascus und Constantinople, und dann wider nacher Venedig. Nuremb., 1624. Mod. hf. vell. (R. Oct.14-18; 1800) DM 850

MURAT, la Comtesse de
- Les Contes des Fées. Paris, 1698. 1st. Edn. 12mo. Lacks 1st. lf. (blank?), 1 lf. browned & a few others slightly browned or spotted. Cont. cf., spine gt. in compartments, defect. at head & foot. (S. Apr.7; 345) *Quaritch.* £220

MURATORI, Lodovico Antonio
- Geschichte von Italien. Ed.:– Chr. G. Jöcher. Leipzig, 1745-50. 1st. German Edn. 9 vols. Lge. 4to. Title stpd., old MS. owner's mark on end-ll. & browned, MS. liby. stp. on vell. spine partly erased, Cont. leath. gt. (vol. 1) & cont. hf. vell. W.a.f. (HK. May 12-14; 656) DM 650

MURAWIEW-APOSTOL, Reise durch Taurien im Jahre 1820
Trans.:– W. v. Oertel. Berlin & Landsberg, 1825. 1st. Edn. in German. Gt.-tooled cf., spine gt. (SG. Oct.9; 175) $600

MURCHISON, Sir Roderick Impey
- Siluria ... 1854. 1st. Edn. Owner's inscr. on title. Orig. cl. (S. Sep.29; 96) *Quaritch.* £80

MURETUS, Marcus Antonius
- Orationes. Venice, 1575. 3 pts. in 1 vol. Lacks(?) final blank, sm. marginal repair to 1st. title, some underlinings & marginal inscrs. in text. 18th. C. cf. gt., jnts. & edges slightly worn. (S. Feb.10; 263) *Ponder.* £60

MURGER, Henri
- Bohemian Life. Phila., [1899]. (5) on Japan vell., with all plts. in 4 states. Orig. lev., gt. arms, wide gt. dentelles enclosing patterned satin doubls. Fore-e. pntg.; from the liby. of Zola E. Harvey. (SG. Mar.19; 155) $400
- Scènes de la Vie de Bohème. Ill.:– Charles Léandre. Paris, 1902. (300); (40) on Arches vell. Lge. 8vo. 2 states of ills., analysis of colours of 1 plt., pencil port. Mor. by Carayon, gt. & blind-tooled decor. on covers, smooth decor. spine, inside dentelle, watered silk end-papers, wrap. & spine preserved. Port. & autograph postcard sigd. by artist. (HD. Jun.25; 352) Frs. 6,700

MURLOCH, Diana Maria
See–CRAIK, nee Murloch, Mrs. Diana Maria

MURNER, Thomas
- Die Gäuchmatt.-Die Schelmen Zunsst. Frankfurt-am-Main, 1565; 1571. 2 works in 1 vol. Some browning, lacks a lf. at beginning & end? (blanks?). Early 19th. C. hf. cf., slightly worn. From liby. of André L. Simon. (S. May 18; 140) *Facchi.* £260

MURPHY, James Cavanagh
- A General View of the State of Portugal. L., 1798. 1st. Edn. Lge. 4to. Blind-tooled cf. Armorial bkplt. of Frederic Straker. (SG. Feb.26; 238) $180
- Travels in Portugal. 1795. 4to. Some ll. soiled. Cont. cf. gt. (SD. Feb.4; 230) £60
- - Anr. Copy. Blind-tooled cf. Armorial bkplt. of Frederic Straker, Newton's port. of Murphy bnd. in. (SG. Feb.26; 237) $325

MURPHY, Robert Cushman
- Oceanic Birds of South America. Ill.:– F.L. Jaques. 1936. 2 vols. 4to. Buckram gt., cased. (PL. Sep.18; 165) *Swann.* £60
- - Anr. Copy. Cl., s.-c. (TA. Jun.18; 107) £55

MURRAY, A.
See–BURLINGTON, Ch. & others

MURRAY, Alexander, D.D., Orientalist
- Account of the Life & Writings of James Bruce, of Kinnaird ... Author of Travels to discover the Source of the Nile ... 1768[-73]. Edinb., 1808. 1st. Edn. (L.P.). 4to. Slight browning. Orig. bds., rebkd., soiled, unc. (S. Nov.4; 567) *Quaritch.* £85

MURRAY, Amelia
- Pictorial & Descriptive Sketches of the Odenwald. [1854?]. Lge. ob. fo. Cont. mor. gt. (C. Jul.15; 79) *Müller.* £3,500

MURRAY, Charles A.
- Travels in North America ... Including a Summer Residence with the Pawnee ... L., 1839. 1st. Edn. 2 vols. Slight foxing. Orig. blind-stpd. cl. From liby. of William E. Wilson. (SPB. Apr.29; 211) $100

MURRAY, George
- The Antarctic Manual for the Use of the Expedition of 1901. 1901. Orig. bdg. (TRL. Dec.10; 97) £54

MURRAY, H.
- The British School of Art. N.d. 2 vols. in 1. Fo. Slight spotting. Cont. cf. (CSK. Oct.17; 32) £120

MURRAY, Hugh
- Historical Account of Discoveries & Travels in North America ... L., 1829. 1st. Edn. 2 vols. Lacks errata lf. called for in Sabin. Cont. cf., gt. spines, upr. covers loose. From liby. of William E. Wilson. [Sabin 51500] (SPB. Apr.29; 212) $300

MURRAY, Sir James & Marston, George
- Antarctic Days. 1913. 4to. Orig. bdg. (TRL. Dec.10; 83) £155

MURRAY-OLIVER, Anthony
- Captain Cook's Artists in the Pacific. Christchurch, New Zealand, 1969. Ltd. Edn. Ob. fo. Orig. hf. rexine, s.-c. (SH. Nov.7; 461) *Weekend Gallery.* £52
- - Anr. Copy. (2,000) numbered. Hf. leath., s.-c. (KH. Nov.18; 446) Aus. $130

MUSAEUS, Johann Karl August
- Die Bücher d. Chronika d. drei Schwestern. Ill.:– H. Lefler & J. Urban. Berlin, 1900. Fo. A few ll. slightly soiled in margin. Orig. wraps, soiled & frayed, linen pasted on spine. (HK. Nov.18-21; 2764) DM 460
- Opusculum de Herone et Leandro. Graece et Latine. Venice, Nov. 1517. Old red mor., gt. fillet & motifs, decor. spine raised bands. (HD. Apr.24; 16) Frs. 3,000
- Popular Tales of the Germans. Trans.:– William Beckford. 1791. 2 vols. 12mo. Cont. spr. cf., gt. (SH. Mar.5; 193) *George's.* £130
- Volksmährchen der Deutschen. Ill.:– after L. Richter. Leipzig, 1842. De Luxe Edn., 1st. Richter Edn. 2 vols. Slightly browned & stained, lacks hf.-title. Cont. hf. leath., gt. spine. (R. 14-18; 1016) DM 800

MUSEE POUR RIRE
Ed.:– M. Alhoy, L. Huart & Ch. Philipon (text). Ill.:– Daumier, Gavarni & others. Paris, 1839. Pts. 1 & 2 (of 3) in 1 vol. 4to. Browned in parts & soiled. Hf. leath. gt. ca. 1880. (HK. Nov.18-21; 2368) DM 850

MUSEE ROYAL DE NAPLES ... avec leur explication par M.C.F.
Paris, 1836. Lge. 4to. Mntd. engraved title on india paper & 60 plts., each dupl., affected by damp, spotting. Cont. cf.-bkd. bds., worn, in mor. portfo., worn. (CSK. Jan.23; 170) £280

MUSEE ROYALE
- Explication des Ouvrages de Peinture, Sculpture, Architecture ... 1838. Mor., fillet, by Ginain. Duchesse de Berry arms. (HD. Oct.10; 261) Frs. 1,650

MUSEN-ALMANACH
Ed.:– Friedrich Schiller. Tübingen, [1796-99]. 1st. Edn. 4 vols. 1 (of 3) frontis., 9 (of 17) folding musical Supps., old MS. owner's mark. Cont. style hf. leath. decor. gt., by Babala., orig. wraps. bnd. in, slightly soiled & worn. (HK. May 15; 4856) DM 980

MUSGRAVE, Sir Richard
- Memoirs of the different Rebellions in Ireland. Dublin, 1801. 2nd. Edn. 4to. Some spotting. Cont. mott. cf. Bkplt. of Sir William Forbes. (SBA. Jul.23; 579) *Emerald Isles Books.* £65

MUSICAL Miscellany
L., 1729-31. 6 vols. 4pp. of advts. in vol. VI. Mod. bds. (SG. Feb.5; 252) $150

MUSIL, Robert
- Der Mann ohne Eigenschaften. Berlin, 1933 & 1943. 1st. Edn. Vol. II & III. Owner's mark. Orig. linen. (H. May 21/22; 1735) DM 1,050

MUSKETT, Joseph J.
- Suffolk Manorial Families. Exeter, Priv. ptd., 1900-14. 3 vols. 4to. Cont. cf. (SH. Nov.6; 52) *College Gateway.* £95

MUSLIH IBN ABD ULLAH, called SA'DI
- Persianische Rosenthal ... Ill.:– Christian Rothgiesser. Schlezwig, 1654. 1st. German Edn. Fo. 9 prelims. with short tear at fore-edge. Cont. vell. (PNY. Mar.26; 289) $1,700

MUSPRATT, John Sheridan
- Chemistry Theoretical, Practical & Analytical as Applied & Relating to the Arts & Manufactures. Glasgow, Edinb., L., N.Y., [1853-61]. 2 vols. 4to. Hf. cf., rebkd. (S. Dec.1; 282) *Music Mart.* £55

MUSSARD, Pierre
[–] Conformités des Cérémonies Modernes avec les Anciennes ... Amst., 1744. New Edn. 12mo.

Cont. mor. by Derome le Jeune with his ticket, triple gt. fillet, flat spine gt. in compartments with single sm. arabesque, inner gt. dentelles, bkplt. of Edouard Rahir. (SM. Oct.7; 1878) Frs. 3,000

MUSSET, Alfred de
- Gamiani oder zwei Nächte der Ausschweifung. Leipzig, Priv. Ptd., 1911. (300). Orig. leath. (D. Dec.11-13; 1992) DM 2,000
- Lorenzaccio. Ill.:– Alexandre Barte. Paris, [1926]. (50) on Japon, with orig. drawing, & plts. in 2 states. 4to. Crushed hf. lev., orig. wraps. bnd. in. (SG. Apr.2; 16) $140
- La Mouche. Ill.:– Lalauze. Paris, 1892. (200) numbered on lge. Arches vell. Ills. in 3 states, clean etching on Holland, 2 prospectus ll. et end. Mor. by Marius Michel, decor. spine, covers framed, wrap. preserved. All ills. sigd. (SM. Feb.11; 267) Frs. 10,000
- - Anr. Copy. (500) out of series copy with ills. in 2 states. Red mor. by P.-R. Raparlier, rococco-style frame on upr. cover & figure on lr., gt. panel. spine, mor. gt. doubls. (SPB. Jul.31; 39) $150
- Nouvelles. Ill.:– Burney, Mordant & Lucas after F. Flameng & O. Corrazo. 1887. (150) numbered on L.P., initialled by publisher. 4to. All etchings in 2 states. Three-qtr. mor., gt. panel. spine by Champs, orig. wraps. bnd. in. (SG. Sep.4; 349) $150
- La Nuit Venitienne ... Ill.:– Brunelleschi. [1913.]. (500) on Jap. 4to. Jansenist mor. by Huser, spine with raised bands, wrap. & spine preserved, bdg. slightly defect. (HD. Jun.25; 353) Frs. 1,700
- Les Nuits. Ill.:– Serge de Solomko. Paris, 1926. De Luxe Edn. on Vel. d'Arches. Mor. sigd. Mireille Magnin, gt., decor., gold fillets, inner dentelles, cold paper s.-c. (D. Dec.11-13; 1154) DM 1,400
- Oeuvres. Paris, 1884-95. Ltd. Edn. 10 vols. 4to. Mor. sigd. by Kauffmann & Horclois, partly unc., orig. wraps. bnd. in. (SI. Dec.3; 417) Lire 1,000,000
- - Anr. Edn. Ill.:– Lalauze. Paris, 1884-95. On Holland. 10 vols. 4to. Hf. mor., corners, spines with raised bands, wraps. & spines preserved. (HD. Feb.27; 189) Frs. 1,950
- Oeuvres Complètes. Paris, 1866. 10 vols. Ills. from 1883 Edn. by Eugene Lami inserted, slight spotting. Red mor. gt., chipping on 1 cover & spine. (SPB. May 6; 334) $600
- - Anr. Copy. Cont. hf. leath. gt. (HK. May 12-14; 1611) DM 580
- - Anr. Edn. Ill.:– Bida. Paris, 1866. Ltd. Edn. 10 vols. Light foxing. Cont. red hf. mor., gt., partly unc. (SM. Oct.8; 2142) Frs. 1,200
- - Anr. Edn. Ill.:– Charles Martin. Paris, 1928-29. Ltd. Edn. 10 vols. 4to. Hf. mor., orig. wraps. bnd. in. (SM. Oct.8; 2223) Frs. 1,000
- On ne Badine pas avec l'Amour. Ill.:– Louis Morin. Paris, 1904. (200) on Marais vell., numbered. Mor. by Charles Meunier, decor. spine, border on covers, wrap. preserved, s.-c. (SM. Feb.11; 268) Frs. 7,000
- Trois Comédies. Ed.:– Ferdinand Fargeot. Lyon, 1944. L.P. Edn. (500) numbered on Papier de Rives. Orig. wraps., sewed, unopened, tissue-wrap., boxed. (PNY. Oct.1; 392) $140

MUSSET, Paul Edme de
- Le Dernier Abbé. Ill.:– Lalauze. Paris, 1891. (315) on Arches vell. 2 states of ills., 1 with comments. Mor. by Canape-Belz, decor. spine, border of 5 fillets on covers, inside dentelle, wrap. preserved. (SM. Feb.11; 269) Frs. 3,000
- Voyage Pittoresque en Italie, Partie Septentionale. Paris, [1864]. Cl., richly gt. (VG. Dec.16; 941) Fls. 500
- Voyage Pittoresque en Italie. [Partie Septentrionale Meridionale et en Sicile.] Paris, 1855-65. 2 vols. Frontis. torn, corner & hole in 2nd. vol. Hf. cf. & publisher's cl., not unif. W.a.f. (CR. Mar.19; 405) Lire 520,000
- - Anr. Copy. Lightly stained. Orig. cl., gt. decor. (SI. Dec.3; 418) Lire 400,000

MUSSIS, Petri Dominici de
- Formularius Instrumetorum. Venice, 1530. 1st. Edn. Fo. Title-p. slightly defect., some discoloration. Old bds. with vell. backstrip, defect. (TA. Oct.16; 187) £100

MUTHER R.
- Die Deutsche Bücherillustration der Gotib und Frührenaissance. Munich, 1884. Text & plt. vol.

Fo. Hf. leath., spine worn. (R. May 21/22; 35) DM 550

MUTIS, Jose Celestino
- Flora de la Real Expedicion Botanico del Nuevo Reino de Granada. Madrid, 1954-57. 3 vols. Fo. Spanish leath. (SG. Sep.18; 269) $300

MUYBRIDGE, Eadweard James
- Animals in Motion. 1899. Ob. 4to. End-papers dust-soiled, hinges worn. Cl., worn. (PD. Feb.18; 22) £75

MYER, Isaac
- Qabbalah. Phila., 1888. 4to. Very slight browning. Cl. (SPB. May 11; 237) $150

MYLIUS, Christian Friedrich
- Malerische Fussreise durch das Südliche Frankreich und einen Theil von Ober-Italien. Carlsruhe, 1818-19. 8 pts. text in 4 vols. & atlas vol., together 5 vols. 8vo & ob. fo. Lacks plts. 35, 60, 72, 79, 86 & 87, plts. 67 & 73 misbnd. Antique style hf. sheep, atlas vol. using old bds. (S. Oct.21; 484) *Brockhaus.* £380

MYLLER, A.M.
- Peregrinus in Jerusalem ... Vienna & Nuremb., 1735. 5 pts. in 1 vol. 68 (of 71) copperplts., 32 folding. Bdgs., linen-bkd. spine. (R. Oct.14-18; 1783) DM 820

MYNSICHT, Hadrianus a
- Thesaurus et Armamentarium Medico-Chymicum ... de Aureo Philosophorum Lapide. Frankfurt, 1675. 2 woodcuts in Testamentum bnd. at beginning. Vell. (S. Dec.2; 563) *Dawson.* £90

MYSINGNER, Joachim
- Apotelesma, Sive Corpus Perfectum Scholiorum. Basle, 1580. Fo. Slight soiling, early ll. dampstained. Cont. vell., blind-stpd., dtd. 1581, soiled. (CSK. Jan.23; 140) £200

N.
- Voyages aux Côtes de Guinée & en Amerique. Amst., 1719. 12mo. 1 or 2 minor tears. 19th. C. cf., upr. cover detchd. [Sabin 51677] (S. Jun.22; 185) *Quaritch.* £260

N., M.
- Anatomy Epitomized & Illustrated. 1737. 1st. Edn. Advt. lf. Marb. bds., new cf. spine, unc. (S. Jun.16; 600) *Phelps.* £65

NA RASPUT'I [At the Cross-Roads]
Ed.:– [S.P. Serebrovsky]. Moscow, 1906. Nos. 1, 2, 4-6 & Bylina (iss. in place of the confiscated no. 3). Fo. A few sm. tears. Unbnd. (SH. Feb.5; 96) *Landry.* £260

NA RAZVETE [At Dawn. Artistic Journal]
Ed.:– [S.F. Mantel']. Ill.:– M. Vrubel'. [Kazan], 1910. 4to. Orig. wraps., torn & soiled. (SH. Feb.6; 339) *Tate Gallery.* £70

NABBES, Thomas
- Hannibal & Scipio. 1637. 1st. Edn. 4to. Last lf. slightly browned. Mor. by Rivière. [STC 18441] (C. Nov.19; 121) *Ludgrove.* £200
- Microcosmus. 1637. 1st. Edn. 4to. Some ll. inkstained. 19th. C. hf. mor. [STC 18342] (C. Nov.19; 122) *Arnold.* £170
- The Unfortunate Mother. 1640. 1st. Edn. 4to. 19th. C. hf. mor. Huth bkplt. [STC 18346] (C. Nov.19; 123) *Sainsbury.* £140

NABOKOV, Vladimir
- Stikhi. Petrograd, 1916. 1st. Edn., (500) numbered. 4to. Stp. on title. Orig. ptd. wraps., soiled, lacks portions of spine. (SPB. Nov.25; 364) $6,400

NACHMAN OF BRAZLAV
- Likutei Maharan Tinyana. Ed.:– Nathan Sternhertz. [?Ostroho], 1809. 1st. Edn. 4to. Slightly browned. Hf. leath. (S. Nov.17; 172) *Rock.* £320

NADRAL, Gabriel
- Essai d'Hematologie Pathologique. Paris, 1843. 1st. Edn. New cl. (S. Dec.2; 441) *Rota.* £70

NAFTALI HURWITZ of Ropshitz
- Ayala Shlucha. Lvov, 1862. 1st. Edn. 4to. Hf. cl. (S. Nov.18; 312) *Goldstein.* £80

NAGAECHKA [Little Whip]
Ed.:– [A.F. Ivanov]. St. Petersb., 1905-06. Nos. 1-4 only (of 5). Fo. Unbnd. (SH. Feb.5; 94) *Landry.* £160

NAGEL, O. & Kollwitz, Käthe
- **Die Handzeichnungen.** Berlin, 1972. Lge. 4to. Orig. linen. (H. Dec.9/10; 2160) DM 450

NAGLER, Dr. George K.
- **Die Monogrammisten.** Munich & Leipzig, n.d. – 1879-1920. 6 vols. including index. Cont. hf. mor. (SH. Jan.29; 129) Dallai. £250
- **Neues Allgemeines Kunstler-Lexicon.** Munich, 1835. 1st. Edn. 22 vols. Spotted. Cont. cl.-bkd. bds. (SH. Jan.29; 130) Berquist. £200
- – **Anr. Edn.** Leipzig, n.d. Reprint of 1835-52 Edn. 25 vols. Orig. linen. (R. Oct.14-18; 709) DM 1,600

NAGPUR WATER WORKS
- **Description of ...** Bombay, 1872. Fo. Each photograph bordered & captioned by hand in ink, images slightly over-exposed from bright sun. Gt.-decor. mor., worn, loose, free end-papers torn. (SG. Apr.23; 109) $300

NALL, John Greaves
- **Great Yarmouth & Lowestoft ...** 1867. (12) on L.P. with additional photographic ills. Cont. hf. mor. From the collection of Eric Sexton. (C. Apr.16; 311) Ferrow. £220

NALSON, John
- **An Impartial Collection of the Great Affairs of State from the beginning of the Scotch Rebellion in the Year 1639, to the Murther of King Charles I.** L., 1682. 2 vols. Fo. Frontis. dust-soiled, text reprd. Rebnd. in mod. cf. (PD. Nov.26; 164) £80
- – **Anr. Edn.** 1682-83. 1st. Edn. 2 vols. Fo. Slight browning. Cont. mott. cf. [Wing N106-107] (S. Sep.29; 59) Parsloe. £55
- – **Anr. Copy.** Cont. cf., rebkd. (SG. Feb.5; 253) $140

NANCE, Ernest Morton
- **Pottery & Porcelain of Swansea & Nantgarw.** 1942. [1st. Edn.?]. Sm. 4to. Orig. cl. (SH. Apr.9; 106) Talerman. £190
- – **Anr. Copy.** A few plts. dampstained & torn. (SH. Jun.4; 92) Hutchings. £160
- – **Anr. Copy.** D.-w. (LC. Feb.12; 107) £130

NANCE, Robert Morton
- **Sailing-Ship Models.** 1924. Ltd. Edn. 4to. Cl. gt. (P. Sep.11; 240) Hughes. £70
- – **Anr. Copy.** (1209) numbered. (TA. Feb.19; 389) £54
- – **Anr. Copy.** (1,750) numbered. (TA. Mar.19; 115) £52
- – **Anr. Edn.** L., 1924. (100) on L.P., specially bnd. Mor. (SG. Feb.26; 287) $150

NANSEN, Fridtjof
- **Farthest North.** 1897. 1st. Edn. 2 vols. Orig. cl., gt., d-w.'s. (SH. Nov.7; 482) Edwards. £70
- – **Anr. Copy.** Hf. mor. (CB. Sep.24; 180) Can. $100
- **The First Crossing of Greenland.** 1890. 2 vols. Cl. (CE. Nov.20; 81) £65
- – **Anr. Copy.** (TRL. Dec.10; 3) £52
- **In Northern Mists.** 1911. 2 vols. 4to. Orig. cl. (TRL. Dec.10; 8) £62
- **Pram over Polhavet den norske Polarfaerd 1893-1896.** Ill.:– after Nansen. Oslo, 1897. 1st. Edn. 2 vols. Orig. cl. (S. Nov.4; 596) Brook-Hitching. £120

NANTES
- **Bulletin Archéologique de Nantes.–Congrès Archéologique de France; Séances tenues à Nantes.** 1859-92; 1857-86. 2 works in 22 vols. 1st. work: cont. hf. chagrin; 2nd. work; no bdg. stated. (HD. Jun.24; 93) Frs. 1,900

NAPIER, E.
- **Scenes & Sports in Foreign Lands.** 1840. 2 vols. Cont. hf. cf. (SH. May 21; 82) Vitale. £50

NAPIER, John
- **A Description of the Admirable Table of Logarithmes.** Trans.:– Edward Wright. 1618. 12mo. Cf., gt. by Rivière, hf. red mor. case. From Honeyman Collection; Gabriel Harvey's copy with his sig. on title-p. [NSTC 18352] (S. Nov.10; 2290) Zeitlin. £1,300
- **Enneades Arithmeticae: the Numbring Nines. Or, Pythagoras His Table Extended to all Whole Numbers under 10000 & the Numbring Rods of the Right Honourable John Lord Nepeer.** 1684. 1 folding engraved table mntd. on linen, slight staining, owners' inscrs. of Edmund Verney & John Jones on verso & recto of title. 19th. C. mor., William Stirling Maxwell's blind-stpd. arms & cipher on covers, with his bkplt. From Honeyman Collection. [Wing E3128] (S. Nov.10; 2293) Quaritch. £280
- **Logarithmorum Canonis descriptio, seu Arithmeticarum Mirabilis abbreviatio [–Sequitur Tabula Canonis Logarithmorum, Mirifici Logarithmorum Canonis constructio].** Lyon, 1620. 1st. Fr. Edn. 3 pts. in 1 vol. 4to. 1st. title stained by ink notats. on verso & with deleted sig., some browning, 19th. C. owner's inscr. & notats. of Charles Fournerat. Bds., jnts. worn, hf. red mor. case. From Honeyman Collection. (S. Nov.10; 2292) Zeitlin. £340
- **Mirifici Logarithmorum Canonis descriptio, eiusque usus, in utraque Trigonometria, ut etiam in omni Logistica Mathematica ... explicatio.** Edinb., 1614. 1st. -Edn., 1st. Iss. 4to. Pp. 14-15 misnumbered 22-23, slight browning, some marginal annots., owners' inscrs. Bnd. in lf. of 14th. C. Italian MS. on vell., worn, hf. red mor. case. From Honeyman Collection. [NSTC 18349] (S. Nov.10; 2288) Zeitlin. £3,000
- **Mirifici Logarithmorum Canonis descriptio [–Mirifici Logarithmorum Canonis constructio].** Edinb., 1619. 1st. Edn. of pt. 2. 2 pts. in 1 vol. 4to. Sm. tear in F3 pt. 2, marginal staining. 19th. C. str.-grd. mor., tooled in blind, hf. red mor. case. Bkplt. & sig of Lord Napier; from Honeyman Collection. [NSTC 18350] (S. Nov.10; 2289) Barchas. £1,800
- **A Plaine Discovery of the Whole Revelation of Saint John.** Edinb., 1593. 1st. Edn. 4to. Al (blank) with sig., 06 inserted from a shorter copy, slight soiling & staining, owner's inscr. on title. 19th. C. red str.-grd. mor., gt. Bkplt. of Lord Napier with his note of purchase; from Honeyman Collection. [NSTC 18354] (S. Nov.10; 2287) Hill. £90
- **Rabdologiae, seu numerationes per virgulas libri duo.** Edinb., 1617. 1st. Edn. 12mo. 1 folding plt. with sm. tear, some staining & discoloration, 17th. C. (?) sig. of Charles Erskine on title. Red mor. by [James Scott of Edinb.], ca. 1776-80, covers gt. with ornamentation, gt. spine, marb. end-papers, hf. red mor. cases, slight wear. From Honeyman Collection; bkplt. & inscr. of Lord Napier with his notation of purchase. [NSTC 18357] (S. Nov.10; 2291) Quaritch. £4,000

NAPIER, Sir William Francis Patrick
- **History of the War in the Peninsular.** 1828-40. 6 vols. Hf. mor. gt. (P. Apr.9; 272) Duran. £50
- – **Anr. Edn.** 1832-40. 6 vols. Tree cf., spines gt. (SKC. Feb.26; 1461) £130

NAPOLEON, I, Emperor
- **Codice di Napoleone il Grande pel Regno d'Italia.** Milan, 1806. 4to. Text in Fr. & Italian. Cont. str.-grd. red mor., elab. stpd. & tooled in gt. & blind, with mor. inlays, slightly soiled & wormed, head of spine reprd., silk doubls., stpd. in gt., affected by damp. (CSK. Dec.12; 154) £65
- **Commentaires.** Paris, 1867. 6 vols. 4to. Cont. red mor. gt., partly unc. (SI. Dec.4; 423) Lire 320,000
- **The Life of Bonaparte, Late Emperor of the French ... By a Citizen of the United States.** Salem, Indiana, 1818. 12mo. Foxed & stained, a few MS. notations on end-papers & blanks. Orig. cf., worn, cracked. From liby. of William E. Wilson. (SPB. Apr.29; 154) $300
- **Le Sacre de sa Majesté l'Empereur Napoleon dans l'Eglise Metropolitaine de Paris.** Ill.:– after Isabey, Percier, Fontaine, etc. Plts. dtd. between 1806-1812. Lge. fo. Early 19th. C. str.-grd. mor. gt. with Napoleonic eagles in centre of covers, gt. border, watered silk end-papers, stpd. Colnaghi & Co., L., jnts. worn. Inscr. 'The Princess Pauline's Copy, Proofs' on 1st. blank in early 19th. C. hand. (BS. Jun.11; 219) £1,250
- **Selection from the Letters & Despatches.** Ed.:– D.A. Bingham. L., 1884. 3 vols. Red mor. gt., Napoleon monog., emblem, raised bands, gt. inner & outer dentelles, by Hatchards. (D. Dec.11-13; 2693) DM 1,200

NAPTON, William B. & others
- **Pro-Slavery Convention of Missouri. Address to the People of the United States ...** St. Louis, 1855. Wraps. (SG. Jun.11; 393) $100

NARBOROUGH, Sir John, Tasman, Capt. J. & others
- **An Account of Several Late Voyages & Discoveries.** 1711. 2nd. Edn. Lacks? hf.-title, repairs to maps, occasional spotting & browning. Mod. spr. cf. [Sabin 72186] (S. Feb.10; 453) Maggs. £160

NARCOTIQUE des Sages (Le), ou le Véhicule de la Folie
Paris, [1790]. Sm. 18mo. Cont. red mor. decor. covers, lge. border & centre floral motif, watered silk fly-ll. & doubls. (HD. Apr.10; 165) Frs. 1,150

NARDI, Giovanni
- **De Igne Subterraneo Physica Prolusio.** Flor., 1641. 1st. Edn. 4to. Text browned, owner's inscr. on title., 18th. C. hf. vell. bds. From Honeyman Collection. (S. Nov.10; 2294) Howell. £170

NARDI, Jacopo
- **Storie della Citta di Firenze.** Flor., 1584. 2nd. Edn. 4to. Fo. A reprd., dupl. stp. of Vienna Hofbibliothek on verso of title. Early 18th C. red mor., gt., by Etienne Boyet, on covers, triple gt. fillet, his cipher & arms, gt., repeated in alternate spine compartments, inner gt. dentelles, 3 sm. wormholes in spine. Dedication copy to Cardinal Alessandro Medici, with his arms on title in red & black bkplt. of Thomas Gaisford. (SM. Oct.7; 1879) Frs. 5,200

NARDINI, Famiano
- **Roma Antica di F.N.** Rome, 1665. 4to. Cf., 7 spine raised bands, tooled decor. gt. on spine. (CR. Mar.19; 319) Lire 220,000
- – **Anr. Copy.** A few ll. torn & reprd., 3D3 with loss of a few letters, some browning. Old vell. (CSK. Apr.24; 126) £55
- – **Anr. Edn.** Rome, 1818-20. 4 vols. in 2. Slight browning. Cont. hf. vell. bds. (S. May 5; 439) Pozzi. £50

NARDINI, Famiano–NARDINI, Nicolo
- **L'Antico Veio ... discorso Investigativo del Sito di Quella Citta.–La Catedra Vescovale di S. Tolomeo in Nepi.** Ed.:– E. Mezzaroma. (2nd. work). Rome, 1647; 1677. 1st. Edns. 2 works in 1 vol. 4to. Some browning, 1st. work with 1 folding plan only (slightly cropped at lr. edge). 18th. C. cf. Edward Gibbon's copy. (S. Jun.9; 33) Ehrman. £150

NARES, George Strong
- **Narrative of a Voyage to the Polar Sea.** 1878. 1st. Edn. 2 vols. Orig. cl., soiled. (SH. Nov.7; 484) Bowes. £75
- – **Anr. Edn.** 1878. 3rd. Edn. 2 vols. Orig. bdg. (TRL. Dec.10; 94) £100
- – **Anr. Edn.** 1878. 4th. Edn. 2 vols. 6 actual photographs mntd. Orig. cl. (SH. Nov.7; 485) Cavendish. £75
- – **Anr. Edn.** Ed.:– H.W. Feilden. L., 1878. 2 vols. Orig. cl., spine slightly discold. (CB. Apr.1; 100) Can. $280

NARJOUX, Felix
- **Notes & Sketches of an Architect taken during a Journey in the North-West of Europe.** Trans.:– John Peto. L., 1876. Slight foxing. Orig. cl. (CB. May 27; 157) Can. $110

NARKISS, B.
See–KATZ, Elias & Narkiss, B.

NARRATIVE OF A MAID LATELY Burnt to Death in a Strange & Wonderful Manner by the Force of Chemical Spirit Seizing upon Her
1678. 4to. Bad inking has affected a few words. Hf. cf. (S. Dec.2; 565) Quaritch. £100

NARSIUS, Joannes–CLEMENS, Venceslaus
- **Gustavidos, sive de Bello Sueco-Austriaco libri tres: Poematum Miscellaneorum Liber Unus. –Francofurtiun Urbis Electoralis Brandenburigica ... Carmine Heroico; Gedanum sive Dantiscum Urbs illustris & Regia; Johanni Wranglio ab Elswert Equestris dignitatis Viro; Johanni Nicodemo ex puta Virtute prognato ... Solemni anniversario die D. Johanni Baptistae.** Hamburg, n.p.; Dantzig; Elbing; n.p., 1632; n.d.; 1630; 1629; n.d. 5 works in 1 vol. 4to. Cont. vell. (S. Oct.20; 167) Fairburn. £90

NARY, C.
- **A Letter to His Grace Edward Lord Arch-Bishop of Tuam.–A Rejoinder to the Reply to the Answer to the Charitable Address.** Dublin, 1728; 1730. 2 vols. in 1. Cont. cf., upr. cover detchd. (GM. Apr.30; 237) £60

NASH, Frederick
- **Series of Views ... of the Collegiate Chapel of St. George at Windsor.** 1805. Lge. 4to. 6 hand-cold. plts., & 3 uncold. plts., very minor dampstaining to title. Cont. hf. cf., rebkd. From

the collection of Eric Sexton. (C. Apr.16; 312)
Traylen. £170

NASH, Frederick & Scott, John
- **Picturesque Views of the City of Paris & its Environs.** Ill.:– after Frederick Nash. 1820. 4to. Text in Fr. & Engl., some spotting. Cont. cf., rebkd., worn. (CSK. Jan.23; 66)   £70
- – **Anr. Copy.** 4to. Cont. str.-grd. mor., smooth decor. spine, bdg. wormed & slightly defect. (HD. Jun.25; 356)   Frs. 2,400
- – **Anr. Edn.** 1823. 2 vols. in 1. 4to. Decor. mor., central embossed arms of Antrim, gt. (CE. Jul.9; 209)   £130
- – **Anr. Copy.** L.P. Fo. Engl. & Fr. text, 35 plts. marked 'Proof', a few slightly spotted plts. Cont. hf. red mor., spines gt., slightly worn. (S. Nov.4; 507)   *Loeb.* £110
- – **Anr. Copy.** L.P. 2 vols. Fo. Ex-liby. Red hf. mor., unc. (SG. Oct.30; 263) $200

NASH, John
- **The Royal Pavilion at Brighton.** 1826. Fo. Red mor.-bkd. cl. bds. Stoke Rochford Liby. bkplt. (C. Mar.18; 80)   *Henderson.* £2,000

NASH, John & Brayley, Edward Wedlake
- **Illustrations of Her Majesty's Palace at Brighton.** Ill.:– A. Pugin & others. 1838. L.P. Lge. fo. Cont. purple str.-grd. mor., gt. blind-tooled borders round Royal arms on sides. Pres. inscr. sigd. Jack Abbey 1943. (C. May 20; 156)   *Rostron.* £2,400

NASH, Joseph
- **The Mansions of England in the Olden Time.** 1839-41. Series I-III only. Fo. Some ll. spotted, many loose. Orig. qtr. mor. gt. (SD. Feb.4; 160)   £80
- – **Anr. Edn.** 1839-49. 4 vols. Fo. Occasional spotting. Cont. mor.-bkd. cl. bds., gt.-lettered on upr. covers. From the collection of Eric Sexton. (C. Apr.16; 313)   *Wood.* £160
- – **Anr. Copy.** Some ll. slightly spotted & soiled. Cont. mor.-bkd. cl. (SH. Mar.5; 103)   *Wallis Clark.* £135
- – **Anr. Edn.** 1869-72. 4 vols. in 1. Mor. by Birdsall, covers with mor. onlay borders enclosing gt. diaper panel of coronets & monogs. of Prince Leopold, Duke of Albany, spine similarly tooled. (C. May 20; 157)   *Sims & Reed.* £180
- – **Anr. Copy.** 4 vols. in 2. Fo. Orig. red mor., jnts. worn. (CSK. Feb.20; 169)   £55
- – **Anr. Copy.** 5 vols. Ex-liby. Red mor. gt. (SG. Oct.30; 264) $475
- – **Anr. Edn.** 1874. 4 pts. in 1 vol. Fo. Some ll. spotted. Orig. mor., gt. (SH. Nov.6; 135)   *Fogg.* £85

NASH, Paul
- **Genesis.** Nones. Pr., 1924. Orig. bds., d.-w., unopened. Ralph Smith's book-label. (SH. Mar.27; 358)   *Loder.* £240
- **Places.** 1922. (55) on Japon, sigd. 4to. Orig. linen-bkd. bds. John Carter's copy, with his sig. (SH. Mar.27; 355)   *Loder.* £270
- – **Anr. Copy.** (210) numbered. Orig. cl.-bkd. ptd. bds., some slight scuffing. (LC. Jun.18; 35)   £58
- **The Sun Calendar for the Year 1920.** Ill.:– Paul & John Nash & Rupert Lee. 1919. 4to. Orig. wraps. Pres. copy to Marjorie & Reginald Wilenski. (SH. Mar.27; 354)   *Music Sales.* £90

NASH or NASHE, Thomas
- **Works.** 1883-85. Ltd. Edn. 6 vols. 4to. Some ll. soiled. Orig. hf. vell. (SH. Jun.25; 103)   *Thorp.* £100

NASH, Treadway Russell
- [–] **Collections for the History of Worcestershire.** 1781-82. 2 vols., including facs. of Domesday & supp. Fo. Cont. cf., rebkd. preserving orig. gt. spine. From the collection of Eric Sexton. (C. Apr.16; 314)   *Temperley.* £180
- – **Anr. Edn.** 1781-99. 3 vols. in 2 including supp. Fo. Cont. hf. mor., jnts. brkn. (SH. Mar.5; 105)   *Russell.* £105
- – **Anr. Edn.** 1799. 2nd. Edn. 2 vols. with Supp. at end of vol. II. Fo. Last few ll. of vol. II slightly browned. Cont. russ., gt. borders on sides, gt. panel. spines. (C. Feb.25; 48)   *Chesters.* £160

NASHI DEPUTATY [Our Deputies]
Ed.:– [V. Panchenko]. St. Petersb., 1906. No. 1. Fo. Torn with some loss of text. Unbnd. (SH. Feb.5; 97)   *Flegon.* £50

NASSARE, P.
- **Escuela Musica, segun la Pratica Moderna, dividida en Primera, y Segunda Parte.** Zaragoza,

1723-24. 1st. Edn. 2 vols. Fo. Browned nearly thro.-out. Cont. vell. (H. May 21/22; 830)   DM 750

NAST, Thomas
[–] **Aunt Louisa's Child's Delight.** Ill.:– Thomas Nast & J.H. Howard. N.Y., ca. 1875. Lge. sq. 4to. Gt. lettered cl., lge. circular area in centre of upr. cover (apparently no label was ever present). (SG. Apr.30; 228) $120

NATAL NATIVE REBELLION (The) as told in Official Despatches, from January 1st to June 23rd, 1906
Pietermaritzburg, 1906. Bds. (SSA. Apr.22; 228)   R. 160

NATALIBUS, Petrus de
- **Catalogus Sanctorum & Gestorum . . .** Ill.:– Urs Graf. Strassburg, 1513. Fo. Cont. wooden bds., blind-stpd. vell. spine, upr. cover brkn. & reprd., lacks clasps. (S. Nov.25; 349)   *Watchman.* £260

NATALIS, Hieronymus
- **Adnotationes et Meditationes in Evangelia . . .** Ill.:– Ant. Wierix. Antw., 1595. Fo. Slightly stained, title lightly browned, with MS. owner's mark. Cont. vell., soiled. (HK. Nov.18-21; 238)   DM 800
- **Evangelicae Historiae Imagines ex Ordine Evangeliorum.** Antw., 1593. Fo. 102 (of 153) copperplts. in same series bnd. in (double). 19th. C. hf. vell., gt. spine. (R. Oct.14-18; 122)   DM 1,900
- – **Anr. Edn.** Antw., 1596. Fo. Margins restored, 6 unnumbered pp., lacks map with Italian trans., 1 unnumbered errata p. Red mor., richly decor. 7 gt. borders, spine reprd., bdg. restored. (CR. Mar.19; 267)   Lire 1,000,000
- **Evangelicae Veritatis Homiliarum Centuriae Quatuor, Tertia vice nuper Excusae.** Ill.:– A. & J. Collaert, Ch. de Mallery, A. Hieron & J. Wierix after B. Passari & M. de Vos. Antw., 1595 [1545]. Fo. Without text, 153 numbered (2nd. series) copperplts. 18th. C. hf. leath. (HK. Nov.18-21; 239)   DM 1,000

NATHAN BEN KALONYMUS, Isaak –CAMERARIUS, J.–BRUSSIUS [BRUCE], W.
- **Concordantiarum Hebraicarum Capita.–De Rebus Turcicis Commentarii Duo.–De Tartaris Diarium.** Basel; Frankfurt; Frankfurt, 1556; 1598; 1598. 1st. Edn.; 1st. Edn.; Edn. unknown. 3 works in 1 vol. Fo. Old owner's mark on title. Cont. vell. (R. Mar.31-Apr.4; 77)   DM 1,000

NATIONAL GALLERY (The)
Ed.:– S.C. Hall. N.d. 3 vols. 4to. Occasional slight spotting. Cont. mor., gt. (CSK. Sep.19; 159)   £120

NATIONAL GALLERY OF PICTURES
Ill.:– after Hogarth & others. L., ca. 1840. 4to. Cont. hf. leath., defect., cover loose. (R. Mar.31-Apr.4; 1595)   DM 500

NATIONAL MUSEUM OF CANADA
- **Collection of Monographs.–Annual Reports of the Museum, 1926-1936/7.** Ottawa, 1900's-1930's. 8 vols.; 2 vols. Buckram. (SG. Mar.5; 75) $210

NATIVELLE, Pierre
- **Nouveau Traité d'Architecture.** Paris, 1729. [1st. Printing?]. 2 vols. Lge. fo. Some spotting & discolouration, minor marginal tears. Cont. mott. cf., worn. (S. Jun.22; 132)   *Weinreb.* £320
- – **Anr. Copy.** Cont. marb. cf., spines decor. with raised bands. (HD. Jun.24; 65)   Frs. 2,000

NATRUS, Leendert van & others
- **Groot Volkomen Moolenboek.** Amst., 1734-36. 2 vols. Fo. Plts., some spotting. Cont. cf., worn, covers detchd. (SH. Oct.9; 131)   *Weinreb.* £580

NATTA, Marcus Antonius
- **De Deo libri XV.** Venice, 1560. 1st. Aldine Edn.; 2nd. Iss. Fo. 1st. gathering loose, old owners' inscrs. on title partly obscured. Old vell., worn. (S. Dec.8; 112)   *Thorp.* £80

NATTER, Laurent
- **Traité de la Methode Antique de Graver en Pierres Fines.** Ill.:– Hemerich. L., 1754. 1st. Edn. Fo. Bookstp. of 'Santo Varui, Scultore' on title. Cont. mor., triple gt. fillet, spine gt. in compartments, inner gt. dentelles, 2 or 3 corners slightly worn. (SM. Oct.7; 1880)   Frs. 1,600

NATTES, John Claude
- **Bath Illustrated by a Series of Views.** 1806. 1st. Iss. Fo. Aquatints wtrmkd. 1801-05. Cont. red hf. mor. (C. Mar.18; 81)   *Taylor.* £1,300
- – **Anr. Copy.** Lacks hf.-title. Cont. hf. mor., upr. cover detchd. From the collection of Eric Sexton. (C. Apr.16; 315)   *Wood.* £800

NATURAL HISTORY
- **A Series of 120 Picture Sheets.** [1850]. Fo. 1st. sheet reprd. Cont. hf.-roan, worn. (SH. Dec.11; 370)   *Wilson.* £95

NATURAL HISTORY of Birds
1815. Vol. 2 only. 82 hand-cold. plts., some spotting. Hf. mor., defect. As a coll. of plts., w.a.f. (P. Apr.30; 85)   *Hill.* £160
- – **Anr. Copy.** 2 vols. Some pp. loose, 2 pp. text & a plt. torn & lacking. Cf., worn. (P. Jul.30; 107)   *Gregory.* £110
- – **Anr. Copy.** Vol. 1 (of 2). 65 cold. plts. (of 152), some tears & stains. Cont. cf., worn. (SH. Jun.18; 147)   *Hill.* £70

NATURAL HISTORY of New York
- Zoology.–Botany.–Mineraology.–Geology. –Agriculture.–Palaeontology. N.Y., 1842-94. Together 16 vols. Some foxing & staining. Hf. mor., worn. As a collection of plts., w.a.f. (SPB. May 6; 229) $375

NATURGESCHICHTE des Thierreichs
Esslingen, 1867. 3 pts. in 1 vol. Fo. Some spotting & marginal tears. Cont. hf. cf., worn. (S. Jan.26; 292)   *Nador.* £150

NAU, M.
- **Almanach Chantant, ou Étrennes Lyriques, Astronomiques et Physiques.** Paris, 1749. 18mo. Cont. white silk, gt. decor. spine & covers. (HD. Apr.8; 8)   Frs. 2,400

NAUDE, Gabriel
[–] **Jugement de tout ce qui a esté Imprimé contre le Cardinal Mazarin, depuis le sixième Janvier, jusques à la Declaration du premier Avril mil six cens quarante-neuf.** [Paris], [1650]. 4to. Lacks last lf. (blank?), waterstained. Early 18th. C. cf., arms of Count Hoym, gt., on covers, & of C.M. Fevret de Fontette, spine gt. in pointillé. (SM. Oct.7; 1881)   Frs. 4,200

NAUGERIUS, Andreas
- **Orationes Duae.** Venice, 1530. 1st. Edn. 4to. Hf. cf. (CR. Jun.11; 515)   Lire 400,000

NAUMANN, J.G.
- **Uber die Vorzüglichsten Theile der Pferdewissenschaft.** Hamburg, 1800. 2 pts. in 1 vol. Orig. hf. leath. (D. Dec.11-13; 2268)   DM 500

NAUMANN, Johann Andreas
[–] **[Naturgeschichte der Land-und Wasser-Vögel des Nördl. Deutschlands u. angrensenden Länder].** Ill.:– J.F. Naumann. [Köthen], [1795-97]. Plt. vol. 1. Fo. Old MS. notes at foot. Hf. linen. (HK. Nov.18-21; 812)   DM 4,800
- **Naturgeschichte der Vögel Deutschlands. Ed.:–** Joh. Fr. Naumann. Leipzig, 1822-60. 13 vols. bnd. in 15. Plts. from vols. 1-10 bnd. separately in 2 plt. vols., vol. 3 lacks uncold. plt. bnd in as title, old liby stp. on title, 1 frontis. cut close & torn, 1 plt. vol. loose. Hf. leath. ca. 1880, slightly worn. (R. Mar.31-Apr.4; 1411)   DM 16,000
- **Naturgeschichte der Vögel Mitteleuropas. Ed.:–** Blasius & C.R. Hennicke. Gera, [1897-1901]. Vols. 2, 4 & 7 in 3 vols. Fo. Cont. hf. leath., spine slightly defect. (R. Mar.31-Apr.4; 1412)   DM 1,300

NAUSEA, Fredericus, Bp. of Vienna
See–BERTHORIUS, Petrus–NAUSEA, Fredericus, Bp. of Vienna–GREGORIUS Nyssenus

NAUTILUS, The
Ill.:– E. Duncan after W.J. Huggins. Priv. Ptd., 1829. Cont. cf., gt. & blind borders on sides, gt. spine. (C. Nov.5; 116)   *Rudge.* £220

NAUWELAERTS, J.
- **Historie de la Ville de Vilvorde.** Brussels, 1941. 2 vols. Publisher's bds. (LM. Mar.21; 320)   B.Frs. 7,000

NAVAL CHRONICLE (The)
1799-1818. 40 vols. Approximately 500 plts. & maps only, some affected by damp or spotted. Mainly cont. hf. cf., worn, several bds. detchd., ex-liby. W.a.f. (CSK. Jul.10; 10)   £370

NAVAL CHRONICLE (The) -*contd.*
– – **Anr. Edn.** [1799-1801]. Vols. 1-6. Cont. hf. cf. (PG. Dec.12; 155) £75

NAVARRE, Marguerite de Valois, Queen of
See-VALOIS, Marguerite de, Queen of Navarre

NAVY Records Society
– Publications. 1894-1928. 62 vols. Unif. cl. gt., unc. W.a.f. (SBA. Jul.23; 588) *Pratt.* £210

NAYLER, Sir George
– The Coronation of His Most Sacred Majesty King George IV. 1839. Lge. fo. Cont. red hf. mor., spine gt. (C. May 20; 42) *Quaritch.* £1,200
– – **Anr. Copy.** (C. Feb.4; 142) *Rosteron.* £520

NAZARI, Giovanni Battista
– Della Tramutatione Metallica sogni tre. Brescia, 1572. 2nd. Edn. 4to. Stained & discoloured thro.-out, tears (reprd.) in quire B & lf. T2, minor flaws in A2, some marginal notations & underscoring, owner's inscr. on title. Cont. limp vell., very soiled, hf. mor. case. From Honeyman Collection. (S. Nov.10; 2295) *Ritman.* £380

NEAL, Daniel
– The History of New-England, containing an Impartial Account . . . of the Country, to the Year of our Lord, 1700. L., 1747. 2nd. Edn. 2 vols. Cont. spr. cf. (SG. Jan.8; 316) $120

NEALE, Adam
– Letters from Portugal & Spain. L., 1809. 4to. Slightly browned & soiled. Cont. style leath., gt. spine. (R. Oct.14-18; 2056) DM 680
– Travels through some parts of Germany, Poland, Moldavia & Turkey. 1818. [1st. Edn.?]. 4to. Hf. cf. gt. (P. Oct.2; 6) *Dupre.* £140
– – **Anr. Copy.** Title-p. torn & reprd., occasional light browning & spotting. Mod. hf. cf. (S. Jun.29; 265) *Dupre.* £80
– – **Anr. Copy.** Some offsetting of text, 4pp. publisher's advts. bnd. in. Later cl. (TA. Nov.20; 396) £85

NEALE, John Preston
– Views of the Seats of Noblemen & Gentlemen, in England, Wales, Scotland & Ireland. 1818-23 ['address' dtd. 1824]. 1st. series. 6 vols. Some ll. foxed. 19th. C. mor., spines gt. (S. Sep.29; 143) *O'Leary.* £180
– – **Anr. Edn.** 1818-29. Together 11 vols. (1st. Series 6 vols., 2nd. Series 5 vols.) Cont. maroon str.-grd. mor. gt. (C. Jul.15; 80) *Sims & Reed.* £650
– – **Anr. Copy.** Russ., bdgs. worn. (BS. Feb.25; 271) £340
– – **Anr. Edn.** L., 1819-23. 6 vols. Lge. 4to. 417 (of 432) engraved plts., each with a mntd. india-proof. Cont. hf. mor. (SG. Feb.26; 256) $350
See-SHEPHERD, Thomas Hosmer–NEALE, John Preston

NEALE, John Preston & Brayley, Edward Wedlake
– History & Antiquities of the Abbey Church of St. Peter's Westminster. 1818-23. 2 vols. 4to. Some ll. slightly browned or spotted. Cont. hf. mor. (SH. Nov.6; 140) *Edwards.* £52
– – **Anr. Edn.** L., Priv. Ptd., 1818-23. L.P. 2 vols. Fo. Some plts. in 2 states & some cold., occasional marginal foxing, extra ill. with 83 plts. (of which 80 hand-cold.) from Ackerman's History of the Abbey Church of St. Peter's, Westminster (L., 1812). Hf. leath., rebkd. (CB. Sep.24; 131) Can. $900

NEANDER, Jean–BORRICHIUS, O.–PETIT, P.
– Tabacologia: h.e. Tabaci . . .–De Somno et Somniferis Maxime Papavereis Dissertatio.–Sive de Sinensi Herba Thee Carmen ad P.D. Hueti . . . Ill.:– Delff after Bailly (1st. work). Leyden; Copen. & Frankfurt; Leipzig, 1626; 1681; 1685. 2nd. Edn. (1st. work). 3 works in 1 vol. 4to. Slightly browned thro.-out, some cont. margin annots. & a few pencil annots. Cont. vell. (VG. Oct.13; 112) Fls. 2,000

NEANDER, M.–BUSSIUS, I.–GLOCERUS, G.
– Menchenspiegel.–Der 147. Psalm.–Wahrhafftige Historia . . . von der Lehr, Leben . . . Docteris M. Lutheri. Leipzig; Frankfurt; Strassburg, 1588; 1568; 1586. 3 works in 1 vol. Blind-tooled pig-bkd. bds., brass clasps. (D. Dec.11-13; 40) DM 1,700

NEBEL, Carl
See-KENDALL, George Wilins & Nebel, Carl

NEBELSPALTER
Zurich, 1925-31. Vols. 51-57 only. 4to. Cont.

cl.-bkd. bds., lacks a few wraps. (SH. Jan.30; 474) *Allan.* £80

NECHUNYA BEN HAKANA, Rabbi
– Ha'temunah. Koretz, 1784. 1st. Edn. 4to. Some discolouration. Hf. vell. Stp. of Etz Chaim of Amst. (S. Nov.18; 390) *James.* £180

NECKER, Jacques
– Compte Rendu au Roi. Paris, 1781. 1st. Edn. 4to. Port. added. Cont. red mor., decor. spine, 3 fillets, inside dentelle. (HD. Dec.5; 157) Frs. 3,500
– De l'Administration des Finances de la France. Paris, 1784. Orig. Edn. 3 vols. Cont. porphy roan, fillet, decor. spines. (HD. Feb.18; 51) Frs. 3,300
– – **Anr. Edn.** Ill.:– Augustin de Saint-Aubin. [Paris], 1784. 1st. Edn., 2nd. Iss. 3 vols. Lacks last lf. in vol. 1 (blank?), inscr. on end-papers & inscr. on fly-lf. of vol. 3. Cont. red mor., triple gt. fillet, flat spines gt. in compartments, inner gt. dentelles. Bkplt. of Alexander Trotter. (SM. Oct.7; 1882) Frs. 4,800
– – **Anr. Edn.** N.p., 1785. 3 vols. 12mo. Cont. cf., gt. spines. (S. Apr.7; 363) *Frost.* £65
– Du pouvoir exécutif dans les grands états. [?Paris], 1792. ?1st. Edn. 2 vols. Slight browning. Mod. red mor.-bkd. marb. bds. (S. Jan.26; 248) *Pharos.* £55
– – **Anr. Copy.** 2 pts. in 1 vol. Slight spotting in places, stp. on 1st. title. Cont. mott. cf., spine gt. & slightly worn. (S. Apr.7; 364) *Drury.* £50
– Lettre et Rapport.–Mémoire.–Mémoire. –Mémoire. Paris (1st. work), [11 Sep. 1789]; 14 Nov. 1789; 29 May 1790; 27 Aug. 1790. 3rd. work browned, others slightly. Mod. bds. (S. Jan.26; 247) *Hendy.* £65

NEDERDUITSCHE Gereformeerde Kerk van Zuid Afrika
– De Handelingen der Zeven Eeerste Vergaderingen. Cape Town, 1857-64. 4to. Cont. hf. mor. (SSA. Jun.18; 223) R. 100

NEDERLAND, HET VERHEERLYKT
Ill.:– after De Beyer, Pronk & others. Amst., 1745-74. Thick paper. 9 pts. in 3 vols. 4to. Some plts. slightly browned. Cont. pol. cf., gt. spines. (VG. Oct.13; 113) Fls. 2,000

NEDERLAND IN BEELD
Buiksloot, ca. 1898. Sm. ob. fo. Cont. hf. leath. (VG. Dec.15; 424) Fls. 500

NEDERLANDSCH BLOEMWERK
Ill.:– H.L. Myling after P.T. van Brussel. Amst., 1794. 4to. Soiled in parts. Hf. linen. (D. Dec.11-13; 141a) DM 3,750

NEEL, L.B.
– Voyage de Paris à Saint-Cloud par Mer, et Retour par Terre. Ed.:– E. Legrand. Ill.:– Gillot after Georges Jeanniot. Paris, 1884. (50) numbered on Japan vell. Crushed lev., triple gt. fillet borders round gt. arabesque with red mor. inlays, unif. gt. spine, gt. dentelles, cold. pict. wraps. bnd. in, by Samblancx-Weckesser. (SG. Sep.4; 55) $275
– – **Anr. Copy.** (SG. Apr.9; 107) $220

NEES VON ESENBECK, Christian Gottfried
– Das System der Pilze und Schwämme. Ill.:– J. Sturm. Würsburg, 1817. 4to. Erased stp. on ptd. title, lightly soiled in parts. Cont. hf. leath. gt. (R. Mar.31-Apr.4; 1427) DM 4,000

NEES VON ESENBECK, Theodor Friedrich Ludwig
– Plantae officnales, oder officineller Pflanzen. Düsseldorf, [1821-] 1828-33. 3 vols. in 5. Fo. Spotted. Variously bnd. From Collection of Massachusetts Horticultural Society, stps. on plts. (SPB. Oct.1; 152) $6,000

NEGLENTIAE et Defectus in Missa Contingentes
Erfurt, [Printer of Hundorn (Marx Ayrer?)], 1494. 4to. 2 capital initials, woodcut on title crudely cold., the work folded across twice, wormhole touching single letter on 2 ll., 1st. & last pp. soiled, some early ink annots. (cropped). Rough vell., from early service book. The copy of E.F. Bosanquet, lately in the collection of Eric Sexton. [Goff D135, H 6079] (CNY. Apr.8; 55) $5,000

NEGOCIATIONS SECRETES touchant la Paix de Munster et d'Osnabrug . . .
The Hague, 1725-26. 4 vols. Fo. Slightly browned in places. Cont. marb. cf., gt. supra-libros of Marquis de Bouzols on upr. cover, spines gt., spine

ends slightly defect. (VG. Dec.17; 1465) Fls. 2,100

NEIDHARDT VON GNEISENAU, A.W.
– The Life & Campaigns of Field-Marshal Prince Blücher, of Wahlstatt. Trans.:– J.E. Marston. L., 1815. Map & some ll. slightly browned. Later cf. gt., slightly worn, 1 sm. repair. (H. May 21/22; 613) DM 420

NELSON, Visc. Horatio
– The Despatches & Letters. 1844-46. 7 vols. Orig. cl., later vols. unc. (CE. Jul.9; 165) £105

NELSON, John
– The History, Topography & Antiquities of the Parish of St. Mary Islington. 1811. 4to. Extra-ill. with 30 ills. Cont. cf., rebkd. Bkplt. of Nathan of Churt, lately in the collection of Eric Sexton. (C. Apr.16; 316) *Lake.* £70
– – **Anr. Copy.** Extra-ill. with 30 ills. Nathan of Churt bkplt. (C. Jul.15; 81) *Weinreb.* £50
See-ROBINSON, William–NELSON, John –PARK, John James

NELSON, Philip
– Ancient Painted Glass in England. L., [1913]. 1 plt. loose. Cl. From the liby. of Clement Heaton. (SG. Mar.12; 345) $110

NENNA, Giovanni Battista
– Nennio. 1595. 1st. Edn. in Engl. 4to. 18th. C. vell.-bkd. bds. [STC 18428] (C. Nov.20; 270) *Money.* £280

NEPTUNE
– Neptune Oriental. Paris, [Brest], 1775. Fo. Hf. cf., upr. cover loose, worn. (PD. Oct.22; 184) £290

NEPTUNE FRANÇOIS ou Atlas Nouveau des Cartes Marines . . .
Paris & Amst., 1693. Pts. 1 & 2 (of 3). Imp. fo. Lacks copper engraved map, 1st. & last ll. slightly stained, some sm. tears. Cont. leath., gt. spine & outer dentelle, very worn. (HK. Nov.18-21; 1058) DM 8,500

NERCIAT, Andréa de
– Le Diable au Corps. Ill.:– after Bornet. N.p., 1803. 6 vols. 16mo. 3 figures (of 20). Cont. marb. cf., spines decor. with gt. fillets. (HD. Apr.10; 355) Frs. 1,150
[-] Les Ecarts du Tempérament, ésquisses Dramatiques. L., 1785. 16mo. Cont. red hf. mor., head gt., unc. (HD. Apr.10; 356) Frs. 1,400
– Félicia . . . Paris, An VI [1798]. 4 vols. 18mo. Slight foxing. Cont. tree cf., gt. fillet around covers, smooth decor. spines. (HD. Jun.24; 66) Frs. 1,510
– – **Anr. Edn.** Ill.:– Borel, engraved by Elluin. L., 1812. 4 vols. 16mo. Cont. red str.-grd. mor., decor. spines, roulette covers, inner dentelle. (HD. Apr.10; 357) Frs. 5,100
– Mon Noviciat, ou Les Joies de Lolotte. [Berlin], 1792. 2 vols. 18mo. 8 supplementary figures from anr. edn. bnd. in. Jansenist mor., inner dentelle, heads gt., unc., by Thierry. (HD. Apr.10; 360) Frs. 3,100
– Monrose, ou Suite de Félicia par le Même Auteur. Ill.:– Queverdo. N.p., 1795. 4 vols. 16mo. Vol. IV port. scratched. Bradel paper bds., ca. 1820. From the liby. of Col. Sickles. (HD. Apr.10; 358) Frs. 1,900
– – **Anr. Copy.** 4 vols. in 2. Old marb. cf., decor. spines, 3 fillets, inner dentelles. (HD. Apr.10; 359) Frs. 1,000
– Pandämonium. N.p., Priv. ptd., ca. 1907. (950). 3 vols. Orig. linen, spine sprung. (D. Dec.11-13; 1993) DM 460

NERESSIAN, S.D.
– The Chester Beatty Library. A Catalogue of the Armenian Manuscripts. Dublin, 1958. 2 vols. Fo. Orig. cl. (SH. Mar.6; 550) *Quaritch.* £110

NERI, Antonio
– L'Arte Vetraria distinta in libri sette. Flor., 1612. 1st. Edn. 4to. Title & some ll. browned. Cont. limp vell., hf. red mor. case. From Honeyman Collection. (S. Nov.10; 2296) *Das Bucherkabinet.* £470
– De Arte Vitraria Libri Septem. Ed.:– Christopherus Merett. Amst., 1659. 12mo. Liby. stp. on title, also inscr. Laurentius Zehweger, M.D., Leiden, 1712. Vell. (S. Apr.7; 334) *Facchinotti.* £180
– – **Anr. Copy.** (S. Dec.1; 284) *Celestial.* £55

NERUCCI, Gh.
- Sette Novelle Montalesi. Ill.:– Dano Cecchi. Verona, 1960. (116) numbered, hand-ptd. on Bütten. 4to. Printer's mark sigd. Orig. pict. wraps., s.-c., slightly defect. (R. Mar.31-Apr.4; 587) DM 1,000

NERUDA, Pablo
- Die Höhen von Macchu Picchu. Trans.:– R. Hagelstange. Ill.:– Hap Grieshaber. Hamburg, [1965]. Ltd. Edn. With accompanying Heft. Fo. Orig. linen. (H. May 21/22; 1593) DM 500
- Residencia en la Tierra. Madrid, 1935. 1st. Edn. 2 vols. 4to. Cl. & leath., not unif., orig. wraps. (DS. Apr.24; 935) Pts. 36,000

NERVAL, Gerard de
- Les Nuits d'Octobre. Ill.:– D. Galanis. Paris, 1920. Slightly spotted. Mor., mor. onlay, sewn with gt. stars on both covers, title incorporated in design on upr. cover, spine slightly worn, watered silk doubls., orig. wraps. bnd. in, s.-c., by G. Schroeder. (SH. Nov.20; 50) Klusmann. £50
- Sylvie. Ill.:– Michel Ciry. 1943. On vell. d'Arches, with suite, orig. ill. Sewed. (HD. Oct.10; 200) Frs. 1,100

NESTOR, Dionysius
- Vocabularius. Venice, Philippus Pincius, 1496. Fo. Slight dampstaining. 18th. C. cf.-bkd. bds., rather worn. From liby. of André L. Simon. (S. May 18; 141) Boyle. £400

NESTROY, Johann
- Sämtl. Werke. Ed.:– Fr. Brubner & O. Rommel. Vienna, 1924-30. 15 vols. Orig. linen. (HK. May 15; 4700) DM 620

NET for the Fishers of Men ...
1687. 3rd. Edn. 24mo. Disbnd., 1 remaining cover detchd. (SG. Feb.5; 254) $130

NETHERLANDS
- Historie, Hedenaagsche, of tegenwoordige staat van alle Volkeren. Amst., 1781-1803. 6 pts. in 4 vols. 8 (of 9) engraved folding views, names & some scribbling on titles, 2 plts. loose & some slight foxing & dampstains in places. Later hf.-cl. (VG. Nov.19; 801) Fls. 1,700
- Vaderlandsche Historie. Ill.:– Houbraken (ports.), & Folkema (copper-plts.). Amst., 1752-59. 20 vols. only (of 21, lacks vol. 1). Cont. vell., buckled, ex-liby. (SG. Feb.5; 126) $300

NETTE
See–POZZI, Carlous Maria–NETTE

NETTER, Thomas, Waldensis
[-] Doctrinale Antiquitatum Fidei Ecclesiae Catholicae. Venice, 1571. 3 vols., vol. III anr. Iss. Fo. Blanks lacking in vols. I & II (3 ll.), slight worming of lr. margins at beginning of vol. I, some reprd., old sig. 'Danes D.S.' on titles. 18th. C. red mor., triple gt. fillet, spines gt. in compartments, arms of Signet Liby. on covers, inner gt. dentelles. (SM. Oct.7; 1886) Frs. 1,600

NETTO, J.
- Zeichen-, Mahler- und Stickbuch zur Selbstlehrung. Leipzig, 1800. Pts. 1 & 3 in 1 vol. Ob. fo. 42 (of 72) partly cold. copperplts., in pt. 1: 7 plts. duplicated, in pt. 3: 10 plts. duplicated, 2 plts. very soiled, 1 with sm. tears. Hf. linen. (D. Dec.11-13; 2226) DM 800

NEUBAUER, Ad
- Catalogue of the Hebrew Manuscripts in Jews' College London. Oxford, 1886. Contents loose. Wraps. (SPB. May 11; 56) $175

NEUE BUCH DER ERFINDUNGEN, Gewerbe und Industrien. Rundschau auf allen Gebieten der Gewerblichen Arbeit
Ed.:– R. Andree, C. Böttger & others. Leipzig & Berlin, 1864-68. 6 vols. in 3, & supp. vol. together in 4 vols. Not collated. Cont. hf. linen. W.a.f. (R. Oct.14-18; 1512) DM 480

NEUE ISRAELITISCHE Tempel zu Leipzig
Berlin, 1859. Fo. Orig. bds., worn. (SH. Jul.23; 117) Fletcher. £130

NEUES CONVERSATIONS-LEXICON
Cologne & Bonn, 1824-30. 12 vols. Not collated. Cont. hf. leath. (R. Oct.14-18; 576) DM 500

NEUES IDEEN-MAGAZIN fur Liebhaber von Garten, Englischen Anlagen und fur Besitzer von Landgutern
Leipzig, 1806-10. 1st. Edn. of 1st. vol., 3rd. Edn. of 2nd. 2 vols. in 1. Lge. 4to. Text in German &

Fr., 232 (of 233) plts., foxed. Cont. sheep, worn. (SPB. May 6; 230) $375

NEUES TASCHENBUCH für Natur-Forst- u. Jagdfreunde
Ed.:– G.V. Schultes. Weimar, 1845. Stpd. Orig. bds., wraps. loose. (HK. Nov.18-21; 1752) DM 540

NEUESTE KUNDE VON AMERICA
Prag, 1818-20. 2 vols. 12 (of 14) maps, 8 outl. cold. & 6 (of 9) copperplts. Cont. bds. [Sabin 52381] (R. Oct.14-18; 1702) DM 480
- - Anr. Edn. Prag, 1819. Vol. 1 only. 6 folding copper maps, 4 outl. cold., 6 copperplts. Cont. bds. (R. Oct.14-18; 1703) DM 480

NEUESTE LANDER-UND VOLKERKUNDE
Prag & Weimar, 1808-12 & 1813. 8 vols.: 3, 4, 6, 7, 10-12, 14. 5 (of 22) copper engraved maps, 109 (of 122) copperplts., 5 supp. plts. bnd. in, some folding plts. defect. Cont. hf. leath., very worn & defect. in parts. (R. Mar.31-Apr.4; 2274) DM 850

NEUFFORGE, Jean-François de
- Recueil Elémentaire d'Architecture. Paris, 1757-80. 10 vols. in 3. Fo. Lacks 2nd. title & 8 additional plts. to plt. VI called for by de Ricci, minor tears, mostly marginal, or slight spotting or staining on a few plts., sm. wormhole on title & table to vol. I. Cont. mott. sheep, some worming, jnts. worn, 1st. vol. stained on upr. cover & reprd. at spine. (SPB. May 6; 231) $1,500

NEUMANN, Arthur H.
- Elephant Hunting in East Equatorial Africa. 1898. Cl. (P. Sep.11; 219) Way. £85

NEUMANN, Caspar
- The Chemical Works Abridged & Methodized with Large Additions ... Ed.:– William Lewis. 1759. 1st. Engl. Edn. 4to. Cont. cf. (S. Dec.1; 285) Quaritch. £55

NEUMANN, F.
- Die Windkraftmaschine. Ed.:– M. Conrad. Leipzig, 1907. 3rd. Edn. Orig. hf. linen. (D. Dec.11-13; 264) DM 450

NEUMANN, J.
- Beschreibung der bekanntesten Kupfermunzen. Prague, 1858-63. 3 vols. in 2. Later cl., soiled. (SH. Mar.6; 410) Christensen. £70

NEVE Y MOLINA, Luis de
- Reglas de orthographia, Diccionario y arte del idioma othomi, Breve Instruccion para los Principiantes. Mexico, 1767. 1st. Edn. Marginal wormhole affecting a few ll. at the beginning. Cont. limp vell. [Sabin 49896] (SPB. May 5; 365) $850

NEVILL, Ralph
- Old English Sporting Prints. 1923. Ltd. Edn. 4to. Orig. cl. gt., d.-w. (P. Mar.12; 4) Cambridge. £70
- - Anr. Copy. Cl., d.-w. (P. Mar.12; 346) Thorpe. £60

NEVILL, Samuel
- Acts of the General Assembly of the Province of New-Jersey, from ... the Second Year of Queen Anne to this Present Time.–ditto, Volume the Second, from 1753 to 1761. [Phila.]; Woodbridge, 1752; 1761. 1st. Edns. 2 vols. Fo. 1st. have ll. of 1st. vol. have margins supplied, some foxing & cover wear. Mod. three-qtr. cf. (SG. Mar.5; 331) $450

NEVILLE, H. 'Cornelius Van Sloetton'
[-] A New & Further Discovery of the Islle of Pines ... Voyage to the East Indies. 1668. 4to. Stained & reprd. with slight loss of text. Cf. [Wing N509] (S. Dec.8; 236) Quaritch. £300

NEVOD [Seine]
Ed.:– [A.A. Pleshcheev]. St. Petersb., 1906. No. 1 Trial (of 2). 4to. Slightly soiled. Unbnd. (SH. Feb.5; 98) De la Casa. £65

NEW ATLAS OF FRANCE
1814. Ob. 4to. Folding cold. map of the Post Roads, 86 hand-cold. maps. Hf. cf. (P. Mar.12; 174) Cambridge. £240

NEW CABINET Album of Entertainment & Instruction
L., ca. 1850. Some foxing. Cont. red str.-grd. mor. gt. Double fore-e. pntg.; from the liby. of Zola E. Harvey. (SG. Mar.19; 156) $650

NEW & COMPLETE DICTIONARY of Arts & Sciences
1754-55. 4 vols. Panel. cf., worn. (CE. Dec.4; 188) £180

NEW CRIES OF LONDON, The
1823 (plts. dtd. 1824). 1st. Edn. 12mo. Lacks front end-lf., 4 pp. of advts. at end. Orig. roan-bkd. bds. (S. Feb.9; 29) Temperley. £130

NEW CYCLOPAEDIA OF BOTANY
Huddersfield, n.d. 2 vols. 4to. Slight spotting. Later bds. (SBA. Oct.22; 640) Spelman. £60

NEW CYCLOPAEDIA of BOTANY & Complete Book of Herbs
[1854]. 2 vols. Plts. etc. hand-cold. Cont. hf.-cf. (SBA. Jul.22; 108) Bisson-Millet. £70

NEW DOLL (the), or Grandmamma's Gift
1826. 1st. Edn. Sq. 12mo. A few ll. loose. Orig. hf. roan, spine defect, 1 plt. repeated on upr. cover. (SH. Mar.19; 222) Notebaart. £160

NEW DRAWING ROOM SCRAPBOOK
Ulm, 1880. 4to. Decor. leath., defect., loose. (R. Oct.14-18; 2520) DM 650

NEW ENGLAND Kitchen magazine: a Domestic Science Monthly
Ed.:– Anna Barrows. Boston, Apr. 1894-Mar. 1899. Vols. I-X in 5 vols. Hf. leath., scuffed. (SG. Jan.8; 320) $100

NEW ENGLISH DICTIONARY, A
Oxford, 1888-1933. 11 vols. in 21, including 1 vol. Supp. Fo. Cont. hf. mor., supp. orig. wraps., worn. (CSK. Apr.3; 21) £180
- - Anr. Copy. 11 vols. in 13. 4to. A few ll. torn. 1 cover loose. (SH. May 28; 75) Howes Books. £140

NEW ENGLISH THEATRE, The
1776-88. 12 vols. Mott. cf. gt. (P. Apr.9; 10) Schapiro. £55

NEW EPICUREAN or the Delights of Sex
1875. In 2 pts. Extra-ill. with 30 early photographs. Orig. bdg. (P. Feb.19; 15) Henderson. £700

NEW & FURTHER Narrative of the State of New-England
1676. 1st. Edn. Fo. Title slightly stained & detchd. from stitching, tear-marks reprd., 2 letters of imprint in pen facs., sigd. at end 'N.S.'. Disbnd. [Wing S120] (C. Nov.20; 271) Quaritch. £450

NEW & GENERAL Biographical Dictionary (A)
L., 1784. New Edn. 12 vols. Hf. cf. (GM. Apr.30; 822) £70

NEW MONTHLY BELLE ASSEMBLEE
L., 1841-43. 3 vols. Lacks 4 steel engrs. Cont. hf. leath., gt. spine. (R. Oct.14-18; 2637) DM 550

NEW NATURALIST Series
- Natural History of the Highlands & Islands. -Snowdonia - The National Park of North Wales. -British Mammals.-The Fulmar.-The Folk Lore of Birds. 1947; 1949; 1952; 1952; 1958. 1st. Edns. 5 vols. Orig. cl., all but 2 vols. in d.-w.'s. (TA. Jun.18; 182) £64

NEW RIDDLE BOOK (A), or a Whetstone for Dull Wits
Derby, ca. 1800. 12mo. Orig. wraps., a further 4 ills. on covers, folder. (SH. Mar.19; 224) Moon. £80

NEW ROYAL & UNIVERSAL DICTIONARY Of Arts & Sciences
Ed.:– M. Hinde. 1769-71. 1st. Edn. 2 vols. Fo. Title in vol. II creased & with several tears, a few plts. frayed & dust soiled in outer edges, occasional spotting & browning. 19th. C. russ., spines gt., slight wear, bkplt. of Eccle Riggs liby. (S. Dec.2; 747) Maggs. £180

NEW SPORTING Magazine
1846-70. 46 vols. Hf. cf., very worn. W.a.f. (SBA. Jul.23; 590) Nicholson. £800
- - Anr. Edn. 1855-69. 28 vols. (lacks vol. for 1857). Cont. hf. cf. gt. As a periodical, w.a.f (C. Nov.5; 114) Cumming. £580

NEW SYDENHAM SOCIETY
- Publications. 1859-1904. 112 vols. (including the fo. atlases). 8vo & fo. Orig. cl. gt., atlas hf. mor., spine torn. As a collection, w.a.f. (S. Jun.18; 606) Pratt. £420
- - Anr. Edn. V.d. 158 vols. 8vo. & fo. Orig. cl., but for Atlas of Pathology in wraps., some vols.

NEW SYDENHAM SOCIETY – Publications.
-contd.
worn. As a collection, w.a.f., from liby. of Dr. E. Ashworth Underwood. (S. Feb.23; 263) *Bickersteth.* £460

NEW SYSTEM OF AGRICULTURE ... by a Country Gentleman
1755. 2nd. Edn. 12mo. Cont. cf. (S. Apr.7; 233) *Morton-Smith.* £65

NEW TESTAMENT
(Alphabetically by Language and chronologically)

NEW TESTAMENT [Anglo-Saxon]
– Quatuor D.N. Jesu Christi Euangeliorum Versiones Perantiquae Duae, Gothica Scil. et Anglo-Saxonica. Ed.:– T. Marshall & F. du Jon. Dordrecht, 1665. 2 pts. in 1 vol. 4to. Owner's inscr. of Benjamin Barnett on fly-lf. Cont. vell. bds., soiled, bkplt. of John Ehrman. [D. & M. 1604] (S. Apr.29; 437) *Goldschmidt.* £500

NEW TESTAMENT [Arabic & Latin]
– Gospels in Arabic. Ill.:– A. Tempesta & others. Rome, 1591. 1st. Edn. Fo. Cont. vell. (C. Jul.16; 318) *Blairman.* £4,500

NEW TESTAMENT [Dutch]
– Dat Nieuuve Testamet. [Antw.], [1525-24]. 5 pts. in 1 vol. 1 prelim. in pt. 1 with minor repair, & corner torn from x3 with slight loss of text. Mod. hf. cf., bkplt. of Frederick J.O. Montagu. W.a.f. due to complexities of collation. (S. Dec.8; 127) *Quaritch.* £1,300
– Testament, het Nieuwe.-Het Boek der Psalmen, nevens de Gezangen.-Evangelische Gezangen.-Catechismus. Amst., 1847-49. 4 pts. in 1 vol. Cont. str.-grd. mor., lge. silver clasps & catches, decor. with flowers, sigd. on inside of lr. clasp L.W.B. & Z.B.B. (VG. Dec.17; 1207) Fls. 700

NEW TESTAMENT [English]
– The New Testament. Trans.:– Gregory Martin & others. Rheims, 1582. 1st. Edn. in Engl. 4to. Some defects patched, blank corners of a1 & a2 renewed, some slight marginal worming. Maroon mor. gt., mor.-tipped s.-c., by Semet & Plumelle. Bkplt. of the General Theological Seminary Liby. [STC 2884] (CNY. Oct.1; 49) $500
– – Anr. Edn. [Colophon: 1583]. 4to. Extensive MS. notes & annots. in 2 near cont. hands, bnd. with 'A Prayer set forth by authoritie to be used for the prosperous successe of her Majesties Forces & Navie' & 'The Whole Book of Psalmes'. Cont. cf. with central gt. lozenge-shaped decor. on covers, together with initials M.M., rebkd. W.a.f. (CSK. May 8; 54) £170
– Text of the New Testament ... translated out of the vulgar Latine by the Papists of the traiterous Seminarie at Rhemes ... 1589. Fo. 1st. few ll. detchd., slightly wormed with loss of a few characters. Old cf., worn. [STC 2888] (CSK. Mar.13; 32) £80
– New Testament.-The Whole Book of Psalms. 1628; 1628. 2 vols. in 1. 12mo. Cont. dos-à-dos needlework bdg., covers worked in cold. silks with design of church on hill, water in front, in oval frame, flowers on spines some wear. [STC 2931; STC 2606] (S. May 5; 296) *Demetzy.* £150
– New Testament. 1633. 2 pts. in 1 vol. 12mo. Some ll. damaged. Cont. embroidered dos-à-dos bdg., worn. [STC 2942 & 2645] (SH. Jul.9; 81) *Stoughton.* £90
– – Anr. Edn. L., [1807]. 24mo. Cont. str.-grd. mor., cl. s.-c. Fore-e. pntg.; from the liby. of Zola E. Harvey. (SG. Mar.19; 110) $250
– – Anr. Edn. N.Y., 1846. 2 vols. Fo. Ptd. in 'raised letters' for the blind. Hf. mor. (SG. May 14; 17) $900
– – Anr. Edn. Trans.:– John Wycliffe. 1848. 4to. Antique-style mor. by Rivière. (C. Feb.4; 81) *Porter.* £130
– New Testament & Psalms. N.d. 32mo. Mor., covers with rows of figures interspersed with white shapes recessed in sm. squares, titled along spine with letraset in similar squares, sigd. with 'key' stp. & dtd. 1961, s.-c., by Philip Smith. (SH. Feb.20; 396) *Melbourne Univ.* £460

NEW TESTAMENT [French]
– New Testament Epistles with Commentary by Jacques Lefevre d'Etaples. Paris, 1515. Fo. Cont. blind-stpd. cf., covers with panels & borders of floral rolls, worn loose in binding. (CNY. Oct.1; 76) $380
– Le Nouveau Testament en François ... avec des reflexions morales sur chaque verset. Trans.:– Pasquier Quesne. Paris, 1692. 4 vols. in 5. Some browning. Cont. Fr. mor., mor. doubls. with gt. inside border. (S. Apr.7; 342) *Maggs.* £95

NEW TESTAMENT [German]
– Das Gantz New Testament. Ed.:– [J. Ditenberger.] Trans.:– [L.H. Emser.] Ill.:– Anton von Worms. [Cologne]. [1529]. Early [6th.] Fo. Edn. Fo. Title-lf. soiled & stpd., browned stain at margin, some pasted tears, wormholes & soiling, lf. 200 corner torn with slight text loss. Cont. cf., blind-tooled metal clasps, carefully restored, worn, some worming & soiling. (H. May 21/22; 913) DM 2,800
– Das new Testamèt so durch Hieronymum Emserseligen verteutscht. Freiburg, 1539. Some side-notes, especially towards end, shaved. Cont. North German pig, over wooden bds., panel of John the Baptist baptising Christ on upr. cover & Annunciation on lr. cover, clasps. (S. Oct.21; 441) *Symonds.* £230
– Das Newe Testament. Trans.:– M. Luther. Wittenberg, 1553. 4to. Cont. blind-stpd. pig-bkd. wood bds. (R. Oct.14-18; 24) DM 2,200
– – Anr. Edn. Trans.:– J. Dietenberger. Cologne, 1567. Fo. Slightly browned. Marb. bds. ca. 1840. (HK. Nov.18-21; 120a) DM 440
– – Anr. Edn. Trans.:– Hieronymus Emser. Neisse, 1571. Bound in H. Emser : Annotationes über Luthers Newe Testament. Browned & stained. Cont. blind-stpd. leath.-bkd. wood bds., clasps, spine & lr. cover defect. (R. Oct.14-18; 25) DM 1,600

NEW TESTAMENT [Greek]
– Novvm Testamentvm Graece. Hagenau, Mar. 1521. 4to. Ink rule thro.-out, owner's mark on title, slightly stained. 18th. C. marb. leath., gt. spine, cover & inner dentelle. (HK. Nov.18-21; 121) DM 750
– Novum Jesu Christo D.N. Testamentum ex Bibliotheca Regia. Paris, 1550. 3rd. R. Stephanus' Edn. Fo. Title soiled. Cont. Parisian cf., rebkd. in 19th. C., upr. jnt. brkn. (S. Nov.25; 358) *Marriott.* £950
– Nouum Iesu Christi D.N. Testamentum. Paris, [Jun. 15], 1550. 1st. Edn. of this text. Fo. Inner blank margins of last 2 ll. strengthened. 17th. C. Fr. red mor. gt., triple gt.-ruled border, gt. arms on covers of Jean-Baptiste Colbert, spine gt. in 7 compartments, head & corners slightly worn. Colbert's ink inscr. on title, bkplts. of A.W. Clifford, William Phelps & WJP, later the copy of John A. Saks. [D. & M. 4622] (CNY. Oct.1; 107) $7,500
– – Anr. Copy. Three 16th. & 17th. C. Fr. owners' inscrs., & 2 ink stps., all on title. Mod. maroon mor. gt. Bkplt. of the General Theological Seminary Liby. (CNY. Oct.1; 47) $1,300
– Novum Testamentum. Ed.:– Robertus Stephanus. Paris, 1569. 2 pts. in 1 vol. 16mo. Ruled. 17th. C. red mor. [by Maitre Doreur?], 3 fillets in fanfare style, decor. with pointillé, spine similarly decor., inside dentelle, mod. cover. (HD. Mar.18; 123) Frs. 19,500
– Novum Testamentum Graecum. Ed.:– A.C.G. Woide. L., 1786. Fo. Red mor. gt., crosses tooled on covers. (P. Jul.2; 208) *Maggs.* £55
– E Kaine Diatheke: Novum Testamentum. L., 1820. Crimson str.-grd. mor. with fillet & floral gt. borders, spine gt., a prize from Wykeham School with label in upr. cover. Fore-e. pntg. of Christ, after Rembrandt. (SG. Aug.7; 315) $200

NEW TESTAMENT [Greek & Latin]
– Iesu Christi D.N. Nouum Testamentum, sive Nouum Foedus [with annotations of Theodore Beza]. Geneva, 1565. Fo. Some ll. slightly browned. Cont. mor. gt. à la fanfare, worn & restored. Bkplts. of Hopetoun House Liby. & the General Theological Seminary Liby. (CNY. Oct.1; 21) $1,600

NEW TESTAMENT [Italian]
– Il Nuovo ed Eterno Testamento di Giesu Christo. Ill.:– Bernard Salomon. Lyon, 1556. 2 pts. in 1 vol. 16mo. Cont. Fr. cf., gt., central empty oval surrounded by panel of arabesque & interlaced decor., arabesque & interlaced corner-pieces on azured ground, ground of panel semé with triple gt. dots, flat spine with alternate ovals filled with gt. arabesque decor. & arabesque panels on ground semé with dots, silk ties, corner slightly worn. [D. & M. 5590] (SM. Oct.7; 1889) Frs. 7,000

NEW TESTAMENT [Latin]
– Novum Testamentum illustratum. Antw., 1545. Cont. blind-stpd. Flemish cf. decor. on covers, worn, inner hinges brkn. (S. Oct.21; 442) *Vrije University.* £120
– Testamenti Novi. Ill.:– G. Reverdy. Lyon, 1548. Vulgate Edn. 2 pts. in 1 vol. Slightly soiled in parts, owner's mark on title. 18th. C. bds. (R. May 12-14; 76) DM 650
– Testamentum Novum. Ed.:– D. Erasmus Roterodamus. Ill.:– H. Brosamer. Frankfurt, 1552. Soiled. Old paper bds., defect. (R. Oct.14-18; 57) DM 1,600

See–BIBLES [Latin]

NEW TESTAMENT [Polyglot]
– Novum Testamentum. Ed.:– Elias Hutter. Nuremb., 1599. 2 vols. Fo. 18th. C. hf. cf., gt. device of the Signet Liby. on covers. The copy of the Munich Royal Liby., lately in the collection of Eric Sexton. [D. & M. 1430] (C. Apr.15; 4) *Gamble.* £130

NEW TESTAMENT [Tongan]
– Koe Tohi Fuakava Foou ... Vavau, 1849. 1st. Edn. Cont. cl., rebkd. [D. & M. 9307] (S. Mar.31; 495) *Quaritch.* £100

NEW TESTAMENT [Yiddish]
– Das Neue Testament dans da werd ginent Evangelien das ist in daitsch ein freuliche Botschaft, glaich wi im evreischen. Trans.:– Johannes Herzuge. Cracow, 1540. Fo. Slight worming affecting letters between B1 & E4, minute wormhole thro.-out, occasional marginal staining. Cont. roll-tooled blind-stpd. cf. over wooden bds., covers detchd., covered with transparent plastic, lacks clasps, bkplt. of Bibliotheca Rosenbergiana. (C. Apr.1; 125) *Jerusalem.* £9,000

NEW TESTAMENT STUDIES. An international Journal
L., 1954-78. Vols. 1-25, pt. 1 in pts. (B. Dec.10/11; 1338) Fls. 600

NEW TESTAMENTIANA [Dutch]
– Historie des Ouden en Nieuwen Testaments. Amst., 1700. 2 vols. Fo. A few sm. tears, mainly marginal. Cont. cf. gt., worn, later wooden case, very sm. defect. (SBA. Dec.16; 19) *Hamilton.* £135
– – Anr. Copy. 2 pts. in 1 vol. Browned & foxed, 1 text lf. reprd. without loss. Cont. hf. cf., worn, spine defect. (VG. Nov.18; 1046) Fls. 1,350

NEW TESTAMENTIANA [English]
– New Week's Preparation for a Worthy Receiving of the Lord's Supper ... Ca. 1750. 36th. Edn. 12mo. Cont. red mor., hollow, mor. onlays on covers, elab. gt., spine gt. in compartments. (S. Nov.25; 387) *Harp.* £580
– The New Week's Preparation for a Worthy receiving of the Lord's Supper ... & a Companion at the Altar. L., [1819]. 12mo. Crimson str.-grd. mor. gt.-tooled with floral & other designs. Double fore-e. pntg. of Chelmsford & Thacksted Church. (SG. Aug.7; 316) $375
– Parables of our Lord. Ill.:– Henry Noel Humphries. 1847. Orig. black papier-mâché covers, mor. spine, largely disbnd. (CSK. Jul.3; 121) £55
– The Parables from the Gospels. Ill.:– Charles Ricketts. Vale Pr., 1903. (310). Orig. limp vell., slightly soiled, unc. Loosely inserted are proof pulls of 6 of the ills. on india paper heightened with white. (S. Jul.31; 51) *Barlow.* £190
– – Anr. Edn. Ill.:– Ricketts. [Vale Pr.] [1903]. (310) Orig. limp vell. (CSK. Apr.3; 71) £100
– – Anr. Copy. Orig. vell., unc., unopened. (SG. Sep.4; 450) $400
– Four Gospels of the Lord Jesus Christ according to the authorized version of King James I. Ill.:– Eric Gill. Waltham Saint Lawrence, Gold Cock. Pr., 1931. (500). Fo. Orig. bdg. Accompanied by T.L.s by Gill, dtd. 1936, regarding Dr. Kahn's bkplt. (sigd. in pencil by Gill on end-paper). (SPB. Nov.25; 288) $2,000
– – Anr. Copy. Partly unc., orig. buckram, hf. mor., card case. (KH. Nov.18; 289) Aus. $1,500
– The Revelation of Saint John. Ill.:– Blair Hughes-Stanton. Gregynog Pr., 1932. (250). Fo. Red mor., s.-c. (C. Jul.22; 74) *Monk Bretton.* £200
– Holy Gospels according to Matthew, Mark, Luke & John. Ill.:– Bruno Bramanti after Bartolomeo di Giovanni. Officina Bodoni, 1962. (155) for Great Britain. Fo. Orig. red mor. gt., s.-c. (SH. Feb.20; 224) *Maggs.* £420
– – Anr. Copy. (SH. Feb.20; 223) *Quaritch.* £380
– – Anr. Copy. (320). Orig. red lev. mor., upr. cover with gt. title in gt. wreath, partly unc., cl. s.-c. (CNY. Oct.1; 201) $1,000

- Durham Gospels. (Early English Manuscripts in Facsimile, vol. XX). Ed.:– C.D. Verey & others. Copen., 1980. Fo. Mod. hf. mor., orig. wraps. bnd. in. (S. Jun.9; 13)   Quaritch. £75

NEW TESTAMENTIANA [Italian]
- Raccolta di Circa 350 Stampe sul Nuovo Testamento. [Italy], 17th. C. 2 vols. 27 × 35 cms. Copper engrs. Vell., defect. (CR. Mar.19; 329)
Lire 1,600,000

NEW TESTAMENTIANA [Mohawk]
- The Gospel According to Saint John. N.Y., 1818. 18mo. Disbnd., ex-liby. (SG. Mar.5; 29) $120

NEW TESTAMENTIANA [Slavonic]
- Evangeliaire du Monastre de Niemstoul. 19th C. Fo. Cont. roan on wooden bds., double border of gt. roll-stps., gt. on upr. cover, silver on lr. cover. (HD. Mar.18; 67)   Frs. 2,000

NEW TOM THUMB (THE) with an Account of his Wonderful Exploits, as related by Margery Meanwell
1822. 2nd. Edn. Page of advts. inserted in lr. cover, fitted case. (SH. Mar.19; 226)
Schiller. £170

NEW UNIVERSAL DICTIONARY of Arts & Sciences
1751. Fo. 59 (of 61) plts., lacks last lf. of text? Old cf., rebkd. (TA. Apr.16; 282)   £60
- - Anr. Copy. (TA. Mar.19; 372)   £50

NEW VERSE
[L.], 1933-39. Numbers 1-31 (a few as double issues) & New Series, Vol. I, numbers 1-2, all publd., in 7 vols. Various colour cl., bkplt. of HDD. (PNY. Mar.26; 28) $160

NEW YORK
- Journal of the First Session of the Senate ... March 4, 1789. N.Y., 1789. 1st. Printing. Fo. Unbnd. [Sabin 15551] (PNY. Oct.1; 514) $950
- Report to the Aqueduct Commissioners, by the President, J.C. Spencer, containing Reports of J.C. Sheehan & Chief Engineer B.S. Church. [N.Y.], [1887]. Fo. Cover title reads 'City of New York Aqueduct Commission Reports on the New Croton Aqueduct, 1883 to 1887.' Cl. (SG. Jan.8; 337) $110

NEW YORK CITY
- An Act for Suppressing Immorality, passed Feb. 23, 1788; to which is added, a Law for the due Observance of the Lord's Day, called Sunday. N.Y., 1795. Sewed. (SG. Mar.5; 341) $160
- Constitution of the St. George's Society of New York, with a List of its Officers & Members, & its Disbursements to 1869. N.Y., 1869. 12mo. Cont. crimson mor. richly gt.-tooled with fillet borders, lettering & lge. design of St. George conquering the dragon, upr. cover lettered 'His Royal Highness Prince Arthur,' this copy specially bnd. for him, gt. cf. doubls. (SG. Mar.5; 345)
£375
- Report of the Select Committee appointed to investigate the Health Department of the City of New York. [Albany], [1859]. Orig. cl., ex-liby. (SG. Mar.5; 349) $110

NEW YORK CRYSTAL PALACE
- The World of Science, Art, & Industry, Illustrated from Examples in the New-York Exhibition, 1853-54. Ed.:– B. Silliman, Jr. & J.R. Goodrich. Ill.:– under superintendence of C.E. Doepler. N.Y., 1854. Fo. Gt.-decor. leath. (SG. Mar.5; 351) $375

NEW YORK ETCHING CLUB
- Twenty Original American Etchings. N.Y., [1884]. (250) numbered on Japan paper. Etchings 8 × 12 ins. 13 (of the 20) etchings, all matted, 3 foxed. In orig. double-compartment 4-way box (brkn.), with metal clasp, ex-liby. Accompanied by 2 lge. etchings by Nicoll & Elten, each sigd. & matted, the 1st. foxed, contained in lge. portfo. (worn), with ties. (SG. May 21; 319) $550

NEW YORK HERALD, The
Ed.:– William Coleman. N.Y., 13 Jul., 1813-28 Dec., 1814. Fo. Ex-liby., some iss's with tears, holes, etc., though generally sound. Mod. buckram. (SG. Jan.8; 336) $275

NEW YORK State
- Documents Relative to the Colonial History of the State of New York. Ed.:– E.B. O'Callaghan & [Berthold Fernow]. Albany, 1856-87. 15 vols., including general index. 4to. 1 map foxed, anr. slightly worn. Orig. cl., spine to index worn,

ex-liby. [Sabin 53653] (CB. Nov.12; 135)
Can. $425

NEW ZEALAND
- Further Papers Relative to the Affairs of New Zealand. L., 1846. Foolscap fo. Stiff wraps., cl. spine. Ingleton bkplt. (JL. Dec.15; 661)
Aus. $210
- Latest Information from the Settlement of New Plymouth ... comprising letters from Settlers there. L., 1842. Orig. wraps. (TA. Nov.20; 222)
£70

NEWBERRY, Arthur St. John
- Another Catch. Cleveland, Priv. ptd., [1914]. 1st. Edn. (75) numbered. Gt.-pict. cl. (SG. Oct.16; 245) $550
- Caught on the Fly. Cleveland, Priv. ptd., 1908. 1st. Edn., (120) numbered. Flexible gt. leatherette. (SG. Oct.16; 244) $475
- A Fisherman's Paradise. Cleveland, Priv. ptd., ca. 1914. (150) numbered. First sig. loose. Gt.-pict. cl. (SG. Oct.16; 246) $110

NEWBERRY, J.S.
See–MACOMB, Capt. John N. & Newberry, J.S.

NEWCASTLE, Margaret Cavendish, Duchess of
- The Description of a New World, called the Blazing World. 1666. 1st. Edn. Fo. Some foxing & soiling, 1 lf. torn in margin. Mod. panel. cf. Cont. owner's inscr. on fly-lf. of Benedicta Kitchen. [Wing N849] (S. Jun.23; 386)   Lawson. £260
- The Philosophical & Physical Opinions. 1655. 1st. Edn. Fo. Some browning, short tear reprd. in title, stubs (indicating cancels?) at X4 & Z4. Hf. red mor., gt., by the Club Bindery. Bkplt. pf Robert Hoe; from Honeyman Collection. [Wing N863] (S. Nov.10; 2297)   Zeitlin. £420
- - Anr. Copy. Lacks port., some browning, short tear reprd. in title, stubs (indicating cancels?) at X4 & Z4. Dupl. from Henry E. Huntinton Collection. [Wing N863] (S. May 20; 3292)
Lawson. £140

NEWCASTLE, William Cavendish, Duke of
- General System of Horsemanship. 1743. 2 vols. Fo. Some browning, mostly in vol. II. Cont. morot. cf., rebkd. (S. May 5; 357)   Traylen. £1,500
- Méthode et Invention Novvelle de Dresser les Chevaux ... Trans.:– [J. de Solleysel]. Antw., 1658. Fo. 41 double-p. engraved plts., plt. 12, text browned. Cont. cf. (S. Nov.25; 417)
Schuster. £850
- - Anr. Edn. [Engraved title reads Antw.], [1658]. 2nd. Edn., L.P. Fo. Very slight spotting. Cont. mott. cf., gt., some wear. (S. Jun.23; 244)
Way. £2,000
- - Anr. Edn. Ill.:– after A. van Diepenbeke. L., 1737. 2nd. Edn. Fo. Lacks plts. 15 & 20, plts. lightly browned in parts, some stains, text slightly browned in parts. Cont. cf., gt. spine, worn, spine torn. (H. Dec.9/10; 363)   DM 4,800
- - Anr. Copy. Old hf. cf., some defects & restored. (LM. Jun.13; 65)   B.Frs. 58,000
- Neueröfnete Reitbahn oder Vollkommener Stallmeister. Nuremb., 1764. New Edn. Fo. Cont. leath., gt., some worming. (R. Oct.14-18; 2768)
DM 9,000

NEWCOME, William
- An English Harmony of the Four Evangelists. 1802. Mor. gt., slightly worn, by Douglas Cockerell, sigd. in gt. 'DC 1901'. (SKC. Feb.26; 1705)   £110

NEWE ZEITTUNG wie key. May. sich mit dem Bapet vereinigt hat
N.p., [1546]. 4to. Wraps., lr. cover fixed to wrap. (HK. Nov.18-21; 241)   DM 440

NEWELL, E.T.
- The Coinage of the Eastern Seleucid Mints. N.Y., 1938. 4to. Cont. cf.-bkd. bds. (SH. Mar.6; 411)
Trade Art. £85
- The Seleucid Mint of Antioch. N.Y., 1918. 4to. Orig. wraps., torn, loose. (SH. Mar.6; 412)
IJL. £80

NEWELL, Peter
- The Hole Book. N.Y., 1908. 1st. Edn. 4to. Orig. cl. (SH. Mar.19; 230)   Fletcher. £75
- The Hole Book.–The Slant Book.–The Rocket Book. N.Y., [1908]; [1910]; [1912]. 1st. Edns. 3 works in 3 vols. All orig. bds. & cl., hinges of 1st. & 3rd. works reinforced with tape. (SG. Apr.30; 233) $260
- The Rocket Book. N.Y., 1912. 1st. Edn. 4to. Orig. cl. (SH. Mar.19; 232)   Fletcher. £75

- A Shadow Show. N.Y., 1896. 1st. Edn. Ob. 8vo. A few ills. loose. Orig. pict. bds., rebkd. preserving part of orig. spine. (SH. Mar.19; 229) Till. £135
- The Slant Book. N.Y., 1910. 1st. Edn. Slanting 4to. Orig. cl.-bkd. pict. bds. (SH. Mar.19; 231)
Fletcher. £95
- Topsys & Turveys.–Topsys & Turveys, (number 2). N.Y., 1893-94. 1st. Edn.; 1st. Engl. Edn. 2 vols. Ob. 8vo. 1st. work with 30 (of 31) ills. Orig. pict. bds., spines worn. (SH. Mar.19; 228)
Fletcher. £75

NEWFOUNDLAND
- An Act to Incourage the Trade to Newfoundland. 1699. Fo. Mod. wraps. (SH. Nov.7; 387)
Remington. £60

NEWGATE CALENDAR (The)
Ed.:– Andrew Knapp, William Baldwin. L., 1824. 4 vols. Orig. bds., cl. spines, 1 bdg. brkn., some foxing, owner's inscr. in vol. 1. (SG. Sep.4; 353)
$130

NEWHOUSE, Charles B.
- The Roadsters Album. L., 1845. Fo. Orig. cl., worn. (SPB. Oct.1; 91) $1,700
- Scenes on the Road. [L.], [1845]. Ob. fo. Lacks engraved title-p. Red hf. mor. gt. As a collection of plts. w.a.f. (SPB. Oct.1; 92) $2,700

NEWLAND, Henry
- Forest Scenes in Norway & Sweden. Ill.:– Dalziel. L., 1854. 1st. Edn. Gt.-decor. cl. (SG. Oct.16; 248) $100

NEWMAN, Cardinal John Henry
- Verses on Various Occasions. 1868. 1st. Edn. Mor. gt., by Benford. A.L.s. from author to Gaisford, pres. inscr. by Gaisford, 3 receipts for Gaisford's school fees loosely inserted, sigd. by Newman. (SH. Apr.9; 306)   Nolan. £70

NEWMAN, Neil
- Famous Horses of the American Turf. 1931-32-33. (750). 3 vols. 4to. Gt.-decor. cl. (SG. Dec.11; 267) $220

NEWMAN & CO.
- Twelve Views in Ireland. L., n.d. Title in photostat, 13 litho. plts., Gap of Dunloe in dupl., a few slight tears reprd. Orig. cl., spine replaced. (GM. Apr.30; 402)   £100

NEWSTEAD, M.S.
See–COULLERY, M.T. & Newstead, M.S.

NEWTON, Alfred Edward
- The Amenities of Book-Collecting, & Kindred Affections. Boston, 1918. 1st. Edn., 1st. Iss., inscr. Laid in is plt. 'A Tour of the Hebrides'. Hf. buckram, orig. d.-w. (SG. Oct.2; 256) $160
See–GUTENBERG, Johann

NEWTON, C.T.
- History of Discoveries at Halicarnassus, Cnidus & Branchidae, being the Results of an Expedition sent to Asia Minor by H.M. Government in 1856. 1862. Vol. I only. (plts.). Lge. fo. Slight foxing, mainly to prelims. Loose in orig. cl., mod. folder. (TA. Dec.18; 420)   £80
- Travels & Discoveries in the Levant. 1865. 2 vols. Some ll. spotted. Hf. crimson mor. gt. (P. Jan.22; 101)   Thorpe. £60

NEWTON, Sir Isaac
[-] Arithmetica Universalis: sive de Compositione et Resolutione Arithmetica Liber. Ed.:– William Whiston. Camb., 1707. 1st. Edn. Short tear in N6. Cont. panel. cf., worn. Bkplt. of Arbury liby.; from Honeyman Collection. (S. Nov.10; 2329)
Quaritch. £400
- - Anr. Edn. Leiden, 1732. 4to. 18th. C. owner's inscr. of Pillon de Lattillaine. Cont. cf. (S. Dec.1; 288)   Quaritch. £60
- The Chronology of Ancient Kingdoms Amended. Ed.:– John Conduitt. 1728. 1st. Edn. 4to. Slight spotting. Cont. cf., gt., hf. red mor. case. Bkplt. of Samuel James, Baron Waring; from Honeyman Collection. (S. Nov.10; 2331)   Hill. £100
- - Anr. Copy. Cont. qtr. cf., worn. (S. Dec.1; 287)
Holdorf. £60
- - Anr. Copy. Cf. gt. (P. Dec.11; 374)
Diba. £55
- De Mundi Systemate. 1728. 1st. Edn. 4to. Some ll. of text & both plts. dampstained. Hf. cf., rebkd., lr. cover stained. From Honeyman Collection. (S. Nov.10; 2306)   Quaritch. £100
- Excerpta Quaedam e Newtoni Principiis Philosophiae Naturalis, cum notis variorum. Ed.:– [John Jebb]. 1765. 1st. Edn. 4to. Sig. 'N. Pym' on

NEWTON, Sir Isaac *-contd.*
title, slight browning. Cont. hf. cf. (S. Jun.29; 413) *Murray-Hill.* £80
– Matematicheskiia nachala natural'noi filosofi. Trans.:– A.N. Kriloff. Petrograd, 1915-16. 1st. Edn. in Russian. Pts. I & II (in: Izvestiia Nikolaevskoi morskoi akademii, Vypusk IV-V). 4to. Orig. pd. wraps., unc., neatly rebkd., Russian bookseller's stp. on upr. cover of each vol., some wear to covers, 1 stained, preserved in buckram box. From Honeyman Collection. (S. Nov.10; 2321) *Quaritch.* £1,800
– The Mathematical Principles of Natural Philosophy. Trans.:– Andrew Motte. 1729. 1st. Edn. in Engl. 2 vols. 2nd. engraved frontis. bound at p. 148 in vol. II, slight soiling & discolouration. Cont. cf., gt., spines worn. L.P.; from Honeyman Collection. (S. Nov.10; 2308) *Norman.* £1,900
– – Anr. Copy. Pol. cf. by Sangorski. (C. Apr.1; 112) *Quaritch.* £850
– – Anr. Copy. 2nd. engraved frontis. bnd. at p. 95 in vol. II, some foxing & soiling. Cont. cf., 1 cover detchd., worn. 19th. C. bkplt. of David Hodgson; from Honeyman Collection. (S. Nov.10; 2309) *Quaritch.* £800
– – Anr. Edn. Trans.:– Robert Thorp. 1777. 1st. Edn. Vol. I (all publd.) 4to. Some foxing & offsetting, printer's ink-smudge on M3r. Mod. hf. cf. From Honeyman Collection. (S. Nov.10; 2312) Quaritch. £240
– – Anr. Edn. Trans.:– Robert Thorp. 1802. 2nd. Edn. 4to. Foxing & damp-staining. Orig. bds., rebkd. in cf., unc. & partly unopened, owner's inscr. on upr. cover. From Honeyman Collection. (S. Nov.10; 2313) *Quaritch.* £90
– – Anr. Edn. Ed.:– W. Davis. Trans.:– Andrew Motte. 1803. 2nd. Edn. 3 vols. Some browning & spotting. Cf.-bkd. bds., vol. I rebkd. Bkplt. of R.S. Milnes in vols. II & III; from Honeyman Collection. (S. Nov.10; 2310) *Phelps.* £90
– Mathematische Principien der Naturlehre. Ed.:– J. Ph. Wolfers. Berlin, 1872. 1st. Edn. in German. 2 ll. of prelims. detchd. Orig. cl., discold., spine defect. From Honeyman Collection. (S. Nov.10; 2319) *Hill.* £260
– – Anr. Copy. Cont. cl.-bkd. bds., spine slightly torn. From Honeyman Collection. (S. Nov.10; 2320) *Das Bucherkabinet.* £140
– – Anr. Copy. Cont. linen. (HK. May 12-14; 387) DM 650
– The Method of Fluxions & Infinite Series; with its Applications to the Geometry of Curve-Lines. Trans.:– John Colson. 1736. 1st. Edn. 4to. Errata/advt. lf., N4 stained, Cont. panel. cf., lr. cover detchd. Lge. copy; from Honeyman Collection. (S. Nov.10; 2327) *Thomas.* £700
– La Méthode des Fluxions, et des Suites Infinies. Trans.:– G.L. Le Clerc, Comte de Buffon. Paris, 1740. 1st. Edn. in Fr. 4to. Cont. cf., gt. spine, slightly worn. From Honeyman Collection. (S. Nov.10; 2328) *Zeitlin.* £150
– – Anr. Copy. Title slightly defect. in margin, slightly dampstained, stp. of Bibliotheque Mathematique des Travailleurs, on title. Cont. mott. cf., worn. (S. Dec.2; 749) *Quaritch.* £110
– Newton's Principia. The Mathematical Principles of Natural Philosophy . . . To which is added Newton's System of the World. Ed.:– N.W. Chittenden. Trans.:– Andrew Motte. N.Y., [1846]. 1st. Amer. Edn. Orig. cl., slightly worn. From Honeyman Collection. (S. Nov.10; 2311) *Quaritch.* £150
– Observations upon the Prophecies of Daniel, & the Apocalypse of St. John. Ed.:– Benjamin Smith. 1733. 1st. Edn. 4to. 1st. 3 ll. detchd., title slightly soiled. Orig. bds., rebkd. with linen, unc., worn. From Honeyman Collection. (S. Nov.10; 2332) *Ritman.* £90
– Opera quae Exstant Omnia. Ed.:– Samuel Horsley. 1779-85. 1st. Coll. Edn. 5 vols. 4to. Some spotting & discolouration. Cont. cf., gt., slightly worn. Bkplt. of Henry Drummond, Albury Park, Surrey from Honeyman Collection. (S. Nov.10; 2299) *Hill.* £650
– Optice: sive de Reflexionibus, Refractionibus, Inflexionibus, & Coloribus Lucis libri tres . . . Trans.:– Samuel Clarke. 1706. 1st. Latin Edn. 4to. Owner's inscr. on title, stp. on verso of R. Gr. von Veltheim. Cont. vell. bds., slightly soiled. From Honeyman Collection. (S. Nov.10; 2326) *Zeitlin.* £500
[–] Opticks: or, a Treatise of the Reflexions, Refractions, Inflexions & Colours of Light. Also Two Treatises of the Species & Magnitude of Curvilinear Figures. 1704. 1st. Edn. 4to. A few pp. slightly soiled. Cont. panel. cf., upr. cover detchd., lacks label, worn, hf. ref mor. case. Pres. copy from Newton to Richard Bentley, inscr. by latter on front free end-paper; from Honeyman Collection. (S. Nov.10; 2324) *Zeitlin.* £4,000
– – Anr. Copy. First 2 gatherings detchd. Rebkd., corners restored, spine brkn., covers detchd. (CNY. May 22; 229) $1,600
– – Anr. Edn. 1718. 2nd. Edn., 2nd. Iss. Most plts. trimmed at foot, advt. lf., some browning. Cont. panel. cf., jnts. reprd., worn. From Honeyman Collection. (S. Nov.10; 2325) *Zeitlin.* £230
– – Anr. Copy. 1 plt. cropped, advt. lf., slight browning. Cf., gt., worn. (S. Dec.2; 748) *Celestial.* £220
– – Anr. Edn. 1730. 4th. Edn. Cont. spr. cf. (CSK. May 22; 100) £75
– – Anr. Edn. 1821. 3rd. Edn. Advt. lf. & 16 pp. advts., sm. stp. on title, bkplt. on verso. Mod. roan, gt. (S. Dec.2; 750) *Phelps.* £100
– Philosophiae Naturalis Principia Mathematica. Prostat, 1687. 1st. Edn., 1st. Iss. 4to. With P3 (pp. 109/110) in its earlier uncorrected state, title a little soiled, owners inscrs., printing flaw at head of 2S4. Cont. panel. cf., rebkd., old spine preserved, cl. case. From Honeyman Collection. [Wing N1048] (S. Nov.10; 2300) *Zeitlin.* £12,500
– – Anr. Copy. Errata lf. bnd. after prelims., damp-stained thro.-out, owners inscrs. on front paste-down, paper flaw in margin of H3. Cont. panel. cf., rebkd. & reprd., hf. red mor. case. From Honeyman Collection. (S. Nov.10; 2301) *Fountain.* £7,000
– – Anr. Edn. Ed.:– Roger Cotes. Camb., 1713. 2nd. Edn. 4to. Errata corrected in MS., owner's inscr., a few sm. holes. Cont. panel. cf., gt., hf. red mor. case. Bkplt. of John Plumptre; from Honeyman Collection. (S. Nov.10; 2303) *Zeitlin.* £750
– – Anr. Edn. Amst., 1714. 4to. Some browning. Cont. vell. bds., hf. red mor. case. Armorial bkplt. of Christian Ernst, Graf zu Stolberg, & stp. of Stolberg liby. at Wernigerode on title; from Honeyman Collection. (S. Nov.10; 2305) *Zeitlin.* £650
– – Anr. Edn. Ed.:– Henry Pemberton. Ill.:– G. Vertue after I. Vanderbank. 1726. 3rd. Edn. (200), 2nd. imp. on writing Royal Paper Wtrmkd. 'CC'. 4to. Rust-hole in X3, offsetting on title. Cont. diced russ., gt., jnts. split. From Honeyman Collection. (S. Nov.10; 2304) *Zeitlin.* £500
– – Anr. Edn. 1726. 3rd. Edn. 4to. Last few ll. reprd. with loss of a few letters, some soiling & dampstaining. Mod. mor., spine gt., gt. inner dentelles. (CSK. Jun.5; 48) £90
– – Anr. Edn. Ed.:– Thomas Le Sueur & Franc. Jacquier. Geneva, 1739-1740-1742. 1st. 'Jesuit' Edn. 3 vols. 4to. In vol. I a printed slip has been pasted over the imprint altering it to: Paris, Carolus Jombert. Cont. cf., worn. (S. Dec.1; 290) *Blackwell.* £65
– – Anr. Edn. Ed.:– T. Le Seur & F. Jacquier. Geneva, 1760. 2nd. Jesuit's Edn. 3 vols. 4to. Some browning, rust-hole in Y3 vol. I, tear reprd. in 2M3 vol. II. 19th. C. hf. russ., gt., jnts. reprd. Bkplt. of Charles Robert Colvile; from Honeyman Collection. (S. Nov.10; 2316) *Hill.* £110
– – Anr. Edn. Ed.:– T. Le Seur & F. Jacquier, & John M.F. Wright. Glasgow, 1822. 1st. Glasgow reissue of Jesuit's Edn. 4 vols. Browned. Orig. bds., unc., worn. From Honeyman Collection. (S. Nov.10; 2318) *Hill.* £90
– – Anr. Edn. Glasgow, 1833. 2 vols. Cont. vell. bds., slightly soiled, prize copy with gt. arms of Edinb. University on covers. (S. Apr.6; 120) *Blackwell.* £60
– – Anr. Edn. Prostant Venales, 1867. 1st. Edn., 2nd. Iss. 4to. Quires 2K & 2Z misbnd., some browning, a few ll. marginally soiled, ink spots on 2M1, slight tears in D1 & H4, paper flaws in R2 & 3I1. Cont. mott. cf., gt. spine, worn, lacks label, hf. red mor. case, epitaph on Newton in Latin in 18th. C. hand on front paste-down. Stp. of Stolberg liby. at Wernigerode on title; from Honeyman Collection. [Wing N1049] (S. Nov.10; 2302) *Quaritch.* £8,000
– Philosophiae Naturalis Principia Mathematica. –Analysis per Quantitatum Series, Fluxiones, ac Differentias. Amst., 1723. 2 works in 1 vol. 4to. Margins browned. Old cf., rebkd. (TA. Mar.19; 368) £72
[–] Principes Mathématiques de la Philosophie Naturelle. Trans.:– Marquise du Chatelet. Paris, 1759. 2 vols. 4to. Slight spotting, owner's inscr. on fly-lf. to vol. I of Du Zillarie Rouviere. Cont. mott cf., worn. Bkplt. of Baron Brougham & Vaux & an A.L.s. to him from Tho. Winter loosely inserted; from Honeyman Collection. (S. Nov.10; 2314) *Hill.* £340
[–] – Anr. Copy. Owner's inscr. of G. Guignard with his notat of purchase, some browning. Cont. mott. cf., gt., arms on upr. covers of Nicolas de La Pinte de Livry, worn. From Honeyman Collection. (S. Nov.10; 2315) *Quaritch.* £280
– Traité d'Optique . . . Trans.:– M. Coste. Ill.:– Hérisset after Chaufourier. Paris, 1722. 4to. Cont. cf., decor. spine, worn. (HD. Dec.5; 158) Frs. 1,300
– A Treatise of the System of the World. 1728. 1st. Edn. in Engl. Cont. cf., hinges worn. (S. Jun.23; 283) *Pickering & Chatto.* £300
– – Anr. Copy. Title slightly soiled & with former owner's name cut from upr. margin, similar piece cut from errata lf. at end, sigs. of J. Barratt (replaced) & Christopher Benson. Cont. cf., rebkd., worn. From Honeyman Collection. (S. Nov.10; 2307) *Ritman.* £220
– – Anr. Copy. Slight worming affecting text, sm. paper flaw in C4. (S. Jun.23; 284) *Fountain.* £140
– – Anr. Edn. 1731. 2nd. Edn. in Engl. Holes in E7-8 affecting text, a few letters erased on Flr, slight soiling, owner's inscr. at head of title. 19th. C. hf. cf., inner hinges defect., hf. red mor. case. From Honeyman Collection. (S. Nov.10; 2323) *Quaritch.* £180
– Two Letters . . . to Mr. Le Clerc, late Divinity Professor of the Remonstrants in Holland. 1754. 18th. C. vell.-bkd. marb. bds., unc., hf. red mor. case. Bkplt. of William Hanbury; from Honeyman Collection. (S. Nov.10; 2333) *Quaritch.* £80
– Two Treatises of the Quadrature of Curves. Trans.:– J. Stewart. 1745. 4to. Spotted. Cont. cf. (SH. Jun.25; 148) *Frognal.* £120

NEWTON, James
– A Compleat Herbal. 1752. Later red str.-grd. mor. gt. (SBA. Jul.22; 109) *Temperley.* £180
– – Anr. Edn. L., 1798. Hf. cf. marb. bd. (HSS. Apr.24; 100) £65

NEWTON, James–LILLIE, John
– A Complete Herbal.–The British Perfumer. Ed.:– C. Mackenzie (2nd. work). 1798; 1822. New Edn.; 2nd. Edn. 2 works in 2 vols. 8vo.; 12mo. 1st. work with some plts. cropped in outer edges, sig. on title of 1st. work. 1st. work: mod. cf.; 2nd. work: mod. hf. cf., unc. (SH. Jul.27; 302) *Fryer.* £90

NEWTON, John
– The Art of Natural Arithmetick, in Whole Numbers & Fractions Vulgar & Decimal. [1671]. 1st. Edn. Repairs to fore-margin of title & to upr. margin of L2 affecting headline, a few rust-spots & sm. holes. Mod. red mor., gt. From Honeyman Collection. (S. Nov.10; 2335) *Schuman.* £240

NEWTON, William
– Human Life: A Poem, In Four Cantos. Jeffersonville, Ind., 1844. 1st. Edn. Slight foxing & soiling, prelims. & early ll. worn, owner's inscrs. of F. Rice McGrew on front end-paper, title & 1st. lf. of text. Orig. wraps., worn, owner's inscrs. of F. Rice McGrew on wraps., stitched as iss., folding cl. case. From liby. of William E. Wilson. (SPB. Apr.29; 214) $600

NIBELUNGE NOT
Darmstadt, Ernst Ludwig Pr. 1926-27. (100). 2 vols. 4to. Orig. hf. vell. (H. Dec.9/10; 1807) DM 460

NIBELUNGEN, Die
Ill.:– J. Sattler. Berlin, 1898-1904. (160) on heavy Bütten special for this Edn. Lge. fo. Wide margin. Mor. gt., decor., gt. vig., end-ll. renewed, some wear, spine torn. (H. May 21/22; 1468) DM 5,100
– – Anr. Edn. Ed.:– F. Keim. Ill.:– C.O. Czeschka. Vienna & Leipzig, [1909]. Orig. hf. linen. (HK. Nov.18-21; 2489) DM 650

NICERON, Jean François
– La Perspective Curieuse ou Magie Artificiele des Effets Merveilleux. Ill.:– Daret. Paris, 1638. 1st. Edn. Fo. G1 & G6 in dupl., text browned. Cont. limp vell., stained, lacks ties. Inscr. by author to Jean Du Rozier; from Honeyman Collection. (S. Nov.10; 2336) *Weinreb.* £380
– Thaumaturgus Opticus, seu Admiranda Optices . . . Catoptrices . . . Dioptrices. Paris, 1646. Pt. 1 (all publd.). Fo. Hf.-title torn in inner margin,

fore-margin of L2 partly renewed, some browning & soiling. 19th. C. hf. cf. From Honeyman Collection. (S. Nov.10; 2337) *Weinreb.* £150
– – **Anr. Edn.** Ill.:– K. Audran after S. Voüet. Paris, 1646. 1st. Edn. (Part 1 all publd.). Minor browning & slight spotting, sm. repair to fore-margin of plt. 7, lf. of directions to binder at end. Cont. vell., slightly worn. (CNY. Oct.1; 19)
$850

NICERON, J.P., Oudin P.F. & others
– **Mémoires pour servir à l'histoire des Hommes illustres dans la République des Lettres.** Paris, 1729-45. 43 vols. in 44. 12mo. Cont. cf., spines worn. (S. Oct.21; 308) *Quaritch.* £140
– – **Anr. Copy.** 44 vols. Orig. cf. (DS. May 22; 797) Pts. 40,000

NICHOL, John
– **Byron.** L., 1880. Extra-ill. with 26 additional plts. Cosway-style mor. gt., gt. lf. design surrounding miniature of Byron, mor.-bkd. folding box. (SPB. Nov.25; 137) $1,100

NICHOLAS, Saint
See Also–SAINT NICHOLAS (Ill.:–Rackham)

NICHOLL, A.
See–PETRIE, George & others

NICHOLLS, Francis
– **De Anima Medica Praelectio.** 1773. 4to. 1 plt. hand-cold., lacks prelim. blank. Cont. hf. cf., very worn. (SBA. May 27; 215) *Phillips.* £180

NICHOLS, John
– **The History of Antiquities of the County of Leicester.** 1795-1811. 4 vols. in 8. Fo. Cont. diced russ., gt. borders. (C. Feb.25; 49) *Thorp.* £1,050
– **Six Old Plays.** L., 1779. 2 pts. in 1 vol. Old cf., rebkd., worn, some foxing. (SG. Aug.21; 466)
$110

NICHOLS, John & Bowyer, William
– **Literary Anecdotes.** 1812-17. 11 vols. with 2 vols. of ills. Cont. hf. cf., some spines worn. (SH. May 21; 13) *Smith.* £55

NICHOLS, John Gough
– **Autographs of Royal, Noble, Learned & Remarkable Personages.** 1829. 3 vols. Fo. Extra-ill. with ports. Cont. mor., gt. W.a.f. (CSK. May 1; 64) £100

NICHOLSON, Ben
– **Zeichnungen. Gemalde. Reliefs. 1911-1968.** Stuttgart, 1969. (10) with orig. etching. 4to. Orig. etching sigd. in pencil inset in upr. cover of folder, text in Engl. & German. Orig. bdg., folder & box. (SPB. Nov.25; 365) $950

NICHOLSON, Francis
– **Six Lithographic Impressions of Sketches from Nature.** 1821. Nos. 2 & 4 only. Ob. fo. Orig. pict. wraps. (SKC. May 19; 455) £50

NICHOLSON, James B.
– **A Manual of the Art of Bookbinding.** Phila., 1856. 1st. Edn. Advts. Three-qtr. cf., ex-libry., covers detchd., foxing. (SG. Oct.2; 277) $850

NICHOLSON, James B.–HORNE, H.P.
– **A Manual of the Art of Bookbinding.–The Binding of Books.** Phila.; L., 1902; 1894. 2 works in 2 vols. 12mo.; 8vo. Cl. (1st. work); a buckram, unopened. (SG. Mar.26; 46) $180

NICHOLSON, Michelangelo
See–NICHOLSON, Peter & Michelangelo

NICHOLSON, Peter
– **The Builder's & Workman's New Directory.** L. & Edinb., 1865. New Edn. 4to. Hf. mor., scuffed. (SG. Dec.4; 259) $100
– **New Carpenter's Guide.** L., 1825. Mod. hf. leath. (R. Oct.14-18; 488) DM 600
[–] **Practical Carpentry, Joinery & Cabinet-Making . . . for the Use of Workmen.** 1826. 2 pts. in 1 vol. 4to. Some ll. spotted. Mod. cf.-bkd. bds. (S. Dec.9; 471) *Talerman.* £110

NICHOLSON, Peter & Michelangelo
– **The Practical Cabinet-Maker, Upholsterer & Complete Decorator.** 1826. 4to. 118 plts., many hand-cold., mostly stained. Hf. cf. (S. Mar.17; 441) *Marlborough Rare Books.* £220
– – **Anr. Copy.** Spotted in places, some marginal tears, 2 corners torn off just affecting plt. edge. Cont. hf. str.-grd. mor., worn. (S. Apr.7; 272)
Sims & Reed. £120

NICHOLSON, William LL.D.
– **History of the Wars Occasioned by the French Revolution.** 1817. Fo. Lacks frontis. Cf., covers detchd. (P. Dec.11; 80) *Reid.* £120

NICHOLSON, William, Artist
– **An Almanac of Twelve Sports.** Ed.:– Rudyard Kipling. 1897. 1st. Edn. 4to. Orig. pict. bds. (C. Feb.4; 78) *Vicurelli.* £90
– – **Anr. Copy.** Unpaginated. Pict. bds. (JL. Mar.2; 800) Aus. $100
– – **Anr. Edn.** Ed.:– Rudyard Kipling. 1898. 4to. Orig. cl.-bkd. pict. bds., worn. (S. Jul.31; 259)
Lord's Gallery. £75
– – **Anr. Copy.** Text loose in bdg. Orig. ptd. bds. (BS. Feb.25; 243) £50
– – **Anr. Copy.** Orig. pict. hf. vell. (H. May 21/22; 1739) DM 420
– – **Anr. Edn.** Ca. 1900. 4to. Orig. cl.-bkd. pict. bds. (SKC. Dec.4; 1497) £55
– **An Alphabet.** 1898. Fo. Orig. pict. cl. (SH. Mar.27; 374) *Greer.* £240
– – **Anr. Copy.** 4to. Orig. cl.-bkd. bds. (SH. Mar.27; 375) *Hancock.* £125
– – **Anr. Copy.** 25 (of 26) cold. ills. (S. Jul.31; 257) *Lord's Gallery.* £95
– – **Anr. Edn.** 1899. 4to. End lf. torn. Orig. cl.-bkd. pict. bds., worn. (SH. Mar.27; 376)
Davidson. £85
– **The Book of Blokes.** [1929]. (50) numbered, sigd. Orig. crayon sketch, & 29 ills. with crayon col. Orig. pict. bds. (SH. Mar.26; 19)
Marks. £210
– – **Anr. Copy.** (SH. Mar.26; 18) *Marks.* £175
– – **Anr. Copy.** Orig. crayon sketch of a bloke by artist, all but 1 of ills. with crayon colouring. (S. Jul.31; 263) *Rota.* £110
– **The Pirate Twins.** [1930]. (60) numbered, sigd. by artist. Ob. 8vo. Orig. pict. bds. (S. Jul.31; 264)
Joseph. £440
– – **Anr. Copy.** Orig. pict. bds., end-papers & cover design by Nicholson. (SH. Mar.26; 20)
Quaritch. £260

NICOLAES de Bruyn
See–STRADANUS, Johannes–DE WITT, F. –NICOLAES de Bruyn

NICOLAI, Christoph Friedrich
[–] **Description des Villes de Berlin et de Potsdam.** Berlin, 1769. 1st. Fr. Edn. Lightly browned or soiled. Cont. leath. gt. (HK. Nov.18-21; 1109)
DM 420

NICOLAS, Sir Nicholas Harris
– **History of the Orders of Knighthood of the British Empire.** 1841-42. 4 vols. 4to. Later red mor., elab. gt., vol. 4 slightly spotted. (SH. Oct.10; 496) *Seaby.* £760
– – **Anr. Edn.** 1842. 4 vols. 4to. Some plts. loose. Cont. cl., vol. 3 brkn., unopened. (C. Jul.15; 139) *Pinches.* £200

NICOLAS, Pierre
– **De Conchoidibus et Cissoidibus Exercitationes Geometricae.** Toulouse, 1697. 1st. Edn. 4to. 1st. plt. with short tear reprd., some browning, 12 ll. from the Phil. Trans. inserted at end, Cf.-bkd. bds., upr. cover detchd, very worn. From Honeyman Collection. (S. Nov.10; 2338)
Howell. £130

NICOLAUS, Damascenus
See–KRAG, Niels–NICOLAUS, Damascenus –HERACLIDES, Ponticus

NICOLAUS DE AQUAEVILLA
– **Sermones Dominicales.** Paris, ca. 1510? Liby. blind-stp. on title, sm. portion of lr. blank margin lacking. 18th. C. cf., head of spine chipped, corners worn. (C. Apr.1; 63) *Yates.* £60

NICOLAUS de Auximo
– **Libro Devoto e Fruttuoso a Ciascun fedel Christiano Chimato Giardino de Orationi.** Venice, 1543. Upr. outer blank corner of N7 cut-away, some ll. with slight browning. Cont. Venetian mor. gt., in the Maioli style, covers with outer gt. & blind-ruled border, lge. rectangular double gt.-ruled panel with outer fleuron cornerpieces, enclosing garland cornerpieces & curved fillet panel in centre & blank escutcheon with star at each side & ornaments above & below, spine blind-tooled & with 7 raised gt.-decor. bands, 3 of them prominent, cl. s.-c. Bkplts. of C.N. Radoulesco & John A. Saks. (CNY. Oct.1; 131)
$2,300
– **Supplementum Summa Pisanellae et Canones Poenitentiales Fratris Astensis.** [Venice] 30 Nov. 1473. Fo. rubricated at beginning, heavily browned, MS. title, some old missing MS. marginalia & underlining. 18th. C. vell. [BMC V209] (HK. Nov.18-21; 242) DM 1,100

– – **Anr. Edn.** Genoa, Mathias Moravus & Michael de Monacho, Jun.22, 14[7]4. Fo. Spaces for initial capitals, supplied in red or blue, lacks final blank, scattered light foxing. Recent qtr. cf. & wood bds. Bkplts. of Jos. Martini, & George Dunn of Wooley Hall, lately in the collection of Eric Sexton. [BMC VII, 901, Goff N59, HC 2152] (CNY. Apr.8; 70) $11,000
– – **Anr. Edn.** Vercelli, Jacobinus Suigus, de Suico, Oct.27, 1485. Spaces for capital initials lacks 1st. blank, some dampstaining at front & back with the final lf. crudely resized & with slight loss of some letters, blank margins restored or slightly defect. at bb2-4, some ll. browned, some early ink annots. Mod. limp vell., lacks leath. ties. Bkplt. of Luigi Cora, lately in the collection of Eric Sexton. [BMC VII, 1106, Goff N77] (CNY. Apr.8; 200)
$6,000
– – **Anr. Edn.** Nuremb., Georg Stuchs for Anton Koberger, 20 Jun. 1488. 4to. Lacks 1st. & last blanks, 1st. initial illuminated, others supplied in red & blue, paragraph-marks in red. Cont. Nuremb. blind-stpd. cf. (by the 'Ornamentale Blute I' Bindery), covers tooled with floral arabesques, rebkd., worn. Later stp. 'Carmelit. Frances'; from liby. of André L. Simon. [BMC II, 467; HC 2168*] (S. May 18; 142) *Zsitva.* £480
– **Supplementum Summae Pisanellae et Canonices Poenitentiales Fratris Astensis.** [Venice], 30 Nov. 1473. Fo. Rubricated at beginning, heavily browned, MS. title, some old MS. marginalia & underlining. 18th. C. vell. [BMC V, 209] (HK. Nov.18-21; 242) DM 1,100

NICOLAUS de Blony
– **Sermones de Tempore et de Sanctis, sive Viridarius.** Strasbourg, [Georg Hussner]. 1494-95. 1st. Edn. 2 pts. in 1 vol. Fo. Initials supplied in red, some rubrication, lacks final blank, e5 reprd. at inner margin with slight text loss, g8 reprd. at fore-margin with slight text loss, but some text masked on verso, many upr. fore-corners damp-stained. Late 16th. C. blind-stpd. pig, top corner on upr. cover worn by damp. [Goff N91, HC 3262*] (S. Feb.10; 212) *Traylen.* £280

NICOLAUS de Lyra
– **Postilla super Biblia cum Additionibus Pauli Burgensis.** Nuremb., 22.1.1481. Pts. 1 & 2. Lge. fo. Rubricated, slightly soiled, 1st. & last ll. stained. Cont. blind-stpd. wood-bkd. bds., wormed, defect., lacks ties. [Hain 10369; BMC II 419] (HK. Nov.18-21; 243) DM 2,400
– **Postilla Super Totam Biblia.** Ed.:– [Johannes Andreae, Bp. of Aleria]. Rome, Conradus Sweynheym & Arnoldus Pannartz, Nov.18, 1471-Mar.13, 1472. 1st. Edn. 5 vols. Fo. Capital spaces, spaces for ills. in vols. 1 & 3, illuminated three-qtr. borders on 1st. text ll. of each vol. incorporating 7-line initials in gold, the design bordered in gold with sprays extending into fore-margin, wreath for coat-of-arms in lr. margin, capital initials supplied in red & blue, ink diagram of the mosaic tablets supplied in space at fo. 131r in vol. 1, MS. headlines, foliation & some notes thro.-out, all these decorations & additions by cont. hands, lacks single final blank lf. in vols. 1 & 2, & 2 1st. & 2 last blank ll. in vol. 4, slight worming affecting 1st. few & last few ll. only of each vol., causing loss of 1 letter to final lf. of vol. 2, sm. tear to upr. portion of fo. 63 in vol. 2, with 5 lines & 5 words partly defect., sm. hole in 1st. lf. of vol. 5 affecting 2 letters, some ll. slightly discold., blank portions of last lf. torn-away. 18th. C. vell., sm. portions of spines of vols. 1 & 2 brkn., head & foot of spines of vols. 2 & 3 reprd., s.-c.'s. Bkplts. of James Edwin Millard, Canon of Winchester & the General Theological Seminary Liby. [BMC IV, 14, Goff N131, HC 10363] (CNY. Oct.1; 51) $48,000
– **Postilla super Totam Bibliam [with Exposition of Paulus Bergensis & Corrections of Matthias Doerling].** Nuremb., Anton Koberger, Jan.22, 1481. 2 vols. Fo. Spaces for capital letters, vol. I with 20-line capital H illuminated in red, blue & gold on a ground of green foliage incorporating a figure & 2 animals, lr. & outer margins with elab. stylized foliage in red, green, yellow & blue, 1st. p. of vol. II with sm. capital in red & blue with marginal penwork ornamentation, some capitals supplied in red & blue, with flourishes, others in red or blue alternately, underlines, paragraph marks & initial strokes added thro.-out in red, all 35 woodcuts cold. by cont. hand, lacks preliminary blank in vol. I & final blanks in both vols., some ll.

NICOLAUS de Lyra -contd.
at beginning & end of both vols. on guards, fo. 1 in vol. I with damp-stain to upr. margin causing running of rubrication, light dampstain to lr. inner margins of some early ll., fo. 101v in vol. I with old stain from rubricator's ink, slight worming to extreme lr. margins of 1 quire, fo. 2 of vol. I with sm. repair to fore-edge margin, fo. 497 with 2 extensive tears to text, reprd. without loss, monastic inscr. on 1st. p. of each vol. Maroon lev. mor. over wood bds., cover with blind-tooled panels, gt.-lettered spines, partly unc., mor.-tipped s.-c.'s, by Gerhard Gerlach. Bkplt. of the General Theological Seminary Liby. [BMC II, 419, Goff N135, HC 10369*] (CNY. Oct.1; 35) $14,000

NICOLAY, John George & Hay, John
- Abraham Lincoln. N.Y., 1890. 10 vols. Crushed red three-qtr. lev. (SG. Sep.4; 354) $130

NICOLAY, Nicolas de
- Les Navigations Peregrinations et Voyages, Faicts en la Turquie. Antw., 1576. Sm. 4to. 19th. C. panel. cf., worn, upr. jnt. split. (S. Nov.24; 220)   *Jonge.* £250
-- Anr. Copy. Mod. vell. (LM. Jun.13; 208)   B.Frs. 20,000
-- Anr. Edn. Antw., 1577. 4to. Title soiled, trimmed & preserved, a2 remargined, occasional worming & other minor defects reprd., a few headlines cropped, occasional light soiling. 19th. C. mor. gt., slightly worn. (SPB. Nov.25; 59) $550

NICOLE PERGAMINUS
[-] Gesta Romanorum cum Applicationibus Moralitatis ac Misticas. N.p., ca. 1511. 16mo. Vell. with bands, by Gruel, double gt. fillet around covers, smooth decor. spine. (HD. Feb.27; 46)   Frs. 1,000

NICOLL, Allardyce
- Shakespeare Survey. Camb., 1948-62. 15 vols. 4to. Orig. cl., minor defects. (SPB. Jul.28; 422) $150

NICOLL, Michael John
- Birds of Egypt. Ed.:- Richard Meinertzhagen. 1930. 2 vols. Lge. 4to. Orig. cl. gt. (C. May 20; 224)   *Hill.* £220
-- Anr. Copy. Orig. cl. (C. Mar.18; 73)   *Schierenberg.* £180
-- Anr. Copy. Orig. cl. gt., inner hinges reprd. with tape. (TA. Sep.18; 90)   £120
-- Anr. Copy. Orig. cl. (CB. Sep.24; 36)   Can. $350

NICOLS, Thomas
- A Lapidary: or, the History of Pretious Stones. Camb., 1652. 1st. Edn. 4to. Lacks A1, T3 defect. & reprd. with some loss of text, minor flaw in V3, title soiled, slight staining. Cont. panel. cf., rebkd. From Honeyman Collection. [Wing N1145] (S. Nov.10; 2339)   *Norman.* £300
-- Anr. Copy. Sig. on recto of 1st. lf. (blank), a little slight browning, sm. hole in 2A3, just affecting text. Early 20th. C. mor., gt. [Wing N1145] (S. Jun.29; 414)   *Lyon.* £260

NICOLSON, Benedict
- Joseph Wright of Derby. 1968. 2 vols. 4to. Orig. cl., d.-w.'s. (CSK. Feb.20; 112)   £55

NICOLSON, J.E.
- Erskine's Institutes. Edinb., 1871. 2 vols. Hf. cf. (CE. Aug.28; 52)   £50

NICOLSON, Joseph & Burn, Richard
- History & Antiquities of Westmorland & Cumberland. 1777. 2 vols. 4to. Cf. gt. (P. Nov.13; 115)   *Steedman.* £60

NICOLSON, William
- The English, Scotch & Irish Historical Libraries. 1776. New Edn. 4to. Cont. cf., scuffed. (PD. May 20; 203)   £50

NICOMACHUS, of Gerasa-Anon.-EUCLID
- Arithmeticae libri duo.- Theologoumena [Greek].- Elementa quaedam Arithmetica. Paris, 1538; 1543; 1554. 1st. Edn. in Greek (1st work). 3 works in 1 vol. 4to. Owner's inscr. on 1st. title, slight staining. 17th. C. cf., gt., rebkd. & restored preserving most of orig. spine, monog. DCM in 5 compartments. From Honeyman Collection. (S. Nov.10; 2340)   *Quaritch.* £400

NICOT, Jean
- Thresor de la Langue Francoyse . . . Paris, 1606. 5 pts. in 1 vol. Fo. Cont. red mor., double fillet border, crowned cipher of Charles II, repeated on

spine, s.-c., jnts. crudely reprd. British Museum stp. (HD. Mar.18; 122)   Frs. 4,000

NIDEK, Mathhaeus Brouerius van
See-BROUERIUS van Nidek, Matthaeus

NIDER, Johann
- De Lepra Morali. 6 Jun. 1511. Slight dampstaining, later inscr. on title, corner torn from i4 without loss of text, lacks last lf. (?) (blank?). 19th. C. red mor.-bkd. marb. bds., spine gt. From liby. of André L. Simon. (S. May 18; 143)   *Goldschmidt.* £60
- Praeceptorium Legis, sive Expositio Decalogi. Ulm, Johann Zainer, [not after 1480]. Fo. Spaces for initial capitals, supplied in red, as are paragraph marks, initial strokes & underlines, lacks 1st. & final blanks, 1st. lf. slightly soiled, light worming at beginning & end, 1 sm. wormhole affecting 1st. 100 ll., scattered light marginal dampstains, monastic inscrs. at fly-lf. & p. 1. Old vell., spine torn. From the collection of Eric Sexton. [BMC II, 527, Goff N205, H 11785*] (CNY. Apr.8; 178) $2,000
- Sermones Aurei de tempore et de sanctis. Ulm, Johann Zainer, [not after 1480]. Fo. Rubricated thro.-out, some initials in green, wormed at beginning & rather less at end, affecting text. Cont. North Austrian blind-stpd. cf. over wooden bds., upr. cover wormed, spine cracked & chipped, metal cornerpieces & 1 clasp-holder remaining. [HC 11802*; BMC II p. 529; Goff N 216] (C. Apr.1; 64)   *Albert.* £620
[-] Die Vierunzwinsig Gulden Harpffen. [Wessobrunn], [1505]. Fo. 1st. 3 ll. heavily soiled & wormed, margins strengthened, sm. margin defects bkd., old MS owner's mark on title, last lf. with slight text loss through worming, slight soiling in parts. Mid 19th. C. hf.-leath., by J.H. Mohr. (HK. May 1274; 153)   DM 580
See-GERSON, Johannes or Nider, Johannes, Attrib. to

NIEBUHR, Barthold Georg
- The Greek Heroes. Ill.:- Arthur Rackham. L., 1903. 1st. Edn. Sm. 4to. Cold. pict. limp cl., worn. Raymond M. Sutton, Jr., copy. (SG. May 7; 221) $220

NIEBUHR, Carsten
- Beschreibung von Arabien. Copen., 1772. [1st. Edn.?]. 4to. 19th. C. hf. leath., spine reprd. (R. Oct.14-18; 1742)   DM 1,400
-- Anr. Edn. Copen., 1772. 1st. Edn. Some text ll. slightly soiled, 2 copper engrs. with sm. tears bkd., some late pencil notes. Cont. cf., very worn, spine torn. (H. Dec.9/10; 532)   DM 1,050
- Description de l'Arabie. 1773. [1st. Edn.?] 4to. Cf. gt. (P. Oct.23; 54)   *Hosain.* £320
-- Anr. Copy. 4 maps with hand-cold. ornams., 1 map loose, ll. partly detchd. from bdg. 19th. C. hf. mor. From Chetham's Liby., Manchester. (C. Nov.27; 310)   *Minerva.* £180
-- Anr. Edn. Amst. & Utrecht, 1774. 2 pts. in 1 vol. 4to. A few ll. slightly soiled, (?) lacks 1st. blank. Cont. bds., unc. (S. Nov.4; 644)   *Quaritch.* £160
-- Anr. Copy. Later hf. cf. (SH. May 21; 220)   *Argyll Etkin.* £95
- Travels through Arabia & other Countries in the East. Trans.:- Robert Heron. Edinb., 1792. 1st. Edn. in Engl. 2 vols. Hf.-titles slightly dust-soiled. 19th. C. hf. mor. From Chetham's Liby., Manchester. (C. Nov.27; 311)   *Taylor.* £150

NIEBUHR, Carsten-MIECHAELIS, Monsieur
- Description de l'Arabie.-Recueil de Questions . . . sa Majesté danoise font le Voyage de l'Arabie. 1774; 1774. 2 works in 1 vol. 4to. Cont. tree cf. gt. (TA. Feb.19; 32)   £210

NIEL, P.G.J.
- Portraits des Personnages Français les plus Illustres du XVIe Siècle. Paris, 1848-56. 1st. Edn. 2 vols. Lge. fo. Cont. cl.-bkd. dyed bds., corners of 1 vol. worn. (PNY. May 21; 300) $150

NIELSEN, Kay
See-ASBJØRNSEN, Peter Christen & Moe, Jorgen I.

NIEMTSCHEK, F.
- Leben des K.K. Kapellmeisters Wolfgang Gottlieb Mozart.-Traurede dem Andenken Mozarts geweiht Academie der Jur. Prag; n.p., 1798; 7 Feb. 1794. 1st. Edn. of 1st. work. 2 works in 1 vol. 4to. Slightly browned, name & monog. stp. on title. Cont. bds. (R. Oct.14-18; 1300)   DM 1,050

NIEREMBERG, Johannes Eusebius
- Historia Naturae, maxime Peregrinae, libris XVI distincta. Antw., 1635. 1st. Edn. Fo. Browned thro.-out, a few dampstains & sm. holes affecting text. Mott. hf. cf. From liby. of Dr. E. Ashworth Underwood. (S. Feb.23; 265)   *Vanhee.* £120

NIERSZESOVICZ, Deodatus
[-] Dictionarium Latino-Armenum. Rome, 1695. 4to. A few ll. loose, some browning & marginal stains. Cont. hf. cf., worn. (S. Apr.29; 441)   *Maggs.* £200

NIETZSCHE, Frederic Wilhelm
- The Antichrist. Trans.:- P.R. Stephensen. Ill.:- Norman Lindsay. Fanfrolico Pr.; 1928. (550) numbered. Fo. Orig. hf. mor., partly untrimmed. (TA. Nov.20; 117)   £100
-- Anr. Copy. (SH. Mar.26; 329)   *Ayres.* £85
-- Anr. Edn. Trans.:- P.R. Stephensen. Ill.:- Norman Lindsay. L., Fanfrolico Pr., ca. 1928. (550) numbered. Fo. Slight offsetting. Orig. hf. mor. (KH. Nov.18; 456)   Aus. $230
-- Anr. Edn. Trans.:- P.R. Stephensen. Ill.:- Norman Lindsay. Franfrolico Pr., n.d. (550) on Arnold's H.M.P. Fo. An out of series copy. Orig. hf. mor. gt., partly unc. (LC. Jun.18; 36)   £52
- Ecce Homo. Ill.:- Henry van de Velde. Leipzig, [1908]. (150) on Japon. 4to. Orig. cf., ex-liby. (HK. Nov.18-21; 2988)   DM 2,200
- Gesammette Werke. Munich, [1922-29]. Musarion Edn. Orig. hf. leath. W.a.f. (HK. May 15; 4710)   DM 1,700

NIEUHOFF, Jan
- L'Ambassade de la Compagnie Orientale des Provinces Unies vers L'Empereur de la Chine. Leiden, 1665. 2 pts. in 1 vol. Fo. Cont. vell., gt., stains to lr. cover, upr. edge slightly worn. (C. Feb.25; 121)   *Maggs.* £550
-- Anr. Copy. 26 engraved plts. (of 35), stained. Cont. cf., worn. (SH. Jun.4; 197)   *Pigeonhole.* £210
- An Embassy from the East-India Company . . . Trans.:- John Ogilby. L., 1669. 1st. Edn. in Engl. Fo. Lacks nearly all the plts., folding map reprd., ex liby. Later hf. leath., worn. (SG. Oct.30; 267) $220
-- Anr. Edn. 1673. 2nd. Edn. in Engl. Fo. A few ll. stained. Old cf. gt., brkn., spine defect. (BS. Jun.11; 175)   £240
- Gedenkweerdige Brasilaense Zee- en Lant-Reize . . . Neerlants Brasil.-Zee en Lant-Reize door Verscheide Gewesten van Oostindien . . . Batavia. Amst., 1682. 1st. Edn. Fo. Cont. vell. [Sabin 55278] (R. Oct.14-18; 1652)   DM 5,600
- Het Gezandschap der Neerlandtsche Oost-Indische Compagne aan den Grooten Tartarushchen Cham, den . . . Keizer van China. Antw., 1666. Fo. Additional engraved title-p. mntd., lf. with instructions to the binder at end, a few tears, some slightly affecting text, slightly spotted or soiled in places. Cont. cf., spine slightly worn. (S. Oct.21; 454)   *Quaritch.* £460
-- Anr. Edn. Amst., 1693. 3rd. Dutch Edn. Fo. Cont. blind-stpd. vell., spine defect. at head & foot. (R. Oct.14-18; 1755)   DM 2,500
- Voyages & Travels into Brasil & the East Indies, Translated from the Dutch Original. 1703. Fo. Cf., rebkd. W.a.f. (S. Dec.2; 568)   *Sawyer.* £120

NIEUWELANDT, Willem van
- Variae Antiquitates Romanae. Amst., 1618. Sm. ob. 4to. Old hf. cf. (CNY. May 22; 231) $300

NIEUWENHUIS, A.W.
- Quer durch Borneo. Ergebnisse seiner Reisen in den Jahren 1894, 1896-97 & 1898-1900. Leiden, 1904-07. 2 vols. Decor. cl. (VG. Dec.16; 886)   Fls. 440

NIGHT-FLYERS (The), series of Moth Pictures
N.d. 4to. Orig. bds. (P. Apr.30; 220)   *De Ste Croix.* £90
-- Anr. Copy. Some plts. loose. Lacquered bds. gt., defect. (P. Jul.2; 37)   *Dillon.* £65

NIGHTINGALE, Florence
- Introductory Notes on Lying-in Institutions. 1871. 1st. Edn. Advt. lf. at end, 8 pp. advts. dtd. Mar. 1871 inserted at end. Orig. cl. (S. Apr.6; 118)   *Studd.* £50

NIGRUS, A.
See-MELANCHTHON, Philip-NIGRUS, A. -CAMERARIUS, J.-CONFESSIO Doctrinae Saxonicarum Ecclesiarum. . . .

NIHELL, Elizabeth
- A Treatise on the Art of Midwifery. 1760. 1st. Edn. Lacks blank end-papers. Cont. cf. (BS. Sep.17; 45) £80

NILSSON, Sven
- Illuminerade Figur til Skandinavisk Fauna. Stockholm, 1831. 4to. 95 cold. litho. plts. only, some lightly browned or stained, 4 with sm. repairs to corners. Late 19th. C. hf. leath., upr. cover of orig. wraps. bnd. in. (HK. Nov.18-21; 813) DM 1,300

NIMMO, R.H., Publisher
- Noxiana.-Wretch's Illustrations of Shakespeare. Edinb., [1829]. 2 series in 1 vol. Fo. Each work with 6 plts., many stains & c. Loosely sewed together. (SG. Nov.20; 384) $175

NIMMO, Rev. William
- History of Stirlingshire. Ed.:– William MacGregor. 1817. 2 vols. Cf. gt. (CE. Jul.9; 127) £90

NIMROD
See-APPERLEY, Capt. Charles James 'Nimrod'

NIN, Anais
- D.H. Lawrence: An Unprofessional Study. Paris, Black Manikin Pr., 1932. (50) reserved for the Press. Cl., d.-w. (SG. Jun.4; 392) $140
- House of Incest. Paris, 1936. 1st. Edn., (249). Fo. Slight browning. Orig. ptd. wraps., slight soiling. Pres. copy. (SPB. Nov.25; 367) $325
- The Hunger. Ill.:– Ian Hugo. N.Y., 1945. 1st. Edn., (50) sigd. Some offsetting. Orig. ptd. bds., spine & upr. portion of cover faded. Pres. Copy, to C.L. Baldwin. (SPB. May 29; 321) $375

NIPHUS, Augustinus, Suessanus
- In Librum Destructio Destructionum Aurerroys Commentationes. [Venice], [Bonetus Locatellus for Octavianus Scotus], [1497?]. Fo. A few wormholes at beginning, blank corners in 1st. 2 sigs. reprd., staining in blank corners. 18th. C. vell.-bkd. bds. (C. Apr.1; 65) Riley-Smith. £400

NISARD, Charles
- Histoire des Livres Populaires ou de la Litterature du Colportage Depuis le XVe Siècle. Paris, 1854. 1st. Edn. 2 vols. Cont. hf. mor. (S. Jul.27; 167) Duran. £80
- – Anr. Copy. Lacks hf.-titles. Late 19th. C. red lev. mor. gt. (S. Nov.24; 221) Forster. £75

NISARD, D.
- [-] Promenades d'un Artiste. Paris, ca. 1850. 2 vols. Orig. elab. gt. bds., vol. 1 in orig. gt. bd. s.-c. (VG. Nov.18; 948) Fls. 1,000

NISBET, Alexander
- Systems of Heraldry. 1722-42. 1st. Edn. 2 vols. Fo. Panel. cf. gt. (CE. Nov.20; 95) £160
- – Anr. Edn. Edinb., 1804. 2nd. Edn. 2 vols. Fo. 2 plts. inlaid, plt. 4 vol. 1 bnd. in vol. 2, no hf.-titles. Mott. cf. gt., by F. Bedford. (S. Nov.24; 222) Traylen. £70

NISBET, John
- Our Forests & Woodlands. Ill.:– Arthur Rackham. L., 1900. 1st. Edn. Deluxe, (150) numbered, on H.M.P. Haddon Hall Liby. series. Gt.-pict. vell., unc. & unopened. Raymond M. Sutton, Jr. copy, extra mntd. proof copy of plt. laid in. (SG. May 7; 223) $130

NISSEN, G.N. v.
- Biogr. W.A. Mozart's. Ed.:– Dr. Feuerstein (preface). Leipzig, 1828. 1st. Edn. Probably lacks 1 lf. of supp., lightly soiled in a few places, 9 folding supps. Cont. hf. leath. (HK. Nov.18-21; 1871) DM 1,000

NISSER, Pedro
- Sketch of the Different Mining & Mechanical Operations employed in some of the South American Goldworks as well ancient as modern . . . particularly those of the province of Antioquia in New Granada. Stockholm, 1834. Orig. ptd. wrap. Pres. inscr. to A.E. Ihre. (S. Oct.20; 170) Bjorck & Borjesson. £200

NITZSCHEWITZ, Hermannus
- Novum Psalterium Beatae Virginis Mariae. Zinna, Pr. of the Cistercian Monastery [Conrad Kachelofen?], [between 1493 & 1496]. 4to. Spaces for capital initials, some with guide letters, floral woodcut border, some fore-edges or upr. margins with short tears, just touching borders in some cases, some reprd., sm. stain touching woodcuts on D1-4, B1 rehinged, some ll. slightly

soiled or browned, corners slightly dampstained. Cont. Italian blind-stpd. mor. over wood bds., a remboitage, covers with lge. panel of knotwork lozenges in border of repeated rectangular flower tool, smaller flower tool repeated as outer border, brass clasps with the leath. renewed, rebkd., spine with slight restorations. The copy of Mrs. A.A. McFall, lately in the collection of Eric Sexton. [BMC III, 700, Goff N260, H 11891*] (CNY. Apr.8; 209) $40,000

NIVELON, F.
- The Rudiments of Genteel Behavior. Ill.:– L.P. Boitard after B. Dandridge. [L.], 1737. 1st. Edn. 4to. Cont. mott. cf., gt., worn. (S. Nov.24; 223) Marlborough. £160

NIXON, Anthony
- A True Relation of the Trauels of M. Bush, a Gentleman: who . . . made a Pynace, in which hee past by Ayre, Land, & Water. 1608. Sm. 4to. A2 soiled, padded with blanks. Later cf., worn, upr. cover detchd. [NSTC 18325] (S. Jun.23; 370) Quaritch. £580

NIXON, Howard M.
- Broxbourne Library Styles & Designs of Bookbindings from 12th-20th Century. Ed.:– Albert Ehrman. 1956. (500). 4to. Qtr. parch. (P. Jan.22; 312) Foster. £460

NIZAMI
- Poems. Ed.:– L. Binyon. L., 1928. Fo. Linen, d.-w. (SG. Dec.4; 260) $160

NOAH OF KAROW
- Kav Chen. [Warsaw-Breslau], 1866. 1st. Edn. 4to. Cl. (S. Nov.18; 315) Maggs. £95

NOAILLES, Comtesse de
- Les Climats. Ill.:– F.L. Schmied. Paris, 1924. (125), this an 'exemplaire de 'mise en page' ', sigd. by artist. 4to. Orig. wraps. with design on upr. cover ptd. in gold, folder & s.-c. Loosely inserted are 2 A.L.s's from Schmied & L. Carteret & M.S. of 1 of the poems sigd. 'Ctesse. de Noailles'. (SH. Nov.21; 471) Scopazzi. £660

NOBBES, Robert
- The Compleat Troller. 1682. 1st. Edn. Spr. cf. gt. by Rivière. From the collection of Eric Sexton. [Wing N1193] (C. Apr.15; 125) Tryon. £380
- [-] – Anr. Edn. L., ca. 1790. Facs. Reprint of 1682 Edn. 18mo. 18th. C. hf. cf. & marb. bds. (SG. Oct.16; 249) $160

NOBILIAIRE DE CHAMPAGNE- Généalogies produites pardevant Mgr D E Caumartin N.d. 474 ll. Old cf., 6 spine raised bands, double blind border, gt. angle fleurons, worn. (LM. Nov.8; 259) B.Frs. 36,000

NOBLE, Thomas
- Blackheath. a Poem . . . and various other Poems. 1808. 4to. Occasional slight spotting. Cont. diced cf. (CSK. Aug.1; 176) £55
- Practical Perspective, Exemplified on Landscapes. Ill.:– John Clark. 1805. 4to. Cont. hf. cf. with old reback, partly untrimmed. (TA. Nov.20; 133) £95

NOBLE, Thomas & Rose, Thomas
- The Counties of Chester, Derby, Leicester, Lincoln & Rutland Illustrated. 1836. 4to. Some plts. spotted. Cont. hf. mor., very worn. (SBA. May 27; 331) Kidd. £88
- – Anr. Edn. Ill.:– Thomas Allom. [1836]. 4to. 70 plts. on 35 ll. only. Hf. cf. gt. (P. Jan.22; 89) Kidd. £100
- – Anr. Edn. 1837. 4to. Some minor defects. Orig. cl., spine torn. (SBA. May 27; 330) Kidd. £90
- Counties of Chester, Derby, Nottingham . . . Illustrated. Ill.:– Thomas Allom. 1836. 4to. Slight spotting. Cl., slightly soiled. (SBA. Oct.22; 286) Nicholson. £120
See-ROSE, Thomas–NOBLE, Thomas & Rose, Thomas

NOBLE, W.B.
- A Guide to the Watering Places . . . between the Exe & the Dart. Ill.:– J. Shury & D. Havell. Teignmouth, 1823. 4 pts. in 1 vol. Title of dedication becoming detchd., the lf. 'Conchology' torn. Later hf. mor., preserving orig. spine. From the collection of Eric Sexton. (C. Apr.16; 318) Hammond. £350

NOCH' [Night]
Ed.:– [Yu. V. Gol'dberg]. St. Petersb., 1906. No. 1. 4to. Unbnd. (SH. Feb.5; 99) Quaritch. £50

NOCQ, Henry
- Poinçon de Paris. Paris, 1968. (400) numbered. 5 vols. 4to. Orig. cl. (SH. Jul.23; 296) Zwemmer. £230

NOCQ, Henry & Dreyfus, Carle
- Tabatières Boites et Etuis . . . des collections du Musée du Louvre. Paris, 1930. 4to. Hf. mor. (CSK. Jan.30; 59) £70
- – Anr. Copy. Sewed, wrap. (HD. Dec.5; 159) Frs. 1,400

NODDER, Frederick P.
See-SHAW, George & Nodder, Frederick P.

NODIER, Charles
- Contes. Ill.:– Tony Johannot (etchings). Paris, 1846. 1st. printing of etchings, on China. Red hf. mor. by Mercier, corners, spine decor. with raised bands, unc., wrap. (HD. Jun.25; 359) Frs. 3,900
- – Anr. Edn. Ill.:– Tony Johannot. Paris, [1852]. Plts. on chine collé. Very foxed. Publishers cl. bds., tooled in gt. & colours. (HD. Apr.9; 605) Frs. 1,100

NOE, Comte Amedée 'Cham'
- L'Art de Engraisser et de Maigrer à Volonté. N.d. Lge. 4to. Buckram. (HD. Jun.24; 164) Frs. 1,750
- Mémoires relatifs a l'Expédition Anglaise. 1826. Slight spotting to text. Disbnd. (P. Apr.9; 92) Kubicele. £70
- – Anr. Copy. Recently rebnd. in hf. mor. (TA. Mar.19; 231) £50
- Series of Lithograph Caricatures by 'Cham'. [Paris], 1868. 4to. Loosely inserted in folder. (SH. Apr.9; 308) Charles. £55
- Tribulations des Bains de Mer d'Ostende. Bruges, ca. 1860. Fo. Orig. embossed cl. (S. Mar.17; 252) Degheldere. £80

NOEHDEN, George Henry
- Specimens of Ancient Coins, of Magna Graecia & Sicily . . . Ill.:– Henry Moses after Del Frate. 1826. 1st. Edn. Fo. Inscr. on front fly-lf. 19th. C. hf. mor., spine gt., partly unc. (S. Sep.29; 217) C.B. Rare Books. £80

NOGARET, François-Félix
- Le Fond du Sac. Ill.:– Durand. Venice, 1780. 2 vols. 18mo. Red mor. by Cazin. (HD. Apr.8; 282) Frs. 2,300

NOGUCHI, Yone
- Hiroshige. 1934. 4to. Orig. wraps., cl. folder. (SH. Jan.29; 132) Walford. £65
- The Ukiyoye Primitives. 1933. Ltd. Edn. sigd. by author. 4to. Orig. wraps, cl. folder. (SH. Dec.29; 131) Ars Artis. £60
- The Ukiyoye Primitives.-Hiroshige. Tokyo; L., 1933; 1934. Ltd. Edns. 2 works in 2 vols. 4to. Slight stain to title-p. of 1st. work. Both pict. laced wraps., cl. folding cases with ivory clasps. (SG. Mar.12; 275) $270

NOGUES, J.
- Manuel du Jeune Marin. Paris, 1814. 12mo. Long-grd. mor., gt. & blind decor. border, inner border, watered silk doubls. & end-ll, gt. dentelle, sigd. by Doll. Dedication. (HD. Jun.10; 190) Frs. 6,000

NOLAN, Dr. E.H.
- The History of the British Empire in India & the East. L., 1855-57. 8 vols. Orig. cl. stpd. in blind & gt. (SG. Oct.30; 268) $120
- The Illustrated History of the War against Russia. L., [1857]. 2 vols. in 8. Orig. linen. (R. Oct.14-18; 1840) DM 420

NOLHAC, Pierre de
- Dauphine Marie-Antoinette. Paris, 1896. On Marais vell. 4to. Red mor. by Durvand, Louvre dentelle around covers, arms of Marie Antoinette, spine decor. with raised bands, inside dentelle, wrap. & spine preserved. (HD. Feb.27; 192) Frs. 2,000
- Les Femmes de Versailles. Paris, ca. 1890. (100). Lge. fo. Hf. mor. gt. Viscount Cowdray's bkplt. (P. Jul.2; 4) Elliot.
- François Boucher . . . Paris, 1907. On Rives paper. 4to. Mor. by Durvand, lge. gt. dentelle around covers, spines decor. with raised bands, inside dentelle, wrap. & spine preserved. (HD. Feb.27; 195) Frs. 2,600
- Madame Vigée-Le Brun, Peintre de la Reine Marie-Antoinette 1755-1842. Paris, 1908. (500) on Rives, numbered. 4to. Some spotting. Mor., decor. spine, rococo border on covers, wrap. preserved. (SM. Feb.11; 270) Frs. 1,000

NOLHAC, Pierre de -*contd.*
- La Reine Marie-Antoinette. Paris, 1890. 1st. Edn. 4to. Chagrin by Durvand Thivet, spine decor. with fleurs-de-lys, 3 fillets, fleurs-de-lys in angles, arms in centre, inside dentelle. (HD. Dec.5; 160) *Frs.* 1,700

NOLLET, Abbé Jean Antoine
- L'Art des Experiences ou Avis aux Amateurs de la Physique, sur le Choix, la Construction et l'usage de Instruments. Paris, 1770. 3 vols. 12mo. New qtr. mor., orig. marb. paper wraps. bnd. in, unc. (S. Dec.1; 298) *Westwood.* £75
- Ensayo sobre la Electricidad de los Cuerpos ... Trans.:- D. Joseph Vazques y Morales. Madrid, 1747. 1st. Spanish Edn. 4to. Marginal stains. Cont. limp vell., remnants of ties.´ From Honeyman Collection. (S. Nov.10; 2344) *Hill.* £80
- Leçons de Physique.-L'Art des Expériences ... de la Physique.-Léttres sur l'Electricité, & Essai sur l'Electricité.-Recherches sur les Causes ... des Phénomènes électriques. Paris, 1775; 1770; 1776/7 & 1771; 1754. 1st. work: 6 vols., 8th. Edn.; 2nd. work: 3 vols., 2nd. Edn.; 3rd. work: 3 pts., together 2 vols.; 4th. work: 1 vol. Cont. marb. cf., a few slightly worn, spine gt. (S. Oct.21; 412) *J. Booth.* £280
- Leçons de Physique expérimentale. Paris, 1771-1777. 12mo. With all instruction ll. to binder, a few ll. slightly spotted. Cont. hf. cf. (S. Feb.23; 83) *Kurzer.* £85
- Lettres sur L'Electricité. Paris, 1764. 2 vols. in 1. Cont. cf. gt. (P. Sep.11; 189) *Henderson.* £70
- Lezioni di Fisica Esperimentale. Venice, 1762-72. 6 vols. 2 plts. in vol. V with dark ink stain, scattered light foxing. Orig. paper bds., unc. From the collection of John A. Saks. (C. Jun.10; 170) *Schio.* £120

NONESUCH Press
Nonesuch Century: an Appraisal, a Personal Note & a Bibliography of the First Hundred Books Issued by the Press, 1923-34. Nones. Pr., 1936. (750) numbered. Fo. A few MS. markings & addenda to bibliography. Orig. buckram, d.-w., worn & reprd. (S. Jul.31; 118) *Monk Bretton-* £200
- - Anr. Copy. (SPB. Nov.25; 377) $425

NONNUS, Ludovicus
- Commentarius in Huberti Goltzi Greciam, Insulas, et Asiam Minorem. Antw., 1644. Fo. Old cf., slightly worn. (SKC. May 19; 219) £120

NOORDKERK, H.
[-] Handvesten; ofte Privilegien ende Octroyen; mitsgaders Willekeuren, Costumien, Ordonnantien en Handelingen der Stad Amsterdam. Amst., 1748. 1st. Edn. 4 vols., 6 pts. & index bnd. in 3 vols. Cont. hf. leath., spine defect. (R. Oct.14-18; 1385) DM 1,000

NOORDUNG, Hermann (Pseud.)
See-POTOCNIC, H.

NORDEN, John
- Speculum Britaniae: An Historical & Chorographical Description of Middlesex & Hertfordshire. 1723. 2 pts. in 1 vol. 4to. Cont. cf., gt. spine. (SH. Oct.10; 312) *Franks.* £320
- - Anr. Copy. 2 engd. titles. engd. arms on dedication verso, 4 folding maps. Cont. cf. (C. May 20; 158) *Maggs.* £240
- Speculum Britanniae.-Speculi Britanniae Pars. 1593; 1598. 1st. Edns. 2 works in 1 vol. Sm. 4to. 1st. work: folding maps bkd. with linen, imprint faint in parts, some slight spotting; 2nd. work: frontis. map bkd. with linen, title short at lr. & outer edges, reprd. just affecting plt., frontis. map slightly spotted. 19th. C. panel. cf. gt., rebkd. preserving orig. spine. From the collection of Eric Sexton. [STC 18635 & 18637] (C. Apr.15; 185) *Crowe.* £600
- The Surveyors Dialogue ... Very Profitable for all men to peruse, that have to do with the revenues of Land. 1607. 1st. Edn. 4to. Lacks blanks A1 & R7-8, lge. hole in Q8 with some text loss, title browned & guarded at inner edge, sig. of Jonathan Maine on A3 recto. Mod. qtr. mor. From Honeyman Collection. [NSTC 18639] (S. Nov.10; 2346) *Maggs.* £500
- - Anr. Copy. Lacks lf. A1 (?privilege). Later hf. cf. (SG. Sep.18; 276) $210

NORDISK NUMISMATISK ARSSKRIFT
Copen., 1936-77. 38 vols. Orig. wraps. & cl. (SH. Mar.6; 414) *Spink.* £310

NORFOLK
- Excursions in the County of Norfolk ... 1818. 2 vols. 12mo. Some slight browning. Cont. hf. cf. Bkplt. of Horatio Austen Smith. (S. May 5; 220) *Quaritch.* £55
- - Anr. Edn. 1818-19. 2 vols. Diced cf. gt. (P. Oct.23; 315) *Hollingsworth.* £120

NORIE, John William
- Directions for Sailing to & From the Coast of Brazil ... L., 1819-25. 3 pts. in 1 vol. Some foxing. Cl. (SSA. Jan.22; 314) R. 200

NORMAN, Don Cleveland
- The 500th Anniversary Pictorial Census of the Gutenberg Bible. Chic., Coverdale Pr., 1961. (985) sigd. by author. Fo. Orig. cl., publisher's box. The John A. Saks copy. (CNY. Oct.1; 199) $220

NORMAN, John
[-] The Town & Country Builder's Assistant ... by a lover of Architect[ure]. Boston, Priv. Ptd., [15 Mar. 1786]. 1st. Edn. Fo. Browning & offsetting. Cont. sheep, worn, upr. cover detchd. (CNY. Oct.1; 20) $2,000

NORMAN, Robert
- The Newe Attractive, contayning a Short Discourse of the Magnes or Lodestone (A Discourse of the Variation of the Cumpas, or Magneticall Needle ... by W. B[orough]). 1581. 1st. Edn. 2 pts. in 1 vol. 4to. Pt. 1 lacks F2-G4 (F2-4 & G4 in photo-facs.), pt. 2 lacks F2-3 & G2 (also in facs.), 1st. title soiled & reprd. at corners slightly affecting border, slight soiling & discolouration. 19th. C. vell., covers warped. From Honeyman Collection, w.a.f. [NSTC 18647] (S. Nov.10; 2347) *Zeitlin.* £1,100

NORMAND, Charles
- Recueil varié de Plans et de Façades. Motifs pour des Maisons de Ville et de Campagne. Paris, 1815. Fo. Cont. bds., defect. spine, unc. (C. Nov.6; 189) *Lyon.* £300

NORMYX
See-DOUGLAS, George Norman 'Normyx'

NORONHA, Freyre Joao (Gio. Gioseppe di S. Teresa, Carmelite)
- Istoria delle Guerre del Regno del Brasilie ... Rome, 1700. 2 vols. in 1. Slight worming in upr. margin, bnd. at front is MS. transcription(?) of E. Stertgenius'(?) 'Brevis succincta ac vera Narratio Expeditionis ... in Brasiliam.'. 19th. C. hf. mor. From Chetham's Liby., Manchester. (C. Nov.27; 312) *Tzakas.* £2,000

NORONHA, Thomas de
- Sermão, que peloz feliz reconhecimento da Indepencia do Imperio do Brasil, na Solemnidade d'Accao' de Graças, celebrada pelo Senado da Camara D'Olinda na Igreja Cathedral. Pernambuco, 1825. Sm. 4to. Mod. cf. (SPB. May 5; 366) $225

NORRIS, Charles
- An Account of Tenby. 1820. Cont. hf. cf., rebkd. preserving orig. gt. spine. From the collection of Eric Sexton. (C. Apr.16; 319) *Maggs.* £180

NORRIS, R. & others
- The African Pilot. n.d. (charts dtd. 1788-94). Tall atlas fo. 12 lge. engraved double-p. charts, some folding, many with cartouches, inset views & coastal profiles, lr. margin of 1st. chart cropped. Cont. cf.-bkd. bds. W.a.f., broadsheet catalogue of compasses, optics, etc. pasted in upr. cover. (C. Nov.6; 266) *Heywood Hill.* £1,000

NORRIS, Thaddeus
- The American Angler's Book. Phila., 1864. 1st. Edn. Gt.-decor. cl. (SG. Oct.16; 251) $150
- - Anr. Edn. Phila., 1886. Memorial Edn., Cl. (SG. Oct.16; 253) $150

NORTH, Alfred John
- Nests & Eggs of Birds found breeding in Australia & Tasmania. Sydney, 1901-14. 4 vols. in orig. 19 pts. 4to. Wraps., slightly worn. (S. Jun.1; 187) *McCormick.* £300

NORTH, Elisha
- A Treatise on a Malignant Epidemic Commonly called Spotted Fever interspersed with Remarks on the Nature of Fever in General. N.Y., 1811. 3 maps of Massachusetts pasted on fly-ll., liby. stp. etc. on title-p., slight foxing. Orig. bds., hinges reprd. Sig. of D.L. Drage 1812 on fly-lf. (S. Jun.16; 611) *Jenner Books.* £160

NORTH, Hon, Roger
[-] A Discourse of Fish & Fishponds. 1713. 1st. Edn. Mod. mor. From the collection of Eric Sexton. (C. Apr.15; 126) *Marlborough.* £150

NORTH-COUNTRY ANGLER, The, or the Art of Angling ...
L., 1786. 1st. Edn. 12mo. Hf. mor., believed by Gosden. Thomas Gosden & Dean Sage bkplts. (SG. Oct.16; 254) $850

NORTH GEORGIA GAZETTE, The
Ed.:- Edward Sabine. 1821. 4to. 19th. C. cl., unc. Pres. Copy from Capt. Parry, from Chetham's Liby., Manchester. (C. Nov.27; 313) *Maggs.* £110
See-PARRY, Sir William Edmund-NORTH Georgia Gazette

NORTHCOTE, James
- One Hundred Fables. 1828-33. 2 vols. 19th. C. hf. mor. gt. (S. Nov.25; 492) *Traylen.* £60

NORTON, John, of New England
- The Orthodox Evangelist ... 1654. 1st. Edn. Sm. 4to. Some ll. stained. Cont. sheep, 1 cover detchd., worn. [Wing N1320; Sabin 55887] (S. Jun.9; 49) *Lachman.* £50

NORWAY ILLUSTRATED
N.Y., n.d. ob. fo. Text in Engl. & Norwegian. Qtr. cf., upr. cover detchd. (P. Jan.22; 262) *Hanas.* £190

NORWOOD, Richard
- Trigonometrie. Or, the Doctrine of Triangles. 1631. 1st. Edn. 4to. Errata on (*)1v, some ll. stained, title soiled, sigs. on title & elsewhere of (Baron.) Cardross. 19th. C. cf., hf. red mor. case. From Honeyman Collection. [NSTC 18692] (S. Nov.10; 2348) *Quaritch.* £650

NORZI, Raphael
See-BECHAYEI, Joseph Ibn Paduka-NORZI, Raphael

NOSTRADAMUS, Michel de
- Les Merveilleuses Centuries et Propheties de Nostradamus. Nice, 1961. (865) on grand vell. de Docelles, filigrané. Lge. 4to. Loose ll. in wrap. & publisher's box. (LM. Nov.8; 118) B.Frs. 9,000
- Le Vrayes Centuries et Propheties de ... Cologne, 1689. 12mo. Vell. (CB. Nov.12; 167) Can. $150
- - Anr. Edn. Rouen, 1691. 12mo. Cont. vell. (HD. Jun.24; 67) *Frs.* 1,300

NOTES & QUERIES for Readers & Writers, Collectors & Librarians
1849-1974. 1st.-12th. series (each in 12 vols.), 13th. series vol. I, continued as vols. 146-217, additional unbnd. iss. of vols. 218 & 219, indexes to 1st.-10th. series, 12th. series, & 15th. general index, together 229 vols. Sm. 4to. Hf. cf., later vols. hf. mor. (lacks labels in some early vols., 3 covers detchd.), all indexes in orig. cl. As a periodical, w.a.f. From the collection of Eric Sexton. (C. Apr.15; 127) *Henderson.* £1,500

'NOTGELD' ALBUM
[München], ca. 1930. Fo. Ca. 1,200 specimens. Hf. cl. (VG. Dec.15; 509) Fls. 650

NOTMAN, William
[-] The Canadian Handbook & Tourist's Guide. Montreal, 1867. Some light offsetting on images, 1 plt. loose. Gt.-decor. cl., worn. (SG. Apr.23; 154) $120
- Portrait of a Period. Ed.:- J. Russell Harper & Stanley Triggs. Montreal, 1967. Fo. Orig. cl., d.-w. (CB. Sep.24; 258) Can. $130

NOTT, Stanley Charles
- Chinese Jade throughout the ages. L., [1936]. 1st. Edn. Cl. (SG. Dec.4; 92) $100
- Chinese Jades in the Stanley Charles Nott Collection. West Palm Beach, 1942. (1000) numbered. 4to. Cl. Sigd. inscr. by Nott & his wife. (SG. Dec.4; 93) $225

NOUVELLE BIOGRAPHIE GENERALE
Ed.:- J.C.F. Hoefer. Paris, 1853-83. 46 vols. Cont. cf.-bkd. bds. (S. Feb.23; 347) *Baker.* £280
- - Anr. Edn. Paris, 1855-83. 46 vols. in 23. Cont. cf. gt., all but last 2 with Rosebery arms in gt. on upr. covers. (SBA. Jul.23; 597) *Dawson.* £220
- - Anr. Edn. Ed.:- J.C.F. Höefer. Paris, 1857-66. 46 vols. Cl., unc., bkplt. of the Duke of Portland. (S. Oct.21; 476) *Lyon.* £260
- - Anr. Copy. 46 vols. in 23. Mod. hf. cf. W.a.f. (SH. Jul.23; 253) *Hannas.* £150

NOUVELLE BIOGRAPHIE UNIVERSELLE
Paris, 1852-70. 46 vols. in 23. Cont. cf. (SH. May 28; 76) *Booth.* £55

NOUVELLE ENCYCLOPEDIE DES ARTS ET METIERS
– Art de la Chaussure considéré dans toutes ses Parties. Paris, 1824. 1 vol. only. (as above). Some plts. cropped at outer margin, affecting borders, some foxing. Cont. bds., mor. spine, worn. (SG. Nov.20; 409) $225

NOVALIS (Pseud.)
See–HARDENBERG, Friedrich Leopold von 'Novalis'

NOVARA, Domenico Maria
– Ad Illustrissimum D. Io. Bentiuolu ... Pronosticon in annum domini MDIIII. [Bologna], 5 Jan. [1504]. 4to. 4 ll. (unsigd.), browned, a few letters supplied. Marb. wraps. From Honeyman Collection. (S. Nov.10; 2350) *Piloboyl.* £150

NOVARINO, A.
– Admiranda Orbis Christiani. Ed.:– J.B. Bagatta. Venice, 1680. 2 vols. in 1. Fo. Lacks 2X6 in vol. I, title & a2 in vol. II, some ll. browned, slight spotting. Cont. blind-stpd. pig. bds., soiled, spine worn, from College of the Soc. of Jesus at Landshuth. (S. Dec.8; 105) *Libris.* £50

NOVELLENBUCH
Ill.:– Arthur Rackham. Zurich, [1925]. 4to. Decor. cl. Raymond M. Sutton Jr. copy. (SG. May 7; 227) $300

NOVERRE, [Jean-Georges]
– Lettres sur la Danse, sur les Ballets et les Arts. St. Petersb., 1803-04. L.P. 4 vols. 4to. Lacks port. by Saunders, very faint dampstain in inner upr. corners of a few ll. in vol. I & III, a few ll. very slightly spotted. Slightly later glazed bds, spine gt. Bkplt. of Arnold Haskell by Michael Ayrton. (S. Dec.9; 447) *Duran.* £400

NOVIOMAGUS, Johannes
– De Numeris libri duo, quorum prior Logisticen & veterum numerandi consuetudinem, posterior Theoremata numerorum complectitur. Paris, 1539. 1st. Edn. Slight staining, a few marginal annots. Mod. vell. bds. From Honeyman Collection. (S. Nov.10; 2351) *Hill.* £170
See–SACROBOSCO, Johannes de –NOVIOMAGUS, Johannes

NOVISSIMA
– Albo d'Arti e Lettere. Milan, 1901-10. 10 vols. Ob. 4to. Orig. decor. cl. (SI. Dec.4; 430) Lire 600,000

NOVUM THEATRUM Pedemonti et Sabaudia
Ill.:– I. Luyken (arms). The Hague, 1726. 4 pts. in 2 vols. Fo. Mntd. on guards thro.-out, some foxing & discoloration at edges, some soiling, 5 additional plts. in vol. II. 19th. C. hf. mor. From Chetham's Liby., Manchester. (C. Nov.26; 40) *King.* £5,200

NOVY LEF [Journal of the Left Front of Art]
Ed.:– [V.V. Mayakovsky & others]. Ill.:– Rodchenko & others. Moscow, 1928. Nos. 1-12 only. Orig. wraps., some slightly soiled & torn. (SH. Feb.6; 340) *Ex-libris.* £420

NOZEMAN, Cornelius & Sepp, Jan Christiaan
– Nederlandsche Vogelen ... Amst., 1770. Atlas fo. 87 (of 250) hand-cold. copperplts. Later hf. cf., unc. (SG. May 14; 158) $6,600
– – Anr. Edn. Amst., 1770-97. 1st. Edn. 3 vols. only (of 5). Fo. Plts. hand-cold., slight soiling & creasing to upr. portion of some text ll. & plts. in vols. 2 & 3. Cont. hf. mor., covers of vol. 1 detchd. W.a.f., from Chetham's Liby., Manchester. (C. Nov.27; 314) *Isley.* £5,000
– – Anr. Edn. Amst., 1770-[97]. Pts. 1-3. Lge. fo. 1 (of 3) hand-cold. engraved titles, lacks printed title & list of plts. vol. 3, with plts. with slight marginal stain. Cont. hf. cf., gt. spines, unc. (VG. Oct.13; 115) Fls. 32,000

NOZZE Colloredo-Maniago
– Componimenti Poetici per lo Sposalizio Solenne. Ill.:– Giacomo Leonardis (frontis. & title). Venice, 1765. Fo. A special copy, with each p. of text in engraved decor. border. Orig. marb. paper bds., buckram s.-c. From the collection of John A. Saks. (C. Jun.10; 172) *Lyon.* £200

NOZZE Foscarini-Barbaro
– Poesie. Venice, Giambattista Albrizzi; Antonio Zatta, 1766; 1766. 2 works in 1 vol. Sm. fo. Cont. Venetian mor., gt.-tooled borders, floral cornerpieces & lge. centrepiece, spine gt. in 6 compartments, buckram s.-c. From the collection of John A. Saks. (C. Jun.10; 174) *Quaritch.* £220

NOZZE Lippomano–Quirini
– Poesie per la Nozze. Ill.:– Giacomo Zatta & Domenico Cagnoni. Venice, 1790. 4to. Cont. flowered paper bds., end-paper renewed, buckram s.-c. From the collection of John A. Saks. (C. Jun.10; 178) *Taylor.* £70

NOZZE Manin-Dolfin–NOZZE Mozenigo-Griman
– Poesie per le Gloriose Nozze . . .; Poesie per le Gloriose Nozze . . .; Poesie per le Felicissime Nozze.– Poesie per le Gloriose Nozze . . .; Poesie . . .
Ed.:– Gasparo Gozzi (1st. work). Venice, 1765; 1766. 5 works in 1 vol. Fo. Vell.-bkd. bds., thongs loosening, mor.-bkd. buckram case. From the collection of John A. Saks. (C. Jun.10; 179) *King.* £340

NOZZE Manin-Pesaro
– Poesie. Ill.:– B. Crivellari & G. Magnini & others. Venice, 1769. Sm. fo. Light staining at beginning. Cont. paste-paper wraps., gt-embossed, with arms of Manin on upr. cover & those of Pesaro on lr., slight wear at edge of lr. cover. From the collection of John A. Saks. (C. Jun.10; 180) *Quaritch.* £240

NOZZE Mozenigo-Griman
See–NOZZE Manin–Dolfin–NOZZE Mozenigo-Griman

NOZZE Pallavicini-Lambertini
– Le Muse in Gara. Ill.:– P. Locatelli (frontis.). Bologna, 1760. Thick paper. Sm. fo. Orig. wraps., embossed in gt, with floral design, buckram s.-c. From the collection of John A. Saks. (C. Jun.10; 182) *Lyon.* £120

NOZZE Porcia-Porcia
– Componimenti Poetici nell' Occasione de' Gloriosi Sponsali. Ill.:– F. Bartolozzi (title). Venice, 1780. 4to. Light browning & minor dampstains to last few ll. Cont. mott. cf. gt., light wear, buckram s.-c. From the collection of John A. Saks. (C. Jun.10; 183) *King.* £110

NUDOW, Heinrich
[–] Anthropolog. Reisen. N.p., 1793. 1st. Edn. Title bkd. at margin. Hf. leath. (HK. May 15; 4715) DM 1,400

NUGENT, M.
– Alla Mostra della Pittura Italiana del '600 e '700 Note e Impressioni. San Casciano, 1925. 2 vols. Orig. wraps. (CR. Mar.19; 450) Lire 200,000

NUIX, Giovanni
– Reflexiones Imparciales sobre la Humanidad de los Espanoles en las Indias. Madrid, 1782. Sm. 4to. Cont. spr. cf. [Sabin 56309] (SPB. May 5; 369) $200

NUMISMATA ANTIQUA
[L.], 1746. Plt. vol. only, comprising 4 series. 4to. Cont. mott. cf., design of gt. coronets, etc. surrounding initials T.P., reprd., & rebkd. Pres Copy from Lord Pembroke to Sir Charles Bingham. (SG. Feb.5; 255) $275

NUMISMATIC CHRONICLE, Seventh Series
1964-75. Vols. 4-15 only. Orig. cl. (SH. Apr.9; 108) *Irwin.* £50

NUNEZ, Hernan
– Refranes O Proverbios en Romance. Madrid, 1619 [colophon: 1618]. Slightly soiled. Old vell., soiled, stitching worn. (CSK. Jan.30; 11) £55

NUNEZ, P. Antonio
[–] Exercicios Espirituales de San Ignacio. Mexico, 1695. Sm. 4to. Title slightly soiled. Later limp vell. (SPB. May 5; 370) $225

NUNEZ, Pedro
– De Crepusculis Liber unus ... Item Allacen ... de Causis Crepusculorum Liber unus, a Gerardo Cremonensi iam olim Latinitate donatus. Lisbon, 1542. 1st. Edn. 4to. Printed slip (corrected table) attached to ol recto, marginal repair to title. Mod. vell.-bkd. bds., hf. mor. case. From Honeyman Collection. (S. Nov.10; 2353) *Rota.* £900
– Libro de Algebra en Arithmetica y Geometria. Antw., 1567. 1st. Edn. Some staining, title slightly soiled, sig. of Thomas Digges & date 1575. Old cf., very worn, from liby. of Marquess of Bute. From Honeyman Collection. (S. Nov.10; 2354) *Hill.* £400

NUNEZ DO LIAO, Duarte
– Orthographia da Lingoa Portuguesa. Lisbon, 1576. 1st. Edn. 4to. Piece cut from blank foot of title & reprd. Cont. limp vell., tears in spine. (C. Apr.1; 157) *Maggs.* £130

NUOVO ATLANTE Portatile
Venice, 1785. Corners of some ll. slightly frayed. Cont. paper wraps., slightly worn, unc. From the collection of John A. Saks. (C. Jun.10; 187) *Taylor.* £55

NUREMBERG CHRONICLE
N.Y., [1966]. Fo. Cl., d.-w. (worn). (SG. Mar.26; 344) $110

NURNBERGER ALBUM
Ill.:– J. Poppel, J. Riegel, E. Rauch & others. [Munich], ca. 1850. MS. dedication on end-paper, some plts. slightly soiled. Orig. linen. (HK. May 12-14; 910) DM 4,800

NURNBERGER PROZESS
– Der Prozess gegen die Hauptkriegsverbrecher. Nuremb., 1947-49. Ltd. Edn. 42 vols. in 41. Erased stp. on end-papers & title, 2 title-ll. replaced by photocopies, lightly browned in parts. Orig. linen & later bnd. linen. (H. May 21/22; 604) DM 2,000

NURNBERGER, J.E.
– Populäres Astronomisches Hand-Wörterbuch. Kempten, 1846-48. 1st. Edn. Stp. on title. Cont. bds. (R. Oct.14-18; 284) DM 500

NUTT, Frederick
– The Imperial & Royal Cook. 1809. Some ll. washed. Mod. hf. cl., mor. case. (S. Dec.2; 752) *Blackwell.* £70

NUTTALL, Thomas
See–MICHAUX, François Andre & Nuttall, Thomas

NUTTER, M.E.
– Carlisle in the Olden Time. 1835. Fo. Extra engraved title with cold. litho. vig., 17 hand-cold. litho. plts., lacks hf.-title & final blank. Orig. cl. bds., rebkd. (C. Jul.15; 82) *Roberts.* £600
– – Anr. Copy. Fo. No bdg. stated. (TRL. Dec.10; 124) £110

NYREN, John
– The Young Cricketer's Tutor ... The Cricketers of My Time. L., 1833. 12mo. Cl. (SSA. Jan.22; 102) R. 260

O [W.B.S.]
See–STEVIN, Simon–O. [W.B.S.]

OAKES, William
– Scenery of the White Mountains. Ill.:– Bufford from drawings by Isaac Sprague. Boston & Camb., 1848. [1st. Edn.?]. Fo. (16¾ × 12½ ins.). Some foxing. Gt.lettered cl. (SG. Jan.8; 342) $220
– – Anr. Copy. Marginal stains on plts. Orig. cl., very worn. (SG. Nov.20; 385) $175

OAKESHOTT, Walter
– Some Woodcuts by Hans Burgkmair. Oxford, Roxburgh Cl., 1960. 4to. Orig. mor.-bkd. cl. (SH. Jan.29; 133) *Forester.* £105

OAKLEY, Edward
– The Magazine of Architecture, Perspective & Sculpture. 1730. Fo. Hf. cf., brkn., some staining thro.-out. (BS. Sep.17; 9) £130

OBADIAH BEN JACOB DE SFORNO
– Biur al Shir ha-Shirim Kohelet. Venice, 1567. Sm. 4to. Mod. bds. (C. Jul.16; 313) *Joseph.* £190

OBERMULLER, A.
– Die Brenner-Bahn. Munich, ca. 1868. Ob. 8vo. Cont. linen. (R. Oct.14-18; 258) DM 1,250

OBERTH, A.
– Wege zur Raumschiffahrt. Munich & Berlin, 1929. 3rd. Iss. Orig. linen. (HK. May 12-14; 201) DM 720

OBICINUS, Thomas
[–] Thesaurus Arabico-Syro-Latinus. Ed.:– D. Germanus. Rome, 1636. Some browning, owner's inscr. in Arabic at end. 18th. C. vell., slightly soiled, s.-c. (S. Apr.29; 443) *Loman.* £160

OBRYV [Precipice]
Ed.:– [Yu. V. Gol'dberg]. St. Petersb., 1907. No. 1. 4to. Unbnd. (SH. Feb.5; 100) *Landry.* £55

OBSERVATIONS on the Present State of Denmark, Russia & Switzerland. In A Series of Letters
L., 1784. Hf. cf. (GM. Apr.30; 680)		£60

O'CALLAGHAN, Edmund Bailley, M.D.
- The Documentary History of the State of New-York. Albany, 1849-1851. 4 vols. Cl., some chipping. (SG. Mar.5; 356)		$100

OCCON, A.
- Pharmacopeia seu Medicamentarium pro. Rep. Augustana. Augsburg, 1580. 18th. C. bds. (R. Mar.31-Apr.4; 1028)		DM 1,800

OCHSENBRUNNER, Thomas
- Priscorum Heroum Stemmata. Rome, Johann Besicken & Sigismundus Mayer, 18 Feb., 1494. Portion of fo. 1 in facs. affecting 7 lines, some sm. wormholes. stained. 19th. C. vell. The copy of Charles John Shoppee & Boies Penrose, lately in the collection of Eric Sexton. [BMC IV, 139, Goff 07, HC 11934*] (CNY. Apr.8; 145)		$900

OCKLEY, Simon
- An Account of South-West Barbary. 1713. [1st. Edn.?]. Folding cold. map with slight marginal dfects. Cont. cf., brkn. (S. Dec.8; 267)		Hosains. £95
- - Anr. Copy. (SH. Jun.18; 138)		Makiya. £90

O'CONNELL, Eileen
[-] A Lament for Art O'Leary. Trans.:- Frank O'Connor. Ill.:- Jack B. Yeats. Cuala Pr., 1940. 1st. Edn., (130) 'K'. 4to. Orig. linen-bkd. bds., unc. (S. Jul.22; 90)		Figgis. £160

O'CONNOR, Jack
- Game in the Desert. Ill.:- T.J. Harter. [1939]. (950) numbered. 4to. Imitation snake, boxed, unopened. Inscr. (SG. Dec.11; 268)		$475

O'CONNOR, M.
- The Scott Gallery of Portraits. L., ca. 1850. Fo. Orig. cl. bds., rebkd., recornered. (C. Jul.16; 333)		Taylor. £380

O'CONOR, Rt. Hon. Charles Owen, the O'Conor Don
- The O'Connors of Connaught. An Historical Memoir. Dublin, [1891]. Inscr. cl. (GM. Apr.30; 398)		£80

O'CURRY, Eugene
- Lectures on the Manuscript Materials of Ancient Irish History. Dublin, 1878. Orig. cl., gt. (GM. Apr.30; 49)		£50

ODDI, Muzio
- Dello Squadro. Milan, 1625. 1st. Edn. 4to. Title stained & slightly wormed in fore-margin. Cont. bds., spine worn, unc. From Honeyman Collection. (S. Nov.10; 2356)		Nox. £80

O'DONOGHUE, F. & Hake, Henry M.
- Catalogue of Engraved British Portraits ... in the British Museum. 1908-25. 6 vols. Orig. cl. (SH. Jan.29; 134)		Forester. £105

O'DONOVAN, Jeremiah
- A Brief Account of the Author's Interview with his Countrymen ... together with a Direct Reference to their Present Location, during his Travels through Various States of the Union in 1854 & 1855. Pittsb., Priv. ptd., 1864. 1st. Edn. 12mo. Orig. hf. leath. (SG. Jan.8; 344)		$160
- A History of Ireland ... with a Direct Reference to her Political Renovation from the Reign of Roderick O'Connor to the Battle of the Boyne. Pittsb., Priv. ptd., 1854. 2 pts. in 1 vol. 12mo. Early binder's hf. leath., orig. ptd. wraps. bnd. in. (SG. Jan.8; 343)		$110

O'DONOVAN, John
- Annals of the Kingdom of Ireland. Dublin, 1856. 2nd. Edn. 7 vols. 4to. Hf. mor., gt. spines. (GM. Apr.30; 393)		£410
- The Tribes & Customs of Hy-Many. Dublin, 1843. Orig. cl. (GM. Apr.30; 390)		£50

OECOLAMPADIUS, Joannes
See-LUTHER, Martin-OECOLAMPADUS, Joannes

OEDER, George Christian (Ed.)
See-FLORA DANICA

OEHLER, R.
See-LANCKORONSKA, Maria & Oehler, R.

OEIL, Revue d'Art Mensuelle
1955-66. Numbers 1-144 in 8 vols. 4to. Mod. hf. mor. gt., gt. ornament on spines. (SH. Oct.9; 16)		Ars Artis. £80

OERSTED, Hans Christian
- [Account of the Discovery of Electromagnetism]. [Copen.], [1821]. In: Oversigt over det Kongelige Danske Videnskabernes Selskabs Forhandlinger. 4to. Disbnd. From Honeyman Collection. (S. Nov.10; 2357)		Quaritch. £380

OERTEL, W. von
See-MURAWIEW-APOSTOL ...

OEUVRES Classiques
Paris, 1878-87. Sm. 12mo. Mor. by Ritter, decor. spine, lyre in centre of covers with border of 3 fillets, s.-c. (SM. Feb.11; 168)		Frs. 4,000

OFENSA y Defensa de la Libertad Eclesiastica. La primera en 24 capitulos, que mando publicar el Exmo, senor Duque de la Palata ... Y la secunda armada con los escudos Catolicos de la Ley y la Razon ...
[Lima], ca. 1684? Fo. Hole affecting last ll., margins of 2 ll. at end defect. Cont. limp vell., soiled. (SPB. May 5; 371)		$275

OFFICE de l'Eglise (L') et de la Vierge
Paris, n.d. Sm. 12mo. Cont. lavallière mor., blind fillet, silver arms of Marie-Louise-Elisabeth d'Orléans, Duchesse de Berry, red mor. doubl. with wide dentelle, dominoe paper end-ll. (HD. Jun.10; 78)		Frs. 1,400

OFFICE de la Semaine Sainte
Paris, 1683. Cont. red mor, fleurs-de-lys & crowned dolphins on spine, 3 fillets & fleurs-de-lys in angles, crowned cypher of Marie-Anne-Christine-Victoire of Bavaria in centre, worn. (HD. Dec.5; 192)		Frs. 1,200
- - Anr. Edn. Paris, 1717. Cont. red mor., gt. fillets & roll-stps. around covers, fleurs-de-lys in corners, arms of Louis XV in centre, raised bands on spine. (HD. Jun.24; 68)		Frs. 1,500
- - Anr. Edn. Ill.:- Scotin. N.p., ca. 1750. Lacks title. Cont. red mor., decor. spine, fillets & lge. roll-stp. with fleurs-de-lys on covers, arms of Marie-Josèphe de Saxe in centre, inside dentelle. (HD. Dec.5; 194)		Frs. 1,200

OFFICE de la Semaine Sainte à l'Usage de la Maison du Roy
Paris, 1727. Cont. red mor., gt. roll-stp. around covers, arms of Louis XV, spine with raised bands & fleurs-de-lys. (HD. Feb.27; 58)		Frs. 1,500

OFFICE de la Semaine Sainte ... dediée a la Reine
Ill.:- Scotin. Paris, 1728. Cont. red mor., gt. roll-stp. around covers, arms of Marie Leczinska, spine with raised bands & fleurs-de-lys, bdg. slightly defect. (HD. Feb.27; 59)		Frs. 1,000

OFFICE de la Semaine Sainte ... pour l'Usage de la Maison de Mme. la Dauphine
Paris, 1745. Cont. red mor., pointillé decor., centre arms, decor. spine raised bands, inner dentelle. (HD. Apr.24; 87)		Frs. 2,800

OFFICE de la Vierge Marie (L')
Paris, 1617. Mor., blind fillet, arms & repeated cyphron spine of Charles-Louis de Bourbon, inner dentelle, by Lortic. Duc Robert de Parme liby. (HD. Jun.10; 77)		Frs. 1,800

OFFICINA BODONI
- Das Werkbuch einer Handpresse in den Ersten Sechs Jahren Ihres Wirkens. Ill.:- Masereel. Paris, 1929. (350) numbered. 4to. Orig. linen. (HK. Nov.18-21; 2836)		DM 1,300

OFFICIUM HEBDOMADAE SANCTAE, caum Psalmiset et Lectionibus secundum Missale et Breviarium Romanum
Madrid, 1616. Fo. Title woodcut cut & replaced by anr. woodcut, old MS. entries on title verso, wormed in parts. Cont. leath., gt., 2 metal clasps, 1 defect. (D. Dec.11-13; 9)		DM 700

OFFROY de la Mettrie, Julien
[-] L'Homme Machine. Leiden, 1748. Early Edn. 12mo. Some browning. Cont. cf., gt. spine, slightly worn. Bkplt. of Herbert McLean Evans; from Honeyman Collection. (S. Nov.10; 2358)		Das Bucherkabinet. £500

O'FLAHERTY, Liam
- Darkness. L., May, 1926. (12) for Copyright. 4to. Patterned paper wraps. Sigd. (SG. Nov.13; 537)		$160
- A Tourist's Guide to Ireland. L., n.d. Some dampstains. Orig. bdg. Inscr., with A Sketch of Galway. (GM. Apr.30; 365)		£62

O'FLAHERTY, R.
- A Chorographical Description of West of H-Iar Connacht. Ed.:- J. Hardiman. Dublin, 1846. 4to. Cl., spine torn. (GM. Apr.30; 391)		£62

O'FLANAGAN, Rev. M.
- Letters Containing information Relative to the Antiquities of County of Clare. Bray, 1928. 3 vols. in l. 4to. Vols. I & III in zerox, vol. II in orig. typescript. Cl. (GM. Apr.30; 413)		£55

O'FLANAGAN, T. Rod.
- The Lives of the Lord Chancellors & Keepers of the Great Seal of Ireland. L., 1870. 1st. Edn. 2 vols. Cl. Pres. copy to author's wife, inscr. (GM. Apr. 30; 9)		£55

OGDEN, James
- Ogden on Fly Tying, Etc. Cheltenham, 1879. 1st. Edn. Lacks errata slip. Cl. (SG. Oct.16; 255)		$130

OGDEN, Peter Skene
[-] Traits of American-Indian Life & Character. L., 1853. With 16 pp. of publisher's advts., liby. stp. on hf.-title. Recent leath., leath. s.-c. (CB. Sep.24; 311)		Can. $700
See-HUDSON'S Bay Record Society

OGEE, Jean
- Dictionnaire Historique et Géographique de la Province de Bretagne. Nantes, 1778, 1780. 4 vols. 4to. Slight foxing. 19th. C. marb. cf., gt. fillet around covers, spines decor. with raised bands, bdgs. defect. (HD. Jun.24; 95)		Frs. 1,900

OGILBY, John
- Africa. 1610. Fo. Lacks pp. 411-412. Old cf. gt., brkn., spine defect. (BS. Jun.11; 176)		£280
- - Anr. Edn. 1670. Fo. Engraved frontis. & 50 engraved maps & plts. only. Old cf., brkn. (BS. Jun.11; 177)		£230
- - Anr. Copy. Lacks plt. of Tangier, plt. of Morocco & Salvador from anr. copy, some plts. torn at inner edge, outer edge of p.99 torn with section missing. Cont. cf., rebkd., spine worn. (SSA. Nov.5; 232)		R. 300
- America; Being the Latest & Most Accurate Description of the New World. L., 1671. 1st. Iss. of Ogilby's translation of Adolphus Montanus. 2nd. Vol. of 'Mr. Ogilby's English Atlas'. Fo. Title & frontis. loose, slight browning & foxing. Cf., covers detchd., worn. (SPB. Nov.24; 43)		$4,750
- - Anr. Edn. 1671. Fo. 7 double-p. maps only (of 19), 24 plts. (of 37), lacks binder's lf., several plts. with fold tears, occasional browning & spotting. Old hf. cf., 1 cover detchd., very worn. W.a.f. [Wing 0165, Sabin 50089] (S. May 5; 249)		Crossley. £1,000
- Asia, the first part ... 1673. 1st. Edn. (all publd.). Vol. I (all publd.). Fo. 1 folding map (of 2), title-p. torn without loss. Old cf. gt., brkn. (BS. Jun.11; 178)		£190
- - Anr. Copy. Vol. I (all publd.). Fo. Lacks 1 plt. listed in the directions to binders & 2 additional engraved folding maps(?), without B1 (but no apparent loss of text), perforation in L2, some ll. slightly stained. Later tree cf. gt. (SBA. May 27; 312)		Temperley. £112
- Britannia. Priv. Ptd., 1675. 1st. Edn. Vol. 1 (all publd.). Fo. 1 map torn 1 laid down. 19th. C. hf. mor. As an atlas, w.a.f. (C. Jul.15; 519)		Taylor. £3,500
- - Anr. Copy. Slight soiling & offsetting, 1 plt. inverted. Later cf., gt. (S. Jun.22; 161)		Traylen. £3,400
[-] - Anr. Edn. [1675]. 1st. Edn. Fo. Lacks 2 maps. W.a.f. (S. Mar.31; 287)		Burgess. £2,600
- - Anr. Edn. 1698. [2nd. Edn.?]. Reprint of the 1675 1st. Edn. Fo. Occasional spotting & discolouration, some edges dust-stained. Old panel. cf., worn. As an atlas, w.a.f. (C. Feb.25; 50)		Burgess. £3,000
- - Anr. Copy. 2 maps defect. W.a.f. (C. Jul.15; 83)		Taylor. £2,400
- - Anr. Copy. Lacks maps 36, 69-71, 90 & 91, some cartouches cold., spotted, dampstained & soiled in places, some sm. tears, some reprd., sm. hole in map l. Cont. hf. roan, slightly worn. As an atlas, w.a.f. (S. Apr.7; 273)		Burgess. £1,200
[-] [-] Anr. Edn. N.d. Fo. 90 double-p. engraved road maps only, various defects. Loose in old hf. leath., worn. W.a.f. (SKC. Feb.26; 1553)		£1,000
- England Exactly Described Or a Guide to Travellers In a Compleat Sett of Most correct Mapps of Counties in England. Ill.:- Hollar. ca. 1710, or later. Agenda 8vo. Plts. 31, 33 & 40 slightly cropped at foot, a few short fold-tears.

Cont. sheep, rebkd. worn. (S. Nov.4; 509) *Shires.* £450
– – **Anr. Edn.** Ca. 1740 or later. Foolscap 8vo. Title & some plts. reprd., mainly in fold, some maps torn in folds, MS. register on fly-ll. Cont. cf., worn upr. cover detchd., clasps. As an atlas, w.a.f. (S. Apr.7; 274) *Mrs. Green.* £320

OGILBY, John & Bowen, Emmanuel
– **Britannia Depicta or Ogilby Improv'd.** 1720. Cont. cf., rebkd. (SH. Mar.5; 107) *Burden.* £360
– – **Anr. Copy.** 4to. A few stains, slight discoloration. Late 19th. C. hf. cf. W.a.f. (S. Nov.3; 37) *Postaprint.* £350
– – **Anr. Edn.** 1724. [4th. Edn.?]. Sm. 4to. Title & following lf. detchd., sm. hole in pp. 129/130, flaw in top fore-corner of pp. 181/182, a few sm. marginal flaws or tears. Cont. cf., worn. W.a.f. (S. Jun.29; 16) *Tooley.* £380
– – **Anr. Copy.** Brownstain to last few ll. Old limp leath., worn. (SG. May 21; 17) £600
– – **Anr. Edn.** 1730. Cont. cf., slightly worn, rebkd. (SKC. May 19; 382) £300
– – **Anr. Edn.** 1736. 4th. Edn. Sm. 4to. Cont. cf. W.a.f. (S. Mar.31; 261) *Martin.* £420
– – **Anr. Copy.** Lacks final plt., sm. section of last lf. torn away slightly affecting text, a number of coats of arms partly or wholly hand-cold. (SKC. Feb.26; 1554) £380
– – **Anr. Copy.** Cf. (P. Sep.11; 126) *Hughes.* £320
– – **Anr. Edn.** 1764. 4to. 19th. C. sheep. (S. Apr.7; 276) *Kidd.* £350

OGILBY, John & Senex, John
– **The Roads through England Delineated.** 1759. Sm. ob. 4to. Cont. limp leath. wallet-type bdg., loose & worn. (SKC. May 19; 364) £150
– – **Anr. Edn.** 1762. Ob. 8vo. Last lf. stained & defect. Cont. limp cf. W.a.f. (C. Jul.15; 97) *Taylor.* £230
– **Roads through England or, Ogilby's Survey.** –Ogilby's Roads of England.–Recueil des Villes, Ports d'Angleterre. Paris; ?Paris; Paris, n.d.; 1766 [3rd. work]. 3 pts. in 1 vol. 4to. 1st. work: engraved title in Fr. & Engl.; 2nd. work: 4 ll. of (Fr.) introductory text & tables, inlaid to size, without title. Cont. cf.-bkd. paper bds., gt., spine worn. W.a.f. (S. Nov.3; 38) *Regent.* £350

OGILVIE-GRANT, W.R. & others (Ed.)
See–GUN at Home & Abroad

OGLE, Nathaniel
– **Colony of Western Australia: a Manual for Emigrants to that Settlement or its Dependencies.** L., 1839. 1st. Edn. 1 plt. soiled. Rebkd. using orig. backstrip, unc. With bkplt. of, & author's pres. inscr. to Sir John Barrow. (KH. Nov.18; 463) *Aus.* $500

OGLE, Nathaniel–WESTGARTH, William
– **The Colony of Western Australia.–The Colony of Victoria.** 1839; 1864. 2nd. iss.; 1st. Edn. 2 works in 2 vols. Occasional dampstaining to 1st. work. Orig. embossed cl. gt., stained, inner hinge brkn.; hf. cf. gt. (C. Nov.6; 9) *Antipodean.* £140

O'GORMAN
– **The Practice of Angling.** Dublin, 1845. 1st. Edn. 2 vols. Three-qtr. cf. by Larkin, spine gt. (SG. Oct.16; 256) $190

O'HANLON, J.
– **Lives of the Irish Saints.** N.d. 9 vols. Orig. cl. (SH. May 28; 77) *Howes Books.* £50

OHM, Georg Simon
– **Die galvanische Kette, mathematisch bearbeitet.** Berlin, 1827. 1st. Edn. Lacks engraved plt. (MS. copy inserted), stp. of W. v. Zahn on fly-lf. Hf. cl., slightly worn, hf. mor. case. From Honeyman Collection. (S. Nov.10; 2359) *Brieux.* £500

OIJEN, A.A. Vosterman van
– **Het Vorstenhuis van Waldeck en Pyrmont.** Utrecht, 1879. (200). Fo. Orig. mor., stpd. in gt. & blind. Bkplt. of H.R.H. The Duke of Albany. (CSK. Jun.19; 92) £50

OJETTI, U.
– **I Macchiaioli Toscani nella Raccolta Enrico Checcucci di Firenze.** Milan, 1928. 4to. Publisher's hf. cl. (CR. Mar.19; 128) *Lire* 220,000

OJETTI, U. & others
– **La Pittura Italiana del Seicento e del Settecento alla Mostra di Palazzo Pitti.** Milan, 1924. Ltd. Edn. 4to. Cf., gt. tooled decor. (CR. Mar.19; 127) *Lire* 240,000

O'KEEFFE, Georgia
– **Georgia O'Keeffe.** N.Y., [1976]. Fo. Cl., d.-w. (SG. Apr.2; 217) $140
– **A Studio Book.** N.Y., [1976]. Fo. Buckram, d.-w. (SG. Oct.23; 245) $200

OKEN, Lorenz
– **Abbildungen zu Oken's allgemeiner Naturgeschichte für alle Stände.** Stuttgart, 1843. Lge. 4to. Slightly soiled in parts. Cont. hf. linen. (R. Oct.14-18; 3036) DM 750
– **Die Zeugung.** Bamberg-Würzburg, 1805. Cont. bds., unc. (D. Dec.11-13; 222) DM 560

OLAUS MAGNUS, Archbishop of Upsala
– **Storia . . . de Costumi de Popoli Settentrionali . . . dove s'ha piena Rotitia delle Genti della Gottia, della Norvegia, della Suevia.** Trans.:– M. Remigio. Venice, 1561. 1st. Edn. in Italian. Cont. limp vell. (S. Oct.21; 276) *Pearson.* £80

OLD CLOSES & Streets of Glasgow
Glasgow, 1900. Fo. Engrs. 1 & 4 lacking. Cl., worn, gt. coat of arms. (CE. Oct.24; 21) £140

OLD COUNTRY HOUSES of the Old Glasgow Gentry
Ill.:– Annan. 1878. (225). 4to. Orig. decor. mor.-bkd. cl. gt. (CE. Apr.23; 251) £125
– – **Anr. Copy.** Mor. spine & decor. bds., worn. (CE. Nov.20; 13) £90

OLD MASTER DRAWINGS. A Quarterly Magazine for Students & Collectors
L., 1927-40. 14 vols. 4to. Linen. (HK. Nov.18-21; 3458) DM 440
– – **Anr. Run.** N.Y., 1970. Collectors' Edn., including index. 14 vols. 4to. Orig. cl. (C. Feb.4; 219) *Higginson.* £65
– – **Anr. Copy.** (SH. Oct.9; 90) *Phillips.* £55

OLD MOTHER GOOSE'S interesting Stories of Past Times
L., [1803]. 12mo. Disbnd. (SG. Apr.30; 242) $180

OLD NICK (Pseud.)
See–FORGUES, Paul Emile Durand 'Old Nick'

OLD WATER-COLOUR Society's Club
1929-49. Vols. 6-27. 4to. Orig. cl.-bkd. bds. (SH. Oct.9; 91) *Fogg.* £350

OLDEN TIME, The; A Monthly Publication Devoted to the Preservation of Documents . . .
Ed.:– Neville B. Craig. Pittsb., 1846-48. 1st. Edn. 2 vols. Slight foxing, marginal repairs. Mod. hf. mor., gt. spine & borders, cover of vol. II loose, unc. From liby. of William E. Wilson. [Sabin 17365] (SPB. Apr.29; 65) $325
– – **Anr. Copy.** 2 vols., separately Iss., & all publd. Walter H. Lourie of Meadville's sig. in both vols. Cont. hf. cf. (PNY. Dec.3; 276) $150
– – **Anr. Run.** Ed.:– Neville B. Craig. Cinc., 1876. 2nd. Edn. 2 vols. Orig. blind-stpd. cl., gt. spine. From liby. of William E. Wilson. [Sabin 17365] (SPB. Apr.29; 66) $150

OLDENDORP, Christian George Andreas
– **Geschichte der Mission der evangelischen Brüder auf den caraibischen Inseln S. Thomas, S. Croix und S. Jan.** Barby [Saxony], 1777. A few spots, faint liby. stp. on title. Cont. bds., slightly worn. [Sabin 57152] (SPB. May 5; 374) $325

OLDFIELD, Thomas
See–SCLATER, Philip Lutley & Oldfield, Thomas

OLDHAM, James
– **A Representation & Description of the last Improved Air Stone Grate . . .** [L.], ca. 1800? Sm. 4to. Engraved title browned, 24 copperplts. on 10 folding sheets. Mod. hf. cl. (SG. May 14; 159) $225

OLDHAM, James Basil
– **English Blind-Stamped Bindings.–Blind Panels of English Binders.** Camb., 1952-58. (750) (1st. work). Fo. Together 2 vols. Orig. cl. (SH. Oct.9; 56) *Thompson.* £130

OLDMIXON, John
[–[**The British Empire in America, Containing the History of the Discovery, Settlement, Progress & State of the British Colonies . . .** L., 1741. 2nd. Edn. 2 vols. Blind-stp. affecting first few ll., slightly stained & browned. Later hf. cf., worn. From liby. of William E. Wilson. [Sabin 57157] (SPB. Apr.29; 217) $375

OLDSTYLE, Jonathan
See–IRVING, Washington

OLEARIUS, Adam
– **Vermehrte Newe Beschreibung der Muscowitischen und Persischen Reyse . . .** Schleswig, 1656. Sm. fo. 23 (of 27) double-p. & folding copperplts., text copperplts. Old hf. cf., brkn. (SG. Oct.9; 182) $650
– **The Voyages & Travells of the Ambassadors . . . containing a compleat History of Muscovy, Tartary, Persia . . .** 1669. 2 pts. in 1 vol. Fo. Lr. margin of frontis. reprd. just affecting engraved surface, 7 folding engraved maps, usually 6, several reprd. & slightly defect. Cont. cf., rebkd. [Wing 0270] (S. Jun.23; 389) *Maggs.* £420
– **Voyages très Curieux et très Renommez faits en Moscovie, Tartarie et Perse.** Amst., 1727. 4 vols. in 2. Fo. Cf., jnts. brkn. (BS. Jun.11; 179) £460
– – **Anr. Copy.** 2 vols. in l. 1 port. reprd. & mntd., last lf. plt. defect. & restored with some loss of text, defects. or repairs to 4 prelims., some browning, slight worming. Mod. qtr. leath. W.a.f. (S. Nov.4; 600) £270
– – **Anr. Copy.** Slightly browned, lacks catalogue of bks. publd. by Le Cene at end. Cont. marb. cf., gt. border, gt. spine raised in compartments, corners defect. (VG. Oct.13; 116) Fls. 2,500

OLEARIUS, Adam–MANDELSLO, J.A. von
– **Vermehrte Newe Beschreibung der Muscowitschen und Persischen Reyse.** –Morgenländische Reyse-Beschreibung. Schleswig, 1656; 1658. 2nd. Edn., 1st. Edn. 2 works in 1 vol. Fo. Slightly browned in margin, lacks 2 plts. Cont blind-stpd. pig-bkd wood bds., clasps, dtd. 1669. (R. Mar.31-Apr.4; 2518) DM 6,200

OLEVSKI, Rafael & others
– **Our Destruction in Pictures.** Bergen-Belsen, Dec., 1946. Ob. fo. Outer hf. of the Yiddish title-p. torn-out. Cold. pict. stiff. wraps., rear blank cover covered with pencil sketches. (SG. Feb.12; 247) $160

OLIPHANT, Laurence
– **Narrative of the Earl of Elgin's Mission to China & Japan.** 1959. 1st. Edn. 2 vols. Cf. gt., arms on covers. (P. Jul.2; 165) *Timmons.* £100
– – **Anr. Copy.** Hf. cf., slightly worn. (BS. Jun.11; 180) £70

OLIPHANT, Mrs. Margaret
– **The Makers of Venice.** L., 1887. Slight foxing to text. Crushed lev., gt.-tooled & inlaid strapwork borders enclosing gt. title with fleur-de-lys, spine unif. gt., wide gt. dentelles with doubls. & end-papers of satin, 2 bkplts on front doubl. Fore-e. pntg.; from the liby. of Zola E. Harvey. (SG. Mar.19; 157) $500

OLIVA, Jean Paul
– **Panegyrique de la Bienheureuse Rose prononcé à Rome dans l'Eglise de la Minerve.** Paris, 1669. 4to. Cont. vell., gt. arms of Cardinal Barberini on covers. (S. Mar.17; 254) *Marriot.* £70

OLIVER, Andrew
– **An Essay on Comets . . . Containing an Attempt to explain the Phaenomena of the Tails of Comets . . . Wherein it is shewn, that . . . Comets may be inhabited Worlds, & even Comfortable Habitations.** Salem, New England, 1772. 1st. Edn. Hf.-title somewhat browned, with inscr. Cont. marb. wraps., spine defect., cl. case. From Honeyman Collection. [Sabin 57199] (S. Nov.10; 2360) *Nebenzahl.* £140

OLIVER, Charles & Laver, James
– **Original Views of London as it is.** Ill.:– after T.S. Boys. Guildford, 1972. 2 vols. Fo. Orig. wraps., upr. cover of 1 vol. slightly soiled. (CSK. Sep.26; 13) £85

OLIVER, Vere Langford
– **The History of the Island of Antigua.** L., 1894. (150). 3 vols. Fo. Slight browning. Cl., lightly stained. (SPB. May 5; 375) $2,800
– – **Anr. Edn.** 1894-99. 3 vols. Fo. Cl., soiled. (BS. Sep.17; 152) £75

OLIVI, Giuseppe–PLANCIUS, Janus–DONATI, Vitaliano
– **Zoologia Adriatica.–De Conchis.–Della Storia Naturale Marina dell' Adriatico.** Bassano; Venice; Venice, 1792; 1739; 1750. 3 works in 3 vols. 4to. Light browning to 2nd. work, occasional minor damp-staining to 3rd. work. 1st. work: mod. qtr. mor., unc.; 2nd. work: orig. paper wraps., unc.; 3rd. work: cont. paper wraps., worn. From the collection of John A. Saks. (C. Jun.10; 192) *Bartoli.* £100

OLIVIER
See–**CHAMPAGNAC & Olivier**

OLIVIER, Eugène & Others
– **Manuel de l'Amateur de Reliures Armoriées Françaises.** Paris, 1924-38. (1000) on vell. 30 Pts. including Tables in 15 vols. 4to. Cl.-bkd. bds. (SM. Oct.7; 1456) Frs. 2,500
– – **Anr. Copy.** 30 vols. Cont. hf. leath. gt. (R. Mar.31-Apr.4; 784) DM 3,200

OLLER Y BONO, Don Mauro Antonio
– **Proclamacion del Rey . . . Carlos III . . . en su fidelissima Ciudad de Valencia.** Valencia, 1759. Fo. 1 plt. with hole in blank margin, some soiling. Disbnd. (S. Jan.27; 430) *Quaritch.* £100

OLLIER, C.
See–**DELAMOTTE, William Alfred & Ollier, C.**

OLRIK, Jorgen
– **Drikkehorn og Sølvtøj.** Copen., 1909. Fo. Later cl. (SH. Jul.23; 297) *Quaritch.* £85

OLSEN, O.T.
– **The Piscatorial Atlas of the North Sea, English & St. George's Channels.** Grimsby, 1883. Fo. Orig. cl., spine worn. (SH. Jan.30; 383) *Quaritch.* £70

OLYMPIUS NEMESIANUS, Marcus Aurelius
See–**CALPURNIUS SICULUS, Titus & Olympius Nemesianus, Marcus Aurelius**

OMAN, Sir Charles
– **A History of the Art of War in the Middle Ages. –A History of the Art of War in the Sixteenth Century.** Boston; L., [1923]; [1937]. Together 3 vols. (2 + 1) Crimson three-qtr. mor., spines gt. (SG. Oct.30; 272) $210
– **A History of the Peninsular War.** Oxford, 1902-30. 1st. Edn. 7 vols. Crimson three-qtr. mor., raised bands. (SG. Oct. 30; 271) $325

OMAR Khayyam
– **Penilion, Rubaiyat in Welsh.** Ed.:– J. Morris-Jones. Gregy. Pr., 1928. Ltd. Edn. Orig. bdg. (P. Oct.2; 15) *Diba.* £70
– **The Rubaiyat.** Trans.:– [Edward Fitzgerald]. L., 1859. 1st. Edn., (250). 4to. Orig. ptd. wraps., upr. cover slightly soiled, silk-lined mor. folding case, unc. From the Prescott Collection. (CNY. Feb.6; 269) $7,500
– – **Anr. Edn.** Trans.:– [Edward Fitzgerald]. L., 1868. 2nd. Edn., (500). 4to. Orig. ptd. wraps., slightly soiled, qtr. mor. s.-c. From the Prescott Collection. (CNY. Feb.6; 270) $1,100
– – **Anr. Edn.** Trans.:– Edward Fitzgerald. 1872. Cont. mor.-bkd. cl., unc., cl. s.-c. John Ruskin's copy, with bkplt., presented by Bernard Quaritch with MS. note in upr. cover, some stanzas annotated with an 'R', preliminary blank inscr. '(J.R's copy.) S.C. Cockerell, from Joan Ruskin Severn . . .', together with an A.L.s. from her to him. (C. Jul.22; 40) *Joseph.* £200
– – **Anr. Edn.** Trans.:– Edward Fitzgerald. N.Y., Grol. Cl., 1885. (2) on vell. Red. lev. mor., elab. gt. decor., mor. onlays, spine in 6 compartments, 5 raised bands, mor. onlaid panels. red mor. doubls. with lge. gt. arabesque of onlaid mor., all gt.-tooled, orig. patterned wraps. bnd. in, sigd., by Rivière & Son, cl. s.-c. Cortlandt F. Bishop book-label. (CNY. May 22; 414) $7,500
– – **Anr. Edn.** L., 1898. Lev., covers & spine gt.-tooled with lge. floral sprays, stems & leaves, gt. dentelles, satin end-papers by Zaehnsdorf. (SG. Mar.19; 12) $180
– – **Anr. Edn.** Trans.:– Edward Fitzgerald. Ill.:– after Gilbert James. [1908]. Rose mor., upr. cover with gt. panel of vine scroll with mor. onlays, enclosing pict. panel. with mor. onlays, lr. cover with panel of double-fillet rules, decor., spine gt., decor., with mor. onlays in compartments, moiré satin end-papers & doubls. in gt. panel, in cl. s.-c., by Bayntum. (C. Feb.4; 190a) *Diba.* £320
– – **Anr. Edn.** Ill.:– Edmund Dulac. [1909]. (750) numbered, sigd. by artist. 4to. Orig. vell. gt., ties. (SH. Mar.26; 165) *Rosenblatt.* £160
– – **Anr. Copy.** 4to. Lacks ties. (SH. Jul.16; 141) *Renard Books.* £140
– – **Anr. Edn.** Ill.:– Edmund Dulac. [1909]. 4to. Orig. buckram gt., orig. box, worn. (SKC. May 19; 22) £65
– – **Anr. Copy.** Orig. gt. cl., publisher's box. (SG. Oct.23; 101) $160
– – **Anr. Edn.** Trans.:– Edward Fitzgerald. Ill.:– René Bull. [1910]. (250). 4to. Orig. vell. gt., lacks ties. Sigd. by artist. (SH. Dec.10; 115) *Joseph.* £155
– – **Anr. Copy.** Fo. Plts. only, individually mntd. on card in floral & gt. frame on floral ground, lettered tissue guards, title soiled. Loose as iss. in orig. cl. portfo., soiled, defect. (C. Jul.22; 64) *Greer.* £100
– – **Anr. Edn.** Ill.:– Anne Harriet Fish. 1922. 4to. Orig. cl.-bkd. bds., unc. (SH. Mar.26; 197) *May.* £60
– – **Anr. Edn.** Ill.:– A.H. Fish. [1922]. 4to. Orig. cl.-bkd. bds . (CSK. Jul.24; 1) £55
– – **Anr. Edn.** L., 1928. Lev. mor., by Rivière, richly gt., quotations in a double fillet border around background of inlaid vines, decor., gt. panel. spine. (SPB. Nov.25; 136) $750
– – **Anr. Edn.** Trans.:– Edward Fitzgerald. Ill.:– Willy Pogany. 1930. (1250) sigd. by artist. 4to. Mor. gt., partly unc., s.-c. (C. Jul.22; 95) *Wood.* £300
– – **Anr. Copy.** (750) sigd. by artist, & with frontis. also sigd. Orig. mor. gt., boxed. (SBA. May 27; 494) *Crook.* £125
– – **Anr. Edn.** Ill.:– Willy Pogany. [1930]. (1250) numbered, sigd. by artist & with etched additional frontis. also sigd. by him. 4to. Orig. mor., discold. (CSK. May 15; 48) £70
– – **Anr. Edn.** Trans.:– Edward Fitzgerald. Ill.:– Valenti Angelo. Ltd. Edns. Cl., 1935. (1500) numbered on Japan paper, & sigd. by artist. 12mo. Tooled cf., orig. box. (SG. Jan.15; 237) $120
– – **Anr. Edn.** Ill.:– John Buckland Wright. Gold. Cock. Pr., 1938. (300) numbered. Fo. Orig. mor.-bkd. cl. (CSK. Apr.3; 53) £185
– – **Anr. Copy.** Orig. mor.-bkd. cl., gt. (SH. Feb.19; 176) *George's.* £180
– – **Anr. Edn.** Trans.:– Edward Fitzgerald. Ill.:– Stephen Gooden. 1940. (125) sigd. by artist. Orig. mor.-bkd. cl., boxed. (SBA. May 27; 475) *Donnithorne.* £160
– – **Anr. Edn.** Ill.:– J. Yunge Bateman. Gold. Cock. Pr., 1958. (200). Sm. fo. Liby. stp. Orig. cl. gt. (SH. Feb.19; 201) *Ayres.* £60
– – **Anr. Edn.** Ill.:– Edmund Dulac. N.d. Ltd. Edn. sigd. by artist. 4to. Orig. vell. gt., ties, carton. (P. Jan.22; 244) *Quaritch.* £250
– – **Anr. Copy.** Mor. gt (CSK. Aug.15; 122) £65
– – **Anr. Copy.** 2 × 1¼ inches. Vell. with flowers & sprays on covers & spine, lacks ties. Miniature. (SG. Sep.4; 332) $100

O'NEILL, Eugene
– **Ah, Wilderness** N.Y., 1933. 1st. Edn. (325) numbered. Cf., spine scuffed. Sigd. (SG. Nov.13; 544) $100
– **Ah, Wilderness.–Days Without End.** N.Y., [1933; 1934]. (325) numbered, sigd. Together 2 vols. Leath., boxed. (SG. Jun.4; 405) $220
– **Days Without End.** N.Y., [1934]. Ltd. L.P. 1st. Edn. (325) numbered, sigd. Sm. 4to. Cf., head of spine very worn, tail of spine & corners worn. Sigd. pres. copy to 'Margaret Mann Again . . .' (PNY. Mar.26; 237) $150
– **Dynamo.** N.Y., 1929. L.P. Edn., (775) numbered on all-rag paper, sigd. 4to. Bds., unc., unopened. (SG. Jun.4; 403) $160
– **The Hairy Ape.** Ill.:– Alexander King. N.Y., 1929. (775) numbered & sigd. 4to. Cl.-bkd. patterned bds., d.-w., unc. & unopened. (SG. Nov.13; 543) $120
– – **Anr. Copy.** Qtr. cl. & batiked bds., d.-w., boxed. (PNY. Dec.3; 278) $110
– **Marco Millions.** N.Y., 1927. L.P. 1st. Edn., (450) sigd. Parch.-bkd. gt.-patterned bds. (SG. Jun.4; 400) $100
– **Mourning Becomes Electra.** N.Y., 1931. 1st. Edn. Cl., d.-w. A.L.s. laid in, to Rabbi Newman. (SG. Jun.4; 404) $850
– – **Anr. Edn.** N.Y., [1931]. Ltd. L.P. 1st. Edn. (550) numbered, sigd. Gt. vell., glassine d.-w., boxed (brkn.). (PNY. Mar.26; 239) $130
– – **Anr. Copy.** Minor defects. Orig. bdgs., box, worn. (SPB. Jul.28; 384) $100
– **The Plays.** N.Y., ca. 1934-35. 'Wilderness Edn.' (700) sigd. 12 vols. Gt. ornamental cl., glassine jackets, boxed. Remains in orig. packing crate. (PNY. Oct.1; 411a) $800
– – **Anr. Copy.** (SG. Dec.18; 323) $375
– **Strange Interlude.** N.Y., 1928. Ltd. L.P. 1st. Edn. (775) numbered, sigd. 4to. Foxed. Gt. & ruled vell., unopened, boxed (box worn). Sigd. pres. copy to former owner from his friend. (PNY. Mar.26; 240) $140
– – **Anr. Copy.** Minor defects. Orig. parch., spotted, browned. (SPB. Jul.28; 386) $125
– **Thirst.** Boston, 1914. 1st. Edn. Slight browning. Orig. bds., linen spine, slight soiling. Pres. copy. (SPB. Nov.25; 382) $700
– – **Anr. Edn.** Boston, [1914]. 1st. Edn. 12mo. Orig. cl.-bkd. bds., d.-w. (slightly soiled), qtr. mor. gt. s.-c. From the Prescott Collection. (CNY. Feb.6; 271) $550
– – **Anr. Copy.** Cl.-bkd. bds., orig. d.-w., pts. torn away. (SG. Jun.4; 399) $150

O'NEILL, Capt. F.
– **The Dance Music of Ireland.** Chic., 1907. Fo. Decor. cl., gt. (GM. Apr.30; 103) £55
– **Music of Ireland.** Chic., 1903. Fo. A few ll. loose. Decor. cl. (GM. Apr.30; 102) £60

O'NEILL, H.
See–**PETRIE, George & others**

O'NEILL, Rose
– **The Kewpies & the Runaway Baby.** Garden City, 1928. 1st. Edn. Cl., loose in bdg. Sigd. Pres. Copy, including sm. sketch of bird. (PNY. Oct.1; 138) $110

ONGANIA, Ferdinando
– **Calli e Canali in Venezia.** 1890-91. Fo. Some plts. detchd., slight spotting. Orig. mor.-bkd. cl. (CSK. Nov.14; 224) £70
– – **Anr. Edn.** [Venice], 1891-96. 2 vols. in 3. Fo. Slight spotting. Orig. cl., soiled. (CSK. May 1; 170) £240

ONOMATOLOGIA MEDICA Completa
Ed.:– A. v. Haller (Preface). Ulm, Frankfurt & Leipzig, 1755. 1st. Edn. Probably lacks 2 ll., supp. probably lacks 1 title-lf., owner's mark on title, slightly soiled in parts. Marb. bds. ca. 1800. (HK. Nov.18-21; 667) DM 480
– – **Anr. Edn.** Ed.:– A. v. Haller (Preface). Ulm, Frankfurt & Leipzig, 1756. 1st. Edn. Slightly browned & soiled, liby stp. on title. Cont. bds. (HK. May 12-14; 388) DM 500

ONTARIO PROVINCIAL MUSEUM
– **First 36 Annual Archaeological Reports.** Toronto, 1886-1928. 6 vols. Buckram. (SG. Mar.5; 77) $130

ONUPHRII PANVINII Veronensis Fratris Eremitae Augustiniani
Venice, 1588. 2 vols. in 1. Fo. Lacks 1 engraved port. Later hf. cf. (TA. Dec.18; 412) £210

OORT, Eduard Daniel van
– **De Vogels van Nederland.** The Hague, 1922-15. 5 vols. 4to. Lacks 1 chromolitho. plt. (no. 298). Orig. hf. leath., sm. tear at head of spine of vol. V. (SM. Feb.11; 39) Frs. 4,500

OPERA DELLA MEDICINA de Cavalli, Composta da Diversi Antichi Scrittori . . . di Greco in Buona Lingua Volgare Ridotta.
Venice, 1559. Spr. cf., [STC Italian p. 475] (S. Dec.1; 300) *Comben.* £50

OPHTHALMOLOGICAL SOCIETY of the United Kingdom
– **Transactions.** 1881-1974. Vols. 1-93, also separate Index vols. for vols. 71-90 (other indices bnd. in), in 99 vols. Cl. As journals, w.a.f. (S. Jun.17; 671) *Levy.* £120

OPIE, Mrs. Amelia
– **New Tales.** 1818. 4 vols. Hf. cf. (P. Jan.22; 3) *Fairweather.* £60
– **Temper.** 1812. 3 vols. Cf. (P. Jan.22; 2) *Cox.* £50

OPPE, Adolf P.
– **The Drawings of Paul & Thomas Sandby . . .** Oxford, 1947. 4to. Buckram, d.-w., boxed. Autograph inscr. to Frank Partridge, & sigd. 'Mary R. Christmas 1946'. (SG. Mar.12; 320) $130
– **Thomas Rowlandson, His Drawings & Water-Colours.** 1923. Fo. Orig. parch. with outer case brkn. (TA. Mar.19; 48) £95
– – **Anr. Copy.** (200) numbered on L.P. Gt.-lettered vell. (SG. Dec.4; 300) $170

OPPENHEIMER Series
– **Government Archives of Southern Rhodesia & Central African Archives.** 1943-54. 9 pts. (nos. 1-9) in 13 vols. Orig. cl., some marked, 2 with d.-w.'s. (SKC. Jul.28; 2475) £120
– – **Anr. Edn.** L., 1945-56. 9 works in 13 vols. Orig. bdgs. (VA. May 8; 482) R. 180

OPPIANUS
– **De Piscibus Libri V.** Venice, Dec., 1517. Some ll. stained, some underlinings, marginal inscrs. on

title & in text. 18th. C. Fr. red mor., gt., slight wear. (S. Feb.10; 454)   *Maggs.* £260
– **De Venatione; De Piscatu.** Ed.:– Conrad Rittershus. Leyden, 1597. 1st. Edn. Old vell. (SG. Oct.16; 259) $130
– **Halieutica, sive De Piscatu.** Colle di Valdelsa, Bonus Gallus, Sep. 12, 1478. 1st. Edn. 4to. Spaces for initial capitals, with guide letters, lacks 1st, lf., supplied in facs., corners of many ll. worn, folios 2 & 3 with corners at lr. edge renewed, some ll. with sm. marginal tears, light foxing & finger-soiling to some early ll. 19th. C. cf. gt., covers with gt. floral borders & central panel of blind-stpd. sm. stars, gt. spine. From the collection of Eric Sexton. [BMC VII, 1079, Goff O 65, HC 12015*] (CNY. Apr.8; 38) $3,000
– **Halieuticks.** Trans.:– W. Draper & J. Jones. Oxford, 1722. 1st. Engl. Edn. Mod. cf. (SG. Oct.16; 260) $180

OPPOLZER, Theodor Ritter von
– **Canon der Finsternisse.** Vienna, 1887. 1st. Edn. 4to. Cont. hf. mor. From Honeyman Collection. (S. Nov.10; 2361)   *Quaritch.* £170

OPPRESSION. A Poem. By an American. With Notes by a North Briton.
L., 1765. 1st. Edn. 4to. Slight soiling, partly unc. Disbnd., folding case. [Sabin 57416] (SPB. Nov.24; 44) $400

ORACLES de Flore . . .
Ill.:– C.F.P. Del . . . Paris, ca. 1810? 18mo. Engraved plts., some cold. Orig. bds. (SG. Sep.18; 279) $200

ORAISON Dominicale
[Paris], [1883]. (100). 4to. Mor. by Weber, lge. blind-tooled border, inside dentelle. (HD. Mar.18; 125)   Frs. 1,880

ORANGE, James
– **The Chater Collection.** 1924. Ltd. Edn. 4to. Orig. cl. (P. Sep.11; 238)   £220
– – **Anr. Copy.** D-w. (SBA. Jul.22; 151)   *Fairbarns.* £160

ORBELIANA, Sulkhan Saba
– **The Book of Wisdom & Lies.** Trans.:– Oliver Wardrop. Hammersmith, Kelms. Pr., 1894. (250). Orig. limp vell, silk ties, unc. & partially unopened. (CNY. Oct.1; 190) $420
– – **Anr. Copy.** (CNY. May 22; 320) $280

ORBELLIS, Nicolaus de
– **Compendium in mathematicam, physicam et metaphysicam.** Bologna, Henricus de Harlem., 1485. 1st. Edn. 2 vols. in 1. 4to. Lacks a blank at beginning of vol. II, some margins damaged by damp & reprd., affecting a few letters in final gathering, some staining & discolouration. Vell. From Honeyman Collection. [BMC VI, 830; Goff O 73] (S. Nov.10; 2362)   *Hill.* £500
– **Expositio super Textu Petri Hispani.** Venice, 10 Mar., 1500. 4to. Later hf. vell. [Goff O 70] (C. Jul.16; 283)   *Maggs.* £180
– **Summule Philosophie Rationalis.** Basle, Michael Furter, 1494. 4to. Rubricated thro.-out, copious marginal notes, many cropped, running title also occasionally cropped, lacks blank portion of title, reprd. Recent vell. bds. [Hain 12044*; BMC II p. 782; Goff O 80] (C. Apr.1; 66)   *Kemp.* £320

ORBIGNY, Alcide Dessalines d'
– **Mollusques Vivants et Fossiles.** Paris, 1845. 35 engraved plts. bnd. in at rear. Cont. hf. mor. (TA. Mar.19; 263)   £58
– **Voyage Pittoresque dans les Deux Amériques.** Paris, 1836. 4to. Soiled in places, some stains. Cont. bds. [Sabin 57458] (D. Dec.11-13; 1343)   DM 450

ORBIGNY, Charles Dessalines d'
– **Dictionnaire d'Histoire Naturelle.** Paris, 1869. 3 vols. 4to. Hf. red chagrin, corners, 5 spine raised bands. (LM. Jun.13; 93)   B.Frs. 41,000

ORBIGNY-EYRIES, d'
See–DUMONT D'Urville, Jules Sebastien César & others

ORCUTT, William Dana
– **Book in Italy, during the 15th & 16th Centuries.** 1928. (750) numbered. 4to. Orig. bds. with vell. backstrip, slightly soiled. (TA. Sep.18; 5)   £64
– – **Anr. Copy.** Orig. parch.-bkd. bds., soiled. (SH. Jan.29; 44)   *Subunso.* £60

ORD, John Walker
See–WHITAKER, Thomas Dunham–ORD, John Walker

ORDEN VOM GOLDENEN VLIES
– **Statutenbuch.** Ed.:– Hans Gerstinger. Vienna, 1934. (300) numbered. 2 vols., facs. reproduction of Codex Vindobonensis 2606. 4to. 196 pp., (14 pp. in colours & gold), & explanatory text with 16 plts. Orig. velvet, clasps, orig mor., in fitted cl. box. (SH. Apr.10; 343)   *Thorp.* £100

ORDENANZA GENERAL Formada de Orden de su Magestada y Mandad a Imprimir y Publicar para el Gobierno e Instruccion de Intendentes, Subdelegados y demas Empleados en Indias
Madrid, 1803. Fo. Liby. stp. removed from title. Cont. red mor., stained and warped. [Sabin 57472] (SPB. May 5; 376) $175

ORDENANZAS del Tribunal del Consulado de esta Ciudad de los Reyes y Renes del Perú, Tierrafirme y Chile
Lima, 1680. Fo. Sm. hole in final lf. with loss of a few letters, margins defect. & stains at beginning & end. Limp vell. (SPB. May 5; 378) $375

ORDERS & ORDINANCES FOR THE BETTER GOVERNMENT of the Hospitall of Bartholomew the Lesse . . . Together with a Briefe Discourse of the Laudible Customes of London
1652. 2 pts. in 1 vol. Some headlines cut into. Hf. mor. British Museum dupl. [Wing 0396] (S. Dec.2; 570)   *Cooke.* £55

ORDNANCE Survey
– **A General Map of Ireland Showing the Poor Law Union & Electoral Division Boundaries.** N.d. 6 pts. Linen-bkd. (GM. Oct.30; 329)   £50

ORDNUNG DES FLEYSCHKAUFFS zu Franckenfurt furgenommen. Anno & c. MDXLI
Frankfurt, a. M., [1541]. 4to. A few marginal annots. & underlinings. Disbnd., cl. case. From Honeyman Collection. (S. Nov.10; 2363)   *Dr. P.C. Martin.* £200

ORDONNANCE de Louis XIV
Paris, 1676. Sm. 12mo. Cont. mor., fleurs de lys semé, inner dentelle. Autograph sig. of J.B. Racine. (HD. Apr.24; 88)   Frs. 2,000

ORDONNANCES de l'Ordre de la Thoyson d'Or (Les)
[Antw.], [Plant. Pr.], ca. 1559. 1st. Edn., on vell. Fo. List of 5 additional chapters of 2nd. Edn. in cont. MS. at foot of H3r & chapters themselves in MS. on last 4 blank ll., bkplt. of A. Bröleman. Red mor., gt. fillet & broad floral border, spine gt. in compartments, narrow gt. onlays of mor. between raised bands & at foot, inner gt. floral dentelles, silk liners. McCarthy-Reagh copy. (SM. Oct.8; 1893)   Frs. 75,000

ORDONNANCES ROYAULX de la Iuridicion de la Prevoste des Marches et Eschivinaige de la Ville de Paris
[Paris], 16 Dec. 1528. 2nd. Edn. 4to. 16 supp. ll., lacks lf. 110 with printer's mark, & lacks 2 supps. slightly stained & browned in parts, cold. woodcut pasted on title verso. Later vell. (D. Dec.11-13; 42)   DM 4,600

ORDONNANCIE ENDE INSTRUCTIE naer de Welcke Voortaen hen moeten reguleren die ghesworen Wisselaers ofte Collecteurs vande Goude ende Silvere penningen, wesende verboden, gheschroyt, te licht oft te teer versleten . . . om de selve te leveren inde Munten van sijne Majesteyt . . ., in penninghen van hunnen slaghe.
Antw., 1633. Very narrow lge. 8vo. A few slight stains at beginning & end, some inner margins with a sm. wormhole. Cont. vell., soiled, some wear, occasionally cropped. (VG. Dec.15; 511)   Fls. 1,500

ORDONNANTIE PROVISIONNAEL ons Heeren des Coninck . . . –DONGHEVALUEERDE GOUDEN ENDE SILVEREN MUNTE
Antw., 1575. Old vell. (LM. Mar.21; 245)   B.Frs. 11,000

ORDRE du Benoist Saint Esprit
– **Le Livre des Statuts et Ordonnances de l'Ordre du Benoist Sainct Esprit . . .** N.p., ca. 1580. 4to. 34 ll. sigd, ruled cont. Cont. mor., 3 fillets, crowned cipher in corners, arms of Henri III of France in centre, surrounded by 4 doves, spine with fleurs-de-lys, sm. stains & repairs. (HD. Mar.18; 105)   Frs. 14,000

ORENDI, J.
– **Das Gesamtwissen üb Antike u Neue Teppiche des Orients.** Vienna, 1930. 2 vols. Slightly stained

in parts, end-ll. stpd, ex-lib. Orig. linen. (HK. Nov.18-21; 3521)   DM 1,100

ORESME, Nicolaus
– **De Latitudinibus formarum [with the Quaestiones of Blasius de Pelicanis de Parma].** Padua, Matthaeus Cerdonis, 18 Feb. 1486. 2nd. Edn. 4to. Lacks final blank, tears reprd. in inner margins thro.-out affecting text, some browning. 19th. C. vell. bds., gt., hf. mor. case. From Honeyman Collection. [BMC VII, 923; Hain 8925; Goff 094] (S. Nov.10; 2364)   *Quaritch.* £850

ORFORD, Horace Walpole, Earl of
See–WALPOLE, Horace, Earl of Orford

ORIENT (L')
Paris, 1852. Fo. Some spotting. Lacks covers. W.a.f. (P. Jul.30; 223)   *Dupont.* £120

ORIENTAL ANNUAL, Or Scenes in India
1834-37. 4 vols. Unif. cont. mor. gt. (TA. Nov.20; 25)   £64

ORIENTAL Ceramic Society
– **Transactions.** 1953-65. Vols. 26-35 (9 vols.). 4to. Lacks vol. 31 for the year 1958. Cl. (C. Feb.4; 265)   *Marks.* £130

ORIENTAL MORALIST (the), or the Beauties of the Arabian Nights Entertainments
Ed.:– Rev. Mr. Cooper [Richard Johnson]. [1791/92?]. 1st. Edn. 12mo. Advts. Orig. sheep. (SH. Mar.19; 237)   *Vincent.* £75

ORIGINAL-ANSICHTEN der Historisch Merkwürdigsten Städte in Deutschland nach der Natur
Ill.:– I. Riegel, M. Kolb, J. Poppel, E. Höfer & others. [Frankfurt], ca. 1880. 4to. Slightly soiled. Orig. linen portfo., defect. (D. Dec.11-13; 1295)   DM 6,000

ORINDA (Pseud.)
See–PHILIPS, Katherine

ORLEANS, Charles d'
– **Poèmes.** Ill.:– Henri Matisse. Paris, 1950. (1230) sigd. by artist, numbered. Fo. Unsewn in orig. wraps., new s.-c. (SH. Nov.21; 413)   *Jamieson.* £470

ORLEANS, F.P. duc d'
– **Lettres 1825-42.** Paris, 1889. (40) numbered. on Japon. Mod. red mor. by Dupré, lavishly gt., mor. & silk doubls., orig. wraps. preserved. (SH. Oct.10; 386)   *James Wilson.* £60

ORLERS, Jan J.
– **Beschrijvinghe der Stadt Leyden . . .** Leyden, 1641. 2nd. Edn. 4to. Plan a little worn in fold. Cont. vell., soiled. (VG. Dec.17; 1473)   Fls. 700
– – **Anr. Copy.** 2 plts. with sm. tear, lacks folding view as usual. (VG. Oct.13; 117)   Fls. 600
– **La Genéalogie des Comtes de Nassau nouvellement imprimée.** Leyden, 2nd. Edn. Priv. Ptd., 1615. 2nd. Edn. Fo. 1 genealogical tree defect. & reprd., some sm. marginal tears reprd., some ll. slightly soiled, some light staining in places. Cont. vell., gt. supra-libros of Signet Liby. on covers (VG. Oct.13; 118)   Fls. 2,600

ORLIK, Emil
– **Aus Agypten.** Berlin, 1922. (10) Privilege Edn. on Jap. with extra etching. Fo. Loose in orig. mor. portfo., slightly soiled. All etchings sigd. by artist, under passepartouts. (H. May 21/22; 1742)   DM 4,200
– **Kleine Aufsätze.** Berlin, 1924. (100) privilege Edn. 4to. Orig. hf. leath., spine worn. Sigd. by artist on etching & cold. woodcut. (H. Dec.9/10; 2271)   DM 480
– **Kleine Holzschnitte.** Berlin, 1920. (100) B Edn. 4to. Slightly stained. Loose, in orig. box. (R. Oct.14-18; 1026)   DM 8,000

ORLOWSKI, Alexandre d'
– **Album Dédié à Son Altesse Impériale Monseigneur le Grand-Duc Michel.** Ill.:– Drouillière after Orlowski. St. Petersb., 1823. 4to. Cont. hf. roan, corners. (HD. Dec.5; 161)   Frs. 5,000
– **Collection de Costumes Persans, Civils et Militaires.** St. Petersb., 1822. Fo. Roan gt., worn, orig. wrap. & explication bnd. in. (BS. Jun.11; 378)   £720

ORME, Edward
– **Collection of British Field Sports.** Ill.:– After Samuel Howitt. L., [1807-08; wtrmkd. 1804-05-06]. Ob. fo. Title inlaid to size, 2 plts.

ORME, Edward – Collection of British Field Sports. *-contd.*
reprd. (no loss), 1 marginal tear, plts. 2 & 9 in earliest state, titles corrected by ptd. overslips, plt. 18 not numbered. Orig. bdg. (SPB. Oct.1; 93)
$13,500
– – **Anr. Edn.** Ill.:– S. Howitt. [Plts. dtd. 1807-08]. Ob. fo. 20 cold. aquatint plts. Cont. hf. cf., mod. mor. box. Schwerdt bkplt. (C. Mar.18; 83)
Crawley. £9,500
– – **Anr. Copy.** 16 cold. aquatints only (of 20). Disbnd. As a collection of plts., w.a.f. (C. Mar.18; 84)
Sabin. £5,000
– – **Anr. Edn.** Ill.:– after Samuel Howitt. [Guildford], n.d. Ob. fo. Orig. wraps., slightly soiled. (CSK. Sep.26; 14)
£70
– **An Essay on Transparent Prints.** 1807. [1st. Edn.?]. Sm. fo. Hf. cf. (P. Jan.22; 250)
Fogg. £400
– – **Anr. Copy.** Lge. 4to. 17 engraved plts., text wtrmkd. 1804, 1 plt. 1802. Orig. bds., rebkd. unc. (S. Nov.25; 435)
Traylen. £340
– – **Anr. Copy.** Text in Engl. & Fr., 1 plt. of specimen papers, without subscription list, a few minor defects. Slightly worn. (SBA. Dec.16; 33)
Baer. £220
– **Foreign Field Sports.** Ill.:– Samuel Howitt & others. 1819. 4to. 110 hand-cold. plts., wtrmkd. 1817, text without wtrmk. Cont. str.-grd. mor. gt. (S. Nov.24; 224)
Traylen. £550
[-][-] **Anr. Edn.** Ill.:– Samuel Howitt. [1819]. Ob. 4to. 57 hand-cold. plts., without wtrmk., no text. Late 19th. C. hf. mor. W.a.f. (S. Nov.24; 225)
Elliott. £190
– **Historic, Military & Naval Anecdotes . . .** L., 1819. 1st. Edn. Fo. Cont. red str.-grd. mor. gt., worn. (CNY. May 22; 170)
$1,000
– – **Anr. Edn.** L., 1819. 4to. List of subscribers, plt. 1 re-inserted. Orig, grd. hf. roan, unc., publisher's ptd. label on front end-paper. (SPB. Oct.1; 205)
$650
– – **Anr. Edn.** [1819]. 4to. Sm. tear in bottom margin of frontis. Cont. hf. mor., worn. (TA. Sep.18; 113)
£360
– – **Anr. Copy.** Margins soiled. Orig. hf. mor., worn. (TA. Sep.18; 322)
£350
– **A Picture of St. Petersburgh.** Ill.:– after Mornay. Priv. Ptd., 1815. Fo. Red hf. mor., gt., by Sangorski & Sutcliffe. (C. Nov.6; 222)
Spencer. £700

See–HOWITT, Samuel–ORME, Edward

ORME, Robert
[-] **Military Transactions . . . in Indostan.** 1775-78. 2 vols. 4to. Cf. gt. (P. Oct.23; 80) *Rogers.* £65

ORMEROD, George
– **The History of Cheshire.** Ed.:– Thomas Helsby. [1875]. Sm. Paper Edn. 3 vols. in 18 orig. pts. (lacks pts. 7 & 17) together 16. Fo. Orig. wraps., slightly spotted. W.a.f. (SBA. Oct.22; 307)
Nicholson. £120
– **The History of the County Palatine & City of Chester.** 1819. [1st. Edn.?]. 3 vols. Fo. Cont. red hf. mor., gt. panel. spines. (C. Feb.25; 51)
Chesters. £280
– – **Anr. Copy.** Slight offsetting, 2 maps & plans hand-cold. in outl., 1 double-p., 2 other plts. of stained glass windows partly hand-cold., 1 heightened with gold. Cont. diced russ. gt. (SBA. Dec.16; 176)
Nute. £250
– – **Anr. Copy.** (65) L.P. Cont. hf. russ. gt., unc. From the collection of Eric Sexton. (C. Apr.16; 322)
Kelsall. £230
– – **Anr. Copy.** Engraved double-p. map, cl.-bkd. Hf. russ., very worn. (SBA. Oct.22; 308)
Nicholson. £140
– – **Anr. Edn.** Ed.:– Thomas Helsby. 1882. L.P. [2nd. Edn.?]. 3 vols. in 6. Fo. Cont. hf. mor. gt. (C. Jul.15; 84)
Traylen. £300
– – **Anr. Copy.** Prelims in vols. 1 & 2 detchd., a few minor defects, doubl-p. map cold. in outl. Orig. cl.-bkd. bds., very worn. (SBA. Dec.16; 175)
Nicholson. £150
– – **Anr. Copy.** Vol. 3 only. Some slight spotting. Cont. hf. mor. (CSK. Mar.13; 59)
£85

ORNEMENT DE LA TOILETTE, ou les Filets de l'Amour
Paris, ca. 1780. 64mo. Leath., isinglass covered miniature painting on each cover, gt.-tooled frame, gt.-tooled s.-c. (SG. Oct.9; 183)
$1,600

OROSIUS, Paulus–DIODORUS SICULUS –[TORRENTINUS, Hermann]
– **Opus Prestantissimum.–Bibliotecae Libri Sex. –Elucidarius Carminum & Historiarum.** Paris, 18 Sep. 1510; ca. 1510; ca. 1510. 3 works in 1 vol. 4to. Some worming in 1st. & 3rd works, affecting text, some browning. Cont. cf., slightly worn. (S. May 5; 17)
West. £85

ORSATO, S.
– **Historia di Padova.** Padua, 1678. 1st. Edn. 1st. pt. Fo. A few stains. Cont. vell., worn. (SH. Jun.11; 222)
Quaritch. £100

ORSCHALL, Jean Christian
[–] **Ars Fusoria Fundamentalis et Experimentalis.** Kassel, 1735. Later Edn. Browned, title reprd. Mod. cont. style leath. (R. Oct.14-18; 207)
DM 1,000

ORTA, Garcia de & Monardes, Nicolo
– **Dell'Historia de i Semplici Aromati.** Venice, 1589. 2 Pts. in 1 vol. Stained in places, ff. 03 & 4 in fac. Cont. limp vell., repd. & recased. (S. Mar.17; 308)
Rosenburg. £60

ORTEGA, Juan de
– **Oeuvre tressubtille & Profitable de l'art & Science de Aristmeticque: & Geometrie translate nouvellement despaignol en fràcoys (by C. Platin).** Lyon, 23 Oct. 1515. 4to. Browned & stained. Old rough cf., worn, hf. mor. case. From Honeyman Collection; stp. of Biblioteca di Pierpaolo Vaccarino. (S. Nov.10; 2365)
Brieux. £740
– **Suma de Arithmetica: Geometrica Practica utilissima.** Rome, 10 Nov. 1515. 1st. Edn. Fo. Last 8 ll. reprd. in upr. inner margins, some foxing., symbolic device incorporating initials SR on fly-lf. Cont. vell. bds., stained, upr. cover almost detchd., lacks ties. From Honeyman Collection. (S. Nov.10; 2366)
Jackson. £520
– **Tratado subtilissimo de Arismetica y de Geometria.** Seville, 1542. 4to. Some staining & soiling, erased inscr. on title leaving 2 sm. holes & a sm. tear in lr. inner border. Vell. bds., soiled. From Honeyman Collection. (S. Nov.10; 2367)
Manning. £240
– – **Anr. Edn.** Ed.:– Goncalo Busto. Seville, 1552. 4to. Some stains, mostly marginal, Spanish owner's inscr., partly deleted, on fly-lf. Vell. bds. From Honeyman Collection. (S. Nov.10; 2368)
Manning. £90
– – **Anr. Edn.** Ed.:– Juan Lagarto & Goncalo Busto. Granada, 1563. 4to. Title restored & mntd., lacks final blank, marginal repairs, slightly affecting text in some cases, printing flaw on verso of 201, some stains. 19th. C. red mor., gt. From Honeyman Collection. (S. Nov.10; 2369)
Manning. £60

ORTELIUS, Abraham
– **Epitome Theatri Orbis Terrarum . . .** Antw., 1612. Ob. 8vo. Lacks 23 engraved maps, & 3 prelims., C4, C5, & Q5 to end, occasional marginal dampstaining & soiling. Red mor., gt. panel. spines & sides. W.a.f. (C. Nov.6; 267)
Hus. £1,000
– **Theatro del Mondo.** Antw., 1608. 1st. Italian Edn. 3 Pts. in 1 vol. Fo. 2 hand-cold. engraved titles, 2 cold. ports., engraved epitaph, hf.-p. conspectus of world, 4 sm. cold. engraved maps, 194 engraved hand-cold. maps on 159 double-p. plts., 5 double-p. plts., many hand-cold. initials & arabesques, some heightening with gold, lacks 2 maps, title torn & reprd., A2, A5 & A6 reprd., 1 plt. reprd. 17th. C. red mor., gt. panel. sides, enclosing cardinal's arms & shield, corners & spine reprd. & restored. (C. Mar.18; 64)
Burgess. £13,000
– **Theatrum Orbis Terrarum.** Ed.:– R.A. Skelton (intro.). Antw. [Cleveland], 1570 [1964]. Facs. Edn. Tall fo. Buckram. (SG. May 21; 153) $130
– – **Anr. Edn.** Antw., [1594]-95. Koeman's Iss. 3 pts. in 1 vol. Fo. 170 names in Catalogus Auctorum, architectural engraved title, port. 146 plts., mostly doubl-p. maps, title to Parergon in woodcut frame, woodcut device on Nomenclator title dtd. 1595, apparently lacks 2 plts., few maps separated at centre fold, 2 inscrs. dtd. 1594. Orig. limp vell., worn. W.a.f. (S. Mar.31; 272)
P. Hillman. £13,000
– – **Anr. Edn.** Antw., 1603. 2 pts. in 1 vol. Fo. 2 hand-cold. engraved titles, 1 heightened with gold, hand-cold. engraved arms on verso, full-p. hand-cold. engraved epitaph & port., 5 double-p. plts., 181 hand-cold. maps on 144 doubl-p. sheets, mntd. on guards, lacks 3 maps, 1 plt. loose from anr. copy, liby. stp. on title & dedication. Late 19th. C. roan, upr. cover detchd. W.a.f. (C. May 20; 159)
Weiss. £16,000
– **Theatrum Orbis Terrarum.** [Nomenclator Ptolemaicus]. Antw., 1579. 2 pts. in 1 vol. Fo. With restorations, lacks map 13, 10 maps with tears, side margin eroded with damp without loss of engr. but for 2 maps. Cont. vell., very defect. with losses. W.a.f. (CR. Mar.19; 321)
Lire 11,500,000
– **Theatrum Orbis Terrarum, with the Parergon & Nomenclator Ptolemaicus.** Antw., 1603. 3 pts. in 1 vol. Fo. (457mm. × 292mm.). 1 port of Ortelius a hand-cold. dupl., mntd. as frontis., 147 (of 151) engraved maps, plus plts. 'Tempe' & 'Daphne' & 2 costume plts., 'De Institutione et Ordine Imperii Germanici', engraved title cut round & remargined, fore-margins of 5 following ll. renewed, wants Koeman's maps 106 & 116-118, repair of clean tear at bottom of centre fold of 1 or 2 maps, a few rust-spots or minor stains, neat MS. numbering on versos of top fore-corners of most maps in 1st. pt. 18th. C. pol. mott. cf. W.a.f. (S. Jun.29; 8)
Burgess. £11,000
– **Thesaurus Geographicus.** Antw., 1596. 2nd. Edn. Fo. Slightly browned thro.-out. 18th. C. leath. gt. (R. Mar.31-Apr.4; 79)
DM 430

ORTELIUS, H.
– **Schöne Bildnusz in Kupfer gestochen der erleuchten berumbtisten Weiber Altes und Neues Testaments.** Nuremb., 1610. 1st. Edn. 2 pts. in 1 vol. 4to. Slightly stained, mainly at ends, a few sm. wormholes, slightly foxed in places, a few sm. tears. 18th. C. hf. vell. (VG. Oct.13; 119) Fls. 800

ORTIZ, Blasius
– **Summi Templi Toletani Perqu[am] Graphica Descriptio.** Toledo, 1549. 1st. Edn. Early inscr. on title referring to author. 18th. C. Fr. mor., triple gt. fillet, spine gt. in compartments, inner gt. floral dentelles. Girardot de Préfond-McCarthy-Reagh copy. (SM. Oct.8; 1896)
Frs. 4,000

ORTOGRAFIA DE LA LENGUA CASTELLANA, compuesta por la Real Academia Espanola.
Madrid, 1792. 7th. Edn. Cont. Spanish tree cf., gt. arms in centre of covers. (C. Apr.1; 158)
Morton-Smith. £60

ORTUTAY, Gyula
– **Nyíri es Rétközi Parasztmesék.** Ill.:– Gyorgy Buday. Gyoma, 1935. (1000) numbered, sigd. by author & artist. Orig. cl.-bkd. bds., slightly worn & soiled. Pres. copy, inscr. by artist. (SH. Nov.20; 245)
Quaritch. £55

ORVILLE, Jacob Ph. de
– **Sicula, quibus Sicilise Veteris, Rudera, Additis Antiquitatum Tabulis, illustrantur.** Amst., 1764. 1st. Edn. 2 vols. in 1. Fo. A few ll. slightly browned & soiled, MS. date & name, later pencil notes in parts. Later vell. gt., gt. arms, ties, slightly soiled. (H. Dec.9/10; 585)
DM 480
– – **Anr. Copy.** 2 pts. in 1 vol. Fo. Old cf., 5 lge. decor. spine raised bands, lge. gt. fillet & dentelle border with arms tooled in centre of covers. (LM. Mar.21; 226)
B.Frs. 9,000

ORVIS, Charles F. & Cheney, A. Nelson
– **Fishing with the Fly.** Manchester, Vt., 1883. 1st. Edn. Gt.-pict. cl. (SG. Oct.16; 263) $160
– – **Anr. Copy.** Pict. cl. (SG. Dec.11; 80) $100

ORWELL, George (Pseud.)
See–BLAIR, Eric Arthur 'George Orwell'

OSA [Wasp]
Ed.:– [M.M. Brodovsky]. St. Petersb., 1906. Trial Iss. & nos. 1-2 only (of 7). 4to. Unbnd. (SH. Feb.5; 101)
De la Casa. £65

OSBALDESTON, George
– **Autobiography.** Ed.:– E.D. Cumming & Cook. 1926. Ltd. Edn. Cl. & bds. (CE. Nov.20; 133)
£54
– **Squire Osbaldeston: His Autobiography.** Ed.:– E.D. Cuming. L. & N.Y., 1926. (100) with 13 extra ill., sigd. by Cook. 4to. Red mor. gt., partly unc., s.-c. (CNY. Oct.1; 109) $350

OSBALDISTON, William Augustus
– **British Sportsman.** 1792. 4to. Cf. gt. (P. Apr.9; 247)
Shapiro. £120
– – **Anr. Edn.** [1792]. 4to. Cont. spr. cf., worn, rebkd. (SBA. Mar.4; 17)
Beverley. £195

OSBORN, Henry Fairfield
– **Proboscidea. A Monograph of the Mastodonts & Elephants.** N.Y., 1936-42. (675) numbered. 2 vols. 4to. Orig. cl. (SH. Jun.4; 188) *Elliott.* £55

OSBORNE, William Godolphin
- The Court & Camp of Runjeet Sing. 1840. 1st. Edn. Orig. cl. (SH. Mar.5; 106)
Glazebrook. £130
– – **Anr. Copy.** 1 or 2 plts. with short tears in margins, some light foxing. Orig. embossed cl., gt., loose unc. (S. Jun.29; 222) *Hossain.* £70

OSBOURNE, Lloyd
See–STEVENSON, Robert Louis & Osbourne, Lloyd

OSENBRUGGEN, Eduard
- Das Berner Oberland. Ill.:– Ludwig Robock. Darmstadt, [1872]. Ob. 4to. Cont. red hf. mor. (C. Jul.15; 85) *Walford.* £180

OSGOOD, Mrs. F.S.
- The Flower Alphabet. Boston, 1845. Sm. 4to. Errata slip. Orig. gt. bds. (SKC. May 19; 41) £65

OSLER, Sir William
- Bibliotheca Osleriana, a Catalogue of Books Illustrating the History of Science & Medicine. Oxford, 1929. [1st. Edn.?]. 4to. Orig. buckram, orig. d.-w. loosely inserted. (S. Jun.16; 621)
Jenner Books. £160
– – **Anr. Copy.** D.-w. (S. Feb.23; 349)
Jenner. £140
- Christmas & the Microscope. 1869. In 'Hardwicke's Science Gossip for 1869'. Hf. cf. (S. Jun.16; 617) *Puech.* £90
- Incunabula Medica, a Study of the Earliest Printed Medical Books 1467-1480. 1923. 4to. Orig. canvas-bkd. bds. (S. Jun.16; 620)
Jenner Books. £130
– – **Anr. Copy.** Slightly soiled. (S. Feb.23; 348) *Way.* £100
– – **Anr. Copy.** Fo. Hf. linen. (SG. Jan.22; 319) $300
- Modern Medicine. Phila., 1907-10. 7 vols. Orig. cl. (CB. Sep.24; 259) *Can.* $200
- The Principles & Practice of Medicine. N.Y., 1892. 1st. Edn. With corrected spelling of 'Gorgias' on p.[vi]. Cl., jnts. crudely reprd. (SG. Aug.21; 348) $220
– – **Anr. Copy.** Sm. 4to. Copy from publisher's liby. (PNY. Mar.26; 241) $150
- The Treatment of Disease.–The Nation & the Tropics.–The Growth of Truth, Harveian Oration.–The Student Life.–Religio Medici.–Michael Servetus. 1906-1909. 6 works in 1 vol. New cl., all orig. wraps. preserved. (S. Jun.16; 627)
Zeitlin & Verbrugge. £80

OSMER, William
- A Dissertation on Horses.–A Treatise on the Diseases . . . of Horses. 1756; 1759. 2 vols. in 1. Hf. cf., worn. (SH. Jun.25; 198) *Way.* £80

OSTELL, Thomas
- New General Atlas. 1807. 4to. Hf. cf., covers detchd. (CSK. Jan.30; 96) £80
– – **Anr. Copy.** Mod. cf.-bkd. cl. (CSK. Sep.12; 106) £55

OSTERREICHISCHE KUNSTTOPOGRAPHIE
Vienna, 1907-47. Vols. 1-30 in 32 vols. 4to. Vol. 30 slightly stained. 10 orig. linen, 11 orig. hf. linen, (R. Oct.14-18; 713) DM 6,600

OTBOI [Retreat]
Ed.:– [M.K. Gurskaya]. St. Petersb., 1906. Nos. 1-5. 4to. Unbnd. (SH. Feb.5; 103)
De la Casa. £90

OTIOT Shel Rabbi Akiva
Constantinople, 1516-19. 1st. Edn. Sm. 4to. Contents loose in bdg., worming not affecting text, lightly stained, owner's sig. on title. Bds. Bkplt. of Elkan Adler. (SPB. May 11; 78) $4,750
[–] – **Anr. Edn.** Venice, 1546. 2nd. Edn. 4to. Slight staining. Cl. (S. Nov.18; 385) *James.* £340
– – **Anr. Edn.** Kracow, 1579. 3rd. Edn. Stained. Hf. cl., spine detchd. (SPB. May 11; 30) $550
– – **Anr. Copy.** Repairs, worming, stained. Wraps. (SPB. May 11; 31) $450

OTTAWA Naturalist, The
Ottawa, 1887/88-1906/07. Vols. I-XX, in 10 vols. Perforated liby. stps. on title-p. & elsewhere. Hf. leath. & cl. (CB. Feb.18; 170) *Can.* $300

OTTENS, Reinier & Josua & Renard, Louis
- Atlas van Zeevaert en Koophandel Door de Geheele Weereldt. Amst., 1744. Atlas fo. Cont. bds., worn, unc. (SG. Oct.9; 20) $13,000

OTTLEY, William Young
- A Collection of 129 Fac-similes . . . 1828. L.P. Fo. Mott. cf., gt., by F. Bedford. (S. Nov.24; 227)
Broseghini. £150
- An Inquiry into the Origin & Early History of Engraving upon Copper & in Wood. Ill.:– after Dürer. 1816. 2 vols. 4to. Late 19th. C. pol. cf. by F. Bedford, spines gt., partly unc. (S. Nov.24; 226)
Talerman. £180
- The Italian School of Design. L., 1823. [1st. Edn.?] Fo. Hf. roan, upr. cover detchd. (P. Jul.2; 217) *Chow.* £190
– – **Anr. Copy.** 1 lf. reprd., a few plts. cropped at head, tear in 2 plts., occasional soiling & spotting. 19th. C. cl., worn, contents loose. Pres. copy from 'D. Colnaghi Esq. 1850' to Bank of England liby., & Literary Association. (S. Sep.29; 223)
Lester. £120

OTTLEY, William Young & Tomkins, P.W.
- Engravings of the Most Noble the Marquis of Stafford's Collection of Pictures. 1818. L.P. 4 vols. Lge. fo. 291 hand-cold. engrs. on 126 card. mounts, ptd. identification slips pasted on versos, some slight discolouration of mounts. Cont. russ., gt., rebkd. preserving most of orig. spines. Bkplt. of Count Hemricourt de Ramioul. (S. Jun.22; 67)
Franklin. £1,200
– – **Anr. Copy.** 4 vols. in 2. Slight spotting. Cont. russ., tooled in gt. & blind, allegorical centre-pieces of Poetry supplying subjects to Paintings & Sculpture, rebkd., slightly marked. (S. Jun.22; 68) *Schuster.* £220
– – **Anr. Copy.** Lacks final blanks, a few ll. spotted, occasional light soiling. 19th. C. mor., elab. gt. (S. Sep.29; 221) *Schuster.* £130
– – **Anr. Copy.** 4 vols. in 2. Tall fo. Cont. red mor. gt., scuffed & worn. (SG. Mar.12; 279) $350
– – **Anr. Edn.** 1818. 4 vols. in 2. 4to. Cl. (C. Jul.22; 158) *Gibbs.* £140

OTTO, Adolph Willhelm
- Monstrorum Sexcentorum Descriptio Anatomica, . . . accedunt CL imagines. Vratislava, 1841. 1st. Edn. Fo. With 2nd. title-p. 'Museum anatomicopathelogicum Vratislavense', spotted, liby. stp. on title. Cont. roan-bkd. bds., slightly worn. (S. Feb.23; 84) *Thybault.* £70

OTTO, J.K.
See–HUTTER, E.–OTTO, J.K.

OTWAY, Thomas
- The Atheist. 1684. 1st. Edn. 4to. Mod. hf. mor. [Wing 0541] (C. Nov.19; 124) *Dunbar.* £60
- Friendship in Fashion. 1678. 1st. Edn. 4to. Recent mor.-bkd. bds. [Wing 0548] (C. Nov.19; 125) *Pickering & Chatto.* £120
- Venice Preserv'd. 1682. 1st. Edn. 4to. Some foxing. Mor. by Sangorski. [Wing 0567] (C. Nov.19; 126) *Quaritch.* £120
– – **Anr. Copy.** Stain on title. Later hf. leath., foxing. (SG. Sep.4; 371) $250

OTZAR ISRAEL
Ed.:– J.D. Eisenstein. N.Y., 1907-13. 1st. Edn. 10 vols. Hf. leath. (S. Nov.18; 537) *Freilich.* £50

OUDIN, P.F.
See–NICERON, J.P., Oudin, P.F. & others

OUGHTRED, William
- Arithmeticae in numeris et speciebus institutio. 1631. 1st. Edn. Stain in fore-margin of prelims., title with partly deleted owner's inscr. Cont. limp vell., soiled, hf. red mor. case. From Honeyman Collection. [NSTC 18898] (S. Nov.10; 2370)
Quaritch. £700
- The Circles of Proportion & the Horizontall Instrument &c. . . . Ed.:– A.H. [Arthur Haughton?]. Oxford, 1660. Some browning. Cont. mott. cf., spine chipped at head. Bkplt. of Earl Fitzwilliam; from Honeyman Collection. [Wing 0572] (S. Nov.10; 2374) *Hill.* £320
- The Circles of Proportion & the Horizontal Instrument . . . [– An Addition unto the Use of the Instrument . . . For the Working of Nautical Questions]. Trans.:– William Forster (1st. pt.) 1633. 2 pts. in 1 vol. 4to. Additional engraved title to pt. 1 dtd. 1632, lacks a blank(?) lf. at end of pt. 2, imprint on 1st. title trimmed with loss of date, slight staining. Cont. sheep, rebkd., hf. red mor. case. Bkplt. of Halsey family of Gaddesden Park; from Honeyman Collection. [NSTC 18899b] (S. Nov.10; 2372) *Hill.* £1,050

- The Circles of Proportion & the Horizontal Instrument; [An Addition unto the Use of the Instrument . . . For the Working of Nauticall Questions; To the English Gentrie . . . The Just Apologie of Wil. Oughtred, against . . . Richard Delamain]. 1633. 3 pts. in 1 vol. Ptd. title to pts. 1 & 2, drop-title to pt. 3, 3 folding plts., woodcut diagrams, 2 errata ll., partly misbnd., some browning & soiling, hole in C4 pt. 2 with loss of p. numbers, a little worming, date on 1st. title shaved, owners' inscrs. of James Sotheran & James Hailes, ptd. label, & sig. on title, of Ch. Cottier., without the engraved title, but apparently complete as issued. Cont. limp vell., stained end-papers from late 16th. C. MS. lf. of accounts, hf. red mor. case. From Honeyman Collection. [NSTC 18899b, 18901a] (S. Nov.10; 2373)
Rogers Turner. £480
- The Key of the Mathematicks new Forged & Filed.–Clavis Mathematica denuo limita, sive potius fabricata. Ill.:– W. Hollar (1st. work). 1647; 1648. 1st. Engl. Edn. (1st. work). 2 works in 1 vol. 1st. work: inscr. on title, sm. tear in pts., 2nd. work: lacks lf. before title (blank?) Cont. blind-tooled cf., jnts. reprd., hf. red mor. case. From Honeyman Collection [Wing 0582, 573] (S. Nov.10; 2371) *Schuman.* £300
- Trigonometria . . . cum Tabulis Sinuum, Tangent. & Secant, & c. ed.:– R. Stokes & A. Haughton. Ill.:– Faithorne (engraved port.). 1657. 1st. Edn. 2 pts. in 1 vol. 4to. Browned almost thro.-out, 2 or 3 ll. soiled in upr. margins. Cont. limp vell., lr. inside hinge brkn., hf. red mor. case. From Honeyman Collection. [Wing 0589]. (S. Nov.10; 2375) *Schumann.* £160

OUIDA (Pseud.)
See–RAMEE, Louise de la 'Ouida'

OULESS, Philip John
See–WALTER, H. & Ouless, Philip John

OUTERBRIDGE, Paul
- Photographing in Color. [N.Y.], [1940]. 1st. Edn. 4to. Colour reproductions tipped-in. Pict. cl., head of spine chipped. (SG. Jul.9; 257) $110

OUTHIER, Reginald
- Journal d'un Voyage au Nord, en 1736 & 1737. Paris, 1744. 1st. Edn. 4to. Some foxing, lr. blank corner of title reprd. Cont. panel. cf., rebkd. From Honeyman Collection. (S. Nov.10; 2376)
Maggs. £130

OUTHWAITE, Ida Rentoul
- Blossom. A Fairy Story. L., 1928. 4to. Foxed. Orig. bdg. (JL. Mar.2; 619) *Aus.* $120
- A Bunch of Wild Flowers. Sydney, 1933. Foxed. Orig. bdg., d.-w. (JL. Mar.2; 618) *Aus.* $130
- Fairyland. Melbourne, 1926. (1000) sigd. Fo. Orig. cl., slightly marked, orig. ptd. & decor. card. s.-c. (KH. Mar.24; 314) *Aus.* $600

OVALLE, Alonso de
- Historica Relacion del Reyno de Chile, y da las Missiones, y . . . la Compagna de Iesus. Rome, 1646. 1st. Edn. 4to. 6 ports. badly damaged by worming, lf. 'Varias y Curiosas Noticis' at beginning, lacks folding map, replaced in photocopy, & text ll. 3H1 & 4, slightly spotted, badly wormed in places with loss of text, some ll. reprd. affecting text. Cont. vell. bds., slightly worn & wormed, soiled. [Sabin 57972] (S. Jun.29; 181) *Gomez.* £80

OVER, Charles
- Ornamental Architecure in the Gothic, Chinese & Modern Taste. 1758. Lacks 1 plt., dampstaining. Cont. cf., worn. (CSK. Sep.26; 51) £50

OVERBEKE, Bonaventura van
- Reliquiae Antiquae Urbis Romae. Ed.:– Michael van Overbeke. Ill.:– M. Pool (frontis.). The Hague, 1763. L.P. 3 vols. in 1l. Lge. fo. Sm. liby stp. on 2nd. title to vol. I, 1st. title slightly soiled. Cont. cf., gt.-panel., slightly worn. (S. Jun.22; 69)
Duran. £500
- Les Restes de l'Ancienne Rome . . . Imprimé aux dépens de Michel d'Overbeke. Amst., 1709. 1st. Edn. in Fr. L.P. 3 vols. Fo. Map & lge. folding plt. browned, a few ll. with slight spotting. Orig. hf. cf., jnts. split, worn, unc. (S. Oct.21; 464)
Teiboulet. £350

OVERBEKE, Bonaventura & Michael Ab
- Reliquiae Antiquae Urbis Romae. 1708. 1st. Edn. 3 vols. in 1l. Fo. Cont. cf., gt. spine. (C. Feb.25; 190) *Sbisa.* £600

OVERBEKE, Bonaventura & Michael Ab – Reliquae Antiquae Urbis Romae. *-contd.*
– – **Anr. Copy.** Wide margins. Hf. leath., worn. (VG. Oct.13; 120) Fls. 1,115

OVERKAMP, D. Heydentryk
See–**VIEUSSENS, Raymond–OVERKAMP, D. Heydentryk**

OVERMEER FISSCHER, J.F. van
– **Bijdrage tot de Kennis van het Japansche Rijk.** Amst., 1833. 4to. 14 (of 15) plts., some stains, & soiling. Cont. hf. cf, spine loose & defect. (VG. Dec.16; 946) Fls. 500

OVERTON, Richard C.
– **Gulf to the Rockies . . . Southern Railways, 1861-1898.** Ill.:– Reginald Marsh. Austin, 1953. 1st. Edn. Pict. cl., d.-w. Pres. Copy sigd. by Overton, orig. sketch inscr. & sigd. by Marsh. (PNY. Oct.1; 456) $130

OVERTON, Thomas Collins
– **The Temple Builder's Most Useful Companion.** 1774. 4to. Hole in 1 margin. Cont. hf. mor., worn. (SBA. Mar.4; 94) *Temperley.* £160

OVIDIUS NASO, Publius
– **Amorum Libri Tres.** Venice, [1518]. Sm. fo. Old staining, lf. 81 defect., restored, old worming. 19th. C. hf. cf. (LM. Mar.21; 288) B.Frs. 13,000
– **L'Art d'Aimer.** Ill.:– Aristide Maillol. Lausanne, 1935. (50) for sale by Zwemmer, sigd. by artist, numbered. Fo. Unsewn in orig. wraps., unc., folder, s.-c., soiled. (SH. Nov.21; 404) *Kawamatsu.* £720
– – **Anr. Edn.** Paris, 1935. (325) on Montgolfier. 4to. Leaves, box. A.L.s. by Maillol to Ludovic Massé. (HD. Apr.24; 168) Frs. 7,000
– **Bellissimum Theatrum . . . ex . . . Libris XV. Metamorphoseos.** Nuremb., 1685. Ob. 4to. Slightly soiled, lacks 2 copperplts., last 9 plts. defect. at margins, 2 very browned, title stpd. 19th. C. hf. leath. gt. (HK. May 12-14; 1614) DM 1,400
– **De Arte Amandi et de Remedio Amoris cum Comento.** Ed.:– [B. Merula]. Lyons, Jean de Vingle, 1495. 4to. 75 ll. (of 76, lacks lf. with device), title reprd. & slightly defect., affecting 7 lines of text on verso, title with tear through device, several ll. near end wormed, affecting some letters, extensive annots. in text, several ll. stained at foot, some browning, blank [k3v] with early polyphonic musical staves & lines of a love song in German. Vell.-bkd. bds. [BMC VIII, 311; C 4559; Goff O 146] (S. Jun.23; 216) *Ponder.* **£220**
– **De Gedaant-Wisselingen.** Ed.:– Banier. Trans.:– Isaak Verburg. Amst., 1732. 2 vols. Fo. Text in Latin & Dutch, lacks hf.-title & final blank in vol. II, a few ll. browned, slight occasional offsetting in text. 19th. C. hf. cf., some wear. (S. Jan.27; 423) *Lester.* £140
– **Elegies.** Trans.:– Christopher Marlowe. Ill.:– John Nash. 1925. (35) numbered, on H.M.P. sigd. by artist. Orig. cl., unc. (SH. Mar.27; 346) *Loder.* £60
– **Epistole . . .** Venice, 1547. Lacks final blank. 19th. C. mor., gt., red mor. onlay. (S. Nov.25; 357) *Marlborough.* £160
– **Epistole Eroiche . . .** Trans.:– Remigio Fiorentino. Ill.:– Carlo Gregori after Zocchi. Paris, 1762. L.P. 4to. Cont. red mor., triple gt. fillet, spine gt. in compartments with sm. bird in foliage, ground semé with dots & stars, inner gt. dentelles. (SM. Oct.8; 1898) Frs. 2,800
– **Epistole Heroides.** Ed.:– Ant. Volsci & Ubertini Clerici. Venice, 1507. Fo. 122 unnumbered ll., sm. restored wormhole. Vell. (CR. Mar.19; 268) Lire 450,000
– **Lehrbuch der Liebe.** Ill.:– Max Slevogt. Berlin. 1921. (320), with extra set of ills. on india paper, numbered. 4to. Orig. pig. gt., slightly soiled, box worn. (SH. Nov.21; 477) *Reed & Sims.* £130
– – **Anr. Copy.** 4to. (100) Privilege Edn. with 2nd. series of lithos. on Japon under passepartouts. Hand-bnd. orig. pig. gt., slightly soiled. All lithos. sigd. by artist. (H. May 21/22; 1811) DM 1,600
– **[Metamorphoses] Herscheppinge [Dutch].** Trans.:– Josse van Vondel. Amst., 1671. 1st. Edn. of this translation. 4to. Slight staining at beginning. Cont. vell. bds., a little stained, fault in upr. cover. (C. Apr.1; 159) *Hendrickx.* £130
– **Metamorphosis [English].** Trans.:– G. S[andys]. Oxford, 1632. Fo. Dampstained. Cont. cf., worn. [NSTC 18966] (S. Sep.29; 63) *Scholz.* £60
– – **Anr. Edn.** Trans.:– George Sandys. 1640. Fo. Sm. hole in 1 plt. Cont. cf., stained. [STC 18968] (C. Feb.25; 170) *Quaritch.* £130
– – **Anr. Copy.** Lacks emblematic extra engd. title. Cont. vell. (SG. May 14; 160) $200
– – **Anr. Edn.** L., 1717. Fo. 14 (of 16) copper-plts., additional plt. at p. 500, some dampstaining thro.-out. 19th. C. hf. cf., worn. (SG. Feb.5; 263) $100
– – **Anr. Edn.** Trans.:– John Clarke. Glocester, 1790. 8th. Edn. Some ll. stpd. Mod. cf.-bkd. bds., ex-liby. (SBA. Oct.22; 344a) *Bargain.* £50
– – **Anr. Edn.** Ill.:– Hans Erni. Ltd. Edns. Cl., 1958. (1500) sigd. by artist & printer. Orig. cl.-bkd. bds., s.-c. (SH. Feb.20; 236) *Quaritch.* £120
– – **Anr. Copy.** Buckram-bkd. patterned bds., boxed. (SG. Apr.2; 108) $160
– – **Anr. Copy.** Monthly letter laid in. Buckram-bkd. bds. (SG. Jan.15; 238) $100
– – **Anr. Edn.** Trans.:– William Caxton. N.Y., 1968. MS. Facs. Edn. 2 vols. Fo. Cf., gt. arms of Samuel Pepys on all covers, spines gt., boxed. (SG. Mar.26; 127) $200
– **Metamorphoses [French].** [Bruges], [Colard Mansion], [May, 1484]. Fo. A fragment of 9 ll. (each matted), comprising folios 19, 22, 25-28, 68-69, & 293, containing 2 lge. & 6 smaller woodcuts, spaces for capital initials, supplied in red, rubricated, corner of 1 lf. defect, slight dampstaining. Disbnd., laid in folding cl. case. The copy of H.P. Kraus, lately in the collection of Eric Sexton. [BMC IX, 134, Goff O 184, HC 12164] (CNY. Apr.8; 30) $14,000
– – **Anr. Edn.** Paris, 1651. Fo. Old cf., 5 spine raised bands, decor. (LH. Jun.13; 166) B.Frs. 11,000
– – **Anr. Edn.** Ill.:– Chauveau. Paris, 1677. 4to. 18th. C. red mor., ornate gt., wide rococo border round royal arms, watered silk end-papers. (SM. Oct.8; 2199) Frs. 5,500
– – **Anr. Edn.** Trans.:– L'Abbé Banier. Ill.:– Picart (frontis.), after Overbeke (vigs.), after Picart, Lebrun, Folkema & others (plts.). Amst., 1732. 2 vols. in 1. Fo. Occasional slight offsetting. Cont. Fr. mor. gt., spine elab. tooled in compartments, slight tear at head & foot of jnts. (C. Feb.25; 191) *Braunschweig.* £300
– – **Anr. Edn.** Trans.:– Abbé Banier. Paris, 1738. 2 vols. 4to. Vol. 1 title reprd. Cont. hf. cf. (S. Mar.17; 255) *Duran.* £60
– – **Anr. Copy.** 1 frontis. sigd. by Humblot, some staining. Cont. marb. roan, decor. spines, bdg. reprd. (HD. Feb.18; 53) Frs. 1,600
– – **Anr. Edn.** Trans.:– M. l'Abbé Banier. Ill.:– Choffard (vig. headpieces), & Basan, Binet, Leroy & others after Boucher, Eisen, Monnet, Moreau & others. Paris, [1767]-1771. 4 vols. 4to. Lacks 1st. title, 4th. hf.-title & [2Y1-4] text ll. in vol. III, plt. 18 reprd., 2X4 in vol. III laid in & reprd., a few sm. stains & repairs, slight soiling. 19th. C. cf., 1 label defect., some wear. (S. Jun.23; 256) *Duran.* £200
– – **Anr. Edn.** Ill.:– after Boucher, Choffard, Eisen, Gravelot, Monnet & others. Paris, [1776-71]. Mor. gt., sigd. by Rivière, emblem, triple gold fillets, floral borders on inner dentelles, gt. outer dentelles, marb. paper end-ll., s.-c. (D. Dec.11-13; 708) DM 3,000
– – **Anr. Edn.** Trans.:– G.T. Villenave. Ill.:– Le Barbier, Monsiau & Moreau. Paris, 1806. 4 vols. 4to. 1st Printing of ills. Later Bordeaux hf. mor., corners, spines decor. with raised bands. (HD. Feb.27; 197) Frs. 1,250
– **La Métamorphose Figvrée.** Ill.:– S. Bernard. Lyon, 1583. 3rd. Edn. Lacks last blank lf. several owners' marks on title, browned thro.-out, stained or soiled in parts, sm. hole in last 3 ll. Cont. leath., gt. spine, gold fillets, 1 jnt. brkn., soiled. (HK. Nov.18-21; 250) DM 1,000
– **Les Metamorphoses Gravées sur les Desseins des Meilleurs Peintres Français.** Ill.:– Choffard (frontis.); ills. after Boucher, Moreau, Eisen, Gravelot & others. Paris, ca. 1770. 'Banier' Edn. 4to. Cont. marb. cf., decor. spine, border of 3 fillets on covers. (SM. Feb.11; 129) Frs. 4,000
– **Les Métamorphoses [French & Latin].** Trans.:– M. l'Abbé Banier. Ill.:– Boucher, Eisen, Gravelot & others. Paris, 1767-71. 1st. Edn. 4 vols. 4to. Cont. diced cf., decor. spines, bdg. reprd. (HD. Feb.18; 54) Frs. 3,500
– **Delle Metamorphosi [Italian].** Ed.:– F. Turchi. Trans.:– Giovanni Andrea dall'Anguillara. Venice, 1579. Lacks corner of table lf. Red mor. by Derome, 3 fillets, decor. spine, inside dentelle. (HD. Mar.18; 128) Frs. 1,300
– – **Anr. Edn.** Trans.:– Gio Andrea dell' Anguillara. Ill.:– Giacomo Franco. Venice, 1584. 4to. Light staining thro.-out. Early 19th. C. hf. vell. (S. Jul.27; 109) *Shapiro.* £60
– **Metamorphoseos Libri XV. [Latin].** Venice, Apr. 1527. Fo. Browned in parts, some ll. bkd., lf. 59 defect. with text loss. 17th. C. vell., defect. (HK. Nov.18-21; 249) DM 450
– – **Anr. Edn.** Venice, 1540. Fo. Slight browning & soiling. 19th. C. vell. bds., soiled. From liby. of André L. Simon. (S. May 18; 144) *Hill.* £100
– – **Anr. Edn.** Antw., [1591]. Probably lacks 2 privilege ll., engr. no. 176 p. 317 'Petrus vander Borcht invent. et facit', typog. mark on p. 361 verso. Cf., 5 spine raised bands decor., centre motif gt. tooled, inner dentelle, by Petit. William Poor ex-liby. (LM. Jun.13; 63) B.Frs. 45,000
– **Metamorphoses [Latin & English].** Ill.:– Picart & others. Amst., 1732. 2 vols. in 1. Fo. Some ll. foxed, P3, I4 & title of vol. II reprd. Cont. russ., gt., by Barratt, Oxford, with his ticket, rebkd., very worn. (S. Jan.26; 112) *Mistrali.* £190
– – **Anr. Copy.** 2 vols. Lge. fo. Slightly browned or soiled in parts. Cont. spr. leath., gt., gt. outer & inner dentelle, marb. end-papers. (HK. Nov.18-21; 2370) DM 2,600
– **Les Métamorphoses [Latin & Fr.].** Ed.:– Abbé Banier. Ill.:– after Lebrun, Leclerc, Maas, Picart & others. Amst., 1732. 2 vols. Fo. Several ll. browned, slight offsetting. Cont. hf. cf., jnts. split, worn, unc. (S. Oct.21; 465) *Quaritch.* £150
– – **Anr. Edn.** Ed.:– Abbé Banier. Ill.:– Baquoy, Duclos & others after Boucher, Eisen, Monnet, Moreau & others. Paris, 1767-70. 4 vols. 4to. Plts. slightly soiled, some lightly browned. Cont. marb. leath., gt. spine, inner & outer dentelle, cover fillets, rubbed. (HK. Nov.18-21; 2371) DM 1,200
– – **Anr. Edn.** Trans.:– L'Abbé Banier. Ill.:– after Eisen, Gravelot, Moreau & others. Paris, 1767-71. 4 vols. 4to. Some spotting. 19th. C. cf., from the Carleton House Liby. with its bkplt. & dupl. stp. in vol. 1, the orig. upr. covers, with arms of the Prince Regent, preserved at the front of each vol. (CSK. Mar.13; 85) £220
– **XV Metamorphoseon [Latin & German].** Ill.:– Crispin van de Pass. Cologne & Arnheim, 1607. 4to. 120 (of 134) ll., defect. Old bds., loose, very worn. (SG. Sep.25; 239) $100
– **Metamorphosis; Epistolae Heroides; De Tristibus; Fastorum Libri; Libri de Ponto; Libri de Arte Amandi; Amorum Libri Tres.** Parma (2nd work); others Venice, 20 Apr., 1517; 15 May, 1517; ca. 1515; 12 Apr., 1520; 9 Oct., 1507; 4 Jan., 1516; Jan., 1518. 7 works in 1 vol. Fo. Lacks 2 ll. from 1st. quire of 1st. work (blank?), lacks last blank lf. in 3rd. & 5th. works, 6th. work lacks 14 ll., & 7th. work lacks about 19 ll., some reprd. worming at front. Cont. blind-stpd. & gt. cf. over bevelled wood bds., dtd. 1523, edges worn, lacks clasps. W.a.f. The copy of John A. Saks. (CNY. Oct.1; 129) $1,100
– **Oeuvres Complètes.** 1834-37. 10 vols. Cont. red hf. mor. (HD. Oct.10; 265) Frs. 1,500
– **Orpheus. 10 Holzschnitte zu den Versen des Ovid.** Ed.:– H. Voss. Trans.:– R. Merckel. Ill.:– G. Marcks. [Hamburg], [1948]. (150). Fo. Orig. hf. linen portfo. 8 full-p. woodcuts & 2 title woodcuts sigd. (H. Dec.9/10; 2212) DM 1,300
[–] **Le Transformation.** Trans.:– Lodovico Dolce. Venice, 1555. 3rd. Giolito Edn. 4to. 18th. C. mor., gt. border incorporating birds & conventional foliage, spine gt. à la grotesque, inner gt. dentelles, 2 tiny wormholes in upr. hinge. (SM. Oct.8; 1900) Frs. 2,400
– **Trois Premiers Livres de la Metamorphose.** Trans.:– Clément Marot (Books 1 & 2); B. Aneau (Book 3). Ill.:– Pierre Eskrich. Lyons, 1556. Ist. Compl. Edn. Title slightly defect. Early 19th. C. Engl. str.-grd. mor., blind-tooled decor., border of 3 fillets, inside border of garland & 3 brkn. fillets, bands on spine, decor. covers, title with scrolls & grotesque heads. Bkplt. of Docteur Desbarreaux-Bernard. (HD. Mar.18; 127) Frs. 3,100
– **Verwandlungen in Kupfern von den Besten Künstlern Deutschlands vorgestellt.** Augsburg, 1802. 3 vols. 4to. Lacks 6 copperplts., including title. Cont. bds. (D. Dec.11-13; 710) DM 500
– **La Vita et Metamorfoso.** Ed.:– M. Gabriello Symeoni. Ill.:– Bernard Salomon. Lyons, 1559. Title dampstained, other slight dampstaining, many side notes in text cropped, woodcut border on 3 ll. torn & reprd. with severe damage to ptd.

area. 17th. C. cf., gt. spine. (C. Feb.25; 15)
Lester. £180

OVIDIUS NASO, Publius–SABINUS, Georgius
– Metamorphoses.–Fabularum Interpretatio Tradita in Academia Regiomontana. Ed.:– Johannes Sprengius (1st. work). Ill.:– Virgil Solis (1st. work). Frankfurt; Wittenburg, 1563; 1555. 2 works in 1 vol. 2nd. work slightly spotted, sm. marginal holes in last lf. 17th. C. vell. bds. (S. Apr.7; 275)
Dr. Kubicek. £380

OVIEDO Y VALDES, Gonzalo Fernandez
– Historia General y Natural de las Indias, Islas y Tierra-Firme del Mar Océano. Ed.:– J. Amador de los Rios. Madrid, 1851-55. 4 vols. 4to. Marb. cf. (SPB. May 5; 381)
$750

OVOD [Gadfly]
Ed.:– [F.K. Zimin & V.M. Ongirsky]. St. Petersb., 1906. Nos. 1-6. Fo. Unbnd. (SH. Feb.5; 104)
Landry. £240

OWEN, Maj. C.H.
– Sketches in the Crimea. Ill.:– after Owen. 1856. Ob. fo. Folding plt. separated at fold, some spotting & soiling. Orig. mor.-bkd. cl., worn & disbnd. (CSK. Sep.26; 32)
£100

OWEN, Charles
– An Essay towards a Natural History of Serpents. 1742. 2 pts. in 1 vol. 4to. Cont. spr. cf. gt. (SBA. Jul.23; 400)
Lawton. £95

OWEN, David Dale
– Report of a Geological Survey of Wisconsin, Iowa, & Minnesota. Phila., 1852. 4to. Orig. cl., ex-liby. (SG. Jan.29; 327)
$120

OWEN, Hugh
– Two Centuries of Ceramic Art in Bristol. 1873. A few ll. spotted. Cont. mor.-bkd. cl. (SH. Jan.29; 192)
Taylor. £65

OWEN, Hugh, of Shrewsbury & Blakeway, J.B.
– A History of Shrewsbury. Ill.:– H. Meyer after P. Corbett [folding mezzotint]. 1825. L.P. 2 vols. 4to. Occasional foxing & offset. Cont. mor., covers with wide gt. ornamental tool panel, spines gt., inner dentelles, by Reeve, spines slightly faded & rubbed. From the collection of Eric Sexton. (C. Apr.16; 323)
Thornhill. £150

OWEN, John
See–OGILBY, John & others

OWEN, Sir Richard
– History of British Fossil Reptiles. 1849-55. 6 pts. in 1 vol. 4to. Hf. mor. gt. (P. Mar.12; 333)
Duran. £100
– Memoir on the Gorilla. 1865. 1st. Edn. 4to. Orig. cl., rebkd. Pres. copy. (S. Dec.2; 571)
Cosby. £140
– On Parthenogenesis. 1849. 1st. Edn. Slight soiling, liby. stp. on title. Orig. bds., faded. (S. Feb.10; 380)
Dawson. £55

OWEN, Prof. Richard & Bell, T.
– Monograph on the Fossil Reptilia of the London Clay. 1949-50. 2 pts. in 1 vol. 4to. Hf. mor. (P. Mar.12; 332)
Duran. £90

OWEN, Robert
– Book of the New Moral World. 1836. 1st. Edn. [Pt. I (all publd.)]. Orig. cl., slightly marked, unopened. Pres. copy to the Queen of Portugal. (S. Jan.26; 249)
Martin. £480

OWEN, Samuel
See–COOKE, William Bernard & Owen, Samuel
See–WESTALL, William & Owen, Samuel

OWEN, Wilfred
– Poems. L., 1920. 1st. Edn. Tissue guard at frontis. loose. Cl. (SG. Nov.13; 548)
$150
– Thirteen Poems. Ill.:– Ben Shahn, & Leonard Baskin after Shahn (port.). Gehenna Pr., 1956. (400) numbered. Fo. Slight wrinkling to hf.-title. Lev. spine. (SG. Apr.2; 274)
$280

OXBERRY'S Dramatic Biography
L., 1825-1826. Vols. I-V. 18mo. Three qtr. cf., 1 cover detchd. (SG. Aug.7; 145)
$100
– –Anr. Edn. L., 1825-1827. 5 vols. & vol. 1 of new series, together 6 vols. 18mo. Old qtr. cf., 1 vol. rebnd. (SG. Aug.7; 146)
$130

OXENHAM, John
– The Book of Sark. Ill.– William A. Toplis. 1908. (500) numbered, sigd. by author & artist. Fo. Orig. vell. bds., lacks 2 ties. (SH. Oct.10; 538)
Hobley. £95

– –Anr. Copy. Orig. vell. gt., partly unc. With an A.L.s. from the artist. (LC. Jun.18; 163)
£50

OXFORD ENGLISH DICTIONARY
Oxford, 1933. 13 vols. 4to. Orig. cl., some spines worn or rebkd. (SH. Jul.23; 113)
Durham University Liby. £130
– –Anr. Copy. (BS. May 13; 209)
£110
– –Anr. Edn. Oxford, 1933-72. 15 vols. with Supps. 4to. Orig. cl. (SH. Jun.11; 96)
Parker. £160
– –Anr. Edn. 1933, 1972, 1976. 15 vols., including bibliography & 3 supps. 4to. Cl. gt., some vols. in d.-w.'s (torn). (PL. Sep.18; 107)
Miles. £120
[–] A New English Dictionary. Oxford, 1888-1933. 13 vols., including supp. 4to. Slight browning. Orig. hf. mor. (SPB. May 29; 325)
$350

OYVED, Moysheh
– Book of Affinity. Ill.:– J. Epstein. L., 1933. Ltd. Edn. sigd. 4to. Orig. cl. gt., orig. box. (P. Jun.11; 43)
£50

OZANAM, Jacques
– Dictionnaire Mathématique. Paris, 1691. 1st. Edn. 4to. Some browning, slightly soiled. Cont. mott. cf., worn. (S. May 5; 132)
Subunso. £50
– La Méchanique où il est traité des Machines simples & composées.–De Rozoi. Essai Philosophique sur l'Establissement des Ecoles Gratuites de Dessein, pour les Arts Méchaniques. Paris; Paris, 1720; 1769. 2 works in 1 vol. Slightly spotted in places, sm. stamps of Henri de Lamargodie, those on title partly removed, slightly damaging blank paper. Cont. mott. cf., slightly worn. (S. Oct.21; 353)
B. Rota. £60
– Récréations Mathématiques et Physiques ... Paris, 1750. New Edn. 4 vols. Cont. mott. cf., worn, spt. spines. (VG. Nov.18; 1316)
Fls. 650
– –Anr. Edn. Ed.:– C.G.F. [Montucla de Chanla]. Paris, 1778. New Edn. 4 vols. Stpd. Cont. cf., slightly worn. (H. Dec.9/10; 319)
DM 420
– Traité des Lignes du Premier Genre Expliquée par une Méthode nouvelle. Paris, 1687. 4to. Title with overslip with publisher's name & address, detchd. Cont. vell. bds., soiled, spine slightly worn. (S. Dec.2; 754)
Quaritch. £75
– L'Usage du Compas de Proportion ... Paris, 1700. New Edn. Slight spotting, inscr. on title. Cont. cf., gt. spine, worn. From Honeyman Collection. (S. Nov.10; 2377)
Veulemans. £70

OZANNE, Nicolas
– Recueil de Combats et d'Expeditions Maritimes. Paris, 1797. Fo. Title slightly defect. in blank margin, fly-lf. torn, some engraved plts. & plans slightly spotted. Cont. hf. cf., worn, upr. cover detchd., lacks portion of spine. (S. Feb.10; 338)
Mistrali. £950

P. & D.
See–COLNAGHI & CO., P. & D., Agnew, Thomas & Sons

P.L.
– Trois Filles de Leur Mère. 1897. 4to. Loosely contained in orig. wraps. (TA. Dec.18; 210)
£80

PABST, G. & Muller, O.
– Cryptogamen-Flora.–Die Flechten und Pilze (Die Lebermoose). 1876-77. 2 pts. in 1 vol. Fo. Hf. cf., reprd. (S. Jun.1; 188)
Junk. £100

PACICIO, Johann Carl
– Allerneueste und bewahrte Historische Nachricht von Allen in ... Regensburg gelegenen Reichs-Stifftern, Hauptkirchen und Clöstern Catholischen Religion ... Regensburg, 1753. 2 pts. in 1 vol. 1 plt. loose, lacks 8 ll. G1-8 in pt. II, 3 ll. torn slightly affecting text, a few wormholes, 1 slightly affecting text. Cont. cf., 2 clasps. (S. Dec.8; 98)
Hyde. £75

PACIFIC RAILROAD
– Narrative & Final Report of Explorations for a Route ... from St. Paul to Puger Sound. Ed.:– Isaac I. Stevens. Wash., 1860. 2 vols. Lge. tall 4to. Orig. cf. & cl. (backstrip very worn) (1st. vol.), & mod. cl. (PNY. May 21; 312)
$275
– Reports of Explorations & Surveys to Ascertain the ... Route for a Railroad from the Mississippi River to the Pacific Ocean. Wash., 1855-58. 1st. House & 1st. Senate Printings. Vols. 1, 2, & 4-9 (of 12 vols.). Lge. tall 4to. 3 vols. in orig. cl. (very worn) or qtr. leath., & 5 vols. in new buckram. W.a.f. (PNY. May 21; 311)
$275

– –Anr. Edn. Wash., 1855. 1856, 1857, 1860, 1861. 5 vols. 4to. Some dampstaining. Publisher's buckram, defect. (HD. Feb.27; 69)
Frs. 8,500

PACINI, Eugène
– La Marine, Arsenaux, Navires, Equipages, Navigation, Atterages, Combats. Paris, 1844. Last sig. slightly browned & loose. Cont. linen. (R. Oct.14-18; 2885)
DM 460

PACIOLI, Luca
– Divina proportione. Ed.:– Antonio Capella. Venice, Jun. 1509. 1st. Edn. Fo. 2 additional plates numbered LX & LXI supplied in pen & ink, marginal repair to title, tears in upr. margins of B6-C4 slightly affecting text, 1st. plt. neatly reprd. 19th. C. cf., gt., rebkd., orig. spine preserved. From Honeyman Collection. (S. Nov.10; 2381)
Weinreb. £7,200
– Somma di Aritmetica Geometria Proporzioni e Proporzionalita. Venice, Paganino de' Paganini, 10-20 Nov. 14[9]4. 1st. Edn. Fo. Title defect. in fore-margin & reprd. affecting a few letters on verso, occasional browning or slight staining. Mod. vell. bds., hf. red mor. case. From Honeyman Collection. [BMC V, 457; Goff L315] (S. Nov.10; 2379)
Martin. £9,800
– Summa de Arithmetica Geometria. Proportioni: et Proportionalita. Toscolano, 20 Dec. 1523. 2nd. Edn. Fo. Strap-work borders trimmed, also a number of marginal diagrams, printed notes & calculations, some staining, tear reprd. in A1, a few ll. with old MS. calculations in margins. 18th. C. cf., gt. spine, some wear. From Honeyman Collection. (S. Nov.10; 2380)
Martin. £3,800

PADOVANI, Giovanni
– De compositione, & usu multiformium Horologiorum Solarium ad omnes totius orbis Regiones. Venice, 1582. 2nd. Edn. 4to. Some browning, lr. inner margins stained towards end. Cont. limp vell. lacks ties, bkplt. of Prince of Lichtenstein. From Honeyman Collection. (S. Nov.10; 2384)
Hill. £140
– –Anr. Copy. 4to. Without 2 ll. of errata, wormed at end, mainly in margins, some stains, title with armorial stp. in upr. margin. Lacks half of spine. From Honeyman Collection. (S. Nov.10; 2385)
Rogers Turner. £90
– De Horis quibuscunque et Horarum Tabulis ad Universas Mundi Regiones supputandis. Verona, 1583. 1st. Edn. 4to. Some ll. browned. Vell., rebkd. From Honeyman Collection. (S. Nov.10; 2386)
McKittrick. £130
– Opera nuova ... tradotta di Latino in volgare, laqual dichiara l'uso del maraviglioso istromento astronomico da lui intitulato Horoscopio. Verona, 1560. 1st. Italian Edn. 4to. Lge. Mod. parch.-bkd. bds., unc. From Honeyman Collection. (S. Nov.10; 2382)
Nox. £160

PADUANIUS, Fabricius
– Tractatus duo alter de Ventis alter perbrevis de Terraemotu. Bologna, 1601. 1st. Edn. Fo. Somewhat browned thro-out, D1 reprd. slightly affecting text. Cont. limp vell., upr. inner hinge defect., lacks ties. From Honeyman Collection. (S. Nov.10; 2387)
Jackson. £850

PAETUS, Lucas
– De Mensuris et Ponderibus Romanis et Graecis. Venice, 1573. 1st. Edn. Fo. Slight browning, title a little soiled, sig. of J.W. Rimington. 17th. C. cf., gt., some wear. Bkplt. of Duke of Sussex; the Phillipps copy, inscr. in pencil MHC; from Honeyman Collection. (S. Nov.10; 2388)
Zeitlin. £200
– –Anr. Copy. 4 ll. of woodcuts (instead of 16 pp.) after p. 56, lge. margins. Red str.-grd. mor. by Lefebvre, lge. border with palm-leaves & lotus flowers, decor. spine, inside dentelle, vell. end-papers. (HD. Mar.18; 129)
Frs. 4,500

PAGAN, Blaise François de, Comte
– Les Dix Livres des Theorèmes Geometriques. Paris, 1654. 1st. Edn. Some browning. Cont. cf., worn. From Honeyman Collection. (S. Nov.10; 2389)
Brieux. £60
– La Théorie des Planètes. Paris, 1657. 1st. Edn. 4to. Slight browning, port. with marginal repair, remains of inscr. on title. Cont. cf.-bkd. bds., spine gt. From Honeyman Collection. (S. Nov.10; 2390)
Quaritch. £340

PAGANI, Francesco
– Arithmetica prattica utilissima ... Con molti Quesiti importanti, & necessarii a Regionieri, a Mercanti, & ad ogni persona, in tutti i Paesi.

PAGANI, Francesco–*contd.*
Ferrara, 1591. 1st. Edn. 4to. Some staining, hole in Z1 slightly affecting text. Cont. limp vell., worn & soiled. From Honeyman Collection. (S. Nov.10; 2391) *Phelps.* £65

PAGE, Augustine
– **A Supplement to the Suffolk Traveller.** 1844. Leath. (O. Jun.3; 112) £80

PAGE, Frank E.
– **Homer Watson.** Ed.:– Ross Hamilton [foreword]. Kitchener, [1939]. (600). Cl. (CB. Apr.1; 110) Can. $100

PAGE, J.L.W.
– **The Church Towers of Somerset.** Ill.:– E. Piper. N.d. (175) numbered. 2 vols. in 1. Fo. Slight marginal staining to some ll. Hf. mor., spine gt., partly unc. Each plt. sigd. in pencil by artist. (LC. Jun.18; 164) £80

PAGE, R.P. (Ed.)
See–**CHRONICLES of the Houghton Fishing Club**

PAGE, Thomas
See–**MOUNT, William & Page, Thomas**

PAGEANT (The)
Ed.:– C.H. Shannon & J.W.C. White. 1896-97. 2 vols., all publd. 4to. Orig. decor. cl. (P. Apr.30; 316) *Henderson.* £60
– – **Anr. Copy.** With the orig. litho. by Whistler, & the Pissarro woodcut. Gt.-decor. cl., designed by Ricketts. (SG. Nov.13; 550) $200
– – **Anr. Edn.** Ed.:– C. Hazlewood Shannon & J.W. Gleeson White. Ill.:– G.F. Watts, Pissarro, Moreau, & others. L., 1897. 4to. Gt.-decor. cl., unc. (SG. Nov.13; 549) $140

PAGES, F.X.
See–**FAUCHET, C., Chamfort, S.R.N., Ginguene, P.L. & Pagès, F.X.**

PAGES, Pierre M.F., Vicomte de
– **Travels Round the World.** 1791-2. 3 vols. Cf. gt. (P. Oct.23; 55) *Quaritch.* £300
– **Voyages autour du Monde et vers les deux Poles.** Paris, 1782. 1st. Edn. 2 vols. Browned, liby. stps. Cont. cl., worn. [Sabin 58168] (SH. Jun.11; 10) *Hannas.* £100
– – **Anr. Copy.** Cont. Fr. mor. [Sabin 58168] (SPB. May 5; 382) $425

PAGET, Major Guy
– **The Althorp & Pytchley Hunt.** 1937. (600). 4to. Orig. parch.-bkd. cl. gt. (SBA. Jul.23; 602) *Way.* £50

PAGET, J. Otho
– **Hunting.** Ill.:– Arthur Rackham. L., 1900. 1st. Edn. Deluxe, (150) numbered on H.M.P. Haddon Hall Liby. series. Gt.-pict. vell., unc., mostly unopened, orig. ribbon bookmark detchd. Extra mntd. proof copy of a photogravure laid in, Raymond M. Sutton Jr. copy. (SG. May 7; 229) $260

PAGNINI, Giovanni
– **Costruzione ed uso del Compasso di Proporzione.** Naples, 1753. 1st. Edn. 4to. Plt. 10 torn & reprd., sm. holes in last lf. of text & a few plts., foxed & stained. Wraps. From Honeyman Collection. (S. Nov.10; 2392) *Fomecon.* £60

PAILTHORPE, Frederick W.
– **Plates to Illustrate 'Great Expectations'.–Plates to Illustrate 'Oliver Twist'.** L., 1885; 1866. 2nd. piece (50) numbered on India-proof in black. 2 pieces. 4to. 1st. piece proof set, 2nd. piece with imitation leaflet. Loose as iss. in cl. folders & inserted in crushed mor. s-c. Bkplts. of Barton Currie, Marion Stuart Gaillard, & Thomas A. McGraw, M.D. (PNY. Mar.26; 96) $1,000

PAIN, William
– **The Practical Builder.** 1776. 4to. Some foxing & staining. Cont. cf., worn, rebkd. (C. Nov.20; 271a) *A. Thomas.* £50
– **The Practical House Carpenter.** 1799. 6th. Edn. Sm. 4to. Later hf. roan. (S. Mar.17; 442) *Traylen.* £50

PAIN, William & James
– **British Palladio.** 1797. Fo. 4 pp. of publisher's advts. at end. Antique-style cf. Sig. of Joshua Plunkitt on title, lately in the collection of Eric Sexton. (C. Apr.15; 75) *Ker.* £120

PAINE or Payne, James
– **Plans, Elevations & Sections, of Noblemen's Houses.** 1767-83. 1st. Edn. 2 vols. Fo. Cont. cf., covers becoming detchd. (C. Feb.25; 192) *Weinreb.* £580

PAINE, Thomas
– **Examination of the Passages in the New Testament, quoted from the Old . . .** N.Y., [1807]. 1st. Edn., 1st. Iss. Mod. wraps. (SG. Jun.11; 351) $100
– **La Independencia de la Costa Firma Justificada por Thomas Paine Treinta Anos ha, extracto de sus Obras.** Trans.:– D. Manuel Garcia de Sena. Phila., 1811. 1st. Edn. Heavily browned thro.-out, some worming. Old mott. cf., worn. (SG. Jan.8; 345) $100
– **Life & Writings.** N.Y., [1908]. Continental Edn., (250). 10 vols. Mor.-bkd. linen bds. (SPB. May 6; 335) $1,000
– **The Political Works.** L., 1817. 2 vols. Some foxing & discolouration. Later hf. mor., worn. (SPB. Jul.28; 394) $125
– **Die Rechte des Menschen.** Copen., 1793. 3 pts. in 1 vol. Cont. style hf. vell. (HK. May 15; 4721) DM 650
– **Rights of Man.** 1791-92. 3rd. Edn; 2nd. Edn. 2 pts. in 1 vol. Cont. tree cf. (SBA. Jul.23; 401) *Frognal Bookshop.* £60

[PAINE, Thomas]–[SMITH, William, D.D.]
– **Common Sense.–Plain Truth . . . Remarks on . . . Common Sense.** 1776; 1776. 1st. L. Edn.; 2nd. Edn. 2 works in 1 vol. Some prelims misbnd., slight browning, censored blank passages in 1st. work supplied in MS., a hf.-title 'Common Sense, & Plain Truth, the Fourth Edition' after title of 1st. work, no other hf.-title. Mod. marb. bds. [Sabin 58214, 10671] (S. Jan.26; 251) *Subunso.* £50

PALAEONTOGRAPHICAL Society (The)
– **Publications.** 1848-70. 24 vols. 4to. Some ll. defect. Orig. wraps., some defect. As periodical, w.a.f. (S. Sep.29; 97) *Schierenberg.* £180

PALAFOX Y MENDOZA, Juan de
– **Constituciones de las Real y Pontificia Universidad de México.** Mexico, 1775. Fo. Sm. marginal wormhole. Cont. cf., slightly worn. (SPB. May 5; 384) $550

PALAMEDE, Le; Revue Mensuelle des Echecs et autres Jeux
Paris, 1841-47. 2nd. Series. Vols. 1-7, in 6. Foxed. Hf. leath. (SG. Apr.9; 133) $240

PALARDY, Jean
– **The Early Furniture of French Canada.** Trans.:– Eric McLean. Toronto, 1963. 1st. Edn. in Engl. Fo. Bdg. not stated, orig. pict. d.-w., sm. tear. (PWP. Apr.9; 245) Can. $100

PALAU Y Dulcet, Antonio
– **Manuel del Librero Hispano-Americano.** Barcelona, 1948-77. 2nd. Edn. 28 vols. 4to. Orig. wraps. (HK. May 12-14; 2271) DM 1,900

PALEI, A.
– **Buben Dnya [Tambourine of Day].** Ekaterinoslav, 1922. Orig. wraps. (SH. Feb.6; 501) *Quaritch.* £100

PALGRAVE, Francis Turner
– **The Golden Treasury.** L., 1898. 2nd. Series. 16mo. Title-p. dampstained. Lev., wide gt. dentelles, by Hatchards. Fore-e. pntg. (SG. Mar.19; 159) $170

PALGRAVE, O.H.C.
– **Trees of Central Africa.** Glasgow, 1957. 2nd. Imp. 4to. Cl., d.-w. (SSA. Jun.18; 232) R. 130

PALGRAVE, William Gifford
– **Narrative of a Year's Journey through Central & Eastern Arabia.** 1865. 2 vols. Folding map, hand-cold. in outl. & 4 folding plans, occasional spotting. Orig. cl. soiled., stitching worn. (CSK. Mar.13; 119) £65

PALINGENIUS, Marcellus (Pseud.)
See–**MANZOLLI, Pietro Angelo 'Marcellus Palingenius'**

PALISOT DE BEAUVOIS, A.M.F.J.
– **Flore d'Oware et de Benin.** Ill.:– After Mirbel, Prêtre & others. Paris, 1804-07[-21.]. 2 vols. in 1. Spotted. Hf. mor. gt. From collection of Massachusetts Horticultural Society, stps. on plts. (SPB. Oct.1; 153) $5,500

PALISSY, Bernard
– **Discours Admirables, de la Nature des Eaux et Fonteines, tant naturelles qu'artificielles, des Metaux, des Sels & Salines, des Pierres, des Terres, du Feu & des Emaux.** Paris, 1580. 1st. Edn. Upr. margins of quire L renewed slightly affecting a few headlines & p.-numbers, sm. repair to E7 touching text. Mod. red mor., by Godillot. From Honeyman Collection. (S. Nov.10; 2393) *Das Bucherkabinet.* £1,700
– **Le Moyen de devenir riche, et la Manière veritable, par laquelle tous les Hommes de la France pourront apprendre à multiplier . . . leurs Thresors & Possesions.** Paris, Lacks a lf. (blank?) at end of each pt., 6 prelim. ll. 2 pts. in 1 vol. Lacks a lf. (blank?) at end of each pt., 6 prelim. ll. to pt. 1 misbnd. in pt. 2, sm. flaw on K6v pt. 1, 1st. title a little soiled. Mod. vell. From Honeyman Collection. (S. Nov.10; 2394) *Brieux.* £200
– **Oeuvres . . .** Ed.:– Faujas de Saint Fond & Gobet. Paris, 1777. 4to. Lacks final lf. (blank?), foxed, sm. stps. on title. Cont. mott. cf., gt. spine., hf. red mor. case. From Honeyman Collection. (S. Nov.10; 2395) *Brieux.* £300

PALLADIO, Andrea
– **The Architecture.** Ed.:– Giacomo Leoni. Ill.:– B. Picart (frontis. & port.), Picart, Vander Gucht, J. Harris & T. Cole (plts.). L., 1721. [2nd. Engl. Edn.?]. 4 pts. in 1 vol. Fo. Cont. spr. cf., spine gt. (C. Feb.25; 194) *Lyon.* £170
– – **Anr. Edn.** Ed.:– Giacomo Leoni. L., 1721. 2nd. Engl. Edn. 202 plts. (of 203), lacks main title to vol. 2, title to First Book in vol. 1, & final blanks. Cont. spr. cf., spines gt. (S. Nov.25; 414) *Lindsay.* £160
– – **Anr. Copy.** 2 vols. Slight browning, staining. Reverse cf. (SPB. May 29; 326) $800
– – **Anr. Copy.** Priv. Ptd. With subscriber's lf., section titles for books 3 & 4 transposed. Disbnd. (SG. Dec.4; 269) $600
– – **Anr. Edn.** Ed.:– Inigo Jones. 1742. 3rd. Edn. 2 vols. Fo. Text foxed. Cont. cf., very worn, covers loose. (S. Jun.22; 133) *Quaritch.* £100
– **Architecture divisée en quatre livres.** Ed.:– Inigo Jones. La Haye, 1726. 4 pts. in 2 vols. Fo. Old cf., worn. (P. Mar.12; 42) *Duran.* £160
– **L'Architettura.** Ill.:– After Vidmani. Venice, 1642. 4 pts. in 1 vol. 4to. Margin torn with a little loss, soiling & marginal browning thro.-out. Old cf., jnts. split & crudely reprd. (CSK. Oct.10; 129) £150
– – **Anr. Copy.** Fo. Plts., some dampstained, sigs. B. & C. reversed. Cont. vell., wormed. (SPB. Oct.1; 238) $750
– – **Anr. Copy.** Sigs. B. & C. bnd. inverted. (DS. May 22; 814) Pts. 80,000
– – **Anr. Edn.** Venice, 1711. Fo. Later vell. From the collection of John A. Saks. (C. Jun.10; 198) *Marlborough.* £350
– **Les Bâtimens et les Desseins. (–Les Thermes des Romains).** Ill.:– Octave Bertotti Scamozzi. Vicenza, 1786-85. Vols. I-IV 2nd. Edns. 5 vols. Fo. Cont. cf.-bkd. bds., vell. corners, gt. spines, worn. (S. Jun.22; 134) *Weinreb.* £550
– **Fabriche Antiche . . . date in luce da Riccardo Conte di Burlington.** Ill.:– Fourdrinier, some after Ware, Vertue after Kent (headpiece). L., 1730. Fo. Some discolouration & slight staining. Cont. cf.-bkd. bds. (C. Feb.25; 193) *Weinreb.* £650
– **Le Fabbriche e i Disegni.** Vicenza, 1776-83. 4 vols. Fo. Disbnd. (SG. Dec.4; 270) $750
– **Le Fabbriche e i Desegni . . .–Le Terme dei Romani . . .** Ill.:– Rossi, Testolini & Vichi (1st. work); Barrera & Testolini (2nd work). Vicenza, 1786; 1785. 2nd. Edn. (1st. work). 4 vols. in 2; 1 vol. Lge. fo. 2nd. work without the frontis. as called for by Fowler. Both cont. hf. cf. & mott. paper bds. From the collection of John A. Saks. (C. Jun.10; 201) *Goldschmidt.* £950
– **The First Book of Architecture.** 1724. 10th. Edn. 4to. Faint stp. at foot, browning & spotting. Mod. hf. cf. (CSK. Feb.13; 17) £55
– – **Anr. Edn.** Trans.:– Godfrey Richards. 1729. 11th. Edn. 4to. Cont. cf., rebkd. (TA. Mar.19; 217) £50
– **Five Orders of Architecture.** Ed.:– Colen Campbell. 1729. Fo. Some spotting, numerous owners' inscrs., including that of Sir Cecil Beaton. Cont. cf., rebkd. (SH. Oct.9; 17) *Longmure.* £160
– – **Anr. Copy.** 29 plts. (numbered 31), 2 additional plts. uncalled for in collation bnd. in at end. (CB. May 27; 159) Can. $800

– I Quattro Libri dell'Architettura. Venice, 1570. 1st. Edn. 4 pts. in 1 vol. Fo. Lev. mor. by Sangorski & Sutcliffe. (C. Nov.6; 223) *Riley Smith.* £2,500
– – **Anr. Edn.** Ill.:– Giorgio Fossati (plts.). Venice, 1769. Fo. Light dampstain to lr. outer portion of early ll. Cont. hf. cf., later marb. paper sides, unc. From the collection of John A. Saks. (C. Jun.10; 199) *Weinreb.* £240

PALLADIUS, [Rutilius Taurus Aemilianus]
See–CATO, Marcus Porcius & others
See–CATO, Marcus Porcius & Varro, M.T.
–PALLADIUS Rutilius Taurus Aemilianus
–VICTORIUS, P.

PALLAS, Peter Simon
– **Flora Rossica.** Ill.:– After Karl Friedrich Knappe. St. Petersb., [Leningrad], 1784-88. Vol. 1, pts. I & II, in 2 vols. Fo. Pt. 1 in presumably pres. bdg. of mott. cf. gt. imperial eagle on sides, spine restored. Vol. 2 in cont. red hf. mor. gt. From Collection of Massachusetts Horticultural Society, stps. on plts. (SPB. Oct.1; 154) $5,250
– **Illustrations plantarum Imperfecte vel. nondum cognitarum, cum centuria iconum.** Leipzig, 1803-[06]. Fo. 59 hand-cold. plts. (all publd.), sm. tear in blank portion of title. Qtr. roan, very worn. From collection of Massachusetts Horticultural Society, stps. on plts. (SPB. Oct.1; 155) $800
– **Travels through the Southern Provinces of the Russian Empire.** 1802-03. 2 vols. 4to. Cont. hf. russ., neatly rebkd. (SBA. Oct.21; 121) *Quaritch.* £320
– – **Anr. Copy.** Hf. cf., worn. (BS. Jun.11; 181) £180
– – **Anr. Copy.** Cont. mott. cf. (SG. May 14; 161) $1,800
– – **Anr. Edn.** 1812. 2nd. Edn. 2 vols. 4to. All but 7 plts. hand-cold., most vigs. cold., sm. marginal stain to 1 plt., sm. hole in anr. in vol. I, offsetting to a few plts. Cont. hf. roan, some wear. (S. Jun.29; 272) *Bonham.* £250
– – **Anr. Copy.** Plt. 4 vol. 2 torn with slight loss, frontis. laid down on to end-papers, some light offsetting & occasional spotting. Hf. cf. (CSK. Jan.30; 84) £180
– **Voyages en Differentes Provinces de l'Empire de Russie et dans l'Asie Septentrionale.** Trans.:– Gauthier de la Peyronie. Paris, 1788-94. 1st. Fr. Edn. 5 vols. & atlas in 6 vols. 4to. & sm. fo. Plts. mostly browned. Cont. leath., gt., atlas cont. style hf. leath. (R. Oct.14-18; 1986) DM 1,900
– – **Anr. Edn.** Paris, 1789-93. 1st. Edn. in Fr. 5 vols. & atlas. 4to. Edges slightly stained. Cont. cf., worn, 2 vols. rebkd., 3 with covers detchd., atlas vol. in cl. From Chetham's Liby., Manchester. (C. Nov.27; 315) *Crete.* £240

PALLAS, Peter Simon & others
[–] **Histoire des Decouvertes Faites par Divers Savans Voyageurs . . .** Berne, 1779; 1781; 1787. 1st. Edn. 3 vols. Lge. 4to. Cont. mott. cf., spines gt. (SG. Oct.9; 184) $275

PALLISER, John
– **Solitary Rambles & Adventures of a Hunter in the Prairies.** L., 1853. 1st. Edn. With advt. lf., stp. on engraved title. Later three-qtr. mor. (SG. Dec.11; 378) $100

PALL MALL BUDGET
Ill.:– Arthur Rackham & others. L., Jan.-Jun. 1892. Vol.24. Fo. Cont. cl., needs rebdg. Raymond M. Sutton Jr. copy. (SG. May 7; 231) $600

PALL MALL Magazine, The
1894-1910. 29 vols., various. Unif. hf. mor., spines gt. (CSK. Jan.30; 103) £120

PALMEDO, Roland
– **Skiing: the International Sport.** Ill.:– F.B. Taylor. N.Y., Derrydale Pr., 1937. De Luxe Edn. (60) numbered, sigd. Lge. 4to. Gt.-decor. red mor., gt. panel. spine. Frontis. sigd. by artist, sigs. of 5 contributors, Peter Lunn, Arnold Lunn, Roger Langley, C.J. Luther & Birger Ruud laid in A.L.s. by Gerald Seligman. (SG. May 14; 55) $1,400
– – **Anr. Copy.** Red mor. gt., partly unc. With a sigd. orig. etching by Frederick B. Taylor. (CNY. Oct.1; 168) $1,300
– – **Anr. Edn.** [1937]. (950). 4to. Cl., elab. gt. border, unopened. (SG. Dec.11; 277) $110

PALMER, Alfred Herbert
– **The Life & Letters of Samuel Palmer.** 1892. [1st. Edn.?]. Hf. cf. gt. (P. Mar.12; 17) *Sedler.* £150

– – **Anr. Copy.** Orig. cl. gt., unc. Sir Cecil Beaton copy, with his sig. (SH. Mar.26; 31) *Ayres.* £80
– – **Anr. Copy.** numbered on L.P. Lge. 4to. Orig. mor. (SG. May 14; 164) $275
– **Life of Joseph Wolf.** 1895. Cl., slightly worn. (P. Mar.12; 292) *Graham.* £60
– **Samuel Palmer, A Memoir.** 1882. 4to. Some ll. creased & slightly soiled. Cont. mor.-bkd. bds., worn, disbnd. (CSK. Sep.12; 11) £60

PALMER, C.J.
– **Perlustration of Great Yarmouth.** 1872-75. 3 vols. 4to. Cf. gt. (P. Jul.30; 11) *Walford.* £75

PALMER, E. & Pitman, N.
– **Trees of Southern Africa.** Cape Town, 1972. (200) sigd. 3 vols. 4to. Qtr. mor., d.-w. Sigd. (SSA. Nov.5; 70) R. 180
– – **Anr. Copy.** Publisher's qtr. leath. (VA. Jan.30; 216) R. 100

PALMER, Harry Clay & others
– **Athletic Sports in America, England & Australia.** Ed.:– Henry Chadwick. Phila., ca. 1889. Cf. (CB. Sep.24; 136) Can. $140

PALMER, Samuel, Printer
– **General History of Printing.** 1733. 4to. Cont. cf. with old reback. (TA. Sep.18; 52) £100

PALMER, Thomas
– **Flores Omnium Pene Doctorum qui cum in Theologia, tum in Philosophia hactenus claruerunt . . .** Paris, 1555. 16mo. Vell. (JL. Jul.20; 562) Aus. $230

PALMERIN DE OLIVA
– **L'Histoire de Palmerin d'Olive, Filz du Roy Florendos de Macedone.** Trans.:– [Ian Maugin]. Paris, 1553. 2nd. Edn. in Fr. Fo. Made up copy with some ll. from 1st. Edn., lacks last lf., ff. 2Y6-2Z5 ruled in red, lr. blank margin of last lf. reprd., stp. of Bibliothèque du Roi, Palais Royale on title, Yemeniz, Henry Hope Edwardes & Henry J.B. Clements bkplts. Early 18th. C. red mor., gt., arms of Duc de Penthievre on covers, triple gt. fillet, spine compartments gt. à la grotesque, inner gt. dentelles. Cisternay du Fay–Yemeniz–Hope Edwardes–Clements copy. (SM. Oct.8; 1903) Frs. 6,500

PALTOCK, Robert
[–] **The Life & Adventures of Peter Wilkins, a Cornish Man, by R.S., a Passenger in the Hector.** Ill.:– Boitard. 1751. 1st. Edn. 2 vols. 12mo. Advts. Cont. cf. gt. (SH. Mar.19; 238) *Goldschmidt.* £450

PAMPHILE DE LA CROIX, Lt.-Gen. Baron
– **Memoires pour servir à la Revolution de Saint-Domingue.** Ill.:– Lapie. Paris, 1819. 1st. Edn. 2 vols. Cont. leath.-bkd. marb. bds. [Sabin 58397] (SG. Oct.30; 275) $100

PAMPHLETEER, The
1813-26. Vols. 1-26 (of 29). Cont. cf., gt., by J.B. Brown of Windsor, crowned gt. initials AS on covers, some jnts. brkn. Liby. stp. of Ernest Augustus of Hanover, Duke of Cumberland at beginning of each vol. (S. Jul.27; 92) *Thorpe.* £170

PAN
Ill.:– Halm. Berlin, 1896-98. Year II, Year III, Pts. 2-4 & Year IV, Pt. 1 & 3 in 9 pts. Fo. 53 (of 56) orig. ills., II, 1 lacks 1 etching, IV, 1 lacks 2 lithos., 2 plts. & 3 ll. loose. Orig. wraps., 1 wrap. very defect. & loose or with sm. tears. (H. May 21/22; 1744) DM 2,900

PANANTI, Filippo
– **Narrative of a Residence in Algiers.** 1818. [1st. Edn.?]. 4to. Some ll. soiled. Mod. hf. cf. (SH. Jun.18; 162) *Makiya.* £95
– – **Anr. Copy.** 2 ll. publisher's advts. bnd. in. Recently rebnd. in qtr. cf. (TA. Sep.18; 296) £52

PANCKOUCKE, André Joseph
[–] **Les Amusemens Mathematiques precedés des Elemens d'Arithmétique, d'Algèbre & de Géometrie.** Lille, 1749. 1st. Edn. Some browning. Cont. cf., spine defect. Bkplts. of Michel Chasles & Henri Viellard; from Honeyman Collection. (S. Nov.10; 2397) *Brieux.* £80

PANCOVIUS, Thomas
– **Herbarium.** Cölln an der Spree [Berlin], 1673. 4to. Slightly soiled or browned. Cont. vell. (HK. May 12-14; 389) DM 3,100

– – **Anr. Copy.** Slightly browned in parts, name on title, last lf. torn in margin. Cont. leath., upr. end-paper defect. (D. Dec.11-13; 223) DM 2,800

PANDECTAE JUSTINIANAE
Paris, 1748. 3 vols. Fo. Marb. cf., 5 decor. spine raised bands. (LM. Nov.8; 63) B.Frs. 7,000

PANNELIER
[–] **L'Hindoustan, ou Religion, Moeurs, Usages, Arts et Métiers des Hindous.** Paris, 1816. 6 vols. 16mo. Cont. bradel paper bds., unc. (HD. Apr.9; 537) Frs. 1,200

PANOFSKY, Erwin
– **Albrecht Dürer.** Princeton, 1943. 2 vols. 4to. Orig. cl. (SH. Jan.29; 135) *Talerman.* £55
– – **Anr. Edn.** 1945. [2nd. Edn.?]. 4to. Orig. cl. (SH. Jan.29; 136) *Phillips.* £55
– – **Anr. Copy.** 2 vols. Buckram. (SG. Dec.4; 129) $110

PANORAMA DER Oesterreichischen Monarchie
Budapest, 1840. 3 pts. in 1 vol. Subscribers' list, no ptd. titles, slightly spotted in places. Cont. str.-grd. mor., gt. (S. Oct.21; 485) *Heald.* £370

PANORAMA DES UNIVERSUMS
Prague, 1839. Vol. 6. 4to. 22 (of 24) views. Cont. hf. linen. (R. Oct.14-18; 2113a) DM 1,200

PANORMITANUS DE TUDESCHIS, Nicolaus
– **Lectura super tertio Decretalium.** Venice, Johannes de Colonia & Johannes Manthen, 4 May, 1478. Fo. 254 ll. (of 256) lacks first & final blanks, sigs., spaces for capital initials with guide letters, all but first initial in alternating blue & red, rubricated in red & blue, early MS. annots 18th. C. blind-stpd. pig., central panel enclosing stp. of a saint, roll-tool border, silk ties. [H. 12327] (CNY. May 22; 233) $3,000

PANTALEON, Heinricus
– **Prosographiae Heroum antque Illustrium Totius Germaniae.** Basel, 1565-66. 1st. Edn. Fo. Later leath., gold-stpd. decor. on both covers, spine renewed with orig. material. (D. Dec.11-13; 43) DM 1,200

PANTHEON des Philantropes (Le), ou l'Ecole de la Révolution
Ill.:– Dorges. Paris, [1790]. 16mo. Cont. white silk, spine & covers decor. with gt. fillet embroidered motifs, centre miniatures under glass with copper round on each cover. (HD. Apr.10; 169) Frs. 7,200

PANTOMIME PICTURES
Ed.:– F.E. Weatherly. [Inscr. dtd. 1896]. Fo. Some text ll. loose. Orig. cl.-bkd. pict. bds. (SH. Mar.19; 213) *Toole-Stott.* £65

PANVINO, Onofrio
– **De Ludis Circensibus, Libri II. De Triumphis, Liber unus.** Ed.:– Ioannis Argoli; Nicolai Pinelli. Padua, 1642. Fo. Sm. stain affecting text on L2r, tiny hole in N1 of Argoli's notes, owner's entry at foot of title, stp. on hf.-title. Cont. vell., gt., fleurons at corners, arabesque centrepieces, saints ties. Bkplt. of Abbey of Vallis Dei; from Honeyman Collection. (S. Nov.10; 2398) *Tzakas.* £400

PANZER, Georg Wolfgang Franz
– **Faunae Insectorum Germanicae Initia.** Nuremb., 1792-1809. 98 pts. only (of 109). Ob. 8vo. 49 pts. in orig. wraps. & s.-c.'s, others in wraps. W.a.f. (C. Nov.5; 118) *Wheldon & Wesley.* £680
– – **Anr. Edn.** [Nuremb.], [1794-1809]. 16 coll. vols., nos. 1-8 & 10-17. Lacks 6 text ll. Cont. hf. leath. gt. (R. Oct.14-18; 3040) DM 2,700

PAOLI, Paulus Antonius
– **Antichita di Pozzuoli.** Flor., 1768 [colophon]. 4to. Slight marginal dampstaining & spotting. 19th. C. hf. roan. From Chetham's Liby., Manchester. (C. Nov.27; 316) *Taylor.* £280
– **Rovine della Città di Pesto.** Rome, 1784. Lge. fo. Hf. vell. (CR. Jun.11; 517) Lire 1,400,000

PAOLO, P.
– **Raccolta degli Scritti.** 1507. 4to. Cont. vell. (P. Mar.12; 93) *Cambridge.* £60

PAPA, Giuseppe del
– **Lettera intorno alla natura del Caldo, e del Freddo, scritta all' illustrissimo sig. Francesco Redi.** Flor., 1674. 1st. Edn. Browned thro-out., some ll. marginally wormed, tiny hole in E8, old owner's inscrs. on title. 18th. C. patterned bds., soiled. From Honeyman Collection. (S. Nov.10; 2399) *Hill.* £60

PAPIAS
– **Vocabularium.** Venice, Theodorus de Ragazonibus, 17 Mar. 1491. Fo. 16th. C. blindstpd. sheep, rebkd. preserving orig. spine, & recornered. [H. 12380*; BMC V p. 477] (C. Apr.1; 67) *Keller.* £650

PAPIN, Denis
– **La Manière d'amolir les Os, et de faire cuire toutes Sortes de Viandes en fort peu de temps, & a peu de frais. Avec une description de la Machine.** Paris, 1682. 1st. Fr. Edn. 12mo. 2nd. folding plt. in facs, partly misbnd., 2 letters of imprint on title defect. 19th. C. mor. From Honeyman Collection. (S. Nov.10; 2401) *Girard.* £170
– **A New Digester or Engine for softning Bones (–A Continuation of the New Digester of Bones).** 1681-87. 1st. Edns. 2 vols. in 1. 4to. 3 folding plts. with slight marginal tears, somewhat browned, vol. II with printing flaw affecting text on P4r, last 6 ll. damp stained, owner's inscr. on fly-lf., stp. on verso of 1st. title. 18th. C. cf.-bkd. bds. From Honeyman Collection. [Wing P309-8] (S. Nov.10; 2400) *Quaritch.* £950

PAPIN, Nicolas
– **Raisonnemens Philosophiques touchant la Salure, Flux & Reflux de la Mer . . . La Mer Lumineuse ou traicté de la Lumière de la Mer.–De pulvère sympathico Dissertatio.** Paris, 1647; 1647. 2 works in 1 vol. (1st. in 2 pts.). Old bds., cf. spine. [BMSTC French p. 182, also 183 with different date] (S. Oct.21; 413) *Phelps.* £65

PAPINI, G. & others
– **Giovanni Fattori (1825-1908).** Flor., 1925. 4to. Publisher's bds. (CR. Mar.19; 135) Lire 520,000

PAPPE, L. & others
– **Synopsis of the Edible Fishes of the Cape of Good Hope.–Florae Capensis Medicae Prodromus. –Synopsis Filicum Africae Australis . . .–Silva Capensis.** Cape Town, 1853; 1858; 1858; 1862. 2nd. & 4th. works 2nd. Edn. Title-p. inscr. 'Bowler 1864'. Cont. hf. cf. (SSA. Nov.5; 171) R. 340

PAPPUS, Alexandrinus
– **Mathematicae Collectiones.** Trans.:– Federicus Commandinus. Bologna, 1660. Fo. Some ll. slightly spotted, tear in folios B1-4 reprd., very slightly affecting text. Cont. cf., rebkd., worn. (S. Jul.27; 234) *Nador.* £70
– **Mathematicae Collectiones [Lib. III-VIII] a Federico Commandino Urbinato in Latinum conversae, et Commentariis illustratae.** Pesaro, 1588. 1st. Edn. Fo. Slight staining, tear in 2I4, some marginal annots. & corrections to text, owner's inscr. on title-p. of Francis Willughby. 17th. C. limp vell., soiled, remains of ties, hf. red mor. case. From Honeyman Collection. (S. Nov.10; 2402) *Howell.* £420

PAPWORTH, John Buonarotti
– **Hints on Ornamental Gardening.** 1823. Cont. hf. cf., rebkd., orig. spine preserved. (C. May 20; 43) *Chambers.* £320
– – **Anr. Copy.** Hf. roan by Lebrun, smooth decor. spine. (HD. Feb.27; 198) Frs. 2,100
– **Rural Residences.** 1818. 4to. Publisher's advts., some text loose. Orig. bds., lacks spine. (P. Nov.13; 311) *Henderson.* £200
– – **Anr. Edn.** 1832. 2nd. Edn. 4to. Bds., lacks spine. (P. Apr.9; 263) *Fogg.* £200
– **Rural Residences, Consisting of a Series of Designs for Cottages, Decorated Cottages, Small Villas . . . Some Observations on Landscape Gardening.–Hints on Ornamental Gardening . . . A Series of Designs for Garden Buildings.** L.; L., 1818; 1823. Both 1st. Edns. 2 works in 1 vol. 4to. Lacks hf.-titles, occasional light spotting & slight offsetting to text. Cont. Engl. red str.-grd. mor., covers gt. & panel., gt. spine. (CNY. Oct.1; 21) $1,200
– **Select Views of London.** 1816. [1st. Edn. in book form?]. Imp. 8vo. Plts. cold., title detchd. Cont. Fr. mor., covers with elab. gt.-tooled panels enclosing the arms of the Duc d'Orleans, gt. spine (slightly faded). From the collection of Eric Sexton. (C. Apr.16; 324) *Quaritch.* £1,500
[–] – **Anr. Copy.** Slight offsetting, 1 plt. loose. Cont. hf. Russ., jnts. & spine slightly torn. (SBA. Oct.21; 70) *Temperley.* £800

PAPWORTH, John Buonarotti & others
– **Poetical Sketches of Scarborough.** Ill.:– T. Rowlandson after J. Green. 1813. 1st. Edn. Plts. hand-cold. Later red mor., gt. panel on covers, spine gt. in compartments, inner dentelles, by Sangorski. From the collection of Eric Sexton. (C. Apr.16; 345) *Foyle.* £100
– – **Anr. Copy.** Hf. cf. (SH. Jul.9; 187) *Ayres.* £80
[–] – **Anr. Copy.** Red lev. mor. gt., spine gt., by J. Larkins. (CNY. May 22; 234) $400
[–] – **Anr. Edn.** Ill.:– T. Rowlandson. 1813. [2nd. Edn.?]. Diced cf. gt. (P. Sep.11; 3) *Schuster.* £85
[–] – **Anr. Copy.** Some ll. slightly spotted or browned, inner margin of frontis. strengthened. Mod. hf. mor., orig. spine preserved, hinges strengthened. (SBA. Jul.14; 183) *Edistar.* £60

PARABLES FROM THE GOSPELS
See–**RICKETTS, Charles**

PARACELSUS, P.A.T. Bombast von Hohenheim
– **Archidoxa . . . Sampt den Buchern Praeparationum, de Tinctura Physicorum, de Renovatione et Restauratione Vitae, und de Vita Longa.** Ed.:– Joannes Albertus Wimpinaeus. Munich, 1570. 4to. Stained thro.-out., title soiled & with old owner's inscrs. Cont. limp vell., stained, lacks ties, inner hinges defect., hf. red mor. case. From Honeyman Collection. (S. Nov.10; 2406) *Das Bucherkabinet.* £350
– **Astronomica et Astrologica . . . Opuscula aliquot, jetzt erst in Truck geben.** Ed.:– Balthasar Flöter. Cologne, 1567. 1st. Edn. Sm. 4to. 18th. C. vell. bds., hf. red mor. case. Armorial bkplt. of Christian Ernst, Graf zu Stolberg; stp. of Stolberg liby. at Wernigerode; from Honeyman Collection. (S. Nov.10; 2404) *Ritman.* £1,400
– **Astronomica et Astrologica . . . Opuscula aliquot. –Das Buch Meteororum . . . Item: liber quartus paramiri de Matrice.–Philosphiae Magnae . . . Tractatus aliquot, jetzt erst in Truck geben.** Ed.:– Balthasar Flöter (1st. & 3rd. works). Cologne, 1567; 1566; 1567. 1st. Edns. 3 works in 1 vol. 4to. Browned thro.-out, some stains, marginal annots. 1st. work: title reprd. where owner's inscr. has been cut out, piece torn from margins of *3 & A3, 2nd. work: title soiled, holes in A1 & B1, 2D1r & 2D2v very soiled, former with tear affecting text. Cont. limp vell., soiled, remains of ties, hf. red mor. case. From Honeyman Collection. (S. Nov.10; 2405) *Ritman.* £800
– **Chirurgische Bücher und Schrifften . . . sambt einem Appendice . . . Durch Johannen Huserum.** Strassburg, 1605. Fo. Holes in 2I1 & 3K4, a few printing flaws, some browning, owner's inscr. on fly-lf. Cont. vell. bds., soiled, 2 ties remaining, hf. red mor. case. From Honeyman Collection. (S. Nov.10; 2409) *Van der Kerckhove.* £1,000
– **Erster [bis vierter] Theil [von 10] der Bücher und Schrifften.** Basle, 1589. Pts. 1-4 (of 10) in 2 vols. 4to. 3 (of 6) repeating woodcut ports & arms & 2 (of 4) woodcut printer's marks, lacks last lf. Later hf. leath. gt. (D. Dec.11-13; 224) DM 4,000
– **The Hermetic & Alchemical Writings of Aureolus Philippus Theophrastus Bombast of Hohenheim.** Ed.:– Arthur Edward Waite. 1894. 2 vols. 4to. Orig. cl. gt., unc. (S. Jun.17; 634) *Jenner Books.* £120
– – **Anr. Copy.** Publisher's advts. bnd. in at rear. Slightly worn on spines, partly untrimmed. (TA. Jun.18; 277) £85
– **[Opera].** Ed.:– John Huser. Basle, 1589-91. 1st. Coll. Edn. 10 vols. in 6. 4to. Folding table at p. 68 vol. X defect., 16 MS. ll. comprising 10th. book of the 'Archidoxis' (not called for) inserted between pp. 98/99 in vol. VI, most vols. badly dampstained in outer margins, especially at beginning & end, title to vol. I stained & with 2 sm. holes, some under-scoring in red ink, marginal annots. etc. Early 18th. C. cf., gt. spines, worn, hf. red mor. cases. From Honeyman Collection. (S. Nov.10; 2407) *Ritman.* £4,000
– **Propheceien und Weissagungen . . . Doctoris Paracelsi, Johan Liechtenbergers, M. Josephi Grunpeck, Joan. Carionis, Der Sibyllen, und anderer.** N.p., 1549. 4to. Somewhat browned, 3 ll. stained. Wraps., hf. red mor. case. From Honeyman Collection. (S. Nov.10; 2403) *Quaritch.* £820
– **Von der Bergsucht oder Bergkranckheiten drey Bucher.–Astronomica et Astrologica.** Ed.:– Samuel Zimmermann (1st. work). Dillingen; Cologne, 1567; 1567. 1st. Edns. 2 works in 1 vol. 4to. Old vell. (C. Nov.20; 201) *Goldschmidt.* £1,500

PARACELSUS, P.A.T. Bombast von Hohenheim–FOSTER, William–ANON
– **A hundred & fourteene Experiments & Cures. –Hoplocrismaspongus: or, A Sponge to wipe away the Weapon-Salve.–(& another).** Trans.:– John Hester (1st. work). 1596; 1631. 1st. Edn. (2nd. work). 3 works in 1 vol. 4to. 1st. work: some head-lines, p.-numbers & side-notes cropped, some staining, last p. very soiled, title frayed, 2nd. work: some catch-words, sigs. etc., cut into, some staining, 3rd. work impft. Cont. sheep, worn, hf. red mor case. From Honeyman Collection. [NSTC 19180 (1st. work); STC 11203] (S. Nov.10; 2408) *Quaritch.* £1,300

PARADIN, Claude
– **Devises Héroiques.** Lyon, 1557. 2nd. Edn. Mor., gt. fillet borders & gt. panel with fleurs-de-lis. (SG. May 14; 166) $1,700

PARADIN, Cl.–FONTAINE, Charles
[–] **Quadrins Historiques de la Bible.–Figures de Nouveau Testament.** Ill.:– Bernard Salamon. Lyon; [1553]-83; 1554. 1st. Edn. 2 works in 1 vol.; 1st. work 2 pts. Title to pt. 1 very soiled, pt. 2 title verso with old MS. notat., soiled & stained; 2nd. work: 1 woodcut cold., old MS. name on title, slightly soiled, lacks some woodcuts. Cont. vell. (HK. Nov.18-21; 124) DM 850

PARADIN, Guillaume
See–**BIBLIANA [English]–PARADIN, Guillaume**

PARALDUS, Guilielmus
– **Sermones de Tempore et de Sanctis.** Tubingen, Johann Otmar, for Friedrich Meynberger, 19 Feb., [14]99. Fo. Spaces for initial capitals, supplied in red, as are paragraph marks, initial strokes & underlines, slight worming at front & back, light dampstaining, mostly marginal. Cont. blind-stpd. pig over bevelled wood bds., covers with central panels divided into lozenge & triangular sections filled with tools (including a thistle, an eagle in circle, an 'ave maria' scroll, & a head of Christ), the outer frames with similar tools (including an IHS) device & a pair of acorns in lozenge), brass clasps & catches, 2 sm. patches to upr. cover. Hand-cold. woodcut bkplt. of Hilprand Brandenburg von Biberach, & 5-line inscr. recording the gift of the book to the Carthusian Charterhouse at Buxheim, bkplt. of J.W. Six de Vromade, lately in the collection of Eric Sexton. [BMC III, 702, Goff P82, H. 8323*] (CNY. Apr.8; 176) $7,500
– – **Anr. Copy.** 3 pts. in 1 vol. Spaces for initial capitals, which are supplied in red, paragraph marks & underlines added in red or blue, pts. 2 & 3 transposed by binder, register of pt. 2 bnd. after register for pt. 1, tear to upr. margin of A1 affecting headline & 2 lines of text, aa2 of pt. 3 with paper flaw to upr. margin affecting headline, 1st. 3 ll. with worming to fore-margins, 1st. & last ll. with extensive browning. Cont. blind-stpd. vell, over wood bds., covers panel, with floral rolls, central panels with stylized foliage & floral tools, brass clasps. Bkplt. of the General Theological Seminary Liby. [BMC III. 702, Goff P82, HC 8323*] (CNY. Oct.1; 63) $1,200

PARCHEMIN (Le) Bulletin Belge d'Entriade et de Documentation Héraldique, Généalogique, Onomastique
Gentbrugge, Apr. 1936-Mar.-Apr. 1980. No. 1-206. In pts. (LM. Nov.8; 231) B.Frs. 8,500

PARDIES, Ignace Gaston
– **Globi Coelestis . . . Opus Postumum.** [Paris], [1693]. 2nd. Edn. Fo. Lacks a port. of John Frederick, Duke of Brunswick Luneburg (?), slight soiling & discolouration, Fr. Jesuit inscr. on title. Cont. cf., worn. From Honeyman Collection. (S. Nov.19; 2410) *Zeitlin.* £650

PARDO, Joseph Ben David
– **Shulchan Tahor.** [Amst.], 1686. 1st. Edn. 12mo. Cropped, tears, some affecting text, browning, stains, owners' sigs. on fly-ll. Blind-stpd. sheep. (SPB. May 11; 173) $600

PARDOE, Julia
– **The Beauties of the Bosphorous.** Ill.:– W.H. Bartlett. 1838. 4to. Lacks port., some spotting. Red mor. (CSK. Mar.20; 71) £60
– – **Anr. Copy.** Ex liby. Red three-qtr. mor., bnd. from pts., wraps. for several pts. bnd. in. (SG. Oct.30; 43) $150
– – **Anr. Copy.** Cont. hf. leath. gt., worn. (D. Dec.11-13; 1612) DM 480
– – **Anr. Edn.** Ill.:– W.H. Bartlett. 1839. 4to. Some plts. spotted. Cont. hf. cf. (C. Nov.5; 119a) *Strufaldi.* £65
– – **Anr. Edn.** Ill.:– after W.H. Bartlet. L., ca. 1840. 4to. No bdg. (R. Mar.31-Apr.4; 2561) DM 480

– – **Anr. Edn.** Ill.:– after W.H. Bartlett. Ca. 1850. 4to. Cont. hf. cf. (TA. Jun.18; 503) £54
– – **Anr. Edn.** N.d. 4to. Hf. cf., upr. cover detchd. (P. Apr.9; 88) *Bookroom.* £85
– – **Anr. Copy.** 77 engraved plts. only (of 78, lacks the 'Fountain & Mosque of Chahzade' plt.). Orig. cl. gt., 'The Bosphorus & Danube' blocked on spine, 1 cover slightly marked, corners & extremities of spine worn. (LC. Feb.12; 203) £50
– **The Court & Reign of Francis the First, King of France.–The Life of Marie de Medici, Queen of France.–Louis the Fourteenth & the Court of France in the Seventeenth Century.** L., 1847. 2 vols.; 3 vols.; 3 vols. Hf. mor. (SSA. Apr.22; 57) R. 100

PARDOE, Julia–BEATTIE, William
– **The Beauties of the Bosphorus.–The Danube.** Ill.:– after W.H. Bartlett. L., ca. 1850. 2 works in 8 vols. 4to. Lightly browned in parts. (H. May 21/22; 391) DM 1,500
– – **Anr. Edn.** Ill.:– after Bartlett. N.d. 2 works in 8 divisions. 4to. Occasional spotting. Orig. cl., spines torn. (CSK. Jul.3; 32) £230
– – **Anr. Copy.** Some foxing, browning. Unif. cl. gt., faded, some repairs, stains. (SPB. May 29; 330) $375
– **The Beauties of the Bosphorus.–Scotland Illustrated.** Ill.:– after W.H. Bartlett. L., 1838. 2 works in 1 vol. 4to. 2nd. work fragment: engraved title & 16 steel engrs., partly soiled. Cont. hf. leath., cover loose. (R. Oct.14-18; 1820) DM 500

PARE, Ambroise
– **Cinq Livres de Chirurgie.–Dix Livres de la Chirurgie.** Paris, (1st. work), 1572; n.d. 1st. work 1st. Edn. 2 vols. in 1. 1st. work: Last lf. slightly defect. & mntd., lacks lf. bearing printer's ornament; 2nd. work: Lacks title, aa2 defect., margins mntd. Old cf. (BS. Feb.25; 332) £320
– **Oeuvres.** Paris, 1575. 1st. coll. Edn. Fo. Old spr. cf., 5 decor. spine raised bands, title defect., 1st. lf. stained, old staining & worming. (LM. Mar.21; 199) B.Frs. 45,000
– – **Anr. Edn.** Paris, 1579. 2nd. Coll. Edn. Fo. Woodcut ports., woodcut text ills., further suite of most ills. on 91 pp. at end, lacks 3 prelim. ll. el-3, first & last 6 ll. reinforced, 3D1 defect., 3C4 damaged. 19th. C. cf., worn, upr. cover with title & first 9 ll. detchd. (S. Mar.17; 360) *Norton.* £400
– – **Anr. Edn.** Lyons, 1685. 13th. Edn. Fo. Lacks ff. 342-5, marginal tears, pt. of last lf. of index missing, slightly soiled & dampstained in places. Old cf. covered with paper, worn. (S. Feb.23; 85) *Vanhee.* £210
[–] **[Les Oeuvres . . . de l'anatomie . . .].** [Paris], ca. 1590. Fo. Very impft. at beginning & end. 19th. C. hf. cf. W.a.f. (SM. Oct.8; 2200) Frs. 2,200
– **Oeuvres Complètes.** Ed.:– J.F. Malgaigne. Paris, 1840-41. 3 vols. Orig. ptd. wraps., unc. (S. Jul.27; 364) *Quaritch.* £95
– **The Works.** Trans.:– Thomas Johnson. 1634. 1st. Edn. in Engl. Fo. Lacks 2 ll. after title with dedication & 'To the reader', 8 ll. of text in photostat facs. (4K 5-5, 4L 1-6), marginal tear in L5 & Q1, sm. hole in M2, corner of M5 & Bb2 torn, sm. rust-hole in Nn1, some ll. after 3A etc. wormed in upr. margin, lr. corner 4N4 & corners of last few ll. of Index reprd., margins of title reprd. Old cf., rebkd. W.a.f. [STC 19189] (S. Jun.17; 635) *Phelp.* £170
– – **Anr. Edn.** Trans.:– Thomas Johnson. 1649. 2nd. Edn. in Engl. Fo. Woodcuts at end mostly cropped & dust-soiled at edges, 2 ll. detchd. with edges dust-soiled, some discolouration. 17th. C. cf., stain on upr. cover. [Wing P349] (C. Feb.25; 16) *Traylen.* £330
– – **Anr. Edn.** Trans.:– Thomas Johnson. 1678. 4th. Edn. in Engl. Fo. Inner margin of title reprd., sm. hole in F6 affecting letters, short marginal tears in 7 ll. New panel. mor. [Wing P351] (S. Jun.17; 636) *Levinson.* £360

PAREDES, Ignacio de
– **Promptuario Manual Mexicano . . . utilissimo a los Parrochos para la Ensenansa . . . y a los que prender la Lengua para la Expedicion.** Mexico, 1759. Sm. 4to. Stain affecting 1 corner of 1st. ll. Bdg. not stated. (SPB. May 5; 389) $1,000
See-CAROCHI, Horacio & Paredes, Ignacio de
See-RIPALDA, Geronymo de & Paredes, Ignacio de

PARETO, Raffaele
– **Italie Monumentale.** Milan & Paris, 1879. 2 vols. Fo. Mod. hf. red mor., unc. (SI. Dec.4; 441) Lire 320,000

PARIS
– **Atlas Municipal des Vingt Arrondissements de la Ville de Paris.** Paris, 1895. Lge. fo. Leath.-bkd. bds. (SG. May 21; 83) $375
– **Collection de Vues de Paris Prises au Daguerreo-type.** Ill.:– Chamouin. [Paris], ca. 1849. Ob. 4to. Some plts. foxed. Hf. leath., worn. (SG. Jul.9; 259) $100
– **Paris dans sa Splendeur.** Ill.:– after Benoist & others. Paris, 1861. 3 vols. Tall fo. 99 (of 100) tinted litho. plts., lacks Facade of the Tuileries, liby. stp. on titles. Hf. mor., slightly worn. (SG. May 21; 413) $280
– **Paris et ses Environs.** Ill.:– Jacottet, Benoist & others. Paris, [1857]. Ob. fo. Gt.-pict. cl., covers detchd. (SG. Oct.30; 279) $225
– – **Anr. Edn.** Paris, ca. 1860. Ob. fo. Title & some plts. slightly browned. Orig. linen with gt. title vig. (H. Dec.9/10; 568) DM 1,600
– – **Anr. Edn.** [Paris], ca. 1867. Ob. 8vo. Orig. cl. (SH. Mar.5; 109) *Cucchi.* £80
– **[Paris Nouveau et ses Environs d'après les Photographies]** [Paris], [1859]. Ob. fo. A few plts. slightly spotted. Orig. cl., gt. (SH. Nov.6; 245) *Shapiro.* £110
– **Principales Vues de Paris et de ses Environs.** Paris, 1832. Ob. 4to. Soiled. Cont. hf. leath. (R. Oct.14-18; 1872) DM 1,200

PARIS, Archbp. of
See-HELVETIUS, Claude Adrien–PARIS, Archbp. of

PARIS, Matthaeus
– **Historia Major.** Ed.:– William Watts. 1639-40. 2 pts. in 1 vol. Fo. Cont. cf., head & foot of spine worn. [NSTC 19210] (S. May 5; 304) *Smith.* £60

PARIS GIRLS–EROS Parisian Girls
Ill.:– Fontan & others. Paris, 1917; 1919. 2 works in 2 vols. Fo. Loose as iss. in cold. pict. bd. folders, cl. spine & ties. (SG. Nov.20; 390) $150

PARIS LONDRES. KEEPSAKE FRANCAIS
Paris, 1837-30. 3 vols. Cont. mor., 3rd. vol. sigd. by Boutigny, gt. spines, partly unc., box. (SI. Dec.4; 445) Lire 240,000

PARIS et Ses Modes
– **Nouvel Almanach rédigé par le Caprice.** Paris, [1821]. 16mo. Cont. paper bds., decor., s.-c. (HD. Apr.10; 170) Frs. 1,400

PARISH REGISTERS
– **Buckinghamshire (Marriages).** 1902-23. Ltd. Edn. Vols. 1-9. Orig. cl., slightly soiled. (SH. Nov.6; 3) *Angle Books.* £55
– **Cambridgeshire, Essex & Hertfordshire.** 18 vols. 8vo. & 4to. Various cont. bdgs. (SH. Nov.6; 4) *Doncaster.* £120
– **Cambridgeshire (Marriages).** 1907-27. Ltd. Edn. Vols. 1-8 & Index to vols. 1-6, together 9 vols. Orig. cl., slightly soiled. (SH. Nov.6; 5) *Heraldry Today.* £55
– **Cornwall (Marriages).** 1900-35. Ltd. Edn. Vols. 1-26 & Index to vols. 1-6, in 27 vols. Orig. cl., slightly soiled. (SH. Nov.6; 10) *Ambra Books.* £260
– **Derbyshire (Marriages).** 1906-22. Ltd. Edn. Vols. 1-15. Orig. cl., slightly soiled. (SH. Nov.7; 14) *Smith.* £100
– **Dorset (Marriages).** 1906-10. Ltd. Edn. Vols. 1-5. Orig. cl., slightly soiled. (SH. Nov.6; 15) *Ambra.* £50
– **Gloucestershire (Marriages).** 1896-1914. Ltd. Edn. Vols. 1-17. Orig. cl., slightly soiled. (SH. Nov.6; 19) *Ambra.* £130
– **Hampshire (Marriages).** 1899-1914. Ltd. Edn. Vols. 1-16. Orig. cl., slightly soiled. (SH. Nov.6; 20) *Heraldry.* £110
– **Leicestershire (Marriages).** 1908-14. Ltd. Edn. Vols. 1-12. Orig. cl., slightly soiled. (SH. Nov.6; 23) *Sowter.* £80
– **Lincolnshire (Marriages).** 1905-21. Ltd. Edn. Vols. 1-11 & Index to vols. 1-6, together 12 vols. Orig. cl., slightly soiled. (SH. Nov.6; 25) *Angle.* £85
– **London.** 23 vols. Various sizes. Cont. bdgs. (SH. Nov.6; 26) *Heraldry.* £150
– **Middlesex (Marriages).** 1909-38. Ltd. Edn. Vols. 1-9. Orig. cl., slightly soiled. (SH. Nov.6; 27) *Frost.* £65

– **Norfolk (Marriages).** 1899-1936. Ltd. Edn. Vols. 1-12. Orig. cl., slightly soiled. (SH. Nov.6; 29) *Heraldry.* £75
– **Nottinghamshire (Marriages).** 1898-1938; 1900-02. Ltd. Edns. Vols. 1-22; Vols. 1-4, together 26 vols. Orig. cl., slightly soiled. (SH. Nov.6; 30) *Angle.* £150
– **Somerset (Marriages).** 1898-1915. Ltd. Edn. Vols. 1-15. Orig. cl., slightly soiled. (SH. Nov.6; 33) *Heraldry.* £100
– **Wiltshire (Marriages).** 1905-14. Ltd. Edn . Vols. 1-14. Orig. cl., slightly soiled. (SH. Nov.6; 37) *Angle.* £85

PARIVAL, Jean Nicolas de
– **Les Délices de la Hollande.** Amst., 1678. 12mo. Lacks 1 folding copper engr., 2 added copper engrs., 2 with sm. tear, a few brownings. Cont. vell. (H. Dec.9/10; 596) DM 540
[–] – **Anr. Edn.** Amst., 1685. 12mo. View & 1 plan slightly torn, browning. Cont. vell. (CSK. Oct.31; 26a) £95

PARK, J.A.
– **A System of the Law of Marine Insurance.** 1787. Cont. cf. (SH. May 21; 90) *Crete.* £80

PARK, John James
– **The Topography & Natural History of Hampstead.** 1818. Slight spotting. Cl.-bkd. bds. (CSK. Feb.6; 32) £80
See-ROBINSON, William–NELSON, John –PARK, John James

PARK, Lawrence
– **Gilbert Stuart. An Illustrated Descriptive List of his Works.** N.Y., 1926. 4 vols. 4to. Orig. cl. (SH. May 28; 218) *Zweller.* £200

PARK, Mungo
– **The Journal of a Mission to the Interior of Africa, in the Year 1805.** 1815. 1st. Edn. 4to. Recent hf. mor. (TA. Feb.19; 13) £60
– **The Journal of a Mission to the Interior of Africa.–Travels in the Interior Districts of Africa . . . with an Appendix.** 1815; 1816. 1st. work 2nd. Edn. 2nd. work, vol. 1 only. 4to. 1st. work: lacks hf.-title; 2nd. work: a few minor defects. Unif. cont. cf. gt. (SBA. Jul.22; 112) *Lovering.* £110
– **Travels in the Interior Districts of Africa.** 1799. 4to. Some offsetting. Cont. cf. (CSK. Aug.22; 100) £80
– – **Anr. Edn.** Ed.:– Major Rennell. 1816. New Edn. 2 vols. 4to. Cont. str.-grd. mor., gt. borders on sides. (C. Feb.25; 123) *Maggs.* £100
– – **Anr. Edn.** 1817-16. New Edn. 2 vols. Lge. engraved folding map, hand-cold. in outl., a few minor defects. Cont. hf. russ. (SBA. Mar.4; 119) *Museum Bookshop.* £55

PARK, Thomas
– **Cupid turned Volunteer . . .** Ill.:– W.N. Gardiner. 1804. 4to. Cont. hf. cf., rebkd., orig. spine preserved. (S. Nov.25; 436) *Broseghini.* £90

PARKER, Dorothy
– **Death & Taxes.** N.Y., 1931. (250) numbered, & sigd. Decor. cl., unc. (SG. Nov.13; 551) $100

PARKER, E.
See-GAY, John, Pope, Alexander & Arbuthnot, John–PARKER, E.

PARKER, Henry
[–] **[Dives & Pauper].** Richard Pynson, 5 Jul. 1493. 1st. Edn. Fo. Lacks blanks a1 & 2a1, & final lf. of Pynson's device, 1st. & last ll. slightly soiled, staining in lr. margin spreading to text, & in outer margin towards end. Late 18th. C. red mor., roll-tooled borders on covers, spine gt. in 6 compartments. Stanesby Alchorne & Chatsworth bkplts. [STC 19212, Goff P117, HC 6109] (C. Nov.19; 18) *A. Thomas.* £8,000

PARKER, John
– **Who's Who in the Theatre.** L. & Boston, 1912-[1972]. 1st.-15th. Edn. (lacks 3rd. & 14th. Edn.). 13 vols. Cl. (SG. Aug.7; 197) $180

PARKER, Samuel
– **Journal of an Exploring Tour Beyond the Rocky Mountains . . . Performed in the Years 1835, '36, & '37 . . .** Ithaca, N.Y., 1838. 1st. Edn. Slight foxing. Orig. blind-stpd. cl., spine gt., upr. jnt. cracked & reprd. From liby. of William E. Wilson. (SPB. Apr.29; 220) $225

PARKER, Thomas N.
– **An Essay on the Construction, Hanging & Fastening of Gates.** 1804. 2nd. Edn. Cont. hf. cf.

PARKER, Thomas N. Gates. -*contd.*
Bkplt. of Sir John Thorold, Syston Park. (S. Jun.22; 72)　　　*McDowell & Stern.* £110

PARKER Society: for the Publication of the Works of the Fathers & Early Writers of the Reformed English Church
- [Edited Texts]. Camb., 1841-53. Compl. run of 53 titles (with some dupls.), & index. 8vo. & 16mo. Orig. cl., some spines lacking, most bdgs. brkn. (SG. Dec.18; 326)　　　$100

PARKES, Samuel
- Chemical Essays Principally Relating to the Arts & Manufactures of the British Dominions. Priv. ptd., 1815. 1st. Edn. 5 vols. 12mo. Orig. bds., unc. (S. Dec.1; 305)　　　*Rota.* £55

PARKIN, Charles
See-BLOMEFIELD, Francis & Parkin, Charles

PARKINSON, James
- An Essay on the Shaking Palsy. 1817. 1st. Edn. Stp. of Medical & Chirurgical Society on title-p. New qtr. mor. From Dr. A. Gilpin's collection. (S. Jun.17; 638)　　　*Jenner Books.* £6,500
- Mad-Houses. Observations on the Act for Regulating Mad-Houses & a Correction of the Statements of the Case of Benjamin Elliott convicted of Illegally confining Mary Daintree. 1811. Paper wraps. (S. Jun.17; 637)
　　　Jenner Books. £170
- Organic Remains of a Former World. L., 1811-08-11. 3 vols. Lge. 4to. Foxed. Old cf., brkn. (SG. Sep.18; 287)　　　$200
- - Anr. Edn. 1820-1808-1811. 3 vols. 4to. Str.-grd. red mor. gt. (S. Dec.2; 862)
　　　Blackwell. £70

PARKINSON, John
- Paradisi in Sole. 1629 [colophon]. 1st. Edn., 1st. Iss. Fo. Woodcut title slightly frayed & detchd., index ll. torn & reprd., with loss of letters. 19th C. cl., lacks spine, covers detchd. From Chetham's Liby., Manchester. [STC 19300] (C. Nov.27; 317)
　　　Sotheran. £520
- - Anr. Edn. L., 1629. 1st. Edn. Fo. Antique-style maroon mor. gt. by Rivière. From the collection of Eric Sexton. [STC 19300] (C. Apr.15; 15)
　　　Figgess. £550
- - Anr. Copy. Title lf. lightly soiled. 18th. C. leath., cover loose (R. Oct.14-18; 3042)
　　　DM 3,400
- - Anr. Edn. 1656. 2nd. imp. Fo. Cont. cf., worn, gt. stp. of an eagle grasping snake & motto on sides. [Wing P495] (S. Dec.3; 1090)
　　　Temperley. £320
- - Anr. Copy. 109 full-p. woodcuts, cold. by cont. hand, offsetting & browning, lr. corner of F6 torn away, L3 reprd. 18th. C. Engl. red mor. gt., spine gt. (CNY. May 22; 209)　　　$2,200
- - Anr. Edn. 1904. Reprint of 1629 edn. Fo. Orig. holland-bkd. bds. (SH. Mar.5; 267)
　　　Blundell. £55
- - Anr. Copy. Three-qtr. lev. (SG. Sep.18; 288)
　　　$130
- Theatrum Botanicum: The Theater of Plantes. 1640. Fo. Margins of last few ll. slightly dampstained & soiled. Recent cf. [STC 19302] (TA. Sep.18; 330)　　　£800
- - Anr. Copy. Lacks additional engraved title, some stains thro.-out. 19th. C. hf. mor. From Chetham's Liby., Manchester. (C. Nov.27; 318)
　　　Sotheran. £580
- - Anr. Copy. Engraved additional title laid down, B2 & L213 holed with loss of a few letters, errata lf. preserved on back end-paper, gathering G6g misbnd. at end. Later reversed cf., worn. (CSK. Aug.22; 138)　　　£460

PARKINSON, Sydney
- A Journal of a Voyage to the South Seas in H.M.S. The Endeavour ... L., 1784. 2nd. Edn. Lge. 4to. 19th. C. hf. cf. (CNY. May 22; 235)
　　　$750

PARKMAN, Francis
- Works. Boston, 1898. 12 vols. Hf. cf., gt. (SPB. Nov.24; 46)　　　$125

PARKMAN, Francis-FARNHAM, Charles H.
- Works.-The Life of Francis Parkman. Boston, 1902; 1902. Frontenac Edn. 16 vols.; 1 vol. Maroon mor. gt. (SPB. Nov.24; 47)　　　$250

PARKS, Fanny
- [-] Wanderings of a Pilgrim ... during Four-& -Twenty Years in the East. 1850. 2 vols. 1 plt. loose in pocket marginally dampstained, a few

ll. slightly spotted. Orig. cl., gt., recased, slightly soiled. (SH. Nov.7; 355)　　　*Glazebrook.* £270
- [-] - Anr. Copy. A few ll. loose. Slightly defect. (S. Jun.22; 187)　　　*Maggs.* £80

PARKYNS, George Isham
- Monastic & Baronial Remains ... 1816. 2 vols. Cont. mor., gt.-panel. spines, inner dentelles, by Rivière. From the collection of Eric Sexton. (C. Apr.16; 326)　　　*Maggs.* £160
- - Anr. Copy. Some ll. slightly soiled. Cont. sheep gt. (SD. Feb.4; 163)　　　£65

PARKYNS, G.J.
See-SOANE, Sir John-PARKYNS, G.J.

PARLIAMENT
- Return of Members of Parliaments of England & Great Britain. [1878]. 2 vols. Fo. Hf. cf., spines gt. in compartments. (LC. Oct.2; 332)　　　£50

PARMACHENEE CLUB, The Story of
Parmachenee Lake, Maine, Priv. Ptd., ca. 1930. 1st. Edn. 4to. Ptd. wraps., unc. (SG. Oct.16; 267)
　　　$100

PARMENTIER, Antoine Auguste
- Discours prononcés à l'Ouverture de l'Ecole Gratuite de Boulangerie le 8 Juin 1870. Paris, 1780. Orig. Edn. MS. corrs. Cont. marb. cf., gt. triple fillet border, centre arms, limp decor. spine. (HD. Apr.24; 90)　　　*Frs.* 2,900

PARNASO Italiano, Ovvero Raccolta de'Poeti Classici Italiani
Venice, 1784-91. 56 vols. 16mo. Cont. red str.-grd. mor., 1 vol. in recent matching bdg., 1 lr. cover detchd. From the collection of John A. Saks. (C. Jun.10; 204)　　　*Greindl.* £400

PARNASSE (Le) des Plus Excellens Poètes de Ce Temps
Lyons, 1618. 3 pts. in 2 vols. 12mo. Mor. by Thouvenin, fillet border on covers & spines, inside dentelle. (HD. Mar.18; 130)　　　*Frs.* 1,600

PARNELL, Thomas
See-GOLDSMITH, Oliver & Parnell, Thomas

PARNY, Evariste, Desiré de Forges, Vicomte
- Chansons Madécasses. L., 1787. 1st. Edn.; on vell. 12mo. Sewed, unc., cont. wrap. (HD. Jun.24; 70)　　　*Frs.* 1,150

PAROLES PEINTES: IV
Ill.:- Henry Moore & others. Paris, 1970. (14) numbered, ptd. on japon nacre, with suite of 7 etchings, each sigd. by artist. Fo. Loose as issued in 7 ptd. folders, cl. folder, s.-c. (SG. Oct.23; 251)
　　　$500

PARQUIN, Capt.
- Récits de Guerre: Souvenirs, 1803-1814. Ill.:- Myrbach, Dupray & others. Paris, 1892. Fo. Gt.-pict. cl. (SG. Oct.30; 281)　　　$100

PARR, Victor G.
- Lives of the Fellows of the Royal College of Surgeons of England. Ed.:- Sir D'Arcy Power etc., continued by W.R. Le Fanu & R.A.O.B. Robinson, 1843-1951. Bristol & L., 1930-70. 4 vols. Cl., not unif. (S. Jun.17; 640)
　　　Hibbott. £130

PARRA, Antonio
- Descripcion de Diferentes Piezas de Historia Natural, las mas del Ramo Maritimo. Havana, 1787. Sm. 4to. Cont. mott. cf. (SPB. May 5; 390)
　　　$1,900

PARRAS, Pedro Joseph
- Gobierno de los Regulares de la America. Madrid, 1783. 2 vols. Sm. 4to. Cont. vell. [Sabin 58841] (SPB. May 5; 392)　　　$175

PARRISH, Maxfield
- [-] Early Venetian Printing Illustrated. N.Y., 1895. Fo. Orig. cl. worn. Parrish's ownership inscr. on front free endpaper, dtd. Phila. Dec. 1897. (SPB. Nov.25; 145)　　　$125

PARRY, Caleb Hillier
- Collections from the Unpublished Writings of the late Caleb Hillier. Ed.:- [Charles Henry Parry]. 1825. 3 vols. Lacks errata slip in vol. I. Hf. cf. (S. Jun.17; 642)　　　*Phillips.* £300

PARRY, J.
- The Coast of Sussex. 1833. Orig. cl., worn. (SH. May 21; 91)　　　*Vitale.* £50

PARRY, Robert Williams
- Cerddi Robert Williams Parry. Ill.:- Peter Reddick. Gregy. Pr., 1980. 1st. Edn., (15)

numbered, specially bnd. Sm. fo. Mor., tree-motif in black & gold on upr. cover, by Sydney Cockerell, unc. (S. Jun.9; 6)　　　*Lord Kenyon.* £350

PARRY, Sir William Edward
- Journal of a Voyage for the Discovery of a North-West Passage ... [1st Voyage]. L., 1821. 2nd. Edn. Lge. 4to. Cont. cf., covers detchd. Armorial bkplt. of Lord Bradford, Weston Park. (SG. Oct.30; 282)　　　$250
- - Anr. Copy. Lacks dedication lf., 1 map with sm. tear, anr. map reprd., lightly dampstained thro.-out. Recent qtr. cf. & marb. bds. (CB. Feb.18; 299)　　　Can. $350
- Journal of a Voyage for the discovery of a North-West Passage from the Atlantic to the Pacific.-Journal of a Second Voyage for the discovery of a ... to the Pacific.-Narrative of an Attempt to reach the North Pole. 1821; 1824; 1828. 1st. Edns. 4to. 1st. work: frontis. spotted, offsetting on title; 3rd. work: title & frontis. spotted, other minor discolouration. Orig. bds. (C. Feb.25; 124)　　　*Morrow.* £420
- Journal of a Voyage for the Discovery of a North-West Passage from the Atlantic to the Pacific. [1st. Voyage]-The North Georgia Gazette, & Winter Chronicle. 1821; 1821. 1st. work: 1st. Edn. 4to. 1st. work: 19 (of 20) engraved charts, coastal profiles & plts., sm. tear in 1, offsetting on title, minor staining at beginning. Orig. bds., 1st. work: spine defect., corners worn. (C. Feb.25; 125)
　　　Bowes. £80
- - Anr. Copy. 2 works in 2 vols. 1st. work: with errata slip, 1 map foxed; 2nd. work: with errata slip. 1st. work: cont. cf.; 2nd. work: cont. hf. cf. Both vols. with sig. of Robert Bell on title-p., bkplt. of John Angerstein in each vol. (CB. Dec.9; 8)
　　　Can. $450
- Journal of a Second Voyage for the Discovery of a North-West Passage from the Atlantic to the Pacific. 1824. 4to. Lacks the Appendix (iss. in 1825), a few plts. & charts slightly wormed, 6 of the 8 folding charts at end bnd. upside down, some fold reinforced, some light browning & offsetting. Later hf. mor. (CSK. Mar.13; 125)　　　£75
- - Anr. Copy. Orig. bdg. (TRL. Dec.10; 90)　　　£75
- - Anr. Copy. Some foxing. Cf., covers detchd. Armorial bkplt. of Lord Bradford, Weston Park. (SG. Oct.30; 283)　　　$325
- Journal of a Second Voyage for the Discovery of a North-West Passage ...-Appendix to a Second Voyage. L., 1824; 1825. 2 vols. 4to. Vol. 2 with the plts. slightly stained, & occasional soiling. Vol. 1: cont. cf.; vol. 2: cont. hf. cf. & marb. bds. Inscr. of J. Hanson on title-p. of vol. 1, sig. of Robert Bell on endpaper of vol. 2. (CB. Dec.9; 9)　Can. $1,600
- Journal of a Third Voyage for the Discovery of a North-West Passage from the Atlantic to the Pacific; Performed in His Majesty's Ships Hecla & Fury, 1824-25. 1826. [1st. Edn.?]. 4to. Recent hf. cf. (TA. Nov.20; 401)　　　£205
- - Anr. Copy. Some foxing. Cont. cf., covers detchd. Armorial bkplt. of Lord Bradford, Weston Park. (SG. Oct.30; 284)　　　$350
- Journal of a [First, Second & Third] Voyage for the Discovery of a North-West Passage ... 1821-26. 1st. Edn. 3 vols. 4to. 70 engraved plts. & charts, some folding. Cont. cf. gt. [Sabin 58860, 58864, 58867] (S. Nov.24; 229)　*Bowes.* £300
- Narrative of an Attempt to Reach the North Pole ... 1828. 1st. Edn. 4to. Cont. cf., gt. (S. Nov.24; 230)　　　*Crete.* £110
- - Anr. Copy. Cont. diced cf. (CSK. May 1; 113)
　　　£90

PARS, A.
- Catti Aborigines Batavorum. Ill.:- P. van den Schelling. Leyden & Amst., 1745. 2nd. Edn. Cont. hf. vell. (VG. Nov.18; 1318)　　　Fls. 550

PARSONS, James
- A Description of the Human Urinary Bladder. 1742. 1st. Edn. Some offsetting. Cont. mott. cf., gt. From liby. of Dr. E. Ashworth Underwood. (S. Feb.23; 269)　　　*Jenner.* £60

PARSON'S HORN-BOOK, The, by the Comet Literary & Patriotic Club
1832. 1st. Edn. Mod. mor., gt. spine & borders, floral onlays, gt. mor. endpapers, s.-c. (C. May 20; 44)　　　*Crow.* £140

PARTINGTON, Charles F.
- Natural History & Views of London. 1834. 2 vols. Contents loose in bdg. Orig. cl. (SH. Jul.23; 209)　　　*Crowe.* £65

– – Anr. Edn. 1835. 2 vols. in 1. Slight foxing. Cont. hf. mor. (TA. Sep.18; 16) £70

PARTINGTON, James Riddick
– A History of Chemistry. 1961-70. 4 vols. Cl. (S. Dec.1; 307a) *Whitehart.* £85

PARTIZAN
Ed.:– [K.P. Koposov]. St. Petersb., 1906. 4to. Slightly soiled. Unbnd. (SH. Feb.5; 105) *Quaritch.* £60

PAS, Crispin de
– Jardin de Fleurs. Utrecht, ca. 1614. Ob. 4to. Some staining, 90 plts. (of 105). Cont. vell. (HD. Jun.30; 61) Frs. 3,100

PASCAL, Adrien
– Histoire de l'Armée et de tous le Regiments. Paris, 1860-64. 5 vols. Cont. qtr. mor. (CNY. May 22; 171) $250

PASCAL, Blaise
[–] Lettres de A. Dettonville contenant quelques-unes de ses Inventions de Géometrie. Paris, 1659. 1st. Coll. Edn. 4to. Plt. I reprd., some browning, sm. stain in some lr. margins, MS. headings in upr. margins. Cont. cf., gt., hf. red mor. case. From Honeyman Collection. (S. Nov.10; 2412) *Quaritch.* £3,600
– Lettres Provinciales. Paris, 1823. 2 vols. Cont. cf., spines decor., covers decor. in gt. & blind, inner dentelles, by Bibolet. (HD. Apr.9; 538) Frs. 1,150
– Oeuvres. 1819. 5 vols. 13 (of 14) plts. Cont. decor. roan. (HD. Jun.30; 62) Frs. 2,200
– Pensées. Paris, 1670. 12mo. Cont. vell., soiled. (S. Oct.21; 286) *Booth.* £55
– – Anr. Edn. [Munich], [Bremer Pr.], [May 1930]. L.P. Edn. (270) numbered. Lge., very tall 4to. Orig. heavy bds., unopened, lacks box portion of s.-c., inner case folder present. (PNY. Mar.26; 57) $100
– – Anr. Edn. Ill:– A. Gleizes. [Casablanca], [1950]. (19) privilege Edn. with 1 aqua, 3 sketches & supp. series of etchgs., initials & vigs. in Bistre, on vel. Montgolfier. Lge. 4to. Lacks series of 50 etchgs., some ll. lightly soiled. Loose ll. in orig. hf. linen covers & s.-c., defect. (H. Dec.9/10; 2080) DM 12,000
– Les Provinciales ou Lettres escrites par Louis de Montalte. [Amst.], 1657. 1st. Edn., 1st. Iss. 12mo. With continuous pagination, with pp. 398 & 111 & reading 'Moines' on p. 3. Cont. vell. (SM. Oct.8; 1905) Frs. 1,200
– – Anr. Edn. [Amst.], 1657. Corrected Edn. 12mo. With pp. 396 & 108 & reading 'Religieux' on p. 3. Early 18th. C. mor., triple gt. fillet, flat spine gt. in compartments, inner gt. dentelles. (SM. Oct.8; 1906) Frs. 1,800
[–] Les Provinciales: or, The Mysterie of Jesuitisme, discover'd in certain Letters. 1657. 1st. Engl. Edn. 12mo. Bkplt. on verso of additional engraved title, advt. lf. Cont. panel. cf., upr. cover nearly detchd. [Wing P643] (S. Dec.9; 342) *Ohern.* £60
– Traité du Triangle Arithmétique, avec quelques autres Petits Traitez sur la mesme Matière. Paris, 1665. 1st. Edn. 4to. Some browning, title slightly soiled. 19th. C. cf., gt., hf. red mor. case. From Honeyman Collection. (S. Nov.10; 2416) *Tzakas.* £3,600
– Traitez de l'Equilibre des Liqueurs, et de la Pesanteur de la Masse de l'Air. Paris, 1663. 1st. Edn. 12mo. Both folding plts. reprd., old owner's inscr. on title. Red mor., gt. inner borders, by H. Alix, s.-c. From Honeyman Collection. (S. Nov.10; 2413) *Zeitlin.* £950
– – Anr. Copy. Both folding plts. with short tears, title a little soiled, cont. owner's inscr. on title. Old-style mor., gt. spine. From Honeyman Collection. (S. Nov.10; 2414) *Brieux.* £600
– – Anr. Copy. Red crushed lev. (SG. May 14; 168) $1,000
– – Anr. Edn. Paris, 1664. 2nd. Edn. 12mo. 1 folding plt. with marginal tear reprd., sm. hole in A3 affecting p.-numbers, title slightly soiled. Cont. cf., worn, bkplt. of Herbert McLean Evans (superimposed on an earlier armorial bkplt.). From Honeyman Collection. (S. Nov.10; 2415) *Quaritch.* £150
– – Anr. Edn. Paris, 1698. Cont. vell., rebnd. (VG. Nov.18; 1319) Fls. 1,200

PASCIN, Jules
– Erotikon. Ill:– Jules Pascin. Brussels, 1933. (41) numbered. 4to. Each plt. numbered in separate

card mount. Orig. wraps. & cl.-bkd. portfo., worn. (SH. Nov.21; 439) *Bradshaw.* £950

PASCOLI, G.
– Tre Poemetti Latini. Trans.:– G.B. Giorgini. Ill.:– A. Ciarrochi. Verona, 1959. (120), hand-printed on Bütten. Printer's mark sigd. Orig. wraps., s.-c. (R. Mar.31-Apr.4; 589) DM 600

PASEMANT, Claude Simeon
[–] Construction d'un Télescope par Reflexion, de Mr. Newton, ayant seize pouces de longueur, & faisant l'effet d'une Lunette de huit pieds. Amst., 1741. 1st. Edn. Folding plt. slightly torn at inner edge, some browning, occasional marginal staining. Cont. cf., worn at corners. From Honeyman Collection. (S. Nov.10; 2419) *Rogers Turner* £240

PASI, Bartolommeo di
– Tariffa de Pexi e Mesure. Venice, 1503. 1st. Edn. 4to. Sm. burn-hole in c4, a few letters erased on G1r, title reprd. in lr. margin, worming reprd. in lr. margins of last few gatherings, some soiling. Mod. mor., gt. From Honeyman Collection. (S. Nov.10; 2417) *Israel.* £340
– – Anr. Copy. Very dampstained & wormed, title & a number of ll. reprd., occasionally affecting text. Vell. bds. From Honeyman Collection, w.a.f. (S. Nov.10; 2418) *Fomecon.* £300

PASQUILLORUM TOMI DUO, quorum primo Versibus ac Rhythmis, altero Soluta Oratione conscripta quamplurima continentur. Eleutheropolis (Basle), 1544. Lacks lr. portions of 5 ll. at beginning, affecting a few lines of text, reprd., cont. owner's inscr. on title. Later vell. (C. Apr.1; 68) *Corby.* £50

PASQUIN, Peter (Pseud.)
See–PYNE, William Henry 'Peter Pasquin'

PASQUINI, J.N.
– Histoire de la Ville d'Ostende et du Port. Ed.:– Delpaire. Brussels, 1843. Hf. roan, limp spine, decor. (LM. Mar.21; 261) B.Frs. 10,000

PASS or Passe, Crispin van de, the Younger
– Les Abus du Mariage . . . [Amst.?], 1641. 1st. Edn. Sm. ob. 4to. Engraved title, 50 engraved ports., 4 extra ll. sigd. L2-5 inserted after H2. Mor. gt., by W. Pratt. Edouard Rahir, John A. Saks & Henry & Alfred Henry Huth bkplts. (CNY. May 22; 236) $3,200
– Hortus Floridus. Ed.:– Eleanour S. Rohde. Ill.:– Margaret Shipton. L., Cresset Pr., 1928-29. (500) numbered. 2 vols. Leath.-bkd. marb. bds., d.-w.'s worn. (SG. Apr.9; 428) $110

PASSAU, Otto von
– Dat Boeck des Gulden Throens. Utrecht, t.C. [device], Mar.30, 1480. 1st. Edn. in Dutch. Fo. Spaces for initial capitals, 1st. p. soiled, marginal repairs to folios 2-3, & 5 & some other ll., fore-edges slightly frayed & stained at front & back, finger-soiling to many ll., ink inscrs. at upr. & lr. margins of 1st. p. Cont. blind-stpd. cf. over wood bds., brass clasps & catches, rebkd. & reprd., church inscr. at front pastedown. From the collection of Eric Sexton. [BMC IX (IB 47094), Goff 0124, HC 12131] (CNY. Apr.8; 182) $18,000
– – Anr. Edn. Haarlem, Jacob Bellaert, 25 Oct., 1484. 2nd. Edn. Fo. Capital spaces, rubricated thro.-out, folios 5-140 numbered i-cxxxvii at foot of recto pp., lacks 1st. & final blanks, some ll. slightly soiled & occasionally stained, scattered early annots., corrections & amendations (including the erasure of several ptd. words), 19th. C. hf. sheep, marb. bds., spine gt., binder's ticket of J. Burio of Ghent. The copy of Jules Capron of Ypres, William H. Crawford of Lakelands, William Morris & Richard Bennett, lately in the Pierpont Morgan Liby. [BMC IX, 101, Goff 0125, HC 12132] (CNY. Apr.8; 74) $14,000

PASSERI, Giovanni Battista
– Vite de' Pittori, Scultori ed Architetti che hanno lavorato in Roma. Rome, 1772. 1st. Edn. 4to. Stain in centre & hole in white margin. Hf. vell. with corners. (CR. Mar.19; 456) Lire 420,000

PASSERIO, G.B.
[–] Thesaurus Gemmarum Antiquarum Astriferarum. Flor., 1750. Sm. fo. Later qtr. cf., worn. (S. Apr.7; 461) *Drury.* £70

PASSIO Domini Nostri Jesu Christi
Ill.:– Eric Gill. Gold. Cock. Pr., 1926. (250). 4to.

Orig. cl., unc., d.-w. (SH. Feb.19; 147) *Marks.* £175

PASTEUR, Louis
– Etudes sur la Bière . . . avec une Théorie nouvelle de la Fermentation. Paris, 1876. 1st. Edn. Cl. printed wraps. (dates on upr. covers those of orig. publication; they are, in fact, later, as per evidence of advts. on the back), unc. & partly unopened, hf. mor. case. From Honeyman Collection. (S. Nov.10; 2427) *Das Bucherkabinet.* £150
– – Anr. Copy. Advts. New cl., roan spine. (S. Jul.27; 118) *Blackwell.* £85
– – Anr. Copy. Lacks advts. Hf. mor., needs rebdg., ex liby. (SG. Sep.18; 293) $110
– Etudes sur la Maladie des Vers à Soie. Paris, 1870. 1st. Edn. 2 vols. in 1. Lacks hf.-title to vol. II. Cont. hf. cf., upr.-cover detchd. Pres. copy; bkplts. of Warren de la Rue & H.C. Plimmer, with his sig.; from Honeyman Collection. (S. Nov.10; 2425) *Norman.* £240
– – Anr. Copy. 2 vols. Orig. printed wraps. (dates on upr. covers are those of orig. publication, wraps are in fact later by evidence of advts. on back), 1 spine defect. at foot, unc., hf. red mor. cases. From Honeyman Collection. (S. Nov.10; 2426) *Blackwell.* £160
– – Anr. Copy. Qtr. mor. (P. Apr.30; 221) *Rota.* £55
– – Anr. Copy. Disbnd., unc. (SG. Sep.18; 292) $100
– Études sur le Vin. Paris, 1866. 1st. Edn. Some foxing. Cl., lr. inner hinge brkn., hf. red mor. case. From Honeyman Collection. (S. Nov.10; 2423) *B. & L. Rottenberg.* £140
– – Anr. Copy. Stp. on title & hf.-title. Mod. Fr. hf. cf., unc. (S. Feb.10; 455) *Crete.* £130
– – Anr. Edn. 1873. 2nd. Edn. Cont. red hf.-chagrin. (HD. Feb.18; 165) Frs. 1,600
– Études sur le Vin.–Études sur le Vinaigre. Paris, 1866; 1868. 1st. Edns. 2 works in 1 vol. Cont. hf. cf. Pres. copies to Warren de la Rue; from Honeyman Collection. (S. Nov.10; 2422) *Norman.* £400
– Études sur le Vinaigre. Paris, 1868. 1st. Edn. Slight marginal staining. Orig. printed wraps., worn & soiled, cl. case. Pres. copy, from Honeyman Collection. (S. Nov.10; 2424) *Norman.* £170
– Examen critique d'un Ecrit posthume de Claude Bernard sur la Fermentation. Paris, 1879. 1st. Edn. Orig. printed wraps., unc., mostly unopened. From Honeyman Collection. (S. Nov.10; 2428) *Quaritch.* £80
– Mémoire sur la Relation . . . entre la Forme Crystaline et la Composition Chimique, et sur la Cause de la Polarisation rotatoire . . . Paris, 1848. In: Comptes rendus . . . l'Academie des Sciences, vol. 26. 4to. Orig. wraps., unc. (S. Oct.21; 414) *Lange & Springer.* £75
– Studies on Fermentation, the Disease of Beer, their Causes & the Means of Preventing Them. Trans.:– Frank Faulkner & D. Constable Robb. 1879. 1st. Edn. in Engl. Advt. lf. Cont. cf., upr. hinge torn, unc. (S. Jun.17; 644) *Stanley.* £55
– Thèses de Physique et de Chimie, presentées à la Faculté des Sciences de Paris, le Aout 1847. Paris, 1847. 4to. Slight spotting. Orig. printed wraps., soiled. From Honeyman Collection. (S. Nov.10; 2420) *Norman.* £1,100

PASTEUR, Louis (Contrib.)
See–COMPTES Rendus Hebdomadaires . . .

PASTONCHI
– Specimen of a New Letter for the Use on the 'Monotypes'. Verona, Bod. Pr., 1928. (200). 4to. Orig. linen. (HK. Nov.18-21; 2837) DM 1,150

PATER, Walter
– Sebastian van Storck. Ill.:– V. Voight Alastair. 1927. (1,050) with 1 plt. sigd. by artist. 4to. Orig. cl., unopened. (SH. Mar.26; 35) *Hatchard.* £70
– – Anr. Copy. Fo. Some foxing. Decor. cl., boxed. (SG. Apr.2; 1) $140
– The Works. L., 1900-01. (775). 9 vols. Frontis.'s hand-cold., extra ill. with many ports. Crushed three-qtr. lev., sm. stain on 1 cover. This set with ptd. title '. . . extra-illustrated . . .', designed and bound for Hon. M.L. Scover'. (SG. Sep.4; 375) $140
– [–] Anr. Edn. L., v.d. 10 vols. Unif. hf. mor. gt. (SPB. Nov.25; 478) $275

PATERSON, Daniel
– British Itinerary. 1785. 2 vols. Vol. 2 slightly dampstained. Cont. marb. cf., worn. Bkplt. of the

PATERSON, Daniel – British Itinerary. *-contd.*
Honourable Shute Barrington, Lord Bishop of Durham. (CSK. Dec.12; 265) £120
– – **Anr. Copy.** Vol. 2 only. Cf., upr. cover detchd. (P. Apr.9; 146) *Green.* £65

PATERSON, George
[–] **The History of New South Wales.** Newcastle-upon-Tyne, 1811. [1st. Edn.]. Sm. section of folding chart defect. & made-up in photostat (with compl. photostat copy also added at end), folding map strengthened, 2 or 3 tears or paper defects, some foxing & discolouration. Mod. mor. (KH. Mar.24; 316) Aus. $130

PATERSON, James
– History of Ayr & Wigton. Edinb., 1863-66. 5 vols. Cl., worn. (CE. Dec.4; 61) £82
– – **Anr. Copy.** Orig. cl., worn. (CE. Jun.4; 199) £52

PATERSON, William
– A Narrative of Four Journeys into the Country of the Hottentots, & Caffraria in the Years One Thousand Seven Hundred & Seventy-Seven, Eight & Nine. L., 1789. 4to. Cf. (SSA. Jan.22; 320) R. 440

PATHOMACHIA
1630. 1st. Edn. 4to. With orig. initial blank. Red mor. by Rivière. [STC 19462] (C. Nov.19; 127) *Quaritch.* £480

PATIN, Guy
– Lettres Choisies . . . sur la Vie et la Mort des Scavans de ce Siècle, sur leurs Écrits. Paris, 1692. 3 vols. Lge. 12mo. Cont. cf. Bkplt. of Cholmondeley liby. (S. Jun.17; 645) *Wood.* £50

PATINA, Carola Catharina
– Tabellae Selectae ac Explicatae. Ill.:– Cochin after Titian & others. Passau, 1691. 1st. Edn. Fo. 34 (of 42) engd. plts., extra engraved title. Cont. cf., worn. (SG. Sep.25; 243) $100

PATMORE, Henry
– Poems. Oxford, Daniel Pr., 1884. (125). Sm. 4to. Orig. parch. Pres. copy from Coventry Patmore to H.E. Watts. (SH. Feb.20; 375) *George's.* £60

PATON, Lucy Allen
– Selected Bindings from the Gennadius Library. Camb., 1924. (300) numbered. 4to. Cl. (SG. Mar.26; 47) $220

PATRICIUS, Franciscus
– La Militia Romana di Polibio . . . Ferrara, 1583. 1st. Edn. Sm. 4to. Vell. bds., spine gt. (C. Jul.16; 284) *Taylor.* £80

PATRIOTISCHES ARCHIV für Deutschland
Ed.:– K.V. Moser. Frankfurt, Mannheim & Leipzig, 1789-90. Vols. 1-12, compl. series, all publd. Cont. bds. (R. Oct.14-18; 1187) DM 2,400

PATTE, Pierre
– Mémoires sur les Objets les plus importans de l'Architecture. Paris, 1769. 4to. Cont. mott. cf., gt. spine. (S. Jun.22; 135) *Weinreb.* £110

PATTERSON, A.W.
– History of the Backwoods; or, The Region of the Ohio . . . Pittsburgh, 1843. 1st. Edn. Folding map foxed, portions of text stained. Orig. blind-stpd. cl., gt. spine, head & foot of spine worn, mod. d.-w., s.-c. From lib. of William E. Wilson; the Littell copy. (SPB. Apr.29; 223) $650

PAUL, James
– Jamaica Physical Journal. Kingston, Apr., May, Jun., & Sept., 1834, & Apr., 1835. Bnd. in 1 vol. Hf. cf., spine gt. (SG. Jan.29; 236) $110

PAUL, Sir James Balfour
– Scots Peerage. Edinb., 1904-14. 9 vols. Ex-liby. copy. Cl. (PD. Oct.22; 42) £200

PAUL, Saint
See–CRINESIUS, Christophorus–PAUL, Saint

PAULI, C. Fr.
– Leben Grosser Helden des Gegenwärtigen Krieges. Halle, 1758-60. 1st. Edn. Vols. II-VI. Vols. I-VI (of 9). Cont. cf., lightly worn. (H. Dec.9/10; 896) DM 440

PAULINUS, Fabius
– Hebdomades, sive Septem de Setenario libri. Venice, 1589. 1st. Edn. 4to. Marginal tear in 2T1. Vell., lacks ties, mod. end-papers. Bkplt. of M.A. Elton; from Honeyman Collection. (S. Nov.10; 2429) *Quaritch.* £140

PAULUS Aegineta
– Opus de Re Medica . . . Trans.:– Ioannem Guinterium Andernacum. Paris, 1532. 1st. Edn. of this translation. 7 pts. in 1 vol. Fo. Prelims. for pts. 6 & 7 misbnd., some marginal repairs to title & sm. holes in margin of following lf., extreme outer upr. blank corners of last ll. reprd., sm. inkstain on p. 15 pt. 3. New vell. (S. Jun.17; 646) *Levinson.* £240

PAULUS, de Middelburgo
– De Recta paschae Celebratione: et de Die Passionis Domini Nostri Iesu Christi. Fossombrone, 8 Jul 1513. 1st. Edn. Fo. Occasional foxing or staining, worming in inner margins near the end. Cont. vell. bds., rebkd. From Honeyman Collection. (S. Nov.10; 2430) *Zeitlin.* £450

PAULUS DE SANCTA MARIA
– Additiones ad Postillam Nicolai de Lyra Super Biblia. Venice, Franciscus Renner, de Heilbronn, 1483. Fo. Rubricated in red & purple thro.-out. 19th. C. mor., rebkd. (C. Jul.16; 223) *Watson.* £90

PAULUS Pergulensis
See–SAVONAROLA, Hieronymous–PAULUS Pergulensis–ARISTOTELES

PAULY, Thomas de
– Description Ethnographique des Peuples de la Russie. St. Petersb., 1862. Lge. fo. Lr. margins, etc., stained. Cl., worn. (BS. Jun.11; 419) £200

PAUQUET, Hippolyte & Polydor
– The Book of Historical Costumes. N.d. Some pp. loose. Cl. gt. (P. Mar.12; 26) £90
– Illustrations of English & Foreign Costume. 1875. 4to. Later cl. (SH. Jan.29; 271) *Litman.* £140
– Modes et Costumes Historiques. Paris, ca. 1860. Fo. Cont. cl. gt., mor. spine, rebkd. (TA. Oct.16; 318) £150
– – **Anr. Edn.** Paris, ca. 1865. 4to. Orig. mor. gt. W.a.f. (TA. Aug.21; 95) £160
– – **Anr. Copy.** (TA. Aug.21; 96) £140
– – **Anr. Edn.** Paris, n.d. 4to. Cont. hf. mor. (SH. Jan.29; 272) *Litman.* £180
– – **Anr. Copy.** Tooled cf. (HSS. Apr.24; 123) £160
– Modes et Costumes Historiques.–Modes et Costumes Historiques Etrangers. [1864]; [1875]. Together 2 vols. 4to. Unif. bnd. in cont. hf. mor. (C. May 20; 161) *Taylor.* £220
– Modes et Costumes Historiques Etrangers. Paris, n.d. 4to. Occasional slight soiling. Cont. hf. mor. (CSK. Dec.12; 21) £170

PAUSANIUS
– The Description of Greece. Trans.:– Thomas Taylor. L., 1824. 3 vols. Cont. diced cf., spines gt. (SG. Mar.19; 258) $130
– Veteris Graeciae Descriptio. Flor., 1551. Fo. Cont. cf., gt., heavily worn, jnts. brkn., supralibros of Jac. Malinfantius. (HK. Nov.18-21; 254) DM 1,200
– Voyage Historique de la Grèce. Trans.:– Abbé Godoyn. Amst., 1733. 4 vols. 12mo. Cont. cf. Royal bkplt. (PNY. Oct.1; 419) $130

PAUW, Corneille de
[–] Recherches Philosophiques sur les Egyptiens et les Chinois. Berlin, 1773. 2 vols. 18th. C. mor. by Derome, gt. spine, corner fleurons, gt. outer dentelles & wide floral inner dentelles. (D. Dec.11-13; 2575) DM 2,200

PAVLOV, Ivan Petroviych
– Die Arbeit der Verdauungsdrusen. Trans.:– A. Walther. Wiesbaden, 1898. 1st. German Edn. Hf. roan. (S. Jul.27; 369) *Smirl.* £300
– – **Anr. Copy.** Orig. ptd. wraps., unc., worn. From Honeyman Collection. (S. Nov.10; 2431) *Norman.* £220
– Dvadtsatiletny opyt ob'ektivnogo izucheniya vysshei nervnoi deyatel'nosti (povedeniya) zhivotnykh [Twenty years' Experience in the objective Study of the higher Nervous Activity (Behaviour) of Animals. Conditioned Reflexes]. Moscow & Petrograd, 1923. 1st. Edn. Orig. wraps. by M.K., slightly torn & soiled, mostly unopened. (S. Oct.21; 415) *Dekker & Noordeman.* £900
– Leçons sur l'Activité du Cortex Cerebral. Trans.:– Dr. I. Trifonoff. Paris, 1929. Hf. mor. From Brooklyn Academy of Medicine. (SG. Jan.29; 332) $100

PAVON, Josepho
See–RUIZ, Hippolyto & Pavon, Josepho

PAXTON, Joseph
– Magazine of Botany & Register of Flowering Plants. L., 1834. Vol. 1. Cont. leath. (HK. Nov.18-21; 673) DM 720
– – **Anr. Run.** 1834-36. Vols. 1 & 2 only. 4to. Some very minor defects. Hf. mor. gt., very worn. (SBA. May 27; 191) *Edistar.* £130
– – **Anr. Run.** 1834-39. 16 vols. (compl. set). Hf. cf. gt. (P. Jan.22; 65b) *Litman.* £1,700
– – **Anr. Run.** 1834-43. Vols 1-10 (of 16). Some imprints trimmed or cropped, occasional light offsetting, a few spots. Cont. hf. roan, spines gt., 1 spine defect., worn. (S. Dec.3; 1093) *Nagel.* £660
– – **Anr. Copy.** Vols. 1-7, 9-10. 4to. Hf. leath., not unif. W.a.f. (S. Dec.3; 1094) *Walford.* £480
– – **Anr. Run.** 1834-46. 5 vols., various. Lacks 1 title, 1 section detchd. Cont. hf. mor. W.a.f. (CSK. Sep.5; 107) £480
– – **Anr. Run.** L., 1834-49. 16 vols. Hf. mor. gt. (P. Jun.11; 324) *Cambridge.* £1,700
– – **Anr. Copy.** 718 (of 719) hand-cold. plts., 2 loose, vol. 3 lacks 1st. plt., some spotting. Vol. 16 cl., worn. (P. Mar.12; 39a) *Cablo.* £1,400
– – **Anr. Run.** L., 1836. Vol. 2. Some plts. lightly soiled. Cont. linen. (HK. Nov.18-21; 674) DM 720
– – **Anr. Run.** L., 1837. Vol. 3. Cont. linen. (HK. Nov.18-21; 676) DM 740
– – **Anr. Run.** 1838. Vol. 4. Cont. leath. (HK. Nov.18-21; 678) DM 720
– – **Anr. Run.** L., 1838. Vol. 5. Slightly soiled in parts, pp. 1-120 bnd. in at end. Cont. hf. leath. (HK. Nov.18-21; 680) DM 860
– – **Anr. Run.** L., 1839. Vol. 6. Some plts. lightly soiled. Cont. linen. (HK. Nov.18-21; 681) DM 720
– – **Anr. Copy.** 44 (of 48) cold. plts., a few plts. with sm. hole in margin, lacks title & 1st. ll. Cont. hf. leath. (HK. Nov.18-21; 682) DM 420
– – **Anr. Run.** L., 1840. Vol. 7. Cont. linen. (HK. Nov.18-21; 683) DM 850
– – **Anr. Copy.** Cont. leath., gt. & blind-tooled. (HK. Nov.18-21; 684) DM 600
– – **Anr. Run.** L., 1841. Vol. 8. Text slightly soiled in parts. Cont. hf. leath. (HK. Nov.18-21; 686) DM 800
– – **Anr. Copy.** Upr. cover loose. (R. Mar.31-Apr.4; 1422) DM 750
– – **Anr. Copy.** Vol. 1. Worn. (HK. Nov.18-21; 672) DM 720
– – **Anr. Run.** L., 1842. Vol. 9. Cont. hf. leath. (HK. Nov.18-21; 688) DM 850
– – **Anr. Copy.** 47 (of 48) cold. plts. Cont. linen. (HK. Nov.18-21; 687) DM 600
– – **Anr. Run.** L., 1843. Vol. 10. Cont. hf. leath. (HK. Nov.18-21; 690) DM 800
– – **Anr. Copy.** Cont. linen. (HK. Nov.18-21; 689) DM 700
– – **Anr. Run.** 1843-49. Vols. 1-15 (of 16). 697 (of 768) plts. Cont. hf. roan, upr. hinge of vol. XV brkn. Bkplt. of St. Chad's College; w.a.f. (S. Jun.1; 190) *Cristiani.* £1,200
– – **Anr. Run.** L., 1844. Vol. 11. Cont. linen. (HK. Nov.18-21; 691) DM 500
– – **Anr. Run.** 1846-49. Vols. 12-16 (of 16). Cont. hf. cf. As periodical, w.a.f. (SBA. Jul.22; 63a) *Schuster.* £500
– – **Anr. Run.** L., 1847. Vol. 13. Cont. hf. leath. (R. Mar.31-Apr.4; 1423) DM 750
– Magazine of Gardening & Botany. L., 1849. Pt. 1. Without text, 22 cold. lithos. Orig. pict. (HK. Nov.18-21; 692) DM 420

PAXTON, Sir Joseph & Lindley, John
– Flower Garden. L., 1850-53. 1st. Edn. 3 vols. 4to. 1 plt. & 1 text lf. loose, foxed. Cont. hf. mor., unc. Armorial bkplts. of De Branteghem, bkplts. of the S.H. Weiss Liby., Constantinople. (PNY. May 21; 316) $350
– – **Anr. Edn.** 1853. 3 vols. 4to. Orig. cl. gt., recased, spine slightly defect. (TA. Feb.19; 535) £300
– – **Anr. Edn.** 1882. 2nd. Edn. 3 pts. in 1 vol. 4to. A few plts. slightly torn. Orig. cl., rebkd. using orig. spine. (S. Dec.3; 1099) *Litman.* £160
– – **Anr. Edn.** 1882-84. 3 vols. 4to. Lacks hf.-title in vol. I, sm. repairs to plts. 8 & 77, short tears in plts. 15 & 68, slight browning. Cont. cf., worn. (S. Dec.3; 1095) *Litman.* £140
– – **Anr. Copy.** Orig. cl. (BS. Sep.17; 139) £90

PAYATS [Clown]
Ed.:– [P.S. Solomko]. St. Petersb., 1905-06. Nos. 1-3 (all publd.). Fo. A few tears. Unbnd. (SH. Feb.5; 106) *De la Casa*. £130
– – **Anr. Copy.** (SH. Feb.5; 180) *Landry*. £65

PAYN, James
– The Lakes in Sunshine. 1868. 2 vols. 4to. Orig. cl. gt. (P. Apr.9; 108) *Henderson*. £80

PAYNE, A.F.
– A Collection of 114 Watercolours and 11 Charcoal, Pencil or Wash Drawings. Ca. 1853-60. 4to. Loosely inserted in an album, many sigd. & dtd. on back. (SH. Apr.10; 633) *Drummond*. £400

PAYNE, Albert Henry
– Book of Art with the Galleries of Munich. Ca. 1850. 3 vols. Hf. mor. (BS. May 13; 260) £200
– – **Anr. Copy.** 4to. Soiled in parts. Cont. linen, defect. (R. Mar.31-Apr.4; 1596) DM 900
– – **Anr. Edn.** Priv. ptd., n.d. 2 vols. 4to. 1 vol. contains 184 engraved guarded plts. Orig. diced cf., decor. gt. backstrip. (PL. Nov.27; 100) *Hyde Park Bookshops*. £95
– Orbis Pictus. Ill.:– H. Leuteman. Dresden & Leipzig, ca. 1840. 4to. Soiled in parts, 'Reynard the Fox (trans. E.W. Holloway) bnd. in. Cont. leath. gt. (R. Mar.31-Apr.4; 1868) DM 700
– – **Anr. Edn.** [Dresden & Leipzig], ca. 1850. Browned in parts. Orig. linen, heavily rubbed & bumped. (R. Mar.31-Apr.4; 2598) DM 750
– – **Anr. Edn.** Dresden & Leipzig, n.d. 4to. Some spotting. Cont. cf. W.a.f. (CSK. Nov.28; 93) £170
– Royal Dresden Gallery. [1845?-50]. 2 vols. 4to. Cont. hf. cf., spines faded. (SBA. Oct.21; 262) *Hyde Park Bookshop*. £180
– – **Anr. Edn.** Dresden & Leipzig, ca. 1860. 2 vols. 4to. Soiled in parts. Cont. linen gt. (R. Mar.31-Apr.4; 1598) DM 850
– – **Anr. Edn.** N.d. 2 vols. 4to. Spotting & dampstaining. Orig. cl. (SH. Jan.29; 137) *Dallai*. £190
– – **Anr. Copy.** Occasional light spotting. Cont. mor., gt. (CSK. May 15; 2) £180
– – **Anr. Copy.** 2 vols. in 1. Chagrin, 5 decor. spine raised bands, gt. border, slightly worn. (LM. Nov.8; 82) B.Frs. 9,500
– Universum. L. & Leipzig, ca. 1845. Vols. 1-3 in 1 vol. 186 (of 191) steel engrs. Cont. hf. leath., defect. & loose, soiled, lacks spine. (R. Mar.31-Apr.4; 2280) DM 1,000
– – **Anr. Copy.** Vol. 1. 4to. Soiled. (R. Mar.31-Apr.4; 2276) DM 600
– – **Anr. Edn.** Leipzig, ca. 1845. Vol. 3, Pt. 2. Lacks title, soiled, text not collated. Cont. linen. (R. Oct.14-18; 2523) DM 650
– – **Anr. Edn.** Leipzig & Dresden, ca. 1860. New series. Vols. 1-4 in 4 vols. 4to. Slightly soiled in parts. Cont. hf. leath. (R. Mar.31-Apr.4; 2282) DM 2,600
– – **Anr. Edn.** Leipzig, n.d. Vol. 9. 4to. Hf. linen, defect. (R. Oct.14-18; 2525) DM 650

PAYNE, Henry Neville
[–] The Morning Ramble. 1673. 1st. Edn. 4to. Mor. by Sangorski. [Wing P892] (C. Nov.19; 128) *Brett-Smith*. £110

PAYNE, James
See–PAINE or Payne, James

PAYNE, John
– A New & Complete System of Universal Geography ... Ed.:– James Hardie. N.Y., 1798-99. 4 vols. Lacks a very few plts., some plts. linen mntd., all with liby. stp. on verso. Hf. linen. (SG. May 21; 85) $300

PAYNE, John Howard
– Clari. L., 1823. 1st. Edn. Title-p. slightly soiled at edges & with offset of bkplt. Old wraps., cl. folding case, unc. The Jerome Kern copy, lately in the Prescott Collection. (CNY. Feb.6; 272) $1,200

PAYNE, William
– Panorama of the Rhine. Ca. 1840? 2nd. Edn. Ob. 4to. Orig. cl. gt. (S. Mar.31; 497) *Schuster*. £190

PAYNE-GALLWEY, R.
– The Book of Duck Decoys. 1886. [1st. Edn.?]. Spotted. Orig. cl. (SH. Jan.30; 385) *Graham*. £80
– – **Anr. Copy.** Cl., spine torn. (SG. Apr.9; 386) $150

– The Diary of Colonel Peter Hawker. 1893. 2 vols. Orig. cl., unc. (SBA. Jul.22; 55) *Coles*. £50

PAYNELL, Thomas
– Regimen Sanitatis Salerni. 1541. 4to. Soiled, lacks ll. 3I-IV. Later panel. cf. gt., some wear to upr. cover. (TA. Oct.16; 184) £85

PAZAUREK, Gustav E.
– Steingut Formgebung und Geschichte. Stuttgart, n.d. Fo. Orig. hf. cl. portfo. (SH. Mar.6; 552) *Schneider-Henn*. £160

PCHELA [Bee]
Ed.:– [N.I. Danishevsky]. St. Petersb., 1906. Nos. 1-5. Ob. 4to. & fo. Unbnd. (SH. Feb.5; 108) *Landry*. £230

PEABODY, George
– Proceedings at the Reception & Dinner in Honor of ...–Proceedings at the Dinner given by Peabody to the Americans connected with the Great Exhibition. Ill.:– Winslow Homer & others. Boston; L., 1856; 1851. Together 2 vols. Cold. litho. plts., extra ill. with 35 engravings. Lev., raised bands, gt. dentelles, by Zaehnsdorf, 2nd. work with orig. cl. covers & spine bnd. in. 6 A.L.s. & 6-p. A.L.s. with orig. envelope by Queen Victoria. (SG. May 14; 169) $1,300

PEACHAM, Henry
– The Gentlemens Exercise ... 1634. 4to. Early 19th. C. cf., Heber liby. stp. on end-paper. [STC 19507] (C. Apr.1; 227) *Marlborough*. £70
– – **Anr. Copy.** 2 vols. in 1. Lacks engraved frontis., 2nd. pt. slightly stained. Cf., rebkd., spine worn, bkplt. of Duke of Portland. [STC 19504 & 19509] (C. Apr.1; 226) *White*. £55

PEACOCK, Thomas Bevill
– On Malformations of the Human Heart etc., with Original Cases & Observations. 1866. 2nd. Edn. 40 pp. advts. dtd. Nov. 1866. Orig. cl. (S. Jun.17; 648) *Gurney*. £85

PEACOCK, Thomas Love
– The Misfortunes of Elphin. Ill.:– H.W. Bray. Gregy. Pr., 1928. (250). Hf. mor. (SH. Feb.20; 207) *Kerrigan*. £130

PEAKE, Mervyn
– Shapes & Sounds. 1941. 1st. Edn. Orig. cl.-bkd. bds., unc., d.-w. with design by author. Pres. Copy. (SH. Dec.18; 21) *Pye*. £65

PEAKE, Mervyn (Ill.)
See–RIDE a Cock-Horse & Other Nursery Rhymes

PEALE, Rembrandt
– An Historical Disquisition on the Mammoth, or, Great American Icognitum ... 1803. A few marginal stains. Orig. wraps., defect., cl. case. From Honeyman Collection. (S. Nov.10; 2433) *Zeitlin*. £90

PEARSE, G.E.
– Eighteenth Century Furniture in South Africa. Pretoria, 1960. (50) sigd. by author. Mor. (SSA. Apr.22; 237) R. 150
– – **Anr. Edn.** Pretoria, 1960. 4to. Cl. (SSA. Apr.22; 236) R. 120

PEARSON, Karl
– The Life, Letters & Labours of Francis Galton. Camb., 1914-30. 3 vols. in 4. 4to. Tables in pocket at end of vol. I & III, 2 ll. detchd. in vol. IV. Orig. cl., gt. From liby. of Dr. E. Ashworth Underwood. (S. Feb.23; 271) *Singleton*. £110

PEARSON, William Henry
– Recollections & Records of Toronto of Old. Toronto, ' 1914. Orig. cl., unopened. (CB. Dec.9; 233) Can. $100

PEART, Edward–WALKER, A.
– The Generation of Animal Heat Investigated. On the Elementary Principles of Nature & the Simple Laws by which they are Governed; On Electricity with Occasional Observations on Magnetism. –Analysis of a Course of Lectures on Natural & Experimental Philosophy. Gainsborough, (1st. work), 1788; 1789; 1791; ca. 1790. 4 works in 1 vol. Pol. cf. (S. Dec.2; 863) *Maggs*. £130

PEARY, Robert E.
– The North Pole. 1910. (500) numbered, sigd. by author & R.A. Bartlett. 4to. Orig. buckram cl. (TRL. Dec.10; 76) £135

PECCETTIUS, Franciscus
– Cheirurgia. Flor., 1616. Fo. Sheet T2/5 duplicated & T3/4 missing, ?lacks 1st. blank, title

& 2 prelims. slightly smaller than rest, dampstained, slightly soiled in places, f. 2T3 torn, slightly affecting text. Cont. vell. bds., spine soiled. (S. Oct.21; 416) *Van der Kerkehove*. £50

PECK, Francis
– Academia Tertia Anglicana. 1727. 1st. Edn., L.P. Fo. Mezzotint port. & MS. biographical sketch inserted, liby. blind-stp. on title. Cont. cf., rebkd. From the collection of Eric Sexton. (C. Apr.16; 327) *Webb*. £100

PECK, R.H., Fincastle, Va.
– Reminiscences of a Confederate Soldier of Co. C. 2nd. Va. Cavalry. [?Fincastle], ca. 1915. Orig. ptd. wraps, stapled. (PNY. Oct.1; 148) $130

PECKHAM, Ann
– The Complete English Cook ... Leeds, ca. 1790. 4th. Edn. 12mo. Cont. 2-toned bds. (SG. Sep.4; 126) $200

PECKHAM, Joannes, Abp. of Canterbury
– Perspettiva ... communis. Ed.:– Andreas Alexander. Leipzig, 1504. Fo. Last 15 ll. a little wormed in outer margins touching 1 or 2 diagrams, a few stains. Mod. vell. From Honeyman Collection. (S. Nov.10; 2434) *Brieux*. £580
– – **Anr. Edn.** Ed.:– L. Gauricus. [Paris], ca. 1510. Fo. Mor. by Zaehnsdorf. From Honeyman Collection. (S. Nov.10; 2435) *Brieux*. £460

PECKHAM, Joannes, Abp. of Canterbury–BACON, Roger
– Perspectivae communis. –Specula Mathematica. –Perspectiva. Ed.:– J. Combach (2nd. & 3rd. works). Cologne; Frankfurt; Frankfurt, 1627; 1614; 1614. 1st. Edns. (2nd. & 3rd. works). 3 works in 1 vol. 4to. Some browning & slight soiling, 2nd. work with sm. tear in upr. margin on title, 3rd. work with 8 pp. of woodcut diagrams stained & annotated. Cont. cf., rebkd., old spine preserved. From Honeyman Collection. (S. Nov.10; 2436) *Hill*. £580

PECQUET, Jean–BARTHOLINUS, Thomas
– New Anatomical Experiments, by which the hitherto unknown Receptacle of the Chyle & the Transmission from thence to the Subclavial Veins by the New Discovered Lacteal Channels ... –An Anatomical Dissertation of the Motion of Blood & Chyle. 1653. 1st. Edn. in Engl. 2 pts. in 1 vol. 12mo. 2 folding plts. with text in Fr., last lf. pt. I blank, but lacks lf. before title (presumably blank), corner of 1st. plt. reprd. just affecting 1 engraved figure, sm. marginal hole in last 2 ll. New spr. cf. With extract of a letter of M. Pecquet to M. Carcavi, concerning a new discovery of the communication of the Ductus Thoracicus with the Emulgent Vein: taken out of the Journal des Scavans, N. VII, 1667, an excerpt, pp. 461-464. [Wing P1045] (S. Jun.17; 650) *Norman*. £850

PECTORALE Dominicae Passionis
[Alost], [Thierry Martens], ca. 1487. 4to. Spaces for initial capitals, unrubricated. Recent vell. From the collection of Eric Sexton. [BMC IX, 127, C 4660, Goff P247] (CNY. Apr.8; 3) $3,500

PEDRINI, Abbate
– Austriborbonide Ovvero Fasti d'Europa. Ill.:– M. Borghi & E. Vasselini. Modena, 1770. 2 vols. 4to. Cont. mott. cf., rebkd. From the collection of John A. Saks. (C. Jun.10; 206) *Taylor*. £55

PEEL, Capt. R.H.
– The Extraordinary Ascent of the Enchanted Mountain ... 1835. 4to. 1 lf. reprd., affected by damp. Mor.-bkd. cl., cover loose. (SH. Mar.19; 247) *Temperley*. £350

PEELE, James
– The Pathe Waye to Perfectnes. 1569. Fo. A1 defect., worm to folios 53-63, not affecting text. Cf. [STC 19548] (P. Sep.11; 60) *Quaritch*. £620

PEETERS, J.
– Cabinet de L'Archduke Leopold 1st. Antw., ca. 1650. Ob. 4to. Old cf. As a collection of plts., w.a.f. (P. Feb.19; 150) *Davies*. £650

PEGIUS, Martin
– Geburtsstunden Buch darinnen eines jettichen Menschens Natur und Eigenschafft. Basel, 1570. 1st. Edn. Fo. Repair to upr. inner corner of title. 18th. C. vell. bds., hf. red mor. case. Bkplt. of Christian Ernst, Graf zu Stolberg; stp. of Stolberg liby. at Wernigerode; from Honeyman Collection. (S. Nov.10; 2437) *Das Bucherkabinet*. £580

PEIGNOT, Etienne Gabriel
– Dictionnaire Raisonné de Bibliologie, [with] Supplement. Paris, 1802-04. 3 vols. Marginal staining, old liby. stps. on versos of titles. New qtr. cf. The John A. Saks copy. (CNY. Oct.1; 202)
$120

PEINTURE MODERNE: et l'Art du Tissu Imprimé
Milan, n.d. (250). Fo. Ptd. flexible bds. (SG. Oct.23; 258)
$170

PELAGIUS, Alvarus, Bp. of Silves
– De Planctu Ecclesiae. 1560. Fo. Inscr. on title 'Colleg. Paris. Societ. Jesu'. 18th. C. red mor., triple gt. fillet, spine gt. in compartments, inner floral gt. dentelles, Stuart de Rothesay arms on covers. (SM. Oct.8; 1907)
Frs. 1,600

PELCOQ, J.
– Prime du Journal: les Modes Parisiennes: Souvenir de l'Exposition Universalle de Vienne. Paris, n.d. 4to. Orig. cl.-bkd. wraps., soiled. (CSK. Sep.19; 22)
£150

PELET, Jean Jaques Germain
– Atlas des Mémoires Militiares Relatifs à la Succession d'Espagne sous Louis XIV. Paris, 1836-48. 6 pts. bnd. in 1 vol. Fo. Occasional spotting. Hf. mor., bkplt. of R.U.S.I. (CSK. Sep.19; 96)
£250

PELET-NARBONNE, G. von
– Geschichte der Brandenburg-Preussischen Reiterei ... Berlin, 1905. 2 vols. Lge. 4to. Three-qtr. mor., spines gt. (SG. Oct.30; 286)
$120

PELETIER, Jacques
– L'Algèbre. Lyon, 1554. 1st. Edn. Some staining & soiling, blank corners torn from c5-6, short tear in kl. Cont. vell., free end-papers renewed, hf. red mor. case. From Honeyman Collection. (S. Nov.10; 2438)
Quaritch. £170
– L'Aritmétique. Poitiers, 1549. 1st. Edn. 4to. Some discolouration, owner's inscr. of Marcus Fugger on front paste-down, liby. stp. of Oettingen-Wallenstein on title. 16th. C. cf., panel. in blind., gt. fleurons at corners, emblematic centre-pieces, hf. mor. case. From Honeyman Collection. (S. Nov.10; 2439) Quaritch. £1,900
– In Euclidis Elementa Geometrica Demonstrationum Libri sex. Lyon, 1557. 1st. Edn. Fo. Some ll. stained, title discold. & with border cropped, worming in outer border of title & 1st. 2 or 3 ll., marginal flaw in cl. Mod. cf., gt., 18th. C. armorial bkplt. of John, Earl of Exeter, Baron Cecil of Burghley (replaced). From Honeyman Collection. (S. Nov.10; 2440) Thomas. £100

PELHAM, Cavendish
– The World. L., 1808-10. Lacks 1 copperplt., slightly soiled. Cont. leath., spine reprd. [Sabin 59572] (R. Oct.14-18; 1516) DM 600
– – Anr. Edn. Ill.:– A.W. Warren & others. 1810-08. 2 vols. 4to. Cont. cf. (C. Feb.25; 126)
Fairbairn. £80

PELLETIER, Capitaine
– Recueil de 369 Aquarelles Originales ... 1828-47. Ob. fo. Cont. hf. chagrin, 1 cover detchd. (HD. Mar.18; 30)
Frs. 38,000

PELLETREAU, William S.
See–ROSS, Peter & Pelletreau, William S.

PELLIOT, Paul
– Les Grottes de Touen-Houang. Paris, 1914-24. 6 vols. Loose as iss. in ptd. bd. folders with linen ties, ex-liby. (SG. Dec.4; 272)
$175
– Jades Archaiques de Chine Appartenant à M.C.T. Loo. Paris & Bruxelles, 1925. Fo. Cont. cl., orig. upr. wrap. bnd. in at end. (S. Sep.30; 426)
£110

PELLOS, Frances
– Compendion de lo Abaco. Turin, Nicolaus de Benedictis & Jacobinus Suigus. 28 Sep. 1492. 1st. Edn. 4to. Lacks folios 73 & 80, (supplied in ptd. facs.), staining, folio 79 defect. & reprd., a few folio numbers cropped, some marginal worming (reprd.). Cont. limp vell., stained, lacks ties, cl. case. From Honeyman Collection. [BMC VII, 1057; Goff P260] (S. Nov.10; 2441)
Martin. £1,400

PELTIER, Jean Gabriel & Others
[–] Les Actes des Apotres. Paris, [1789-91]. 1st. Edn. 311 pts. (all publd.) in 10 vols. Lacks number 5 of 'Petits-Pacquets' in vol. X, 4-lf. prospectus in vol. III, 2-lf. prospectus in vol. X, supps. to pts.

94-5 & 99, bkplt. of Laurence Currie. Cont. cf. by Antoine Chaumont with his ticket, triple gt. fillet, flat spine semé with sm. spearhead tool, inner gt. dentelles. W.a.f. (SM. Oct.8; 1908) Frs. 5,500

PELZER, Louis
– Marches of the Dragoons in the Mississippi Valley. Iowa City, 1917. 1st. Edn. Gt.-decor. buckram. (SG. Oct.30; 287)
$110

PEMBERTON, Henry
[–] A View of Sir Isaac Newton's Philosophy. 1728. [1st. Edn.?]. 4to. Some margins slightly browned. Cont. mott. cf., rebkd. (CSK. Nov.14; 147) £95
– – Anr. Copy. Cont. panel. cf., rebkd. (S. Dec.1; 296) Celestial. £80
– – Anr. Copy. Slight browning. Cont. cf., worn. From liby. of Dr. E. Ashworth Underwood. (S. Feb.23; 272) Thorp. £55
See–MACLAURIN, Colin–PEMBERTON, Henry

PENA, Ignacio de la
– Trono Mexicano, en el Convento de Religiosas Pobres Capuchinas ... la Insigne Ciudad de Mexico. Madrid, 1728. 1st. Edn. 4to. Ex liby. Cont. vell., leath. ties defect. (SG. Jun.11; 224)
$250

PENA, Petrus & Lobel, Matthias de
– Nova Stirpium Adversaria. Antw., 1576. 3 pts. in 1 vol. Fo. Sm. rust hole on Q2, title slightly cropped at head, some ll. stained in lr. margins, a few ll. browned. Mod. spr. cf., inscr. in the hand of Robert Travers, Trinity College, Dublin. 1836. [STC 19595.3] (S. Jun.1; 274)
Van Haverbeke. £360
– – Anr. Copy. Ptd. slips tipped-in at pp. 33 & 150, hole affecting title border, marginal staining thro.-out. 19th. C. hf. mor. From Chetham's Liby., Manchester. (C. Nov.27; 319) Junk. £100
– Plantarum seu Stirpium Historia. Antw., 1576. 1st. Edn. Fo. With the 'Appendix', 'Formulae' & indices to the 'Nova Stirpium Adversaria' inserted at end, a few ll. with slight marginal worming cutting a few letters, a few marginal stains, some browning, index in 18th. C. hand on blanks at beginning & end. Cont. vell. bds., slight soiling. Sig. of Henry Swann, Oriel College, 1753 on front free end-paper. (S. Jun.1; 273) Joseph. £540

PEÑA Y MONTENEGRO, Alonso de la
– Itinerario para Parochos de Indios. Antw., 1698. Sm. 4to. Owner's inscrs. on title, minor wormholes affecting a few catchwords, a few ll. slightly soiled. Cf. 18th. C. owner's inscr. of Juan Ignacio Bustamente, parish priest at Aezontepec. [Sabin 59624] (SPB. May 5; 394)
$200

PENDASIO, Federico
– De Natura Corporum Coelestium. Mantua, 1555. 1st. Edn. Old owners' inscrs. on title (partly deleted). Bds. From Honeyman Collection. (S. Nov.10; 2443) Hill. £140

PENHALLOW, Samuel
– The History of the Wars of New-England. Boston, 1726. 1st. Edn. Several ll. torn, stains & burn-holes in text, many gutter tears, owner's sig. dtd. 1727 on upr. fly-lf. Old cf. (SG. May 14; 170)
$1,800
– – Anr. Edn. Cinc., 1859. 2nd. Edn. 4to. Foxed. Orig. blind-stpd. cl., gt. spine, head & foot of spine slightly worn. From liby. of William E. Wilson. [Sabin 59655] (SPB. Apr.29; 225)
$100

PENITEAS CITO Libellus iste nuncupatur Tractans compendiose de Penitentia
[Metz], [Caspar Hochfeder], ca. 1500. 4to. Lacks final blank, a few sm. wormholes slightly affecting text, some sheets becoming detchd. Paper wraps. [Hain 13158*; BMC III p. 664; Goff P 848] (C. Apr.1; 69) Daye. £120

PENITENCE (La) des Beuvers
Paris, 1673. 1st. Edn. 12mo. Slight browning. Mod. panel. cf., spine gt. From liby. of André L. Simon. (S. May 18; 148) Veul. £160

PENITENT Hermit, The
1679. 1st. Edn. 12mo. Cont. cf., rebkd. [Wing P1233] (C. Nov.19; 19) Quaritch. £600

PENN, Irving
– Moments Preserved. N.Y., [1960]. 1st. Edn. Tall 4to. Cl., masked owner's inscr. on front free end-paper, orig. s.-c. & d.-w., both scuffed. (SG. Jul.9; 262)
$350
– – Anr. Copy. Lge. 4to. English publisher's label mntd. to title-p. Boxed. (SG. Apr.23; 158) $325

PENN, William
– The Frame of the Government of the Province of Pennsilvania in America ... [L.], 1682. Fo. Stained, soiled & worn. Disbnd. (SPB. Jun.22; 109)
$2,000
[–] Some Account of the Province of Pennsylvania in America; Lately Granted under the Great Seal of England to William Penn. L., 1681. Fo. Disbnd. [Sabin 59733] (SPB. Jun.22; 107)
$1,400

PENNA, Agostino
– Viaggio Pittorico della Villa Adriana. Rome, 1833. 2 vols. Ob. 4to. Hf.-titles, some stains. Cl. (SI. Dec.4; 453) Lire 300,000

PENNANT, Thomas
[–] Arctic Zoology. L., 1784-87. 3 vols. in 2, including supp. 4to. The 2 folding maps of the supp. misbnd. in vol. 1, sm. tear in 1 map. Cont. cf. [Sabin 59757] (CB. Sep.24; 5) Can. $700
– British Zoology. 1776. 2 vols. (3 pts. plus Appendix). 4to. Cont. mor. (TA. Apr.16; 94)
£100
– – Anr. Edn. 1776-77. 4 vols. 4to. Cf. gt. (P. May 14; 311) £130
– – Anr. Edn. 1812. L.P. 4 vols. Cf. gt., ties. (P. Mar.12; 322) Kestrel. £230
– History of London, Westminster & Southwark ... L., 1814. 2 vols. 4to. Slight browning, extra-ill. with views & ports. Cf. gt., stained. (SPB. May 29; 334) $120
– The History of the Parishes of Whiteford & Holywell. 1796. [1st. Edn.?]. 4to. Some very minor defects. Later hf. cf. (SBA. May 27; 441)
Jones. £74
– – Anr. Copy. Browned. Cont. cf. (SH. Jul.16; 200) Frost. £55
– A History of Quadrupeds. 1793. 3rd. Edn. 2 vols. 4to. A few ll. slightly spotted. Cont. tree cf. (SBA. Jul.14; 252) Dauncey. £75
[–] Indian Zoology. 1790 [1791]. 2nd. Edn. 4to. Engraved title with cold. vig., 16 hand-cold. engraved plts., lacks errata, but facs. loosely inserted, 'An Essay on India' trans. from Latin of J.R. Forster by John Aikin & list Indian Faunula bnd. at the end. Later cf. gt. (C. Jul.15; 197)
Taylor. £240
[–] Journey from Chester to London. L., 1872. 1st. Edn. 4to. Cont. cf. gt., rebkd. (P. Jun.11; 351)
Lawton. £75
– A Journey from London to the Isle of Wight. 1801. 1st. Edn. 2 vols. 4to. Some browning & spotting, advt. lf. at end of vol. II. Cont. red hf. mor., gt. spines. (S. Jun.22; 73) Traylen. £90
– London Illustrated; Or A Series of Plates to Illustrate the History of London & Westminster. 1805. 4to. Some foxing. Cont. bds., rebkd. (TA. Feb.19; 634) £52
– Of London. 1790. 1st. Edn. 1 vol. in 3. 4to. Extra-ill., some tears, spotted. Later hf. mor., 1 cover loose. (SH. Jul.23; 124) Ord. £200
– – Anr. Copy. A few ll. slightly spotted. Cont. tree cf. (SBA. Dec.16; 178a) Weiniger. £65
– Of London.–The Journey from Chester to London.–A Tour in Wales.–The Journey to Snowdon. 1790; 1782; 1778; 1781. 4 works in 4 vols. 4to. Non-unif. cont. cf. From the collection of Eric Sexton. (C. Apr.16; 328) Maggs. £130
– Some Account of London, Westminster & Southwark ... together with an appendix & Index. 1814. 4 vols. 4to. Extra-ill. with 267 ports., some interleaving, slightly spotted. Cont. russ., gt. borders on sides, spines worn. (C. Feb.25; 52)
Bentham. £220
– – Anr. Edn. N.d. 3 vols. 4to. Cont. mor. gt. (SD. Feb.4; 234) £75
– Thiergeschichte der Nördlichen Polarländer. Trans.:– E.A.W. Zimmermann. Ill.:– P. Mazell. L., 1787. 1st. German Edn. 2 pts. in 1 vol. 4to. Lightly browned, in pt. 2 mostly only in margin. Cont. bds. (R. Mar.31-Apr.4; 1424) DM 550
– A Tour in Scotland [in 1772]. 1774. 4to. Cont. hf. cf., worn. (SH. Nov.6; 141) Mullett. £50
– – Anr. Edn. 1776. 3 vols. Bdg. not stated. W.a.f. (CE. Jun.4; 60) £110
– A Tour in Scotland.–A Tour in Scotland & Voyage to the Hebrides. 1769; 1790. 5th. Edn. (1st. Work). 2nd. work Pt. 1 only, together 2 vols. Sm. 4to. Some foxing & fingering thro.-out. Cont. tree cf., stained & worn. (PD. Aug.20; 69) £80
– – Anr. Edn. N.d. 4th. Edn.; 2nd. Edn. 1 vol.; 2 vols., together 3 vols. 4to. Cont. cf., some covers detchd. (SH. Jun.4; 130) Ayres. £60
– A Tour in Scotland.–A Tour in Wales.–The Journey from Chester to London. 1776; 1778; 1782.

1st. work 4th. Edn. 3 vols.; 2 vols.; 1 vol. 4to. Cont. unif. cf. (SH. Mar.5; 112) *Crowe.* £260
- **Tours in Scotland & Voyage to the Hebrides.** 1776. 3 vols. 4to. Bds. & cf. spine. (CE. Nov.20; 129) £180
- **Tours in Wales.** 1810. 3 vols. Some very minor defects, owner's inscr. cut from upr. margin of title in vol. I. Cont. russ. gt., slightly worn. (SBA. May 27; 442) *Vitkovitch.* £90
- - **Anr. Copy.** Occasional slight spotting. Cont. str.-grd. cf. (CSK. Oct.24; 1) £60
- **[Works].** Chester & L., 1774-1800. Various Edns. 20 vols. 4to. Lacks A Tour from Dawning to Alston Moor & A Tour from Alstom Moor to Harrowgate, slight offsetting. Unif. in early 19th. C. str.-grd. mor., gt., head & foot of some spines & most corners slightly worn. (S. Nov.4; 482) *Wills.* £500

PENNELL, Elizabeth Robins & Joseph
- **Life of James McNeill Whistler.** 1908. (150) numbered on Japanese vell. 2 vols. 4to. Hf. mor. (RBT. Jan.22; 27) £52
- **The Whistler Journal.** Phila., 1921. 1st. Edn., (500) for America, with additional plts. Qtr. vell. & cl. 2 port. plts. of Pennells sigd. by both. (PNY. Mar.4; 206) $130

PENNELL, Joseph
- **The Adventures of an Illustrator.** Boston, 1925. Ltd. Edn., numbered & sigd. 4to. Pol. hf. cf., d.-w., orig. box, partly unc. (SG. Dec.4; 275) $120
- **Etchers & Etching.** N.Y., 1919. (105) numbered on Lge. H.M.P. & sigd. Fo. Qtr. mor., slightly worn, unc. (SG. Dec.4; 274) $130
- **The Glory of New York.** .:- Elizabeth Pennell (intro.). N.Y., 1926. 1st. Edn., (355) numbered on L.P., & sigd. by E. Pennell. Tall fo. Publication broadside inserted. Gt.-pict. cl. (PNY. May 21; 318) $125
- **Lithographs of New York in 1904.** N.Y., 1905. Tall fo. Each of 12 orig. lithos. mntd. on paper mats. Loose as iss. in ptd. wraps. Each plt. sigd. by Pennell. (SG. Nov.20; 391) $950
- **Pen Drawing & Pen Draughtsmen.** N.Y. & L., 1920. (150) on Japan paper, sigd., & with orig. sigd. drawing. 4to. Hf. leath., worn. (SG. Mar.12; 286) $130

PENNETHORNE, John
- **The Geometry & Optics of Ancient Architecture.** 1878. Fo. Cont. hf. roan, worn. (SH. Jan.29; 274) *Fletcher.* £120

PENNYSYLVANIA PACKET, or the General Advertiser
10 Apr. 1783. Fo. Restored at fold. (SPB. Nov.24; 59) $850

PENOTUS, Bernardus Georgius
- **Tractatus Varii de Vera Praeparatione et Usus Medicamentorum Chymicorum.** Ober-Ursel, 1602. Paper discold., some headlines & marginalia cut into. Pol. cf. (S. Dec.1; 310) *Ribi.* £80

PENROSE'S PICTORIAL ANNUAL: an Illustrated Review of the Graphic Arts
Ed.:- William Gamble. Ill.:- Arthur Rackham & others. L., 1905-6; 1921. 2 vols. 4to. Cold. pict. & decor. cl. Raymond M. Sutton Jr. copy. (SG. May 7; 232) $100
- - **Anr. Edn.** Ed.:- William Gamble. L., 1921; 1923; 1925; 1928. Vols. 23, 25, 27 & 30 only. 4to. Orig. cl. Ingleton bkplt. (JL. Jul.20; 597) Aus. $140

PENTHER, Johann Friedrich
- **Gnomonica Fundamentalis et Mechanica.** Augsburg, 1733. 1st. Edn. Fo. First 5 ll. slightly stained & soiled. Cont. leath. (HK. Nov.18-21; 757) DM 950
- - **Anr. Edn.** Augsburg, 1752. Fo. Cont. cf.-bkd. bds., worn, spine reprd. From Honeyman Collection. (S. Nov.10; 2446) *Rogers Turner.* £220
- **Praxis Geometriae.** Augsburg, 1776 & 1768. 2 vols. in 1. Fo. Old MS. notes on end-paper. Cont. cf., very worn. (H. Dec.9/10; 299) DM 460
- - **Anr. Edn.** Augsburg, 1788. 2 pts. in 1 vol. Fo. Occasional cont. notations in ink. Marb. paper bds., worn. (CNY. Oct.1; 22) $200
- **Praxis Geometriae.-Zugabe zur Praxi Geometrie.** Augsburg, 1738; 1749. 2nd. Edn. (1st. work). 2 vols. in 1. Fo. Title & frontis. of 1st. work slightly stained. Liby. bdg., hf. cl., bkplt. of John Crerar liby. (with perforated stp. on title-p.).

From Honeyman Collection. (S. Nov.10; 2444) *Howell.* £170
- **Praxis Geometriae [-Zugabe zur Praxi Geometriae]-Gnomonica Fundemantalis et Mechanica.** Augsburg, 1749; 1733. 3rd. Edn.; 1st. Edn. (1st. work 2 pts.). 2 works in 1 vol. Fo. Some damp staining, lr. margin cut from 1st. title of 1st. work, in 2nd. work plts. 5 & 13 with holes in margins. Cont. vell. bds., soiled, upr. cover defect. From Honeyman Collection. (S. Nov.10; 2445) *Rota.* £220

PENTON, Stephen
- **The Guardian's Instruction, or The Gentleman's Romance.-New Instructions to the Guardian.** 1688; 1694. 2 works in 1 vol. 12mo. Cont. cf. (CSK. Oct.31; 177) £55

PEOPLE OF ALL NATIONS, a Useful Toy for Girl or Boy
1806. 55mm. × 44mm. Title & a few other ll. ink-stained. Orig. roan-bkd. bds., 2 sm. holes in spine. (SH. Mar.19; 196) *Fletcher.* £200

PEOPLE'S GALLERY OF ENGRAVINGS
Ill.:- after Thomas Allom & others. Ca. 1840. 2nd. Series. 4to. Some minor defects. Cont. cf. gt. (SBA. May 27; 492) *Hyde Park Bookshop.* £52

PEPLER, Douglas
- **The Devil's Devices.** Ill.:- Eric Gill. 1915. (200) sigd. by author & artist. Some very minor defects. Orig. cl.-bkd. bds., faded, liby. stp. on front paste-down, unopened. (SBA. May 27; 473) *Donnithorne.* £120
[-] **In Petra.** Ed.:- Eric Gill. Ill.:- Eric Gill & David Jones. St. Dominic's Pr., 1923. Sm. 4to. Orig. linen. From liby. of Guild of St. Joseph & St. Dominic. (SH. Feb.19; 76) *Donnithorne.* £85

PEPYS, Samuel
Diary. Ed.:- Henry B. Wheatley. 1893-99. 10 vols. Extra-ill. with some 330 engraved views, ports., etc., many hand-cold. Purple mor. gt. by Bayntun for Brentano's. (C. Jul.22; 25) *Chelsea Rare Books.* £550
- - **Anr. Copy.** 10 vols. including Index & Pepysiana. Cont. hf. mor. by Henry Sotheran, slightly soiled, spines gt. (CSK. Jan.14; 143) £85
- - **Anr. Copy.** (250) L.P. Orig. vell.-bkd. cl., unc. (SBA. May 27; 95) *Bollingier.* £70
- - **Anr. Edn.** Ed.:- Henry B. Wheatley. N.Y., ca. 1900. Brampton Edn., (250) numbered. 18 vols. Hf. lev. (SG. Sep.4; 376) $120
- - **Anr. Edn.** Ed.:- Henry B. Wheatley. Trans.:- Mynors Bright. Ill.:- William Sharp. Ltd. Edns. Cl., 1942. (1500) numbered, & sigd. by artist. 10 vols. Cl.-bkd. pict. bds., orig. box. (SG. Jan.15; 240) $130
- **Memoirs.** Ed.:- Lord R. Braybrooke. 1825. 1st. Edn. 2 vols. 4to. Cont. cf. (P. Apr.9; 233) *Lewis.* £55
- - **Anr. Copy.** Lacks advt. lf. at end of vol. I, offsetting to titles, occasional spotting. 19th. C russ. gt., 2 covers partly detchd., some wear. (S. May 5; 382) *Blundell.* £50
- - **Anr. Copy.** Mor. gt., each cover with orig. port. miniature of Pepys & wife in frames of sm. pearls & lge. gt. ornaments, spines similarly tooled, hf. mor. gt. boxes, by Bayntun. (CNY. May 22; 340) $600
- - **Anr. Copy.** Some foxing. Recent bds., qtr. mor. gt. s.-c.'s, unc. The Jerome Kern copy, with bkplts., lately in the Prescott Collection. (CNY. Feb.6; 274) $550
- - **Anr. Copy.** Offsetting from plts. Later str.-grd. red three-qtr. mor., spines gt. (SG. May 14; 171) $300

PERABO, Gabrio
- **Ammirabile Promozione all'Arcivescovato di Milano (di) ... Giuseppe Pozzobonelli.** Milan, 1744. Sm. fo. 2 sm. wormholes, hf.-title. Mod. cf., gt., partly unc. (SI. Dec.4; 454) Lire 260,000

PERACCHI, Antonio
*See-*ROMANI, Felice & Peracchi, Antonio

PERALTA BARNUEVO, Pedro de
- **Passion y Triumpho de Christo.** Lima, 1738. Sm. 4to. Corner of title & dedication burned with some loss to border of title, inscr. on title dtd. 1786 relating to the condemnation of this work by the 'Santo Tribunal de la Inquisicion'. Cont. vell., detchd. (SPB. May 5; 395) $350

PERCEAU, Louis
- **Bibliographie du Roman Erotique au XIXe Siècle.** Paris, 1930. 2 vols. Tall 8vo. Orig. wraps., vol. 1 unc. & unopened. (SG. Mar.26; 363) $110

PERCIER, Charles & Fontaine, Pierre François Leonard
- **Chateau de la Malmaison.** Paris, ca. 1900. Fo. Hf. mor., worn, ptd. wraps. bnd. in. (SG. Mar.12; 288) $100
- **Choix des plus célèbres Maisons de Plaisance de Rome et de ses Environs.** Paris, 1824. Fo. Some spotting, liby.-stp. on title. Cl. (SPB. Oct.1; 239) $1,000
- **Recueil de Décorations Interieures.** Paris, 1812. 1st. Edn., L.P. Fo. Some foxing. Hf. leath. (SG. Dec.4; 277) $325
- - **Anr. Edn.** Ed.:- F. Lazzari; J. Borsato (supps.). Venice, 1843. Fo. Fr. & Italian text, lightly soiled & browned in parts, last plts. soiled in margin. Later hf. vell. (H. May 21/22; 287) DM 600

PERCIVAL, Capt. Robert
- **Account of the Island of Ceylon.** 1803. [1st. Edn.?]. 4to. Cf. gt., upr. cover detchd. (P. Oct.2; 83) *Ad Orientem.* £80
- - **Anr. Copy.** 4to. Cont. cf. (P. Mar.12; 68) *Lawson.* £75

PERCIVALE, Richard
- **A Dictionarie in Spanish & English.-A Spanish Grammar ... & Pleasant & Delightful Dialogues in Spanish & English.** Ed.:- John Minsheu. 1599; 1599. 1st. Edn. (1st. work). 2 works in 1 vol. Fo. Minor repair to title, & some slight browning to 1st. work. Old vell. bds., rebkd., new end-papers. [STC 19620; 19622 & 17948] (LC. Feb.12; 540) £110

PERCKHAMMER, Heinz von
*See-*SIREN, Osvald–PERCKHAMMER, Heinz von

PERCY, Sholto & Reuben
- **The Percy Anecdotes.** 1820. 40 vols. in 20. 12mo. Plts. spotted. Cont. hf. mor. (SH. May 28; 80) *Wade Gallery.* £50

PERCY, Thomas
[-] **Reliques of Ancient English Poetry.** 1765. 1st. Edn. 3 vols. Lacks blank A1 in vol. 1, occasional spotting & browning. Cont. spr. cf., slight wear. (S. Feb.10; 456) *Traylen.* £110
- - **Anr. Copy.** Cont. pol. cf. gt. (TA. Nov.20; 30) £90
- - **Anr. Copy.** Advt. ll. in vol. III. Cont. cf., rebkd. (SH. Jun.18; 139) *Frost.* £65

PERECYVELLE
- **Syr Perecyvelle of Gales.** Ed.:- Frederick S. Ellis & J.O. Halliwell. Hammersmith, Kelms. Pr., 1895. (350). Orig. holland-bkd. bds., unc. (CNY. May 22; 323) $350
- - **Anr. Copy.** 4to. Slight spotting. Orig. bds., soiled. (SPB. May 29; 239) $300

PEREFIXE, Hardouin de Beaumont de
- **The Life of Henry the Fourth of France.** Trans.:- M. le Moine. Paris, 1785. L.P. Sig. on title of 'Eustace', inscr. on fly-lf. 'Rob Robertson'. Cont. red mor., gt., arms of Philippe Henri, Marquis de Segur, fleuron in each corner, triple gt. fillet, flat spine gt. in compartments, inner gt. dentelles, 2 wormholes in hinges, 18th c. bkplt. of col. John Skey Eustace, (SM. Oct.8; 1909) Frs. 4,800

PEREGRINUS, Peter
- **Epistle ... to Sygerus of Foncaucourt ... concerning the Magnet.** Trans.:- S.P. Thompson. 1902. 1st. Edn. in Engl., (240) numbered. 4to. 1st. initial in red with blue penwork extending into margin, other initials supplied in red, red & blue chapter marks. Orig. canvas-bkd. bds., spine slightly worn. (S. Oct.21; 417) *Thomas.* £60
- **Sermones.** Strassburg, 1493. 4to. 2 ll. torn without loss. Orig. wood bds. with leath. backstrip reprd., later crude brass clasp. (TA. Apr.16; 360) £400

PEREGRINUS, Petrus, Maricurtensis -DOUGLAS, David
De Magnete, seu Rota Perpetui Motus, Libellus ... per Achillem P. Gasserum ... nunc primum promulgatus.-De Naturae Mirabilibus Opusculum. Augsburg; Paris, 1558; 1524. 1st. Edn. (2nd. work). 2 works in 1 vol. 4to. 1st. work with some passages underscored. 18th. C. cf., gt. panel. covers with arms of Jean Bouhier, head & foot of spine chipped, bkplt. of Henry Beaufoy, hf. red

**PEREGRINUS, Petrus, Maricurtensis
–DOUGLAS, David Naturae Mirabilibus
Opusculum.** *-contd.*
mor. case. From Honeyman Collection. (S.
Nov.10; 2447) *Quaritch.* £11,00

PEREIRA DA SILVA, J.M.
**– Os Varoes Illustres do Brazil durante os Tempos
Coloniaes.** Paris, 1858. 2 pts. in 1 vol. Slightly
soiled thro.-out. Spr. leath. gt., gt. stpd. fillets.
[Sabin 60887] (D. Dec.11-13; 1456) DM 700

PERELLE, Adam D.
[–] Collection de Vues de Paris. [Paris], ca. 1681.
Ob. fo. 123 engraved views (of 139), most with
marginal browning, plt. 72 torn & reprd., some
spotting. Cont. cf., very worn, upr. cover detchd.
W.a.f. (SM. Feb.11; 131) Frs. 2,900
– Collection des Petits Paysages. Ill.:– Gabriel,
Nicolas or Adam Perelle. [Paris], ca. 1750, or
later. Ob. fo. Imprint erased from title, occasional
slight spotting. Cont. paper bds., worn. (S.
Jun.23; 332) *Broseghini.* £550
[–] [Vues des Belles Maisons de France]. Paris, n.d.
Ob. 4to. 30 engraved plts. of Versailles only,
without prelims. 18th. C. parch.-bkd. bds., worn.
(SBA. Dec.16; 78) *Broseghini.* £210

PERELLE, Gabriel, Nicolas & Adam
– Architectural Views of France . . . Paris, 1688.
Ob. fo. 8 suites of engrs. (240 etchings on 220 ll.),
65 plts. before all letters, cont. ink captions, 4-pp.
cont. MS. index, 1 sheet stained, margins thro.-out
stained. Cont. cf., restored. W.a.f. (CNY. May
22; 237) $2,600

PERERIIS, Guillermus de
– Oratio super Electione Innocentii VIII. [Rome,
Stephen Plannck, after Aug. 26, 1484]. 4to. Mod.
bds. [Goff P271] (C. Jul.16; 286) *Tzakas.* £50

PERESVET [Through Light]
Moscow, 1921. (3,000). No. 1 (all publd.). Orig.
wraps., spine torn, loose. (SH. Feb.6; 504)
Lempert. £50

PEREZ, Manuel
– Arte de el Idioma Mexicano. Mexico, 1713. Sm.
4to. Light stain affecting a few ll., lacks the 2 ll.
comprising index & errata, sm. hole in last lf.
Disbnd. (SPB. May 5; 396) $700

PEREZ BOCANEGRA, Juan
**– Ritual Formulario e Institucion de Curas, para
administar a los Naturales de este Reyno.** Lima,
1631. Sm. 4to. Lacks 11 ll. of prelims. or the
folding map, tear in 2A2 affecting letters, some
stains, margins reprd. at beginning & end. Later
cf. (SPB. May 5; 397) $350

PEREZ DE BARRADAS, Jose
– Orfebreria Prehispanica de Colombia. Madrid,
1954-58. 2 vols. text & 1 vol. plts. 4to. Cl., d.-w.'s.,
slight wear. (SG. Dec.4; 278) $100

PEREZ DE MOYA, Juan
– Arithmetica . . . intitulada manuel de contadores.
Alcala, 1582. 1st. Edn. Woodcut diagrams
dampstained & browned, piece torn from Z2 with
slight text loss, a few sm. holes in quire S affecting
text, a few headlines cut into. Cont. limp vell.,
stained. From Honeyman Collection. (S.
Nov.10; 2450) *Manning.* £60
– Tratado de Geometria Practica, y Speculativa.
Alcala, 1573. 1st. Edn. Fo. Some staining &
discolouration, title mntd. & with lr. fore-corner
reprd., hole in R3. Mod. Spanish cf., gt., bkplt. of
Luis Bardon. From Honeyman Collection. (S.
Nov.10; 2449) *Manning.* £100
See–GUTIERREZ DE GUALBA, Juan–PEREZ
DE MOYA, Juan

PEREZ DE VALENTIA, Jacobus
**– Cantica Canticorum Salomonis cum Expositione
Disertissima et Questionis Finalis Discussione
Fecundissima.** Paris, 1507. Fo. Slight browning,
some early (cont.?) MS. notes. 19th. C. hf. cf.
From liby. of André L. Simon. (S. May 18; 149)
Kesel. £125
– Commentaria in Psalmos. Valencia, [Gabriel
Luis de Arinyo & Alfonso Fernandez de Cordoba],
6 Sep., 1484. 1st. Edn. 2 vols. Fo. Lacks blank fo.
192 in vol. 1 & 2 final blanks in vol. 2, light
worming, wormhole to last 40 ll. of vol. 1 catching
some text, anr. at front of vol. 2 affecting
headlines, dampstains to upr. & inner portions of
much of vol. 2, occasional cont. ink marginalia.
Cont. Spanish goat, blind-tooled in the mudejar
style, covers divided by multiple parallel fillets
into narrow central panel & 2 frames, panel filled

with repetitions of a square 8-pointed star, inner
frame with imps. of a looped knot-work tool, outer
frame with repetitions of an 'ave' stp., spines in 5
compartments, orig. clasps & catches, rubbed.
Bkplts. of Louis Alexandre de Bourbon, Comte de
Toulouse, lately in the collection of Eric Sexton.
[BMC X, 17, Goff P276] (CNY. Apr.8; 183)
$21,000

PEREZ DE VARGAS, Bernardo
**– De Re Metalica en el qual se tratan muchos y
Diversos Secretos del Conocimiento de Toda
Suerte de Minerales.** Madrid, 1569. 1st. Edn.
Lacks final lf. (presumably blank), browned &
stained thro.-out, some marginal worming. 19th.
C. russ., covers detchd., spine very worn. Bkplt. of
William Stirling; from Honeyman Collection. (S.
Nov.10; 2453) *Hill.* £360

PEREZ DE VILLA-AMIL, Genaro
**– Espana Artistica y Monumental, Vistas y
Descripcion.** Paris, 1842-50. 1st. Edn. 3 vols. Fo.
Foxing, browning & some staining. Hf. roan,
badly worn. (SPB. May 6; 233) $2,600

PEREZ-ROSALES, V.
– Essai sur le Chili. Hamburg, 1857. Later hf.
leath. [Sabin 60917] (D. Dec.11-13; 1457)
DM 450

PERFECT, William
**– Cases of Insanity, the Epilepsy, Hypochondriacal
affection, Hysteric Passion & Nervous Disorders
successfully treated.** Rochester, Priv. ptd., [1780?].
2nd. Edn. New cl. (S. Jun.17; 651)
Gurney. £300

PERGAUD, Louis
– La Guerre des Boutons. 1912. (19) on Hollande.
Jansenist red mor. by Marius Michel. Note. (HD.
Oct.10; 134) Frs. 8,000

PERGER, A.R.
[–] Die Kunstschätze Wiens. Triest, 1854. 4to.
Lightly soiled, lacks ptd. title. Cont. leath. (R.
Mar.31-Apr.4; 1600) DM 520

PERGOLESE, Giovanni Battista
– La Serva Padrona. Paris, 1752. 1st. Edn. Ob. fo.
Mod. hf. leath. (H. Dec.9/10; 1236) DM 900

PERGOLESI, Michelangelo
[–] Designs for Various Ornaments. [L.], [plts. dtd.
1777-85]. Fo. 55 plts. (of 70), plt. 46 slightly torn,
some spotting. Cont. hf. cf., gt. spine. W.a.f. (S.
Jun.22; 74) *Brosseghini.* £130
– Original Designs of Vases. Ill.:– Bartolozzi after
J.B. Cipriani. [Plts. dtd. 1777-92]. Fo. No ptd.
title or text, orig. ptd. sheet 'proposals for
publishing' mntd. in place of title (with MS.
corrections in cont. hand), engraved dedication to
Hugh Percy, Duke of Northumberland bnd. with
plt. 56. Maroon hf. mor., gt., by Sangorski &
Sutcliffe. (C. Nov.6; 224) *McQueen.* £580

PERIER, Gilberte
[–] The Life of Mr. Paschal. Trans.:– [William
Andrews]. 1744. 2 vols. Cont. mor., elab. mor.
onlays, gt. tools, spine gt., mott. cf. doubl. gt.
tooled. (S. Nov.25; 386) *Maggs.* £180

PERINGSKIOLD, Johannes
**– Monumentorum Sveo-Gothicorum.–Historia
Hialmari.** Stockholm, 1710; 1701. 2 works in 2
vols. Fo. 1st. work: last 2 ll. detchd., some
marginal staining. 19th. C. hf. roan; 19th. C. cl.
From Chetham's Liby., Manchester. (C.
Nov.27; 320) *Cash.* £100

PERIODICALS PUBLISHING COMPANY
– Ballarat & District in 1901; A Concise History.
Melbourne, [1901]. Square 8vo. Not collated.
Early hf. mor., slightly worn. (KH. Nov.18; 476)
Aus. $120

PERITSOL or FARISSOL, Abrahamo
– Itinera Mundi. Trans.:– Thomas Hyde. Oxford,
1691. Sm. 4to. Early vell. [Sabin 60934] (SG.
Oct.9; 185) $850

PERKINS, Henry
– The Perkins Library: A Catalogue of . . . [1873].
4to. Litho. plts., MS. prices. Cont. red hf. mor. (S.
Nov.24; 234) *Dawson.* £50

PERKINS, Simeon
See–CHAMPLAIN Society

PERKINS, William
– A Discourse of the Damned Art of Witchcraft.
Camb., 1608. 1st. Edn. Lacks final blank, titles
soiled affecting line-border, hole in A1 & A5

affecting some letters, piece torn from margin of
F1 affecting line-border, a few ll. near end
marginally wormed cutting some letters, some ll.
stained. Cont. sheep, worn. [NSTC 19697] (S.
Jun.23; 371) *Maggs.* £60

PERLIN, E.
**– Description des Royaulmes d'Angleterre et
d'Escosse . . . 1558. Histoire de l'entrée de la Reine
Mère dans la Grande Bretagne. Par P. de la Serre
. . . 1639.** 1775. 4to. Short tear in folding map,
some browning, bkplt. of Sir J. Ayloffe on verso of
title & of 5th. Earl of Rosebery. Cont. red mor. in
the style of (by?) Roger Payne, gt., covers with
1-line fillet border, spine divided by flat bands, gt.
inside borders. Pres. copy, inscr. by ed. (R.
Gough). (S. Apr.7; 398) *Way.* £100

PERNAMBUCO
**– Carta do Conselheiro Abrantes, a Sir William
A'Court, sobre a Regencia de Portugal e a
authoridade do Senhor Dom Pedro IV.** 1827. Sm.
4to. Ptd. overslip on title to correct orig. error in
spelling of Regencia. Mod. cf. (SPB. May 5; 400)
$275

PERNAU, F.A. von
[–] Gründl. Anweisung, alle Arten Vögel zu fangen.
Nuremb., 1754. 1st. part stained. Cont. hf. vell.,
lacks lr. half of spine. (HK. Nov.18-21; 1748)
DM 1,000

PERNETY, Antoine Joseph Dom
**– History of a Voyage to the Malouine (or
Falkland) Islands . . . & of two Voyages to the
Streights of Magellan with an Account of the
Patagonians.** 1773. 2nd. Edn. in Engl. 4to. A few
ll. slightly soiled or dampstained. Mod. hf. mor.,
unc. [Sabin 60997] (S. Jun.22; 188)
Maggs. £220

PERON, François & Freycinet, Louis
**– Voyage de Découvertes aux Terres Australes.
Historique. Atlas Deuxième Partie.** Paris, 1811.
4to. A few marginal stains. Red mor.-bkd. bds., w.a.f.
From Honeyman Collection, w.a.f. (S.
Nov.10; 2454) *Hinchliffe.* £320

PEROTTUS, Nicolaus
– Cornucopiae Linguae Latinae. Ed.:– [Aldus
Manutius]. Venice, Aldus Manutius, Jul., 1499.
1st. Aldine Edn. Fo. Capital initial spaces with
guide letters, lacks final blank, fore-margin of 1st.
lf. restored affecting text, H5 severely torn &
reprd., some ink staining & holes filled,
occasionally touching text, dampstained. Mod. cf.
gt. to a 'Canevari' design, vell. paste-downs, by
Gozzi of Modena. Bkplt. of Baron Horace de
Landau, lately in the collection of Eric Sexton.
[BMC V, 561, Goff P296, H. 12706*] (CNY.
Apr.8; 198) $3,500
– – Anr. Edn. Basle, 1526. Fo. Title slightly
defect., without loss of text, reprd., some
dampstaining. 18th. C. cf.-bkd. bds., very worn,
covers detchd. From liby. of André L. Simon. (S.
May 18; 150) *Poole.* £60

PERRAULT, Charles
**– La Belle au Bois Dormant et Le Petit Chaperon
Rouge.** Ill.:– Lucien Pissaro. Eragny Pr., 1899.
(224). Orig. bds., unc. (S. Jul.31; 18)
Maggs Brothers. £210
**– La Belle au Bois Dormant, et quelques autres
Contes de Jadis.** Ill.:– Edmund Dulac. Paris, 1910.
4to. Cont. hf. mor., decor. spine gt., slightly worn,
orig. wraps. bnd. in. (S. Jul.31; 204)
Hadfield. £90
– Cendrillon. Ill.:– Arthur Rackham. Paris, n.d.
(500) numbered sigd. by artist. 4to. Orig. bds.,
slightly browned. (CSK. May 29; 131) £110
– Cinderella.–The Sleeping Beauty. Ill.:– Arthur
Rackham. L., [1919]; [1920]. Both (850) sigd. by
artist. 2 works in 2 vols. 4to. Frontis. removed
from each vol., offsetting. Both orig. bdgs. worn,
cf.-bkd. case. (SPB. May 29; 363) $100
– Contes de Fées . . . Ill.:– Annedouche & Rebel.
Lyon. 1865. 2nd. Edn. Cont. chagrin, decor.
double fillet borders, central motif, fleurons,
decor. spine, inner dentelle. (HD. Feb.18; 168)
Frs. 1,300
**– Courses de Testes et de Bague faittes par le Roy
et par les Princes et Seigneurs de sa Cour en
l'année 1662.** Ill.:– Rousselet, Chauveau, Israel
Silvestre, etc. Paris, 1670. Fo. A few ll. loose.
Cont. mott. cf., arms of Louis XIV gt. on sides,
worn. (S. Oct.21; 287) *Favre.* £1,600
– Fairy Tales. Ill.:– Henry Clarke. [1922]. 4to.
Orig. cl. (CSK. May 15; 9) £65

– **Festiva ad Capita Annulumque Decursio, a Rege Ludovico XIV . . . anno MDCLXII . . .** Trans.:– Spiritus Fletcher. Paris, 1670. Lge. fo. 1 plt. mntd., some reprd., a few marginal tears, slightly soiled in places, slightly dampstained at beginning. Cont. red mor. gt., arms of Louis XIV & his cyphers on sides, spine gt. incorporating the cypher, slightly worn. (S. Apr.7; 277) *Veulemans.* £700

– **Histoire de Peau d'Ane.** Ill.:– Lucien Pissarro & T. Sturge Moore. Eragny Pr., 1899. (230). Orig. bds., unc. (SH. Feb.19; 33) *Ayres.* £110

– – **Anr. Edn.** Ill.:– Lucien Pissarro & T. Sturge Moore. Eragny Pr., 1902. (230). Orig. bds., slightly stained, unc. (S. Jul.31; 24) *Duchnes.* £60

– **Les Hommes Illustres qui ont paru en France.** Ill.:– Gerard Edelinck & others. Paris, 1696-1700. 1st. Edn., 1st. Iss. 2 vols. Fo. 2 engraved ports. with MS. text tipped in, MS. verses on verso of Arnauld's port., 1 lf. reprd. 18th. C. red mor., triple gt. fillet, spine gt. in compartments, inner gt. floral dentelles, upr. cover of vol. 1 reprd. (SM. Oct.8; 1910) Frs. 4,500

– **The Sleeping Beauty.** Ill.:– Arthur Rackham. L., [1920]. (625) sigd. by artist, & with an extra plt. 4to. Offsetting. Orig. vell.-bkd. parch., soiled, front free end-paper cut away. (SPB. May 29; 362) $175

– **Trois Contes.** Ill.:– H. Lemarié. 1950. Sewed. On vell. de Rives, 2 separate suites. (HD. Oct.10; 201) Frs. 2,100

PERRAULT, Claude
[–] **De l'origine des Fontaines.** Paris, 1674. 1st. Edn. 12mo. Some spotting & discolouration, owner's entry on front paste-down. Cont. cf., gt. spine, some wear. From Honeyman Collection. (S. Nov.10; 2458) *Quaritch.* £260

[–] **Description Anatomique d'un Caméléon, d'un Castor, d'un Dromadaire, d'un Ours, et d'une Gazelle.** Paris, 1669. 1st. Edn. 4to. Title soiled. Mod. vell. From Honeyman Collection. (S. Nov.10; 2455) *Zeitlin.* £360

[–] **Mémoires pour servir à l'Histoire Naturelle des Animaux.** Ill.:– Goyton after Sebastien le Clerc. Paris, 1671-76. 2 vols., 2 pts. in vol. 1. Fo. Heraldic book-stp. of Count Buturlin (Russ.). Cont. red mor., gt. arms of Louis XIV on covers, gt. panel with royal cipher at corners, triple gt. fillet, spine gt. in compartments with royal cipher & fleur-de-lis, inner gt. fleur-de-lis dentelles. (SM. Oct.8; 1911) Frs. 26,200

[–] **Memoirs for a Natural History of Animals . . . To which is added an Account of the Measure of a Degree of a great Circle of the Earth . . .** Trans.:– Alexander Pitfield; Richard Waller. 1688. 1st. Engl. Edn. Fo. A few MS. corrections to text, title slightly discold. Cont. red mor., panel. in gt., slightly worn, bkplt. of Herbert McLean Evans. From Honeyman Collection. (S. Nov.10; 2456) *J. & J. House.* £440

[–] **Natural History of Animals.** Trans.:– A. Pitfield & R. Waller. 1702. 4to. All engrs. with a liby. stp. Mod. mor. (P. Apr.9; 99) £170

– **Ordonnances des Cinq Espèces de Colonnes selon la Methode des Anciens.** Paris, 1683. 1st. Edn. Fo. Cont. spr. cf., gt. spine, foot of spine slightly torn. (C. Feb.25; 195) *Weinreb.* £200

– **Recueil de Plusieurs Machines, de Nouvelle Invention. Ouvrage Posthume.** Paris, 1700. 1st. Edn. 4to. Slight soiling & discolouration, fly-lf. with inscr. Cont. cf., gt. spine, some wear. 19th. C armorial bkplt. of Courtenay-de-Bauffremont family; from Honeyman Collection. (S. Nov.10; 2457) *Rogers Turner.* £290

– **A Treatise of the Five orders in Architecture.** Trans.:– John James. Ill.:– John Stuart. 1708. 1st. Engl. Edn. Fo. Final tail-piece on last lf. cut away. Cont. panel. cf., upr. cover detchd. (TA. Sep.18; 148) £56

– – **Anr. Edn.** Trans.:– John James. 1722. 2nd. Engl. Edn. Fo. Lr. hf. of plt. VI apparently from anr. copy. Cf., very worn, covers detchd. (S. Jun.22; 137) *Weinreb.* £70

– – **Anr. Edn.** N.d. Sm. fo. Some spotting & soiling. Cont. cf., rebkd. (CSK. Jul.10; 129) £80

PERRIN, Ida S.
*See-*BOULGER, Prof. George S. & Perrin, Ida S.

PERROT, A.M.
– **Historische Sammlung aller noch bestehenden Ritter-Orden der Verschiedenen Nationen . . .** Leipzig, 1821. 1st. & only German Edn. 3 pts. 4to.

Stained thro.-out. Orig. wraps. (R. Oct.14-18; 2852) DM 1,000

PERRY, Charles
– **A Mechanical Account & Explication of the Hysteric Passion . . . a General Account & Explication of all other Nervous Diseases . . . to which is added an Appendix being a Dissertation on Cancers in General . . .** 1755. 1st. Edn. Cont. cf. (S. Jun.17; 677) *Quaritch.* £180

PERRY, Charles
– **A View of the Levant.** 1743. [1st. Edn.?]. Fo. Cont. cf., worn. (CE. Jun.4; 88) £150
– – **Anr. Copy.** Stp. of Birmingham Liby. on title & recto of plts., plt. 23 reprd. 19th. C. hf. cl., jnts. split, upr. cover detchd. (S. Nov.25; 537) *Crete.* £100

PERRY, Charles–CHISHULL, Edmund
– **A View of the Levant.–Travels in Turkey & back to England.** 1743; 1747. 2 works in 2 vols. Fo. Slight dampstaining to 2nd. work. 1st. work: cont. cf., worn, covers detchd.; 2nd. work: cont. hf. cf., worn, covers detchd. From the collection of Eric Sexton. (C. Apr.15; 42) *Ross.* £60

PERRY, George
– **Conchology, or the Natural History of Shells.** 1811. 1st. Edn. Fo. 59 hand-cold. engraved plts. (of 61, lacks plts. 33 & 35), some soiling, remargined at inner edge. Cont. hf. mor., worn. (S. Jun.23; 306) *Gilbert's.* £300
– – **Anr. Edn.** [1823 or later]. Fo. Text wtrmkd. 1823, plts. 1810, some slight soiling & offsetting onto text. Cont. str.-grd. mor., gt. (S. Jun.1; 191) *Carr.* £600

PERRY, Capt. Matthew Calbraith
– **Narrative of the Expedition of an American Squadron to the China Seas & Japan.** Ed.:– Francis L. Hawks. Wash., 1856. 1st. Edn. 4 vols. including vol. of maps. 4to. Orig. embossed cl., gt. (C. Feb.25; 127) *Thorp.* £420
– – **Anr. Copy.** Rebnd. cl. gt. (P. Jan.22; 264) *Quaritch.* £140
– – **Anr. Copy.** 3 vols. Orig. cl. (SG. Oct.30; 288) $650
– – **Anr. Copy.** Lacks nude bathing plt. (SG. Feb.26; 267) $275
– – **Anr. Copy.** Without the suppressed bather's plt. in vol. I. Orig. blind-pict. cl., corners slightly frayed. (PNY. May 21; 342) $225
– – **Anr. Copy.** Vol. 1 only. Orig. cl. (SG. Feb.26; 268) $200
– – **Anr. Copy.** Vol. I only. Lacks some tinted litho. plts., but with the nude bathing plt. W.a.f. (SG. May 21; 415) $140
– – **Anr. Edn.** N.Y., 1857. 2nd. Edn. 4to. Without appendix?, slightly spotted. Cont. hf. mor. (SBA. Oct.21; 248) *Quaritch.* £170
– – **Anr. Copy.** Orig. blind-stpd. mor. (SG. Feb.26; 269) $400

PERS, A. van
– **Nederlandsch Oost-Indische Typen. Types Indiens Neerlandais. Verzameling van groote gelithografieerde Platen in Kleurdruk.** Ill.:– A. van Pers. The Hague, 1853-56. Lge. fo. Lacks 1 text lf., marginal tears in some plts., a few stains. Orig. wraps., mostly defect. (VG. Dec.16; 888) Fls. 950
– – **Anr. Edn.** Ill.:– after A. van Pers. The Hague, [1853-62]. Fo. Orig. hf. chagrin, defect. (VG. Oct.13; 123) Fls. 2,200

PERSE, Saint John
– **Anabasis.** Trans.:– Thomas Stearns Eliot. 1930. 1st. Engl. Edn., (350) numbered, sigd. This copy 'Out of Series'. Orig. cl., s.-c. (SH. Dec.18; 142) *Subunso.* £60
– – **Anr. Copy.** Cl., boxed. (SG. Jun.4; 130) $250
– **L'Ordre des Oiseaux.** Ill.:– Georges Braque. Paris, 1962. (100) sigd. by author & artist. Ob. fo. Orig. mor.-bkd. & edges silk, cut paper bird mntd. on upr. cover, unc., s.-c., worn. (SH. Nov.20; 238) *Fauré.* £1,200

PERSIA
– **Secret History of.** 1745. Cf. gt. (P. Oct.23; 56) *Diba.* £100

PERSIUS FLACCUS, Aulus
– **[Satyrae VI].** Trans.:– Francesco Stelluti. Ill.:– Matthaeus Greuter (engraved title). Rome, 1630. 4to. Some ll. browned, single wormhole in lr. margins at end, paper flaw in Q1. Cont. mott. cf., rebkd. preserving orig. spine, gt. arms of Pierre Séguier on covers, his cipher combined with that of his wife in compartments of spine. From

Honeyman Collection. (S. May 20; 3293) *Zeitlin & Verbrugge.* £480

*See-*JUVENALIS, Decimus Junius & Persius Flaccus, Aulus

PERSOY, Pieter
– **Generaale Wissel en Munt Reductie.** Ill.:– R. de Hoog. Amst., 1694. 4to. Cont. old cf. (LM. Mar.21; 250) B.Frs. 16,000

PERSOZ, J.
– **Traité Théorique et Pratique de l'Impression des Tissus.** Paris, 1846. 4 vols. only, lacks atlas vol. Mott. three-qtr. cf. (SG. Mar.12; 291) $220

PERVIGILIUM VENERIS
Hammersmith, Doves Pr., 1910. (12) on vell. Sm. 4to. Lev. mor., gt. borders & ornaments, spine in 6 compartments, 5 raised bands, gt. panel., sigd. by Doves Bindery, 1913, qtr. mor. s.-c. (CNY. May 22; 391) $3,500

PESTALOZZI, Jean Henri
– **Buch der Mütter.** Zürich, 1803. 1st. Edn. Pt. 1 (all publd.). Title multi-stpd., lightly soiled at beginning. Cont. hf. linen. (HK. May 15; 4724) DM 450
– **Vaterlehren.** Trogen, 1829. 1st. Edn. Cont. hf. leath. (HK. May 15; 4726) DM 850

PETACHIA, of Regensburg
– **Sibuv.** Prague, 1595. 1st. Edn. Sm. 4to. Margins reprd. without text loss, some worming, discoloration, owners' sigs. Cl. Sigs. of the printer & J.C. Wagenseil. (SPB. May 11; 174) $3,750

PETAU, Denis
– **Uranologion sive Systema Variorum Authorum, qui de Sphaera, ac Sideribus, eorumque Motibus Graece commentati sunt.** Paris, 1630. 2 pts. in 1 vol. Fo. Some browning, title stained & with lr. margin renewed. Cont. blind-stpd. vell. bds., lacks ties, some gatherings in middle sprung. From Honeyman Collection. (S. Nov.10; 2460) *Brieux.* £360

PETAU, Paul
– **Explication de plusieurs Antiquités.** Amst., 1757. Sm. 4to. Cont. bds. (S. Jun.22; 75) *Weinreb.* £50

PETER II
*See-*CATHERINE I, Empress of Russia & Peter II

PETER PIPER'S PRACTICAL PRINCIPLES OF PLAIN & PERFECT PRONUNCIATION
Phila., 1836. 16mo. Orig. ptd. wraps. with 3 further ills., discold., short split at top of spine, mor.-bkd. case. (SH. Mar.19; 249) *Maggs.* £160

[PETER PRIM'S PROFITABLE PRESENT TO THE LITTLE MISSES & MASTERS OF THE UNITED KINGDOM]
1809 (wtrmkd. 1811). 16mo. Ills. cold. by former owner?, soiled. Roan-bkd. bds., fitted case. (SH. Mar.19; 250) *Moon.* £210

PETERKIN, Alexander
– **Notes on Orkney & Zetland . . .** Edinb., 1822. Vol. 1 (all publd.). Foxing thro.-out. Hf. mor. (PD. Feb.18; 113) £80

PETERMANN, Wilhelm Ludwig
– **Deutschlands Flora mit Abb. Sämmtl. Gattungen.** Leipzig, 1849. 4to. Lightly soiled in places. Cont. hf. leath. (HK. Nov.18-21; 694) DM 550

PETERS, Harry Twyford
– **America on Stone . . .** Garden City, 1931. (751) numbered. Lge. 4to. Linen, d.-w. (SG. Oct.9; 188) $500
– **America on Stone.–Currier & Ives . . .** Garden City, 1931. 1st. Edns., (751) & (501). 2nd. work vol. 1 only, together 2 vols. Lge. 4to. Orig. cl., d.-w.'s, boxed. (CNY. May 22; 238) $300
– **Currier & Ives . . .** Garden City, N.Y., 1929-31. (501) numbered. 2 vols. 4to. Orig. cl., vol. 2. with d.-w. & box. (SPB. Jun.22; 113) $550
– – **Anr. Copy.** Cl. (SG. Oct.9; 187) $350
– – **Anr. Copy.** (SG. May 14; 173) $225
– **Currier & Ives; America on Stone; California on Stone.** N.Y., 1976. 4 vols. 4to. Orig. cl. (SH. Oct.9; 93) *Grosvenor Prints.* £110

PETERSBURGSKY Sbornik [Petersburg Collection]
Ed.:– [N. Nekrasov]. Ill.:– Agin & Gavarni. St. Petersb., 1846. A few ll. slightly spotted. Cont. hf. cf. (SH. Feb.5; 9) *Bjorck.* £600

PETHER, Thomas
– A Book of Ornaments, Suitable for Beginners. 1773. Stitched as issued in folding cl. portfo. (S. Mar.17; 443) *Quaritch.* £220

PETIT, Jean Louis
– Traité des Maladies Chirurgicales, et des Opérations qui leur Conviennent. Paris, 1774. 1st. Edn. 3 vols. Engraved port. detchd. & frayed in margin, a few short tears, slight spotting. Cont. cf., worn, bkplt. of C.G. Lemerchier, M.D. From liby. of Dr. E. Ashworth Underwood. (S. Feb.23; 273) *Dawson.* £110

PETIT, Petrus
– Dissertations Académiques sur la Nature du Froid et du Chaud. Paris, 1671. Later leath., defect., inner hinge brkn., gt. spine. (VG. Nov.18; 1320) Fls. 450

PETIT, Victor
– Souvenirs des Pyrenées. Pau, ca. 1860. 5 pts. in 1 vol. Fo. Folding plt. detchd. at fold. Cont. cf.-bkd. bds. (C. Mar.18; 155) *Duran.* £140
– – Anr. Edn. Pau, n.d. 1 plt. torn at fold, occasional slight spotting. Orig. cf.-bkd. cl., worn. (CSK. Mar.6; 113) £120

PETIT ATLAS des Environs de Paris
Paris, ca. 1780. 12mo. MS. notes at end. 19th C. hf. roan, smooth spine. (HD. Jun.24; 5) Frs. 1,300

PETIT ATLAS MODERNE
Paris, 1793. 4to. Lacks engraved contents ll. after copper title, 2 maps slightly stained at foot. Hf. leath. (HK. Nov.18-21; 1059) DM 500

PETIT BIJOU [LE] DES ENFANS, Année 1816
Paris, [1815]. 26mm × 16mm. Orig. roan gt. (SH. Mar.19; 197) *Gregory.* £80

PETIT CHANSONNIER DE L'ENFANCE 1830
Paris, [1829]. 25mm. × 16mm. Orig. roan gt. (SH. Mar.19; 198) *Gregory.* £70

PETIT COURRIER DES DAMES
Paris, 1839-40. 2 vols. (pt. of vol. 38 & vol. 39). Hf. mor. W.a.f. (S. Dec.9; 518) *Mistrali.* £140

PETIT JOURNAL POUR RIRE
Ill.:– Grévin (lithos), Bertall, Cham, Daumier & others. Paris, ca. 1865. 3rd. Series., Year I-V, Nos. 1-261 in 5 vols. Lge 4to. Cont. hf. leath. (HK. Nov.18-21; 2355) DM 650

PETIT MESSAGER, Le
Paris, Apr., 1865-Jul., 1866. Vol. I, no. 1-Vol. II, no. 4, in 1 vol. 4to. Lacks portions of 2 folding plts., some offsetting, plts. slightly dust-soiled. Leath.-bkd. cl., slightly worn. (CB. Feb.18; 214) Can. $160

PETIT NEPTUNE FRANCAIS; or, French Coasting Pilot.
1793. 4to. Engraved frontis. slightly soiled. Cont. marb. cf., rebkd. (CSK. Nov.14; 144) £180
– – Anr. Edn. Ed.:– J.F. Dessiou. 1805. 4to. Cont. cf., slight wear. (TA. Sep.18; 295) £95

PETITE ANTHOLOGIE Poétique du Surréalisme
Ed.:– George Hugnet. Paris, 1934. Wraps. Sigd. by Paul Eluard, Salvador Dali, Hugnet, & E.L.T. Mesens. (SG. Jun.4; 471) $190

PETITE VOLIERE, La
Paris, n.d. 2½ × 1¾ ins. Orig. ptd. paper-covered bds., of neo-classical design, orig. s.-c. (LC. Feb.12; 291) £110

PETITES ETRENNES Spirituelles Dédiées à Madame La Dauphine
Paris, ca. 1780. 18mo. Cont. cl., decor., embroidered centre lyre gt. with fleurettes, gt. & cold. fillets & spangles. (HD. Apr.10; 176) Frs. 2,900

PETITES FILLES (les) ET LES POUPEES, ...
Merveilleuse, La Poupée Parlante, La Poupée de Linge, La Poupée Invalide, Les Poupées du Jour del'An, La Tante de Carton
Paris, ca. 1840 6 vols. Ob. 8vo. 2 vols. slightly spotted. Orig. embossed bds., orig. s.-c. (SH. Mar.19; 251) *Sanger.* £210

PETITES MISERES DE LA VIE HUMAINE
Ill.:– after Grandville. Paris, 1843. Some plts. spotted. Mor.-bkd. bds. (SH. Nov.20; 165) *Droller.* £55

PETITOT (Ed.)
See–REPERTOIRE DU THEATRE FRANCOIS

PETITOT, Claude Bernard
– Collection Complete des Mémoires Relatifs à l'Histoire de France. Paris, 1820-29. 1st. & 2nd. series. 131 vols. Cont. mott. cf., gt., sm. gt. arms of John Earl of Clare on sides., lacks many labels. W.a.f. (SBA. Jul.23; 614) *Konuma.* £350

PETITOT, Ennemond Alexandre
– Suite des Vases Tirée du Cabinet de Monsieur du Tillot . . . Ill.:– Bossi after Petitot. Milan, [1764]. Fo. Some margins soiled. Cased bds., lacks spine, slightly worn. (SM. Feb.11; 132) Frs. 2,200

PETITE CONTEURS de XVIIIe Siècle [Collection de]
Ed.:– O. Uzanne. Ill.:– P. Avril, Lalause & others. Paris, 1878-81. 6 vols. Vari-cold. hf. mor., decor. spines, unc., wrap., lacks spine, by Pagnant. (HD. Jun.10; 192) Frs. 1,250

PETITS MONTAGNARDS, Les
[Paris], [1821]. Title soiled, 23 × 16mm. Orig. roan gt. (SH. Dec.12; 564) *Gregory.* £50

PETITS VOYAGES Pittoresques dans l'Asie, l'Afrique, l'Amérique, la Polynesie et les Terres Australes . . .
Paris, 1813. 2 vols. Square 16mo. Cont. marb. roan, decor. spines & covers, roulette border. (HD. Apr.9; 540) Frs. 2,200

PETIVER, James
– English Herbal. Ca. 1860. Fo. 1 lf. only of text. Recent cl. (TA. Nov.20; 454) £65
– Opera Historiam Naturalem Spectantia.–Musei Petiveriana.–Gazophylacii Naturae. 1764; 1695-[1703]; 1702-[1704]. 2 vols.; 2 works in 1 vol. Fo. Cont. cf., rebkd. From Chetham's Liby., Manchester. (C. Nov.27; 321) *Jones.* £1,700

PETRAMELLARI, Io. Antoni
– Ad Librum Onvphrii Panvinii de Summis Pontif et S.R.E. Cardinalibus . . . Bononiae, 1599. 4to. Cont. vell. (CR. Mar.19; 271) Lire 260,000

PETRARCA or PETRARCH, Francesco
– De Remediis Utiusche Fortunae. Cremona & Parmensis, 1492. Fo. Vell. [Hain 12793] (CR. Jun.11; 518) Lire 1,600,000
– – Anr. Edn. Paris, 1557. Slightly stained at beginning, pp. 41-44 with sm. tears. Cont. Fr. cf., gt. centrepiece & corner fleurons, slightly worn. (HK. Nov.18-21; 254) DM 1,200
– Opera. Basle, 1496. Fo. 367 ll. (of 389), extensively wormed thro.-out in inner margins, often with text loss, piece torn from folio 299, secured with pin, browning & staining, other tears. Blind-stpd. cf.-bkd. wood bds., lacks clasps, rebkd. [BMC III 757; Goff P365; HC 1274d] (SM. Oct.8; 2203) £2,800
– Opera con il Com[m]enti sopra il Triumphis: Soneti: & Canzone. Ed.:– Nicolo Peronzone. Venice, 1508. 2 pts. in 1 vol. Fo. Some ll. slightly browned, some old MS. marginalia. Later vell. (R. Oct.14-18; 129) DM 1,700
– Il Petrarca. Venice, 1532. Stain on last p., cancelled owners sig. on title, cont. margin notes. Mod. vell. (SI. Dec.4; 458) Lire 220,000
– – Anr. Edn. Ed:– Alessandro Vellutello. Vinegia, 1538. 4to. Slight marginal dampstaining at end. Cont. Venetian mor., blind-tooled fillet border, 2 borders with sm. flowers in outside corners, lge. fleurons in corners of inside border, gt. motif in centre, angelot heads between borders, spine decor. & blind-tooled, bdg. reprd. (HD. Mar.18; 132) Frs. 9,500
– – Anr. Edn. Venice, 1546. 19th C. mor., gt. fillet borders by Wright. (SG. Sep.25; 15) $600
– Le Rime . . . Esposte per Lodovico Castelvetro. Ill.:– Crivellari, Magnini, Moreti, & others. Venice, 1756. 2 vols. 4to. Light foxing to some ll. at beginning & end. Cont. Fr. mor. gt. The Lamoignan copy, bkplts. of Lord Auckland, Earl of Cromer & Maurice Baring, lately in the collection of John A. Saks. (C. Jun.10; 208) *Greindl.* £150
– Sonetti. Ed.:– K. Vietor. Frankfurt, 1923. (250) numbered. 4to. Orig. mor., fillet cover & inner & outer dentelle, by Ernst Rehbain, Darmstadt, bd. s.-c. (HK. Nov.18-21; 2714) DM 420
– Sonetti Canzoni e Triomphi . . . con la Spositione di Bernardo Daniello da Lucca. Venice, 1549. Stained at beginning, a few ll. slightly soiled. Mod. hf. cf. (S. Dec.8; 113) *Pearson.* £90
– Sonetti, Canzoni, et Triomphi.–I Sonetti, le Canzoni, et i Triomphi di M. Laura in riposta di M. Francesco Petrarca. Venice, 1548; 1552. 2 works in 1 vol. Inscr. on titles by Rase des Neux,

surgeon of Charles IX of France 'degli libri del Scorello(?) . . . 1575', loosely inserted sheet of 2 vig. ports. of Petrarch & Laura. 18th. C. mor., gt., with arms of Count Hoym, spine gt. in compartments, wide inner gt. dentelles. Vernon-Holford copy. (SM. Oct.8; 1913) Frs. 7,000
– Trionfi e Canzoniere. Ed.: Bernardo Lapini da Siena. Venice, 1481. 2 pts. in 1 vol. Fo. Wants last lf. in Pt. I & 1st. 2 ll. in Pt. II, stained & discold. thro.-out, a few ll. wormed, blank portion of final lf. torn away. Vell. [H. 12768; Goff P382] (SPB. Nov.25; 60) $350
– Trostspiegel in Glück und Unglück. Ill.:– Hans Weiditz. Frankfurt, 1572. 2nd. Edn. Fo. 2 longish tears in title reprd., hole in 1 text lf. reprd. Cont. style leath. (R. Oct.14-18; 131) DM 3,800
[–] [–] Anr. Edn. Late 16th C. Fo. Lacks title & some ll., some slight soiling. Old cf., blind-stpd., wormed, rebkd. W.a.f. (CSK. Apr.10; 151) £160
See–GERSON, Johannes–PETRARCA, Francesco & others

PETRASANTA, Silvester
– Symbola Heroica. Ill.:– C. Galle after Rubens. Amst., 1682. 2nd. Edn. 4to. E1 wormed. Cont. vell., slightly stained. (S. Oct.21; 455) *Quaritch.* £170

PETRI, B.
– Das Ganze der Schafzucht. Vienna, 1815. 1st. & only Edn. Slightly soiled in parts. Cont. cf. gt. (R. Oct.14-18; 2725) DM 650

PETRIDES, Paul
– L'Oeuvre Complet de Maurice Utrillo. Paris, 1959-66. (1000). 4 vols. 4to. Orig. wraps., s.-c.'s (SH. Oct.9; 94) *Scandecor.* £360

PETRIE, George
– The Complete Collection of Irish Music. Ed.:– C.V. Stanford. L., ca. 1902. 3 pts. Orig. wraps. (GM. Apr.30; 403) £65

PETRIE, George & others
– Illustrations of the Landscape & Coast Scenery of Ireland. Dublin, 1835. Pts. 1-6. 4to. Plts. hand-cold., publisher's advts. bnd. into 1st. pt. Stitched in orig. ptd. paper wraps. as iss., mod. lev. mor. case. From the collection of Eric Sexton. (C. Apr.16; 329) *Maggs.* £8,500

PETRONIUS Arbiter, Titus or Gaius
– Satyricon. Amst., 1677. 16mo. Cont. vell. Sig. of John Wilkes on title. (LC. Jun.18; 312) £100
– – Anr. Edn. Trans.:– Héguin de Guerle. Ill.:– André Derain. Paris, 1951. (326) on Arches. Fo. In sheets, s.-c. (HD. Jun.25; 366) Frs. 2,900
– – Anr. Copy. (HD. Feb.18; 226) Frs. 2,100
– Works. Trans.:– Jack Lindsay. Ill.:– Norman Lindsay. Franfrolico Pr., [1927]. (650) numbered, sigd. by translator. 4to. Some slight soiling. Cont. hf. cf. (CSK. Feb.27; 133) £70
– – Anr. Copy. Fo. Three-qtr. vell., worn. (SG. Jan.15; 29) $180

PETRUCCI, Giosefo
– Prodomo Apologetico alli Studi Chicheriani. Amst., 1677. 4to. Spr. cf., upr. cover loose, bkplt. of Earl of Marchmont dtd. 1725. (S. Dec.2; 582) *Rota.* £75

PETRUM, Henricum
– Sedulii Scoti Hyberniensis in Omnes Epistolas Pauli Collectaneum. 1528. 1st. Edn. Fo. Numbered on verso of pp. only, front end-paper pasted to inner of 1st. bd., last end-paper wormholed in 2 places without loss of text. Cont. vell., lacks label on spine. (JL. Dec.15; 833) Aus. $350

PETRUS Comestor
– Historia Scholastica. [Chambery], [Printer of the Sion Breviary], [1482, not after 1486]. Fo. Spaces for capital initials with guide letters, some initials supplied in red & blue, rest in red, rubricated, 1st. lf. stained & mntd., fo. 6 rehinged, some dampstaining, mostly to 1st 9 ll., annots. to table in black & red (this & MS. foliation cropped), 17th. C. church inscr. on title & fo. 7r. 17th. C. Fr. cf., spine gt. (reprd.). From the collection of Eric Sexton. [BMC VIII, 384, Goff P464] (CNY. Apr.8; 35) $6,500
– – Anr. Edn. Leyden, 1543. Sm. 4to. Lacks final blank, slight soiling. Later mor. with cf. panel. in upr. cover. (SPB. Jul.28; 397) $150

PETRUS, Lombardus
– Sententiarum Libri IV. [Strassburg], [Printer of the Henricus Ariminensis], [not after 1468]. 1st.

Edn. Fo. Spaces for initial capitals, some supplied in red & blue, rest in alternate red or blue, headings, underlinings, initial strokes & paragraph marks in red, folios 1-18 with 2 wormholes at inner margin, 3 ll. with clean tear to margin, folios 1, 12, & 162 with sm. portion of blank margin torn away, light browning. Cont. German blind-stpd. cf. over wood bds., covers with central panel of lozenge & triangular compartments filled with floral & sm. eagle stps., borders with repeated rosette tools & griffin stps. at corners, brass catches, vell. paste-downs from 14th. C. antiphonal, rebkd. preserving orig. spine, reprd. at corners, lacks clasps & bosses. The copy of Dr. Bertalan Nemenyi, lately in the collection of Eric Sexton. [BMC I, 76, Goff B478, H 10184*] (CNY. Apr.8; 162) $11,000
– – **Anr. Edn.** Venice, Vindelinus de Spira, Mar. 10, 1477. 1st. Dtd. Edn. Fo. Capital spaces, initials supplied in alternating red & blue, paragraph marks & initial strokes mostly in red, some blue, some lines with yellow highlights, all by a cont. hand, lacks 1st. & last blank ll., title soiled & with reprd. marginal worming extending through 1st. 12 ll., some marginal annots. in a cont. hand. 18th. C. Italian vell. gt., gt. arms on covers of Pope Pius VI. Bkplt. of the General Theological Seminary Liby. [BMC V, 248, Goff P480, HC 10186] (CNY. Oct.1; 69) $1,600
– **Sententiarum Libri IV.-Tabula super Libros Sententiarum.** Ed.:– [Johann Beckenbaum (1st. work].) [Nuremb.], Anton Koberger; [Anton Koberger], after May 2, 1491; n.d. 2 works in 5 vols. Fo. Spaces for initial capitals, many with guide letters, vols. 1-4 each with a 19-line opening capital illuminated in cols. & gold on a blue ground, Tabula with similar 10-line capital, other capitals & paragraph marks supplied in red, lacks preliminary blank in vols. 1-3, & final blank in tabula, puncture to extreme fore-edges of some 50 ll. in vol. 1, worming at beginning & end of vol. 1, end of vol. 3 & some margins elsewhere, browning, some ll. darkened, stain to upr. inner margins of 1st. 40 ll. of tabula, owner's inscrs. on title. Lev. mor., covers & spine panel. in gt. & blind, by Sangorski & Sutcliffe, orig. covers of blind-stpd. cf. over wood bds. preserved in cl. folding box. Bkplt. of the General Theological Seminary Liby. [BMC II, 433 (with variant tabula), Goff P486, HC 3540*] (CNY. Oct.1; 39) $2,800
– **Sententiarum Textus.** Ed.:– [D. Agricola]. Ill.:– Urs Graf. Basel, 20 Jan. 1516. 2nd. Edn. Fo. Cont. blind-tooled pig-bkd. wood bds., clasps, ties renewed. (R. Oct.14-18; 132) DM 1,200
*See–*CALVIN, John–PETRUS LOMBARDUS
*See–*ROLEWINCK, Werner–PETRUS LOMBARDUS

PETRUS [Pallagari] Tranensis
– **De Ingenius Puerorum et Adolescentium Moribus.** Ferrara, Laurentius de Rubeis, Oct. 7, 1496. 4to. Spaces for capital initials, some upr. margins wormed at end, slight dampstaining affecting upr. portions of last 16 ll., some early marginal ink annots. Mod. decor. paper bds. Bkplt. of C.W. Dyson Perrins, lately in the collection of Eric Sexton. [BMC VI, 613, Goff P535] (CNY. Apr.8; 58) $900

PETRUS de Palude
– [–] **Sermones Thezauri Novi de Sanctis.** Nuremb., Anton Koberger, 1496. Fo. 194 ll. (Copinger gives only 170 ll.), some ll. slightly dampstained, cont. marginalia. 17th. C. vell. bds., soiled, extremities of spine damaged. [C 5429, Goff P517] (S. Jul.27; 104) Sterling. £280

PETTER, Nicolaes
– **Klar Onderrichtinge der . . . Worstel-Konst.** Ill.:– Romeyn de Hooge. Amst., 1674. 1st. Edn. 4to. 18th. C. blind-stpd. vell. bds. (S. Mar.17; 309) Robinson £680

PETTERSSON, Carl Anton
– **Lappland, dess Natur och Folk.** Stockholm, 1866. Ob. fo. Loose sheets, as issued. Orig. gt. decor. cl. folder, upr. cover. faded. (S. Oct.20; 182) Van Kempen. £100
– – **Anr. Copy.** (S. Jun.22; 189) Remmington. £70

PETTIGREW, Thomas Joseph
– **Bibliotheca Sussexiana, a descriptive catalogue . . . of the manuscripts & printed books contained in the library of the Duke of Sussex in Kensington Palace.** 1827-39. L.P. 2 vols. in 3. Cf.-bkd. bds. (C. Feb.4; 143) Dawson. £120

– **A History of Egyptian Mummies.** Ill.:– after G. Cruikshank & others. 1834. [1st. Edn.?]. 4to. Orig. cl.-bkd. bds. From the collection of Eric Sexton. (C. Apr.15; 43) McBride. £100
– – **Anr. Copy.** Spotted. (SH. Mar.5; 113) Seaby. £65
– – **Anr. Copy.** L.P. 4-p. subscribers list, lacks hf.-title. Three-qtr. mor., spine gt., by Rivière. (SG. May 14; 174) $400
– [–] **Lucien Greville.** Ill.:– George Cruikshank. 1833. 1st. Edn. 3 vols. Late 19th. C. pol. cf. by F. Bedford, spines gt. (S. Nov.24; 235) Sawyer. £90

PETTUS, Sir John
– **Fleta Minor. The Laws of Art & Nature, in Knowing, Judging, Assaying, Fining, Refining . . . Metals.** Priv. ptd., 1683. 1st. Edn. 2 pts. in 1 vol. Fo. Slight worming in some inner margins, sm. flaw in Y2 pt. 2 affecting text, 18th. C. sig. at head of title of Francis Gregor. Cont. cf., gt. spine, defect., reprd. at head, hf. red mor. case. Later bkplt. of G.W.E. Gregor; from Honeyman Collection. (S. Nov.10; 2461) Schuman. £340
– – **Anr. Copy.** Lacks 2 ills., some browning & soiling, lacks port. & 2Bl. 19th. C. cf.-bkd. marb. bds., worn. Verso of title inscr. 'Wm. Colvile his booke/presented to him by ye Author Sr John Pettus/Valued at –£1.5s.0d/No. 30:83'. (S. Nov.4; 569) Sekuler. £80

PETTY, Sir William
– **The Discourse made before the Royal Society the 26 of November 1674. Concerning the Use of Duplicate Proportion . . . Together with a New Hypothesis of Springing or Elastique Motions.** 1674. 1st. Edn. 12mo. Stab-holes in inner margins. Cont. panel. cf., rebkd. From Honeyman Collection. [Wing P1919] (S. Nov.10; 2462) Quaritch. £150
– [–] **England's Guide to Industry.** 1683. 12mo. Some ll. torn with slight text loss. Cont. cf., very worn, upr. cover detchd. [Wing P1922] (SBA. May 27; 102a) Subunso. £65
– **Hiberniae Delineatio.** [1685]. Fo. (448mm. × 300mm.]. Port. a little discold., early sig. on title. Cont. hf. cf., marb. bds., worn. W.a.f. (S. Jun.29; 102) Duyck. £2,400
– **Political Arithmetick, or a Discourse concerning the Extent & Value of Lands, People, Buildings; Husbandry, Manufacture, Commerce, Fishery . . . Publick Revenues, Interest, Taxes, [etc].** 1690. 1st. Edn. Advt. lf., slight soiling & foxing, catchword defect. on G7r, owner's inscr. of H.L. Wood. Cont. mott. cf., worn, upr. jnt. reprd. From Honeyman Collection. [Wing P1932] (S. Nov.10; 2463) Norman. £460
– – **Anr. Edn.** 1691. 2nd. Edn. Cont. panel. cf., rebkd. [Wing P1933.] (C. Jul.16; 359) Dawson. £480

PEUCER, Caspar
– **De Dimensione Terrae et Geometrice Numerandis Locorum Particularium Intervallis.** Wittenberg, 1554. 1st. Edn. Marginal flaw in T7, sm. hole in last 3 ll. Mod. mor., bkplts. of Scheepvaart Museum, & C.E. Kenney. From Honeyman Collection. (S. Nov.10; 2464) McKittrich. £190

PEURBACH, Georg
– **Novae Theoricae Planetarum . . . a Petro Apiano . . . redactae.** Venice, 1551. Slight worming just touching text, marginal staining. Wraps., worn, stitching loose. From Honeyman Collection. (S. Nov.10; 2467) Phelps. £130
– **Tabulae Eclypsium . . . Tabula Primi mobilis Joannis de Monte Regio.** Vienna, 1514. 1st. Edn. Fo. 2 woodcuts hand-cold., badly wormed towards end, slight marginal staining, initial scraped on 2A5. Cont. blind-stpd. vell.-bkd. wooden bds., reprd., lacks clasps, hf. red mor. case. From Honeyman Collection. (S. Nov.10; 2465) Norman. £600
– **Theoricarum Novarum [Planetarum] . . . cu utili ac preclarissima Expositione Domini Francisci Capuani de Manfredonia.** Paris, 1515. Fo. Worming, mainly marginal, reprd., with a few letters in pen facs., tear reprd. in d6. Mod. cl. From Honeyman Collection. (S. Nov.10; 2466) Manning. £380
*See–*RINGELBERGIUS, Joachimus Fortius –PEURBACH, Georg von

PEUTINGER, Conrad
– **Peutingeriana Tabula Itineraria, quae in Augusta Bibliotheca Vindobonensi nunc servatur adcurate exscripta, dicata a F.C. Scheyb.** Vienna, 1753. 1st.

Edn. Fo. Minor staining. Cont. cf., worn, covers detchd. (C. Apr.1; 160) Nuncio. £230

PEVERLY, Charles A.
– **American Pastimes: The Book of . . .** N.Y., Priv. ptd. 1866. 1st. Edn. Orig. gt.-pict. cl. (PNY. Mar.26; 11) $150

PEVERONE, Giovanni Francesco
– **Due Brevi e Facili Trattati, il primo d'Arithmetica: l'altro di Geometria.** Lyon, 1558. 1st. Edn. 4to. Some browning, cont. owner's inscr. (cropped & crossed through) at foot of title. Mod. limp vell. From Honeyman Collection. (S. Nov.10; 2469) McKittrich. £100

PEYER, Johann Conrad
– **Exercitatio Anatomico-Medica de Glandulis Intestinorum . . . cui subjungitur Anatome Ventriculi Gallinacei.** Schaffhausen, 1677. 1st. Edn. Without the 3 engraved plts. that should be present(?), an early owner, almost certainly before 1700, has added 3 drawings in red with explanatory text presumably copied from the engraved plts. when they were eventually made, inscr. 'Matthaeus Hay, M.D., 1884' on title-p. New vell., dust-soiled. (S. Jun.17; 676) Norman. £800

PEYRE, Marie Joseph
– **Oeuvres d'Architecture.** Paris, 1765. 1st. Edn. Fo. 19th. C. qtr. mor. (S. Jun.22; 138) Weinreb. £280

PEYRON, Bernardinus
– **Codices Hebraici in Regiae Bibliothecae in Taurinensi Athenaeo Asservatur.** Turin, 1880. 4to. Bds. (S. Nov.17; 90) Quaritch. £110

PFINTZING, Melchior
– [–] **Die Geuerlicheiten und eins teils der Geschichten des Lobliche Streit-Baren und Hochberumbten Helds und Ritters Tewrdanncks.** Ill.:– L. Beck, Hans Burgkmair & Hans Schaufelein. Augsburg, 1519. 2nd. Edn., Panzer's Version A. Fo. Lacks P5 blank, title reprd. in margin, owner's inscr. removed. 18th. C. vell. bds. Lge. copy, with all the flourishes intact. (S. Feb.10; 259a) Loubeyre. £3,200
– [–] – **Anr. Edn.** Ill.:– Beck, Schaüfelein, Burghmair & others. Augsb., 1519. 2nd. Edn. Fo. Lacks 6 ll. & 2 wdcts., title-lf. very defect., reprd. with owner's mark, some ll. with margin reprs. & tears pasted, heavily browned in places, soiled. 19th. C. hf. leath., worn. (H. May 21/22; 949) DM 2,500
– [–] **[Theuerdank].** Ill.:– Leonhard Beck, Wolfgang Traut, & others. Nuremb., [1517]. 1st. Edn. Fo. With 3 paste-over errata slips on A6r, A6v & A8, text lf. p5 in ptd. facs., occasional slight spotting, rustmarks & staining, sm. liby. stp. in margin of 1st. & last ll. Cont. German blind-stpd. vell. over wood bds., gt.-stpd. arabesque inserted in centre panel of covers. From Chetham's Liby., Manchester. (C. Nov.20; 284) Adams. £4,800

PFISTER, Kurt
– **Deutsche Graphiker der Gegenwart.** Leipzig, 1920. 4to. 1 plt. loose. Orig. hf. linen, defect. (D. Dec.11-13; 1164) DM 4,600
– – **Anr. Copy.** (R. Mar.31-Apr.4; 908) DM 4,300

PFLAUM, Jacob
– [–] **Kalendarium [Tables in Latin for 1477-1552].** Ulm, Johann Zainer. 1478. 1st. & only Latin Edn. Fo. Rubricated, cont. MS. p. of tables at end. Mod. vell.-bkd. bds., hf. red mor. case. From Honeyman Collection. (S. Nov.10; 2471) McKittrich. £1,800

PFLUGER, Eduard
– **Untersuchungen über die Physiologie des Electrotonus.** Berlin, 1859. Hf. cl., upr. wrap. bnd. in. (S. Jun.17; 678) Maggs. £120

PFNOR, Rodolphe
– **Architecture Decoration et Ameublement Epoque Louis XVI.** Paris, 1865. Fo. Cont. mor.-bkd. bds. (S. Nov.25; 407) Booth. £100

PHAEDRUS, Gaius Julius
– **Ezopische Fabelen.** Trans.:– D. van Hoogstaate. Ill.:– J. van Vianen. Amst., 1704. 4to. Lacks port. & f.2B4 (?blank). Cont. vell. bds. (S. Mar.17; 277) R. Barker. £65
– – **Anr. Copy.** Cont. blind-stpd. vell., slightly soiled, some staining in prelims. (VG. Oct.13; 126) Fls. 800

PHAEDRUS, Gaius Julius -contd.
- **Fabularum Aesopiarum.** Ed.:– J. Laurentio. Amst., 1667. Some age-browning. Old vell. (SG. May 21; 315) $140
- – – **Anr. Edn.** Amst., 1701. 4to. Cont. cf., rebkd. (SH. Jul.16; 201) *Ayres.* £60

PHAIR, Charles
- **Atlantic Salmon Fishing.** Ed.:– Richard C. Hunt [foreword]. N.Y., [1937]. 1st. Edn., (950). 4to. Gt.-pict. cl. (PNY. Dec.3; 104) $200
- – – **Anr. Edn.** N.Y., Derry Pr. [1939]. De Luxe Edn., (40) numbered sigd. by author on hf.-title. 2 vols. 4to. Hf. mor. gt., partly unc., partly unopened, s.-c. (CNY. Oct.1; 170) $7,500

PHALARIS [Pseud.]
- **Epistolae.** Sant'Orso, Johannes de Reno, 1475. 4to. Spaces for initial capitals, unrubricated, 4 ll. guarded, 2 wormholes at front, 1 extending to fo. 24 & catching some text. Early Italian blind-stpd. mor., recased, covers worn. From the collection of Eric Sexton. [BMC VII, 1027, Goff P555, HC[Add] 12894] (CNY. Apr.8; 152) $3,000
- – – **Anr. Edn.** Messina, Henricus Alding, ca. 1478. 4to. Spaces for initial capitals, unrubricated, lacks 1st. blank, p. 1 torn at lr. inner margin, foxing to some ll., occasional cont. marginalia, erased inscr. at lr. margin of p. 1, bnd. at rear is the 1st. lf. (with dedicatory epistle) from the 1498 Venice Edn. Old vell., worn. Bkplt. of Bibliotheca Richteriana, lately in the collection of Eric Sexton. [BMC VII, 1076, Goff P556] (CNY. Apr.8; 102) $8,000

PHARMACOPOEIA
- **Pharmacopoeia Augustana renovata, revisa et appendica aliquot Medicamentorum selectiorum aucta.** Augsburg, 1734. Fo. Cont. hf. cf., back gt. (VG. Dec.17; 1485) Fls. 850
- **Pharmacopoea Borussica, oder Preussische Pharmacopoea.** Ed.:– Carl Wilhelm Juch. Nuremb., 1817. Lge. 4to. 18-p. 'Neue Arzney Taxe' 1805 bnd. in. Old bds. Juch's annots. (SG. Sep.18; 298) $375
- **Pharmacopoea Bremensis.** Bremen, 1792. 1st. Edn. Slightly browned. Cont. bds., soiled. (R. Oct.14-18; 374) DM 1,100
- **Pharmocopoea Bruxellensis jussu amplissimi Senatus edita.** Ed.:– J. Jocquet, P. de Hullegarde etc. Brussels, 1641. 4to. A few stains. Qtr. cf. (S. Dec.2; 583) *Asher.* £190
- **Pharmacopoea Helvetica.** Schaffhausen, 1872. Cont. linen, spine defect. (R. Mar.31-Apr.4; 1029) DM 550
- **Pharmacopoea Saxonica.** Dresden. 1837. Sm. 4to. Lightly soiled. Cont. hf. leath. (R. Mar.31-Apr.4; 1030) DM 650
- **Pharmacopoeia of the United States of America.** Boston, Dec. 1820. 1st. Edn. Heavily brownstained thro.-out. Orig. bds., early rebkd., unc. (SG. Sep.18; 300) $160
- **Pharmakopoe fürdas Königreich Bayern.** Munich, 1859. 4to. Slightly soiled. Cont. bds. (HK. Nov.18-21; 697) DM 650

PHEBE, ou la Piété Filiale
Paris, 1817. Sm. 8vo. Decor. bds., decor bds. s.-c. (worn). (VG. Dec.16; 1071) Fls. 560

PHELPS, Rev. William
- **The History & Antiquities of Somersetshire . . .** 1836-39. 3 vols. in 1. Thick 4to. Cont. hf. mor. (TA. Jun.18; 255) £80
- – – **Anr. Copy.** (TA. May 21; 495) £70
- – – **Anr. Edn.** 1839. 2 vols. 4to. Extra ill. with 7 plts., from Rutter's Delineation of Somersetshire, some foxing. Cont. hf. mor. (TA. Oct.16; 87) £110

PHILADELPHIA
- **Views of Philadelphia & its Vicinity.** Phila., 1848. Fo. Lacks title & other prelims., a few extra plts., drawings, etc. inserted, some slight spotting. Cont. str.-grd. red mor., inscr. on front free end-paper, from John McAllister to James Black. W.a.f. [Sabin 62366] (S. Apr.7; 480) *Church.* £220

PHILADELPHIA PHOTOGRAPHER, The
Ed.:– Edward Wilson. Phila., 1869; 1870. Vols. VI & VII. (Numbers 61-84). Three-qtr. mor., both vols. worn, 1 disbnd. (SG. Apr.23; 159) $800

PHILALETHES, Eirenaeus (Pseud.)
See–STARKEY, George 'Eirenaeus Philalethes'

PHILALETHES, Eugenius (Pseud.)
See–SAMBER, Robert 'Eugenius Philalethes'

PHILATELY
- **Billig's Philatelic Handbook.–Billig's Philatelic Specialized Catalogues, Volume 6.** Jamaica, N.Y., [1943-55]. 1st. work vols. 1-24 (but lacks vol. 23). Cl. (SG. Feb.12; 308) $100

PHILATHES (Pseud.)
See–LESLIE, Charles

PHILBY, Harry
- **Arabia of the Wahhabis.** 1928. 1st. Edn. Mod. hf. mor. (S. Mar.31; 498) *Ghani.* £60

PHILELPHUS, Johannes Marius
- **Epistolarium Novum.** Basle, Johann Amerbach, 1489. 2nd. Amerbach Edn. 4to. Lacks final blank, crudely sewn with 3 tears to u3, title soiled, sm. wormhole to 1st. 34 ll. Old hf. vell., spine gt. Bkplt. of the General Theological Seminary Liby. [BMC III, 752, Goff P619, HC 12974] (CNY. Oct.1; 10) $750

PHILIDOR, François Andre Danican
- **L'Analyse des Echecs.–Analyse de Jeu des Echecs.** L., 1748; 1777. 1st. Edn.; New Edn. 2 works in 2 vols. Slight paper fault to title of 1st. work, affecting 2 letters. Both cont. cf., rebkd. Bkplt. of the Earl of Sandwich in 1st. work, bkplt. of Lord Northwick in the 2nd., both lately in the collection of Eric Sexton. (C. Apr.15; 16) *Macdonald Ross.* £400
- **Analysis of the Game of Chess.** 1790. Cont. cf. gt. (P. Jan.22; 5) *Weininger.* £70
- – – **Anr. Copy.** 2 vols. in 1. Some foxing. Cont. cf., centre panels with initials 'C.P.' & a vase, in oval floral borders, spine gt. with vases, both covers detchd. Fore-e. pntg. of chessboard & game; from the liby. of Zola E. Harvey. (SG. Mar.19; 160) $2,000
- **Studies of Chess; containing Caissa, a Poem by Sir. W. Jones.** L., 1803. Orig. leath. (D. Dec.11-13; 2300) DM 480

PHILIP, G.
- **Library Atlas.** 1856. 4to. Engraved maps cold. in outl., 1 torn. Cont. hf. mor. (SH. Mar.5; 114) *Lilburn.* £60

PHILIP, H.R.H., The Prince, Duke of Edinburgh & Fisher, James
- **World Wildlife Crisis.** Arcadia Pr. 1971. (265) sigd. by Prince Philip. 4to. Orig. mor. (CSK. Sep.5; 37) £55

PHILIPON, Ch. (Ed.)
See–MUSEE POUR RIRE

PHILIPON de la Madeleine
- **L'Orléanais . . .** Ill.:– Baron, Français, C. Nanteuil & Rouargue. Paris, 1845. 1st. Printing. Lge. 8vo. Cont. chagrin, gt. tools on covers & spine. (HD. Jun.25; 368) Frs. 1,300

PHILIPPI, H.
See–KEPLER, J.–SCHEINER, C. & Locher, J.G. –SCHEINER, C.–PHILIPPI, H.–MARTILIN-GEN, J.

PHILIPPI, R.A.
- **Los Fósiles Terciarios i Cuartarios de Chile.** Santiago, 1887. 4to. Publisher's mor., gt. (SPB. May 5; 401) $325
- **Viage al Desierto de Atacam.** Halle, 1860. 4to. Some foxing. Orig. cl. (SPB. May 5; 402) $325

PHILIPPS, Henry
- [–] **The Grandeur of the Law.** 1684. Old sheep, worn. [Wing P2022] (CSK. Mar.27; 53) £50

PHILIPPSON, Johannes 'Sleidanus'
- **A Famouse Cronicle of Oure Time . . .** Trans.:– Jhon Daus. L., 1560. 1st. Edn., 1st. Iss. 18th. C. cf., rebkd. [STC 19848] (SG. Sep.25; 285) $250

PHILIPS, Katherine 'Orinda'
- **Poems . . .** Ill.:– Faithorne. 1669. 2 Pts. in 1 vol. Fo. Lacks last blank. Cont. mott. cf., gt. panel. [Wing P2034] (S. Nov.24; 236) *Sanders.* £160

PHILIPS JACOBSZ, C.
- [–] **Verzaameling van alle de Huizen en prachtige Gebouwen langs de Keizers en Heere-Grachten der Stadt Amsteldam, beginnende van den Binnen Amstel en eindigende aan de Brouwers-Gracht.** Amst., [1767]. Fo. Some plts. a little browned or foxed, all with a fold across. Cont. hf. cf. (VG. Dec.17; 1486) Fls. 1,700

PHILLIP, Arthur
- **The Voyage of Governor Phillip to Botany Bay with an account of the establishment of the colonies of Port Jackson, & Norfolk Island.** 1789.

1st. Edn. 4to. Title slightly stained, very minor discolouration. Cont. cf., corners worn. (C. Feb.25; 128) *Quaritch.* £520
- – – **Anr. Copy.** 52 (of 53?) engraved plts. & charts. Cont. tree cf., slightly worn, covers detchd. (SBA. Oct.21; 120) *Terra Australis.* £400
- – – **Anr. Copy.** 53 plts. (nos. 33 & 45 loose & torn). Cf. gt. (P. Oct.23; 57) *Fenfert.* £220
- – – **Anr. Edn.** 1790. 3rd. Edn. 3 ports., 3 folding maps & 12 folding plts. only, some soiling. Cont. hf. vell. (SD. Feb.4; 200) £60

PHILLIPS, Arthur S.
- **My Wilderness Friends.** Fall River, Munroe Pr., 1910. 1st. Edn. Cl. (SG. Oct.16; 281) $100

PHILLIPS, Henry
- **Floral Emblems.** 1825. 1st. Edn. Slight offsetting. Cont. cf., rebkd., orig. spine preserved. (S. Jun.1; 279) *Portmeirion.* £70
- – – **Anr. Edn.** L., 1825. Cf. (P. Jul.2; 174) *Cavendish.* £60
- **The True Enjoyment of Angling.** L., 1843. 1st. Edn., Subscriber's Copy (100). First sig. loose, rebkd. with binder's tape. Cl. Front. sigd. in pencil, A.L.s. tipped in. (SG. Oct.16; 282) $170

PHILLIPS, John Artist & Rider, A
- **Mexico Illustrada.** Mexico, 1965. (1,000) numbered, facs. reprint. Fo. Text in Engl. & Spanish. Orig. cf. (SH. Mar.5; 115) *De Velasco.* £220
- **Mexico Illustrated.** 1848. Fo. Occasional light spotting, slight marginal soiling & a few tears, litho. title & 24 plts. only, lacks the 'Covent de Merced'. Orig. mor.-bkd. cl., worn, disbnd. (CSK. Sep.26; 46) £520

PHILLIPS, John C.
- **A Natural History of the Ducks.** 1922. 4 vols. 4to. Hf. red mor. gt. (P. Nov.13; 217) *Traylen.* £1,350
- – – **Anr. Edn.** Ill.:– after Frank W. Benson, Allan Brooks & others. 1923-26. 4 vols. 4to. Some minor spotting, mainly marginal. Orig. bds. with buckram backstrips, unc. (TA. Jun.18; 104) £800

PHILLIPS, John C. & Hill, Lewis Webb
- **Classics of the American Shooting Field.** Ill.:– Frank W. Benson. Boston & N.Y., 1930. 1st. Edn. (150), sigd. by Phillips, Hill & Benson. Cl., unc. (SG. Oct.16; 285) $100

PHILLIPS, Philip A.S.
- **Paul de Lamerie Citizen & Goldsmith of London.** 1935. (250). Fo. Orig. cl. gt., d.-w., torn. (SBA. Mar.4; 274) *Chesters.* £120

PHILLIPS, Philip Lee
- **A List of Geographical Atlases in the Library of Congress, Volumes I-IV.** Wash., 1909-20. 4 vols. 4to. Cl., ex-liby. (SG. Mar.26; 364) $220
- **A List of Maps of America in the Library of Congress.** Wash., 1901. 4to. Cl. (SG. May 21; 154) $150

PHILLIPS, Philip Lee–LEGEAR, Clara Egli
- **A List of Geographical Atlases in the Library of Congress, Volumes I-IV.– . . . Volumes V & VI.** Wash., 1909-20; 1958 & 1963. 6 vols. 4to. Cl. (SG. Mar.26; 365) $550

PHILLIPS, Sir Richard, publisher
- **Book of English Trades.** 1821. 12mo. Slight browning. Cont. sheep. (S. Jan.26; 253) *Martin.* £160
- **Modern London; being the History & Present State of the British Metropolis.** 1805. 4to. Slight foxing, text slightly browned. Cont. hf. mor., some wear. (TA. Nov.20; 432) £280
- [–] – **Anr. Copy.** Some soiling, lacks map. Cont. cf., rebkd. (CSK. Sep.26; 83) £250
- – – **Anr. Copy.** Later hf. cf., gt. (SH. Mar.5; 116) *George's.* £230

PHILLIPS, T.
- [–] **Scenes & Occurences in Albany & Caffer-Land, South Africa.** L., 1827. Some light foxing, with correct title pasted over incorrect one. Orig. cl.-bkd. bds., slightly worn, light liby. stp. partially removed. (VA. Jan.30; 234) R. 110

PHILLIPS, U.B. (Ed.)
See–AMERICAN INDUSTRIAL SOCIETY . . .

PHILLIPS, William
- **A Selection of Facts . . . arranged so as to form an Outline of the Geology of England & Wales.** 1818. 1st. Edn. 12mo. Folding table slightly torn

& reprd., advt. lf. Orig. bds., unc., ticket of J.W. Jackman, head of spine reprd. From Honeyman Collection. (S. Nov.10; 2472) *Zeitlin.* £80

PHILLPOTTS, Eden
- A Dish of Apples. Ill.:– Arthur Rackham. 1921. Ltd. Edn. (500) sigd. by Ill. Orig. cl. gt. (P. Oct.23; 140) *Gerrard.* £210
– – Anr. Edn. Ill.:– Arthur Rackham. L., [1921]. (500) numbered, sigd. by author & artist. 4to. Gt.-pict. cl. Raymond M. Sutton Jr. copy. (SG. May 7; 233) $475
- The Girl & the Faun. 1916. 1st. Edn., (350) sigd. by author & artist. 4to. Orig. vell.-bkd. bds., upr. cover stained. (SH. Mar.26; 114) *Ayres.* £55

PHILOMATHEAN Society of the University of Pennsylvania
- Report of the Committee appointed . . . to translate the Inscription on the Rosetta Stone. Ill.:– L.N. Rosenthal. [Phila.], [1858]. 1st. Edn. Sq. 4to. Mor. (SG. Mar.26; 396) $130

PHILOSOPHICAL THERESA
N.d. 2 vols. Early photograph inserted at end. Cl. (P. Feb.19; 12) *Bibn.* £250

PHILOSTRATUS, Flavius
- De la Vie d'Apollonius Thyaneen en VIII Livres. Paris, 1611. 2 vols. in 1. 4to. Stps. on title of Bibliothèque Prytanée & Bibliothèque du Roi, St. Cloud. Cont. pol. cf., arms of Louis XIII, gt. on covers, side & spine compartments semé with fleurs-de-lis, broad gt. border, 1 or 2 wormholes in spine. (SM. Oct.8; 1919) Frs. 16,000

PHIPPS, Constantine John
- Reise nach dem Nordpol.–Engels Neuer Versuch. Ed.:– Engel. Bern, 1777. 4to. Lightly soiled in parts. Cont. hf. leath., slightly worn. (H. Dec.9/10; 599) DM 820
- Voyage au Pole Boréal. Paris, 1755. 1st. Fr. Edn. 4to. Cont. mott. cf., gt.-panel. back. (PNY. May 21; 346) $125
- A Voyage towards the North Pole. 1774. 1st. Edn. 4to. Margins spotted. 19th. C. cl. From Chetham's Liby., Manchester. (C. Nov.27; 322) *Marshall.* £220
– – Anr. Copy. Mod. cf. (TRL. Dec.10; 91) £110
– – Anr. Copy. Browned, foxing, hf.-title & front free end-paper loose. Disbnd. [Sabin 62572] (SPB. May 6; 235) $450
– – Anr. Copy. 12 (of 14) plts., ex-liby., stnd. Old hf. cf., rebkd., worn. (SG. Feb.26; 28) $140
– – Anr. Edn. Dublin, 1775. 2nd. Edn. Sm. tear in map. Recent buckram, unc. [Sabin 62572] (CB. Feb.18; 300) Can. $260

PHIPPS, Col. Ramsay Weston
- The Armies of the First French Republic . . . L., 1926-39. 5 vols. Cl. (SG. Feb.26; 272) $160

PHIZ (Pseud.)
See–BROWNE, Hablot Knight 'Phiz'

PHOCYLIDES
See–PHYTHAGORAS & PHOCYLIDES

PHOEBE, THE COTTAGE MAID
1811. 1st. Edn. 7 aquatinted figures, 3 (of 5) hats, & interchangable. Orig. ptd. wraps., s.-c. reprd. (SH. Mar.19; 64) *Gregory.* £190

PHOEBUS, Nathan Feitel Ben Shmeul
- Drushim Le'chol Chefzeihem.–O Ha'drush Asher Darash & Drush Na'eh. Kracow, 1609; [1613?]. 2 works in 1 vol. 4to. 2nd. work ptd. without title, light staining, browning. Cl.-bkd. bds. (SPB. May 11; 169) $1,200

PHOTOGRAPHIC History of the Civil War
Ed.:– Francis Trevelyan Miller. N.Y., 1911-12. 10 vols. 4to. Blind-stpd. cl., stained. (SG. Jul.9; 81) $250
– – Anr. Edn. Ed.:– F.T. Miller. N.Y., 1912. 10 vols. 4to. Cl. (SG. Apr.23; 59) $175

PHOTOGRAPHIE DU NU (La)
Ed.:– C. Klary. 1902. Frontis. & title defect. Moire cl. (SG. Apr.23; 156) $110

PIARRON DE CHAMOUSSET, C.H.
- Oeuvres. Paris, 1783. 1st. Edn. 2 vols. 9 ptd. folding tables. Cont red mor., gt., arms of M.J.L.B. de Savoie, Comtesse de Provence, triple gt. fillet, corner sprays, spine gt. in compartments, Signet Liby. label & arms on covers, inner gt. dentelles. (SM. Oct.8; 1915) Frs. 2,800

PIAZZI, Giuseppe
- Della Specola Astronomica de' Regi Studi di Palermo. Palermo, 1792-94. 1st. Edn. 2 vols. in 1. Fo. Vol. I apparently lacks 3 prelim. ll. (pp. III-VIII). Cont. hf. cf., worn. Pres. copy to Jérôme Lalande; sm. slip with notes about the book in Lalande's hand tipped in beneath pres. inscr., marginal annots. in Lalande's hand; 2nd. pres. inscr. on blank lf. preceding 2nd. vol.; owner's stp. of Raspail (François-Vincent Raspail?); from Honeyman Collection. (S. Nov.10; 2473) *Hill.* £550
– – Anr. Copy. Pres. copy to Jérôme Lalande; sm. slip with notes about the book in Lalande's hand tipped in beneath pres. inscr., marginal annots. in Lalande's hand; 2nd. pres. inscr. on blank lf. preceding 2nd. vol.; owner's stp. of Raspail (François-Vincent Raspail?); from Honeyman collection; w.a.f. (S. May 20; 3294) *Roberts.* £450

PIBRAC, Guy Du Faur, Seigneur de
- Les Quatrains des Sieurs Pybrac, Favre, et Mathieu . . . Paris, 1646. 18th. C. red mor., 2 fillets, sm. fleuron in corners, decor. spine. (HD. Mar.18; 133) Frs. 1,400

PICA, V.
- Giuseppe de Nittis. L'uomo e l'Artista. Milan, 1914. (600) numbered. 4to. Sewed. (CR. Jun.11; 327) Lire 250,000
– – Anr. Edn. Milan. 1914. 4to. Publisher's bds. (CR. Mar.19; 140) Lire 220,000

PICARD, Jean
- Traité du Nivellement . . . Et un Abbregé de la Mésure de la Terre . . . Mis en lumière par les Soins de M. de La Hire. Paris, 1684. 1st. Edn. 12mo. Slight staining. Cont. cf., gt. spine. From Honeyman Collection. (S. Nov.10; 2474) *Hill.* £240

PICARD, Capt. L.
- Album d'Hippiatirque et d'Equitation de l'Ecole de Cavalerie. Paris, ca. 1892. Lge. fo. Gt. hf. mor. & bds. (PNY. Oct.1; 284) $180

PICART, Bernard
- Ceremonies et Coutumes Religieuses de tous les Peuples du Monde. Amst., 1723-33. 1st. Edn. Vol. 1 in 2 vols., vol. II, Vol. III, Vol. V, & supp. vol. 1 (of 2). Fo. 6 engraved title vigs., 7 text copper engrs., 200 partly double-p. copperplts. Cont. vell. (D. Dec.11-13; 2220) DM 2,800
– – Anr. Edn. Amst. & L., 1723-56. 11 vols. & Boydell's vol. of counterfeits. Fo. Old cf. (rebkd.) & hf. cf. From liby. of Baron Dimsdale. (MMB. Oct.8; 12) *Leicester Galleries.* £360
– – Anr. Edn. Amst., 1736-43. 9 pts. in 11 vols. Lge. Fo. 265 (of 266?) partly folding copperplts., lightly soiled in places. Cont. marb. leath., 6 raised bands, floral decor., inner gt. dentelle, spine with defects at head & foot. (HK. May 12-14; 1169) DM 2,100
– – Anr. Edn. Bael, 1750. Fo. Interleaved Dutch Trans., 18th. C. MS. preface & explanations, finely calligraphed in style of printing types, some plts. mntd., sm. stains near end, some reprd. tears. 19th. C. hf. cf., gt. spine. (VG. Oct.13; 127) Fls. 2,400
- Ceremonies et Coutumes Religieux de tous les Peuples du Monde . . .–Nouveau Supplement. Amst., 1733-43; 1784. 11 vols., Supp. 4 vols. in 1, together 12 vols. Tall fo. Cont. mott. cf., worn. (SG. May 14; 175) $1,100
- Ceremonies & Religious Customs of the . . . World. L., 1731-39. 7 vols. in 6. Fo. Some browning & tears. Old cf., worn, covers detchd. (SPB. Nov.25; 112) $700
– – Anr. Copy. Vol. 2 lacks 6 plts., some folding plts. frayed. Cont. leath. (HK. Nov.18-21; 1975) DM 2,400
– – Anr. Edn. L., 1733. Vol. I only: Ceremonies of the Jews. Fo. Mod. hf. cf. (S. Nov.17; 34) *Gmesh.* £420
– – Anr. Edn. 1733-39. 7 vols. in 6. Fo. Lacks plt.-lists in vols. I-V, slight marginal worming in vols. I-II, occasional browning & spotting. Cont. spr. cf., gt., worn. W.a.f.; C. Beauchamp Cooper's bkplt. (S. Jan.26; 114) *Mistrali.* £550
– – Anr. Copy. Lacks final blank in vol. 5, several ll. in vol. 5 marginally wormed, slight staining at some edges. Bkplt. of Edward Davenport; w.a.f. (S. Feb.10; 400) *Hirschler.* £420
- Histoire Générale des Cérémonies . . . de tous les Peuples du monde. Paris, 1741. 2 vols. Fo. Early

19th. C. red mor. bkd. bds., gt. (SM. Oct.8; 2360) Frs. 5,100
- Impostures innocentes, ou Recueil D'Estampes. Amst., 1734. Fo. Cont. cf. gt. (P. Nov.13; 307) *Erlini.* £55
- Neureöffneter Musen-Tempel . . . Amst./Leipzig, 1754. L.P. Fo. Explanations to plts. in Fr., Engl., German & Dutch, title, introduction, text & plts. loose in bdg. Orig. covers, bds., unc. (VG. Nov.18; 448) Fls. 650
- Pierres Antiques Gravées. Ed.:– Philippe de Stosch. Amst., 1724. L.P. Lge. fo. Cont. Fr. red mor. gt., spine tooled in compartments, covers with 3-line roll border. Bkplts. of Dr. Charles Chauncy & Robert Stearne Tighe; extra plt. by Bartolozzi after Cipriani inserted. (S. Nov.24; 237) *Watchman.* £220
- Tafereel, of Beschchryving van den Prachtigen Tempel der Zang-Godinnen. Amst., 1733. Lge. fo. 58 (of 60) copperplts., lightly soiled. 19th. C. leath., lightly soiled, unc. (R. Oct.14-18; 2526) DM 500
[-] Le Temple des Muses. Amst., [1730-32]. Fo. Loose in cl. folder. As a Collection, w.a.f. (S. Oct.21; 459) *Hyde Park Books.* £110
– – Anr. Edn. Amst., 1749. Fo. Cont. mott. cf., worn. (S. Nov.25; 381) *Marshall.* £240

PICASSO, Pablo
- Carnet de la Californie. Paris, 1959. (1500). Fo. Slight browning. Orig. bdg., soiling, some tears. (SPB. May 29; 339) $150
- Linogravures. Trans.:– Jacques Chavy. Paris, [1962]. Ob. fo. Cl., box. (SG. Aug.21; 438) $100
- Oeuvres. Paris, [1942-52]. Ltd. 1st. Edns. Vols. I-V in 6 vols., separately iss. Sm. fo. Unif. ptd. wraps., tissue guards. (PNY. Mar.4; 208) $850
- 40 Dessins au Marge du Buffon. Paris, 1957. (226) on vélin d'Arches with orig. lino-cut sigd. by artist. 4to. Unsewn in orig. wraps., folder & s.-c., rather worn. (SH. Nov.21; 451) *Simons.* £310
- Suite de 180 Dessins, 1954-54. N.Y., [1955]. 1st. Edn. in Engl. Sm. fo. Cold. pict. bds., d.-w. (PNY. Mar.4; 209) $100
- Trente-deux Reproduction des Maquettes en Couleurs d'après les Originaux des Costumes & Decor . . . pur le Ballet 'Le Tricorne'. Paris, 1920. 1st. Edn., (250) numbered. 4to. Plts. loose, as iss., in ptd. wraps., inserted in cl.-bkd. bd. folder & inserted in blind-pict. mor. s.-c., upr. cover of folder separated, lacks cl. ties. (PNY. Mar.4; 212) $550
- Le Tricorne. Paris, 1920. (250). Sm. 4to. In sheets, publisher's portfo. (HD. Dec.5; 164) Frs. 3,900

PICASSO, Pablo (Ill.)
See–KOCHNO, Boris & Luz, Maria

PICCHA, Gregoria
- Oratio ad Sixtum V. Pont. Max. Aliosq. Christianos Principes, et Respubl. pro Britannico Bello Indicendo. Rome, 1588. 4to. Slight spotting, sm. hole in B2, restored, outer margins just cropped. Mod. mor. (S. Dec.8; 111) *Maggs.* £100

PICCOLOMINI, Alessandro
- De La Sfera del Mondo . . . Dele Stelle Fisse. Venice, 1540. 1st. Edn. 2 pts. in 1 vol. 4to. Some staining, extensive marginal annots. & underscoring in 1st. pt., owners' inscrs. on title. Cont. vell., stained, mod. bkplt. with name erased, hf. red mor. case. From Honeyman Collection. (S. Nov.10; 2477) *Phelps.* £550
– – Anr. Copy. From Honeyman Collection. (S. May 20; 3295) *McKittrick.* £350
- Instrumento della Filosofia Naturale.–Parte Prima [Parte Seconda] della Filosofia Naturale. Venice, 1576; 1576. 2 works in 1 vol. 4to. Some ll. browned or marginally stained, MS. corrections to text. Cont. limp vell. From Honeyman Collection. (S. Nov.10; 2480) *Rogers Turner.* £55
- La prima parte delle Theoriche, overo Speculationi de i Pianeti. Venice, [1558]. 4to. Some staining. 18th. C. cf., spine worn at head. From Honeyman Collection. (S. Nov.10; 2478) *McKittrick.* £55
- La Sfera del Mondo.–[De le Stelle fisse]. Venice, ca. 1580. 2 pts. in 1 vol. 4to. Slightly spotted, soiled or dampstained in places. Wraps., worn. (S. Oct.21; 418) *Elliot.* £70

PICCOLOMINI, Arcangelo
- Anatomicae Praelectiones. Rome, 1586. 1st. Edn. Fo. Slight staining at beginning, occasional minor discolouration. Cont. limp vell. (C. Apr.1; 70) *Mediolanum.* £460

PICCOLPASSO, Cipriano
- **Three Books of the Potter's Art.** 1934. (750). Fo. Orig. cl., d.-w. (SH. Oct.9; 148) *Rosewood.* £85

PICHON, Baron Jerome
- **Bibliophiles et Relieurs.** Ed.:– Georges Vicaire. Paris, 1907. (80). 4to. Lev., gt. floral borders with lge. gt. cornerpieces, gt.-lettered title in wreath, spine gt., gt. dentelles, by Gruel. (SG. Oct.2; 292) $500

PICHON, T. J. & Gobet, N.
[–] **Sacre et Couronnement de Louis XVI . . . à Rheims, le 2 Juin, 1775.** Ill.:– Patas (folding map). Paris, 1775. 4to. Cont. Fr. mott. cf., gt. arms on covers, lacks front end-paper. (BS. Jun.11; 220) £400

PICHON, Thomas
[–] **Lettres et Memoires pour Servir à l'Histoire Naturelle, Civile, et Politique du Cap Breton.** L., 1760. 12mo. Cont. cf., bkplts. [Sabin 62610] (CB. Nov.12; 113) Can. $320

PICINELLO, Philip
- **Mondo Simbolico.** Ill.:– Simon Durello. Milan, 1669. 2 pts. in 1 vol. Fo. 'Bibliotheca Colbertina. l.' written on title, bkplt. of Marchese d'Adda. Cont. red mor., gt., arms of Jean-Baptiste Colbert, Marquis de Seignelay, on covers & his monog., gt., in each spine compartment, triple gt. fillet. (SM. Oct.8; 1917) Frs. 3,200

PICKARD, Samuel T.
See–WHITTIER, John Greenleaf–PICKARD, Samuel T.

PICKARD-CAMBRIDGE, F.O.
- **Biologia Centrali-Americana. Arachmida-Araneidea.** 1889-1905. 2 vols. 4to. Binder's cl. (S. Jun.1; 10) *Maggs Brothers.* £260

PICKEN, Andrew
- **Madeira Illustrated.** 1840. Fo. Most plts. foxed. Hf. mor., worn & soiled. (PD. Oct.22; 110) £140

PICKERING, Miss Ellen
- **The Quiet Husband.–The Fright.–The Prince & the Pedlar.** 1840; 1839; 1839. Each 3 vols., together 9 vols. 12mo. Some spotting. Cont. unif. hf. cf. (CSK. May.8; 110) £110

PICKERING, Harold G.
- **Angling of the Test.** N.Y., Derrydale Pr., 1936. (197) numbered, sigd. Cl. (SG. Apr.9; 351) $225
– – **Anr. Copy.** (SG. Dec.11; 271) $170
- **Dog-Days on Trout Waters.** 1933. (199) numbered & sigd. 12mo. Bds. (SG. Dec.11; 270) $600
- **Merry Xmas, Mr. Williams. 20 Pine St. N.Y.** Ill.:– Harry L. Timmins. 1940. (267) numbered & sigd. 12mo. Cl. Inscr. to Henry Ingraham. (SG. Dec.11; 274) $280
– – **Anr. Copy.** Silver-decor. cl. (SG. Dec.11; 273) $260
- **Neighbors have my Ducks.** Ill.:– Harry L. Timmins. 1937. (227) numbered & sigd. 12mo. Gt.-decor. leatherette. Inscr. to Henry A. Ingraham. (SG. Dec.11; 272) $260
- **Trout Fishing in Secret.** 1931. (99) numbered & sigd. 12mo. Bds. (SG. Dec.11; 269) $1,200

PICRO, A.
- **Album Militaire.** Ill.:– H. Meyer after P. Corbett (folding mezzotint). 1860-90. 4to. Title lf. sigd. & dtd. 1860, 5 ll. sigd. or with monog. & dtd. 1887-90, all ll. with MS., 2 ll. loose, some sm. tears, slightly soiled or browned in parts. Cont. hf. leath., slightly worn. (H. Dec.9/10; 824) DM 2,800

PICTON, J.A.
See–HERDMAN, William Gawin & Picton, J.A.

PICTORIAL ALBUM (The) or Cabinet of Paintings
Ill.:– George Baxter. 1837. 4to. Orig. mor. gt., various repairs. (SKC. May 19; 5) £75

PICTORIAL HISTORY OF ENGLAND
1855-58. New Edn. 7 vols. Some spotting. Cont. cf., spines gt. (CSK. Jan.16; 165) £50

PICTORIAL HUMPTY DUMPTY
Ill.:– Alquis. 1843. 87mm. × 1600mm. Folds strengthened behind. Orig. cl.-bkd. pict. bds., stained & worn. (SH. Mar.19; 243) *Libris.* £120

PICTURE POST
1938-57. Vol. 1 no. 1-vol. 75 no. 9, 973 Iss. 4to. Orig. wraps. (SKC. May 19; 129) £290

– – **Anr. Copy.** Vols. 1-75. A few special numbers included. First 7 vols. in publishers cl., rest in orig. wraps., a few slightly soiled. (SH. Oct.10; 501) *Landry.* £270

PICTURESQUE AMERICA
N.Y., [1872]. Vol. 1. Fo. Frontis. & title soiled. Orig. linen. (D. Dec.11-13; 1345) DM 1,200
– – **Anr. Edn.** Ed.:– William Cullen Bryant. N.Y., [1872-1874]. 2 vols. 4to. Some foxing. Orig. blind-stpd. & gt. mor. (SG. Mar.5; 366) $260

PICTURESQUE CALIFORNIA: the Rocky Mountains & the Pacific Slope
Ed.:– John Muir. Ill.:– Moran, Rix, Darley, Remington, & others. N.Y. & California, [1888]. 2 vols. Fo. A few extreme corners dampstained. Orig. gt.-pict. cl., new buckram spines. (SG. Jan.8; 362) $260

PICTURESQUE CANADA
See–GRANT, George Munro

PICTURESQUE Description of North Wales
1823. Ob. 4to. Views cold. Cont. red hf. mor. From the collection of Eric Sexton. (C. Apr.16; 320) *Maggs.* £280

PICTURESQUE EUROPE
Ill.:– Birket Foster, Harry Fenn & others. 1816. 5 vols. 4to. Some foxing. Orig. pict. & gt. decor. cl. (PL. Jul.11; 137) *Fairburn.* £50
– – **Anr. Edn.** Ca. 1860. 5 vols. 4to. Cont. hf. mor. (TA. Feb.19; 653) £80
– – **Anr. Edn.** Ca. 1870. 4 vols. 4to. Orig. gt. decor. cl. (TA. Feb.19; 654) £70
– – **Anr. Copy.** Vols. 1 & 2-The British Isles. Some spotting. Orig. hf. mor., gt. decor. spines. (TA. Feb.19; 655) £50
– – **Anr. Edn.** Ed.:– Bayard Taylor. N.Y., 1875. 3 vols. 4to. Hf. leath. (D. Dec.11-13; 1279) DM 1,100
– – **Anr. Edn.** Ill.:– after Birket Foster & others. Ca. 1875. 10 vols. 4to. Orig. cl. gt. (SBA. Oct.21; 73) *Sommewald.* £130
– – **Anr. Copy.** 5 vols. 4to. Cont. hf. leath. gt. (R. Oct.14-18; 1844) DM 800
– – **Anr. Edn.** Ed.:– Bayard Taylor. N.Y., 1875-79. 3 vols. Lge. 4to. Orig. hf. leath. (HK. May 12-14; 793) DM 660
– – **Anr. Edn.** Ed.:– Bayard Taylor. N.Y., [1875-79]. 3 vols. 4to. Some foxing. Orig. blind-stpd. & gt. embossed mor. (SG. Mar.19; 260) $260
– – **Anr. Copy.** Sm. fo. Disbnd. (SG. May 21; 418) $180
– – **Anr. Copy.** 3 vols. 4to. Cont. hf. leath. (R. Oct.14-18; 1842) DM 850
– – **Anr. Copy.** Orig. leath., gt. cover & inner dentelle. (HK. Nov.18-21; 1423) DM 820
– – **Anr. Copy.** Cont. hf. leath. (R. Oct.14-18; 1843) DM 800
– – **Anr. Edn.** N.Y., [1877-78]. 3 vols. 4to. Some foxing, few pp. loose in 1 vol. Orig. gt. pict. cl. (SPB. Nov.25; 127) $150
– – **Anr. Edn.** Ca. 1880. 5 vols. 4to. Cont. mor.-bkd. cl. gt., slightly worn. (SBA. Oct.22; 272a) *Dupont et Fils.* £60
– – **Anr. Edn.** N.d. 5 vols. 4to. Cont. mor. (SH. Jun.4; 60) *Blanks.* £160
– – **Anr. Copy.** A few ll. slightly soiled. Orig. roan-bkd. cl. (SH. Nov.6; 246) *Kundlatsch.* £130
– – **Anr. Copy.** 3 vols. Some spotting. Orig. cl. (CSK. Apr.24; 41) £90
– – **Anr. Copy.** Vols. 1-5 (of 6). Hf. mor. (P. Jun.11; 68) *Dolcetia.* £65

PICTURESQUE & LANDSCAPE VIEWS of European & American Scenery
Phila., 1852. Lge. ob. 8vo. Slightly soiled, stp. on engraved title, 2 plts. torn, text browned, Cont. linen, spine renewed. (R. Oct.14-18; 1517) DM 850

PICTURESQUE Views of the Principal Seats of the Nobility & Gentry in England & Wales
1787-88. Ob. fo. Some plts. stained. Old cf., worn. W.a.f. as a collection of prints. (BS. Sep.17; 41) £130
– – **Anr. Edn.** L., [1787-88]. Ob. 8vo. Some foxing. Hf. cf., very worn. (SPB. May 29; 343) $125

PICUS de Mirandula, Johannes
- **Heptaplus de Septiformi sex Dierum Geneseos Enarratione.** [Flor.], [Bartholommeo di Libri], ca. 1490. 1st. Edn. Fo. Spaces for some capital initials, & spaces for Hebrew, 4-line initial M supplied in ink on a2, lacks final blank (but

supplied), gutter margins reprd. in sig. a, traces of old staining, some early ink annots. washed faint. Mor. gt., to a Maioli design, gt.-lettered, vell. paste-downs, by Gozzi of Modena, covers bowed. From the collection of Eric Sexton. [BMC VI, 662, Goff P641, HC 13001*] (CNY. Apr.8; 61) $2,400
- **Oratio de Hominis Dignitate.** Trans.:– Elizabeth L. Forbes. [Lexington], [1953]. Fo. Bds., unc., liby. bkplt. (SG. Jan.15; 1) $120

PIEDAD, Francisco de la
- **Teatro Iesuitico.** Coimbra, 1654. 4to. Last lf. reprd., old sig. of ?S. Chivido on title, ptd. book labels of Girardot de Préfond. 18th. C. mor., wide gt. dentelles of fleurons & tassels, gt. fillet & 'drawer-handle' border, spine gt. in compartments, inner gt. floral dentelle between borders, pink silk liners, names of Girardot de Préfond & Renouard, gt., on upr. cover. (SM. Oct.8; 1918) Frs. 8,500

PIERCE, Danny
- **Little No Name.** Kent, Wash., 1959. Ltd. numbered & sigd. Edn. 4to. Buckram, with woodcut of an antelope. (SG. Apr.2; 239) $100

PIERS, Harry
- **Biographical Review.** Boston, 1900. 4to. Orig. embossed leath. (CB. Apr.1; 37) Can. $260
- **Robert Field.** N.Y., Priv. Ptd., 1927. (325). Orig. bds., boxed. (CB. Sep.24; 301) Can. $380
– – **Anr. Copy.** Cl.-bkd. bds. (CB. Apr.1; 111) Can. $300
– – **Anr. Copy.** 4to. Orig. cl.-bkd. bds., unc. & unopened. (CB. Nov.12; 114) Can. $220

PIGAFETTA, Antonio
See–BRY, Theodore de & others

PIGANIOL DE LA FORCE, Jean Aymar
- **Nouvelle Descriptions de la France.** Amst., 1719. 6 vols. Cont. cf. (P. Jan.22; 56) *Balham.* £65
– – **Anr. Edn.** Ill.:– Herisset & others after Delamonce. Paris, 1722. 2nd. Edn. 7 vols. in 8. Maps, hand-cold. in outl. Cont. mott. cf., spines gt. (C. Feb.25; 129) *Shapiro.* £130

PIGAULT-LEBRUN, Guillaume Charles Antoine
- **L'Enfant du Bordel.** Paris, 1800. 2 pts. in 1 vol. 16mo. Mod. Jansenist mor. (HD. Apr.10; 366) Frs. 1,350
[–] **L'Enfant du Bordel.–Les Putains Cloitrées.** Paris; Bicêtre, 1800; 1797. 2 works in 1 vol., 1st. work 2 vols. 18mo. Cont. roan, gt. fillets on spines. (HD. Apr.10; 365) Frs. 3,600

PIGHIUS, Albertus
- **Adversus prognosticatorum vulgus, qui annuas praedictiones edunt, & se astrologos mentiuntur, Astrologiae Defensio.** Paris, 1518 [1519]. 1st. Edn. 4to. Title soiled, minor imperfections affecting a few letters. 19th. C. mor.-bkd. bds. From Honeyman Collection. (S. Nov.10; 2481) *Hill.* £160

PIGNORIUS, Lamentius
- **De Servis, et eorum apud Veteres Ministeriis Commentarius.** Amst., 1674. 12mo. Cont. mott. cf. (PNY. Oct.1; 432) $100

PIGOT, James
- **The Isle of Wight.** Ill.:– Percy Roberts after F. Calvert. 1846. 4to. Plts. hand-cold., tinted litho. frontis. spotted. Mod. hf. mor., orig. red mor. gt. covers bnd. in at end. From the collection of Eric Sexton. (C. Apr.16; 227) *Maggs.* £420

PIGOT, James & Co.
- **British Atlas.** [1840, or later]. Fo. 3 engraved cold. folding maps, 1 torn, 39 full-p. maps, hand-cold. in outl., folding circular map torn in 1 fold, Orig. cl. gt., lacks spine, worn. (S. Mar.31; 262) *Martin.* £380

PIIS, Chevalier de
- **Chansons Nouvelles.** Paris, [1787]. Sm. 18mo. Cont. silk, covers decor. with gold or other col. embroidery, centre floral motif. (HD. Apr.10; 177) Frs. 1,900

PIIS & Barré
- **Théâtre.** L., 1785. 2 vols. 18mo. Red mor. by Cazin. (HD. Apr.8; 288) Frs. 1,100

PIKE, Zebulon Montgomery
– **Exploratory Travels through the Western Territories of North America, comprising a Voyage from St. Louis, on the Mississippi, to the Source of that River, & a Journey through the Interior of Louisiana, & the North-Eastern Provinces of New Spain, Performed in the Years 1805, 1806, 1807.** L., 1811. 1st. Engl. Edn. 4to. Lacks hf.-title, some foxing. Disbnd. (SG. Mar.5; 368) $350
– – **Anr. Copy.** 1 map cropped & with occasional spotting. Hf. leath., upr. bd. detchd. [Sabin 62837] (CB. Sep.24; 181) Can. $500
– **Reise durch die Westlichen Gebiete von Amerika** . . . Trans.:– P.C. Weyland. Weimar, 1813. 1st. German Edn. Cont. bds. [Sabin 62839] (R. Oct.14-18; 1716) DM 520

[PILES, Roger de]–LECLERC, Sebastian
– **Les Premiers Elemens de la Peinture Pratique. –Figures d'Academie pour apprendre à Désiner.** Paris, 1684; [1673]. 1st. work 1st. Edn. 2 works in 1 vol. 12mo. 1st. work: 1 plt. reprd., 2nd. work: lacks text. Cont. cf., worn. (SH. Jun.11; 78) *Sims & Reed.* £75

PILKINGTON, G.
See–**BEDWELL, W.–PILKINGTON, G.**
See–**BUTCHER, Richard–BEDWELL, W. –PILKINGTON, G.**

PILLEMENT, Jean
– **Album containing 237 ornament designs & other engravings.** L. & Paris, ca. 1765-75. Fo. Some discolouration. 18th. C. Fr. cf., worn, jnts. brkn. As a collection of plts, w.a.f. (SPB. Nov.25; 113) $3,700

PILLING, James Constantine
– **Bibliography of the Chinookan Languages. –Bibliography of Eskimo Language.–Bibliography of the Salishan Languages.–Bibliography of the Algonquian Languages.** Wash., 1893; 1887; 1893; 1891. 4 works in 1 vol. Title & last few pp. of 4th. work torn. Crude buckram. (SG. Jan.22; 325) $110
– **Siouan.–Muskhogean.–Iroquoian.–Wakashan. –Athapascan.** Wash., 1887-92. All (100) L.P. 5 works in 1 vol. 4to. Mod. buckram. (SG. Jan.22; 324) $110

PIL'NYAK, Boris
– **Povest' Peterburgskaya [Petersburg Tale].** Ill.:– V. Masyutin. Moscow & Berlin, 1922. Orig. wraps. (SH. Feb.6; 506) *Lemos.* £50

PILOTE (Le) des Iles Britanniques
Paris, ca. 1800. Lge. fo. 29 folding engraved charts, MS. contents list, stained thro.-out, 5 extra maps loosely inserted. Cont. mott. cf. gt., rebkd. & restored, worn. W.a.f. (S. Mar.31; 263) *Potter.* £150

PILSBRY, H.A.
See–**TRYON, George W. Jr. & Pilsbry, H.A.**

PIMENTERL, Manoel
– **Arte de Navegar . . . e Roteiro das Viagens, e Costas Maritimas de Guinee, Angola, Brazil, Inias, e Ilhas Occidentaes, e Orentaes.** Lisbon, 1762. Fo. Stained thro.-out, title soiled. Cont. cf., worn. (SPB. May 5; 404) $300

PINCHAS, Shapiro, of Koretz & Yitzhak, Isaac, of Koretz
– **Kodesh Hilulim-Nofet Zufim.** Lvov, 1864. 1st. Edn. With notes by Joseph Weiss. Hf. cl. (S. Nov.18; 316) *Maggs.* £85

PINCKARD, George
– **Notes on the West Indies . . .** L., 1806. 1st. Edn. 3 vols. Slight spotting. Hf. cf. gt. [Sabin 62893] (SPB. May 5; 405) $275
– – **Anr. Copy.** Cont. cf., rebkd. (SPB. May 5; 406) $150

PINDAR
– **Odes.** Trans.:– R. Toulet. 1818. 4 pts. in 2 vols. Cont. mor., gt. dentelle. (HD. Jun.30; 63) Frs. 1,000
– **Olympia, Nemea, Pythia, Isthmia.** Ed.:– N. Sudorius. Oxford, 1697. Fo. Cont. red mor. gt. Bkplt. & label of Sophia Streatfield. [Wing P 2245] (C. Jul.16; 334) *Maggs.* £260
– **Olympia, Pythia . . . Graece.** Venice, Jan. 1513. 1st. Edn. Old. vell. (HD. Apr.24; 12) Frs. 3,800
See–**CARMINUM Poetarum Novem–PINDAR**

PINDAR, Peter (Pseud.)
See–**WOLCOT, John 'Peter Pindar'**

PINDER, Ulrich
– **Speculum Passionis Domini Nostri Ihesu Christi.** Ill.:– H. Schäufelein, H. Baldung Grien & others. Nuremb., 1507. 1st. Edn. Fo. Lacks last blank lf., title-lf, with cont. owner's note in brown ink, 2 ll. with sm. stains, some ll. wormed, rubricated in parts. 19th. C. leath., blind-tooled, slightly worn, jnts. renewed. (H. Dec.9/10; 1362) DM 19,000

PINE, John
– **The Procession & Ceremonies . . . of the Installation of the Knights Companion . . .–The Tapestry Hangings of the House of Lords.** 1730; 1739. 2 works in 1 vol. Fo. Some plts. slightly spotted in 2nd work. Cont. hf. cf., corners scuffed. Bkplts. of Lord Roseberry & J. Hely-Hutchinson, lately in the collection of Eric Sexton. (C. Apr.15; 76) *Burgess.* £2,300
– **The Tapestry Hangings of the House of Lords.** 1739. Fo. 15 double-p. maps & plts. (of 18). Old sheep, worn. (P. Mar.12; 172) *Burgess.* £1,000

PINEIRO, Juan Bautista
– **Les Descriptions Merveilleuses.** Ill.:– Léonor Fini. Paris, 1973. (35) exemplaires d'artiste, numbered. 4to. Unsewn in orig. wraps., unc., box, slightly worn. Each plt. sigd. by artist. (SH. Nov.20; 47) *Mark Gallery.* £250

PINEL, Philippe
– **A Treatise on Insanity in which are Contained the Principles of a New & More Practical Nosology of Maniacal Disorders.** Trans.:– D.D. Davis. Sheffield, 1806. 1st. Engl. Edn. Orig. bds., spine worn, unc. Pres. copy from the Trans. to Mr. Earnest & photostat of a letter by the Trans. referring to the publication of the book. (S. Jun.17; 680) *Norman.* £200

PINELLI, Bartolomeo
[–] **Il Carnevale di Roma.** Rome, 1820. Ob. fo. Orig. wrap. (S. Oct.20; 184) *Pallai.* £260
[–] **[Cinquanta Vedute dei Costumi Popolari e piu Interessanti di Roma].** [Rome], ca. 1836. Fo. Some plts. slightly soiled. Cont. wraps., torn. (SH. Nov.6; 247) *L'Aquaforte.* £300
– **Costumes & Moeurs.** Carlsrouhe, n.d. 12mo. Hf. mor. (P. Nov.13; 303) *Erlini.* £65
– **Istoria Romana.** Rome, [1820]. Lge. ob. fo. Lr. fore-corners of last few plts. stained. Mod. red hf. mor., retaining orig. cl. covers, gt. spine. (S. Jun.22; 76) *Duran.* £120
– – **Anr. Edn.** Rome, n.d. Ob. fo. Some plts. slightly spotted. Cont. hf. mor. (SH. Oct.9; 95) *Walford.* £70
– **Nuova Raccolta di Cinquanta Costumi Pittoreschi.** Rome, 1816. Ob. fo. Title creased, some spotting. Cont. mor.-bkd. bds., soiled. (CSK. Jan.23; 149) £320
– – **Anr. Copy.** Lr. margins dampstained thro.-out affecting some plts. Orig. wraps., soiled. (CSK. Apr.10; 119) £260
– – **Anr. Copy.** Ob. 4to. Some plts. & frontis. stained. Lacks covers. (CR. Mar.19; 325) Lire 800,000
– **Raccolta de'Costumi di Roma.** Rome, 1819. Ob. fo. Plts. stained, mostly in margins, some spotting & soiling. Disbnd. (SKC. Jul.28; 2612) £200
– **Raccolta di Cinquanta Costumi Pittoreschi.** Rome, 1809. [1st. Edn.?]. Ob. fo. Cont. bds., rebkd. & cornered, new end-papers. (SBA. Mar.4; 112) *Fletcher.* £375
– – **Anr. Copy.** Hf. mor. gt., by Bedford. (S. Nov.24; 238) *Broseghini.* £250
– – **Anr. Copy.** 49 plts. (of 50), lr. outer corner dampstained slightly affecting plts. Orig. wraps., slightly worn, unc. (SKC. Feb.26; 1748) £230
– – **Anr. Edn.** Rome, 1817. 2 works in 1 vol. Ob. 8vo. Slight spotting. Cont. hf. mor., worn. (CSK. Apr.10; 120) £260

PINELLI, Maffeo
– **Bibliotheca . . .** Ed.:– Jacopo Morellio. Ill.:– Francesco Bartolozzi. Venice, 1787. 6 vols. Appendix bnd. in at end of vol. II, MS. catalogue bnd. in at end of vol. II. Cont. mor., triple gt. fillet, spine gt. in compartments with central roundels with border, inner gt. dentelles, pink silk liners. A.L.s. from Jacopo Morelli loosely inserted, MS. note loosely inserted, single ptd. sheet & supp. loosely inserted. (SM. Oct.7; 1468) Frs. 14,500

PINGRÉ, A.G.
– **Cometographie ou Traité Historique et Théorique des Comètes.** Paris, 1783-84. 1st. Edn. 2 vols. 4to. Cont. cf.-bkd. bds. From Honeyman Collection. (S. Nov.10; 2484) *Quaritch.* £360

PINGRET, Edouard
– **Voyage de Louis-Philippe 1er Roi . . .** Paris & L., 1846. Lge. fo. 1 corner dampstained. Publisher's bds. (HD. Feb.27; 202) Frs. 1,000

PINKERTON, John
– **A General Collection of the Best & Most Interesting Voyages & Travels in all Parts of the World.** 1808-14. 17 vols. 4to. Some plts. & maps offset. Cont. cf. (C. Feb.25; 130) *Traylen.* £270
– **A Modern Atlas.** 1815. Fo. Maps hand-cold. in outl., margins slightly soiled, a few maps torn in folds. Disbnd. (S. Jan.27; 526) *Franks.* £350
– **Modern Geography.** L., 1802. 2 vols. 4to. Early cf., 1 cover detchd., some sm. bdg. defects. (KH. Mar.24; 324) Aus. $210

PINTER VON DER AU, Johann Christoph
– **Vollkommener Pferd-Schatz.** Frankfurt, 1664. 3 pts. in 1 vol. including appendix. Fo. 1 plt. torn & reprd., some MS. annots. at end. Cont. vell. bds., lacks ties. (S. Jun.1; 37) *Joseph.* £300

PINTO, F. Mendez
– **Les Voyages Adventureux . . .** Trans.:– Sieur Bernard Figuier. Paris, 1765. 2nd. Edn. 4to. Yellowed. Cont. vell. (HD. Jun.24; 72) Frs. 1,500

PINTO, M.
– **Don Pirlone a Roma.** Torino, 1850. 3 vols. 4to. Lacks last text pp. Hf. cl. with corners. (CR. Mar.19; 326) Lire 200,000

PINTO GUEDES, Rodrigo
– **Echec et Mat a' Impostura do Illustrissima e Excellentissimo Senhor Joao Severiano Maciel da Costa.** Rio de Janeiro, 1830. A few light marginal stains. Mod. qtr. cf. (SPB. May 5; 408) $125

PIOZZI, Hester Lynch
– **Anecdotes of the late Samuel Johnson.** 1786. 1st. Edn. A few ll. slightly spotted. Cont. hf. cf. (SH. Oct.10; 388) *Frazer.* £120
– – **Anr. Copy.** Cont. cf., upr. cover detchd. From the collection of Eric Sexton. (C. Apr.15; 131) *Symonds.* £100
– – **Anr. Edn.** L., 1786. 4th. Edn. 1st. 2 gatherings loose. Cont. cf., worn, jnts. brkn., qtr. mor. gt. s.-c. Autograph marginal annots., etc., by author; from the Prescott Collection. (CNY. Feb.6; 276) $1,700
– **Observations & Reflections made in the course of a Journey through France, Italy & Germany.** L., 1789. 1st. Edn. 2 vols. Cont. mott. cf., rebkd. orig. spines preserved. (PNY. Oct.1; 435) $130

PIPER, John
– **Brighton Aquatints.** Ed.:– Lord Alfred Douglas. 1939. Ob. 4to. Orig. cl.-bkd. bds. Sir Cecil Beaton copy. (SH. Mar.26; 32) *Sherlock.* £155

PIPER, John (Ill.)
See–**INDIA LOVE POEMS**

PIRANESI, Giovanni Battista
– **Il Camp Marzio dell' Antica Roma.** Rome, 1762. Fo. Mod. hf. cf. gt. (P. Jul.2; 2) *Hammond.* £1,150
– **Campus Martius Antiquae Urbis.** Rome, 1762. 1st. Edn. Lge. fo. Cont. hf. vell. (R. Oct.14-18; 1928) DM 5,000
– **Della Magnificenza ed Architettura de' Romani Opera.** Rome, 1761. Fo. Lacks port. of Pope Clement XIII, supp. generally found with this is not present, some tears, reprd. Hf. cf. (SPB. Nov.25; 127a) $2,000
– **Della Magnificenza e d'Architettura de'Romani. –Osservazione . . . sopra La Lettre de M. Mariette . . .** Rome, 1761; 1765. 2 pts. 1 vol. Lge. fo. 1st. pt.: lacks hl (pp. xxix-xxx), 1 title creased & soiled; some ll. a little discold. Cont. hf. russ., marb. bds., covers detchd., worn. (S. May 5; 185) *Cristani.* £750
– **Lettere di Giustificazione scritte a Milord Charlemont e a' di lui agenti di Roma . . . Socio della Real Societa degli Antiquari di Londra intorno la Dedica della sua opera . . .** Rome, 1757. 4to. 4-pp. letter ptd. in Italian & Fr. dtd. Rome 15 Mar., 1758 bnd. at end. Cont. Engl. hf. red mor. & marb. bds. Sir Henry FitzHerbert, Bart., 19th. C. bkplt. (CNY. May 22; 244) $3,500
– **Roman Architecture.** Ed.:– William Young. 1900. 5 vols. Fo. Orig. wraps., slightly soiled, a few tears with loss. (CSK. Jul.3; 136) £50
– **Vasi, Candelabri, Cippi, Sarcofagi, Tripoli, Lucerne ed Ornamenti Antichi.** [Rome], 1778. [1st. Edn.?]. 2 vols. Fo. 1st. engraved title torn with loss, 111 plts. only, all mntd. on linen, some

PIRANESI, Giovanni Battista -contd.
soiling. Hf. mor., worn. W.a.f. (CSK. Jul.24; 101)
£240
– – Anr. Copy. Later leath.-bkd. bds., needs rebdg.
(SG. Oct.9; 191) $1,600

PIRIENNE, H.
– Histoire de Belgique. Brussels, n.d. (200) on
Chiffon d'Arches. 4 vols. 4to. Loose ll. in wrap &
publisher's box. (LM. Nov.8; 126) B.Frs. 7,000

PIRON, Alexis
– Ode à Priape. N.p., n.d. Sm. 12mo. Mod. hf.
mor., spine with gt. fillet, unc. (HD. Apr.10; 367)
Frs. 2,000
– Oeuvres. Ill.:– Charles Nicolas Cochin. Paris,
1758. 1st. Coll. Edn. 3 vols. 12mo. 12-p.
publisher's catalogue in vol. 1, lacks 1-lf. Avis au
relieur, bkplt of Laurence Currie. Cont. red mor.,
triple gt. fillet, spine gt. in compartments, inner gt.
dentelles. Beckford copy. (SM. Oct.8; 1923)
Frs. 2,000
– Oeuvres Choisies. L., 1782. 3 vols. 18mo. Red
mor., probably foreign. (HD. Apr.8; 289)
Frs. 2,600
– – Anr. Edn. Paris, 1810. Sterotype Edn., on vell.,
L.P. 2 vols. 12mo. Cont. cf., spines gt., inner
dentelle. (HD. Apr.9; 542) Frs. 1,200
– Oeuvres Complètes. Amst., 1776. 9 vols. 16mo.
Cont. marb. cf., limp decor. spine. (LM.
Mar.21; 281) B.Frs. 7,000
– – Anr. Edn. Ill.:– Saint-Aubin. Paris, 1776. On
Holland paper. 7 vols. (of 8). Privilege &
approbation ll. in vol. 1. Cont. red mor., triple gt.
fillet, spines gt. in compartments, inner gt.
dentelles, 1 or 2 wormholes in some hinges. (SM.
Oct.8; 1924) Frs. 12,000
– – Anr. Edn. Neuchatel, 1777. 7 vols. Cont. cf.
(SH. Jul.9; 188) Wagner. £55

PISANELLI, Baldassare
– Trattato della Natura de'cibi e del Bere.
Bergamo, 1587. Slight browning & soiling, a few
ll. loose, tear in Cl, lacks A8. 17th. C. limp vell.,
soiled. Bkplt. of Auchincruive liby.; from liby. of
André L. Simon. (S. May 18; 151) Bozzo. £50
– – Anr. Edn. Venice, 1629. Inscr. on title 'Domus
civitatis Plebis/Scolarum Piarum', slight
browning, a little worming, slightly affecting text.
Mod. pol. cf. by Rivière, gt. From liby. of André
L. Simon. (S. May 18; 152) Duran. £60
– – Anr. Edn. Venice, 1649. 12mo. Slight
browning, some worming, affecting text. Cont.
limp vell., soiled. From liby. of André L. Simon.
(S. May 18; 153) Bozzo. £50

PISANO, G.
– Per la Ricostrusione del Pergamo di G. Pisano.
Pisa, 1926. (300) De Luxe Edn. 4to. Publisher's
bds. (CR. Jun.11; 332) Lire 200,000

PISO, Willem
– De Indiae Utriusque Re Naturali et Medica.
Amst., 1658. 1st. Edn. Fo. Engraved title rubbed.
19th. C. hf. mor., worn. From Chetham's Liby.,
Manchester. [Sabin 63029] (C. Nov.27; 324)
Quaritch. £400
– Historia Naturalis Brasiliae. Leyden, Amst.,
1648. 1st. Edn. 2 pts. in 1 vol. Fo. Engraved title
slightly soiled, some dampstaining in 1st. pt. &
1st. pp. of 2nd. pt. Cont. cf., rebkd., covers detchd.
From Chetham's Liby., Manchester. (C.
Nov.27; 323) Tzakas. £400

PISSARRO, L. R. & Venturi, L.
– Camille Pissarro. Paris, 1839. (1000) numbered.
2 vols. 4to. Hf. leath, wraps. bnd. in. (HK.
Nov.18-21; 2858) DM 1,000

PISSARRO, Lucien
See–RICKETTS, Charles & Pissarro, Lucien

PISTOFILIO, Bonaventura
– Oplomachia. Sienna, 1621. 4to. Slightly
browned in parts, last ll. soiled, 2 text ll. reprd.,
lacks sm. port after ded. Cont. leath. (R.
Oct.14-18; 2853) DM 600

PIT, A. & Others
– George Hendrik Breitner. Indrukken en
Biographische Aantekeningen. Amst., ca. 1910.
4to. Orig. decor. cf. gt., by C.A. Lion Cachet.
(VG. Nov.17; 402) Fls. 700

PITATI, Pietro
– Almanach Novum . . . Superadditis annis quinque
supra ultimas hactenus in lucem editas Ioannis
Stoefleri Ephemeridas 1551 ad . . . annum MDLVI.
Venice, 1542. 1st. Edn. 4to. Some staining,
owners' inscrs. on title, old MS. notats. & a

diagram on end-papers. Cont. limp vell., soiled,
lacks ties. From Honeyman Collection. (S.
Nov.10; 2485) Quaritch. £140

PITCAIRN, Archibald & others
– Selecta Poemata.–Poems in English & Latin on
the Archers. Edinb., 1727; 1726. 2 works in 1 vol.
Cont. mor. gt. (SH. Jul.23; 96) Rhys-Jones. £50

PITCAIRN, Robert
– Ancient Criminal Trials in Scotland. Edinb.,
Bannat. Cl. 1833. 5 vols. in 3. Hf. mor. by Rivière.
(CE. Nov.20; 165) £90

PITISCUS, Bartholomeo
– Thesaurus Mathematicus sive Canon Sinuum ad
Radium 1.00000.00000.00000. Frankfurt, 1613.
1st. Edn. Fo. Browned & stained thro.-out, some
ll. wormed in upr. inner margins, owner's entry at
head of title. 19th. C. cf.-bkd. bds., worn, hf. red
mor. case. From Honeyman Collection. (S.
Nov.10; 2488) Barchas. £200
– Trigonometriae sive de Dimensione
Triangulorum libri quinque, item Problematum
Variorum. Augsburg, 1600. 4to. 1st. gathering
loose, title stained & holed in upr. margin, owner's
inscrs. on title. Cont. cf., spine very worn, owner's
inscr. on end pastedown. Bkplt. of John, Earl of
Bute; from Honeyman Collection. (S.
Nov.10; 2486) Quaritch. £260
– Trigonometriae sive de Dimensione
Triangulorum libri quinque, item Problematum
Variorum.–Canon Triangulorum Emendatissimus,
et ad usum Accomodatissimus. Frankfurt, 1612.
3rd. Edn. (1st. work). 2 vols. in 1. 4to. Browned
thro.-out, 1st. lf. of errata reprd. in upr. margin in
2nd. work. Cont. vell., Armorial bkplt. of
Francesco Vargas Macciuca; from Honeyman
Collection. (S. Nov.10; 2487) Degraeve. £90
– Trigonometry. Trans.:– R. Handson. [1642?],
Sm. 4to. Lr. corner of title border defect. &
reprd., stain on A2 with some letters inked over,
slight staining & soiling, MS. insertions at pp. 22
& 23. Mod. cf. The Kenney copy. [NSTC 19968a]
(S. Jul.27; 250) Quaritch. £90

PITMAN, Capt. Charles R.S.
– A Guide to the Snakes of Uganda. Kampala,
1938. Sm. 4to. Orig. cl., soiled. (TA. Jun.18; 42)
£90

PITMAN, N.
See–PALMER, E. & Pitman, N.

PITOU, Louis Ange
– Voyage à Cayenne. Paris, 1805. 1st. Edn. 2 vols.
Cont. cf.-bkd. bds., slightly worn. [Sabin 63057]
(SPB. May 5; 410) $200

PITT, Moses
– The English Atlas. Oxford, Priv. Ptd.,
1680-83-82. 4 vols. Lge. fo. Title vig. in vol. I,
headpieces, initials, plt., & all maps hand-cold.,
on guards thro.-out, map no. 14 of vol. I bnd. in vol.
II, 45 maps in vol. III (numbered to 47, without
nos. 43 & 46), 1 map in vol. IV bnd. inverted,
world map slightly torn at centre with sm. defects.
Cont. mott. cf., covers with blind-tooled panels &
cornerpieces, spines gt. (reprd.). W.a.f. From the
collection of Eric Sexton. [Wing P2306] (C.
Apr.15; 44) Traylen. £13,000
– – Anr. Edn. Oxford, 1680-81-83-82. 4 vols. Lge.
fo. Title vigs., 3 frontis./ports., 175 maps
hand-cold. in outl., 1 plt., cartouches, etc. &
engraved titles fully cold., some maps defect.
Cont. cf., 3 covers detchd., spines defect., very
worn. W.a.f. (S. Mar.31; 289) Burgess. £7,000
– – Anr. Edn. Oxford, 1680-83. Vols. II-IV only.
Fo. With 4 disbnd. maps, with full later colouring.
Cont. cf., upr. cover detchd. on vol. III. As an
atlas, w.a.f. (SPB. Oct.1; 277) $10,000

PITT, William
– Plano Sabio Profferido no Parliamento de
Inglaterra. Trans.:– Throno de Portugal. Lisbon,
1808. Sm. 4to. Some discolouration. Mod. cf.
(SPB. May 5; 411) $100

PITTMAN, Philip
– The Present State of the European Settlements
on the Mississipi [sic]; With a Geographical
Description of that River . . . L., 1770. 1st. Edn. 2
vols. 4to. Owner's inscr. on title. Mod. hf. mor., gt.
spine & borders. Inscr; from liby. of William E.
Wilson; the Littell copy. (SPB. Apr.29; 226)
$2,500

PITT-RIVERS, Gen. Augustus H.L. Fox
– Antique Works of Art from Benin. 1900. 4to.
Orig. wraps., torn. (SH. Apr.9; 112)
Lord Congleton. £130
– – Anr. Copy. Priv. Ptd. 4to. Orig. cl., soiled, liby.
stp. on front-end-paper. (CSK. Mar.13; 115) £85

PIUS II, Pope Aeneas Silvius Piccolomini
– Epistolae in Cardinalatu Editae. Rome, Johannes
Schurener, de Bopardia, 14 Jul. 1475. 4to. A few
cont. marginal notes in ink, staining in outer
margin. Cont. blind-stpd. cf. over wooden bds.,
worn, clasps (1 lacking). [H. 166*; BMC IV p. 57;
Goff P. 710] (C. Apr.1; 71) Rosenthal. £620
– Historia Bohemica. Rome, Johannes S. de
Bopardie & Johannes N.H. de Oppenheym, 10
Jan., 1475. 1st. Edn. 4to. Spaces for initial
capitals, some with guide letters, without the sm.
deaths-head woodcut at colophon found in some
copies, sm. wormhole affecting last 3 ll., faint
traces of dampstaining to fore-margins. Red mor.,
spine gt.-lettered, by Sangorski & Sutcliffe. From
the collection of Eric Sexton. [BMC IV, 56, Goff
P728, HC 255*] (CNY. Apr.8; 143) $4,000
– Oratio . . . Coram Calixto Papa Tertio de
Obedientia Frederici Tertii Imperatoris. [Rome],
[Stephan Plannck], ca. 1488-90. 4to. Mod. bds.
[HC 208*; BMC IV p. 95; Goff P 731] (C.
Apr.1; 72) Crum. £120

PIUS V, Pope
– Extensio, Ampliatio nova Concessio, et
Confirmatio Privilegiorum . . . in Sacros Ordines,
et Congregationes Claustrales. Rome, 1567. On
vell. 4to. Sigd. at end by Papal Notary responsible
for publication, sm. earlier inscr. '1907 P' in lr.
corner of free end-paper, book-label of Chandon
de Briailles. 18th. C. mor., single gt. fillet, spine
gt. with title & single fillets close to bands, inner
gt. dentelles. Pinelli-MacCarthy-Reagh copy.
(SM. Oct.8; 1925) Frs. 3,400

PIVATI, Gianfrancesco
– Nuovo Dizonario Scientifico e Curioso
Sacro-Profano. Ill.:– Giuseppe Filosi. Venice,
1746-51. 1st. Edn. 10 vols. Fo. Some vols. lightly
stained. Orig. paper bds., some vols. slightly
scuffed or stained, unc. From the collection of
John A. Saks. (C. Jun.10; 209) Bozzolato. £750

PIVIDOR, G.
See–CECCHINI, G.B., Pividor, G. & Viola, T.

PIX, Mary
[–] The Spanish Wives. 1696. 1st. Edn. 4to. Some
stains towards end. Recent mor.-bkd. bds. [Wing
P2332] (C. Nov.19; 129) Quaritch. £90

PIZARRO Y ORELLANA, Fernando
– Varones Ilustres del Nuevo Mundo. Madrid,
1639. Fo. All after prelims. browned, sm. holes
affecting 1st. 3 ll., a few side-notes cropped. Later
cf. (SPB. May 5; 413) $1,200
– – Anr. Copy. Some wormholes affecting text, a
no. of ll. browned or stained. Later hf. cf., wormed.
[Sabin 63189] (SPB. May 5; 414) $325

PLAISIR de la Vie (Le)
N.p., [1773]. Sm. 16mo. Lacks title. Cont. decor.
bds., gt. fillet with spangle bands, centre figure on
each cover, watered silk fly-ll. & doubls. (HD.
Apr.10; 178) Frs. 1,350

PLAISIRS de l'Amour (Les), ou Recueil de Contes,
Histoires et Poèmes Galans
Mont Parnasse, 1782. L.P. 3 vols. 12mo. Cont.
limp decor mor., decor. spine, 3 fillets & angle
motifs, by Cazin. (HD. Apr.8; 290) Frs. 2,000

PLAISIRS (Les) de l'Ancien Régime et de Tous les
Âges
L., 1795. 16mo. Hf. mor., spine decor. with
fleur-de-lys, ca. 1860. (HD. Apr.10; 368)
Frs. 3,300

PLAMYA [Flame]
Ed.:– [G.B. Agraev & A.I. Gessen]. St. Petersb.,
1905. Nos. 1-3 only. Fo. No. 1 torn, slightly soiled.
Unbnd. (SH. Feb.5; 182) De la Casa. £55
– – Anr. Run. Ed.:– [G.V. Agraev & A.I. Gessen].
St. Petersb., 1905-06. Nos. 1-4. Fo. Unbnd. (SH.
Feb.5; 112) De la Casa. £65

PLANCHE, James Robinson
– A Cyclopaedia of Costume; Or, Dictionary of
Dress. 1876-79. 1st. Edn. 2 vols. 4to. Cont. tree
cf., gt., rebkd. (TA. Nov.20; 96) £95
– – Anr. Copy. A few slightly affected by
adherence of tissue guards. Mor.-bkd. cl., slightly

soiled, upr. cover of vol. 2 affected by damp at foot. (CSK. Feb.20; 155) £55
-- **Anr. Edn.** 1876. 2 vols. 4to. Orig. mor.-bkd. cl. (SH. Apr.9; 113) *Crete.* £60
- **Lays & Legends of the Rhine.** N.d. Orig. bdg. (DWB. May 15; 372) £60
- **Souvenir of the Bal Costumé.** 1842. 4to. 33 chromolitho. plts. only, lacks plt. list, occasional foxing. Cont. hf. mor., gt. spine. (C. Nov.6; 190) *Marsland.* £90
-- **Anr. Edn.** Ill.:– Coke Smyth. 1843. Disbnd. (DWB. Mar.31; 37) £80
See–TOMKINS, C.F. & Planche, J.R.

PLANCIUS, Janus
See–OLIVI, Giuseppe–PLANCIUS, Janus –DONATI, Vitaliano

PLANCK, Max
- **Das Princip der Erhaltung der Energie. (& 3 other works).** 1887. 1st. Edn. 4 works in 1 vol. Some ll. dampstained at foot, title browned. Cl.-bkd. bds., worn. From Honeyman Collection. (S. Nov.10; 2490) *Lascelles.* £150
- **Zur Theorie des Gesetzes der Energieverteilung im Normalspectrum.** In Verhandlungen der Deutschen Psysicalischen Gesellschaft, Erster [–Zweiter] Jahrgang. Ed.:– Arthur König. Leipzig, 1899-1900. 1st. Edn. 2 Pts. in 1 vol. Cont. hf. cl. (S. Mar.17; 362) *Samueli.* £75
- **Vorlesungen uber Thermodynamik.** Leipzig, 1897. 1st. Edn. A few crayon markings, sig. of G.L. Voermans on title. Orig. cl. From Honeyman Collection. (S. Nov.10; 2491) *Rootenburg.* £140
-- **Anr. Edn.** Leipzig, 1900. Mod. bds. From Honeyman Collection. (S. Nov.10; 2492) *Zeitlin.* £500

PLANISCIG, Leo
- **Andrea Riccio.** Vienna, 1927. 4to. Hf. linen. (HK. May 12-14; 2439) DM 800
- **Collezione Camillo Castiglioni, Catalogo Dei Bronzi.** Vienna, 1923. Ltd. Edn. 4to. Cont. hf. mor. Pres. copy, inscr. by Camillo Castiglioni. (C. Feb.4; 221) *Rosewood.* £320
- **Piccoli Bronzi Italiani del Rinascimento.** Milan, 1930. 4to. Publisher's cl. (CR. Mar.19; 229) Lire 360,000

PLAT or PLATT, Sir Hugh
- [-] **Delights for Ladies.–Closet for Ladies & Gentlewomen.** 1628; [?1636], 2 works in 1 vol. 12mo. 2nd. work: lacks title & C12, 1st 3 ll. slightly frayed, affecting border of 1st lf.; slightly brown or soiled in places. Cont. limp vell. [NSTC 19983.7; STC ?5440] (S. May 5; 297) *Bridge.* £420
The Jewel House of Art & Nature. 1653. 2nd. Edn. 4to. Later cf., worn. [Wing P2390] (SH. Jun.18; 11) *Ball.* £130
-- **Anr. Copy.** Some stains & spots, printing flaw on G4. 19th. C. hf. cf. From Honeyman Collection. (S. Nov.10; 2494) *Blackwell.* £110
-- **Anr. Edn.** 1653. 4to. Some headline rules cropped, lr. margin of R1 defect., sm. piece torn from upr. margins of R2-4, slight browning, owner's inscr. on title. Cont. cf., rebkd., lr. cover a little wormed. Bkplt. of Bibliothèque Hammer, Stockholm; from Honeyman Collection. [Wing P2391] (S. Nov.10; 2495) *Travis.* £150

PLATEA, Franciscus de
- **Opus Restitutionum Usurarum et Excommunicationum.** Venice, Johannes de Colonia & Johannes Manthen, 25 Mar. 1474 [22 Jan., 1477]. 4to. Lacks 1st. & last 2 blanks, initials & chapter-marks supplied in red, in last quire in red or blue, some marginalia, slightly spotted & soiled in places, wormholes, some slightly affecting text, some reprd., some inner margins reprd. slightly affecting some letters, old owner's inscr. at beginning. Mod. antique-style cf. [BMC V, 225, 227; HC 13038, 13040; Goff P755, 758] (S. Apr.7; 289) *Thorp.* £500

PLATH, Sylvia
- **Crystal Gazer & other Poems.** Rainbow Pr., 1971. 1st. Edn., (400) numbered. 4to. Mor., geometric design of raised crumpled mor., extending round spine, enclosing silver kid & palladium-tooled mor. onlays, suede doubls., palladium edges, fitted case, sigd. with initials in lr. cover by Sally Lou Smith [1978]. (SH. Feb.20; 397) *Smith.* £450
-- **Anr. Copy.** Fo. Orig. buckram-bkd. decor. bds., s.-c. (S. Jul.22; 242) *Blackwell.* £50

- **Lyonnesse.** Rainbow Pr., 1971. 1st. Edn., (400) numbered. 4to. Orig. cf.-bkd. decor. bds., s.-c. (S. Jul.22; 243) *Blackwell.* £60
- **Pursuit.** Ill.:– Leonard Baskin. Rainbow Pr., 1973. 1st. Edn., (100) numbered, with orig. sigd. etching. 4to. Orig. mor., s.-c. (S. Jul.22; 244) *Quaritch.* £110

PLATINA or Sacchi, Bartholomaeus
- **De Honeste Voluptate et Valetudine.** Cividale, Gerardus de Lisa de Flandria, Oct. 24, 1480. 4to. Spaces for initial capitals, with guide letters, unrubricated, lacks final blank, minor dampstains to some fore-margins. 19th. C. hf. cf., spine gt.-lettered. From the collection of Eric Sexton. [BMC VII, 1094, Goff P763, HC(Add) 13052*] (CNY. Apr.8; 37) $7,000
-- **Anr. Edn.** Venice, 2 Jan. 1517. Sm. 4to. Inscr. on title, slight dampstaining, a little worming, slightly affecting text, sm. portion torn from last lf. without loss of text. Mod. pol. hf. cf. by Rivière, spine gt., slightly rubbed. From liby. of André L. Simon. (S. May 18; 155) *Birsner.* £160
- **De Vita et Moribus Summorum Pontificum Historia** . . . [Cologne], 1529. Fo. Slight browning. Cont. cf., worn, covers detchd. (S. May 5; 25) *McNulty.* £55
- **De Vita et Moribus Summorum Potificum Historia; De Falso & Vero Bono Dialogi** . . . **De Optimo cive; De Honesta Voluptate** . . . **De Natura.** [Paris], 1530. 3 works in 1 vol. Cont. cf., head & foot of spine & corners worn. (S. Apr.7; 279) *Facchinotti.* £90
- **Vitae Pontificum.** Nuremb., Anton Koberger, Aug. 11, 1481. Fo. Wormhole in text at beginning. 19th. C. mor. Falconer Madan liby. stp., cont. pres. inscr. of Dominus Tilemannus Swedtstorpp. [Goff P769] (C. Jul.16; 287) *Franklin.* £180
- **Von Speisen. Naturlichen und Kreuter wein aller Verstandt.** Frankfurt-am-Main, 1531. 3rd. Edn. in German. Sm. 4to. Some browning & soiling, tear in blank. Mod. vell.-bkd. decor. bds., slightly soiled. From liby. of André L. Simon. (S. May 18; 158) *Bucherkabinet.* £420
See–THEOPHRASTUS–LUSCINIUS, Ottomar –RINGELBERGIUS, Joachimus–MARULUS, Marcus–PLATINA, Bartholomaeus

PLATO
- **Chalcidii** . . . **luculenta Timaei Platonis traductio, &** . . . **explanatio.** Ed.:– Aug. Giustiniani. [Paris], 1520. Fo. 19th. C. mott. cf., worn. From Honeyman Collection. (S. Nov.10; 2496) *Quaritch.* £170
- **Théâtre.** 1831-38. 9 vols. Cont. red hf. mor. (HD. Oct.10; 269) Frs. 1,800
- **Works.** 1578. 3 vols. Parallel Greek & Latin text. 18th. C. cf. tooled & gt. (HSS. Apr.24; 399) £125

PLATT, Sir Hugh
See–PLAT or PLATT, Sir Hugh

PLATTER, Felix
- **De Corporis Humani Structura et Usu.** Basle, 1583. 1st. Edn. Fo. Old vell., liby. bkplt. (SG. Oct.9; 192) $1,600

PLATTES, Gabriel
- **A Discovery of Subterraneall Treasure, viz. of all manner of Mines & Mineralls, from the Gold to the Coale.** [1639]. 1st. Edn. 4to. Cropped thro.-out, last p. soiled. 18th. C. cf.-bkd. marb. bds., hf. red mor. case. From Honeyman Collection. [NSTC 20000; Sabin 63360] (S. Nov.10; 2497) *Norman.* £140

PLAUTUS, Titus Maccius
- **Comedies.** 1694. 1st. Coll. Edn. in Engl. 19th. C. red str.-grd. mor., rebkd. [Wing P2415] (C. Nov.19; 130) *Blackwell.* £90
-- **Anr. Edn.** Trans.:– Bonnell Thornton. 1769-74. 2nd. Edn. vols. 1-2, 1st. Edn. vols. 3-5. Cont. red mor. gt., vol. 5 not quite unif., spines tooled in compartments. Vol. 1 with David Garrick's bkplt. (S. Nov.24; 241) *Quaritch.* £280
- **Comoediae vigi[n]ti.** Venice, 12 Aug. 1518. Fo. Lacks final blank, slight browning & soiling. 18th. C. mott. cf., rebkd. (S. Jan.27; 360) *Symonds.* £240
-- **Anr. Copy.** Lacks title, 2 woodcuts defect. Cf. W.a.f. (BS. Jun.11; 273) £110
-- **Anr. Copy.** Wormhole in 1st. 4 ll., lacks last blank. Recent vell. (CR. Mar.19; 273) Lire 1,000,000
-- **Anr. Edn.** Venice, Jul. 1522. Fairly severe worming (expertly reprd.) in top margins from *6-b6 occasionally touching headlines, some

waterstaining. 17th. C. cf., rebkd. (S. Oct.21; 314) *Ponder.* £80
-- **Anr. Edn.** Ed.:– J. Sambucus. Basle, 1568. 2 pts. in 1 vol. Ruled. Cont. vell. with cover, gt. plaque, oval in centre, decor. spine. MS. bkplts., including that of Claude(?) Joly, Oct. 1645. (HD. Mar.18; 135) Frs. 2,000
- **Comoediae XX [with commentary of Bernard Saracensus & others].** Venice, Aug. 14, 1511. Fo. Sm. hole in title-p., some ll. browned, some slight dampstaining at end. Old vell., tightly bnd., rebkd. with orig. backstrip preserved. Sigs. of Sylvius Pontruici & Bern. Baldi, 18th. C. bkplt. of Giuseppe C. Belforti, bkplt. of John A. Saks. [Goff T95] (CNY. Oct.1; 128) $700
- **Comoediae viginti, olim a Ioachimo Camerario emendatae.** Antw., 1566. 12mo. Later sig. 'Habier' at foot of title. Mid-17th. C. Parisian mor., gt., slightly marked, in cl. folder & mor.-bkd. cl. s.-c. (S. Oct.21; 443) *Symonds.* £95
- **Ex Plauti Comoediis.** [colophon: Venice], [colophon: 1522]. 4to. Title slightly soiled. Early 19th. C. hf. cf. (CSK. Apr.24; 131) £100

PLAW, John
- **Ferme Ornée; Or Rural Improvements.** 1795. 4to. Some soiling. Cont. hf. mor. (CSK. May 15; 120) £100
- **Rural Architecture; or Designs, from the simple Cottage to the decorated Villa.** 1802. 4to. Some spotting, 8-p. publisher's list inserted at end. Cont. hf. cf., worn, unc. (S. Jun.22; 78) *Quaritch.* £230

PLAYFAIR, John
- **Illustrations of the Huttonian Theory of the Earth.** Edinb., 1802. 1st. Edn. Some discolouration. Orig. bds., spine worn & crudely reprd., unc., cl. case. Pres. copy to Sir William Herschel, with his sig. on title; from Honeyman Collection. (S. Nov.10; 2498) *Norman.* £280
-- **Anr. Copy.** Some pencil marginalia. 19th. C. cf.-bkd. bds., hf. red mor. case. From Honeyman Collection. (S. Nov.10; 2499) *Brook-Hitching.* £220

PLAYFAIR, William
- **British Family Antiquity.** 1809-11. 9 vols. Orig. bds., worn & torn. (CE. Jul.9; 138) £130

PLAYFORD, John
- **The Musical Companion.** L., 1673. 1st. Edn. Ob. 4to. Mod. spr. cf. [Wing 2490] (SG. May 14; 177) $1,200

PLEASANT & Delightful History of Jack & the Giants
Nottingham, ca. 1780. 2 pts. in 1 vol. 12mo. 2 ll. with tears. Old hf. roan, worn. (SG. Apr.30; 195) $150

PLEMPIUS, Vopiscus Fortunatus
- **Opthalmographia sive Tractatio de Oculi Fabrica, Actione & Usu.** Amst., 1632. 1st. Edn. 4to. Limp vell. (S. Dec.2; 590) *Maggs.* £170

PLENCK, Joseph Jacob
- **Bromatologia seu Doctrina de Esculentis et Potulentis.–Physiologia et Pathologia Plantarum.** Vienna, 1784; 1794. 1st. Edns. 2 works in 1 vol. Slight browning. Cont. mott. cf. From liby. of André L. Simon. (S. May 18; 159) *Bucherkabinet.* £85
- **Icones plantarum medicinalium.** Vienna, 1788-94. 6 vols. (vols. 1-5, vol. 6 pts. 1-3 of 8) Fo. Lacks plt. 100, 1 plt. from anr. work bnd. after plt. 14, a few stains. Vols. 1-3 hf. roan, vols. 4-5 cont. German hf. cf., unc., vol. 6 cl.-bkd. bds., unc., fascicule wraps. bnd. in. From Collection of Massachusetts Horticultural Society, stps. on plts. (SPB. Oct.1; 156) $8,250

PLESCHEEF, Sergey
- **Survey of the Russian Empire.** Trans.:– James Smirnove. 1792. Lacks 1st. lf. (?blank). Cont. mott. cf. by C. Kalthoeber, with his ticket, gt., spine tooled in compartments. William Beckford's copy, MS. notes 'Fonthill copy' & 'from Lord Gosfords Library'. (S. Nov.24; 242) *Quaritch.* £200

PLESKE, Theodore
- **Birds of the Eurasian Tundra.** Boston, Priv. Ptd., 1928. 4to. Orig. wraps. (CB. Sep.24; 41) Can. $140

PLINIUS, Gaius Secundus, The Elder
- **Bücher und Schrifften von der Natur.** Trans.:– J. Heyden. Ill.:– J. Amman, V. Solis & others. Frankfurt, 1565. 1st. Edn. Fo. Wood bds., partly

PLINIUS, Gaius Secundus, The Elder – Bücher und Schrifften von der Natur. *-contd.*
renewed, cont. blind-stpd. pig spine. (R. Oct.14-18; 133a) DM 3,500
– **Histoire de la Peinture Ancienne, extraite de l'Hist. Naturelle de Pline.** Trans.:– Durand. L., 1725. Fo. Cont. mott. cf. gt. Elden Hall bkplt. (C. Jul.16; 335) *Poole.* £50
– **Histoire Naturelle.** 1829-1838. 20 vols. Cont. red hf. mor. (HD. Oct.10; 270) Frs. 2,200
– **Historia Mundi.** Basle, Mar. 1525. 1st. Edn. of Erasmus' Edn. Fo. Minor staining & other marks at beginning, mostly in margins, lacks final lf. C6 (presumably blank), a few cont. MS. notes in ink, owner's inscr. & quote on title. Cont. blind-stpd. vell. over wooden bds., elaborate roll-tools, worn & stained, especially on lr. cover, corners, head & foot of spine worn, lacks 1 clasp. (C. Apr.1; 161) *Hendrickx.* £110
– **Historia Mundi Naturalis.** Ill.:– J. Ammann, Petrarcameister & others. Frankfurt, 1582. Fo. Some ll. slightly browned & soiled. Red-brown mor. ca. 1860, gt. spine & inner & outer dentelles, gold fillets & gold-stpd. arms on both covers. (HK. Nov.18-21; 261) DM 2,600
– **Historia Naturale . . .** Trans.:– Christophoro Landino. Venice, 30 Oct. 1501. Fo. Some dampstaining, a few ll. slightly defect., reprd., lacks title. Mod. hf. vell. bds., slightly soiled. From liby. of André L. Simon. (S. May 18; 160) *Bennett.* £90
– – **Anr. Edn.** Ed.:– Antonio Brucioli. Trans.:– Christophorus Landinus. Venice, 1543. 4to. Lacks last lf. with device, title reprd. & mntd., some staining. 18th. C. cf., spine defect., hf. red mor. case. From Honeyman Collection. (S. Nov.10; 2502) *Lamm.* £50
– **Historia Naturalis.** Ed.:– Bp. Joannes Andreae. Venice, Nicolaus Jenson. 1472. Lge. Copy. Fo. Lacks folios 1, 357 & 358 (all blank), 1st. p. of Book I decor. with fine illuminated border, at bottom of p. are arms of orig. owner [Granfioni], at beginning of each book is lge. initial in burnished gold on decor. ground, interstices filled with red, green & blue, other initials in alternating red & blue, folio 348 detchd., 10 ll. of Book VII stained in outer margins where some cont. marginalia have been painted over with lead white, a few other marginal stains & minor wormholes at beginning & end. 18th. C. red mor., panel. in gt., bkplt. of Charles & Mary Lacaita, Selham House, Sussex. From Honeyman Collection. [BMC V, 172; HC 13089; Goff P788] (S. Nov.10; 2501) *Thomas.* £9,200
– **Historiae Naturalis Libri XXXVII.** Leiden, 1635. 3 vols. 12mo. Vell. gt. (S. Dec.1; 316) *H. & F.* £60
– **Naturae Historiarum Libri XXXVII.** Lucca, 1518. Fo. Slight browning, slight dampstaining to a few ll., some ll. loose. Cont. Netherlands bdg. of cf. over wooden bds. blindstpd. with 'pineapple' tool in diaper fillets in floral roll, lacks clasps & most of spine. (S. May 5; 441) *Cristani.* £190
See–**BUNTING, H.–PLINIUS, Caius Sedundus**

PLINIUS, Gaius Secundus, the Elder–PLINIUS, Gaius Caecilius Secundus, the Younger
– **Historiae Naturalis Libri XXXVII.–Epistolarum Libri X & Panegyricus.** Ed.:– Jean du Laet (1st work). Leyden, 1635; 1640. Elvevir Edn.; 1st. Elzevir Edn. 3 works in 4 vols. 12mo. Early 19th. C. str.-grd. mor., chain between gt. fillets, decor. spines with gold pointillé background, inside dentelle. (HD. Mar.18; 136) Frs. 1,050

PLON, Eugene
– **Benvenuto Cellini: Orfevre, Medailleur, Sculpteur.** Ill.:– Le Rat & others. 1883. Fo. Old liby. stp. on title. Disbnd. (SG. Mar.12; 64) $190

PLOT, Robert
– **The National History of Oxfordshire.** Oxford, [1677]. Fo. Cont. mott. cf. (SH. Oct.9; 19) *Burgess.* £260
– – **Anr. Edn.** Oxford, 1705. 2nd. Edn. Fo. Folds reinforced along versos, slight spotting & staining. Cont. cf., crudely rebkd. (CSK. Nov.14; 5) £120
– **The Natural History of Staffordshire.** Oxford, 1686. [1st. Edn.]. Fo. Folding map mntd. on linen, lacks list of subscribers, title reprd. with 1 letter in facs., dupl. stp. of Trinity College, Camb., on final lf. 19th. C. red mor., gt. [Wing P2588] (CSK. Jun.26; 28) £420
– – **Anr. Copy.** Title slightly stained. 19th. C. diced cf. (C. Feb.25; 53) *Marlborough.* £380
– – **Anr. Copy.** 2 plts. with short tears, dampstain to lr. corner thro.-out. Cont. cf., rebkd. From the collection of Eric Sexton. (C. Apr.16; 332) *Burgess.* £260
– – **Anr. Copy.** 34 (of 37) engraved plts., lacks 'Armes omitted' (as usual), folding engraved map linen-bkd., 1 plt. damaged, some other plts. reprd., title creased, corner of 1 lf. reprd. Spr. cf., rebkd. (LC. Jun.18; 167) £160
– – **Anr. Copy.** Cont. panel. cf., rebkd. (TA. Nov.20; 428) £90

PLOTINUS
– **Operum Philosophicorum Omnium . . .** Ed.:– Marsilius Ficinus. Basle, 1580. Fo. Slightly dampstained in parts. 18th. C. cf., rebkd. (S. May 5; 46) *Poole.* £100

PLUCHE, Noel Antoine
[–] **Schau-Platz der Natur.** Vienna & Nuremb., 1750-54. 9 vols. including plt. vol. 200 engraved plts. (of 203, lacks pt. 2, plts. 14 & 16, pt. 4, plt. 4), 1 torn apart & loosely inserted. Cont. hf. cf. (S. Mar.17; 258) *Frick.* £160
[–] – **Anr. Edn.** Frankfurt ,& Leipzig, 1764-66. Vols. II & IV-VII (of 8). Vol. IV lacks hf. plt., vol. VII lacks 1 plt. & 1 plt. holed, lightly browned in parts, especially text. Cont. hf. leath. (H. May 21/22; 241) DM 680
– [–] **Le Spectacle de la Nature.** The Hague, 1743-53. 8 vols. Lightly browned in parts, some stains, owner's mark on title. Cont. cf., gt. spine, slightly worn. (H. Dec.9/10; 397) DM 900

PLUKENET, Leonard
– **Phytographia (in 4 pts.), with Almagestum Botanicum, Almagesti Botanici Mantissa, & Almatheum Botanicum.** 1691-1705. 1st. Edns. 7 works bnd. in 5 vols. Fo. & 4to. Lacks 8 prelims. in the 'Mantissa', titles dust-soiled. 19th. C. hf. mor. or cf. (rebkd., non-unif.). From Chetham's Liby., Manchester. (C. Nov.27; 325) *Taylor.* £680

PLUMIER, Charles
– **L'Art de Tourner, ou de faire en perfection toutes sortes d'ouvrages au tour.** Paris, 1701. Fo. Slight browning, Jombert's imprint pasted over orig. Lyon imprint, but date unchanged. Cont. cf., rebkd., old spine preserved., monog. of Earl of Essex gt. on upr. cover. From Honeyman Collection. (S. Nov.10; 2504) *McKittrich.* £400
– – **Anr. Edn.** Paris, 1749. Fo. 2 plts. bnd. inverted, plt. 23 torn & reprd., some margins discold. 19th. C. hf. mor. From Chetham's Liby., Manchester. (C. Nov.27; 327) *Taylor.* £440
– – **Anr. Copy.** Cont. cf., worn & corroded. (SG. Sep.25; 255) $140
– – **Anr. Copy.** Hf. cf. (VG. Nov.18; 1327) Fls. 750
– **Description des Plantes de l'Amerique.** Paris, 1693. 1st. Edn. Fo. Hf.-title soiled, plts. slightly discold., F3 & Ii in uncancelled state(?). 19th. C. hf. mor. From Chetham's Liby., Manchester. (C. Nov.27; 326) *Cucchi.* £420
– **Nova Plantarum Americanarum Genera.** Ill.:– P. Giffart after author. Paris, 1703. 1st. Edn. 4to. Sm. tear in A1, partly erased owner's inscr. on title. Cont. cf., gt. spine., worn, armorial bkplt., hf. red mor. case. From Honeyman Collection. [Sabin 63457] (S. Nov.10; 2505) *Zeitlin.* £320
– **Plantarum Americanarum facsiculus Primus [–Decimus].** Ed.:– Joannes Burmann. Amst., 1755-60. 10 pts. in 1 vol. Fo. 1 plt. slightly torn, affecting plt., linnean names added in pencil. Cont. cf., reprd. & rebkd. [Sabin 63459] (S. Dec.3; 1102) *Asher.* £950
– **Traité des Fougères de l'Amérique.** Paris, 1705. Fo. Plts. slightly discold. 19th. C. hf. mor. From Chetham's Liby., Manchester. (C. Nov.27; 328) *Junk.* £580

PLUS VIELLE HISTOIRE (La) DU MONDE, mise en images par Françoise
Paris, ca. 1930. Ob. 4to. Outer pp. forming cover, slightly soiled & stained. (SH. Mar.19; 258) *Schiller.* £65

PLUTARCH
– **De Tranquillitate.** Trans.:– Guillielmo Budeo. Rome, 1510. Vell. (P. Dec.11; 114) *Marlborough.* £65
– **De Virtute Morali.** Trans.:– Andreus Mattheus Acquaviva. Naples, Jun. 1526. Fo. Lacks A1, quires B-D, 2A1, M3-4, Z2-3, &1, &4, the last blank, portion of lr. inside corner in 1st. quire lacking, 1st. lf. & last few quires stained & wrinkled, several other ll. stained. Disbnd. in cl. box. (C. Apr.1; 73) *Manners.* £750
– **Liues of the Noble Grecians & Romaines . . .** Trans.:– [Sir Thomas North]. 1603. 3rd. Edn. 2 pts. in 1 vol. Fo. Slight dampstaining, a few sm. holes, slightly affecting text, lacks 1st. & final blanks, 17th. C. sig. on recto of 3S5, a few MS. lines of verso on other ll. 17th. C. cf., worn. [NSTC 20068] (S. Sep.29; 65) *Parker.* £80
– – **Anr. Edn.** Trans.:– John Dryden. Ill.:– Van der Gucht. 1727. 8 vols. Cont. panel. cf. (SBA. Jul.22; 27) *Ghani.* £55
– – **Anr. Edn.** Trans.:– J. & W. Langhorne. 1792. 6 vols. Mott. cf., decor. spine gt. (CE. Jul.9; 164) £80
– – **Anr. Edn.** Nones. Pr. 1929-30. (1050). 5 vols. 4to. Orig. cl. (SH. Jan.30; 479) *Maggs.* £95
– – **Anr. Copy.** Orig. cl. (SH. Jan.30; 480) *Curtis.* £90
– – **Anr. Copy.** Fo. Buckram, partly untrimmed. (SG. Jan.15; 69) $120
– – **Anr. Copy.** Buckram. (VA. Aug.29; 114) R. 120
– **Oeuvres Complètes.** Ed.:– L'Abbé Brotier. Trans.:– J. Amiot. Ill.:– Borel, de Fraine, Le Barbier & others. Paris, 1783-87. On papier de Hollande. 22 vols. Some browning. Cont. cf., gt. roulette border, limp decor. spines, sm. faults. (HD. Apr.24; 92) Frs. 4,700
– – **Anr. Edn.** Ill.:– Borel, Le Barbier, Marillier & others. Paris, 1801-05. 25 vols. 131 wood engrs. & 22 ills. from 1783-1805 edn. Cont. grained roan, decor. spines. (HD. Feb.18; 58) Frs. 4,100
– **Les Oeuvres Morales et Meslées–Les Hommes Illustre Grecs & Romains.** Ill.:– Boulander. Paris, 1645. Armorial bkplts., ribbed spines, ties, soiled & a few worm holes. (CE. Apr.23; 132) £120
– **Opuscula LXXXXII, Index Moralium omnium [Greek]** Venice, 1509. Fo. Cont. London bdg. of blind-stpd. cf. on wooden bds. [by John Reynes?], rebkd., upr. cover reprd. (C. Jul.15; 225) *Dimakarakos.* £150
– **The Philosophie.** Trans.:– Philemon Holland. 1603. 1st. Edn. in Engl. Fo. Slight browning & soiling, some worming, occasionally affecting text. Cont. cf., gt., rebkd., old spine preserved, slightly worn. [NSTC 20063] (S. Sep.29; 66) *Maggs.* £150
– **Regum & Imperatorum Apophtegmata Raphaele Regio Interprete . . .** Venice, 1508. 1st. Edn. 4to. Cont. bdg., worn, strengthened. (DS. May 22; 812) Pts. 20,000
– **Les Vies des Hommes Illustres.–Decade contenant les Vies des Emereurs.–Les Oeuvres Morales et Meslées.** Ill.:– After Marillier & others. Paris, 1567; 1567; 1574. 6 vols.; 1 vol.; 7 vols.; together 14 vols. 'Hannibal & Scipio' with separate title bnd. at end of Vol. 6 of 1st. work.; 3rd. work includes the 'Table, rubricated, 22 plts. from 1783 Edn. inserted. Late 18th. C. Fr. red mor., gt. Charles Nodier copy with bkplt. (SM. Oct.8; 2416) Frs. 29,000
– **Les Vies des Hommes Illustres . . .–Les Oeuvres Morales et Meslées . . .** Trans.:– Jacques Aymot. Paris, 1567 [1574]. 3rd Edn.; 2nd. Edn. 2 works in 12 vols. Ruled. Old vell. with covers. (HD. Mar.18; 137) Frs. 3,600
– **Vitae Illustrium Virorum.** Trans.:– Alfonso de Palencia. Seville, Paulus de Colonia, Johannes Pregntzer, Magnus Herbst & Thomas Glockner. 2 Jul. 1491. Vol. II only (of II). Fo. Lacks title & end blank, outer margins of folios 136 & 176 extended, slight worming affecting text. 18th. C. cf., some wear. [Goff P837; H 13133] (SPB. Nov.25; 66) $250
– – **Anr. Edn.** Venice, Bartholomaeus de Zanis, Jun. 8, 1496. Fo. Title-p. slightly stained & with a sm. tear reprd., minor marginal worming to some 50 ll., sm. wormhole in quires b & c affecting some letters, some ll. browned. Stiff vell. [BMC V, 432, Goff P798, H 13130] (CNY. Oct.1; 121) $1,400

PLUVINEL, Antoine de
– **L'Instruction du Roy en l'Exercice de Monter à Cheval.** Ill.:– Crispin van de Pas. Paris, 1625. 2nd. Edn. (1st. with this title). Fo. 1 dupl. port. of Roger de Bellegarde loosely inserted from anr. copy, other of Roger de Bellegarde pasted over a dupl. of port. of Louis XIII, lacks plts. 48BBB, 49EEE & also 4*, 1 loosely inserted from anr. copy, 2 early MS. notes. 18th. C. mor., triple gt. fillet, spine gt. in compartments, inner gt. dentelles. Contains plts. of Maneige Royal of 1623, with revised text. (SM. Oct.8; 1928) Frs. 19,000

– – **Anr. Edn.** Ill.:– M. Merian. Frankfurt, 1628. 1st. Edn. Fo. Fr.-German parallel text, text browned, some plts. stained lightly in upper corners, 15 more heavily, 1 plt. with sm. tear. Cont. vell., gt. borders & arms, soiled, upr. cover with sm. defect., new ties. (H. May 21/22; 220) DM 6,000

– – **Anr. Edn.** Paris, 1629. Fo. A few splits in folds of double-p. plts., 2 plts. of harness slightly defect., some ll. slightly soiled, stained or loose. Cont. blind-stpd. cf. (S. Jun.23; 240) *Goldschmidt*. £1,000

– **Maneige Royal.** Brunswick, 1626. 3rd. Edn. Fo. Ptd. title with engraved arms torn & bkd., engraved title with lr. margin renewed & tears reprd., 2 ll. with engraved ports. torn, 6 plts. stained, 7 with tears, few wormed. 18th. C. sheep., spine gt. (CNY. May 22; 246) $2,000

PLUVINEL, Antoine de & Charnizay, Rene Marou de
– **L'Exercice de monter à Cheval, ensemble le Maneige Royal.** Paris, 1660. All plts. with borders slightly cropped. Cont. cf., gt. spine. (C. Feb.25; 18) *Way*. £100

PLYMOUTH COMPANY
– **A Patent for Plymouth in New-England; To which is annexed, Extracts from the Records of that Colony.** Boston, 1751. 1st. Edn. 4to. Stitched, unc., as issued. Document corrected & sigd. in MS. by Josiah Cotton. [Sabin 59034] (SPB. Jun.22; 116) $400

POACHER'S Progress . . . from paintings by C. Blake
[L.], [1826]. Ob. fo. Lacks ptd. title, prospectus mntd. at beginning. Red hf. mor. (SPB. Oct.1; 94) $3,300

POCOCK, J.I.
See–COLLYER, J.N. & Pocock, J.I.

POCOCKS, Richard
– **Beschreibung des Morgenlandes u. einiger anderer Länder.** Trans.:– Chr. E.V. Windheim & v. Mosheim. Erlangen & Leipzig, 1754-55. 1st. German Edn. 2 vols. 4to. Slightly soiled, wormed in fold, some worming & defects. Cont. leath. gt. (HK. Nov.18-21; 1322) DM 700
– **Description of the East, & some other Countries.** 1743-45. 1st. Edn. 2 vols., 2 pts. in vol. II. Fo. 1 plt. cropped at head, light staining to outer edges of a few plts., slight browning. Cont. cf., spines gt., Emile Hoet's bkplt. (S. Nov.4; 609) *Cawthorn*. £380
– – **Anr. Edn.** 1743-45. 2 vols. (3 pts.) in 3. Vol. 1 lacks 3 plts. & with extra plt. not called for. Cont. mott. cf. gt. W.a.f. (C. May 20; 162) *Taylor*. £280

PODEWILS, O. Chr.
– **Friedrich der Grosse und Maria Theresia.** Ed.:– C. Hinrichs. Berlin, 1937. (100) privilege Edn. on Bütten. 4to. Orig. mor. gt., silk end-papers & doubl., by Spamer. (H. Dec.9/10; 1817) DM 620

POE, Edgar Allan
– **Arthur Gordon Pym** [Armenian]. Trans.:– Father E. Chakejian. Vienna, 1857. 12mo. Wraps. (SG. May 14; 178) $350
– **The Bells & Other Poems.** Ill.:– Edmund Dulac. [1912]. (750) numbered, sigd. by artist. 4to. Orig. parch. gt., discold., lacks ties. (S. Jul.31; 212) *Jones*. £110
– – **Anr. Copy.** Vell., s.-c. (HSS. Apr.24; 208) £80
– **Les Cloches, et Quelques Autres Poèmes.** Trans.:– J. Serruys. Ill.:– Edmund Dulac. Paris, 1913. 4to. Cont. hf. mor., orig. wraps. bnd. in. (S. Jul.31; 213) *Hughey*. £70
– – **Anr. Edn.** Trans.:– J. Serruys. Ill.:– Edmund Dulac. 1913. (400) numbered. 4to. Cont. hf.-mor., orig. wraps. bnd. in. (SH. Dec.10; 190) *Aubrée*. £130
– – **Anr. Copy.** 4to. Spine decor. with onlays, slightly worn, by Samblanx. (S. Jul.31; 206) *Subunso*. £85
– **The Conchologist's First Book: A System of Testaceous Malacology.** Phila., 1840. 2nd. Edn. Tall 12mo. Orig. roan-bkd. ptd. bds., covers & blanks loose, spine cracked, minor spotting at sides. (PNY. Mar.26; 259) $150
– **Eureka.** N.Y., 1848. 1st. Edn. 12mo. 16 pp. of advts. Orig. cl., rebkd. Inscr. by publisher. (SG. Nov.13; 555) $210

'– – **Anr. Copy.** Ends of spines & corners worn, qtr. mor. s.-c. From the Prescott Collection. (CNY. Feb.6; 279) $140
– **Mesmerism 'In Articulo Mortis'.** L., 1846. 1st. Separate Edn. 12mo. Occasional discolouration. Sewn as iss., cl. folding case. From the Prescott Collection. (CNY. Feb.6; 278) $450
– **Les Poèmes.** Trans.:– Stéphane Mallarmé. Ill.:– Edouard Manet (port. & fleuron). Brussels, 1888. 1st. Edn.; (850); (800) on Holland. Jansenist mor. by L. Couard, spine with raised bands, watered silk doubls. & end-papers, wraps. preserved. (HD. Jun.25; 372) Frs. 1,000
– **The Poems.** Ill.:– William Heath Robinson. 1900. A few ll. slightly spotted. Orig. pict. cl. gt., spine slightly torn. (SBA. Jul.14; 424) *Subunso*. £50
– **The Raven & other Poems.** N.Y., 1845. 1st. Edn., (750). 12mo. With 12 pp. of advts. at end. Orig. ptd. wraps., qtr. mor. s.-c. From the Prescott Collection. (CNY. Feb.6; 277) $24,000
– – **Anr. Edn.** Ill.:– Doré. 1883. Fo. Orig. cl. (SH. May 21; 259) *Le Clercq*. £55
– **Silence.–Ombre.–L'Ile de la Fée.** Ill.:– Jean Bruller. 1942. No. 1. Cf. by Cretté. Orig. ills., many orig. study sketches. (HD. Oct.10; 202) Frs. 3,800
– **Tales.** N.Y., 1845. Clean tear in title reprd., some browning, advts. at back. Mor., covers detchd., orig. bdg. preserved at end. (CSK. Mar.13; 148) £100
– **Tales of Mystery & Imagination.** Ill.– Harry Clarke. 1919. 4to. Orig. pict. cl., d.-w. worn. (SH. Mar.26; 133) *Ayres*. £60
– – **Anr. Edn.** Ill.:– Harry Clarke. [1923]. 4to. Cl., preserving orig. pict. label. (SH. Dec.10; 134) *Hancock*. £68
– – **Anr. Edn.** Ill.:– Harry Clarke. 1928. 4to. Orig. cl. (SH. Mar.26; 135) *Hatchard*. £55
– – **Anr. Edn.** Ill.:– Arthur Rackham. 1935. 1st. Trade Edn. 4to. Orig. cl., d.-w. (SH. Mar.27; 444) *Fletcher*. £80
– – **Anr. Copy.** Cl. gt., d.-w. Raymond M. Sutton Jr. copy. (SG. May 7; 236) $450
– – **Anr. Edn.** Ill.:– Arthur Rackham. [1935]. (460) numbered, sigd. by artist. 4to. Orig. parch., s.-c. (CSK. Feb.13; 180) £380
– – **Anr. Copy.** Vell. gt., partly unc. & unopened. Raymond M. Sutton Jr. copy. (SG. May 7; 235) $1,500
– – **Anr. Edn.** Ill.:– Harry Clarke. L. & N.Y., n.d. Orig. cl. (CSK. May 22; 131) £60
– **Tales & Poems.** 1884. 4 vols. Hf. mor. gt., by Bickers & Son. (P. Mar.12; 36) *Hemsworth*. £110
– **The Works.** N.Y., [1884]. Ltd. L.P. Edn. (315) numbered. sigd. by publisher (Amontillado Edn.). 8 vols. Crushed mor., gt.-panel. backs, gt.-ruled covers, silk place-markers, by Morrell, 3 vols. rebkd. preserving orig. backstrips. Bkplts. of M.C.D. Borden; extra-ill. with etched plts. on mntd. India-proof, by F.S. Church & others. (PNY. Mar.26; 261) $425
– – **Anr. Edn.** Ed.:– E.C. Stedman & George E. Woodberry. Ill.:– Albert Edward Sterner & Aubrey Beardsley. Chic., 1894-1895. (250) numbered on L.P. 10 vols. Orig. vell. with lge gt. floral designs, unc., ex-liby. (SG. Aug.7; 380) $350
– – **Anr. Copy.** Unopened. (SG. Sep.4; 383) $325
– **Complete Works.** N.Y., n.d. Tamerlane Edn., (300). 10 vols. Crimson mor. elab. gt., floral inlays, mor. doubls., dentelles. (SPB. Nov.25; 479) $3,100
– – **Anr. Copy.** Plts. in 2 states. Hf. mor. gt. (SPB. Nov.25; 480) $1,500

POE, Edgar Allan–DANA, Richard Henry, Jnr. –DOUGLAS, George Norman
– **The Narrative of Arthur Gordon Pym.–Two Years before the Mast.–South Wind.** Ill.:– R. Clarke (1st. work); H.A. Mueller (2nd. work) & Carlotta Petrina. Ltd. Edns. Cl., 1930; 1947; 1932. Each (1500) numbered, & sigd. by artist. 3 works in 3 vols. 4to. Various bdgs., in orig. boxes (all worn). (SG. Jan.15; 336) $100

POEDINOK [Duel]
Ed.:– [V.M. Onigirsky). St. Petersb., 1906. Nos. 1-3. 4to. No. 3 slightly torn. Unbnd. (SH. Feb.5; 113) *De la Casa*. £100

POELLNITZ, Carl Ludwig, Baron von
[–] **Les Amusemens de Spa.–Perspectives ou Vues des Fontaines de Spa.** Amst., 1745; 1734. 2 works,

together 3 vols. (2 & 1). Cont. cf., rebkd. (C. May 20; 45) *Crow*. £65

POEPPIG, Eduard
– **Reise in Chile, Peru und auf dem Amazonenstrome.** Leipzig, 1835. 2 vols., without atlas. 4to. Cont. hf. cf., reprd. (SPB. May 5; 415) $100
– – **Anr. Edn.** Leipzig, 1835-36. 3 vols. including atlas. 4to. & lge. fo. Text in cont. hf. cf., atlas in orig. wraps. (C. Jul.15; 119) *Burton-Garbett*. £1,300

POESIA: IL FUTURISMO
Ed.:– F.T. Marinetti. Milan, 1909. Anno V, nos. 3-6 in 1. Ob. 4to. Orig. pict. wraps., unc. Declaration of Futurism & editorial note loosely inserted. (SH. Nov.21; 459) *Tate Gallery*. £50

POESIAS DE GUERRA I. Documentos Históricos
N.d. 4to. Mor., orig. wraps. (DS. Apr.24; 981) Pts. 20,000

POESIES Satirique du XVIIIe Siècle
Ill.:– Marillier. L., 1782. 2 vols. 18mo. Marb. cf., by Cazin. 2 frontis. sigd. by artist, piece addressed by Dorat to Mademoiselle Raucourt. (HD. Apr.8; 291) Frs. 600

POETAE GRAECI Principes Heroici Carminis . . .
Ed.:– H. Stephanus. [Geneva], 1566. 2 vols. in 1, 4 Pts. Fo. 19th. C. russ., spine defect., covers detchd. (S. Nov.25; 539) *Karakos*. £120

POETICAL REGISTER, The, & Repository of Fugitive Poetry, for 1801-1811
Ed.:– [Thomas Park]. L., 1802-14. 1st. Edns., but for Vol. I: 2nd. Edn. 8 vols. (All publd.?). 12 mo. Cont. marb bds., roan backs & tips. 2 vols. inscr. pres. copies to 'The Rev. J. Whitehouse' from ed., each with armorial bkplt. & sig. of J. Lee Colworth. (PNY. Mar.26; 263) $240

POETS
– **The British Poets.** Edinb., 1773. Vols. III-XXIX, XXXI-XLII. (39 vols.). 12mo. Some slight browning. Cont. cf., spines gt. Bkplt. of John Randall. (S. May 5; 419) *Byrne*. £75
– – **Anr. Edn.** 1822. 100 vols. Cont. cf., spines soiled. (SH. Jun.11; 205) *Wade Gallery*. £140
– – **Anr. Edn.** 1890-95. Aldine Edn. Orig. cl., soiled. (SH. May 28; 12) *Walford*. £70
– **Poets of Great Britain . . . from Chaucer to Churchill.** Ed.:– John Bell. L. & Edinb., 1782-78-88-1793. Various Edns. 109 vols. 12mo. Cont. tree cf., covers with gt. Greek key geometric borders, the spines with lyres stpd. in gt., in 2 mod. cf.-boxes in the form of 4 lge folio's labelled 'Bell's British Poets'. (CSK. May 8; 61) £1,000

POETS & ETCHERS
Ill.:– A.F. Bellows, S. Colman, H. Farrer, & others. Boston, 1882. Sm. fo. Gt.-pict. cl., partly unc. (SG. May 21; 420) $190

POEYDAVANT, Abbé
– **Histoire des Troubles Survenus en Béarn dans le 16e et la Moitié du 17e Siècles.** Pau, 1819. 3 vols. Glazed hf. cf. (HD. Jun.29; 202) Frs. 1,300

POGGIO, Iacopo
– **Historia Florentina.** Venice, 8 Mar. 1476. 1st. Edn., L.P. Fo. Lacks final blank, spaces left for rubrication of initials, some with guide letters. 18th. C. mor., triple gt. fillet, spine gt. in compartments, inner gt. dentelles. [HC (+Add) 13172*; BMC V 215; Goff P. 873] (SM. Oct.8; 1929) Frs. 10,000

POGGIUS, Braccolinus Florentinus
– **Orationes Invectivae Epistolae Descriptiones quaedam: et Faceciarum Liber.** [Strasb.], 11 Feb. 1511. Fo. Title strengthened in margins, slightly damp-stained or soiled in places, some wormholes, slightly affecting text. 19th. C. vell. bds., d. (S. Apr.7; 280) *Dr. Kubicek*. £80
– **Reise im Innern von Brasilien.** Vienna, 1832-37. 3 vols. including atlas vol. 4to. & lge. fo. Text in cont. hf. cf., atlas in orig. ptd. bds. (C. Jul.15; 120) *Quaritch*. £1,400

POHL, Johann Baptist Emanuel
– **Plantarum Brasiliae.** Ill.:– after Wilhelm Sandler. Vienna, [1826-] 1827-31 [-33.]. 2 vols. Fo. A few text ll. spotted. Hf. mor. gt. From collection of Massachusetts Horticultural Society, stps. on plts. (SPB. Oct.1; 157) $7,000

POHLIG, J.W.
– **Album der Herrschaftlichen Landsitze und Schlösser im Kaiserthum Oesterreich.** Ill.:– W.

POHLIG, J.W.-*contd.*
Rau. Pohlig, 1852-53. Pts. 1-111 in 1 vol. Ob. fo. Cont. linen, cover & spine loose. (R. Oct.14-18; 1958) DM 2,800

POINSETT, Joel R.
- Notes on Mexico. 1825. Folding map mntd. on linen. Mod. cf.-bkd. bds. (SH. Nov.7; 389) *Porruas.* £90

POINTES, Sieur de
A Genuine & Particular Account of the Taking of Carthagena by the French & Buccanneers, in 1697. Ill.:– P. Harrison (folding plan). L., 1740. Lf. of Advts., with plan of Carthagena. Mod. three qtr. buckram. [Sabin 63704] (SG. Jan.8; 364) $220

POIRET, Paul
- Les Choses de Paul Poiret Vues par Georges Lepape. N.p., 1911. Ltd. Edn. 4to. Publisher's decor. cl. s.-c. Inscr., sigd. (HD. Dec.5; 162) Frs. 6,500
- Deauville. Ill.:– Maccard after Van Dongen. Paris, 1931. (12) on Jap. Fo. Publisher's s.-c. Each plt. sigd. by artist. (HD. Dec.5; 163) Frs. 5,500
- - Anr. Copy. (297) on velin d'Arches. In sheets, pict. cover. hf. cl. publisher's portfo. (HD. Feb.18; 229) Frs. 2,000

POISSON, S.D.
- Traité de Mécanique.-Nouvelle Théorie de l'Action Capillaire. Paris, 1811; 1831. 1st. Edns. 2 vols. + 1. 8vo. & 4to. 1st. work: some ll. stained, orig. wraps, very worn, 1 cover missing, stitching loose, unc., 2nd. work: lacks port. (?), a few ll. stained in lr. margins, some spotting, orig. wraps., worn, unc., hf. red mor. case. From Honeyman Collection. (S. Nov.10; 2507) *Zeitlin.* £70

POITIER DE COURCY, Pol.-RECUEIL DES BLASONS DE BRETAGNE
- Nobiliaire et Armorial de Bretagne. Ill.:– Alexandre de la Bigne. Rennes, 1890; 1895. (320) numbered & sigd. by author. 3 vols.; 1 vol. 4to. Etude Historique by Arthur de la Borderiei. Hf. cf., 4 decor. spine raised bands, arms. (LM. Nov.8; 165) B.Frs. 14,000

POKORNY, A.
See-ETTINGSHAUSEN, C. von & Pokorny, A.

POLACCO, Giorgio-FRANCISCUS, Torrensis
- Anti-Copernicus Catholicus, seu de Terrae Statione, et de Solis Motu, contra Systema Copernicanum, Catholicae Assertiones.-De Sola Lectione Legis, & Prophetarum Iudaeis cum Mosaico Ritu, & Cultu Permittenda. Venice; Rome, 1644; 1555. 1st. Edn. (1st. work). 2 works in 1 vol. 4to. Marginal staining in 2nd. work. Vell. bds., hf. red mor. case. Bkplt. of Gilbert Redgrave, with his notes on fly-lf.; from Honeyman Collection. (S. Nov.10; 2508) *Hill.* £850

POLAIN, Louis
- Catalogue des Livres Imprimés au Quinzième Siècle des Bibliothèques de Belgique. Brussels, 1922. On Hollande. 4 vols. Orig. bdg. (LM. Mar.21; 53) B.Frs. 10,000
- - Anr. Edn. Brussels, 1932. Sewed. (LM. Mar.21; 52) B.Frs. 9,000

POLAR SCENES, exhibited in the Voyages of Heemskirk & Barenz to the Northern Regions etc. 1823. Orig. bds. (TRL. Dec.10; 56) £62

POLE, Matthew
- Synopsis criticorum aliorumque Sacrae Scripturae. Utrecht, 1684-86. 5 vols. Fo. Wormhole at beginning of vol. I. Cont. blind-stpd. vell., vol. I not unif., gt. arms added on covers of vols. II-V, spines soiled. (S. Dec.8; 126) *Heyndericks.* £60

POLE EVANS, I.B. & others
- The Flowering Plants of South Africa. L. & Pretoria, 1922-77. Vols. 1-44, & dupl. copies of vol. 33 pt. 1-vol. 36 pt. 2, & vol. 37 pt. 1-vol. 37 pt. 4, & 2 copies of index to vols. 1-36. Hf. cf. (vols. 1-19 & 33-34), cl. (vols. 20-31), indexes & vol. 32 in orig. pts. (SSA. Nov.5; 72) R. 2,450

POLENI, Giovanni
- Epistolarum Mathematicarum Fasciculus. Padua, 1729. 1st. Edn. 4to. Cont. vell. bds. Bkplt. of Marquess of Bute; from Honeyman Collection. (S. Nov.10; 2510) *Howell.* £80
- - Anr. Copy. Cont. vell., upr. cover a little stained. Pres. Copy, inscr. 'ex dono Auctoris'. (CNY. Oct.1; 23) $250
- Memorie Istoriche della gran Cupola del Tempio Vaticano. Padua, 1748. Fo. Cont. red Fr. mor. gt.,

lge. gt. arms of the Writers to the Signet added to sides. From the collection of John A. Saks. (C. Jun.10; 213) *Weinreb.* £400
- Miscellanea, hoc est I. Dissertatio de Barometris & Thermometris. II. Machinae Aritmeticae . . . III. De Sectionibus Conicis Parallelorum in Horologiis Solaribus Tractatus. Venice, 1709. 1st. Edn. 4to. Cont. bds. From Honeyman Collection. (S. Nov.10; 2509) *Norman.* £320

POLENI, Giovanni & others
- Sopra l'Aurora Boreale comparsa il di 16 Dicembre, l'Anno 1737. Venice, 1738. 1st. Edn. 4to. Stain on upr. fore-corner of title. Wraps., owner's inscr. of Tnomas Temanza. From Honeyman Collection. (S. Nov.10; 2511) *Hill.* £50

POLIPHILO
See-COLUMNA, Franciscus, Dominican

POLITE ACADEMY (the), or School of Behaviour for Young Gentlemen & Ladies, intended as a Foundation for Good Manners & Polite Address in Masters & Misses
Ill.:– Cannot. Ca. 1790. 10th. Edn. 12mo. Mod. cf. gt. (SH. Mar.19; 259) *Maggs.* £170

POLK, James K.
- Message from the President to the Two Houses of Congress . . . Wash., 1847. 2 vols. Badly foxed in parts. Hf. leath. (SG. Jun.11; 265) $120

POLLARD, Alfred William
- Cobden-Sanderson & the Doves Press . . . & a list of the Doves Press printings. San Franc., 1929. (27) with an inserted Doves Pr. lf. ptd. on vell. Fo. Orig. vell. gt., partly unc., s.-c.'s by Hübel & Denck of Leipzig. The John A. Saks copy. (CNY. Oct.1; 196) $1,200
See-BARTLETT, Henrietta C.

POLLARD, Alfred William, Redgrave, G.R., & others
- A Short Title Catalogue of Books Printed in England, Scotland & Ireland, etc. 1475-1640. 1946. 4to. Orig. bds. with linen backstrip. (TA. Sep.18; 39) £64

POLLARD, Alfred William, Redgrave, G.R., & others - - WING, Donald
- A Short-Title Catalogue of Books Printed in England, Scotland & Ireland, etc. 1475-1700. 1926-76. Together 6 vols., including Index & vol. 2 of 2nd. edn. of Pollard & Redgrave. 4to. Orig. cl., 1 worn. (SH. Mar.6; 555) *Dawson's.* £270

POLLARD, Graham
See-CARTER, John & Pollard, Graham
See-HILL, George Francis & Pollard, G.

POLLARD, Hugh Bertie Campbell
- Game Birds. Ill.:– Philip Rickman. 1929. (99) sigd. by the author & artist. 4to. Slight staining. Qtr. vell. (P. Oct.2; 36) *Smith.* £70
- - Anr. Copy. Some lr. margins slightly dampstained. Vell.-bkd. buckram, slightly soiled. (SG. Dec.11; 383) $130

POLLARD, Hugh Bertie Campbell & Barclay-Smith, Phyllis
- British & American Game Birds. Ill.:– Philip Rickman. N.Y., Derry Pr., 1939. (10) numbered, sigd. by artist. 4to. Pig, gt., partly unc., s.-c. with an orig. watercolour sigd. by artist. (CNY. Oct.1; 171) $10,000
- - Anr. Edn. Ill.:– Phillip Rickman. 1945. Ltd. Edn. Mor. spine. (CE. Nov.20; 44) £70

POLLARD, Richard
- The New & Complete Angler. L., [1802]. 1st. Edn. 12mo. Ex-liby. Later three-qtr. mor. (SG. Oct.16; 290) $325

POLLOCK, W.H. & others
- Fencing.-Boxing.-Wrestling. L., 1889. Orig. linen, slightly soiled. Badminton liby. HK. Nov.18-21; 1583) DM 700

POLLOK, Robert
- The Course of Time. Edinb., 1849. Cont. mor. with wide gt. border round blind-tooled centres with arabesques. Double fore-e. pntg. (SG. Sep.4; 190) $110

POLLUX, Julius
- Vocabularium. Flor., Nov., 1510. Fo. Late 16th. C. Engl. cf., gt., centrepiece on covers, rebkd. (SH. Jul.27; 118) *Maggs.* £90

POLO, Marco
- Le Livre de Marco Polo. Ill.:– after Mariette Lydis. Paris, 1932. (111), numbered. 4to. Red mor. by Gruel, geometrique motifs in gold & black on covers, silk doubls., wrap. preserved, s.-c.

Bkplts. of D. Lesourd & Paul Jeffrain. (SM. Feb.11; 247) Frs. 9,000

POLONSKY, Vyacheslav
- Russky Revolytusionny Plakat [Russian Revolutionary Poster]. Moscow, 1925. (3000). Fo. Orig. bds. (SH. Feb.5; 252) *Reed & Sims.* £240

POLOTSKY, Semen
See-AFANAS'EV-SOLOV'EV, I. & others
See-LANE, Ary & others

POLYBIUS
- Ex Libris Polybii Megalopolitani Selecta De Legationibus, et alia . . . nunc primum in lucem edita, ex bibliotheca Fulvi Ursini. Antw., 1582. 4to. Red str.-grd. mor. by C. Lewis, gt. spine. The Bedford-Hoe copy. (C. Apr.1; 162) *Carter.* £340
- Histoire. Trans.:– Dom Vincent Thuillier. Amst., 1759. New Edn. 7 vols. 4to. Light dampstain thro.-out, slight marginal worming in Supp. Cont. cf. (CSK. Dec.12; 124) £50
- Historiae. Trans.:– [Nicolaus Perottus]. Rome, C. Sweynheym & A. Pannartz, 31 Dec. 1473 [i.e. 1472]. 1st. Edn. Fo. 149 ll. (of 156) lacks 7 ll. including first & last blanks, 11 ll. reprd., coat-of-arms added in pen & ink on last page, cont. marginal annots. 19th. C. vell. bds. [BMC IV, 16] (S. Nov.25; 397) *Kreuzer.* £400
- Römische Historien. Trans.:– W. Xylander. Basle, 1574. 1st. German Edn. Fo. Slightly browned & stained, 6 ll. reprd., sm. hole in last lf. 19th. C. bds. (R. Oct.14-18; 135) DM 1,750
See-SOPHOCLES–POLYBIUS

POMARDI, S.
- Viaggio nella Grecia fatto negli Anni 1804, 1805 e 1806. Rome, 1820. 2 vols. Publisher's cl. (CR. Mar.19; 230) Lire 550,000

POMEROY, R.L.
- The Story of a Regiment of Horse. 1924. 2 vols. Orig. cl. (SH. Jun.4; 82) *Craig.* £60

POMET, Pierre
- A Compleat History of Drugs. 1725. 2nd. Edn. 4to. Upr. pt. of A2 cut away with loss of text, a few plts. cropped, some soiling. Rebnd. hf. cf. (S. Apr.6; 125) *Demetzy.* £120
- - Anr. Copy. 85 (of 86) copperplts. Cont. leath. (R. Mar.31-Apr.4; 1033) DM 650
- - Anr. Edn. 1748. 4th. Edn. 4to. Some first ll. wormed in upr. inner margins. Cont. cf., worn. (S. Jul.27; 372) *Hollingsworth.* £100
- - Anr. Copy. 2 vols. in 1. Lacks title to vol. 2, a few ll. detchd. & margins slightly soiled or torn, a few other minor defects. Very worn, rebkd. (SBA. Mar.4; 164) *Fletcher.* £75
- Histoire Générale des Drogues. Paris, 1694. 1st. Edn. Fo. Some marginal tears. Old cf., very worn. (SG. Jan.29; 344) $400

POMMERAYE, Dom J.-Fr.
[-] Histoire de l'Abbé Royale de S. Ouen de Rouen . . . Ill.:– J. David, Audran & R. Harel. Rouen, 1662. 1st. Edn. Fo. Lacks 1 plt. Cont. cf., decor. spine, worn, stained. (HD. Feb.18; 59) Frs. 1,000

POMODORO, Giovanni
- Geometria prattica tratta dagl'Elementi d'Euclide et alteri Auttori . . . Dichiaratu da Giovanni Scala. Rome, 1599. 1st. Edn. Fo. Some browning & occasional marginal staining, K3 reprd., cont. MS. annots. & calculations on a few ll. Mod. bds. From Honeyman Collection. (S. Nov.10; 2512) *Quaritch.* £220
- - Anr. Edn. Rome, 1624. Fo. A few wormholes at beginning, inner margins of M1 & M4 reprd. & stained, tear mended in N6, some browning, title with ex libris inscr. Cont. vell. bds., later gt. arms of Maximilian, Abbot of Benedictine Monastery at Lambach, & stp. of Blessed Virgin, its patron saint, on covers, slightly worn, 2 corners reprd., lacks ties. From Honeyman Collection. (S. Nov.10; 2513) *Dr. Strauss.* £230
- - Anr. Edn. Rome, 1772. Fo. Some spotting & discolouration. Cont. vell., slightly worn. From Honeyman Collection. (S. Nov.10; 2514) *Weinreb.* £140

POMOLOGICAL MAGAZINE
L., 1828. Vol. 1 (of 3). 1 double-p. plt. wormed. Cont. hf. leath., worn. (R. Mar.31-Apr.4; 1363) DM 3,100
- - Anr. Run. Ed.:– John Lindley. Ill.:– after C.M. Curtis & Mrs. Withers. 1828-30. 3 vols. Cont. hf. cf. (C. Mar.18; 67) *Marshall.* £1,700

POMOLOGIE de la France . . .
Ed.:– [C.F. Willermoz]. Lyons, 1863-65. 3 vols. Cont. hf. roan. (SM. Feb.11; 108) Frs. 2,400

POMPADOUR, Jeanne Antoinette Poisson le Normant d'Etoiles, Marquise de
- Catalogue des Livres de la Bibliothèque. Paris, 1765. Lacks 1st. lf. (blank?), priced thro.-out in ink. Cont. cf., spine gt., corners worn. (SM. Oct.7; 1469) Frs. 2,200
- Mémoires . . . Liege, 1766. 2 vols. 12mo. 19th. C. mor., triple fillet, decor. spines, inner dentelle. (HD. Jun.10; 85) Frs. 1,500

POMPONAZZI, Pietro
- De Naturalium Effectuum Causis, sive de Incantationibus.–Tractatus de Immortalitate Animae. Basle, [Paris], 1556; 1534 [ca. 1634]. 2 vols. 8vo.; 12mo. 1st. work with slight worming in upr. outside corner, reprd., just affecting pagination in some ll. Cont. cf., worn; 17th. C. cf. (C. Apr.1; 74) Quaritch. £520

POMPONIUS LAETUS
See–LAETUS, Pomponius

PONCE, Nicolas
- Collection des Tableaux et Arabesques Antiques . . .–Arabesques Antiques des Bains de Livie, et de la Ville Adrienne. Paris, 1805; 1789. 2nd. work: 1st. Edn. 2 works in 1 vol. Fo. Some ll. stained, touching a few plt.-margins. Old bds., worn. (S. May 5; 186) Booth. £130

PONCET DE LA GRAVE, Guillaume
- Project des Embellissemens de la Ville et Fauxbourgs de Paris. Ill.:– after Lucas, Eisen, Lorrain. Paris, 1756. 1st. Edn. 3 vols. 12mo. A few pp. spotted. Cont. mott. cf. gt., gt. spines, head of 1 spine slightly chipped. (CNY. Oct.1; 24) $200

PONCETTON, François
- Les Erotiques Japonais. Paris, 1925. (225) on Madagascar. Fo. In sheets, publisher's folder. (HD. Dec.5; 166) Frs. 2,900

POND, Arthur & Knapton, Charles
[–] [Les Estampes qui imitent les Desseins Gravées]. Ill.:– after Raffael, Parmiggiano, Claude Lorrain, etc. [Prints dtd. 1734-35]. Fo. 65 mntd. 'chiaroscuro' etchings only (of 70?), lacks engraved & text, first few ll. slightly spotted. Cont. hf. cf. gt., worn. W.a.f. (SBA. Jul.14; 188) Hamilton. £200
- Estampes qui imitent les Desseins . . . d'après les Tableaux originaux des Maîtres.–Les Caricatures de M. Pond. [Plts. dtd. 1734-47]. 2 works in 1 vol. Fo. Slight spotting & soiling. Cont. cf., gt., rebkd. W.a.f. (S. Jun.22; 79) Franklin. £420

POND, James L.
- The History of Life-Saving Appliances . . . & Military & Naval Constructions. Invented & Manufactured by Joseph Francis. N.Y., 1885. 1st. Edn. Sm. 4to. Orig. gt.-pict. cl. (PNY. Mar.26; 184) $140

PONGE, Francis & Mourlot, Fernand
- Braque Lithographie. Ill.:– Georges Braque. Monte Carlo, 1963. (4125) numbered. 4to. Orig. wraps., s.-c., cover design by artist. (SH. Nov.20; 239) Scopazzi. £85

PONIATOWSKI COLLECTION: PHOTOGRAPHIC FACSIMILES OF THE ANTIQUE GEMS
Ed.:– J. Prendeville. 1859. 2 vols. Cont. hf. mor. (SH. Jan.29; 276) Drury. £330

PONOFSKY, Erwin & others
- Die Deutsche Plastik. Leipzig, Flor. & Munich, [1924-26]. 5 vols., various. 4to. Orig. bds. & unif. cl. (CSK. Nov.7; 131) £75

PONSONBY, John H.
- Album containing Notices of Cricket Events, etc. 1871-75. 4to. Hf. cl. (SH. Apr.10; 605) Sanders. £170

PONT, Timothy & Dobie, J.
- Cuninghame 1604-08. Glasgow, 1876. 2 vols. 4to. Hf. cf. (CE. Nov.20; 132) £148

PONT-DE-VESLE, le Comte de
- Catalogue des Livres . . . une Collection Presque Universelle de Pieces de Théâtre.–Catalogue des Livres, Estampes, & c. 1774; [1773]. 2 Catalogues in 1 vol. 2nd. priced in MS., table of authors & plays by title. Cont. cf., flat spine gt. in compartments. (SM. Oct.7; 1473) Frs. 1,100

PONTA, Gioachino
- Il Trionfo della Vaccinia Poema. Parma, 1810. (250). Vell., unc., qtr. red mor. gt. s.-c. Author's pres. copy inscr. on fly-lf. to Il Signor Duca de Laurenzana, Napoli, 20 Giugno 1814, bkplt. of

Francesco Paolo Ruggiero, the John A. Saks copy. (CNY. Oct.1; 154) $150

PONTANUS, Johannes Isaac
- Rerum et Urbis Amstelodamensium Historia. Amst., 1611. 1st. Edn. Fo. Sm. gouge at outer margin of first 30 or so ll., some age-browning, etc. Cont. vell., reprd. [Sabin 64002] (SG. Feb.5; 276) $1,300

PONTANUS, Joannes Jovianus
- Opera. Venice, 1513. 2 pts. in 1 vol. 1st. title slightly soiled, some marginal wormholes to beginning. Old limp vell., spine slightly worn & soiled. (S. Jul.27; 108) Maggs. £100
– – Anr. Edn. Venice, 1513-18. 2 vols. Cont. blind-stpd. cf., decor. (HD. Apr.24; 10) Frs. 1,800
– – Anr. Edn. Flor., 1514. 2 vols. Mor., gt. borders, spines & dentelles gt., satin doubls. & end-ll., by Bozerian. (SG. Oct.9; 193) $1,200
- [Opera]. Urania seu de Stellis . . . Meteororum . . . De Hortis Hesperidum. Ed.:– Marianus Tuccius. Flor., 1514. 19th. C. cf., gt. Bkplt. of Pierre Duhem; from Honeyman Collection. (S. Nov.10; 2516) Rogers Turner. £160

PONTCHARTRAIN, Jerôme Phelypeaux, Comte de
- Catalogue des Livres et Estampes. Paris, 1747. Prices in cont. hand, last lf. reprd., 2 ll. of MS. notes bnd. in, MS. note on verso of title dtd. 1847. Cont. mott. cf., flat spine, gt., each compartment semé with different charge of de Bourgevin de Vialart de Moligny arms. Bkplt. of de Bourgevin de Vialart de Moligny. (SM. Oct.7; 1471) Frs. 1,300

PONTEY, W.
- The Forest Pruner. Huddersfield, ca. 1805. 1st. Edn. Browned. Cont. hf. cf., rebkd. (SH. Jun.18; 49) Armstrong. £55

PONTIFICALS
- Pontifical [Use of Rome]. Rome, Stephan Plannck, 16 Aug., 1497. Fo. Most capitals ptd. in red, spaces for others, 6 woodcut capitals illuminated by mod. hand, full border added to capital at 1st. p., 12 smaller capitals similarly illuminated, lacks 4 prelims. of Table & Epistle, some sm. wormholes to margins of last ll., scattered spotting & foxing. Late 19th. C. red lev. mor., covers gt.-panel., gt. spine. Bkplt. of the General Theological Seminary Liby. [BMC IV, 99, Goff P934, HC 13287*] (CNY. Oct.1; 53) $900
- Pontificale. Collio di Val Trompia, 12 Aug. 1503. Fo. Musical notation, title slightly stained & soiled & with repair to lr. margin, some marginal staining, a few ll. slightly wormed in inner margins just catching text. Old cf., very worn, covers detchd. (S. Jun.23; 218) Quaritch. £220
- Pontificale Romanum Clementis VIII. Antw., 1627. Fo. Preliminary & final margins strengthened. Mod. reversed cf. (SBA. May 27; 102) Hamilton. £54
- Pontificale Romanum, Gregorio XIII. Pont. Max. Venice, 1582. Fo. Title & some ll. slightly soiled, first 16 ll. with old marginalia, some sm. corrections, some pp. with old MS. text pasted over. Hf. leath. ca. 1800, worn & defect. (HK. Nov.18-21; 262) DM 500

PONTOPPIDAN, Erich
- The Natural History of Norway. 1755. Fo. Cont. mott. cf., spine worn. (CE. Jun.4; 47) £290
– – Anr. Copy. (TA. Dec.18; 107) £140

PONZIANI, Domenico Lorenzo
[–] Il Gioco Incoparabile degli Scacchi. Modena, 1769. 1st. Edn. Hf. leath. (D. Dec.11-13; 2302) DM 1,150

POOL, R. & Cash, John
- Views of the most remarkable Public Buildings . . . in the city of Dublin. 1780. 4to. Cont. cf. (P. Mar.12; 224) Crow. £480

POOLE, R.S.
- Catalogue of the Coins of Alexandria & the Nomes. 1892. Orig. cl. (SH. Mar.6; 424) Quedar. £100
- A Catalogue of the Greek Coins in the British Museum, Italy. 1873. Orig. cl. (SH. Mar.6; 425) Quedar. £100

POOLE, Thomas W.
- A Sketch of the Early Settlement . . . of the Town of Peterborough. Peterborough, 1867. Advts. at end. Orig. wraps. (CB. Dec.9; 48) Can. $110

POOR LAW COMMISSIONERS
- Report . . . on an Inquiry into the Sanitary Conditions of the Labouring Population of Great Britain. 1842. Orig. cl. (SH. Oct.10; 502) Bunsei. £160

POOT, Hubert Kornelizoon
See–HUYGENS, Constantin–POOT, Hubert Kornelizoon

POP-UP PINOCCHIO (The)
Ill.:– Harold Lentz. N.Y., 1932. 4to. Orig. pict. bds. (SH. Mar.19; 215) Fletcher. £60

POPE, Alexander
- Complete Poems. Ed.:– John Butt & others. L., v.d. Twickenham Edn. 11 vols. (in various edns.), without index vol. Cl., d.-w.'s. (SG. Dec.18; 336) $325
- Essai sur l'Homme, Poëme, Philosophique. Strassburg, 1772. Cont. red mor. gt. (S. Nov.24; 243) Watchman. £60
- An Epistle to the Right Honourable Richard Lord Cobham. 1733. Fo. Publisher's advt. at end. Mod. qtr. mor. gt. (P. Apr.30; 40) Jarndyce. £70
- Les Pastorales. Trans.:– De Lustrac. Paris, 1753. Orig. Edn. 12mo. Cont. grd. cf., arms of Elisabeth Farnèse, decor. spine, inner dentelle, mor. s.-c., by Rivière. (HD. Jun.10; 86) Frs. 1,800
- The Rape of the Lock. An Heroi-Comical Poem. Ill.:– Du Garnier after Du Bose. L., 1714. 1st. Separate & 1st. Compl. Edn. Lev. mor. gt. by Rivière. (CNY. Oct.1; 112) $420
– – Anr. Copy. Prelims. browned, slight stains, minor paper repairs to margin of frontis., some offsetting from plts. Hf. sheep, folding cf.-bkd. box. (SPB. May 6; 236) $375
– – Anr. Edn. Ill.:– Aubrey Beardsley. 1896. [1st. Edn.?]. 4to. Orig. decor. cl. gt., unc., partly unopened. (SH. Mar.26; 57) Fletcher. £160
– – Anr. Copy. Orig. cl. gt., unc. (SH. Mar.26; 58) Fogg. £65
– – Anr. Copy. Gt.-pict. cl., unc. 4-page prospectus laid-in, Spoor bkplt. (SG. Oct.23; 26) $170
- Works. 1717-1735. 1st. 4to. Edn., 1st. iss. of vol. I. 4to. Some marginal soiling, short tear in port. Cont. cf., worn, upr. cover of vol. 2 detchd. (S. Apr.7; 391) Traylen. £75
- The Works.–The Works of Alexander Pope in Prose. 1717-35; 1737-41. 1st. Coll. Edn. (1st. work). Together 4 vols. (2 + 2). 1st. work lacks binder's directions in vol. II. Unif. cont. spr. cf. (SBA. Jul.22; 28) Ghani. £100
- The Works. Ed.:– William Warburton. L., 1760. 9 vols. Cf. (SSA. Apr.22; 60) R. 110
– – Anr. Edn. L., 1804-1806. 18 vols. Pol. cf., triple filleted borders, spines gt., by Worsfold. (SG. Sep.4; 386) $175
– – Anr. Edn. Ed.:– Rev. Whitwell Elwin & William John Courthope. 1871-86. 10 vols. Mor., spines gt., for Sotheran. (SKC. Feb.26; 1514) £200
– – Anr. Copy. Orig. cl. (SH. May 28; 84) Howes Books. £70

See–GAY, John, Pope, Alexander & Arbuthnot, John

POPE, Alexander & others
- A Collection of 23 Poems by Pope, Swift, & others. 1731-39. Most 1st. Edns. Fo. Slight browning & soiling. Late 19th. C. mott. cf. by Roger de Coverly, gt., upr. cover detchd., partly unc. Bkplt. of Austin Dobson. (S. Jun.23; 399) Quaritch. £1,300

POPE, Arthur Upham & Ackermann, Phyllis
- A Survey of Persian Art. L. & N.Y., 1938-39. 6 vols., without index, 3 vols. of plts. Orig. cl., d.-w.'s, slightly torn. (SBA. Jul.14; 378) Simms & Reed. £350
– – Anr. Copy. 6 vols., lacks index. Fo. A few ll. torn. Soiled. (SH. Jan.29; 277) Rastegar. £580
– – Anr. Edn. 1938-58. 7 vols. including Index. Fo. & 8vo. Orig. cl. (SH. Oct.9; 182) Zwemmer. £750
– – Anr. Edn. Tokyo, etc., 1964-65, & 1967. 12 vols., & vol. XIV. 4to. Hf. leatherette. (SG. Mar.12; 296) $500

POPE, John A.
- Chinese Porcelains from the Ardebil Shrine. Wash., 1954. 4to. Orig. cl., d.-w. (S. Sep.30; 430) £75

POPE-HENNESSY, John
- Catalogue of Italian Sculpture in the Victoria & Albert Museum. 1964. 3 vols. 4to. Cl., d.-w.'s & s.-c. (C. Feb.4; 222) *Du Boulay.* £65

POPERT, C.
- Costumi e Tipi Sardi. Rome, 1901. (50). Fo. Publisher's vell. (CR. Mar.19; 231) Lire 800,000

POPISIL, M. & F.
- Guglielmo Ciardi. Flor., 1946. (250) numbered. 4to. Publisher's bdg. (CR. Mar.19; 147)
Lire 700,000

POPLIMONT, Charles
- La Belgique Héraldique. Paris, 1863-67. 11 vols. Hf. chagrin. (LM. Jun.13; 83) B.Frs. 20,000
- - Anr. Edn. Paris, 1867. 10 vols. (of 11), lacks vol. 8. Orig. bdg. (LM. Nov.8; 206) B.Frs. 7,000

POPPERS, Meir
- Meorot Nathan. Frankfurt am Main, 1709. 1st. Edn. Sig. of former owner on title. Hf. cl. (S. Nov.18; 452) *Stern.* £90

PORCACCHI, Tomaso
- L'Isole piu Famose del Mondo. Ill.:- Girolamo Porro. Padua, 1620. Fo. A few ll. with sm. owner's stps. Limp vell. (CSK. Jun.5; 152) £550

PORCELLA, Vincenzo
- Iscrizione delle Chiese e degli Altri Edifici di Milano. Milan, 1889-93. 12 vols. Mod. hf. cf., orig. wraps. bnd. in, partly unc. (SI. Dec.4; 466)
Lire 380,000

PORCUPINE, Peter (Pseud.)
See–COBBETT, William 'Peter Porcupine'

PORDAGE, Samuel
- The Siege of Babylon. 1678. 1st. Edn. 4to. Recent hf. mor. [Wing P2977] (C. Nov.19; 131)
Ritman. £200

PORT OF NAGASAKI; Based On: (1) Jap. H.O. Chart 197 . . . & AMS Map 340961. (2) Interpretation of Photographs . . . (3) Ground Intelligence
Wash., May 1945. (1000?). Sm. fo. Orig. ptd. wraps., stapled. (PNY. Mar.26; 351) $130

PORTA, Carlo
- Brindes de Meneghin all'Ostaria per el Sposalizzi de S.M. l'Imperator Napoleon con Maria Luisa. Milan, 1810. 1st. Edn. Mod. bds., orig. wraps. bnd. in. (SI. Dec.4; 467) Lire 520,000
- Opere Complete in Dialetto Milanese. Milan, 1865. Red mor. sigd. by Gruel, gt., centre gt. medal on upr. cover, box. (SI. Dec.4; 468)
Lire 3,000,000
- Poesie in Dialetto Milanese. Milan, 1821. 2 vols. 12mo. Hf.-titles. Red mor. sigd. by Gruel, orig. wraps. bnd. in. (SI. Dec.4; 469) Lire 500,000
- Il Romanticismo.-Brindes de Meneghin a l'Ostaria per l'Entrada in Milan de . . . Franzesch Primm . . . Milan, 1819; 1815. 1st. Edn. 2 vols. Mod. bds., orig. wraps. bnd. in. (SI. Dec.3; 474)
Lire 780,000

PORTA, Giovanni Battista della
- De Distillatione Lib. IX. Rome, 1608. 1st. Edn. 4to. On blue paper, title & last p. very soiled, former strengthened. Mod. vell. bds., gt., bkplt. of J. Campbell Brown, Liverpool. From Honeyman Collection. (S. Nov.10; 2521) *Jackson.* £380
- - Anr. Copy. Slight worming in inner lr. margins towards end, also a very sm. wormhole in last few ll., hardly affecting letters, liby. stp.: Bibliotheca Giovannini at end. Old rough bds. (S. Dec.1; 317)
Quaritch. £270
- Della Celeste Fisonomia Libri sei nei quali Ributtata la Vanita dell'astrologia Giudiciaria. Padua, 1616. 4to. Lr. outer corner of title defect. with loss of date & a few letters. Cf. gt. (S. Dec.2; 591) *Broseghini.* £70
- Della Fisonomia dell' Huomo . . . Padua, 1613. 4to. Folios 2M2 & 3 with 2 ills. in facs. Old pig, spine reprd. (S. Mar.17; 310) *Vitale.* £100
- Magiae Naturalis, sive de Miraculis Rerum Naturalium Libri IIII. Naples, 1558. 1st. Edn. Fo. Sm. repair to last lf. with several letters supplied in pen, 1st. 2 quires loose, title slightly stained with piece missing from lr. inner margin, slight spotting. Cont. limp vell., stained, lr. cover reprd., hf. red mor. case. From Honeyman Collection. (S. Nov.10; 2518) *Quaritch.* £520
- - Anr. Copy. Slightly stained in parts. Cont. paper bds. (HK. Nov.18-21; 264) DM 1,300
- - Anr. Edn. Antw., 1567. 16mo. Slightly browned & soiled, some worming, affecting text,

later sig. 'Alexr. Murray' on title. Cont. cf., very worn. (S. Apr.6; 127) *Libris. Antik.* £80
- Magiae Naturalis Libri XX. Naples, 1589. Fo. A few ll. slightly wormed affecting text, some spotting, occasional stains, marginal annots. on a few ll. Old limp vell., new end-papers, hf. red mor. case. From Honeyman Collection. (S. Nov.10; 2519) *Jackson.* £380
- - Anr. Edn. Leiden, 1650. 12mo. Cf., worn. (S. Dec.1; 318) *Ribi.* £50
- Magia Naturalis, Oder: Hauss,-Kunst- und Wunder-Buch. Trans.:- Chr. Peganius [Rautner]. Nuremb., 1713. 1st. German Edn. 4to. Title lf. with owner's mark pasted over, 1 copper engr. newly pasted in with slight text loss, lacks Books VIII & IX with 2 copper engrs., some browning & soiling. Cont. vell., slightly soiled. (H. May 21/22; 243) DM 650
- Phytognomica. Naples, 1589. 1st. Edn., 2nd. Iss. Fo. Some browning & spotting, short tear in 2R2. Cont. limp vell., upr. cover stained, lacks ties. From Honeyman Collection. (S. Nov.10; 2520)
Jackson. £540

PORTAFOGLIO Necessario a tutti quelli che fanno il giro d'Italia
1774. General map of Italy & 26 sectional maps, all engraved folding & hand-cold. in outl., map 9 slightly torn & soiled. Cont. red mor., gt. borders & cornerpieces on sides, gt. panel. spine. W.a.f. (C. Nov.6; 258) *Wood.* £260

PORTAL, Antoine
- Histoire de l'Anatomie et de la Chirurgie. Paris, 1770-73. 1st. Edn. 6 vols. Slight browning. Cont. cf., very worn, lacks some labels, owner's inscr. on fly-ll. (S. Apr.6; 128) *Brieux.* £70

PORTALIS, J.E.M.
- De l'Usage et de l'Abus de l'Esprit Philosophique durant le XVIIIe Siècle. Ill.:- Pigeot (port.). Paris, 1820. 1st. Edn. 2 vols. Cont. str.-grd. red mor., decor. spines, fillets & roll-stps. gt. on covers, inside dentelle, watered silk end-papers & doubls. Bkplt. of Marcel Bernard. (HD. Dec.5; 167)
Frs. 2,200

PORTALIS, Baron Roger & Beraldi, H.
- Les Graveurs du Dix-huitième siècle. N.Y., 1970. Reprint of Paris 1880-82 Edn. 3 vols. Orig. linen. (HK. May 12-14; 2274) DM 460

PORTEFEUILLE des Fouteurs (Le) ou La Lyre gaillarde et Libertine du Jour
Boulingrain, 1793. 18mo. Mod. bradel hf. chagrin, unc. (HD. Apr.10; 369) Frs. 1,100

PORTEFEUILLE Historique de l'Ornement
- Ornaments of the Classical Masters . . . Watteau, Vriese, Alb. Durer, Lepôtre, Berain, Morisson, De Bry, etc. Paris, 1841. Fo. Cont. red mor.-bkd. bds. (S. Jan.27; 463) *Orssich.* £55

PORTEFEUILLE du XVIIIe Siècle
N.d. Sm. 12mo. Cont. red mor., gt. dentelle, gt. metal lock. White-paper notebook & almanac for 1770 inserted. (HD. Apr.10; 179) Frs. 1,650

PORTER, Anna Maria
- The Recluse of Norway. 1814. 1st. Edn. 4 vols. 12mo. Lacks hf.-titles, a few minor defects. Cont. hf. mor. (SBA. Jul.14; 3) *Laywood.* £65

PORTER, Arthur Kingsley
- Romanesque Sculpture of the Pilgrimage Roads. Boston, 1923. (500). 1 vol. text & 9 vols. plts. Text in cl., plts. loose in portfos. boxed as orig. iss. (SG. Dec.4; 282) $300

PORTER, Katherine Anne
- French Song-Book. [Paris], Harrison of Paris, [1933]. 1st. Edn., (595) numbered, sigd. Buckram-bkd. bds., partly unc. & unopened. (SG. Jun.4; 415) $190
- Noon Wine. Detroit, 1937. L.P. 1st. Edn., Sm. 4to. Patterned bds., glassine guard, boxed, end-paper with some soiling. (PNY. Mar.26; 266)
$130

PORTER, Sir Robert Ker
- Letters from Portugal & Spain written during the March of the British Troops.–A Narrative of the Campaign in Russia, during the Year 1812. 1809; 1815. 1st. Edn.; 4th. Edn. 2 vols. 1st. vol.: lacks plan, a few ll. slightly dampstained, 2nd. vol.: a few ll. slightly spotted. Cont. cf. or hf. cf., worn, upr. cover of 1st. vol. detchd. (SBA. Jul.14; 6) *Santos.* £55
- Travelling Sketches in Russia & Sweden. 1809. 1st. Edn. 2 vols. in 1. 4to. Some plts. offset. Mod.

hf. cf., earlier spine preserved. (SH. Nov.6; 248)
Strufaldi. £310
- - Anr. Copy. Light foxing & offsetting. Cont. qtr. cf., rebkd. with orig. spine preserved. (S. Nov.4; 598) *Lind.* £250
- - Anr. Copy. 2 vols. Mod. hf. cf., spines gt. (S. Mar.31; 499) *Foyles.* £250
- - Anr. Copy. Cont. russ. gt., rebkd. (SPB. Oct.1; 206) $450
- - Anr. Edn. 1813. 2nd. Edn. 2 vols. in 1. 4to. Cont. hf. cf., some wear. (S. Jun.29; 279)
Cumming. £190
- - Anr. Copy. 2 vols. 40 (of 41) plts. Cont. hf. cf. gt., rebkd. (SBA. Mar.4; 122) *Ghani.* £120
- - Anr. Copy. 2 vols. in 1. A former owner's label on title. Cl. (BS. Jun.11; 184) £100
- - Anr. Copy. 39 engraved plts. only (of 41), 1 defect., a few tears, some ll. soiled. Cont. hf. mor. (SH. Feb.5; 253) *Harris.* £50
- Travels in Georgia, Persia, Armenia, Ancient Babylonia. 1821. 1st. Edn. 2 vols. 4to. 1 folding map cl.-bkd. in folding pocket at front of vol. 1, the other slightly torn but reprd., margins of 1 preface lf. strengthened, a few other minor defects. Cont. russ., worn, 1 jnt. strengthened. (SBA. Jul.14; 7) *Dimakrakos.* £170
- - Anr. Edn. 1821. Vol. 1 only. Cont. cf. (SH. Jul.16; 172) *Maggs.* £100
- - Anr. Edn. 1821-22. 1st. Edn. 2 vols. Cont. pol. cf., gt. borders on sides, gt. panel. spines, rebkd. with orig. spines preserved. (C. Nov.5; 122)
Maggs. £450
- - Anr. Copy. 2 vols. Cont. cf. (SG. May 14; 180)
$850

PORTER, Thomas
- The Carnival. 1664. 1st. Edn. 4to. Sm. tear in title reprd., slight staining thro.-out. Mod. hf. mor. [Wing P2988] (C. Nov.19; 132)
Pickering & Chatto. £130

PORTER, Thomas Cunningham
- Impressions of America. L., 1899. Hand-stp. on title-p. Cl., stereoviewer in sleeve in lr. cover. (SG. Apr.23; 184) $350

PORTER, William Sydney 'O. Henry'
- The Complete Writings. Ill.:- Gordan Grant. Garden City, 1917. Ltd. Memorial Edn., 14 vols. Two-tone bds., cl. d.-w.'s. (PNY. Oct.1; 439)
$160
- The Voice of the City, & other Stories. Ed.:- Clifton Fadiman. Ill.:- George Grosz. Ltd. Edns. Cl., 1935. (1500) numbered, & sigd. by artist. 4to. Buckram. (SG. Jan.15; 203) $180
- - Anr. Copy. Badly spotted. (SG. Oct.23; 151)
$130
- - Anr. Copy. Orig. bdg., boxed. (SPB. Jul.28; 296) $100

PORTFOLIO, (The)
1823-24. 4 vols. Cont. mor., gt. (SH. Jun.18; 50)
Lenton. £80
- - Anr. Run. 1870-1886. 17 vols. Cont. hf. mor. gt. (P. Sep.11; 174) *Lott & Gernish.* £380
- - Anr. Run. Ed.:- Philip Gilbert Hamerton. Ill.:- Whistler & others. 1870-93. Vols. 1-21 & 24 only. Fo. A few ll. dampstained. Cont. mor., 1 cover detchd. Some orig. etchings by artists. (CSK. Jul.3; 129) £300
- - Anr. Run. 1873-95. 22 vols. Some hf. cf. (DWB. May 15; 93) £260
- - Anr. Run. 1875-84. Vols. 6, 7, 8, 10-15, together 10 vols. 4to. Hf. mor., worn. (P. Apr.9; 8)
Schuster. £140
- - Anr. Run. Ed.:- P.G. Hamerton. 1876-81. 75 vols. Fo. Cl., gt., 1 vol. stained. (BS. Nov.26; 171)
£180
- - Anr. Run. 1894-1902. 11 vols. only. Cont. hf. mor. (SH. Jan.29; 278) *Lenton.* £75

PORTIGIANI, Girolamo
- Prospettiva di Fortificationi. [Rome], [1648]. Ob. 8vo (6½ × 18 inches). Engraved title-p. & 15 plts. only, foxed & stained, liby. stp. on verso of title inked out. New bds. (SPB. May 6; 237) $125

PORTIO, S. Camillo
- La Conguira de'Baroni del Regno di Napoli. Rome, 1565. 4to. Early 17th. C. red mor., probably by Simon Corberan at Aix, with monog., gt., of N.-C. Fabri de Peiresc on covers, triple gt. fillet, spine gt. with sm. flower in compartments. Soubise copy, with press-mark on front paste-down, bkplt. of Conte della Trinita. (SM. Oct.8; 1932) Frs. 10,000

PORTIS, Leonardus de
- De Sestertio Pecuniis Ponderibus et Mensuris antiquis libri duo. [Venice], [after 1500]. 1st. Edn. 4to. Lr. margin of title reprd. Mod. vell.-bkd. bds. Bkplt. of Dallas Bache Pratt; from Honeyman Collection. (S. Nov.10; 2524)   *Maggs.* £130
- – Anr. Edn. Basle, 1530. Stained at end, some browning thro.-out. Cont. limp vell. (C. Apr.1; 163)   *Michael.* £60

PORTIUS, Simon
- De Conflagratione Agri Puteolani. Flor., 1551. 1st. Edn. Sm. 4to. A few marginal inscrs. Mod. vell.-bkd. bds. (S. Jun.29; 334)   *Solner.* £60

PORTLOCK, J.E.
- Report on the Geology of the County of Londonderry & of Parts of Tyrone & Fermanagh. Dublin, 1843. Orig. cl., unopened. (GM. Apr.30; 300)   £55

PORTLOCK, Nathaniel
- A Voyage Round the World. L., 1789. 1st. Edn. Lge. 4to. Disbnd. (SG. Feb.26; 273) $1,000

PORTRAIT DE LA FRANCE
Paris, 1926-30. 29 vols. Sm. 4to. Mor.-bkd. bds., orig. wraps. bnd. in. (SM. Oct.8; 2224) Frs. 1,200

PORTRAITS & CHARACTERS OF THE KINGS OF ENGLAND, from William the Conqueror to George the Third
1823. 1st. Edn. 2 pts. 12mo. Advts. Orig. pict. wraps., worn, backstrip of 2nd. restitched. (SH. Mar.19; 260)   *Burmand.* £50

PORTRAITS DES GRANDS HOMMES, FEMMES ILLUSTRES . . . DE FRANCE
Paris, [1787]. Fo. 64 (of 192) plts., foxing & a few creases, strengthened in plt. 49. Cont. Engl. str.-grd. mor., gt. spine, lacks front free end-paper. (S. Dec.9; 488)   *Mistrali.* £400

PORTRAITS OF BROOD MARES belonging to the Royal Stud at Hampton Court. By C.W.
L., 1837. Lge. fo. Orig. wraps., loose. (R. Mar.31-Apr.4; 1702)   DM 3,200

PORTRAITS OF CURIOUS CHARACTERS IN LONDON, with Descriptive & Entertaining Anecdotes
[1806]. Advts. Orig. ptd. wraps., soiled & worn. (SH. Mar.19; 261)   *Rota.* £90

PORZEL, E.
- [–] Gantz neue Biblische Bilder-Ergötzung dem Alter u.d. Jugend, aus dem Alten [u. Neuen] Testament angestellet. Ill.:– Porzel after J.J. van Sanrrart. Nuremb., ca. 1700. 2 pts. in 1 vol. Ob. 8vo. Mod. hf. cf., antique style. (VG. Dec.17; 1145)   Fls. 900

PORZIO, L.A.
- De Militis in Castris Sanitate Tuenda. Ed.:– J.C. Prieger. Den Haag, 1739. Latest Edn. Cont. leath., gt. spine. (R. Oct.14-18; 378)   DM 540

POSL, F.J.
- Die Bienenzucht. München, 1807. Cont. hf. leath., spine defect. (R. Oct.14-18; 2685)   DM 480

POSSELT, E.L.
- Unparteyische, Vollständige und Actenmäsige Geschichte des Peinlichen Prozesses gegen Ludwig XVI König von Frankreich. Basel, 1793. 2 pts. in 1 vol. Stained. Cont. hf. leath., gt. spine. (R. Oct.14-18; 1362)   DM 580

POST, P.J.
- [–] [Begraeffemisse van Frederick Henrick . . . Prince van Orange]. [1651]. Fo. Plts. only. Disbnd. W.a.f. (BS. Jun.11; 221)   £260

POST BOY (The)
Phila., ca. 1807. 12mo. Slightly stained. Orig. wraps., backstrip reprd. (SH. Mar.19; 262)   *Schiller.* £230

POSTANS, T.
- Personal Observations on Sindh. 1843. 1st. Edn. Early 20th. C. red hf. mor. by Sangorski & Sutcliffe. (S. Mar.31; 500)   *Hosains Books.* £70

POSTEL, Guillaume
- De Cosmographica Disciplina et Signorum Coelestium vera Configuratione. Leiden, 1636. 2 pts. in 1 vol. 12mo. A few stains. Cont. cf., worn. [Sabin 64523 for American references] (S. Dec.1; 319)   *Dix.* £60
- De Magistratibus Atheniensium Liber. Basle, 1551. 18th. C. mor., triple gt. fillet, flat spine gt. in compartments, inner gt. dentelles. Bkplt. of

Brancas de Lauraguais. (SM. Oct.8; 1933)   Frs. 1,600
- – Anr. Edn. Basle, [1551]. 16mo. MS. ex-libris on title, dtd. 1582. Mod. bds. (SG. Feb.5; 278) $100
- De Originibus, seu, de Varia et Potissimum Orbi Latino. Basel, 1553. Title with owner's mark. Cont. MS. vell., sm. spine tear. (HK. Nov.18-21; 266)   DM 520
- De Universitate Liber, in quo Astronomiae Doctrinaeûe Coelestis Compêdium Terrae aptatum, & secundum Coelestis influxus Ordinem precipuarûmque. Paris, 1563. 2nd. Edn. 2 pts. in 1 vol. 4to. 1st. title browned & soiled, slight spotting. Cf., very worn, lâcks spine, upr. cover loose. From Honeyman Collection. (S. Nov.10; 2526)   *Rota.* £110
- Liber de Causis seu de Principis et Originibus Naturae Utriusque. Paris, 1552. 16mo. 18th. C. red mor. by Derome le Jeune with his ticket, triple gt. fillet, spine gt. with single roundel in compartments, inner gt. dentelles. Girardot de Préfond–William Beckford copy, bkplts. of Cortland Bishop & William Loring Andrews. (SM. Oct.8; 1936)   Frs. 2,800
- La Loy Salique Livret de la Première Humaine Verité. Paris, 1553. 2nd. Edn. 16mo. Dampstained. 18th. C. red mor., triple gt. fillet, flat spine gt. with longitudinal title, inner gt. dentelles. Girardot de Préfond-MacCarthy-Reagh-Chardin-William Beckford copy. (SM. Oct.8; 1935)   Frs. 1,400
- Quatuor Librorum de Orbis Terrae Concordia Primus. [Paris], [1543]. 18th. C. mor., triple gt. fillet, flat spine gt. in compartments, inner gt. dentelles, single wormhole in upr. hinge. (SM. Oct.8; 1937)   Frs. 4,000

POSTES IMPERIALES
- Etat Général des Postes et Relais de l'Empire Français. 1806. Red. mor. Napoleon I arms. (HD. Oct.10; 272)   Frs. 3,600

POSTL, K.A. 'Ch. Sealsfield'
- Gesammelte Werke. Stuttgart, 1846. 1st. German Coll. Edn. 18 pts. in 8 vols. Title stpd., slightly soiled. Cont. hf. linen gt. W.a.f. (HK. May 15; 4896)   DM 440

POSWICK, Eugène
- Histoire Biographique et Généalogique de la Noblesse Limbourgeoise. Liège. 1873. Vol. 1, all publd. 4to. 1 errata lf. Hf. red chagrin. (LM. Jun.13; 156)   B.Frs. 9,000

POSWICK, Guy
See-ARMORIAL D'ARY-TABLE DES MEUBLES HERALDIQUES

POTE, Capt. William, Jnr.
- Journal during his Captivity in the French & Indian War. Ed.:– V.H. Paltsits. N.Y., De Vinne Pr., 1896. (375) numbered, on Holland H.M.P. Together 2 vols. Orig. hf. leath. (SG. Jun.11; 361) $110

POTIER de Courcy
- Nobiliaire et Armorial de Bretagne. Nantes & Paris, 1862. 2nd. Edn. 3 vols. in 1. 4to. Cont. hf. chagrin, spines decor. with raised bands. (HD. Jun.24; 97)   Frs. 1,200

POTOCNIC, M. 'Hermann Noordung'
- Das Problem der Befahrung des Weltraums der Raketen-Motor. Berlin, 1929. 1st. Edn. Orig. linen. (HK. Nov.18-21; 368)   DM 520

POTONNIEE, Georges
- The History of The Discovery of Photography. Trans.:– Edward Epstean. N.Y., 1936. (300). 4to. Buckram. (SG. Apr.23; 170) $225
- – Anr. Copy. Ex-liby. (SG. Jul.9; 280) $130

POTT, Percival
- The Chirurgical Works. Ed.:– Sir James Earle. Ill.:– Sir Joshua Reynolds (port.). 1808. 3 vols. Some foxing. Hf. cf. (S. Jun.17; 685) *Pratt.* £100

POTTER, Beatrix
- The Story of a Fierce Bad Rabbit. 1906. 1st. Edn. 16mo. Orig. cl., wallet-type bdg., slightly soiled. (SBA. Jul.14; 426)   *Amikliariat.* £60
- The Tale of Jemima Puddle-Duck. 1908. 1st. Edn. 16mo. Orig. bds., spine soiled. (SH. Dec.11; 401)   *Phillips.* £50
- The Tale of Mr. Tod. 1912. 1st. Edn. 16mo. Frontis. loose. Orig. bds., worn. Pres. Copy. (SH. Dec.11; 396)   *Carter.* £320
- The Tale of Peter Rabbit.–The Tale of Benjamin Bunny. Ca. 1912. 2 vols. 16mo. Orig. bds. Pres. Copies. (SH. Dec.11; 397)   *Phillips.* £170

- The Tale of Pigling Bland. L., 1913. 12mo. Orig. paper bds. Author's dummy proof copy, ptd. text & blank slips for ills. pasted in, with printer's pencil notes, & with holograph corrections & additions in author's hand. From the Prescott Collection. (CNY. Feb.6; 280) $4,000

POTTER, Francis
- An Interpretation of the Number 666. Oxford, 1642. 1st. Edn. 4to. Cont. limp vell., gold-stpd. centre-piece & fillets. [Wing P3028] (D. Dec.11-13; 180)   DM 2,200

POTTER, John
- Griechische Archäologie, oder Alterthümer Griechenlandes. Trans.:– J.J. Rambach. Halle, 1775-78. 1st. Edn. of this trans. 3 vols. In II J.A. Ernesti Archaeologia Literaria, Leipzig, 1768, 127 pp. with engraved title vig. bnd. in, lightly browned in parts, sm. corrections. Cont. cf., slightly worn. (H. Dec.9/10; 926)   DM 420

POTTER, Paulus
- Suite Complète de Six Gravures de Chevaux. Amst., 1650. Ob. 4to. Mod. bds. (LM. Jun.13; 95)   B.Frs. 7,500

POTTER, Woodburne
- [–] The War in Florida. Balt., 1836. 1st. Edn. 12mo. Orig. cl., rebkd., part of orig. spine laid down. (SG. Oct.30; 292) $100

POTTIER
See-DAREMBERG, Charles Victor, Saglio & Pottier

POTTINGER, Lieut. Henry
- Travels in Beloochistan & Sinde. L., 1816. 1st. Edn. Lge. 4to. Ex liby., foxed. Hf. leath., crudely reprd. (SG. Oct.30; 293) $190

POTTNER, E.
- Der Garten am Wasser. Berlin, 1918. (25) privilege Edn. on Bütten. Fo. Text by O. Bie. Orig. vell. portfo. sigd. aquarelle as cover vig., soiled, browned. Printer's mark & many woodcuts sigd. by artist. (H. Dec.9/10; 2307)   DM 1,150

POTTS, Thomas
- The British Farmers Cyclopaedia. 1808. 4to. Vig. title spotted. Hf. cf., spine defect. (P. Apr.30; 244a)   *Campbell.* £70

POUCHET, F.A.
- The Universe. L., 1882. 6th. Edn. Elab. blind-stpd. mor. Fore-e. pntg. (SG. Mar.19; 162) $200

POUCHKINE, Alexandre Sergyeevich
See-PUSHKIN or Pouchkine, Alexandre Sergyeevich

POUGET, Jean
- Dictionnaire de Chiffres et de Lettres Ornées. Paris, 1767. 4to. Orig. cf. (D. Dec.11-13; 2351)   DM 700

POUJOULAT, J.J.F.
See-MICHAUD, J.F. & Poujoulat, J.J.F.

POULSON, George
- Beverlac; or, The Antiquities & History of the Town of Beverley. 1829. 2 vols. in 1. 4to. Engraved frontis. trimmed & mntd. to strengthen. Cont. diced russ. gt., neatly rebkd. (SBA. Oct.22; 485)   *Spelman.* £70
- The History of Antiquities of the Seigniory of Holderness. Hull, 1840 & 1841. 2 vols. Hf. cf. marb. bds. (HSS. Apr.24; 113)   £145

POUNCY, B.T.
See-HEARNE, Samuel–POUNCY, B.T.
-BYRNE, Letitia–GILPIN, William & Alken, Samuel

POUND, Ezra
- Canto Pisan LXXVI. Ill.:– Zao Wouki. Paris, 1972. (180) sigd. by artist. Fo. Leaves, publisher's cl. box. (HD. Apr.24; 169)   Frs. 2,500
- Cavalcanti Poems. Verona, 1968. (10) on Japanese paper lettered B, sigd. 4to. Orig. mor-bkd. bds., s.-c. (SH. Dec.18; 238)   *House of Books.* £500
- Exultations. L., 1909. 1st. Edn. Sm. 12mo. 10-pp. advts. Bds., unc., cl. s.-c. (SG. Jun.4; 417) $300
- Lustra. [1916]. 1st. Edn., (200). Orig. cl., unc. (C. Feb.4; 310)   *Minerva Books.* £130
- – Anr. Copy. Buckram. (SG. Jun.4; 421) $200
- Quia Pauper Amavi. [1919]. 1st. Edn. Printers typography corrections in last part for 1st. separate Edn. of Homage to Sextus Propertius: Orig.

POUND, Ezra -contd.
cl.-bkd. bds., unc. Error on p. 34 not corrected. (SH. Dec.18; 237) *Rota.* £105
– – **Anr. Copy.** Unopened. Error on p. 34 not corrected. (SH. Dec.18; 236) *Stevens.* £65
– **Ripostes.** 1912. 1st. Edn., 1st. Iss. Lacks publisher's advts. Orig. cl., unc. Pres. Copy. (SH. Dec.18; 23) *Scott.* £210

POUQUEVILLE, François Charles Hugues Laurent
– **Voyage dans la Grèce.** 1820-21. 1st. Edn. 5 vols. Cont. spr. cf., spines slightly defect., Signet arms on covers. (S. Nov.25; 540) *Drakatos.* £170
– – **Anr. Edn.** 1826-27. 2nd. Edn. 6 vols. Cf., blind plaque, gt. & blind decor. spine, by Thouvenin. (HD. Feb.18; 170) *Frs.* 2,800
– **Voyage en Morée à Constantinople en Albanie** . . . Paris, 1805. 1st. Edn. 3 vols. 1 folding map or plan reprd., liby. stp. on a few pp. Cf. gt. (P. Jul.2; 171) *Timmons* £180

POUTEAU, Calude
– **Oeuvres Posthumes.** Paris, 1783. Sig., erased, & date 1819 on fly-ll., bkplt. of Mercantile Liby. Association. Cont. red mor., gt., arms of A.J. Amelot de Chaillou, but with one of father's stps., triple gt. fillet, spine gt. in compartments, inner gt. dentelles. (SM. Oct.8; 1940) *Frs.* 1,800

POWELL, Anthony
– **A Dance to the Music of Time.** 1951-75. 12 vols. Orig. cl., d.-w.'s. 3rd. vol. sigd. subsequent vol. pres. copies to Handasyde Buchanan, 4 T.L.s., 3 autograph postcards. (S. Jul.22; 311) *Words, etc.* £900

POWELL, George
[–] **The Cornish Comedy.** 1696. 1st. Edn. 4to. Title slightly stained, cont. owners' inscr. on title. Mod. mor.-bkd. bds. [Wing P3048] (C. Nov.19; 133) *Pickering & Chatto.* £90
[–] **The Imposture Defeated.** 1698. 1st. Edn. 4to. Some staining thro.-out, occasionally heavy. Mod. mor.-bkd. bds. [Wing P3051] (C. Nov.19; 134) *Quaritch.* £280

POWELL, J.
[–][**Views in Egypt**]. Ca. 1810. Fo. Soft-ground etchings, a few slightly torn, no text, a few ll. slightly spotted. Orig. bds., worn. (SH. Nov.7; 431) *Walford.* £100

POWELL, Thomas
[–] **Humane Industry.** 1661. 1st. Edn. Without sig. B (not called for), several ll. stained from margins, occasional browning & soiling, sig. on title. Mod. cf. (S. Feb.10; 457) *Fletcher.* £160

POWER, Henry
– **Experimental Philosophy, in Three Books: containing New Experiments Microscopical, Mercurial, Magnetical.** 1664. 1st. Edn. 4to. Slight soiling & staining, cont. owner's inscrs. of Hugh Fortescue. 19th. C. cf., over which has been laid an early 16th. C. Flemish blind-stpd. bdg., rather wormed, hf. red mor. case. From Honeyman Collection. [Wing P3099] (S. Nov.10; 2529) *Zeitlin.* £720
– – **Anr. Copy.** Extreme upr. corner of 1st. 2 ll. slightly wormed. Cont. cf., head & foot of spine chipped. (CSK. Jun.26; 131) £250

POWER, Tyrone
– **Impressions of America.** Ill.:– A. Hervieu. L., 1836. 1st. Edn. 2 vols. Mod. three-qtr. leath. (SG. Jun.11; 362) $120

POWNALL, Thomas
– **Hydraulic & Nautical Observations on the Currents in the Altantic Ocean.** L., 1787. 4to. Folding map reprd., some foxing, ex liby. Hf. cf., rebkd., orig. spine laid down. [Sabin 64822] (SPB. Jun.22; 117) $425

POWYS, Llewelyn
– **Glory of Life.** Ill.:– Robert Gibbings. Gold. Cock. Pr., 1934. (277). 4to. Orig. vell.-bkd. cl. Compl. set of 14 wood-engraved blocks & compl. set of proofs on japanese paper in 3 fo. cases by Sangorski & Sutcliffe, mor. spines with Gold. Cock. device. (SH. Feb.19; 165) *Marks.* £2,200

POWYS, Thomas Littleton, Baron Lilford
See–LILFORD, Thomas Littleton Powys, Baron

POYNTING, Frank
– **Eggs of British Birds.** 1895-96. 4to. Hf. mor. gt. (P. Mar.12; 293) *Park.* £85
– – **Anr. Copy.** Pts. I-IV (all Iss.). Cont. hf. mor., orig. wraps. bnd. in at rear. (TA. Jun.18; 56) £70

POZZI, Carlous Maria–NETTE
– **Artis Sculptoriae, vulgo Stuccatoriae paradigmata.–Adelich Land- und Lust-Haüser nach Modernen Gout.** Ill.:– 1st. work: Johann August Corvinus after C.M. Pozzi; 2nd. work: Carl Remshardt & Andreas Geyer. Augsburg, 1708; ca. 1710. 2 works in 1 vol. Fo. Additionally hand-cold. engraved plan of Augsburg by Johann Baptist Homann, Nuremb., & 3 folding engraved plts., 1st. work: wormholes in centre fold, slightly affecting plt., lacks title; 2nd. work: lacks 1 plt. Cont. hf. vell. gt., arms of the Counts Sinzendorf, on sides. (S. Jan.27; 346) *Marlborough.* £300

POZZO, Agostino
– **Gnomices biformis, Geometricae, scilicet, & Arithmeticae Synopsis.** Venice, 1679. 1st. Edn. 4 pts. in 1 vol. 4to. Some staining & soiling, several ll. with tears. Cont. vell. bds., stained. From Honeyman Collection. (S. Nov.10; 2530) *McKittrich.* £160

POZZO, Andrea
– **Der Mahler U. Baumeister Prospectiv.** Augsburg, 1800. 2 vols. Fo. A few plts. slightly frayed. Cont. hf. linen. (HK. Nov.18-21; 1983) *DM* 520
– **Perspectiva Pictorum et Architectorum.** Rome, 1693-1737. 1st. Edn.; 3rd. Edn. 2 vols. Fo. Text in Latin & Italian, slight worming, some plts. discold. Vell. W.a.f. (SPB. Jul.28; 402) $200
– – **Anr. Edn.** Romae, 1702-1700. 2 vols. Fo. Some staining, mostly marginal. Cont. plain flexible bds., slightly wear. (SG. Dec.4; 283) $800
– – **Anr. Edn.** Ill.:– Georg Bodenehr. Augsburg, 1719 (1st. vol.), 1711 (2nd. vol.). 2 vols. Fo. 218 engraved plts. (of 222, without plts. 64, 80, 103 & 105 in vol. 2), browning to some text, last 2 quires & plts. in vol. 1 misbnd., plt. 60 dampstained, plt. 95 in vol. 2 with repair at inner lr. corner with slight loss to border. Cont. cf., spines gt. & gt.-lettered. (CNY. Oct.1; 25) $600
– – **Anr. Edn.** Augsburg, after 1720. 4th. German [Augsburg] Edn. 2 vols. Fo. Parallel Latin/German text, slightly soiled. Cont. leath., gt. spine. (R. Oct.14-18; 622) *DM* 1,600
– – **Anr. Edn.** Rome, 1723. 2 vols. Fo. Vol. 1 1st. Edn. [1693]. frontis. & 102 plts., this copy lacks plt. 100, vol. II frontis. dtd. 1700, 118 plts. Cont. vell. (HD. Jun.10; 87) *Frs.* 3,100
– – **Anr. Copy.** Fo. Vol. II lacks 4 plts., vol. I with folding plt. no. 100. Cont. roan, guarland & sm. centre motif, decor. spines. (HD. Jun.10; 88) *Frs.* 2,300
– **Prospettiva de Pittori e Architetti.** Rome, 1700. Vol. 2 only. Fo. Text in Italian & Dutch. Cont. vell., worn, soiled. (SBA. Mar.4; 95) *Pilo.* £80
– **Rules & Examples of Perspective.** Trans.:– John James. Ill.:– John Sturt. 1707. 1st. Edn. in Engl. Fo. C. hf. mor. The Approbation of this Edition on recto of 1st. plt. is sigd. by C. Wren, J. Vanbrugh & N. Hawksmoor; from Chetham's Liby. Manchester. (C. Nov.27; 329) *Weinreb.* £240
– – **Anr. Copy.** Taylor's 4-p. 'Catalogue of Modern Books on Architecture' ca. 1800 bnd. in at end. Early cf.-bkd. marb. bds. (SG. Oct.9; 194) $600
– – **Anr. Edn.** N.d. Fo. 100 plts. only, lacks plt. 71, text in Latin & Engl., a few ll. detchd. Old hf. cf., worn. W.a.f. (CSK. Feb.20; 88) £100

PRACTICAL ENGINEER (The)
1887-98. Vols. 1-17. 4to. Hf. mor., 2 vols. with spines defect., worn. (TA. Apr.16; 394) £52

PRACTICE of the High Court of Chancery
L., 1672. 16mo. Dampstained in parts. Old cf., worn. (SG. Feb.5; 206) $225

PRAG IM 19. JAHRHUNDERTE
Prag, ca. 1830. Some plts. slightly soiled or browned. Orig. linen. (HK. Nov.18-21; 1123) *DM* 620
– – **Anr. Edn.** Prag, ca. 1850. Ob. 4to. Slightly soiled. Cont. hf. leath. (R. Mar.31-Apr.4; 2704) *DM* 1,000

PRANTL, K.
See–ENGLER, A. & Prantl, K.

PRASSE, Leona E.
– **Lyonel Feininger: a Definitive Catalogue of his Graphic Work.** [1972]. 4to. Pict. cl., d.-w. With catalogue of the A.A.A. exhibition, Mar.-Apr. 1972. (SG. Oct.23; 115) $110

PRATEIUS, P.
– **Lexicon Iuris Civilis et Canonici.** Ill.:– J. Amman. Frankfurt, 1581. 4th. Edn. Fo. Lacks 2

blank ll. Cont. style mod. hf. leath. (R. Oct.14-18; 1426) *DM* 600

PRATT, Anne
– **Flowering Plants of Great Britain.** N.d. 6 vols. Occasional slight spotting. Orig. cl. (CSK. Jan.9; 64) £55
– **The Flowering Plants, Grasses, Sedges & Ferns of Great Britain.** L., [1850-70]. Orig. linen. (D. Dec.11-13; 143) *DM* 590
– – **Anr. Edn.** Warne, ca. 1860. 6 vols. Slight foxing. Cont. cl., some wear to spines. (TA. Oct.16; 303) £100
– – **Anr. Copy.** (TA. Sep.18; 350) £65
– – **Anr. Edn.** L. & N.Y., 1889. 4 vols. Orig. cl. gt. (SBA. Oct.21; 161) *Mediolanum.* £70
– – **Anr. Copy.** A few ll. slightly spotted. (SBA. Dec.16; 149) *Loose.* £60
– – **Anr. Edn.** 1891. 4 vols. Plts., a few detchd., occasional slight soiling, 1 lf. torn. Orig. cl., spines rubbed. (CSK. Sep.12; 126) £65
– – **Anr. Edn.** 1899-1900. 4 vols. Orig. cl. (SKC. Feb.26; 1603) £70
– – **Anr. Copy.** Cont. hf. cf. (CSK. Sep.19; 53) £50
– – **Anr. Edn.** N.d. 6 vols. Orig. cl. gt., worn. (P. Jul.30; 252) *McDonnell.* £110
– – **Anr. Copy.** Hf. mor. gt. (P. Oct.23; 225) *Robert.* £70
– **Wild Flowers.** 1852-53. 2 vols. Orig. cl., slightly soiled. (CSK. Mar.27; 5) £65
– – **Anr. Edn.** 1853. 4to. A few ll. slightly spotted. Orig. cl. gt., slightly worn. (SBA. Mar.4; 165a) *L'Acquaforte.* £85
– – **Anr. Copy.** Orig. blind-stpd. cl. (LC. Feb.12; 149) £75

PRATT, Orson
– **A Series of Pamphlets.** L'pool., 1851. Port. dampstained. Crude hf. sheep. (SG. Jan.8; 308) $110

PRATT, Samuel
– **The Regulating Silver Coin.** L., 1696. 1st. Edn. Later three-qtr. mor. (SG. Feb.5; 259) $110

PRATT, Samuel Jackson
– **Family Secrets & Domestick.** 1897. 1st. Edn. 5 vols. Cf. gt. (P. Jan.22; 9) *Hannas.* £95

PRATTENT, T. & Denton, M.
– **The Virtuoso's Companion & Coin Collector's Guide.** 1795-97. Vols. 1-6 & Continuation in 1 vol. 1 plt. slightly torn. Later hf. cf. (SH. Jan.29; 279) *Drury.* £50

PRATTICA CIOE nuova inventione di conteggiare
Milan & Bologna, 1637. 16mo. Rather browned & stained, a few short tears, hole in D2, some ll. partly loose. Cont. vell. with flap & tie, owner's name 'Boccabadati' on cover. From Honeyman Collection. (S. Nov.11; 2531) *Jackson.* £85

PRAYER BOOKS [English]
– **Book of Common Prayer.** 1549; 1552; 1637; 1662; 1844. Facs. Reprints. 5 vols. 4to. Cont. mor., 1 cover detchd. (SH. May 28; 10) *Howes Books.* £50
– **A Prayer & Thanksgiving.** 1587. Sm. 4to. Mor. by Sangorski, partly unc. From the collection of Eric Sexton. [STC 16518] (C. Apr.15; 134) *Quaritch.* £400
– **Books of Christian Prayers.** 1590. 4to. Cont. vell., slightly worn. [STC 6431] (S. May 5; 268) *Quaritch.* £340
– **Certaine Praiers to be used at this present time . . . for the good Successe to the French King.** 1590. Sm. 4to. Worming in lr. margin, affecting 4 words. Mor. by Sangorski, unc. From the collection of Eric Sexton. [STC 16523.3] (C. Apr.15; 136) *Quaritch.* £300
– **A Fourme of Prayer.** 1590. Sm. 4to. Some cont. MS. notes & emendations. Mor. by Sangorski. From the collection of Eric Sexton. [STC 16522] (C. Apr.15; 135) *Quaritch.* £320
– **A Fourme of Prayer with Thanksgiving, to be used . . . every Yeere the Fift of August.** 1603. 1st. Edn. 4to. Lacks final blank. Mor. limp vell., gt. fillet border on covers, central gt. floral device, lacks ties. From the collection of Eric Sexton. [STC 16489] (C. Apr.15; 137) *Quaritch.* £240
– **Certaine Prayers Collected out a Forme of Godly Meditation . . .–A Forme of Prayer . . . to bee used in these Dangerous Times of Warre.** 1603. 2 works in 2 vols. Sm. 4to. Title dust-soiled in 1st. work. 1st. work; buckram-bkd. bds.; 2nd. work; 19th. C. hf. mor. From the collection of Eric Sexton. [STC

16532 & 16547.5] (C. Apr.16; 138)
Burgess. £120
- **Prayers . . . for the Queenes Safe Deliverance.**
1605. 1st. Edn. Sm. 4to. Mor. by Sangorski. From
the collection of Eric Sexton. [STC 16534] (C.
Apr.15; 139)
Quaritch. £260
- **A Booke of Christian Praiers.** Ed.:– [Richard
Daye?]. 1608. Sm. 4to. Sm. stain in 1st. few ll.
Cont. cf., gt. device in centre of covers, flanked
with blind-stpd. initials 'MT', rebkd., new ties, s.-c.
Bkplt. of Henry Yates Thompson, lately in the
collection of Eric Sexton. [STC 6432] (C.
Apr.15; 133)
Thorp. £260
- **Book of Common Prayer.** Oxford, 1679. Cf. with
silver corners & clasps, spine decor. with acorns.
(P. Apr.9; 201)
£55
- **The Book of Common Prayer.–Book of Psalms.**
1704; 1705. 2 works in 1 vol. 1st. work rubricated
thro.-out. Cont. chagrin, silver corner pieces &
clasps, centre pieces engraved with coat of arms (a
lozenge quarterly 1 & 4 argent a lion rampant
gules, 2 & 3 azure) on upr. cover, & initials
(MP?) on lr. cover, 1 cornerpiece missing, loosely
inserted a bifolium from a 15th. C. Italian Book of
Hours. (S. Dec.8; 69)
Heyndericks. £78
- **Book of Common Prayer.** 1711. Ruled in red
thro.-out, slight browning. Cont. black mor., gt.,
spine tooled in compartments, covers with
elaborate floral border & panel, silver clasps &
corner & centre-pieces, rather worn, rebkd., old
spine preserved. (S. Apr.7; 390)
Traylen. £75
- – Anr. Edn. 1717. 18th C. Scottish wheel
binding of red mor., gt., spine tooled in
compartments, elab. decor. covers. (S. Nov.24; 38)
Breslauer. £500
- **Book of Common Prayer . . . According to the
use of the Church of England.–The Whole Book of
Psalms.** 1717; 1724. 2 works in 1 vol. 1st. work
with title & dedication lf. slightly soiled, 2nd.
work ruled in red. Cont. panel. mor. gt. (C.
Apr.1; 195)
Pierson. £90
- **Book of Common Prayer.** Camb., 1760. Lacks
blank lf. preceding title, ex-liby. Old suede, rebkd.
(SG. Sep.25; 65)
$120
- – Anr. Edn. Camb., 1761. 2nd. Baskerville Edn.
Title, B7, C3 & C6 are cancels. Red mor. gt. by
Bedford. W.E. Gladstone's copy, inscr. to him by
Charles Tennant, stp. of St. Deiniol's Liby.,
Hawarden. (S. Nov.25; 478)
Sotheran. £85
- **The Book of Common Prayer [with Psalms].**
Camb., 1764-66. 4to. Cont. Engl. red mor. gt.,
mor. gt. onlaid medallion 'JHS' centrepieces,
dentelle borders, ornamental gt. spine in 6
compartments, hf. red mor. gt. drop-box. With
double fore-e. pntg.; from the Prescott Collection.
(CNY. Feb.6; 112)
$900
- **The Book of Common Prayer, with the Psalter.**
Oxford, 1784. 12mo. Cont. crimson str.-grd. mor.
gt. Fore-e. pntg.; from the liby. of Zola E. Harvey.
(SG. Mar.19; 115)
$275
- **Book of Common Prayer.** 1792. 2 vols. 4to. Red
mor. gt. with central crosses surrounded with
flames, decor. spine with green bands, booksellers
label of S. Bagster. (CE. Jul.9; 151)
£90
- **Book of Common Prayer . . . Psalms of David.**
Oxford, 1793. Fo. Cont. mor. gt. Duchess of
Chandos's copy, her name gt. stpd. on covers. (S.
Nov.25; 482)
Traylen. £65
- **The Collects from the Book of Common Prayer.
–Holy Communion from the Book of Common
Prayer.** Bedford Park, Chiswick. Caradoc Pr.,
1901; 1904. (18) on vell. Together 2 vols. 12mo.
Orig. limp vell., upr. cover of 2nd. work with sm.
painted symbol, both with painted spine lettering,
silk ties, unc., qtr. mor. case. Charles C.
Kalbfleisch bkplts. (CNY. May 22; 367) $500
- **The Book of Common Prayer. Use of the Church
of England.** Ill.:– Charles Robert Ashbee. L.,
Essex. Ho. Pr., [1903]. (400) numbered. Fo.
Wood bds., leath. spine, lacks clasps. Supp.
'showing variants from the Prayer Book . . . of the
American Church' loosely inserted. (SG.
Sep.4; 174)
$260
See–BIBLES [English]–PRAYER BOOKS
[English]
*See*BIBLES [English]–PRAYER BOOKS [English]
–PSALMS, PSALTERS & PSEUMES

PRAYER BOOKS [English & Mohawk]
- **Book of Common Prayer.** Ed.:– Rev. Abraham
Nelles. Hamilton. 1842. Cont. leath. (CB.
Dec.9; 281)
Can. $150

PRAYER BOOKS [Hebrew]
- **Machzor Nusach Barcelona Minhag Catalonia.**
Salonica, 1526. Sm. 4to. 161 ll. only (of 201, lacks

---

all prelim. prayers, title, & last section with the
colophon), 9 ll. towards end written in 16th. C.
script, some repairs to margins without loss, short
tears in 3 ll. without loss, cropped, soiled, stained.
Cf., warped, worn, end-papers torn. (SPB. May
11; 150)
$4,500
- **Machzor Lechol Ha'shanah, with the
commentary Hadrat Kodesh.** Sulzbach. 1709. 2
pts. in 1 vol. Fo. Discolouration. Leath. (SPB.
May 11; 147)
$275
- **Tikun Chatzot.** Ed.:– Moshe Sacuto. Mantua,
ca. 1710. Staining & browning. Mod. cl. (SPB.
May 11; 206)
$125
- **Leket Ha'omer.** Ed.:– Abraham Mordo. Venice,
1718. 16mo. Staining & browning, soiled. Bds.,
worn. (SPB. May 11; 22)
$475
- **Tikun Se'udah Ve'sefer Yetzirah.** Venice,
[1725?]. 24mo. Some spotting, soiling. Wraps.,
slightly soiled. (SPB. May 11; 208)
$275
- **Tikun Shovavim.** Ed.:– Moshe Zacuto. Mantua,
1732. Staining, repairs. Wraps. (SPB. May
11; 241)
$125
- **Sidur Shaar Hashamayin.** Amst., 1742. 2nd. Edn.
2 pts. in 1 vol. 4to. Several ll. reprd., some text
loss, cropped, browned, stained. Cl. (SPB. May
11; 200)
$350
- **Ziduk Ha'din.** Venice, 1758. 24mo. Stained.
Wraps., worn. (SPB. May 11; 221)
$175
- **Selichot.** Venice, 1792. 16mo. Tears, stitching
loose, some repairs, lightly stained, browning.
Cl.-bkd. bds., wormed, soiled. (SPB. May 11; 189)
$225
- **Tikun Chatzot Lomar Bein He'mezarim.** Livorno,
1797. 16mo. Browned, stains. Bds., soiled. (SPB.
May 11; 207)
$100
- **Prayer Book.** Vienna, 1850. 12mo. Silver bdg.
repousse & chased with flowers, scrolls, &
trelliswork, similar clasp. As a bdg., w.a.f. (CNY.
Oct.9; 31)
$1,200
- **Sidur Zichron Jerusalem.** Jerusalem, 1899. 32mo.
Cropped, slightly browned. Cl. (SPB. May
11; 201)
$100

PRAYER BOOKS [Welsh]
- **Llyfr Gweddi Gyffredin.** 1664. Fo. Recent qtr. cf.
(TA. Jan.22; 84)
£55

**PRECIS Elementaire et Méthodique de la Nouvelle
Géographie de la France**
See–ATLAS NATIONAL Portatif de la France
–PRECIS Elementaire et Méthodique de la
Nouvelle Géographie de la France

PREECE, Louisa
See–SYMONDS, Mary & Preece, Louisa

PREETORIUS, Emil
- **Exlibris und Signete.** Munich, 1924. (40) on
echte Japan, sigd. by artist, numbered. Orig.
blind-stpd. mor., box, slightly defect. (SH.
Nov.20; 73)
Ayres. £55

PRESCOTT, William Hickling
- **Geschichte der Eroberung von Mexico.** Leipzig,
1845. 1st. German Edn. 2 vols. Slightly soiled.
Cont. linen. [Sabin 65271] (R. Oct.14-18; 1696)
DM 680
- **History of the Conquest of Mexico.** N.Y., 1843.
1st. Edn. 3 vols. Orig. cl. (SG. Oct.9; 195) $400
- – Anr. Copy. Cl. (SG. Jun.11; 225)
$170
- **Works & Life.** Ed.:– George Ticknor. 1864. 13
vols. Cf. gt. by Maclehose. (CE. Mar.19; 232)
£60
- **Works.** Ed.:– John Foster Kirk. Phila.,
1892-1893. (250) numbered. [Ill. liby. Edn.]. 12
vols. Orig. hf. leath., chiefly unopened. (SG.
Sep.4; 390)
$125
- **Complete Works.** Ed.:– John Foster Kirk. L.,
1896-97. Lge. Type Edn. 12 vols. Three-qtr. mor.,
spines gt., partly unopened. (SG. Dec.18; 337)
$200
- **Works.** Phila., [1904]. Aztec Edn., (250). 22
vols. Hf. mor. gt., gt. panel. spines with mor. gt.
diamond shape inlays. With clipped sig. tipped in.
(SPB. May 6; 336)
$2,400
- **The Complete Works.** N.d. 12 vols. Cont. hf.
mor. (SH. May 28; 85)
Walford. £50

**PRESCOTT, William Hickling–TICKNOR,
George**
- **Conquest of Peru; Reign of Charles the 5th;
Reign of Phillip the 2nd; Conquest of Mexico;
Reign of Ferdinand & Isabella; Biographical &
Critical Miscellanies.–Life of William H. Prescott.**
L., 1847; 1857; 1855-59; 1843; 1839; 1845; 1864.
Together 15 vols. Some foxing, spotting, offsetting.
Unif. cf. gt., by Zaehnsdorf. (SPB. Nov.25; 481)
$350

PRESTON, Margaret
- **Recent Paintings . . .** Ed.:– S. Ure Smith &
Leon Gellert. Sydney, 1929, (250) numbered.
Orig. hand-cold. woodcut. Plts. 1-9 in orig. ptd.
wraps., 10-23 in individual mounts, dupl. set of the
15 plts. in wrap., all in cl. bnd. case. (JL.
Jul.20; 690)
Aus. $1,450

PRESUHN, Emil
See–STEEGER, Victor–PRESUHN, Emil

**PRETTY, PLAYFUL, TORTOISE-SHELL CAT
(The), a New Game of Questions & Commands**
1817. 1st. Edn.(?). Orig. stiff wraps., engraved
label on inside of upr. cover for James Izzard's
Juvenile Repository. (SH. Mar.19; 266)
Pendennis. £240

PRETTY POLLY: a Novel Book for Children
Ed.:– F.E. Weatherley (intro.). L. & N.Y., ca.
1900. Tall 8vo. Cl.-bkd. cold. pict. bds. (SG.
Apr.30; 250)
$160

PREUSS, Jacob
- **Ordnung, Namen, unnd Regiment alles Kriegs
Volcks. Von Geschlechten, Namen un Zal aller
Büchsen, in ein gantze Aerckelei eins Feldtzugs un
Zeughauss gehörig.** Strassburg, 1530. 1st. Edn. 4to.
Mod. bds. Bkplt. of Prince of Lichtenstein; from
Honeyman Collection. (S. Nov.11; 2532)
Israel. £300

PREUSSLER, J.P.C.
- **Deutliche und Ausführliche Auseinandersetzung
der Schachspielgeheimnisse des Arabers Philipp
Stamma . . .** Berlin, 1823. Cont. bds., worn. (D.
Dec.11-13; 2303)
DM 710

PREVERT, Jacques
- **L'Atelier.** Ill.:– I. Pougny. Paris, [1964]. (140)
on Bütten. Fo. Orig. wraps. & linen box. (H.
Dec.9/10; 2308)
DM 840
- **Les Chiens ont Soif.** Ill.:– Mourlot after Max
Ernst. Paris, [1964]. (320) numbered, with 2 orig.
etchings sigd. by Ernst. Fo. Unsewn, orig. wraps.,
folding cl. case. (SG. Oct.9; 90)
$1,300
See–ERNST, Max & Prevert, Jacques

PREVERT, Jacques & Calot, F.
- **Contes de Boccace.** Ill.:– Marc Chagall. [Paris],
[1950]. Fo. Pict. wraps. by Chagall. (SG.
Oct.23; 54)
$100

PREVOST, Sir George
- **Some Account of the Public Life of, Particularly
of his Services in the Canadas.** L., 1823.
Dampstains, mostly marginal. Hf. cf. (SG.
Jan.8; 70)
$110
- – Anr. Copy. Occasional foxing, penned sig. on
title-p. Qtr. leath., end-papers slightly
dampstained & foxed. (CB. Apr.1; 295)
Can. $320

PREVOST, Paul Emile (Contrib.)
See–GIL BLAS: Illustre Hebdomadaire

PREVOST d'Exiles, Abbé Antoine François
- **Histoire de Manon Lescaut.** Ill.:– Jules Adolphe
Chauvet. Paris, 1867. (2) on vell. with 16 orig.
sigd. drawings by Chauvet. Mor., triple gt. fillet
borders, gt. spines & dentelles, by Rivière. (SG.
Oct.9; 196)
$650
- – Anr. Edn. Ill.:– Jacquemart, L. Flameng,
Pannemaker. Paris, 1875. (50) numbered on
China paper. Three-qtr. lev., spine gt., orig. wraps.
bnd. in, by Rivière, partly untrimmed. (SG.
Dec.18; 39)
$160
- [–] **Histoire du Chevalier des Grieux, et de Manon
Lescault.** Ill.:– Pasquier & Le Bas after Gravelot.
Amst., 1753. Definitive Edn. 2 vols. 12mo. With
usual N3 cancel in vol. 1, some ll. slightly spotted,
sm. inscr. on verso of final lf. in vol. 2. Red mor.,
gt., by Chambolle-Duru. (S. Feb.10; 458)
Klusmann. £500
- – Anr. Copy. Errata lf. Cont. marb. cf., decor.
spines, bdg. reprd. (HD. Feb.18; 60)   Frs. 2,200
- – Anr. Edn. L., 1782. 2 vols. 18mo. Marb. cf. by
Cazin. (HD. Apr.8; 293)
- – Anr. Edn. Ill.:– Lelong. Paris, 1927. (75)
numbered on imperial Japon. 4to. Mor. by Ysieux,
decor. spine, rococo border on covers, red mor.
doubls., wrap. preserved, s.-c. (SM. Feb.11; 272)
Frs. 8,000
- **Histoire Générale des Voyages.** La Haye,
1747-49. Vols. 1-9. 4to. Cf., bdgs. badly defect. As
a collection of prints, w.a.f. (BS. Jun.11; 185)
£260

PRICE, Edward
– Norway. Views of Wild Scenery, & Journal. 1834. 4to. Some spotting. Recent hf. mor. (TA. Feb.19; 659) £80

PRICE, F. Newlin
– Horatio Walker. N.Y. & Montreal, 1928. 1st. Edn., (1024). Orig. paper bds. & cl. spine, s.-c. (CB. Feb.18; 152) Can. $100

PRICE, Francis
– The British Carpenter: or, a Treatise on Carpentry. 1753. 3rd. Edn. 2 pts. in 1 vol., including Supp. 4to. Some spotting & soiling, marginal repair to 1 plt. Mod. hf. cf. (S. Jun.22; 81) Quaritch. £90

PRICE, Capt. George F.
– Across the Continent with the Fifth Cavalry. N.Y., 1883. 1st. Edn. Gt.-pict. cl. (SG. Oct.30; 294) $130

PRICE, Harry
– Short-Title Catalogue of Works on Psychical Research ... for the Scientific Investigation of Alleged Abnormal Phenomena. 1929-35. 2 vols. including supp. Orig. wraps. (SH. Oct.23; 187) Carpenter. £70

PRICE, Sir John
– An Historical Account of the City of Hereford. Hereford, 1796. Cont. hf. russ. (SBA. Oct.22; 361) Davies. £70
See–CARADOC, of Llancarfan–PRICE, Sir John

PRICE, Owen
See–RUSSELL, P. & Price, Owen

PRICE, Richard
– Observations on the Importance of the American Revolution. Boston, 1784. 1st. Amer. Edn. Mod. cl. (SG. Jun.11; 363) $100
– Observations on Reversionary Payments. 1771. 1st. Edn. 1st. gathering a little loose. Cont. cf. (SH. Oct.10; 314) Traylen. £95
– – Anr. Edn. 1772. 2nd. Edn. Cf. gt. (P. Jan.22; 10) Waterfield. £60

PRICE, Capt. Robert Kenrick
– Astbury, Whieldon, & Ralph Wood Figures, & Toby Jugs. 1922. (500). 4to. Orig. hf. mor. (SKC. May 19; 223) £130
– – Anr. Copy. Orig. cl.-bkd. bds., d.-w. (SBA. Mar.4; 273a) Quaritch. £120

PRICE, Sarah
– Illustrations of the Fungi of Our Fields & Woods. 1865. 4to. Cl. gt. (P. May 14; 253) Walford. £50

PRICES OF CABINET WORK, The, with Tables & Designs ...–The Prices of Cabinet Work, Agreed to by the Master Cabinet-Makers of Nottingham
L.; Nottingham, 1797; 1805. 2 works in 1 vol. Cont. reverse cf. (S. Mar.17; 444) Marlborough Rare Books. £220

PRICHARD, James Cowles
– On the Different Forms of Insanity in Relation to Jurisprudence. 1842. Title-p. written on. Hf. cf. (S. Dec.2; 594) Phelps. £70
– Researches into the Physical History of Man. L., 1813. 1st. Edn. Disbnd., ex-liby. (SG. Jan.29; 347) $160
– A Treatise on Insanity & Other Disorders affecting the Mind. 1835. 1st. Edn. 16pp. advts. dtd. Apr. 1844. Orig. cl., spine & hinges reprd., label worn, unc., in cl. box. (S. Jun.17; 686) Jenner Books. £160

PRICKE, Robert
– [–] An Excellent Introduction to Architecture being a Book of Geometrical-Practice. 1670. Fo. Fresh imprint advertising Pricke's most recent work laid down over orig., & advts. for his books on verso of final text lf., lacks final lf. (blank?), a few perforations on title, stab marks in inner margins. 18th. C. parch.-bkd. bds., slightly worn, spine torn. (SBA. Dec.16; 79) Marlborough Rare Books. £220

PRIDEAUX, Humphrey
– Marmora Oxoniensia. Oxford, 1676. 1st. Edn. 2 pts. in 1 vol. Fo. Browned. Cont. cf., rebkd. [Wing 0896] (SH. Jun.11; 79) Book Room, Cambridge. £50

PRIDEAUX, Mathias
– An Early & Compendious Introduction for reading all sorts of Histories. Oxford, 1862. 6th. Edn. 4to. Cont. cf. (CB. Sep.24; 139) Can. $110

PRIDEAUX, Sarah T.
– Bookbinders & their Craft. N.Y., 1903. 1st. Edn. Mod. hf. mor. (CNY. May 22; 247) $120

PRIEST, Capt. Cecil D.
– The Birds of Southern Rhodesia. 1933-36. [1st. Edn.?]. 4 vols. Orig. cl., slightly soiled. (TA. Jun.18; 45) £130
– – Anr. Copy. 4to. Slightly worn. (SKC. May 19; 430) £100
– – Anr. Copy. 4 pp. loose. (SKC. Jul.28; 2428) £50
– – Anr. Copy. Cl. (SSA. Nov.5; 145) R. 290

PRIESTLEY, Joseph
– Directions for Impregnating Water with Fixed Air in Order to Communicate the Peculiar Spirit & Virtues of Pyrmont Water. 1772. 1st. Edn. New cl. (S. Dec.1; 323) Quaritch. £170
– Discourses relating to the Evidence of Revealed Religion. 1794. 3 vols. Cont. hf. cf. (SBA. Jul.14; 190) Waterfield Ltd. £55
– An Essay on the First Principles of Government & on the Nature of ... Liberty.–An Examination of Dr. Reid's Inquiry into the Human Mind on the Principles of Common Sense, Dr. Beattie's Essay on Nature. 1771; 1775. 2nd. Edns. 2 vols. 1st. work with advt. New bds., cl. spine, unc.; cont. cf. (S. Dec.1; 350) Waterfield. £85
– Examination of Dr. Reid's Enquiry. 1774. Cf. gt. (P. Jan.22; 11) Wakefield. £95
– Experiences et Observations sur Differentes Especes d'Air. Trans.:– [Gibelin]. Berlin & Paris, 1775. 1st. Edn. in Fr. 12mo. Cont. qtr. cf. (S. Dec.1; 326) Whitehart. £140
– Experiments & Observations on Different Kinds of Air. 1774. 1st. Edn. 1st. folding plt. offset onto title-p. Cont. cf., spine chipped at head, hf. red mor. case. Pres. copy to Professor Hahn(?); from Honeyman Collection. (S. Nov.11; 2536) Zeitlin. £430
– – Anr. Edn. 1774-75-77. 1st. Edn. 3 vols. 4 pp. for errata & advts. in vol. I, 4 pp. advts. in vols. II & III. New cf. (S. Jun.17; 687) Pritchard-Jones. £280
– – Anr. Edn. 1775-77. Vol. 1 2nd., vols. 2 & 3 1st. Edns. 3 vols. Cont. cf., spines gt. (S. Dec.1; 327) Dawson. £180
– – Anr. Copy. Slight browning & offsetting. Vols. I & II cont. cf., gt., vol. III orig. bds., unc. From liby. of Dr. E. Ashworth Underwood. (S. Feb.23; 275) Bickersteth. £150
– – Anr. Edn. Bg'ham., 1790. 3 vols. Dupls. of all plts. but no. 7, a few ll. slightly spotted. Cont. tree cf., gt. (S. Dec.2; 760) Barnet. £120
– Experiments & Observations on Different Kinds of Air.–Philosophical Empericism Containing Remarks on a Charge of Plagiarism Respecting Dr. H ... s.–Experiments & Observations Relating to Various Branches of Natural Philosophy. Bg'ham., (last Work), 1781-1776-1777-1779; 1775; 1781. 1st. work: vol. 1 3rd., vol. 2 2nd., vol. 3 1st. Edn; 2nd. work: 1st. (& only) Edn.; 3rd. work: 1st. Edn. 1st. work: 3 vols. (2nd. work bnd. in); 3rd. work: vols. 1 & 2. In 2nd. work text ends on p. 85, followed by 6 unnumbered pp. of catalogue of author's works. Unif. cont. tree cf., spines gt. (S. Dec.1; 330) Quaritch. £100
– Forms of Prayer & other Offices for the Use of Unitarian Societies. Bg'ham., 1783. 1st. (& only?) Edn. New cl., unc. (S. Dec.1; 332) Maggs. £50
– A Free Discussion of the Doctrines of Materialism & Philosophical Necessity in a Correspondence Between Dr. Price & Dr. Priestley. 1778. 1st. (& only?) Edn. 1 advt. lf. with list of Price's & Priestley's books at end only (of 2). Hf. cf., worn. (S. Dec.1; 329) Waterfield. £100
– A General History of the Christian Church to the Fall of the Western Empire. Bg'ham, L., 1790. 1st. Edn. 2 vols. Cont. tree cf. (S. Dec.1; 336) Traylen. £60
– Geschichte und Gegenwartiger Zustand der Optik ... Trans.:– Georg Simon Klugel. Leipzig, 1776. 1st. German Edn. 2 pts. in 1 vol. 4to. Tear in U3 affecting letters. Cl., cf. spine. (S. Dec.1; 328) Whitehart. £150
– Hartley's Theory of the Human Mind on the Principle of the Association of Ideas. 1775. 1st. Edn. 4 pp. of advts. Cont. cf. (S. Dec.1; 325) Traylen. £90
– Heads of Lectures on a Course of Experimental Philosophy Particularly Including Chemistry Delivered at the New College of Hackney. Dublin,

1794. Some dampstains at end. Cf., rebkd. (S. Dec.1; 340) Rota. £65
– Histoire de l'Electricité. Trans.:– [Nollet & Brisson]. Paris, 1771. 3 vols. 12mo. Cont. Fr. cf. (S. Dec.1; 322) Quaritch. £100
– Historical Account of the Navigable Rivers, Canals & Railways of Great Britain.–Map of the Inland Navigation. 1831; 1830. 1st. work L.P. 2 works. 4to.: 193cm. X 156cm. The map is engraved & folding. Orig. cl.; map mntd. on linen, cont. cf. s.-c. (SH. Jun.18; 109) Edelhardt. £390
– The History & Present State of Discoveries relating to Vision, Light, & Colours. 1772. 1st. Edn. 2 vols. 4to. Some browning & spotting, without subscriber's list of errata lf. Early 19th. C. hf. cf., rather worn, hf. red mor. cases. From Honeyman Collection. (S. Nov.11; 2534) Rootenberg. £270
– The History & Present State of Electricity, with Original Experiments. 1767. 1st. Edn. 4to. Some spotting & offsetting onto text, Honeyman's annot. of purchase on front paste-down. Cont. cf., very worn, hf. red mor. case. Armorial bkplt. of Philip Puleston, Esclusham, Denbighshire; from Honeyman Collection. (S. Nov.11; 2533) Zeitlin. £410
– – Anr. Edn. 1769. 2nd. Edn. 4to. Errata slip at end, 3 pp. catalogue of books on electricity & 2 pp. of works of Priestly. Cont. cf., worn. (S. Dec.1; 321) Blackwell. £70
– – Anr. Edn. L., 1794. 4to. Heavily browned in parts & soiled, especially plts. Linen. (HK. Nov.18-21; 482) DM 800
– Lectures on History & General Policy to which is Prefixed an Essay on a Course of Liberal Education for Civil & Active Life. Bg'ham., 1788. 1st. Edn. 4to. Advts. New hf. mor., unc. (S. Dec.1; 334) Traylen. £75
– Memoirs ... to the year 1795 ... with a continuation ... by his son, Joseph Priestly: & observations on his writings, by Thomas Cooper ... & the Rev. William Christie. 1806. 1st. Edn. ptd. in England. 2 vols. 10 pp. of advts. & an errata lf. at end of vol. II, some foxing. Orig. bds., unc., spine of vol. I worn, hf. red mor. cases. From Honeyman Collection. [Sabin 65511] (S. Nov.11; 2538) Hill. £55
– Observations on Different Kinds of Air. [1772]. Extract from: Phil. Trans., vol. 62. 4to. Wraps., worn & soiled, unc., hf. red mor. case. From Honeyman Collection. (S. Nov.11; 2535) Zeitlin. £110
– Observations on the Increase of Infidelity. Phila., 1797. 3rd. Edn. Bds., mor. spine. (S. Dec.1; 341) Traylen. £75
– Original Letters by the Rev. John Wesley & his Friends ... with other Curious Papers Communicated by the Late Rev. S. Badcock to which is Prefixed an Address to the Methodists. Bg'ham., L., 1791. 1st. (& only) Edn. Cont. hf. cf. (S. Dec.1; 337) Lawson. £110
– Sperienze ed Osservazioni Sopra Diverse Specie di Aria. Naples, 1784-85. 5 vols. Hf.-title in vol. I only, some stains, bad at end on vol. 1 affecting last pp. of text & plts, liby. stps. Bds., cf. spine. (S. Dec.1; 333) Barnet. £150

PRIJS, Joseph
– Die Basler Hebraeischen Drucke [1492-1866]. Ed.:– Bernhard Prijs. Olten-Freiburg, 1964. Fo. Buckram. (S. Nov.17; 91) Lutz. £75

PRIME, Wendell
– Fifteenth Century Bibles. N.Y., 1888. Tall 8vo. Cl. (SG. Mar.26; 266) $120

PRIME, William C.
– Pottery & Porcelain ... N.Y., 1878. 1st. Edn. 4to. Contents loose in bdg. Gt.-pict. cl. (SG. Dec.4; 84) $225

PRIMEROSIUS, Jacobus
– Exercitationes, et Animadversiones in Librum, De Motu Cordis, et Circulatione Sanguinis, Adversus Guilielmum Harveum. 1630. 1st. Edn. 4to. Some rule-borders cropped at head, title with marginal tear reprd. & a few tiny holes, last 2 ll. reprd. in inner margins. Red mor. gt. by Zaehnsdorf. From Honeyman Collection. [NSTC 20385] (S. Nov.11; 2539) Zeitlin. £620

PRINCE, J.
– The Worthies of Devon. Exeter, 1701. 1st. Edn. Fo. Browning. Cont. cf. (SH. Jun.25; 109) Smith. £60

PRINCE, J.H.
- Neville Cayley: His Royal Zoological Society of NSW Collection of Parrots & Cockatoos of Australia. [Sydney], [1980]. (250) numbered, & sigd. Fo. Leath. (KH. Mar.24; 329) Aus. $170

PRINGLE, Jacob Farrand
- Lunenburgh or the Old Eastern District. Cornwall, 1890. Orig. cl. (CB. Sep.24; 265) Can. $100

PRINGLE, John
- Observations on the Diseases of the Army, in Camp & Garrison. 1752. 1st. Edn. 3 pts. in 1 vol. Cont. cf. gt. (SBA. Dec.16; 36) Rota. £120

PRINT COLLECTOR'S QUARTERLY
N.Y., 1911-40. 27 vols. in 54. Stitching loose in a few vols., slight browning. Cl., soiled, orig. wraps. bnd. in. As a periodical, w.a.f. (SPB. May 6; 238) $500

PRIOR, D.H.
- Gli Ex Libris Italiani. Milan, 1902. (300). 4to. Sewed. (CR. Jun.11; 48) Lire 300,000

PRIOR, Henry
- Il Biglietto di Visita, contributo alla Storia del Costume e dell Incisione. Bergamo, [1920?]. De Luxe Edn. 4to. Cl. (CR. Jun.11; 548) Lire 220,000

See-BERTARELLI, Achille & Prior, Henry

PRIOR, James
See-BURKE, Edmund-PRIOR, James

PRIOR, Matthew & Montagu, Charles
[-] The Hind & the Panther Transvers'd to the Story of the Country Mouse & the City-Mouse. 1687. 1st. Edn. Sm. 4to. Lacks final blank, a few spots. Mod. hf. sheep. Bkplt. of Fairfax of Cameron. [Wing P3511] (S. Jun.9; 49a) Blackwells. £160

PRIORATO, G.G.
- Historia di Ferdinando terzo Imperatore. Vienna, 1672. Fo. Some ports. cropped, dampstains. Vell. (P. Dec.11; 102) Harling Hausen. £65

PRISCIANUS
- Opera. Venice, [Jacobus de Fivizano, Lunensis], 1476. Fo. 349 ll. (of 350), lacks first blank, fo. 2 & 3 rubricated & initials supplied, some cont. marginalia, very faded. Red Engl. 18th. C. mor., elab. gt. border on sides, spine gt., upr. jnt. split. Chatsworth bkplt. [BMC V, 242] (S. Nov.25; 333) Maggs. £1,500

PRISSE, Emile & St. John, James Augustus
- Oriental Album. Ill.:– after E. Prisse. 1848. Fo. Some spotting. Cont. hf. mor. (CSK. Sep.26; 43) £180
– – Anr. Edn. 1851. Fo. Some dampstains. Orig. hf. mor., new end-papers. (CSK. Sep.5; 220) £250
– – Anr. Copy. Plts. & text loose in bdg. Cl., spine defect. (BS. Jun.11; 186) £160

PRISSE D'AVENNES, Achille Constant T. Emile
- La Décoration Arabe. Paris, 1885. Fo. Index ll. slightly spotted. Orig. cl., soiled. (SBA. Oct.21; 187) Fogg. £130
- Oriental Album. 1846. Fo. Slightly spotted. Cont. hf. mor. (SH. Nov.7; 432) Walford. £220

PRITCHARD, W.
- Picturesque Scenery in North Wales. N.d. Ob. 4to. 29 extra ills., some dampstains. Hf. mor., worn, lacks pt. of spine. W.a.f. (CSK. Jan.30; 162) £135

PRITT, Thomas Evan
- Book of the Grayling. Leeds, 1888. [1st. Edn.?]. 4to. Orig. cl. gt. (P. Sep.11; 21) Shaw. £50
– – Anr. Copy. L.P. 4to. Cl. Frank M. Buckland's bkplt. (SG. Oct.16; 303) $170
– – Anr. Copy. (SG. Oct.16; 304) $140
- North Country Flies. L., 1886. 2nd. Edn. Liby. blind-stp. on title-p. Cl. (SG. Oct.16; 302) $240
- Yorkshire Trout Flies. Leeds, 1885. 1st. Edn. (200). Cl. (SG. Apr.9; 302) $230

PRITZEL, George August
- Thesaurus Literaturae Botanicae Omnium Gentium. Milan, [1950]. Facs. of 1877 Edn. 4to. Linen. (SG. Jan.22; 333) $220

PRITZLAFF, John, Hardware Co.
- Catalogue. Milwaukee, ca. 1926. 4to. Orig. leatherette, upr. inner cover eroded. (SG. Dec.4; 170) $110

PRIVATE EYE
1962-77. Nos. 1-418 & Private eyeballs, together 412 Iss. only (lacks nos. 408-409 & 411). 4to. & 8vo. Orig. wraps., some soiled. (SH. Apr.9; 312) Landry. £200

PRIVILEGIA Ordinis Cisterciensis
Dijon, Petrus Metlinger, 4 Jul., 1491. 1st. Edn. 4to. Woodcut calligraphic capitals, lacks first & 2 final blanks, 2 sm. repairs to extreme inner margin of fo. 1, light dampstaining to some quires, browning & soiling. Cont. deer over paste-bds., worn at extremities, cl. folding case. From the collection of Eric Sexton. [BMC VIII, 409, Goff P976, HC 13367*] (CNY. Apr.8; 54) $14,000

PROBA Falconia
- Carmina, sive Centones Virgilii. [Paris], [Guy Marchant] for Alexander Alyate, 3 Mar., 1499. 4to. Rubricated, inner portions dampstained thro.-out, sm. tear to blank margin of title. Recent mor., spine gt. From the collection of Eric Sexton. [BMC VII, 66, Goff P989, HC 6908] (CNY. Apr.8; 122) $1,100

PROBIER BÜCHLEIN, auff Gold, Silber, Kupffer, und Bley, Auch allerlay Metall wie man die zü nutz arbayten uñ Probieren soll
[Augsburg?], [1515?]. Title soiled & with fore-margin strengthened, a few marginal worm-holes. Mod. vell. From Honeyman Collection. (S. Nov.11; 2540) Norman. £1,250

PROBIERKUNST. Kurze und deutliche Vorstellung der edlen Probierkunst
Nuremb., ca. 1700. Foxed & stained, title soiled & with date erased. Hf. cf., worn. From Honeyman Collection. (S. Nov.11; 2541) Das Bucherkabinet. £55

PROCEEDINGS of a General Court Martial of the Line . . . for the Trial of Major General Arnold
Phila., 1780. 1st. Edn., (50). Fo. Title browned, slightly browned thro.-out, lr. right corner of final lf. reprd. Hf. mor., ex-liby. (SPB. Nov.24; 51) $1,700

PROCESSIONARIUM Ordinis Fratrum Praedicatorum
Seville, Meinardus Ungut & Stanislaus Polonus, 3 Apr., 1494. 4to. Spaces for initial capitals, with guide letters, some ornamental woodcut initials, lacks 1st. & final blanks, first 3 ll. partly detchd., a7 with reprd. tear at lr. margin affecting 1 line of text, 4 ll. guarded, el & f5 with corner renewed, 6 ll. with slight marginal repairs, scattered spotting. Old vell. From the collection of Eric Sexton. [BMC X, 39, Goff P997, HC 13380] (CNY. Apr.8; 155) $3,500

PROCHASKA, Georg
- Disquisitio anatomico-physiologica Organismi Corporis Humani Ejusque Processus Vitalis. Vienna, 1812. 4to. Numerous liby. stps. Cont. marb. bds., slightly worn. (S. Feb.23; 90) Dawson. £50

PROCLUS, Diadochus
- Hypotyposis Astronomicarum Positionum. Ed.:– S. Grynaeus. Basle, 1540. 4to. Greek text, stained. Later Fr. red mor., gt., arms of J.A. De Thou on covers & his cipher in compartments of spine, spine slightly worn & reprd. at head. Bkplt. of Baron Holland; from Honeyman Collection. (S. Nov.11; 2542) Manning. £480
- In primum Euclidis Elementorum librum Commentariorum. Trans.:– Francesco Barozzi. Padua, 1560. 1st. Edn. in Latin. Fo. Cont. limp vell., lacks ties, hf. red mor. case, bkplt. of the Prince of Lichtenstein. From Honeyman Collection. (S. Nov.11; 2543) Maggs. £210
- La Sfera . . . Trans.:– Egnation Danti. Flor., 1573. 2 pts. in 1 vol. 4to. Slight browning. Mod. bds. From Honeyman Collection. (S. Nov.11; 2544) Mursia. £90
- Sphaera, Ptolemaei de Hypothesibus Planetarum . . . Canon Regnorum. Trans.:– J. Bainbridge. 1620. 4to. Slight soiling & discolouration, Sir George Shuckburgh's sig, dtd. 1779 on fly-lf., earlier owner's inscr. on title. Cont. limp vell., stained, bkplt. of Librairie Centrale des Sciences, Paris. From Honeyman Collection. [NSTC 20398] (S. Nov.11; 2545) Rogers Turner. £65

PROCOPIUS, of Caesarea
[-] De Bello Italico Adversus Gothos Gesto. Trans.:– Leonardus Brunus Arentinus. Foligno, Johann Neumeister & Aemilianus de Orfinis, 1470. 1st. Edn. Fo. Spaces for capital initials, lacks 1st. blank, 1st. lf. browned & rehinged (possibly inserted from anr. copy), inner blank margin of fo. 14 cut, traces of old staining, marginal annots. washed faint. Vell., spine gt. Bkplt. of Ger. Msl. d'Adda, lately in the collection of Eric Sexton. [BMC VI, 599, Goff B1234, HC 1558] (CNY. Apr.8; 66) $7,000
- The Secret History of the Court of the Emperor Justinian. 1674. Cont. cf., spine gt. [Wing P3641] (SH. Jul.9; 190) Gratsos. £50

PROCTOR, Robert George Collier
- Bibliographical Essays. 1905. (200) numbered. Orig. mor.-bkd. cl. (SH. Jan.29; 48) Lister. £85
– – Anr. Copy. Orig. qtr. mor., partly unc. Initialled by Alfred W. Pollard, who wrote Memoir. (TA. Sep.18; 125) £74

PROGNOSTICON, Opusculum repertorii pronosticon in mutationes aeris (with: Hippocrates. Libellus de medicorum astrologia, translated by Petrus de Abano)
Venice, Erhard Ratdolt. [before 4 Nov.] 1485. 4to. Lacks 1st. blank, a few folio numbers trimmed, some marginal spotting. 19th. C. cf.-bkd. bds. Bkplt. of J.L.E. Dryer; from Honeyman Collection. [BMC V, 291; Goff P1006] (S. Nov.11; 2546) Schuman. £540

PRONTI, Domenico
- Nuova Raccolto di 100 Vedutine antiche della Citta di Roma . . . Rome, ca. 1795. 2 vols. in 1. Later gt. qtr. leath. & marb. bds. (PNY. Oct.1; 463) $200

PROPERT, Walter Archibald
- The Russian Ballet, 1909-1920. 1921. (500) numbered. 4to. Orig. cl.-bkd. bds. (SH. May 21; 95) Facchinetti. £140
– – Anr. Copy. Slightly worn. (SH. Nov.20; 131) Mackenzie. £100
– – Anr. Edn. Ill.:– Leon Bakst, Matisse, Picasso, et al. N.Y., 1921. Ltd., L.P. 1st. Amer. Edn. (450) numbered. Sm. fo. Gt. cl.-bkd. colour-designed bds. (PNY. Mar.4; 224) $300

PROPERTIUS, Sextus
See-CATULLUS, Caius Valerius, Tibullus, Albius & Propertius, Sextus

PROPYLAEN-KUNSTGESCHICHTE
Berlin, 1923-27. 6 vols. 4to. Orig. hf. mor. (SH. Oct.9; 184) Zwemmer. £55
– – Anr. Edn. Berlin, 1923-29. 15 (of 16) vols., lacks vol. 9. 4to. Orig. hf. leath. (HK. Nov.18-21; 3473) DM 1,000
– – Anr. Edn. Berlin, [1923-29]. Vols. 1-16 & 3 related vols., 19 vols. Hf. mor., slightly worn. (SPB. Nov.25; 106) $750

PROUD, Robert
- The History of Pennsylvania in North America, from . . . 1681 till after the Year 1742. Phila., 1797-98. 1st. Edn. 2 vols. Orig. 2-toned bds., worn, spines partly cracked, unc. & partly unopened. (SG. Mar.5; 377) $120

PROUDHON, P.J.
- Die Gerechtigkeit in der Revolution und in der Kirche. Neue Principien Prakt. Philosophie. Trans.:– I. Pfau. Hamburg & Zürich, 1858-60. 1st. German Edn. Slightly browned. Cont. hf. linen. (R. Oct.14-18; 1363) DM 800

PROUST, Marcel
- A La Recherche du Temps Perdu. Paris, 1913-27. 1st. Edns. 13 vols. Various bdgs. (SG. Oct.9; 198) $5,000
– – Anr. Edn. 1919-27. 1st. Edn. (except 'Du Côté de chez Swann'). 13 vols. Sm. 8vo. Sewed. (HD. Jun.25; 441) Frs. 4,600
- A la Recherche du Temps Perdu. Du Côté de chez Swann. 1914. 1st. Edn., 1st. Printing. 12mo. With publisher's catalogue. Sewed. Stp. 'Hommage de l'auteur' & author's visiting card. (HD. Jun.25; 373) Frs. 3,500
- 47 Unpublished Letters to Walter Berry. Paris, Black Sun Pr., 1930. (200) numbered, on velin d'Arches. 4to. Wraps., boxed. (SG. Jun.4; 426) $100
- Oeuvres Complètes . . . Ill.:– Hermine David. 1929-36. 1st. Coll. Edn.; on Japon. 18 vols. 15 frontis.'s (of 18) on China. Sewed. (HD. Jun.25; 441) Frs. 6,100
- Les Plaisirs et Les Jours. Ill.:– Madelaine Lemaire. Paris, 1896. 1st. Edn. 4to. Mod. hf. mor. (SH. Nov.20; 119) Trocchi. £100
– – Anr. Copy. (30) on Chine. Sewed. (HD. Oct.16; 141) Frs. 3,500

PROSSER, George Frederick
- Select Illustration of . . . Surrey . . . 1828. Foxed. Hf. cf., gt. spine. (WW. May 20; 1) £115
-- Anr. Edn. 1828. L.P. Fo. Some spotting. Mor. gt. by Clarke. From the collection of Eric Sexton. (C. Apr.16; 334) *Kitz.* £550

PROUT, John Skinner
- Antiquities of York. ca. 1835? Fo. A few margins slightly dampstained, barely affecting matter. Orig. mor.-bkd. cl. gt., slightly worn. (SBA. Dec.16; 157) *Chester.* £115

PROUT, Samuel
- Facsimilies of Sketches made in Flanders & Germany. Ill.:– Hullmandel. [1833]. L.P. Fo. Mod. red hf. lev. mor. Sigd. MS. receipt & note by Prout inlaid, receipt ill. with sepia drawing. (C. Nov.6; 225) *Martell.* £2,400
-- Anr. Copy. Sigd. Ms. receipt. ill. with orig. sepia drawing, & note inlaid at front. (C. Jul.15; 89) *Müller.* £2,000
- Illustrations of the Rhine. L., 1853. Fo. 3 plts. stpd. Orig. hf. leath., worn. (R. Oct.14-18; 2444) DM 3,500
- Prout's Microcosm. The Artist's Sketch-Book. 1841. Fo. Advt. lf., 1 imprint slightly cropped. Orig. cl., spine faded. A.L.s. from Prout to [Sir] Charles Tilt (publisher), dtd. Hastings, Jan. 9, 1834, tipped in at front. (S. Nov.4; 512) *Quaritch.* £65
- Sketches at Home & Abroad. 1884. 1st. Edn. Fo. Plts. on india paper, some minor foxing, mainly marginal. Cont. hf. mor., gt. decor. spine. (TA. Jan.22; 114) £110
- Sketches in France, Switzerland & Italy. L., 1839. Fo. Foxed, several plts. stpd. in margins. Leath.-bkd. gt.-lettered cl., disbnd., ex-liby. (SG. Dec.4; 286) $650
-- Anr. Copy. Slightly soiled, title & 2 plts. stpd. Cont. hf. leath., very worn & loose. (R. Oct.14-18; 2021) DM 2,200
[–]– Anr. Edn. [1839]. Lge. fo. 23 (of 25) litho. plts. only, hand-cold., loose as iss. Orig. hf. mor. portfo., worn. (SKC. Jul.28; 2553) £650
-- Anr. Edn. N.d. Fo. Dampstains in lr. margins, 1 torn. Qtr. mor. gt. (P. Jul 30; 120) *Walford.* £550
-- Anr. Copy. 1 plt. with clean tear, staining to several lr. margins affecting some plts. at lr. corner, with 2 advt. ll., contents loose in bdg. Orig. cl. As a collection of plts., w.a.f. (KH. Mar.24; 331) Aus. $550

PROUT, VARLEY & WILSON
- Picturesque Sketches of Rustic Scenery including Cottages & Farm Houses. 1815. Fo. Cont. cl., recased. (TA. Nov.20; 132) £80

PROVERBES . . .
ca. 1820/40. Fo. Slight internal foxing. Orig. qtr. mor., worn. W.a.f. (TA. Aug.21; 18) £120

PROVISIONAL CONGRESS
- Provisional & Permanent Constitutions, of the Confederate States.–Acts & Resolutions of the First Session of the Provisional Congress.–Ditto, 2nd. Session.–Ditto, 3rd. Session. Richmond, 1861. 4 pieces in 1 vol. Orig. sheep, covers detchd. (SG. Jan.8; 108) $180

PRUDEN, Dunstan
- Silversmithing, its Principles & Practice in Small Workshops. St. Dominic's Pr., 1933. Unbnd., unc., unopened. With MS. agreement drawn up between Pruden & the press regarding the book, & paper for the covers. (SH. Feb.19; 80) *Quaritch.* £90

PRUDENTIUS, Aurelius
- Opera omnia. Parma, 1788. 1st. Bodini Edn. 2 vols. in 1. 4to. Cont. diced russ. gt., gt. spine. (CNY. Oct.1; 151) $220

PRUTZ, G.
- Illustriertes Mustertauben-Buch. Hamburg, ca. 1895. 4to. Lacks 3 chromolitho. plts., 7 plts. loose. Orig. linen. (D. Dec.11-13; 310) DM 620

PRYCE, William
- Mineralogia Cornubiensis; a Treatise on Minerals, Mines, & Mining. Priv. ptd., 1778. 1st. Edn. Fo. Cont. cf., slightly worn, hf. red mor. case. From Honeyman Collection. (S. Nov.11; 2547) *Conklin.* £440
-- Anr. Copy. Cont. cf.-bkd. bds., bkplt. From the collection of Eric Sexton. (C. Apr.16; 335) *Lloyd.* £120

PRYNNE, William
- Histrio-Mastix. 1633. 1st. Edn., 2nd state. 2 pts. in 1 vol. Sm. 4to. With 'Errataes' on verso of 3*4, cont. inscr. at head of title, a few marginal annots. in text, a few sm. stains. Cont. spr. cf., rebkd., orig. spine laid down. [NSTC 20464A] (S. May 5; 300) *Smith.* £160

PSALMS, Psalters & Pseumes [English]
- Psalter, or Psalmes of David . . . 1617. 16mo. 18th. C. black mor. gt. Aldenham bkplt. & sig. of Henry H. Gibbs, first Baron Aldenham. (S. Nov.25; 456) *Stoughton.* £450
- The Whole Booke of Psalmes. 1635. 32mo. Cont. needlework bdg. in cold., gt. & silver thread, satin liners. [STC ⋅ 2262] (S. Mar.16; 143) *Stoughton.* £240
-- Anr. Edn. 1636. 12mo. Cont. embroidered cl., a heart surrounded by stylised foliage on covers, flowers on spine, worked in silk & metal thread. (CSK. Sep.12; 76) £120
-- Anr. Edn. Ed.:– Thomas Starhold, Jo. Hopkins. 1637. 12mo. Lacks at least 1 index lf. at end. Cont. velvet, openwork silver cornerpieces, stpd. with cherubs' heads in strapwork, clasps reprd., cl. box. J.R. Abbey bkplt., his arms on cl. box. (SM. Oct.8; 2436) Frs. 2,800
-- Anr. Edn. 1641. Cont. needlework bdg. in silver thread. [?Wing B2384] (S. Mar.16; 230) *Temperley.* £140
- Psalms of David. Ed.:– Isaac Watts. L., 1719. 1st. Edn. Sm. 12mo. Black mor. gt., gt. dentelles, by Jenkins & Cecil. Samuel F. Barger bkplt. by E.D. French. (SG. May 14; 222) $450
- Psalms of David Imitated . . . L., 1719. 1st. Edn. 12mo. Black gt. lev. mor., by Francis Bedford. (SG. Sep.25; 326) $375
- A Liberal Version of the Psalms into Modern Language . . . Ed.:– W.R. Wake. Bath, 1793. 2 vols. in 1. Cont. red str.-grd. mor. Fore-e. pntg. (SG. Mar.19; 163) $240
- Psalms of David. Ill.:– Owen Jones. [1861]. Fo. Orig. elab. embossed cl., rebkd., orig. spine preserved. (SH. Mar.26; 305) *Slade.* £150
- The Psalter or Psalms of David. Ill.:– C.R. Ashbee & W. Hooper. L., Essex House Pr., 1902. (250). Fo. Orig. limp vell., silk ties, unc. (CNY. May 22; 309) $150
-- Anr. Copy. Orig. limp vell., silk ties, unc. (CNY. May 22; 310) $140
-- Anr. Edn. Ill.:– C.R. Ashbee. Essex House Pr., 1902. (260). Fo. Orig. pig gt., tooled border, monogram A.P. within date 1902 & Guild of Handicraft initials. (SH. Mar.26; 43) *Sanders.* £95
- The Rutland Psalter. Ed.:– E.G. Millar. Roxb. Cl., 1937. Loose in buckram folder, s.-c. (C. May 20; 49) *Quaritch.* £380

See–BIBLES [English]–PRAYER BOOKS [English]–PSALMS, Psalters & Pseumes [English]
See–BIBLES [English]–PSALMS, Psalters & Pseumes [English]

PSALMS, Psalters & Pseumes [French]
- Les Pseaumes de David . . . Trans.:– Clemént Marot & Theodore de Beze. Charenton, 1644. Cont. red mor., slightly spotted, Du Seuil decor., motif with sm. tools in centre, decor. spine with sm. tools, inside dentelle. (HD. Mar.18; 139) Frs. 1,300
-- Anr. Edn. Paris, 1691. Cont. red mor., 3 fillets, decor. spine, red mor. doubls., decor. with 1 dentelle. (HD. Mar.18; 140) Frs. 1,600
- Les CL Pseaumes de David. Amst., n.d. 2.7 × 1.6 inches (miniature book). Cont. cf., gt. on wooden bds., metal clasp & corners. (CSK. May 2; 107) £75

PSALMS, Psalters & Pseumes [Hebrew]
- Tehilim. Ed.:– Vitt Eliano. Rome, 1581. 12mo. Some outer margins reprd. without loss, slight discolouration, owners' sigs. on fly-lf. Mod. leath. (SPB. May 11; 53) $1,300

PSALMS, Psalters & Pseumes [Latin]
- Psalter. [Wurzburg], [Georg Reyser], ca. 1485-86. Fo. Spaces for important initial capitals, supplied in red & blue, lacks blank folios 231 & 280, dampstaining to lr. inner portions of many ll., with reprd. marginal tears (extending into text at folios 201-2, 204, 214, 221, 241 & 259, reprd. without loss), portion of blank margin renewed at folios 196-7, 204, 225-6, 230, 268-9 & 277-8, sm. wormholes at extreme inner margins of folios 33-56, sm. wormtrack to last 4 ll. slightly affecting text, inscr. at head of p. 1. Mor., covers & spine blind-tooled, spine gt.-lettered. Bkplts. of Charles

Harry St. John Hornby & Clifford Rattey, lately in the collection of Eric Sexton. [BMC II, 571, Goff P1046, HC 4011*] (CNY. Apr.8; 207) $3,500
- Psalterium et Hymni. [Venice], ca. 1490. 4to. Rubricated, calendar slightly defect., slightly stained, slightly soiled thro.-out. 19th. C. hf. vell. (HK. Nov.18-21; 269) DM 1,300
- Psalterium Davidis cum Hymnis. Leipzig, Conrad Kachelofen, 1497. Fo. 4-line music staves provided for antiphons (some with notation supplied in MS.), many ll. with extensive wear & sm. tears to lr. outer corners, some 45 ll. with sm. portions of corners of margins renewed, reprd. tears to some 50 ll., affecting text at 10 places, with slight loss at folios 1, 101, 132, 140, & 164, some 15 ll. with lge. portions of margins renewed (including last lf. with printer's mark cut round & mntd.), spotting to many ll., finger-soiling. Cont. blind-stpd. cf. over wood bds., brass cornerpieces, centrepieces & clasps, rebkd. & reprd. From the collection of Eric Sexton. [Goff P1056] (CNY. Apr.8; 80) $6,000
- Psalterion. Ed.:– [Junstinus Decadyus]. Venice, Aldus Manutius, Romanus, [early 1498]. 1st. Edn., 1st. Iss. 4to. With top line of fo. title omitted by printer & supplied in pen & ink, title on alr overwritten in gold, fore-margin of vl reprd. with loss of 2 letters of text, 2 sm. wormholes at beginning, 1 as far as B2. Late 18th. C. Engl. str.-grd. mor., sm. gt. ornaments in panels of spine, geometrical pattern on covers, inner dentelle of Greek key pattern. Bkplt. of Edward Herbert, Viscount Clive, circular mor. bkplt. of Phyllis Walter Goodhart. [BMC V, 563; Goff P1033] (S. Jun.9; 29) *Thomas.* £4,000
- Sacrorum Psalmorum Libri Quinque . . . Trans.:– Aretius Felinus. Strassburg, 1532. Fo. Cont. blind-stpd. pig., border of roll-stps. (HD. Mar.18; 149b) Frs. 1,500
- Psalmorum Davidis . . . libri quinque . . . Theodoro Beza Vezelio. Antw., 1580. Some slight dampstaining. Cont. limp vell., rather soiled, parts of a 14th. C. Italian legal MS. used as end-papers. Bkplt. of George Lockhart of Carnwath pasted in on verso of title. (S. Apr.7; 311) *Vrije Univ.* £70
- Psalmi Penitentiales. Ed.:– F.S. Ellis. Hammersmith, Kelms. Pr., 1894. (300). Orig. holland-bkd. bds., unc. Inscr. by Emery Walker to Bird Williams Stair. (CNY. May 22; 321) $420
- Mainz Psalter, 1457. [Vienna], [1968]. (295) numbered, on H.M.P. from Richard-de-Bas mill in Auvergne. Fo. Cf. tooled in medieval style, metal bosses, lacks 1 clasp, cl. folding case. (SG. May 14; 136) $325

PSALMS, PSALTERS & PSEUMES [Latin & Arabic]
- Liber Psalmorum Davidis Regis et Prophetae. Trans.:– V. Scialac & G. Sionita. Rome, 1614. 1st. Edn. 4to. Cont. owner's inscr. on title (slightly soiled), a few marginal stains. Cont. limp vell., soiled s.-c. (S. Apr.29; 451) *Poggiori.* £360

PSALMS, Psalters & Pseumes [Latin & German]
- Psalter. Ed.:– [Nicolaus de Lyra (commentary)]. [Strassburg], [Printer of the Henricus Ariminensis], ca. 1474. Fo. Spaces for initial capitals, opening capital P supplied in red & blue, other capitals, paragraph marks & initial strokes in red, blank fo. 5 misbnd. at front, 1st. & 2nd. quires transposed (the former inserted from anr., slightly shorter, copy), portion of inner margin of 1st. lf. renewed, fo. 205 with marginal tear affecting 4 lines of text, reprd. without loss, worming at beginning & end, scattered light browning. Mod lev. mor., gt. spine, by Gerhard Gerlach. Bkplt. of the General Theological Seminary Liby. [BMC I, 79, Goff P1066, HC 13508*] (CNY. Oct.1; 59) $3,000
- Psalterium Ca. 1500 4to. Many cont. marginalia, lacks Sept./Oct. ll. of kalendar, ll. 106 & 108, lr. p. 105, lightly soiled in parts. Cont. wood bds., blind-stpd. leath.-bkd., gt. centrepiece, 2 clasps, spine renewed. (HK. Nov.18-21; 268) DM 1,100

PSALMS, Psalters & Pseumes [Latin & Greek]
- Psalmorum Davidis Paraphrasis Poetica . . . Trans.:– George Buchanan. [Geneva], ca. 1565. 17th. C. red mor., gt. fillet borders & panels. Gt. bkplt. of Ambroise Firmin-Didot, 1850, sig. on title of 'Christian Florent, precepteur de Henri IV'. (SG. Sep.25; 70) $240

PSALMS, Psalters & Pseumes [Polyglot]
– Psalterium Hebreum, Grecum, Arabicum & Chaldeum. Ed.:– Augustino Giustiniani. Genoa, Oct. 1516. Fo. Some inner margins wormed, few reprd., stains, sm. burn hole to E3, many ink annots. Mod. vell. [Sabin 66468] (CNY. May 22; 248) $1,000

PSALMS Psalters & Pseumes [Swiss]
– Des Konigs und Propheten Davids Psalmen . . . Anhang der jenigen Neuen Comunions-Catochismus. Trans.:– Ambros. Lobwasser. Basle, 1738. Title slightly defect. Cont. silver bdg. over blue cl., embossed & pierced with strapwork & decor. scrolls round plaque on covers, clasps, blue silk & gt. floral end-papers, cl. box. J.R. Abbey bkplt., his arms on cl. box. (SM. Oct.8; 2432) Frs. 20,000

PSALMS, Psalters & Pseumes [Syriac & Latin]
– Psalmi Davidis. Ed.:– T. Erpenius. Leiden, 1625. 4to. Slight browning & staining. Cont. limp vell., some wear, s.-c. (S. Apr.29; 452) *Brill.* £70

PSELLUS, Michael
– Arithmetica, Musica, et Geometria: Item Procli Sphaera. Tournon, 1592. 12mo. Dampstained, title torn at head, flaw in a6, sig. on title. Cont. limp vell. Bkplt. of Michael Chasles; from Honeyman Collection. (S. Nov.11; 2548) *Fenyves.* £190

PTOLEMAEUS, Claudius
– Almagestum. Venice, 10 Jan. 1515. 1st. Compl. Edn. Fo. Sm. repair to fore-margin of title. Mod. hf. mor. From Honeyman Collection. (S. Nov.11; 2550) *McKittrich.* £1,200
– – Anr. Edn. Ed.:– Lucas Gauricus. Venice, 1528. Fo. Title browned & with sm. repairs, some ll. slightly stained at end, sm. hole in hl. Bnd. in vell. lf. of a medieval antiphonal, new end-papers. From Honeyman Collection. (S. Nov.11; 2551) *Zeitlin.* £360
– Composition Mathématique. Ed.:– M. Delambre. Trans.:– M. Halma. Paris, 1813-16. (400). 2 vols. 4to. Some spotting & marginal staining, 4 p. prospectus dtd. 1811 inserted at beginning of vol. I, a few ll. detchd. in vol. I. Roan-bkd. bds., worn. From Honeyman Collection. (S. Nov.11; 2556) *Brieux.* £180
– Cosmographia. Trans.:– [Jac. Angelus]. Rome, 4 Nov. 1490. 2nd. Rome Edn. Fo. Lacks 5 ll. & 6 copper engraved maps, 1st. & last ll. soiled, wormed, tears at margins, plts. slightly stained, especially in margins. Lacks bdg. [HC 13541; BMC IV, 133; Goff P-1086] (R. Mar.31-Apr.4; 2324) DM 5,700
– La Geografia de Claudio Ptolemeo. Ed.:– Sebastian Munster. Trans.:– P.A. Mattiolo. Ill.:– Jacopo Gastaldo (maps). Venice, 1548 [colophon dtd. 1547]. 1st. Edn. in Italian. 58 (of 60) double-page copperplt. maps, some dampstaining, mostly affecting maps. Cont. limp vell., partially disbnd. As an atlas, w.a.f. [Sabin 66502] (SPB. Oct.1; 278) $2,500
– – Anr. Copy. Lacks 8 ll. title & prelims. & 214 ll. ptd. text, index cut narrow at head & foot, lightly soiled in parts, 1 map with sm. tear at margin, 1 bkd. Old (later) vell. (R. Mar.31-Apr.4; 2326) DM 8,000
– – Anr. Edn. Trans.:– Girolamo Ruscelli. Venice, 1561. 4to. Some foxing & stains. Unbnd. in orig. sigs. (SG. May 14; 182) $2,500
– – Anr. Copy. 3 pts. in 1 vol. Slightly browned in parts, underlining in index & last lf. 19th. C. hf. leath., loose, spine slightly torn at foot. (HK. Nov.18-21; 1060) DM 3,200
– – Anr. Edn. Trans.:– Ieronimo Ruscelli. Venice, 1564. 2nd. Edn. of Ruscelli's trans. 3 pts. in 1. 4to. (233mm × 163mm). Lacks numbers xi & xii, piece cut from blank lr. margin of 1st. title, map of Italy (vi bis) defect., pt. 2 worming in centre folds of maps Asia 5 & 6, Africa 1 separated in fold, slight staining of some upr. & lr. margins. Cont. patterned paper bds., worn. W.a.f. (S. Nov.3; 3) *Arader.* £1,400
– – Anr. Edn. Ed.:– G. Malombra. Trans.:– G. Ruscelli. Venice, 1574-73. New Edn. 3 pts. in 1 vol. 4to. Slightly dampstained, some browning. Parch.-bkd. bds. (CSK. Mar.6; 42) £580
– – Anr. Edn. Ed.:– G. Rosaccius. Trans.:– G. Ruscellus. Venice, 1598-99. 2 pts. in 1 vol. 4to. Wide margin. Cont. vell. (HK. Nov.18-21; 1063) DM 3,600
– – Anr. Edn. Ed.:– G.A. Magini. Trans.:– L. Cernoti. Padua, 1620-21. 2nd. Edn. of Cernoti's trans. 2 pts. in 1 vol. Fo. Old name on title, notes & old stp. on end-papers. Cont. vell. [Sabin 66508] (R. Oct.14-18; 1556) DM 4,300
– – Anr. Copy. Lightly browned in parts, 1st. text ll. soiled slightly, lacks double-p. world map as often. Spine defect. thro. heavy worming. (R. Mar.31-Apr.4; 2327) DM 3,000
– Geographia. Ed.:– J. Moletio. Trans.:– B. Pirckheimius. Venice, 1562. 1st. Moletius Edn. 4to. 18th. C. bds. [Sabin 66489] (R. Oct.14-18; 1555) DM 3,400
– – Anr. Copy. Maps slightly stained especially at margins, MS. owner's mark. 18th. C. hf. vell. (HK. Nov.18-21; 1061) DM 2,800
– Geographicae Enarrationes libri octo. Ed.:– Ioannis de Regio Monte (notes). Trans.:– Bilibaldo Pirckheimero. Ill.:– Albrecht Dürer. Strassburg, 30 Mar. 1525. Fo. (392mm × 260mm). Title restored & tissued, without loss, map 50 reprd. adjoining fold, with some loss, numbers 44 & 49 similarly reprd., with very slight loss, a few other repairs, 2 sm. wormholes in maps 37-50, with occasional minimal loss. Mod. mor. gt., 2-line border & panel, decor. upr. cover, silk end-ll. W.a.f. [Sabin 66482] (S. Nov.3; 2) *Terry.* £3,200
– – Anr. Copy. Fo. 40 (of 50) maps, title a little thumbed, some ll. with traces of use, some slight staining. 18th. C. vell. (VG. Dec.17; 1180) Fls. 5,600
– – Anr. Edn. Ed.:– Michael Villanovanus. Trans.:– Willibald Pirckheimer. Lyons, 1535. Fo. 49 maps (of 50), all on guards. Cont. limp vell., worn, later end-papers. [Sabin 66483] (C. Jul.15; 90) *Cash.* £4,500
– – Anr. Edn. Ed.:– M. Villanovano. Trans.:– B. Pirckeymheri. Lyon, 1541. Worming. Fo. 17th. C. vell. [Sabin 66485] (R. Oct.14-18; 1554) DM 27,000
– Geographiae Vniversae tvm Veteris tvm Novae. Ed.:– Magini. Ill.:– H. Porro after Ortelius, world map after Mercator. Cologne, 1597. 2nd. Edn. 2 pts. in 1 vol. Browned. Cont. limp vell., 2 ties, cockled. (HK. Nov.18-21; 1062) DM 3,200
– Liber de analemmate, a Federico Commandino . . . Instauratus . . . Eiusdem Federici Commandini liber de Horlogiorum Descriptione. Rome, 1562. 1st. Edn. 4to. Slight spotting, a few marginal stains. Cont. limp vell., soiled, lacks ties. Bkplt. of [Sebastiano] Canterzani; from Honeyman Collection. (S. Nov.11; 2558) *Zeitlin.* £400
– Liber Geographiae cum Tabulis et Universali Figura et cum Additione Locorum quae a recentioribus reperta sunt diligenti cura emendatus et impressus. Ed.:– Sylvanus of Eboli. Trans.:– J. Angelus. Venice, 20 Mar. 1511. Fo. (425mm × 280mm). 3 prelims. bnd. after maps, title restored & inlaid, without loss of text, slight cropping of text in W. margin of 1st. map, 1 or 2 maps cut close, some cropping of various headings added above the text in an early hand, a few other MS. marginalia. W.a.f. [Sabin 66477] (S. Nov.3; 1) *Hardy-Dodd.* £7,500
– Magnae Constructionis, Id est Perfectae coelestium motuum pertractationis, lib. XIII. Theonis Alexandrini in eosdem Commentariorum lib. XI. Ed.:– Simon Grynaeus. Basel, 1538. 1st. Edn. 2 pts. in 1 vol. Fo. Pt. 1 lacks quire a, title & last p. soiled, a few marginal stains. 17th. C. cf., worn, hf. red mor. case. From Honeyman Collection. (S. Nov.11; 2552) *Poole.* £180
– Mathematicae constructionis Liber primus graece & latine editus. [& another work]. Ed.:– Erasmus Rheinhold. Wittenberg, 1549. 2 works in 1 vol. Lacks table, some ll. stained at foot, sig. of Philip Melanchthon on title-p. & 3 lines of Greek in his hand, title-p. of Latin text with inscr. in anr. hand recording Rheinhold's gift of the book. Cont. blind-stpd. pig. over bds., worn, lacks clasps & catches. 2 quotations in margins in hand of ed., both sigd., from Honeyman Collection. (S. Nov.11; 2553) *Israel.* £820
– – Anr. Edn. Ed.:– Erasmus Rheinhold. Paris, 1556. 2 folding tables with sm. holes, title-p. soiled, some browning. Disbnd., hf. red mor. case. From Honeyman Collection. (S. Nov.11; 2554) *Quaritch.* £65
– Planisphaerium. Iordani Planisphaerium. Federici Commandini . . . Commentarius. Venice, 1558. 2 pts. in 1 vol. 4to. General title slightly stained. Mod. red mor., gt. Bkplt. of Giorgio di Veroli; from Honeyman Collection. (S. Nov.11; 2557) *Zeitlin.* £330
– Quadripartium [with other tracts]. Ed.:– Hieronymus Salius. Venice, Bonetus Locatellus, for Octavianus Scotus, 20 Dec. 1493. Fo. Last 10 ll. wormed in inner margins, a few single wormholes at beginning & end affecting text, slight marginal staining, tear in N1, old MS. annots. on a few ll. Cont. blind-stpd. cf.-bkd. wooden bds., 4 clasps & catches. From Honeyman Collection. [BMC V, 442; Hain 13544; Goff P1089] (S. Nov.11; 2549) *Schuman.* £700
– Tabulae Geographicae Orbis Terrarum Veteribus Cogniti. Amst. & Utrecht, 1704. Fo. Mod. cl. W.a.f. (S. Mar.31; 295) *Burgess.* £500
– Theatrum Geographiae Veteris . . . Ed.:– Peter Bertius. Leiden, 1618-19. 2 vols. in 1. Fo. (430mm × 270mm). Dedication lf. with port. of Bertius (not called for by Phillips) on verso, engraved plt. facing 003 not called for by Phillips, inscr. on title, various early MS. marginalia in Greek or Latin in text, with some underscoring, a few MS. annots. on versos of maps, MS. translation of Latin place-names on 2F6/2G1, pp. 190/191 of vol. 1 dust-soiled, some slight spotting, a few ll. in vol. 2 discoloured, top edge of dedication lf. restored. 18th. C. russ. gt., outer & inner panels, compartments formed in centre panel, gt. spine, rebkd. & restored. W.a.f. (S. Nov.3; 4) *Cohen.* £1,300

PTOLOMAEUS, Claudius-RUSCELLIUS, Girolamo
– La Geografia di Claudio Alessandrino. –Espositioni et Introductioni Universali; Discorso Universale Matematico al Signor Federigo Morando. Trans.:– Girolamo Ruscelli. Venice, 1561. Sm. 4to. Later vell. (LM. Mar.21; 29) B.Frs. 90,000

PUBLIC EDIFICES OF THE BRITISH METROPOLIS; With Historical & Descriptive Accounts of the Different Buildings
1825. Fo. Slight foxing. Old bds. (TA. Nov.20; 85) £105

PUBLICIUS, Jacobus
– Ars Oratoria Ars Epistolandi. [Augsburg], [Erhard Ratdolt], 20 Jan., 1490. Sm. 4to. 65 ll. (of 68), lacks title, fo. a3 & last blank. 19th. C. hf. cf. W.a.f. [BMC II, 384] (S. Nov.25; 322) *Andrews.* £240
– Artes Orandi Epistolandi Memorandi. Venice, Erhard Ratdolt, 31 Jan., 1485. 2nd. Edn. Sm. 4to. Volvelle lacks pointer. Red mor. gt. by Bedford. [BMC V, 289] (S. Nov.25; 321) *Boyl.* £1,300

PUCELLE D'ORLEANS (La)
L., 1780. Old gt. leath. in card case. (HY. Jan.14; 64) £90

PUCHOWITCHER, Yehuda Leib
– Divrei Chachamim. [Hamburg], 1692-93. 1st. Edn. 4to. Margins of 1st. 4 ll. reprd., slight discolouration. Hf. cl. (S. Nov.18; 453) *Stern.* £130

PUCKLE, James
– The Club: in a Dialogue between Father & Son. Ill.:– Thirston. L., 1817. 4to. Mntd. hf.-title, title & limitation ll., mntd. port., some ills. on mntd. India-proof, some pp. on Chinese paper, 1 lf. on satin, 1 on blue paper, etc. Cont. panel. cf., rebkd. in cf., covers brittle, burn-mark at inner edge of covers. Apparently a proof copy, marked in pencil at upr. blank 'Only 40 of this printed when the block was destroyed'. (PNY. Mar.26; 269) $100

PUEHLER, Christoff
– Ein kurtze und grundliche Anlaytung zů dem rechten Verstand Geometriae. Dilingen, 1563. 1st. Edn. 4to. Stained, tear in I3. Mod. hf. cf. From Honeyman Collection. (S. Nov.11; 2559) *Martin.* £200

PUFENDORF, Samuel, Baron von
– De Rebus a Carolo Gustavo Sueciae Rege gestis Commentariorum libri septem. Ill.:– Lombart, Cochin, Perelle & others. Nuremb., 1696. 1st. Edn. Fo. Some browning & light staining thro.-out. Cont. spr. cf., gt. spine. (S. Nov.4; 595) *Jackson.* £1,000
– De Rebus Gestis Friderici Wilhelmini Magni, Electoris Brandenburgici. Berlin, 1695. 1st. Edn. Fo. Title restored & browned. Cont. cf., slightly defect. & worn. (H. Dec.9/10; 897) DM 720
– Introduction à l'Histoire Moderne Générale et Politique de l'Univers. Ed.:– Bruzen de la Martinière. Ill.:– Charles Dominique Joseph Eisen. Paris, 1753-59. On Holland paper. 8 vols. in 16. Fo. Bkplt. of Joshua Smith, Stoke Park. Cont. mor., triple gt. fillet, flat spines tooled to design of ornamental foliage in style of Gravelot, arms at foot of Jean du Barry, arms of Duke of Newcastle

PUFENDORF, Samuel, Baron von -contd.
on covers, spine dulled to brown. (SM. Oct.8; 1945) Frs. 11,000
- **Sieben Bücher von denen Thaten Carl Gustavs Königs in Schweden.** Trans.:- S.R. Nuremb., 1697. 1st. German Edn. Fo. Hf.-title with later inscr., lacks last ll., others slightly defect. Cont. cf., worn. W.a.f. (S. Jun.23; 247) *Schmidt.* £700
- - **Anr. Copy.** 4 (of 12) engraved ports., 92 double-p. engraved plts., views & plans (of 115 & lacking panorama of Stockholm), 1st. gathering detchd. Loose in cont. vell. (S. Oct.20; 192) *Bjorck & Borjesson.* £600
- - **Anr. Copy.** Wide margin, plts. bnd. together at end, 10 ports. soiled, lightly browned. Later vell. (R. Mar.31-Apr.4; 1869) DM 12,500
- - **Anr. Copy.** Slightly browned or soiled, 3 (of 12) copper ports., 87 (Of 115) double-p. or folding copperplts. Cont. leath., very defect., upr. cover loose. (R. Oct.14-18; 1845) DM 7,000

PUFENDORF, Samuel Baron von & Bruzen de la Martinière, Antoine Augustin
- **Introduction à l'Histoire Moderne** . . . Ed.:- M. de Grace. Ill.:- Eisen. Paris, 1753-59. New Edn. 8 vols. 4to. Spr. cf., arms of Chancelier Lamoignon de Malesherbes on covers, spines decor. with raised bands & crossed maces. (HD. Jun.29; 251) Frs. 5,380

PUGET DE LA SERRE, Jean
- **Paralèlles et Eloges Historiques D'Alexandre le Grand, et de Monseigneur le Prince duc d'Anguien.** Paris, 1647. 2nd. Edn. (L.P.) 4to. Mourning bdg., covers blind-stpd. with arms of Montmorency in palm wreath, the whole in blind-stpd. panel with the eagles from the arms at each corner & single fleur de lis at head, foot & each side, flat spine blind-stpd. with fleur de lis, worn, lacks ties, slight surface worming on upr. cover, piece missing from head of spine. From the Knowsley liby., with press mark. (S. Apr.7; 329) *Temperley.* £240

PUGH, Edward
[-] **Cambria Depicta.** Ill.:- T. Cartwright. 1816. [1st. Edn.?]. 4to. Cont. cf., rebkd. preserving orig. spine. From the collection of Eric Sexton. (C. Apr.16; 336) *Maggs.* £260
[-] - **Anr. Copy.** Title damaged, restored & mntd., fo. H2 torn in inner margin & slightly frayed, H3 nearly torn out & tear in outer margin slightly affecting text, anr. lf. slightly torn in margin, slight offsets. Rebkd. (S. May 5; 223) *Burgess.* £180
- - **Anr. Copy.** Some dampstaining affecting top corner of some plts. Cont. hf. mor., gt. decor. spine. (TA. Oct.16; 293) £85

PUGH, John
- **A Treatise on the Science of Muscular Action.** 1794. [1st. Edn.?]. 4to. Plts. in 2 states, 2 text ll. with MS. notes in ink. Cont. pol. hf. cf. (C. Nov.6; 191) *Walford.* £80
- - **Anr. Copy.** Additional engraved title foxed. 19th. C. hf. cf., upr. cover detchd. From Chetham's Liby., Manchester. (C. Nov.27; 330) *Phelps.* £75
- **Specimens of Gothic Architecture.** Ill.:- E. Turrell & others after Pugin. Plts. dtd. 1820-22 [1825]. 3 pts. in 2 vols. 4to. Cont. mor.-bkd. cl. (C. Feb.25; 197) *Mortensan.* £150
- - **Anr. Edn.** Ed.:- E.J. Wilson. L., 1821-23. 1st. Edn. 2 vols., separately iss. Lge., tall 4to. Orig. qtr. leath. (PNY. Mar.26; 20) $130

PUGIN, Augustus Charles & others
- **Modern Furniture.** Ca. 1845. Sm. 4to. Plts. wtrmkd. 1821-43. Mod. qtr. cl. (S. Mar.17; 447) *Sims & Reed.* £260

PUGIN, Augustus Charles & Augustus Welby
- **Examples of Gothic Architecture.** Edinb., 1895. 3 vols. 4to. 1 plt. loose. Cont. buckram. (CB. May 27; 168) Can. $110

PUGIN, Augustus Welby
- **Details of Antient Timber Houses.-Gothic Furniture.-Designs for Gold & Silversmiths. -Designs for Iron & Brass Work.** 1836 [1837]; [?1835]; 1830; 1836. 4 works in 1 vol. 4to. Hf. mor., very slightly worn, spine gt. (SKC. Feb.26; 1466) £55
- **Details of antient timber houses.-The Style of Gothic Furniture of the 15th Century.-Designs for gold & silver-smiths.-Designs for iron & brass work.** 1836; 1835; 1836; 1836. 4 works in 1 vol. 4to. No text, advt. lf. at end. Cont. hf. mor., gt. panel. spine. (C. Feb.25; 196) *Cooper.* £90

- **Glossary of Ecclesiastic Ornament & Costume.** 1844. 4to. Cont. hf. mor. (TA. Mar.19; 97) £56
- - **Anr. Edn.** Ed.:- Rev. Bernard Smith. 1846. 2nd. Edn. 4to. Red mor., elab. gt. borders & central lozenge on sides, gt. spine, by J. Wright. (C. Nov.5; 123) *Traylen.* £160
- - **Anr. Copy.** Plts. numbered 2-71, 72 misnumbered 69, frontis. & last plt. not numbered but are included in list of plts. as 1 & 73. Cont. gt. decor. cl., crudely rebkd. (CB. May 27; 169) Can. $350
- **Gothic Furniture.** Ca. 1828. 4to. Last lf. torn across, some tears & marginal defects. Cont. hf. roan, spine gt. (S. Mar.17; 445) *Sims & Reed.* £170
- **The True Principles of Pointed or Christian Architecture: set forth in Two Lectures delivered at St. Marie's, Oscott.** L., 1841. 1st. Edn. Sm. 4to. Orig. cl. & mor. spine. (CB. May 27; 170) Can. $260
- **The True Principles of Pointed or Christian Architecture.-An Apology for the Revival of Christian Architecture in England.** L., 1853; 1843. 1st. Edn. (2nd. work). 2 works in 1 vol. 4to. Gt. cl., light wear & cover soiling. (SG. Dec.4; 289) $130
See-BRITTON, John & Pugin, Augustus Welby

PUGIN, Augustus Welby & Heath, Charles
- **Paris & its Environs.** 1829-31. 1st. Edn. 2 vols. in 1. 4to. Some Plts. & ll. spotted, some offsetting to text. Cont. cl., spine defect., worn. (S. Sep.29; 203) *Sermoneta.* £60
- - **Anr. Edn.** Ed.:- L.T. Ventouillac. L. & Paris, 1829 & 1831. Foxed thro.-out. Cont. cf., worn & crudely reprd., ex-liby. (SG. Nov.20; 389) $160
- - **Anr. Edn.** Ill.:- Augustus Charles & Augustus Welby Pugin & others. 1831. 2 vols. 4to. Mor., blind-stpd. on both covers with elab. decors., by Remnant & Edmonds. (SH. Apr.9; 164) *Blundell.* £110
- - **Anr. Copy.** Plts. on india paper, some foxing. Cont. hf. cf., some wear to spines. (TA. Jan.22; 383) £66
- - **Anr. Copy.** Text in Engl. & Fr., 2 ll. detchd. (TA. Nov.20; 439) £54
- - **Anr. Copy.** 2 vols. in 1. Orig. bdg. (TA. Sep.18; 299) £52
- - **Anr. Copy.** Lacks engraved & ptd. titles for vol. 1. Mod. leatherette, some foxing. (SG. Aug.21; 430) $130
- - **Anr. Edn.** L., 1833. L.P. (? 26 X 35 cms.). 2 vols. in 1. 101 engraved plts. proofed before (or with partial) letterpress & mntd. in, 2 engraved titles of the same nature dtd. 1829 & 1831, ptd. titles dtd. 1833, 1 additional plt. not called for, with additional p. of text. Cont. maroon mor. with gt. dentelles front & back & inside & outside, upr. bd. detchd. (CB. May 27; 166) Can. $800
- - **Anr. Edn.** Ca. 1840. 2 vols. in 1. 4to. Lacks title to vol. II, slightly spotted. Orig. embossed cl. (S. Dec.8; 223) *Heyndericks.* £70
- - **Anr. Edn.** N.d. 4to. Engraved title & plts. on India Paper, some ll. slightly spotted. Cont. mor., gt. (SH. Mar.5; 117) *Vitale.* £60

PUGIN, Augustus Welby & others
- **Specimens of the Architecture of Normandy, from the XIth to the XVIth Century.** Ed.:- Richard Phené Spiers & John Britton. Ill.:- John & Henry Le Keux. L., 1874. New Edn. 4to. Occasional slight foxing. Hf. leath. & buckram. (CB. May 27; 165) Can. $450

PUG'S VISIT, or the Disasters of Mr. Punch
1806. 1st. Edn. 16mo. Sm. hole in 1 lf., 1 lf. crudely reprd., 2 ll. loose. Wraps. (SH. Mar.19; 267) *Hirsch.* £75

PULCI, Luigi
- **Il Morgante.** Flor., 1574. 4to. Wormhole through corner of last 2 ll. touching 1 catchword, sig. of Fredk: Nicolay on title, bkplt. of Comte de Lauraguais. 18th. C. Fr. red mor., gt. border comprising birds & foliage, flat spine gt. à la grotesque, inner gt. dentelles, 2 fore-corners slightly worn. (SM. Oct.8; 1948) Frs. 1,200
- **Morgante Maggiore.** Venice, 1551. 4to. Lacks final blank, burnhole in B1 affecting text, old sig. on title, 1 flaw & 1 sm. glue mark affecting 1 or 2 letters. 18th. C. Fr. red mor., triple gt. fillet, spine gt. in compartments, inner gt. dentelles. (SM. Oct.8; 1949) Frs. 2,000

PULEMET [Machine-Gun]
St. Petersb., 1905. Finnish Edn. No. 1. 4to. Browned, sm. marginal tears. Unbnd. (SH. Feb.5; 116) *Landry.* £80

- - **Anr. Edn.** Ed.:- [N. Shebuev]. St. Petersb., 1905-06. Nos. 1-5 & Express no. Ob. fo. No. 1. torn. Unbnd. (SH. Feb.5; 115) *Landry.* £230

PULMAN, George P.R.
- **The Book of the Axe.** L., 1854. Tinted litho. plts., folding map reprd. on verso. Cl., stpd. in blind & gt. Henry A. Portong's bkplt. (SG. Oct.16; 313) $110
- **Rustic Sketches.** L., 1853. 2nd. Edn., L.P. 4to. Cl. (SG. Oct.16; 311) $160
- **Vade Mecum of Fly-Fishing for Trout.** Axminster, 1841. 1st. Edn. 12mo. Cl. (SG. Oct.16; 309) $300
- - **Anr. Edn.** L., 1851. 3rd. Edn. 12mo. Cl. (SG. Oct.16; 310) $100

PUNCH
L., 1841-1860. Vols. 1-39 in 20 vols. 4to. Hf. mor., spines gt. (SG. Sep.4; 393) $250
- - **Anr. Run.** 1841-89. Vols. 1-96 in 24. 4to. Cont. cl. gt., spines slightly worn. (TA. Dec.18; 253) £56
- - **Anr. Run.** 1841-1917. Vols. 1-152 (lacks vol. 128), 77 vols. 4to. 25 vols. in cont. hf. cf., others in orig. cl. (SH. Apr.9; 314) *Phillips.* £150
- - **Anr. Run.** 1841-1920. Vols. 1-100 & various later vols. in 51. 4to. Various bdgs., most worn. (CSK. Jan.30; 1) £110
- - **Anr. Run.** 1841-1938. 110 vols: vols. 1-4, 7, 40-48, 50-59, 64, 65, 68-99, 102-195. 4to. 1st. 58 vols. in orig. cl., others in cont. hf. mor. (SH. Apr. 9; 315) *Primrose Hill Books.* £130
- - **Anr. Run.** L., 8 Dec., 1915, 4to. With (on p.468) 'In Flanders Field' by John McRae. Orig. pict. wraps., buckram folding case. Carroll A. Wilson bkplt. (SG. Nov.13; 445) $100
- **Snapdragons for Christmas.** Ill.:- John Leech. L., 1844. 1st. Edn. Cf., multiple gt. fillet borders, spine gt., by Zaehnsdorf, orig. wraps. bnd. in, bkplt. (SG. Mar.19; 233) $100

PUNCH & London Charivari
1841-1937. Vols. 1-193. 4to. Orig. cl., gt. decor. spines, some slight wear to earlier vols. (TA. Jun.18; 382) £230

PUNCTUATION PERSONIFIED, or Pointing Made Easy, by Mr. Stops
N.Y., ca. 1830. A few ll. stained. Orig. pict. wraps., backstrip split, soiled. (SH. Mar.19; 268) *Schiller.* £190

PUNIN, N.N.
- **Noveishie Techeniya v Russkom Iskusstve [Newest Tendencies in Russian Art].** Leningrad, 1927-28. (3000); (2000). 2 vols. Orig. wraps. after Tatlin & Bruni, slightly soiled. (SH. Feb.6; 347) *Rosenthal.* £60
- **Percy Tsikl Lektsy [First Cycle of Lectures].** Petrograd, 1920. Title slightly soiled. Orig. wraps. by Malevich, torn & soiled, loose. (SH. Feb.5; 254) *Dembeck.* £260

PURCELL, Henry
- **Orpheus Britannicus.** L., 1698-1702. 2 books in 1 vol. Fo. Headlines cropped, minor tears & repairs, foxed. Old cf., very worn, upr. cover detchd. From the New York Public Liby. (SPB. Jul.28; 404) $275
- - **Anr. Edn.** 1702. Fo. Engraved frontis. port. laid down, pp. 171-4 misnumbered 143-6. Cont. reversed cf. (C. Jul.16; 342) *Henderson.* £75
- **The Vocal & Instrumental Musick of the Prophetess, or the History of Dioclesian.** 1691. 1st. Edn. Fo. Lr. margin of D2 cut into affecting text. Hf. roan, brkn. (BS. Jun.11; 80) £420

PURCELL, John
- **A Treatise of Vapours, or Hysterick Fits.** 1702. 1st. Edn. New panel. cf. (S. Jun.17; 690) *Jenner Books.* £180

PURCHAS, Samuel, the Elder
- **Purchase his Pilgrimage** . . . 1626. 4th. Edn. Fo. Double-p. engraved map, 22 engraved text maps, 1 plt. Old cf. [STC 20508] (C. May 20; 163) *Weiss.* £280
- - **Anr. Copy.** 24 maps, 1 plt., lacks Q2 & Q5, ex liby. Cf., scarred, rebkd. [Sabin 66682] (SPB. Jun.22; 118) $400
- **Purchas His Pilgrimes. In Five Bookes.** L., 1624-26. 1st. Edn., 2nd. Iss. of 1st. Vol. 5 vols. Fo. Lacks John Smith's map from vol. 4, pp. 1692-93, slight discolouration, a few tears. 18th. C. cf., worn covers detchd. [Sabin 66686] (SPB. Nov.24; 52) $2,500
- - **Anr. Edn.** 1625-26. 1st. Edn. (4th. Edn. of 'Purchas his Pilgrimes'). 5 vols. 5 double-p.

engraved maps only (of 7), 1 map slightly torn, engraved title soiled, some margins dampstained, occasional sm. holes or minor marginal tears. 19th. C. hf. mor., worn, some covers detchd., vol. 1 brkn. with ll. loose. W.a.f., from Chetham's Liby., Manchester. [STC 20509 & 20508.5; Sabin 66686] (C. Nov.27; 331) *Arkway.* £2,000
– Purchas his Pilgrimes.–Purchas his Pilgrimage. 1625-26. 1st. work 1st. Edn., 2nd. work 4th. Edn., iss. with dedication to King Charles. 1st. work. 4 vols., together 5 vols. Fo. Vol. 4 lacks 1st. blank. Late 18th, C. pol. cf., spines gt., jnts. split. [STC 20509. 20508.5] (S. Nov.24; 245) *Traylen.* £3,600

PURMANN, J.G.
[–] **Sitten und Meinungen der Wilden in Amerika.** Vienna, 1790. Latest Edn. 4 vols. Cont. hf. leath., spine partly brkn. [Sabin 66712] (R. Oct.14-18; 1683) DM 1,600

PURMANN, Matthaeus Gottfried
– **Der Rechte und Wahrhafftige Feldscher oder die rechte . . . Feldshers-Kunst . . . nebst Bayfügung des Pest-Barbierers.** Frankfurt & Leipzig, 1715. 2 pts. in 1 vol. Vell. (S. Jun.17; 691) *Preidel.* £60

PUSCHMANN, Theodor
– **Handbuch der Geschichte der Medizin . . . herausgegeben von . . . Max Neuberger, und . . . Julius Pagel.** Jena, 1902-05. 3 vols. Slight browning. Cl.-bkd. marb. bds. (S. Apr.6; 132) *Studio Books.* £50

PUSHKIN, Aleksandr Sergeevich
– **Boris Godunov.** St. Petersb., 1831. 1st. Edn. Lacks final blank, occasional foxing thro.-out. Later marb. paper bds. (C. Nov.20; 202) *Quaritch.* £520
– – **Anr. Edn.** Trans.:– J. Schiffrin. Ill.:– V. Choukhaeff. Paris, 1925. (390) numbered on Vergé à la Forme paper. Tall 4to. Orig. ornamental wraps., slightly worn. (PNY. May 21; 353) $125
– – **Anr. Edn.** Ill.:– Vassili Choukhaeff. Paris, 1925. (430) numbered. 4to. Decor. wraps., boxed. (SG. Apr.2; 71) $180
– **Le Coq D'Or, et d'Autres Contes.** Trans.:– N. Andreieff. Ill.:– B. Zworykine. Paris, 1925. (955) numbered. 4to. Orig. decor. wraps., foot of backstrip slightly worn. (SH. Mar.19; 331) *Fletcher.* £260
– **Gavriiliada.** Ed.:– [B. Tomashevsky]. St. Petersb., 1922. 1st. Complete Edn. 4to. Orig. wraps. (SH. Feb.6; 348) *Nijhoff.* £65
– **The Golden Cockerel.** Ill.:– Edmund Dulac. N.Y., Ltd. Edns. Cl., 1950. (1500) numbered. Sm. fo. Cl., gt. medallion on cover scratched, orig. box. Sigd. by artist. (SG. Apr.9; 518) $175
– – **Anr. Copy.** Bd. folder & box. (SG. Jan.15; 246) $100
– **Kapitanskaya Dochka [Captain's Daughter].** –**Evgeny Onegin.** Ill.:– Pavel Sokolov. Moscow, 1891-93. (1000) numbered (1st. work). 2 vols. Cont. hf. mor. (SH. Feb.5; 10) *Flegon.* £60
– **Pikovaya Dama [Queen of Spades].** Ill.:– A. Benois. St. Petersb., 1911. 4to. Orig. cf., spine worn. (SH. Feb.5; 11) *Lempert.* £80
– **Shazka o Tsare Saltane [Tale of Tsar Saltan].** Ill.:– I. Ya. Bilibin. St. Petersb., 1904. Ob. 4to. Loose in orig. pict. wraps., backstrip worn. (SH. Mar.19; 29) *Fletcher.* £110
– – **Anr. Edn.** Ill.:– Ivan Bilibin. St. Petersb., 1905. Ob. 4to. Orig. pict. wraps. (CSK. Jun.12; 125) $100
– **Skazka O Zolotom Pjetushkje [The Tale of the Golden Cockerel].** Ill.:– Ivan Bilibin. St. Petersb., 1907. Ob. 4to. Orig. pict. wraps. (CSK. Jun.12; 127) £120
– **Zolotoi petushok [Golden Cockerell for the Opera by S.I. Zimin].** Ill.:– I. Bilibin. St. Petersb., 1909. Orig. wraps., slightly soiled. (SH. Feb.5; 12) *Reisler.* £110

PUTEANUS, Erycius
– **De Cometa (1618). Novo Mundi Spectaculo, libri duo. Paradoxologia.** Cologne, 1619. 12mo. Cont. vell. From Honeyman Collection. (S. Nov.11; 2561) *Hill.* £65

PUTTI, Vittorio
– **Berengario da Carpi: Saggio Biografico e Bibliografico seguito dalla Traduzione del 'De Fractura Calvae sive Cranei'.** Bologna, 1937. 1st. Edn. 4to. Orig. cl., d.-w. From liby. of Dr. E. Ashworth Underwood. (S. Feb.23; 277) *Mistrali.* £60

PÜTTMANN, H.
– **Deutsches Bürgerbuch für 1845.** Darmstadt, 1845. Cont. bds. Pp. III-VI rehinged. Cont. bds. (R. Oct.14-18; 1365) DM 1,300

PUYDT, Paul Emile de
– **Les Orchidées.** Paris, 1880. Cont. mor.-bkd. cl. (C. Jul.15; 198) *Junk.* £320

PYE, Charles
– **Provincial Copper Coins or Tokens issued between the years 1787 & 1796.** L. & Bg'ham., n.d. Engraved title, spotted, some general spotting. Cont. hf. cf., rebkd., with old spine preserved. (CSK. Jan.16; 109) £60

PYLE, Howard
– **Book of Pirates.–Book of the American Spirit.** N.Y., 1921; 1923. 1st. Edns. 2 vols. Tall 4to. Qtr. cl. & bds., portions of d.-w.'s. present. (PNY. Mar.26; 270) $100

PYNE, James B.
– **The English Lake District.** 1853. Edges soiled, light stains. (JN. Apr.2; 854) £165

PYNE, William Henry 'Peter Pasquin'
– **The Costume of Great Britain.** 1804. Fo. Plts. wtrmkd. 1823, text 1821, some offsetting, slightly soiled. 19th. C. str.-grd. mor., gt. (S. Oct.21; 506) *Walford.* £530
– – **Anr. Edn.** 1808. Fo. Cont. red str.-grd. mor., wide gt. scallop-shell borders & central gt. lozenge on sides, gt panel. spine. (C. Nov.5; 124) *Davidson.* £450
– – **Anr. Copy.** 55 (of 60) plts. Cont. hf. cf. (SH. Jan.29; 282) *Nolan.* £340
– **A Day's Journal of a Sponge.** L., 1824. Ob. 4to. Orig. wraps. (SSA. Jan.22; 103) R. 210
– **Etchings of Rustic Figures.** 1815. Hf. cf. (P. Feb.19; 216) *Davies.* £65
– **History of the Royal Residences . . .** 1819. [1st. Edn.?]. 3 vols. 4to. 100 cold. aquatint plts., most with a dupl. uncold. etching. Crimson str.-grd. mor., sides panel. in gt. & blind, spines gt. (C. Mar.18; 86) *Chelsea.* £1,500
– – **Anr. Copy.** Cont. str.-grd. mor., sides with wide gt. & blind roll tooled borders, gt. ornament., gt. panel. spine. (C. Mar.18; 87) *Henderson.* £1,200
– – **Anr. Copy.** Plts. hand-cold., & wtrmkd. 1818. Cont. maroon mor. gt., gt. cathedral pattern on covers. Bkplt. of George Godwin, lately in the collection of Eric Sexton. (C. Apr.16; 338) *Rostron.* £850
– – **Anr. Copy.** L.P 3 vols. 4to. 100 uncold. plts., text & plts. wtrmkd. 1816-18, 2 ll. in vol. 2 inlaid vols. 2 & 3 titles misbnd. 19th. C. hf. red mor., spines gt., worn. Inscr. to Edward P. Tennant from Sir Arthur & Lady Hayter. (S. Nov.24; 246) *Maggs.* £200
– – **Anr. Copy.** Lf. of instructions to binder in vol. 3. Cont. red str.-grd. mor. gt. lettered on upr. covers. (SPB. Oct.1; 207) $1,800
– – **Anr. Copy.** Some tears, slight discolouration. Hf. red mor. (SPB. Nov.25; 120) $900
– **Microcosm or a Picturesque Delineation of the Arts, Agriculture, Manufactures.** 1806. Vol. 2 only. Ob. fo. Orig. bds. W.a.f. (P. Dec.11; 81) *Trevor.* £150
– – **Anr. Edn.** 1808. 2 vols. in 1. Fo. Aquatint frontis., 120 plts., some browned & foxed, index & text partly misbnd. 19th. C. hf. roan, upr. jnt. split. (C. Mar.18; 85) *Gibbs.* £500
– – **Anr. Edn.** [1822-24]. 2 vols. in 1. Ob. fo. Spotted & stained. Cf.-bkd. bds., lacks upr. bd., lr. bd. detchd. W.a.f. (CSK. Mar.6; 45) £340

PYNE, William Henry & Wylie, D. & others
– **Lancashire Illustrated.** 1831. 4to. Cont. moiré cl. (CSK. Sep.5; 5) £90

PYNE, William Henry & others
– **Picturesque Groups for the Embellishment of Landscape.** 1845. 2 vols. in 1. Fo. Title & a few plts. slightly soiled or spotted. Mod. leath. (S. Dec.9; 506) *Crossley.* £280

PYRARD DE LAVAL, François
– **Voyage . . . contenant sa Navigation aux Indes Orientales, Maldives, Moluques, & au Bresil.** Paris, 1679. 4to. A few sm. stains. Cont. cf. (SPB. May 5; 420) $550

PYTHAGORAS & PHOCYLIDES
– **Poemata . . . cum duplici interpretatione Viti Amerbachij.** Leipzig, 1578. Texts in Greek & Latin, some woodcut initials hand-cold., soiled & dampstained, some worm-holes slightly affecting

text, old owners' inscrs. NS. notes on paste-downs, last blanks & blank versos of last lf. Wooden bds., blind-stpd. pig. spine, dtd. 1589, some wormholes, slightly worn, lacks clasp. (S. Dec.8; 93) *Harley.* £55

QUACKENBOS, John D.
– **Geological Ancestors of the Brook Trout & Recent Saibling Forms from which it Evolved.** N.Y., Priv. Ptd. 1916. 1st. Edn., (300) numbered sigd. Leath., unc. (SG. Oct.16; 315) $300

QUAD, Matthew
– **Geographicae Tabulae.** 1600? 4to. Lacks title, 53 maps (of 82), several in bad condition. Old hf. roan. (HD. Jun.24; 4) Frs. 18,000

QUAD, Matthew & Bussemecher, J.
– **Europae Totius Orbis Terrarum Partis Praestantissimae . . . Descriptio.** Cologne, 1594-96 [Colophon]. Fo., (272mm × 185mm). Text in Latin on versos, underscoring of place-names on some maps, early MS. note in margin of map of Bradenburg, port. crudely cold. Cont. cf., line & roll-tooled borders, elliptical centre ornaments, traces of gilding, rebkd., worn. W.a.f. (S. Nov.3; 5) *Schuster.* £3,000

QUADRAGESIMAL SPIRITUEL (Le) ou Caresme Allégorié, pour enseigner le simple Peuple a deuément & salutaireme(n)t ieuner & voyager Paris, 1565. Slight browning & soiling, later inscr. on title. 18th. C. cf., worn, upr. cover detchd. From liby. of André L. Simon. (S. May 18; 164) *Hill.* £80

QUADRI, Gio. Lodovico
– **Tavole gnomoniche per delineare orologi a sole, –Tavole per regolare di giorno in giorno gli Orologi a ruote.** Bologna, 1733; 1736. 1st. Edns. 2 works in 1 vol. 4to. 1st. work with title a little soiled & hinged at inner edge. Cl.-bkd. bds., worn. From Honeyman Collection. (S. Nov.11; 2562) *Nox.* £160

QUAGLIO, Dominicus
– **Merkwürdige Gebäude des Teutschen Mittelalters.** Ed.:– S. Schreiber. Karlsruhe, [1821-26], 2 vols. in 1. Fo. Some lithos. soiled, 3 ll. loose. Cont. linen, spine torn. (H. Dec.9/10; 732) DM 6,800

QUAIN, Jones & Wilson, William J.E.
– **The Muscles-Vessels-Nerves-Viscera of the Human Body.** 1836-40. 4 vols. Fo. Some marginal dampstains, some spotting & stains, a few short tears in margins, some reprd. Hf. cf., vol. 4 not unif. (S. Jun.17; 692) *Norman.* £140
– **A Series of Anatomical Plates . . . of the Human Body.** 1836-42. 2 vols. in 3 (5 pts.). Fo. Mod. hf. cf. (C. May 20; 47) *Elstein.* £220
– – **Anr. Edn.** L., 1842. 2 vols. Tall fo. Approx. 200 litho. plts., many cold., lacks at least 1 plt. Mod. buck. Erratically bnd., possibly incompl., w.a.f., ex liby. (SG. Sep.18; 311) $450

QUARANTE MANIÈRES de Foutre (Les)
[L.], [1790]. Sm. thin 16mo. Lacks title. Bradel paper bds., ca. 1830. (HD. Apr.10; 370) Frs. 2,000

QUARENGHI, Giacomo
– **Fabriche e Disenni.** Milan, 1821. Fo. 1 plt. stained. Cont. hf. cf., rather worn, upr. cover stained, unc. (SI. Dec.4; 478) Lire 520,000

QUARLES, Francis
– **Divine Fancies Digested into Epigrammes . . .** 1641. Sm. 4to. Mod. cf. [Wing Q62] (S. Mar.16; 150) *Lam.* £70

QUARTA Centuria Ecclesiasticae Historiae Basle, 1562. Fo. Cont. embossed vell. over bds., soiled, lacks 1 orig. clasp. MS. exlibris of Pastor Christophorus Pfefflem. (SG. Feb.5; 282) $110

QUARTERLY JOURNAL of Agriculture Edinb. & L., 1829-45. Vols. 1-13, New Series, vol. 1, together 14 vols. A very few spots. Cont. hf. cf. (SBA. Jul.23; 274) *Brian.* £75

QUARTERLY REVIEW, The 1809-29. Vols. 1-39. Some ll. spotted. Orig. cf. gt. (SD. Feb.4; 58) £130

QUATRAINS (Les) du Quatrain Ill.:– Luc Lafnet. Paris, 1927. 1st. Edn., copy no, 1. (400) numbered on Annam. 5 vols. 4to. Jansenist mor., sigd. by Affolter & Augoyat, mor. doubls., triple gold fillet border, silk end-ll., double cold. end-ll., orig. wraps. bnd. in, s.-c. Ms. ded. & Beraldi ex-lib. (D. Dec.11-13; 1169) DM 2,200

QUATRE Fils Aymon, Histoire des
Ill.:– Eugène Grasset. Paris, 1883. 4to. Hf. mor., spine decor. with raised bands, wraps. (HD. Feb.27; 146) Frs. 1,500

QUEBEC Mercury
[Quebec], Jan.6-Dec.29, 1812. Vol. III, nos. 1-52. 4to. 3 ll. with minor tears. Cont. hf. leath. & marb. bds. (CB. Dec.9; 238) Can. $350

QUEEN, The
1862-63. Vols. 1-3. 4to. Orig. cl. gt. (P. Apr. 9; 275) Walford. £70

QUEEN MARY'S PSALTER
– Miniatures & Drawings by an English Artist of the 14th Century reproduced from Royal Ms. 2 B. VII in the British Museum. Ed.:– Sir George Warner. 1912. Fo. Rebnd. in hf. mor. (TA. Sep.18; 49) £75

QUEENY, Edgar M.
– Prairie Wings. Ill.:– Richard E. Bishop. Phila., 1947. Lge. 4to. Buckram. (SG. Apr.9; 389) $220

QUELLENBUCHER DER LEIBESUBUNGEN
Ed.:– M. Schwarze & W. Limpert. Dresden, [1927-34.] Vols. 1-8, all publd. Hf. leath. (R. Oct.14-18; 2902) DM 950

QUELLINUS, A.
See–CAMPEN, Jacob van–QUELLINUS, A.

QUENTIN, Jean
– Examen de Conscience pour soy Congnoistre (&) abien se confesser. [Paris], ca. 1500. A little slight browning. Late 19th. C. mor. by Cape, gt. From Liby. of André L. Simon. (S. May 18; 165) Hill. £350

QUENTIN BAUCHART, Ernest
– Les Femmes Bibliophiles de France. Paris, 1886. (300) on Holland paper, 1st. Edn. 2 vols. 4to. 20th. C. mor. by Yseux, ptly. unc., orig. wraps. preserved. (SM. Oct.7; 1477) Frs. 3,200

QUERARD, Joseph Marie
– La France Litteraire. Paris, 1827-39. 10 vols., lacks Supps. Cont. cf. (SH. May 28; 86) Booth. £55

QUERLON, Meunier de
[–] Les Graces. Ill.:– Moreau (title), Simonet after Boucher (Frontis.) plts. Massard, Simonet & others after Moreau. Paris, 1769. Cont. marb. leath., gt. spine, gold-stpd. floral borders, outer gt. dentelle. (D. Dec.11-13; 715) DM 650

QUESNAY, Fr.
[–] Physiocratie. Yverdon, 1768. 1st. Edn. Vols. I & II in 1 Vol. Lightly browned. Cont. hf. leath., spine slightly torn. (H. May 21/22; 662) DM 1,400

QUESNAY, Fr. & others
– Recherches Critiques et Historiques sur l'origine, sur les divers Etats et sur les Progres de la Chirurgie. Paris, 1744. 1st. Edn. 4to. A few additional pieces between pp. 524 & 533. Cont. cf., spine gt., worn. (S. Dec.2; 598) Norris. £90

QUEVEDO, Francisco de
– Plabo de Segovie. Ill.:– Daniel Vierge. Paris, 1902. (455) numbered on L.P. Fo. Chagrin, orig. wraps preserved. Sigd. by artist. (DS. May 22; 876) Pts. 30,000

QUEVEDO Y VILLEGAS, Don Francisco de
– Les Oeuvres . . .–Voyages Récréatifs du Chevalier de Quevedo. Ecrits par lui-mesme. Trans.:– Sr. Raclots. (1st. work). Ill.:– Harrewijn (1st. work). Brussels; [Paris], 1718; 1756. 3 vols. 12mo. Cont. mor. (by Derome le Jeune), triple gt. fillet, flat spines gt. in compartments, inner gt. dentelles. (S. Apr.7; 348) Foyles. £140

QUILLER-COUCH, Sir Arthur
– In Powder & Crinoline: Old Fairy Tales. Ill.:– Kay Nielsen. [1913]. 4to. Orig. cl.-bkd. pict. bds., slightly stained & soiled. (SKC. Feb.26; 1291) £85
– – Anr. Copy. 1 p. cut away at front, slight browning. Orig. vell. gt., warped, spots. (SPB. May 29; 314) $400
– – Anr. Copy. Lin.-bkd. bds. (SG. Oct.23; 242) $260
– – Anr. Edn. Ill.:– Kay Nielsen. n.d. 4to. Cl.-bkd. bds. (P. Dec.11; 209) Spake. £130
– – Anr. Copy. Orig. cl.-bkd. bds., in orig. ptd. box. (C. Feb.4; 79) Joseph. £50
– The Sleeping Beauty & Other Fairy Tales from the Old French. Ill.:– Edmund Dulac. L., [1910].

(100) numbered sigd. by Dulac. 4to. Orig. gt.-ornamental mor. (PNY. Dec.3; 130) $160
– – Anr. Copy. Publisher's mor., fillets & gt. motifs on covers, decor. spine. (HD. Jun.25; 377) Frs. 1,000
– – Anr. Edn. Ill.:– Edmund Dulac. [1911]. 4to. Orig. cl. gt. (SH. Dec.10; 185) Smith. £50
– – Anr. Edn. Ill.:– Edmund Dulac. n.d. (1,000) numbered De Luxe Edn. sigd. by Dulac. 1 vol. 4to. Tipped in cold. plts. Hf. red mor. (RBT. Jan.22; 13) £82
– – Anr. Copy. Mor., gt., worn. Sigd. (CE. Aug.28; 289) £60
– The Twelve Dancing Princesses & other Fairy Tales Retold. Ill.:– Kay Nielsen. N.Y., ca. 1915. Gt.-pict. cl. (SG. Apr.2; 214) $325

QUINCEY, Thomas de
– L'Assassinat Considéré comme un des Beaux-Arts. Ill.:– Gus Bofa. Paris, 1930. (100) on Rives. In sheets, publisher's s.-c. (HD. Dec.5; 168) Frs. 1,750

QUINCY, Marquis de
– Histoire Militaire de Louis le Grand, Roy de France. Paris, 1726. 1st. Edn. 8 vols. Lge. 4to. Cont. cf., spines gt. Pict. bkplt. of President Henault, with port. of him bnd. in. (SG. Oct.9; 200) $550

QUINCY, John
– Compleat English Dispensatory. 1722. Cf. gt. (P. Sep.11; 64) Chelsea. £60

QUINTILIANUS, Marcus Fabius
– Institutio Oratoria. Paris, 1541. Fo. Cf., gt. roundel on covers. (P. Jun.11; 103) £60
– Institutionum Oratoriarum. Venice, 1513. 12mo. Stained. Cf. (SH. Jul.9; 86) Dampaloni. £60

QUINTINYE, Jean de la
– Complete Gard'ner. 1701. 2 vols. in 1. Some worming, not affecting text. Cf. gt. (P. Oct.2; 81) Park. £55

QUIRINO, Carlos
– Philippine Cartography [1320-1899]. Manila, [1959]. (100) numbered copies. 4to. Cl. (SG. Oct.2; 301) $110

QUIVER; an Illustrated Magazine . . .
Ill.:– Arthur Rackham & others. L., 1897-98. 2 vols. 4to. Cont. cl. Raymond M. Sutton Jr. copy. (SG. May 7; 241) $120

QUIVER OF LOVE, The
– A Collection of Valentines ancient & modern. Ill.:– Walter Crane & Kate Greenaway. 1876. 4to. Gt. pict. cl. (CE. Mar.19; 155) £75
– – Anr. Copy. 1 text lf. with short tears. Orig. cl., gt. (C. Feb.4; 71) Harcourt/Williams. £50

QUIZEM, Caleb
– Annals of Sporting. Ill.:– Thomas Rowlandson after Bunbury & Woodward. 1809. 1st. Edn. Orig. ptd. bds., crushed mor. s.-c. (C. Nov.6; 330) Way. £75

R., L.N.
– The Book & its Story. L., 1856. Blind-stpd. mor. Fore-e. pntg. of Samson & Deliah (extending along fore-edge & continuing along both other edges). (SG. Mar.19; 114) $500

R.B.
– The Kingdome of Darkness. L., 1688. 12mo. Cont. cf. [Wing C 7342] (VG. Oct.13; 130) Fls. 1,000

RABANUS Maurus
– De Laudibus Sancte Crucis opus erudicione versu prosaqz mirificum. Pforzheim, 1503. Fo. Lacks final blank C4, title soiled & reprd in margins, some staining. 18th. C. cf., worn. (S. Jun.23; 219) Rota. £420
– De universo. [Strassburg], [Adolph Rusch]. [Before 20 Jul. [or Jun.], 1467]. 1st. Edn. Fo. Lacks 1st. & last blanks, initials & paragraph marks in red, slight discolouration, wide margins. 18th. C. Dutch cl., panel. in gt., royal couronnes fermées surmounted by orb & cross at corners, lge. ornamental centre-pieces, spine gt. with cockerel in 7 compartments, hf. red mor. case. From liby. of Pierre-Antoine Bolongaro-Crevenna; from Honeyman Collection. [BMC I, 60; Goff R1] (S. Nov.11; 2563) Meijer. £9,200

RABBINOWITCH, Raphael Nathan Nata
– Maamar Al Hadpasat Hatalmud. Munich, 1877. 1st. Edn. Mor.-bkd. bds. Extensive MS. notes by Aron Freimann. (SPB. May 11; 175) $150

RABBULA GOSPELS
Ed.:– C. Cecchelli & others. Olten & Lausanne, 1959. Ltd. Edn. Fo. Orig. cf. (SH. Mar.6; 560) Erasmus. £80

RABEL, Daniel
[–] Theatrum Florae. Paris, 1633. Fo. Lacks frontis. & plts. 25 & 59, 1 plt. torn, another with sm. hole, occasional marginal spotting. Old cf., rebkd. W.a.f., from Chetham's Liby., Manchester. (C. Nov.27; 332) Antiqua Libri. £680

RABELAIS, François
– Les Oeuvres. Lyons, 1588. 3 pts. in 1 vol. 12mo. Slight dampstaining. Cont. limp vell., worn. From liby. of André L. Simon. (S. May 18; 167) Claridge. £260
– – Anr. Copy. Closely cut affecting most head-lines & some sigs. etc., sm. marginal repair to blank margin of last lf., some discolouration. Vell., rebkd., in s.-c., bkstp. of Benjamin Bayfield on fly-lf. (S. Jun.23; 232) Duran. £100
– – Anr. Edn. Ill.:– after L.F. Du Bourg (plts.), Bernard Picart (head & tail-pieces). Amst., 1741. New Edn. 4to. Occasional foxing, plts. browned. Cont. marb. cf., slightly worn, spines richly gt. (VG. Nov.18; 1341) Fls. 800
– – Anr. Edn. Ill.:– De Launay after Sarabat (port.). Geneva, 1782. 4 vols. 18mo. Marb. sheep. by Cazin. (HD. Apr.8; 295) Frs. 2,300
– – Anr. Edn. 1823. 9 vols. Red hf. cf. by Niedrée. (HD. Oct.10; 273) Frs. 2,000
– – Anr. Edn. Ill.:– Gustave Doré. Paris, 1873. [1st. Edn.?]. 2 vols. Fo. Publisher's cl., limp decor. spine, special gt. tools, sigd. A. Souze, 1 corner reprd. (LM. Mar.21; 96) B.Frs. 9,000
– – Anr. Copy. On vell., Lge. 4to. (LM. Jun.13; 177) B.Frs. 8,500
– – Anr. Copy. (25) on Chine. Fo. Hf. grenate mor., corners, s.-c., publisher's cl. wrap. preserved, by Devanchelle. (HD. Jun.10; 197) Frs. 12,500
– – Anr. Edn. Ill.:– Doré. Paris, n.d. 2 vols. 4to. Later hf. mor., by Vermorel, spines gt., mor. overlays. (SM. Oct.8; 2242) Frs. 2,000

RACANATI, Manachem
– Piskei Halachot. Bologna, 1538. 1st. Edn. Sm. 4to. Some sigs. loose, lightly stained. Sheep, worn, backing torn. (SPB. May 11; 177) $1,500

RACCOLTA DE' VIAGGI Piu Interessanti Esequiti nelle Varie parti del Mondo
Milan, 1816-20. 20 vols. 12mo. Cont. leath.-bkd. marb. bds. (SG. Oct.30; 299) $280

RACCOLTA DEI PRIMI VENTINOVE CATALOGHI Dell'Espozione Internazionale della Citta di Venezia
Venice, 1895-1958. 16mo. Orig. wraps. (CR. Mar.19; 148) Lire 650,000

RACCOLTA della Gerarchia Ecclesiastica
Rome, 1834. Roan-bkd. bds. (BS. Jun.11; 382) £75

RACCOLTA DI FIGURINI DI MODO
N.d. 4to. 50 plts. Cl. (CR. Mar.19; 330) Lire 650,000

RACCOLTA DI LIBRETTI D'OPERA della Prima Meta del Secolo XIX
Milan & Modena, ca. 1820-40. Orig. wraps. W.a.f. (SI. Dec.3; 328) Lire 380,000

RACER, J.W.
– Overijsselsche Gedenkstukken. Leiden; Kampen, 1781-93. 7 vols. Liby.-stp. on verso of title-pp. Cont. marb. cf. (VG. Nov.18; 818) Fls. 700

RACINE, Jean
– Bérénice. Ill.:– Decaris. Priv. ptd., 1948. (135); (15) on Lana vell. 4to. Copper-engr., corresponding orig. drawing, engrs. in 3 states. Mor. by J. Lambert, gt. & silver fillets, chevrons in relief on covers, smooth decor. spine, cf. doubls. with leath. plaque, watered silk end-papers, wrap. & spine preserved, s.-c. (HD. Feb.27; 216) Frs. 2,000
– Oeuvres. Ill.:– De Sève. 1760. 1st. Printing. 3 vols. 4to. Cont. cf. (HD. Jun.30; 67) Frs. 4,800
– – Anr. Edn. Ed.:– M. Luneau de Boisjermain. Ill:– Santerre engraved by Gauchet (port), Gravelot engraved by Flipart, Lemire. Paris, 1768. 1st. Printing. 7 vols. 1sm. wormhole. Cont. porphyr. cf., gt. triple fillet border, limp decor. spines, some defects & reprs. (HD. Apr.24; 95) Frs. 2,300
– – Anr. Edn. Ed.:– M. Luneau de Boisjermain. Ill:– After Gravelot. Paris, & L., 1768. Mixed Edns. 7 vols. Light spotting. Cont. cf., gt. spines

designed by Gravelot. (SM. Oct.8; 2150)
Frs. 1,500
– – **Anr. Edn.** L., 1782. 3 vols. 18mo. Red mor. by Cazin. (HD. Apr.8; 296) Frs. 3,200
– – **Anr. Edn.** Paris, 1783. (200). 3 vols. 4to. Approbation lf. in vol. 1. Cont. str.-grd. mor., gt., narrow concentric roll borders incorporating stars, fleur-de-lis, circles within squares & fillets, spine gt. in compartments with repeated lozenges, inner gt. dentelles, purple silk liners. Malmesbury Copy. (SM. Oct.8; 1952) Frs. 4,200
– – **Anr. Copy.** Minimal browning. Cont. mor., blind-stpd., gt. inner & outer dentelle, slightly soiled & lightly defect. (H. May 21/22; 1245)
DM 2,600
– – **Anr. Edn.** Paris, 1784. 3 vols. Red mor. by Derôme, triple gt. fillet around covers, smooth decor. spines, inside dentelle. (HD. Feb.27; 49)
Frs. 4,500
– – **Anr. Copy.** (450) on vell., 5 vols. 16mo. Cont. red str.-grd. mor., spines decor., fillet on covers, inner dentelle. From the 'Collection des Auteurs Classiques Francais et Latin', ptd. for the Education of M. le Dauphin. (HD. Apr.9; 545)
Frs. 1,900
– – **Anr. Edn.** Ed.:– M. Luneau de Boisjermain. Ill.:– Gaucher after Santerre, Gravelot. Paris, 1796. 7 vols. Cont. hf. roan, false spine raised bands gt., some defects. (HD. Apr.9; 606)
Frs. 1,300
– **Oeuvres Complètes.** Paris, 1796. 1st. printing, on L.P. vell. 4 vols. Light browning. Red mor., decor spines, wtrd. silk end-ll., by Bozérian. (HD. Jun.10; 89) Frs. 11,500
– – **Anr. Edn.** Ill.:– Prudhon, Gérard, Giraudet & others. 1820. On vell. 6 vols. With extra set of 57 figures before the letter, for Didot's edn. of 1801, foxed. Cont. Bradel str.-grd. red hf. mor., smooth decor. spines. (HD. Feb.27; 212) Frs. 2,550
– **Phèdre & Hippolyte.** Ill.:– Le Clerc after Le Brun (frontis.). Paris, 1677. Some sm. wormholes. Old red bkpl., spine with decor. bands, lge. dentelle border on covers. (SM. Feb.11; 133) Frs. 1,600
– **Théâtre.** Ill.:– Hillemacher. Paris, 1873-74. (100) on Holland. 4 vols. Red mor. by Rivière, triple gt. fillet around covers, fleurons in corners, spines decor. with raised bands, inside dentelles. From liby. of Lord Battersea. (HD. Feb.27; 215)
Frs. 1,600
– **Théâtre Complet.** Parma, 1813. 3 vols. Fo. With the 'imprime' lf. in each vol. & lf. of contents at end of vol. III. Cont. hf. vell., unc. (S. Jul.27; 159)
Quaritch. £400
– – **Anr. Copy.** Some engraved plts. loosely inserted. Cont. str.-grd. red hf. mor., unc. (SM. Feb.11; 134) Frs. 3,500

RACINET, Auguste
– **Le Costume Historique.** Paris, 1888. 6 vols. 4to. Later mor.-bkd. bds. (SH. Oct.9; 20)
Duran. £360
– – **Anr. Copy.** Marb. hf. roan, decor. spines. (HD. Dec.5; 171) Frs. 4,600
– – **Anr. Copy.** 4 vols. Fo. Cont. red chagrin, decor. spine raised bands, 1 vol. disbnd. (HD. Apr.24; 178) Frs. 3,400
– – **Anr. Copy.** 6 vols. Hf. red mor., slightly worn, partly unc. (SI. Dec.4; 483) Lire 850,000
– – **Anr. Copy.** 4to. Chagrin. (DS. May 22; 872)
Pts. 90,000
– – **Anr. Edn.** Paris, n.d. 2 folios. Hf. cl. (P. Apr.9; 189D) Horesh. £150
– **L'Ornement Polychrome.** Paris, ca. 1870-85. 2 vols. Fo. Cont. hf. red mor. (SI. Dec.4; 484)
Lire 350,000
– – **Anr. Edn.** Paris, 1885-6. 2nd. series. 10 vols. Fo. Orig. cl. (SH. Jan.29; 285) Gilbert. £105
– – **Anr. Edn.** Paris, 1888. Fo. Some plts. slightly soiled. Mod. three-qtr. leath. (SG. Mar.12; 304)
$300
– – **Anr. Edn.** Paris, n.d. Fo. Cont. hf. mor. (SH. Jan.29; 286) Gilbert. £95

RACING Calendar, The
1769-1966. 198 vols. Cf., defect. W.a.f. (SBA. Jul.23; 623) Dawson. £650
– – **Anr. Run.** 1773-1971. Vols. 1-199. Cont. cf. (CSK. Feb.27; 100) £300

RACKHAM, Arthur
– **Book of Pictures.** 1913. [1st. Edn.?]. 4to. Orig. cl. gt., spine slightly discold. (S. Jul.31; 286)
Ross. £65
– – **Anr. Copy.** 44 cold. plts. tipped in. (TA. Jun.18; 441) £50

– – **Anr. Copy.** (1030) numbered, sigd. Red three-qtr. mor., by Zaehnsdorf. (SG. Oct.9; 202)
$375
– – **Anr. Edn.** Ed.:– Sir A. Quiller-Couch (introduction). L., [1913]. (1030) numbered, & sigd. 4to. Title-p. foxed. Gt.-pict. cl., discold., hf. lev. folding case. (SG. Apr.2; 249) $450
– – **Anr. Copy.** Raymond M. Sutton Jr. copy. (SG. May 7; 13) $400
– – **Anr. Edn.** Ed.:– Sir Arthur Quiller-Couch. 1923. 4to. Orig. cl. gt. (SH. Dec.11; 440)
Mundy. £60
– – **Anr. Copy.** Some foxing. Orig. bdg., d.-w. (JL. Mar.2; 611) Aus. $100
[–] **Catalogue of an Exhibition of Water-Colour Drawings Illustrating 'Peter Pan in Kensington Gardens'.** L., Nov.-Dec. 1906. Sm. 4to. Wraps. Raymond M. Sutton Jr. copy. (SG. May 7; 54)
$100
– **Fairy Book.** L., [1933]. (460) numbered, sigd. 4to. Vell. gt., unc., unopened, cl. s.-c. Raymond M. Sutton Jr. copy. (SG. May 7; 12) $750
– – **Anr. Copy.** Parch. gt., minor wear, publisher's box, worn. (SPB. May 29; 353) $475
– – **Anr. Copy.** Gt. decor. vell., spine wrinkled, boxed, unc. (SG. Apr.30; 264) $450
– **Oeuvres.** Paris, n.d. (460), numbered; (400) on vell. 4to. Publisher's Bradel bds. Sigd. (HD. Jun.25; 379) Frs. 1,400
– **Peter Pan Pictures.** L., Dec., 1907. Cold. pict. wraps. Raymond M. Sutton Jr. copy. (SG. May 7; 23) $260
– **The Peter Pan Portfolio.** L., [1912]. (500). Fo. 12 plts., matted, some light stains on matting, inscr. on end-paper. Orig. vell. gt., soiled, orig. ptd. box, worn. (SPB. May 6; 239) $2,300
– **Some British Ballads.** [1919]. (575) sigd. 4to. Orig. vell.-bkd., slightly soiled, recornered, s.-c. (SBA. May 27; 497) Rosenblatt. £140
– – **Anr. Copy.** Some foxing. Vell.-bkd. vell.-style bds., gt. Raymond M. Sutton Jr. copy, Shipton Court bkplt. (SG. May 7; 269) $500
– – **Anr. Copy.** Vell.-bkd. parch., soiled, orig. front free end-paper cut away, end-papers browned. (SPB. May 29; 354) $225
– – **Anr. Edn.** N.d. (575) numbered, sigd. 4to. Orig. parch.-bkd. bds., soiled. (CSK. Aug.15; 126)
£130
– – **Anr. Copy.** This copy unnumbered? Lr. corners worn. Sigd. (PD. Apr.1; 19) £90

RACKHAM, Arthur (Ill.)
See–AESOP
See–ALLIES' Fairy Book
See–ANDERSEN, Hans Christian
See–BARHAM, Rev. Richard Harris 'Thomas Ingoldsby'
See–BARRIE, James Matthew
See–BERLYN, Mrs. Alfred
See–BEST BOOKS of the Season
See–BIANCO, Margery Williams
See–BOOKMAN SPECIAL CHRISTMAS NUMBERS
See–BROWN, Abbie Farwell
See–BROWNE, Maggie
See–BROWNING, Robert
See–BYRON, May
See–COOPER, Anice Page
See–COSTUME Through the Ages
See–COYKENDALL, Frederick
See–DEWAR, George A.B.
See–DICKENS, Charles
See–DODGSON, Charles Lutwidge 'Lewis Carroll'
See–DORAN BOOKS FOR CHILDREN
See–DRURY, Maj. W.P.
See–EVANS, Charles Seddon
See–FITZGERALD, S.J. Adair
See–FORD, Julia Ellsworth & Bynner, Witter
See–FRIEDERICHS, Hulda
See–GARDENS OLD & NEW ...
See–GEISTERGESCHICHTEN
See–GOLDSMITH, Oliver
See–GRAHAME, Kenneth
See–GRIMM, Jacob Ludwig Carl & Wilhelm Carl
See–GUYOT, Charles
See–HAMER, S.H.
See–HARBOUR, Henry
See–HARMSWORTH Monthly Pictorial Magazine
See–HAWTHORNE, Nathaniel
See–HENLEY, William Ernest
See–HOLME, Geoffrey
See–HOPE, Anthony
See–HORN BOOK: Magazine of Books
See–HUTTON, Edward

See–IBSEN, Henrik
See–IRVING, Washington 'Dietrich Knickerbocker'
See–KENYON, C.R.
See–KIPLING, Rudyard
See–LAMB, Charles & Mary
See–LA MOTTE Fouque, Baron Friedrich Heinrich Karl
See–LAND OF ENCHANTMENT
See–LATIMORE, Sarah Briggs & Haskell, Grace Clark
See–LIMITED EDITIONS CLUB
See–LITTLE FOLKS ...
See–MAERCHENWALD
See–MALORY, Sir Thomas
See–MERRIMAN, Henry Seton
See–MILTON, John
See–MOORE, Clement C.
See–MORLEY, Christopher
See–MOTHER Goose
See–NIEBUHR, Barthold Georg
See–NISBET, John
See–NOVELLENBUCH
See–PAGET, J. Otho
See–PALL MALL BUDGET
See–PENROSE'S PICTORIAL ANNUAL ...
See–PERRAULT, Charles
See–PHILLPOTTS, Eden
See–POE, Edgar Allan
See–QUIVER ...
See–ROLY POLY STORIES ...
See–ROSSETTI, Christina
See–RUSKIN, John
See–SAGENBUCH
See–SELOUS, Edmund
See–SHAKESPEARE, William
See–SHAND, A.I.
See–SPIELMANN, Mrs. Mabel H.
See–STEEL, Flora Annie
See–STEPHENS, James
See–STILLE Volk, Das
See–SUNDAY STRAND ...
See–SWIFT, Jonathan
See–SWINBURNE, Algernon Charles
See–VENTURE ...
See–WAGNER, Richard
See–WALTON, Isaac
See–WALTON, Izaak & Cotton, Charles

RACKHAM, Bernard
– **The Glaisher Collection of Pottery & Porcelain in the Fitzwilliam Museum, Cambridge.** Camb., 1935. [1st. Edn.?]. 2 vols. (1 vol. of plts.). 4to. Orig. cl. in d.-w.'s. (C. Feb.4; 267) Morris. £370
– – **Anr. Copy.** 2 vols. Red hf. mor., spines gt. (S. Feb.9; 171) Traylen. £280
– **Islamic Pottery & Italian Maiolica.** 1959. Orig. cl., d.-w. (S. Sep.30; 431) £60
See–HOBSON, Robert Lockhart & others

RACKHAM, Bernard & Read, Herbert
– **English Pottery.** 1924. (75) sigd. by authors. Mor. (BS. May 13; 273) £55

RACZYNSKI, Edward, Count
– **Malerische Reise in einigen Provinzen des Osmanischen Reichs.** Trans.:– F.H. von der Hagen. Breslau, 1824. Fo. 72 engrs. (of 83), but with 28 bis, lacks title, slightly soiled & dampstained in places. Cont. hf. cf., spine & corners worn. (S. Apr.7; 370) Hyde Park. £120

RADCLIFFE, Alexander
– **The Ramble: an anti-heroick poem.** Priv. ptd., 1682. 1st. Edn. Lacks blank A1, rust-hole in D4. Red mor., by Rivière. [Wing R129] (S. Dec.9; 344) Quaritch. £85

RADCLIFFE, Ann
– **Gaston de Blondeville.** L., 1826. 1st. Edn. 4 vols. 12mo. Lacks hf.-titles to vols. 1 & 11. Three-qtr. lev., spines gt., chiefly untrimmed, by Zaehnsdorf. (SG. Sep.4; 394) $140
– **The Italian.** 1797. 1st. Edn. 3 vols. 12mo. Some pp. loose. Cf. gt. (P. Jan.22; 13) Cox. £80
– **The Mysteries of Udolpho.** L., 1794. 1st. Edn. 4 vols. 12mo. Three-qtr. mor., gt. spines, by Zaehnsdorf. (SG. Oct.9; 206) $350

RADCLIFFE, Delme
– **The Noble Science.** 1875. Hf. mor. gt. (CE. Nov.20; 126) £55

RADCLYFFE, Charles W.
– **Memorials of Westminster School.** N.d. Fo. Litho. title loose, spotting. Orig. hf. cf., worn, upr. cover detchd. (SH. Nov.6; 142) Crowe. £100

RADD, Dr. Gustav
- Ornis Caucasica. Kassel, 1884. 4to. Cont. hf. leath. gt., slightly worn. (R. Mar.31-Apr.4; 1430) DM 560

RADDATZ, Fritz J.
- Lithographies 1959-73. Paris, 1974. (1090). 4to. Orig. bdgs., d.-w.'s. (SPB. Nov.25; 427) $175

RADEMAKER, Abraham
- Fifty of the Pleasantest Landscape Views in Holland. L., ca. 1760. Ob. Sm. 8vo. Minor marginal worming. Cont. cf., slightly worn. (S. May 5; 251) Quaritch. £200
- Hollands Arcadia of de vermaarde Rivier Den Amstel; vertonende alles deszelfs Lustplaatzen, Herenhuizen en Dorpen zig uitstrekkende van Amsterdam af door Ouderkerk, Abcoude, Baembrug tot Loendersloot. Amst., 1730. Fo. Mod. hf. mor. (VG. Dec.17; 1498) Fls. 1,700
- Kabinet van Nederlandsche Outheden en Gezichten. 1725. [1st. Edn.?] 2 vols. 4to. Cont. cf. (SH. May 21; 96) Forum. £1,000
- - Anr. Copy. Pt. 1. 150 hf.-p. engraved views printed on 1 side only, Dutch, Fr. & Engl. legends, lacks engraved title, some marginal staining at beginning. Cont. hf. cf. (VG. Oct.13; 132) Fls. 2,150
- - Anr. Edn. Amst., 1725-31. 2 vols. 4to. 1st. title in Fr., text in Dutch, Fr. & Engl. Later russ. gt., non-unif. (SBA. Dec.16; 80) Baer. £1,200
- Versameling van 100 Nederlantse Outheden en Gesigten. Amst., ca. 1726. 4to. 98 (of 100) views on 61 plts. Cont. hf. cf., jnts. torn. (SBA. Oct.21; 249) Hyde Park Bookshop. £420
- - Anr. Edn. Amst., ca. 1730. 4to. Engraved pict. title & 99 views, including 1 dupl. Hf. leath., unc. (SKC. Feb.26; 1672) £220
- Versameling van 150 Nederlantse Outheeden en Gesigten. N.p., before 1770. Pt. 2. 4to. 115 (of 150) engraved views, plts. ptd. without text, in cont. MS. in this copy. Cont. vell., spine defect., slightly soiled, stained. (VG. Oct.13; 133) Fls. 2,000

RADERUS, Matthaeus
- Bavaria Sancta. Ill.:- R. Sadeler. 1615-24-27. 3 pts. in 1 vol. Fo. Crimson mor. gt. (P. Oct.2; 18) Weston. £85
- Heiliges Bayer-Land. Augsburg, 1714. 3 vols. in 1. Fo. Cf., very worn. (S. Dec.8; 97) Bart. £180

RADI, Archangelo Maria
- Nuova Scienza di Horologi a polvere. Rome, 1665. 4to. Engraved title, torn & reprd. without loss, soiled. Wraps., soiled, stitching slightly shaken. (CSK. Jan.23; 132) £180

RADIGUET, Raymond
- Le Bal du Comte d'Orgel. Ill.:- J. Cocteau. Monaco, 1953. 4to. Ll. in bd. cover & bd. s.-c. (HK. Nov.18-21; 2482) DM 750
- - Anr. Copy. (277). In sheets, publisher's s.-c. (HD. Dec.5; 173) Frs. 1,400

RADISSON, Pierre Esprit
- Voyages. Ed.:- Gideon D. Scull. Boston, 1885. (250). 4to. Orig. red hf. mor. Bkplt. & sig. of Thomas Balch. (CB. Feb.18; 41) Can. $260

RADLOV, N.E.
- O Futurizme [On Futurism]. St. Petersb., 1923. (1000). Orig. wraps., slightly soiled. (SH. Feb.6; 349) Bjorck. £65

RADLOW, N.
- Der Moderne Buchschmuck in Russland. St. Petersb., 1914. 4to. Orig. wraps., spine torn. (SH. Feb.5; 255) Flegon. £50

RADOWSKY, Hartwig Hundt von
- Die Judenschule oder Gruendliche Anleitung in Kurzer Zeit ein Vollkommener Schwarzer oder Weisser Jude zu Werden. [Jerusalem], 1822. 2 vols. Bds. (S. Nov.18; 681) Valmadonna. £220

RAEI, Joannes de
- Clavis Philosophiae Naturalis, seu Introductio ad Naturae Contemplationem, Aristotelico-Cartesiana. Leiden, 1654. 1st. Edn. 4to. Sig. on title of Anthony Murray. Cont. vell., soiled. Bkplt. of J.B. Craven of Kirkwall; from Honeyman Collection. (S. Nov.11; 2566) Hill. £75

RAEMAEKERS, Louis
- The Great War. L., 1916-19. Ltd. Edns. 3 vols. Orig. hf. cl. gt. 2 vols. sigd. by artist. (VG. Dec.16; 813) Fls. 575
- The Great War in 1916.-The Great War Victory Volume.-The Great War-A Neutral's Indictment.

1917; 1919; 1916. (1050) sigd. by artist; (1030) sigd. by artist; (1050). 3 vols. Fo. Orig. hf. buckram, slightly soiled. (CSK. Jun.19; 97) £80

RAFALOVICH, S.
*See-*BURLYUK, David & others

RAFFALD, Elizabeth
- The Experienced English Housekeeper. 1793. New Edn. Some spotting. Cont. sheep, worn. (CSK. Mar.13; 36) £75
- - Anr. Edn. 1794. 11th. Edn. Orig. bds. Sigd. (S. Mar.16; 182) Thorp. £60

RAFFET
*See-*COGNIET, Leon & Raffet

RAFFLES, Lady Sophia
- Memoir of Sir Thomas Stamford Raffles. 1830. 1st. Edn. 4to. Publisher's advts. (dtd. Jan. 1831). Cont. cl. (MMB. Oct.8; 29) Gooch. £190
- - Anr. Copy. Port. slightly foxed. Cont. pol. cf., gt. (C. Nov.5; 125) Ad Orientem. £110
- - Anr. Copy. Hf. mor. (SBA. Jul.23; 624) Grosvenor Prints. £90
[-] - Anr. Copy. Hf. cf., worn, reprd. (SG. Oct.30; 301) $150

RAFFLES, Sir Thomas Stamford
- The History of Java. L., 1817. 1st. Edn. 2 vols. 4to. Hf. cf., brkn. (SG. Oct.9; 207) $900
- - Anr. Copy. Folding map present, slightly browned or foxed in places. Cont. cf., rebkd., vol. 2 loose & slightly defect. (VG. Oct.13; 134) Fls. 600
- - Anr. Edn. L., 1844. Lge. 4to. Some foxing. Hf. mor. (SG. Oct.30; 300) $300

RAGUSE, August Frederick Louis Viesse, Duc de
- Memoires. Paris, 1857. 1st. Edn. 9 vols. Cf.-bkd. marb. bds. Rosebery liby. stp. on hf.-titles. (SBA. Jul.23; 625) Clavreuil. £60

RAILROAD ALPHABET
L., ca. 1860. Bds., orig. pict. wraps., upr. wrap slightly defect. with reprd. tear, 2 text ll. bkd. (R. Mar.31-Apr.4; 1159) DM 440

RAILROADS
- Report of Explorations in California for Railroad Routes . . .-Reports of Explorations & Surveys to Ascertain the Most Practicable . . . Route for a Railroad . . . Mississippi River to the Pacific Ocean . . . Vol. V. Wash., 1853; 1856. 4to. Some ll. loose, some foxing. Orig. cl., spine reprd. [Sabin 69946] (CB. Nov.12; 139) Can. $200
- Reports of Explorations & Surveys . . . for a Railroad from the Mississippi River to the Pacific Ocean. Wash., 1855-61. Senate Iss. Vols. 1, 2, 4, 6-9, & 11. 4to. Orig. sheep or cl., 2 loose. (SG. Nov.20; 425) $600

RAILWAY CALENDAR for 1840
[1839]. 890 × 565mm. Lge. sheet with litho. map, & letterpress tables, soiled, mntd. on linen. (S. Oct.17; 136) £75

RAILWAY MAGAZINE
1897-1975. Vols. 1-121, lacks vols. 92 & 93, in 119 vols. 8vo & 4to. Orig. or cont. cl. (SH. Oct.9; 276) Humm. £1,000

RAILWAYS, later Railway World
1939-71. Vols. 1-32. 4to & 8vo. Mod. cl. (SH. Oct.9; 277) Humm. £80

RAIMONDI, Eugenio
- Le Caccie delle Fiere armate . . . et de gl'Animali Quadrupedi, Volatili, et Acquatici. Brescia, 1621. 1st. Edn. Full cf. gt. (P. Oct.23; 287) Rogers. £290
- - Anr. Copy. Title reprd. & inscr., stained thro.-out from margins, final 2 ll. reprd. in outer edges, a few sm. repairs in text. Mod. spr. cf. (S. Jun.9; 37) Quaritch. £130
- - Anr. Copy. Lightly browned in parts, sm. erased stp. on title lf. Cont. vell. (R. Mar.31-Apr.4; 1706) DM 800
- Delle Caccie . . . Naples, 1626. 2nd. Edn. 4to. Cont. mott. cf., spine & corners worn. (S. Nov.25; 372) Broseghini. £220
- - Anr. Edn. [Venice], [1630]. [3rd. Edn.?]. Vell., gt. (CE. Aug.28; 241) £180
- - Anr. Copy. 4to. Copperplts. slightly soiled, lightly browned in parts, some sigs. loose. Cont. limp vell., soiled. (R. Mar.31-Apr.4; 1707) DM 1,200

RAINERIUS de Pisis
- Pantheologia, sive Summa Universae Theologiae. Nuremb., Anton Koberger, 14 Feb., 1477. 2 vols.

Fo. Spaces for initial capitals, fo. 34r of vol. 1 with 14-line capital A fully illuminated in green on red & white ground with frame in blue & yellow & lge. foliate sprays extending into margins, 18 other lge. capitals illuminated in blue, red & green with penwork flourishes, many smaller capitals in red & blue, smallest capitals in alternate red or blue, underlinings, initial strokes & paragraph marks supplied in red, lacks blank folios 32 & 190 in vol. 1, & 441 & 863 in vol. 2, penultimate lf. of vol. 1 with 2 minor marginal tears, last lf. with a reprd. tears, 1 affecting 1 column of text, 1st. p. of vol. 2 soiled, marginal worming to last lf. of vol. 2, long monastic inscr. in both vols. Cont. German blind-stpd. cf. over bevelled wood bds., brass bosses, cornerpieces, clasps (3 replaced) & catches, rebkd., spines gt.-lettered. From the collection of Eric Sexton. [BMC II, 413, Goff R8, H 13018*] (CNY. Apr.8; 111) $9,000

RAINSFORD, Marcus
- An Historical Account of the Black Empire of Hayti: Comprehending a View of the Principle Transactions in the Revolution of St. Domingo. 1805. 4to. Recent hf. cf., untrimmed. (TA. Nov.20; 399) £190

RAINSSANT, Pierre, Garde des Médailles du Roi
- Explication des Tableaux de la Galerie de Versailles et de ses deux Salons. Versailles, 1687. 4to. Sig. on fly-lf. of Comte d'Eu, stp. on title of Bibliothèque du Roi, Palais Royale. Cont. red mor., gt., arms of Louis XIV on covers, single gt. fillet, spine gt. in empty compartments, inner gt. dentelles. (SM. Oct.8; 1953) Frs. 5,600

RALEIGH, Sir Walter
- The Discoverie of the Large, Rich, & Bewtiful Empyre of Guina, with a Relation of the Great & Golden Citie of Manoa. 1596. 1st. Edn. 3rd. iss. 4to. 1st. word of title cropped, running-titles of several other ll. cropped, title laminated with blank corners reprd. Mod. hf. cf. [STC 20636; Sabin 67554] (C. Apr.1; 228) Quaritch. £110
- The Historie of the World. L., 1614 (colophon dtd. 1634). 2 pts. in 1 vol. Fo. Old cf., crudely rebkd. (SG. Sep.25; 266) $180
- - Anr. Edn. 1617 [1621]. Fo. With the 'Minde' lf., titles & a few prelims. slightly frayed in lr. outer corners, slight spotting. Cont. spr. cf., rebkd., old spine preserved, cl. box. Bkplt. of John Blackburne (1690-1786, botanist). [NSTC 20638a] (S. May 5; 294) Quaritch. £200
- - Anr. Edn. 1666. Fo. Cf., rebkd. (P. Jul.30; 291) Georges. £70
- - Anr. Edn. 1677. Fo. 'The Mind of the Front' lf. loose. Old cf., worn. (SKC. May 19; 226) £55
- - Anr. Edn. 1687. Fo. Additional engraved title with accompanying lf. 'The mind of the front'. Cont. cf., head of spine worn. [Wing R168] (S. May 5; 334) Franks. £80
- - Anr. Copy. Slight worming in margins only. Cont. panel cf. (TA. Nov.20; 105) £60

RALEIGH, Walter & Jones, H.A.
- The War in the Air. Oxford, 1922-37. 9 vols. (vols. 1-6, 1 appendix vol. & 2 boxes of maps). Orig. cl., 1 vol. slightly dampstained, spine of 1 box slightly worn. (SKC. Jul.28; 2485) £300

RALFE, James
- The Naval Chronology of Great Britain. 1820. 3 vols. Frontis. port. in vol. I hand-cold. & aquatint plts. cold. Cont. pol. cf. gt. From the collection of Eric Sexton. (C. Apr.15; 45) Hammond. £920
- - Anr. Copy. Offsetting on the text. Hf. mor., gt. spines, a little worn. (SPB. Oct.1; 208) $3,200

RALFS, John
- British Desmidieae. Ill.:- after Edward Jenner. 1848. Fo. 16pp. publisher's advts. bnd. in. at rear. Orig. blind-stpd. cl., spine defect. (TA. Nov.20; 59) £56

RALPH, Julian
- On Canada's Frontier: Sketches of History, Sport & Adventures. Ill.:- Frederic Remington. N.Y., 1892. 1st. Edn. Decor. cl. (SG. Jan.8; 380) $110

*See-*FRIEND, The

RAMAL, Walter (Pseud.)
*See-*DE LA MARE, Walter 'Walter Ramal'

RAMANN, G.H.W.
- Die Schmetterlinge Deutschlands und der Angrenzenden Länder. Arnstadt, [1870-76]. Text & plt. vol. Cont. hf. leath. (R. Oct.14-18; 3065) DM 550

RAMASWAMY, C.V., Pundit
- A Digest of the Different Castes of India.
Madras, 1837. 12mo. 1 lf. torn, several plts. reprd.
Orig. leath., worn. (SG. Feb.26; 275) $600

RAMAZZINI, Bernardinus
- Abhandlung v.d. Krankheiten d. Künstler u.
Handwerker. Ed.:- J.C.G. Ackermann. 1780-83.
2nd. German Edn. 2 vols. Slightly soiled. Cont.
bds., spine browned, unc. (HK. Nov.18-21; 708)
DM 1,550
- Opera Omnia Medica et Physiologica ... Ed.:-
Barthol[omaeo] Ramazzino. N.p., 1742. 2 pts. in
1 vol. 4to. Slightly spotted, name on title. Cont.
vell. bds., worn & soiled. (S. Oct.21; 419)
Phelps. £65

RAMEAU, J. Ph. Zais
- Ballet Heroique. Paris, ca. 1750. 1st. Edn.? Ob.
fo. Slightly browned. Cont. cf. (H.
Dec.9/10; 1246)   DM 780

RAMEE, Louise de la 'Ouida'
[-] A Tale of a Toad. Corvinus Pr., 1939. 1st. Edn.
(25). Lge. 4to. Orig. mor.-bkd. linen, unc. (S.
Jul.22; 73)   *Rota.* £70

RAMEL, Jean Pierre–HILL, S.S.
- Narrative of the Deportation to Cayenne of
Barthelemy, Pichegru, Willot ... & c.–Travels in
Peru & Mexico. 1799; 1860. 1st. Engl. Edn. (1st.
work). 2 works in 2 vols. Hf. roan; cont. embossed
cl. gt. [Sabin 67630] (1st. work). (C. Nov.6; 226)
Eccles. £110

RAMELLI, Agostino
- Le Diverse et Artificiose, Machine. Paris, Priv.
ptd. 1588. 1st. Edn. Fo. Text in Italian & Fr.,
some staining & discolouration, extensively
annotated in Engl. in two cont. hands. Cont. limp
vell., gt., soiled. From the Kenney & Honeyman
Collections. (S. Nov.11; 2567)   *Zeitlin.* £2,700
– – Anr. Copy. Plt. XX not ptd. & inserted in
early water-col., slight stains in some lr. margins.
19th. C. hf. mor. From Chetham's Liby.,
Manchester. (C. Nov.27; 333)   *Wienreb.* £2,400
– – Anr. Copy. Priv. Ptd. Title & port. slightly
damaged & soiled, nearly detchd., 178 engravings
(of 195, lacks numbers 74, 86, 87, 104, 140, 142,
144, 146, 148/9, 150-153, 157, 162, 191, 193),
lacks some text ll. including 2 ll. at end, some ll.
soiled, bkplt. of Cholmley Turner & the
Kirkleatham Liby. 18th. C. cf., spine worn. W.a.f.
(S. Oct.21; 355)   *Thoemmes.* £900

RAMESEY, William
- Elminthologia (grece) or some Physical
Considerations of the Matter, Origination &
Several Species of Wormes. 1668. 1st. Edn. Tear
in lr. margin of engraved frontis. port. reprd., advt.
lf. Mott. cf. gt. by De Coverly. [Wing R205] (C.
Apr.1; 115)   *Lawson.* £50

RAMHOFFSKY, Johann Heinrich
- Drey Beschreibungen ... Ill.:- J.D. Herz
(frontis.); J.A. Pfeffel, M. Tyroff & others after
J.J. Dietsler (plts.) Prague, [1743.] Fo. Slightly
brown in places. Cont. cf., worn, arms of Bavaria
in centre of covers. (S. May 5; 77)
Rheinbuch. £520

RAMIRO, E. i.e. E. Rodrigues
- L'Oeuvre Lithographié de Felicien Rops. Paris,
1891. Orig. Edn., (50) Privilege Edn. on Jap. 4to.
Etchings & ills. in 2 states, some ll. slightly soiled.
Vell., orig. wraps. bnd. in, soiled. (H.
Dec.9/10; 1644)   DM 620

RAMLER, Karl Wilhelm
[-] Lieder der Deutschen. Ill.:- J.W.M. Meil.
Berlin, 1766. 1st. Edn. Cont. leath., sm. spine
defect. (HK. May 15; 4756)   DM 520

RAMM, S.L.
- Abbildungen von allen Uniformen der Königl.
Preus. Armee. [Berlin], [1800]. Without 45 text
pp., all copper engrs. with MS., all with sm. stp. on
verso, slightly soiled in parts. Later hf. leath. (H.
Dec.9/10; 833)   DM 7,400

RAMMINGER, Jacob
- Vom Fass Visieren Kurtze und eigentliche
Beschreibung auss Rechtem Fundament der
Löblichen Freyen Kunst Geometria. Stuttgart,
1598. 1st. Edn. Piece torn from margin of A5.
Cont. limp vell. From Honeyman Collection. (S.
Nov.11; 2568)   *Das Bucherkabinet.* £200

RAMON Y CAJAL, Santiago
- Degeneration & Regeneration of the Nervous
System. Trans.:- Raoul M. May. N.Y., 1959. 2
vols. Orig. cl. (S. Jun.17; 701)   *Whitehart.* £110
- Histologie du Système Nerveux de l'Homme et
des Vertébrés. Trans.:- Dr. L. Azoulay. Madrid,
Priv. ptd. 1952-55. Fr. Edn. 2 vols. Orig. cl.,
d.-w.'s slightly torn. (S. Jun.17; 700)
Jenner Books. £85
- Les Nouvelles Idées sur la Structure du Système
Nerveux chex l'Homme et chez les Vertébrés.
Trans.:- Dr. Azoulay. Paris, 1894. 1st. Fr. Edn.
Hf.-title stained. Cl.-bkd. bds. (S. Jun.17; 694)
Jenner. £170
- Die Retina der Wirbelthiere. Untersuchungen mit
der Golgi-Cajal'schen Chromsilbermethode und de
Ehrlich'schen Methylenblaufärbung ... Trans.:-
Richard Greeff. Wiesbaden, 1894. Sm. fo. Orig.
ptd. wraps., unc., rebkd. (S. Jun.17; 695)
Jenner Book. £260
- Studien ueber die Hirnrinde des Menschen.
Trans.:- J. Bresler. Leipzig. 1900-03. 4 vols. Ptd.
wraps., torn & loose, unc. & mostly unopened.
(SG. Jan.29; 351) $130
– – Anr. Edn. Trans.:- Dr. J. Bresler. Leipzig,
1900-06. 5 pts. Orig. ptd. wraps., unc. &
unopened, in cl. box. (S. Jun.17; 697)
Jenner Books. £170
- Textura del Sistema Nervioso del Hombre y de
los Vertebrados. Madrid, 1899-1904. (800). 2 vols.
in 3. Cl., roan spine. (S. Jun.17; 696)
Norman. £650

RAMOS DEL MANZANO, Francisco
[-] Respuesta de España al Tratado de Francia ...
N.p., 1667. Fo. Orig. vell. (DS. May 22; 878)
Pts. 32,000

RAMSAY, Allan
- The Ever Green. Edinb., 1724. 1724. 1st. Edn. 2
vols. Late 19th. C. red lev. mor. by F. Bedford, gt.
(S. Nov.24; 247)   *Thorp.* £240
– – Anr. Copy. A few ll. slightly soiled. Cont. cf.,
John Rutherford of Edgerston's bkplt., 1 lettering
piece worn. (S. Jan.26; 13)   *Thorp.* £100
- Gentle Shepherd. 1794. Fo. Mott. cf. gt. (P. May
14; 234)   *Way.* £130
- Poems. Ill.:- R. Cooper (frontis. ports.). Edinb.,
1728. 2 vols. 4to. Cont. diced cf., covers with gt.
floral & foliate roll-tool panel, spines gt. From the
collection of Eric Sexton. (C. Apr.15; 141)
Dewar. £190

RAMSAY, Andrew Michael
[-] Histoire du Vicomte du Turenne. Paris, 1735. 2
vols. 4to. Vol. I dampstained in lr. margins. Cont.
mott. cf., worn. (S. Dec.8; 151)   *Booth.* £60
- The Travels of Cyrus. Dublin, 1728. 2 vols. in 1.
Cont. sig. of Martha Corry on title. Cont. red mor.
gt., gt. panels on covers, spine gt. in compartments.
(C. Apr.1; 229)   *Henderson.* £110

RAMSAY, David
- Histoire de la Revolution d'Amérique, par rapport
à la Caroline méridionale. L. & Paris, 1787. 1st.
Edn. in Fr. 2 vols. Advt. ll. Cont. tree cf., gt.
spines. [Sabin 67692] (S. Jun.29; 188)
Arader. £50
- The History of the Revolution of South Carolina.
Trenton [New Jersey], 1785. 1st. Edn. 2 vols. Sm.
tear & hole in 1 folding map, liby. stps. on titles.
19th. C. hf. mor., vol. II using old cf. bds. [Sabin
67691] (C. Nov.20; 272)   *Quaritch.* £150
– – Anr. Copy. Cont. hf. cf. (SH. May 21; 97)
Lawson. £100
- The History of South Carolina, from Its First
Settlement in 1670 to the Year 1808. Charleston,
1809. 1st. Edn. 2 vols. 1 map hand-cold. in outl.,
both maps foxed. Cont. cf., vol. 1 disbnd., other
lacks upr. cover. Pres. copy to Abiel Holmes
(father of Oliver Wendell Holmes). (PNY.
Dec.3; 343) $180
- A Sketch of the Soil, Climate, Weather &
Diseases of South-Carolina ... Charleston, 1796.
1st. Edn. 2 ports. inserted later, slight soiling &
foxing. Disbnd., folding cl. case. From liby. of
William E. Wilson. [Sabin 67707] (SPB.
Apr.29; 230) $500

RAMSAY, Phillip A.
- Views of Renfrewshire. Edinb., 1839. 4to. Emb.
bds. & roan spine, worn. (CE. Nov.20; 8)   £80

RAMSEY, James B.
- True Eminence Founded on Holiness.
Lynchburg, Va., 1863. 1st. Edn. Wraps. (SG.
Jun.11; 115) $170

RAMUS or Ramée, P.
- Arithmeticae Libri Dvo: Geometriae Septem et
Viginti. Basel, 1569. 1st. Edn. 4to. Printer's mark
on title. Cont. limp vell., lacks ties. (HK.
Nov.18-21; 275)   DM 950
- Arithmeticae libri duo: Geometriae Septem et
Viginti.–Scholarum Mathematicarum, libri unus et
Triginta. Basel, 1569. 2 works in 1 vol. 4to. Some
stains & discolouration, marginal annots. on a few
ll., 1st. work with slight adhesion affecting text on
pp. 128-9. Cont. vell., soiled, lacks ties. Armorial
bkplt. of Count Chorinsky; from Honeyman
Collection. (S. Nov.11; 2570)   *Nador.* £240
- Arithmetices Libri duo, et Algebrae totidem: a
Lazaro Schonero Emendati ... Eiusdem Schoneri
... De Numeris Figuratis ... De Logistica
Sexagenarie. Frankfurt, 1586. Deleted owner's
inscr. on title of Wilhelm Dilich, 1587, later sig. of
'Reichard'. Cont. blind-stpd. sheep, figures of
Justice & Lucretia on covers, worn. Bkplt. of
Christian Ernst, Graf zu Stolberg; stp. of Stolberg
liby. at Wernigerode; from Honeyman Collection.
(S. Nov.11; 2573)   *Nador.* £50
- Scholarum Mathematicarum, libri unus et
triginta. Basel, 1569. 4to. Dampstained, especially
towards end, C4 crudely reprd., owner's inscr. on
title-p. Cont. pig-bkd. vell. bds. (stained green),
worn. From Honeyman Collection. (S.
Nov.11; 2571)   *Nador.* £130
- Via Regia ad Geometriam. The Way to
Geometry ... Trans.:- William Beadwell. 1636.
4to. Some ll. stained in margins, A1r & A2v
dust-soiled, holes in B3 & C6. Cont. sheep., worn.
Armorial bkplt. of Marquess of Tweeddale; from
Honeyman Collection. [NSTC 15251] (S.
Nov.11; 2575)   *Mrs. Slade.* £80

**RAMUS, Petrus–FINCK, Thomas–PECKHAM,
John, ArchBp. of Canterbury**
- Arithmeticae Libri duo: Geometriae septem et
viginti.–Geometriae Rotundi Libri XIII.
–Perspectivae communis Libri tres. Basel; Basel;
Cologne, 1580; 1583; 1580. 3 works in 1 vol. 4to.
Some staining & discolouration, folding table to
1st. work bnd. at end of 3rd., extensive marginal
annots. & scoring through of text, bnd. at end are
6 ll. of MS. 'De Logistica Astronomica' inscr. to
Nicolaus Hommer of Copenhagen by Johannes
Coppius of Leisnig, written at Leipzig, 1589,
several owners' inscrs. at beginning. Cont. hf.
blind-stpd. pig., worn, upr. cover with initials
MKG & date 1586. From Honeyman Collection.
(S. Nov.11; 2572)   *Quaritch.* £160

**RAMUS, Petrus–TALAEUS, Audomarus
–SCRIBONIUS, G.A.**
- Dialecticae Libri duo.–Rhetorica, e P. Rami
Praelectionibus Observata.–Rerum Physicarum
iyxta leges logicas methodica explicatio. Ed.:-
Rolandus Makylmenaeus (1st. work); Claudus
Minos. (2nd work). Frankfurt, 1579. 3 works in 1
vol. Some browning & marginal staining,
microscopic annots. in cont. hand, some in spiral
form, 3rd. work with lr. hf. of last lf. cut away
affecting word 'Finis'. Bnd. in fragment of old vell.
MS., very worn. From Honeyman Collection. (S.
Nov.11; 2569)   *Radzievsky.* £110

RANDALL, M.
- The Canadian Reader. Stanstead, 1834. Cf., bds.
warped, dampstained & wormed. (CB. Apr.1; 298)
Can. $100

RANDOLPH, Thomas
[-] Aristippus, or the iouiall Philosopher ... (with)
The Conceited Pedlar. 1630. 2nd. Edn. Sm. 4to.
Slight browning & soiling, A4 cropped at foot
with loss of catchword & 1 or 2 letters shaved,
rust-hole in D1, lacks final blank. Mod. wraps.
From liby. of André L. Simon. [NSTC 20686.5]
(S. May 18; 168)   *Lawson.* £120
- Poems.–The Jealous Loves.–Aristippus. Oxford
[1st. work], Camb. [2nd. work]. 1638; 1634; 1635.
1st. Edn.; 2nd. Edn.; 5th. Edn. 3 works in 1 vol.,
1st. work 3 pts. 4to. Some dampstaining, bkplt. of
Algernon Capell, Earl of Essex, 1701, pasted on
verso of title of 1st. work. Cont. cf., rebkd., spine
gt. [NSTC 20694; 20693; 206689] (S.
Sep.29; 104)   *Pickering & Chatto.* £220

RANJITSINHJI, K.S.
- The Jubilee Book of Cricket. 1897. (350)
numbered, sigd. 4to. Orig. cl., soiled, torn at top of
spine. (TA. Jun.18; 402)   £60

RANKING, John
- Historical Researches on the Conquest of Peru, Mexico . . . in the 13th Century, by the Mongols, accompanied with Elephants. 1827. Without supplement, a little offsetting, fore-margin of 1 lf. reprd. Mod. hf. mor. Author's pres. inscr. on title (cropped). [Sabin 67891] (CSK. Oct.31; 27)   £55

RANSOM, John Crowe
- Chills & Fever.–New Criticism.–Two Gentlemen in Bonds. N.Y.; Norfolk; N.Y., 1924; [1941]; 1927. 3 vols. Orig. bdgs., worn. 1st. vol.: Pres. copy to Untermeyer, last work; 3 letters to him tipped in, 2 autograph letters, other typed. (SPB. Nov.25; 388) $200

R[ANSOM], R.
- The Invited Alphabet, or Address of A to B, containing his Friendly Proposal for the Amusement & Instruction of Good Children. Ill.:– Charles Knight after author. Ca. 1815. Sq. 12mo. A few plts. slightly stained at lr. corner. Marb. paper wraps. (SH. Mar.19; 271)   Vincent. £95

RANSOM, Will
- Private Presses & their Books. N.Y., 1929. (1200). Orig. cl. (CSK. May 15; 50)   £75
- – Anr. Copy. Cl., d.-w. (SG. Oct.2; 305) $110

RANTZAU, Heinrich
- Tractatus Astrologicus de Genethliacorum thematum iudiciis pro singulis nati accidentibus. Frankfurt, 1593. 1st. Edn. Sig. Q misbnd., tears reprd. in D5-8, some spotting, recto of last lf. stained by 17th. C. inscr. on verso. Bnd. in fragment of vell. MS., with ties, spine defect. Armorial bkplt. of Count von Nostitz; from Honeyman Collection. (S.   Nov.11; 2576)   Quaritch. £130

RANTZAU, Heinrich–FABER, Jac, Stapulensis
- Diaruim sive Calendarium Romanum, Oeconomicum, Ecclesiasticum, Astronomicum & fere perpetuum.–In Sex Primos Metaphysicorum Aristotelis Libros Introductio. Leipzig; Paris, 1596; 1563. 4th. Edn. 2 works in 1 vol. Lightly browned in parts. Cont. vell., gold & blind-stpd., lacks ties. (HK. May 12-14; 411)   DM 700

RANVIER, Louis Antoine
- Leçons sur l'Histoire du Système Nerveux. Ed.:– Edward Weber. Paris, 1878. 1st. Edn. 2 vols. Blank strip cut from title of each vol. removing name. Qtr. mor. (S. Jun.17; 706)   Harding. £200

RAO, Cesare
- I Meteori. Venice, 1582. 1st. Edn. 4to. Browned, marginal stains at beginning, old annots. Cont. limp vell., rebkd., lacks ties. From Honeyman Collection. (S. Nov.11; 2577)   Howell. £110

RAOUL-ROCHETTE, Desire
- Lettres sur la Suisse. Ill.:– after König & others. Paris, 1823. 6 vols. 16mo. Cont. Russ. leath., spines decor. (HD. Apr.9; 549)   Frs. 4,700
- Mes Souvenirs d'Égypte, par Madame la Baronne de Minutoli. Ill.:– after Cassas. Paris, 1826. 2 vols. 16mo. Publisher's bds., decor. with Egyptian motif, unc. (HD. Apr.9; 550)   Frs. 1,300
- Monumens Inedits d'Antiquité Figurée. Paris, 1833. L.P. Pt. 1 only (all publd.). Fo. Red qtr. mor. (SG. Dec.4; 292) $100

RAPHAEL, Sanzio
- Castrioto Lusitano. Lisbon, 1679. 1st. Edn. Fo. Stained, wormed. Mod. vell. (SH. Jul.16; 193)   Tzakas. £130
- Imagines Veteris ac Novi Testamenti. Rome, 1675. Fo. Cont. spr. cf. (C. Jul.16; 336)   Taylor. £120

RAPHAEL DE NORICA
- Sea Solet-Marpe la-Nefesh-Orach Hayim. Venice, 1579. 2nd. Edn. 3 vols. in 2. Sm. 4to. Mod. mor. & cl., not unif. (C. Jul.16; 315)   Stein. £240

RAPHELT, M.
- Einfeltiger und Kurtzer Unterricht, Von den Kläglichen Brandschäden . . . Leipzig, [1592]. 4to. Slightly browned, old 1592 MS on title. Bds., linen pasted on spine. (HK. Nov.18-21; 276)   DM 580

RAPIN, Rene
- [Of] Gardens. Trans.:– J[ohn] E[velyn, Jnr.]. 1673. 1st. Edn. in Engl., 2nd. iss. Errata lf. inserted after preface, lacks last blank, title reprd. at head & foot, affecting 1st. word of title. 19th. C. panel. cf. Bkplt. of John Evelyn. [Wing R269A] (S. Dec.8; 176)   Quaritch. £220

RAPIN de Thoyras, Paul
- [–] [Atlas] for Mr. Tindal's Continuation of Mr. Rapin's History. [L.], ca. 1745. Tall fo. 71 double-p. maps, &, bnd. in, Dorret's lge. folding map of Scotland (with cold. boundaries). Old hf. cf., shabby. (SG. Nov.20; 104) $800
- Histoire D'Angleterre. The Hague, 1724-27. 10 vols. 4to. Cont. cf., armorial motif on spines. (GM. Apr.30; 627)   £120
- – Anr. Edn. Ill.:– Boucher. The Hague, 1749. New Edn. 16 vols. 4to. Some browning. Cont. mor., gt. triple fillet border, centre arms, decor. spine raised bands, sm. faults. (HD. Apr.24; 96)   Frs. 12,500
- The History of England. Trans.:– N. Tindal. 1728-31. 15 vols. Cont. cf. (CSK. Jan.23; 103)   £60
- – Anr. Edn. Trans.:– N. Tindall. 1732-47. 4 vols. in 5. Fo. Slight marginal worming to 1st. few ll. of vol. I. Old cf. gt., worn, leath. leaving some bds. (LC. Jun.18; 316)   £170
- – Anr. Edn. Trans.:– Nicholas Tindal. 1732-51. 2nd. Engl. Edn. 5 vols. Fo. Cont. tree cf. gt. W.a.f. (SBA. Jul.22; 115)   Shotton. £550
- – Anr. Edn. Trans.:– N. Tindal. L., 1743-44. 3rd. Edn. 3 vols. Lge. fo. Cont. panel. cf., worn. W.a.f. (SG. Oct.30; 302) $750
- – Anr. Edn. Ed.:– Nicholas Tindal. 1743-47. 3rd. Edn. 4 vols. in 5. Fo. Cont. cf. gt., worn. W.a.f. (SBA. Jul.23; 403)   Shotton. £500
- [–] – Anr. Edn. Trans.:– Rev. Nicholas Tindal. [1745 or later]. Atlas only. Fo. Soiled & browned. Partially disbnd., lacks covers. W.a.f. (CSK. Oct.3; 119)   £400
- – Anr. Edn. Trans.:– N. Tindal. Ill.:– J. Mynde, Vertue, Proud, & others. 1757-59. 21 vols. Cont. pol. cf. (C. Jul.22; 195)   Traylen. £70
- – Anr. Edn. 1785. Fo. With ptd. title to vol. 1 but without text. Cont. cf., rebkd. & cornered. W.a.f. (SBA. Oct.21; 250)   Burgess. £450

RAPIRA [Foil]
Ed.:– [Yu. V. Goldberg]. St. Petersb., n.d. No. 1. 4to. Unopened. Unbnd. (SH. Feb.5; 118)   De la Casa. £65

RARITATEN BUREAU FUR GUTE KNABEN UND MADCHEN: Der Kleine Vaterlandische Landschaftmahler; Die Menschenracen; Marchen aus der Fabelwelt; Das Fuhrwesen; Naturwunder; Geographische Merkwurdugkeiten aus allen Weltheilen; Kleine Naturgeschichte fur kleine Leute (3 pts.); Kleine Erzahlungen; Unterhaltungen aus der Naturlehre; Kunstaltenthumer; Kleine Schauplatz der Kunste und Handwerker (2 pts.).
Chemnitz, 1809. 14 (of 16) vols. 32mo. Vol. 12 lacks 1 plt. Orig. marb. wraps. (SH. Mar.19; 272)   Maggs. £400

RASHLEIGH, Philip
- Specimens of British Minerals. 1797-1802. 2 vols. in 1. 4to. Cont. diced cf., gt., rather worn. (S. Apr.6; 228)   Lloyd. £340

RASI, L.
- I Comici Italiani. Flor., 1897-1905. 2 vols. Hf. cf., col. not unif. (CR. Jun.11; 606)   Lire 350,000

RASPE, Rudolph Erich
- [–] Gulliver Revived, or the Vice of Lying Properly Exposed . . .–A Sequel to the Adventures of Baron Munchausen. 1799; 1796. 8th. Edn. (1st. work). 2 vols. 12mo. 1st. work lacks hf.-title, 2nd, work has some captions cropped or cut away. Unif. cont. hf. cf. (SH. Mar.19; 273)   Rota. £270
- Munchausen at Walcheren. Ill.:– Isaac & George Cruikshank. 1811. 1st. Edn. 12mo. Frontis. reprd. Mor. gt., by Rivière. (SH. Dec.10; 22)   Ferret Fantasy. £160
- Specimen Historiae Globi Terraquei, praecipue de Novis e Mari Natis Insulis. Amst. & Leipzig, 1763. 1st. Edn. Browned. Cont. cf., gt. spine, worn. Armorial bkplt. of Antoine Lavoisier; mod. bkplt. of Herbert McLean Evans; from Honeyman Collection. (S. Nov.11; 2578)   Zeitlin. £580
- Surprising Adventures of the Renowned Baron Munchausen. Ill.:– Thomas Rowlandson. L., 1811. 12mo. Mod. cf. by Bayntun. (SG. Sep.4; 409) $210
- [–] – Anr. Copy. Text browned. Cf. gt. by Rivière. (SPB. Jul.28; 417) $150

RASTALL, W. Dickinson
- A History of the Antiquities of the Town & Church of Southwell. 1787. 4to. Lge. folding plt. of Haughton in Nottingham by Jan Kip loosely inserted, with slight tear in fold. Cont. cf.-bkd. bds., slightly worn, upr. cover detchd. (SBA. Oct.22; 486)   Chesters. £70
- – Anr. Copy. Some spotting. Cont. cf., rebkd. (SH. Nov.6 143)   Quaritch. £60

RASTELL, John
- [–] The Grete Abregement of the Statutys of England. N.d. Title & following lf. reprd. 16th. C. cf., rebkd., upr. cover blind-stpd. with design depicting the Annunciation, lr. cover with floral design incorporating 6 winged beasts. [STC 9521] (CSK. Aug.22; 139)   £500

RATHBORNE, Aaron
- The Surveyor. 1616. 1st. Edn. Fo. 03-4 inserted from anr. copy, both ports. slightly defect., some staining, early 17th. C. owner's inscr. of Edward Miller on 1st. blank lf. Cont. cf., rebkd. & reprd. From Honeyman Collection. [NSTC 20748] (S. Nov.11; 2579)   Howell. £460

RATHIER, L.
See–BEAUNIER, F. & Rathier, L.

RATTA, Cesare
- Gli Adornatori del Libro in Italia. Bologna, 1923-27. Ltd. Edns. 9 vols. Fo. Many cold. plts., some mntd. Hf. vell., orig. wraps. bnd. in. (SI. Dec.4; 489)   Lire 1,200,000
- L'Arte del Libro e della Rivista nei Paesi D'Europa e D'America. Bologna, 1927. Ltd. Edn. 2 vols. 4to. Loose, ready for bdg. (SI. Dec.4; 490)   Lire 300,000

RATTO, R.
- 2 Auction Catalogues of Greek & Roman Coins including the Sydenham Collection. Lugano, 1927. 4to. Some ll. browned. Cont. hf. cl. (SH. Mar.6; 430)   Trade Art. £280
- Duplicati di un Museo Straniero. Lugano, 1925-27. 3 vols. Orig. wraps. (SH. Mar.6; 429)   Spink. £60

RATTRAY, James
- Scenery, Inhabitants & Costumes of Afghanistan. 1847. Fo. Some offsetting of plts. on text, dampstaining affecting 1 plt. Hf. mor., worn. (BS. Jun.11; 384)   £280

RATZEBURG, J.T.C.
See–BRANDT, F.J. & Ratzeburg, J.T.C.

RAUBNACHT
- 13 Steinzeichnungen. Berlin, 1925. Ob. fo. Text ll. lightly stained. Orig. hf. linen portfo. Printer's mark sigd. by artist. (H. Dec.9/10; 2164)   DM 800

RAUCH, Nicolas
- Catalogue no. 6 & 7: Les Peintres et le Livre. –Livres Precieux, including 'Livres de Peintres'. Geneva, 1957; 1961. (1500) numbered; (1100). Orig. wraps. (SH. Nov.21; 461)   Tate Gallery. £50
- La Photographie des Origines au Debut du XXe Siècle. Genève, 1961. Many annots. Pict. wraps. (SG. Apr.23; 21) $280

RAUMER, Friedrich von
- Die Herbstreise nach Venedig. Berlin, 1816. 1st. Edn. 2 vols. Soiled lightly in places, title more heavily. Cont. hf. leath. gt., worn, ex-lib. (HK. May 15; 4759)   DM 620

RAUWOLF, Leonhart
- Aigentliche Beschreibung der Raiss . . . inn die Morgenländer . . . Alles in drey underschidliche Tail . . . abgethailet. Lauingen, 1582. (1st. edn.?). 3 pts. in 1 vol. 4to. Dampstained at beginning, slightly soiled or spotted in places. Cont. German blind-stpd. pig. over wooden bds., lacks bosses & clasps. Loosely inserted is offprint from Deutsche Medizinische Wochenschrift with article proving that fact by F.W. Rieppel. (S. Feb.23; 92)   Dawson. £260
- – Anr. Edn. Lauingen, 1583. 1st. Edn. of 4 pts. together. 4 pts. in 1 vol. 4to. Lacks final blank, lr. margin of general title renewed, a few ll. wormed in pt. 1 affecting text, tear reprd. in B1 pt. 4, cont. marginalia on some ll. 19th. C. hf. mor., blind-stpd. arms & bkplt. of William Stirling Maxwell. From Honeyman Collection. (S. Nov.11; 2580)   Das Bucherkabinet. £980

RAVENEAU de Lussan
- Journal du Voyage fait à la Mer du Sud. Paris, 1690. 1st. Edn. 12mo. Browned. Cont. bds. [Sabin 67984] (SH. Jun.25; 3)   Klee. £80

RAVENSCROFT, Edward
- The Canterbury Guests. 1695. 1st. Edn. 4to. 2 natural paper faults slightly affecting text, final line of text cropped, 1 catchword cropped, some stains in text. Mor. by Sangorski. [Wing R327] (C. Nov.19; 136) *Brett-Smith.* £120
- The Careless Lovers. 1673. 1st. Edn. 4to. Mor. by Sangorski. [Wing R328] (C. Nov.19; 137) *Brett-Smith.* £260
- The English Lawyer. 1678. 1st. Edn. 4to. Lacks corner of 1 lf., affecting text. Mor. by Sangorski. [Wing R2211] (C. Nov.19; 141) *Sotheran.* £120
- The Italian Husband. 1698. 1st. Edn. 4to. Sm. hole in 1 lf. reprd., affecting 3 words, slight foxing. Mor. by Sangorski. [Wing R330] (C. Nov.19; 139) *Pickering & Chatto.* £120
- King Edgar & Alfreda. 1677. 1st. Edn. 4to. Mor. by Sangorski. [Wing R331] (C. Nov.19; 140) *Pickering & Chatto.* £170
- Scaramouche a Philosopher.-Dame Dobson. 1677; 1684. 1st. Edns. 2 works in 2 vols. 4to. 2nd. work: title mntd. with loss of some of imprint, pagination cropped at beginning, staining thro-out. Both works in mor. by Sangorski. [Wing R337; R329] (C. Nov.19; 138) *Quaritch.* £280

RAVENSCROFT, Edward & Motteux, Peter
- The Anatomist ... with The Loves of Mars & Venus. 1697. 1st. Edn. of the Anatomist. 4to. Title & last p. slightly stained, lacks portion of 1 blank margin of 1 lf., affecting catchword. Mor. by Sangorski. [Wing R326] (C. Nov.19; 135) *Brett-Smith.* £220

RAVENSCROFT, Edward James & others
- The Pinetum Britannicum. Ill.:– After Robert Kaye Greville & others. L., [1863-] 1884. 3 vols. 4to. Hf. mor. From collection of Massachusetts Horticultural Society, stps. on plts. (SPB. Oct.1; 158) $2,700

RAVICHIO DE PERETSDORF
- Traité de Pyrotechnie Militaire ... Paris, 1824. 2 vols. 8vo. 4 to. Long-grd. mor., gt. fillet & blind border, gt. fillet border, angle fleurs de lis & on spine, inner guarland, arms of Duc. d'Angoulême, by Bibolet. (HD. Jun.10; 199) Frs. 6,500

RAVILIOUS, Eric
- The Wood Engravings. Lion & Unicorn Pr. 1972. Ltd. Edn. Fo. Orig. cl., s.-c. (SH. Oct.9; 39) *Quaritch.* £70
- - Anr. Edn. Lion & Unicorn Pr., 1972. (188). Fo. Orig. buckram. (SH. Feb.20; 325) *George's.* £55
- - Anr. Edn. Ed.:– J.M. Richards. Lion & Unicorn Pr. 1972. Fo. Orig. cl. (P. Oct.2; 20) *Sims & Reed.* £65

RAWLINSON, George
- The History of Herodotus. L., 1858-60. 4 vols. extended to 8. Some browning, minor defects. Hf. crimson mor. gt., soiled. Litchfield copy. (SPB. Jul.28; 407) $100

RAWSON, R.W.
See–PAPPE, L. & others

RAWSON Thomas James
- Statistical Survey of the County of Kildare. Ill.:– Taylor (folding map). Dublin, 1807. Cl.-bkd. bds., unc. Inscr. 'For Arthur Young Esq. With Gen. Vallenceys Compl.' (GM. Apr.30; 278) £90
See–WELD, Isaac–TOWNSEND, Horatio –RAWSON, Thomas James

RAWSTORNE, Lawrence
- Gamonia. L., 1837. Errata slip, stained. Orig. mor. gt. (SPB. Oct.1; 95) $1,000

RAY or REA, John
- A Collection of Curious Travels. 1693. 1st. Edn. 2 pts. in 1 vol. Licence lf. & 2 folios of Catalogus Stirpium torn & reprd. with some text loss. 19th. C. hf. roan, worn, covers detchd. From Chetham's Liby., Manchester. [Wing R385] (C. Nov.19; 335) *Wheldon & Wesley.* £50
- A Collection of English Words. 1674. 1st. Edn. Lacks 1st. blank lf., title stained, slight browning. Mod. hf. cf., spine gt. [Wing R388] (S. Feb.10; 459) *Bicker.* £110
- Flora: seu de Florum Cultura. Or a Complete Florilege. Ill.:– D. Loggan (engraved frontis.). 1665. 1st. Edn. Fo. Cf upr. cover loose, Ditton Park bkplt. [Wing R421] (S. Dec.2; 603) *Rota.* £110
- - Anr. Edn. Ill.:– D. Loggan. 1676. 2nd. Edn. Fo. Slight marginal worming, S4v soiled. Mod. hf. cf. [Wing R422] (S. Jun.1; 281) *Rota.* £70

- L'Histoire Naturelle. Trans.:– Françoise Salerne. Ill.:– Martinet. Paris, 1767. 4to. Some minor discolouration to plts. Cont. spr. cf., rebkd. From Chetham's Liby., Manchester (C. Nov.27; 337) *Wheldon & Wesley.* £100
- Historia Insectorum. 1710. 1st. Edn. 4to. Title & some text ll. dust-soiled. 19th. C. mor.-bkd. cl., stitching brkn. From Chetham's Liby., Manchester. (C. Nov.27; 336) *Junk.* £80
- Historia Plantarum. 1686-1704. 1st. Edns. 3 vols. Fo. Lacks 1st. blank in vol. I, a few sm. holes & flaws in text, title to vol. I in both states. Cont. cf., rebkd., upr. cover of vol. I loose. Bkplt. of Herbert McLean Evans; from Honeyman Collection. [Wing R394] (S. Nov.11; 2582) *Hill.* £700
- - Anr. Copy. Some foxing in vol. 3. 19th. C. hf. mor., worn, 1 cover detchd. From Chetham's Liby., Manchester. (C. Nov.27; 334) *Wheldon & Wesley.* £70
- Miscellaneous Discourses Concerning the Dissolution & Changes of the World. 1692. 1st. Edn. Slight soiling, stp. of W. Barker, 1779, on title. Cont. cf., rebkd. From Honeyman Collection. [Wing R397] (S. Nov.11; 2583) *Hill.* £100
- Narrative of an Expedition to the Shores of the Arctic Sea. L., 1850. Orig. cl., rebkd. & recased, orig. spine pasted on. (CB. Dec.9; 10) *Can.* $1,000

RAY or REA, John & Willoughby or Willughby, Francis
- The Ornithology ... all the Birds Hitherto Known. 1678. 1st. Engl. Edn. Fo. Includes 2 plts. of snares often missing. Cont. cf., gt. spine. (S. Dec.3; 1114) *Blackwell.* £400

RAYE, Charles
- A Picturesque Tour through the Isle of Wight. 1825. 1st. Edn. Ob. 4to. Tissues wtrmkd. 1822, plts. 1824. 1st. plt. slightly loose. Orig. hf. red roan, slightly worn. (S. Nov.4; 537) *Maggs.* £350

RAYER, Pierre François Olive
- A Theoretical & Practical Treatise on the Diseases of the Skin. Trans.:– [R. Willis]. Paris, 1835. 2nd. Edn. 1 vol. text & atlas with 26 hand-cold. plts. 8vo. & fo. Hf.-title in atlas, but missing in text vol. Hf. cf. (S. Jun.17; 707) *Bickersteth.* £180
- Traité des Maladies des Reins & des Altérations de la Secrétion Urinaire. 1839-41-1837. 3 vols. & fo. atlas with 60 cold. plts. Text qtr. roan, atlas red qtr. mor. (S. Jun.17; 708) *Norman.* £260

RAYLEIGH, John William Strutt, Baron
- Collection of 23 Offprints of Scientific Papers. 1885-96. Cl. Inscr.; from liby. of Herbert E. Ives; from Honeyman Collection. (S. Nov.11; 2584) *Zeitlin.* £95

RAYMOND, Daniel
- Thoughts on Political Economy, in Two Parts. Balt., 1820. 1st. Edn. Disbnd., ex-liby. (SG. Mar.5; 382) $190

RAYMOND, Jean Arnaud
- Projét d'un Arc de Triomphe. Paris, 1812. Lge. fo. Slight spotting, sm. marginal tears in 2 plts. Orig. wraps., defect. (S. Jun.22; 82) *Weinreb.* £70

RAYMOND, Jean Paul (Pseud.)
See–RICKETTS, Charles 'Jean Paul Raymond'

RAYMOND, Rev. Oliver
- The Art of Fishing on the Principle of Avoiding Cruelty. L., 1866. 1st. Edn., L.P. Sm. 4to. Three-qtr. mor. Pres. copy. (SG. Oct.16; 318) $130

RAYNAL, Abbé Guillaume Thomas
[-] Atlas de Toutes les Parties Connues du Globe Terrestre ... [Paris], ca. 1776. 4to. 50 engraved double-p. maps, mntd. on guards, tables, many folding. Cont. mott. cf., spine gt. As an atlas, w.a.f. (C. Jul.15; 122) *Wilson.* £450
[-] Histoire Philosophique et Politique des Etablissements & du Commerce des Européens dans les Deux Indes. Maastricht, 1777-81. 5th. Edn. 10 vols., lacks atlas. Browned in parts. Cont. cf., gt., slightly worn. [Sabin 68110] (H. May 21/22; 518) DM 520
- - Anr. Edn. Ill.:– Cochin (port.), Moreau. Geneva, 1780. 5 vols. 4to. Some browning. Cont. red mor., gt. roulette borders, decor. spine raised bands, inner dentelles. (HD. Apr.24; 97) Frs. 6,500

- - Anr. Copy. Cont. cf., gt., arms of Preseau, sm. fleuron in centre of covers & at each corner, spine compartments gt., inner gt. dentelles, purple silk liners. [Sabin 68081] (SM. Oct.8; 1955) Frs. 4,200
- - Anr. Edn. [Geneva], ca. 1780. Atlas vol. only. 4to. Cont. tree cf. (CSK. Apr.10; 38) £110
- Histoire Philosophique.-Atlas ... pour l'Histoire Philosophique. Ill.:– Moreau; M. Bonne. Geneva, 1780; n.d. 2 works in 5 vols. 4to. Occasional minor staining & offsetting in 1st. work. Unif. 19th. C. hf. mor. From Chetham's Liby., Manchester. (C. Nov.27; 338) *Cucchi.* £280
- Philosophical & Political History of the Settlements & Trade of the Europeans in the East & West Indies. Trans.:– John Obadiah Justamond. 1798. 2nd. Edn. 6 vols. 1st. title dust-soiled. Cont. cf., worn. [Sabin 68089] (S. Sep.29; 166) *Subunso.* £60

RAYNAUD, Maurice
- De l'Asphyxie Locale et de la Gangrène Symétrique des Extrémités. Paris, 1862. 1st. Edn. Hf. mor., upr. wrap. bnd. in, a note on this cover probably by the author & initialled by him. (S. Jun.17; 709) *Phillips.* £420

RAZZI, D. Silvano
- Vita di Piero Soderini Gonfaloniere Perpetuo della Repubblica Fiorentina. Ill.:– P. Pilaja after G. Odam (borders). Padua, 1773. Fo. Scattered light foxing & slight browning. Cont. Italian cf. gt., sides gt.-panel. & with shaped corners, the broad borders with gt. flowers, urns, sm. star tools, & lge. masks in the classical style, rubbed. From the collection of John A. Saks. (C. Jun.10; 219) *Breslauer.* £240

RAZZI, Père Seraphin
- Les Vies des Saincts, et Sainctes, bien-heureux, et Hommes illustres de l'Ordre sacré de S. Dominique. Trans.:– Rev. Père Frère Iean Blancons. Paris, 1616. 2 pts. in 1 vol. 4to. Lacks pp. 361-432 of pt. 1, engraved port. of Aquinas pasted over pt. of text of pp. 360 & 433, ptd. ticket of letter H in red with 115 in ink below, bkplt. of Viscount Bruce of Ampthill. 17th. C. mor., gt., lozenge in centre of covers made up of sm. tools, gt. panel border, fleur-de-lis at each corner, flat spine gt. with long panel, sm. ornament in centre & fleur-de-lis at each corner. (SM. Oct.8; 1956) Frs. 11,500

REA, John
See–RAY or REA, John

READ, Alexander
- Chirurgorum Comes or the Whole Practice of Chirurgery begun by the Learned Mr. Read, Continued & Completed by a Member of the College of Physicians in London. 1687. 1st. Edn. Sm. marginal hole in Cc7, tiny paper flaw in Xx3 affecting letters, some worming in lr. margin in last section touching some letters. Cont. cf., purchase entry Sep. 1687. [Wing R427] (S. Jun.17; 710) *Levinson.* £380

READ, Grantly Dick
- Natural Childbirth. 1933. 1st. Edn. Cl. (S. Jun.17; 711) *Quaritch.* £55

READ, Herbert
- English Stained Glass. 1926. (50) numbered on H.M.P., sigd., 1st. Edn. 4to. Orig. vell. (TA. Mar.19; 22) £65
- - Anr. Edn. L. & N.Y., [1926]. Advance prospectus laid in. Buckram, spotted. From the liby. of Clement Heaton. (SG. Mar.12; 348) $120
See–RACKHAM, Bernard & Read, Herbert

READE, Charles
- Christie Johnstone.-Cream.-White Lies.-The Cloister & the Hearth.-Griffith Gaunt.-Put yourself in his place.-A Terrible Temptation.-A Woman-Hater. 1853; 1858; 1857; 1861; 1866; 1870; 1871; 1877. 5th. work 2nd. Edn., most 1st. Edns. Together 21 vols. Soiled. Cont. hf. cf. (SH. Jan.30; 354) *Jarndyce.* £200
- [Works]. L., 1884-1927. 21 vols. Slight browning. Unif. hf. cf. gt. by Sangorski & Sutcliffe. (SPB. Nov.25; 482) $250

READE, T.S.B.
[-] Christian Retirement. L., 1831. 12mo. Diced cf. gt. Fore-e. pntg. (SG. Dec.18; 186) $160

REAGAN, Oliver
- American Architecture of the Twentieth Century. N.Y., [1927]. 7 pts. Tall fo. Loose in bd. covers, all loose. (SG. Dec.4; 10) $220

REALENCYKLOPADIE FUR PROTESTANT-ISCHE THEOLOGIE Und Kirche Ed.:– A. Hauck. Leipzig. 1896. Orig. hf. leath. (D. Dec.11-13; 2611) DM 650

REALES ORDENANZAS Para la Dirección, Regimen y Gobierno du importante cuerpo de la Mineria de Nueva-España. Real orden de 8 Diciembre de 1785, y Declaraciones en su cumplimienento hechas para adaptar la Ordenanza de Mineria de Nueva Espana a el Virreinato de Lima Lima, 1786. 2 pts. in 1 vol. Fo. Title slightly soiled. Cont. limp vell., new end-papers. (SPB. May 5; 422) $375
– – **Anr. Copy.** Sm. 4to. Soiled & worn thro.-out. Soiled & detchd. (SPB. May 5; 421) $225

REALLEXIKON zur Deutschen Kunstgeschichte Ed.:– O. Schmitt & others. Stuttgart, 1937-67. Vols. 1-5. 4to. Orig. linen. (R. Mar.31-Apr.4; 919) DM 730

REAUMUR, René Antoine Ferchault de
– **L'Art de convertir le Fer forgé en Acier, et l'Art d'adoucir le Fer fondu.** Paris, 1722. 1st. Edn. 4to. Some browning. Cont. cf., gt. spine, hf. red mor. case. Stp. of Count R. von Veltheim; from Honeyman Collection. (S. Nov.11; 2585) *Das Bucherkabinet.* £420
– – **Anr. Copy.** A few ll. slightly damaged on surface, slightly affecting text. Cont. mott. cf., spine gt. (S. Oct.21; 420) *Maggs.* £140
– **The Art of Hatching & Bringing Up Domestick Fowls.** L., 1750. Mod. cf.-bkd. bds. (P. Feb.19; 162) *Thorp.* £170
– **Bees. Natural History of Bees.** 1744. Cont. cf. gt. (P. Jan.22; 65) *Book Room.* £75
– **Mémoires pour servir à l'histoire des Insectes.** Paris, 1734-42. 1st. Edn. 6 vols. 4to. 2 wormholes in plts. to vol. III, occasional marginal stains in vol. VI. Cont. Fr. mott. cf., gt., some wear. Bkplt. of Herbert McLean Evans; from Honeyman Collection. (S. Nov.11; 2586) *Howell.* £520
– – **Anr. Copy.** Titles dust-soiled, 1 plt. in vol. 5 frayed & reprd., many plts. browned, vol. 1 slightly stained. 19th. C. hf. mor. From Chetham's Liby., Manchester. (C. Nov.27; 339) *Junk.* £240
– – **Anr. Edn.** Paris, 1734-36. Vols. 1 & 2 (of 6). 4to. Cont. cf. gt. (P. Apr.30; 222) *Dillon.* £65
– **Oeconomische Abhandlung von den Bienen.** Frankfurt & Leipzig, 1759. 1st. German Edn. 4to. Slightly soiled. Cont. vell., new back. (R. Mar.31-Apr.4; 1608) DM 900

REAVEY, George
– **Faust's Metamorphoses.** Ill.:– Stanley William Hayter. Fontenay-Aux-Roses, [1931]. (100) -numbered, sigd. by author & artist, with extra suite of 5 sigd. & numbered etchings. 4to. 6 orig. etchings. Orig. wraps., d.-w. (SG. May 14; 97) $650
– – **Anr. Copy.** Orig. ptd. wraps. Accompanied by 2 orig. sigd. etchings (plts. V & VI, dtd. 1932 & 1931 respectively). (SG. Apr.2; 132) $425
– – **Anr. Copy.** (6) Priv. Ptd. sigd. by author & artist. Buckram, orig. wraps. bnd. in. Author's Copy, 3rd. plt., which should be on p. 27 (left blank in this copy) is over-ptd. onto p. 29. With working proof of this plt., marked up by printer & sigd. & captioned by artist. (SG. Jun.4; 428) $150

REBELL, Hugues
– **Les Nuits Chaudes du Cap Français.** 1902. (15) on Hollande. Jansenist mor., wrap., by Cretté. (HD. Oct.10; 142) Frs. 1,650

REBHUN, P.
– **Hausfried.** Wittenberg, 1552. 19th. C. vell. (R. Mar.31-Apr.4; 83) DM 950

RECHENBUCH AUFF NYDERLAND auff Sylber und Goltt probyren und auff Geldt an Flemysch pfund [Nuremb.?], 1527. 4to. Cont. marginalia on last p., stp. of G. Loos. 19th. C. hf. cf., worn. From Honeyman Collection. (S. Nov.11; 2588) *Martin.* £340

RECHTEN ende Costumen van Antwerpen. [suivi de] Ordonnantie ende Verhael vanden Stijl Antw., 1582. Fo. Old cf., 5 spine raised bands, decor. (LM. Nov.8; 2) B.Frs. 24,000

RECKLINGHAUSEN, Friedrich Daniel von
– **Ueber die Multiplen Fibrome der Haut und ihre Beziehung zu den Multiplen Neuromen, Festschrift . . . Herrn Rudolf Virchow dargebracht.** Berlin,

1882. 1st. Separate Edn. Hf. mor., upr. wrap. bnd. in. (S. Jun.17; 712) *Jenner Books.* £160

RECLUS, Elisée
– **Géographie de l'Afrique.** Paris, 1885-88. 4 vols. 1 cold. map on linen. Cont. hf. leath., not collated. (R. Oct.14-18; 1611) DM 420
– **Géographie de l'Europe.** Paris, 1875-80. 5 vols. Cont. hf. leath. (R. Oct.14-18; 1846) DM 600
– **Nouvelle Geographie Universelle. Tome III [Europe Centrale] & IV.** Paris, 1878-79. 2 vols. Cont. hf. leath. (R. Oct.14-18; 2116) DM 450
– **The Universal Geography.** L., ca. 1875-95. 27 vols. Orig. linen. (R. Oct.14-18; 1519) DM 1,500

RECOPILACION de Leyes de los Reynos de las Indias Madrid, 1774. 4 vols. Fo. Previous owners' inscrs. & stps. erased from titles, 1 sm. owner's inscr. remaining. Later cf., slightly worn. [Sabin 68388] (SPB. May 5; 423) $1,000

RECORD, Robert
– **Arithmetick, or, the Ground of Arts.** 1636. Title soiled, some staining, last gathering loose & with lr. blank corners torn off, slight defect to P4 recto, paper flaw in 2B4, hole in 2H3 affecting text. Cont. limp vell., inner hinges brkn., 1 tie remaining, hf. red mor. case. From Honeyman Collection. [NSTC 20810] (S. Nov.11; 2592) *Quaritch.* £110
– – **Anr. Edn.** Ed.:– M. John Dee. [1646; title to 'third part' dtd. 1648]. Cont. sheep. [Wing R650] (C. Feb.25; 168) *Laywood.* £80
– – **Anr. Edn.** Ed.:– John Dee & John Mellis. 1654. Lacks 1st. lf. (? blank), slightly spotted or soiled. Cont. cf. [Wing R466] (S. Jan.26; 294) *Quaritch.* £65
– – **Anr. Edn.** 1668. Paper flaw in C4 affecting text. Cont. sheep, rebkd. Bkplt. of Tixall liby.; from Honeyman Collection. [Wing R647] (S. Nov.11; 2594) *Quaritch.* £65
– **The Castle of Knowledge.** 1556. 1st. Edn. Fo. Slight soiling, blank corner torn from last lf., rust-hole in H5, early sig. of William Gyfford on title, cont. marginal annots. at beginning. Mod. hf. mor. From Honeyman Collection. [NSTC 20796] (S. Nov.11; 2590) *Quaritch.* £1,700
– **The Pathway to Knowledge containing the First Principles of Geometrie . . . both for use of instrumentes Geometricall, & astronomicall & also for proiection of plattes in euerye kinde.** 1551. 1st. Edn. 2 pts. in 1 vol. 4to. Slight soiling, some ll. stained. Cont. panel. cf., gt., rebkd. & reprd., lacks ties, hf. red mor. case. From Honeyman Collection. [NSTC 20812] (S. Nov.11; 2589) *Quaritch.* £2,600
[-] **The Whetstone of Witte, whiche is the seconde parte of Arithmetike.** 1557. 1st. Edn. 4to. 1 folding table bnd. upside down, some soiling & discolouration, stain on A1, 17th. C. owner's inscrs. Cont. cf. rebkd. & reprd. From Honeyman Collection. [NSTC 20820] (S. Nov.11; 2591) *Quaritch.* £2,700

RECREATIONS FRANCOISES . . . Utopia [Holland], 1681. 2 pts. in 1 vol. 12mo. English red mor., ca. 1820, fillet, fleurons in corners, inside dentelle, decor. spine. (HD. Mar.18; 142) Frs. 1,000

RECREATIONS LUBRIQUES des Fouteurs de Tout Sexe, de Tout Age et de Tout Parti Foutropolis [Paris], 1791. Sm. thin 12mo. Frontis. & 4 figures in the Gravelot style. Hf. mor., unc., ca. 1850. (HD. Apr.10; 371) Frs. 3,300

RECUEIL DE CALEMBOURGS Ill.:– Thierry. Paris, ca. 1820. Lightly browned thro.-out, slightly soiled in parts. Hf. linen with orig. wraps. bnd. in, soiled. Paul Gavarni ex-libris. (H. Dec.9/10; 1748) DM 750

RECUEIL DE COIFFURES et D'Habillements N.p., [1779]. Thick 18mo. Cont. red mor., decor. spine, 3 fillets, worn. (HD. Apr.10; 181) Frs. 1,450

RECUEIL DE QUELQUES PIECES Nouvelles et Galantes Cologne [Amst.], [1667]. 3rd. Elz. Edn. 2 vols. in 1. 12mo. Early 19th. C. str.-grd. mor., triple gt. fillet round spine & cover compartments. From Charles Pieters collection with ex-libris. (SM. Oct.8; 2417) Frs. 4,000

RECUEIL DES BLASONS *See*–POITIER DE COURCY, Pol.

RECUEIL DES MEILLEURS CONTES EN VERS [Paris], 1778. 1st. Edn. (60). 4 vols. Minimal browning, slight soiling. Cont. marb. cf., gt. spine, gold borders on covers, inner & outer dentelles. (H. Dec.9/10; 1635) DM 2,800
– – **Anr. Edn.** Ill.:– Duplessis-Bertaux. L. [Paris], 1778. 4 vols. 18mo. Old red mor. by Cazin. (HD. Apr.8; 298) Frs. 7,500
– – **Anr. Copy.** 4 vols. 18mo. Old red mor. by Cazin. (HD. Apr.8; 299) Frs. 6,100
– – **Anr. Copy.** 4 vols. 18mo. Mor. by Lortic, decor. spines, 3 gt. fillets on covers, inside dentelle. Bkplt. of James Hartmann. (HD. Dec.5; 174) Frs. 4,800

RECUEIL D'OBSERVATIONS CURIEUSES, sur les Moeurs, les Coutumes, les Usages, les Differentes Langues . . . de l'Asie, de l'Afrique, & de d'Amérique Paris, 1749. 1st. Edn. 4 vols. 12mo. Some stains, 1 lf. in vol. II transposed with 1 in vol. IV. Later hf. cf., unc., bkplts. [Sabin 68424] (SG. Jan.8; 378) $160

RED MAGIC Ed.:– Romer Wilson. Ill.:– Kay Nielsen. 1930. Orig. cl. (SH. Mar.27; 384) *White.* £100

RED RIVER SETTLEMENT
– **Papers Relating to . . .** 1819. Fo. Disbnd. (SH. Mar.5; 119) *Remington.* £130

REDGRAVE, Gilbert R. *See*–POLLARD, Alfred William, Redgrave, G.R. Wing, D. & others

REDI, Francesco
– **Esperienze Intorno a Diverse Cose Naturali.** Flor., 1671. 1st. Edn., L.P. 4to. Some browning & spotting. 19th C. hf. vell. (S. Jul.27; 304) *Mediolanum.* £75
– – **Anr. Copy.** Vell. (S. Dec.1; 363) *Tzakas.* £60
– – **Anr. Edn.** Naples, 1687. 6 engraved plts. browned. Vell. bds. [Sabin 68516] (SPB. May 5; 424) $100
– **Esperienze Intorno a diverse Cose Naturali, e particolarmente a quelle, che ci son Portate dall'Indie.–Lettera . . . sopra alcune Opposizioni fatte alle sue Osservazioni intorno alle Vipere.** Flor., 1671; 1670. 1st. Edns. (L.P.) 2 works in 1 vol. 4to. 1st. work with some browning & spotting, liby. stp. on title. 19th. C. hf. roan, worn. From Honeyman Collection. (S. Nov.11; 2599) *Gurney.* £160
– **Esperienze intorno alle Generazione degl'Insetti.** Flor., 1668. 1st. Edn. 4to. Stained. Cont. limp bds., defect., unc., bkplt. of Dukes of Arenberg at Nordkirchen. From Honeyman Collection. [BMC (Nat. Hist.] VIII, p. 1056 [28 plts.]] (S. Nov.11; 2598) *Gurney.* £240
– **Opere.** Venice, 1712-28. 6 vols. Later hf. cf. (CSK. Apr.24; 51) £60
– – **Anr. Edn.** Ill.:– A. Luciani (folding plt.). Venice, 1742-60. 7 vols. Sm. 4to. Occasional light browning. Orig. paper bds., in 2 folding buckram cases, unc. From the collection of John A. Saks. (C. Jun.10; 221) *Quaritch.* £140
– **Osservazioni . . . intorno agli Animali viventi che si trovano negli Animali viventi.** Flor., 1684. 1st. Edn. 4to. 19th. C. hf. cf., slightly worn. Pres. copy; from Honeyman Collection. (S. Nov.11; 2600) *Schuman.* £340
– – **Anr. Copy.** Plt. 21 misbnd., tear in fold of plt. 8, lacks port., sm. stp. on hf.-title. Cont. vell. bds., lr. cover stained. From Honeyman Collection. (S. Nov.11; 2601) *Pilo Boyl.* £170
– **Osservazioni intorno alle Vipere.** Flor., 1664. 1st. Edn. 4to. Hf. vell. From Honeyman Collection. (S. Nov.11; 2596) *Gurney.* £160
– – **Anr. Edn.** Flor., 1686. 2 pts. in 1 vol. 4to. D1 pt. 2 reprd., a few stains. Cont. vell. Bkplt. of Giacomo Manzoni; from Honeyman Collection. (S. Nov.11; 2597) *Gurney.* £70
– **Osservazioni Intorno alle Vipere.–Lettera . . . sopra alcune Opposizioni Fatte alle sue Osservazioni Intorno alle Vipere.** Flor., 1664; 1670. 1st. Edns. 2 works in 1 vol. 4to. Hf.-title & title of 1st. work rehinged. Cont. cf., gt. spine. (S. Jul.27; 303) *Dekker & Nordemann.* £220

REDING, H. *See*–MENDEL, P.H. & Reding, H.

REDOUTE, Pierre Joseph
- Fruits & Flowers.-The Best of Redouté's Roses.
Ed.:– Eva Mannering. 1955; 1959. Fo. Orig. pict.
wraps. (SBA. Jul.22; 117) *Schwarz.* £50
- Les Liliacées. Paris, 1802-16. Lge. copy. 8 vols.
Fo. Plt. 95 in 1st. state, 370/371 on 1 folding lf., 2
versions of plt. 428, plt. 429 numbered 427 & 263
numbered 163, occasional minor foxing affecting
hf.-titles to vols. 3, 4, 5, & 7, titles to vols. 4 & 7,
tissues, 1 or 2 plts. & some text ll., sm. stain
affecting some ll. of general table. Orig. bds., unc.
(C. Nov.5; 126) *Urquhart.* £14,00
- Les Roses ... Ed.:– C.A. Thory. Paris, 1828.
3rd. Edn. 3 vols. Cont. long-grd. hf. mor., sm.
corners, decor. spines, unc. (HD. Jun.10; 200)
Frs. 62,000

REECE, Robert
[-] Hints to Young Barbados-Planters. Bridge
Town, Barbados, [1857]. 1st. Edn. Orig. cl. stpd.
in blind & gt., rebkd. with orig. spine laid down.
(SG. Oct.30; 36) $100

REED & BARTON
- Illustrated Catalogue & Price List of Electro
Silver Plate ... Taunton, Massachusetts, [1877].
Fo. Orig. cl. (SG. Dec.4; 322) $170

REES, D.
See–BURLINGTON, Charles

REEVE, Emma
See–ALLOM, Thomas & Reeve, Emma

REEVE, J. Arthur, Architect
- A Monograph of the Abbey of St. Mary of
Fountains. Yorkshire, 1892. Lge. fo. Orig. hf. mor.
(TA. Dec.18; 1) £55

REEVERELL, James
- Les Délices de la Grand'Bretagne et de l'Irlande.
Leiden, 1727. 7 vols. (of 8). 12mo. 1 vol. sewed,
rest old cf. (LM. Mar.21; 310) B.Frs. 10,000

**REFLECTOR. Revista Ultraista de la que
apareció ...**
Madrid, Dec. 1920. 4to. Wraps. (DS.
Apr.24; 1044) Pts. 20,000

REFORMATION der Stadt Worms
[Speier], [Peter Drach], 27 May, 1499. Fo. Initial
capitals, underlines, paragraph marks & initial
strokes supplied thro.-out in red, stain to upr.
margins thro.-out, affecting most headlines &
foliation, causing slight disintegration of paper at
extreme upr. edge. Cont. oak bds., rebkd. in
blind-stpd. mor. antique, orig. end-papers
preserved. Bkplt. of the General Theological
Seminary Liby. [BMC II, 510, Goff R40, HC
13719*] (CNY. Oct.1; 54) $4,000

REGENFUSS, Franz Michael
- Auserlesene Schnecken, Muscheln ... Copen.,
1758. Vol. 1 only (of 2, all publd.?). Lge. fo. Plts.
& ills. hand-cold., occasional light foxing &
soiling. 19th. C. hf. mor., covers detchd. W.a.f.,
from Chetham's Liby., Manchester. (C.
Nov.27; 340) *Douwma.* £1,600
– – Anr. Copy. Imp. fo. Minimal soiling of last 4
text ll., last lf. stained in margin, plt. 1 slightly
soiled, plts. 7, 9, 10 with stain at head. Cont. red
mor., slightly soiled & worn, floral gt., gt. outer
dentelle & inner dentelle. (HK. May 12-14; 357)
DM 20,000

REGGIO, Pietro
[-] Songs. [L.], [1680]. 1st. Printing. 2 vols. in 1.
Fo. Lacks title, some margins soiled, some sm.
repairs. Cf., defect. (H. May 21/22; 848)
DM 720

REGINALDETUS, Petrus
See–JOHANNES de Lapide–GREGORIUS I, Pope
–REGINALDETUS, Petrus

REGIOMONTANUS, Johannes
- De Triangulis Omnimodis libri quinque ...
Accesserunt ... D. Nicolai Cusani De Quadratura
Circuli. Nuremb., 1533. 1st. Edn. 2 pts. in 1 vol.
Fo. Lacks blank at end of pt. 2, marginal repairs
to F1 & F4, some discolouration. Mod. hf. vell.,
soiled. From Honeyman Collection. (S. May
20; 3299) *Norman.* £650
– – Anr. Copy. Mod. hf. vell., soiled. From
Honeyman Collection. (S. Nov.11; 2607)
Cooper. £580
- Ephemerides sive Almanach Perpetuum. Ed.:–
J.L. Santritter. Venice, Petrus Liechtenstein, 15
Oct. 1498. 1st. Edn. 4to. Last lf. guarded &
slightly soiled on verso. Hf. vell., worn. From

Honeyman Collection. [BMC V, 578; Goff R110]
(S. Nov.11; 2604) *Hill.* £620
- Epitoma in Almagestum Ptolemaei. Venice,
Johannes Hamman, 31 Aug. 1496. 1st. Edn. Fo.
Without inserted 2 ll. letter of Abioscus, a little
worming, mostly marginal, slight marginal stains.
19th. C. hf. russ., gt. From Honeyman Collection.
[BMC V, 427; Goff R111] (S. Nov.11; 2602)
Jackson. £3,000
– – Anr. Copy. Slight marginal staining & soiling,
title with lr. margin reprd. & partly erased
owner's inscr. & stp. leaving sm. holes. Cont.
blind-stpd. cf., rebkd., very worn. Bkplt. of
Herbert McLean Evans; from Honeyman
Collection. (S. Nov.11; 2603) *Nox.* £2,100
- In Ptolemaei magnam compositionem, quam
Almagestum vocant, libri tredecim. Nuremb., 1550.
Fo. Lacks blank T8, fore-margin of T5 reprd.,
printing flaws on E1v, N3 & P1r, title browned,
slight marginal spotting. 18th. C. hf. vell., worn.
Bkplt. of Dr. Sydney Ross; from Honeyman
Collection. (S. Nov.11; 2608)
Rogers Turner. £170
- Kalendar Maister Johannes Künisperger.
Augsburg, 1489. 1st. Ratdolt German Edn. 4to.
Rubricated, after 28 text ll. 4 ll. with instrument
ills. bnd. in, letters LVNE printed out of order,
another 5 ll. with letter LVNE correct & moving
parts, many cont. notes, last 2 ll. with sm.
corrections, some worming & holes in parts,
slightly soiled, mostly in fold, title stained. Cont.
old MS. vell. [H. 13787] (H. Dec.9/10; 261)
DM 450
- Naturlicher kunst der Astronomei ... kurtzer
begriff. Strassburg, 1529. 1st. Edn. 4to. Stained,
title soiled, a few wormholes. Mod. hf. mor. From
Honeyman Collection. (S. Nov.11; 2605)
Lamm. £160
- Tabulae Directionum Profectionumque, non tam
Astrologiae Iudiciariae, quam Tabulis
Instrumentisque Innumeris fabricandis Utiles ac
Necessariae. Tübingen, 1559. 4to. Last few ll.
wormed in inner margin, some marginal staining,
title browned. Cont. limp vell., worn & stained.
Bkplt. & stp. of H. Silva; from Honeyman
Collection. (S. Nov.11; 2610) *Nox.* £80
- Temporal ... Natürlicher Kunst der Astronomy
kurtzer Begriff. Frankfurt a. M., [1550?]. 4to.
Some marginal staining & soiling. Wraps., hf. red
mor. case. Stp. of Stolberg liby. at Wernigerode;
from Honeyman Collection. (S. Nov.11; 2609)
Das Bucherkabinet. £240
See–SACROBOSCO, Johannes de
–REGIOMONTANUS, Johannes

REGIOMONTANUS, Johannes–FINE, Oronce
- De Triangulis omnimodis libri quinque ...
Accesserunt ... D. Nicolai Cusani de Quadratura
circuli.–Quadratura Circuli, tandem inventa &
clarissime demonstrata. Ed.:– J. Schoener (1st.
work). Nuremb.; Paris, 1533; 1544. 1st. Edns. 2
works in 1 vol. (first 2 pts.). Fo. Some staining &
soiling in 1st. work, slight staining in 2nd. 17th. C.
cf., spine gt., worn. Thomas Digges' copy, with his
sig. & marginal annots. & diagrams; from liby. of
Marquess of Bute & Honeyman Collection. (S.
Nov.11; 2606) *Thomas.* £1,450

**REGIOMONTANUS, Johannes–REINHOLD,
Erasmus**
- Tabulae directionum profectionumque.
–Prutenicae tabulae coelestium motuum.
Wittenberg, 1584; 1585. 2 works in 1 vol. 4to.
Some discolouration. 17th. C. vell., gt. (oxidised),
emblem of Fortune on upr. cover, with ties,
end-papers renewed. Bkplt. of Dukes of Arenberg
at Nordkirchen; from Honeyman Collection. (S.
Nov.11; 2611) *Hill.* £260

REGIOMONTANUS, Johannes–SANTBECK, D.
- De Triangulis Planis et Sphaericis Libri Quinque.
–Problematvm Astronomicorvm et Geometricorvm
Sectiones Septem. Ed.:– D. Santbeck (1st. work).
Basle, [1561]; 1561. 2nd. Edns. 2 works in 1 vol.
Fo. 1st. title lf. with old owners' inscrs., correction,
both works slightly browned & soiled in parts.
Cont. blind-stpd. pig., soiled, spine slightly defect.,
lacks clasps. [BMC German Books 631] (H.
Dec.9/10; 262) DM 2,600

REGISTRUM Honoris de Richmond
1722. Fo. Decor. initials, all hand-cold. &
heightened or emblazoned with gold. Cont. cf.,
rebkd. From the collection of Eric Sexton. (C.
Apr.16; 340) *Traylen.* £220

REGIUS, Hudalrich
- Utriusque arithmetices epitome ex variis
authoribus concinnata. Strassburg, 1536. 1st. Edn.
Title slightly soiled, some staining, single
wormhole running through text towards end. 19th.
C. mor. From Honeyman Collection. (S.
Nov.11; 2612) *Hill.* £130

REGIUS, Ph.
- Von Lutherischen Wunderzaychenn. [Augsburg],
[1524?]. 4to. Wraps. (R. Oct.14-18; 137)
DM 450

**REGLAMENTO y Aranceles Reales para el
Comercio libre de España a Indias de 12. Octubre
de 1778**
Madrid, [1779]. 4to. Wide margins. Cont. tree cf.
[Sabin 68890] (SPB. May 6; 425) $225

**REGLEMENT de la Confrerie de l'Adoration
Perpetuelle du S. Sacrement**
Montreal, 1776. 2nd. Edn. 16mo. Orig. light bds.,
covered with damask wall paper. (CB. Apr.1; 96)
Can. $850

REGNARD, Jean-François
- Oeuvres. Ill.:– after Moreau. Paris, 1789-90. 4
vols. Ills. slightly spotted. Cont. tree cf., decor.
spines, border of 2 interlaced fillets on covers, 1
with gold dots & the other with olive leaves. (SM.
Feb.11; 98) Frs. 1,000
– – Anr. Edn. Ill.:– Vignet, Duhamel, Halbou &
others, 9 after Borel. Paris, 1790. On vell. 4 vols.
Cont. red mor., gt., in Bradel style. (SM.
Oct.8; 2418) Frs. 13,000
– – Anr. Copy. Extra-illustrated with 1 port. after
Rigaud & 7 plts. after Jean Michel Moreau le
Jeune, 2 before letter, from 6-vol. edn. of 1789-90,
some ll. slightly browned, bkplt. of John Kettle.
Cont. mor., gt., perhaps by Bradel or Bisiaux,
dentelle borders, flat spine gt. in compartments,
inner gt. dentelles. (SM. Oct.8; 1961) Frs. 1,000
- Oeuvres Complètes. Ed.:– Garnier. Ill.:– after
Rigaud (port.), Moreau & Marillier. Paris, 1790.
6 vols. Inserted suite of unsigd. port. & 12 figs. by
Borel & Bornel & port. after Rigaud engraved by
Ficquet. Long-grd. red mor., inner dentelle,
watered silk doubls. & end-ll., by Bozérian. (HD.
Jun.10; 92) Frs. 10,500
– – Anr. Edn. Ill.:– Rigaud, Moreau & Marillier.
1820. 6 vols. Cont. porphyr cf., dentelle border,
decor. spines. (HD. Feb.18; 174) Frs. 1,200

REGNAULT, Nicolas F.
- La Botanique mis à la Portée de tout le Monde.
Paris, 1774. Vol. 2 [only]. Fo. Ca. 90 plts. (only),
some additional plts. partly defect., some stains &
soiling. Hf. cf., very worn, covers detchd. W.a.f.
(S. Jun.1; 193) *Cristiani.* £230

REGNE de la Mode (Le)
- Nouvel Almanach des Modes, rédigé par Le
Caprice. Paris, [1823]. 16mo. Some spotting.
Cont. paper bds., spine decor., lge. gt. border, s.-c.
(HD. Apr.10; 184) Frs. 1,100

REGNIER, Henri de
- Le Bon Plaisir. Ill.:– Drésa. Paris, 1919. (250);
(30), numbered. 4to. 3 states of etchings, some sm.
stains. Mor. by Kieffer, pointillé fillet in
compartments of spine & on covers, orig. wrap.
(SM. Feb.11; 274) Frs. 2,800
– – Anr. Edn. Ill.:– de Becque. Paris, 1922. (1200);
(60) on Van Gelder Holland. 4to. Mor. by
Flammarion, inside dentelle, wrap. preserved, s.-c.
(SM. Feb.11; 275) Frs. 3,000
– – Anr. Edn. Ill.:– Sylvain Sauvage. Paris, 1929.
(31). 4to. 20 etchings in 2 states (black-&-white
with comments & cold.). Red hf. mor. by Georges
Grette, wrap. preserved, s.-c. Specially printed for
Sylvain Sauvage, bkplt. of Louis Vigoureux. (SM.
Feb.11; 276) Frs. 2,000
- La Cité des Eaux. Ill.:– Jouas. Paris, 1912.
(250); (180). 4to. 1 state of etchings. Mor. by
David, decor. spine, border of 3 fillets on covers,
orig. wrap. A.L.s. by author loosely inserted. (SM.
Feb.11; 277) Frs. 5,000
- Contes à soi-même. 1894. (15) on vergé des
Vosges. Hf. mor., wrap., by Merienne. Note. (HD.
Oct.10; 143) Frs. 2,900
- L'Escapade. Ill.:– George Barbier. Paris, 1931.
(75) priv. ptd., numbered. 4to. Mor., cover design
by artist, orig. wraps. bnd. in. (SH. Nov.20; 7)
Klusmann. £160
– – Anr. Copy. (1075) numbered. 4to. Orig.
wraps., unc., unopened, cover design by Barbier.
(SH. Nov.20; 217) *Monk Bretton.* £120

REGNIER, Henri de -contd.
- **Lui ou les Femmes et l'Amour Suivi de Donc . . . et Paray-le-Monzal.** Paris, 1929. Coll. Edn., (44) on Jap. Imp. Long-grd. mor., 5 decor. spine raised bands, triple border, triple gt. fillet, inner border of 6 fillets, gt. & 1 pointillé, wrap. preserved, by Canape & Corriez s.-c. (LM. Mar.21; 291) *B.Frs.* 14,000
- **Le Médaillier.** Ill.:– Adolphe Giraldon. Paris, 1923. (118) numbered. 4to. Mor. by Affolter, gt. arms., gt. mor. doubls., orig. wraps. bnd. in, s.-c. For Duchesse de Massa. (SM. Oct.8; 2364) *Frs.* 1,800
- **La Pécheresse.** 1920. Hf. mor., wrap. Dedication copy, A.N., on Hollande. (HD. Oct.10; 148) *Frs.* 2,600
- **– Anr. Edn.** Ill.:– Antoine Calbet. Paris, 1922. (500) on Arches vell., numbered. 4to. 1 state of all compositions. Red mor. by Flammarion Vaillant, mor. doubls. with very ornate gt., wrap. preserved, folder & s.-c. (SM. Feb.11; 278) *Frs.* 12,000
- **– Anr. Edn.** Ill.:– George Barbier. Paris, 1924. (99) on Rives hors commerce, numbered. Hf. mor., orig. pict. wraps. bnd. in. (SH. Nov.20; 215) *Ayres.* £160
- **Les Rencontres de Monsieur de Bréot.** Ill.:– George Barbier. Paris, 1930. (91) priv. ptd. numbered. 4to. Mor. cover design by artist, orig. wraps. bnd. in. (SH. Nov.20; 5) *Lutrin.* £120
- **Scènes Mythologiques.** Ill.:– A.-E. Marty. 1924. Orig. Edn. Mor., red mor. doubls., copper engr. on covers, by Canape. On vergé de Hollande. (HD. Oct.10; 203) *Frs.* 3,500
- **– Anr. Copy.** Ll., box. Letter from artist. (HD. Jun.30; 68) *Frs.* 950

REGRA Y STATUTOS: Da Ordem de Santiago
Lisbon, 15 Jun., 1548. Sm. 4to. Some worming at ends slightly affecting text & woodcuts, some reprd., 1 lf. slightly soiled & stained. 18th. C. red str.-grd. mor., panels of borders & fillets, blind-stpd. covers & spine, gt. inside border. From collections of Pereira Laloas, relief stps. in margin, Moreira Cabral, Conde de Sucena & Boies Penrose, with bkplts. (S. Nov.25; 370) *Thomas.* £380

REGULATIONS & Instructions relating to His Majesty's Service at Sea
1808. 4to. Cont. tree cf., slightly worn. (SBA. Dec.16; 38) *Lawson.* £55

REHBERG, Frederick
- **Drawings . . . at Naples . . .** Ill.:– Thomas Piroli. 1794. 4to. Some spotting. Hf. mor. (CSK. Mar.6; 153) £65
- **– Anr. Copy.** Fo. Hf. cf., rebkd. (S. May 5; 134) *King.* £60
- **[Lady Hamilton's Attitudes].** 1797-1801. 2 pts. Fo. Wraps., worn. (S. Jun.22; 83) *Franklin.* £130

REIBISCH, Friedrich Martin
- **Eine Auswahl merkwürdiger Gegenstände aus der Königl. Sächs. Rüstkammer.** Dresden, [1825-27]. Ob. 4to. Newer hf. leath. in cont. style, gt., old pict. cover material used. (D. Dec.11-13; 2784) DM 1,000

REICHENBACH, Anton Benedict
- **[–] Die Naturgeschichte in getreuen Abbildungen. Fische.** Leipzig, [1838-]40. 4to. Lacks 6 plts., quite soiled in parts. Cont. hf. leath. (R. Oct.14-18; 2959) DM 420
- **Neueste Volks-Naturgeschichte des Pflanzenreiches für Schule u. Haus.** Leipzig, ca. 1845. 4to. Most plts. bkd., slightly soiled, lacks 1 plt. Cont. hf. leath., worn. (HK. Nov.18-21; 711) DM 440

REICHENBACH, Hans
- **Relativitätstheorie und Erkenntnis apriori. –Axiomatik der relativistischen Raum-Zeit-Lehre. –Philosophie der Raum-Zeit-Lehre.–Philosophic Foundations of Quantum Mechanics.** Berlin; Brunswick; Berlin/Leipzig; Berkeley & Los Angeles, 1920; 1924; 1928; 1944. 1st. Edns. Hf. roan; orig. cl.-bkd. bds.; orig. cl.; orig. cl. From Honeyman Collection. (S. Nov.11; 2614) *Rootenberg.* £55

REICHENBACH, Heinrich Gottlieb Ludwig
- **Iconographia Botanica . . . Kupfersammlung Kritischer Gewächse.** Leipzig, 1823-32. 10 vols. 4to. A few stains. 19th. C. hf. cf., a few repairs. From collection of Massachusetts Horticultural Society, stps. on plts. (SPB. Oct.1; 159) $3,400

REICHENBACH, Heinrich Gottlieb Ludwig & Heinrich Gustav
- **Icones Florae Germanicae et Helveticae.** Leipzig, 1837-[1903]. Vol. 1 2nd. Edn. Vols. I-XXII (of 25) in 17 vols. 4to. Vol. XXII lacks title. Hf. mor., gt., slightly stained. W.a.f. (S. Jun.1; 194) *Junk.* £1,000
- **– Anr. Edn.** Leipzig (Vol. I), Leipzig & Gera (Vols. 2-25), 1850 (Vol. I), 1837-1912 (Vols. 2-25). Vol. I 2nd. Edn., rest Edns. 25 vols. in 24 (i.e., I-XIX; XIX pt. 2, 3 vols.; XX-XXV pt. 2). 4to. Vol. 7 lacks plts. LXXII-LXXXII, vol. I has 11 extra plts. with these numbers (in 2nd. Edn. state), which appear to tally with those missing in vol. 7, 1st. Edn. text bnd. at end of vol. I, some stains. Hf. mor., some covers loose. As a periodical, w.a.f., from collection of Massachusetts Horticultural Society, stps. on plts. (SPB. Oct.1; 160) $7,750

REICHENTHAL, Ulrich von
- **Das Concilium. So zu Constanz gehalten ist Worden des Jars . . .** Augsburg, 1536. 2nd. Edn. Fo. Tailpieces, woodcut ills. & coats of arms crudely cold. by early hand, lacks M3 & 4 (replaced with 3 ll. from the 1483 edn.), title-p. defect. & mntd. with portion of ill. painted in by hand & with all the text on verso masked, top inner corners rotted away thro.-out, reprd. but occasionally affecting text or ill., top fore-corner of d4 torn away & reprd. with partial loss of fo. number, tears in d1, k3 & m3, sm. hole in n1, some soiling & staining. Mod. vell. (S. Feb.10; 227) *Thomas.* £450

REID, Thomas
- **Essays on the Active Powers of Man.** Edinb., 1788. 1st. Edn. 4to. Probably lacks hf.-title, MS. notes in margins, etc. Hf. cf. (S. Jun.17; 714) *Thoemines.* £70
- **– Anr. Copy.** Cont. tree cf., backstrip very worn. (PNY. Dec.3; 319) $240
- **Essays on the Intellectual Powers of Man.** Edinb., 1785. 1st. Edn. 4to. Cont. tree cf., worn, upr. cover loose. (PNY. Dec.3; 318) $200
- **Travels in Ireland in the Year 1822.** L., 1823. 1st. Edn. Orig. bds., spine reprd., unc. (GM. Apr.30; 42) £52
- **A Treatise on Clock & Watch Making.** N.d. 2nd. Edn. 1 plt. torn with loss, spotting & soiling. Mod. cl. (CSK. Dec.12; 271) £50
- **Two Voyages to New South Wales & Van Diemen's Land.** 1822. 1st. Edn. Orig. paper-bkd. bds., unc. (C. Jul.15; 91) *Maggs.* £200
- **– Anr. Copy.** Slight foxing, errata slip. Rebnd., hf. cf., marb. bds., gt. decor. spine, gt. titling piece. (JL. Dec.15; 722) *Aus.* $330

REIMANN, Johann Baptist
- **Samlung alter und neuer Melodien Evangel.: Lieder.** Ill.:– C.H. Lau. Hermsdorf, [1747]. Soiled, some MS. marginalia, 7 ll. Chorale bnd. in. 19th. C. hf. leath. (H. Dec.9/10; 1251) DM 650

REINEKE FUCHS
Rostock, 1650. Some lines p. 19 with green ink strokes, woodcut on p. 50 with cold. scribble, 2 sm. tears on title. 18th. C. hf. leath. gt. (HK. May 15; 4760) DM 1,500

REINHARD, Andreas
- **Drey Register Arithmetischer Anfeng zur Practic, Reguliret, unnd Reime verfasset.** Leipzig, 1599. 1st. Edn. Colophon dtd. 1600, very browned, some ll. trimmed, H3 reprd. affecting text, a few other ll. with marginal repairs. Disbnd. From Honeyman Collection. (S. Nov.11; 2616) *Lamm.* £70

REINHARD, Count of Solms-Lich
See-[REISNER, Adam]–REINHARD, Count of Solms-Lich-[FRONSPERGER, Leonhard]

REINHARDT, Joseph
- **A Collection of Swiss Costumes, in Miniature.** L., [1828]. 2nd. Engl. Edn. Sm. 4to. Cont. roan, corners, unc. (HD. Dec.5; 172) *Frs.* 10,800
- **– Anr. Edn.** Ca. 1830. 4to. Cont. hf. mor., gt. (S. Dec.9; 519) *Rostron.* £1,200

REINHOLD, Erasmus
- **Gründlicher und Warer Bericht vom Feldmessen . . . Desgleichen vom Marscheiden kurtzer und gründlicher Unterricht.** Erfurt, 1574. 2 pts. in 1 vol. 4to. 2 folding diagrams/tables reprd., some browning, former owner's inscr. cut from title. Disbnd. Stp. of Stolberg liby. at Wernigerode; from Honeyman Collection. (S. Nov.11; 2620) *Fomecon.* £120

- **Prutenicae Tabulae Coelestium Motuum.** Tübingen, 1551. 1st. Edn. 4to. 2 folding tables torn, dampstained, 2 or 3 ll. shaved, several ll. with tears in lr. margins. 17th. C. vell., spine stained & gt. in cf. style. From Honeyman Collection. (S. Nov.11; 2618) *Hill.* £780
- **– Anr. Edn.** Tübingen, 1562. 2nd. Edn. 4to. 1 folding table (of 3), some damp staining, title with deleted owners' inscrs. & margin reprd., old annots. Cont. blind-stpd. cf., worn. From Honeyman Collection. (S. Nov.11; 2619) *Quaritch.* £210
- **Themata quae continent Methodicam Tractationem de Horizonte Rationali ac Sensili, deque Mutatione Horizontium & Meridianorum.** Wittenberg, 1541. 1st. Edn. Cont. inscr. of Erasmus Floeck on title. Red mor., by Sangorski & Sutcliffe. From Honeyman Collection. (S. Nov.11; 2617) *Quaritch.* £540
See-REGIOMONTANUS, Johannes
–REINHOLD, Erasmus

REISBOEK, Algemeen, door Berlyn en Potsdam . . . ten dienste van alle derwaards reizenden
Amst., 1792. A few light stains at end. Cont. hf. cf., back gt. (VG. Dec.17; 1504) *Fls.* 650

REISCH, Gregorius
- **Aepitoma Omnis Phylosophiae. Alias Margarita Phylosophica Tractans de Omni Genere Scibili.** Strassburg, Feb. 23, 1504. 2nd. Edn. Sm. 4to. Several ills. or diagrams cold. by cont. hand, folding map of world slightly torn & restored. Mod. red mor. gt. (S. Jul.27; 253) *Potter.* £1,500
- **– Anr. Copy.** Folding map of the world slightly torn & restored. Red mor., gt., by S. David. From Honeyman Collection. (S. Nov.11; 2621) *Israel.* £1,000
- **[–] Margarita Philosophica.** Freiburg, [before 13 Jul.], 1503. 1st. Edn. Sm. 4to. Lacks folding map. 18th. C. cf.-bkd. bds. (C. Jul.16; 325) *Maggs.* £500
- **Margarita Philosophica nova.** Strassburg, 1512. 2 pts. in 1 vol. 4to. Folding lf. with 2 woodcut diagrams with sm. tear, lacks the world map, somewhat damp stained, 1st. title soiled. Mod. mor.-bkd. cl. From Honeyman Collection. [Sabin 69127] (S. Nov.11; 2622) *Pilo Boyl.* £380
- **– Anr. Edn.** Strassburg, 1515. 2 pts. in 1 vol. 4to. Folding sheet with 2 woodcut diagrams loosely inserted (reprd. & mntd.), lacks world map, Appendix lacks folding diagram 'Spera in plano' & folded sheet sigd. P. at end containing the new map 'Typus universalis terre' (a smaller version, defect., from a later edn. is loosely inserted), slight soiling, a few stains. 19th. C. blind-stpd. pig. over wooden bds. in cont. South German style, clasps & catches. From Honeyman Collection. [Sabin 69128] (S. Nov.11; 2623) *Schuman.* £480

REISET, Gustav Armand Henri, Vicomte de
- **Marie-Caroline, Duchesse de Berry.** Paris, 1906. (130) on Japon. 4to. Double series of plts. Mor. by Stroobants, triple gt. fillet around covers, fleurons in corners, arms of Duchesse de Berry, spine decor. with raised bands, inside dentelle, wrap. & spine preserved. (HD. Feb.27; 220) *Frs.* 1,650
- **Modes et Usages au Temps de Marie-Antoinette.** Paris, 1885. 2 vols. Hf. chagrin, arms. (LM. Jun.13; 204) *B.Frs.* 10,000
- **– Anr. Copy.** On Japon. 4to. Hf. mor., corners, spines decor. with raised bands. (HD. Feb.27; 219) *Frs.* 2,900

REISSNER, Adam
- **Jerusalem . . .** Trans.:– I. Heydenus. Ill.:– Virgil Solis. Frankfurt, 1563. Fo. Lightly browned & stained in parts. Cont. blind-stpd. pig.-bkd. wood bds., worn & slightly torn, lacks 2 ties. (HK. Nov.18-21; 279) DM 1,100

[REISSNER, Adam]–REINHARD, Count of Solms-Lich-[FRONSPERGER, Leonhard]
- **Historia Herrn Georgen und Herrn Casparn von Fründsberg; Absolutae Historiae Dominorum a Frundsberg.–Beschreibung vom Ursprung Anfang und Herkhomen des Adels.–Ein kurtzer Bericht, wie Stätt, Schlösser, oder Flecken, mit Kriegs Volck sollen besetz sein . . .** Frankfurt am Main, 1568; 1568; 1564; 1564. 4 works in 1 vol. (1st. work pt. 1 only?). Fo. 1st. work: tears in L6 & g6, holes in T1 & b4, lacks 4th. lf., blank; 3rd. work: lacks B2, lge. piece torn from fore-margin of B3 with very slight loss of text, piece cut from fore-margins of C4-D1 with slight loss of text, C1-3 cut into, piece torn from fore-margin of D2. 2nd. work misbound, cont. blind-stpd. pig over

wooden bds. with clasps, lr. bd. brkn. W.a.f. (S. May 5; 42)   *Hyde*. £110

REISSIG, K.
- Sozvezdiya ... dlya Uchebnyh Zavedenii i Lyubitelei Astronozii [Constellations ... for Educational Institutions & Lovers of Astronomy]. St. Petersb., 1829. 4to. Slightly soiled. Cont. cf.-bkd. bds. (SH.   Feb.5; 259) *Livres des Cinq Cents*. £50

RELACION de las Diversiones Festejos Publicos, etc.
Barcelona, 1802. 4 pts. in 1 vol. Sm. 4to. Old cf., worn. (BS. Jun.11; 222)   £400

RELACION de Ultimo Viage al Estrecho de Magallanes de la Fragata de S.M. Santa Maria de la Cabeza ...
Madrid, 1788-93. 4to. Tears reprd. in 5 folding engraved maps, later inscr. on title. Cont. cf. [Sabin 16765] (SPB. May 5; 426) $350

RELAND, Adrian
- Palestina ex Monumentis Veteribus illustrata. Utrecht, 1714. 2 pts. in 1 vol. 4to. 2 maps/plts. slightly torn, 1 marginal tear. 19th. C. cf., gt., upr. cover   dampstained.   (S.   Dec.8; 234) *Leverton*. £120
-- Anr. Copy. 2 vols. Vol. 2 dampstained. Cont. vell. (CSK. May 8; 22)   £70
-- Anr. Edn. Nuremb., 1716. 4to. 2 maps slightly torn. Cont. vell. bds. (S. Nov.4; 643)   *Hus*. £240

RELATION DE LA RECENTE CAPTIVITE DE MME. JANE ADELAINE WILSON PARMI LES INDIENS CAMANCHES
Trans.:- Mme. Leonie d'Aunet. [Paris], [1854]. From Les Modes Parisiennes Illustrées, no. 567, Jan.7, 1854. 4to. Mod. bds. (SG. Jan.8; 211) $160

RELATION d'un Voyage du Pole Arctique, au Pole Antarctique
Amst., 1721. Later hf. roan, defect. [Sabin 69249] (SPB. May 5; 427) $300

RELIGION IN GESCHICHTE UND GEGENWART
Tübingen, 1957-65. 3rd. Edn. 5 vols. & index, together 6 vols. Orig. hf. mor. (B. Dec.10/11; 1362)   Fls. 600

RELLY, James & John
- Christian Hymns, Poems, & Spiritual Songs. Burlington, 1776. Some ll. torn. Crude hf. linen, ex-liby. (SG. Mar.5; 337) $120

REMAK, Robert
- Observationes Anatomicae et Microscopicae de Systematis Nervosi Structura. Berlin, 1838. 4to. Paper wraps. From the collection of Sir Thomas Phillips. (S. Jun.17; 716)   *Jenner Books*. £120

REMESAL, Antonio de
- Historia de la Provincia de S. Vincente de Chyapa y Guatemala de la Orden de nro. glorioso Padre Sancto Domingo. Madrid, 1619. Fo. Minor repair to 1 lf., a few sm. stains. Later cf., spine detchd. (SPB. May 5; 428) $5,000

REMIGIUS, Nicolaus
- Daemonolatria. Hamburg, 1693. 3 pts. in 1 vol. Cont.   vell.   bds.   (S.   Mar.17; 260) *Hyde Park Books*. £120
- Fundamentum Scolarium. Basel, Michael Furter. 1499. 4to. Scattered worming in text at beginning. Old paper bds. [HC 13863*; Goff R141] (C. Apr.1; 77)   *Summers*. £450

REMINGTON, Frederic
- Done in the Open; Drawings, Introduction & Verses by Owen Wister & others. N.Y., 1903. Fo. Cold. pict. bds., cl. spine, worn. (SG. Mar.5; 387) $100
- Drawings. N.Y., 1897. (250) sigd. by publisher. Ob. fo. Orig. bdg. (SPB. Jun.22; 120) $400

REMIZOV, Aleksei
- Chasy [Clock]. St. Petersb., 1908. Orig. wraps. by M. Dobuzhinsky, slightly soiled & torn, unopened. (SH. Feb.6; 352)   *Quaritch*. £85
- Elektron. St. Petersb., 1919. Orig. wraps. by the author, loose. (SH. Feb.6; 353)   *Lempert*. £75
- O sud'be ognennoi [About Fiery Fate]. Ill.:- E. Turova. Petrograd, n.d. Hand-cold. wraps. by E. Turova. (SH. Feb.6; 511)   *Lempert*. £50
- Povest' o Ivane Semenoviche Stratilatove [The Story of Ivan Semenovich Stratilatov]. -Chakkchygys-Tassu [A Siberian Tale]. Berlin,

1922. 2 vols. Orig. wraps., 1st. slightly torn. (SH. Feb.6; 354)   *Lempert*. £55
- Sibirsky Pryanik [Siberian Gingerbread]. St. Petersb., 1919. (3000). Orig. wraps. by the author, spine torn. (SH. Feb.6; 355)   *Quaritch*. £110
- Snezhok [Snowball]. Ill.:- E. Turova. Petrograd, n.d. (125) numbered. Orig. wraps. by E. Turova. (SH. Feb.6; 512)   *Quaritch*. £160

REMUS, Favinus
See-LOCHER,   Jacobus-REMUS,   Favinus -UGUITON-WIMPHELING,   Jacobus -VALLIBUS, Hieronymus de

REMY, Jules & Brenchley, Julius
- A Journey to Great-Salt-Lake City ... with a Sketch of the History & Customs of the Mormons. 1861. 1st. Engl. Edn. 2 vols. Orig. cl., loose. [Sabin 69594] (S. Jun.29; 196)   *Ginsberg*. £60
-- Anr. Copy. A few sigs. sprung. Orig. gt.-decor. cl., shelf worn, a bit shaken, spine of vol. I torn. (SG. Jan.8; 381) $220
-- Anr. Copy. Mod. hf. leath. (SG. Mar.5; 388) $190

RENAN, Ernest
- Histoire du Peuple d'Israël. Paris, 1887-93. 1st. Edn., (30) on Japon. 5 vols. Red hf. mor. by Septier, corners, unc., wraps. & spines. (HD. Dec.5; 175)   Frs. 3,300
- Prière   sur   l'Acropole.   Ill.:-   H. Bellery-Desfontaines. Paris, 1899. (45) on thick China. 4to. 3 prospectus ll. at end. Mor. by Noulhac, spine & covers decor. with mosaic motifs, owl on upr. cover, circular symbol on lr. cover, mor. doubls., wrap. preserved, s.-c. Bkplt. of Marcel Pognon. (SM. Feb.11; 279)   Frs. 9,500

RENARD, Jules
- Les Oeuvres Complètes Paris, 1925-27. Ltd. Edn. 17 vols. Hf. mor., partly unc. (SM. Oct.8; 2154)   Frs. 1,200

RENARD, Louis
- Poissons, Ecrevisses et Crabes ... Amst., [1718-19]. 1st. Edn. 2 vols. in 1. Fo. Cont. cf. gt. on wooden bds., rebkd. [Sabin 69600] (C. Jul.15; 199)   *Quaritch*. £8,000
See-OTTENS, Reinier & Josua & Renard, Louis

RENAUDOT, Eusebe
- A General Collection of Discourses of the Virtuosi of France.-[-Another Collection of Philosophical Conferences of the French Virtuosi]. Trans.:- G. Havers & J. Davies. 1664-65. 1st. Edn. in Engl. 2 pts. in 1 vol. Fo. Lacks blank lf. at end of pt. I (?), slightly dampstained at beginning & end, owner's inscr. on fly lf. Antique style cf. [Wing R1034 & 1033A] (S. Dec.2; 762)   *Quaritch*. £120

RENAULT, Jules
- La Legion d'Honneur. Paris, [1932]. (100) numbered, on papier Madagascar. 4to. Maroon mor., gt. dentelles, by Charles Benoit, orig. s.-c., lacks bronze plaque. (SG. Oct.30; 165) $110

RENDLER, J.
[-] Beschreibung einer anatomischen Uhr. Ill.:- I.G. Gruber. Vienna, 1771. 4to. Text slightly browned, stpd., plt. versos stpd. 19th. C. hf. linen. (R. Mar.31-Apr.4; 1309)   DM 600

RENESSE, Comte Théodore de
- Dictionnaire des Figures Héraldiques. Brussels, 1894-1903. 7 vols. Sewed. (LM. Jun.13; 85)   B.Frs. 18,500
-- Anr. Copy. (LM. Nov.8; 207)   B.Frs. 16,000

RENNBRAND, J.C.V.
- Der Geschickte und Erfahrne Jäger. Lunz, 1825. 2nd. Edn. Title stpd. Orig. wraps., spine defect. (R. Mar.31-Apr.4; 1710)   DM 520

RENNELL, James
- Memoir of a Map of Hindoostan. 1788. 2 pts. in 1 vol. 4to. Some ll. slightly spotted. Cont. hf. mor. gt., slightly worn. (SBA. May 27; 314)   *Pugh*. £65

RENNELL,   James-EDWARDS,   B.-FADEN, William
- A Map of Hindoostan.-General Map ... between the Black Sea & the Caspian.-The Southern Countries of India; The Sea of Marmara or Propontis. 1788; 1788; 1791; 1786. 4 works in 1 vol. 4to. Sm. liby. stp. on each map of 4th. work. 19th. C. hf. mor. From Chetham's Liby., Manchester. (C. Nov.27; 341)   *Maggs*. £120

RENOIR, Pierre Auguste
- L'Atelier de Renoir. Ed.:- Albert André & Marc Elder. Paris, 1931. (500). 2 vols. Lge. 4to. Sewed, wraps. (HD. Dec.5; 176)   Frs. 9,500
-- Anr. Edn. Ed.:- A. André & M. Elder. Paris, [1931]. (500). 2 vols. Orig. wraps., lightly browned. (HK. Nov.18-21; 2870)   DM 3,200

RENOUARD, Antoine Augustin
- Annales de l'Imprimerie des Alde. Paris, 1825. 3 vols. Cf. gt., Hon. G.M. Fortescue's arms on covers. Autograph list by Renouard of Aldines bought in Paris inserted, 1820. (P. Jul.2; 124)   *North*. £85

RENOUVIER, Jules
- Des Gravures sur Bois dans les Livres de Simon Vostre ... avec un Avant-propos par Georges Dupleiss. Paris, 1862. Mor. gt., by Chambolle Duru dtd. 1864. The John A. Saks copy. (CNY. Oct.1; 203) $420

RENOWNED HISTORY (The) of Primrose Prettyface, who by her Sweetness of Temper & Love of Learning was raised from being the Daughter of a poor Cottager to great Riches, & the Dignity of Lady of the Manor
Ca. 1785. 12mo. Most ills. cold. by former owner, advts. at end reprd. Orig. Dutch floral bds., rebkd. (SH. Mar.19; 274)   *Moon*. £100

RENTSCH, Johann Wolfgang
- Brandenburgischer Ceder-Hein. Bareut, 1682. 1st. Edn. Cont. vell., lacks front fly-lf. (SG. Feb.5; 283) $450
-- Anr. Copy.   Later   pencil   notes.   (H. Dec.9/10; 1636)   DM 700

REPERTOIRE DU THEATRE FRANCOIS
Ed.:- M. Petitot. Paris, 1803-04. 22 (of 23 vols.). Cont. cf., gt. (SM. Oct.8; 2155)   Frs. 1,200

REPERTORIO DEL TEATRO MILANESE
Milan, 1873-1913. Approximately 170 pts. in 9 boxes. 12mo. Orig. wraps. (SI. Dec.4; 491)   Lire 750,000

REPERTORIO PINTORESCO, o Miscelanea Instructiva y Amena ...
Ed.:- Crescenio Carrillo. Ill.:- J.D. Espinos Rendon. Merida, 1863. Disbnd., ex-liby. (SG. Jun.11; 226) $120

REPERTORY OF ARTS & Manufactures: Consisting of Original Communications, Specifications of Patent Inventions ...
1794-1801. Vols. 1-7, 12-15. Lacks 1 engr. Orig. tree cf. (TA. Oct.16; 237)   £94

REPORT OF COLLEGE of Engineering Imperial University of Tokyo No. 7. Decoration of Palace Buildings of Peking
Tokyo, 1906. (1000) numbered. Ob. fo. Some plts. mntd. & cold. Unbnd. as iss., in orig. portfo. (CSK. Nov.14; 212)   £85

REPORT together with the Minutes of Evidence & an Appendix of Papers from the Committee Appointed to consider the Provision being made for the Better Regulation of Madhouses in England
Ed.:- James Birch Sharpe. 11 Jul. 1815. Orig. bds., rebkd., unc. (S. Jun.17; 717)   *Clay*. £70

REPORTS des Cases en Ley
1678-80. 11 vols. Fo. Several vols. lack? prelim. 'Preface' lf., 2 titles slightly defect., some spotting & browning. Later hf. russ., very worn. W.a.f. (S. May 5; 324)   *Thorp*. £420

REPORTS FROM COMMISSIONERS: Charities in England & Wales
1821-25. Vols. 5-13, together 9 vols. Fo. Cont. hf. mor. (SH. Oct.10; 508)   *Bunsei*. £50

REPORTS OF EXPLORATIONS & Surveys to Ascertain the Most Practicable & Economical Route for a Railroad from the Mississippi River to the Pacific Ocean
Wash., 1855-61. House Iss. (Vol. II Senate Iss.). 13 vols. 4to. Cont. hf. cf., worn, some brkn., some covers detchd. W.a.f. as a collection. (SPB. Nov.24; 53) $1,000

REPORTS OF Tax Cases
1875-1975. 49 vols. Cl. (CE. Feb.19; 30)   £420

REPSOLD, J.A.
- Zur   Geschichte   der   Astronomischen Messwerkzeuge (1450-1900). Leipzig, 1908-14. 2 vols. Fo. Vol. II badly dampstained at beginning. Hf. cl., vol. II defect. From Honeyman Collection. (S. Nov.11; 2627)   *Das Bucherkabinet*. £120

REPTON, Humphrey
- Designs for the Pavilion at Brighton. 1808. 1st. Edn. Fo. 9 plts., 5 with overslips, 11 aquatint vigs. & headpieces, 3 cold., 2 with overslips. Cont. hf. russ., lr. cover detchd. (C. Jul.15; 160)
Maggs. £1,300
- - Anr. Copy. 12 cold. or tinted aquatint & litho. plts., 3 with movable overslips, double-p. plt. & folding plt. each with 2 movable overslips & 1 full-p. overslip, 7 uncold. litho. vigs., paper wtrmkd. 1808. Cont. mod.-bkd. cl. (C. Mar.18; 91)
Sims & Reed. £750
- Observations on the Theory & Practice of Landscape Gardening. 1803. 1st. Edn. 4to. Engraved port. & 27 cold. or tinted plts., some with hinged overslips. Hf. mor. gt. (C. Jul.15; 92)
Rodgers. £1,500
- - Anr. Copy. 13 plts. hand-cold., 14 plts. with overslips, port mntd., 2 plts. mntd. on linen, 1 extra plt. inserted, some repairs. Mod. hf. mor. (P. Sep.11; 83)
Hatchards. £900
- - Anr. Copy. 1 plt. with sm. tears at folds. Hf. mor. & vell., part of orig. upr. wrap. preserved on end-paper, vell. slightly spotted, binder's title misdtd. '1802'. (CB. May 27; 175) *Can.* $4,200
- - Anr. Edn. 1805. 4to. 12 plts. & 2 text ills. with hinged overslips. Orig. bds., unc. (C. Mar.18; 89)
Rodgers. £1,900
- Odd Whims & Miscellanies. 1804. 2 vols. Cont. cf., key pattern borders on covers, rebkd. (C. Feb.4; 145)
Breman. £100

REPTON, Humphrey & Repton, John Adey
- Fragments on the Theory & Practice of Landscape Gardening. 1816. 4to. 42 aquatint plts., some cold. or tinted, 14 plts. & 2 text ills. with hinged overslips. Orig. bds., unc. 4 orig. pen & ink drawings of Lodge at Luscombe loosely inserted, sig. of Charles Hoare, Luscumbe. (C. Mar.18; 90)
Rodgers. £2,600
- - Anr. Copy. 42 plts., some cold., 14 plts. & 2 text ills. with hinged overslips. Hf. mor. gt. (C. Jul.15; 93)
Harcourt Williams. £1,700

RERESBY, Sir John
- Memoirs ... L., 1734. 1st. Edn. 1st. 2 gatherings loosening. Cont. cf., rebkd. Sigd. 'W. Cornwallis' on title-p. (CB. Nov.12; 169)
Can. $110

RERUM ANGLICARUM SCRIPTORES POST BEDAM PRAECIPUI
Ed.:– [Sir Henry Savile]. Frankfurt, 1601. Fo. MS. folding table of kings from Saxon Heptarchy to Elizabeth I bnd. in at front, numerous cross-references in text, browned thro.-out, some ll. near end marginally wormed, several ll. stained from margins, a few rustholes. Cont. vell. bds., rebkd., worn. Thomas Gale's copy, with annots. & marginal notes in pen & ink in his hand; dispersal stp. of Royal Institution. (S. Jun.9; 35)
Pickering & Chatto. £50

RERUM MOSCOVITICARUM Auvtores Varii, unum in Corpus nunc Primum Congesti
Frankfurt, 1600. 1st. Edn. Fo. 19th. C. hf. leath. (SG. Oct.9; 215)
$500

RESENBERGER, Nikolaus
- Astronomia Teutsch. Augsburg, 1569. 1st. Edn. 4to. Loosely inserted sheet at end describing astronomical instrument of author's design with 2 woodcuts, a few ll. marginally stained, title slightly soiled. Cont. blind-stpd. pig. over wooden bds., rolls of medallion heads & the Virtues enclosing the figures of Fortune & Justice on upr. & lr. covers respectively, upr. cover stpd. 'WEGZS 1577', spine defect., lacks clasps, lr. red mor. case. Armorial bkplt. of Christian Ernst, Graf zu Stolberg; stp. of Stolberg liby. at Wernigerode; from Honeyman Collection. (S. Nov.11; 2626)
Quaritch. £780

RESTA, Sebastiano
- True Effigies of the Most Eminent Painters, & Other Famous Artists that have Flourished in Europe. L. & Antw.?, 1694. 1st. Engl. Edn. Fo. Lacks plt. 46, 1 other plt. at end, apparently not in series, plt. 18 torn, each port. neatly numbered in ink on engraved surface, slight spotting. Cont. spr. cf., spine defect., covers detchd., worn. Blantyre bkplt.; as a collection, w.a.f. [Wing R1174] (S. May 5; 339)
Cristani. £320
[-] - Anr. Copy. Cont. pol. cf. (C. Feb.25; 198)
Hermans. £80

RESTIF DE LA BRETONNE, Nicolas Edme
- La Confidence Necessaire. The Hague, 1769. 2 pts. in 1 vol. Cont. vell. (S. Mar.17; 282)
Norton. £75
[-] Les Contemporaines. Paris, 1781-92. 1st. Edn., vols. 1, 5, 13, 14, 17, 18 & 19 2nd. Edn. 3 series in 42 vols. Lacks 1 copperplt., slightly soiled in places. Late 19th. C. hf. leath., mostly unc., slightly worn. (H. Dec.9/10; 1637)
DM 3,200
- Contes. Ill.:– Mongin (figures), de More (port.). Paris, 1881. Ltd. Edn. Mor. by Pagnan, decor. spine, inside dentelle. Bkplt. of Francis Kettaneh. (SM. Feb.11; 169)
Frs. 3,000
[-] Le Drame de la Vie. Ill.:– Berthet after Binet. Paris, 1793. 1st. Edn. 5 pts. in 5 vols. 19mo. C. red qtr. mor. by Pagnant, partly unc. (S. Mar.17; 290)
Nat. Art Inst. £260
[-] L'Ecole des Pères. Paris, 1776. 3 vols. Lacks last lf. of vol. 3. 19th. C. hf. mor. by Vailly. (S. Mar.17; 286)
Norton. £95
- La Famille Vertueuse. Paris, 1767. 1st. Edn. 4 pts. in 2 vols. 12mo. I5-6 in pt. 1 reprd. 19th. C. hf. mor., spines gt. (S. Mar.17; 280)
Norton. £260
[-] Les Françaises ... Neuchatel & Paris, 1786. 1st. Edn. 4 vols. 12mo. 19th. C. mor.-bkd. bds. (S. Mar.17; 287)
H.D. Lyon. £240
[-] Ingenue Saxancour, ou la Femme Séparée. Liege & Paris, 1789. 1st. Edn. 3 vols. in 1. 12mo. 19th. C. cf., gt., unc. (S. Mar.17; 288)
Norton. £280
[-] Le Menage Parisien ... The Hague, 1773. 1st. Edn. 2 pts. in 1 vol. 12mo. 19th. C. cf., gt. (S. Mar.17; 284)
Royal Liby. of Holland. £220
[-] La Mimographe, ou Idées ... du Theâtre National. Amst. & The Hague, 1770. 1st. Edn. Hf.-title misbnd. Cont. hf. cf. (S. Mar.17; 283)
J. Booth. £80
[-] - Anr. Copy. Ink stain on some outer margins. Hf. vell. (BS. Jun.11; 274)
£70
- Monument du Costume Physique et Moral de la Fin du Dix-Huitieme Siècle. Ill.:– J.M. Moreau le Jeune & Freudeberg. Neuwied, 1789. 1st. Edn. Lge. fo. Text & plts. mntd. on stubs, some ll. or plts. very slightly soiled or spotted. Red mor., gt. 5 line border on covers, floral cornerpieces, spine gt.-tooled, gt. in border, by Pagnant, corners slightly rubbed, in cl.-bkd. sleeve. Bkplt. of G. de Berny. (S. Feb.10; 322)
Klusmann. £3,500
[-] - Anr. Edn. Neuwied, 1789. New Edn. Lge. fo. 19th. C. hf. leath., soiled, spine defect. (H. Dec.9/10; 1614)
DM 7,200
- Le Palais Royal. Paris, 1790. 3 vols. 12mo. Mod. marb. hf. roan, spines decor., unc. (HD. Apr.9; 553)
Frs. 2,800
- La Paysanne Pervertie. Ill.:– Binet. The Hague & Paris, 1784. 8 pts. in 4 vols. 12mo. Hf. chagrin by Pagnant, corners, decor. spines, unc. (HD. Dec.5; 177)
Frs. 7,500
[-] Le Pied de Fanchette. The Hague & Paris, 1769. 1st. Edn. 3 pts. in 1 vol. 12mo. Cont. cf. (S. Mar.17; 281)
Bouillier. £240
[-] Tableaux de la Vie. Ill.:– Moreau le Jeune & Freudeberg. Neuwied & Strassburg, [1790]. 1st. Edn. 2 vols. 12mo. Cont. sheep., gt. Bkplt. of J.N. Arrachart, surgeon. (S. Mar.17; 289)
H.D.Lyon. £190
- - Anr. Copy. 2 vols. in 1. Red mor., fillet, decor. spine, inner dentelle, by Raparlier. (HD. Jun.10; 94)
Frs. 2,100

RETTE, A.
See-EUDEL, Paul-GAUSSERON, B.H.-RETTE, A.

RETURNS for His Majesty's Land Forces
1805-08. 4 vols. Ptd. forms with MS. additions, title-pp., indexes, & abstracts, together 185 ll. (32 pp. blank). Red mor. gt. (C. Oct.22; 65)
Franks. £120

RETZIUS, Gustav
- Das Menschengehirn, Studien in der Makrosckopischen Morphologie. Stockholm, 1896. 2 vols. Sm. fo. Hf. cl. (S. Jun.17; 722)
Norman. £160
See-KEY, Axel & Retzius, Gustav

RETZSCH, M.
[-] Gedichte. Stuttgart & Tübingen, 1829. Lightly soiled in places. Cont. hf. leath. gt. (HK. May 15; 4296)
DM 750

REUCHLIN, Johann
- De Arte Cabalistica. Hagenau, 1517. 1st. Edn. Fo. Vell. covers from early MS. with cold. initials. (SG. Oct.9; 208)
$2,700

REUSNER, Nicolaus–REUSNER, Elias –FABRICIUS, G.
- Icones sive Imagines Impp Regum, Principum, Electorum et Ducum Saxoniae.–Genealogia sive Enucleatio Inclyti Stemmatis VVitichindei.–Rerum Misnicarum. Jena, 1597. 3 works in 1 vol. Fo. Lacks final blank to last work, stained thro.-out in lr. outer corners, some browning, sm. inscr. on 1st. title. Cont. spr. cf., gt. arms on covers, 'Hic Liber Est Ex Bibliotheca Gulielmi Antonii Pieterson' round border, spine gt. (S. Feb.10; 272)
Harling. £70

REUSNER, Nicolaus–SABINUS, G.
- Icones Imagines Vivorvm Literis Illvstrivm.–Poemata. Strassburg; Leipzig, 1587; 1581. 1st. Latin Edn. 2 works in 1 vol. Worming at beginning, light browning. Cont. cf., blind-tooled, slightly worn, sm. wormholes & spine torn. (H. Dec.9/10; 1366)
DM 1,100

REUSS, Chr. Fr.
- Dispensatorium Universale seu Lexicon Chemico-Pharmaceuticum. Strassburg, 1791. 2 vols. Title stpd., slightly soiled in parts. Cont. bds. (HK. May 12-14; 416a)
DM 520

REUSS, Ch. G.
- Anweisung zur Zimmermannskunst. Leipzig, 1789. 3rd. Edn. Fo. Cont. bds. (R. Mar.31-Apr.4; 1291)
DM 1,400

REUSSE, H.
- Die Deutschen Eisenbahnen in Beziehung auf Geschichte, Technik und Betrieb. Kassel, 1844. 1st. Edn. Old liby. stp. on title. Cont. bds. (R. Oct.14-18; 259)
DM 1,000

REUVEN, Hoeschke
- Yalkut Reuveni. Prague, 1660. 1st. Edn. 4to. Lacks title & 2 ll., soiled, staining, browning. Vell., worn, stained. Bkplt. of Samuel Dresner. (SPB. May 11; 179)
$225

REVENTLOW-FARVE, Ernst & Warmstedt, H.A.V.
- Beiträge zur Land-und Forstwirthschaftlichen Statistik der Herzogthümer Schleswig und Holstein. Altona, 1847. Extra hand-cold. engraved title heightened with gold, 21 litho. plts., 18 cold. Cont. embossed cl., gt., spine gt., watered silk end-papers. (C. Mar.18; 92)
Temperley. £420

REVEREND, Vicomte Albert & Villeroy, Comte Eugène
- Album des Armoires Concédées par Lettrespatents de Napoléon ler ... Paris, 1911. Fo. In sheets, publisher's portfo. (HD. Dec.5; 178)
Frs. 3,100

REVERIES ORIENTALES (Les) ou Les Miracles de l'Ancien Monde
Ill.:– Dorgez. Paris, [1793]. 18mo. Cont. silk bds., decor. with gold spangles of embroidery, painted centre motif on each cover. (HD. Apr.10; 189)
Frs. 2,500

REVETT, Nicholas
See-STUART, James & Revett, Nicholas

REVUE DE LA NUMISMATIQUE BELGE
Tirlemont [Brussels], [1845]-1978. Vols. 1-124 + 1 table bnd. in 78 vols., lacks 69th. year (1913). Hf. chagrin & hf. cl., from 1955 sewed. (LM. Mar.21; 252)
B.Frs. 320,000

REVUE DE PHOTOGRAPHIE, La
Paris, 1903. Numbers 1-5 & 7-12 (lacks number 6, Jun.). 4to. Ptd. wraps., moderate to heavy wear, 3 spines badly chipped. (SG. Apr.23; 171)
$200

REY, Jean
- Essays ... sur la Recherche de la Cause pour laquelle l'Estain & le Plomb augmentent de poids quand on les calcine. Ed.:– N. Gobet. Paris, 1777. New Edn. Some browning. Cont. cf., gt. spine. From Honeyman Collection. (S. Nov.11; 2628)
Quaritch. £780

REYBAUD, Louis
- Jérome Paturot à la Recherche d'une Position Sociale. Ill.:– after Grandville. Paris, 1846. Orig. pict. bds. (SH. Nov.20; 155)
Droller. £120
- Jérôme Paturot à la Recherche d'une Position Sociale.–Jérome Paturot à la Recherche de la Meilleure des Républiques. Ill.:– Grandville; Tony

Johannot. Paris, 1846; 1829. 2 vols. Foxing in 1st. vol. Publisher's cl. bds., specially tooled. (HD. Apr.9; 608)   Frs. 1,600

REYD, E. VAN & Sande, J. van
- **Historie der Nederlantscher Oorlogen tot 1601 ... tot 1641.** [Gron.], Leeuwarden, 1650. 2 pts. in 1 vol. Fo. 1st. 200 pp. with some stains. Vell., some stains on upr. cover. (VG. Oct.13; 135)   Fls. 600

REYES, Jose de los
- **Margarita Seraphica.** Mexico, 1734. Sm. 4to. Owner's brand on top edge (S.F.). Cont. limp vell., fragment of ptd. paper label. (SPB. May 5; 430) $150

REYGERSBERG, Jan
- **Chroniik van Zeelandt.** Ed.:– M. Zuerius van Boxhorn. Middelburg, 1644. 2 vols. 4to. Stained in places. Cont. vell. (VG. Dec.17; 1506)   Fls. 825

REYHER, Samuel–SEELANDER, Nicolas
- **Monumenta Landgraviorum Thuringiae et Marchionum Misniae ...–Des Muentz-Schatzer Mittlerer Zeiten.** Kiloni; n.p., 1692; 1725. 2 works in 1 vol. Fo. Old cf., new leath. spine. (SG. Feb.5; 285) $130

REYNARDSON, Charles Thomas Samuel Birch
- **'Down the Road', Or, Reminiscences of a Gentleman Coachman.** 1875. 2nd. Edn. Sm. 4to. Orig. cl. gt. (TA. May 21; 434)   £68
- – **Anr. Copy.** Orig. spine on free end-paper, tooled red mor. (CE. Nov.20; 171)   £60
- – **Anr. Edn.** L., 1887. New Edn. Orig. linen. (R. Oct.14-18; 2529)   DM 620

REYNOLDS, G.W.
- **The Aloes of South Africa.** Johannesburg, 1950. (500) sigd., in leath., Subscriber's Edn. Leath. Bkplt. of Mrs. Buchanan, formerly of Lanzerac, Stellenbosch. (VA. May 8; 353)   R. 105
- – **Anr. Copy.** 4to. Publisher's leath., d.-w. Compliments slip inserted dtd. 12/12/50. (VA. Jan.30; 279)   R. 90

REYNOLDS, J.H.
See–HOOD, Thomas & Reynolds, J.H.

REYNOLDS, John
- **The Pioneer History of Illinois, Containing the Discovery, 1673, & the History of the Country to the Year Eighteen Hundred & Eighteen ...** Belleville, 1852. 1st. Edn. Slightly foxed & browned, a few minor printing flaws. Mod. hf. mor., by Bennett, gt. spine & borders. From liby. of William E. Wilson. (SPB. Apr.29; 233) $125

REYNOLDS, Sir Joshua
- [–] **A Collection of 8 Discourses delivered at the Royal Academy between 1774 & 1778.** 1775-89. 1st. Edns. 4to. Lacks 1st. hf.-title, 1st. title browned at edges. Cont. tree cf., spine gt., slightly worn. 5 Discourses inscr. 'From the Author'; bkplt. of William Hodgson. (S. Jun.23; 408)   Maggs. £140
- – **Anr. Edn.** Ed.:– John Burnet. 1842. 4to. Late 19th. C. red lev. mor. gt., by J. White of Pall Mall. Watercolour in style of Rowlandson pasted-in at end. (S. Nov.24; 248)   Lyon. £260
- **Collection of 139 Engraved Plates.** Ill.:– Samuel William Reynolds, the Younger, after Reynolds. [Plts. dtd. 1820-38]. 4 vols. Fo. Slight discolouration. Mott. cf., orig. ptd. wraps. (stained) bnd. in. As a coll., w.a.f. (S. Sep.29; 228)   Pinto. £260
- **Engravings from the Works.** [1833-39]. 3 vols. Fo. Very slightly spotted. Cont. hf. cf., spine of vol. III slightly worn & jnt. brkn. (S. Apr.7; 443)   Sanders of Oxford. £380
- – **Anr. Edn.** N.d. 3 vols. Fo. Spotted. Cont. hf. mor. (SH. Jan.29; 141)   Fogg. £240

REYNOLDS, Samuel William
- **Engravings from the Pictures & Sketches painted by Sir Joshua Reynolds.** Bayswater, Jul. 1820. Port. detchd., some spotting & light dampstains. Cont. hf. mor., worn, upr. cover detchd., spine torn with loss. W.a.f. (CSK. Jan.30; 144)   £150

REYNST, Gerard
- **Variarum Imaginium a celeberrimis artificibus pictarum caelaturae elegantissimis tabulis repraesentatae.** Ill.:– Cornelis Vischer, Blotelin, Van Dalen & Matham. Amst., ca. 1661. Fo., (465 X 355mm.). 1 plt. possibly inserted later, the names of the artists & engravers inserted in MS. Cont. mott. cf. (C. Feb.25; 199)   Marlborough. £650

REYRAC, Abbé de
- **Hymne au Soleil.** Paris, 1783. Cont. red mor., triple gt. fillet borders, enclosing on both covers gt. arms of 'Imprimerie Royale', spine gt., gt. dentelles. (SG. Sep.25; 46) $1,000

RHEAD, George Wooliscroft
- **History of the Fan.** 1910. Ltd. Edn. Fo. Some spotting. Orig. cl. (SH. Oct.9; 185)   Sanders. £260
- – **Anr. Copy.** (450). (SH. Jan.29; 287)   Sanders of Oxford. £250
- – **Anr. Copy.** Orig. decor. cl. (CE. Jul.9; 210)   £240

RHEAD, Louis
- **American Trout Stream Insects.** N.Y., [1916]. 1st. Edn. Cl., unc. (SG. Oct.16; 326) $130
- **How to Fish the Dry Fly.** Brooklyn, Priv. Ptd. [1921]. 1st. Edn. Pict. wraps. Pres. copy, with orig. sketch. (SG. Oct.16; 328) $150

RHEEDE tot Draakestein, Hendrik Adrian van
- **Hortus Indicus Malabaricus.** Amst., 1678-73-1703. 1st. Edn. 12 vols. Fo. 790 plts. only (of 793, lacks 17 in vol. 11 & 37 & 38 in vol. 12), some plts. cropped with loss of plt. numbers, slight discolouration & spotting thro-out (mostly marginal), 1 plt. with sm. wormholes. Old cf., panel. cf. & hf. mor., non-unif. W.a.f., from Chetham's Liby., Manchester. (C. Nov.27; 342)   Weldon & Wesley. £2,200

RHEIN, Der
Wiesbaden, ca. 1840. 38 steel engrs. Cont. linen, spine renewed. (HK. Nov.18-21; 1343)   DM 700
- – **Anr. Edn.** Frankfurt am Main, n.d. Ob. 4to. Some plts. marginally dampstained. Orig. cl.-bkd. bds. (SH. Mar.5; 121)   Henderson. £580

RHENANUS, Johann
See–[GRASSHOFF, Johann]–RHENANUS, Johann

RHETICUS, Georg Joachim
- **De Libris Revolutionum ... Doctoris Nicolai Copernici ... Narratio prima.** Danzig, 1540. 1st. Edn. 4to. Limp vell., hf. red mor. case. On title-p. is written author's name, beneath which is inscr.: 'Ex dono Laurentii Vuirt (?) ciue Babenberg[e]n[sis]' a further inscr. at foot, from Honeyman Collection. (S. Nov.11; 2630)   Quaritch. £75,00
- **Opus Palatinum de Triangulis ... L. Valentinus Otho ... consummavit.** [Neustadt a.d. Hardt], 1596. 1st. Edn. 6 pts. in 1 vol. Fo. Cont. blind-stpd. pig. over wooden bds., soiled, lacks clasps & catches. From Honeyman Collection. (S. Nov.11; 2631)   Barchas Lib. £1,600

RHIND, William
- **A History of the Vegetable Kingdom.** Glasgow, 1860. 4to. Occasional slight soiling. Cont. hf. mor. (CSK. Feb.20; 107)   £60

RHINGIER, Innocent
- **Cinquante Jeus divers d'honnête Entretien.** Lyon, 1555. 1st. Edn. in Fr. 4to. Lacks last lf., blank except for fleuron on verso, some old underlinings on f.a. 18th. C. red mor., triple gt. fillet, flat spine gt. with sm. bird in each compartment within pattern of foliage & stars, inner gt. dentelles. (SM. Oct.8; 1965)   Frs. 2,000

RHODE, Eleanour Sinclair
- **The Old English Herbals.** 1922. 1st. Edn. 4to. Orig. buckram, slightly soiled. (S. Apr.6; 197)   Talerman. £50

RHODIGINUS, Ludovicus Coelius
- **Sicuti Antiquarum Lectionum Commentariat.** [Colophon: Venice], [colophon: 1516]. Fo. Early 19th. C. hf. cf. (CSK. Apr.24; 151)   £160

RHYNE, W. ten
See–BREYN, Jacob & Rhyne, W. ten

RHYS, John David
- **Cambrobrytannicae Cymraecaeve Linguae Institutiones et Rudimenta ... cum exacta Carmina Cymrraeca condendi Ratione, & Cambrobrytannicorum Poematum.** 1592. 1st. Edn. Fo. 1 ptd. folding table torn, with errata & last blank. 18th. C. cf., very worn. [NSTC 20966] (S. Oct.20; 197)   P. Grinke. £250

RHYS, John & Evans, J. Gwenogvryn, editors
- **The Text of the Mabinogion (&) The Bruts & other Welsh Tales from the Red Book of Hergerst.** Oxford, 1887-90. (80) numbered on H.M.P.

initialled by editor. 2 vols. Facs. Cont. hf. red mor. gt. (SBA. Oct.22; 752)   Simon. £56

RIAT, George
- **Gustave Courbet, Peintre.** Paris, 1906. 4to. Cont. hf. mor., orig. wraps. bnd. in. (SH. Nov.20; 140)   Klusmann. £50

RIBADENEYRA Y BARRIENTOS, Antonio Joachin de
- **Manual Compendio de el Regio Patronato Indiano.** Madrid, 1755. 4to. A few light stains. Cont. cf., slightly defect. at head of spine. [Sabin 70785] (SPB. May 5; 431) $275
- – **Anr. Copy.** Engraved vig. on title stained. Some wear. (SPB. May 5; 432) $250

RIBEYRO, J.
- **Histoire de L'Isle de Ceylan.** Amst., 1701. Cont. cf. gt. (P. Dec.11; 98)   Weston. £55

RICARD, Samuel
- **Traité Général du Commerce.** Amst., 1700. 1st. Edn. 4to. Some browning. Cont. cf., gt. spine, some wear. (S. Oct.21; 468)   Quaritch. £70

RICARDO, David
- **On the Principles of Political Economy & Taxation.** Georgetown, 1819. 1st. Amer. Edn. Dampstained in parts. Hf. linen, ex-liby. (SG. Feb.12; 333) $110
- – **Anr. Edn.** 1821. 3rd. Edn. Lacks(?) hf.-title. Prize bdg. of cont. cf. with gt. arms of Trinity College Dublin on covers, spine & upr. jnt. damaged. Dedication label to Francis Dunne, dtd. 1820. (S. Jul.27; 222)   Bickersteth. £130

RICAUTI, T.J.
- **Sketches for Rustic Work.** 1848. 4to. Plts., rather spotted & dampstained. Orig. cl., rebkd. (SH. Oct.9; 135)   Meyer. £95
- – **Anr. Copy.** 18 plts., spotted & dampstained. (SH. Apr.9; 115)   Fogg. £50

RICCARDI, Pietro
- **Biblioteca Matematica Italiana.** Milano, [1952]. 2 vols. 4to. Cl. (SG. Jan.22; 339) $120

RICCATI, Vincenzo
- **De Seriebus Recipientibus Summam Generalem Algebraicam aut Exponentialem Commentarius.** Bologna, 1756. 1st. Edn. (Lge.). 4to. Slight discolouration. Orig. limp bds., soiled. From Honeyman Collection. (S. Nov.11; 2635)   Zeitlin. £85
- – **Anr. Copy.** Slight spotting, fly-lf. torn. Cont. vell., soiled. From Honeyman Collection. (S. Nov.11; 2636)   Zeitlin. £70
- **De Usu Motus Tractorii in Constructione Aequationum Differentialium Commentarius.** Bologna, 1752. 1st. Edn. 4to. Stp. cut from title leaving hole touching engraved device. Cont. vell. bds. Stp. of Convent of St. Peter & Vincula on title; from Honeyman Collection. (S. Nov.11; 2634)   Zeitlin. £75
- **Dialogo ... dove ne' congressi di piu giornate delle Forze Vive e dell'azioni delle Forze morte si tien Discorso.** Bologna, 1749. 1st. Edn. 4to. 1st. quire detchd. Orig. wraps., spine worn, unc., bookseller's label on upr. cover. From Honeyman Collection. (S. Nov.11; 2633)   Zeitlin. £50
- **Opusculorum ad Res Physicas, & Mathematica pertinentium.** Bologna, 1757-62. 1st. Edn. 2 vols. in 1. 4to. Some foxing. 19th. C. roan-bkd. bds. Stp. & sig. of Prof. Ettore Bortolotti, Bologna; from Honeyman Collection. (S. Nov.11; 2637)   Nador. £100

RICCATI, Vincenzo & Saladini, G.
- **Institutiones Analyticae.** Bologna, 1765-67. 1st. Edn. 2 vols. in 3. 4to. Foxed thro.-out, stab-hole through a few ll. near beginning of vol. III, plt. 41 adhering to text, hole in 4V2. 19th. C. vell. bds., unc. From Honeyman Collection. (S. Nov.11; 2638)   Howell. £170

RICCI, Bartolomeo, S.J.
- **Considerationi sopra tutta la Vita di N.S. Giesu Christo.** Rome, 1607. 1st. Edn. Early mor., worn. (SG. Sep.25; 269) $210

RICCI, Elisa
- **Antiche Trine Italiane: Trine ad Ago.** Bergamo, [1910]. Fo. Publisher's cl. (CR. Mar.19; 233)   Lire 260,000
- **Old Italian Lace.** 1913. 2 vols. 4to. Cl., worn. (BS. Jun.11; 421)   £75

RICCI, Matteo
- **Histoire de l'Expedition Chrestienne au Royaume de la Chine ...** Ed.:– Nicolas Trigault. Lille, 1617.

RICCI, Matteo -*contd.*
1st. Fr. Edn. 4to. Cont. cf., blind, armorially stpd.,
cl. ties. Armorial bkplt. of M. de Contagnet.
(PNY. Oct.1; 142) $ 400
See-RODRIGUEZ, J.-RICCI, Matteo

RICCIOLI, Giambattista
- **Almagestum novum Astronomiam veterem
novamque complectens.** Bologna, 1651. 1st. Edn.
Vol. I (all publd.), in 2 vols. Fo. Some browning &
spotting, holes in A4 & B4 vol. I. Cont. red mor.,
panel. in gt., tear at head of spine. Bkplt. of Dr.
J.L.E. Dreyer; the Hamilton liby. copy; from
Honeyman Collection. (S. Nov.11; 2642)
                                            Jackson. £980
- - **Anr. Copy.** Some browning, owner's inscr. on
1st. fly-lf. Cont. cf., gt., rebkd., old spines
preserved, worn. From Honeyman Collection. (S.
Nov.11; 2641)   *Zeitlin.* £820
- **Argomento fisicomattematico ... contro il moto
diurno della terra.** Bologna, 1668. 1st. Edn. 4to.
Prelims. a little stained. Cont. limp vell., spine
worn, hf. red mor. case. Sig. of G.V. Marelini; stp.
of Galletti liby., Flor.; from Honeyman Collection.
(S. Nov.11; 2644)   *Hill.* £210
- **Astronomiae Reformatae Tomi duo.** Bologna,
1665. 1st. Edn. 2 vols. in 1. Fo. Lr. margins
stained at beginning, faded Jesuit inscr. at foot of
1st. title. Cont. vell. bds., rebkd., soiled. From
Honeyman Collection. (S. Nov.11; 2643)
                                            Zeitlin. £420
- **Chronologiae et ad Certas Conclusiones redactae.**
Bologna, 1669. 1st. Edn. 3 vols. in 1. Fo. Some
damp staining, a few ll. wormed at head affecting
headlines, etc., owner's inscrs. of 'Peragallo',
Lisbon, 1887. 19th. C. red mor.-bkd. bds., worn.
From Honeyman Collection. (S. Nov.11; 2645)
                                               Hill. £300
- **Chronologiae Reformatae et ad Certas
Conclusiones redactae.** Bologna, 1669. 1st. Edn. 3
vols. in 1. Fo. Engraved frontis to vol. I only, some
worming, mostly marginal, occasional marginal
staining, some ll. browned. Cont. limp vell. From
Honeyman Collection. (S. Nov.11; 2646)
                                            Zeitlin. £280
- **Geographiae et Hydrographiae Reformatae.**
Venice, 1672. Fo. Some browning, piece torn from
fore-margin of 2D4. Mod. vell. bds., unc. Stp. of
Biblioteca Queriniana (Martinengro Bequest);
from Honeyman Collection. (S. Nov.11; 2647)
                                               Nox. £130
- **Geographicae crucis fabrica et usus.** Bologna,
1643. 1st. Edn. Fo. A4 reprd. at foot affecting
border on verso, additional errata slip pasted to
G3v, a few MS. corrections (by author?) to 1st. 8
ll. of text causing slight corrosion holes, title
slightly dampstained. Wraps., defect. Bkplts. of
Riccardi & Carlo Vigano; from Honeyman
Collection. (S. Nov.11; 2640)   *Zeitlin.* £130

RICCIUS, B.
- **Apparatus Latinae Locutionis.** Strassburg, 1535.
4to. Some stains. Cont. blind-stpd. cf., spine worn,
lacks clasps. (SH. Jun.11; 161)   *Bondy.* £70

RICCOBONI, Louis
- **Histoire du Théâtre Italien.** Ill.:– Joulain after
Watteau. [colophon dtd. 1728]. Cont. cf., worn.
(CSK. Nov.28; 184)   £95
- **Histoire du Théâtre Italien.–Dell'Arte
Rappresentativa.** Paris, 1730-31; 1728. 2 works in
1 vol., 2nd. work 2 vols. Cont. cf. (BS. Jun.11; 276)
                                                      £160

RICE, N.L.
- **An Account of the Law-Suit Instituted by Rev.
G.A.M. Elder ... Against Rev. N.L. Rice ...**
Louisville, 1837. 1st. Edn. 12mo. Foxed & soiled,
some MS. notations. Orig. cl. & remnants of orig.
ptd. label, soiled & worn, upr. cover loose., folding
cl. case. From liby. of William E. Wilson. [Sabin
70848] (SPB. Apr.29; 234) $300

RICE, William
- **Tiger-Shooting in India.** 1857. Orig. cl. gt.
(SBA. Oct.21; 162a)   *Gopinath.* £110

RICH, Claudius James
- **Narrative of a Residence in Koordistan.** 1836. 2
vols. 1 plt. slightly torn, advt. ll., soiled. Later
cf.-bkd. bds., recased. (SH. Nov.7; 356)
                                             Hosain. £95

**RICH STOREHOUSE or Treasurie for the
Diseased, Wherein are many approved Medicines
... set foorth for the ... poorer sort ... by G.W.
And now fifthly augmented ... by A.T.**
1612. 4to. Some early MS. notats., staining, some

headlines shaved, upr. corners of 1st. & last 2 ll.
chewed with loss of some letters, last 3 ll. detchd.,
their margins worn, Hh1 holed with loss of letters.
Hf. cf., worn. [STC 23608] (CSK. Nov.28; 201)
                                                       £50

RICHARD, Edouard
- **Acadie.** Ed.:– Henri d'Arles (i.e. Henri Beaude).
Quebec & Boston, 1916-21. 3 vols. 4to. Orig. ptd.
wraps., unc. & unopened. (CB. Apr.1; 32)
                                            Can. $300

RICHARDS, Walter
- **Her Majesty's Army.** [1888-91]. 6 vols. 4to.
Orig. cl. (SH. Jul.9; 191)   *Bookroom.* £80
- - **Anr. Edn.** Ca. 1890. 4 vols. plus 2 vols.
Supp.–Indian & Colonial Forces. 4to. Advts. to
each vol. Orig. decor. cl., slightly soiled. (TA.
Apr.16; 271)   £60
- - **Anr. Copy.** 3 vols. Cl. (SG. Oct.30; 304) $180
- **Her Majesty's Army.–Her Majesty's Indian &
Colonial Forces.** Ca. 1890. 2 vols.; 1 vol. 4to. Orig.
decor. cl. (TA. Mar.19; 662)   £90

RICHARDS, William
- **The Universal Library of Trade & Commerce.**
1747-53. 7 pts. in 1 vol. 4to. Lacks gathering *I, a
few ll. slightly stained. Cont. cf., slightly worn.
(SH. Oct.10; 315)   *Henderson.* £70

RICHARDSON, Sir Albert Edward
- **Monumental Classic Architecture.** Ill.:– [E.
Dockree]. L., [1914]. Fo. Gt.-pict. buckram. (SG.
Mar.12; 311) $200
- - **Anr. Copy.** Lge. 4to. Orig. cl. (CB. May
27; 176)   Can. $180

RICHARDSON, Charles, Sportsman & others
- **Racing at Home & Abroad.** 1923-31. Ltd. Edn.
3 vols. 4to. Orig. mor. (SH. Jan.30; 387)
                                              Way. £70

RICHARDSON, Charles James
- **Architectural Remains of the Reigns of Elizabeth
& James I.** 1838-40. Fo. Litho. title, 37 plts. on 34
ll., some tinted or partly hand-cold., including 3
repeats with plts. in uncold. or partly cold. state &
cancelled plt., with explanatory slip, 1 plt. loose.
Orig. mor.-bkd. bds. (C. May 20; 48)
                                          Quaritch. £200
- **The Englishman's House, a practical guide for
selecting or building a house.** L., [1883]. 3rd. Edn.
Slight foxing. Orig. gt. decor. cl. (CB. May
27; 180)   Can. $130
- **Studies from Old English Mansions.** 1841-48.
1st.-4th. Series. 4 vols. Fo. Cont. mor.-bkd. cl.,
loose. (SH. Nov.6; 144)   *Cavendish.* £80

RICHARDSON, George
- **A Book of Ceilings.** Ill.:– Richardson. 1776. Fo.
Title in Engl. & Fr. Cont. bds., unc., soiled, lacks
spine. (C. Feb.25; 200)   *Quaritch.* £380
- **Iconology; or, a Collection of Emblematical
Figures ...** 1778-9. 1st. Edn. 2 vols. in 1. 4to.
Apparently lacks a title for vol. II, slight browning.
Cont. mott. cf., rather worn, jnts. reprd. (S.
Apr.7; 401)   *Parikian.* £160
- **A Treatise on the Five Orders of Architecture.**
1778. Fo. Engl. & Fr. text, dampstained. Cont. hf.
cf., covers detchd. (TA. Jan.22; 108)   £65
- - **Anr. Edn.** 1787. 1st. Edn. Lge. fo. Slight
spotting. Hf. russ., gt. From Belton House Liby.
(S. Jun.22; 139)   *Maggs.* £110

RICHARDSON, J.
- **Narrative of a Mission to Central Africa.** 1853. 2
vols. Orig. cl. (SH. Nov.7; 321)   *Edwards.* £155

RICHARDSON, John, Brewer
- **The Philosophical Principles of the Science of
Brewing.** York, 1805. 3rd. Coll. Edn. Orig. bds.,
rebkd., new end-papers. (SBA. Oct.22; 645)
                                            Spelman. £54

RICHARDSON, John, of Clark County, Illinois
- **A New Theory on the Causes of the Motions of
the Planetary Bodies, Belonging to the Solar
System.** Vincennes, 1829. 1st. Edn. 12mo. Sig. of
James McBride on title & 1st. p. of text, foxed &
stained, a few marginal tears. Disbnd., folding cl.
case. From liby. of William E. Wilson. [Sabin
71034] (SPB. Apr.29; 235) $650

RICHARDSON, Maj. John
- **War of 1812.** Ed.:– A.C. Casselman. Toronto,
1902. Orig. cl., unc. & unopened. Pres. Copy. to
J.P. Whitney, Premier of Canada, 1905-14. (CB.
Sep.24; 197)   Can. $100

**RICHARDSON, Sir John, M.D. & Swainson,
William**
- **Fauna Boreali Americana.** L., 1829. 1st. Edn. Pt.
1 only (of 4). 4to. Embossed liby. stp. on title.
Cont. cf. gt., covers with gt. arms, spine gt. (CNY.
May 22; 210) $320
- - **Anr. Edn.** L., 1831. Pt. 2 only ('The Birds').
4to. 49 plts. only (of 50, lacks no. 63). Completely
disbnd. (SG. Nov.20; 413) $475

RICHARDSON, Samuel
[-] **Clarissa.** L., 1748. 1st. Edn. 7 vols. 12mo.
Misprint 'all owed' in vol. IV corrected, trimmed,
with occasional cropping at lr. edges. Cf., gt. fillet
borders, spines gt., by Rivière. (SG. Feb.5; 287)
                                                      $275
- **Complete Novels.** L., 1902. (375). 19 vols. Slight
browning. Hf. mor. gt., some stains. (SPB. May
6; 337) $650
- **The Correspondence.** Ed.:– A.L. Barbauld. 1804.
[1st. Edn.?]. 6 vols. 8 facs. letters. Cont. cf. gt. (P.
Jan.22; 16)   *Jarndyce.* £110
- - **Anr. Copy.** Cont. hf. red mor. gt., spines gt.
(CNY. May 22; 254) $150
- **Lettres Angloises, ou Histoire de Miss Clarisse
Harlove.** Ill.:– Duponchel (port.). L., 1784. 11 vols.
18mo. Grained cf. by Cazin, some defects. (HD.
Apr.8; 300)   Frs. 1,400
- **The Novels.** 1902. Ltd. Edn. 19 vols. Orig. cl.
(SH. May 28; 87)   *Pankhurst.* £130
- **Pamela.–Clarissa Harlowe.–The History of Sir
Charles Grandison.** 1742; 1751; 1754. Various
Edns. 4 vols.; 7 vols.; 6 vols. Unif. 18th. C. diced
cf., blind-stpd. floral border, spines gt. (LC.
Feb.12; 563)   £80

RICHARDSON, T.M.
- **Architectural Antiquities of Northumberland.**
Ill.:– D. Havell & T. Sutherland. N.d. Fo. Bdg.
not stated. (DWB. May 15; 375)   £220
- **Sketches in Italy, Switzerland & France.** L.,
1837. Imp. fo. Slightly soiled in pts., titles & 4
plts. stpd. Cont. leath., gt., spine defect., 1 cover
loose. (R. Oct.14-18; 1847)   DM 3,600

**RICHARDSON, William & Churnton, Rev.
Edward**
- **The Monastic Ruins of Yorkshire.** 1843. 2 vols.
in 1. Fo. Some ll. slightly spotted. Cont. hf. cf.,
worn, loose. (SH. Nov.6; 145)   *K. Books.* £180
- - **Anr. Copy.** Gt. spine. (SH. Mar.5; 122)
                                            Fairburn. £115

RICHARDSON, Lt.-Col. William H.
- **A Manual of Infantry & Rifle Tactics.**
Richmond, 1861. 1st. Edn. 18mo. Disbnd., upr.
cover retained. (SG. Jun.11; 111) $100

RICHENTHAL, Ulrich von
- **Das Concilium. So zu Constanz gehalten.**
Trans.:– R.M. Buck. Meersburg, 1936. Facs. of
1536 Augsburg Edn. Sm. fo. Hf. leath. (R.
Mar.31-Apr.4; 788)   DM 750
[-] - **Anr. Copy.** Lge. 4to. Orig. hf. vell. (HK. May
12-14; 2220)   DM 460

RICHEPIN, Jean
- **Les Blasphèmes.** Ill.:– E. Liphart, E. Dufour.
Paris, 1884. (575), (350) on vell. 4to. Mor.,
vertical mor. borders, blind-tooled, motif decor.,
gt. & silver, limp decor. spine, unc., wrap.
preserved, s.-c., by Kieffer. A.N., 3 verses sigd. &
dtd. by author, MS. note by binder. (HD.
Apr.24; 180)   Frs. 4,500
- **La Chanson des Gueux.** Paris, [1876]. 1st. Edn.
12mo. Cont. hf. chagrin, spine decor. with raised
bands, cipher of Francisque Sarcey on spine.
Autograph dedication & lge. autograph letter
from author to Francisque Sarcey. (HD.
Jun.25; 381)   Frs. 1,700
- - **Anr. Edn.** Ill.:– Steinlen. Paris, 1910. (325),
(267) numbered on velin du Marais. 4to. Red
mor., 5 decor. spine raised bands, lge. gt. fillet
border, pointillé & angle fleurons, mor. doubls.,
inner gt. border, double paper board, wrap.
preserved, s.-c., by Affolter 1910. Sigd. by ed. with
prospectus. (LM. Mar.21; 299)   B.Frs. 33,000
- **Les Débuts de César Borgia.** Ill.:– Avril,
Courboin, Manesse & Fornet. Paris, 1890. Ltd.
Edn. 2-7 states of decors., orig. water colour ill.
Mor. gt., by Marius Michel, floral silk end-papers,
orig. wraps. bnd. in. (SM. Oct.8; 2366)   Frs. 5,000
- **Les Litanies de la Mer.** Ill.:– Henri Carruchet.
Paris, 1903. (100) on Jap. Lge. 8vo. Orig.
watercolours. Mor. by H. Asper, spine & covers
with floral mosaic decor., wrap. (HD. Jun.25; 383)
                                            Frs. 1,600

RICHMOND, Leigh
- Annals of the Poor. Ed.:– John Ayre. L., 1846. New Edn. 16mo. Mor., gt.-tooled borders enclosing black-stpd. geometric design. Fore-e. pntg.; from the liby. of Zola E. Harvey. (SG. Mar.19; 164) $200

RICHOTTI, Vladimir
See–AFANAS'EV-SOLOV'EV, I. & others

RICHTER, August Gottlieb
- Anfangsgruende der Wundarzneykunst. Goettingen, 1782-1804. 7 vols. Old liby. stps. on titles. Cont. cf.-bkd. bds, worn. (SG. Sep.18; 317) $275

RICHTER, J.W.O.
- Bilder aus dem Westlichen Mitteldeutschland. Leipzig, [1882]. 1st. lf. soiled, 1 map defect., lacks series title. Orig. linen. (R. Oct.14-18; 2452) DM 650

RICHTER, Jean Paul
- Blumen-Frucht- und Dornenstükke ... Berlin, 1796-97. 1st. Edn. 3 vols. Slightly browned & soiled, title ll. with owner's mark, MS. note in inner cover regarding bdg. Later hf. leath., 1 sm. tear. (H. Dec.9/10; 1553) DM 440
- – Anr. Copy. New cf. gt., slightly worn, 1 spine loose. (H. Dec.9/10; 1555) DM 420
- Die Unsichtbare Loge. Ill.:– Chodowiecki (title). Berlin, 1793. 1st. Edn. 2 vols. With printer's errors, with title vig., slightly soiled. Cont. paper bds., worn, spine browned. (H. Dec.9/10; 1558) DM 480
- Sämtliche Werke. Ed.:– [R.O. Spazier & H. Förster]. Berlin, 1826-38. 1st. Coll. Edn. 65 in 27 vols. Lightly browned thro.-out. Later hf. leath., gt. spine, slightly soiled, several spine tears, vol. 65 not unif., unc. (H. Dec.9/10; 1550) DM 1,500
- – Anr. Copy. Cont. hf. leath., 4 spines reprd., several sm. tears., 2 vols. rebnd. (H. Dec.9/10; 1552) DM 1,050
- – Anr. Copy. Cont. paper bds., worn, spine browned. (H. Dec. 9/10; 1551) DM 770
- – Anr. Edn. Weimar, 1927-63. Pt. I, vols. I-XIX; Pt. 2. vols. I-V, together 24 vols. Orig. hf. leath. & 2 wraps., some spines worn. (H. Dec.9/10; 1849) DM 1,800

RICIUS, Alphonsus
- Eruditiones Christiane Plurimum Utiles & Cuilibet Christiano ad Modum Necessarie. –Dialogus quo ex Sacre Scripture.–Questio Perpulchra qua Inuestigatur. Paris, Nov. 11, 1512; ca. 1512; ca. 1512. 1st. Edns? 3 works in 1 vol. 4to. Some very slight spotting, a2 & 7 of 1st. work creased with break in print. Red lev. mor., spine gt.-lettered, by M. Godillot. The copy of John A. Saks. (CNY. Oct.1; 103) $1,600

RICIUS, Augustinus
- De Motu Octave Sphere: Opus Mathematica atque Philosophia Plenum. Trino, 10 Sep. 1513. 1st. Edn. Marginal spotting. Limp vell., hf. red mor. case. From Honeyman Collection. (S. Nov.11; 2648) Quaritch. £340

RICIUS, Paulus
See–SCHONER, Johann–HEYLL, Christophorus –FUCHS, Leonhard–RICIUS, Paulus

RICKENBACKER, Capt. Edward V.
See–LINDBERGH, Charles–RICKENBACKER, Capt. Edward V.

RICKETT, Henry William
- Wild Flowers of the United States. N.Y., [1966-72]. 5 vols. only, lacks vol. 6 & index. 4to. Orig. cl., in s.-c.'s. (CB. Sep.24; 240) Can. $240

RICKETTS, Charles 'Jean Paul Raymond'
- Beyond the Threshold. Curwen Pr., 1929. Orig. mor. gt. (S. Jul.31; 300) Maggs. £190
- – Anr. Edn. Curwen Pr., [1929]. 4to. Gt.-decor. red mor. (SG. Jan.15; 75) $130
- A Defence of the Revival of Printing. Vale Pr., 1899. (250) on paper. Orig. bds., short split & slight chipping of spine, unc. Bkplt. of Thomas B. Mosher. (S. Jul.31; 46) Warrack & Perkins. £110
- Oscar Wilde: Recollections. Nones. Pr., 1932. (800) numbered. Orig. pict. cl. gt., cover design by author, d.-w. reprd. (S. Jul.31; 116) Maggs. £90
- Pages on Art. 1913. Orig. cl. gt. Pres. copy to Hamilton Minchin, with accompanying A.L.s. (S. Jul.31; 299) Henderson. £65

RICKETTS, Charles (Ill.)
See–APULEIUS, Lucius

See–DRAYTON, Michael
See–GRAY, John
See–LONGUS
See–MARLOWE, Christopher & Chapman, George
See–MILTON, John
See–NEW TESTAMENTIANA (English)
See–SHAKESPEARE, William
See–SHAW, Bernard
See–SIDNEY, Sir Philip
See–TENNYSON, Alfred Lord
See–WILDE, Oscar

RICKETTS, Charles & Pissarro, Lucien
- De la Typographie et de l'Harmonie de la Page Imprimée. Vale Pr., 1898. (250) on paper. Errata slip loosely inserted. Orig. bds., corners slightly chipped, unc., unopened. (S. Jul.31; 44) Warrack & Perkins. £140
- – Anr. Copy. Bdg. ink-stained, soiled. (S. Jul.31; 45) Warrack & Perkins. £55

RICKETTS, Major
- Narrative of the Ashantee War. 1831. Later hf. cf. (SH. Nov.7; 322) Lloyd. £75

RICKMAN, Philip
- A Bird-Painter's Sketch Book. L. & N.Y., 1931. 1st. Edn. Sm. fo. Cl. (SG. Oct.16; 329) $110
- A Selection of Bird Paintings & Sketches. Ed.:– H.R.H. the Duke of Edinburgh. 1979. (500) numbered, sigd. Fo. Cold. plts. tipped in. Orig. hf. mor. gt. with s.-c. (TA. Jun.18; 130) £250

RICO, Juan P.
- Reales Exequias, que por el Fallecimiento del Senor Don Carlos III, Rey de España y de las Indias, mando celebrar en la Ciudad de Lima. –Oracion Funebre que ... dixo en la Iglesia Catedral de Lima Fr. Bernardo Rueda. Lima, 1789. 2 pts. in 1 vol. Fo. 1st. pt. lacks engraved plt. Cont. vell. (SPB. May 5; 434) $100

RICORDI & C.
- Gli Avvisi delle Officine G. Ricordi & C. Milano. Milan, n.d. Ob. 4to. Portfo. & box. (SI. Dec.4; 495) Lire 780,000

RICTUS, Jehan
- Les Soliloques du Pauvres. Ill.:– Steinlen. Priv. ptd., 1897. 1st. Edn., (80) on imperial Japon. Sewed, unc., spine yellowed, sm. tear on upr. cover. (HD. Jun.25; 385) Frs. 1,200

RIDE a Cock-Horse & Other Nursery Rhymes
Ill.:– Mervyn Peake. 1940. 1st. Edn. 4to. Orig. bds. with 2 of the ills. repeated on covers. Pres. Copy to Mrs. de la Mare. (SH. Dec.18; 20) Steenson. £95

RIDER, A.
See–PHILLIPS, John & Rider, A.

RIDER, William
See–BRADSHAW, T. & Rider, William

RIDGWAY, Robert
- The Birds of North & Middle America. Wash., 1901-19. 8 vols. Cont. buckram, orig. upr. wrap. preserved in each vol., lr. wrap. preserved in most. (CB. Sep.24; 43) Can. $150
- Color Standards & Color Nomenclature. Wash., Priv. ptd., 1912. 1st. Edn. Orig. cl., orig. upr. cold. wrap. bnd. in. (PNY. Dec.3; 92) $100

RIDING, Laura
- Though Gently. Majorca, The Seizin Pr., 1930. 1st. Edn., Orig. cl.-bkd. pict. bds. (S. Jul.22; 152) Babcock. £95
- Twenty Poems Less. Paris, Hours Pr., 1930. 1st. Edn., Orig. mor.-bkd. pict. bds., unc. (S. Jul.22; 153) Babcock. £130

RIDINGER, Joh. Elias
- Lehrreiche Fabeln aus dem Reiche der Thiere. Augsburg, 1744. 1st. Edn. Fo. Lacks 4 copperplts. as often, margins slightly soiled, 1 sm. tear, upper margin stained thro.-out, blind-stp. on title-lf. Cont. cf., very worn, spine torn. (H. May 21/22; 1254) DM 4,200
- Neue Reit-Kunst. Ill.:– J.D. Hertz & others after Ridinger. Augsburg, 1744. Ob. fo. Lacks plts. 3, 7, 18 & 20, MS. owner's mark on title, plt. 13 sm. defect., plts. partly backed. Cont. hf. leath. (HK. Nov.18-21; 1962) DM 10,000

RIDLEY, Henry, i.e. Humphrey
- Anatomia Cerebri Complectens ejus Mechanismum et Physiologiam Simulque nova quaedam inventa ... Leiden, 1725. Advt. lf. Vell. (S. Jun.17; 727) Phelps. £110

- The Anatomy of the Brain containing its Mechanism & Physiology. 1695. 1st. Edn. Short tear in 1 plt. Cont. cf., unpressed copy. (S. Jun.17; 726) Phillips. £1,100

RIDLEY, James 'Sir Charles Morell'
- The Tales of the Genii. 1805. L.P. 2 vols. Cont. red str.-grd. mor., tooled in gt. & blind. (S. Nov.24; 165) Dosson. £120

RIDLEY, Mark
- A Short Treatise of Magneticall Bodies & Motions. 1613. 1st. Edn., 1st. Iss. 4to. Without errata on X3r, A1 (blank) defect., X3 restored in upr. & inner margins with headline & p.-number in pen facs., some staining, title slightly soiled, a few letters in O1v erased, a few marginal tears in O4, sm. tear in K3. Cont. limp vell., reprd., hf. red mor. case. From Honeyman Collection. (S. Nov.11; 2649) Stillings. £2,400

RIDOUT, W.
- Catalogue ... of Italian & other Maiolica, Mediaeval English Pottery, Dutch, Spanish & French Faience. 1934. Ltd. Edn. Cl. (P. Feb.19; 344) Talerman. £55

RIDPATH, George
- The Border History of England & Scotland. 1776. 1st. Edn. 4to. Cont. cf. (SH. Nov.6; 146) Sykes. £70

RIEDESEL, Generalin von
- Die Berufs-Reise nach America: Briefe auf dieser Reise und waehrend ihres Sechsjaehrigen Aufenthalts in America zur Zeit des dortigen Krieges, 1776-1783. Berlin, 1800. 1st. Publd. Edn. Cont. marb. bds., cf. spine & tips. (SG. Mar.5; 390) $170

RIEDRER, Friedrich
- Spiegel der wahren Rhetorik. Freiburg im Breisgau, Friedrich Riedrer, Dec. 11 1493. 1st. Edn. Fo. Wormed thro.-out slightly affecting text, dampstained at beginning, title soiled & with inner margin strengthened. Old cf. over wooden bds. From Honeyman Collection; the Phillipps copy; inscr. in pencil 'MHC'. [BMC III, 696; HC 13914; Goff R197] (S. Nov.11; 2650) Martin. £1,600
- – Anr. Copy. Woodcut calligraphic initial S at fo. 2r, spaces for other capitals, sm. wormhole to 1st. lf. slightly affecting title woodcut & extreme edge of woodcut on verso, slight repairs to inner blank margin of same lf., 3 ll. with sm. portions of margin torn away. Cont. bevelled wood bds., recased, blind-stpd. pig spine supplied. From the collection of Eric Sexton. [BMC III, 696, Goff R197, HC 13914] (CNY. Apr.8; 68) $7,000

RIEFENTHAL, Otto von
- Die Raubvögel Deutschlands. Kassel, [1876-78]. 1st. Edn. Fo. Magins slightly soiled in places, sm. plts. with sm. stain in lower corner, text ll. slightly defect in margins. Loose in orig. linen portfo. (R. Mar.31-Apr.4; 1431) DM 950

RIEGEL, Christoff
[-] Ausführliche und Grundrichtige Beschreibung der Vier Weltberühmten Ströme Mosel, Saar, Neckar und Mayn. Frankfurt & Leipzig, 1690. Slightly browned in parts. Cont. leath., ties. (R. Mar.31-Apr.4; 1872) DM 16,000
- Bilder-Geographie. Nuremb., 1770. Some foxing thro.-out. Old cf., worn. (BS. Jun.11; 386) £180

RIEMANN, Georg Friedrich Bernhard
- On the Hypotheses which lie at the Bases of Geometry. Trans.:– W.K. Clifford. 1873. 1st. Engl. trans. In: Nature, vol. VIII, nos. 183 & 184. 4to. Mod. bds., John Carter's pencil annot. in upr. cover. From Honeyman Collection. (S. Nov.11; 2651) The Teachers Charity. £70

RIEMER, J.
- Die Mittel ... zu einer Angenehmen Heyrath ... Frankfurt [Augsburg], 1722. Title stpd., some lr. corners browned. Hf. leath. (HK. May 15; 4781) DM 1,200

RIENZI, G.L.D. de
- Oceanien. Trans.:– C.A. Mebold. Stuttgart, 1837-40. 3 vols. Lacks plts. 171-200 in vol. 3, this vol. slightly soiled. Cont. bds. (HK. Nov.18-21; 1071) DM 460

RIESE, Adam
- Rechenung nach der Lenge, auff den Linihen und Feder. Leipzig, [1550]. 1st. Edn. 4to. Text browned & stained, sm. hole in title & following 2 ll., owner's inscr. on last p. 19th. C. hf. parch., hf.

RIESE, Adam – Rechenung nach der Lenge, auff den Linihen und Feder. *-contd.*
red mor. case. From Honeyman Collection. (S. Nov.11; 2652) *Martin.* £850
See–STIFEL, Michael–RIESE, Adam

RIESE, Isaac
– Ein newes Nutzbar gerechnetes Rechenbuch ... auff die Meissnische Muntze und Wehrunge gestellet und gerechnet. Leipzig, 1580. 1st. Edn. Sm. 4to. Dampstained & browned, last few ll. wormed affecting borders, 2 sm. holes in title, tear in D4, lge. hole in M4, corner torn from n1, owner's inscrs. of Matteus Widiger, 1611. Vell. Stp. of Stolberg liby. at Wernigerode; from Honeyman Collection. (S. Nov.11; 2653) *Martin.* £240

RIETSTAP, J.B.
– Armorial General. Gouda, n.d. 2nd. Edn. 2 vols. Hf. chagrin. (LM. Mar.21; 137) B.Frs. 14,000
– Wapenboek van den Nederlandschen Adel. Groningen, 1883. 2 pts. Lge. 4to. Linen, gold & silver decor., polychromatic arms. (LM. Jun.13; 87) B.Frs. 26,000

RIGBY, Edward
[–] Letters from the Shores of the Baltic. L., 1842. 2 vols. Slightly soiled. Cont. linen. (R. Mar.31-Apr.4; 2143) DM 550

RIGEL, Franz Xavier
– Der Siebenjährige Kampf auf der Pyrenäischen Halbinsel vom Jahre 1807 bis 1814. Rastatt, 1819-21. 3 vols. Slightly stained. Cont. hf. leath. (R. Oct.14-18; 1191) DM 550

RIGENERATIONE dell'Olanda
Venice, 1799. Fo. Occasional light marginal staining. Orig. ptd. paper bds., slightly stained, buckram s.-c. From the collection of John A. Saks. (C. Jun.10; 223) *Goldschmidt.* £350

RIGHETTI, Pietro
– Descrizione del Campidoglia. Rome, 1833-36. 2 vols. Fo. Hf. cf. gt. (P. Nov.13; 285) *Kestel.* £55
– – Anr. Copy. Cont. hf. cf., gt. spines. (SI. Dec.4; 496) Lire 300,000

RILEY, James
– Loss of the American Brig Commerce. 1817. 4to. Cont. cf., worn. (SH. Jun.18; 8) *Walford.* £50

RILEY, James Whitcombe 'Benjamin F. Johnson'
– The Old Swimmin'-Hole, & 'Leven More Poems. Indianapolis, 1883. 1st. Edn. 12mo. Dust-soiled. Orig. ptd. wraps., qtr. mor. gt. s.-c. Pres. Copy, to Ben S. Parker, inscr. with the poem 'Hail & Farewell'; lately in the Prescott Collection. (CNY. Feb.6; 283) $650

RILKE, Rainer Maria
– Duineser Elegien, Elegies from the Castle of Duino. Trans.:– V. & Edward Sackville West. Ill.:– Eric Gill. Weimar, Cranach Pr., for Hogarth Pr., 1931. (250), this out of series. 4to. Orig. vell.-bkd. bds. (SH. Nov.20; 33) *Scopazzi.* £90
– – Anr. Edn. Trans.:– V. & Edward Sackville-West. Ill.:– Eric Gill. [L.], Cranach Pr., [1931]. (230) 'Out of Series' on H.M.P. Qtr. vell., partly unc. (SG. Oct.9; 70) $500
– Gesammelte Gedichte. Ill.– Eric Gill & Aristide Maillol. Weimar, 1931. Vol. 3. 4to. Loose ll. (HK. May 12-14; 1815) DM 440
– Larenopfer. Prag, 1896. 1st. Edn. Title lf. restored in part (⅓), upr. margin with sm. tear. Mod. bds., orig. wraps. bnd. in. (H. May 21/22; 1767) DM 460
– Lettres à une Amie Vénitienne. Verona, 1941. 1st. Edn., hand-printed, (420) numbered on Bütten. 4to. Orig. vell., vell. s.-c. (R. Mar.31-Apr.4; 590) DM 1,450
– Sämtliche Werke. Ed.:– Ruth Sieber-Rilke & E. Zinn. Wiesbaden, 1955-66. 6 vols. Orig. cf. (H. Dec.9/10; 2316) DM 550
– Das Stundenbuch. Ill.:– W. Tiemann. Leipzig, 1905. 1st. Edn., (500) on Bütten. Orig. vell. (HK. May 12-14; 2034) DM 1,900

RINALDI, Orazio
– Specchio di Scienze, et Compendio delle Cose. Venice, 1583. 1st. Edn. 4to. Some browning, title stained & with untidily deleted inscr. at foot. Cont. limp vell., soiled. From Honeyman Collection. (S. Nov.11; 2654) *Howell.* £90

RINALDIS, Aldo de
– La Pittura del Seicento nell'Italia Meridional. Verona, 1929. 4to. Publisher's hf. cf. (CR. Mar.11; 65) Lire 320,000

RINDER, Frank
– D.Y. Cameron. An Illustrated Catalogue of His Etched Work. Glasgow, 1912. 4to. Steel-faced sigd. etching (State V) as frontis., partly untrimmed. Orig. qtr. parch., slightly soiled. Pres. copy. (TA. Feb.19; 436) £68

RINGELBERGIUS, Joachimus Fortius
– Lucubrationes. Basel, 1541. Lacks 2D8 (blank?), title defect. & reprd. with loss of a few letters, some marginal staining, occasional marginal annots. Cont. blind-stpd. cf., recased & restored. From Honeyman Collection. (S. Nov.11; 2656) *Allan.* £50
See–THEOPHRASTUS–LUSCINIUS, Ottomar –RINGELBERGIUS, Joachimus–MARULUS Marcus–Platina, Bartholomaeus

RINGELBERGIUS, Joachimus Fortius –PEURBACH, Georg von
– Opera.–Elementa Arithmetices. Lyon; Wittenburg, 1531; 1534. 1st. Coll. Edn. (1st. work). 2 works in 1 vol. (1st. work 2 pts.). 1st. work with some browning & staining, 1st. gathering loose, owner's inscr. on title-p., 2nd. work with some staining. Cont. blind-stpd. pig. over bds., date 1534 on upr. cover, soiled, lacks clasps, hf. mor. case. From liby. of Andreas Goldschmidt, called Aurifaber with his owner's inscr. on both title-pp. (struck out on 1st.); from Honeyman Collection. (S. Nov.11; 2655) *Goldschmidt.* £380

RINGHIERI, Innocenzo
– Cento giuochi liberali, et d'ingegno. Bologna, 1551. 1st. Edn. 4to. Some ll. stained, minor wormholes in title, inscr. on title. Cont. limp vell., soiled. From Honeyman Collection. (S. Nov.11; 2658) *Nox.* £90
– Cinquante ieus divers d'honnete entretien. Trans.:– Hubert Philippe de Villiers. Lyon, 1555. Some browning, bleached owner's inscr. on title. Cont. limp vell., lr. cover defect., lacks ties. From Honeyman Collection. (S. Nov.11; 2660) *Manning.* £60
– Il Sole. Rome, 1543. 1st. Edn. 4to. Lacks last lf. (blank?), some staining, last gathering loose, title with inscr. 19th. C. roan-bkd. bds. From Honeyman Collection. (S. Nov.11; 2657) *Nox.* £70

RINGLER, F.A., & Co.
– Specimens of Fine Engravings. N.Y., ca. 1880's. Fo. Cl., worn. (SG. Mar.26; 374) $100

RINGWALT, J. Luther (Ed.)
See–AMERICAN ENCYCLOPAEDIA of Printing

RIO, Andrés Manuel del
– Elementos de Orictognosia, o del Conocimiento de los Fosiles ... Primera parte. Mexico, 1795. 1st. Edn. 4to. Disbnd. From Honeyman Collection. (S. Nov.11; 2661) *Zeitlin.* £150

RIO DE JANEIRO
– Contrato Novo Dos Direytos dos Escravos, que vam Paras Minas do Porto do Rio de Janeyro, que le Fez no Concelho Ultra-marino, com Jeronymo Lobo Guimaraes, por Tempo de Tres Annos. [Lisbon], [1725?]. Fo. Sm. burnhole affecting several letters in 1st. lf., marginal annots. Mod. cf. (SPB. May 5; 435) $250
– Decreto. Exigindo as Circunstancias em que se acha a Monarchia justas y Adecuadas Providencias para consolidar a Throno ... [Rio de Janeiro], 1821. Sm. fo. 2 ll., fold reprd. Unbnd. (SPB. May 5; 437) $125
– Relacao dos Publicas Festejas que tiverão lugar do I. de Abril até 9. Pelo Feliz Regresso de SS. MM. II., e A.I. voltando da Bahia a Corte Imperial do Rio de Janeiro. Rio de Janeiro, 1826. Slight discolouration, orig. ptd. wraps. (stained) bnd. in. Mott.cf. (SPB. May 5; 436) $275

RIOLAN
[–] Gigantologie. Histoire de la Grandeur des Géants. Paris, 1618. Sig. on title of Jean Ballesdens, dtd. 1675, bibliophile. 18th. C. red mor. by Derome le Jeune with his ticket, triple gt. fillet, flat spine gt. with single fleuron in compartments, inner gt. dentelles. (SM. Oct.8; 1969) Frs. 2,900

RIOLAN, Jean, the Younger
– Schola Anatomica Novis et Raris Observationibus Illustrata. Geneva, 1624. A few ll. stained, slight marginal worming, inscr. on title 'Ex Libris Huberti Barbier Doctoris medici 1687'.

Cont. limp vell. bds., lacks ties. (S. Jun.29; 298) *Bennett.* £50

RIORDAN DE MUSCRY, D.
See–MENTET DE SALMONET, Robert & Riordan de Muscry, D.

RIOU, Stephen
[–] The Grecian Orders of Architecture. 1768. 1st Edn. Fo. Some browning & slight soiling. Hf. cf., rebkd. (S. Dec.9; 465) *Weinreb.* £180

RIPA, Cesare
– Iconologia. Ill.:– I. Fuller & others. 1709. 1st. Engl. Edn. 4to. Mott. cf. gt. by F. Bedford. (S. Nov.24; 249) *Quaritch.* £220

RIPALDA, Geronymo de
– Catecismo Mexicano ... Mexico, 1758. 1st. Edn. of this trans. Corner of title torn & reprd., worming in inner margin spreading to text, lacks last lf. (possibly advts.?) Cont. Spanish cf., spine defect. (C. Apr.1; 78) *Cavendish.* £60
– – Anr. Edn. Trans.:– Ignacio de Paredes, S.J. Mexico, 1758. Stp. on verso of frontis., text in Spanish & Nahuatl, sm. restoration to border of title, slightly soiled. Mod. vell. bds. (SPB. May 5; 439) $650
– – Anr. Copy. 16mo. (in 4's). Title-p. soiled Later hf. roan. (SG. Jan.8; 294) $260
– – Anr. Copy. Lacks copperplt. port. of St. Francis Xavier, ll. Y & Y2 have outer lr. corner torn away, with loss of a few words, photostats of the pp. are laid in, index lf. laid in, presumably from anr. copy. Cont. vell., leath. ties (lacks 1). (SG. Mar.5; 313) $100

RIPLEY, S. Dillon
– Rails of the World. Toronto, 1977. (400). Fo. 1 litho. laid in. Hf. mor., s.-c. (S. Jun.1; 196) *White.* £120

RIPLEY, S. Dillon & Scribner, Lynette L.
– Ornithological Books in the Yale University Library ... New Haven, 1961. Buckram. (SG. Jan.22; 318) $150

RIPPENHAUSEN, E.
– Sammlungen mit 149 Rokoko-Modekupfern. Late 18th. C. 4to. Some plts. dtd. 1785-1790, slightly soiled in parts. 19th. C. hf. leath. (R. Mar.31-Apr.4; 1571) DM 500

RISE OF LEARNING (The), or Ground-Work of Science, Shewing how Good Boys & Girls, by attending to the Rules may acquire Wisdom, Riches & Honour, by Mrs. Winlove
Edinb., 1819. 12mo. Orig. ptd. wraps., backstrip partly split., ill. on lr. cover. (SH. Mar.19; 277) *Maggs.* £55

RISE & Progress of the Game of Billiards
N.Y., 1860. 12mo. Ptd. wraps. (SG. Dec.11; 176) $130

RISSO, A.
– Histoire Naturelle des Principales Productions de l'Europe Meridionale et Particulièrement de Celles des Environs de Nice et des Alpes Maritimes. Paris, 1826. 5 vols. Some spotting. Cont. mott. cf., recently rebkd. with new end-papers. (TA. Jan.18; 157) £325

RIST, Joh.
[–] Das Friedewünschende Teutschland. Hamburg, 1649. 1st. sigs. lightly soiled. Cont. hf. leath. gt. (HK. May 15; 4782) DM 2,300

RITCHIE, Leitch
– Wanderings by the Seine. Ill.:– after J.M.W. Turner. 1834-35. 2 vols. Orig. mor., 1 spine worn. (SH. May 28; 191) *Crete.* £65

RITI NUZIALI DEGLI ANTICHI ROMANI PER LE NOZZE di ... Giovanni Lambertini con ... Lucrezia Savorgnan
Bologna, 1762. Fo. Mod. hf. vell. (SI. Dec.4; 499) Lire 220,000

RITSON, Joseph
[–] A Select Collection of English Songs. Ill.:– William Blake & others. L., 1783. 1st. Edn. 3 vols. Cont. mott. cf., gt.-decor. spines. (SG. May 14; 183) $400
[–] – Anr. Copy. Cont. tree cf., some covers detchd. (SG. Feb.5; 289) $130

RITTER, C.
– The Comparative Geography of Palestine & the Sinaitic Peninsula. Edinb., 1866. 4 vols. Orig. cl., spines worn, mostly unopened. (SH. Nov.7; 434) *Chesterman.* £60

- **Die Erdkunde.** Berlin, 1822-59. Pts. 1-19 in 21 vols. & 2 index vols. Some titles stpd. & with MS. entries, lightly browned & slightly soiled in parts. Cont. hf. leath. gt., slightly rubbed. W.a.f. (HK. Nov.18-21; 1353) DM 550

RITTER, Georges
- **Les Vitraux de la Cathédrale de Rouen.** Cognac, 1926. Tall fo. Loose in hf. cl. folder with linen ties. From the liby. of Clement Heaton. (SG. Mar.12; 349) $250

RITTER Pontus von Adelichen Tugenten
N.p., [1548]. Sm. fo. Lacks prelims. (excepting 1 lf. of the Vorrede), some heavy dampstains. Later bds. (SG. May 21; 364) $100

RITTER-PLATZ Geoffnete (Der)
Hamburg, 1706-11. 20 pts. in 3 vols. 12mo. Slightly spotted or browned in places. Vols. I & III cont. vell. bds., vol. II cont. cf. (S. Jun.1; 40) *Leisten Books.* £260

RIVE, Abbé Jean Joseph
[-] **La Chasse aux Bibliographes et Antiquaires mal-advisés . . . par un des Elèves que M. l'Abbé Rive a laissés dans Paris.** L., 1789. 2 vols. 2nd. title in vol. 1 mntd. & partly detchd. Cont. red hf.-mor., red glazed bds., flat spines gt. in compartments, partly unc., wormholes in spines. (SM. Oct.7; 1487) Frs. 1,600

RIVERA, Diego & Wolfe, Bertram D.
- **Portrait of America.** N.Y., [1934]. Cl. Sigd. (SG. Oct.23; 302) $210

RIVERO, Mariano Eduardo de & Tschudi, Juan Diego de
- **Antiguedades Peruanas.** Vienna, 1851. 2 vols. including atlas vol. 4to & atlas fo. Orig. bds., spine of 1 vol. stained. [Sabin 71642] (C. Feb.25; 131) *Burton-Garbett.* £800
- - **Anr. Copy.** Atlas vol. only. Ob. fo. Margin of plt. 53 cleanly torn, slight spotting. Orig. cl.-bkd. bds., soiled. (CSK. Jan.30; 14) £200
- - **Anr. Copy.** 2 vols. 4to, Atlas ob. fo. Upr. blank margins slightly damp defect., some spotted or soiled. Orig. ptd. bds., atlas worn & contents loose. (SPB. May 5; 440) $800

RIVERS, Augustus Henry Lane Fox Pitt
See—FOX, Augustus Henry Lane, afterwards Rivers, A.H.L. Fox Pitt

RIVERSIDE Press—HOUGHTON Mifflin & Co.
- **Specimens of Type, Ornaments, Borders, & Corners.–A Sketch of the Firm of . . .; Catalogue for 1889-90.** Camb.; n.p.; n.p., 1887; 1889; [1889]. 3 works in 1 vol. Three-qtr. mor. (SG. Mar.26; 387) $110

RIVIERA, Cesare della
- **Il Magico Mondo de gli Heroi.** Mantua, 1603. 4to. Vell. (S. Dec.1; 367) *Pythagoras.* £160

RIVIERE, Georges
- **Le Maître Paul Cezanne.** Ill.:– Cezanne. Paris, 1923. 1st. Edn. Buckram, cold. pict. wrap. bnd. in. (SG. Oct.23; 51) $150
- **Renoir & ses Amis.** 1921. 4to. Cl. (P. Feb.19; 317) *Phillips.* £90

RIVIERE, Henri
- **Les Trente-Six Vues de la Tour Eiffel.** 1888-1902. (500). Ob. 4to. Publisher's decor. bds., s.-c. (HD. Jun.25; 387) Frs. 8,000

RIVIERE, P.–Louis Poh-Deng
- **Scènes de la Vie Siamoise.** Ill.:– H. de la Nésière. Paris, 1913. (50) on Jap. 4to. Black state. Mor. gt. by Affotter, mor. doubls., interlacing geometrical gt. border, orig. wraps. bnd. in, s.-c. (SM. Oct.8; 2367) Frs. 1,500

RIVINUS, August Quirinus
- **Introductio Generalis in rem Herbariam.** Leipzig, 1690. 2 vols. (only, of 6) in 1. Lacks general title, some discolouration thro.-out. 19th. C. hf. mor. W.a.f., from Chetham's Liby., Manchester. (C. Nov.27; 343) *Lester.* £100

RIVIRIUS, J.N.
See—ARISTOTELES–RIVIRIUS, J.N.

RIZZETTI, Conte Luigi
- **Riforma de' Carri di Quattro Ruote.** Trevigi, Priv. Ptd., 1785. 1st. Edn. Cont. limp bds., vell. spine, unc. (SG. Feb.12; 140) $325

RIZZI-ZANNONI, Giovanni Antonio
- **Atlas Géographique.** Paris, 1762. 24mo. Cont. red mor., jnts. & covers slightly worn. (SPB. Jul.28; 355) $225

- **Atlas Géographique et Militaire.** Paris, [1763]. 16mo. 4 p. publisher's catalogue, dtd. 1763. Cont. red mor., gt. borders, spine gt. with floral design. (SG. Nov.20; 106) $100

ROBAUT, Alfred
- **L'Oeuvre Complet de Eugène Delacroix.** Ed.:– [Ernest Chesneau]. Paris, 1885. [1st. Edn?]. 4to. Slight foxing. Cont. hf. mor. (S. Jul.27; 182) *Nakajima.* £100
- - **Anr. Copy.** Hf. leath. (HK. Nov.18-21; 3320) DM 750
- - **Anr. Copy.** 4to. Hf. leath., slightly worn. (H. May 21/22; 90) DM 620

ROBBE, Jacques
- **Methode Pour Apprendre Facilement la Géographie.** Paris, 1771. 2 vols. Various maps. No bdg. stated. (JN. Apr.2; 807) £72

ROBBERDS, J.W.
See—STARK, James & Robberds, J.W.

ROBERT-HOUDIN, Jean Eugène
- **Memoirs of Robert-Houdin, Ambassador, Author & Conjuror.** 1859. 1st. Engl. Edn. 2 vols. Orig. cl., worn. (SH. Oct.23; 189) *Meyer.* £70
- **The Secrets of Conjuring & Magic.** Ed.:– 'Professor Hoffman', A.J. Lewis. 1878. 1st. Engl. Edn. Orig. pict. cl. gt., worn. (SH. Oct.23; 88) *Tigner.* £80

ROBERT DE VAUGONDY, [Giles & Didier]
- **Abregé des Differens Systèmes du Monde; de la Sphere, et des Usages des Globes.** Paris, 1745. Cont. cf. (S. Dec.2; 764) *Dix.* £50
- **Atlas Universel.** Paris, 1757. Lge. 4to. Engraved pict. title, 108 double-p. engraved maps, hand-cold. in outl., mntd. on guards, 5pp. subscribers list. Old cf., worn. W.a.f. (C. Jul.15; 94) *Wilson.* £3,000
- - **Anr. Edn.** Paris, 1757 [-58]. 1st. Edn. Lge. fo. A few maps lightly browned, 4 maps with sm. tears. Cont. leath. gt., 1 corner slightly defect. (R. Mar.31-Apr.4; 2329) DM 7,500
- - **Anr. Edn.** Ed.:– C.F. Delamarche. Paris, [1785-99]. Lge. fo. Lacks 3 maps, engraved title soiled, approx. 40 maps with corrections & tears bkd., slightly stained thro.-out, especially in last part. Newer hf. leath., worn. (H. Dec.9/10; 451) DM 6,400

ROBERTI, Gaudenzio
- **Miscellanea Italica Physico-Mathematica.** Bologna, 1692. 1st. Edn. 4to. Some staining in fore-margins, C4 torn in fore-margin, single wormhole in first 2 ll., inscr. on title. Cont. limp. vell. From Honeyman Collection. (S. Nov.11; 2663) *Zeitlin.* £260

ROBERTS, Dr. A.
- **The Birds of South Africa.** Ill.:– N.C.K. Lighton. L., 1940. (125) sigd. by author & artist. Hf. mor. (SSA. Jan.22; 334) R. 170
- **The Mammals of South Africa.** Johannesburg, 1951. 4to. Cl., d.-w. torn. (SSA. Jun.18; 245) R. 150
- - **Anr. Copy.** Orig. bdg., d.-w. (VA. Jan.30; 301) R. 120

ROBERTS, Alexander
- **A Treatise of Witchcraft.** 1616. 4to. Sm. hole in E3 affecting 2 words, worming in last lf. infilled slightly affecting text, some slight stains. Cf. gt. by Roger de Coverly, covers loose, spine worn. [STC 21075] (C. Nov.20; 274) *Maggs.* £300

ROBERTS, C.H.
See—BELL, H.I. & Roberts, C.H.

ROBERTS, David
- **Egypt & Nubia.** L., 1846. [Vol. I only]. Fo. First 16 plts. of Vol. II bnd. in, lacks frontis. & litho. title for Vol. II, foxed & stained. 19th. C. hf. mor., worn. (SPB. May 6; 244) $850
- - **Anr. Edn.** Ed.:– William Brockendon. Ill.:– L. Haghe after Roberts. 1846-49. 3 vols. Lge. fo. Lithos. mntd. as originals, 2 plts. detchd. in vol. 1. Cont. maroon mor., only 1 side with elab. gt. panels, spines gt., bdgs. becoming detchd. (C. Nov.5; 131) *Marshall.* £6,000
- - **Anr. Copy.** Occasional foxing. Cont. maroon hf. roan, gt. (C. Nov.5; 132) *Asmail.* £2,200
- - **Anr. Copy.** Vol. 1 bnd. in 1 bnd. vol. & 5 orig. unstitched pts. (nos. XI-XVIII). Occasional minor foxing. Cont. hf. mor., gt. & cl.-bkd. ptd. wraps., soiled & torn. (C. Feb.25; 132) *Burgess.* £1,800
- - **Anr. Copy.** 3 vols. in 2. A few plts. spotted. (SH. May 21; 190) *Russell.* £1,050
- - **Anr. Copy.** 3 vols. Slightly foxed. Mor. gt. (SPB. May 6; 245) $4,500

- - **Anr. Copy.** 3 vols. in 2. Sm. liby. stp. on plts. & title-p. Orig. three-qtr. mor., brkn. & worn. (SG. May 14; 185) $3,800
- - **Anr. Edn.** 1849. Vols. II & III. Fo. 55 plts. only (of 79), all mntd., a few ll. slightly spotted. Cont. hf. mor. (SH. Nov.7; 439) *Irani.* £3,200
- - **Anr. Copy.** Vol. 2 only (of 3). Cold. litho. title, engraved map, 42 cold. lithos. Cont. maroon hf. mor., gt. W.a.f. (C. Mar.18; 95) *Burgess.* £1,700
- **Egypt & Nubia.–The Holy Land . . .** L., ca. 1840. 1st. work vols. 1 & 3, 2nd. work, pts. 1 & 2, together 3 vols. Atlas fo. 1st. work, vol. 1, 43 plts., vol. 3, 37 (of 38) plts., 2nd. work, pts. of vols. 1 & 2 comprising plts. 35-83, lacks numbers 43, 44, 80 & 81, together 125 cold. litho. plts. mntd. on stiff bds. Cont. red mor. gt., worn, partly loose. (SG. Oct.30; 305) $13,000
- **The Holy Land, Syria, Idumea, Arabia & c.** Ed.:– Rev. George Croly. Ill.:– L. Haghe after Roberts. 1842. Vol. 1 only (of 3). Lge. fo. Lithos. cold. & mntd. as originals, port. of author detchd. Cont. maroon mor., sides with elab. gt. panels, spines gt., bdg. loose & becoming detchd. (C. Nov.5; 127) *Colnaghi.* £5,400
- - **Anr. Copy.** 3 vols. Some foxing & staining. 19th. C. hf. mor. gt., worn. (SPB. May 6; 246) $4,500
- - **Anr. Edn.** 1842-43. Proof copy on thicker paper. Vols. I & II only. Fo. Some ll. spotted. Cont. hf. mor. (SH. Nov.7; 435) *Walford.* £1,500
- - **Anr. Edn.** Ed.:– Rev. George Croly. Ill.:– L. Haghe. 1842-45. Orig. 20 pts. (in 18). Lge. fo. Port., cold. litho. titles to vols. 1 & 2, 120 cold. mntd. lithos. Loose in orig. roan-bkd. cl. fescicules, gt. (C. May 20; 167) *Joseph.* £12,000
- - **Anr. Copy.** 3 vols. in 2. Without map & title to vol. 3, sm. blind-stp. on plts. in vol. 2. 19th. C. hf. mor. From Chetham's Liby., Manchester. (C. Nov.27; 344) *Homasei.* £2,500
- - **Anr. Edn.** Ed.:– Rev. George Croly & William Brockendon. 1842-[46]. 20 orig. pts. in 18. Fo. Without Egypt & Nubia, without map. Loose, orig. mor.-bkd. folders gt. Subscribers proof copy, w.a.f. (SBA. Oct.21; 100) *Lester.* £13,000
- - **Anr. Edn.** Ed.:– George Croly. Ill.:– L. Haghe after Roberts. 1842-49. 20 orig. pts. in 18. Fo. 113 (of 120) litho. views, cold. & mntd. as orig., 1 plt. with short tear in edge, lacks plts. 4, 8, 26, 34, 36, 55, 59. Loose in roan-bkd. orig. cl. fescicules, gt. W.a.f. (C. Feb.25; 133) *Hoare.* £12,500
- - **Anr. Copy.** 6 vols. in 4. A few ll. slightly spotted. Cont. hf. mor., gt. (SH. Nov.7; 438) *Irani.* £4,200
- - **Anr. Copy.** 6 vols. Plts. on guards thro.-out, some ll. slightly spotted. (SBA. Oct.21; 99) *Burgess.* £3,800
- - **Anr. Copy.** 3 vols. Occasional foxing. Cont. hf. roan, gt. (C. Nov.5; 128) *Asmail.* £2,100
- - **Anr. Copy.** Vols. I-III, V & VI only. Spotted, 3 vols. dampstained. Cont. hf. mor., worn, loose. (SH. Nov.7; 437) *Heald.* £1,150
- - **Anr. Copy.** 3 vols. in 2. 124 litho. plts. only including 2 titles (of 3) & port., lacks map, 1 lf. loose, spotted. Cont. mor. (SH. May 21; 191) *Ayres.* £1,000
- - **Anr. Copy.** Sm. liby. stp. on plts. Orig. three-qtr. mor., very worn & brkn. (SG. May 14; 186) $4,800
- - **Anr. Edn.** 1855. 6 vols. in 3. 4to. Some spotting. Cont. mor., gt. (SH. Nov.7; 440) *Walford.* £500
- - **Anr. Copy.** (P. Jan.22; 71) *Leverton.* £420
- - **Anr. Copy.** Hf. leath., worn. (S. Mar.17; 389) *Bailey.* £320
- - **Anr. Copy.** 4to. Minor internal foxing. Loose in cont. hf. mor., gt. decor spines. (TA. Jan.22; 359) £300
- - **Anr. Copy.** 2 vols. (only) in 1. Occasional slight spotting. Cont. hf. mor., slightly dampstained. (CSK. Sep.26; 22) £60
- - **Anr. Edn.** Ed.:– Rev. George Croly. 1855-56. 6 vols. in 2. 4to. Cont. maroon mor., gt. panel. sides, spines gt. (C. May 20; 165) *Hancock.* £550
- - **Anr. Copy.** 6 vols. in 3. 250 litho. plts., later hand colouring, some ll. spotted. Cont. hf. mor., gt. spines. (SH. May 21; 192) *Winer.* £500
- - **Anr. Copy.** Some plts. & maps loose or spotted. Cont. hf. mor. (SH. Jun.18; 110) *Frick.* £380
- - **Anr. Copy.** 4 vols. in 2 (of 6), lacks vols. 1 & 2. Tinted litho. titles, 2 engraved maps, 157 tinted litho. plts. Cont. russ. W.a.f. (C. May 20; 166) *Kassis.* £300
- - **Anr. Copy.** 6 vols. in 3. Cont. mor., gt. fillet borders, inner dentelles, spines gt. in 6 compartments. (SG. Oct.9; 209) $2,200

ROBERTS, David -contd.
- - **Anr. Copy.** Map on plt. 212 misbnd., foxed. Mor. gt. (SPB. May 6; 247) $750
- - **Anr. Edn.** [Vols. I-II] L., [Vol. III] N.Y., [Vols. IV-VI] L., 1855-56; n.d.; 1855-56. 6 vols. in 3. 4to. Minor browning. Hf. mor. gt. (SPB. May 6; 248) $1,000
- - **Anr. Edn.** Ed.:- Rev. George Croly. L., n.d. 3 vols. in 2. 4to. 120 tinted litho. plts. Cont. hf. mor. (C. Jul.15; 132)   Dewar. £240
- - **Anr. Copy.** 3 vols. in 1. Title of vol. 1 detchd. Orig. cl., slightly soiled, upr. jnt. slightly holed. (CSK. Jan.23; 174)   £170
- - **Anr. Copy.** 3 vols. only (of 6). 1 litho. plt. stained. Cont. mor., gt. (CSK. Aug.22; 17)   £120
- - **Anr. Copy.** Some foxing, stains. Hf. mor., stains. (SPB. May 29; 372) $275
- **Picturesque Sketches in Spain.** 1837. Fo. 26 plts., some tears. Cont. mor.-bkd. cl., worn, loose. (SH. Jul.16; 116)   Duran. £230
- - **Anr. Edn.** [1837]. Lge. 4to. 26 litho. plts., cold. & mntd. on card. Loose in cont. mor.-bkd. cl. portfo., ties, spine reprd. (C. Mar.18; 156)
                                          Rodgers. £800
- - **Anr. Copy.** Lacks text & dedication. (C. May 20; 164)   Davidson. £700
- - **Anr. Edn.** N.d. Fo. 4 page prospectus (dtd. 1837) giving description of plts. bnd. in after dedication lf. Cont. mor.-bkd. cl., disbnd. (CSK. Aug.1; 135)   £380
- **La Terre Sainte, Vues & Monuments.** Brussels, 1843. Fo. Cont. hf. mor. (C. Mar.18; 93)
                                          Cohen. £650
- - **Anr. Copy.** Foxed thro.-out. Cont. cf., sides with elab. gt. & blind tooled borders, by Schaefer R. de la Reine. (C. Mar.18; 94)   Lester. £600
- - **Anr. Copy.** Cont. hf. leath., linen box. (HK. Nov.18-21; 1038)   DM 1,400
- **Views in Spain: comprising Granada & Andalusia, with the Palace of the Alhambra.** 1836. Fo. Plts. from Jennings' Landscape Annuals for 1835 & 1836. Cont. hf. mor., soiled. (CSK. Nov.21; 154)   £85

ROBERTS, Col. David
[-] **The Military Adventures of Johnny Newcombe.** Ill.:- Thomas Rowlandson. 1815. Disbnd. (P. Feb.19; 28)   Rostron. £90
- - **Anr. Edn.** Ill.:- Thomas Rowlandson. L., 1816. 2nd. Edn. 15 hand-cold. plts., wtrmkd. 1812, margin of p.66 torn away & renewed. Mor. gt., spine gt. (CNY. May 22; 255) $100

ROBERTS, Emma
See-ELLIOTT, Commander Robert & Roberts, Emma

ROBERTS, Capt. Joseph-[MAURY, D.H.]
- **The Hand Book of Artillery.-Skirmish Drill for Mounted Troops.** Richmond, 1861. 12mo. Orig. limp cl. (SG. Jan.8; 110) $250

ROBERTS, Lewis
- **The Merchants Mappe of Commerce.** 1638. 1st. Edn. Fo. Sm. rust hole in last lf. affecting 2 letters, cont. sig. of George Legatt on end-paper. Cont. cf. [STC 21094] (C. Feb.25; 169)   Traylen. £2,100
- - **Anr. Edn.** 1700. 4th. Edn. Fo. Soiled & slightly dampstained. Cf.-bkd. bds. [Wing R1601] (CSK. Mar.6; 49)   £60

ROBERTS, Peter
- **The Cambrian Popular Antiquities.** 1815. 10 plts., 9 cold., lacks hf.-title, dedication & advts. Hf. cf. (C. Jul.15; 95)   Taylor. £90

ROBERTS, Thomas S.
- **The Birds of Minnesota.** 1932. 1st. Edn. 2 vols. 4to. Orig. cl. (SH. Jul.23; 34)   Lenton. £50
- - **Anr. Copy.** Cl. gt., damp-spotted. (PNY. Dec.3; 47) $150
- - **Anr. Copy.** Orig. bdg. Pres. Copy with inscr. to Stanley A. Mickel in vol. 1, both vols sigd. (CB. Sep.24; 44)   Can. $150

ROBERTSON, A.S.
- **Roman Imperial Coins in the Hunter Coin Cabinet.** 1962-71. 2 vols. Orig. cl. (SH. Mar.6; 432)   Trade Art. £280

ROBERTSON, Archibald
- **A Topographical Survey of the Great Road from London to Bath & Bristol.** 1792. 2 vols. Plt. imprints cropped, some offsetting onto text, stp. of the Schlossbibliothek Dessau on verso of titles. Cont. str.-grd. mor., gt. (S. Jun.22; 85)
                                          Quaritch. £260
- - **Anr. Edn.** N.d. 1st. Edn. 2 vols. 19th. C. hf. vell. & marb. bds. (PJ. Jun.6 ('80); 117)   £200

ROBERTSON, David
- **A Tour through the Isle of Man.** Priv. ptd., 1794. L.P. Cont. tree cf., gt., slightly worn. (SBA. Oct.22; 764)   Chesters. £76

ROBERTSON, Edward Graeme & Craig, Edith N.
- **Early Houses of Northern Tasmania.** Melbourne, 1964. (1000) numbered, sigd. by authors. 2 vols. 4to. No bdg. stated. (JL. Dec.15; 633)   Aus. $320

ROBERTSON, George
- **Ayrshire Families.** 1823-27. 4 vols. Extra data in Vol. IV. Hf. red mor. gt. Pres. inscr. to James Dobie. (CE. Nov.20; 187)   £210
- **Description of Ayrshire.** 1820. Folding map. Marb. bds., worn. (CE. Dec.4; 57)   £62
See-CRAWFURD, George & Robertson, George

ROBERTSON, Mrs. Hannah
- **The Young Ladies School of Arts.** Edinb., 1766. Cf.-bkd. bds. (PD. May 20; 109)   £70

ROBERTSON, J.C. & Byerley T.
[-] **The Percy Anecdotes. Original & Select by Shotto & Reuben Percy.** 1823. 40 pts. in 20 vols. 12mo. A few pts. without their individual titles, (not called for?). 19th. C. hf. mor. (CSK. Sep.19; 182)   £65

ROBERTSON, John, Librarian
- **The Elements of Navigation.** 1796. 2 vols. Slight browning, sm. hole in P1, vol. II. Cont. cf., very worn. (S. Apr.6; 229)   Talerman. £55

ROBERTSON, Robert
- **Observations on the Jail, Hospital or Ship Fever.** 1783. Cont. cf. (P. Apr.9; 312)   Kossow. £70

ROBERTSON, W.
See-FLAXMAN, J. & Robertson, W.
See-GYFFORD, E.-ROBERTSON, W.

ROBERTSON, Walford Graham
- **French Songs of Old Canada.** L., 1904. (350) numbered. Fo. Some occasional foxing. Orig. gt.-lettered cl. spine & paper bds. (CB. Feb.18; 156)   Can. $260

ROBERTSON, Dr. William
- **L'Histoire de l'Amérique.** Paris, 1778. 1st. Edn. in Fr. 2 vols. 4to. Cont. cf., spines gt. (SG. Mar.5; 391) $110
- **Histoire du Règne de l'Empereur Charles-Quint. -Histoire de l'Ecosse.-Recherches Historiques sur l'Inde Ancienne.** 1817; 1821; 1821. 4, 3 & 1 vol. Hf. strawberry cf., blind ornamental spines, by Thouvenin. Marquis de Lespine liby. (HD. Oct.10; 279)   Frs. 2,100
- **The History of America.** L., 1777. 1st. Edn. Books 1-8 in 2 vols. 4to. Tree cf. [Sabin 71973] (SPB. Jun.22; 121) $125
- - **Anr. Edn.** 1777. 2 vols. Cont. cf. (SH. May 21; 101)   Cooley. £60
- **A Tour through the Isle of Man.** 1794. 1st. Edn., L.P. Some spotting. Cont. cf., rebkd., covers worn. With seditous passage later supressed. (CSK. Oct.24; 94)   £70
- **Works.** 1851. 6 vols. Port. offset. Mor., slightly marked, spines gt. (SKC. Feb.26; 1473)   £50

ROBERTSON, William & Flaxman, John
- **Anatomical Studies of the Bones & Muscles for the Use of Artists.** Ill.:- after John Flaxman. 1833. 1st. Edn. Fo. Some plts. dampstained, spotted. Cont. bds., worn. (SH. Jun.11; 72)   Tropper. £55
- - **Anr. Copy.** Some spotting. Cl. (SH. Jun.25; 168)   Tropper. £50

ROBERTUS, Anglicus
[-] **Astrolabii quo primo mobilis motus deprehenduntur Canones.** Venice, 1512. 4to. Bnd. in fragment of 14th. C. Italian medical MS. on vell. over bds. From Honeyman Collection. [BMC V, 458] (S. Nov.11; 2664)   Hill. £440

ROBERVAL, Gilles Personne de
- **Traite de Machenique, des Poids soustenus par des Puissances sur les Plans inclinez a l'horizon.** Paris, 1636. 1st. Edn. Fo. Marginal repair to C5, some browning & marginal staining. Old mott. vell. Stp. of Charles-Marie de la Condamine; from Honeyman Collection. (S. Nov.11; 2665)
                                          Brieux. £240

ROBESPIERRE, Maximilien Marie Isidore
- **Le Comité de Salut Public à la Convention Nationale.** Paris, 1794. 2 vols. in 1. Lightly soiled thro.-out. Later hf. linen, worn. (H. May 21/22; 555a)   DM 420

ROBIDA, Albert
- **Poèmes et Ballades du Temps Passé.** Ed.:- Jules de Marthold (preface). Paris, 1902. (115). 4to. Orig. sigd. watercolour on hf.-title, 2 pencil drawings. Marb. Bradel hf. roan, corners, wrap. & spine. A.Ls., dtd., Jules de Marthold's copy. (HD. Jun.25; 389)   Frs. 1,200

ROBINEAU, A.L.B.
- **Voyage sur le Rhin, depuis Mayence jusqu'à Dusseldorf.** Ill.:- Cranz, Dupuis & others. Neuwied, 1791. Cont. leath., gt. spine, worn. (R. Oct.14-18; 2455)   DM 3,200

ROBINSON, Cmndr. Charles N.
- **Old Naval Prints.** 1924. Ltd. Edn. Orig. cl. gt., d.-w. (P. Mar.12; 2)   Green. £95
- - **Anr. Copy.** (1500) numbered. 4to. Gt.-lettered cl. (SG. Mar.12; 313) $160

ROBINSON, Edwin Arlington
- **The Children of the Night.** Boston, 1897. 1st. Edn., (50) on Imperial Japan vell. 12mo. Orig. ptd. paper-vell. wraps., spine slightly wrinkled, stitching tender between 3rd. & 4th. quires, qtr. mor. gt. folding case, mostly unopened. Pres. Copy, to W.S. Braithwaite, lately in the Prescott Collection. (CNY. Feb.6; 284) $1,000

ROBINSON. F. Cayley (Ill.)
See-BIBLIANA [English]

ROBINSON, Henry Crabb
- **Diary, Reminiscences & Correspondence.** Ed.:- Thomas Sadler. L., 1869. 3 vols. extended to 9. Extra-ill. with plts., ports. & india proofs, some foxing & browning. Red mor. by R.W. Smith, some mildew. (SPB. Nov.25; 483) $225

ROBINSON, Herbert Chris
- **The Birds of the Malay Peninsular.** L., 1927-39. 4 vols. 4to. Orig. cl. (CB. Sep.24; 45)   Can. $600

ROBINSON, Mary
- **Memoirs of the late Mrs. Robinson, written by herself.** 1801. 1st. Edn. 4 vols. 12mo. Orig. bds. (new labels?), unc., in mor.-bkd. s.-c. (C. Feb.4; 83)   Mackenzie. £55

ROBINSON, Peter Frederick
- **Rural Architecture; Or, A Series of Designs for Ornamental Cottages.** 1836. 4th. Edn. 4to. Margins discold. Cont. qtr. mor., slightly worn. (TA. Mar.19; 297)   £55

ROBINSON, Thomas
[-] **The Anatomie of the English Nunnery at Lisbon in Portugal.** 1623. 2nd. Edn. 4to. Hole in last lf. reprd., affecting several words, rules at head of title & elsewhere cropped or shaved. Mor. by Rivière. From the collection of Eric Sexton. [STC 21124] (C. Apr.15; 144)   Lyon. £380

ROBINSON, William
- **Gravetye Manor.** 1911. Fo. Orig. vell. with ties, partly untrimmed, soiled. A.Ls. from author. (TA. Jun.18; 35)   £55

ROBINSON, William-NELSON, John-PARK, John James
- **The History & Antiquities of the Parish of Tottenham.-The History, Topography & Antiquities of the Parish of St. Mary.-The Topography . . . of Hampstead.** 1840; 1811; 1814. 2 vols.; 1 vol.; 1 vol. 8vo.; 4vo.; 8vo. Hand-cold. folding maps in 1st. work mntd. on linen, 2nd. work with 28 extra ills., & MS. plt. list by W. Boyne. 1st. work: cont. cf. gt., panel spines: 2nd. work: 19th. C. hf. mor. gt.; 3rd. work: cont. hf. cf. From the collection of Eric Sexton. (C. Apr.16; 342)   Traylen. £240

ROBINSON, William E.
- **'Chung Ling Soo' Spirit Slate Writing & Kindred Phenomena.** N.Y., 1898. 1st. Edn. Orig. pict. cl., worn. (SH. Oct.24; 403)   Masters. £120

ROBINSON, William Heath
- **Absurdities.** [1934]. (250) numbered, sigd. by artist. 4to. Orig. hf. roan gt. (S. Jul.31; 307)
                                          Joseph. £85
- **Bill the Minder.** 1912. 4to. Orig. cl. gt., stained & worn. (S. Jul.31; 305)   Joseph. £50
- **Humours of Golf.** 1923. 1st. Edn. 4to. Margins slightly browned. Later cl. (TA. Mar.19; 337)
                                          £56

ROBLES, Lucas de
- **Sermon del Dulcissimo nombre de Maria, que predico en la Cathedral de la Ciudad del Cuzco.** Lima, [1653]. Sm. 4to. 1st. & last ll. preserved, sidenotes cropped, pt. of title border trimmed

ROBLEY, Augusta J.
- **A Selection of Madeira Flowers.** 1845. Fo. 8 hand-cold. litho. plts., all ll. detchd. in gutta-percha bdg. Orig. embossed cl. gt. (C. Jul.15; 200) *Pillar.* £300
- - **Anr. Copy.** Slightly soiled. Orig. linen, blind-stpd. upr. cover with decor. figure, end-ll. renewed. (HK. May 12-14; 417) DM 700

ROBLEY, Maj.-Gen. Horatio Gordon
- **Moko.** L., 1896. 1st. Edn. 4to. Orig. cl. (P. Jul.2; 84) *Elliott.* £80

ROBSON, Albert H.
- **Canadian Landscape Painters.** Toronto, [1932]. Ills. mntd. thro.-out. Orig. cl., light spotting. (CB. Nov.12; 117) Can. $100

ROBSON, George Fennell
- **Scenery of the Grampian Mountains.** 1819. Fo. Orig. gt.-lettered ribbed cl., slightly worn. From the collection of Eric Sexton. (C. Apr.16; 343) *Traylen.* £390
See-BRITTON, J. & Robson, George Fennell

ROBSON, Joseph
- **An Account of Six Years Residence in Hudson's-Bay, From 1733 to 1738, & 1744 to 1747.** L., 1752. 1st. Edn. Browned & stained. 19th. C. hf. cf., new end-papers. From liby. of William E. Wilson. [Sabin 72259] (SPB. Apr.29; 239) $500

ROCA, Antich
- **Arithmetica ... de varios Auctores recopilada ... Va anadido un Compendio, para tener y regir los Libros de Cuenta.** Barcelona, 1565. 2 pts. in 1 vol. Lacks 1st. lf. (blank?), N1 wormed & inserted from a shorter copy, title stained & with heavily deleted inscr., 2nd. pt. wormed in lr. margins at end, some browning & staining. Cont. limp vell., worn & stained. From Honeyman Collection. (S. Nov.11; 2667) *Manning.* £55

ROCHAS, Albert de
- **Les Sentiments, la Musique, et le Geste.** Ill.:- Alphonse Mucha. Grenoble, 1900. 4to. Orig. pict. wraps., slightly worn. (SH. Nov.21; 435) *Hancock.* £50

ROCHAS, Henri de
- **La Physique Reformé, contenant la Refutation des Erreurs Populaires, et le Triomphe des Veritez Philosophiques.** Paris, 1648. 1st. Edn. 4to. Some staining, mostly marginal, lacks final lf. (blank?). Cont. cf., gt. spine, worn. From Honeyman Collection. (S. Nov.11; 2668) *Hill.* £160

ROCHE, E.
- **L'Italie de Nos Jours.** Paris, [1845]. Cl., gt. stpd. (CR. Mar.19; 471) Lire 280,000

ROCHEFORT, Charles
- **Historische Beschreibung der Antillen Inseln in America gelegen in sich begreiffend deroselben Gelegenheit ... nunmehr in die Teutsche uebersetzet.** Franckfurt. 1668. 1st. Edn. in German. Vol. 1 only. 24mo. Old vell. [Sabin 72321] (SG. Mar.5; 394) $325

ROCHESTER, John Wilmot, Earl of
- **Collected Works.** Ed.:- John Haywood. Nones. Pr., 1926. (975). Mod. mor., elab. gt., partly unc. (S. Jun.9; 8) *Sawyer.* £80

ROCHON, Alexis Marie
- **Recueil de Memoires sur la Mecanique et la Physique.** Paris, 1783. 1st. Edn. Sigs. R & Q transposed, sm. stain on title. Cont. cf.-bkd. bds. From Honeyman Collection. (S. Nov.11; 2669) *Brieux.* £320

ROCKSTUHL, A.
See-CILLE, F. & Rockstuhl, A.

ROCKWELL, Norman
- **The Album.** Garden City, 1961. Special De Luxe Edn. with a separate print in inserted envelope. Sm. fo. Mor. gt., boxed. (PNY. May 21; 360a) $110

ROCOLES, Jean Baptiste de
- **The History of Infamous Imposters.** 1683. 1st. Edn. in Engl. Cont. cf., rebkd., worn, upr. cover loose. [Wing R1766] (C. Nov.19; 36) *Blackwell.* £70

ROCQUE, John
- **An Exact Survey of the City's of London, Westminster & Borough of Southwark & Country near Ten Miles round.** Ill.:- Richard Parr (1ge. map) & J. Wallis (folding map). 1746. 1st. Edn.

Fo. Folding map reprd., mntd., & bnd. in at end, litho. map of Pimlico loosely inserted. 19th. C. hf. mor. As an atlas, w.a.f. (S. Jul.27; 41) *Crowe.* £480
- - **Anr. Copy.** Republd. by Edward Stanford, 1878, quarterised on linen, (16 sheets). Orig. cl. wallet. (TA. Oct.16; 161) £70
- - **Anr. Edn.** Ill.:- R. Parr (engraved map). [1747]. 2nd. Iss. Fo. Mod. cl. From the Collection of Eric Sexton. (C. Apr.16; 344) *Burgess.* £320
- **A Topographical Survey of the County of Berks.** Priv. Ptd., 1761. Fo. Hf. roan. (C. Nov.6; 227) *Marsden.* £240
- - **Anr. Copy.** There is no plt. numbered 15. Cont. marb. bds., cf. spine. (S. Dec.2; 865) *McAlpine.* £100

RODD, Rennell
- **Rose Leaf & Apple Leaf ...** Ed.:- Oscar Wilde (intro.). Ill.:- after J.E. Kelly. Phila., 1882. 1st. Edn., Ltd. De Luxe Iss. Ptd. on rectos only on thin H.M.P. & interleaved with tissue. Orig. vell., slightly soiled, gt. inner dentelle border, mor. gt. s.-c., partly unc. Sigd. by Wilde on upr. cover; bkplt. of Jerome Kern, lately in the Prescott Collection. (CNY. Feb.6; 365) $950
- - **Anr. Copy.** Sm. tears to end-ll. & pastedowns, qtr. mor. gt. s.-c., partly unc. Publisher's Pres. Copy, to H.H. Kimball; with 2 A.L.s. from Mosher to Stoddart, & T.L.s. to Mosher from Stoddart; from the Prescott Collection. (CNY. Feb.6; 366) $220
- - **Anr. Edn.** Portland, Thomas B. Mosher, 1906. (5) on vell., sigd. by Mosher. 12mo. Mor., s.-c. (SG. Oct.9; 172) $275

RODERICUS Zamorensis
- **Speculum Vitae Humanae.** Rome, Conradus Sweynheym & Arnoldus Pannartz, 1468. 1st. Edn. 4to. Fo. 5 with initial in burnished gold on ground of white vine decor. filled with red, blue & green, at head is added 8 line dedication to Pope Paul II in romanesque hand in red ink, 1 similar initial, other initials & paragraph marks in red & blue alternatively, 3 or 4 ll. at beginning & end with wormholes reprd. & a few letters in pen facs., 1st. & last pp. soiled, some spotting, a few marginal stains, cont. annots. Old vell. bds., wormed & stained, new end-papers. From Honeyman Collection. [BMC IV, 4; HC 13939; Goff R214] (S. Nov.11; 2670) *Jackson.* £4,000
- - **Anr. Edn.** Augsburg, Günther Zainer, 11 Jan., 1471. 2nd. Edn. Fo. Rubricated, initials on fo.'s 1 & 69 supplied in green & red respectively with red pen-work decor., a few ll. marginally stained, occasional annots. Cont. blind-stpd. cf. over wooden bds. by Ambrosius Keller of Augsburg, panel. covers in compartments with repeated tool & binder's name in a scroll, worn, chain-hole in lr. cover, 'maria'-stpd. catches, lacks clasps, hf. red mor. case. From Honeyman Collection. [BMC II, 316; HC 13940; Goff R215] (S. Nov.11; 2671) *Schoman.* £2,300
- - **Anr. Edn.** Beromunster, Helias Heliae, 30 Jul., 1473. 2nd. Edn. Fo. Spaces for initial capitals, 8-line capital S at 1st. p. illuminated in gold on red, blue & green ground, other capitals & paragraph marks supplied in red or blue, upr. corner of last lf. renewed with portion of 3 lines in facs., worming at front & back, mostly marginal, but catching some letters of text on several ll. Mor., covers & spine gt.-tooled, by Rivière. From the collection of Eric Sexton. [BMC III, 799, Goff R219, HC 13942] (CNY. Apr.8; 25) $5,200
- - **Anr. Edn.** Besançon, [Petrus Metlinger], 1488. 4to. Spaces for some initial capitals, occasionally with guide letters, some woodcut initials touched with yellow, some sm. patches & marginal repairs to first & last ll., some other ll. with minor restorations, bnd. without the additional tracts found in some copies. Mor., covers & spine blind-tooled, by Chambolle-Duru. Bkplt. of H. & A.H. Huth, bkplt. of Cortlandt F. Bishop, lately in the collection of Eric Sexton. [BMC VIII, 405, Goff R228, HC 13947] (CNY. Apr.8; 26) $2,200
- **Spejo Dela Vida Humana.** Zaragoza, Paulus Hurus, 13 May, 1491. Fo. 122 ll. (of 124), lacks title, replaced in fac. & last lf. (?blank) wormed, reprd. Mor. gt. by Brugalla, sigd. & dtd. 1944, s.-c. [H. 13954] (S. Nov.25; 339) *Quaritch.* £1,100

RODOLFI, Volumnio
- **De Proportione Proportionum Disputatio.** Rome, 1516. 1st. Edn. Sm. 4to. Slight marginal worming touching a few side-notes, 1st. quire loose. Cont.

blind-stpd. cf., very worn. From Honeyman Collection. (S. May 20; 3301) *McKittrick.* £110

RODO-PISSARRO, L. & Venturi, Lionello
- **Camille Pissarro. Son Art. Son Oeuvre.** Paris, 1939. (100). 2 vols. 4to. Publisher's decor. cl. s.-c. (HD. Dec.5; 181) Frs. 8,100

RODRIGUEZ de Almela, Diego
- **Tractado que se llama Valerio de las Estorias Escolasticas y de España.** Murcia, Lope de la Roca, 6 Dec., 1487. Fo. Spaces for initial capitals, with guide letters, lacks the 2 ll. of table at front, & f8, t8, & v1 (the latter 3 replaced with ll. f8, g4, & g1 from Roca's 'Copilacion de las Batallas'), portion of upr. corner of fo. 145 torn & reprd., lr. corner of fo. 153 torn & reprd. affecting sig., sm. stain to fo.'s 9v & 10r. Mod. blind-stpd. cf., spine gt.-lettered. From the collection of Eric Sexton. [BMC X, 72, Goff R236] (CNY Apr.8; 109) $6,000

RODRIGUEZ DELGADO, Agustin
- **Constituciones Synodales.** Lima, 1739. Fo. Pagination erratic & altered in MS., lacks frontis. Cont. limp vell. (SPB. May 5; 444) $225

RODRIGUEZ d'Oliveira, Cristovao
- [-] **Summario.** Lisbon, [1551]. 1st. Edn. 4to. Title reprd. at head & foot, & border cropped in outer margin, paper fault in D7, occasional creasing of paper & minor tears, later annots. in ink & occasional inkstains. 18th. C. spr. cf., gt. spine. (C. Nov.20; 203) *Fellner.* £200

RODRIGUEZ, J.-RICCI, Matteo
- **Litterae Japonicae Anni M.DC. VI.-[Litterae] Chinenses Anni M.DC. VI. & M.DC:VII.** Antw., 1611. 2 pts. in 1 vol. Cont. vell. (R. Oct.14-18; 1791) DM 750

RODRIGUEZ JORDAN, S.
- **Escuela de a Cavallo.** Madrid, [1751]. 4to. Engraved title & ll. slightly soiled. Cont. vell. (H. Dec.9/10; 366) DM 1,100

ROE, F. Gordon
- **Sea Painters of Britain.** Leigh-on-Sea, 1947-48. (500). 2 vols. Orig. cl., d.-w.'s. (SH. Oct.9; 97) *Tate Gallery.* £80
See-GRUNDY, C. Reginald & Roe, F.G.

ROE, Fred
- **Ancient Coffers & Cupboards.** L., 1902. 1st. Edn. 4to. Gt.-pict. buckram. (SG. Mar.12; 315) $100

ROEDERER, le Comte P.-L.
- **Mémoire ... Société polie en France.** 1835. Cont. long-grd. mor., decor. gold & silver borders & angle motif, decor. spine, silver paper end-papers & painted. 2 A.L.s. (1 dtd. 26 Nov. 1832). (HD. Feb.18; 177) Frs. 1,750

ROELOFS, W.
- **100 Lichtdrukken naar zijn Werken. Met een inl. woord d. H.P. Bremmer.** Amst., 1909. Fo. Loose in hf. cl. portfo. (VG. Dec.15; 251) Fls. 475

ROEMER, Johann Jakob
- **Genera Insectorum Linnaei et Fabricii.** Winterthur, 1789. 4to. Most plts. with pencil annots. giving Engl. Cont. hf. cf., rebkd. With bkplt. of W. Sowerby & a related cont. invoice & letter tipped in. (CSK. Oct.24; 211) £150

ROERICH, N. & Makovsky, Serge
- **Talachkino. L'Art Décoratif des Ateliers de la Princesse Ténichef.** St. Petersb., 1906. 4to. Orig. wraps., slightly torn. (SH. Feb.5; 261) *Archer.* £75
- - **Anr. Edn.** St. Petersb., 1906. Sodrougestvo Edn. 4to. Orig. pict. sewed. wraps. (D. Dec. 11-13; 488) DM 600

ROESEL von Rosenhof, Augustus Johannes
- **Historia Naturalis Ranarum Nostratium.** Nuremb., [1753]-58. Fo. Plts. in 2 states, 1 state hand-cold., frontis. offset, some light staining & discolouration of plts. 19th. C. hf. mor. From Chetham's Liby., Manchester. (C. Nov.26; 346) *Kistner.* £580
- **De Naturlijke Historie der Insecten.** Trans.:- C.F.C. Kleemann. Harlem/Amst., [1765]. 1st. Pt. (of 5). 4to. Lacks frontis. & 3 plts., many pts. loose. Bds., lacks spine. (VG. Nov.18; 1349) Fls. 1,000
- - **Anr. Edn.** Ill.:- C.F.C. Kleemann. [Harlem/Amst.], ca. 1780? 4to. Dutch, Fr. & Latin text, possibly a fragment, plts. in 2 series: of

ROESEL von Rosenhof, Augustus Johannes -contd.
40 numbered plts. & of 8 plts. In orig. bd. bdg. case, unbnd., unc. (VG. Oct.13; 136) Fls. 1,100

ROESEL von Rosenhof, Augustus Johannes -KLEEMAN, Christian Friedrich Carl
- Der Monatlich-Herausgegebenen Insecten-Belustigung.-Beytrage zur Natur-u. Insecten Geschichte. Nuremb., 1746-61; 1761-76. 1st. Edn.(1st. work). 2 works in 4 vols. 4to. Plts. hand-cold. in both works, lacks 28 pp. in 2nd. work, & 2 plts. 19th. C. hf. mor. W.a.f., from Chetham's Liby., Manchester. (C. Nov.27; 345) *Kistner.* £1,600

ROESLIN, Helisaeus
- De Opere Dei Creationis seu de Mundo Hypotheses. Frankfurt, 1597. 1st. Edn. 4to. I diagram on inserted lf. with margins cut down, cont. MS. annots. & a diagram at end staining last lf. Mod. red mor.-bkd. cl. From Honeyman Collection. (S. Nov.11; 2672) *McKittrich.* £210

ROESSLER, Balthazar
- Speculum Metallurgiae Politissimum. Oder: Hellpolierter Berg-Bau-Spiegel. Ill.:- J.C. Boldberger. Dresden, 1700. 1st. Edn. Fo. Hf.-title slightly torn & stained, paper flaw in 2C1, printing flaw affecting sig. 2S, some browning. Bds., crudely rebkd. with cl., worn, hf. red mor. case. From Honeyman Collection. (S. Nov.11; 2673) *Henderson.* £500

ROESSLIN, Eucharius
- The Birth of Mankind. Trans.:- T. Raynalde. 1545. Lacks lf., also Y8-Y10 at end, 4 ll. inserted with early woodcuts preserved. Old panel. cf. W.a.f. [STC 21154] (P. Sep.11; 7) *Schapiro.* £210
- - Anr. Edn. 1565. 4to. Some stains. Limp vell., s.-c. [STC 21157] (S. Jun.17; 732) *Studd.* £400

ROGER-MARX, Claude
- Bonnard Lithographe. Ill.:- Pierre Bonnard. Monte-Carlo, 1952. 4to. Orig. wraps., s.-c. (SH. Nov.20; 233) *Reed & Sims.* £70
- - Anr. Copy. Cold. pict. wraps. (SG. Oct.23; 40) $400
- - Anr. Copy. Sewed. (HD. Dec.5; 182) Frs. 1,500
- Dunoyer de Segonzac. Geneva, 1951. (200) numbered, with 4 orig. numbered etchings. 4to. Cold. pict. wraps. (SG. Apr.2; 103) $400
- La Loïe Fuller. Ill.:- Peignot. Evreux, 1904. (130). Sm. 4to. Cont. hf. mor., decor. spine, wrap. (HD. Feb.18; 230) Frs. 7,200
- L'Oeuvre Gravé de Vuillard. Monte-Carlo, [1948]. (2500). 4to. Orig. cl., d.-w. (CSK. Aug.15; 216) £75
- - Anr. Copy. Orig. paper bds. (H. Dec.9/10; 2388) DM 420

ROGERS, Charles
- A Collection of Prints in Imitation of Drawings . . . [with] Lives. L., 1778. 2 vols. Lge. fo. L.P., 1 plt. with slight dampstain. Hf. cf., rebkd., marb. bds. (GM. Apr.30; 731) £800
- - Anr. Copy. Cont. hf. cf., spines defect., corners worn. (C. Feb.25; 201) *Litman.* £750

ROGERS, Major Robert
- A Concise Account of North America. L., 1765. 1st. Edn. Mod. mor., marb. bds., unc. [Sabin 72723] (SPB. Nov.24; 54) $750
- - Anr. Copy. Some discolouration at margins of title & end-papers. Cont. cf., rebkd., inner hinges reprd. From liby. of William E. Wilson. (SPB. Apr.29; 236) $700
- - Anr. Copy. Remains of stp. at top of B1, tear at bottom of P3 slightly affecting text, foxed & soiled. Mod. mor.-bkd. buckram, gt. spine, floral design. From liby. of William E. Wilson. (SPB. Apr.29; 237) $475
- - Anr. Edn. Dublin, 1769. 12mo. Lacks title-p. Recent buckram with cont. cf. pasted on bds. [Sabin 72724] (CB. Sep.24; 182) Can. $100
- Journals . . . Containing an Account of the Several Excursions he Made Under the Generals Who Commanded Upon the Continent of North America During the Late War . . . L., 1765. 1st. Edn. Advts., slightly stained at inner margins thro.-out. Orig. mott. cf., gt. spine, upr. cover loose. From liby. of William E. Wilson. (SPB. Apr.29; 238) $950
- - Anr. Copy. Slight spotting. Later cf., gt., lr. cover detchd., upr. cover loose. [Sabin 72725] (SPB. Nov.24; 55) $900

- Eine Kurze Nachricht von Nord-Amerika. Trans.:- J.T. Köhler. Göttingen & Gotha, 1767. 1st. German Edn. Cont. bds. [Sabin 38223] (R. Mar.31-Apr.4; 2459) DM 750

ROGERS, Samuel
- Italy.-Annuaire pour l'An 1853 . . . augmente de Notices Scientifiques par M. Arago. Paris (2nd. work), 1830; [1852]. Mor., gt., worn, fore-e. pntg.; mor., gt., fore-e. pntg. W.a.f. (S. Dec.8; 70) *Chelsea.* £110
- Poems. Ill.:- after Stothard & Turner. L., 1834. Str.-grd. mor., gt. borders & ornamental central panel, spine gt. Fore-e. pntg. (SG. Mar.19; 165) $280
- - Anr. Edn. Ill.:- after Stothard & Turner. L., 1860. New Edn. Mor., gt. fillet borders enclosing a vase in gt., gt. panel. spine. Fore-e. pntg. (SG. Mar.19; 166) $140

ROGERS, Capt. Woodes
- A Cruising Voyage round the World. 1718. 2nd. Edn. 1 map torn. Mod. cf. [Sabin 72754] (S. Jun.18; 163) *Walford.* £100
- Voyage Autour du Monde . . . Amst., 1745. 1st. Fr. Edn. 2 vols. Cont. cf., worn. [Sabin 72757] (SPB. May 5; 445) $175

ROGISSART, Le Sieur de
- Les Délices de l'Italie. Leiden, 1706. 1st. Edn. 3 vols. Later mott. cf. gt., gt. monogs. of Earl of Rosebery on covers. (SBA. Jul.23; 635) *L'Acquaforte.* £260
- - Anr. Copy. Cont. cf. gt. (P. Mar.12; 98) *Davies.* £210

ROH, Franz & Tschichold, Jan
- Photo-Eye. Stuttgart, 1929. 4to. Disbnd., with orig. wraps. (torn & shabby). (SG. Apr.23; 173) $275

ROH, Franz & Tschichold, Jan (Ed.)
See-FOTO-AUGE

ROHAN, Henri, Duc de
- Les Mémoires . . . Amst., 1693. 16mo. Cont. cf. (HD. Jun.29; 215) Frs. 1,710

ROHAULT, Jacques
- Oeuvres Posthumes. Paris, 1682. 1st. Coll. Edn. 4to. Title stained & with owner's inscr. cut from margin. 18th. C. patterned bds. From Honeyman Collection. (S. Nov.11; 2675) *Howell.* £120
- Traité de Physique. Paris, 1671. 1st. Edn. 2 vols. in 1. 4to. Browned, some upr. margins wormed at beginning catching a few letters of text, owner's inscr. on fly-lf. Cont. cf., very worn. From Honeyman Collection. (S. Nov.11; 2674) *Zeitlin.* £170

ROHDE, Eleanour Sinclair
- The Old English Gardening Books. L., 1924. 1st. Edn. Some foxing. Hf. linen. (SG. Mar.26; 392) $120
- The Old English Herbals. L., 1922. 1st. Edn. Buckram. (SG. Mar.26; 391) $110

ROHR, Julius Bernhard von
- Vollständiges Hauss-Haltungs-Recht. Leipzig, 1738. 4to. Slight trace of worming at beginning. Cont. vell. (HK. Nov.18-21; 1702) DM 720

ROHRBACH, Carl
See-KRETSCHMER, Albert & Rohrbach, Carl

ROIZ, Pedro
- Libro del reloges solares. Valencia, 1575. 1st. Edn. 4to. Colophon dtd. 1576, some stains. Cont. limp vell., lacks ties, bookseller's label. From Honeyman Collection. (S. Nov.11; 2676) *Rogers Turner.* £200

ROIZMAN, Matvei
- Khevronskoe Vino [Hebron Wine]. Moscow, 1923. (1000). Orig. wraps. by G. Egeistov, slightly soiled. (SH. Feb.6; 513) *Quaritch.* £55

ROIZMAN, Matvei & Shershenevich, Vadim
- My chem kaemsya. Moscow, 1922. (1000). Orig. wraps. by E. Spassky, torn & reprd. (SH. Feb.6; 514) *Quaritch.* £50

ROJANKOVSKY, Fedor
- Daniel Boone. Ed.:- Esther Averill & Lila Stanley. Ill.:- Mourlot Frères after author. Paris, [1931]. 1st. Edn. Fo. Cold. pict. bds., spine worn. Inscr. (SG. Apr.30; 279) $180

ROJAS SARMIENTO, Juan de
- Commentariorum in Astrolabiem, quod Planisphaerium vocant, libri sex. Paris, 1551. 2nd. Edn. 4to. Some marginal worming, prelims. &

---

some other ll. detchd. Cont. vell., upr. inner hinge brkn., hf. red mor. case. From Honeyman Collection. (S. Nov.11; 2677) *Rogers Turner.* £180

ROLANDO, Luigi
- Cenni fisico-patologici sulle differenti specie d'Eccitabilita' e d'Eccitamento sull' irritazione . . . Turin, 1821. Orig. ptd. wraps., unc. & unopened, rebkd. (S. Jun.17; 733) *Norman* £300

ROLEWINCK, Werner
- Fasciculus Temporum. Louvain, Johann Veldener, 29 Dec., 1476 [i.e. 1475]. 1st. Dutch Edn. Fo. Spaces for capital initials, supplied in red, rubricated, 1st. lf. stained & with sm. reprd. hole affecting 3 words & numerals, final lf. badly dampstained, with slight loss of the printing in red & with reprd. hole affecting 1 or 2 letters on 3 lines, some other slight dampstaining. 19th. C. qtr. cf. gt. From the collection of Eric Sexton. [BMC IX, 136, Goff R256, HC 6920*] (CNY. Apr.8; 83) $4,600
- - Anr. Edn. Ed.:- [Henricus Wirtzburg]. Rougemont, Henricus Wirtzburg, 1481. Fo. Variant containing the line at foot of fo. 81r noting the foundation of the Abbey of Rougemont, 6-line initial G on fo. 6 supplied in red ink (faded), margins of several ll. reprd. & extreme lr. outer corners of some ll. slightly frayed, sm. hole in fo.'s 56 & 92 affecting 1 or 2 letters, sm. wormholes in some other ll., discold. Mor., spine gt.-lettered, mor. solander case, by Rivière. Bkplt. of Lessing J. Rosenwald, & gift label of the Liby. of Congress, lately in the collection of E. Sexton. [BMC VIII, 383, Goff R266] (CNY. Apr.8; 150) $8,500
- - Anr. Edn. Venice, 28 May 1484. Fo. Mod. leath. in cont. style. [BMC V, 288] (R. Mar.31-Apr.4; 57) DM 4,200
- - Anr. Edn. [Strassburg], after 1490. Sm. fo. 96 ll. (of 98), title-p. defect., few tears & repairs, stained. 19th. C. hf. cf., worn. [BMC I, 127] (S. Mar.16; 44) *Panadero.* £210

ROLEWINCK, Werner-LOMBARDUS, Petrus
- Fasciculus Temporum.-Sententiarum Libri IV. Venice; Nuremb., 28 May 1484; 10 May 1481. 4th. Edn. (1st. title). 2 works in 1 vol., 2nd. title bnd. first. Fo. Cont. blind-tooled pig-bkd. wood bds. [HC 6934; Goff R-270] [HC 10188; Goff R-481] (D. Dec.11-13; 46)

ROLFE, Frederick William S. 'Baron Corvo'
- Stories Toto Told Me. L. & N.Y., 1898. 1st. Edn. 16mo. Orig. wraps., worn, folder, s.-c. (S. Jul.22; 249) *Asher.* £60
- The Weird of the Wanderer . . . L., 1912. 1st. Edn. With Rider's 12-p. cat. Cl. (SG. Jun.4; 82) $280
- - Anr. Copy. With publisher's 12-p. catalogue. Spine slightly worn. (SG. Nov.13; 107) $200
- Without Prejudice. 100 Letters to Jon Lane. 1963. (600). Orig. bds. (SH. May 28; 192) *Stevens.* £55

ROLL, Timotheus von
See-GABRIEL, Peter-ROLL, Timotheus von -MONTIF, Lucian-M[ULLER], M.J.G.

ROLLIN, Charles
- Histoire Ancienne des Egyptiens . . . Ill.:- Le Bas; Coypel (frontis). Paris, 1740. 6 vols. 4to. Maps heightened with colours. Cont. glazed cf., gt. fillets on covers, spines decor. with raised bands. (HD. Jun.29; 254) Frs. 2,300
- Oeuvres Complètes. Paris, 1807. 1st. Compl. Edn., (525). 60 vols. Glazed cf. by Bozérian jeune, gt. roll-stps. around covers, smooth decor. spines. (HD. Feb.27; 221) Frs. 4,000

ROLLIN, Charles & Crevier
- Histoire Romain . . . Paris, 1752. 8 vols. 4to. Cont. glazed cf., triple gt. fillets on covers, decor. spines. (HD. Jun.29; 255) Frs. 1,610

ROLLINAT, Maurice
- Les Névroses. 1883. (50) on hollande. Cont. hf. chagrin. Note. (HD. Oct.10; 149) Frs. 2,600

ROLLINS, William
- Notes on X-Light. Boston, Massachusetts, 1904. 1st. Edn. Orig. cl., partly unc. From Honeyman Collection. (S. Nov.11; 2678) *Rootenberg.* £65
- - Anr. Copy. Cl. From Brooklyn Academy of Medicine. (SG. Jan.29; 453) $100

ROLY-POLY STORIES; a Picture Story-Book for Little Folks
Ill.:- Arthur Rackham & others. L., ca. 1917. 4to.

Cl.-bkd. pict. cold. bds. Raymond M. Sutton Jr. copy. (SG. May 7; 243) $220

ROMA. Rivista di Studi e di Vita Romana, Organo Uff. dell'Ist. di Studi Romani
Ed.:– C. Galassi Paluzzi. Rome, 1923-40. 19 vols. Cl. (CR. Mar.19; 475)   Lire 220,000

ROMAINE, Lawrence B.
– A Guide to American Trade Catalogs, 1744-1900. N.Y., 1960. Tall 8vo. Two-tone cl., ex-liby. (SG. Mar.26; 393) $120

ROMAN, A.
[–] **Samen-Spraeck, tusschen Waermondt ende Gaergoedt, nopende de Opkomste ende Ondergangh van Flora.–Tweede Samen-Spraeck . . . zijnde het Vervolgh van den op ende Ondergangh van Flora. –Register van de Prijsen der Bloemen.** Harlem, 1637. 3 vols. in 1. 4to. Some light stains, mainly in last part. Mod. hf. cf. (VG. Oct.13; 157)   Fls. 2,000

ROMAN DE RENART, Le
Ill.:– Lucien Boucher. 1942. Mosaic cf., by Anthoine Legrain. On hollande, suite of wood engrs. on chine, long ill. (HD. Oct.10; 204)   Frs. 1,800

ROMAN Y CARDENAS, Juan
– Noticias Genealógicas del Linage de Segovia, continuados por Espacio de Seiscientos Años. [Madrid], [1690]. Cf. (DS. May 22; 827)   Pts. 32,000

ROMANI, Felice & Peracchi, Antonio
– Dizionario d'Ogni Mitologia e Antichità. Milan, 1809-27. 8 vols. including 2 vols. supp. Cont. hf. cf., unc. (SI. Dec.4; 503)   Lire 680,000

ROMANIN, Isaiah
– Musar Melachim. Venice, 1744. Slight staining. Leath. (S. Nov.18; 455)   *James.* £75

ROMANIS, Antonio
– Le antiche Camere Esquiline dette comunemente delle Terme di Tito. Rome, 1822. Fo. Orig. ptd. bds., soiled, spine worn. (S. Jun.22; 86)
Goldschmidt. £120

ROMANO, A.
*See–*STEMPEL, G. & Zelst, A.–ROMANO, A. –HORCHER, Phillipus

ROMANO, Giulio
– [Frieze depicting the entry of the Emperor Sigismund into Mantua]. Ill.:– Antoinette Bouzonnet Stella. Paris, 1675. Ob. fo. Pict. dedication to Colbert, but without title. 18th. C. cf.-bkd. bds., very worn. (SBA. Dec.16; 82)
Quaritch. £120

ROMANUS, Adrianus
– Speculum Astronomicum, sive Organum forma mappae expressum. Louvain, 1606. 1st. Edn. 4to. Some ll. browned, marginal repair to title, rust-hole in S1, owner's inscr. (deleted) on fly-lf. Cont. limp vell., soiled, spine cracked. From Honeyman Collection. (S. Nov.11; 2680)
Hill. £140

ROMBERCH, Johann
– Congestorium Artificiose Memorie . . . [Venice], [1533]. 2nd. Edn? Lacks A2, 17 & 8 & the last, fore-margin of last lf. slightly defect. Old limp vell. (S. Jul.27; 111)   *Rhys Jones.* £150

ROMBERG, Moritz Heinrich
– Lehrbuch der Nervenkrankheiten des Menschen. Berlin, 1840-43. 1st. Edn. 2 vols. Hf. leath., not unif. (SG. Sep.18; 321) $150

ROME
– Nuova Raccolta delle Principali Vedute Antiche et Moderne dell' Alma Citta di Roma . . . Ill.:– P.A. Parboni, P. Ruga & Cottavi. Rome, ca. 1829. Ob. fo. Sewed. (HD. Feb.27; 199)   Frs. 1,500
– – **Anr. Edn.** Early 19th. C. Ob. 8vo. Hf. cf. (P. Jan.22; 305)   *Cambridge.* £65
– Nuova Raccolta di 25 Vedute Antiche e Moderne di Roma e sue Vicinanze. Rome, ca. 1800. Ob. 4to. Lightly soiled. Later linen. (R. Oct.14-18; 1925)
DM 600
– Nuova Raccolta di 100 Vedutine Antiche della Citta di Roma.–Nuova Raccolta delle Vedutine Moderne . . . Ill.:– Dominico Pronti. Rome, n.d. 2 works in 2 vols. 4to. Sewed. (HD. Feb.27; 206)   Frs. 2,300
– Principali Vedute di Roma. Ill.:– A. Moschetti. Rome, 1857. Ob. fo. Lightly soiled in places, mostly only in margins. Cont. bds., orig. wrap.

title pasted on, soiled. (R. Mar.31-Apr.4; 2673)
DM 950
– Raccolta della Citta di Roma. Ob. 4to. Hf. cf. (P. Jan.22; 249a)   *Zanazzo.* £65
– Raccolta di XXXX: Vedute Antiche e Moderne della Citta' di Roma e sue Vicinanze . . . Rome, ca. 1800. Ob. fo. New buckram. (SG. Oct.30; 306)
$325
– Vedute Antiche e Moderne le piu interessanti della Cita di Roma. N.d. 4to. 100 views, 2 per plt. on 50 plts. Late 18th. C. blank wraps. (LM. Mar.21; 301)   B.Frs. 9,000
– Views of Rome. [Rome], ca. 1840. Ob. fo. Plts. captioned in Engl. & Italian. Cont. mor., gt. (S. Nov.4; 586)   *Lawford.* £110

ROME & Bologna
– Architectural Views of. Ill.:– Giuseppe Antonio Landi, Pio Panfili & others. Bologna & Rome, ca. mid 18th. C. Ob. fo. Cont. vell.-bkd. patterned bds. (PNY. Oct.1; 32) $450

ROME DE L'ISLE, J.B.L. de
– Cristallographie, ou Description des Formes propres à tous les Corps du Regne Minéral. Paris, 1783. 4 vols. Some spotting & offsetting. Cont. hf. cf., hf. red mor. cases. From Honeyman Collection. (S. Nov.11; 2682)   *Conklin.* £420
– Essai de Cristallographie, ou Description des Figures Géométriques, propres à differens Corps du Regne Mineral. Paris, 1772. 1st. Edn. Slight spotting. Cont. mott. sheep, gt. spine, slightly worn. From Honeyman Collection (S. Nov.11; 2681)   *Krotki.* £180

ROMEIN, Jan & others (Ed.)
*See–*GESCHIEDENIS, Algemeene der Neder- landen

ROMERO DE LA CABALLERIA, Francisco Diego
– Phanal Chronologico. Indispensable para la mas facil, y perfecta inteligencia de las Historias, e Instrumentos Antiguos de España. Madrid, 1752. 1st. Edn. Vol. I (all publd.). 4to. Cont. limp vell., remnants of ties, bkplts. of Armando Cotarelo Valledor & bookseller Luis Bardón. From Honeyman Collection. (S. Nov.11; 2683)
Hill. £110

ROMME, Prof. Charles
– Description de l'Art de la Nature. 1778. Fo. Mod. bds. with vell. backstrip. (TA. Dec.18; 364)
£90

ROMMEL, Chr.
– Geschichte von Hessen. Kassel, 1820-58. 10 vols. Slightly soiled. Cont. hf. leath. & bds., Vol. 10 bnd. in after. (R. Oct.14-18; 2300)   DM 1,150

ROMNEY, J.
– Chester & its Environs Illustrated. Chester, 1853. 4to. Some plts. slightly spotted. Orig. cl. gt. (SBA. May 27; 348)   *Chesters.* £100
– – **Anr. Copy.** A few minor details. (SBA. Jul.14; 283)   *Grosvenor Museum.* £85
– – **Anr. Edn.** [1853]. Cont. hf. mor. gt. (SBA. Oct.22; 312)   *Nicholson.* £190

RONALDS, Alfred
– Fly-Fisher's Entomology. 1836. 1st. Edn. Cl. (P. Sep.11; 22)   *Thorp.* £140
– – **Anr. Copy.** Unc., rebkd. (SG. Oct.16; 343)
$700
– – **Anr. Copy.** Some foxing, many pencil notes thro.-out by early owner. Old hf. mor., worn, hf. mor. s.-c. (SG. Dec.11; 92) $280
– – **Anr. Edn.** 1844. [3rd. Edn?]. Orig. cl. (P. Apr.30; 223)   *Boland.* £60
– – **Anr. Copy.** 32-p. cat. dtd. 1847. Cl. (SG. Oct.16; 344) $220
– – **Anr. Edn.** L., 1849. 4th. Edn. Cl., unc. (SG. Oct.16; 345) $200
– – **Anr. Edn.** L., 1856. 5th. Edn. Cl. Frank M. Buckland's bkplt. (SG. Oct.16; 346) $160
– – **Anr. Edn.** 1862. 6th. Edn. Slightly soiled. Orig. cl. (SH. Jan.30; 388)   *Head.* £50
– – **Anr. Edn.** 1868. 7th. Edn. A few plts. slightly soiled. Cont. cl., soiled, spine slightly torn. (CSK. Jun.19; 53)   £60
– – **Anr. Copy.** 24-p. cat. dtd. March 1872. Cl., unc. (SG. Oct.16; 347) $160
– – **Anr. Edn.** L., 1877. 8th. Edn. 30-p catalogue dtd. Sep 1877. Cl., unc. (SG. Oct.16; 348) $110
– – **Anr. Edn.** L., 1901. 10th. Edn. Cl. (SG. Oct.16; 350) $100
– – **Anr. Edn.** 1913. [11th. Edn?] (250) numbered. 2 vols. 4to. Mod. mor., mor. onlay on upr. covers. (SH. Mar.5; 281)   *William.* £550

– – **Anr. Edn.** L'pool., 1913. 11th. Edn., (250) numbered, sigd. by publishers. 2 vols. 4to. Gt. decor. cl., gt. leath. spines, unc., s.-c. (SG. Oct.16; 351) $2,000
– – **Anr. Copy.** Cyril Sturla bkplt. (SG. Apr.9; 304) $900
– – **Anr. Copy.** (270) Lacks a few fly specimens. Orig. mor.-bkd. cl., gt. (SH. Oct.9; 244)
Angle Books. £460

RONALDS, Sir Francis
– Catalogue of Books & Papers relating to Electricity . . . & c. Ed.:– Alfred J. Frost. L., 1880. Three-qtr. mor., worn. (SG. Jan.22; 344)
$250
– Descriptions of an Electrical Telegraph, & of some other Electrical Apparatus. 1823. 1st. Edn. A few ll. wormed affecting text, some foxing & offsetting. Orig. bds., spine missing, upr. cover detchd., unc., hf. red mor. case. From Honeyman Collection. (S. Nov.11; 2685)
Das Bucherkabinet. £85
– – **Anr. Copy.** 1 folding plt. foxed, some offsetting onto text, lacks errata lf., sig. on title of J.C. Carter. Cont. hf. cf. From Honeyman Collection. (S. Nov.11; 2684)   *Rogers Turner.* £80

RONALDS, Hugh
– Pyrus Malus Brentfordiensis . . . selected Apples. 1831. 4to. Some foxing. Hf. mor. (S. Jun.1; 197)
Harris. £280

RONCHI, Luigi
– Vivandiere dell'Armata d'Italia. N.p., ca. 1850. Panorama of 20 plts., lithographed & hand-cold. Orig. cl. gt. (SI. Dec.4; 505)   Lire 620,000

RONDELET, Guillaume
– Libri de Piscibus Marinis. Lyon, 1554. 1st. Edn. Fo. Ruled thro.-out in red, lacks 2nd. pt. publd. in 1555, some ll. browned, several ll. with sm. stains in inner margins, liby. deletion in lr. title margin, release stp. of the Public Liby., Geneva, on verso of title. Cont. cf., rebkd., worn. (S. Jun.1; 283)
Sbisa. £400
– – **Anr. Edn.** Lyon, 1554-55. 1st. Edn. 2 pts. in 1 vol. Fo. Cont. annots., 1st. title very soiled, some browning & marginal staining, rust-hole in N3. Old cf., very worn. From liby. of Dr. E. Ashworth Underwood. (S. Feb.23; 280)   *Symonds.* £310
– – **Anr. Copy.** Marginalia by early owner. 18th. C. mott. cf., worn. (SG. Oct.9; 211) $1,600
– Libri de Piscibus Marinis, in quibus verae Piscium effigies expressae sunt [–Universae aquatilium Historiae pars altera]. Lyon, 1554-55. 1st. Edn. 2 pts. in 1 vol. Fo. Occasional slight staining or browning, tear in lr. fore-corner of 1st. title, 2 ll. detchd. in final gathering, cont. owner's inscr. on titles (deleted on 1st.). 18th. C. Fr. mott. cf., gt. spine, slightly worn. Bkplt. of Herbert McLean Evans; from Honeyman Collection. (S. Nov.11; 2687)   *Israel.* £1,000
– – **Anr. Copy.** 2 pts. in 2 vols. Some browning, a few stains, cont. owners' inscrs. on titles. Old vell. bds., rebkd. From Honeyman Collection. (S. Nov.11; 2688)   *Israel.* £600
– La Première [et la Seconde] Partie de l'Histoire Entière des Poissons. Trans.:– Laurent Joubert. Ill.:– G. Reverdy (text woodcuts) & P. Vase (ports.). Lyon, 1558. 2mo. Pencil MS. notes. Old vell. (D. Dec.11-13; 299)   DM 3,900

RONDOT, Natalis
– Notice du Vert de Chine et de la Teinture en Vert chez les Chinois. Paris, 1858. 1st. Edn. Inscr. by the author of hf.-title, 2 ll. 'Sur le Wei-Hwa, plate tinctoriale de la Chine' by J.L. Hénon tipped in at end, spotted & dampstained, upr. hinge brkn. Cont. hf. cf. (S. Oct.21; 421)   *Artico.* £60

RONSARD, Pierre de
– Abrégé de l'Art Poétique François. Ill.:– Lucien Pissarro. Eragny Pr., 1903. (226). Orig. bds., unc., unopened. With letterpress bkplt. of Joseph Manuel Andreini, & a reduced version of pict. wood-engraved bkplt. designed for him by Lucien Pissarro. (S. Jul.31; 25)   *Heringa.* £130
– Choix de Sonnets. Ill.:– Lucien Pissarro, Esther Pissarro after Lucien Pissarro. Eragny Pr. 1902. (226) Orig. decor. bds., soiled, unc. (SH. Dec.18; 22)   *Elliott.* £60
– Discours des Misères de ce Temps. Ill.:– A. Decaris. Paris, 1930. (300) numbered on Vergé de Montval. 4to. Loose ll. in wrap. & publisher's box. 2 full-p. sigd. wash ills. (LM. Nov.8; 133)
B.Frs. 12,000
– – **Anr. Copy.** 2 extra suites of ills. at each on Chine & vergé de Montval, orig. pencil ill. at

RONSARD, Pierre de -contd.
beginning. Mor. by Aussourd, mor. onlay doubls., geometrical patterns, orig. wraps. bnd. in, s.-c. (SM. Oct.8; 2372)						Frs. 4,500
- **Oeuvres.** 1609. 11th. Coll. Edn., Orig. Edn. of 9 poems. 2 pts. in 1 vol. Fo. Frontis. in 1st. state remntd., some sm. repairs, worming & staining. Cont. cf. (HD. Jun.30; 70)						Frs. 3,500
- **Les Quatre Premiers Livres des Odes.** Paris, 1555. Partly 1st. Edn. Sm. 8vo. Lacks prelims., title reprd. Mod. chagrin. (HD. Dec.5; 183)						Frs. 2,200

RONSSE, Jozef
See–VAN LERBERGHE, Lodewijk & Ronsse, Jozef

RÖNTGEN, Wilhelm Conrad
- **Eine neue Art von Strahlen.** Wurzburg, [1895]. Pt. 1 only. (From Sitzungsberichte der Physik.-Med. Gesellschaft zu Würzburg). Offprint, withdrawal stp. of Smithsonian Institution in upr. margin of 1st. p. Disbnd, cl. case. Pres. copy; from Honeyman Collection. (S. Nov.11; 2691)						*Rootenberg.* £880
- - **Anr. Edn.** Wurzburg, 1895-96. Pts. I & II. (From Sitzungsberichte der Physik.-Med. Gesellschaft zu Würzburg). Offprints. Orig. printed wraps., slightly soiled, hf. mor. case. Included with lot is photographic print of 1st. X-ray performed in public by Röntgen, from Honeyman Collection. (S. Nov.11; 2690)						*Norman.* £2,900
- - **Anr. Edn.** Würzburg, 1896. 2nd. Edn.; 1st. Edn. 2 pts. Orig. ptd. wraps., name Dr. Ernst Cohen stpd. on upr. covers, in cl. box. Loosely inserted in Dr. E. Wunschmann's 'Die Röntgen' schen X-Strahlen gemeinverständlich dargestellt, viertes Tausend', Berlin, 1896, with orig. wraps., rebkd. (S. Jun.17; 731)						*Phelps.* £380

RONZANI, Fr. & Luciolli, G.
- **Le Fabbriche Civilii Ecclesiastiche e Militari di Michele Sanmicheli.** Venice, 1831. 2nd. Edn. Fo. Port. & hf.-title with tear bkd., 1st. ll. lightly browned & soiled, 1 plt. browned. Loose, unc., in mod. hf. linen portfo., worn. (H. May 21/22; 293)						DM 900

ROO, Gerardus de
- **Annales oder Historische Chronick der Durchleuchte . . . Ostereiche.** Augsburg, 1621. Sm. fo. Old vell. (BS. Jun.11; 114)						£85

ROOPER, George
[-] **The Autobiography of the Late Salmo Salar, Esq.** L., 1867. 1st. Separate Edn. Foxed. Leath.-bkd. marb. bds., orig. wraps. bnd. in, worn. J.C. Lynn's bkplt. (SG. Oct.16; 352)						$130

ROOSES, Max
- **Dutch Painters of the Nineteenth Century.** 1898-1901. 4 vols. 4to. Orig. cl. gt. (P. Feb.19; 231)						*Sims & Reed.* £50
- - **Anr. Copy.** Fo. Decor. cl. (PWP. Apr.9; 131)						Can. $220

ROOSEVELT, Eleanor & Hickok, Lorena A.
- **Ladies of Courage.** N.Y., [1954]. 1st. Edn. Cl., d.-w. Pres. Copy, inscr. in Hickok's hand & sigd. by both authors. (PNY. May 21; 361)						$100

ROOSEVELT, Theodore, President of the U.S.A.
- **Address . . . on the Occasion of the Celebration of the Hundredth Anniversary of the Birth of Abraham Lincoln.** Wash., 1909. 1st. Edn. Orig. ptd. wraps., qtr. mor. s.-c. Pres. Copy, to Major Loeffler, lately in the Prescott Collection. (CNY. Feb.6; 285)						$600
- **Big Game Hunting in the Rockies & on the Great Plains.** Ill.:– Remington, Frost, Beard, & others. N.Y., 1899. (1000) numbered & sigd. on L.P. 2 pts. in 1 vol. 4to. Three-qtr. mor., covers detchd. (SG. Dec.11; 393)						$160
- **The Winning of the West.** N.Y., 1900. (200). 4 vols. Orig. lev. mor. gt., partly unc., red suede doubls. & end-pp. With page of Roosevelt's orig. autograph MS. bnd. at front of vol. 1. (CNY. Oct.1; 114)						$320
- **The Works.** N.Y., 1923-26. The Memorial Edn. (1050) numbered sets, sigd. by Edith Kermit Roosevelt. 4to. Gt. cl., unc., boxed. (PNY. Oct.1; 464)						$700

ROOSEVELT, Theodore & Heller, Edmund
- **Life Histories of African Game Animals.** L., 1915. 2 vols. Pict. cl. (SG. Dec.11; 394)						$170

ROQUES, Joseph
- **Phytographie Medicale.** Paris, 1821. 2 vols. 4to. Cont. hf. mor., gt. spines. (S. Jun.1; 198)						*Joseph.* £1,100

ROQUETTE, Louis-Frederic
- **Le Grand Silence Blanc.** Ill.:– Andre Collet. Paris, [1944]. (1000) numbered. 4to. Orig. pict. wraps. Sigd. (CB. Sep.24; 298)						Can. $240

ROSA, José Antonio da
- **Compendio das Minas.** Lisbon, 1794. 2nd. Edn. 4to. Some worming affecting text. Orig. wraps., spine worn. (S. Oct.21; 422)						*Barnet.* £50

ROSA, P.
See–LANDESIO, E. & Rosa, P.

ROSA, Salvator
[-] **[Fifty-Nine Etched Plates of Single Figures & Groups of Soldiers].** [Rome?], [1640]. 4to. Mod. hf. cf. (C. Nov.6; 333)						*Schuster.* £190
- **Has Ludentis Otii.** N.d. 4to. Later cf.-bkd. bds. (SH. Jul.16; 118)						*Schwing.* £360
- **Salvator Rosa Invenit Liber Primus.** Paris, n.d. Ob. 8vo. Some plts. stained. Disbnd. (SKC. May 19; 518)						£85
- **Twenty Four Figures by Benjamin & Sarah Green.** 1789. Ob. 4to. Cont. hf. mor. (SH. Jun.11; 197)						*Erlini.* £95

ROSACCIO, Giuseppe
- **Viaggio da Venetia, a Constantinopoli.** Venice, 1606. Ob. 4to. Browned & soiled. Cont. limp vell., worn, lacks spine. (S. Oct.1; 613)						£780

ROSAIN, Domingo
- **Necropolis de la Habana: Historia de los Cementerios de esta Ciudad, con Multitud de Noticias Interesantes.** Habana, 1875. Square 4to. Mod. buckram, ex-libry. (SG. Mar.5; 163)						$130

ROSAMOND, DOLLY'S NEW PICTURE BOOK
Trans.:– Madame de Chatelain. Ill.:– Rudolph Geissler. Ca. 1860. 3rd. Edn. 54mm. × 80mm. Orig. decor. bds., rebkd., or spine preserved. (SH. Mar.19; 278)						*Nador.* £55

ROSARIO de la Giiosa Vgime Maria
Venice, ca. 1540. 3 unnumbered pp., lacks last p. with sig. Vell., some sm. stains on some pp. (CR. Mar.19; 276)						Lire 420,000

ROSARIUS, Simon
- **Antitheses Christi et Antichristi, iv-delicet Papae, versibus & figuris illustrata.** Geneva, 1578. 19th. C. mor., parch. end-ll. (SPB. Oct.1; 240)						$1,000

ROSCHI, Johann Jakob
- **Vorschrift zum Nutzen der Bernerischen Jugend.** Ill.:– Brupbacher. [Berna?], 1780. Ob. 4to. Cont. hf. cf. (SI. Dec.4; 506)						Lire 400,000

ROSCIO, Guito, Mascardi, Agostino & others
- **Ritratti et Elogii di Capitani Illustri.** Rome, 1646. 4to. 19th. C. hf. cf. (CSK. Apr.24; 56)						£70

ROSCOE, Thomas
- **The London & Birmingham Railway.** [1839?]. Spotted. Cont. hf. cf. (SKC. Feb.26; 1769)						£65
- **Roscoe's Novelists Library.** Ill.:– George Cruikshank. (17 vols.). L., 1831-33. 19 vols. Cf. gt. by Zaehnsdorf, slightly worn. (SPB. Nov.25; 445)						$450
- **The Tourist in Italy.** L., 1831. Mor. (CR. Mar.19; 279p)						Lire 260,000
- **The Tourist in Switzerland & Italy.** Ill.:– Samuel Prout. L., 1830. Orig. mor. (SG. Oct.30; 307)						$100
- **Views of Cities & Scenary in Italy, France, & Switzerland.** N.d. 3 vols. 4to. Text in Engl. & Fr. Cont. hf. mor., spines gt. (SKC. Feb.26; 1674)						£130
- **Wanderings & Excursions in North [& South] Wales.** [?1836-37]. 2 vols. 4to. Slight spotting. Orig. roan. (S. Jan.27; 609)						*Mistrali.* £50
- - **Anr. Edn.** Ca. 1840. 2 vols. Orig. cl., 1 inside hinge brkn., a little worn. (S. Jun.29; 255)						*Cumming* £50
- - **Anr. Edn.** N.d. 2 vols. Cont. hf. cf. (SBA. Jul.14; 331)						*Morgan* £50
- **Wanderings & Excursions in South Wales; including the Scenery of the River Wye.** Ca. 1845. Slight foxing. Cont. hf. mor. (TA. Nov.20; 17)						£58
- - **Anr. Copy.** (TA. Sep.18; 9)						£52

ROSCOE, Thomas
See–LANDSCAPE ANNUAL

ROSCOE, William
- **Monandrian Plants . . .** Ill.:– after drawings by Thomas Allport & others. L'pool., 1828. (150). Fo. Plts. hand-cold. (Unsigd. & unnumbered), title detchd. 19th. C. hf. mor., worn, upr. cover detchd. From Chetham's Liby., Manchester. (C. Nov.27; 347)						*Marshall.* £1,200
- - **Anr. Copy.** Title page soiled, plt. 83 heavily spotted, offsetting from text on some plts., without lf. of directions to the binder. Cont. russ., heavily restored. Inscr. by Sir William Jackson Hooker to Robert Wight, from collection of Massachusetts Horticultural Society, stps. on plts. (SPB. Oct.1; 162)						$2,500

ROSE, Alfred
- **Register of Erotic Books.** N.Y., 1965. 2 vols. Orig. cl. (CSK. Jan.9; 100)						£80

ROSE, Rt. Hon. George
See–FOX, Charles James–ROSE, Rt. Hon. George

ROSE, J.N.
See–BRITTON, Nathaniel Lord & Rose, J.N.

ROSE, Thomas
- **British Switzerland or Picturesque Rambles in the English Lake District.** Ill.:– after Allom & others. L., [1858-60?]. Vols. 1 & 2. 4to. Hf. cf. gt. (P. Jul.2; 65)						*Kidd.* £90
- - **Anr. Copy.** 2 vols. in 1. Slightly spotted. Cont. cl., worn. (SBA. Oct.22; 318)						*Wilson.* £80
- **British Switzerland.–Westmorland, Cumberland, Durham & Northumberland.** Ca. 1835. 2 vols. in 1. 4to. Hf. cf. (P. Feb.19; 115)						*Russell.* £85
- **The Northern Tourist . . . Views in Westmoreland, Cumberland, Durham & Northumberland.** L., 1834-35. 2 vols. 4to. 146 (of 173) plts., foxing. Orig. cl. (SPB. May 29; 374)						$100
[-] **Wanderungen im Norden von England . . . in den Grafschaften Westmorland, Cumberland, Durham und Northumberland.** Trans.:– James Edwin Stahlschmidt. Ill.– after T. Allom. 1836. 4to. Some ll. spotted or browned. Orig. hf. mor. gt. (SBA. May 27; 318)						*Seddon.* £50
- **Westmorland, Cumberland, Durham & Northumberland Illustrated.** Ill.:– Thomas Allom. 1832. Cont. hf. mor. lacks head of spine. (SH. Nov.6; 63)						*Sennitt.* £100
- - **Anr. Edn.** Ill.:– Thomas Allom & others. 1832-[35]. 3 vols. 4to. Slight spotting. Cont. mor.-bkd. cl. (SBA. Oct.22; 554)						*Nicholson.* £130
- - **Anr. Copy.** 3 vols. Some earlier plts. hand-cold. by previous owner, some ll. spotted. Cont. cf.-bkd. cl., worn, spines torn, 1 with covers detchd. (SBA. Jul.14; 302)						*Morland.* £105
- - **Anr. Copy.** 3 vols. in 1. Lacks 12 (of 110) engraved plts., lacks titles to vols. 2 & 3, preliminary lf. of text (the description of the frontis.) to each vol., & pp. 5-12 of vol. 3, occasional light foxing. Cont. mor., gt. spine. (C. Nov.5; 133)						*Price.* £80
- - **Anr. Edn.** 1833-[35]. 2 vols. 4to. Lacks 2 plts., a few margins slightly stained. Cont. hf. mor. gt. (SBA. Dec.16; 177a)						*Moreland.* £110
- - **Anr. Edn.** N.d. 4to. Occasional spotting, 213 views on 108 ll. only. Cont. cl. W.a.f. (CSK. Sep.26; 104)						£160
- - **Anr. Copy.** 3 vols. Orig. cl., spines slightly torn. (CSK. Oct.24; 33)						£140
- - **Anr. Copy.** 2 vols. Cont. hf. cf., jnts. cracked. (CSK. Nov.7; 194)						£95
See–NOBLE, Thomas & Rose, Thomas

ROSE, Thomas–NOBLE, Thomas & Rose Thomas
- **Vues Pittoresques des Comtes de Westmorland, Cumberland, Durham et Northumberland.** -**Itineraire Pittoresque aux Comtes de Chester, Derby, Leicester . . .** Ed.:– 1st. work, J.F. Gerard. Trans.:– 2nd. work, A. Sosson. Ill.:– Thomas Allom & others. L., ca. 1835; 1837-8. 1st. work, 3 vols., 2nd. work 1 vol., together 4 vols. 4to. Orig. cl., 1st. work bdgs. brkn. (SG. Oct.30; 309) $190

ROSEL VON ROSENHOE, August Johann
- **Der Monatlich-herausgegebenen Insecten-Belustigung.** Nuremb., [1740-]46. 1st. Edn. 6 pts. in 1 vol. Lightly soiled in patches, 1st pt. torn, lightly stained at beginning, sig. 1 lacks pp. 9-16, lacks 5 old cold. copper engrs. Cont. leath., spine reprd. (R. Mar.31-Apr.4; 1442)						DM 1,500
- - **Anr. Edn.** Nuremb. 1755. 4to. Lacks 1 cold. copperplt., some plts. slightly soiled & torn. Cont. leath. (HK. Nov.18-21; 495)						DM 1,200

ROSELLIS, Antonius de
- Tractatus de Jejuniis. [Rome], [Stephan Plannck], ca. 1491. 4to. Mod. mor. [Goff R 325] (C. Apr.1; 79)   *Walton.* £120

ROSEN, Peter
- Pa-Ha-Sa-Pah or the Black Hills of South Dakota. St. Louis, 1895. 1st. Edn. Orig. cl., blind-stpd. with elab. designs. (SPB. Jun.22; 123) $125

ROSENBACH, Abraham Simon Wolf
- An American Jewish Bibliography . . . [Phila.], [1926]. Orig. Edn. Cl. (SG. Jan.22; 345) $100
- Books & Bidders. Boston, 1927. (785) L.P., sigd. Orig. cl.-bkd. bds., slightly worn. (SPB. Jul.28; 411) $100

ROSENBERG, Adolf
- Geschichte des Kostüms. Ed.:– E. Heyck (text). Berlin, 1905. 5 vols. Fo. Portfos. (D. Dec.11-13; 2221)   DM 500
- - Anr. Edn. Ed.:– Eduard Heyck. Berlin, n.d. 5 vols. Lge. 4to. Hf. mor., worn. (SG. May 21; 429) $130
- - Anr. Copy. 4 vols. 4to. Mod. hf. mor. (SI. Dec.4; 508)   Lire 280,000

ROSENBERG, Isaac
- Collected Works.–Collected Poems. 1937; 1949. 1st. Edn.; 1st. Separate Edn. 8vo. & 4to. Orig. cl., d.-w.'s. With Leeds University Rosenberg Exhibition catalogue, 1st. work with Jacob Isaacs' A.N.s. loosely inserted. (S. Jul.22; 148)   *Sawyer.* £90
- Moses. Stepney Green, Paragon Printing Works, 1916. 1st. Edn. Sm. 4to. Orig. wraps., unc. MS. corrections, pres. copy to J. Isaacs. (S. Jul.22; 145)   *Sawyer.* £660
- Night & Day. Priv. ptd., [1912]. 1st. Edn. Orig. wraps. MS. corrections, Israel Zangwill/Jacob Isaacs copy. (S. Jul.22; 143)   *Sawyer.* £1,800
- Poems. 1922. 1st. Edn. Orig. cl., unc., d.-w. (S. Jul.22; 147)   *Blackwell.* £85
- - Anr. Copy. Jacob Isaacs' copy, with transcript of 'Epilogue' below inscr. on end-lf., autograph MS. of 'Poetry of Isaac Rosenberg' & other MS. material loosely inserted. (S. Jul.22; 146)   *Sawyer.* £60
- Youth. 1915. 1st. Edn. Orig. wraps. Pres. copy to J. Isaacs 1917. (S. Jul.22; 144) *Sawyer.* £500

ROSENBERG, Jakob
See–FRIEDLANDER, Max J. & Rosenberg, Jakob

ROSENBERG, Mary Elizabeth
- The Museum of Flowers. 1856. Orig. cl. gt. (C. Jul.15; 201)   *Pillar.* £150

ROSENBURG, Harold
See–BUTOR, Michel & Rosenburg, Harold

ROSENGARTEN
Ed.:– [H. Nestel]. 1866-[69]. Lge. 4to. Lacks title, soiled. Cont. linen, upr. cover gt. (HK. Nov.18-21; 716)   DM 600

ROSENTHAL, Leonard
- The Kingdom of the Pearl. Ill.:– Edmund Dulac. L., [1920]. (675) numbered. 4to. Orig. cl.-bkd. bds. (SH. Mar.26; 173)   *Ayres.* £80
- - Anr. Copy. L.P. Gt. & silver-pict. qtr. cl., lr. corner of upr. cover bruised. (PNY. Dec.3; 131) $125
- - Anr. Edn. Ill.:– Edmund Dulac. N.Y., [1920]. (675) numbered, for America. Lge. 4to. Cl.-bkd. gt.-pict. bds., d.-w. frayed. (SG. Oct.23; 103) $140
- Au Royaume de la Perle. Ill.:– Edmund Dulac. Paris, n.d. 4to. Orig. wraps., backstrip worn & torn with loss. Pres. Copy. (CSK. Sep.26; 198)   £55

ROSE'S BREAKFAST (The)
1808. 1st. Edn. 16mo. Orig. ptd. wraps., mor.-bkd. case. (SH. Mar.19; 280)   *Reisler.* £290

ROSEVEAR, D.S.
See–BANNERMAN, David Armitage–HALL & Moreau–ROSEVEAR, D.S.

ROSEY, Gui
- Electro-Magie. Ill.:– Man Ray. Paris, 1969. (150) numbered, on velin de Rives, each etching numbered & sigd. 4to. 6 orig. cold. etchings, each sigd. by artist. Loose sheets in ptd. wraps., cl. folder & s.-c. (SG. Oct.23; 202) $2,400

ROSICRUCIANS
- Secret Symbols of the Rosicrucians . . . Ed.:– H. Spencer Lewis (preface). Chic., 1935. (50) numbered. Fo. Qtr. mor., gt. title & raised bands on spine, cl. bds., taffeta end-papers. Inscr. by H. Spencer Lewis. (JL. Jul.20; 830)   Aus. $575

ROSIERES (Les)
Paris, ca. 1820. 18mo. Foxed. Cont. red str.-grd. mor., spine decor. in gold & blind-stpd., covers with lge. roulette decor. & blind-stpd. in gt. fillet border, centre motif gt. & blind pointillé, 2 inner gt. fillets. (HD. Apr.10; 192)   Frs. 1,150

ROSIUS, Jacobus
- Ephemeris perpetua: hoc est, generale calendarium Astronomicum et Astrologicum. –Calendarium ostendens dies cuius libet Mensis . . . Ortus et occasus Solis. [& an imperfect work by Kepler]. Basel, [1628]; 1630. 3 works in 1 vol. 4to. Vell.-bkd. bds., worn. Armorial bkplt. of Count Chorinsky; from Honeyman Collection. (S. Nov.11; 2694)   *Quaritch.* £100

ROSNEL, Pierre de
[-] Le Mercure Indien, ou le Tresor des Indes. Paris, 1667. 2 pts. in 1 vol. Pt. 1 slightly wormed affecting text, lacks sub-title at p. 137 pt. 2, some browning & slight soiling, liby. stp. removed from 1st. title. Vell. From Honeyman Collection. (S. Nov.11; 2695)   *Zeitlin.* £170

ROSS, Alexander
[-] The Schollers Companion, or a Little Library, Containing all the Interpretations of the Hebrew & Greek Bible. 1648. 1st. Edn. Head of 2nd. lf. cropped. Cont. cf. [Wing R1982] (C. Apr.1; 231)   *Quaritch.* £100

ROSS, Sir John
- Narrative of a Second Voyage in Search of a North-West Passage. 1835. [1st. Edn.?]. 4to. 1 folding steel-engraved map hand-cold. in outl., torn & reprd., slight spotting & soiling, 1 plt. cleanly torn along plt. mark. Cont. hf. cf. (CSK. Feb.6; 112)   £100
- - Anr. Copy. Orig. cl., upr. bd. detchd. (TRL. Dec.10; 38)   £72
- - Anr. Copy. Spine torn, stitching brkn. (S. Nov.5; 134)   *Bowes.* £55
- - Anr. Copy. Unc. Sm. tipped-in slip offering subscribers various bdgs. (SG. Oct.30; 311) $350
- - Anr. Copy. Ex-liby. (SG. Feb.26; 282) $220
- - Anr. Copy. Cont. blind-stpd. mor. (CB. Nov.12; 247)   Can. $110
- Narrative of a Second Voyage in Search of a North-West Passage . . . –Appendix to the Narrative of a Second Voyage. L., 1835. L.P. 2 vols. 4to. Some ll. loose, some foxing to vol. 1. Cont. cl., vol. 1 rebkd., spine to vol. 2 nearly detchd. (CB. Sep.24; 183)   Can. $450
- Voyage of Discovery . . . Baffin's Bay. 1819. 1st. Edn. 4to. Cont. cf. gt., jnts. split. [Sabin 73376] (S. Nov.24; 251)   *Brooke.* £260
- - Anr. Copy. Orig. bds., unc., spine stained. (C. Feb.25; 134)   *Bowes.* £240
- - Anr. Copy. Hf. cf. gt. (P. Apr.30; 2)   *Ryman.* £210

ROSS, Martin
See–SOMERVILLE, Edith Oenone & Ross, Martin

ROSS, Martin C.
- Russian Porcelain . . . the Collections of Marjorie Merriweather Post. Norman, Oklahoma, [1968]. Two-tone cl., d.-w. Sigd. & inscr. to Kouchakjis. (SG. Mar.12; 76) $110

ROSS, Peter & Pelletreau, William S.
- A History of Long Island, from its Earliest Settlement to the Present Time. N.Y., 1903. 3 vols. 4to. Disbnd. (SG. Mar.5; 279) $110

ROSS, Thomas
See–MacGIBBON, David & Ross, Thomas

ROSSET, Pierre Fulcrand de
- L'Agriculture poème [First Part]. Ill.:– Saint-Quentin, Marillier & Loutherbourg. Paris, 1774. 1st. & Orig. Edn. 4to. Cont. marb. cf., triple fillet, inner dentelle, decor. spine. (HD. Feb.18; 69)   Frs. 1,100

ROSSETTI, Christina
- Goblin Market. Ill.:– Laurence Housman. 1893. (160) on L.P. Cont. mor., partly unopened. (SH. Mar.26; 282)   *Ayres.* £140
- - Anr. Edn. Ill.:– Arthur Rackham. L., [1933]. (410) numbered, sigd. by artist. Limp vell., s.-c.

- - - Raymond M. Sutton Jr. copy. (SG. May 7; 245) $500
- - Anr. Copy. Gt. lettered vell., partly unc. (SG. Apr.30; 270) $400
- - Anr. Edn. Ill.:– Arthur Rackham. Phila., [1933]. 1st. Amer. Trade Edn. Cl., cold. pict. d.-w. Raymond M. Sutton Jr. copy. (SG. May 7; 247) $170
- Sing-Song, a Nursery Rhyme Book. Ill.:– George & Edward Dalziel after Arthur Hughes. 1872. Orig. pict. cl. (SH. Dec.11; 471) *Reisler.* £50
- Verses, reprinted from G. Polidori's Edition of 1847. Ed.:– J.D. Symon. Ill.:– L. & E. Pissarro. Eragny Pr., 1906. (175). 12mo. Errata slip tipped in. Flowered bd. covers, bd. spine, end-papers discold., unc. & unopened. (SG. Jan.15; 25) $200

ROSSETTI, Dante Gabriel
- Hand & Soul. Hammersmith, Kelms. Pr., 1895. (525). Mor., gt. tooled with iris & heart pattern, stpd. & dtd. E.G.S. 1900, s.-c. (SPB. Nov.25; 315) $600
- - Anr. Copy. Vell., slight warping. (SPB. Nov.25; 316) $200
- - Anr. Edn. [Kelms Pr.], [1895]. [(525)]. 16mo. Orig. vell. (CSK. May.15; 30)   £130
- Poems. Ed.:– W.M. Rossetti. L., 1904. L.P. Edn. 2 vols. 4to. Mor., gt.-stpd. overall with roses inlaid in red & decor., gt.-panel. spine with similar tooling, inner dentelles gt., unc., by C. & C. McLeish for the Doves Bindery. (PNY. Dec.3; 111) $180
- Sonnets & Lyrical Poems. Hammersmith, Kelms. Pr., 1894. (310). Orig. limp vell., lacks 1 silk tie. (CNY. May 22; 318) $350

ROSSETTI, Donato
- Dimostrazione Fisico-Matematica delle Sette Proposizioni; [Lettera . . . al Signor Dottor Carlo Fracassati]. Flor., 1668. 1st. Edn. 2 pts. in 2 vols. 4to. Cont. limp vell., gt. From Honeyman Collection. (S. Nov.11; 2696)   *Hill.* £60

ROSSI, Domenico de
- Raccolta di Statue Antiche e Moderne. Rome, 1704 [1742]. Fo. 162 plts. (of 163, lacks plt. 60), some plts. browned, title slightly soiled & spotted. 19th. C. hf. russ., upr. cover detchd., worn. (S. Feb.10; 340)   *Mistrali.* £90
- Studio d'Architettura civile sopra gli Ornamenti di Porte e Finestre tratti da alcune Fabbriche insigni di Roma. Ill.:– after Bernini, Michelange, Borromini & others. Rome, 1702-21. 3 pts. in 2 vols. 4to. 281 plts. (of 282, lacks plts. 51 in pt. III). Cont. vell. bds. (C. Feb.25; 223) *Canning.* £400
- - Anr. Copy. Vols. 1 & 3 only (of 3). Fo. Unif. cont. cf. (C. Feb.25; 202)   *Mediolanum.* £150

ROSSI, Domenico de–ROSSI, Giovanni Giacomo de
- Studio d'Architettura Civile . . .–Insignium Romae Templorum Prospectus . . . Rome, 1702; 1684? Together 2 vols., 1st. work vol. 1 only. Fo. 2nd. work lacks title, wrong title of vol. 3 from previous work bnd. in. 18th. C. cf. (C. May 20; 95a)   *Elstein.* £127

ROSSI, Giovanni Giacomo de
- Insignium Romae Templorum Prospectus. Ill.:– Vincenzo Francischini, Filipo Vasconi & others. Rome, 1684. [1st. Edn.?] 4to. Cont. spr. cf., spine gt. in compartments. (C. Feb.25; 203)   *Quaritch.* £220
- - Anr. Copy. Fo. Some plts. & title slightly torn, spotted, marginal dampstaining. Cont. hf. cf., worn. (S. Oct.21; 323)   *Marlborough Rare Books.* £150

ROSSI, Giovanni Giacomo & Falda, Giovanni Battista
- Il Nuovo Teatro delle Fabriche, et Edificii, in Prospettiva di Roma Moderna. Rome, 1699. 4 pts. in 1 vol. Ob. fo. Cont. spr. cf., slightly worn. (SBA. Dec.16; 83) *Morten's Bookshop.* £460
- Vedute Delle Fabriche, Piazze et Strade Fatte Fare Nuovamte in Roma Dalla . . . Alessandro VII. Rome, 1665. 1st. Edn. 3 pts. in 1 vol. Ob. fo. Title & some plts. slightly soiled or spotted. Cont. cf., spine slightly worn. (S. Apr.7; 281)   *Mistrali.* £500

ROSSI, Shlomo de
- Otavo Ha'shirim Asher Lishlomo. Frankfurt a. M., Aug., 1925. Facs. of 1st. Edn., (3) on vell. Sm. 4to. Vell., s.-c., reprd. This copy specially ptd. for A. Freimann. (SPB. May 11; 181) $1,900

ROSSINI, Giovanni
- **Guillaume Tell.** Paris, [after 1830]. Fo. Slightly soiled thro.-out. Cont. hf. leath. (H. Dec.9/10; 1256)   DM 600

ROSSINI, Luigi
- **Antichità Romane in Cento Tavole.** Rome, 1823. 1st. printing. Ob. fo. Cont. hf. cf. (CR. Jun.11; 608)   Lire 5,500,000
- – **Anr. Edn.** Rome, 1829. [2nd. Edn.?]. Lge. ob. fo. Last plt. foxed. Cont. hf. mor. (C. Nov.6; 228)   *Henderson.* £3,200
- – **Anr. Copy.** Ptd. title-lf. loose. Cont. hf. vell. gt. (R. Mar.31-Apr.4; 2675)   DM 8,500
- **Vedute di Roma.** Rome, 1821-23. Fo. No title. 19th. C. hf. mor. As a collection, w.a.f. (S. Nov.25; 422)   *Henderson.* £650
- **Viaggio Pittoresco da Roma a Napoli.** [Rome], [1839]. Fo. Cont. hf. vell., gt. (S. Nov.4; 585)   *Colnaghi.* £1,700

ROSSLIN, E.
- **Ehestands Arzneibuch.** Frankfurt, 1544? Leaves 2-120, 20 text woodcuts, lacks title, 1544 at end of Index, slightly browned, stained & soiled, some ll. with sm. holes. Old MS. vell. (H. May 21-22; 205)   DM 850

ROSTAND, Edmond
- **Cyrano de Bergerac.** 1898. Orig. Edn. Hf. mor., cover & wrap., by Lortic. (HD. Jun.30; 71)   Frs. 1,300
- – **Anr. Edn.** Trans.:– Humbert Wolfe. Ill.:– Humphrey Waterfield. Corvinus Pr., Dec. 1937. (30) numbered, sigd. by translator. Orig. buckram-bkd. linen. (S. Jul.31; 143)   *Updike.* £60
- – **Anr. Copy.** (S. Jul.22; 68)   *Rota.* £50
- **La Dernière Nuit de Don Juan.** Ill.:– Malassis. Paris, 1921. (1000) on imperial Jap., numbered. Sm. 4to. Mor. by Noulhac, mosaic arms on upr. cover, and mor. doubls., wrap. preserved, s.-c. (SM. Feb.11; 280)   Frs. 9,000
- **La Princesse Lointaine.** Ill.:– J. Germain after Desvallières & Reyre. Paris, 1920. (150). 4to. Pol. cf. by Bruel, upr. cover decor. with multi-cold. mosaic cf. sailing ship, wrap. preserved, s.-c. (SM. Feb.11; 281)   Frs. 2,500

ROSVINIEN, Marquis de Piré
See–DESFONTAINES, Abbé & others

ROTH, E.R.
- **Memorabilia Europae.** Ulm, 1714. Slightly soiled. Cont. vell., lacks spine. (HK. Nov.18-21; 1357)   DM 650.

ROTH, Henry Ling
- **Aborigines of Tasmania.** L., 1890. 1st. Edn., (200) numbered & initialled. Orig. cl. (KH. Nov.18; 513)   Aus. $220
- **Great Benin, its Customs, Art & Horrors.** Halifax, 1903. 4to. Orig. cl. (SH. Jul.23; 46)   *Johnson.* £70
- **The Natives of Sarawak & British North Borneo.** 1896. (700). 2 vols. Orig. cl. (SH. Nov.7; 464)   *Randall.* £110
- **Oriental Silverwork, Malay & Chinese.** 1910. 4to. Orig. cl. (SH. Oct.9; 186)   *Maggs.* £70

ROTH, Johann Michael
- **Augspurgisches Friedens-Gedächtnis das ist Alle so genannte Friedens-Gemahlde.** Augsburg, 1748. Ob. 4to. Hf. cf. W.a.f. (P. Dec.11; 25)   *Frankel.* £120

ROTH, Walter E.
See–SCHIDLOFF, B. & others

ROTH-SCHOLTZ, F.
- **Deutsches Theatrum Chemicum, auf welchem der Berühmtesten Philosophen und Alchymisten Schriften, die von dem Stein der Weisen, von Verwandelung der Schlechten Metallen in Bessere, von Edelgesteinen [etc.] handeln, vorgestellet werden.** Nuremb., 1732. Only Edn. Pt. 3 (of 3). Cont. leath. (R. Oct.14-18; 212)   DM 1,200

ROTHE, Gottfried
- **Introduction à la Chymie Accompagné de deux Traités . . .** Trans.:– J.L. Clausier. Paris, 1741. 12mo. Cont. Fr. cf., spine gt. (S. Dec.1; 369)   *Phelps.* £60

ROTHENBURG, Fr. D. von
- **Schlachten Atlas.** Leipzig, 1842-44. Text & plt. vol. Slightly soiled. Cont. hf. leath. (R. Oct.14-18; 2117)   DM 2,300
- **Die Schlachten der Preussen u. Ihrer Verbündeten.** Berlin, 1848. 3rd. Edn. Ob. 4to. Pp.

hand-numbered, soiled thro.-out, plts. mostly browned, owner's mark on title in old hand. Pages hand-numbered, soiled thro.-out, plts. mostly browned, (HK. Nov.18-21; 1851)   DM 1,700

ROTHSCHILD, Baron James de
- **Catalogue des Livres composant la Bibliothèque de.** Paris, 1884-1920. 5 vols. Hf. mor., gt., orig. wraps. bnd. in, unc. (SI. Dec.4; 511)   Lire 420,000

ROTHSCHILD, Baron Victor
- **The Rothschild Library.** 1969. 2 vols. Orig. cl. (SH. Mar.6; 564)   *Haut.* £100

ROTHSCHILD, Hon. Walter
- **Extinct Birds.** Ill.:– after Keulemans Lodge & Frohawk. 1907. (300). Fo. Mod. hf. mor. (S. Dec.3; 1119)   *Old Hall.* £700
- – **Anr. Copy.** Lge. 4to. Cont. hf. mor., sm. piece torn from lr. cover. (C. Mar.18; 147)   *Duran.* £550

ROTTBOELL, Christian Friis
- **Descriptiones et Icones Rariores et pro Maxima Parte Nova Plantas.** Copen., 1773. Fo. 19th. C. hf. mor., upr. cover detchd. From Chetham's Liby., Manchester. (C. Nov.27; 348)   *Quaritch.* £160

ROUARGUE Frères
- **Album Pittoresque du Jardin de la France . . .** Paris, n.d. 1st. Printing. Ob. 4to. Some foxing, 46 plts. (of 50). Publisher's decor. buckram. (HD. Jun.25; 393)   Frs. 1,400

ROUART, Denis
See–DEGAS, Edgar & Rouart, Denis

ROUAULT, Georges
- **Divertissement.** [1493]. (40) on papier de Chine Ancien. Fo. Lacks hf.-title. Ll., wrap., box. (HD. Jun.30; 72)   Frs. 1,500

ROUEN, Le Colonel
- **L'Armée Belge.** Brussels, [1896]. 4to. Hf. red chagrin, corners, 5 decor. spine raised bands, unc. (LM. Jun.13; 18)   B.Frs. 22,000

ROUILLE D'ORFEUIL, Auguste
[-] **L'Ami des François.** Constantinople; [Paris], 1771. 1st. Edn. Cont. MS. marginalia on f.14v & V8v, textual corrections on f. V7 & 2A4, bkplt. of Comte de Saint Paul, dtd. 1759. Cont. red mor., floral corner sprays, gt., double gt. fillet, flat spine gt. with central thistle in compartments, inner gt. dentelles, pink silk liners. (SM. Oct.8; 1973)   Frs. 1,000

ROUILLIARD, Sebastian
- **Capitulaire auquel est traicté qu'un Homme nay sans Testicules apparens . . . est capable des Oeuvres du Mariage.** Paris, 1603. Inscr. on fly-lf. 'tres curieux. P'. 18th. C. red mor., triple gt. fillet, spine gt. à la grotesque, inner gt. dentelles. Radziwill–Béhague copy. (SM. Oct.8; 1974)   Frs. 1,100
- **Parthénie, ou Histoire de la très Auguste et très Dévote Eglise de Chartres . . .** Paris, 1609. Cont. cf. (HD. Jun.29; 175)   Frs. 1,050

ROUILLON-PETIT, F.
- **Campagnes Memorables des Français.** Paris, 1817. 2 vols. Fo. Slight internal spotting. Orig. qtr. mor. W.a.f. (TA. Aug.21; 12)   £170

ROULLET
- **Notice Historique des Evenements . . . l'Opéra la nuit du 13 février.** Ca. 1820. Cont. grenate hf. roan, decor. spine. (HD. Jun.10; 201)   Frs. 1,500

ROUPELL, A.E.
[-] **Specimens of the Flora of South Africa.** L., 1849. Fo. Orig. cl., lacks spine. (SSA. Nov.5; 77)   R. 2,200

ROUQUETTE, Louis Frederic
- **Le Grand Silence Blanc.** Ill.:– Clarence Gagnon. Paris, 1928. (725). On Rives, numbered. 4to. Sewed. (HD. Feb.27; 222)   Frs. 3,000

ROURA, J.
- **Memoria sobre los Vinos y su Destilacion y sobre los Aceites.** Barcelona, 1839. Cont. hf. leath., gt. spine, gold-stpd. floral cover borders, silk end-papers, gold-stpd. name on cover. (D. Dec.11-13; 145)   DM 510

ROUSSEAU, Jean Baptiste
- **Odes, Cantates, Epitres et Poésies diverses . . . pour l'Education de Monseigneur le Dauphin.** Paris, 1790. 4to. Cont. mor., gt., arms of Louis Philippe Joseph d'Orléans, Philippe Egalite, on covers, concentric roll borders, with corner sprays, including leafy branch entwining a double fillet,

spine gt. in compartments with lge. central fleuron, inner gt. dentelles, including 'drawer-handle' border. (SM. Oct.8; 1975)   Frs. 16,000
- **Oeuvres.** 1820. 5 vols. Long-grd. mor; oriental style, ornamental spines, by Doll. (HD. Oct.10; 282)   Frs. 3,100

ROUSSEAU, Jean Jacques
- **La Botanique.** Ill.:– P.J. Redouté. Paris, 1805. 4to. Title with engraved vig., 65 engraved plts., col.-ptd. & hand finished, 9 plts. stained. Cont. Fr. red str.-grd. mor., sides with gt. roll tool & fillet borders & cornerpieces, spine gt. (C. Mar.18; 96)   *Christopher.* £880
- – **Anr. Edn.** 1822. No bdg. stated. (DWB. Mar.31; 262)   £800
- **Les Confessions.** L., 1782. 3 vols. 18mo. Red mor. by Cazin. (HD. Apr.8; 301)   Frs. 1,100
- – **Anr. Edn.** Trans.:– Leloir. Paris, 1889. (48) Grand Luxe Edn. on Jap. 2 vols. 4to. Hf. red mor. sigd. by V. Champs, gt. spines, partly unc. (SI. Dec.4; 514)   Lire 580,000
- **Les Confessions.–Seconde Partie des Confessions.** Geneva, 1782; 1789. 2 works in 4 vols. Unif. cont. spr. cf., decor. spines, cold. pieces, 3 gt. fillets on covers, (HD. Dec.5; 186)   Frs. 6,500
- **Discours sur l'Origine . . . de l'Inégalité parmi les Hommes.** Ill.:– Eisen. Amst., 1755. 1st. pirated Edn. With lf. 'Adverissement', lacks 1st. blank lf., a few ll. slightly spotted. Mod. hf. mor. (S. Oct.21; 463)   *Braeklein.* £50
- **Emile, ou De l'Education.** Amst., 1762. 1st. Edn. 4 vols. Mott. cf. gt. (P. Jul.30; 311)   *Quaritch.* £170
- – **Anr. Copy.** 12mo. Cont. hf. cf., spines gt., worn. (S. Jul.27; 145)   *Maggs.* £80
- – **Anr. Copy.** Cont. spr. cf., decor. spines, cold. pieces, 3 fillets. (HD. Dec.5; 184)   Frs. 4,000
- **Lettres de Deux Amans.** Amst., 1761. New Edn. 6 vols. 12mo. Cont. cf., spines gt. (CSK. May.15; 106)   £60
- **La Nouvelle Héloise ou Lettres de Deux Amans.** Ill.:– Moreau. L., 1781. 1st. Printing. 7 vols. Cont. cf., gt. fillets around covers, smooth decor. spines, bdgs. defect. From Beraldi liby. (HD. Feb.27; 53)   Frs. 1,400
- – **Anr. Edn.** Ill.:– Tony Johannot, Lepoitevin, Baron & others. 1845. 1st. Edn. 2 vols. Cont. red. hf. mor., decor. spines, unc. (HD. Feb.18; 178)   Frs. 1,200
- **Oeuvres.** Geneva, 1782. 15 vols. including 3 vol. supp. 4to. Lacks 2 vol. 1789 supp., lacks final blanks in vols. III, IV & V, 1 hole affecting text in vol. 1, 12 (of 13) plts. from 1774 Brussels quarto coll. edn. loosely inserted in vols. II & III, 4 in 1st. state, 8 in 3rd. state. Cont. red mor. by Derome le Jeune with his 1785 ticket in vol. 1, later cipher of Lord Brougham (?) blind-stpd. on upr.-covers, triple gt. fillet, spines gt. with single urn in each compartment, inner gt. dentelles, vol. III reprd. (SM. Oct.8; 1976)   Frs. 1,000
- – **Anr. Edn.** Geneva, 1782-89. 17 vols. 4to. Added plts. by Moreau (from the 1774-83 edn.). Cont. cf., gt., some wear, some minor repairs. As an extra-ill. work, w.a.f. (S. Dec.8; 87)   *Bart.* £320
- – **Anr. Edn.** Paris, 1801. 20 vols. Cont. cf., cover defect. (H. May 21/22; 1256)   DM 420
- **Oeuvres Complètes . . .** Paris, 1788-89. New Edn. 38 vols. Cont. cf., gt. fillets on covers, spines richly decor. (HD. Jun.29; 72)   Frs. 5,200
- – **Anr. Edn.** Ed.:– Sebastien Mercier. Ill.:– Moreau, Marillier, Le Barbier, Leclerc, Boucher & others. 1788-93. New Edn. 39 vols. Some ll. yellowed, some plts. defect. Cont. tree cf., smooth decor. spines, bdgs. slightly defect. (HD. Jun.24; 110)   Frs. 7,200
- – **Anr. Edn.** Paris, 1793. Vols. 1-37 only. Later hf. cf. (SH. Mar.5; 282)   *Wade.* £80
- – **Anr. Edn.** Ill.:– Devéria. 1824-25. 27 vols. Hf. mor., sm. corners, gt. & blind ornamental spines, unc. On vell. (HD. Oct.10; 283)   Frs. 6,200
- **Le Testament.** 1771. Cont. cf., worn. (CE. Jul.9; 186)   £80

ROSSEAU, Jean-Jacques–TRONCHIN, J.R.–LA VERITE
- **Du Contrat Social.–Lettres Ecrites de la Campagne.–Ode à Mr de Voltaire.** Amst.; Proche Genève; L., 1762; 1765; 1765. 1st. Edn. (1st work). 3 works in 1 vol. Cont. red mor., smooth decor. spine, 3 fillets, inside dentelle. (HD. Dec.5; 185)   Frs. 13,000

ROUSSEL, Abbé
- Le Diocès de Langres ... Langres, 1873-79. 4 vols. Sm. fo. Hf. mor. (HD. Jun.29; 192)
Frs. 2,820

ROUSSEL, Raymond
- Locus Solus. Paris, 1914. 1st. Edn.; on imperial Jap. Sewed, unc. (HD. Jun.25; 394)   Frs. 3,600
- La Poussière de Soleils. Paris, 1927. Ltd. Edn. Mor.; gt., by Vermorel, partly unc. Inscr. to Paul Imbert. (SM. Oct.8; 2276)   Frs. 1,200

ROUSSET DE MISSY, Jean
See-DUMONT, Jean & Rousset de Missy, Jean

ROUVEYRE, André
- Apollinaire. Ill.:- Henri Matisse. Paris, 1952. (350) on Arches vell. 4to. In sheets, publisher's s.-c. (HD. Dec.5; 188)   Frs. 1,600
- Repli. Ill.:- Henri Matisse. Paris, 1947. (280); on Arches vell., numbered, sigd. by author & artist. In sheets, wrap., publisher's s.-c. (HD. Dec.5; 187)   Frs. 1,400

ROUVEYRE, Edouard
- Connaissances nécessaires à un Bibliophile. Paris, 1899. 5th. Edn., (50) on Jap. Imp. 10 vols Jansenist grenate mor., inner dentelle, wrap., by Jaffin. (HD. Jun.10; 202)   Frs. 2,900
- - Anr. Edn. Paris, [1899]. 5th. Edn., on papier velin tiente. 10 vols. Red hf. mor., spines faded. (SG. Mar.26; 397) $150
- - Anr. Edn. Paris, n.d. On vell. 10 vols. Hf. red mor., gt. spines, orig. wraps. bnd. in, unc. (SI. Dec.4; 515)   Lire 260,000

ROUX, Joseph
- Carte de la Mer Mediterranée. Marseilles, 1764. Fo. Some dampstains causing slight loss of engraved surface, mainly of upr. margins. Cont. cf., very worn. (SBA. Jul.14; 48)   Shapiro. £70
- Receuil des principaux Plans des Ports et Rades de la Mer Mediterranée estraits de ma Carte en Douze Feuilles. Marseilles, 1764. Ob. 8vo. Occasional staining, 1 plt. loose. Cont. mott. cf. As an atlas, w.a.f. (SPB. Oct.1; 209) $450
- - Anr. Copy. Cont. marb. cf., limp spine. (HD. Apr.24; 100)   Frs. 3,700

ROUX, Marcel
See-COURBOIN, François & Roux, Marcel

ROUX DE ROCHELLE, J.B.G.
- Historia de las Ciudades Anseaticas. Barcelona, 1844. Cont. hf. leath., gt spine. (R. Oct.14-18; 2342)   DM 680

ROWE, Elizabeth
- Friendship in Death: In Twenty Letters from the Dead to the Living ... L., 1741. Title re-set at inner margin. 19th. C. gt.-ornamental roan. Bnd. in are 22 orig. watercolour plts., with MS. captions, sigd. M. Pigot, ca. 1840. (PNY. Mar.26; 282) $125

ROWE, Jacob
- All Sorts of Wheel-Carriage, improved. 1734. 1st. Edn. 4to. Some foxing, a few marginal stains. 18th. C. hf. cf., worn, hf. red mor. case. Bkplt. of Peter Nouaille; from Honeyman Collection. (S. Nov.11; 2699)   Quaritch. £180

ROWLANDS, Henry
- Mona Antiqua Restaurata. An Archaeological Discourse on the Antiquities ... of the Isle of Anglesey. Dublin, 1723. 1st. Edn. 2 pts. in 1 vol. 4to. Slight spotting. Cont. panel. cf., rebkd. & cornered. (SBA. Oct.22; 753)
Teachers Charity. £70
- - Anr. Edn. 1766. 2nd. Edn. 4to. Some cont. marginal MS. notes. Cont. spr. cf. gt., slightly worn. (SBA. Jul.14; 333)   Richard. £90

ROWLANDS, Richard 'Richard Verstegan'
[-] A Restitution of Decayed Intelligence: In Antiquities. Concerning the Most Noble & Renowned English Nation. 1634. 4to. Recent panel. cf. gt. in traditional style by Bayntun of Bath. (TA. Mar.19; 495)   £95
- - Anr. Copy. 4to. Mod. spr. cf. by Bayntun. [STC 21363] (CSK. Nov.14; 4)   £80

ROWLANDSON, Thomas
- Advice to Sportsmen ... L., 1809. 1st. Edn. 16mo. Crimson three-qtr. mor., spine gt. (SG. Sep.4; 407) $180
- The Grand Master or Adventures of Qui Hi? in Hindostan. 1816. Errata slip at end but lacks cancel lf. C8. Cf. by Zaehnsdorf, gt. spine. (C. Feb.4; 84)   Chelsea Rare Books. £120

- - Anr. Copy. Hand-cold. aquatint title-p. & 25 plts. only. Mod. cl. folder. (TA. Oct.16; 181) £50
- Loyal Volunteers of London & Environs ... in their Respective Uniforms. L., 1798-99. 1st. Edn. Lge. 4to. Old hf. russ. gt. Baron de Marbot bkplt. (CNY. May 22; 172) $2,200
- - Anr. Edn. [L.], [1798-99]. 1st. Edn., early iss. 4to. Without 2 additional plts., slight offsetting, occasional foxing. Cont. russ., rebkd., worn. (SPB. Oct.1; 210) $3,250
[-] Poetical Sketches of Scarborough. Ill.- Thomas Rowlandson after James Green. L., 1813. 2nd. Edn. Cf. (SG. Sep.4; 410) $175
- Sketches from Nature. Ill.:- Stadler. N.d. Ob. 4to. Plts. dtd. 1822 & wtrmkd. 1818. Mod. red hf. mor. From the collection of Eric Sexton. (C. Apr.16; 346)   Edmonds. £1,500
See-GREEN, James & Rowlandson, Thomas

ROWLANDSON, Thomas (Ill.)
See-ACKERMANN, Richard
See-BRITTON, John
See-COMBE, William
See-EGAN, Pierce
See-ENGLEBACH, Lewis
See-GOLDSMITH, Oliver
See-GRAY, Thomas
See-ILLUSTRATED POCKET LIBRARY of Plain & Coloured Books
See-MITFORD, John, Journalist 'A. Burton'
See-PAPWORTH, John Buonarotti & others
See-QUIZEM, Caleb
See-RASPE, Rudolph Erich
See-ROBERTS, Col. David
See-SHOBERL or Schoberl, Frederic
See-WIGSTEAD, Henry

ROWLANDSON, Thomas & others
[-] Poetical Magazine. L., 1809-11. 4 vols. (all publd.). 49 (of 50) cold. aquatints, lacks ll. 'To the Reader' in vols. III & IV as usual & advts. in vols. I & IV. Str.-grd. mor. gt. by Wallis, jnts. worn, s.-c. (SPB. Jul.28; 416) $350

ROWLEY, George Dawson
- Ornithological Miscellany. 1875-78. 14 Pts. in 3 vols. 4to. 135 litho. plts. & 3 maps, 104 plts. cold., with orig. drawing for lge. folding plt. in vol. 2 loosely inserted, 2 uncold. litho. plts. stpd. & addressed to author also inserted. Red mor. gt., gt. panels & gt. fillet borders & cornerpieces, author's initials in gt. on upr. covers, by R.H. Porter, orig. wraps., title-p., list of plts., etc. to orig. pts. bnd. in. Author's copy, with sig. & A.N. (C. Mar.18; 97)   Evans. £1,900
- - Anr. Edn. Ill.:- some by Keulemans. 1876-78. 3 vols. Lge. 4to. Late 19th. C. hf. mor. with gt. crowned monog. CSF [or FSC] in bottom compartment of spine. (S. Jun.1; 199)
Milner. £850
- - Anr. Copy. Cl., worn. (CE. Oct.24; 159) £550

ROWLEY, William
- A New Wonder, a Woman never Vext ... 1632. 1st. Edn. 4to. 2 headlines cropped, slight dampstaining. 19th C. cf., gt., by Rivière. Bkplt. of 'A.K.' [NSTC 21423] (S. May 5; 299)
Quaritch. £220

ROXBURGH, William
- Plants of the Coast of Coromandel. 1795-[1819?]. 3 vols. Fo. Vol. 3 incompl. (lacks pts. 2 & 3), lacks 75 plts. (of 300), index lf. & 3 plts. loose, 1 plt. spotted. Orig. paper bds., covers of vol. 2 detchd., unc. W.a.f. (C. Nov.5; 135)
Henderson. £2,600

ROY, Claude
- Hans Erni. Zurich, 1964. (100). 4to. Orig. bdg. & publisher's box. (SPB. Nov.25; 265) $150

ROY, William
- The Military Antiquities of the Romans in Britain. 1793. 1st. Edn. Fo. Slight marginal spotting to a few plts., title slightly soiled. Cont. hf. cf., some wear. (S. Dec.9; 399)   Weinreb. £90
- - Anr. Copy. Cont. panel. cf. (PG. Dec.12; 50)
£52

ROYAL ACADEMY
- A Commemorative Catalogue of the International Exhibition of Chinese Art. 1936. 4to. Orig. cl. (S. Sep.30; 385)   £80
- - Anr. Edn. L., [1936]. 4to. Gt.-lettered cl., some soiling on spine, unc. & mostly unopened. (SG. Mar.12; 97) $180
- Pictures. 1892-1906. 15 vols. only. Cont. hf. cf. (CSK. Dec.12; 111)   £50

ROYAL AGRICULTURAL SOCIETY of England
- Journal. 1840-65. Vols. 1-25 & General Index. Cont. hf. cf. (SD. Feb.4; 265)   £80

ROYAL ANTHROPOLOGICAL INSTITUTE
- Journal. 1940-65. Vols. 70-95, in 41 vols. 4to. Orig. wraps. (SH. Jan.30; 487)   Funabiki. £80

ROYAL ARTILLERY INSTITUTION
- Minutes of the Proceedings (the Journal). N.d. Vols. 1-44. Bdg. not stated, ex-liby. As a periodical, w.a.f. (LC. Jun.16; 221)   £140

ROYAL CUCKOLD, The
L., 1693. 1st. Edn. 4to. Sm. hole in some ll. affecting text. Mor. by Sangorski. [Wing R2125] (C. Nov.19; 142)   Brett-Smith. £480

ROYAL GALLERY OF ART
Ed.:- S.C. Hall. Ca. 1850. 4 vols. Fo. A few plts. detchd., some other very minor defects. Cont. hf. mor. gt. (SBA. May 27; 501)   Edistar. £160
- - Anr. Edn. Ed.:- Samuel Carter Hall & others. L., ca. 1862. Lge. fo. Some plts. loose. Orig. cl. Inscr. by editors. (GM. Apr.30; 741)   £65

ROYAL GEOGRAPHICAL SOCIETY of London
The Journal. L., 1861. 31st vol Orig. bdg., unopened. (JL. Mar.2; 622)   Aus. $140
- - Anr. Edn. L., 1862. 32nd. vol. Orig. bdg., unopened. (JL. Mar.2; 623)   Aus. $170

ROYAL ILLUSTRATED ATLAS (The) of Modern Geography
L. & Edinb., 1864-65. Fo. 1 corner of engraved title stained, cold. maps on guards thro.-out, some prelims. spotted or slightly stained but text only. Orig. mor. gt., slightly worn. As an atlas, w.a.f. (SBA. Jul.14; 13)   Shapiro. £100

ROYAL IRISH ACADEMY (The)
- Transactions of ... Dublin, 1787-97. Vols. 1-6. 4to. Orig. bds. & cf., worn, unc. & partly unopened. (TA. May 21; 305)   £55

ROYAL KALENDAR (The), or ... Annual Register for England, Scotland, Ireland & America, for ... 1799-HERALDRY in Miniature -COMPANION (A) to the Royal Kalendar-EAST INDIA Kalendar (The)
L., 1799; 1798; n.d.; 1799. 4 works in 1 vol. 12mo. Cont. str.-grd. crimson mor., tooled gt. border. (GM. Apr.30; 226)   £70

ROYAL MILITARY CHRONICLE
L., Nov. 1810-Apr. 1817. 1st. Series in 7 vols., New Series in 6 vols., tog. 13 vols. Crimson three-qtr. mor., spines gt., by Morrell. (SG. Oct.9; 213) $700

ROYAL NAVY, The
Ill.:- after W.F. Mitchell. Portsmouth, 1881. 4to. Slightly soiled. Orig. linen. (R. Mar.31-Apr.4; 1795)   DM 1,200
- Regulations & Instructions relating to His Majesty's Service at Sea. 1808. 4to. Owner's inscr. 'Captain Christian. H.M. Ship Heroine April 1809'. Cf., spine gt. (LC. Oct.2; 215)   £60

ROYAL SOCIETY OF LONDON
- Catalogue of Scientific Papers (1800-83). 1867-1902. Vols. I-XII. 4to. Vols. I-VIII cont. red hf. mor., rest cl., some wear. (S. Apr.6; 198)
Pratt. £110
- The Philosophical Transactions ... Abridged. (1665-1800). Ed.:- Charles Hutton & others. 1809. 18 vols. 4to. Cont. hf. cf. From liby. of Dr. E. Ashworth Underwood. (S. Feb.23; 282)
Stewart. £130

ROYAL SOCIETY OF NEW SOUTH WALES
- Journal. 1881-1932. 33 vols., lacks some vols. Bnd. & unbnd. vols. (JL. Dec.15; 895)   Aus. $125

ROYALL, Mrs. Anne
- Sketches of History, Life & Manners in the United States ... New Haven, 1826. 1st. Edn. 12mo. Slight paper loss not affecting image at frontis., text browned & foxed. Cont. hf. cf., scarred, gt. spine, worn. From liby. of William E. Wilson. (SPB. Apr.29; 240) $325

ROYAUMONT, Sieur de
See-FONTAINE, Nicolas, Sieur de Royaumont

ROYEN, Jacob van
[-] Amsterdamsche Secretary, bestaende in Formulieren van Schepenen-kennissen, Quijtscheldeningen, Schat-brieven, en andere. Amst., 1700. Cont. vell. (C. Jul.15; 227)
Quaritch. £150

ROZANTAL, A.
– Arts Antiques de l'Asie Occidentale et les Origines des Motifes de le Céramique Islamique Arquaique. Nice, 1948. (1000) numbered. 4to. Orig. bds. (SH. Mar.6; 565) *Diba.* £110

RUBEIS, Domenico de
See–ROSSI, Domenico de

RUBEIS, Giovanni Giacono de
See–ROSSI, Giovanni Giacono de

RUBENS, Sir Peter Paul
– La Gallerie du Palais Luxembourg peinté par Rubens. Ill.:– after Van Dyck by Audran (frontis.), after Rubens by Audran, Picart & others (plts.). Paris, 1710. Fo. Cont. mott. cf., gt. spine. (C. Feb.25; 204) *Cucci.* £420
– Palazzi Antichi di Genova. Antw., 1663. 2 pts. in 1 vol. Lge. fo. Last plt. in pt. 1 & some plts. in pt. II mntd., lacks (?) dedication lf. in pt. I, title of pt. I reprd., a few marginal tears, some plts. slightly stained or soiled. Old. cf., very worn. (S. Jun.29; 287) *Duran.* £350

RUCHAT, Abraham & others
– Etat et Délices de la Suisse. Neuchatel, 1778. 2 vols. 4to. Cont. cf., spines gt. (C. Jul.15; 126) *Mohler.* £1,950

RÜCKERT, Friedrich
– Gedichte. Frankfurt, 1841. 1st. Edn. Cont. hf. leath. gt. (HK. May 15; 4788) DM 440
– Gesammelte Politische Werke. Frankfurt, 1868-69. 1st. Coll. Edn. 12 vols. Slightly browned in parts. Cont. hf. leath., slightly worn. (H. Dec.9/10; 1650) DM 640

RUCKERT, R. (Ed.)
See–MEISSNER PORZELLAN

RUDBECK, Olaus
– Atland eller Manheim dedan Japhets afkomne . . . Upsala, 1679-86. 1st. Edn. 2 vols. & Atlas. Fo. Atlas with engraved frontis. preserved, some marginal repairs, vol. 1 lacks last lf. (as in most known copies), vol. 2 with the Emendanda & Index. 19th C. qtr. cf., gt. (S. May 5; 64) *Hannas.* £500

RUDD, Thomas
– Practicall Geometry, in Two Parts . . . for Surveyors of Land, Engineers, Military Architects. 1650. 1st. Edn. 4to. Stained & soiled, prelims. loose & frayed, slight marginal worming, owner's inscr. of Tho. Wilkinson, 1835, with a few annots. in his hand. Sheep, spine reprd., very worn. From Honeyman Collection. (S. Nov.11; 2700) *Dr. Strauss.* £70

RUDDER, Samuel
– A New History of Gloucestershire. Cirencester, 1779. Fo. Lev. mor. gt. by Rivière. From the collection of Eric Sexton. (C. Apr.16; 347) *Traylen.* £380
– – Anr. Copy. Title soiled. Cont. cf. with old reback. (TA. Mar.19; 599) £140
– – Anr. Copy. Lacks 1 single-p. plt. Disbnd. W.a.f. (TA. Aug.21; 295) £105
– – Anr. Edn. Ill.:– J. Cary. 1801. Fo. Lacks 3 engrs. & sm. portion of title-p. Old panel. cf. W.a.f. (TA. Aug.21; 296) £100

RUDING, Rev. Rogers
– Annals of the Coinage of Great Britain. 1840. 3rd. Edn. 3 vols. 4to. Cont. hf. mor. (SH. Jun.18; 111) *Barra.* £70

RUDNICKI, Leon
– Original Designs for 'Feminies'. Ill.:– Rudnicki & Gaston Noury. [1894?]. Suite of finished article at end, orig. watercolour drawing by Noury. Red hf. mor. (SM. Oct.8; 2309) *Frs. 3,800*

RUDOLF von Osterreich
– Eine Orientreise. Vienna, 1884. Fo. Some plts. spotted. Orig. cl. gt. (SH. May 21; 257) *Crete.* £110

RUDOLFF, Christoff
– Kunstliche Rechnung mit der Ziffer und mit den Zal Pfennigen, sampt der Wellischen practica, und allerley Vorteil auff die Regel de Tri. Nuremb., 1532. Lacks final blank, slight staining & soiling. Mor., by Leighton. From Honeyman Collection. (S. Nov.11; 2701) *Martin.* £290
– – Anr. Edn. Vienna, Priv. ptd., 1574. Text browned, wax stain of fore-edges. Cont. blind-stpd. vell. bds., rolls of medallion heads & figures of Erasmus, Luther, Melancthon & Calvin, some wear, clasps & catches. From

Honeyman Collection. (S. Nov.11; 2702) *Martin.* £320

RUDOLPHI, J.A.
– Neu-Vermehrte Heraldica Curiosa. Leipzig, 1718. 2nd. Edn. 2 pts. in 1 vol. Cont. leath., spine defect. (R. Oct.14-18; 1233) DM 800

RUDOLPHI, Karl Asmund
Anatomisch-Physiologische Abhandlungen. Berlin, 1802. 1st. Edn. Old marb. bds., ex-liby. (SG. Aug.21; 362) $110

RUELLIUS, Joannes
– De Natura Stirpium. Paris, 1536. 1st. Edn. Fo. 19th. C. hf. mor. From Chetham's Liby., Manchester. (C. Nov.27; 349) *Junk.* £320
– – Anr. Copy. Title in woodcut border, detchd. & very worn, stained thro.-out, some ll. holed, old marginalia, cont. inscr. on remains of fly-lf. Cont. Fr. mor., gt., arms of Cosse, Comptes de Brissac in oval in wide gt. dentelle border, worn, wide scratches. (S. Nov.25; 384) *Stewart.* £50

RUEMANN, Arthur
– Alte Deutsche Kinderbuecher. Wein, 1937. Ltd., numbered Edn. Buckram, d.-w. (SG. Jan.22; 120) $250

RUET, Noel
– Femmes. Ill.:– Armand Rassenfosse. Liège, 1928. (121) numbered. 4to. Orig. wraps., slightly discold. (SH. Nov.20; 74) *Monk Bretton.* £85

RUGE, A.
[–] Die Polit. Lyriber unserer Zeit. Leipzig, 1847. Soiled. Cont. hf. leath. gt. (HK. May 15; 4797) DM 700

RUGGIERI, Ferdinando
– Scelta di Architecture Antiche e Moderne della Citta di Firenze. Flor., 1755. 2 vols. only in 1. Fo. Dampstained thro.-out. Later hf. mor., soiled. (CSK. Nov.28; 27) £75

RUGGLE, George
See–RAVENSCROFT, Edward (or Ruggle, George)

RUIZ, Hippolyto & Pavon, Josepho
– Systema Vegetablium Florae Peruvianae et Chilensis. [Madrid], 1798. Vol. 1 (all publd.). Sm. 4to. Stained at beginning & end. Cf.-bkd. bds. (SPB. May 5; 447) $550

RUIZ DE MONTOYA, Antonio
– [Works]. Ed.:– J. Platzmann. Leipzig, 1876. 4 vols. Sm. 4to. A few light stains. Cont. qtr. mor. (SPB. May 5; 449) $300

RUIZ VILLEGA, Ferdinando
– Opera. Ill.:– Cattini, Nicolai, & O[rsolini] (head & tail-pieces). Venice, 1734. 4to. Paste-paper bds. From the collection of John A. Saks. (C. Jun.10; 225) *Lyon.* £180

RULAND, Martin
– Lexicon Alchemiae sive Dictionarium Alchemisticum. Frankfurt, 1612. 1st. Edn. 4to. 1st. p. of dedication repeated on verso of last lf., some browning & staining, slight worming affecting text, owner's inscr. on fly-lf, sig. on title. 19th. C. parch.-bkd. bds. From Honeyman Collection. (S. Nov.11; 2703) *Das Bucherkabinet.* £260
– – Anr. Copy. Slight stain thro.-out, some pp. heavily browned. Cont. leath. (D. Dec.11-13; 2252) DM 1,200
– – Anr. Edn. Frankfurt, 1661. Sm. 4to. Mod. hf. leath. (R. Oct.14-18; 213) DM 900

RUMANN, Martin
See–LANCKORONSKA, Maria & Rümann, A.

RUMFORD, Benjamin Thompson, Count
– Recherches sur la Chaleur developpée dans la Combustion et dans la Condensation des Vapeurs. (& 11 other pieces). Paris, 1812. 12 pieces in 1 vol. Mor.-bkd. bds. From Honeyman Collection; w.a.f. (S. Nov.11; 2704) *Rota.* £110

RUMPF, Fritz
– Primitive Japanese Woodcuts. Ed.:– Curt Glaser. Berlin, n.d. Fo. Loose as iss. in vell.-bkd. patterned bd. folder, torn. (SG. Dec.4; 285) $200

RUMPH, George Eberhard
– Herbarium Amboinense . . . Ed.:– Jan Burman. Amst., [1741]-50-55. 6 vols. Fo. 2 pts. loosening in vol. 2, some plts. at end discold., margins of text ll. spotted in vol. 6, 'Auctarium' bnd. in at end of vol. 6. Old cf., rebkd. From Chetham's Liby., Manchester. (C. Nov.27; 350) *Junk.* £2,200
– Thesaurus Imaginum Piscium Testaceorum . . . Cochlearum . . . Conchylia . . . Mineralia. The

Hague, 1739. [2nd. Edn.?]. Slim fo. Engraved title with sm. portion of bottom corner torn away. Cont. cf. with central gt. armorial, worn. (TA. Jul.16; 149) £220
– – Anr. Copy. Lacks plt. no XXII, with the additional engraved title normally found in the 1st. edn., some plts. browned. 19th. C. hf. mor. From Chetham's Liby., Manchester. (C. Nov.27; 351) *Taylor.* £140
– – Anr. Copy. Extra engraved title dtd. 1711, 58 (of 60) copperplts., all stpd. on rectos. Old cf.-bkd. bds., worn, ex-liby. (SG. Sep.18; 323) $100

RUNGE, Friedlieb Ferdinand
– Einleitung in die Technische Chemie für Jedermann. Berlin, 1836. 1st. Edn. Cont. linen. (HK. Nov.18-21; 719) DM 650
– Farbenchemie. Berlin, 1834-50. 1st. Edn. 3 vols. Some browning & offsetting. Bds., very worn, vol. I not unif. From Honeyman Collection. (S. Nov.11; 2705) *Henderson.* £170

RUNGE, Heinrich
– Die Schweiz in Original Ansichten ihrer Interessantesten Gegenden. Darmstadt, 1866-70. Vols. 2 & 3 (of 3). 4to. Slightly browned in parts, steel-engraved title & vol. 2 dtd. 1870. Cont. linen. (HK. May 12-14; 778) DM 9,800

RUNGE, Philip Otto
– Von dem Fischer un Syner Fru. Berlin, 1914. (180). 4to. Orig. hf. linen, orig. bd. s.-c., defect. Printer's mark sigd. by artist, ex-liby. (HK. May 12-14; 1781) DM 1,650
– [–] Anr. Edn. Ill.:– G. Marcks. [Hamburg], [1955]. Orig. bds. With 13 supp. loose woodcuts on various Japan-Bütten-papers, printer's mark sigd. by artist. (H. Dec.9/10; 2214) DM 1,300

RUNKEL, Shlomo Zalman
– Chatan Damim. Prague, 1605. Sm. 4to. Stained, reprd., cropped, browning. Hf. cl., label torn. (SPB. May 11; 182) $750

RUPIN, Ernest
– L'Oeuvre de Limoges. Paris, 1890. 4to. Cont. hf. mor. (SH. Oct.9; 151) *Talerman.* £55

RUPP, Israel Daniel
[–] Early History of Western Pennsylvania, & of the West, & of Western Expeditions & Campaigns from 1754-1833. Pittsb., 1846. 1st. Edn. Sig. of Walter H. Lourie, Pittsburgh, 1848. Cont. cf., backstrip badly worn. (PNY. Dec.3; 290) $170
– The Geographical Catechism of Pennsylvania & the Western States. Harrisburg, 1836. 1st. Edn. 18mo. Orig. cl. (SG. Jun.11; 373) $140

RUSCA, Antonio
– De Inferno et Statu Daemonum. Milan, 1621. 1st. Edn. 4to. Inscr. at foot of p. 33 'Ex Libris Stae genovesae parisiensis 1696' & same on title, bkplts. of Girardot de Préfond, Marquess of Crewe & Evan, Viscount Tredegar. 18th. C. mor., triple gt. fillet, spine gt. in compartments with initials PGDP for Girardot de Préfond at foot, inner gt. dentelles. (SM. Oct.8; 1980) *Frs. 1,600*

RUSCA, Louis
– Recueil des Dessins de différens Batimans construits à Saint-Petersbourg. St. Petersb., 1810. 2 pts. in 1 vol. Fo. Text in Fr. & Italian, dampstained, mostly marginal. Cont. cf.-bkd. bds. (SH. Feb.5; 263) *Weinreb.* £1,500

RUSCELLI, Girolamo 'Piemontese Alessio'
– Precetti della Militia Moderna, tanto per Mare, quanto per Terra. Venice, 1568. 1st. Edn. 4to. Lacks final blank, browned & stained, lr. fore-margins wormed at end, tear in H4, data in colophon imperfectly printed, owners' inscrs. on title. 18th. C. patterned wraps., spine defect., upr. cover wormed. From Honeyman Collection. (S. Nov.11; 2706) *Mursia.* £130
– The Secrets of Alexis. 1615-14. Sm. 4to. Hole in title with slight textual loss, repair to N1, rust-holes in O5 & T4, clean tear in 2E4. Old-style panel. cf. [STC 299] (S. Jul.27; 66) *Thorpe.* £90
– Weiber Zierung des Hocherfarnen . . . Trans.:– Hans Jacob Wecker. Basle, 1575. 1st. Edn. in German. Some browning, lacks J3-8 & K1. Early 19th. C. hf. cf., worn. From liby. of André L. Simon. (S. May 18; 14) *Hoppen.* £50
See–PTOLOMEUS, Claudius–RUSCELLIUS, Girolamo

RUSH, Benjamin
– Medical Inquiries into Observations upon the Diseases of the Mind. Phila., 1830. 4th. Edn.

Advts. at beginning & 2 pp. at end. Cont. cf. Bkplt. of the M. Blumenthal collection. (S. Jun.17; 738) *Jenner Books.* £75
– Report of an Action for a Libel, brought by Dr. Benjamin Rush, against William Cobbett . . . Phila., 1800. 1st. Edn. Foxed. Disbnd. (SG. Jan.29; 368) $250

RUSHTON, Edward
– Expostulatory Letter to George Washington, of Mount Vernon, in Virginia, on his Continuing to be a Proprietor of Slaves. L'pool., 1797. 1st. Edn. 12mo. Title a little spotted. Disbnd. [Sabin 72480] (C. Apr.1; 185) *Nicholas.* £110

RUSIUS, L.
– Hippiatria sive Marescalia. Ill.:– H.S. Beham (title & 2 text woodcuts). Paris, Jul. 1532. 2nd. Wechel Edn. Fo. Lacks ll. 2 & 3 at beginning, title slightly soiled & with defects. bkd., lightly browned in parts, wormed in parts. 17th. C. vell. (HK. May 12-14; 165) DM 800

RUSKIN, John
– The Architecture of Venice. Ill.:– T.S. Boys & others. 1851. 3 pts. Fo. Loose in orig. wraps. Subscriber's copy. (C. May 20; 50) *Boyd.* £400
– Deucalion. Orpington, Kent, 1879. 2 vols. in 1. Mor. gt., rebkd. With a fore-e. pntg.; as a fore-e. pntg., w.a.f. (SPB. May 29; 162) $275
[–] The King of the Golden River. Ill.:– after Richard Doyle. L., 1851. 1st. Edn. Square 8vo. Cf., triple gt. fillet borders, spines gt., by Bayntun, orig. pict. wraps. bnd. in (almost faded to illegibility), in cl. s.-c. (SG. Apr.30; 281) $110
– – Anr. Edn. Ill.:– Arthur Rackham. 1932. (570), this copy marked 'Special' & sigd. by artist. Orig. parch., unopened, s.-c. worn. With pen & ink drawing by Rackham under limitation statement, sigd. & dtd. 1932. (S. Jul.31; 293) *Hatchards.* £320
– – Anr. Copy. Inscr. on hf.-title. Orig. vell. gt., box, soiled. (SPB. May 29; 364) $275
– – Anr. Edn. Ill.:– Arthur Rackham. L., [1932]. 1st. Trade Edn. Cold. pict. wraps., d.-w. Raymond M. Sutton Jr. copy. (SG. May 7; 251) $100
– – Anr. Edn. Ill.:– Arthur Rackham. L., [1932]. (570) numbered, sigd. by artist. Limp vell. wrinkled, partly unopened, s.-c. damaged. Raymond M. Sutton Jr. copy. (SG. May 7; 250) $375
– The Laws of Fésole. Orpington, Kent, 1879. Mor. gt. Fore-e. pntg. of a town or village; as a fore-e. pntg., w.a.f. (SPB. May 29; 161) $225
– Letters . . . to Ernest Chesneau.–Letters on Art & Literature.–Letters . . . to Rev. J.P. Faunthorpe, M.A. . . . Ed.:– Thomas James Wise. L., Priv. ptd. 1894-1903. Together 6 vols. Cl., each with gold-lettered buckram d.-w. with hf. mor. s.-c. with simulated spines. (SG. Oct.2; 320) $400
– Modern Painters. L., 1851-60. 1st. Edns. (Vols. III-V); 5th. Edn. (Vol. 1); 3rd. Edn. (Vol. II). 5 vols. 4to. Gt. ruled mor., by Bacster's Bindery. (PNY. Oct.1; 467) $130
– – Anr. Edn. L., 1867-9. 7th. Edn.; 5th. Edn.; 2nd. Edn.; 2nd. Edn. 4 vols. Royal 8vo. Unif. ribbed cl., blind decor. bds. & gt. decor. spines, dampstain on bd. of 3rd. vol. (TW. Sep.19; 168) £52
– The Nature of Gothic. Kelms. Pr., 1892. (500). Orig. ll., silk ties, unc. (SH. Feb.19; 1) *Fletcher.* £170
– – Anr. Copy. 4to. Minor defects. Slight soiling. (SPB. Jul.28; 208) $225
– Notes on his Collection of Drawings by J.M.W. Turner. L., 1878. 1st. Edn., L.P. 4to. Orig. mor.-bkd. cl. (SH. Oct.9; 100) *Esterow.* £50
– – Anr. Copy. Vell., gt. borders with hand-painted design, matching spine, gt. dentelles. (SG. May 14; 189) $525
– St. Mark's Rest: The History of Venice. Sunnyside, Orpington, Kent, 1884. 1st. Edn. 12mo. Crushed lev. mor. gt., single fillet panels, flat spine in 6 compartments, 5 raised bands, by Doves Bindery, sigd. & dtd. 1912, red mor. solander case by Rivière. Edith Rockefeller McCormick bkplt. (CNY. May 22; 342) $600
– Sesame & Lilies. L., [1906]. Mor., covers gt.-tooled with lge. spray of roses on pointillé grounds in border of sm. stars with heart in each corner, spine unif. gt., unif. gt. dentelles with doubls. & end-ll. of moire satin, by Ramage. (SG. Feb.12; 110) $120
– The Seven Lamps of Architecture.–Modern Painters.–The Stones of Venice. 1849; 1873; 1873-74. 1st. work 1st. Edn. 1 vol.; 5 vols.; 3 vols. 2 vols. of 3rd. work spotted. Unif. red mor. gt., slightly worn. 1st. vols. of 2nd. & 3rd. works sigd. (SKC. Feb.26; 1475) £130
– The Stones of Venice. Sunnyside, Orpington, 1886. 4th. Edn., L.P. 3 vols. 4to. Lev., triple gt. fillet borders, spines gt., gt. dentelles, by Bickers. (SG. Mar.12; 319) $130
– – Anr. Copy. Slightly soiled in parts. Linen. (D. Dec.11-13; 1531) DM 700
– Unto This Last: Four Essays on the First Principles of Political Economy. Hammersmith, Doves Pr., 1907. (12) on vell. Sm. 4to. Dull-pol. mor., covers with double gt.-ruled border, lge. tooled central panel, spine in 6 compartments, raised bands, gt. panel. in 3, ornament in the rest, sigd. by Doves Bindery 1907, qtr. mor. s.-c. (CNY. May 22; 382) $3,200
– – Anr. Copy. (300) Orig. limp vell., unc. (CNY. May 22; 302) $180
– Works. 1871-87. 26 vols. Unif. tree cf. gt. (CE. Jul.9; 39) £270
– [–] Anr. Edn. 1871-1901. 30 vols. Various sizes. Cont. cf. (SH. May 28; 88) *Harrington.* £160
– – Anr. Edn. Ed.:– E.T. Cook & A. Wedderburn. 1903-12. Liby. Edn. 39 vols. Orig. cl. with liby. marks on spines, unopened. (P. Mar.12; 226) *Lincoln College.* £660
– – Anr. Copy. Hf. mor. by Bickers & Son. (CSK. Sep.26; 55) £580
– – Anr. Copy. Orig. cl. (SH. Jul.23; 101) *Subunso.* £300
– – Anr. Edn. Ed.:– E.T. Cook & Alexander Wedderburn. L., 1903-13. Liby. Edn. 39 vols. Orig. blind-stpd. maroon mor. (SG. Oct.9; 214) $1,500
– Works.–Fors Clavigera.–Arrows of the Chace.–A Joy for Ever. 1st. work: Kent, 1872-78; 1871-77; 1880; 1880. 10 vols.; 7 vols.; 2 vols.; 1 vol. Some offsetting. Mor. gt., gt. panel. covers. (SPB. Nov.25; 484) $300

RUSSEGGER, J.v.
– Reisen in Europa, Asien und Afrika, mit Besonderer Rücksicht auf die Naturwissenschaftlichen Verhältnisse. Stuttgart, 1841-49. 4 vols. in 6 & atlas., together 7 vols. Atlas lge. fo. Soiled. Cont. hf. leath. (R. Mar.31-Apr.4; 2541) DM 1,200
– – Anr. Edn. Stuttgart, 1841-48. 4 vols. in 6, without atlas vol. Mostly browned & soiled, title-lf. stpd. Cont. hf. leath., worn. (H. May 21/22; 322) DM 420

RUSSELL, Alexander
– The Natural History of Aleppo. 1756 (mis-ptd. 1856). 1st. Edn. 4to. Mor.-bkd. cl. From Chetham's Liby., Manchester. (C. Nov.27; 352) *Armstrong.* £140
– – Anr. Edn. 1794. 2 vols. 4to. Cf. gt. (P. Feb.19; 111) *Maggs.* £120

RUSSELL, Bertrand
See–**WHITEHEAD, Alfred North & Russell, Bertrand**

RUSSELL, George
– A Tour through Sicily in the Year 1815. 1819. Some ll. slightly spotted. Cont. hf. cf. (SD. Feb.4; 203) £65

RUSSELL, George William 'A.E.'
– Collected Poems, by A.E. L., 1913. 1st. Edn. Cl., hf. mor. s.-c. Sigd. as Russell & A.E., with cold. pencil sketch, Crosby Gaige bkplt. (SG. Jun.4; 439) $260
– Deirdre. Dublin, 1907. 1st. Edn. Square 16mo. Wraps., unc., unopened, hf. mor. s.-c. Sigd. as Russell & A.E. (SG. Jun.4; 438) $160
– The Divine Vision, & Other Poems, by A.E. L., 1904. 1st. Edn. Cl., unc., partly unopened, hf. mor. s.-c. Sigd. both as George W. Russell & A.E.; Crosby Gaige & A.B. Spingarn bkplts. (SG. Jun.4; 437) $100
– Voices of the Stones, by A.E. L., 1925. 1st. Edn. Cl., d.-w., hf. mor. s.-c. Sigd. in both names & with sm. cold. drawing, Crosby Gaige bkplt. (SG. Jun.4; 440) $220

RUSSELL, Sir Gordon
– Designer's Trade. 1968. Mor., blind-tooled frame dividing covers into 15 squares, similar bands on spine, sigd. with monog. & dtd. 1968, s.-c., by Bernard Middleton. (SH. Feb.20; 400) *Quaritch.* £260

RUSSELL, Hastings William
See–**RUSS, Karl F. Otto–RUSSELL, Hastings William**

RUSSELL, James
– A Practical Essay on a Certain Disease of the Bones termed Necrosis. Edinb., 1794. Last 2 plts. slightly stained. Cf., rebkd. (S. Jun.17; 739) *Quaritch.* £150

RUSSELL, John
– Ben Nicholson, Drawings, Paintings & Reliefs. 1969. (60) with sigd. etching. 4to. Orig. linen, d.-w., s.-c. (SH. Mar.27; 373) *Thomson.* £160

RUSSELL, John, of Cambridge
– The Two Famous Pitcht Battels of Lypsich & Lutzen. 1634. 1st. Edn. Sm. 4to. 19th. C. hf. cf. Huth bkplt., lately in the collection of Eric Sexton. [STC 21460] (C. Apr.15; 145) *Hannas.* £280

RUSSELL, P. & Price, Owen
– England Displayed. 1769. 2 vols. Fo. Some engraved maps or plts. defect. Cont. cf., 2 covers detchd. W.a.f. from the collection of Eric Sexton. (C. Apr.16; 251) *Kidd.* £300

RUSSELL, Patrick
– An Account of Indian Serpents collected on the Coast of Coromandel. 1796. 1 vol. only. Fo. Cont. mor.-bkd. cf., worn, covers detchd. W.a.f. (C. Mar.18; 98) *Negro.* £300
– – Anr. Copy. Lacks later Supp. Hf. cf. Lge. copy, bkplt. of Sir John Smith, Bart. (S. Jun.1; 200) *Wheldon & Wesley.* £190
– A Treatise of the Plague. 1791. 1st. Edn. (L.P.) 2 pts. in 1 vol. 4to. Slight browning. Orig. bds., worn, unc. (S. Dec.2; 608) *Gurney.* £50

RUSSELL, Richard
– A Dissertation Concerning the Use of Sea Water in Diseases of the Glands. Oxford, 1753. 2nd. Edn. A few tears, browned. Mod. hf. cf. (SH. Jun.18; 52) *Ball.* £75

RUSSELL, William Howard
– The Atlantic Telegraph. [1865]. 4to. Cont. hf. cf. (C. May 20; 169) *Maggs.* £60
– Memorial . . . Marriage of H.R.H. Albert Edward & Alexandra. Ill.:– Robert Dudley. 1863. Fo. Orig. cl. gt., jnts. worn. (SH. Apr.10; 323) *Balour.* £135
– – Anr. Edn. 1864. Fo. 2 plts. detchd., a few other very minor defects. Orig. cl. gt. (SBA. Jul.14; 194) *Temperley.* £72
– – Anr. Edn. N.d. Fo. Loose, some spotting. Orig. cl., gt. (SH. Oct.10; 513) *Lenton.* £60

RUSSIA
– Atlas Leningradskoi Obglasti i Karelskoi ASSR. [Leningrad], [1934]. Fo. 55 double-p. maps, numbered 1-49, 57-60, 64 & 65. Cl., spine torn. (SG. Nov.20; 108) $140
– Das Veraenderte Russland, in Welchem die Jetzige Verfassung des Geist- und Weltlichen Regiments, der Kriegs-Staat zu Lande und zu Wasser . . . Frankfurt & Leipzig; Hannover, 1738; 1739-40. 3 pts. in 1 vol. 4to. Cont. vell. (SG. Oct.30; 319) $170

RUSSIAN ACADEMY OF SCIENCES
– [Transactions]. St. Petersb., 1728-1830. 1st. to 5th. Series. 72 vols. in 65. 4to. Mostly unif. in 19th C. hf. mor., covers of about 12 vols. detchd., sides partly cont. cf. or cl. As a periodical, w.a.f., from Chetham's Liby., Manchester. (C. Nov.27; 353) *Taylor.* £3,200

RUSSKAYA IKONA [Russian Ikon]
St. Petersb., 1914. Pts. 1-3 (all publd.). Fo. Orig. wraps., spines reprd. (SH. Feb.6; 358) *Reed & Sims.* £80

RUSSKAYA KHUDOZHESTVENNAYA Letopis [Russian Chronicle of the Arts]
[St. Petersb.], 1912. 20 Iss. in 1 vol. 4to. Cont. hf. mor. (SH. Feb.6; 359) *Tate Gallery.* £80

RUSSKOE ISKUSSTVA [Russian Art]
Moscow & Petersb., 1923. (3000). Nos. 1-2 in 2 vols. (all publd.). 4to. Lacks 2 plts. Mod. cl., orig. wraps. by Chekhonin mntd. (SH. Feb.5; 265) *Rutter.* £70

RUSSO-JAPANESE WAR
- **Official History (Naval & Military) of the Russo-Japanese War.** L., 1910-20. 3 text vols. & 3 loose-lf. portfos., together 6 vols. Cl. (SG. Feb.26; 285) $350

RUSSOW, Balthasar
- **Chronica der Provintz Lyfflandt ... mit velen Historien vermehret durch den autoren Sulvest.** Barth, 1584. 1st. Edn. 4to. Some orig. notes in an 18th. C. hand. Cont. cf., gt. arabesque on both covers, worn with some worm damage to upr. cover. (S. Oct.20; 207)
Bjorck & Borjesson. £420

RUSSOW, K.E.
- **Bruno Liljefors.** 1929. Ltd. Edn. 4to. Mod. hf. cf. mor., gt., orig. wraps. bnd. in. (P. May 14; 263)
Grahame. £55

RUST, Margaret
- **The Queen of the Fishes.** Ill.:- Lucien Pissarro. Eragny Pr., 1894. (150) numbered, initialled by artist. Dampstained. Orig. limp vell., dampstained. Loosely inserted are proofs in black of 2 of the ills., numbered 9/20 & 11/20, both sigd. with monog. stp. (S. Jul.31; 15) *Matthieson Fine Arts.* £230

RUTHERFORD, Sir Ernest
- **A Collection of 10 offprints of scientific papers.** 1908-24. Wraps., hf. red mor. case. From Honeyman Collection. (S. Nov.11; 2710)
Norman. £240
- **Radio-activity.** Camb., 1904. 1st. Edn. Orig. cl., lr. inner hinge brkn. From Honeyman Collection. (S. Nov.11; 2708) *House.* £140
- - **Anr. Copy.** Radcliffe liby. dupl. with stps. (S. Dec.1; 371) *Rota.* £75

RUTHERFORTH, Thomas
- **A System of Natural Philosophy, Being a Course of Lectures in Mechanics, Optics, Hydrostatics, & Astronomy.** 1748. 1st. Edn. 2 vols. 4to. Cont. spr. cf., spines gt. Bkplt. of Francis Pym. (S. Jun.29; 429) *Murray-Hill.* £70

RUTHERSTON, Albert
- **Sixteen Designs for the Theatre.** Oxford, 1928. (475) numbered. 4to. Orig. cl., d.-w. (CSK. Apr.24; 13) £50
*See-*DRINKWATER, John & Rutherford, Albert

RUTILII, Paladii
*See-*VARRO, Marcus Terentius, Moedrati, L. Iunii & Rutilii, Paladii

RUTTER, John
- **Delineations of Fonthill & its Abbey.** Shaftesbury & L., Priv. ptd., 1823. [1st. Edn.] L.P. 4to. Proof plts. & ills. on India paper. Orig. hf. cf. (SH. Mar.5; 194) *Kossow.* £200
- - **Anr. Copy.** Plts. 6, 7 & 8 (title) in plain & cold. states, 4 other plts. in 2 states, plt. 5 in dupl., some staining, stitching brkn. Hf. roan, very worn, unc. (S. Jun.22; 142) *Hatchwell.* £150
- - **Anr. Copy.** B2-3 & 1 plt. sprung, slight spotting. Mod. hf. mor., retaining orig. bds., unc. (S. Jun.22; 88) *Shaw.* £70

RUTTY, John
- **A Methodical Synopsis of Mineral Waters, Comprehending the Most Celebrated Mineral Waters, Both Cold & Hot ... Interspersed with Tables.** 1757. 4to. Minor dampstaining to last few ll. Recently rebnd. in qtr. cl. (TA. Mar.19; 592) £75

RUVIGNY & Raineval, Marquis of
- **The Blood Royal of Britain.-The Plantagenet Roll of the Blood Royal.** 1903; 1908. 2 works in 2 vols. 4to. Both orig. cl. (C. Jul.22; 197)
Heraldry. £60

RUXNER, Georg
[-] **Anfang, Ursachen, Ursprung u. Herkommen, der Thurnier im Heyligen Röm. Reich.** Ill.:- J. Amman. Frankfurt, 1566. 1st. Edn. Pt. 1 of 3. Fo. Slightly browned in parts, old MS. owner's marks on title, near end some ll. slightly wormed in margin. Late 18th. C. leath. Ex-liby. Comitis Antonii de Pergen. (HK. May 12-14; 164a)
DM 850
- **Anfang, Ursprung unnd Herkomen des Thurnirs in Teutscher Nation.** Simmern, 31 Oct., 1530. 1st. Edn. Fo. Many woodcut arms in text cold. (but lacks 6 owing to mutilation), lacks title, next 3 ll., lge. portion of x4 & 3H6 (the latter with total loss of woodcut ill.) & some qtr. of t1 & 3A5, lacks lge. piece from ff4, with slight text loss, & loss of 1 coat-of-arms, lge. piece torn from lr. margin of vv2

& a tear in same lf., several tears & other defects (affecting text at e4, x2, tt4, & vv5), some wormholes slightly affecting text, some staining. Cont. blind-stpd. pig over wood bds., ex-liby. (S. Feb.10; 220) *Robinson.* £280
- - **Anr. Copy.** Double-p. woodcut enlarged & mntd., 6 ll. only 1 privilege enlarged & loose, 1st. & last ll. very spoiled, defect. & reprd., 8 ll. with sm. corrections, 1 lf. torn, full-p. arms mntd., lightly browned & with soiling in parts, some ll. with MS. notes. 19th. C. hf. leath., gt. spine, worn. (H. Dec.9/10; 785) DM 11,500
[-] - **Anr. Edn.** Simmern, 1532. 2nd. Edn. Fo. Lightly soiled in parts, some pp. slightly browned, some worming. Cont. blind-tooled pig-bkd. wood bds., clasps brkn. (R. Mar.31-Apr.4; 85) DM 3,000
- **Thurnierbuch.** 1530. Fo. Lacks title, 7 ll. of introduction & double-plt. Vell. W.a.f. (BS. Jun.11; 115) £240
- - **Anr. Edn.** Simmern, 1532. 2nd. Edn. Fo. Slightly wormed at end with minimal loss, first 3 ll. after title torn, lacks 8 unnumbered ll. at beginning, title-lf. from anr. (ca. 17th. C.) Edn. 17th. C. leath., worn, wormed. (HK. May 12-14; 164) DM 2,400
[-] - **Anr. Edn.** Ill.:- Jost Amman & others. Frankfurt, 1566. 3rd. Edn. (1st. with these ills.). 2 pts. in 1 vol. Fo. 2 folding woodcut plts., both mntd. & reprd. slightly affecting woodcut, slightly soiled or spotted in places, ll. 2B6 & 2C1 damaged affecting text, bkplt. on verso of title. 19th. C. antique style blind-stpd. leath. over wooden bds., brass clasps. (S. May 5; 41) *Kubicek.* £420
[-] - **Anr. Edn.** Ill.:- Jost Amman. Frankfurt, 1579 & 1578. 2nd. Frankfurt Edn. 2 pts. in 1 vol. Fo. Some old MS. marginalia, lightly stained, owner's mark on last lf. Cont. vell., soiled, spine defect. (HK. Nov.18-21; 285) DM 2,600

RUYSCH, Fredericus
- **Observationum Anatomico-chirurgicarum Centuria accedit Catalogus Rariorum quae in Museo Ruyschiano asservantur.** Amst., 1691. 2 pts. in 1 vol. 4to. Tears in folding plts. Vell., dust-soiled. (S. Jun.17; 742) *Levinson.* £55
- **Thesaurus Anatomicus Primus [-Decimus], -Curae posterioris [-renovatae] seu Thesaurus Anatomicus ... maximus.-Tractatio Anatomica de Musculo.-Operum Anatomico-medico-chirurgiorum Index.-& 6 other tracts by or on Fredericus Ruysch.** Amst., 1725-44. 1st. work: 10 pts.; 2nd. work: 2 pts.; 4th. work: 2 pts. 4to. 1 plt. slightly torn in fold, some ll. & a few plts. slightly spotted. Cont. cf., head of spine slightly worn. As a collection, w.a.f. (S. Feb.23; 97) *Brienx.* £320

RUYSDALE, Philip
[-] **A Pilgrimage Over the Prairies.** L., 1863. 1st. Edn. 2 vols. in 1, as iss. 12mo. Some sigs. sprung. Gt.-pict. cl., worn. (SG. Jan.8; 390) $160

RUYTER-BRANDT, Gerard de
*See-*BRANDT, Gerard

RYAN, V.J.E.
- **Catalogue of Greek, Roman, English & Scottish Coins.** 1950-52. 5 vols. 4to. Orig. wraps. (SH. Mar.6; 436) *Campbell.* £85

RYCAUT, Sir Paul
- **The Present State of the Ottoman Empire.** 1668. 2nd. Edn. Fo. Lacks both ports. Late 17th./early 18th. C. cf., gt. arms on covers of Bertie, Earl of Abingdon, rebkd., corners reprd. [Wing R2413] (S. Jun.29; 248) *Diba.* £80
- - **Anr. Edn.** 1670. 3rd. Edn. Fo. Title reinforced at inner margin. Cont. sheep, gt. spine. [Wing R2414] (S. Nov.4; 639) *Nadir.* £110
*See-*KNOLLES, Richard

RYFF, Petrus
- **Quaestiones Geometricae, in Euclidis & P. Rami Stoiceiosin [Greek].** Frankfurt, 1600. 1st. Edn. Browned, marginal repairs to title & last lf., sm. hole in A2. 18th. C. sheep-bkd. bds., worn. From Honeyman Collection. (S. Nov.11; 2711)
Quaritch. £80

RYFF, Walter Hermann
- **Anatomica Omnium Humani Corporis Partium Descriptio.** Paris, 1545. Fo. Lacks 2 full-p. woodcuts (of 19), pp. 39-42 supplied in Xerox facs., some marginal soiling, 2 corners reprd. Mod. vell. gt. (SG. Jan.29; 371) $1,900

- **Der Architectur furnembsten, notwendigsten, angehorigen Mathematischen und Mechanischen, engentlicher Bericht.** Nuremb., 1558. Fo. Lge. armorial device sigd. 'SG' at end, lacks last lf. (blank?), some browning & soiling, marginal repair to title, sm. hole affecting text in following 2 ll., single wormhole towards end slightly affecting text, corner of last lf. reprd., owners' inscrs. on title of P. Romanus & Monastry of S. Emmeram. Cont. hf. pig. bds., with initials 'GS', covers very worn. From Honeyman Collection. (S. Nov.11; 2715) *Hamilton.* £410
[-] [**Confect-Buch und Hauss Apothek.** Ill.:- Jost Amman. [Frankfurt], [1567]. Lacks title & ll. 1-24 & 8 unnumbered index ll., slightly browned & soiled. Hf. linen. (HK. Nov.18-21; 720)
DM 470
- **Der furnembsten, notwendigsten, der gantzen Architectur angehorigen Mathematischen und Mechanischen Kunst, eygentlicher Bericht.** Ill.:- Peter Floetner. Nuremb., 1547. 1st. Edn. Fo. Some marginal worming & soiling at beginning & end. Cont. blind-stpd. pig. over wooden bds., upr. cover dtd. 1547, soiled, metal corner-pieces & clasps. From Honeyman Collection. (S. Nov.11; 2713) *Bresslauer.* £4,400
- - **Anr. Copy.** Lacks last lf., dampstained thro.-out, title defect. & reprd. (outer third missing), lr. margins of prelims. & some ll. at end reprd., 4 other ll. reprd. with some loss of text. Mod. cf., orig. panel. covers preserved. From Honeyman Collection, w.a.f. (S. Nov.11; 2714) *Zeitlin.* £200
- **New gross Distillier-Buch, Wolgegrundter Kunstlicher Distillation.** Frankfurt, 1556. Fo. Lacks last lf. (blank?), some browning, title soiled, corner torn from *4. 18th. C. cf., worn. From Honeyman Collection. (S. Nov.11; 2716)
Hill. £680
*See-*THURNEYSSER zum Thurn, Leonhardt

RYLANDS & SON LTD.
- **Textile & Fancy Goods Merchants.** Manchester, 1923 4to. Cl. gt. (P. Apr.9; 254)
Manchester. £60

RYMER, Thomas
- **Edgar, or the English Monarch.** 1678. 1st. Edn. 4to. Slight browning at edges. Recent mor.-bkd. bds. [Wing R2423] (C. Nov.19; 143)
Brett-Smith. £140
- **A Short View of Tragedy, with some Reflections on Shakespeare.** 1693. Old cf. [Wing R2431] (BS. Jun.11; 278) £100

S., I.
- **A Brief & Perfect Journal of the late Proceedings & Success of the English Army in the West-Indies.** L., 1655. 1st. Edn. Sm. 4to. Lacks final blank, text foxed, ex-liby. with stp. on title, browning, soiling. Red hf. mor., rebkd., soiled. [Sabin 74616; Wing S35] (SPB. May 5; 450)
$650

S., M.
- **Letters from France: written by a Modern Tourist in that country.** 1815. 1st. Edn. Light foxing. Cont. red bds., partly unc. William Beckford's copy with his pencilled number on front free end-paper, Lord Rosebery's bkplt. (S. Nov.4; 588) *Quaritch.* £95

S., Th. N.
*See-*LINEUS Buscimducis, Thomas-S., Th. N.

S.E.
[-] **The Magic Lantern, or Amusing & Instructive Exhibitions for Young People.** [Frontis. & watermark dtd. 1806]. 1st. Edn. 12mo. Slight spotting, advts. Orig. roan-bkd. bds., rebkd. & recorrened. (SH. Mar.19; 282) *Hackhofer.* £80

S.J.D.C.
[-] **Voyage dans la Haute Pensylvanie ... de New York.** Paris, 1801. 3 vols. Cf. (P. Sep.11; 31)
Cook. £120

SAALMULLER, Max & Heyden, L. von
- **Lepidopteren von Madagascar.** Frankfurt, 1884-91. 2 vols. 4to. Cont. hf. mor., orig. wraps. bnd. in (C. May 20; 236)
Wheldon & Wesley. £100

SAAR, J.J.
*See-*BALDAEUS, Philippus-SAAR, J.J.

SAAVEDRA FAJARDO, Diego de
- **Idea de un Príncipe Político Christiano.** Ill.:- John Sadlier. Mónaco [Munich], 1640. 1st. Edn. 4to. Orig. cf. (DS. May 22; 867) Pts. 120,000

– – Anr. Edn. Amst., 1659. 12mo. Cont. vell. bds., reprd., lacks clasps. (S. Nov.25; 377)
Duran. £110
– – Anr. Copy. Vell. (DS. May 22; 820)
Pts. 30,000
– Idea Principis Christiano-Politic. Cologne, 1650. Slightly stained. Cont. vell., lacks ties. (HK. Nov.18-21; 1573)
DM 520

SAAZ, J. von
– Der Ackermann und der Tod. Ed.:– A. Bernt. Leipzig, 1919. (320) numbered, facs. reprint of 1st. 1461 Wolfenbüttel printing). Orig. vell. (R. Oct.14-18; 947)
DM 520

SABADINO DE GLI ARIENTE BOLOGNESE, [Giovanni]
– Porretane ... Dove si Narra Novelle Settana Una. Venice, 1531. Old sig. of de Monharville Malier on title & pencilled on last lf., old 'No. 73' in ink on fly-lf. Bkplt. of Wilmot, Viscount Lisburne, 18th. C. mor., triple gt. fillet, spine gt. in compartments with, in the 5th., label with crest of Joseph Gulston & the date of the book, inner gt. dentelles, gt. starred end-papers. (S. Apr.7; 301)
Facchinotti. £350

SABARTES, Jaime
– A Los Toros mit Picasso. Monte Carlo, 1961. Lge. ob. 4to. Orig. linen, pict. s.-c. (HK. May 12-14; 2017)
DM 500
– – Anr. Edn. Trans.:– U.R. Hemmerich. Ill.:– Picasso. Monte Carlo, [1961]. Ob. 4to. Orig. linen, orig. pict. s.-c. (D. Dec.11-13; 1165)
DM 600
– – Anr. Copy. (H. Dec.9/10; 2300) DM 520
– Picasso: Toreros. Trans.:– Patrick Gregory. Ill.:– Pablo Picasso. L. & Monte Carlo, 1961. Ob. 4to. Orig. decor. cl., s.-c. (SH. Nov.21; 453)
Ayres. £85
– – Anr. Edn. Trans.:– Patrick Gregory. Ill.:– Pablo Picasso. N.Y. & Monte Carlo, [1961]. Ob. 4to. Pict. cl., d.-w. (SG. Oct.23; 265)
$150
– – Anr. Edn. Ill.:– Picasso (lithos). L. & Monte Carlo, [1961]. Ob. 4to. Pict. cl., unif. bd. s.-c. (SG. Apr.2; 232)
$180
– – Anr. Edn. N.Y., [1961]. Ob. 4to. Orig. cl., d.-w., some fading, chipping to d.-w. (SPB. May 29; 342)
$200

SABATINI, Rafael
– Works. Boston, 1924-37. Autograph Edn., sigd., (750). 34 vols. Minor defects. Orig. cl.-bkd. bds. (SPB. Jul.28; 420)
$200

SABELLICUS, Marcus Antonius
– De Venetis Magistratibus. Venice, Antonius de Strata, de Cremona, 19 Jan., 1488/89. 1st. Edn. 4to. Spaces for capital initials with guide letters, 1st. lf. reprd. & with sm. holes filled, some other margins strengthened, some sm. wormholes. Mor. gt. to a Padeloup design, vell. paste-downs, s.-c., by Gozzi of Modena. From the collection of Eric Sexton. [BMC V, 295, Goff S9, H. 14057*] (CNY. Apr.8; 188)
$1,700
– Rerum Venetarum Decades. Venice, Andreas de Torresanus, de Asula, 21 May, 1487. 1st. Edn. Fo. Spaces for initial capitals with guide letters, light dampstain to lr. margins of first 6 ll., & to fore-margins of last 15 ll., early Engl. ink inscr. at fo. 1r. Cont. blind-stpd. cf. over wood bds., central panels of covers diapered by triple fillets & filled with repeated imps. of 3 lozenge-shaped tools including a sm. unicorn, a stylized flower & 2 fighting birds, the panels flanked by narrow bands filled with floral tool, the unicorn & a sm. griffin tool, broad outer borders with floral tool & an 'ihs' scroll repeated, by Walter Hatley (the 'Unicorn Binder'), slight repairs to head & tail of spine. The copy of Major John Roland Abbey, lately in the collection of Eric Sexton. [BMC V, 308, Goff S5, H. 14053*] (CNY. Apr.8; 186)
$9,000

SABIN, Joseph
– Dictionary of Books Relating to America. N.Y., 1868-1936. 29 vols. Cl. (SH. Mar.6; 566)
Pelizzi. £450
– – Anr. Edn. N.Y., n.d. 29 vols. in 1. Readex Microprint, some ll. soiled. Orig. cl. box. (SH. Apr.9; 119)
Duran. £50

SABINE, Edward
*See–*NORTH Georgia Gazette, The

SABINUS, Georgius
– De Electione et Coronatione Caroli V Caesaris Historia, Ecloga eiusdem ... de Gallo ad Ticinum capto. Mainz, 1543. Owner's inscr. on title. Cont. red mor. gt., double fillet borders on sides, centre

& corner-pieces, title at head of upr. cover, spine gt. in 5 compartments with flower, sm. fault on upr. cover. (C. Apr.1; 166)
Maggs. £240
*See–*OVIDIUS NASO, Publius–SABINUS, Georgius
*See–*REUSNER, N.

SABOUREUX DE LA BONNETRIE, C.F.
[–] Constitutions des Jésuites, avec les Declarations. 1762. Holland Paper. 3 vols. Hf.-titles in vol. 1 inscr. 'Par M. Baudouin, Maitre des Requetes au Conseil du Roy'. Cont. mor., triple gt. fillet, spine gt. in compartments, with birds at foot, inner gt. dentelles, red silk liners. (SM. Oct.8; 1984)
Frs. 1,500

SABRETACHE (Pseud.)
*See–*BARRON, Albert 'Sabretache'

SACCHI, Bartholomaeus
*See–*PLATINA or Sacchi, Bartholomaeus

SACERDOTALE SECVNDVM VSVM S.R. ECCLESIAE Alierumque Ecclesiarum
Venice, [1588]. 4to. Some stains & light browning. Cont. pig-bkd. wood bds., blind-tooled, some worming, end-ll. detchd. (H. Dec.9/10; 1262)
DM 650

SACHER-Masoch
– Contes Juifs, Récits de Famille. Paris, 1888. (125) numbered. 4to. Plts. in 2 states. Hf. brown mor. by Wood, orig. cold. upr. wrap. bnd. in. (SBA. Jul.23; 639)
Temperley. £70

SACHEVERELL, William
– An Account of the Isle of Man. 1702. 1st. Edn. Some ll. spotted. Cont. cf. Pres. copy, inscr. to 'Tho: Harley London 16th Dec 1703'. (S. Apr.7; 507)
Foyles. £75

SACHS, Hans
– Ausgewählte Werke. Ed.:– P. Merker & R. Buchwald. Leipzig, 1923-24. With mus. supp. Orig. pig, blind-stpd. (R. Oct.14-18; 948)
DM 420
– Eyn Gesprech Vö[n] den Scheinwercke[n] der Geystlichen. [Nuremb.], 1524. 4to. Disbnd. (S. Dec.8; 177)
Maggs. £130
– Im Gewande seiner Zeit ... Ed.:– R.Z. Becker. Gotha, 1821. Lge. 4to. Bds. Dupl. from the Metropolitan Museum of Art. (BS. Jun.11; 83)
£280
– Der Klagent Waldtbruder vber alle Stend auff Erden. Nuremb., n.d. 1st. Edn. 4to. Browned & soiled, title-lf. with 2 sm. corrections, sm. hole in title woodcut. Wraps. (H. Dec.9/10; 1368)
DM 420

SACHS, Maurice
– Le Sabbat ... 1946. 1st. Edn., (41) numbered; 12mo. Sewed. (HD. Jun.25; 395)
Frs. 17,000

SACHSENSPIEGEL
Ed.:– Chr. Zobel. Leipzig, 1561. 2nd. Zobel Edn. Fo. Some browning. Cont. pig-bkd. wood bds., blind-tooled, corners defect., lacks clasps. (H. Dec.9/10; 1369)
DM 1,950

SACK, Baron Albert von
– Beschreibung einer Reise nach Surinam und des Aufenthaltes ... Berlin, 1818. 1st. Edn. 2 vols. in 1. 4to. Cont. red mor. Front fly-lf. gt.-lettered 'Ihro Koenigliche Hoheit der Prinzessin Charlotte von Preussen ...', royal bkplts. in covers. (SG. Oct.9; 217)
$3,200

SACK, E.
– Giambattista u. Domenico Tiepolo. Hamburg, 1910. (312) numbered. 2 pts. in 1 vol. Lge. 4to. 1 lf. torn. Orig. linen, lightly browned. (HK. Nov.18-21; 3527)
DM 420

SACKVILLE-WEST, Victoria
– Challenge.–The Heir. N.Y., [1923]; 1922. 1st. Edn.? (1st. work). 2 works in 2 vols. Cl. Inscr. on dedication-p. of 1st. work. (SG. Nov.13; 578)
$160
– The Garden. [1946]. (750) sigd. Orig. cl. (CSK. Sep.5; 201)
£55
– Poems of West & East. 1917. 1st. Edn. Mor., view of Pera inlaid in black mor. on upr. cover, gt. inner borders, by Bumpus. (SH. Dec.19; 614)
Sawyer. £80
– Sissinghurst. Hogarth Pr. 1931. 1st. Edn., (500) numbered, sigd. Sm. 4to. Orig. bds. (SKC. May 19; 341)
£50
– – Anr. Copy. Ptd. bds., spine defect. (SG. Nov.13; 579)
$100

SACRE de Charles X
Ill.:– Langlumé & Engelmann after Adam, Chapius, Chauvin etc. Paris, 1825. Fo. Some browning & staining. Cont. hf. red mor., corners, limp decor. spine. (HD. Apr.24; 182)
Frs. 1,300

SACRE de Louis XV (Le) ...
Ill.:– Audran, Beauvais, Cochin Père, Desplaces, Duchange, Dupuis, Larmessin, Tardieu & others. Paris, 1723. Lge. fo. Cont. cf., arms of Louis XV on covers, triple dentelles & fleurs-de-lys in corners, spine with raised bands & fleurs-de-lys, bdg. slightly defect. (HD. Jun.29; 50)
Frs. 4,200

SACRE de sa Majesté Charles X ...
Paris, 1825. Fo. Litho. vig., 10 lge. photographs. Str.-grd. hf. mor., corners, dentelle & gt. fleurons on covers, spine decor. with royal arms & gt. fillets. (HD. Jun.29; 51)
Frs. 2,100

SACROBOSCO, Johannes de
– Libellus de Sphaera. Accessit eiusdem Autoris computus Ecclesiasticus ... Wittenberg, 1543. 2 pts. in 1 vol. Lacks volvelle on D5v, no folding tables, marginal tear on last lf., sig. of Johannes Pollicarius of Zwickau dtd. 1544 on title-p., many annots. in his hand, slight soiling. Hf. cl. From Honeyman Collection; Gilbert Grave's copy, with his bkplt. & owner's inscr. dtd. 1900. (S. Nov.11; 2732)
Quaritch. £130
– – Anr. Edn. Wittenberg, 1629. Folding sheet with volvelles to be cut out, browned thro.-out. Cont. vell. From Honeyman Collection. (S. Nov.11; 2738)
Moskowitz. £65
– La Sfera ... Trans.:– Pier-Vincentio Dante de Rinaldi. Perugia, 1574. 4to. Histor. initial L partly inked out on A2r, D3v & E3r, in 2nd. case causing hole affecting text, some browning. Bds., worn. From Honeyman Collection. (S. Nov.11; 2736)
Mursia. £60
– – Anr. Edn. Trans.:– Francesco Giuntini. Lyon, 1582. Volvelles attached to woodcut diagrams on pp. 74, 75 & 210, inserted woodcut diagram at p. 143, browned thro.-out, slight staining, title with inscr. Vell., spine defect. at foot. From Honeyman Collection. (S. Nov.11; 2737)
Mursia. £70
– Sphaera Emendata. Venice, 1562. Stained. Mod. hf. vell. (S. Mar.17; 262)
Lockwood. £75
– Sphaera Emendata.–Libellvs de Anni Ratione: seu, vt vocatur vulgò, computus Ecclesiasticus. Antw., 1566. 2 works in 1 vol. Cont. blind-stpd. pig., lacks ties. (HK. Nov.18-21; 290) DM 450
– Sphaera Mundi. [Venice], [Type of Filippo di Pietro], ca. 1476. 4to. Lr. third of a2 torn away with 2 lines of text missing on recto & verso (photostat of complete lf. loosely inserted), some spotting, a few stains. 19th. C. hf. vell., end-ll. from a defect. vell. MS. preserved. From Honeyman Collection; bkplt. of Hans Ludendorff. [C. 5206; Goff J401 New York Public liby. only] (S. Nov.11; 2718)
Dr. Honig. £280
– – Anr. Edn. Venice, 1519. 4to. Some stains, obscuring text in 2 or 3 places. 19th. C. hf. mor., gt. From Honeyman Collection; bkplt. of Wilbraham Egerton. (S. Nov.11; 2728)
Thomas. £260
– Sphaera Mundi [–Gerardi Cremonensis Theorica planetarum]. Venice, Franciscus Renner, de Heilbronn. 1478. 2 pts. in 1 vol. 4to. Some spotting & soiling, slightly wormed in a few inner margins. Hf. vell. bds. From Honeyman Collection. [BMC V, 195; HC 14108; Goff J402] (S. Nov.11; 2719)
Hill. £840
– Sphaera Mundi cum Tribus Commentis ... Cicchi Esculani, Francisci Capuani de Manfredonia, Jacobi Fabri Stapulensis [–Theoricae Novae Planetarum Georgii Purbachii]. Venice, Simon Bevilaqua, 23 Oct. 1499. 2 pts. in 1 vol. Fo. Some ll. browned, single wormhole runs thro.-out (but for 1st. 2 ll.), cont. marginal annots. 19th. C. hf. vell., worn. Bkplts. of Prof. Riccardi & Teodoro Becu; bkplt. & stp. of Prof. Pedro N. Arata; from Honeyman Collection. [BMC V, 524; H. 14125; Goff J419] (S. Nov.11; 2723)
Hill. £350
– Sphaera Mundi [with other tracts]. Bologna, Dominicus Fuscus, 1480. Sm. 4to. 36 ll. (of 40, lacks last 4 ll.), rubricated, spike-hole through 1st. hf. reprd. but text slightly affected. Vell. bds. [BMC VI, 820; Goff J404; HC 14109] (S. Jun.23; 211)
Faurre. £160
– – Anr. Edn. Venice, [Before 4 Nov.] 1485. 4to. Some browning & staining. Bnd. in fragment of MS. antiphonal on vell. From Honeyman Collection. [BMC V, 290; HC 14111; Goff J406] (S. Nov.11; 2720)
Nebenzahl. £460

SACROBOSCO, Johannes de -*contd.*
- - **Anr. Edn.** Venice, [Bonetus Locatellus] for Octavianus Scotus, 4 Oct., 1490. 4to. Damp-stain to 1st. 4 ll., 23 ll. with reprd. or patched wormhole to lr. inner blank margin, b1 & b8 with upr. margin renewed, d1 with upr. & fore-margin renewed, 1st. & last ll. with sm. marginal restorations, other repairs. Old vell., worn. From the collection of Eric Sexton. [BMC V, 438, Goff J409, HC 14113*] (CNY. Apr.8; 190) $1,400
- - **Anr. Edn.** Venice, Guilelmus Anima Mia, Tridinensis. 14 Jan. 1491. 4to. Some diagrams partly printed or stencilled in colours, some staining, browned & soiled, 16th. C. owner's inscr. on title of Joannes Baptista Gualterius of Picardy, copious marginal annots. in his hand (some trimmed). Mod. vell. From Honeyman Collection. [BMC V, 412; HC 14114; Goff J410] (S. Nov.11; 2722) *Nox.* £380
- - **Anr. Edn.** Ed.:– Jacobus Faber Stapulensis. Paris, [Johannes Higman, for] Wolfgang Hopyl. 1st.Sep. 1500. Fo. Washed. Red mor. gt. by Emile Rouselle. From Honeyman Collection. [Goff J423] (S. Nov.11; 2724) *Nebenzahl.* £320
- **La Sphera** ... Trans.:– Rodrigo Saenz de Santayana y Spinosa. Valladolid, 1568. 4to. Very dampstained, 1 prelim. lf. & 5 ll. at end remargined, owner's inscr. on title, a few insignificant wormholes. 18th. C. Spanish cf. From Honeyman Collection. (S. Nov.11; 2735) *Moskowitz.* £55
- **Sphere Textum una cum Additionibus non Aspernandis Petri Cirvelli ... Intersertis Praeterea Questionibus Domini Petri de Alliaco.** Paris, Aug., 1515. Fo. Some browning & slight staining, marginal tear in c4 affecting headline, cont. annots. & underscoring. Mod. Spanish cf. From Honeyman Collection. (S. May 20; 3302) *Pichler.* £220
- - **Anr. Copy.** From Honeyman Collection. (S. Nov.11; 2726) *Holler.* £120
- **Textus Sphaerae.** Ed.:– Jacobi Frabri Stapulensis. Venice, 1508. Fo. iv + separate paginations-folios 1-94/1-65, some annots. to margins of 1st. few ll. Old vell., slightly worn. (TA. Mar.19; 475) £180
- **Textus de Sphaera (& other tracts).** Ed.:– Jacobus Faber Stapulensis. Paris, 1527. Fo. Mod. hf. cf. From Honeyman Collection. (S. Nov.11; 2729) *Meijer.* £420
- **Trattato della Sphera** ... Trans.:– Antonio Brucioli. Venice, 1543. 4to. Tear reprd. in d2, slight staining. Old vell. bds. From Honeyman Collection. [Sabin 74810] (S. Nov.11; 2730) *Nox.* £210
- - **Anr. Copy.** Wormed at end affecting last 2 ll., some staining & spotting, 1st. 2 ll. detchd. Cont. owner's inscr. of Benedetto Montacuto & liby. stps. of Count Raimondo Cardelli of Rome; from Honeyman Collection. (S. Nov.11; 2731) *Rogers Turner.* £90
- **Uberrimum Sphere Mundi commetum [Petri Cirvelli] Intersertis etia Questionibus Domini Petri de aliaco.** Paris, Aug. 1508. Fo. Lacks quire o at end (4 ll., last a blank), slight worming affecting text, some upr. margins stained, lr. inner corner of b1 reprd., textual flaw on m3v. Cont. blind-stpd. cf., roll borders with figures of Virtues, worn. From Honeyman Collection; bkplt. of Luis Bardon. (S. Nov.11; 2725) *Moskowitz.* £95.

SACROBOSCO, Johannes de-**FABER Stapulensis, Jacobus**-**JORDANUS, Nemorarius**
- **Textus de Sphera (with other tracts).**
-**Introductorium Astronomicum Theorias Corporum Coelstium duobus Libris complectens.**
-**Arithmetica Decem Libris demonstrata. Musica Libris demonstrata quatuor (& other tracts).** Ed.:– Jacobus Faber Stapulensis; J. Clichtoveus; Jacobus Faber Stapulensis. Paris, 1516; 1517; 1514. 3 works in 1 vol. Fo. 1st. work with single wormhole through 1st. 9 ll. 17th. C. revrsed cf., spine worn. From Honeyman Collection; bkplt. of Thomas Frognall Dibdin. (S. Nov.11; 2727) *Fenyves.* £1,100

SACROBOSCO, Johannes de-**NOVIOMAGUS, Johannes**
- **Libellus de Sphaera ...**-**De numeris libri II.** Wittenberg; Cologne, 1545; 1544. 2 works in 1 vol. 1st. work: lacks 2 folding tables, stained in lr. margins at beginning, a few wormholes, owner's inscr. & a liby. stp. on title, 2nd. work: lr. blank corners torn from F3-4, last quire slightly stained. Cont. mor., panel. in blind, gt. fleurons at corners, 'Io de Sacro Busto' stpd. in gt. on upr. cover. From

Honeyman Collection. (S. Nov.11; 2733) *Quaritch.* £70
- **Sphaera Mundi (with other tracts).**-**Kalendarium.** Venice; Augsburg, J.L. Santritter & Hieronymus de Sanctis; Erhard Ratdolt. 31 Mar. 1488; 21 Mar. 1489. 2 works in 1 vol. 4to. 1st. work: 1st. paragraph on A2r printed in red, several diagrams partly ptd. with colours, cont. annots. in miniscule hand, slight soiling, a few stains, 2nd. work: 40 sm. woodcuts in red & black, 2 sheets of last quire pasted together to form 2 stiff ll., brass pointer on last diagram, lacks 2 volvelles or 2nd., somewhat stained & soiled. 19th. C. vell., soiled, sig. of W.M. Grimshaw on front pastedown. From Honeyman Collection. [1st. work: BMC V, 462; HC 14112; Goff J407; 2nd. work: BMC II, 383; HC 13780; Goff R97] (S. Nov.11; 2721) *Hill.* £920

SADE, Donatien Alphonse François, Marquis de
- **Aline et Valcour** ... Paris, 1795. 1st. Edn. 8 pts. in 4 vols. 18mo. 1 lf. reprd. on last p. of vol. 8. Marb. roan, smooth decor. spines, bdgs. worn. (HD. Jun.24; 111) Frs. 3,000
- - **Anr. Edn.** Paris, 1795. 8 pts. in 4 vols. 16mo. 15 figures (of 16). Hf. cf., spines decor. with gold or blind-stpd. fillets, ca. 1820. (HD. Apr.10; 374) Frs. 2,200
- **La Nouvelle Justine, ou Les Matheurs de la Vertu.** Holland [Paris?], 1797. 10 vols. 12mo. Vols. V & VI hf. titles very faint. Mor. (P. Feb.19; 10) *Klusman.* £880
- - **Anr. Copy.** 4 vols. 18mo. With 38 19th. C. figures. Cl. bds., ca. 1880. (HD. Apr.10; 376) Frs. 3,800
- **La Nouvelle Justine ou Les Malheurs de la Vertu, suivi de l'Histoire de Juliette, sa Soeur.** Ill.:– Bornet. Holland [Paris], 1797. 10 vols. 16mo. Mor., decor. spines, 2 fillets on covers, mor. doubls. gt. decor., by Lafontaine. (HD. Apr.10; 375) Frs. 24,000
- **La Philosophie dans le Boudoir.** L., 1805 (vol. 2). 2 vols. 12mo. Cl. (P. Feb.19; 11) *Bibn.* £230

SADELER, G.
- **Vestigi delle Antichita di Roma, Tivoli, Pozzuolo et altri Luochi.** Ill.:– M. Sadeler. Rome, 1660. 16 × 28 cms. 50 plts. Album, defect., lightly soiled. (CR. Mar.19; 333) Lire 650,000

SADI, Gulistan
- **Musladini Sadi Rosarum Politicum, sive Amoenum Sortis Humanae Theatrum.** Ed.:– Georgius Gentius. Amst., 1651. 1st. Edn. Fo. Title dust-soiled, 1st. gathering partly detchd. 19th. C. hf. mor., upr. cover detchd. (C. Apr.1; 167) *Ad Orientem.* £400

SADLEIR, Michael
- **XIX Century Fiction.** 1951. Ltd. Edn. 2 vols. Cl., d.-w.'s. (WW. May 20; 36) £82
- - **Anr. Edn.** N.Y., 1969. 2 vols. 4to. Orig. cl. (CSK. May 29; 95) £70

SADLIER, Thomas U. & Dickinson, P.L.
- **Georgian Mansions in Ireland.** Dublin, 1915. Ltd. Edn. Lge. 4to. Buckram. (GM. Apr.30; 91) £70

SADOLETUS, Cardinal Jacobus
- **Epistolae Quotquot Extant.** Rome, 1759-67. 5 vols. including Appendix & Epistolae Pontificae. Early red mor., gt.-tooled borders enclosing arms of Cardinal Borghese, spines gt. Armorial bkplt. of Sir Thomas North Dick Lauder, 1882. (SG. Oct.9; 218) $1,000

SADOVSKY, Boris
- **Samovar.** Moscow, 1914. 4to. Orig. wraps., spine torn. (SH. Feb.6; 515) *Quaritch.* £50

SAGE, [Balthazar Geo.]
- **Analyse Chimique et Concordance des Trois Règnes.** Paris, 1786. 3 vols. Ptd. folding table in vol. II, sig. of Thomas Brande on title, old pr. mark on fly-lf. with (possibly) name cut out. Cont. red mor., gt., arms of Charles Alexandre de Calonne on covers, triple gt. fillet, spines gt. in compartments with royal cipher of interlaced Ls enclosing royal arms, surmntd. by couronne fermée, fleur-de-lis in each corner, inner gt. dentelles, 2 lr. corners worn. (SM. Oct.8; 1985) Frs. 2,800

SAGENBUCH
Ed.:– Martha De Haas. Ill.:– Arthur Rackham. Zurich, 1920. 1st. Edn., (1000) numbered. 4to. Gt. pict. cl. Raymond M. Sutton, Jr., copy. (SG. May 7; 253) $220

SAGLIO
See-**DAREMBERG, Charles Victor, Saglio & Pottier**

SAHACHIRO, Hata
See-**EHRLICH, Paul & Sahachiro, Hata**

SAHAGUN, Bernardino de
- **Historia General de las Cosas de Nueva España.** Mexico, 1829-30. 3 vols. Sm. 4to. Liby. stps. removed from titles, affecting 1 or 2 letters. Cf.-bkd. bds., 1 cover detchd. [Sabin 74950] (SPB. May 5; 451) $550

SAHULA, Isaac
- **Sefer ha-tappuah, & Mashal ha-kadmoni.** Frankfurt, [1693]. Some restoration to text. Later bds. (CNY. Oct.9; 33) $1,000

SAINBEL, Charles Vial de
- **Works; with a Short Account of his Life ...** L., 1795. 1st. Edn. 4to. With lf. of publisher's advts. at end, 1 folding plt. torn, blank corner of 1 lf. torn away, some foxing. Disbnd., unc. (SG. Dec.11; 397) $170

SAINT-ALLAIS, Nicolas Viton de
- **Nobiliaire Universel de France.** Paris, [1872 reprint]. 20 vols. bnd. in 16. Hf. chagrin, 4 spine raised bands, decor lys, unc. (LM. Nov.8; 260) B.Frs. 17,000

SAINT-AUBIN, Gabriel de
- **L'Oeuvre Gravé de. Notice Historique et Catalogue Raisonné par Emile Dacier.** Paris, 1914. (425) on Velin d'Arches. 4to. Cont. cl., orig. wraps. bnd. in. (PNY. Mar.26; 290) $175

SAINT-CLAIR, Arthur
- **A Narrative of the Manner in Which the Campaign Against the Indians ... Was Conducted** ... Phila., 1812. 1st. Edn. Owner's inscr. on hf.-title, some soiling & offsetting. Later bds., unc. & largely unopened. From liby. of William E. Wilson. (SPB. Apr.29; 241) $300
- - **Anr. Copy.** Pts. of title, A1 & 2N1 torn away & renewed, engraved port. & litho. inserted. Hf. mor. gt., partly unc., by MacDonald. [Sabin 75020] (CNY. May 22; 259) $200

SAINT-EVREMOND, Charles de Saint Denis
- **Oeuvres Meslées.** L., 1709. 2nd. Edn. 3 vols. 4to. 6 pp. in vol. 2 stained. 18th. C. Fr. red mor. gt. by Derome le Jeune, with his ticket. Lamy copy. (S. Nov.25; 398) *Watchman.* £450

SAINT-FOIX, Germain François Poullain de
- **Catalogue des Chevaliers, Commandants et Officiers de l'Ordre du Saint-Esprit.** Ill.:– Gravelot (vigs.); frontis. after Boucher. 1760. Fo. Some ll. yellowed. Cont. marb. cf., gt. fillets, arms in corners surrounding emblem, spine decor. with raised bands, bdg. slightly defect. (HD. Jun.24; 112) Frs. 1,300

SAINT-FOND, B.F.
- **Travels in England, Scotland & the Hebrides.** 1799. 2 vols. Rebnd. cl. (CE. Nov.20; 188) £120

SAINT-GAUDENS, Augustus
- **The Reminiscences.** Ed.:– Homer Saint-Gaudens. N.Y., 1913. 1st. Edn. 2 vols. Gt. ornamental qtr. cl., covers slightly soiled. Inscr. & sigd. at title by Homer & Augusta H. Saint-Gaudens, Cornish, New Hampshire, 1915. (PNY. Mar.4; 227) $160

SAINT-GERMAIN, Christopher
[-] **The Dialogue in English, betweene a Doctor of Divinitie, & a Student in the Lawes of England.** 1598. Outer margin of title & 1st. lf. cut down, slightly soiled. Old vell., soiled. [STC 21576] (CSK. Mar.13; 23) £90
[-] - **Anr. Edn.** 1638. Corner of title torn away, slightly affecting border, sm. wormhole affecting text, slight browning. Cont. sheep, worn. Early (? cont.) sig. 'Jo Hyndman de/Grey's-Inn' on title. [NSTC 21582] (S. May 5; 303) *Frost.* £60

SAINT-GRAAL
- **C'est l'Hystoire du Sainct Greaal.** Ill.:– Geoffroy Tory after Urs Graf (title). Paris, Oct.24, 1523 (title dtd. 1519). 2nd. Edn. 2 pts. in 1 vol. Fo. 1st. 8 ll. with sm. patch at lr. blank margin, slight tear to h5, j6 torn & reprd. touching 4 lines, L1 remargined at 3 sides & probably inserted. Late 19th. C. mor., gt.-ruled, upr. cover with lge. central panel of onlaid cold. mor. depicting 1 of the woodcuts, lr. cover with mor. gt. onlay with monog. & motto of Pickering & Chatto (for whom the book was bnd.), spine gt. & gt.-lettered, replacing bdg. by Duru (his stp. on fly-lf.), mor.

gt. solander case. The copy of Andre Massena, Prince d'Essling, bkplts. of E.V. Utterson & William Morris (with the 2 lf. catalogue by his secretary Sydney Cockerell, later A.L.s. from Cockerell laid in), bkplt. of Edith R. McCormick, later the copy of Maurice & Edward Schenk, bkplt. of John A. Saks. (CNY. Oct.1; 104) $12,000

SAINT-HILAIRE, Emile Marco
- Histoire . . . de la Garde Impériale. Paris, 1847. Hf.-title & last p. lightly stained. Cont. hf. cf., unc. (SI. Dec.4; 517)   Lire 520,000
– – **Anr. Copy.** Lge. 8vo. Hf. chagrin, corners. (HD. Jun.29; 47)   Frs. 1,350

SAINT-HILAIRE, Isidore Geoffroy
See–GEOFFROY SAINT-HILAIRE, Isidore

SAINT HILAIRE, Jaume de
- L'Anatomie du Corps Humain avec ses Maladies & les Remèdes pour les Guerir. Paris, 1684. New Edn. Cont. cf. (S. Dec.2; 614)   Rota. £70

SAINT-HYACINTHE, Themiseul de
See–LABADIE, Dom–SAINT-HYACINTHE, Themiseul de

SAINT-JOHN, James Augustus
See–PRISSE: Emile & St. John, James Augustus

SAINT-JOHN, John (Pseud.)
See–GALSWORTHY, John

SAINT-JOHN, Spencer
- Life in the Forests of the Far East. 1862. 2 vols. 2 folding maps torn, some ll. spotted. Later hf. mor., slightly soiled. (SH. Nov.7; 358)   Maggs. £60

SAINT-JORY, Rustaing de
[–] Les Femmes Militaires. Ill.:– Fessard after Riquard. Paris, 1750. 12mo. Inkstain on 1st. 3 or 4 ll. Cont. mott. cf., spine gt., 2 bkplts. Double fore-e. pntg.; from the liby. of Zola E. Harvey. (SG. Mar.19; 134) $600

SAINT-JUIRS, René Delorme
- La Seine à Paris. Ill.:– G. Fraipont. 1890. Lge. 8vo. Orig. watercolour. Hf. chagrin, corners, spine with raised bands, wrap. & spine preserved. Autograph dedication by artist. (HD. Jun.25; 399)   Frs. 1,250

SAINT-JULIEN, M. Charles de
- Voyage Pittoresque en Russie . . . suivi d'un Voyage en Siberie par M.R. Bourdier. Paris, 1854. 1st. Edn. Tall 8vo. Minor spotting. Orig. decor. cl. gt., top & bottom of spine slightly defect. (TA. Apr.16; 424)   £50
– – **Anr. Copy.** Orig. romantic publisher's bds., special tool decor., by Liebherre. (LM. Mar.21; 302)   B.Frs. 7,500

SAINT-JULIEN, Pierre de
- De l'Origine des Bourgongnons, et Antique des Estats de Bourgongne. Paris, 1581. Fo. Slight tear to view of Tournus, 17th. C. Engl. sig. on title. 18th. C. cf. gt., gt. arms on sides. Chiswick House bkplt. of the Duke of Devonshire, bkplt. of John A. Saks. (CNY. Oct.1; 109) $2,600

SAINT-LEGER, S.E.
- War Sketches in Colour. L., 1903. (250) sigd. by artist. 4to. Cl. (SSA. Jun.18; 272)   R. 120

SAINT-MARC, Jean Paul André de
- Oeuvres. Ill.:– After Danloux, Jean Michel Moreau le Jeune, Charles Nicolas Cochin, Charles Dominique Eisen & Others. Paris, 1785. 3rd. Edn. 2 vols. (of 3?). Cont. red mor., by Derome le Jeune, with his 1785 ticket, triple gt. fillet, flat spine gt. with repeated sm. ovals interspersed with dots, inner gt. dentelles. Bkplts. of Baron de Breteuil & Laurence Currie. (SM. Oct.8; 1988)   Frs. 1,600

SAINT-MARTIN, Louis Claude de
[–] Tableau Naturel des Rapports qui existent entre Dieu, L'Homme et l'Univers. Edinb., 1782. 1st. Edn. Hf. leath., gt., marb. end-ll. (D. Dec.11-13; 2612)   DM 720

SAINT-MICHEL, Maurile de
- Voyages des Isles Camercanes. En l'Amerique. Le Mans, 1652. 1st. Edn. Cont. cf., upr. cover detchd. [Sabin 46987] (S. Jun.22; 191)   Nixon. £400

SAINT-NON, l'Abbé Richard de
- Voyage pittoresque, ou Description du Royaume de Naples et de Sicile. Ill.:– after Fragonard. Paris, 1781-86. 1st. Edn. 4 vols. in 5. Fo. A few ll.

browned, vol. III lacks last lf. (blank?). Cont. red mor., triple gt. fillet, spines gt. in compartments, inner gt. dentelles, head & foot of spine of vol. I slightly worn, a few corners slightly worn. Bkplt. of 'Paris d'Illens'. (S. Jun.22; 192)   Lyon. £3,400
– – **Anr. Copy.** Lacks the unnumbered plt. of Phallus antiques & the 14 plts. of doubles medailles in vol. 4, repeats of ills. in the same vol., 2 plts. in vol. 3 strengthened with tape on verso, occasional light soiling. 19th. C. hf. mor., covers detchd. W.a.f. from Chetham's Liby., Manchester. (C. Nov.27; 354)   Cornaro. £3,000
– – **Anr. Copy.** Some plts. stained, unnumbered plt. stained & loosely inserted. Cont. cf. gt., spines & corners worn. (CNY. May 22; 260) $3,800

ST. PETERSBURG
- Nouvelle Collection de Quarante Vues de Saint-Petersbourg et de ses Environs. St. Petersb., 1825. Ob. fo. Lacks 4 lithos. Mod. hf. leath. (H. Dec.9/10; 617)   DM 1,000
– – **Anr. Edn.** St. Petersb., 1826. Ob. fo. Lacks plts. 17-20, added plt., soiled, tears backed, some stains, title-lf. loose. Unbnd. (H. Dec.9/10; 618)   DM 800
- [Views]. N.p., n.d. Ob. 8vo. Captions in Fr. & Russian, no text. Cont. roan-bkd. bds., worn. (SH. Feb.5; 266)   De Velasco. £70

SAINT-PIERRE, Jacques Henri Bernardin de
- Oeuvres Complètes. Paris, 1825-26. 12 vols. Hf. mor. On vell. (HD. Oct.10; 284)   Frs. 1,900
- Paul & Virginia. Trans.:– Helen M. Williams. L., 1819. 12mo. Some foxing. Cont. str.-grd. mor., gt. vine-leaf borders, spine gt. worn. Fore-e. pntg.; from the liby. of Zola E. Harvey. (SG. Mar.19; 167) $220
- Paul et Virginie. Ill.:– Pelée after Lafitte (port.); Tony Johannot (plts.). Paris, 1863. Lge. 8vo. Mor. by Bertrand, decor. spine, border of 3 gt. fillets on covers, s.-c. (SM. Feb.11; 192)   Frs. 2,500
– – **Anr. Edn.** Ill.:– Brunelleschi. [Paris], [1943]. (525) numbered. 4to. Orig. wraps. (HK. Nov.18-21; 2468)   DM 440
- Paul et Virginie.–La Chaumière Indienne. Ill.:– after Tony Johannot, Français, Marville Isabey & others. Paris, 1838. 1st. Printing. Lge. 8vo. Woodcuts & ports. on China. Mor., gt. fillets & blind-tooled roll-stp. around covers, spine decor. with raised bands, inside dentelle, watered silk doubls. & end-papers. (HD. Jun.25; 401)   Frs. 1,350
– – **Anr. Edn.** Paris, 1838. 4to. Mor. gt., arabesque centrepiece on cover enclosing red mor. onlay, by Zaehnsdorf. (SH. Nov.20; 181)   Klusmann. £50
– – **Anr. Edn.** Paris, 1839. 12mo. Mor. lie-de-vin, limp decor. spine, triple border, gt. fillet & sm. tools, mosaic centre medallion oriental decor., unc., wrap. lined & reprd. prsvd., by De Samblancx. (LM. Mar.21; 294)   B.Frs. 10,500

SAINT PIERRE, Michel de
- Les Côtes Normandes. Ill.:– after Raoul Dufy. Paris, 1961. (50) on grand vélin d'Arches. 2 vols. Fo. Unsewn in orig. pict. wraps., cl. boxes. 11 separations of 1 colour plt., 2 unused double-p. plts. & extra suite of the 9 double-p. plts. (SH. Nov.21; 311)   Haarlem. £80

SAINT-REAL, César Vichard, Abbé de
- Conjuration des Espagnols contre Venise, en 1618. Paris, 1781. (25) on Holland Paper. 18mo. Old inscr. & sig. of W. Rees Mogg, 1957, on fly-lf. Cont. red mor. by Derome le Jeune with his ticket, triple gt. fillet, flat spine gt. with sm. roundel in compartments, inner gt. dentelles. (SM. Oct.8; 1991)   Frs. 1,500

SAINT-SAENS, Charles C.
- Printed Score for Soir Romantique. Paris, 1907. Fo. Self-wraps. Inscr. & sigd. (PNY. Mar.26; 446) $350

SAINT-SAUVEUR, J.G.
- Voyages Pittoresques dans les Quatre Parties du Monde. Paris, 1806. 2 vols. Sm. 4to. Frontis. & title-p. of vol. 1 reprd., 1 map reprd. & 1 plt. defect. Tree cf., rebkd. As a collection of prints, w.a.f. (BS. Jun.11; 191)   £420

SAINT-SIMON, Louis, Duc de
- Mémoires Publiés Par MM. Chéruel et A. Régnier. Paris, 1873-77. 20 vols. 12mo. Cont. hf. chagrin, corners, spines decor. with raised bands. (HD. Feb.27; 224)   Frs. 2,200
- Mémoires.–Supplement. 1788; 1789. 3 vols., 4 vols. Cont. grd. roan. (HD. Oct.10; 285)   Frs. 2,500

SAINT-VICTOR, J.M.B. De
[–] Tableau Historique et Pittoresque de Paris . . . Paris, 1808-11. 1st. Edn. 3 vols. 4to. Cont. cf., rebkd., orig. spines preserved. (SG. Oct.9; 219) $500

SAINTE BEUVE, Charles Augustin
- Livre d'Amour. 1843. (500). Three quarter mor., by Petit. (HD. Oct.10; 151)   Frs. 2,000
- Volupté. 1834. Orig. Edn. 2 vols. Title-page of vol. 2 short, some browning. Hf.-cf., corners decor. spines, by Meslant. (HD. Feb.18; 180) Frs. 1,050

SAINTE Marie Magdeleine, Pierre de
- Traité d'Horlogiographie . . . Paris, 1701. 12mo. Cont. marb. cf., spine decor. with raised bands, bdg. defect. (HD. Feb.27; 56)   Frs. 1,300

SAINTE PALAYE, Jean Baptiste de la Curne de
- Memoirs of Ancient Chivalry. Trans.:– [Mrs. S. Dobson]. 1784. 1st. Edn. in Engl. Cont. Engl. red mor., gt., spine tooled in compartments, covers with motto of Order of the Bath (?for Viscount Molesworth), surmounted by an earl's coronet, at the foot less the badge of the Order. (S. Nov.24; 253)   Howes. £90

SAINZ DE VALDIVIESO Y TOREJON –MERLO, Diego Joseph
- Parentacion Real. Luctuosa Pompa. Sumptuoso Cenotaphio, que . . .–Oracion Funebre a las Reales Exequias del Rey Nuestro Senor Don Phelipe V. [Lima], [1748]. 2 pts. in 1 vol. Sm. 4to. No engraved plt. Vell. bds. (SPB. May 5; 453) $110

SAKISIAN, Armenag Bey
- La Miniature Persan . . . Paris & Brussels, 1929. Lge. 4to. Sewed, wrap. (HD. Dec.5; 189)   Frs. 1,500

SALA, Angelo
- Opera Medico-Chymica, quae extant omnia. –Tractatus Duo: De Variis tum Chymicorum, tum Galenistarum Erroribus, in Praeparatione Medicinali commissis. Frankfurt, 1647; 1649. 1st. Coll. Edn. (1st. work). 2 works in 1 vol. 4to. Browned thro-out, slightly stained in extreme lr. margins, owner's entry on title, 'Joh. Jac. Renniger MFr'. Cont. vell. bds., soiled, Joh. Jac. Renniger's initials with date 1669 stpd. on upr. cover., hf. red mor. case. From Honeyman Collection. (S. Nov.11; 2740)   Das Bucherkabinet. £420

SALADINI, F.
See–TETTONI, L. & Saladini, F.

SALADINI, G.
See–RICCATI, Vincenzo & Saladini, G.

SALAMAN, Malcolm C.
- The Etchings of James McBey. 1929. (100) numbered, sigd. by McBey. 4to. Orig. vell.-bkd. buckram, slightly soiled. (CSK. Feb.20; 58)   £65

SALAZAR, Juan Jose de
- Vida de V.P. Alonso Messia de la Compañia de Jesús, fervoroso Misionero y Director de Almas en la Ciudad de Lima. Lima, 1733. Sm. 4to. A few stains & marginal wormholes. Cont. limp vell. (SPB. May 5; 454) $200

SALCANTENTIUS, H.B.
See–GODELMANN, J.G.–SALCANTENTIUS, H.B.

SALE, George (Trans.)
See–KORAN

SALERNO, School of
- Magistri Salernitani Nondum Editi. Torino, 1901. 1st. Edn. 2 vols. Tall fo. atlas & 8vo. Cl.-bkd. bds., worn. (SG. Sep.18; 334) $130

SALFELD, Siegmund
- Martyrologium des Nuernberger Memorbuches. Berlin, 1898. Slight browning. Vell.-bkd. bds. (SPB. May 11; 184) $125

SALHULA, Isaac Ibn
- Mashal Ha'Kadmoni. Venice, ca. 1546-50. 3rd. Edn. 4to. Title probably from anr. copy, repairs to margins with text loss, cropped, 1 woodcut altered, staining. Mod. hf. leath. (SPB. May 11; 183) $4,750

SALIS, Baptista de
- Summa Casuum Conscientiae quae Baptistiniana nuncupatur. Nuremb., Anton Koberger, 14 Apr. 1488. Fo. Lacks 1st. lf., a few ll. at beginning defect. at inner corner of head, with loss of a few letters of text, reprd., a little worming, slightly affecting text. 18th. C. vell. bds., rebkd., slightly

SALIS, Baptista de – Summa Casuum Conscientiae quae Baptistiniana nuncupatur. *-contd.*
soiled. From liby. of André L. Simon. [BMC II, 432; Goff S46; HC 14181*] (S. May 18; 174)
Hill. £150

SALISBURY GUIDE & Mashonaland Directory
Salisbury, 1909. Map slightly torn. Decor. cl. (VA. Jan.30; 323)
R. 110

SALLENGRE, Alb. Hendrik
[–] **Mémoires de Literature.** The Hague, 1715-17. L.P. 2 vols. Vol. 1 lacks last lf. (blank?). Red mor. by Derome le Jeune with his ticket, triple gt. fillet, flat spines gt. with single lozenge in compartments, inner gt. dentelles. Apley liby. & Rosebery bkplts., blind-stp. of Durdans, Epsom. (SM. Oct.8; 1993)
Frs. 1,600

SALLUSTIUS CRISPUS, Caius
– **La Conjuracion de Catilina y la Guerra de Jugurta.** Madrid, 1772. 4to. Cont. tree cf., Greek key border, gt. spine with urns in compartments, inner gt. border. (S. Oct.20; 210)
Beres. £900
– – **Anr. Copy.** Fo. Lacks plt. Red mor. by Derome le Jeune, with his 1785 ticket, wide roll-tooled borders, gt., including fleur-de-lis & entwined stems with rows of dots, spine gt. with sm. fountain in each compartment on pointillé ground, inner gt. dentelles. Tatton Park bkplt. (SM. Oct.8; 1994)
Frs. 1,300
– – **Anr. Edn.** [colophon: Madrid], [1772]. Fo. Cont. marb. sheep, lge. sections excised from covers. (CSK. Jan.30; 12)
£260
– **Ex Libris Historiarum Orationes et Epistolae.** [Mantua], [Johannes Schallus], [after Sep. 1475]. 4to. Arms & inner & upr. margin illuminated in colours & gold. Paper bds. [Hain 14243; BMC VII p. 933; Goff S 92] (C. Apr.1; 80)
Medoilanum. £500
– **Opera [with Valla's commentary on the Catalina].** Ed.:– [Pomponius Laetus]. Venice, Joannes Tacuinus, de Tridino, 5 Aug., 1493. Fo. Rubricated, ll. at end marginally wormed, affecting some letters, sm. hole in colophon, affecting 2 letters, title spotted. Old panel. cf., rebkd. [BMC V, 528; HC 14226; Goff S78] (S. May 5; 8)
Stewart. £280
– [–] **Anr. Edn.** Ed.:– Laurentius Valla, Joannes Chrysostomus Soldus, Pomponius Laetus & Joannes Britannicus. [Venice], [Christophorus de Pensis, de Mandello], [after 1494]. Fo. 103 ll. (of 110, lacks f1 & 6 ll. at end, supplied in facs.), some wormholes. 18th. C. wraps. [HC 14229; BMC V474; Goff S81] (SPB. May 6; 250) $250

SALLUSTIUS CRISPUS, Caius & Florus, Lucius Annaeus
– **Opera.** Bg'ham., 1774. 2nd. Baskerville Edn. 12mo. Mid-19th. C. red mor. gt., gt. rococo borders, partly unc. (CNY. May 22; 299) $150

SALMON, André
– **Venus dans la Balance.** Ill.:– Jules Pascin. Paris, [1926]. (300) numbered, on verge á la cuve de Montval, sigd., & with orig. etching sigd. by artist. Ptd. wraps., unc., unopened. (SG. Oct.23; 257)
$300

SALMON, Nathaniel
– **The History of Hertfordshire; Describing the County & Its Antient Monuments.** 1728. Fo. Browned. Old panel. cf., recently rebkd. (TA. Feb.19; 337)
£60

SALMON, Richard
– **Trout Flies.** N.Y., 1975. De Luxe Edn., (29) numbered, sigd. & with orig. sketch. Gt.-stpd. leatherette, s.-c. (SG. Oct.16; 360) $650

SALMON, Thomas
– **Modern History: or, The Present State of all Nations.** Ill.:– Herman Moll. 1739. 3 vols. 4to. Vol. 1 slightly wormed at end, title to vol. III slightly defect. Cont. cf., worn, 2 covers detchd. (S. Jun.23; 400)
Diba. £600
– – **Anr. Edn.** Ill.:– Herman Moll (maps). 1745-46. 3rd. Edn. 3 vols. Fo. Vol. I damaged by damp thro.-out. Cont. cf., scuffed. W.a.f. (LC. Feb.12; 568)
£100
– **The Universal Traveller.** 1752. Vol. 1 only. Fo. Cont. cf. W.a.f. (CSK. Aug.22; 101) £550
– – **Anr. Edn.** 1752-53. 2 vols. Fo. Some ll. & plts. & maps defect., dampstained. Orig. bds., defect. W.a.f. (S. Sep.29; 164)
Gibbs. £560

SALMON, William
– **Botanologia; The English Herbal: Or, History of Plants.** L., 1710. [1st. Edn.?]. Fo. Index Morborum (3 ll.) bnd. in, last few ll. slightly affected by worm, margins generally browned, a few mod. annots. & underlinings in ink on prelims. 19th. C. hf. cf. (TA. Sep.18; 329)
£375
– – **Anr. Copy.** Some ll. slightly browned, a few margins frayed. Cont. cf., worn. W.a.f. (SBA. Oct.21; 164)
L'Acquaforte. £220
– – **Anr. Copy.** Several ll. torn & crudely reprd., lacks Index Morborum–not often present. Old cf., worn. (TA. Feb.19; 371)
£200
– – **Anr. Copy.** Lacks 'Index morborum', margin of 8D in index torn with loss of some letters, last 2 ll. of index torn out (supplied loose from another copy, cut-down & mntd.), last lf. of index pasted on endpaper, occasional light dampstaining to corners. 19th. C. hf. sheep, worn. From Chetham's Liby., Manchester. (C. Nov.27; 356)
Sotheran. £160
– – **Anr. Copy.** Lacks engraved title, pp. 1281-1296 & a lf. of Index Morborum, last 2 ll. of Index Latinus defect., ptd. title soiled. Hf. cf., worn. W.a.f. (S. Jun.1; 285)
Erlini. £120
– – **Anr. Copy.** Reversed cf. (HSS. Apr.24; 7)
£100
– – **Anr. Edn.** 1710-[11]. 1st. Edn. Fo. 'Index Morborum' at end, holes in 4 ll., some worming, mainly marginal, occasionally affecting a few letters, some ll. stained in inner margins or fore-edges, some ll. browned, several ll. near end loose. Cont. panel. cf., rebkd., worn, upr. cover detchd. (S. Dec.3; 1120)
Traylen. £220
– **Iatrica: seu praxis mendendi, the Practice of Curing Diseases being a Medicinal History of near Two Hundred Famous Observations . . .** 1694. 4to. Sm. marginal tear in H2 & 3L2, sm. hole in 8H1, upr. margin m2 torn, slight worming affecting text in some places. Cf. [Wing S433] (S. Jun.17; 743)
Sargeant. £100
– **Polygraphice.** 1685. 5th. Edn. Additional engraved title probably from anr. copy, title stained, minor spotting & staining thro.-out. Mod. hf. mor. [Wing S448] (C. Nov.5; 137)
Smith. £60
– **Seplasium, the Compleat English Physician, or the Druggist's Shop Opened.** 1693. 1st. Edn. Hf.-title & title lack corners, slightly affecting text, browned thro.-out. Recent hf. mor. [Wing S452] (C. Apr.1; 116)
Lawson. £120

SALMSON, A.J.
– **Rikssalen pa Gripsholms Slott.** Stockholm, 1854. Fo. Orig. cl., rebkd. (SH. Jun.18; 197)
Fairburn. £60

SALOMON III, Bp.
– **Glossae ex Illustrissimis Collectae Autoribus.** [Augsb.], ca. 1475. 1st. Edn. Fo. Lightly stained & soiled in parts, some sm. faults. 19th. C. bds., worn. (HK. Nov.18-21; 292)
DM 4,000

SALOMON, Dr. Erich
– **Beruehmte Zeitgenossen in Unbewachten Augenblicken.** Stuttgart, [1931]. 4to. Cl. (SG. Apr.23; 174)
$240

SALOMONSEN, Finn
– **Birds of Greenland.** Ill.:– Gitz-Johansen. Copen., 1950. Fo. Red mor., mor. & cl. box. (CE. Nov.20; 88)
£180
– – **Anr. Copy.** 4to. Parallel text in Danish. Decor. cl. (CE. Mar.19; 161)
£50
– **Grønlands Fugle, The Birds of Greenland.** Ill.:– Gritz-Johansen. 1950. 4to. Hf. cf. gt. (P. Nov.13; 219)
Quaritch. £120
– – **Anr. Edn.** Ill.:– Gitz-Johansen. Copen., [1950-51]. 3 vols. 4to. Orig. wraps., boxes. (CSK. May 22; 11)
£110

SALT, Sir Henry
– **Twenty-Four Views of St. Helena, The Cape, India, Ceylon, Abyssinia, & Egypt.** Ill.:– D. Havell & others, after Salt. 1809. Fo. Slight spotting to some plts., 2 plts. cropped at foot just within platemark. Cont. hf. cf. gt. over marb. bds. (LC. Oct.2; 197)
£1,000
– **A Voyage to Abyssinia . . .** 1814. 1st. Edn. 4to. 1 or 2 maps/plts. cold. in outl., a few ll. lightly discold. Cont. (orig.?) hf. roan, unopened. (S. Jun.29; 212)
Maggs. £350
– – **Anr. Copy.** Mod. cf. (SG. Feb.26; 2) $300
– – **Anr. Edn.** 1814. 1st. Edn. L.P. Lge. 4to. Mod. three-qtr. mor., unc. (SG. Feb.26; 289) $650

– **Voyage en Abyssinie.** Trans.:– P.F. Henry. Paris, 1816. 1st. Fr. Edn. 2 vols. & atlas vol. Cont. qtr. cf. & marb. bds. (PNY. May 21; 372) $150

SALTBERGER, C.
– **Hier Innen volgen etlich Müntz Vergleichungen Gericht auf allerlay Bezalungen.** N.p., 1576. 4to. Lightly soiled & stained, old note on arms & title, engraved arms ex libris on inner upr. cover, MS. Italian trans. on each table head. Leath. ca. 1576, gt., gold-stpd. arms supralibros on both covers, MS. ex libris, defect. (HK. Nov.18-21; 293)
DM 3,000

SALTEN, Felix
– **Bambi.** Berlin, 1923. 1st. Edn. 4 pp. of advts. at end. Cl.-bkd. pict. bds. (SG. Apr.30; 286) $600

SALTER, Thomas Frederick
– **The Angler's Guide.** L., 1814. 1st. Edn. Mod. three-qtr. cf., orig. wraps. bnd. in, unc. (SG. Oct.16; 362)
$325
– – **Anr. Edn.** L., 1815. 2nd. Edn., L.P. Extra ill. with 6 additional plts. Mod. three-qtr. mor., unc. (SG. Oct.16; 363)
$400

SALTMARSHE, Christopher (Ed.)
See–CAMBRIDGE POETRY

SALUSBURY, Thomas
– **Mathematical Collections & Translations.** 1967. Facs. Edn. (200) numbered. 2 vols. Fo. Orig. cf., by Zaehnsdorf, a little rubbed, s.-c. From Honeyman Collection. (S. Nov.11; 2743)
Whitehart. £55

SALUSBURY, Thomas–DUILLIER, N. Facio
– **Mathematical Collections & Translations. –Navigation Improv'd.** 1661; 1728. 1st. Edn., 1st. Iss. (1st. work). Vol. I (of 2). Fo. For 1 set of diagrams cut out & hinged to text, lacks hf.-title, errata lf. inserted in facs., prelims. misbnd., title to Galileo's 'System of the World' bnd. at front (soiled) & with lr. blank corners renewed), marginal stains, a few sm. repairs to text, owner's inscr. on 1st. title. Mod. mor. From Honeyman Collection, w.a.f. [Wing S517] (S. Nov.11; 2742)
Zeitlin. £190

SALVAGE, Jean-Galbert
– **Anatomie du Gladiateur Combattant.** Paris, 1812. Fo. Slight soiling. Later hf. cl. (CSK. Jan.23; 95)
£130

SALVATOR, Archduke Ludwig
– **Die Balearen.** Würzburg & Leipzig, 1897. Vol. II only. Fo. Cl. (DS. May 22; 831) Pts. 34,000

SALVERTE, Eusebe
– **The Occult Sciences.** Trans.:– Anthony Todd Thomson. L., 1846. 2 vols. Ex liby. Cl., very worn. (SG. Apr.9; 222)
$120

SALVIN, Francis H. & Broderick, William
– **Falconry in the British Isles.** 1855. [1st. Edn.?]. 4to. Hf. mor. gt. Wagstaff Armorial Label, A.L.s. by Francis Henry Salvin, 2½ pp., 12mo., 6 January, 1866 to Mr. Hincks, on matters of natural history. (P. Oct.2; 264) *McEwan.* £340
– – **Anr. Copy.** Occasional spotting. Orig. cl., gt., slight spotting. (C. Nov.5; 138)
Wheldon & Wesley. £280
– – **Anr. Edn.** 1873. [2nd. Edn.?]. Orig. cl. gt. (C. Mar.18; 182)
Henderson. £520
– – **Anr. Copy.** 4to. 1 plt. loose. Unopened. (P. Apr.9; 264)
Hill. £420

SALVIN, Osbert & Godman, Frederick Ducane
– **Biologia Centrali-Americana.** 1879-1904. 4 vols. (3 of text & 1 of plts.). Royal 4to. Hf. mor. cf. (S. Jun.1; 201)
Maggs Brothers. £850
– – **Anr. Copy.** Mod. cl. gt. (P. Nov.13; 220)
Marks. £360
– **Biologia Centrali-Americana. Lepidoptera-Rhopalocera.** L., 1879-1901. 3 vols. 4to. Some plts. loose. Red mor. gt. (SPB. Oct.1; 183) $1,900

SALZMANN, Chr. G.
– **Denkwürdigkeiten aus dem Leben ausgezeichneter Teutscher des Achtzehnten Jahrhunderts.** Schepfenthal, 1802. 1st. Edn. 18th. C. bds., unc., worn. (D. Dec.11-13; 2737)
DM 1,100
– **Elements of Morality for the use of Children, with an Introductory Address to Parents.** Trans.:– [Mary Wolstonecraft]. Ill.:– William Blake (16 plts., attributed to). 1791. 3 vols. 12mo. Advts. in vol. 3. Cont. cf., lacks upr. cover of vol. 1, upr. covers of vols. 2 & 3 loose. (SH. Mar.19; 284)
Schiller. £260

SAMAIN, Albert
- **Au Jardin de l'Infante.** Ill.:– J.G.C.M. Beltrand after Carlos Schwabe. Paris, 1908. (120) numbered. 4to. Cont. tree cf., orig. wraps. bnd. in. 3 variant proofs of frontis. bnd. in. (SH. Nov.21; 472) *Bergquist.* £78
- **– Anr. Edn.** Ill.:– Giraldon. Paris, 1920. (50) numbered on Arches vell. 3 states, including black-&-white separate printing. Mor. by Joly fils, mosaic spine & covers, wrap. preserved, s.-c. (SM. Feb.11; 283) Frs. 6,500
- **Hyalis.** Ill.:– Mossa. Paris, 1918. (55) on Jap. Imp. Sm. 4to. Three states of plts. Hf. mor., corners, decor. & mosaic spine, unc., pict. wrap., by Flammarion-Vaillant. (HD. Jun.10; 204) Frs. 1,600

SAMBER, Robert 'Eugenius Philalethes'
[-] **Long Livers.** 1722. Cf. (P. Sep.11; 70) *Phelps.* £65

SAMBUCUS, Joannes
- **Veterum Aliquot ac Recentium Medicorum Philosophorumque Icones.** [Leiden], 1603. Fo. Title cut round & mntd., lacks K5, slight marginal staining, a few printing flaws. Disbnd. (S. Dec.2; 767) *Harlinghausen.* £120
- **– Anr. Edn.** Amst., 1615. Fo. 62 numbered plts. (of 67), additional plts. 5 & 60 loosely inserted, slight discolouration, title slightly soiled. Cf., worn, upr. cover detchd. W.a.f. (S. Jun.23; 239) *Harlinghausen.* £170

SAMMLUNG der Besten und Neuesten Reisebeschreibungen
Ed.:– J.F. Zückert. Berlin, 1768-80. Vols. 1-20 (Vol. 1-2 2nd. Edn.) Cont. leath., gt. spine, fillets & corner fleurons. (R. Oct.14-18; 1520) DM 3,400

SAMPSON, George Vaughan
- **Memoir, Explanatory of the Chart & Survey of ... Londonderry.** 1814. 4to. Mod. marb. bds., unc. (P. Mar.12; 264) *Crowe.* £120
- **Statistical Survey of the County of Londonderry** Dublin, 1802. Some finger marks. Str.-grd. mor. (GM. Apr.30; 276) £85

SAMS, William
- **A Tour through Paris.** [plts. dtd. 1822]. Fo. Sm. stain affecting lr. blank margins of last 2 plts. & accompanying text ll. Mod. hf. mor. (C. Feb.4; 148) *Hackhaffer.* £850
- **– Anr. Copy.** 16 plts. (of 21, lacks title). Hf. roan. (BS. Feb.5; 256) £50
- **– Anr. Edn.** [1824]. Fo. 17 cold. aquatint plts. only some foxing thro.-out not affecting plts. Hf. mor. (BS. Jun.11; 192) £140
- **– Anr. Edn.** L., n.d. [wtrmkd. 1825]. Fo. Orig. red hf. mor. (SPB. Oct.1; 211) $1,400

SAMUEL, William, Attrib. to
- **Arte of Angling.** Ed.:– G.E. Bently & C.O. von Kienbusch. 1956. Facs. of 1577 Edn. 16mo. Antique-style vell. bds. A.L.s. from Kienbusch to H.A. Ingraham laid in. (SG. Dec.11; 7) $120

SANADON, Noel Etienne
- **Carmina in Regalem Partum Mariae Ludovicae Hispaniarum Reginae.** Ill.:– Rochefort after Desmaretz. Paris, 1707. Partly erased stp. on title. Cont. red mor., gt., arms of Louis de France, Le Grand Dauphin, on cover, triple gt. fillet, spine gt. in compartments, inner gt. dentelles, gt. flowered end-papers, apparently lacks rear free end-paper, lr. edges worn slightly. Bkplt. of Lord Grantham. (S. Apr.7; 346) *Quaritch.* £220

SÁNCHEZ RECIENTE, Juan
- **Tratado de Trigonometria nautica, y de la Construccion, y Uso de las Escalas Plana, y Artificial.** Madrid, 1759. Paper flaws at foot of I2 & M8. Mod. hf. red mor. From Honeyman Collection. (S. Nov.11; 2744) *Armero.* £50

SANCHO DE MELGAR, Estevan
- **Arte de la Lengua del Ynga Hamada Qquechua.** Lima, 1691. Title loose, old stp. erased slightly affecting letters, recent liby. stp., blank portion of last lf. cut away, some ll. shaved affecting headlines, slight discolouration. Cl. (SPB. May 5; 455) $750

S[ANCTINUS] L[UCENSIS], A[ntonius]
See–VIETA, Franciscus–S[ANCTINUS] L[UCENSIS], A[ntonius]

SANCTO GEORGIO, Johannes Antonius de
- **Oratio in exequijs Reuerendissimi D. Cardinalis Tornacensis.** [Rome], [Stephan Plannck], [after

16 Oct. 1483]. 4to. Paper bds. [H. 7597*; Goff S 134] (C. Apr.1; 81) *Wade.* £150

SAND, George (Pseud.)
See–DUPIN, Amandine Aurore Lucie, Baronne Dudevant 'George Sand'

SAND, Maurice
- **Masques et Boufons.** Paris, 1862. 2 vols., hf.-titles, some slight marks, vol. II title slightly defect. Mod. red mor., gt. spines. (SI. Dec.4; 520) Lire 650,000

SANDBURG, Carl
- **In Reckless Ecstasy.** Ed.:– Philip Green Wright. Galesburg, Illinois, Asgard Pr., 1904. 1st. Edn. 12mo. Orig. wraps., stitched with red ribbon, unc., piece chipped from upr. cover & spine. Pres. copy to Vella Martin. (CNY. May 22; 261) $4,500
- **Incidentals.** Galesburg, Illinois, Asgard Pr., [Nov. 1907]. 1st. Edn. 12mo. Orig. pict. wraps., stitched with red ribbon. (CNY. May 22; 262) $1,600
- **Steichen the Photographer.** N.Y., [1929]. (925) numbered, sigd. by Steichen & Sandburg. Lge. 4to. Blank corner of 1 plt. torn away. Gt.-lettered buckram. (SG. Apr.23; 183) $400

SANDBY, Paul
- **Virtuosi's Museum Select View of England, Scotland & Wales.** 1778. Ob. 4to. Cf. gt. (P. Sep.11; 288) *Crowe.* £280
- **– Anr. Copy.** No bdg. stated. (GT. Oct.2; 199) £130
- **Virtuoso's Museum.–Collection of One Hundred & Fifty Select Views in England, Scotland & Ireland.** 1781. 2 works in 1 vol., 2nd. work vol. 1. Ob. 4to. Cont. cf. gt., Kenneth Rae's bkplt. designed by R. Whistler. (P. May 14; 66) *Walford.* £210

SANDBY, Paul & Chatelain, M.
- **A Collection of Landskips & Figures.** 1773. Fo. Some soiling & spotting. Wraps., disbnd. W.a.f. (CSK. Mar.6; 157) £260

SANDE, J. Van
See–REYD, E. Van & Sande, J. Van

SANDE, J.B. van den & Hahnemann, S.
- **Die Kennzeichen der Güte u. Verfälschung der Arzney Mittel.** Dresden, 1787. 1st. German Edn. Cont. bds. (HK. Nov.18-21; 723) DM 1,060

SANDEBERG-VAVALA, E.
- **La Croce Dipinta Italiana e l'Iconografia della Passione.** Verona, 1929. 4to. Publisher's cl. (CR. Mar.19; 156) Lire 280,000

SANDEMAN, Fraser
- **By Hook & By Crook.** L., 1892. 1st. Edn., (100) numbered on L.P., sigd. Gt.-decor. cl., unc. (SG. Oct.16; 372) $120

SANDER, Henry F.C.
- **Reichenbachia, Orchids Illustrated & Described** ... 1886-95. 4 vols., 1st. & 2nd. Series. Lge. fo. 192 chromolitho. plts. & 5 extra unissued chromolitho. plts. loosely inserted. Mor. gt. by Zaehnsdorf. (C. Jul.15; 202) *Traylen.* £3,500

SANDERSON, J.
- **Memoranda of a Trading Trip into the Orange River [Sovereignty] Free State & the Country of the Transvaal Boers, 1851-52.** L., [1860]. Orig. bdg., ptd. wraps. (VA. Jan.30; 328) R. 105

SANDERSON, Robert
- **Physicae Scientiae Compendium.** Oxford, 1671. 1st. Edn. Last 2 ll. cropped at foot, sm. tear in H5, slight browning. Old-style cf. From Honeyman Collection. [Wing S620] (S. Nov.11; 2747) *Haller.* £55

SANDERUS, Antonio
- **Flandria Illustrata.** Cologne, 1641. 1st. Edn. 2 vols. Lge. fo. 1 plan reprd. Old vell., 7 spine raised bands. (LM. Jun.13; 253) B.Frs. 340,000

SANDFORD, Francis
- **A Genealogical History of the Kings of England.** Priv. ptd., 1677. Fo. 5 engraved double-p. plts. mntd. on guards. Cont. cf., worn. [Wing S 651] (CSK. Aug.15; 196) £55
- **The History of the Coronation of ... James II.** 1687. 1st. Edn. Fo. Panel. cf., brkn. (BS. Jun.11; 225) £200
- **– Anr. Copy.** 27 engraved plts. (of 30). Old cf., Signet Arms on covers, brkn. (BS. Jun.11; 226) £110
- **– Anr. Copy.** Chagrin, worn. (LM. Nov.8; 81) DM 14,000

SANDIFORT, Ed.
- **Observationes Anatomico-Pathologicae.** Leiden, 1777-81. 1st. Edn. 4 pts. in 2 vols. 4to. Old MS. owner's note on title, slightly soiled. Cont. hf. leath. (HK. Nov.18-21; 724) DM 1,200

SANDRART, Joachim von
- **L'Academia Todesca della Architectura, Scultura & Pittura, oder Deutsche Academie.** Nuremb., 1675-79. 6 pts. in 2 vols. Fo. Old vell. (BS. Jun.11; 129) £460
- **Sculpturae Veteris Admiranda sive Delineatio vera Perfectissimarum Eminentissimarumque Statuarum.–Romae Antiquae et Novae Theatrum Illustratum** ... Ill.:– Raphael Collin after Joachim von Sandrart. Nuremb., 1680; 1684; 1685; 1683. 1st. Edns. 4 works in 3 vols. Fo. 1 or 2 ll. browned. 18th. C. mor., triple gt. fillet, spines gt. in compartments, inner gt. dentelles. (SM. Oct.8; 1997) Frs. 26,000

SANDS & KENNY
- **Commercial & General Melbourne Directory for 1857** ... Melbourne, 1857. Mod. mor. (KH. Mar.24; 346) Aus. $150

SANDWICH, John Montagu, Earl of
- **A Voyage round the Mediterranean.** 1799. 1st. Edn. 4to. Browned. Mod. hf. cf. (SH. Jun.18; 91) *Dimakarakos.* £80

SANDYS, George
- **A Relation of a Journey ... containing a Description of the Turkish Empire.** 1615. 1st. Edn. Fo. Tall copy. Cf., gt., by Bedford. Bkplts. of William Gott & Sir C.E.H. Chadwyck Healey, lately in the collection of Eric Sexton. [STC 21726] (C. Apr.15; 46) *Kossow.* £500
- **– Anr. Copy.** Engraved title, folding map loose, text ills., G4 & I5 torn, lacks I6, scorch-marks on few ll. Cont. cf., worn. (S. Mar.31; 501) *Scott.* £120
- **Travailes.** L., 1658. 6th. Edn. Fo. With the genital area of Father Nile clipped, & consequent text loss on p. 73. Old cf., badly scuffed, newly rebkd. (SG. Feb.5; 296) $120
- **– Anr. Edn.** 1670. 6th. Edn. Fo. Lacks engraved title & plt., some dampstains. Later cf.-bkd. bds. [Wing S679] (S. Jun.18; 64) *Makiya.* £70
- **– Anr. Copy.** Lightly soiled, map with restored tear. Cont. leath., spine reprd. (R. Mar.31-Apr.4; 2542) DM 420

SAN GIOVANNI, Antonio
- **Seconda Squara Mobile, et Aritmetica ... Con Aggionta d'un Breve Trattato d'Agricoltura.** Vicenza, 1686. 1st. Edn. 2 pts. in 1 vol. 4to. Some browning. Orig. limp bds., worn. From Honeyman Collection. (S. Nov.11; 2748) *Nox.* £100

SANGUINETI, Edoardo
- **Baj. The Biggest Art Book in the World.** Ill.:– Enrico Baj. Milan, 1968. (400) numbered, & sigd. by artist. Fo. Orig. bdg., d.-w. (SPB. Nov.25; 218) $200

SAN MARCO
- **La Basilica di San Marco in Venezia, Seconde Partie.–Documenti per la Storia dell'Augusta Ducale Basilice di San Marco in Venezia.** Venice, 1883; 1886. 2 vols.; 1 vol. Fo. Some tissue-guards occasionally adhering to face of chromolithos. 1st. work: loose in ptd. wraps. 16 pts. in 2 folding portfos., as iss., worn, soiled, ex-liby.; 2nd. work: ptd. wraps. (SG. Dec.4; 262) $180

SANMICHELI, Michele
- **Li Cinque Ordine dell' Architettura Civile.** Ill.:– A. Balestra & A. Pompei. Verona, 1735. 1st. Edn. Fo. Cont. vell. From the collection of John A. Saks. (C. Jun.10; 227) *Marlborough.* £220

SANNAZARO, Jacopo
- **De Partu Virginis.** Rome, 1526. 17th. C. bds., solander case. Henry A. Sherwin's bkplt. (SG. Oct.16; 376) $475
- **El Parto de la Virgen ...** Trans.:– Gregorio Hernandez. Salamanca, 1569. 2nd. Edn. in Castellan. Wormhole in margin of title, slightly soiled, 1 lf. torn, slightly affecting text. 18th. C. cf., slightly worn. (S. Dec.8; 91) *Quaritch.* £80

SANQUIRICO, Alessandro
- **Incoronandosi in Milano la Sacra Cesarea Reale Apostolica Maesta di Ferdinando I, Imperatore d'Austria.** N.p., [1838]. Ob. fo. Title & dedication detchd., slightly dampstained thro.-out. Cont. blind-stpd. mor. gt., worn, jnts. brkn. (C. Nov.5; 139) *Marlborough.* £110

SANQUIRICO, Alessandro -contd.

- Inocoronazione de S.M.J.R.A. Ferdinando I a Re des Regno Lombardo-Veneto. Milan, [1838]. Ob. fo. Bds., gt., imperial arms, cf. spine, Principe Borghesi ex-libris. (SI. Dec.4; 522) Lire 900,000

SANSON, Nicholas

- Atlas Nouveau, Contenant Toutes les Parties du Monde. Paris, 1692. Fo. Hf. cf., worn. (CE. Nov.20; 38) £1,600
- - Anr. Edn. Paris, 1693-96. Fo., 625mm×530mm. Some maps with tears at central fold, browned, lacking 18 maps., maps cold. by cont. (?) hand. Late 19th. C. qtr. mor., worn. W.a.f. (CNY. Oct.1; 32) $6,000
- L'Etat de la Republique de Venise. Amst., ca. 1740, or later. Fo. 17 double-p. engraved plts., hand-cold. in outl., without title or text. Mod. cf.-bkd. bds. W.a.f. (S. Mar.31; 297)
Gibbs. £750
See-JAILLOT, Hubert & Sanson, Nicholas

SANSON, Nicholas & Berry, William

- Atlas. Ca. 1689. Fo. No ptd. title, 37 hand-cold. maps, some repairs. Bdg. not stated. (P. Mar.12; 166) *Cambridge.* £2,200

SANTACILLA, Jorge Juan y

See-ULLOA, Antonio de & Santacilla, Jorge Juan y

SANTA CLARA, Abraham a [Johann Ulrich Megerle]

- Etwas für Alle. Würzburg, 1699. 1st. Edn. Pt. 1 of 3. Lacks plt. 38 & 65 & pp. 327-330, stained thro.-out, slightly browned & soiled in parts, owners mark on title in old MS. Endpapers renewed, cont. vell. (HK. May 12-14; 949) DM 6,500
- - Anr. Copy. Cont. hf. leath., worn, spine torn & lacks leath. in 2 places. (D. Dec.11-13; 2109) DM 4,700
- - Anr. Edn. Würzburg, 1699. 1st. Edn. 2nd. printing, pt. 1 (of 3). Lacks 2 copperplts., frontis. & last index lf., slightly soiled & stained thro.-out, 3 plts. torn, 1st. 3 text ll. half missing. Cont. vell. (HK. Nov.18-21; 1470) DM 5,200
- - Anr. Edn. Würzburg, 1711. 1st. Edn. Pt. 3 (of 3). Frontis. & title stpd., upr. cover loose, text slightly browned towards end. Cont. leath.-bkd. wood bds., rubbed, lacks 2 clasps. (HK. Nov.18-21; 1471) DM 7,200
- Heilsames Gemisch Gemasch. Würzburg, 1704. Sm. 4to. Front. by C. Luyken, front & title slightly defect. Cont. vell., upr. cover stained. (R. Oct.14-18; 798) DM 920
- Iets voor Allen. Trans.:- J. Le Long. Amst., 1758-59 & n.d. 3 vols. Light wear, mainly marginal, stained in places. 19th. C. hf. cl., gt. spines, slightly loose. (VG. Oct.13; 2) Fls. 6,800

SANTA CLAUS & JENNY LIND

N.Y., 1850. 4to. Orig. pict. wraps., backstrip partly split, slightly worn. (SH. Mar.19; 285) *Schiller.* £190

SANTA MARIA, Antonio Francisco Javier

- Vida Prodigiosa de la Venerable Virgen Juana de Jesus, de la Tercera. Lima, 1756. Sm. 4to. Lacks engraved plt., light stains at beginning & end. Cont. vell., defect. (SPB. May 5; 456) $150

SANTANDER, Sebastian de

- Oracio Funebre declamada en las Honras y Exequias de Capitan Don Miguel Raboso de la Plaza, Alguacil Mayor desta Ciudad de los Angeles, . . . Puebla de los Angeles, 1693. Sm. 4to. Scorch-marks in margins from owner's brand, stains. Rebnd. in old limp vell. (SPB. May 5; 457) $175

SANTAREM, Visconde de

- Estudos de Cartographia Antiga. Lisbon, [1919]. 2 vols. Purple hf.-mor. gt. (SG. Oct.2; 322) $130

SANTA TERESA, Giovanni Giuseppi di

- Istoria delle Guerre del Regno del Brasile accadute tra la Corona di Portogallo e la republica de Olanda. Rome, 1698. 1st. Edn. 2 pts. in 1 vol. Fo. A few charts & maps & plts. with short tears, lr. fore-corner torn from B1 & lr. margins of K3 & R4 cut away, with no loss of text, occasional light spotting & browning. Late 18th. C. hf. cf., reprd. & with the insertion of new end-papers. [Sabin 76793] (S. Nov.4; 657) *Soublin.* £3,500
- - Anr. Copy. Engraved frontis., 2 ports., 21 (of 23) folding engraved plts., 1 plt. reprd., 1 torn at inner margin, early MS. notes to binder on plt. versos. 18th. C. blind-panel. parch., spine wormed

& defect. Bkplt. of Girolamo Durazzo. (S. Mar.31; 502) *Mistrali.* £550

SANTAYANA, George

- The Works. N.Y., 1936-40. Triton Edn., (940) numbered & sigd. 15 vols. Cl.-bkd. bds. with sm. gt. medallions, mostly unopened. (SG. Dec.18; 365) $350

SANTBECK, D.

See-REGIOMONTANUS, Johannes
-SANTBECK, D.

SANTIAGO DE CHILE

- Reglamento del Panteon General de Santiago de Chile, dictado por el Supremo Gobierno. [Santiago de Chile], 1824. Sm. 4to. Slight discolouration. Cl.-bkd. bds. (SPB. May 5; 458) $250

SANTISTEBAN OSORIO, Diego de

- Quarta y quinta Parte de la Araucana. Barcelona, 1598. 12mo. Marginal repairs at beginning & end, a few ll. slightly soiled. Mod. vell. [Sabin 57802] (SPB. May 5; 459) $500

SANTO BARTOLI, Pietro-[BARTHE'LEMY, L'Abbé]-SANTO BARTOLI, Pietro

- Recueil de Peintures Antiques.-[La Mosaique de Palestine.]-Recueil de Peintures Antiques. Paris, 1757-60; 1783-87. 1st. Edns. [1st. 2 works] (30), 2 works in 1 vol. & vols II & III of 2nd. Edn. in 1 vol. Fo. 1st. work lettering in MS., 1 p. MS. explanation, 2nd. work title in 2 states, 3 single ll. in Mariette's hand tipped in. Cont. mor. gt., tooling in spine compartments, not quite unif., inner gt. dentelles. Pierre Jean Mariette's copy, his sig., Library of Thomas Johnes of Hafod. (SM. Oct.7; 1998) Frs. 48,000

SANTO BARTOLI, Pietro & [Rive, l'abbé]

- Recueil de Peintures Antiques Trouvées à Rome. -[Histoire Critique de la Pyramide de Caius Cestius]. Paris, 1783-87. On vell. 2 works in 3 vols. Fo. Cont. mor. by Derome le Jeune with his ticket, wide gt. borders, spines gt. in compartments, inner gt. dentelles, pink silk liners. (SM. Oct.8; 1999) Frs. 40,000

SANVITALE, Jacopo Antonio

- Poema Parabolico Diviso in Morale, Politico, e Fisico. Ill.:- F. Marcello & P. Monaco. Venice, 1746. 4to. Some sm. wormholes to extreme lr. inner margins of some ll. Cont. cf., gt. spine. From the collection of John A. Saks. (C. Jun.10; 228) *Lyon.* £190

SAPPHO

See-ANACREON & others-MUSAEUS

SARASIN, Jean François

- Les Oeuvres. Ill.:- R. Nanteuil. Paris, 1656. 1st. Edn. 2 vols. 4to. Port. placed at beginning of vol. 2, heads of several ll. dampstained. Cont. marb. cf., arms of Marie-Anne de Bourbon-Condé, decor. spines, ex-liby. (HD. Mar.18; 152) Frs. 1,600

SARCEPHALUS, Christophorus

- Duodecim Domiciliorum Coelestium Tabula Nova. Breslau, 1600. 1st. Edn. 4to. Browned, stp. of University of Wratislavia (Breslau) on verso of title. Wraps. From Honeyman Collection. (S. Nov.11; 2750) *McKittrich.* £70

SARMIENTO DE LOS SALVADORES, Agustin

- Clarin de la Aurora y Excelencias de la Purissima Reyna de los Angeles. Lima, 1669. Sm. 4to. Folding engraved port. with short tears reprd., last lf. loose, sm. piece torn from inner margin affecting letters, sm. marginal stains. Cont. cf., gt., some wear. (SPB. May 5; 460) $175

SAROYAN, William

- A Collection of Works. 1936-61. All but 1 1st. Edns. 27 vols. Orig. cl., d.-w.'s. (SH. Dec.18; 255) *Sheldon.* £65
- Harlem as Seen By Hirschfeld. Ill.:- Al Hirschfeld. N.Y., [1941]. (1,000) numbered. Fo. Pict. covers, dented. (SG. Jun.4; 441a) $275

SARPI, Paolo

- [-] Historia del Concilio Tridentino. 1619. 1st. Edn. Fo. Royal arms on title. Antique style mor., gt., lacks clasps. [NSTC 21760] (S. Nov.25; 367) *Mediolanum.* £130
- - Anr. Copy. Sig. of L. Puy on title, red ptd. ticket 'F' with MS. number 23 of liby. of Louis Henri de Loménie de Brienne. Late 17th. C. cf., arms of Loménie de Brienne & his cipher, gt., in spine compartments. [NSTC 21760] (SM. Oct.8; 2000) Frs. 1,200

SARRATT, J.H.

- The Works of Damiano, Ruy-Lopez, & Salvio, on the Game of Chess. L., 1813. 1st. Edn. Cont. cf. (SG. Sep.4; 103) $100

SARRE, Friedrich

- Islamic Bookbindings. L., [1923]. (550) numbered. 4to. Owner's sig. on title & some other pp. Buckram. (SG. Mar.26; 50) $425

SARRE, Friedrich & Martin, F.R.

- Die Ausstellung v. Meisterwerken Muhammedan. Kunst in München. Munich, 1911-12. (430) numbered. Lge. fo. Lacks plts. 199 & 254-7. Orig. linen portfo. (HK. Nov.18-21; 3489) DM 2,100

SARTAIN, John

- The Reminiscences of a Very Old Man. N.Y., 1899. Extra ill. with extensive series of Sartain mezzotints, & other plts., contents partly loose in bdg. Three-qtr. lev., spine & top gt. (SG. Dec.4; 310) $175

SARTON, George

- Introduction to the History of Science. Baltimore, Md., 1927 [1946]-31-48. 3 vols. in 5. 4to. Orig. cl. From liby. of Dr. E. Ahsworth Underwood. (S. Feb.23; 284) *Whitehart.* £100

SARTORIUS, C.

- Mexico Landscapes & Popular Sketches. N.Y., ca. 1859. 4to. Cont. hf. mor., worn. [Sabin 77121] (SH. Jun.18; 198) *De Velasco.* £500

SARZOSA, Francisco

- In Aequatorem Planetarum, Libri duo. Paris, 1526. 2nd Edn.? Fo. 4 full-p. woodcut diagrams cut out & folded at outer edge. 19th. C. panel. cf. From Honeyman Collection; the Dyson Perrins copy. (S. Nov.11; 2751) *Nox.* £320

SASSOON, David Solomon

- Ohel Dawid. Descriptive Catalogue of the Hebrew & Samaritan Manuscripts in the Sassoon Library. Oxford, 1932. 2 vols. 4to. Cl. (S. Nov.17; 99) *Kingsgate.* £380
- - Anr. Copy. Spines faded. (SPB. May11; 57) $1,000

SASSOON, Sir Ellice V.

- The Catalogue of Sassoon Chinese Ivories. Ed.:- S.E. Lucas. 1950. (250). 3 vols. Fo. Orig. hf. vell. gt. (P. May 14; 225) *Sims & Reed.* £180

SASSOON, Siegfried 'Saul Kain'

- Collected Poems. 1947. 1st. Edn. Orig. cl. Pres. copy to Dorothy Wallis. (S. Jul.22; 263) *Blackwell.* £95
- Common Chords. 1950. 1st. Edn., (107). Orig. cl. Inscr. to Richard [Seymour]. (SH. Dec.19, 617) *Maggs.* £50
- [-] The Daffodil Murderer. 1913. 1st. Edn. Orig. wraps. (S. Jul.22; 252) *Maggs.* £65
- [-] - Anr. Copy. (S. Jul.22; 253) *Sherlock.* £50
- [-] Early Morning Long Ago. 1941. 1st. Edn., (50). Orig. wraps., unc. Inscr. by Geoffrey Keynes for Richard de la Mare. (SH. Dec.18; 281) *Sherlock.* £50
- The Heart's Journey. N.Y., & L., 1927. 1st. Edn., (599). Orig. cl.-bkd. bds., d.-w., unc. Inscr. to Dick de la Mare, sigd. on title, autograph deletion & correction by author. (SH. Dec.18; 266) *Chelsea.* £120
- - Anr. Copy. (C. Feb.4; 312) *Hook.* £85
- [-] Lingual Exercises for Advanced Vocabularians. Camb., Priv. Ptd. 1925. 1st. Edn., (99). Orig. buckram, unc. Inscr. to W[alter] de la M[are], A.L.s. from author. (SH. Dec.18; 261) *Baldur.* £210
- [-] - Anr. Copy. S.-c. Inscr. to 'Dick de la Mare (the perfect publisher)'. (SH. Dec.18; 262) *Sherlock.* £140
- [-] Melodies. 1912. 1st. Edn. Orig. wraps., paint on pt. of fore-e., unc. (SH. Dec.18; 258) *Baldur.* £720
- [-] - Anr. Edn. [L.], [Priv. Ptd.]. 1912. 1st. Edn., (35). 12mo. Orig. ptd. wraps., stitched as iss. (slightly loose). Sigd.; from the Prescott Collection. (CNY. Feb.6; 286) $700
- Memoirs of a Fox-Hunting Man. 1928. (260) sigd. Orig. buckram. (SH. Dec.18; 267) *Radmall.* £75
- - Anr. Edn. Ill.:- William Nicholson. 1929. [1st. Ill. Edn.?] Orig. pict. cl., unc., d.-w. Advance Copy of 1st. Ill. Edn. (SH. Dec.18; 269) *Henderson.* £480
- - Anr. Copy. Port.-frontis., 7 plts., text ills. Orig. pict. cl., unc., d.-w. (S. Jul 22; 14) *Mimpriss.* £350

- - Anr. Copy. (300) numbered, sigd. by author & artist. Orig. vell. (SKC. Feb.26; 1517) £90
- - Anr. Copy. (300) numbered, sigd. by author & artist. (S. Jul.22; 256) *Sotheran.* £65
- - Anr. Edn. Ill.:– William Nicholson. [1929]. Lacks 1st. gathering. Orig. wraps. Proof Copy of 1st. Ill. Edn. (SH. Dec.18; 268) *Henderson.* £880
[-] Memoirs of an Infantry Officer. 1930. 1st. Edn., (750). Orig. buckram. Sigd. (SH. Dec.18; 271) *Ellerton.* £68
[-] - Anr. Copy. (SH. Dec.18; 272) *Williams.* £65
- - Anr. Edn. Ill.:– Barnett Freedman. 1931. 1st. Ill. Edn. (320)., unnumbered. Orig. parch. over pict. designs, d.-w., orig. box. (SH. Dec.18; 273) *Williams.* £65
- Memoirs of an Infantry Officer.–The Heart's Journey. L.; N.Y. & L., 1930; 1927. 1st. Edn., (750) sigd.; (590) sigd. 2 works in 2 vols. Cl. (1st. work); & cl.-bkd. bds., d.-w.; both unopened & unc. (C. Jul.22; 27) *Maggs.* £110
- Meredith. 1948. 1st. Edn. Orig. cl., d.-w. worn. Pres. copy to Dorothy Wallis. (S. Jul.22; 264) *Maggs.* £55
- Nativity. N.Y., 1927. 1st. Amer. Edn. 12mo. One of 27 copies (12 for sale) ptd. to secure Amer. copyright. Orig. ptd. wraps., lr. cover wrinkled, qtr. mor. gt. s.-c. From the Prescott Collection. (CNY. Feb.6; 287) $320
- On Poetry, being the Arthur Skemp Memorial Lecture. 1939. 1st. Edn. Orig. wraps. (SH. Dec.18; 279) *Sherlock.* £70
- The Path to Peace. Stanbrook Abbey Pr. 1960. 1st. Edn., (500). 4to. Orig. vell-bkd. bds. Inscr. to Richard [Seymour]. (SH. Dec.19; 620) *Maggs.* £50
- Picture Show. Camb., Priv. Ptd. 1919. 1st. Edn., (200). Orig. bds., unc. Inscr. to Walter de la Mare. (SH. Dec.18; 259) *Mimpress.* £250
[-] Poems. [1911]. 1st. Edn. Orig. wraps., unc. Author's name under last poem. (SH. Dec.18; 257) *Quaritch.* £820
- Recreations. Priv. ptd. 1923. 1st. Edn., (81). Orig. vell-bkd. bds. Inscr. to Walter de la Mare. (SH. Dec.18; 260) *Chelsea.* £270
- Rhymed Ruminations. Ill.:– Laurence Whistler. 1939. 1st. Edn., (75). Orig. decor. bds., unc. Inscr. to W[alter] de la M[are]. (SH. Dec.18; 280) *Sherlock.* £105
- Sequences. Priv. Ptd. 1956. 1st. Edn., (25). Orig. buckram-bkd. bds. Inscr. to R[ichard] d[e] l[a] M[are]. (SH. Dec.18; 283) *Sherlock.* £125
- - Anr. Copy. Pres. Copy, sigd. with monog. & inscr. 'Richard' under limitat. statement. (SH. Dec.19; 619) *Lincoln.* £65
- Sherston's Progress. 1936. 1st. Edn. (300) sigd. Orig. buckram. 'Out of Series'. (S. Jul.22; 16) *Maggs.* £55
- The Tasking. Camb., 1954. 1st. Edn., (100). Orig. buckram-bkd. bds. Inscr. to R[ichard] d[e] l[a] M[are]. (SH. Dec.18; 282) *Sherlock.* £75
- Vigils. Ill.:– Stephen Gooden (title vig.). 1934. (303) numbered, & sigd. MS. correction in pencil, lacks the loosely inserted limitation lf. Buckram-bkd. bds., partly unc., by Gray. Pres. Copy, to S. Cockerell, with inscr. on preliminary blank, & an A.L.s. from Sassoon to Cockerell tipped-in. (C. Jul.22; 42) *Taylor.* £170
- - Anr. Copy. Orig. niger mor. Record of edns. loosely inserted. (SH. Dec.18; 276) *Baldur.* £50

SATCHELL, T.
See–WESTWOOD, Thomas & Satchell, T.

SATIRA
Ed.:– [V.M. Arnol'd]. St. Petersb., 1906. Nos. 1-2. 4to. Unbnd. (SH. Feb.5; 119) *Lempert.* £60

SATIRICHESKAYA GAZETA [Satirical Paper]
St. Petersb., 1906. No. 1. Fo. Slightly soiled & torn. Unbnd. (SH. Feb.5; 120) *Quaritch.* £50

SATIRICHESKOE OBOZRENIE [Satirical Review]
Ed.:– [H.K. Di-Sen'i]. St. Petersb., 1906. Nos. 1-3. Fo. Unbnd. (SH. Feb.5; 121) *Landry.* £130

SATIRIK
Ed.:– [Yu. V. Gol'dberg]. St. Petersb., 1907. No. 1. Unbnd. (SH. Feb.5; 122) *Quaritch.* £50

SATURDAY BOOK (the)
Ed.:– Leonard Russell & others. 1941-75. Vols. 1-34. Orig. cl., lacks 3 d.-w.'s., slightly soiled, 18 boxed. (SH. Oct.10; 514) *Brailey.* £70

SAUER, Martin
- An Account of a Geographical & Astronomical Expedition to the Northern Parts of Russia . . . by Commodore Joseph Billings . . . 1785 . . . to 1794. 1802. 1st. Edn. 4to. Lacks errata lf./list of plts., occasional light spotting. Cont. hf. cf., worn. Bkplt. of 1st. Baron Londesborough. [Sabin 77152] (S. Jun.29; 276) *Maggs.* £380

SAUERBRUCH, F.
- Die Willkürlich Bewegbare Künstl. Hand. Ed.:– G. Ruge, W. Felix, A. Stadler. Berlin, 1916. 1st. Edn. Orig. wraps. (HK. May 12-14; 421) DM 600

SAUL, Edward
- An Historical & Philosophical Account of the Barometer, or Weather- Glass. 1730. 1st. Edn. Disbnd. From Honeyman Collection. (S. Nov.11; 2753) *Rogers Turner.* £100

SAULAT DE MAREZ, Jacob
- Mutus Liber, in quo tamen tota Philosophia Hermetica, Figuris Hierogly'hicis depingitur. La Rochelle, 1677. 1st. Edn. Fo. With printed lf. 'Au Lecteur' at beginning (slightly stained & with marginal tear), owner's inscr. on recto of 1st. lf. Orig. wraps., worn & soiled, hf. mor. case. From Honeyman Collection. (S. Nov.11; 2754) *Ritman.* £4,400

SAULCY, F. de
- Recherches sur les Monnaies des Ducs Héréditaires de Lorraine.–Recherches sur les Monnaies des Comtes et Ducs de Bar. Metz; Paris, 1841; 1843. 2 works in 1 vol. 4to. Hf. chagrin. (LM. Mar.21; 253) B.Frs. 7,000

SAULNIER, René
See–DUCHARTRE, Pierre Louis & Saulnier, René

SAUNDERS, C.
See–LE CORDEUR, B. & Saunders, C.

SAUNDERS, John Cunningham
- A Treatise on Some Practical Points relating to the Diseases of the Eye. Ed.:– J.R. Farre. 1811. 1st. Edn. Hf. cf. (S. Jun.17; 745) *Pratt.* £60

SAUNDERS, Louise
- The Knave of Hearts. N.Y., 1925. 1st. Edn., Advance copy. Fo. Publisher's rubberstp. on pres. plt., title & margins of 3 pp. Cl. (SG. May 14; 167) $275
- - Anr. Edn. Ill.:– Maxfield Parrish. N.Y., 1925. 4to. Orig. cl.-bkd. pict. bds., slightly soiled, stitching shaken. (CSK. Mar.20; 46) £130
- - Anr. Edn. [1925]. 4to. Spiral bnd. cold. pict. wraps., some wear. (SG. Apr.2; 224) $200

SAUNDERS, Richard (Pseud.)
See–FRANKLIN, Benjamin 'Richard Saunders'

SAURIN, Jaques
- Discours Historiques, Critiques . . . du Vieux et du Nouveau Testament. Ill.:– Hoet, Houbraken & B. Picart. La Haye, 1728-36. 4 vols. Fo. Old cf., brkn. (SG. Sep.25; 276) $325
- - Anr. Edn. Paris, 1728-39. 6 vols. Fo. Cont. mott. cf., spines gt., worn. (S. Mar.17; 279) *Booth.* £150

SAUSSURE, Horace Bénédict de
- Essais sur l'Hygrométrie. Neuchatel, 1783. 1st. Edn. 4to. Tear in 2K1, slight discolouration. Orig. bds., unc., stain on upr. cover, red hf. mor. case. From Honeyman Collection. (S. Nov.11; 2759) *Schuman.* £150
- - Anr. Copy. A few ll. slightly dampstained in margin. Orig. wraps., worn, upr. cover nearly detchd., unc., partly unopened. (S. Oct.21; 423) *Maggs.* £120
- - Anr. Copy. Some browning, quires X, 2T & 2X misbnd. Cont. mott. cf., gt. spine, some wear, red hf. mor. case. From Honeyman Collection. (S. Nov.11; 2760) *Zeitlin.* £95
- Recherches Chimiques sur la Végétation. Paris, 1804. 1st. Edn. Some foxing, 1st. few ll. stained. 19th. C. hf. cf. From Honeyman Collection. (S. Nov.11; 2763) *Schuman.* £220
- Versuch über die Hygrometrie. Leipzig, 1784. Some browning, stp. of Odense Kathedr. Skoles Bibliothek on title. Cont. bds. From Honeyman Collection. (S. Nov.11; 2762) *Schuman.* £55
- Voyages dans les Alpes, précédés d'un Essai sur l'Histoire Naturelle des Environs de Genève. Neuchatel & Geneva, 1779-96. 1st. Edn. 4 vols. 4to. Slight browning, a few marginal tears & sm. holes. Cont. bds., worn, largely unopened, spines

of vols. 3 & 4 misnumbered. From Honeyman Collection. (S. Nov.11; 2757) *Schuman.* £880
- - Anr. Edn. Neuchatel, 1803-04-1796. 4 vols. 4to. Most folding plts. & map laid down on linen. 19th. C. mor.-bkd. cl. From Chetham's Liby., Manchester. (C. Nov.27; 357) *Mediolanum.* £450

SAUVAN, Jean Baptiste Balthazar
- Picturesque Tour of the Seine. 1821. 1st. Edn. Fo. Early 20th. C. maroon mor. by Birdsall, gt., gt. panel decorations, gt. floral decorations to sides, spine tooled in compartments. (S. May 5; 262) *Traylen.* £1,200
- - Anr. Copy. 4to. Upr. left-hand corner slightly dampstained thro.-out. Red mor., spine gt. (S. Feb.10; 355) *Mistrali.* £750
- - Anr. Copy. Fo. Cf. gt., worn, covers detchd. (CE. Nov.20; 5) £550
- - Anr. Edn. N.d. [plts. dtd. 1821]. (50) on L.P. 4to. Red lev. mor. gt. by Zaehnsdorf. (C. Mar.18; 99) *Quaritch.* £2,600

SAUVIGNY, Edme Louis Billardon de
- Les Après-Soupers de la Société . . . Ill.:– Eisen, Binet & Martinet. Paris, priv. ptd., 1782-83. 2nd. Printing (1st. 2 vols.). 23 pts. in 1 vol. 18mo. Lacks 3 figures. Mod. vell., triple gt. fillet around covers, smooth decor. spines. (HD. Jun.24; 8) Frs. 1,050
- Essais Historiques sur les Moeurs des François . . . Paris, 1785. On L.P. 6 vols. 4to. Cont. hf. roan. (HD. Jun.29; 257) Frs. 3,100

SAVAGE, William
- Dictionary of the Art of Printing. 1841. Rebnd. hf. cf. gt. (P. Feb.19; 60) *Weiniger.* £90
- Practical Hints on Decorative Printing. 1822 [1823]. 1st. Edn., L.P. Lge. 4to. 19th. C. red mor. by Clarke & Bedford, gt. (S. Nov.24; 254) *Henderson.* £1,350
- - Anr. Copy. Some spotting. Mod. hf. mor. Bkplt. of John Leighton. (S. May 5; 442) *Quaritch.* £880

SAVARY, Claude Etienne
- Grammaire de la Langue Arabe Valgaire et Littérale. Ed.:– L.M. Langlés. Paris, 1813. 1st. Edn. (L.P.) 4to. Slightly foxed. Cont. red hf. mor., spine gt., covers soiled & reprd., unc. (S. Apr.29; 454) *Loman.* £300
- Lettres sur l'Egypte. Paris, 1786. 3 vols. Lacks last lf. in vol. 1 & last in vols. II & III (blanks?). Cont. red mor., triple gt. fillet, flat spines gt. with floral ornams., inner gt. dentelles. (SM. Oct.8; 2001) Frs. 16,000
- Morale de Mahomet, ou Recueil des plus Pures Maximes du Coran. Constantinople & Paris, 1784. 18mo. Cont. mor., decor. spine, gt. roulette, inner dentelle. From Russian Liby. of Comte Chérémétiev. (HD. Apr.9; 562) Frs. 1,150

SAVARY, J.T.
- Venationis Cervinae, Capreolinae, Aprugnae, et Lupinae Leges. Caen, 1659. 1st. & only Edn. Fr. marginalia, slightly browned in parts, lacks last lf. blank. Cont. vell., slightly soiled. (R. Oct.14-18; 2807) DM 480

SAVARY, [Jacques]
- The Universal Dictionary of Trade & Commerce. 1751-55. 2 vols. Fo. Some tears reprd., a few ll. slightly soiled. Cont. hf. cf., worn. (SH. Oct.10; 515) *Maggs.* £140
- - Anr. Edn. Trans.:– Malachy Postlethwayt. 1766. 3rd. Edn. 2 vols. Fo. Some ll. & plts. in vol. II slightly stained in outer edges, occasional offsetting, a few short tears. Cont. spr. cf., gt, 1 spine defect., worn. [Sabin 77276] (S. Jan.26; 254) *Subunso.* £70

SAVE-ALLS, The
ca. 1710. Fo. 2 pp. (S. Oct.17; 13) £130

SAVERIEN, Alexandre
- Dizionario Istorico, Teorico e Pratico di Marina. Ill.:– after L. Carlevaris (frontis.). Venice, 1769. Sm. 4to. Frontis. in 2nd. state. Cont. hf. roan. From the collection of John A. Saks. (C. Jun.10; 229) *Mediolanum.* £90

SAVERY, Thomas
- The Miner's Friend; or, an Engine to raise Water by Fire, described. 1702. 1st. Edn. Lacks final blank, title loose & slightly soiled. Recent hf. cf. From Honeyman Collection; bkplt. of Franklin Institute. (S. Nov.11; 2766) *Quaritch.* £1,200

SAVERY, Thomas -contd.
- Navigation Improv'd: or, the Art of Rowing Ships ... in Calms ... Also, a Description of the Engine that performs it. 1698. 1st. Edn. 4to. Final errata lf., folding plt. & 3 textual engravings in facs., browned. 19th. C. vell., hf. red mor. case. From Honeyman Collection. (S. Nov.11; 2765)
Schuman. £80

SAVI, Gaetano
- Flora Italiana. Ill.:– Antonio Serantoni. Pisa, 1818-24. 3 vols. Fo. Publisher's announcement & general title dtd. 1817 bnd. in before title of vol. 1, some spotting. Cont. Italian hf. cf., spines gt., unc. From collection of Massachusetts Horticultural Society, stpds. on plts. (SPB. Oct.1; 163) $7,000

SAVIGNON, André
- Les Filles de la Pluie ... Ill.:– M. Méheut. 1934. (65) on imperial Jap. Square 8vo. Orig. sketch. Hf. mor. by Léonard, corners, spine with raised bands, wrap. & spine preserved. (HD. Jun.24; 100)
Frs. 1,250

SAVILE, Sir George
See-MARTYN, Benjamin–SAVILE, George

SAVILLE-KENT, W.
- The Great Barrier Reef of Australia; Its Products & Potentialities. 1893. Fo. Ex-liby. copy with stp. to title only. Orig. cl. gt., spine defect. (TA. Mar.19; 642) £60

SAVONAROLA, Girolamo
- Compendio di Revelatione. Flor., Francesco Bonaccorsi, 18 Aug., 1495. 1st. Edn. Variant with 33 lines on a1. Mod. cf.-bkd. bds. [Goff S179b] (C. Jul.16; 292) *Maggs.* £120
- Epistola Contro la Scomunica Surrettizia nuovamente fatta. Flor., Bartolommeo di Libri, after 19 June, 1497. 4to. 2 ll., both remargined. Mod. vell., vell. end-papers. [Goff S192] (C. Jul.16; 293) *Maggs.* £120
- Operetta del Amore di Jesu. [Flor.]. [Bartolommeo di Libris], ca. 1495. 4to. Lr. corner of last lf. renewed, not affecting text. Mod. qtr. mor., marb. paper covers. The copy of William Mitchell, lately in the Pierpont Morgan Liby. [BMC VI, 659, Goff S170] (CNY. Apr.8; 63) $2,800
- Operetta Nuova composta da frate Girolamo da Ferrara. [?Flor.], [Bartolommeo di Libri]. Ca. 1497/8. Sm. 4to. Author's name in text deleted in ink on title & 4 other pp., some stains, mostly in blank margins. Later stiff wraps., sewn. (S. Jun.23; 217) *Quaritch.* £220
- Operetta Sopra i Dieci Comandamenti di Dio. Flor., [Bartolommeo di Libris], Oct.24, 1495. 1st. Edn? 4to. Mod. qtr. mor., marb. paper covers. The copy of William Mitchell, lately in the Pierpont Morgan Liby. [BMC VI, 650, Goff S224] (CNY. Apr.8; 62) $2,500
- Tractato Diuoto & Tutto Spirituale in Defensione & Commendatione dell'Oratione Mentale. [Flor.], [Lorenzo Morgiana], ca. 1496. 4to. Mod. qtr. mor., marb. paper covers. The copy of William Mitchell, lately in the Pierpont Morgan Liby. [BMC VI, 689, Goff S234] (CNY. Apr.8; 64) $2,500

SAVONAROLA, Girolamo or Hieronymous –ARIOSTIS, Alexander de
- Confessionale pro Instructione Confessorum. –Enchiridion, sive Interrogatorium. Venice; Pavia, Aug. 1517; Jun. 1516. 2 works in 1 vol. Some staining at beginning & end of 1st. work, a few marginal stains in 2nd. work. Cont. blind-stpd. cf., spine defect., covers wormed & worn. (C. Apr.1; 82) *Ridge.* £120

SAVONAROLA, Girolamo or Hieronymous –PAULUS Pergulensis–ARISTOTELES
- Compendium Logicae.–Compendium Logicae [with De Sensu Composita et Diviso].–Thesaurus Veteris et Novae Logicae. Pescia; Venice; [Cologne], [Eponymous Pr.]; Baptista de Tortis; [Heinrich Quentell], Aug. 24, 1492; Sep.13, 1486; ca. 1497. 3 works in 1 vol. 4to. 1st. work: spaces for initial capitals; 2nd. work: sm. woodcut initial capitals; slight dampstaining to margins of some quires, light foxing. Cont. blind-stpd. cf. over wood bds., orig. clasps & catches, jnts. & spine reprd. The copy of John Francis Neylen, lately in the collection of Eric Sexton. [Goff S176; P192 & T158a] (CNY. Apr.8; 135) $10,500

SAVOY, The, an Illustrated Monthly
Ed.:– Arthur Symons. Ill.:– Aubrey Beardsley.

1896. No. 1-8 (all publd.) in 3 vols. 4to. Orig. cl. gt., unc. (SH. Mar.26; 56) *Quaritch.* £180
- - Anr. Copy. 4to. With the Beardsley Christmas card bnd. in at rear of no. 2. Orig. gt. pict. cl., orig. pict. wraps. bnd. in. (PNY. Dec.3; 325) $425
- - Anr. Copy. Orig. gt.-pict. cl. designed by Beardsley, orig. pict. wraps. bnd. in, unopened. (PNY. Mar.26; 294) $400
- - Anr. Copy. Christmas card & prospectus tipped in, minor tears, some foxing. Orig. bds. & wraps., soiled & chipped. (SPB. May 29; 410) $175

SAWARD, Blanche C.
See-CAULFIELD, S.F.A. & Saward, Blanche C.

SAWYER, Charles W. & Darton, F.J. Harvey
- English Books 1475-1900. 1927. 2 vols. Orig. buckram, d.-w.'s. (CSK. May 29; 125) £50
- - Anr. Edn. Westminster, 1927. Ltd. Edn. Buckram. (SG. Mar.26; 182) $150
- - Anr. Copy. Cl., unc., d.-w.'s., worn. (SG. Oct.2; 324) $130

SAX, F.
- Bau-Technologie und Bau-Oekonomie. Ed.:– J.F. Jäckel. Vienna, 1843. 2nd. Edn. 4 vols. 4to. Soiled in parts, stpd. on title & plt. versos. Cont. hf. linen, spine lightly defect. (R. Mar.31-Apr.4; 1293) DM 1,000

SAXE, Maurice, Comte de
- Mes Reveries. Amst. & Leipzig, 1757. 2 vols. 4to. Cont. mott. cf. (CSK. Jan.30; 6) £110
- - Anr. Copy. Stp. of Herzoglicher S. Meiningischer Bibliothek on verso of titles Cont. cf., triple gt. fillet, spines gt. in compartments. (SM. Oct.8; 2002) Frs. 5,800
- Les Rêveries ou Mémoires sur l'Art de la Guerre. The Hague, 1756. Fo. Slight browning, short tear in 1 plt. Cont. cf., spine gt., worn. Keppel bkplt. (S. Apr.7; 355) *Veulemans.* £120
- - Anr. Copy. Keppel bookplate. (S. Oct.21; 303) *Vankempen.* £55
- Les Reveries ou Memoires sur l'Art de la Guerre [–Supplement aux Reveries]. Ed.:– C. de Bonneville (supp.), Ill.:– O. Sibelius (11 plts.). The Hague, 1758. (Supp.) 1st. Edn. 2 pts. in 1 vol. Fo. 4 ll. misbnd. Cont. mott. cf., spine gt., slightly worn. (S. Apr.7; 357) *Maggs.* £140

SAXONIA: Museum fuer Saechsische Vaterlandskunde
Dresden, 1835. The 24 fascicules in 1 vol. Tall 8vo. With all plts., some foxing thro.-out. Orig. ptd. bds., spine very worn. (SG. May 21; 430) $160

SAXTON, Christopher
- An Atlas of England & Wales. 1979. Facs. of 1579 Edn., (500) sigd. by R.V. Tooley. Fo. Qtr. of gt. s.-c. (P. Apr.9; 149) *Burgess.* £140
- Map of England. 1749. 36 maps & 7 folding maps. Cf., torn, wormholes. (WW. May 20; 19) £6,800

SAY, Thomas
- American Entomology.–A Glossary to Say's Entomology. Phila.; Phila., 1824-28; 1825. 4 vols. Some foxing, offsetting, each plt. with liby-stp. Hf. mor., ex-liby. with labels, marks, glossary in orig. bds. (SPB. Oct.1; 212) $1,000

SAYER, R.
- The Florist. L., ca. 1760. Some plts. slightly soiled. Cont. hf. leath., detchd., cover loose. (R. Oct.14-18; 3050) DM 2,000

SAYERS, Dorothy L. & Simpson, Helen
[–] Papers relating to the Family of Wimsey. Ed.:– Matthew Wimsey. Priv. Ptd. [1936]. 1st. Edn., (500). Orig. wraps. Inscr. by Helen Simpson. (SH. Dec.18; 287) *Rota.* £80

SAYLE, C.E.
- Early English Printed Books in the University Library Cambridge, 1475-1640. 1900-07. 4 vols. Unif. cl. gt. (TA. Sep.18; 86) £80

SAZERAC, J.M.H.
- Un Mois en Suisse ou Souvenirs d'un Voyageur. Ill.:– Edouard Pingret. Paris, 1825. Fo. Slightly soiled in parts. Hf. leath. (R. Mar.31-Apr.4; 2760) DM 4,000

SAZERAC, J.M.H. & Engelmann, E. & others
- Lettres sur la Suisse. Paris, 1823-32. 5 vols. Sm. fo. Foxed & stained. Cont. cf.-bkd. bds., chipped & worn. (SPB. May 6; 251) $2,700

SCADDING, Henry
- Toronto of Old. Toronto, 1873. Owner's sig. on title-p. Orig. cl., lr. free end-paper torn away, bkplt. (CB. Feb.18; 173) Can. $110

SCALE, Bernard
- An Hibernian Atlas; or general description of the Kingdom of Ireland. 1st. Feb. 1776. 4to. Lf. of description text to each map, inscr. on title. 19th. C. parch., gt. W.a.f. (S. Nov.3; 21) *Quaritch.* £300

SCALI, Pietro Paolo
[–] Introduzione alla Practica del Commercio ovvero Notizie necessarie per l'Esercizio della Mercatura. Livorno, 1751. 1st. Edn. Fo. Some spotting, title slightly soiled & with wormhole in upr. margin. Cont. vell. bds., worn. From Honeyman Collection, (S. May 19; 2769) *Riley-Smith.* £110

SCALICHIUS VON LIKA, Paulus
- Oration an de[n] ... Herrn Ferdinandum Römischen Keyser ... Von der Genealogie unnd gar alten herrlichsten Ursprung und herkömen der Scalichern. Strassburg, 25 Jan. 1561. 4to. Some old underlinings. 18th. C. marb. bds. (S. Jan.27; 350) *Parikian.* £100

SCALIGER, Joseph Juste
- Cyclometrica Elementa duo (–Mesolabium). Leiden, 1594. 1st. Edn., iss. without Appendix. 2 pts. in 1 vol. Fo. Browned, slight marginal staining. 18th. C. vell. bds., spine defect. at head, bkplts. removed from upr. pastedown. From Honeyman Collection. (S. May 19; 2771) *McKittrick.* £70
- Opus novum de Emendatione Temporum. Paris, 1583. 1st. Edn. Fo. Some marginal staining thro.-out, short tear in upr. margins of 1st. 3 ll., title inscr. 'Ex Bibli episcop Beluae'. Cf., gt., very worn, upr. cover detchd. From Honeyman Collection. (S. May 19; 2770) *Zeitlin & Verbrugge.* £220

SCAMMON, Charles M.
- The Marine Mammals of the North-Western Coast of North America ... San Franc., 1874. 1st. Edn. Lge. 4to. Some foxing thro.-out. Gt.-pict. cl. (SG. May 14; 190) $1,500

SCAMOZZI, Ottavio Bertotti
- Le Fabriche e i Disegni di Andrea Palladio. Vicenza, 1786. 2nd. Edn. 2 vols. in 1 (of 4 vols. in 2). Slight foxing on port. & 2 plts. Disbnd. (CB. May 27; 158) Can. $380

SCAMOZZI, Vincenzo
- Les Cinq Ordres d'Architecture. Trans.:– A.D. d'Aviler. Paris, 1685. Fo. Cont. cf., spine gt., worn. (S. Jun.22; 144) *Goldschmidt.* £130
- Dell' Idea della Architettura Universale. Piazzola, 1687. 2 pts. in 1 vol. Fo. 1st. engraved title reprd. & loose, tear in K5 & hole in 2C5 pt. 2, pt. 1 ?lacks prelim. lf. A6. Old cf., worn, covers loose or detchd. (S. Jun.22; 143) *Weinreb.* £150
- Oeuvres d'Architecture. Leiden, 1713. Fo. Sm. hole in B2, a few marginal stains. 18th. C. cf., gt. spine. (S. Jun.22; 145) *Goldschmidt.* £240

SCANAVACCA, Bartolomeo
- Novissima inventore per dissegnare Horologi Solari, Italiana, Babilonici e Francesi. Padua, 1688. 1st. Edn. Sm. 4to. G4 slightly defect., liby. stp. Cont. vell., soiled. (SH. Jun.11; 224) *Rogers Turner.* £90

SCANLAN, R.R.
- My Book of Curs. (Tog. with vol. of Pencil Drawings based on ills.). 1840. Fo. Some plts. spotted. Hf. mor., pict. upr. cover for pts. 1 & 2 bnd. in. (SH. Apr.10; 326) *Doggie Hubbard.* £ 260

SCANTLEBURY, C.B., Publisher
- A Souvenir of Belleville. [Belleville], ca. 190-? Ob. 8vo. Orig. wraps. (CB. Sep.24; 67) Can. $120

SCARELLA, Giambattista
- De Magnete libri quatuor. Brescia, 1759. 1st. Edn. 2 vols.in 1. 4to. Vol. II with sm. hole in E1 with loss of sig. & marginal repairs to 2N1 & 2X1. Orig. bds., worn, unc., hf. red mor. case. From Honeyman Collection. (S. May 19; 2772) *Zeitlin & Verbrugge.* £140

SCARPA, Antonio
- Practical Observations on the Principal Diseases of the Eyes. Ed.:– James Briggs. 1806. 1st. Edn. in Engl. Plts. spotted. Orig. bds., unc. (S. Jun.17; 749) *Norman.* £130

– Saggio di Osservazioni e d'Esperienze sulle Principali Malattie degli Occhi. Pavia, 1801. 1st. Edn. Fo. Cl. (S. Dec.2; 618) *Albert.* £180
– Sull' aneurisma, Riflessioni ed Osservazioni Anatomico-Chirurgiche. Ill.:– Pietro Anderloni. Pavia, 1804. 1st. Edn. Lge. fo. 15 engraved plts., 10 finished & outl. plts. for nos. 1, 3, 4, 5 & 7, light stain on last few plts. New hf. cf. (S. Jun.17; 748) *Jenner Books.* £1,000
– Tabulae Neurologicae ... Ill.:– F. Anderloni. Pavia, 1794. 1st. Edn. Lge. fo. With 7 outline & 7 finished plts. New hf. cf. (S. Jun.17; 747) *Norman.* £550
– A Treatise on Hernia. Trans.:– John Henry Wishart. Edinb., 1814. 1st. Edn. in Engl. 8pp. advts. dtd. Mar. 1814. New marb. paper bds., unc. (S. Jun.17; 750) *Norman.* £80
– A Treatise on the Principal Diseases of the Eyes. Trans.:– James Briggs. L., 1818. 2nd. Edn. Plts. foxed & stained. Cont. hf. leath. (CB. Nov.12; 171) Can. $190

SCARPA, Antonio & Leveille, Jean Baptiste François
– Memoires de Physiologie ... Paris, An XIII-Dec., 1804. Faint stps. on verso of plts. Liby. buckram. From Brooklyn Academy of Medicine. (SG. Jan.29; 374) $160

SCARRON, Paul
– Recueil des Oeuvres Burlesques.–La Suite des Oeuvres Burlesques.–Typhon ou la Gigantomachie.–La Relation Veritable.–Le Iodelet ou le Me Valet ... Paris, 1648-50. 1st. Edn. 2 pts. in 1 vol., 8 pts. in 2 vols. 4to. Lacks engraved frontis., that for 'Relation veritable' supplied, sig. 'Gersaint' on 1st. title of vol. 1. Early 18th. C. mott. cf., arms of Henri Louis de Loménie de Brienne, triple gt. fillet, arms of Loménie, gt., in spine compartments, inner gt. dentelles, spines defect., corners slightly worn. (SM. Oct.8; 2003) Frs. 1,100
– Le Roman Comique. L., 1781. 4 vols. 18mo. Porphyre cf. by Cazin. (HD. Apr.8; 304) Frs. 1,100

SCARUFFI, Gasparo
– L'Alitinonfo ... per fare Regione, et Concordanza d'oro, e d'argento, che Servira in Universale [–Breve Instruttione sopra il Discorso fatto dall Mag. M. Gasparo Scaruffi]. Reggio, 1582. 1st. Edn. 2 pts. in 1 vol. Fo. 19th. C. roan-bkd. bds. From Honeyman Collection. (S. May 19; 2773) *Quaritch.* £750

SCATTAGLIA, Pietro
See–ALESSANDRI, Innocente & Scattaglia, Pietro

SCAVIZZI, G.
See–FERRARI, Oreste & Scavizzi, G.

SCELTA di Facezie, Tratti, Buffonerie, Motti, e Burle cavate da diversi Autori
Flor., 1586. Inscr. on flylf. possibly in Heber's hand. 18th. C. red mor. by A.-M. Padeloup le Jeune with his ticket, triple gt. fillet, double fillet round spine compartments, inner gt. dentelles. Book-label of Charles Nodier, bkplts. of Comte de Lurde with his arms, Baron de Ruble & Cutcliffe of Ilfracombe with his arms. (SM. Oct.8; 2004) Frs. 3,600

SCENERY
– A Collection of 482 Scenes & Views of Canada, France, the Rhine, Russia, Italy, Sicily & other places. Ill.:– After W.H. Bartlett, T. Allom, W. Leitch & others. ca. 1832-45. In 4 vols. 4to. Some staining in Constantinople vol., several imprints cropped, occasional spotting & soiling at edges, some plts. loose or detchd. Cont. hf. red mor., slightly worn. As a collection, w.a.f.; bkplt of Jasper Holmes. (S. Nov.4; 515) *Loeb.* £480
– A Collection of 259 Scenes & Views of England, Ireland, Scotland & Wales. Ill.:– After J. Neale, T. Allom, W. Tombleson, N. Whittock & others. ca. 1829-39. 2 vols. 4to. A number of scenes on india paper, several plts. loosely inserted or detchd., occasional spotting or browning. Cont. hf. mor., spines faded. As a collection, w.a.f.; bkplt. of Jasper Holmes. (S. Nov.4; 514) *Schuster.* £130

SCEPPER, Cornelius Duplicius
– Assertionis fidei Adversus Astrologos. Sive de Significationibus Coniunctionum Superiorum Planetarum anni Millesimi Quingentesimi Vicesimi Quarti. Antw., 16 May, 1523. 1st. Edn. Fo. Slight worming at foot affecting text, stain on 1 lf., inscr. erased from title. Cont. Parisian cf., covers richly

stpd. with Renaissance ornament, rebkd., name 'Pomerii' in ink on covers. From Honeyman Collection. (S. May 19; 2774) *Quaritch.* £700

SCHADE, Abraham
– Promptuarii Musici, Sacras Harmonias sive Motetas. Strassburg, 1611-17. 1st. Edn. Cont. MS. music bnd. in after the 1st. 3 pts., browned & soiled, sm. wormholes in 3rd. & 4th. pts., slight marginal wear to title-p. & prelims. of pt. I. Cont. blind-stpd. pig, soiled & worn, front end-papers chewed. (SPB. May 6; 252) $300

SCHADT-KISTE, de, der Philosophen ende Poeten ... Porphyre en Cyprine Treurspel ...
See–THEUILLIER, J. & Fay-d'Herbe, H.
–SCHADT-KISTE, de, der Philosophen ende Poeten ... Porphyre en Cyprine Treurspel ...

SCHAEBAELJE, Jan Philipsz
– Emblemata Sacra ... Bybelsch Figueren. Amst., 1653. Ob. fo. Lacks 4 plts. & all of sig. B, some plts. loose & soiled at edges, a few stained. Cont. vell. bds., stained. W.a.f. (C. Apr.1; 168) *Hendrickx.* £650

SCHAEFFER, August
– Lene Stelling. [Berlin], [1923]. (100) Privilege Edn. numbered. 4to. Slightly soiled in parts. Orig. pict. hf. leath. Printer's mark sigd. by publisher. (HK. Nov.18-21; 2752) DM 640

SCHAEFFER, Jacob Christian
– Entwurff, einer Allgemeiner Farbenverein. Regensburg, 1769. Only Edn. 4to. Stitched. (R. Oct.14-18; 422) DM 950
– Fungorum. Regensburg, 1762-[74]. 1st. Edn. 4 vols. 4to. Plts. hand-cold., some margins discold. 19th. C. hf. mor. From Chetham's Liby., Manchester. (C. Nov.27; 358) *Kistner.* £1,800
– – Anr. Edn. Ed.:– C.H. Persoon. Erlangen, 1800. Latest Edn. 4 text vols., commentary & plts. 3 vols. & 1 portfolio. Lge. 4to. Interim sewed bdg., plts. in mod. bd. portfolio. (R. Oct.14-18; 3045) DM 4,000
– Icones Insectorum ...–Elementa Entomologia. Regensburg, 1766-79; 1766. 1st. Edns. 5 pts. in 3 vols; 1 vol. together 5 vols. 4to. Plts. hand-cold. in both works, engraved port. of 2nd. work misbnd. in 1st. 1st. work: qtr. mor. & cont. cf. (rebkd. in mor.); 2nd. work: qtr. mor., misnumbered 3 on spine. From Chetham's Liby., Manchester. (C. Nov.27; 359) *Weldon & Wesley.* £200

SCHÄFER, Sir Edward Albert Sharpey
– Text-Book Physiology. Edinb. & L., 1898-1900. 1st. Edn. 2 vols. No advt. ll. Cf., gt., bnd. as a prize of Merchant Taylors' school. (S. Jun.17; 754) *Trimble.* £75
– – Anr. Edn. Edinb. & L., 1898-1900. 1st. Edn. Advt. ll. Orig. cl. (S. Jun.17; 753) *Wood.* £55

SCHALDACH, William J.
– Coverts & Casts ... N.Y. [1943]. 1st. Edn., (160) numbered, sigd. 4to. Buckram-bkd. bds., s.-c. (SG. Oct.16; 382) $170
– Currents & Eddies. West Hartford, Vermont, 1944. 1st. Edn. (250) numbered, sigd. 4to. Cl., s.-c. brkn. (SG. Oct.16; 384) $110
– Fish: Collected Etchings ... of Trout, Salmon & Other Game Fish. Phila., 1937. De Luxe 1st. Edn. (157) numbered, sigd., with orig. sigd. etchg. 4to. Gt.-decor. vell. (SG. Oct.16; 380) $1,100
– – Anr. Copy. (1560) numbered. (SG. Dec.11; 93) $150
– – Anr. Copy. (SG. Oct.16; 381) $120

SCHARD, Simon
– Schardius Redivivus. Sive Rerum Germanicarum Scriptores Varii. Ed.:– H. Thomae. Giessen, Ca. 1500. 4 pts. in 1 vol. Fo. Cont. vell. (R. Mar.31-Apr.4; 154) DM 500

SCHAUFFELEIN, Hans
[–] Doctrina Vita et Passio Jesu Christi Artificiosissime Affigiata. Frankfurt, 1637. 1st. Edn. 67 (of 79) full-p. woodcuts on 35 (of 40) ll. Old wraps., lacks lr. cover. (R. Oct.14-18; 149) DM 2,000

SCHEDA, J.
– Fortsetzung der Generale Karte des Osterreichischen Kaiserstaates. N.p., [1850?]. 27 Parts. Approx. 50 × 40cms. Mntd. on cl., hf. cf. box, defect., gt. tools. (CR. Jun.11; 612) Lire 200,000

SCHEDEL, Hartmann
– Buch d. Chroniken. Leipzig, 1933. Facs. of 1493 Nuremburg Edn., Ltd. Edn. on Hadern Bütten.

Lge. fo. Loose ll. (HK. May 12-14; 2222) DM 450
– Das Buch der Croniken vnnd Geschichten. Augsburg, J. Schönsperger. 1496. 2nd. German Edn. [1st. Schönsperger Edn.]. Fo. Heavily soiled in a few parts, heavy faults in index, several tears, some with light text loss bkd., some worming, 2 ll. with heavy text loss, title & 6 ll. with slight text loss. 16th. C. leath.-bkd. wood bds., lacks ties, loose, worn, slightly wormed, jnts. partly brkn. [H 14511*; Goff S310] (HK. Nov.18-21; 297) DM 6,000
– – Anr. Edn. Trans.:– G. Alt. Augsburg, J. Schönsperger. 1500. Fo. Lightly browned, soiled in parts, 1st. & last ll. slightly stained, 18 ll. with reprd. marginal tears, lf. 208 with some loss, 1st. 3 ll. bkd., map defect. & bkd. in parts, lacks woodcut title & part of preface verso & last blank lf. Cont. blind-tooled pig-bkd. wooden bds., clasps brkn. [HC 14512*; BMC II 375; Goff S311] (R. Mar.31-Apr.4; 2291) DM 9,000
– Liber Chronicarum. Ill.:– Wohlgemuth & Pleydenwurff. Nuremb., Anton Koberger, 12 Jul. 1493. 1st. Edn. Fo. Lacks final blank, fine painted initial in divided red & blue, with elaborate full-length penwork & other painted floral initials, title & 17 ll. remargined, a few with sm. repairs slightly affecting text, outer corners of 5 ll. of 'Tabula' restored, ills. between fo. 83v & fo. 86v, crudely cold. in part, repair to fo. 99, map & a few other ll., ills. on fo. 29 & fo. 103 slightly affected, some ll. at beginning & end with light worming cutting text, a few ll. browned or with stains, a few penmarks & inscrs. 19th C. cf., rebkd., some wear Bkplt. of W.H. Watts. [HC 14508*; BMC II, 437; Goff S307] (S. May 5; 91) *Symonds.* £6,800
– – Anr. Copy. 322 ll. (of 326), lacks final blank & ff. 259-61 (blank except for headline & foliation) lge. double-p. map of Europe at end wormed, initials to Index supplied in red, 1st. lf. of text with lge. illuminated initial C with three-qtr. floral border cropped, missing 'blanks' replaced by unnumbered ll. 'De Sarmacia' normally found at end, f. 257 wormed & inserted, title soiled & reprd., Index & illuminated lf. affected by damp or cleaning, margins of final ll. restored affecting letters, early 17th. C. owners' inscrs. on verso of title 19th. C. cf., worn. (S. Jun.23; 215) *Burgess.* £6,300
– – Anr. Copy. Lacks final blank & folio 280 (blank except for running-title), natural paper fault in folio 249 affecting text, title lacks portion at head affecting text, folios 321-5 misbnd. after folio 286, liby. stps. on about half of the larger woodcuts, other sm. defects. 19th. C. hf. mor. From Chetham's Liby., Manchester. (C. Nov.20; 285a) *Schuster.* £5,400
– – Anr. Copy. Spaces for capital initials in the tabula, supplied in red, ptd. capitals elsewhere, 3 woodcuts cold., reprd. tears affecting text or woodcuts at 7 folios, some marginal repairs elsewhere, lr. margin of fo. 170 patched with slight loss of last line, some sm. holes or wormholes, slight staining, early inking to a figure on fo. 184. Mor. gt. by Bedford, slight defect to lr. cover. Bkplts. of Henry & Alfred H. Huth, & Herschel V. Jones, lately in the collection of Eric Sexton. (CNY. Apr.8; 114) $28,000
– – Anr. Copy. Title soiled with inscr. erased, some dampstaining to several ll. affecting upr. outer or inner corners, some marginal repairs, particularly folios 159 & 160. 16th. C. blind-stpd. cf. over wood bds., rebkd. & corners renewed, folding cl. box. Bkplt. & sig. of A.F.B. Williams, bkplts. of William Bateman & the General Theological Seminary Liby. (CNY. Oct.1; 40) $18,000
– – Anr. Copy. Lacks final blank & 2 blanks preceding 'De Sarmacia', approx. 40 ll. with tape repairs, last 3 index ll. very worn, 5 ll. with tears & repairs, title-p. trimmed & mntd. Early 19th. C. maroon str.-grd. mor., gt. borders & spines. Armorial bkplts. of Syston Park, Michael Tomkinson & Hayne. [HC 14508] (SG. May 14; 191) $9,400
– – Anr. Copy. 1st. ll. wormed, initials in index painted red & blue, some ll. at end heavily soiled, lacks 2 blank ll. Wood bds. ca. 1500, blind-stpd. leath. bkd., spine renewed 19th. C., worn, reprd. (HK. Nov.18-21; 295) DM 25,000
– – Anr. Edn. [Nuremb.], [1493]. 17⅓ × 12 inches). Browned on many pp. Orig. vell. (JN. Apr.2; 806) £6,300
[–] – Anr. Edn. Ill.:– M. Wohlgemut & W. Pleydenwurff. Augsburg, Johann Schönsperger, 1 Feb., 1497. 2nd. Latin Edn. Iss. with dbl.-p. map

SCHEDEL, Hartmann -contd.
at end. Fo. 364 ll. (of 366) lacks 2 blanks, few ll. added from smaller copy, some wormholes affecting some letters & woodcuts, all before N2 rubricated. Cont. German blind-stpd. pig., wormed, 2 clasps, straps renewed. [BMC II, 370] (S. Nov.25; 323)　　　　　　　　*Zanesco*. £3,200

SCHEELE, Carl Wilhelm
- **The Chemical Essays . . . Translated from the Transactions of the Academy of Sciences at Stockholm.** Ed.:– Thomas Beddoes. 1786. 1st. Engl. Edn. Slight discolouration. Bds., worn, unc., hf. red mor. case, stained. From Honeyman Collection. (S. May 19; 2777)　　*Percy*. £220
- **Chemical Observations & Experiments on Air & Fire . . .** Ed.:– Richard Kirwan. Trans.:– J.R. Forster. 1780. 1st. Engl. Edn. 1 plt. cropped, inner margin of title slightly stained. Cont. cf., worn, hf. red mor. case. From Honeyman Collection. (S. May 19; 2776A)　　　　　　　*Percy*. £360
- **Chemische Abhandlung von der Luft und dem Feuer. Nebst einem Vorbericht von Torbern Bergman.** Uppsala & Leipzig, 1777. 1st. Edn. 2 ll. of Foreword misbnd. in quire K. Cont. hf. cf., gt. spine, hf. red mor. case. Stp. of Count R. von Veltheim; from Honeyman Collection. (S. May 19; 2775)　　　　　　　　*Percy*. £6,200
- - **Anr. Edn.** Ed.:– J.G. Leonhardt. Leipzig, 1782. 2nd. Edn. Cont. bds., hf. red mor. case. Stp. of Count R. von Veltheim; from Honeyman Collection. (S. May 19; 2776)　　　　　*Hill*. £700

SCHEEN, Pieter A.
- **Lexicon Nederlandse beeldende Kunstenaars 1750-1950.** The Hague, 1969. 2 vols. Cl. (VG. Nov.17; 168)　　　　　　　　Fls. 1,300
- - **Anr. Edn.** The Hague, 1969-70. 2 vols. Cl. gt. (VG. Dec.16; 578)　　　　　　　Fls. 1,100

SCHEERBART, Paul
- **Glasarchitektur.** Ill.:– H. Vogeler. Berlin, 1914. 1st. Edn. Orig. wraps., slightly soiled, spine defect. MS. dedication from author to A.W. Heymel, 25.V.1914, his ex-libris. (H. Dec.9/10; 2327)　　　　　　　　　　　　　DM 640
- **Das Paradies.** Berlin, 1889. 1st. Edn. Lightly browned, Hf. vell. MS. dedication from author to A.W. Heymel 25.XI.1899, his ex-libris. (H. Dec.9/10; 2330)　　　　　　　DM 680
- **Rakkóx der Billionaer.–Die Wilde Jagd.** Ill.:– Jossot & F. Vallotton. Berlin & Leipzig, 1900. 1st. Edn. 2 vols. in 1. Slightly soiled in parts. Orig. hf. linen. A.W. Heymel ex-libris. (H. Dec.9/10; 2331)　　　　　　　DM 500

SCHEFFER, Jean-Gabriel
- **Choix de Costumes Italiens.** Paris, 1832. 4to. Cont. hf. cf., orig. engraved wrap. serving as title bnd. in. (S. Jun.23; 333)　*Studio Books*. £350

SCHEFFER, Johannes
- **Histoire de la Laponie.** Paris, 1678. 1st Edn. in Fr. 4to. ? Lacks engraved title. Cont. spr. cf., top of spine & upr. cover wormed, corners worn. (S. May 5; 252)　　　　　　　　*Lind*. £100
- - **Anr. Copy.** 18 plts. (of 21), map reprd., some tears, soiled. Mod. hf. cf. (SH. Jun.18; 194)　　　　　　　　　　　　*Lind*. £80
- - **Anr. Copy.** Cont. style leath. (R. Mar.31-Apr.4; 2778)　　　　　　DM 600
- **The History of Lapland.** L., 1704. Ex liby. Old cf., crudely rebkd. (SG. Oct.30; 324)　　$130
- **Lapponia.** Frankfurt, 1673. 1st. Edn. Slightly soiled in parts, sm. tear reprd. on ptd. title verso, pp. 137/138 torn. Cont. vell. (R. Oct.14-18; 2045)　　　　　　　　　　　　　DM 750

SCHEINER, Christoph
- **Oculus hoc est: Fundamentum Opticum.** Innsbruck, 1619. 1st. Edn. Sm. 4to. Some browning, partly erased stp. & cropped Jesuit inscr. on title. Cont. limp vell., stained. From Honeyman Collection. (S. May 19; 2780)　　　　　　　　　　　*Quaritch*. £900
- - **Anr. Edn.** L., 1652. 4to. Slightly browned in parts, title stpd. Leath. (HK. Nov.18-21; 725)　　　　　　　　　　　DM 1,800
- **Pantographice, seu Ars Delineandi Res Quaslibet per Parallelogrammum Lineare seu Cavum, Mechanicum, Mobile.** Rome, 1631. 1st. Edn. 4to. Some browning, a few marginal repairs (1 touching side-note), sm. tear in last lf., owner's entry of Tommaso Guateri. Cont. vell., covers warped. From Honeyman Collection. (S. May 19; 2781A)　　　　　　　　　*Hill*. £140
- **Refractiones Coelestes, sive Solis Elliptici Phaenomenon Illustratum.** Ingolstadt, 1617. 1st.

Edn. Sm. 4to. Slight staining, minor repair to S4. Bnd. in fragment of MS. antiphoner on vell., owner's inscr. on title, & stp. erased in margin. From Honeyman Collection. (S. May 19; 2779)　　　　　　　　　　*Hill*. £400
- **Rosa Ursina sive Sol ex Admirando Facularum & Macularum suarum Phoenomeno varius.** Bracciano, 1626-30. 1st. Edn. Fo. Errata lf. slightly torn & with sm. repair, title soiled & stained, some staining, mostly marginal, 2il book III reprd. 18th. C. cf., worn. From liby. of Dukes of Arenberg at Nordkirchen; from Honeyman Collection. (S. May 19; 2781)　　*Riley-Smith*. £2,000
See–KEPLER, J.–SCHEINER, C. & Locher, J.G. –SCHEINER, C.–PHILIPPI, H. –MARTILINGEN, J.

SCHELIHA, V.E.R. von
- **A Treatise on Coast-Defence, based on the Experience gained by Officers of the . . . Confederate States.** L., 1868. 1st. Edn. Gt.-pict. cl. (SG. Jan.8; 393)　　　　　　　$200

SCHELLING, Friedrich Wilhelm Joseph
- **Philosophische Schriften.** Landshut, 1809. 1st. Edn. Slightly soiled. New Romantic cont. leath., gt. (HK. May 15; 4818)　　　　DM 460
- **Sämmtliche Werke.** Stuttgart & Augsburg, 1856-61. 1st. Coll. Edn. 14 vols., (pt. 1 10 vols. & pt. 2 4 vols). Hf. leath. (R. Mar.31-Apr.4; 281)　　　　　　　　　　　DM 2,200

SCHEMERL, J.v.
- **Ausführliche Anweisung zur Entwerfung, Erbauung und Erhaltung Dauerhafter und Bequemer Strassen.** Vienna, 1819. 1st. Edn. 3 vols. Title multi-stpd., lightly soiled in parts. Cont. leath. gt. (R. Mar.31-Apr.4; 1300)　　　　DM 850

SCHENK, Pieter
- **Atlas Saxonicus Novus.** Ca. 1755. Approx. 560 × 490mm. Title, table & 15 cold. maps loose. (P. Jun.11; 242)　　　　　　　*Baumer*. £250
See–VALCK, Gerard & Schenk, Pieter

SCHENKMAN, J.
- **Het Nieuwe Apenspel. Zonder Weerga. Nooit Gezien** Amst., ca. 1840. Lge. 8vo. Fly-ll. foxed, browned. Orig. hf. cl. (VG. Dec.16; 1080)　　　　　　　　　　　　　Fls. 600

SCHETKY, John Christian & Manners, Lord John
- **Sketches & Notes of a Cruise in Scotch Waters . . .** 1850. Fo. Cont. mor.-bkd. woods bds., gt. & gt.-lettered on upr. cover, spine gt. (C. Nov.5; 139a)　　　　　　　*Crowe*. £950

SCHEUBEL, Johann
- **Algebrae Compendiosa Facilisque Descriptio, qua Depromuntur Magna Arithmetices Miracula.** Paris, 1551. 1st. Edn. Sm. 4to. Some marginal staining, sm. dark stain on title. Cont. limp vell., worn, lr. inside hinge brkn., front fly-lf. from vell. MS., hf. red mor. case. From Honeyman Collection. (S. May 19; 2782)　　　　　*Rota*. £70

SCHEUCHZER, Johann Jacob
- **Helvetiae Historia Naturalis, oder Natur-Historie des Schweitzerlandes.** Zürich, 1716-18. 3 pts. in 1 vol. 4to. Slightly soiled in parts, frontis. slightly defect, 1 plt. pt. 3 torn. Cont. hf. vell., spine defect. (R. Oct.14-18; 2022)　　　　　　　　　　　DM 4,200
- **Herbarium Diluvianum.** Zurich, 1709. 1st. Edn. Fo. A large copy, stp. on verso of title. Orig. bds., worn, unc. From Honeyman Collection. (S. May 19; 2786)　　　　　　　*Percy*. £400
- - **Anr. Edn.** Ill.:– J. Nutting after M. Fussli (port.). Leiden, 1723. 2nd. Edn. Fo. Some browning, single wormhole in some inner margins. Cont. mott. cf., worn. From Honeyman Collection. (S. May 19; 2787)　　　*Crete*. £280
- - **Anr. Edn.** Leiden, 1723. Margins spotted. Cont. cf., rebkd. From Chetham's Liby., Manchester. (C. Nov.27; 362)　　　　　　　　　*Weldon & Wesley*. £200
- **Itinera per Helvetiae Alpinas Regiones.** Leiden, 1723. 4 vols. in 1. Some plts. with overslips, margins slightly spotted. Cont. vell., spine torn. From Chetham's Liby., Manchester. (C. Nov.27; 360)　　　　*Wenner*. £4,600
- **Kupfer-Bibel, in Welcher die Physica Sacra . . .** Augsburg & Ulm, 1731-35. 3 vols. Fo. Cont. red mor., spines gt. in 8 compartments with raised bands. (C. May 20; 53)　　*Quaritch*. £3,200
- **Naturhistori des Schweitzerlands.** Ill.:– J.M. Füssli. Zürich, 1716-18. 3 vols. 4to. All titles with old MS. owner's mark, title & pt. 1 with ex-lib.

removed & defect with text loss, sm. faults. Cont. hf. leath., gt. spine, defect & worn. (HK. Nov.18-21; 728)　　　　　　　DM 3,000
- **Ouresiphoites. Helveticus, sive Itinera per Helvetiae Alpinas Regiones.** Leiden, 1723. 4 vols. in 1. 4to. A few minor tears, slight discolouration collation note sigd. 'RCH' on fly-lf. Cont. vell. bds., soiled, hf. red mor. case. From Honeyman Collection. (S. May 19; 2788)　　　*Mughini & Nesa*. £4,800
- **Physique Sacrée ou Historie-Naturelle de la Bible.** Ill.:– Jean André Pfeffel. Amst., 1737. 8 vols. Fo., Frontis., 2 ports., 758 engd. plts. Mor. gt. (P. Jun.11; 282)　　　*Cambridge*. £1,000

SCHEUCHZER, Johann Jacob–HALLER, A. von
- **Agrostographia sive Graminum . . .–Synonyma Nuperiora . . .** Zürich, 1775. 2 works in 1 vol. 4to. Cont. bds., unc. (HK. Nov.18-21; 727)　DM 750

SCHEWITZER, Christopher
See–FRYKE, Christopher & Schewitzer, Christopher

SCHEYB, Franz Christoph von
- **Peutingeriana tabula Itineraria.** 1753. Fo. 12 engraved plts., all double-p., mntd. on guards. Hf. cf., worn, covers detchd. (CSK. Apr.10; 41)　£55

SCHIAPARELLI, G.V.
- **Osservazioni Astronomiche e Fisiche . . . del Pianeta Marte.–Il Pianeta Marte.** Rome; Milan, 1878-99; 1893. 2nd. title is offprint from review 'Natura ed Arte'. 6 pts.; 1 pt. 4to. Orig. ptd. wraps., unc., lacks 1 cover & 1 spine, 2 others brkn.; orig. ptd. wraps., cl. case. Pres. copy to Prof. E[rnst] Mach; from Honeyman Collection. (S. May 19; 2789)　　　　　*Norman*. £320

SCHICKFUSS, Jacobus
- **New Vermehrte Schlesische Chronica und Landes Beschreibung.** Jena, [1625]. Fo. Cont. black mor.-bkd. wood bds., gt. spine & cover, 2 clasps, lightly worn, some worming, clasps reprd. (R. Oct.14-18; 2377)　　　　　DM 4,400

SCHIDLOF, Leo
- **The Miniature in Europe.** Graz, 1964. Ltd. Edn. 4 vols. 4to. Orig. cl. (SH. Jun.11; 97)　　　　　　　　*Sims & Reed*. £75

SCHIDLOFF, B. & others
- **Venus Oceanica: The Sexual Life of South Sea Natives. Erotic Rituals of Australian Aboriginals . . . Ethnopornographia.** Ed.:– R. Burton. N.Y., Priv. ptd. 1935. (925). Orig. bdg. (KH. Nov.18; 526)　　　　　　　Aus. $160

SCHIEFLER, G.
- **Emil Nolde. Das Graphische Werk.** Ill.:– Christel Mosel. Cologne, [1966-67]. 2 vols. 4to. Orig. linen. (H. Dec.9/10; 2269)　　DM 740

SCHIELE, Egon
- **Watercolours & Drawings.** Ed.:– Erwin Mitsch. 1970. (100) numbered for Thames & Hudson Ltd., L. Lge. fo. Orig. cl. gt., s.-c. (SBA. Jul.14; 384)　　　　　　　*Ursus Books*. £120

SCHIFF, Mortimer L.
- **Catalogue of . . . the famous Library.** 1938. 3 pts. in 1 vol. 4to. Pt. 1 priced in pencil, pt. 3 ptly. priced with ptd. price-list bnd. in, index to each pt. Mod. cl. (SM. Oct.7; 1494)　　　　Frs. 1,800

SCHILLER, Johann Christoph Friedrich von
- **Demetrius.** [Munich], [1922]. (500) numbered on Bütten. 4to. Orig. vell., orig. bd. s.-c. (HK. Nov.18-21; 2463)　　　　　　　DM 420
- **Dom Karlos. Infant v. Spanien.** Leipzig, 1787. 1st. Individual Edn. Lacks end-p., a few ll. stained. Cont. style hf. leath., gt., by Bakala. (HK. May 15; 4839)　　　　　　　DM 650
- **Der Geisterseher.** Ill.:– E. Oppler. Berlin, [1922]. (100) Privilege Edn. on Bütten. 4to. Hand-bnd. orig. mor. gt. (H. May 21/22; 1476)　DM 900
- **Gedichte.** Leipzig, 1800-03. 1st. Authorised Edn. 2 vols. Several sm. margin tears bkd. Cont. style hf. leath. gt., by Bakala. (HK. May 15; 4841)　　　　　　　DM 480
- - **Anr. Edn.** Leipzig, 1807-08. 3rd Edn. Cont. red mor., gt. cover, spine & inr. & outer dentelle. (HK. May 15; 4842)　　DM 1,400
- **Kabale und Liebe.** Mannheim, 1784. 1st. Edn. Lacks 2nd. title, title with sm. fault bkd. Cont. style hf. leath. gt., by Bakala. (HK. May 15; 4844)　　　　　　　DM 850
- **Musen-Almanach für das Jahr 1796.** Ill.:– Fr. Bolt (title). Neustrelitz, [1795]. 1st. Edn. Heavily soiled at beginning & end, title copper engr. torn

at corner with slight loss, MS. notes on Kalendarium, lacks 4 mus. supps., old owner's note on end paper. Cont. paper bds. (H. Dec.9/10; 1655) DM 420
– **Musen-Almanach für das Jahr 1799.** Ill.:– after H. Meyer by H. Guttenberg (title). Tübingen, [1798]. 1st. Edn. Lacks 7 ll. Kalendarium, lightly browned in parts. Orig. pict. wraps., light soiling. (H. Dec.9/10; 1656) DM 500
– **The Piccolomini.** Trans.:– S.T. Coleridge. L., 1800. 1st. Edn. Hf.-title replaced by general title for both pts., stipple port. of Wallenstein (with Longman's 1800 imprint) inserted, without advts. at end, some foxing. Old qtr. cf. John Livingston Lowe's copy, with his sig., presented to him by H.T.S. (SG. Dec.18; 366) $130
– **Sämmtliche Werke.** Vienna, 1819-20. Orig. Edn. 18 vols. 3 engraved titles lightly soiled. Cont. bds. W.a.f. (HK. May 15; 4827) DM 700
– – **Anr. Edn.** Stuttgart & Tübingen, 1838. 12 vols. Slightly spotted in pts. Cont. hf. cf., a few spines worn at top. (S. Jan.27; 449) Wagner. £110
– – **Anr. Edn.** Ed.:– M. Hecker & A. Köster. Leipzig, 1905-06. 6 vols. Orig. cf., 2 covers slightly worn. (H. Dec.9/10; 1893) DM 620
– **Wallenstein.** Tübingen, 1800. 1st. Edn. 2 vols. Vol. 2 lacks pp. 1/2, title reprd. 2 ll. with tears reprd., vol. 1 slightly soiled. Cont. style hf. leath. gt., by Bakala. (HK. May 15; 4864) DM 500
– – **Anr. Edn.** Berlin, [1915-18]. (300) on Bütten, for Maximilian Gesellschaft. 4to. Hand-bnd. orig. mor., silk end-papers & doubls. (E.A. Enders)., spine lightly worn. (H. Dec.9/10; 1870) DM 640
– **Wallensteins Lager.** Ill.:– L. Corinth. Berlin, 1922. (80) numbered. On H-m-p. Fo. Priv. vell. (D. Dec.11-13; 1033) DM 2,200
– – **Anr. Copy.** Hand-bnd. vell., sm. fault on lr. cover. by O. Herfurth. 5 (of 6) etchgs. sigd. by artist. (H. Dec.9/10; 2011) DM 1,800

SCHILLER, Julius
– **Coelum Stellatum Christianum.** Ill.:– L. Kilian. Augsburg. 1627. 1st. Edn. Ob. fo. Some soiling & spotting, mostly marginal, lacks a lf. (ll.?) of tables at end, minor repairs to title, owner's inscr. of Jesuit College at Ingolstadt in upr. margin of title, title. stp. on verso, sig. of L.A. Kunze on fly.-lf. Cont. vell., soiled & scratched, lacks ties, hf. red mor. case. From Honeyman Collection. (S. May 19; 2790) Hillman. £1,400

SCHILPEROORT, T.O.
See–HAAS, H. de–DE KANTER, J. –SCHILPEROORT, T.O.

SCHIMMUSCH TEHILIM
Trans.:– Gottfried Selig. Berlin, 1788. Without the 5 plts., slight discolouration. Bds. (S. Nov.18; 457) Rapoport. £85

SCHIMPFFER, B.–TREU, A.–SCHORER, C.
– **Kurtze Beschr. des Dunckelen Cometen.** –Deckwürd., u mehrentls. Neue Observationes von Grossen Conjunctionibus u. Oppositionibus . . .; Observationes . . jüngst ersch. Cometen . . . –Bedenchen von der Cometen . . . vnd Erdbewegung . . . Frankfurt; Nüremb; Nuremb.; Basel, 1653. 4 works in 1 vol. 4to. Lightly browned thro'-out, title I defect. & bkd. Cont. vell. (HK. Nov.18-21; 729) DM 500

SCHINKEL, Carl Friedrich
– **Sammlung Architektonischer Entwürfe.** Berlin, [1819-35]. 1st. Edn. Pts. 1-24 (of 28) in 2 vols. Lge. ob. fo. Some browning. Cont. hf. leath., spine worn & defect. in parts. (H. Dec.9/10; 940) DM 5,400
– – **Anr. Edn.** Berlin, [1819]-40. 1st. Edn. Pts. 1-28 (Pts. 25-28 New Series Pts. 1-4.) Lge. ob. fo. All text ll. & plts. with sm. liby. stps., 174 mostly engraved plts., some at end also in litho. Loose, from pt. 13 in Orig. pt. wraps., hf. linen portfolio. (R. Oct.14-18; 761) DM 6,300
– – **Anr. Edn.** Ill.:– Berger, Jügel, Thiele & others after Schinkel. Berlin, 1843/47. Fo. Lacks title lf. Orig. hf. linen gt., rubbed. (D. Dec.11-13; 395) DM 4,800
– **Sammlung von Theater-Dekorationen.** Ill.:– Dietrich, Jügel & Thiele after Schinkel. Berlin, 1862. Ob. fo. Some erased stps. in margin, slightly soiled in parts. Hf. leath. (HK. Nov.18-21; 2083) DM 9,200

SCHINZ, H.R.
– **Naturgeschichte und Abbildungen der Menschen und der Saeugethiere.** Zurich, 1840. 2nd. Improved Edn. Fascicules 1-3, 5, 7, 8, & 10-12.

14¾ × 10¾ ins. Occasional light foxing & staining. Orig. wraps. (SG. May 21; 432) $130

SCHINZ, Sal.
– **Anleitung zu der Pflanzenkenntniss und derselben Nützlichsten Anwendung.** Ill.:– J.B. Bullinger after Schinz (2 cold. copperplts), 104 cold. woodcuts from L. Fuchs. Zürich, 1774[-1777]. Fo. Lacks title & 1 ded. lf. Hf. leath. ca. 1820. (HK. May 12-14; 320) DM 5,800

SCHIOPPALALBA, Joan Baptista
– **In Perantiquam Sacram Tabulam Graecam . . . Dissertatio.** [Venice], 1767. Sm. fo. 2 plts. torn & reprd. Cont. Italian red mor., gt. spine, buckram s.-c. From the collection of John A. Saks. (C. Jun.10; 231) Taylor. £60

SCHIPPERIUS, P.A.
See–CRAANDIJK, J. & Schipperius, P.A.

SCHKUHR, Chretien
– **Histoire des Carex ou Laiches.** Leipzig, 1802. 4to. Occasional slight staining. Cont. cf., worn. (CSK. Nov.7; 9) £50

SCHLECHTENDAL, Diedrich Franz Leonhard von & others
– **Flora von Deutschland.** 1880-87. 5th. Edn. Vols. III-XXX. Slight browning. Orig. cl., rebkd. with cf. (S. Jun.1; 202) Joseph. £260
– – **Anr. Edn.** Ed.:– E. Hallier. Gera-Untermhaus, 1880-88. Latest Edn. 30 vols. & Index vol. Orig. hf. leath., spine slightly defect. (H. May 21/22; 228) DM 3,200

SCHLEGEL, Gustave
– **Uranographie Chinoise ou Preuves directes que l'Astronomie Primitive est Originaire de la Chine.** The Hague & Leiden, 1875. 1st. Edn. 3 vols. including Atlas. Lge. 8vo. & ob. fo. Slight discolouration, sig. of W. Stahlman. Mod. buckram. From Honeyman Collection. (S. May 19; 2791) Quaritch. £130

SCHLEGEL, Hermann
– **De Vogels van Nederlandsch Indie.** Leyden/Amst., [1863-66]. 3 pts. in 1 vol., all publd. Fo. Some plts. sigd. by J. Smit, text Dutch & Fr., 1 lf. loose & frayed. Orig. cl. gt., slightly worn. (VG. Oct.13; 140) Fls. 1,600

SCHLEGEL, Hermann & Verster de Wulverhorst, A.H.
– **Traité de Fauconnerie.** Ill.:– J. Wolf, J.B. Sonderland & others. Leiden & Dusseldorf, 1844-53. Elephant fo. Dedication & preface ll. with lge. tears reprd. Mod. pol. cf. (C. May 20; 238) Taylor. £3,500

SCHLEIDEN, Jacob Mathias
– **Grundzüge der Wissenschaftlichen Botanik.** Leipzig, 1842-43. 1st. Edn. 2 vols. Advt. lf. in vol. II. Cont. bds. Bkplt. of Herbert McLean Evans; from Honeyman Collection. (S. May 19; 2792) Percy. £550

SCHLEIERMACHER, F.
[–] **Über die Religion. Reden an die Gebildeten unter Ihrem Verächtern.** Berlin, 1799. 1st. Edn. 19th. C. linen. (R. Mar.31-Apr.4; 282) DM 620

SCHLEMMER, O. (Ed.)
See–STAATLICHES BAUHAUS WEIMAR

SCHLICKUM, O.
– **Die Wissenschaftl Ausbildung des Apothekerlehrlings.** Leipzig, 1878. 1st. Edn. Cont. hf. leath. (R. Mar.31-Apr.4; 1038) DM 475

SCHLIEBEN, W.E.A.v.
– **Vollständiges Hand-und Lehrbuch der Gesammten Feldmess Kunst.** Ed.:– J.B. Montag. Quedlinburg & Leipzig, 1857. 4th. Edn. Bds., orig. wraps. (R. Mar.31-Apr.4; 1295) DM 450

SCHLIEMANN, Dr. Henry
– **Mycenae.** 1878. Advts., slight spotting. Orig. cl. gt. (SBA. Oct.21; 76) Leget. £90

SCHLOSS, A.
See–ALMANACS

SCHLOSSER, Johann
– **Carminum Libellus.** Wittenberg, 1558. 1st. Edn. Slight browning, 1 or 2 scrape-marks, affecting a few letters of text. Mod. pol. hf. cf. by Wood. From liby. of André L. Simon. (S. May 18; 176) Overton. £40

SCHLUETER, Christoph Andreas
– **De la Fonte des Mines, des Fonderies, & c.** Trans.:– M. Helot. Paris, 1764-53. Vol. I 2nd.

Edn., Vol. II 1st. Edn. 2 vols. 4to. Some browning. Cont. mott. cf., gt. spines, worn at edges, hf. red mor. cases. From Honeyman Collection. (S. May 19; 2793) Zeitlin & Verbrugge. £240
– – **Anr. Copy.** 2 vols. in 1. Some browning & staining, 1st. title slightly soiled, sm. tear in 1st. plt. Cont. mott. sheep, worn. From Honeyman Collection. (S. May 19; 2794) Elliott. £90
– **Grundlicher Unterricht von Hutte-Werken . . .** Braunschweig, 1738. Fo. 19th. C. hf. mor. From Chetham's Liby., Manchester. (C. Nov.27; 363) Marcus. £400

SCHLUMBERGER, Gustave
– **Sigillographie de l'Empire Byzantin.** Paris, 1884. 1st. Edn. 4to. Buckram, orig. wraps. bnd. in, ex-liby. (SG. Dec.18; 68) $110

SCHMEIZEL, M.
– **Einleitung zur Wappen-Lehre.** Jena, 1734. 2nd. Edn. Lacks some copperplts. Old bds. (R. Mar.31-Apr.4; 185) DM 520

SCHMID, Herman & Stieler, Karl
– **Aus Deutschen Bergen.** Stuttgart, 1873. 4to. Orig. decor. cl., gt. (SH. Nov.6; 251) Walford. £75
– **Wanderungen im Bayrischen Gebirge.** Stuttgart, Ca. 1880. 2nd. Edn. Fo. Orig. linen. (R. Oct.14-18; 2214) DM 800
– – **Anr. Copy.** Lacks title. Cont. linen. (R. Mar.31-Apr.4; 1988) DM 650

SCHMID, Karl
– **Naturhistorische Beschreibung der Vögel.** Munich, 1818. 4to. Text slightly soiled, lacks plt. 81, includes plt. 21. Cont. leath. gt., worn. (R. Mar.31-Apr.4; 1445) DM 700

SCHMID, Wolffgang
– **Das erst [–viert] Buch der Geometria.** Nuremb., 1539. 1st. Edn. Sm. 4to. Soiling. Old limp vell., stained, lr. inside hinge brkn. From Honeyman Collection. (S. May 19; 2795) Israel. £170

SCHMIDEL
See–BRY, Theodore de & others

SCHMIDEL or Schmiedel, Casimir Christoph
– **Erz Stüffen und Berg Arten mit Farben genaü abgebildet.** Ed.:– Johann Michael Seligmann. Nuremb., 1753. 4to. 26 hand-cold. engraved plts. only., lacks all after p. 36 of text. Cont. cf.-bkd. bds., worn. W.a.f.; from Honeyman Collection. (S. May 19; 2796) Offenbacher. £200
– **Fossilium Metalla et Res Metallicas . . .** Nuremb., 1753. 4to. Plts. hand-cold. & unc. Mod. cl. From Chetham's Liby., Manchester. (C. Nov.27; 364) Taylor. £450
– **Icones Plantarum . . .** Ed.:– J.C. Keller. Ill.:– after N. Gabler, J.C. Keller, & V. Bishoff. [Nuremb.], 1762. Pt. 1 only (of 3). Fo. Plts. hand-cold., title detchd. 19th. C. hf. mor., upr. cover detchd. W.a.f., from Chetham's Liby., Manchester. (C. Nov.27; 365) Lester. £300

SCHMIDL, A. Adolf
– **Wien u. s. Nächsten Umgebungen.** Vienna, 1847. Romantic cont. hf. leath. gt. (HK. Nov.18-21; 1312) DM 700

SCHMIDLAP, Johannes
– **Künstliche und rechtschaffene Fewerwerck zum Schimpff.** Nuremb., 1564. 1st. Edn. (?). Title soiled & defect. in inner margin touching 2 letters, some browning & marginal staining, sm. hole in E2, lacks final blank. Mod. buckram-bkd. bds. From Honeyman Collection. (S. May 19; 2797) Interlibrum. £500

SCHMIDLIN, Ed.
See–KONIG, L.F.C.–SCHMIDLIN, Ed.

SCHMIDT, Adolf
– **Atlas der Diatomaceenkunde . . .** Aschersleben & Leipzig, 1885-1904. 63 Pts. & Indices for Pts. 1-36 (Series I-III) & for plts. 1-240 (Series I-V). Fo. Plts. defect. at margin. Orig. ptd. wraps, Indices mostly disbnd., approx. 4 Pts. lack lr. wrap. (PNY. Oct.1; 477) $440

SCHMIDT, Fechtmeister in Berlin
– **Lehrbuch für die Kavallerie zum vortheilhaften Gebrauch des Säbels.** Berlin, 1797. Ob. 4to. Spotted, MS. annots. in Fr. inside upr. cover. 18th. C. wraps. (S. Jun.1; 42) Hinersdorff. £150

SCHMIDT, Robert
– **Early European Porcelain.** Munich, 1953. Ltd. Edn. 4to. Orig. cl., d.-w. (S. Sep.30; 439) £60

SCH

428

SCH

SCHMIDTMEYER, Peter
- Travels into Chile. 1824. 4to. Lacks 5 plts., some spotting. Hf. mor., worn. W.a.f. (P. Dec.11; 66)
Waterloo Investments. £100

SCHMIED, F.L Lucien-Graux, Doctor
[-] L'agneau du Moghreb. Paris, 1942. (125). 4to. Orig. wraps, folder & box, slight wear & soiling. (SPB. Oct.1; 242) $800
[-] Le Cantique des Cantiques. Paris, 1925. (110) sigd. by author. Mor. with elaborate geometric inlaid design, geometric mor. doubls., by Gruel, hf. mor. chemise, s.-c. (SPB Oct.1; 243) $2,800

SCHMIT, Robert
- Eugene Boudin. Paris, 1973. [1,300] numbered. 3 vols. 4to. Orig. cl. (CSK. Nov.21; 66) £130

SCHMITZ, H.
- Deutsche Möbel des Klassizismus. Stuttgart, 1923. 2 vols. 4to. Orig. cl.-bkd. bds. (SH. Jul.16; 180) *Lustenberger.* £90

SCHNEEVOGT, G. Voorhelm
- Icones Plantarum Rariorum. Ed.:– S.J. van Geuns. Ill.:– Haaricus Schwegman. Haarlem, 1793. 2 pts. in 1 vol. Fo. 19th. C. hf. cf. (VG. Oct.13; 141) Fls. 14,500

SCHNEUR Salman of Liadi–MENDEL of Lisko –AZULAI, Chaim Joseph David
- Luach Birchat Ha'nehenin.-Darchei Zedek. -Avodat Ha'kodesh. Lvov; [Zolkiev]; Zolkiev, 1804; [1800?]; 1809. 2nd. Edn.; 2nd. Edn.; 9th. Edn. 3 works in 1 vol. 1st. work: slightly browned. Hf. cl. (S. Nov.17; 209) *Zysblat.* £70

SCHNEURSON, Joseph Yitzhak, of Lubavitch
- Ma'amarim (13 Kuntrasim). 'Riga', 1931-33. 1st. Edn. Hf. cl. (S. Nov.17; 219) *Maggs.* £50

SCHOBERL, Frederic
See-SHOBERL, Frederic

SCHOENBERG
- Standard Atlas of the World. N.Y., 1864. Tall fo. Orig. cl., worn & loose. (SG. May 21; 95) $160

SCHOEPFF, Johann David
- Historia Testudinum, Iconibus Illustrata. Erlangae, 1792. Lge. 4to. 34 (of 37) copperplts., 32 fully hand-cold., unc. Disbnd. (SG. Sep.18; 333) $350
- - Anr. Edn. Erlangen, 1792 [–1801]. 1st. Edn. 4to. Plts. numbered 1-32, in orig. sheets. Orig, wrap. of pt. 1-2, unopened, preserved in cl. box. (S. Dec.3; 1122) *Asher.* £190
- Materia Medica Americana Potissimum Regni Vegetabilis. Erlangen, 1787. 1st. Edn. Lightly browned in parts. Cont. interim bds., unc. [Sabin 77756] (R. Mar.31-Apr.4; 1042) DM 8,500

SCHOKKER, H.W.
- Handboek voor de Kennis Van den Scheepsbouw. Amst., 1861. 2 vols. 4to. Cont. hf. leath. (R. Oct.14-18; 2888) DM 420

SCHOLEFIELD, E.O.S. & Howay, F.W.
- British Columbia, from the Earliest Times to the Present. Vancouver, etc., 1914. 4 vols. 4to. Orig. hf. mor. (SG. Mar.5; 53) $160

SCHOLZ, Joseph
-De Kleine Huisvrouw. Ments, [inscr. dtd. 1837]. 12mo. Orig. stiff pict. wraps., backstrip partly split. (SH. Mar.19; 287) *Nador.* £120

SCHOMBURGK, Sir Robert Hermann
- Twelve Views in the Interior of Guiana: from Drawings Executed by Mr. Charles Bentley. L., 1840-41. Fo. Some foxing, minor soiling, slight marginal tears. Mor.-bkd. bds., covers detchd. [Sabin 77796] (SPB. May 5; 462) $650
- - Anr. Edn. Ill.:– Charles Bentley. 1841. Fo. Some ll. spotted. Cont. hf. mor. (SH. May 21; 240) *Faupel.* £750
- - Anr. Copy. Hf. leath. & cl., worn. (CE. Dec.4; 207) £400

SCHONE, W.
- Die Deutsche Zeitung des Siebzehnten Jahrhunderts in Abbildungen. Leipzig, 1940. 400 pp. facs. Hf. vell. (R. Oct.14-18; 611) DM 750

SCHONER, Andreas
- Gnomonice . . . hoc est: de Descriptionibus Horologiorum Sciotericorum Omnis Generis, proiectionibus circulorum Sphaericorum ad superficies . . . libri tres. Nuremb., 1562. 1st. Edn. Fo. Folding plt. in MS. inserted at fo. 30, title very soiled & with partly erased inscrs. (margins strengthened on verso), wormhole in inner margins

towards end, occasionally catching text., cont. annots. Mod. vell. bds., hf. red mor. case. From Honeyman Collection. (S. May 19; 2800) *Rogers Turner.* £360

SCHONER, Johann
- Coniectur odder ab Nemliche Auslegung Joannis Schoners uber den Cometen so im Augstmonat, des MCCCCCXXXI. Leipzig, 1531. Sm. 4to. Last 3 ll. slightly wormed in margins. Vell.-bkd. bds., soiled. From Honeyman Collection. (S. May 19; 2801) *Veron.* £180
- Opera Mathematica. Nuremb., 1551. 1st. Edn. 3 pts. in 1 vol. Fo. Inner margins of title & a few other ll. strengthened, blank corner torn from E4 pt. 1. Cont. German blind-stpd. pig. over wooden bds., outer roll containing Crucifixion (dtd. 1541) & other scenes, inner roll containing Justitia, Lucretia, Caritas (sig. I.F.) & Suavitas (dtd. 1556), later stp. of school of Altenburg impressed on each cover, soiled, clasps & catches. The Harmsworth copy; from Honeyman Collection. [Sabin 77805] (S. May 19; 2802a) *Hill.* £800
- - Anr. Edn. Nuremb., 1561. 2nd. Edn. 3 pts. in 1 vol. Fo. No volvelles, ink stain on 2K5 recto pt. 1, a few other sm. stains, slight browning, cont. MS. list of famous astronomers on fly-lf., a few marginal notes, liby. stp. on title. Cont. blind-stpd. pig over wooden bds., rolls of medallion heads, soiled, lacks 1 clasp, front pastedown inscr. 'Ex libris M. Vicendelini Bulfingeri Leomontani. 1589. 8 Octobris. From Honeyman Collection. [Sabin 77806] (S. May 19; 2803) *Zeitlin & Verbrugge.* £440
- Tabulae Astronomicae. Nuremb., 1536. 1st. Edn. 4to. Preface: Ph. Malacnthonis, old monog. stp. on title & end-lf. Cont. limp MS. vell. wraps. (R. Oct.14-18; 287) DM 1,200

SCHONER, Johann–HEYLL, Christophorus –FUCHS, Leonhard–RICIUS, Paulus
- Ephemeris . . . pro anno domini MDXXXII accuratissime supputata.–Hoc in volumine haec continentur. Artificialis Medicatio, constans paraphrasi in Galeni Librum de Artis Medicae Constitutione (etc.).–Errata Recentiorum Medicorum.–De Anima Coeli Compendium. Nuremb.; Mainz; Hagenau; Augsburg, [1532]; 1534; 1530; 1519. 1st. Edns. 4 works in 1 vol. Sm. 4to. 1st. work with a few wormholes; 2nd. work with some worming, marginal repairs to title & el; 3rd. work with marginal repair to A2, a few ll. stained in fore-margins; 4th. work with slight marginal staining, a few insignificant wormholes. Cont. German blind-stpd. pig over wooden bds., wormed & stained, metal clasps & catches. From Honeyman Collection. (S. May 19; 2802) *Quaritch.* £420

SCHONHEINTZ, Jakob
- Apologia Astrologie. Nuremb., 1502. 1st. Edn. Sm. 4to. Some sig. letters cropped, title slightly browned & soiled. 19th. C. bds. Bkplts. of George Kloss, M.D. of Frankfurt a. M., & Robert, Earl of Crewe; from Honeyman Collection. (S. May 19; 2804) *Goldschmidt.* £260

SCHOOL (The) OF GOOD MANNERS
N.Y., ca. 1820. 16mo. Spotted. Orig. ptd. wraps. (SH. Mar.19; 288) *Schiller.* £190

SCHOOL Mistress, The
Ca. 1790. 32mo. Mor.-bkd. cl., orig. pict. wraps. bnd. in. (SH. Dec.10; 5) *Rota.* £70

SCHOOL FOR MOTHERS, The, with the Politics of a Village
1823. 1st. Edn. 3 vols. 12mo. Orig. cl.-bkd. bds., unc. (C. May 20; 54) *Hannas.* £130

SCHOOLCRAFT, Henry Rowe
- Historical & Statistical Information Respecting . . . the Indian Tribes of the United States. Ill.:– Seth Eastman & others. Phila., 1851-60. 6 vols. Lge. 4to. Ex-liby., stp. on verso of all plts. Cl., reprd., brkn. (SG. Jun.11; 383) $750
- Information, respecting the History, Condition & Prospects of the Indian Tribes of the United States. Phila., 1853-54. Vols. I-IV only (of 6). Lge. tall 4to. Orig. gt.-pict. cl., corners frayed. W.a.f.; 2 vols. are Sigd. Pres. Copies to William Tweed from George W. Manypenny. (PNY. May 21; 378) $400
- - Anr. Edn. Phila., 1853-56. 5 vols., 4to. Three-qtr. mor., gt.-panel. spines, by Morrell. (SG. Oct.9; 220) $550
- Narrative Journal of Travels . . . in the Year 1820. Albany, 1821. 1st. Edn. With errata slip,

folding map torn & reprd., title defect. Cont. tree cf., spine defect. (PNY. Oct.1; 476) $130
- - Anr. Copy. Badly foxed, map reprd. on verso, old liby. stp. on title. Later sheep. A.L.s. tipped in, torn & linen-mntd. (SG. Jun.11; 381) $120

SCHOONEBEEK, Adrien
- Courte Description des Ordres des Femmes et Filles Réligieuses. Amst., [1695]. 12mo. Mod. cf., 4 spine raised bands, blind border. (LM. Mar.21; 176) B.Frs. 8,500
- Courte & Solide Histoire de la Fondation des Ordres Religieux . . . Amst., 1688. 12mo. Cont. spr. cf., decor. spine. (HD. Feb.18; 72) Frs. 1,000
- Histoire de tous les Ordres Militaires . . . Amst., 1699. 2 vols. Later glazed cf., double gt. fillets on covers, decor. raised bands on spine. (HD. Jun.29; 131) Frs. 1,610

SCHOOTEN, Frans van
- De Organica Conicarum Sectionum in Plano Descriptione, Tractatus . . . Cui subnexa est Appendix, de Cubicarum Aequationum Resolutione. Leiden, 1646. 1st. Edn. Sm. 4to. Some spotting, a few stains, cancelled liby. stp. of Bibliothèque Municipale, Nimes, on title & in margins of 3 or 4 other ll. Cont. vell., soiled. From Honeyman Collection. (S. May 19; 2807) *Hughes.* £70
- Exercitationum Mathematicarum libri quinque . . . Quibus accedit Christiani Hugenii Tractatus, de Ratiociniis in Aleae Ludo. Leiden, 1657. 1st. Edn. Sm. 4to. First few ll. stained, title to Book 1 with liby. stps. & short tear reprd., similar tear in following lf., a few ll. wormed at head. Cont. vell., soiled. From Honeyman Collection. (S. May 19; 2808) *Stigler.* £180
- - Anr. Copy. Text dampstained & browned. Spine defect. From Honeyman Collection. (S. May 19; 2809) *Hughes.* £80
- Tabulae Sinuum Tangentium Secantium, ad Radium 10000000. Amst., 1627. 1st. Edn. 16mo. Some staining. Cont. vell., soiled, lacks 1 tie, hf. red mor. case. From Honeyman Collection. (S. May 19; 2805) *Hughes.* £70

SCHOPENHAUER, Arthur
- Die Welt als Wille und Vorstellung. Leipzig, 1819. 1st. Edn. Text browned. Bds., worn, hf. red mor. case. Dupl. stp. of liby. of University of Breslau; from Honeyman Collection. (S. May 19; 2810) *Norman.* £750
- - Anr. Copy. Browned thro.-out, soiled in parts. Cont. bds. (H. May 21/22; 1277) DM 2,200

SCHOPF, J.D.
- Reise durch Einige der Mittlern und Südlichen Vereinigten Nordamerikanischen Staaten nach Ost-Florida und den Bahama-Inseln. Erlangen, 1788 1st. Edn., 1st. printing. 2 pts. 19th. C. hf. leath. [Sabin 77757] (R. Mar.31-Apr.4; 2461) DM 3,800

SCHOPPER, Hartmann
- De Omnibus Illiberalibus sive Mechanicis Artibus. Ill.:– Jost Amman. Frankfurt, 1574. Slight browning, some underlinings on title. Cont. limp vell. bds., spine slightly worn, soiled, lacks ties. (S. Feb.10; 460) *Quaritch.* £1,700
- Speculum Vitae Aulicae. Reineke Fuchs. Ill.:– Jost Amman. Frankfurt, 1574. 2nd. Latin Edn., 1st. Edn. ill. Amman. Lacks title, lightly browned or soiled in parts. Cont. vell., very defect., lacks ties. (HK. Nov.18-21; 278) DM 800
- - Anr. Edn. Ill.:– J. Amman. Frankfurt, 1584. 12mo. Lightly browned, sm. stain at end, title-lf. very soiled & defect., lacks last lf. blank. Cont. vell., cockled, wormed, spine torn. (H. Dec.9/10; 1365) DM 520

SCHOPPER, Jacob
- Comoediae et Tragoediae Sacrae et Novae, Accuratissime recognitae. Cologne, 1562. 6 in 1 vol. Annots. on title, lacks lr. corners to few pp., some staining. Old cf. (BS. Jun.11; 279) £60

SCHORER, C.
See-SCHIMPFFER, B.-TREU, A.-SCHORER, C.

SCHOTT, Gaspar
- Anatomia Physico-Hydrostatica Fontium ac Fluminum . . . Accedit in fine Appendix de vera Origine Nili.–Arithmetica Practica Generalis ac Specialis. Wurzburg, 1663; 1663. 1st. Edn.; 2nd. Edn. 2 works in 1 vol. 1st. work with plt. 1 imperfectly ptd. Cont. vell. From Honeyman Collection. (S. May 19; 2815) *Hill.* £300

- **Cursus Mathematicus, sive Absoluta Omnium Mathematicarum Disciplinarum Encyclopaedia ... Accesserunt in fine Theoreses Mechanicae Novae.** Ill.:– A. Frolich (engraved frontis.). Würzburg, 1661. 1st. Edn. Fo. Last lf. detchd., rust-hole in plt. at p. 203. Cont. cf., worn, upr. cover detchd., bkplt. removed from front pastedown. From Honeyman Collection. (S. May 19; 2811) *Quaritch.* £260
- **- Anr. Copy.** Frontis. torn & soiled at outer edge, text browned, rust-hole in M5, partly deleted owner's inscr. on title, name 'Lutterloh' at foot of frontis. Cont. vell., soiled. From Honeyman Collection. (S. May 19; 2812) *Rogers Turner.* £100
- **- Anr. Edn.** Frankfurt a. M., 1674. Fo. Engraved frontis. slightly defect. & reprd., text browned, some ll. marginally stained. Cont. cf., gt. arms on covers, very worn. From Honeyman Collection. (S. May 19; 2813) *De Graeve.* £50
- **Magia Universalis Naturae et Artis ... Pars I. Optica. II. Acoustica. III. Mathematica. IV. Physica.** Bamberg, 1677 (Vol. II 1674). 4 vols. 4to. Very browned, vol. IV stained at beginning, sm. holes in title to vol. II, frontis. inscr. 'B. de Heresi', Cont. mott. cf., gt. spines, worn, lacks 2 labels. Bkplt. of Aquilla Smith; from Honeyman Collection. (S. May 19; 2819) *Hackhofer.* £350
- **Mechanica Hydraulico-Pneumatica ... Opus Bipartitum.** Würzburg, 1657. 1st. Edn. 4to. 1 plt. slightly torn in fold, some ll. slightly spotted. Cont. spr. cf., slightly worn. (S. Feb.23; 100) *Pilo.* £440
- **- Anr. Edn.** Würzburg, 1657 [-8]. 1st. Edn. 4to. Lf. 'instruction vor den Buchbinder', some ills. spotted. Cont. mott. cf., slightly worn. Bkplt. of Ludovicus de Puge, 1709. (S. Oct.21; 356) *Licini.* £480
- **Organum Mathematicum libris IX.** Würzburg, 1668. 1st. Edn. 4to. 4 plts. detchd., a few ll. & plts. wormed. Cont. vell. bds., initials I.B.G.V.H. & date 1678 on upr. cover. Armorial bkplt. of Count von Nostitz; from Honeyman Collection. (S. May 19; 2818) *Goldschmidt.* £280
- **Pantometrum Kircherianum, hoc est, Instrumentum Geometricum Novum, à ... P. Athanasio Kirchero.** Würzburg, 1665. Sm. 4to. Very browned thro.-out, printing flaw on 2M4. Cont. vell., soiled. From Honeyman Collection. (S. May 19; 2817) *Hill.* £80
- **Pysica Curiosa, sive mirabilia naturae et artis.** Würzburg, 1667. 2nd. Edn. 4to. Hf.-title torn & creased, 60 engraved plts. (of 61, lacks plt. 44), corner torn from 4 plts., slightly affecting engr., corner torn from 5F4 affecting 7 lines of text, a few sm. tears, some ll. slightly spotted or soiled, a few ll. slightly defect. in inner margin. Cont. vell., nail damage in spine. (S. Feb.23; 101) *Hackhofer.* £200
- **Technica Curiosa, sive Mirabilia Artis, libris XII Comprehensa.** Würzburg, 1664. 1st. Edn. 4to. Lacks 1 plt. at p. 926, a few plts. with short tears or sm. holes, some browning & slight soiling, owner's inscr. on engraved title. Cont. vell., soiled, hf. red mor. case. From Honeyman Collection. (S. May 19; 2816) *Zeitlin & Verbrugge.* £260
- **- Anr. Copy.** Stained, lightly soiled in pts. Lacks ties, stained. (HK. Nov.18-21; 743) DM 2,000

SCHOTT, Gaspar–HORNIGK, L.V.
- **Magia Optica.–Politica Medica.** Bamberg; Frankfurt, 1671; 1638. 1st. German Edn. (1st. work). 2 works in 1 vol. 4to. 1st. title defect. at margin & bkd., 2 index ll. to 1st. work with sm. tears at foot, minimal text loss, index ll. to 2nd. work half lacking & title lf. & 1st. lf. with reprd. tears, lightly soiled thro.-out, some sm. stains or browning. Later vell. (D. Dec.11-13; 228) DM 1,000

SCHOUTEN, William Corneliszoon
See–BRY, Theodore de & others

SCHRAEMBL, F.A.
- **Allgemeiner Grosser Atlas.** Vienna, 1800. Imp. fo. Maps slightly soiled, 1 map defect., 1 bnd. in twice. Cont. leath., defect., spine reprd. at head & foot. (R. Oct. 14-18; 1561) DM 4,500

SCHRAG, Karl
- **By the Sea.** Priv. Ptd., [1966]. (18) numbered on velin d'arches, & with an orig. cancelled metal plt. 4to. Loose as iss. in folding cl. box. Each etching numbered & sigd. by Schrag. (SG. Apr.2; 272) $1,300

SCHREBER, Johann Christian Daniel
- **Beschreibung der Graser nebst ihren Abbildungen nach de Natur.** Leipzig, 1769-74. 1st. Edn. 2 pts. (fascicules 1 & 2 only of 2nd. pt.). Fo. 29 hand-cold. plts. only (of 40) 19th. C. hf. mor. W.a.f.; from Chetham's Liby., Manchester. (C. Nov.27; 366) *Lange.* £60
- **[-] [Die Säugethiere nach der Natur mit Beschreibungen].** Ill.:– A. Fleischmann, I. Nussbiegel, H.I. Tyroff & others. [Erlangen], [1776-78 & 1827/28]. Plt. vol 2. Lge. 4to. Cont hf. leath., gt. spine. (HK. Nov.18-21; 744) DM 460

SCHRECKENFUCHS, Erasmus Oswald
- **Commentaria, in Novas Theoricas Planetarum Georgii Purbachii. (& two other works).** Basle, 1556. 1st. Edn. 3 works in 1 vol. Fo. 1 double-p. diagram slightly wormed, title soiled & with author's name struck out, lge. hole in a2 affecting text, some browning, a few ll. marginally stained. 18th. C. cf., worn. W.a.f.; bkplt. of Earl of Kinnoul; from Honeyman Collection. (S. May 19; 2820) *McKittrick.* £240

SCHREIBER, C. von
- **Beyträge zur Geschichte und Kenntniss Meteorischer Stein- und Metallmassen.** Wien, 1820. Only Edn. 9 litho plts., 1 double-p., 1 engraved map, liby. stps. on title recto & verso & plt. versos. Cont. hf. leath. (R. Oct.14-18; 236) DM 620

SCHREIBER, Lady Charlotte
- **Journals.** Ed.:– Montague Guest. 1911. 2 vols. A few margins soiled. Orig. cl. gt. (SBA. Mar.4; 280) *Knight.* £160
- **- Anr. Copy.** Orig. cl. (SH. Jan.29; 194) *Reed & Sims.* £55

SCHREIBER, George
- **Buchsenmeister-Discurs; eine Neuerfundene Kugel-Taffel, Abtheilung der Stücke, Laveten und Visir-Stäbe, sambt einem Wohlbestellten Feuerwercks-Laboratorio.** Brieg, 1662. Fo. A few plts. slightly defect. & reprd., engraved title remargined & with key plt. mntd. on verso, some text browning, marginal annots. 19th. C. cf., rebkd., worn. Sir William Stirling's copy, with his lge. armorial bkplt. & blind-stps. on covers; from Honeyman Collection. (S. May 19; 2821) *Goldschmidt.* £1,000

SCHREIBER, H.
- **Freiburg im Breisgau mit seinen Umgebungen.** Freiburg, 1838. 8 (of 9) steel engrs., slightly soiled. Orig. bds. (R. Oct.14-18; 2151a) DM 750

SCHREIBER, Heinrich
- **Behend unnd Khunstlich Rechnung nach der Regel und Welhisch Practic, mit sambt Zuberaittung der Visier ym Quadrat und Triangel.** Nuremb., 1521. 1st. Edn. A8 misbnd. at end of quire D, slight soiling & discolouration. 19th. C. cf., gt. From Honeyman Collection. (S. May 19; 2823) *Dr. Martin.* £440
- **Libellus de Compositione Regularum pro Vasorum Mensuratione. Deque arte ista tota theoricae & practicae.** Vienna, 1518. 1st. Edn. Sm. 4to. Some stains & soiling, last lf. reprd. slightly affecting text, title guarded at inner edge. Mod. parch. bds., spine defect. From Honeyman Collection. (S. May 19; 2822) *Schaffer.* £170
- **Ein New Kunstlich Behend und Gewiss Rechenbuchlin, uff alle Kauffmanschafft.** [Frankfurt], [1544]. Some browning & staining, mostly marginal, single wormhole in last gathering. Mod. hf. vell. From Honeyman Collection. (S. May 19; 2824) *Dr. Martin.* £360

SCHREIBER, J.F.
- **Recueil d'Estampes ...** Esslingen, ca. 1840. Sm. fo. Plts. hand-cold., with captions in German. Old hf. mor. (SG. Apr.30; 287) $110

SCHREIBER, Johann, Georg
- **Atlas selectus von allen Königreichen und Ländern der Welt.** Ill.:– H. Moll. Leipzig, ca. 1750. Ob. 4to. Maps numbered with ink, first 10 approx. strengthened, slightly soiled. Limp orig. leath., defect. (R. Oct.14-18; 1562) DM 16,000
- **Geograph. Atlas zum Gebrauch f. Schulen.** Leipzig, [1816]. Lge. ob. 4to. Title soiled, maps stained in margins. Hf. linen. (HK. Nov.18-21; 1064) DM 460

SCHREIBER, Wilhelm Ludwig
- **Handbuch der Holz- und Metallschitte.** Leipzig, 1926-29. 8 vols. 4to. Orig. hf. linen, defect. (HK. May 12-14; 2280) DM 600

SCHREINER, William H.
- **Sporting Manual.** Phila., 1841. 1st. Edn. 12mo. Cl. Eugene V. Connett's copy, with early South Orange bkplt. (SG. Oct.16; 386) $1,600

SCHRODER, Johann
- **The Compleat Chymical Dispensatory ...** Trans.:– William Rowland. 1669. Fo. Lacks 1st. & last blanks. rust-hole in cl, slight marginal worming, some browning, stain on pp. 492-3, title slightly soiled. Cont. cf., worn, reprd. [Wing S898] (S. Jul.27; 379) *Kurzer.* £100
- **Pharmacopoeia Medico-Chymica.** Ulm, 1655. 4th. Edn. 4to. Lightly browned, old notes & underlining. Cont. vell. (HK. Nov.18-21; 745) DM 650
- **- Anr. Edn.** Ulm, 1662. 4to. Lightly stained & browned in parts. Cont. blind-tooled pig-bkd. wood bds. (R. Oct.14-18; 389) DM 1,000
- **[-] [Vollst. u. Nutz-Reiche Apotheke].** [Frankfurt & Leipzig,] [1709]. Fo. Lacks frontis., port., title & 3 ll. preface, slightly browned & soiled, slightly wormed in parts, first ll. defect. at margins. Cont. vell., soiled. (HK. Nov. 18-21; 746) DM 1,300

SCHRODER, Johanna
- **Allg. Hannoversches Koch- u. Wirtschafts- Buck. –Recept-Buch.** Hannover, 1842. 1st. Edn. Cont. linen gt., slightly soiled. (HK. Nov.18-21; 1638) DM 450

SCHRODER, Rudolf Alex
- **Neue Gedichte.** [Olten], [1949]. 1st. Edn. (40) numbered Privilege Edn. on Bütten. Oasis goat leath., gt. cover, spine, inner & outer dentelle, bd. s.-c. (HK. Nov.18-21; 2909) DM 420

SCHROT, Martini
- **Wappenbuch des Heiligen Römischen Reichs und Allgemeiner Christenheit in Europa.** Ill.:– Joh. Nell. München, 1580. 2nd. Edn. Fo. Old cold. title woodcut, 1 hf.-p. figurative woodcut, uncold. 1 double-p. woodcut plt., approx. 1,000 mostly old arms woodcuts, including 2 ports. Cont. leath., gt., spine reprd., very worn. (R. Oct.14-18; 151) DM 5,500
- **Wappenbuch des Heiligen Römischen Reichs ... Daneben auch der Geistliche Stand.** Munich, 1580. Fo. Double-p. woodcut plts. torn in fold, lacks last lf. (blank?), 1 lf. torn slightly affecting text, slightly spotted or soiled & dampstained in places. 18th. C. cf., gt. borders, arabesque centre-pieces & cornerpieces on covers, slightly worn & wormed, lacks 3 (of 4) ties. (S. Apr. 7; 310) *Burgess.* £1,000
- **Wappen Buch des Hohen Geistlichen vnd Weltlichen Stands der Christenheit in Europa, des Apostolischen Stuels zu Rom ...** Munich, 1576. 1st. Edn. 4to. Cont. MS. entries on end-paper, some pencil notes. Cont. limp vell., lacks 3 of 4 ties. Hupp exlibris. (HK. Nov.18-21; 298) DM 2,000

SCHROTER, J.F.
- **[-] Allgemeine Geschichte der Länder und Völker von America.** Ed.:– S.J. Baumgarten. Halle, 1752-53. 1st. Edn. 2 vols. 4to. Vol. 2 with some worming, 2 folding maps very defect., 1 lf. reprd. Cont. leath. [Sabin 77989] (R. Oct.14-18; 1725) DM 620
- **[-] - Anr. Copy.** Tear in frontis. reprd., minor marginal wormholes. Cont. cf., jnts. reprd. (SPB. May 5; 463) $325

SCHROTER, Johann Hieronymus
- **Aphroditographische Fragmente, zur genauern Kenntniss des Planeten Venus.** Helmstedt, 1796. 1st. Edn. 4to. Some browning. Cont. hf. cf., worn. Bkplt. of Radcliffe Observatory, Oxford, with cancel stp. on title; from Honeyman Collection. (S. May 19; 2825) *Quaritch.* £260

SCHUBART, Christian Friedrich Daniel
- **Sämmtliche Gedichte.** Stuttgart, 1842. 2 vols. Cont. hf. leath. gt., unc. (R. Mar.31-Apr.4; 650) DM 420

SCHUBERT, Fr.
- **Vier Gedichte von Rückert und Graf Platen.** Vienna, [1826]. 1st. Edn. Ob. fo. Title lf. with old owner's mark. New bds. (H. Dec.9/10; 1272) DM 420

SCHUBERT, G.H.
- **[-] Bilder aus dem Heiligen Lande.** [Stuttgart], [1839]. Ob. sm. fo. 38 lithographic plts., all but

SCHUBERT, G.H. [ ] Bilder aus dem Heiligen Lande. -contd.
1st. with accompanying ll. of text. Cont. marb bds. (PNY. Mar.26; 148) $200

SCHUBLER, Johann Jacob
- Ars Inveniendi . . .-Nützliche Vorstellung wie man Bequeme Repositoria, Compendiose Contoirs und neu-faconirte Medaillen-Schränke ordiniren kan. Nuremb., 1734; 1730. 1st. Edn. 2 works in 1 vol. Fo. Text of 1st. title lightly browned. Cont. leath., gt. spine. (R. Oct.14-18; 479) DM 1,800

SCHUCKING, Christoph B. Levin
See–FREILIGRATH, Ferdinand & Schücking, Christoph B. Levin

SCHUERMANS, L.W.
- Algemeen Vlaamsch Idioticon. Louvain, 1865-70, 1883. 2 vols. including supp. Orig. bdg. (LM. Nov.8; 96) B.Frs. 12,000

SCHULT, Fr.
- Ernst Barlach. Das Graphische Werk. Ill.:– after Barlach. Hamburg, [1957]. (600) 4to. Orig. paper bds. (H. Dec.9/10; 1942) DM 1,050

SCHULTENS, A.
- Haririi eloquentiae Arabicae principis tres priore consessus.–Consessus Haririi Quartus, Quintus & Sextus.–Monumenta vetustiora Arabiae. Franecker; Leiden; Leiden, 1731; 1740; 1740. 3 works in 1 vol. Sm. 4to. Slight browning & soiling, 1st. work with owner's stps. on title. Later hf. cf., worn. (S. Apr.29; 455) Loman. £90

SCHULTZ, Christian
- Travels on an Inland Voyage Through the States of New-York, Pennsylvania, Virginia, Ohio, Kentucky & Tennessee, & Through the Territories of Indiana, Louisiana, Mississippi & New-Orleans ... 1807 & 1808. N.Y., 1810. 1st. Edn. 2 vols. Some offsetting, slight foxing. Later marb. bds., covers loose. From liby. of William E. Wilson. (SPB. Apr.29; 244) $300

SCHULTZ, J.C.
- Danzig und seine Bauwerke. Berlin, 1872. 3 pts. in 1 vol. Fo. Margins slightly soiled & stained. Hf. linen portfo., defect. (HK. Nov.18-21; 1143) DM 2,500

SCHULZ, Benjamin
- Conspectus litteraturae Telugicae vulgo Warugicae. Halle, 1747. 1st. Edn. 4to. Some foxing. Bds., s.-c. (S. Apr. 29; 456) Maggs. £100

SCHULZE, J.H.
- Chemische Versuche nach dem eigenhänd. Manuscript Des Verfassers. Ed.:– Ch. C. Strumpf. Halle, 1745. 1st. Edn. Slightly soiled. Cont. sewed. (R. Oct.14-18; 288) DM 420

SCHURMANN, C.W.
See–TEICHELMANN, C.G. & Schurmann, C.W.

SCHUTZ, C.
- Historia Rerum Prussicarum. Zerbst, 1592. 1st. Edn. Fo. Some ink underlining, bnd. in D. Chytraeus Historica Continuation Rerum Prussicarum, Eisleben, 1599. 17th. C. leath. (R. Oct.14-18; 2381) DM 5,500

SCHUTZ, K.D. von
- Texas. Rathgeber für Auswanderer nach diesem Lande. Mit bes. Unterstützung des Vereins zum Schutze Deutscher Einwanderer in Texas herausgegeben. Wiesbaden, 1846. Slightly browned. Cont. linen, orig. wraps. bnd. in, unc. (R. Oct.14-18; 1735) DM 3,100

SCHUYLKILL FISHING COMPANY, Members of
- A History of the Schuylkill Fishing Company ... 1732-1888. Phila., 1889. Cl., gt. mor. spine, unc. Bkplt. of John Burgess Camac. (SG. Oct.16; 387) $300
- A History of the Schuylkill Fishing Company ... 1888-1932. Phila., 1932. 1st. Edn. Wraps., unc. (SG. Oct.16; 388) $140

SCHWAB, G.
- Die Argonauten. Ill.:– R. Seewald. Berlin, 1923. (300) numbered. Lge. 4to. Orig. hf. leath. Printer's mark & 1 litho. sigd. (HK. Nov.18-21; 2922) DM 520

SCHWAB, Gustav. Benj.
- Wanderungen durch Schwaben. Leipzig, ca. 1840. Ptd. title & 30 steel engrs. from 1st. Edn., no text, slightly stained in places. Loose in portfo. (R. Oct.14-18; 2168) DM 2,300

- - **Anr. Edn.** Ed.:– K. Klüpfel. Tübingen, 1879. Slightly soiled in parts, lacks 1 steel engr. Orig. linen, slightly worn & loose. (R. Oct.14-18; 2169) DM 2,100

SCHWAB, Moise
- Vocabulaire de l'angeologie d'après les Manuscrits Hébreux de la Bibliothèque Nationale. Paris, 1897. 4to. Title in facs. Cl. (S. Nov.18; 520) Rapaport. £70

SCHWABE, J.J. & others
[–] Allgemeine Historie de Reisen zu Wasser und zu Lande. Ill.:– after Gravelot, J. Punt. Leipzig, 1747-74. 21 vols., lacks vol. 2. 4to. Cont. cf. gt., vol. 6 spine slightly defect. at head, all vols. slightly soiled. [Sabin 3209] (D. Dec.11-13; 1402) DM 5,400
[–] – **Anr. Edn.** Leipzig, 1751. Vol. 9. 4to. Cont. leath., gt. spine. [Sabin 36810] (R. Oct.14-18; 1727) DM 750
[–] – **Anr. Copy.** Vol. 8. Lightly browned in parts, title recto & plt. versos stpd. Joints brkn. (R. Mar.31-Apr.4; 2548) DM 420
[–] – **Anr. Edn.** Leipzig, 1755. Vol. 13. 4to. Lightly browned, lacks plt. 10, title recto & plt. versos stpd. Cont. leath. gt., lacks upr. cover. (R. Mar.31-Apr.4; 2463) DM 750
[–] – **Anr. Edn.** Leipzig, 1756. 1st. German Edn. Vol. 14. 4to. Slightly browned in parts, some 10 pp. soiled, title recto & plt. versos stpd. Cont. leath. gt., spine & upr. cover defect. [Sabin 12138] (R. Mar.31-Apr.4; 2464) DM 750
[–] – **Anr. Edn.** Leipzig, 1757. Vol. 15. Lightly browned in parts, title recto & plt. versos stpd. Cont. leath. gt., spine & 1 corner slightly defect. (R. Mar.31-Apr.4; 2465) DM 500
[–] – **Anr. Edn.** Leipzig, 1758. Vol. 16. 4to. Lightly browned in parts, stp. on title recto & plt. versos. Cont. leath. gt., spine slightly defect. (R. Mar.31-Apr; 2466) DM 430

SCHWANDTNER, Johann Georg
- Scriptores Rerum Hungaricarum. Ed.:– M. Belius. Ill.:– A. Nunzer. Vienna, 1746-48. 3 vols. Fo. Slightly soiled or browned. Cont. vell. (R. Oct.14-18; 1201) DM 1,000

SCHWANN, Theodor
- Mikroskopische Untersuchungen uber die Uebereinstimmung in der Struktur und dem Wachsthum der Thiere und Pflanzen. Berlin, 1839. 1st. Edn. Some foxing, slight adhesion affecting inner margin of title-p. Mod. buckram, unc., orig. upr. wrap. (mntd.) bnd. in. From Honeyman Collection. (S. May 19; 2827) Friedman. £1,400

SCHWARZ, Arturo
The Large Glass & Related Works. Ill.:– Marcel Duchamp. Milan, [1967; 68]. (95) on specially wtrmkd. H.M.P., each vol. sigd. by author & artist. 2 vols. Loose as issued in cl. folder & 2 wooden crates with plastic slide-tops. (SG. Oct.23; 92) $3,200

SCHWARZENBERG, Johann von
- Memorial der Tugend. Ill.:– Hans Leonhardt Schaeufelein & others. 1534. Fo. Fragment from R2 to Dd5 only. Old marb. paper bds. W.a.f. (C. Nov.20; 205) Leath. £200

SCHWEGLER, J.
- Gemälde der Kapellbruecke in Luzern. Luzerne, ca. 1840. Ob. 4to. 74 triangular lithos. (1 defect.). Hf. cf., worn, orig. upr. wrap. bnd. in. (P. Jul.30; 3) Christoff. £230

SCHWEITZER, Albert
- Message de Paix. Ill.:– Hans Erni. 1958. (40) numbered on Velin d'Arches, & with extra suite of the orig. cold. lithos. on Holland paper. Fo. Loose as iss. in pict. wraps., folding cl. box. (SG. Apr.2; 109) $600

SCHWENCKFELD, Caspar von
[–] Vom Erkantnus Christi ... Drei Christliche Sendbriefe. [Ulm], 1555. 1st. Edn. 4to. Red ink underlining, some light browning. Bds., covered with paper from old printing, sm. stain. (H. Dec.9/10; 1371) DM 560

SCHWENTER, Daniel
- Deliciae Physico-Mathematicae. Oder Mathemat. und Philosophische Erquickstunden. Nuremb., 1636. 1st. Edn. Sm. 4to. Engraved title inlaid, lacks last blank, browned thro.-out, 3F1 reprd., a little marginal worming. Hf. cf., worn. From Honeyman Collection. (S. May 19; 2828) Hackhofer. £1,000

- - **Anr. Edn.** Nuremb., 1651-53. 3 vols. in 2. 4to. Some unif. browning, 3G4 vol. 1 reprd., a few minor paper & printing flaws. 18th. C. vell., hf. red. mor. cases. From Honeyman Collection. (S. May 19; 2829) Hackhofer. £1,400

SCHWENTER, Daniel–APIANUS, Petrus –URSINUS, P. SCHWENTER, D.–APIANUS, P. –URSINUS, P.
- Geometriae Practicae.–Centiloquium Circini Proportionum. Ein newer Proportionalcirckel; Organor Catholicum.–Trigonometria cum Magno Logarithmorum Canone; Magnus Canon Triangulorum Logarithmicus. Nuremb.; Nuremb.; Nuremb.; Cologne; Cologne. 1641; 1626; 1626; 1625; 1624. 5 works in 1 vol. Cont. vell. (R. Mar.31-Apr.4; 1195) DM 2,500

SCHWERD, Friedrich Magnus
- Die Beugungserscheinungen aus den Fundamental-gesetzen der Undulationstheorie Analytisch entwickelt und in Bildern dargestellt. Mannheim, 1835. 1st. Edn. 4to. Loosely inserted advt. lf., some foxing, 2 ll. with stps. Orig. ptd. bds., spotted, hf. red mor. case. Pres. copy; from Honeyman Collection. (S. May 19; 2830) Goldschmidt. £90
- - **Anr. Copy.** No advt. lf., some foxing & light staining. Pres. copy; bkplt. of Herbert McLean Evans; from Honeyman Collection. (S. May 19; 2831) Zeitlin & Verbrugge. £70

SCHWERDT, Charles Francis George Richard
- Hunting, Hawking, Shooting. L., 1928. (300). 4 vols. 4to. Orig. hf. mor. (SPB. Oct.1; 96) $2,700
- - **Anr. Edn.** L., priv. ptd., 1928-37. (300) numbered, sigd. 4 vols. 4to. Prospectus loosely inserted. Hf. mor. gt., partly unc. Moncure Biddle bkplt. (CNY. May 22; 212) $2,600
- - **Anr. Copy.** John A. Saks copy. (CNY. Oct.1; 204) $2,400

SCHWIEDLAND, F.A.
- Esquisses de la Vie Populaire en Hongrie. Pesth, [1856]. Fo. Some foxing, etc. affecting a few plts., some plts. from a smaller copy? Cl. gt. (BS. Jun.11; 390) £85
- - **Anr. Copy.** Foxed thro.-out. Hf. mor. (BS. Jun.11; 389) £50

SCHWITTERS, Kurt
- Merz 6. Hannover, 1923. Orig. wraps., owner's mark on verso wraps. (H. Dec.9/10; 2340) DM 640

SCHWITTERS, Kurt & Steinitz, Käte
- Die Märchen von Paradies. Hannover, 1924. Vol. 1, all publd. 4to. Orig. bds. (HK. May 12-14; 2054) DM 1,600

SCHWOB, Marcel
- La Croisade des Enfants. Ill.:– Daragnès. Paris, 1930. (100) on Arches vell., numbered & sigd. 4to. Mor. by Jacques Anthoine Legrain after Pierre Legrain, covers & spine decor. with mosaic geometrical figure, watered silk doubls. & end-papers, wrap. & spine preserved, s.-c. (HD. Jun.25; 407) Frs. 5,200

SCHWOB, Sigismundus
See–SUEVUS or SCHWOB, Sigismundus

SCHYRELLUS DE RHEITA, Antonio Maria
- Oculus Enoch et Eliae sive Radius Sidereomysticus; [sive Theo-Astronomia]. Antw., 1645. 1st. Edn. 2 pts. in 1 vol. Fo. Some ll. browned, a few ll. wormed in lr. margins. Cont. cf., gt., rebkd. preserving old spine, covers worn. From Honeyman Collection. (S. May 19; 2832) Wynter. £1,100

SCILLA, Agostino
- De Corporibus Marinis Lapidescentibus ... Rome, 1752. 2nd. Edn. 4to. Lf. to readers inserted from previous edn.(?). 19th. C. buckram. From Chetham's Liby., Manchester. (C. Nov.27; 367) Taylor. £70
- La Vana Speculazione Disingannata sal Senso. Naples, 1670. 4to. Dampstained. Cont. vell. (SH. Jun.18; 18) King. £75

SCLATER, Philip Lutley
- A Monograph of the Birds forming the Tanagrine Genus Calliste. 1857. Mod. red hf. mor. (C. Jul.15; 203) Taylor. £580
- A Monograph of the Jacamars & Puff-Birds. Ill.:– J.G. Keulemans. [1879]-82. 4to. Cont. hf. mor. (C. Mar.18; 100) Pillar. £1,400
- - **Anr. Copy.** Cont. red hf. mor., spine gt. (C. Nov.5; 140) Quaritch. £1,100

SCLATER, P.L. (Ed.)
See–IBIS

SCLATER, Philip Lutley & Oldfield, Thomas
– The Book of Antelopes. 1894-1900. 4 vols. 4to. 1 plt. loose. Hf. mor. gt. (P. May 14; 310)
Quaritch. £2,000
– – **Anr. Edn.** 1899-1900. 4 vols. 4to. Cont. hf. mor., spines gt. (C. Mar.18; 101)
Quaritch. £2,600

SCLATER, William Lutley & Stark, Arthur C.
– The Birds of South Africa. 1900-06. 4 vols. Orig. cl. (P. Nov.13; 224)
Quaritch. £360
– – **Anr. Copy.** Sm. repair to title of vol. 1, a few marginal tears to vol. 3. Hf. mor. gt. (TA. Jun.18; 40) £240

SCORESBY, William Jnr.
– Journal of a Voyage to the Northern Whale-Fishery ... Edinb., 1823. 1st. Edn. Cf.-bkd. bds., upr. cover detchd., spine torn. Pres. copy from James B. Ford to Frederick S. Dellenbaugh. [Sabin 78171] (SPB. Jun.22; 124) $375
– – **Anr. Copy.** Folding maps backed with linen, plts. cropped at fore-edge. Recent hf. mor. & marb. bds. (CB. Dec.9; 11)
Can. $550

SCORESBY, William–FELLOWS, William Dorset.
– Narrative of the Loss of the Esk & Liveley, Greenland Whalers.–Narrative of the Loss of the Lady Hobart Packet. 1826; 1803. 2nd. work with crudely hand-cold. frontis. Paper wraps., stitched; cont. hf. mor., unc. (C. Nov.6; 334)
Quaritch. £170

SCOT, Reginald
– The Discoverie of Witchcraft. 1584. 1st. Edn. 4to. With the unpaginated ll. between sigs. 2d & 2e, worming at head of 1st. sig., slightly affecting running-title. Mor. by Ramage. [STC 21864] (C. Nov.19; 20) *Huber.* £2,000
– – **Anr. Copy.** Lacks G1-H2, Q8-R8, T2-T3, ll. containing woodcut ills., some shaving with loss of headline, some corners torn away, some ll. loose & soiled, some browning. Early 19th C. hf. cf., worn. W.a.f. (S. May 5; 287) *Rix.* £130

SCOT, Thomas
– Philomythie or Philomythologie, wherin outlandish Birds, Beasts & Fishes are taught to speake true English. 1616. 2nd. Edn. 2 pts. in 1 vol. Spotted. Cont. cf. [NSTC 21870] (SH. Jun.11; 41) *Bennett.* £100
– Philomythie or Philomythologie.–The Second Part of Philomythie or ... 1622 [1612]; 1625. 1st. Edn. (2nd. pt.). 2 pts. in 1 vol. 1st. work: margins restored, pt. of plt. area in facs., margins & corners of 10 other ll. restored, 1 touching text, 2nd. work: margins of last lf. restored. 19. C. mor. (STC 21871; 21871a.7) (C. Nov.19; 37)
Quaritch. £140

SCOTLAND
– Atlas of Scotland. Ill.:– William Home Lizars. Edinb., 1832. Fo. Cont. hf. roan. W.a.f. (C. Nov.6; 239) *Gable.* £300
– Lawes & Actes of Parliament Maid be King James the First & his Successours. Ed.:– Sir J. Skene. Edinb., 1597. 3 Pts. Fo. Title with lf. 'In libri frontespicium' mntd., folding table reprd., early owners inscrs. & marginalia. Early 18th. C. cf., rebkd. [STC 21877] (S. Mar.16; 76)
Thomas. £170
– The Principal Acts of the General Assembley of the Church of Scotland. Edinb., 1691-1709. 17 pts. in 1 vol. Fo. Cont. cf., worn. (SH. Jul.23; 202)
Murray-Hill. £70

SCOTO, Francesco
– Itinerario overo Nova Descrittione de Viaggi Principali d'Italia. Padua, 1659. 3 vols. in 1. Pt. 1, R4 & 5 lacking. Cont. vell., soiled. W.a.f. (CSK. Jun.5; 26) £240
– – **Anr. Copy.** 3 pts. in 2 vols. Title of pt. 2 torn with loss. Old cf., rebkd. (CSK. Apr.24; 130) £220

SCOTS LAW TIMES
Edinb., 1893-94 (vol. 1) -1978. 100 vols. Cl., pt. of 1976 & 1978 in wraps. (PD. Apr.1; 46) £700
– – **Anr. Run.** 1914-79. 74 vols. Cl. (CE. Aug.28; 54) £600
– – **Anr. Run.** 1948-66. 19 vols. Cl. (CE. Aug.28; 56) £50

SCOTS LAW TIMES & Statutes
Times 1896-1968; Statutes 1911-28. 81 pts. Times

& 38 pts. Statutes, together 119 pts. Cl. gt. (CE. Feb.19; 13) £680

SCOTT, Alex Walker
– Australian Lepidoptera & their Transformations. L., 1864. Vol. 1 (of 2). Fo. Orig. linen, orig. pt wraps. bnd. in. (HK. Nov.18-21; 738) DM 680

SCOTT, J.E.
– Sir Henry Rider Haggard: A Bibliography. Takely, Herts., 1947. (500) numbered. Cl. (SG. Jan.22; 193) $110

SCOTT, James L.
– A Journal of a Missionary Tour Through Pennsylvania, Ohio, Indiana, Illinois, Iowa, Wisconsin & Michigan ...·Providence, 1843. 1st. Edn. 12mo. Some foxing & discolouration. Orig. blind-stpd. cl., gt. flower on panels, gt. spine, mor.-bkd. box. From liby. of William E. Wilson; the Littell copy. (SPB. Apr.29; 246) $750

SCOTT, John
See–NASH, Frederick & Scott, John

SCOTT, John, of Indianapolis
– The Indiana Gazetteer ... Centreville, 1826. 1st. Edn. 12mo. Browned & foxed. Orig. upr. wrap., lacks backstrip & bottom, restitched, worn, hf. mor. s.-c. From liby. of William E. Wilson; the Littell-Jones copy. (SPB. Apr.29; 247) $425

SCOTT, John, Poet, of Amwell
– Amwell: a descriptive poem.–Four Elegies, descriptive & moral. 1776; 1760. 1st. Edns. 2 works in 1 vol. 4to. Slight spotting & offsetting, cont. sig. of Bab. Arthington on hf.-titles. Mod. hf. mor. (S. Jun.22; 89) *Hannas.* £70

SCOTT, Peter Markham
–Morning Flight. [1914]. 4to. Orig. cl. With pen & ink drawing of a goose on front free end-paper inscr. by author. (CSK. May 8; 78) £60
– – **Anr. Edn.** 1935. (750) sigd. 4to. Orig. cl., d.-w. (C. May 20; 239) *Maggs.* £110
– – **Anr. Copy.** Cl., d.-w. (P. Jul.2; 214)
Ackermann. £70
– – **Anr. Copy.** Orig. cl., slightly soiled, d.-w. slightly worn. (S. Jul.31; 311) *Drabeck.* £50
– – **Anr. Edn.** N.d. Ltd. Edn., sigd. 4to. Cl., d.-w. (CE. Dec.4; 18) £115
– Wild Chorus. 1938. Ltd. 1st. Edn. 4to. Hf. mor. (S. Jun.1; 206) *Langmead.* £120
– – **Anr. Copy.** Cl., slightly marked. (S. Dec.3; 1123) *W. & W.* £90
– – **Anr. Edn.** L., [1938]. (1250) numbered on L.P., sigd. Lge. 4to. Gt.-decor. buckram, partly unc., d.-w., box. (SG. Apr.9; 394) $300

SCOTT, Robert Falcon
– Voyage of the Discovery. 1905. 2 vols. Folding maps in pockets, a few ll. slightly spotted. Orig. cl. (SH. Nov.7; 492) *Barnett.* £85
– – **Anr. Copy.** Orig. bdg. (TRL. Dec.10; 107) £72

SCOTT, Sir Sibbald David
– The British Army: its Origin, Progress & Equipment.–From the Restoration to the Revolution. L., 1868; 1880. 1st. Edns. 1st. work 2 vols., together 3 vols. Cl. (SG. Oct.30; 327) $100

SCOTT, Dr. Thomas
– The Anglers. L., 1758. 1st. Edn. 12mo. Mor.-bkd. marb. bds. (SG. Oct.16; 396) $250

SCOTT, Thomas B.D., Minister of Utrecht
[–] An Experimental Discoverie of Spanish Practises. 1623. 1st. Edn. 4to. 2nd. iss?, with the 'faire opportunities' & 'attaine' readings on p. 1. Later three-qtr. cf., worn. [STC (new edn.) 22077.3, Sabin 78363] (SG. Feb.5; 299) $130

SCOTT, Thomas, Secretary to the Earl of Roxburgh
– The Mock-Marriage. 1696. 1st. Edn. 4to. Tear in 1 lf. reprd., minor worming in title affecting text, reprd. Mor. by Sangorski. [Wing S2089A] (C. Nov.19; 144) *Arnold.* £60

SCOTT, Sir Walter
– The Border Antiquities of England & Scotland. 1814. [1st. Edn.?] 2 vols. 4to. Cont. red str.-grd. mor., covers with gt. & blind-tooled borders enclosing diamond-shaped ornament. From the collection of Eric Sexton. (C. Apr.16; 351) *Sawyer.* £130
– – **Anr. Copy.** L.P., 2 vols. Fo. Additional engraved titles & plts. on india paper, some offsetting onto text. Cont. russ. gt., 1 corner defect. (S. Apr.7; 421) *Symington.* £100

– – **Anr. Copy.** Cont. mor. (SH. Jul.9; 193)
Scott. £60
– – **Anr. Edn.** 1814-17. L.P. 2 vols. 4to. Cont. red mor., gt. (S. Mar.17; 390) *Vitale.* £100
– Ivanhoe. Trans.:– A.J.D. Defaucompret. Paris, 1827. 6 vols. 18mo. Cont. hf. russ., decor. spines by Meslant. (HD. Apr.9; 563) Frs. 1,300
– The Lady of the Lake; a Poem. Ill.:– Heath after Saxon (port.). Edinb., 1810. 1st. Edn. 4to. Cont. mor., fillet & border, richly decor. spine, inside dentelle. (HD. Apr.18; 155) Frs. 2,800
– The Lay of the Last Minstrel, a Poem. L., 1805. 1st Edn. 4to. Slight foxing. Cont. mor., fillet & border, spine richly decor., inside dentelle. (HD. Mar.18; 153) Frs. 2,800
– – **Anr. Edn.** L., 1806. 3rd. Edn. Crimson str.-grd. mor., gt. borders & spine. Fore-e. pntg. (SG. Mar.19; 168) $250
– Letters on Demonology & Witchcraft. Ill.:– George Cruikshank. 1830. 1st Edn. Mod. red mor., decor. in gt. with cat, moon, imps etc. on covers & spine. (S. May 5; 202)
Somerville. £110
– – **Anr. Copy.** 12 plts., each in 3 states–plain, hand-cold. & on india paper. Mod. red mor. decor. on sides & spine. (S. Jan.26; 208) *Durell.* £90
– The Life of John Dryden. L., 1808. 1st Edn., (50) on L.P. 2 vols. Lge. 4to. Extra ill. with over 100 engraved ports., inlaid to size. Mor., triple gt. fillet borders, rebkd. (SG. Apr.9; 250) $130
– The Life of Napoleon Bonaparte. Edinb., 1827. [1st. Edn.?] 9 vols. Without hf.-title in vol. I. Cont. hf. mor., spines slightly faded. (SBA. May 27; 109) *Armstrong.* £55
[–] – **Anr. Copy.** 9 vols. Extra-ill. with ports. Crushed three-qtr. mor., spines gt., raised bands. A.N.s. tipped in. (SG. Oct.9; 221) $325
– The Lord of the Isles. Edinb., 1815. 1st. Edn. 4to. Slight spotting, a few ll. loose, torn in margin. Orig. bds., unc., spine very worn, covers detchd. (S. Jan.26; 207) *Rhys Jones.* £50
– Marmion: a Tale of Flodden Field. Edinb., 1808. 1st Edn. Cont. mor., fillet & border, spine richly decor., inside dentelle, upr. cover slightly spotted. (HD. Mar.18; 154) Frs. 2,800
– – **Anr. Edn.** Edinb., 1808. 2nd. Edn. Old diced cf., rebkd., cl. s.-c. Fore-e. pntg.; from the liby. of Zola E. Harvey. (SG. Mar.19; 169) $190
– – **Anr. Edn.** Ill.:– Thomas Annan. 1866. Sm. 4to. 15 mntd. photographs by Annan, 1 on title. Orig. embossed mor., gt. (S. Apr.7; 422) *Fletcher.* £65
[–] Minstrelsy of the Scottish Border. Edinb., 1812. 5th. Edn. 3 vols. Cont. red str.-grd. mor., gt. & blind-tooled borders, spines gt. with lyres. Fore-e. pntg. in each vol.; from the liby. of Zola E. Harvey. (SG. Mar.19; 170) $900
– Oeuvres Complètes. Trans.:– L. Vivien. Ill.:– Marckl. Paris, 1845. 25 vols. Lacks title-pp. of vols. 8 & 23, foxed. Mod. hf. roan, corners, spine with raised bands. (HD. Jun.25; 409) Frs. 1,100
– The Pirate.–Woodstock; or, The Cavalier.–Anne of Geierstein; or, the Maiden of the Mist. Edinb., 1822; 1826; 1829. 1st. Edns. 3 vols.; 3 vols.; 3 vols. Cont. hf. mor. (SBA. Dec.16; 88) *Smith.* £50
– Poetical Works. Ed.:– J.L. Robertson. L., 1894. Tree cf., spine gt., 1 cover partly loose. Fore-e. pntg. (SG. Dec.18; 187) $210
– Provincial Antiquities & Picturesque Scenery of Scotland. 1826. L.P. 2 vols. Fo. Engd. titles, plt. on india paper in 2 states. Mor. gt. by F. Bedford. (S. Nov.24; 256) *Forster.* £130
– – **Anr. Copy.** 2 vols. in 1. 4to. Foxing. Hf. cf., central embossed Coat of Arms of Antrim. (CE. Jul.9; 205) £80
– Rokeby; The Lord of the Isles. Edinb., 1813-15. 1st. Edns., L.P. 2 vols. 4to. Later mor., gt. (SH. Jun.11; 212) *Forster.* £110
– Tales & Romances. 1824-33. 14 vols. Cf., worn. (BS. Feb.25; 316) £50
– Waverley. Edinb., 1814. 1st. Edn. 3 vols. Recent hf. mor., unc. (TA. Jan.22; 53) £140
– Waverley–Guy Mannering.–Rob Roy. Edinb., 1814; 1815; 1818. 1st. Edns. 3 vols.; 3 vols.; 3 vols. 12mo. 2nd. work with inserted engrs. from the 1836 edn. Old hf. cf., worn, qtr. mor. gt. s.-c.'s. (1st. work); hf. mor., partly unc., by Reilly, cl. case (2nd. work); & orig. bds., spines worn, qtr. mor. gt. s.-c.'s, unc. From the Prescott Collection. (CNY. Feb.6; 289) $350
– Waverley Novels. Edinb., 1814-32. 1st. Edns. 24 works in 78 vols. 12mo. Crushed crimson three-qtr. mor., by Rivière. (SG. Oct.9; 222) $2,000
[–] – **Anr. Edn.** Edinb., 1816-29. 1st. Edns. 49 vols. 12mo & 8vo. Some browning & soiling, a few ll.

SCOTT, Sir Walter -contd.
loose. Orig. bds., worn, some spines defect., a few covers detchd., unc. (S. Jan.26; 206) *Thorp.* £170
– – **Anr. Edn.** 1829-33. 48 vols. Prelims. spotted. Cont. hf. cf., gt. decor. spines, by M. Bell, Richmond. Ex-libris Lord Tyrconnel, with gt. ducal crests to spines. (TA. Jun.18; 267) £75
– – **Anr. Copy.** (TA. May 21; 456) £64
– – **Anr. Copy.** Hf. cf., worn & marb. bds. (CE. Dec.4; 184) £50
– – **Anr. Edn.** 1830-33. 47 vols. only. Plts., most spotted & soiled. Cont. hf. cf., slightly worn. (SD. Feb.4; 94) £60
– – **Anr. Edn.** 1836-39. 48 vols. Some spotting. Cont. hf. mor. (TA. Jun.18; 234) £50
– – **Anr. Edn.** 1839-33. 48 vols. Some title labels worn. Hf. cf., gt. (PD. Nov.26; 8) £60
– – **Anr. Edn.** Edinb., 1851. 48 vols. Cont. cf., some covers detchd. (SH. Jul.9; 111) *Wade.* £65
– – **Anr. Edn.** Edinb., 1852. Liby. Edn. 25 vols. Gt. panel. cf. (PG. Sep.3; 137) £80
– – **Anr. Edn.** Edinb., 1852-57. 25 vols. Cf., gt. (PD. Apr.1; 43) £220
– – **Anr. Edn.** Edinb., 1856-57. 48 vols. Cont. hf. mor. (TA. Nov.20; 470) £54
– – **Anr. Edn.** Boston, 1864. Household Edn. 50 vols. 12mo. Cont. hf. cf., spines worn. (SG. Aug.7; 399) $100
– – **Anr. Edn.** Edinb., 1865-68. 48 vols. Hf. cf. (MMB. Oct.8; 80) *Harrington.* £92
– – **Anr. Edn.** 1871. Centenary Edn. 25 vols. Hf. cf. gt. (P. Apr.9; 304) *De Metzy.* £60
– – **Anr. Edn.** Edinb., 1877. 48 vols. Slight browning. Rose cf. gt. by Tout. (SPB. May 6; 339) $1,000
– – **Anr. Edn.** Edinb., 1877-79. 48 vols. Spotted. Cont. hf. cf., spines gt. (CSK. Nov.21; 41) £120
– – **Anr. Edn.** L., 1892. Border Edn. 48 vols. Hf. red mor. gt. (SPB. Nov.25; 486) $500
[–] – **Anr. Edn.** 1895-96. 44 vols. Some spotting. Mod. mor.-bkd. bds. (CSK. Jun.19; 9) £70
– – **Anr. Edn.** Ed.:– A. Lang. 1906-01. 24 vols. Hf. mor. gt. (P. May 14; 227) *Wolfson.* £120
– – **Anr. Edn.** N.d. 48 vols. Hf. mor. gt., worn. (CE. Feb.19; 253) £75
– **The Waverley Novels.–The Poetical Works.** 1829-34. 48 vols.; 12 vols. Later cf. (SH. May 28; 91) *Howes Books.* £200
– **The Waverley Novels.–The Prose Works.–The Poetical Works.** Edinb., 1829-33; 1834-36; 1833-34. 48 vols.; 28 vols.; 12 vols. 12mo. Unif. hf. mor., spines gt. in compartments. (LC. Jun.18; 325) £220
– **Woodstock.** Edinb., 1826. 1st. Edn. 3 vols. Later cf., gt. fillet borders, spines gt., gt. dentelles. (SG. Mar.19; 272) $100
– **Works.** Paris, 1821-29. 70 vols. Cont. hf. cf. (CSK. Aug.15; 28) £80
– **The Poetical Works.** Ill.:– Charles Heath after R. Smirke & others. Edinb., 1830. 11 vols. 12mo. Three-qtr. cf., spines gt. (SG. Mar.19; 275) $120
– **Works.** Boston, River. Pr., 1912-1913. L.P. Edn. (375) numbered. 51 vols. Buckram, unc., unopened. (SG. Sep.4; 415) $150
– – **Anr. Edn.** N.d. 17 vols. Hf. red cf., gt. spine. (BS. Nov.26; 131) £110

SCOTT, Sir Walter–LOCKHART, John
– **Waverley Novels.–The Life of Sir Walter Scott.** Edinb., 1901-03; 1902. 48 vols.; 10 vols. Unif. hf. mor. gt., cl. bubbled, some stains. (SPB. May 29; 382) $450

SCOTT, William Bell
– **William Blake Etchings from his Works.** Ill.:– William Blake. 1878. Fo. A few spots, 4 dupl. plts. on India proof paper loosely inserted. Orig. cl.-bkd. bds. (SBA. Oct.21; 203) *Kawamatsu.* £65
– – **Anr. Copy.** Loose in cl.-bkd. pict. bds. (SG. Dec.4; 42) $100

SCOTT, William Henry (Pseud.)
*See–*LAWRENCE, John 'W.H. Scott'

SCOTT, Zachary
– John Emery. N.Y., Nov. 18, 1964. 1st. Edn., (200) not for sale. Orig. mor.-bkd. bds. (SPB. Nov.25; 405) $550

SCOTTISH CURRENT Law Statutes –SCOTTISH Current Law Year Book-Citators 1963-79; 1953-79; (ex 1969); 1948-56, 1948-71, 1948-76 & 79. 20 pts.; 26 pts.; 4 pts. Cl. gt., except 1979 Citator. (CE. Feb.19; 36) £55

SCOTTISH HISTORY SOCIETY
V.d. 1st. & 3rd. Series. 31 vols. only. Orig. cl. (SH. Mar.5; 287) *George's.* £115

SCOTTISH LAW REVIEW
1885-1963. [ex 1941]. 78 vols. Hf. cf. (CE. Feb.19; 35) £50

SCOTTISH NATIONAL ANTARCTIC EXPEDITION Report on the Scientific Results of the Voyage of S.Y. Scotia, 1902-04, under the Leadership of William S. Bruce
Edinb., 1907-15. Vols. 2, 3, 4 (2 pts.). 4to. Orig. cl. gt. (TA. Oct.16; 292) £150

SCOTTISH NATURAL HISTORY
– **The Annals.** 1892-1909. Vols. 1-18. Hf. cf. (CE. Apr.23; 324) £90

SCOTTISH NOTES & QUERIES
Aberdeen, Ca. 1891-1907. 1st. & 2nd. Series. Orig. bdg. (PD. Nov.26; 68) £55

SCOTUS, Michael
[–] **[Liber Physiognomiae].** [Venice], [Jacobus de Fivizano, Lunensis]. 1477. 1st. Edn. 4to. 36 ll., last blank (of 78), lacks all before fl, initials, chaptermarks & initial strokes supplied in red, slightly dampstained. Cont. limp vell., worn, upr. hinge brkn. [BMC V, 242; HC 14550; Goff M551] (S. Dec.8; 103) *Music.* £60
– – **Anr. Edn.** Venice, 23 May, 1508. 4to. Lacks last blank, slightly soiled in places, name removed from title, numerous blank sheets bound in at end, bkplt. of James, Earl of Southesk, a few old marginalia cropped. Early 20th. C. mor., gt. (S. Oct.21; 424) *Mediolarium.* £130

SCOURGE, The
Ed.:– [Thomas Lewis]. [4 Feb.]-25 Nov. 1717. Nos. I-XLIII (complete set) in 1 vol. Fo. Some dampstaining & soiling, etc., 1st. 2 Iss. torn & reprd., short tear reprd. in no. XXXI, holes in upr. margins. Cont. cf., worn. As a periodical, w.a.f. (S. Jan.26; 89) *Heron.* £190
– – **Anr. Edn.** 1811-16. Vols. 1-11. Cf., most bdgs. brkn. As a periodical, w.a.f. (BS. Jun.11; 85) £320

SCOWEN, P.H.
*See–*VOLPI, Charles de & Scowen, P.H.

SCRIBNER, Lynette L.
*See–*RIPLEY, S. Dillon & Scribner, Lynette L.

SCRIBONIUS, G.A.
*See–*RAMUS, Petrus–TALAEUS, Audomarus –SCRIBONIUS, G.A.

SCROPE, William
– **Art of Deer-Stalking.** 1838. Few ll. soiled. Mod. hf. mor. (SH. Apr.10; 332) *Hubbard.* £50
– – **Anr. Edn.** 1839. Red mor. gt., orig. cl. bnd. in. (P. Apr.30; 81) *Old Hall.* £130
– **Days & Nights of Salmon Fishing.** Ill.:– Haghe, Landseer & Williams. 1843. [1st. Edn.?] Panel. red mor. gt., worn. (CE. Nov.20; 174) £130
[–] – **Anr. Copy.** Lacks a blank tissue-guard. Gt.-decor. cl., unc. (SG. Oct.16; 398) $550
– – **Anr. Copy.** Plts. slightly foxed. Gt. mor. by Mansell. (SG. Dec.11; 96) $300
– – **Anr. Copy.** Some foxing etc. Gt.-pict. cl., unc. (SG. Dec.11; 97) $100

SCUDDER, Samuel Hubbard
– **The Butterflies of the Eastern United States & Canada.** Camb., Massachusetts, 1889. 3 vols. 4to. Hf. mor., gt. spines. (SPB. Oct.1; 213) $650

SCUDERY, Madelaine de
– **Almahide, or the Captive Queen.** Trans.:– J. Phillips. L., 1677. 1st. Edn. in Engl. Fo. Slight marginal worming in some ll. Cont. red mor., crowned cipher of Charles II repeated on spine. MS. bkplt. of Sall Sanders. (HD. Mar.18; 157) Frs. 4,000
– **Amaryllis to Tityrus . . .** 1681. 1st. Edn. in Engl. 12mo. Publisher's advts. at end, catchwords & sigs. occasionally shaved. Mor. by Sangorski. [Wing S2143] (C. Nov.19; 21) *Quaritch.* £700

SCULTET, Abraham–BELLARMINE, Card. Robert
– **Medulae Theologiae Patrum.–Commonitorium . . .** Neustadt; Strassburg, 1605; 1606. 2 works in 1 vol. 4to. Cont. mor., fillet, arms of J.A. de Thou & Gasparde de La Chastre, cipher repeated on spine. (HD. Mar.18; 156) Frs. 3,500

SCULTETUS Ulmensis, Johannes
– **L'Arcenal de Chirurgie . . . augmenté de plusieurs reflexions.** Lyons, 1712. 2 pts. in 1 vol. 4to.

Slightly soiled in places, slightly dampstained at end. Mod. bds. (S. Feb.23; 102) *Tybbalt.* £180
– **Armentarium Chirurgicum.** Hagae-Comitum, 1656. Vell., spine reprd. (LM. Mar.21; 198) B.Frs. 9,000
– – **Anr. Edn.** Venice, 1665. 5th. Edn. Slight soiling & offsetting. Bds., upr. inner hinge brkn. (S. Jul.27; 380) *Nagel.* £140
– – **Anr. Edn.** Amst., 1741. Sm. burn hole in last lf. Cont. cf. (TA. Jan.22; 201) £68

SCUPOLI, Lorenzo
– **Combattimento Spirituale.** Ill.:– Rousselet after Loyre. Paris, 1660. Fo. Cont. red mor., gt., with ermine in centre of covers & at each corner, ermine in each spine compartment with pointillé decor., inner gt. dentelles. (SM. Oct.8; 2005) Frs. 1,800

SEABURY, Samuel
[–] **Free Thoughts, on the Proceedings of the Continental Congress, held at Philadelphia Sept. 5, 1774; wherein their Errors are Exhibited, their Reasonings Confuted . . . By a Farmer.** [N.Y.], 1774. 1st. Edn. (24 p. iss.). Gt.-lettered cf. by Rivière. (SG. Mar.5; 405) $250

SEALSFIELD, Ch. (Pseud.)
*See–*POSTL, K.A.

SEAVER, James E.
– **A Narrative of the Life of Mrs. Mary Jemison, who was Taken by the Indians, in the Year 1755.** Canandaigua, 1824. 1st. Edn. 16mo. Copyright notice laid onto verso of title, final lf. in facs., browned & soiled thro.-out. Mod. cf. (SG. Jan.8; 212) $160
– – **Anr. Edn.** Howden, 1826. 1st. Engl. Edn. 16mo. Slight foxing & soiling, top of p. 5 burned affecting 1 word of text, pp. 5-8 detchd. Orig. ptd. bds., rebkd., upr. cover reprd., new end-papers, unc. From liby. of William E. Wilson. [Sabin 78678] (SPB. Apr.29; 248) $325

SEBA, Albertus
– **Locupletissimi Rerum Naturalium Thesauri Accurata Descriptio . . .** Amst., 1734-65. 4 vols. Fo. Some titles soiled, hf.-title to vol. 4 loose, some foxing. Cont. diced russ., gt. urn & floral borders on covers, later spines, covers detchd. From Chetham's Liby., Manchester. (C. Nov.27; 368) *Marcus.* £1,200
– – **Anr. Copy.** 4 vols. Lge. fo. All plts. & ills. with cont. hand-colouring., some unimportant foxing or browning in places, Latin & Fr. text, on thick paper. Cont. pol. cf., spines richly gt., some repairs to spines & corners. (VG. Dec.17; 1528) Fls. 52,000

SEBASTIANI, Antonio
– **L'Arte Poetica.** Venice, 1563. 1st. Edn. 4to. Later vell., gt. Signet arms on covers. (S. May 5; 40) *Crete.* £50

SEBEZIUS, Melchior ie Joh. Libaltus
[–] **[XV Bücher von dem Feldbaw].** [Strassburg], [1592]. Fo. Lacks title & some ll. at end, old MS. notes on end-ll., slightly browned or soiled in parts. Cont. blind-tooled pig-bkd. wood bds., 2 clasps, lacks ties. (HK. Nov.18-21; 1704) DM 650

SECCOMBE, Joseph
– **A Discourse Utter'd in Part at Ammauskeeg-Falls, in the Fishing Season.** Manchester, 1892. Wraps., folding. cl. case. (SG. Oct.16; 400) $150

SECKENDORFF, Vitus Ludovicus
– **Christen-Stat, in Drey Bücher Abgetheilet.** Leipzig, 1686. 1st. Edn. Slightly browned. Cont. vell., upr. cover soiled. (R. Oct.14-18; 1070) DM 650

SECRET HISTORY OF THE Most Renowned Queen Elizabeth & the Earl of Essex, by a Person of Quality
Cologne, 1695. 2 pts. in 1 vol. 12mo. Several ll. reprd., publishers advts. bnd. in. Old cf., recased. *(TA. Dec.18; 188)* £58

SEDAINE, Michel Jean
– **La Tentation de Saint-Antoine.** Ill.:– Borel, engraved by Elluin. L., 1782. 18mo. Red mor. by Cazin. (HD. Apr.8; 305) Frs. 2,100
– **La Tentation de Saint-Antoine.–Le Pot-pourri de Loth.** Ill.:– Elluin after Borel. L., 1781. 2 works in 1 vol. Cf., ca. 1810, decor. spine, gt. chain on covers, Greek inside. (HD. Dec.5; 190) Frs. 3,100

SEDDON, John P.
- Rambles in the Rhine Provinces. 1878. 4to. 14 actual photographs mntd. Orig. cl., loose. (SH. Nov.6; 252) *Kundlatsch.* £85

SEDER CHAMISHA TAANIOT Keminhag Sephradim
Amst., 1728. 1 tear. Leath., spine defect. (S. Nov.18; 698) *Kingsgate.* £50

SEDER Ha'ma'amadot Lifnei Rosh Ha'shanah Ve'yom Ha'-kimpurim Ve'sukkot
Venice, 1526. Pt. 2 only. 16mo. 379 ll. only (of 456), 2 ll. in dupl., title & last lf. in facs., tears, some affecting text, some staining. Blind-tooled leath., rebkd. (SPB. May 11; 185) $1,900

SEDER Hatarat Nedarim
Pisa, 1805. 12mo. Slight browning, stain. Wraps., slightly browned. Bkplt. of Samuel Dresner. (SPB. May 11; 186) $175

SEDER Me'ah Berachot-Orden de Bendiciones
Amst., 1687. 12mo. Some lr. margins reprd., browned, cropped, 3 ll. of index with holes, not affecting text, 5 words on p. 187 in MS. Hf. sheep, wormholcs. (SPB. May 11; 187) $800

SEDER SELIGHOT Le'chevra Kadisha Ve'takanot Le'chavura Kdosha
Kracow, 1810. All pp. mntd., upr. margins reprd. with loss of some letters. Mod. hf. leath. (SPB. May 11; 190) $175

SEDER TIKUN Shetarot Han'hugot Bimdinat Ashkenaz U'polin U'bisher Tefuzot Israel
Ed.:– Shmuel Ben David, of Kracow. Amst., ca. 1697. 24mo. Outer margins, reprd., cropped, browning, stains, index written in. Old sheep, worn. (SPB. May 11; 191) $1,600

SEDGEWICK, O.
- The Universal Masquerade: or, The World Turn'd Inside Out. 1742. 2 vols. 12mo. G7 of vol. 2 torn with loss of a few letters. Near cont. cf., jnts. worn. (CSK. May 8; 115) £70

SEEBOHM, Henry
- The Geographical Distribution of the Family Charadriidae . . . Ill.:– J.G. Keulemans. [1887-88]. 4to. Cont. hf. mor. gt. (C. Mar.18; 149) *Quaritch.* £450
– – Anr. Copy. Plts. hand-cold. Orig. cl. (CB. Sep.24; 46) *Can.* $650
- History of British Birds. 1883-85. 4 vols. in 3. Hf. mor. gt. (P. Nov.13; 221) *Graham.* £75

SEEBOHM, Henry & Sharpe, Richard Bowdler
- A Monograph of the Turdidae or Family of Thrushes. Ill.:– J.G. Keulemans. [1898-]1902. 2 vols. Lge. 4to. Cont. hf. mor., spines gt., partly unc. (C. Mar.18; 148) *Duran.* £1,600
– – Anr. Copy. Cont. red hf. mor., partly unc. (C. Jul.15; 204) *Weldon & Wesley.* £1,300

SEELANDER, Nicolas
See-REYHER, Samuel–SEELANDER, Nicolas

SEELEY, John
- Stowe: a description of the magnificent House & Gardens of . . . Earl Temple, Viscount & Baron Cobham. Buckingham, 1777. New Edn. 21 plts. & plans, 2 reprd., some browning of text. Cont. sheep, rebkd. (S. Jun.22; 90) *Weinreb.* £80

SEELEY, L.B.
- Horace Walpole & his World. L., 1884. Rebnd. in 2 vols. 4to. Extra-ill. Gt.-pict. & gt.-ornamental bdg., crushed red mor., unc., by Stikeman. (PNY. Oct.1; 529) $100

SEEMANN, Berthold
- Narrative of the Voyage of H.M.S. Herald. L., 1853. 2 vols. in 1. Orig. cl., gt. [Sabin 78867] (SPB. Jun.22; 125) £65
- Viti. 1862. 1st. Edn. Orig. hf. cf. decor. gt. spine. Complete with related letter. (PL. Nov.27; 125) *Turner.* £65

SEER, THE (Pseud.)
See-YAKOV YITZHAK Ha'levi of Lublin [The Seer']-CHAIM of Mohilev

SEFER Yetzirah
Koretz, 1779. 11th. Edn. 4to. Soiled, repairs, slight worming. Mod. bds. Bkplt. of Samuel Dresner, formerly in the liby. of Michael Sachs. (SPB. May 11; 192) $425

SEGAR, Sir William
- The Booke of Honor & Armes. 1590. 1st. Edn. Sm. 4to. Some ll. slightly torn & soiled. Mod. cf.

[NSTC 22163] (SH. Jun.4; 210) *Armstrong.* £80

SEGAR, William & Edmondson, Joseph
- Baronagium Genealogicum. Ill.:– F. Bartolozzi [titles]. [1764]-1784. 6 vols., including supp. Fo. MS. index to the Pedigrees mntd. at end of vols. I-V, many cont. & later MS. additions & corrections, some inserted. Cont. pol. tree cf., spines gt., rebkd. Bkplt. of Charles George Young, lately in the collection of Eric Sexton. (C. Apr.16; 352) *Traylen.* £620
– – Anr. Copy. Hf. mor. Not collated, w.a.f. (SG. Sep.25; 278) $675

SEGARD, Sir William & Testard, F.M.
- Picturesque Views of Public Edifices in Paris. 1814. 1st. Edn. 4to. Lacks hf.-title, occasional minor marginal foxing. Mor. gt., partly unc., by Morell. (C. Feb.4; 170) *Rose.* £210
– – Anr. Copy. All plts. somewhat foxed. Cont. diced cf., rebkd. with orig. spine preserved. (S. Jun.29; 261) *Elliott.* £50

SEGATO, G.
See-VALERIANI, D. & Segato, G.

SEGOING, Charles
- Mercure Armorial . . . Paris, 1652. 4to. Many arms in text heightened with colours. Cont. vell. (HD. Jun.29; 132) *Frs.* 1,400

SEGUIERIO, J.F. & Bumaldi, J.A.
- Bibliotheca Botanica. The Hague, 1740. 4to. Cont. cf. gt. (P. Feb.19; 163) *Dawsons.* £90

SEGUIN, A.
- De L'Influence des Chemins de Fer et de l'Art de les tracer et de les construire. Lüttich, 1839. Old MS. note on end-lf., wrap stpd. Old. hf. leath., orig. wraps. bnd. in. (R. Mar.31-Apr.4; 1162) DM 780

SEGURA, Juan
- Mathematicae quaedam Selectae Propositiones, ex Euclidis, Boetii, & Antiquorum Aliorum libris decerptae. Alcares, 1566. 1st. Edn. Sm 4to. Some dampstaining & discolouration, deleted inscr. at foot of title. Cont. sheep, gt. ornaments at corners & arms in centre of covers, worn. From Honeyman Collection. (S. May 19; 2834) *McKittrick.* £280

SEGUR-CABANAC, Comte Victor de
- Histoire de la Maison de Ségur dès son Origine 876 . . . Priv. ptd., 1908. Fo. Hf. cl., corners. (HD. Jun.29; 133) *Frs.* 1,100

SEGUY, E.A.
- Bouquets et Frondaisons. Paris & N.Y., ca. 1925. Tall fo. Loose as issd. in orig. bd. portfo. with cold. decor., linen ties. (SG. Oct.9; 223) $475
- Suggestions pour Etoffes et Tapis. Paris, ca. 1925. Tall fo. Loose as issd. in orig. bd. folder, linen ties. (SG. Oct.9; 224) $600

SEIDA UND LANDENSBERG, Baron Franz Eugen von
- Denkbuch der Franzoesischen Revolution von dem Todestage Ludwigs XVI . . . bis zur Einfuhrung der Konsularregierung, den 9ten November 1799. Memmingen, 1817-19. Vol. I 2nd. Edn. 2 vols. Ob. 4to. 4 wood engravings pasted into margins, 1 onto verso of a plt., newspaper cutting pasted on verso of title, slightly spotted, liby. stps. on titles & some ll., a few slightly affecting text. Cont. hf. roan. (S. Dec.8; 100) *Robinson.* £100

SEIDLITZ, Woldemar von
- History of Japanese Colour-Prints. L., 1910. 1st. Edn. 4to. Gt.-decor. cl., worn. (SG. Dec.4; 195) $120
– – Anr. Copy. Frontis. loose. (SG. Mar.12; 215) $110
- Die Radierungen Rembrandts. Leipzig, 1922. 4to. Orig. hf. leath., end-ll. soiled, worn, spine defect. (HK. Nov.18-21; 3478) DM 450

SEITZ, Dr. Adalbert
- Macrolepidoptera of the World; The African Rhopalocera. 1925. Vol. 13 in 2 vols. (including 1 of plts.). 4to. Hf. mor. (P. Oct.23; 217) *Dillon.* £70

SEKAI Toji Zenshu
- Catalogue of World's Ceramics. 1955-56. Vols. 4-6, 11 & 12 only (of 16). Orig. cl., s.-c.'s. (S. Sep.30; 440) £110

SEKIRA [Pole-Axe]
Ed.:– [M.M. Brodovski]. St. Petersb., 1905-06.

Nos. 1-14. Fo. Unbnd. (SH. Feb.5; 123) *De la Casa.* £100

SELBY, Prideaux John
- Illustrations of British Ornithology. [1819]-34. 4 vols. Fo. & 8vo. 2 engd. titles, 219 hand-cold. plts., 4 uncold. plts. Hf. cf. gt., covers loose. (P. Jun.11; 25) *Traylen.* £7,000
– – Anr. Edn. [Wtrmkd. 1821-27]. 1st. Series: Land Birds, 4 pts. only; 2nd. Series: Waterbirds, 1 pt. only. Fo. Some plts. affected by damp, mainly marginal, text of pt. 5 of 'Waterbirds' loosely inserted. Orig. wraps., worn. W.a.f. (CSK. Sep.26; 221) £420
– – Anr. Edn. Edinb. & L., n.d.-1834 [wtrmarked. 1818-33]. 2 vols. Fo. Occasional spotting, possibly vol. 1 lacks a plt., whilst vol. 2 contains an additional one not normally called for. Mid. 19th. C. hf. cf., covers detchd. (CSK. Oct.24; 179) £1,600
- The Natural History of Parrots. Ill.:– Lear. Edinb., 1836. Embossed leath., reprd. (S. Dec.3; 1124) *Hill.* £65
See-JARDINE, Sir William & Selby, Prideaux John

SELDEN, John
- Historical & Political Discourse on the Laws & Government of England. Ed.:– Nathaniel Bacon. 1689. Fo. Advt. lf., sm. tear in 2F1 just affecting 1 line. Cont. spr. cf., spine slightly worn. [Wing S2428] (S. May 5; 337) *Frost.* £65
– – Anr. Copy. Old cf., rebkd. (SG. Sep.25; 279) $180
- Mare Clausum seu de Dominio Maris . . . 1635. 1st. Edn. Sm. fo. Cont. spr. cf. [STC 22175] (S. Mar.16; 142) *Fletcher.* £380
– – Anr. Edn. Leiden; 1636. 12mo. 1 or 2 ll. slightly browned, sig. of 'Buckinghamshire' on fly.-lf. Early 18th. C. Fr. mor., red mor. only on covers shaped to irregular 'carved design, semé with sm. fleurons, gt., pomegranate, gt., at each corner in wide border of quadrilobes & double ogees semé with fleurons, flat spine gt. in alternate compartments with tulip head & red mor. onlay, each of different shape, seme with fleurons, inner gt. dentelles, gt. & cold. flowered endpapers with design, 1 lr. corner worn, mod. mor.-bkd. s-c. [NSTC 22175.3] (SM. Oct.8; 2006) *Frs.* 10,100
- Opera Omnia. 1726. 3 vols. in 6. Fo. Cont. cf., worn, some covers detchd. (SH. May 28; 195) *Pharos.* £60
- Table-Talk. 1696. 2nd. Edn. A few ll. foxed. Cont. panel. cf., spine reprd., worn. [Wing S2438] (S. Jan.26; 64) *Pharos.* £50
- Titles of Honor. 1614. 1st. Edn. 4to. Recent mor. gt. Pres. Copy; 17th. C. owner's inscr. of Charles Herrick, lately in the collection of Eric Sexton. [STC 22177] (C. Apr.15; 187) *Thorp.* £70

SELECT VIEWS OF LONDON & Its Environs
1804-05. 2 vols. Fo. Ex-liby copy with blind stps. thro.-out, mostly to margins. Cont. diced cf., rebkd., upr. cover of vol. 2 detchd. (TA. Jan.22; 398) £65

SELECTA Epigrammata ex Florilegio et alia . . .
Rome, 1608. Cont. red mor., gt.-tooled decors. on upr. cover enclosing sacred monog., arms of Nicolaus Donus on lr. cover, spine gt. (SG. Feb.5; 48) $130

SELENUS, Gustavus [i.e. Herzog August II von Braunschweig Lüneburg]
- Cryptomenytices et Cryptographiae Libri IX. Lüneburg, 1624. 1st. Edn. Fo. 1 endlf. loose, lacks 1 lf. Cont. vell., defect. (D. Dec.11-13; 2253) DM 1,800
– – Anr. Copy. 5 or 6 pp. partly smeared with ink, not obliterating text. Old vell., spine loose. (SG. Feb.5; 302) $160
- Das Schach- oder König-Spiel. In Vier Unterschiedene Bücher. Leipzig, 1616. 1st. Edn. Lacks 2 copperplts., including lf. with printer's mark, double-p. plt. at end nearly detchd., pp. 459-66 loose, slightly browned. Cont. vell., reprd. tear in middle of spine. (D. Dec.11-13; 2292) DM 2,900

SELIGMANN, J.M. & Houttuyn, M.
[-] Verzameling van Uitlandsche en Zeldzaame Vogelen. Trans.:– G. Edwards & M. Catesby, J.M. Seligmann, M. Houttuyn. [Amst.], [1776]. 3rd. vol. Fo. 61 (of 105) engraved hand-cold. plts., some loose, some tears, some stained, some with names in Dutch written in right upr. corner, some

SELIGMANN, J.M. & Houttuyn, M. [–]
Verzameling van Uitlandsche en Zeldzaame
vogelen. -contd.
childish scribbling, mainly on versos of plts. Hf.
roan, badly defect. W.a.f. (VG. Nov.18; 1384)
Fls. 2,750

SELKIRK, Thomas Douglas, Earl of
– **Obscrvations on the Present State of the**
Highlands of Scotland. 1805. [1st. Edn.?]. Cont.
cf. Pres. copy. (CE. Jul.9; 191) £170
– – **Anr. Copy.** Gt.-stp. spr. cf. (CB. Dec.9; 243)
Can. $260

See-CHAMPLAIN Society

SELL, Godefried
See-KLEIN, Jacob Theodor–VINCENT, Levinus
–SELL, Godefried

SELLER, John
– **The English Pilot. Part I . . . Southern**
Navigation. 1709. Fo. 1 or 2 charts cropped at
edges, lge. chart creased & slightly torn at fold,
some dampstaining thro.-out, slight worming
through 2 charts. Cont. sheep, spine torn. W.a.f.
(C. Nov.6; 268) *Franks.* £160
– **The English Pilot. [Part III] . . . Mediterranean**
Sea. 1736. Fo. Disbnd. (P. May 14; 133)
Franks. £280
– – **Anr. Edn.** 1786. Fo. Lacks 4 (of 17?) double-p.
engraved charts, 2 halves of charts (other portions
excised), lacks 14 text ll. Cont. sheep, covers detchd.
W.a.f. (C. Nov.6; 269) *Franks.* £120

SELOUS, Edmund
– **Bird Watching.** Ill.:– Arthur Rackham. L., 1901.
1st. Edn. Deluxe. (150) numbered on H.M.P.
Haddon Hall Liby. series. Gt.-pict. vell., unc.,
unopened, orig. ribbon bookmark detchd.
Raymond M. Sutton, Jr. copy, extra cold. copy of
frontis. laid in. (SG. May 7; 258) $280

SELOUS, Frederick Courtney
– **A Hunter's Wanderings in Africa.** 1890. Cl.,
soiled. (CE. Nov.20; 79) £50
– **Travel & Adventure in South-East Africa.** 1893.
Orig. cl. gt. (P. Jul.2; 99) *Timmons.* £55

SEL'VINSKY, Il'ya
– **Zapiski Poeta [Notes of a Poet].** [Moscow &
Leningrad], [1928]. (3,000). Lacks title & folding
lf., a few tears, rather soiled. Orig. decor. wraps.
by El Lisitsky, worn, lacks spine. Inscr. (SH.
Feb.6; 360) *Lempert.* £65

SEMEDO, F. Alvares
– **The History of the Great & Renowned**
Monarchy of China . . . 1655. 1st. Engl. Edn. Fo.
Lacks lf. of advt. at end. Cont. sheep, worn. [Wing
S2490] (S. Sep.29; 182) *Remington.* £190
– – **Anr. Copy.** Cont. cf., mostly covered with later
cf., worn & recased. (S. May 5; 313)
Quaritch. £170
– **Imperia de la China y Cultura Evangelica en el,**
por los Religiosos de la Compaña de Jesus. Ed.:–
M. de Faria y Sousa. Lissabon, 1731. 2nd. Edn.
Fo. Some slight worming in lr. margin. Cont.
leath. gt., traces of worming, spine slightly defect.
(R. Mar.31-Apr.4; 2489) DM 620

SEMMELWEISS, Ignaz Philipp
– **Gesammelte Werke.** Ed.:– Tiberius von Gyory.
Jena, 1905. Orig. wraps., unc. & unopened. (S.
Jun.17; 760) *Pratt.* £60
– **Offener Brief an Sämmtliche Professoren der**
Geburtshilfe. Ofen, 1862. 1st. Edn. Slightly soiled
in parts. Hf. linen. (HK. May 12-14; 441a)
DM 700

SEMPLE, Miss
– **Costume of the Netherlands.** Ill.:– after Bartlett.
L., [1817]. Fo. Slightly soiled in parts. Liby. linen.
(R. Mar.31-Apr.4; 2654) DM 1,100
– – **Anr. Edn.** Ill.:– William Henry Bartlett. [1818
or later]. Fo. Text wtrmarked 1815-16, plts. 1818,
a few plts. browned. Cont. bds., worn & loose. (S.
Sep.29; 272) *Traylen.* £240

SEMPLE, Robert
– **Observations on a Journey through Spain &**
Italy to Naples. 1807. 2 vols. Cf. gt. (P. Oct.23; 60)
Brooke-Hitching. £55

SEMS, Johan & Jan Dou
– **Practijck des Landmetens . . . Vermeerdert met**
hondert Geometrische Questien met haer Solutien.
Door Sybrant Hansz.–Van het Ghebruyck der
Geometrische Instrumenten.–Tractaet van maken
ende Gebruycken eens nieu Gheordonneerden
Mathemtischen Instruments. Amst., ca. 1620; ca.

1620; 1620. 3 works in 1 vol. 3rd. work with 1
short tear (reprd.) in folding plt., pt. 2 of 1st. work
bnd. after 3rd., slight staining & discolouration.
Vell. W.a.f.; from Honeyman Collection. (S. May
19; 2835) *Rogers Turner.* £460

SENAC de Meilhan, Gabriel
– **La Foutromanie, Poème Lubrique.** Ill.:– Borel.
Sardanapalis, [1778]. 18mo. Foxcd, 6 figurcs (of
8). Imitation cont. marb. cf., decor. spine & covers.
(HD. Apr.10; 377) Frs. 1,900

SENANCOUR, Etienne Pivert de
– **Rêveries sur la Nature Primitive de l'Homme.**
1802. 2nd. Edn. (with new title dtd. 1802). Cont.
hf.-roan, marb., minimal worming. (HD.
Feb.18; 189) Frs. 1,220

SENCKENBERG, H.C. von
– **Gedanken von dem jederzeit Lebhaften Gebrauch**
des Uralten Deutschen Burgerlichen und
Staatsrechts. Frankfurt, 1759. 1st. Edn. Cont. hf.
leath., gt. spine. (R. Oct.14-18; 1435) DM 430

SENDAK, Maurice
– **Pictures.** N.Y., [1971]. (500) numbered, with a
sigd. reproduction. Loose as iss. in lge. cl.-bkd. &
floral design folding box. (PNY. May 21; 379)
$200

SENDIVOGIUS, Michael
[–] **Tractatus de Sulphure altero Naturae Principio.**
Cologne, 1616. 1st. Edn. Browned & stained, sm.
holes in F2-3, stp. & inscr. in margins of title.
Cont. limp vell. From Honeyman Collection. (S.
May 19; 2836) *Quaritch.* £260

SENECA, Lucius Annaeus
– **Opera Philosophica.** Treviso, Bernardus de
Colonia. 1478. Fo. 19th. C. paper bds., in
mor.-bkd. s.-c. [H14591*; BMC VI p. 892; Goff S
369] (C. Apr.1; 83) *Fletcher.* £500
– **[Opera Philosophica] Lucubratioes omnes.** Ed.:–
Desiderius Erasmus. Basle, 1515. Fo. Title brown,
a few ll. very slightly dampstained, a few
wormholes slightly affecting text. 17th. C. cf, over
wooden bds., spine worn, lacks clasps. (S.
Apr.7; 297) *Dr. Kubicek.* £100
– **Pistole del Moralissimo Seneca Nuovamente**
fatte volgare [by Sebastiano Manilio]. Venice,
Sebastiano Manilio with Stefano & Bernardino di
Nalli. 14 Apr. 1494. 1st. Edn. in Italian. Fo. Mod.
mor.-bkd. bds. [H. 14606; BMC V p. 545; Goff S
382] (C. Apr.1; 84) *Fletcher.* £340
– **Proverbios.** Trans.:– Pedro Diaz de Toledo.
Seville, Meinardus Ungut & Stanislaus Polonus.
22 Oct., 1495. Sm. fo. Blindstpd. cf. by Brugalla,
sigd. & dtd. 1959, s.-c. [BMC X, 41] (S.
Nov.25; 340) *Maggs.* £1,400

SENEFELDER, Alois
– **A Complete Course of Lithography.** 1819. 1st.
Edn. in Engl. 4to. Slight soiling, a few liby. stps. in
text. Mod. cf.-bkd. bds. (S. Jun.23; 334)
Quaritch. £420
– – **Anr. Copy.** Soiling thro.-out. Cont. hf. cf.
(CSK. Jun.19; 54) £220
– – **Anr. Copy.** Port. discold., slight spotting, liby.
stp. on title & plts. 19th. C. hf. mor., covers
detchd. From Chetham's Liby., Manchester. (C.
Nov.27; 369) *Dawson.* £200
– – **Anr. Copy.** Lacks frontis., title-p. mntd., 1 plt.
& text lf. partly brownstained. Mod. three-qtr. lev.
(SG. Mar.26; 409) $225

SENES MANEGG DI SPADA
Bologna, 1660. Roan spine, worn. (CE.
Nov.20; 73) £80

SENEX, John
– **An Actual Survey of all the Principal Roads of**
England & Wales. 1742. 2 pts. in 1 vol. Ob. 8vo.
Lacks title to pt. 1, several ll. reprd., some soiling.
Mod. rough cf. (S. Feb.10; 363) *Clark.* £140
– **[Atlas].** Ill.:– Senex & G. De L'Isle. [Senex maps
dtd. 1709-14]. Lge. fo. World map by Senex
defect. at fold with text loss, several maps with
tears & soiling at folds, all maps linen-bkd., most
with liby. stps. (sometimes on verso). 19th. C. hf.
mor. As an atlas, w.a.f., from Chetham's Liby.,
Manchester. (C. Nov.27; 370) *Taylor.* £900
– **A New General Atlas.** 1721. Lge. fo. 12
double-p. maps only (of 34), edges foxed at
beginning, some soiling & creasing (mostly to
text), map of Africa soiled & creased at edges, all
maps with sm. liby. stps. 19th. C. cl., upr. cover
partly detchd., spine torn. As an atlas, w.a.f., from
Chetham's Liby., Manchester. (C. Nov.27; 371)
Taylor. £450

– – **Anr. Copy.** 512mm × 305mm. Title page
detchd., browned & spotted in places. Cont.
cf.-bkd. bds., worn, covers detchd. W.a.f. (CNY.
Oct.1; 33) $3,200
– **New Geography.** Ca. 1740. 4to. Hand-cold.
engraved maps, most with engraved cartouches.
Old hf. cf., worn. (TA. Feb.19; 109) £120
See-OGILBY, John & Senex, John

SENGHOR, L.S.
– **Elégie des Allizés.** Ill.:– M. Chagall. [Paris],
[1960]. (420). 4to. Loose ll. in orig. wraps. (H.
Dec.9/10; 1993) DM 440

SENGUERDIUS, Wolferdus
– **Inquisitiones Experimentales. Quibus . . .**
Atmosphaerici Aeris Natura Explicatius traditur
. . . Adjectae sunt Ephemerides. Leiden, 1699. 2nd.
Edn. Sm. 4to. 8 engrs. mntd., slight spotting &
discolouration. Cont. vell. bds., hf. red mor. case.
Bkplt. of J.W. Six; from Honeyman Collection.
(S. May 19; 2837) *Crete.* £190

SENIOR, Nassau W.
– **Four Introductory Lectures on Political**
Economy. 1852. 1st. Edn. Slight spotting. Cont.
cf.-bkd. marb. bds., bkplt. of the Baker Liby.,
Harvard Business School, with cancellation stp.
(S. Jan.26; 256) *Bickersteth.* £55
– **Political Economy.** 1827. Cont. hf. cf. (CSK.
Sep.5; 14) £50

SEPP, Anton & Bohm, A.
– **Reisbeschreibung wie die selbe aus Hispanien in**
Paraguariam kommen. Nuremb., 1698. 12mo.
Later marb. bds. [Sabin 79165] (SPB. May
5; 465) $325

SEPP, Christiaan Andreas, Entomologist
– **Beschouwing der Wonderen Gods in de**
Minstgeachtte Schepzelen. Of Nederlandsche
Insecten. Amst., Priv. Ptd. 1762. 1st. Edn. Pt. 1
only (of 8). 4to. Plts. hand-cold., margins
somewhat discold., plts. with liby. blind-stps. 19th.
C. qtr. roan. From Chetham's Liby., Manchester.
(C. Nov.27; 372) *Junk.* £650
– – **Anr. Copy.** Vol. 1, Pts. 1-6 only. 30 hand-cold.
engraved plts., most with liby. blindstp. Qtr. roan.
(C. Mar.18; 102A) *Weldon & Wesley.* £55
– – **Anr. Edn.** Amst., 1762-1836. 1st. series. 5 vols.
4to. 4 (of 5) handcold. engraved frontis. & 245 (of
250) engraved plts., light stains in places. Cont. hf.
cf., slightly worn & loose, 2 spines slightly defect.,
unc. (VG. Oct.13; 144) Fls. 4,000
– **Beschouwing der Wonderen Gods, in de**
Minstgeachte Schepselen. of Nederlandsche
Insecten.–Beschrijvingen en Afbeeldingen van
Nederlandsche Vlinders.–Nederlandsche Vlinders
Beschreven en Afgebeeld . . . Amst.; The Hague.
[1728?-1860]; 1860-1900; 1905-27. 1st., 2nd. &
3rd. Series, together 17 vols. (8 + 4 + 5). 4to. 1st.
& 2nd. Series cont. hf. cf., some vols. rebkd.
preserving orig gt. spines, 1 upr. cover detchd.,
3rd. Series orig. wraps., unc., lacks 1 upr. cover.
(C. Mar.18; 102) *Junk.* £5,200

SEPP, Jan Christian
– **A Representation of Different Sorts of Marble.**
Amst., Priv. Ptd. 1776. 1st. Edn. 4to. Plts.
hand-cold., bkplt. pasted on to Dutch title. 19th.
C. hf. mor. From Chetham's Liby., Manchester.
(C. Nov.27; 373) *Angus.* £1,500
See-NOZEMANN, C. & Sepp, Jan Christiaan

SEPULVEDA, Juan Gines de
– **Opera.** Madrid, 1780. 4 vols. 4to. Cont. limp
vell., slightly soiled & loose. [Sabin 79180] (SPB.
May 5; 466) $175

SEQUEIRA, Angelo de
– **Livre do Vinde, e Vede e do Serman do Dia do**
Juizo Universal, em que se lhama a todos los
Viventes para Virem, e verehumas les Sombras.
Lisbon, 1758. 1st. Edn. Sm. 4to. Slightly soiled.
Qtr. vell. (SPB. May 5; 467) $125

SERA, Yosuke
– **Old Imari Blue & White Porcelain.** Kyoto, 1959.
4to. Orig. bds., s.-c. (S. Sep.30; 441) £60

SERANTONI, Giuseppe Maria
– **Dialogo Intorno alla Cagione della Celebre**
Aurora Boreale . . . 16 Decembre dell' Anno 1737.
Lucca, 1740. 1st. Edn. 4to. Cont. marb. wraps.,
worn. From Honeyman Collection. (S. May
19; 2838) *Crete.* £110

SERE, Ferdinand
See-LACROIX, Paul & Seré, Ferdinand

SERIMAN, Zaccaria
[-] **Viaggi di Enrico Wanton** ... Berna [i.e. Bassano]. 1764. 2nd. Edn. 4 vols. Cont. cf., gt. spine. From the collection of John A. Saks. (C. Jun.10; 232) *Quaritch.* £300

SERLE, Percival
- **A Bibliography of Australasian Poetry & Verse** ... Melbourne, 1925. (250) numbered. Bds. & qtr. cl., slightly worn, unc. (KH. Mar.24; 351) Aus. $190

SERLIO, Sebastiano
- **Regoli Generali Architettura [libro quarto].** Venice, 1540. 2nd. Edn. Fo. Lacks G2 & G3, H3 torn & reprd., some ll. soiled. Cont. cf., worn. (S. Apr.7; 445) *Weinreb.* £150

SERMONES Sensati
Gouda, Gerard Leeu. Feb. 20, 1482. Fo. 12-line woodcut capital initial S on fo. 21r, spaces for other capital initials, supplied in red & blue, rubricated, faint dampstaining affecting B1-3. Old hf. sheep. From the collection of Eric Sexton. [BMC IX, 34, C 5376, Goff S442] (CNY. Apr.8; 72) $11,000

SERRA, Junipero
- **Torrens y Nicolau, Francisco. Bosquejo Historico del Insigne Franciscano V.P.F. Junipero, Fundador y Apostol de la California Septentrional.** Felanitae, 1913. 1st. Edn. Rebnd. in cl., orig. wraps. bnd. in, unopened. (SG. Jan.8; 396) $100

SERRA, L.
- **L'Arte nelle Marche dalle Origini Cristiane alla Fine del Gotico.** Pesaro, 1929. Fo. Publisher's cl. (CR. Mar.19; 237) Lire 240,000

SERRE DE RIEUX, J. De
[-] **Les Dons des Enfans de Latone, la Musique et la Chasse du Cerf. Poèmes.** Paris, 1734. 2nd Edn. Offsetting on 1 plt. Antique-style cf., old endpapers, gt. spine, Chateau de Rosny bkplt. (C. Apr.1; 169) *Hough.* £220

SERRES, Jean de
[-] **Recueil des Choses Memorables Avenues en France sous le Regne de Henri II** ... N.p. 1598. 10th. Edn. 16mo. Old spr. cf., spine gt. (SG. Sep.25; 281) $220

SERRES, Marcel de
- **L'Autriche, ou Moeurs, Usages et Costumes des Habitans de cet Empire.** Paris, 1821. 6 vols. 16mo. Cont. cf., spines decor. in gt. & blind, lge. plaque in blind on covers with gt. fillet, lightly worn. (HD. Apr.9; 564) Frs. 1,300

SERRURE, Raymond
See-ENGEL, Arthur & Serrure, Raymond

SERVICE Géographique de l'Armée
- **[Environs de Paris 1-10000].** Late 1890's. 4 vols. Lge. fo. Containing 288 maps, each with stp. in lr. right offering the map for 6 frs. Mor.-bkd. gt.-stpd. cl. (SG. May 21; 84) $425

SERY VOLK [Grey Wolf]
Ed.:- [S.A. Iznar]. St. Petersb., 1907; 1908. Nos. 1-26; nos. 1-23 in 22. Unbnd. (SH. Feb.5; 124) *Quaritch.* £380

SESTI, Giovanni Battista
- **Piante delle Citta, Piazze, e Castelli Fortificati in questo Stato di Milano.** Milan, [1718]. 4to. Mod. hf. vell. (SI. Dec.4; 530) Lire 650,000

SET OF INDIAN MINIATURES showing the different Castes & costumes of the Madras Presidency
Ca. 1840. 20 pts. Hand-painted on tulk (a clear cellophane-like material). Contained in booklet. (TA. Sep.18; 229) £100

SETON, Ernest Thompson
- **The Birch-Bark Roll of the Woodcraft Indians.** N.Y., 1906: Orig. ptd. wraps., slightly tattered. Pres. Copy. (CB. Sep.24; 312) Can. $100
- **Blazes on the Trail.** Greenwich, Connecticutt. Nov., 1928. Last ll. dampstained. Orig. wraps., lr. wrap. dampstained. Sigd. & inscr. (CB. Dec.9; 245) Can. $110
- **Life Histories of Northern Animals.** N.Y., 1909. 1st. Edn. 2 vols. 4to. Buck., worn, ex liby. (SG. Sep.18; 339) $120
- - **Anr. Copy.** 4to. Liby. stps. Orig. cl. (CB. Dec.9; 246) Can. $260
- - **Anr. Edn.** 1910. 1st. Engl. Edn. 2 vols. 4to. Slight spotting. Orig. cl., partly unc. (S. Dec.3; 1125) *Silver.* £75

- **Studies in the Art Anatomy of Animals.** L., 1896. Fo. Foxed. Orig. gt.-decor. cl. (CB. Dec.9; 244) Can. $260

SETON, G.
- **A History of the Family of Seton.** 1896. (12) numbered, on L.P. 2 vols. 4to. Orig. cl., mor. rebkd. (SH. Jul.16; 173) *MacLaren.* £55

SETTLE, Elkanah
- **The Female Prelate.** 1680. 1st. Edn. 4to. Some lines cropped at foot, staining & some tears at edges affecting text. Recent mor. [Wing S2684] (C. Nov.19; 38) *Dutt.* £50
[-] **The World in the Moon.** 1697. 1st. Edn. 4to. Recent mor.-bkd. bds. [Wing S2729] (C. Nov.19; 145) *Quaritch.* £280

SEUME, Johann Gottlieb
- **Mein Leben.** Leipzig, 1813. 1st. Edn. Lightly browned. Cont. bds. (HK. May 15; 4898) DM 560
- **Mein Sommer.** [Leipzig], 1806. 1st. Edn. Title & p.3 stpd. 's', lightly soiled. Cont. style bds. (HK. May 15; 4899) DM 420

SEURAT, Georges
- **Les Dessins de Georges Seurat.** Ed.:- G. Kahn. Paris, [1928]. 2 portfolios. Fo. Orig. linen portfolios, slightly torn. (H. May 21/22; 1794) DM 520

SEUTTER, Matthias
- **Atlas Minor Praecipua Orbis Terrarum Imperia.** Augsburg, ca. 1750. Ob. fo. 20 (of 50?) engraved cold. maps. Bds. (HK. Nov.18-21; 1065) DM 2,200
- **Atlas Novus: Grosser Atlas Worinnen Enthalten alle die Geographische ... Mappen.** Augsburg, ca. 1730, or later. Thick Paper. Ob. lge. fo. Engraved pict. title/frontis., 2 engraved dedications, 237 engraved plts. 167 maps, 3 celestial & planisphere plts., 67 plans, G.J. Haupt's map, maps hand-cold. in outl., principal areas of most maps, plans, views, celestial plts. & frontis. fully cold., some staining, all plts. bnd. without centre fold, numbered in MS. thro.-out. Cont. cf., very worn. W.a.f. (S. Mar.31; 268) *Burgess.* £24,00
- **Atlas Novus sive Tabulae Geographicae Totius Orbis** ... Augsburg, ca. 1730, or later. Fo. Pict. engraved title, 103 double-p. engraved maps, plan, 2 tables, lge. engraved folding maps, the maps hand-cold. in outl., most principal areas & title fully cold., some maps reprd., numbered in Ms. on map versos, not bnd. in order, new end-ll., later guards thro.-out. Cont. hf. cf. marb. bds., marb. cl. pull-off case, worn. W.a.f. (S. Mar.31; 269) *Span.* £6,500
- - **Anr. Edn.** Augsburg, ca. 1732. Fo. Engd. title-p., engd. & ptd. dedication, privilege 1f., 2 text ll., engd. table of contents 1f., 170 (of 171) hand-cold., double-p. engd. maps, plans, views & tables, several stained, approx. 20 maps reprd.with tape. Cont. panel. cf., very worn. (CNY. May 22; 29) $22,000

SEVEN YEARS WAR IN CANADA, 1756-1763: a Volume of Records & Illustrations together with a Pictorial Travelogue
Toronto, [1934]. 1st. Edn. 4 folding maps in cover pocket. Buckram. (SG. Mar.5; 81) $120

SEVEREN, Gilliodts, Van
- **Coutumes des Pays et Comté de Flandre. Coutume du Franc de Bruges.-Coutume de la Ville de Bruges.** Brussels, 1880; 1874-75. 3 vols. + 2 vols. 4to. Sewed. (LM. Mar.21; 67) B.Frs. 7,000

SEVERIM DE FARIA, M.
- **Noticias de Portugal.** Lisbon, 1655. 1st. Edn. Fo. Browned thro.-out. Cont. cf. (SH. Nov.6; 253) *Duran.* £100
- - **Anr. Copy.** Cf. (DS. May 22; 879) Pts. 23,000

SEVERINUS, Marcus Aurelius
- **Vipera Pythia id est de Viperae Natura, Veneno etc.** Padua, 1650. 4to Tear in N2, corner of Eel torn with loss of text. Vell. (S. Dec.2; 620) *Elliot.* £65

See-FABRICIUS Hildanus, Guilelmus
-SEVERINUS, Marcus Aurelius

SEVIGNE, Marie de Rabutin Chantal, Marquise de
- **Letters from the Marchioness de Sevigné to her Daughter the Countess de Grignan.** L., 1927. (1,000). 10 vols. Hf. mor. gt. (SPB. Nov.25; 487) $325
- **Lettres.** Ill.:- after Devéria. Paris, 1823. 12 vols. Some foxing. Cont. hf. cf., spines decor. with raised bands. (HD. Jun.25; 410) Frs. 1,200

- - **Anr. Edn.** Paris, 1862-66. 15 vols., including album. Cont. mor.-bkd. marb. bds. (SBA. Jul.23; 653) *Cuenca.* £120
- **Lettres ... à ... sa Fille.** [Rouen], 1726. 2 pts. in 1 vol. 12mo. Lacks errata. Cont. spr. cf., decor. spine. (HD. Dec.5; 195) Frs. 1,850
- **Lettres à Mme. la Contesse de Grignan ...** -
Lettres ... nouvellement recouvrées ... Rouen, 1780. 9 vols. (8 & 1). Cont. marb. roan, decor. spines. (HD. Feb.18; 73) Frs. 1,600

SEWALL, Thomas
- **The Pathology of Drunkenness.** Ill.:- J.H. Hall. Albany, 1841. Fo. Orig. marb. bds., leath. spine brkn., Delavan's endorsement in upr. cover obscured by insertion of several cont. election tickets. (SG. Jan.29; 380) $120

SEWEL, W.
- **Die Geschichte von dern Ursprung Zunehmen und Fortgang des Christlichen Volcks, so Quäcker genennet werden.** [Jena], 1742. 1st. German Edn. Fo. Title slightly browned. 19th. C. hf. leath. (R. Mar.31-Apr.4; 232) DM 460

SEWELL, Anna
- **Black Beauty.** L., [1877]. 1st. Edn. 16mo. 8 pp. of advts. at end. Gt. decor. green cl., upr. cover with title on 1 line & sm. circular gt. vig. (Carter's bdg. variant state C), cl. s.-c. (SG. Apr.30; 289) $550

SEXTON, J.J. O'B
See-BINYON, Robert Lawrence & Sexton, J.J. O'B

SEXTUS, Empiricus
- **Adversus Mathematicos ... Gentiano Herveto Aurelio interprete. Eiusdem Sexti Pyrrhoniarum Hypotyposeon libri tres ...** Trans.:- Henrico Stephano. Paris, 1569. 1st. Edn. 2 pts. in 1 vol. Fo. Some browning, a few ll. stained, mostly in margins. Cont. vell., worn at corners. Armorial bkplt. of Joseph Estienne; from Honeyman Collection. (S. May 19; 2839) *Somma.* £100

SEYFRIED, J.H.
- **Poliologia, das ist Beschreibung aller Beruhmten Städte in der Ganzen Welt.** Sulzbach, 1683. 1st. Edn. 2 Pts. in 1 vol. 2nd. pt. lacks A1, engraved title torn, sm. wormholes. Cont. parch. bds. [Sabin 79635] (S. Mar.31; 503) *Warren Smith.* £130

SEYMOUR, Robert
- **A Survey of the Cities of London & Westminster** ... 1735. 2 vols. Fo. Cont. cf., rebkd. Bkplt. of Nathan of Churt, lately in the collection of Eric Sexton. (C. Apr.16; 353) *Elliott.* £65

SFONDARTUS, Pandulphus
- **Causa Aestus Maris.** Ferrara, 1590. 1st. Edn. Sm. 4to. Some browning & marginal staining, owner's entries on title. Cont. limp vell., spine worn. Armorial bkplt. of Turriana liby.; from Honeyman Collection. (S. May 19; 2840) *Roberts.* £140

SFORTUNATI, Giovanni
- **Nuovo lume. Libro di Arithmetica ... Co uno Breve Trattato di Geometria.** Venice, 1534 1st. Edn. Sm. 4to. 2 sm. holes in title & following 1f., some staining, old owners' inscrs. on title & annots. in margins & on last 2 ll. 19th. C. cf.-bkd. bds., worn. From Honeyman Collection. (S. May 19; 2841) *Pilo.* £110

SFORZIONO, F.
- **I Tre Libri de Gli Uccelli da Rapina con un Trattato de' Cani da Caccia.** Vicenza, 1622. 16mo. Hf. cf. (CR. Mar.19; 238) Lire 220,000

SHACKLETON, Ernest Henry
- **Heart of the Antarctic.** 1909. 1st. Edn. 2 vols. 4to. Orig. cl., d.-w.'s. (SH. Nov.7; 494) *Edwards.* £110
- - **Anr. Copy.** Orig. bdg. (TRL. Dec.10; 24) £50
- - **Anr. Copy.** Slight foxing. Some wear. (KH. Mar.24; 35.) Aus. $100
- - **Anr. Edn.** L., 1909. (300) with additional The Antarctic Book sigd. by party. Sm. amount of silverfish damage to 1 map & a free end-paper. 2 vols. in vell. & 1 qtr. vell., partly unc., backstrips spotted, papering of the bds. of 1 vol. defect. (KH. Nov.13; 535) Aus. $950

SHADWELL, Thomas
- **The Amorous Bigotte: with the second part of Tegue O Divelly.** 1690. 1st. Edn. 4to. Lacks portion of title affecting 1 word. Mor. by Sangorski. [Wing S2835] (S. Nov.19; 146) *Franks.* £110

SHADWELL, Thomas *-contd.*
– Epsom-Wells. 1693. 1st. Edn. 4to. Mor. by Sangorski. [Wing 2843] (C. Nov.19; 147) *Franks.* £90
– The Humorists. 1671. 1st. Edn. 4to. Slight dampstaining thro.-out. Mor. by Sangorski. [Wing S2851] (C. Nov.19; 148) *Arnold.* £130
– The Lancashire Witches & Tegue O Divelly the Irish Priest. 1682. 1st. Edn. 4to. Recent Mor.-bkd. bds. [Wing S2853] (C. Nov.19; 149) *Quaritch.* £120
– The Libertine. 1676. 1st. Edn. 4to. Mor. by Sangorski. [Wing S2857] (C. Nov.19; 150) *Pickering & Chatto.* £170
– The Scowrers. 1691. 1st. Edn. 4to. Lf. of advts. at end. Hf. mor. by Sangorski. [Wing S2872] (C. Nov.19; 151) *Arnold.* £60
– The Volunteers. 1693. 1st. Edn. 4to. Natural paper fault in 1 lf. affecting a few letters, slight foxing. Mor. by Sangorski. [Wing S2885] (C. Nov.19; 152) *(C. Nov.19; 152) Arnold* £60
– The Woman-Captain. 1680. 1st. Edn. 4to. Mod. mor.-bkd. cl. [Wing S2887] (C. Nov.19; 153) *Arnold.* £140
– The Works. 1693. 1st. Coll. Edn. 17 pts. in 1 vol. 4to. Some browning, a few ll. cropped at foot with some loss of text. Cont. mott. cf., worn. [Wing S2834] (S. Sep.29; 72) *Quaritch.* £950
– – Anr. Edn. Ed.:– M. Summers. L., Fortune Pr., 1927. Ltd. Edn. 5 vols. Orig. cl., unopened. (P. Jul.2; 25A) *Meadows* £55

SHAFTESBURY, Rt. Hon. Anthony, Earl of
– Characteristicks of Men, Manners, Opinions, Times. 1737. 6th. Edn. 3 vols. Cont. mott. cf. with gt. decor. spines. (TA. Mar.19; 257) £52

SHAHN, Ben
– The Alphabet of Creation.–Sweet Was the Song the Virgin Sung. N.Y., [1954]. 1st. work (550) numbered, sigd., 2nd. work, (275) numbered. Tog. 2 vols. 1st. work 8vo., 2nd. work ob. 32mo. 1st. work, gt.-stpd. cl., boxed, 2nd. work, vell. wraps. (SG. Oct.23; 311) $280

SHAKESPEARE, William
[Separate Pieces]
– Anthony & Cleopatra. Hammersmith, Doves Pr. 1912. (15) privilege Edn. on vell. Hand-bnd. red orig. mor., gold fillets on spine, cover, inner and outer dentelles. (H. Dec.9/10; 1798) DM 3,900
– – Anr. Copy. Sm. 4to. Crushed lev. mor., gt.-ruled, spine in 6 compartments, 5 raised bands, gt.-panel., sigd. by Doves Bindery, 1913, qtr. mor, s.-c. (CNY. May 22; 397) $2,500
– Coriolanus. Hammersmith, Doves Pr., 1914. (15) on vell. Sm. 4to. Lev. mor., gt.-ruled border & panel, gt. tools, spine in 6 compartments, 5 raised bands, gt.-panel., sigd. by Doves Bindery, 1914, qtr. mor. s.-c. (CNY. May 22; 402) $2,800
– – Anr. Edn. Doves Pr., 1914. (200). 4to. Orig. limp vell., unc. (C. Jul.22; 63) *Maggs.* £150
– – Anr. Copy. Hammersmith, Doves Pr., 1914. (200) Lev., raised bands, by René Kieffer, s.-c. (SG. May 14; 66) $250
– – Anr. Copy. 4to. Minor browning. Orig. vell., slight soiling. (SPB. Jul.28; 116) $200
– – Anr. Edn. Doves Pr., [1914]. (200). 4to. Niger mor., gt., by the Doves bindery after a design by Cobden-Sanderson, cl. portfo. in mor.-bkd. s.-c. (C. Jul.22; 62) *Joseph.* £320
– Cymbeline.–Macbeth. Ed.:– H. Granville Barker. Ill.:– A. Ruthbertson & Charles Ricketts. L., Shakes. Hd. Pr. 1923; 1923. Both (100) on Batchelor's Kelmscott H.M.P., sigd. by artist & Ed. 2 vols. Fo. Mor., gt. panels on covers, by Zaehnsdorf. (SPB. Nov.25; 395) $350
– Hamlet. Ill.:– Edward Johnston. Hammersmith, Doves Pr., 1909. (15) on vell. Sm. 4to. Orig. vell., unc., inscr. by T.J. Cobden-Sanderson 'Doves Bindery/C.W. 1909', qtr. mor. s.-c. Thomas B. Lockwood bkplt., ex-libris stp. of J. Visser, Rotterdam. (CNY. May 22; 387) $3,800
– Hamlet. Ill.:– Edward Johnston. Doves Pr., 1909. 1909. 4to. 1 initial. Orig. limp vell., unc. (SH. Feb.19; 45) *John.* £190
– – Anr. Copy. Doves Pr. 1909. (250) on paper. 4to. Orig. limp vell. Sigd. & dtd. by William Russell Flint. (CSK. Dec.10; 25) £140
– – Anr. Copy. Unc. (SH. Feb.19; 44) *Fermoy.* £125
– – Anr. Copy. Doves Bindery. (VG. Dec.16; 763) Fls. 800
– – Anr. Edn. [Hammersmith]. [Doves Pr.]. [1909]. (250). 4to. Silver-ruled crushed mor., silver-panel spine, inner dentelles silver-ruled, by C. & C. McLeish at Doves Bindery. (PNY. Dec.3; 125) $450
– – Anr. Edn. Trans.: Georges Vidal. Ill.:– Georges Bruyer. Paris, 1913. (180) numbered. 4to. Mor. with embossed designs in five lozenges, gt. dentelles enclosing lin. stpd. with figures, marb. flyll., by René Kieffer, cold. pict. wraps. bnd. in, s.-c. (SG. Oct.9; 226) $650
– – Anr. Edn. Ed.:– J. Dover Wilson. Ill.:– Edward Gordon Craig, Eric Gill. Weimar, Cranach Pr., 1930. (322) numbered. Fo. Notes by editor inserted in pocket on inside.lr. cover. Orig. cl.-bkd. bds., slightly worn, unc. (S. Jul.31; 196) *Bertram Rota.* £1,400
– – Anr. Edn. Ill.:– Eric Gill. Ltd. Edns. Cl. 1933. (1500) numbered, & sigd. by artist. Pig., orig. box. (SG. Jan.15; 249) $130
– Julius Caesar. L., 1684. 1st. Separate Edn. 4to. Lacks 1st. blank lf. before title, catchwords & sigs. cropped on last 2 ll., 3 cont. MS. changes to the Dramatis Personae p. Red mor. gt. The John L. Clawson, Herschel V. Jones copy, lately in the Prescott Collection. (CNY. Feb.6; 291) $1,800
– – Anr. Edn. Hammersmith, Doves Pr., 1913. (15) on vell. Sm. 4to. Orig. vell., unc., qtr. mor. s.-c. (CNY. May 22; 400) $2,200
– – Anr. Edn. N.Y., n.d. Orig. ptd. wraps., mor. case. John W. Booth's inscr. on upr. cover. (SPB. Nov.24; 5) $900
– King Henry V; King Henry VI. L., 1663. Fo. Cf., gt. dentelles, by Bayntun, buckram s.-c. (SG. May 14; 193) $425
– King Lear. Ed.:– N. Tate. 1689. 4to. Cont. panel. cf., rebkd. [Wing S2919] (C. Nov.19; 157) *Quaritch.* £320
– Lucrece. Hammersmith, Doves Pr., 1915. (10) on vell. Sm. 4to. Crushed lev. mor., gt.-ruled border, spine in 6 compartments, 5 raised bands, gt.-panel., sigd. by Doves Bindery, 1915, qtr. mor. s.-c. (CNY. May 22; 405) $2,500
– Macbeth. Ill.:– Ron King. Circle Pr., 1970. (150) sigd. by artist. Lge. fo. 10 screenprints, each captioned & initialled in pencil by artist. Unbnd. as issued in orig. folder & s.-c. (SH. Feb.20; 401) *Smith.* £60
– Macbeth. [German] Trans.:– Friedrich von Schiller. Tübingen, 1801. 1st. Edn. Slightly soiled at beginning. Cont. hf. leath. gt., slightly soiled. (HK. May 15; 4845) DM 580
– Measure for Measure. 1700. 1st. Separate Edn. 4to. Hf. mor. by Sangorski. [Wing S2936] (C. Nov.19; 158) *Quaritch.* £600
– The Merchant of Venice.–Cymbeline.–A Midsommer Nights Dreame.–Love Labour's Lost. –Julius Caesar. Ill.:– Lowinsky, Rutherson, Nash, Wilkinson, & Stern. L., Shakes. Head Pr. 1923-25. Each (450) numbered, on pure rag paper. 5 works in 5 vols. Fo. Linen-bkd. bds., d.-w.'s. (SG. Jan.15; 99) $130
– The Merry Wives of Windsor. Dreams.–Love Labour's Lost.– Julius Caesar. Ill.:– Hugh Thomson. 1910. (350). 4to. Orig. vell. gt., lacks ties. Sigd. by artist. (SH. Dec.12; 505) *Vincent.* £65
– – Anr. Copy. Slightly spotted. Worn & stained, silk ties. (S. Jul.31; 325) *Beetles.* £60
– A Midsummer Nights Dream. Ill.:– Arthur Rackham. 1908. 4to. Orig. cl. (CSK. Mar.20; 31) £60
– – Anr. Copy. Orig. cl. gt. (SH. Mar.27; 427) *Hatchard.* £52
– – Anr. Copy. (SH. Dec.11; 422) *Mundy.* £50
– – Anr. Edn. Ill.:– Arthur Rackham. 1908. (1000) sigd. by artist. 4to. 1 plt. loose. Orig. vell., lacks ties. (SH. Dec.11; 421) *Ayres.* £150
– – Anr. Copy. Orig. vell. gt., slightly soiled. (P. Apr.30; 186) £80
– – Anr. Copy. Slight browning. Warped, some soiling, front free end-paper cut away. With orig. Rackham ink drawing, sigd., on a blank preceding hf.-title. (SPB. May 6; 241) $1,500
– – Anr. Copy. Gt.-pict. vell. Raymond M. Sutton, Jr. copy. (SG. May 7; 259) $750
– – Anr. Edn. Ill.:– Arthur Rackham. Munchen, 1909. Ltd. Edn. German text. Vell., ties torn. (PD. Feb.18; 185) £75
– – Anr. Edn. Ill.:– W. Heath Robinson. 1914. 4to. Orig. cl., d.-w. (SH. Mar.27; 464) *Barnard.* £70
– – Anr. Copy. Hf. mor., spine gt. by Bayntun (Rivière). (SKC. May 19; 58) £50
– – Anr. Edn. Ill.:– Paul Nash. Shakes. Hd. Pr., 1924. (106) sigd. by Harley Granville-Barker, Albert Rutherston & artist. 4to. Mor. gt., s.-c., by Rivière. (SH. Mar.27; 359) *Brook.* £90
– The Passionate Pilgrim & the Songs in the Plays. Ed.:– T. Sturge Moore. Ill.:– Charles Ricketts. L., Vale Pr. 1896. Mor., upr. cover with lge. gt. design of flowers, gt. dentelles, by Bumpus, writing & bkplt. in upr. cover. (SG. Feb.12; 111) $120
– Romeo & Juliet. [1623]. 1st. Fo. Edn. Fo. 11 pp., some repairs. Qtr. cf. (P. Jan.22; 331) *Dubin.* £80
– Ein Sommernachtstraum. Trans.:– W.v. Schlegel. Ill.:– A. Rackham. Munich, 1909. (1001). 4to. Orig. vell., gt. spine, unc. (R. Oct.14-18; 1042) DM 600
– – Anr. Edn. Trans.:– A.W. Schlegel. Frankfurt, 1923. (250) on Bütten numbered. 4to. Orig. vell., inner gt. dentelle, cover fillets, bd. s.-c. (HK. Nov.18-21; 2716) DM 800
– Le Songe d'une Nuit d'Eté. Ill.:– Arthur Rackham. Paris, 1909. (300) on vell., numbered. 4to. Orig. gt. parch. with ties, s.-c. (SM. Feb.11; 104) Frs. 1,600
– The Tempest. 1676. 4to. Hf. mor. by Wood. [Wing S2946] (C. Nov.19; 159) *Quaritch.* £300
[–] – Anr. Copy. Without the misprint in the imprint as mentioned by Wing. Mod. cf. gt. spine slightly worn. (SM. Jul.27; 72) *Pickering & Chatto* £200
– – Anr. Edn. Ill.:– Edmund Dulac. [1907]. (500) numbered, sigd. by artist. 4to. Orig. vell. gt., lacks ties. (SH. Dec.10; 180) *Mirdan.* £180
– – Anr. Edn. Ill.:– Edmund Dulac. 1908. (500) sigd. by artist. 4to. Orig. vell., gt., partly unc., silk ties. (C. Feb.4; 56) *Innes.* £190
– – Anr. Edn. Ill.:– Edmund Dulac. [1908]. (500) numbered sigd. by artist. 4to. Orig. vell., lacks ties. (SH. Mar.26; 163) *Mirdan.* £140
– – Anr. Copy. Orig. vell. gt., 1 tie detchd., s.-c. worn. (SH. Mar.26; 164) *Joseph.* £100
– – Anr. Edn. Ill.:– A. Schinnerer. Munich, 1921. (205) numbered. Lge. 4to. Slightly soiled. Orig. vell., gold stpd, gt. inner dentelle, by Knorr & Hirth, slightly soiled. (HK. Nov.18-21; 2902) DM 540
– – Anr. Edn. Ill.:– Arthur Rackham. 1926. 4to. Orig. cl. gt. (SH. Mar.27; 440) *Razzall.* £55
– – Anr. Edn. Ill.:– Arthur Rackham. L., [1926]. 1st. Trade Edn. Cl., d.-w. Raymond M. Sutton, Jr. copy. (SG. May 7; 261) $350
– – Anr. Edn. Ill.:– Arthur Rackham. L., [1926]. (520) numbered, sigd. by artist. Lge. 4to. Vell.-bkd. vell.-style bds., gt. stpd., d.-w. Raymond M. Sutton, Jr. copy. (SG. May 7; 260) $800
– – Anr. Edn. Ill.:– Edmund Dulac. N.d. Ltd. Edn. sigd. by Ill. 4to. Orig. vell. gt., ties. (P. Oct.23; 135) *Bailey.* £130
– – Anr. Copy. 1 p. torn away. Orig. vell.-bkd. parch., soiled, front free end-paper torn away. (SPB. May 29; 365) $275
– – Anr. Edn. Ill.:– Edmund Dulac. L., n.d. 4to. Publisher's bds., unc. (HD. Jun.25; 397) Frs. 1,700
– Titus Andronicus. 1687. 1st. Edn. of this version. 4to. Mor. by Sangorski. [Wing S2949] (C. Nov.19; 160) *Quaritch.* £600
– Venus & Adonis. Hammersmith, Doves Pr., 1912. (15) on vell. Sm. 4to. Lev. mor., covers with double gt.-ruled borders, gt.-tooled mor. onlay on upr. cover, spine in 6 compartments, 5 raised bands, gt.-panel., by Bumpus, qtr. mor. s.-c. Thomas B. Lockwood bkplt. (CNY. May 22; 398) $1,000
– – Anr. Edn. Doves Pr., 1912. (200) on paper. 4to. Orig. limp vell., discold., unc. (S. Jul.31; 62) *Duchnes.* £80
– – Anr. Edn. Paris, 1930. (10) on japon priv. ptd. Orig. hf. mor., s.-c. (SH. Nov.21; 340) *Monk Bretton.* £50
– – Anr. Edn. Ill.:– Rockwell Kent. Rochester, 1931. (1250) numbered, & sigd. by artist. 4to. Hf. cf., boxed, partly untrimmed. Sigd. by artist. (SG. Nov.13; 398) $110
– – Anr. Copy. Mor.-bkd. linen, boxed. (SG. Apr.2; 158) $100
– The Winter's Tale. 1632. Extracted from an iss. of the 2nd. Fo. Edn. Fo. Mod. three-qtr. crushed mor. (PNY. Mar.26; 297) $375
– – Anr. Edn. [L.], [1632]. Fo. Gt.-decor. pol. cf., gt. dentelles, by Bayntun, buckram s.-c. (SG. May 14; 192) $425

[Poems, Songs & Sonnets]
(Arranged Chronologically)
– Poems. Ill.:– Marshall (port.). 1640. Remargined at lr., outer & inner edges, undtd. title misbnd. before dtd. title, B3-6 & M2-3 misbnd. Mor. gt. by C. Smith, rebkd. preserving orig. spine. Bkplt. of John Pierpont Morgan. [STC 22344] (C. Nov.20; 275) *Grove.* £5,500

- Sonnets & a Lover's Complaint. L., 1870. Reprnt. of 1609 Edn. Red crushed lev. mor., elab. gt. decor., rounded spine in 6 compartments with gt. tools, 5 raised bands, Japanese vell, endpapers, sigd. by T.J. Cobden-Sanderson 'C.S.1890' & inscr., mor. solander case. John A. Spoor & John A. Saks bkplts., 2 A.L.s. to Saks by Mrs. Stella Cobden-Sanderson. (CNY. May 22; 358) $16,000
- Poems. Hammersmith, Kelms. Pr. 1893. (500). Prepared for rebinding, in stitched bds. (SPB. Nov.25; 317) $250
- - Anr. Edn. [Kelms. Pr.]. [1893]. [(510)]. Orig. vell., soiled. (CSK. May 29; 116) £85
- - Anr. Edn. L., Essex Ho. Pr. 1899. [450]. 4to. Niger mor. gt., covers with decor. borders, gt. spine. (CNY. Oct.1; 177) $280
- - Anr. Copy. Vell., silk ties, unc. (SG. Sep.4; 416) $140
- The Poems, including the Lyrics, Songs, & Snatches found in his Dramas. L., Essex Ho. Pr. 1899. (450) numbered. Orig. vell., linen ties, unc. (SG. Sep.4; 176) $130
- Sonnets. New Rochelle, N.Y. Elston Pr., 1901. (210). Mor. gt., spine & upr. cover with cold. mor. onlays, silk linings, partly unc., by Cuneo. (CNY. May 22; 305) $220
- - Anr. Edn. Ill.:- Noel Rooke & Eric Gill. Hammersmith, Doves Pr., 1909. Tercentenary Edn., (15) on vell. Sm. 4to. Lev. mor., covers with double gt.-ruled border & gt. tooled ornaments, spine in 6 compartments, 5 raised hands, gt.-panel., sigd. by Doves Bindery, 1910, qtr. mor. s.-c. Cortlandt Field Bishop bkplt. (CNY. May 22; 388) $5,000
- - Anr. Edn. [Hammersmith], [Doves Pr.]. 1909. (250). 4to. Vell., upr. cover warped. (PNY. Dec.3; 124) $220
- Songs & Sonnets. Ill.:- Charles Robinson. [1917]. 4to. Orig. pict. cl. gt. (SH. Dec.11; 460) Jones. £50
- The Sonnets. Ed.:- Robert Graves. Ill.:- Clarke Hutton. Swallow Pr., 1975. (300) sigd. by Ed., designer & artist. Fo. Orig. mor. gt., s.-c. (SH. Feb.20; 379) Itkin. £70
- - Anr. Edn. Ed.:- Keith Michell. [Melbourne]. 1979. (500) numbered. & sigd. by Michell. Fo. Mor., gt. & ornamented. (KH. Mar.24; 353) Aus. $180

[Collected Works]
(Arranged Chronologically)
- Comedies, Histories, Tragedies. Ill.:- Martin Droueshout (port.). L., 1623. 1st. Fo. Edn. Fo. Port. in 3rd. state, earlier state of [pp5] in Hamlet, with p. 277 numbered 273, & 1st. column, line 9 from the bottom reading 'iowlos' for 'iowles', lf. 02 inserted, lf. 'To the Reader' cut round & mntd., title-p. with the 1st. 2, hf. of the 3rd., & a sm. portion of last line in facs., some letters in facs. on B1, d2, g2, t6, & ff2, 116 with lr. margin restored & the ptd. rule & some letters in facs., sm. reprd. tear to port., ss5 with sm. reprd. tear in text, H3, Aa3, & f2 torn & reprd., without affecting text, final lf. bbb6 dust-soiled & with inner blank margin restored, some other minor stains & rust spots. Late 18th. C. Engl. diced russ. gt., rebkd. with orig. backstrip preserved, red mor. gt. solander case (by Rivière). The 7th. Earl of Newcastle's copy (by descent), lately in the Prescott Collection. [STC 22273] (CNY. Feb.6; 290) $210,000
- - Anr. Edn. L., 1632. 2nd. Fo. Edn. [2nd. Imp.] Fo. Greg's 1st. variant imprint, 1st. lf. & title remargined with some letters on title in facs., lacks corner of u5 affecting 3 lines, sm. hole in 2g5 touching 1 letter, last 2 ll. remargined with pagination of last lf. in facs. Red mor. gt. by Rivière. [STC 22274a] (C. Nov.19; 154) Quaritch. £5,800
- - Anr. Copy. 'Effigees' lf. in corrected state, first 3 ll. reprd. Early 19th. C. russ. gt. [by Roger Payne], worn & reprd. A.L.s. from Alexander Chalmers to Thomas Caldecott tipped in. (S. Nov.25; 467) Hilman. £4,200
- - Anr. Edn. L., 1663, 1664. 3rd. Fo. Edn. Fo. Title & lf. 'To the Reader' in both principal states, stabmarks thro.-out prelims., natural paper faults or tears affecting text in A2, A5, G1, G3, H5, K1, O5, R3, X3, Y2, 2B1, 2G6, 2I4, & 3C3, most reprd., other minor faults & sm. holes slightly affecting text. Cont. cf., both covers rehinged, in mor.-bkd. case. [Wing S2913-4] (C. Nov.19; 155) Quaritch. £16,00
- - Anr. Edn. L., 1685. 4th. Fo. Edn. Fo. Cont. spr. cf., rebkd. preserving orig. gt. spine, in

mor.-bkd. case. [Wing S2915] (C. Nov.19; 156) Quaritch. £7,000
- - Anr. Copy. Early 19th. C. str.-grd. mor., later matching box. Bkplts. of Charles Mildmay & the Dogmersfield Liby., lately in the collection of Eric Sexton. (C. Apr.15; 146) Burgess. £5,200
- - Anr. Copy. Fo. Slight stain thro.-out, some worming, port. & title backed, margin of YY3-4 trimmed. Recent mor. by Lamacraft & Laurence, scratches on upr. cover. Bkplt. of Edmund de Pentheny O'Kelly. (S. Nov.25; 470) Sotheran. £2,400
- - Anr. Copy. Lacks port., 8 prelim. ll. & 4 ll. at end. 18th. C. tree cf., rebkd., upr. cover detchd. W.a.f. (S. Nov.25; 468) Sotheran. £650
- Works. Ed.:- Sir T. Hanner. Oxford, 1744. 6 vols. 4to. Cf. gt., with initials F.B. in back compartments, jnts. worn. (BS. Jun.11; 282) £50
- The Plays & Poems. Dublin, 1771. 12 vols.; 1 vol. Cont. mor. gt., prize bdgs., from Trinity College, Dublin. (SKC. Feb.26; 1522) £75
- The Works. Ed.:- Lewis Theobold. 1772. 12 vols. 12mo. Cont. cf. (CSK. Aug.15; 33) £65
- Schauspiele. Trans.:- J.J. Eschenburg. Ill.:- C. Verelst (port.) Strassb., 1778-80. New Edn. 22 pts. in 11 vols. 6 titles with cont. MS. owner's mark, some defects, some thro. worming. Cont. cf. gt. W.a.f. (HK. May 15; 4900) DM 760
- Works. Ed.:- George Steevens. 1802. L.P. 9 vols. Fo. A few ll. very slightly browned. Hf. cf. gt. (SBA. Jul.14; 201) Salinas. £120
- Plays. Ed.:- Samuel Johnson, George Steevens & Isaac Reed. 1803. 21 vols. Cont. red str.-grd. mor., gt. roll-tooled borders, spines gt. in compartments. (C. Feb.4; 86) Traylen. £560
- - Anr. Copy. Some ll. slightly spotted. Cont. cf., worn, some covers detchd. (SH. Oct.9; 22) Ghani. £50
- - Anr. Edn. 1809. 12 vols. in 6. Hf. mor., spines gt. (SKC. Sep.9; 1485) £65
- - Anr. Edn. 1813. 21 vols. 1 vol. with a few plts. spotted. Vell. gt. (SKC. Feb.26; 1521) £280
- The Plays & Poems. Ed.:- Edmund Malone. L., 1821. 21 vols. 2 engraved ports. spotted. Cont. str.-grd. mor; gt. (SM. Oct.8; 2160) Frs. 2,100
- Dramatische Werke. Trans.:- A.W. von Schlegel & L. Tieck. Berlin, 1825-33. 1st. Edn. 9 vols. Soiled in parts. Decor. hf. leath., slightly worn. (H. Dec.9/10; 1665) DM 780
- Plays & Poems. 1832-34. 15 vols. 19th. C. red mor., ruled in gt., contained in a velvet lined late Victorian ebonised & crossbanded box. (CSK. Nov.14; 69) £120
- The Plays. 1856. 8 vols. Cont. vell. gt., spines gt. (SKC. Sep.9; 1486) £50
- The Works. Ed.:- William George Clarke & John Glover. Camb. & L., 1863-65. 7 vols. Cont. hf. lev. by Rivière. (CSK. Jul.10; 133) £65
- - Anr. Edn. 1891-93. 9 vols. Cont. hf. mor. (SH. May 28; 93) Howes Books. £90
- - Anr. Edn. Ed.:- T.S. Moore. Ill.:- Charles Ricketts. 1900-03. Vale Edn. 36 vols. Orig. cl., slightly soiled, unc. & partly unopened. (TA. May 21; 372) £115
- - Anr. Copy. (TA. Apr.16; 42) £105
- - Anr. Edn. Ed.:- W.E. Henley. 1901-04. (50) numbered, sigd. by Grant Richards. 10 vols. Fo. Cont. hf. Mor. (SH. Oct.10; 392) Traylen. £110
- - Anr. Edn. Ill.:- William Aldis Wright. 1902-4. 9 vols. Cont. hf. cf. (CSK. Aug.15; 137) £55
- - Anr. Edn. Ed.:- William Aldis Wright. L., 1902-05. 9 vols. Gt.-ruled three-qtr. crushed red mor., gt.-panel. spines. (PNY. Dec.3; 329) $180
- - Anr. Edn. Shakes. Hd. Pr., 1904-07. Ltd. Edn. 10 vols. Red hf. mor. by Frost, partly unc. (C. Jul.22; 29) Joseph. £320
- - Anr. Copy. 4to. Orig. cl. gt., unc. With envelope containing a poem, a brochure on the Press, 3 copies of the prospectus, 1904, an A.L.S. by one of the publishers to Kearns, 1908, etc. (SH. Feb.19; 53) Subunso. £90
- The Complete Histories, Tragedies & Poems. Boston, 1912. New Great White Shakespeare Book Lovers Edn., (1,000). 18 vols. Hf. mor. gt., gt. spines with mor. inlays. (SPB. May 6; 341) $2,100
- [Plays]. L., 1922-30. Temple Shakespeare. 39 (of 40) vols. Sm. square 12mo. Hf. red cf. by Sangorski & Sutcliffe. (SPB. Nov.25; 488) $150
- Works. Darmstadt, Ernst. Ludwig Pr. 1925-31. [200]. 7 vols. 4to. Orig. niger mor. gt., partly unc. The John A. Saks copy. (CNY. Oct.1; 176) $1,000
- - Anr. Edn. Ed.:- H. Farjeon. Nones. Pr.,

1929-32. Ltd. Edn. 7 vols. Niger mor. gt. (P. Oct.23; 247) Goodwin. £330
- - Anr. Edn. Ed.:- Herbert Farjeon. Nones. Pr., 1929-33. (1050) numbered. 7 vols. Orig. niger mor., s.-c.'s. (S. Jul.31; 113) Lory. £310
- - Anr. Edn. Nones. Pr. 1929-33. (1,600) numbered. 7 vols. Orig. mor., some endpapers browned. (CSK. Apr.3; 51) £290
- - Anr. Copy. Niger mor. (SG. May 14; 157) $700
- - Anr. Copy. Orig. niger mor. gt., partly unc. The John A. Saks copy. (CNY. Oct.1; 198) $550
- - Anr. Edn. Ed.:- Herbert Farjeon. L., Nones. Pr., 1929-33. Ltd. Edn., numbered. 7 vols. Niger mor., unc. (SG. Oct.9; 227) $450
- Les Tragédies. Trans.:- Suzanne Bing & Jacques Copeau. Ill.:- Edy-Legrand. Paris, 1939. (70) on mother-of-pearl Jap. 5 vols. 4to. Jansenist mor., unc., s.-c. (HD. Dec.5; 196) Frs. 1,700
- Comedies, Histories & Tragedies. Ed.:- Herbert Farjeon. Ill.:- Arthur Rackham, Eric Gill & others. Designed: Bruce Rogers. N.Y., Ltd. Edns. Cl., 1939-40. 37 vols. Sm. fo. Linen-bkd. decor. bds., partly unopened. Raymond M. Sutton Jr. copy. (SG. May 7; 262) $700
- - Anr. Edn. Ill.:- Arthur Rackham & others. N.Y., Ltd. Edns. Cl., 1939-40. (1,950) numbered sets designed by Bruce Rogers. 37 vols. Sm. fo. Buckram-bkd. patterned bds. (SG. Apr.9; 521) $275
- Comedies, Histories, & Tragedies.- Poems. Ed.:- Herbert Farjeon. Ill.:- Arthur Rackham, Eric Gill, & others. Ltd. Edns. Cl. 1939-41. 39 vols. Fo. Buckram-bkd. patterned bds, partly untrimmed. (SG. Jan.15; 250) $190
- Works. Ed.:- Charles Knight. n.d. Pictorial Edition. 8 vols. Cont. mor., gt. (CSK. Jan.9; 49) £60
- - Anr. Copy. 10 vols. Hf. mor. gt. (SPB. Nov.25; 490) $275

SHAKESPEARE, William-KNIGHT, Charles
- The Works.-William Shakespeare: A Biography. L., 1867. 2nd. (pict.) Edn.; 3rd. Edn. 7 vols.; 1 vol. 4to. Hf. mor. (SSA. Jun.18; 27) R. 130

SHAKESPEARIANA
- The Flowers of Shakespeare. [L.], ca. 1840. 4to. Orig. linen, defect., upr. cover & 1st. lf. loose. (D. Dec.11-13; 725) DM 500
- Songs from the Plays. Ill.:- After Paul Woodroffe, hand-cold. by Gloria Cardew. 1898. (10) on vell. for Guild of Women Binders. Orig. buckram by the Guild of Women Binders, soiled. Sigd. by Gloria Cardew. (CSK. Oct.17; 94) £110
- - Anr. Edn. Ill.:- Paul Woodroffe & Gloria Cardew. L., 1899. (100) on Japan Vell. Sm. 4to. Mor. gt., covers with centre & corners in sm. mor. onlays gt. with repeated foliage tool, mor. doubls., padded cl. case, by Guild of Women-Binders. (CNY. May 22; 344) $1,200

SHAND, A.I.
- Shooting. Ill.:- Arthur Rackham, J. Smit & others. L., 1902. 1st. Edn. Deluxe, (150) numbered on H.M.P. Haddon Hall Liby. series. Orig. ribbon bookmark detchd. Gt.-pict. vell., unc., unopened. Extra cold. copy of frontis. laid in, Raymond M. Sutton, Jr. copy. (SG. May 7; 263) $280

SHANNON, Richard
- A Practical Treatise on Brewing, Distilling, & Rectification, with the Genuine Process of Making Brandy, Rum & Holland Gin . . . with a Copious Index on the Culture . . . 1805. 4 pts. in 1 vol. 4to. Lacks hf.-title, some foxing. Recent hf. cf. (TA. Feb.19; 506) £95

SHARF, G. (Ill.)
See-COSTUME

SHARP, Granville
- The Gilbert Prize Essay on the Adaptation of Recent Discoveries & Inventions in Science & Art to the Purpose of Practical Banking . . . L.; Norwich, 1854. 3rd. Engl. Edn. (Ill. Edn.). Recent hf. mor. W.a.f. for possible imperfections in specimens & ills.; from Honeyman Collection. (S. May 19; 2844) Dr. Martin. £600

SHARP, Mrs. Jane
- The Midwives Book. 1671. 1st. Edn. Engraved plt. with printed lf. of explanation with hf.

SHARP, Mrs. Jane – The Midwives Book. *-contd.*
missing, both plts. with minor defects. Cont.
sheep, worn. (S. Dec.2; 769)   *Maggs.* £150

SHARPE
See–VERNOR, Hood & Sharpe

SHARPE, Richard Bowdler
– Catalogue of African Birds in the Collection of
R.B. Sharpe. L., 1871. Inscr. 'A.B. Brooke
Esq./from his friend/the author'. Hf. cf. & marb.
bds. (VA. Jan.30; 346)   R. 360
– A Monograph of the Alcedinidae. Ill.:– J.G.
Keulemans. 1868-71. 4to. Cont. hf. mor., spine gt.
(C. Mar.18; 103)   *Sotheran.* £3,200
– Monograph of the Paradiseidae, or Birds of
Paradise ... Ill.:– J.G. Keulemans & W. Hart.
1891-98. 2 vols. Fo. 79 hand-finished litho. plts.
Cont. hf. mor., partly unc., by Sotheran. (C.
Mar.18; 150)   *Ortleep.* £7,200
– – Anr. Copy. Orig. upr. wraps. preserved, mod.
lev. mor. gt., spines tooled in compartments with
arabesque ornaments, covers with alaborate
borders of arabesque & foliage ornaments, gt.
inner borders. (S. Dec.3; 1126)   *Nielson.* £6,400
– – Anr. Copy. Cont. mor., sides with gt. tooled
borders. (C. Jul.15; 206)   *Marks.* £4,400
See–DRESSER, Henry Eeles & Sharpe, Richard
Bowdler
See–GOULD, John & Sharpe, Richard Bowdler
See–SEEBOHM, Henry & Sharpe, Richard
Bowdler

SHARPE, Richard Bowdler & Wyatt, Claude W.
. – A Monograph of the Hirundinidae or Family of
Swallows. 1885-94. 2 vols. Lge. 4to. Orig. cl.,
partly unc. (C. Jul.15; 205)   *Peach.* £1,600

SHARROCK, Robert
– The History of the Propagation & Improvement
of Vegetables by the Concurrence of Art & Nature.
Oxford, 1660. 1st. Edn. Advt. lf., paper discold. in
places. Cont. cf., upr. cover loose. [Wing S3010]
(S. Dec.2; 621)   *Quaritch.* £60

SHAW, G.F.
– The Panorama of Nature. L., 1819. 4to. Hf. cf.
& marb. bds. (SSA. Nov.5; 83)   R. 90

SHAW, George
– General Zoology. 1800-26. 24 vols. only.
Spotting. Cont. hf. mor. W.a.f. (CSK.
Nov.21; 213)   £170
– Zoological Lectures Delivered at the Royal
Institution. 1809. 1st. Edn. 2 vols. Cont. diced cf.,
spines gt. (C. May 20; 243)   *Klein.* £220

SHAW, George & Nodder, Frederick P.
– Naturalist's Miscellany. 1790. 24 vols. Some
plts. loose. Orig. parch.-bkd. bds., not unif., unc.
As periodical, w.a.f. (SBA. Jul.22; 122)
          L'Acquaforte. £2,200
– – Anr. Copy. 23 vols. only (of 24, lacks vol. 18).
Some very minor defects. Cont. cf., worn & rebkd.
As a periodical, w.a.f. (SBA. May 27; 194)
          Hyde Park Bookshop. £1,250

SHAW, George Bernard
– The Doctor's Dilemma. L., 1911. 1st. Edn. 12mo.
Orig. cl., qtr. mor. s.-c. With A.C.s to Miss Edith
Craig (L., May 19, 1908, 12mo., 2 pp.), & A.N.s.
('Mother') to her from Ellen Terry; from the
Prescott Collection. (CNY. Feb.6; 292) $500
– John Bull's other Island & Major Barbara. L.,
1908. Cl., cl. s.-c. Inscr. (SG. Nov.13; 593) $150
– Man & Superman.–The Philanderer. L., 1903;
1913. 1st. Edns. 2 works in 2 vols. 12mo. Orig. cl.,
lr. cover slightly blistered, qtr. mor. gt. s.-c. (1st.
work); & orig. cl., qtr. mor. gt. s.-c. 1st. work
inscr. to E.S. Sutro, with his owner's sig., 2nd.
work inscr., & with A.P.C.s (with initials) to
Philip Carr, & A.N.s. (with initials) to (John?)
Drinkwater; both works from the Prescott
Collection. (CNY. Feb.6; 293) $650
– Nine Answers. Ed.:– Christopher Morley
(introduction). N.Y., [1923]. 1st. Edn. (62)
numbered, on L.P. Orig. ptd. bds., d.-w. (PNY.
Dec.3; 330) $160
– Saint Joan. Ill.:– Charles Ricketts. L., [1924].
(750). Fo. Linen-bkd. decor. bds., unc., d.-w. (SG.
Oct.23; 301) $110
– Shaw Gives Himself Away, an Autobiographical
Miscellany. Gregy. Pr. 1939. (300) on H.M.P.,
numbered. Orig. mor. with inlays. (SBA.
Oct.22; 729)   *Simon.* £220
– Statement of the Evidence in Chief ... before the
Joint-Committee on Stage Plays. [L.], Priv. Ptd.
[1909]. 1st. Edn. 12mo. Ptd. wraps. (SG.
Nov.13; 595) $110

– What a Playwright Should do with his First Play.
N.p., n.d. 2 ll. on one sheet, undivided. Sigd. (SG.
Jun.4; 446) $200
– Works. 1930-32. (1025) numbered. Vols. 1-30
(of 33). Orig. cl., d.-w.'s. (SH. Oct.10; 393)
          Lenton. £55
– Collected Works. N.Y., 1930-32. Ayot St.
Lawrence Edn., (1,790) numbered. 30 vols
Linen-bkd. bds., d.-w.'s., unopened. (SG.
Jun.4; 452) $300

SHAW, Henry
– The Decorative Arts ... of the Middle Ages. L.,
1851. 1st. Edn. 4to. Cont. cf. gt., jnts. brkn. (SG.
Dec.4; 314) $190
– Dresses & Decorations of the Middle Ages.
1843. 2 vols. 4to. Mor. gt., ties. (P. Nov.13; 281)
          Henderson. £210
– – Anr. Copy. Fo. Cont. hf. mor. (SH.
Mar.6; 571)   *Henderson.* £170
– – Anr. Copy. Occasional light foxing. Cf., gt.
spines, by J. Clarke. (C. Nov.5; 142)
          Kaplan. £140
– – Anr. Copy. 4to. 92 plts. (of 93). Orig. cl., 1 vol.
loose, worn, lacks spines. (SH. Jan.29; 294)
          Baer. £120
– – Anr. Copy. Some lr. margins slightly
dampstained. Cont. hf. mor., spines gt. (CSK.
Sep.26; 65)   £85
– – Anr. Edn. 1858. 2nd. Edn. 2 vols. 4to. Cont. hf.
mor. (SH. Jan.29; 296)   *Baer.* £100
– – Anr. Copy. Spotted. (SH. Jan.29; 295)
          Crete. £85
– The Encyclopaedia of Ornament Illustrated by a
Series of Fifty-Three Plates of Ironwork,
Lacework ... Edinb., 1904. 4to. Orig. cl. (CB
May 27; 184)   Can. $120

SHAW, Henry & Madden, Sir Frederick
– Illuminated Ornaments ... 1833. Fo. Hf. mor.,
spine gt. in compartments, by Hayday. (LC.
Feb.12; 58)   £320

SHAW, John Robert
– A Narrative of the Life & Travels ... Lexington,
1807. 1st. Edn. 2 plts. in facs., paper losses to title,
not affecting text, marginal tears & slight paper
losses to early ll., browned, slight foxing &
staining, lacks front free endpaper, with
subscriber's list. Cont. cf., worn, folding cl. s.-c.
From liby. of William E. Wilson. (SPB.
Apr.29; 250) $2,200

SHAW, Richard Norman
– Architectural Sketches from the Continent. 1872.
Fo. A few ll. slightly spotted. Orig. roan-bkd. cl.,
worn. (SH. Nov.6; 254)   *Foster.* £110

SHAW, Stebbing
– The History & Antiquities of Staffordshire.
1798-1801. L.P. Vols. I & II, pt. 1 (all publd.). Fo.
2 folding pedigrees only, lacks 1 from vol. 1, lacks
hf.-title. Later hf. mor. (CSK. Jun.26; 29)   £350
– – Anr. Copy. Later hf. mor., gt. panel. spines,
unc. (C. Feb.25; 57)   *Chesters.* £260
– – Anr. Copy. Maps with tears at fold, lr. portion
of vol. II damp-stained. Cont. hf. mor., bdg. to vol.
I detchd. From the collection of Eric Sexton. (C.
Apr.16; 354)   *Walker.* £160
[–] History of the Staffordshire Potteries. Hanley,
1829. 1st. Edn. 12mo. Orig. cl.-bkd. bds., spine
worn. (SH. Jun.11; 81)   *Sims & Reed.* £80

SHAW, T.E. (Pseud.)
See–LAWRENCE, Thomas Edward 'T.E. Shaw'

SHAW, Thomas
– Travels, Or Observations Relating to Several
Parts of Barbary & the Levant. Oxford, 1738. 1st.
Edn. Fo. 1 map with sm. portion torn away. Old
cf., rebkd. (TA. Jan.22; 99)   £225
– – Anr. Copy. Minor inkstain on title, a few pp.
slightly spotted. Cont. cf., rebkd., corners reprd.
(S. Nov.4; 640)   *Jackson.* £160
– – Anr. Copy. Old cf., brkn. (BS. Jun.11; 193)
          £90
– – Anr. Edn. Ill.:– Gravelot, 1757. 2nd. Edn. 4to.
Cont. spr. cf. Bkplt. of James Brodie of Brodie. (S.
Jun.29; 244)   *Minerva.* £120

SHAW, Vero
– The Illustrated Book of the Dog. N.d. 4to. Cont.
hf. mor., covers worn. (SKC. Feb.26; 1787) £120

SHEARER, Thomas
– The Cabinet-Makers London Book of Prices.
1793. 4to. Old sheep. (P. Jan.22; 109)
          Allen. £220

SHEBBEARE, John
– The Practice of Physic. 1755. 1st. Edn. 2 vols. A
few ll. foxed. Cont. cf.-bkd. bds., worn, unc. Vol.
II inscr. 'Ex dono Authoris. 1758 G[eorge]
P[aterson]', from liby. of Dr. E. Ashworth
Underwood. (S. Feb.23; 288)   *Lawson.* £60

SHEFFER, Joannes
– Histoire de la Laponie traduite du Latin. Ill.:–
Michault. Paris, 1678. 1st. Edn. in Fr. 4to. Map
with short tear. Cont. spr. cf. (C. Feb.25; 135)
          Braunschweig. £200

SHEIL, Teresa
– Poems. Cuala Pr., 1930. 1st. Edn. Orig.
linen-bkd. bds. (S. Jul.22; 80)   *Quaritch.* £95

SHELDON, Col. Harold P.
– Tranquillity. Ed.:– Nash Buckingham. Ill.:–
Ralph L. Boyer. [1936]. (950) numbered. Gt. cl.,
bkplt. (SG. Dec.11; 275) $110
– Tranquillity Revisited. Ill.:– A. Lassell Ripley.
N.Y., Derrydale Pr. [1940]. (485) numbered. 4to.
Gt.-decor. cl., boxed. (SG. Apr.9; 352) $400

SHELDRAKE, Timothy, the Elder
– Botanicum Medicinale. [1768?]. Fo. Figures on
plts. hand-cold., engraved title detchd., piece torn
from lr. outer corner of folding table, not affecting
text, some plts. slightly discold. Old cf., covers
detchd. From Chetham's Liby., Manchester. (C.
Nov.27; 373a)   *Angus.* £1,500

SHELDRAKE, Timothy, the Younger
– Useful Hints to those who are Afflicted with
Ruptures. Priv. ptd. 1803. Orig. bds., unc. (S.
Jun.17; 767)   *Phillips.* £70

SHELLEY, George Ernest
– A Handbook to the Birds of Egypt. Ill.:– J.G.
Keulemans. 1872. Cont. cl., stained. (C.
Mar.18; 104)   *Schierenberg.* £280
– – Anr. Copy. Orig. cl. (TA. Jun.18; 59)   £250
– – Anr. Copy. Slight marginal soiling. Covers
stained, slightly worn. (S. Dec.3; 1127)
          Clarendon. £140
– A Monograph of the Nectariniidae, or Family of
Sun-Birds. Ill.:– J.G. Keulemans. 1876-80. 4to.
121 hand-finished cold. litho. plts., shelf mark to
title, sm. liby. stp. on title & verso of each plt.
Cont. hf. cf. (C. Mar.18; 151)   *Ortleep.* £3,000
– – Anr. Copy. Cont. red mor. gt. Inscr. (S.
Nov.25; 399)   *Schrire.* £2,200
– – Anr. Copy. Cont. hf. mor., gt., inner hinge
brkn.   (C. Nov.5; 143)
          Weldon & Wesley. £1,700

SHELLEY, Percy Bysshe
[–] History of a Six Weeks' Tour through a Part of
France. L., 1817. 1st. Edn. Old cf., cover detchd.
(SG. Dec.18; 372) $200
– Laon & Cynthia. L., 1818. 1st. Edn., 2nd. Iss.
Without the fly-title lf. to 'Laon & Cynthia', &
lacks advt. lf. at front, & cancelled errata lf. at
end, some ll. slightly spotted. Orig. bds., upr. jnt.
reprd., lr. jnt. brkn., some wear & staining to
covers & spine, red mor. gt. solander case. The
W.T. Wallace, Robert J. Hanershlag copy, with
bkplts., lately in the Prescott Collection. (CNY.
Feb.6; 296) $420
– Poems. Hammersmith, Doves Pr., 1914. (12) on
vell. Sm. 4to. Crushed lev. mor., covers with triple
gt.-ruled border & tools, spine in 6 compartments,
5 raised bands, gt.-panel., gt. ornaments, sigd. by
Doves Bindery, 1914, qtr. mor. s.-c. (CNY. May
22; 403) $2,500
[–] – Anr. Copy. (200). Ms. inscr. 'Maisie Alderly
1 November, 1914 C.S.'. Orig. vell. (CSK.
Aug.22; 207)   £90
– Posthumous Poems. L., 1824. 1st. Edn. Some
foxing, without the errata lf. Cont. str.-grd. mor.,
worn & defect. (SG. Nov.13; 607) $100
– Prometheus Unbound. L., 1820. 1st. Edn., 2nd.
Iss. Lacks advts. Crimson lev., gt.-tooled, satin
doublures & endll., by Rivière, upr. cover detchd.,
hf. lev. s.-c. Kalbfleisch bkplt. (SG. May 14; 194)
          $200
– – Anr. Edn. L., Essex House Pr., 1904. (200). Fo.
Orig. limp vell., silk ties, unc. (CNY. May 22; 311)
          $150
– Queen Mab. L., 1821. 1st. Publd. Edn. Without
lf. of publisher's advts. Mor. gt. by Tout, unc.
Mor. owners' label of C.B. Tinker, & bkplt. of
Frank L. Hadley. (SG. Nov.13; 604) $275

– – Anr. Edn. L., 1822. 1st. Carlile Edn. Orig. bds., covers detchd., hf. mor. s.-c., unc. Shelley bkplt. of Buxton Forman, & his initialled 12-line pencil note. (SG. Nov.13; 603) $250
– Rosalind & Helen, A Modern Eclogue; with Other Poems. 1819. 1st. Edn. Lacks hf.-title & advt. ll., repair to p. 83. Red mor., gt., by Rivière. (S. Jun.9; 61)   *Thomas.* £70
– The Sensitive Plant. Ill.:– Charles Robinson. N.d. 4to. Some ll. slightly soiled. Orig. vell., gt., slightly soiled. (CSK. Mar.20; 51)   £50
– Shelley at Oxford. Ed.:– Walter Sidney Scott. Gold. Cock. Pr. 1944. (500) numbered, sigd. 4to. Orig. smooth mor. gt. by Leighton Straker, s.-c. (TA. May 21; 377)   £58
– Zastrozzi. Ill.:– Cecil Keeling. Gold. Cock. Pr. 1955. (60) specially bnd. 4to. Extra set of 8 engrs. Mor. with elab. gt.-pict. design, gt. spine, marb. box. (SG. Sep.4; 211) $150
– The Poetical Works. L., 1839. 4 vols. 12mo. Pink crushed lev., gt.-tooled, raised bands on spines, covers with elab. geometric borders in gt., doubls., by Bayntun. (SG. Sep.4; 419) $170
– – Anr. Copy. Slight browning. Rose mor. gt., by Bayntun, browning to silk end-papers, spines slightly chipped. (SPB. May 29; 395) $125
– The Works. Ed.:– Harry Buxton Forman. 1880. 8 vols. Orig. cl. (CSK. Jun.12; 40)   £50
– Complete Poetical Works. Camb., 1892. (250), L.P. 8 vols. Slight offsetting. Hf. mor. gt. (SPB. May 6; 342) $800
– Poetical Works. Ed.:– F.S. Ellis. Kelms. Pr., [1894]-95. (250). 3 vols. Orig. limp vell., unc. (SH. Feb.19; 9)   *J.L. Scott.* £390
– – Anr. Copy. Vell. (SG. May 14; 118) $900
– – Anr. Copy. Orig. limp vell., unc. (CNY. May 22; 322) $750

SHELLEY, Percy Bysshe & others
– The Athenians. Ed.:– Walter Sidney Scott. Gold. Cock. Pr. 1943. (350) numbered, this 1 of first 50 specially bnd. & sigd. by editor. 4to. Orig. smooth mor. gt., by Leighton Straker, s.-c., partly untrimmed. (TA. May 21; 375)   £58
– Harriet & Mary. Ed.:– Walter Sidney Scott. Gold. Cock. Pr. 1944. (500) numbered, sigd. 4to. Orig. smooth mor. gt. by Leighton Straker, s.-c. (TA. May 21; 376)   £58

SHELVOCKE, Capt. George, the Elder
– A Voyage Round the World ... 1726. 1st. Edn. Cont. panel. cf., rebkd. [Sabin 80158] (S. Mar.31; 504)   *Foyles.* £180

SHEPARD, Ernest Howard
– Fun & Fantasy. Ed.:– A.A. Milne (intro.). L., [1927]. (150) numbered, & sigd. Sm. fo. Cl.-bkd. batik bds., d.-w. (worn), hf. mor. s.-c., unc. (SG. Apr.30; 290) $300

SHEPARD, William A.
– City of Hamilton directory, containing a Full & Complete List of Householders ... Hamilton, 1858. Advts., (some pict.), map loose. Orig. cl., head & tail of spine slightly worn. (CB. May 27; 316)   Can. $350

SHEPHARD, Charles
*See–*McCLELLAND, John–HOLMES, Samuel –SHEPHARD, Charles

SHEPHERD, J.C. & Jellicoe, G.A.
– Italian Gardens of the Renaissance. 1925. Fo. Hf. mor. gt. (P. Oct.2; 32)   *Park.* £75

SHEPHERD, Thomas Hosmer
– Modern Athens: displayed in a Series of Views: or Edinburgh in the Nineteenth Century. 1829. 4to. Some spotting. Cont. hf. roan, slightly worn. (S. Nov.4; 575)   *Traylen.* £65
– – Anr. Copy. Cont. hf. mor. (TA. Mar.19; 629)   £56
– – Anr. Edn. Ca. 1830. 2 vols. 4to. Hf. cf. gt. (P. Apr.9; 6)   £75
– – Anr. Edn. 1831. Engraved title & 87 plts. only, some ll. soiled. Cont. cf., gt., worn, upr. cover detchd. (SH. Mar.5; 129)   *Watt.* £55
– Modern Athens or Edinburgh in the Nineteenth Century.–Scotland Illustrated. 1829. 2 works in 1 vol. 4to. Spotted & soiled, 2nd. work: lacks title & prelims. Cont. cf., worn, covers detchd. (SH. Nov.6; 152)   *Elliott.* £55

SHEPHERD, Thos. Hosmer & Elmes, James
– London & its Environs in the Nineteenth Century. 1804-5. 2 vols. in 1. 4to. Lacks final text lf? Cont. hf. cf. W.a.f. (SBA. Jul.23; 278)   *Nicholson.* £140

– – Anr. Copy. Orig. bds. worn. L.P. (CSK. Sep.19; 59)   £60
– – Anr. Edn. 1829. Sm. 4to. Hf. cf. (P. Oct.23; 313)   *Tallerman.* £150
– – Anr. Copy. Upr. cover detchd. (P. May 14; 80)   *Kenyon.* £130
– – Anr. Copy. Slightly soiled, no text. Cont. hf. mor. (SH. Nov.6; 153)   *Trotter.* £60
– London & its Environs in the 19th. Century. –Metropolitan Improvements. 1827-29. 2 vols. 4to. All views on india paper, some plts. in vol. I dtd. 1830-31, some plts. in vol. II 1828-29, lacks ptd. titles in both vols., & ?B1-C2 in vol. II, slight spotting. Orig. cl., rebkd., orig. spines preserved. (S. Nov.4; 516)   *Elliot.* £90
– – Anr. Edn. n.d.; 1827. 2 works in 1 vol. 4to. 1st. work: imprints 1830-31-n.d., title & frontis. spotted. Cont. hf. cf., gt. (S. May 5; 224)   *Byrne.* £130
– Metropolitan Improvements; Or, London in the Nineteenth Century. 1827. 4to. Foxing, prelims. detchd. Cont. gt. decor. cf. W.a.f. (TA. Aug.21; 245)   £110
– – Anr. Copy. Additional engraved title & 79 plts. on India P., slight foxing. Hf. cf., gt. spine. (S. Sep.29; 152)   *Quaritch.* £80
– – Anr. Edn. [1827]. 4to. Some spotting. Hf. cf. (P. May 14; 81)   *Kenyon.* £60
– – Anr. Edn. 1827-29. 2 vols. in 1. 4to. Vig. titles & plts. on india paper, 1st. few ll. detchd. Orig. bdg., brkn. (TA. Feb.19; 663)   £75
– – Anr. Edn. 1827-30. 1st. Edn. Pts. 1-42 (all publd.?). 4to. Orig. ptd. paper wraps., some slightly frayed or worn, lr. wrap. of pt. 27 missing, cl.-bkd. folder. (S. Apr.7; 283)   *Fletcher.* £140
– – Anr. Edn. 1828. 4to. Browning & spotting. Hf. cf. (CSK. Jun.26; 31)   £85
– – Anr. Copy. Cont. hf. roan. (C. Mar.18; 183)   *Traylen.* £75
– – Anr. Copy. Spotting. Cont. hf. cf., worn. (CSK. Aug.15; 183)   £65
– – Anr. Edn. 1829. 4to. Occasional slight spotting. Orig. hf.-mor., spine worn. (CSK. Sep.12; 132)   £85
– – Anr. Copy. Some ll. spotted. Cont. hf. cf., worn. (SBA. Jul.14; 305)   *Bailey.* £60
– – Anr. Edn. 1830. 4to. Some dampstains. Orig. pict. bds. (P. Apr.9; 74)   *Park.* £100
– – Anr. Edn. N.d. & 1829. 2 vols. 4to. Lacks a few ll., plts. rather spotted or stained. Cont. hf. cf., worn. W.a.f. (SKC. Dec.4; 1635)   £100
– – Anr. Edn. N.d. 4to. Orig. cl., lacks spine. (CSK. May 15; 64)   £80

SHEPHERD, Thomas Hosmer–NEALE, John Preston
– Modern Athens Displayed in a Series of Views: Or, Edinburgh in the Nineteenth Century ... –[Views ... of Scottish Seats]. 1829; 1830. 2 works in 1 vol. 4to. 1st. work: vig. title foxed; 2nd. work: lacks title, some spotting. Cont. cl., rebkd. (TA. May 21; 498)   £70
– – Anr. Copy. 1st. work: vig. title foxed; 2nd. work: some spotting. (TA. Jun.18; 501)   £65

SHEPHERD, Thomas Hosmer & others
– London Interiors, with their Costumes & Ceremonies. 1841. 4to. Cont. gt. (SBA. Dec.16; 90)   *Quaritch.* £70

SHERATON, Thomas
– The Cabinet Dictionary. 1803. 1st. Edn. 88 engd. plts., many folding, few torn, many stained. Cont. reverse cf., unc. (S. Mar.17; 450)   *Allan.* £380
[–] The Cabinet-Maker & General Artist's Encyclopaedia. 1803-07. Nos. 1-30. Fo. 67 engraved plts., 1 torn & reprd., no title-p. Cont. cf., rebkd., cl. s.-c. W.a.f. (S. Mar.17; 451)   *Sims & Reed.* £1,100
– The Cabinet-Maker & Upholsterer's Drawing-Book. 1793-96. 3 pts. in 2 vols. 4to. Lacks 2 plts. (supplied in facs.), some folding plts. with reprd. tears, 1 plt. detchd. Old reversed cf., rebkd. (C. Nov.5; 144)   *Harcourt-Williams.* £150
– The Cabinet-Maker & Upholsterer's Drawing Book.–Appendix ... 1791-93. 1st. Edn. Together 4 pts. in 1 vol. 4to. Engd. frontis., 98 engd. plts., 2 plts. reprd., some stained. Mod. mor. by Sangorski. (C. Jul.16; 337)   *Henderson.* £340
– – Anr. Edn. L., Priv. Ptd. 1794. 2nd. Edn. 4 pts. in 1 vol. 4to. Foxing. Cont. diced cf., gt. arms of a Royal Duke (Connaught?) on both covers, rebkd. (SG. Mar.12; 322) $850
– – Anr. Edn. 1802. 1st. work 3rd. Edn. 2 works in 1 vol. 4to. 1st. work 88 plts. (of 122). Cont. reverse cf. W.a.f. (S. Mar.17; 452)   *Fogg.* £100

– Model- und Zeichnungsbuch für Ebenisten, Tischler, Tapezirer und Stuhlmacher ... Trans.:– Gottfried Traugott Wenzel. Leipzig, [1794]. 1st. German Edn. 3 vols. in 2. 4to. 94 engraved plts., should be 93 but vol. 2 lacks plt. 27, replaced by plt. 19 of vol. 3, & vol. 3 plts. not corresponding to list of contents. Orig. bds., largely unopened, cl. s.-c. (S. Mar.17; 453)   *Weinreb.* £280

SHERER, Col. J.M.
– Recollections of the Peninsula. L., 1825. 4th. Edn. Early str.-grd. mor., gt. borders & spine, worn. Double fore-e. pntg.; from the liby. of Zola E. Harvey. (SG. Mar.19; 171) $475

SHERER, John
– The Classic Lands of Europe: embracing Italy, Sicily, & Greece. Ill.:– William Bartlett & others. L., ca. 1875. 2 vols. Fo. Stpd. mor., jnts. & edges defect., 1 cover partly separated. (PNY. Oct.1; 95) $550
– – Anr. Edn. n.d. 2 vols. 4to. Cont. hf. cf. (SH. Nov.6; 256)   *Strufaldi.* £150
– – Anr. Copy. 2 vols. Cont. hf. cf. gt. (SBA. Oct.21; 125)   *Hyde Park Bookshop.* £110
– Rural Life. Ca. 1860. 4to. Hf. cf. gt. (P. Oct.2; 35)   *Freeman.* £120
– – Anr. Copy. 2 vols. Cont. hf. mor., worn. (TA. Jan.22; 268)   £70

SHERIDAN, Mrs. Frances
[–] The History of Nourjahad. 1767. 1st. Edn. Cf., rebkd. (P. Apr.30; 31)   *Jarndyce.* £100

SHERIDAN, Richard Brinsley
– The School for Scandal. Ill.:– Hugh Thomson. [1911]. (350) numbered, sigd. by artist. 4to. Orig. vell. gt., lacks ties. (SH. Mar.27; 523)   *Donnithorne.* £80

SHERIDAN, Richard Brinsley–CHAUCER, Geoffrey
– The School for Scandal.–The Complete Poetical Works. Ill.:– Hugh Thompson (1st. work); W. Goble (2nd. work). N.p.; N.Y., n.d.; 1912. 2 works in 2 vols. 4to. Both vols. in orig. cl. gt. (SKC. Dec.4; 1523)   £60

SHERSHENEVICH, Vadim
– Komu ya zhmu ruku [Whose Hand do I Shake]. [St. Petersb.], n.d. Liby. stp. on title. Orig. wraps., slightly soiled. (SH. Feb.6; 517)   *Quaritch.* £200
*See–*ESENIN, Sergei & others
*See–*ROIZMAN, Matvei & Shershenevich, Vadim
*See–*ZEMEMKOV, Boris & others

SHERWOOD, William A.
– Anvers un Jour parmi le Peuple. Anvers, 1913. (35) numbered. 11×13½ ins. Portfo., brkn. (SG. May 21; 436) $180

SHEVCHENKO, Aleksahdr
– Printsipy Kubizma [Principles of Cubism & other Trends in Painting]. Ill.:– Larionov, Goncharova, Shevchenko & others. Moscow, 1913. Ptd. on recto only. Orig. wraps., slightly torn & soiled, spine reprd. (SH. Feb.5; 268)   *Reed & Sims.* £190

SHIMON, of Cairo
– Halachot Gedolot. Venice, 1548. 1st. Edn. Fo. Sigd. by censors in 1577 & 1618, slight foxing. Cf. with blind-tooled triangles in rectangles. (SPB. May 11; 194) $1,000

SHIMON BEN MEIR
*See–*KITZUR Sefer Mitzvot Gadol–OVER Orach

SHIMON BEN YOCHAL, Rabbi
[–] Zohar (Genesis only). Cremona, 1559-60. 2nd. Edn. Fo. Lacks title, margins of 1st. 6 ll. reprd. with loss of text, slight staining. Orig. bdg. (S. Nov.18; 480)   *Elberg.* £140
[–] – Anr. Edn. Amst., 1715. 5th. Edn. 5 pts. in 3 vols. Lacks title to pt. III, slight staining. Varied bdgs. (S. Nov.18; 481)   *James.* £100

SHIPLEY, M.A.
– Artificial Flies & How to Make Them. Phila., 1888. 1st. Edn. 12mo. Gt.-decor. cl. (SG. Oct.16; 418) $200

SHIPLEY, William
– A True Treatise on the Art of Fly Fishing. Ed.:– Edward Fitzgibbon. L., 1838. L.P. Iss. Mod. buck., unc. (SG. Oct.16; 420) $100

SHIPP, John
- Cases in Farriery. Leeds, [1806]. 4to. Cont. hf. cf. From the collection of Eric Sexton. (C. Apr.15; 17) *Way.* £90

SHIRLEY, Evelyn Philip
- Catalogue of the Library of Lough Fea. Chiswick Pr., 1872. 4to. Cont. mor. gt. (SBA. Jul.23; 654) *Wilson.* £95
- The History of the County of Monaghan. 1879. Fo. Cont. lev. mor., richly gt. From the collection of Eric Sexton. (C. Apr.16; 355) *Gamble.* £400

SHIRLEY, Henry
- The Martyr'd Souldier. 1638. 1st. Edn. 4to. Mor. by Rivière. [STC 22435] (C. Nov.19; 162) *Dunbar.* £170

SHIRLEY, James
- The Lady of Pleasure. 1637. 1st. Edn. 4to. Staining to inner margins at beginning. Recent mor. [STC 22448] (C. Nov.19; 161) *Brett-Smith.* £1,200
- The Maides Revenge. 1639. 1st. Edn. 4to. Minor worming in upr. inside corner affecting some text letters only. Recent cf.-bkd. bds. [STC 22450] (C. Nov.19; 163) *Dunbar.* £240

SHIRLOW, John
- Six Etchings comprising 'The Melbourne Set'. 1918 & 1919. Ltd. Edn., numbered. Fo. Orig. bds., upr. cover slightly stained, cl. spine, worn. (JL. Dec.15; 725) *Aus.* $740

SHIROKOV, P.
- Rozy v vine [Roses in Wine]. St. Petersb., 1912. Orig. wraps. (SH. Feb.6; 518) *Quaritch.* £70

SHIRREFF, John
- General View of the Agriculture of the Orkney Islands.–Agriculture of Shetland Islands. Edinb., 1814. 2 vols. in 1. Most ll. dusty. Orig. bdg. (PD. Feb.18; 130) £170

SHLOMO OF LUTZK
- Divrat Shlomo. Lvov, 1859. 2nd. Edn., on blue paper. 4to. Hf. leath. (S. Nov.18; 328) *Stern.* £65

SHLOSA Peirushim Al Shir Ha'shirim
Ed.:– Yitzhak Ibn Akrish [preface]. Constantinople, [1575-78]. 1st. Edn. Sm. 4to. Lacks ll. 13-16, inner margins reprd., without text loss, worming, staining. Mod. bds. (SPB. May 11; 89) $2,400

SHMEREL'SON, Grigory
- Goroda Khmur [The City of Gloom]. Petersb., 1922. (1,000). Orig. wraps. by V. Grigoriev. (SH. Feb.6; 520) *Quaritch.* £60
See–AFNAS'EV-SOLOV'EV, I. & others

SHMUEL SHMELKE HURWITZ of Nicolsburg
- Divrei Shmuel (on the Pentateuch). [Lvov], 1862. 1st. Edn. 4to. With notes by Joseph Weiss. Orig. bdg. (S. Nov.18; 331) *James.* £60

SHNEUR SALMAN of Liadi
- Likutei Torah (on Genesis; Chasidut). Wilno, 1884. 1st. Edn. 4to. Hf. leath. (S. Nov.17; 207) *Maggs.* £80
- Seder Tephilah Al Pi'nusach Ari. Ed.:– Maharid of B. Shneurson. Berditchev, 1913. 1st. Edn. 2 vols. 4to. Notes by Joseph Weiss. Hf. leath. (S. Nov.17; 211) *Zysblat.* £85
- Tanya-Likutei Amarim. Zolkiev, 1799. 2nd. Edn. 1st. 5 ll. & title in facs., slightly browned, slight worming. Hf. leath. (S. Nov.17; 213) *Zysblat.* £85
– – Anr. Edn. Tel-Aviv, 1943. Extensive notes by Joseph Weiss. Cl. (S. Nov.17; 214) *Quaritch.* £60

SHNEUR SALMAN of Liadi & Dov Ber of Lubavitch
- Kuntras Peirush Ha'milot Ha'nikra Mahadura Batra (La'sidun). Warsaw, 1867. 1st. Edn. 4to. Hf. leath. (S. Nov.17; 206) *Zysblat.* £100
- Likutei Torah (on Leviticus, Numbers & Deuteronomy). Wilno, 1903. 5th. Edn. 3 pts. in 2 vols. 4to. Orig. bdg. (S. Nov.17; 208) *Farro.* £50
- Torah Or. Lvov, 1851. 1st. Edn. 4to. Hf. cl. (S. Nov.17; 216) *Zysblat.* £75
– – Anr. Edn. Zhitomir, 1862. 3rd. Edn. 2 pts. in 1 vol. 4to. Notes by Joseph Weiss. Leath. (S. Nov.17; 217) *Rock.* £130
- Torat Chaim (on Genesis). Warsaw, 1866. 2nd. Edn. 2 pts. in 1 vol. 4to. Hf. leath. (S. Nov.17; 218) *Rock.* £120

SHNEURSON, Menachem Mendel [Zemach Zedek]
- Inyan Ha'histat-chut al Kivrei Ha'zaddikim (Chasidut). Warsaw, 1864. 2nd. Edn. 4to. Orig. wraps. (S. Nov.17; 221) *Maggs.* £85

SHNEURSON, Shneur Salman, of Kopyst
- Magen Avot. Berditchev, 1902. 1st. Edn. 7 pts. in 2 vols. Fo. Hf. leath. (S. Nov.17; 222) *Quaritch.* £130

SHOBERG & Geisler
- Description des Planches Relatives aux Crieurs Publics de St. Petersbourg . . . St. Petersb., 1794. 4to. Cont. Bradel paper s.-c., unc. (HD. Dec.5; 197) *Frs.* 14,300

SHOBERL or Schoberl, Frederic
- Ackermann's Juvenile Forget Me Not. [1830]. 12mo. Orig. bds., very slightly soiled. Inscr. by Mary Louisa Victoria, Duchess of Kent to her daughter, later Queen Victoria 'my dearly beloved Victoria from her affectionate Mother Victoria 24th Decem. 1830'. (CSK. Jun.19; 81) £90
- Austria. Phila., 1828. 12mo. 11 (of 12) hand-cold. engraved plts. Orig. leath.-bkd. bds., foxed. (SG. Oct.30; 31) $120
- Descripcion Abreviada del Mundo, Persia. Trans.:– J.J. de Mora. 1824. 2 vols. 12mo. Some offsetting. Mod. buckram. (BS. Jun.11; 195) £55
- Forget Me Not, 1846 & 1847. Ca. 1845-46. 2 vols. Red mor. gt., both covers elab. decor. with Garter ribbon encircling cipher of Queen Victoria, inside borders gt., silk doubls. & end-ll., fitted cl. cases. (SH. Apr.9; 5) *Simpson.* £125
- Picturesque Tour from Geneva to Milan by way of the Simplon. Ill.:– J. & J. Lory. L., 1820. 4to. Map heavily soiled, otherwise lightly soiled in places. Publishers cont. hf. leath., head of spine slightly defect. (R. Oct.14-18; 2013) DM 3,200
- Topographical & Historical Description of the County of Suffolk. 1820. Tree cf. gt. (P. Nov.13; 331) *Ackermann.* £70
- The World in Miniature. [Paris], 1811-21. 7 titles in 33 vols. 18mo. Unif. cont. red mor., gt.-tooled borders & spines. (SG. Oct.9; 257) $3,600
- The World in Miniature: Africa. N.d. 4 vols. 12mo. Some ll. detchd. Orig. bds., worn. (CSK. Nov.7; 20) £55
- The World in Miniature: Asiatic Islands & New Holland. Ill.:– Thomas Rowlandson. L., n.d. 2 vols. 12mo. Plts. dtd. 1824. Cont. cf. (CB. Sep.24; 140) Can. $160
- The World in Miniature: Austria. L., [1823]. 2 vols. in 1. 12mo. Without the 10 pp. of inserted advts. at end. Cont. cl., slightly faded. (CB. Apr.1; 251) Can. $160
- The World in Miniature: England, Scotland & Ireland. Ed.:– W.H. Pyne. L., 1827. 4 vols. 18mo. 77 (of 84) hand-cold. plts. Later three-qtr. mor., spines gt. (SG. Oct.30; 381) $300
- The World in Miniature: Hindoostan. L., [1822]. 6 vols. 18mo. Pol. cf., triple gt. fillet borders, spines gt., gt. dentelles, by Morrell, orig. pict. wraps. (1 upr. wrap. lacking) bnd. into each vol. (SG. May 14; 196) $900
- The World in Miniature: Japan. Japan, 1823. 12mo. Slightly soiled, 1 lf. torn, some plts. spotted. Cont. blind-stpd. cf., worn. (CSK. Nov.28; 54) £50
- The World in Miniature . . . Persia. L., [1822]. 3 vols. 16mo. Cont. red str.-grd. mor., spines & covers, roulette, inner dentelle. (HD. Apr.9; 566) Frs. 2,300
- The World in Miniature: Spain & Portugal. [1825]. 1st. Edn. 12mo. Lacks Courier plt. in vol. I. Orig. cl., inside hinge brkn. (S. Sep.29; 211) *Crete.* £85
- The World in Miniature: Turkey. N.d. 6 vols. 12mo. Some spotting, vol. 2 slightly wormed. Orig. bds., worn, upr. cover of vol. 2 lacking. (CSK. Nov.7; 21) £55

SHOEMAKER, R.M.
- Reports of Preliminary Surveys from the Union Pacific Railway, Eastern Division from Fort Riley to Denver City. Cinc., 1866. 1st. Edn. Orig. ptd. wraps., sewed (minor soiling), in mor.-bkd. folding case. (PNY. Mar.26; 245) $425

SHORT, Richard
- Peru Psychroposiac. 1656. 1st. Edn. Lacks final blank, 1 headline & p. number cropped, sm. marginal tear to title, occasional browning. Cont. sheep, reprd., some wear. [Wing S3528] (S. Feb.10; 385) *Waterfield.* £50

SHORT, Thomas
- A Comparative History of the Increase & Decrease of Mankind in England, & Several Countries Abroad. 1767. 1st. Edn. 4to. Some ll. stained, A1-2 frayed & soiled in upr. margins. Orig. bds., unc. (S. Apr.6; 147) *Rota.* £50
- Discourses on Tea, Sugar, Made-Wines, Spirits, Punch, Tobacco, etc. 1750. 1st. Edn. Advt. ll., slight browning. Cont. cf., rebkd. & reprd. From liby. of Dr. E. Ashworth Underwood. (S. Feb.23; 291) *Bickersteth.* £130
- The Natural, Experimental, & Medicinal History of the Mineral Waters of Derbyshire, Lincolnshire, & Yorkshire. 1734. 1st. Edn. 4to. Slight soiling. Cont. panel. cf., rebkd., corners reprd. From liby. of Dr. E. Ashworth Underwood. (S. Feb.23; 290) *McDowell.* £55
– – Anr. Edn. L. & Sheffield, 1734-40. 2 vols. in 1. 4to. Slight dampstaining, mainly marginal. Later hf. cf. (SBA. Oct.22; 648) *Rase.* £105
- The Natural, Experimental & Medicinal History of the Mineral Waters of Derbyshire, Lincolnshire & Yorkshire.–An Essay Towards the Natural, Experimental & Medicinal History of the Principle (sic) Mineral Waters of Cumberland, Northumberland etc. Sheffield (2nd. work), priv. ptd., 1734; 1740. 2 works in 1 vol. 4to. Cont. cf. (S. Dec.1; 381) *Whitehart.* £75
- New Observations . . . on City, Town, & Country Bills of Mortality. 1750. 1st. Edn. Sm. imperfections affecting B1-2, some browning. Cont. cf., worn. From liby. of Dr. E. Ashworth Underwood. (S. Feb.23; 292) *Dawson.* £160.

SHORT ANSWER (A) to a Late Book entitled Tentamen Medicinale, in which are Reprinted Several Papers . . . touching the Rise, Growth & Usefulness of the Dispensaries erected by the College of Physicians for the Benefit of the Sick Poor
1705. 3 pts. in 1 vol. Cont. panel. cf., rebkd. (S. Jun.17; 770) *Palinvrus.* £50

SHORTRIDGE, Capt. G.C.
- The Mammals of South West Africa. L., 1934. 2 vols. 4to. Cl. (SSA. Jun.18; 264) R. 120

SHORTT, Adam & Doughty, Arthur George
- Canada & its Provinces. Toronto, 1913-17. Authors' Edn., (875) numbered. 23 vols. 4to. Perforated stp. on title-pp., bkplt. & Circulation label of Detroit News in each vol. Lev., lge. gt. medallions on upr. covers round arms of Canada & Provinces. (SG. May 14; 39) $275
– – Anr. Edn. Toronto, 1914-17. Edinburgh Edn., (1875) numbered, on all-rag wtrmkd. paper. 23 vols. 4to. Buckram. (SG. Jun.11; 71) $160

SHOWER, Sir Bartholomuw
[–] Cases in Parliament Resolved & Adjudged upon Petition, & Writs of Error. 1698. 1st. Edn. Fo. Sig. dtd. 28 Jan. 1698, extensive MS. notes by Joseph Keble, barrister, owner's inscr. dtd. 1710, Maurice Johnson's bkplt. Cont. cf. [Wing S3650] (S. Jan.26; 66) *Bennett.* £90

SHRAPNEL'
Ed.:– [V.E. Milyaev]. Moscow, 1905. Nos. 1-2. 4to. Slightly stained. Unbnd. (SH. Feb.5; 125) *Quaritch.* £70

SHUNAMI, Shlomo
- Bibliography of Jewish Bibliographies, with Supplement. Jerusalem, 1965, Supp.: 1975. 2nd. Edn. 4to. Cl. (S. Nov.17; 108) *Israel.* £50

SIBLY or Sibley, Ebenezer
- Magazine of Natural History. [1795-98]. Vols. 1-4. Cf., worn, loose. W.a.f. (SH. Jul.9; 119) *Crossley.* £210
- The Medical Mirror. Ill.:– W. Newman. L., [1796]. New Edn. Mod. three-qtr. cf. (SG. Sep.18; 341) $150

SIBNAL
Ed.:– [K.I. Chukovsky]. St. Petersb., 1905. Nos. 1-4. 4to. Unbnd. (SH. Feb.5; 127) *De la Casa.* £75

SIBTHORP, John, Smith, Sir James Edward & Lindley, John
- Flora Graeca. Ill.:– James Sowerby & James de Carle Sowerby after Ferdinand Bauer. L., 1806-40 (wtrmkd. 1845). (Bohn's Iss.). 10 vols. Fo. Colophon lf. in vols. 1 & 10, 2 engraved titles slightly foxed. Cont. hf. mor. gt. by Hammond. From collection of Massachusetts Horticultural Society, stps. on plts. (SPB. Oct.1; 164) $120,000

SIDNEY, Sir Philip
- The Countesse of Pembroke's Arcadia. Dublin, 1621. Fo. Tear in pp. 263-4, corner cut at pp. 239-40, not affecting text, sig. on p. 539. Old cf., spine with raised bands. (LC. Feb.12; 588) £85
- - Anr. Edn. 1725. 2 vols. in 3. Cont. Engl. red mor., gt., spine tooled in compartments, covers with elab. border. (S. Nov.24; 258) *Quaritch*. £110
- - Anr. Copy. L.P. Fo. Some foxing. Old cf., loose, needs rebdg. (SG. Feb.5; 308) $150
- The Sonnets. Ill.:– Charles Ricketts. Vale Pr., 1898. (210). Orig. bds., unc., unopened. With pict. wood-engraved bkplt. of John Quinn. (S. Jul.31; 42) *Monk Breton*. £60

SIDNEY, Samuel
- The Book of the Horse. Ca. 1885. 4to. Orig. cl. (P. Apr.9; 32) *Schapiro*. £60
- - Anr. Copy. Hf. mor. (P. Apr.9; 30) *Reid*. £55
- - Anr. Edn. N.d. 4to. Cont. hf. mor., worn. (SH. Jan.30; 392) *Russell*. £75
- - Anr. Copy. Hf. buckram. (PG. Sep.3; 30) £60

SIDUR Mi'beracha
Ferrara, 1693. Tears, repairs, stains, browning. Hf. parch., wormholes. (SPB. May 11; 199) $950

SIEBMACHER, Johannes
- Das Erneuerte Teutsche Wappenbuch. Nuremb., 1655-57. 4th. Edn. 5 pts. in 3 vols., lacks pt. V supp. Ob. 4to. MS. notes on end-ll., ink & pencil notes, lightly soiled in parts, pt. IV browned at end. Bds. (HK. Nov.18-21; 1664) DM 1,700

SIEBOLD, A.E.v.
- Ausführl. Beschreibung der Heilquellen zu Kissingen und Ihrer Wirkungen, bes bei Frauenzimmerkrankheiten nebst einer Abhandlung über die Quellen zu Bocklet und Brückenau. Berlin, 1828. Cont. bds. (R. Mar.31-Apr.4; 1952) DM 1,200

SIEBOLD, M. & Kuyper, J.
- De Mensch, zoo als hij Voorkomt op den Bekenden Aardbol. Ill.:– L. Portman after Kuyper. Amst., 1802-07. L.P. 6 vols. Some minor foxing. Orig. wraps., loose & frayed, defect. (VG. Dec.16; 951) Fls. 800

SIEBOLD, Philipp Franz von
- Fauna Japonica. Aves. Leiden, 1850. Fo. Some spotting. Mod. mor. (S. Dec.3; 1129) *W. & W.* £1,500
- - Anr. Edn. Tokyo, 1975. Reprint Edn. 6 vols. Fo. Hf. leath., gt. (S. Jun.1; 210) *Nixon*. £440
- Nippon. Ed.:– A. & H. von Siebold. Würzburg & Leipzig, 1897. 2 vols. 4to. Orig. hf. linen. (R. Oct.14-18; 1792) DM 820

SIECLE DES MODES FEMININES
Paris, 1896. Cont. cf., orig. wraps. bnd. in, partly unc. (SI. Dec.4; 531) Lire 200,000

SIEGEL, R.
- Die Flagge. Berlin, 1912. 4to. Orig. pict. linen. (H. Dec.9/10; 484) DM 430

SIEGEMUNDIN, Justinen
- Die Chur-Brandenburgische Hoff-Wehe-Mutter, das ist, ein Hoechst-Noethiger Unterricht von Schweren und Unrecht-Stehenden Geburten ... Coeln an der Spree, 1690. 1st. Edn. 4to. Cont. vell., browned. (SG. May 14; 197) $1,900
- Die Königle. Preussische und Chur-Brandenburg. Hof-Wehe-Mutter. Berlin, 1756. 4to. Lacks port. Cont. leath., upr. cover loose. (R. Oct.14-18; 392) DM 2,200

SIELEN TROEST
[Saint Maartensdijk], [Pieter Werrecoren], [Nov., 1478]. 1st. Edn. in Dutch. 2 qtr. ll. only (of 90 ll.), rubricated, removed from a binding, holes from old stitching just affecting text, worming to blank portions, stained. Folding mor. case, gt., by Sangorski & Sutcliffe. From the collection of Eric Sexton. (CNY. Apr.8; 151) $2,400

SIENKIEWICZ, Henryk
- Quo Vadis? Ill.:– Salvatore Fiume. Ltd. Edns. Cl., 1959. (1500) sigd. by artist & printer. Orig. cl., d.-w., s.-c. (SH. Feb.20; 238) *George*. £50

SIEVEKING, L. de Giberne
- Bats in the Belfry. Ill.:– John Nash. 1926. (50) numbered, sigd. by author & artist. Orig. mor.-bkd. cl. gt. (SH. Mar.27; 347) *Quaritch*. £65

SIGAUD DE LA FOND, Jean René
- Essai sur Differentes Espèces d'Air qu'on signe sous le nom d'air fixe pour servir de suite ... aux Elemens de Physique du même auteur. Paris, 1779. 1st. Edn. Cont. bds., cf. spine gt. (S. Dec.1; 382) *Poulton*. £50

SIGNAL
Ed.:– [K.I. Chukovsky]. St. Petersb., 1905. Nos. 1-4 (all publd.). Fo. Unbnd. (SH. Feb.5; 185) *De la Casa*. £85

SIGNALY [Signals]
Ed.:– [V.E. Turok]. St. Petersb., 1906. Nos. 1-4 & Supp. (all publd.). Fo. A few sm. tears. Unbnd. (SH. Feb.5; 186) *Landry*. £170
- - Anr. Copy. 4to. (SH. Feb.5; 128) *De la Casa*. £130

SIGNATURE, The
1915. Nos. 1-3 (all publd.). Orig. wraps., in folding case. (C. Feb.4; 305) *Ross*. £170
- - Anr. Run. 1935-54. Nos. 1-12 & 14; New Series no. 1-18, together 31 vols. 4to. Orig. wraps., a few spines torn. (SH. Mar.6; 572) *Weston Gallery*. £180
- - Anr. Run. Nos. 1-18; New Series Nos. 1, 3-11 & 13 only. (SH. Jan.29; 52) *Weston*. £140
- - Anr. Run. 1946-54. New Series no. 1-18. Orig. wraps., 6 cl.-bkd. portfos. (SH. Jan.29; 53) *Forster*. £90

SIGNORELLI, A.
- Collezione [of Italian Coins]. Rome, 1952-55. Pts. 2-6 only. Orig. wraps. (SH. Mar.6; 441) *Spink*. £110

SIGUENZA Y GONGORA, Carlos de
- Libra Astronomica, y Philosophica. Mexico, 1690. 1st. Edn. Sm. 4to. Lr. blank corner of title reprd., some ll. stained or spotted. Mod. cf. Stp. of University of Mexico with note on A1r; mod. bkplt. with name removed; from Honeyman Collection. (S. May 19; 2846) *Zeitlin & Verbrugge*. £900

SILBERSCHLAG, J.E.
- Ausführliche Abhandlung der Hydrotechnik oder des Wasserbaues. Leipzig, 1772-73 2 pts. in 1 vol. Pt. 1 lightly browned, 1 title lf. stpd. Cont. leath. gt. (R. Mar.31-Apr.4; 1298) DM 720

SILHON, Jean de
- Esclaircissement de quelques Difficultez touchant l'Administration du Cardinal Mazarin. Paris, 1650. 1st. Edn. Pt. 1 (all publd.). Fo. Cont. red mor., gt., royal arms surmntd. on upr. cover, by gt. inscr., surrounded by broad decor. & leafy border incorporating cornerpieces of fleur-de-lis & couronne fermée, arms probably cont., lettering ca. 1800 or later, wide border probably cont. with lettering, except for cornerpieces which appear cont. with arms, spine gt. in compartments with single fleur-de-lis & couronne fermée, inner gt. dentelles. (SM. Oct.8; 2008) Frs. 4,500

SILLIMAN, Benjamin
- Elements of Chemistry. New Haven, 1830-31. 1st. Edn. 2 vols. Sm. hole in title to vol. 1, slight spotting & discolouration. Orig. cl.-bkd. bds., worn, unc., cl. case. From Honeyman Collection. (S. May 19; 2847) *Bennett*. £180

SILTZER, Capt. Franc.
- The Story of British Sporting Prints. N.d. Spotted. Orig. cl. (SH. Jan.29; 149) *Dallai*. £75
- - Anr. Copy. (CSK. Jan.30; 161) £50

SILVA, Ercole
[-] Dell'Arte dei Giardini Inglesi. Milan, 1801. 4to. Last lf. of errata, hf.-title, 1 plt. torn & reprd. Mod. hf. mor., partly unc. (SI. Dec.4; 532) Lire 320,000

SILVATICUS, Matthaeus
- Pandectae Medicinae. Ed.:– [Georgius de Ferrariis after Matthaeus Moretus]. Venice, Philippus Pincius for Bernardinus Fontana, 16 Jun. 1492. Fo. Lacks first 4 ll. with title, table & dedication & last blank lf., capital spaces, some with guide letters, a few very sm. wormholes at end, liby. stp. of St. Bride's Foundation. New cf. [BMC V493; Goff Census S516; H. 15201] (S. Jun.17; 772) *Jenner Books*. £180

SILVESTRE DE SACY, Antoine Isaac, Baron
- Mémoires d'Histoire et de Littérature Orientale. Paris, 1832. 4to. Some spotting. 19th. C. hf. mor., s.-c. From Bibliotheca Lindesiana. (S. Apr.29; 458) *Loman*. £140

SILVIUS, Aeneius
See–AENEIUS SILVIUS

SIM, T.R.
- The Ferns of South Africa. Camb., 1915. 2nd. Edn. Cl. (SSA. Nov.5; 86) R. 130
- The Forests & Forest Flora of the Colony of the Cape of Good Hope. Aberdeen, 1907. 4to. Some ills. crudely cold. Cl., stained. (SSA. Jun.18; 266) R. 100
- Sketch & Check-List of the Flora of Kaffraria. Cape Town, 1894. Orig. wraps., spine reprd. (SSA. Nov.5; 85) R. 90

SIMCHA BUNIM of Pshischa
- Chedvat Simcha (on Genesis). Warsaw, [1930]. 1st. Edn. Hf. cl. (S. Nov.18; 332) *Maggs*. £55
- Kol Sincha. Breslau, 1859. 1st. Edn. 2 pts. in 1 vol. 4to. Slight staining. Hf. leath. (S. Nov.18; 333) *James*. £70

SIMCOE'S MILITARY JOURNAL: a History of a Partisan Corps called The Queen's Rangers, Commanded by Lieut. Col. J.G. Simcoe, during the War of the American Revolution
N.Y., 1844. 1st. Amer. Edn. 12mo. Stp. on verso of maps. Later three-qtr. linen, ex-liby. (SG. Mar.5; 83) $160

SIMEONI, Gabriel
- Le Imprese Heroiche et Morali. Lyon, 1559. 1st. Edn. 4to. Slight spotting. Modern limp vell. (S. May 5; 37) *King*. £160
- La Vita et Metamorfoseo d'Ovidio. Ill.:– Bernard Salomon. Lyons, 1559. 19th. C. leath.-bkd. bds. Bkplt. & blindstp. of Francisco Poey, Havanna. (SG. Sep.25; 240) $425

SIMEONI, Gabriel–[FAUCHET, Claude]
- Les Illustres Observations Antiques.–Recueil des Antiquitez Gauloises et Françoises. Lyon; Paris, 1558; 1579. 1st. Edn. in Fr.; 1st. Edn. 2 works in 1 vol. 4to. 1st. work lacks final blank, sm. flaw in title-margin; 2nd. work with marginal inscr. on title. 17th. C. vell. bds., mott. in cf. style, covers sprung. (S. Jun.9; 31) *Marlborough*. £95

SIMI, Niccolo
- Theoricae Planetarum in Compendium Redactae. Basle, 1555. Slight staining & soiling. Mod. bds. From Honeyman Collection. (S. May 19; 2848) *Quaritch*. £260

SIMLER, Josias
- De Helvetiorum Republica, Pagis, Foederatis, Stipendiariis, Oppidis (etc.). Paris, 1577. 17th. C. cf., upr. cover detchd. (C. Apr.1; 170) *Davidson*. £600
- De Republica Helvetiorum. Zurich, 1576. Title inscr., lacks final blank, slight dampstaining. 19th. C. hf. cf., worn. (CSK. Mar.13; 29) £75

SIMMS, Frederick W.
- Public Works of Great Britain. 1838. 4 pts. in 1 vol. Fo. 138 (of 151) un-cold. aquatint plts. Cont. hf. mor. (TA. Jan.22; 107) £110
- - Anr. Copy. Spotted. Worn, covers detchd. (SH. Nov.6; 155) *Weinreb*. £100

SIMMS, William Gilmor
[-] Michael Bonham: or, The Fall of Bexar, A Tale of Texas. Richmond, 1852. 1st. Edn. Tall 4to. Corrected thro.-out in cont. hand. Orig. ptd. wraps., sewed, wraps. chipped at extremities, in mor.-bkd. 4-way folding case. [Sabin 81239] (PNY. Mar.26; 314) $100

SIMON, Andre L.
- Bibliotheca Gastronomica. L., 1953. (750) numbered. 4to. Cl., d.-w. (SG. Jan.22; 357) $110
- Wines of the World. 1969. Ltd. sigd. Edn. 4to. Crimson mor. gt., overlay on upr. cover, by Zaehnsdorf, buckram box. (P. Sep.11; 28) *Chelsea Rare Books*. £50

SIMON, Henry
- Armorial Général de l'Empire Français. Ill.:– B. Turlure. Paris, priv. ptd., 1812. 2 vols. Fo. First 3 ll. vol. 2 reprd. Hf. red mor., spine-raised bands, by Loisellier. (HD. Apr.24; 185) Frs. 2,300

SIMON, Sir John
- Public Health Reports . . . Ed.:– Edward Seaton. 1887. 1st. Edn. 2 vols. Some spotting. Orig. cl., end-paper of vol. II with release stp. of Manchester Medical Society. From liby. of Dr. E. Ashworth Underwood. (S. Feb.23; 294) *Jenner*. £55

SIMON, Oliver
- A Specimen Book of Types & Ornaments in Use at the Curwen Press. 1928. Ltd. Edn. 4to. Orig. cl. (SH. Jan.29; 54) *Henderson.* £180

SIMON, Oliver (Ed.)
See-FLEURON, The

SIMOND, Louis
- Journal of a Tour & Residence in Great Britain. Edinb., 1815. 2 vols. Cf. gt. (P. Oct.23; 62) *Brooke-Hitching.* £70

SIMONOFF, Leonid de & Moerder, Jean de
- Les Races Chevalines. Paris, ca. 1894. Some marginal foxing. Qtr. mor. (CB. Dec.9; 132) *Can.* $130

SIMONS, Anna
- Titel und Initialen fur die Bremer Presse. Munich, 1926. (220). Fo. Loose as iss. in cl.-bkd. bd. portfo., linen ties. (C. Jul.22; 125) *Sims & Reed.* £80

SIMONS, Menno
- Opera, ofte Groot Sommarie, etc. [Haarlem], [1646]. 2nd. Edn. 4to. 4 ll. ptd. on 1 side only & misbnd. Cont. blind-stpd. cf.-bkd. wood bds., lacks clasps, top of spine defect. (VG. Oct.13; 146) *Fls.* 1,050

SIMPLICISSIMUS
Ed.:– Th. Heine & A. Langen. Ill.:– Heine, Reznicek, Steinlen & others. Munich, 1896-97. Yr. I. Fo. 1 issue double, 3 ll. with tear, 4 ll. reprd., browned. Cont. linen, 2 tears in spine, lightly worn, orig. wraps. bnd. in. (H. Dec.9/10; 2344) *DM* 450
- - Anr. Edn. Munchen, 1904-43. 14 iss. only. 4to. Orig. wraps. (SH. Oct.9; 40) *Lamm.* £70

SIMPLON (Le)
- Promenade Pittoresque de Genève à Milan. Paris, ca. 1825. 16mo. Cont. paper bds., spine decor., covers gt., s.-c. (HD. Apr.9; 567) *Frs.* 3,600

SIMPSON, Christopher
- A Compendium of Practical Musick. 1678. Some ll. soiled. Cont. cf., worn, split, lacks upr. cover. [Wing S3811] (S. Apr.7; 383) *Bickersteth.* £120

SIMPSON, Sir George
- Narrative of a Journey round the World. L., 1847. 1st. Edn. 2 vols. Port. slightly foxed. Orig. cl., ex-liby. (CB. Dec.9; 250) *Can.* $320

SIMPSON, Helen
See-SAYERS, Dorothy L. & Simpson, Helen

SIMPSON, James H.
- Journal of a Military Reconnaisance, from Santa Fe, New Mexico, to the Navajo Country. Phila., 1852. 1st. Separate Edn. Ex-liby. stp. on many plts. Orig. cl. (SG. Mar.5; 410) $190

SIMPSON, Sir James Y.
- Acupressure: a New Method of Arresting Surgical Haemorrhage & of Accelerating the Healing of wounds. Edinb., 1864. 1st. Edn. Orig. cl., stain on upr. cover. Pres. copy, A.L.s to Dr. McGavin (to whom book is inscr.) dtd. 24 Dec. 1864. (S. Dec.2; 622) *Studd.* £85
- Anaesthesia or the Employment of Chloroform & Ether in Surgery, Midwifery, etc. Phila., 1849. [1st. Amer. Edn.?]. Slight foxing. Orig. cl. (S. Jun.17; 776) *Gurney.* £90
- - Anr. Copy. Orig. stpd. cl. (SG. Sep.18; 342) $375
- The Works of. Ed.:– J. Watt Black & Sir Alexander R. Simpson. Edinb., 1871-72. 3 vols. Orig. cl. (S. Jun.17; 777) *Hammond.* £70

SIMPSON, John
- A Complete System of Cookery. L., [1813]. 3rd. Edn. Old bds., brkn., unc. (SG. Dec.18; 124) $120

SIMPSON, T.
See-WETHERED, H. Newton & Simpson, T.

SIMPSON, Thomas
- The Doctrine of Annuities & Reversions. 1742. 1st. Edn. Some browning, sig. on title-p. Cont. tree cf. From Honeyman Collection. (S. May 19; 2850) *Riley-Smith.* £150
- The Doctrine of Annuities & Reversions.–An Appendix. 1742-43. 2 works in 1 vol. Mod. bds. (SH. Oct.10; 319) *Frognal.* £85
- The Doctrine & Application of Fluxions. 1750. 1st. Edn. 2 vols. Some foxing, owner's inscr. of S. Stonehouse, 1843, with sm. pen & ink sketch dtd. 1871 on fly-lf. to vol. I. Cont. cf., worn. From

Honeyman Collection. (S. May 19; 2851) *Quaritch.* £70

SIMPSON, William
- Hydrologia Chymica. 1669. Cont. cf. [Wing S3833] (SH. Jul.16; 214) *Lawson.* £95
- - Anr. Copy. From the Tittenhanger liby. (S. Dec.1; 383) *Poulton.* £80

SIMPSON, William
- The Seat of the War in the East. 1855. 2 vols. in 1. Fo. Dampstains, marginal soiling & tears, some plts. with slight loss. Orig. hf. mor., worn & partly disbnd., upr. cover detchd. (CSK. Jan.9; 134) £80
- - Anr. Edn. 1855-56. 1st. & 2nd. Series. 2 vols. Lge. fo. 78 cold. litho. plts. only (of 79), some foxing, all plts. loose in gutta-percha bdgs. Cont. hf. mor., worn. W.a.f. (C. Mar.18; 105) *Arader.* £480
- - Anr. Copy. Some ll. spotted. (SH. Nov.7; 359) *Heald.* £420
- - Anr. Copy. 79 tinted litho. plts., all interleaved, most interleaves carrying keys, some foxing. Cont. red mor. gt. (C. Mar.18; 106) *Hammond.* £240
- - Anr. Copy. Litho. titles & 79 plts. tinted in 2 cols. Cont. hf. mor. (C. May 20; 171) *Hardy.* £220
- - Anr. Copy. In 1 vol. Spotted. Cont. hf. mor., gt. (SH. Jun.4; 154) *Erlini.* £160
- - Anr. Copy. 2 vols. in 1. Spotted. (SH. Nov.7; 360) *Cookey.* £120
- - Anr. Copy. Litho. title to 2nd. pt. & 79 (of 81) litho. plts., some ll. loose, lacks title to 1st. Series & all before plt. 2, a few short tears. Cont. cf., lacks covers & most of spine. W.a.f. (S. Jun.23; 335) *Elliott.* £100
- - Anr. Edn. 1856. 2nd. Series only. Lge. fo. 38 cold. litho. plts., 1 torn, some interleaves carrying keys. Cont. hf. mor., worn. (C. Mar.18; 107) *Crisp.* £350
- - Anr. Copy. 1 plt. torn, plts. loose in gutta-percha bdg., foxed thro.-out. Mor.-bkd. cl., worn. (C. Nov.5; 145) *Simpson.* £60
- - Anr. Copy. 2 vols. Titles foxed, minor foxing at other plts. (mostly marginal). Orig. mor.-bkd. gt.-stpd. cl., disbnd., needs rebacking. (PNY. Mar.26; 298) $700
- - Anr. Edn. N.d. Fo. 38 hand-cold. litho. plts. only & some odd plts., loose. Orig. cl.-bkd. bds., worn & soiled. (SD. Feb.4; 236) £170

SIMROCK, Karl
- Das Malerische u. Romantische Rheinland. Leipzig, ca. 1840. Soiled towards end. Cont. hf. leath. gt. (HK. May 12-14; 736) *DM* 2,300
- - Anr. Edn. Leipzig, ca. 1850. Vol. 9. Loose in parts, text soiled in parts. Cont. red mor. gt. (HK. Nov.18-21; 1345) *DM* 2,100

SIMS, James Marion–SOUCHON, Edmond
– Silver Sutures in Surgery, the Anniversary Discourse before the New York Academy of Medicine.–Reminiscences of Dr. J. Marion Sims in Paris. N.Y., 1858; 1894. 2nd. work offprint. 2 works in 1 vol. New cl. (S. Jun.17; 780) *Pratt.* £65

SIMSON, Robert
- Opera Quaedam Reliqua. Ed.:– James Clow. Glasgow, 1776. 1st. Edn. 4to. Colophon lf. dtd. 1774 at end, offsetting on title. Cont. tree cf., gt., worn. Stp. of Société de Lecture de Genève on title; from Honeyman Collection. (S. May 19; 2853) *Quaritch.* £80

SIMSON, Thomas
- An Inquiry how Far the Vital & Animal Actions of the More Perfect Animals can be Accounted for Independent of the Brain, being the Substance of the Chandos Lectures. Edinb., 1752. Hf. cf. (S. Jun.17; 781) *Quaritch.* £80

SINCLAIR, Mrs. Francis
- Indigenous Flowers of the Hawaiian Islands. L., 1885. 1st. Edn. Fo. Orig. cl. (CNY. May 22; 213) $850
- - Anr. Copy. Disbnd. & loose. (SG. Nov.20; 353) $375

SINCLAIR, Sir John
- An Account of the System of Husbandry. 1813. 2 vols. Cont. cf. gt. Pres. copy. (CE. Jul.9; 126) £190
- The Code of Health & Longevity. 1816. Foxed. Orig. cl.-bkd. bds. A.L.s from author requesting acceptance of his book to Sir Evan John Murray. (CE. Jul.9; 94) £78

- History of the Public Revenue of the British Empire. 1785-90. 1st. Edn. 4to. Cf. gt. (P. Oct.23; 85) *Brooke-Hitching.* £130
- Statistical Account of Scotland. Edinb., 1793-98. 1st. Edn. 12 vols. (VI, VIII-XII, XIV-XVI, XVIII-XX) of 21. Some slight browning. Cont. hf. cf., rather worn. (S. May 5; 225) *Aberdeen.* £120

SIND, Baron J.B. von
- Vollständiger Unterricht in den Wissenschaften eines Stallmeisters. Göttingen & Gotha, 1770. Fo. A few marginal wormholes at beginning & end. Cont. cf., spine gt. (S. Jun.1; 45) *Joseph.* £280
- - Anr. Copy. Göttingen, 1775. Title copper engr. with sm. tear behind. Cont. hf. leath., sm. tear at spine pasted. (R. Mar.31-Apr.4; 1712) *DM* 800

SINGER, Charles Joseph
- The Earliest Chemical Industry. 1948. 1st. Edn. (Ltd.). Fo. Engraved colophon device by Stephen Gooden. Orig. buckram. From liby. of Dr. E. Ashworth Underwood. (S. Feb.23; 295) *Subunso.* £60
- A History of Technology. Ed.:– [C. Singer, E.J. Holmyard & A.R. Hall & others]. Oxford, 1954-58. 5 vols. 4to. Vol. II mor. gt., specially bnd. for pres. to Dr. Singer on his 80th. birthday, rest orig. cl., d.-w.'s. From liby. of Dr. E. Ashworth Underwood. (S. Feb.23; 299) *Pilo.* £80

SINGER, Hans Wolfgang
See-MULLER, Hermann Alexander & Singer, Hans Wolfgang

SINJOHN, John (Pseud.)
See-GALSWORTHY, John 'John Sinjohn'

SINNER, J.R.
- Catalogus Codicum Mss. Bibliothecae Bernensis. Berne, 1760. 4 folding engraved facs.'s bnd. in at rear. Cont. hf. cf. (TA. Mar.19; 223) £54

SINTENIS, Renee
- Junge Tiere. [Hamburg], [1942]. (30) Privilege Edn. on Japon. Fo. Under passepartouts. Loose in orig. hand-bnd. hf. linen portfo. by J. Gerbers, Hamburg, slightly soiled. All etchings sigd. by artist. (H. May 21/22; 1799) · *DM* 3,400
- Sappho. Figurae. [Munich], [1921]. Fo. Upr. cover with printed note, C. copy, separate portfo. of etchings. Orig. hf. linen portfolio. (HK. May 12-14; 2063) *DM* 1,800

SIONITA, Gabriele
[-] Arabia seu Arabum Vicina. Amst., 1635. 16mo. Lr. right corner of engraved title reprd., margins shaved with loss of a few letters. Old cf., rebkd. (CSK. Oct.17; 150) £70

SIONITA, Gabriele & Hesronita, Johannes
- Grammatica Arabica Maronitarum. Paris, 1616. 1st. Edn. 4to. Text cropped at foot on several ll., sm. wormhole thro.-out, title & last lf. a little stained. 18th. C. cf., gt. spine, head & foot of spine chipped. (C. Apr.1; 85) *Riley-Smith.* £330

SIQUEIROS, David Alfaro
- Prison Fantasies. N.Y., [1973]. (70) numbered on Japan paper. Portfos. I & II. Lge. fo. Loose as iss. in wraps. (SG. Apr.2; 276) $1,200

SIR GWAIN & the Green Knight
Ed.:– Gwyn Jones. Ill.:– Dorothea Braby. Gold. Cock. Pr., 1952. (360) numbered, sigd., nos. 1-60 specially bnd. Sm. fo. Orig. mor., partly untrimmed, with s.-c. (TA. Jul.16; 235) £110

SIREN, Osvald
- Chinese Sculpture from the Fifth to the Fifteenth Century. N.Y., 1925. Fo. Gt.-decor. buckram, liby. label in covers & on title-pp. (SG. Dec.4; 324) $650
- Early Chinese Paintings from A.W. Bahr Collection. 1938. (750) numbered. Fo. Orig. cl. (SH. Mar.6; 574) *George's.* £90
- - Anr. Copy. Gt.-lettered buckram, partly unc. (SG. Mar.12; 331) $200
- A History of Early Chinese Painting. L., [1933]. 2 vols. Fo. Buckram, ex-liby. (SG. Mar.12; 330) $325
- Les Palais Impériaux de Pékin. Paris & Brussels, 1926. 3 vols. 4to. Orig. wraps. (SH. Oct.9; 137) *Quaritch.* £200

SIRET, Henri & Louis
- Les Premiers Ages du Metal dans le Sud-Est de l'Espagne. Antw., 1887. 2 pts. in 1 vol. 4to. 27 plts. (but without additional atlas of plts.). Orig. mor.-bkd. cl., spine torn. (SBA. Dec.16; 64) *Duran.* £80

SIRIA, Antonio de
- Vida Admirabile y Prodigiosas Virtudes de la Ven. Sierva de Dios D. Anna Guerra de Jesus. Guatemala, 1716. 4to. Title soiled & frayed, outer margin strengthened, port. rebkd. & soiled, inner margin strengthened, a few other ll. torn or with marginal repairs, with some loss, dampstaining, etc. Old vell., leath. ties. (SG. Jan.8; 183) $250

SIRTORI, Girolamo
- Telescopium: sive ars Perficiendi Novuum illud Galilaei Visorium Instrumentum ad Sydera. Frankfurt, 1618. 1st. Edn. Sm. 4to. 1 folding plt. (of 2), slight worming affecting text & plt., a few MS. corrections, pencilled owners' inscr. of Jesuits at Vienna, on slip pasted in upr. margin. Vell. Pres. copy to Tommaso Mingoni; from Honeyman Collection. (S. May 19; 2854) *Roberts.* £570

SISMONDI, Jean Charles Leonard Simonde de
- Nouveaux principes d'économie Politique, ou de la Richesse dans ses Rapports avec la Population. Paris, 1827. 2nd. Edn. 2 vols. Slight spotting, liby. stps. on titles & hf.-titles. Mod. cf.-bkd. marb. bds. (S. Jan.26; 257) *Subunso.* £100

SITWELL, Edith
- The Collected Poems. Ill.:– Pavel Tchelitchew (Port.). L., 1930. L.P. 1st. Edn. Errata slip tipped-in. Buckram, unc. & unopened. Sigd. (SG. Nov.13; 609) $100
- Five Poems. 1928. 1st. Edn., (275). 4to. Orig. cl., unc., partly unopened. Sigd., inscr. to Cecil Beaton. (SH. Dec.19; 376) *Maggs.* £80
- Green Song & Other Poems. 1944. Orig. cl., d.-w. Pres. Copy to Walter de la Mare. (SH. Dec.18; 25) *Blackwell.* £55
- Rustic Elegies. 1927. 1st. Edn. Orig. cl., d.-w. Inscr. by Siegfried Sassoon 'Taplow de la Mares'. (SH. Dec.18; 291) *Maggs.* £65

SITWELL, Sir George R.
- The Sitwell Pedigree.–The Barons of Pulford. Scarborough; Scarborough, priv. ptd., ca. 1890; [1889]. (20) numbered; (250) numbered, sigd. 2 works in 1 vol. 4to. 1st. lf. slightly browned, 2nd. work facs. Red mor.-bkd. cl. gt. (SBA. Oct.22; 649) *Chambers.* £65

SITWELL, Sir Osbert & Sacheverell
- All at Sea. 1927. 1st. Edn. Orig. cl., d.-w. designed by Cecil Beaton, worn. Inscr. to Cecil Beaton. (SH. Dec.19; 382) *Vaughan.* £65

SITWELL, Sacheverell
- Exalt the Eglantine & other Poems. Ill.:– Thomas Lowinsky. 1926. (370) numbered. 4to. Orig. decor. cl. bds., some pink staining to covers, unc. (LC. Jun.18; 51) £60
See–BEAUMONT, Cyril W. & Sitwell, Sacheverell

SITWELL, Sacheverell & Blunt, Wilfred
- Great Flower Books, 1700-1900. Ed.:– P.M. Synge. 1953. Ltd. Edn. Fo. Orig. hf. cf., slightly soiled. (S. Jan.26; 295) *Clarendon.* £340
- - **Anr. Edn.** 1956. Fo. Hf. cl., d.-w. (torn & reprd.) *Peters.* £200
- - **Anr. Copy.** Cl., d.-w. (SSA. Nov.5; 88) R. 280
- - **Anr. Edn.** 1956. (295) special copies numbered. Fo. Hf. mor., s.-c. (S. Dec.3; 1131) *Quaritch.* £300
- - **Anr. Edn.** 1956. Ltd. Edn., numbered copy, sigd. by authors. Lge. fo. Orig. hf. mor. gt., sm. graze on spine, cl. s.-c. (S. Jun.1; 213) *Langmead.* £240
- - **Anr. Edn.** 1956. (1750) unnumbered, sigd. by authors; bnd. as Ltd. Iss. (195). Fo. Orig. hf. mor. by the Wigmore Bindery, slightly rubbed at head & foot. (S. Jun.9; 18) *Forum Books.* £180

SITWELL, Sacheverell & Madol, Roger
- Album de Redoute. 1954. Facs. of 1824 Edn., sigd. by authors. Fo. Hf. mor. gt., s.-c. (P. Nov.13; 245) *Forster.* £160
- - **Anr. Edn.** 1954. (250), this copy unnumbered. Lge. fo. Orig. hf. mor. with s.-c. by Mansell of L. Pres. copy. (TA. Jun.18; 128) £75
- Album de Redoute.–New Redoute Bibliography. 1954, Facs. of the 1824 Edn. (250) numbered, sigd. Fo. Orig. hf. mor., s.-c. (TA. Feb.19; 487) £85

SITWELL, Sacheverell & others
- Fine Bird Books 1700-1900. 1953. Fo. Hf. buckram. (S. Jun.1; 215) *Beynon.* £240
- - **Anr. Copy.** Orig. hf. buckram. Inscr. 'My own copy, Handasyde Buchanan'. (S. Jun.1; 211) *Hill.* £220
- - **Anr. Copy.** Hf. cl. (S. Dec.3; 1130) *Dawson.* £190
- - **Anr. Edn.** L. & N.Y., 1953. Ltd. Edn. Tall fo. Review copy, with laid-in message from publishers. Buckram-bkd. marb. bds. (SG. May 14; 198) $475

SIX Ages de Leontine (Les)
Paris, ca. 1825. 6 pts. in 1 vol. 12mo. Cont. romantic cf., blind & gt. decor. inner dentelle. (HD. Jun.10; 208) Frs. 2,200

SIXTUS IV, Pope
- De Sanguine Christi ... de Potencia Dei. Nuremb., Friedrich Creussner, 1474. Fo. Lacks blank fo. 89, initials & head-lines in red, rubricated thro.-out, some stps. in margins. 18th. C. cf., spine gt., worn. Thomas Welton bkplt. [H. 14798] (S. Nov.25; 324) *Fletcher.* £260
See–BOETHIUS, Anicius Manilius Torquatus Severinis–SIXTUS IV, Pope

SIXTUS VON SIENA
- Bibliotheca Sancta. Cologne, 1586. 3rd. Edn. Fo. Lightly soiled, 2 cont. MS. owner's marks on title dtd. 1586 & 1616. Cont. blind-tooled pig-bkd. wood bds., owner's monog., 2 clasps, slightly worn & soiled. (HK. Nov.18-21; 299) DM 560

SKAZKI [Tales]
Ed.:– [V.E. Solodilov]. St. Petersb., 1907. Nos. 1-2. 4to. Unbnd. (SH. Feb.5; 129) *Quaritch.* £90

SKEAT, Walter William & Blagden, Charles Otto
- Pagan Races of the Malay Peninsula. 1906. 2 vols. Orig. cl. (SH. Mar.5; 290) *Randall.* £75

SKELTON, Sir John
- Charles I. Goupil, 1898. (500) on Japanese paper. 4to. Cont. mor., gt. (SH. Jun.11; 213) *Armstrong.* £50

SKELTON, Sir John–CREIGHTON, Mandell
- Mary Stuart.–Queen Elizabeth. L. & Paris, 1893; 1896. (100) numbered on Japan vell. (1st. work). Fo. 1st. work without the dupl. set of plts. Both lev. gt., gt. dentelles, orig. wraps. bnd. in (SG. Mar.19; 247) $130

SKELTON, Joseph
- Engraved Illustrations of the Principal Antiquities of Oxfordshire. 1823. 4to. Plts. on india paper mntd., end-papers browned, some edges slightly dampstained, occasional light foxing. Cont. mor., gt. borders & arms on upr. cover. (C. Feb.25; 58) *Old Hall.* £120
- - **Anr. Copy.** Occasional light spotting. Cont. hf. mor. (CSK. Sep.26; 120) £55
- Engraved Illustrations of the Principle Antiquities of Oxfordshire, from Original Drawings by Frederick Mackenzie.–Pietas Oxoniensis, Or, Records of Oxford Founders. 1823; 1828. 2 vols. Fo. Matching cont. hf. mor. (TA. Jul.16; 267) £130
- Etchings of the Antiquities of Bristol from Original Sketches by the late Hugh O'Neill. 1825. 4to. Recent hf. imitation mor. (TA. Feb.19; 631) £50
- Oxonia Antiqua Restaurata. Ill.:– after J. Skelton, J.M.W. Turner & others. Oxford, 1823. 2 vols. Fo. Some marginal foxing & tears. Cont. hf. cf., rebkd., orig. spines preserved. (C. Mar.18; 184) *Kentish.* £320
- Oxonia Antiqua Restaurata.–Engraved Illustrations of the Principal Antiquities of Oxfordshire. Ill.:– after F. Mackenzie (2nd. work). Oxford, 1823. L.P. (1st. work). 2 vols.; 1 vol. Lge. 4to. Title & frontis. of 2nd. work with minor marginal spotting. 1st. work: cont. hf. mor.; 2nd. work: cont. maroon mor. gt. Bkplts. of E.G. Baldwyn Childe & S.P.B. Mais in 1st. work, both works lately in the collection of E. Sexton. (C. Apr.16; 356) *Kentish.* £220
See–MEYRICK, Sir Samuel Rush & Skelton, Joseph

SKENE, Sir John of Curriehill
- Regiam Majestatem. Trans.:– Sir John Skene. Edinb., 1609. 1st. Edn. in Engl. Fo. Title slightly soiled, margin defect. 17th. C. cf. [NSTC 22626] (S. Jan.26; 11) *Crowe.* £110

SKETCH (The). A Journal of Art & Actuality 1893-1918. Vols. 1-4, 64-84, 91-102. (37 vols. in

29). Fo. 2 vols. in cont. hf. roan, 21 vols. in orig. cl. gt., 6 vols. in later hf. mor gt., with name of Sir Cecil Beaton gt.-stpd. at foot of spine. (SH. Oct.9; 23) *Jeffery.* £115

SKETCHES of Germany & the Germans
Ill.:– George Baxter (cold. frontis.). L., 1836. 2 vols. Folding map mntd. on linen, sm. stain at lr. edge of 1 frontis. Cont. hf. mor. (CB. Apr.1; 252) Can. $140

SKETCHLEY, Rose E.D.
- English Book-Illustration of To-day. Ed.:– Alfred W. Pollard. L., 1903. 1st. Edn. Deluxe, Vell. gt., moire taffeta box. Raymond M. Sutton Jr. copy. (SG. May 7; 260) $260

SKIFF, F.J.V.
See–DAWSON, Thomas Fulton & Skiff, F.J.V.

SKIING. The International Sport
See–PALMEDO, Roland

SKINNER, Andrew
See–TAYLOR, George & Skinner, Andrew

SKINNER, Joseph
[-] The Present State of Peru. 1805. 1st. Edn. 4to. Some sm. tears, slight offsetting. Hf. cf., spine crudely reprd. with tape. [Sabin 81615] (S. Jan.27; 567) *Burton Garbett.* £160
- - **Anr. Copy.** Text discold. Cont. hf. cf., worn. (TA. Nov.20; 400) £105
[-] - **Anr. Copy.** Lacks hf.-title, some staining & offsetting thro.-out. Cl. (BS. Jun.11; 391) £60
- - **Anr. Copy.** Mod. hf. mor., corners, decor. spine, unc. (HD. Dec.5; 198) Frs. 2,800

SKINNER, Stephan
- Linguae Anglicanae. 1671. Fo. Privilege lf., 'Bibliotheca Colbertina' on title. Cont. red mor., gt., arms of Jean Baptiste Colbert on covers, triple gt. fillet, spine gt. in compartments with his cipher. Bkplt. of Charles de Brosses. [Wing S3947] (SM. Oct.8; 2010) Frs. 3,600

SKODA, Joseph
- Abhandlung über Perkussion und Auskultation. Vienna, 1839. 1st. Edn. Orig. hf. mor., orig. ptd. wraps. bnd. in, unc. (S. Jun.17; 784) *Palinvrus.* £380
- - **Anr. Edn.** Vienna, 1842. 2nd. Edn. Old hf. cl. (SG. Sep.18; 345) $110

SKORPION
Ed.:– [Yu. S. Idel'son]. St. Petersb., 1906. Nos. 1-2. 4to. Unbnd. (SH. Feb.5; 130) *Landry.* £100

SKOTNES, Cecil & Gray, S.
- The Assassination of Shaka. Ill.:– Cecil Skotnes. Johannesburg, 1974. (250) sigd. by artist & author, De Luxe Edn. Fo. All plts. marked 'trial'. Orig. bdg., in orig. linen box. (VA. Jan.30; 354) R. 260

SLADE, Adolphus
- Records of Travels in Turkey, Greece, etc. 1833. 2 vols. Cont. hf. cf. (SH. May 21; 109) *Maggs.* £75

SLATER, Rev. M.
- Introductory Essay to a New System of Civil & Ecclesiastical Topography ... of Ireland. Dublin, 1806. Mod. bds., unc. (GM. Apr.30; 249) £52

SLEEMAN, William Henry
- Rambles & Recollections of an Indian Official. 1844. 1st. Edn. 2 vols. Hf. cf. by Bayntun, orig. cl. covers bnd. in. Extra-ill. with 9 watercolour drawings of the Taj Mahal & other buildings & monuments. (S. Jun.29; 233) *Plant.* £220
- - **Anr. Copy.** Occasional spotting. Orig. cl., gt. (CSK. Sep.26; 53) £50

SLEIDANUS, Johannes
- Commentariorum de Statu Religionis & Reipublicae, Carolo Quinto Caesare Libri XXVI. Strassburg, 1576. Old MS. names. Cont. blind-tooled pig-bkd. wood bds., monog. on upr. cover & date 1585 on lr. cover, brass clasps, lacks l. (D. Dec.11-13; 47) DM 600
- A Famouse Cronicle of oure Time, called Sleidanes Commentaries ... 1560. 1st. Edn. in Engl. Fo. Title a little soiled & mntd., lacks blank A6, A4-5 & A2-3 misbnd. 17th. C. cf., covers warped. [STC 19848] (C. Apr.1; 233) *Fletcher.* £120

SLEIGH, Burrows Willcocks Arthur
- Pine Forests & Hacmatack Clearings. L., 1853. 1 p. torn & reprd., occasional stains to margins. Recent qtr. leath. (CB. Apr.1; 306) Can. $170

SLESSOR, Kenneth
- **Thief of the Moon.** Ill.:– Norman Lindsay. Sydney, 1924. (150) numbered, sigd. 4to. 3 mntd. wood-engraved plts., numbered & sigd. or initialled by artist. Orig. mor. (SH. Mar.26; 324)
Lott & Gerrish. £300

SLEVOGT, Max
- **13 Federlithographien zu dem Märchen Der Gelernte Jäger.** Berlin, [1924]. (100) Privilege portfolio Edn. Sm. fo. Guarded, loose, orig. hf. vell. decor., defect. Pen lithos. printed in China, all sigd. by artist. (R. Mar.31-Apr.4; 654) DM 1,450
- **Ein Liederbuch mit Steinseichsungen.** Berlin, [1919]. (100) numbered. Lge. ob. 4to. Orig. hf. leath., upr. cover loose. 1st. litho. sigd. (HK. Nov.18-21; 2932) DM 480
- **Schatten u Traüme.** [Berlin], [1926]. (50). Ob. fo. Orig. hf. vell., etching on upr. cover. (HK. May 12-14; 2065) DM 2,700

SLEZER, John
- [–] **Theatrum Scotiae . . .** 1718. Fo. Lge. folding plan slightly torn, 8 plts. cut shorter & mntd., few ll. reprd. in margin. Cont. diced cf., worn, rebkd. W.a.f. (S. Mar.17; 392) *Cumming.* £380

SLICHTENHORST, A. Van
- **XIV Boeken ven de Geldersse Geschiedenissen.** Trans.:– J.I. Pontanus. Arnhem, 1654. 2 pts. in 1 vol. Fo. 15 (of 21) double-p. engraved maps & plans. Cont. vell., stained. W.a.f. (VG. Oct.13; 147) Fls. 2,200

SLIMAN-BEN-IBRAHIM
- **Rabia et Kouloub ou le Printemps des Legendes Sahariennes.** Trans.:– E. Dinet. Ill.:– Dinet. Paris, 1902. (260) on Vélin à la Cuve, numbered. Sm. 4to. Mor. gt. by Aussourd, decor. mor. onlays in centre panel of spine, silk end-papers, orig. wraps. bnd. in, s.-c. Pres. copy from translator, 2pp. note by him bnd. at end. (SM. Oct.8; 2374) Frs. 8,000

SLOANE, B.L.
See–WHITE, A. & Sloane, B.L.

SLOANE, Sir Hans
- **An Account of a most Efficacious Medicine for Soreness . . . of the Eyes.** 1745. 1st. Edn. Lacks hf.-title. Later mor.-bkd. cl. (SBA. Jul.23; 655) *Laywood.* £50
- **A Voyage to the Islands Madera, Barbados, Nieves, S. Christophers & Jamaica.** Ill.:– G. van der Gucht after Kickius. 1707-25. 1st. Edn. 2 vols. Fo. Text & plts. of vol. 1 mntd. on guards, 4 plts. of the 1st. series in vol. 1 detchd. Cont. cf. gt., & cont. spr. cf., gt. Vol. 1 with engraved armorial bkplt. of Viscount Weymouth, vol. 2 with bkplt. of Marquis Le Tellier de Courtanvaux, & his liby. stp. on title. [Sabin 82169] (C. Nov.5; 147) *Bath.* £1,600
- – **Anr. Copy.** Mntd. on guards thro.-out, vol. 1 errata lf. torn & reprd. Cont. cf., spines gt. in 7 compartments. (C. Jul.15; 99) *Taylor.* £1,200
- – **Anr. Copy.** Some plts. stained, ll. bnd. on guards thro.-out. 19th. C. hf. leath. From Chetham's Liby., Manchester. (C. Nov.27; 274 *Wheldon & Wesley.* £1,000
- – **Anr. Copy.** Panel. cf. gt. W.a.f. (CE. Nov.20; 41) £200
- – **Anr. Copy.** Some fold tears. Cont. cf. gt., reprd. From collection of Massachusetts Horticultural Society, plts. unstpd. (SPB. Oct.1; 165) $13,500

SMALL, Henry Beaumont
See–CANADIAN HANDBOOK & Tourist's Guide . . .

SMEATON, John
- **Experimental Enquiry Concerning the Natural Powers of Wind & Water to Turn Mills.** 1794. Orig. bds. (SH. Jun.18; 113) *Weinreb.* £180
- **Experimental Enquiry Concerning the Natural Powers of Wind & Water to Turn Mills & Other Machines.–An Historical Report on Ramsgate Harbour.** 1794; 1791. 2nd. work 2nd. Edn. 2 works in 1 vol. 1st. work with offsetting on plts.; 2nd. work with 1 folding plt. spotted, offsetting on title, sig. on 1st. title. Mod. hf. cf. From liby. of E.N. da C. Andrade; from Honeyman Collection (S. May 19; 2857) *Sims & Reed.* £150
- **A Narrative of the Building & a Description of the Construction of the Edystone Lighthouse with Stone.** 1791. 1st. Edn. Lge. fo. 1 plt. with tear, upr. inner margins stained & frayed by damp thro.-out, 'Advertisement to the Reader' slip tipped in. Hf. cf., covers detchd., spine defect.

W.a.f.; from Honeyman Collection. (S. May 19; 2856a) *Sims & Reed.* £160
- – **Anr. Edn.** 1813. 2nd. Edn. Fo. Spotted. Cont. hf. mor., worn, covers detchd. (SH. Oct.10; 521) *Weinreb.* £140
- **A Narrative of the Building of the Edystone Lighthouse.–Reports on Various Occasions. –Miscellaneous Reports.** 1812-14. 5 vols.; 2nd. & 3rd. works 4 vols. together. Fo. & 4to. 1st. work lacks some plts., stained & liby. stpd. Hf. leath.; cont. cf., 1 cover detchd. W.a.f. (SH. Jun.18; 115) *Weinreb.* £280

SMEDLEY, Frank E.
- **Frank Farlegh.–Harry Coverdale's Courtship. –Lewis Arundel.** Ill.:– George Cruikshank & 'Phiz'. 1901. Unif. hf. mor., spines gt. (SKC. May 19; 19) £60

SMEDLEY, Harold Hinsdill
- **Fly Patterns & their Origins.** Muskegon, [1943]. 1st. Edn. Cl., d.-w. Sigd., & with inserted typed list sigd. 'Dilo' by author. (SG. Oct.16; 432) $120

SMEE, William, & Sons
- **Designs for Furniture.** Ca. 1850. 4to. Without title, 185 (of 374?) engraved plts., contents loose due to gutta percha bdg. Orig. leath.-bkd. cl., ptd. sheet with Smee's name & address pasted in lr. cover. (LC. Feb.12; 116) £55

SMELLIE, William
- **A Set of Anatomical Tables with Explanations & an Abridgment of the Practice of Midwifery.** Ill.:– Grignion after Rymsdyk, Smellie & Camper. 1754. 1st. Edn. Fo. Plt. 35 with lf. of text inserted from a slightly shorter copy. Hf. vell., marb. paper covers. (S. Jun.17; 785) *Studd.* £750
- – **Anr. Edn.** Ed.:– A. Hamilton. Edinb., 1787. New Edn. Fo. Lf. of text to plts. 3 & 4 torn across, corners of plt. 25 stained. Bds., very worn, bdg. brkn. (S. Dec.2; 867) *Westwood.* £160
- – **Anr. Edn.** Edinb., 1792. Upr. margin of title reprd. with loss of 1st. letter, a few stains. Cf., rebkd. (S. Jun.17; 788) *Studd.* £100
- **A Treatise on the Theory & Practice of Midwifery, (vol. II: A Collection of Cases & Observations, vol. III: A Collection of Preternatural Cases & Observations) to which is now added a Set of Anatomical Tables.** 1779. 1st. vol. New Edn. 3 vols. Strip cut from upr. margin of title-pp. removing name, liby. stps., stains at end of vol. 1 affecting plts. Cont. cf., rebkd. (S. Jun.17; 787) *Studd.* £70
- **A Treatise on the Theory & Practice of Midwifery.–A Collection of Cases & Observations in Midwifery to Illustrate his former Treatise or First Volume on that Subject.** 1766; 1768. 5th. Edn.; 4th. Edn. 2 vols. 1st. title dust-soiled. New cf. (S. Jun.17; 786) *Studd.* £50

SMET, Pierre Jean de
- **Missions de l'Oregon et Voyages aux Montagnes Rocheuses . . .** Gent, [1848]. Lightly browned in parts & soiled, maps with sm. tears. Cont. hf. leath., worn. [Sabin 82265] (H. Dec.9/10; 516) DM 460

SMIDS, L.
- **Schatkamer der Nederlandsse Oudheden; of Woordenboek behels. Nederlands Steden en Dorpen, Kasteelen, Sloten en Heeren Huysen . . . [etc.].** Ill.:– R. Rochman. Amst., 1711. A few plts. with a sm. tear in the fold. Cont. vell., stained. (VG. Dec.17; 1533) Fls. 580

SMINOWSKY, Levi Yitzhak
- **Netiv Rashi Al Masechet Shabbat [Ma'amar Hillel Ha'levi of Paritch].** Jerusalem, 1895. Hf. cl. (S. Nov.17; 202) *Maggs.* £105

SMIRKE, Miss
- **Six Welsh Views.** N.d. [plts. wtrmkd. 1805]. Ob. fo. Stitched as iss. lacks ptd. wraps. (C. Jul.15; 100) *Quaritch.* £380

SMIRKE, Sydney
- **Illustrations of the Architectural Ornaments & Embellishments & Painted Glass, of the Temple Church, London, from drawings specially made, by permission, by W.R.H. Essex.** L., 1845. 4to. Marginal staining in some plts. Cont. hf. leath. & bds., worn & loose. (CB. May 27; 239) Can. $100

SMIRNOV, J.I.
- **Der Schatz von Achalgori.** Tiflis, 1934. Fo. Mod. buckram, orig. wraps. bnd. in, ex-liby. (SG. Dec.4; 163) $175

SMITH, Miss
- **Studies of Flowers from Nature.** Doncaster, priv. ptd., ca. 1820. 4to. 20 aquatint plts. in 2 states, cold. & uncold., lacks errata slip sometimes found. Hf. mor., worn. (S. Jun.1; 286) *Rostron.* £1,900

SMITH, A.
- **Illustrations of the Zoology of South Africa . . .** L., 1838. 4to. Cl. (SSA. Nov.5; 180) R.180
- – **Anr. Edn.** Ed.:– R.F. Kennedy. Johannesburg, 1976. Facs. Reprint, (350) numbered. 3 vols. 4to. Orig. bdgs. (VA. May 8; 495) R. 370
- – **Anr. Edn.** Johannesburg, 1977. (350). 3 vols., 4to. Publisher's leath. (VA. Aug.29; 371) R. 320
- – **Anr. Copy.** This set numbered 'P'. Qtr. publisher's leath. (VA. Jan.30; 361) R. 270

SMITH, A.H.
- **Commemorative Medals of the Z.A.R.** Johannesburg, 1958. 4to. Duplicated typescript. Cl.-bkd. wraps. (SH. Mar.6; 443) *Spink.* £55

SMITH, A.W. & Hallett, M.W.
- [–] **The Thames Angler.** L., 1846. 2nd. Edn. 16mo. Publisher's cl. stpd. in blind & gt. (SG. Oct.16; 434) $220

SMITH, A. Croxton
- **Sporting Dogs.** Ed.:– Duchess of Newcastle. Ill.:– G. Vernon Stokes L. & N.Y., [1938]. (250) numbered on L.P., sigd. by author & artist. 4to. Cl. (SG. Apr.9; 398) $130

SMITH, Adam
- **Essays on Philosophical Subjects.** 1795. 1st. Edn. 4to. A few very minor defects., stp. on verso of title. Later hf. cl. (SBA. Mar.4; 4) *Riley-Smith.* £240
- – **Anr. Edn.** Ed.:– Dugald Stewart, F.R.S.E. Dublin, 1795. 1st. Dublin Edn. Bds. (GM. Apr.30; 498) £80
- **An Inquiry into the Nature & Causes of the Wealth of Nations.** Dublin, 1776. 3 vols. Cont. cf., 2 upr.-covers detchd. (CSK. Oct.17; 226) £280
- – **Anr. Copy.** MS. annots., most in vol. 1. (CSK. Feb.27; 116) £240
- – **Anr. Edn.** 1789. 5th. Edn. 3 vols. Slight spotting. Cont. spr. cf., gt., some wear. (S. Jan.26; 172) *Subunso.* £110
- – **Anr. Copy.** Cont. tree cf., slightly worn. (S. Oct.21; 436) *Riley-Smith.* £50
- – **Anr. Edn.** 1791. 3 vols. Cf. gt. (P. May 14; 243) *Nelson.* £60
- – **Anr. Edn.** Dublin, 1793. 2 vols. Cf., stained. (PD. May 20; 7) £70
- – **Anr. Edn.** 1793. 7th. Edn. 3 vols. Cont. tree cf., gt., worn. (S. Jan.26; 179) *Subunso.* £70
- **The Theory of Moral Sentiments.** 1790. 2 vols. Cont. cf., worn. (SH. Jul.16; 202) *Subunso.* £60

SMITH, Adolphe
- **Street Incidents: A Series of Twenty-One Permanent Photographs, with Descriptive Letter-Press.** L., 1881. 4to. Title & last p. of text stained. Gt.-pict. cl., wrinkled. (SG. Apr.23; 197) $2,400

SMITH, Albert
- **The Story of Mont Blanc.** 1853. Tree cf. gt. (P. Apr.30; 322) *Cavendish.* £50

SMITH, Rev. Alfred
- **Sketches in Norway & Sweden.** 1847. Fo. Cont. hf. mor. (C. May 20; 172) *Hannas.* £700

SMITH, C.
- **Actual Survey of the Roads from London to Brighthelmstone, also London to Worthing.** 1800. Advt. Orig. bdg., covers detchd. (P. Apr.30; 324) *Cummings.* £65

SMITH, Charles, Cartographer
- **New General Atlas.** 1808. Fo. Cont. hf. cf., rebkd., worn. (SH. Jun.18; 122) *Jeffrey.* £100
- – **Anr. Edn.** 1809. 4to. Slight staining & offsetting. Cont. hf. cf., worn & almost disbnd. (CSK. Nov.28; 84) £110
- – **Anr. Copy.** Engraved title soiled, 14 maps cold. in outl. Hf. cf., upr. cover detchd. (P. Apr.9; 148) *Horesh.* £55

SMITH, Charles, Irish County Historian
- **The Ancient & Present State of the County & City of Cork.** Dublin, 1750. 1st. Edn. 2 vols. Cont. cf. (GM. Apr.30; 270) £110
- – **Anr. Edn.** Cork, 1815. New Edn. 2 vols. A few plts. rebkd. New hf. cf. (GM. Apr.30; 40) £60
- **The Ancient & Present State of the County & City of Waterford.** Dublin, 1746. 1st. Edn. Mott. cf. (GM. Apr.30; 272) £80

- The Ancient & Present State of the County of Kerry. Dublin, 1774. 1st. Edn. Cont. cf. (GM. Apr.30; 271) £95

SMITH, Charles Hamilton
- The Ancient Costume of Great Britain & Ireland. 1814. Fo. Cont. maroon str.-grd. mor., sides with gt. & blind tooled borders, spine gt. (C. Mar.18; 108) *Shafto.* £220
- - Anr. Copy. Engraved title (soiled), dedication & 60 plts., all hand-cold. Cont. hf. mor. (SH. Apr.9; 121) *Nolan.* £130
- - Anr. Copy. 1 plt. wtrmkd. 1824, a few slight stains. Cont. str.-grd. mor., gt., some wear. (S. May 5; 203) *Blundell.* £90
- - Anr. Edn. N.d. Fo. Lacks front free end-paper. Cont. hf. mor., upr. cover partly detchd., spine defect. (S. Sep.29; 264) *Gilbert.* £160
See-MEYRICK, Samuel Rush & Smith, Charles Hamilton

SMITH, Charlotte
- Celestina. 1791. 1st. Edn. 4 vols. 12mo. Lacks hf.-titles, last lf. of vol. II slightly torn affecting text. Cont. cf., gt., worn, lacks 3 labels. Bkplt. of Ragley Hall. (S. Jan.26; 226) *Traylen.* £60
- Emmeline, the orphan of the castle. 1789. 3rd. Edn. 4 vols. 12mo. Lacks hf.-titles(?), slight foxing. Cont. spr. cf., worn, lacks labels, lge. label of J. Fryer, bookseller, Bath, on front pastedown of each vol. (S. Jan.26; 224) *Rota.* £70
- Ethelinde. 1789. 1st. Edn. 5 vols. Cf. (P. Oct.23; 102) *Brooke-Hitching.* £160
- The Old Manor House. 1793. 1st. Edn. 4 vols. 12mo. Lacks hf.-titles(?), sig. on title to vol. I. Cont. cf. (S. Jan.26; 227) *Traylen.* £75
- Rural Walks: in dialogues.-Rambles Farther: a continuation of rural walks. 1795; 1796. 1st. Edns. 2 vols.; 2 vols. 12mo. 1st. work: slight foxing, a few gatherings loose; 2nd. work: owner's inscr. on titles. Unif. vell.-bkd. bds., some wear. (S. Jan.26; 228) *Somerville.* £155

SMITH, David Nichol
See-COURTNEY, William Prideaux & Smith, David Nichol

SMITH, Edmund Ware
- The Further Adventures of the One-Eyed Poacher. Ill.:- A. Lassell Ripley. N.Y., [1947]. (750) numbered, sigd. Cl. (SG. Oct.16; 435) $100
- The One-Eyed Poacher of Privilege. Ill.:- A.L. Ripley. [1941]. (750) numbered. Gt.-decor. cl. (SG. Dec.11; 279) $140
- A Tomato Can Chronicle. Ill.:- Ralph. L. Boyer. [1937]. (950) numbered. Gt.-pict. cl., bkplt. (SG. Dec.11; 278) $140

SMITH, Edward
- Account of a Journey through North-Eastern Texas Undertaken in 1849 for the Purposes of Emigration Embodied in a Report. L. & Bg'ham, 1849. Orig. cl., spine torn. [Sabin 82444] (S. Dec.8; 254) *Ginsberg.* £220

SMITH, Elizabeth
- The Compleat Housewife ... L., 1746. 13th. Edn. Cont. cf. (SG. Sep.4; 127) $220

SMITH, G.
See-WETSTENIOS, R. & J. & Smith, G.

SMITH, Garden G.
See-HILTON, Harold H. & Smith, Garden G.

SMITH, George
- The Laws of Grenada, from the year 1763 to the year 1805. L., 1808. 4to. Browning. Cont. diced cf. gt. [Sabin 28755] (SPB. May 5; 240) $150

SMITH, Capt. George
- An Universal Military Dictionary. L., 1779. 1st. Edn. 19th. C. hf. mor. gt., worn. (CNY. May 22; 173) $120

SMITH, George, Upholsterer
- Cabinet-Maker's & Upholsterer's Guide. [Plts. dtd. 1804-07]. 4to. Lacks title-p., prelims. soiled & defect., 145 (of 158) uncold. aquatint plts. Cont. bds., worn. (TA. Nov.20; 191) £60
- - Anr. Edn. 1826. [1st. Edn.?]. 4to. Mod. hf. cf. gt. (P. Feb.19; 180) *Hammond.* £240
- - Anr. Copy. 38 plts. hand-cold., 2 plts. reprd., some browned. Mor. by Sangorski. (C. Jul.16; 338) *Taylor.* £200
- - Anr. Copy. Cont. tree cf., rebkd. W.a.f. (S. Mar.17; 454) *Allan.* £150
- Collection of Designs for Household Furniture & Interior Decoration. 1808. 1st. Edn. 4to. Orig.

---

bds., lr. cover detchd., unc., folding buckram box. (S. Mar.17; 455) *Hammond.* £1,700
- - Anr. Copy. Red three-qtr. mor. by Sangorski & Sutcliffe. (SG. May 14; 199) $1,000
- - Anr. Copy. 3 pts. in 1 vol. Lacks compl. text except for 3 ll. plt. index, & lacks 1 plt. in pt. 3. No bdg. (R. Oct.14-18; 464) DM 2,500

SMITH, George & John
- A Collection of Fifty-Three Prints. 1770. Fo. Later hf. mor. gt., slightly soiled. (SBA. May 27; 118) *Swann.* £120

SMITH, Godfrey
- The Laboratory, or School of Arts ... 1738. 1st. Edn. Slight spotting & offsetting onto text. Cont. cf. Bkplt. of John, Earl of Bute. (S. Dec.2; 771) *Barnet.* £90
[-] - Anr. Edn. 1739. Cont. cf. Bkplt. of Lord Minto. (S. Dec.1; 389) *Quaritch.* £65
- - Anr. Edn. 1810. 7th. Edn. 2 vols. in 1. Additional plt. in vol. II also numbered 16. Hf. cf. (S. Dec.1; 390) *Whitehart.* £55

SMITH, Grafton Elliot
- The Royal Mummies. Cairo, 1912. Fo. Mod. hf. mor., upr. wrap. preserved. (SH. Mar.5; 132) *Loman.* £125

SMITH, Harry B.-ADAM, Robert Borthwick
- A Sentimental Library.-The Library relating to Samuel Johnson & his Era. L. & N.Y. (2nd. work), Priv. Ptd. (1st. work), 1914; 1929. 1 vol.; 3 vols. Fo.; 4to. Orig. qtr. vell. & cl., partly unc. (1st. work); & orig. cl. gt., partly unc. From the Prescott Collection. (CNY. Feb.6; 357) $280

SMITH, J.J.
- Remarks on Rural Scenery. [1797]. 4to. 5 orig. watercolours by author bnd. in at end. Hf. cf., upr. cover detchd. (P. Sep.11; 252) *Park.* £110

SMITH, J.L.B.
- The Sea Fishes of Southern Africa. Cape Town, 1949. Subscriber's Edn., (200) sigd. 4to. Hf. mor., d.-w. Sigd. (SSA. Nov.5; 183) R. 180
- - Anr. Copy. Hf. leath., d.-w. slightly torn. (VA. May 8; 374) R. 100

SMITH, James
- The Mechanic, or, Compendium of Practical Inventions ... with a copious Index. L'pool., [1813-18]. 2 vols. 1 frontis. (of 2, lacks that in vol. 1), sm. stp. of the Liby. of the Clockmakers' Company on verso of plts. & titles. Cont. suede, spines & jnts. worn. (S. Oct.21; 357) *B. Bopp.* £70

SMITH, Col. James
- A Treatise, on the Mode & Manner, of Indian War, their Tactics, Discipline & Encampments, the Various Methods they practise, in order to obtain the Advantage by Ambush, Surprise, Surrounding, &c ... also a Brief Account of Twenty-Three Campaigns ... Paris, 1812. Lacks last 8 pp., heavily dampstained in part, title-lf. wrinkled. Unc., stitched. (SG. Mar.5; 417) £550

SMITH, James, of Melbourne
- The Cyclopedia of Victoria ... Melbourne, 1903-04. Vols. I & II only (of 3). 4to. Hf. roan, rebkd. (KH. Mar.24; 361) Aus. $110

SMITH, Sir James Edward
- Grammar of Botany, Illustrative of Artificial, as well as Natural Classification with an Explanation of Jussieu's System. N.Y., 1822. 1st. Amer. Edn. Slight spotting, sig. on title. Orig. bds., spine defect., unc., sig. on upr. cover of Dr. Van Rensselaer. From Honeyman Collection. (S. May 19; 2859) *Phelps.* £140
- A Specimen of the Botany of New Holland. Ill.:- after Sowerby. 1793. 1st. Edn. Vol. I (all publd.). 4to. Some spotting. Cont. hf. cf. (S. Jun.1; 216) *McCormick.* £650
See-ABBOT, John & Smith, Sir James Edward
See-WHITE, John, Surgeon-General-SMITH, Sir James Edward

SMITH, Sir James Edward & Sowerby, James
- English Botany. 1790-96. 1st. Edn. Vols. I-V only. Cont. hf. cf., some wear. (TA. Jan.22; 77) £310
- - Anr. Edn. 1790-98. 7 vols. Cf. (DWB. May 15; 367) £320
- - Anr. Edn. 1790-99. 8 vols. Cf. gt., some covers detchd. (P. Dec.11; 124) *L'Aquaforte.* £500
- - Anr. Edn. 1790-1801. Vols. 1-12. Hf. cf., worn, all covers loose. As a collection, w.a.f. (S. Jun.17; 793) *Mellor & Baxter.* £300

[-] - Anr. Edn. [1790-1806]. 1st. Edn. Vols. I-XII only. Lacks titles, text & plts. haphazardly bnd. Cont. hf. cf., a few covers detchd. Bkplt. of William Selwyn; w.a.f. (S. May 5; 443) *Cristani.* £850
- - Anr. Edn. 1790-1813. 1st. Edn. 36 vols. in 18. Some foxing & staining. Cf., gt. spines, some bds. detchd. (WW. May 20; 83a) £1,200
- - Anr. Edn. L., 1790-1814. 1st. Edn. 36 vols. & 4 supp. vols. in 40 vols. Plts. soiled in parts, plt. 1488 bnd. in double for plt. 2088. Cont. hf. leath., gt., leath. corners. (R. Oct.14-18; 3075) DM 13,000
- - Anr. Copy. 36 vols. in 25 vols. Unc. (H. Dec.9/10; 388) DM 5,800
- - Anr. Edn. 1790-1849. Vols. 1-36 in 18 & 4 Supps. Marb. bds., & hf. cf., worn. (CE. Mar.19; 195) £1,650
- - Anr. Edn. L., 1796. Vol. 5. Cont. tree cf. (SG. Sep.18; 357) $140
- - Anr. Edn. 1796-1809. 9 vols. only. Without text, some plts. slightly soiled. Cont. hf. cf., worn. W.a.f. (CSK. Nov.7; 15) £1,100
- - Anr. Edn. [1832]. 12 vols. Some spotting, 1 plt. loose. Cl. (P. Feb.19; 90) *Nagel.* £460
- - Anr. Edn. [1832]-39. 2nd. Edn. 6 vols. (1-6 only of 12). Cl.-bkd. bds. worn. W.a.f. (C. May 20; 246) *Taylor.* £380
- - Anr. Copy. Vols. 1-3 & 5-6 in 5 vols. A few plts. slightly soiled. Cont. hf. leath., spine slightly defect. (R. Mar.31-Apr.4; 1454) DM 3,000
- - Anr. Edn. [1832]-40. 2nd. Edn. 7 vols. (1-7 only of 12). Cont. cl., 1 spine & few covers detchd., anr. spine defect. W.a.f. (C. May 20; 245) *Taylor.* £420
- - Anr. Edn. 1832-43. 2nd. Edn. (matched set). Vols. 1-10. Lacks 1 plt. in vol. 9. Orig. cl., some wear to spines. (TA. Sep.18; 349) £700
- - Anr. Edn. [1832]-46. 2nd. Edn. 12 vols. Cf., very worn. W.a.f. (S. Dec.3; 1135) *Symonds.* £280
- - Anr. Edn. [1832]-54. 7 vols. (of 12) Cl. W.a.f. (C. Jul.15; 211) *Loose.* £500
- - Anr. Edn. 1835-54. Vols. I-VII '3rd.' Edn., vols. VIII-XII 2nd. Edn. 12 vols. Cont. hf. cf., worn, lacks some labels. W.a.f. (S. Dec.3; 1136) *W. & W.* £300
- - Anr. Edn. 1836-40. Vols. 3-7 only (of 12). A few ll. slightly spotted, some detchd. Orig. cl., very worn. W.a.f. (SBA. Dec.16; 151) *Hyde Park Bookshop.* £210
- - Anr. Edn. 1842. Vols. 1-9 & 12. Orig. cl. defect. As a collection, w.a.f. (P. Apr.9; 259) *Loose.* £460
- - Anr. Edn. 1863-72. 3rd. Edn. Vols. 1-11 (of 13). Cl., slightly worn. W.a.f. (S. Jun.1; 217) *Carr.* £300
- - Anr. Edn. 1863-73. 3rd. Edn. 11 vols. Cont. hf. mor., lr. cover to vol. 1 detchd. (TA. May 21; 542) £500
- - Anr. Copy. Vols. 1-10 (of 12 vols.) Lacks 7 cold. lithos., most plts. loose. 4 vols. cont. hf. leath., 6 vols. orig. linen, 2 vols. defect. (R. Oct.14-18; 3076) DM 1,100
- - Anr. Edn. 1863-1886. 3rd. Edn. 12 vols. 4to. 1937 hand-cold. plts. only, plt. number 1174 lacking, title to vol. 9 lacking, some ll. detchd., some margins torn. Orig. cl. W.a.f. (CSK. Sep.19; 49) £320
- - Anr. Copy. Vols. I-XII only, lacks final supp. A few spots, several plts. loose. Orig. cl., gt., slight wear. (S. Dec.3; 1138) *Erlini.* £240
- - Anr. Edn. Ed.:- J.T. Boswell Syme. 1863-92. 3rd. Edn. 13 vols. including Supp. 1 lf. shaken, a few reinforced & slightly marked. Ex-libris, mainly hf. cf. (PL. Jul.11; 48) *Miles.* £300
- - Anr. Edn. Ed.:- John T. Boswell Syme. 1863-99. 3rd. Edn. 13 vols. including supp. Most plts. with owner's stp. on reverse, 1 folding plt. reprd. Cont. hf. mor. (CSK. Aug.29; 112) £360
- - Anr. Edn. Ed.:- John T. Boswell Syme. 1864. 3rd. Edn. Vol. II only. Cont. hf. mor. (TA. Sep.18; 348) £62
- - Anr. Edn. Ed.:- J.T. Syme. 1865-66. 6 vols. Vol. 1 lacks title-p., some spotting. Hf. cf. As a collection of plts., w.a.f. (P. Jan.22; 349) *Cambridge.* £420
- - Anr. Edn. Ed.:- John T. Boswell Syme. L., 1865-73. 3rd. Edn. Vols. 2, 4-7 & 10 only. Hf. leath., scuffed, last vol. loose in orig. cl. (SG. Nov.20; 327) $750
- - Anr. Edn. 1873. 3rd. Edn. Vols. I-XI only, lacks vol. XII & supp. Some plts. loose or detchd., slight spotting. Orig. cl., gt., slight wear. (S. Dec.3; 1139) *Verekamp.* £220

SMITH, Sir James Edward & Sowerby, James – English Botany. *-contd.*
– – **Anr. Edn.** 1873-86. 3rd. Edn. 12 vols. without Supp. 1918 hand-cold. plts. only. Cont. hf. mor., worn, 2 vols. disbnd., bds. detchd. W.a.f. (CSK. Jul.10; 11) £340
– – **Anr. Edn.** L., 1877-86. 3rd. Edn., various Iss. 12 vols. 1,885 hand-cold. plts. (of 1,922). Orig. gt.-decor. cl., all brkn. in spine & hinges, & loose. (CB. Sep.24; 6) Can. $475
– – **Anr. Edn.** 1878-87. 3rd. Edn. Vols. I-XII only, lacks final supp. Slight spotting & occasional browning. Cont. hf. mor., some wear, 1 cover detchd. (S. Dec.3; 1137) *Varekamp.* £260
– – **Anr. Edn.** Ed.:– John T. Boswell Syme 1899. 3rd. Edn. 13 vols. including Supp. Plt. & text ll. in some vols. detchd. from gutta-percha bdg. Hf. mor. gt., spine in compartments. (C. Mar.18; 161) *Wheldon & Wesley.* £450
– – **Anr. Edn.** N.d.-1835-46. 2nd. Edn. 13 vols. (including a vol. with the Supplementary Plts.). Occasional spotting. Cont. hf. cf., spines varnished. (CSK. Nov.21; 55) £650
– – **Anr. Edn.** N.d. & 1837-50. 2nd. & 3rd. Edns. Vols. 1-7. Hf. mor. (SKC. Feb.26; 1605) £280
See–**ANDREWS, Henry C.–SMITH, Sir James Edward & Sowerby, James–ANON**

SMITH, Jerome V.C.
– **Natural History of the Fishes of Massachusetts.** Boston, 1843. 2nd. Edn. Cl.-bkd. bds. Daniel Webster's bkplt. (SG. Oct.16; 441) $130

SMITH, John
– **A System of Modern Geography.** 1810-11. 2 vols. 4to. Cont. tree cf. (SBA. Jul.22; 123) *Shapero.* £60

SMITH, Capt. John
– **Generall Historie of Virginia.** 1626. Fo. Engraved title loose & frayed affecting engr., 1 folding plt. (of 2) reprd. & part replaced in pen facs., mntd., hf. the map of New England, lacks folios A3 & 4, contents ll., & text lf. 2A2, also lacks 2 ports. & map of Virginia, apparently replaced by Mercator's map of Virginia 1636, hand-cold., engraved port. of author inserted, some ll. from anr. copy, spotted or soiled in places. 18th. C. hf. cf., worn, upr. cover detchd. W.a.f. [NSTC 22790; Sabin 82826] (S. Jun.29; 200) *Quaritch.* £170
– – **Anr. Copy.** 4 folding maps in facs., V3 reprd., stain on lr. corner of last few gatherings, front free end-papers detchd. Later cf., rebkd., cl. s.-c. From liby. of William E. Wilson. [NSTC 22790b] (SPB. Apr.29; 252) $550
– **The True Travels, Adventures, & Observations . . .** 1630. 1st. Edn., early iss. Fo. With the misprints uncorrected, lacks plt. Disbnd. [Sabin 82851; NSTC 22796] (S. Jun.29; 201) *Quaritch.* £220
– **The True Travels of Capt. John Smith.–The Generall Historie of Virginia, New-England, & the Summer Iles . . .** Richmond, 1819. 2 vols. 2 frontis., 2 folding plts., 1 folding map, map loose & torn, 1 plt. with slight paper loss, text browned & soiled, some foxing. Cont. cf., worn, upr. cover of vol. I detchd. From liby. of William E. Wilson. [Sabin 82852] (SPB. Apr.29; 253) $100

SMITH, John, Artist
– **Select Views in Italy.** 1792. Vol. 1 only. Ob. fo. Engl. & Fr. text. Cont. str.-grd. mor. gt., worn. (SBA. Jul.23; 407) *Shotton.* £110
– – **Anr. Edn.** L., Priv. Ptd., 1792-96. 1st. Edn. 2 vols. Ob. fo. 2 plts. with sm. stain, 1 marginal, plts. foxed, mostly marginal, minor text foxing, cont. sig. on title. Cont. marb. bds., roan back & tips, corners & edges very worn. (PNY. May 21; 384) $200
– – **Anr. Edn.** L., 1792-96. 2 vols. in 1. Ob. 4to. Foxed. Mod. three-qtr. mor. (SG. Oct.9; 230) $300

SMITH, John, Chronologist
[–] **Horological Dialogues . . . Shewing the Nature, Use, & right Managing of Clocks & Watches.** 1675. 1st. Edn. Lacks blank A1, inner margin of title renewed. Mod. citron mor., gt., red hf. mor. case. From Honeyman Collection. [Wing S4105] (S. May 19; 2860) *Sotheran.* £440
– **Horological Disquisitions Concerning the Nature of Time, & the Reasons why all Days . . . are not Alike Twenty Four Hours Long.** 1694. 1st. Edn. Occasional underlining of text, MS. table copied from that of 'Mr. Barclay spectacle-maker' loosely inserted. Cont. spr. sheep, worn. The Trotter copy, with purchase note, Edinb. 1695, from Thomas Caruthers; from Honeyman Collection. [Wing S4106] (S. May 19; 2861) *Quaritch.* £440
See–**DERHAM, William–SMITH, John, Chronologist**

SMITH, John, Picture Dealer
– **A Catalogue Raisonné of the Works of the Most Emminent Dutch, Flemish & French Painters . . .** L., 1829-42. Orig. Edn. 9 vols., including supp. New leatherette, unc. & mostly unopened. (SG. Dec.4; 325) $300
– – **Anr. Edn.** 1908. (1250). 9 vols. including Supp. Orig. cl. (SH. Oct.9; 103) *Scandecor.* £115
– – **Anr. Copy.** (CSK. Nov.21; 71) £85
– – **Anr. Copy.** (CSK. Jan.30; 54) £70

SMITH, John, Picture Dealer–SMITH, John Chaloner
– **A Catalogue Raisonné of the Works of . . . Dutch, Flemish & French Painters.–British Mezzotinto Portraits.** 1908; 1883. 1st. work (1250). 9 vols.; 4 vols. Both orig. cl. (SH. Jan.29; 151) *Larsen.* £110

SMITH, John Calvin
[–] **The Western Tourist & Emmigrant's Guide through the States of Ohio, Indiana, Illonois, Missouri, Iowa, & Wisconsin.** N.Y., 1851. 12mo. 16 pp. bookseller's catalogue. Gt.-decor. cl. (SG. Jan.8; 406) $110

SMITH, John Chaloner
– **British Mezzotint Portraits.** 1884. 4 vols. Hf. mor. gt. by Zaehnsdorf. (C. Jul.22; 164) *Taylor.* £220

SMITH, John Guthrie
– **Parish of Strathblane.** 1886. Ltd. Edn. 4to. Cl., worn. (CE. Apr.23; 9) £68

SMITH, John Russell
– **A Bibliographical Catalogue of English Writers on Angling & Ichthyology.** L., 1856. 12mo. Three-qtr. mor. (SG. Dec.11; 103) $100
– **Bibliotheca Cantiana.** 1837. Cont. mor. (SH. Jul.9; 47) *Talerman.* £60
– – **Anr. Edn.** 1838. 1 vol. in 2. Hf. cl. The copy of Dr. Frederick W. Cock, interleaved, with many cuttings from booksellers' catalogues & many MS. annots. thro.-out by Cock & a previous owner. (C. Jul.22; 126) *Chamberlain.* £250

SMITH, John Thomas
– **Antiquities of London.** 1791. 4to. Orig. bds., spine defect. (P. Jul.30; 132) *Thorp.* £60
– – **Anr. Edn.** L., 1791 [& later]. 4to. Plts. dtd. 1791-1800. Leath.-bkd. marb. bds. (SG. Feb.26; 304) $130
– **Antiquities of Westminster.** 1802. With supp. of 62 additional plts. 4to. Cont. mor. gt. From liby. of Baron Dimsdale. (MMB. Oct.8; 3) *Traylen.* £185
– – **Anr. Edn.** 1807. 4to. Engraved title to additional plts. bnd. before plt. 39, some plts. & plans hand-cold, a few marginal tears. Cont. diced russ., rebkd. (CSK. Feb.6; 172) £140
– – **Anr. Edn.** 1807-[09]. 1st. Edns., 1st. vol. 1st. Iss. 2 vols. in 1, including the supp. of plts. Fo. 1st. vol. lacks 8-p. 'Vindication'. Hf. mor., gt., by Rivière. (S. Nov.24; 259) *Marlborough.* £140
– – **Anr. Copy.** 2 vols. in 1, including supp. 4to. 62 additional plts. in vol. II, some hand-cold. Mod. buckram, partly unc. From the collection of Eric Sexton. (C. Apr.16; 357) *Burgess.* £110
– **The Cries of London.** 1839. L.P. 4to. Some ll. spotted & loose. Cont. cl., worn. (SH. Jun.4; 171) *Adams.* £70
– – **Anr. Copy.** Some foxing thro.-out. Cl. (BS. Jun.11; 87) £65
– **Etchings of Remarkable Beggars.** L., 1815. Etched title & 23 plts. only, spotting. Cf., lacks 1 label from spine, s.-c. (SPB. Jul.28; 425) $150
– – **Anr. Copy.** 4to. Some foxing, a couple of wormholes not affecting etchings. Hf. mor. (SSA. Apr.22; 75) R. 95
– **Vagabondia, Etchings of Remarkable Beggars.** 1817. 4to. Hf. mor., covers detchd. (P. Oct.2; 9) *Geotetner.* £65

SMITH, Joseph, Bookseller
[–] **Catalogus Librorum Rarissimorum ab Artis Typographiae Inventoribus . . . ante Annum Millesimum Quingentesimum Excusorum.** [Venice], [1737]. 2nd. Edn. Lists 248 items, inscr. on front fly-lf. Cont. red mor., triple gt. fillet, flat spine gt., inner gt. dentelles, spine worn. Bkplt. of Lucius Wilmerding. (SM. Oct.7; 1500) Frs. 3,200

– **Ecclesiarum Anglicae.** 1719. Fo. Cont. panel. cf., worn. (MMB. Oct.8; 29a) *Cumming.* £150

SMITH, M.J. & Ganf, R.W.
– **Marsupials of Australia. Volume I: Possums, the Koala & Wombats.** Melbourne &c., [1980]. (1000) numbered, & sigd. Fo. Canvas bds., mor. titling piece & panel on upr. cover. (KH. Mar.24; 362) Aus. $300

SMITH, Nathan
– **A Practical Essay on Typhous Fever.** N.Y., 1824. 1st. Edn. Old cf.-bkd. bds., upr. cover loose. (SG. Sep.18; 349) $120

SMITH, Pamela Coleman (Ed.)
See–**GREEN SHEAF, The**

SMITH, Pemberton
– **A Research into Early Canadian Masonry.** Montreal, 1939. (300) numbered, & sigd. Orig. cl. (CB. Feb.18; 45) Can. $110

SMITH, Robert, of Cambridge
– **A Compleat System of Opticks.–The Elementary Parts of Dr. Smith's Compleat System of Opticks.** Camb., 1738; 1778. 2 vols.; 1 vol. 4to. Cont. cf., brkn. (1st. work); & mod. cl.-bkd. bds. From the collection of Eric Sexton. (C. Apr.15; 18) *Acadia.* £50

SMITH, Sydney Ure
See–**URE-SMITH, Sydney**

SMITH, T.J.
– **Nollekens & his Times.** 1829. 2 vols. Extra-ill. with 135 ports. & plts., 2 hand-cold., & 2 orig. watercolours. Mod. mor. by Rivière. (SH. Mar.5; 294) *Blundell.* £160

SMITH, William
– **Journal of a Voyage in the Missionary Ship Duff, to the Pacific Ocean . . .** N.Y., 1813. 1st. Edn. 12mo. Ex liby. Mod. buckram. (SG. Oct.30; 334) $160

SMITH, William, D.D.
See–**PAINE, Thomas–SMITH, William, D.D.**

SMITH, William, of the Canadian Public Archives
– **The History of the Post Office in British North America.** Camb., 1920. 1st. Edn. Orig. cl. (CB. Dec.9; 252) Can. $120
– – **Anr. Copy.** Recent buckram, with orig. spine label pasted on. (CB. Nov.12; 294) Can. $100

SMITH, William, Geologist
– **A Memoir to the Map & Delineation of the Strata of England & Wales, with part of Scotland.** 1815. 1st. Edn. 4to. Offsetting, a few ll. slightly creased, 2nd. folding table in 2nd. state. Orig. wraps., spine defect., cl. case. From Honeyman Collection. (S. May 19; 2863) *Percy.* £620
– **Observations on the Utility, Form & Management of Water Meadows, & the Draining & Irrigation of Peat Bogs.** Norwich, 1806. Cont. tree cf. (S. May 5; 138) *Hitching.* £110

SMITH, William, Provost of Philadelphia
[–] **Relation historique de l'expédition contre les Indiens de l'Ohio.** Trans.:– C.F.G. Dumas. Ill.:– after Benjamin West. Amst., 1769. 1st. Edn. in Fr. Orig. marb. paper wraps., unc., wraps. worn, chipped at spine. [Sabin 84647] (CNY. Oct.1; 50) $550

SMITH, William & Andrew
– **Authenticated Tartans of the Clans & Families of Scotland.** Mauchline, [1850]. 1st. Edn. 4to. Slight spotting. Cont. maroon hf. mor., spine gt. (S. Nov.4; 572) *Grossmith.* £80
– – **Anr. Copy.** Cont. hf. mor. (SH. Jul.16; 207) *Thorp.* £75

SMITH, William Henry
– **Canadian Gazeteer.** Toronto, 1846. 1st. Edn. 1st. iss., with map dtd. 1846, key to map locations bnd. before title-p., map slightly foxed with dampstain at top, 8 pp. of advts. at end. Orig. cl., slightly spotted, bkplt. [Sabin 84780] (CB. Feb.18; 46) Can. $130

SMITH REVIEW Exam Blues Issue
Northampton, Massachusetts, Jan. 1955. Orig. ptd. wraps. Sylvia Plath's copy with her sig. on cover. (SPB. Nov.25; 385) $200

SMITHSONIAN ANNUAL REPORTS
Wash., 1872-1906. 55 vols. Lacks pt. 1 for 1885. Cl., some vols. defect. & worn. (SG. Jun.11; 394) $140

SMOLLETT, Tobias

- **The Adventures of Ferdinand Count Fathom.** 1753. 1st. Edn. 2 vols. Cont. cf., worn. Stirling of Craigbarnet's bkplt. (CE. Mar.19; 239) £55
[–] **The Adventures of Pergrine Pickle.** 1751. 1st. Edn. 4 vols. 12mo. Vol. 3 with cancel L12, tear in K3 of vol. 2, some ll. of vol. 4 near end slightly frayed in outer edges, occasional browning. Cont. spr. cf., gt., recent labels, some wear at head & foot of spines. (S. Feb.10; 461) *Waterfield.* £120
[–] **Anr. Copy.** L12 of vol. 3 a cancel, with the blank at end of vol. 2, but lacks blank at end of vol. 3, some slight spotting. Cont. cf., spines gt., new labels, corners worn, some restoration to spines, qtr. mor. gt. s.-c.'s. From the Prescott Collection. (CNY. Feb.6; 299) $320
[–] **The Adventures of Roderick Random.** 1748. 1st. Edn. 2 vols. 12mo. 1st. iss., with Locke's name mentioned among the philosophers on I9 in vol. 1, slight browning, marginal sig. on titles. Cont. spr. cf., gt., blind-stpd. arms of Stuart de Rothesay on covers. (S. Feb.10; 462) *Quaritch.* £150
[–] **– Anr. Edn.** Ill.:– Grignion after Hayman. L., 1748. 2nd. Edn. 2 vols. 12mo. Mod. mott. cf. gt. by Bayntun. (SG. Sep.25; 286) $160
[–] **The Adventures of Sir Launcelot Greaves.** 1762. 1st. Edn. in book form. 2 vols. 12mo. Titles & some ll. browned at edges. Cont. spr. cf., rebkd., slight wear. (S. Feb.10; 463) *Maggs.* £380
- **The Expedition of Humphry Clinker.** L., 1771. 1st. Edn., mixed states. 3 vols. 12mo. Mod. mott. cf., elab. gt. borders, spines gt. (SG. May 14; 200) $225
[–] **– Anr. Edn.** L., 1771. 1st. Edn. 3 vols. 12mo. Vol. 1 misdtd. 1671, ll. stained. Cont. cf., gt. spines worn, qtr. mor. gt. s.-c.'s. Bkplt. of George B. McCutcheon, lately in the Prescott Collection. (CNY. Feb.7; 300) $100
- **Novels.** Boston & N.Y., Shakes. Hd. Pr., 1926. L.P. 11 vols. Orig. vell. spine, silk bds., slight stain on lr. portion of spines, publisher's wraps., soiled. (SPB. Nov.25; 397) $200
- **Works.** 1747. 8 vols. Cont. cf., decor. spine gt. (CE. Jul.9; 161) £120
– – Anr. Edn. Ed.:– J. Moore. 1797. 8 vols. Cf. gt. (P. Jan.22; 25) *Traylen.* £100
– – Anr. Copy. Cont. diced cf. gt. (SD. Feb.4; 102) £60
– – Anr. Edn. N.Y., Jenson Society, 1911. (1000). 12 vols. Hf. mor. gt., floral inlays on spine. (SPB. May 6; 343) $550
- **Works & Memoirs of his Life.** 1872. 8 vols. Hf. mor. gt. by Bickers. (CE. Mar.19; 234) £85

SMOLLETT, Tobias (Ed.)
*See–*HUME, David

SMYTH, George Lewis
- **The Monuments & Genii of St. Paul's Cathedral & of Westminster Abbey.** L., 1826. 2 vols. Browned. Cont. mor., gt. floral borders enclosing design of vine & flowers, spines gt. Fore-e. pntg. in each vol.; pres. label in each cover, to Sir Thomas Cochran, with his bkplt., from the liby. of Zola E. Harvey. (SG. Mar.19; 172) $500

SMYTH, Sir James Carmichael
- **The Effect of the Nitrous Vapour, in Preventing & Destroying Contagion.** 1799. 1st. Edn. Folding engraved plan stained, folding table torn in inner margin. Orig. bds., slightly stained, unc. Pres. copy; from liby. of Dr. E. Ashworth Underwood. (S. Feb.23; 300) *Temperley.* £60
- **Precis of the Wars in Canada.** L., 1862. Cl. [Sabin 85237] (CB. Apr.1; 309) Can. $130

SMYTH, W. & Lowe, F.
- **Narrative of a Journey from Lima to Para.** L., 1836. Spotting, advt. ll. at end. Orig. cl., reprd. [Sabin 85346] (SPB. May 5; 476) $175

SMYTH, William Henry
- **Memoir Descriptive of . . . Sicily & its Islands.** 1824. 4to. Some ll. slightly soiled. Mod. hf. mor. (SH. Mar.5; 133) *George's.* £100

SMYTHE, Elizabeth Anne
- **The Adventures of Orphan Henry, or the Sure Road to Wealth & Happiness.** Ill.:– Abel Bowen(?). Boston, [Inscr. dtd. 1831]. 12mo. Orig. pict. wraps., 2 ills. repeated on covers. (SH. Mar.19; 294) *Schiller.* £100

SMYTHIES, Bertram E.
- **The Birds of Borneo.** Ill.:– A.M. Hughes. 1960. 1st. Edn. Cl. gt., pict. d.-w. (PL. Sep.18; 166) *Wheldon & Wesley.* £100

- **Birds of Burma.** Ill.:– A.M. Hughes. Rangoon, 1940. Orig. cl. (CSK. Jan.16; 134) £130
– – Anr. Edn. 1953. Buckram gt., d.-w.'s. (P. Nov.13; 222) *Hill.* £85
– – Anr. Edn. Ill.:– A.M. Hughes. 1953. Orig. cl. gt., pict. d.-w., unc. (PL. Sep.18; 167) *Chilton.* £75
– – Anr. Edn. Edinb. & L., [1953]. 2nd. Edn. Orig. cl. (CB. Sep.24; 47) Can. $170

SMYTHSON, Hugh
- **The Compleat Family Physician.** 1785. 1st. Edn. 4to. Slight browning. Cont. mott. cf., worn. From liby. of Dr. E. Ashworth Underwood. (S. Feb.23; 301) *Miller.* £50

SNAPE, Andrew
- **The Anatomy of a Horse . . .** 1686. 2 pts. in 1 vol. Fo. Cont. cf., rebkd. with orig. gt. spine preserved. [Wing S4384] (C. Nov.5; 149) *Comber.* £320

SNELGRAVE, William
- **A New Account of Some Parts of Guinea & the Slave-Trade.** 1734. 1st. Edn. Folding engraved map with 2 short tears, slight soiling. Mod. hf. mor. [Sabin 85380] (S. Jun.22; 194) *Rota.* £100

SNELL, Willebrord
- **Cyclometricus, de Circuli Dimensione Secundum Logistarum Abacos, & ad Mechanicem Accuratissima.** Leiden, 1621. 1st. Edn. Sm. 4to. Some browning. Mod. vell.-bkd. bds. From Honeyman Collection. (S. May 19; 2865) *McKittrick.* £220
- **Descriptio Cometae, qui anno 1618 mense Novembri Primum Effulsit. Huc Accessit Christophori Rhotmanni . . . Mathematici Descriptio Accurata Cometae anni 1585.** Leiden, 1619. 1st. Edn. Sm. 4to. Stained & browned, sm. tear at foot of O3, coroneted stp. on title-p. Cont. limp vell., soiled. From Honeyman Collection. (S. May 19; 2866) *Hill.* £320
- **Doctrinae Triangulorum Canonicae libri quatuor. –Canon Triangulorum.** Leiden, 1627; 1626. 1st. Edns. 2 works in 1 vol. Browned thro.-out, 1st. work with title browned & soiled, inner margin reprd., sm. rust-hole affecting 2 or 3 letters, 8 reprd., short tear in D3, 2nd. work with last few ll. stained, inner margin of M3 reprd. Mod. vell. From Honeyman Collection. (S. May 19; 2869) *Hughes.* £70
- **Eratosthenes Batavus, de Terrae Ambitus vera Quantitate.** Leiden, 1617. 1st. Edn. Sm. 4to. Some marginal staining, upr. margins of pp. 241-250 slightly defect., blank corner torn from 2Kl. 18th. C. cf., gt., worn, lacks label. Bkplt. of Marquess of Bute; from Honeyman Collection. (S. May 19; 2864) *Zeitlin & Verbrugge.* £850
– – Anr. Copy. Upr. pt. of title in pen facs., some marginal staining & discolouration, Q2 reprd. slightly affecting text, marginal repair to 2D3. Vell., soiled. From Honeyman Collection. (S. May 19; 2865) *De Graeve.* £190
- **Tiphys Batavus, sive Histiodromice, de Navium Cursibus, et Re Navali.** Leiden, 1624. 1st. Edn. 2 pts. in 1 vol. Sm. 4to. Title & a few ll. at beginning marginally stained, ptd. slip pasted at foot of title: 'Ex Bibliotheca Viri Illust. Isaaci Vossii'. Cont. vell., slightly soiled, hf. mor. case. From Honeyman Collection. (S. May 19; 2868) *Israel.* £340

– – Anr. Edn. Strassburg, 1624. 4to. Title & prelims foxed. Cont. Engl. red mor., double border of fillets, crowned cypher of Charles II in corners, repeated on spine. British Museum stp. (HD. Mar.18; 160) *Frs.* 4,100

SNELLEN, Dr. Maurits
- **De Nederlandsche Pool-Expeditie 1882-83.** Utrecht, 1886. Fo. Some spotting. Orig. cl. gt., slightly soiled. (TA. Dec.18; 103) £56

SNELLING, Thomas
- **View of the Coinage of Great Britain, Ireland, etc.** 1762-74. 7 vols. in 1. 4to. A few minor defects. Cont. diced russ. gt., upr. cover detchd. (SBA. Jul.14; 86) *Laywood.* £55
- **A View of the Gold Coin & Coinage of England. –Miscellaneous Views of the Coins Struck by English Princes in France.–A View of the Silver Coin & Coinage of Scotland.** 1763; 1769; 1774. 3 works in 1 vol. 4to. Later hf. mor. (SH. Mar.6; 444) *Barra Books.* £60
- **A View of the Silver Coin & Coinage of England. –A View of the Copper Coin & Coinage of England.–A View of the Silver Coin & Coinage of Scotland.–A View of the Origin, Nature & Use of Jettons or Counters.** 1762; 1766; 1774; 1769. 4

works in 1 vol. 4to. Occasional spotting, last work with 6 plts. only. Cont. hf. cf., rebkd. (CSK. Oct.24; 210) £60
[–] **A View of the Silver Coin & Coinage of England.–A View of the Gold Coin & Coinage of England.** 1762; 1763. 1st. Edns. 2 works in 1 vol. Fo. Cont. reverse cf., gt. crest pasted to covers. (S. Jul.27; 211) *Barra Books.* £60

SNOW, David & others
- **Raymond Ching: the Bird Paintings.** 1978. (360) sigd. by the artist. Fo. Sigd. print loosely inserted. Cont. mor., gt. (SH. Oct.9; 246) *Way.* £95

SNOW, Jack
- **Who's Who in Oz.** Ill.:– John R. Neill, Frank Kramer & 'Dirk'. Chic., [1954]. 1st. Edn. Cl., d.-w. (SG. Apr.9; 63) $150

S[NOW], T.
- **Arts Improvement, or choice Experiments and Observations.** 1703. 1st. Edn. with this title. Cont. cf., rebkd. J.B. Findlay's bkplt. (SH. Apr.10; 454) *Roberts.* £110

SNOW, William Parker
- **A Two Years' Cruise off Tierra Del Fuego, The Falkland Islands, Patagonia & in the River Plate. –A Narrative of Life in the Southern Seas.** L., 1857. 2 vols. in 1. Cl. (SSA. Jan.22; 120) R. 100

SNOWMAN, A. Kenneth
- **Eighteenth Century Gold Boxes.** 1966. 4to. Orig. cl. (SH. Jul.23; 304) *Wilson.* £55

SOANE, Sir John
- **Description of the House & Museum on the North Side of Lincoln's Inn Fields, the residence of Sir John Soane.** L., [1835]. (150) on L.P. Lge. 4to. Some minor foxing. Cont. blind-stpd. cl., gt. lettering & gt. inner dentelles, mor. spine with gt. floral pattern & title on spine. Pres. copy, sigd., to George Rennie. (CB. May 27; 187) Can. $850

SOANE, Sir John–PARKYNS, G.J.
- **Sketches in Architecture.–Six Designs for Improving & Embellishing of Grounds.** 1793. 1st. Edns.? 2 works in 1 vol. Fo. 49 (of 54) plts., publisher's catalogue bnd. in at end, that & 1 other lf. torn, latter with no loss of text, some other defects., but barely affecting text. Cont. hf. cf., very worn. (SBA. Mar.4; 78) *L'Acquaforte.* £70

SOBY, James Thrall
- **The Prints of Paul Klee.** Ill.:– Paul Klee. N.Y., 1945. (1000). 4to. Text in ptd. wraps., plts. loose as issued in cl. portfo. (SG. Oct.23; 189) $100

SOCIETA PROMOTRICE DELLE BELLE ARTI IN TORINO
- **Album della Pubblica Esposizione del 1857.** Ed.:– Luigi Rocca. Turin, 1857-66. 10 vols. 4to. Publisher's cl. (CR. Jun.11; 524) Lire 500,000
- **Album della Pubblica Esposizione.–Ricordo della XLVI-XLVIII Esposizione.** Turin, 1866-71; 1887-89. 6 vols.; 3 vols. Ob. 4to. All orig. cl. (SI. Dec.4; 536) Lire 340,000

SOCIETE D'AQUARELLISTES FRANCAIS
- **Texte par les Principaux Critiques d'Art.** Paris, 1883. 2 vols. Fo. Many lithographic plts. on India. Hf. red mor., unc. (SI. Dec.4; 537) Lire 160,000

SOCIETE D'ETUDES DE LA PROVINCE DE CAMBRAI
- **Recueils 9 a 16, 22, 43 a 50, 52 et 53.** N.d. 18 vols. together. Sewed. (LM. Nov.8; 278) B.Frs. 8,000

SOCIETE Royale de Médecin
- **Histoire et Mémoires . . .** Paris, 1779-90. 9 vols. 4to. Cont. tree cf., gt. roll-stp. around covers, smooth decor. spines, vol. 2 defect. (HD. Jun.24; 63) Frs. 1,400

SOCIETY OF ANTIQUARIES
- **Vetusta Monumenta.** 1747, 1789, 1796 [reprint, 1799], 1815. Vols. 1-4. Fo. Old hf. leath., unc., worn. As a periodical, w.a.f., bkplt. of Sir Gore Ouseley. (S. Dec.9; 492) *Weinreb.* £190
– – Anr. Edn. 1747-1835. Vols. 1-5 only (of 6). Fo. Minor browning to a few plts. Cont. mott. cf., spines gt., rebkd., hinges worn, upr. cover of vol. 4 detchd. (C. Feb.25; 59) *Thornton.* £70
– – Anr. Edn. 1747-[1842]. 6 vols. in 5. Fo. Vol. VI lacks all plts. before plt. XVIII, slight spotting

SOCIETY OF ANTIQUARIES – Vetusta Monumenta. *-contd.*
& marginal soiling. Recent red hf. mor., gt., unc. W.a.f. (S. Dec.9; 491) *Weinreb.* £260
– – **Anr. Edn.** L., 1835. 1 vol. Fo. 165 ll. of text & 58 plts. only, plts. dtd. from 1718-1829. Cont. qtr. cf., bds., loose. (CB. May 27; 189) Can. $180

SOCIETY OF THE CINCINNATI
Trenton, 1808. Some browning, end-papers wormed. Crimson-str. grd. mor., gold rolled border, gt.-tooled spine, 'Cincinnati' gt. stpd. on upr. cover, 'David Brearley' on lr. cover, bdg. attributed to Benjamin Olds of Newark, N.J. (SPB. Jun.22; 2) $175

SOCIETY FOR THE DIFFUSION of Useful Knowledge
– **[Atlas].** 1830-35. 4to. Engraved maps & town plans, hand-cold. in outl. Cont. hf. mor. (TA. Oct.16; 177) £80
[–] [–] **Anr. Edn.** 1830-37. 4to. 123 engraved maps, 2 double-page city plans, all hand-cold. in outl., lacks title, MS. index on end-P. Cont. hf. cf. W.a.f. (SBA. Jul.23; 299) *Baer.* £220
– [–] **Anr. Edn.** Ca. 1835. 4to. Maps etc. cold. in outl. Orig. wraps. (P. Sep.11; 134) *Smith.* £95
– [–] **Anr. Edn.** L., 1844. Vol. 1 only. Maps cold. (JN. Apr.2; 818) £65
– **Maps.** [1830-]. Lge. 4to. Title to vol. 1 only but index ll. to vols. 1 & 2 bnd. in, 106 engraved maps & 23 city plans only, some other minor defects. Cont. hf. mor., worn. As an atlas, w.a.f. (SBA. Jul.14; 40) *Morten's of Manchester.* £110
– – **Anr. Edn.** 1844. 2 vols. in 1. Fo. 192 engraved maps & townplans only, occasional spotting. Partly disbnd., lacks covers. W.a.f. (CSK. Jul.3; 15) £270
– – **Anr. Copy.** 4to. Mainly loose in orig. hf. mor. (TA. Feb.19; 112) £200
– – **Anr. Copy.** 2 vols. Fo. Hf. cf. (PJ. Jun.6 ('80); 60) £155
– – **Anr. Copy.** 2 vols. in 1. Mod. maroon three-qtr. mor. (SG. May 21; 96) $800
– **The Penny Magazine.** Boston, 1832-36. Vols. 1-5 in 5 vols. 4to. Cont. leath. & linen, 1 spine defect. (R. Oct.14-18; 1841) DM 500

SOCIETY for the Improvement of Medical & Chirurgical Knowledge
– **Transactions.** 1793-1812. 3 vols. Orig. bds., unc., from the Medico-Chirurgical Society, Aberdeen. (S. Jun.17; 832) *Norman.* £220

SOCIETY OF DILETTANTI, The
– **Antiquities of Ionia.** Ed.:– William Wilkins & W.R. Lethaby. 1821-1797-1840-1881-1915. 1st. Edns. vols. 2-4, 2nd. Edn. vol. 1. Pts. 1-5, 5 vols. Fo. Mod. bds., unc. (S. Nov.24; 260) *Weinreb.* £650
– **Ionian Antiquities.** 1769. Fo. Orig. bdg. (HY. Jan.14; 83) £70
– **Specimens of Antient Sculpture Aegyptien . . .** 1809-35. L.P. 2 vols. Lge. fo. Cont. red str.-grd. mor., gt. Bkplt. of John, Duke of Bedford. (S. Nov.25; 437) *Weinreb.* £150
– **The Unedited Antiquities of Attica.** 1817. 1st. Edn. Fo. A few plts. foxed, occasional spotting. Cont. hf. russ., spine gt. (S. Sep.29; 193) *Pintic.* £180
– – **Anr. Copy.** Occasional browning. Cont. cf., gt. & blind-tooled key-pattern borders, spine reprd. at head & foot. From the Coole Liby., with bkplt. & notes of Richard Gregory. (S. Jun.22; 92) *Neil.* £160
– – **Anr. Copy.** Slight spotting & soiling. Orig. bds., worn, lacks spine, unc. (S. Jun.22; 147) *Dimakrakos.* £100

SOCIETY of Dilettanti–KNIGHT, R.P.
– **Specimens of Antient Sculpture, Aegyptian, Etruscan, Greek & Roman.–An Inquiry into the Symbolical Language of Antient Art & Mythology.** L., 1809-35; 1818. 2 works in 1 vol. Fo. A few marginal tears, some spotting, title to vol. I torn & mntd. Mod. hf. cf. gt. (SPB. May 6; 255) $375

SOCIETY of Jesus
– **Institutum Societatis Jesu, auctoritate Congregationis Generalis XVIII.** Prague, 1757. 2 vols. Fo. Cont. red mor., wide gt. dentelle border incorporating sunflowers, thistles & shell-like rococo ornament, single fillet & 'drawer-handle' border, spine gt. in compartments, surface of mor. in 2nd. compartment from foot completely removed, inner gt. dentelles, corners slightly worn. (SM. Oct.8; 2011) Frs. 2,800
– **Règles de la Compagnie de Iesus.** Paris, 1620. 12mo. Slightly browned, 19th. C. (?) stp. on title 'BAE', old note on rear end-paper, states that this is Gaignat copy. 18th. C. red mor., triple gt. fillet, spine gt. in compartments, inner gt. dentelles. (SM. Oct.8; 2012) Frs. 2,500

SOCIETY OF UPHOLSTERERS
– **The IId Edition of Genteel Household Furniture . . .** Ca. 1760. Cont. red mor. gt. (C. Jul.16; 326) *Henderson.* £650

SODDY, Frederick
– **Radio-Activity: an Elementary Treatise, from the Standpoint of the Disintegration Theory.–The Interpretation of the Atom.** 1904; 1932. 1st. Edns. 2 vols. Orig. cl., slightly worn; orig. cl., d.-w. (worn). 1st. work with stps. of Samuel Jacobsohn, bkplt. of Barry H. Jones; 2nd. work Jacobsohn's copy; from Honeyman Collection. (S. May 19; 2871) *Howell.* £70

SOEMMERRING, Samuel Thomas
– **Abbildungen des Menschlichen Auges.** Frankfurt, 1801. 1st. Edn. Fo. 8 engraved plts., 7 with dupls. in outl., foxed. Old bds., brkn. (SG. Sep.18; 354) $550
– **Abbildungen und Beschreibungen Einiger Misgeburten die sich ehemals auf dem Anatomischen Theater zu Cassel befanden.** Mainz, 1791. 1st. Edn. Fo. Cont. bds. (S. Feb.23; 104) *Goldschmidt.* £260
– **Icones Oculi Humani.** Frankfurt, 1804. 1st. Latin Edn. Fo. 16 copperplts., 2 cold. Cont. hf. leath., fo. (R. Oct.14-18; 303) DM 1,800
– **Ueber die Koerperliche Verschiedenheit des Negers vom Europaer.** Frankfurt, 1785. 1st. Edn. Later three-qtr. mor., worn, ex liby. (SG. Sep.18; 353) $220
– **Vom Hirn und Rückenmark.** Mainz, 1788. 1st. Edn. Cont. bds. (R. Mar.31-Apr.4; 1045) DM 750

SOFIYA [Journal of Art & Literature]
Ed.:– [P.P. Muratov]. Moscow, 1914. Nos. 1-6 (all publd.). 4to. 1st. few ll. of no. 1 torn. Orig. wraps., slightly torn & soiled, upr. wrap. of no. 1 reprd. (SH. Feb.6; 362) *Lempert.* £80

SOKOLOV-MIKOTOV, I.
– **Zasuponya.** Ill.:– N. Lyubavina. Petrograd, n.d. (125) numbered. Orig. wraps. by N. Lyubavina. (SH. Feb.6; 521) *Quaritch.* £75

SOKOLOW, N.
– **History of Zionism.** 1919. 2 vols. Orig. cl. (SH. Jul.9; 5) *Rosenbaum.* £90

SOLANDER, Dr. Daniel
See–**BANKES, Sir Joseph & Solander, Dr. Daniel**

SOLDATEN-FREUND
Ed.:– L. Schneider. Berlin, Jul. 1848-Jun. 49. Year 16. 12 pts. in 1 vol. Text browned in parts. Cont. hf. leath., spine defect. (R. Oct.14-18; 2858) DM 500

SOLDIER'S MANUAL, for Cavalry, Artillery, Light Infantry, & Infantry
Phila., 1824. Some offsetting. Orig. bds., upr. cover loose, unc. (SPB. Nov.24; 41) $2,400

SOLDO, Mauro
– **Descrizione degl'instrumenti, delle Macchine, a delle Suppellittili raccolte ad Uso Chirurgico e Medico dal P. Don Ippolito Rondinelli Ferrarese.** Ill.:– Savoja after Lindemain (engraved vig. on title); Lindemain. Faenza, 1766. 4to. Folding plan of the Museum torn across, lacks plt. 29, liby. stp. on title & at end. Cont. paper bds. (S. Dec.2; 625) *Dix.* £130

SOLE, Francesco dal
– **Libretti nuovi con le Regole . . . con Additioni Astronomice.** Ferrara, 1546. Sm. 4to. Slight discolouration. Bnd. in vell. lf. of Italian MS. gradual over bds. From Honeyman Collection. (S. May 19; 2872) *Parikian.* £220

SOLE, William
– **Menthae Britannicae.** Bath, 1798. Fo. Sm. ink liby. stp. on Preface, text lf. G1 torn. Old hf. cf. (CNY. May 22; 216) $300

SOLEINNE, de
– **Catalogue de la Bibliothèque Dramatique [by 'P.L. Jacob', Charles Brunet & Others].** N.Y., ca. 1970. Photolitho, Reprint. 8 vols. in 7. Orig. cl. (SM. Oct.7; 1501) Frs. 2,000

SOLENNE PROCESSIONE VATICANA DEL CORPUS DOMINI
Ill.:– S. Busuttil. Rome, [1838-39]. Ob. fo. Most plts. dtd. with monog., some sigd., 6 ll. soiled, 3 more heavily. Mod. linen portfo. (H. Dec.9/10; 790) DM 1,100

SOLER, R.
– **Araldica.** N.p., n.d. 4to. Occasional light foxing & dust soiling. Orig. gt. leath. (CB. Nov.12; 175) Can. $220

SOLINUS, Caius Julius
– **De Mirabilibus.** Venice, 13 Jan. 1493. 4to. Dampstained, MS. inscrs. on end-papers. Cont. Italian mor., blind-stpd. fillets, roll-stps., repeated, with lozenge motifs, bdg. defect. [Goff S-621; BMC V, 412] (HD. Mar.18; 161) Frs. 2,100
– **De Mirabilibus Mundi.** Ed.:– Bartolinus Atriensis. Brescia [Venice], [Petrus de Quarengiis?], 20 Nov. 1498 [after 1500]. Fo. Some browning, cont. marginal annots. Mod. blind-stpd. cf. From Honeyman Collection. [HC 14883; Goff S624] (S. May 19; 2873) *Pilo.* £400
– **Polihistor, Rerum toto orbe memorabilium Thesaurus Locuplentissimus.** Basle, 1543. Fo. Some wormholes slightly affecting a few letters, slightly dampstained in places, sm. stps. on title. Cont. limp vell., slightly worn, upr. cover torn. (S. Oct.21; 279) *Pearson.* £60
– **Polyhistor, sive De Mirabilibus Mundi.** Parma, Andreas Portilla, 22 Dec. 1480. Sm. 4to. Spaces for capital initials with guide letters, some staining, old MS. foliation cropped away, early ink marginal annots. washed faint thro.-out. Cf. gt. by Mackenzie. Bkplt. of Henry B.H. Beaufoy, lately in the collection of Eric Sexton. [BMC VII, 937, Goff S619, HC 14878] (CNY. Apr.8; 129) $1,500
See–**MELA, Pomponius–SOLINUS, Caius Julius**

SOLIS y Ribadeneyra, Antoine de
– **Histoire de la Conqueste du Mexique . . .** Paris, 1730. 5th. Edn. 2 vols. 12mo. Cont. cf., arms of Roujault President au Parlement in centre of covers, spines decor. with raised bands, bdgs. slightly defect. Bkplts. of Fourqueux & Maynon de Farcheville. (HD. Jun.24; 115) Frs. 1,800
– **Historia de la Conquista de Mexico.** Madrid, 1704. Sm. fo. Some stains thro.-out. Mod. buckram, ex-liby. (SG. Jun.11; 232) $140
– – **Anr. Edn.** Madrid, 1783-84. 2 vols. 4to. Mod. cf. (SPB. May 5; 479) $1,300
– – **Anr. Copy.** Cont. tree cf., gt. lines, spines gt. raised in compartments. [Sabin 85465] (VG. Oct.13; 148) Fls. 800
– **The History of the Conquest of Mexico.** Trans.:– Thomas Townsend. Ill.:– George Vertue (frontis. port.). 1724. 1st. Edn. in Engl. Fo. Short tear to fold of 1 plt., anr. frayed, frontis. browned. Mod. hf. mor., spine slightly faded. From the collection of Eric Sexton. (C. Apr.15; 47) *Traylen.* £140
– **Tesoro de la Iglesia Catolica.** Lima, 1650. Sm. 4to. 1st. & last margins reprd. or re-inforced with loss to border of woodcut lf. before title, stains at beginning & end. Limp vell. (SPB. May 5; 479) $175

SOLIS, Virgil
– **Biblische Figuren Dess Alten Testaments. –Biblische Figuren Dess Neuwen Testaments.** Ill.:– Solis. Frankfurt, 1562; 1562. 2 works in 1 vol. Ob. 4to. Some ll. torn & neatly reprd., soiling, staining. Later cf., worn, spine crudely reprd. W.a.f. (CSK. Oct.3; 41) £100
– **Wappenbüchlein.** [Köln], ca. 1590. 4th. Edn.? 4to. Ca. 1900 leath., gt. spine cover & outer dentelle, by Zaehnsdorf. O. Hupp ex-libris. (HK. Nov.18-21; 300) DM 2,400

SOLLEYSELL, Jacques Sieur de
– **Le Parfait Mareschal.** Amst., 1723. 20th. Edn. 2 vols. in 1. 4to. Lightly browned in parts, folding plt. torn. Cont. leath. (R. Mar.31-Apr.4; 1714) DM 450
– – **Anr. Edn.** Paris, 1723. New Edn. Cont. cf., spine gt. (VG. Nov.18; 1390) Fls. 500

SOLLY, Samuel
– **The Human Brain, its Structure, Configuration, Development & physiology.** 1836. 1st. Edn. Hf. mor. Sir Charles Sherrington's copy inscr. 'Gonville & Caius College, Camb., 1886' (S. Jun.17; 792) *Whitehart.* £75

SOLOMON, King of Israel
– **Song of Solomon.** Ill.:– Ronald King. Guildford, 1968. (150), sigd. by artist, numbered. Fo.

Unsewn in orig. buckram folder gt., spine slightly soiled, s.c. (SH. Nov.21; 355)
Monk Bretton. £380

SOLOMON BEN ELIEZER, ha-Levi
– Avodas ha-Levy. Venice, 1546. Sm. 4to. 18th. C. vell.-bkd. bds. (C. Jul.16; 316) *Stein.* £350

SOLON, Louis M.
– The Ancient Art Stoneware. 1892. Ltd. Edn. 2 vols. Fo. Orig. wraps. (SH. Jan.29; 196)
Tropper. £60

SOLORZANOY PEREYRA, Juan de
– De Indiarum Iure. Lyon, 1672. 2 vols. Fo. Sm. hole through bdg. of vol. 1, also affecting some ll. of text, browned or spotted thro.-out. Cont. vell. bds., slightly defect. [Sabin 86528] (SPB. May 5; 480) $225

SOLTAU, G.W.
– Trout Flies of Devon & Cornwall. Plymouth, [1856]. 2nd. Edn. (unrecorded variant). 100 pp., 4 advt. pp. Cl. (SG. Oct.16; 443) $110

SOLTYKOFF, Prince Alexis
– Indian Scenes & Characters. 1858. Fo. Hf. mor. gt. (P. Jul.30; 9) *Ewart.* £150

SØLVER, A.
– Danske Guldsmede. Copen., 1929. 4to. Orig. hf. leath. (SH. Jul.23; 305) *Zwemmer.* £90

SOLVYNS, François Baltazar
[–] [A Collection of ... coloured etchings descriptive of the Manners, Customs, & Dresses of the Hindoos by Batt. Solvyns]. [Calcutta], [1796-99]. Fo. 185 mntd. cold. plts. only, some slight soiling, 1 plt. torn & reprd., lacks titles. Old cf., badly worn. W.a.f. (CSK. Mar.6; 123) £340
– The Costume of Hindostan. 1807. Fo. Text wtrmkd. 1803-04, plts. 1819, lacks text lf. for plt. 39. Lacks covers, spine worn. (S. Sep.29; 266)
Doran. £150
– – Anr. Copy. 4to. Title & text in Engl. & Fr., dedication torn but reprd., a few margins slightly stained. Cont. hf. mor. (SBA. Mar.4; 124)
Quaritch. £115
– – Anr. Copy. 4to. Title & last lf. foxed. Orig. cl., covers detchd., lacks spine. (C. Nov.5; 150)
Hosain. £70
– – Anr. Edn. 1807: (plts. dtd. 1804-05). Fo. Titles in Engl. & Fr. Cont. hf. mor., spine gt. (C. Feb.25; 226) *Browning.* £150
– – Anr. Edn. L., ca. 1835. Fo. Paper wtrmkd. 1823-30. Cont. maroon mor., gt.-stpd. borders, rebkd. in panel. cf. (PNY. May 21; 148) $350
– – Anr. Edn. N.P., n.d. Fo. Bnd., lacks covers. (DS. May 22; 875) Pts. 46,000
– Les Hindous. Paris, 1808-11. Privilege Edn. Vols. 1-3 (of 4). Slightly soiled. Mid 19th. C. hf. leath. (HK. May 12-14; 541) DM 1,800
– – Anr. Edn. Paris, 1808-12. 4 vols. Fo. Plts. hand-cold., lacks hf.-titles, 4 plts. with tear in fold, occasional marginal foxing. Cont. hf. cf. From Chetham's Liby., Manchester. (C. Nov.27; 375)
Davidson. £1,000

SOMARE, E.
– I Maestri Italiani dell'Ottocento nella Raccolta Marzotto. Milan, 1937. 4to. Publisher's cl. (CR. Mar.19; 170) Lire 200,000
– Storia dei Pittori Italiani dell'Ottocento. Milan, 1928. (100) numbered. 2 vols. 4to. Publisher's vell. (CR. Mar.19; 167) Lire 500,000

SOME Short Stories, written by a Lady to Amuse a Young Friend
1825. 2nd. Edn. 16mo. Orig. roan-bkd. bds. (SH. Dec.10; 6) *Reisler.* £100

SOMERS or Sommers, Lord John
[–] Jura Populi Anglicani.–The History of the Kentish Petition. 1701; 1701. 2 works in 2 vols. 4to. Title & other ll. browned. Hf. cf. over marb. bds. Both from collection of Sir Thomas Neame with armorial bkplt., & sigd. in pencil in both vols. (LC. Oct.2; 310) £65

SOMERSETSHIRE Archaeological & Natural History Society
– Proceedings. 1849-1964. 82 vols. 26 vols. in hf. cf., 56 vols. in ptd. wraps. As a periodical, w.a.f. From the collection of Eric Sexton. (C. Apr.16; 358) *Burgess.* £110

SOMERVILE, William
See–SOMERVILLE, William

SOMERVILLE, Edith Oenone
– Slipper's ABC of Fox Hunting. L., 1903. 4to. Contents loose in bdg. Orig. decor. bdg., worn. Sigd. (SPB. May 29; 397) $100

SOMERVILLE, Edith Oenone & Ross, Martin
– Sporting Works. Ed.:– H.W. Smith. Ill.:– Somerville. 1927. Hitchcock Edn., (750) numbered. 7 vols. Gt.-pict. cl., partly untrimmed, most vols. unopened, bkplts. Sigd. by Somerville. (SG. Dec.11; 280) $380

SOMERVILLE, William
– The Chase. Ill.:– Thomas Bewick after John Bewick. L., 1796. 4to. Mod. cf., mod. s.-c. (SG. Apr.9; 400) $120
– The Chase.–Hobbinol. Bg'ham., 1767. Title & some ll. slightly browned. Cont. red mor., triple gt. fillet, spine gt. in compartments, inner gt. dentelles. (SM. Oct.8; 2014) Frs. 2,000

SOMMER, H. Oskar
– The Arthurian Legends. Wash., 1909-1916. Vulgate Edn. 8 vols. 4to. Mod. buckram, orig. wraps. bnd. in. (SG. Oct.2; 15) $220

SOMMERARD, Alexandre du
– Les Arts au Moyen Age. Paris, 1838-46. Bnd. in 2 vols. Atlas fo. Comprising 154 plts. & 4 illuminated titles only, most plts. cold. & in gold & silver. Leath., disbnd., worn, ex-liby. (SG. May 21; 212) $160

SOMMERING, Samuel Thomas
– Vom Baue d. Menschl. Körpers. Frankfurt, 1791 & 1801. 1st. Edn. (except vol. 4). 5 vols. Title with owner's mark., 1st. sigs. of vol. 3 soiled, slightly soiled in parts. Cont. hf. leath., gt. spine, blind-stpd. (HK. Nov.18-21; 754) DM 800

SOMNER, William–JUNIUS, Franciscus–LYE, Edward
– Dictionarium Saxonico-Latino-Anglicum.–Etymologicum ...–Dictionarium Saconico et Gothico-Latinum ... Ed.:– Edward Lye (2nd. work); & Owen Manning (3rd. work). Oxford; Oxford; L., 1659; 1743; 1772. 2 pts. in 1 vol.; 1 vol.; 2 vols. Fo. Slight marginal worming to 2nd. work. 1st. work: cont. cf. gt.; 2nd. work: hf. cf., liby. stp. at on upr. cover; 3rd. work: lev. mor. by Sangorski. From the collection of Eric Sexton. [Wing S4663] (1st. work) (C. Apr.15; 189)
Morton-Smith. £260

SOMOFF, C.
[–] Le Livre de la Marquise. Venice, [St. Petersb.], 1918. L.P. Hollande. 1st. Edn. 4to. Hf. leath., cover fillets, upr. orig. wrap. bnd. in, unc. Hand-cold. by artist, MS. dedication by author on end-paper dtd. 19.2.1919. (HK. Nov.18-21; 2938) DM 4,200

SONDERMANN, A.
– Der Wilddieb, Schmuggler und Falschmünzer Ignaz Diedrich ... Dresden, ca. 1860. 3 pts. in 1 vol. Slightly soiled in parts, pp. 1199/1200 with 2 small holes & loss. Cont. hf. linen. (R. Oct.14-18; 2808) DM 700

SONG of Roland, The
Riverside Pr. 1906. (220) numbered. Fo. Vell.-bkd. patterned bds., several light stains on covers. (SG. Jan.15; 85) $400
– – Anr. Copy. Patterned bds., vell. spine. (SG. Sep.4; 404) $190

SONG OF SONGS
Ill.:– W. Russell Flint. Riccardi Pr., 1901. Ltd. Edn. 4to. Orig. bds., d.-w., unc. (P. Sep.11; 210)
Sawyer. £65
– – Anr. Edn. Ill.:– Sir William Russell Flint. Riccardi Pr., 1909. (517) numbered. 4to. Orig. cl.-bkd. bds., d.-w. reprd. (S. Jul.31; 220)
Joseph. £55
– – Anr. Edn. Ill.:– Eric Gill. Gold. Cock. Pr., 1925. (750) numbered. 4to. Buckram, unc. (SG. Jan.15; 40) $240
– – Anr. Edn. Trans.:– W.O.E. Oesterley. Ill.:– Lettice Sandford. Gold. Cock. Pr., 1936. (64) specially bnd., with 6 extra sigd. etchings. Fo. Orig. hf. mor. gt., s.-c. (SH. Feb.19; 171)
Maggs. £300
– – Anr. Edn. Ill.:– Lettice Sandford. Gold. Cock. Pr. 1936. (204) numbered. Fo. Occasional slight soiling. Orig. cl. (CSK. Dec.10; 23) £55

SONNERAT, Pierre
– Voyage aux Indes Orientales ... Paris, 1782. 2 vols. 4to. 19th. C. hf. mor. From Chetham's Liby., Manchester. (C. Nov.27; 376) *Maggs.* £430

– – Anr. Edn. 1806. 5 vols., including Atlas. Text 8vo., Atlas 4to. (P. Oct.23; 63) *Rogers.* £190

SONNETS d'Amour
Ill.:– Dunoyer de Segonzac, Galanis, Marie Laurencin, Goerg, Brayer & others. Paris, 1943. (326); (26) on Arches vell. 4to. In sheets, publisher's s.-c. (HD. Dec.5; 199) Frs. 1,450

SONNINI, Charles Sigisbert
– Travels in Upper & Lower Egypt. 1799. 3 vols. Cont. hf. cf. (SH. May 21; 112)
Museum Books. £55

SONNINI, Parmentier, & others
[–] Nouveau Dictionnaire d'Histoire Naturelle. Paris, 1803-4. 24 vols. (? lacks atlas vol.). Liby. stps. Cont. cf., slightly worn, 1 spine defect. W.a.f. (S. May 5; 139) *Duran.* £100

SOPHOCLES
– Antigone. Ill.:– Hans Erni. Lausanne, n.d. (230) sigd. by artist & ed. 4to. Orig. wraps., folder & box, slight wear & soiling. (SPB. May 29; 145) $325
– King Oedipus. Trans.:– Edward Watling. Ill.:– Giacomo Manzu. N.Y., [1968]. (114) ptd. at Officina Bodoni, Verona, sigd. by artist. Fo. Mor.-bkd. parch. bds., unsewed, folding cl. case. (SG. Oct.23; 208) $650
– Oedipe Roi. Ill.:– Hans Erni. Lausanne, 1949. (230) sigd. by artist & ed. 4to. Orig. wraps., folder & box, box worn. (SPB. May 29; 146) $325
– Le Trachiniensi, L'Ajace Flagellifero, ed Il Filottete. Trans.:– Tommaso Giuseppe Farsetti. Venice, 1773. L.P. Cont. vell.-bkd. bds. From the collection of John A. Saks. (C. Jun.10; 66)
Quaritch. £160
– Tragaediae ... Venice, Aug. 1502. Mod. hf. vell. (HD. Apr.24; 5) Frs. 3,700

SOPHOCLES–POLYBIUS
– Commentarii in septem Tragedias Sophoclis. –Frangmenta [sic] duo ...–De Diversis Rerum Publicarum formis. [Rome]; Bologna, [1518]; 1543. 2 works in 1 vol. 1st. work lacks head of title, affecting 3 words on verso, replaced in pen facs., occasional browning & staining, cont. marginal MS. notes. 16th. C. cf., gt. fillet borders on covers, spine defect. at head & foot, reprd. (C. Apr.1; 86) *Summers.* £55

SOPWITH, Thomas
– Eight Views of Fountains Abbey. Ill.:– after R. Metcalf & J.W. Carmichael. Ripon, n.d. (plts. dtd. 1832). Some dampstaining, mainly marginal. Orig. wraps., soiled. (CSK. Jan.16; 181) £50

SOREL, Albert
– Vieux Habits, Vieux Galons. Ill.:– Maurice Leloir, Leon Boisson. Paris, 1915. (80) numbered on Japan vell. 8 plts., 17 head & tail-pieces, all in 2 states. Str.-grd. mor., gt. interlocking floral borders, gt.-panel. spine, gt. dentelles, by Chambolle-Duru, bkplt. (SG. Sep.4; 305) $150

SOREL, Charles
[–] The Extravagant Shepherd, or the History of the Shepherd Lysis, an anti-romance. 1660. 3rd. Edn. Fo. Engraved frontis. slightly cropped, blank margins of title cut short. Cont. cf. [Wing S4704A] (C. Feb.25; 172) *Hannas.* £100

SORIA VELASQUEZ, Jeronimo de
– Los Capitanes D. Miguel Diaz de la Mora ... Don Juan de Larrea ... Mexico, 1696. Fo. A few wormholes. Vell. bds., sprung. (SPB. May 5; 481) $125

SORLIER, C.
See–CAIN, Julien, Mourlot, Fernand & Sorlier, C.
See–MOURLOT, Fernand & Sorlier, Charles

SOTHEBY, William
– A Tour through Parts of Wales. Ill.:– J. Smith. 1794. 4to. Cont. hf. cf., worn. (C. Nov.6; 335)
Catchpole. £60
– – Anr. Copy. Cont. cf., worn. (SH. Jun.18; 7)
Rennard. £55

SOTHEBY & CO.
– Catalogue of the Celebrated Library of the Late Major J.R. Abbey. 1965-78. 10 vols. 4to. & fo. Orig. bds., stiff wraps., spines worn. (TA. Sep.18; 42) £60
– Mentmore Catalogue. 1977. 5 vols. 4to. Orig. bds., d.-w. (P. Mar.12; 363) *Cambridge.* £50
– Sotheby's Review. 1956-78. 20 vols. various. 4to. Orig. bdgs. (CSK. Jan.9; 115) £90
– – Anr. Edn. 1960-78. 14 vols. various. 4to. Orig. bdgs. (CSK. Feb.13; 49) £60

SOTHERAN, Henry
- Bibliotheca Chemico-Mathematica. L., 1921-52. 2 vols., & supps. 1-3, together 6 vols. Cl. (SG. Jan.22; 361) $850

SOUBISE, Charles de Rohan, Prince de
- Catalogue des Livres, Imprimés et Manuscrits, de la Bibliothèque. Paris, 1788. Table of authors, priced thro.-out in ink, marginalia. Cont. cf.-bkd. bds., later vell. corners. E.P. Goldschmidt's copy. (SM. Oct.7; 1502)   Frs. 3,200

SOUCHON, Edmond
See-SIMS, James Marion-SOUCHON, Edmond

SOUCIET, Etienne
- Observations Mathématiques, Astronomiques, Géographiques, Chronologiques, et Physiques, tirées des anciens livres Chinois; ou faites nouvellement aux Indes et à la Chine, par les Pères de la Campagnie de Jesus. Paris, 1729. Vol. I only. Cont. spr. cf., gt. (S. Dec.8; 143)   Lindsay. £120

SOULE, Frank & others
- The Annals of San Francisco ... N.Y., 1855. 1st. Edn. Cont.-gt. Mor., upr. covers loosened, ex-liby. (PNY. Oct.1; 124) $150

SOULES, François
- Histoire des Troubles de l'Amérique Anglaise ... Paris, 1787. 4 vols. Cont. marb. cf., spines decor. with raised bands. (HD. Jun.24; 116)   Frs. 2,000

SOULIER
- Histoire ... du Calvinisme en France. Paris, 1689. 2nd. Edn. 4to. Cont. cf., arms of J.J. Charron, Marquis de Menars, cypher repeated on spine. (HD. Mar.18; 162)   Frs. 1,600

SOURCES CHRETIENNES
Ed.:– H. de Lubac & J. Danielou. Paris, 1943-76. 65 vols. (B. Dec.10/11; 1301)   Fls. 1,200

SOUSA, Fr. Luis de
- Plans, Elevations, Sections & Views of the Church of Batalha, in the Province of Estremadura in Portugal. Ed.:– James Murphy (intro.). 1795. Lge. fo. Cont. russ., panel. in blind. Bkplt. of the Earl of Leitrim. (S. Jun.22; 93)   Quaritch. £140
- - Anr. Copy. Cont. bds., rebkd. & recornered with cf., unc. From the collection of Eric Sexton. (C. Apr.15; 48)   Marlborough. £130
- - Anr. Copy. Rather stained. Hf. cf., new spine & corners. (S. Dec.9; 470)   Dupont. £60

SOUTH, Theophilus (Pseud.)
See-CHITTY, Edward

SOUTH AUSTRALIAN Government Gazette
Jan.4-Dec.27, 1849. Nos. 1-54, in 1 vol. 4to. Pagination slightly irregular, some fore-margins stained. Old qtr. roan, slightly worn. (KH. Mar.24; 369)   Aus. $350

SOUTHARD, Frank B.
- Constructive Cover Designing. Holyoke, 1923. Fo. Hf.-mor. (SG. Oct.2; 89) $100

SOUTHERNE, Thomas
- The Fatal Marriage. 1694. 1st. Edn. 4to. Some minor stains. Mod. cf. [Wing S4756] (C. Nov.19; 164)   Terry. £90
- The Maids Last Prayer. 1693. 1st. Edn. 4to. Tear in title reprd., some stains, once affecting imposition. Mor. by Sangorski. [Wing S4760] (C. Nov.19; 165)   Wisbech. £50
- Oroonoko. 1696. 1st. Edn. 4to. Mor. by Sangorski, partly unc. [Wing S4761] (C. Nov.19; 166)   Brett-Smith. £150
- Sir Anthony Love. 1691. 1st. Edn. 4to. Some stains, especially at end, natural paper fault affecting catchword. Mor. by Sangorski. [Wing S4766] (C. Nov.19; 167)   Maggs. £90

SOUTHEY, Robert
- Historia do Brazil. Rio de Janeiro, 1862. 6 vols. Occasional spotting. Orig. cl., slight wear. (SPB. May 5; 482) $175
- History of Brazil. L., 1810-17-19. 1st. Edn. 3 vols. Lge. 4to. Mod. hf. buckram. (SG. May 14; 201) $750
- The Life of Nelson. L., 1813. 1st. Edn. 4to. Early crimson str.-grd. mor. gt., cl. s.-c. Triptych-style fore-e. pntg. in each vol.; from the liby. of Zola E. Harvey. (SG. Mar.19; 173) $850
- Roderick, the Last of the Goths. L., 1816. 4th. Edn. 2 vols. 12mo. Cont. crimson str.-grd. mor., wide gt. floral borders, spines gt., bkplt. Fore-e. pntg. in each vol.; from the liby. of Zola E. Harvey. (SG. Mar.19; 174) $425

SOUTHGATE, R.
- Museum Southgatianum. 1795. 3 pts. in 1 vol. Cont. hf. cf., lacks head of spine. (SH. Mar.6; 451)   Seaby. £110

SOUTHWART, Elizabeth
- Brontë Moors & Villages from Thornton to Haworth. Ill.:– T. Mackenzie. 1923. (75) numbered, with etched front. sigd. by artist. Orig. buckram gt. (SH. Mar.27; 334)   Marks. £50

SOUVENIR DE MOSCOU
[Moscow], ca. 1909. Ob. fo. 15 actual photographs mntd., slightly soiled. Orig. cl., soiled. (SH. Feb.5; 275)   Lyon. £170

SOUVENIR de Saint-Petersbourg
St. Petersb., 1828. Fo. Cont. diced cf., wide gt. ornam. borders, rebkd. (SG. Feb.26; 306) $800

SOUVENIR DU RHIN
Ill.:– J.J. Tanner. Bad Ems, ca. 1840. Ob. 4to. Slightly soiled in margin. Orig. hf. linen gt., lacks ties. (HD. Nov.18-21; 1346)   DM 1,700

SOUVENIRS DE LA SUISSE
Geneva, ca. 1860. Ob. 8vo. Orig. cl. gt. (P. Apr.9; 36)   Walford. £500
- Lac de Genève. Geneva, n.d. Ob. 8vo. 21 cold. litho. views, 4 double-p., 1 reprd. Orig. cl. gt. (P. Jun.11; 100)   Baumer. £160

SOUVENIRS de la Suisse-Dessinés d'après Nature
Geneva, n.d. Ob. 8vo. Some plts. detchd. Orig. mor., s.-c. (CSK. Jun.19; 38)   £750

SOUVENIRS PITTORESQUES DU RHIN
Ill.:– Arnoud, Bichebois & Deroy. Frankfurt, 1826. Ob. 4to. Plts. on india paper, title & some ll. slightly soiled. Orig. bds., soiled, lacks ties. (CSK. Feb.6; 66)   £130

SOWERBY, Geo. Brettingham
- The Conchological Illustrations. L., 1841. Lacks plts. 137, 138. Cont. hf. leath. (HK. Nov.18-21; 760)   DM 500
- Conchological Manual. 1852. 4th Edn. Orig. cl., spine worn & stuck down. (S. May 5; 159)   Wesley. £60
- - Anr. Copy. Cont. cf., worn, spine reprd. (H. Dec.9/10; 360)   DM 450
- Illustrated Index of British Shells. 1859. 1st. Edn. 4to. Orig. cl. gt. soiled. (SBA. Mar.4; 166)   Rochdale Bookshop. £50
- Thesaurus Conchyliorum. 1844-86. Pts. 4-6, 12-26, 31, 43 & 44 in 3 vols. Numerous marginalia & occasional writing on plts. Hf. leath., soiled & worn, most orig. wraps. preserved. W.a.f. (S. May 5; 140)   Cristani. £220

SOWERBY, James
- A Botanical Drawing-Book. Priv. ptd. N.d. Ob. 4to. Advt. lf. Bds. (S. Dec.2; 626)
                                    Marlborough. £80
- The British Miscellany. L., 1804-06. 1st. Edn. Hf. mor., spine gt., partly unc., by Bumpas, orig. wraps. of 12 pts. bnd. in. (CNY. May 22; 217) $180
- - Anr. Edn. 1806. [1st. Edn.?] Vol. 1 only (all publd.). Cont. str.-grd. mor., upr. cover detchd. (TA. Apr.16; 95)   £90
- Exotic Minerology: or Coloured Figures of Foreign Minerals, as a Supplement to British Mineralogy. L., 1811-17. 2 vols. Lacks plt. 73, slightly browned & soiled. Cont. hf. leath., spine very defect. (R. Mar.31-Apr.4; 1142)   DM 550
- The Mineral Conchology of Great Britain. L., 1829. Vol. 6. Liby. linen. (R. Oct.14-18; 3033)   DM 650
- A New Elucidation of Colours, Original Prismatic, & Material ... with Some Observations on the Accuracy of Sir Isaac Newton. 1809. 1st. Edn. 4to. Orig. bds., unc., spine defect., covers detchd., cl. case. From Honeyman Collection. (S. May 19; 2876)   Norman. £320
See-SMITH, Sir James Edward & Sowerby, James

SOWERBY, James & George Brettingham
- The Genera of Recent & Fossil Shells ... [1820-25]. 42 pts. in 2 vols. 264 (of 267) hand-cold. engraved & litho. plts., lacks titles & indexes. Cont. hf. cf. W.a.f. (C. Jul.15; 209)
                            Wheldon & Wesley. £150

SOWERBY, James de Carle & Lear, Edward
- Tortoises, Terrapins & Turtles. 1872. Fo. Few ll. loose in gutta-percha bdg. Cont. mor.-bkd. cl. (C. Mar.18; 109)   Wheldon & Wesley. £1,000

SOWERBY, John Edward & Johnson, Charles Pierpont
- British Wild Flowers. Ed.:– C.P. Johnson. 1863. Mor. gt. (P. Dec.11; 217)   Ayres. £65

SPAAN, G. van
- Het Koddig en Vermakelyk Leven van Louwtje van Zevenhuizen, of het Schermschool der Huislieden. Waar agter de Afrikaansche en Aziaansche Wegwyzer. Rotterdam, 1752. 4 pts. in 1 vol. Cont. marb. cf., bkd. (VG. Oct.13; 149)   Fls. 500

SPACH, Edouard
- Histoire Naturelle des Vegetaux-Phanerogames. 1846. Atlas only. Plts., mostly hand-cold. Cont. qtr. cf. (TA. Sep.18; 27)   £130

SPALART, R.V.
- Versuch über das Kostüm ... Völker des Althertums. Vienna, 1796-1804. 1st. Edn. 2 vols. Sm. ob. fo. Only copper engrs. to Section 1, pts. 1-3 & Section 2, pts. 1-3, 194 (of 218?) cold. copperplts., no text & sm. 8vo. plts. Unc., cont. hf. leath. & cont. wraps (2). (R. Mar.31-Apr.4; 1573)   DM 600
- - Anr. Edn. [Vienna], [1796-1837]. Ob. fo. 232 plts., some plts. slightly soiled, spine defect. Cont. hf. leath. (HK. May 12-14; 1172)   DM 800
- Versuch über das Kostum ... des Alterthums ... Ersten Abtheilung. Vienna, ca. 1800. Atlas vol. only. Ob. 4to. Lacks text vols. & atlas to 2nd. pt. iss. in 1811. Cont. hf. mor., worn. W.a.f. (CNY. Oct.1; 84) $380

SPALLANZANI, Lazzaro
- De'Fenoneni della Circolazione Osservata nel Giro Universale de'vasi. Modena, 1773. 1st. Edn. Some spotting & discolouration, ink stains on O2r. 19th. C. roan-bkd. bds., spine wormed, red hf. mor. case. From Honeyman Collection. (S. May 19; 2878)   Zeitlin & Verbrugge. £120
- Dissertations Relative to the Natural History of Animals & Vegetables. 1789. 2 vols. Some spotting & offsetting. 19th. C. hf. roan. (S. Apr.6; 153)   Gurney. £85
- Dissertazioni di Fisica Animale, e Vegetabile. Modena, 1780. 1st. Edn. 2 vols. 1 folding plt. with marginal tear, some browning. Orig. bds., slightly soiled. Pres. copy; blind-stp. of Dr. Luciano Aragona; from Honeyman Collection. (S. May 19; 2880)   James. £400
- Experiments upon the Circulation of the Blood. Ed.:– J. Tourdes. Trans.:– R. Hall. L., 1801. 1st. Edn. in Engl. Stain on title-p. Crude hf. leath., brkn. From Brooklyn Academy of Medicine. (SG. Jan.29; 388) $150
- Fisica Animale e Vegetabile. Venice, 1782. 1st. Edn. 3 vols. 12mo. Cont. vell. From the collection of John A. Saks. (C. Jun.10; 234)   King. £80
- - Anr. Edn. Venice, 1782. 2nd. End. 3 vols. 12mo. Bds., cl. spine. (S. Dec.1; 393)
                                    Gurney. £50
- Opuscoli di Fisica Animale, e Vegetabile. Modena, 1776. 1st. Edn. 2 vols. Text foxed, pp. 174/175 soiled in vol. II. 19th. C. roan-bkd. bds., red hf. mor. cases. From Honeyman Collection. (S. May 19; 2879)   Quaritch. £240
- Prodromo di un'Opera da Imprimersi Sopra le Riproduzioni Animali. Modena, 1768. 1st. Edn. Sm. 4to. Dampstained at end. Cont. patterned wraps., slightly worn & discold. From Honeyman Collection. (S. May 19; 2877)   Norman. £360
- Travels in the Two Sicilies, & Some Parts of the Apennines. 1798. 1st. Engl. Edn. 4 vols. Some plts. slightly torn or cut at upr. inner edge where folded, 1 with caption cropped, lr. inner margin of last lf. in vol. III reprd., slight browning. Cont. tree cf., gt. spines, red hf. mor. cases. Owner's inscrs. of R. Guy Evered & Arthur Parker Hitchens; from Honeyman Collection. (S. May 19; 2882)   Zeitlin & Verbrugge. £280
- - Anr. Copy. Some browning & spotting, last 2 plts. stained in vol. IV, L8 misbnd. before L1 in vol. II. Cont. cf., rebkd., corners reprd. From Honeyman Collection. (S. May 19; 2883)
                                    Prichard-Jones. £180
- - Anr. Copy. Plts. cropped, 1 or 2 with short tears, occasional light foxing. Cont. diced cf., rebkd. (S. Nov.4; 583)   Wills. £140
- Versuche über d. Erzeugung d Thiere u. Pflanzen. Trans.:– C.F. Michaelis. Leipzig, 1786. 1st. German Edn. Vol. 1, all publd. Slightly soiled & browned. Cont. bds., unc. (HK. Nov.18-21; 762)   DM 700
- Viaggi alle due Sicilie e in Alcune Parti dell' Appennino. Pavia, 1792-97. 1st. Edn. 6 vols. Slight

spotting & discolouration. Orig. limp bds., unc., spine of vol. I reprd., lr. cover of vol. II stained, cl. cases. From Honeyman Collection. (S. May 19; 2881) *Sotheran.* £800
- Voyages dans les deux Siciles. Paris, An VIII [1800]. 6 vols. Some staining. Orig. paper wraps., unc., some vols. slightly torn. Proof Copy, with extensive corrections (by Trans.). in vols. 2-6. (C. Nov.5; 151) *Wheldon & Wesley.* £50

SPAMER, A.
- Das Kleine Andachtsbild vom 14. bis zum 20. Jahrhundert. Munich, 1930. Lge. 4to. Orig. linen. (R. Mar.31-Apr.4; 847) DM 750
- - Anr. Copy. Sm. fo. Slightly stained. (R. Oct.14-18; 767) DM 680

SPAMER, O.
- Illustriertes Konversations-Lexikon. Leipzig & Berlin, 1870-80. 8 vols. 4to. Browned, some pp. loose, not collated. Cont. linen. W.a.f. (R. Oct.14-18; 2534) DM 1,600
- Illustrirtes Handels-Lexikon. Leipzig, 1876-79. 4 vols. Slightly soiled in parts, vol. 3 lacks title lf. Hf. linen, 2 spines renewed. W.a.f., not collated. (R. Mar.31-Apr.4; 1876) DM 1,050

SPAMPANI, Giambattista & Antonini, Carlo
- Il Vignola illustrata. Rome, 1770. Fo. Dampstained & slightly spotted. 19th. C. hf. cf. (S. Feb. 23; 105) *Licini.* £75

SPAN, S.
- Speculum Iuris Metallici. Dresden, 1698. Fo. Slightly browned. Cont. style hf. leath. (R. Oct.14-18; 238) DM 600

SPANGENBERG, Cyriacus
- Mansfeldische Chronica. Eisleben, 1572. 1st. Edn. Fo. Lacks 2 end-ll. with Imprint, text, index & errata complete, hole in title, some text loss on 3 ll. Cont. vell., soiled. (R. Oct.14-18; 157) DM 520

SPANGENBERG, J.
- Ausslegunge der Episteln und Evangelien ... Nuremb., 1559. Early Edn. Fo. Pref.: M. Luther, 3 woodcut title borders, 1 old cold., many larger text woodcuts, the 1st. 4 old cold., printer's mark at end, slightly browned. Cont. blind-tooled pig-bkd. wood bds., 1 (of 2) clasps. (R. Oct.14-18; 158) DM 950

SPANISCHE SCHACHZABELBUCH des Königs Alfons des Weisen vom Jahre 1283
Ed.:– G. White. Leipzig, 1913. 2 vols. Fo. Loose ll. in orig. linen portfo., 1 defect. (H. Dec.9/10; 97) DM 800

SPANISH BAWD, (The) represented in Celestina, or, the Tragicke-Comedy of Calisto & Melibea
Trans.:– James Mabbe. 1631. 1st. Edn. Fo. Outer margin of title restored with rules & 2 letters in pen facs., a few minor stains. Cf. by Rivière. [STC 4911-2] (C. Apr.1; 223) *Storne.* £110

SPANLIN, Gallus
- Arithmetica, Künstlicher Rechnung lustige Exempel, Mancherley schoener Regeln auff Linien und Ziffern, vormals nie gesehen. Augsburg, 1546. 1st. Edn. Lacks final blank, sm. holes in B8 & Q4, some browning, title a little soiled. Sheep, very worn, lr. cover & spine loose. From Honeyman Collection. (S. May 19; 2885) *Dr. Martin.* £460

SPARE, Austin Osman
- Earth Inferno. 1905. (265) numbered, sigd. Fo. Orig. parch., unc., stained. (SH. Mar.27; 498) *Ayres.* £60

SPARLING, Henry Halliday
- The Kelmscott Press & William Morris Master-Craftsman. Kelms. Pr., 1924. 1st. Edn. Orig. linen-bkd. bds. (SH. Feb.19; 16) *Libris.* £60
- - Anr. Copy. (SH. Feb.19; 15) *Dawson.* £55
- - Anr. Edn. L., 1929. Slight wear. Orig. cl.-bkd. bds., soiled. (SPB. May 29; 241) $100

SPARRMAN, Andrew
- A Voyage to the Cape of Good Hope. 1786. 2nd. Edn. 2 vols. 4to. Some ll. slightly spotted. Hf. cf. (S. Jul.27; 9) *Maggs.* £420
- - Anr. Copy. Cf. (P. Oct.23; 64) *Rogers.* £160

- - Anr. Copy. 2 vols. P. 25, vol. 1 torn, pp. 179 & 267 vol. 2 slightly torn but not affecting text, light foxing. Hf. mor., marb. bds. (SSA. Jan.22; 319) R. 450
- - Anr. Edn. Perth, 1789. 2 vols. Qtr. cf. & marb. bds. by Bumpus. Bkplt. of Hans Sauer. (VA. Jan.30; 393) R. 210

SPARROW, Geoffrey
- The Crawley & Horsham Hunt. [1931]. (500) numbered, sigd. by author. 4to. Map in pocket at end. Orig. vell.-bkd. cl. gt., slightly worn. (SKC. Feb.26; 1798) £70

SPARROW, Walter Shaw
- Angling in British Art. 1923. 1st. Edn. 4to. Mod. cl. (SH. Oct.9; 105) *Grosvenor Prints.* £80
- - Anr. Copy. Orig. cl. gt., partly unc. (LC. Oct.2; 62) £50
- - Anr. Copy. Cl., unc., unopened. (SG. Oct.16; 449) $130
- - Anr. Edn. Ill.:– Norman Wilkinson. L., [1923]. 1st. Edn., L.P., (125) numbered, sigd., with orig. sigd. etching by artist. Lge. 4to. Cl., unc. (SG. Oct.16; 448) $300
- Frank Brangwyn & his Work. 1910. (160) numbered sigd. by Brangwyn. Fo. Cont. hf. vell. by Bayntun. 2 orig. etchings sigd. by Brangwyn. (CSK. May 22; 105) £85
- Henry Alken ... with an Introduction by Sir Theodore Cook. 1927. (250) numbered, sigd. by Cook. 4to. Orig. cl., slightly spotted. (SH. Oct.9; 247) *Way.* £65
- John Lavery & his Work. N.d. (160) numbered. Fo. Orig. vell.-bkd. bds., soiled. (SH. Jan.29; 152) *Villiers.* £60
See–BRANGWYN, Frank & Sparrow, Walter Shaw

SPECCHI, Alessandro
- Il Quarto Libro del Nuovo Teatro delli Palazzi Prospettiva di Roma Moderna. Rome, 1699. Ob. fo. Engraved title & 28 plts. only, spotted. Cf.-bkd. bds., worn, upr. cover loose. (SKC. May 19; 468) £85

SPECTACLES EN PLEIN VENT
Paris, ca. 1850. 145mm. × 2435mm. In panoramic form, some folds reprd. Orig. bds., rebkd. (SH. Mar.19; 245) *Till.* £280

[SPECULUM HUMANAE SALVATIONIS]–DER SPIEGEL MENSCHLICHER BEHALTNUSS
Augsburg, Johann Schonsperger, 2 Mar. 1500. Fo. Lacks title, a3 & 2 final blanks, most ll. in first 3 quires cut down & remargined, usually not affecting text, these & last 3 quires detchd. from bdg., many ll. with tears & holes, sm. portions lacking, some with text loss, stained & thumbed, particularly at beginning, x3-4, y3-4 & C3-4 misbnd. Cont. German blind-stpd. cf. over wooden bds., lacks spine & clasps, covers partly detchd. [HC 14940*; Goff S669] (C. Apr.1; 123) *Kleinwort.* £2,200

SPEECHLY, William
- A Treatise on the Culture of the Vine. [1789]. 2nd. Edn. Hf. cf. (P. Sep.11; 190) *Denniston.* £55

SPEEDE, John
- England. Ed.:– John Arlott. 1953-54. Facs. of 1st. Edn. 4 vols. Fo. Hf. cl., s.-c. (P. Sep.11; 2) *Singleton.* £100
- England, Wales, Scotland & Ireland.–Prospect of the Most Famous Parts of the World. 1666; 1668. 2 works in 1 vol. Ob. 8vo. 1st. work: map of Yorkshire folding & laid down, title browned with sm. tears & marginal defects reprd.; some spotting & browning thro.-out both works (mostly marginal). Mod. hf. mor. W.a.f. (C. Nov.6; 271) *Shires.* £1,200
- - Anr. Edn. N.d.; 1668. 2 works in 1 vol. Ob. 8vo. 1st. work lacks title & all before A3, lacks 1st. map of 'England, Scotland & Ireland', & 'Yorkshire', 1 map torn, 2 maps with sm. piece torn from blank margins, 1 map with sm. hole, 2nd. work with occasional spotting. Old cf., worn, covers cracked. As an atlas, w.a.f. (C. Apr.1; 234) *Burgess.* £350
[–] [The English Atlas]. 1770. Fo. 41 engraved maps, & 16 engraved maps from England fully described (1743), & 1 engraved plt. 'Prospect of

Shrewsbury', no text, some maps cut down, all mntd., map of Nottingham cropped, some staining of maps. Loose in hf. mor. folder. W.a.f. (C. Nov.6; 272) *Crossley.* £3,000
- An Exact Geography of the Kingdom of England, Scotland & Ireland. Also a Prospect of the Most Famous Parts of the World ... Asia, Africa, Europe & America. [L.], [1676]. Fo. Maps uncold., some with tears & defect., stains in margins. Leath. on bds., loose. (JN. Apr.2; 806b) £12,500
- The Theatre of the Empire of Great Britaine. 1611-12. [1st. Edn.?]. 4 pts. in 1. Fo. 67 double-p. maps mntd. on guards. Diced russ., Mark Masterman Sykes crest & monog. in gt. on upr. cover. As an atlas, w.a.f. (C. Jul.15; 161) *Hammond.* £8,800
- - Anr. Copy. 475mm × 280mm. Without the 'Prospect', publd. later, maps of Dorset & Devon from anr. copy, margins renewed to size, repairs of centre fold of some maps, with loss, map of Hertfordshire stained, paper of some maps slightly dis-cold., 2 sm. wormholes in top blank margins at beginning. 19th. C. russ., gt. line-border, blind-tooled panel decor. with border of repeated tool, fleuron at corners, circular composite centre ornament, gt. spine, worn. W.a.f. (S. Nov.3; 10) *Kentish.* £6,000
- Theatre of the Empire of Great Britain. -Prospect of the Most Famous Parts of the World. L., 1627-31. Fo. No title or prelims., 85 maps (of 96), many frayed & torn. Disbnd. (P. Jul.2; 230) *Burgess.* £4,000
- - Anr. Edn. 1676. 5 pts. in 1 vol. Fo., (432mm. × 290mm.). Maps on later guards thro.-out, map of Oxford from the 1627 Edn., repairs to blank inner margin of frontis. & to a number of bottom margins, in a few cases affecting engraved surface, several maps separated at centre fold, top engraved border of Bermuda shaved, natural flaw in engraved surface at 1 side of world map, tear in maps of Greece & Roman Empire, a few rust spots or stains. Cont. panel. cf., rebkd. & restored. W.a.f. (S. Nov.3; 11) *Arader.* £7,500
- - Anr. Copy. Hand-cold. frontis., engraved title, 96 partly cold. maps, many with tears, some margins frayed. Cf., covers loose. (P. Jun.11; 204) *Burgess.* £7,000
See–BIBLES [English]–PRAYER BOOKS –PSALMS, PSALTERS & PSEUMES –SPEEDE, John

SPEEDE, John–[KEER, Peter]
- England, Wales, Scotland & Ireland Described & Abridged.–[A Prospect of the most famous parts of the World]. 1676; [1676?]. 2 works in 1 vol. Ob. sm. 8vo. (111mm. × 170mm.). 1st. work: lacks numbers 38, 61, 62, wanting contents lf., map 59 torn, ink-stains on 41, natural flaw in G7, without loss; 2nd. work: 27 engraved maps, (20 only are called for), wanting title A1, stain in margin of map of Barbados, last lf. S4 reprd. in margin. Mod. mott. cf. W.a.f. (S. Nov.3; 12) *Gibbons.* £1,200

SPEER, A.
- Die Neue Reichskanzlei. Munich, n.d. 4to. Cl. gt. (P. Oct.23; 166) *Ars Artis.* £50

SPEKE, John Hanning
- Die Entdeckung der Nilquellen. Leipzig, 1864. 1st. German Edn. 2 vols. Some browning. Cont. red hf. leath., lightly worn. (H. May 21/22; 346) DM 460
- Journal of the Discovery of the Source of the Nile. 1863. 1st. Edn. Hf. mor. gt. (SBA. Jul.23; 659) *Francis.* £130
- - Anr. Copy. 1 lf. advts., 32-p. Blackwood catalogue. Gt. decor. cl., recased. (SG. Oct.30; 335) $175

SPENCE, Joseph
- A Parallel, in the Manner of Plutarch ... Strawberry Hill, 1758. 1st. Edn., (700). Cont. Engl. red mor., gt., spine tooled in compartments. Bkplt. of J.G. Teed. (S. Nov.24; 262) *Maggs.* £240
- Polymetis ... L., 1747. 1st. Edn. Fo. Mod. hf. leath. (SG. Sep.25; 289) $140

SPENCER, Baldwin
- Native Tribes of the Northern Territory of Australia. 1914. Hf. mor. gt. (P. Oct.23; 222a) *Bonham.* £55

SPENCER, Baldwin – Native Tribes of the Northern Territory of Australia. *-contd.*
– – **Anr. Copy.** Orig. decor. cl. (JL. Dec.14; 85) Aus. $125
– – **Anr. Copy.** Orig. bdg. (KH. Nov.18; 552) Aus. $120
– **Report on the Work of the Horn Scientific Expedition to Central Australia.** L. & Melbourne, 1896. 4 vols. 4to. in 8's. Orig. cl., gt., vol. 1 bnd. from wraps. in later cl., therefore not unif. (KH. Nov.18; 554) Aus. $820
– **Wanderings in Wild Australia.** 1928. [1st. Edn.?]. 2 vols. Cl. gt. (P. May 14; 297) £60
– – **Anr. Copy.** Orig. cl., d.-w. (P. Oct.23; 222b) *Bonham.* £50
– – **Anr. Copy.** Slight foxing, mainly to fore-edges. Orig. cl. gt., d.-w.'s. (KH. Mar.24; 373) Aus. $120

SPENCER, Baldwin & Gillen, F.J.
– **The Arunta.** 1927. 2 vols. Orig. cl., d.-w. (SH. Mar.5; 135) *Remington.* £80
– – **Anr. Copy.** Cl., gt. title to spine. (JL. Dec.14; 84) Aus. $130
– **Native Tribes of Central Australia.** 1899. Orig. cl. gt. (P. Oct.23; 222) *Burke.* £50
– – **Anr. Copy.** Slight foxing, inscr. sigd. by Edward H. Sugden. Buckram. (KH. Nov.18; 555) Aus. $210
– **The Northern Tribes of Central Australia.** L., 1904. Orig. decor. cl. (JL. Dec.14; 86) Aus. $125

SPENCER, Nathaniel
– **The Complete English Traveller.** 1771. Fo. Cf. (DWB. May 15; 250) £195
– – **Anr. Edn.** [1771?]. Fo. Frontis. mntd. Hf. cf. (SBA. May 27; 320) *Nolan.* £140
– – **Anr. Edn.** L., 1772. Fo. 59 (of 60) copperplts., ex liby. Cont. cf. (SG. Oct.30; 336) $300

SPENCER, Thomas
– **Instructions for the Multiplication of Works of Art in Metal, by Voltaic Electricity.** Glasgow, 1840. 1st. Edn. Hf. cl., red hf. mor. case. Bkplt. of Alexander Watt; from Honeyman Collection. (S. May 19; 2888) *Zeitlin.* £50

SPENDER, Stephen
– **Twenty Poems.** Oxford, [1930]. 1st. Edn. Orig. wraps., soiled, unc. Inscr. to Mr. de la Mare. (SH. Dec.18; 299) *Blackwell.* £220

SPENDLOVE, F. St. George
– **The Face of early Canada.** Toronto, [1958]. 4to. Orig. cl., d.-w. slightly tattered. (CB. May 27; 317) Can. $130

SPENSER, Edmund
– **Faerie Queene.** Ed.:– John Upton. 1758. 2 vols. 4to. Pp. 466-7 & 470-1 in vol. 1 not pd., lacks last ll. (blanks?), old sig. of Mary Benest on fly-lf. Cont. red mor., gt., arms of Marie Charlotte Hippolyte de Campet de Saujon, Marquise de Boufflers-Rouverel, gt. dentelle border incorporating charges from arms, floral roll border, spine gt. in compartments with charges from arms & semé with stars & dots, inner gt. dentelles, upr. cover of vol. 11 detchd. (SM. Oct.8; 2018) Frs. 2,100
– – **Anr. Edn.** Ed.:– T.J. Wise. Ill.:– Walter Crane. 1894-97. 6 vols. 4to. Orig. upr. covers bnd. in, orig. cl., soiled. (PD. Oct.22; 86) £75
– – **Anr. Edn.** Ed.:– Thomas J. Wise. Ill.:– Walter Crane. 1897. (1000). 6 vols. 4to. Orig. iss. upr. wraps. bnd. in, partly untrimmed. Cont. cl. gt., slightly soiled. (TA. Jan.22; 348) £100
– – **Anr. Edn.** Ash. Pr., 1923. (192), (180) on paper. Fo. Orig. cf.-bkd. vell., unc., s.-c. (S. Jul.31; 64) *Duchnes.* £240
– – **Anr. Edn.** Ed.:– John Hayward. Ill.:– Agnes Miller Parker & John Austen. Ltd. Edns. Cl., 1953. (1,500) sigd. by Parker. 2 vols. 4to. Orig. buckram, d.-w.'s, s.-c. (SH. Feb.20; 232) *Wavey.* £65
– **Faerie Queene [Second Part].** 1596. 1st. Edn. Sm. 4to. Cont. limp vell., gt. arms on sides, reprd., lacks ties. [STC 23082] (S. Mar.16; 129) *Claridge.* £300
– **Faerie Queen.–Shepheards Calendar (with the other works).** 1617. Sm. fo. Light marginal staining thro.-out. Cf. by Rivière, slightly worn. [STC 23085] (S. May 5; 293) *Thomas.* £95
– – **Anr. Copy.** Some MS. notes (not by Cotton), slight browning & soiling, a few short tears, lacks blank A1, V6 of the 2nd. pt., C3, & M2 of last pt., title of Prothalamium detchd., bkplt. of George Stanhope, Dean of Canterbury on verso of general title, & a note by his daughter on verso of

dedication. 18th. C. hf. cf., worn. Charles Cotton's copy. (S. Apr.7; 373) *Shapero.* £60
– **Minor Poems.** Ash. Pr., 1925. (200) on paper. Fo. Orig. cf.-bkd. vell., unc., s.-c. (S. Jul.31; 65) *Jonathan.* £280
– – **Anr. Copy.** Orig. mor.-bkd. vell., soiling. (SPB. Nov.25; 217) $700
– – **Anr. Edn.** Ash. Pr., 1925. (215). Fo. Orig. cf.-bkd. vell., slightly soiled. Sigd. & dtd. by William Russell Flint. (CSK. Dec.10; 27) £200
– [–] **The Shepheardes Calender.** 1579. 1st. Edn. 4to. With the 'tun' device on verso of last lf. (frayed at edges with long tear, affecting printer's device & touching 1 letter of text, & almost detchd. from bdg.), sm. stain in some ll. at beginning. Disbnd., in mor.-bkd. box. The Houghton Copy. [STC 23089] (C. Nov.20; 276) *Brett-Smith.* £38,000
– – **Anr. Edn.** Ed.:– F.S. Ellis. Ill.:– A.J. Gaskin. Kelms. Pr., 1896. (225) on paper. Sm. 4to. Mor. gt., rule borders with floral decor. at corners, by Sangorski & Sutcliffe. (S. Jul.31; 12) *Seibu.* £520
– – **Anr. Copy.** Orig. cl.-bkd. bds., slightly soiled. Sigd. & dtd. twice by William Russell Flint. (CSK. Dec.10; 28) £160
– – **Anr. Copy.** 4to. Orig. holland-bkd. bds., unc. (CNY. May 22; 328) $480
– – **Anr. Copy.** (CNY. May 22; 329) $320
– **Shepherd's Calendar . . . Calendarium Pastorale** . . . Trans.:– Theodore Bathurst. L., 1653. 1st. Edn. Lacks last 2 ll. comprising Glossary. Three qtr. lev., spine gt., by Stikeman. (SG. Sep.25; 290) $200
– **Works.** 1611. 1st. Coll. Edn., 1st. Iss. Fo. Lacks Prosopopoia, or Mother Hubbard's Tale, title & first few ll. detchd. & slightly defect, some dampstaining. Cont. cf., worn, upr. cover detchd. [NSTC 23083.3] (S. May 5; 444) *Rix.* £60
– – **Anr. Edn.** Ill.:– Hilda Quick. Shakes. Hd. Pr., 1930-32. (375) numbered. 8 vols. 4to. Orig. mor.-bkd. bds., unc. (SH. Feb.19; 58) *Subunso.* £150
– – **Anr. Copy.** Gt. qtr. leath. & marb. bds., unopened. (PNY. Oct.1; 482) $280
– – **Anr. Edn.** Ed.:– Greenlaw & others. Balt., [1966]. Variorum Edn. 10 vols. Cl. (SG. Aug.7; 413) $130

SPERATUS, Paulus
See–ETLICH Christliche Lyeder Lobgesang und Psalm

SPERONI, S.
– **Canace Tragedia [Guidicio Sopra la Tragedia di Canace, et Macareo].** Venice, 1566. 2 pts. in 1 vol. 17th. C. mor., wide pointillé border, spine compartments gt. in pointillé, inner red mor. doubl., gt. border, s.-c. The MacCarthy-Reagh-Soleine-La Roche Lacarelle-Schiff copy, with bkplts. of La Roche Lacarelle & Schiff. (S. Apr.7; 308) *Maggs.* £160

SPICILEGIUM Botanicum
See–ANDREWS, Henry C.–SMITH, Sir James Edward & Sowerby, James–ANON

SPIELMANN, Mrs. Mabel H.
– **Littledom Castle.** Ed.:– Marion Harry Spielmann. Ill.:– Arthur Rackham, Kate Greenaway & others. L. & N.Y., 1903. 1st. Edn. Sm. 4to. Gt.-pict. cl. Raymond M. Sutton Jr. copy. (SG. May 7; 271) $120
– **The Rainbow Book.** Ill.:– Arthur Rackham, Hugh Thomson & others. L., 1909. 1st. Edn. Gt.-pict. cl., worn. Raymond M. Sutton Jr. copy. (SG. May 7; 273) $160

SPIELMANN, Marion Harry
– **Henriette Ronner, the painter of Cat Life & Cat Character.** 1891. 4to. Orig. cl., soiled. (P. Jan.22; 110) *Meyer.* £80
– **The Iconography of Andreas Vesalius.** 1925. 4to. Plts. include 1 of title of 'De humani corporis fabrica', 2nd. edn., 1555, ptd. from orig. woodblock, inserted in pocket at front. Orig. cl., d.-w. (S. Feb.23; 355) *Bennett.* £50

SPIELMANN, Marion Harry & Layard, G.S.
– **Kate Greenaway.** L., 1905. 1st. Edn., 1st. Iss. 4to. Lev., vari-cold. mor. inlay on cover, wide gt. dentelles, spine gt. with basket of flowers, by Bayntun-Rivière, wallpaper end-papers bnd. in at end, cl. s.-c. (SG. Apr.30; 175) $325
– – **Anr. Edn.** 1905. 1st. Edn. Orig. decor. cl. (SH. Dec.10; 253) *Smith.* £50
– – **Anr. Copy.** Water colour drawing inlaid. Mor. gt. by Rivière. (SPB. Nov.25; 298) $325

– – **Anr. Edn.** 1905. (500) with orig. pencil sketch laid in & sigd. by John Greenaway. 4to. Frontis. just spotted. Orig. cl. gt., slightly soiled. Pres. Copy, inscr. by Spielmann. (SBA. May 27; 503) *Taylor.* £180
– – **Anr. Copy.** Ex-liby. copy with stps. to title only. (TA. Feb.19; 404) £150
– – **Anr. Edn.** N.d. (500) numbered, sigd. by John Greenaway & with orig. pencil sketch by Kate Greenaway. 4to. Orig. cl., slightly soiled. (CSK. Jul.17; 41) £250

SPIERA, Ambrosius de
– **Quadragesimale de Floribus Sapientiae.** [Venice], [Vindelinus de Spira], [18 Dec., 1476]. 1st. Edn. Fo. 126 ll. (of 512), lacks 18 prelims., fo. N6, n1 & all after n9, including 3 blanks, initials in red or blue, with green, brown, red or yellow penwork, chaptermarks in red, cont. marginalia. 19th. C. vell. wraps. W.a.f. (S. Nov.25; 325) *Lister.* £150
– – **Anr. Edn.** Venice, Gabriel de Grassis, 1485. 4to. A few cont. annots. to margins thro.-out. Later vell., slightly soiled. (TA. Dec.18; 182) £400
– – **Anr. Edn.** Venice, Bonetus Locatellus for Octavianus Scotus, 20 Feb. 1488/89. 4to. Rubricated thro.-out, 1st. gathering almost detchd. Cont. dyed cf. on wooden bds., upr. cover with blindstp. border, upr. cover almost detchd., orig. clasps. [BMC V 436] (C. Jul.16; 229) *Taylor.* £340

SPIGELIUS, Adrianus
– **Anatomica Operum Omnium.** Trans.:– J.A. van der Linden. Ill.:– after J. Casserius & Daniel Bucretius. Amst., 1645. 2 vols. in 1. Fo. 112 (of 117) engraved plts., some marginal tears & stains. 19th. C. hf. mor. From Chetham's Liby., Manchester. (C. Nov.27; 377) *Preidel.* £350
– **Isagoges in Rem Herbariam Libri Duo.** Leyden, 1633. 1st. Elz. Edn. 24mo. Cont. vell., decor. (D. Dec.11-13; 149) DM 800

SPILBERGEN, Joris van
See–BRY, Theodore de & others

SPILBURY, John
– **A Collection of Fifty Prints from Antique Gems.** N.d. 4to. Slight marginal browning & spotting. Cont. mor., stpd. in gt. & blind. (CSK. Oct.10; 159) £85

SPILLER, Burton L.
– **Firelight.** Ill.:– Lynn Bogue Hunt. [1937]. (950) numbered. 4to. Cl., multiple gt. fillet borders enclosing cold. bird medallion on upr. cover, bkplt. (SG. Dec.11; 283) $200
– **Grouse Feathers.** Ill.:– Lynn Bogue Hunt. [1935]. (950). 4to. Leatherette, elab. gt. borders enclosing cold. bird medallion on upr. cover. (SG. Dec.11; 281) $120
– **More Grouse Feathers.** Ill.:– Lynn Bogue Hunt. [1938]. (950) numbered. 4to. Cl., elab. gt. border enclosing cold. bird medallion on upr. cover. (SG. Dec.11; 284) $120
– **Thoroughbred.** Ill.:– Lynn Bogue Hunt. [1936]. (950) numbered. 4to. Pict. leatherette. (SG. Dec.11; 282) $200

SPILSBURY, Francis B.
– **Picturesque Scenery in the Holy Land & Syria.** 1803. Fo. Hf. mor. gt. (P. Oct.2; 5) *Groffen.* £400
– – **Anr. Edn.** 1819 [plts. wtrmkd. 1823]. 2nd. Edn. Fo. Orig. cl.-bkd. bds. (C. Feb.25; 136) *Hughes.* £350

SPILSBURY, John
– **A Collection of Fifty Prints from Antique Gems, in the Collections of the Right Honourable Earl Percy . . . C.F. Greville, & T.M. Slade.** 1785. 4to. Slight spotting & soiling. 19th. C. str.-grd. mor., gt. (S. Apr.7; 462) *Drury.* £55

SPINDLER, N.
– [–] **Experiment: Gewisse, Rechte, und bewährte Erfahrung allerhand Artzney . . .** Frankfurt, 1566. Lacks lf. 177, last index lf. with fault in margin, old MS. entry on title, soiled. Cont. pig-bkd. wood bds., defect., 2 clasps. (HK. Nov.18-21; 763) DM 1,600

SPINK & SON
– **Numismatic Circular.** 1893-1939. Vol. 1-47 (lacks vol. 38 & 41). Fo. Cont. bdgs., some worn. (SH. Mar.6; 452) *Spink.* £220
– – **Anr. Edn.** 1947-76. Vol. 55-84 (lacks vol. 65 pt. 2). 4to. Orig. wraps. & cont. cl. (SH. Mar.6; 453) *Spink.* £170

SPINOLA, Francesco
- De Intercalandi Ratione Corrigenda, & de Tabellis Quadratorum, Numerorum a Pythagoreis Dispositorum. Venice, 1562. 1st. Edn. A few marginal stains. Cont. limp vell., gt. arms of Jacques-Auguste de Thou as bachelor on covers. Bkplt. of William Poidebard of Lyon; from Honeyman Collection. (S. May 19; 2980)
Hughes. £220

SPINOZA, Baruch de
- Tractatus Theologico-Politicus ... Pace Reipublicae ... Hamburg [Amst.], 1670. 1st. Edn. 4to. Cont. bds. (D. Dec.11-13; 2581) DM 4,200

SPINOZA, Benedictus de
- Renati Des Cartes Principiorum Philosophiae Pars I, & II, more Geometrico Demonstratae ... Accesserunt ... Cogitata Metaphysica. Ed.:– Ludovicus Meyer. Amst., 1663. 1st. Edn. Sm. 4to. Slight soiling, owners' inscrs. of Thomas Fjuke, with his note of purchase, Charles Leeson Prince & Charles Singer. Mod. cf., hf. mor. case. From Honeyman Collection. (S. May 19; 2891)
Ritman. £700

SPIRIT OF '76, The
Frankfort, Ky., 10 Mar.-Aug. 1826. Vol. 1, 22 issues. Foxed. Cont. cf.-bkd. bds., worn, folding cl. s.-c. From liby. of William E. Wilson. (SPB. Apr.29; 142) £700

SPIRITUALI VINEA (De) siue Religionis Profectu: necnon de Perfectiore Nouitiorum Institutione
- Tractatuli duo Nuremb., 14 May 1513. 1st. Edn. Sm. 4to. Slight browning & soiling, wormhole, not affecting text. Mod. pol. hf. cf. by Wood, spine gt. From liby. of André L. Simon. (S. May 18; 180)
Kesel. £350

SPITZER COLLECTION
Paris, 1890-92. (600). 6 vols. Fo. Loose as iss. in orig. cl. portfos., 1 worn. (SH. Oct.9; 191)
Rosewood. £850
– – **Anr. Copy.** Lacks 1 plt., 1 duplicated. Lacks ties. (SH. Jan.29; 300) *Reed & Sims.* £150

SPIX, Dr. Johann B. de
- Selecta Genera et Species Piscium quos in Itinere per ... Brasiliam Annis MDCCCXVII-MDCCCCXX jussu et Auspiciis Maximiliani Joseph I. Ed.:– Dr. F.C. Ph. de Martius. Ill.:– Dr. L. Agassiz. Munich, 1829. Lge. 4to. Late 19th. C. red hf. mor. by Pijnaker Brothers of the Hague, with their ticket. (S. Jun.1; 222) *Schierenberg.* £1,400
- Testacea Fluviatilia quae in Itinere per Brasiliam Annis MDCCCXVII-MDCCCXX Jussu et Auspiciis Maximiliani Josephi I. Ed.:– Dr. F. a Paula de Schrank & Dr. C.F.P. de Martius. Ill.:– Dr. J.A. Wagner. Munich, 1827. 29 cold. plts. (only 27 called for in list of plts.). Late 19th. C. red hf. mor. by Pijnaker Brothers of The Hague, with their ticket. (S. Jun.1; 223)
Schierenberg. £500

SPIX, J.B. von & Martius, C. Fr. Ph. von
- Reise in Brasilien in den Jahren 1817 bis 1820. Munich, 1823-31. 1st. Edn. 3 text & 1 atlas vol. 4to. & lge. ob. fo. Vol. 3 slightly soiled or browned, liby. stp. on title versos, engraved title with sm. stp., some sm. tears, some bkd., some plts. slightly soiled in parts. Cont. paper bds., slightly worn & hf. leath., spine, corners & end-papers renewed. [Sabin 89549] (H. Dec.9/10; 529) DM 8,200

SPOLVERINI, Giovanni Battista
- La Coltivazione del Riso. Ill.:– D. Cunego after F. Lorenzi. Verona, 1758. Sm. fo. cont. paper bds., stitching loosening from bdg., buckram s.-c. From the collection of John A. Saks. (C. Jun.10; 235)
Burgess. £130

SPON, Isaac Jacob
- Histoire de Genève. Geneva, 1730. 2 vols. 4to. 5 folding song sheets bnd. at back of vol. 2., light dampstaining. Cont. cf., jnts. worn. (CSK. Apr.24; 72) £260
- The History of the City & State of Geneva. 1687. 1st. Edn. in Engl. Fo. Slight browning & soiling. Cont. cf. [Wing S5017] (S. Sep.29; 75)
Scot. £100
– – **Anr. Copy.** Covers detchd. (CSK. Jun.19; 129) £95
- Recherches Curieuses d'Antiquité. Lyons, 1683. 1st. Edn. 4to. A few very minor defects. Cont. spr. cf., worn. (SBA. Mar.4; 96) *O'Neil.* £65

SPONS, Jacob
See-TAVERNIER, Jean Baptiste–SPONS, Jacob

SPONTINI, G.L.
- Fernand Cortez ou la Conquête du Mexique. Paris, [1809]. 1st. Edn. Fo. Cont. red mor., floral & decor. gt., monog. (H. Dec.9/10; 1285)
DM 1,600

SPORTING Magazine
L., 1792-1870 [index ca. 1892]. 157 vols., lacks vol. for Jul. to Dec., 1839. Many plts. & most engraved titles in dupl. state, light foxing thro.-out, some vols. charred &/or dampstained. Red three-qtr. mor., worn. (SG. Dec.11; 411)
$6,600
– – **Anr. Run.** L., 1793-1870. 157 vols. including Index vol. Mod. hf. mor., spines gt. in 6 compartments with 5 raised bands with gt. tools, by Bartlett. Edward Motley Weld bkplts., as a periodical, w.a.f. (CNY. May 22; 218) $6,000
– – **Anr. Run.** 1796-1858. 11 vols., various. Some browning. Various bdgs., some worn. W.a.f. (CSK. Feb.6; 153) £250
– – **Anr. Run.** L., 1810-15. Vols. 36-45 in 10 vols. Text minimal browning, plts. slightly soiled. Cont. hf. leath., spine slightly defect. (R. Mar.31-Apr.4; 1715) DM 1,800

SPORTING MAGAZINE & The New Sporting Magazine
L., 1841-70. 60 vols. 58 (of 60) engraved or litho titles & 734 (of 741) steel engraved plts., most plts. soiled, & in 1st. vol. some browned, 4 plts. very defect., 4 mntd. on linen. Cont. hf. leath., very worn, some spines defect., lacks 2 spines. (R. Oct.14-18; 2811) DM 6,500

SPORTING Repository (The)
Ill.:– after H. Alken & J. Barenger. 1822. 1st. Edn. Vol. 1 nos. 1-6. Some spotting. Cont. hf. cf., worn. (S. Jun.23; 336) *Harley Mason.* £160
– – **Anr. Edn.** Ill.:– Henry Alken & others. L., 1904. (500). Gt.-decor. cl. (SG. Apr.9; 404) $100

SPORTSMAN & Breeder's Vade-Mecum
York, 1787-1800, & 1802. 15 vols. Cont. bds., unc., some wear to spines. (TA. Oct.16; 269) £75

SPORTSMAN'S CABINET (The)
Ed.:– J. Scott. 1804. 2 vols. 4to. Slight foxing. Mor. gt. Bkplt. of Antrim. (CE. Jul.9; 217) £200

SPORTSMAN'S Kennel, The
Ill.:– T. Fairland after E. Landseer, Hancock, & others. L., [1834]. Fo. Some hand-soiling & foxing, early inscr. on title-p. Mod. cl. (SG. Dec.11; 412) $260

SPRAT, Thomas
- The History of the Royal Society of London, for the Improving of Natural Knowledge. Ill.:– Hollar (frontis.). 1667. 1st. Edn. 4to. Frontis. cut round & mntd., minor marginal worming, a few ll. slightly gnawed at lr. edge. Cont. cf., rebkd., old spine preserved, worn. From Honeyman Collection. (S. May 19; 2892) *Porter.* £130
– – **Anr. Copy.** Lacks folding engraved frontis. [Wing S5032] (S. Dec.2; 775) *Bopp.* £90
– – **Anr. Copy.** Lacks frontis., cont. verse inscr. on verso of licence lf. Cont. mott. cf. (C. Feb.25; 19) *Midmer.* £50
– – **Anr. Edn.** 1722. 3rd. Edn. 4to. D2-3 slightly spotted. Cont. panel. cf., worn. (S. Apr.6; 154) *Morton-Smith.* £60

SPRENGEL, Christian Konrad
- Das Entdeckte Geheimniss der Natur im Bau und in der Befruchtung der Blumen. Berlin, 1793. 1st. Edn. 4to. All plts. hinged to blanks bearing MS. explanations, slight soiling. Cont. cf.-bkd. bds., worn. Blind stp. of Dr. Hermann Muller (notes presumably in his hand); bkplt. of Herbert McLean Evans; from Honeyman Collection. (S. May 19; 2893) *Percy.* £1,400

SPRENGEL, Kurt Polycarp Joachim
- Institutiones Medicae. Amst.; Leipzig & Altenburg, 1809; 1816. 7 pts. in 6 vols. Advt. ll. in vol. I. Cont. hf. cf., gt. arms on upr. cover. (S. Feb.23; 106) *Frick.* £50

SPRIGGE, Joshua
- Anglia Rediviva. L., 1647. Fo. 19th. C. mor., tooled in blind, rebkd. (SG. Sep.25; 291) $180

SPRINGETT, W.S.P.
- Recollections of Maderia. 1843. Fo. Most plts. heavily foxed, loose. Cl., soiled & worn. (PD. Oct.22; 111) £50

SPRUNER, Dr. Carl von
- Historisch-Geographischer Hand-Atlas. Gotha, 1846. 4to. Hf. cf. gt. (P. May 14; 136) £65

– – **Anr. Edn.** Gotha, 1854. Vol. 2 only. Fo. Cont. hf. cf., spine preserved. (CSK. May 8; 28) £90

SPRUT [Octopus]
Ed.:– [M.I. Titov]. St. Petersb., 1905-06. Nos. 1-9, 11-15 only (of 15). 4to. Unbnd. (SH. Feb.5; 131) *De la Casa.* £95

SPURZHEIM, Johann Gaspar
- Phrenology ... Part I. Characters. 1826. 1st. Edn. Several plts. & ll. stained, some browning. Old paper-bkd. bds., stained, contents loose, unc. (S. May 5; 164) *Cooper.* £65
See–GALL, Franz Joseph & Spurzheim, Johannes Caspar

SQUIER, Ephraim George
- Catalogue of the Library. Ed.:– Joseph Sabin. N.Y., 1876. Priced thro.-out, 8 p. bibliography bnd. in. Later hf. cl. (SG. Mar.26; 421) $200
- Travels in Central America. N.Y., 1853. 2 vols. A few ll. slightly spotted. Orig. cl. (SH. Nov.7; 391) *House.* £70

ST. SERNIN
- Healthful Sports for Young Ladies, interspersed with Original Poetry & Anecdotes. Ill.:– after J. Dugourc. [Plts. dtd. 1822]. Ob. 8vo. Slightly stained. Orig. bds., rebkd., mor.-bkd. case. (SH. Mar.19; 283) *Schierenberg.* £170

STAATLICHES BAUHAUS WEIMAR
Ed.:– W. Gropius (text), W. Kandinsky, P. Klee, L. Moholy-Nagy & O. Schlemme. Weimar & Munich, [1923]. Ob. 4to. 225 pp. with 9 cold. lithos., 11 cold. plts. & 147 ills. Orig. cold. pict. bds., spine slightly defect., upr. cover loose. (HK. Nov.18-21; 2418) DM 2,400

STACKHOUSE, Thomas
- Copies of Drawings illustrating a Course of Lectures on the Architectural & Other Remains of Britain. L., 1833. 1st. Edn. of Lecture II (of 2). 4to. Cont. hf. cf. & marb. bds. (PNY. Oct.1; 492) $160
- Two Lectures on the Remains of Ancient Pagan Britain. Priv. ptd., 1833. (75). 4to. Orig. cl. (SBA. Jul.22; 66) *Thompson.* £55
- An Universal Atlas. 1790. 4th. Edn. Fo. Maps hand-cold., title creased & slightly soiled, all maps with sm. liby. stps. on versos. Cont. hf. cf. As an atlas, w.a.f., from Chetham's Liby., Manchester. (C. Nov.27; 378) *Cash.* £250
– – **Anr. Edn.** [1798?]. 6th. Edn. Lge. 4to. 37 hand-cold. maps (of 40). Cont. hf. cf. As an atlas, w.a.f. (C. May 20; 174) *Schuster.* £150

STADIUS, Johannes
- Tabulae Bergenses Aequabilis et Adparentis Motus Orbium Coelestium. Cologne, 1560. 1st. Edn. Fo. Sigs. M & N transposed, wormed at upr. outer corners towards end, mainly in margins, sm. hole in title affecting a few letters & a few similar holes in text, browned thro.-out, a few marginal annots. Cont. limp vell., soiled. From Honeyman Collection. (S. May 19; 2894) *Hill.* £150
See–BRY, Theodore de & others

STAEHLIN von Storcksburg, Jacob–LE ROY, Pierre Louis
- An Account of the New Northern Archipelago.–A Narrative of the Singular Adventures of Four Russian Sailors ... 1774. 2 pts. in 1 vol. Advt. lf. at end. Hf. mor. From the collection of Eric Sexton. [Sabin 90063] (C. Apr.15; 49)
Traylen. £380

STAEL-HOLSTEIN, Anna Louise Germaine de Necker, Baronne de
- De l'Allemagne. L., 1813. 1st. Edn. 3 vols. Lightly browned, slightly soiled in parts. Later hf. linen, partly unc., soiled. (H. Dec.9/10; 1669) DM 620
- Mémoires. Ill.:– Leon Boisson, Charles Delort. Paris, 1891. (400) numbered on velin du Marais. All etchings in 2 states. Three-qtr. vell., spine gt. with floral devices, ptd. wraps. bnd. in. Inscr. to Monsieur Launetie. (SG. Sep.4; 429) $110
- Oeuvres Complètes. Paris, 1820-21. 1st Coll. Edn. 17 vols. Slight foxing. Cont. hf. cf., corners, decor. spines, bdgs. slightly defect. (HD. Feb.27; 233) Frs. 2,300

STAFFORD GALLERY
- Album containing 68 proof impressions of engravings. N.d. 4to. Some engrs. in 2 states, mntd. on tinted paper. Early 19th. C. str.-grd. mor. gt., wide inside borders with gt. fillets, by Charles Lewis. Note on end-paper stating this to

STAFFORD GALLERY – Album containing 68 proof impressions of engravings. -contd.
have been in the Hamilton Palace Sale no 2,185. (C. Feb.4; 224) *Doll.* £110

STAFFORD, Hugh
– A Treatise on Cyder-Making. L., 1753. 1st. Edn. 4to. 64 (of 68) pp., lacks last 2 ll., title reprd. 19th. C. three qtr. cf. Armorial bkplt. of Henry Thomas Ellacombe. (SG. Sep.18; 358) $110

STAFFORD, Ignacio
– Historia de la celestial Vocacion, Missiones apostolicas ... del Padre Marcello Franco Mastrili. Lisbon, 1639. 1st. Edn. 4to. Engraved title & engraved plt. slightly soiled & each with sm. hole, approbation lf. soiled, some staining. Cont. cf. (SPB. Oct.1; 214) $1,200

STAHL, G.C.
– Neu aufgeführter Ingenieur: oder Kriegs-Bau-Kunst. Nuremb., 1687. 2nd. Edn. 3 pts. in 1 vol. Cont. vell., monog. & arms on upr. cover. (R. Oct.14-18; 2860) DM 1,600

STAHL, Georg Ernst
– Fundamenta Chymiae Dogmaticae & Experimentalis. Nuremb., 1723. 1st. Edn. Sm. 4to. A few lr. margins badly wormed just touching text, browned, title a little soiled, sig. of J. Crowther on title. Vell. bds., soiled, new end-papers. Bkplts. of Sir Benjamin Collins Brodie & Denis Duveen; from Honeyman Collection. (S. May 19; 2895) *Quaritch.* £240

STAHL, J.F. (Ed.)
See–ALLGEMEINE OECONOMISCHES Forst-Magazin

STAINTON, H.T.
– The Natural History of the Tineina. 1855-73. [1st. Edn.?]. Vols. 1-4, 6-13, together 12 vols. Slight foxing to a few vols. Ex-libris, orig. embossed moire cl., partly unc. (PL. Jul.11; 60) *Wheldon & Wesley.* £70
– – Anr. Copy. 13 vols. German-Engl.-Fr.-Latin parallel text, slightly soiled in parts. Cont. linen. (R. Mar.31-Apr.4; 1455) DM 900

STALKER, John
– A Treatise of Japaning & Varnishing. Oxford, 1688. 1st. Edn. Fo. Cont. mott. cf., rebkd. [Wing S5187A] (S. Mar.17; 456) *Allan.* £1,200

STALLENGE, William
[–] Instructions for the Increasing of Mulberie Trees. 1609. 1st. Edn. Sm. 4to. 3 pp. with 1st. line of text cropped, slightly stained thro.-out. Hf. mor. by Sangorski. From the collection of Eric Sexton. [STC 23138] (C. Apr.15; 19) *Pullen.* £240
[–] – Anr. Copy. 3 full-p. woodcuts, title ornament, headlines & text on A2 & A3 cropped. (C. Jul.16; 361) *Taylor.* £120

STALLKARTT, Marmaduke
– Naval Architecture. L., 1803. 3rd. Edn. 2 vols. Fo. & atlas fo. Hf. cf., atlas unc., by Sangorski & Sutcliffe. (CNY. May 22; 174) $1,400

STAMMA, Phillip
– The Noble Game of Chess. L., 1745. 1st. Edn. 2 pts. in 1 vol. 12mo. Cont. cf., rebkd. Sigd. by author in last page a guarantee of authenticity, armorial bkplt. of G.J.W.A. Ellis. (SG. Sep.4; 104) $240

STAMPED INDELIBLY
Ed.:– William Katz. Ill.:– Robert Creeley, Tom Wesselman, Red Grooms & Kenneth Koch, Marisol, Robert Indiana, Josef Levi, Gerald Malanga, Allen Jones, Andy Warhol, Peter Saul, Claes Oldenburg, Allen Ginsberg, & John Willenbecher. Bowery, N.Y.C., 1967. (225) sigd. by Ed., numbered. 4to. Orig. cl., unc. All but 1 print sigd. by artist. (SH. Nov.21; 508) *Fogg.* £120
– – Anr. Copy. All but 1 print sigd. by artist. (SH. Nov.21; 507) *Wylam.* £105

STAMPTIOEN DE JONGHE, Johan
– Algebra. Ill.:– Queborn (port.) 's-Grav., priv. Ptd., 1636. 1st. Edn. 4to. 1 lf. frayed with short tear, some light stains & wear. Cont. vell., soiled. (VG. Oct.13; 150) Frs. 1,000

STANDARD ENCYCLOPAEDIA of Southern Africa
Cape Town, 1970-76. 12 vols. Orig. bdgs. (VA. Jan.30; 398) R. 180

STANDISH, Miles, Jr.
– The Times: a Poem Addressed to the Inhabitants of New-England, & of New-York, particularly on the Subject of the Present Anti-Commercial System of the National Administration. Plymouth, priv. ptd., 1809. 1st. Edn. Foxed. Disbnd. (SG. Mar.5; 421) $130

STANFIELD, Clarkson
– Coast Scenery. 1836. 1st. Edn., L.P. 4to. 37 engraved plts. on india paper (of 40). Cont. hf. roan, spine gt. (S. Mar.31; 506) *Regent Gal.* £90
– – Anr. Copy. 38 plts. (of 40), lacks nos. 34 & 35. Orig. hf. roan spine, defect., foxed (LA. Mar.5; 60) £76
– Sketches on the Moselle, the Rhine & the Meuse. Ill.:– after Boays, Haghe, Gauci, Pikken & others. L., 1838. Fo. 29 (of 30) tinted lithos., some plts. stpd., soiled. Orig. hf. leath., defect. & loose. (R. Oct.14-18; 2439) DM 6,000

STANFIELD, Clarkson–COOKE, William
– Coast Scenery.–A New Picture of the Isle of Wight. 1847; 1808. 2nd. Edn. (1st. work). 2 works in 2 vols. Occasional light foxing in 1st. work. Orig. cl., gt. spine; cont. mor., gt. borders on sides, gt. spine. (C. Nov.6; 336) *Clarkson.* £100

STANFORD, Sir William
– An Exposicion of the Kinges Prerogative. 1567. 1st. Edn. Sm. 4to. Mod. mott. sheep. [STC 23213] (S. Mar.16; 123) *Frognal Books.* £280
– – Anr. Edn. [Colophon: 1577]. 4to. Blank margins wormed, a few ll. stained. Mod. bds. [STC 23216] (CSK. Mar.13; 22) £95

STANHOPE, Lady Hester
– Memoirs.–Travels. L., 1846. 1st. work 2nd. Edn., 2nd. work 1st. Edn. Each work 3 vols., together 6 vols. Three-qtr. cf., spines gt., by Zaehnsdorf. (SG. Oct.30; 339) $130
– Travels ... narrated by her Physician. 1846. 1st. Edn. 3 vols. Orig. blind-stpd. cl. (TA. Sep.18; 81) £60

STANHOPE, Philip Dormer, Earl of Chesterfield
See–CHESTERFIELD, Philip Dormer Stanhope, Earl of

STANLEY, Henry Morton
[–] The Congo & the Founding of Its Free State. N.Y., 1885. 1st. Amer. Edn. 2 vols. 5 partly hand-cold. folding maps. Gt. & cold.-pict. cl. (PNY. Dec.3; 6) $140
– In Darkest Africa. 1890. (250) sigd. 2 vols. 4to. Orig. mor.-bkd. vell., partly unc. (C. May 20; 175) *Maggs.* £380
– – Anr. Copy. Some wear, some browning to fore-edges, inscr. on hf.-title. Orig. hf. mor., warped, very rubbed, soiled, some browning of end-papers. (SPB. May 29; 401) $130
– Through the Dark Continent. 1878. 1st. Edn. 2 vols. Slight spotting. Orig. pict. cl., slight wear. (S. Jun.9; 65) *Spink.* £60

STANTON, Elizabeth Cady, Anthony, Susan B. & Gage, Matilda Joslyn
– History of Woman Suffrage. N.Y. & Rochester, 1881-[1902]. 1st. Edns. 4 vols. Orig. leath., worn. Vols. I, II, & IV inscr. by Anthony. (SG. Feb.12; 60) $450

STAPFER, Phil.-Alb.
[–] Voyage Pittoresque de L'Oberland. Ill.:– S. Weibel after G. Lory, the younger. Paris & Strasbourg, 1812. 4to. Cont. cf.-bkd. bds., unc. (C. Nov.5; 152) *Larocque.* £4,000

STAPULENSIS, Jacobus Faber
See–RANTZAU, Heinrich–STAPULENSIS, Jacobus Faber
See–SACROBOSCO, Johannes de –STAPULENSIS, Jacobus Faber–JORDANUS, Nemorarius

STARCK, Johann August von
[–] Saint Nicaise oder eine Sammlung Merkwürdiger Maurerischer Briefe ... [?Frankfurt], 1785. 1st. Edn. Cont. hf. cf. (S. Mar.17; 313) *Weiner.* £65

STARFORTH, John
– The Architecture of the Farm. Edinb. & L., 1853. 4to. Publishers' advts. loosely inserted, ownership inscr. of Earl of Kintore. Orig. cl. gt. (SBA. Jul.23; 282) *Cummings.* £60

STARK, Arthur C.
See–SCLATER, William Lutley & Stark, Arthur C.

STARK, James & Robberds, J.W.
– Picturesque Views on & Near the Eastern Coast of England. 1834. 1st. Edn., L.P. Fo. Mor. gt., by Wright. (S. Nov.24; 265) *Quaritch.* £300
– – Anr. Edn. Ill.:– Cooke & others after Stark. L. & Norwich, 1843. L.P. Fo. 1 lf. (with a vig.) with piece torn out but still present. Early cl., worn . (S. Dec.9; 421) *Crowe.* £130
– Scenery of the Rivers of Norfolk ... Ill.:– after Stark. Norwich, 1834. L.P. 4to. Engraved title & some margins spotted. Cont. hf. mor., corners worn, partly unc. From the collection of Eric Sexton. (C. Apr.16; 360) *Ferrow.* £150
– – Anr. Edn. 1834. 4to. Some spotting. Hf. mor. (P. Apr.30; 279) *Morrow.* £90

STARKEY, George
– Die Behaupt-und Erlauterte Pyrotechnie oder die vortreffliche Kunst das Philosophische Feuer zu halten und darinnen zu arbeiten ... durch einem Freund in das Hochteutsche gebracht. [Frankfurt], [1711]. 12mo. Closely cut in lr. margin removing imprint & some sigs. & catchwords, lacks 1st. 2 blank ll. Bds., cl. spine. (S. Dec.1; 399) *Weiner.* £160
– Enarratio Methodica Trium Gebri Medicinarum in Quibus Continetur Lapidis Philosophici vera Confectio. [L.], 1678. Mod. buckram. [Wing S5273] (S. Jul.27; 382) *Quaritch.* £95
[–] A True Light of Alchymy. Containing I. A Correct Edition of the Marrow of Alchymy etc. Priv. ptd., 1709. 12mo. Sm. tear in lr. outer corner of title affecting letters, a few short marginal tears. Hf. roan. (S. Dec.1; 398) *Quaritch.* £200

STARTER, J.J.
– Friesche Lust-Hof, Beplant met verscheyden stichtelijcke Minne-Liedekens, Gedichten, ende Boertighe Kluchten. Ill.:– J. Vande Velde. Amst., 1634. 5th. Printing [8th. Edn.]. 2 pts. in 1 vol. Ob. 4to. Lr. margin of ptd. title, frontis. & 1st. lf. a bit short, blank inner margins of a few quires with wormhole, some light staining in places, especially in upr. margins, browned in places. Cont. spr. vell. (VG. Dec.17; 1542) Fls. 4,800

STASSOF, Vladimir
See–GUNZBURG, David & Stassof, Vladimir

STATIUS, Publius Papinus
– [Opera]. Venice, Octavianus Scotus., 2 Dec. 1483. 1st. Edn. Fo. 60 ll. of 260, lacks all before sig. a, sig. b & 2 sigs. at end, some ll. supplied in facs., washed & stained. Mod. vell. bds. [HC 14976; BMC V 278; Goff S691] (SPB. May 6; 257) $200

STATON, Frances M. & Tremaine, Marie
– A Bibliography of Canadiana, with Supplement. Ed.:– Gertrude M. Boyle & Marjorie Colbeck (supp.). Toronto, 1934 & 1959. 1st. Edns. 2 vols. With errata slip. Orig. cl. (CB. Sep.24; 157) Can. $280

STATUTA or Statutes
(Arranged Chronologically)
– Statuta Communis Veronae. Vicenza, Hermannus Liechtenstein [Levilapis], 20 Dec. 1475. 1st. Edn. Fo. Spaces for initial capitals, quire E misbnd., some wormholes, mainly at beginning & end, catching text on several ll., some 20 ll. with very minor repairs to margins or to wormholes, slight foxing. Crushed gt.-panel. mor., gt. spine, by Leighton. Inscrs. of Sebastianus de Gregoriis, later the copy of C. Fairfax Murray, cancelled ink stp. of the London Liby., recently in the collection of Eric Sexton. [BMC VII, 1036, Goff S726, H 10000] (CNY. Apr.8; 202) $4,200
– Statuta hec Magnifice Ciutatis Parme. Parma, Angelus Ugoletus, 16 Sep. 1494. Fo. Some later MS. notes, some browning & soiling, a few tears, slightly affecting text, reprd. Mod. antique-style cf. From liby. of André L. Simon. (S. May 18; 146) *James.* £1,200
– Statuta Synodalia Eystettensia cum Statutis Provincialibus Moguntinis. [Basle, Michael Furter, not after 1496]. 4to. 95 ll. (of 96) lacks L1. 19th. C. hf. cf. cf. G. Kloss bkplt. [Goff S735] (C. Jul.16; 297) *Taylor.* £320
– Abbreviamentum Statutorum. L., Richard Pynson, 9 Oct. 1499. Lacks 1st. blank, 1st. & last pp. soiled, clean tear to lr. blank margin of l6, staining to some ll. at beginning & end, light finger-soiling. 19th. C. qtr. cf. & marb. paper bds., gt. arms of the Society of Writers to the Signet on covers, worn, rebkd. From the collection of Eric Sexton. [Goff A4] (CNY. Apr.8; 82) $6,000

– In this volume are contained the Statutes made & established from the time of Kyng Henry the thirde ... [L.], [1543]. Vol. 1 only (of 2). Fo. Lacks colophon lf., browned & soiled, some worming, affecting text. Cont. cf., defect., 1 cover detchd. [STC 9301] (S. Sep.29; 26) *Rix.* £180

– Statuta Magnificae Communitatis Regii. –Constitutiones, Privilegia et Reformationes Additionesque Statutorum Civitatis Regii. –Raccolta di Diversi Ordini Ducali.–Elenchus Alphabeticus Rubri carum, ac Notabilium Statuti Regiensis a Prospero Ferretto ... **Confectus.** Reggio, 1582; 1611; 1690; 1682. In 1 vol. with a few similar but later & minor items. 4to. Slight browning. 18th. C. vell. bds., worn. As a collection, w.a.f.; from liby. of André L. Simon. (S. May 18; 171) *King.* £150

– Statuta Communitatis S. Columbiani et sue Iurisdictionis. Lodi, 1586. Fo. Slight dampstaining, a few tears, reprd. 19th. C. hf. cf. From liby. of André L. Simon. (S. May 18; 147) *Lyle.* £220

– The Whole Volume of Statutes at large.–Anno xxxi. Reginae Elizabethae. 1587; 1589. 2 works in 1 vol., Fo. Early (?cont.) MS. notes, some dampstaining, wormhole, slightly affecting text. Cont. cf., defect. [STC 9316; 9488]. (S. Sep.29; 27) *Traylen.* £280

– Corpus Statutorum Universitatis Oxon. Oxford, 1634. Fo. Slight soiling & signs of use in lr. margin, many early insertions, marginal notes & additions in an 18th. C. hand. Cont. cf., rebkd. preserving orig. spine, hf. mor. case. Owner's stp. of Falconer Madan on title verso, lately in the collection of Eric Sexton. [STC 19005] (C. Apr.15; 186) *Murray-Hill.* £220

– Statuti del Principato di Monaco distinti in Quattro Libri ... 1678. Fo. Old vell., lacks part of spine. (SG. Feb.5; 246) $250

– Statutes of the Most Honourable Order of the Bath. L., 1725, reprinted 1812. 4to. Cont. crimson str.-grd. mor., jnts. brkn. Fore-e. pntg.; from the liby. of Zola E. Harvey. (SG. Mar.19; 158) $475

– Takanot De'chevra Kadisha Gemilut Chasadim De'kehila Kedosha Ashkenazim Be'Amsterdam. Amst., 1776. Some sigs. loose, some staining. Bds., very worn. (SPB. May 11; 202) $850

– The Statutes at Large from Magna Carta to William VI. 1786-1832. 26 vols. 4to. Mod. cl. (P. Apr.9; 57) *Tunkel.* £270

– Statutes of the Province of Upper Canada, together with such British Statutes, etc., as relate to the said Province. Ed.:– H.C. Thomson & James Macfarlane; James Nickalls Jr. Kingston, U.C., 1831. 4to. Foxed, last few ll. dampstained, upr. portion of title-p. lacking, with loss of 1st. word. New hf. cf. (SG. Mar.5; 85) $100

– Scottish Current Law Statutes. 1948-77 (except 1954 & 1957). Cl. gt. & unbnd. pts. to 1978. (CE. Feb.19; 6) £105

– – Anr. Run. 1948-78. Cl. (CE. Feb.19; 26) £300

– Scottish Current Law Statues ... plus Scottish Law Citator. Edinb., 1949-77; 1948-71. 32 vols. Cl. (PD. Apr.1; 52) £70

STAUNTON, Sir George
– An Authentic Account of an Embassy ... to the Emperor of China. 1797. [1st. Edn.?]. 2 vols. & atlas. 4to. & fo. Slight offsetting to text. Cont. diced russ., gt. borders on sides, gt. panel. spines, & cont. hf. russ. (C. Nov.5; 153) *Quaritch.* £900

– – Anr. Copy. Advt. lf. in vol. II. Cont. spr. cf., spines gt., atlas hf. cf., worn. (S. Sep.29; 181) *Quaritch.* £580

– – Anr. Copy. 3 vols., lacks atlas. Cf. gt. (P. Oct.23; 65) *Brooke-Hitching.* £75

– – Anr. Copy. 2 vols. only, lacks atlas. 4to. Advt. lf. at end of vol. II, lacks final blank in vol. I, offsetting to titles, occasional spotting. Mod. cl.-bkd. bds. [Sabin 90843] (S. Jan.27; 543) *Fairbairns.* £55

– – Anr. Copy. 2 vols. & atlas vol. 4to. & lge. fo. Text vol. lightly browned thro.-out & slightly soiled in parts, some soiled in margins. Cont. hf. leath. gt. (R. Mar.31-Apr.4, 2490) DM 4,500

– – Anr. Edn. Ca. 1797. Atlas only. Fo. 43 (of 44) plts. & maps, badly dampstained. Disbnd. (P. Mar.12; 31) *Davies.* £110

STAUPITZ, Johann von
[–] Ain Säligs Newes Jar. Von der Lieb Gottes. [Munich], 1518. 1st. Edn. 4to. Slightly soiled. 18th C. bds. (S. Jan.27; 351) *Goldschmidt.* £120

STEARN, W.T.
– The Australian Flower Paintings of Ferdinand Bauer. Basilisk Pr., 1976. Ltd. Edn. Lge. fo. Hf. cl. (SH. Jul.16; 204) *Morrow.* £130

STEBBING, Henry & Bartlett, William Henry
– Christian in Palestine. N.d. 4to. Hf. mor. gt., stained. (MMB. Oct.8; 138) £60

– – Anr. Copy. Cf. gt. (DWB. May 15; 351) £50

STEDMAN, Charles
– History of the Origin ... American War. 1794. 2 vols. Tree-cf. gt. (P. Oct.23; 66) *Monk.* £400

STEDMAN, Edmund C.
– Poets of America. Camb., 1885. 6 vols. Extra-ill. with letters & plts., some browning. Red mor. elab. gt. (SPB. May 6; 344) $2,300

STEDMAN, Fabian
[–] Campanalogia. 1677. 1st. Edn. Slightly soiled in places, old MS. inscr. of bell ringing changes on blank versos of title & last lf. 19th. C. cf. [Wing S5374] (S. Jun.29; 324) *Rhys-Jones.* £140

STEDMAN, Capt. John Gabriel
– Narrative of a Five Years' Expedition against the Revolted Negroes of Surinam. Ill.:– William Blake & others. L., 1796. 1st. Edn. 2 vols. 4to. With the plt.-lists & errata ll., 65 plts. & maps only (of 80, lacks nos. 1, 6, 11, 15, 21, 26, 30, 35, 38, 39, 45, 56, 63, 64, & 79), some foxing & staining. Disbnd. (SG. Nov.20; 411) $110

– – Anr. Edn. Ill.:– William Blake & others. 1806. 2nd. Edn. 2 vols. 4to. Cont. diced cf., gt., Earl of Derby's crest gt. stpd. on upr. covers, rebkd. (C. Mar.18; 110) *Maggs.* £750

– – Anr. Copy. Piece torn from corner of R4 in vol. 2 with slight text loss, reprd., occasional light foxing. Cont. hf. cf. (C. Nov.5; 154) *Carter.* £200

– – Anr. Copy. Some spotting, offsetting, inner hinges reinforced. Cont. cf., gt., worn. [Sabin 91075] (SPB. May 5; 484) $600

– – Anr. Copy. Cont. hf. cf., rebnd., 4to. (VG. Oct.13; 151) Fls. 1,300

– – Anr. Edn. Ill.:– William Blake & others. 1813. 2 vols. 4to. Mod. hf. mor., s.-c. (C. May 20; 177) *Taylor.* £380

– – Anr. Copy. Cont. gt. & blind-panel. pol. cf., spines gt. (C. Feb.25; 139) *Maggs.* £180

– Voyage à Surinam ... Collection des Planches. Trans.– P.F. Henry. Paris, An VII [1797/98]. 4to. Cont. hf.-leath. [Sabin 91083] (R. Mar.31-Apr.4; 2472) DM 750

– Voyage to Surinam. [1799]. Atlas only. 4to. Bds. (P. Apr.30; 272) *Warrell.* £80

STEEDMAN, Charles J.
– Bucking the Sagebrush. Ill.:– Charles M. Russell & others. N.Y., 1904. 1st. Edn. Pict. cl. (PNY. May 21; 392) $105

STEEGER, Victor–PRESUHN, Emil
– The Most Beautiful Walls of Pompeii.–I Piu' Recenti Scavi di Pompei ... Turin; Leipzig, 1877; 1878. Together 7 pts. (3 & 4), in 1 vol. 4to. Cont. cl. gt. (C. May 20; 178) *Taylor.* £70

STEEL, Flora Annie
– English Fairy Tales. Ill.:– Arthur Rackham. L., 1918. 1st. Edn. Deluxe, (500) numbered, sigd. by artist. Lge. 4to. Some foxing. Vell. gt. Raymond M. Sutton Jr. copy. (SG. May 7; 277) $550

– – Anr. Edn. Ill.:– Arthur Rackham. N.Y., 1918. (250) L.P. 4to. Cf., slight soiling, sm. tear to spine. (SPB. Jul.28; 405) $250

STEELE, David
[–] The Elements & Practice of Rigging & Seamanship. 1794. 1st. Edn. 2 vols. Cont. cf., rebkd. Bkplt. of Lord Willoughby de Broke. (C. Nov.6; 337) *Maggs.* £850

[–] – Anr. Copy. Lacks 5 plts. W.a.f. (C. May 20; 57a) *Taylor.* £120

STEELE, Isaac
See–FRY, Edmund & Steele, Isaac

STEELE, Sir Richard
[–] [The Tatler] The Lucubrations of Isaac Bickerstaff Esq., L., 1710, 1711, 1709-10. 1st. Edn., Orig. Iss. Nos. 1-271. Fo. With 2 titles, indices, ll. of dedication & preface, mezzotint port. (trimmed) inserted as frontis., no. 227 supplied in facs., some early nos. cropped at head, foxing. 18th. C. cf., rebkd. preserving orig. spine, new labels. From the Prescott Collection. (CNY. Feb.6; 301) $550

STEELE, Robert
– Some Old French & English Ballads. Ill.:– Lucien Pissarro. Eragny Pr., 1905. (210). Orig. bds., unc. Pres. copy inscr. by artist. (S. Jul.31; 30) *Quaritch.* £260

STEENHOFF, W.
See–PIT, A. & others

STEENKAMP, A.E.
– Gedenschrift of Journaal van Onzen uittogt uit Ons Moedertaal tot hier dan Port Natal, 'Overgedrukt uit 'Elpis', deel IX, No. 2'. Pietermaritzburg, 1886. Foxing. Ptd. wraps, spine strengthened. (VA. Aug.29; 379) R. 110

STEGMANN, C.J.
[–] Fragmente über Italien, aus dem Tagebuche eines Jungen Deutschen. N.p., 1798. 2 vols. Pages 271-272 vol. 1 counted double, 1st. ll. lightly soiled. Cont. hf. leath. (H. May 21/22; 1283) DM 520

STEGMANN, J.G.
– Beschreibung einer Kleinen Luftpumpe. Kassel, 1783. Cont. marb. bds. (R. Oct.14-18; 462) DM 540

STEHELIN, J.P.
– Rabbinical Literature, or the Tradition of the Jews Contained in their Talmud & other Mystical Writings. L., 1748. 2nd. Edn. 2 vols. Slight staining. Mod. vell. (S. Nov.18; 684) *Kingsgate.* £120

STEIDELE, Joh.
– Abhandlung v. dem unvermeidl. Gebrauch d. Instrumente in der Geburtshülfe ... Vienna, 1774-75. 3 works in 1 vol. Soiled, 2 plts. torn, all plts. multi-stpd. Cont. hf. leath. gt. (HK. May 12-14; 325) DM 420

STEIN, Sir Marc Aurel
[–] Les Documents Chinois Decouvertes ... dans les Sables du Turkestan Oriental. Trans.:– Edouard Chavannes. Oxford, 1913. 1st. Edn. Fo. Ex liby. Buckram. (SG. Oct.30; 341) $120

– On Alexander's Track to the Indus. 1929. Orig. cl. (SH. Mar.5; 136) *Diba.* £130

STEIN, Gertrude
– The Autobiography of Alice B. Toklas. N.Y., [1933]. 1st. Edn., 1st. Iss. Inscr. & sig. 'Misia Sert ... Long Life' at upr. blank, anr. sigd. pres. statement in French at upr. fly by unidentified personality. Cl., d.-w. Pres. copy from Stein & Toklas, 'For Bobsie' [Goodspeed]. (PNY. Mar.4; 233) $700

– – Anr. Edn. N.Y., [1933]. 1st. Literary Guild Edn. Sigd. pres. copy from Toklas. 'To dear Bobsy & Geo.' [Goodspeed]. (PNY. Mar.4; 234) $200

– A Book Concluding With As A Wife Has A Cow: A Love Story. Ill.:– Juan Gris. Paris, [1926]. 1st. Edn., (102) numbered on vergé d'Arches. 4to. Orig. ptd. stiff wraps., glassine d.-w. Sigd. by Stein & Gris. (PNY. Mar.4; 235) $2,200

– Composition as Explanation.–Narration: Four Lectures by Gertrude Stein.–What Are Masterpieces. L.; Chic.; Los Angeles, 1926; [1935]; [1940]. 1st. Edns., 2nd. work: (872). 3 vols. 12mo. Decor. bds., & cl., d.-w.'s. (PNY. Mar.4; 236) $100

– First Reader & Three Plays. Ill.:– Francis Rose. Dublin & L., 1946. 1st. Edn. Orig. cl.-bkd. bds. Inscr. to Cecil Beaton by artist, with pen & ink port. of Gertrude Stein. (SH. Dec.19; 392) *Rota.* £85

– Four Saints in Three Acts. N.Y., 1934. 1st. Edn. With 10 line autograph, Poem To Peter who drank Milk as 1st. line, sigd. Orig. cl. (SPB. Nov.25; 403) $950

– – Anr. Copy. Cl., d.-w., minor wear to jacket. Pres. copy. (PNY. Mar.4; 237) $350

– – Anr. Copy. Sigd. pres. copy to Nancy Custer Chewfie(?). (PNY. Mar.4; 238) $220

– The Geographical History of America or the Relation of Human Nature to the Human Mind. [N.Y.], [1936]. 1st. Edn. 2-tone cl., d.-w. (PNY. Mar.4; 239) $130

– How to Write. Paris, [1931]. 1st. Edn., (1000). 12mo. Two-tone bds. Sigd. pres. copy 'For Barney [Goodspeed]'. (PNY. Mar.4; 240) $450

– – Anr. Edn. Paris, [1931]. 12mo. Two-tone bds. Sigd. pres. copy 'For Bobsie ... '[Goodspeed]. (PNY. Mar.4; 241) $425

– Lectures in America. N.Y., [1935]. 1st. Edn., 1st. binding. Glazed cl., d.-w. (sm. piece off at head & tail of spine fold). Sigd. pres. copy 'For dear Bobsie' [Goodspeed]. (PNY. Mar.4; 242) $500

STEIN, Gertrude -contd.
- **Lucy Church Amiably.** Paris, 1930. 1st. Edn., (1000). Orig. ptd. bds., lr. hinge brkn. Sigd. pres. copy 'For Bobsy . . .' [Goodspeed]. (PNY. Mar.4; 243) $425
- **The Making of Americans.** Paris, 1925. 1st. Edn. 4to. Orig. wraps. loose & reprd., unc., partly unopened, cl. folder, mor.-bkd. s.-c. (S. Jul.22; 293) *House of Books.* £80
- - **Anr. Edn.** Paris, [1925]. 1st. Edn., (500). 4to. Most unopened. Orig. wraps. bnd. in, mor.-bkd. bds., with Shakespeare & Co. label on back end-paper. (SPB. Nov.25; 402) $600
- - **Anr. Edn.** N.Y., [1934]. 1st. Abridged Edn. Cl. Sigd. pres. copy 'To Bobsy . . .' [Goodspeed]. (PNY. Mar.4; 244) $300
- **Matisse, Picasso & Gertrude Stein. With Two Shorter Stories.** Paris, [1933]. 1st. Edn., (500). Ptd. wraps., boxed. Sigd. pres. copy to 'Bobsie' [Goodspeed]. (PNY. Mar.4; 245) $475
- **Morceaux Chosis de la Fabrication des Americains.** Paris, 1929. (100). Orig. ptd. wraps., slight soiling, cl. folding box. Sigd. (SPB. Nov.25; 404) $175
- **Operas & Plays.** Paris, [1932]. 1st. Edn., (500). 12mo. Wraps., boxed. Sigd. (SG. Jun.4; 456) $300
- **Picasso.** Paris, 1938. 1st. Edn. Orig. pict. wraps., spine worn, upr. wrap. held in place with 1 length of clear tape. Sigd. pres. copy to 'Bobsy' [Goodspeed]. (PNY. Mar.4; 247) $325
- **Portraits & Prayers.** N.Y., 1934. 1st. Edn. Photo-pict. cl., heavy woven cl. backstrip, glassine d.-w. retaining paper flaps. Sigd. pres. copy 'For Bobsy . . .' [Goodspeed]. (PNY. Mar.4; 248) $400
- **Tender Buttons: Objects, Food, Rooms.** N.Y., Claire Marie, 1914. 1st. Edn., (1000). 12mo. Advt. lf., sm. ptd. sheet laid in 'For Review, from Claire Marie . . .' Bds., hf. mor. s.-c. Inscr. to Jack Thompson, recipient's bkplt. (SG. Jun.4; 454) $1,500
- - **Anr. Copy.** Orig. bds., later glassine guard, normal soiling. Sigd. pres. copy 'For Bobsie . . .' [Goodspeed]. (PNY. Mar.4; 249) $700
- **Three Lives.** N.Y., 1909. 1st. Edn. Slight browning. Orig. cl., folding mor.-bkd. box. (SPB. Nov.25; 401) $600
- - **Anr. Edn.** N.Y., [1933]. 1st. Modern Library Edn. 12mo. Flexible cl., d.-w. Sigd. pres. copy, also inscr. & sigd. by Alice B. Toklas. (PNY. Mar.4; 250) $190
- **Useful Knowledge.** L., [1929]. 1st. Engl. Edn. Cl., d.-w. Sigd. pres. copy 'For Bobsie . . .' (Goodspeed). (PNY. Mar.4; 252) $325
- **The World is Round.** Ill.:– Sir Francis Rose. L., [1939]. 1st. Engl. Edn. Publisher's 4 p. prospectus laid in, as iss. Cl., d.-w. Sigd. pres. copy. 'To Bobsy & Barney' (Goodspeed). (PNY. Mar.4; 254) $350

STEINBECK, John
- **East of Eden.** N.Y., 1952. 1st. Edn., (1500) numbered, sigd. Buckram, boxed. (SG. Jun.4; 464) $275
- **Nothing So Monstrous.** Ill.:– Donald McKay. N.Y., 1936. 1st. separate Edn., (370). Orig. bds. (SPB. Jul.28; 427) $350
- **Of Mice & Men.** N.Y., [1937]. 1st. Edn., 1st. Iss. 12mo. Cl., d.-w. (SG. Jun.4; 463) $140
- **The Red Pony.** N.Y., 1937. 1st. Edn., (699) numbered, sigd. by author. 4to. Pict. cl., boxed. (PNY. Dec.3; 349) $320
- **Saint Katy the Virgin.** [N.Y.], [1936]. (199) numbered on H.M.P. 16mo. Without the greeting slip. Patt. bds., gt. spine, unc. Sigd. (SG. Nov.13; 618) $700

STEINER, Johann
- **Der Reisegefaehrte durch die Oesterreichische Schweitz.** Linz, 1820. 1st. Edn. Red mor., gt. inlaid borders, spines gt., gt. dentelles, satin doubls. & end-papers. (SG. Oct.30; 347) $325

STEINITZ, Käte
See–SCHWITTERS, Kurt & Steinitz, Käte

STEINITZ, W. (Ed.)
See–INTERNATIONAL CHESS MAGAZINE, The

STEINLEN, Theophile Alex.
- **Des Chats, Images sans Paroles.** Paris, [1898]. Fo. Liby. stp. on title. Orig. cl.-bkd. pict. bds., creased. (SH. Nov.21; 479) *Arts Anciens.* £50

STEINMETZ, Mauricius
- **Arithmeticae Praecepta, in Quaestiones Redacta.** [Leipzig], 1568. 1st. Edn. Some browning & marginal staining. Mod. wraps. From Honeyman Collection. (S. May 19; 2898) *Schaffer.* £50

STEINSCHNEIDER, Moritz
- **Catalogus Codicum Hebraeorum Bibliothecae Academiae Lugduno-Batavia.** (Hebrew Manuscripts in Leiden). Leiden, 1858. Orig. wraps., unc. (S. Nov.17; 110) *Valmadonna.* £65
- **Hebraeische Bibliographie. Blätter Fuer Neure und Aelter Literatur des Judenthum,** Berlin 1858-81/82. Hildesheim, 1972. 21 vols. in 4. Orig. bdg. (S. Nov.17; 113) *Gradenwitz.* £85
- **Hebraeische Ueberestzungen des Mittelalters.** Berlin, 1893-95. 1st. Edn., (300). 4to. Slight browning. Vell.-bkd. bds. (SPB. May 11; 60) $250
- **Die Hebraeischen Handschriften der K. Hof und Staatsbibliothek in Muenchen.** Munich, 1895. 2nd. Edn. 4to. Cl. (S. Nov.17; 114) *Valmadonna.* £65
- **Schach bei Den Juden.** Berlin, 1873. 1st. Edn., (50). Hf. cl. (S. Nov.17; 116) *Waechter.* £60

STELLA, Jacques & Bouzounet, Claudine
- **Stella, les Jeux et Plaisris '[sic] de l'Enfance.** Paris, 1657. 1st. Edn. 4to bnd. into 8vo. Lacks ptd. dedication & privilege lf., 19th. C. Engl. pres. inscr. on flylf. 18th. C. mor. in Jansenist style, flat spine with title, gt., & sm. blindstpd. fleurons, inner gt. dentelles. (SM. Oct.8; 2020) *Frs.* 3,800

STELLA CLERICORUM
Cologne, Heinrich Quentell, ca. 1496. Sm. 4to. Marb. bds. [BMC I, 295] (S. Nov.25; 346) *Maggs.* £220

STELLER, Georg Wilhelm
- **Beschreibung von dem Lande Kamatschatka . . .** Ed.:– J.B. S[cherer]. Frankfurt & Leipzig, 1774. 1st. Edn. Early 19th. C. bds. (R. Oct.14-18; 1796) DM 2,600

STEMPEL, G. & Zelst, A.–ROMANO, A. –HORCHER, Phillipus
- **Vtrivsqvo Astrolabii tam Particvlaris . . . –Theoria Calendariorum; Svppvtatio Ecclesiastica. –Libri Tres . . .** Lüttich; Würsburg;–; Mainz. 1602; 1594; 1595; 1605. 1st. Edn. [1st. work]. 4 works in 1 vol. 4to. 1st. title browned, 4th. work lightly browned. Cont. blind-tooled pig–bkd. wood bds., 2 clasps. (HK. Nov.18-21; 768) DM 1,000

STENBERGER, M.
- **Die Schatzfunde Gotlands. Der Wikingerzeit.** Stockholm & Lund, 1947. 2 vols. 4to. Orig. wraps. (SH. Mar.6; 455) *Spink.* £65

STENDHAL, M. de
See–BEYLE, Henri 'M. de Stendhal'

STENGEL, Johannes P.
- **Ausführlicher Beschreibung der Sonnen-Uhren.** Ulm, 1755. New Edn. Slightly soiled, stpd. on title verso & all plt. versos. Cont. hf. leath. gt. (R. Mar.31-Apr.4; 1310) DM 650
- **Gnomonica Universalis . . . Horlogia Solaria.** Ulm, 1680. P. 103 with sm. hole from paper flaw with loss of a few letters, directions to binder at end. Cont. vell. (CNY. Oct.1; 27) $300

STENGELIUS, Georgius
- **Exempla in Septem Capitalium Vitiorum Detestationem.** Ingolstadt, 1649. 1st. Edn. Slight browning. Cont. mor., tooled in gt. & blind, gt. floral endpapers. From liby. of André L. Simon. (S. May 18; 182) *Parikian.* £70

STENO, Nicolaus
- **De Musculis et Glandulis Observationum Specimen, cum Epistolis duabus Anatomicis.** Amst., 1664. 12mo. New bds. (S. Jun.17; 798) *Quaritch.* £280
- **De Solido Intra Solidum Naturaliter Contento Dissertationis Prodromus.** Flor., 1669. 1st. Edn. Sm. 4to. Lacks 1st. blank, browned & spotted. Cont. vell., spine wormed, hf. red mor. case. Owner's stps. on title of Dr. Federico Castelli; from Honeyman Collection. (S. May 19; 2900) *Percy.* £3,200
- **Dissertatio de Cerebri Anatome.** Ed.:– Guido Fanoisius. Leiden, 1671. 12mo. Vell. (S. Jun.17; 799) *Maggs.* £240
- **Elementorum Myologiae Specimen, seu Musculi Descriptio Geometrica.** Flor., 1667. 1st. Edn., L.P. 4to. 2 plts. with minor tears in folds, G4 reprd., some marginal staining, slight spotting. Cont. red mor., gt., slightly worn. Bkplt. of Baron Landau; stp. of Galletti liby., Flor., on title; from Honeyman Collection. (S. May 19; 2899) *Norman.* £1,300
- **The Prodromus to a Dissertation Concerning Solids Naturally Contained Within Solids** Trans.:– H[enry] O[ldenburg]. 1671. 1st. Engl. Edn. Errata/advt. lf. inserted from a smaller copy. Mod. cf. Bkplt. of Herbert McLean Evans; from Honeyman Collection. [Wing S5409] (S. May 19; 2901) *Percy.* £1,600

STEP, Edward
- **Favourite Flowers of Garden & Greenhouse.** Ed.:– William Watson. 1896-97. 4 vols. Lacks 2 plts. Cont. hf. mor. (CSK. Jan.9; 65) £150
- - **Anr. Copy.** Light spotting. Cont. hf. mor., spines gt. (S. Dec.3; 1142) *Litman.* £120
- - **Anr. Copy.** Cont. mor.-bkd. cl. (CSK. Oct.10; 47) £80
- - **Anr. Copy.** Hf. mor. gt. (P. Jul.30; 253) *Schapiro.* £55

STEPHANUS, Henricus (Pseud.)
See–ESTIENNE, Henri

STEPHEN, John
[-] **The Land of Promise . . . South Australia.** Ill.:– W. Westall & others. 1839. 1st. Edn. Orig. cl., gt. vig. on covers, unc. (C. Jul.15; 101) *Walford.* £60

STEPHENS, Charles
See–ESTIENNE or Stephens, Charles, Printer 1504-64 & Liébault, Jean

STEPHENS, Henry L.
- **The Comic Natural History of the Human Race.** Phila., [1851]. 1st. Edn. Cont. mor. gt., spine gt. (CNY. May 22; 219) $260

STEPHENS, James
- **The Crock of Gold.** Ill.:– Thomas MacKenzie. L., 1926. (525). 4to. Vell.-bkd. bds., d.-w. (some tears), unc. & unopened, bkplt. Sigd. (SG. Nov.13; 626) $100
- **The Hill of Vision.** Dublin, 1912. 1st. Dublin Edn. 12mo. Cl.-bkd. bds. Inscr. to Witter Bynner. (SG. Jun.4; 465) $160
- **Irish Fairy Tales.** Ill.:– Arthur Rackham. 1920. 1st. Edn. Cl. (GM. Apr.30; 387) £65
- - **Anr. Edn.** Ill.:– Arthur Rackham. L., 1920. 1st. Trade Edn. 4to. Gt.-pict. cl., pict. d.-w., gt. hf. mor. box. E.E. Taylor bkplt.; Raymond M. Sutton Jr. copy. (SG. May 7; 279) $225
- - **Anr. Edn.** Ill.:– Arthur Rackham. L., 1920. (520) sigd. by artist. Lge. 4to. End-papers foxed. Gt.-decor. vell. spine, vell.-style bds., partly unc. & unopened. Raymond M. Sutton Jr. copy. (SG. May 7; 278) $650

STEPHENS, James Francis
- **Illustrations of British Entomology.** 1828-34. 4 vols. Hf. mor. (P. Apr.30; 225) £80

STEPHENS, John Lloyd
- **Incidents of Travel in Central America, Chiapas, & Yucatan.** Ill.:– F. Catherwood. N.Y., 1841. 1st. Edn. 2 vols. Some foxing & staining. Orig. gt.-pict. cl., neatly rebkd., orig. spines preserved. (SG. Mar.5; 426) $325
- - **Anr. Copy.** gt.-pict. cl., owner's rubberstp. on end-papers. (SG. Jan.8; 412) $250
- - **Anr. Copy.** 12mo. Liby. bkplt. & stp. on title-pp. versos. Mod. buckram. (SG. Jun.11; 236) $200
- - **Anr. Copy.** Foxed, sig. on title-pp. Hf. cf., spines gt. (SG. Mar.5; 427) $180
- - **Anr. Edn.** 1842. 2 vols. Orig. decor. cl. gt. (CE. Jul.9; 87) £50
- - **Anr. Edn.** Ed.:– Frederick Catherwood. L., 1854. 1st. 3 ll. rehinged, old private rubberstp. on title. New marb. bds., three qtr. lev. (SG. Jan.8; 416) $210
- - **Anr. Copy.** Cont. cf., rebkd. (SG. Mar.5; 429) $170
- **Incidents of Travel in Yucatan.** Ill.:– F. Catherwood. N.Y., 1843. 1st. Edn. Some foxing. Orig. gt.-decor. cl., 2nd. vol. partly loose in bdg., & lacks top & bottom of spine. (SG. Mar.5; 428) $260
- - **Anr. Copy.** 2 vols. Foxed, 4 p. publisher's catalogue at end of vol. ll. Backstrips badly worn. (PNY. Mar.4; 256) $120
- - **Anr. Edn.** Ill.:– Frederick Catherwood. N.Y., 1860. 2 vols. Ex liby. New buckram. (SG. Jun.11; 237) $100

STEPHENSON, George
- A Description of the Safety Lamp, Invented by ... To Which is Added, an Account of the Lamp Constructed for Sir Humphrey Davy. 1817. 1st. Edn. Some spotting & offsetting. Wraps., red hf. mor. case. From Honeyman Collection. (S. May 19; 2902) *Quaritch.* £280

STEPHENSON, John & Churchill, James M.
- Medical Botany. Ed.:– G. T. Burnett. 1834-36. New Edn. 3 vols. A few plts. with stab-marks in outer edges. Cont. hf. cf., slightly worn. (S. Jun.1; 287) *Joseph.* £600
- – Anr. Copy. Cont. russ. gt., spines torn. (SBA. May 27; 196) *Hutchinson.* £240

STEPHENSON, Robert
- Report on the Atmospheric Railway System. 1844. 4to. A few plts. spotted. Orig. mor.-bkd bds. (SKC. Feb. 26; 1771) £85

STERN, Frederick Claude
- Study of the Genus Paeonia. Ill.:– L. Snelling. 1946. 4to. Cl. gt. (P. Nov. 13; 241) *Ashwell.* £100

STERN, I.F. (i. e J.F.S. Holzschuher)
- Lexicon der Jüdischen Geschäfts- und Umgangs-Sprache Vom Jüdischen in's Deutsche und vom Deutsche in's Jüdische. Munich, 1833. 2 pts. Partly soiled. Mod. bds., orig. wraps. bnd. in. (R. Oct.14-18; 1263) DM 700

STERNE, Laurence
- A Sentimental Journey through France & Italy 1768. 1st. Edn. 2 vols. 12mo. Cont. mott. cf., gt. (S. Feb.10; 464) *Millet.* £250
- – Anr. Copy. L.P. Sig. F in vol. 1 misbnd., some spots. Cont. cf., spines gt., slight wear, 1 label defect. (S. Feb.10; 465) *Whitby.* £230
- – Anr. Copy. 'Vous' reading on p. 140 in vol. I & misprint on p. 133 in vol. II, sigs. in ink on titles. Spines worn, old bkplts. of William Spooner, Doncaster in each vol. (C. Apr.1; 235) *Marlow.* £180
- [–] – Anr. Copy. Lacks hf.-titles, slight browning. Early 19th. C. hf. cf., jnts. split, 1 cover detchd. (S. Oct.1; 632) £75
- – Anr. Copy. Rothschild's variant state 2 (vous) of line 12, p. 150 of vol. 1, & state 2 (whho) of last line of p. 133 in vol. 2, without the inserted advt. 1f. in vol. 1. Cont. hf. cf. & marb. bds., Smith's Circulating Liby. label on upr. cover of vol. 1, removed from vol. 2, mor. gt. solander case, unc. From the Prescott Collection. (CNY. Feb.6; 303) $600
- [–] – Anr. Copy. 16mo. Lacks hf.-titles. Later mott. cf. gt., jnts. brkn. Armorial bkplt. of Anthony Trollope in each vol. (SG. Sep.25; 293) $350
- – Anr. Copy. Lacks advt. lf., slight browning. Cont. cf., cf.-bkd. s.-c. (SPB. May 6; 258) $275
- – Anr. Edn. Ill.:– Maurice Leloir. Paris, 1885. 4to. Hf. mor. (SH. Nov.20; 176) *Kaufmann.* £50
- – Anr. Edn. Ill.:– J.E. Laboureur. Gold. Cock. Pr., 1928. (500) Orig. buckram. (SH. Feb.19; 153) *Ayres.* £75
- – Tristram Shandy. 1760-67. 1st. Edn. 9 vols. Tree cf. gt. (P. Apr.30; 30) *Southern.* £1,250
- – Anr. Edn. L., 1760-67. 2nd. Edns. of 1st. 2 vols., 1st Edns. of others. 9 vols. in 4. 12mo. Inserted lf. with marb. papers as called for. Cont. cf., worn, some repairs. Author's sig. on Chapter I in vols. V, VII, IX. (SPB. Nov.25; 166) $650
- – Anr. Edn. L., 1760-67. 1st. Edns. (except vols. 1 & 2: 3rd. Edn.) 8 vols. only (of 9, lacks vol. 8). 16mo. Vols. 4, 5, 6, & 9 with hf.-titles. Old cf. Vols. 5, 7, & 9 sigd. (SG. Dec.18; 378) $140
- – Anr. Edn. Ill.:– J.E. Laboureur. Gold. Cock. Pr. 1929-30. (500) numbered. 3 vols. Buckram. (SG. Jan.15; 41) $150
- Works. 1793. 10 vols. Mott. cf. gt. by F. Bedford. (CE. Mar.19; 235) £160
- – Anr. Edn. Edinb., 1803. 8 vols. 12mo. Cont. tree cf., covers warped, 1 detchd. (PNY. May21; 394) $100
- – Anr. Edn. Oxford & Boston, Shakes. Hd. Pr. 1926. L.P. 7 vols. Orig. vell. spine, silk bds., slight stain on 1r. portions of spine, publisher's wraps., soiled. (SPB. Nov.25; 398) $200

STERNHERTZ, Nathan
- Ma'sa'ot Ha'yam of Rabbi Nachman. Jozefov, 1846. 1st. Edn. 12mo. Orig. wraps. (S. Nov.17; 175) *Valmadonna.* £85

STERRE, Jean Chrysost. van der
- Vita S. Norberti Ill.: Corneille Galle. Antw., [1622]. 1st. Edn. 4to. Mod. full mor., 5 spine raised bands, decor., lge. inner dentelle (LM. Jun.13; 164) B. Frs. 18,000

STEUART, Sir James
- Enquiry into the Principles of Political Economy. 1767. 2 vols. 4to. Bkplts. Cf., worn. (CE. Nov.20; 12) £780
- – Anr. Edn. Basel, 1796. 5 vols. Slightly soiled in parts. Cont. hf. leath., slightly worn. (H. May21/22; 663) DM 620

STEUART, John Robert
- A Description of some Ancient Monuments, with Inscriptions ... in Lydia & Phrygia. 1842. Fo. Some spotting & marginal staining, blank corner torn from frontis. Roan-bkd. bds. (S. Jun.22; 95) *Marlborough Rare Books.* £90

STEVENS, Benjamin Franklin
- Facsimilies of Manuscripts in European Archives relating to America, 1773-1783. 1889-95. Ltd. Edn. Vols. 1-5, 13-16, 21-24, & dupl. of vol. 22. Fo. Cont. hf. mor. (SH. Jul.23; 115) *Wade Gallery.* £110

STEVENS, John
See–DUGDALE, Sir William & Stevens, John
See–WARE, Sir James–STEVENS, John

STEVENS, Kaerle & Libaut, Ian
- De Veltbouw ofte Lantwinninghe. Ed.:– Melchior Sebizidor. Amst., n.d. Fo. Engraved title restored, some pp. restored. Mod. marb. vell. (LM. Mar.21; 143) B.Frs. 14,000

STEVENS, Wallace
- Man with the Blue Guitar & Other Poems. N.Y., 1937. 1st. Edn. Orig. cl., d.-w. (SPB. Nov.25; 406) $900
- Three Academic Pieces. [Cummington], 1947. 1st. Edn., (250). In sewn bds. with ties. (SPB. Nov.25; 407) $400

STEVENS-NELSON Paper Company
- Catalogue. [N.Y.], ca. 1950. 4to. Price list [dtd. 1953] laid in. Lev.-bkd. marb. bds. (SG. Mar.26; 419) $300

STEVENSON, Henry
- The Birds of Norfolk. 1866-70-90. 3 vols. Orig. cl., vols. 1 & 2 slightly worn. (P. May. 14; 121) *Goodfellow.* £55

STEVENSON, Matthew
- The Twelve Moneths. 1661. 1st. & only Edn. 4to. Mor., gt. by Rivière, gt. falcon on upr. cover. The Schwerdt copy. [Wing S5510] (S. Dec.3; 1143a) *Maggs.* £2,700

STEVENSON, Robert Louis
- A Child's Garden of Verses. 1885. 1st. Edn. Blind-stpd. 'Presented by Publishers' on title. Orig. cl., partly unc., in cl. box. (C. Feb.4; 88) *Basket/Day.* £110
- – Anr. Copy. 12mo. mor.-bkd s.-c. (C. Feb.4; 313) *Maggs.* £85
- – Anr. Copy. Ptd. on heavy H.M.P., with blind-stp. 'Presented by the Publishers' on title-p. Orig. cl. gt. over bevelled bds., upr. cover slightly spotted, qtr. lev. mor. s.-c., partly unc. From the Prescott Collection. (CNY. Feb.6; 305) $500
- – Anr. Copy. 12mo. Bevelled cl., head & foot of spine worn, partly untrimmed, 2 armorial bkplts. (SG. Nov.13; 640) $200
- – Anr. Copy. 16mo. Cl., owner's sig. on free end-paper, hf. lev. s.-c., partly unc. (SG. Apr.30; 294) $140
- Father Damien. Edinb., Priv. Ptd. 1890. (30) numbered on Japan vell., & sigd. by T. & A. Constable. Pres. port. of Father Damien laid in, with slip noting it is 'not to be bound in.'. Unbnd. loose sheets laid into gt.-lettered vell., lacks ties. (SG. Nov.13; 646) $110
- An Inland Voyage. L., 1878. 1st. Edn. Cl. gt., armorial bkplt. (SG. Nov.13; 631) £110
- The Novels & Tales. N.Y., 1911. 25 vols. Hf. maroon mor. gt. by Sangorski & Sutcliffe. (SPB. Nov. 25; 492) $850
- [–] The Pentland Rising. Edinb., 1866. 1st. Edn. Orig. wraps., in mor. solander box. (CSK. Apr.3; 84) £360
- St. Ives. L., 1898. 1st. Engl. Edn. Orig. cl. gt., qtr. red mor. gt. s.-c., unc. With 1 lf. of the autograph MS., with several corrections in author's hand (corresponds to p. 90 in the publd. book); from the Prescott Collection. (CNY. Feb.6; 306) $1,300

- Some College Memoirs. Edinb., 1886. Wise Forgery. 12mo. Ptd. wraps., bkplt. removed from upr. wrap., hf. lev. s.-c. Cheque, sigd. by Stevenson, tipped in upr. wrap.; bkplt. of J.W.R. Crawford (SG. Mar.19; 280) $425
- – Anr. Copy. Wraps., hf. mor. s.-c., unc. (SG. Nov.13; 643) $225
- The Story of a Lie. L., 1882. Wise Forgery. Orig. sheets. Unbnd. Cheque, sig., by Stevenson laid in. (SG. May 14; 206) $325
- The Strange Case of Dr. Jekyll & Mr. Hyde. 1886. 1st. Edn. Orig. cl. (S. Jul.22; 298) *Fletcher.* £110
- – Anr. Copy. Cl., spine soiled & slightly wrinkled. (SG. Nov.13; 641) $160
- To F.J.S. [1881]. 1st. Edn. Single lf. poem only. Silk folder, mor. pull-off case, by Sangorski. (C. Jul.22; 30) *Wood.* £140
- Treasure Island. 1883. 1st. Edn. 4pp. advts. Orig. cl. (S. Jul.22; 296) *Fletcher.* £260
- – Anr. Copy. Early iss., with '7' stpd. in at p. 127, 'Dead Man's Chest' not capitalized on pp. 2 & 7, 'a' lacking in line 6 of p. 63, 'period' dropped in line 20 of p. 178, 'worse' for 'worst' in line 3 of p. 197, '8' dropped in pagination of p. 83, frontis. map in 3 cols., 4 pp. of advts. at end (dtd. 5R 1083). Orig. cl., gt. spine, qtr. mor. s.-c., unc. From the Prescott Collection. (CNY. Feb.6; 304) $2,800
- – Anr. Copy. Advts. at end. Silked cl. (SG. Nov.13; 637) $240
- Virginibus Puerisque & Other Papers. L., 1881. 1st. Edn. Cl., hf. mor. s.-c. 2-p. A.L.s. tipped in. (SG. Oct.9; 233) $475
- The Works. Ed.:– Edmund Gosse. 1906-07. Pentland Edn., (1550). 20 vols. Hf. mor., spines gt. in compartments, partly unc., by Bickers. (C. Jul.22; 31) *Traylen.* £260
- – Anr. Edn. 1911-12. Swanston Edn. 25 vols. Cl. gt. (P. Sep.11; 88) *Traylen.* £60
- – Anr. Copy. 25 vols. Orig. cl. (SH. May 28; 96) *Rhys-Jones.* £55
- – Anr. Edn. N.Y., 1921-22. Vailima Edn., (1030). 26 vols. Maroon mor. gt., gt. panel. spines. (SPB. May 6; 345) $3,250
- – Anr. Edn. N.Y., 1921-23. Ltd. numbered Vailima Edn. on L.P. initialed by Lloyd Osbourne. 26 vols. Three-qtr. lev., spines gt. with repeated thistles, by Whitman Bennett. (SG. Aug.7; 403) $375
- – Anr. Edn. 1922-3. Vailima Edn., 26 vols. Orig. cl. (CSK. Aug.15; 101) £130
- – Anr. Edn. 1922-23. Ltd. Vailima Edn. Cl. gt., d.-w. (CE. Oct.24; 17) £75
- – Anr. Edn. L. & N.Y., 1922-23. Vailima Edn. (1030). 25 vols. Tall 8vo. Buckram, partly untrimmed. (SG. Nov.13; 656) $200

STEVENSON, Robert Louis & Osbourne, Lloyd
- The Wrong Box. L., 1889. 1st. Edn. 16 p. catalogue at end. Cl. Inserted are: money order sigd. by Stevenson, receipt from the Orient Line to Osbourne, & folding cabin-plan for the ship 'Australia', bkplt. of H. Buxton Forman. (SG. Feb.12; 51) $300

STEVIN, Simon
- L'Arithmétique ... Contenant les Computations des Nombres Arithmétiques ou Vulgaires. Leiden, 1585. 1st. Edn. in Fr. 2 pts. in 1 vol. Many headlines cropped, title & prelims. stained, some browning, owner's inscrs. of 'Delpech' on title. 19th. C. cf.-bkd. bds., spine defect. From Honeyman Collection. (S. May 19; 2904) *Israel.* £480
- De Beghinselen des Waterwichts [–De Beghinselen der Weeghconst. De Weeghdaet]. Leiden, 1586. 1st. Edn. 3 pts. in 1 vol. 4to. 15 11. from pt. 2 misbnd. at beginning of pt. 1. Cont. cf., gt. arabesque stp. on covers, upr. cover lettered 'Haerlem 1586' & 1r. cover 'T' Iaer 1586, rebkd. preserving orig. gt. spine, mor. gt. case From Honeyman Collection. (S. May 19; 2905) *Israel.* £6,200
- Castrametatio, dat is Legermeting. Rotterdam, 1617. 1st. Edn. Fo. 2 11. inserted from a shorter copy containing a full-p. engraved port. of Maurice, Prince of Orange, & a full-p. engraved coat of arms, title a little soiled & with stp. removed from 1r. margin. Cont. vell., gt., soiled & slightly defect., lacks ties. From liby. of Dr. Max Jähns; from Honeyman Collection. (S. May 19; 2908) *Elte.* £360
- La Castrametation ... – Nouvelle Manière de Fortification par Escluses. Leiden, 1618; 1618. 2nd. Edn. 2 works in 1 vol. Fo. Some

STEVIN, Simon -contd.
dampstaining & browning, 2nd. work with folding sheet comprising sig. E (pp. 33-34) misbnd. at p. 42, last 2 ll. with 1r. fore-corners eaten away without text loss. Cont. limp vell., stained, spine defect., inside hinges brkn. From Honeyman Collection. (S. May 19; 2909) *Elte.* £320
– **Hypomnemata Mathematica.** Trans.:– Willebrord Snell. Leiden, 1608-05. 1st. Coll. Edn. in Latin. 5 vols. in 2. Fo. Somewhat browned, vol. I stained at beginning & end, sm. repair to C2 (Canon Sinuum) vol. I. Cont. mott. cf., rebkd., vol. number labels transposed. From Honeyman Collection. (S. May 19; 2906)
– **Les Oeuvres Mathématiques . . .** Ed.:– Albert Girard. Leiden, 1634. 2 pts. in 1 vol. Fo. Browned, a few wormholes at beginning & end, b2, 13-4, & 3f6 pt. 2 reprd., without correction 1f. to pp. 529 & 532. Cont. vell. bds., soiled, upr. cover slightly wormed, lacks ties, red hf. mor. case. From Honeyman Collection. (S. May 19; 2910) *Quaritch.* £1,100
– **Problematum Geometricorum . . . Libri V.** Antw., (1583). 1st. Edn. Sm. 4to. Some 11. very browned, sm. holes in H4 & Il affecting 2 or 3 letters, old annots. on a few ll. Cont. vell., rebkd. From Honeyman Collection. (S. May 19; 2903) *Israel.* £420

STEVIN, Simon–O.[W.B.S.]
– **Festung-Bawung, das ist, Kurtze und Eygentliche Beschreibung, wie man Festungen bawen, unnd sich wider allen Gewaltsamen Anlauff der Feinde zu Kriegszeiten Auffhalten, fichern und Verwahren Möge.–Ursachen und Eigentliche Endschuldigung, beyder der Armbrust und Büchsenschützen.** Trans.:– G. Arthus (1st. work). Frankfurt; Strassburg, 1608; 1606. 1st. German Edn. (1st work). 2 works in 1 vol. Sm. 4to. 1st. work with some dampstaining. Cont. vell., gt., arms & initials of Johann Casimir Herzog zu Sachsen Gotha or Gülich (Jülich) Cleve und Berg, 1616, slightly soiled, lacks ties. From Honeyman Collection. (S. May 19; 2907) *Elte.* £420

STEWART, A.T.
– **Catalogue of [his] Collection of Paintings, Sculptures & other Objects of Art.** Ill.:– Chase, Moran, Gifford, & others. N.Y., 1887. (500) numbered. 4to. Orig. bds., worn & soiled, lacks spine. (SG. Mar.12; 357) $150

STEWART, Basil
– **Subjects Portrayed in Japanese Colour-Prints.** 1922. Fo. Orig. cl.-bkd. bds. (SH. Jul.9; 34) *Ars Artis.* £110

STEWART, Donald W.
– **Old & Rare Scottish Tartans.** 1893. (300) numbered. 4to. Hf. mor. gt. (CE. Jun.4; 167) £105

STEWART, Douglas
See–LINDSAY, Norman & Stewart, Douglas

STEWART, John
– **An Account of Prince Edward Island in the Gulph of St. Lawrence, North America.** 1806. 1st. Edn. Engraved folding map, hand-cold. in outl. Cont. hf. cf. [Sabin 91696] (C. Feb.4; 171) *Monk Bretton.* £200
– **A View of the Past & Present State of the Island of Jamaica; with Remarks on the moral & physical conditions of the Slaves, & on the Abolition of Slavery in the Colonies.** Edinb., 1823. Hf. cf., very worn. (PD. May 20; 6) £120
– – **Anr. Copy.** Slight browning. Blind-stpd. cf. (SPB. May 5; 486) $150

STEWART, John
– **The Resurrection.–Genevieve.** L., 1808; 1810. 2 works in 2 vols. 12mo. Unif. crimson mor., gt.-tooled with borders & corner-pieces enclosing, on all covers, sm. gt. coronet with 3 plumes, spines gt., wide gt. dentelles with mor. inlaid cornerpieces, doubls. & end-papers of moire satin. Bloomfield armorial bkplt. in each work. (SG. Mar.19; 13) $150

STIBBERT, Federigo
– **Abiti e Fogge Civili e Militari dal I al XVIII Secolo.** Bergamo, 1914. 4to. cl. (SI. Dec.4; 545) Lire 200,000

STIEGLITZ, Alfred
– **America & Alfred Stieglitz.** Ed.:– Frank, Waldo, et al. Garden City, 1934. 1st. Edn. Cl., d.-w. Sigd. pres. copy from Gertrude Stein. 'For Bobsy . . .' (Goodspeed). (PNY. Mar.4; 257) $325
– **Memorial Portfolio.** Ed.:– Dorothy Norman. N.Y., 1947. (1500) Fo. Orig. hf. linen portfo. (H. May 21/22; 1753) DM 480

STIEGLITZ, Christian Ludwig
– **Encyklopädie der Bürgerlichen Baukunst.** Ill.:– J. G. Klinger & Liebe. Leipzig. 1792-98. 5 text & 1 plt. vol. Ob. 4to. Some plts. lightly browned, title stpd. 19th. C. hf. linen, slightly defect, vol. 1 spine sprung & loose. (R. Mar.31-Apr.4; 1299) DM 1,200
– **Zeichnungen aus der Schönen Baukunst.** Leipzig, 1805. 2nd. Edn. Cont. hf. leath., spine reprd. (R. Oct.14-18; 769) DM 1,100

STIELER, A.
– **Hand-Atlas über alle Theile der Erde.** Ed.:– Stieler, Reichardt, Hübbe & others. Gotha, 1845. Ob. fo. Cont. hf. leath. (R. Oct.14-18; 1566) DM 1,000
– **Karte von Deutschland, dem Königr. der Niederlande und der Schweiz mit den angränzenden Länder in XXV Blatt.** Gotha, 1829-[1832]. 1st. Edn. Ob. fo. Cont. hf. leath. (R. Mar.31-Apr.4; 1877) DM 550

STIELER, Karl
See–SCHMID, Herman & Stieler, Karl

STIELER, Karl, Wachenhusen, K.S.H. & Hackländer, Friedrich Wilhelm
– **Rheinfahrt.** Ill.:– Stieler, H. Wachenhusen & F.W. Hackländer. Stuttgart, ca. 1880. Fo. Linen. (HK. Nov.18-21; 1347) DM 1,900
– – **Anr. Edn.** Stuttgart, [1885]. Sm. fo. Slightly soiled in parts. Cont. hf. leath. (R. Oct.14-18; 2466) DM 2,500
– – **Anr. Copy.** Orig. linen gt. (R. Mar.31-Apr.4; 2210) DM 2,300
– **The Rhine from its Source to the Sea.** 1878. Fo. Orig. cl., slightly soiled. (CSK. Aug.1; 157) £350
– – **Anr. Copy.** Defect., upr. cover loose. (R. Mar.31-Apr.4; 2211) DM 1,800
– – **Anr. Edn.** Trans.:– G. C. T. Bartley. L., Ca. 1880. Sm. fo. Orig. linen loose. (R. Oct.14-18; 2468) DM 1,800

STIFEL, Michael
– **Arithmetica Integra . . .** Ed.:– Philippi Melanchthonis. Nuremb., 1544. 1st. Edn. 4to. Prelims. stained, title slightly soiled & with deleted inscrs. Cont. blind-stpd. cf., rebkd., end-ll. from 13th. C. Engl. MS. on vell. of a glossed philosophical text. Bkplt. of Earl of Hopetoun; from Honeyman Collection (S. May 19; 2912) *Quaritch.* £480
– **Die Coss Christoffs Rudolfis. Mit Schönen Exempeln der Coss.** Amst., 1615. 3rd. Edn. Some browning, slight staining, mostly marginal. Cont. vell. From Honeyman Collection. (S. May 19; 2817) *Mrs. Nador.* £65
– **Die Coss Christoffs Rudolffs mit schonen Exempeln der Coss.–Ein sehr Wunderbarliche Wortrechnung Sampt einer Mercklichen Erklerung Etlicher Zalen Danielis und der Offenbarung Sanct Johannis.** Konigsberg; (Konigsberg), 1553 (-1554); 1553. 1st. Edns. 2 works in 1 vol. Sm. 4to. 1st. work lacks penultimate lf. with colophon & woodcut, 1st. title soiled; browned & stained. Old blind-panel. cf., worn, lacks ties. From Honeyman Collection. (S. May 19; 2916) *Dr. Martin.* £700
– **Deutsche Arithmetica, inhaltend, die Haussrechnung, Deutsche Coss, Kirchrechnung.** Nuremb., 1545. 1st. Edn. Sm. 4to. Some browning, minor repair to X1. Mod. hf. red mor. Bkplt. of Baron Landau; from Honeyman Collection. (S. May 19; 2913) *Dr. Martin.* £400
– **Ein Rechen Buchlin vom End Christ.** Wittenberg, 1532. 1st. Edn. 2 pts. in 1 vol. Old inscrs. on 1st. title. Mod. vell., red hf. mor. case. From Honeyman Collection. (S. May 19; 2911) *Schaffer.* £200
[–] **Ein sehr Wunderbarliche Wortrechnung, Sampt einer Mercklichen Erklerung Eticher zalen Danielis und der Offenbarung Sanct Johannis.** [Konigsberg], 1553. 1st. Edn. Sm. 4to. Slightly browned & soiled, title & following lf. remargined at head, former with sm. tears reprd., 2 or 3 wormholes running thro-out. Mod. mor., gt., by A(lice) P(aterson), 1905, covers tooled representing author's 'word calculus' hf. mor. case.

From liby. of Rev. Walter Begley, with his note at end; from Honeyman Collection. (S. May 19; 2915) *Ritman.* £1,000

STIFEL, Michael–RIES, Adam
– **Rechenbuch von der Welschen und Deutschen Practick, auff allerley Vorteyl und Behendigkeit.–Rechenung nach der lenge, auff den Linihen und Feder.** Nuremb.; Leipzig, 1546; (1550). 1st. Edns. 2 works in 1 vol. 4to. Bnd. in reverse order, some browning & spotting, sig. of D.G. Seidel on 1st. title. Cont. German blind-stpd. pig. over wooden bds., roll-borders of biblical figures, inner frame & panel decor. with flowers, leaves & acorns, upr. cover stpd. 'Adam Ries' & with owner's initials 'C F' & date 1551, metal corner-pieces & clasps, slightly worn & soiled. Bkplt. of Comte de Solms; from Honeyman Collection. (S. May 19; 2914) *Das Bucherkabinet.* £2,800

STIFTER, Adalbert
– **Der Nachsommer.** Ill.:– after Geiger. Pest, 1857. 1st. Edn. 3 vols. Slightly soiled. Cont. hf. leath. gt. (HK. May 15; 4924) DM 3,900
– – **Anr. Edn.** Pesth, [1857]. 1st. Edn. Lacks ptd. title, slightly soiled in parts. Cont. linen. (H. May 21/22; 1285) DM 700
– **Studien.** Pest & Leipzig, 1844-50. 1st. Edn. Lacks 4 sub-titles & 2 ll. in vol. 6., vols. 5 & 6 stained, stp. eradicated, hole in 1 lf. Cont. lin. (R. Oct.14-18; 1088) DM 1,250

STIGAND, Capt. Chauncy Hugh
– **The Game of British East Africa.** L., 1913. 2nd. Edn. 4to. Some light foxing. Decor. cl., lacks front free end-paper. (VA. May 8; 497) R. 90

STILES, John R.
– **Portrait of The Assassin.** N.Y., (1965). 2nd. printing. Cl., d.-w. Composed at upr. fly-lf. is autograph MS. statement, sigd., by Gerald R. Ford. (PNY. Mar.26; 381) $3,000

STILLE Volk, Das
Ill.:– Arthur Rackham. Zurich. 1923. (1000). 4to. Orig. cl. gt. (SH. Dec.11; 439) *Goblins.* £65

STILLINGFLEET, Benjamin
[–] **Principles & Power of Harmony.** 1771. 4to. Hf. cf. From liby. of William Ayrton, the musicologist, with autograph MS. annots. in ink & pencil. (P. May.14; 83) £50

STILLMAN, Jacob D.B.
– **The Horse in Motion . . .** Ed.:– Leland Stamford. Ill.:– Eadweard Muybridge, Boston, 1882. [1st. Edn.?] 4to. Orig. cl., spine & corners worn. (S. Dec.3; 1145) *Way.* £85
– – **Anr. Copy.** Gt.-pict. cl., cover heavily spotted. (SG. Apr.23; 186) $175
– – **Anr. Copy.** Liby. stps. on some plts. (SG. Jul.9; 308) $120

STIRLING, Charles
– **Twelve Views in the Grounds of Woburn Farm, near Chertsey.** Ill.:– C. Hullmandel after Stirling. n.d. Fo. Orig. cl.-bkd. bds. (CSK. Oct.17; 228) £70

STIRLING, Patrick James
– **The Australian & Californian Gold Discoveries, & their Probable Consequences.** Edinb., 1853. Cl. (PD. May 20; 8) £55

STIRLING, William
– **Some Apostles of Physiology.** Priv. ptd. 1902. Fo. Orig. cl. gt., soiled. From the liby.'s of W. Bulloch & Sir Geoffrey-Jefferson. (S. Jun.17; 803) *Wood.* £75

STIRRUP, Thomas
– **The Description & Use of the Universall Quadrat . . . Also the Resolution of Such Propositions as are Most Usefull in Astronomic, Navigation, & Dialling.** 1655. 1st. Edn. 4to. 1 plt. with sm. tear, text browned, sm. tears in title & M2. Cont. sheep, worn, upr. cover detchd. From Honeyman Collection. [Wing S5687] (S. May 19; 2918) *Rogers Turner.* £340

STISSER, Friedrich Ulrich
– **Forst. u. Jagd-Historie d. Teutschen.** Jena, 1737. 1st. Edn. Soiled. Cont. leath. (HK. Nov.18-21; 1750) DM 1,200

STITH, William
– **History of the First Discovery & Settlement of Virginia.** Williamsburg. 1747. 1st. Edn., 3rd iss. Mott. cf., triple gt. fillet borders, spines gt. with fleurons, gt. dentelles, by Rivière, qtr. mor. s.-c. (SG. Oct.9; 234) $650

STOBO, Maj. Robert
– Memoirs of . . . of the Virginia Regiment. Pittsb., 1854. 16mo. Orig. gt. & blind cl. (PNY. Dec.3; 351) $150

STOCHOVE, Vincent de
– Voyage du Sieur de Stochove . . . Brussels, 1643. 1st Edn. Sm. 4to. Lacks additional engraved title, inscrs. on title, several ll. slightly stained from margins, title & 4 ll. detchd. 19th C. cf.-bkd. bds., lacks spine, covers detchd., worn. (S. May 5; 58) Habibis. £80

STOCKDALE, John
– Geographical, Historical & Political Description of Germany, Holland . . . Sardinia. 1800. 4to. Cf. (P. Oct.23; 68) Brooke-Hitching. £260
[–] – Anr. Copy. 27 maps & town plans, liby. stp. on title. Diced cf., spine defect. (P. Mar.12; 215) £220
– – Anr. Copy. 2 double-p. maps or plans torn at fold, 4 ll. of table at end spotted. Cont. tree cf., spine gt., rebkd. preserving orig. spine. From the collection of Eric Sexton. (C. Apr.15; 50) Dawson. £190

STOCKDALE, John Joseph
[–] The History of the Inquisitions. L., 1810. 1st. Edn. 4to. Heavily foxed. Crude hf. leath. (SG. Feb.12; 219) $110

STOCKDALE, Percival
– Memoirs . . . Ill.:– Fittler. 1809. 1st. Edn. 2 vols. Engd. port. in 2 states, the 2nd. offset onto title-p. Cont. hf. mor., gt. ornaments in panels of spines. William Beckford's copy, with 5½pp. pencilled notes, bkplt. of Lord Rosebery. (S. Nov.25; 486) Traylen. £100

STOCKLEIN, J.
– Allerhand so Lehr- als Geist-reiche Brief, Schrifften und Reis-Beschreibungen, welche von den Missionariis der Gesellschafft Jesu . . . Augsburg & Graz, 1726-35. Vol. 1, pts. 5-8 & Index; Vol. II, Pts. 9-16 & Index; Vol. III, Pts. 17-24 & Index, Together 5 vols. Fo. Slightly soiled, lacks title & 2 prelim. ll. to Pts. 21/22, pp. 141-144 in Pts. 23/24 & last Index lf. Vol. III, 1 Index lf. defect. 2 vols. cont. leath., gt., 3 vols. cont. vell., 2 spines defect. [Sabin 91981] (R. Oct.14-18; 1732) DM 1,400

STODART'S PICTURESQUE VIEWS OF SCOTLAND
N.d. 33 cold. plts. in folder. Worn & detchd. at spine. (CE. Nov.20; 93) £100

STODART, Robert Riddle
– Scottish Arms. Edinb., 1881. Ltd. Edn. 2 vols. Fo Orig. cl. (SH. Oct.10; 529) Heraldry Today. £90
– – Anr. Edn. Edinb., 1881. Cl. gt., worn. (CE. Dec.4; 179) £60

STODDART, John
– Remarks on Local Scenery & Manners in Scotland. 1799. 2 vols. Cf. gt. (CE. Jun.4; 211) £130
– – Anr. Edn. [1801]. Cf. gt. (CE. Nov.20; 130) £190
– – Anr. Copy. 2 vols. Mor. gt., soiled. (CE. Nov.20; 131) £50

STOEFFLER, Johann
– Almanach noua Plurimis annis Venturis Inseruientia. Venice, Jan.3, 1506. Early Edn. 4to. Slight staining in upr. margins, single wormhole thro. 1st. few ll., sm. repairs to title & last lf. affecting a few letters etc., lf. of MS. tables inserted after title. Cont. hf. blind-stpd. pig. over wooden bds., some wear, clasps & catches. From Honeyman Collection. (S. May 19; 2920) Hill. £560
– – Anr. Copy. Some staining & spotting, title soiled & with marginal tear, MS. annots., owner's inscr. of Justus Jacobus Leibnitz, Nuremb., 1658 on title. Cont. hf. pig. over wooden bds., worn, lacks clasps. Bkplt. of Michel Chasles; from Honeyman Collection; w.a.f. (S. May 19; 2921) Quaritch. £80
– Elucidatio Fabricae Ususque Astrolabii. Oppenheim, 1512-13. 1st. Edn. Fo. Extension slips to those at A6, B3, C4 & D3, woodcut initials, title-border & some ills. & initials cold., by cont. hand, some browning & staining, wormholes towards end, single wormhole thro.-out, sm. portion erased from upr. border of title, cont. marginalia in red & black ink. Mod. vell., hf. mor.

case. From Honeyman Collection. (S. May 19; 2922) McKittrick. £1,000
– In Procli Diadochi . . . Sphaeram Mundi, Omnibus Numeris longe Absolutissimus Commentarius. Tübingen, 1534. 1st. Edn. Fo. Woodcut port. of author on last lf. slightly soiled & mntd., some browning, slight staining, title a little soiled & with marginal repair, owners' inscrs. of Arbogast Hocker & Jesuit College at Freiburg in Bresigau, 1648 & '64. Cont. limp vell. From Honeyman Collection. [Sabin 91983] (S. May 19; 2924) Hughes. £200
– Der Newe gross Romisch Calender, mit seinen Ausslegungen, Erclärungen, unnd Regeln. Oppenheim, 1522-18. 1st. Edn. in German. Fo. Slight marginal staining & soiling, lr. fore-corner of title a little frayed, owner's inscrs. of Franciscans at Passau. Cont. hf. blind-stpd. cf. over wooden bds., later rebacking, very worn, lacks clasps. From Honeyman Collection. (S. May 19; 2923) Dr. Martin. £1,100

STOER, Lorenz
– Geometria et Perspectiva. Hierjnn Etliche Zerbrochne Gebew, den Schreiner jn eingelegter Arbait dienstlich. [Augsburg], 1567. 1st. Edn. Sm. fo. Title stained & slightly torn, colophon cut away at foot of last lf., a little worming, barely affecting woodcuts, stained in upr. margins. Disbnd., red hf. mor. case. From Honeyman Collection. (S. May 19; 2925) Goldschmidt. £3,200

STOFFEL, Col.
– Historie de Jules César: Guerre Civile. Paris, 1887. 3 vols. Lge. 4to. & fo. Red three-qtr. mor. (SG. Oct.30; 342) $120

STOKE, Melis
– Rijmkronijk. Ed.:– B. Huydecoper. Leyden, 1772. L.P. 3 vols. 4to. Cont. marb. cf., spines gt. Bkplt. of Albert Verwey. (VG. Dec.17; 1447) Fls. 450

STOKER, Bram
– Dracula. Ltd. Edns. Cl., 1965. Ltd. Edn. Orig. bdg., box. (SPB. Jul.28; 312) $100

STOKES, Hugh
– Belgium. Ill.:– Frank Brangwyn. 1916. (160), sigd. by artist. 4to. Orig. cl. gt. (SH. Mar.26; 113) Ayres. £60

STOKES, Isaac Newton Phelps
– The Iconography of Manhattan Island. N.Y., 1915-28. (360) on Engl. H.M.P. 6 vols. 4to. Orig. hf. vell. & cl. bds., unc., cl. jackets & s.-cs., a few cases worn, vell. slightly spotted. (CNY. Oct.1; 116) $1,600

STOKES, Isaac Newton Phelps & Haskell, Daniel C.
– American Historical Prints. N.Y., 1933. Cl. (SG. Jan.22; 13) $150

STOKES, J.
– The Complete Cabinet Maker & Upholsterer's Guide. [1829]. 12mo. Orig. bds., rebkd., unc. (S. Mar.17; 458) Henderson. £180

STOKES, William
– The Diseases of the Heart & the Aorta. Dublin, 1854. 1st. Edn. Lacks hf.-title. Cf. gt., upr. hinge worn. (S. Jun.17; 806) Pratt. £160
– An Introduction to the Use of the Stethoscope with its Application to the Diagnosis in Disease of the Thoracic Viscera. Edinb., 1825. 1st. Edn. Hf. mor. Photograph of the author dtd. 1863 inserted. (S. Jun.17; 804) Norman £600
– A Treatise on the Diagnosis & Treatment of Diseases of the Chest. 1837. 1st. Edn. Pt. I-Diseases of the Lung & Windpipe (all publd.). Lacks hf.-title, port. inserted. Hf. cf. (S. Jun.17; 805) Silver. £110

STOLBERG, Frederic Leopold, Count
– Travels through Germany, Switzerland, Italy & Sicily. Trans.:– Thomas Holcroft. 1797. 2nd. Edn. of this translation. 4 vols. A few sm. tears & other minor defects, mainly marginal. Cont. tree cf., slightly worn. Earl of Wicklow's bkplts. (SBA. Mar.4; 125) Edwards £90

STOLLWERCK'S SAMMEL-ALBUM
Berlin, 1889-1905. Nos. 1-5 & 7 in 5 vols. Fo. Orig. paper bds. & 1 orig. hf. linen, worn. (H. Dec.9/10; 2122) DM 1,150

STONE, Reynolds
– The Old Rectory. [L.], 1976. (150) proof sets, with engrs. numbered, sigd. & separately mntd.

With the associated booklet 'Little Cheney, 1877'. Orig. lettered cl. case. (KH. Mar.24; 382) Aus. $200

STONE, Wilbur Macey
[–] The Triptych's Penny Toys. Ill.:– Jay Chambers. N.Y., Priv. Ptd. 1924. (99) numbered. Ob. 12mo. Prospectus for this work & 3 p. article on Chambers laid in. Cold. pict. bds. by William Jordan. Limitation handwritten & sigd. by Stone, & inscr. to Franklin Lüdington. (SG. Dec.18: 380) $160

STONES, Margaret
See–CURTIS, Winifred & Stones, Margaret

STONEY, Capt. H. Butler
– A Residence in Tasmania. 1856. Occasional spotting. Cont. cf. (CSK. Feb.20; 150) £85
– – Anr. Copy. Slight soiling. Orig. cl., unc., soiled. (KH. Nov.18; 561) Aus. $150

STONHAM, Charles
– Birds of the British Islands. Ill.:– after L. Medland. 1906. 5 vols. Lge. 4to. Cl. gt., slight spotting. (P. Jan.22; 268) Fisher. £100
– – Anr. Edn. Ill.:– Lilian M. Medland. 1906-11. 1st Edn. 5 vols. 4to. Mod. hf. mor. gt. (C. Mar.18; 111) Hill. £3,000
– – Anr. Copy. Ill.:– Lilian M. Medland. 1906-11. 1st. Edn. 5 vols. in 20 orig. pts. 4to. Orig. ptd. wraps., unc. (C. Jul.15; 212) Traylen. £1,100
– – Anr. Edn. 1906-11. 5 vols. 4to. Cont. buckram, gt. (SBA. Jul.23; 286) Nicholson. £120
– – Anr. Copy. Orig. cl., slightly soiled. (SH. Oct.9; 248) Bookroom. £65

STOPENDAAL, Daniel
[–] De Vechtstroom van Utrecht tot Muiden. Amst., 1791. Fo. Cont. hf. cf., gt. spine, slightly worn & corners slightly defect. (VG. Oct.13; 153) Frs. 2,300
– De Zegepraalende Vecht, Vertoonende verschiedene Gezichten van Lustplaatsen, Heeren Huysen en Dorpen . . . –La Triomphante Rivière De Vecht. Amst., 1719. 2 pts. in 1 vol. Fo. The 2 ll. with extra-ills. folded due to longer size. Mod. hf. mor. (VG. Dec.17; 1546) Fls. 1,800

STOPENDAAL, Daniel & Brouerius van Niedek, M.
– Het Verheerlykt Watergraefs- of Diemer-Meer, by Amsterdam, . . . Ill.:– After D. Stopendaal. Amst., ca. 1730. Fo. Cont. vell., soiled, spine renewed. (VG. Dec.17; 1547) Fls. 650

STORCH, Henri
– Tableau Historique et Statistique de l'Empire de Russie . . . Basle & Leipzig, 1802. 1st. Edn. in Fr. 2 vols. Cont. red mor. (SG. Oct.30; 318) $190

STORER, Horatio Robinson
– Medicina in Nummis. Ed.:– Malcolm Storer. [Boston], Priv. Ptd. [1931]. 1st. Edn. 4to. Cl., crudely reprd. From Brooklyn Academy of Medicine. (SG. Jan.29; 393) $170

STORER, James Sargent
– A Description of Fonthill Abbey, Wiltshire. 1812. 1st. Edn., L.P. 4to. 5 additional plts. (dtd. 1824) with accompanying text to Fonthill from Neale's 'Views of Seats' bnd. at end, some spotting & offsetting. 19th. C. hf. mor. (S. Jun.22; 96) Nester. £90
– History & Antiquities of the Cathedral Churches of Great Britain. 1814-19. 4 vols. Hf. cf. gt. (P. Oct.2; 11) Tulloch. £50

STORER, James Sargent & Henry
– Views in Edinburgh & its Vicinity . . . Edinb., 1820. 2 vols. Cont. cf., blind-stpd. & gt., elab. gt. borders & blind central panels, spines gt., by R. Hamilton, with his ticket. (CNY. May 22; 275) $100

STORER, James Sargent & Greig, John
– Antiquarian & Topographical Cabinet, Containing a Series of Elegant Views . . . in Great Britain. 1807-11. 10 vols. Cont. hf. mor. (TA. May 21; 49) £75
– – Anr. Copy Cont. hf. cf., spines gt., with raised bands. (C. Nov.5; 155) Townshend. £50

STORM, Theodor
– Sommer-Geschichten u. Lieder. Berlin, 1851. 1st. Edn. Soiled. Cont. linen., slightly stained. (HK. May 15; 4934) DM 850

STORY, George Walter
[-] A True & Impartial History of The Most Material Occurances in the Kingdom of Ireland during the Two Last Years. L., 1691. 4to. Hf. title reprd., advt. on end-lf. liby. stp. on title-p., Disbnd. [Wing S5750] (GM. Apr.30; 339) £95

STOSCH, M. Philippe de
- Pierres Antiques Gravées Ill.:– Bernard Picart. Amst., 1724. Fo. Bkplt. of Robert Henry Clive. Red mor. by Derome le Jeune with his ticket, triple gt. fillet, spine gt. with fleurons in compartments, inner gt. dentelles. (SM. Oct.8; 1920) Frs. 2,500

STOTHARD, Mrs. Charles
- Letters Written During a Tour through Normandy, Britanny & other parts of France in 1818. Ill.:– after the author. 1820. 4to. Cont. cf., some wear, rebkd. (SKC. Feb.26; 1682) £65

STOTHARD, Charles Alfred
- The Monumental Effigies of Great Britain. 1817. [1832]. Fo. Occasional slight spotting. Near cont. hf. mor., worn. Bkplt. & owner's inscr. of R. Almack. (CSK. Jul.3; 116) £170
– – Anr. Copy. Frontis. & 145 hand-cold. plts., ex liby. Red hf. mor. (SG. Oct.30; 344) $275

STOTHARD, Thomas (Ill.)
See–AKENSIDE, Mark
See–BUNYAN, John
See–DEFOE, Daniel
See–ROGERS, Samuel

STOTSCH, Melchior Friedrich von
- Genealogia des Hoch-Graeflich. Ill.:– Strahowsky after Bernhardi (port.). Bresslau & Leipzig, 1736. Fo. Old cf., worn. (SG. Feb.5; 313) $300

STOTT, Raymond Toole
- Circus & Allied Arts. Derby, [1958-71]. Ltd. 1st. Edn. 4 vols. 4to. Cl., d.-w.'s Last vol. sigd. (SG. Jan.22; 124) $130

STOUT, Rex
- Champagne for One.–The Mother Hunt.–A Family Affair. N.Y., (1958-75). 1st. Edns. 3 vols. Cl. & cl.-bkd. bds., d.-w.s. 1st. 2 titles pres. copies. to Mr & Mrs Chapman. 3rd. title pres. copy from author's wife. (PNY. Mar.4; 258) $240

STOW, G.W.
- Rock-Paintings in South Africa. L., 1930. 4to. Orig. bdg. (SSA. Nov.5; 271) R. 150

STOW, John
- Annales, or, A Generall Chronicle of England. 1631-32. 5th. Edn. Fo. Later cf. (SH. May 21; 231) Ayres. £120
– – Anr. Copy. Extra-ill, engraved title of 'Basiliologia' (Greek) & 25 plts. inserted, browned, some tears & holes, with slight loss of text, bkplt. of John Ward, & Inner Temple, pasted on verso of title. Cont. cf., worn, foot of spine defect. [NSTC 23340] (S. Sep.29; 111) Fletcher. £70
- A Summarie of the Chronicles of England. 1598. 16mo. Cont. cf., rebkd., preserving orig. spine, new label. From the collection of Eric Sexton. [STC 23328] (C. Apr.15; 191) Thorp. £90
- A Survey of the Cities of London & Westminster. Ed.:– John Strype. 1720. 1st. Strype Edn. 2 vols. Fo. 1 plan with tears at folds., 1 double-p. plan damp-stained. Old. panel. cf., worn, rebkd. (C. Nov.5; 156) Marks. £300
– – Anr. Copy. 2 vols. Fo. 69 engraved plts. (Upcott calls for only 68), 1 plt. with short tear, some minor paper flaws. Cont. panel. cf., rebkd. (S. Jul.27; 42) Franks. £280
– – Anr. Copy. 19th. C. hf. cf. (reprd. & restored by Sotheran). Bkplt. of Nathan of Churt, lately in the collection of Eric Sexton. (C. Apr.16; 361) Heraldry Today. £50
– – Anr. Edn. Ed.:– John Strype. 1754-55. 2 vols. Fo. Cont. cf., gt., rebkd. Bkplt. of Nathan of Churt, lately in the collection of Eric Sexton. (C. Apr.16; 362) Kentish. £220
- A Survey of London. 1598. 1st. Edn. Sm. 4to. Old cf., rebkd. Bkplts. of F.G. Howard & Nathan of Churt, lately in the collection of Eric Sexton. [STC 23341] (C. Apr.15; 193) Traylen. £280
– – Anr. Edn. 1603. Sm. 4to. Staining in 1st. 20 ll. Cont. cf. Cont. owner's mark of Roger Harris on title, bkplt. of Nathan of Churt, lately in the

collection of E. Sexton. [STC 23343] (C. Apr.15; 195) Quaritch. £130
– – Anr. Edn. 1618. 4to. A few ll. very slightly stained. Old cf., worn. (SKC. Feb.26; 1683) £120
– – Anr. Copy. Cont. cf. Bkplt. of Nathan of Churt, lately in the collection of Eric Sexton. [STC 23344] (C. Apr.15; 196) Traylen. £100
– – Anr. Edn. Ed.:– A. M[unday] & H. D[yson]. 1633. Fo. Prelim. with armorial woodcut reprd. in lr. corner. Cont. cf., rebkd. From the collection of Eric Sexton. [STC 23345] (C. Apr.15; 197) Traylen. £120
– – Anr. Edn. L., 1633? 4to. Lacks all before p. 3, many repairs, stains, etc., with some text loss, with the 4 p. sheet between pp. 20 & 21 'Rivers & other waters serving this Citie'. 19th. C. hf. cf. Fore-e. pntg. of Old Fleet Bridge by John T. Beer, sigd. by him & with his bkplt., sig. of John Camden, lately in the liby. of Zola E. Harvey. (SG. Mar.19; 175) $825

STOWE, Harriet Beecher
- Uncle Tom's Cabin. Boston, 1852. 1st. Edn., 1st. Iss. 2 vols. Orig. cl., some wear, qtr. mor. s.-c. Pres. Copy., to Mr. Fleece, laid in are an autograph quotation (sigd. by Stowe), & 7 lines in her hand on a sm. slip of paper; from the Prescott Collection. (CNY. Feb.6; 307) $7,500
– – Anr. Copy. 12mo. Pict. wraps. reprd., hf. mor. s.-c. (SG. Oct.9; 235) $800
– – Anr. Copy. With Hobart & Robbins imprint on title verso, shaken, some spotting. Orig. cl., worn, some stains. (SPB. Nov.25; 211) $600
– – Anr. Copy. 12mo. Orig. cl., worn, qtr. cf. s.-c. A.L.s. laid in. (CNY. May 22; 276) $200
– – Anr. Edn. Boston, 1852. 1st. Edn. 2 vols. 12mo. Some foxing. Lev., gt.-tooled with floral design, spines unif. gt., by MacDonald, orig. cl. covers used as lining papers, & spines mntd. on blank ll. Sig. of H.M. Robbins on fly-lf. (SG. Dec.18; 381) $325

STOWE, Harriet Beecher–FIELDS, Annie
- The Writings.–The Life & Letters of Harriet Beecher Stowe. Camb., 1894; 1897. (250) sigd. by Mrs. Stowe. 17 vols. Unif. hf. red mor., gt. A.L.s. by Mr. Stowe tipped in. (SPB. May 6; 346) $1,300

STOWE: A Description of the Magnificent House & Gardens
1773. New Edn. 1 plt. cleanly torn, slight browning. Cont. sheep, worn. (CSK. Mar.13; 1) £75

STOWITTS, Hubert
- Le Oeuvre de . . . Paris, [1927]. (200) numbered. Sq. fo. Gold-decor. simulated limp leath. wraps. (SG. Apr.2; 281) $400

STRABO
- De Situ Orbis. Venice, 1510. Fo. Slight worming & staining, contents loose in bdg., full-p. Latin poem in early hand before title. Old vell. (SG. Feb.5; 314) $260
- Geographicarum. Ed.:– Thomas Falconer. Oxford, 1867. 2 vols. Fo. 19th. C. hf. cf., jnts. split. (S. Nov.25; 544) Crete. £95
- Rerum Geographicarum libri XVII . . . Amst., 1707. Fo. Cont. decor. ivory vell., fillet & centre oriental style plaque. Old MS notes. (HD. Feb.18; 74) Frs. 1,100

STRACK, [C.F.L.]
- Naturgeschichte in Bildern. Düsseldorf, [1819-26]. 1st. Edn. 56 pts. in 4 vols. Ob. 4to. Slightly soiled or browned in parts. Cont. leath. & hf. leath. (vol. 4). Not collated. (HK. May 12-14; 444) DM 6,200

STRADA, Famianus
- De Bello Belgico. The History of the Low Country Wars. Trans.:– Sir Richard Stapylton. 1650. 1st. Engl. Edn. 4to. A few holes, slightly affecting text. Mod. mor.-bkd. bds., gt. arms on upr. cover. [Wing S5777] (S. Sep.29; 116) Trotman. £60
- Histoire de la Guerre de Flandre.–Supplement à l'Histoire des Guerres Civiles de Flandre sous Philippe II. Trans.:– P. Du-ryer. Brussels, Amst., 1712; 1729. 1st. work 3 vols., 2nd. work 2 vols., together 5 vols. 12mo; fo. 2nd. work, title-p. defect. 1st. work, old cf. gt., 2nd. work cf., brkn. (SG. Oct.30; 345) $200

STRADA FERRATA DA VENEZIA A MILANO
Venice, 1837. 4to. Some stains. Mod. hf. vell. (SI. Dec.4; 548) Lire 200,000

STRADA, Jacobus de
- Imperatorum Romanorum Omnium Orientalium et Occidentalium Verissimae Imagines. Ill.:– P. Flötner [decor.]. Zürich, 1559. Lge. fo. 1st. ll. with sm. hole & margin stain, title slightly soiled, lf. 88 stained in port., upr. margin cut short in places. Cont. blind-tooled pig, soiled & wormed, worn. Lf. 50 sigd. & dtd. by Flötner. (H. May 21/22; 956) DM 4,200

STRADANUS, Johannes
- Equile Ioannis Austriaci Caroli V. N.p., ca. 1620. Ob. fo. Engraved dedication cut down & mntd., 26 engraved plts., 2 cut down & mntd., some loose. 18th. C. bds., worn. As a collection, w.a.f. (S. Nov.25; 369) Broseghini. £450
– – Anr. Edn. N.p., ca. 1680. Fo. Engraved title & 37 engraved plts., all cut down & mntd. 19th. C. hf. str.-grd. mor. As a collection, w.a.f. (S. Nov.25; 418) Broseghini. £600
- Venationes Ferarum, Avium Piscium. Ill.:– after Straet. [Antw.], [1580]. Ob. fo. Lacks title-p., bnd. with an additional 17 various plts., some margins torn & soiled, many rebkd., some other defects. Later cf.-bkd. bds., very worn. (SBA. Dec.16; 41) Broseghini. £1,200

STRADANUS, Johannes–DE WITT, F.–NICOLAES de Bruyn
- Venationes Ferrarum, Avium, Piscium.–Jacht en Veld-Tuych.–Libellus Varia Genere Piscium Complectens. Ed.:– Philippo Gallaeo [1st. work]. [Antw. (1st. work)], ca. 1580; n.d.; n.d. 3 works in 1 vol. Ob. fo. 1st. work: minor stains, some plts. slightly browned towards edges; 2nd. work: 11 plts. numbered 2-12; 3rd. work: 10 plts. (only?); all plts. trimmed & mntd. on larger sheets. Old hf. cf., worn, upr. cover detchd. As a coll. of prints, w.a.f., from Chetham's Liby., Manchester. (C. Nov.20; 285) King. £950

STRADLING, Sir John
- Divine Poems. 1625. 1st. Edn. 4to. Lacks initial blank, a few blank margins just frayed. Old vell., very worn. Early inscrs., MS. inscrs. (Charles Kenney (?), Mrs. Katherine Vaughan). [STC 23353] (S. May 5; 275) Quaritch. £400

STRAHLHEIM, C.
- Die Wundermappe. Frankfurt, 1834-36. Bd. 1; Italy; 3 vols. in 2. Pt. 2 lacks 2 plts. Cont. hf. linen. (R. Oct.14-18; 1933) DM 600
– – Anr. Edn. Frankfurt, 1835-37. Vols. 6 & 9 together in 1 vol. Lightly soiled. Cont. hf. linen., loose. (R. Mar.31-Apr.4; 2564) DM 520
– – Anr. Edn. Frankfurt, 1836. Lge. 8vo. Slightly soiled, lacks 1 plt. No bdg. (R. Oct.14-18; 2026) DM 1,400
– – Anr. Edn. Frankfurt, 1837. Band 5: Norddeutschland. Lightly soiled. Cont. hf. linen. (R. Oct.14-18; 2124) DM 7,500
– – Anr. Copy. Band 4: Süd-Deutschland. 61 (of 67) engrs., lightly soiled. (R. Oct.14-18; 2123) DM 4,000

STRAHORN, Carrie Adell
- Fifteen Thousand Miles by Stage. Ill.:– Charles M. Russell. N.Y., 1911. 1st. Edn. Gt. cl. (PNY. Mar.26; 309) $100

STRANA MECHTY [Land of Dreams]
Ed.:– [S.M. Federov]. St. Petersb., 1906. No. 1. 4to. Unbnd. (SH. Feb.5; 132) Landry. £95

STRAND, Paul
- The Mexican Portfolio. [N.Y.], [1967]. (1,000), numbered, sigd. Fo. Loose as iss. in buckram portfo. & bd. s.-c. (SG. Apr.23; 190) $600
- A Retrospective Monograph: The Years 1915-1946.–. . . The years 1950-1968. [Millerton], [1971]. Together 2 vols. Lge. 4to. Both cl., d.-w.'s (reprd.). (SG. Jul.9; 311) $150
- Tir a'Mhurain: Outer Hebrides. Ed.:– Basil Davidson [commentary]. L., [1962]. 1st. Edn. 4to. Cl. (SG. Apr.23; 189) $130

STRAND MAGAZINE (The)
1891-1917. Vols. 1-54. Orig. cl., some soiling. (CSK. May 29; 39) £60
– – Anr. Run. Ed.:– George Newnes. L., Jul. 1891-Dec. 1896. Vols. 2-12. Slight browning. Orig. decor. bdgs., soiled. (SPB. May 29; 317) $175

STRANGE, Edward F.
- The Colour-Prints of Hiroshige. N.d. (250) numbered. 4to. Orig. vell. bds. (SH. Jan.29; 154) George's. £125

– – Anr. Copy. Slightly spotted. (CSK. Feb.20; 187) £100

STRANGE, Sir Robert
– A Collection of Historical Prints . . . [1787 or later]. Fo. 50 engraved plts., some dbl.-p., some plts. dtd. from 1753-1787, engd. plt. loosely inserted. Cont. hf. russ., spine gt., upr. cover detchd., worn. (S. Nov.24; 267) *Honan.* £500
– – Anr. Edn. [L.], ca. 1790. Lge. fo. Knife-slit in plt. 42, slight spotting. Cont. red str.-grd. mor., gt., Greek key-pattern to borders, flat spine gt., slightly worn. (S. Jun.22; 97) *Erlini.* £320

STRANGEWAYS, Thomas
– Sketch of the Mosquito Shore. Edinb., 1832. 1st. Edn. Lev. mor. by Sangorski & Sutcliffe. [Sabin 92722] (C. Nov.6; 230) *Burton Garbett.* £150

STRAPAROLA, Giovanni Francesco
– Les Facecieuses Nuicts . . .–Le Second et Dernier Livre des Facecieuses Nuicts . . . Trans.:– Louveau (book 1); De Larivey (book 2). Lyons, 1596. 2 vols. 16mo. Red mor. by Lortic, blind-tooled fillets on covers & spines, inside dentelle. (HD. Mar.18; 164) Frs. 2,800

STRATTON, Arthur
See–GARNER, Thomas & Stratton, Arthur

STRATTON, Ezra M.
– The World on Wheels. N.Y., Priv. Ptd. 1878. 1st. Edn. Mod. buckram, ex-liby., remainder of circulation slip on front end-paper. (SG. Dec.11; 197) $180

STRATTON, R(oyal) B.
– Captivity of the Oatman Girls . . . Chic., 1857. 1st. Chic. printing. 12mo. Remnants of pencil tracings on port. & title, tear at pp. 83-86, affecting text & 2 plts., slight foxing. Orig. blind-stpd. cl., upr. cover gt., rebkd. From liby. of William E. Wilson. (SPB. Apr.29; 256) $275

STRAUCH, Egidius
See–WEIGEL, Erhard–TAUST, J.G.–MADWEIS, F.-STRAUCH, Egidius

STRAUSS, Richard
– Printed Score of Arabella. Berlin, 1933. Sm. fo. Wraps., disbnd. Sigd. & dtd. Sep. 9 1945. (PNY. Mar.26; 453) $300

STRAUSS, W.
– Von Eisernem Pferden und Pfaden. Hannover, 1924. 4to. Orig. linen. (R. Mar.31-Apr.4; 1163) DM 580

STRECKER, C.C.
– Auf den Diamanten und Goldfeldern Südafricas. Freiburg, 1901. Pict. cl. (SSA. Jan.22; 366) R. 110

STREET, George Edmund
– Brick & Marble in the Middle Ages: notes of a Tour in the North of Italy. L., 1855. 1st. Edn. Orig. cl., spine torn. (CB. May 27; 193) Can. $160
– The Cathedral Church of the Holy Trinity. 1882. Plts. & ills., some mntd., slightly spotted. Orig. decor. vell., soiled. Pres. copy from the publishers. (CSK. Mar.27; 94) £60

STREETE, Thomas
– Astronomia Carolina. A New Theorie of the Coelestial Motions. 1661. 1st. Edn. Sm. 4to. Some browning & slight soiling. Cont. sheep, stitching loose, worn, red hf. mor. case. Bkplt. of Francis North, Baron of Guilford, 1703; from Honeyman Collection. (S. May 19; 2926) *Quaritch.* £400

STREETER, Thomas Winthrop
– Bibliography of Texas. Camb., 1955-60. (600). 5 vols. Cl., d.-w.'s. (SG. Jan.22; 367) $650
– The Celebrated Collection of Americana. N.Y., 1966-1969. 7 vols. & index, tog. 8 vols. 4to. Facs. title-pp. Bds. (SG. Oct.2; 342) $350
– – Anr. Edn. N.Y., 1966-70. 9 vols. including dupl. of vol. 4 & index. 4to. Orig. bds. (SH. Jul.9; 198) *Talerman.* £140
– – Anr. Copy. 8 vols. (including Index). Bds. (SG. Jun.11; 401) $450

STREETON, Arthur
– The Art of Arthur Streeton. Ed.:– S. Ure Smith, B. Stevens & C. Lloyd Jones. Sydney, 1919. (1500). 4to. Pp. foxed. Bds. stained. (JL. Jul.20; 702) *Aus.* $140

STREETT, William B.
– Gentlemen Up. N.Y., Derry Pr. 1930. [75] numbered on L.P. 4to. Hf. mor. gt., cl. very

slightly soiled. With an orig. dry-point sigd. by Paul Brown, sigd. on hf.-titles. (CNY. Oct.1; 162) $1,100

STREICH, T.F. & Gerstenberg, K. von
– Arbeitsstätten der wichtigsten Handwerker. Ill.:– after T.F. Streich. Esslingen, 1875. 4to. Lacks 4 pp. Cont. hf. linen. (R. Oct.14-18; 2649) DM 2,100

STRELY [Arrows]
Ed.:– [I.M. Knorozovsky]. St. Petersb., 1905-06. Nos. 1-9. 4to. Unbnd. (SH. Feb.5; 133) *Landry.* £200

STRICKLAND, Agnes
– Lives of the Queens of England. L., 1841. 12 vols. Hf. cf. gt. Edward Lear's copy with his sig. & dtd. 'Roma Apr. 1844' on front free end-paper. (SPB. Nov.25; 493) $225
– – Anr. Edn. 1842-48. 12 vols. Hf. mor., spines gt. (SKC. Feb.26; 1482) £50
– – Anr. Edn. L., 1866. 8 vols. Mor. (SSA. Apr.22; 78) R. 100

STRICKLAND, Hugh Edwin & Melville, A.G.
– The Dodo & its Kindred, or the history, affinities, & osteology of the Dodo, Solitaire & other extinct birds. 1848. 4to. Orig. cl. (C. Feb.25; 140) *Henderson.* £130

STRIGELIUS, Victorinuš
– Arithmeticus Libellus. Leipzig, [1563]. 1st & only Edn. 1629 dtd. owner's mark on title-lf. Mod. bds. (R. Mar.31-Apr.4; 1198) DM 450
– Epitome Doctrinae de Primo Motu Aliquot Demonstrationibus Illustrata. Leipzig, [1564]. 1st. Edn. Lacks last lf., some fore-margins slightly stained. Mod. bds. From Honeyman Collection. (S. May 19; 2928) *Howell.* £140

STRIGELIUS, Victorinus–FRISIUS, Gemma
– Arithmeticus libellus continens non modo praecepta nota et usitata, sed etiam demonstrationes praeceptorum.–Arithmeticae Practicae Methodus Facilis. Leipzig, [1563]; 1565. 1st. work 1st. Edn. 2 works in 1 vol. 1st. work lacks final blank, title slightly soiled, sm. tear in B2, hole in Cl. affecting a few letters. 18th. C. hf. cf. Bkplts. of Christian Friedrich Eberhard of Leipzig & Michael Chasles; from Honeyman Collection. (S. May 19; 2927) *Schaffer.* £80

STRINDBERG, A.
– Werke. Trans.:– E. Schering. Munich, 1917-21 Orig. hf. leath. (H. Dec.9/10; 2360) DM 500

STROEHLIN, P.C.
– Collections Numismatiques. Geneva & L., 1909-11. 3 vols. 4to. Orig. wraps., torn, vol. 1 in mod. cl. (SH. Mar.6; 456) *Spink.* £85

STROMER, Heinrich
– Algorithmus Linealis Numerationé Additionez Subtractioné: Duplationé: Mediationé . . . Leipzig, 1512. Sm. 4to. Mod. wraps., red hf. mor. case. From Honeyman Collection. (S. May 19; 2929) *Goldschmidt.* £160

STRONG, A.B.
– The American Flora. N.Y., 1848-50. 1st. Edn. 4 vols. Lacks 55 plts., some foxing, stains, & marginal fraying. Orig. gt.-stpd. roan, crudely rebkd. W.a.f. (SG. Jan.29; 395) $400

STRONG, Leonard Alfred George
– Common Sense about Drama. Corvinus Pr., Jan. 1937. 1st. Edn., (30) numbered, sigd. Orig. limp vell., silk ties, s.-c. (S. Jul.31; 138) *Bertram Rota.* £65
– The Hansom Cab & the Pigeons. Ill.:– Eric Ravilious. Gold. Cock. Pr., 1935. (212) sigd. Mor., circular inset panel on both covers with onlaid figure, front view on upr. cover, rear view on lr. cover, cf. doubls., palladian edges, sigd., fitted case, by Angela James. (SH. Feb.20; 403) *Quaritch.* £500
– Two Stories. Corvinus Pr., [1936]. 1st. Edn., (60) numbered, sigd. Orig. vell.-bkd. linen, s.-c. (S. Jul.31; 136) *Foyles.* £70

STROOBANT, François
– Vues de la Belgique. [?Brussels], Mid-19th. C. Ob. 4to. 41 tinted litho. plts., no title or text, loose. Cont. red hf. roan, worn. W.a.f. (S. Nov.24; 268) *A. Stewart.* £170

STROTHER, David H.
[–] The Blackwater Chronicle. N.Y., 1853. 1st. Edn. Lge. 12mo. Mod. three-qtr. mor. (SG. Oct.16; 466) $170

STROZZI COLLECTION
– Médailles Grecques et Romaines. Rome, 1907. Orig. wraps., spine torn. (SH. Mar.6; 457) *Trade Art.* £65

STRUCK, Hermann
– Die Kunst des Radierens. Ill.:– Baum, Liebermann, Munch, Struck & Zorn. Berlin, [1908]. 1st. Edn. Sm. 4to. Orig. paper bds. spine pasted over, sm. tear. (H. Dec.9/10; 2362) DM 520
– – Anr. Edn. Ill.:– P. Baum, M. Liebermann, E. Munch, A. Zorn, M. Slevogt. Berlin, [1912]. 2nd. Edn. 4to. Orig. ills. Orig. bds. (R. Oct.14-18; 770) DM 480
– – Anr. Edn. Berlin, 1919. Orig. bds., head of spine slightly defect. (R. Mar.31-Apr.4; 922) DM 460
– – Anr. Edn. Ill.:– M. Liebermann, P. Baum, H. Meid, E. Munch & H. Struck (etchings), M. Slevogt (litho.). Berlin, [1919]. 3rd. Iss. Orig. bds. 6 orig. ills. (H. May 21/22; 1828) DM 420
– – Anr. Edn. Ill.:– Liebermann, Baum, Meid & others. Berlin, [1920]. 4to. Orig. pict. bds. 6 orig. ills. (HK. May 12-14; 2076) DM 540
– – Anr. Copy. Orig. paper bds., lacks lr. cover. (H. Dec.9/10; 2363) DM 470
– – Anr. Edn. Ill.:– Liebermann, Kokoschka & Barlach. 1923. Sm. 4to. Orig. linen. (H. Dec.9/10; 2364) DM 500

STRUTT, Jacob George
– Sylva Britannica. 1822-[26]. Fo. Light foxing. Cont. hf. mor., gt. (S. Dec.3; 1146) *Litman.* £180
– Sylva Britannica . . . [with Sylva Scotica]. 1826. 2 pts. in 1 vol. fo. India proofs, no title to 2nd pt. Cont. hf. russ. gt., unc. (SBA. Jul.23; 352) *Astair.* £120
– Sylva Britannica; or, Portraits of Forest Trees. –Deliciae Sylvarum. 1822; [1828]. 2 works in 1 vol. Fo. Slight marginal foxing. Cont. hf. mor., gt. by B. Hunt of Birmingham with his ticket, worn. (S. Jun.1; 224) *Maggs Brothers.* £320

STRUTT, Joseph
– A Biographical Dictionary. 1785-86. 1st. Edn. 2 vols. 4to. Cont. spr. cf., gt. key-pattern borders on sides, gt. spines. (C. Nov.5; 157) *Rota.* £60
– A Compleat View of the Manners, Customs, Arms, Habits, & c. of the Inhabitants of England. 1775-76. 3 vols. Lacks 9 ills., 1 or 2 trimmed at fore-e. Cont. Fr. mor., triple gt. fillet, spine gt. in compartments with sm. single fleuron in circle, inner gt. dentelles. Bkplt. of Henry Drummond of Albury Park, Surrey. (SM. Oct.8; 2021) Frs. 1,100
– – Anr. Edn. 1796-99. 1st. Edn. 2 vols. 4to. Frontis's. & 1 title detchd., some spotting & browning, some offsetting to titles. Cont. cf., gt., spines gt., 2 covers detchd., worn. (S. Sep.29; 270) *Sereni.* £160
– – Anr. Edn. 1842. 2 vols. 4to. Plts. loose. Cont. hf. mor. (SH. Nov.6; 159) *Matthews.* £100
– Glig-Gamena Angel-Deod. 1801. 1st. Edn. 4to. Str.-grd. mor. gt. by A.S. Colley. (C. May 20; 58) *Traylen.* £110
– – Anr. Copy. Cont. cf., spine gt., front end-papers dampstained. (C. Nov.5; 158) *McKenzie.* £75
– – Anr. Copy. Wide margins. Cont. diced cf. gt., gt. inner dentelles. (LC. Feb.12; 157) £50
– – Anr. Edn. [1801]. 4to. Lacks title-p. & 1st. lf. of introduction. Cont. cf., gt. decor. spine. (TA. Nov.20; 97) £60
– – Anr. Edn. 1810. 2nd. Edn. 4to. Red mor. gt., slightly worn & discold. (SKC. May 19; 533) £50
– – Anr. Copy. Hf. cf., rebkd. Grahame Pollard's bkplt. (P. Jul.2; 50) *Laughton.* £50
– Horda Angel-Cynnan. 1775-76. 3 vols. 4to. Cont. cf., spines gt., lacks some labels. (C. Nov.5; 159) *Allan.* £50
– The Regal & Ecclesiastical Antiquities of England.–A Complete View of the Dress & Habits of the People of England. 1793; 1796-99. 1 vol.; 2 vols. 4to. Some ll. spotted. Cont. cf., worn, covers detchd. (SH. May 21; 114) *Ayres.* £60
– Works. [Collection of] 1774-1842. 9 vols. 4to. Engraved & litho. plts., some heightened with silver & gold. Unif. mor., sides with elab. gt. borders, spines gt. in compartments, by Clarke. (C. Mar.18; 112) *Traylen.* £1,400

STRUVE, Friedrich Georg Wilhelm
– Catalogus Novus Stellarum Duplicium et Multiplicium. Dorpat, 1827. 1st. Edn. Fo. Cont. hf. russ., spine defect., cl. case. Sir John

STRUVE, Friedrich Georg Wilhelm – Catalogus Novus Stellarum Duplicium et Multiplicium. *-contd.*
Herschel's copy, tables interleaved thro.-out with many additions in his hand; from Honeyman Collection. (S. May 19; 2931) *Quaritch.* £580
– **Description de l'Observatoire Astronomique Central de Poulkova.** St. Petersb., 1845. 1st. Edn. 2 vols. including atlas of plts. 4to. Plt. 34 reprd., a few plt. numbers cropped, slight foxing. Text in hf. cf., jnts. brkn., very worn; plts. in new cl. Columbia University liby. dupls. with stps.; from Honeyman Collection. (S. May 19; 2933)
Zeitlin & Verbrugge. £180
– **Etudes d'Astronomie Stellaire. Sur la Voie Lactée et sur la Distance des Etoiles Fixes.** St. Petersb., 1847. 1st. Edn. Foxed thro.-out. Cont. cf.-bkd. cl., rebkd., old gt. spine preserved, cl. case. Stp. of Bibliotheque de San Donato; bkplt. of Prince Rolan Bonaparte; from Honeyman Collection. (S. May 19; 2934) *Quaritch.* £160
– **Stellarum Duplicium et Multiplicium Mensurae Micrometricae.** St. Petersb., 1837. 1st. Edn. Fo. Text browned. Cont. tree cf., gt. spine, worn. From Honeyman Collection. (S. May 19; 2932)
Quaritch. £320

STRUYS, Jan
– **Reysen, door Italien, Griekenlandt, Lijsland, Moscovien, Tartarijen, Meden, Persien, Oost-Indien, Japan, en verscheyden andere Gewesten.** Amst., 1686. 2 pts. in 1 vol. 4to. Sm. holes in Tenos & Scamachie plts., slight worming in upr. inner margins from Z3 to end. Cont. vell. bds., some wear & soiling. (S. Nov.4; 465)
Crete. £160
– **Les Voyages ... en Moscovie, en Tartarie, en Perse, aux Index.** Amst., 1720. 3 vols., 2 pts. in vol. III. 12mo. Lacks 1st. ll. (blanks?), 2 plts. reprd. on blank verso, single wormhole affecting catchwords in vol. III. Cont. spr. cf., triple gt. fillet, spines gt. in compartments with wheatsheaf motif, inner gt. dentelles, single wormhole thro. covers of vol. III & upr.-cover of vol. II. (SM. Oct.8; 2022) Frs. 2,800

STRYPE, John
– **Historical & Biographical Works.** Oxford, 1812-28. L.P. Edn., (50). 26 vols. Mor., multiple gt. fillet borders, gt. panel. spines, 2 bdgs. brkn. (SG. Dec.18; 382) $130

STUART, Alexander
– **Dissertatio de Structure et Motu Musculari.** 1738. 4to. Stp. of the Edinb. Medical Society with inscr. on title & stps. on plts. Marb. bds., rebkd. mor. (S. Jun.17; 807) *Norman.* £50

STUART, Charles B.
– **The Naval & Mail Steamers of the United States.** N.Y., 1853. 4to. Lacks 1 diagram. Cont. hf. cf., brkn. (TA. Jan.22; 231) £95

STUART, Charles Edward
See–STUART, John Sobieski Stolberg & Stuart, Charles Edward

STUART, Gilbert
– **View of Society in Europe.** 1778. 4to. Cf. gt. (P. Jan.22; 30) *Traylen.* £120

STUART, James A.B. of Armagh
– **Historical Memoirs of the City of Armagh.** Newry, 1819. Orig. bds., unc. (GM. Apr.30; 248)
£52

STUART, James, Architect & Revett, Nicholas
– **Die Alterthumer zu Athen.** Ca. 1840. 2nd. Edn. Fo. Some plts. on india paper, some spotting. Orig. cl., spine defect. (TA. Mar.19; 603) £60
– **Les Antiquités d'Athènes ...** Trans.:– [Laurent François Feuillet]. Paris, 1808-12. 1st. Edn. in Fr. Vols. 1-3, lacks vol. 4. Fo. Sm. liby. blind-stp. on titles. Cont. cf.-bkd. bds., worn. (S. Nov.25; 545) *Finopoulos.* £200
– **The Antiquities of Athens.** 1762-94. 1st. Edns. Vols. I-III only (of 4). Fo. Cont. cf., gt. Bkplts. of Dogmersfield Liby. & C.M.G. Keeping. (S. Jun.22; 148) *Dimakrakos.* £850
– – **Anr. Edn.** 1762-87-94. 1st. Edn., 2nd. Iss. 3 vols. (of 5), without supps. Fo. Without subscription list, 230 (of 232) engraved maps & plts. 1 map hand-cold. in outl., a few ll. slightly spotted, a few minor defects. Cont. russ. gt., 1 cover detchd. (SBA. Dec.16; 95) *Santa.* £600
– – **Anr. Edn.** L., 1762-87-94-1816. 1st. Edn., 2nd. Iss. 4 vols. Fo. 317 (of 319) copper-plts., errata correctly spelt, some plts. stpd. 3 vols. in mod.

buckram, vol. 2 disbnd., ex-liby. (SG. Dec.4; 332) $1,300
– – **Anr. Edn.** 1762-1816. 1st. Edn. 4 vols. (of 5, lacks 1830 'Supplement'). Fo. Plts. V-VI in Chapter X of vol. III, neither called for in plt.-list or index, lacks. plt. 29 in Chapter I of vol. II, occasional spotting & light offsetting. 19th. C. russ, spines gt., 5 covers detchd., others loose, worn. (S. Sep.29; 190) *Elmassian.* £900
– – **Anr. Copy.** 4 vols., lacks final Supp. vol. Occasional offsetting & light foxing, edge of frontis. in vol. IV dampstained. Cont. pol. russ., gt. spines. (C. Feb.25; 206) *Demacaraco.* £850
– – **Anr. Edn.** Ill.:– J. Basire. L., 1762-1830. 1st. Edn. 5 vols. Fo. Foxed, ink smudge affecting 1 plt. in vol. I. Hf. cf. W.a.f. (SPB. May 6; 260) $1,700
– – **Anr. Edn.** 1762-1830. 1st. Edn., L.P. 5 vols. including Supp. Lge. fo. Late 19th. C. mor. by Bedford, gt., spines tooled in compartments, covers with elab. borders, gt. inside borders. (S. Nov.24; 269) *McCabe.* £2,800
– – **Anr. Edn.** 1825-30. New Edn. 4 vols. including Supp. Fo. Additional 'corrected plt.' of number 3 in Cockerell section in vol. 4, some plts. & text sections misbnd., lacks hf.-title to vol. 2, 1 plt. partly detchd. Cont. hf. russ., spines defect., worn. (S. Nov.25; 546) *Karakos.* £280
– – **Anr. Copy.** Lacks 3 (of 193) engraved plts. Orig. bds., cl. spines, vol. 2 brkn. (C. Nov.6; 193) *Mondale.* £180
– – **Anr. Copy.** Engraved titles, 2 ports., frontis. & 180 plts. only, dampstained. Cont. hf. mor. W.a.f. (CSK. Mar.6; 106) £100
– – **Anr. Copy.** Foxed, some plts. stpd. Three-qtr. mor., ex-liby. (SG. Dec.4; 333) $425

STUART, John McDouall
– **Explorations in Australia: The Journals ... during the years 1858, 1859, 1860, 1861 & 1862.** Ed.:– William Hardman. L., 1864. Occasional foxing or soiling. Orig. cl., unc., soiled, jnts. reprd. (KH. Nov.18; 566) *Aus.* $450

STUART, John Sobieski Stolberg
– **Vestiarium Scoticum.** Edinb., 1842. [1st. Edn.?]. Fo. Crimson mor. with gt. coat of arms. (CE. Nov.20; 139) £110
– – **Anr. Copy.** Short tear in hf. title. Orig. red mor., gt. arms on covers, rebkd., slightly worn. (S. Jun.23; 340) *Lord Dacre.* £100
– – **Anr. Copy.** Fo. 2 plts. with slight soiling. Cont. hf. red mor., covers worn. (S. Jun.23; 341) *Elliott.* £120

STUART John Sobieski Stolberg & Stuart, Charles Edward
– **Costume of the Clans.** Edinb., 1845. Fo. Hf. mor., worn. (CE. Nov.20; 26) £200
– – **Anr. Copy.** Atlas fo. Cl., blind stp., upr. cover loose, badly worn. (PD. Aug.20; 10) £50
– – **Anr. Edn.** Edinb., 1892. (500). Atlas fo. Cl. mor. bkd., sm. tear on spine, head & tail of spine frayed. (PD. Aug.20; 257) £100

STUART, Martinus & Kuyper, Jaques
– **De Mensch.** Amst., 1802-18. 6 vols. Mod. hf. cl. (SH. Jul.23; 134) *Van der Wijk.* £160

STUART, Robert
– **Historical & Descriptive Anecdotes of Steam-Engines.** 1829. 1st. Edn. 2 vols. 12mo. Plts. in vol. I slightly stained. Orig. cl., stained, unc., vol. I detchd. from bdg. From Honeyman Collection. (S. May 19; 2935) *Dr. Martin.* £90

STUBBS, George
– **The Anatomy of the Horse.** Priv. Ptd. 1766. 1st. Edn., 1st. Iss.(?). Ob. fo. Plts. on thick paper (not wtrmkd.), title with 18th. C. watermark of Strasburg lily & bend, title & some text ll. creased, minor offset to a few key plts. Cont. diced russ., worn. From Chetham's Liby., Manchester. (C. Nov.27; 379) *Fletcher.* £1,500
– – **Anr. Edn.** 1766. Ob. fo. Some plts. wtrmkd. 1823, some staining, mostly marginal, title & 1 plt. creased & with marginal tears. Hf. roan, worn. (SH. Jul.27; 307) *Franks.* £340
– – **Anr. Edn.** 1853. Fo. Slight spotting. Orig. cl., worn. (SKC. Jul.28; 2502) £65
– – **Anr. Edn.** Ed.:– J.C. McCunn & C.W. Ottaway. L., 1938. Fo. Qtr. cl., covers slightly soiled, sm. stains on spine. (CB. Dec.9; 133) Can. $140

STUBBS, George & others
– **A Comparative View ... of the English Racer & Saddle-Horse during the Last & Present Centuries.** L., 1836. 4to. Some plts. foxed, some ll. loose.

Orig. cl., brkn. in spine. (CB. Dec.9; 131) Can. $240

STUCKIUS, Johannes Guilelmus
– **Operum Tomus Primus ... [Tomus Secundus ...].** Leiden & Amst., 1695. 2 vols. in 1. Fo. Cont. vell. bds., gt. statuesque emblem of The Hague on covers, soiled. From liby. of André L. Simon. (S. May 18; 185) *Thomas.* £55

STUDER, Gottlieb
– **Die Eis-Wuesten und Selten-Betretenen Hochberge und Bergspitzen des Cantons Bern.** Bern & St. Gallen, 1844. 2nd. Edn. 2 vols. including atlas. 12mo. Pict. bds., orig. box. (SG. Feb.26; 314) $450

STUDIA PATRISTICA
Berlin, 1957-76. 14 vols. (B. Dec.10/11; 1277) Fls. 725

STUDIO, The – **An Illustrated Magazine of Fine & Applied Art.** 1893-1907. Vols. 1-42 but lacks 6 vols. Fo. Orig. cl., bds. with linen backstrip. (TA. Sep.18; 205) £195
– – **Anr. Run.** 1893-1913. Vols. 1-58 in 233 orig. pts. 4to. Lacks pts. 28, 78, 83, 84, 141, 146 & 148. Orig. wraps., some soiled & worn, together with 8 dupl. pts., 3 'Studio Special Numbers', & unused cl. case for pt. 1. (CSK. Nov.28; 163) £350
– – **Anr. Run.** 1901-09. 21 vols. Fo. Bnd. for the Chelsea Arts Club in cont. unif. hf. mor., worn. W.a.f. (TA. Apr.16; 354) £110
– – **Anr. Run.** 1908-30. Vols. 56-75, 81-100, & 2 other part vols., together in 32 vols. 4to. No advts. 1 vol. disbnd., rest in cont. cl. (SH. Oct.9; 193) *Ars Artis.* £120
– – **Anr. Run.** Jul.-Dec. 1934, 1935-38, Jan.-Jun. 1939. 10 vols. 4to. Cont. cf. gt. (SD. Feb.4; 150) £60

STUDIO Year Book of Applied Art
L., Paris, N.Y., for 1906-19, & 1921. 15 vols. 4to. Liby. stps. Liby buckram, first 2 vols. need rebdg. (SG. Mar.12; 359) $300

STUKELEY, William
– **Itinerarium Curiosum.** 1776. 2nd. Edn. 2 vols. 4to. 19th. C. russ. gt., 2 covers detchd. Wadham Wyndham bkplt. (S. Nov.24; 272) *Weinreb.* £300
– – **Anr. Copy.** 2 vols. in 1. Fo. Cont. cf., gt. panel on covers enclosing Greek urn device at head of curciform central ornament, spine worn, upr. cover detchd. (C. Feb.25; 60) *Crowe.* £200
– **Palaeographia Britannica: or, Discourses on Antiquities in Britain.** Stamford, 1746. Number II. 4to. Cont. cf. gt. Pres. copy with author's autograph corrections in text. (SBA. Oct.22; 426) *Quaritch.* £75
– **Stonehenge.** 1740-43. 1st. Edn. 2 vols. in 1. Fo. Vol. 1 lacks directions to binder lf., tear in 1 lge. plt., marginal tear in another. 19th. C. russ. gt., 2 jnts. split, slightly defect. at head. Wadham Wyndham bkplt. (S. Nov.24; 271)
Quaritch. £300

STUMPF, Johann
– **Gemeiner Loblicher Eydgnoschafft Stetten Landen und Volckeren Chronick widriger Thaaten Beschreybung.** Zurich, 1548. 6 pts. (only, of 13, but with dupl. of pt. 4) in 2 vols. Fo. Lacks Z2, Ii5 & Kk2 (dupls.), & EE3, lge. piece cut from lr. fore-corner of title, & the whole mntd., numerous defects, many crudely reprd., several affecting text, some browning & staining. Cont. blind-stpd. pig over wood bds. with clasps, spine worn (1st. vol.), & later cf., worn. W.a.f. (S. Feb.10; 242) *Ancien.* £400

STUMPF, P.
– **Bayern.** München, 1853. Cont. hf. leath. (R. Oct.14-18; 2217) DM 4,000

STURGE, Joseph & Harvey, Thomas
– **The West Indies in 1837.** L., 1838. 2nd. Edn. Mod. three-qtr. mor., spine gt. (SG. Feb.26; 309) $180

STURM, Johann Christoph
– **Collegium Experimentale sive Curiosum.** Nuremb., 1676. 1st. Edn. 2 pts. in 1 vol. Sm. 4to. 3 folding plts. with tears, partly reprd., some marginal stains, without the Appendices or Epistola. 18th. C. hf. cf., worn. (S. Jul.27; 383) *Rota.* £75
– **Mathesis Juvenilis; or a Course of Mathematicks.** 1709-08. 3 vols. A few tears, browned. Cont. cf., spines worn. (SH. Jun.11; 225) *Quaritch.* £50

- **Project de la Resolution du Fameux Probleme Touchant la Longitude sur Mer.** Nuremb., 1720. 1st. Edn. 4to. Mod. bds. From Honeyman Collection. (S. May 19; 2938) *McKittrick.* £280

STURT, Capt. Charles
- **Narrative of an Expedition into Central Australia.** L., 1849. 2 vols. No tipped-in advt. slip, long tear in blank inner margin of folding map. Early qtr. mor. (KH. Nov.18; 568) Aus. $700
- **Two Expeditions into the Interior of Southern Australia.** 1833. 1st. Edn. 2 vols. Orig. bds., unopened, rebkd. with cf. (S. Mar.31; 507) *Ryman.* £280

STURTEVANT, Simon
- **Metallica, or the Treatise of metallica . . .** 22 May, 1612. 1st. Edn. 4to. Cont. limp vell., gt. [NSTC 23411] (S. Jun.23; 290) *Goldschmidt.* £420

STYLES, John
- **An Essay on the Character, Immoral, & Antichristian Tendency of the Stage.** Newport, Isle of Wight, priv. ptd., 1806. 1st. Edn. Interleaved thro.-out, for Style's corrections, corrected thro.-out, 6 pp. of MS. notes at upr. & lr. blanks in Styles hand, retitled in his hand. Orig. 2-tone bds., worn. (PNY. Dec.3; 355) $150

SUARES, André
- **Le Crépuscule sur la Mer.** Ill.:– Maurice Denis. Paris, 1933. (225) on Rives. 4to. In sheets, portfo. (HD. Feb.27; 235) Frs. 1,100
- **Hélène chez Archimède.** Ill.:– G. Aubert after Pablo Picasso. Paris, 1955. (140) numbered. Fo. Loose as iss. in wraps., bd. folder. (SG. Apr.2; 237) $220
- **Le Livre de l'Emeraude.** Ill.:– A. Brouet. 1927. (200) 50 on Imp. Japan paper. 4to. Ll. in s.-c. (HD. Feb.18; 231) Frs. 1,500

SUAREZ de Rivera, Francisco
- **Ilustracion, y Publicacion de los Diez y Siete Secretos.** Madrid, 1732. 1st. Edn. Sm. 4to. Some headlines, etc., cut into, browned & stained. Mor.-bkd. bds. (S. Jul.27; 384) *Duran.* £60

SUASSO, Antonio
- **Theory of the Infantry Movements.** L., 1825. 3 vols. Long-grd. mor., gt. fillet border, blind palmette border, important angle motifs, Duc d'Angoulêone arms, gt. & decor. spines, inner fillet, watered silk end-ll., by Simier. (HD. Jun.10; 211) Frs. 6,300

SUBERTI, Petrus, Bp. of Saint Papoul
- **De Cultu Vinee d[omi]ni liber inumere plenus co[m]moditatis [etc.].** Ed.:– Jean Chappuis. Paris, 8 Mar. 1508. Sm. 4to. Slight browning & soiling. Mod. pol. hf. cf. by Rivière. From liby. of André L. Simon. (S. May 18; 186) *Hill.* £130

SUBERVILLE, Henry de
- **L'Henry-Metre, Instrument Royal, et Universal, avec sa Théorique, Usage, et Pratique Demonstrée par les Propositions Elementaires d'Euclid . . . Lequel prend toutes Mesures Géometriques, & Astronomiques.** Paris, 1598. 1st. Edn. 4to. Lacks port. of Henry IV, fore-margins of first 6 ll. renewed, some other ll. with marginal repairs, sm. tear in title reprd. without loss, slight dampstaining. Mod. limp vell. From Honeyman Collection. (S. May 19; 2940) *De Graeve.* £200

SUCKLING, Rev. Alfred
- **History & Antiquities of the County of Suffolk.** 1846-48. 2 vols. 4to. Some plts. spotted. Cont. mor., rebkd. (SH. Nov.6; 164) *College Gateway.* £75
- - **Anr. Edn.** 1846-48-1952. 3 vols., including Ltd. edn. index. 4to. A few plts. in 2 states, some spotting. Cont. hf. cf., orig. cl. (SH. Nov.6; 56) *Hayward.* £170
- **Memorials of the Antiquities & Architecture of the County of Essex.** 1845. 4to. 1 plt. with MS. caption, some plts. spotted, a few ll. torn & reprd. Cont. hf. roan. (SH. Nov.6; 55) *Lamb.* £60

SUCKLING, Sir John
- **Fragmenta Aurea.** 1646. 1st. Edn. 1st. variant titlee. Cont. cf., rebkd. [Wing S6126] (C. Nov.19; 39) *Finch.* £150
- - **Anr. Copy.** 1st. state of title to 'Aglaura' with Moseley's Christian name incorrectly spelt, sm. stain on port. & title. 18th. C. hf. cf., worn, upr. cover loose. Bkplt. of Birket Foster. (S. Dec.9; 356) *Thomas.* £70

SUDEK, Josef
- **Profyl/I.** Ed.:– Petr Tausk (introduction). Prague. [1980]. Sm. portfo. Loose as iss. in pict. folder. (SG. Apr.23; 192) $140

SUE, Eugène
- **Le Juif Errant.** 1844. Orig. Edn. 10 vols. (in 5). Vol. 5 on 357 pp. instead of 419, vol. 2 lacks hf.-titles, some staining. Hf.-cf., decor. spines, by Kleinhans. (HD. Feb.18; 193) Frs. 3,300
- - **Anr. Edn.** Ill.:– Gavarni. Paris, 1845. 4 vols. Hf.-titles. Cont. hf. mor. (SI. Dec.4; 549) Lire 220,000
- **Mystères de Paris [Les].** 1843-1844. Orig. Edn. 10 vols. (in 5). Vol. 1 on 385 pp. instead of 421, vol. 2 lacks hf.-titles. Hf.-cf., decor. spines, by Kleinhans. (HD. Feb.18; 193a) Frs. 3,300
- **The Mysteries of Paris.** L., 1845-46. 3 vols. Tall 8vo. Extra-ill. with 10 plts., port. & engraved title, by Thomas Onwhyn, from a smaller format edn., each plt. inlaid to size. Three-qtr. lev., spines gt. with floral designs, by Bayntun. Bkplt. of John Francis Neylan. (SG. Mar.19; 286) $100
- **Works.** Boston, [1899]. Edn. des Amateurs, (50). 20 vols. Plts. in 2 states, the proofs sigd. in pencil by the artists. Mor. gt., gt. panel. spines, watered silk end-papers. With A.N.s. inserted. (SPB. May 6; 347) $850

SUESS, Eduard
- **Das Antlitz der Erde.** Prague, Leipzig, Vienna, 1885-1909. 1st. Edn., vol. I 2nd. Iss. dtd. 1885. 3 vols. in 4. Some spotting, quires 33 & 34 transposed in vol. II, 2 maps detchd. Hf. cl., marb. bds. From Honeyman Collection. (S. May 19; 2942) *Pilcher.* £60

SUETONIUS Tranquillus, Gaius
- **De la Vie des XII Cesars.** Trans.:– George de la Boutière. Lyons, 1556. 4to. Sm. wormhole in first 2 ll., some stains. Cont. vell., soiled, new end-papers at front. (S. Jul.27; 125) *Pearson.* £80
- **[De Vita Duodecim Caesarum] Ex Recognitione Des. Erasmi . . . Dion Cassius Nicaeus. Aelius Spartianus [& others].** Cologne, 1527. Fo. Wormed near end, wormhole in title & first 5 ll., a few ll. stained in margins, title with inscr. at head. 18th C. mott. cf., gt., spine worn. (S. Jan.27; 367) *Pearson.* £85
- **Duodecim Caesares.** Paris, 1527. Cont. Engl. blind-sptd. cf. on wooden bds., pastedowns from Engl. legal MS., of ca. 1300, lacks clasps, spine worn. (S. Mar.17; 269) *Maggs.* £190
- **The Historie of Tvvelve Caesers.** Trans.:– Philemon Holland. 1606. 1st. Edn. in Engl., 1st. Iss. 2 pts. in 1 vol. Fo. Letterpress title, the variant which includes translator's name, slight browning & soiling, 1 or 2 sm. holes, slightly affecting text, a few ll. loose. Cont. limp vell. [NSTC 23423] (S. Sep.29; 77) *Quaritch.* £100
- **[Vitae XII Caesarum.]** Ed.:– Philippus Beroaldus & Marcus Antonius Sabellicus. Venice, 1506. Fo. Early vell. Bkplts. of William Morris & the Sunderland liby. (SG. May 14; 207) $750

SUEVUS or SCHWOB, Sigismundus
- **Arithmetica Historica. Die Lobliche Rechenkunst.** Breslau, 1593. 1st. Edn. Sm. 4to. Text browned & spotted, title inscr. 'Ex Bibliotheca Wenceslai Bergmanni 1647', later sig. of D.G. Seidel. Cont. hf. blind-stpd. pig., hf. red mor. case. From Honeyman Collection; bkplt. of Comte de Solms. (S. May 19; 2943) *Das Bucherkabinet.* £160

SUFFERINGS OF THE ICE-BOUND Whalers; containing copious extracts from a Journal taken on the spot by an officer of the Viewforth of Kirkcaldy
Edinb., 1836. 2nd. Edn. Title-p. soiled, light soiling thro.-out. Orig. bdg. (PD. Nov.26; 87) £65

SUFFOLK DOMESDAY
1889. 2 vols. Qtr. cf. (O. Jun.3; 109) £54

SUHR, Christoph
- **Hanburgische Trachten Gezeichnet und Gestochen.** [Hamburg?], 1815. Fo. Title & table in Fr. & German, 36 hand-cold. aquatint plts., with 'C. Suhr' stpd. in blind beneath each one, blank margins of title & plts. no. 7 & 23 cleanly torn, slightly soiled. Cont. hf. mor. (CSK. May 22; 63) £2,700

SUHR, Christoph & Cornelius
- **Sammlung Verschiedener Spanischer National Trachten und Uniformen der Division des Marquis de la Romana.** Hamburg, ca. 1808 Fo. Mor.-bkd. bds. (C. May 20; 180) *Maggs.* £300

SUIDAS
- **Lexicon.** Camb., 1705. Lge. fo. Cont. vell. bds. (S. Jun.29; 435) *Dimakarakos.* £65

SUIKERS, Geerlof & Verburg, Isaak
- **Algemene Kerkelyke en Wereldlyke Geschiedenissen des Bekenden Aardkloots . . .** Amst., 1728. 10 pts. in 5 vols. Fo. Completely disbnd., ex-liby. (SG. Feb.5; 315) $350

SUISETH, Ricardus
- **Calculationes.** Ed.:– [Joannes de Cipro]. Padua, [N.T.S.P.], ca. 1477. 1st. Edn. Fo. Lacks final blank, initials & paragraph marks supplied in red & blue, 1st. initial in blue with red penwork decor., lr. margins of last quire defect., very minor flaw in 1st. lf., a few wormholes in upr. margins, slight soiling & discolouration, inscr. 'Darwinii'. 16th. C. vell., inside hinges breaking, hf. mor. case. Bkplts. of Michael Chasles & Constantin Le Paige; from Honeyman Collection. [BMC VII, 919; Goff S830; HC 15136] (S. May 19; 2944) *Sbisa.* £2,300

SUISSE ILLUSTREE
Paris, 1851. [1st. Edn.?]. 2 vols. in 1. 4to. Some steel engrs. slightly soiled, several text pp. loose in vol. II, slightly soiled. Cont. hf. leath. (H. Dec.9/10; 629) DM 3,200
- - **Anr. Copy.** Lacks 4 cold. lithos., steel engrs. & text slightly soiled in parts, several ll. loose in vol. 2. (H. May 21/22; 440) DM 2,400

SULIVAN, Richard Joseph
- **A Tour through parts of England, Scotland, Wales.** 1785. 2nd. Edn. 2 vols. Some spotting. Cont. tree cf., gt., by Kalthoeber, with his ticket. The Beckford copy, bkplt. of William Hopetoun, 7th. Earl of Northesk. (S. Jun.22; 98) *Crowe.* £120

SULLIVAN, Arthur
See–KIPLING, Rudyard

SULLIVAN, Dennis
- **A Picturesque Tour through Ireland.** 1824. Ob. 4to. Views cold. Mod. red hf. mor., orig. gt. label. From the collection of Eric Sexton. (C. Apr.16; 363) *Maggs.* £1,900

SULLIVAN, James
- **History of the District of Maine.** Boston, 1795. [1st. Edn.?]. Slightly browned. Cont. cf., rebkd. & reprd. (SH. Nov.7; 392) *Remington.* £60
- - **Anr. Copy.** Cont. tree cf., De Witt Clinton's armorial bkplt., his sig. at title. (PNY. Dec.3; 229) $180

SULLIVAN, Louis H.
- **A System of Architectural Ornament according with a Philosophy of Man's Powers.** N.Y., 1924. (1000). Fo. Orig. bds. & cl. spine, bds., slightly dust-soiled. (CB. May 27; 196) Can. $1,200

SULLY, Henri
- **Régle Artificielle du Tems. Traite de la division naturelle & artificielle de Tems, des Horloges & des Montres.** Paris, 1717. Cont. cf.-bkd. bds. (CSK. Jan.23; 131) £110

SULLY, Maximilien, Duc de Bethune
- **Memoires des Sages et Royales Oeconomies d'Estat.** [Amst.]; [Angers]; Paris, [1638]-62. 1st. Edn., 1st. Iss. 4 vols. in 3. Fo. Blank before title of vol. IV, cancel slip on 4R4 of vol. 1, 2 inner margins strengthened. Cont. red mor., gt., arms of Duc de Sully, on covers, surrounded by gt. panel with pointillé corner sprays, triple gt. fillet, arms repeated in each spine compartment, arms of Earl of Derby blind-stpd. on covers. (SM. Oct.8; 2024) Frs. 7,000
- - **Anr. Edn.** Ed.:– Abbé de l'Eeluse des Loges. Ill.:– Tardieu, Lecherie engraved by Baudet, Gravelot engraved by Fessard. L., [Paris], 1747. 3 vols. 4to. Cont. red. mor., triple fillet border, limp spines, decor., inner dentelle. (HD. Apr.24; 104) Frs. 11,800
- - **Anr. Copy.** Staining & worming. Cont. mor., dentelle (HD. Jun.30; 75) Frs. 3,800

SULTE, Benjamin
- **Histoire des Canadiens-Français 1608-1880.** Montreal, 1882-1884. 8 vols. Fo. Orig. cl., gt. (PWP. Jun.4; 107) $140

SULZBERGER, Cyrus
- The Resistentialists. N.Y., [1962]. 1st. Edn. Cl.-bkd. bds., d.-w., s.-c. (SG. Jun.4; 219) $110

SULZER, J. H.
- Die Kennzeichen der Insekten nach Anttg. des . . . K. Linnaeus Ed.:– J. Gessner (preface). Ill.:– J. R. Schellenberg. Zürich, 1761. 1st Edn. Sm. 4to. Cont. leath. gt. spine & outer dentelle. (HK May 12-14; 305)   DM 6,200

SUMNER, Hon. Charles
- Speech . . . on the Cession of Russian America to the United States. Wash., 1867. 1st. Edn. Ptd. wraps., some wear & soiling, upr. wrap. nearly detchd. Tipped in before title is pres. slip, sigd. by William H. Seward. (SG. Jan.8; 6) $400
- Complete Works. Boston, 1900. Statesman Edn., (1000). 20 vols. Hf. red mor. gt. With 3-p. A.L.s. (SPB. May 6; 348) $600

SUNDAY STRAND: an Illustrated Home Monthly
Ill.:– Arthur Rackham & others. L., 1900. Vols. 1 & 2. 4to. Old three-qtr. cf. Raymond M. Sutton Jr. copy. (SG. May 7; 282) $100

SUNDER, called Cranach, Lucas, the Elder
- Einblattholzschnitte. Munich, [1972]. (250) numbered. 3 vols. Lge. fo. Loose as iss. in orig. roan-bkd. folders, in s.-c.'s. (S. Jul.27; 174)   *Maggs.* £90

SUNDERLAND, Charles S., Earl of
- Bibliotheca Sunderlandiana. Ed.:– John Lawler. L., 1883. L.P. 2 vols. 4to. With compl. list of buyers & prices, contents loose in bdg. Hf. mor., worn. (SG. Mar.26; 430) $120

SUNDEVALL, C. J. & Kinberg, J. G. H.
- Svenska Foglarna. 1856; 1886. 2 vols. Ob. 4to. Hf. mor. gt. (P. Nov.13; 225)   *Quaritch.* £250

SUNTHEIM, Ladislaus
- Der Lolichen Fursten und des Landes Oesterreich Altherkommen und Regierung. Basle, [Michael Furter], [not after 1491]. 1st. Edn. Fo. Woodcut initial capitals, spaces for other capitals with guide letters, lacks final blank. Red mor. gt.-lettered spine. From the collection of Eric Sexton. [BMC III, 782, Goff S868, H. 879*] (CNY. Apr.8; 22) $6,500

SUN-TSE & others
[-] Art Militaire des Chinois. Trans.:– P. Amiot. Paris, 1772. 1st. Edn. 4to. Slight soiling. Cont. cf., worn. (S. Jun.23; 257)   *Henderson.* $340

SURIREY DE SAINT REMY, Pierre
- Mémoires d'Artillerie. Paris, 1697. 1st. Edn. 2 vols. 4to. Pp.135-8 excised. Cont. spr. cf., rebkd., orig. gt. spine preserved. (CNY. May 22; 176) $320
- - Anr. Edn. Paris, 1707. 2nd. Edn. 2 vols. 4to. Cont. cf., spines gt. Armorial bkplt. by Albert Du Thon, cont. sig. of J. Du Thon. (SG. Feb.26; 310) $350

SURPRISES (Les), ou le Bien et le Mal
Ill.:– C. Haeberlin. Paris, ca. 1880. Fo. Loose in orig. cl.-bkd. bds. (SH. Mar.19; 216)   *Temperley.* £170

SURR, T. S.
- Magic of Wealth. 1815. 3 vols. 12mo. Cf. gt. (P. Jan.22; 31)   *Scott.* £75

SURREALISME EN 1947, Le
Ed.:– André Breton & Marcel Duchamp. Ill.:– Max Ernst, Joan Miro & others. Paris, [1947]. (999) numbered. 4to. Pict. wraps., glassine d.-w., s.-c. worn. (SG. Oct.23; 320) $500

SURREY PARISH REGISTER
- Publications. 1903-17. Vols. 1-15 in 14. Orig. cl., slightly soiled. (SH. Nov.6; 36)   *Cummings.* £85

SURTEES, Robert
- The History & Antiquities of the County Palatine of Durham. Ill.:– after J.M.W. Turner & others. 1816-40. [1st. Edn.?]. 4 vols. Fo. Sepia aquatint by Turner inserted. 19th. C. mor. gt. From the collection of Eric Sexton. (C. Apr.16; 364)   *Chesters.* £220
- - Anr. Copy. Occasional foxing. Later russ., gt. spines. (C. Feb.25; 61)   *Traylen.* $200
- - Anr. Copy. Some spotting & offsetting in text, some ll. loose. Cont. hf. russ., spines defect, covers loose or detchd., very worn. Lge. copy, w.a.f. (S. Jan.27; 611)   *Keating.* £120

SURTEES, Robert Smith
- Ask Mama.-Mr. Sponge's Sporting Tour. -Handley Cross.- Mr. Romford's Hounds.-Plain or Ringlets?- Ill.:– John Leech. 1853; 1852; 1854; n.d.; n.d. 5 vols. A few minor defects. Unif. hf. red mor. gt. (SBA. Dec.16; 132a)   *Allen & Co.* £100
- - Anr. Edn. Ill.:– John Leech. L., 1853; 1854; 1858; 1860; 1865. 1st. Edns. 5 works in 5 vols. Unif. hf. mor. gt., unc. (PNY. May 21; 397) $325
- - Anr. Edn. Ill.:– John Leech & others. N.d. 5 vols. Some very minor defects. Unif. hf. red mor. gt. (SBA. May. 27; 120a)   *Taylor.* £95
[-] - Anr. Copy. Unif. hf. mor., spines gt. (CSK. Jan.16; 172)   £85
[-] Ask Mama.-Plain or Ringlets?-Mr. Romford's Hounds.-Mr. Sponge's Sporting Tour. Ill.:– John Leech & H. K. Browne. N.d. 4 vols. Some ll. slightly spotted. Unif. hf. cf., spines gt., soiled. (SKC. May. 19; 36)   £50
- Hawbuck Grange.-Mr Sponge's Sporting Tour. -Handley Cross.-Ash Mamma.-Plain or Ringlets. -Mr Facey Romford's Hounds.-Hillingdon Hall. Ill.:– John Leech, H. K. Browne, Wildrake, Heath & Jellicoe. 1847; 1853; 1854; 1858; 1860; 1865; 1888. All 1st. Editions or 1st. Illustrated Editions. Together 7 vols. 1st. & 6th. with orig. cl. covers & spine bnd. in at end, unif. later gt.-tooled mor. by Bayntun of Bath. (SH. Oct.9; 249)   *Way.* £580
[-] Hillingdon Hall. L., 1845. 1st. Edn. 3 vols. 12mo. Cf. Armorial bkplt. of Gordon of Aikenhead. (SG. Apr.9; 407) $120
[-] Jorrock's Jaunts & Jollities.-Handley Cross. -Hillingdon Hall. Ill.:H. Alken (1st. work); John Leech (2nd. work). N.d.; 1854; 1888. 3 works in 3 vols. 1 plt. detchd. from 1st. work. Orig. embossed cl., gt.; cont. hf. cf.; orig. cl., gt. (C. Nov.5; 160)   *Allan.* £70
- Plain or Ringlets?-Mr. Sponge's Sporting Tour. -Ask Mamma.-Hawbuck Grange.-Mr. Romford's Hounds.-Handley Cross. Ill.:– mostly by John Leech. N.d. 6 vols. Cont. cf. gt., all but 1 unif. (SBA. Mar.4; 20)   *Udall.* £110
- - Anr. Copy. Hf. cf. (DWB. May. 15; 383)   £70
[-] Sporting Novels. Ill.:– John Leech & others. L., ca. 1890. Subscriber's Edns. 6 vols. Crimson str.-grd. mor. with sm. gt. cornerpieces, repeated on spines, gt. dentelles, by Bayntun. (SG. Dec.11; 419) $350
- - Anr. Edn. 1892. Jorrocks Edn. 6 vols. Cont. hf. mor.   (SH. Jul.16; 147) *Trocch* £55
- - Anr. Edn. Ill.:– John Leech. 1899. 11 vols. Hf. mor. gt. by Riviére. (CE. Nov.20; 124)   £230
[-] - Anr. Edn. Ill.:– John Leech & others. L., ca. 1900. Subscriber's Edn. 6 vols. Gt.-pict. cl., all but 1st. col. unopened. (SG. Dec.11; 420) $120
[-] [-] Anr. Edn. Bath, 1926. 6 vols. Orig. pict. cl. (CSK. Jun.26; 27)   £50
- - Anr. Edn. N.d. & 1888. 7 vols. Some spotting, 1 title reprd. Orig. cl., worn. W.a.f. (CSK. Jan.30; 93)   £110
[-] [-] Anr. Edn. Ill.:– after John Leech, H. K. Browne & W. T. Maud. Bradbury, n.d. 6 vols. Orig. pict. cl. (CSK. Jun.26; 49)   £100
- - Anr. Edn. Ill.:– John Leech & H. K. Browne. N.d. Subscription Edn. 6 vols. Decor. cl. gt. (CE. Jun.4; 163)   £90

SURVILLE, Clotilde de
- Poésies. 1824 [1827]. New Vanderbourg Edn. (100) on Annonay vell. 2 vols. Cont. red hf. mor., decor. spines, unc. (HD. Feb.18; 194)   Frs. 1,100

SUSANE, Gen. L.
- Histoire de L'Infanterie Française. Paris, 1876. 1st. Edn. 5 vols. 18mo. Mod. buckram. (SG. Feb.26; 311) $325

SUSO, Henricus
- Horologium Sapiente. Venice. Petrus de Quarengiis, 24 Jan. 1492/3. 4to. Scattered worming thro.-out text, a few wormholes filled in. Recent vell. bds. [C. 3170; BMC V p. 510; Goff S 875] (C. Apr.1; 87)   *Sharpe.* £260
- - Anr. Edn. Paris, Antoine Verard, 15 Jul. 1499. Fo. Spaces for some initial capitals, lacks a2 & 5, f3-4, & final blank y4, first 6 ll. with portions of lr. & upr. blank margins renewed or patched, some other ll. with corners renewed, 10 ll. with reprd. marginal tears, 3 ll. with tears affecting text reprd., wormholes to last 2 ll. reprd. with loss of some letters of text, browned. Early blind-stpd. cf., rebkd. & reprd. The copy of C. W. Dyson Perrins, lately in the collection of Eric Sexton. [Goff (Supp.) S877a] (CNY. Apr.8; 123) $1,000

SUTCLIFF, Robert
- Travels in Some Parts of North America. York, 1815. 2nd. Edn. Cont. pol. cf., gt. spine. The Beckford-Rosebery copy. [Sabin 19 (S. Jun.29; 190)   *Crete.* £55

SUTHERLAND, Duchess, Countess of Sutherland
- Views on the Northern & Western Coasts of Sutherland. Ill.: Frederick Christian Lewis. N.d. Fo. Foxed, 14 only (of 20) hand-cold. mezzotints mntd. on card. Loose in cl. (CE. Jun.4; 205)   £50

SUTHERLAND, C.H.V. & others
- The Roman Imperial Coinage. 1967-66. Vols. 6-7 only. Orig. cl. (SH. Mar.6; 458)   *Trade Art.* £110

SUTHERLAND, Peter C.
- Journal of a Voyage in Baffin's Bay & Barrow Straits. L., 1852. 2 vols. Sm. tears in folding maps., 2 plts. loose, some light foxing. Orig. cl. (CB. Apr.1; 315)   *Can.* $600

SUTTOR, George
- The Culture of the Grape-Vine & the Orange, in Australia & New Zealand. L., 1843. Catalogue of Smith, Elder & Co., Jan. 1843, bnd. in. Orig. blind-stpd. cl., gt. title on spine. Inscr. (JL. Jul.20; 825)   *Aus.* $340

SUYIN, Han
See–CARTIER-BRESSON, Henri

SVENSK FOERFATTNINGS-SAMLING, 1856, No. 78
Stockholm, Mar. 26. 1857. Sm. 4to. Some dampstaining. Unbnd. (PNY. Mar.26; 136) $120

SVERDRUP, Otto
- New Land, Four Years in the Arctic Regions. 1904. 2 vols. Orig. bdg. (TRL. Dec.10; 10)   £52

SVETAET [Day is Breaking]
Ed.:– [A.P. Khotulev]. St. Petersb., 1906. Nos. 1-2. Fo. Unbnd. (SH. Feb.5; 134)   *Lempert.* £140

SVETLOFF, Valerian
- Le Ballet Contemporain. St. Petersb., 1912. (520) numbered. 4to. Orig. cl. (SH. May 21; 116)   *Facchinetti.* £230
- - Anr. Copy. Mod. cl. (SH. Oct.10; 531)   *Mackenzie.* £140
- Sovremennyi Balet. Ill.:– Bakst & others. N.p., 1911. Lge. 4to. Gt.-decor. satin, unc. (SG. May 14; 208) $325
- Thamar Karsavina. Ed.:– Cyril W. Beaumont. Ill.:– Claud Lovat Fraser. 1922. (350) numbered. 4to. Orig. buckram-bkd. bds., spine soiled. (SH. Nov.20; 136)   *Henderson.* £70

SVININE, Paul Petrovitch
- Sketches of Russia. 1814. 12 extra mntd. hand-cold. plts., slightly soiled, a few ll. loose. Cont. hf. cf. (SH. Feb.5; 281)   *Bjorck.* £150
- - Anr. Edn. 1843. 2nd. Edn. Orig. cl., gt. decor. spine, slightly worn. (TA. Dec.18; 47)   £62

SVOBODA [Freedom]
Ed.:– [S.M. Usas]. St. Petersb., 1905. No. 1 only (of 2). Fo. Unbnd. (SH. Feb.5; 135)   *De la Casa.* £55

SVOBODNY SMEKH [Free Laughter]
Ed.:– [E.M. Adamov]. St. Petersb., 1905-06. Nos. 1-24. Fo. Unbnd. (SH. Feb.5; 136)   *Quaritch.* £400

SWAINSON, William
- Zoological Illustrations. 1820-33. 6 vols. Cont. hf. mor., ex liby. with labels removed. (S. Dec.3; 1148)   *W. & W.* £1,400
See–RICHARDSON, Sir John, M.D. & Swainson, William

SWAMMERDAM, Jan.
- Bibel der Natur. Leipzig, 1752. 1st. German Edn. Fo. Slightly soiled in parts. Cont. vell. (H. Dec.9/10; 294)   DM 700
- The Book of Nature or the History of Insects reduced to Distinct Classes. Ed.:– John Hill. Trans.:– Thomas Flloyd. 1758. 1st. Edn. in Engl. 2 pts. in vol. Fo. Cont. cf., rebkd. (S. Jun.17; 810)   *Rootenberg.* £300
- Bybel de Natuure . . . Historie der Insecten . . . Biblia Naturae; sive Historia Insectorum . . . [Dutch & Latin]. Ed.:– Hermann Boerhaave. Trans.:– Hieronimus David Gaubius. Leiden, 1737-38. 1st. Edn. 2 vols. in 3. Fo. Plts. 1-52 (all folding) bnd. at end of 3rd. vol., plt. 53 bnd. in vol II, slight spotting & browning, a little marginal soiling, tear reprd. in 2H1 vol. I. Cont. hf. cf., spines worn. Mod. bkplt. of Arno B.

Luckhardt; from Honeyman Collection. (S. May 19; 2946) *Zeitlin & Verbrugge.* £600
– – **Anr. Copy.** 2 vols. Some foxing, particularly to edges in vol. 2. 19th. C. hf. mor. From Chetham's Liby., Manchester. (C. Nov.27; 380) *Taylor.* £450
– **Historie Générale des Insectes.** Utrecht, 1682. 1st. Edn. 4to. Cont. cf., worn, rebkd. From Chetham's Liby., Manchester. (C. Nov.27; 381) *Taylor.* £140
– **Tractatus Physico-Anatomico-Medicus de Respiratione Usuque Pulmonum.** Leiden, 1667. 1st. Edn. Vell., soiled. (S. Jun.17; 809) *Rootenberg.* £360
– – **Anr. Edn.** Leiden, 1679. Browned & stained thro.-out. Cont. vell., stained. 18th. C. bkplt. of Dr. De Superville; mod. bkplt. of John S. Ely; from Honeyman Collection. (S. May. 19; 2945) *Zeitlin & Verbrugge.* £160

SWAN, Abraham
– **The British Architect: or, The Builder's Treasury of Stair-Cases.** 1745. Fo. Some plts. with letterpress descriptions on same lf., title soiled. Later hf. mor., worn. (CSK. Nov.14; 218) £130
– – **Anr. Edn.** [1780]. Fo. Cont. reverse of cf., rebkd., orig. spine preserved. (S. Mar.17; 460) *Woodruff.* £190
– – **Anr. Edn.** N.d., Fo. Advts., some soiling. Cont. reversed cf., worn. (S. Dec.9; 463) *Talerman.* £210

SWAN, Joseph
– **A Demonstration of the Nerves of the Human Body.** Ill.:– Finden after West. 1834. Re-Iss. in smaller size of the lge. fo. publd. in 1830. 4to. Index & advt. ll. at end. Bnd. as a prize in cf., worn, spine torn at bottom, gt. inscr. on upr. cover 'Presented to Mr. George Bower Thorpe in testimony of his having obtained the first prize in anatomy awarded by Mr. Shaw at the Middlesex Hospital School, April 1839'. (S. Jun.17; 812) *Wood.* £55
– **Observations on Some Points relating to the Anatomy, Physiology & Pathology of the Nervous System.** 1822. 1st. Edn. 10 pp. advts. dtd. Mar. 1822, errata slip, stain in inner blank corners of 1st. 2 ll. Cl.-bkd. bds. (S. Jun.17; 811) *Jenner Books.* £120

SWAN, Joseph, Engraver & Leighton, John M.
– **Select Views of Glasgow.** Glasgow, 1828. 4to. 4-p. subscribers list inserted at end. Late 19th. C. mor. gt. (S. Nov.24; 273) *Traylen.* £50

SWANEPOEL, D. A.
– **Butterflies of South Africa.** Cape Town, 1953. 4to. Mor. Pres. Copy. SSA. Nov.5; 186) R.150

SWANN, Harry Kirke
– **A Monograph of the Birds of Prey.** Ed.:– Alexander Wetmore. Ill.:– after H. Gronvold. 1924-45. 1st. Edn. 2 vols. 4to. cont. cf., orig. wraps. bnd. in. (C. Nov.5; 161) *Clarchy.* £260
– – **Anr. Edn.** Ed.:– Alexander Wetmore. 1930-45. 2 vols. 4to. Hf. crimson mor. gt., orig. wraps. bnd. in. (P. Nov.13; 226) *Traylen.* £240
– – **Anr. Copy.** (412). Later cl., soiled, orig. wraps. bnd. in at rear of each vol. (TA. Jun.18; 103) £180

SWARBRECK, Samuel D.
– **Sketches in Scotland.** 1839. Fo. Some plts. slightly spotted. Hf. mor. gt., worn. (CE. Apr.23; 127) £320
– – **Anr. Copy.** 1 plt. detchd. Roan-bkd. cl. (S. Nov.24; 274) *Marsden.* £240.
– – **Anr. Copy.** Spotted. Cont. mor.-bkd. cl., worn. loose. (SH. Nov.6; 165) *Remington.* £210

SWAYSLAND, W.
– **Familiar Wild Birds.** 1883. 4 vols. Hf. mor. gt. (P. Mar.12; 33) *Hill.* £75

SWEDENBORG, Emmanuel
– [–] **De Coelo et eius Mirabilibus, et de Inferno, ex Auditis & Visis.** 1758. 1st. Edn. 4to. Slight browning. Cont. cf., rebkd., hf. red mor. case. From Honeyman Collection. (S. May 19; 2947) *Ritman.* £90
– [–] **De Nova Hierosolyma et eius Doctrina Coelesti: ex Auditis e Coelo.** 1758. 1st. Edn. 4to. Slight browning. Cont. cf., spine reprd. at head, hf. red mor. case. From Honeyman Collection. (S. May 19; 2948) *Ritman.* £160
– **Opera Philosophica et Mineralia.** Dresden & Leipzig, 1734. 1st. Edn. Fo. Without the port., plt. at p. 169 in vol. 3 with tear, browned. Cont.

blind-stpd. vell. bds., soiled. Swedenborg Soc. stps. on some ll. (S. Feb.10; 318) *Hannas.* £360
– **Principia Rerum Naturalium.** Dresden & Leipzig, 1734. 1st. Edn. 3 vols. Fo. Lacks port., & plts. 45, 46, 47 & 82 in vol. 3, lacks general hf.-title to vol. 1, description of map in vol. 2, & directions to binder, in vol. 3 map misbnd. in vol. 1, titles & some edges dust-soiled. 19th. C. hf. mor., spines misnumbered. W.a.f., from Chetham's Liby., Manchester. (C. Nov.27; 383) *Schmidt.* £500
– **Principia Rerum Naturalium.–Regnum Subterraneum.** Dresden & Leipzig, 1734. 2 vols. Fo. 1st. vol.: port., 28 copper engrs. on 26 plts., 2nd. vol.: 92 (of 93) copper engrs. on 71 (of 72) plts. Cont. hf. leath. (R. Oct.14-18; 291) DM 1,000
– **Regnum Animale Anatomice, Physice et Philosophice Perlustratum.** The Hague/L., 1744-45. 1st. Edn. 3 vols. in 1. 4to. 1st. title dust-soiled. 19th. C. hf. mor. From Chetham's Liby., Manchester. (C. Nov.27; 382) *Taylor.* £140
– **A Theosophic Lucubration of the Nature of Influx.** 1770. 1st. Edn, in Engl. 4to. Advt. 19th. C. red str.-grd. mor. gt., gt. corner & centre-pieces. (C. Apr.1; 117) *Wade.* £120

SWEENEY, James Johnson
– **Marc Chagall.** N.Y., [1946]. 1st. Edn. 4to. Pict. cl., d.-w. Contains orig. watercolour drawing, inscr. & sigd. by Chagall 'pour Bobsy'. [Goodspeed]. (PNY. Mar.4; 122) $7,000

SWEERT, Emanuel
– **Florilegium . . .** Amst., 1620. 2 pts. in 1 vol. Fo. Lacks author's port., engraved title dust-soiled & strip cut from upr. margin, plts. spotted or slightly discold., 1 rubbed affecting letters, anr. bnd. inverted. 19th. C. hf. mor., upr. cover detchd. From Chetham's Liby., Manchester. (C. Nov.27; 384) *Schmidt.* £700

SWEERTS, François
– **XII Caesarum Romanorum Imagines, e Numismatibus Expressae, et Historica Narratione illustratae.** Antw., 1603. 4to. 17th. C. cf., gt. spine, spine chipped at head. Bkplt. of Philip Carteret Webb. (C. Apr.1; 171) *Hendrickx.* £140

SWEET, Robert
– **British Flower Garden.** 1823-33. Vols. 1-3, 1st. Series, vols. 1 & 2, 2nd. Series. Hf. cf. defect. (P. Jan.22; 309) *Cambridge.* £1,100
– – **Anr. Edn.** 1831. Vol. 1 only (of 4), 2nd. series. A few ll. slightly spotted. Mod. red hf. mor. (S. Dec.3; 1151) *Litman.* £340
  The British Warblers. 1823[-32]. Note tipped in at end, lacks(?) 1st. lf. (blank?), last lf. nearly detchd. Cont. hf. cf., worn. upr. cover detchd., lr. cover nearly detchd. (S. Jun.29; 289) *Hill.* £180
– **Cistineae. The Natural Order of Cistus, or Rock-Rose.** 1825-30. Some offsetting onto text, title slightly spotted. Hf. cf. (S. Jun.1; 226) *Traylen.* £580
– – **Anr. Copy.** Mod. hf. leath. (R. Oct.14-18; 2974) DM 2,600
– **Flora Australasica.** 1827-28 [but wtrmkd. 1846]. Orig. cl., slightly worn. (S. Jun.1; 227) *McCormick.* £800
– **Geraniaceae.** 1820-24. Vols. 1-2 (of 5). Disbnd. (S. Dec.3; 1150) *Walford.* £540
– – **Anr. Edn.** 1820-26. Vols. I-III only (of 5). Occasional light offsetting to text & some plts. Mod. mor.-bkd. bds., unc. (S. Dec.3; 1149) *Litman.* £900

SWIFT, Jonathan
– [–] **A Complete Collection of Genteel & Ingenious Conversation . . . by Simon Wagstaffe.** 1738. 1st. Edn. Some ll. stained in margins, advt. lf. Mod. cf. (S. Feb.10; 469) *Waterfield.* £55
– [–] **Directions to Servants.** 1745. 1st. L. Edn. Bnd. with 8 other pamphlets dtd. 1745-46, contents list in a cont. hand on fly-lf. & individual comments on titles. Cont. hf. sheep, worn. (S. May 5; 277) *Hill.* £480
– – **Anr. Edn.** Ill.:– John Nash. Gold. Cock. Pr., 1925. (380) numbered. Cont. vell. gt. by Mansell & Co., L., s.-c. Sigd. by artist. (TA Nov.20; 100) £85
– **Gullivers Reise ins Land der Riesen. Eine. Reise nach Brobdingnag.** Ill.:– L. Corinth. Berlin, 1922. (200) privilege Edn. Lge. 4to. Orig. hf. leath. 1 sigd. etching by Corinth & printer's mark sigd. by artist. (HK. May 12-14; 1812) DM 900

– **Gulliver's Travels** 1726. 1st. Edn., [Teerink's 'A' Edn.]. 4 pts. in 2 vols. Engraved port. in 2nd. state, slight browning, short tears in general title & in D8 of pt. III, slightly affecting text, reprd. Late 19th. C. red lev. mor. by F. Bedford, gt. (S. Jun.23; 397) *Hosain Books.* £1,100
– – **Anr. Copy.** 1st. title & some following ll. wormed in lr. margins, some early ll. in vol. 2 slightly stained in upr. outer corners. Cont. spr. cf., gt., some wear. (S. Feb.10; 470) *Hannas.* £650
[–] – **Anr. Copy.** 2 vols. Port. in 2nd. state, text in 1st. state. Cont. panel. cf., red hf. mor. s.-c. (SG May 14; 210) $3,100
– – **Anr. Edn.** L., 1726. '2nd. 8vo. Edn'. [Terrink's 'AA' Edn.]. 2 vols. Port. in 2nd. state, some foxing & browning, worming in margin of 4 ll., staining in margin of vol. I. Old panel. cf., rebkd. (SPB. Nov.25; 167) $400
– – **Anr. Edn.** 1726. 1st. Edn., [Teerinks 'B' Edn.]. 2 vols. Some worming. Old cf. Sheridan's bkplt. (P. Oct.23; 260) *Riaz.* £90
[–] – **Anr. Edn.** 1726. '3rd. 8vo. Edn.'. 2 vols. Mod. cf., gt. spines. (SH. Nov.7; 525) *Figgis.* £300
[–] – **Anr. Edn.** L., 1726. 1st. Edn. 2 vols. Some browning & spotting. Late 18th. C. tree cf., spines gt., upr. cover of vol. 1 detchd., qtr. mor. s.-c. From the Prescott Collection. (CNY. Feb.6; 310) $3,800
– – **Anr. Edn.** 1726 & 1727. 2 vols. Some slight browning. Panel. cf., slightly disparate. (LC. Jun.18; 338) £50
– – **Anr. Edn.** L., 1727-26. 2nd. Edn., [Teerink's 'AA' Edn.]. 2 vols. Some discolouration. Cf. gt. by Riviére. (SPB. Nov.25; 169) $150
– – **Anr. Edn.** L., ca.1772? 24mo. Badly frayed at many margins, with 4 pp. of advts. Disbnd., unc. (SG. Apr.30; 301) $400
– – **Anr. Edn.** Ed.:– George Saintsbury (prefatory memoir). L., 1886. Pol. cf., orig. cl. preserved at end. (CB. Feb.18; 236) Can. $120
– – **Anr. Edn.** Ill.:– Arthur Rackham. L., 1909. 1st. Trade Edn. 4to. Cl. gt., pict. end-papers browned. d.-w. Raymond M. Sutton, Jr. copy. (SG. May 7; 285) $130
– – **Anr. Edn.** Ill.:– Arthur Rackham. L. & N.Y., 1909. Three-qtr. cf., gt., by Zaehnsdorf. (SG. Oct.23; 292) $150
– – **Anr. Edn.** Ill.:– Arthur Rackham. L. & N.Y., 1909. (750) numbered, sigd. by artist. Orig. cl. gt., soiled, ties. (SH. Dec.11; 425) *Joseph.* £190
– – **Anr. Copy.** Some ills. cold. by previous owner. Orig. buckram gt., ties. (SBA. Jul.22; 193) *Chesters.* £85
– – **Anr. Copy.** Cl. Raymond M. Sutton Jr. copy. (SG. May 7; 284) $475
[–] – **Anr. Edn.** Ill.:– David Jones. Gold. Cock. Pr., 1925. (450) numbered. 2 vols. 4to. Hf. cl., unc. (SH. Feb.19; 145) *Libris.* £350
– – **Anr. Copy.** 2 vols. 4to. Orig. hf. cl., worn, unopened. (S. Jul.31; 77) *Lam.* £170
[–] – **Anr. Copy.** Orig. hf. buckram, soiled. (CSK. Jul.3; 126) £150
[–] – **Anr. Copy.** Bds., three-gtr. buckram. (KH. Nov.18; 575) Aus. $170
– – **Anr. Edn.** Ill.:– Rex Whistler. Cresset Pr., 1930. (205) numbered. 2 vols. Fo. Orig. hf. mor. with vell. cover, s.-c. worn. (S. Jul.31; 331) *Toynbee Clarke.* £850
– **The History of the Four Last Years of the Queen.** L., 1758. 1st. Edn. Cont. cf., worn. (SG. Feb.5; 317) $110
[–] **Miscellaneous Works.** L. [The Hague], 1720. Unauthorised 1st. Edn. 2 pts. in 1 vol. Cont. cf. (LC. Feb.12; 592) £50
[–] **Miscellanies in Prose & Verse.** 1711. 1st. Edn., 2nd. state. Cont. panel. cf., head & foot of spine chipped. (C. Apr.1; 236) *Croft.* £100
[–] **A Tale of a Tub,** 1704. 1st. Edn. 'Advertisement' lf. at beginning p.320, with space for 'uterinus' left blank. Late 19th. C. red lev. mor. by F. Bedford, gt. (S. Nov.24; 275) *Howes.* £400
– – **Anr. Copy.** Title & several other ll. with early pen scribbles, marginal worming in the 1st. gathering, just touching a few letters, the lf. 'Treatise writ . . .' bnd. at end. Cont. cf., worn. (S. May 5; 276) *Traylen.* £260
– – **Anr. Copy.** Cont. panel. cf., hf. mor. s.-c. upr. cover detchd. (SG. Sep.25; 295) $600
[–] – **Anr. Edn.** 1704. 2nd. Edn. 'Advertisement' lf. at beginning, slight browning. Cont. panel. cf., spine gt. Sir William Hustler, (S. Jan.26; 71) *Subunso.* £65

SWIFT, Jonathan -contd.
- - **Anr. Copy.** Bkplt. of Sir William Hustler. (S. Sep.29; 130) *Colbeck.* £50
- **Voyage to Lilliput; Voyage to Brobdingnag.** Ltd. Edns. Cl., [1950]. (1500) numbered, & sigd. (with initials) by B. Rogers. 2 vols. 48mo. & atlas fo. Cl.-bkd. bds., in specially designed box. (SG. Apr.30; 302) $120
[-] **Voyages de Gulliver.** Paris, 1727. 2nd. [1st. Paris] Edn. in Fr. 2 vols. 12mo. Late 19th. C. red lev. mor. by Cuzin, gt. (S. Nov.24; 277) *Watchman.* £140
- - **Anr. Edn.** Ill.:- Masquelier after Le Febvre. Paris, 1797. L.P., on vell. 4 vols. 16mo. Cont. red hf. mor., gt. decor. spines, ca. 1820. (HD. Apr.9; 570) Frs. 3,100
[-] - **Anr. Edn.** Ill.:- Masquelier after Le Febvre. Paris, An V [1797]. 2 vols. in 4. 18mo. Wide margins. Cont. cf., gt. Greek-key borders & spines, spines very worn. (SG. Feb.5; 318) $120
- - **Anr. Edn.** Ill.:- Grandeville. Paris, 1838. 1st. Printing. 2 vols. Hf. cf. by Capé, gt. fillets & blind-tooled decor. on spines. (HD. Dec.5; 200) Frs. 1,900
- **The Works.** 1768-79. Vols. I-XXV. Cont. cf., gt. spines. Armorial bkplt. of George Paterson of Castle Huntly. (S. Feb.23; 357) *Wade.* £110
- - **Anr. Edn.** Edinb., 1778. 18 vols. Tree cf., gt. (CE. Aug.28; 226) £85
- - **Anr. Edn.** Ed.:- J. Hawkesworth & others. Edinb., vol. IX Dublin, 1778, except Vol. IX, 1774. Vols. 1-18, lacks Vol. 13. 12mo. Cf., all but Vol. IX with Trinity Prize Stamp. (GM. Apr.30; 229) £60
- - **Anr. Edn.** 1784. 17 vols. Cont. cf., spines gt. (SH. Apr.10; 348) *Kauffman.* £160
- - **Anr. Edn.** Ed.:- John Nichols. Ill.:- James Basire (frontis. port.). 1801. 19 vols. Cont. diced russ. (C. Jul.22; 33) *Quaritch.* £130
- - **Anr. Edn.** Ed:- Sir Walter Scott. Edinb., 1824. 18 vols. Mor., spines gt., 1 cover loose. (SKC. Sep.9; 1489) £65

SWINBURNE, Algernon Charles
- **Atalanta in Calydon.** L., 1865. 1st. Edn. Sm. 4to. Lev. mor. gt., rounded spine in 6 compartments, 5 raised bands, dtd. at foot, silk linings, in Doves Bindery style, orig. buckram covers & spine preserved, unsigd. cl. case. (CNY. May 22; 362) $700
- - **Anr. Edn.** Kelms. Pr., 1894. (250). Lge. 4to. Orig. limp vell., silk ties, one defect., unc. (SH. Feb.19; 6) *Pickering.* £290
- - **Anr. Copy.** Fo. (CNY. May 22; 319) $500
- **A Century of Roundels.** L., 1883. 1st. Edn. Sm. 4to. Crushed lev. mor., elab. gt. tooled, rounded spine in 6 compartments, gt.-lettered & tooled, 5 raised bands, silk brocade doubls. & free end.pp., by T.J. Cobden-Sanderson, inscr. & dtd. 1891., qtr. maroon mor. gt. s.-c. M. C. D. Borden bkplt., Cortlandt Field Bishop booklabel. (CNY. May 22; 359) $18,000
- **Laus Veneris.** Ill.:- John Buckland-Wright. Gold. Cock. Pr., 1948. (750). Orig. cl.-bkd. bds. (SH. Feb.19; 184) *Blond.* £52
- **Pasiphae.** Ill.:- John Buckland-Wright. Gold. Cock. Pr., 1950. (500) numbered, (100) with extra ills. Orig. buckram gt., s.-c. (S. Jul.31; 103) *Jonathan.* £60
- **Poems & Ballads.** L., 1866. 1st. Edn., 2nd. Iss. Without advts. Red mor., gt.-decor. on both covers & spine, & repeated on dentelles, by the Doves Bindery, & sigd. 'C-S, 1904'. (SG. Jan.15; 21) $240
- **Poems & Ballads.-A Song of Italy.** L., 1866; 1867. 1st. Edn., 1st. Iss. (1st. work). 2 works in 2 vols. 8 pp. of advts. in each work, title-p. of 1st. work with knife-slit up lr. third (for cancellation?). Cl. Stp. & sig. of F. G. Palmer, Soho, on title. (SG. Nov.13; 657) $180
- **The Springtide of Life.** Ill.:- Arthur Rackham. 1918. (765) numbered, sigd. by artist. 4to. Orig. parch. gt. (SH. Mar.27; 436) *Renard.* £85
- - **Anr. Copy.** Orig. parch. gt., soiled. (SH. Dec.11; 438) *Katzer.* £70
- - **Anr. Edn.** Ed:- Edmund Gosse. Ill.:- Arthur Rackham. L., [1918]. (765) numbered, sigd. by artist. Lge. 4to. Vell.-bkd. vell.-style bds., gt.-decor., foxed. Raymond M. Sutton Jr. copy. (SG. May 7; 287) $325
- - **Anr. Copy.** Tall 4to. Owner's sig. Vell.-bkd. gt.-decor. bds., soiled. (SG. Apr.2; 258) $150
- **William Blake.** 1868. 1st. Edn. Orig. cl. gt., slightly worn. (P. Apr.30; 317) *Scott.* £55

- **Collection of 19 Works.** 1880-1905. In 21 vols. All in cont. hf. mor., spines gt. (SH. Apr.10; 349) *Kauffman.* $260

SWINBURNE, Henry
- **Picturesque Tour through Spain.** 1810. Ob. fo. Occasional spotting. Orig. bds., worn. (S. Sep.29; 212) *Denniston.* £220
- - **Anr. Copy.** Cont. cf., worn, upr. cover dtchd. (S. Nov.24; 278) *Nolan.* £160
- - **Anr. Edn.** 1823. Fo. Some plts. slightly soiled. Hf. roan, defect. (P. Mar.12; 44) *Cambridge.* £160
- **Travels Through Spain.** 1779. 1st. Edn. 4to. Some tears & stains. Cont. cf., worn. Hispaniae'. Extra-ill. with 52 plts. from 'Theatrum (SH. Jun.18; 187) *Browne.* £100
- **Travels through Spain.-Supplement: a Journey from Bayonne to Marseilles.** L., 1779: 1787. 2 works in 1 vol. 4to. 1st. work, folding map mntd., 13 plts., plus 6 etched plts. not called for in plt.-list. Cont. cf., rehinged. (SG. Feb.26; 312) $200
- **Travels in the Two Sicilies.** 1783-85. 2 vols. 4to. 1 engraved map detchd. Cont. cf., rebkd. preserving old spines. (CSK. Jun.5; 156) £160
- **Travels in Two Sicilies.-Travels in Spain.** 1783; 1787. 2 vols.; 2 vols. Cf. (DWB. May 15; 344) £50
- **Voyage ... dans les deux Siciles, en 1777, 1778, 1779 et 1780.** Trans.:- [Louise-Felicité Kéralio]. Paris, 1785. 4 vols. Some ll. browned, bkplt. 'Ex Bibliotheca Warclanensi Comit: de Borch'. Cont. red mor., gt., by Derome le Jeune, triple gt. fillet, flat spine gt. with sm. horizontal lozenge in compartments, divided by 'Greek key' roll border, inner gt. dentelles. (SM. Oct.8; 2026) Frs. 14,500

SWINDEN, Jan Hendrik van
- **Dissertation sur la Comparaison des Thermométres.** Amst., 1778. 1st. Edn. Table badly torn in 2 pts., liby. stp. on title. Cont. bds. From Honeyman Collection. (S. May 19; 2950) *Rademaker.* £90

SWINHOE, Robert
- **Notes on the Island of Formosa.-Notes on the Ethnology of Formosa.-The Ornithology of Formosa.-On the Mammals of the Island of Formosa.-A List of the Formosan Reptiles.** 1863. 5 offprints in 1 vol. 1 actual photograph mntd. Later cl. (SH. Mar.5; 137) *Kossow.* £160

SWINTON, George
- **Eskimo Sculpture/Sculpture Esquimaude. -Sculpture of the Eskimo.** Toronto & Montreal; Toronto, [1965]; [1972]. 2 works in 2 vols. Ob. 8vo.; 4to. Orig. cl., d.-w.; orig. canvas, d.-w. (CB. Nov.12; 44) Can. $100

SWITZERLAND
- **A Collection of Swiss Views.** Mid-19th. C. Ob. 4to. 62 litho., engraved or aquatint plts. Cont. mor. gt. Booklabel of Mrs. M. Tennant Wallace, 1856-57. (S. Nov.24; 279) *Nolan.* £950
- **Souvenir de la Suisse.** [Zurich], ca. 1860. Ob.12mo. No title or text, foxed. Cl., lacks spine. (SG. Feb.26; 313) $475
- **La Suisse Pittoresque.** Ill.:- Heisinger & Riegel. Zurich, ca. 1860. Ob. 4to. Bds., ex liby. (SG. Oct.30; 348) $1,400

SWITZERLAND & THE BAVARIAN HIGHLANDS
N.d. Some ll. detchd., slight soiling. Orig. cl., soiled. (CSK. May 1; 107) £300

SWOBODA, M.
- **Zähmung und Abrichtung der wildfänge. Ein Handbuch für den Reiter.** Vienna, 1824. 2 vols. 1 plt. slightly browned. Orig. bds. (R. Mar.31-Apr.4; 1726) DM 480

SWORD OF SONG called by Christians The Book of the Beast
Benares, 1904. 1st. Edn. 4to. Orig. ptd. wrap. (BS. Nov.26; 245) £55

SYDENHAM, Thomas
- **Epistolae Responsoriae duae ... prima De Morbis Epidemicis ... 1675 ... 1680 ... Secunda De luis Venereae Historia & Curatione.** 1680. 1st. Edn. Slight dampstaining, sm. holes in Bl, slightly affecting text. Mod. bds. [Wing S6310] (S. Dec.2; 630) *Rota.* £75
- **The Whole Works ...** Ed.:- John Pechey. 1705. 4th. Edn. Advt. lf. Mor. (S. Jun.17; 817) *Jenner Books.* £60

SYDENHAM SOCIETY [New Sydenham Society]
- **Publications.** 1844-54. 40 vols. Orig. cl. gt. As a collection, w.a.f. (S. Jun.17; 819) *Pratt.* £550
- - **Anr. Run.** 1844-83. 45 vols. 1 vol. cont. hf. cf., rest orig. cl. (SH. Oct.10; 532) *Walford.* £180
- - **Anr. Run.** V.d. 72 vols. 8vo. & fo. Orig. cl., some vols. worn. As a coll., w.a.f., from liby. of Dr. E. Ashworth Underwood. (S. Feb.23; 304) *Bickersteth.* £760

SYDERFF, Sir Thomas
- **Tarugo's Wiles.** 1668. 1st. Edn. 4to. Mor. by Sangorski. [Wing S6322] (C. Nov.19; 168) *Quaritch.* £320

SYDNEY MORNING HERALD (The)
Sydney, [1 Oct.-31 Dec. 1851]. Vol. XXXI. Lge. fo. Orig. bds. with leath. spine, worn, inner hinges reprd. With the Ingleton bkplt. (JL. Mar.2; 651) Aus. $120
- - **Anr. Run.** Sydney, [2 Jan.-30 Jun. 1852]. Vol. XXXII. Lge. fo. Orig. bds. with leath. spine, worn. With the Ingleton bkplt. (JL. Mar.2; 652) Aus. $200
- - **Anr. Run.** Sydney, [1 Jul.-31 Dec. 1852]. Vol. XXXXIII. Lge. fo. Orig. bds. with leath. spine, worn. With the Ingleton bkplt. (JL. Mar.2; 653) Aus. $200
- - **Anr. Run.** Sydney, 2 Jan.-31 Mar. 1854. Vol. XXXV. Lge. fo. Orig. bds., leath. spine, worn. Ingleton kbplt. (JL. Jul.20; 589) Aus. $160
- - **Anr. Run.** Sydney, 2 Oct.-30 Dec. 1854. Vol. XXXV. Lge. fo. Orig. bds., leath. spine, worn. Ingleton bkplt. (JL. Jul.20; 590) Aus. $190
- - **Anr. Run.** Sydney, 1 Jan.-30 Apr. 1855. Vol. XXXVI. Lge. fo. Orig. bds., leath. spine, worn. Ingleton bkplt. (JL. Jul.20; 591) Aus. Pds300
- - **Anr. Run.** Sydney, 1 May-31 Aug. 1855. Vol. XXXVI. Lge. fo. Orig. bds., leath. spine, worn. Ingleton bkplt. (JL. Jul.20; 592) Aus. $300

SYKES, Sir Mark Masterman
- **Catalogue of Library of.** 1824. 3 pts. in 1 vol. Port. frontis. inserted. 19th. C. hf. cf. (S. Nov.24; 280) *Dawson.* £90

SYLVANUS OF EBOLI, Bernardus
See-PTOLOMAEUS, Claudius & Sylavanus of Eboli, Bernardus

SYLVESTER, Charles
- **An Elementary Treatise on Chemistry ... with tables of Decomposition on a New Plan.** L'pool, 1809. Orig. bds., rebkd., unc. (S. Dec.1; 403) *Maggs.* £100

SYLVESTER, Joshua
- **Lachrymae Lachryum.** 1613. 3rd. Edn., 2nd. Iss. 4to. Title & most ll. cropped or slightly defect., reprd. Recent hf. mor. [STC 23578] (C. Nov.19; 40) *Quaritch.* £110

SYLVESTRE, Armand
- **Le Conte de l'Archer.** Ill.:- A. Poirson. Paris, 1883. (50) on Japon, numbered. Red mor. by Chambolle-Duru, spine & covers richly gt., wrap. preserved, s.-c. (SM. Feb.11; 171) Frs. 5,000

SYLVIA'S HOME JOURNAL
1883-92. Vols. 6, 8-15 only. 4to. Some ll. soiled & torn. Various cont. bdgs., some loose. (SH. Jun.4; 74) *Erlini.* £65

SYLVIUS, Franciscus de la Boe
- **Opera Medica ... cum duplici indice.** Amst., 1679. 1st. Coll. Edn. 4to. Additional port. inserted. Cont. cf., spine gt., slightly worn. (S. Feb.23; 114) *Gurney.* £55

SYME, Patrick
- **Practical Directions for Learning Flower-Drawing.** 1810. 4to. 12 plts. hand-cold., many pp. loose. Orig. bds., upr. cover detchd. (P. Sep.11; 58) *Fogg.* £170
[-] **A Treatise on British Song-Birds.** Edinb. & L., 1823. Cont. hf. cf., rebkd., recornered, orig. mor. label preserved. Pres. copy to Prof. Jameson. (C. Jul.15; 213) *Hill.* £200

SYMONDS, John A.
- **Renaissance in Italy.** L., 1920. 7 vols. Hf. cf. gt., gt. panel. spines, by Sangorski & Sutcliffe, slightly worn. (SPB. Nov.25; 494) $150
- **Works [Collection of].** L., 1872-95. 31 works in 43 vols. 16mo., 12mo. & 8vo. 5 vols. dampstained. Crushed three-qtr. mor., by Stikeman. (SG. Oct.9; 237) $1,700

SYMONDS, Mary & Preece, Louisa
- **Needlework through the Ages.** 1928. 4to. Orig. cl. (CSK. Oct.31; 129) £60

– – **Anr. Copy.** (SBA. Oct.21; 189) *Laywood.* £50
– – **Anr. Copy.** (D. Dec.11-13; 2223) DM 600

SYMONDS, Robert Wemyss
– **English Furniture from Charles II to George II.** 1929. (1000) numbered. 4to. Orig. cl. gt. (SBA. Oct.21; 190) *Wheatley.* £65
– **Furniture Making in the Seventeenth & Eighteenth Century England.** 1955. Orig. cl., slightly affected by damp, d.-w., publisher's box. Sigd. (CSK. Jun.12; 91) £130
– – **Anr. Copy.** 4to. Cl. gt. (P. Oct.23; 255) *Sims & Reed.* £55
– **Masterpieces of English Furniture & Clocks.** 1940. (1250). Fo. Orig. cl. (SH. Oct.9; 139) *Rosewood Inn.* £70
– – **Anr. Copy.** 4to. Orig. cl. gt. (SBA. Oct.21; 191) *Wheatley.* £60
– **Thomas Tompion.** 1951. Ltd. Edn. 4to. Orig. hf. mor. (SH. Mar.6; 578) *Haut.* £110
– – **Anr. Edn.** 1951. 4to. Orig. cl. (SH. Jan.29; 304) *George's.* £65

SYMONS, Alphonse James Albert & others
– **The Nonesuch Century.** 1936. Ltd. Edn. Fo. Orig. cl. (SH. Jun.4; 134) *Shack.* £190
– – **Anr. Copy.** Nones. Pr., 1936. Orig. buckram, covers slightly dampstained, unc. Pres. copy inscr. to André Simon; from liby. of André L. Simon. (S. May 18; 187) *Quaritch.* £80

SYMONS, Arthur (Ed.)
See–SAVOY, The

SYMONS, G.J.
– **British Rainfall.** 1865-1921. 54 vols. Lacks only Iss. for 1889. Unif. cl. gt. (TA. Mar.19; 365) £115

SYMONS, W. Christian & Mitchell, W. Frederick
– **The British Navy, Past & Present.** 1905. 4to. Lacks front end-paper. Orig. decor. cl., front inner hinge brkn. (TA. Feb.19; 644) £60

SYMPSON, Samuel
– **A New Book of Cyphers.** 1736. Title & 1st. plt. cut out & mntd., tear in list of engravers. Cont. reverse cf., rebkd. (S. Jul.27; 210) *Libris.* £60

SYNESIUS
– **Synesii Episcopi Cyrenes Opera quae extant Omnia.** Paris, 1612. 1st Edn. Fo. Old mor. (from Lyons?), lge, border of fillets & sm. gt. tools with thistles in corners, arms & cipher of Charles de Neuville, Governor of Lyons, decor. spine, some repairs. Bkplts. of Comte Chandon de Briailles & Esmerian. (HD. Mar.18; 165) *Frs.* 20,500

SYNGE, John Millington
– **The Aran Lands.** Ill.:– Jack B. Yeats. Dublin & L., 1907. L.P. Edn. (150). 4to. Buckram, worn, unc. Sigd. by author & artist. (SG. Nov.13; 659) $550

SZYK, Arthur
– **Ink & Blood.** Ed.:– Struthers Burt (preface). N.Y., 1946. (1000) sigd. Fo. Mor., batik bd. s.-c. (lr. edge loose). Recipient's name hand-written by Szyk. (SG. Apr.2; 282) $260
– **The Ten Commandments.** Phila., [1947]. (1000) numbered, & sigd. Cold. pict. cl. (SG. Apr.2; 283) $180

T., A.
– **A Rich Storehouse, or Treasurie for the Diseased.** 1630 [colophon dtd. 1631]. Sm. 4to. Some browning, title slightly soiled, printing flaw on Rlv. Cf., worn, rebkd. [NSTC 23610] (S. Jul.27; 385) *Temperley.* £100

T., R.
– **De Templis, A Treatise of Temples.** 1638. 1st. Edn. 12mo. Edges slightly frayed at beginning. Cont. sheep, corners worn. From the collection of Eric Sexton. [STC 23625] (C. Apr.15; 150) *Marlborough.* £90

TABARIN–GRATTELARD, Baron de
– **Inventaire Universel des Oeuvres de Tabarin . . . –Les Rencontres . . . du Baron de Grattelard.** Paris, 1622; n.d. 2nd Edn.; 3rd Edn. 2 works in 1 vol. 16mo. Red mor. by Trautz-Bauzonnet, fillet, decor. spine. inside dentelle. (HD. Mar.18; 166) *Frs.* 2,800

TABERNAEMONTANUS, Jacobus Theodorus
– **Neuw, vnd vollkommenlich Kreuterbuch.** Frankfurt, 1591. 1st. Edn. Pt. 2 (of 2). Lge. fo. Title defect at margin & bkd., slightly browned at end, last lf. lacks corner, lightly soiled, Cont blind-tooled pig-bkd. wd. bds., 2 clasps, lacks 1 tie, other tie defect. (HK. Nov.18-21; 778) DM 4,200
– – **Anr. Copy.** Lacks ll. 5 & 6 (blank) at beginning, pp. 1-10 & 753-64 (752-63), 1st- & last ll. defect. & reprd, lacks most of title. Cont. blind-tooled leath.-bkd. wood bds., soiled, end-ll. renewed 19th. C., 2 clasps, lacks ties. (HK. May 12 74; 448) DM 4,000
– – **Anr. Edn.** Ed.:– Caspar Bauhinus. Frankfurt, 1625. 3rd. Edn. 3 pts. in 1 vol. Fo. slightly browned thro.-out, slightly soiled in parts in margins, some sm. margin tears. Cont. decor. blind-tooled pig.-bkd. wood bds. 8 corner & 2 centre bosses, remains of ties. (R. Mar.31-Apr.4; 1460) DM 3,600
– – **Anr. Edn.** Basle, 1664. Fo. Staining, browned. Cont. blind-stpd. pig. (SPB. Nov.25; 96) $1,600
– – **Anr. Edn.** Ed.:– C. Bauhin. [Basel] [1664] 2 pts. in 1 vol. Fo. Lacks 1 lf. after typographical title, several index ll., 7 index ll. from a later Edn., slightly soiled thro.-out, fault in typog. title & text loss, worming. Cont. pig-bkd. wd. bds., very worn, wormed, lacks 2 clasps. (HK. Nov.18-21; 779) DM 3,200
– – **Anr. Edn.** Ed.:– Casp & Hier. Bauhin. Basel, 1687. Later Edn. Pt. 1 (of 3). Fo. Some old MS. marginalia, sm. fault bkd., browned in parts & slightly soiled. Cont. leath., spine & jnts. defect. (HK. May 12-14; 449) DM 1,500

TABLE DES MEUBLES HERALDIQUES
See–ARMORIAL D'ABRY–TABLE DE MEUBLES HERALDIQUES

TABLEAU de la Croix . . .
Paris, 1651. Cont. red mor., borders, 2 fillets, corner-pieces, central motif decor. with pointillé tools, central cartouches with 'Claudine' on upr. cover & 'Dupré' on lr., traces of metal clasps. (HD. Mar.18; 167) *Frs.* 2,500
– – **Anr. Copy.** Lr. margin soiled & some browning, some ll. with sm. tears in margin. Cont. mor., dentelle, sm. stps., decor., fillet outer dentelle. (D. Dec.11-13; 731) DM 1,200

TABLEAUX HISTORIQUES des Campagnes d'Italie, depuis l'an IV jusqu'a la bataille de Marengo
Paris, 1806. L.P. Fo. Mod. crimson mor., gt., Napoleonic emblems on sides & in 5 compartments of spine. (S. Oct.21; 478) *C.E. King.* £500

TABLEAUX HISTORIQUES DE LA REVOLUTION FRANÇAISE
Ill.:– Berthault. Paris, 1804. 3 vols. Fo. Hf.-title. Later hf. cf. (SI. Dec.4; 554) Lire 1,400,000

TABLEAUX, STATUES . . . Galerie de Florence
[Paris], 1819. 2 vols. Fo. Hf. mor., worn. (P. Feb.19; 48) *Mamos.* £80
– – **Anr. Copy.** Foxed & dampstained, 2 ll. badly torn. Orig. hf. mor., worn. (TA. Oct.16; 157) £55

TABLEAUX VIVANTS
N.d. Ltd. Edn. Extra-ill. with 3 ill. Orig. parch. gt. (P. Feb.19; 18) *Bibn.* £210

TABLETTES DES FLANDRES
Bruges, 1948-73. 18 vols. Orig. bdg. (LM. Nov.8; 283) B.Frs. 7,000

TABOUROT, Etienne
– **Les Bigarrures et Touches du Seigneur des Accords. Avec les Apophtegmes du sieur Gaulard, et les Escraignes Dijonnoises.** Paris, 1585. 1st Edn. 3 pts. in 1 vol. 12mo. Red mor. by Blanchetiere-Bretault, fillet border on spine, mor. doubls. with border of tools in 16th C. style, Flemish silk end-papers. (HD. Mar.18; 168)
– – **Anr. Edn.** Rouen, 1620. 5 pts. in 1 vol. 12mo. Jansenist mor. by Raymann, inside dentelle. (HD. Mar.18; 170) *Frs.* 1,200
– – **Anr. Edn.** Rouen, 1621. 5 pts. in 1 vol. 12mo. Cont. vell. (HD. Mar.18; 171) *Frs.* 1,150
– – **Anr. Edn.** Rouen, 1640. 5 pts. in 2 vols. Cont. red mor., fillet, spines decor. with pointillé. Bkplt. of Firmin-Didot. (HD. Mar.18; 172) *Frs.* 1,250

TABOUROT, Jehan 'Thoinot Arbeau'
– **Compot et Manuel Calendrier par lequel toutes personnes peuvent facilement apprendre & scavoir les Cours du Soleil & de la Lune.** Paris, 1588.

Mor. by Lortic. Stp. 'Bibliothèque de Mr. L. Dufruit' on title; from Honeyman Collection. (S. May 19; 2953) *Hughes.* £460

TABULA CHRISTIANE RELIGIONIS
[Venice], [Manfredus de Bonellis], [after 1500?]. Some inner margins reprd. Mod. paper bds. (C. Apr.1; 88) *Goldschmidt.* £80

TABULATED PEDIGREES of Thoroughbred Horses
1932. Lge. fo. Cl., s.-c., front pp. taped & torn. (JL. Dec.14; 479) Aus. $280

TACHARD, Gui
– **Second Voyage du Père Tachard et des Jesuites envoyez par le Roy au Royaume de Siam.** Ill.:– Vermeulen. Paris, 1689. 1st. Edn. 4to. Cont. mott. cf. (C. Feb.25; 142) *Feldman.* £200
– **Voyage to Siam, des Péres Jesuites . . . together with Second Voyage.** Paris, 1686; 1689. 4to. Margins slightly soiled, top right-hand corner of vol. 1 slightly affected by worm. Old mott. cf., rebkd. (TA. Jan.22; 26) £160

TACHE, Joseph Charles
– **Des Provinces de l'Amérique du Nord et d'une Union Fédérale.** Quebec, 1858. 1st. Edn. 12mo. Mor. gt., upr. cover gt.-lettered 'Presented to H.R.H. Prince Arthur by the Province of Quebec'. (SG. Mar.5; 117) $220

TACITUS, Publius or Gaius Cornelius
– **The Annales . . .–The Ende of Nero & Beginning of Galba.** Trans.:– [R. Greneway] (1st. work); & [Sir H. Savile]. 1598. 1st. Edn. in Engl.; 2nd. Edn. 2 works in 1 vol. Fo. Lacks 1st. lf. of 1st. work (blank except for sig.). Cont. cf., gt. arms of Dr. Roger Goad on upr. cover, spines reprd. Bkplts. of Gerard Moultrie & J.R. Abbey, lately in the collection of Eric Sexton. [STC 23644 & 23643] (C. Apr.15; 151) *Maggs.* £110
– – **Anr. Copy.** 2 vols. in 1. Wormed. Mod. qtr. cf. (SG. Sep.25; 299) $120
– – **Anr. Edn.** L., 1640. 2 vols. in 1. Fo. Old cf. Sigd. inscr. by Charles Whibley to Frank Bond, 1916, on fly-lf. (SG. Sep.25; 300) $110
– **De Vita et Moribus Iulii Agricolae Liber.** Hammersmith, Doves Pr., 1900. (5) on vell. Sm. 4to. Orig. vell., unc., qtr. mor. s.-c. (CNY. May 22; 372) $1,800
– – **Anr. Edn.** L., Doves Pr., 1900. (225). 4to. Orig. vell., slight soiling. (SPB. May 29; 126) $200
– – **Anr. Edn.** Ed.:– J.W. Mackail. Hammersmith, Doves Pr., 1900. 5 vols. Mor. by Cobden-Sanderson, gt., fillets, decor., gt. inner dentelles & spine. (D. Dec.11-13; 1051) DM 5,000
– **Les Oeuvres.** Paris, 1582. Fo. Ruled in red thro-out, old inscr. 'Par. Pyr' de Gandole' on title. Cont. red mor., gt., covers with central wreath of olive sprays, cornerpieces of same sprouting from roundel enclosing double lily-head, flat spine gt. à la fanfare, including apples, lilies & daisies, lacks silk ties. (SM. Oct.8; 2029) *Frs.* 5,500
– [Opera.] Venice, Nov. 1534. 4to. 1st & last ll. torn & reprd., not affecting text, slight browning. 19th C. str.-grd. mor., gt. foliate decorations to corners. Bkplt. of John Wyndham Bruce. (S. May 5; 447) *Thorp.* £90
– – **Anr. Edn.** Parma, 1795. (30). 3 vols. 4to. Cont. qtr. cf., rebkd., orig. spines preserved. (S. Nov.25; 383) *Quaritch.* £130
– [Opera] **libri quinque noviter inverti atque relinquis eius operibus edita.** Ed.:– Philippus Beroaldus. Rome, 1 Mar. 1515. 1st. Compl. Edn. Fo. 10 ll. 'Vita Agticlae' bnd. after f.2N4, slightly spotted & dampstained, some marginalia in old hand, bkplts. Antique style pig, gt. arms of the Cole family on covers, worn, covers detchd. (S. Oct.21; 319) *Quaritch.* £290

TAFEREEL DER DWAASHEID, HET GROOTE
Ed.:– Johr Law. [Amst?]. 1720. Fo. Cont. Dutch red mor. gt., spine tooled in compartments, covers elab. decor., jnts. split, gt. inside borders. (S. Nov.24; 184) *S. & R.* £1,300
– – **Anr. Copy.** Without 5th. text pt., title in 3rd. version, 72 engraved plts., a few plts. with an insignificant tear, or worn in fold, some a bit browned. Cont. gt.-stpd. & panel. cf., spine gt., top & foot of spine slightly defect. (VG. Dec.17; 1552) *Fls.* 2,350

TAFEREELEN, Nederlandsche . . .
Ill.:– H. Spilman after C. Pronk, J. Bulthuis, J. de Beijer, & others. Amst., 1792. 3 vols. Impressions of some plts. weak, some foxing & browning,

TAFEREELEN, Nederlandsche . . . *-contd.*
occasional soiling. Cont. hf. cf., top of spine a bit defect. (VG. Dec.17; 1553) Fls. 13,000

TAGART, Edward
– Memoir of the late Captain Peter Heywood, R.N., with Extracts from his Diaries & Correspondence. L., 1832. Inked notes on some pp. Recased in orig. bds., qtr. cl., with remains of backstrip label unc. (KH. Nov.18; 580) Aus. $140

TAGLIAFERRI, Filippo
– Corso Completo di Calligrafia. Ill.:– N. Pasinati. Ca. 1860. 4to. Cont. hf.-cf. (SH. Dec.12; 499) *Schierenberg.* £50

TAGLICHE ERBAUNG eines wahren Christen
Ill.:– after J.W. Baumgartner, Fr. Sigrist & others. Vienna & Augsburg, 1755. 4to. Cont. leath. (HK. Nov.18-21; 1446) DM 900

TAGLIENTE, Girolamo
– Libro de Abaco il quale insegna fare ogni ragione mercantile: & pertegare le terre con larte di la Geometria. Ill.:– L(uc') A(ntonio degli Uberti). Venice, 1544. Disbnd., vell. s.-c. From Honeyman Collection. (S. May 19; 2954) *Zeitlin & Verbrugge.* £480

TAGLINI, Carlo
– Libri duo de aere eiusque Natura et effectis cum notis et animadversionibus. Flor., 1736. 1st. Edn. 4to. Cont. mott. cf., gt. spine, worn. From Honeyman Collection. (S. May 19; 2955) *Howell.* £60

TAINE, Hippolyte A.
– Les Origines de la France Contemporaine. Paris, 1876-94. Orig. Edn. 6 vols. Long-grd. hf. lavallière mor., corners, decor. spines, gt. fillets, unc., wrap., by Noulhac. (HD. Jun.10; 214) Frs. 4,700

TAIROV, Aleksandr
– Zapiski rezhissera [Notes of a Director]. [Moscow], 1921. Some plts. & ills. offset. Orig. ptd. upr. wrap. by A. Ekster, reprd., rebkd. with mod. lr. wrap. (SH. Feb.6; 366) *Reed & Sims.* £80

TAISNIER, Joannes
– De Annuli Sphaerici Fabrica & usu libri tres Geometrici. Antw., 1560. Sm. 4to. Lge. piece torn from G1 with loss of text, a few ll. cropped at foot, title browned & with old inscrs. Disbnd., hf. red mor. case. From Honeyman Collection. (S. May 19; 2956) *Rogers Turner.* £170
– Opsculum . . . de Natura Magnetis. Cologne, 1562. 1st. Edn. 4to. Lacks last lf. with the port. dupl., some ll. slightly spotted, old name 'Cyneliy Clementis' on title. 19th. C. hf. cf., slightly worn. (S. Oct.21; 426) *Ellison.* £190
– Opus Mathematicum Octo Libros Complectens . . . Cologne, 1562. 1st Edn. Fo. Slight worming, not affecting text, some foxing. Cont. cf., worn. (HD. Jun.24; 117) Frs. 1,800
– – Anr. Edn. Cologne, 1583. Fo. Browned thro.-out, some marginal staining, a few wormholes at beginning & end, occasional marginal repairs, MS. notes on a few ll. Cont. vell., stained. From Honeyman Collection. (S. May 19; 2957) *Hughes.* £130

TAJIMA, Schücki
– Masterpieces selected from the Ukiyoye' School. Tokyo, 1906-09. 5 vols. fo. Publisher's silk bds., box. (HD Jun.10; 215) Frs. 6,500
– Selected Relics of Japanese Art. Kyoto, 1899-1903. 10 vols. Fo. Pict. linen, laced. (SG. Dec.4; 336) $350

TALAEUS, Audomarus
See–**RAMUS, Petrus–TALAEUS, Audomarus –SCRIBONIUS, G.A.**

TALAVERA, Fernando de, Archbp. of Granada
– Breve e Muy Provechosa Doctrina delo que Deue Saber todo Christiano con Otros Tractados. [Granada]. [Meinerdus Ungut & Johann Pegnitzer], ca. 1496. 1st. Edn. 4to. Rubricated, lacks a3-6 & 4 blank ll., 1st. 10 & last 5 ll. wormed affecting text, some other marginal worming, some slight soiling. 17th. C. limp vell., upr. hinge brkn., paste-down torn, cl. box. From the collection of Eric Sexton. [C(Add) 1244b, Goff T11] (CNY. Apr.8; 73) $6,500

TALBOT, Catherine
– Essays. L., 1820. 24mo. Gt.-tooled cf., cl. s.-c. Fore-e. pntg.; from the liby. of Zola E. Harvey. (SG. Mar.19; 176) $170

TALBOT, Edward Allen
– Five Years Residence in the Canadas. 1824. 1st. Edn. 2 vols. Frontis.'s slightly foxed & offset on titles. Later pol. hf. cf. [Sabin 94229] (C. Nov.6; 231) *Shore.* £90

TALBOT, William Henry Fox
[–] Affidavits made by Sir D. Brewster & Sir J. Herschel respecting the Calotype Photographic process invented by H.F. Talbot, Esq. [L.], [1854]. Lightly foxed, iss. without title-p. 2 loose sheets as iss. (SG. Apr.23; 194) $550
– The Process of Calotype Photogenic Drawing, Communicated to the Royal Society, June 10th, 1841. [L], [1841]. Reprint of Fox Talbot's paper to Royal Society. Mod. marb. bds. (S. Dec.2; 779) *Quaritch.* £260
– – Anr. Edn. [L.], n.d. 4to. On 1 loose sheet as iss. (SG. Apr.23; 195) $190

TALFOURD, Sir Thomas Noon
– Tragedies. L., 1844. 16mo. Red mor. gt. Fore-e. pntg. (SG. Mar.19; 177) $160

TALLEMANT DES REAUX, Gédéon
– Geschichten. Trans.:– O. Falke. Munich, 1913. (100) Privilege Edn. 2 vols. Orig. leath., gt. (R. Oct.14-18; 1014) DM 680
– Les Historiettes. Paris, 1854. 1st. Compl. Edn. 9 vols. Mor. gt., gt. monogs. on covers. (SBA. Jul.23; 665) *Lavigne.* £240

TALLEYRAND, Charles Maurice, Duc de
– Mémoires . . . Ed.:– Duc de Broglie. Paris, 1891-92. 5 vols. Lge. 8vo. Hf. cf. (HD. Jun.29; 218) Frs. 3,200

TALLIS, John
– History & Description of the Crystal Palace, & the Exhibition of the World's Industry in 1851. Ed.:– J.G. Strutt. Ill.:– after drawings & daguerreotypes, by Beard, Mayall, etc. L., ca. 1855. 3 vols. in 2. 4to. Some foxing. Hf. mor., worn. (SG. Apr.23; 196) $200
– – Anr. Edn. N.d. 3 vols. 4to. Spotted. Cont. cf. (SH. Mar.5; 141) *Reed & Sims.* £70
– – Anr. Copy. 2 vols. Some foxing, Mor. gt. (P. Sep.11; 49) *Crowe.* £50
– Illustrated London. Ed.:– W. Gaspey. ca. 1850. 2 vols. Hf. cf. gt. (P. Nov.13; 41) *Jeffreys.* £60
– Topographical Dictionary of England & Wales. Ed.:– E.L. Blanchard. Ca. 1860. 6 vols. Orig. blind-stpd. cl., spines worn. (TA. Jun.18; 245) £60

TALMUD
– The Living Talmud. Ed.:– Judah Goldin. Trans.:– Judah Goldin. Ill:– Ben-Zion. Ltd. Edns. Cl., 1960. (1500) numbered, & sigd. by artist. Fo. Monthly letter laid in. Vell.-bkd. buckram. (SG. Jan.15; 270) $110

TALMUD Babli
– Masechet Eiruvin. Pesaro, ca. 1510-11. 1st. Edn. Fo. 135 ll. only (of 140, lacks ll. at beginning & end), some ll. loose, 1 lf. defect. & reprd. with word loss, worming, stained. Sheep-bkd. bds., torn, hinges brkn. (SPB. May 11; 203) $2,200
– Masechet Yebamot. Pesaro, 1508. 1st. Edn. Fo. 150 ll. only (of 169), outer margins reprd. without text loss, some ll. detchd., some worming, stained. Cl., spine torn, stained. (SPB. May 11; 204) $4,500

TAMAYO, Rufino
–Apocalypse de Saint Jean. Monaco, [1959]. (255) numbered on velin de Rives. 4to. Loose as iss. in wraps., boxed. (SG. Apr.2; 287) $1,100

TAMBIMUTTU (Trans.)
See–**PIPER, John**

TANA DE'VEI Eliyahu Rabba Ve'zuta
Venice, 1598. 1st. Edn. 4to. Staining, slight worming, repairs. Hf. cl. (SPB. May 11; 205) $650

TANNER, Henry Schenk
– The American Traveller. Phila., 1837. 3rd. Edn. 18mo. Lge. folding map torn, some foxing, ex-liby. Orig. cl. (SG. Jun.11; 406) $110
– Atlas of the United States. Phila., priv. ptd., 1835. 4to. Cont. hf. roan. W.a.f. (C. Nov.6; 275) *Evans.* £320
– New Universal Atlas. Phila., 1845. New Edn. 4to. Some prelim. lr. margins just stained not affecting matter. Cont. hf. str.-grd. mor. gt., slightly worn. (SBA. Oct.21; 126) *Nicholson.* £340

TANNER, John
– The Hidden Treasures of the Art of Physick Fully Discovered. 1667. 2nd. Edn. 1 prelim. blank, but no blank before title, some headlines, sigs etc. just touched. New cl. [Wing T137] (S. Dec.2; 634) *Phelps.* £60

TANNER, Matthias
Societas Jesu Apostolorum Imitatrix. Ill.:– W.P. Kilian after J.G. Heinsch. Prague, 1694. Fo. Ill. 108 on 3V4 trimmed & mntd. over misprinted ill. 135, slight browning, a few rust holes, sm. flaw in ill. 110. Mod. red mor. by J. Mackenzie, gt., spine gt., inside dentelles, 1 jnt. split. From liby. of the discalced Carmelite monks of ?Rasne. (S. Oct.21; 458) *Thomas.* £130

TANNER, Thomas
– Bibliotheca Britannico-Hibernica. 1748. 1st. Edn. Fo. Offsetting on title, slight spotting. Cont. spr. cf., worn. (S. Jan.26; 128) *Crowe.* £50

TANSILLO, Luigi
– The Nurse, a Poem. Trans.:– William Roscoe. L'pool, 1798. 4to. Cont. str.-grd. mor. (SH. Jan.30; 495) *Williams.* £85

TANSILLO, Luigi & Bernia, Francesco
[–] Stanze Amorose, sporta gli Horti delle Donne et in Lode della Menta. La Caccia d'Amore del Bernia. Venice, 1574. 2 pts. in 1 vol. 12mo. Lacks 3rd. (?) blank, stp. of J. Richard de Montbard on title, bkplt. of Thomas Gaisford. 18th. C. Fr. red mor., triple gt. fillet, flat spine gt. with longitudinal title, inner gt. dentelles. (SM. Oct.8; 2030) Frs. 3,800

TÄNTZER, Joh. & Pärson, Joh. W. von
– Der Dianen Hohe und Niedere Jagdgeheimnisse. Leipzig, 1734. 2nd. Leipzig Edn. Fo. Lightly browned in parts, some stains. Cont. vell., worn, slightly soiled. (H. Dec.9/10; 303) DM 4,000

TANZI, Carlo Antonio
– Alcune Poesie Milanesi, e Toscane. Milan, 1766. 4to. Mod. hf. mor., partly unc. (S. Dec.4; 556) Lire 320,000

TAPIA ZENTENO, Carlos de
– Arte Novissima de Lengua Mexicana. Mexico, 1753. Sm. 4to. Some spotting. Limp vell. (SPB. May 5; 491) $1,600
– Noticia de la lengua Huasteca, que en Beneficio de sus Nacionales. Mexico, 1767. Sm. 4to. Lacks sig. H. (pp. 49-56). Limp vell. (SPB. May 5; 492) $750

TAPISSERIES DU ROI . . . Les Quatre Elemens et Les Quatres Saisons
Ill.:– C. Le Brun. Paris, 1670. Lge. fo. Title strengthened. Old cf., gt. arms on covers. (BS. Jun.11; 91) £400
– – Anr. Edn. [Paris], [1670]. Fo. Some foxing & staining. Red mor. gt., with arms & devices of Louis XIV. (SPB. May 6; 207) $1,200

TAPLIN, Rev. George
– Folklore, Manners, Customs & Languages of the South Australian Aborigines. Adelaide, 1879. 1st. Series. Several ll. detchd., soiling. Cl., shaken. (KH. Nov.18; 581) Aus. $150

TAPLIN, William
[–] The Sportsman's Cabinet. L., 1803. 1st. Edn. 2 vols. in 1. 4to. Some foxing & minor stains. Three-qtr. mor. (SG. Dec.11; 421) $550
[–] – Anr. Edn. Ill.:– Bewick. 1803-04. 1st. Edn. 2 vols. 4to. Cont. red str.-grd. mor. gt. Bkplt. of Eliza Gulston. (S. Nov.24; 281) *Steedman.* £350
[–] – Anr. Copy. Advts., some slight spotting. Cont. panel. cf., rebkd. (S. May 5; 204) *Demetzy.* £240
[–] – Anr. Edn. 1803-04. Margin of 1 plt. torn & reprd., slight soiling. Later hf. mor. (CSK. May 8; 160) £190
[–] – Anr. Copy. Plts. soiled. Orig. leath. (R. Oct.14;18; 2816) .DM 1,400

TAPSTERS Downfall, The, & the Drunkards Joy
[L], 1641. Sm. 4to. Tree cf. by Rivière, rebkd., orig. spine preserved. [Wing T165] (S. Nov.25; 461) *Quaritch.* £130

TARAPHA, Franciscus
See–**TARRAFA, Franciscus**

TARAN [Ram]
Ed.:– [Yu. V. Gol'dberg]. St. Petersb., 1907. No. 1. 4to. Unbnd. (SH. Feb.5; 137) *De la Casa.* £65

TARDY
- La Pendule Française.-La Montre. Paris, 1974; n.d. 3 vols.; 1 vol. 4to. Orig. wraps. (SH. Jun.25; 10) *Hill.* £60

TARENTE, Alexandre Charles Macdonald, Duc de
- Recollections. Ed.:- Camille Rousset. Trans.:- S.L. Simeon. N.Y., 1892. 2 vols. Cl. (SG. Oct.30; 229) $120

TARIF POUR LA JAUGE DES VAISSEAUX PROPRES A CONTENIR DES LIQUEURS,
avec une Explication de son usage
1742. 12mo. Slight browning & soiling. Cont. Fr. red mor., gt. From liby. of André L. Simon. (S. May 18; 189) *James.* £130

TARLETON, Sir Banastre
- A History of the Campaigns of 1780 & 1781, in the Southern Provinces of North America. L., 1787. 1st. Edn. 4to. A few top edges worn, paper losses to later ll. Mod. red hf. mor., gt. spine. From liby. of William E. Wilson. [Sabin 94397] (SPB. Apr.29; 260) $800
- - Anr. Copy. Old cf., rebkd. (SPB. Jun.22; 127) $425

TARRAFA, Franciscus
- De Origine, ac Rebus Gestis Regum Hispaniae. Antw., 1553. 1st. Edn. Ruled in red thro-out, a little worming, slightly affecting text. Cont. (?Fr.) cf., gt. ornaments, double fillet panels, rebkd., wormed & worn, bkplt of Baron Landau Liby. [Sabin 94398] (S. Oct.21; 535) *Quevedo.* £130
- De Origine, ac Rebus Gestis Regum Hispaniae Liber multarum Rerum cognitione refertus.-De Vitis Principum et gestis Venetorum liber. Antw.; Venice, 1553; 1554. 1st. Edn. (1st. Work). 2 works in 1 vol. Slight browning. Cont. blind-stpd. pig. over oak bds., covers with central panels with acorn motifs, soiled, lacks clasps. From liby. of André L. Simon. (S. May 18; 188) *Maggs.* £150

TARTAGLIA, Niccolo
- L'Arithmétique. Trans.:- G. Rosselin. Paris, 1578. 1st. Fr. Edn. 2 pts. in 1 vol. A few ll. misbnd. Old cf., rebkd., hasp mark on upr. cover. Bkplt. of liby. of Cathedral Chapter at St. Peter's Exeter; from Honeyman Collection. (S. May 19; 2964) *Riley-Smith.* £150
- Nova Scientia. Venice, 1537. 1st. Edn. Sm. 4to. Title cut into at head with partial loss of some letters, some browning & staining. 18th. C. vell., hf. mor. case. Bkplts. of Marbury Hall liby.; from Honeyman Collection. (S. May 19; 2958) *Offenbacher.* £560
- Nova Scientia.-Quesiti, et Inventioni Diverse. Venice, 1537; 1546. 1st. Edns. 2 works in 1 vol. 4to. 1st. work with a few stains; 2nd. work lacks folding plt., very stained at beginning & near end; bnd. in reverse order. Cont. cf., rebkd. & reprd., worn, hf. mor. case. From Honeyman Collection. (S. May 19; 2959) *Riley-Smith.* £520
- - Anr. Copy. Lr. outer margins dampstained & frayed at beginning & end, slight soiling, etc., 1st. work with title cut into at head with partial loss of some letters; 2nd. work lacks folding plt., & has a few marginal repairs & tears. From Honeyman Collection. (S. May 19; 2959A) *Zeitlin & Verbrugge.* £460
- La Prima [-sesta] parte del General Trattato di Numeri, et Misure. Venice, 1556-60. 1st. Edn. 6 pts. in 2 vols. Fo. Some staining, occasional browning, prelims. to pt. 1 slightly wormed in lr. margins. Cont. limp vell., vol. I a little defect., inscr. 'Franci cerregi liber' on end-papers, hf. red mor. cases. From Honeyman Collection. (S. May 19; 2962) *Quaritch.* £1,700
- Quesiti, et Inventioni Diverse. Venice, 1546. 1st. Edn. 1st. 5 lines of A2 recto heightened in gold, lacks 2 lf. table & folding plt., slip with ptd. arms pasted on verso of title. Cont. Italian mor., richly gt. with interlaced panels, fleurons & lf. tools, sm. hand-painted royal arms in centre of covers, spine & corners reprd., lacks ties. From Honeyman Collection. (S. May 19; 2960) *Norman.* £900
- - Anr. Copy. later vell. gt. (TA. Sep.18; 212) £190
- Regola Generale da Sulevare con Ragione e Misura non Solamente ogni Affondata Nave: ma una Torre Solida di Metallo (-Ragionamenti ... sopra la sua Travagliata Inventione). Venice, 1551. 1st. Edn. 2 pts. Sm. 4to. Lacks blank e4 at end of 1st. pt., 2nd. pt. marginally stained. Wraps., 1 spine defect. From Honeyman Collection. (S. May 19; 2961) *James.* £360

- Three Books of Colloquies Concerning the Arte of Shooting in Great & Small Peeces of Artillerie ... a Treatise Named Lucar Appendix. 1588. 1st. Engl. Edn. 2 pts. in 1 vol. Fo. 3 folding woodcut plts. (of 4, 1 defect. & reprd.), lacks title, errata lf. & final blank, some soiling, short tears in 2 ll., owner's inscr. Cont. sheep, worn, rebkd. 19th. C. bkplt. of Lt. Gen. Sir Henry Lefroy; from Honeyman Collection. [NSTC 23689] (S. May 19; 2965) *Armouries.* £360
- Tutte l'Opere d'Arithmetica. Venice, 1592-93. 2nd. Edn. 2 pts. in 1 vol. 4to. Some ll. in pt. 2 wormed in lr. fore-corners touching text in places, some staining, title inscr. 'Ad uso di Filippo Sachini' & with stp. on end-papers. Hf. cf., spine defect., MS. index on end-papers. From Honeyman Collection. (S. May 19; 2963) *Riley-Smith.* £70

TARTINI, G.
- Trattato di Musica secondo la Vera Scienza dell'armonia. Padova, 1754. 1st. Edn. 4to. Cont. paper bds., spine reprd., defect. (H. Dec.9/10; 1292) DM 900

TASCHENBIBLIOGRAPHIEN FUR BUCHERSAMMLER
Stuttgart, [1924-27]. 5 vols., all publd. Orig. linen, 1 spine torn. (H. Dec.9/10; 49) DM 420

TASMAN, Capt. J.
See–NARBOROUGH, Sir John, Tasman, Capt. J. & others

TASSIN, Nicolas
- Les Plans et Profils de Toutes les Principles Villes ... de France. [1638]. 2 vols. in 1. Ob. 4to. Lacks ptd. title. Disbnd. W.a.f. (P. Jul.30; 292) *Braunschweg.* £520

TASSO, Torquato
- Aminta. Paris, 1781. Slight spotting. Cont. vell. bds., gt., red mor. lettering & border-pieces, spine tooled in compartments with flower, vase & lyre ornaments, covers with floral border & cornerpieces, gt. in borders, by Kalthoeber(?), slightly rubbed & soiled, mod. cl. box. Bkplt. of T.N. Parker (S. Feb.9; 116) *Kossow.* £130
- - Anr. Edn. Parma, 1789. 4to. Cont. mor. (SH. Jan.30; 496) *Fletcher.* £150
- - Anr. Edn. [Parma], 1796. 4to. Mod. hf. mor., orig. wraps. bnd. in, partly unc. (SI. Dec.4; 557) Lire 320,00
- - Anr. Copy. L., 1800. Hand-painted vell., soiled & buckled. Fore-e. pntg.; from the liby. of Zola E. Harvey. (SG. Mar.19; 179) $150
- L'Aminta Boschereccia. Ill.:- F. Fambrini after P.A. Novelli. Venice, 1762. 12mo. Cont. cf. From the collection of John A. Saks. (C. Jun.10; 240) *Quaritch.* £90
- Aminta, Favola Pastorale. Paris, 1781. On vell. Cont. mor., gt., by Derome le Jeune with his ticket, arms of 'Paris d'Illens' on covers, wide gt. dentelle border including bird with outspread wings at corners, flat spine gt. in compartments, inner gt. dentelles, pink silk liners, s.-c. with arms on covers, lined with pink silk, head of s.-c. slightly brkn. Bkplt. of Edward Herbert. (SM. Oct.8; 203) Frs. 41,000
- Aminte. Trans.:- Sieur de la Brosse. Ill.:- Champollion, Ranvier, Maurice Chol - on vell.) Paris, 1882. (10) with 3 printings of vig. Mor. sigd. by Carayon, gt. & decor. 1st. plt. sigd. by Champollion. (SI. Dec.4; 558) Lire 520,000
- Delle Rime ... Insieme con altri Componimenti del Medesima. Venice, Ald. Pr., 1582. 2 vols. 24mo. Later mor., gt. borders, gt.-panel spines. (SG. Sep.25; 16) $450
- La Gierusalemme Liberata. Genova, 1590. 4to. Lacks folios G4 & G8, replaced in cont. facs., some sm. tears, some stains & other sm. imperfections. Cont. vell. (SI. Dec.4; 559) Lire 550,000
- - Anr. Copy. 1 blank, 1 unnumbered p., lacks 4 last pp. with allegory of poem & plt. Vell. (CR. Mar.19; 277) Lire 400,000
- - Anr. Edn. Venice, 1673. 4to. Slight soiling. Old cf., corners reprd. (CSK. Jan.9; 224) £80
- - Anr. Edn. Parma, 1707. 2 vols. 4to. Extra ill. with 36 plts. by Cochin for Paris Didot Edn., 1784. Mod. hf. mor., partly unc. (SI. Dec.4; 560) Lire 1,000,000
- - Anr. Edn. Ill.:- J. Polanzani & M. Schedl. Venice, 1745. 1st. Printing. Lge. fo. 2 ll. with sm. marginal tear reprd., very slight light dampstains to extreme upr. edges of final ll. Orig. vell. bds., gt., outer fillet border, central mor. onlays with gt.

arms of Consul J. Smith, corners slightly scuffed, sm. tear at spine reprd., qtr. mor. gt. box. Subscriber's Copy, with bkplt. of Consul Joseph Smith, bkplts. of Wrest Park, O. & S. Sitwell, & Osbert Sitwell (with his A.N. inserted), lately in the collection of John A. Saks. (C. Jun.10; 238) *Breslauer.* £9,000
- - Anr. Copy. 1 double plt. p. 103 & anr. at end, hf.-title. 19th. C. vell gt., sm. fault in spine, unc. (SI. Dec.4; 561) Lire 3,600,000
- - Anr. Edn. Ill.:- Jean Charles Baquoy & others after Hubert François Bourguignon Gravelot. Paris, 1771. Holland Paper. 2 vols. Sig. on fly-lf. of J. Boothby. Cont. red mor., triple gt. fillet, flat spine gt. with tools designed by Gravelot for the edn., inner gt. dentelles. (SM. Oct.8; 2033) Frs. 6,700
- - Anr. Edn. Paris, [1785-86]. 2nd. Edn. 2 vols. 4to. 1 plt. in double state. 19th. C. red chagrin, 5 spine raised bands, triple gt. fillets, triple gt. inner fillet. (LM. Jun.13; 261) B.Frs. 8,500
- - Anr. Edn. Parma, 1794. 2 vols. bnd. in 1. Fo. Cont. cf., (CR. Jun.11; 526) Lire 1,300,000
- - Anr. Edn. Brussels, 1844. Occasional spotting. Cont. vell., elab. gt., soiled. Fore-e. pntg. of a view of Rome with the Castel St. Angelo & Ponte St. Angelo in the foreground & St. Peter's in the background. (CSK. May.15; 57) £55
- La Gerusalemme Liberata [Plates only]. Ill.:- Bartolommeo Pinelli. [Rome], [1826-27]. Ob. fo. Sm. strip cut from blank lr. margins of engraved frontis. & plt. 43. Stitched & sewn, mostly unc., inserted in imitation mor. gt. folder, silk linings. (CNY. May 22; 240) $400
- Godfrey of Boulogne: or the Recouerie of Ierusalem. Trans.:- Edward Fairefax. 1624. 2nd. Edn. of this trans. Fo. With extra lf. of verses 'The Genius of Godfrey to Prince Charles', title soiled & with rust hole, some ll. stained in lr. margins, last lf. spotted & soiled on verso. Later 17th. C. mor., panel. in gt., some wear, rear pastedown with inscr. 'Francesse Teressa Stuart', mor. pull-off case. [NSTC 23699] (S. Dec.9; 359) *Claridge.* £170
- [-] - Anr. Edn. Trans.:- Edward Fairfax. 1687. Cont. cf., spine gt., bkplt. of John Evelyn. [Wing T174B] (S. Dec.9; 360) *Thorp.* £60
- Il Goffredo Ovvero Gierusalemme Liberata. Ed.:- Scipione Gentili & Giulio Gustavini. Ill.:- J. Leonardis after P.A. Novelli & B. Castello. Venice, 1760-61. 2 vols. 4to. Cont. vell. From collection of John A. Saks. (C. Jun.10; 239) *Breslauer.* £420
- Jerusalem Delivered. Trans.:- John Hoole. L., 1787. 2 vols. Crimson str.-grd. mor. gt. Fore-e. pntg.; from the liby. of Zola E. Harvey. (SG. Mar.19; 178) $400
- Jérusalem délivreée ... Ill.:- H. Gravelot. Paris, 1774. 2 vols. Name cut from title of vol. I, title of vol. II with stp., slightly soiled in places. Cont. red mor., gt., vol. I discoloured. (S. Oct.21; 289) *Ledbury.* £75
- - Anr. Copy. Late 18th. C. str. grd. red mor., gt. roll-stp. around covers, arms of Comte Duriez de Verninac (added later), spines decor. with raised bands, watered silk end-papers, gt. inside Greek. (HD. Feb.27; 39) Frs. 3,000
- - Anr. Copy. 7 extra plts., slight marginal dampstaining at beginning. Cont. marb. cf., gt. roll-stp. around covers, spines decor. with raised bands. (HD. Jun.24; 54) Frs. 1,150
- - Anr. Edn. Trans.:- Philipon de la Madelaine & M. de Lamartine. 1844. Cont. mor., lge. gt. decor. à la cathédrale. (HD. Jun.30; 76) Frs. 1,750

TASSONI, Alessandro
- Memoirs ... Ed.:- Samuel Waker. L., 1814. Early crimson mor., elab. gt.-tooled borders enclosing stpd. design, spine gt., gt. dentelles, doubls. & end-ll. of satin. Fore-e, pntg.; from the liby. of Zola E. Harvey. (SG. Mar.19; 180) $280
- La Secchia Rapita. Modena, 1744. 4to. Cont. mor. gt., head of spine lightly worn. (SI. Dec.4; 564) Lire 550,000

TASTEVEN, Genrikh
- Futurizm [Futurism (Towards a new Symbolism)]. Moscow, 1914. Liby. stps. on title & 1 p. Cont. hf. cl., orig. wraps. mntd. (SH. Feb.6; 367) *Chalk.* £50

TASTU, Amable
- Voyage en France. Ill.:- after Ledoux (frontis.). Tours, 46. Orig. pict. cl., gt., by Haarhaus. (S. Jun.29; 262) *Crete.* £120

TATHAM, Charles H.
- Etchings Representing ... Ancient Ornamental Architecture ... in Rome, 1794-96. 1803. [2nd. Edn.?]. Fo. Mod. hf. cf. (BS. Jun.11; 131) £75
-- Anr. Copy. 101 plts. only, a little soiling & staining. Cont. hf. mor., worn & rebkd., front inner hinge brkn. (CSK. Jan.23; 80) £50
- Etchings Representing the Best Examples of Grecian & Roman Architectural Ornament. 1843. Fo. With number 47 bis plt., no plt. 101 (lacking?), additional inserted litho. title. Mor.-bkd. cl. (S. Dec.8; 34) *Talerman.* £55

TATTERSALL, George
[-] The Cracks of the Day. [L.], ca. 1840. Title-p. heavily browned. Orig. cl. (SG. Dec.11; 422) $180
[-] The Pictorial Gallery of English Race Horses. 1844. Pict. title detchd. Orig. cl. gt., spine torn, slightly loose, unc. (SBA. Jul.23; 666) *Shapero.* £80
-- Anr. Edn. Ill.:- Alken, Cooper, Herring, Hancock, & others. L., 1850. 3rd. Edn. Foxed. Three-qtr. mor., ex-liby. (SG. Dec.11; 423) $475
-- Anr. Copy. Red hf. mor., gt. (R. Oct.14-18; 287) DM 1,700
-- Anr. Edn. 1856. Cl., defect. (PJ. Dec.5; 115) £90
- Sporting Architecture. 1841. 4to. Some foxing. Orig. cl. (S. Dec.8; 1) *Breman.* £110
-- Anr. Edn. L., [1841?]. 4 pts. 4to. Marginal dampstaining on some plts. Cont. cl. with gt.-stpd. title. (CB. May 27; 199) Can. $380

TAUBER-ARP, Sophie
See-ARP, Jean, Delaunay, Sonia & others

TAUCHNITZ
- Collection of British Authors [16 titles]. 1871-1924. 17 vols. Sm. 4to. Cont. unif. qtr. cf., gt. decor. spines. (TA. Dec.18; 70) £50

TAULER, Johannes
- [Sermonen und Historia]. Leipzig, 17 Mar. 1498. 1st. German Edn. 4to. Initial spaces, lf. 60 numbered double, title-lf. bkd., 1 lf. torn at corner, lf. 280 completed in MS, lightly browned in places or stained. Hf. leath., soiled, spine torn. (H. May 21/22; 957) DM 4,200

TAUNTON, Thomas Henry
- Portraits of Celebrated Racehorses. L., 1887. 4 vols. 4to. Hf. red mor. gt., partly unc., by Morrell. (CNY. May 22; 221) $280
-- Anr. Edn. 1887-88. 4 vols. 4to. A few ll. detchd. Orig. mor.-bkd. cl. (CSK. May.1; 152) £240
-- Anr. Copy. Orig. cl., soiled, rebkd. preserving orig. spine. (CSK. Jun.19; 34) £180

TAUST, J.G.
See-WEIGEL, Erhard-Taust, J.G.-MADWEIS, F.-STRAUCH, Egidius

TAUT, Bruno
- Die Auflösung der Städte. Hagen, 1920. 4to. 3 ll. loose, text ll., end-papers slightly soiled. Orig. paper bds., lightly soiled. (H. Dec.9/10; 1926) DM 440

TAVERNER, Eric
- Trout Fishing from all Angles. L., 1929. 1st. Edn. Interleaved thro.-out. Cl. Author's copy, sigd. & with many MS. corrections, A.L.s. from H. Marshall Webb Loosely insrtd. (SG. Oct.16; 470) $300

TAVERNER, Eric & others
- Salmon Fishing. L., 1931. De Luxe 1st. Edn. (275) numbered on H.M.P., sigd. Gt.-stpd. mor. (SG. Apr.9; 309) $650
-- Anr. Copy. Unc. & unopened. (SG. Oct.16; 476) $600

TAVERNER, John
- Certaine Experiments Concerning Fish & Fruite. Ed.:- Eric Parker. Manchester, 1928. Reissue of the 1928 sheets. 4to. Ptd. notice beneath title date 'Eugene V. Connett ... New York City ... 1961'. Hf. cl. (SG. Dec.11; 106) $1,200

TAVERNIER, Jean Baptiste, Baron d'Aubonne
- Beschr. der Sechs Reisen ... in Türckey, Persien und Indien, innerhalb Viertsig Jahren, durch alle Wege. Genf, 1681. 5 pts. in 1 vol. Fo. Lacks 5 pp. at end, browned & slightly soiled in parts, slightly stained at head at beginning. Cont. leath.-bkd. wood bds., 2 brass clasps. (HK. May 12-14; 515) DM 900
- A Collection of Several Relations & Treatises Singular & Curious. 1680. 1st. Edn. in Engl. 2 pts.

in 1 vol. Fo. 7 plts. only (of 8), 1 folding engraved map, with advt. lf. [a]2 & at end, slight browning. Cont. cf., slightly worn. [Wing T250] (S. Sep.29; 79) *Crete.* £120
- Les Six Voyages ... en Turquie, en Perse, et Aux Indes. Amst?, 1679. 2 vols. 12mo. 1 plt. with several tears, title & several ll. in vol. II stained, liby. stp. on titles, occasional browning. Cont. vell. bds., 2 hinges brkn., soiled. (S. May 5; 63) *Russell.* £80
-- Anr. Edn. Paris, 1679. 16mo. Old cf., worn. (SG. Feb.26; 316) $150
- The Six Voyages ... through Turkey into Persia, & in the East Indies. Trans.:- J. Philips. 1677-78. 1st. Edn. in Engl. 3 pts. in 1 vol. Fo. Occasional spotting, tear in ll. *L2 & 3 reprd. without loss, some outer margins slightly frayed. Cont. cf., rebkd. [Wing T255] (C. Nov.5; 162) *Diba.* £500
-- Anr. Copy. 2 pts. in 1 vol. Some browning & staining, a few ll. cropped with loss of p. numerals, etc., short tears in H3, BB4 & *K1-*L3. Cont. cf. (S. Mar.31; 508) *Bertall.* £100
-- Anr. Edn. 1678. Fo. 22 plts. (of 23), some tears. Bdg. not stated, worn, 1 cover detchd. [Wing T256] (SH. Jul.16; 191) *Murray.* £80
- Six Voyages through Turkey into Persia. -Collection of Several Relations & Treatises not Printed among his First Six Voyages. Trans.:- J. Phillips. L., 1678; 1680. 1st. Edn. in Engl. 2 works in 1 vol. Fo. 2nd. work lacks map. Disbnd. (SG. Oct.30; 349) $600
- Six Voyages ... through Turkey into Persia & East Indies.-A New Relation of the Inner-Part of the Grand Seignor's Seraglio. L., 1678; 1677. 2 works in 1 vol. Fo. Cf., rebkd. (P. Jul.2; 173) *Timmons.* £320
- Vierzig-Jährige Reise-Beschreibung. Trans.:- J. Menudier. Nuremb., 1681. Coll. Edn. 5 pts. in 1 vol. Fo. Slightly browned in parts. Cont. vell. (R. Mar.31-Apr.4; 2556) DM 2,300

TAVERNIER, Jean Baptiste-SPONS, Jacob
- Vierzig-Jaehrige Reise-Beschreibung ... durch Tuerken, Persien, Indien ... und andere Oerter [pts. I-III].-Italienische Dalmatische, Greichische & Orientalische Reise-Beschreibung. Ill.:- J.J. Schollenberger, J.J. Vogel, P. Troschel & G. Hiyschman. Nuremb., 1681. 1st. Edn. in German. 5 pts. in 1 vol. Fo. Cont. vell., worn at spine. (CNY. Oct.1; 51) $850

TAXE de la Chancellerie Romaine ...
Rome [Holland], 1744. 12mo. Cont. mor., by Derome, 3 fillets, decor. spine, inside dentelle, stained. (HD. Mar.18; 173) Frs. 1,500

TAXIL, Jean
- L'Astrologie et Physiognomie en leur Splendeur. Tournon, 1614. 1st. Edn. Some browning, marginal staining at beginning & end, last 2 ll. marginally wormed. Cont. cf., very worn. From liby. of Fr. astronomer Pierre Gassendi; from Honeyman Collection. (S. May 19; 2966) *Hill.* £380

TAYLOR, Alexander S.
- About Grasshoppers & Locusts in California & the World. San Franc., 1858. 4to. Mod. red mor. Author's corrected proof copy, inscr. to John Henry Gurney; from Honeyman Collection. (S. May 19; 2967) *Zeitlin & Verbrugge.* £110

TAYLOR, Alister & Glen, Jan
- C.F. Goldie, his Life & Paintings.-Prints, Drawings & Criticism. 1977-79. Ltd. Edns. 2 vols. 4to. Orig. mor.-bkd. cl., preserved in cl. boxes. (SH. Oct.9; 106) *Daly.* £50

TAYLOR, Bayard (Ed.)
See-PICTURESQUE Europe

TAYLOR, Brook
- Methodus Incrementorum Directa & Inversa. 1715. 1st. Edn. 4to. Some browning, wormed in upr. outer corners. Cont. cf., worn, hf. mor. case. Bkplt. of Earl of Kinnoul; from Honeyman Collection. (S. May 19; 2968) *Quaritch.* £140
- A New Book of Chinese, Gothic & Modern Chairs, with a manner of putting them in Perspective. [1751]. 12mo. Stitched as issued. (S. Mar.17; 461) *Marlborough Rare Books.* £220

TAYLOR, C.
- The Public Edifices of the British Metropolis; with Historical & Descriptive Accounts of the Different Buildings. 1825. Slim fo. Orig. hf. mor. (TA. Dec.18; 361) £60

TAYLOR, Conyngham Crawford
- Toronto 'Called Back' from 1886 to 1850 ... Toronto, 1886. Orig. cl., head & tail of spine slightly worn, upr. cover slightly stained, end-papers slightly foxed. (CB. May 27; 318) Can. $120

TAYLOR, Deems
- Walt Disney's Fantasia. N.Y., 1940. 4to. With the programme for the film inserted. Cl., d.-w. reprd. With Disney's bold, lge. autograph sig. on card pasted to front free end-paper. (SG. Nov.20; 315) $100

TAYLOR, Frederick Winslow
- Principles of Scientific Management. N.Y. & L., 1911. 1st. Edn., 1st. Iss. Cl., gt. spine, folding cl. case. (SG. Oct.9; 239) $375

TAYLOR, G.
- With Scott, The Silver Lining. 1916. Orig. bdg. (TRL. Dec.10; 100) £56

TAYLOR, Sir George (Ed.)
See-JONES, Paul

TAYLOR, George & Skinner, Andrew
- Maps of the Roads of Ireland. 1778. [1st. Edn.?]. Tears to fold of lge. map. Cont. cf. Bkplt. & sig. of John Pollock, lately in the collection of Eric Sexton. (C. Apr.16; 366) *McGee.* £160
-- Anr. Copy. Hf. cf., upr. cover detchd. (GM. Apr.30; 372) £140
- Survey & Maps of the Roads of North Britain or Scotland. 1776. General map reprd., some dust-soiling at edges. Cont. tree cf. (S. Jun.22; 99) *Bunsel Smoin.* £80
-- Anr. Copy. 8½ × 20 inches. Lacks general map. Cont. limp leath. CSK. Nov.7; 187) £65
- Survey of the Roads of Scotland on an Improved Plan. Edinb., ca. 1810? Orig. bds., spine worn. (SKC. Jul.28; 2395) £50

TAYLOR, I. & J.
- Ideas for Rustic Furniture ... [1790?]. Hf. cf. by Harley. (S. Mar.17; 462) *Weinreb.* £280

TAYLOR, Isaac, Engraver, & others
- Voyages Pittoresques et Romantiques dans l'Ancienne France. Ill.:- after Fragonard, Bonnington, Isabey, Bergeret & others. Normandy, Paris, 1820-25. 1st. Printing. 2 vols. Fo. Compl. with sketches of plts. I, II, IV, V, VI, XII, XIII, plts. 13 & 138 repeated, some foxing, slight dampstaining in margins of vol. 1. Mor. by R.P. Badiejous, lge. borders of dentelles & gt. blind-tooled fillets on covers, inside dentelles, watered silk doubls. & end-papers, spines with raised bands. (HD. Jun.24; 101) Frs. 17,000

TAYLOR, Jane & Ann
- City Scenes or a Peep into London. 1828. Slim cf., by Root. (CE. Dec.4; 226) £135
- Little Ann & other Poems. Ill.:- Kate Greenaway. [1883?]. 1st. Edn. Orig. decor. bds., cl. spine & corners, orig. d.-w. (C. Feb.4; 70) *Harcourt/William.* £55
- Rural Scenes, or a Peep into the Country for Children. [Plts. wtrmkd. 1822 & 1823; plts. dtd. 1813 & 1818]. 12mo. Mor.-bkd. bds. (SH. Mar.19; 304) *Moon.* £60

TAYLOR, Lieut.-Col. John
- Letters on India, Political, Commercial & Military, Relative to Subjects Important to the British Interests in the East. 1800. 4to. Recent hf. cf. (TA. Mar.19; 345) £56

TAYLOR, John, Water Poet
[-] [The Booke of Martyrs]. N.d. B3-El0 of pt. 2 only. 64mo. in 16's (1 × 1½ inches), miniature book. Soiled & dampstained. Crudely bnd. in 17th. C. kid, covered in silk, design in yellow thread incorporating the initials I R on covers, worn. (CSK. Apr.3; 41) £100
- Works. 1630. 1st. Edn. 3 pts. in 1 vol. Fo. Lacks first blank, extra engraved title & last lf. slightly defect., reprd. & remargined, corner torn from 3L1, reprd. Early 19th. C. russ., gt., jnts. split. [NSTC 23725] (S. Nov.24; 283) *Whitby.* £320

TAYLOR, John Richard
[-] Furniture Designs. Ca. 1823. 50 numbered & hand-cold. engraved plts., one wtrmkd. 1823, no text. Cont. hf. roan. (S. Mar.17; 463) *Marlborough Rare Books.* £140

TAYLOR, Joseph H.
- Sketches of Frontier & Indian Life on the Upper Missouri & Great Plains. Pottstown, Pa., Priv.

Ptd., 1889. 1st. Edn. 12mo. Later hf. leath. (SG. Jan.8; 423) $130

TAYLOR, Capt. Philip Meadow
– Confessions of a Thug. 1839. 1st. Edn. 3 vols. Cont. hf. cf. (SH. May 21; 119)   *Cavendish.* £55

TAYLOR, Samuel
– Angling in All its Branches. L., 1800. 1st. Edn. Extra-ill. with 10 engraved plts., 9 hand-cold. Later three-qtr. mor. Dean Sage's bkplt. (SG. Oct.16; 480) $200

TAYLOR, Thomas
[–] A Dissertation on the Elusinian & Bacchic Mysteries. Amst., [1790]. 1st. Edn. Hf. cf., unc. (S. Dec.2; 637)   *Weiner.* £200

TAYLOR, Tom
– Pictures of English Landscape. Ill.:– Dalziel brothers after Birket Foster. 1881. (1000) numbered. Fo. Orig. red mor. gt. (SH. Mar.26; 214)   *Salinas.* £105
– – Anr. Copy. This copy unnumbered? Orig. parch., slightly worn. (S. Jul.31; 225)
  Salinas. £50

TAYLOR, Zachary
– Letters from the Battle-Fields of the Mexican War. Rochester, Priv. Ptd., 1908. (300) numbered. 4to. Cl.-bkd. bds., unc. Inscr. by W.K. Bixby, owner of the orig. letters. (SG. Oct.30; 350) $120

TCHEMERZINE, Avenir
– Bibliographie d'Editions Originales et Rares d'Auteurs Français. Paris, 1927-34. Ltd. Edn. 10 vols. Mod. cl., orig. wraps. bnd. in. (SM. Oct.7; 1509)   Frs. 4,000

TCHERNYKHOV, Jacob
– Architectural Fictions. Ed.:– 'Meshdunarodnaja Kniga'. Leningrad, 1933. 1st. Edn. Tall 4to. Orig. blind-stpd. cl., minor spotting at extremities. (PNY. Mar.26; 22) $4,750

TCHOU-KIA-KIEN
– Le Théâtre Chinois. Pekin, 1927. (500) numbered. 4to. 5 woodcut hand-cold. plts., mntd. as folding plts., few sm. repairs, ills. (1 hand-cold), anr. on upr. cover. Orig. bds., unc. (SH. Apr.10; 430)   *Crete.* £85

TE, M.
See–AZAREVICH, Valentin & Te, M.

TEATE, Faithful
– Ter Tria: or the doctrine of . . . Father, Son, & Spirit. 1669. 2nd. Edn. Lacks final blank, some soiling, a few ll. slightly stained. Cont. sheep, worn. [Wing T618] (S. Dec.9; 362)   *Laywood.* £60

TEERINK, Herman
– Bibliography of Jonathan Swift. Ed.:– A. H. Scouten. Phila., [1963]. Cl., d.-w. (SG. Jan.22; 371) $140

TEESDALE, Henry
– New British Atlas. 1832. 4to. 2 maps torn along folds, a few other sm. tears, 2 spotted, contents lf. lacking. Hf. cf., 1 cover detchd. (CSK. Sep.19; 94)   £220
– – Anr. Edn. 1842. Fo. Maps on guards thro.-out, a few sm. tears. Cont. str.-grd. mor. gt., by J. Martin. As an atlas, w.a.f. (SBA. Jul.14; 51)   *Mizon.* £185
– A New General Atlas of the World. 1831-32. Fo. (470mm × 370mm). 46 cold. engraved maps, including 1 double-p. numbered as 2, bottom margin of title & lr. fore-corner of contents lf. reprd. Orig. cf.-bkd. paper bds., spine defect., worn. W.a.f. (S. Nov.3; 29)   *Maggs.* £130
– – Anr. Edn. 1838. Fo. 33 hand-cold. maps (of 47), loose. Orig. cl., worn. (SH. Jul.9; 29)   *Jeffery.* £120
– – Anr. Edn. 1841. Impressed panel bds. (LA. Mar.5; 115)   £95
– – Anr. Edn. 1852. Fo. Diced cf., gt., worn. (S. May 5; 236)   *Franks.* £55

TEGETMEIER, William Bernhard
– The Poultry Book. Ill.:– Harrison Weir. L., 1867. Hf. cf., worn, covers detchd. (SG. Sep.18; 307) $160

TEHILIM [Psalms, with commentaries of Rashi & Elieser Ha'levi Hurwitz & Ma'amadot of Aron of Apta]
Zhitomir, 1856. Hf. leath. (S. Nov.18; 335)   *Stern.* £150

TEICHELMANN, C.G. & Schurmann, C.W.
– Outlines of a Grammar, Vocabulary, & Phraseology of the Aboriginal Language of South Australia. Adelaide, 1840. Title-p. slightly soiled. Without plain wraps. in mod. hf. mor., gt. (KH. Nov.18; 584)   Aus. $240
– – Anr. Copy. Irregularly paginated. Early qtr. roan gt. (KH. Mar.24; 391)   Aus. $100

TEJEDA, Gaspar de
– Suma de Arithmetica practica y de todas Mercaderias. Con. la horden de contadores. Valladolid, 1546. 1st. Edn. Sm. 4to. Some browning & spotting. Mod. cf., blind-tooled borders & panel. From Honeyman Collection. (S. May 19; 2969)   *Dr. Martin.* £640

TELEKI, Paul Graf
– Atlas zur Geschichte der Kartographie der Japanischen Inseln. Budapest, 1909. 1st. Edn. Atlas fo. Hf. mor., rehinged preserving orig. spine. Pres. copy. (SG. Oct.2; 350) $450

TELESCOPIO BRASILIENSE Nos, Açores, ou o Brasileiro emigrado. Em fins do anno de 1831
Oporto, 1833. No. 1 (all publd.). Sm. 4to. Sm. hole in final lf. without loss, stains. Mod. cl. [Sabin 94612] (SPB. May 5; 493) $325

TELFORD, T.
– The Life. Ed.:– J. Rickman. 1838. 2 vols. including atlas of plts. 4to. & fo. Spotted. Cont. hf. mor., leath. d.-w.'s. (SH. Jun.18; 117)   *Weinreb.* £720

TEMANZA, Tommaso
– Vite dei piu Celebri Architetti, Scultori Veneziani . . . nel Secolo Decimesesto. Venice, 1778. 1st. Edn. 4to. Mod. spr. cf., gt. arms on sides, gt. spine. From the collection of John A. Saks. (C. Jun.10; 242)   *Weinreb.* £160
– – Anr. Edn. Venice, 1778. Sm. fo. A few margins stained. Hf. cf., worn, upr. cover loose. (S. Jun.22; 150)   *Weinreb.* £130

TEMERLES, Yakov
– Safra Diznuta De'yakov. Amst., 1669. Hf. leath., with stp. of Etz Chaim Liby. of Amst. on cover. (S. Nov.18; 461)   *Morris.* £130

TEMMINCK, Conrad Jacob
– Verhandelingen over de Natuurlijke Geschiedenis der Nederlandsche Overzeesche Bezittingen. Leiden, 1839-44. (250). 3 vols. (Zoologie, Land-en Volkenkunde, & Botanie). Fo. A few marginal stains. Cont. Dutch hf. cf., spines gt. with bird in compartments. (S. Jun.1; 228)   *Maggs.* £2,600
See–KNIP, Antoinette Pauline Jacqueline & Temminck, Conrad Jacob

TEMMINCK, Conrad Joseph & Laugier de Chartrouse
– Nouveau Recueil des Planches Colorié d'oiseaux pour server de Suite aux Planches illuminées de Buffon. Paris, [1820]/1838. 5 vols. Lge. fo. Lacks 17 plts., last p. of index vol. 1 defect & reprd., some marginal stains. Cont. gt. hf. leath., Pijnaker Frères, La Haye. (VG. Oct.13; 155)   Fls. 16,000

TEMPEST, P. [& Lauron, M.]
– The Cryes of the City of London. Ca. 1700. Fo. 74 engraved plts. including title tipped in, title plt. damaged. Orig. bdg. (P. Oct.2; 288)   *Cumming.* £400

TEMPLE, Alfred George
– The Wallace Collection, Paintings. 1902. Ltd. Edn. 2 vols. Fo. Hf. mor. gt. (P. Jan.22; 133)   *Cambridge.* £75

TEMPLE, Edmund
– Travels in Various Parts of Peru. 1830. 2 vols. Orig. cl., worn. (SH. May 21; 120)   *Crete.* £65

TEMPLE, Sir John
– The Irish Rebellion, or An History . . . of the General Rebellion . . . in the Year 1641. L., 1646. 1st. Edn. 4to. Old cf., bkplt. of Philip Earl of Hardwicke. (GM. Apr.30; 313)   £90
– – Anr. Copy. Cont. cf. [Wing T627] (S. Sep.29; 117)   *O'Leary.* £50
The Irish Rebellion . . . 1641.–Letters . . . from the Earl of Ormond to Michael Jones . . . Rebellion . . . in the Year 1641. 1646; 1649. 1st. Edn. 2 works in 1 vol. 4to. Cont. owners' inscrs., some ll. with perforations slightly affecting text, 2nd. work: slight loss of text on 1 lf. Later cf. Rosebery liby. stp. on title-p. of 1st. work. (SBA. Jul.23; 667)   *Emerald Isles Books.* £120

TEMPLE des Muses (Le)
Ill.:– B. Picart le Romain & others. Amst., 1749. Lge. fo. Cont. spr. cf., worn. (HD. Jun.29; 52)   Frs. 1,350

TEMPLEMAN, Thomas
See–MOLL, Herman–TEMPLEMAN, Thomas

TEMPLIN, Hugh
See–BYERLY, A.E.–TEMPLIN, Hugh

TEMPSKY, Gustav Ferdinand von
– Mitla. A Narrative of . . . a journey in Mexico, Guatemala, & Salvador. 1858. [1st. Edn.?]. Folding map, cold. in outl., liby. stp. on verso of title. Cont. hf. cf. (CSK. Mar.13; 132)   £150
– – Anr. Copy. Red hf. mor. gt. (R. Mar.31-Apr.4; 2446)   DM 1,000

TEN FOLDING CHARTS recording the tracks of His Majesty's Sloop Discovery & Armed Tender Chatham . . . in the year 1791
N.d. Fo. Hf. cf., worn, upr. cover loose. (PD. Oct.22; 182)   £110

TENCH, Capt. Watkins
– A Complete Account of the Settlement at Port Jackson, in New South Wales. 1793. [1st. Edn.?]. 4to. Title slightly soiled & spotted, occasional foxing affecting map & some text ll. Orig. bds., worn, spine defect., unc. Sig. of Bryan Cooke, Owston, 1793, on title, lately in the collection of Eric Sexton. (C. Apr.15; 52)   *Burgess.* £1,400
– – Anr. Copy. Some foxing & offsetting of map. 19th. C. hf. hard-grd. mor. (KH. Nov.18; 585)   Aus. $2,300

TENGLER, Ulrich
[–] Layenspiegel. Ed.:– Sebastian Brandt & Jacobus Locher. Strassburg, Johann Albrecht, 7 Mar. 1538. Fo. Lacks last blank, title & 5 ll. reprd. 18th. C. bds., worn. (S. Nov.25; 355)
  Broseghini. £350

TENIERS, David
– Schilder-Thooneel. Brussels, 1660. Fo. Final port. of artist cut down & mntd. Cont. cf., gt. spine. (C. Nov.20; 206)   *Bonometti.* £650

TENISON, Lady Louisa
– Castile & Andalucia. 1853. Orig. cl., slightly soiled. (CSK. Jul.3; 106)   £90
– – Anr. Copy. Lge. 8vo. Spotting. Rebkd., old spine preserved. (CSK. Oct.17; 13)   £70

TENNIEL, Sir John (Ill.)
See–AESOP
See–DODGSON, Rev. Charles Lutwidge 'Lewis Carroll'

TENNYSON, Alfred Lord
[–] The Charge of the Light Brigade. N.p., [dtd. at end 8 Aug. 1855]. 1st. Separate Edn. [1st. Edn. of the final version]. 4to. Horizontal crease to both ll. & slight tear to fold at blank fore-margins. Red mor., spine gt.-lettered, by Rivière, upr. cover detchd. Pres. Copy, to Major M'Crea, sig. of William K. Bixby on free end-paper, bkplts. of Roderick Terry & Frank J. Hogan, lately in the Prescott Collection. (CNY. Feb.6; 311) $18,000
– Idylls of the King. Ill.:– Gustave Doré. 1868. 4 pts. in 1 vol. Fo. Later cf., gt., cold. miniatures mntd. on covers with pol. semi-precious stones. (SH. Oct.10; 396)   *Arts Anciens.* £160
– – Anr. Copy. Mntd. engraved plts. on india-paper, occasional slight spotting. Cont. red mor., ruled in gt., upr. cover with crossed spears, surmounted by a crown, supporting a shield, design in gt. with mor. inlays, upr. cover warped. (CSK. Jan.23; 167)   £70
– In Memoriam. Ill.:– Charles Ricketts. Vale Pr., 1900. (320). Orig. buckram, unc. & unopened. (S. Jul.31; 48)   *Foyles.* £50
– – Anr. Edn. Ill.:– C.S. Ricketts. Ballantyne Pr., 1900. Ltd. Edn. Lev. mor. gt. with wide border of stylised flower sprays, sigd. with initials M.R. & dtd. 1905. (BS. Sep.17; 153)   £65
– – Anr. Edn. Nones. Pr., 1933. (1250). Mor. gt. (SH. Feb.19; 132)   *Lincs. County Liby.* £60
– Maud. Hammersmith, Kelms. Pr., 1893. (500). 4to. Mor. gt. by Bradford, mor. solander case. (SPB. Nov.25; 320) $650
– – Anr. Copy. Orig. vell., spotted, lacks ties. (SPB. May 29; 242) $250
– Poems. 1842. 2 vols. Later mor. by Rivière, spines gt. (SH. Apr.10; 351)   *Prof. Swales.* £75
– – Anr. Edn. Ill.:– C.S. Ricketts. [L.], [Ballantyne Pr.], [1911]. Mor., gt.-stpd., leaf-sprays at corners of sides & at panel. spine, covers multiply gt.-ruled, inner dentelles gt., by

TENNYSON, Alfred Lord -contd.
Charles McLeish at the Doves Bindery, dtd. 1911. (PNY. Dec.3; 112) $280
- **Seven Poems & Two Translations.** Hammersmith, Doves Pr., 1902. (25) on vell. Sm. 4to. Crushed lev. mor., gt. tooled borders, spine in 6 compartments, 5 raised bands, gt. tooled designs on covers & spine, sigd. 'Doves Bindery 19 C-S 09', qtr. mor. gt. s.-c. (CNY. May 22; 375) $5,000
- - **Anr. Edn.** Doves Pr., 1902. (325) on paper. Sm. 4to. Orig. limp vell., unc. (SH. Feb.19; 37) *Lincolnshire County Liby.* £150
- - **Anr. Copy.** Very slight staining to fore-edges of 3 early ll. Cont. mor. gt., covers with outer border of line in blind with a gt. fillet on either side, inner border of 3 fillets connected with cornerpieces, spine with raised bands, by Sangorski & Sutcliffe, with their stp. on turnover. Bkplt. of Lily Antrobus. (LC. Jun.18; 53) £90
- **Works.** 1872-73. 8 vols. Cont. red mor., gt. with the arms of Exeter College, Oxford, stpd. in gt. on upr. & lr. covers. (CSK. Jan.16; 148) £50
- - **Anr. Edn.** L., 1883. Maroon mor. Panoramic fore-e. pntg. on all edges. (SG. Mar.19; 181) $350
- - **Anr. Edn.** L., 1897. Maroon mor. Fore-e. pntg. (SG. Sep.4; 191) $300
- - **Anr. Edn.** L., 1898. Lev., gt. border of fleurons, spine unif. gt., gt. dentelles, by Bickers. Fore-e. pntg. (SG. Mar.19; 182) $250
- - **Anr. Edn.** L., 1899. Edn. De Luxe, (1050). 12 vols. Mor. gt., 1 cover detchd. (SPB. Nov.25; 495) $425
- - **Anr. Edn.** N.Y., [1909]. Poet Laureate Edn., (50). 8 vols. Mor. gt., elab. gt. spines with red mor. inlays. A.L. tipped in. (SPB. May 6; 349) $1,700

TENNYSON, Alfred & Charles
- **Poems by Two Brothers.** 1827. 1st. Edn. Cont. cf., rebkd. (SH. Oct.10; 398) *Swales.* £200

[TENNYSON, Alfred & Charles]-HOOD, Thomas
- **Poems by Two Brothers.-The Plead of the Midsummer Fairies.** 1827; 1827. 1st. Edns. 2 works in 1 vol. 1 p. advt. at end of 2nd. work. Cont. cf. (C. Feb.4; 151a) *Bickersteth.* £300

TENSINI, Agostino
- **La Vera Regola Dello Scrivere, utile a Giovani.** Bassano, ca. 1680? Ob. 4to. Slight stain on title. Mod. vell. bds. (C. Apr.1; 89) *Goldschmidt.* £380

TENTZEL, W.E.
- **Saxonia Numismatica.** Frankfurt & Leipzig, Amstadt., 1705-11 & 1713 (Index). 3 pts., supp. (?pt. 4) & index in 1 vol. 4to. Cont. vell. (R. Mar.31-Apr.4; 189) DM 2,150

TENUE DES TROUPES DE FRANCE à toutes les Epoques
Ill.:- Job. Paris, n.d. 4to. Orig. cl., gt. decor. (SI. Dec.4; 565) Lire 220,000

TERCERO CATHECISMO y Exposicion de la Doctrina Christiana
Cuidad de los Reyes [Lima], 1585. Sm. 4to. Sm. hole in title affecting 1 letter on verso, inscrs. on 2A7 verso & several other ll., some light stains, a few short tears reprd. Limp vell., soiled. (SPB. May 5; 496) $7,500
- - **Anr. Edn.** [Lima], [1773]. Sm. 4to. 1 gathering loose, light stains. Cont. vell., soiled. (SPB. May 5; 497) $125

TERENTIUS Afer, Publius
- **Andria oder das Mädchen von Andros.** Ed.:- G. Mardersteig. Trans.:- F. Mendelsschn-Bartholdy. Ill.:- F. Kredel after A. Dürer. Verona, 1971. (160). Hand-bnd. orig. hf. vell., orig. linen s.-c. (HK. Nov.18-21; 2840) DM 1,200
- - **Anr. Copy.** Fo. (HK. May 12-14; 2006) DM 900
- **Les Comedies ...** Ed.:- Mme. Dacier. Rotterdam, 1717. Fine Paper. 3 vols. 12mo. 18th. C. mor., double gt. fillet, flat spines gt. with narrow bands of fillets & foliage, inner gt. dentelles, pink silk liners. (SM. Oct.8; 2036) Frs. 1,000
- - **Anr. Edn.** Trans.:- Abbé Le Monnier. Ill.:- Cochin. 1771. 1st. Printing. 3 vols. Cont. porphyr. cf., dentelle. (HD. Jun.30; 77) Frs. 1,600
- **A Comedy called Andria.** Ill.:- Fritz Kredel after Albrecht Dürer. 1971. (170) numbered. Fo. Orig. vell.-bkd. bds., s.-c. (SH. Feb.20; 225) *Appleton.* £240

- **Comoediae.** Ed.:- A. Bonato. 1524. Fo. Some worming thro.-out. Wooden bds., cf. spine, lacks hf. upr. cover. (BS. Jun.11; 288) £90
- - **Anr. Edn.** Paris, 1552. Fo. Margins slightly browned. Old panel. cf. (TA. Nov.20; 111) £150
- - **Anr. Edn.** Ed.:- G. Sandby. Ill.:- Miller. L., 1751. L.P. 2 vols. in 1. Cont. vell., tooled gt. border with armorial badge, gt., tooled gt. spine, T.C.D. Prize bdg., inscr., bkplt. of Cotton Liby. (GM. Apr.30; 505) £210
- - **Anr. Edn.** Bg'ham., 1772. 4to. Cont. red mor. gt., spine tooled in compartments. Bkplt. of W.H. Wilmot. (S. Nov.24; 285) *Traylen.* £160
- - **Anr. Copy.** Extra ill. with some 50 plts. dtd. 1716, inlaid to size. Early 19th. C. red str.-grd. mor. gt. (C. Jul.16; 339) *Beck.* £60
- - **Anr. Copy.** Red mor. early gt.-armorial bdg., stpd. with arms of Lord Brownlow. Early inscr. to Eton College by B. Drury at blank. (PNY. Oct.1; 97) $300
- **Comoediae Sex.** Ed.:- Heinz. Strassburg, 1635. 1st. Edn. 12mo. Slight foxing. 18th. C. red mor., 3 fillets, decor. spine, inside dentelle. (HD. Mar.18; 174) Frs. 1,000
- - **Anr. Edn.** Glasgow, 1742. Lightly spotted at beginning & end. Cont. Fr. red mor. gt. (S. Jul.27; 161) *Laywood.* £60
- **Le Grant Thérèce en Francoys ...** Trans.:- G. Rippe & G. Cybille. Paris, 1539. Fo. Ruled thro.-out in red, large cutting through wood-cuts, piece torn from outer edge of I6, sm. repairs to lr. outer corners of a3, z8, & M7, some ll. with slight marginal staining. 19th. C. mor. gt., arms on sides of J. Gomez de Cortina, & with his bkplt. (S. Feb.10; 471) *Israel.* £1,700
- **Vulgaria in Theutonicam Linguam Traducta.** Deventer, [Richardus Pafraet], 4 Nov. 1489. 1st. Edn. 4to. Spaces for initial capitals, paragraph marks, capitals, & underlines supplied in red, slight restorations to extreme inner margin of 1st. lf., sm. liby. stp. erased from margin of title-p. Mor. gt., gt. spine, by Zaehnsdorf. From the collection of Eric Sexton. [C 5760, Goff T109] (CNY. Apr.8; 53) $17,000

TERESA, Saint
- **The Flaming Hart.** Antw., 1642. Lacks final (probably blank) lf., sm. hole in title-p., marginal flaw in Ii7. Cont. vell., 1 hinge worn, covers warped, lacks ties. [Wing T753] (S. May 5; 305) *Duran.* £50

TERESA DE JESUS, Saint
- **Die von der Heiligen Seraphischen Jungfrau und Mutter Theresia ... Uber das Vatter unser gemachte Betrachtungen.-Geistliche Wasser-Quelle.** Trans.:- Maria Eleonora Francisca Cajetana Aloisia Grafin von Sporck. Prag, 1707. 1st. Edn.; 2nd. Edn. 2 works in 1 vol. Cont. leath., gt. spine. (R. Oct.14-18; 1085) DM 400

TERRASSE, Charles
- **Bonnard.** Paris, 1927. Sm. 4to. Sewed, ill. wrap. (HD. Dec.5; 201) Frs. 1,000

TERRY, Daniel
- **British Theatrical Gallery.** 1825. Fo. Mod. hf. mor. gt. (SBA. Mar.4; 80) *McKenzie.* £250

TERZIO, Fr.
- **Austriacae Gentis Imaginum Pars Prima [-Quinta].** Innsbruck, 1569-73. Fo. Some ll. slightly wormed in fold, owner's mark, stp. on title with sm. woodcut initials pasted over on both sides. Cont. vell., lacks ties, soiled & slightly wormed. (HK. Nov.18-21; 304) DM 6,500

TESORO DELLE GIOIE, NEL QUALE ... Virtu, Qualita, & Proprieta delle Gioie, come Perle, Gemme Auori [etc.]. Padua, 1630. 12mo. Very minor staining. Hf. vell. (C. Apr.1; 90) *Goldschmidt.* £90

TESSEREAU, Abraham
- **Histoire Chronologique de la Grande Chancellerie de France.** Paris, 1710. 2 vols. Fo. Cont. red. mor., triple fillets on covers, spines decor. with raised bands, bdgs. defect. (HD. Jun.29; 259) Frs. 2,300

TESTARD, F.M.
See-SEGARD, Sir W. & Testard, F.M.

TESTI, L.
- **La Storia della Pittura Veneziana.-** Bergamo, 1909. 2 vols. 4to. Publisher's cl. gt. (CR. Mar.19; 176) Lire 280,000

TESTORI, C.G.
- **La Musica Ragionata.** Venice, 1767-82. 1st. Edn. 4 pts. in 1 vol. 4to. Slightly browned in parts, especially pt. II. Cont. cf., worn. (H. Dec.9/10; 1293) DM 750

TETTI, Carlo
- **Discorsi delle Fortificazioni.** Venice, 1575. 4to. 4 unnumbered pp. Mod. vell. (CR. Mar.19; 278) Lire 350,000

TETTONI, L. & Saladini, F.
- **Teatro Araldico ovvero Raccolta Generale delle Armi ed Insegne Gentilizie delle pie Illustri e Nobili Casate.** Lodi, 1841-46. 6 vols. 4to. Lacks 6 plts. Cont. hf. mor. (SI. Dec.4; 566) Lire 550,000

TEUBER, O.
- **Die Osterreichische Armee von 1700 bis 1867.** Vienna, 1895. 2 vols. Fo. Hf. mor., corners, unc. (HD. Dec.5; 202) Frs. 2,000

TEVO, Zaccaria
- **Il Musica Testore.** Venice, 1706. Sm. 4to. Crushed mor. by John Saks, unc. From the collection of John A. Saks. (C. Jun.10; 245) *Robison.* £50

TEWSON, Roland Stuart
See-FRY, Sir Frederick Morris & Tewson, Roland Stuart

THACHER, James
- **A Military Journal during the American Revolutionary War.** Boston, 1823. 1st. Edn. Early mott. sheep. (SG. Jun.11; 409) $160

THACKERAY, Francis
- **History of the Honorable William Pitt, Earl of Chatham.** Ill.:- Finder. L., 1827. 1st. Edn. 2 vols. Fo. Cl., gt. fillets, spine raised bands. (DS. May 22; 858) Pts. 36,000

THACKERAY, William Makepeace 'M.A. Titmarsh'
- **The Book of Snobs.** L., 1848. 1st. Edn. Some foxing, etc. Three-qtr. mor., orig. upr. wrap. bnd. in. A.N.s to Sir William tipped-in, & calling-card mntd. on rear end-paper. (SG. Dec.18; 394) $100
- [-] **Christmas Books.** L., [1847]-55. 6 vols. 4to. Crimson lev., triple gt. fillet borders, gt. spines & dentelles, by Root, 4 vols. with orig. pict. wraps. bnd. in, cl. s.-c. (SG. May 14; 211) $1,100
- **The Letters & Private Papers.** Ed.:- Gordon N. Ray. 1945-46. 4 vols. Orig. buckram. (SKC. Feb.26; 1528) £55
- **Mrs. Perkin's Ball.** 1847. 1st. Edn. Sm. 4to. Remains of tissue wrap. adhering to inside covers, orig. ptd. bds., lacks spine. (SH. Apr.10; 352) *Johns.* £50
- [-] **The Newcomes.** Ill.:- Richard Doyle. L., Oct. 1853-Aug. 1855. 1st. Edn. Orig. 24 pts. in 23. 'Newcomes Advertiser' in each pt. Pict. wraps., unc., cl. folding case, some spines reprd. (SG. May 14; 212) $225
- - **Anr. Copy.** Some slight repairs, with the Newcomes Advertiser in each pt. (1 defect.), & other inserted advts. Orig. pict. ptd. wraps., qtr. mor. gt. s.-c. From the Prescott Collection. (CNY. Feb.6; 313) $180
- - **Anr. Edn.** Ed.:- Arthur Pendennis. Ill.:- Richard Doyle. L., 1854. 1st. Edn. Vol. I only, bnd. from the pts. Many advts. bnd. in, plts. heavily foxed. Red lev., raised bands, wide gt. dentelles, orig. wraps bnd. in. (SG. Nov.13; 674) $110
- - **Anr. Edn.** Ill.:- Edward Ardizzone. 1954. (1500) numbered, sigd. by artist. 2 vols. 4to. Orig. pict. cl. bds., s.-c. (P. Dec.1; 138) £50
- **The Orphan of Pimlico.** L., 1876. Ltd. Edn., with plts. in 2 states. Fo. Cf., gt. floral cornerpieces, spine gt., orig. upr. wrap. bnd. in. (SG. Mar.19; 290) $150
- **Our Street.-Mrs. Perkins Ball.-Doctor Birch. -Rebecca & Rowena.-Kicklebury's on the Rhine.** L., 1848; 1847; 1849; 1850; 1850. 1st. Edns. 5 vols. Various sizes. Advts. where called for. Mor. gt. by Rivière, orig. bdgs. bnd. at end. (SPB. Nov.25; 212) $475
- **The Paris Sketch Book.-The Second Funeral of Napoleon.-The History of Henry Esmond.** L., 1840; 1841; 1852. 1st. Edns. (2nd. work 1st. Iss.) 2 vols.; 1 vol.; 3 vols. 12mo; 16mo; 12mo. Some spotting to 3rd. work. Orig. cl., spines gt. (faded & slightly worn), upr. inner jnt. of vol. 1 brkn. (1st. work); orig. ptd. wraps., slightly soiled, mor. gt. s.-c. (2nd. work); & orig. cl., spines discold., qtr. mor. gt. s.-c. 1st. & 3rd. works with the bkplts. of

Jerome Kern, all lately in the Prescott Collection. (CNY. Feb.6; 315) $300

- **Rebecca & Rowena.** Ill.:– Richard Doyle. L., 1850. 1st. Edn. Sq. 8vo. With hf.-title & advt. lf. Orig. decor. bds., in red str.-grd. mor. solander case. Bkplt. of Henry S. van Duzer. (SG. Nov.13; 673) $240

- **Vanity Fair.** L., Jan. 1847-Jul. 1848. 1st. Edn., 1st. Iss. 20 orig. pts. in 19. Some slight foxing, with the Vanity Fair Advertiser in nos. 1, 12, 16-18, & 19/20, other inserted advts., & the slip advts. in nos. 3, 13, 14, & 19/20, 2 orig. owners' inscrs. on 3 of the pts. Orig. pict. ptd. wraps., slight wear & repairs to spines of 3 nos., sm. spots on 3 wraps., mor. gt. solander case. From the Prescott Collection. (CNY. Feb.6; 312) $7,000

- **– Anr. Edn.** Ill.:– Lewis Baumer. N.d. Ltd. Edn. sigd. by artist. 4to. Vell. gt., lacks ties. (P. Mar.12; 207) *Welby.* £50

- **The Virginians.** Nov., 1857-Oct., 1859. 1st. Edn. In 24 orig. pts. Advts. Orig. wraps., cl. box. (SH. Jul.23; 67) *Thorp.* £150

- **– Anr. Copy.** Some foxing, with the Virginian Advertiser in each pt. (excepting no. 15), & other inserted advts. Orig. pict. wraps., many spines reprd., some covers dust-soiled, qtr. mor. gt. s.-c. From the Prescott Collection. (CNY. Feb.6; 314) $350

- **– Anr. Copy.** 'Virginians Advertiser' in each pt. Pict. wraps., unc., hf. lev. s.-c. E. Hubert Litchfield bkplt. (SG. May 14; 213) $275

- **The Virginians.-The History of Henry Esmond.** L., 1858-59; 1852. 1st. Edns. Together 5 vols. (2 & 3). Orig. cl., 2nd. work qtr.-mor. box defect. (CNY. May 22; 278) $150

- **The Works.** 1869. 22 vols. Cont. hf. mor., spines gt. (SKC. May 19; 351) £140

- **– Anr. Edn.** 1869-74. 22 vols. Hf. cf. (BS. Nov.26; 127) £55

- **– Anr. Edn.** 1869-86. 24 vols. Hf. cf. (C. Feb.4; 91) *Traylen.* £280

- **– Anr. Edn.** 1879. 24 vols. Some spotting. Cont. hf. mor. (CSK. Oct.24; 24) £65

- **– Anr. Copy.** Hf. cf., spines gt., ex-liby. (SG. Aug.7; 423) $100

- **– Anr. Edn.** 1879-87. 26 vols. Some ll. slightly spotted. Cont. hf. mor., spines gt. (SKC. May 19; 352) £170

- **– Anr. Edn.** 1883-86. 26 vols. Hf. crimson mor. gt. (P. Apr.9; 49) *Rhys-Jones.* £55

- **– Anr. Edn.** 1894. 26 vols. Hf. cf., spines gt. in compartments. (CSK. Sep.5; 241) £85

- **– Anr. Edn.** 1898-99. Biographical Edn. 13 vols. Red mor. gt. (SKC. Feb.26; 1527) £200

- **– Anr. Edn.** N.Y., 1903-1904. Kensington Edn. in lge. type. 32 vols. Three-qtr. lev., gt., worn, some covers detchd. (SG. Aug.7; 424) $175

- **– Anr. Edn.** 1910-11. 26 vols. Cont. red hf. mor. (SH. Jun.11; 214) *Lady Wolfson.* £160

- **– Anr. Edn.** Boston, n.d. Ill. Cabinet Edn. 20 vols. Slight browning. Hf. burgundy mor. (SPB. Nov.25; 496) $250

THAER, A.
- **Grundsätze der Rationellen Landwirtschaft.** Berlin, 1853. 4 vols. Orig. hf. leath. (D. Dec.11-13; 174) DM 500

THALERGROSCHEN
N.p., 1567. Ob. 4to. Slightly stained. Linen box. (HK. Nov.18-21; 305) DM 900

THARAUD, Jérome & Jean
- **Un Royaume de Dieu.** Ill.:– Lucien Madrassi. Paris, 1925. (20) on vergé Hollande pur chiffon numbered alphabetically. 4to. Suite of etchings with remarques on Japon, orig. watercolour ill. Decor. mor., gt., by Kieffer, orig. wraps. bnd. in, s.-c. (SM. Oct.8; 2376) Frs. 1,200

THAXTER, Celia
- **An Island Garden.** Ill.:– Childe Hassam. Boston, 1894. 1st. Edn. Tall 8vo. Gt.-pict. cl. (SG. Apr.2; 131) $350

THAYER, Emma Homan
- **Wild Flowers of Colorado.** N.Y., [1885]. 1st. Edn. 4to. Orig. decor. cl. (CNY. May 22; 222) $120

THEAKSTON, Michael
[-] **A List of Natural Flies that are Taken by Trout ... in the Streams of Ripon.** Ripon, 1853. 1st. Edn. 12mo. Cl. (SG. Oct.16; 481) $350

THEAL, G.M.
- **Records of the Cape Colony, 1793-1831.** Cape Colony, 1897-1905. 36 vols. Some browning. Orig. bdgs., some marked. (VA. Jan.30; 440) R. 1,000

THEATER-ZEITUNG, Allg., u. Originalblatt f. Kunst...
Ed.:– A. Baüerle. Vienna, 1833. Year 26. 4 vols. 4to. Some plts. browned. Cont. marb. bds. (HK. Nov.18-21; 2084) DM 900

THEATRE
Paris, 1898-1913. 30 vols. (1st.-16th. year), lacks Year 3 vol. 2 & Year 4 vol. 2, dupl. Year 16 vol. 2. Orig. cl. (SH. Oct.9; 25) *Shane-Taylor.* £300

THEATRE ARTS MAGAZINE continued as Theatre Arts Monthly, then Theater Arts
N.Y., 1939-62. 191 Iss. only & 6 dupls. Vol. VII, no. 4-XLVI, no. 10. Orig. wraps., some worn or detchd. (SH. Apr.10; 432) *Harvey.* £50

THEATRE DE LA GUERRE PRESENTE EN ALLEMAGNE
Paris, ca. 1760. Bds. (R. Oct.14-18; 2126) DM 1,000

THEATRUM DANUBII Exhibens Varios Perspectus... quae Danubio Adjacent
Augsburg, ca. 1750. Ob. fo. Cont. wraps., spine slightly torn. (SBA. Dec.16; 97) *Reiss.* £3,200

THEBES, Georg
- **Liegnitzische Jahr-Bücher ... als such die Geschichte der Piastischen Hertzoge in Schlesien.** Ed.:– G.B. Scharff. Jauer, [Silesia], 1733. 2 pts. in 1 vol. Fo. 27 engraved plts. (? of 29, lacks plts. 3 & 10), all but 1 trimmed & mntd., several sm. marginal repairs, affecting a few letters, some browning & spotting. Cont. vell. bds., soiled, Earl of Crawford's bkplt. W.a.f. (S. Jan.27; 424) *Wohler.* £110

THEION kai Ieron Evangelion -EVANGELISTARION...
Venice, 1588. 2 pts. in 1 vol. 4to. gl & z2 imperfect, a few lr. corners reprd. some worming & staining, title & some headlines of 2nd. pt. cropped. Cont. blind-panel cf., gt. composite cruciform ornament on upr. cover, tool of virgin & child on lr., fleurons at corners, rebkd. & restored, lacks clasps & catches, a monastic binding, perhaps by Monks of the Armenian community in Venice. W.a.f. (S. May 5; 2) *Cout.* £120

THEMMINCK, Conrad Jacob
See–TEMMINCK, Conrad Jacob

THENARD, Louis Jacques, Baron
- **Traité de Chimie Elementaire, Théorique et Pratique.** Paris, 1813-16. 1st. Edn. 4 vols. Bds., spine gt. (S. Dec.1; 405) *Quaritch.* £80

THEOCRITUS
- **Eidyllia [etc.].** Trans.:– Eobanus Hess. Paris, 1546. 4to. Minor stains. Cont. limp vell. (S. Dec.8; 141) *Bart.* £75

- **Idylles et autres Poésies.** Trans.:– M. Gail. 1792. Fr. & Greek text. Cont. red mor., gt. dentelle border. (HD. Jun.30; 78) Frs. 1,200

- **L'Oaristys.** Ill.:– Georges Bellenger. Paris, 1896. (100) on vell. Mor. by Noulhac, mor. doubls., wrap. preserved. (SM. Feb.11; 287) Frs. 2,200
See–ANACREON & others–MUSAEUS

THEOCRITUS, Bion & Moschus
- **The Idylls.** Trans.:– Andrew Lang. Ill.:– Sir William Russell Flint. Riccardi Pr., 1922. (500) numbered. 2 vols. Orig. linen-bkd. bds., d.-w.'s. (S. Jul.31; 221) *Jones.* £100

- **– Anr. Copy.** Linen-bkd. bds., partly unc. (S. Oct.23; 130) $190

- **– Anr. Copy.** 2 vols. 4to. Orig. cl.-bkd. bds., slightly soiled. (CSK. Jan.30; 66) £55

THEODORE
- **Grammatices Libri IV ... Graece.** Venice, Jun. 1525. Cont. havanna cf., blind-stpd. centre motif, fillet decor., decor. spine raised bands, worn. (HD. Apr.24; 23) Frs. 3,500

THEODORE, Jasper
- **The Birds of North America.** Columbus, Ohio, 1878. 4to. 1st. plt. reprd. Hf. mor. gt. (SPB. Oct.1; 201) $175

THEODORUS, Saint, Archbp. of Pavia
- **Vita de Sancto.** Trans.:– [Giovanni Matteo Migliardi]. Pavia, Giovanni Andrea de Boscho, 10 Apr. 1500. 1st. Edn. 4to. Spaces for initial capitals, with guide letters, unrubricated, 2 sm. wormholes to extreme blank fore-margins. 18th.

C. vell. bds., worn. Sig. & notes of J. Martini, later the copy of H.P. Kraus, recently in the collection of Eric Sexton. [Goff T147] (CNY. Apr.8; 133) $3,800

THEODOSIUS, of Bithynia
- **De Sphaericis libri tres, a Ioanne Vogelin ... restituti, & scholiis non improbandis illustrati.** Vienna, 1529. Sm. 4to. 19th. C. hf. red mor., spine defect. Stp. of University of Landshut; armorial bkplt. of William Stirling Maxwell; from Honeyman Collection. (S. May 19; 2971) *Maggs.* £220

- **Sphaericorum libri III. A. Christophoro Clavio ... illustrati. Item Eiusdem Christophori Clavii Sinus. Lineae Tangentes et Secantes. Triangula Rectilinea atque Sphaerica.** Rome, 1586. Sm. 4to. Wormed in some inner margins catching occasional letters of text, 2S3-4 possibly inserted from anr. copy, some browning & slight staining. Cont. Italian red mor., panel. in gt., outer frame decor., inner with decor. corners enclosing on upr. cover sacred monog. with attributes of the Cross, on lr. cover the crest of a griffin, surmounted by crown, of Prince Giacopo Boncompagni (the dedicatee), a smaller version of the crest in compartments of spine, reprd. at head & foot, stain on upr. cover. From liby. of Prince Pignatelli; from Honeyman Collection. (S. May 19; 2973) *Hughes.* £420

THEODOSIUS TRIPOLITA
See–CLAVIUS, Chris.–THEODOSUS TRIPOLITA–CASTELLANUS, L.

THEOPHRASTUS
- **Characterum Ethicorum ...** Ill.:– Cagnoni (port.). Parma, 1786. 4to. With errata lf. at end, title soiled. Red crushed mor. by Maltby, upr. cover detchd. (S. Jul.27; 156) *Thorp.* £55

- **De Historia Plantarum ...** Amst., 1644. Fo. Slightly browned. Cont. mott. cf., recased with old spine relaid. (TA. Jun.18; 92) £675

- **– Anr. Copy.** 19th. C. hf. mor. From Chetham's Liby., Manchester. (C. Nov.27; 385) *Antiqua Libri.* £450

- **Historam de Plantis de Causis Plantarum ...** Venice, 1552. Vol. 6. Lacks blank fo. 8 & the last lf. Red mor., rebkd. Sig. R. Bentley (ca. 1700) on title-p. (S. Jun.17; 822) *Korn.* £52

- **History of Stones.** 1774. 2nd. Edn. Cont. cf., worn. (SH. Jun.11; 23) *Edwards.* £260

- **– Anr. Copy.** Slightly dampstained at end. Rebkd. (S. Dec.2; 783) *Poole.* £60

THEOPHRASTUS–LUSCINIUS, Ottomar –RINGELBERGIUS, Joachimus–MARULUS, Marcus–PLATINA, [Bartholomaeus]
- **Characteres.–Seria iocique.–Chaos.–Quinquaginta parabolae.–De Honesta voluptate.** Trans.:– 1st. work: Willibald Pirckheimer. Nuremb.; Antw.; [Strassburg?]; Cologne; Cologne, 1527; [1529]; 1529; Sep. 1529; 1529. 5 works in 1 vol. 5th. work: errata lf. at end, slightly damaged & reprd., affecting text, rest: a few ll. slightly soiled. 18th. C. cf., slightly worn. (S. Oct.21; 447) *Artico.* £300

THEOPHYLACTUS
- **Ennarationes on Epistolas S. Pauli.** Trans.:– [Christophorus de Persona]. Rome, Ulrich Han, 25 Jan. 1477. 1st. Edn. Fo. Spaces for initials at beginning of each epistle, final lf. torn & reprd., some ll. marginally stained at front, the 1st. 4 & last 3 strengthened at hinges & with minor marginal defects at lr. inner corners. Mod. mor., gt.-lettered, by MacDonald. Bkplt. of the General Theological Seminary Liby. [BMC IV, 25, Goff T156, H 1902] (CNY. Oct.1; 52) $1,500

THERRY, R.
- **Reminiscences of Thirty Years Residence in New South Wales & Victoria with supplementary chapter on Transportation & the Ticket-of-Leave** Sydney. L., 1863. Pages 1 & 2 loose. Hf. mor., marb. bds., gt. (JL. Dec.15; 763) Aus. $180

THERSNER, Ulric
- **Fordna och Narvarande Sverige. La Suède Ancienne et Moderne.** Stockholm, [1817-67]. 3 vols. Fo. Hf. cf., pts. stitched in orig. ptd. wraps., numbered in ink 26, 29, 31, 33-4, 36, 38, 40, 42-5, 47-72, 74-76, 79-91 with 83 & 87 bis. W.a.f. (S. Oct.20; 240) *Lyon.* £2,200

THESAURUS CORNUCOPIAE-HORTI Adonidis
Ed.:– [Varinus Camers & others]. Venice, Aldus Manutius, 1496. Fo. Inner margin of title & of a

THESAURUS CORNUCOPIAE–HORTI Adonidis -contd.

few ll. at end renewed, repairs (without loss) to lr. fore-corners of 17 ll. following title, & to outer corners of some ll. at end, colophon lf. mntd., preceding 2 ll. reprd. without loss, occasional worming, sometimes reprd., slightly affecting text of folios 78-91 & 209-213, some other repairs, mostly to worming of blank margins, MS. marginalia in Greek in a small neat hand (some extensive) & notes on title, dampstaining at beginning & end. 19th. C. mor.-bkd. bds., orig. blind-tooled sides laid down, portion of old spine preserved. [BMC V, 555; HC 15493] (S. May 5; 1)   *Quaritch.* £600

THESAURUS GEOGRAPHICUS, A New Body of Geography, or, a compleat Description of the Earth
1695. 1st. Edn. Fo. Cont. panel. spr. cf. [Wing T869] (C. Feb.25; 143)   *Burgess.* £160

THEUILLIER, J. & Fay-d'Herbe, H. –SCHADT-KISTE, de, der Philosophen ende Poeten . . .
- Porphyre en Cyprine Treurspel . . . Mechelen, 1621; 1621. 2 works in 1 vol. Sm. fo. Bnd. in reverse order. Cont. blind-stpd. vell., soiled. (VG. Dec.17; 1520)   Fls. 4,400

THEUPOLUS, Laurentius & Federicus
- Musei Theupoli: Antiqua Numismata. Ill.:– A. Visentini (title & head & tail-pieces). [Venice], 1736. 2 vols. 4to. Cont. vell., edges of bds. frayed. From the collection of John A. Saks. (C. Jun.10; 246)   *Bartoli.* £55

THEURIET, André
- Nos Oiseaux. Ill.:– Giacomelli. Lille & Paris, ca. 1880. Pict. cl. gt. (GM. Apr.30; 514)   £50
- La Secret de Gertrude. Ill.:– Emile Adan. Paris, 1890. (25) on China. 4to. Etchings in various states, portfo. containing 85 orig. drawings (5 watercold.) & 18 studies & sketches. Mor. by Marius Michel, decor. spine, border of 4 gt. fillets on covers, with 3 fleurons in corners, mor. doubls., s.-c. Bkplts. of Paul Gavault. (SM. Feb.11; 288)   Frs. 28,000
- Sous Bois. Ill.:– H. Giacomelli. Paris, 1883. (75) for subscribers. With the woodcuts before the letter inserted. Crushed mor. by E. Carayon, mor. panel. doubls. with multi-cold. inlays in floral pattern, brocade & marb. end-papers, s.-c., orig. wraps. bnd. in. Orig. watercolour sigd. by artist. (SPB. Jul.28; 41) $350
– – **Anr. Edn.** Ed.:– Jules Claretie. Ill.:– H. Giacomelli. Paris, 1883. (150) numbered, L.P. on Japan vell. Extra proof imps. of all 78 wood-engrs., 4-p. prospectus bnd. in. Lev., gt. & cold. inlays on covers, spines gt., gt. dentelles, by Marius Michel, cold. pict. wraps. bnd. in. (SG. Apr.9; 108) $325

THEVENOT, Jean de
- The Travels of . . . into the Levant. 1687. 1st. Edn. in Engl. Fo. Old cf., worn. (LC. Jun.18; 180)   £85
- Les Voyages. Paris, 1689. 3 vols. Some ll. loose. Vell., 1 bdg. defect. (BS. Jun.11; 200)   £180

THEVENOT, Melchisedek
- The Art of Swimming. 1764. 12mo. Disbnd. (P. May 14; 205)   *Evelyn.* £50

THEVET, André
- Histoire des plus illustres et scavans Hommes de leurs Siècles. Paris, 1670. 8 vols. 12mo. Browned thro.-out. Early 18th. C. red mor., gt. arms of Philippe Bon, on covers, double gt. fillet, spine compartments gt. in pointillé, sm. inkstain on upr. cover of vol. III. (SM. Oct.8; 2037)   Frs. 3,500
- Les Vrais Pourtraits et Vies des Hommes Illustres . . . Paris, 1584. 1st. Edn. 2 pts. in 1 vol. Fo. Lacks title & following lf. of pt. 2 (ll. 173 & 174). Old cf., very worn. [Sabin 95341] (SG. May 14; 214) $900
– – **Anr. Copy.** Title cut-round & mntd., with slight loss, port. of author slightly defect. at border, some dampstaining, mostly marginal. 17th. C. cf., spine gt., rebkd., jnts. & corners reprd. but worn. Bkplt. of the General Theological Seminary Liby. (CNY. Oct.1; 48) $750
– – **Anr. Copy.** Rebkd., worn. Elden Hall bkplt. (CNY. May 22; 279) $600

THEWALT, H.E. von (Trans.)
*See–*MAERCHENWALD

THIEBAULD, J.
- Bibliographie des Ouvrages Français sur la Chasse. Paris, 1934. (1000) numbered. 4to. Ptd. wraps. (SG. Jan.22; 376) $130

THIELE, A.F.
- Die Juedischen Gauner in Deutschland. Berlin, 1841. 1st. Edn. Vol. I only. Cont. bds. (SG. Feb.12; 67) $180

THIENEMANN, Fr. A.L.
- Einhundert Tafeln Colorirter Abbildungen von Vogeleiern. [Leipzig], [1856]. 4to. Some plts. soiled, text mostly soiled, at beginning with stain. Cont. hf. leath., worn. (H. May 21/22; 254)   DM 800

THIERS, Adolphe
- Histoire du Consulat et de l'Empire. 1845; 1862. Orig. Edn. 20 vols. Hf. cf., ornamental spines, wraps., by Champs. (HD. Oct.10; 289)   Frs. 2,400
- Histoire de la Révolution Française. 1823-27. Orig. Edn. 10 vols. Cont. Fr. hf cf., ornamental spines. (HD. Oct.10; 288)   Frs. 1,500

THIERY DE MENONVILLE, N.J.
- Traité de la Culture du Nopal, et de l'education de la Cochenille dans les Colonies Françaises de l'Amerique; Précédé d'un Voyage à Guaxaca. Cap Français [Santo Domingo, but probably Paris], 1787. 2nd. Edn. but 1st. with voyage to Guaxaca. 2 vols. 4 hand-cold. plts., 1 affected by adhesion. Cont. cf. (SPB. May 5; 499) $400

THIMM, Carl A.
- A Complete Bibliography of Fencing & Duelling. L. & N.Y., 1896. 1st. Edn. 4to. Cl.-bkd. pict. buckram. (SG. Oct.30; 352) $110

THIOUT, A.
- Traité de l'Horlogerie. Paris, 1741. 1st. Edn. 2 pts. in 1 vol. 4to. Lacks plt. 46, the 2 additions at corrections ll. bnd. in twice at end. Cont. leath., gt. spine. (HK. Nov.18-21; 789)   DM 1,000

THIRD CHAPTER (The) OF ACCIDENTS & REMARKABLE EVENTS, containing Caution & Instruction for Children
Phila., 1807. 12mo. Orig. wraps. (SH. Mar.19; 307)   *Schiller.* £160

THOELDE, Johann
- Haliographia, das ist: Gründliche unnd eigendliche Beschreibung aller Saltz-mineralien. [Leipzig], 1612. 2nd. Edn. Printing flaw on T3, Y5 reprd., both affecting text, browned thro.-out, slight marginal staining. Cont. vell. Bkplt. of Count Chorinsky; from Honeyman Collection. (S. May 19; 2974)   *Globe Bookstore.* £110

THOINAN, Ernest
- Les Relieurs Français, (1500-1800). Paris, 1893. 1st. Edn., (80) on Vélin du Marais paper. 4to. Cont. mor.-bkd. bds., orig. upr. wrap. & spine preserved. Bkplt. of J.J. Simon. (SM. Oct.7; 1511)   Frs. 1,600

THOMAS, Antoine Jean Baptiste
- Un An à Rome et dans ses Environs. Paris, 1823. Fo. 71 (of 72) cold. litho. plts., foxed. Cont. hf. roan, corners, worn. (HD. Dec.5; 203)   Frs. 4,900

THOMAS, Arthur Hermann & Thornley, I.D.
- The Great Chronicle of London. 1938. (500) numbered. 4to. Orig. mor. (SH. Mar.5; 138)   *Thorp.* £85

THOMAS, Arthur, Sieur d'Embry
[-] Description de l'Isle des Hermaphrodites, Nouvellement découverte. Cologne, [Brussels], 1724. Red mor. gt., by Chambolle-Duru. Genard Copy. (SM. Oct.8; 2282)   Frs. 3,000

THOMAS, Corbinianus
- Mercurii Philosophici Firmamentum Firmianum Descriptionem et Usum Globi Artificialis Coelestis. Ill.:– A.C. Fleischmann (engraved frontis.). Frankfurt & Leipzig, 1730. 1st. Edn. Ob. sm. 4to. Text browned, marginal repair to 2C4, a few ll. cut into, title stained & mntd. (remains of Franciscan owner's inscr.). 19th. C. cf. From Honeyman Collection. (S. May 19; 2975)   *Zeitlin & Verbrugge.* £950

THOMAS, David
- Travels Through the Western Country in the Summer of 1816 . . . Auburn, N.Y., 1819. 1st. Edn. Errata slip preserved on back blank, browned & slightly foxed. Cont. tree cf., worn, gt. spine, upr. cover loose. From liby. of William E. Wilson. (SPB. Apr.29; 261) $175

THOMAS, Dylan
- 18 Poems. L., [1934]. 1st. Edn., 1st. Iss. Cl. (SG. Jun.4; 480) $250
- Twenty-Five Poems. L., [1936]. 1st. Edn. Bds., d.-w. (SG. Jun.4; 481) $425

THOMAS, Edward
- British Country Life. L., 1907. 4to. Cl. (GM. Oct.30; 169)   £50
- Chosen Essays. Ill.:– R.A. Maynard & H.W. Bray. Newtown, Montgomeryshire, Gregy. Pr., 1926. (350). 4to. Orig. cl. gt. (P. Jul.2; 131)   *Sawyer.* £55
- The Happy-Go-Lucky Morgans. 1913. 1st. Edn. Orig. cl. Inscr. to Walter de la Mare. (SH. Dec.18; 308)   *Sawyer.* £175
- Lafcadio Hearn. 1911. Orig. wraps. Inscr. to Walter de la Mare, Proof Copy. (SH. Dec.18; 306)   *Sawyer.* £330
- Poems. 1917. 1st. Edn. Bds. (S. Apr.7; 439)   *Clements.* £75
- Richard Jeffries. N.d. Port. slightly spotted. Orig. cl. Inscr. to Walter de la Mare (1911), with a few annots. & sketches in pencil by de la Mare. (SH. Dec.18; 307)   *Sawyer.* £130
- Selected Poems. Ed.:– E. Garnett. Newtown, Montgomeryshire, Gregy. Pr., 1927. (275). Cl. gt. (P. Jul.2; 132)   *Lawrence.* £50
- The Woodland Life. L., 1897. 1st. Edn. Decor. buckram. (SG. Nov.13; 678) $280

THOMAS, Frederick W.
- The Emigrant, or Reflections while Descending the Ohio. A Poem. Cinc., 1833. 1st. Edn. Title soiled, text slightly foxed, title loose. Disbnd., folding cl. case. From liby. of William E. Wilson. [Sabin 95393] (SPB. Apr.29; 262) $275
- Sketches of Character & Tales Founded on Facts. Louisville, 1849. 1st. Edn. 12mo. Foxed. Orig. bds., covers detchd., lacks backstrip, folding cl. case. From liby. of William E. Wilson. (SPB. Apr.29; 263) $100

THOMAS, Gabriel
- An Historical & Geographical Account of the Province & Country of Pennsylvania; & of West-New-Jersey in America . . . L., 1698. 1st. Edn. 16mo. Map reprd. in fold., almost all the imprint shaved in rebdg., last 2 pp. in early crude photostat, heavily browned thro.-out. 19th. C. cf. W.a.f. (SG. Mar.5; 438) $900

THOMAS, Hugh Owen
- Cases in Surgery Illustrative of a New Method of Applying the Wire Ligature in Compound Fracture of the Lower Jaw. L'pool., 1875. Orig. cl. As an association copy, w.a.f.; appears to be the author's copy with extensive alterations & additions in preparation for anr. Edn. (S. Jun.17; 825)   *Phillips.* £220

THOMAS, Isaiah
- Catalogue of Books to be sold by Isaiah Thomas . . . History, Voyages, Travels, Geography, Antiquities . . . Worcester, 1787. 12mo. Mod. cl., dampstained, liby. hand-stp. on title-p. [Sabin 95400] (SG. Oct.2; 353) $400

THOMAS, Joseph B.
- Hounds & Hunting Through the Ages. N.Y., Derry. Pr., 1928. De luxe Edn., (50). 4to. Red mor. gt., partly unc., s.-c. Sigd. (CNY. Oct.1; 158) $1,200
– – **Anr. Edn.** Ed.:– Earl of Lonsdale. 1928. (750). 4to. Gt.-decor. cl., owner's blind-stp. on front end-paper. (SG. Dec.11; 286) $200

THOMAS, Michael R. Oldfield
*See–*SCLATER, Philip Lutley & Thomas, Michael R. Oldfield

THOMAS, Thomas
- Dictionarium. 1610. 8th. Edn. Slight browning & soiling, a few short tears. Cont. cf., worn. [NSTC 24014] (S. Jun.29; 441)   *Riddell.* £50

THOMAS, William
[-] The Historye of Italye. 1561. 2nd. Edn., iss. with catchword on A1v enough. 4to. Title soiled & reprd. in upr. margin, some ll. slightly spotted, last few ll. slightly soiled, last lf. reprd. in upr. margin & sm. hole just affecting a few letters. Antique-style cf. [NSTC 24019] (S. Dec.9; 279)   *Elliott.* £100

THOMAZ, Alvaro
- Liber de Triplici Motu Proportionibus Annexis . . . Philosophicas Suiseth Calculatoes ex parte declaras. Paris, [1509]. 1st. Edn. Fo. Slightly wormed thro.-out (partly reprd. at beginning),

some browning, slight marginal staining. 18th. C. vell. From Honeyman Collection. (S. May 19; 2976) *Hughes.* £480

THOMPSON, Benjamin E.
- History of Long Island . . . to the Present Time. Ed.:– Charles J. Werner. N.Y., 1918. 3rd. Edn. (600) on Berkshire linen. 3 vols. Buckram. (SG. Jan.8; 247) $100

THOMPSON, David
See–CHAMPLAIN Society

THOMPSON, Edward G.
See–WOODWARD, George E. & Thompson, Edward G.

THOMPSON, Edward P.
- Roentgen Rays & Phenomena of the Anode & Cathode (concluding chapter by William A. Anthony). N.Y., 1896. 3 ll. advts. of apparatus. Orig. cl. (S. Jun.17; 823) *Rota.* £60

THOMPSON, Francis Benjamin
- The Angler's Manual. L., ca. 1860. 1st. Edn. 12mo. Title-p. worn & rebkd. Mod. cl. (SG. Oct.16; 485) $260

THOMPSON, G.
- Travels & Adventures in Southern Africa . . . Comprising a View of the Present State of the Cape Colony . . . Progress & Prospects of British Emigrants. L., 1827. 2nd. Edn. 2 vols. Some light foxing. Hf. cf. & marb. bds. (VA. Jan.30; 449) R. 140

THOMPSON, Robert
See–GIRAULD, Jane Elizabeth–THOMPSON, Robert

THOMPSON, Thomas
- An Account of Two Missionary Voyages . . . L., 1758. 1st. Edn. Disbnd. (SG. Oct.30; 353) $350

THOMSEN, J.
- Arcana Naturae. Paris, 1859. Vol. 1 (all publd.). Fo. 11 cold. & 2 uncold. steel engrs., slightly browned in parts. Loose in orig. wraps., very defect. (H. Dec.9/10; 296) DM 800

THOMSEN, R.
- Early Roman Coinage. Aarhuus, 1974-61. 3 vols. 4to. Orig. wraps. (SH. Mar.6; 461) *Spink.* £80

THOMSON, David Croal
- Life & Labours of Hablot Knight Browne: 'Phiz'. Ill.:– C.O. Murray after Walter G. Browne (frontis.). L., 1884. Ltd. L.P. 1st. Edn., (1200) numbered, initialed by author. Sm. fo. Crushed mor., multiply gt.-ruled, gt.-panel. back, by Rivière. Frontis. sigd. by Murray & Browne. (PNY. Mar.26; 255) $250
- The Life & Works of Thomas Bewick. 1882. 4to. Orig. cl. (P. Jul.30; 303) *Sanders.* £70
- Water Colour Drawings of Thomas Bewick. 1930. Decor. cl. (CE. Nov.20; 69) £110
– – **Anr. Edn.** 1930. (525) numbered. 4to. Orig. cl. gt. (LC. Feb.12; 631) £75

THOMSON, J.
- Retreats. L., 1827. 4to. Some plts. slightly browned, 1 plt. loose. Cont. hf. leath., worn, spine torn. (H. Dec.9/10; 941) DM 560

THOMSON, James
- The Poetical Works. Glasgow, 1784. L.P. 2 vols. in 1. Fo. Lacks dedication lf. in vol. 1. Cont. mor., triple gt. fillet, spine gt. in compartments, broad floral inner gt. dentelles. (SM. Oct.8; 2039) Frs. 2,000
– – **Anr. Edn.** Ed.:– Thomas Park. L., 1805. 2 vols. in 1. 16mo. Cont. red mor., Greek-key gt. borders. Fore-e. pntg.; from the liby. of Zola E. Harvey. (SG. Mar.19; 183) $200
– – **Anr. Edn.** Boston, 1854. 2 vols. 12mo. Three-qtr. cf., spines gt. Double fore-e. pntg. in each vol. (SG. Mar.19; 186) $750
- The Seasons. Ed.:– J. Aikin. Ill.:– Caldwell after Allan & Hamilton. 1789. Cont. gt. vell., each cover with view drawn in sepia under the vell., spine gt. in compartments, cl. case. Fore-e. pntg. (S. Nov.25; 388) *Traylen.* £380
– – **Anr. Edn.** Ill.:– Bartolozzi & Tomkins after W. Hamilton. 1797. Fo. A little slight browning & staining. Cont. russ., gt., rebkd., old spine preserved. (S. Apr.7; 405) *Shapero.* £170
– – **Anr. Copy.** Red mor. gt., worn. (BS. Feb.25; 293) £120
– – **Anr. Copy.** 4to. Some ll. slightly dampstained, mostly marginal. Cont. diced russ., gt., slightly worn. (SBA. May 27; 124) *Barker.* £95

– – **Anr. Edn.** Ill.:– F. Bartolozzi & P.W. Tonkins after W. Hamilton. 1807. L.P. Fo. Mor. gt. by Ramage, spine gt. in 6 compartments, partly unc. (S. Nov.24; 286) *Klusmann.* £260
– – **Anr. Edn.** Ed.:– John Williams (notes). L., 1824. New Edn. 12mo. Cf., gt. floral borders. Fore-e. pntg.; from the liby. of Zola E. Harvey. (SG. Mar.19; 185) $220
– – **Anr. Edn.** Ed.:– Patrick Murdoch. L., 1852. 3rd. Edn. Mor. gt. with fillet borders, floral cornerpieces, & lge. central fleurons, spine gt., by J. Wright. Fore-e. pntg. (SG. Dec.18; 188) $290
- The Seasons, Hymns, Ode, & Songs. L., 1809. Heavily foxed thro.-out. Cont. vell., gt.-tooled floral cornerpieces enclosing, on upr. cover, an oval painted port., spine gt. with floral design, bnd. by Taylor & Hessey gt.-stpd. along edge of upr. cover. Fore-e. pntg. (crudely executed). (SG. Mar.19; 184) $160

THOMSON, John, Cartographer
- General Atlas. Edinb., 1819. 4to. Slightly spotted. Mod. cf., slightly soiled. (CSK. Jan.16; 104) £200
– – **Anr. Edn.** Edinb., n.d. [Cabinet Edn.]. 4to. Cont. hf. cf. W.a.f. (CSK. Aug.15; 209) £120
- A New General Atlas. Edinb., 1817. Lge. fo. Occasional spotting, slight dampstaining affecting text. Cont. cf., worn, upr. cover detchd. (CSK. Jun.5; 28) £550
– – **Anr. Copy.** Occasional staining. Cont. hf. cf., 1 cover detchd. W.a.f. (CSK. Aug.15; 211) £450
– – **Anr. Copy.** Hand-cold. double-p. engraved maps, lacks Turkey in Europe/Attica, a few edges dampstained, hardly affecting engraved surfaces. Loose in cont. hf. cf. (TA. Oct.16; 179) £425
– – **Anr. Copy.** 65 engraved maps of 74, 4 defect., some soiling. Orig. bdg., defect. As an atlas, w.a.f. (GM. Apr.30; 726) £260
– – **Anr. Edn.** Edinb., Priv. ptd., 1821. Fo. All maps hand-cold. in outl, slight offsetting, some ll. at end dis-cold., fore-margins stained. Mod. crimson hf. mor. (S. Jan.27; 530) *Jeffery.* £450
- World Atlas. Edinb., 1817. Lge. fo. Lacks 1 map, others cold. No bdg. stated. (JN. Apr.2; 812) £430

THOMSON, John, F.R.G.S.
- Illustrations of China & its People. 1873-74. Vols. II, III & IV only. Cl. gt., worn. (CE. Apr.23; 121) £390

THOMSON, Sir Joseph John
- Conduction of Electricity through Gases. Camb., 1903. 1st. Edn. Orig. cl. (S. Dec.1; 409) *Ohern.* £60

THOMSON, Peter G.
- A Bibliography of the State of Ohio. Cinc., Priv. Ptd., 1880. 4to. Cl. (SG. Jan.22; 315) $100

THOMSON, Robert
- Statistical Survey of the County of Meath. Dublin, 1802. Errata slip. Hf. mor. (GM. Apr.30; 282) £105

THOMSON, T.R.H.
See–ALLEN, William & Thomson, T.R.H.

THOMSON, Thomas
- Travels in Sweden. 1813. 4to. Mod. cf.-bkd. bds. (P. Feb.19; 160) *Hannas.* £65

THOMSON, Sir William, Baron Kelvin
- Notes of Lectures on Molecular Dynamics & the Wave Theory of Light. Delivered at the John Hopkins University Baltimore. Balt., 1884. 1st. Edn. 4to. Cl.-bkd. bds. From Honeyman Collection. (S. May 19; 2979) *Norman.* £90
– – **Anr. Copy.** Cont. hf. mor. From Honeyman Collection. (S. May 19; 2978) *Norman.* £80

THON, C.F.G.
- Ueber Klavierinstrumente, deren Ankauf, Behandlung und Stimmung. Sondershausen, 1817. 1st. Edn. 2 folding mus. supps., slightly browned. Cont. bds., unc. (R. Oct.14-18; 1303) DM 580

THORBURN, Archibald
- British Birds. 1915-16. 1st. Edn. 4 vols. 4to. Cont. red hf. mor. gt. by Root & Son. (TA. Jun.18; 114) £400
– – **Anr. Copy.** 4 vols., lacks Supp. Several ll. near end of vol. I marginally wormed & slightly stained from foot. Orig. cl., spotted. (S. Jun.1; 231) *Old Hall Books.* £200
– – **Anr. Copy.** 4 vols. Without 2 supp. plts. Cl., stained & slightly soiled. (S. Dec.3; 1155) *W. & W.* £240

– – **Anr. Copy.** Gt.-lettered cl., ex-liby. (SG. Sep.18; 367) $350
– – **Anr. Edn.** 1916. 4 vols. 4to. Red cl. gt. (CE. Nov.20; 140) £400
– – **Anr. Copy.** Orig. cl., dampstained. (CE. Jun.4; 17) £120
– – **Anr. Edn.** 1918. 3rd. & 4th. Edn. 4 vols. 4to. Some marginal stains. Hf. red mor. (S. Dec.3; 1156) *W. & W.* £260
– – **Anr. Copy.** Vols. 1-3 only (of 4). Orig. cl., gt., vol. 1 slightly stained. (C. Nov.5; 163) *Clarchy.* £100
– – **Anr. Edn.** 1918. 4 vols. (lacks Supp.). Lge. 4to. 82 cold. plts. Orig. cl. (C. May 20; 249) *Wessely.* £220
– – **Anr. Edn.** 1925-26. New Edn. 4 vols. Orig. cl. (CSK. Apr.3; 24) £120
– – **Anr. Copy.** Recent red hf. mor., gt. (S. Jun.1; 234) *Wakeling.* £100
– – **Anr. Copy.** 4 vols. Orig. cl. (TA. Jun.18; 115) £75
– – **Anr. Copy.** Cl. gt. (P. Apr.9; 214) *Dartmoor.* £55
– – **Anr. Edn.** 1925-26. New Edn., (205) numbered. 4 vols. Hf. mor. gt., ties. (P. Apr.30; 82) *Hill.* £340
– – **Anr. Copy.** Orig. cl. (S. Jun.1; 233) *Old Hall Books.* £210
– – **Anr. Copy.** Orig. cl. gt. (SBA. Mar.4; 168) *Langmead.* £180
– – **Anr. Edn.** 1926-34. 4 vols. Cl. (S. Dec.8; 182) *Roberts.* £50
– – **Anr. Edn.** 1931-33-26. 4 vols. Orig. cl. (C. May 20; 252) *Joseph.* £55
- British Mammals. 1920-21. [1st. Edn.?]. 2 vols. Red cl. gt. (CE. Nov.20; 141) £320
– – **Anr. Copy.** 4to. Orig. cl. gt., spine of vol. 2 slightly stained. (PL. Sep.18; 146) *Hobson.* £260
– – **Anr. Copy.** 2 vols. in 1. Cl. gt. (CE. Nov.20; 142) £210
– – **Anr. Edn.** 1920-21. (155) numbered, L.P. 2 vols. Lge. 4to. Orig. cl., covers slightly marked. (S. Jun.1; 235) *Head.* £500
- Game Birds & Wild-Fowl of Great Britain & Ireland. 1923. [1st. Edn.?]. Fo. Orig. cl., worn. (P. Oct.2; 106) *Mitwar.* £320
– – **Anr. Copy.** (S. Dec.3; 1157) *Lugger.* £210
– – **Anr. Copy.** Prelims. spotted, margins slightly browned. Soiled. (TA. Jun.18; 113) £155
– – **Anr. Edn.** 1923. Ltd. Edn. Fo. Red cl. gt. (CE. Nov.20; 158) £500
- A Naturalist's Sketch Book. 1919. [1st. Edn.?]. 4to. Hf. mor. (CSK. Jan.23; 109) £320
– – **Anr. Copy.** Orig. cl. (TA. Jun.18; 112) £320
– – **Anr. Copy.** (C. May 20; 250) *Joseph.* £150
– – **Anr. Copy.** Orig. cl., gt., lr. cover slightly stained. (C. Nov.5; 165) *Maggs.* £120
– – **Anr. Copy.** Some spotting & staining. Orig. cl., worn. (SKC. May 19; 432) £60

THOREAU, Henry David
[-] Euripidis Tragoediae. Leipzig, 1828. Vol. 3. 4to. Hf. cf., marb. bds., in gt. mor. case. Sigd. (SPB. Nov.25; 213) $200
- Excursions. Boston, 1863. 1st. Edn. 12mo. With 27 p. biographical sketch. Cl. Bkplt. of H.A. Ingraham. (SG. Nov.13; 683) $130
- The Maine Woods. Boston, 1864. 1st. Edn. Lacks publisher's advts. Orig. cl. E.R. Hoar's copy. (SPB. Jul.28; 439) $300
- The Maine Woods.–Cape Cod.–A Yankee in Canada. Boston, 1864; 1865; 1866. 1st. Edns., 1st. work 1st. Iss. 3 works in 3 vols. 12mo. Advts. in 1st. & 2nd. works. Orig. cl., spines worn, bkplts. (SG. Nov.13; 685) $140
- Walden. Boston, 1854. 1st. Edn. Cl., s.-c. (SG. Oct.9; 240) $625
– – **Anr. Copy.** 12mo. With map opposite p. 307, 8 p. publisher's catalogue at end dtd. May, 1854. Qtr. mor. s.-c. From the Prescott Collection. (CNY. Feb.6; 317) $450
– – **Anr. Copy.** Publisher's advts. dtd. Apr. 1854, browning. Head of spine chipped. (SPB. Jul.28; 441) $375
– – **Anr. Copy.** 12mo. With 8 pp. of advts. dtd. Sep. 1854. Spine torn with some sm. pts. lacking, some sigs. partly sprung. (SG. Dec.18; 399) $280
– – **Anr. Copy.** Considerable foxing, 8 pp. of advts dtd. May, 1854. Bookseller's label in cover. (SG. Mar.19; 293) $240
– – **Anr. Copy.** 8 pp. of advts. Lev. gt., 1 orig. cl. cover & spine bnd. in, bkplt. (SG. Nov.13; 681) $200

THOREAU, Henry David -contd.

- – **Anr. Edn.** Boston, 1909. (9) on Japanese vell. 2 vols. Minor defects. Mor. gt., gt. spine, aqua mor. doubls. with floral inlays. (SPB. Jul.28; 440) $325
- – **Anr. Edn.** Ed.:– H.S. Canby (Introduction). Ill.:– Edward Steichen. Ltd. Edns. Cl., 1936. (1500) numbered, sigd. by artist. Sm. 4to. Qtr. cl., tissue d.-w., boxed. (PNY. Mar.26; 191) $240
- **A Week on the Concord & Merrimack Rivers.** Boston & Camb., 1849. 1st. Edn. 12mo. Some foxing. New mor., blind-tooled border, orig. cl. covers & spine bnd. in. (SG. Mar.19; 292) $600
- **Writings.** Boston, 1898. Riverside Edn. 11 vols., with supp. vol. of 'Familiar Letters'. Crimson three-qtr. mor., spines gt., with floral designs. (SG. Sep.4; 443) $150
- – **Anr. Edn.** Boston, 1906. MS. Edn., (600) numbered, containing lf. of MS. 20 vols. This copy unnumbered? Hf. mor. gt. by Sangorski & Sutcliffe. (SPB. Nov.25; 497) $1,600
- – **Anr. Copy.** Buckram, unc., unopened. (SG. May 14; 216) $950
- **A Yankee in Canada.** Boston, 1866. 1st. Edn. 12mo. Without advts. Cl., bkplt. (SG. Mar.19; 295) $100
- **Yankee in Canada.–Letters to Various Persons.** Boston; Boston, 1866; 1865. 1st. Edns. 2 vols. Slight browning. Orig. cl. (SPB. Nov.24; 58) $150

THOREAU, Henry David–CANBY, Henry Seidel

- **A Week on the Concord & Merrimack Rivers.** –Thoreau. Boston; n.p., 1862; 1939. 2nd. Edn.; 1st. Edn. 12mo. 1st. work with advt. lf. at end. 1st. work in orig. cl., 2nd. work with d.-w. Bkplt. of Henry A. Ingraham in 1st. work. (SG. Nov.13; 682) $230

THORESBY, Ralph

- **Ducatus Leodiensis.** 1715-[1713]. 1st. Edn. 2 pts. in 1 vol. Fo. Cont. cf. From the collection of Eric Sexton. (C. Apr.16; 367) *Kelsall.* £90

THORESBY, Ralph & Whitaker, Thomas Dunham

- **Ducatus Leodiensis.–Loidis & Elmete.** Leeds, 1816; 1816. 2nd. Edn. (1st. work). 2 pts. in 1 vol.; 1 vol. Fo. Cont. russ., gt., worn. (C. Nov.6; 338) *K. Books.* £80
- – **Anr. Copy.** 2 vols. Cont. hf. mor. (SH. Nov.6; 176) *K. Books.* £70

THORN, Major William

- **Memoirs of the Conquest of Java** ... 1815. 4to. 1 map reprd., some spotted, some ll. soiled. Cont. cf., slightly worn. (SD. Feb.4; 229) £190

THORNBURY, Walter

- **The Life of J.M.W. Turner.** 1862. 2 vols. Extra-ill. with 45 plts. including early etching at pp. 6-7. Cf. gt. by L. Broca. (P. Mar.12; 18) *Chelsea Rare Books.* £100

THORNDIKE, Lynn

- **A History of Magic & Experimental Science.** N.Y., 1923-41. 1st. Edn. Vols. I-VI (of 8). Orig. cl. From liby. of Dr. E. Ashworth Underwood. (S. Feb.23; 306) *Goldschmidt.* £55
- – **Anr. Edn.** N.Y. & L., 1964-66. 8 vols. Orig. linen. (HK. May 12-14; 2295) DM 500

THORNHILL, Richard B.

- **The Shooting Directory.** 1804. 1st. Edn. 4to. Lacks some ll., browned. Cont. hf. cf. (SH. Jul.16; 123) *Hollis.* £160

THORNLEY, I.D.

See–THOMAS, Arthur Hermann & Thornley, I.D.

THORNTON, Alfred

[–] **The Adventures of a Post Captain, by a Naval Officer.** Ill.:– Mr. Williams. [1817]. Some spotting. Recently rebnd. in hf. cf. (TA. Feb.19; 571) £72
- **Don Juan.** 1821-22. 2 vols. Slight browning. Late 19th. C. red mor., gt., rebkd., preserving orig. spines. (S. Jun.23; 337) *Armstrong.* £110

THORNTON, Robert John

- **Botanical Extracts.** L., 1810. 2 vols. in 3. Fo. Cont. leath.-bkd. bds. W.a.f. (SG. Sep.18; 368) $325
- **New Family Herbal.** Ill.:– Thomas Bewick. 1810. 1st. Edn. Publisher's list (dtd. 1809). Hf. mor. (MMB. Oct.8; 36) *Traylen.* £50
- – **Anr. Edn.** Ill.:– Bewick after Henderson. 1814. 2nd. Edn. Slight browning. 19th. C. hf. cf. (S. Jun.1; 288) *Fryer.* £70
- **A New Illustration of the Sexual System of Linnaeus.** 1799-1802. 3 pts. in 2 vols. Fo. 14 plts.

ptd. cold. & hand-finished (only, of 32), frontis. to vol. 1 detchd. 19th. C. hf. cf., worn, upr. cover of vol. 1 detchd. W.a.f., from Chetham's Liby., Manchester. (C. Nov.27; 387) *Quaritch.* £2,600
- **Temple of Flora.** 1812. 4to. 27 hand-cold. engraved plts. & 2 uncold. plts. Cont. cf., worn, rebkd. (C. Nov.5; 166) *Larnark Jones.* £800
- – **Anr. Copy.** 28 hand-cold. stipple & aquatint plts., including the plt. of the Persian Cyclamen, cold. frontis. detchd. Cont. cf., gt., worn, poorly rebkd. From Chetham's Liby., Manchester. (C. Nov.27; 386) *Burden.* £650
- – **Anr. Edn.** [1812]. 4to. Inner margins slightly obscured by stitching, without printed title or engraved dedication. Cont. red str.-grd. mor., gt. (S. Dec.3; 1160) *Dr. Pike.* £700
- – **Anr. Edn.** Ed.:– Geoffrey Grigson. 1951. Fo. Hf. mor., gt., box. (CE. Nov.20; 20) £60

THORNTON, Col. Thomas

- **Sporting Tour through the Northern Part of England** ... 1804. 1st. Edn. 4to. Str.-grd. mor., ca. 1920 gt., crowned coat of arms of the Marquis of Beauffort (Belgium) inlaid & gt. on upr. cover, unc. Lge. Copy. (S. May 5; 205) *Traylen.* £160
- – **Anr. Copy.** Cont. cf. (SG. Oct.16; 486) $350
- **Sporting Tour through Various Parts of France.** 1806. 1st. Edn., L.P. 2 vols. 4to. (340mm. × 260mm.). Str.-grd. mor., ca. 1920, gt., crowned inlaid & gt. coat of arms of the Marquis of Beauffort (Belgium) on upr. covers, unc. (S. May 5; 206) *Maggs.* £420
- – **Anr. Copy.** 2 vols. in 1. Lacks hf.-titles, lf. of Directions to Binder & 2 advt. ll. Cont. str.-grd. mor. by C. Hering, with his ticket, gt., spine tooled in compartments. Bkplt. of George Gostling. (S. Nov.24; 287) *Way.* £140
- – **Anr. Copy.** 2 vols. Mod. three-qtr. cf., marb. bds. (SG. Oct.16; 487) $550

THORNTON, William

- **The New, Complete & Universal History, Description & Survey of the Cities of London & Westminster.** 1784. Fo. Some plts. & maps torn. Cont. hf. mor., rebkd. (SH. Nov.6; 166) *Shapero.* £75
- – **Anr. Edn.** N.d. Fo. 2 engraved folding maps, defect., maps & plts. slightly spotted. Hf. mor., covers loose. (SKC. Jul.28; 2555) £55

THOROTON, Robert

- **The Antiquities of Nottinghamshire.** 1677. 1st. Edn. Fo. Slip with further engraved coats-of-arms inserted, slight dampstaining, a few rust-holes. Cont. mott. cf., bkplt. of Downing Liby., bkplt. of Lord Esher. [Wing T1063] (S. Apr.7; 509) *Blackwell.* £320
- – **Anr. Edn.** Nottingham, 1790. 2nd. Edn. 3 vols. 4to. Slight discolouration. 19th. C. hf. cf. (C. Feb.25; 62) *Laywood.* £140
- – **Anr. Copy.** Some ills. spotted. 19th. C. mor., spines gt. (SKC. Sep.9; 1633) £95
- – **Anr. Edn.** 1790-96. 2nd. Edn. 3 vols. 4to. Engraved titles & 95 plts. only (of 97, lacks 1 port. & 1 map), 1 plt. torn & reprd., some ll. slightly spotted. Cont. hf. mor., 1 cover detchd. (SH. Nov.6; 167) *Fairburn.* £55
- **The History & Antiquities of the town & county of Nottingham.** 1795. 4to. Cont. diced cf. (CSK. Apr.3; 103) £70
- – **Anr. Edn.** Ed.:– John Throsby. 1797. 3 vols. 4to. Slight spotting. Later hf. cf. gt. (SBA. Oct.22; 494) *Jermy & Westerman.* £140
- – **Anr. Copy.** Ex-liby. copy with stp. in each vol., cont. russ. gt., worn, covers detchd. (SBA. Oct.22; 495) *Jermy & Westerman.* £80

THORPE, Francis Newton

See–LEE, Guy Charleton & Thorpe, Francis Newton

THOU, Jacques Auguste de

- **Il Falconiere ... coll' Uccellatura a Vischio di Pietro Angelio Bargeo.** Ill.:– Filosi (frontis.). Venice, 1735. 4to. Scattered spotting. Cont. vell. From the collection of John A. Saks. (C. Jun.10; 247) *Maggs.* £90

THROSBY, John

- **The History & Antiquities of the Ancient Town of Leicester.** 1791-1888. 4to. Some ll. spotted, extra-ill. with engravings, maps, photos, etc. Later cf. W.a.f. (SH. Jun.18; 149) *Chesters.* £180

THUCYDIDES

- **De Bello Peloponnesiaco.** Ed.:– I. Bekkeri. Oxonii, 1824. Cont. cf., covers detchd. Thackeray's copy, with owner's inscr. on fly-lf.,

also sm. note tipped onto fly-lf. & 16 line poem in lr. cover may be in his hand. (SG. Mar.19; 291) $100
- **Eight Bookes of the Peloponnesian Warre.** Trans.:– Thomas Hobbes. Ill.:– T. Cecill. L., 1629. 1st. Edn. Fo. 4 (of 5) plts. Mod. cf. (SG. Sep.25; 310) $280
- – **Anr. Edn.** Trans.:– Thomas Hobbes. 1634. 1st. Edn., 2nd. Iss. Fo. Slight browning & soiling, some tears & holes, slightly affecting title, plts. & maps & 1 or 2 ll. of text. Cont. cf., rebkd., old spine preserved, slightly worn. [NSTC 24059] (S. Sep.29; 115) *Armstrong.* £130
- **History of the Peloponnesian War.** Trans.:– Benjamin Jowett. Ash. Pr., 1930. (260) on paper. Fo. Orig. pig, unc. (S. Jul.31; 65a) *Maggs Brothers.* £650
- **Hystory** ... Trans.:– Thomas Nicholls. 1550. 1st. Edn. in Engl. Fo. Lacks final blank, lacks head & foot of title-p. with concomitant loss of border, stab-holes at beginning & end affecting text, a few lr. margins cut or torn away with slight loss of text on Oo5. Cont. Engl. blind-stpd. cf., worn. [STC 24056] (S. May 5; 282) *Pfefferkorn.* £180

THUDICHUM, J.L.W. & Dubré, August

- **A Treatise on the Origin, Nature & Varieties of Wine.** L. & N.Y., 1871. 1st. Edn. Orig. cl., worn & slightly stained, loose. (S. Jun.17; 827) *Norman.* £170

THUILE, J.

- **Histoire de l'Orfevrerie du Languedoc.** Paris, 1964-69. 3 vols. 4to. Orig. cl. (SH. Jul.23; 307) *Sims & Reed.* £90

THUNBERG, Carolus Petrus

- **Plantarum Brasiliensium.** Upsalla, 1817-21. 3 pts. in 1 vol. 4to. Mod. bds. (S. Dec.3; 1161) *Quaritch.* £65
- **Travels in Europe, Africa & Asia.** N.d. & 1795. 4 vols. Vols. 1-3 cont. tree cf., vol. 4 mod. cf. (S. Mar.31; 509) *Remington.* £220
- **Voyages ... au Japon, par le Cap de Bonne-Espérance, les îles de la Sonde, & c.** Ed.:– J.B. Lamarck. Trans.:– L. Langes. Paris, 1796. 4 vols. No last blanks. Cont. cf. gt., top of 1 spine slightly worn. (S. Nov.4; 606) *Maggs.* £220
- – **Anr. Copy.** Later hf. leath. (D. Dec.11-13; 1494) DM 875

THURAH, Lauritz de

- **Den Danske Vitruvius.** Copen., 1746-49. 1st. Edn. 2 vols. Fo. Cont. mott. sheep, gt. panel. spines. (C. Nov.6; 194) *Lyon.* £3,200
- [–] – **Anr. Copy.** 280 (of 281) engrs., 3 plts. cropped in Pt. 1, plts. in Pt. 2 reprd. thro-out, touching ptd. surface of 41 plts. Mod. panel. cf., initials V.G. in centres, spines gt. Paul Mellon/Pierpont Morgan Liby. copy, w.a.f. (CNY. May 22; 280) $1,500

THURET, Gustave

- **Etudes Phycologiques: analyses d'algues marines.** Paris, priv. ptd., 1878. (200). Fo. Hf. mor., unc. From collection of Massachusetts Horticultural Society, stps. on plts. (SPB. Oct.1; 166) $1,000

THURLOE, John

- **A Collection of the State Papers.** Ed.:– Thomas Birch. Ill.:– George Vertue. 1742. 7 vols. Fo. Cont. mott. cf. gt., worn. (SBA. Jul.23; 411) *Moseley.* £140

THURLOW, Edward, Lord

- **Moonlight (& other poems).** 1814. Str.-grd. mor., gt., silk liners, later leath. s.-c. Fore-e. pntg. (S. Dec.8; 71) *Chelsea.* £190

THURNEYSSER, Leonhard

- **Dess Menschen [Der Sonnen, Dess Mons, Dess Saturni, Dess Jupiters, Dess Martis, Der Veneris, Dess Mercuri] Circkel und Lauff.** Berlin, 1575. 1st. Edn. Lge. fo. Lacks plt. Dess Menschen & Dess Mons, hand-cold. thro-out, no title, 3 plts. a little wormed, slightly stained & soiled. Cont. blind-stpd., panel. rolls of biblical figures, lozenge-shaped centre-pieces, worn & reprd. hf. red mor. cases. From Honeyman Collection. (S. May 19; 2981) *Rogers Turner.* £5,500
- **Pison, das erst Theil. Von Kalten, Warmen Minerischen und Metallischen Wassern, sampt der Vergleichung der Plantarum und Erdgewechsen 10. Bücher.** Frankfurt a.d. Oder, 1572. 1st. Edn. Fo. Browned, a few stains. 18th. C. cf., gt. spine, worn. From Honeyman Collection. (S. May 19; 2980) *Neville.* £600

- **Prognosticon Eller Practica, Paa det Aar, effter vor Herris Jesu Christi Naaderige Fodsel MDXCI.** Copen., 1591. 16mo. Slight staining. Mod. vell., unopened. From Honeyman Collection. (S. May 19; 2982) *McKittrick.* £70
- **Prokatalepsis oder Praeoccupatio.–Quinta Essentia.–Pison, das erst Theil von Kalten.–Besaiosis Agonismon, das ist Confirmatio Concertationis.** Frankfurt; Leipzig; Frankfurt; Berlin, 1571; 1574; 1572; 1576. 1st. Edn. (1st. work). 4 works in 1 vol. Fo. 2nd. work lacks author's port. but inserted in photostat; 4th. work: 2 lge. folding woodcuts with overslips (2nd. laid down with slight loss of print area), W.H. Ryff's 'Des aller Fuertrefflichsten Hochsten unnd Adelichsten Gschopffs aller Creaturen' (Strassburg, 1541, 1st. Edn., slightly stained and thro.-out) bnd. at end. 18th. C. vell. (C. Nov.20; 207) *Leather.* £3,300

THURNHEIM, Lulu
- **Mein Leben.** Trans.:– R. van Rhyn. [Ph. v. Bittersdorff]. Munich, 1913-14. (150) Privilege Edn. on Bütten. 4 vols. Orig. mor. gt. (H. May 21/22; 1484) DM 1,400

THWAITES, Reuben Gold
- **Early Western Travels.** Cleveland, 1904-07. (750) numbered sets, sigd. by publisher. 32 vols. Crimson three-qtr. lev., raised bands, by the Atelier Bindery. (SG. May 14; 69) $2,800
- – **Anr. Copy.** 31 (of 32) vols. (SG. Oct.30; 142) $700

THWROCZ, Johannes de
- **Chronica Hungariae.** Brünn, [Conrad Stahel & Mathias Preunlein], 20 Mar. 1488. Fo. 16th. C. marginal notes, occasional browning, washed. Cf. [BMC III 815, Goff T360, H. 15517] (SPB. Oct.1; 245) $15,000

TIBULLUS, Albius
See–CATULLUS, Caius Valerius, Tibullus, Albius & Propertius, Sextus

TICKELL, Rev. John
- **The History of the Town & County of Kingston upon Hull.** Ill.:– after Hollar. 1798. 4to. 1 plt. slightly torn. Later hf. cf., slightly worn, unc. (SBA. Oct.22; 497) *Chesters.* £75

TICKNOR, George
See–PRESCOTT, William Hickling–TICKNOR, George

TICOZZI, S.
- **Dizionario degli Architetti, Scultori, Pittori, Intagliatori in Rame ed in Pietra, Coniatori di Medaglie, Musicisti, Niellatori ed Intarsiatori d'Ogni eta e d'Ogni Nazione.** Milan, 1830-33. 4 vols. in 3. Hf. cf. (CR. Mar.19; 177) Lire 220,000

TIDEMAND, A.
See–TONSBERG, Christian & Tidemand, A.

TIECK, Ludwig
- **Der Aufruhr in den Cevennen.** Berlin, 1826. 1st. Edn. Pts. 1 & 2, all publd. 1st. & last ll. browned in corners. Cont. hf. leath. gt. (HK. May 15; 4958) DM 420
- **Gesammelte Novellen.** Breslau, 1838-42. 14 pts. in 7 vols. End-papers browned in corners, MS. note. Cont. hf. leath. gt., decor. (HK. May 15; 4956) DM 1,550
- **Kaiser Octavianus.** Jena, 1804. 1st. Edn. 2 pts. in 1 vol. Slightly soiled. Cont. mor., gt. spine, cover & outer dentelle. (HK. May 15; 4963) DM 1,050
- **Minnelieder aus d. Schwäb. Zeitalter.** Ill.:– Ph. O. Runge. Berlin, 1803. 1st. Edn. Lacks 30 pp. preface. Cont. hf. leath. gt. Erzherzogin Sofie von Osterreich copy with crowned initials on title verso. (HK. May 15; 4964) DM 1,500
- **Phantasus.** Berlin, 1812-16. 1st. Edn. 3 vols. Cont. hf. leath. gt. From liby. of Gräfin Lanckorońska. (HK. May 15; 4969) DM 2,000
- **Schriften.** Berlin, 1828-54. 1st. Coll. Edn. 28 vols. Some staining, minimal browning & soiling. Cont. hf. leath., slightly worn, not unif. (H. Dec.9/10; 1679) DM 2,000

TIERNEY, Rev. Mark A.
- **History of Arundel.** 1834. 1st. Edn. 2 vols. Extra ill. Hf. mor. (MMB. Oct.8; 34) £58

TIFFANY, John K. & others
- **The Stamped Envelopes, Wrappers & Sheets of the United States.** N.Y., 1892. Fo. Gt.-lettered leatherette, shabby. (SG. Feb.12; 324) $100

TIFFANY, Louis C.
- [–] **The Art Work of Louis C. Tiffany.** Garden City, 1914. (492) on Japan vell. Sm. fo. Patterned gt. bds. Inscr. to Dr. F.S. Meara. (SG. Oct.9; 241) $750

TIGHE, William
- **Statistical Observations relative to the County of Kilkenny.** Dublin, 1802. Cl. (GM. Apr.30; 67) £90

TIGNY, F.M.G.T. de
- **Histoire Naturelle des Insectes.** Paris, 1802. 1st. Edn. 10 vols. Vol. 10 lacks pp. 421-24 in index. Cont. bds. (HK. Nov.18-21; 496) DM 1,150

TILKE, Max
- **Orientalische Kostüme in Schnitt und Farbe.** Berlin, 1923. 4to. Orig. cl. (SI. Dec.4; 569) Lire 200,000
- – **Anr. Edn.** Berlin, [1923]. 4to. Cl. (SG. Aug.21; 426) $100

TILLI, Michele Angelo
- **Catalogus Plantarum Horti Pisani.** Flor., 1723. 1st. Edn. Fo. Cont. cf., rebkd. From Chetham's Liby., Manchester. (C. Nov.27; 388) *Antiqua Libri.* £500

TILT'S Hand-Books for Children
- **Little Book of English History & Biography.** L., ca. 1840. 3 × 2½ ins. Contents partly loose in bdg. Orig. gt.-decor. cl. From Franklin D. Roosevelt's Liby., with bkplt., & initials on fly-lf. (SG. Feb.12; 276) $100
- **Little Picture Bible & New Testament.** L., ca. 1840. 3 × 2½ ins. Orig. gt.-decor. cl., worn. From Franklin D. Roosevelt's Liby., with bkplt., & initials on fly-lf. (SG. Feb.12; 272) $130

TIME LIFE BOOKS
- **The World's Wild Places.** N.d. 28 vols. Orig. bdgs., s.-c.'s. (JL. Dec.15; 610) Aus. $110

TIMLIN, William M.
- **The Ship that Sailed Away.** N.d. 4to. Orig. vell.-bkd. bds. (LC. Feb.12; 598) £260

TIMPERLEY, C.H.
See–WRIGHT, George Newnham & Timperley, C.H.

TINAN, Jean de
- **La Petite Jeanne Pâle.** Ill.:– Edouard Chimot (etchings). Paris, 1922. (8) numbered on Van Gelder Holland vell. 4to. Orig. drawings, trial-proofs, all plts. in 3 states (black-&-white & cold.). Mor. by Flammarion Vaillant, 2 mosaic mor. clematises on upr. cover, 1 clematis on lr. cover, marb. cf. doubls., wrap. preserved, s.-c. (SM. Feb.11; 290) Frs. 28,000

TINAYRE, Marcelle
- **La Maison du Peche.** Ill.:– Henri Jourdain. Paris, 1909. (130), numbered. 4to. Mor. by Meunier, decor. spine, border of 3 fillets & gt. leaves on covers, wrap. preserved, s.-c. (SM. Feb.11; 291) Frs. 8,500

TINDAL, Rev. Nicholas (Trans.)
See–RAPIN de Thoyras, Paul

TINDAL, William
- **History & Antiquities of the Abbey & Borough of Evesham.** Evesham, 1794. 4to. Some ll. spotted, lacks hf.-title. Mod. cf.-bkd. bds. (SH. Nov.6; 168) *Quaritch.* £50

TINDALE, Thomas Keith & Harriet Ramsay
- **The Handmade Papers of Japan.** Rutland, 1952. 1st. Edn. 4 vols. 4to. Japanese-style decor. paper wraps., sewn, stencilled paper end-ll., folding cl. case. (CNY. Oct.1; 207) $1,500

TINKER, Chauncey Brewster
- **Tinker Library: a Bibliographical Catalogue of the Books & Manuscripts Collected by ...** Ed.:– Robert F. Metzdorf. New Haven, [1959]. (500). Buckram. (SG. Jan.22; 378) $170

TINTI, Mario
- **Il Mobilio Fiorentino.** Milan, 1928. 4to. Publisher's cl. (CR. Mar.19; 239) Lire 250,000
- – **Anr. Edn.** Milan/Rome, ca. 1930. 4to. Cl. (SG. Dec.4; 343) $100

TINYAKOV, Aleksandr
- **Navis Nigra.–Trigol'nik [Three-Cornered Hat].–Ego sum qui sum.** Moscow; Petersb.; Leningrad, 3rd. vol.: priv. ptd., 1912; 1922; 1925. 3rd. vol.: (2000). 3 vols. All in orig. wraps., the 1st. slightly torn & spotted. (SH. Feb.6; 528) *Quaritch.* £80

TIPPING, Henry Avray
- **English Homes.** 1922-21-20. 3 vols. only. Fo. Orig. cl., affected by damp. (CSK. Jun.12; 144) £90
- – **Anr. Edn.** 1929. 2 vols. only. Fo. Orig. cl., slightly soiled. (CSK. Sep.26; 132) £50
- – **Anr. Edn.** L., n.d. & 1920. 2 vols. Fo. Some lr. blank margins dampstained. Buckram. (SG. Dec.4; 344) $260
- **English Homes. Period III–Period IV.** 1922-28. 1st. Edns. Vol. I; Vol. II; 2 vols. only (of 9). Fo. Orig. cl. Bkplt. of Geoffrey Harmsworth. (S. Jun.9; 22) *Allan.* £80
- **English Homes, Period IV, 1649-1714.** 1928-29. Vols. I & II. Fo. Orig. cl., vol. 1 in d.-w. (TA. Nov.20; 128) £82

TISCHBEIN, Joh. H., der Jüngere
- **Sammlung von Einhundert und Siebenzig Kupferstichen.** Zwickau, ca. 1800. Fo. Cont. bds., slightly soiled. (R. Oct.14-18; 2818) DM 2,400

TISCHER, F.
- **Bohemisches Zinn und Seine Marken.** 1928. 4to. Cl. gt., d.-w. (P. Feb.19; 349) *Sims & Reed.* £65

TISSANDIER, Gaston
- **Histoire des Ballons et des Aeronautes Célèbres.** Paris, 1887-90. De Luxe Edn. 2 vols. Slight foxing. Hf. red gt. mor. (SPB. May 6; 265) $700
- – **Anr. Copy.** 4to. Marb. hf. roan by R. Collet, unc., wraps. 2 A.L.'s. (HD. Dec.5; 204) Frs. 2,300
- **History & Handbook of Photography.** Ed.:– J. Thomson. N.Y., 1877. 2nd. Edn. Tipped-in erratum slip, advts. Cl. (SG. Apr.23; 198) $140

TISSERAND, Francois Felix
- **Traite de Mécanique Céleste.** Paris, 1889-96. 1st. Edn. 4 vols. 4to. Some foxing. Stitching loose in vol. I, hf. leath., worn. From Honeyman Collection. (S. May 19; 2984) *Rogers Turner.* £55

TISSOT, Joseph James
- **The Old Testament.–Life of Our Saviour Jesus Christ.** Paris; N.Y., 1904; 1899. 2 vols.; 2 vols. 4to. Many plts. in 2 states, minor defects. Both hf. mor., spines faded, some wear. (SPB. May 29; 421) $200

TISSOT, S.A.D.
See–COE, Thomas–TISSOT, S.A.D.

TITAN
- **Komischer Anhang zum Titan.** Berlin, 1800-03. 1st. Edn., 1st. printing. 6 vols. in 4. Pp. 97-128 vol. I transposed for same pp. supp. 1, lightly browned thro.-out. Some hf. leath., gt. spines, 2 spines loose. (H. Dec.9/10; 1560) DM 620

TITFORD, William Jowit
- **Sketches Towards a Hortus Botanicus Americanus.** 1811. 1st. Edn. 4to. Slightly dampstained, some ll. slightly spotted, tear in title neatly reprd. slightly affecting text. Mod. mor.-bkd. cl. bds. (S. Dec.3; 1162) *Varekamp.* £100
- **Sketches towards a Hortus Botanicus Americanus; ... New & Valuable Plants of the West Indies & North & South America ...** L., 1811; 1812. 1st. Edn. 4to. Foxed. Mod. maroon hf. mor. (SPB. May 5; 501) $850

TITIS, Placidus de
- **Physiomathematica, sive Coelestis Philosophia Naturalibus hucusque; desideratis ostensa prinicipiis.** Ill.:– And. Salminicus. (Engraved frontis.). Milan, [1650]. 1st. Edn. 4to. Folding plts. numbers 1 & 5 imperfectly ptd., some browning & staining, 1 lf. creased, a few ll. with MS. calculations in margins. 18th. C. bds. From Honeyman Collection. (S. May 19; 2985) *Hill.* £120

TITMARSH, M.A. (Pseud.)
See–THACKERAY, William Makepeace 'M.A. Titmarsh'

TITSINGH, Isaac
- **Illustrations of Japan.** Trans.:– Frederick Shoberl. 1822. 2 pts. in 1 vol. 4to. Cont. cf. gt., rebkd. (C. May 20; 181) *Ad Orientam.* £720

TITTMANN, E.
- **Gründliche Nachricht wegen des Ohnweit der Stadt Meissen, bey dem Dorff Gasern im vorigen 1714 Jahr gefunden ... Mineralischen Gesundheit-Wassers ...** Dresden, [1715]. Cont. bds., cover loose. (D. Dec.11-13; 236) DM 500

TOALDO, Giuseppe
– Dell'uso de'Conduttori Metallici a Preservazione degli Edifizi Contro de'Fulmini. Venice, 1774. 4to. Paper bds. (S. Dec.2; 640) *Quaritch*. £55
– Della vera Influenza degli astri, delle Stagioni, e Mutazioni di Tempo, saggio Meteorologico Fondato sopra lunghe Osservazioni, ed Applicato agli usi dell' Agricultura, Medicina, Nautica, etc. Padua, 1770. 1st. Edn. 4to. Some staining. Cont. vell., soiled, hf. red mor. case. From Honeyman Collection. (S. May 19; 2986)
Zeitlin & Verbrugge. £120

TOBAR Y BUENDIA, Pedro
– Verdadera Historica Relacion del Origen, Manifestacion, y Prodigiosa Renovacion por si misma, y milagros de la Imagen de la Sacratissima Virgen Maria ... Madrid, 1735. Sm. 4to. A few marginal inscrs., blank portion of ¶5 cut away, lacks final lf. of prelims., stains. Cont. cf., worn. (SPB. May 5; 502) $650

TOCQUEVILLE, Alexis de
– L'Ancien Régime et la Révolution. Paris, 1856. 1st. Edn. Cont. hf. cf., smooth decor. spine. (HD. Feb.27; 237) Frs. 1,700
– De La Democratie en Amérique. Paris, 1835. 1st. Edn. 2 vols. Sm. tears, stains, browning, spotting. Mod. mor.-bkd. bds. [Sabin 96069] (SPB. Jun.22; 128) $500
– – Anr. Edn. Paris, 1835-40. 1st. Edn. 4 vols. Stained in parts. Cont. cf., gold-stpd. border, spine renewed. (D. Dec.11-13; 2716) DM 1,400
– – Anr. Edn. Paris, 1850. 13th. Edn. 2 vols. Hf. chagrin. (HD. Jun.29; 76) Frs. 1,000

TOD, George
– Plans, Elevations & Sections, of Hot-Houses, Green-Houses, an Aquarium, Conservatories, etc. 1823. Slim fo. Some discolouration. Orig. hf. roan, some wear, unc. (TA. Jun.18; 34) £280

TOD, James
– Annals & Antiquities of Rajasthan. Ill.:– J. & C. Walker (map), Edward Finden (plts.). 1829-32. 1st. Edn. 4to. Folding engraved map hand-cold. in outl., 79 engraved plts., including 24 in 2 states, short tear in fold of map. Cont. red mor., elab. gt. broad panel on covers enclosing foliate arabesque in entwined cartouche roll, spines gt. in compartments, edges with triple gt. rule, inner dentelles, by J. Wright. (C. Feb.25; 145)
Ad Orientem. £580

TODD, Frederick P.
See–KREDEL, Fritz & Todd, Frederick P.

TODD, John Henry
– Historical Tablets & Medallions ... L., 1827. 1st. Edn. 4to. Orig. bds., brkn., lacks spine. (SG. Dec.18; 400) $110

TODD, Robert B.
– The Cyclopaedia of Anatomy & Physiology. 1835-59. 5 vols. in 6, vol. 4 in 2 pts. & including Supp. Hf. mor. Woburn Abbey bkplt. (S. Jun.17; 831) *Norman*. £70

TOELTIUS, J.G.
– Coelum Reseratum Chymicum oder Philosophischer Tractat worinne nicht allein die Materien und Handgriffe, woraus und wie der Lapis Philosophorum in der Vor- und Nach-Arbeit zu bereiten. Ed.:– J.C. von Friesau. Frankfurt & Leipzig, 1737. 1st. Edn. Some browning, text partly ruled in ink, marginal annots. Vell., fore-edges uneven. From Honeyman Collection. (S. May 19; 2988) *Ritman*. £380

TOEPFFER, Rudolphe
– Collection des Histoires en Estampes, vol. 3-6: Mr. Pencil; Le Docteur Festus; Mr. Albert; Mr. Vieux Bois.–Histoire de Monsieur Crytogame. –Monsieur Crepin. Geneva, 1846; 1896; 1900. 1st. work: 3rd. vol. 2nd. edn., rest 5th. Edns. 4 vols.; 1 vol.; 1 vol. All slightly spotted. Mod. cl., orig. wraps. bnd. in. (SH. Nov.20; 188)
Henderson. £90

TOESCA, Pietro
– La Pittura e la Miniatura nella Lombardia dai piu Antichi Monumenti alla meta del Quattrocento. Milan, 1912. 4to. Publisher's cl. (CR. Mar.19; 178) Lire 380,000

TOFINO DE SAN MIGUEL, Vicente
– Atlas Maritimo Espano. Madrid, 1789. Fo. 47 maps, plans & vistas, old dampstain at lr. corner affecting most plts. but only affecting a few

engraved surfaces. Orig. sheep-bkd. bds. (P. Mar.12; 167) *Burgess*. £350
– Derrotero de las Costas de Espana en el Mediterraneo. Madrid, 1787. 1st. Edn. 4to. Cont. red mor., gt. borders round gt. arms of Charles III, King of Spain, spine gt., author's monog. (SG. Sep.4; 60) $260

TOFT, Mary, the Rabbit Woman
[–] The Discovery or the Squire Turn'd Ferret. Westminster, 1727. 3rd. Edn. Fo. Unbnd. (S. Dec.2; 870) *Quaritch*. £65

TOKLAS, Alice B.
– What is Remembered. N.Y., [1963]. 1st. Edn. Cl., d.-w. Pres. copy., 'For Bobsie ...' [Chapman]. Orig. MS. envelope & clipping inserted. (PNY. Mar.4; 261) $300

TOLAND, John
– Adeisidæmon sive Titus Livius-Annexae Sunt Ejusdem Origines Judaicae. The Hague, 1709. 12mo. Slight staining, stp. on title. Cl. (S. Nov.18; 685) *Valmadonna*. £170
[–] Pantheisticon sive Formula Celebrandae Sodalitatis Socraticae, in Tres Particulas Divisa. 'Cosmopoli', 1720. 1st. Edn. 18th. C. mor., triple gt. fillet, flat spine gt., inner gt. dentelles bkplts. of Wallace Heaton & Otto Reich. (SM. Oct.8; 2040)
Frs. 2,000

TOLEDO, Piero Giacomo da
– Ragionamento del Terremoto, del nuovo Monte, del Aprimento di Terra in Pozuolo, nel anno 1538, e, dela Significatione d'Essi. Ed.:– G.B. Pino. Naples, 1539. Sm. 4to. Some ll. slightly wormed & stained in margins. Loose, 18th. C. patterned wraps., stained. From Honeyman Collection. (S. May 19; 2989) *James*. £380

TOLHURST, Rogers
– In the Emperor's Garden ... Cuala Pr., 1928. 1st. Edn. (50). Orig. linen-bkd. bds., unc. (S. Jul.22; 77) *Quaritch*. £95

TOLKIEN, John Ronald Renel
– The Hobbit. 1937. 1st. Edn. Orig. cl., d.-w. slightly frayed & soiled. (SH. Dec.19; 649)
Sawyer. £520
– – Anr. Edn. [1937]. 1st. Edn. Orig. cl., slightly soiled, maps on end-papers, d.-w. a little torn. (CSK. Jul.3; 127) £320
– The Lord of the Rings. 1954-55. 1st. Edn. 3 vols. Mor. gt., eye of Sauron composed of red mor. onlays in circles on each cover, linked with line tooling round spines, by Bayntun. Inserted are A.N.s. from author, 4 A.L.s.s, port. in vol. 1, author's sig. in vols. 1, 2 & 3, 2 reviews of final vol. (SH. Dec.19; 650) *Ash*. £2,700

TOLDEO, Mariano Angel de
– Methodus divin. Offic. Recitandi, Missasque Celebrandi pro Anno Domini 1814. N. Guatemala, [1814]. 16mo (in 4's). Plain paper wraps. (SG. Jan.8; 184) $130

TOLLER, Ernst
– Masse-Mensch. Potsdam, 1922. Orig. paper-bkd. bds. With a typed postcard sigd. by Toller. (SPB. Nov.25; 412) $150

TOLMER, Alexander
– Reminiscences of an Adventurous & Chequered Career at Home & at the Antipodes. L., 1882. 2 vols. Orig. cl., some wear & spotting, unc. (KH. Nov.18; 595) *Aus*. $120

TOLNE, David Twersky
– Kohelet David. Lublin, 1881. 1st. Edn. 4to. Hf. leath. (S. Nov.18; 341) *Maggs*. £75

TOLOMEI, Claudio 'Adriano Franci'
[–] De le Lettere Nuovamente aggiunte Libro ... intitolato, Il Polito. Rome, [1525]. 1st. Edn. 4to. 18th. C. mor., triple gt. fillet, flat spine gt. in compartments, inner gt. dentelles, bkplt. of Wilmot, Viscount Lisburne. (SM. Oct.8; 2041)
Frs.3,800

TOLSTAYA, T.
See–BURLYUK, David & others

TOLSTOI, Leo Nikolayevich
– Anna Karenina. Moscow, 1878. 1st. Edn. 3 vols. A few ll. slightly soiled. Cont. hf. cf. (SH. Feb.5; 14) *Quaritch*. £2,700
– Voina i Mir [War & Peace]. Moscow, 1868-69. 1st. Edn. 6 vols. in 3. Pp. 127 & 225 in vol. III & 253 in vol. IV misnumbered, some ll. spotted or soiled. Cont. hf.-cf. (SH. Feb.5; 16)
Quaritch. £4,000

– – Anr. Edn. Moscow, 1868-69. 2nd. Edn. 6 vols. in 3. Some ll. spotted, a few sm. tears. Orig. cl., loose, vol. 1 lacks spine. (SH. Feb.5; 17)
Bjorck. £150
– – Anr. Edn. N.Y., 1886. 1st. Edn. in Engl. 6 vols. Orig. decor. cl., in 3 s.-c.'s. (SH. Feb.5; 18)
Dawsons. £210
– – Anr. Edn. Trans.:– Louise & Aylmer Maude. Ill.:– Barnett Freedman. Ltd. Edns. Cl., 1938. (1500) numbered, & sigd. by artist. 6 vols. Linen, lithographed with designs by Freedman. (SG. Jan.15; 273) $100
– Works. 1904-05. 24 vols. Orig. cl. (SH. May 28; 11) *Walford*. £110
– – Anr. Edn. 1929-37. Centenary Edn. 21 vols. Orig. cl. (SH. Jun.4; 11) *Hall*. £55

TOMASINI, Giacomo Filippo, Bp. of Citta Nuova
– Illustrium Virorum Elogia, Iconibus Exornata. Passau, 1640. 4to. Old vell.-bkd. bds. (SG. Feb.5; 322) $120

TOMASO di Giesu, Francesco
– Compedio dell Oratione Mentale. Rome, 1652. Cont. Italian red mor., double fillets, fan motifs, leaves & spirals, arms of Cardinal Federigo Cornaro, slightly defect., decor. spine. Dedication copy. (HD. Mar.18; 179) Frs. 1,300

TOMBLESON, William
– Picturesque Memorials of Winchester. Ill.:– John Le Keux. 1830. Tall fo. On india paper, some marginal dampstaining. Orig. cl. (TA. Dec.18; 360) £56
– Thames. N.d. 4to. Text in Fr. Cl. (P. Oct.2; 294) *Whatmore*. £220
– Die Themse. L., ca. 1850. 4to. Lightly browned & slightly soiled in parts. Cont. hf. leath., spine torn. (H. Dec.9/10; 558) DM 420

TOMBLESON, William, & Fearnside, William Gray
– Eighty Picturesque Views on the Thames & Medway. 1834. 4to. Slight spotting. Orig. cl., worn, contents detchd. (S. Nov.4; 535)
Map Setters. £260
– – Anr. Copy. Dampstained. Orig. cl., gt., rebkd. & reprd. (S. Sep.29; 136) *Reid*. £210
– – Anr. Edn. [1834]. 4to. 73 plts. (of 79), some spotting. Hf. mor. gt., lacks spine. (P. May 14; 204) *Donovan*. £230
– – Anr. Copy. Spotting, 1 lf. of text inlaid. Orig. cl., worn, inner hinges reprd. (S. Nov.4; 536)
Hyde Park Books. £220
– – Anr. Edn. L., ca. 1845. 4to. Orig. embossed bds. (SG. Feb.26; 318) $375
– – Anr. Edn. N.d. 4to. Orig. cl. gt. (P. Sep.11; 4a) *Grove*. £340
– Picturesque Beauties of the Rhine. Ca. 1834. 79 (only) engraved plts., some ll. slightly spotted. Cont. hf. mor. (SBA. May 27; 325)
Schuster. £220
– – Anr. Edn. N.d. Lacks engraved title?, slight spotting. Orig. cl. gt., jnts. torn. (SBA. Oct.21; 127) *Baily*. £200
– Rhein Ansichten. L., 1832. 2 vols. Vol. II lacks 2 steel engrs., browned & slightly soiled. Cont. hf. leath. (H. Dec.9/10; 710) DM 2,300
– – Anr. Copy. Vol. 2 lightly soiled. Cont. hf. linen. (HK. May 12-14; 739) DM 1,800
– – Anr. Copy. Lacks folding leporells, title stpd., lightly browned in parts. Cont. hf. leath. gt., worn. (HK. Nov.18-21; 1350) DM 1,100
– – Anr. Edn. L., [1832]. Lacks map & 6 steel engrs., soiled. Cont. linen. (R. Oct.14-18; 2470)
DM 1,000
– Upper Rhine. L., [1832]. Slightly soiled. Orig. linen. (R. Mar.31-Apr.4; 1942) DM 2,300
– – Anr. Copy. Slightly soiled. Cont. hf. leath., gt. spine. (R. Oct.14-18; 2171) DM 2,000
– – Anr. Edn. [1834]. Some spotting. Cont. cf. gt. (P. Jul.30; 112) *Dupont*. £300
– – Anr. Copy. Hf. cf. gt. (P. May 14; 57)
Kestel. £320
– – Anr. Copy. 69 engrs., folding plan. Hf. mor. gt. (P. Jun.11; 319) *Fairburn*. £290
– – Anr. Edn. L., ca. 1835. Hf. cf., spine gt. (SG. Feb.26; 277) $650
– – Anr. Edn. N.d. Engraved title, folding map & 67 plts. only, text in Fr., some spotting. Cont. mor.-bkd. bds. W.a.f. (CSK. Feb.13; 105) £300
– Views of the Rhine. Ill.:– R. Bodmer after T.A. Lasinstoy, C. Richter after F.W. Dolkeskamp. 1832. 1st. Edn. Extra-ill. with 17 plts., 7 hand-cold., several with Frankfurt imprint 'Friedr Wilmans', cont. elevation & plan of the Convent of Nonnenworth loosely inserted, 2 advts. tipped

in, slight soiling & marginal dust-soiling. Orig. cl., rebkd., preserving orig. spine, unc. (S. Nov.4; 518)
Loeb. £620
- - **Anr. Copy.** Hf. cf. gt. (P. May 14; 58)
Walford. £270
- - **Anr. Copy.** A few ll. slightly spotted. Cont. cf., worn, lacks spine. (SH. Nov.6; 259)
Dupont. £240
- - **Anr. Copy.** Lacks 1 steel engr., slightly soiled. Cont. hf. leath., gt. spine. (R. Oct.14-18; 2471)
DM 1,000
- - **Anr. Copy.** Slightly soiled. Cont. cf. (D. Dec.11-13; 1307)
DM 900
- - **Anr. Edn.** L., 1832 & n.d. 2 vols. Lacks 15 steel engraved plts. & 1 folding engraved panorama map, soiled, some plts. browned, text more heavily. Cont. bds. (HK. May 12-14; 740)
DM 1,700
- - **Anr. Edn.** [1832]. Folding panorama worn at folds, some spotting, lacks prelims. & title. Hf. mor. (P. Apr.30; 281) *Schapiro.* £210
- - **Anr. Edn.** Ca. 1860. Text in Fr., contents stained thro.-out. Cont. hf. mor. W.a.f. (TA. Aug.21; 259)
£170
- **Views of the Rhine [& Upper Rhine].** 1832[-34]. 2 vols. Slight browning. Cont. cf., bkplt. of Russell of Ashysteel. (S. Apr.7; 493)
Loeb Larocque. £700
- - **Anr. Copy.** Some slight dampstaining, mostly marginal. Both cont. mor. (SBA. May 27; 324)
Nagel. £540
- - **Anr. Edn.** 1832; ca. 1840. 2nd. work 2nd. series. 2 vols. A few plts. slightly spotted, 2nd. work: engraved map with sm. tear. Cont. hf. cf. (S. Jan.27; 592)
Dupont. £500
- **Vues du Rhin.** N.d. Lacks map, spotted. Cont. cl., worn. (SH. Jun.4; 193) *Dupont.* £250

TOMKINS, C.F. & Planche, J.R.
- **Twelve Designs for the Costume of Shakespeare's Richard the Third.** 1830. Fo. Hf. roan, worn at head & foot of spine, unc. (S. Dec.8; 47) *Mistrali.* £90

TOMKINS, Charles
- **Tour of the Isle of Wight.** L., 1796. 2 vols. in 1. 4to. Hf. cf., spine worn. (P. Jun.11; 16)
Quaritch. £160
- - **Anr. Edn.** [1796]. Hf. cf. (P. Jul.30; 69)
Dupre. £75

TOMKINS, Peltro William
See—OTTLEY, William Young & Tomkins, Peltro William

TOMKINS, Thomas
- **Rays of Genius.** L., 1806. 2 vols. 12mo. Cont. str.-grd. mor. gt., gt. dentelles, satin doubls. & end-ll., by C. Hering, with his ticket, worn. Fore-e. pntg. in each vol.; from the liby. of Zola E. Harvey. (SG. Mar.19; 187)
$600

TOMKIS, Thomas
[-] **Lingua.** 1657. 4to. Publisher's advts. at end, title slightly stained. 19th. C. cf., lr. cover stained. Bridgewater Liby. dupl. stp. on title verso. [Wing T1842] (C. Nov.19; 169) *Quaritch.* £100

TOMLINSON, Henry Major
- **Ports of Call.** Corvinus Pr., Jan. 1942. 1st. Edn. (31) numbered, sigd., reserved for Mrs. Everard Gates. Orig. buckram, s.-c. (S. Jul.31; 154)
Updike. £80
- **The Sea & the Jungle.** L., [1912]. Gt. decor. cl., hf. mor. s.-c. Advance Copy inscr. on fly-lf. 'Early copy for review. H.M. Tomlinson', stp. on title 'To be published on 15 Nov. 1912' & (in pencil) '7/6 net'. (SG. Nov.13; 688)
$120

TOMS, W., Jnr., Carver in General
- **Thirty-six New Original & Practical Designs for Chairs, Adapted for the Drawing & Dining Room, Parlour & Hall, to be had of W. Evans.** Bath, ca. 1820-30. 4to. Prelims. spotted. Orig. ptd. bds. with linen backstrip. (TA. Nov.20; 192)
£150
- - **Anr. Edn.** Bath, ca. 1830. 4to. Orig. ptd. bds., cl. rebkd. (S. Mar.17; 465)
McDowell & Stern. £140

TOMS, William Henry
See—BADESLADE, Thomas & Toms, William Henry

TONSBERG, Christian
- **Billeder af Norges Natur og Folkeliv.** Christiania, 1875. Ob. fo. Cl., worn. (BS. Jun.11; 396) £120
- **Norge Fremstillet i Tegninger.** Christiania, 1855? Ob. fo. Cont. mor., gt., worn. (SKC. Jul.28; 2556)
£300

- **Norske Nationaldragter.** 1852. 4to. Cold. litho. title, 33 cold. litho. plts. Hf. mor. gt. (P. Jun.11; 306) *Rosenberg.* £270
- - **Anr. Copy.** 22 cold. plts. (of 33), with 10 litho. views of Norwegian scenery inserted at end. Cl., slightly worn. W.a.f. (BS. Jun.11; 395) £100

TONSBERG, Christian & Tidemand, A.
- **Norske Folkelivsbilleder.** Christiania, 1854. Ob. fo. Some browning & foxing thro.-out. Mor. gt. (BS. Jun.11; 397)
£110
- - **Anr. Copy.** Bds. (BS. Jun.11; 398) £75
- **Udvalgte Norske Folkelivsbilleder.** Christiania, 1864. Ob. fo. Title soiled, some foxing. Hf. roan, worn, spine defect. (BS. Jun.11; 399) £70

TOOKEY, James
See—IBBETSON, Julius & Tookey, James

TOOLEY, Ronald Vere
- **English Books with Coloured Plates, 1790-1860.** 1954. 1st. Edn. 4to. Orig. cl. in d.-w. (TA. Sep.18; 26)
£50
- - **Anr. Edn.** L., [1954]. Cl., d.-w. (SG. Jan.22; 379)
$240
- - **Anr. Copy.** 4to. Orig. cl., d.-w., chipped. (SPB. May 29; 422)
$100

TOOLEY, Ronald Vere & Bricker, Charles
- **A History of Cartography.** 1969. Fo. Cl., s.-c. (C. Feb.4; 208)
Russell. £95

TOOVEY, James
- **A Catalogue of . . . the Productions of the Aldine Press . . .** 1880. Cont. mor.-bkd. marb. bds. (S. Nov.24; 288)
Dawson. £60

TOPELIUS, Zacharias
- **Finland Framstalld I Teckningar.** Helsingfors, 1845. 30 pts. in 19. Ob. fo. Orig. ptd. wraps., lacks 1 lr. wrap. & some loose. W.a.f. (S. Jun.22; 195)
Loebe. £420
- - **Anr. Copy.** (S. Oct.20; 243) *Delmonte.* £300
- **Eine Reise in Finnland.** Trans.:— H. Paul. Helsingfors, 1884. Sm. ob. fo. Soiled in parts. Orig. linen gt. (R. Mar.31-Apr.4; 2779) DM 530

TOPFFER, Rudolphe
- **Voyage en Zigzag.** N.p., n.d. 1st. pp. lightly browned. Cl., gt. stpd. (CR. Mar.19; 487)
Lire 200,000

TOPOGRAPHIA Alsatiae
Frankfurt, 1644. German Lang. Edn. 4to. Lacks part of 1 double-p. map. Cont. vell. (HD. Jun.10; 104)
Frs. 15,000

TOPSELL, Edward—MOFFET, Thomas
- **The History of Four-footed beasts & Serpents, . . . collected out of the writings of Gesner & other authors . . . Whereunto is now added, the Theater of insects; or lesser living Creatures . . .** 1658. 2nd. Edn.; 1st. Edn. in Engl. Fo. Kk3-4 lacking, I, Cc, RR, SS, & SS2 torn & reprd. with loss of a few letters, last few ll. heavily soiled, some soiling & browning. Later mor. W.a.f. [Wing G624] (CSK. Oct.24; 219)
£240
- - **Anr. Copy.** Cf. (HSS. Apr.24; 251) £50
- - **Anr. Copy.** 3 pts. in 1 vol. (2 works). Fo. 3 title-pp., text woodcuts, browned, woodcuts offset to text. Cont. sheep., worn, rebkd. (CNY. May 22; 223)
$1,000

TORCHET DE BOISMELE & others
- **Histoire Générale de la Marine.** Paris & Amst., 1744-58. 1st. Edn. 3 vols. 4to. Old cf., worn. [Sabin 6158] (SG. Oct.30; 355)
$100

TORFAEUS, Thormodus
- **Gronlandia Antiqua.—Historia Vinlandiae Antiqua.** Copen., Priv. ptd., 1706-05. 1st. Edns. Some worming in inner margin at end of 1st. vol., occasionally affecting text. From Chetham's Liby., Manchester. [Sabin 96192 & 96193] (C. Nov.27; 389)
Hannas. £360
- **Historia Rerum Norvegicarum.** Copen., 1711. 1st. Edn. 4 vols. in 2. Fo. Lightly browned & slightly soiled in parts. Hand-bnd. cf. gt. & blind-tooled, upr. cover loose, by C. Hering. (H. Dec.9/10; 600)
DM 2,400

TORIO DE LA RIVA, Torquato
- **Arte de Escribir por Reglas y con Muestras, segun la Doctrina de los Mejores Autores.** Madrid, 1802. 2nd. Edn. Slight discolouration. Cont. cf. (C. Apr.1; 92)
Henderson. £85

TORONTO City Directory for 1892
Toronto, [1891?]. Many advts. inserted. Orig. bds., jnts. & spine reprd. (CB. Dec.9; 221)
Can. $110

TORONTO Public Library
- **A Bibliography of Canadiana.–The First Supplement to . . .** Ed.:– F.M. Staton & M. Tremaine; G.M. Boyle & M. Colbeck (supp.). Toronto, 1934; 1959. 2 vols. Both orig. cl. (CB. Feb.18; 248)
Can. $320

TORQUATUS A FRANGIPANI, Alexander Julius
- **Panegyricus aeternaturae Gloriae . . . Joanni Christophero Königsmarcho.** [?Amst.], 1663. Fo. 3 folding plts., 3 torn in fold. Cont. vell. bds., spine defect., pt. missing at foot. (S. Jan.27; 352)
Goldschmidt. £180

TORQUEMADA, Juan de
- **Primera [-Segunda y Tercera] de los Veinte i un Libros Rituales i Monarchia Indiana, con el Origen y Guerras de los Indios Ocidentales.** Madrid, 1723. 3 vols. Fo. Light stains in vol. II. Cont. limp vell., vol. II not quite unif. & soiled. [Sabin 96212] (SPB. May 5; 503)
$1,600

TORRE, Carlo
- **Il Ritratto di Milano.** Milan, 1674. 4to. Mod. hf. vell. (SI. Dec.4; 571)
Lire 600,000
- - **Anr. Edn.** Milan, 1714. 2nd. Edn. 4to. Red mor. sigd. by Gruel, gt., box. (SI. Dec.4; 572)
Lire 520,000

TORRE, Georgio Dalla
- **Dryadum, Amadryadum, Cloridisque Triumphus.** Padua, 1685. 1st. Edn. Fo. Engraved title slightly browned & soiled, last lf. slightly soiled, sm. area of dampstaining in upr. margins at beginning. Cont. blind-stpd. vell., slightly soiled. From Chetham's Liby., Manchester. (C. Nov.27; 390)
Taylor. £320

TORRE DI REZZONICO, Conte Carlo Costone Gastana della
- **Alessandro e Timoteo: Dramma per Musica . . .** Parma, Bod. Pr., [1782]. 4to. Cont. mor., gt. borders & spine. (SG. Sep.25; 54)
$220

TORRENS, [Henry D.]
- **Travels in Ladâk, Tartary & Kashmir.** 1862. Some ll. slightly soiled. Orig. cl. (SH. Nov.7; 361)
Enfield. £100

TORRENS, R.
- **An Essay on the External Corn Trade.** 1815. Cont. russ., 3 bkplts. including that of the Earl of Munster. MS. inscr. on title to 'His Royal Highness the Duke of Clarence'. (CSK. May 22; 113)
£180

TORRENTINUS, Hermann
See—OROSIUS, Paulus–DIODORUS SICULUS –[TORRENTINUS, Hermann]

TORREY, John
- **A Flora of the State of New York.** Albany, 1843. 2 vols. 4to. Some marginal staining, offsetting & spotting. Hf. roan, very defect. (S. Dec.8; 183)
Mistrali. £130
- - **Anr. Copy.** Plts. uncold. & unnumbered in vol. II. Cl., lacks spines. (SG. Nov.20; 417) $110
- **Superstition on his Last Legs, a Poetical Tragicomedy . . .** America, 1797. 1st. Edn. 12mo. Stitched, unc. (CNY. May 22; 281) $1,800

TORRIANO, Giovanni
- **Mescolanza Dolce di Varie Historiette . . .** 1673. Last p. stained & reprd. Mod. mor. gt. [Wing T1921] (S. Mar.16; 166) *Thomas.* £50

TORRICELLI, Evangelista
- **Lezioni Accademiche.** Ed.:– Tommaso Bonaventuri. Flor., 1715. 1st. Edn. 4to. 19th. C. hf. cf., gt. spine, a little wormed, red hf. mor. case, unc. Stp. of Biblioteca Raineri-Biscia; bkplt. of Francesco Bracchini; from Honeyman Collection. (S. May 19; 2993)
Percy. £650
- - **Anr. Copy.** Cont. vell.-bkd. bds., jnts. wormed. (S. Nov.25; 380)
Quaritch. £80
- **Opera Geometrica.** Flor., 1644. 1st. Edn. 4to. Some browning & staining. Cont. limp vell., spine torn, covers stained, owners' inscrs. on front pastedown including Vincenzo Biancalana. From Honeyman Collection. (S. May 19; 2991)
Rota. £360
- - **Anr. Copy.** General title bnd. after 1st. sectional title, some browning, owners' inscrs. of Joan. Jos. LaMontre & James Wilson. Cont. cf., worn. From Honeyman Collection. (S. May 19; 2992)
Pilo. £340
- - **Anr. Copy.** Slightly stained or soiled. Late 17th. C. leath., worn. Andrew Fletcher of Saltoun copy. (HK. Nov.18-21; 784)
DM 2,000

TORRY, Alvin
- **Autobiography.** Ed.:– Rev. William Hosmer. Auburn, 1861. Some foxing on 1st. few ll. & port. Orig. blind-stpd. buckram. (CB. Feb.18; 107) Can. $260

TORTELLIUS, Johannes
- **De Orthographia Dictionum e Graecis Tractarum.** Ed.:– [Hieronymus Bononius]. Treviso, Hermannus Liechtenstein, for Michael Manzolus, 2 Apr. 1477. Fo. & 4to. Spaces for initial capitals, paragraph marks, capitals, underlines & initial strokes in red, rubricator's ink spilled at M1r, worming at beginning & end, catching some text, slight finger-soiling, lacks 1st. & last blanks. Cont. blind-stpd. pig over wood bds., central panel of upr. cover with floral diaper, outer frame with repetitions of lozenge showing heart pierced by arrow, lr. cover with multiple intersecting fillets & scattered imps. of a circular double-headed eagle, a griffin in lozenge & a sm. rosette, rubbed, lacks bosses & clasps. Purchase inscr. & numerous marginalia of Hieronymus Munzer, inscr. of Valentin Kriss, lately in the collection of Eric Sexton. [BMC VI, 887, Goff T396, HC 15565] (CNY. Apr.8; 175) $6,000

TORY, Geofroy
- **Champfleury.** Trans.:– George B. Ives. Ill.:– Bruce Rogers. [N.Y.], Grol. Cl., 1927. (390) on Wove Rag Paper, sigd. by artist. Fo. Hf. mor. gt., spine gt., partly unc., orig. pastepaper covers of fleur-de-lis & thistle design bnd. in. (CNY. May 22; 339) $250

TOSCANA, Leopoldo
- **Saggi di Naturali Esperienze.** Firenze, 1691. 2nd. Edn. Fo. 75 plts., many dupls. Later panel. cf. (TA. Feb.19; 638) £80

TOSI, P. Fr.
- **Anleitung zur Zingkunst.** Berlin, 1757. 1st. Edn. 4to. Lightly browned. Cont. hf. leath., slightly worn. (H. Dec.9/10; 1295) DM 1,050

TOSINI, A.
- **Oggetti piu Interessanti della R. Citta di Venezia.** Ill.:– A. Lazzari after author. Venice, 1834. Ob. 4to. Stained at beginning & end. Cont. hf. leath., defect. (R. Oct.14-18; 1938) DM 1,200

TOUCHEMOLIN, Aegidius & Erhard, Johann C.
- **Neu eröffnete Reitschule.** Ill.:– Erhard after Touchemolin. Nuremb., ca. 1818. 1st. Edn. 4to. Some ll. slightly spotted. 19th. C. mor.-bkd. bds. (S. Jun.1; 47) Koch. £300

TOUCHSTONE, S.F.
- **History of Celebrated English & French Thorough-Bred Stallions.** L., 1890. Ltd. Edn. Ob. 4to. 2 hand-cold. vig. titles, cold. dedication plt., 60 cold. plts., hand-cold. vigs. Qtr. mor. Signet Liby. copy. (P. Jun.11; 274) Way. £160

TOULET, Jean-Paul
- **Les Contrerimes.** 1921. (40) on vell. Sewed. (HD. Oct.10; 162) Frs. 2,400
- **Monsieur du Paur.** 1898. Jansenist mor., by Cretté. Note. (HD. Oct.10; 161) Frs. 1,800

TOULMIN, Henry
- [–] **A Description of Kentucky, in North America: To Which are Prefixed Miscellaneous Observations Respecting the United States.** [L.], 1792. 1st. Edn. Map with explanatory lf. in facs. Mor. gt. by Zaehnsdorf, gt. borders. From liby. of William E. Wilson. (SPB. Apr.29; 264) $425

TOURNAMENT, The; or Days of Chivalry
1823. Plts. 10 & 12 misbnd. Early 20th. C. red mor., gt., by Zaehnsdorf. (S. Apr.7; 456) Bickersteth. £160
- – **Anr. Edn.** 1873. Hf. cf. gt. (P. Apr.30; 297) Cummings. £75

TOURNEFORT, Joseph Pitton de
- **Complete Herbal; Or, The Botanical Institutions.** 1719. Vol. I only. Square 4to. Cont. cf., worn. (TA. Nov.20, 289) £58
- **Institutiones Rei Herbariae.** Ill.:– after Claude Aubriet. Paris, 1700. 2nd. Edn. 3 vols. 4to. Cont. cf., rebkd. From Chetham's Liby., Manchester. (C. Nov.27; 391) Taylor. £240
- – **Anr. Edn.** 1719. 3 vols. 4to. Title-p. for Vol. 3 inserted in Vol. 2. Old cf. gt. spines, worn. (BS. Nov.26; 190) £280
- **Relation d'Un Voyage du Levant, fait par Ordre du Roy.** Paris, 1717. Fine Paper. 2 vols. 4to. Some ll. spotted or slightly browned. 18th. C. red mor., triple gt. fillet, spines gt. in compartments, inner

gt. dentelles. William Beckford's copy, Rosebery bkplt. (SM. Oct.8; 2042) Frs. 12,500
- – **Anr. Edn.** Lyon, 1727. 3 vols. Cont. cf., worn, ex-liby. (SG. Oct.30; 356) $275
- **Voyage into the Levant.** 1718. 2 vols. Cf. (DWB. May 15; 314) £180
- – **Anr. Edn.** 1746. 3 vols. 149 plts. (lacks 3?). Cf. gt. W.a.f. (P. Oct.23; 69) Hosain. £110

TOURTEL, Mary
- **The Matchless ABC, (A was an Apple Pie).** Ca. 1910. 38mm.×25mm. Orig. cl. with cover label resembling a Bryant & May matchbox. (SH. Mar.19; 201) Bromer. £55

TOUSSAINT, Franz
- **Le Jardin des Caresses.** Paris, 1914. (400) on Papier velin à la Cuve. 4to. Mor., cold. mor. onlays on covers, panel cornerpieces of tooled mor., spine in 6 compartments, 5 raised bands, mor. doubls. with corner ornaments, watered silk endpapers, orig. wraps. preserved, qtr. mor. chemise, by Leon Gruel, with his ticket. (CNY. May 22; 343) $1,500

TOUSSAINT, V.
- [–] **Les Moeurs.** Paris, 1748, 1st. Edn., L.P. 'Arrest de la Cour du Parlement' bnd. in at end, bkplt. of Laurence Currie. Cont. mor. by J.A. Derome with his ticket, triple gt. fillet, spine gt. in empty compartments, inner gt. dentelles. La Bedoyere–Beckford copy. (SM. Oct.8; 2044) Frs. 3,000

TOUSSAINT DE CHARPENTIER
See–ESPER, E.J.-Ch. & Toussaint de Charpentier

TOWNLEY, Thomas–ANON
- **Apology for the Servants by Oliver Grey.**
–**Adventures of a Hackney Coach.** 1760; 1781. 2nd. work (1st. Edn.?). 2 works in 1 vol. 1st. work with title soiled & cropped, some pp. numbers cropped, 2nd. work slightly soiled, a few marginal tears. Cont. hf cf., rebkd. (S. Apr.7; 231) Murray Hill. £200

TOWNSEND, Rev. Horatio
- **Statistical Survey of the County of Cork.** Dublin, 1810. A few finger marks, liby. stp. Cf., spine reprd. (GM. Apr.30; 283) £75
See–WELD, Isaac–TOWNSEND, Horatio
–RAWSON, Thomas James

TOWNSEND, Rev. Joseph
- **Journey through Spain.** L., 1791. 3 vols. 4to. Cf. (DS. May 22; 865) Pts. 34,000

TOWNSHEND, Thomas, of Gray's Inn
- **Poems.** L., 1797. 2nd. (1st. London) Edn. Cont. red str.-grd. mor. gt. Bkplt. of Alexander Davison, Swarland. (S. Nov.24; 289) Quaritch. £80

TOWNSLAND SURVEY of the County of Limerick
Dublin, 1844. Atlas fo. Hand-cold. index map & 60 double-p. maps. Cf., armorial motif, Castlegarde, some slight soiling. (GM. Apr.30; 197) £300

TOWNSON, Robert
- **Travels in Hungary.** 1797. [1st. Edn.?]. 4to. Cf. gt. (P. Oct.23; 70) Rogers. £95
- – **Anr. Copy.** Cont. cf. (SG. Feb.26; 321) $250

TOYE, Nina & Adair, A.H.
- **Drinks–Long & Short.** Ill.:– Rex Whistler. 1925. Orig. bds., jnts. & d.-w. torn. Pen & ink sketch sigd. by artist. (SH. Mar.27; 543) Sawyer. £90

TOYNBEE, J.M.C.
- **Roman Medallions.** N.Y., 1944. 4to. Orig. wraps. (SH. Mar.6; 463) Thibaut. £200

TOYS Catalogue for Britains Ltd.
Ca. 1935. 4to. Orig. wraps. Few additions loosely inserted. (SH. Apr.10; 565) Burley. £50

TRACTATUS Brevis et Utilis pro Infirmis Visitandis
Passau, Benedictus Mayr & Johannes Alakraw, 14 Nov. 1482. 4to. Spaces for initial capitals, which are supplied in red, as are paragraph marks, underlines & initial strokes. Limp vell. From the collection of Eric Sexton. [BMC II, 614, Goff 176, HC(+Add) R 9182] (CNY. Apr.8; 131) $1,300

TRACTATUS HISTORICO–THEOLOGICUS de Jubilaeo
See–THEODORO A SPIRITU SANCTO

TRACTATUS DE JUDEORUM et Christianorum Communione et Conversatione
[Basel], ca. 1474. 1st. Edn. Fo. Initials hand

painted in red & blue. Mod. marb. bds. [HC 9464] (SG. Oct.9; 242) $4,800
- – **Anr. Edn.** [Strassb.], ca. 1476. Fo. Hand-painted rubricated initials, damp-stained. Mod. stiff vell., 2 vell. clasps. MS. description of this edn. written & initialed by G.P. Winship tipped in. [HC 9465] (SG. Oct.9; 243) $1,800

TRACTATUS de Verbo Rei Collectus ex Doctore Sancto
[Merseburg], [Marcus Brandis], ca. 1479-80. Fo. (in 8's). Spaces for initial capitals, slightly wormed. Disbnd., laid in folding cl. case. From the collection of Eric Sexton. [Goff T421, H 15593] (CNY. Apr.8; 101) $11,000

TRAILL, Catherine Parr
- **The Canadian Settler's Guide.** Toronto, 1855. 5th. Edn. 12mo. Many ll. loose, occasional spotting. Orig. cl., lacks spine, bds. loose. (CB. Sep.24; 272) Can. $450
- **Canadian Wild Flowers.** Ill.:– Agnes Fitzgibbon. Montreal, 1869. [2nd. Edn.?]. Fo. Orig. cl. gt. (C. Mar.18; 185) Weldon & Wesley. £220
- – **Anr. Copy.** Plt. no. V misnumbered VI & VI misnumbered V. Orig. panel. gt.-stpd. cl., with gt.-stpd. floral decors. Sig. of Dr. John Bell on front free endpaper. (CB. Dec.9; 262) Can. $850
- **Studies of Plant Life in Canada.** Ill.:– Agnes Chamberlin. Ottawa, 1885. 1st. Edn. Some plts. retouched by hand by unknown artist. Orig. cl., gt.-stpd. decors. on upr. cover & spine. (CB. Feb.18; 49) Can. $350

TRAINS ILLUSTRATED
1946-68. Vols. 1-14, and 1 other vol., together in 14 vols. Cont. cl. (SH. Oct.9; 279) McAlpine. £140

TRANSFORMATION BOOK
- **Miss Rose.** Ca. 1845. 1 lf. lacks corner. Orig. pict. wraps., backstrip reinforced. (SH. Mar.19; 311) Libris. £55
- **Table Book.** N.Y., ca. 1850. Soiled. Orig. pict. wraps., slightly worn, backstrip restitched. (SH. Mar.19; 312) Ashton. £85

TRANSITION
Paris, etc., 1927-38. 1st. Printings. Numbers 3, 13, 14, 16-17, 24-27 (number 26 dupl.). Pict. wraps., number 3 unbnd., number 13 lacks lr. cover & spine. Number 3 has long sigd. pres. inscr. from Gertrude Stein & double number 16-17 has pres. inscr. from Alice B. Toklas, for 'Bobsy' (Goodspeed). (PNY. Mar.4; 263) $300
- – **Anr. Edn.** Paris, [1948-50]. Together 6 iss., numbered 1-6. 12mo. Pict. wraps., one by Matisse. (SG. Jun.4; 483) $260

TRANSPORTATION
- **Report from the Select Commitee on the State of Gaols, &c. Ordered, by the House of Commons, to be printed, 12 July 1819.** [L.], [1819]. Fo. Old hf. roan, upr. bd. almost detchd. (KH. Nov.18; 598) Aus. $820

TRANSVAAL
- **Sixty-Three Views (of Pretoria & Johannesburg).** Cape Town, ca. 1906. Ob. 8vo. Without title-p. (as iss.) Decor. & photographic covers, soiled. (VA. Oct.31; 414) R. 520

TRAPNELL, Alfred
- **A Catalogue of Bristol & Plymouth Porcelain, with Examples of Bristol Glass & Pottery.** 1912. (250) numbered. 4to. Cont. hf. cf. by Zaehnsdorf, slightly rubbed, orig. wraps. bnd. in. Pres. copy inscr. by publisher. (CSK. Aug.29; 212) £60

TRAPP, Oswald Graf
- **Armoury of the Castle of Churburg.** Trans.:– J.G. Mann. 1929. Ltd. Edn. Fo. Cl. (CE. Nov.20; 91) £300

TRAQUAIR, Ramsay
- **The Old Architecture of Quebec.** Toronto, 1947. 4to. Orig. cl. With A.L.s. from Traquair to A.W. Wallace, dtd. Sep. 10, 1947. (CB. May 27; 320) Can. $550

TRATTINNICK, Leopold
- **Thesaurus botanicus.** Ill.:– After Strentzel & others. Vienna, [1805-]1819. Fo. 19th. C. qtr. cf., worn. From collection of Massachusetts Horticultural Society, stpd. on plts. (SPB. Oct.1; 167) $11,000

TRAU, F.
- **Sammlung. Münzen der Römischen Kaiser.** Vienna & Lucerne, 1935. 4to. Orig. wraps. (SH. Mar.6; 464) Sapori. £95

TRAVELS OF Cosmo the Third, Grand Duke of Tuscany, through England.
1821. 4to. Cont. tree cf., covers detchd. (TA. Aug.21; 106) £160
– – Anr. Copy. Some plts. affected by off-setting of text. (TA. Oct.16; 285) £130

[TRAVERSARI], Ambrosius, Camaldulensis
– Hodoeporicon ... ex Bibliotheca Medicea ad Illustrissimum ... Antonium Magliabechi. Flor., [1680]. 4to. Inner margin of title reprd., faded inscr. on verso of title 'Ex dono Clarissimi ... D. Ant. Magliabechi Florentiae 27 May 1710', bkplts. of Earl of Guildford & Sir Thomas Phillips. 18th. C. red mor. by Derome le Jeune with his ticket, triple gt. fillet, flat spine gt. with zig-zag of double fillets interspersed with dots, inner gt. dentelles. Dedication copy to Magliabechi. (SM. Oct.8; 2046) Frs. 1,000

TREASURE of Poor Men
[–] Here Begynneth a Good Booke of Medecines called the Treasure of Pore Men. 12 Dec. 1544. Thro.-out 2nd. hf. of book are sm. tears in upr. margins affecting letters, but with hardly any loss of text (most of them are tissued), short tear in centre of G4 with no loss. New mor. In lr. blank margin written in faded ink (probably 19th. C.) a record of the gift of the book of one Bezet (?) to Southam. [STC 24203] (S. Jun.17; 834) Levinson. £1,500

TREATIES
– Articuli Pacis & Confoederationis inter ... Carolum II ... et Celsos ac Praepotentes Dominos Ordines Generales Foederatarum Belgii Provinciarum, 1667. L., 1667. 4to. Some dampstaining. Old vell. Includes 3 other treaties, with separate title-pp., those with Louis XIV & Frederick III, & naval & commercial treaty with the Dutch. [Wing C2919; Sabin 2154c] (SG. Mar.5; 444) £260
– Indian Treaties Printed by Benjamin Franklin, 1736-1762. Ed.:– Julian P. Boyd. Phila., 1938. (500) numbered. Fo. Buckram, endpapers discold. in inner margins. (SG. Mar.5; 240) £70

TREATY of Paris
– Tratado Definitivo de Paz. Lisbon, 1763. 1st. Portuguese Edn. Marb. wraps., light waterstain through at head. (CB. Dec.9; 53) Can. $220

TREBECK, G.
See–MOORCROFT, W. & Trebeck, G.

TREDGOLD, Thomas
– The Steam Engine ... 1827. 1st. Edn. 4to. Advts. at beginning & end, some foxing & offsetting. Orig. bds., rebkd., unc. Label & release stp. of Essex Institute, liby. of Francis Peabody (Salem, Mass.), with latter's sig.; from Honeyman Collection. (S. May 19; 2994) Zeitlin & Verbrugge. £140
– – Anr. Edn. Ed.:– W.S.B. Woodhouse. L., 1838. 4to. Some sm. stains. Orig. cf. (D. Dec.11-13; 274) DM 800
– – Anr. Edn. 1838-43. 2 vols. including Atlas of plts. from a later Edn. 4to. & fo. Spotted thro.-out. Orig. cl.-bkd. bds. (SH. Oct.9; 284) Corbett. £75
– – Anr. Edn. N.d. 2 vols. 4to. Hf. cf. (P. Feb.19; 182) Busch. £85

TREMAINE, Marie
See–STATON, Frances M. & Tremaine, Marie

TREMBLEY, Abraham
– Memoires, pour servir à l'Histoire d'un genre de Polypes d'eau douce, à Bras en Forme de Cornes. Leiden, 1744. 1st. Edn. 4to. Lf. of directions to binder at end, some marginal staining, slight soiling. Cont. mott. cf., spine reprd. new endpapers, unc. Bkplt. of Herbert McLean Evans; from Honeyman Collection. (S. May 19; 2995) Goldschmidt. £160
– – Anr. Edn. Paris, 1744. 2 vols. Cont. cf. (TA. Jun.18; 78) £92
– – Anr. Copy. 4to. Cont. marb. cf., gt. spine. (VG. Oct.13; 156) Fls. 650

TRENCHANT, Jan
– L'Arithmetique ... Avec l'art de calculer aux Getons ... Reueue & augmentée pour la quartième edition. Lyon, 1578. Stained & soiled, piece torn from margin of 2A4, sm. tears in last 2 ll., owner's inscrs. of 'Salissar' & Charles Barry, 1862. 19th. C. vell. From Honeyman Collection. (S. May 19; 2996) Hill. £220

TRESHAM, Henry & others
– British Gallery of Pictures. L., 1818. Lge. fo. Cont. hf. leath., defect & loose. (R. Mar.31-Apr.4; 1601) DM 650

TRESOR DE NUMISMATIQUE ET DE GLYPTIQUE
Paris, 1836-44. 13 vols. 4to. Hf. cf. (LM. Mar.21; 256) B.Frs. 33,000

TRESOR des Almanachs (Le), Etrennes Nationales
Paris, 1784. 32mo. Cont. red mor., covers decor. with sm. tools. (HD. Apr.10; 201) Frs. 1,350
– – Anr. Edn. Paris, [1785]. Sm. 18mo. Cont. red mor., gt. decor. covers, lge. gt. decor. border with mor. centre medallion, watered silk fly-ll. (HD. Apr.10; 202) Frs. 3,700

TRESSAN, Comte Louis Elisabeth de la Vergne de Braussin
– Oeuvres Choisies. Ill.:– Clement-Pierre Marillier. ca. 1788. 12 fine ink & wash drawings only, all sigd., for Tressan's 'Oeuvres', guarded. Red mor. gt., by Chambolle-Duru, upr. jnt. brkn. (SM. Oct.8; 2422) Frs. 45,000

TRET'YAKOV, Sergei
– Zheleznaya Pausa [Ferrous Pause]. Vladivostok, 1919. Orig. wraps., torn & soiled. (SH. Feb.6; 529) Lempert. £100
See–MAYAKOVSKY, Vladimir & others

TREU, Abdias
– Grundlicher Bericht von deme, in dem Ende verwichenen Januarii Alten, und Anfang dess Februarii Neuen Calenders erschienenen Cometen. Nuremb., 1661. Sm. 4to. Mod. bds. From Honeyman Collection. (S. May 19; 2997) Hill. £55
See–SCHIMPFFER, B.–TREU, A.–SCHORER, C.

TREVELYAN, G.M.
– Garibaldi's Defence of the Roman Republic. L., 1914. Diced cf. gt., sm. arrows in corners, spine gt., prize bkplt. of Harrow School. Fore-e. pntg. (SG. Mar.19; 188) $170

TREVELYAN, Robert Calverley
– Polyphemus & other Poems. Ill.:– Roger Fry. 1901. Sm. 4to. Orig. cl.-bkd. bds., unc., partly unopened, worn. (SH. Mar.26; 227) Slade. £50

TREVERS, Joseph
– An Essay to the Restoring of our Decayed Trade, wherein is Described, the Smuglers, Lawyers, & Officers Frauds, & c. 1675. 1st. Edn. 4to. Recent cf.-bkd. bds., partly unc. [Wing T2129] (C. Apr.1; 187) Quaritch. £260

TREVOR, Robert, Viscount Hampden
– Britannica, Lathmon, Villa Bromhamensis. Parma, 1792. (115?). Fo. Cont. russ. gt., lacks lettering pieces. (C. Nov.20; 276a) Lyon. £70

TREW, Christoph Jakob
– Hortus Nitidissimis. Nuremb., 1768-72. 2 vols. (only, of 3) in 1. Lge. fo. 118 hand-cold. engraved plts. only (lacks 2 plts. in vol. 2), upr. & lr. edges of plt. 97 cropped with loss of title, plt. no. & publisher's imprint, some spotting & browning in vol. 2, Latin title & final 3 ll. Old vell.-bkd. bds., worn, upr. cover detchd. From Chetham's Liby., Manchester. (C. Nov.27; 393) Marshall. £6,000
– – Anr. Edn. 1768-86. 3 vols. in 2. Lge. fo. 175 hand-cold. engraved plts. (of 178), 1 plt. cropped. Mod. hf. mor. (C. Mar.18; 113) Quaritch. £17,00
– Plantae Selectae. Ill.:– After Georg Dionysius. [Nuremb.], [1750-]1771[-73.] Fo. Without general title & 4th. port. found in some copies, 2 ports. supplied from a smaller copy. Cont. diced russ. gt., rebkd., portions of orig. spine preserved. From collection of Massachusetts Horticultural Society, stps. on plts. (SPB. Oct.1; 168) $13,500
– – Anr. Edn. Ill.:– J.J. & J.E. Haid after G.D. Ehret. [Nuremb.], 1750-73. Fo. Plts. hand-cold., without the 4th. port. or the general title found in some copies, nor the supp. 19th. C. hf mor. From Chetham's Liby., Manchester. (C. Nov.27; 394) Fletcher. £5,000

TRIAL & EXECUTION OF THE SPARROW FOR KILLING COCK ROBIN
N.d. 16mo. Inscr., dtd. 1831. Orig. ptd. wraps. (SH. Mar.19; 313) Schiller. £270

TRIALS
– Case & Appeal of James Ashley of Bread Street, London, addressed to the public in general in relation to the apprehending of Henry Simons, the Polish Jew, on a warrant issued out against him for perjury. L., 1753. Slight discolouration, stp. of the Mocatta Liby. Hf. leath. (S. Nov.18; 640) Laurie. £220
– A Collection of the Most Remarkable & Interesting Trials ... L., 1775-76. 2 vols. 4to. Cont. marb. bds., cf. rebkd. (SG. Sep.25; 312) $240
– Nuremburg Trials. The Trial of German Major War Criminals. 1946-51. 26 vols. including Opening & Closing Speeches & Judgement. Mod. cl. (SH. Mar.5; 264) Verby. £165
– Proceedings of a General Court-Martial for the Trial of Lieut.-Col. Geo. Johnston on a Charge of Mutiny for Deposing William Bligh. 1811. 1st. Edn. With errata slip. Cl.-bkd. bds., unc. Inscr. by Bligh to Henry Barker, with an A.L.s. from a descendant of the recipient loosely inserted, presenting the book to Owen Rutter. (SH. Jul.27; 1) Brook-Hitching. £1,900
– Recueil Général des Pièces concernant le Procez entre la Demoiselle Cadière de la Ville de Toulon et le Pere Girard, Jesuite, Recteur du Seminaire Royal de la Marine de ladite Ville. N.p., 1781. 2 vols. Fo. Cf., 6 spine raised bands, decor. (LM. Mar.21; 289) B.Frs. 8,000
– Report of the State Trials, before a General Court-Martial held at Montreal in 1838-39. Montreal, 1839. 2 vols. Slight foxing thro.-out. Gt.-edged mor. (CB. Sep.24; 103) Can. $800
– Reports of the Trials of Colonel Aaron Burr ... For Treason & For a Misdeameanor ... Taken in Short Hand by David Robertson ... Phila., 1808. 1st. Edn. ('Fine Paper'). Browned & foxed. Orig. bds., spines split & mostly perished. From liby. of William E. Wilson. [Sabin 9434] (SPB. Apr.29; 44) $200
– Sacco-Vanzetti Case: Transcript of the Record of the Trial ... N.Y., 1928-29. 6 vols. 4to. Ex liby. Buckram. (SG. Jun.11; 378) $140
– Trial of George Crowninshield, J.J. Knapp, Jnr. & John Francis Knapp ...–Appendix to the Report of the Trial of J.F. Knapp, containing the New Evidence ... Boston; Salem, 1830. Together 2 vols. Disbnd. (SG. Jun.11; 278) $120
– The Trial of Mrs. Mary Reed, for Petit Treason, in Poisoning her Husband, William Reed ... Gloucester, [1796]. 4to. With 2-pp. testimony of Dr. Edward Jenner. Later hf. leath. (SG. Sep.18; 201) $110
– Trial of Samuel Chase ... Taken in Short Hand by Samuel H. Smith & Thomas Lloyd. Wash., 1805. 1st. Edn. 2 vols. Portions of text browned & foxed. Orig. bds., soiled, lacks backstrip on vol. II. From liby. of William E. Wilson. [Sabin 12205] (SPB. Apr.29; 51) $175

TRICASSO, Patricio, da Ceresari
– Chyromantia ... ingeniosamente extratta dai Libri de Aristotile, et altri Philosophi Naturali. Venice, 1535. Amherst bkplt. 18th. C. Fr. red mor., triple gt. fillet, flat spine, longitudinal title, gt., inner gt. dentelles. (SM. Oct.8; 2047) Frs. 3,600

TRIGGS, Henry Inigo
– Formal Gardens in England & Scotland Ill.:– Charles Latham & Triggs. 1902. Fo. Hf. mor., spotted. (SG. Mar.12; 367) $240

TRIGGS, Stanley
See–HARPER, Russell J. & Triggs, Stanley

TRIMEN, Henry
– A Hand-Book to the Flora of Ceylon. 1893-1900. 6 vols. (including folder of plts. but lacks Supp. of 1931). 8vo & 4to. Lacks vols. 6, 10, 21, 32, 33, 37, 49, 51, 64, 71, & 78. Loose as iss., slight spotting, orig. cl., soiled. (S. Jan.26; 298) Wheldon & Wesley. £160

TRIMEN, R.
– South African Butterflies. L., 1887-89. 3 vols. Some foxing. Mod. cl., ex-liby. (SSA. Nov.5; 187) R. 140

TRINIDADE, Bento da
– Sermão sobre a Religiao pregado na Igreja de Saõ Salvador dos Campos. Rio de Janeiro, 1811. Some discolouration. Mod. cf. (SPB. May 5; 505) $200

TRIOMPHE de la Ligue, ou la France à la Veille de Soucrire à la Paix
Paris, 1696. 24mo. Crimson mor., triple gt. fillet

TRIOMPHE de la Ligue, ou la France à la Veille de Soucrire -contd.
borders, gt. dentelles & spine, by Derome, s.-c., spine title is 'Alcoran de L.XIX' a misprint for L.XIV, the title under which the work appeared in 1695. Mor. bkplts. of Charles Nodier & Mortimer Schiff. (SG. Sep.25; 47) $700

TRIOMPHE HERMETIQUE ou la Philosophale Victorieuse
Amst., 1689. 1st. Edn. in Fr. Folding plt. slightly torn in fold. Cont. cf. (S. Dec.1; 416)
Quaritch. £600

TRIPPAULT, Leon
- Celt-Hellenisme, ou Etymologic des Mots François tirez du Grace. Plus preuves en Général de la Descente de nostre Langue. Orleans, 1581. 1st. Edn. Slight foxing. Cont. vell., worn & lacking ties. (S. Oct.20; 249) *P. Beres.* £250

TRISSINO, Giovanni Giorgio
- La Italia Liberata di Gotthi. Rome [Venice], 1547 [1548]. 1st. Edn. 3 vols. Vol. II lacks woodcut device, title with old MS. addition 'Tom II' inserted in vol. II, woodcut border inserted in vol. III, centre cut away & old MS. transcript of vol. I title supplied with 'Tom III' in anr. hand, lacks last blank in each vol. & 1 lf. of errata in vol. III, inscr. on blank *6 recto. 18th. C. red mor., triple gt. fillet, spine gt. in compartments, inner gt. dentelles. (SM. Oct.8; 2048) Frs. 1,100
- La Poetica. Vicenza, Apr. 1529. 1st. Edn. 4to. Lacks 2 errata ll. at end (publd. later), ownership inscr. on title of Benedictine monastery at Saint Maur, bkplt. & sig. of Walter W. Gregg. 18th. C. mott. cf., gt. fillets & corner sprays, spine slightly worn. (SM. Oct.8; 2049) Frs. 1,400

TRISSMOSIN, Salomon
- Aurei Velleris oder Der Gulden Schatz und Kunstkamer. Tractus III. Rorschach, 1599. 1st. Edn. Vol. III (of 3). 4to. A few ll. loose, 2 blank corners torn away, slightly spotted or soiled in pts., slightly dampstained at beginning, cont. marginalia. Cont. vell. bds., soiled, upr. cover slightly worn. (S. Jan.27; 353)
Globe Book Store. £180

TRISTRAM, Ernest William & Bordswell, Monica
- English Medieval Wall Painting, The Twelfth Century; The Thirteenth Century. (Text vol. only). 1944-50. 2 vols. 4to. Orig. cl. (SH. Mar.6; 579) *George's.* £85

TRISTRAM, Henry Baker
- Survey Western Palestine . . . Fauna & Flora. 1884. 4to. Buckram gt. (P. Nov.13; 229)
Cohen. £150

TRISTRAM, W. Outram
- Coaching Days & Coaching Ways. Ill.:– Hugh Thomson & Herbert Railton. 1893. (250) on L.P. Orig. cl. (SH. Mar.27; 512) *Johns.* £160
- - Anr. Edn. Ill.:– Hugh Thomson & Herbert Railton. L., 1924. 12mo. Crimson mor., gt. borders, enclosing figure in vari-cold. mor. inlays, spine gt., by Kelliegram. (SG. Apr.9; 413) $275

TRITHEIM, Johann
- De Vanitate et Miseria Humanae Vitae. Mainz, Peter von Friedberg, 1495. 1st. Edn., on vell. 4to. Spaces for initial capitals, supplied alternately in red & blue, underlines & initial strokes in red, lacks final blank, lr. fore-margin of c2 with slight natural vell. flaw. Mor., covers blind-tooled. From the collection of Eric Sexton. [BMC I, 48, Goff T457, HC 15635*] (CNY. Apr.8; 97) $7,500
- Liber de Scriptoribus Ecclesiasticis. Basle, Johann Amerbach, [after Aug. 28], 1494. 1st. Edn. Fo. Spaces for initials with guide letters, lge. initials in blue with red penwork tracery at inner margins on A2 & a1r, other initials supplied in red & in red & blue with line strokes in red in the 6 prelims., by a cont. hand, fo. 135 inserted from anr. copy, but lacks the conjugate final blank lf., marginal worming to last 3 ll. Mod. qtr. mor., gt.-lettered, by MacDonald. Bkplts. of Dr. Georg Kloss & the General Theological Seminary Liby. [BMC III, 755, Goff T452, HC 15613] (CNY. Oct.1; 12) $2,000
- Polygraphiae libri six [–Clavis Polygraphiae]. [Oppenheim], 1518. 1st. Edn. 2 pts. in 1 vol. Fo. Lacks 1st. b6 (blank), tear in q3 reprd., 1st. title slightly soiled, prelims. a little wormed in upr. margins, a few marginal stains, inscr. 'Ex libris Sti. Martini a Campis'. 19th. C. cf., gt. From

Honeyman Collection, with his note of purchase. (S. May 19; 2998) *Percy.* £900

TRIUMPH OF GOOD NATURE EXHIBITED IN THE HISTORY OF MASTER HARRY FAIRBORN & MASTER TRUEWORTH
Glasgow, [Wtrmkd. 1818]. 12mo. Orig. wraps., backstrip worn, folder. (SH. Mar.19; 314)
Vincent. £55

TROIANI, Filippo
- Vent'otto Vedute della Grecia. Rome, 1830. Ob. fo. Cont. hf. leath. (SI. Dec.4; 576) Lire 250,000

TROIL, Uno von
- Letters on Iceland. 1780. 1st. Engl. Edn. Lge. folding map with sm. tear. 19th. C. hf. mor., worn. From Chetham's Liby., Manchester. (C. Nov.27; 395) *Maggs.* £80

TROILI da Spilamberto, Giulio
- Paradossi per Pratticare la Prospettiva Senza Saperla, fiori, per Facilitare l'Intelligenza, frutti, per non operare alla cieca. Bologna, 1683. 2nd. Edn. Fo. Corner torn from B3 pt. 2, a little worming in lr. margins of last quire, title & some ll. browned. Mod. hf. vell. bds. From Honeyman Collection. (S. May 19; 3000) *Schaffer.* £340
- - Anr. Copy. 2 pts. in 1 vol. Vell. (BS. Jun.11; 132) £190
- - Anr. Copy. 2 vols. (3 pts.) in 1. C4 & H4 with reprd. tears affecting text, scattered light dampstaining & spotting. Hf. vell. & paper bds. (CNY. Oct.1; 28) $300

TROJAN, Giuseppe
- [-] Notizie Istoriche sulla Vita della B. Giuliana Vollalto. Venice, 1756. On vell. Sm. 4to. Cf.-bkd. bds., spine defect. The Beckford copy, bkplt. of Henry J.B. Clements, lately in the collection of John A. Saks. (C. Jun.10; 251) *Lyon.* £200

TROLLOPE, Anthony
- An Autobiography. 1883. 1st. Edn. 2 vols. Hf. mor. gt. (SBA. Jul.23; 673) *Hemker.* £90
- Ayala's Angels. 1881. 3 vols. Orig. cl., faded. (SH. Apr.10; 356) *Merrion Book Co.* £250
- Barchester Towers. L., 1857. 1st. Edn. 3 vols. 2-pp. publisher's advts. in Vols. I & III, slight browning. Cont. hf. cf., marb. bds. (SPB. Nov.25; 24) $325
- - Anr. Copy. Without hf.-title in vol. I, occasional light foxing, bnd. without advts. Early hf. cf. gt. (KH. Mar.24; 402) Aus. $140
- The Barsetshire Novels. Ed.:– Michael Sadleir. Oxford, Shakes. Hd. Pr., 1929. (525). 14 vols. Orig. buckram. (CSK. Apr.3; 88) £480
- - Anr. Copy. (S. Jul.31; 126a) *Lord.* £380
- The Claverings. 1867. 1st. Engl. Edn. 2 vols. Orig. cl. (SH. Jan.30; 364) *Old Hall.* £140
- Duke's Children. 1880. 1st. Edn. 3 vols. Lacks adverts. Orig. cl. (SH. Apr.10; 355) *Boyle.* £260
- - Anr. Copy. (SH. Jul.9; 53) *Scott.* £90
- How the 'Mastiffs' went to Iceland. 1878. 1st. Edn. 4to. 1 Photographic ill. unstuck, occasional minor spotting. Orig. cl. gt., 2 photographic views with MS. captions mntd. on verso of front free end-paper. Sigd. & dtd. inscr. of John Burns on hf.-title, the Roseberry copy, with bkplt., lately in the collection of Eric Sexton. (C. Apr.15; 53)
Foyle. £150
- Hunting Sketches. L., 1865. 1st. Edn. With 36 pp. of advts. at end. Orig. cl., upr. cover stained, bkplt. (SG. Dec.11; 424) $130
- The Last Chronicle of Barset. Ill.:– George H. Thomas. L., 1867. 1st. Edn. 2 vols. Three-qtr. cf. (SG. Mar.19; 300) $120
- The Macdermots of Ballycloran. L., 1847. 1st. Edn., 1st. Iss. 3 vols. 12mo. With the title-p. variants in vols. 2 & 3 as noted by Sadleir, with the correct pagination on p. 437 of vol. 3, & with all the other misprints listed by Sadleir, at end of text in each vol. (in cont. hand) is pencil check mark & the phrase 'Penrith./June 1847.'. Hf. mor., gt. panel. spines, by Macdonald. Pres. Copy, to his Mother, title-pp. of vols. 2 & 3 inscr. by her(?); James F. Drake's copy (with T.L.s. from Michael Sadleir to him laid in), lately in the Prescott Collection. (CNY. Feb.6; 319) $11,000
- Marion Fay. 1882. 1st. Edn. 3 vols. Orig. cl. (SH. Apr.10; 357) *Boyle.* £230
- North America. 1862. 2 vols. Map torn. Orig. bdg. (SH. May 21; 122) *Jarndyce.* £60
- Saint Pauls. A Monthly Magazine. 1868-73. Vols. 1-12 only. Cont. hf. cf. Bkplt. of H.R.H. The Duke of Albany. (CSK. Jun.19; 118) £50
- The Three Clerks. L., 1857. [1st. Edn.]. 3 vols. 12mo. Some light foxing, mostly to ll. at beginning

& end of each vol. Early hf. cf. gt. (KH. Mar.24; 403) Aus. $160
- The Way We Live Now. Ill.:– Sir John Everett Millais. 1875. 1st. Edn. in Book form. 2 vols. 1 ill. strengthened & misbound. Orig. cl. gt. (SBA. Jul.23; 676) *O'Hern.* £55
- Works. Phila., 1900. Collector's Edn., (250). 30 vols. Mor. gt., unopened. With a clipped sig. of Trollope inserted. (SPB. May 6; 350) £2,300
- [-] - Anr. Edn. N.Y., 1925-31. 42 vols. Hf. mor. gt. by Sangorski & Sutcliffe, slightly worn. (SPB. Nov.25; 498) $750

TROMMSDORFF, J.B.
- Systematisches Handbuch der Pharmacie für Arzte und Apotheker. Erfurt, 1827. 3rd. Edn. Cont. hf. leath. (R. Oct.14-18; 400) DM 420

TRONCHIN, J.R.
See–ROUSSEAU, Jean-Jacques–TRONCHIN, J.R.–LA VERITE

TRONCHIN DE BREUIL, J.
[-] Relation du Voyage de sa Majesté Britannique en Hollande, et de la Reception qui luy a été faite. Ill.:– Romayn de Hooghe. The Hague, 1692. Fo. Lacks frontis. port., 3 plts. with sm. tears at folds just affecting plts., 1 with margin reprd. not affecting plt., occasional spotting or staining. Cont. cf., recornered, rebkd. with gt. spine. (C. Apr.1; 172) *Hendrickx.* £100

TROTSKY, Leon
- The History of the Russian Revolution. N.Y., 1936. 3 pts. in 1 vol. Orig. cl. Inscr. to 'M. Puntervold des Verfaner'(?). (SH. Feb.5; 38)
Crete. £90
- Moya zhizn' [My Life]. Berlin, 1930. 1st. Edn. 2 vols. Slightly browned. Cont. cl., slightly soiled. (SH. Feb.5; 39) *Bjorck.* £140
- Nasha Revolyutsiya [Our Revolution]. St. Petersb., 1906. Orig. wraps., head of spine slightly torn. (SH. Feb.5; 40) *Quaritch.* £520
- Novaya Ekonomicheskaya Politika [New Economic Politics of Soviet Russia & Perspectives of World Revolution]. Moscow, 1923. Orig. wraps., spotted. (SH. Feb.5; 41) *Bjorck.* £55

TROTTER, William Edward
- Views of the Environs of London. N.d. Sm. 4to. 1 plt. detchd. & with margins soiled, some ll. slightly spotted. Orig. cl. gt. (SBA. May 27; 326)
Postaprint. £60

TRUE ACCOUNT (A) of the Present State of Ireland, giving a full relation of the New Establishment made by the late King James . . .
[L.], 1689. Sm. 4to. Disbnd. [Wing W349] (GM. Apr.30; 332) £60

TRUE LATTER DAY SAINTS' HERALD
Plano, Ill., Jul. 1-Dec. 15, 1865. Vol. 8, numbers 1-12. Mod. buckram. (SG. Jan.8; 307) $110

TRUSLER, John
[-] The Honours of the Table, or Rules for Behaviour During Meals, with the Whole Art of Carving, for the Use of Young People. Ill.:– after John Bewick. 1791. 12mo. Orig. cf.-bkd. bds. (SH. Mar.19; 316) *Quaritch.* £180
[-] The Progress of Man & Society. Ill.:– John Bewick. [1810]. 12mo. Sm. hole in T2. Cont. cf. gt. (SH. Mar.19; 317) *Vincent.* £90
[-] Proverbs in Verse. Ill.:– John Bewick. [1814]. Orig. bds., lacks pt. of backstrip, unc., partly unopened. Bkplt. of Rev. Thomas Hugo. (SH. Dec.10; 14) *Maggs.* £95

TRYON, George W. Jr. & Pilsbry, H.A.
- Manual of Conchology. Phila., 1885-1935. 2nd. Series: Pulmonata. 28 vols. in 112 pts. Additionally in vols. 24 & 28: 67 plts. in 2nd. cold. state, some marginal tears, loose, some in 2nd. cold. sheets, some stitched. Orig. ptd. paper wraps., many wraps. torn or slightly defect. (S. Jun.1; 238)
Junk. £550

TRYON, Thomas
- The Way to Health, Long Life & Happiness: Or, a Discourse of Temperance, & the Particular Nature of . . . all Sorts of Meats, Drinks, Air, Exercises, etc . . . 1697. 3rd. Edn. Title slightly soiled, publisher's advts. bnd. in at rear. Later cf., rebkd. (TA. Jun.18; 212) £55

TSCHACBASOV, Nahum
- Twelve Color Etchings. Ed.:– Rosamund Frost. N.Y., 1947. (50) numbered, each plt. sigd. & numbered by artist. Fo. Loose as issued in portfo., brkn. (SG. Oct.23; 325) $1,300

TSCHEINER, D.J.
- Der Wohlerfahrene Fischmeister. Pest, 1821. Slightly soiled, 2nd. part with slight worming. Mod. hf. leath. (R. Oct.14-18; 2759) DM 520

TSCHICHOLD, Jan
See–ROH, Franz & Tschichold, Jan

TSCHUDI, Don Juan Diego de
See–RIVERO, Mariano Eduardo de & Tschudi, Don Juan Diego de

TSCHUDI, Hugo von
- Adolph von Menzel. Abbildungen seiner Gemälde und Studien. Munich, 1905. Fo. Orig. bds. (R. Oct.14-18; 701) DM 650

TSVI BEN SHIMSHON TUCHFUERER
- Nachlat Tsvi. 1659. 4to. Sigs. & stps. of previous owners on title & fly-lf., slight worming. Vell. (S. Nov.18; 755) James. £110

TUANO, J.A.
- Il Falconiere. Ed.:– G.P. Bergantini. Venice, 1735. 4to. Publisher's bds., unc. (CR. Jun.11; 527) Lire 280,000

TUCK, Edward
- Some Works of Art belonging to Edward Tuck in Paris. L., priv. ptd. 1910. (50). 4to. Red mor. by Durvand, gt. geometrical patterns in panels, s.-c. Inscr. to Sir Basil Zaharoff. (SM. Oct.8; 2210) Frs. 3,200

TUCKER, Andrew G.C.
- Ornithologia Danmoniensis. 1809. 2 orig. pts. (all publd.) 4to. 6 engraved & aquatint plts. in 2 states, 1 cold. & extra uncold. plt. Unc. as issued in orig. ptd. wraps., stitching brkn., cl. box. (C. Jul.15; 214) Quaritch. £500

TUCKER, Beverley
- Address to the People of the United States, with Appendix relating to President Johnson's Proclamation of 2nd. May, 1865. Montreal, 1865. 1st. Edn. 24mo. Sewed. (SG. Mar.5; 447) $325

TUCKER, St. George
- A Dissertation on Slavery . . . Phila., 1796. 1st. Edn. Disbnd. (SG. Mar.5; 448) $200

TUCKEY, Capt. James Kingston
- An Account of a Voyage to Establish a Colony at Port Philip in Bass's Strait. 1805. 1st. Edn. Slight browning & staining near end. Orig. bds., covers loose, spine defect., unc. (S. Feb.10; 472) Remington. £600
- Narrative of an Expedition to explore the River Zaire. 1818. [1st. Edn.?]. 4to. Some ll. spotted. Mod. cl. (SH. Nov.7; 329) Enfield. £130
- - Anr. Copy. 13 engraved plts., 1 folding chart, all spotted, lacks hf.-title, occasional spotting to text. Cont. hf. cf. (CSK. Apr.24; 90) £70
- - Anr. Copy. Wide margin, plts. slightly soiled. Unc., cont. hf. leath., spine & covers restored. (R. Mar.31-Apr.4; 2374) DM 1,050

TUDOR-CRAIG, Sir Algernon
- Armorial Porcelain of the Eighteenth Century. Ed.:– Sir Henry F. Burke (foreword). L., 1925. (1000) numbered. 4to. Gt.-decor. buckram, partly unc. (SG. Mar.12; 369) £110

TUER, Andrew W.
- Bartolozzi & his Works. [1882]. (50) numbered, sigd. 2 vols. in 4. Fo. Interleaved, some plts. loose. Orig. parch. (SH. Jun.11; 215) Erlini. £50
- - Anr. Edn. N.d. 2 vols. 4to. Some spotting. Orig. parch., soiled. (CSK. Jan.30; 50) £55
- History of the Horn-Book. 1896. 1st. Edn. 2 vols. 4to. Orig. vell. gt. (SH. Dec.12; 536) Vincent. £210
- - Anr. Copy. 6 (of 7) facs. specimens in front compartment of each vol. Orig. vell. gt., slightly soiled, partly untrimmed. Author's pres. copy. (TA. Nov.20; 181) £160
- - Anr. Copy. 7 facs. horn-books contained in flaps in front of each vol. Vell. (SSA. Jun.18; 29) R. 390
- - Anr. Edn. 1897. 4to. 3 actual specimens contained in rear compartment, partly unc. Orig. cl., spine worn. (TA. Sep.18; 96) £105
- - Anr. Copy. Worn. (SH. Dec.12; 537) Subunso. £85
- - Anr. Copy. Pict. bds., ex-liby. (SG. Apr.30; 308) $220
- London Cries. L., [1883]. (250) numbered & sigd. proof copies. 4to. With an extra suite of engrs., ptd. in brown, & some 40 other text ills.,

reproduced in facs. from various edns. Hf. cl., disbnd. (SG. May 21; 399) $150
- Pages & Pictures from Forgotten Children's Books.–Stories from Old Fashioned Children's Books. L., 1898-99; 1899-1900. 1st. Edn., 1st. Iss.; 1st. Edn. 2 works in 2 vols. 1st. work with a specimen of late 18th. C. Dutch floral gt. paper mntd. on p. 8 (later substituted by a woodblock design). Both gt. pict. cl., some wear. (SG. Apr.30; 309) $130
- - Anr. Copy. (SG. Jan.22; 121) $110

TUFANOV, A.
- K zaumi [Phonic Music & Phonematic Functions of Consonants]. Ill.:– B. Ender. St. Petersb., priv. ptd. 1924. (1,000). Orig. wraps. by B. Ender, unopened. (SH. Feb.6; 532) Sackner. £150

TUKE, Daniel Hack
- A Dictionary of Psychological Medicine. 1892. 1st. Edn. 2 vols. Advt. lf. in vol. I. New hf. cf. (S. Jun.17; 836) Jenner Books. £70
See–BUCKNILL, Sir John Charles & Tuke, Daniel H.

TUKE, John
- General View of the Agriculture of the North Riding of Yorkshire. 1800. Lacks hf.-title, engraved folding map, hand-cold. Cont. hf. russ., worn. (SBA. Mar.4; 197) Waggett. £90

TUKE, Samuel
- Description of the Retreat, an Institution near York for Insane Persons of the Society of Friends. York, 1813. Orig. bds., spine defect., unc. (S. Jun.17; 838) Whitehart. £190

TUKE, Sir Samuel
[-] The Adventures of Five Hours. 1663. 1st. Edn. Fo. Slight browning thro-out. Mor.-bkd. cl. by Sangorski. [Wing T3229] (C. Nov.19; 170) Blackwell. £150

TULLY, Richard
[-] Narrative of a Ten Years' Residence at Tripoli in Africa. [Letters written during a Ten Years' Residence . . .]. 1816. [1st. Edn.?]. Cont. hf. cf., lacks 1 spine label. (CSK. May 1; 105) £150
- - Anr. Copy. 4to. Lacks advt. lf. at end, 1st. few ll. reprd. in inner margin, a few ll. slightly soiled, sm. hole in margin of title & 1st. 2 ll. Mod. poldd. cf. (S. Nov.4; 646) Scott. £60
- - Anr. Copy. Ex liby. Mod. cl. (SG. Oct.30; 359) $120
- - Anr. Edn. 1817. 4to. Cf. (P. Oct.23; 71) Holmes. £60
[-] - Anr. Edn. 1819. 3rd. Edn. 2 vols. Soiled, 7 hand-cold. aquatint plts., each stpd. 'N.S.L.', 1 torn. Mod. cf.-bkd. cl. (CSK. Jan.9; 23) £50
- - Anr. Copy. Str.-grd. mor. gt., spines gt., by R. Storr of Grantham. Sir John Thorold, Syston Park, bkplts. (CNY. May 22; 284) $200

TULPINCKE, Camille
- Les Arts Anciens de Flandre. Bruges, ca. 1906-13. (75). Vols. 2-6. Fo. Three-qtr. mor., orig. parch. wraps. bnd. in (each with orig. subscriber's name on upr. wrap.). (SG. Dec.4; 142) $800

TULPIUS, Nicolaus
- Observationes Medicae . . . libro Quarto Auctior. Amst., 1652. New Edn. Cont. cf. (S. Dec.2; 872) Nador. £90
- - Anr. Edn. Amst., 1685. New Edn. with Book 4 added. Upr. outer corners of M2-4 damaged by a burn affecting 2 numerals. Cont. vell. (S. Jun.17; 840) Jenner Books. £60

TUNNARD, W.H.
- A Southern Record: the History of the Third Regiment Louisiana Infantry. Baton Rouge, 1866. 1st. Edn. 12mo. Cl., stained. (SG. Jun.11; 112) $150

TUNNICLIFFE, C.F.
- Shorelands Summer Diary. [1952]. (150) numbered, sigd. by author. 4to. Orig. cl.-bkd. bds., s.-c. (CSK. Feb.20; 157) £110

TUNSTALL, Cuthbert
- De Arte Supputandi libri quattuor. Ill.:– after Holbein (woodcut title border). 1522. 1st. Edn. 4to. Marginal worming thro-out, rather worse near beginning, 2 tiny holes just affecting title-border, some soiling & staining, piece torn from outer margin of title, MS. calculations in lr. margins of several ll., owner's inscr. of Dominus Topping on title-p. Cont. cf., gt. ornament on covers, very worn & defect., hf. mor. case. From

Marbury Hall liby.; from Honeyman Collection. [NSTC 24319] (S. May 19; 3001) Thomas. £900
- - Anr. Edn. Paris, 1529. 2nd. Edn. Sm. 4to. A little marginal staining, title browned & slightly soiled. Cf., lr. cover replaced with bd., jnts. reprd., hf. mor. case. From Honeyman Collection. (S. May 19; 3002) Hughes. £260
- - Anr. Edn. Paris, 1538. Sm. 4to. Title with device rather stained & spotted. Cont. limp vell, panel. in gt., new endpapers. From Honeyman Collection. (S. May 19; 3003) Prichard-Jones. £110

TURBERVILLE, George
- The Booke of Falconrie or Hawking.–The Noble Art of Venerie or Hunting. 1611. 2nd. Edn. 2 works in 1 vol. Sm. 4to. Mor. gt. by Rivière. [STC 24325; 24329.] (C. May 20; 60) Maggs. £1,100

TURGENIEV, Ivan
- Neschastnaya [The Unhappy Woman].–Stuk . . . . i Strannaya Istoriya [Knock . . . & a Strange Story].–Stepnoi Korol' Lir [King Lear of the Steppes].–Razskaz Otta Alekseya [The Tale of Father Aleksei]. Leipzig, 1869; 1873; 1873; 1877. 1st. Edns. (?) 4 works in 1 vol. Cont. roan-bkd. bds. (SH. Feb.5; 20) Bjorck. £100

TURKEY
- Neu-eröffnetes Amphitheatrium Turcicum. Erfurt, 1724. Fo. Hf. cf. (P. Oct.2; 16) Ad Orientem. £150

TURNBULL, George
- A Treatise on Ancient Painting. 1740. 1st. Edn. Fo. Sm. margin repair to plt. 29, slight spotting. Cont. spr. cf., spine gt., worn, bkplt. of Sir James Dashwood. Lge. copy. (S. Jan.27; 464) Weinreb. £100
- - Anr. Copy. Cont. mott. cf., gt. spine, slightly worn. (S. Jun.22; 101) Ars Artis. £50

TURNBULL, J.R.
- Sketches of Delhi. 1858. Fo. Orig. cl., loose. (SH. Nov.7; 362) Hosain. £105

TURNBULL, John
- A Voyage round the World in the years 1800, 1801, 1802, 1803 & 1804; In which the author visited . . . the English Settlements of Port Jackson & Norfolk Island. Phila., 1810. 1st. Amer. Edn. 12mo in sixes. Discoloured, occasional staining. Old cf. or sheep, rebkd. (KH. Nov.18; 603) Aus. $200
- - Anr. Edn. 1813. 4to. Mott. cf. (P. Oct.23; 72) Brooke-Hitching. £400

TURNBULL, Robert J.
- Bibliography of South Carolina. Charlottesville, [1956], [1960]. 6 vols., including index. Cl. (SG. Jan.22; 362) $160

TURNER, C.
See–EARLOM, R., Turner, C. & Dunkarton, R.

TURNER, Daniel
- Apologia Chyrugica. 1695. Dampstains. Later cf., worn. (CE. Jun.4; 217a) £130

TURNER, Dawson
- Account of a Tour in Normandy. 1820. 1st. Edn. 2 vols. Plts. on india paper, proof copies. Cont. bds., gt. spines, unc., Lord Rosebery's bkplt. William Beckford's copy with 3½pp. of pencilled notes in his hand. (S. Nov. 24; 587) Holler. £190
- - Anr. Copy. Plts. on india paper, some foxing. Cont. cf. gt. (TA. Nov.20; 22) £104
- - Anr. Copy. Some marginal dampstains. Orig. cl. (SH. Mar.5; 145) Roolephiero. £50

TURNER, Henry
See–COXE, Daniel W. & Turner, Henry

TURNER, Joseph Mallord William
- Liber Fluvium or River Scenery of France. 1843. 4to. Cl. gt., rebkd., worn. (P. Nov.13; 166) Schapiro. £65
- - Anr. Edn. Ill.:– after Turner. 1853. A few ll. slightly spotted. Orig. cl. gt. (SBA. Mar.4; 217) Spencer. £65
- - Anr. Copy. 4to. Orig. cl., worn. (SH. Mar.5; 146) Strufaldi. £50
- - Anr. Copy. Red mor., gt., loose. (SG. Nov.20; 418) $110
- Picturesque Views in England & Wales. 1838. L.P. 2 vols. in 1. Lge. fo. Bk.-stp. of Bibliothèque du Roi, Neuilly, on titles. Mid-19th. C. Engl. red mor. by Francis Bedford, gt., spine tooled in compartments with cartouches & mor. onlays,

TURNER, Joseph Mallord William -contd.
covers with elab. border. (S. Nov.24; 290) *L. & G.* £1,800
– – **Anr. Edn.** 1838. Vol. 2 only (of 2). 4to. A few ll. slightly soiled. Cont. hf. mor. gt. (SBA. Jul.14; 52) *Salinas.* £140
– **Picturesque Views on the Southern Coast of England.** 1826. 2 vols. in 1. 4to. A few ll. slightly browned or spotted. Cont. mor. gt. (SBA. Mar.4; 128) *Duran.* £280
– **Rivers of France.** 1837. [1st. Edn.?] 2 pts. in 1 vol. 4to. 1st title & last 2 plts. spotted. Cont. hf. mor., gt. (S. May 5; 263) *Cristani.* £75
– – **Anr. Copy.** Some spotting, text in Engl. & Fr. Hf. mor. (CSK. Sep.12; 217) £50
– – **Anr. Copy.** Jewelled bdg., mor. gt., covers with lge. recessed arabesque centrepieces, the upr, with oval ornamental onlays, the lr. circular, the panels set with 39 stones & pearls., elab. decor., spine with 6 compartments, 5 raised bands, mor. doubls., by Sangorski & Sutcliffe. (CNY. May 22; 350) $3,200
– – **Anr. Copy.** Cf., gt. borders & spine. (SG. Feb.26; 322) $140
– **Rivers of France–The Loire.** Ca. 1840. Lacks ptd. title. Recent mor. gt. (TA. Apr.16; 449) £55
– **The Southern Coast of England.** N.d. Fo. 37 (of 38) loose engraved plts. Orig. cl. gt. (P. Apr.30; 48) *Philips.* £190
– **The Turner Gallery.** N.Y., ca. 1860. 2 vols. 4to. 120 steel engraved plts. Cont. leath. (R. Oct.14-18; 2674) DM 1,500
– – **Anr. Copy.** Cont. hf. leath., very defect. (R. Mar.31-Apr.4; 1602) DM 1,100
– – **Anr. Copy.** 1875. 2 vols. Lge. fo. Port. & plts. on India Proof paper. Orig. hf. red mor. gt. (SBA. Jul.22; 37) *Studio.* £220
– – **Anr. Copy.** Hf. mor., worn and disbnd. (CSK. Sep.5; 218) £150
– – **Anr. Copy.** Cont. hf. leath., gt., worn. (R. Oct.14-18; 2677) DM 950
– – **Anr. Edn.** Ed.:– R.N. Wornum. Ca. 1875. L.P. Fo. 60 plts. on india paper, title reprd. Hf. mor. (P. Mar.4; 38) *Duran.* £300
– – **Anr. Edn.** Ed.:– W. Cosmo Monkhouse. N.Y., ca. 1880. 2 vols. Fo. Orig. mor., needs rebdg. (SG. Dec.4; 346) $325
– – **Anr. Copy.** 4 vols. 4to. Plts. loose. Orig. linen. (D. Dec.11-13; 1255) DM 800
– – **Anr. Copy.** 2 vols. Orig. leath. (D. Dec.11-13; 1254) DM 600
– – **Anr. Edn.** Ed.:– William Cosmo Monkhouse. N.d. Vols. I & III only (of 3). Fo. 80 plts. only (of 81), soiled. Orig. cl., worn. (SH. Jan.29; 156) *Roberts.* £130
– – **Anr. Copy.** 1 vol only ? Engraved title & 60 plts. only. Cont. hf. mor. W.a.f. (CSK. Jan.9; 194) £100

TURNER, Joseph Mallord William & Girtin, Thomas
– **Picturesque Views, Sixty Years Since.** Ed.:– T. Miller. 1854. Cl. gt., soiled. (BS. Jun.11; 94) £50
– **River Scenery.** 1827. 4to. 21 mezzotint plts. on india paper, spotting, mainly marginal. Cont. hf. cf., s.-c., bkplt. of George Creswell Turner. (CSK. Sep.12; 133) £90

TURNER, Joseph Mallord William & Huish, M.B.
– **The Seine & the Loire.** 1895. New Edn. Occasional spotting Cont. mor.-bkd. cl. (CSK. Oct.31; 173) £50

TURNER, Joseph Mallord William & others
– **An Antiquarian & Picturesque Tour round the Southern Coast of England.** Ill.:– After Turner & others. 1849. 4to. 46 plts. only, mntd. ills. on India paper, slight spotting. Cont. hf. mor., worn. W.a.f. (CSK. Oct.24; 35) £100

TURNER, Rev. Richard
– **A View of the Earth.** L., 1798. 4to. Qtr. cf. (P. Jun.11; 207E) *Leviton.* £95

TURNER, Capt. Samuel
– **Account of an Embassy to the Court of the Teshoo Lama, in Tibet.** 1800. 1st. Edn., L.P. 4to. Some spotting. Cf., rebkd. (P. Apr.30; 75) *Morrow.* £260
– – **Anr. Copy.** Plts. slightly foxed. 19th. C. cl. From Chetham's Liby., Manchester. (C. Nov.27; 396) *Taylor.* £120
– – **Anr. Copy.** Text rather browned. Cf., slightly wormed. (S. Dec.8; 247) *Hosains.* £100

TURNER, Thomas
– **Narrative of a Journey, Associated with a Fly, from Gloucester to Aberystwyth.** Ill.:– after D. Cox & others. Priv. ptd. 1840. Errata slip. Orig. cl Pres. copy. (TA. Aug.21; 40) £54

TURNER, William
[–] **[The Herball].** Cologne, 1568. 4 pts. in 1 vol. Fo. Lacks 1st. title & 4 prelims., 6 ll. in sig. C. in 1st. pt., 2 sections reversed, some staining thro.-out, 1st. few ll. frayed, several ll. reprd. in margin (mostly without text loss). Binder's cl. W.a.f., from Chetham's Liby., Manchester. [STC 24367] (C. Nov.27; 397) *Sotheran.* £620
– – **Anr. Copy.** 5 pts. in 1 vol. Lacks title to pt. 1, & a few ll. thro.-out, some damp staining, latter pp. reprd. Later panel. cf. Impft. copy, w.a.f. (TA. Feb.19; 370) £155
– **A New Boke of the Natures & Properties of all Wines that are Commonly Vsed Here in England** ... 1568. 1st. Edn. Slight browning, a cont. MS. correction on verso of E3. Cont. cf. by Bedford, spine worn, covers detchd. The Heber-Huth copy, with Huth bkplt.; from liby. of André L. Simon [NSTC 24360] (S. May 18; 192) *Quaritch.* £3,500

TURNER, William–[BRUNSCHWIG, Hieronymus]
– **A New Herball.– The Seconde Parte of William Turner's Herball [A Booke of the Bath of Baeth in Englande].–A Most Excellent & Perfecte Homish Apothecarye or Homely Physicke Booke** ... Trans.:– John Hollybushe (3rd. work). Cologne (2nd. & 3rd. works), 1551; 1562; 1561. 1st. Edn.; 1st. Edn.; 1st. Edn. in Engl. 3 works in 1 vol., 2nd. 2 pts. in 1. Fo. 1st. work: inner margin of title strengthened, some sm. wormholes in 1st. few quires, 2nd. work: errata slip tipped in, 1 lf. torn & reprd., just affecting text, minor worming in blank margin, 3rd. work: a few wormholes, mostly in margins, lacks final blank lf., margins of last 3 ll. strengthened, slight discolouration in all 3 works. 17th. C. mott. cf., rebkd. [STC 24365; STC 24366; STC 13433] (C. Apr.1; 118) *Quaritch.* £1,800

TURNLEY, J.
[–] **Reveries of Affection, in Memory of ... His Royal Highness, the late Prince Consort.** [1868]. Foxed. Red mor. Inscr. to Wm. Creswick. (SG. Apr.9; 90) $250

TURNOR, Christopher Hatton
– **Astra Castra. Experiments & Adventures in the Atmosphere.** 1865. 1st. Edn. 4to. Orig. cl., worn. Inscr. to Manley Hopkins. (S. Dec.8; 184) *Henderson.* £125
– – **Anr. Copy.** Cl., worn. (S. Dec.2; 787) *Dr. Pile.* £80

TURNOR, Edmund
*See–*HOWETT, Bartholomew–TURNOR, Edmund

TURNOR, Philip
*See–*CHAMPLAIN Society

TURPIN DE CRISSE, Lancelot
– **Commentaires sur les Memoires de Montecuculi.** Amst. & Leipzig, 1770 3 vols. 1st. vol. lacks hf.-title. Mod. mott. three-qtr. cf. (SG. Feb.26; 325) $130

TURRECREMATA, Johannes de
– **Quaestiones Evangeliorum de Tempore et de Sanctis.** Vienne, Eberhard Frommolt, Jul.24, 1481. Fo. Spaces for initial capitals, 3 supplied in red & blue, other capitals, paragraph marks, initial strokes & underlines in red, lacks 1st. blank, very light worming at beginning & end, light foxing & minor marginal dampstains to some ll., monastic inscr. at head of fo. 1. Mor. gt., gt. spine, silk doubls. & end-papers. From the collection of Eric Sexton. [BMC VIII, 374, Goff T551, HC 15716*] (CNY. Apr.8; 204) $4,000

TURTLE DOVE'S WEDDING (the), a Poem
[Wtrmkd. 1834]. Colouring smudged on 1 plt. Orig. wraps., slightly soiled. (SH. Mar.19; 318) *Schiller.* £190

TURTON, John
– **The Angler's Manual.** L., 1836. 1st. Edn. Cl. Eric Taverner's copy, with pencil sig. (SG. Oct.16; 490) $260

TURTON, William
– **Conchylia Insularum Britannicarum.** [1822]. 4to. Orig. cl., head of spine torn. (C. Nov.5; 168) *Weldon & Wesley.* £55

TUSSAC, F. Richard de
– **Flore des Antilles.** Ill.:– After Redouté & others. Paris, 1808-27. (150). 4 vols. Fo. 1st. hf.-title reprd., a few of larger plts. in vol. 3 cut into by binder. Cont. Fr. qtr. red mor. gt., royal arms of France at head of spine with legend 'Pairs de France'. From collection of Massachusetts Horticultural Society, stps. on plts. (SPB. Oct.1; 169) $24,000

TWAIN, Mark (Pseud.)
*See–*CLEMENS, Samuel Langhorne 'Mark Twain'

TWAMLEY, Louisa Anne
*See–*MEREDITH, Louisa Anne, neé Twamley

TWEEDDALE, Arthur, Marquis of
– **The Ornithological Works reprinted from the Originals.** Ed.:– Robert G. Wardlaw Ramsay. Priv. ptd. 1881. 2 vols. Lge. 4to. Some plts. inlaid to size, title-lf. in both vols. Red hf. mor. (S. Jun.1; 239) *Joseph.* £500

TWEEDIE, Maj.-Gen. William
– **The Arabian Horse.** L., 1894. (100) numbered. on L.P. 4to. Orig. hf. mor. gt., partly unc. (CNY. May 22; 224) $320

TWINING, Elizabeth
– **Illustrations of the Natural Order of Plants.** 1849-55. 2 vols., fo. Cont. hf. mor. (CSK. Aug.1; 137) £2,100

TWISS, R.
– **Chess.** L., 1787. Cont. leath., decor. spine. (D. Dec.11-13; 2304) DM 1,100

TWYNE, Brian
– **Antiquitatis Academiae Oxoniensis Apologia.** Oxford, 1608. 1st. Edn. 4to. Slight staining on title & towards end. Cont. limp vell., soiled & worn. Cont. inscr. of Thomas Monro, bkplt. of Henry Latham, lately in the collection of Eric Sexton. [STC 24405] (C. Apr.15; 198) *Morton-Smith.* £100
*See–*HOWSON, John–TWYNE, Brian

TYARD, Pontus de
[–] **L'Univers, ou, Discours des Parties, et de la Nature du Monde.** Ill.:– [Bernard Salomon, woodcut port, of author attributed to]. Lyon, 1557. 1st. Edn. 4to. Last few ll. dampstained, ink-stain in inner margin of d2v, some underscoring of text. Vell. From Honeyman Collection. (S. May 19; 3004) *Hill.* £450

TYAS, Robert
– **Beautiful Birds.** 1850. 2 vols. Orig. cl. (P. Sep.11; 291) *Wakeline.* £110
– – **Anr. Edn.** 1854-56. 3 vols. Some plts. cropped. Cont. mor. gt. (SKC. Feb.26; 1608) £150
– **Favourite Field Flowers.** 1850. 2nd. Series. Inscr. on title. Orig. cl., gt., worn. (S. Jan.26; 299) *Edistar.* £50
– **The Wild Flowers of England.** Ill.:– James Andrews. 1860. 2 pts. in 1 vol. Cont. embossed cl., elab. gt. (C. May 20; 254) *Taylor.* £95

TYLDEN, Major G.
– **The Armed Forces of South Africa.** Johannesburg. 1954. Cl. (SSA. Jun.18; 291) R. 140

TYMMS, William Robert
*See–*WARING, John Burley & Tymms, William Robert

TYNDALL, John
– **Essays on the Floating-Matter of the Air in Relation to Putrefaction & Infection.** 1881. 1st. Edn. Orig. cl. (S. Apr.6; 161) *Phillips.* £90

TYPOGRAPHIC ADVERTISER
L., Jul.-Jun. 1866-67; Jul.-Feb. 1867-68. Vol. 5, nos. 52-63; vol. 6, nos. 64-71. Slim 4to. Generally foxed, some marginal dampstaining. Cont. hf. cf., some wear. (TA. Sep.18; 177) £50

TYRO, The
Ed.:– Wyndham Lewis [1921]. Nos. 1 & 2. 4to. & fo. No. 1 as issued, No. 3 in orig. wraps., cl. case. (SH. Mar.26; 320) *Thomson.* £65

TYRRELL, Henry
– **The History of the Present War with Russia.** L., ca. 1856. 1st. Edn. 9 vols. Tall 4to. 1 plt. loose, plts. foxed. Unif. gt.-pict. cl., most vols. unopened. (PNY. May 21; 408) $125
*See–*WRIGHT, Thomas–TYRRELL, Henry

TYSON, Edward
- Orang-Outang . . . or, the Anatomy of a Pygmie compared with that of a Monkey, an Ape & a Man . . . 1699. 1st. Edn. 2 pts. in 1 vol. 4to. Some spotting, sm. hole in E3 affecting footnote. Cont. panel. cf., rebkd. Donor's inscr. from William Cowper, surgeon & anatomist to Phineas Fowke on flylf., a few other MS. notes in text by Cowper & anr. [Wing T3598] (S. Jun.1; 240) White. £2,000
- - Anr. Copy. Imprimatur 1f. reprd., advt. 1f., some plts. cut into by binder & with sm. tears or wormholes, 1st. few ll. wormed in lr. inner margins (partly reprd.), some soiling & spotting. Cont. panel. cf., rebkd. preserving old spine, worn, front pastedown inscr. 'E Libris Wilhelmi Musgrave Med. Exon. July 1 (16)99'. From Honeyman Collection. (S. May 19; 3007) Zeitlin & Verbrugge. £400
- - Anr. Copy. Advt., lacks final blank, plts. torn, reprd. & stained, some browning & spotting, sm. hole in H4 affecting text, old owner's inscrs. on title, liby. stps. on verso. Mod. cf.-bkd. bds., covers detchd. From Honeyman Collection. (S. May 19; 3008) Laywood. £340
- - Anr. Copy. With final advt. 1f., lacks plts. 1 & 2, spotting thro.-out, liby. stp. on title. 19th. C. hf. mor. From Chetham's Liby., Manchester. (C. Nov.27; 398) Phelps. £220

TYSSOT DE PATOT, Simon
[-] Voyages et Aventures de Jacques Massé. Bordeaux. 1710. Orig. Edn. 12mo. Cont. cf., decor. spine. MS. note on endpaper. (HD. Feb.18; 78) Frs. 1,000

TYTLER, Sarah
- Landseer's Dogs & their Stories. Ill.:– after Landseer. L., 1877. Gt.-pict. cl. (SG. Dec.11; 348) $100

TZARA, Tristan
- L'Arbre des Voyageurs.–Morceaux Choisis. Paris, [1930; 1947]. 1st. Edns. 12mo. Wraps., unc., unopened. Both vols. inscr. to George Reavey. (SG. Jun.4; 486) $100
- Entre-Temps. Ill.:– Henri Laurens. [Paris], 1946. (300) numbered, & sigd by author & artist. Ptd. wraps., unc. & unopened. (SG. Apr.2; 172) $130

TZOREF, Shmuel
- Kur La'zahav. Ed.:– Yehuda Al-Harizi (summary of Tachkemoni). Offenbach, 1716. 2nd. Edn. Sm. 4to. Cropped, browning. Cl.-bkd. bds. (SPR. May 11; 197) $175

UBALDUS, Guidus
- De Cochlea libri Quatuor. Venice, 1615. 1st. Edn. Fo. Slight worming in fore-margins, a few ll. stained. Cont. limp vell, upr. cover stained. From Honeyman Collection. (S. May 19; 3013) Hill. £90
- In Duos Archimedis Aequeponderantium Libros Paraphrasis Scholiis Illustrata. Pesaro, 1588. 1st. Edn. Fo. Some browning & spotting, title slightly soiled & with tear in inner margin. Cont. limp vell., soiled, rebkd. From Honeyman Collection. (S. May 19; 3011) Pilo. £180
- Le Mechaniche . . . Trans.:– Filippo Pigafetta. Venice, 1615. Sm. 4to. A few marginal stains, sm. tear affecting headlines on D4. Stiff wraps., worn & soiled, hf. red mor. case. From Honeyman Collection. (S. May 19; 3012) Hill. £160
- Mechanischer Kunst Kammer Erster Theil. Frankfurt, 1629. Fo. Some dampstaining. Later vell. (TA. Mar.19; 374) £110
- Mechanorum Liber. Pesaro, 1577. 1st. Edn. Fo. Last lf. of prelims. & 2K4 blank, l3 reprd. without loss, some browning, sig. of N. Lagomaggiore. Cont. limp vell., soiled, worn at fore-edges. Bkplt. of Herbert McLean Evans; from Honeyman Collection. (S. May 19; 3009) Pilo. £480
- Planisphaeriorum Universalium Theorica. Pesaro, 1579. 1st. Edn. Fo. Some ll. browned, owners' inscrs. on title including Gio. Pietro Piattelli. Limp bds., unc. From Honeyman Collection. (S. May 19; 3010) Rogers Turner. £190

UBER LAND UND MEER
Stuttgart, 1871. Vols. 25 & 26. Cont. hf. linen. Not collated, w.a.f. (R. Oct.14-18; 2131) DM 600
- - Anr. Edn. Stuttgart, 1871-80. Vols. 26, 41-44 in 5 vols. Cont. hf. leath. Not collated, w.a.f. (R. Oct.14-18; 2132) DM 1,100
- - Anr. Edn. Ed.:– F.W. Hackländer. Stuttgart, 1877-89. Vols. 38-40 & 62. Fo. Vols. 38 & 39 hf.

leath., vol. 62 orig. wraps. W.a.f. (HK. Nov.18-21; 2089) DM 850

UDALL, William
[-] The Historie . . . of Mary Stuart Queen of Scotland. 1636. 2nd. Edn. Mor. gt. [STC 24510] (S. Nov.25; 460) Armstrong. £110

UEBER LANDES-KULTUR UND BEVOLKERUNG des Kónigreichs Pressen Gätopien (Königsberg), 1800. Cont. bds. (R. Oct.14-18; 1379) DM 420

UFANO, Diego–BASTA, G.–ERRARD de Bar-le Duc, J.
- Artillerie.– Le Govvernement de la Cavallerie legière.–La Fortification. Ill.:– T. Bry. Frankfurt; Hanau; Frankfurt. 1614; 1614; 1604. 3 works in 1 vol. Fo. 2nd. work: 12 engraved double-p. or folding plts., 1 slightly defect. Cont. vell. (S. Jun.23; 238) Lyon. £600

UGUITON
See– LOCHER, Jacobus REMUS Favinus
–UGUITON–WIMPHELING, Jacobus
–VALLIBUS, Hieronymous de

UHSE, Erdmann
- Wohl-informierter Redner. Leipzig. 1719. Cont. hf. leath. gt. (D. Dec.11-13; 844) DM 470

ULITA, [Almanach of the Ural Literary Association] Ekaterinburg, 1922. Orig. wraps. by V. Gerasimov. (SH. Feb.6; 534) Lempert. £50

ULLOA, Alfonso de
- Historie del S.D. Fernando Colombo . . . Venice, 1571. Stain on title, title & following folio reinforced on verso, some worming in 1st. ll. with slight text loss, some slight stains. Cont. vell. (SI. Dec.4; 578) Lire 320,000
- Historie, ende het Leven can den Keyser Caerle de Vijfde. Trans.:– P. Beelaert. Amst., 1610. Fo. Some inner corners slightly stained. Cont. vell. [Sabin 97678] (VG. Oct.13; 40) Fls. 940

ULLOA, Antonio de
- Noticias Americanas: engre-tenimientos phisicos-historicos, sobre la America Meridional y la Septentrional Oriental. Madrid, 1772. 1st. Edn. Sm. 4to. A few liby. stps. Cont. vell. bds., reprd. [Sabin 97687] (SPB. May 5; 507) $275

ULLOA, Antonio de & Juan, Jorge
- Noticias Secretas de America. L., 1826. L.P. 2 pts. in 1 vol. Fo. Liby. stp. at head of title. Cont. hf. vell., partly unc. (SPB. May 5; 510) $500
- Observaciones Astronomicas, y Phisicas Hechas de Orden de S. Mag en los Reynos del Peru. Madrid, 1748. Lge. tall 4to. Cont. vell. (PNY. May 21; 409) $450
- Relacion Historica del Viage a la America Meriodional, (with Observaciones Astronomicas, y Phisicas). Madrid, 1748. 1st. Edn., L.P. 5 vols. in 3. Fo. Cont. cf., rebkd., covers detchd. From Chetham's Liby., Manchester. [Sabin 36811 & 36808] (C. Nov.27; 221) Magnes. £380
- - Anr. Copy. 4 vols. 4to. Some stains & discolouration. Cont. cf., except for vol. II in mor.-bkd. bds. (SPB. May 5; 509) $850
- - Anr. Copy. Madrid, 1748. 5 vols. 4to. Some plts. browned, wormed at beginning & end. Cont. cf., wormed & reprd., last vol. bnd. recently to match. (SPB. May 5; 508) $700
- - Anr. Edn. Madrid, 1748. 1st. Edn. Vols. I & II, Pts. 1-4, 4 vols. 4to. A few plts. lightly soiled & browned. Cont. leath. gt., slightly defect. & worn, some worm-holes in spine. [Sabin 97689] (D. Dec.11-13; 1467) DM 2,200
- Voyage Historique de l'Amerique Meridionale. Amst. & Leipzig. 1752. 1st. Fr. Edn. 2 vols. 4to. Some browning & spotting. Mod. mor.-bkd. cl. Bkplt. of Charles Atwood Kofoid; from Honeyman Collection. [Sabin 36812] (S. May 19; 3014) Somma. £180
- - Anr. Copy. 1 map badly defect. at fold. 19th. C. hf. mor. From Chetham's Liby., Manchester. (C. Nov.27; 222) Tzakas. £160
- A Voyage to South America. 1760. 2nd. Edn. in Engl. 2 vols. Cont. cf., rebkd., spines gt. [Sabin 36813] (S. Mar.31; 481) Richter. £220

ULMANN, Doris
- Roll, Jordan, Roll. Ed.:– Julia Peterkin (text). N.Y., [1933]. (350) numbered, sigd. by Ulmann & Peterkin. 4to. Edges lightly spotted. Two-toned cl., boxed (box stained). Laid in is sigd. photogravure of image appearing on p. 31. (SG. Apr.23; 200) $1,100

ULSTADT, Philipp
- Coelum Philosophorum. Von Heimlichkeit der Natur . . . Item Marsilii Vicini Regiment des Lebens. Frankfurt a.M., 1551. Fo. Some browning & staining. Bnd. in 2 ll. of a German incunabula over bds. From Honeyman Collection. (S. May 19; 3015) Quaritch. £360
- - Anr. Edn. Lyons, 1553. 16mo. Lr. blank margin of title cut away, & lr. section of A6, probably blank, just affecting a few letters. Limp vell., defect. [STC French 431] (S. Dec.1; 418) Ribi. £100

ULTRA
Madrid, 1921. 16 issues (of 24). Lge. fo. Orig. wraps. (DS Apr.24; 1035) Pts. 60,000

UNANUE, Joseph Hiplito
- Guia Politica, Ecclesiástica y Militar del Virreynato del Perú, para el año 1979. [Lima], 1797. Sm. 4to. Short tear & ink stain. Cont. mott. cf. (SPB. May 5; 512) $125
- Observaciones sobra el Clima de Lima y sus Influencias. Madrid, 1815. Sm. 4to. Slight worming affecting a few letters, title discold. with repairs to margins. Hf. cf. (SPB. May 5; 513) $200

UNCLE'S PRESENT, The
Phila., ca. 1810. 12mo. Orig. pict. stiff wraps. (SG. Apr.30; 314) $275

UNDERHILL, Francis T.
- Driving for Pleasure N.Y., 1897. 4to. Frontis. & several plts. loose & frayed in margins. Gt. suede covers, leath. spine & tips, owner's blind-stp. on endpaper. (SG. Dec.11; 201) $170

UNICORNO, Giuseppe
- De l'Arithmetica Universale. Venice, 1598. 1st. Edn. 2 pts. in 1 vol. 4to. Piece torn from lr. margin of 4F2 with loss of sig., some staining. Hf. vell. bds. From Honeyman Collection. (S. May 19; 3016) Pilo. £60

UNION STEAMSHIP COMPANY
- The Emigrants Guide to South Africa, including Cape Colony, The Diamond Fields . . . L., 1880. 6th. Edn. Pict. cl. (SSA. Jan.22; 375) R. 160

UNITED STATES OF AMERICA
- Declaration of Independence. Salem, Mass., [1776]. Fo. Broadsheet. Torn along central vertical & horizontal folds, with loss of several letters & one word. (CNY. May 22; 81) $6,000
- - Anr. Edn. Wash., 1823. (200), this copy on parch. Lge. fo. 17 sm. abrasions at top & left edges, not affecting image. Mntd. on heavy bd. & F. Pres. inscr., possibly in the hand of John Quincy Adams, later the copy of Margaret T. Weems. (PNY. May 21; 163) $8,000
- Geological Survey to the Secretary of the Interior. Wash., 1883-1904. Vols. III, IV & VI-XXVI in 64, with dupl. of vol. IV & a vol. of cold. folding maps. Cont. red hf. leath. (excepting 2 vols.). (SH. Jul.23; 139) Jeffery. £170
- House of Representatives: William T.G. Morton, M.D.– Sulphuric Ether. [Wash.], 1852. Folding facs. MS., foxed. Disbnd. (SG. Sep.18; 14) $100
- Return of the Whole Number of Persons within the Several Districts of the United States . . . Phila., 1791. Cont. wraps. (SG. Oct.9; 54) $500

UNITED STATES Treasury Department
- American Bond Detector, & Complete History of the United States Government Securities. Wash., 1869. Ob. 4to. 9 plts on brown paper, embossed. Gt. lettered cl., crudely rebkd., worn, ex-liby. (SG. Sep.4; 362) $1,600

UNITED STATES War Department
- Survey of the North & Northwestern Lakes. [Wash?], 1905. 4 vols. Lge. fo. Maps mntd. on linen. Orig. bdg., very worn, jnts. brkn. (CB. Sep.24; 171) Can. $220

UNIVERSAL History (An)
1747-48. 20 vols. Cont. cf. (P. Oct.2; 64) Broen. £70
- - Anr. Edn. 1747-54. 21 vols. Some folding plts. & maps torn. Later vell. bds. (SH. Mar.5; 298) Womersley. £80

UNIVERSAL-LEXIKON DER KOCHKUNST
Leipzig, 1909. 8th. Edn. 3 vols. 1 plt. loose vol. 1.
Orig. hf. linen. (R. Mar.31-Apr.4; 1648) DM 420

UNIVERSO O Storria E Descrizione di Tutti I Popoli.
Venice, 1834-50. 28 vols. Minor worming in margins of most vols., occasional spotting. Cont. hf. cf. W.a.f. (C. Feb.4; 173) *Russell.* £380

UNNA, Paul Gerson
– The Histopathology of the Diseases of the Skin.
Trans.:– Sir Norman Walker. Edinburgh., N.Y., 1896. 1st. Engl. Edn. Cl. (S. Jun.17; 844)
Bickersteth. £65

UNTERMYER, Irwin
– Meissen & other Continental Porcelain.–Chelsea & other English Porcelain. 1956; 1957. 2 vols. 4to. Orig. cl., d.-w's. (C. Feb.4; 271) *Morris.* £380

UNWINS, Thomas
– The Costume of the University of Oxford. Ill.:– J. Agar after Unwins. 1815. 1st. Edn. 4to. Lacks port., a few plts. spotted. Cont. cf., rebkd., worn. (S. Nov.4; 519) *Yateley Gallerys.* £75
– – Anr. Copy. Some offsetting & slight foxing. Bds. (BS. Jun.11; 403) £50

UPCOTT, William
– A Bibliographical Account of the Principal Works Relating to English Topography. 1818. 1st. Edn., L.P. Iss. 3 vols. Later 19th. C. russ. gt. (S. Nov.25; 489) *Quaritch.* £420
– – Anr. Copy. Light foxing at beginning of each vol. Cont. hf. mor., gt., unc. (S. Nov.4; 545) *Lawford.* £95
– – Anr. Copy. Spotted thro.-out. Cont. cf., rebkd. From the collection of Eric Sexton. (C. Apr.16; 372) *Puddle.* £70
– – Anr. Copy. Spotted thro.-out. (C. Jul.22; 127) *Wilson.* £50
– Catalogue of the Library. 1846. (31) for the Roxburghe Cl., L.P. 3 pts. in 1 vol., as iss. Fo. Orig. cl., worn. (C. Jul.22; 128) *Quaritch.* £90

UPDIKE, Daniel Berkeley.
– Printing Types. Camb., 1937. 2nd. Edn. 2 vols. Cl., d.-w.'s. (SG. Jan.22; 381) $150

UPHAM, Charles W.
– Lectures on Witchcraft, Comprising a History of the Delusion in Salem ... Boston, 1831. 1st. Edn. 16mo. Shortened hf.-title, heavily foxed & stained. Cont. cl., soiled, upr. cover loose. From liby. of William E. Wilson. [Sabin 98039] (SPB. Apr.29; 269) $125

UPPER CANADA; HOUSE OF ASSEMBLY
– Journal. York, U.C., 8 Jan.-20 Mar. 1829. Fo. Foxed & brownstained. Old hf. cf. (SG. Mar.5; 72) $180
– – Anr. Edn. York, 8 Jan.-6 Mar. 1830. Fo. Foxed. Marb. bds., cf. spine. (SG. Mar.5; 73) $180

UPTON, Florence K. & Bertha
– Golliwogg Books. 1896-1902. 8 vols. Ob. 4to. Orig. pict. bds., worn. (TA. Feb.19; 617) £75

URBANUS Bellunensis [Bolzanio]
– Institutiones Graecae Grammatices. Venice, Aldus Manutius, Jan., 1497/98. 1st. Edn. Sm. 4to. Spaces for lge. initials thro.-out with guide letters, upr. portion of diagram cropped, some slight staining, mostly at front & at end. 18th. C. Fr. red mor. gt., spine gt.-lettered & with flower tools, slight wear to corners & jnts., head of spine slightly torn. The copy of Michael Wodhull (with his sig., date of acquisition & price, & further notes on fly-lf.), later the copy of Henry J.B. Clements, recently in the collection of Eric Sexton. [BMC V, 588, Goff U66, HC 16098*=2763*] (CNY. Apr.8; 194) $5,000

URE-SMITH, Sydney
– The Art of Arthur Streeton. Sydney, 1919. 4to. Slight browning to some blank pp. Orig. bdg., d.-w. (JL. Mar.2; 715) Aus. $180

URFE, Honoré d'
– L'Astrée. Pastorale Allégorique avec la Clé ...
Ill.:– Gravelot & Rigaud. Paris, 1733. Latest Edn., 1st Printing. 5 vols. in 10. 12mo. Ills. slightly defect. Cont. marb. cf., spines decor. with raised bands. (HD. Jun.24; 119) Frs. 1,400

URQUHART, Beryl Leslie
– The Camellia. Ill.:– after Raymond Booth & Paul Jones. [1956-60]. 1st. Edn. 2 vols. Fo. Orig.

hf. cl. & cl., vol. II with d.-w. (S. Dec.3; 1166)
Marks. £50

URSUS, Nicolaus Raimarus
– Fundamentum Astronomicum: id est, Nova Doctrina Sinuum & Triangulorum. Strassburg., 1588. 1st. Edn. Sm. 4to. 3 double-p. ptd. tables mntd., inserted pen & ink diagram, some browning, title slightly soiled. Disbnd., cl. case. From Honeyman Collection. (S. May 19; 3017)
McKittrick. £500

URY, Lesser
– Der Künstlerische Nachlass von Lesser Ury. Versteigerungskatalog. Berlin, 1932. 4to. Orig. sewed. (D. Dec.11-13; 466) DM 450

U.S. CAMERA
N.Y., 1935; 36; 40. 3 vols. 4to. Bds. & wraps., spiral bnd. (SG. Apr.23; 203) $100

USHER, James
– Strange & remarkable prophesies & predictions of the holy learned & excellent James Usher ... written by the person who heard it from this excellent persons own mouth. 1679. 4to. Sm. holes & tears affecting letters & p. numerals in last 2 ll. 19th. C. hf. cf. (C. Feb.4; 153) *Quaritch.* £130

USHER, James Ward
– An Art Collector's Treasures. 1916. [300]. 4to. Orig. mor., gt. Inscr. to Sheriff of Lincoln dtd. 18th. Oct. 1922 stpd. in gt. on red mor., preserved on upr. inner cover. (CSK. Nov.28; 195) £60

UTKIN, Iosif
– Poves' o Ryzhem Motele [Story of the Ginger Model, Mister Inspector, Rabbi Issai & Commissar Blokh]. Ill.:– K. Rotov. Moscow, [1926]. 4to. Orig. wraps. by K. Rotov. (SH. Feb.6; 535) *Quaritch.* £50

UTTENHOFER, Caspar
– Circulus Geometricus, zu Teutsch Mess-Circkel, nemlich: ein Geometrisch Instrument, durch welches gar leicht, gewiss unnd Künstliche, so wol ohne, als durch die Rechnungen, alle höhe ... Abzumessen. Nuremb., 1626. 1st. Edn. Sm. 4to. Lacks plt., slight soiling & discolouration, rust-hole in B2. Disbnd. From Honeyman Collection (S. May 19; 3018)
Rogers Turner. £100

UZANNE, Octave
– Anactodes sur la Comtesse Du Barry.–Les Moeurs Secrètes du XVIIIe Siècle. Paris, 1880; 1883. (100) on Whatman. 2 vols. Hf. vell., orig. wraps. bnd. in. (SI. Dec.4; 580) Lire 220,000
– La Chronique Scandaleuse. Ill.:– Adolphe Lalauze. Paris, 1879. Crimson crushed lev., triple gt. fillet borders, spine gt. with floral design, gt. dentelles, by Thirbaron-Joly. (SG. Sep.4; 446) $250
– – Anr. Copy. (SG. Apr.9; 274) $120
– Dictionnaire Bibliophilosophique ... Paris, 1896. Mor., 4 spine raised bands, gt. & mosaic, 2 fillet border & pointillé with mosaic angle fleurons, gt. pointillé, 6 fillet inr. border, wrap, preserved, box, by Weckesser, 1914. (LM. Mar.21; 313) B.Frs. 30,000
– L'Eventail.–L'Ombrelle. Ill.:– Paul Avril. Paris, 1882; 1883. 2 works in 1 vol. Three quarter red mor., 5 spine raised bands decor. in compartments with special tools, unc. wraps. preserved by Champs. (LM. Mar.21; 314) B.Frs. 10,000
– Fashion in Paris ... 1797-1897. 1898. 4to. Orig. cl. (CSK. Oct.17; 62) £55
– – Anr. Copy. 4to. Disbnd. (SG. Nov.20; 419) $100
– La Femme à Paris. Ill.:– Masse, Vidal. Paris. 1894. Ltd. Edn. Orig. decor wraps., silk portfolio. unc. (SI. Dec.4; 583) Lire 280,000
– La Française du Siècle, Modes, Moeurs, Usages. Ill.:– E. Gaujean after Lynch. Paris, 1886. (100) numbered ptd. on Japon, with extra suite of ills. Orig. pict. wraps., s.-c., ties. (SH. Apr.10; 361)
Marks. £55
– The French Bookbinders of the Eighteenth Century. Trans.:– Mabel McIlvaine. Chic., Caxton Cl. 1904. (252). Fo. Cl.-bkd. bds. Orig. prospectus laid in. (SG. Oct.2; 364) $375
– – Anr. Copy. 4to. Orig. cl.-bkd. bds., unc., bkplt. of Henry W. Poor. The John A. Saks copy. (CNY. Oct.1; 208) $180
– Le Livre Moderne. Paris, 1890-92. 5 vols. including index. Cont. hf. mor., orig. wraps bnd. in, partly unc. (SI. Dec.4; 585) Lire 220,000
– La Locomotion à travers l'Histoire et les Moeurs. Paris, 1900. Ltd. Edn. 4to. Plts., some double-p. &

hand-cold, partly unc. (SI. Dec.4; 586)
Lire 260,000
– La Locomotion à Travers le Temps, les Moeurs, et l'Espace. Paris, [1912]. 1st. Edn. 4to. Cont. red mor.-bkd. bds., some wear, 'College Stanisla' on upr. cover. (S. Jun.9; 67) *Duran.* £70
– Le Miroir du Monde. Ill.:– Paul Avril. Paris, 1888. (100) on Japan Vell. 4to. Mor. gt., mor onlays on covers, spine with 4 raised bands, gt. turn-ins, with mor. onlays, silk brocade doubls., orig. wraps. & spine bnd. in, unc., by Charles Meunier. (CNY. May 22; 347) $650
– Les Modes de Paris ... Ill.:– François Courbin. Paris, 1898. (90) on imperial Jap., numbered. 4to. Hf. mor. by Meunier, mosaic woman's head & thistles on spine, wrap. preserved. (SM. Feb.11; 292) Frs. 5,000
– L'Ombrelle. Paris, 1883. Crushed lev. mor. gt., spine gt. with emblems in compartments, orig. wraps. & spine bnd. in, by Pagnant. (CNY. May 22; 285) $100
– L'Ombrelle : le Gant : le Manchon.–L'Eventail. Ill.:– Paul Avril. Paris, 1883; 1882. 2 vols. Cont. cf. gt, orig. silk wraps. bnd. in. (SI. Dec.4; 588) Lire 350,000
– La Reliure Artistique et Fantaisiste. Ill.:– Paul Avril. Paris, 1887. 1st. Edn., (1500) numbered copies on Papier Velin. 4to. Red lev., geometric gt. design of fillets & dots round gt. arms, gt.-panel, spine, gt. dentelles, orig. pict. wraps., by Rivière. (SG. Oct.2; 363) $225
– Voyage autour de sa Chambre. Ill.:– Henri Caruchet & Frederic Masse. Paris, 1896. (200). 4to. Hand-cold. copper engraved ills. & calligraphic text. Hf. mor., floral gt., marb. paper over & end-ll., orig. wraps. bnd. in, sigd. by Meurier. L. to Raisin, Uzanne ex-lib. & Maurice Quarre ex-lib. (D. Dec.11-13; 1203) DM 2,500

UZTARIZ, Jeronimo de
– The Theory & Practice of Commerce & Maritime Affairs. 1751. 1st. Edn. in Engl. 2 vols. Slight foxing. Cont. cf., spines & corners worn. (C. Apr.1; 188) *Lawson.* £110

V., V.C.
– The Google Book. N.d. (100). 4to. Cl.-bkd. bds. (P. Mar.12; 27) *Marks.* £75

VADÉ, Jean Joseph
– Oeuvres Complettes. Ill.:– Boily after Richard. 1777. 4 vols. 18mo. Red mor. by Cazin. (HD. Apr.8; 308) Frs. 1,500
– Oeuvres Poissardes. Ill.:– Monsiau. 1796. Lge. 4to. Browning. Cont. hf. mor. (HD. Jun.30; 81) Frs. 2,500

VAENIUS, Ernestus
– Tractatus Physiologicus de Pulchritudine. Brussels, 1662. 18th. C. red mor., gt. (SH. Jun.4; 114) *Marlborough Rare Books.* £90

VAENIUS i.e. Veen, Otto van
– Amoris Divini emblemata. Antw., 1660. 2nd. Edn. 4to. Text in Latin, Spanish, Dutch & Fr., slightly soiled, 2 corners & 1 tear reprd., slightly affecting 1 engr. Cont. vell. bds. (S. Dec.8; 128) *Duran.* £100
– – Anr. Copy. Soiled, last 2 ll. torn. Old vell., soiled. (TA. Dec.18; 194) £64
– Batavorum cum Romanis Bellum ... Antw., 1612. 1st. Edn. Ob. 4to. Considerable foxing & soiling. Old vell., unc. (SG. Feb.5; 327) $150
[–] The Doctrine of Morality ... Trans.:– T.M. Gibbs. Ill.:– Daret. L., 1721. 2 pts. in 1 vol. Fo. Browned in places. Cont. panel. cf. (VG. Dec.17; 1304) Fls. 1,000
– Emblemata Horatiana, imaginibus in aes incisis atque Latino, Germanico, Gallico et Belgico Carmine Illustrata. Amst., 1684. Single gt. fillet, spine gt. in compartments, inner gt. dentelles. (SM. Oct.8; 2052) Frs. 2,700
– Quinti Horatii Flacci Emblemata ... Brussels, 1683. 4to. Slight marginal dampstaining to a few ll. Cont. vell. bds., soiled. (S. Jun.23; 246) *Norton.* £100

See–HUGO, Hermann & Veen, Otto van

VAERST, Baron E.
– Gastrosophie oder Lehre von den Freunden der Tafel. Ed.:– C.G. von Maassen. Munich, 1922. (50) numbered on Van-Gelder. 2 vols. Orig. leath., gt. spine & cover. (R. Oct.14-18; 2737) DM 650

VAILLANT, Jean
– Selectiora Numismata in Aere Maximi Moduli. Paris, 1695. 4to. Lacks 1 plt., a few minor defects. Cont. cf., worn. (SBA. Mar.4; 84)
Stutzmann. £50

VAILLANT, Sebastien
- Botanicon Parisiense ou Denombrement ...
Ill.:– after Claude Aubriet. Leiden & Amst., 1727.
Fo. Lacks port. Cont. cf., rebkd. From Chetham's
Liby., Manchester. (C. Nov.27; 399)
Taylor. £120
– – Anr. Copy. Lacks engraved port. (C.
Mar.18; 114) *Weldon & Wesley.* £80

VAISSETTE, Joseph
See–VIC, Claude de & Vaissette, Joseph

VALENS, Evans G.
- Magnet.–Motion. Ill.:– Berenice Abbott.
Cleveland, [1964; 1965]. 1st. Edns. 2 vols. 4to. Cl.,
d.-w.; pict. cl. (SG. Apr.23; 3) $110

VALENTA, E.
See–EDER, J.M. & Valenta, E.

VALENTIA, George Annesley, Viscount
- Beautiful & Rare Trees & Plants ... L., 1903.
(300) numbered. Fo. Cl. gt. (GM. Apr.30; 406)
£75
- Voyages & Travels to India, Ceylon, the Red Sea
& Egypt. 1809. [1st. Edn.?]. 4to. Orig. cf. (P.
Oct.23; 73) *Brooke-Hitching.* £520
– – Anr. Copy. 3 Vols. 69 engraved maps & plts.,
sm. stp. on titles. Cont. vell. gt., blind-stpd. arms
on covers. (C. Jul.15; 106A) *Quaritch.* £400
– – Anr. Copy. 9 folding maps & plans, some
reprd. Cont. panel. cf. (CSK. May 1; 102) £280
– – Anr. Copy. Sm. stp. on each title. Cont. vell.
gt., blind-stpd. arms on covers. From Chetham's
Liby., Manchester. (C. Nov.27; 400)
Edwards. £220

VALENTIJN, Fr.
- Oud en Nieuw Oost-Indien. Dordr./Amst.,
1724-26. 5 vols. bnd. in ll. Fo. 234 (of 243) maps
& plts., some marginal repairs, some tears reprd.,
slightly browned & foxed in places. 19th. C. hf. cl.
(VG. Oct.13; 160) Fls. 3,700
– – Anr. Edn. Dordrecht/Amst., 1726. 2 vols. Fo.
Browned in places, some wormholes, affecting a
number of text ll. & plts., a few ll. loose. Cont.
marb. cf., backs gt., spine ends defect., gt. supra
libros of Isaac de Pinto on covers. (VG.
Dec.17; 1569) Fls. 750

VALENTINE, Basilius
[-] The Last VVill & Testament. 1671. 4th. Edn.
Slight tear in table reprd., rust hole in L2, printing
flaw on 2H1r affecting headline, some browning
& staining. 19th. C. hf. cf. [Wing B1018] (S.
Dec.9; 364) *Quaritch.* £85

VALENTINE, David Thomas
- Manual of the Corporation of the City of New
York. N.Y., 1851-70. 19 vols. 12mo. Orig. cl., 2
vols. in orig. leath., brkn. (SG. Oct.9; 245) $750

VALENTINI, Michel Bernard
- Museum Museorum ... Frankfurt, 1714. 3 pts.
in 2 vols. Fo. Lacks 1 unnumbered plt., plt. IV of
pt. 1 & plt. I of pt. 2, lacks 2 ll. of text in pt. 1, hf.
title of pt. 3 reprd. Cont. vell. (HD. Mar.18; 179)
Frs. 5,900

VALENTYN, François
- Oud en Nieuw Oost-Indien. Dordrecht & Amst.,
1724-26. 5 vols. in 7. Fo. Lacks several plts., &
possibly text at end of last vol., some foxing. Cont.
cf., spines gt. W.a.f. (SG. Feb.5; 328) $2,000

VALERA, Jernómino
- Comentarii ac Quaestiones in Universam
Aristotelis ac Subtilissimi Doctoris Ihoannis Duns
Scoti Logicam. Lima, 1610 [colophon 1609]. Fo.
Some stains, top edge with 17th. C. owner's brand
'SF.'. Limp vell. with ties, worn. (SPB. May
5; 516) $250

VALERI, Franceso Malagiozzi
- La Corte di Lodovico il Moro. Milan, 1913. 4to.
Orig. wraps., vol. 1 spine defect. (CR.
Mar.19; 102) Lire 900,000
– – Anr. Copy. Vol. 1. Hf. vell. (CR. Mar.19; 434)
Lire 200,000
– – Anr. Edn. Milan, 1913-23. 4 vols. 4to. Orig.
ptd. cl. with medal on upr. cover, metal ornaments
in angles, boxes. (SI. Dec.4; 590) Lire 1,000,000
– – Anr. Edn. Milan, 1917. Vol. III. 4to. Orig.
wraps., loose. (CR. Mar.19; 436) Lire 200,000

VALERIANI, D. & Segato, G.
- Atlanto Monumentale del Basso e dell'Alto
Egitto. Flor., 1840. Fo. Last 2 plts. torn, a few ll.
slightly soiled. Orig. cl., lacks spine, worn, loose.
(SH. Nov.7; 444) *Walford.* £200

VALERIANO BOLZANI, Giovanni Pierio
- De Fulminum Significationibus. Rome, [1517].
1st. Edn. On vell., numerous text markings in red
ink, a few ll. discold. 19th. C. mor., gt., pink
watered silk linings. Bkplts. of Sir John Thorold
(Sÿston Park liby.); from Honeyman Collection.
(S. May 20; 3019) *Goldschmidt.* £1,250
- Hieroglyphica sive de Sacris Aegyptiorum Literis
Commentarii. Basle, 1556. 1st. Edn. Fo. Short tear
in fo. 352, single sm. wormhole in 1st. 4 ll.,
worming reprd. in fore-margins of fos. 315-338,
some browning, deleted inscr. on title. 18th. C. hf.
vell. (S. Feb.10; 254) *Thomas.* £220
– – Anr. Edn. Lyon, 1579. 2 vols. in 1. Fo. Some
browning, last vol. title slightly soiled, a little marginal
staining at end. Mod. hf. vell. bds. From
Honeyman Collection. (S. May 20; 3020)
Sbisa. £240

VALERIO, Luca
- De Centro Gravitatis Solidorum Libri tres. Rome,
1604. 1st. Edn. Sm. 4to. Somewhat browned &
spotted thro.-out, lacks last lf. (blank?), 2 sm.
holes affecting title device, marginal wormholes in
last quire, liby. stp. on title. Cont. vell., worn.
From Honeyman Collection. (S. May 20; 3021)
Nador. £80

VALERIO, Samuel
- Yad ha'melech. Venice, 1586. 1st. Edn. Sm. 4to.
Liby. stp. on title. Antique style mor. (C.
Jul.16; 316a) *Stein.* £220

VALERIO, T.
- Costumes du Grand-Duché de Bade. Paris,
[1841]. Fo. Foxing thro.-out. Roan-bkd. bds. (BS.
Jun.11; 405) £280

VALERIUS FLACCUS, Caius
- Argonautica. Venice, Ald. Pr., priv. ptd., May
1523. Late Fr. bdg. of gt.-ruled crushed mor. 2 Fr.
& 1 Engl. armorial bkplts., 2 other bkplts. (1 of
Charles Dexter Allen). (PNY. Oct.1; 515) $100

VALERIUS Maximus, Gaius
- Collections of the Memorable Acts & Sayings of
Orators, Philosophers, Statesmen ... 1684.
Frontis. plt. laid down, some light browning to
early ll. 19th. C. hf. mor. The Meyerstein copy,
with bkplt. [Wing V33A] (LC. Feb.12; 600)
£100
- Dictorum et Factotum Memorabilium Rubricae.
[Venice], Vindelinus de Spira, 1471. 3rd. [1st.
Italian] Edn. Fo. Gold & illuminated 7-line initial
V amidst background of red, blue & green
extending to upr. & inner margins on fo. 3 (this lf.
is sometimes found with ptd. border), other initials
& paragraph marks supplied in alternate red &
blue, lacks final blank lf., some light dampstaining
affecting 1st. 12 ll. & with some fading of blue
initials on these ll. Early 18th. C. Engl. red mor.
gt., broad gt. border of thistle & floral tools,
central gt. lozenges of stylized flowers, spine gt.,
qtr. red mor. gt. s.-c. Bkplt. of John A. Saks.
[BMC V, 156 (also without border), Goff V24]
(CNY. Oct.1; 112) $7,500
– – Anr. Edn. Venice, Johannes de Colonia &
Johannes Manthen, 1474. [2nd. or 3rd. Italian
Edn.]. Fo. Gold & illuminated 6-line initial V
incorporating a vine-scroll ascender & descender
against a green, blue & red ground, arms of the
Visconti family painted in lr. margin, on fo. 4,
other initials supplied thro.-out over guide letters
in alternating red & blue, lacks final blank lf.,
some slight soiling to a few initials. Red mor. gt.,
gt. arms on sides of Baron Seilliere, by C. Hardy,
qtr. red mor. gt. s.-c. Bkplt. of John A. Saks.
[BMC V, 230, Goff V26, HC 15776] (CNY.
Oct.1; 114) $3,000
– – Anr. Edn. Paris, Ludovicus Symonell & others,
1475. Fo. Initials & chapter marks supplied in red
or blue (the blue faded), cont. marginalia,
wormholes at beginning & end, some slightly
affecting text. 19th. C. red mor., gt. 3-line border
on covers, spine gt. [BMC VIII, 17; HC 15778;
Goff V28] (S. May 5; 449) *Lyon.* £1,600
– – Anr. Edn. Ed.:– Oliverius Arzignanensis.
Venice, Guilelmus Anima Mia Tridinensis,
Aug.12, 1491. Fo. Some ll. browned, sm. marginal
hole in last 2 ll. affecting 2 letters. Mott. cf.
antique, worn, upr. cover loosening. [BMC V, 412,
Goff V39, HC 15791*] (CNY. Oct.1; 119) $850

See–CICERO, Marcus Tullius–GELLIUS, Aulus
& VALERIUS Maximum, Gaius

VALERY, Paul Ambroise
- Le Cimitière Marin. 1920. Hf. cf., mor. ornam.,
wrap., lacks spine, by Anthoine Legrain. On
Mittineigue-Mill. (HD. Oct.10; 163) Frs. 1,800
- Degas. Danse. Dessin. Ill.:– after Edgar Degas.
Paris, 1936. (325) on Rives vell. 4to. In sheets,
wrap. (HD. Dec.5; 205) Frs. 2,500
- Gedichte. Trans.:– R.M. Rilke. Ill.:– E. Gill.
Leipzig, 1925. (450) numbered 1st. Edn. 4to. MS.
owner's note on end-paper & erased entry. Orig.
hf. vell. (HK. Nov.18-21; 2878) DM 650
- Oeuvres. Paris, n.d. 1st. Coll. Edn.; (10) on Jap.,
numbered (vol. XI on Rives vell., numbered). 12
vols. Sewed, wraps. (HD. Dec.5; 206) Frs. 2,500
- Propos sur l'Intelligence. Paris, 1926. Orig.
Edn., on hollande. Cf., angle decor., mosaic motifs
of mor. bands., vari-cold., inner fillet, wrap., hf. cf.
s.-c., box, by Canape & Corriez. A.L. by author.
(HD. Jun.10; 217) Frs. 3,300

VALÉRY, Paul & others
- Paul Bonet. Paris, 1945. (300) on Arches vell.
Fo. In sheets, publisher's s.-c. (HD. Dec.5; 21)
Frs. 1,050

VALIN, R.J.
- Nouveau Commentaire sur l'Ordonnance de la
Marine du Mois d'Août 1681. La Rochelle, 1776.
2 vols. 4to. Cont. marb. roan, spines decor. with
raised bands, bdgs. defect. (HD. Jun.24; 103)
Frs. 1,100

VALK, Gerard & Leonard
[-] Atlas. [Amst.], ca. 1660-1740. Atlas fo.
Composite atlas containing: engraved port. of
Johann Baptist Homann, Gerard & Leonard
title-p., 194 double-p. hand-cold. copperplt. maps
(a few folding, by Homann (over 70, including 5
maps from his Star Atlas following title), the
Valks (approximately 16), Nicholas Visscher
(approximately 21), F. De Witt (approximately
19), J. Covens & C. Mortier (approximately 20),
Pierre Mortier (approximately 5), De Lisle
(approximately 6), Peter Schenk, & others by
Blaeu (Iceland), J.C. Mueller, Gerard van Keulen,
de Fer, H. Jaillot & a few others, atlas is indexed
in MS. in cont. Fr. hand as having once contained
198 maps (4 missing maps at rear are among those
of the ancient world), each map numbered on
verso in hand matching that of index, 3 maps with
repairs, 1 with short recent tears at 1 intersecting
fold. Cont. gt.-fillet cf., elab. gt.-stpd. on covers,
corners stpd. with astrolabes (gt.-lettered),
rebacking recorrering in later cf., orig. backstrip
preserved. Apparently compiled & sold by the
Valks to a collector whose widow has written long
pres. inscr. to Marquis Ferdinand Herns (?).
(PNY. Dec.3; 30) $26,000

VALLA, Laurentius
- De Latinae Linguae Elegantia ... Iodici Badii
Ascensii in sex de Latinae Linguae Elegantia
Libros. Paris, 27 Sep. 1541. Fo. Lacks last blank,
title slightly soiled & dampstained, some ll.
slightly dampstained in lr. margin, John Evelyn's
owner's inscr. on title, press mark obliterated.
17th. C. cf., gt. centre ornament & corner pieces,
spine cracked & worn, piece missing at head,
bkplt. (S. Dec.8; 138) *Fletcher.* £80

VALLANCE, Aymer
- The Art of William Morris. Ed.:– Gleeson White.
L., Chis. Pr. 1897. [220]. Fo. Cl., partly unc.,
hinges reinforced. Bkplt. of editor, initialed by him
on limitation p., the John A. Saks copy. (CNY.
Oct.1; 194) $650

VALLE, Genera del
- Anales de la Inquisición. Madrid, 1841. 4to.
Cont. linen. (DS. Apr.24; 850) Pts. 42,000

VALLE, Pietro della
- Reiss-Beschreibung in unterschiedliche Theile
der Welt. Genf., 1674. 1st. German Edn. 4 vols. in
1. Fo. Cont. leath., gt., upr. cover reprd. (R.
Oct.14-18; 1823) DM 2,600
– – Anr. Copy. Cont. vell., slightly defect. (R.
Mar.31-Apr.4; 2567) DM 1,900
- The Travels ... into East-India & Arabia
Deserta ... whereunto is added a relation of Sir
Thomas Roe's voyage into the East-Indies. 1665.
1st. Edn. in Engl. Fo. Cont. mott. cf., rebkd. with
orig. spine preserved, Edward Howes bkplt. [Wing
V48A (4to)] (S. Nov.4; 642) *Traylen.* £160

VALLE-INCLAN, Ramón del
- Cenizas. Madrid, 1899. Wraps. (DS.
Apr.24; 923) Pts. 40,000

VALLEMONT, Abbé Pierre Le Lorrain de
– La Physique Occulte, ou Traité de la Baguette Divinatoire . . . aves des Principes qui Expliquent les Phenomènes les plus Obscurs de la Nature. Paris, 1709. 12mo. Cont. cf. (C. Apr.1; 118A)
Goldschmidt. £130

VALLERY-RADOT, J.
See–LUGT, Frits & Vallery-Radot, J.

VALLES, Jules 'Jules La Rue'
[–] L'Argent par un Homme de Lettres devenu de Bourse. 1857. Three qtr. mor., wrap., doubl., by Champs-Stroobants. (HD. Oct.10; 165)
Frs. 1,250
– Jacques Vingtras. 1879. Three quarter mor., wrap, double spine. (HD. Oct.10; 166) Frs. 1,050
– Jacques Vingtras.–L'Insurgé. 1871. Three quarter mor., double wrap. (HD. Oct.10; 168)
Frs. 1,050

VALLET, L.
– A Travers L'Europe Croquis de Cavalerie. Paris, 1893. 4to. Hf. mor. gt. (P. Jul.2; 27) *Lenton.* £60
– A travers l'Europe. Croquis de Cavalerie.–La Chic à Cheval. Paris, 1893; 1891. 2 vols. 4to. Orig. wraps. bnd. in 2nd. work, unif. hf. mor., partly unc. (SI. Dec.4; 591) Lire 340,000

VALLET, P.
– Le Iardin dv Roy tres Chrestien Henry IV. Ill.:– Pierre Vallet. [Paris], 1608. 1st. Edn. Fo. Lacks port & plts. R.-D. 193 & 206, title & 1 text lf. bkd., washed. Mod. paper bds. (H. Dec.9/10; 389)
DM 4,500

VALLIBUS, Hieronymous de
See–LOCHER, Jacobus–REMUS Favinus –UGUITON–WIMPHELING, Jacobus –VALLIBUS, Hieronymous de

VALLISNIERI, Antonio
– Opera Diverse. Ill.:– Ant. Luciani (engraved port.). Venice, 1715. Vols. I & II (of 3) in 1 vol. 4to. A few minor tears, slight soiling & spotting, ink-stain on X1, owner's inscr. of Dr. Luigi Moriani, 1821. Cont. vell., soiled, spine worn. From Honeyman Collection. (S. May 20; 3022)
Beaver. £50
– [Opere]. Venice, Padua & Modena, 1710-28. Some 2nd. Edns. 12 works in 8 vols. 4to. Cont. mott. cf., 3 vols. rebkd., some jnts. worn. W.a.f. (CSK. Apr.24; 52) £160
– Opere Diverse . . .–Istoria della Generazione dell' Uomo e degli Animali. Ill.:– A. Luciani (1st. work). Venice, 1715; 1721. 3 pts. in 1 vol.; 1 vol. 4to.; sm. 4to. Cont. paper bds. (1st. work); & paper wraps. From the collection of John A. Saks. (C. Jun.10; 253) *Rota.* £190
– Opere Fisico-Mediche. Ill.:– A. dalla Via, A. Luciani, & others. Venice, 3 vols. Fo. Wormhole in title & 1st. ll. of vol. I. Orig. paper bds., buckram s.-c.'s, unc. From the collection of John A. Saks. (C. Jun.10; 254) *Burgess.* £160

VALOIS, Marguerite de, Queen of Navarre
See–MARGUERITE DE VALOIS, Queen of Navarre

VALSALVA, Antonius Maria
– De Aure Humana Tractatus. Utrecht, 1707. 4to. Marb. bds., cf. spine, unc. (S. Jun.17; 857)
Chatham Books. £80
– – Anr. Edn. Utrecht, 1717. 4to. Slight browning & soiling. Cont. panel. cf., bkplt. of George Paterson of Castle Huntly. From liby. of Dr. E. Ashworth Underwood. (S. Feb.23; 311)
Bennett. £120
– – Anr. Copy. Imprint on plt. 4 cut away. Hf. cf., upr. cover loose. (S. Dec.2; 645) *Phelps.* £60

VALSECCHI, G. Bagatti
– La Casa Bagatti Valsecchi in Milano. Milan. 1918. Lge. fo. Orig. decor. cl., unc. (SI. Dec.4; 592) Lire 350,000

VALTURIUS, Robertus
– De Re Militari. [Verona], Joannes Nicolai de Verona, 1472. 1st. Edn. Fo. Illuminated initials on folios 1 & 7 in violet, green & blue on burnished gold ground with decoration extending into inner margin, other initials supplied in red or blue, some with penwork decoration in contrasting colour, tears reprd. in folios 171 & 176, lr. blank fore-corner of folio 179 renewed, several other ll. with marginal tears reprd., folio 1 soiled, last few ll. slightly stained, slight marginal soiling & spotting, annots. in 2 or more hands, 1 apparently cont. Citron mor., by Birdsall of Northampton, lge. gt. ornaments in centre of covers, author, title,

printer & date in decorative cartouches at head & foot, gt. inside borders. From Honeyman Collection. [BMC VII, 948; HC 15847; Goff V88] (S. May 20; 3023) *James.* £32,00
– – Anr. Edn. Paris, 1532. 1st. Fr. Edn. Fo. Slight marginal staining, title & last p. a little soiled, marginal tear in T4, old owners' inscrs. on title of Andre Hurault, Theod. Taborot, & Stephanus Guyot. Vell., hf. red mor. case. From Honeyman Collection. (S. May 20; 3024) *Simonin.* £550
– – Anr. Edn. Paris, 1535. Fo. A few wormholes & 1 sm. hole, just affecting some letters, last few ll. reprd. with some slight loss of text, colophon Sep. 1534. Antique style limp vell. (S. Oct.21; 283)
Licini. £310

VALVERDE DE HAMUSCO, Juan
– Anatomia del Corpo humano. Rome, 1560. 1st. Edn., 2nd. Iss. of Italian translation. Fo. Title stained & occasional staining thro.-out. Cont. limp vell., fleece-lined case. (SPB. Nov.25; 107) $700

VAMBERY, Arminius
– Travels in Central Asia. 1864. 1st. Edn. Orig. cl. (SH. Mar.5; 147) *Morton-Smith.* £85

VAMPIR
Ed.:– [B.A. Katlovker]. St. Petersb., 1906. Nos. 1-8. Fo. Unbnd. (SH. Feb.5; 138) *Landry.* £330

VAN BRAGHT, Tileman Jansz
– T Merg van de Historien des Martelaren . . . uit de groote Martelaars Spiegel der Doopsgezinden . . . door J.B. de derde Druk. Amst., 1769. Price dedication lf. at beginning to Klass Sansz from Vereenigde Doopsgezinde Gemeente te Westzaandam, dtd. 1781. Cont. vell. bds. (S. Apr.7; 286) *Forum.* £70

VANBRUGH, Sir John
[–] A Short Vindication of the Relapse & the Provok'd Wife from Immorality & Phophaneness. 1698. 1st. Edn. Cont. cf. gt. [Wing V59] (C. May 20; 61) *Murray-Hill.* £140
See–COLLIER, Bp. Jeremy–CONGREVE, William–VANBRUGH, Sir John

VANCOUVER, George
– Voyage de Découvertes à l'Océan Pacifique du Nord. Paris, 1800. 3 vols. 4to. & atlas lge. fo. Stains, liby. stps. on titles. Later hf. mor. (SPB. May 5; 517) $1,700
– – Anr. Edn. Paris, [1800]. 6 vols. Cont. cf.-bkd. bds., slightly worn. [Sabin 98442] (SPB. May 5; 518) $600
– A Voyage of Discovery to the North Pacific Ocean, & Round the World. 1798. 1st. Edn. 3 vols. & atlas. 4to. & fo. Titles spotted, plts. browned & offset in text vols., some spotting in atlas. Text bnd. in cont. diced cf. (rebkd.) & 1 vol. rebnd. in hf. roan, most covers detchd., atlas in hf. roan. From Chetham's Liby., Manchester. [Sabin 98443] (C. Nov.27; 401) *Bowes.* £1,800
– – Anr. Edn. 1798-n.d. 4 vols. including reprint of Atlas. 4to. & fo. Some ll. slightly soiled. Cont. cf., rebkd. & orig. hf. cl. (SH. Nov.7; 526)
Bowes. £700

VAN CUYK, P., Jnr.
– Lyk-Staetsie. The Hague, 1755. Fo. 27 engraved plts. only, double-p. & mntd. on guards, some detchd. & with upr. & lr. margins cropped, occasional slight soiling. Cont. hf. mor., worn. W.a.f. (CSK. Nov.21; 247) £110

VANDERMAELEN, Philip M.G.
– Atlas Universal de Géographie. Brussels, 1827. 6 pts. in 3 vols. Ob. fo., 675mm. X 540mm. Last map in vol. 1 torn & reprd., chart at end of vol. 3 badly torn & loose, a few maps with offsetting or light browning. Cont. qtr. cf., worn, covers detchd. W.a.f. (CNY. Oct.1; 34) $750

VAN DE VELDE, C.W.M.
– Le Pays d'Israel. Paris, 1857. Fo. Orig. hf. leath. (D. Dec.11-13; 1349) DM 500

VAN DIEMEN'S LAND
– Copy of a Despatch from Lieut.-Governor Sir John Franklin, to Lord Glenelg, dated 7 October, 1837, relative to the Present System of Convict Discipline in Van Dieman's Land. [L.], 1838. Fo. Pp. 110+186. Disbnd. (KH. Nov.18; 609)
Aus. $210

VAN DYCK, Anthony
– Icones Principum Virorum Doctorum Pictorum Chalcographorum . . . Antw., [1646]. Fo. Interleaved thro.-out. 19th. C. red mor. by Chambolle-Duru. Pierre Mariette's copy with his

dtd. sig. on verso of many plts., later in J.F. Chéreau collection, his long MS. note. (SM. Oct.8; 2423) Frs. 25,000
– Iconographie ou Vies des Hommes Illustres du XVII Siècle Ecrites par M. V**. Ill.:– Pontius, Vosterman, Hendricx, van Voerst, du Pont & others after Van Dyke & Rubens. Amst. & Leipzig. 1759. 1st. Edn. 2 vols. in 1. Fo. Slight browning. Cont. hf. cf., slight wear, unc., s.-c. As a collection of prints, w.a.f. (S. May 5; 189)
Edmunds. £280
– – Anr. Copy. 120 plts. only (4 lacking), a few ll. cleanly torn, occasional slight soiling. Later hf. cf., worn. W.a.f. (CSK. Sep.19; 57) £180
– – Anr. Copy. Mor., 6 decor. spine raised bands, lge. gt. border, gt. triple fillet, inner dentelle. (LM. Jun.13; 100) B.Frs. 100,000
– De Kouse-Kamer Der Allerschoonste Portraiten van Versheide Prinssen en Prinsessen. Amst., 1732. Fo. A few light stains & spots, title tipped in. Cont. parch., soiled. (CSK. Mar.6; 154) £85

VAN DYKE, Henry
– The Travel Diaries of an Angler. Ill.:– R.L. Boyer. 1929. (20) for presentation. Hf. cl. Author's bkplt., inscr. to Henry Ingraham, frontis. sigd. by artist. (SG. Dec.11; 288) $400

VAN DYKE, Theodore S.
– The Still-Hunter. Ill.:– Carl Rungius & author. N.Y., 1919. 12mo. Three-qtr. lev., spine gt. with stag head. (SG. Dec.11; 425) $130

VANE, Charles William, Marquis of Londonderry
See–LONDONDERRY, Lt. Gen. Charles William Vane, Marquis of

VANEGAS, Alejo
– Primera parte de las Diferècias de libros q´ ay enl Universo . . . Nuevamente Emendada y Corregida. Toledo, 1546. 2nd. Edn. Sm. 4to. Upr. fore-corner of title reprd. 19th. C. mor., gt., arms on covers of J. Gomez de la Cortina, (Marqués de Morante). From Honeyman Collection. (S. May 20; 3027)
Hughes. £450

VAN ESPEN, Zegero Bernardo
– Jus Ecclesiasticum Universum.–Supplementum. Louvain, Brussels, 1735, 1769. 4 vols. & 1 vol. supp. Fo. Marb. cf., 6 decor. spine raised bands, slightly worn. (LM. Nov.8; 64) B.Frs. 13,000

VAN ESVELDT, S.
See–VAN HUISTEEN, A. & G., Crajenschot, T., Van Esveldt, S. & other publishers

VAN GALEN, Christofle Bernard
– La Vie et les Faits Memorable de Chr stofle Bernard van Galen, Evêque de Munster. Leyden, ca. 1680. Frontis. slightly stained. Cont. cf., spine gt., defect. Inscr. in pencil to Le Lorrain. (VG. Nov.18; 1169) Fls. 500

VAN GESTEL, Cornelius
– Historia Sacra et Profana Archiepiscopatus Mechliniensis. [The Hague], 1725. 2 vols. in 1. Fo. Cont. cf., 6 spine raised bands. (LM. Nov.8; 112)
B.Frs. 16,000

VAN GOGH, Vincent
– The Letters of Vincent Van Gogh to his Brother. –The Complete Letters.–Letters to Emile Bernard. L.; Greenwich, Ct.; L., 1872-1889; 1927-30; [1958]; 1938. 1st. Edns. in Engl. 3 vols.; 3 vols.; 1 vol. Thick tall 8vo. & sm. 4to. Cl., 1st. title with glassine wraps., 1st. & 2nd. titles boxed. (PNY. Mar.4; 264) $150

VAN GOIDSENHOVEN, J.P.
– La Céramique Chinoise sous les Ts'ing. 1936. Ltd. Edn. 4to. Mor. gt., s.-c. (P. Nov.13; 322)
Tallerman. £85
– – Anr. Edn. Brussels, 1936. 4to. Publisher's cl. (LM. Mar.21; 83) B.Frs. 14,000

VAN HELMONT, J.B.
– Oriatrike or, Physick Refined. 1662. Fo. First few ll. wormed, some with slight loss. Cont. cf., rebkd. [Wing H1400] (CSK. May 1; 156) £130

VANINI, Giulio Cesare
– Amphitheatrum Aeternae Providentiae Divino-Magicum.–De Admirandis Naturae Reginae Deaeque Mortalium Arcanis. Lyon, Paris, 1615; 1616. 1st. Edns. Inscr. on 1st. title 'Collegii Paris, Societ. Jesu . . . Guillemi dies (?)', note on fly-lf. in Fr. 18th. C. mor., triple gt. fillet, flat spine gt. in compartments, inner gt. dentelles, corners slightly worn, bkplt. of Baron de Bellet. (SM. Oct.8; 2053) Frs. 5,200

- De Admirandis Naturae Reginae Deaeque Mortalium Arcanis . . . Paris, 1616. Crushed mor., triple gt. fillet border, spines gt., gt. dentelles, by Derome le Jeune. Auchincruive bkplt. & Mortimer Schiff's mor. bkplt. (SG. Sep.25; 48) $550

VANISHING PICTURES: a Novel Picture Book with Dioramic Effects
L. & N.Y., ca. 1900. Square 8vo. 1 movable picture slightly defect. Cl.-bkd. cold. pict. bds. (SG. Apr.30; 315) $275

VANITY FAIR
Nov. 14 1868-Dec. 28 1872. 8 vols. Fo. Lacks a few plts. in the 1st. vol., 7th. vol. spotted. Orig. cl. gt. (SKC. Feb.26; 1800c) £380
– – **Anr. Run.** 1870-71. Vols. IV & V. Fo. Orig. cl. gt., slight wear to tops & bottoms of spines. (TA. Sep.18; 119) £56
– – **Anr. Run.** 1896-98. 6 vols. only. Fo. Hf. cf., worn. W.a.f. (SH. Jul.9; 10) *Reid.* £320

VANITY FAIR ALBUM (The)
Ill.:– Ape, etc. L., 1871. 3rd. Series. Fo. Some loosening. Orig. cl., defect. (GM. Apr.30; 563) £52
– – **Anr. Edn.** 1873-78. 2 vols. Fo. Lacks titles. Cont. hf. mor. W.a.f. (SBA. Jul.22; 39) *King.* £220
– – **Anr. Edn.** 1903. Vol. 35. Sm. fo. Orig. cl. (SH. Apr.9; 40) *Vaughan.* £75
– – **Anr. Edn.** Ill.:– after 'Spy' & others. N.d.-1888. Vols. 1-20. Orig. cl., spines torn. W.a.f. (CSK. Apr.24; 31) £1,000

VAN KAMPEN, Prof. N.G. & Bartlett, W.H.
- The History & Topography of Holland & Belgium. Trans.:– W.G. Fearnside. L., ca. 1850. Some slight foxing. Cont. mor., richly gt. in romantic style. (VG. Dec.16; 927) Fls. 900
– – **Anr. Edn.** Trans.:– William Gray Fearnside. N.d. Lacks 1 engr., general foxing. Disbnd. (TA. Oct.16; 276) £120
– – **Anr. Copy.** Short tear in map. Cont. embossed cf. gt. (SD. Feb.4; 222) £90

VAN LERBERGHE, Lodewijk & Ronsse, Jozef
- Audenaerdsche Mengelingen. Audenaarde, 1845-54. 6 vols. Cont. hf. roan, 4 decor. spine raised bands. (LM. Mar.21; 31) B.Frs. 32,000

VAN LOEN, Alfred
- Origin of Structure & Design. Ed.:– A. Silver & S. Levine (introductory text). [1966]. (200) numbered. Fo. Padded mor., boxed. Inscr., & with orig. self-port. sketch & A.L.s. (SG. Mar.12; 373) $100

VAN LOON, Gerard
- Histoire Metallique des XVIII Provinces des Pays-Bas. Ill.:– Houbraken after Van Mieris, Bernaris. The Hague, 1732-26. 4 vols. Lge. fo. Some browning. Cont. marb. cf., 6 decor. spine raised bands, worn. (LM. Nov.8; 120) B.Frs. 27,000

VAN LUYKEN, Johannes
- Figures du Vieux et du Nouveau Testament. Amst., ca. 1700. Fo. 18th. C. mor. by Derome le Jeune with his 1785 ticket, triple gt. fillet, dos à l'urne, inner gt. dentelles. W.a.f. (SM. Oct.8; 2054) Frs. 1,200

VAN MARLE, Raimond
- The Development of the Italian Schools of Painting. N.Y., 1970. Reprint. 19 vols. Orig. cl. (SH. Mar.6; 581) *Chaplin.* £150
– – **Anr. Copy.** (CSK. Jan.9; 108) £130

VAN PRAET, Joseph B.B.
[-] Catalogue des Livres Imprimés sur Vélin de la Bibliothèque du Roi . . . Paris, 1822-28. 1st. Edns. 10 vols. in 9. Advt. ll. before title in 2 vols. Later bds., unc. (SM. Oct.7; 1514) Frs. 2,000

VAN REENEN, J.
- Narrative of the Loss of the Grosvenor Indiaman, which was wrecked on the Coast of Caffraria on the 4th August, 1782 . . . N.p., n.d. Cl. (SSA. Apr.22; 267) R. 160

VAN RIEBEECK SOCIETY
Cape Town, 1918-69. 1st. Series. Vols. 1-50. Vol. 2 in Society bdg. & somewhat 'handled', vol. 14 rebnd. in near matching cl. (VA. May 8; 385) R. 880
– – **Anr. Edn.** Cape Town, 1931-49. Vols. 12-30. Cl. (SSA. Jan.22; 396) R. 100

- The Reports of Chavonnes & His Council, & of Van Imhoff, on the Cape, with Incidental Correspondence. Ed.:– Rt. Hon. J.X. Merriman (introduction). Cape Town, 1918. Vol. 1. Cl., lr. cover slightly stained. (SSA. Jun.18; 296) R. 540
– – **Anr. Copy.** Pres. copy from Ed. (SSA. Jan.22; 379) R. 450

VAN SINDEREN, Adrian
- Christmas Books. N.Y., priv. ptd., 1935-57. Ltd. Edns. 21 vols. only. 8vo & 4to. Cl. & bds., most in orig. s.-c.'s. Most vols. with Henry A. Ingraham's bkplt. (SG. Sep.4; 453) $130

VAN SLOETTON, Cornelius
See–NEVILLE, H. 'Cornelius Van Sloetton'

VAN VECHTEN, Carl
- Music After the Great War & Other Studies.
- Interpreters & Interpretations.–The Merry-Go-Round. N.Y., 1915-17-18. 1st. Edns. 3 vols. Cl., 3rd. title in bds. (lr. jnt. lifted). Each vol. with pres. inscr. to Mrs. Goodspeed. (PNY. Mar.4; 265) $150

VARCHI, Benedetto
- Storia Fiorentina. Cologne, 1721. Fo. 1st. imp. of pp. 639-40 & 51 lines per p. in sig. 4L. Cont. red mor., triple gt. fillet, spine gt. in compartments, inner gt. dentelles. (SM. Oct.8; 2055) Frs. 2,000

VARENIUS, Bernhard
- Cosmography & Geography. Ed.:– Richard Blome. Ill.:– Francis Lamb. 1683-80. 2 pts. in 1 vol. Fo. Lacks pp. 335/336, pp. 189-194 not consecutively bnd., 4 plts. with sm. tear in fold, some ll. & plts. slightly browned. 19th. C. roan-bkd. cf., worn, upr. cover detchd. W.a.f., from Chetham's Liby., Manchester. [Wing V103a] (C. Nov.27; 402) *Nicholson.* £260
– – **Anr. Edn.** Ed.:– Richard Blome. Ill.:– Nicolas Sanson. 1693. 3rd. Impression. Fo. Lacks 2 engraved maps (of 63), all hand-cold. in outl. with cartouches, inset arms, etc., amended dedication to maps of Great Britain & North & South America on overslip. 19th. C. hf. roan. (C. Nov.20; 277) *Bonometti.* £900
- Descriptio Regni Japoniae et Siam. 1673. 1st. Engl. Edn. Slight dampstaining. 19th. C. hf. cf., worn. [Wing V105] (S. Jun.29; 443) *Bunsei Shoin.* £70
- Geographia Generalis. Amst., 1650. 1st. Edn. 12mo. Slightly dampstained at beginning & end, wormhole, slightly affecting a few letters. Cont. limp vell. (S. Nov.4; 469) *Rawson.* £50
- Geographia Generalis, in qua Affectiones Generales Telluris Explicantur. Ed.:– Sir Isaac Newton. Camb., 1672. 1st. Edn. Cont. mott. cf. From Honeyman Collection. [Wing V106] (S. May 20; 3028) *Zeitlin & Verbrugge.* £280

VARENNES, Pierre Gaultier de
See–CHAMPLAIN Society

VARGAS Alphonsus de, Toletanus
- Lectura super primo Sententiarum. Venice, Paganinus de Paganinis, 31 Oct. 1490. Fo. Lacks final blank, some minor worming slightly affecting text. Cont. limp vell., in mor.-bkd. box. [H. 876*; BMC V p. 455; Goff V 91] (C. Apr.1; 93) *Corby.* £260

VARIARUM IMAGINUM A CELEBERRIMIS ARTIFICIBUS PICTARUM . . . Ipsae Picturae partim extant apud viduam Gerardi Reynst
Amst., n.d. Fo. 1 additional plt. Old vell.-bkd. bds., slightly soiled. (CSK. Apr.3; 17) £320

VARIGNON, Pierre
- Eclaircissemens sur l'Analyse des Infiniment Petits. Paris, 1725. 1st. Edn. 4to. Slight spotting. Cont. cf., worn. From Honeyman Collection. (S. May 20; 3032) *Goldschmidt.* £130
- Nouvelle Mécanique ou Statique. Ill.:– G. Vertue (engraved port.). Paris, 1725. 1st. Edn. 2 vols. 4to. Plt. 49 repeated, text browned, slight staining in vol. I. Cont. mott. cf., worn. Stp. of College of S. Alessandro, Milan; from Honeyman Collection. (S. May 20; 3033) *Norton.* £140
- Projet d'une Nouvelle Mechanique. Avec un Examen de l'Opinion de M. Borelli sur les Proprietez des Poids Suspendus par des Cordes. Paris, 1687. 1st. Edn. 4to. Lacks a1 (hf.-title?), some browning, title slightly soiled. 18th. C. cf.-bkd. bds. From Honeyman Collection. (S. May 20; 3031) *Hill.* £130

VARILLAS, [Antoine]
- Histoire de François Premier. Paris, 1685. L.P. 2 vols. 4to. Cont. red mor., gt., arms of Michel le

Tellier, triple gt. fillet, spine compartments gt. in pointillé incorporating lizards from arms, inner gt. dentelles, bkplt. of Thomas Anson. (SM. Oct.8; 2056) Frs. 2,800

VARLEY
See–PROUT, VARLEY & WILSON

VARLEY, John
- A Practical Treatise on Perspective . . . Ill.:– J. Gleadah, G. & F.C. Lewis after Varley. L., 1820. Fo. Slight discolouration. New hf. mor. (SPB. May 29; 427) $200

VARON MILANES de la Lengua de Milan e Prissian de Milan de la Parnonzia Milanesa
Milan, 1750. 19th. C. hf. vell. (SI. Dec.4; 595) Lire 320,000

VARRO, Marcus Terentius
See–CATO, Marcus Porcius & Varro, Marcus Terentius–PALLADIUS Rutilius Taurus Aemelianus–VICTORIUS, P.
See–CATO, Marcus Porcius & others

VARRO, Marcus Terentius, Moedrati, L. Iunii & Rutilii, Paladii
- Scriptores Rei Rusticae. Libri De Re Rustica. Paris, [Feb. 1533]. Fo. Title slightly browned. Old. cf., rebkd., worn. (S. Feb.10; 222) *Fletcher.* £80

VASARELY, Victor
- Naissances. [Koeln], [1963]. (450) numbered. 4to. 37 etchings & 1 sigd. serigraph (of 2). Wraps. (SG. Oct.23; 328) $130

VASARI, Giorgio
- Lives of the Most Eminent Painters, Sculptors, & Architects. Trans.:– Gaston duc. de Vere. L., 1912-15. 10 vols. 4to. Buckram, slightly worn, vols. 8 & 10 supplied from the de luxe edn. in gt.-decor. vell. (SG. Dec.4; 350) $425
– – **Anr. Edn.** Ltd. Edns. Cl., 1966. (1500) sigd. by printer. 2 vols. 4to. Orig. cl. gt., unc., s.-c. (SH. Feb.20; 248) *Kerrigan.* £75
- Trattato della Pittura. Ed.:– Giorgius Vasarus III. Florenz, 1619. 2nd. Edn. 18th. C. leath., gt., some sm. wormholes in spine. (R. Oct.14-18; 778) DM 650
- Le Vite de Piu Eccellenti Architetti, Pittori, et Sculptori Italiani. Firenze, 1550. 1st. Edn. 4to. Many ll. rehinged, considerably foxed & stained. Mod. linen. (SG. Mar.12; 375) $650
- Le Vite d'piu Eccellenti Pittori, Scultori et Architette. Bologna, 1647. Reprint of 2nd. (1st. only 1 compl.) Edn. of 1568. 3 vols. Hf. vell. (R. Oct.14-18; 779) DM 600
– – **Anr. Edn.** Livorno, Flor., 1767; 1772. 7 vols. 4to. Cont. vell. (SI. Dec.4; 596) Lire 600,000
– – **Anr. Edn.** Milan, 1928. 3 vols. 4to. Hf. vell. with corners. (CR. Mar.19; 489) Lire 260,000

VASCONCELLOS
- Archivo Nobiliarchico Brasileiro. Lausanne, 1908. 4to. Orig. cl. (SPB. May 5; 519) $160

VASI, Giuseppe
- Delle magnificenze di Roma antica e moderna. Rome, 1747-61. 10 vols. in 5. Ob. fo. Lr. margin of a few titles enlarged to size, apparently by publisher. Cont. sheep-bkd. marb. bds., unc. (SPB. Oct.1; 246) $5,000
– – **Anr. Copy.** Text slightly browned in parts. Cont. hf. leath. (R. Mar.31-Apr.4; 2676) DM 10,500
– – **Anr. Edn.** Rome, 1773. Ob. fo. 19th. C. hf. leath. (HK. Nov.18-21; 1231) DM 9,000
[-] [Views of Rome]. N.d. Ob. 4to. Lacks title, 56 engraved plts. only?, marginal annots. Cont. bds., worn. W.a.f. (CSK. Jun.12; 150) £220

VASI, Mariano
- Itinerario Istruttivo di Roma Antica e Moderna. Rome, 1816. 2 vols. Recent hf. cf. (TA. Jul.16; 286) £60

VASON, George
[-] An Authentic Narrative of Four Years' Residence at Tongataboo. 1810. 1st. Edn. Cont. cf., rebkd. (C. Jul.15; 107) *Lawson.* £150

VATOUT, J.
- Galerie Lithographiée . . . Paris, ca. 1825-29. 20 × 13½ ins. Over 60 mntd. litho. proofs on india paper, loose, some foxing. (SG. Nov.20; 420) $100

VAUBAN, Sebastien le Prestre de
- Der Angriff und die Vertheidigung der Festungen. Berlin, 1744-45. 1st. German Edn. 2 pts. in 1 vol.

VAUBAN, Sebastien le Prestre de – **Der Angriff und die Vertheidigung der Festungen.** *-contd.*
Some plts. with long tear & text loss. Cont. hf. leath. (R. Mar.31-Apr.4; 1784) DM 700
– **Traité de l'Attaque et de la Defense des Places.** The Hague, 1737; 1742. 2 vols. Lge. 4to. Cont. mott. cf., spines gt. (SG. Oct.30; 363) $475
– – **Anr. Edn.** The Hague, 1742-43. 2 vols. 4to. Some sm. tears, slightly browned or soiled in parts. Cont. cf., not unif., worn, 2 sm. tears in spine. (H. May 21/22; 715) DM 450

VAUGHAN, David
See–SAUTHIER, Claude Joseph & Vaughan, David

VAUGHAN, Henry
– **Poems.** Ill.:– R.A. Maynard & H.W. Bray. Gregy. Pr., 1924. (500). Orig. cl.-bkd. bds., unc. (SH. Feb.20; 205) *Maggs.* £80

VAUGHAN, William
– **The Golden Grove** . . . 1608. Sm. hole in 1 lf. affecting text, last lf. torn & reprd. affecting text, verso soiled. Mod. mor. [STC 24611] (C. Nov.19; 41) *Quaritch.* £350
– **The Narrative of Captain David Woodard & Four Seamen, who . . . Surrendered themselves up to the Malays** . . . 1804. 2 pts. in 1 vol. Cont. russ. gt., jnts. torn. (SBA. Jul.14; 53) *Ad Orientem.* £62

VAUGONDY, Robert de
– **Nouvel Atlas Portatif.** Paris, 1790. Engraved title & 16 maps only cold. in outl., including Britain, England, 4 Mappe-Mondes, etc. Orig. bdg. (P. Feb.19; 138) *Short.* £50

VAURIE, C.
– **Tibet & its Birds.** 1972. Ltd. Sigd. Edn. Hf. red mor. gt. by Sangorski. (P. Nov.13; 230) *Hosain.* £50

VAUTS, Moses à
– **The Husband's Authority Unvail'd** . . . 1650. 1st. Edn. Sm. 4to. Some dampstaining, lacks last (blank?) lf.?, M2 torn & reprd. Disbnd. [Wing V163] (S. Apr.7; 377) *Laywood.* £70

VAUX, Calvert
– **Villas & Cottages.** N.Y., 1857. 1st. Edn. 1 chromolitho. plt. of advts., occasional light foxing. Orig. gt. decor. cl. (CB. May 27; 205) Can. $130

VAZ, Thomé
See–CORREA, Joâe de Medeiros–VAZ, Thomé

VECCHIA MILANO
– **Una Raccolta di 10 Portafogli.** N.d. 4to. 10 ll., 8 with photos, 1 with A.L.s., sigd. ports. etc., 1 with cheques, etc. Hf. red mor. (SI. Dec.4; 597) Lire 2,600,000

VECELLIO, Cesare
– **Costumes Anciens et Modernes. Habiti Antichi et Moderni di Tutto il Mondo.** Paris, 1859-60. 2 vols. Cont. hf. mor. (SI. Dec.4; 599) Lire 200,000
– – **Anr. Edn.** Paris, 1860. 2 vols. Qtr. mor. (SG. Oct.30; 364) $160
– **De gli Habiti Antichi.** Venice, 1590. 1st. Edn. Lacks final blank lf., slight blank marginal defects at F7, K1, T2 & Q'2, slight browning. Early 19th. C. Fr. str-grd. mor. gt., border of crossed drawer handle tools, spine gt. with 5 raised bands. Bkplts. of Henry J.B. Clements & John A. Saks. (CNY. Oct.1; 135) $2,300
– **Habiti Antichi et Moderni di Tutto il Mondo.** Venice, 1598. 2nd. Edn. 19th. C. cf. [Sabin 98732] (S. Nov.25; 365) *Zanesco.* £700
– – **Anr. Copy.** Lacks A8 & 18, title & some headlines cropped, some stains & a few minor repairs. Vell. gt. (SPB. Jul.28; 450) $275
– – **Anr. Copy.** Stain on last p., some borders lightly torn, 3 ll. from smaller copy(?). 19th. C. hf. mor., spine worn. (SI. Dec.4; 598) Lire 1,600,000
– – **Anr. Edn.** Venice, 1664. 3rd. Edn. A few ll. slightly soiled. Mod. red mor. [Sabin 98732 [note]] (S. Feb.23; 363) *Sinistri.* £370
– – **Anr. Copy.** Sm. 8vo. 413 (of 415) plts. Old roan, decor. spine. (HD. Dec.5; 207) Frs. 2,000
– – **Anr. Copy.** Later leath., blind-stpd. decor., narrow border, gt. spine. [Sabin 98732] (D. Dec.11-13; 1270) DM 1,700
– – **Anr. Copy.** 411 (of 415) lge. text woodcuts, some light soiling, some ll. narrower trimmed probably from anr. copy, lacks pp. 7-10 each with 1 figure. Old leath., spine old renewed, mostly unc. (R. Mar.31-Apr.4, 1575) DM 850

VEDUTE ANTICHE e Moderne le piu interessanti della Citta di Roma–Raccolta di Vedute Antiche e Moderne della Citta di Roma
Rome, ca. 1800; 1816. 2 works in 1 vol. 4to. Cont. hf. russ. (SBA. Mar.4; 97) *L'Acquaforte.* £50

VEEN, Otto van
See–VAENIUS i.e. Veen, Otto van

VEER, Gerrit de
– **Tre Navigationi Fatte dagli Olandesi, e Zelandesi.** Trans.:– Giovanni Giunio. Venice, 1599. 1st. Italian Edn. Sm. 4to. Last 4 ll. slightly defect. in inner margin, lacks last blank, some ll. slightly spotted. Disbnd. (S. Jun.22; 197) *Quaritch.* £60

VEGA, Garcilasso de la
See–GARCILASSO de la Vega

VEGA CARPIO, Lope Felix de
– **The Star of Seville.** Ill.:– Charles Thomas. Gregy. Pr., 1935. (175). Orig. mor., stpd. in blind & gt. (SH. Feb.20; 212) *Maggs.* £210

VEGETIUS RENATUS, Flavius
– **De Re Militari.** Rome, 29 Jan. 1487. 4to. Mod. wraps. [Goff S343] (SG. May 14; 219) $425
– **De Re Militari Libri quatuor [with works by Frontinus, Aelianus Tacticus, & Modestus].** Ed.:– G. Bude. Paris, 1535. 3rd. Wechel Edn. Fo. A few letters erased on A3r & A4v. 18th. C. cf., gt., slightly worn, fly-lf. inscr. 'de la Bibliothèque de P.D. Lemazurier . . .' Bkplt. of Dr. Lucien-Graux; from Honeyman Collection. (S. May 20; 3034) *Hughes.* £900
– **Du Fait de Guerre et Fleur de Chevalerie Quatre Livres [und Andere Werke].** Trans.:– N. Volkyr de Serouville. Paris, 1536. 1st. Fr. Edn. Fo. Cont. style old vell., sigd. Devauchelle. [BMSTC 436] (D. Dec.11-13; 52) DM 18,000
– **Vier Bücher der Ritterschafft.** [Augsburg], 1534. 2nd. German Edn. Fo. 137 woodcuts, most full-p. 19th. C. leath., gt. spine, soiled. (R. Oct.14-18; 168) DM 6,000

VEGETIUS Renatus, Flavius; Aelianus Tacticus; Frontinus, Sextus Julius–MODESTUS
– **De Re Militari; De Instruendis Aciebus; Strategematicon.**–De Vocabulis Rei Militaris. Rome, Eucharius Silber, 29 Jan., 15 Feb., 1 Jun. 1487; 7 Jun. 1487. 4 works in 1 vol., 1st. 3 iss. as 1 4to. 1st. work lacks blank (hl), slight browning thro.-out. Cont. vell., slightly wormed & worn. [H. 15913*; BMC IV p. 107; H. 11444; BMC IV 108] (C. Apr.1; 94) *Maggs.* £680

VEHSE, Eduard
– **Geschichte der Deutschen Höfe seit der Reformation.** Hamburg, 1851-60. 48 vols. in 22. Soiled in parts. Cont. hf. leath. & 2 cont. hf. linen. (R. Mar.31-Apr.4; 1889) DM 2,700

VEITCH, James H.
– **Hortus Veitchi.** 1906. Ltd. Edn. for Private Circulation. L.P. 4to. Hf. mor., s.-c. (SBA. Jul.23; 679) *Chesters.* £75

VELASCO, Alfonso Alberto de
– **Exaltacion de la Divina Misericordia en la Milagrosa Renovacion de la Soberana Imagen de Christo que se venera en la Iglesia . . . de esta Ciudad de Mexico.** Mexico, 1807. Reprint. 4to. Cont. vell., leath. ties. [Sabin 98788] (SG. Mar.5; 315) $140

VELAZAUEZ MINAYA, Francisco
– **Esfera, forma del Mundo, con vna breue Descripcion del Mapa.** Madrid, 1628. Wormhole affecting title & first ll., fore-margins stained & defect., many reprd., obscuring or affecting text, corner of 2Fl missing with loss of text. Cont. limp vell., detchd. [Sabin 49191] (SPB. May 5; 520) $300

VELDE, C.W.M. van de
– **Le Pays d'Israel.** Paris, map dtd. 1858. Ob. fo. Lacks plt. no. 74 (of 100). Hf. mor. gt. As a collection of plts., w.a.f. (P. Sep.11; 11) £800

VELIKAYA MOSKVA [Great Moscow]
Ed.:– [B.F. Geier]. St. Petersb., 1905. Trial no. Fo. Unbnd. (SH. Feb.5; 139) *De la Casa.* £55

VELIUS, D.
– **Chroniick van Hoorn** . . . Hoorn, 1648. 4th. printing. 3 pts. in 1 vol. 4to. Cont. vell. (VG. Dec.17; 1571) Fls. 1,700
– – **Anr. Copy.** Browned, a few blank margins lightly stained. Cont. mott. cf., back gt. (VG. Dec.17; 1572) Fls. 1,600

VELPEAU, Alfred Armand Louis Marie
– **Embryologie.** Ill.:– A. Chazal. Paris, 1833. 1st. Edn. Fo. Stp. on verso of plts., some foxing thro.-out. Ptd. bds., spine very worn. From Brooklyn Academy of Medicine. (SG. Jan.29; 415) $100

VELSCHIUS, Georgius Hieronymus
– **Commentarius in Ruzname Naurus sive Tabulae Aequinoctiales Novi Persarum & Turcarum Anni.** Ill.:– Melchior Haffner. Augsburg, 1676. 1st. Edn. Sm. 4to. Mod. hf. mor. From Honeyman Collection. (S. May 20; 3036) *Hughes.* £380

VENABLES, Col. Robert
– **The Experienced Angler.** L., 1825. 1st. Gosden Edn. 12mo. Cont. cf. (SG. Oct.16; 497) $180
– – **Anr. Edn.** L., 1825. L.P. reprint of 1662 Edn. With a 23 p. memoir of author. Cont. hf. mor., worn, ex-liby. (SG. Dec.11; 109) $100
See–MARKHAM, Gervase & Venables, Robert
See–WALTON, Izaak, Cotton, Charles & Venables, Col. Robert

VENAULT DE CHARMAILLY, Col.
See–BURGOYNE, Lieut. Gen. John–VENAULT DE CHARMILLY, Col.

VENEGAS, Miguel
– **A Natural & Civil History of California.** 1759. 1st. Edn. in Engl. 2 vols. Liby. stp. on plts. & titles. 19th. C. hf. mor. From Chetham's Liby., Manchester. [Sabin 98845] (C. Nov.27; 405) *Arkway.* £170
– – **Anr. Copy.** Cont. cf., jnts. brkn. [Sabin 98845] (SG. Oct.9; 247) $800

VENERES UTI Observantur in Gemmis Antiquis.
N.d. 2 pts. in 1 vol. Text in Fr. & Engl., outer margin of 1 lf. reprd. Later marb. cf., gt. (CSK. Mar.13; 5) £60

VENETTE, Nicolas
– **Abhandlung von denen Geheimnissen Keuscher Liebes-Wercke im gesegneten Kinder-Zeugen.** Dresden & Leipzig, 1729. Slightly dampstained & browned in places. Cont. blind-stpd., reprd. (S. Feb.23; 120) *Leisten.* £50
[–] **The Art of Pruning Fruit-Trees.** 1685. Some dampstaining & worming with loss of a few letters. Old cf., lacks spine, upr. cover detchd. [Wing V187] (CSK. Feb.20; 108) £65

VENGROV, Natan
– **Khvoi.** Ill.:– E. Turova. Petrograd, [1919]. (?Ltd. numbered Edn.). Orig. wraps. by E. Turova, spine torn. (SH. Feb.6; 537) *Quaritch.* £75
– **Sebe samomu [To Myself].** Ill.:– N. Lyubavina. [Petrograd], n.d. (125) numbered. Orig. wraps. by N. Lyubavina. (SH. Feb.6; 539) *Quaritch.* £100
– **Segodnya [Today].** Ill.:– V. Ermolaeva. Petrograd, n.d. (125). Orig. wraps. by V. Ermolaeva. (SH. Feb.6; 540) *Quaritch.* £140

VENICE
– **Album delle Principali Vedute di Venezia.** Ill.:– M. Moro. [Venice], ca. 1854. Ob. fo. Slightly browned in parts. Orig. hf. linen, worn, soiled. (H. May 21/22; 412) DM 600
– **Forestière Illuminato . . . della Citta di Venezia.** Venice, 1761. Plts. slightly offset, a few prelim. margins dampstained. Cont. vell. (SBA. Mar.4; 129) *Spencer.* £155
– **Il Gran Teatro di Venezia, ovvero raccolta delle principali Vedute e Pitture che in essa si contengono.** Ill.:– after Tiepolo, Manaigo & others. [Venice], ca. 1720. Fo. 1 plt. defaced at foot, 2 shaved or cropped, sm. faults in 2 others, a few spots, 2 other doubl-p. views inserted from anr. work. Cont. hf. cf., bds., worn. W.a.f. (C. Feb.25; 228) *Hammond.* £3,800
– **Venezia Monumentale Pittoresca.** Ill.:– after M. Moro. Venice, ca. 1850. 2 vols. Ob. fo. A few text ll. & plts. soiled in margins. Orig. linen. (R. Mar.31-Apr.4; 2681) DM 6,000

VENN, Capt. Thomas & others
– **Military & Maritime Discipline.** 1672. 3 pts. in 1. Fo. Slightly browned or stained in places, a few minor repairs to margins. Old cf., rebkd. (TA. Jul.16; 364) £250

VENNE, Adrian van de
– **Sinne-Vonck op den Hollandtschen Turf** . . . Ill.:– D.v. Bremden (engraved port. of author). The Hague, priv. ptd., 1634. 2 pts. in 1 vol. Sm. 4to. Some light stains, owners' entries. Cont. vell. (VG. Dec.17; 1574) Fls. 850

– Tafereel van de Belacchende Werelt, en des Selfs Geluckige Eeuwe . . . The Hague, 1635. 1st. Edn. 4to. Extra engraved title. Early mott. cf. gt. (SG. Sep.25; 313) $950

VENNER, Tobias
– Via Recta ad Vitam Longam . . . (with) a . . . **Treatise of the Famous Baths of Bathe** . . . (and) an **Accurate Treatise Concerning Tobacco.** 1650. 5th. Edn. 4to. Some browning, slight dampstaining, a little worming, not affecting text. Cont. cf., slightly worn, rebkd. [Wing V195; Sabin 98890] (S. Apr.7; 378) *Targett.* £60

VENTURE: an Annual of Art & Literature.
Ed.:– Laurence Housman & W. Somerset Maugham. Ill.:– Arthur Rackham, Charles Ricketts & others. L., 1903; 1905. 2 vols. 4to. Linen-bkd. pict. bds. stained, & cold. pict. cl., 1st. vol. unc., unopened. Raymond M. Sutton, Jr., copy. (SG. May 7; 293) $140

VENTURI, Adolphe
– La Galleria Crespi in Milano. Milan, 1900. 4to. Publisher's bdg. (CR. Mar.19; 181) Lire 400,000
– La Pittura del Quattrocento nell'Emilia. Bologna, 1931. (300) numbered. 4to. Publisher's hf. cf. gt. (CR. Mar.19; 186) Lire 220,000
– Storia dell'Arte Italiana. Milan, 1901-40. 11 vols. in 25. Mod. mor., gt. spines, s.-c.'s. (SH. Oct.9; 197) *Zwemmer.* £1,050
– – **Anr. Edn.** Milan, 1907. Publisher's bdg., orig. wraps. preserved. (CR. Mar.19; 182) Lire 240,000
– Storia dell'Arte Italiana, vol VII la Pittura del Quatrocento. Milan, 1911-15. 4 vols. Orig. wraps. (CR. Mar.19; 183) Lire 400,000
– Storia dell'Arte Italiana. Vol. IX la Pittura del 500. Milan, 1925-34. 7 vols. Orig. wraps. (CR. Mar.19; 184) Lire 700,000

VENTURI, Giambatista
– Commentari sopra la Storia e le Teorie dell'Ottica . . . Bologna, 1814. 1st. Edn. Vol. 1, [all publd.]. 4to. 4 ll. (pp. 79-86) misbnd., some foxing & marginal staining, sm. repair to foot of title where stp. has been removed. Orig. wraps., worn. From Honeyman Collection. (S. May 20; 3037) *Zeitlin & Verbrugge.* £190

VENTURI, Lionello
– Cezanne, Son Art, Son Oeuvre. Paris, 1936. [1st. Edn.?]. (1000) 2 vols., including plt. vol. 4to. Orig. ptd. wraps., slightly soiled, partly unopened, unc. (C. Jul.22; 169) *Sims & Reed.* £850
– – **Anr. Copy.** Numbered. Gt. cl. (PNY. Mar.4; 117) $1,700
– – **Anr. Edn.** Paris, 1936. 2 vols. 4to. Publisher's decor. cl. s.-c. (HD. Dec.5; 208) Frs. 10,000
– La Collezione Gualino. Rome, 1926. (350) numbered. 1 vol. Fo. Publisher's vell. (CR. Jun.11; 418) Lire 600,000
– Marc Chagall. N.Y., 1945. 1st. 'Ordinary' Edn., (1450) numbered. 4to. Errata slip is inserted. Wraps. over bds., d.-w. Contains at upr. blank lf. orig. watercolour drawing, inscr. & sigd. 'For Mrs. [Bobsy] Goodspeed . . .' (PNY. Mar.4; 123) $4,000
– – **Anr. Edn.** Ill.:– Marc Chagall. Lausanne, 1956. Orig. cl., d.-w., s.-c. Pres. copy inscr. by artist, with ink drawing. (SH. Nov.21; 265) *Droller.* £95

See–PISSARRO, L.R. & Venturi, Lionello

VERA, Gerardus de
– Tre Navigationi . . . Trans.:– Giovan Guinio Parisio. Venice, 1599. Sm. 4to. Old vell. (HD. Dec.5; 209) Frs. 3,000

VERACRUZ, Alfonso de
– Speculum Coniugiorvm. Mexico, 1556. Sm. 4to. All but a fragment of title torn away, worming affecting some ll., lacks pp. 275-87. 19th. C. cf.-bkd. bds., covers detchd. (SPB. May 5; 522) $2,700

VERARDUS, Carolus
– Historia Baetica [with Marcellinus Verardus, Elegiae]. [Valladolid], [Pedro Giraldi & Miguel de Planes], ca. 1497. 4to. Woodcut initial capitals, spaces for some initials, with guide letters, lacks title-p., supplied in facs., ink inscrs. on blank verso of final lf. Mor., spine gt.-lettered, by Sangorski & Sutcliffe. From the collection of Eric Sexton. [Goff V126, H. 15843] (CNY. Apr.8; 184) $9,500

VERBURG, Isaak
See–SUIKERS, Geerlof & Verburg, Isaak

VERCELLENSIS, Johannes
– Sermones Vademecum . . . [Strassburg], [J. Pruss], ca. 1488-93. 4to. Capitals supplied in red, some browning, slight dampstaining to last few ll. Cont. blind-stpd. cf., rather worn, lacks clasps, spine defect. From Heber liby. with stp. [BMC I, 128; Goff J443; HC 9431*] (S. May 5; 6) *Quaritch.* £320

VERDIZOTTI, Giovanni Mario
– Cento Favole Morali. Venice, 1577. 2nd. Edn. 4to. Worming of 5 blank fore-corners reprd., Ragley Hall bkplt. 18th. C. red mor. by Derome le Jeune with his ticket, triple gt. fillet, flat spine gt. with sm. lozenge in each compartment, inner gt. dentelles. (SM. Oct.8; 2058) Frs. 3,800
– – **Anr. Edn.** Venice, 1599. 4to. Title reprd., 3 blank fore-e's. reprd., 2 marginal tears reprd., some ll. browned, 18th. C. Fr. inscr. on fly-lf. Late 17th. C. red mor., gt. fillet. (SM. Oct.8; 2059) Frs. 1,200
[–] – **Anr. Edn.** [Ven], [1613?]. Slightly browned, lacks title. Cont. vell. (HK. May 12-14; 1627) DM 420

VERDUN DE LA CRENNE, J.R.A., Marquis de & Others
– Voyage fait par Ordre du Roi en 1771 et 1772 en diverses Parties de l'Europe, de l'Afrique et de l'Amerique. Paris, 1778. 2 vols. 4to. Lacks map, sig. of J.T. Stanley of Alderley, 1789, on Fly-lf. & his bkplt. Cont. red mor., arms of C.A. de Calonne, triple gt. fillet, spines gt. in compartments, inner gt. dentelles. [Sabin 98960] (SM. Oct.8; 2060) Frs. 3,200

VERE, Sir Francis
– The Commentaries. Camb., 1657. 1st. Edn. Cont. cf., rebkd. [Wing V420] (C. Nov.20; 277a) *Malkiewicz.* £160
– – **Anr. Copy.** Sm. fo. Upr. blank margin of hf.-title defect. & renewed, some ll. stained from inner margins, a few spots. Cont. mott. cf., recased & rebkd., clasps. Inscr. to Hon. Philip Skippon, Major-General, from 'W.D.' [Wing V240] (S. Jun.9; 40) *Forum.* £75

VERGERIO, Pietro Paulo, the Younger, Bp. of Capo d'Istria
[–] **Sopra le Letere volgari di M. Claudio Tolomei Vescovo di Curzola.–Delle Commissioni e Faculta che Papa Giulio 111 ha daro a M. Paolo Odescalco Comasco suo Nuncio** . . . [Basle], 1554; 1553; 1553; 1552; 1553. 6 works in 1 vol. Blank margins with 1 or 2 repairs. 18th. C. mor. by Derome le Jeune with his ticket & bdr's. note on verso of last blank, triple gt. fillet, spine gt. in compartments, inner gt. dentelles. Gaignat–Girardot de Préfond copy. (SM. Oct.8; 2062) Frs. 2,800

VERGIER, Jacques
– Oeuvres. L., 1780. 3 vols. 18mo. Red mor. by Cazin. From the Liby. of Guy Pellion. (HD. Apr.8; 309) Frs. 1,300

VERGILIUS, Polidorus
– An Abridgement of the Notable Works of . . . Ed.:– Thomas Langley. Ca. 1560. Lacks blank portions of title, just touching woodcut, reprd., title dust-soiled, upr. margin of A2 reprd., touching 1 letter, some staining, dust-soiling, etc. 19th. C. cf., rebkd., spine brkn. & lr. cover detchd. From the collection of Eric Sexton. [STC 24658] (C. Apr.15; 154) *Elliott.* £50
– Adagiorum Opus. Basle, 1525. Fo. Bds., Signet liby. gt. stp. on covers. (C. Jul.16; 230) *Taylor.* £70
– De Inuentoribus Reru(m). Venice, 13 Jul. 1503. Sm. 4to. Heavily corrected in later (late 16th. or early 17th. C.?) hand, presumably for new edn., slight browning, a little worming & a few holes slightly affecting text. Mod. decor. bds. From liby. of André L. Simon. (S. May 18; 194) *Facchi.* £160
– – **Anr. Edn.** Venice, 1507. Sm. 4to. Some worming, mainly marginal, stained at beginning & end. cont. marginalia, inscrs. on title. Old limp bds. From Honeyman Collection. (S. May 20; 3038) *Hoppen.* £180
– – **Anr. Edn.** Amst., 1671. 24mo. Crimson str.-grd. mor., triple gt. fillet borders, spines gt., gt. dentelles, by Bradel. Armorial Dogmersfield Liby. bkplt., Mortimer Schiff's mor. bkplt. (SG. Sep.25; 49) $475
– De Rerum Inventoribus Libri VIII. Et de Prodigiis libri III. Leiden, 1644. 12mo. 18th. C. red. str.-grd. mor., gt., by Roger Payne. The

Syston Park-Robert Hoe copy; from Honeyman Collection. (S. May 20; 3040) *Williams.* £50

VERGNAUD, N.
– L'Art de Créer les Jardins . . . Ill.:– Sabattier, Leborne & others. Paris, 1839. Fo. 26 hand-finished cold. lithos., some double-p., 5 with moveable overslips. Cont. mor.-bkd. bds., spine gt., rebkd., orig. spine preserved. (C. Jul.15; 108) *Maggs.* £950

VERHAEREN, Emile
– Helenas Heimkehr. Nachgedichtet von St. Zweig. [Leipzig], [1909]. (270) Orig. hf. vell. Stefan Zweig's MS. ded. to Fritz Engel of 1 Aug. 1909 on end-paper. (H. May 21/22; 1402a) DM 950
– Les Petits Vieux. Ill.:– Lucien Pissarro. Eragny Pr. 1901. (230). Ob. 16mo. Orig. bds. Front paste-down with ptd. ex-libris of Harry Graf Kessler. (S. Jul.31; 22) *Appleton.* £170

VERHANDLUNGEN Der Zusammenkunft der Prediger und Almosenpfleger der Mennonisten Gemeinden des Waterloo Berzerks
Berlin, Apr.13, 1844. Some foxing. Unbnd. (CB. Feb.18; 123) Can. $130

VERHEERLYKT KLEEFSCHLAND of Kabinet van Kleefsche Oudheden en Gezigten
Ill.:– P. van Liender after J. de Beyer. Amst., 1792. 2nd. Edn. 4to. Lacks 4 engraved views, sm. hole in lower corner of 1 plt. reprd. Cont. hf. cf. (VG. Oct.13; 92) Fls. 14,000

VERHEIDEN, Jacobus
– Praestantium aliquot Theologorum . . . **effigies.** Ill.:– Hondius. The Hague, 1602. 1st. Edn. Fo. 45 engraved ports. (of 50, 4 loosely inserted in facs.), 1 additionally in MS. facs.), lacks Cl & 3, D2, E1, 2B2 & 3 & last blank, quires G & H misbnd. Cont. limp vell., Sutherland arms on upr. cover, bkplt. of Marquis of Stafford. (S. Dec.8; 124) *Harlinghausen.* £70

VERHEYEN, Philipp
– Anatomiae. Brussels, 1710. 2nd. Edn. 2 vols. 4to. Sig. removed from titles, slightly browned in places. Cont. cf., spines gt. (S. Feb.23; 122) *Rota.* £90

VERKLEINERTER HAND-ATLAS In LX Karten über alle Theile der Erde
Weimar, 1806. Ob. fo. 42 (of 60) outl. cold. copper engraved maps. Loose, no bdg. (R. Oct.14-18; 1569) DM 500

VERLAINE, Paul
– Les Amies. Segovia, 1870. (100) on papier verge, 2nd. Edn. 12mo. Ex-libris. Mor. gt. sigd. by Lepretre. (D. Dec.11-13; 974) DM 1,500
– – **Anr. Edn.** Ill.:– Gustave Buchet. Paris, 1921. (475), numbered. 4to. Unsewn in orig. wraps., backstrip defect., unc. (SH. Nov.20; 17) *Schaller.* £240
– Amour. Paris, 1888. 1st. Edn. 12mo. Occasional spotting, sig. on title. Crushed mor., gt., orig. sraps. bnd. in, by Zaehnsdorf, partly unc. (S. Feb.10; 473) *Crete.* £80
– La Bonne Chanson. 1870. Mor., ornam. mor. doubl., by Marius Michel. A.N., on tinted vell. (HD. Oct.10; 169) Frs. 3,800
– Elégies. Paris, 1893. 1st. Edn. Mor., gt., by Kieffer, orig. wraps. bnd. in, s.-c. (SM. Oct.8; 2283) Frs. 1,200
– Fêtes Galantes. Paris, 1869. 1st. Edn. Sm. 12mo. Red mor. by Blanchetière, triple gt. fillet round covers, spine decor. with raised bands, wrap. slightly defect., wrap. & spine preserved, s.-c., inside dentelle. (HD. Jun.25; 425) Frs. 1,800
– – **Anr. Edn.** Paris, 1903. (125); on vell., numbered. 4to. With separate black-&-white set of all engrs. Bradel tree cf., wrap. (HD. Jun.25; 432) Frs. 1,000
– – **Anr. Edn.** Ill.:– George Barbier. Paris, 1928. (1025). 4to. Orig. pict. wraps. by Barbier, spine torn, unc. (SBA. Mar.4; 204) *Fletcher.* £520
– – **Anr. Edn.** Ill.:– Marie Laurencin. Paris, 1944. (263) numbered. 4to. Red mor., upr. cover with embossed design with mor. onlays tooled in gt., mor. onlays at edge of cover, cf. doubls., red watered silk end ll., orig. wraps. bnd. in, cf.-bkd. folder, s.-c., by Bonfils. (SH. Nov.21; 384) *Klusmann.* £450

– Odes en son Honneur. Paris, 1931. (100) on Hollande. 4to. Orig. bds. 16 orig. ills. (LM. Nov.8; 142) B.Frs. 23,000
– Parallèlement. Ill.:– Chimot (etchings). Paris, 1934. (23) on old Jap., numbered. 4to. 1st state (comments in blood-red), 2nd state (comments in

VERLAINE, Paul -*contd.*
black), & definitive state, complete dossier of 1 plt., 2 orig. drawings. Mor. by Trinckvel, wrap. preserved, s.-c. Copy reserved for artist & his friends. (SM. Feb.11; 294)   Frs. 13,000
– – **Anr. Edn.** Ill.:– Lobel-Riche. Paris, [1947]. (230); (170) on Arches vell. 4to. With extra plt. Red mor. by Durand, mosaic with bands & gt. fillets, smooth spine similarly decor., wrap. & spine preserved, s.-c. Sigd. dedication by artist. (HD. Feb.27; 240)   Frs. 2,500
– **Poèmes d'Amour.** Ed.:– André Suarès (Preface). Ill.:– Édouard Chimot. Paris, 1937. (515) numbered. 4to. Hf. mor., orig. wraps. bnd. in, s.-c., worn. (SH. Nov.20; 27)   Ayres. £130
– **Poèmes Saturniens.** Paris, 1866. 1st. Edn. 12mo. Some foxing. Hf. chagrin, smooth decor. spine, wrap. reprd., wrap. & spine preserved. (HD. Jun.25; 424)   Frs. 1,300
– **Romances sans Paroles.** Sens, [Paris], 1874. [300]. Mor., inner gt. dentelles, partly unc. Inscr. to M. Grandmorigues. (SM. Oct.8; 2285)   Frs. 3,200
– – **Anr. Edn.** 1874. 1st. Edn. 12mo. Hf. chagrin by Ronleu, smooth decor. spine, wrap. & spine preserved. (HD. Jun.25; 427)   Frs. 2,700
– **Sagesse.** Paris, 1881. [1st. Edn.?]. Vell., by Paul Vié. Ernest Chausson's copy, port of Verlaine on Japon mince & note of author bnd. in, Chausson's sig. on wrap. (HD. Oct.10; 170)   Frs. 5,000
– – **Anr. Copy.** Sewed, folder, s.-c. (HD. Jun.25; 428)   Frs. 2,500
– – **Anr. Edn.** Ill.:– Maurice Denis. Paris, 1911. (250). 4to. With no. 244 of 'Hommes d'aujourd'hui' about Paul Verlaine. In sheets, wrap., publisher's folder. (HD. Dec.5; 210)   Frs. 2,200
– – **Anr. Edn.** Ill.:– Maurice Denis engraved by Beltrand. 1916. On Hollande. 4to. Ll., box. (HD. Jun.30; 83)   Frs. 2,700

VERLET, Pierre & others
– **Sèvres.** Paris, 1953. 2 vols. & prospectus. 4to. Orig. cl., d.-w.'s., prospectus in orig. ring-bkd. rexine. (S. Sep.30; 447)   £200

VERMIGLI, Pietro
See–MARTYR or Vermigli, Pietro

VERMOREL, V.
See–VIALA, P. & Vermorel, V.

VERNAY, F.J. & others
– **The Motograph Moving Picture Book.** Ill.:– Vernay, Yorick & others. 1898. Lge. 4to. 1 plt. cleanly torn, with the 'Transparency' loosely inserted. Orig. cl.-bkd. pict. bds., cover design by H. de Toulouse Lautrec, slightly soiled. (CSK. May 15; 72)   £110

VERNE, Jules
– **Robur-le-Conquérant- Un Billet de Loterie. Fritt-Flacc.** Ill.:– Bennet & Roux. Paris, n.d. 1 lf. torn. Buckram by Engel, elephant on cover, lighthouse on spine. A.L.s. dtd. 14 Jan. 1886. (HD. Feb.27; 246)   Frs. 2,000
– **Les Voyages Extraordinaires.** Paris, ca. 1890-1910. 14 works in 10 vols. 4to. Orig. linen. (R. Mar.31-Apr.4; 676)   DM 1,200
– **Works.** N.Y., [1911]. 15 vols. Slight browning. Hf. red mor., gt., heads of spines chipped. (SPB. Jul.28; 451) $250
– – **Anr. Edn.** N.Y., n.d. Edn. Couronnée, (50). 15 vols. Mor. gt., red fleur de lis inlays on gt. panel, spine & corners. (SPB. May 6; 351) $1,900

VERNER, Capt. Willoughby W.C.
– **History & Campaigns of the Rifle Brigade 1800-13.** 1912-19. 2 vols. Sm. 4to. Orig. cl. (P. Oct.23; 264)   Delotz. £50
– **Sketches in the Soudan.** 1885. Ob. fo. Publisher's advt. lf. bnd. in at rear. Orig. ptd. bds., soiled & worn. (TA. Jan.22; 232)   £60
– – **Anr. Copy.** Ob. 4to. Orig. bds., worn. (CSK. Nov.7; 215)   £50

VERNET, Carle
– **Campagnes des Français sous le Consulat et l'Empire.** Paris, ca. 1860. Lge. fo. Orig. linen, slightly loose. (R. Mar.31-Apr.4; 1890)   DM 1,700
– **Cris de Paris.** Paris, ca. 1820. 2 vols. Fo. Ptd. on blue india paper & mntd. on grey bd., all on guards, lacks title. 19th. C. red hf. mor., gt. title on spine. (S. Oct.21; 502)   Lockwood. £1,200
– – **Anr. Edn.** Paris, n.d. Fo. 50 plts. (numbered 51-100) only, 1 detchd., margins soiled, some

slightly dampstained, lacks cold. title. Orig. mor.-bkd. bds. W.a.f. (CSK. Sep.26; 121)   £280

VERNET, Carle & Lami, Horace & Eugene
– **Collection des Uniformes des Armées Françaises.** 1822. 4to. Red mor., ivory plaque set in upr. cover, gt. inner dentelle, silk doubls. & end-ll., by Pagnant. (HD. Jun.30; 84)   Frs. 3,600
[–] **Collection Raisonnée des Uniformes Francais.** Paris, 1825. 4to. Hf. mor. Rubberstps. of the Tsarskoye-Selo Palace Liby. & the Czarevitch on hf.-title. (SG. Oct.30; 365) $750

VERNET, Claude Joseph & Hue, J.
– **Les Ports de France.** Paris, 1812. Orig. bds. (P. Jun.11; 321)   Schapiro. £70

VERNEUIL, Ad. & M.P.
– **Kaleidoscope.** Ill.:– J. Saude (colouring). Paris, n.d. Fo. 15 (of 20) plts. Loose in orig. cl.-bkd. portfo., slightly worn & soiled, ties. (SH. Nov.20; 229)   Ayres. £80

VERNEY, Frances Parthenope
– **Memoirs of the Verney Family during the Civil War . . . /During the Commonwealth . . .** 1892-99. 4 vols. Hf. mor. with gt. decor. spines by Bickers & Son Ltd. (TA. Mar.19; 253)   £50

VERNIER, Charles
– **Au Quartier Latin.** Charivari, n.d. Fo. Cl., worn. (BS. Jun.11; 201)   £60

VERNOR, Hood & Sharpe
– **British Atlas.** 1810. 4to. Cold. county maps, town plans. Hf. mor. gt., upr. cover detchd. (P. Dec.11; 159)   Kidd. £360

VERRI, Pietro
[–] **Storia di Milano.** Milan, 1783-98. 1st. Edn. 2 vols. 4to. Mod. hf. mor., cont. wraps bnd. in, partly unc. (SI. Dec.4; 601)   Lire 600,000

VERRUE, la Comtesse de
– **Catalogue des Livres.** Paris, 1737. Some ll. wormed at end. Later mor. by Galwey of Dublin with his ticket. (SM. Oct.7; 1516)   Frs. 1,600

VER SACRUM. Organ der Vereinigung Bildender Künstler Osterreichs
Ed.:– W. Schrermann & A. Roller. Vienna, 1898. Year 1, Pts. 1-12, no special issues. In pts. with orig. wraps., loose in orig. hf. leath., spine defect. (R. Oct.14-18; 1103)   DM 460

VERSAILLES GARDEN STATUARY
Ill.:– Le Potre, Edelinck & Chauveau. [Prints dtd. 1672-81]. Fo. 56 engraved plts. depicting statues & ornaments in the gardens of Versailles, 1 torn. 18th. C. cf.-bkd. bds., worn, edges unc. (C. Feb.25; 207)   Marlborough. £240

VERSCHAFFELT, Ambroise
– **Nouvelle Iconographie des Camellias.** Ghent, 1853-54. 2 vols. only (of 11) in 1. Orig. hf. mor. gt. (SBA. Mar.4; 169)   Coke. £800

VERSTEGAM, Richard
See–ROWLANDS, Richard

VERSTER DE WULVERHORST, A.H.
See–SCHLEGEL, Hermann & Verster de Wulverhorst, A.H.

VERTES, Marcel
– **Complexes.** Ed.:– Pierre Mac Orlan (preface). Monte Carlo, [1948]. (890) numbered. 4to. Edge of title lightly foxed. Loose as iss. in pict. wraps., unif. bd. folder, boxed. (SG. Apr.2; 299) $130

VERTOT, René Aubert, Abbé de
– **Histoire des Chevaliers Hospitaliers de St Jean de Jérusalem . . .** Paris, 1726. 4 vols. 4to. Cont. spr. cf. (HD. Jun.29; 137)   Frs. 4,200
– **Histoire des Revolutions arrivées dans le Gouvernement de la Republique Romaine.** Paris, 1727. 3rd. Edn. 3 vols. 12mo. Sig. of John Shaw Kennedy on fly-ll. Cont. red mor., gt., arms of Louise Anne de Bourbon-Condé, surmntd. by name 'Atis', triple gt. fillet, spine gt. in compartments, inner gt. dentelles. (SM. Oct.8; 2063)   Frs. 2,200
– **The History of the Knights of Malta.** 1728. 2 vols. Fo. Some dampstaining, mostly marginal. Cont. cf. gt. W.a.f. (SBA. Jul.23; 413)   Carruthers. £110

VERULAM, Baron, Sir Francis Bacon
See–BACON, Sir Francis, Baron Verulam

VERVE: an Artistic & Literary Quarterly
Paris, 1937; [1938]. Numbers 1 & 2, tog. 2 vols.

Fo. Cold. pict. wraps. by Matisse & Bonnard, orig. boxes brkn. (SG. Oct.23; 336) $150
– – **Anr. Run.** Ill.:– after Chagall, Derain, Leger, Klee, Matisse, Miro & others. Paris, 1937-39. Nos. 1, 3, 4, & 5/6. 4to. Nos. 1, 3, & 4 with Engl. text. Orig. wraps., cover designs by Matisse, Bonnard, Roualt & Maillol. (SH. Nov.21; 495)   Graziani-Levy. £80
– – **Anr. Run.** Nos. 1-4 in 1 vol. 4to. Cold. pict. cl., orig. upr. wraps. (by Matisse, Braque, Bonnard, & Rouault) bnd. in. (SG. Apr.2; 302) $325
– – **Anr. Run.** Ed.:– E. Terade. Ill.:– Matisse, et al. Paris, 1937-45. 1st. Edns. in Engl. of numbers 1-8 & 1st. Edn. of number 13. Numbers 1-8 & 13, 8 vols. Sm. fo. Pict. wraps., 2 boxed, 1 in s.-c. (PNY. Mar.4; 266) $425
– – **Anr. Run.** Ill.:– Bonnard, Braque, Chagall, Matisse, Picasso & others. Paris, 1937-60. 26 vols. (nos. 1-38). Lge. 4to. Complete collection, contains only the nos. with Fr. text. Sewed, ill. wraps. (HD. Dec.5; 212)   Frs. 27,500
– – **Anr. Run.** Paris, 1938-39. Numbers 2, 3 & 4. Fo. Publisher's silver-stpd. buckram, orig. cold. wraps. by Braque, Bonnard & Rouault bnd. in. (SG. Oct.23; 337) $140
– – **Anr. Run.** Paris, 1945-48. Nos. 13, 19/20, & 21/22, 3 iss.'s. 4to. Orig. wraps., slightly worn, 1 cover design by Matisse. (SH. Nov.21; 497)   Schouvaloh. £52

See–CHAGALL, Marc

VESALIUS, Andreas
– **Anatomia.** Amst., 1617. Fo. Double-p. plt. with tears in centre fold & margin, lacks E2 & E5, plt. M defect., a few plts. with marginal tears, some soiling & staining, text browned, cont. owner's inscr. on title. Vell. bds., stained. (S. Dec.8; 185)   Heynderickx. £210
– **De Humani Corporis Fabrica Libri Septem.** Basel, 1543. 1st. Edn. Fo. With the double lf. & unpaged lf. (both sigd. m3) in quire m & the double lf. (sigd. p4) in quire p, title reprd. in extreme lr. margin & with sm. hole, slightly wormed at end affecting text, lr. blank portion of colophon lf. holed, tear reprd. in H2, sm. repair to I4, some dampstains in quires O & P (text slightly affected on P2), slight marginal soiling & staining. Cont. blind-stpd. cf. over wooden bds., outer roll of medallion heads, central panel divided into 8 squares enclosing rolls of flowers & figures, rebkd., some wear, clasps (1 brkn.), red mor. case. From Honeyman Collection. (S. May 20; 3043)   Percy. £44,000
– – **Anr. Copy.** Double ll. m3 'Venarum arteriarumque' & p4 'nervarum' both present, title slightly stained, clean tear & fraying reprd., & laid down, inner blank margin of 1st. 14 ll. affected by damp & reprd., minor staining at beginning & worse at end. 17th. C. mott. cf., rebkd., orig. spine preserved, corners restored. (C. Apr.1; 119)   Walton. £6,500
– – **Anr. Copy.** Lacks title, port., all but *5 of the other prelim. ll., O4-4, P1, P3, P5, R1, h4, p5, s1, 2L6, folding lf. m3 torn in 2 & slightly defect., a few other ll. torn & slightly defect. Early 19th. C. hf. roan, worn, upr. cover detchd. (S. Apr.6; 163)   Veulemans. £800
– – **Anr. Edn.** Ill.:– probably Stephen van Calcar. Basle, 1555. 3rd. (2nd. Ill.) Edn. 7 Books. Fo. (406 X 274mms). Very sm. wormhole in title & following 11 ll. affecting letters, sm. marginal wormhole through pp. 797-808 hardly affecting marginalia, insignificant paper flaw in blank margin B3. 17th. C. panel. cf., rebkd. Tall copy. (S. Jun.17; 845)   Quaritch. £3,200
– – **Anr. Edn.** Venice, 1568. 4th. Edn. 7 Books. Fo. Lacks 7 ll., title stained, defect. in margin affecting letters (supplied in pen facs.), & mntd., T1 defect. in inner portion with text missing, last 2 ll. of index defect. in upr. margin & roughly reprd. with loss of letters, some stains & a few sm. wormholes. Cf., soiled. (S. Jun.17; 846)   Wood. £450
– **Icones Anatomicae.** N.Y. & Munich, Bremer Pr. 1934. (615) numbered. Fo. Hf. pig, unc. (SG. Sep.18; 375) $1,500
– – **Anr. Copy.** (SG. May 14; 220) $1,400
– – **Anr. Copy.** Orig. hf. leath., by Frieda Thirsch. (H. May 21/22; 1381)   DM 3,600
– – **Anr. Edn.** Ed.:– [Drs. Wiegand, Lambert, Archibald Malloch]. Munich, Bremer Pr., 1934 [-35]. Facs. reprint, (615) numbered. Fo. Hf. parch., in box. (S. Jun.17; 848)   Norman. £700
– **Opera Omina Anatomica & Chirurgica.** Ed.:– Hermann Boerhaave & Bernardus Siegfried Albinus. Ill.:– J. Wandelaar. Leiden, 1725. 1st.

Compl. Edn. 2 vols. Fo. Lacks sub-title before dedication in vol. I, the first in vol. II misbnd. before title, ll. in sigs. 4Z vol. II misbnd. Cont. cf., rebkd. (S. Jun.17; 847) *Quaritch.* £1,000
– – **Anr. Copy.** 78 (of 79) engraved plts., some spotting & browning. Very worn. From liby. of Dr. E. Ashworth Underwood. (S. Feb.23; 314) *Duran.* £300

VESENNY SAKIB POETOV [Spring Salon of Poets]
Moscow, 1918. Orig. wraps. by G. Yakulov, slightly soiled. (SH. Feb.6; 542) *Quaritch.* £120

VESLING, Johann
– **Syntagma Anatomicum.** Passau, 1647. 4to. 23 plts. only (of 24), without fly-ll., some stains, 7 pp. MS. bnd. in, embossed armorial stps. on titles. Cont. stiff. vell. Early bkplt. of Jacobus Godard. (SG. Jan.29; 417) $130
– – **Anr. Edn.** Ed.:– Gerardo Leonardi Blasio. Amst., 1659. 2 vols. in 1. 4to. Liby. bkplt. Old vell. (SG. Sep.18; 376) $380
– – **Anr. Edn.** Ed.:– G. Blasius. Amst., 1666. Ed. II., 6th. Edn., 3rd. Edn. with Appendix. 4to. Sm. stp. on title. Cont. vell. (R. Oct. 14-18; 403) DM 1,500

VESPUCCI, Amerigo
See–BRY, Theodore de & others

VESTIARIUM Scoticum
Ed.:– John Sobieski Stuart. 1842. Fo. Mor., gt. coat of arms, worn. (CE. Jun.4; 165) £100

VET, J. & others
See–PIT, A. & others

VETANCOURT, Agustin
– **Arte de Lengua Mexicana.** Mexico, 1673. Sm. 4to. A few light stains. Limp vell. (SPB. May 5; 523) $2,100

VETCH, John
– **A Practical Treatise on the Diseases of the Eye.** L., 1820. 1st. Edn. Old hf. cf., covers detchd. Casey A. Wood bkplt. (SG. Sep.18; 377) $100

VETTER, A.
– **Theoretisch–pract. Handbuch d. allg. u. Speciellen Heilquellenlehre.** Berlin, 1845. Soiled thro.-out. Cont. linen, loose. (HK. Nov.18-21; 378) DM 420

VEVER, Henri
– **La Bijouterie Française au XIXe Siècle.** Paris, 1906-08. (1000). 3 vols. 4to. Hf. mor. by Durvand, corners, unc., wraps. & spines. (HD. Dec.5; 213) Frs. 1,900
– **Catalogue of Highly Important Japanese Prints, Illustrated Books, Drawings & Fan Paintings.** 1975-77. Vols. 2 & 3 only. 4to. Orig. bds., d.-w.'s. (SH. Oct.9; 198) *Talerman.* £55

VIALA, P. & Vermorel, V.
– **Traité Général de Viticulture. Ampelographie.** Paris, 1901-09. 7 vols. 4to. Hf. leath. (D. Dec.11-13; 152) DM 3,000
– – **Anr. Edn.** Paris, 1901-10. 7 vols. Sm. fo. Mod. hf. leath. (R. Oct.14-18; 3085) DM 3,300
– – **Anr. Copy.** (R. Mar.31-Apr.4; 1465) DM 2,600

VIALART, Charles, Bp.
– **Geographia Sacra.** Amst., 1704. 2 pts. in 1 vol. Fo. Annotated by Lucas Holstein, sm. liby. stp. on hf.-title, & title, a few ll. slightly spotted, sm. hole in fo. 12 affecting pagination. Old bds., slightly worn. (S. Oct.21; 469) *Murphy.* £75
See–MARIANA, Juan de–VIALART, Charles

VIAU, Théophile de
– **Les Oeuvres ...** Paris, 1629. 3 pts. in 1 vol. Cont. mor., 2 borders of fillets & pointillés, 2 motifs with sm. tools & rosettes, central motif with oval & 'A Mr le comte' on upr. cover, 'de Largouet' on lr. cover, spine decor. (HD. Mar.18; 176) Frs. 2,600

VIC, Claude de & Vaissette, Joseph
– **Histoire Générale de Languedoc ...** Ill.:– J.B. Nolin, Rolin & others. Paris, 1730-45. 5 vols. Fo. Cont. cf., decor. spine raised bands, very worn. (HD. Apr.24; 108) Frs. 5,500
– – **Anr. Edn.** Toulouse, 1772-76. 14 vols. 4to. Orig. ptd. paper bds., unc. & unopened. (C. Nov.5; 43) *Rota.* £100

VICAIRE, Georges
– **Manuel de l'Amateur de Livres du XIXe Siècle.** Paris, 1894-1920. 8 vols. Orig. bds. (HK. May 12-14; 2297) DM 500

– – **Anr. Edn.** N.Y. 1973. Reprint of Paris 1894-1920 Edn. 8 vols. Orig. linen. (HK. Nov.18-21; 3243) DM 450

VICARY, Thomas
– **The English-Mans Treasure with the True Anatomy of Mans Body.** Ed.:– W. B[oraston]. 1633. 8th. Edn. 4to. Lacks 3 prelims. after title, some stains mainly on last few ll., sm. hole in N3-4. New rough cf., top of spine worn. [STC 24712] (S. Jun.17; 850) *Joslen.* £80

VICENTIUS, Bellovancensis
– **Speculum Doctrinale.** [Strassburg], [The R-Printer (Adolf Rusch)], [before 11 Feb. 1478]. 1st. Edn. Fo. Variant with the reading 'ambulet' for 'abulet' in the last line of fo. 403r, spaces for initial capitals, un-rubricated thro.-out, some 20 ll. slightly browned, a very few ll. with minor marginal worm tracings. Old blind-tooled mor., brass clasps & catches, rebkd. preserving orig. spine. The copy of Herschel V. Jones, lately in the collection of Eric Sexton. [BMC I, 65, C 6242, Goff V279] (CNY. Apr.8; 166) $6,000
– **Speculum Morale.** Strassburg, Johann Mentelin, 9 Nov. 1476. 1st. Edn. Fo. Spaces for initial capitals, unrubricated, lacks blank folios 1, 5, & 477, without the 12-line colophon at fo. 473r, clean tear to lr. margin of fo. 434, some 25 pp. with finger-soiling & ink smudges, some quires slightly browned, occasional cont. marginalia. 16th. C. German blind-stpd. pig over wood bds., lacks clasps & catches, worn at corners, torn at head of spine, engraved monastic bkplt. The copy of Herschel V. Jones, lately in the collection of Eric Sexton. [BMC I, 58, C.6252, Goff V288] (CNY. Apr.8; 164) $9,500
– **Speculum Naturale.** [Strassburg], [The R-Printer (Adolf Rusch)], [not after 5 Apr. 1477]. 1st. Edn. 2 vols. Fo. Spaces for initial capitals, thirty-one 12-line capitals supplied in red & blue, capitals at text openings of both vols. illuminated in red & blue with floral decor. in yellow, green & purple extending into margins, smaller capitals, paragraph marks & initial strokes in red, lacks 1st. & final blank in vol. 1, & final blank in vol. 2, reprd. tears slightly affecting text at folios 221 & 333 in vol. 1, some other ll. with marginal tears, last few ll. in both vols. wormed, catching some letters at final 2 ll., scattered browning. Cont. blind-stpd. cf. over wood bds., both vols. similarly but not unif. bnd., vol. 1 with scattered tools including a circular 'ihs' tool, vol. 2 with interlocking fillets at covers, rebkd. preserving orig. spines. The copy of Herschel V. Jones, lately in the collection of Eric Sexton. [BMC I, 64, C.6253, Goff V292 (1973 edn.) (CNY. Apr.8; 165) $25,000
– – **Anr. Copy.** Capital spaces, initials & paragraph strokes supplied by cont. hand, lacks 1st. & last blank ll. in vol. I & 1st. blank in vol. II, margins of vol. I with traces of dampstaining, 2 ll. in vol. II discold. Antique-style blind-stpd. pig. [BMC I, 64, C.6253 & 6256, Goff V292] (CNY. Oct.1; 111) $10,000

VICKERS, A.G.
– **Gallery of 100 British Engravings.** L., ca. 1850. 2 vols. in 1. 4to. Orig. leath., defect. (R. Oct.14-18; 2138) DM 1,450

[VICKERS, V.C.] 'V.C.V.'
– **The Google Book.** Ill.:– Vickers. 1913. (100) numbered, sigd. 4to. Margins browned. Orig. cl.-bkd. bds., slightly soiled, d.-w. (CSK. Feb.13; 66) £160

VICO, Enea
– **Ex Libris XXIII Commentariorum in vetera imperatorum Romanorum Numismata ... liber primus (Discorsi ... sopra le Medaglie de gli Antichi).** Paris, 1619. 2 pts. in 1 vol. (all publd.). 4to. 1 plt. inserted from anr. work. Cont. red mor., gt. borders on covers, spine gt. in 6 compartments, spine reprd. at foot. (C. Apr.1; 173) *Hewitt.* £120

VICOMERCATUS, Franciscus
– **In Octo libros Aristotelis de Naturali Auscultatione Commentarii.** Venice, 1564. Fo. Some staining & browning, wormed at beginning & end, corrosion hole in X5-6. Vell.-bkd. bds., soiled. From Honeyman Collection. (S. May 20; 3044) *Howell.* £55

VICQ D'AZYR, Felix
– **Traité d'Anatomie et de Physiologie.** Ill.:– Briceau (afterwards Angelique Allais). Paris,

1786. 2 vols. Fo. Lacks hf.-title in vol. 1, all plts. in vol. II accompanied by an outl. plt. except plt. 18 in black & white only (being taken from Blumenbach's De Basi Encephali). Hf. cf. (S. Jun.17; 851) *Norman.* £3,200

VICTOIRES, CONQUETES, DESASTRES, Revers et Guerres Civiles des Française de 1792 à 1815
Paris, 1817-21. 27 vols. Some ll. spotted. Cont. cf.-bkd. bds. (SH. Oct.10; 543) *Fairburn.* £75

VICTOR, Benjamin
– **The History of the Theatres of London & Dublin.** 1761. 2 vols. only. 12mo. Mod. cf.-bkd. bds. (CSK. May 8; 120) £95
[–] **The Widow of the Wood.** 1755. 1st. Edn. Advt. lf. for lottery bnd. in at end. Cont. cf. (C. Nov.20; 214) *Hannas.* £50

VICTORIA COUNTY HISTORIES
– **Durham.** Ed.:– William Page. 1905-28. 3 vols. 4to. Orig. cl. (CSK. Aug.1; 107) £50
– **Hertfordshire.** 1902-23. Vols. I-IV & index vol. 4to. Orig. hf. mor., spines gt., index vol. in cl. (LC. Jun.18; 185) £80
  A History of the County of Surrey. Ed.:– H.D. Doubleday. 1902-12. 4 vols., no index vol. 4to. Orig. cl. gt. (P. May 14; 18) £60
– **Rutland.** 1908-35-36. 3 vols. (including the index). Fo. Orig. cl. (CSK. Oct.27; 83) £90
– **Surrey.** 1902-14. 1st. Edn. 4 vols. & index. Fo. Mor. (MMB. Oct.8; 62) £100
– **Wiltshire.** 1957-65. Vol. 1, pt. 1 (all publd.) & vols. 2-8. Fo. Vols. 1-7 in hf. cf., vol. 8 in cl. From the collection of Eric Sexton. (C. Apr.16; 374) *Dawson.* £300

VICTORIA ILLUSTRATED
Victoria, 1891. Lge. 4to. Orig. cl. (CB. May 27; 321) Can. $160

VICTORIA, Queen of England
– **Landscape Illustrations to the Bubbles from the Brunnens of Nassau by An Old Man.** Frankfurt, 1834. Ob. 8vo. Orig. hf. mor. Inscr. by Queen Victoria 'From My dear Sister Feodore 17th Sept: 1834'. (CSK. Jun.19; 80) £260
– **Leaves from the Journal of Our Life in the Highlands.** Ed.:– Sir A. Helps. Priv. ptd., 1865. 1st. Edn., (63). Illustrations, spotted, 1 loose. Orig. cl., gt., s.-c. Pres. copy, inscr. by the author to her son. (SH. Oct.10; 401) *Fairburn.* £210

VICTORIUS, P.
See–CATO, Marcus Porcius & Varro, M.T.
–PALLADIUS Rutilius Taurus Aemilianus
–VICTORIUS, P.

VICUNA MACKENNA, Benjamin
– **La Campaña de Tarapaca.–La Campaña de Lima.–Vida del General Bernardo O'Higgins. –Dictadura del General Bernardo O'Higgins.–Las dos Esmeraldas.–Historia de la Jornada del 20 de April de 1851.** Santiago de Chile, 1879-1882. 2 vols.; rest 1 vol, together 7 vols. Some discoloration. Unif. mor.-bkd. cl., slightly worn. (SPB. May 5; 525) $175
– **Esploración de las Lagunas Negra i del Encañado en las Cordilleras de San José in del Yeso.** Valparaiso, 1874. 4to. Hf.-title with owner's inscr., inner margin of title soiled by old adhesive tape, hf.-title loose. Cont. mor.-bkd. bds., worn. (SPB. May 5; 524) $175

VIDAL, A.
– **Les Instruments à Archet.** Ill.:– Frédéric Hillemacher. Paris, 1876-78. 1st. Edn., (500). 3 vols. 4to. Hf. chagrin, corners, unc. (HD. Dec.5; 214) Frs. 2,700

VIDIUS, Vidus
– **Ars Medicinalis.** Ed.:– Vidus Vidius Jr. Venice, 1611. 3 vols. Fo. Title in vol. I mntd. & defect. at inner upr. corner affecting text, lr. blank corner reprd., upr. margins of following ll. stained, upr. margins towards end stained & brittle with some inner margins roughly reprd. affecting letters, last lf. in vol. II bkd. with defect in upr. margin & loss of text, lacks section 'De curatione membratim' by Vidius Jr., 76 anatomical plts. in vol. 3 (of 78), lacks engraved title. Hf. leath. W.a.f. (S. Jun.17; 852) *Rota.* £110

VIE PARISIENNE
Paris, 1918. 52 nos. in 1 vol. Lge. 4to. Without table of contents. Cl., cold. covers bnd. in. (SG. May 21; 445) $180

VIE PARISIENNE -contd.
- - **Anr. Edn.** Paris, 1919. 52 nos. in 1 vol. Lge. 4to. General title-p. in 2 states. Hf. leatherette, cold. covers bnd. in. (SG. May 21; 444) $200

VIE PRIVEE, Libertine et Scandaleuse de feu Honoré Gabriel Riqueti, ci-devant comte de Mirabeau
Paris, 1791. 16mo. Mod. red mor., decor. spine, 2 fillets, inner dentelle. (HD. Apr.10; 383)
Frs. 5,500

VIE PRIVEE, Libertine et Scandaleuse de Marie-Antoinette d'Autriche, ci-devant Reine des Français Gabriel Riqueti, ci-devant comte de Mirabeau
Paris, 1793. 4 pts. in 3 vols. 16mo. Most plts. unstpd. Porphyre roan, decor. spines & covers, roulette round. With 2nd. Printing of several engrs. (HD. Apr.10; 384)   Frs. 5,000

VIEH ARTZNEY ... auss Varrone, Plinio, Virgilio, Palladio, und andern bewerten naturkündigern . . . gezogen
Frankfurt, 1580. Some blank paper bnd. in. 18th. C. limp vell. (S. Jun.1; 48)   Junk. £150

VIEILLOT, Louis Jean Pierre
- Histoire Naturelle des plus Beaux Oiseaux Chanteurs de la Zone Torride. Paris, 1805. Fo. 72 hand-cold. engraved plts. Orig. bds., unc. (C. Jul.15; 162)   Rodgers. £2,800
See-AUDEBERT, Jean Baptiste & Vieillot, Louis Jean Pierre

VIEN, Joseph-Marie
- Caravane du Sultan à la Mecque ... [Paris], [1749]. 1st. Printing. 4to. Mod. red mor., decor. spine, 3 fillets, inside dentelle, watered silk doubls. & end-papers. (HD. Dec.5; 215)   Frs. 95,500

VIENNA
- Der stat Wienn ordu[n]g vnd Freyhaiten. Vienna, [1526]. Sm. fo. Lacks final blank, some browning. Mod. hf. cl. From liby. of André L. Simon. (S. May 18; 205)   Goldschmidt. £350

VIERI, Francesco de'
- Trattato delle Metheore. Flor., 1573. 1st. Edn. Some browning & staining. Cont. vell. Mod. bkplt. of Joseph Martin Luc; from Honeyman Collection. (S. May 20; 3045)   Roberts. £70

VIETA, Franciscus
- Canon Mathematicus seu ad Triangula cum Adpendicibus (-Universalium Inspectionum ad Canonem Mathematicum, Canonem Triangulorum Laterum Rationalium). Paris, 1579. 1st. Edn. 3 pts. in 1 vol. Fo. Some ll. misbnd., marginal staining, title inscr. 'Ex libris Hurtaldi' & with owner's entries of Nicholas Souciet. 18th. C. cf., rebkd. & reprd., worn. From Honeyman Collection. (S. May 20; 3046)   Howell. £4,000
- - **Anr. Copy.** Pt. 2 bnd. first, browned & stained thro.-out, some worming, mostly marginal, occasionally affecting tables, owners' inscrs. of College of St. Balsius, Rome, & Ant. Santini. Cont. limp vell., spine defect., upr. inside hinge brkn. Lge. copy. From Honeyman Collection. (S. May 20; 3047)   Norman. £1,500
- De Aequationum Recognitione et Emendatione Tractatus duo. Ed.:– Alexander Anderson. Paris, 1615. 1st. Edn. Sm. 4to. Some browning, stp. on title. Cont. limp vell., hf. red mor. case. From Honeyman Collection. (S. May 20; 3049)   Gurney. £260
- Opera Mathematica. Ed.:– Franciscus a Schooten. Leiden, 1646. Fo. Inserted lf. with volvelles for cutting out at 3L3, some ll. browned or spotted, a little worming in last 2 ll. affecting text, title guarded. 18th. C. cf.-bkd. bds., spine gt. From Honeyman Collection. (S. May 20; 3050)   Quaritch. £320
- Varia Opera Mathematica. Paris, 1609. 3 pts. in 1 vol. Fo. Some browning, title a little soiled. Cont. vell. bds., worn & soiled, hf. mor. case. From Honeyman Collection. (S. May 20; 3048)   Rota. £550

VIETZ, Ferdinand Bernhard
- Icones Plantarum Medico-Oeconomico-Technologicarum ... Vienna, 1800; 1804. 2 vols. in 1. 4to. Old hf. cf., brkn. Accompanied by bi-lingual text, about 500 pp., for the 222 plts., disbnd. (SG. Oct.9; 248) $1,300
- - **Anr. Edn.** Vienna, [1800-1806]. Vols. I-III (of 10), together 3 vols. 4to. Text in Latin & German, a few ll. very slightly soiled. Cont. hf. cf., spine gt.,

marb. paper on covers of vol. II renewed. (S. Feb.23; 124)   Frick. £800

VIEUSSENS, Raymond–OVERKAMP, D. Heydentryk
- Neurographia Universalis.–Oeconomia Animalis. Frankfurt; Leipzig, 1690; 1690. 2 works in 1 vol. 1st. work: a few plts. with short tears, plts. 23 torn in folds & reprd. with very sm. section in fold missing, sm. tear in N5 reprd. affecting a few letters, a few letters on Ff4 scraped. Cont. cf. Purchase entry by Philip Brandhorsten (?) at Halle Jul. 1740, bkplt. of Ralph H. Major, the medical historian. (S. Jun.17; 853)
Chatham Books. £350

VIEWS OF ALL THE COLLEGES, Halls & Public Buildings in the University & City of Oxford
Oxford, [1824]. Ob. 16mo (4½ × 5¼ inches). Some views slightly spotted. Cont. hf. cf. (CSK. Sep.26; 126)   £80

VIGANI, Johannes Franciscus
- Medulla Chymiae Variis Experimentis Aucta. 1685. New bds. [Wing V373] (S. Dec.1; 421)   Mediolanum. £60

VIGER, Denis Benjamin
- Siège de Quebec, en 1759. Quebec, 1836. Orig. plain wraps., dampstained. (CB. Feb.18; 53)   Can. $100

VIGERIUS de la Rovere, Cardinal Marcus
- Decachordum Christianum. Fano, 10 Aug. 1507. 1st. Edn. Fo. Some lge. initials supplied in red & blue, others with later pencil outls., all with guide letters, 1 full-p. block cold., lacks blank lf. aa8, 16 ll. AA to BB mis-bnd. after title-p., BB2 & BB7 inlaid with slight loss of text, first 19 ll. washed, some slight dampstaining to outer blank margins of last 70 ll., some marginal repairs & slight worming not affecting text. Mott. cf. antique. Bkplts. of Jacobi P.R. Lyell, George Dunn, & John A. Saks. (CNY. Oct.1; 85) $3,400

VIGIL OF VENUS: Pervigilium Veneris
Trans.:– F.L. Lucas. Ill.:– John Buckland-Wright. Gold. Cock. Pr., 1939. (100) numbered. 4to. Orig. blind-tooled mor., unc. Christopher Sandford's copy, with separate folder with first pencil layout, annotated paste-up of galley proofs, compl. set of wash drawings, proofs for vigs. & tail-pieces & many other items. (SH. Feb.19; 177)   Dowd. £1,900
- - **Anr. Copy.** Orig. mor. by Sangorski & Sutcliffe, & cl. s.-c. (SBA. Dec.16; 126)   Emerald Isle Books. £200

VIGNE, Godfrey Thomas
- A Personal Narrative of a Visit to Ghuzni, Kabul & Afghanistan. 1840. 1st. Edn. Orig. cl. (SH. Mar.5; 148)   Ad Orientem. £105
- - **Anr. Copy.** (SH. May 21; 126)   Hosein. £85

VIGNEAUX, Ernest
- Souvenirs d'un Prisonnier de Guerre au Mexique. Paris, 1863. 18mo. Hf. mor. (SG. Oct.30; 366) $120

VIGNOLA, Giacomo Barozzi da
- Le Due Regole della Prospettiva Pratica ... Ed.:– Egnatio Danti. Rome, 1583. 1st. Edn. Fo. Lr. corners dampstained & frayed at beginning, lacks final blank. Hf. cf., very worn. (S. Jun.22; 112)   Brosseghini. £220
- Grand et Nouveau Vignole ...–Livre Nouveau ... Ed.:– Blondel (2nd. work). Paris, n.d.; 1767. 3rd. Edn. (2nd. work). 2 works in 1 vol. Fo. Lacks 3 last plts. Cont. roan, worn. (HD. Jun.10; 108)   Frs. 1,900
- Livre Nouveau ... Ed.:– Blondel. Paris, 1767. 3rd. Edn. Fo. Lacks plt. 72, 2 added plts. Hf. roan. (HD. Jun.10; 109)   Frs. 1,400
- Regles des Cinq Ordres d'Architecture. Amst., ca. 1690. Fo. Dampstained & slightly soiled in pts., owner's inscr. on title, dtd. 1727 deleted. Cont. cf. bds., worn & soiled, hf. mor. case. From Honeyman Collection. (S. Jan.27; 308)   Booth. £110
- - **Anr. Edn.** Paris, n.d. 4to. Sm. wormhole through margin of 25 plts., prelims. slightly stained at head. Recent qtr. cl. (CB. Dec.9; 109)   Can. $280
- Regola delli Cinque Ordini d'architettura ... –Alcune Opere d'architettura. Rome, n.d.; 1617. 1st. work 1st. Book, 2 works in 1 vol. Fo. 1 plt. in 2nd. work slightly torn. Cont. vell. bds., soiled. (S. Jun.22; 113)   Licini. £180
- Regole della Prospettiva Prattica ... Ill.:– Giorgio Fossati (plts.). Venice, 1743. Lge. fo. Sm.

marginal stain to 1 plt. Cont. paper bds., slightly worn, unc. From the collection of John A. Saks. (C. Jun.10; 256)   Weinreb. £220
- Il Vignola illustrato proposto da Giambattista Spampani, e Carlo Antonini. Rome, 1770. Fo. Some spotting. Hf. roan, very worn. (S. Jun.22; 116)   Ars Artis. £50

VIGNOLA, Giacomo Barozzi da–LABACCO, A.
- Regola delli Cinque Ordini d'Architettura.–Libro appartenente a l'Architettura nel quale si figurano alcune Notabili Antiquita di Roma. Rome, 1559. 1st. Edn. 2 works in 1 vol. Stained. Cont. limp vell., soiled & worn. (S. Oct.14-18; 2522)   DM 5,500

VIGNY, Alfred de
- Cinq-Mars on une Conjuration sous Louis XIII. Ill.:– Gaujean after Dawant. Paris, 1889, (50) on Jap., numbered. 2 vols. 4to. Hf. mor. by Champs, decor. spines, wraps. preserved. (SM. Feb.11; 295)   Frs. 2,200
- Les Destinées. Ill.:– C. Bellenger engraved by Froment. 1898. (15) on Japon with 2nd. state on Chine. Mor., gt. dentelle. (HD. Jun.30; 86)   Frs. 2,100
- - **Anr. Edn.** Ill.:– Alberto Martini. Paris, 1930. (290) numbered, on papier d'Arches. Fo. 30 orig. watercolrs. Mor., geometric patterned in mor. onlays, gt. dentelles with doubls. & end-ll. of satin, by A. Weber, s.-c. (SG. Oct.9; 249) $1,500
- Les Destinées Precedées de Moise. Ill.:– G. Bellenger. Paris, 1898. (50); on China. Lge. 8vo. Mor. by Viau y Zona, mor. doubls., wrap. preserved, folder & s.-c. Pres. copy, specially printed for Anatole France. (SM. Feb.11; 296)   Frs. 4,500
- Poèmes. 1829. 2nd. Edn., part orig. Three-qtr. vell., wrap., doubl., by Gruel. Note. (HD. Oct.10; 172)   Frs. 3,300
- Servitude et Grandeur Militaires. 1835. Cont. hf. cf., ornam. spine. (HD. Oct.10; 173)   Frs. 1,600
- - **Anr. Edn.** Ill.:– Clement Bellenger after L. Dunki. Paris, 1898. (350) numbered. 2 vols. 4to. Ills. in 2 states. Red mor. by Marius Michel, red mor. doubls., wraps. preserved, s.-c. Bkplt. of Louis Barthou. (SM. Feb.11; 297)   Frs. 11,000
- Stello. Ill.:– Edgar Vieuxblé. Paris, 1953. (438); (17), numbered. 4to. Double-p. copper-engr. with corresponding orig. drawing, set with comments in 3 states on Annam (black-&-white, red & blue, & 1 ready for press). Folder, s.-c. (SM. Feb.11; 120)   Frs. 2,400

VIGO, Johannes de
- The Most Excellent Workes of Chirurgerye. 1543. Fo. Slight worming to first & last few margins. Cont. blind-stpd. cf., spine torn with loss. [STC 24720] (CSK. Mar.27; 1)   £2,100
- - **Anr. Edn.** Trans.:– [Bartholomew Traheron]. 1571. 3rd. Edn. in Engl. Fo. Lacks 2 ll. of text (Aa2 & Aa5). Cont. blind-stpd. cf., roll-stp. borders, rebkd., new end-papers, 2 clasps. [STC 24722] (S. Jun.17; 854)   Joslen. £140
- The Whole Worke ... Ed.:– Thomas Gale. 1586. 3 plts. in 1 vol. Sm. 4to. 2nd. lf. reprd., some browning & staining. Mod. hf. cf. [STC 24723; 11529a & 11531] (S. Mar.17; 369)   Dawson. £1,500

VIJVER, C. van der
- Geschiedkundige Beschrijving der Stad Amsterdam, sedert hare Wording tot op den Tegenwoordigen Tijd. Amst., 1844-48. 4 vols. Slightly foxed & browned thro.-out. Orig. cl. (VG. Dec.16; 959)   Fls. 550

VILLA & COTTAGE ARCHITECTURE: select examples of country & surburban residences recently erected
1868. Fo. Mod. cl. (CSK. Mar.20; 78)   £55

VILLAFANE, Juan de Arphe Y.
- Varia commensuracion para la escultura y arquitectura.– Ed.:– Don Pedro Enguera. Madrid, 1795. 7th. Edn. of the 1585 work. Sm. fo. Browned & foxed. Cont. tree sheep, spine reprd., worn. (SPB. May 6; 268) $200

VILLAGOMEZ, Pedro de–AVENDANO, Fernando de
- Carta Pastoral de Exortacion e Instruccion contra los Idolatrias de los Indios del Arzobispado de Lima.–Sermones de los Misterios de Nuestra Santa Fe Catolica, en Lengua Castellana y la General del Inca. Lima, 1649; [1648]. 2 works in 1 vol. Fo. Marginal stains at end inner margin of 1st. title guarded with tissue, first & last ll.

slightly soiled. Cont. limp vell. (SPB. May 5; 532)
$1,100

VILLAGUTIERRE SOTOMAYOR, Juan de
- Historia de la Conquista de la Provincia de el Itza. Madrid, 1701. Pt. 1 (all publd.). Fo. Inner margins guarded, some discolouration, sm. liby. stps. Later cf., slightly worn. (SPB. May 5; 534)
$1,100
– – **Anr. Copy.** Imprimatur lf. & 2 ll. at end with margins ragged or defect., spotting & a few sm. stains. Mod. cl. (SPB. May 5; 533) $1,000

VILLALON, Cristobel de
- Provechoso Tratado de Cambios y Contrataciones de Mercaderes y Reprouacion de Usura. Valladolid, 1541. 1st. Edn. Sm. 4to. Title in woodcut border trimmed & remargined at fore-edge, lacks final blank, some staining. 19th. C. hf. mor., gt., worn, blind-stpd. arms of William Stirling. Stp. on title of W.B. Chorley; bkplt. of William Stirling; from Honeyman Collection. (S. May 20; 3052) *Marques.* £450

VILLARROEL, Gaspar de, Bp. of Santiago
- Govierno Eclesiastico Pacifoco y Union de los dos Cuchillos, Pontificio y Regio. Madrid, 1656-57. 2 vols. Fo. Some discolouration, final lf. of vol. II guarded with tissue. Cont. limp vell. [Sabin 99668] (SPB. May 5; 535) $175

VILLARS, Louis Hector, Duc de
- Vie du Maréchal Duc de Villars. Ed.:– Anquetil. Paris, 1784. 1st. Edn. 4 vols. 12mo. 1 lf. nearly loose, a few liby. stps. Cont. mott. cf., spines gt. (S. Jan.27; 438) *Booth.* £50

VILLE E CASTELLI D'ITALIA
Milan, 1907-17. 4to. Mod. hf. mor. (SI. Dec.4; 606) Lire 240,000

VILLEFOSSE, Antoine Marie Heron de
- Eaux-de-Vie. Paris, 1954. (300) Orig. Edn., (200) numbered on Arches. 4to. Loose ll. in wrap. & publisher's box. A.l. by author. (LM. Nov.8; 86) B.Frs. 8,000

VILLE-HARDOUIN, Geoffroy de
- L'Histoire . . . de la Conqueste de Constantinople . . . Paris, 1585. 1st. Edn. Sm. ob. 4to. Decor. spine, cold. pieces, 3 gt. fillets, inside dentelle, bdg. ca. 1860. (HD. Dec.5; 216) Frs. 6,000

VILLEROY, Comte Eugène
See–REVEREND, Vicomte Albert & Villeroy, Comte Eugène

VILLIERS, George, Duke of Buckingham
See–BUCKINGHAM, George Villiers, Duke of

VILLIERS DE L'ISLE ADAM, Jean Marie Mathias Philippe Auguste, Comte de
- Nouveaux Contes Cruels. Ill.:– E. Georg. N.p., 1947. (90) numbered on pur fil de Lana. Lge 4to. In loose ll. in wrap. & publisher's box. (LM. Nov.8; 144) B.Frs. 7,000

VILLON, François
- Autres Poésies. Ill.:– Lucien Pissarro. Eragny Pr., 1901. (226). Last few ll. uncut. Orig. bds., unopened. (S. Jul.31; 21) *Monk Bretton.* £70
- Les Ballades. Ill.:– Lucien Pissarro. Eragny Pr., 1900. (226). Orig. bds., slightly worn, unopened. (S. Jul.31; 19) *Appleton.* £100
- Les Ballades.–Autres Poésies. Ill.:– Esther & Lucien Pissarro. L., Eragny Pr., 1900; 1901. (226) each vol. 2 vols. Bds., unc. (SG. Oct.9; 89) $500
- Les Oeuvres. Paris, 1532. Lacks final blank (t4), t1 misbnd. before s1, slight browning. 18th. C. Fr. red mor., gt. (S. Feb.10; 474) *Israel.* £3,400
– – **Anr. Edn.** Ill.:– Charles Martin. Paris, 1932. (15) numbered. 4to. Mor. by Creuzevault, suede doubls., wrap. preserved, s.-c. Bkplt. of Francis Kettaneh. (SM. Feb.11; 172) Frs. 8,500
– – **Anr. Edn.** Ill.:– Henri Lemarié. Paris, [1943]. In sheets, ill, wrap., publisher's s.-c. (HD. Dec.5; 217) Frs. 2,300
– – **Anr. Edn.** Ill.:– H. Lemarié. N.d. Sewed. On vell. d'arches, 1 suite & 10 unedited plts. (HD. Oct.10; 209) Frs. 2,200

VIMAR, A.
See–GUIGOU, P. & Vimar, A.

VINCENT, Augustine
- A Discoverie of Errours . . . 1622. Fo. Cont. cf., gt., arms of Sir John Paulet gt. on covers, lacks ties. Pres. Copy, to John Philipott, bkplt. of J.R. Abbey, lately in the collection of Eric Sexton. [STC 24756] (C. Apr.15; 199) *Quaritch.* £260

VINCENT, Levinus
See–KLEIN, Jacob Theodor–VINCENT, Levinus –SELL, Godefried

VINDEL, Francisco
- El Arte Tipográfico en Espana durante el Siglo XV. Madrid, 1945-51. (500). 8 vols. & index. 4to. Orig. wraps. (HK. May 12-14; 2298) DM 2,200
- Mapas de America em los Libros Espanoles de los Siglos XVI al XVIII (1503-1798). Madrid; Gongora, 1955. (520) numbered copies. Fo. Cf., gt. arms on upr-cover, orig. wraps. bnd. in. (SG. Oct.2; 367) $230

VIOLA, T.
See–CECCHINI, G.B., Pividor, G. & Viola, T.

VIOLLET-le-Duc, Eugène Emmanuel
- Dictionnaire Raisonné de l'Architecture Française du XIe au XVIe siècle. Paris, 1854-68. 10 vols. Cont. hf. chagrin, bdgs. slightly defect. (HD. Feb.27; 249) Frs. 1,050
– – **Anr. Edn.** Paris, 1861-75. 10 vols. Some ll. slightly spotted. Cont. mor.-bkd. bds. (SBA. Mar.4; 97a) *Duran.* £120
– – **Anr. Edn.** Paris, 1867-69. 10 vols. Recent red qtr. mor. & marb. bds. (CB. May 27; 208) Can. $350
– – **Anr. Edn.** Paris, 1867-70. 10 vols. in 5. Hf. mor. (SG. Dec.4; 355) $180
– – **Anr. Edn.** Paris, 1868. 10 vols. Some foxing. Red hf. mor., ex-liby. (SG. Dec.4; 356) $160
– – **Anr. Edn.** Paris, 1875. 10 vols. 4to. Cont. gt. hf. mor. (PNY. Oct.1; 523) $160
- Dictionaire Raisonné du Mobilier Française de l'Epoque Carlovingienne à la Renaisance. Paris, 1858-75. 6 vols. Old hf. mor., worn. (SG. Dec.4; 354) $200
– – **Anr. Edn.** Paris, 1868-75. 1st. Edn., except vol. 1 2nd. Edn. 6 vols. Lacks 4 steel engrs. or woodcut plts. & 1 chromolitho, some plts. & text ills. with monog. stp., slightly soiled in parts, 1st. title defect. & bkd., last lf. with hole, other titles defect. through erased stp. Hf. leath., spine very defect. (H. May 21/22; 694) DM 720
– – **Anr. Edn.** Paris, 1871-75. 6 vols. Hf. cf. (CR. Jun.11; 529) Lire 260,000
– – **Anr. Edn.** Paris, 1872-75. 6 vols. Cont. dyed bds., mor. spine, unc. (PNY. Oct.1; 524) $160
– – **Anr. Copy.** (100) numbered. Cont. hf. mor., partly unc. (SI. Dec.4; 607) Lire 460,000
- Lectures on Architecture. Trans.:– Benjamin Bucknall. L., 1977. 2 vols. Occasional foxing on 2nd. vol. Orig. qtr. leath. & cl., spines chipped at head. (CB. May 27; 210) Can. $170

VIRCHOW, Rudolf
- Die Cellularpathologie in ihrer Begründung auf Physiologische und Pathologische Gewebelehre. Berlin, 1858. 1st. Edn. Cont. hf. leath., worn. From Honeyman Collection. (S. May 20; 3055) *Percy.* £1,000
– – **Anr. Copy.** 28pp. advts. at end, a few liby. stps. Cont. cf., worn, covers loose. (SKC. May 19; 270) £480

VIRGILIAE CHRISTIANAE. A Review of Early Christian Life & Language
Amst., 1947-78. Vols. 1-32 pt. 1 in pts. No bdg. stated. (B. Dec.10/11; 1344) Fls. 1,500

VIRGILIUS Maro, Publius
- L'Aneide . . . del Commendatore Annibal Caro. Padua, 1612. Sm. 4to. Some sm. holes, occasional light staining. 19th. C. hf. cf., slightly worn. (S. Jul.27; 116) *Shapiro.* £50
- Aeneidos. 1793. Lib. 1-6. Red mor. gt. Cont. fore-e. pntg. of Caernarvon Castle. (BS. May 13; 213) £50
- The Aeneis. Trans.:– Joseph Trapp. 1718. 2 vols. 4to. Later hf. cf. Vol. I inscr. 'Ex Libris T. Warton', Tollemach bkplts. (SBA. Jul.22; 69) *O'Hern.* £80
- Bucolica. Ecloga I-X. Ill.:– R. Seewald. Munich, 1918-19. (300). Lge. fo. Orig. hf. vell. (HK. May 12-14; 2059) DM 1,000
– – **Anr. Edn.** Ill.:– R. von Seewald. Munich, 1919. (300). Lge. fo. Orig. paper bds., defect. (H. Dec.9/10; 2343) DM 420
– – **Anr. Copy.** Lge. 4to. Paper bds., spine reprd., inner hinges slightly stained. (VA. May 8; 261) R. 100
- Bucolica, Georgica, et Aeneis. Bg'ham., 1757. 1st. Baskerville Edn. 4to. Lacks blank lf. before title. Mod. red mor. gt., by de Coverley. (S. Nov.24; 291) *Howes.* £130

– – **Anr. Copy.** Cont. red mor. gt., gt. tooled borders, spine gt., mor. onlays. Richard Crofts 18th. C. bkplt. (CNY. May 22; 296) $500
– – **Anr. Edn.** Rome, 1763-65. De Luxe Edn., on vell., wide margin. 3 vols. Fo. Slightly soiled in some margins, pp. 171/172 vol. 3 with sm. tear. Mod. bds. (R. Mar.31-Apr.4; 675) DM 1,150
– – **Anr. Edn.** Ed.:– G.A. Monaldini. Rome, 1764-65. 3 vols. Fo. 3 facs. plts. on 1 lf., hole in C1 of vol. 1, slight spotting. 18th. C. tree cf., 1 cover detchd., some wear, bkplt. of John Rutherford of Edgerston. (S. Jan.27; 433) *Rebecchi.* £80
– – **Anr. Edn.** Glasgow, 1778. 2 vols. in 1. Fo. Lacks 4A2 blank. Cont. red mor. gt., spine tooled in compartments, covers with 3-line roll border. Bkplt. of Richard Harington. (S. Nov.24; 292) *Traylen.* £220
– – **Anr. Edn.** Ill.:– Baquoy, Godefroy, & others after Gerard & Girodet. Paris, 1798. (200) numbered. Lge. fo. 22 (of 24) copperplts. only. Cont. red mor., wide gt. floral borders, spine elab. gt., satin end-papers, by Le Febvre. With MS. notation by the printer. (SG. Feb.5; 333) $350
– – **Anr. Edn.** Ill.:– Bartolozzi & others. L., 1800. 2 vols. Outer margins of some plts. stained. Cont. red str.-grd. mor., gt.-tooled panel borders, richly tooled spines. (C. Feb.4; 153a) *Elstein.* £130
- Bucoliques. Trans.:– M. Henri Goelzer. Ill.:– Andre Beaudin. Paris, 1936. (110) numbered, sigd. by artist. 4to. Unsewn in orig. wraps., folder. (SH. Nov.20; 223) *Andrews.* £210
- Die Eclogen. Trans.: R.A. Schröder. Ill.:– Eric Gill & A. Maillol. Leipzig, Cranach Pr. [1926]. (250) on H.-m.-P. 4to. Slightly soiled in places. Loose ll. in wraps. (D. Dec.11-13; 1206) DM 2,500
- The Eclogues. Trans.:– Samuel Palmer 1883. 4to. Orig. cl. gt. (P. Mar.12; 15) *Craddock & Barnard.* £320
– – **Anr. Copy.** Later vell. (SH. Mar.27; 389) *Ayres.* £250
– – **Anr. Edn.** Trans. & ill.:– Samuel Palmer. L., 1883. (135) numbered, on L.P. Fo. Gt.-decor. vell., unc. (SG. May 14; 162) $850
– – **Anr. Edn.** Trans. & ill.:– Samuel Palmer. 1884. 2nd. Edn. of this trans. Sm. fo. Orig. vell. gt. (C. Jul.22; 92) *Fine Art Society.* £280
– – **Anr. Edn.** Trans.:– Marc Lafargue. Ill.:– Aristide Maillol. Weimar, Cranach Pr., 1926. (292) numbered. 4to. Spotted. Unsewn, unc., unopened, in orig. vell.-bkd. folder, slightly defect., ties. Prospectus inserted. (SH. Nov.20; 65) *Graziani-Levy.* £400
- L'Eneide di Virgilio recata in Versi Italiani. Trans.:– Annibal Caro. Rome, 1819. 2 vols. Fo. A few ll. slightly spotted. Cont. vell. gt., slightly soiled. (SBA. Mar.4; 85) *Erlini.* £140
- The Georgics. Trans.:– John Dryden. Ill.:– Bruno Bramanti. Ltd. Edns. Cl. 1952. (1500) numbered, & sigd. by artist & printer. 4to. Cl. & bds., orig. box. (SG. Jan.15; 282) $100
- Les Géorgiques . . . Ill.:– Christophe de Longueil after Casanova & Charles Dominique Joseph Eisen. Paris, 1770. 3 plts. mntd. possibly from anr. edn(?). Cont. mor. by Derome le Jeune with his ticket, triple gt. fillet, flat spine gt. with sm. interlocking semicircles, inner gt. dentelles. Bkplt. of Thomas Courtenay Theydon Warner. (SM. Oct.8; 2067) Frs. 2,800
- Les Oeuvres de Virgile. Paris, 1540. Fo. Typographic mark on last blank lf. Mod. cf., 5 spine raised bands, blind decor. (LM. Jun.13; 163) B.Frs. 27,000
– – **Anr. Edn.** Ill.:– Eisen, Moreau le jeune & others. Paris, 1796. 4 vols. Cont. mott. cf., gt. (SM. Oct.8; 2380) Frs. 2,500
- Opera. Ed.:– C. Landino. Venice, 1491. Fo. Lacks title, 353 ll. (of 356), initials supplied in red or blue, rubricated, many annots. in an early hand. Vell. W.a.f. (P. May 14; 271) *Grossfield.* £240
– – **Anr. Edn.** Ill.:– after Sebastien Brandt. Strassburg, 1502. 1st. Ill. Edn. Fo. Orig. blind-stpd. hf. pig. over wooden bds., traces of clasps. (HD. Mar.18; 185) Frs. 42,000
- [-] **Anr. Edn.** Venice, Oct. 1514. Old vell. (HD. Apr.24; 13) Frs. 3,000
– – **Anr. Edn.** Ed.:– [J. Badius Ascensius]. Lyons, Aug. & Dec., 1517. 1st. Lyons Badius Edn. 2 pts. in 1 vol. Fo. Rubricated, woodcuts (with 1 or 2 exceptions) lightly cold. by cont. hand. Cont. cf. over bevelled wood bds., ruled central panel with lattice pattern filled with oval lozenges, brass clasps, vell. fly-ll., old vell. MS. upr. paste-down, rebkd. & restored. Bkplt. of John A. Saks. (CNY. Oct.1; 92) $2,000

VIRGILIUS Maro, Publius -contd.
- [-] **Anr. Edn.** Ill.:– After Brant in the Strassburg Edn. of 1502. Venice, 20 Nov. 1522. Fo. Dampstained, title & a few ll. at end defect., lacks last lf. Cont. blind-stpd. cf., very worn. W.a.f. (S. Oct.21; 317) *Broseghini.* £200
- – **Anr. Edn.** Lugdini, 1529. Fo. Upr. margin of title reprd., a few outer margins stained. Cont. stpd. cf. over oak bds., brkn. (BS. Jun.11; 116) £340
- – **Anr. Edn.** Venetia, 1544. Fo. 1st. title-p. & a few ll. defect. Old bds., worn. W.a.f. (BS. Jun.11; 117) £160
- – **Anr. Edn.** Antw., 1572. Cf., front hinge reprd., free end-paper inserted. Owner's inscr. on title of Sir Thomas Knyvett. (LC. Jun.18; 344) £50
- – **Anr. Edn.** Paris, 1641. Fo. Cont. red mor. (SG. Sep.25; 316) $325
- – **Anr. Edn.** Ed.:– Nicolaus Heinsius. Amst., 1676. 12mo. Ruled. Late 17th. C. red mor., fillet, decor. spine, arms of Michel-Andre Jubert de Bouville. (HD. Mar.18; 186) Frs. 1,450
- – **Anr. Edn.** Ed.:– Petrus Burmannus. Amst., 1746. 4 vols. 4to. Cont. vell., soiled. (CSK. Oct.31; 5) £60
- – **Anr. Edn.** Ed.:– Henricus Justice. [The Hague], [1757]. 2nd. Iss. 5 vols. Cont. tree cf. gt., spines worn. The John A. Saks copy. (CNY. Oct.1; 117) $200
- **Opera Vergiliana Calderinus, Jodocus Badius & others.** Ed.:– Servius Donatus Mancellinus & Pedro Probo, Beroaldus, L., [1517]. 2 vols. in 1. Fo. 1st. title remntd. & restored, torn without text loss on LIIII 2nd. pt., old staining, some ink stains, MS. inscrs. on titles. Old vell. (LM. Mar.21; 177) B.Frs. 65,000
- **Quinq[ue] Carmina Pulcherrima ... Fratris Baptiste Mantuani Carmen Votiuu[m] ad Beatam Virginem.** Leipzig, 1514. Sm. 4to. Copious cont. MS. notes glossing text, some browning & soiling. Mod. bds., slightly soiled. From liby. of André L. Simon. (S. May 18; 206) *Schaeffer.* £80
- **The Works.** Trans.:– John Ogilby. 1668. Fo. 1 engr. with sm. hole, 1 lf. torn, slightly affecting text. Cont. mott. cf., bnd. for John Evelyn, with his bkplt. & gt. arms on covers, slightly worn. [Wing V613] (S. Dec.9; 365) *Braunschweig.* £300
- – **Anr. Edn.** Trans.:– John Dryden. 1698. 2nd. Edn. Fo. Staining thro.-out. 19th. C. hf. cf. Fore-e. pntg. of the Bay of Naples. [Wing V617] (C. Feb.4; 129) *Sotheran.* £140
- – **Anr. Edn.** Trans.:– John Dryden. 1810. 4 vols. in 2. Cont. red str.-grd. mor., covers with gt. panel, spines gt. Fore-e. pntg. in each vol. (C. Jul.22; 186) *Maggs.* £100

See–MORRIS, William

VIRIBUS UNITIS
- **Das Buch vom Kaiser.** Ill.:– Kolomon Moser, Josef Hoffman & others. Budapest, Vienna, Leipzig, ca. 1908. Fo. Orig. mor. inset panel on upr. cover with design tooled in gt. & blind, centrepiece a gt. metal crown with enamelling & stones, white enamelled monog. below, similarly decor. clasp, hinged portion brkn. off but present, narrow metal border to upr. cover & circular studs on lr. cover, after design by Josef Hoffman, orig. cl. case, jnts. reprd. (SH. Nov.21; 432) *Ex Libris.* £115

VIRTUE, George, publishers
- **Picturesque Beauties of Great Britain–Kent.** Ill.:– after Shepherd, Gastineau & others. 1831. 4to. Lacks 1 plt., publisher's advt. lf. bnd. in at front. Cont. hf. mor., rebkd. (TA. Dec.18; 395) £155

VISCONTI, Ennio Quirino
- **Il Museo Pio Clementino Descritta.** Rome, 1782-92. Vols. 1, 3, 4 & 6, together 4 vols. Atlas fo. Not collated. Disbnd. (SG. Sep.25; 317) $110

VISENTINI, Antonio
See–GALLACINI, Teofile–VISENTINI, Antonio

VISSCHER, Nikolaas, the Younger
- **Historiae Sacrae Veteris et Novi Testamenti.** Amst., ca. 1700. Fo. Engraved title & 91 engraved double-p. plts., most with Dutch text, some with text in 4 languages, 3 with Dutch text added in MS., 2 corners torn off. 18th. C. cf., worn. As a collection w.a.f. (S. Nov.25; 419) *Leverton.* £220

VISSCHER, Nicolaus Joannes, the Elder
- **Atlas Minor.** Amst., n.d., after 1705. Fo. Engraved & ptd. title, 36 (of 40) hand-cold. double-p. engraved maps, some folding, engraved title reprd., ptd. title laid down. Cont. cf. As an atlas, w.a.f. (C. May 20; 183) *Taylor.* £2,500

VISSCHER, Nicolaus Joannes the Elder–JACOB MARTSZ. DE JONGE
- **Theatrum Praecipuarum Urbium Ducatus Brabantiae nec non Comitatuum Flandriae et Zelandiae.–[The Spaniards · & their Garrison leaving Gennep for Venlo on 29 July 1641].** Ill.:– Pieter Nolpe. Amst., 1660; ca. 1641. 2 works in 1 vol. Lge. ob. 4to. Old hf. vell. (VG. Oct. 13; 162) Fls. 15,000

VITA BEATI P. Ignatii Loiolae Societatisies V. Fundatoris
Rome, 1609. A few plts. torn & crudely reprd. Vell., slightly soiled, stitching slightly shaken. (CSK. Apr.24; 33) £65

VITA di S. Filippo Neri
Ill.:– Innocente Alessandri after P.A. Novelli. Venice, 1793. Fo. Cont. hf. cf., worn, head of spine chipped. From the collection of John A. Saks. (C. Jun.10; 260) *Taylor.* £60

VITA Seraphicae Virginis S. Mariae Magdalenae de Pazzis
Ill.:– after Abraham van Diepenbeeck. Ca. 1700. 4to. Title slightly soiled, last plt. slightly defect in text & reprd. Cont. spr. cf., spine gt. (S. May 5; 72) *Hyde.* £55

VITAL, Chaim
- **Etz. Chaim.** Shklow, 1800. Fo. Outer & inner margins reprd. with some text loss, staining. Mod. hf. leath. (SPB. May 11; 210) $250
- **Shaare Kedusha.** Amst., 1745. 3rd. Edn. 12mo. Slight discolouration. Vell. (S. Nov.18; 472) *Waiman.* £50

VITE DE GLI RE DI FRANCIA, & DE GLI DUCA DI MILANO
Rome, 1525. 4to. Mod. hf. vell. (SI. Dec.4; 611) Lire 320,000

VITELLIO
- **[Opticae] id est de Natura, Ratione, & Proiectione Radiorum Visus, Luminum, Colorum atque Formarum, quam vulgo Perspectivam vocant, Libri X.** Nuremb., 1535. 1st. Edn. Fo. Slight marginal staining. Cont. German blind-stpd. cf. over wooden bds., rolls of medallion heads, classical figures & ports., sigd. H.B., worn, 1 corner defect., lacks 1 clasp. Bkplt. of Count Chorinsky; from Honeyman Collection. (S. May 20; 3057) *Zeitlin & Verbrugge.* £1,300

VITRIACO, Jacobus de
- **Historia Orientalis ... Occidentalis.** Douai, 1596. Vell. gt. The Heber copy. (P. Oct.2; 2) *Ad Orientem.* £130

VITRING, Campegius
- **De Synagoga Vetere Libri Tres.** Franequer, 1696. 1st. Edn. 2 vols. 4to. In Hebrew & Latin. Vell. (S. Nov.18; 687) *Ganz.* £240

VITRUVIUS POLLIO, Marcus
- **De Architectura.** Ed.:– [Joannes Sulpitius]. [Rome], [Eucharius Silber], [1483-95]. 1st. Edn. Fo. Folios 1, 4, 6 (& others?) possibly in good facs. or from anr. copy, some dampstaining, a number of neat marginal repairs, fo. 3 reprd. with a few letters in facs., sm. flaw affecting 1 word on recto of fo. 70. Maroon mor., gt., by Zaehnsdorf, red hf. mor. case, owner's inscr. on fly-lf of Robert Mylne, with his purchase note. From Honeyman Collection. [BMC IV, 124; Goff V306] (S. May 20; 3058) *Weinreb.* £4,800
- [-] **Anr. Edn.** Ed.:– G. Giocondo. Venice, 1511. 1st. Giocondo Edn. Fo. Lacks final blank, some worming, affecting text & ills. & several headlines near beginning (lge. holes reprd.), upr. margin of title reprd., slight marginal staining & spotting. Mod. hf. cf., worn. From Honeyman Collection. (S. May 20; 3059) *Weinreb.* £2,000
- – **Anr. Edn.** Trans.:– C. Cesariano. Como, 1521. 1st. Edn. in Italian. Fo. Errata lf. possibly inserted from a shorter copy, tear reprd. in X5, a few marginal repairs, slight soiling & staining. 18th. C. cf., some wear. Mod. bkplt. of Silvio Zipoli; from Honeyman Collection. (S. May 20; 3060) *Weinreb.* £7,000
- – **Anr. Copy.** Stained slightly, minimal worming at beginning. 17th. C. gt. spine. (HK. Nov. 18-21; 318) DM 19,000

- – **Anr. Edn.** Lyon, 1552. 1st. De Tournes Edn. 4to. A few margins very lightly stained. Cont. vell., slightly reprd. (PNY. Mar.26; 329) $1,200
- – **Anr. Edn.** Ed.:– Danielis Barbari. Venice, 1567. Fo. Some ll. dampstained. Old vell., soiled, upr. cover loose. (S. Jun.22; 151) *Mediolanum.* £170
- **Architectura ... cum Exercitationibus ... Joannis Poleni et Commentariis Variorum, additis nunc primum studiis Simonis Stratico.** Udine, 1825-30. 8 pts. in 4 vols. 4to. Slight spotting. Cont. russ., rebkd., 'Ralph Sneyd' gt.-stpd. on covers. Stp. of Dominican Fathers, Edinb. (S. Jun.29; 286) *Weinreb.* £280
- **The Architecture.** Trans.:– W. Newton. 1791. [1st. Compl. Edn. in Engl.?]. 2 vols. in 1. Fo. Printers' cancel on title-pp. Cont. cf., worn. (PD. May 20; 107) £190
- – **Anr. Copy.** 2 vols. Imprint on both title-pp. inlaid to replace another. Old qtr. cf., needs rebdg. (SG. Dec.4; 357) $300
- **Architecture Générale.** Paris, 1681. 12mo. Cont. cf. (SH. Jul.16; 35) *Hawkins.* £65
- **I Dieci Libri Dell'Architectura ...** Trans.:– Monsig. Daniel Barbaro. Venice, 1629. Fo. Dampstained at end, MS. note an acquisition of this book, on fly-lf. Mod. cl.-bkd. bds. (S. Dec.8; 121) *Weinreb.* £180
- – **Anr. Copy.** 4to. A few stains. 19th. C. cf., worn. (SH. Jun.4; 151) *Elliott.* £85
- **Les Dix Livres d'Architecture.** Trans.:– C. Perrault. Paris, 1684. 2nd. Edn. Fo. Lacks final blank, tear in 3G1, some ll. slightly stained at head, slight soiling & spotting. Cont. mott. cf., very worn. (S. Feb.10; 342) *Paine.* £160
- – **Anr. Copy.** Some dampstaining, wormed in lr. inner margins at beginning. Old cf., very defect. (S. Jun.22; 152) *Faurre.* £90
- **Iterum [de Architectura] et Frontinus [de Aqueductibus].** Flor., 1513. 2 pts. in 1 vol. Cont. limp vell., pastedowns from incunable ll., spine lining from 13th. C. MS. (S. Nov.25; 409) *Breslauer.* £600
- **M. Vitruvius per Iocundum Solito castigatior factus cum Figuris.** Ed.:– G. Giocondo. Venice, 22 May 1511. 1st. Ill. Edn. Sm. fo. Stain on last p., lacks last blank lf., sm. wormhole in last 9 ll. 19th. C. vell. (SI. Dec.4; 613) Lire 5,200,000

VITRUVIUS Pollo, Marcus–FRONTINUS, Sextus Julius
- **De Architectura.–De Aquaeductibus.** Ed.:– [Johannes Sulpitius] (1st. work); & [Pomponius Laetus & Johannes Sulpitius]. [Rome], [Eucharius Silber], ca. 1487. 1st. Edns. 2 works in 1 vol. Fo. 1st. work: capital spaces, most with guide letters, spaces for diagrams & Greek verses, woodcut diagram on fo. 13r, fo. 39 remargined; 2nd. work: capital spaces with guide letters, spaces for Greek, sm. paper flaw on final lf., affecting 2 or 3 letters; some ll. at beginning & end slightly soiled, some others stained, early marginalia bleached out on several ll. Italian mott. sheep. The copy of Girolamo Caratti & Paul Mellon, lately in the Pierpont Morgan Liby. [BMC IV, 125 & 123, Goff V306 & F324] (CNY. Apr.8; 144) $50,000

VITRY, Paul
- **Hotels & Maisons de la Renaissance Française.** Ill.:– Clive Chevojon. Paris, ca. 1912. 1st. Edn. 3 vols. Later binder's cl. (PNY. Oct.1; 29) $125

VITRY, Urbain
- **Le Proprietaire Architecte.** Paris, 1827. 2 vols. 4to. Mod. cl., orig. wraps. bnd. in, partly unc. (SI. Dec.4; 614) Lire 650,000

VITTOVA PLYASKA [St. Vitus Dance]
Ed.:– [B.V. Nikol'sky]. St. Petersb., 1905-06. 7 Iss. in 1 vol. Fo. 1 iss. loose, a few sm. tears. Mod. cl.-bkd. bds. (SH. Feb.5; 141) *Quaritch.* £150

VIVALDUS, J.L.
- **Aureum Opus de Veritate Contritionis.** 24 Apr. 1509. Old inscrs., partly deleted, on title & last lf. verso. Cont. cf., reprd. (SH. Jul.9; 153) *Lee.* £70

VIVES, Joannes Ludovicus
- **Von gebührlichem thun und lassen eines Christlichen Ehamanns ... De Officio Mariti [–De Instituione Christianae Foeminae ... Von underweisunge und anfürung einer Christlichen Junkfrawen].** Trans.:– Christopher Bruno. Frankfurt, 1566. 2 pts. in 1 vol. Fo. A few marginal wormholes, title & a few ll. soiled, lacks last blank of pt. I. Old bds., slightly worn. (S. Jan.27; 354) *Wenner.* £550

VIVIAN, A. Pendarves
- Wanderings in the Western Land. Ill.:- Albert Bierstadt after the author. L., 1879. 1st. Edn. New leatherette. Pres. copy. (SG. Jan.8; 441) $160

VIVIAN, George
- Views from the Gardens of Rome & Albano. Ill.:- J.D. Harding after Vivian. 1848. Fo. Orig. mor.-bkd. cl. (C. May 20; 184) *Davidson*. £380

VIVIANI, Vincenzo
- De Locis Solidis Secunda Divinatio Geometrica in quinque Libros Iniuria Temporum Amissos Aristaei Senioris Geometriae. Ill.:- F.A. Lorenzini. Flor., [1701]. 1st. Edn. Fo. Some foxing & staining. Cont. Italian red mor., panel. in gt., arms of Pope Clement XI on covers, gt. spine, reprd. at head & foot. Pres. copy; bkplt. of Petrus-Stephanus Dutour de Salvert; from Honeyman Collection. (S. May 20; 3063) *Hughes*. £1,100
- - Anr. Copy. Some spotting, title reinforced in inner margin. Cont. vell. bds. Bkplt. of Biblioteca Banzil; from Honeyman Collection. (S. May 20; 3064) *Howell*. £170
- De Maximis, et Minimis Geometrica Divinatio In Quintum Conicorum Apollonii Pergaei. Flor., 1659. 1st. Edn., L.P. 2 pts. in 1 vol. Fo. Some MS. corrections to text, others on paste-in ptd. slips. Cont. cf., gt. From Honeyman Collection. (S. May 20; 3061) *Hill*. £350

VIVIEN, Renée
- Etudes et Préludes.-Cendres et Poussières. 1901-02. 1st. Edns. 2 works in 2 vols. Square 12mo. Limp Bradel mor. by Lavaux, wraps. Autograph dedication by author (1st. work). (HD. Jun.25; 435) Frs. 1,050
- Une Femme m'apparut.-A l'Heure des Mains Jointes.-Flambeaux Eteints. Paris, 1905-06; 1907. 1st. Edns. (except 1st. work). 3 works in 2 vols. 12mo/8vo. Limp Bradel mor. by Lavaux, wraps. 2 works with author's visiting card & autograph dedication. (HD. Jun.25; 437) Frs. 1,550

VLAAMSE STAM
Mar. 1965-1980. Yr. 1, no. 1-Yr. 16, no. 4. In pts. (LM. Nov.8; 292) B.Frs. 7,500

VLACQ, Adriaan
- Thesaurus Logarithmorum Completus ... Ed.:- Georgio Vega. Leipzig, 1794. Fo. Browned & spotted. Hf. cf., sig. 'Burckhardt' on front pastedown. Stps. of Royal Astronomical Society & Mathematical Society; from Honeyman Collection. (S. May 20; 3067) *Birch*. £50
- Trigonometria Artificialis: sive Magnus Canon Triangulorum Logarithmicus. Gouda, 1633. 1st. Edn. Fo. First 29 ll. guarded at inner edge, title & last lf. mntd., title & several other ll. soiled or stained. 18th. C. mott. cf., covers loose, very worn, red hf. mor. case. John Flamsteed's copy with sigs. of his wife & John Weston; as an association copy, w.a.f.; bkplts. of Alexander Lord Polwarth & J.W.L. Glaisher; from Honeyman Collection. (S. May 20; 3065) *Zeitlin & Verbrugge*. £170

VLADERACKEN, Chr.
- Polyonyma Ciceroniana. Antw., 1604. Biographical annots. on end-papers. Cont. blind-stpd. vell. (VG. Nov.18; 1421) Fls. 700

VLAMINCK, Maurice de
- Notre Pain Quotidien. Paris, 1963. (50) numbered on H.M.P. from Moulin Richard de Bas, & with 7 orig. etchings & engrs. Fo. Loose as iss. in linen pict. folding box. (SG. Apr.2; 306) $600

VODOLAZ [Diver]
Ed.:- [Yu. V. Gol'dberg]. St. Petersb., 1906. Nos. 1-5. 4to. Last no. stained. Unbnd. (SH. Feb.5; 142) *De la Casa*. £90

VODOVOROT [Whirlpool]
Ed.:- [S.N. Mendel'son]. St. Petersb., 1906; 1907. Nos. 1-6, 8 & 9 only (of 9); 1-3 (? only). Various sizes. Unbnd. (SH. Feb.5; 143) *De la Casa*. £230

VOERHOFF
See-BRY, Theodore de & others

VOGEL, F.C.
- Panorama des Rheins. Frankfurt-am-Main, ca. 1840. 2 pts. Ob. lge. 8vo. In 2 orig. portfos., bds., s.-c., bds. covered with red leath., decor. with gt. borders & blind-stpd. flower decor., defect. (VG. Nov.18; 964) Fls. 2,600

VOGEL, Julius
- Studien und Entwuerfe Aelterer Meister im Staedtischen Museum zu Leipzig. Ill.:- Max Klinger & Otto Greiner (orig. ills.). Leipzig, ca. 1895. Tall lge. fo. Loose as iss. (SG. May 21; 412) $110

VOGEL, Z.
- Anatomische, Chirurgische und Medicinische Beobachtungen und Untersuchungen. Rostock, 1759. Title stpd., slightly soiled. Cont. leath. gt. (D. Dec.11-13; 239) DM 800

VOGELSANG, W.
See-PIT, A. & others

VOGELWEIDE, Wather von der
- [Gedichte]. Ed.:- C. v. Kraus. Munich, 1931. (250). Orig. vell., s.-c. (R. Mar.31-Apr.4; 414) DM 1,000

VOGTER, Bartholomeus
See-BRUNSCHWIG, Hieronymus–VOGTER, Bartholomeus

VOGUE
N.Y., Jul.-Dec. 1920. Vol. 56, 12 nos. in 1 vol. 4to. Advts. Buckram, worn, with all the cold. pict. covers. (SG. May 21; 446) $150

VOIGHT, Hans Henning 'Alastair'
- Fifty Drawings. Ed.:- Carl Van Vechten. N.Y., 1925. 1st. Edn. (1250) on L.P. Lge. tall 4to. Cl., boxed. (PNY. Oct.1; 11) $110
- Forty Three Drawings. L., 1914. (500). 4to. Many pp. loose, slight soiling. Orig. bdg., soiled. (SPB. May 29; 3) $150
- - Anr. Edn. Ed.:- Robert Ross. L., 1914. (500) numbered on L.P. Tall 4to. Gt. pict. cl. (PNY. Oct. 1; 12) $140

VOIGT, C.
[-] Gespräch von der Musik. Erfurt, 1742. 4to. Cont. paper bds., heavily defect. (H. Dec.9/10; 1298) DM 920

VOIGTEL, Nicolaus
- Geometria Subterranea, oder Marckscheide-Kunst. Eisleben, 1686. 1st. Edn. Fo. Browned thro.-out. 19th. C. bds., red hf. mor. case. From Honeyman Collection. (S. May 20; 3068) *Zeitlin & Verbrugge*. £480

VOINA KOROLEI [War of Kings, from the series 'Petrushka'. Obolensky Puppet Theatre]
Moscow, 1918. Ob. fo. Orig. wraps., slightly soiled, loose. (SH. Feb.6; 544) *Reed & Sims*. £100

VOISENON, Claude Henri de Fusée, Abbé de
- Contes. Ill.:- Lalauze after Cochin (port.); Gery-Bichard (figures). Paris, 1878. Ltd. Edn. Figures in 2 states. Mor. by Pagnan, decor. spine, inside dentelle. Bkplt. of Francis Kettaneh. (SM. Feb.11; 173) Frs. 2,000

VOLCKHAMER, Johann Georg
- Flora Noribergensis. Nuremb., 1700. 1st. Edn. 4to. 24 engraved plts. (of 25?), minor staining at end, minor tears at outer edges. 19th. C. hf. mor. From Chetham's Liby., Manchester. (C. Nov.27; 405a) *Quaritch*. £140

VOLCKMER, Tobias
- Tabulae Proportionum Anglorum Geometriae. Augsberg, 1617. 4to. Wormhole at beginning slightly affecting text & engrs. Wraps., sm. hole in upr. cover. (S. Jan.27; 355) *Wagner*. £95

VOLK [Wolf]
Moscow, 1906. 4to. Unbnd. (SH. Feb.5; 144) *Quaritch*. £75

VOLKMANN, Daniel G.
- Memories of a Fishing Journey to New Zealand. San Franc., Westgate Pr., 1950. (100). Bds., unc. (SG. Oct.16; 502) $225

VOLKMANN, J.J.
- Historisch-kritische Nachrichten von Italien. Leipzig, 1770-71. 1st. Edn. 3 vols. Slightly soiled in places, ex-lib. inside cover. Cont. hf. leath. gt., slightly worn. (H. May 21/22; 1114) DM 1,400

VOLKOVYSKY, Arnold
- Solnsta Potselui [Kiss of the Sun]. Ill.:- N. Al'tman. St. Petersb., 1914. Orig. wraps., slightly torn & soiled. (SH. Feb.6; 545) *Quaritch*. £80

VOLLARD, Ambroise
- Paul Cezanne. Paris, 1914. (200) 'sur velin à la forme'. 4to. Bdg. not stated, orig. wraps. bnd. in, partly unc. (C. Jul.22; 170) *Fletcher*. £250
- - Anr. Edn. Paris, 1914. (600) numbered, on papier teinte. Lge. 4to. Mod. leatherette, orig. pict. wraps bnd. in. (SG. Oct.23; 52) $600
- - Anr. Edn. Paris, 1914. 4to. Hf. roan, wrap. (HD. Dec.5; 219) Frs. 2,400
- Sainte Monique. Ill.:- Pierre Bonard. 1930. Sewed. On papier de lin à la cuve, suite of lithos. & etchings on vell. d'Arches. (HD. Oct.10; 210) Frs. 3,500
- - Anr. Edn. Ill.:- after Pierre Bonard. Paris, priv. ptd., 1930. (390) on vell. 4to. Sewed, wrap. (HD. Dec.5; 220) Frs. 2,700
- Tableaux, Pastels & Dessins de Pierre-Auguste Renoir. Paris, 1954. Facs. Reprint, (100). 2 vols. Sm. fo. Orig. wraps. pasted onto mor. (S. Jul.27; 200) *Ursus Books*. £1,400
- La Vie & l'Oeuvre de Pierre-Auguste Renoir. Ill.:- Renoir (1 etching). Paris, 1919. (1000) numbered on vel. d'Arches. Lge. 4to. Orig. pict. sewed, s.-c., lightly soiled. (HK. Nov.18-21; 2872) DM 1,600

VOLLSTANDIGE VOLKERGALLERIE
Meissen, [1830-39]. 5 pts. in 4 vols. Plts. slightly soiled, text more heavily. Cont. hf. leath. (R. Mar.31-Apr.4; 1576) DM 2,200
- - Anr. Copy. 5 pts. in 3 vols. Lacks 3 old cold. litho. plts., lacks 2 ll. text, vol. 2 slightly soiled in parts. Cont. hf. leath., very worn, 2 spines defect. (R. Oct.14-18; 2652) DM 2,000

VOLMARIUS, M.
- Newe Zeitung vom Schröcklichen Erdbidm, den 15. nach dem Newen, aber den 5. Tag Septembris, nach dem Alten Calender des 1590 Jars, zu Wien ... N.p., 1591. 4to. Lightly soiled or browned. Later hf. vell. (D. Dec. 11-13; 55) DM 600

VOLNEY, Constantin François
- Oeuvres. 1825-1826. 8 vols. Cont. decor. hf. cf., fillet decor. (HD. Feb.18; 199) Frs. 1,100
- Travels through Syria & Egypt. 1788. 2 vols. Cf. gt. (P. Oct.23; 76) *Brooke-Hitching*. £70
- View of the Climate & Soil of the United States. Phila., 1804. 1st. L. Edn. Mod. hf. mor., gt. spine & borders, unc. & unopened, marb. bds. & end-papers. From liby. of William E. Wilson. [Sabin 100694] (SPB. Apr.29; 271) $100

VOL'NITSA [Freeman]
Ed.:- [B.N. Nelidov]. St. Petersb., 1906. No. 1. Orig. wraps., spine torn, loose. (SH. Feb.5; 145) *Quaritch*. £50

VOLPI: Annali della Tipografia Volpi-Cominiana
Padua, 1809. L.P. Orig. ptd. wraps., unc. From the collection of John A. Saks. (C. Jun.10; 281) *Quaritch*. £220

VOLPI, Charles de & Scowen, P.H.
- The Eastern Townships. Montreal, [1962]. 4to. Cl., d.-w. (slightly torn). (CB. Apr.1; 113) Can. $110

VOLSHEBNY FONAR' [Magic Lantern]
Ed.:- [I.N. Potopenko]. St. Petersb., 1905; 1906. Nos. 1-3; nos. 1-5. 4to. Unbnd. (SH. Feb.6; 146) *Landry*. £150

VOLTA, Alessandro
[-] Biblioteca Fisica d'Europe. Ed.:- L.V. Brugnatelli. Pavia, [1788]. Vols. I & II. Orig. ptd. wraps., spines defect., unc. From Honeyman Collection. (S. May 20; 3074) *Quaritch*. £120
- Collezione dell' Opere. Ed.:- Vincenzio Antinori. Flor., 1816. 1st. Coll. Edn. 3 vols. in 5. Some staining, lacks port. Orig. wraps., spines defect., unc., red hf. mor. cases. From Honeyman Collection. (S. May 20; 3078) *Zeitlin & Verbrugge*. £140
- De Vi Attractiva ignis Electrici, ac Phaenomenis inde Pendentibus ... ad Joannem Baptistam Beccariam ... Dissertatio Epistolaris. Como, 1769. 1st. Edn. Slight marginal soiling, title partly circled in ink. Cont. limp bds., rebkd., unc. From Honeyman Collection. (S. May 20; 3070) *James*. £3,000
- L'Identita del Fluido Elettrico col cosi detto Fluido Galvanico vittoriosamente dimostrata ... Memoria Communicata al signore Pietro Configliachi. Ed.:- Pietro Configliachi. Ill.:- G. Garavaglia. Pavia, 1814. 1st. Edn., L.P. 4to. 7 pp. catalogue of author's works at end with slip 'Aggiunta' pasted on last p., neat marginal repairs to pp. 43/44 & last lf. Mod. bds. From Honeyman Collection. (S. May 20; 3076) *James*. £340
- - Anr. Copy. 7 pp. catalogue of Volta's works at end, without the 'Aggiunta' slip. Hf. cl., worn, orig. wrap. (stained) bnd. in. Pres. copy from ed.

VOLTA, Alessandro *-contd.*
to Dr. [Johann Friedrich] Meckel of Halle; from Honeyman Collection. (S. May 20; 3077) *Offenbacher.* £260
– Lettere . . . sull'aria Infiammabile Nativa delle paludi. Milan, 1777. 1st. Edn. Inserted lf. at end with Latin quotation, last 2 ll. of text a little wormed at head, slight stain in lr. margin of title. Cont. bds., covers wormed, sig. on fly-lf. of Giovanni Cristofano Amaduzzi. From Honeyman Collection. (S. May 20; 3072) *Quaritch.* £280
– – Anr. Copy. Without inserted lf. at end. Worn. From Honeyman Collection. (S. May 20; 3073) *Zeitlin & Verbrugge.* £220
– Novus ac Simplicissimus Electricorum Tentaminum Apparatus: seu de Corporibus Eteroelectricis quae fiunt Idioelectrica. Como, 1771. 1st. Edn. Sm. 4to. Mod. wraps. From Honeyman Collection. (S. May 20; 3071) *James.* £1,200
– Schriften über die Thierische Elektrizitat . . . Aus dem Italiänischen Ubersetzt. Ed.:– D. Johann Mayer. Prague, 1793. Title spotted & with verso hinged at inner margin to following lf. Cont. bds. Bkplt. of Herbert McLean Evans; from Honeyman Collection. (S. May 20; 3075) *Zeitlin & Verbrugge.* £260

VOLTAIRE, François Marie Arouet de
– Candide. 1759. 1st. Engl. Edn? 12mo. Additional engraved port. laid down on A1 blank, some ll. slightly soiled. Cont. hf. cf., worn. (SBA. May 27; 127) *Claridge.* £120
– – Anr. Edn. Trans.:– Mr. le Docteur Ralph. N.p., [Fr.?], 1759. 12mo. Some browning & soiling. Cont. sheep, worn. (S. Oct.21; 537) *Lyon.* £85
[–] – Anr. Edn. [L.], 1759-61. 2 vols. 12mo. Cont. hf. mor., jnts. reprd. William Morris's copy. (SH. Jan.30; 365) *Subunso.* £50
– – Anr. Edn. Ill.:– Rockwell Kent. N.Y., 1928. (95) numbered, sigd. by artist. Mor.-bkd. patterned linen. (SG. Oct.23; 181) $800
– – Anr. Edn. Ill.:– Rockwell Kent. N.Y., 1928. (1470) numbered on Fr. rag paper, sigd. by artist. 4to. Gt.-embossed buckram. (SG. Dec.18; 261) $100
– – Anr. Edn. Ill.:– Maillart after S. Sauvage. Paris, 1928. (12), numbered. 4to. Red mor. by Saulnier, decor. spine, border of 4 gt. fillets on covers, wrap. preserved, s.-c. Collaborator's copy. (SM. Feb.11; 298) Frs. 6,000
– – Anr. Edn. Ill.:– Clave. Paris, [1948]. (250) on Bütten. 4to. Loose ll. in orig. wraps. (H. Dec.9/10; 2006) DM 800
– Elemens de la Philosophie de Neuton. Ill.:– Jacob Folkema (frontis. & port.). Amst., 1738. 1st. Edn. Browned & spotted. Cont. cf., gt., rebkd. preserving old spine, hf. red mor. case. From Honeyman Collection. (S. May 20; 3079) *Zeitlin & Verbrugge.* £220
– – Anr. Edn. L. [Paris], 1738. 2nd. Edn. Some browning. Cont. cf., gt., slightly worn. Pres. copy; from Honeyman Collection. (S. May 20; 3080) *Maggs.* £500
– – Anr. Edn. 'L.', [Paris], 1741. New Edn. No port. of Voltaire. Cont. cf., worn. (S. Dec.2; 788) *Phelps.* £50
– – Anr. Copy. 12mo. Cont. mott. cf., gt. spine. (SG. Sep.25; 318) $275
– Letters concerning the English Nation. Trans.:– John Lockman. 1733. 1st. Edn. Advt. lf. Cont. panel. cf. (S. May 5; 353) *Quaritch.* £90
– Lettres Chinoises, Indiennes et Tartares à Monsieur Paw par un Benedictin avec Plusieurs autres Pieces Intéressantes.–Un Chrétien Contre Six Juifs.–Le Taureau Blanc. Paris; L.; [Paris?], 1776; 1777; 1774. 1st. Edns. 3 works in 1 vol. Cf. (S. Nov.18; 688) *Kreuzer.* £180
[–] Lettres écrites de Londres sur les Anglois et autres sujets. Basle [L.], 1734. 1st. Fr. Edn. Cont. cf., spine gt. (S. Feb.23; 364) *Pythagoras.* £60
– Oeuvres. Paris, 1864. 13 vols. Some spotting. Unif. cf.-bkd. bds. (CSK. Jan.30; 101) £70
– Oeuvres Complètes. Paris, 1784-89. 70 vols. Later cf., some spines worn. (SH. May 28; 103) *Booth.* £160
– – Anr. Copy. Red mor. by Bisiaux, gt. fillets & roll-stps. around covers, smooth decor. spines, inside dentelle, watered silk end-papers, some sm. stains on covers. (HD. Feb.27; 60) Frs. 64,000
– – Anr. Copy. Lacks 1 port., soiled or browned in parts, vol. 44 (without copper engr.) & 54 double. Cont. cf., not. unif., worn. (H. May 21/22; 1316) DM 800
– – Anr. Edn. Ill.:– after Moreau. [Kehl], 1785-89. 70 vols. Some very minor defects. Cont. tree cf. gt., some vols. slightly worn. Bkplts. of the Earl of Wicklow. (SBA. May 27; 136) *Barock Museum.* £760
– – Anr. Copy. Cont. hf. cf., worn, some covers detchd. (S. May 5; 81) *Duran.* £400
– – Anr. Copy. Lacks frontis. (replaced by port. of Voltaire after Largillière). Cont. marb. roan, decor. spines, inner dentelles. (HD. Feb.18; 80) Frs. 12,500
– – Anr. Edn. Paris, 1821-22. 60 vols. 12mo. Some vols. spotted. Later hf. cf., decor. spines. (SM. Feb.11; 40) Frs. 2,600
– – Anr. Edn. Paris, 1825-32. 95 vols. Foxed thro.-out. Hf. cf. by Boutigny, decor. spines, some vols. slightly worn. (SM. Feb.11; 136) Frs. 3,500
– – Anr. Edn. 1826-30. Vols. 1-70. Hf. cf., some spotting. (P. Apr.30; 90) *Horsh.* £85
– Le Philosophe Ignorant.–Les Questions de Zapota.–Le Diner du Comte de Boulainvilliers. Trans.:– Tamponet (2nd. work). 1766; 1766; n.d. Orig. Edn. of 1st. 2 works. 3 works in 1 vol. Cont. red mor., inner dentelle. (HD. Jun.10; 111) Frs. 3,000
– La Pucelle d'Orléans. L., 1761. Some foxing. Cont old red mor., spine very decor., 3 fillets on covers, inner dentelle. (HD. Apr.10; 386) Frs. 1,700
– – Anr. Edn. Ill.:– Drake. [Geneva], 1762. [1st. Edn.?]. 16mo. 25 figures (of 26), foxing. Cont. cf., spine decor., 3 gt. fillets, 3 inner gt. fillets. From the Liby. of Victor Cousin. (HD. Apr.10; 387) Frs. 2,300
– – Anr. Copy. Cf. (DS. May 22; 862) Pts. 30,000
– – Anr. Edn. Ed.:– M. de Morza. L., 1775. Some ills. loose. Cont. spr. cf., decor. spine, worn. (HD. Dec.5; 221) Frs. 1,300
[–] [–] Anr. Edn. Ill.:– Charles Monnet. 1777-79. Fo. Suite of 22 fine ink & wash drawings prepared for unpubld. edn., mntd. in album with calligraphic red & gt. title-p. by J. Lundy. Red mor., elab. gt., mor. doubls., silk liners. Savigny de Moncorps copy, his arms on doubls., later in Lord Carnarvon Collection. (SM. Oct.8; 2424) Frs. 97,000
– – Anr. Edn. Ill.:– Duplessi-Bertaux. L., 1780. 2 vols. 18mo. Red mor. by Cazin, worn. (HD. Apr.8; 310) Frs. 2,100
– – Anr. Edn. Ill.:– Marillier. Geneva, 1788. 18mo. Foxing, plts. generally found in 1777 Edn. Marb. sheep, by Cazin. (HD. Apr.8; 311) Frs. 1,600
[–] – Anr. Copy. 12mo. Slightly soiled. Cont. red leath. (R. Oct.14-18; 1109) DM 2,400
– – Anr. Edn. Ill.:– after Moreau le Jeune, engraved by Dambrun, Delaunay, Duclos & others. [Kehl], 1789. On vell. 2 vols. 4 ports. Cont. red mor., decor., narrow gold border, centre-piece of gold fillets with sm. round gold stp., wide gold border on inner dentelles, silk end-ll., outer gt. dentelle. (D. Dec.11-13; 747) DM 2,000
– – Anr. Edn. Ill.:– A. Romanet, C.L. Lingée, N. Ponce, Chaffard, Delvaux & others after Monnet, Marillier & others. Paris, [1795]. On vell. Lge. 4to. Slightly soiled, engraved port. by Ponce slightly stained at margin. Cont. leath. gt. (HK. Nov.18-21; 2397) DM 3,600
– – Anr. Edn. Paris, An VII, ca. 1796. 2 vols. Cont. gt.-ornamental spr. cf. (PNY. Oct.1; 526) $190
– – Anr. Edn. Paris, An VII [1798-99]. 2 vols. Cont. tree cf., gt. (S. Mar.17; 291) *Greenwood.* £50
– Romans et Contes. Ill.:– Duponchel after Chevaux. (frontis.). L., 1781. 3 vols. 18mo. Marb. cf. by Cazin. (HD. Apr.8; 313) Frs. 1,400
– Traité sur la Tolérance. N.p., 1763. Early (1st. ?) Edn. Lightly browned. Cont. vell., slightly soiled. (H. Dec.9/10; 1693) DM 420
– Works. [1901-03]. (1000). 43 vols. Cont. hf. mor. (CSK. Aug.29; 175) £55
– – Anr. Edn. N.d.-1903. 43 vols. Orig. cl. (SH. May 28; 104) *Makey.* £50

VONDEL, Joost van den
– Gysbrecht van Aemstel. Ed.:– L. Simons. Ill.:– A.J. Derkinderen. Harlem, 1893-1901. 2 vols. 4to. Slight foxing, vol. II loosening. Later cl. (VG. Nov.18; 849) Fls. 500
– [Works]. Amst., Rotterdam, Franeker, 1643-1703. 63 pts. in 11 vols. 4to. A few quires slightly foxed or browned. Cont. vell., some vols. slightly stained. (VG. Oct.13; 163) Fls. 1,200
– [–] Anr. Edn. Amst., 1682-1768. 18 works in 10 vols. 4to. 18th. C. marb. cf., gt. spine & raised in compartments. (VG. Oct.13; 164) Fls. 1,800

VON FERSMANN, A. & Goldschmidt, V.
– Der Diamant. Heidelberg, 1911. 2 vols. Pencil notes in margins. Hf. mor. Pres. copy from V. Goldschmidt. (SSA. Jan.22; 138) R. 95

VON GERNING, Baron Johann Isaac von
– A Picturesque Tour along the Rhine. 1820. Fo. Some ll. loose & soiled. Orig. cl., worn. (SH. Mar.5; 149) *Symonds.* £1,400

VON MUELLER, Baron Ferdinand
See–**MUELLER, Baron Ferdinand von**

VORAGINE, Jacobus de
[–] [The Golden Legend]. Trans.:– William Caxton. [Wynkyn de Worde], [20 May, 1493]. 3rd. Edn. in Engl. Fo. Lacks 35 ll., lacks pt. of a5 affecting 10 lines of text, portions of woodcuts on folios n7, B4, I3, & 2c2 excised, some ll. at beginning & end frayed, some staining, some 16th. C. notes in ink. 19th. C. mor. over wood bds. [STC 24875; Goff J149] (C. Nov.19; 23) *Stewart.* £5,000
[–] [–] Anr. Copy. 217 ll. of 463, first & last lf. replaced in facs., 47 woodcuts from 35 blocks (of a possible 61 blocks), some ll. slightly defect., mostly in margin, ff. o8, z3, 98 & Q2 defect. with some loss, some old marginalia, some ll. soiled. 19th. C. antique-style cf., upr. cover detchd. W.a.f. [Goff J105; NSTC 24875] (S. Jun.23; 210) *Sotheran.* £2,000
– – Anr. Edn. Westminster, Wynkyn de Worde, 8 Jan. 1498. Fo. 2 lf. fragment, comprising folios 299 & 303. Red mor. gt. by Sangorski & Sutcliffe. From the collection of Eric Sexton. [Goff J151] (CNY. Apr.8; 205) $700
– – Anr. Edn. L., 15 Feb. 1512. Fo. Incompl., lacks prelims. before 'Folio primo', final lf. supplied in early photographic facs. Later cf., rebkd. [STC 24879] (SG. Feb.5; 336) $1,900
– – Anr. Edn. Trans.:– William Caxton. Kelms. Pr., 1892. (500). 3 vols. 4to. Orig. holland-bkd. bds. (SH. Jan.30; 366) *Subunso.* £210
[–] [Legenda Aurea]. Nuremb., 1481. Fo. Lightly soiled, slightly wormed at end. 18th. C. hf. leath. [BMC II, 419] (HK. Nov. 18-21; 320) DM 900
– [Legenda Aurea] Passionael, Somerstuck. Delft, Christian Snellaert, 7 Oct. 1489. Pt. 2 only (of 2). Fo. Spaces for initial capitals, paragraph marks, capitals & initial strokes supplied in red, lacks title-p. & s7 (both supplied in facs.), sm. marginal repairs to fo. 2-4, lr. margin of e1 renewed, patch of abrasion at k1r with loss of some letters, marginal tear at p7 reprd., long tear from lr. margin at u7 reprd. without loss, last lf. rehinged with sm. tear to extreme inner margin, soiling & traces of use, monastic inscr. on blank verso of last lf. & rear paste-down, with later censor's note dtd. 1753. Cont. blind-stpd. cf. over wood bds., worn, spine reprd. Bkplt. of Thedoro Becu, lately in the collection of Eric Sexton. [BMC IX, 23, C. 6518, Goff J141] (CNY. Apr.8; 52) $9,000
– Legendario delle Vite de'Santi. Venice, 1585. Fo. 4 unnumbered pp. Mod. hf. vell. (CR. Mar.19; 279a) Lire 300,000
– Legendario di Sancti. Venice, 2 Aug. 1518. Fo. Short tear in LL2, stain on lr. margin of title-p. necessitating repair on verso, a few minor stains & repairs towards end, occasional very light worming with infinitesimal loss of text. 19th. C. cont.-style cf. (S. May 5; 20) *Stewart.* £420
[–] Lombardica Historia. Strassburg, 19 Dec. 1486. Sm. fo. Rubricated, old MS. underlining, old MS. arms on title & owner's mark, title slightly wormed, some loss, several sigs. stained, 1 lf. bkd. at head & 2 other sm. places. 16th. C. pig-bkd. wood bds., blind-tooled, decor. roll stps., lines, 2 brass bosses, lr. cover slightly soiled. [BMC I/135; 6444] (D. Dec.11-13; 29) DM 6,800
– Sermones de Tempore, Sermones de Sanctis. Deventer, Richardus Pafraet, 1483 & 6 Mar. 1483. 2 vols. in 1. Fo. Spaces for capital letters, those at head of each book supplied in red, green & yellow, others in red, paragraph marks, underlines & initial strokes in red, lacks the 2 blanks preceding text in vol. 1, first & last pp. soiled, portion of lr. corner of a2 in vol. 1 torn away, g2 in vol. 1 with clean tear to lr. margin, slight spotting to some ll. Cont. blind-stpd. cf. over wood bds., covers with central panels diapered with fleur-de-lys & Agnus Dei stps., brass clasps, worn, rebkd. Bkplt. of the General Theological Seminary Liby. [C. 6546, Goff J196] (CNY. Oct.1; 19) $7,000

VORBERG, Gaston, ed.
– **Die Erotik der Antike in Kleinkunst und Keramik.** Munich, 1921. Fo. Introductory text & 111 plts. (of 113). Loose as iss. in orig. box, slightly worn at corners. (S. Feb.23; 126) *Diba.* £160

VORON [Raven]
Ed.:– [N.A. Basin]. St. Petersb., 1905. No. 1. Fo. Unbnd. (SH. Feb.5; 147) *Landry.* £85
– – **Anr. Copy.** A few tears. (SH. Feb.5; 188) *Lempert.* £80
– – **Anr. Edn.** Ed.:– [K.E. Solodilov]. St. Petersb., n.d. No. 1 (?all publd.). Unbnd. (SH. Feb.5; 148) *Landry.* £180

VORSTERMAN VAN OIJEN, A.A.
– **Stam- en Wapenboek van Aanzienlijke Nederlandsche Familiën, met Genealogische en Heraldische Aanteekeningen.** Groningen, 1885-90. 3 vols. Lge. fo. Hf. of 1 plt. torn away in middle, altogether 621 (of 624) coats of arms depicted. Hf. leath., 1 vol. stained & defect. (VG. Dec.15; 447) Fls. 800
– – **Anr. Copy.** Minor foxing. Orig. cl. gt., loose & defect. W.a.f. (VG. Dec.15; 448) Fls. 600

VOSBURG, Walter S. & others.
Cherished Portraits of thoroughbred Horses. 1929. Fo. Orig. gt.-lettered red mor., spine gt., by Sangorski & Sutcliffe. Inscr. to Camilla Lippincott from William Woodward. (SG. Dec.11; 290) $1,500
– **Thoroughbred Types.** N.Y., 1926. (250) numbered. 4to. Linen-bkd. bds. (SG. Apr.9; 412) $130
– – **Anr. Edn.** Ill.:– Andrew R. Butler (etched frontis.). N.Y., Priv. ptd., 1926. (75) numbered, on Strathmore Old Stratford paper. Mor., rebnd., orig. covers. (JL. Dec.14; 429) *Aus.* £105

VOSSIUS, Gerardus, Canon of Canterbury
– **De Quatuor Artibus Popularibus, de Philologia, et Scientiis Mathematics . . . libri tres.** Amst., 1660. 4to. Short tear in N2 pt. 1. Cont. cf., worn. Armorial bkplt. of Sir Lister Holte, Aston, Warwickshire; from Honeyman Collection. (S. May 20; 3081) *Poole.* £55

VOYAGE EN ITALIE
Ca. 1817. 4to. Atlas; 2 folding maps, 27 town plans, 7 plts. Wraps. (P. May 14; 134) *Walford.* £120

VOYAGE PITTORESQUE Dans les Ports et sur les Côtes de France
[Paris], [1823-25?]. Fo. 45 cold. aquatint plts. Cont. hf. cf., cover detchd. (C. Mar.18; 163) *Hammond.* £4,800

VOYAGE PITTORESQUE . . . de Rome, Naples
1823-24. Fo. Hand-cold. title, 57 hand-cold. plts. & charts. Mod. hf. mor. gt. (P. Jun.11; 252) *Traylen.* £620

VOYAGES
– **A Compendium of Authentic & Entertaining Voyages . . .** 1766. 2nd. Edn. 7 vols. 12mo. 23 maps, 24 plts. Cont. cf., lacks some labels. [Sabin 20518] (C. May 20; 185) *Allen.* £100

VOYAGES Imaginaires . . .
Ed.:– M. Garnier. Ill.:– Marillier. Amst. & Paris, 1787-89. 39 vols. Some foxing. Cont. spr. roan, spines decor. with raised bands, some vols. in pastiche bdgs., bdgs. slightly defect. (HD. Jun.24; 123) Frs. 2,900

VREDIUS, Olivarius
– **Sigilla Comitum Flandriae et Inscriptiones Diplomatum.** Brussels, 1639. 1st. Edn. 2 pts. in 1 vol. Fo. Title slightly soiled, some short marginal tears. Cont. mott. cf., worn. Liby. bkplt. of Kimbolton Castle. (S. Feb.10; 347) *Haverbeke.* £130
– **Sigilla Comitum Flandriae et Inscriptiones Diplomatum ab iis Editorum cum Expositione Historica.–La Généalogie des Comtes de Flandre. –Historiae Comitum Flandriae. Pars Secunda.** Brugis Flandorum; Bruges; Bruges, 1639; 1642; 1650. 1 vol.; 2 vols.; 1 vol. Fo. Old cf., worn. (LM. Nov.8; 277) B.Frs. 18,000

VRIES, David Pietersz. de
– **Korte Historiael.** 1655. 1st. Edn. 4to. Sm. repair to port., title with several repairs & backed in inner margin, some sm. holes, folding fore-edges of some ills. with sm. repairs, slightly affecting engraved surfaces, several headlines slightly cropped or trimmed, some ll. smudged, other sm. repairs, washed thro.-out, view of New

Amsterdam by Ogilby inserted. Mod. citron mor., spine slightly discold. Bkplt. of Samuel Pennypacker. [Sabin 100852] (S. Feb.10; 475) *Israel.* £850

VRIES, Hugo de
– **The Mutation Theory . . .** Trans.:– J.B. Farmer & A.D. Darbishire. 1910-11. 2 vols. Orig. cl., slightly marked. (S. Apr.6; 166) *Blackwell.* £65
– **Die Mutationstheorie. Versuche und Beobachtungen uber die Entstehung von Arten im Pflanzenreich.** Leipzig, 1901-03. 1st. Edn. 2 vols. Cont. hf. leath. From Honeyman Collection. (S. May 20; 3082) *Percy.* £350

VRIES, Jan Vredeman de–MAROLOIS, Samuel
– **Perspectiva Theoretica ac Practica . . . Opus Opticum (2 pts.)–Architectura.–Artis Muniendi sive Fortificationis (2 pts.).–Geometrica Theoretica ac Practica.–Opticae sive Perspectivae.** Ill.:– Samuel Marolois [1st. & 2nd. works]. All Amst., 1633-32; 1647; 1644; 1647; 1647. 5 works in 2 vols. Fo. 1st. work: lacks plt. 34, general engraved title-page dtd. 1651; 2nd. work: apparently lacking some text, engraved title-page dtd. 1628; 3rd. work: engraved title-page dtd. 1662; 4th. work. lacks plt. 34, engraved title-page dtd. 1662. Cont. cf., gt. spines. W.a.f. (CNY. Oct.1; 29) $300

VRIES, Simon de
– **De Geheele Weereld.** Amst., 1686-94. 1st. Edn. 5 vols. 4to. Cont. vell., ex-liby. (SG. Feb.5; 337) $350

VUES DE PARIS au Daguerreotype
N.d. Cl. gt., worn. (CE. Oct.24; 213) £62

VUES DE ROME
Rome, 1876. Ob. fo. Dampstain thro.-out upr. margins. Orig. wraps., soiled, almost disbnd. (CSK. Dec.12; 119) £60

VUES PITTORESQUES DE LA BELGIQUE
Brussels, ca. 1870. Sm. fo. Orig. hf. leath. (R. Oct.14-18; 1907) DM 750

VUES PITTORESQUES DU RHIN
[1847]. Ob. fo. 27 engraved plts., without text(?), some margins slightly soiled or spotted, bnd. in are a panorama of the Rhine on 20 sheets, & a folding map. Cont. cf. gt., worn. W.a.f. (SBA. May 27; 315) *Hyde Park Bookshop.* £360

VUILLEMIN, A.A.
– **La France et Ses Colonies . . .** Paris, n.d. 1877 Edn. Fo. 108 hand-cold. maps (? only). Cont. mor.-bkd. bds. W.a.f. (CSK. Aug.29; 81) £110

VULSON, Marc de, Sieur de la Colombière
– **Le Vray Théâtre d'Honneur et de Chevalerie . . .** Paris, 1648. 2 vols. Fo. Cont. mott. sheep., Charles X arms gt.–stpd. on sides at later date, rebkd. with orig. backstrips, s.-c. M le Baron ed Warengheim & Edward Burne-Jones bkplts. (CNY. May 22; 286) $400

WAAGEN, Dr. Gustav Friedrich
– **Treasures of Art in Great Britain.** 1854-57. 4 vols., including Supp. Cont. hf. cf. gt. (SH. Oct.9; 199) *Bennett.* £65

WACHENHUSEN, K.S.H.
See–STIELER, Carl, Wachenhusen, K.S.H. & Hackländer, Friedrich Wilhelm

WACHTER, Leo De
– **Repertorium van de Vlaamse Gouwen en Gemeenten.** Antw., 1952. 5 pts. Orig. bdg. (LM. Nov.8; 19) B.Frs. 7,500

WADDINGTON, George & Hanbury, Barnard
– **Journal of a Visit to Ethiopia.** L., 1822. 1st. Edn. 4to. Three-qtr. cf. (SG. Oct.30; 4) $210

WADE, Henry
– **Halcyon; or Rod Fishing with Fly, Minnow & Worm.** L., 1861. 1st. Edn. Blind-stpd. cl. (SG. Oct.16; 503) $160

WADSWORTH ATHENEUM
– **Pablo Picasso, February-March, 1934, Hartford.** [Hartford], [1934]. Sm. 4to. 8 p. addenda leaflet inserted. Pict. wraps. Inserted is A.L.s., 12mo., 2 pp. from Alice B. Toklas to Bobsy Goodspeed, undtd. (PNY. Mar.4; 262) $100

WAELCKL, Georg
– **Die Walsch Practica, Gezogen auss der Kunst der Proportion, lernt gar Gruntlich unnd Behend Rechnen alle Kauffmans Handel und der Gleichen Furgab.** [Strassburg], 1536. 1st. Edn. A little worming in upr. margins of last few ll., slight dampstaining. Bnd. in fragment of incunable lf.

From Honeyman Collection. (S. May 20; 3083) *Dr. Martin.* £260

WAFER, Lionel
See–DAMPIER, William & Wafer, Lionel

WAGENAAR, Jan
– **Amsterdam . . .** Amst., 1760-67. 3 vols. Fo. Light soiling in some margins. Cont. hf. leath. gt., spine(s?) lightly defect., unc. (R. Mar.31-Apr.4 2657) DM 850
– – **Anr. Copy.** L.P. Lacks 1 engraved map. Cont. hf. cf. (VG. Oct.13; 166) Fls. 1,900
– – **Anr. Copy.** Includes the 52 extra plts. from Commelin, tear in author's port., some plts. with a short tear in the fold, foxed or browned in places, especially in vol. I. Cont. hf. roan, worn & defect., 3 jnts. brkn., unc. (VG. Dec.17; 1597) Fls. 1,600
– **Vaderlandsche Historie . . . noord-Americaansche Onlusten.** Amst., 1786-1811. 47 vols. & index. Vol. 35 lacks all after p. 216, some vols. heavily dampstained. Old hf. cf., all need rebdg., ex-liby. W.a.f. (SG. Feb.5; 339) $350
– **Vaderlandsche Historie, vervattende de Geschiedenissen, der nu Vereenigde Nederlanden, inz. die van Holland.** Amst., 1749-59. 21 vols. in 20. Cont. pol. cf., spines richly gt., raised in compartments. (VG. Dec.17; 1595) Fls. 1,525
– – **Anr. Copy.** 21 vols. Some slight browning, 125 (of 131) engrs. Cont. hf. leath., worn. (VG. Nov.18; 1439) Fls. 1,050
– **Vaderlandsche Historie.–Byvoegsels en Aanmerkingen.** Amst., 1790's; 1797 & 1801. 25 vols.; 2 vols. Some dampstaining to 1st. work. Old hf. cf., all need rebdg., ex-liby. (1st. work); & orig. wraps., unc. (SG. Feb.5; 338) $350

WAGENAAR, Jan & others
– **Amsterdam in zyne Opkomst, Aanwas, Geschiedenissen . . . (etc.). Om te dienen ten Ommiddelyken Vervolge op het Werk van Jan Wagenaar. Vierde Stuk.** Amst., ca. 1794. 4th. vol. Fo. Title & last lf. browned, marginal stains in few ll., ample margins, thick paper. Cont. hf. cf., top & foot of spine defect. (VG. Dec.17; 1598) Fls. 1,650

WAGENSEIL, Johann Christof
– **Belehrung der Juedisch Teutschen Red Und Schreibart. (Containing also Masechet Negaim, Drey Lieder Welche die Juden zu Singen Pflegen, & Ein Schoen Maase von Koehnig Artishof).** Koenigsberg, 1699. 4to. Slight staining. Hf. leath. (S. Nov.18; 690) *Waechter.* £500

WAGHENAER, Lucas Jansz
– **Speculum Nauticum Super Navigatione Maris Occidentalis Confectum . . .** Ill.:– Baptista & Joannes van Deutecom. Leiden, 1586. 1st. Edn. with Latin text. 2 pts. in 1 vol. Fo. (398mm. × 282mm.). Engraved general title dtd. 1583, pt. 1 engraved margins of map of Europe cropped, 2. sm. perforations in plt. 19, slightly affecting engraved surface & text on verso. Cont. pig., blind-tooled borders, panel & lozenge-shaped centre ornament, very worn, restored. W.a.f. (S. Jun.29; 8) *Hillman.* £19,00

WAGINGER, Johannes
See–LEONARDUS, Deacon of Salxburg & others

WAGNER, F.
[–] **Einleitung in die Alte und Neuerer Georgraphia.** Vienna, 1737. Cont. leath. (R. Oct. 14-18; 1571) DM 900

WAGNER, Henry R.
– **The Plains & the Rockies.** Ed.:– Charles L. Camp. San Franc., Grabhorn Pr. 1937. (600). Facs. title-pp. Cl. (SG. Oct.2; 369) $350

WAGNER, Richard
– **Lohengrin.** Leipzig, [1858]. Lge. 4to. 1st. ll. stpd., slightly browned in parts. Hf. leath. (H. Dec.9/10; 1301) DM 2,800
– **Die Meistersinger von Nürnberg.** [Munich], [1922]. (410) Lge. 4to. Orig. hand-bnd. red mor. gt. (H. Dec.9/10; 1302) DM 800
– – **Anr. Edn.** Mainz, n.d. 1st. Separate Edn. of the full score. Fo. Sewn. (C. Oct.22; 272) *Emery.* £55
– **Parsifal.** Trans.:– T.W. Rolleston. Ill.:– Willy Pogany. 1912. (525) numbered, sigd. by artist. 4to. Orig. vell. gt., slightly soiled. (S. Jul.31; 275) *Jones.* £110
– – **Anr. Copy.** 4to. Orig. gt.-pict. vell., partly unc. (SG. Apr.2; 246) $260

WAGNER, Richard -*contd.*
- **Das Rheingold.** Mainz, [1873]. 1st. Edn., numbered. Lge. 4to. Leath., defect., loose. (H. Dec.9/10; 1304) DM 1,500
- **The Rhinegold & the Valkyrie.** Ill.:– Arthur Rackham. 1910. [1st. Edn?] (1150) numbered, sigd. by artist. Vell. gt., lacks 1 tie. (WW. May 20; 85) £145
- - **Anr. Copy.** 4to. Orig. parch. gt., lacks ties. (SH. Mar.27; 431) *Primrose Hill.* £125
- - **Anr. Copy.** Soiled, backstrip torn, lacks ties. (S. Jul.31; 283) *Beetles.* £95
- - **Anr. Copy.** Lacks ties. (SH. Jul.16; 142) *Ayres.* £85
- - **Anr. Copy.** Slightly spotted. Orig. cl. gt. (S. Jul.31; 284) *Davidson.* £50
- - **Anr. Copy.** Some browning & spotting. Soiled, front free end-paper cut away. With orig. watercolour & ink drawing, sigd. on a blank preceeding title. (SPB. May 6; 242) $1,500
- - **Anr. Copy.** Gt.-pict. vell., orig. silk ties. Raymond M. Sutton, Jr., copy. (SG. May 7; 294) $800
- - **Anr. Copy.** Gt. vell., lacks ties, worn. (SG. Oct.23; 293) $425
- - **Anr. Copy.** Orig. decor. gt. cl., worn. (SPB. Jul.28; 406) $150
- - **Anr. Copy.** Gt.-pict. buckram. (SG. Oct.23; 294) $110
- **The Rhinegold & the Valkyrie.–Siegfried & the Twilight of the Gods.** Ill.:– Arthur Rackham. 1910-11. 2 vols. 4to. Orig. pict. cl. gt., slightly soiled. (SD. Feb.4; 127) £50
- **Das Rheingold & die Walkuere.** Ill.:– Arthur Rackham. Frankfurt, 1910. 1st. Edn. in German. 4to. Foxed. Vell.-bkd. bds., gt., warped., d.-w., box worn. Raymond M. Sutton, Jr., copy. (SG. May 7; 296) $425
- **Der Ring des Nibelungen.** Mainz, [1873-76]. 1st. Edn. 4 vols. Lge. 4to. Pig. (H. Dec.9/10; 1305) DM 5,600
- - **Anr. Edn.** Ill.:– A. Rackham. Frankfurt, 1910-11. 4to. Orig. hf. vell., spine slightly torn. (R. Mar.31-Apr.4; 631) DM 500
- **The Ring of the Niblung: The Rhinegold & the Valkyrie.–Siegfried & the Twilight of the Gods.** Ill.:– Arthur Rackham. 1910-11. 2 vols. 4to. Orig. pict. cl. gt., slightly worn. (S. Jul.31; 285) *Wangermee.* £120
- - **Anr. Copy.** Orig. decor. cl. covers bnd. in at end, unif. red hf. mor., gt. panel. spines, by Sotheran. (C. Feb.4; 203a) *Basket & Day.* £90
- **Siegfried.** Mainz, [1875]. 1st. Edn. (88) numbered. Lge. 4to. Slightly soiled. Vell. (H. Dec.9/10; 1307) DM 1,500
- **Siegfried & Goetterdaemmerung.** Ill.:– Arthur Rackham. Frankfurt, 1911. 1st. Edn. in German. 4to. End-papers foxed. Hf. vell. gt., warped, d.-w. foxed, box worn. Raymond M. Sutton, Jr., copy. (SG. May 7; 301) $110
- **Siegfried & the Twilight of the Gods.** Ill.:– Arthur Rackham. 1911. (1150). 4to. Orig. vell. gt., soiled. Sigd. by artist. (SH. Dec.11; 430) *Hatchard's.* £150
- - **Anr. Copy.** Numbered. Some ll. slightly discold. Spine discold., lacks ties. (SKC. May 19; 52) £90
- - **Anr. Copy.** Foxed. Gt.-pict. vell., warped , orig. silk ties. Raymond M. Sutton, Jr., copy. (SG. May 7; 298) $650
- - **Anr. Copy.** 4to. Stpd. pict. limp suede. Raymond M. Sutton, Jr., copy. (SG. May 7; 300) $170
- **Siegfried & the Twilight of the Gods.–The Rhinegold & the Valkyrie.** Ill.:– Arthur Rackham. 1911; 1910. 2 vols. 4to. Some ll. soiled. Orig. cl. (CSK. Feb.6; 52) £85
- - **Anr. Edn.** Ill.:– Arthur Rackham. 1911-18. Together 2 vols. 4to. Orig. cl. gt. (SH. Mar.27; 432) *Baddiel.* £70
- **The Tale of Lohengrin.** Trans.:– T.W. Rolleston. Ill.:– Willy Pogany. L., [1913]. De Luxe Edn., (525) numbered, & sigd. by Pogany. 4to. Orig. gt.-decor. vell., upr. cover spotted, partly worn. (SG. Apr.2; 247) $210
- **Tannhäuser.** Ill.:– Willy Pogany. 1911. (525) numbered, sigd. by artist. 4to. Orig. cf., tooled in blind, orig. box. (SH. Mar.27; 410) *Black.* £160
- - **Anr. Copy.** Orig. blind-stpd. mor. (S. Jul.31; 274) *Hancock.* £80
- - **Anr. Edn.** Trans.:– T.W. Rolleston. Ill.:– Willy Pogany. L., [1911]. (525) numbered, & sigd. by artist. 4to. Disbnd. (SG. Apr.2; 245) $190
- **Tristan und Isolde.** Ill.:– Alois Koilbe. Vienna, 1919. (100) on japon paper, each plt. sigd. by

artist, numbered. Orig. vell. (SH. Nov.21; 358) *Simon.* £70

WAGSTAFFE, John
- **The Question of Witchcraft Debated.** L ., 1671. 2nd. Edn. 16mo. Title soiled, & with old liby. stps. Crude hf. leath. (SG. Feb.5; 348) $110

WAHL, F.G.
[–] **Aus Erfahrungen Gesammelter theoret-prakt. Unterricht in dem Strassen-u. Brückenbau.** Zweibrücken, 1786. Cont. bds. (R. Mar.31-Apr.4; 1302) DM 600

WAHL, Dr. Hans
- **Die 92 Holzschnitte der Luebecker Bibel aus dem Jahre 1494 von einem unbekannten Meister.** Weimar, 1917. (550) numbered. Fo. Vell-bkd. bds. (SG. Mar.26; 270) $100
- - **Anr. Edn.** Weimar, 1917. (25) numbered, on Van Gelder H.M.P. Sm. fo. Pig. in medieval style, clasps with silver finials, bnd. by Walter Tiemann. (SG. May 14; 110) $600

WAHL, Jean
See–CHAGALL, Marc

WAHLEN, Auguste
- **Moeurs, Usages et Costumes de tous les Peuples du Monde.** Brussels, 1843-44. 4 vols. Ex liby., lacks all tissue-guards. Hf. cf., 2 vols. brkn. W.a.f. (SG. Oct.30; 368) $400
- **Ordres de Chevalerie et Marques d'Honneur.** Brussels, 1844. Many plts. col. heightened. Romantic hf. roan, limp spine, decor. (LM. Mar.21; 264) B.Frs. 9,000

WAIDDER, S.
- **Das Schachspiel in seinem Ganzen Umfange ...** Vienna, 1837. Vol. II, pts. 1 & 2. Cont. hf. leath. (D. Dec.11-13; 2305) DM 650

WAIFS & STRAYS
Ed.:– Harold Edwin Boulton. Oxford, Jun., 1879 & Mar., 1880. Nos. 1 & 3. Containing 2 poems by Oscar Wilde. Orig. paper wraps., qtr. mor. gt. s.-c. From the Prescott Collection. (CNY. Feb.6; 362) $200

WAILES, G.H.
See–CASH, J. & others

WAIN, Louis
- **Cats & Dogs.** L., n.d. 4to. Pict.bds. (P. Jun.11; 109c) *Reisler.* £70
- **Days in Catland.** N.d. Ob. 4to. 14 cut-out figures, (complete) in folder at end. Pict. upr. cover, some sellotape reinforcements & repairs, mainly to edges. (SKC. Sep.9; 1454) £55
- **Pa Cats, Ma Cats & their Kittens.** L., n.d. 4to. Pict. bds. (P. Jun.11; 109d) *Reisler.* £65

WAIN, Louis & others
- **A Book of Drawings.** Ill.:– Hugh Thomson & others. Priv. Ptd., 1891. (100) numbered, sigd. by publisher. 4to. Pp. 36 & 37 stuck together, & plt. may be missing. Orig. parch. wraps. gt. (SH. Mar.27; 536) *Greer.* £130

WAIT, Benjamin
- **Letters from Van Dieman's Land.** Buffalo, 1843. Folding map with sm. tear. Cont. cf., some foxing on end-papers. [Sabin 100969] (CB. Nov.12; 305) Can. $310
- - **Anr. Copy.** Map tattered along outer edge with sm. piece lacking, foxed. Orig. qtr. leath. & cl., cl. faded. (CB. Feb.18; 54) Can. $120

WAIT, W.E.
- **Coloured plates of the Birds of Ceylon.** Ill.:– G.M. Henry. 1927-35. 4 pts. in 1 vol. 4to. Some spotting, mostly marginal. Cont. cl. (CSK. Jan.16; 106) £110

WAITT, M.M., & Co.
- **Views of British Columbia & Alaska.** [Victoria], ca. 189-? Orig. cl., slightly dust-soiled. (CB. Feb.18; 268) Can. $110

WAKEFIELD, Edward Jerningham
- **Adventure in New Zealand.** 1845. 2 vols. of text, & atlas of plts. 8vo. & fo. Text in orig. embossed cl., atlas in orig. ptd. bds., roan spine (torn), slightly soiled. (C. Nov.6; 341) *Israel.* £1,800

WAKEFIELD, Gilbert
- **Memoirs of the Life of Gilbert Wakefield.** 1804. Slight browning, note at beginning of vol. I 'This copy of Wakefield's Memoirs ... (was) sold by me at Fonthill Abbey Septr 1823. H. Phillips'. Cont. str.-grd. mor., spines gt. William Beckford's

copy, with 4 pp. of notes by him. (S. Apr.7; 408) *Traylen.* £160

WAKEFIELD, John A.
- **History of the War between the United States & the Sac & Fox Nations of Indians, & Parts of other Disaffected Tribes of Indians, in 1827, 31 & 32.** Jacksonville, Illinois, 1834. 1st. Edn. 18mo. Foxed. Orig. linen, worn & stained, tiny fragment of orig. label retained on spine. (SG. Jan.8; 443) $475
- - **Anr. Copy.** 12mo. Stains, browning, foxing, faint liby. marks on title. Cf.-bkd. bds., head of spine chipped. From liby. of William E. Wilson. [Sabin 100978] (SPB. Apr.29; 274) $300

WAKEMAN, N.F.
- **Dublin Delineated.** Dublin, 1831. Slightly spotted. Mod. cl. (CSK. Dec.12; 95) £50

WALBRAN, Francis M.
- **British Angler.** Leeds, 1889. 1st. Edn. Wraps. (SG. Oct.16; 504) $100

WALCH, Joh.
- **Allgemeiner Atlas nach den Bewührtesten Hülfsmitteln u. Astronomischen Ortsbestimmungen ...** Augsburg, 1803. Ob. 4to. Old stp. on title, slightly soiled in margin. Cont. hf. leath. (HK. Nov.18-21; 1067) DM 1,000

WALCKENAER
[–] **Le Monde Maritime, ou Tableau Géographique et Historique de l'Archipel d'Orient, de la Polynesie et de l'Australie.** Paris, 1818. 4 vols. in 2. 16mo. Cont. hf. chagrin, gt. decor. spines, raised bands, ca. 1850. (HD. Apr.9; 580) Frs. 3,300

WALCOTT, John
- **Synopsis of British Birds.** L., 1789. (25). 2 vols. 4to. Lacks 1 plt. 19th. C. hf. cf. (VG. Oct.13; 167) Fls. 2,200

WALDMANN, Emil
- **Edouard Manet.** Ill.:– Manet. Berlin, 1923. Ltd. Edn. with 2 orig. etchings & specially bnd. 4to. Vell.-bkd. bds. (SG. Oct.23; 207) $300
- **Wilhelm Leibl. E. Darst. s. Kunst Gesamtverz seiner Gemälde.** Berlin, 1930. (400). Lge. 4to. Orig. hf. vell., orig. bd. s.-c. (HK. May 12-14; 2404) DM 650
- - **Anr. Copy.** Orig. hf. leath. (D. Dec.11-13; 449) DM 500

WALES ILLUSTRATED
1830. Orig. bdg. (DWB. Mar.31; 138) £62
- - **Anr. Edn.** Ill.:– Henry Gestineau. L., ca. 1830. 2 pts. in 1 vol. 4to. 90 plts. (of 112, with 30 in pt. 1 & 60 in pt. 2). Cont. str.-grd. mor., gt.-lettered title in gt. borders, back gt. (SG. May 21; 447) $100

WALEY, Arthur
- **An Introduction to the Study of Chinese Painting.** 1923. (50) numbered, sigd. 4to. Spotting. Orig. pig. (SH. Jan.29; 158) *Fine Books Oriental.* £65

WALKER, A.
See–PEART, Edward–WALKER, A.

WALKER, Adam
- **A Journal of Two Campaigns of the Fourth Regiment of U.S. Infantry, in the Michigan & Indiana Territories, under the Command of Col. John P. Boyd, & Lt. Col. James Miller ... 1811, & 12.** Keene, Priv. ptd. 1816. 1st. Edn. 12mo. Orig. wood bds., paper covering badly eroded, crudely rebkd. (SG. Jan.8; 444) $400

WALKER, Alexander
[–] **Colombia: being a Geographical, Statistical, Agricultural, Commercial & Political Account of that Country.** 1822. 1st. Edn. 2 vols. Lge. folding map torn at fold. Orig. bds., worn. (S. Dec.8; 263) *Garbett.* £120

WALKER, Francis A.
- **Statistical Atlas of the United States.** [N.Y.], 1874. Fo. Hf. mor., brkn. (SG. Nov.20; 122) $160

WALKER, George
- **The Voyages & Cruises of Commodore Walker.** 1760. 1st. Edn. 2 vols. 12mo. Pol. hf. cf. [Sabin 101044] (C. Nov.6; 233) *Remington.* £150

WALKER, George, Artist
[–] **Costume of Yorkshire.** [1813-] 1814. 1st. Edn. Fo. Cont. hf. red mor. (S. Sep.29; 155) *Faber.* £750
[–] - **Anr. Edn.** 1814. L.P. Fo. Cont. crimson str.-grd. mor., covers with gt. fillet borders &

blind-stpd. cornerpieces, spine gt. (C. Mar.18; 115)
Burton. £3,200
[-] – **Anr. Copy**. Cont. hf. cf., gt. (C. May 20; 186)
Howard. £1,200
– – **Anr. Edn**. Ed.:– Edward Hailstone. Leeds, 1885. (600) numbered. Fo. Frontis. & text in Fr. & Engl. Orig. mor.-bkd. cl. gt. (SBA. Mar.4; 198)
Kelsall. £180
– – **Anr. Copy**. Orig. qtr. mor., gt. W.a.f. (TA. Aug.21; 3)
£140
– – **Anr. Copy**. Spotted. Orig. parch., worn, loose. (SH. Mar.5; 150)
Capes. £120

WALKER, Isaac P.
– Report . . . [Wash.], 1853. Mod. marb. wraps. (SG. Sep.18; 15)
$100

WALKER, James
See–ATKINSON, John Augustus & Walker, James

WALKER, Rev. John
– Oxoniana. 1809. 4 vols. 12mo. Slightly spotted. Cont. hf. red mor. (SBA. Oct.22; 505)
Quaritch. £90

WALKER, John & Charles
– [Admiralty Charts of the St. Lawrence River from Montreal to the Gulf of St. Lawrence]. L., [1860-65]. Fo. Several maps loose, some slightly dust-soiled. Orig. bdg., worn. (CB. Dec.9; 16)
Can. $400
– The British Atlas. 1835-37. 4to. Lacks 1 engraved map, without title, maps hand-cold. in outl. Cont. hf. mor. (SBA. Dec.16; 67)
Nicholson. £130
– – **Anr. Edn**. 1837. Fo. A few maps soiled, loose. Cont. hf. cf., worn. (SH. Mar.5; 151)
Wallis Clark. £100
– – **Anr. Edn**. 1870. Fo. Contents loose. Cont. hf. cf., backstrip defect. (TA. May 21; 85) £120

WALKER, Joseph C.
– Historical Memoirs of the Irish Bards. Dublin, 1818. 2nd. Edn. 2 vols. Hf. mor. (GM. Apr.30; 244)
£52

WALKER, Robert
– An Inquiry into the Small-Pox, Medical & Political. 1790. 1st. Edn. Occasional spotting, liby. inscr. on title. Orig. paper bds., some wear, unc. (S. Feb.10; 391)
McDowell. £55

WALKER, Sayer
– A Treatise on Nervous Diseases in which are Introduced some Observations on the Structure & Functions of the Nervous System. 1796. Orig. Edn. Cont. tree cf. (S. Jun.17; 860)
Wood. £50

WALKOWITZ, Abraham & Lichtenstein, Isaac
– Ghetto Motifs. N.Y., 1946. 1st. Edn., inscr. by Walkowitz. 4to. Cl. Lichtenstein's 6-p. biography of Walkowitz, inscr. & sigd. by Walkowitz, loosely inserted. (*SG*. Oct.23; 346) $110

WALLACE, Alfred Russel
– Darwinism, an Exposition of the Theory of Natural Selection. L., 1890. Cl. Postcard to E.B. McCormick tipped-in. (SG. Sep.18; 380) $110
– The Geographical Distribution of Animals. 1876. 1st. Edn. 2 vols. Orig. cl. gt., ex-liby. (PL. Jul.11; 64)
Miles. £75
– The Malay Archipelago. L., 1869. 1st. Edn. 2 vols. Gt.-decor. cl., worn. (SG. Sep.18; 379) $210

WALLACE, Harold Frank
– British Deer Heads. N.d. 4to. Cl., slightly dust-soiled. (PD. May 20; 166) £60

WALLACE, Lew
– Ben-Hur. N.Y., 1880. 1st. Edn. 12mo. Orig. decor. cl., some light stains on lr. cover, qtr. mor. s.-c. With 2 A.L.s.'s from Mrs. Wallace to the publishers (regarding the change to the dedication), 1 letter foxed, in qtr. mor. s.-c., & with 8 other A.L.s.'s to publishers (5 by Wallace & 3 by his wife); bkplt. of George B. McCutcheon, lately in the Prescott Collection. (CNY. Feb.6; 320)
$1,400

WALLER, Edmund (contributor)
See–CAMBRIDGE UNIVERSITY

WALLER, Erik
– Bibliotheca Walleriana. Ed.:– Hans Sallander. Stockholm, 1955. 2 vols. Cl. (S. Jun.17; 862)
Heuer. £100
– – **Anr. Copy**. Orig. buckram, d.-w.'s. Pres. copy to Dr. E. Ashworth Underwood. (S. Feb.23; 367)
Temperley. £85

– – **Anr. Copy**. Buckram, ptd. wraps. bnd. in. (SG. Jan.22; 391)
$210

WALLERIUS, Johan Gottschalk
– Systema Mineralogicum, quo Corpora Mineralia in Classes, Ordines, Genera et Species suis cum Varietatibus Divisa Describuntur . . . Vienna, 1778. 2nd. Edn. 2 vols. Some browning & staining, printing flaw on 1 lf. vol. I. Cont. bds., soiled, unc., hf. red mor. case. Stp. of Bibliothèque Cantonale; from Honeyman Collection. (S. May 20; 3084)
Hill. £220

WALLHAUSEN, Jacob Johann von
– Art Militaire à Cheval. Ed.:– Johann Theodor de Bry. Frankfurt, 1616. 1st. Edn. in Fr. Fo. Mod. cf.-bkd. bds. (S. Nov.25; 415)
Moxon. £650
– L'art Militaire pour l'Infanterie. [1638]. Fo. Slightly wormed & 2 plts. slightly defect. Cont. vell., lacks 3 ties, upr. cover & some ll. wormed slightly. (HK. May 12-14; 1202)
DM 650
See–BOCKLER, Georg Andreas–FELIBIEN, Andre–WALLHAUSEN, Johann Jacob von

WALLICH, Nathaniel
– Plantae Asiaticae Rariores. Ill.:– Gauci after C.M. Curtis, Vishnu Prasad, & others. 1830-32. 3 vols. Lge. fo. Plts. hand-cold., 1 plt. in vol. 2 cropped with loss of plt. no., very occasional minor spotting in vol. 1. Later cl. From Chetham's Liby., Manchester. (C. Nov.27; 406)
Taylor. £2,500
– – **Anr. Copy**. Plt. 31 oxydized & plt. 50 slightly so, imprint of folding plt. 222/223 trimmed away (if ever present). Hf. mor. gt. Pres. copy inscr. to Mr & Mrs Lushington, from collection of Massachusetts Horticultural Society, stps. on plts. (SPB. Oct.1; 170)
$6,500

WALLING, Henry F.
– Atlas of the Dominion of Canada. Montreal, Toronto & L., 1875. Fo. Map at p. (180-81) misnumbered 98-99. Orig. hf. leath. & buckram, lacks spine, jnts. brkn. but reinforced. (CB. Nov.12; 121)
Can. $130

WALLING, Henry F. & Gray, O.W.
– New Topographical Atlas of the State of Pennsylvania. Phila., 1872. Fo. With 19pp. business directory of Phila. Disbnd. (SG. Aug.21; 270)
$160

WALLIS, Henry
– The Godman Collection. 1894. (200) numbered. Fo. Orig. cl. (CSK. Aug.29; 127) £65

WALLIS, James
– British Atlas. 1814. Lacks 13 maps, slightly stained, some ll. disbnd. Hf. mor., upr. cover detchd. (CSK. Nov.7; 206)
£85
– New British Atlas. 1812. 4to. Hf. roan, covers detchd. (P. Sep.11; 121)
Greenaway. £90

WALLIS, John
– Grammatica Linguae Anglicanae. 1672. Vell. (P. Jan.22; 39)
Hanas. £50
– – **Anr. Edn**. 1765. Advt. lf. at end. Cont. red mor., gt., caduceus on spine, ornaments on covers, bnd. by Mathewman for Thomas Hollis. Inscr. to Linnaeus on front fly-lf. 'An Englishman, Citizen of the World is desirous of having the honor to present this Book to Charles Linnoeus, of Upsal, in Sueden, noble above all parchment, London, jan. 1 1765'. (S. Oct.20; 262)
Lyon. £450
– Mechanica: sive, de Motu, Tractatus Geometricus. 1670-71. 1st. Edn. 3 pts. in 1 vol. 4to. Lacks port. by Faithorne, upr. margin of 4D1. 18th. C. vell., hf. red mor. case. Armorial bkplt. of Count Chorinsky; from Honeyman Collection. [Wing W593] (S. May 20; 3085)
Barchas Library. £380
– Opera Mathematica. Oxford. 1695-93-99. 1st. Edn. 4 vols. in 3. Fo. Some browning & spotting, occasional marginal staining, a few repairs, stp. removed from margin of title leaving sm. holes, former owner's name 'Gartz' on titles. Cont. sheep-bkd. bds., spines defect., covers worn, unc. From Honeyman Collection. [Wing W596] (S. May 20; 3087)
Quaritch. £1,100
– A Treatise of Algebra, both Historical & Practical. Ill.:– D. Loggan (engraved port.). 1685. 1st. Edn. Fo. A few short tears & sm. holes of flaws affecting text, slight marginal staining, title slightly soiled. Cont. cf., rebkd., worn. From liby. of Baron Gerard, Eastwell Park, Ashford, Kent; from Honeyman Collection. [Wing W613] (S. May 20; 3086)
Barchas Library. £220

WALLIS, John–MACKENZIE, E.
– The Natural History & Antiquities of Northumberland & . . . of the County of Durham.
– An Historical, Topographical, & Descriptive View of the County of Northumberland . . . Priv. Ptd. [1st. work], 1769; 1825. 2 vols.; 2 vols. 4to. Frontis. of 2nd work offset onto titles. 1st. work: cont. tree cf., rebkd. preserving orig. gt. spines & labels; 2nd. work: cont. tree cf. gt. From the collection of Eric Sexton. (C. Apr.16; 375)
Cole. £90

WALLIS, N.
– The Carpenter's Treasure. 1773. Orig. wraps., unc., folding cl. portfo. (S. Mar.17; 466)
Marlborough Rare Books. £200
– The Complete Modern Joiner. [1772]. Ob. 4to. Mod. qtr. cl. (S. Mar.17; 467)
Clements Liby. £350

WALMSEY, Edward
[-] Physiognomonical Portraits. One Hundred Distinguished Characters. 1824. L.P. 4to. Engl. & Fr. text. proofs on india paper, some plts. spotted. 19th. C. mor., gt. (S. Dec.8; 49)
Music. £90

WALPOLE, F.
– The Ansayrii or Assassins, with Travels in the Further East. 1851. 3 vols. Mod. cf.-bkd. cl. (SH. Nov.7; 363)
Diba. £95

WALPOLE, Horace, Earl of Orford
– Anecdotes of Painting in England . . . Collected by the Late Mr. George Vertue (& a Catalogue of Engravers). Strawberry Hill, 1762-71-[80]. 1st. Edn. 5 vols. 4to. Lf. of directions to binder at beginning of vol. V, some spotting. Cont. blind-stpd. str.-grd. mor., gt., covers with coroneted arms of Earl of Mountmorris. (S. Apr.7; 395)
Maggs. £620
– – **Anr. Edn**. Ed.:– Dallaway. 1828. 5 vols. Engraved plts. & wood-engraved ills., all in 2 states. Mor. gt., 1 vol. recased with spine preserved, by Rivière. (SKC. May 19; 249) £120
[-] The Castle of Otranto. Parma, 1790. 6th. Edn. (300). 4to. Lacks first blank. Cont. vell. by Edwards of Halifax, gt. Fore-e. pntg. (S. Nov.24; 294)
Thomas. £550
[-] – **Anr. Edn**. Parma, 1791. 6th. Edn. 4to. Without plts. or blanks at beginning & end. Early tree cf., rebkd. (SG. Feb.5; 340)
$250
– – **Anr. Edn**. 1796. Cont. mott. cf. gt. (C. Feb.4; 154)
Henderson. £100
– – **Anr. Edn**. 1796. Some foxing. Cont. red str.-grd. mor. gt., recased, later end-papers. (S. Jul.27; 155)
Shapiro. £50
– Catalogue of the Classic Contents. of Strawberry Hill. 1842-83. 3 Pts. in 2 vols. 4to. 1 vol. mod. cl., the other cont. hf. cf., worn, upr. cover detchd. (S. Mar.17; 459)
Marlborough Rare Books. £170
– Catalogue of the Royal & Noble Authors of England. L., Straw. Hill Pr., 1758. 1st. Edn. 2 vols. Vol. 2 has 18-p. Postscript with foldg. front, 1786, bnd. in. Mor., triple gt. fillet borders, spines gt., by Rivière. Fly-titles are used as hf.-titles, & the Indexes precede the text, the copyright p. precedes the text in vol. 1. (SG. Sep.25; 324)
$225
– – **Anr. Edn**. Ed.:– Thomas Park. 1806. 5 vols. 4to. Cont. mor. gt., recased, spines preserved. (SKC. May 19; 248)
£75
– – **Anr. Copy**. Str.-grd. mor., gt. (P. Oct.2; 22)
Forster. £55
– Correspondance. 1937-74. Yale Edn. 39 vols. in 38. Orig. cl. (SH. Mar.5; 299)
Chaplin. £200
[-] A Description of the Villa of Mr. Horace Walpole . . . at Strawberry Hill. Straw. Hill Pr., 1784; 1786-91. 4to. Engraved frontis., 26 plts., some folding. Cont. diced russ., rebkd. (C. May 20; 63)
Marlborough. £180
– A Description of the Villa . . . at Strawberry Hill.
– A Catalogue of the Classic Contents of Strawberry Hill. 1784; 1842. L.P. [1st. work]. 2 works in 2 vols. 4to. 19th. C. hf. mor. (1st. work); & orig. ptd. paper wraps., frayed, lr. wrap. detchd. From the collection of Eric Sexton. (C. Apr.15; 156)
Wood. £220
– Essay on Modern Gardening. Trans.:– Le Duc de Nivernois. Strawberry Hill, 1785. 1st. Edn. 4to. Stp. of Bibliothèque Prytanée on Fr. title, bkplt. of John Hely-Hutchinson, 1946. Cont. red mor., gt., arms on covers of Duchesse de Levis-Mirepoix, decor. initials W & N in alternate corners for Walpole & Nivernois, flat spine gt. in compartments with cross within panel in pointillé, inner gt. dentelles. (SM. Oct.8; 2068) Frs. 16,000
[-] A Letter to the Editor of the Miscellanies of Thomas Chatterton. Strawberry Hill, 1779. 1st.

WALPOLE, Horace, Earl of Orford -contd.

Edn. (200). With misprint on p. 22 corrected in ink by Walpole, & by 'Horace Walpole Esqr', in ink on title. Mod. mor. (SH. Jan.30; 367)
George's. £100

- **Letters.** Ed.:– Peter Cunningham. L., 1857. 18 vols. Extra-ill., some folding plts., some stains, foxing. Hf. red mor. gt. (SPB. May 6; 353) $900
- – **Anr. Edn.** Ed.:– Peter Cunningham. 1866. 9 vols. Cont. hf. mor., unc. (SBA. Jul.23; 686)
Weller. £50
- – **Anr. Edn.** Ed.:– Mrs. Paget Toynbee. Oxford, 1903-05 & 1918-25. 19 vols., including 3 vol. supp. Cl., supps. in d.-w.'s. (SG. Dec.18; 421) $140
- **Letters to the Countess of Ossory.** L., 1903. 3 vols. Maroon mor., gt. with floral designs, unif. gt. spines, gt. dentelles, by Morrell. (SG. Sep.4; 62)
$100
- [-] **Miscellaneous Antiquities.** Strawberry Hill, 1772. 1st. Edn. Nos. I & (II) (all publd.). Sm. 4to. Stitched in orig. wraps., as iss. From the collection of Eric Sexton. (C. Apr.15; 157)
Murray-Hill. £90
- [-] – **Anr. Copy.** In 1 vol. Cont. hf. cf. (TA. Sep.18; 49) £75
- **Works.** 1798. [1st. Edn.?]. 5 vols. 4to. Cf. gt. (P. Jan.22; 40) *Jarndyce.* £180
- – **Anr. Copy.** Hf.-titles in vols. 2, 4 & 5 only. Cont. tree cf. (SBA. Jul.23; 416)
Barock Museum. £70
- – **Anr. Copy.** 165 engraved plts., 1 stained, some foxing & offsetting. Hf. mor., by MacDonald. Caroline Norton's copy, her sig. in each vol. (CNY. May 22; 287) $150

WALPOLE, Horace–G[UIDICKIUS], F.W.

- **Historic Doubts on the Life & Reign of King Richard the Third.–An Answer to Mr. Horace Walpole's Late Work.** L., 1768. 2 works in 1 vol. 4to. Slight offsetting, minor marginal tears. Sheep gt. (SPB. May 29; 431) $150

WALPOLE, Rev. Robert

- **Travels in Various Countries of the East.** Ill.:– after J[ohn?] Martin. 1820. 1st. Edn. 4to. Cont. diced cf., rebkd. orig. spine preserved. (S. Jun.29; 231) *Dimakarakos.* £50

WALPOLE, Sir Robert

- **Memoirs.** 1798. 3 vols. 4to. Cont. cf. gt. (P. Jan.22; 42) *Jarndyce.* £60

WALPOLE, Thomas, Franklin, Benjamin & others

- **Report of the Lords Commissioners for Trade & Plantations on the Petition of Thomas Walpole . . . for a Grant of Lands on the River Ohio . . .** L., 1772. 1st. Edn. Lacks hf.-title. Mod. hf. tree cf., gt. spine, new endpapers. From liby. of William E. Wilson. [Sabin 101150] (SPB. Apr.29; 273)
$ 650

WALPOLE SOCIETY

Oxford, 1912-39. Vols. 1-27. 4to. Orig. cl.-bkd. bds. As a periodical, w.a.f. (C. Jul.22; 171)
Ransford. £280

WALPOLE-BOND, John

- **A History of Sussex Birds.** Ill.:– P. Rickman. 1938. [1st. Edn.?]. 3 vols. Cl. gt. (P. Nov.13; 231)
Traylen. £120
- – **Anr. Copy.** 4to. Orig. buckram. (SKC. Feb.26; 1610) £110

WALPOOLE, George Augustus

- **The New British Traveller.** Ill.:– Kitchen & others. 1784. Fo. Sm. hole in 1 plt. Cont. mott. cf., worn, new end-papers, hinges & jnts. strengthened. (SBA. Oct.22; 276) *Nicholson.* £300
- – **Anr. Copy.** Soiled. Cont. hf. cf. (CSK. Oct.24; 173) £260
- – **Anr. Edn.** Ca. 1785. Fo. 1 map torn. Cont. cf., worn, rebkd. (CSK. Feb.6; 23) £280
- – **Anr. Edn.** Ill.:– Thornton after Hamilton. Ca. 1800. Fo. Cont. spr. cf. (C. Feb.25; 63)
Hughes. £250
- – **Anr. Edn.** N.d. Fo. Maps of Nottinghamshire & Derbyshire lacking, some soiled. Cont. cf., worn. W.a.f. (CSK. Nov.7; 50) £180

WALSER, R.

- **Kleine Dichtungen.** Leipzig, 1914. 1st. Edn. MS. owner's mark & stp. on endlf., some ll. lightly soiled. Orig. pict. bds., by Karl Walser, soiled & minimal defect. at spine head. (HK. Nov.18-21; 3006) DM 850

WALSH, J.

- **Journal of the late Campaign in Egypt.** 1803. 4to. Title of 1 map cropped, slight worming, spotting. Hf. cf. (P. May 14; 101) *Primrose.* £70

WALSH, James J.

- **History of Medicine in New York.** N.Y., 1919. 5 vols. Cl. (SG. Sep.18; 381) $100

WALSH, John Henry

- **Dogs of the British Islands.** L., 1878. 3rd. Edn. 4to. Gt.-pict. cl., very chippcd, cx-liby. (SG. Apr.9; 356) $160

WALSH, Rev. Robert

- **Constantinopel und die Malerische Gegend der Sieben Kirchen in Kleinasien nach der Natur gezeichnet.** Trans.:– J.Th. Zenker. Braunschweig, 1841. 2 vols. in 1. 4to. Cont. leath. (R. Oct.14-18; 1814) DM 500
- **Constantinople & the Scenery of the Seven Churches of Asia Minor Illustrated.** Ill.:– after Thomas Allom. 1838. 2 vols. in 1. 4to. Minor foxing. Disbnd. (TA. Jan.22; 360) £54
- – **Anr. Edn.** Ill.:– Thomas Allom. 1840. 1st. & 2nd. Series in 2 vols. 4to. Cont. hf. roan, spines gt. (S. Nov.25; 548) *Karakos.* £50
- – **Anr. Edn.** N.d. 2 vols. 4to. Some foxing. Hf. cf. gt. (P. Sep.11; 246) *Sambos.* £75
- – **Anr. Copy.** Mor., worn. (P. Oct.2; 17)
Weston. £65
- – **Anr. Copy.** 2 vols. 4to. Slight spotting. Cont. mor. (CSK. Oct.3; 29) £55
- **Illustrations of Constantinople & its Environs.** Ill.:– after Allom. L., ca. 1840. 4to. Lightly soiled. Cont. hf. leath., upr. cover loose. (R. Mar.31-Apr.4; 2565) DM 520
- **Notices of Brazil in 1828 & 1829.** 1830. 1st. Edn. 2 vols. Cont. cf., gt. [Sabin 101153] (S. Jun.29; 179) *Burton-Garbett.* £150
- – **Anr. Copy.** Mod. cf. (SPB. May 5; 538) $350

WALSH, Capt. Thomas

- **Journal of the Late Campaign in Egypt.** 1803. 2nd. Edn. 4to. Later hf. mor., gt. decor. spine. W.a.f. (TA. Aug.21; 62) £150
- – **Anr. Copy.** Some maps & plans cold., text wtrmkd. 1801, plts., 1801-02, lacks directions lf., some offsetting to text & plts. Cont. russ., rebkd. (S. Sep.29; 183) *Remington* £90
- – **Anr. Copy.** Some plts. full or partly hand-cold. Cont. hf. red mor. gt. (SBA. Jul.23; 290)
Shapero. £55
- – **Anr. Copy.** Cont. mott. cf., rebkd. (SG. Feb.26; 332) $325

WALSINGHAM, Lord

See–DRUCE, Herbert & Walsingham, Lord

WALSINGHAM, Thomas

- **Histoire Tragique et Mémorable de Pierre Gaverston.** [Paris?], 1588. Red ruled thro.-out. Cf. gt. by Antoine Chaumont. Hamilton Palace copy. (C. Jul.16; 300) *Maggs.* £100
- **Historia Brevis ab Edwardo Primo.–Ypodigma Neustriae vel Normanniae.** 1574. 2 works in 1 vol. Fo. Sm. hole to side of 1st. work reprd. Antique-style mor. by Rivière. Bkplt. of Edward Halctone, lately in the collection of Eric Sexton. [STC 25004 & 25005] (C. Apr.15; 200)
Morton-Smith. £300

WALTER, Caspar

- **Zimmerkunst oder Anweisung wie Allerley Arten von Deutschen und Welschen Thurnhauben, auch Kugelhelme, nach der Neuesten Manier, zu Bedeckung der Kirchenthurme nicht nur zu Entwefern, Sondern auch mit Holz zu Verbinden.** Augsburg, 1769. 1st. Edn. Fo. Bds., worn. From Honeyman Collection. (S. May 20; 3088)
Goldschmidt. £260

WALTER, H. & Ouless, Philip John

- **The Royal Jersey Album.** 1847. Fo. Margins slightly soiled. Loose in orig. cl. gt., soiled. (TA. Feb.19; 332) £230

WALTER, Johann Gottlieb

- **Observationes Anatomicae.** Berlin, 1775. Fo. Title slightly soiled. Cont. hf. cf. (S. Feb.23; 127)
Phillips. £60
- **Tabulae Nervorum Thoracis et Abdominis.** Berlin, 1783. 4 plts. in 2 states. Hf. cf. (S. Jun.17; 863)
Chatham Books. £100

WALTER, Ph. A.F.

- **Der Darmstädter Antiquarius.** Darmstadt, 1857. Cont. bds. (R. Oct.14-18; 2277) DM 800

WALTON, Elijah

- **Flowers from the Upper Alps.** 1869. 4to. Cl. gt. (BS. Nov.26; 158) £50

WALTON, Elijah, & Bonney, Thomas George

- **The Bernese Oberland.** 1874. Fo. Lacks 2 text ll. Orig. cl., worn, loose. (SH. Jul.9; 1)
Lamm. £110
- **Lake & Mountain Scenery from Swiss Alps.** Ill.:– after Closs & Froelicher. 1874. Fo. Orig. mor. cl. gt. From liby. of Baron Dimsdale. (MMB. Oct.8; 8) £58

WALTON, Isaac

- **The Life of Mr. Rich Hooker.** 1665. 1st. Edn. Very minor worming to some ll., mostly in blank margins, just touching text, sm. rust-hole in 1 lf. affecting 2 letters. 19th. C. cf. gt., rebkd. preserving orig. spine, mor. pull-off case. Pres. Copy, to Philip King (& with MS. corrections in Walton's hand), 19th. C. sig. of J.D. Scripps, bkplt. of John Gribbel, lately in the collection of Eric Sexton. [Wing W670] (C. Apr.15; 158)
Burgess. £480
- **Lives of Donne, Wotton, Hooker & Herbert.** 1670. 1st. Coll. Edn. Slight browning. Cont. panel. cf., worn, covers detchd. [Wing W671] (S. May 5; 319) *Hill.* £65
- **Wallet Booke.** Ill.:– Crawhall. L., 1885. L.P., (100) numbered & sigd. by Field & Tuer. 2-tone vell., with ties, soiled, unc. Bkplt. of H.A. Ingraham. (SG. Dec.11; 148) $160

WALTON, Isaac & Cotton, Charles

- **The Compleat Angler.** 1676. 1st. Edn. Pt. 2 only. F3 cancellans, licenced on front-endpaper, some ll. cropped, some browning & staining. Mott. cf. gt. [Wing C6381] (PL. Sep.18; 300)
Angle Books. £70
- – **Anr. Edn.** Ed.:– Hawkins. 1766. A few minor flaws. Early 19th. C. hf. mor., emblematically gt. spine. (S. Dec.8; 12) *Thorp.* £65
- – **Anr. Edn.** Ed.:– Moses Browne. L., 1772. 8th. Edn. 12mo. 19th. C. three-qtr. mor., spine gt. (SG. Oct.16; 508) $200
- – **Anr. Edn.** Ed.:– John Hawkins. L., 1775. 3rd. Edn. 2 Pts. in 1 vol. Mod. cf., spine gt. (SG. Apr.9; 310) $140
- – **Anr. Copy.** Later mor., spine decor. gt. bkplt. (SG. Dec.11; 123) $110
- – **Anr. Edn.** Ed.:– Sir J. Hawkins. 1815. 2nd. Bagster Edn. Cf. gt. (P. Jan.22; 43)
Cavendish. £65
- – **Anr. Edn.** 1823. Mntd. India paper plts. Later mor. by J. Wright, gt. (CSK. Jan.23; 193) £50
- – **Anr. Edn.** L., 1825. Extra-ill. by Thomas Gosden with 60 engrs. (mostly india paper proofs), & with his 1825 replacement title-p. Orig. mor. over thick wood bds., bevelled edges, blind & gt.-tooled with creel ornams. on covers in decor. frames, set with circular bronze port. medals on upr. & lr. covers, & a total of 8 smaller circular bronze medals of a creel with the IWCC monog. accompanied by net, line, & fish as cornerpieces on raised plinths, bd. edges partly gt., spine with ornam. in upr. & lr. compartments, central compartment with the IWCC initials against the arms of Stafford, London, & Winchester, compartment above with lettered title, & below with interlaced IWCC joint monog., orig. maroon mor. s.-c. (worn), by Thomas Gosden. From the Prescott Collection. (CNY. Feb.6; 131) $8,000
- – **Anr. Edn.** L., 1825. Diamond Classics Edn. 64mo. With the advt. lf. at front. Orig. cl., slightly worn, unc. (SG. Dec.11; 129) $100
- – **Anr. Edn.** Ed.:– Sir Harry Nicolas. L., 1860. 2nd. Nicolas Edn., L.P. 2 vols. 4to. Engraved plts. & text ills. all mntd. india-proofs. Mor., triple gt. fillet borders, spines gt. with fleurons, gt. dentelles. (SG. Dec.11; 136) $200
- – **Anr. Edn.** Ed.:– R.B. Marston. 1888. (500) sigd. by editor. 4to. Cl. gt. (P. Jul.30; 1)
Lott & Gerrish. £210
- – **Anr. Copy.** 2 vols. Slight spotting. Hf. mor. (CSK. Sep.5; 224) £180
- – **Anr. Edn.** Ed.:– R.B. Marston. Ill.:– from photographs by P.H. Emerson & George Bankart. L., 1888. (250) Lea & Dove De Luxe Edn. 2 vols. Lge. 4to. 1 plt. loose, light foxing thro.-out, affecting some images. Mor.-bkd. cl. (SG. Apr.23; 206) $850
- – **Anr. Copy.** 54 photogravure plts. on India paper. Orig. qtr. cl. & bds., unc. (CNY. May 22; 225) $800
- – **Anr. Copy.** Lr. edge of some plts. stained. (CNY. May 22; 226) $180

– – **Anr. Edn.** Ed.:– George A.B. Dewar. Ill.:– William Strang & D.Y. Cameron. L., 1902. Winchester Edn., (150) numbered, L.P., sigd. by artists & plts. in 2 states. 2 vols. 4to. Vell., unc. (SG. Oct.16; 515) $675

– – **Anr. Edn.** Ill.:– James Thorpe. [1911]. (250) numbered, sigd. by artist. 4to. Orig. vell. gt., lacks ties, spine slightly soiled. (SBA. Mar.4; 230) *Angle Books.* £56

– – **Anr. Copy.** Gt.-pict. lev., partly unc., worn. (SG. Apr.9; 319) $130

– – **Anr. Edn.** Ill.:– Arthur Rackham. Phila., 1931. 1st. Amer. Trade Edn. 4to. Gt.-pict. cl., cold. pict. d.-w. reprd., publisher's box. Raymond M. Sutton Jr. copy. (SG. May 7; 304) $200

– – **Anr. Edn.** Ill.:– Arthur Rackham. 1931. (750) numbered, sigd. by artist. 4to. Orig. parch. gt., unopened, s.-c. (SH. Dec.11; 443) *Black.* £280

– – **Anr. Edn.** Ill.:– Arthur Rackham. 1931. (775) numbered, sigd. by artist. 4to. Vell., s.-c. (PJ. Jun.6 (80); 55) £160

– – **Anr. Copy.** Raymond M. Sutton Jr. copy. (SG. May 7; 302) $600

– – **Anr. Edn.** Ill.:– Arthur Rackham. [1931]. (775), this out-of-series, sigd. by artist. 4to. Orig. cl., slightly soiled. (CSK. May 29; 130) £150

– – **Anr. Edn.** Ill.:– James Thorpe. N.d. (250) numbered, sigd. by artist. 4to. Occasional slight spotting. Cont. mor., spine faded. (CSK. Oct.24; 6) £50

– Memoirs. Ed.:– Sir Harris Nicolas (notes). L., 1836. 1st. Pickering Edn. 4to. Extra-ill., with some 83 engraved plts., some mntd., some inlaid. Cont. gt.-floral patterned mor., gt. dentelles, by the Tout Bindery. (PNY. May 21; 417) $350

WALTON, Izaac & Cotton, Charles–WALTON, Izaac
– The Complete Angler.–The Lives of Donne, Wotton, Hooker, Herbert & Sanderson. Ill.:– Charles Sigrist & Thomas Poulton. Nones. Pr., 1929. (1,600). Orig. niger mor. (SH. Feb.19; 127) *S. Lawson.* £60

– – **Anr. Copy.** Niger mor., unc., marb. bds., s.-c.'s. (SG. Sep.4; 457) $110

WALTON, Izaak, Cotton, Charles & Venables, Col. Robert
– The Universal Angler. 1676. 3 Pts. in 1 vol. Mor. by Rivière. [Wing W674] (S. Nov.24; 295) *Angle.* £620

WALTON, James
See–FIELDING, Theodore Henry & Walton, James

WALTON, William
– The Army & Navy of the United States. Boston, ca. 1896. De Luxe Edn. 2 vols. Fo. Roan, worn. (SPB. May 29; 433) $150

WALTZ, Jean-Jacques 'Hansi'
– Le Paradis Tricolore . . . 1918. Publisher's ptd. cl. (HD. Jun.24; 213) Frs. 1,150

W[ALVIS], J.
– Beschryving der Stad Gouda. Gouda/Leyden, [1714]. 2 pts. in 1 vol. 4to. Between pp. 122/3 of 1st. pt. is ptd. slip inserted, concerning fraud of Jan van Dam, browned &/or foxed, 1 folding plt. torn in fold. Cont. cf., back gt. (VG. Dec.17; 1600) Fls. 800

WANDERINGS of a Pilgrim in Search of the Picturesque
1850. 2 vols. 4to. Orig. decor. cl., gt. (CE. Jul.9; 173) £80

WANG HUI-MING
– The Birds & the Animals. [Northampton, Massachusetts], Gehenna Pr., [1969]. (200). Loose sheets in mor.-bkd. cl. folder. (SG. Apr.9; 442) $120

WANN, Paulus
– Sermones de Preservatione Hominis. Munich, Johann Schobsser, ca. 1501. 4to. Spaces for initial capitals, lacks final blank, 1st. lf. with 2 reprd. marginal tears & sm. patch to lr. margin, fo. 18 with reprd. tear to margin, folios 70, 72, 75, & 102-105 with sm. portions at corners renewed, staining to last few ll. 16th. C. three-qtr. blind-stpd. cf. over wood bds., covers tooled with pict. rolls, incl. the Salvador Mundi frame bearing the date 1536, & a roll of port. medallions, with upr. cover lettered 'IMPERATO IMA', clasps & catches. Armorial woodcut bkplt. of Franciscus Godefridus Troilin Lessot, lately in the collection

of Eric Sexton. [BMC III, 662, Goff W4, H 16148*] (CNY. Apr.8; 108) $1,100

WANOSTROCHT, Nicholas
[–] Felix on the Bat. 1845. 4to. Occasional slight spotting. Orig. cl. by Remnant & Edmonds, covers detchd., spine lacking. (CSK. Dec.12; 262) £200

WANTON Widow, The
1769. 1st. Edn. Cont. sheep. (C. Nov.20; 215) *Quaritch.* £180

WAR PICTURES BY BRITISH ARTISTS
1942; 1943. 8 vols. Orig. pict. paperback. 4 vols. sigd. by Edward Ardizzone. (P. Dec.1; 143) £50

WARD, Edward
[–] A Hue & Cry after a Man-Midwife, who has lately delivered the Land-Bank of their Money. 1699. Fo. 2 pp., stained. [Wing W737] (S. Oct.17; 17) £180

WARD, H. Snowden & Catherine
– The Real Dickens Land. L., 1904. 4to. Extra-ill. with 110 plts. Hf. cf., gt. Pres. Copy. (SPB. May 29; 434) $110

WARD, Henry George
– Mexico in 1827. 1828. 2 vols. Lacks hf.-titles, some light dampstains & spotting. Cont. hf. cf., spines torn, 1 with loss. (CSK. Oct.3; 213) £85

– – **Anr. Copy.** Orig. bds., mod. linen s.-c. [Sabin 101302] (R. Oct.14-18; 1698) DM 1,400

WARD, John
– First Set of English Madrigals . . . Bassus [only]. 1613. 4to. Disbnd., cl. case. [STC 25023] (S. May 5; 414) *Macnutt.* £140

WARD, Madeline
See–COLLINSON, John–WEAVER, F.W. & Bates, E.H.–WARD, Madeline

WARD, Roland
– A Naturalist's Life Study. Priv. ptd. 1913. 4to. Orig. cl. (P. Nov.13; 244) *Way.* £50

WARD, Seth, Bp. of Salisbury
– Astronomia Geometrica. 1656. 1st. Edn. 3 pts. in 1 vol. Tear at foot of B1, some browning, owner's inscr. of J. Patrick. Cont. cf., upr. cover detchd. Bkplt. of Marquess of Bute; from Honeyman Collection. [Wing W816] (S. May 20; 3090) *'Roberts'.* £220

– Idea Trigonometriae . . . item praelectio de Cometis et Inquisitio in Bullialdi Astronomicae. Oxford, 1654. 3 pts. in 1 vol. 4to. Slightly spotted. 19th. C. mor. with snake-skin panels inlaid in covers & spine. [Wing W821] (S. Dec.2; 789) *Celestial.* £90

WARD, Wilfrid
– The Life of John Henry Cardinal Newman. 1912. 2 vols. Extra-ill. with approximately 70 ports., including 2 actual photos of Newman, 12 A.L.s.'s, 2 by Newman, others by W.E. Gladstone, Matthew Arnold, Sara Coleridge, Robert Southey, James Bryce, Cardinals Herbert Vaughan, Henry Manning & Nicholas Wiseman, Rev. John Lingard, & J.A. Froude. Cont. red mor., by Macdonald, covers elaborately gt. with lge. central cross & decor., mor. doubls., watered silk end-papers, partly unc. (S. Dec.8; 21) *S.P.C.K.* £220

WARDEN, David Baillie
[–] Bibliotheca Americo-Septentrionalis. Paris, May 1820. Orig. ptd. wraps., unc., partly unopened, foxing. [Sabin 101354] (SG. Oct.2; 373) $200

WARE, Francis M.
– Driving. N.Y., 1903. 1st. Edn. 4to. Some foxing. Ornate gt.-decor. cl., lacks front free endpaper, unc. & unopened, bkplt. (SG. Dec.11; 202) $140

WARE, Isaac
– A Complete Body of Architecture. Adorned with Plans & Elevations, from Original Designs. 1756. 1st. Edn. Fo. Frontis. partly detchd. Cont. cf. (TA. Apr.16; 320) £160

– – **Anr. Copy.** Cf., worn. (S. Mar.16; 183) *Demetry.* £100

– – **Anr. Copy.** Plt. 100 torn & laid down without loss of print area. Mor. by Morell. Bkplt. of Chesterfield House, lately in the collection of Eric Sexton. (C. Apr.15; 79) *Litz.* £75

– – **Anr. Edn.** Ill.:– after Roberts, Grignion & others. 1767. Fo. Cont. spr. cf. (C. Feb.25; 209) *Quaritch.* £300

WARE, James, Surgeon, 1756-1815.
– Chirurgische Beobachtungen ueber das Auge. Ed.:– Dr. Karl Himly. Trans.:– J.G. Runde. Goettingen, 1809. 1st. Edn. in German. 2 vols. Cont. bds. (SG. Sep.18; 382) $120

WARE, Sir James
– The Antiquities & History of Ireland. Dublin, 1705. 1st. Edn. Panel. cf., defect. (GM. Apr.30; 92) £65

– The Whole Works. 1739-45. 3 vols. in 2. Fo. Panel. suede. (GM. Apr.30; 423) £160

WARE, Sir James–STEVENS, John
– De Hibernia et Antiquitatibus eius Disquisitiones. –Monasticon Hibernicum. 1654; 1722. 1st. Edn. (1st. work). 2 works in 2 vols. Recent mor. gt. (1st. work); & cont. panel. cf. From the collection of Eric Sexton. [Wing W843] (1st. work) (C. Apr.15; 200a) *Wilson.* £160

WARE, William Rotch
– The Georgian Period. N.Y., 1923. 3 vols. Fo. Orig. cl. (CB. May 27; 212) Can. $100

WARHOL, Andy
– A Gold Book. [N.Y.], [1957]. (100) numbered, sigd. Fo. Gt. bds. (SG. Oct.23; 348) $1,400

– Index. Random House, 1967. 4to. Contents loose in bdg. Three-dimensional trompe l'oeil upr. cover, buckram spine. Sigd. by Warhol on cover, & initialled twice in text. (SG. Apr.2; 309) $180

WARING, Edward Scott
– A Tour to Sheeraz. L., 1807. 1st. Edn. 4to. Disbnd. (SG. Oct.30; 370) $250

WARING, John Burley
– Art Treasures of the United Kingdom. 1858. 4to. Cont. mor. (SH. Jan.29; 309) *Edwards.* £105

– – **Anr. Copy.** Fo. Cont. tooled & decor. cf. gt., resewn & rebkd. (TA. Jun.18; 319) £60

– Masterpieces of Industrial Art & Sculpture at the International Exhibition. 1862. 3 vols. Fo. Text in Engl. & Fr. Qtr. cf. (P. Jan.22; 269) *Trigg.* £90

– – **Anr. Edn.** 1863. 3 vols. Fo. Text in Engl. & Fr. Orig. red mor., gt. (C. Feb.25; 210) *Quaritch.* £180

– – **Anr. Copy.** Orig. bevelled decor. cl. gt., mor. spine. (C. Nov.5; 170) *Traylen.* £110

– – **Anr. Copy.** Generally loose. Orig. gt. decor. mor. (TA. Oct.16; 103) £85

– – **Anr. Copy.** Orig. gt.-tooled mor. (SG. Mar.12; 380) $800

WARMSTEDT, H.A.V.
See–REVENTLOW-FARVE, Ernst & Warmstedt, H.A.V.

WARNER, Charles Dudley
See–CLEMENS, Samuel Langhorne & Warner, Charles Dudley

WARNER, Sir George Frederic
– Queen Mary's Psalter. 1912. 4to. Cont. hf. mor. (SH. Jan.29; 58) *George's.* £65

– – **Anr. Copy.** (SH. Jan.29; 60) *George's.* £50

WARNER, Pelham F.
– The Cricketer. May 1922-Sep. 1927. Vols. 2-8. 4to. Advts. Cont. qtr. mor. (TA. Apr. 16; 125) £75

– Imperial Cricket. 1912. (900) numbered. 4to. Some ll. slightly spotted. Orig. buckram-bkd. cl., soiled. (SD. Feb.4; 157) £75

WARNER, Ralph
– Dutch & Flemish Flower & Fruit Painters of XVIIth & XVIIIth Centuries. 1928. 4to. Cl., d.-w. (P. Jan.22; 273) *Sims & Reed.* £80

WARNER, Rev. Richard
– Collections for the History of Hampshire. N.d. 5 vols in 3 only. 4to. Cont. cf.. gt., worn. (SD. Feb.4; 226) £75

– The History of Bath. 1801. 2 pts. in 1 vol., including Appendix. 4to. Occasional offsetting. Cont. cf., rebkd. From the collection of Eric Sexton. (C. Apr.16; 376) *Wood.* £130

– The History of the Isle of Wight. Southampton, 1795. Tree cf. (P. Jun.11; 22) *Lacy.* £60

WARNER, Robert & Williams, B.S.
– The Orchid Album. 1882-83. Vols. 1 & 2 only (of 11). 4to. Prelims. of 2nd. vol. detchd. & slightly frayed, some other very minor defects. Orig. cl. gt., very worn. (SBA. May 27; 202) *Nagel.* £260

WARNER, Robert & Williams, B.S. – The Orchid Album. -contd.
– – **Anr. Edn.** L., 1883. Vol. 2 (of 11). Lge. 4to. Cont. hf. leath. gt., spine reprd. (HK. Nov.18-21; 817) DM 1,300
– – **Anr. Edn.** Ill.:– after J.N. Fitch. L., 1884. Vol. 3. 4to. Lacks bdg. & loose. (R. Mar.31-Apr.4; 1414) DM 1,400
– – **Anr. Edn.** Ill.:– J.N. Fitch. L., 1893. Vol. 10. Lge. 4to. Orig. linen. (HK. Nov.18-21; 818) DM 1,400
– – **Anr. Edn.** L., 1897. Vol. 11. Lge. 4to. Linen. (HK. Nov.18-21; 819) DM 1,000

WARNER BROTHERS, INC.
– **Story Catalog.** [Los Angeles], Nov. 1, 1937. 4to. Multigraphed, date of release of all completed films & encyclopaedic information. Leatherette, stabbed & bolted. (PNY. Mar.26; 226) $400

WARNERY, Gen. Chas Emmanuel von
– **Remarques sur la Cavalerie.** 1828. New Edn. 12mo. Long-grd. red mor., double fillet border, spiral angle motifs, Duc d'Angoulême arms, decor. spine gt. & blind, inner garland, by Devillers. (HD. Jun.10; 220) Frs. 4,200

WARREN, H.B.
– **Reports on the Birds of Pennsylvania.** Harrisburg, priv. ptd. 1890. 2nd. Edn. Leath. (D. Dec.11-13; 313) DM 460

WARREN, John C.
– **A Comparative View of the Sensorial & Nervous Systems in Men & Animals.** Boston, 1822. 1st. Edn. Ex-liby. with rubber stp. on each plt. Disbnd. (SG. Aug.21; 384) $220

WARREN, Mrs. Mercy
– **History of the Rise, Progress & Termination of the American Revolution ...** Boston, 1805. 1st. Edn. 3 vols. Hf. linen, ex-liby. (SG. Mar.5; 464) $180

WARTON, Thomas
– **The Union.** Edinb., 1753. 1st. Edn. Cont. Engl. mor [by Ed. Moore of Cambridge], spine tooled in compartments. (S. Nov.24; 296) Quaritch. £280

WASHINGTON, George
– **President's Address to the People of the United States announcing his Intention of retiring from Public Life.** Phila., 1796. 1st. Edn. Some staining & foxing, unc. Orig. wraps., stabbed & sewn as Iss. (SPB. Nov.24; 60) $9,000

WASSON, R. Gordon
– **Soma, Divine Mushroom of Immortality.** Ill.:– Charles Poluzzi. Verona, Stamperia Valdonega, 1968. (680). 4to. Orig. mor.-bkd. cl., s.-c. (SH. Feb.20; 385) Thorp. £70

WATELET, Claude Henri
– **L'Art de Peindre. Poème.** Paris, 1760. Lacks lf. 'Explication des Figures'. Cont. red mor., decor. gt., decor. borders, gt. inner & outer dentelles. (D. Dec.11-13; 748) DM 800

WATERHOUSE, Benjamin
– **The Botanist.** Boston, 1811. 1st. Edn. Orig. bds., spine very worn, lacks most of label. (SG. Sep.18; 388) $110
– **Information Respecting the Origin ... of the Kine Pock Inoculation ...** Camb., Massachusetts, 1810. 1st. Edn. Mod. marb. wraps. (SG. Sep.18; 387) $280
– **The Rise, Progress & Present State of Medicine.** Boston, 1792. 1st. Edn. Foxed. Mod. marb. wraps. Inscr. to Dr. Mitchel. (SG. Sep.18; 385) $180
– **A Synopsis of a Course of Lectures on the Theory & Practice of Medicine in Four Parts, Part the First.** Boston, 1786. [1st. Edn.?] (All published?). Paper wraps. sewn into bds. (S. Dec.2; 650) Quaritch. £90
– – **Anr. Copy.** Disbnd., ex liby. Inscr. to General Brooks. (SG. Sep.18; 384) $275

WATERHOUSE, Professor E.G.
– **Camellia Quest.** Ill.:– after Adrian Feint & Paul Jones. Sydney, [1947]. 1st. Edn. (550), sigd. by author & artist. Fo. Orig. cl., d.-w. (S. Dec.3; 1170) W. & W. £150
See–JONES, Paul

WATERING PLACES of Great Britain, & Fashionable Directory
Ill.:– after W.H. Bartlett & others. L., 1831. 4to. No ptd. title. Hf. leath., needs rebdg. (SG. Nov.20; 423) $130

WATERMAN, Thomas Tileston
See–JOHNSTON, Francis Benjamin & Waterman, Thomas Tileston

WATERTON, Charles
– **Wanderings in South America, the North-West of the United States, & the Antilles.** L., 1825. 1st. Edn. 4to. Engraved frontis. spotted, liby. stp. removed from title. Orig. bds., unc., worn, backstrip reprd. [Sabin 102094] (SPB. May 5; 539) $225

WATHEN, James
– **Journal of a Voyage, in 1811 & 1812, to Madras & China.** 1814. 1st. Edn. 4to. Lacks 1st. lf. of plt. list, short tear in 1 plt., several stabbed in outer edges, 1st. plt. with marginal stain, occasional spotting & soiling. Cont. hf. russ., very worn, upr. cover & title detchd. (S. Jun.22; 196) Quaritch. £300
– – **Anr. Copy.** Slightly soiled, last 2 ll. slightly torn in margin. Cont. style hf. leath. gt. (R. Mar.31-Apr.4; 2570) DM 1,000
– **A Series of Views Illustrative of the Island of St. Helena.** Sep. 1821. 1st. Edn., 1st. Iss. 4to. Port., marked 'Private Plate', dupl. set of title & un-cold. plts. on india paper, the latter marked 'Only 35 Proofs on India Paper', 1 plt. in 1st. series wtrmkd. 1821, text in 2nd. series 1818, 1 plt. 1820, correction slip tipped in at front, lacks port. & text for 1st. series & folding plt. of St. Helena for 2nd. series, port. & india title slightly stained in inner margin, title inscr. at head, slightly soiled. Cont. hf. cf. (S. Nov.4; 619) Coffin. £340

WATNEY, Vernon
See–KENNETT, White–WATNEY, Vernon

WATSON, Frank John Bagolt
– **Wrightson Collection.** N.Y., 1966-73. 5 vols. 4to. Orig. cl. Vol. 1 inscr. to Cecil Beaton. (SH. Apr.9; 41) Heald. £110

WATSON, Frederick
– **A Brief History of Canberra.** Canberra, 1927. 1st. Edn., (50) on special P., & sigd. Pig gt. (SBA. Jul.23; 291) Frognal. £110

WATSON, Joseph
– **Instruction of the Deaf & Dumb.** L., 1809. 1st. Edn. Some plts. misbnd., all stpd. on versos, foxed. Later hf. linen, ex-liby. (SG. Feb.12; 163) $100

WATSON, Bp. Richard
– **Chemical Essays.** Camb. & L., 1781-86; 1787. 1st. Edn. 5 vols. Cont. mott. cf., gt., some lettering pieces missing, bkplt. Inscr. (S. Dec.2; 790) Quaritch. £140
– – **Anr. Copy.** General hf.-title in vol. 3. Cont. cf., not unif. (S. Dec.1; 423) Maggs. £95

WATSON, William
See–STEP, Edward & Watson, William

WATT, James
– **Supplement to the Description of a Pneumatic Apparatus for Preparing Fractitious Airs Containing a Description of a Simplified Apparatus & of a Portable Apparatus.** Bg'ham., 1796. New cl., unc. (S. Dec.1; 428) Whitehart. £190
– **Thoughts on the Constituent Parts of Water & of Depthlogisticated Air.** 1784. Offprint from Philosophical Transactions of the Royal Society. 4to. Title slightly spotted, anr. paper bnd. at end. Bds., red hf. mor. case. From Honeyman Collection. (S. May 20; 3092) Pickering & Chatto. £320

WATT, Robert
– **Bibliotheca Britannica; or a General Index to British & Foreign Literature.** Edinb., 1824. [1st. Edn.?]. 4 vols. 4to. Russ. gt. by Stamper. (C. Feb.4; 155) Faustus. £180
– – **Anr. Copy.** Some spotting & marginal staining. Mod. hf. mor. (S. Feb.23; 368) Whipple. £75
– – **Anr. Edn.** 1824. 2 vols. in 4. Recent buckram with orig. labels replaced. (TA. Mar.19; 160) £50

WATTEAU, Jean Antoine
– **Figures de Differents Caractères, de Paysages & d'Etudes.** Paris, ca. 1740. 2nd. Edn. Fo. Short tears reprd. in lr. margins of 2 text ll. & plt. 5 cahier III & plts. 2 & 4 cahier XXIV to engrd.

area, 1 or 2 plts. lightly soiled. Late 19th./early 20th. C. mor. gt. (SM. Oct.8; 2425) Frs. 45,000
– **Livre de Différents Caractères de Têtes.** Paris, 1752. Glased cf., gt. triple fillet border, decor. spine raised bands, inner dentelle, by Pagnant. (HD. Apr.24; 109) Frs. 3,800
– **L'Oeuvre.** Ill.:– after author. Paris, n.d. 20½ × 14 ins. Loose in portfo. (SG. Dec.4; 361) $150

WATTS, Henry Edward
See–CERVANTES Saavedra, Miguel de–WATTS, Henry Edward

WATTS, Isaac
– **The Psalms of David.–Hymns & Spiritual Songs.** L., 1810; 1808. 2 works in 1 vol. 24mo. Old crimson str.-grd. mor., worn. Two-way fore-e. pntg.; from the liby. of Zola E. Harvey. (SG. Mar.19; 190) $925
See–PSALMS, PSALTERS & PSEUMES [English]

WATTS, William, Engraver
– **The Seats of the Nobility & Gentry.** 1779. Ob. fo. Spotting. Cont. cf., worn. Cont. MS. inscr. on front free end-paper verso. (CSK. Oct.3; 145) £190
– – **Anr. Copy.** 4to. Foxed. Cf., central embossed arms of Antrim, decor. spine gt. (CE. Jul.9; 215) £130
– – **Anr. Copy.** Cont. str.-grd. mor., gt. (SM. Oct.8; 2212) Frs. 3,800
– – **Anr. Edn.** 1779-83. Ob. 4to. 48 (of 52?) plts., a few damp stained to margins only. Later cl., spine defect. (TA. Dec.18; 392) £54
– – **Anr. Edn.** 1779-[1786]. Ob. 4to. Occasional minor spotting. Cont. tree cf., gt. spine. (C. Nov.5; 171) Henderson. £160
– – **Anr. Copy.** Cont. russ., worn, covers detchd. (S. Nov.24; 297) P. Roberts. £140
– – **Anr. Edn.** N.d. Ob. 4to. Most plts. spotted. Cont. tooled sheep gt., soiled. (SD. Feb.4; 228) £95

WATZDORF, Erna von
– **Johann Melchior Dinglinger Der Goldschmied des Deutschen Barock.** Berlin, 1962. 2 vols. Lge. 4to. Orig. cl., d.-w.'s, s.-c. (CSK. Jun.12; 92) £50

WAUGH, Arthur
– **Oxford.** Ill.:– Sir William Nicholson. 1905. Ltd. Edn. 2 vols. Fo. 24 plts., some cold., each sigd. & numbered by artist. Loose as issued in cl.-bkd. portfos., worn, 3 (of 4) ties defect. (SH. Mar.27; 377) Henderson. £520
– – **Anr. Copy.** 19 (of 24) plts., each sigd. & numbered by artist, in separate mounts, titles & a few ll. spotted. (S. Jul.31; 262) Henderson. £250
– **The Square Book of Animals.** Ill.:– Sir William Nicholson. N.Y., 1900. 4to. End-lf. loose. Orig. cl.-bkd. pict. bds., slightly worn. (S. Jul.31; 261) Newman. £140

WAUGH, Evelyn
– **Basil Seal Rides Again, or the Rake's Regress.** 1963. (750) numbered, sigd. by author. 4to. Bdg. not stated, partly unc. (SKC. May 19; 355) £70
– **Black Mischief.** 1932. 1st. Edn., (250). Orig. cl. gt. Pres. Copy. (SH. Dec.19; 491) Barry Scott. £230
– **The Holy Places.** Ill.:– Reynolds Stone. L., 1952. Ltd. L.P. 1st. Edn. (50) numbered, specially bnd., sigd. by author & artist. Sm. 4to. Gt.-ptd. niger mor. (PNY. Mar.26; 333) $400
– **The Life of the Right Reverend Ronald Knox.** 1959. 1st. Edn. (29) specially ptd. & bnd. Orig. buckram. Pres. copy. (S. Jul.22; 315) Words, etc. £440
– **A Little Learning ...** 1964. 1st. Edn. Orig. cl., d.-w. Pres. copy. (S. Jul.22; 317) Elliott. £180
– **The Loved One.** Ill.:– Stuart Boyle. [1948]. (250) numbered, sigd. by author & artist. Orig. cl., orig. cellophane d.-w. (CSK. Apr.3; 81) £110
– **Men at Arms.** 1952. 1st. Edn. Orig. cl. Pres. copy. (S. Jul.22; 313) Elliott. £200
– – **Anr. Copy.** D.-w. Inscr. to J.L. Naimaster, inserted are autograph postcard & ptd. card from author, 2 T.L.s's. from Mr. Naimaster, & other items. (SH. Dec.19; 651) Barry Scott. £135
– **The Ordeal of Gilbert Pinfold.** 1957. 1st. Edn. (30) specially ptd. & bnd. Orig. buckram, unc. Pres. copy. (S. Jul.22; 314) Greig. £680
– – **Anr. Edn.** 1957. 1st. Edn. Orig. cl., unc. Inscr. to Cecil Beaton. (SH. Dec.19; 397) Wilson. £370
– **Unconditional Surrender.** 1961. 1st. Edn. Orig. cl., d.-w. Pres. copy. (S. Jul.22; 316) Sotheran. £240

- **Wine in Peace & War.** Ill.:– Rex Whistler. [1948]. 1st. Edn. Orig. pict. bds. Pres. copy to H. Buchanan. (S. Jul.22; 312) *Marks.* £260

WAUTERS, Alphonse
- **Les Délices de la Belgique.** Brüssels, 1844. Orig. bds., lacks spine. (R. Oct.14-18; 1900) DM 4,200
- – **Anr. Copy.** Pict. spine reprd. (LM. Nov.8; 16) B.Frs. 21,000

WAUTHIER, Herbert & others
- **Artwork.** 1924-31. Vols. 1-28. 4to. Orig. wraps., some lightly soiled. (CSK. Jul.24; 44) £70

WAY of the Cross
Ditchling, St. Dominics Pr. 1917. 16mo. Price-list for 6 publications of the pr. tipped in. Linen-bkd. bds., d.-w., bkplt. (SG. Jan.15; 94) $120

WAYTH, C.
- **Trout Fishing: or, the River Darent.** L., 1845. 1st. Edn. Blind-stpd. cl. (SG. Oct.16; 525) $100

WEALE, John
- **Designs of Ornamental Gates. Lodges, Palisading, & Iron Work of the Royal Parks.** L., 1841. 4to. Blind liby. stp. on title & 1 plt. Orig. cl., worn, mor. spine. (SPB. Nov.25; 128) $150
- **The Theory, Practice & Architecture of Bridges.** 1843. 4 vols. in 3. Cont. mor.-bkd. cl. (SH. Jun.18; 118) *Weinreb.* £320

WEALE, Putnam
- **The Pageant of Peking.** Ill.:– after photographs by Donald Mennie. Shanghai, 1920. 1st. Edn. (1,000) numbered. Fo. Light foxing thro.-out, most images not affected. Orig. gt. decor. silk over bds., orig. ribbon bookmark, bdg. slightly rubbed, worn at ends of spine. (SG. Apr.23; 134) $325

WEATHERLEY, Frederic Edward
- **A Happy Pair.** Ill.:– Beatrix Potter. Ca. 1890. 16mo. Orig. pict. wraps., soiled, worn. Ills. with initials H.B.P. (SH. Dec.11; 395) *Andrews.* £1,850

WEAVER, F.W. & Bates, E.H.
See–COLLINSON, John–WEAVER, F.W. & Bates, E.H.–WARD, Madeline

WEAVER, Sir Lawrence
See–BENSON, Arthur Christopher & Weaver, Sir Lawrence

WEAVER, William D.
- **Catalogue of the Wheeler Gift of Books, Pamphlets & Periodicals in the Library of the American Institute of Electrical Engineers.** Ed.:– Brother Potamian. N.Y., 1909. 2 vols. Orig. buckram, slightly soiled. Pres. copy; from Honeyman Collection. (S. May 20; 3307) *Simonin.* £95

WEBB, John
- **A Vindication of Stone-Heng Restored: in which the orders & rules of Architecture, observed by the Ancient Romans, are discussed.** 1665. [1st. Edn.?]. Cont. cf. [Wing W1203] (CSK. Feb.20; 184) £110
- – **Anr. Copy.** Fo. Sm. hole in title & D1 but barely affecting text. Rebkd., slightly worn. [Wing W1203] (SBA. Oct.22; 560) *Gasson.* £90

WEBB, Peter
- **The Erotic Arts.** Ill.:– David Hockney & Allen Jones. 1975. (126), with ill. by each artist, both sigd. & numbered. Mor., s.-c. (SH. Mar.26; 276) *R. Jones.* £170

WEBER, Carl J.
- **Fore-edge Painting.** Irvington-on-Hudson, 1966. Tall 8vo. Cl., d.-w. (frayed). (SG. Mar.19; 196) $170
- **A Historical Survey of a Curious Art in Book Decoration.** Irvington-on-Hudson, 1966. Cl., d.-w. Fore-e. pntg. (SG. Oct.2; 132) $100
- **A Thousand & One Fore-edge Paintings.** Waterville, Maine, 1949. 1st. Edn., (1000) rag paper. Tall 8vo. Buckram, d.-w. (frayed). (SG. Mar.19; 195) $300

WEBER, Ernst Heinrich & Wilhelm
- **Wellenlehre auf Experimente Gegrundet oder uber die Wellen tropfbarer Flussigkeiten mit Anwendung auf die Schall-und Lichtwellen.** Leipzig, 1825. 1st. Edn. Hf. roan, worn. Bkplt. of Herbert McLean Evans; from Honeyman Collection. (S. May 20; 3093) *Norman.* £260

WEBER, F.A.
See–DECKER, J.M. & Weber, F.A.

WEBER, G.A.
- **Systemat Darstellung der Reinen Arzneiwirkungen . . .** Braunschweig, 1831. 1st. Edn. Cont. hf. leath. gt. (R. Mar.31-Apr.4; 1069) DM 680

WEBER, J.
- **Neue Erfahrungen Idiolektrische Körper ohne einiges Reiben zu elektrisieren.** Augsburg, 1781. 1st. Edn. Partly stained. Cont. bds. (R. Oct.14-18; 294) DM 650

WEBER, J.C.
- **Die Alpen-Pflanzen Deutschlands und der Schwiez.** München, 1872. 4 vols. Hf. mor. (SSA. Apr.22; 85) R. 200
- – **Anr. Edn.** Munich, 1880. 4th. Edn. 4 vols. Orig. linen, gold stpd. (R. Oct.14-18; 3084) DM 1,400

WEBER, Max
- **Woodcuts & Linoleum Blocks.** N.Y., [1956]. (225) numbered, & sigd. Linen, s.-c. (SG. Apr.2; 310) $325

WEBER, Wilhelm
- **Elektrodynamische Maassbestimmungen.– Elektrodynamische Maassbestimmungen insbesondere Widerstandsmessungen.** Leipzig; [Leipzig], 1846; [1852]. 1st work 1st. Edn.; 2nd. work from the Abhandl. d. K.S. Ges. d. Wissench. 2 works in 1 vol. 4to. Slight discolouration. Hf. cl., worn, hf. mor. case. Bkplt. & sig. of Dr. Heinrich Lehmann, Hamburg, 1898; from Honeyman Collection. (S. May 20; 3094) *Zeitlin & Verbrugge.* £180

WEBER, Wilhelm & Eduard
- **Mechanik der Menschlichen Gehwerkzeuge. Eine Anatomisch-Physiologische Untersuchung.** Göttingen, 1836. 1st. Edn. Some spotting & staining, pp. XVII-XXIV of prelims. bnd. after pp. 418 & 422. Cont. hf. mor. From Honeyman Collection. (S. May 20; 3095) *Norman.* £360

WEBSTER, John
- **The Displaying of Supposed Witchcraft.** 1677. 1st. Edn. Fo. Cont. panel. cf., rebkd. (C. Jul.16; 363) *Taylor.* £220
- **Metallographia: or, an History of Medals.** 1671. 1st. Edn. Sm. 4to. Advt. lf., browned thro.-out, title & E2 with fore-margins reprd., some worming in lr. margins, slightly affecting text, piece torn from D3 with loss of a few words, owner's inscr. 'Rad. Thoresby'. 19th. C. hf. cf., worn, upr. cover detchd. From Honeyman Collection. [Wing W1231] (S. May 20; 3096) *Rogers Turner.* £120

WEBSTER, M.R.
See–CESCINSKY, Herbert & Webster, M.R.

WEBSTER, Noah
- **A Brief History of Epidemic Pestilential Diseases.** Hartford, 1799. 1st. Edn. 2 vols. Foxed. Disbnd. (SG. Sep.18; 389) $250

WEBSTER, Pelatiah
- **An Essay on Credit . . .** Phila., 1786. 1st. Edn. Sewed, unc. (SG. Mar.5; 470) $220

WEBSTER, W.
- **Webster's Tables.** 1634. 3rd. Edn. Browned. Mod. cl. [NSTC 25183.5] (SH. Jun.11; 44) *Quaritch.* £100

WEBSTER, William Henry Bayley
- **Narrative of a Voyage to the Southern Atlantic Ocean, in the Years 1828, 29, 30, Performed in H.M. Sloop Chanticleer . . .** 1834. 1st. Edn. 2 vols. Some foxing, offsetting & dampstaining in vol. 1, 1 contents lf. detchd. Hf. cf., rebkd., covers worn. Author's copy, with numerous notes in his hand; from Honeyman Collection. [Sabin 102429] (S. May 20; 3097) *Crete.* £450

WECKER, Johannes & Jacobus
- **Antidotarivm Generale.–Antidotarivm.** Basel, 1576; 1574. 1st. Edn; 2nd. Edn. 2 works in 1 vol. 4to. 1st. & last sigs. stained, owner's mark on title & last lf. & inner & outer covers. Cont. blind-tooled leath.-bkd. wd. bds., 2 clasps. (HK. Nov.18-21; 820) DM 1,600

WEDEKIND, Frank
- **Die Buechse der Pandora.** Ill.:– Alastair. Munich, n.d. (500) numbered. 4to. Patterned bds. (SG. Apr.2; 3) $140
- **Erdgeist.** Ill.:– Alastair. Munich, n.d. (500) numbered. 4to. Patterned bds. (SG. Apr.2; 2) $140

WEDEL, George Wolfgang
- **Introductio in Alchimiam.** Jena, 1706. 1st. Edn. 4to. Some stains. New cl. (S. Dec.1; 430) *Weiner.* £80

WEDGEWOOD, Josiah
- **Catalogue of Cameos, Intaglios, Medals (etc.) formed in different Kinds of Porcelain & Terra Cotta.** Etruria, 1787. 6th. Edn. Orig. wraps., rebkd., cl. case. Holland House copy. (S. Jan.27; 485) *Drury.* £400

WEDMORE, Frederick
- **Turner & Ruskin.** 1900. Ltd. de luxe Edn. 2 vols. Fo. Plts. in 2 states, some spotting. Cont. hf. mor., gt. (SH. Oct.9; 107) *Harding.* £85

WEEGEE (Pseud.)
See–FELLIG, Arthur 'Weegee'

WEEMS, Mason L.
- [–] **The Life & Memorable Actions of George Washington.** [Balt.], [1800]. 24mo. Old bds., frontis. woodcut pasted in upr. cover. (SG. Apr.30; 320) $150

WEEVER, John
- [–] **An Agnus Dei.** 1606. 3rd. Edn. 31×25 mm. Lacks C7 & N1., soiled. Cont. cf. gt., worn. Miniature Book. [STC 25222] (SH. Dec.12; 567) *Fletcher.* £1,250

WEGELIN, D.
See–DIELMANN, J. & Wegelin, D.

WEIBEL, A.
- **Two Thousand Years of Textiles.** 1952. 4to. Orig. cl. (SH. Apr.9; 42) *Quaritch.* £95

WEICKHMANN, C.
- **New-erfundenes Grosses Königs-Spiel.** Ulm, 1664. Fo. Lacks title lf. & 3 folding maps. Hf. linen. (D. Dec.11-13; 2306) DM 1,200

WEIDENFELD, Johannes Segerus
- **Four Books Concerning the Secrets of the Adepts or of the Use of Lully's Spirit of Wine.** 1685. 1st. Edn. in Engl. 4to. Pagination jumps from 264 to 293, some stains & discolourations. New cl. [Wing W1253] (S. Dec.2; 652) *Quaritch.* £200

WEIDENSEE, Eberhardt
- **Eyne Alte Prophecey von der Verstorung des Keyserlichen Bapstumbs.** Magdeburg, 1541. 1st. Edn. 4to. Lacks last (?)blank. Disbnd. (S. Dec.8; 187) *Hyde.* £70

WEIGEL, Christian Ehrenfried
- **Grundriss der reinen und angewandten Chemie.** Griefswald, 1777. 1st. Edn. 2 vols. Orig. bds., unc., mostly unopened, red hf. mor. cases. From Honeyman Collection. (S. May 20; 3100) *Hill.* £220

WEIGEL, Christoph
- **Abbildung der Gemein-Nuetzlichen Hauptstaende von denen Regenten . . . Kuenstler und Handwerker . . .** Regensburg, 1698. 4to. Without the brandy-distilling plt., lacks title-p. & preliminary text, 3 or 4 ll. defect. 19th. C. bds., cl. spine. (SG. Feb.5; 343) $6,000
- **Biblia Ectypa.** Ill.:– G.C. Eimmart & J.J. v. Sandrart. Regensburg, 1697. Later Edn. 2 vols. with 2 pts. in each vol. Sm. ob. fo. Slightly soiled especially at beginning of vols., some plts. with sm. margin tears, 1 longer. Cont. leath., vol. 1 spine & corners reprd. (R. Mar.31-Apr.4; 1481) DM 3,400
- **Columnae Militantis Ecclesiae.** [Nuremb.], [1725]. Fo. Lacks title, frontis. & probably 1 lf. (printer's mark?) at end, slightly soiled. Cont. leath., worn. (HK. Nov.18-21; 2098) DM 500
- **Descriptio Orbis Antiqui.** Nuremb., ca. 1720. Fo. 19th. C. hf. cf. As an atlas, w.a.f. (SPB. Oct.1; 279) $1,200
- **Historiae Celebriores Veteris [Novi] Testamenti Iconibus representatae.** Ill.:– C. & J. Luykens, F.A. Meloni, P. Decker. Nuremb., 1712. 2 pts. in 1 vol. Lge. fo. O.T. lacks plt. 1, 2 & 26. Cont. cf., gt. spine, cover & outer dentelle, arms on both covers. (HK. Nov.18-21; 1513) DM 2,800
See–KOEHLER, Johann David & Weigel, Christoph

WEIGEL, Erhard–FRISIUS, D.F.
- **Speculum Uranicum Aquilae Romae Sacrum.–Kurtzer und Gründtlicher Bericht von Erscheinung und Bedeutung des Grossen Newen Wunder-Sterns, welcher den 1. October 1604 . . .** Frankfurt; Goslar, 1661; 1662. 1st. Edn.; 2nd. Edn.

WEIGEL, Erhard–FRISIUS, D.F. Gründtlicher Bericht von Erscheinung und Bedeutung des Grossen Newen Wunder-Sterns . . . -contd.
2 works in 1 vol. 4to. Browned, worming at end. Mod. hf. leath. (R. Oct.14-18; 296) DM 450

WEIGEL, Erhard–TAUST, J.G.–MADEWEIS, F. –STRAUCH, Egidius
– Unterschiedliche Beschreibung und Bedeutungen, so wohl der Cometen ins Gemein, als isonderheit des bissanhero . . . erschienenen . . . Wunder-Cometen.–Der von Abend gegen Morgen lauffende Unglücks-Prophete; Cometa redivivus. –Die Wieder-Erscheinung der ungewöhnlich grossen Stern-Ruthe, verstehe den Neuen Cometen; De sydere Crinito.–Von der Weisen aus Morgenlande Alten, und dem jetzigen Neuen Wünder-Sternen.–Observatio Cometae Stetinensis. [Jena]; Halle; ib.; Berlin; ib.; Danzig; Stettin. 1681; 1681; 1681; 1681; 1681; [1681]; 1665. 7 works in 1 vol. Sm. 4to. Some browning, 1st. work lacks plt., 7th. work with 1 plt. cropped. 18th. C. vell., red hf. mor. case. Bkplt. of Christian Ernst Graf zu Stolberg, & stp. of Stolberg liby. at Wernigerode; from Honeyman Collection. (S. May 20; 3101) Vernon. £180

WEIGLE, C. (Ed.)
See–ARCHITEKTONISCHE RUNDSCHAU

WEILAND, Carl Ferdinand
[–] Allgemeiner Hand-Atlas der Erde und des Himmels . . . Weimar, 1857. Lge. fo. 70 double-p. engraved maps, hand-cold. in outl. Cont. hf. cf., gt. decor. spine, worn. (TA. Feb.19; 102) £50

WEINBERGER, Bernhard W.
– Dental Bibliography. N.Y., [1929], 1932. 2nd. Edn. 1 vol., & index, together 2 vols. Wraps. (SG. Jan.22; 147) $130

WEINTHAL, Leo
– The Story of the Cape to Cairo Railway & River Route, from 1887-1922. 1923. 3 vols. plus General Index bnd. with Maps. 4to. Orig. hf. mor., gt. decor. spines. (TA. Feb.19; 647) £85

WEINWIRTH, Der Vollkommene, und Weinkellermeister
Graz, 1791. Slightly stained in parts. Cont. bds. (HK. Nov.18-21; 1647) DM 450

WEISLINGER, Johann Nicolaus
– Ausserlesene Merckwürdigkeiten von Alten und Neuen Theologischen Marckschreyeren . . . Augsburg & Freiburg, 1750. 4 vols. 19th. C. bds. (S. Mar.17; 264) Hackofer. £130

WEISS, Erich 'Harry Houdini'
– The Unmasking of Robert-Houdin. 1909. 1st. Engl. Edn. Orig. cl. gt., worn. (SH. Oct.23; 165) Huber. £80

WEISS, Fr.
– Die Malerische und Romantische Rhein-Pfalz. Ed.:– W. Kuby. Neustadt, [1856]. Lacks engraved title, soiled, lightly browned in parts. Later hf. linen. (H. Dec.9/10; 713) DM 6,400
– – Anr. Edn. Ed.:– W. Kuby. Neustadt/H., [1885]. 3rd. Edn. Orig. gold-stpd. linen, spine pasted over. (R. Oct.14-18; 2478) DM 8,000

WEISS, H.M.
– Li. Berlin, ca. 1920. (850). Sm. 4to. Orig. linen gt. (H. Dec.9/10; 2273) DM 500

WEISS, J.H.
– Atlas Suisse. Ill.:– Guerin, Eichler & Scheurmann. Aarau, 1786-1802. Lge. partly outl. cold. copper engraved map in 16 ll. & 1 supp. map in 6 segments on linen, folding. 2 cont. bd. s.-c.'s. (R. Oct.14-18; 2030) DM 3,700

WEISSMANN, Adolf
– Der Klingende Garten. Ill.:– Michel Fingesten. Berlin, 1920. (10) with dupl. set of etchings on Japan vell. 4to. 10 etchings & dupl. set on Japan vell., all sigd. by artist. Vell.-bkd. bds. (SG. Oct.23; 116) $240

WELBY, Adlard
– A Visit to North America & the English Settlements in Illinois, with a Winter Residence in Philadelphia . . . L., 1821. 1st. Edn. Some offsetting, slight foxing. Cont. cf., rebkd., gt. spine & borders, head of spine slightly chipped, mor.-bkd. cl. s.-c. From liby. of William E. Wilson; the Littell copy. (SPB. Apr.29; 276) $425

WELCH, D'Alte A.
– A Bibliography of American Children's Books Printed Prior to 1821. 1963-68. 6 pts. Wraps., spines crudely labelled. (SG. Jan.22; 123) $130

WELCOME (A): Original Contributions in Poetry & Prose
Ed.:– Emily Faithfull. 1863. Occasional light spotting. Orig. kid, stpd. & ruled in gt. & blind. Pres. copy inscr. 'Presented to His Royal Highness Prince Leopold by Miss Faithfull', bkplt. of H.R.H. Prince Leopold. (CSK. Jun.19; 82) £80

WELD, Isaac
– Illustrations of the Scenèry of Killarney. L., 1807. L.P. 4to. Dampstain thro.-out. Hf. cf. (GM. Apr.30; 108) £60
– – Anr. Edn. L., 1812. Orig. bdg. (GM. Apr.30; 381) £65
– Statistical Survey of the County of Roscommon. Dublin, 1832. Cl., spine defect., unc. & unopened. (GM. Apr.30; 277) £90
– Travels through the States of North America. 1799. 1st. Edn. 4to. Engraved folding map hand-cold. in outl., erratum slip pasted onto plt. list. plts., erratum slip pasted onto plt. list. Cont. tree cf. gt. [Sabin 102541] (C. Jul.15; 135) Heald. £280
– – Anr. Copy. Lacks 1 plt., some ll. slightly browned, liby. stp. on title. Cont. cf., rebkd. & reprd. (SH. Nov.7; 393) Deacon. £65
– – Anr. Copy. Errata slip pasted to list of plts., slip of ptd. verse tipped onto title, plts. foxed. Orig. bds., spine cracked & largely perished. From liby. of William E. Wilson. (SPB. Apr.29; 277) $850
– – Anr. Copy. 1 map partly hand-cold., plts. slightly foxed & lacks most of tissue guards, lacks errata slip & advts. Cont. hf. cf., disbnd. (PNY. Dec.3; 369) $350
– – Anr. Edn. 1807. 4th. Edn. 2 vols. Some spotting. Cont. hf. cf., rebkd. (TA. Feb.19; 46) £55
– – Anr. Copy. Sm. repairs on 2nd. title-p., some foxing. Cont. str.-grd. mor., spines gt. (SG. Jan.8; 453) $150

WELD, Isaac TOWNSEND, Horatio–RAWSON, Thomas James
– Statistical Survey of the County of Roscommon. –Survey of Cork.–Survey of Kildare. Dublin, 1832; 1810; 1807. 2nd. work with slight spotting to text. Unif. bnd. in hf. roan. From the collection of Eric Sexton. (C. Apr.16; 289) McGee. £220

WELLCOME ARCHAEOLOGICAL RESEARCH EXPEDITION TO THE NEAR EAST
1938-53. 7 vols. 4to. Orig. cl. (SH. Mar.5; 301) George's. £50

WELLER, Emil
– Die Falschen und Fingirten Druckorte. Leipzig, 1864. 3 vols. Some dampstains & foxing. Mod. hf. buckram. (SG. Jan.22; 398) $110

WELLER, Karl Heinrich
– A Manual of the Diseases of the Human Eye . . . from the Best National & Foreign Works. Trans.:– G.C. Monteath. Glasgow, 1821. 1st. Edn. in Engl. 2 vols. Disbnd., old bd. covers detchd., ex-liby. Bkplt. of Casey A. Wood. (SG. Jan.29; 429) $650

WELLING, Georgius von
– Opus Mago-Cabbalisticum et Theosophicum. Homburg v.d. Hohe, 1735. 1st. Edn. 4to. Text evenly browned. 18th. C. bds., worn, red hf. mor. case. From Honeyman Collection. (S. May 20; 3102) Nador. £180

WELLINGTON, Arthur Wellesley, Duke of
[–] Campaigns. Paris, [1817]. Fo. Many ll. browned. Hf. mor. (BS. Jun.11; 96) £200
– The Dispatches . . . Ed.:– Lieut. Col. Gurwood. 1837-39. Vols. 1-9 New Edns. 13 vols. Some spotting. Mod. hf. mor. (CSK. May 1; 165) £80
– – Anr. Edn. Ed.:– Lieut. Col. Gurwood. 1837-39. New Edn. 13 vols. Mor. (PD. Nov.26; 15) £65
– Orders of Knighthood. N.d. Ob. fo. Some spotting. Orig. hf. mor. (CSK. Mar.6; 122) £50

WELLS, Edward
– An Historical Geography of the Old Testament. –. . . New Testament. L., 1711; 1712. 3 vols.; 1 vol. Some maps or plts. linen-bkd. Both 19th. C. hf. mor., worn. ex-liby. (SG. May 21; 110) $350
– New Set of Maps both of Ancient & Present Geography. Oxford, 1701. Fo. Slight tear in map of Europe, 2 maps worn at centre fold. Cont. cf., worn & defect. As an atlas, w.a.f. (SPB. Nov.25; 117) $1,500
– – Anr. Edn. Ill.:– Sutton, Nicholls & others. L., 1718. Lge. fo. Cont. hf. leath., worn, spine partly defect. (HK. Nov.18-21; 1068) DM 1,550

WELLS, Herbert George
– Door in the Wall & other stories. Ill.:– after A.L. Coburn. 1911. Ltd. 1st. Edn. Fo. Some plts. offset. Orig. bds., stained, unc. (P. Sep.11; 205) Kent. £100
– The Invisible Man.–The War of the Worlds. 1897; 1898. 1st. Edns. Together 2 vols. Orig. cl. (S. Jul.22; 325) Maggs. £65
– The Invisible Man.–War of the Worlds/Time Machine.–Tono-Bungay. Ltd. Edns. Cl., 1967; 1964; 1960. 1 vol.; 2 vols.; 1 vol., together 4 vols. Orig. bdgs., boxed. (SPB. Jul.28; 319) $200
– The Secret Places of the Heart. 1922. 1st. Edn. Orig. cl. Pres. copy to Norman Flour, with pen & ink drawing. (S. Jul.22; 323) Quaritch. £65
– The Time Machine. 1895. 1st. Edn. Orig. cl. (S. Jul.22; 321) Korn. £55
– The Works. 1924-27. Atlantic Edn., (620) numbered, sigd. 28 vols. Orig. cl. (SH. Mar.5; 302) Kenyushu. £340
– – Anr. Copy. (CSK. Sep.26; 57) £170
– – Anr. Edn. N.Y., 1924-27. Atlantic Edn., (1050) sigd. Hf. red mor. gt. (SPB. May 6; 354) $3,500

WELLS, William Charles
– An Essay on Dew, & Several Appearances Connected with it. 1814. 1st. Edn. Some foxing at beginning & end, slight adhesion affecting a few letters on pp. 62/63. Later hf. cf., red hf. mor. case. Pres. copy (inscr. crossed out); bkplt. of Sir Andrew Noble; from Honeyman Collection. (S. May 20; 3103) Lawson. £60
– Two Essays: One Upon Single Vision with Two Eyes; the Other on Dew. L., 1818. Lacks hf.-title. Cont. hf. cf. From Honeyman Collection. (S. May 20; 3104) Zeitlin & Verbrugge. £140
– – Anr. Copy. Buckram-bkd. hf. cf., worn. Sigd. by Howard A. Kelly. (SG. Sep.18; 391) $100

WELLSTED, James Raymond
– Travels to the City of the Caliphs. 1840. 2 vols. Cont. hf. cf. (SH. May 21; 130) Nelwood. £310

WELPIUS, Heinrich
– Libellus de Minutiis Physics, & Practicis Astronomicae Arithmeticae Regulis. Cologne, 1544. 1st. Edn. Sm. 4to. Wraps., torn. From Honeyman Collection. (S. May 20; 3105) Hill. £130

WELSER, Marcus
– Opera Historica et Philogia. Nuremb., 1682. Fo. Vell. bds., slightly soiled. [Sabin 102615] (SPB. May 5; 540) $275

WELT-GEMALDE-GALLERIE
Trans.:– C.A. Mebold. Stuttgart, 1837-40. 3 vols. Orig. mor. gt. (D. Dec.11-13; 1498) DM 1,250

WELWOD, William
– An Abridgement of all Sea-Lawes. 1613. 1st. Edn. 4to. Cont. limp vell. gt., arms of King James I gt.-stpd. on covers. Dedication Copy? to James I. [STC 25237] (C. Nov.20; 280) Quaritch. £550

WEMMERS, J.
– Lexicon Aethiopicum. Rome, 1638. 1st. Edn. 4to. 14 ll. defect. with some textual loss, some browning & staining. Cont. vell., upr. inside hinge brkn., s.-c. (S. Apr.29; 467) Brill. £170

WENDINGEN
– Maandblad voor Bouwen en Sieren van Architectura en Amicitia. Ill.:– El Lissitsky. Amst., 1918-21. 4 vols. in 34 (of 35) pts., lacks vol. 2, nos. 7/8. 4to. Japanese bdg., orig. wraps. (VG. Nov.17; 698) Fls. 1,600
– – Anr. Edn. Ed.:– Th. Wijdeveld & others. Ill.:– El Lissitzky. Amst., 1921 & 1930. 2 pts. Fo. Orig. wraps., 1 with cold. litho. by Lissitzky, lightly soiled with sm. tears. (H. Dec.9/10; 1930) DM 800
– – Anr. Edn. Ed.:– Th. Wijdeveld. Amst., 1925. 7 special numbers. Fo. Title slightly soiled. Orig. wraps. (H. Dec.9/10; 1931) DM 620

WENTWORTH, Lady Judith Anne Dorothea Blunk-Lytton
– Thoroughbred Racing Stock. N.Y., 1938. 1st. Amer. Edn. 4to. Gt.-decor. buckram, d.-w. (SG. Dec.11; 427) $120
– Thoroughbred Racing Stock & Its Ancestors. –The Authentic Arabian Horse & His Descendants. 1938; 1945. 1st. Edns. 2 vols. 4to. With stps. to prelims. only. Orig. cl. gt. ex-liby. Sigd. copies. (TA. Jan.22; 387) £120

WENTWORTH, T.
[–] **The West India Sketch Book.** 1834. 1st. Edn. 2 vols. Slight spotting & offsetting. 19th. C. hf. cf., bnd. at Mayo Constitution Office, with ticket, spines gt. with crest at head. [Sabin 102634] (S. Dec.8; 262)   *Kossow.* £100

WENTWORTH, William Charles
[–] **A Statistical, Historical & Political Description of the Colony of New South Wales & Van Diemen's land.** L., 1819. [1st. Edn.]. Rebnd., hf. cf., gt. decor. spine. (JL. Dec.15; 723)   Aus. $280
– – **Anr. Edn.** L., 1820. 2nd. Edn. Slight foxing, sm. hole in 1 lf. (pp. 565/6), tear in folding map reprd. Recent mor., unc. (KH. Nov.18; 631)   Aus $190
– **A Statistical, Historical & Political Description of the Colony of New South Wales.–A Statistical Account of the British Settlements in Australasia.** 1819; 1824. 1st. work 1st. Edn., 2nd, work 3rd. Edn. Together 3 vols. (1 & 2). 1st. work cont. hf. cf., rebkd., 2nd. work cont. cf., Signet Liby. gt. stp. on covers. (C. May 20; 187)   *Maggs.* £200

WENZEL, Michael Johann Baptist, Baron
– **Traité de la Cataracte avec des Observations.** Paris, 1786, 1st. Edn. Liby. stps. Cont. hf. cf. (S. Dec.2; 654)   *Quaritch.* £80

WEPFER, Johann Jacob
– **Observationes anatomicae ex cadaveribus eorum ... Schaffausen**, 1675. New Edn. Mor.-bkd. bds. (S. Jun.17; 870)   *Norman.* £160
– **Observationes Medico-Practicae, de Affectibus Capitis Internis et Externis.** Ed.:– Bernardinus & Georg Michael Wepfer. Schaffhausen, 1727. 4to. Liby. stp. on title. New hf. cf. (S. Jun.17; 871)   *Norman.* £80

WERDENHAGEN, Johannes Angelius
– **De Rebuspublicis Hanseaticis Tractatus.** Frankfurt, Matthew Merian, 1641. Fo. Lacks port. of author & possibly ptd. title, some staining thro.-out. Cont. vell. As an atlas, w.a.f. (C. Jul.15; 77)   *Weinreb.* £10,00

WERNER, Abraham Gottlob
– **Neue Theorie von der Enstehung der Gänge.** Freiberg, 1791. 1st. Edn. Cont. hf. cf., gt. spine. Stp. of Count R. von Veltheim; bkplt. of Herbert McLean Evans; from Honeyman Collection. (S. May 20; 3107)   *Hill.* £110
– – **Anr. Copy.** Cont. leath, gt. spine. Author's Pres. copy. (R. Oct. 14-18; 240)   DM 750
– **Von den Äusserlichen Kennzeichen der Fossilien.** Leipzig, 1774. 1st. Edn. Slight browning. Cont. bds., stained, inititals 'M.L.F.B.' on upr. cover. From Honeyman Collection. (S. May 20; 3106)   *Hill.* £520

WERNER, F.
– **Die Galvanoplastik in Ihrer Technischen Anwendung.** St. Petersb., 1844. 1st. Edn. Linen. (R. Oct. 14-18; 486)   DM 780

WERNER, Joannes, of Nuremberg
– **Canones ... Complectentes Praecepta & Observationes de Mutatione Aurae.** Nuremb., 1546. 1st. Edn. Sm. 4to. Cont. marginalia in red. Mod. bds. From Honeyman Collection. (S. May 20; 3109)   *Goldschmidt.* £380

WERNER, Nicolaus
– **Rechen Buch von allerley Kauffmannschlag, auff Sonderlichen Vorthel der Regel Detri.** Frankfurt a. M., 1569. 1st. Edn. Short tear reprd. in A3. Cont. German blind-stpd. pig over wooden bds., rolls incorporating figures, clasps & catches, cont. owner's inscr. on fly-lf. of Johannes Kremer of Ulm, his initials in ink on upr. cover. From Honeyman Collection. (S. May 20; 3110)   *Dr. Martin.* £550

WERNER, R.
– **Atlas des Seewesens.** Leipzig, 1871. Separate Edn. from 2nd. Iss. of Bilder-Atlas. Ob. fo. Slightly soiled, text browned. Cont. linen. (HK. Nov.18-21; 1833)   DM 620

WERNHERUS, Abbas Monasterii S. Blasii
– **Libri Deflorationnum suie Exceptionum ex Melliflua Diuersorum Patru[m].** Basle, [Michael Furter?], 1494. Fo. Lacks final blank, some worming slightly affecting text, slight browning. Mod. vell. bds., covers decor. with fragments from late medieval theological MS., soiled. From Liby. of André L. Simon. [BMC III, 788; Goff W12; HC 16158*] (S. May 18; 207)   *Thomas.* £320

WERTH, Leon
See–MIRBEAU, Octave & others

WESKETT, J.
– **A Complete Digest of the Theory, Laws & Practice of Insurance.** 1781. Fo. Cont. cf. (SH. May 21; 131)   *Pharos.* £170

WESLEY, Charles
– **Short Hymns on Select Passages of the Holy Scriptures.** Bristol, 1762. 1st. Edn. 2 vols. Minor defects. Mor. gt. by Zaehnsdorf. The Herschel V. Jones copy. (SPB. Jul.28; 455) $225
– **A Short Latin Grammar.** Bristol, 1748. 1st. Edn. Marginal tears & paper repairs, soiled. Mor. by Zaehnsdorf. The Herschel V. Jones copy. (SPB. Jul.28; 456) $200

WESLEY, John
– **Explanatory Notes upon the New Testament.** L., 1842. Cont. gt.-tooled mor. Fore-e. pntg. (SG. Mar.19; 191) $220

WESLEY, Samuel
– **The History of the New Testament.** Ill.:– J. Sturt. L., 1701. Red mor. gt., very worn. (SG. May 14; 224) $300

WEST, Anthony
– **John Piper.** 1979. (10) with orig. sigd. watercolour by the artist. 4to. Mor., s.-c. (P. Apr.9; 291)   *Marks.* £110
– – **Anr. Edn.** [1979]. (10) with orig. watercolour by Piper sigd. & numbered, tipped in. 4to. Orig. mor., s.-c. (CSK. Oct.31; 155)   £200

WEST, Charles
– **Lectures on the Diseases of Infancy & Childhood.** 1848. 1st. Edn. Advts., dtd. Oct. 1847, inserted. Orig. cl. From liby. of Dr. E. Ashworth Underwood. (S. Feb.23; 316)   *Dawson.* £90
– – **Anr. Copy.** 16pp. advts. Rebkd. (S. Jun.17; 873)   *Rootenberg.* £60

WEST, Edward
– **Emigration to British India.** L., 1857. 1st. Edn. Cl. (SG. Feb.26; 338) $110

WEST, Dr. G.S.
See–WEST, W. & others

WEST, H.A.
– **Six Views of Gibraltar.** 1828. 2 pts. Ob. fo. Orig. ptd. wraps., upr. wrap. of pt. 2 lacking, spines brkn. (C. Nov.6; 343)   *Traylen.* £260

WEST, John
– **History of Tasmania.** Tasmania, 1852. 1st. Edn. 2 vols. Later hf. cf. (C. Nov.5; 172)   *Traylen.* £160

WEST, Rev. John
– **The Substance of a Journal during a Residence at the Red River Colony, British North America.** L., 1824. 1st. Edn. Cont. bds., rebkd., new end-papers. (SPB. Jun.22; 131) $225

WEST, Leonard
– **The Natural Trout Fly & its Imitation.** Ravenhead, St. Helens. ca. 1912. Cl., covers badly discold. (SG. Apr.9; 323) $110
– – **Anr. Edn.** Ravenhead, St. Helens, n.d. 1st. Edn. Cl. (SG. Oct.16; 533) $130

WEST, Thomas
– **The Antiquities of Furness.** 1774. 1st. Edn. 4to. Map with sm. tear. Cont. cf., spine worn at head & foot. (S. Jun.22; 105)
                    McDowell & Stern. £70

WEST, W. & others
– **A Monograph of the British Desmidaceae.** 1904-23. 5 vols. Orig. embossed cl., ex-liby. (PL. Jul.11; 88)   *Wheldon & Wesley.* £80

WEST, William
– **The History, Topography & Directory of Warwickshire.** Bg'ham., 1830. Mod. cl. (SBA. Oct.22; 549)   *Davies.* £90
– – **Anr. Copy.** 1 folding hand-cold. map cleanly torn, 26 trade advts., 27 pp. of publisher's advts. Orig. cl., rebkd. in mor. (CSK. Apr.10; 132)   £80

WESTALL, William
– **Drawings by William Westall, Landscape Artist on Board H.M.S. Investigator during the circumnavigation of Australia by Captain Matthew Flinders, R.N., in 1801-03.** L., 1962. (1000). Fo. Orig. cl., slight wear. (KH. Nov.18; 633)   Aus. £160
– **The Mansions of England.** Ill.:– after Westall, Shepherd, Gendall & others. N.d. [plts. dtd. 1823-28]. 2 vols. Hf. mor. gt. by Riviére. Sig. of

William Day on title, bkplt. of Sir Davic̄ Salomons, lately in the collection of Eric Sexton. (C. Apr.16; 378)   *Wood.* £1,600
– – **Anr. Copy.** Red hf. mor., spines gt. (C. Mar.18; 116)   *Hammond.* £1,400

WESTALL, William & Moule, Thomas
– **Great Britain Illustrated.** 1830. 1st. Edn. (L.P.) 4to. Most plts. on india paper, additional title & 13 plts. also in unlettered proof state, 2 other plts. in final but unlettered state, slight spotting. Cont. red hf. mor., spine gt. A.L.s. from Westall to John Martin (the publisher), dtd. L., Jul.7 tipped in at front. (S. Nov.4; 520)   *Jeudwine.* £200
– – **Anr. Copy.** Cont. qtr. mor. (TA. May 21; 496)   £170
– – **Anr. Copy.** On India-paper, some spotting. Cont. blind-stpd. mor. by Remmant & Edmonds, covers with central circular panels depicting the 3 muses, sigd. D.N. (CSK. Feb.20; 67)   £120
– – **Anr. Copy.** Spotting. Cont. hf. russ., worn. (CSK. Oct.3; 56)   £105
– – **Anr. Copy.** 58 (of 59) plts., some tears, spotted. Cont. hf. mor. (SH. Jun.11; 133)   *Kidd.* £60
– – **Anr. Copy.** Occasional foxing, mostly marginal. Cont. mor. & marb. bds., gt., rebkd. in cl. (PNY. May 21; 290) $100
– – **Anr. Edn.** Ca. 1835. 4to. A few views spotted. Cl., spine defect. (P. Apr.30; 69)   *Kidd.* £80

WESTALL, William & Owen, Samuel
– **Picturesque Tour of the River Thames.** 1828. L.P. 4to. Red lev. mor. gt., by Zaehsndorf. (C. Mar.18; 117)   *Spencer.* £2,500
– – **Anr. Edn.** 1828. 4to. Views cold. Mod. red str.-grd. mor., covers with triple gt. fillet border enclosing gt. diamond-shaped ornament, partly unc. From the collection of Eric Sexton. (C. Apr.16; 379)   *Reid.* £1,900

WESTCOTT, Frederic
See–KNOWLES, G.B. & Westcott, Frederic

WESTERN RAILROAD
– **Reports of Explorations & Surveys ... from the Mississippi River to the Pacific Ocean ... 1853-4.** Wash., 1855-1856. Senate Iss. 4 vols. (I, III, IV & V). 4to. Cl., 3 vols. brkn., ex-liby. (SG. Aug.21; 500) $140

WESTGARTH, William
– **Victoria: late Australia Felix.** Edinb., 1853. Orig. cl. Inscr. (SH. Mar.5; 152)   *Cavendish.* £85
See–OGLE, Nathaniel–WESTGARTH, William

WESTHEIM, Paul
– **Das Holzschnittbuch.** Ill.:– Hecbel, Feiringer, Compendonk. Potsdam, 1921. Special Iss. 4to. 4 sigd. woodcuts from (100) privilege edn. (full vell.), Feininger woodcut on thin Japan. Orig. linen. (HK. Nov.18-21; 3019)   DM 6,400

WESTHEIM, Paul & Rathenau, E.
– **Kokoschka. Drawings.** L., 1962. (50) Privilege Edn. with 2 col. lithos. on Japan sigd. by artist. 4to. Orig. linen. (H. Dec.9/10; 2155)   DM 500

WESTLAKE, Nathaniel Hubert John
– **History of Design in Painted Glass.** L. & Oxford, 1881-94. 4 vols. Fo. Contents partly loose in bdg. Cl., worn. From the liby. of Clement Heaton. (SG. Mar.12; 350) $350

WESTMACOTT, Charles Molloy 'Bernard Blackmantle'
– **The English Spy.** Ill.:– George Cruikshank. L., 1825-26. 1st. Edn., 1st. Iss. 2 vols. Mor. gt. by Riviére. (P. Sep.11; 275)   *Traylen.* £620
– – **Anr. Copy.** Slight offsetting, foxing. Red mor. gt. by Bedford (SPB. Oct.1; 217) $1,100
– – **Anr. Copy.** Browned & stained. Mor. gt. by Stikeman. (SPB. Nov.25; 123) $950
– – **Anr. Copy.** 1 plt. cropped. Red crushed lev. mor. gt., spines gt., by Riviére & Son. (CNY. May 22; 288) $380
– – **Anr. Copy.** Occasional foxing & 1 plt. offset. Mor. by Riviére. (KH. Nov.18; 68)   Aus. $980
– **Sketches in Australia.** Exeter, [1848]. Pts. 1-3. Fo. Some ll. detchd., a few marginal tears. Orig. wraps., backstrips worn. (CSK. Jun.12; 151)   £3,000

WESTMINSTER ABBEY
[1966]. Ltd. numbered Edn. Fo. Mor., gt.-lettered, by Zaehnsdorf, cl. folding case. Sigd. by Dean Eric S. Abbott. (SG. Aug.21; 502) $110

WESTON, Edward
– **50 Photographs.** Ed.:– Merle Armitage, Robinson Jeffers & Donald Bear (text). N.Y.,

/ESTON, Edward – 50 Photographs. -contd.
[1947]. (1500) numbered, with initials of Weston
tipped in. Lge. 4to. Ptd. bds., cl. spine, d.-w. (SG.
Apr.23; 211) $500
- **My Camera on Point Lobos: 30 Photographs &
Excerpts from E.W.'s Daybook.** Yosemite
National Park, 1950. 1st. Edn. Fo. Ptd. bds., spiral
bdg., 1 lr. corner bumped. (SG. Apr.23; 212)
$250

WESTWOOD, Anthony
- **De Variolis & Morbillis: of the Small Pox &
Measles.** [1656]. 12mo. Sm. hole in blank portion
of title & stain in 1st. few ll., date & part of
imprint cropped from title, some foxing Cont.
sheep, worn. [Wing W1486] (C. Feb.25; 173)
Hammond. £190

WESTWOOD, John Obadiah
- **Arcana Entomologica.** 1845. 2 vols. Minor
foxing. Hf. cont. mor., slightly worn. (S.
Jun.1; 244) _Beaver._ £400
- **The Butterflies of Great Britain.** 1855. 1st. Edn.
Hf. cf. (SH. Jun.18; 174) _Frick._ £90
- - **Anr. Copy.** 4to. Slight soiling. Orig. cl., worn.
(CSK. Nov.7; 3) £60
- - **Anr. Edn.** 1857. Some ll. slightly soiled. Orig.
cl., rebkd. (SH. Oct.9; 26) _Elkin Mathews._ £55
- - **Anr. Edn.** N.d. Cont. cl. (SH. Jun.18; 175)
Book Room Camb. £65
- **Cabinet of Oriental Entomology.** 1848. 4to. Hf.
mor. gt. (P. Oct.2; 265) _Quaritch._ £300
- **A Descriptive Catalogue of the Fictile Invories in
the South Kensington Museum.** L., 1876. Leath.
spine, worn. (SG. Mar.12; 200) $110
- **Illuminated Illustrations of the Bible Copies from
Select Mss of the Middle Ages.** 1846. 4to.
Leath.-bkd. cl., spine gt., new end-papers. (LC.
Jun.18; 55) £50
- **Palaeographia Sacra Pictoria.** 1843-45. 4to.
Cont. hf. mor. (SH. Oct.10; 545) _Russell._ £60
See–HUMPHREYS, Henry Noel & Westwood,
John Obadiah

WESTWOOD, Thomas & Satchell, Thomas
- **Bibliotheca Piscatoria.** L., 1883. 1st. Edn. Cl.
Pres. Copy from Satchell to Charles B. Reynolds.
(SG. Apr.9; 326) $120
- - **Anr. Edn.** L., 1883; 1901. 1 vol. & supp. Cl., &
wraps. (SG. Dec.11; 115) $100

WETENHALL, Edward
[-] **Enter into Thy Closet; or a Method & Order
for Private Devotion.** 1676. 5th. Edn. 12mo. Some
browning. Cont. Engl. red mor., gt., drawer handle
& floral tools on covers, spine gt. in compartments.
[Wing 1499] (S. Dec.9; 369) _Fletcher._ £120

WETHERED, H. Newton & Simpson, T.
- **The Architectural Side of Golf.** 1929. No bdg.
stated. (CSK. Jul.20; 102) £130

WETMORE, Alexander
See–SWANN, H.K. & Wetmore, Alexander

WETSTENIOS, R. & J. & Smith, G.
- **Orbis Antiqui Tabulae Geographicae secundum
C.I. Ptolemaeum.** Amst., 1730. Fo. 28 double-p.
maps, mntd. on guards, slight browning. Cf., worn.
(CSK. Apr.10; 34) £220

WETZEL, Charles M.
- **Trout Flies.** Harrisburg, [1955]. Ltd., numbered
& sigd. Edn. 4to. 29 plts. (12 hand-cold. by
author). Gt.-lettered padded mor., bkplt. (SG.
Dec.11; 116) $500

WEY, Francesco
- **Roma Descrizione e Ricordi.** Milan, 1879. Fo.
Hf. cf. (CR. Mar.19; 279Q) Lire 220,000

WEYER, Edward Moffat
- **The Eskimos.** New Haven, L., & Oxford, 1932.
Cl., d.-w. (worn). (CB. Apr.1; 317) Can. $120

WEYGAND, James Lamar
[-] **A Collection of Pressmarks.–A Second Book.
–A Third Book.** Nappanee, Priv. Ptd., 1956, 1959,
1962. 3 vols. 12mo. All cl. (SG. Mar.26; 467)
$100

WEZLAR, Sholomo
- **Chakirat Ha'lev.** Amst., 1731. In old Yiddish,
lacks title, tear in last lf., with loss of text. Vell.,
Chaim Spivak's bkplt. (S. Nov.18; 473)
Elberg. £60

WHARNCLIFFE, Lord
- **Sketches in Egypt & in the Holy Land.** 1855. Fo.
Slightly spotted, 1 plt. loose. Orig. mor.-bkd. cl.
(SH. Nov.7; 445) _Heald._ £130

- - **Anr. Edn.** N.d. Fo. Spotted, some ll.
marginally soiled. Orig. mor.-bkd. cl., worn. loose.
(SH. Nov.7; 446) _Primrose Hill._ £100

WHARTON, Edith & Codman, Ogden
- **The Decoration of Houses.** N.Y., 1897. 1st. Edn.
Marb. bds., cl. s.-c. (SG. Dec.4; 364) $100

WHARTON, Thomas
- **Adenographia ...** Nymwegen, 1664. 12mo.
Slight worming. Cont. cf. (S. Jun.17; 874)
Gurney. £65

WHATELY, Richard
[-] **Account of an Expedition to the Interior of New
Holland.** Ed.:– Lady Mary Fox. 1837. 1st. Edn.
Without advts. Cont. tree cf. gt., spine gt. in
compartments, by Rivière. (C. Jul.15; 110)
Quaritch. £80

WHATLEY, Hewett
- **The Rod & Line.** L., 1849. 1st. Edn. 12mo.
Blind-stpd. cl. Armorial bkplt. of Edward Pering
Henslowe. (SG. Oct.16; 535) $200

WHEAT, Carl I.
- **Mapping the Trans-Mississippi West.** San
Franc., 1957-63. 5 vols. in 6. Fo. Orig. mor.-bkd.
buckram, unc. (S. Dec.8; 260) _Way._ £240
- - **Anr. Edn.** San Franc., Grab. Pr., 1957-1963.
(1000). 5 vols. Fo. Lacks 2nd. pt. of vol. V.
Buckram covers, leatherette spines. (SG.
Mar.5; 473) $700
- - **Anr. Edn.** San Franc., 1963. (1000). Vol.5. pt.
1 only. Leatherette-bkd. buckram. (SG.
Jun.11; 423) $110

WHEATLEY, Henry B.
- **London Past & Present.** L., 1891. 3 vols. Hf.
niger mor. gt. (P. Jun.11; 61) _Crowe._ £55
- **Les Reliures Remarquables du Musée
Britannique.** Trans.:– Janet M. Barwick. Paris &
L., 1889. Fr. Edn. 4to. Hf.-mor., spine torn. (SG.
Oct.2; 377) £110
- **Samuel Pepys: & the World He Lived In.** L.,
1880. Extra ill. with 10 engraved ports., 3
hand-cold. Crushed lev., gt.-tooled fillet & floral
borders, spine gt., high raised bands, gt. dentelles,
satin doubls. & end-papers, by Bayntun,
upr.-cover with port. of Pepys painted on ivory,
inlaid under glass. (SG. May 14; 172) $475

WHEATLEY, Phillis
- **Poems on Comic, Serious & Moral Subjects.** L.,
1773. 2nd. Edn. Some staining at end, advt. lf. at
end. Hf. mor. gt., partly unc. (Sabin 103137)
(CNY. Oct.1; 119) $550
- **Poems on Various Subjects Religious & Moral.**
L., 1786. 12mo. Slight foxing. Disbnd., ex-liby.
(SPB. Nov.24; 65) $225

WHEELER, C.G.
- **Hand-coloured Illustrations of the Beautiful &
Wonderful in Animated Nature.** N.p., ca. 1860. Fo.
Loose in cont. hf. linen portfo., spine defect. (R.
Oct.14-18; 3086) DM 460

WHEELOCK, Rev. Eleazar
- **A Brief Narrative of the Indian Charity School in
Lebanon in Connecticut, New England.** 1766. 1st.
Edn. Paper wraps. [Sabin 103202] (S. Dec.8; 253)
Ginsberg. £50

WHELER, George
- **A Journey into Greece ... in Company of Dr.
Spon of Lyons.** 1682. 1st. Edn. Fo. Slight
browning & soiling, a little worming, affecting a
few ll. of text. Cont cf., worn, 1 cover detchd.
[Wing W1607] (S. Sep.29; 84) _Crete._ £190
- - **Anr. Copy.** Folding map reprd., cont. sig. on
title, some discolouration thro.out. 19th C. hf. cf.
(S. Sep.29; 196) _Remington._ £150

WHEWELL, William
- **History of the Inductive Sciences.** 1837. 1st. Edn.
3 vols. Errata ll. at end of vol. I & II, label inside
upr. cover reading 'Telford Premium awarded to
William Worby Beaumont ... by the Institution
of Civil Engineers ... 1877'. Cont. hf. mor.
cypher CE on covers, 3 detchd. (S. Oct.21; 358)
Quaritch. £70

**WHIMSICAL JESTER (The): or, Rochester in
High Glee**
1784. Hf. cf. (BS. Jun.11; 292) £50

WHISHAW, Francis
- **Analysis of Railways.** L., 1837. 1st. Edn. Cont.
linen, slightly soiled, spine pasted. (R.
Mar.31-Apr.4; 1166) DM 950

WHISTLER, James A. NcNeill
- **The Gentle Art of Making Enemies.** L., 1890.
1st. Authorised Edn. Mor. gt., central onlaid mor.
emblems, silk linings, partly unc., upr. wraps. &
spine preserved, by Sangorski & Sutcliffe, upr.
cover detchd. W.a.f. A.L.s. inserted. (CNY. May
22; 289) $150

WHISTLER, Laurence
- **The Burning-Glass.** Priv. ptd., 1941. 1st. Edn.,
(50). Orig. wraps., Pres. Copy to Walter de la
Mare. (SH. Dec.18; 30) _Chelsea._ £80
- **Rex Whistler.** 1948. 1st. Edn. Orig. cl., d.w.
Inscr. to Walter de la Mare. (SH. Dec.18; 318)
Barry Scott. £80

WHISTLER, Laurence & Fuller, Ronald
- **The Work of Rex Whistler.** 1960. 4to. Orig. cl.,
d.-w. Pres. copy sigd. by Laurence Whistler &
with A.L.s. from him loosely inserted. (CSK.
Jul.17; 49) £95
- - **Anr. Copy.** Sir Cecil Beaton copy. (SH.
Mar.26; 34) _Wood._ £85
- - **Anr. Copy.** (CSK. Aug.22; 190) £75

WHISTLER, Rex
- **The Konigsmark Drawings.** Ed.:– Laurence
Whistler. 1952. (1000) numbered. 4to. Orig. cl.,
s.-c. (CSK. Jan.9; 171) £55
- - **Anr. Copy.** (CSK. Jul.17; 50) £50

WHITAKER, Joseph I.S.
- **The Birds of Tunisia.** Ill.:– H. Grönvold. 1905.
(250). 2 vols. Liby. stps. on titles. Recent red hf.
mor., spines emblematically tooled in gt. (S.
Jun.1; 245) _Hill._ £380

WHITAKER, Thomas Dunham
- **The History & Antiquities of the Deanery of
Craven in the County of York.** 1812. 2nd. Edn.,
L.P. Fo. Including 22 aquatints in 2 states. Cont.
cf., gt. panel. sides, rebkd. Fore-e. pntg. (C.
Jul.15; 111) _Burton._ £900
- - **Anr. Copy.** Cf. spine, marb. bds. (HSS.
Apr.24; 33) £60
- - **Anr. Edn.** Ed.:– A.W. Morant. Leeds, 1878.
3rd. Edn. 4to. Lacks Sigilla plt., 1 folding table
bkd. Crushed red mor., gt. borders, by F. Bedford,
gt. floral dentelles, spine gt. with design in five
compartments. (S. Nov.24; 298) _Quaritch._ £240
- - **Anr. Copy.** Some dampstains. Orig. mor.-bkd.
cl. (CSK. Nov.7; 185) £110
- - **Anr. Copy.** Hf. cf. & cl. (HSS. Apr.24; 115)
£65
- - **Anr. Copy.** 4to. Mor. gt. (SBA. Mar.4; 199)
Kelsall. £62
- **A History of the Original Parish of Whalley &
Honor of Clitheroe.** Ed.:– J.G. Nichols & Rev.
P.A. Lyons. 1872. 4th. Edn. 2 vols. Cf. (HSS.
Apr.24; 32) £85
- **A History of Richmondshire in the North Riding
of the County of York.** Ill.:– Lowry & others after
Buckler & others. 1823. 2 vols. Hf. cf., cl. & gt. by
J. Bland, Preston. (HSS. Apr.24; 200) £145
- - **Anr. Copy.** Fo. Slight spotting. Cont. hf. russ.,
worn. (CSK. Oct.31; 108) £95
- - **Anr. Copy.** L.P. Vol. 1 only (of 2). Cont. mor.
gt., slightly faded. (SBA. Oct.22; 659)
Inskip. £50

See–THORESBY, Ralph & Whitaker, Thomas
Dunham

WHITE, Alain & others
- **The Succulent Euphorbieae.** 1941. 4to. Orig.
buckram gt. (PL. Sep.18; 190)
Wheldon & Wesley. £75
- - **Anr. Copy.** Orig. bdg. (VA. May 8; 507)
R. 300
- - **Anr. Copy.** Cl. (SSA. Nov.5; 115) R. 230

WHITE, Alain & Sloane, Boyd L.
- **The Stapelieae.** California, 1937. 2nd. Edn. 3
vols. Sm. fo. Orig. cl. (TA. Jun.18; 134) £90
- - **Anr. Copy.** Orig. bdg. (VA. May 8; 508)
R. 150

WHITE, B.
– Ode Written for the Opening of the Grahamstown South African Exhibition of Arts & Industries, 1898, set to Music of Chorus & Orchestra by Theophil Wendt. L., 1898. Wraps. (SSA. Jan.22; 404)	R. 100

WHITE, Charles
– Account of the Regular Gradation in Man, & in Different Animals & Vegetables & from the Former to the Latter. 1799. 1st. Edn. 4to. Lacks errata lf.(?). Cont. cf.-bkd. bds. (S. Dec.2; 791)	*McBride.* £60
– An Inquiry into the Nature & Cause of that Swelling in one or both of the Lower Extremities which sometimes Happen to Lying-In Women. Manchester (1st. pt.), 1792; 1801. 2nd. Edn.; 1st. Edn. 2 pts. in 1 vol. Pt. II bnd. first, some worming in upr. outer corners in pt. I, liby. stps. on title-pp. Hf. cf. Inscr. in pt. II 'from the author', possibly the author's hand. (S. Jun.17; 876)	*Norman.* £200
– A Particular Narrative of What has Happened relative to a Paper ... entitled An Account of a Remarkable Operation on a broken Arm.–On the regeneration of Animal Substances.–Observations on Gangrene & Mortifications Accompanied with ... Convulsive Spasms. Warrington (2nd. & 3rd. vols.), 1762; 1785; 1790. 3 vols. Unif. new cl., parch. spine. (S. Jun.17; 877)	*Phillips.* £130
– A Treatise on the Management of Pregnant & Lying-In Women ... 1773. 1st. Edn. Cont. cf., rebkd. (S. Jun.17; 875)	*Studd.* £180
– – Anr. Edn. 1777. 2nd. Edn. Lr. blank margin of title torn, 1st. p. of dedication soiled. Cf., worn. (S. Dec.2; 655)	*Studd.* £60
– – Anr. Edn. 1785. 3rd. Edn. Some offsetting to 2 folding engraved plts., slightly browned. Orig. bds., sm. tear in spine, unc. From Liby. of Dr. E. Ashworth Underwood. (S. Feb.23; 317)	*Thorp.* £80

WHITE, Chr. & Boon, K.G.
– Rembrandt's Etchings. Amst., [1969]. 4to. Orig. linen. (HK. May 12-14; 2438)	DM 900

WHITE, Diana
– The Descent of Ishtar. Ill.:– Lucien Pissarro. Eragny Pr., 1903. (226). Orig. bds., unc. (S. Jul.31; 27)	*Maggs.* £140

WHITE, Frederick
– The Spicklefisherman & others. Ill.:– A.B. Frost & others. N.Y., 1928. (750). Parch.-bkd. marb. bds., partly unc. Inscr. to H.A. Ingraham. (SG. Dec.11; 117)	$600

WHITE, George
– Historical Collections of Georgia. N.Y., 1854. 1st. Edn. Some foxing. Cf., state arms stpd. on covers. (SG. Jun.11; 160)	$100

WHITE, George Francis
– Views in India, chiefly among the Himalaya Mountains. 1838. 4to. Slightly spotted. Orig. mor. (SH. Nov.7; 364)	*House.* £65
– – Anr. Copy. 1 plt. detchd., others loose, a few margins slightly stained. Orig. mor. gt. (SBA. Oct.21; 128)	*Dr. A.K. Sengupta.* £55
– – Anr. Edn. L. & Paris, [1838]. 4to. Slight foxing. Cont. diced cf., gt. (S. Jun.29; 230)	*Plant.* £75

WHITE, Gilbert
– [–] The Natural History & Antiquities of Selborne. 1789. 1st. Edn. 4to. 2 folding plts. rebkd. with linen, slight browning, sm. hole in 2E4 with loss of p. numerals. Mor. by Zaehnsdorf, 1901, spine tooled in compartments, elab. gt. floral decor. to corners, partly unc., gt. inside borders, silk end-papers. (S. Jun.1; 246)	*Traylen.* £580
– – Anr. Copy. Lev. mor. gt., by Rivière. Hugh Walpole's bkplt. (C. Mar.18; 186)	*Sotheran.* £520
– – Anr. Copy. Late 19th. C. lev. mor. gt., spine tooled in compartments. (S. Nov.24; 299)	*Traylen.* £450
– – Anr. Copy. Spotted. Cont. cf., rebkd. (SH. Jul.23; 35)	*Matthews.* £340
– – Anr. Copy. A2 loose, some spotting & offsetting. Old spine preserved. (S. Dec.3; 1173)	*Primrose.* £250
– – Anr. Copy. 4 extra plts. inserted at end, some spotting & offsetting, 1 plt. cropped. 19th. C. cf., lf. cover missing, upr. cover detchd. (S. Dec.3; 1174)	*Walford.* £220

– – Anr. Copy. Cont. cf., worn, rebkd. Thomas Pennant's copy with armorial bkplt. & 2-p. A.L.s. laid in. (SG. May 14; 225)	$750
– – Anr. Edn. 1813. 4to. Browned. Mod. hf. cf. (SH. Jul.23; 36)	*Subunso.* £55
– – Anr. Edn. Ill.:– John Nash. Ltd. Edns. Cl., 1972. (1500) sigd. by artist. 4to. Orig. mor.-bkd. bds., s.-c. (SH. Feb.20; 257)	*Thorp.* £90
– The Natural History & Antiquities of Selborne & A Garden Kalendar. Ed.:– R. Bowdler Sharpe. Ill.:– E.J. Sullivan, H. Railton & J.G. Keulemans. 1900. (160) sigd. by Ed. & Illustrators. 2 vols. 4to. Some spotting. Orig. vell., slightly soiled. (CSK. Oct.17; 43)	£75
– The Writings. Nones. Pr., 1938. Ltd. Edn. 2 vols. Orig. cl., s.-c. (SH. Jul.23; 39)	*Henderson.* £120

WHITE, Henry
– Gold Regions of Canada. Toronto, 1867. 12mo. Orig. cl., slightly faded. (CB. Feb.18; 55)	Can. $120

WHITE, Henry Kirke
– Remains. Ed.:– Robert Southey (life). L., 1811 2 vols. Contents loose, heavily foxed. Old str.-grd. mor., worn. Double fore-e. pntg. in each vol. (SG. Mar.19; 192)	$660

W[HITE], J.
– A Rich Cabinet, with Variety of Inventions. 1668. Browned. Cont. cf., worn, covers detchd. [Wing W1791] (SH. Jun.25; 199)	*Orskey.* £190

WHITE, J. G.
See–SPANISCHE SCHACHZABELBUCH DES KONIGS ALFONS DES WEISEN

WHITE, James
– A New Century of Inventions: being Designs & Descriptions of one Hundred Machines, Relating to Arts, Manufactures, & Domestic Life. Manchester, 1822. 2nd. Edn. 4to. 'Directions to Binder' slip, plt. 49 detchd., some offsetting onto text. Bds., unc., backstrip almost detchd. From Honeyman Collection. (S. May 20; 3112)	*Offenbacher.* £130
– – Anr. Copy. Plts. slightly dampstained & soiled at beginning. Mod. cl. (S. Oct.21; 359)	*D. Vine.* £50

WHITE, James
See–LAMB, CHARLES & White, James

WHITE, John
– Art Treasury. 1658. 2 vols. in 1. 12mo. 4 pp. advts. Hf. mor. (CE. Mar.19; 238)	£110

WHITE, John, Surgeon-Gen.
– Voyage à la Nouvelles Galles du Sud, à Botany Bay ... Trans.:– C. Pougins. Paris, 1795. Mod. hf. mor. (P. Jul.30; 99)	*Burden.* £55

[WHITE, John, Surgeon-General]–SMITH, Sir James
– [A Small Collection of Drawings of Australian Fauna & Flora associated with White].–A Specimen of the Botany of New Holland Ill.:– ?Thomas Watling (1st. work). [1790-95]; 1793. 2 works in 1 vol. 4to. 1st. work: ink captions & annots. probably in author's hand, a few pencil annots. by Richard Pulteney (1730-1801, botanist), the next owner; 2nd. work: 15 (of 16) cold. plts., lacks plt. 12, 6 cold. plts. & text from Andrew's Botanists Repository, a Linnean Society List of 1799 & offprint by Maton presented to Pulteney bnd. in. Cont. bds., bnd. (S. Jun.1; 253a)	*McCormick.* £1,400

WHITE, W. C.
– Tombs of Old Lo-Yang. Shanghai, 1934. (500) numbered. 4to. Orig. cl. (CSK. May 29; 91)	£90

WHITE HOUSE Gallery of Official Portraits of the Presidents
[1901]. Ltd. numbered Edn. Fo. Three-qtr. leath., worn, covers detchd. (SG. May 21; 448)	$175

WHITEHEAD, Alfred North & Russell, Bertrand
– Principia Mathematica. 1910-13. 1st. Edn. 3 vols. Orig. bds., slightly marked. From Honeyman Collection. (S. May 20; 3113)	*Percy.* £2,500

WHITEHEAD, Peter James Palmer & Edwards, Phyllis I
– Chinese Natural History Drawings. L., 1974. (400) numbered. Fo. Cased, goat. (JL. Dec.15; 746)	Aus. $340
– – Anr. Copy. Buckram gt. & qtr. mor., lined box. (KH. Mar.24; 424)	Aus. $310

WHITEHURST, John
– An Inquiry into the Original State & Formation of the Earth. 1778. 1st. Edn. 4to. Old hf. vell. From the collection of Eric Sexton. (C. Apr.15; 21)	*Snellenberg.* £110

WHITELEGGE, Thomas
– Scientific Papers. Sydney, 1890-1907. 11 papers bnd. together. Cl. Ingleton bkplt. (JL. Dec.15; 681)	Aus $170

WHITESIDE, J.
See–AYLIFF, J. & Whiteside J.

WHITFIELD, H.
– Plymouth & Devonport. 1900. (20). 4to. Cont. mor. (SH. May 21; 133)	*Crowe.* £75

WHITMAN, Walt
– An American Primer. Ed.:– Horace Traubel. Boston, L.P. 1st. Edn., (500). Cont. gt. hf. mor., orig. upr. wrap. & vell. backstrip bnd. in. Tipped-in is orig. MS., corrected, in Whitman's hand, composed on verso of letter received by Whitman, 16mo. (PNY. Mar.26; 339)	$1,150
– Complete Poems & Prose ... [Phila], [Priv. Ptd.], [1888]. 1st. Coll. Edn., (600) numbered, & sigd. Orig. cl. & marb. bds., mor.-bkd. s.-c., unopened. Pres. Copy, to Talcott Williams, lately in the Prescott Collection. (CNY. Feb.6; 324)	$1,100
– Drum-Taps. N.Y., [Priv. Ptd.], 1865. 1st. Edn., 1st. Iss. 12mo. Text ends on p. 72, without the 24 p. 'Sequel to Drum-Taps', sm. tear at fore-edge of title-p. Orig. cl., spine faded, thin fly-ll. From the Prescott Collection. (CNY. Feb.6; 322)	$650
– – Anr. Edn. N.Y., [Priv. Ptd.]. 1865. 1st. Edn., 2nd. Iss. With the addition of the 24 p. 'Sequel to Drum-Taps'. Orig. brown cl., slight wear at ends of spine. From the Prescott Collection. (CNY. Feb.6; 323)	$280
– An 1855-56 Notebook toward the Second Edition of Leaves of Grass. Ed.:– Harry G. Blodgett, & C. E. Feinberg (foreword). Carbondale, [1959]. (12) numbered, with 14 orig. items of memorabilia. Tall 8vo. Gt. lettered cf. spine, memorabilia in marb. bd. folder, together in marb. bd. box. Sigd. by Feinberg. (SG. Mar.19; 314)	$130
– Franklin Evans. N.Y., Nov., 1842. 1st. Edn. Fo. Minor hand-soiling & foxing. Disbnd. (SG. Nov.13; 724)	$280
[–] Good-Bye My Fancy. Phila., 1891. 1st. Edn., L.P. Orig. cl., partly unc. Inscr. to Clarence Darrow from Horace Traubel, with Traubel's note below, envelope (addressed by Traubel to Darrow) pasted in lr. cover, & containing autograph memorandum of Whitman's, & 4 photographs of him, lately in the Prescott Collection. (CNY. Feb.6; 325)	$480
[–] Leaves of Grass. N.Y., 1855. 1st. Edn., 1st. Iss. Fo. Frontis. port. with orig. tissue guard, title & 1st. few ll. foxed, some newspaper clippings laid in or pasted to front end-paper. Orig. cl., gt.-lettered & decor. in blind on covers, in triple gt. rule, gt.-lettered & decor. spine, marb. end-papers, spine reprd., mor. solander case. From the Prescott Collection. (CNY. Feb.26; 321)	$5,000
– – Anr. Edn. Brooklyn, 1855. 1st. Edn., 2nd. Iss. Fo. Foxed. Orig. cl. (SPB. Jun.22; 132)	$3,250
– – Anr. Edn. Brooklyn, N.Y., 1855. 1st. Edn., Early Iss. Sm. fo. Port. foxed, title-p. loose, no advts. or reviews. Cl., blind-tooled rules on cover. (SG. May 14; 226)	$1,100
– – Anr. Edn. Camden, 1876. Author's Edn. Port. tipped-in before title, not part of pagination. Orig. mor. & marb. bds., rebkd. in cf. & recornered in vell., later pastedowns. Sigd. (PNY. Mar.26; 343)	$425
– – Anr. Edn. Phila., 1891-92. 9th. Separate Edn., 2nd. Iss. Orig. wraps., unopened. Dr. Alexander MacAlister (Whitman's doctor) copy, with later bkplt. & note by family member. (CNY. Oct.1; 120)	$1,400
– – Anr. Copy. Dr. Alexander MacAlister copy. (CNY. May 22; 290)	$1,200
– – Anr. Edn. Ill.:– Edward Weston. N.Y., Ltd. Edns. Cl., 1942. (1500) sigd. by artist. 2 vols. 4to. Orig. bdg., publisher's box. (SPB. Nov.25; 419)	$750
– – Anr. Copy. Pict. bds., orig. box. (SG. Jan.15; 287)	$375
– November Boughs. Phila., 1888. Orig. cl., orig. spine laid down & gt.-ruled, qtr. mor. s.-c. Interleaved with 15 Whitman MSS. & 3 corrected proofs (most for November Boughs); inscr. on

WHITMAN, Walt -contd.

fly-lf. by T. Harned, lately in the Prescott Collection. (CNY. Feb.6; 328) £13,000
- Pionery [Pioneers]. Ill.:– V. Ermolaeva. Petrograd, n.d. Orig. wraps. by V. Ermolaeva. (SH. Feb.6; 548) *Lempert.* £50
[–] Two Rivulets. Camden, New Jersey, 1876. 1st. Edn. Slight spotting. Cont. hf. cf. Pres. Copy, inscr., sigd. & mntd., albumen port. (CSK. Oct.3; 129) £70

WHITNEY, Geoffrey

- A Choice of Emblems, & other Devices; [The Second Part of Emblemes]. Leiden, 1586. 1st. Edn. 4to. Iss. with **3 recto line 18 ending 'and', & the emblem 'Ex damno alterius' on p. 119, lacks? final blank, 2 sm. holes in margin of d2, sm. repairs to lr. inner margins of f2-3. Mor., gt., by Bedford, rebkd., with orig. spine laid down. [NSTC 25438] (S. Feb.10; 478) *Quaritch.* £1,800

WHITNEY, John

- The Genteel Recreation. 1700 [1800]. (100). 12mo. Early 19th. C. red mor. Bkplt. of Edwin F. Snow. (S. Nov.25; 300) *Thorp.* £60
- – Anr. Edn. L., 1820. (100) reprinted from 1700 Edn., with facs. title-p. 12mo. Bds., unc. Frank M. Buckland's bkplt. (SG. Oct.16; 538) £220

WHITTAKER, John

- Ceremonial of the Coronation of His Most Sacred Majesty King George the Fourth. 1823. Elephant fo. Cold. aquatint frontis., 42 plts. on thick paper, many with figs. heightened with gold, title, dedication & text elab. embossed in gt. in gt. armorial frames, folding plt. mntd. & varnished. Cont. red hf. mor. gt., brass clasps. (C. Jul.15; 112) *Taylor.* £5,800

WHITTIER, John Greenleaf

- The Pennsylvania Pilgrim. Boston, 1872. Lev. gt., gt. dentelles, by Sangorski & Sutcliffe, orig. cl. covers & spine bnd. in. A.L.s. to Brewer tipped in (Amesbury, May 15, 1871, 12mo., 3 pp.). (SG. Mar.19; 315) £230
- Writings. Ed.:– S.T. Pickard (life). Camb., Riverside Pr., 1888-1894. (400) numbered on L.P. 9 vols. Cl.-bkd. bds., unc. & unopened. (SG. Mar.19; 316) £180

WHITTIER, John Greenleaf–PICKARD, Samuel T.

- Works.–Life & Letters of John Greenleaf Whittier. Boston, 1892; 1894. Artists Edn., (750). 9 vols. Hf. mor. gt. (SPB. Nov.25; 499) $250

WHITTLE, James

See–LAURIE, Robert & Whittle, James

WHITTOCK, Nathaniel

- Art of Drawing & Colouring Flowers, Fruit & Shells. 1829. Some foxing. Hf. cf. gt. (P. Sep.11; 56) *Fogg.* £170
- The Decorative Painters' & Glaziers' Guide . . . L., 1827. 4to. Heavily foxed. Mod. hf. cf. (SG. Dec.4; 370) $300
- The Oxford Drawing Book . . . Oxford, ca. 1825. Ob. 4to. Z2 torn. Cont. cf., reprd., upr. cover loose. (S. Nov.25; 438) *Tate.* £90
- A Topographical & Historical Description of the University & City of Oxford. 1828. 1st. Edn. 4to. Extra-ill. with plts. from Pugin's 'Ecclesiastical Collegiate Architecture' & 2 hand-cold. costume plts. from Harraden's 'Costume of the University of Cambridge' bnd. in at end, frontis. & additional title stained in lr. inner margins, 3 Pugin plts. with short tears, occasional light spotting. 19th. C. cl. (S. Nov.4; 521) *Kentish.* £130
- – Anr. Copy. Costume plts. hand-cold. Hf. mor., gt. From the collection of Eric Sexton. (C. Apr.16; 380) *Kentish.* £80
- – Anr. Copy. 42 (of 43) litho. plts., 5 cold., some browning, minor tears. Mor. gt. (SPB. May 29; 439) $250
- – Anr. Edn. 1829. 4to. Lacks plt. of St. Edmund Hall, slight foxing. Cont. hf. mor. (TA. Dec.18; 394) £125
- – Anr. Edn. N.d. 4to. Some spotting. Cont. hf. mor. (TA. Mar.19; 248) £140
- The Youths' New London Self-Instructing Drawing-Book, in Colours. 1836. 1st. Edn. Ob. 8vo. 41 aquatint plts., all but frontis. in cold. & uncold. states, piece torn from upr. edge of 1st. plt. with loss of number, a few spots. Cont. hf. roan, slightly loose. (S. Jun.23; 338) *Traylen.* £200

WHITTY, M.J.

[–] Tales of Irish Life. Ill.:– George Cruikshank. L., 1824. 1st. Edn. 2 vols. Some foxing. lf. of advts.

---

before preface & at end of vol. II. Later three-qtr. cf., spines gt. Bkplt. of W.H. Woodin. (SG. Mar.19; 65) $100

WHITWORTH, Lord Charles

- An Account of Russia. Strawberry Hill, 1758. 1st. Edn. Late 18th. C. red str.-grd. mor. gt., spine tooled in compartments. Bkplt. of J.G. Teed. (S. Nov.24; 301) *Maggs.* £180
- – Anr. Copy. Cont. cf., rebkd. & reprd. (S. Jul.27; 23) *Thorpe.* £70
- – Anr. Copy. Slight offsetting, inkspots on title. Mod. cf., unc. (S. Jan.27; 576) *Lister.* £50

WHOLE Art of Fishing, The

1714. 1st. Edn. Frontis. cut down & mntd. Early 19th. C. cf., worn, upr. cover detchd. (S. Nov.24; 302) *Thorp.* £130

WHYMPER, Edward

- The Ascent of the Matterhorn. 1880. Orig. cl. (CSK. Jul.3; 104) £52
- Travels Amongst the Great Andes. 1891-92. 2 vols. Mor. gt. with lions rampant, by Zaehnsdorf. (CE. Nov.20; 121) £100
- – Anr. Edn. 1892. Lge. folding chart in pocket at end. Orig. cl., unc. (S. Jun.29; 183) *Crete.* £55

WHYTE-MELVILLE, George John

- Works. 1898-1902. (1050). 24 vols. Mod. hf. mor., gt. decor. on spines. (SH. Apr.10; 366) *Thorp.* £260

WHYTT, Robert

- An Essay on the Vital & other Involuntary Motions of Animals. Edinb., 1751. 1st. Edn. Cont. cf., rebkd. (S. Jun.17; 878) *Norman.* £350
- Observations on the Dropsy in the Brain, to which are added his other Treatises never hitherto published. Edinb., 1768. 1st. Edn. Cf., rebkd. (S. Jun.17; 881) *Maggs.* £220
- Observations on the Nature, Causes & Cure of those Disorders which have been commonly called Nervous, Hypochondriac or Hysteric. Edinb., 1765. 1st. Edn. Cont. cf. (S. Jun.17; 879) *Sargeant.* £170
- – Anr. Edn. Edinb., 1765. 2nd. Edn. Cf., rebkd. (S. Jun.17; 880) *Jenner Books.* £75
- The Works. Edinb., 1768. 1st. Edn. 4to. Dampstained thro.-out. Cont. cf., rebkd. & corners reprd., orig. spine preserved. From liby. of Dr. E. Ashworth Underwood. (S. Feb.23; 318) *Whitehart.* £150

WICQUEFORT, Abraham de

- Advis . . . aux Véritables Hollandois . . . Ill.:– Romain de Hooghe. [Amst.], 1673. 1st. Printing. 4to. Cont. mor., spine grotesquely decor., 3 fillets, inside dentelle. (HD. Dec.5; 222) Frs. 14,500

WIDMAN, Johannes

- Behend und hüpsch Rechnung uff allen Kauffmanschafften. Hagenau, 1519. 4th. Edn. 2 wormholes thro. 1st. 34 ll., some staining & discolouration, owners' inscrs. Bnd. in lf. of vell. MS., wormed, lacks ties. From Honeyman Collection. (S. May 20; 3116) *Dr. Martin.* £600
- Rechnung auf alle Kaufmannschaft. Leipzig, Conrad Kachelofen, 1489. 1st. Edn. Lacks 6 ll. including last blank, hand-cold. woodcut arms of Leipzig on title, single wormhole thro. 1st. 19 ll. of text, last line on d3r partly failed to print, short tear in C7, some staining, title slightly soiled. 19th. C. vell., rebkd. hf. mor. case. From Honeyman Collection. [BMC III, 624; HC 13712; Goff W14] (S. May 20; 3115) *Dr. Martin.* £2,000

WIDOWSON, Henry

- Present state of Van Diemen's Land; comprising an account of its agricultural capabilities . . . & other important matters connected with emigration. 1829. 1st. Edn. Folding engraved map, somewhat spotted & offset onto title-p. Mod. hf. mor., unc. (S. Nov.4; 624) *Lawson.* £150

WIEGLEB, Johann Christian

- Geschichte des Wachsthums und der Erfindungen in der Chemie (1651-1790). Berlin & Stettin, 1790-91. 1st. Edn. 2 vols. in 1. Some browning & marginal staining. Cont. hf. sheep; red hf. mor. case. From Honeyman Collection. (S. May 20; 3117) *Quaritch.* £160

WIELAND, Christoph. Martin

- Histoire du sage Danischmend . . . ou l'Egoïste et le Philosophe. Ill.:– Schwebach. Paris, 1800. Orig. Edn. 2 vols. Cont. str.-grd. hf. cf., decor. spines. (HD. Feb.18; 81) Frs. 1,700
- Sämmtliche Werke. Leipzig, 1794-1805. 1st. Coll. Edn., 'wohlfeile Edn.' 38 (of 39) vols. & 6

---

supp. vols. in 44 vols. Lacks last vol., heavily soiled & browned in parts. Cont. bds., very worn, 3 vols. bnd. later in cont. style. (H. May 21/22; 1322) DM 450
- – Anr. Edn. Trans.:– J.G. Gruber. Leipzig, 1818-28. 53 vols. Lightly browned in parts, sm. stains. Cont. hf. leath., 3 spines torn. (H. Dec.9/10; 1695) DM 1,300
- – Anr. Edn. Ed.:– J.G. Gruber. Leipzig, 1824-27. 1st. Gruber Edn. Vols. 1-51 (of 53). Soiled. Cont. hf. leath. gt., decor. W.a.f. (HK. May 15; 5013) DM 750
- – Anr. Edn. Leipzig, 1853-58. Later hf. leath. gt. (D. Dec.11-13; 849) DM 440

WIELANDSLIED DER AELTEREN EDDA

Trans.:– K. Simrock. Ill.:– G. Marcks. Munich & Weimar, 1923. (110). Fo. Woodcuts individually monogrammed, dated. Loose ll. in orig. hf. vell. portfo. (H. Dec.9/10; 2215) DM 3,800

WIENER ZEITSCHRIFT für Kunst, Literatur, Theater und Mode

Ed.:– Fr. Witthauer. Vienna, 1838. 3rd. Quartal. Cont. bds. (D. Dec.11-13; 2229) DM 420

WIENMANN, J.W. & Dietrichs, J.G. & others

- Phytanthoza Iconographia. Ill.:– after Ehret & others. Regensburg, [1735-] 1737-45. 5 vols. (including index dtd. 1735). Fo. Latin & German title-pp. in each vol. (except index), Latin version of Haller's German foreword bnd. in index vol., not present are list of subscribers, a lf. of testimonials, 2 ll. of verse, 3 indexes are present, some spotting & a few stains. Cont. stpd. pig over wooden bds., device of Jesuit house in centre of covers. From collection of Massachusetts Horticultural Society, stps. on plts. (SPB. Oct.1; 171) $30,000

WIER, Johannes

- De Praestigiis Daemonum, et Incantationibus ac Ueneficiis, libri V. Basle, Mar. 1566. 3rd. Edn. Slight dampstaining, late 17th. C. inscr. on title. 17th. C. panel. cf., soiled. (S. Apr.6; 170) *Symonds.* £140
- De Praestigiis Daemonum, & Incantationibus ac ueneficiis Libri sex . . . Access. liber Apologeticus et Pseudomonarchia Daemonum.–De Lamiis Liber. Basel, 1577; 1577. 2 works in 1 vol. 4to. Title & port. on verso in 1st. work replaced in facs. Cont. vell. (VG. Dec.17; 1615) Fls. 480

WIERX, Hieronymus

- [Engravings]. [Antw.], Late 16th. C. Slight browning & soiling. Cont. limp vell., soiled, bkplt. of Holland House, front pastedown end-paper inscr. 'E[lizabeth] V[assall] [Lady] Holland/bought at Parma/1814'. W.a.f. (S. Jan.27; 465) *Mendez.* £240

WIESBADEN UND SEINE UMGEBUNG

Darmstadt, ca. 1850. Browned in parts & heavily soiled, text incompl. Cont. paper bds. (H. Dec.9/10; 714) DM 1,400

WIGGIN, Kate Douglas

- The Birds' Christmas Carol. San Franc., 1887. 1st. Edn. Sq. 12mo. Accompanied by anr. edn. of the work (Boston, [1912], ill. by Kate Wireman). Lacks wraps. & most of spine, orig. stitching present, the later edn. in orig. cl. Both edns. inscr. to Bertha Coolidge, both lately in the Prescott Collection. (CNY. Feb.6; 333) $3,800
- Rebecca of Sunnybrook Farm. Boston, 1903. 1st. Edn., 1st. Iss. 16mo. Pict. cl., publisher's name in sm. type on spine, extremities of spine worn. Inscr. to Joseph Brooks. (SG. Apr.30; 323) $180
- The Story of Patsy.–The Birds' Christmas Carol. San Franc., Priv. Ptd. (1st. work), 1883; 1887. 1st. Edns. 2 works in 1 vol. Sq. 12mo. Specially bnd. in plain white wraps., covers slightly soiled. Pres. Copy, to Bertha Coolidge, with author's ink sketches on upr. cover, & titles gt.-lettered by her, lately in the Prescott Collection. (CNY. Feb.6; 334) $950
- Writings. Boston, n.d. Autograph Edn., with MS. quote sigd. by Wiggin. 10 vols. Mor. gt., silk end-papers, mor. doubls. (SPB. May 6; 355) $1,800

WIGHT, John

- More Mornings at Bow Street. Ill.:– George Cruikshank. L., 1827. 1st. Edn. Later bds., orig. spine label preserved, unc. Bkplt. of John Byram. (SG. Mar.19; 66) $100
- Sunday in London . . . with a copy of Sir Andrew Agnew's Bill. Ill.:– George Cruikshank. 1833. 1st. Edn. 3 dupls. plts. (proofs before letters). Late 19th.

C. lev. mor. by Zaehnsdorf, gt., orig. wraps. preserved. A.L.s. by Agnew inserted, bkplts. of Albert M. Cohn & Lord Nathan of Churt. (S. Nov.24; 92) *Sawyer.* £120

WIGSTEAD, Henry

– Remarks on a Tour to North & South Wales. Ill.:– after Rowlandson & others. 1800. Plts. cold., lacks ptd. title & hf.-title. Pol. cf. gt., by Root. From the collection of Eric Sexton. (C. Apr.16; 382) *Maggs.* £240

– – Anr. Copy. Lacks hf.-title, frontis. cropped & soiled, occasional foxing. Mod. red hf. mor. (C. Nov.5; 173) *Larnark Jones.* £100

WILBERFORCE, William

– Letter on the Abolition of the Slave Trade. 1807. 1st. Edn. 4 pp. advts. Orig. wraps., unc. (S. Nov.4; 632) *Brook-Hitching.* £240

– – Anr. Edn. 1807. Lacks advts., prelims. slightly spotted. Cont. hf. cf., upr. cover detchd. (TA. Nov.20; 341) £60

WILCOCKE, Samuel Hull

– History of the Viceroyalty Buenos Aires. L., 1807. Slightly soiled. Later hf. leath., worn, spine defect. & loose. (D. Dec.11-13; 1471) DM 800

[–] Recit des Evenemens qui ont eu lieu sur la Territoire des Sauvages dans l'Amérique Septentrionale. Montreal, 1818. 1st. Fr. Edn. Cont. linen-bkd. bds. [Sabin 68367] (SPB. Jun.22; 134) $300

WILD, Charles

[–] [English & Foreign Cathedrals]. N.d. 2 vols. Fo. No titles or text, slightly soiled. Orig. hf. cf. folders, worn. (SH. Nov.6; 262) *Foster.* £180

– Foreign Cathedrals. Ca. 1826. Fo. Unbnd. as issued in orig. portfo., worn. (CSK. Oct.17; 203) £110

WILD FLOWERS OF THE ALPHABET, a Poem for Children

1858. 4to. Orig. decor. cl. gt., spine neatly reprd. (SH. Mar.19; 323) *Fletcher.* £210

WILD or Ferus, Johann

– Wintertheil[–Sommertheil] der Postill de Sanctis. Mainz, 1568. 2 pts. in 1 vol. Fo. Some wormholes, a few slightly affecting text, dampstained, occasional slight spotting, owners' inscrs. on title. Cont. German blind-stpd. cf. over wood bds., gt., initials FHIB & arms of Bavaria on upr. cover. Dedication inscr. by Ferdinand, Duke of the Palitine & Bavaria on fly-lf., dtd. 1591. (S. Feb.10; 209) *Rota.* £120

WILD, Frank

– Shackleton's Last Voyage. 1923. 1st. Edn. Orig. decor. cl. (SH. Nov.7; 498) *Barnett.* £55

WILD, John James

– At Anchor, a Narrative of Experiences Afloat & Ashore During the Voyage of H.M.S. Challenger from 1872 to 1876. 1878. Fo. Orig. cl., gt. (S. Dec.2; 656) *Cawthorn.* £90

WILDE, Oscar

– After Berneval. Ed.:– More Adey [intro.]. Ill.:– Marcel Schwabe. [L.], [Beaumont Pr.], [1922]. 1st. Edn., (5) numbered for presentation, on Japan vell. & sigd. by printer & artist Orig. qtr. vell. & decor. paper bds., spine gt.-lettered, unc. From the Prescott Collection. (CNY. Feb.6; 402) $380

– After Reading. Ill.:– Ethelbert White. [L.], [Beaumont Pr.] [1921]. 1st. Edn., (75) numbered on Japan vell., sigd. by printer & artist. Orig. qtr. vell. & decor. paper bds., spine gt.-lettered, unc. From the Prescott Collection. (CNY. Feb.6; 400) $140

[–] The Ballad of Reading Gaol. L., 1898. 1st. Edn., (30) numbered on Japan vell. Tall 8vo. Orig. qtr. vell. & cl., spine gt.-lettered, mor. solander case, partly unc. Pres. Copy, to Mr. & Mrs. Dal Young, lately in the Prescott Collection. (CNY. Feb.6; 389) $4,800

– – Anr. Edn. L., 1898. 1st. Edn., (800). Orig. buckram-bkd. cl. (C. Feb.4; 322) *Blackwell.* £65

– – Anr. Copy. Orig. cl., unc. Author's pres. copy, inscr. on verso of hf.-title 'Cyril, from his friend the author. Paris, March. 98. Oscar Wilde'. (CNY. Oct.1; 124) $1,400

– – Anr. Edn. Trans.:– Henry D. Davrey. Paris, 1898. 1st. Fr. Edn. 12mo. Hf. maroon mor. gt., qtr. mor. gt. s.-c., partly unc. Pres. Copy, to Frank Harris, lately in the Prescott Collection. (CNY. Feb.6; 390) $2,800

– – Anr. Edn. 1898. 3rd. Edn., Cont. red mor. gt., by Hampstead Bindery. (S. Jul.22; 332) *Estorick.* £210

– – Anr. Edn. Ill.:– R. Schlichter. [Munich], [1923]. (10) Privilege Edn., on old Holländischen Bütten. Sm. 4to. 61 sigd. etchings (60 on printer's mark). Hand-bnd. orig. vell., gold fillets, by Frieda Thirsch. (H. May 21/22; 1790) DM 2,200

– – Anr. Edn. Ill.:– Frans Masareel. Munich, [1923]. (70) on H.M.P., sigd. by artist. Cont. parch. (SH. Nov.21; 409) *Reed & Sims.* £145

– – Anr. Edn. Ill.:– Frans Masereel. L., [1925]. (450) numbered. Tall 8vo. Some staining. Linen-bkd. bds., end-papers foxed. (SG. Apr.2; 190) $110

– – Anr. Edn. Portland, n.d. (10) numbered on vell. 12mo. Gt.-ptd. vell., unopened. Sigd. by printer. (PNY. Mar.4; 269) $375

– – Anr. Edn. Ill.:– Isabel Lyndall, F.V. Wilson, George Gibbs, L. Horter & others. N.Y., n.d. 4to. Text & ills. inlaid thro.-out. Mor. gt., panel. spine with mor. inlays, mor. panel inlaid on upr. cover with scene of prison & prisoners in gt., mor. inlays on panel, mor. doubls. depicting scenes from vol. in gt., by Hyman Zucker. (SPB. Nov.25; 421) $900

– Ballade de la Geôle de Reading. Ill.:– Tavy Notton. Paris, 1951. 4to. Hf. chagrin, corners, unc., wrap. (HD. Dec.5; 223) Frs. 1,000

[–] Catalogue of the Library of Valuable Books . . . L., Apr. 24, 1895. Interleaved with additional blank ll., some remargining at gutter edges, other repairs. Qtr. mor. & paper bds. C.S. Millard's copy, with bkplt., annotated & priced thro.-out by him, lately in the Prescott Collection. (CNY. Feb.6; 409) $4,200

– De Profundis. L., [1905]. 1st. Edn., (50) on Japan vell. Tall 8vo. Orig. limp vell. bds., upr. cover with 3 sm. gt. medallion devices after designs by Ricketts, spine gt.-lettered, qtr. mor. gt. s.-c., partly unc. From the Prescott Collection. (CNY. Feb.6; 394) $1,000

– – Anr. Edn. L., [1905]. 1st. Edn., (200) on Engl. H.M.P. Tall 8vo. Orig. buckram, upr. cover with 3 sm. gt. medallion devices after designs by Ricketts, spine gt.-lettered, partly unc. From the Prescott Collection. (CNY. Feb.6; 393) $220

– – Anr. Edn. Milan, 1945. (125) numbered. Orig. hf. vell., s.-c. (S. Jul.31; 158) *Bertram Rota.* £260

– The Duchess of Padua. L., [1908]. 1st. Edn., (1000) on H.M.P. Inserted are several clipped newspaper reviews, & a brief A.L.s. of Adele Schuster (the dedicatee). Orig. buckram bds., covers with 3 gt. medallion devices after designs by Ricketts, spine gt.-lettered, partly unc. Inscr. by Ross (1 of Wilde's literary executors) to C.S. Millard, with his bkplt. & pencil notes, lately in the Prescott Collection. (CNY. Feb.6; 395) $180

– The Happy Prince & other Tales. Ill.:– Walter Crane. L., 1888. 1st. Edn., (75) numbered on L.P., & sigd. by author & publisher. Fo. With the 4 plts. present in dupl. as mntd. india-paper proofs, ptd. in both brown & black. Orig. Japan vell., upr. cover with blocked design, soiled, end-ll. foxed, unc. From the Prescott Collection. (CNY. Feb.6; 369) $1,400

– – Anr. Edn. L., 1888. 1st. Edn., (1000). 4to. Orig. Japan vell., upr. cover with blocked design (after J. Hood), soiled & worn, qtr. mor. gt. s.-c., unc. Pres. Copy, to Mrs. Bernard Beere, lately in the Prescott Collection. (CNY. Feb.6; 368) $1,800

– – Anr. Edn. Ill.:– Walter Crane & Jacomb Hood. Boston, 1888. 1st. Amer. Edn. 12mo. Pict. cl. (SG. Nov.13; 727) $110

– – Anr. Edn. Ill.:– Charles Robinson. 1913. (250) sigd. by artist. 4to. Orig. bds. (MMB. Oct.8; 150j) £72

– The Harlot's House. Ill.:– Althea Gyles. L., 1904. (12) Privilege Edn. on Vell., De Luxe with 3 series of plts. Fo. Hand-bnd. red mor. gt., double gold fillets on covers & inner dentelles, orig. wraps. (H. May 21/22; 1871) DM 3,000

– A House of Pomegranates. Ill.:– after Shannon & Rickets. L., 1891. 1st. Edn., (1000). 4to. Orig. linen bds., gt.-decor. cl. spine, upr. cover with design in gt. & red, cl. spotted, qtr. mor. gt. s.-c. From the Prescott Collection. (CNY. Feb.6; 370) $350

– – Anr. Edn. Ill.:– Charles Ricketts & C.H. Shannon. L., 1891. 1st. Edn. 4to. Gt.-pict. cl., unc. (SG. Jun.4; 495) $150

– – Anr. Copy. Sq. 4to. Gt.-pict. cl., soiled, end-papers loose. (SG. Dec.18; 422) $110

– – Anr. Edn. Ill.:– Jessie M. King. 1915. [6th. Edn.?]. 4to. Orig. cl. gt. (SBA. Oct.21; 226) *Temperley.* £110

– – Anr. Copy. Decor. cl. (PJ. Jun.6; ('80);54) £85

– – Anr. Copy. Orig. decor. cl., rebkd. (SKC. Dec.4; 1485) £55

[–] An Ideal Husband. L., 1899. 1st. Edn., (100) numbered on Lge. H.M.P., & sigd. 4to. Prelims. & free end-ll. foxed. Orig. linen bds., covers & spine gt. with designs after Shannon, worn, qtr. mor. s.-c., unc. From the Prescott Collection. (CNY. Feb.6; 392) $1,400

[–] The Importance of Being Earnest. L., 1898. 1st. Edn., (100) numbered on Lge. H.M.P., & sigd. 4to. Orig. linen bds., covers & spine with gt.-stpd. designs after Shannon, free end-papers spotted, qtr. mor. gt. s.-c., unc. With A.L.s. (with initials) to Leonard Smithers (ca. Feb. 2, 1899, 8vo., 4 pp., with orig. envelope in Wilde's hand); from the Prescott Collection. (CNY. Feb.6; 391) $8,500

– – Anr. Edn. 1899. 1st. Edn. (1000) numbered. Orig. cl. gt., unc. (S. Jul.22; 333) *Ghani.* £80

– – Anr. Edn. N.Y., 1956. (500) numbered. 2 vols. 4to. Gt.-ornamental vell. bds., tissue guards, s.-c. (PNY. Mar.4; 270) $250

– Intentions. L., 1891. 1st. Edn. Browning. Orig. cl., soiled. (SPB. Jul.28; 459) $250

– Lady Windermere's Fan. L., 1893. 1st. Edn., (50) on Lge. H.M.P. 4to. Orig. buckram, gt. spine, covers with gt. decors. after Shannon, cl. soiled, qtr. mor. gt. s.-c., unc. With James Shepherd's sig. on limitation p., lately in the Prescott Collection. (CNY. Feb.6; 377) $1,000

– – Anr. Edn. 1893. 1st. Edn. 4to. Orig. cl. Inscr. by publisher John Lane to F. Harrison. (SH. Dec.19; 656) *Sganzela.* £80

– – Anr. Copy. Orig. cl., gt. spine, covers with gt.-decors after Shannon, slightly soiled, qtr. mor. gt. s.-c., unc. Pres. Copy, to Marion Terry, lately in the Prescott Collection. (CNY. Feb.6; 375) $5,500

– – Anr. Copy. Spine slightly soiled. Pres. Copy, to Edmund Gosse, lately in the Prescott Collection. (CNY. Feb.6; 376) $4,200

– Lord Arthur Savile's Crime & Other Stories. 1891. 1st. Edn. Orig. bds., worn. (SH. Dec.19; 655) *Sganzela.* £50

– – Anr. Copy. 12mo. Orig. pict. bds., spine worn, later cl. s.-c., bkplt. of Lewis Alsberg. (PNY. Mar.4; 271) $130

[–] Oscariana. L., Priv. Ptd., 1895. 1st. Edn., 1st. Iss., (50). Orig. paper wraps., slightly worn at edges, qtr. mor. gt. s.-c., unc. From the Prescott Collection. (CNY. Feb.6; 387) $350

– Pan . . . & Desespoir. Boston & L., 1909. 1st. Edn., (30) numbered for copyright. 2nd. lf. with slight dampstain. Orig. self-wrap. with title & imprint, qtr. mor. gt. s.-c., unc. From the Prescott Collection. (CNY. Feb.6; 397) $380

– The Picture of Dorian Gray. L., N.Y., & Melbourne, 1891. 1st. Edn., (250) numbered on L.P., & sigd. 4to. Orig. parch.-bkd. paper bds., cover & spine with gt.-decors. after Ricketts, qtr. mor. gt. s.-c., unc. From the Prescott Collection. (CNY. Feb.6; 373) $1,700

– – Anr. Copy. Sq. 4to. Gt. decor. bds., vell. spine (torn), partly unc. (SG. Nov.13; 729) $325

– – Anr. Edn. L., N.Y., & Melbourne, [1891]. 1st. Edn. Some pp. at end & some fore-margins foxed. Orig. parch.-bkd. paper bds., cover & spine with gt.-decors. after Ricketts, ptd. d.-w. (frayed), qtr. mor. folding case, unc. From the Prescott Collection. (CNY. Feb.6; 371) $2,200

– – Anr. Copy. Orig. parch.-bkd. paper bds., gt.-decor., worn & soiled, qtr. mor. gt. s.-c., unc. Pres. Copy, to Luther Munday, lately in the Prescott Collection. (CNY. Feb.6; 372) $1,000

– – Anr. Edn. Ill.:– Jim Dine. L., [1968]. (200) numbered, sigd. by artist. Fo. Lacks added suite of lithos. Velvet, title blocked in silver on upr.-cover, s.-c. (SG. Oct.23; 89) $425

– The Picture of Dorian Gray.–De Profundis.–The Trial of Oscar Wilde. Phila.; L.; Paris, Jul., 1890; [1905]; 1906. 3 works in 3 vols., 1st. work: in 'Lipponcott's Monthly Magazine'; 2nd. work: 1st. edn., scattered foxing to some ll.; 3rd. work: Ltd. edn. Orig. ptd. paper wraps., slight wear & fraying, qtr. red mor. gt. s.-c., unc. (1st work); orig. gt.-decor. cl., qtr. mor. gt. s.-c., unc. (2nd. work); & orig. paper wraps., qtr. mor. gt. s.-c., unc. From the Prescott Collection. (CNY. Feb.6; 404) $400

– The Picture of Dorian Gray.–The Short Stories. Ltd. Edns. Cl., 1957; 1968. Ltd. Edns. 2 vols. Orig. bdgs., boxed. (SPB. Jul.28; 320) $100

WILDE, Oscar *-contd.*
– **Poems.** L., 1881. 1st. Edn., (250). Orig. Japan vell., qtr. mor. gt. s.-c. Pres. Copy, to John Addington Symonds, lately in the Prescott Collection. (CNY. Feb.6; 363) $2,500
– – **Anr. Copy.** Orig. gt.-decor. Japan vell., minor soiling to vell., qtr. mor. gt. s.-c., partly unc. From the Prescott Collection. (CNY. Feb.6; 364) $420
– – **Anr. Edn.** 1892. (220) numbered, & sigd. Orig. cl. gt. (SBA. May 27; 131) *National Library of Wales.* £160
– – **Anr. Copy.** Orig. cl., covers & spine elab. blocked in gt. design, slightly faded & soiled, qtr. mor. gt. s.-c., partly unc. From the Prescott Collection. (CNY. Feb.6; 374) $1,000
– – **Anr. Edn.** L., [1908]. 1st. Coll. Edn., (1000) on H.M.P. Inserted are proof sheets of the 1st. quire of the 1908 edn. with note of Robert Ross, 2 typed lists of corrections for the 1909 revised edn., & publisher's 4 p. announcement of the unif. corrected edn., with brief notations in Stuart Mason's hand. Orig. buckram bds., upr. cover with 3 gt. medallion devices after designs by Ricketts, qtr. mor. gt. s.-c., partly unc. The Robert Ross copy, with his notes & corrections, bkplt. of Stuart Mason, with some notes by him, lately in the Prescott Collection. (CNY. Feb.6; 396) $750
– **Ravenna.** Oxford, 1878. 1st. Edn. Orig. ptd. paper wraps., upr. portion of lr. wrap. defect. with some loss of paper surface & print, mor. gt. s.-c. Pres. Copy, to Harold Edwin Boulton, bkplt. of Jerome Kern, lately in the Prescott Collection. (CNY. Feb.6; 361) $1,600
– **Salome.** Ill.:– Felicien Rops (title vig.). Paris & L., 1893. 1st. Edn., (50) on van Gelder H.M.P. 4to. Orig. paper wraps., upr. cover silver-lettered, qtr. mor. gt. s.-c., unc. From the Prescott Collection. (CNY. Feb.6; 379) $750
– – **Anr. Edn.** Ill.:– Felicien Rops (title vig.). Paris & L., 1893. 1st. Edn., (600) on wove paper. 4to. Orig. paper wraps., upr. cover silver-lettered, spine & outer portion of wraps. faded, qtr. mor. gt. s.-c., unc. Pres. Copy, to Oswald Sickert, lately in the Prescott Collection. (CNY. Feb.6; 378) $2,000
– – **Anr. Edn.** L. & Boston, 1894. 1st. Edn. in Engl., (100) L.P., with ills. on Japan vell. 4to. Orig. silk bds., covers with central gt. design, gt.-lettered spine, silk faded, qtr. mor. gt. s.-c., unc. From the Prescott Collection. (CNY. Feb.6; 381) $3,800
– – **Anr. Edn.** Trans.:– Lord Alfred Douglas. Ill.:– after Aubrey Beardsley. L. & Boston, 1894. 1st. Edn. in Engl., (500). 4to. Orig. cl., covers with central gt. design. gt.-lettered spine, qtr. mor. gt. s.-c., unc. From the Prescott Collection. (CNY. Feb.6; 380) $600
– **Salomé, Drame en un acte.** Ill.:– after Aubrey Beardsley. Paris, 1907. 4to. Orig. paper wraps., unc., hf. mor. s.-c., rebkd. with tape, wraps discoloured. (CNY. Oct.1; 125) $220
– **Salome: Drame en un Acte.-Salome.** Trans.:– 2nd. work: Lord Alfred Douglas. Ill.:– 1st. work: Andre Derain. 2nd. work: Aubrey Beardsley. N.Y., Ltd. Edns. Cl., 1938. Together 2 vols. 4to. Ptd. wraps. & gt.-pict. cl., boxed together, 1st. title foxed. 1st. work sigd. by Derain. (SG. Oct.23; 79) $200
– **Some Letters . . . to Alfred Douglas, 1892-1897.** Ed.:– A.S.W. Rosenbach. San. Franc., 1924. (225). Fo. With frontis. port. of Douglas & 26 facs. letters tipped in, with transcriptions. Orig. qtr. vell. & paper bds., s.-c., lr. edges unc. From the Prescott Collection. (CNY. Feb.6; 403) $220
– **The Soul of Man [Under Socialism].** L., Priv. Ptd. 1895. 1st. Edn., (50). 4to. Orig. paper wraps., qtr. mor. gt. s.-c., unc. From the Prescott Collection. (CNY. Feb.6; 388) $450
– **The Sphinx.** Ill.:– Charles Ricketts. L., 1894. 1st. Edn., (25) L.P. 4to. 4 p. announcement of the publication laid in at front. Orig. gt.-decor. vell., slightly soiled, cl. ties, qtr. mor. gt. s.-c., unc. From the Prescott Collection. (CNY. Feb.6; 385) $4,000
– – **Anr. Edn.** Ill.:– Charles Ricketts. L., 1894. 1st. Edn., (200). 4to. Spotted at front. Orig. gt.-decor. vell., slightly soiled, qtr. mor. gt. s.-c., unc. From the Prescott Collection. (CNY. Feb.6; 384) $1,300
– – **Anr. Copy.** Orig. vell. decor. in gt. after design by Rickett, unc., slightly soiled. (CNY. Oct.1; 123) $1,000
– – **Anr. Edn.** Ill.:– Alastair. L. & N.Y., 1920. (1000). 4to. Gt.-pict. buckram. (SG. Oct.23; 3) $275
– **The Suppressed Portion of 'De Profundis' . . .** N.Y., 1913. 1st. Edn., (15) for copyright. Tall 8vo. Orig. linen bds., slight soiling, qtr. mor. gt. s.-c. From the Prescott Collection. (CNY. Feb.6; 398) $500
[–] **To M.B.J.** Ed.:– C.S. Millard (preface). [L.], [1920]. 1st. Edn., (65) numbered. 12mo. Folded as iss., qtr. mor. gt. s.-c., unc. From the Prescott Collection. (CNY. Feb.6; 399) $200
– **Vera.** [N.Y.?], 1882. 2nd. Edn. Orig. ptd. wraps., slightly foxed, mor. gt. solander case. Pres. Copy, to Eleanor Calhoun; bkplt. of Jerome Kern, lately in the Prescott Collection. (CNY. Feb.6; 367) $2,200
– **A Woman of No Importance.** L., 1894. 1st. Edn., (50) Lge. H.M.P. 4to. Orig. buckram, covers & spine gt. after a design by Shannon, soiled, qtr. mor. gt. s.-c., unc. Sig. of James Shepherd at limitation, lately in the Prescott Collection. (CNY. Feb.6; 386) $550
– **[Works].** L., 1908. (1000) on H.M.P. 14 vols. Mor., dentelles. (SPB. Nov.25; 500) $600
– **Works.–For Love of the King.** [Paris, 1 vol. of works], 1908; 1922. (1000) on H.M.P. (1st. work). 14 vols. + 1. 1 vol. of works a little yellowed. Unif. orig. buckram. (C. Feb.4; 95) *Traylen.* £250
– – **Anr. Edn.** L., [1908]; [1922]. (1000); 1st. Edn., (1000). 14 vols.; 1 vol. Linen, both soiled. (SG. Feb.12; 406) $160
– **Writings.** Ed.:– Richard le Gallienne & others. N.Y., 1925. L.P. Edn., (575) numbered. 12 vols. Crushed lev., gt. fillet & floral borders, gt. panel. spines, gt. dentelles with doubls. of red mor., moire satin end-ll. (SG. Sep.4; 460) $100
See–**CHAMELEON, The**
See–**KOTTABOS**
See–**WAIFS & STRAYS**

WILDE, Oscar–MILLARD, Christopher Sclater 'Stuart Mason'
– **[Works].–A Bibliography of the Poems of Oscar Wilde.** 1908; 1907. (1000); (475). 14 vols.; 1 vol. Slightly soiled. Orig. cl., slightly soiled. (CSK. May 15; 25) £120

WILDENSTEIN, Georges
– **Chardin.** Paris, [1933]. 4to. Orig. wraps., slightly soiled, marb. bd. s.-c. (SG. Mar.12; 88) $130
– **Un Peintre de Paysage au XVIIIe Siècle: Louis Moreau.** Paris, 1923. (275). 4to. In sheets, folder. (HD. Dec.5; 224) Frs. 1,400

WILDER, Thornton
– **The Bridge of San Luis Rey.** Ill.:– Rockwell Kent. N.Y., 1929. [1100] numbered & sigd. by author & artist. 4to. Cold. pict. bds., boxed. (SG. Nov.13; 735) $150
– – **Anr. Copy.** Pict. cl. (SG. Nov.13; 399) $100
– **Our Town.** Ill.:– Robert J. Lee. Ltd. Edns. Cl., 1974. (2000) numbered, sigd. by Wilder & Lee. 4to. Corduroy, boxed. Inserted is autograph postcard, sigd., ob. 12mo., to Bobsy Chapman. (PNY. Mar.4; 277) $200
– **The Woman of Andros.–The Long Christmas Dinner.–The Cabala.** N.Y., 1930; 1931; [1927]. 1st. Edns. & later printing. 3 vols. Cl. Sigd. Pres. copies to Bobsy [Goodspeed]. (PNY. Mar.4; 278) $240

WILDMAN, Thomas
– **A Treatise on the Management of Bees.** Priv. ptd., 1768. 1st. Edn. 4to. Name deleted from title, sm. stain on recto, bkplt. removed from verso, orig. flaw in X1 affecting 1 letter of catchword. Orig. cf., spine reprd. (S. Jun.23; 417) *Hodson.* £160

WILHELM, Gottlieb T.
– **Unterhaltungen aus der Naturgeschichte. [Insecten. Amphibien].** Augsburg, 1794-98. 6 text & 2 plt. vols. Some plts. soiled, 1 mntd. Cont. hf. leath. portfo. gt. (R. Oct.14-18; 3087) DM 1,000
– **Unterhaltungen aus der Naturgeschichte Insekten.** Augsburg, 1796-97. 3 vols. Vol. 1 some plts. a little soiled & text. Cont. hf. leath., 1 spine defect. (R. Mar.31-Apr.4; 1444) DM 850
– – **Anr. Edn.** Vienna, 1796-98. 1st. Edn. Vols. 6-8. Stp. on title. Cont. hf. leath., gt. spine. (HK. Nov.18-21; 498) DM 1,500
– **Unterhaltungen aus d. Naturgeschichte d. Mineralreichs.** Augsburg, 1834. New Edn. 2 vols. 125 (of 132) copperplts., copper title stpd. Cont. bds. (HK. May 12-14; 383) DM 420
[–] **Unterhaltungen aus d. Naturgeschichte d. Pflanzenreichs.** Augsburg, 1810-20. Vols. 2, 4 & 8 (of 10). Slightly soiled in parts. Cont. bds. (HK. Nov.18-21; 826) DM 750

WILKES, Benjamin
– **One Hundred & Twenty Copperplates of English Moths & Butterflies . . .** 1773. 2nd. Edn. 4to. Occasional spotting. Diced cf., gt., rebkd. with orig. spine preserved. (C. Nov.5; 174) *Carter.* £1,600
– – **Anr. Copy.** Plts. hand-cold., margins slightly discold., occasional spotting, plts. with liby. blind-stps. Cont. cf., brkn., covers detchd. From Chetham's Liby., Manchester. (C. Nov.27; 408) *Marshall.* £850

WILKES, Charles
– **Narrative of the United States Exploring Expedition.** Phila., 1845. 1st. Publd. Edn. 6 vols. including Atlas vol. Orig. gt.-decor. cl., unc. (SG. Oct.9; 254) $1,100
– – **Anr. Copy.** 5 vols. plus atlas, together 6 vols. Orig. cl., gt.-pict. spines. (SG. Feb.26; 340) $650

WILKIE, Sir David
– **Sketches in Turkey, Syria & Egypt.** 1843. Fo. Spotted. Cont. mor.-bkd. cl. (SH. Nov.7; 447) *Irani.* £350
– **The Wilkie Gallery. A Selection of the Best Pictures . . .** Ca. 1860. Fo. Some spotting of prelims. Later hf. cf. (TA. Sep.18; 141) £80
– – **Anr. Copy.** 4 divisions. 61 (of 65) engraved plts. Contents loose in orig. cl. gt. (TA. Sep.18; 142) £58

WILKINS, John, Bp. of Chester
[–] **The Discovery of a World in the Moone. Or, a Discourse Tending, to Prove, that 'tis Probable there may be Another Habitable World in that Planet.** 1638. 1st. Edn. Wormholes in first few ll. slightly affecting text, last lf. defect. affecting rule-borders. Cont. cf., red hf. mor. case. Bkplt. of John Camp Williams, from Honeyman Collection [NSTC 25640] (S. May 20; 3119) *Norman.* £550
– **An Essay Towards a Real Character & a Philosophical Language.** 1668. 1st. Edn. 2 pts. in 1 vol. Fo. Slight browning & soiling, title sigd. 'Charles Herrick', with errata-lf. d2. Cont. cf., worn. [Wing H2196] (S. Dec.2; 657) *Elliot.* £70
– – **Anr. Copy.** Lacks final blank, some tears. Covers detchd. (SH. Jul.16; 192) *Quaritch.* £50
– **Mathematicall Magick. Or, the Wonders that may be Performed by Mechanicall Geometry.** 1648. 1st. Edn. 2 pts. in 1 vol. Old cf., rebkd. (TA. May 21; 361) £125
– – **Anr. Copy.** Lacks blank A1, slight staining & soiling, sm. hole in E2, owners' inscrs. on title & end-ll. Hf. cf., very worn, upr. cover detchd., red hf. mor case. From Honeyman Collection. [Wing W2198] (S. May 20; 3120) *Goldschmidt.* £120
– – **Anr. Copy.** Sm. stains on title & dedicatory ll. Cont. cf., spine worn. (SPB. Nov.25; 108) $400
[–] **Le Monde dans la Lune . . .** Trans.:– Sr. de la Montagne. Rouen, 1655. 1st. Edn. in Fr. 2 vols. in 1. Cont. Fr. mor. gt. William Beckford's copy. (S. Nov.24; 303) *Watchman.* £260

WILKINS, William
– **The Antiquities of Magna Graecia.** 1807. 1st. Edn. Fo. Spot on Agrigentum plt., some marginal soiling, slight spotting or foxing to several plts., a few imprints cropped. Cont. hf. cf., covers detchd., worn. (S. Apr.7; 495) *Maggs.* £200
– – **Anr. Copy.** Some staining., title foxed. Cl.-bkd. bds., worn, unc. L.P. (S. Sep.29; 192) *Pintico.* £170

WILKINSON, G.
– **Five Lithographic Views of the Isle of Man.** N.d. Ob. fo. Without title (not called for), some slight marginal spotting. Orig. ptd. wraps. with vig. (LC. Jun.18; 186) £90

WILKINSON, Gen. James
– **Memoirs of My Own Times.** Phila., 1816. 3 vols. & atlas. 8vo. & 4to. Spotted, foxed, stains & tears. Hf. sheep, worn, atlas in cl., stained. From liby. of William E. Wilson. [Sabin 104028] (SPB. Apr.29; 279) $150

WILKINSON, James Vere S.
– **The Lights of Canopus.** [L.], ca. 1930. Cl. (SG. Dec.4; 372) $120

See–Arnold, Sir Thomas W. & Wilkinson, James Vere S.

WILKINSON, Sir John Gardner
– Manners & Customs of the Ancient Egyptians.
–Modern Egypt & Thebes. 1837-43. 1st. work:
1st. & 2nd. Series. Together 8 vols. A few ll. soiled.
Cont. cf. (SH. Jun.4; 87) *Blanks.* £100

WILKINSON, Rev. Joseph
– Select Views in Cumberland, Westmorland &
Lancashire. 1810. 1st. Edn. Fo. Some spotting.
Cont. hf. cf., worn. (SH. Jun.18; 186)
Abacus. £270
– – Anr. Edn. 1821. Fo. Orig. str.-grd. crimson
mor. gt., worn. (TA. May 21; 421) £600

WILKINSON, Neville R.
– Wilton House Pictures. 1907. (300) sigd. 2 vols.
Lge. 4to. Orig. cl. gt., upr. cover of vol. 2 stained,
partly unc. (C. Jul.22; 172) *Tate Gallery.* £75

WILKINSON, Robert
– Atlas Classica. 1830. 4to. Cont. hf. cf., worn,
covers detchd. (CSK. May 8; 18) £70
– A General Atlas. 1794. 4to. Title stained,
marginal soiling. Cont. hf. cf., lr. bd. detchd.
(CSK. Jun.5; 38) £110
– – Anr. Edn. L., 1800. 48 cold. maps, first few
soiled. No bdg. stated. (JN. Apr.2; 809) £50
– – Anr. Edn. 1809. 4to. Title stained. Cont. hf.
cf., worn. (SH. Jul.16; 177) *Frost.* £70
– – Anr. Edn. 1822. 3rd. Edn. 4to. 1 folding map
torn at fold, some dampstaining. Cont. hf. cf.,
worn. (CSK. Feb.13; 119) £100
– Londina Illustrata; Theatrum Illustrata. 1819-25.
2 vols. 4to. Several plts. dtd. 1826-34, occasional
light spotting, 1st. title & a few plts. with slight
fore-e. staining. Cont. hf. red mor., slightly worn,
unc. (S. Nov.4; 522) *Marsden.* £170
– Scotch Views & a New Map of Scotland. 1797.
Fo. 65 cold. plts. (title-p. notes '35' but all are
listed), crayon addition to sky in plts. & margins
slightly soiled & spotted. Orig. bds., paper spine,
worn. (CE. Jul.9; 69) £1,600

WILKINSON, Tate
– Memoirs of His Own Life. York, 1790. 4 vols.
Tree gt. (P. Jan.22; 47) *Traylen.* £180
– The Wandering Patentee; or, a History of the
Yorkshire Theatres. York, 1795. [1st. Edn.?]. 4
vols. 12mo. Cont. hf. cf. (SH. May 21; 134)
Hannas. £220
– – Anr. Copy. Without hf.-title in vol. IV. 19th.
C. hf. cf., gt. spines. (C. Nov.20; 281)
Traylen. £190
– – Anr. Copy. 12mo. Lacks hf.-titles. Later
three-qtr. cf., spine gt. (SG. Aug.7; 199) $300

WILKOMM, E.
– Wanderungen an der Nord- und Ostsee. Ill.:–
Sander & Peeters. Leipzig, 1850. Later hf. leath.
(D. Dec.11-13; 1299) DM 2,100

WILKOMM, Heinrich Moritz
– Illustrationes florae Hispaniae insularumque
Balearium. Stuttgart, [1880]- 1881-92. 2 vols. Fo.
With slip announcing termination of work
'parce-que son auteur n'a plus les matériaux ni les
forces nécessaires pour pouvoir le continuer'. Hf.
mor. From collection of Massachusetts
Horticultural Society, stps. on plts. (SPB.
Oct.1; 173) $2,200

WILLAN, Leonard
– Astrae. 1651. 1st. Edn. Remargined, staining in
outer margin. 19th. C. cf., rebkd. Sig. of W.C.
Hazlitt on title verso. [Wing W2262] (C.
Nov.19; 24) *Quaritch.* £200

WILLAN, Robert
– On Vaccine Inoculation. 1806. 1st. Edn. 4to. A
few ll. foxed. Cont. cf., upr. cover detchd. From
liby. of Dr. E. Ashworth Underwood. (S.
Feb.23; 319) *Jenner.* £100
– – Anr. Copy. Advt. lf., cont. MS. notes on p. 75
referring to Dr. Jenner, on p. 85 referring to cases
of smallpox accompanied by a sketch of a tumour,
& on slip criticising Mr. Knowles; also some other
marginal notes & scribblings. Orig. bds., rebkd.,
unc. (S. Dec.2; 658) *Jenner.* £80

**WILLDENOW, Karl Ludwig & Hayne, Friedrich
Gottlieb**
– Abbildung der deutschen Holzarten. Ill.:– by &
after Friedrich Guimpel. Berlin, 1815-20. 2 vols.
4to. Cont. hf. roan gt. From collection of
Massachusetts Horticultural Society, stps. on plts.
(SPB. Oct.1; 172) $3,000

WILLEM I OF ORANGE
– Apologie ou Deffense de très illustre Prince
Guillaume par la Grace de Dieu Prince d'Orange,
Conte de Nassau, [etc.] contre le Ban et edict publié
par le Roy d'Espagne, [etc.]. Delft, 1581. 1st. Edn.
4to. Liby. stp. on verso of title, sm. hole in last 2 ll.,
with loss of a few letters, a few insignificant stains.
18th. C. hf. cf., back gt., some staining. (VG.
Dec.17; 1618) Fls. 450
– Apologie, ofte Verantwoordinghe der Vorsts
Wilhelms Prince van Orangien . . . Leyden, 1581.
1st. Dutch Edn. 4to. Page from 'De Oranje
Nassau-boekerij en de Oranje-penningen in de
K.B. 1898' added in photocopy. Cont. vell., lge. gt.
arms of Prince Maurits on upr. cover & arms of
Holland on lr. cover, recased, lr. cover
dampstained, oxidating orig. silver stp. into black,
19th. C. Pro Patria paper end-papers. (VG.
Dec.17; 1617) Fls. 5,000

WILLIAM, Paul
– The Rose Garden. In Two Divisions. 1848. 1st.
Edn. 2 pts. in 1 vol. Orig. cl., spine defect., worn,
Dorfold bkplt. (S. Dec.3; 1091) *Schuster.* £110

WILLIAMS, A.F.
– The Genesis of the Diamond. L., 1932. 2 vols.,
4to. Orig. bdg. (VA. Aug.29; 410) R. 280

WILLIAMS, B.S.
See–WARNER, Robert & Williams, B.S.

WILLIAMS, Caroline Ranson
– Gold & Silver Jewelry. N.Y., 1924. 4to. Ptd.
wraps., frayed, ex-liby. Inscr. (SG. Dec.4; 205)
$175

WILLIAMS, David & Gardnor, John
– The History of Monmouthshire. 1796. (32) with
hand-cold. plts. 4to. 19th. C. hf. mor. Sig. of
Charles Hardwick, lately in the collection of Eric
Sexton. (C. Apr.16; 383) *Maggs.* £1,600

WILLIAMS, H. M.
– Poems. 1786. 2 vols. Cont. cf. (P. Jan.22; 49)
Waterfield. £80

WILLIAMS, Sir Harold
– Book Clubs & Printing Societies of Great
Britain & Ireland. First Edn. Club, 1929. (750).
4to. Orig. decor. cl. (SH. Feb.19; 116)
Sherlock. £50

WILLIAMS, Hugh W.
– Select Views in Greece. L., 1829. 1st. Edn., L.P.,
2 vols. in 1. 4to Lacks hf.-titles. Mor., elab. gt., by
Clarke & Bedford. (S. Nov.24; 304)
Traylen. £180
– – Anr. Copy. No text. Disbnd. (CSK.
Nov.28; 14) £85
– – Anr. Copy. 2 vols. 4to. Cont. mor., gt. borders
& spines. Inscr. (SG. Feb.26; 342) $425
– Travels in Italy, Greece, & the Ionian Islands.
1820. 2 vols. Hf. cf. gt. (P. Oct.23; 79)
Brooke-Hitching. £120
– – Anr. Edn. Edinb., 1820. 1st. Edn. 2 vols. Old
cf., rebkd. (SG. Feb.26; 343) $160

WILLIAMS, Iolo A.
– Points in Eighteenth Century Verse. 1934. (500).
Orig. bds. (CSK. May 29; 93) £50

WILLIAMS, Isaac
[–] The Baptistery. Oxford, 1846. Mor., wide gt.
floral borders, spine gt., by J. MacKenzie. Fore-e.
pntg. (SG. Dec.18; 189) $140

WILLIAMS, John S.
– The American Pioneer . . . Sketches Relative to
the Early Settlement & Successive Improvement of
the Country. Cinc., 1844, 1843. Vol. 1 3rd. Edn.,
Vol. II 2nd. (?) Edn. 2 vols. Some staining. Later
cf., gt. spines. From liby. of William E. Wilson.
(SPB. Apr.29; 280) $325

WILLIAMS, Jonathan
– Memoria sobre el Usu del Termometro en la
Navegacion Presentada a la Sociedad Filosofica
Americana de Filadelfia . . . Madrid, 1794. Sm.
4to. Red mor., royal arms of Spain gt. on covers.
From Honeyman Collection. (S. May 20; 3122)
Hughes. £110

WILLIAMS, R.S.
See–HOBSON, Robert Lockhart & others

WILLIAMS, Roger
– The Bloody Tenent. L., 1644. 'Tenent' Edn. 4to.
Red mor., gt. spine & panels, by Bradford. Brinley
Copy. [Sabin 104332] (SPB. Nov.24; 67) $9,000
– Bloody Tenent Yet More Bloody. L., 1652. 4to.
Slight worming to final 11. Mor., gt. spine &

panels, initials J.C.B. in gt. on upr. cover. The
John Carter Brown Copy. [Sabin 104333] (SPB.
Nov.24; 69) $5,750
– Key to the Language of America: Or, An help to
the Language of the Natives in that part of
America, called New England. L., 1643. Some
foxing. Mod. mor., blind-stpd. centre ornament on
covers, gt. spine, mor. box. Inscr. to William
Masham on verso of front free end-paper. (SPB.
Nov.24; 68) $15,000

WILLIAMS, Sidney Herbert & Madan, Falconer
– A Handbook of the Literature of the Rev. C.L.
Dodgson. L., 1931. (734) numbered. Errata slip &
24 p. supp. of 1935 tipped in. Cl., d.-w. (SG.
Jan.22; 98) $110

WILLIAMS, Tennessee
– Grand. N.Y., House of Books, 1964. 1st. Edn.,
(300) numbered, sigd. 12mo. Cl. (SG. Jun.4; 503)
$100
– One Arm & Other Stories. N.Y., New
Directions, [1948]. (50) numbered, sigd. Gt.
parch.-bkd. bds., box defect. (SG. Jun.4; 501)
$800
– – Anr. Edn. [Mount Vernon], [1948]. (50)
numbered on Virgil Paper. Tall 8vo. Decor. bds.,
parch. gt. spine, s.-c. Sigd. (SG. Nov.13; 737)
$280

WILLIAMS, William Carlos
– The Clouds, Aigeltinger, Russia, & c. 1968.
(310). No bdg. stated. (SPB. Jul.28; 461) $125
– The Great American Novel. Paris, 1923. 1st.
Edn., (300) numbered. Erasure of hf.-title, picture
of author pasted on blank lf. Cl. spine, cl. bds.,
lettering on spine stpd. in gt., worn. Pres. copy.
(SPB. Nov.25; 422) $250

WILLIAMS, William Carlos & others
– Poets & the Past. N.Y., 1959. 1st. Edn. (50)
sigd., inscr. by publishers. Orig. cf.-bkd. bds. (S.
Jul.22; 339) *Sawyer.* £230

**WILLIAMS, Col. William Freke & Gaspey,
Thomas**
– The Life & Times of the Late Duke of
Wellington. Ill.:– J. Tallis. Ca. 1860. 4 vols. 4to.
Hf. cf. (P. Apr.9; 269) £95
– – Anr. Edn. Ill.:– Tallis (maps). L., n.d. 4 vols. in
2. 4to. Maps cold. in outl., town plan, ports. &
battle scenes. Hf. cf. (P. May 14; 82) *Kidd.* £60

WILLIAMS, William Frith
– An Historical & Statistical Account of the
Bermudas. L., 1848. Ex liby., folding map torn,
some foxing. Blindstpd. cl., spine heavily chipped,
hinges brkn. (SG. Oct.30; 375) $275

WILLIAMSON, Gen. Adam
See–CHARMILLY, Col. Venault de &
Williamson, Gen. Adam

WILLIAMSON, George C.
– Andrew & Nathaniel Plimer. 1903. (365). 4to.
Cl. gt. (P. Mar.12; 7) *Lawson.* £70
– The Book of Famille Rose. 1927. (12) sigd. 4to.
Orig. linen-bkd. bds., some wear. (Sp.Sep.11; 193)
Tallerman. £60
– – Anr. Edn. [1927]. 4to. Orig. cl. (CSK.
Mar.27; 131) £110
– The History of Portrait Miniatures. 1904. (520).
2 vols. Fo. Orig. cl., gt., slightly soiled. (SH.
Oct.9; 108) *Quaritch* £80
– – Anr. Copy. (P. Jun.11; 36) *Leicester.* £60
– – Anr. Edn. 1904. Ltd. Edn. 2 vols. 4to. Red hf.
mor. gt. by Sotheran. (CE. Jun.4; 131) £230
– – Anr. Copy. Fo. Cl. gt. (BS. Sep.17; 102) £60
– The Imperial Russian Dinner Service. L., 1909.
(10) ptd. on japan vell., this copy unnumbered. 4to.
Orig. publisher's vell. gt., partly unc. (CNY.
Oct.1; 126) $300
– – Anr. Edn. 1909. (310). 4to. Orig. vell.-bkd. cl.,
slightly soiled. (CSK. Jul.31; 71) £110
– Life & Works of Ozias Humphry. 1918. (400).
4to. Qtr. buckram gt. (P. Mar.12; 8)
Lawson. £75

WILLIAMSON, George C. & Engleheart, H. L. D.
– George Engleheart 1750-1929. Priv. ptd., 1902.
(53) numbered. 4to. Occasional slight soiling.
Orig. cl., soiled, Alfred & Geoffrey Harmsworth's
bkplts. (CSK. Feb.20; 139) £55

WILLIAMSON, Henry
– The Linhay on the Downs. 1934. 1st. Edn. Orig.
cl., spine worn. Inscr. to Walter [de la Mare].
(SH. Dec.18; 322) *Minerva.* £55

WILLIAMSON, Henry -contd.
- The Star-Born. Ill.:– C. F. Tunnicliffe. 1933. Autograph revisions, typog. corrections & pencil notes. Stapled or stitched gatherings loose in paper wrap. Proof Copy of 1st. Edn., 1st. gathering with limitation statement unnumbered, but sigd. (SH. Dec.18; 321) *Lincoln.* £150

WILLIAMSON, John, Angler
- The British Angler. L., 1740. 1st. Edn. Cont. cf. (SG. Oct.16; 543) $150

WILLIAMSON, John, of Kentucky
- Fern Etchings. Louisville, 1879. 2nd. Edn. Gt.-pict. cl., worn. (SG. Jan.29; 440) $150

WILLIAMSON, Capt. Thomas
- Agricultural Mechanism or a Display of ... the Vehicles, Implements & Machinery Connected with Husbandry. 1810. May lack hf.-title. Hf. cf., rebkd. (S. Dec.1; 432) *Comben.* £85
- The Complete Angler's Vade-Mecum. L., 1808. 1st. Edn. Mod. cf.-bkd. old bds., unc. (SG. Oct.16; 544) $160
– – Anr. Copy. Cont. hf. cf. (SG. Oct.16; 545) $140
– – Anr. Edn. L., 1822. 2nd. Edn. Linen-bkd. old bds. (SG. Oct.16; 546) $110
See–DOYLEY, Charles & Williamson, Capt. Thomas

WILLIAMSON, Capt. Thomas & Blagdon, F.W.
- The European in India. 1813. 4to. Some marginal worming. Mor. (S. Dec.8; 244) *Hosains.* £100

WILLIAMSON, Capt. Thomas & Howitt, Samuel
- Oriental Field Sports. 1807. 1st. Edn. Ob. lge. fo. Additional hand-cold. aqua. title, 40 hand-cold. aqua. plts., text wtrmkd. E. & P. 1804 & Hall & Taplin 1804, plts. E. & P. 1804. Cont. russ. gt., upr. cover detchd. (S. Nov.24; 305) *Old Hall.* £1,000
– – Anr. Copy. Rebkd., worn. (SPB. Oct.1; 98) $4,600
– – Anr. Edn. 1807. Ob. fo. Some ll. including title torn, affecting text, corner of title torn away, a few plts. marginally torn, some reprd. at margin with some loss of text, some soiling. Cont. hf. cf., worn, upr. cover & spine loose. (S. May 5; 207) *Burgess.* £800
– – Anr. Edn. [1807]. 2nd. Edn. 4to. Some foxing. Red mor. gt., tooled emblems, panel. spine. (CE. Dec.4; 227) £620
– – Anr. Edn. 1808. 2 vols. 4to. Hf. russ., spines worn. (P. Feb.19; 65) *Bookroom.* £90
– – Anr. Copy. Orig. bdg. (DWB. May 15; 350) £88
– – Anr. Edn. Ill.:– Samuel Howitt. 1819. [2nd. Edn.?] Ob. fo. 40 cold. aquatint plts., lacks cold. hf.-title, title, dedication, index ll. & few text ll. with marginal tears reprd., 1st. plt. laid down. Hf. cf., rebkd., s.-c. (C. Mar.18; 118) *Carlton.* £1,500
– – Anr. Copy. Captions in Engl. & Fr., some repairs & some slight soiling or finger marks. Cont. str.-grd. mor., tooled gt. borders, by Andrews. (GM. Apr.30; 737) £1,350
– – Anr. Copy. 2 vols. 4to. Cont. str.-grd. mor., sides with gt. & blind tooled borders, spines gt. in compartments. (C. Mar.18; 119) *Negro.* £450
– – Anr. Copy. Cont. str.-grd. maroon mor., gt., rebkd. & recornered preserving orig. gt. spines. (C. Feb.4; 172) *Russell.* £200
– – Anr. Copy. 2 vols. 4to. 30 hand-cold. plts. (of 40), slightly soiled or dampstained in places, a few ll. slightly torn in margin. Cont. str.-grd. mor., gt., upr. hinge of vol. 1 brkn. (S. May 5; 208) *Schuster.* £80

WILLIS, Nathaniel Parker
- Sacred Poems. Ill.:– after Lumley, T. Moran, T. Nast, & others. N.Y., 1860. Orig. mor., title gt. on both covers. (SG. Mar.19; 317) $125

WILLIS, Nathaniel Parker & Bartlett, William Henry
- American Scenery. 1840. [1st. Edn.?]. 2 vols. in 1. 4to. Engraved port., 2 engraved titles with vigs., map, 117 engraved plts., port., title vigs. & all views hand-cold. Cont. red mor., sides elab. gt., rebkd. (C. Jul.15; 114) *Elstein.* £380
– – Anr. Copy. 2 vols. Cont. hf. mor. (C. Feb.25; 69) *Bouwma.* £240
– – Anr. Copy. Additional vig. titles & some plts. spotted, some with marginal staining in lr. inner margin. Orig. cl., gt.-stpd. vig. on covers, worn. (SPB. Nov.25; 523) *Sekuler.* £170

– – Anr. Copy. 114 (of 117) engraved plts. Orig. cl. gt. (P. Oct.2; 318) *Grossfield.* £130
– – Anr. Copy. 4to. Spotting, Cont. hf. mor. (CSK. Sep.19; 220) £100
– – Anr. Copy. Foxed, browned. Hf. cf. (SPB. Jun.22; 136) $375
– – Anr. Copy. A few plts. soiled at margin, lightly browned in parts. Cont. mor gt. [Sabin 3784] (H. May 21/22; 361) DM 820
– – Anr. Edn. Ill.:– W. H. Bartlett N.d. 2 vols. in 1. 4to. Hf. cf. gt. (P. Jul.30; 55) *Walford.* £150
- American Scenery.–Canadian Scenery. L., 1840-42. 2 vols. in 13 pts. 4to. Publisher's advts., occasional foxing &/or staining, a few sm. dampstains in lr. corner of margins, a few pp. loose. Unif. orig. pict. bds., leath. spines, a few covers detchd., spines worn. (CB. May 27; 287) *Can.* $2,400
- Canadian Scenery. Ill.:– after W.H. Bartlett. L., [1840]-42. Compl. in the orig. 6 pts. 4to. Plts. foxed in pts. 2, 3, & 6. Orig. pict. bds., bds. loose in pts. 3 & 4. (CB. Feb.18; 1) *Can.* $1,500
– – Anr. Edn. 1842. Ill.:– [1st. Edn.?]. 2 vols. 4to. Cont. cf. gt. (C. Feb.25; 70) *Mitchell.* £400
– – Anr. Copy. Occasional spotting & staining. Cont. hf. cf., worn. (CSK. Jan.23; 177) £380
– – Anr. Copy. Vol.1 only (of 2). Cont. hf. mor., spine gt. (S. Nov.25; 501) *Bowes.* £130
– – Anr. Copy. 2 vols. Port., map, 119 steel-engraved plts. with tissue-guards. Cont. maroon mor. gt. (SG. Oct.9; 50) $1,200
– – Anr. Copy. Later hf. mor. (SG. May 14; 40) $650
– – Anr. Copy. Lacks 1 plt., 4 others loose, foxed. Cont. red hf. mor. [Sabin 3786] (CB. Apr.1; 31) *Can.* $1,400
– – Anr. Edn. N.d. 2 vols. in 1. 4to. Hf. cf. gt. (P. Oct.2; 319) *Boland.* £360

WILLIS, Nathaniel Parker & Coyne, J. Stirling
- Scenery & Antiquities of Ireland. Ill.:– after W. H. Bartlett. 1841. 2 vols. 4to. Lacks port., some plts. spotted, a few with stains in outer edges. Cont. hf. cf., rebkd., worn. (S. Nov.4; 524) *Kentish* £80
– – Anr. Edn. Ill.:– after W. H. Bartlett. [1841]. 2 vols. in 1. 4to. Lacks 4 plts. & port. Cont. hf. mor. (SBA. Oct.22; 672) *Hayden.* £95
– – Anr. Copy. 2 vols. A few ll. spotted. Orig. cl. gt., slightly worn. (SBA. Jul.14; 318) *Mortens of Manchester.* £80
– – Anr. Copy. Lacks port.?, a few ll. slightly spotted, 1 plt. loose. Slightly worn. (SBA. Jul.14; 317) *Neptune Gallery.* £75
– – Anr. Edn. L., ca. 1845. 6 pts. 4to. Orig. mor.-bkd. bds. (GM. Apr.30; 397) £155
– – Anr. Copy. 2 vols. in 5. Without port.(?), indexes bnd. in, slight spotting. Orig. cl. gt. (SBA. Oct.22; 671) *Maynet.* £120
– – Anr. Edn. Ill.:– W.H. Bartlett. L., ca. 1850 2 vols. in 1. 4to. Map & 120 steel-engraved plts. Gt.-pict. hf. mor. (SG. Oct.30; 45) $140
– – Anr. Edn. Ca. 1860. 2 vols. in 1. Cont. hf. mor. gt. (S. Jun.29; 258) *Egan.* £140
– – Anr. Edn. Ill.:– after William Henry Bartlett. N.d. & 1875. 2 vols. 4to. Orig. embossed cl. gt. (LC. Oct.2; 171) £90
– – Anr. Edn. N.d. 2 vols. 4to. Badly foxed. Hf. mor. gt. (P. Oct.2; 30) *Postaprint.* £90
– – Anr. Copy. 2 vols. in 1. Cont. hf. cf. (CSK. Aug.22; 182) £70

WILLIS, Robert
- Illustrations of Cutaneous Disease. 1841. Fo. A few spots. Hf. roan. (S. Jun.17; 883) *Norman.* £80

WILLIS, Prof. Robert & Clarke, J.W.
- Architectural History of the University of Cambridge. 1886. 4 vols. (including 1 of plans). Hf. mor. gt., unc. & unopened. (P. Sep.11; 108) *Traylen.* £60

WILLIS, Thomas
- De Anima Brutorum quae Hominis Vitalis ac Sensitiva est Exercitationes duae. Amst., 1674. 12mo. Short tear in plt. 5. Cont. vell. (S. Jun.17; 886) *Phelps.* £130
- Diatribae duae medico-philosophicae quarum prior agit de Fermentatione ... The Hague, 1662. 3rd. Edn. 12mo. Engraved frontis. soiled, upr. corner cut off. Cl. (S. Jun.17; 884) *Jenner Books.* £65
- The London Practice of Physick of the Whole, Practical Part of Physick Contained in the Works of Dr. Willis. 1685. 1st. Edn. Sm. paper flaw in

3Q1, short tear in upr. margin 4el & 2. Cont. cf. [Wing T2838] (S. Dec.2; 873) *Dawson.* £240
- Opera Omnia. Amst., 1682. 4to. Disbnd. (SG. Sep.18; 395) $300
- Practice of Physick being the Whole Works ... 1684-83. 2 vols. Fo. Short tear in vol. I. New hf. cf. Sig. of James Blew 1689 on verso of 1 title-p. [Wing W2854] (S.Jun.17; 887) *Norman.* £350

WILLIS, Thomas–CROONE, William
- Cerebri Anatome cui accessit Nervorum Descriptio & usus.–De Ratione motus Musculorum. Amst., 1667. Latest Edn. (1st work). 2 works in 1. vol. 12mo. No bdg. stated. (S. Jun.17; 885) *Jenner Books.* £220

WILLIUS, Frederick A. & Keys, Thomas E.
- Cardiac Classics. 1941. Cl., ex-liby. (S. Jun.17; 889) *Hubbard.* £55

WILLMOT, Ellen Ann
- The Genus Rosa. 1914. 2 vols. Fo. Cont. cl., partly unc., wraps. to orig. pts. bnd. at end of each vol. (C. Jul.15; 215) *Taylor.* £400
– – Anr. Copy. 4to. Orig. hf. mor., worn. From collection of Massachusetts Horticultural Society, stps. on plts. (SPB. Oct.1; 174) $1,200

WILLOUGHBY or Willughby, Francis
- De Historia Piscium. Oxford, 1686. 1st. Edn. Fo. Lacks frontis. & plt. R5, title slightly soiled, occasional light staining. 19th. C. hf. mor., vell. corners. W.a.f., from Chetham's Liby., Manchester. (C. Nov.27; 409) *Wagner.* £200
- The Ornithology. 1678. Fo. 78 plts. only, lacks the 2 unnumbered ones, plt. 78 torn at foot with loss, some soiling & staining. Later cf., lr. cover wormed. [Wing W2880] (CSK. Jul.3; 140) £170
– – Anr. Copy. 2 unnumbered plts., the first mntd., the second inlaid, several plts. short & possibly inserted from anr. copy, plt. 26 reprd., slight soiling, other minor imperfections, sm. holes, etc. Cont. cf., rebkd., covers worn. (S. Jun.1; 293) *Wheldon & Wesley.* £160
– – Anr. Edn. Trans.:– John Ray. 1778. 1st. Engl. Edn. Fo. Some repairs. Old cf. [Wing W2880] (TA. Jun.18; 91) £300
See–RAY or Rea, John & Willoughby or Willughby, Francis

WILLS, William John
- Successful Exploration through the Interior of Australia, from Melbourne to the Gulf of Carpentaria, [edited] from the Journals & Letters of William John Wills. L., 1863. Slight soiling. Orig. cl., unc., slight wear. (KH. Nov.18; 644) *Aus.* $400

WILLSFORD, Thomas
- Arithmetick, Naturall, & Artificiall: or, Decimalls. Containing the Science of Numbers. 1656. 1st. Edn. Nail-hole through pp. 261-314 affecting text, port. & title soiled & frayed, former with hole in border, some prelims. marginally stained, a little worming in some lr. margins, short tear in last lf., sig. of William Saunders written several times on verso of port. Cont. sheep, worn. The Bute-Kenney copy; from Honeyman Collection. [Wing W2874] (S. May 20; 3125) *Lawson.* £70

WILLUGHBY, Francis
See–WILLOUGHBY or Willughby, Francis

WILLUMSEN, J.F.
- La Jeunesse du Peintre El Greco. Paris, 1927. (1100) numbered. 2 vols. Hf. vell. (CR. Mar.19; 190) Lire 200,000

WILLYAMS, Rev. Cooper
- Selection of Views in Egypt, Palestine, Rhodes, Italy, Minorca, & Gibraltar. 1821. Fo. Plts. only, 4 defect. Loosely contained in orig. hf. mor., worn. (TA. Dec.18; 366) £260
– – Anr. Edn. 1822. 1st. Edn. Fo. 2 plts. with short reprd. tears in the margins, a little marginal dust-soiling. Mod. hf. mor. (S. Nov.4; 637) *Russell.* £400
– – Anr. Copy. 36 hand-cold. plts., wrtmkd. 1820. Cont. red hf. mor. (S. Nov.25; 550) *Duran.* £300
– – Anr. Copy. Offsetting of plts. on text. Hf. mor., worn, upr. jnt. brkn. (BS. Jun.11; 204) £200
– – Anr. Copy. Engl.-Fr. text. Linen. (DS. May 22; 866) Pts. 75,000
- Voyage up the Mediterranean ... with a Description of the Battle of the Nile. 1802. [1st. Edn.?]. 4to. Some tissue guards heavily foxed.

WILSON

Crimson str.-grd. mor. gt. by Bayntun, Bath. (TA. Nov.20; 397) £600
– – **Anr. Copy.** Engraved hand-cold. dedication lf., 42 hand-cold. plts. Mod. hf. mor. (C. Jul.15; 115) *Traylen.* £260
– – **Anr. Copy.** Qtr. cf. gt., spine defect. (P. Jul.30; 135) *Habibis.* £140

WILSON
See–PROUT, VARLEY & WILSON

WILSON, Alexander
– **Poems.** Paisley, 1790. Red mor. gt. by Rivière. (CE. Nov.20; 170) £220

WILSON, Alexander & Bonaparte, Charles Lucian
– **American Ornithology.** Phila., 1808-1814; 1825-1833. 1st. Edns. 9 vols.; 4 vols. Fo. Some browning, foxing, offsetting, some tears affecting 1 plt., some ll. loose or detchd. Orig. hf. mor., scarred, chipped, worn. From liby. of William E. Wilson. (SPB. Apr.29; 282) $3,500
– – **Anr. Edn.** Phila., 1825-33. 1st. Edn. 4 vols. Fo. Spotted in places, some offsets, liby. stps. & labels of Harvard University, including release stp. Cont, red hf. str.-grd. mor., vol. 1 reprd. & rebkd. preserving orig. spine, vols. II & III unc. [Sabin 6264] (S. Jun.1; 75) *Arader.* £520
– – **Anr. Edn.** Phila., 1828-29. 3 vols. 8vo & Fo. atlas. Sm. liby.-stp. on each plt. Hf. mor., atlas vol. rebkd., ex-liby. with labels, marks. (SPB. Oct.1; 216) $3,600
– – **Anr. Edn.** N.Y. & Phila., 1829. Lge. 4to. 76 cold. plts., lacks 3 text vols. Mod. hf. cf. (S. Mar.17; 372) *Robinson.* £720
– – **Anr. Copy.** Plt. vol. only. Fo. 76 hand-cold. plts. (SG. May 14; 7) $1,900
– – **Anr. Edn.** 1832. 3 vols. Cf. gt. (P. Nov.13; 232) *Wagner.* £220
– – **Anr. Copy.** Hf. mor., worn. (S. Dec.3; 1176) *W. & W.* £140
– – **Anr. Copy.** 97 full-p. hand-cold. plts., 12 foxed. Mor. gt., by Tout. (CNY. May 22; 227) $400
– – **Anr. Edn.** Ed.:– Sir William Jardine. Ill.:– Lizars. 1876. 3 vols. 4to. Red str.-grd. mor., gt., spines with onlaid gt. eagles, by Bayntun-Rivière. (C. Nov.5; 177) *Carter.* £320
– – **Anr. Copy.** Slight foxing, mainly affecting prelims. Orig. qtr. mor., gt. decor. spines. (TA. Sep.18; 29) £90
– – **Anr. Copy.** Hf. leath., disbnd. (SG. Sep.18; 10) $300
– – **Anr. Edn.** Ed.:– Sir William Jardine. Ill.:– Lizars. L., ca. 1880. 3 vols. Orig. hf. mor., spines gt., worn. (SG. Jan.29; 13) $200
– – **Anr. Edn.** Phila., n.d. Plt. vol. only. Fo. 1 plt. torn, some soiling, chipping. Orig. cl. folder, worn. (SPB. May 29; 441) $175

WILSON, Charles Henry
– **The Beauties of Tom Brown.** Ill.:– Thomas Rowlandson. L., 1808. 1st. Edn. Mod. crushed rose mor., gt.-panel. back, unc. (PNY. Mar.26; 284) $425

WILSON, Capt. Sir Charles William, K. C. B.
– **Picturesque Palestine, Sinai & Egypt.** Ca. 1870. 4 vols. plus Supp. 4to. Orig. cl. gt. (TA. Feb.19; 652) £66
– – **Anr. Edn.** [1880-84]. 5 vols. including Supp. 4to. Orig. cl. (C. May 20; 188) *Jones.* £110
– – **Anr. Copy.** 4 vols. (lacks supp.). Orig. cl. gt. (SBA. Jul.22; 42) *Museum Bookshop.* £50
– – **Anr. Edn.** [1881-83]. 4 vols. (without supp.). 4to. Orig. cl. gt. (SBA. Oct.21; 130) *Studd.* £90
– – **Anr. Copy.** (SBA. Oct.21; 131) *Studd.* £80
– – **Anr. Copy.** 2 vols. Considerable foxing. Disbnd. (SG. May 21; 419) $100
– – **Anr. Copy.** 2 vols. Orig. leath., worn. (R. Mar.31-Apr.4; 2535) DM 800
– – **Anr. Edn.** N.d. 5 vols. including supp. 4to. A few ll. slightly spotted. Orig. cl. (SH. Nov.7; 448) *Hosain.* £105
– – **Anr. Copy.** 4 vols. in 2. Cl. (P. Mar.12; 255) *Cambridge.* £80
– – **Anr. Copy.** 4 vols. Orig. cl. gt. (SKC. Oct.8; 1475) £55

WILSON, Edward
[–] **Rambles at the Antipodes; A Series of Sketches.** L., 1859. 2 clean tears in 1 folding map, 1 plt. detchd. without damage. Orig. cl., slight wear. (KH. Nov.18; 645) *Aus.* $200

WILSON, Erasmus
See–QUAIN, Jones & Wilson, Erasmus

WILSON, H.
– **Ariana Antiqua. A Descriptive Account of the Antiquities & Coins of Afghanistan.** 1841. 4to. Orig. cl. (SH. Mar.5; 156) *Kossow.* £320
– – **Anr. Copy.** Cont. cf., rebkd. (SH. Nov.7; 449) *Diba.* £90

WILSON, Hardy
– **Collapse of Civilization.** [Kew], [1936]. 4to. Process dupl. on versos only, [2] + 19 sheets. Binder's cl. (KH. Nov.18; 647) *Aus.* $130
– **Eucalyptus.** Wandin, 1941. (25). 2 ll. detchd. Reversed cf. (KH. Nov.18; 649) *Aus.* $270
– **Old Colonial Architecture in New South Wales & Tasmania.** Sydney, Priv. Ptd., 1924. (1000) numbered. Fo. Batik bds., bdg. torn. (SG. Dec.4; 374) $300
– **Solution of Jewish Problem.** Wandin, 1941. A few stains & marks. Stapled in wraps. (KH. Nov.18; 650) *Aus.* $140

WILSON, Harriette
– **Memoirs.** L. & Phila., 1825-26. 4 vols. 12mo. Extra-ill. with 300 engraved ports ports., views & rare theatrical programmes inserted. Lev. gt., by Thiery. 5pp. 4to, A.L.s. to the Earl of Craven, sigd. Harriette Beaufort late Wilson, dtd. Mar.24, 1824, asking for financial assistance, some folds torn. (BS. Jun.11; 294) £260

WILSON, Henry
– **A Compleat Universal History of the Several Dominions throughout the Known World.** L., 1738. Fo. Disbnd. (SG. Oct.30; 376) $110

WILSON, Herbert Wrigley
– **With the Flag to Pretoria.–After Pretoria the Guerilla War.** L., 1900-02. 4 vols. 4to. Decor. cl., covers slightly stained at edges, slightly shaken. (VA. Jan.30; 541) R. 210

WILSON, J.
– **Works.** 1866-67. 12 vols. Cont. hf. cf. (SH. May 28; 110) *Booth.* £70

WILSON, James
[–] **Considerations on the Bank of North-America.** Phila., 1785. 1st. Edn. 12mo. Mor. gt., unc., by Zaehnsdorf. From the Prescott Collection. [Sabin 15967] (CNY. Feb.6; 338) $420
– – **Anr. Edn.** L., 1799. [1st. Edn.]. 4to. Some light foxing. Old. cf., brkn., bds. detchd. (KH. Mar.24; 427) *Aus.* $120

WILSON, James Grant (Ed.)
See–APPLETON'S CYCLOPAEDIA . . .

WILSON, James William
– **Sketches of Louth.** Louth, 1840. Fo. Some soiling. Orig. cl., spine torn. Inscr. on title 'Henry Chaplin, Esq. M.P. with the sketchers compliments'. (CSK. Apr.3; 120) £80

WILSON, Sir John
– **The Royal Philatelic Collection.** Dropmore Pr., 1952. Fo. Orig. mor., box. (SH. Jun.11; 217) *Thorp.* £60
– – **Anr. Edn.** Dropmore Pr., [1952]. Fo. Orig. bdg., s.-c. (CSK. Feb.20; 178) £70

WILSON, Sir Robert
– **Brief Remarks on the Character . . . of the Russian Army.** L., 1810. 1st. Edn., L.P. Lge. 4to. Mod. bds. (SG. Oct.30; 377) $110

WILSON, Sir Robert Thomas
– **History of the British Expedition to Egypt.** 1802. 4to. Cont. cf., covers detchd. (SH. May 21; 136) *Joughin.* £50

WILSON, Romer (Ed.)
See–RED MAGIC

WILSON, T.L. Rodney
– **A Catalogue Raisonné . . . Petrus van der Velden.** Sydney, 1979. (1500). 2 vols. Fo. Canvas bds. (KH. Mar.24; 429) *Aus.* $180

WILSON, Rev. T. M.
– **The Rural Cyclopedia.** Edinb., 1847-49. 4 vols. Orig. hf. cf. (GM. Apr.30; 812) £75

WILSON, W.
– **The Post-Chaise Companion, or Travellers Directory through Ireland.** Dublin, 1786. 1st. Edn. Old cf., upr. cover loose. (GM. Apr.30; 45) £60
– – **Anr. Copy.** Cf., lacks lr. cover. (P. Jul.30; 297) *Bickersteth.* £50

WILSON, William
– **A Missionary Voyage to the Southern Pacific Ocean, Performed in the Years 1796-98, in the Ship Duff.** 1799. 1st. Edn. 4to. Margins untrimmed & slightly browned. Orig. bds. with linen backstrip, some wear. (TA. Jan.22; 374) £190
– – **Anr. Copy.** Some foxing. Cont. tree cf., rebkd. From the collection of Eric Sexton. (C. Apr.15; 54) *Frum.* £160
– – **Anr. Copy.** Some plts. & charts dampstained, occasional spotting. Old bds., rebkd. & covered in mor. (CSK. Mar.13; 128) £95

WILSON, William J.E.
See–QUAIN, Jones & Wilson, William J.E.

WILTHEMIO, R. P. Alexandro
– **Luciliburgensia. Se Luxemburgum Romanum.** Luxemburg, 1842. 4to. Cont. bds., spine slightly defect., unc. (LM. Jun.13; 186) B.Frs. 7,000

WIMPHELING, Jacobus
See–LOCHER, Jacobus–REMUS Favinus
–UGUITON–WIMPHELING, Jacobus
–VALLIBUS, Hieronymus de

WIMPINA, Conradus
– **Precepta Coaugmentande Rethorice Oracionis Comodissia.** [Leipzig], [Printer of Capotius], ca. 1485-90. 4to. Some margins strengthened. Mod. bds. [H. 13315] (C. Apr.1; 95) *Maggs.* £380

WINCKELL, G. Fr.D. aus dem
– **Handbuch für Jäger, Jagdberichte und Jagdliebhaber.** Neudamm, 3rd. Edn. 3 vols. Orig. linen. (R. Mar.31-Apr.4; 1732) DM 520

WINCKELMANN, Johann Joachim
[–] **Anmerkungen über die Geschichte der Kunst des Alterthums.–Abhandlung der Fähigkeit der Empfindung des Schönen in der Kunst. –Sendschreib von der Herculanischen Endeckungen.** Dresden, 1767; 1771; 1762. 1st. Edn; 2nd. Edn.; 1st. Edn. 3 works in 1 vol. 4to. Cont. hf. leath., spine defect. (D. Dec.11-13; 381) DM 450
– **Geschichte der Kunst des Alterthums. Erster [–Zweiter] Theil.** Dresden, 1764. 1st. Edn. 4to. Mod hf. mor. (S. Oct.21; 474) *Artico.* £220
– **Monumenti Antichi.** Rome, 1767. 2 vols. Fo. Cont. cf., cardinal arms, decor., mod. box. (CR. Jun.11; 622) Lire 650,000
– **Storia delle Arti del Disegno.** Trans.:– Tedesco. Rome, 1783-84. 3 vols. 4to. Some margins slightly wormed, barely affecting matter, a few minor defects. Cont. vell., slightly worn. (SBA. Mar.4; 88) *Pelizzi.* £170

WINCKELMANN, Johann Joachim–FEA, Carlo
– **Storia delle Arti del Disegno Presso gli Antichi. –Riposta . . . alle Osservazione del Sig. Cav. Onofrio Boni . . .** Ed.:– Carlo Fea (1st. work). Rome, 1783-84; 1786. 2 works in 3 vols. A few ll. with sm. marginal stains; 1st. work has 52 plts. & plans (of 53?). Cont. vell. bds., spines gt., slightly soiled. (S. May 5; 190) *Duran.* £120

WINCKELMANN U. SOHNE, Publishers
– **Vorlege-Blatter zum Thier-Zeichen.** [Berlin], n.d. 1 pt. only. Fo. 10 litho. plts. only, some spotting. Unbnd. as iss. in orig. portfo., worn. (CSK. Feb.13; 133) £95

WINDELER, Bernard
– **Sailing Ships & Barges of the Western Mediterranean & Adriatic Seas.** Ill.:– Edward Wadsworth. 1926. 1st. Edn. (450) numbered. Fo. Orig. cl., unc., s.-c. (SH. Mar.27; 535) *Marks.* £125
– – **Anr. Copy.** Orig. buckram-bkd. linen, gt., spine slightly soiled, unc. (S. Jul.31; 329) *Campus.* £110

WINDUS, John
– **Reise nach Mequinetz, der Residentz des . . . Kaysers von Fetz und Marocco . . .** Trans.:– F.C. Weber. Hanover, 1726. 4to. Some ll. of text lightly browned & foxed. Cont. cf. (S. Jun.29; 206) *Quaritch.* £85

WING, Donald

– Short-Title Catalogue of Books Printed in England, Scotland, Ireland, Wales & British America & of English Books Printed in Other Countries, 1641-1700. N.Y., 1945-51. 3 vols. 4to. Orig. cl. (TA. Sep.18; 41) £460
– – Anr. Copy. (CSK. Nov.28; 97) £300
– – Anr. Edn. N.Y., 1951. 3 vols. Orig. cl. (P. Mar.12; 365) *Dawsons.* £300
*See-*POLLARD, Alfred William, Redgrave, G.R. & others – – WING, Donald

WINGFIELD, Henry

– A Compendious or Shorte Treatise ... conteynynge Certayne Preceptes necessary to the Preservation of Healthe. [1551]. Lacks last lf. (presumably blank). New cf., gt. panel. sides. [STC 25852] (S. Jun.17; 892)
Jenner Books. £1,500

WINGFIELD, Rev. W. & Johnson, George William

– Poultry Book. Ill.:– after Harrison Weir. 1853. 4to. Some foxing. Cont. mor. gt. (TA. Nov.20; 416) £85
– – Anr. Copy. Mor. gt. (P. Jun.11; 304)
MacDonnel. £55

WINKLER, Ed.

– Getreue Abbildung aller in d. neuem Pharmacopöen ... auf genommenen Officienellen Gewaechse. Leipzig, ca. 1850. Plt. vol. 4to. Slightly browned. Cont. bds., defect. & worn. (HK. Nov.18-21; 828) DM 1,000
– Sämmtl. Giftgewächse Deutschlands. Ill.:– Ad. & C.E. Menzel. 1831. 1st. Edn. Heavily soiled & browned. Bds. ca. 1850, spine worn & defect. (HK. May 12-14; 478) DM 1,400

WINKLER, Friedrich

– Die Zeichnungen Albrecht Durers. Berlin, 1936-38. Vols. I-III (of 4). 4to. Orig. cl. (S. Jul.27; 177) *Pilkington.* £60
– – Anr. Edn. Berlin, 1936-39. Definitive Edn. 4 vols. 4to. Publisher's cl. (CR. Jun.11; 429) Lire 400,000

WINKLER, Johann Heinrich

– Gedanken von den Eigenschaften, Wirkungen und Ursachen der Electricität.-Die Eigenschaften der Electrischen Materie und des Electrischen Feuers. -Die Stärke der Electrischen Kraft des Wassers in Gläsernen Gefässen. Leipzig, 1744; 1745; 1746. 1st. Edns. 3 works in 1 vol. Browned thro.-out, 1st. work lacks 3 plts. Cont. mott. cf., gt. spine. Bkplt. of Herbert McLean Evans; w.a.f.; from Honeyman Collection. (S. May 20; 3129) *Rota.* £260

WINKLES, B. & Henry

– Architectural & Picturesque Illustrations of the Cathedral Churches of England & Wales. 1835-42. 3 vols. Orig. cl., vol. 1 rebkd. with old spine relaid. (TA. Mar.19; 664) £60
– – Anr. Copy. Sm. fo. Lacks 1 plt., margins slightly browned, slight foxing. Spines defect. (TA. Dec.18; 74) £52
– – Anr. Copy. L.P. 4to. Occasional light spotting. Cont. hf. mor. (CSK. May 29; 9) £50

WINKLES, B. & Henry-WINKLES, B.

– Architectural & Picturesque Illustrations of the Cathedral Churches of England & Wales.-French Cathedrals. 1836-42; 1837. 3 vols.; 1 vol. Qtr. cf. (O. Jun.3; 97) £130
– – Anr. Copy. 3 vols.; 1 vol. 8vo. & 4to. A few spots. Unif. later cf. gt. (SBA. Jul.22; 148)
Stanyer. £70

WINLOVE, Samuel

– Moral Lectures ... 1781. 32mo. Orig. Dutch floral bds., backstrip loose & upr. cover loose, fitted case. (SH. Mar.19; 205) *Quaritch.* £370

WINNECKE, Charles

– Journal of the Horn Scientific Exploring Expedition, 1894. Adelaide, 1897. 2 folding maps in rear pocket. Without wraps. in old semi-limp binder's cl., qtr. roan, slightly worn. (KH. Nov.18; 651) Aus. $240

WINSEMIUS, Pierius

– Chronique ofte Historische Geschiedenisse van Vrieslant. Franeker, 1622. Fo. Lacks general map & port., engraved title cut to plt. & mntd., slightly browned in places, plans with sm. repairs, margins of some ll. at end reprd. & a few light marginal stains. Cont. cf., gt. spine, foot of spine slightly defect. (VG. Oct.13; 170) Fls. 800

WINSHIP, George Parker

– William Caxton, a Paper Read at a Meeting of the Club of Odd Volumes. Hammersmith, Doves Pr., 1909. (15) on vell. Sm. 4to. Lev. mor., gt.-ruled, gt. ornaments, spine in 6 compartments, 5 raised bands, gt.-panel., sigd. by Doves Bindery 1911, qtr. mor. s.-c. (CNY. May 22; 389) $3,200
– – Anr. Copy. Mor. gt., sigd. by the Doves Bindery. (CNY. May 22; 304) $1,000
– – Anr. Edn. Doves Pr., 1909. (300) on paper. 4to. Mor. gt., line tooled border to covers with rose spray at corners, centre compartment with repeated flower tool, after a design by D.J. Cobden-Sanderson, 1911. (S. Jul.31; 60)
Foyles. £620
– – Anr. Copy. 4to. Vell.-bkd. bds. (PNY. Dec.3; 126) $150
*See-*HIGDEN, Ranulphus

WINSTON, Charles

[-] An Inquiry into the Difference of Style Observable in Ancient Glass Paintings. Oxford, 1847. 1st. Edn. 2 vols. Gt.-pict. cl., worn. From the liby. of Clement Heaton. (SG. Mar.12; 353) $130

WINTER VON ADLERSFLUGEL, Georg Simon

– Bellerophon, sive Eques Peritus ... Nuremb., 1678. 1st. Edn. Fo. Latin & German text. Cont. cf., covers worn. (S. Jun.1; 51)
Brooke-Hitching. £3,000
– – Anr. Copy. 168 engraved plts. (of 170, lacks plts. 16 & 82), 1 plt. slightly defect. in margin, lacks hf.-title, ptd. Latin title & plts. misbnd. 19th. C. hf. vell. (S. Jun.1; 52) *Robinson.* £1,100
– Neuer Tractat von der Reith-Kunst. Ulm, 1674. Fo. Browned & spotted. 19th. C. hf. cf. bds. (S. Jun.1; 53) *Way.* £80
– Tractatio ... de Re Equaria ... Neuer und vermehrter Tractat von der Stuterey oder Fohlen-Zucht. Nuremb., 1703. Fo. Latin, German, Italian & Fr. text, many plts. reprd., lacks f. 2D4 of index, slightly spotted. Hf. cf., preserving old bds. w.a.f. (S. Jun.1; 54) *Erlini.* £300
– Wohlerfahrner Pferd-Artzt, Welcher Gruendlich Lehret, wie man der Pferde Complexion, Natur und Alter Erkennen. Ed.:– Valentin Frichter. Nürnburg, 1757. Revised Edn. 44 plts., 1 folding, 1 unnumbered, bnd. erratically. Cont. leath. on wood bds., leath. clasps, worn. W.a.f. (SG. Sep.25; 329) $250

WIRSING, A.L. & Gunther, F.C.

– Collection de Figures de Nids et d'Oeufs de differents Oiseaux, tirés des Cabinets de Mr. de Schmidel, Cahier I. Nuremb., 1777. All publd. Fo. Text describes 1st. 25 plts. only. Hf. cf. (S. Dec.3; 1177) *Evans.* £1,100

WIRTZUNG, Christoph

– The General Practise of Physick. Trans.:– Jacob Mosan. 1654. 4th. Edn. Fo. Cont. blind-ruled cf., rebkd. [Wing M2850a & W3100 or W3101] (C. Jul.16; 364) *Taylor.* £130

WISDEN, John

– Cricketers' Almanack. 1879-1943. Vols. 16-76 & 80 only, in 55 vols. Photographs mntd., lacking in 1st. 10 years. Later cl. & orig. wrap. (SH. Oct.9; 255) *Mackenzie.* £600
– – Anr. Edn. 1879-1979. Nos. 1-15 facs. Edns. Vols. 1-116, lacks vol. 17 (1880), 4 duplicates (1876, 87, 1929, 58), together in 122 vols. Most in orig. wraps. & cl., 15 rebnd., many worn, vol. 18 (1881) misdtd. 1880 on spine. (SH. Oct.9; 254) *Mackenzie.* £1,100
– – Anr. Edn. 1905-11; 1922-36; 1938-40; 1947-78. 58 vols. Various bdgs. (HSS. Apr.24; 193) £320
– – Anr. Edn. For 1907-15, 1920-36 & 1946-80. 51 vols. only. Orig. bdgs., some worn. (SH. Jul.23; 196) *Baldur.* £640
– – Anr. Edn. 1911-80. 70 vols. only. Orig. bdgs., some worn. (SH. Jul.9; 58) *McKenzie.* £650
– – Anr. Edn. 1947-79. 33 vols. Orig. bdgs., 16 in limp covers, some spines soiled, some with cellophane covers. (SKC. Jul.28; 2519) £180

WISE, Francis

– Letter to Dr. Mead concerning ... the White Horse.-Further Observations upon the White Horse. Oxford, 1738-42. 2 vols. in 1. 4to. Some ll. spotted. Cont. hf. cf. (SH. Nov.6; 180)
Sanders. £50

WISE, George

[-] History of the Seventeenth Virginia Infantry, C.S.A. Balt., 1870. 1st. Edn. 12mo. Gt.-pict. cl. (SG. Jun.11; 114) $140

WISE, John

– A System of Aeronautics. Phila., 1850. 1st. Edn. Orig. cl. (S. Nov.25; 551) *Stewart.* £280

WISE, Thomas James

– Alfred Lord Tennyson: Bibliography of the Writings. L., priv. ptd. 1908. (100). 2 vols. Cl., unc. Ashley Liby. colophon. (SG. Oct.2; 351) $150
– The Ashley Library. L., 1922-30. (200). 10 vols. 4to. Orig. buckram gt., some covers slightly spotted, partly unc. From the Prescott Collection. (CNY. Feb.6; 358) $650
– A Byron Library.-A Bibliography of the Writings ... of Byron.-Bibliographical Catalogue of first editions, proof copies & manuscripts of books by Lord Byron. 1928; 1932-3; 1924. (30) on H.M.P. (1st. work); (180) on antique paper (2nd. work). 4 vols. together. 4to. All orig. cl. Issued with the lot is set of p. proofs, corrected in MS., of Byron section of Wise's Ashley liby. Catalogue & correspondence between Wise & O.N. Chadwick-Healy, with some carbon copies of replies from the latter, also 3 letters with copies of replies from A.W. Evans of Elkin Mathews & 1 from John Murray. (C. Feb.4; 97) *Forster.* £400

WISE, Thomas James & Wyndham, H. Saxe

– Reference Catalogue of British & Foreign Autographs & Manuscripts. L., 1893-1900. (200) (pt. 1 only), & (100). Pts. I-IX in 9 vols. Tall fo. Ptd. wraps. (those of pt. 1 soiled), unc. (SG. Mar.26; 472) $275

WISEMAN, Richard

– Eight Chirurgical Treatises. 1705. 4th. Edn. Fo. Cont. cf., rebkd. (S. Jun.17; 895) *Phelp.* £140
– A Treatise of Wounds. 1672. 1st. (? & only) Edn. F5 blank except for sig., short marginal tear in ll. Cont. sheep worn, torn at top of spine. Dr. George Mitchell's copy. [Wing W3110] (S. Jun.17; 894)
Phillips. £800

WISHAW, Francis

– The Railways of Great Britain & Ireland. 1842. 2nd. Edn. 4to. 1 plt. worn, 1 lf. reprd. Cl., unc. (SKC. Feb.26; 1772) £65

WISSET, Robert

*See-*DAVY, Sir Humphrey-WISSET, Robert

WIT, Frederick de

– Atlas. Amst., [1680?], Fo. Engraved frontis., 51 double-p. engraved maps, hand-cold. in outl., frontis., cartouches, etc. fully cold., some maps torn at bottom of centre fold. Orig. vell. gt., roll borders, inner panel, cornerpieces, centre ornament. W.a.f. (S. Mar.31; 288)
Burgess. £5,000
– – Anr. Copy. Crudely cold. title, all maps dampstained, some repairs. Bds. (P. Jan.22; 186)
Kentish. £850
– – Anr. Edn. Amst., [after 1688]. Fo., (525mm×315mm). Maps hand-cold. in outl., principal areas of some fully cold., historiated & other cartouches, Hungary dtd. 1688, other maps undated, wanting map of Scandinavia, but with 5 maps not called for in index, including Russia & the Holy Land, map of Germany very defect., pt. of map of the Low Countries torn away, a number of maps reprd. in centre fold, several maps with tears, perforations or repairs, some stained, frontis. reprd. affecting surface, title reprd., ptd. tables (some defect.), to some of the maps, interleaved on later guards thro.-out. Cont. paper bds., later cl. spine. W.a.f. (S. Nov.3; 13)
Nagle. £500
– – Anr. Edn. Amst., ca. 1710. Lge. fo. Lacks map 14 (Poland), 14 maps partly cont. hand-cold., map of France dtd. 1709. Cont. hf. vell., worn, soiled. (VG. Dec.17; 1182) Fls. 10,000
*See-*STRADANUS, Johannes-WIT, Frederick de -NICOLAES de Bruyn

WITHER, George

– Select Lyrical Poems. Kent, Lee Piory Pr., 1815. (100). Sm. 4to. Hf. cf. gt., by Wood, orig. wraps. preserved. (CNY. May 22; 333) $120

WITHERBY, Harry Forbes & others

– Handbook of British Birds. 1938. 5 vols. Buckram gt. (P. Nov.13; 233) *Holmes.* £60
– – Anr. Edn. 1938-41. 1st. Edns. 5 vols. Orig. cl. Ex-libris Lord Hurcomb, with some related correspondence loosely inserted. (TA. Jun.18; 1) £80
– – Anr. Copy. (C. May 20; 257) *Joseph.* £75
– – Anr. Edn. 1938-41. 5 vols. Orig. cl. gt., d.-w.'s. (PL. Sep.18; 157) *Hobson.* £100
– – Anr. Copy. Some spotting. Orig. cl., worn. (CSK. May 22; 10) £80

– – Anr. Copy. Slight spotting. Cl. (P. Apr.30; 83) *Graham.* £70
– – Anr. Edn. 1943. 5 vols. Bdg. not stated. (GT. Oct.2; 166) £65
– – Anr. Edn. 1945. 5 vols. Cl. gt., d.-w.'s. (P. Oct.2; 80) *Hatchards.* £100
– – Anr. Edn. N.d. 5 vols. Orig. bdg. (DWB. Mar.31; 269) £85

WITHERING, William
– An Account of the Foxglove, & some of its Medical Uses: with Practical Remarks on Dropsy, & other Diseases.-An Account of the Scarlet Fever & Sore Throat. Bg'ham., 1785; 1793. 1st. Edn.; 2nd. Edn. 2 works in 1 vol. 1st. work with cold. folding plt. in 1st. state (reprd.), a few ll. slightly damp-spotted; 2nd. work lacks hf.-title. Cont. hf. cf., very worn, cl. case. From Honeyman Collection. (S. May 20; 3131) *Norman.* £1,900
– An Account of the Scarlet Fever & Sore Throat of Scarlatina Anginosa particularly as it Appeared at Birmingham in 1778. 1779. 1st. Edn. Hf.-title & last p. dust-soiled. New cl., unc. (S. Jun.17; 896) *Zeitlin & Verbrugge.* £380
– A Botanical Arrangement of All the Vegetables Naturally Grown in Great Britain. 1776. 1st. Edn. 2 vols. Some margins just browned. Cont. spr. cf., slightly worn. (SBA. May 27; 206) *Studd.* £100
– The Miscellaneous Tracts. 1822. 2 vols. Sm. liby. stp. on titles. Hf. cl. (S. Jun.17; 897) *Maggs.* £240

WITHERS, Alexander S.
– Chronicles of Border Warfare, or A History of the Settlement by the Whites of North-Western Virginia... Clarksburg Va., 1831. 1st. Edn. 12mo. Advt., foxed. Cont. cf., worn, rebkd. From liby. of William E. Wilson; the Littell copy. (SPB. Apr.29; 284) $300
– – Anr. Copy. Owners' inscrs. Cont. tree cf., some scarring on upr. cover, folding cl. s.-c. From liby. of William E. Wilson; bkplts. of James McBride & Carl R. Bogardus. (SPB. Apr.29; 283) $225

WITHWORTH, Charles, Baron
– An Account of Russia as It was in the Year 1710. Strawberry Hill, 1758. 1st. Edn. Cont. gt. mott. cf., in gt. mor. & cl. s.-c. (PNY. Mar.26; 288) £110

WITLAM, Thomas
– Oriental & Western Siberia. 1858. Cont. cf. (SH. Apr.9; 136) *Crete.* £50

WITNASH Rectory
– A Collection of 20 Christmas Recitation Programmes from Witnash School. Witnash, 1851-70. Pict. general title, frontis. Cont. diced cf. gt., orig wraps. bnd. in. (SBA. Oct.22; 550) *Spelman.* £76

WITS MUSEUM, or the New London Jester
Ca. 1780. Cf., rebkd. (BS. Jun.11; 297) £60

WITSEN, Nicolas
– Aeloude en Hedendaegsche Scheeps-Bouw en Bestier. Amst., 1671. 1st. Edn. Fo. Engraved title-p., port., 113 engraved plts., 3 reprd., Tt4 reprd., a few ll. on guards. Early Dutch vell., lr. cover reprd. & recased, end-ll. renewed, bds. warped. (CNY. May 22; 177) $1,500
– – Anr. Copy. 112 (of 114) engraved plts., with the plt. (very often lacking) of a man-of-war, frontis., port. & 2 lacking plts. supplied in facs., title & 1st. 4 pp. slightly browned & foxed. Old vell., soiled, spine reprd. (VG. Nov.18; 1450) Fls. 3,000

WITT, Carl
– Die Tapferen Zehntausend. Ill.:– M. Slevogt. Berlin, [1921]. (500) Portfo. Plate on Bütten. 4to. Loose in orig. vell. box. All lithos. sigd. by artist. (H. May 21/22; 1814) DM 1,600

WITT, Jan de
– Brieven...-Secrete Resolutien van... Holland en Westvriesland. The Hague; Utrecht, 1723-25; 1717. 6 vols.; 2 vols. 4to. Some foxing & dampstaining to 1st. work. Unif. cont. vell., ex-liby. (SG. Feb.5; 114) $350

WITTE, C.
See–LUDEMAN, Wm. von & Witte, C.

WITTE, Fritz
– Die Liturgischen Gewänder und Kirchlichen Stickereien des Schnütgenmuseums Köln. Berlin, 1926. (400). Fo. Orig. linen. (R. Oct.14-18; 776) DM 420

– Skulpturen der Sammlung Schnütgen in Cöln. Berlin, 1912. (300) numbered. Fo. Orig. linen. (D. Dec.11-13; 361) DM 800

WITTICH, J.
– Aphoristischer Extract und Kurzer Bericht, des Mineralischen Sauerbruns zu Kissingen, im Fürstenthumb Francken. Erfurt, 1589. 4to. Hf. vell. (R. Oct.14-18; 309) DM 1,900

WITTKOWER, R.
See–BRAUER, H. & Wittkower, R.

WITTY, Robert
– Ograuoskopia. Or, a Survey of the Heavens ... by the Telescope ... To which is Added the Gout-Raptures ... in English, Latine, & Greek Lyrick Verse. Priv. ptd., 1681. 1st. Edn. Advt. lf., some dampstaining, a little worming, mainly marginal. Stitching loose, cont. sheep, worn, head of spine defect. Pres. copy; inscr. 'Donu Authoris Septemb. 22 1682'; sig. on fly-lf. (possibly in same hand) of Charles Beaumont; from Honeyman Collection. [Wing W3229] (S. May 20; 3133) *Crete.* £190

WOCHENBLÄTTER für Freiheit und Gesetz
Karlsbad, 1848. Year 1, Nos. 1-85, probably all publd. Cont. bds., orig. wraps. pasted on. (R. Oct.14-18; 1384) DM 600

WODEHOUSE, Pelham Grenville
– The Code of the Woosters. [1938]. 1st. Engl. Edn. Margins slightly browned. Orig. cl. Inscr. (CSK. Mar.20; 59) £50
– A Gentleman of Leisure. 1910. 1st. Edn. Orig. cl., gt. lettered. (C. Feb.4; 103) *Irene Editions.* £180
– The Gold Bat. 1904. 1st. Edn. Orig. pict. cl., spine soiled. (SH. Dec.19; 664) *Irene Books.* £280
– – Anr. Copy. Spotted. Worn. (SKC. Feb.26; 1532) £60
– The Pot-Hunters. 1902. 1st. Edn. [2nd. Iss?]. Orig. pict. cl., some wear. (C. Feb.4; 99) *Murphy.* £95
– – Anr. Edn. Ill.:– R. Noel Pocock. 1902. 1st. Edn. Orig. cl., worn. (SH. Dec.19; 662) *Old Hall.* £280
– A Prefect's Uncle. Ill.:– Noel Pocock. 1903. [1st. Edn.?]. Orig. pict. cl., worn. (S. Jul.22; 343) *Irene Editions.* £230
– – Anr. Copy. Orig. pict. cl., gt. spine. (C. Feb.4; 100) *Irene Editions.* £200
– Psmith in the City. Ill.:– T.M.R. Whitwell. 1910. 1st. Edn. Orig. pict. cl. (S. Jul.22; 344) *Irene Editions.* £160
– Psmith in the City.-Psmith Journalist. 1910; 1915. 1st. Edns. 2 vols. Orig. pict. cl., spine lettered gt. (C. Feb.4; 104) *Blackwell.* £170
– Psmith Journalist. Ill.:– T.M.R. Whitwell. 1915. 1st. Edn. Orig. pict. cl. (S. Jul.22; 345) *Irene Editions.* £150
– Tales of St. Austin's. 1903. 1st. Edn. 1 plt. loose. Orig. pict. cl., soiled. (SH. Dec.19; 663) *Hughes.* £220
– The White Feather. 1907. 1st. Edn. Orig. pict. cl., gt. spine (stained). (C. Feb.4; 102) *Quaritch.* £260
– William Tell Told Again. Ill.:– after Phillip Dadd. 1904. 1st. Edn. 4to. Advt. lf. bnd. in at rear. Orig. cl. decor. in green, brown & gt., slightly spotted. (TA. Mar.19; 483) £95
– – Anr. Edn. Ill.:– Phillip Dadd. [1904]. Orig. pict. cl. (C. Feb.4; 101) *Aldridge.* £65

WODHULL, Michael
– Poems. 1772. (150?) for presentation. Cont. cf., spine gt. Inscr. to Fiennes Trotman. (LC. Jun.18; 350) £65

WOELMONT DE BRUMAGNE, Baron de
– Notices Généalogiques. 1925-35. 3rd.-8th. Series. 7 vols. Mod. bdg. (LM. Nov.8; 294) B.Frs. 26,000

WOHLERFAHRENE JAGER
Ulm, 1834. Only Edn. Hf. leath., ca. 1890. (R. Oct.14-18; 2826) DM 1,200

WOLCOT, John 'Peter Pindar'
– Works. 1794-1801. 5 vols. Cont. cf., gt. spines. (SH. Jul.23; 68) *Thorp.* £60

WOLF, Johann
– Lectionum Memorabilium et Reconditarum Centenarii XVI. Ill.:– Jost Amman & others. Lauingen, 1600. 1st. Edn. Vol. I only (vol. 2 publd. later). Fo. Spotted, some ll. brown, old

---

marginalia. Old stained vell., worn. (S. Jul.27; 137) *Studio Books.* £110

WOLF, Joseph
– Life & Habits of Wild Animals ... with descriptive letter-press by Daniel Giraud Elliot. 1874. L.P. 4to. Lev. by Zaehnsdorf. (CSK. Nov.28; 80) £90

WOLF, Joseph Christopher
– Bibliotheca Hebraea. Hamburg-Leipzig, 1715-33. 4 vols. 4to. Glosses in margins, sigs. of previous owners. Orig. vell. except vol. II. (S. Nov.17; 123) *Kingsgate.* £380

WOLF, W.
– Fahrrad und Radfahrer. Leipzig, 1890. Orig. pict. linen. (R. Mar.31-Apr.4; 1811) DM 450

WOLFE, Bertram D.
See–RIVERA, Diego & Wolfe, Bertram D.

WOLFE, Thomas
– From Death to Morning.-Of Time & the River. -The Web & the Rock.-You Can't Go Home Again.-The Hills Beyond.-A Stone, A Leaf, A Door. N.Y., 1935-45. 1st. Edns. 6 vols. Cl., d.-w.'s. (PNY. Dec.3; 378) $120
– Look Homeward, Angel. N.Y., 1930. 12mo. Cl., d.-w. (defect.). Inscr. (SG. Nov.13; 744) $300

WOLFE TONE, William Theobald
– Life of Theobald Wolfe Tone. Wash., 1826. 1st. Edn. 2 vols. Cf., reprd., s.-c. (GM. Apr.30; 59) £80

WOLFF, Christian Friedrich von, Baron
– Allerhand Nützl. Versuche, Dadurch zu Genauer Erkäntniss der Natur und Kunst der Weg gebähnet wird ... Halle, 1737-38. 3 vols. Cont. bds. (HK. Nov.18-21; 661) DM 480
– Elementa Matheseos Universae. Halle a. S., 1717-15. 1st. Edn. 2 vols. in 6. 4to. Some browning of text. Panel. cf., spines worn, 1 cover detchd., lacks 1 label. Bkplt. of Duke of Somerset; from Honeyman Collection. (S. May 20; 3134) *Nador.* £130
– – Anr. Edn. Ill.:– Daudet (engraved port.). Geneva, 1732-41. New Edn. 5 vols. 4to. Some browning, occasional stains or soiling. Cont. vell. bds., red hf. mor. cases. Stp. of Cologne Gymnasium; from Honeyman Collection. (S. May 20; 3135) *Hill.* £130
– Jus Gentium. Halle, 1749. 1st. Edn. 4to. Text browned & foxed. Cont. vell., a little soiled. (VG. Oct.13; 171) Fls. 1,200
– [-] Vollständiges Mathematisches Lexicon. Leipzig, 1742-47. New Edn. 2 pts. Lightly browned. Cont. leath. (R. Mar.31-Apr.4; 1200) DM 520

WOLFF, Jens
– Sketches on a Tour to Copenhagen. 1816. 2nd. Edn. 4to. Cont. hf. roan. (C. Nov.5; 178) *Fredrikstad.* £80

WOLFF, Jeremias
– [-] [Berliner Bauten]. Ill.:– after J.A. Corvinus & A. Meyer, additional engrs. by Martin Engelbrecht & Johann Georg Merz. [Augsburg], ca. 1700. Fo. Lacks 2 plts., 1 plt. mntd., additional plts. mntd. at end. 18th. C. bds., corners worn. As a collection, w.a.f. (S. Jan.27; 358) *Marlborough.* £280

WOLFF, Oscar Ludwig Bernhard
– Belgien und Holland. Leipzig, 1873. New Edn. Loose, some pp. & plts. very loose, prelims lack 2 text pp. Cont. hf. leath. (R. Oct.14-18; 1908) DM 600
– – Anr. Copy. Some pp. & plts. loose, lacks 2 ll. prelims. Loose. (R. Mar.31-Apr.4; 2658) DM 450

WOLFF, Oscar Ludwig Bernhard & Doering, Heinrich
– The German Tourist. Ill.:– after A.G. Vickers. L., 1837. Slightly soiled, plts. lightly browned. Orig. leath. (R. Oct.14-18; 2139) DM 1,700

WOLFFHUGEL, Gustav
See–KOCH, Robert-KOCH, Robert & others –KOCH, Robert & Wolffhugel, Gustav

WOLFIUS, H. & Fillingerus, C.
– Suidae Historica, Caeterague omni que ulla ex Porte ad Cignitionem Rerum Spectant. Basle, 1581. Fo. Some staining. 17th. C. mor. gt., fully tooled with monog. P.S. & fleur de lis on covers & spine, slightly worn, 2 corners slightly defect. (BS. Jun.11; 205) £120

WOLFRAM, L.F.
- Vollständiges Lehrbuch der Gesammten Baukunst. Stuttgart & Vienna, 1833-45. 1st. Edn. 3 vols., tog. 11 pts. in 11 vols. 4to. Soiled in parts, title stpd. Later hf. linen. (R. Mar.31-Apr. 4; 1314)   DM 1,850

WOLLEY, Hannah
[-] The Accomplish'd Ladies Delight in Preserving, Beautifying, & Cookery. 1683. 3rd. Edn. 3 pts. in 1 vol. 12mo. 1 figure in Angling woodcut partly cut round from behind, sm. tears in K12, L1 & 1 woodcut, single wormhole from 17 to end, cutting some letters, occasional browning & spotting. 19th. C. cf., spine gt. & discold. [Wing W3270] (S. Feb.10; 479)   Thomas. £550
[-] New & Excellent Experiments & Secrets in the Art of Angling. L., 1683. 16mo. Later crude hf. cf. (SG. Oct.16; 553) $475
- The Queen-like Closet ... [with a Supplement]. 1681-84. 3 pts. in 1 vol. 12mo. Advt. lf. at end of 2nd. pt., slight browning & soiling, some ll. frayed with some loss of text. Cont. cf. worn. [Wing W3285; 3288] (S. Sep.29; 100)   Bridge. £400

WOLLSTONECRAFT, Mary
- Original Stories from Real Life. Ill.:– William Blake. L., 1791. 12mo. Some foxing. Disbnd. (SG. Dec.18; 423) $325
- A Vindication of the Rights of Woman. L., 1792. 1st. Edn. Some ll. slightly spotted or soiled. Cont. sheep-bkd. bds., spine reprd., bd. edges worn, qtr. mor. gt. s.-c., unc. From the Prescott Collection. (CNY. Feb.6; 339) $750

WOLTERS, Fr.
- Herrschaft und Dienst. Berlin, 1909. (500) on Bütten. 4to. Orig. vell. Printer's mark monogrammed & numbered by artist. (H. May 21/22; 1877)   DM 600

WOLVERIDGE, James, M.D.
- Speculum Matricis or the Expert Midwives Handmaid. 1671. (?)2nd. Edn. 4 prelims. (a3-6) & C8 in photostat facs., extreme outer blank margin of 1st. few ll. reprd., last 4 ll. on guards, sm. hole in plt. 1 with sm. loss of engraved surface, tear in plt. 2, outer section of plt. 5 reprd. hardly affecting engraved surface, a few stains. New cf. Dr. Alistair Gunn's copy. (S. Jun.17; 899)   Korn. £450

WONDERFUL PIG (The) who exhibits every day near Charing Cross, with new Music
Ca. 1800. 4to. 2 engraved ll., with ills., mus. notat. & words. (SH. Apr. 10; 503)   Temperly. £110

WONDERS: DESCRIPTIVE OF SOME OF THE MOST REMARKABLE OF NATURE & ART
Balt., ca. 1830. 12mo. Orig. ptd. wraps., stained, backstrip worn & restitched. (SH. Mar.19; 326)   Schiller. £130

WONG, K. Chimin & Lien-Teh, Wu
- History of Chinese Medicine ... from Ancient Times to the Present Period. Tientsin, [1932]. 1st. Edn. Orig. cl., slightly soiled. From liby. of Dr. E. Ashworth Underwood. (S. Feb.23; 249)   McDowell. £60
- - Anr. Copy. Plts. stpd. on versos. Cl. From Brooklyn Academy of Medicine. (SG. Jan.29; 448) $100

WOOD, Aaron
- Sketches of Things & People in Indiana. Indianapolis, 1883. 1st. Edn. Sig. of A.G. Porter on title, a few MS. notations in text. Orig. ptd. wraps., upr. wrap. torn & reprd., erasure & slight soiling, title repeated in Porter's hand at top of title, MS. index lf. added, spine partially perished, boxed, cut sig. of J.B. Dillon laid in pocket in box. From liby. of William E. Wilson; the Littell copy. (SPB. Apr.29; 285) $400

WOOD, Anthony à
- Athenae Oxonienses. 1721. 2nd. Edn. 2 vols. Fo. Cont. cf., rebkd. (SH. Jan.30; 504)   Blundell. £50
- Historia et Antiquitates Universitatis Oxoniensis. Oxford, 1674. 2 pts. in 1 vol. Lge. fo. Some browning & soiling, a little dampstaining. Mod. cl., soiled. [Wing W3385] (S. Apr.6; 204)   Hendrickson. £50

WOOD, Arnold
- A Bibliography of the 'Complete Angler' ... N.Y., 1900. (120) numbered. 4to. Hf. vell., unc. Bkplt. of H.A. Ingraham. (SG. Dec.11; 154) $200

WOOD, Hugh
- Views in France, Switzerland, The Tyrol, & Italy. N.d. Ob. fo. Litho. title stained at corner. Cont. red hf. mor. gt., some light staining. (LC. Jun.18; 188)   £320

WOOD, John
- An Essay towards a Description of Bath. 1749. 2nd. Edn. 4 pts. in 2 vols. Cont. cf. gt., slightly worn. (SBA. Mar.4; 98)   Chesters. £70
- - Anr. Copy. 2 vols. Cf. (PJ. Jun.6 (80); 105)   £65
- Plans of Scottish Towns. Ill.:– T. Clerk, W. Murphy, & others. Edinb., 1818-28. Fo. No title or text. Cont. hf. roan. W.a.f. (C. Nov.6; 277)   Ludgrove. £2,000
- - Anr. Copy. 14 engraved plans partly hand-cold. in outl. Cont. hf. roan. (C. Jul.15; 116)   Tooley. £1,900
- - Anr. Copy. Fo. No title or text. Cont. hf. roan. W.a.f. (C. Nov.6; 278)   Traylen. £800

WOOD, John George
- Principal Rivers of Wales. 1813. 2 vols. Lge. 4to. Cf. gt. (P. Jan.22; 72)   Evans. £550
- - Anr. Copy. Some spotting. Cont. cf., recased. (TA. Jun.18; 259)   £525
- The Principles & Practice of Sketching Landscape Scenery from Nature. 1820. 3rd. Edn. 4 pts. in 1 vol. Ob. 4to. Plt. 2 in pt. IV with hand-cold. overslips, a few plt.-numbers & imprints cropped, sig. in title-margin. Cont. hf. russ., worn, covers & last plt. detchd. (S. Dec.9; 503)   Lancey. £80

WOOD, Lambert (Pseud.)
See–BOS or Bosch, Lambert van den 'Lambert Wood'

WOOD, Nicholas
- A Practical Treatise on Rail-Roads ... with Original Experiments, & Tables of the Comparative Value of Canals & Rail-Roads. 1825. 1st. Edn. Pages 95-98 misbnd. at p. 112, some foxing & offsetting, marginal tear in last lf. Hf. russ., very worn, upr. cover detchd., hf mor. case. From Honeyman Collection. (S. May 20; 3137)   Weinreb. £140
- Traité Pratique des Chemins de Fer. Brussels, [1834]. Hf. leath., orig. wraps. bnd. in. (R. Mar.31-Apr.4; 1167)   DM 1,400

WOOD, Robert
-The Ruins of Balbec. 1757. 1st. Edn. Fo. Cont. cf., worn, covers detchd. From Chetham's Liby., Manchester. (C. Nov.27; 410)   Wordie. £220
[-] - Anr. Copy. Title & some plts. browned or spotted. Cont. hf. cf., worn. L.P. (S. Sep.29; 188)   Maggs. £190
[-] - Anr. Copy. Plt. 41 partly detchd., occasional spotting. Cont. cf., spine gt., worn. (S. Sep.29; 187)   Weinreb. £100
[-] - Anr. Copy. Spotting & dampstaining. Cont. cf., very worn, covers detchd. (S. Dec.8; 231)   Elliott. £50
- The Ruins of Palmyra. 1753. 1st. Edn. Fo. Sm. tear in the folding plt. Cont. cf., worn, covers detchd. From Chetham's Liby., Manchester. (C. Nov.27; 411)   Taylor. £100
- - Anr. Copy. Cont. bds., backstrip defect. (TA. Jan.22; 368)   £94
[-] - Anr. Copy. Some plts. foxed. Cont. cf., gt., worn, covers loose. (S. Sep.29; 185)   Lester. £70
- The Ruins of Palmyra, otherwise Tedmor, in the Desert.–The Ruins of Balbec, otherwise Heliopolis in Coelosyria. 1753; 1757. L.P. 2 works in 1 vol. Lge. fo. 1st. work: double-p. plt. of Dawkins & Wood discovering Palmyra inserted, Abbé Barthelemy's 'Reflections' (1755), 8 pp., with plt., bnd. at end; 2nd. work: last plt. foxed. 19th. C. red mor., gt. by J. Clarke, broad floral borders, spine gt. in compartments, slightly worn. (S. Jun.22; 107)   Traylen. £420

WOOD, Samuel S. & William
- Catalogue of Books on Anatomy, Medicine, Surgery, Midwifery, Dentistry, Chemistry, Agriculture ... N.Y., 1848. 12mo. Ptd. wraps., lacks lr. wrap., worn, some foxing. (SG. Oct.2; 381) $230

WOOD, Silas
- A Sketch of the First Settlement of the Several Towns on Long Island. Ed.:– Alden J. Spooner. Brooklyn, 1865. Atlas fo. Mod. cl. (SG. Jun.11; 338) $130

- - Anr. Edn. Ed.:– Alden J. Spooner. Brooklyn, 1865. (30) numbered on L.P. Lge. 4to. Three-qtr. mor. (SG. Jun.11; 337) $100

WOOD, William
- New England's Prospect. 1639. 3rd. Edn. Woodcut map dtd. 1639. Mor. by Sangorski. From the collection of Eric Sexton. [STC 25959, Sabin 105076] (C. Apr.15; 56)   Burgess. £950

WOOD, William, F.R.S.
- A Complete Illustrated Catalogue ... of the Lepidopterous Insects of Great Britain. 1854. Cont. hf. mor., lacks spine, covers detchd. (CSK. Oct.10; 139)   £60
- Index Testaceologius. 1828. 2nd. Edn. 2 pts. in 1 vol. Cont. cf., worn, upr. hinge brkn. (S. May 5; 161)   Crete. £65
- - Anr. Edn. Ed.:– S. Hanley. L., 1856. Hf. mor. (GM. Apr.30; 685)   £85
- Zoography, or The Beauties of Nature Displayed. Ill.:– W. Daniell. L., 1807. 3 vols. Cont. diced cf., tooled gt. borders, with armorial motif in centre. (GM. Apr.30; 619)   £150
- - Anr. Edn. Ill.:– after W. Daniels. 1807. L.P. 3 vols. Cont. cf. gt. (P. Jul.30; 78) Bickersteth. £80

WOOD, William Charles Henry
- Select British Documents of the Canadian War of 1812. Toronto, Champlain Society, 1920-28. (530). 3 vols. in 4. Buckram. (SG. Feb.26; 333) $350

WOODALL, John
- The Surgeons Mate or a Treatise discovering faithfully ... 1617. 1st. Edn. 4to. Pagination jumps from 310 to 313, lacks 2 ll. of text, folding table largely torn away, last few ll. defect. in upr. section & roughly reprd. affecting text, some stains. New limp vell. with ties. Inscr. 'G. Lydall' on title, inscr. on verso with initials J.W. dtd. 1620. [STC 25962] (S. Jun.17; 901)   Joslen. £240

WOODBERRY, George E.
See–HAWTHORNE, Nathaniel–WOODBERRY, George E.

WOODCRAFT Magazine
N.Y., 1900-05. Vols. I-VI., & dupl. copies of vols. I & II. 12mo. Cl. (SG. Dec.11; 429) $100

WOODCUT (The), an Annual
Ed.:– H. Furst. 1927-30. Vols. 1-4 (all publd.). Facs., some cold. Bds., in d.-w.'s. (BS. Jun.11; 98)   £160
- - Anr. Copy. Nos. 1-4. 4to. Orig. cl.-bkd. bds. (SH. Jan.29; 64)   Bennett. £125
- - Anr. Copy. No. 1, 2 & 4. 4to. Orig. cl.-bkd. bds., d.-w.'s. (SH. Mar.27; 551)   Forster. £80

WOODFIN, Mrs.
[-] Northern Memoirs. N.d. 2 vols. 12mo. Slight dampstaining. Near cont. cf., jnts. worn. (CSK. May 8; 102)   £120

WOODS, John
- Two Years Residence ... in the Illinois Country ... L., 1822. 1st. Edn. Traces of blind-stp. & slight foxing on title. Mod. red hf. mor., marb. bds. & end-papers, gt. spine & borders. From liby. of William E. Wilson. (SPB. Apr.29; 287) $400

WOODS, Rev. Julian Edward Tenison
- Geological Observations in South Australia. 1862. 1st. Edn. Orig. cl. (SH. Jul.27; 12)   Hook. £50

WOODS, FOREST & LAND REVENUES
- 4th (5, 7, 13-18, 20-22, 24, 26, 28 to 36th) Report of the Commissioners; & 6 vol. of Reports from the Select Committee. 1823-58. Together in 29 vols. Fo. Disbnd., some soiled. (SH. Mar.5; 158)   Bunsei. £220

WOODVILLE, W.
See–NORRIS, R. & others

WOODVILLE, William
- Medical Botany. 1790. 1st. Edn. Vol. I (of 4). 4to. Cont. hf. cf., worn. (SH. Jun.4; 175)   Vitale. £130
- - Anr. Edn. Priv. Ptd. 1790-93. 1st. Edn. 3 vols. (lacks supp.). 4to. Lacks plt. 83 in vol. 2. Cont. tree cf., spines gt. W.a.f. (C. Nov.5; 180)   Schuster. £60
- - Anr. Edn. 1790-94. [1st. Edn.?]. 3 vols. & Supp. in 2 vols. 4to. MS. notes in text. Hf. mor., partly unc. (SKC. Feb.26; 1614)   £650
- - Anr. Copy. 4 vols., including supp. Sm. piece torn away from upr. outer edge of title-p. to vol. 3,

sm. tear in 1 lf., pen sigs. on title-pp. Qtr. leath. & marb. bds., rebkd. (CB. Dec.9; 127) Can. $2,800
– – **Anr. Edn.** Ed.:– W.J. Hooker & G. Spratt. 1832. 3rd. Edn. 5 vols. in 2. 4to. Slight spotting & offsetting. Mor., gt. by J. Clarke. (S. Jun.1; 251)
Cristiani. £1,000
– – **Anr. Copy.** 5 vols. 36 lithographs in vol. V (of 39?), plts. between 105 & 113 misnumbered, ending vol. II with 140 plts. but with plt. 181* in vol. III for correct total, advt. lf. in vol. V, lacks last blank in vol. IV, occasional spotting & light offsetting. Orig. cl., 4 spines defect. 6 covers detchd., worn. W.a.f. due to plt. variants. (S. Dec.3; 1179) *Litman.* £360

WOODWARD, Bernard Bolingbroke
– **The History of Wales.** 1853. Some foxing, mainly to margins. Cont. cf. (TA. Feb.19; 350)
£58
– **The History of Wales.–The Tourist in Wales.** Ill.:– W.H. Bartlett & others. L., & N.Y., 1853; ca. 1850's? 2 works in 3 vols. (2 + 1). 1st. work: minor foxing; 2nd. work: stained thro.-out. Unif. cont. hf. leath. (CB. Nov.12; 192) Can. $180

WOODWARD, Bernard Bolingbroke & others
– **A General History of Hampshire.** [1861-69]. 3 vols. 4to. Spotted, plts. on India paper. Cont. cf., gt., worn. (SH. Jun.4; 172) *Chernington.* £160

WOODWARD, George E. & Thompson, Edward G.
– **National Architect.** N.Y., Priv. ptd. [1869?]. 4to. Orig. cl. (CB. May 27; 219) Can. $260

WOODWARD, George Moutard
– **Eccentric Excursions . . .** Ill.:– Isaac Cruikshank. Ca. 1817. 4to. Red str.-grd. mor. gt. by Rivière. (S. Nov.24; 308) *Sawyer.* £190
[–] **Something Concerning Nobody.** 1814. 1st. Edn. Late 19th. C. lev. mor. by Rivière, gt. (S. Nov.24; 307) *Traylen.* £110

WOODWARD, John
– **An Essay Toward a Natural History of the Earth: & Terrestrial Bodies, Especially Minerals.** 1695. 1st. Edn. Cont. MS. note in upr. margin of imprimatur lf., stpd. monog. in lr. margin of title. Cont. vell. bds. From Honeyman Collection. [Wing W3510] (S. May 20; 3138) *Hill.* £140

WOODWARD, R.B. & J.D.S.
– **Natal Birds.** Pietermaritzburg, 1899. Orig. cl. (SSA. Nov.5; 153) R. 330
– – **Anr. Copy.** Cl. (VA. Jan.30; 550) R. 140
– – **Anr. Copy.** (VA. Jan.30; 549) R. 110

WOOLF, Virginia
– **Jacob's Room.** Hogarth Pr., 1922. 1st. Edn. Orig. cl. (SH. Dec.18; 325)
Bloomsbury Bookshop. £65
– **Monday or Tuesday.** Ill.:– Vanessa Bell. Hogarth Pr., 1921. 1st. Edn. Orig. cl.-bkd. decor. bds. (S. Jul.22; 347) *Hosain.* £85
– **Mrs. Dalloway.** Hogarth Pr., 1925. 1st. Edn. Orig. cl. (S. Jul.22; 348) *Hosain.* £85
– – **Anr. Copy.** Worn, unc. Inscr. to Cecil Beaton, with recipient's ownership inscr. inside lr. cover. (SH. Dec.19; 400) *House of Books.* £55
– **On Being Ill.** [L.], Hogarth Pr., 1930. (250) numbered. Hf. vell., d.-w. Sigd. (SG. Nov.13; 747)
$350
– **Orlando.** N.Y., 1928. 1st. Edn., (800) sigd. Orig. cl. (C. Feb.4; 323) *Basket & Day.* £190
– – **Anr. Edn.** N.Y., 1928. 1st. Edn. (861) numbered, sigd. Orig. cl. (S. Jul.22; 349)
Hosain. £150
– **A Room of One's Own.** Hogarth Pr., 1929. 1st. Engl. Edn. Orig. cl., d.-w. (S. Jul.22; 350)
Gal. Sq. Books. £50

WOOLLEY, Charles Leonard
*See–*LAWRENCE, Thomas Edward & Wooley, Charles Leonard

WOOLNOTH, W.
– **A Graphical Illustration of the Metropolitan Cathedral Church of Canterbury.** 1816. L.P. Fo. With 6 additional engraved plts. by I. Kip, some plts. foxed, some offset, sm. liby. stp. at lr. margin of ptd. title & other pp. Cont. str.-grd. mor., covers with alternate gt. & blind roll tool panels enclosing gt. vig., spine gt. in compartments. From the collection of Eric Sexton. (C. Apr.16; 386)
Taylor. £70

WOOSTER, David
– **Alpine Plants.** 1872. 1st. Edn. A few spots, lacks the 2nd. Series. Orig. cl. gt. (SBA. Jul.22; 68)
Archer. £50

– – **Anr. Edn.** 1872-74. 2 vols. 1 vol. spotted. Orig. cl. gt. (SKC. Feb.26; 1615) £85
– – **Anr. Edn.** 1874. 2nd. Edn. 2 vols. Cold. plts. Orig. pict. cl. gt. (SBA. Jul.23; 362)
Chesters. £160
· – **Anr. Copy.** Cl., loose. (S. Dec.3; 1180)
Elliot. £70

WORCESTER, Edward Somerset, Earl of
[–] **A Century of the Names & Scantlings of such Inventions, as at Present I can Call to Mind to have Tried & Perfected.** 1663. 1st. Edn. 12mo. Without 34 p. supp., lacks blanks A1 & E6, title very soiled & browned, some staining, a few rule-borders touched by binder. 18th. C. cf., spine chipped at head, red hf. mor. case. From Honeyman Collection. [Wing W3532] (S. May 20; 3139)
Weinreb. £50

WORDSWORTH, Christopher
– **Greece: Pictorial, Descriptive, & Historical.** 1844. 2nd Edn. 4to. Some spotting, steel engraved additional title. Cont. cf. (CSK. Feb.13; 191) £60
– – **Anr. Edn.** 1853. New Edn. 4to. Cont. mor., elab. gt., 'Fretherne House School' stpd. on upr. cover. (S. Nov.25; 552) *Drakatos.* £55
– – **Anr. Copy.** Later hf. mor. by W. Worsfold. (CSK. Oct.17; 165) £50
– – **Anr. Edn.** Ed.:– H.F. Tozer. L., 1882. New Edn. Cont. leath., gt., defect. (R. Oct.14-18; 1142)
DM 420

WORDSWORTH, William
– **A Decade of Years.** Hammersmith, Doves Pr., 1911. (12) on vell. Sm. 4to. Lev. mor., gt.-ruled border & panel, spine in 6 compartments, 5 raised bands, gt.-panel., sigd. by Doves Bindery, 1912, qtr. mor. s.-c. (CNY. May 22; 394) $2,000
– – **Anr. Edn.** Doves Pr., 1911. (200) on paper. 4to. Orig. limp vell., unc., cl. folder & s.-c. (S. Jul.31; 61) *Foyles.* £150
– – **Anr. Copy.** Orig. vell. MS. inscr. by Cobden-Sanderson. (CSK. Aug.22; 208) £90
[–] **The Little Maid & the Gentleman; or, We are Seven.** York, [1820?]. 1st. Separate Edn. 24mo. Orig. ptd. wraps., mor. folding case. From the Prescott Collection. (CNY. Feb.6; 340) $250
– **Poems.** Ed.:– Matthew Arnold. L., 1898. 16mo. Lev., gt. dentelles, by Hatchards, spine faded. Fore-e. pntg. (SG. Mar.19; 193) $225
– – **Anr. Edn.** Ed.:– T. Sturge Moore. Vale Pr., 1902. (300). Orig. buckram. unc. With letterpress bkplt. of Joseph Manuel Andreini & his pict. bkplt. with wood-engraved design by Lucien Pissarro. (S. Jul.14; 50) *Quaritch.* £70
– **The Prelude.** Hammersmith, Doves Pr., 1915. (10) on vell. Sm. 4to. Gt.-decor. lev. mor., spine in 6 compartments, 5 raised bands, sigd. 'Rivière & Son . . . 1931', & pencilled diagram worksheet, with instructions, sigd. by John Barrymore July 1931. (CNY. May 22; 406) $2,500
– – **Anr. Edn.** Doves Pr., 1915. (155). Orig. vell. MS. inscr. by Cobden-Sanderson. (CSK. Aug.22; 209) £90
– **The River Duddon.** L., 1820. 1st. Edn. Lf. M6 a cancel, advt. after title, some foxing. Cont. red hf. mor., spine gt. Fore-e. pntg. (S. Dec.18; 190)
$275
– **Complete Poetical Works.** Boston, 1910. (500), L.P. 10 vols. Mor. gt., elab. gt. spines. (SPB. May 6; 356) $3,250

WORDSWORTH, William & Coleridge, Samuel Taylor
[–] **Lyrical Ballads, with a few other poems.** 1798. 1st. Edn., 2nd. Iss. Advts., title spotted. Cf., gt. by Rivière. (S. Jun.23; 413) *Hosain Books.* £1,000
[–] – **Anr. Copy.** Sm. reprd. tear to title-p., some blank fore-margins slightly damaged by damp. Orig. bds., spine reprd., hf. mor. gt. s.-c., unc. From the Prescott Collection. (CNY. Feb.6; 341)
$2,200
[–] – **Anr. Copy.** 16mo. Blank pt. of title & following lf. stained. Cont. mott. cf., rebkd., gt.-decor. spine laid down, mor. s.-c. (SG. May 14; 227) $600

WORLD, The
Ed.:– 'Adam FitzAdam' (i.e. Edward Moore). L., 1753-56. 4 vols., 208 iss. (lacks iss. no. 66). Sm. fo. Lacks last lf. of index, tears, repairs, some browning & spotting, stitching loose. Cont. sheep-bkd. bds. (SPB. May 29; 307) $150

WORLD DISPLAYED, The
L., 1762-93. Various Edns. 20 vols. in 10. 18mo. Cont. cf., spines gt., worn. (SG. Apr.30; 325)
$325

– – **Anr. Edn.** Dublin, 1779. 6th. Edn. 20 vols. 12mo. Cont. cf. (SH. Mar.19; 328)
Quaritch. £170
– – **Anr. Edn.** Dublin, 1814-15. 9 vols. (of 10), lacks vol. IX. Sig. on titles, 2 plts. detchd., some offsetting to text, browning & soiling. Cont. cf., spines gt., worn. W.a.f. [Sabin 105485] (S. Sep.29; 170) *Lamm.* £100

WORLD IN MINIATURE
*See–*SHOBERL, Frederic

WORLD OF FASHION
Jan.-Dec. 1828. Vol. 5. 4to. Cf. gt. (P. Nov.13; 272) *Kestel.* £130
– – **Anr. Edn.** 1828-30. Vols. 5-7 only. 4to. 129 hand-cold. plts. only, lacks some ll. of text, some loose, a few tears. Cont. cl.-bkd. bds., worn. (SH. May 21; 138) *Cumming.* £270
– – **Anr. Edn.** 1829-35. Vols. 6 & 12. Disbnd. (SH. Jul.9; 216) *Ayres.* £440
[–] – **Anr. Edn.** 1831-33. 4to. Some spotting & browning. Hf. mor. W.a.f. (CSK. Jan.30; 91)
£180
– – **Anr. Edn.** 1835-51. Vols. 12-34 only, in 2 vols. 4to. 256 plts. only, a few ll. soiled & spotted. Cont. hf. cf. (SH. Jan.29; 313) *Fletcher.* £230
– – **Anr. Edn.** 1837-39. 3 vols. 4to. Hf. cf., spines defect. (P. Apr.9; 273) *Fairburn.* £160

WORLD'S COLUMBIAN EXPOSITION:
– **Art Portfolio.** Ill.:– Childe Hassam. [Chic.]. [1892]. Ob. 4to. Each plt. identified in MS by architect & sculptor in neat hand at bottom margins. Pict. wraps., stabbed & tied, light cover-soiling. Inscr. 'To Jack . . . a votive offering from 'his E', F.B.D.' (PNY. Mar.26; 17) $220

WORLIDGE, John
– **Systema Agriculturae; The Mystery of Husbandry Discovered.** 1675. 2nd. Edn. Sm. fo. Engraved title & explanation lf. both re-laid, margins browned. Recent qtr. cf. (TA. May 21; 527) £70
– – **Anr. Edn.** 1681. 3rd. Edn. 3 pts. in 1 vol. Fo. Soiled. Cont. cf., worn. [Wing 3600] (TA. Jun.18; 19) £120

WORLIDGE, Thomas
– **A Select Collection of Drawings from Curious Antique Gems.** 1768. [1st. Edn.?]. Slight foxing. 19th. C. str.-grd. mor., gt. (S. Apr.7; 463)
Drury. £90
– – **Anr. Copy.** 2 vols. Plts. including the head of Medusa (1 lacking?), some marginal spotting, without text. Early 19th. C. red str.-grd. mor., soiled. (CSK. Oct.3; 234) £75
– – **Anr. Copy.** Occasional light foxing. 19th. C. mor. gt. (S. Jul.27; 216) *Ricklefs.* £60
– – **Anr. Copy.** With the 2 extra plts. of Medusa & Hercules & the Lion, some upr. margins corroded by inked numbers. Later hf. mor., rebkd. in buckram. (SG. Dec.4; 376) $140

WORM, Ole
– **Danicorum Monumentorum Libri Sex.–Regum Daniae Series Duplex.** Copen., 1643; 1642. 2 works in 1 vol. Fo. Cont. cf., jnt. reprd. From the collection of Eric Sexton. (C. Apr.15; 57)
Quaritch. £130
– **Museum Wormianum.** Leiden, 1655. 1st. Edn. Fo. 19th. C. hf. mor., spine worn. From Chetham's Liby., Manchester. (C. Nov.27; 412) *Junk.* £100
– – **Anr. Copy.** Lacks port., dampstained, 1 or 2 short tears & sm. holes. Cont. mott. cf., worn. (S. Dec.2; 660) *Lindahall.* £80

WORSLEY, Sir Richard
– **The History of the Isle of Wight.** 1781. 1st. Edn. 4to. Mid 19th. C. mor. gt., gt. roll-tooled borders on sides, spine gt. (C. Feb.25; 66) *Crowe.* £220
[–] – **Anr. Copy.** Some plts. folding & mntd. on guards. Cont. diced cf., covers detchd. (CSK. Mar.20; 91) £170
– – **Anr. Copy.** Old russ., jnts. worn. From liby. of Baron Dimsdale. (MMB. Oct.8; 7) £95
– – **Anr. Copy.** Folding map torn, partly reprd. Cont. hf. cf., rebkd., worn. (C. May 20; 189)
Warner. £55
– **Museum Worsleyanum or a Collection of Antique Basso Relievos . . . with Views of Places in the Levant taken on the spot.** Ill.:– after A. Cardon. 1794-[1803]. [1st. Edn.?] L.P. copy. 2 vols. Fo. With the letter to the University of Camb. ptd. on vell. at end of vol. I, offset to some ll. facing plts., minor browning. Cont. red str.-grd. mor., gt. 'Greek-key' panel to covers, spines gt. with raised bands. (C. Feb.25; 213) *Sbisa.* £500

WORSLEY, Sir Richard -contd.

[-] - **Anr. Copy.** 2 plts. in vol. 2 cropped, Cambridge Letter & 1 lf. detchd. Cont. diced russ. by Comte de Caumont, elab. gt., spines defect., worn., arms of Earl of Chesterfield on covers. (S. Sep.29; 215) *Weinreb.* £260

[-] - **Anr. Copy.** Cont. str.-grd. red mor. gt., spines gt. Pres. Copy to Richard Bull, 2 MS. letters to Bull loosely inserted. (S. Nov.25; 439) *Weinreb.* £240

[-] - **Anr. Copy.** 1 plt. in vol. II cropped, titles & some ll. foxed, some offsetting to text. 19th. C. mor., elab. gt. (S. Sep.29; 216) *Weinreb.* £220

- - **Anr. Edn.** 1824. 2nd. Edn. 2 vols. Fo. Cont. hf. roan, worn, lr. cover of vol. II detchd. (S. Jun.22; 155) *Duran.* £160

WORTHINGTON, A.M.

- **A Study of Splashes.** 1908. 1st. Edn. Cl. The Andrade copy, with sig. & bkplt.: from Honeyman Collection. (S. May 20; 3140) *Offenbacher.* £85

WORTLEY, Lady Emmeline Stuart

- **Travels in the United States etc. During 1849 & 1850.** L., 1851. 1st. Edn. 3 vols. Orig. blind-stpd. cl., gt. spine. From liby. of William E. Wilson. [Sabin 93220] (SPB. Apr.29; 288) $175

WOTTON, Thomas

[-] **The English Baronetage.** 1741. 1st. Edn. 5 vols. Lacks hf.-titles & final blanks in vols. 1 & 3. Mod. hf. Mor. (S. Nov.24; 310) *Smith.* £110

WRANGHAM, Francis
See-PAPWORTH, John B. & others

WREDE, Friedrich W. von

- **Lebensbilder aus den Vereinigten Staaten von Nordamerika und Texas . . .** 1844. 1st. Edn. Orig. marb. bds., spine worn. (PNY. Mar.26; 315) $375

WREN, Christopher

- **Bicentenary Memorial Volume.** 1923. 4to. Orig. cl. (SH. Jun.18; 100) *Weiner.* £50

- **Life & Works of Sir Christopher Wren.** [Strand & N.Y.], Essex House Pr., [1903]. (250) numbered from 1750 Edn. Sm. fo. Orig. cl., spine label slighty chipped. (CB. May 27; 220) *Can.* $120

WREN, Matthew (contributor)
See-CAMBRIDGE UNIVERSITY

WREN SOCIETY (The)
Oxford, 1924-43. Vols. 1-20. 4to. Orig. cl. (P. May 14; 325) *Sims & Reed.* £200

WRIGHT, Edward

[-] **Sketches in Bedlam or Characteristic Traits of Insanity as Displayed in the Cases of 140 Patients of Both Sexes now, or Recently, Confined in New Bethlem.** 1823. 1st. Edn. Cf., top of spine torn. (S. Jun.17; 903) *Lawson.* £120

WRIGHT, Edward

- **Some observations Made in Travelling through France, Italy, etc., in the Years 1720-22.** 1730. 2 vols. in 1. 4to. Recent cf. (TA. Feb.19; 45) £50

- - **Anr. Edn.** 1764. 2nd. Edn. 2 vols. 4to. Cont. cf., 1 cover detchd. (SH. Nov.6; 265) *Duran.* £70

- - **Anr. Copy.** Upr. cover detchd. (CSK. Feb.6; 26) £50

- - **Anr. Copy.** 2 vols. 4to. 1 map loose. Orig. cf. (DS. May 22; 821) Pts. 22,000

WRIGHT, Fanny

- **Views of Society & Manners in America, in a Series of Letters during 1818, 1819, & 1820.** N.Y., 1821. 1st. Amer. Edn. Writing on title. Later hf. linen, ex-liby. (SG. Mar.5; 479) $120

WRIGHT, Frank Lloyd

- **An Autobiography.** L., N.Y. & Toronto. 1932. 1st. Edn. Square 8vo. Extra-ill. with 23 mntd. & identified orig. photographs of houses by F.L. Wright taken by Arthur Wallace, ca. 1920's, also 17 additional orig. photographs by Wallace preserved loosely in an envelope, also 8 mntd. photo reproductions of Wright's work mntd. in with the orig. photos. Orig. cl., d.-w. slightly soiled & chipped, slightly shaken. (CB. May 27; 224) *Can.* $400

- **Drawings for a living Architecture.** N.Y., 1959. 1st. Edn. Ob. fo. Orig. cl. & pict. d.-w. (CB. May 27; 226) *Can.* $525

- **The Japanese Print: An Interpretation.** Chic., 1912. L.P. 1st. Edn., on Rice Paper. 4pp. with pencil corrections to text apparently in Wright's hand. Orig. pict. bds. Pres. copy to William Norman Guthrie. (PNY. Dec.3; 383) $725

WRIGHT, Rev. George Newnham

- **China.** L., ca. 1840. 4 vols. in 2. 4to. Hf. cf. (P. Jun.11; 257) *Campbell.* £180

- - **Anr. Edn.** Ill.:- Thomas Allom. 1843. 4to. Cont. hf. cf. gt. (SBA. Dec.16; 70) *Philatelist.* £400

- - **Anr. Copy.** 4 vols. in 2. Cont. mor., gt. & blind borders on sides, gt. spines. (C. Nov.5; 181) *Larnark Jones.* £170

- - **Anr. Copy.** 4 vols. in 1. Lacks ptd. titles, 1 engraved title & 84 plts. only, a few margins slightly spotted. Cont. mor. gt. (SBA. Mar.4; 132) *Holiday.* £155

- - **Anr. Edn.** Ill.:- from orig. sketches by Thomas Allom. [1843]. Vols. III & IV only bnd. together. 4to. Slight foxing thro.-out. Cont. hf. cf., gt. decor. spine. (TA. Sep.18; 297) £70

- - **Anr. Edn.** Ill.:- Thomas Allom. Ca. 1860. 4 vols. in 2. 4to. 120 (of 124) engrs. Recent hf. cf. (TA. Feb.19; 671) £150

- - **Anr. Edn.** Ill.:- Thomas Allom. N.d. 4 vols. in 2. 4to. Spotting. Cont. hf. mor. (CSK. Jul.31; 78) £200

- - **Anr. Copy.** 4 vols. Slightly soiled. Slightly worn. (SH. Nov.7; 333) *K. Books.* £180

- - **Anr. Copy.** 2 vols. Some dampstaining, maps hand-cold. in outl. Orig. cl. gt. (TA. May 21; 72) £140

- - **Anr. Copy.** 1 engraved title & 85 plts. only, lacks prelims. & some ll. of text. Cont. mor., gt. (SH. Mar.5; 2) *Campbell.* £100

- - **Anr. Copy.** 4 vols. in 2. Some foxing, tears, marginal stains. Mor. gt. (SPB. May 29; 445) $275

- **The Chinese Empire Illustrated.** Ill.:- Thomas Allom. L., ca. 1845. 4 vols. in 2. 4to. Partly soiled. Cont. hf. leath. (R. Oct.14-18; 1750) DM 600

- - **Anr. Edn.** N.d. 2 vols. 4to. A few ll. slightly spotted. Cont. hf. mor. (SH. Nov.7; 335) *Beddow.* £240

- **France Illustrated.** Ca. 1840. 4 vols. in 2. 4to. 141 engraved plts. only. Cont. hf. mor. gt., slightly worn. (SBA. Mar.4; 132a) *Spencer.* £125

- - **Anr. Edn.** Ill.:- Thomas Allom. [1845-47]. 1st. Edn. 4 vols., including supp. 4to. Some plts. foxed. Cont. maroon mor., gt., spines gt., 2 spines worn, 1 cover detchd. (S. Sep.29; 207) *Bailey.* £130

- - **Anr. Copy.** 3 vols. in 1. 92 (of 93) plts., lacks Angouleme plt., lacks supp., ptd. titles & index ll., some plts. foxed. Cont. maroon mor., spine gt., covers detchd. (S. Sep.29; 206) *Bailey.* £90

- - **Anr. Edn.** Ill.:- Thomas Allom. N.d. 4 vols. 4to. Some ll. spotted. Cont. mor., gt. (SH. Nov.6; 185) *Loeb.* £150

- - **Anr. Copy.** Some slight spotting. Cont. hf. cf. (CSK. Jan.22; 21) £130

- **Ireland Illustrated.** Ill.:- Petrie, Bartlett & others. 1831. 4to. Mor.-bkd. cl. (PD. May 20; 158) £70

- - **Anr. Copy.** Some ll. spotted or stained. Cont. hf. cf., worn. (SBA. May 27; 389) *Bonar Law.* £55

- - **Anr. Edn.** Ill.:- after William Henry Barlett & others. 1833. 4to. Occasional spotting. Cont. cf. (CSK. Sep.26; 113) £75

- - **Anr. Edn.** N.d. 4to. Hf. mor. (P. Mar.12; 222) *Donovan.* £95

- **The Rhine, Italy & Greece.** L., 1841. 2 vols. in 1. 4to. Lacks 2 steel engrs. Cont. hf. leath. (R. Oct.14-18; 2480) DM 950

- **The Shores & Islands of the Mediterranean.** [1839]. 4to. Orig. mor. gt., rebkd. (TA. May 21; 69) £80

- - **Anr. Edn.** [1840]. 4to. Cont. mor. gt. (SD. Feb.4; 220) £60

- - **Anr. Copy.** Soiled, slightly stained in outer margin. Cont. leath., lacks upr. cover. (R. Mar.31-Apr.4; 2684) DM 420

- - **Anr. Edn.** Ca. 1843. 4to. Some plts. dtd. 1841-43. Cont. hf. mor., spine gt. (S. Nov.25; 555) *Nash.* £120

- - **Anr. Edn.** N.d. 4to. Slight spotting. Cont. hf. mor. (CSK. Mar.27; 17) £85

- - **Anr. Copy.** Some plts. spotted. Cont. cf., gt., upr. cover detchd. (SH. Mar.5; 162) *Pittsillidis.* £75

- - **Anr. Copy.** Some spotting. Cont. hf. mor. (CSK. May 1; 116) £65

- - **Anr. Copy.** No bdg. (DS. May 22; 796) Pts. 20,000

See-ALLOM, Thomas & Wright, George Newnham

WRIGHT, George Newnham & Buckingham, L.F.A.

- **Belgium, the Rhine, Italy & Greece.** L., 1850. 2 vols. only. 4to. Cont. leath., gt., spine torn. (R. Oct.14-18; 1943) DM 500

- - **Anr. Edn.** L., ca. 1850. 2 vols. Slightly browned. Cont. hf. leath. (R. Oct.14-18; 2481) DM 1,300

- - **Anr. Edn.** L., n.d. 2 vols. 4to. 151 (of 152) plts., vol. II stained, foxing. Hf. cf., very worn. (SPB. May 29; 444) $225

- - **Anr. Copy.** Vol. 1 (of 2). Title with cut out stp., bkd., slightly soiled. Cont. hf. leath. (HK. Nov.18-21; 1433) DM 700

WRIGHT, Rev. George Newnham [& C.H. Timperley]

- **Gallery of Engravings.** 1844-45. 3 vols. 4to. Some foxing. Cont. hf. mor. (TA. Sep.18; 144) £95

- - **Anr. Edn.** 1844-46. Cont. gt. decor. mor. (TA. Jan.22; 153) £65

- - **Anr. Edn.** N.d. 3 vols. 4to. Some plts. spotted. Cont. mor., gt. (SH. Mar.6; 585) *Questor.* £50

WRIGHT, Harold James Lean

- **Etchings & Drypoints of Sir William Russell Flint.** Colnaghi. 1957. (135) numbered, (20) specially bnd. & sigd. by artist. 4to. Lacks loose crayon figure study. Orig. red mor. gt., slightly marked. Sigd. drypoint frontis. (S. Jul.31; 222) *Marks.* £110

WRIGHT, James

- **The History & Antiquities of the County of Rutland.** 1684. Fo. Title mntd. on stub, some marginal tears reprd. Mod. hf. mor. From the collection of Eric Sexton. [Wing W3696] (C. Apr.16; 387) *Temperley.* £110

- - **Anr. Copy.** Cont. cf., slightly worn, upr. cover detchd. (SBA. Oct.22; 506) *Quaritch.* £90

- - **Anr. Copy.** Fo. Some stains. Hf. cf., worn. (S. Dec.9; 422) *Crowe.* £70

WRIGHT, John, Horticulturist

- **The Fruit Grower's Guide.** [1891-94]. 6 vols. 4to. Cl. (S. Dec.3; 1181) *Litman.* £140

- - **Anr. Copy.** Orig. cl. (SH. Jul.9; 202) *Midwest.* £110

- - **Anr. Edn.** [1896-1901]. 3 vols. in 6. (SH. Jun.25; 139) *Kouchak.* £85

- - **Anr. Edn.** N.d. 3 vols. in 6. 4to. Orig. pict. cl. (SD. Feb.4; 268) £120

- - **Anr. Copy.** 3 vols. 2 conjugate ll. detchd. without loss, some foxing. Old hf. mor., some wear. (KH. Mar.24; 433) *Aus.* $150

WRIGHT, Rev. John

- **Spiritual Songs for Children: or, Poems on several subjects & Occasions.** 1793. 12mo. Woodcut frontis. detchd. Orig. patterned bds., lacks backstrip. (CSK. Jun.26; 94) £120

WRIGHT, Jonathan

- **The Nose & Throat in Medical History.** N.p., ca. 1910? 1st. Edn. Cl. From Brooklyn Academy of Medicine. (SG. Jan.29; 451) $120

WRIGHT, Joseph

- **The English Dialect Dictionary.** 1898-1905. 6 vols. 4to. Orig. cl. (SH. Jan.30; 505) *Linden.* £110

- - **Anr. Copy.** 30 pts. in 18. Fo. D.-w.'s as iss., some torn. (CE. Jul.9; 170) £65

WRIGHT, Lewis

- **The Illustrated Book of Poultry.** 1880. 4to. Orig. cl. gt., recased preserving orig. spine. (SKC. Feb.26; 1616) £100

- - **Anr. Edn.** 1890. Hf. mor. gt. (P. Dec.11; 6) *Demetzy.* £80

- - **Anr. Edn.** Ill.:- J.W. Ludlow. N.d. 4to. A few plts. detchd., tissue guard adhering to 2, a lf. of text to anr. with loss of letters. Orig. cl., worn. (CSK. Dec.12; 121) £75

WRIGHT, M.

- **An Account of His Excellence Roger Earl of Castlemaine's Embassy to His Holiness Innocent XI.** Ill.:- Westerhout, port. by White. 1688. 1st. Edn. in Engl. Fo. Cont. spr. cf. gt., slightly worn, in mor. s.-c. with arms. (BS. Jun.11; 207) £320

WRIGHT, Magnus, W. & F. von & Lönnberg, E.

- **Svenska Faglar.** Stockholm, 1924-29. 3 vols. Fo. 356 cold. litho. ornithological plts. (of 364, lacks 4 plts. in vol. 1 & 4 in vol. 2). Orig. decor. pig, heads of spines worn. W.a.f. (S. Jun.23; 308) *Marks Ltd.* £260

- – Anr. Copy. Orig. decor. pig, worn. (S. Dec.3; 1185) *W. & W.* £220

WRIGHT, Thomas, of Durham
- Clavis Coelestis. Being the Explication of a Diagram, Entitled a Synopsis of the Universe: or, the Visible World Epitomized. Priv. ptd., 1742. 1st. Edn. 4to. A few short tears in folds, etc., of plts., some soiling & dampstaining. Cont. cf., gt., rebkd. preserving old spine, worn. Signet liby. copy, with arms on covers; from Honeyman Collection; included with lot is copy of facs. edn., 1967, prepared from this copy. (S. May 20; 3142) *Zeitlin & Verbrugge.* £2,800
- An Original Theory or New Hypothesis of the Universe. Priv. ptd., 1750. 1st. Edn. 4to. Plts. 21 & 22 repeated, but no plt. numbered 23, plt. 19 inverted, lr. inner blank corners wormed at beginning, some offsetting onto text. Cont. cf., worn, upr. cover detchd. From Honeyman Collection. (S. May 20; 3143) *Quaritch.* £850
- The Use of the Globes: or, the General Doctrine of the Sphere. 1740. 1st. Edn. Advts., marginal repair to title. Cont. cf., gt., jnts. reprd., new label, sig. of Will. Cooper on fly-lf. From Honeyman Collection. (S. May 20; 3141) *Wynter.* £140

WRIGHT, Thomas, M.A., F.S.A.
- The History of Ireland. Ill.:– after H. Warren. L., ca. 1855. 3 vols. 4to. Hf. cf. (SG. Mar.19; 217) $130
- The History & Topography of the County of Essex. Ill.:– after W.H. Bartlett. 1831-35. 2 vols. 4to. 98 plts. (of 100) on India paper, map spotted. Cont. mor.-bkd. cl., worn. (SH. Jun.11; 158) *Mathews.* £80
- The Picturesque Beauties of Great Britain – Essex. Ill.:– after W.H. Bartlett. 1834. 4to. Some spotting. Cont. hf. mor., rebkd. (TA. Feb.19; 353) £160
- Universal Pronouncing Dictionary . . . [1852-56]. 6 vols. including atlas. 4to. Orig. hf. roan, corners & spines worn, 1 cover detchd. (S. Mar.16; 194) *Hyde Park Books.* £520
- – Anr. Copy. 5 vols. Maps hand-cold. in outl. Orig. hf. cf. gt., a little worn. W.a.f. (S. Jun.29; 175) *Faupel.* £480
- – Anr. Edn. Ill.:– J. Rapkin [maps only]. N.d. 24 vols. only (vol. 8 lacking). Maps mntd. on guards & hand-cold. in outl., occasional slight spotting. Orig. cl. W.a.f. (CSK. Sep.19; 129) £280

WRIGHT, Thomas, M.A., F.S.A., & Evans, Robert
- Works of James Gillray the Caricaturist. Ill.:– James Gillray. Ca. 1862. 4to. Extra ill. with approx. 60 etched plts. by Gillray, most hand cold., some double-p. Mor., orig. wraps bnd. in by Rivière. (SH. Apr.9; 10) *Neale.* £320
- – Anr. Edn. Ill.:– James Gillray. L., ca. 1873. 4to. Gt.-ornamental mor. with red inlays, by Hammond binders. Armorial bkplt. of Cornelius Paine. (PNY. Oct.1; 238) $100

WRIGHT, Thomas, M.A., F.S.A. & Longueville Jones, T.
- Memorials of Cambridge. Ill.:– Le Keux. 1847. 2 vols. Some spotting. Orig. cl., spines faded & slightly torn. W.a.f. (CSK. Oct.24; 60) £130

WRIGHT, Thomas, M.A., F.S.A.–TYRELL, H.
- The History of France.–The History of the Present War with Russia. L., ca. 1860. 1 vol. 4to. Plts. only for 2 works, together in 1 vol. Cont. hf. leath. (R. Oct.14-18; 1852) DM 650

WRIGHT, Thomas, Theatrical Machinist
- The Female Vertuoso's. 1693. 1st. Edn. 4to. Catchwords & sigs. frequently cropped, slight foxing thro.-out. Mor. by Sangorski. [Wing W3711] (C. Nov.19; 171) *Franks.* £60

WRIGHT, Wilbur
- Experiments & Observations on Soaring Flight; Some Aeronautical Experiments. Chic., Dec. 1901-Aug. 1903. Offprints from Journal of Western Society of Engineers (Vol VI, no. 6, & vol. VIII, no. 4). Orig. wraps., 1 upr. cover with stp. of North Western University liby., Evanston, Illinois, buckram folder. (S. Dec.2; 792) *Dawson.* £720
- Some Aeronautical Experiments. Wash., 1903. Offprint from Smithsonian Report for 1902. Orig. ptd. wraps., cl. case. From Honeyman Collection. (S. May 20; 3144) *Phillips.* £180

WRONSKI, St[anislaus], artist
- 'Scenery Around Lake Bikal Road in Eastern Siberia, 1873-4'. N.p., n.d. Ob. tall fo. Each plt.

sigd., on mntd., pol. bd. Mor., title stpd. in gt. at upr. cover. (PNY. Mar.26; 288a) $1,300

WROTH, Lawrence C.
- A History of the Printed Book. Ltd. Edns. Cl., 1938. 4to. Cl., ex-liby., lacks end-paper. (SG. Oct.2; 383) $150
- A History of Printing in Colonial Maryland. Balt., 1922. (500). Rebnd. in buckram. (SG. Mar.26; 477) $150
See–DOLPHIN, The

WROTH, W.
- Catalogue of the Greek Coins of Crete & the Aegean Islands. 1886. Orig. cl. (SH. Mar.6; 473) *Spink.* £120
- Catalogue of the Greek Coins of the Troas, Aeolis, & Lesbos. 1894. Orig. cl. (SH. Mar.6; 474) *Laskaris.* £100

WULFF, Lee
- The Atlantic Salmon N.Y., 1958. De Luxe 1st. Edn. (200) numbered, with extra sigd. water-colour. 4to. Mor.-bkd. marb. bds., s.-c. (SG. Oct.16; 560) $275
- Leaping Silver: Words & Pictures on the Atlantic Salmon. N.Y., [1940]. De Luxe 1st. Edn., (540) numbered, sigd. 4to. Mor.-bkd. cl., s.-c. (SG. Oct.16; 559) $220

WU LIEN-TEH
See–WONG, K. Chimin & Wu Lien-Teh

WUNDT, Wilhelm
- Grundzüge der Physiologischen Psychologie. Leipzig, 1874. 1st. Compl. Edn. Slight discolouration. Cont. bds., worn. Bkplt. of Herbert McLean Evans; from Honeyman Collection (S. May 20; 3145) *Offenbacher.* £350

WURSUNG, Christoph
- General Practice of Physicke contayning all Inward & Outward Parts of the Body . . . Trans.:– Jacob Mosan. 1605. Fo. Lacks 3D8 (1 lf. of index), 3D1 & last lf. of index in photostat facs., title cut round & mntd. with loss of 1st. word & damage to a few letters, following lf. inlaid, following few ll. stained & reprd. in outer lr. corners, short tear to inner margin G2, tear & hole in 2 ll. of index with loss of text, some marginal repairs & stains to last few ll. of index affecting some letters. New cf. [STC 25864] (S. Jun.17; 893) *Wood.* £70

WURZBACH, Alfred von
- Niederländisches Künstler-Lexicon. Vienna & Leipzig, 1906-11. 3 vols., including additions. Numerous sig. facs. in text. Cont. hf. vell. (S. Oct.21; 486) *Beres.* £60

WYATT, Claude W.
- British Birds. 1894-99. 2 vols. in 1. A few ll. slightly soiled. Cont. hf. mor., gt. spine. (SH. Oct.9; 257) *Way.* £400
See–SHARPE, Richard Bowdler & Wyatt, Claude W.

WYATT, Sir Matthew Digby
- The Art of Illuminating. 1860. 4to. Orig. cl. rebkd. (P. Oct.2; 118) *Roberts.* £60
- The Industrial Arts of the Nineteenth Century. 1851. 5 orig. parts. Fo. 2 chromolitho. titles & 155 plts. only (of 158), some ll. soiled & spotted, a few tears. Orig. cl.-bkd. bds., worn, loose. (SH. Jan.29; 315) *Edwards.* £120
- – Anr. Edn. 1851-53. 2 vols. Fo. Vol. 1 lacks chromolitho. title. Cont. mor. gt. (C. May 20; 65) *Elstein.* £210
- – Anr. Copy. Soiled, a few ll. loose. Cont. hf. mor. (SH. Jan.29; 316) *Edwards.* £110
- – Anr. Copy. With only 1 ptd. title, some plts. slightly spotted. Orig. hf. mor. gt. (SBA. May 27; 267) *National Library of Wales.* £80
- – Anr. Edn. L., 1853. 2 vols. Fo. Title-p. to vol. 2 bnd. in vol. 1 & slightly torn. Hf. mor. (SSA. Nov.5; 346) *R.* 300
- Specimens of Ornamental Art Workmanship. 1852. Fo. Cont. hf. mor. (SH. Jul.23; 311) *Quaritch.* £80

WYATVILLE, Sir Jeffry
- Illustrations of Windsor Castle. 1841. 2 vols. in 1. Fo. 3 extra engrs. inserted, some ll. spotted. Cont. hf. mor. (SH. Nov.6; 182) *Quaritch.* £120

WYCHERLEY, William
- Miscellany Poems. Ill.:– after Lely (frontis.). 1704. 1st. Edn., 1st. Iss. Fo. Cont. panel. cf., rebkd. L.P. Autograph Pres. Copy, with 2 inscrs., to Anthony Englefeild & Dr. Charlton, the latter

deleted by author. (C. Nov.20; 282) *Maggs.* £400
- – Anr. Copy. Cont. panel. cf. (C. Apr.1; 240) *Lawson.* £260

WYETH, Andrew
- [Works.] Ed.:– Richard Merryman (text.) Boston, 1968. 1st. Edn. Ob. tall fo. Ptd. two-tone cl., d.-w. (PNY. Mar.4; 279) $240

WYLD, James
- A General Atlas. Ill.:– N.R. Hewitt. Edinb., 1819. Sm. fo. Orig. qtr. cf., detchd. (SG. May 21; 144) $400
- – Anr. Edn. Ill.:– N.R. Hewitt. Edinb., ca. 1820. Sm. fo. Engraved vig. title, frontis., table & 44 maps, hand-cold. in outl., 7 text engrs., 4 hand-cold. Cont. hf. cf., worn. W.a.f. (S. Mar.31; 266) *Martin.* £130
- – Anr. Edn. Edinb., [1825?] Sm. fo. (357mm. × 265mm.). Maps hand-cold. in outl. Cont. qtr. russ., worn. W.a.f. (S. Jun.29; 14) *Jeffery.* £100
- – Anr. Edn. Edinb., ca. 1830. 4to. 43 (of 44) engraved maps. Cont. cl. (TA. May 21; 86) £80
- – Anr. Edn. N.d. 4to. Occasional staining. Cf.-bkd. bds., worn (CSK. Jun.5; 24) £100
- A New General Atlas of Modern Geography. [1842]. Fo. 44 engraved maps only (of 58), 8 additional maps including 4 charts of China by James Horsburgh 1823-40 & map of Poland by William Faden 1799 bnd. in, some torn or soiled. Cont. hf. cf., worn & disbnd. W.a.f. (CSK. May 8; 47) £110
- – Anr. Edn. Ca. 1850. Lge. fo. 59 (of 61) engraved maps, hand-cold. in outl., 1 comparative plt. torn, lacks maps of Britain & Scotland, World map & some others soiled & torn, title, contents lf. & celestial ll. stained. Cont. hf. mor., lacks spine, covers detchd. (S. Apr.7; 475) *Remington.* £480

WYLIE, D.
See–PYNE, William Henry & Wylie, D. & others

WYLIE, Elinor
- Mr. Hodge & Mr. Hazard. N.Y., 1928. 1st. Edn., (145) numbered, on L.P., sigd. Silver-decor. buckram, unc., unopened, boxed. (SG. Jun.4; 506) $110

WYLIE, Rev. J.A.
- The History of Protestantism. N.d. 3 vols. Hf. mor. & cl. (HSS. Apr.24; 4) £50

WYLLY, Col. H.C.
- XVth [The King's] Hussars, 1759-1913. 1914. (250) L.P. 4to. Mor. gt. (C. Jul.22; 201) *Browning.* £80

WYN, Ellis
See–BORROW, George 'Ellis Wyn'

WYNDHAM, Henry Penruddocke
- A Tour through Monmouthshire & Wales. Salisbury, 1781. 2nd. Edn. 4to. Slight offsetting. Cont. cf., slightly worn, rebkd. (SBA. Oct.22; 717) *Morgan.* £120

WYNNE, Giustinia, Countess of Rosenberg
- Alticchiero. Ill.:– G. de Pian & A. Sandi. Padua, 1787. 4to. Circular owner's stp. on title. Cont. marb. paper wraps., worn, in buckram s.-c., unc. From the collection of John A. Saks. (C. Jun.10; 261) *Weinreb.* £180

WYRLEY, William
- The True Use of Armorie. 1592. 1st. Edn. Sm. 4to. 19th. C. mor. gt. Aldenham House bkplt., lately in the collection of Eric Sexton. [STC 26062] (C. Apr.15; 200b) *Maggs.* £190

WYSE, F.
- Die Vereinigten Staaten von Nord-Amerika. Ed.:– E. Amthor. Leipzig, 1846. 3 vols. Cont. hf. leath. (R. Oct.14-18; 1739) DM 900

WYSS, Johann David
- The Family Robinson Crusoe. Trans.:– [William Godwin?]. Ill.:– Springsguth & J. Dadley after H. Corbould. L., 1814. 1st. Edn. in Engl., 1st. Iss. 2 vols. 12mo. Some ll. slightly spotted in vol. 1, cont. owner's inscr. on 1st. paste-down. Orig. bds., spines slightly defect., qtr. mor. gt. s.-c., unc. From the Prescott Collection. (CNY. Feb.6; 342) $4,000
- Le Robinson Suisse. Ed.:– Charles Nodier. Trans.:– Elise Voiart. Ill.:– after Lemercier. Paris, 1841. Sewed, box. (HD. June.10; 221) Frs. 1,900

WYTFLIET, Cornelius
- Descriptionis Ptolemaicae Augmentum. Douay, 1603. 3rd. Edn. Sm. fo. Lightly browned, 1 map bnd. inverted. Leath. gt., gold fillets. [Sabin 105698] (R. Mar.31-Apr.4; 2295) DM 11,000

WYTSMAN, P. & others
- Genera Avium. Ed.:– R. Bowdler Sharpe & others. Brussels, 1905-14. 26 pts. in 1 vol. Fo. Mod. qtr. cf., orig. wraps. bnd. in. (S. Jun.1; 252) Hill. £220

XAVIER, Hieronymus
- Historia Christi Persice Conscripta (–Historia S. Petri Persice conscripta, Rudimenta Linguae Persicae). Ed.:– L. de Dieu. Leiden, 1639. 3 pts. in 1 vol. Sm. 4to. Some browning & spotting, 1st. title with inscr. 'E Bibliothecâ Theologicâ Edinensi' & with liby. stp. Old mott. cf., gt., worn. (S. Apr.29; 469) Goldschmidt. £220
- – Anr. Copy. Stp. of the Bibliothèque de L'Arsenal on title & at end, slight browning without the 'Rudimenta Linguae Persicae'. Cont. vell. bds. soiled, s.-c. (S. Apr.29; 470) Hosain's Books. £180

XENOPHON of Ephesus
- Cyrupaedia, or, the Institution & Life of Cyrus, King of the Persians. Trans.:– Philemon Holland. 1632. 4to. Cont. spr. cf. (SH. Nov.7; 450) Diba. £160
- – Anr. Edn. Ill.:– Loyd Haberly. Shakes. Hd. Pr., 1936. (150) numbered. 4to. Mor., centrepiece & corners composed of mor. onlays, tooled with arabesque designs, s.-c. (S. Jul.31; 131) Foyles. £520
- The Ephesian Story. Ill.:– Eric Fraser. Gold. Cock. Pr., 1957. (300), this number 12 of 75 specially bnd. 4to. With an additional 7 plts. loosely inserted. Orig. mor., s.-c. (CSK. Oct.31; 71) £55
- Oeuvres . . . Trans.:– Citoyen Gail. Paris, An III. 4to. Cont. spr. cf., gt. fillet around covers, smooth decor. spine, cipher P.B. in gold letters on spine. Josephine's copy. (HD. Jun.24; 125) Frs. 3,450
- Quae extant Opera . . . Ed.:– Henrici Stephan. [Geneva], 1581. 2nd. Edn. 2 pts. in 1 vol. Fo. Latin & Greek text, lacks last blank. 17th. C. cf., spine gt., bkplt. of John Evelyn. (S. Dec.8; 85) Fletcher. £85
- – Anr. Edn. Ed.:– J. Leunclavius, Aemilius Portius. Frankfurt, 1596 [1594]. Latest complete Leunclavius Edn. 2 vols. in 1. Fo. Cont. pig-bkd. blind-tooled with centre stp. & date 1619, slightly soiled. (R. Oct.14-18; 170) DM 800
- – Anr. Edn. Paris, 1625. Fo. Cont. red mor., gt. border on sides, crowned arms of Henry II d'Orléans, Duc de Longueville in centre, spine gt. tooled in compartments. (S. Mar.17; 265) Maggs. £160

XYLANDER, Guilielmus
- Opuscula Mathematica. Heidelberg, 1577. 1st. Edn. Sm. 4to. Bds. From Honeyman Collection. (S. May 20; 3146) Quaritch. £170

YAARI, Abraham
- Bibliography of the Passover Haggadah. Jerusalem, 1960. Fo. Linen, d.-w. (slightly soiled). (SG. Mar.26; 480) $150

YAD [Poison]
Ed.:– [A.M. Petrov]. St. Petersb., 1905. No. 1 (all publd.). 4to. Unbnd. (SH. Feb.5; 189) Lempert. £80
- – Anr. Copy. (SH. Feb.5; 149) Lempert. £60

YAKOV Ben Asher
- Arba'ah Turim. Augsburg, 1540. 7th. Edn. 4 vols. Sm. fo. Lacks hf.-title to pt. 2, margins reprd. with occasional loss of words, lr. corner of last lf. torn with loss of 2 line of poetry, lightly stained. Mod. vell. (SPB. May 11; 213) $3,500
- Peirush Ha'torah. Constantinople, 1514. 1st. Edn. 4to. 71 ll., 32-mntd., tears, staining, some words underlined. Mod. buckram. (SPB. May 11; 90) $6,500
- Tur-Orach Chaim & Yore De'ah. Venice, 1522-23. 5th. Edn. 2 pts. in 2 vols. Sm. fo. 1st. & last ll. of pt. 1 in facs., stained, reprd., cropped. Vell. by M. Katz, boxed. (SPB. May 11; 212) $2,100

YAKOV Joseph Ben Meir Sofer, of Elsas
- Even Israel. Metz, 1766. Pt. 1. 4to. Some staining & soiling. Decor. wraps., lacks backing. (SPB. May 11; 242) $140

YAKOV YITZHAK Ha'levi of Lublin ('The Seer')
- Zikaron Zot. Warsaw, 1869. 1st. Edn. Slight staining. Hf. cl. (S. Nov.18; 349) Maggs. £220
- Zot Zikaron. Zolkiev, 1865. 1st. Edn. 4to. With notes by Joseph Weiss. Bds. (S. Nov.18; 351) Rock. £85

YAKOV YITZHAK Ha'levi of Lublin ['The Seer']-CHAIM of Mohilev
- Divrei Emet.–Shaar Ha'tefila. Sudzilkow, 1835; 1836. 2nd. Edns. 2 works in 1 vol., 2nd. on blue paper. 4to. Bds. (S. Nov.18; 346) Stern. £70

YAROSLAVSKY, Aleksandr
- Svoloch' Moskva [Swine Moscow]. Moscow, 1922. Orig. wraps., slightly soiled. (SH. Feb.6; 552) Quaritch. £85

YARRELL, William
- A History of British Birds. 1843. L.P. 3 vols. Hf. mor., spines gt., by F. Bedford. (C. Mar.18; 121) Bosworth. £400
- – Anr. Copy. Str.-grd. mor., spines gt. (SKC. Jul.28; 2432) £60
- – Anr. Edn. L., 1843; 1845; 1856. L.P. Iss. 4 vols. including 2 Supplements. Mor., gt. borders, spines gt., gt. dentelles. Robert Hoe bkplt. (SG. Oct.9; 258) $400
- – Anr. Edn. 1845. 3 vols. Cf. gt. (P. May 14; 116) Payne. £50
- – Anr. Edn. 1856. 3rd. Edn. 3 vols. Cont. mor. gt. (C. May 20; 259) Wheldon & Wesley. £50
- A History of British Birds.–A History of British Fishes. L., 1856; 1859. 3rd. Edns. Together 5 vols. (3 & 2). Mor. gt., gt. spines with tools in compartments, by Hayday. (CNY. May 22; 228) $120
- On the Growth of the Salmon in Fresh Water. L., 1839. 1st. Edn. Ob. 4to. Leath.-bkd. cl., worn. (SG. Oct.16; 562) $100

YARROW, Joseph
- Love at First Sight, or the Wit of a Woman; A Ballad Opera, (Trick upon trick or the Vintner out-witted, a farce). York, 1742. 1st. Edn. Slightly spotted thro.-out. Old hf. russ., upr. cover detchd. (C. Apr.1; 242) Hannas. £160

YASHIRO, Yukio
- Sandro Botticelli. 1925. (600) numbered. 3 vols. 4to. Orig. cl., soiled. (SH. Jan.29; 164) Subunso. £95
- – Anr. Copy. Cl. gt., d.-w.'s. (P. Jan.22; 260) Thorp. £55

YATES, Richard
- An Illustration of the Monastic History & Antiquities of the Town & Abbey of St. Edmund's Bury. Ill.:– after William Yates. 1805. 4to. 1 plt. torn at inner margin, browning, 4pp. prospectus for Blomfield's Norfolk at back. Mod. bds., old label pasted down on upr. cover. (CSK. Apr.3; 22) £75
- – Anr. Copy. Spotted. Cont. hf. cf., rebkd. (SH. Nov. 6; 60) Frost. £55

YEATS, Grant David
- Observations on the Claims of the Moderns to some Discoveries in Chemistry & Physiology. Priv. ptd. 1798. Hf. cf., gt. Pres. copy to Earl Spencer. (S. Jun.16; 565) Maggs. £120

YEATS, William Butler
- The Cat & the Moon, & Certain Poems. Dublin, Cuala Pr. 1924. (500). Cl.-bkd. bds., unc. & unopened. Inscr. (SG. Nov.13; 300) $300
- The Celtic Twilight. Ill.:– J.B. Yeats. 1893. 1st. Edn. Orig. cl., unc. (S. Jul.22; 361) Figgis. £60
- Collected Works. Shakes. Hd. Pr. 1908. 8 vols. Vell.-bkd. cl., stained, lr. cover of vol. 1 soiled. (PD. May 20; 167) £50
- – Anr. Copy. Hf. mor., some slight scuffing. (SPB. May 6; 357) $1,400
- Dramatis Personae. Cuala Pr., 1935. 1st. Edn. (400). Orig. linen-bkd. bds., unc. (S. Jul.22; 82) Thomson. £50
- The Dublin University Review. Dublin, 1886. Cf.-bkd. bds. (S. Jul.22; 358) Thomson. £130
- Essays.–Plays in prose & verse.–Later Poems. –Early Poems & Stories. N.Y., 1924; 1924; 1924; 1925. (250) sigd. by author. 4 vols. Unif. cl.-bkd. bds., d.-w.'s, slightly torn. (C. Feb.4; 315) Edrich. £210
- The Hour Glass & Other Plays. 1904. (100) numbered on Japan vell. Ptd. wraps. over bds., wraps. slightly stained at upr. edge, unc. Inscr. (SG. Nov.13; 755) $130
- Irish Fairy & Folk Tales. Ill.:– James Torrance. L. & N.Y., [1892]. 1st. Edn. 12mo. 7 ll. of advts.

at end. Pict. cl. Inscr., bkplt. of John Quinn laid in. (SG. Nov.13; 753) $250
- The King's Threshold. N.Y., priv. ptd. 1904. 1st. Edn., (100) sigd. Orig. bds., s-c. (SH. Dec.19; 535) Edrich. £160
- Last Poems & Two Plays. Dublin, Cuala Pr. 1939. [500]. Cl.-bkd. bds., unc. & unopened. Sigd. by Elizabeth Yeats under colophon, & inscr. by George Yeats on 1st. fly-lf. (SG. Nov.13; 764) $150
- Mosada. Dublin, Cuala Pr., 1943. (50) numbered, sigd. by George B. Yeats. Orig. wraps., unc., unopened. (S. Jul.22; 382) Quaritch. £170
- New Poems. Cuala Pr., 1938. 1st. Edn. (450). Orig. linen-bkd. bds., unc. (S. Jul.22; 85) Subunso. £60
- Poems. 1949. (375) numbered, sigd. by author. 2 vols. Orig. cl., s.-c. (CSK. Apr.3; 80) £150
- – Anr. Edn. Ed.:– Peter Allt & Russell K. Alspach. N.Y., 1957. [825] numbered. Tall 8vo. 2-tone cl., boxed. With lf. containing Yeat's sig. (SG. Nov.13; 765) $120
- The Poetical Works. N.Y., 1913-09. 2 vols. Hf.-title & title show browning from newspaper clippings. Gt.-pict. cl. Sigd. pres. copy. (PNY. Mar.4; 280) $350
- Seven Poems & a Fragment. Dundrum, Cuala Pr., 1922. 1st. Edn., (500). Cl.-bkd. bds (SG. Jun.4; 510) $100
- Stories of Michael Robartes & his Friends. Cuala Pr., 1931. 1st. Edn. (450). Orig. linen-bkd. bds., unc. (S. Jul.22; 81) Thomson. £55
- Three Things. Ill.:– Gilbert Spencer. 1929. 1st. Edn., (500), unnumbered. Ariel Poem no.18. Orig. bds., unc. Sigd. (SH. Dec.18; 327) White. £50
- The Tower. Ill.:– Thomas Sturge Moore. 1928. 1st. Engl. Edn. Orig. pict. cl. gt., d.-w., unc. (SH. Dec.18; 326) Quaritch. £80
- – Anr. Copy. Orig. pict. cl. gt. by T. Sturge Moore, unc., unopened, d.-w. (S. Jul.22; 381) Foley. £60
- – Anr. Copy. (S. Jul.22; 368) Treadwell. £50
- The Trembling of the Veil. Priv. ptd., 1922. 1st. Edn. (1,000) numbered, sigd. Orig. bds., unc. (S. Jul.22; 367) Thomson. £70
- The Wanderings of Oisin . . . 1889. 1st. Edn. (500). Orig. cl., unc. (S. Jul.22; 360) Thomson. £210
- The Winding Stair . . . 1933. 1st. Edn. 'Advance Review Copy. Special Notice' loosely inserted. Orig. pict. cl. by Sturge Moore, spine gt., d.-w. worn, lacks back. (S. Jul.22; 369) Maggs. £50

YEATS, William Butler & others
- The Book of the Rhymers' Club.– The Second Book of the Rhymers' Club. 1892; 1894. 1st. work (50) on L.P., 2nd. work; (70). Together 2 vols. sm. 4to. Orig. parch.-bkd. bds., unc., 2nd. unopened (S. Jul.22; 378) Sawyer. £120

YEDAYAH OF BEZIERS
- Bechinat Olam. Ed.:– Shimshon Morpurgo & Yakov Frances. Venice, 1703-04. 12th. Edn. 4to. Slight staining. Bds. (S. Nov.18; 474) Kornbluth. £60

YEHUDA Ben Shmuel Chasid–RECANATI, Menachem
- Sefer Chasidim.–Ta'amei Ha'mitzvot. Basle, 1580-81; 1581. 2nd. Edns. 2 works in 1 vol. Sm. 4to. Staining, browning, repairs. Sheep, torn, worming. (SPB. May 11; 216) $1,200

YEHUDA LEIB BEN MOSHE Chazan
- Shirei Yehuda. Amst., 1697. 4to. In Hebrew & old Yiddish, slight staining & worming. Hf. vell. (S. Nov.18; 476) Elberg. £160

YEHUDA LEIB Ha'cohen of Hanipolye
- Or Ha'ganuz-Ve'zot Liyehuda. Lvov, 1866. 1st. Edn. 2 pts. in 1 vol. 4to. Hf. cl. (S. Nov.18; 355) James. £70

YEHUDA LEIB of Zakilkow
- Likutei Maharil. [Lvov?], 1862. 1st. Edn. 4to. Hf. cl. (S. Nov.18; 356) Maggs. £85

YEHUDA Loew Ben Bezalei
- Tiferet Israel. Venice, 1599. 1st. Edn. Fo. Lightly stained. Cf.-bkd. bds. (SPB. May 11; 218) $800

YELLOW BOOK, The, an Illustrated Quarterly
Ill.:– Aubrey Beardsley & others. 1894-97. 13 vols. 4to. Orig. pict. cl. (SH. Mar.26; 52) Maggs. £270
- – Anr. Copy. (S. Jul.31; 181) Quaritch. £200
- – Anr. Copy. Orig. cl., some vols. slightly soiled. (CSK. Aug.1; 163) £150

- - **Anr. Copy.** Orig. pict. cl., unc. (SH. Mar.26; 53) *Jones.* £130
- - **Anr. Copy.** A few light dampstains. (CSK. Jul.24; 116) £85
- - **Anr. Copy.** Some marginal soiling. (CSK. Mar.13; 143) £70
- - **Anr. Copy.** Pict. cl., mostly unopened. (PNY. Mar.26; 354) $700
- - **Anr. Copy.** Minor occasional soiling. (PNY. Dec.3; 386) $400
- - **Anr. Copy.** Sm. 4to. Slight browning. Orig. cl., some wear & soiling. (SPB. Jul.28; 462) $250
- - **Anr. Copy.** 2 spines with sm. tears, lightly browned. (H. Dec.9/10; 1960) DM 1,400

YERRINTON, J.M.W.
- **Report of the Case of Geo. C. Hersey, indicted for Murder** ... Boston, 1862. 1st. Edn. Cl. (SG. Jun.11; 279) $120

YETTS, W. Perceval
- **The George Eumorfopoulos Collection Catalogue of Chinese & Corean Bronzes, Sculpture, (etc.).** 1932. (590), this copy unnumbered. Vol. 3 only. Fo. Orig. three-qtr. cl., unc. (SKC. Feb.26; 1487) £150

YITZHAK, of Corbill
- **Amudei Golah, Sefer Mitzvot Katan.** Constantinople, [1510]. 1st. Edn. Sm. 4to. Extensive glosses in 16th. C. Sefardi cursive Rabbinic script, tears, repairs, corners cropped, owners' sigs. on title. Blind-tooled leath., rebkd., worming. (SPB. May 11; 92) $7,500

YITZHAK Bar Sheshet Barfat
- **She'eilot U'teshuvot.** Riva di Trento, 1559. 2nd. Edn. Sm. 4to. Last 4 ll. of register in 16th. C. MS., stained, repairs, worming. Mod. vell., end-paper detchd. Bkplt. of Samuel Dresner. (SPB. May 11; 219) $600

YITZHAK Ben Meir, of Duren
- **Shaarei Dura.** Constantinople, 1553. 4th. Edn. 4to. Without title, worming towards end affecting text & colophon, staining. Hf. leath., very worn, cover detchd. (SPB. May 11; 91) $3,500

YITZHAK EISIK of Zidachev
- **Likutei Torah Ve'Hashass.** Lvov, Munkacs, Lvov, Marmoresch-Szigat, 1877; 1833; 1889; 1892. 1st. Edns. 4 vols. (lacks vol. III). 4to. Varied bdgs. (S. Nov.18; 357) *Maggs.* £70

YITZHAK, Isaac, of Koretz
See–PINCHAS, Shapiro, of Koretz & Yitzhak, Isaac, of Koretz

YONGE, Charlotte Mary
[-] **The Instructive Picture Book, or Lessons from the Vegetable World.** Edinb., 1857. Fo. Text spotted. Orig. pict. bds., worn. (SKC. Feb.26; 1617) £80
[-] - **Anr. Edn.** Edinb., 1858. Fo. Orig. pict. bds., slightly soiled, spine slightly torn. (SKC. Dec.4; 1533) £60
- **The Victorian Half Century.** L., 1886. 12mo. Cl., brown-spotted. Inscr. on fly-lf. 'Victoria R & I, Jan.16-1887', & below, sig. of F.L. Calder, A.L.s. by Sir Henry F. Ponsonby (Victoria's private secretary) to Miss Calder, with orig. envelope in his hand. (SG. Feb.12; 57) $140

YORK, Philip, Earl of Hardwicke & others
- **Athenian Letters** ... 1810. 3rd. Edn. 2 vols. 4to. Slight browning, map torn along fold. Cont. diced cf., gt., slightly soiled, fly-lf. in vol. I with sig. 'C. Yorke.' (S. Apr.7; 414) *Thorp.* £50

YORKE, James
- **The Union of Honour.** 1641. 1st. Edn. Fo. 18th. C. cf., rebkd., buckram s.-c. From the collection of Eric Sexton. (C. Apr.15; 200c) *Heraldry Today.* £65

YORKE, Philip, of Erthig
- **The Royal Tribes of Wales.** Wrexham, 1799. 4to. Offsetting onto text. Cont. mor., gt. (S. Dec.9; 409) *Maggs.* £75

YORKSHIRE NUMISMATIC SOCIETY
- **Transactions.** Hull etc., 1915-66. Vols. 1-3, New Series vols. 1-2 pt. 2, in 9 vols. 1st. series in cont. cl., others in orig. wraps. (SH. Mar.6; 476) *Seaby.* £58

YORKSHIRE PARISH REGISTER SOCIETY
- **Publications.** 1899-1979. Vols. 1-142 (lacks vols. 132 & 133). Cont. hf. mor. or cl., & orig. wraps. (SH. Nov.6; 40) *K. Books.* £300

YOSY, A.
- **Switzerland.** 1815. [1st. Edn.?]. 2 vols. Hf. cf., worn, spine defect. (CE. Jul.9; 234) £950
- - **Anr. Copy.** 2 vols. in 1. Hf. mor., brkn., upr. jnt. crudely reprd. (BS. Jun.11; 410) £660

YOUNG, Arthur
[-] **The Farmer's Guide in Hiring & Stocking Farms.** 1770. 1st. Edn. 2 vols. Orig. bds., spines slightly torn, unc. (SBA. Mar.4; 100) *Way.* £85
- **The Farmer's Guide.–The Farmer's Tour through the East of England.** 1770; 1771. 1st. Edns. 2 vols.; 4 vols. 2nd. work: slight marginal worming in vol. 2. Unif. cf. gt. (SBA. Jul.23; 690) *Subunso.* £130
- **The Farmer's Tour through the East of England.** 1771. 4 vols. Cf. (O. Jun.3; 113) £100
[-] **Political Essays concerning the Present State of the British Empire.** 1772. 1st. Edn. 4to. Slight browning, front free endpaper sigd. 'James Grant 1772'. Cont. spr. cf. [Sabin, vol. 29, p. 228] (S. Jan.26; 258) *Traylen.* £95
[-] **Rural Oeconomy.** 1770. 1st. Edn. Cont. cf. (P. Jul.30; 299) *Walford.* £95
[-] **A Six Months Tour through the North of England.** 1770. [1st. Edn.?]. 4 vols. Cont. cf. (CSK. Sep.26; 118) £100
- - **Anr. Copy.** Cf. gt. rebkd. (P. Oct.2; 76) *Park.* £95
[-] **Six Weeks Tour through the Southern Counties of England & Wales.** 1768. 1st. Edn. Cont. cf. (S. Dec.3; 1189) *Mathews.* £110
- - **Anr. Edn.** 1769. Cf. gt. (P. Sep.11; 74) *Walford.* £70
- **A Tour in Ireland.** 1780. 1st. Edn. 4to. Cont. hf. cf. From the collection of Eric Sexton. (C. Apr.16; 388) *Crowe.* £160
- **Travels, During the Years 1787, 1788 & 1789 ... with a View of Ascertaining the Cultivation, Wealth, Resources ... of the Kingdom of France.** Bury St. Edmunds, 1792-94. 1st. Edn. (Vol.I), 2nd. Edn. 2 vols. 4to. 1 map with short tears. Cont. cf. (S. Apr.7; 494) *Morton-Smith.* £110
- - **Anr. Edn.** Bury St. Edmunds, 1794. 1st. Edn. vol. 1, 2nd. Edn. vol. 2. 2 vols. 4to. Slight browning. Cont. mott. cf., worn, covers detchd. (S. Sep.29; 86) *Subunso.* £60

YOUNG, Edward
[-] **The Complaint & the Consolation.** Glasgow, 1776. 2 vols. in 1. 12mo. Cont. vell. gt., covers with medallion ink drawings, gt.-key pattern borders, gt. lattice-pattern spine, silk linings, str.-grd. mor. s.-c., in the style of Edwards of Halifax. With fore-e. pntg.; from the Prescott Collection. (CNY. Feb.6; 113) $800
- - **Anr. Edn.** L., 1795. New Edn. Cont. red str.-grd. mor. gt., spine worn. Fore-e. pntg.; from the liby. of Zola E. Harvey. (SG. Mar.19; 194) $220
- - **Anr. Edn.** Ill.:– William Blake. L., 1797. [1st Edn.?]. Fo. 19th C. hf. mor., spine gt. (S. Nov.24; 30) *Robinson.* £900
- - **Anr. Copy.** Three-qtr. lev., raised bands, by Rivière. (SG. Oct.9; 35) $1,600

YOUNG, George, 1777-1848
- **A History of Whitby & Streoneshalh Abbey.** Whitby, 1817. 1st. Edn., L.P. 2 vols. Extra ill. with 14 etched plts., 7 hand-cold., & 2 folding maps. Orig. bds., spines torn, unc. 3 A.L.s. loosely inserted (from the author). (C. Nov.6; 345) *Burton.* £190

YOUNG, George, 1777-1848 & Bird, John
- **Geological Survey of the Yorkshire Coast.** Whitby, 1822. 1st. Edn. 4to. Slight offsetting in text. Cont. hf. cf., some wear. (S. May 5; 149) *Quaritch.* £70

YOUNG, George
- **A Treatise on Opium Founded upon Practical Observations.** 1753. 1st. Edn. Advt. lf. Cont. cf. (S. Jun.17; 904) *Bickersteth.* £55

YOUNG, George
See–CHARLTON, Lionel–YOUNG, George

YOUNG, John
- **A Series of Designs, for Shop Fronts, Porticoes, & Entrances to Buildings.** 1843. 1st. Edn. 4to. Some spotting. Mod. hf. cf. (S. Jun.22; 109) *Traylen.* £130

YOUNG, John, of Halifax, N.S.
- **The Letters of Agricola on the Principles of Vegetation & Tillage.** Halifax, 1822. Some ll. loose, some staining & browning. Orig. paper bds., loose. (CB. Sep.24; 280) *Can.* $100

YOUNG, Richard
[-] **The Drunkard's Character, or a True Drunkard with such Sinnes as Raigne in him ... Together with Compleat Armour Against Evill Society ...** 1638. 1st. Edn. Cont. owner's inscr. on title, slight browning & soiling, a little worming scarcely affecting text, lacks 3A2. Cont. cf., rebkd., slightly worn. From liby. of Andrée L. Simon. [NSTC 26111] (S. May 18; 208) *Matthews.* £100
See–BROWNE, Hablot Knight & Young, Robert

YOUNG, Sidney
- **The Annals of the Barber-Surgeons of London.** 1890. [1st. Edn.?]. 4to. Hf. mor. Pres. copy to J.C.S. Benham, who painted his port. (S. Jun.17; 906) *Canale.* £80
- - **Anr. Copy.** Rubber-stp. on verso of plts. From Brooklyn Academy of Medicine. (SG. Jan.29; 454) $225

YOUNG, Thomas, 1773-1829, M.D., F.R.S.
- **De Corporis Humani Viribus Conservatricibus Dissertatio.** Gottingen, 1796. Liby. stp. on title. New cl. (S. Dec.2; 662) *Rota.* £95
- **A Course of Lectures on Natural Philosophy & the Mechanical Arts.** 1807. 1st. Edn. 2 vols. 4to. Some plts. in vol. II with p. directions at upr. right-hand corner cropped. Cont. hf. cf., rebkd. preserving old spines with crest at foot, slightly worn. From Honeyman Collection. (S. May 20; 3147) *Barchas Library.* £350
See–BINION, Samuel Augustus–YOUNG, Thomas

YOUNG, Maj. William
- **The Old Closes & Streets of Glasgow.** Ill.:– Annan. Glasgow, 1900. Fo. Orig. cl. gt. with city arms. (PG. Dec.12; 110) £250

YOUNG ALBERT, THE ROSCIUS
1811. 2nd. Edn. 12mo. 7 aquatinted cut-out figures & 1 head (of 3, normal head & that of Falstaff supplied in facs.), all hand-cold., lacks the 2 hats. Orig. ptd. wraps., s.-c. reprd. (SH. Mar.19; 63) *Reisler.* £300

YOUNG ANGLER, Naturalist, & Pigeon & Rabbit Fancier ...
L., 1860. 1st. Edn. 12mo. Gt.-decor. cl. (SG. Oct.16; 566) $100

YOUNGER, John
- **On River Angling for Salmon & Trout.** Edinb., 1840. 1st. Edn. 16mo. Cl. (SG. Oct.16; 569) $260

YOUTHFUL RECREATIONS
Phila., ca. 1810. Orig. wraps., covers loose, fitted case. (SH. Mar.19; 330) *Maggs.* £75

YSAMBRACE, Sir
Ed.:– F.S. Ellis. Kelms. Pr., 1897. (350). Orig. holland-bkd. bds., unc. (SH. Feb.19; 11) *George's.* £130

YURKUN, Yu.
- **Durnaya kompaniya [Bad Company].** Ill.:– Yu Annenkov. Petrograd, 1917. Plts. in 2 states, some hand-cold. Orig. wraps. by Yu. Annenkov. (SH. Feb.6; 553) *Hall.* £100

YUVENAL
Ed.:– [A.F. Domontovich]. St. Petersb., 1906. No.1. Fo. Unbnd. (SH. Feb.5; 150) *Lempert.* £60

ZABAGLIA, Nicolo
- **Castelli, e Ponti ... con la Descrizione del Trasporto dell' Obelisco Vaticano, e di altri del Cavaliere Domenico Fontana.** Ill.:– Girolamo Rossi after P.L. Ghezzi. Rome, 1743. 1st. Edn. Lge. fo. Some browning & spotting, sm. tear in text to plt. 2, unnumbered plt. of design by Tomasso Albertini. Cont. cf., elab. panel. in gt., some wear. Stp. of Empress Marie Louise; from Honeyman Collection. (S. May 20; 3149) *Elstein.* £1,400
- - **Anr. Copy.** Some margins lightly stained. 19th, C. hf. vell. (SI. Dec.4; 617) Lire 2,600,000

ZABIYAKA [Squabbler]
Ed.:– [L.M. Zuzerovich-Klebansky]. St. Petersb., 1905-06. No. 1, 2nd. Year, no. 1-3. 4to. & fo. Unbnd. (SH. Feb.6; 151) *De la Casa.* £60

ZACH, Fr. von (Ed.)
See–MONATLICHE CORRESPONDENZ ZUR BEFORDERUNG DER ERD–UND HIMMEL-SKUNDE

ZACUTO, Moshe
- **Shuda De'dayanei.** Mantua, 1678. Sm. 4to. Stained, cropped, slight worming. Cl.-bkd. Bkplt.

ZACUTO, Moshe – Shuda De'dayanei. -contd.
of Rabbi Nachum David Freidman of Sadagur.
(SPB. May 11; 220) $1,300

ZAEHNSDORF, Joseph W.
– Art of Bookbinding. 1880. (50), L.P. Qtr. mor.
(P. May 14; 15) *Tallerman.* £100
– – Anr. Edn. 1880. 1st. Edn. Orig. cl., soiled.
(SH. Jan.29; 66) *De Simon.* £70
– – Anr. Copy. Slight browning. (CSK.
Jun.19; 144) £50
– – Anr. Edn. 1890. Some ll. soiled. Orig. cl.
(CSK. May 29; 40) £75

ZAHN, Joannes
– Specula Physico-Mathematico-Historica
Notibalium ac Mirabilium Sciendorum. Ill.:– G.C.
Eimmart. Nuremb., 1696. 1st. Edn. 3 vols. in 1.
Fo. 40 (of 55) plts. & maps, 15 (of 16) double-p.
tables, stain in lr. margins at end, some browning
& slight soiling, a few ll. sprung. Cont. cf., very
worn, red hf. mor. case. W.a.f.; from Honeyman
Collection. (S. May 20; 3150) *Franks.* £300

ZAKHAROV-MENSKY, N.N.
– Chernaya rosa [Black Rose]. Moscow, 1917.
Orig. wraps. by E. Buchinsky. (SH. Feb.6; 554)
Quaritch. £100

ZALP [Volley]
Ed.:– [P.V. Bebutov]. St. Petersb., 1906. No. 1.
Fo. Unbnd. (SH. Feb.5; 152) *Lempert.* £60

ZAMBONI, Baldassare
– Memorie Intorno alle Pubbliche Fabbriche piu
Insigni dells Citta di Brescia. Ill.:– P. Beceni & F.
Zucchi. Brescia, 1778. Fo. Cont. paper bds.,
soiled, unc. From the collection of John A. Saks.
(C. Jun.10; 262) *Weinreb.* £320

ZAMORANO, Rodrigo
– Cronologia y Reportorio de la Razon de los
Tiempos. Seville, 1594. Sm. 4to. Some browning
& staining, last lf. reprd. affecting 1 word, piece
missing from lr. margin of P4 affecting a few
letters, a few other marginal repairs & tears. 19th.
C. cf., blind-stps. on covers & bkplt. of William
Stirling. From Honeyman Collection. (S. May
20; 3151) *Hughes.* £160

ZAMOYSKI, Stefan
See–BOBINSKI, Capt. Kazimierz & Zamoyski,
Stefan

ZAMYATIN, Evg.
– O tom kak istselen byl ofrok Erazm.–Bich
Bozhyz. Ill.:– B. Kustodiev. Berlin; Paris, 1922;
n.d. 1st. work: (1,000). 2 vols. Orig. wraps. by B.
Kustodiev; orig. wraps. (SH. Feb.6; 555)
Flegon. £60
– Vereshki. Ill.:– N. Lyubavina. Petrograd, n.d.
(125) numbered. Orig. wraps. by N. Lyubavina.
(SH. Feb.6; 556) *Lempert.* £75

ZANETTI, Antonio Maria, the Elder & Younger
– Delle Antiche Statue Greache e Romane. Ill.:–
Sartori, Pitteri, Faldoni, & others. Venice, 1740. 2
vols. Lge. fo. Cont. hf. cf., corners scuffed. From
the collection of John A. Saks. (C. Jun.10; 263)
Elstein. £400
– – Anr. Edn. Ill.:– after Piazzetta (port.). Venice,
1740-43. 2 pts. in 1 vol. Lge. fo. Cont. red mor.,
decor. spine. (HD. Mar.18; 188) Frs. 6,200
– Le Gemme Antiche ... Illustrate. Trans.:–
Francesco Goti (Latin commentary). Venice, 1750.
L.P. Fo. Cont. vell. bds., gt. spine. From the
collection of John A. Saks. (C. Jun.10; 265)
Lyon. £220

ZANETTI, Antonio Maria, the Younger
– Varie Pittura a Fresco de' Principali Maestri
Veneziani. Ill.:– after Zanetti (port. & plts?).
Venice, 1760 [i.e. 1788]. Lge. 4to. Cont. qtr. cf.,
rebkd., covers worn. From the collection of John
A. Saks. (C. Jun.10; 266) *Marlborough.* £120

**ZANETTI, Antonio Maria, the Younger &
Bongiovanni, A.**
– Graeca [Latina et Italica] D. Marci Bibliotheca
Codicum Manuscriptorum ... Ill.:– G.B. Moretti
after G. Patrini (port.). Venice, 1740-41. 2 vols.
Fo. Cont. spr. cf., gt. spines. From the collection of
John A. Saks. (C. Jun.10; 267) *Breslauer.* £140

ZANGWILL, Israel
– Works. 1925. De Luxe Edn., 14 vols. Hf. mor.
Sigd. (BS. Nov.26; 178) £50

ZANNONI, Giovanni Antonio Rizzi
– Atlas Géographique contenant la Mappemonde et
les Quatre Parties avec les Differents Etats
d'Europe. Ill.:– Legrand (title). Paris, 1782.
Square 16mo. Cont. red mor., spine decor., 3
fillets, inner dentelle. (HD. Apr.10; 208)
Frs. 2,100
– Atlas Géographique et Militaire, ou théâtre de la
Guerre présente en Allemagne. Ill.:– Choffard
(frontis.). Paris, [1761]. Sm. 12mo. 3pp. advts.
Cont. red mor., decor. spine, 3 fillets, angle
fleurons, inner dentelles. (HD. Apr.10; 206)
Frs. 1,400

ZANOLI, Alessandro
– Sulla Milizia Cisalpino-Italina Cenni
Storico-Statistici dal 1796 al 1814. Ill.:– Corbetta
da Focosi. Milan, 1845. 1st. Edn., Ltd. Edn.
numbered. 3 vols. including atlas. Slight staining,
1 defect. & reprd. plt. 2 plts. with sm. tears. Cont.
hf. cf., unc. Lf. at front of vol. with limitation note
& long dedication. (SI. Dec.4; 618) Lire 750,000

ZANONI, Giacomo
– Istoria Botanica. Bologna, 1675. 1st. Edn. Fo.
19th. C. qtr. mor. From Chetman's Liby.,
Manchester. (C. Nov.27; 413)
Antiqua Libri. £300

ZANOSA [Splinter]
Ed.:– [P.L. Antropov]. St. Petersb., 1906. Nos.
1-14. Fo. Unbnd. (SH. Feb.5; 153)
De la Casa. £90

ZANOTTI, Francesco Maria
– Della Forza de' Corpi che Chiamano Viva Libri
Tre. Bologna, 1752. 1st. Edn. Sm. 4to. Cont. vell.
Bkplt. of Marquess of Bute; from Honeyman
Collection. (S. May 20; 3152) *Elstein.* £65
– Das Malerische, Monumentale, Historische und
Artistische Venedig. Trans.:– A. Müller. Ill.:– M.
Moro & J. Rebellato. Venice, 1857. Ob. fo. Some
plts. lightly soiled, some plts. loose, lacks birds eye
panorama as usual. Cont. hf. leath., gt. (R.
Oct.14-18; 1940) DM 4,000
– Storia Veneta. Ill.:– A. Viviani & others after G.
Gatteri. Venice, 1860. 2 vols. in 1. Ob. fo. Recent
hf. linen, orig. wraps. pasted on. (R.
Oct.14-18; 1941) DM 450

ZANOTTI, Giampietro
– Le Pitture di Pellegrino Tibaldi e di Niccolo
Abbati Esistenti nell' Instituto di Bologna. Ill.:–
G.B. Brustolon & B. Crivellari (plts.). Venice,
1756. Lge. fo. Minor foxing to some fore-margins.
Mod. buckram. From the collection of John A.
Saks. (C. Jun.10; 269) *Taylor.* £140

ZAPF, Hermann
– Pen & Graver. Ed.:– Paul Standard (preface).
Ill.:– August Rosenberger. N.Y., [1952]. (2000)
on Fabriano paper. Ob. 4to. Vell.-bkd. bds. (SG.
Mar.26; 119) $140
– Specimen Pages from the Manuale
Typographicum'. Frankfurt, ca. 1952. Ltd. Edn.
(30) numbered. Ob. 4to. Ptd. in German & Fr. on
rectos only of 11 ll. Vell.-bkd., gt. initialled bds.
Pres. Copy sigd. by Zapf to Walter Howe. (PNY.
Oct.1; 508) $140

ZARAGOZA, Jose
– Esphera en Comun Celeste, y Terraquea. Madrid,
1675. Sm. 4to. Minor defects to a few plts., sm.
repair to 2B4, a few stains & spots, owner's inscr.
of Dno. Jose Deogracias Sanchez. Cont. limp vell.,
stained, new endpapers. From Honeyman
Collection. (S. May 20; 3154) *Hughes.* £110

ZARATE, Agustin de
– Histoire de la Découverte et de la Conquête du
Pérou. Amst., 1700. 1st. Fr. Edn. 2 vols. 12mo.
Blank margins of 2 plts. slightly defect. Cont. cf.,
slightly worn. (SPB. May 5; 550) $150
– – Anr. Edn. Paris, 1716. 2 vols. Sm. stain in 1 vol.
Cont. mott. cf. (SPB. May 5; 551) $175
– Historia del Descubrimiento y Conquista de las
Provincias del Peru. Seville, 1577. Fo. Lacks
errata lf., liby. stp. removed from title & reprd.,
title & a few other ll. stained. Mod. cf. [Sabin
106269] (SPB. May 5; 549) $800
– Le Historie ... dello Scoprimento et Conquista
del Peru ... Trans.:– S. Alfonso Ulloa. Venice,
1563. Sm. 4to. Later cf., spine gt., Henry Stevens'
& Clarence S. Bement's bkplts. [Sabin 106271]
(SPB. May 5; 548) $400
– – Anr. Copy. Hf. vell. (SPB. May 5; 547) $350

ZAREVO [Glow]
Ed.:– [V.V. Trofimov]. St. Petersb., 1906. Nos.

1-4. Fo. & 4to. Unbnd. (SH. Feb.5; 154)
Landry. £200
– – Anr. Copy. Nos. 1-2. Fo. Slightly soiled. (SH.
Feb.5; 155) *Quaritch.* £85

ZARNITSY [Summer Lightning]
Ed.:– [L.I. Zarnityn & others]. St. Petersb., 1906.
Nos. 1-6, 8-9 (of 9). Fo. Unbnd. (SH. Feb.5; 156)
Landry. £270

ZASTREL'SHCIK [Pioneer]
Ed.:– [M.K. Mukalov]. St. Petersb., 1906. Nos.
1-2 only (of 3). 4to. Unbnd. (SH. Feb.5; 157)
De la Casa. £75

ZATTA, Antonio
– Atlante Novissimo. Venezia, 1775-85. Vols. 1, 2
& 4. Fo. 135 partly cold. double-p. maps. Cont. cf.
gt. (P. Mar.12; 168) *Cambridge.* £2,600
– – Anr. Copy. 4 vols. Cont. hf. leath., spine defect.
(R. Oct.14-18; 1573) DM 15,000
– – Anr. Edn. Venice, 1779. Vol. I only (of 4). Fo.
Double-p. pict. frontis. misbnd., all maps
hand-cold. in outl., decor. or vig. title cartouches,
& some other features fully cold., slight browning,
on guards thro.-out. Cont. hf. cf., spine gt.,
wormed. (S. Dec.8; 196) *Burden.* £1,200
– – Anr. Edn. Ill.:– G. Zuliana after P.A. Novelli
(titles). Venice, 1779-84. 4 vols. Fo. Mntd. on
guards thro.-out, maps & charts hand-cold. in outl.
Cont. hf. cf. & marb. bds., spines gt., mod.
buckram boxes. As an atlas, w.a.f.; from the
collection of John A. Saks. (C. Jun.10; 271)
Burgess. £3,800
– – Anr. Edn. Venice, 1779-85. 4 vols. Fo.,
(385mm × 275mm). A few sm. marginal tears, on
guards thro.-out. Cont. vell. bds., spines & edges
slightly worn. W.a.f. (S. Nov.3; 22)
Turri. £3,200
– – Anr. Edn. Venice, 1782. 2 vols. only. Fo. Cont.
hf. leath. (R. Oct.14-18; 1574) DM 4,700
– L'Augusta Ducale Basilica dell'Evangelista San
Marco. Ill.:– Visentini (plts.). Venice, 1761. Atlas
fo. With the port. of Procuratore Foscarini,
without the additional lf. of dedication to
Foscarini, accompanied by a copy of Gregg's facs.
edn. of 1964. Cont. hf. cf. From the collection of
John A. Saks. (C. Jun.10; 272) *Quaritch.* £950

ZAUNMUELLER, Wolfram
– Bibliographisches Handbuch der
Sprachwoerterbuecher. Stuttgart, 1958. 4to. Cl.,
d.-w. (SG. Jan.22; 412) $140

ZAUNSCHLIFER, P.
– Tafereel van overdeftige Zinnebeelden ... Ed.:–
C. Ripa, P. Valerianus, Oros Apollo & others.
Ill.:– A. Houbraken. Amst., 1722. 4to.
Occasionally foxed. Cont. cf. (VG. Dec.17; 1305)
Fls. 530

ZA ZHIZN' [For Life]
Ed.:– [S.M. Prokhorov]. St. Petersb., n.d. No. 1.
Fo. Unbnd. (SH. Feb.5; 158) *Flegon.* £50

ZDRAVY SMYSL [Common Sense]
Ed.:– [M.K. Gurskaya]. St. Petersb., 1907. Nos.
1-2. Fo. Unbnd. (SH. Feb.5; 159) *Lempert.* £90

ZEICHNUNG, Die
Ill.:– Klemm, Unold & others, after Kubin,
Liebermann Franck & others. Berlin, [1922-23].
Pts. 1-20 (all publd.?) 8vo. & 4to. Orig. pict.
wraps., 1 loose. (H. May 21/22; 1879) DM 420

ZEIDLER, P.
– Insignia Vrbivm of Vicorvm Svperioris
Palatinatvs Electoralis in Bauaria, Carminis
Genere Diuerso Descripta. Regensburg, 1585.
Sewed. From Otto Hupp collection. (HK.
Nov.18-21; 322) DM 420

ZEILLER, Martin
– Topographia Alsatiae &c. Ill.:– Matthew
Merian. Frankfurt, 1663. Fo. Some plts. slightly
discold. Old hf. vell. From Chetham's Liby.,
Manchester. (C. Nov.27; 279) *Maggs.* £1,600
– Topographia Archiepiscopatum Moguntinensis
... Ill.:– Matthew Merian. Frankfurt, 1646. Fo.
Old hf. vell. From Chetham's Liby., Manchester.
(C. Nov.27; 289) *Kurka.* £3,500
[–] – Anr. Edn. Ill.:– Matthew Merian.
[Frankfurt], 1646 [?ca. 1720]. Latest Edn. Fo.
65 (of 67) views on 39 (of 40) double-p. or folding
copperplts. Hf. leath. (R. Oct.14-18; 2437)
DM 11,000
– Topographia Bavariae ... Ill.:– Matthew
Merian. Frankfurt, 1644. [1st. Edn.?]. Fo. Tear in
1 plt., paper fault affecting plt. of Rosenheim. Old

hf. vell. From Chetham's Liby., Manchester. (C. Nov.27; 281) *Kistner.* £2,400
– – **Anr. Copy.** Fo. Lightly browned in parts, some soiling, title-lf. bkd. Hf. leath., worn. (H. May 21/22; 314) DM 21,000
[–] – **Anr. Copy.** 19th C. linen (R. Oct. 14-18; 2200a) DM 14,500
– **Topographia Bohemiae, Moraviae et Silesiae.** Ill.:– Matthew Merian. Frankfurt, 1650. Fo. Lacks the plts. of Laun & Leutmeritz. Old hf. vell. From Chetham's Liby., Manchester. (C. Nov.27; 282) *Weinreb.* £1,900
– **Topographia Electorati Brandenburgici et Ducatus Pomeraniae & c.** Ill.:– Matthew Merian. Frankfurt, [1652]. 3 pts. in 1 vol. Fo. Some plts. slightly discold. Old hf. vell., head of spine defect. From Chetham's Liby., Manchester. (C. Nov.27; 283) *Bauer.* £1,800
– – **Anr. Edn.** Ill.:– Matthias Merian. [Frankfurt], [1690]. 2nd. Edn. 3 vols. in 1. Fo. Lacks ptd. title & 3 copper engrs., 3 added copper engrs., engraved title reprd. on verso, 1 copper engr. pasted, 1 bkd., light soiling. Cont. cf., very worn. (H. Dec.9/10; 464) DM 10,000
– **Topographia Franconiae.** Ill.:– Matthew Merian. Frankfurt, [1648]. Fo. Printing fault to Wultzburg with lr. corner not impressed, worming to inner margin of sigs. D & E slightly affecting 3 plts., some sm. tears & staining. Old hf. vell. From Chetham's Liby., Manchester. (C. Nov.27; 285) *Rheinbuch.* £4,000
– **Topographia Galliae.** Frankfurt, 1655-61. 13 vols. in 4. 4to. Extra engraved title to vol. 1, engraved titles to vols. 2-9, over 300 engd. maps, plans & views mntd. on guards. Old spr. cf., spines gt. W.a.f. (C. Jul.15; 158) *Weinreb.* £2,000
[–] – **Anr. Edn.** Frankfurt, 1656. 1st. Edn. Fo. Browned & stained, wormed. No bdg., loose. (R. Oct.14-18; 1866) DM 2,200
– – **Anr. Edn.** Ill.:– Matthew Merian. Frankfurt, 1656-61. 13 vols. in 4. Fo. Minor stain in centrefold of 1st. 60 pp. of vol. 1, stain in upr. corner of pt. of vol. 3 & in vol. 4, some staining in vols. 11-13. Old hf. cf. W.a.f., from Chetham's Liby., Manchester. (C. Nov.27; 295) *Maggs.* £2,200
– – **Anr. Edn.** Ill.:– Matthew Merian. Amst., 1660-63. 4 vols. Some browning. Cont. vell., blind fillet frame, stpd. centre motif, spine raised bands, engraved clasps. (HD. Apr.24; 110) Frs. 30,000
– **Topographia Germaniae-Inferioris vel Circulibergundici.** Ill.:– Matthew Merian. Frankfurt, [1659]. Fo. 107 plts. only (of 108). Old hf. vell. From Chetham's Liby., Manchester. (C. Nov.27; 286) *Forum.* £1,600
– **Topographia Hassiae** . . . Ill.:– Matthew Merian. Frankfurt, [1646]. [1st. Edn.?] Fo. Lacks plt. of the Bridge at Frankfurt, tear in 1 plt., paper fault in another. Old hf. vell. From Chetham's Liby., Manchester. (C. Nov.27; 287) *Reiss.* £4,200
[–] – **Anr. Edn.** Some light soiling. Cont. vell., worn. (R. Mar.31-Apr.4; 2084) DM 19,000
[–] – **Anr. Edn.** Ill.:– Matthew Merian. Frankfurt, 1665. [= after 1700]. Last Edn. Fo. Cont. style hf. leath. (R. Oct.14-18; 2296) DM 14,000
– **Topographia Helvetiae.** Ill.:– Mathias Merian. 1642. Sm. fo. 2 maps & 67 views etc. on 53 sheets only, many double-p., lacks titie most plts. preserved & loose in bdg., map of Germany lacking corner affecting cartouche, some foxing thro.-out. Vell. W.a.f. (BS. Nov.26; 238) £3,200
– **Topographia Helvetiae, Rhaetiae et Valesiae.** Ill.:– Matthew Merian. Frankfurt, 1654 [engraved title dtd. 1642]. Fo. 51 plts. only (of 78), pp. 55-58 bnd. inverted, double-p. maps cropped at foot, slight paper fault in plt. of Einsiedeln, minor staining in some blank outer margins Old hf. vell. From Chetham's Liby., Manchester. (C. Nov.27; 288) *Wenner.* £7,000
– – **Anr. Edn.** Ill.:– Matthias Merian. Frankfurt, ca. 1654. Fo. Text & Index compl., lacks engraved title & lr. blank, 56 double.-p. plts. present, some defect., plts.' all cropped to borders & mntd. on later blanks, few ll. partly defect. Later vell., shaken in bdg. W.a.f. (PNY. Oct.13; 365) $3,100
– **Topographia Palatinus Rheni** . . . Ill.:– Matthew Merian. Frankfurt, 1645. Fo. 55 plts. only (of 60). Old hf. vell. From Chetham's Liby., Manchester. (C. Nov.27; 290) *Rheinbuch.* £5,600
[–] – **Anr. Edn.** Ill.:– Matthew Merian. Frankfurt, ca. 1720. 3rd. Edn. Fo. 95 (of 98) views on 59 (of 60) partly double-p. or folding copperplts. Hf. leath. (R. Oct.14-18; 2438) DM 19,000
[–] **Topographia Provinciarum Austriacarum.** Frankfurt, [1736]. 3 pts. in 1 vol. Fo. 150 (of 154)

views on 102 (of 106) partly double-p. copperplts, some slightly soiled. Bnd. in Topographia Bohemiae without copperplts. Cont. hf. leath. (R. Oct.14-18; 1955) DM 15,500
[–] **[Topographia Provinciarum Austriacarum].** Ill.:– Matthias Merian. ca. 1650. Fo. Collection of 224 engraved ills. & plans mostly of Austria, a few of Bavaria & Bohemia, & 13 maps of Austria, Bavaria, Savoy, Bohemia & Italy, cut out & mntd. on 96 sheets. In cont. album, 17th. C. mott. cf., lettered 'Villes Allem'. (C. Apr.1; 155) *Davidson.* £2,400
– **Topographia Provinciarum Austriacarum . . . Oesterreichischen.-Anhang zu dess M.Z. anno 1649 gedruckter Topographia Provinciarum Austriacarum.-Topographia Windhagiana** . . . Ill.:– Matthew Merian. Frankfurt, 1649; 1656; 1656. 3 vols. in 1. Fo. Lr. margin of title to vol. 3 reprd., not affecting text. Old hf. vell. From Chetham's Liby., Manchester. (C. Nov.27; 280) *Rheinbuch.* £3,800
– **Topographia Saxoniae Inferioris** . . . Ill.:– Matthew Marian. Frankfurt, 1653. [1st. Edn.?] Fo. 35 (of 36) plts. only, light spotting & foxing thro.-out. Old hf. vell. From Chetham's Liby., Manchester. (C. Nov.27; 291) *Henderson.* £2,800
[–] – **Anr. Copy.** lacks ptd. title. Cont. blind-tooled vell. (R. Oct.14-18; 2338) DM 15,000
– **Topographia Superioris Saxoniae, Thuringiae, Misniae, Lusatiae** . . . Ill.:– Matthew Merian. Frankfurt, 1650. Fo. Old hf. vell. From Chetham's Liby., Manchester. (C. Nov.27; 292) *Bauer.* £1,900
– **Topographia Superioris Saxoniae.-Topographia Saxoniae Inferioris.** Ill.:– Matthew Merian. Frankfurt, 1650; 1653, [ca. 1720]. 1st work 1st. Edn., 2nd work reprint of 1653 Edn. Fo. 1st work lacks 2 plts. Old cf. (SG. Oct.9; 166) $8,000
– **Topographia Sveviae.** Ill.:– Matthew Merian. Frankfurt, 1643. Fo. Old hf. vell. From Chetham's Liby., Manchester. (C. Nov.27; 293) *Rheinbuch.* £5,800
– **Topographia vnd Eigentliche Beschreibung der Vornembsten Stäte, Schlösser auch anderer Plätze vnd Oerter in denen Hertzogthümer Braunschweig vnd Lüneburg etc.** Ill.:– Matthias Merian. Frankfurt, 1654. 1st. Edn. Fo. Lacks pp. 215-220, 4 ll. index, 1 lf. copper engr. index & 5 copper engrs., added Grundriss Nienburg & Ansicht Haelen an der Weser bnd. in, 2 ll. text with tears, 1 copper engr. with torn corner & loss, other plts. torn, soiled. Cont. vell., lacks spine & lr. cover. (H. Dec.9/10; 463) DM 20,000
Anr. Edn. Ill.:– Matthew Merian. Frankfurt, 1654. Fo. 129 plts. only of (132), caption on plt. of Eimbeck defect., slight tear in plt. of Seesen. Old hf. vell. From Chetham's Liby., Manchester. (C. Nov.27; 284) *Wenner.* £6,000
– – **Anr. Copy.** Sm. fo. Engraved title, 2 double-p. maps, 2 double-p. family trees, 129 copperplt. views, mostly double-p., lacks plt.-list & Wolffenbuettel map. Old vell. (SG. May 14; 146) $8,400
– **Topographia Urbis Romae.** Ed.:– Dietrich de Bry. Ill.:– Matthew Merian. Frankfurt, 1681 [ca. 1700]. Fo. 91 (of 99) plts., 3 mntd., 2 strengthened in margin, many headlines cropped, lacks last lf. 18th. C. hf. cf. (S. Jan.27; 343) *Baer.* £140
– **Topographia Westphaliae.** Ill.:– Matthew Merian. Frankfurt, 1648. Fo. Lacks 3 plts., lacks sm. corner from ill. of Tongren, minor tear in fold of 2 plts. Old hf. vell. From Chetham's Liby., Manchester. (C. Nov.27; 294) *Braun.* £5,000
– – **Anr. Edn.** Ill.:– Matthaeus Merian. [Frankfurt], [1648]. Fo. Engraved title, double-p. map, 50 plts., lacks ptd. title, about 14 plts. stained, 1 reprd. Mod. vell. gt. (C. May 20; 152) *Schuster.* £4,500

ZEILLER, Martin–MERIAN, Matthew
– **Topographia Italiae.-Das Lang Bestrittene Konigreich Candia.** Ill.:– Matthew Merian. Frankfurt, 1688; 1670. 2 works in 1 vol. Fo. 1st. work: foot of ptd. title slightly cropped, some maps slightly discold., occasional spotting. Old hf. vell. From Chetham's Liby., Manchester. (C. Nov.27; 296) *Crete.* £1,600

ZEILLER, Martin & Simler, Josias
– **Topographia Helvetiae, Rhaetiae et Valesiae.** Amst., 1644. 2 pts. in 1 vol. Fo. Cont. leath., gt. spine, spine slightly defect. (R. Oct.14-18; 2016) DM 34,000

ZEISBERGER, David
– **Indian Dictionary: English, German, Iroquois, & Algonquin.** Ed.:– Eben N. Horsford. Camb., Massachusetts, 1887. 4to. Red three-qtr. mor., spine gt. (SG. Mar.5; 482) $130

ZEIT-ECHO, ein Kriegs-Tagebuch der Kunstler
Ill.:– Unold, Klee & Kokoshka. Munich, 1914-15. Nos. 1-24 in 23 pts., the last a double iss. Loosely contained in a cl.-bkd. portfo. case, worn, inside flaps detchd. (SPB. May 6; 271) $800

ZEITSCHRIFT fuer Geschichte und Wissenschaft des Judenthums
Ed.:– Leopold Zunz. Berlin, 1822-23. 4 nos. in 1 vol. (all publd.). Browning. Bds., spine torn & reprd. with losses, covers loose. (SPB. May 11; 223) $100

ZEITUNG FUR DIE ELEGANTE WELT
Leipzig, 1802-04. Years 2-4. 4to. Slightly soiled. Cont. bds. (R. Oct.14-18; 2640) DM 480

ZELINSKY, Kornely
– **Poeziya kak smysl [Poetry as Sense. A Book about Constructivism].** Moscow, 1929. (3,000). Orig. bds., slightly worn. (SH. Feb.5; 287) *Quaritch.* £55

ZELST, A.
*See-*STEMPEL, G. & ZELST, A.–ROMANO, A. –HORCHER, Phillipus

ZEMENKOV, Boris
– **Undarnoe iskusstvo [Persuasive Art of Windows of Satire].-Grafika v bytu [Graphics in Life].** Moscow, 1930. Both (5,000). 2 vols. Orig. wraps., the 2nd. torn. (SH. Feb.5; 288) *Quaritch.* £65

ZEMENKOV, Boris & others
– **Ot Mamy na Pyat' Minut [From Mama for Five Minutes].** [Moscow], [1920]. Orig. wraps., unopened. (SH. Feb.6; 557) *Quaritch.* £120

ZENKER, F.G.
– **Vollst, Theoret.-Praktische Anleitung sur Feineren Kochkunst.** Vienna, 1824. 2nd. Edn. Pt. 1. Lightly soiled, erased stp. on 4 ll. Cont. hf. linen; spine defect. (R. Mar.31-Apr.4; 1657) DM 550

ZENTNERS
– **Engravings after Drawings made by him from Original Paintings of Old Masters.** 1791. Square 4to. Hf. cf. (PJ. Mar.7 (80); 83) £175

ZEPPELIN, Ferdinand von, Count
– **Erfahrungen beim Bau von Luftschiffen.** Berlin, 1908. Orig. ptd. wraps., slightly soiled. From Honeyman Collection. (S. May 20; 3155) *Dr. Martin.* £110

ZERBE, Jerome
*See-*CONNOLLY, Cyril & Zerbe, Jerome

ZERBI, Giovanni Antonio
– **Discorseo in Forma di Dialogo intorno al Banco S. Ambrosio della Citta di Milano.-Delle Leggi Contratti et Governe del Banco Santo Ambrosio della Citta di Milano.** Milan, 1599; 1601. 1st. Edn. 2 works in 1 vol. 4to. Stp. on 1st. title, & bank stp. on 2nd. title. 18th C. hf. cf. (SI. Dec.4; 619) Lire 350,000

ZERVOS, Christian
– **L'Art en Grèce des Temps Préhistoriques au debut du XVIIIe Siècle.-Les Oeuvres du Greco en Espagne.** Paris, 1934; 1939. 1st. Edns. 2 vols. Sm. fo. Orig. bds. (PNY. Mar.4; 281) $100
– **Pablo Picasso, Volume 14.** Paris, [1963]. Fo. Ptd. wraps. (SG. Apr.2; 238) $100

ZEVECOTE, Jacob van
– **Poematum.** Amst., 1640. Latest Edn. 12mo. Commendatory verses ptd. on shorter sheets, single wormhole slightly affects approximately three-qtrs. of text, inscr. on title, possibly with stp. removed from pastedown, inscr. on pastedown. Cont. pol. cf., possibly prize bdg., gt. semé with fleurs de lis, dentelle border, fleur de lis gt. in spine compartments. (S. Apr.7; 325) *Forum.* £70

ZHALO [Sting]
Ed.:– [I.I. Vlasov]. Moscow, 1905. No. 1. 4to. Unbnd. (SH. Feb.5; 160) *De la Casa.* £65

ZHGUT [Plait]
Ed.:– [I.I. Klang]. Moscow, 1906. No. 1. 4to. Unbnd. (SH. Feb.5; 162) *Quaritch.* £60

ZHUPEL [Bugbear]
Ed.:– [Z.I. Grzhebin]. St. Petersb., 1905-06. Nos. 1-3. Fo. Unbnd. (SH. Feb.5; 163) *Landry.* £190
– – **Anr. Edn.** Ed.:– [A. Schastlivtsev]. St. Petersb., 1906. Finnish Edn.(?). No. 1. 4to. Unbnd. (SH. Feb.5; 164) *Quaritch.* £55

ZHURNAL ZHURNALOV [Journal of Journals]
Ed.:– [N.P. Malinovsky]. St. Petersb., 1905-06. Nos. 1-9. Fo. Unbnd. (SH. Feb.5; 165)
Landry. $310

ZICHY, Michael von
– **Liebe.** Leipzig, Priv. ptd., 1911. (300) numbered for Subscribers only. Ob. fo. Gt.-ornamental hf. vell. & patterned bds., unc. (PNY. Oct.1; 207) $475

ZIEGLER, Jacob
– **Quae intus Continentur. Syria, Palestina, Arabia (etc.).** Strassburg, 1532. 1st. Edn. Sm. fo. 8 maps, title & 2 maps in facs., dampstained, wormholes. Later vell., soiled. [Sabin 106330] (SH. Jun.18; 196) *Leverton.* £520

ZIEGLER-KLIPHAUSEN, Heinrich Anselm von
– **Continuirter Historische Schau-Platz.** Leipzig, 1718. 1st. Edn. Lge. fo. Leath. (HK. Nov.18-21; 2104) DM 1,100
– **Historisches Labyrinth der Zeit, darinnen die Denckwürdigkeiten Welt-Händel, Lebens-Beschreibungen aller Könige ...** Leipzig, 1701. 1st. Edn. Fo. Sm. wormholes at foot, last index lf. soiled. Cont. vell., soiled. (R. Oct.14-18; 1119) DM 600
– **Täglicher Schau-Platz der Zeit.** Frankfurt, 1695. 1st. Edn. Lge. fo. Some ll. at beginning reprd., some margins bkd., defect. title mntd. on china, slightly soiled. Leath. (HK. Nov.18-21; 2103) DM 1,000

ZIENKOWICZ, L.
– **Les Costumes du Peuple Polonais.** Paris, 1841. Some slight foxing thro.-out. Bds., mor. spine. (BS. Jun.11; 411) £280

ZILLE, Heinrich
– **Die Landpartie. Aus meiner Jungszeit.** [Berlin], Priv. Ptd. [1920]. (400) 4to. Last lf. with sm. tear. Bds. (H. May 21/22; 1880) DM 1,700

ZIMMERMAN, A.F.
– **Der Bier-Brauer als Meister in seinem Fach.** Berlin, 1842. Orig wraps., unc. (R. Oct.14-18; 2691) DM 440

ZIMMERMANN, Eberhardt August Wilhelm von
– **Frankreich und die Freistaaten von Nordamerika: Vergleichungen beider Laender.** Berlin; Braunschweig, 1795; 1799. 1st. Edn. 2 vols. Vol. II comprises 32 prelims., errata lf., 612 pp., 72 pp. of 'Erlaeuterungen und Zusaetze', & anr. lf. of errata. Red mor., spines richly gt. (SG. Jan.8; 468) $1,200

ZIMMERMANN, Ernst
– **Chinesisches Porzellan und die übrigen Keramischen Erzeugnisse Chinas.** Leipzig, 1923. 2nd. Edn. 2 vols. 4to. Cl. (C. Feb.4; 273) *City.* £75
– – **Anr. Copy.** 4to. Sigs. & marks. (VG. Dec.15; 301) Fls. 550
– – **Anr. Copy.** 2 vols. Both vols. slightly stained towards end. Orig. linen. (HK. May 12-14; 2388) DM 520

ZIMMERMANN, Johann Georg
– **Von der Erfahrung in der Arzneykunst.** Zürich, 1763-64. 1st. Edn. 2 vols. Cont. hf. leath. gt. (HK. Nov.18-21; 831) DM 550

ZIMRA, David Ibn [Radbaz]
– **Magen David.** Amst., 1713. 1st. Edn. 4to. Bds. (S. Nov.18; 479) *Stern.* £80

ZINANNI, Guiseppe
– **Della Uova e dei Nidi degli Uccelli.** Venice, 1737. 4to. 19th. C. hf. mor. From Chetham's Liby., Manchester. (C. Nov.27; 414)
Antiqua Libri. £110

ZINCGREF, J.W.
– **Emblematum Ethico-Politicorum Centuria ... Hundert Sitten–und Politischen Sinnenbilder.** Ed.:– G. Greflinger. Ill.:– M. Merian. Heidelberg, 1681. New Edn. Ob. 8vo. Text Latin, Fr. & German, lacks hf.-title, 8 ll. with tears, heavily soiled & browned in parts. Cont. vell., soiled & worn. (H. Dec.9/10; 1464) DM 950

ZINN, Johannes Gottfried
– **Descriptio Anatomica Oculi Humani Iconibus Illustrata.** Göttingen, 1755. 1st. Edn. 4to. Text heavily soiled in parts. Cont. leath. gt. (R. Mar.31-Apr.4; 965) DM 1,050
– **Dissertatio Inauguralis Medica Sistens Experimenta quaedam circa corpus callosum ...** Göttingen, 1749. Sm. 4to. Disbnd. From the liby. of Carl Gustav Carus with bkplt. (S. Jun.17; 908) *Ragel.* £55

ZINNER, Ernst
– **Geschichte und Bibliographie der Astronomischen Literatur in Deutschland zur Zeit der Renaissance.** Stuttgart, 1964. 2nd. Edn. Orig. cl., d.-w. From Honeyman Collection. (S. May 20; 3309) *Roberts.* £80

ZITTAUISCHES TAGEBUCH
Ed.:– K.G. Grohmann. Zittau, 1828-29, 1831. 2 vols. Sm. 4to. Das Dampschiff, Zittau 1831 bnd. in. Cont. bds. (R. Oct.14-18; 2140) DM 1,700

ZLOI DUKH [Wicked Spirit]
Ed.:– [S.A. Pataraki]. St. Petersb., 1906. No. 1 only (of 2). Fo. 1 tear. Unbnd. (SH. Feb.5; 167) *Quaritch.* £60

ZNAMYA [Banner]
Ed.:– [A.G. Galach'ev]. St. Petersb., 1906. No. 1. Fo. Unbnd. (SH. Feb.5; 168) *Landry.* £150

ZOBEL, Chr.
See–SACHSENSPIEGEL

ZOEGA, G.
– **De Origine et Usu Obeliscorum.** Rome, 1797. Fo. Hf. cf. (CR. Jun.11, 532) Lire 450,000

ZOLA, Emile
– **L'Attaque du Moulin.** Ill.:– Favire after Boutigny. Paris, 1901. (20) numbered on old Japan. 4 states of plts., Red mor., by Affolter, mor. doubls., gt. arms, orig. wraps. bnd. in, s.-c. (SM. Oct.8; 2381) Frs. 2,800
– **La Curée.–Nana.–Au Bonheur des Dames.–La Joie de Vivre.–Germinal.–L'Oeuvre.–Le Rêve.–Les Soirées de Médan.** 1871; 1880; 1883; 1884; 1885; 1886; 1888; 1880. 1st. Edns. 8 works in 8 vols. 12mo. Mod. red hf. mor., corners, spines decor. with raised bands, wraps. slightly defect. (HD. Jun.25; 440) Frs. 4,100
– **La Fortune des Rougon.** 1871. Jansenist mor., wrap., sigd. (but not bound) by Marius Michel, washed. (HD. Oct.10; 175) Frs. 1,350
– **Germinal.** 1885. (150) on Hollande. Three quarter mor., wrap., by Champs. (HD. Oct.10; 176) Frs. 3,100
– – **Anr. Edn.** Ill.:– Jean Oberlé. Paris, 1928. (60) on imperial Jap. 4to. Orig. watercolour, black-&-white set replaced with 24 pencil drawings. Bordeaux mor. by Vermorel, brkn. gt. fillet on covers, surrounding mosaic motif, spine decor. with raised bands, wrap. & spine preserved, s.-c. Printed specially for Jean Oberlé, watercolour & drawings sigd. by artist. (HD. Feb.27; 250) Frs. 4,500
– **Oeuvres Complétes.** Ed.:– M. le Blonde. Paris, 1927-29. Hand-bnd. hf. leath., orig. wraps preserved. (H. Dec.9/10; 2404) DM 420
– **Les Rougon-Macquart.** Phila., n.d. (1000). 12 vols. Red hf. mor. gt. (SPB. Nov.25; 501) $225
– **The Soil.** Paris, n.d. 'Suppressed Engl. Edn.'. 12mo. Lev. gt., orig. ptd. wraps. bnd. in, by the Atelier Bindery, rehinged. Inscr. to M.J. Young, sm. mor. bkplts. of Arthur M. Brown & Zola E. Harvey. (SG. Feb.12; 61) $100

ZOMPINI, Gaetano
– **Le Arti che Vanno per Via nelle Citta di Venezia.** Venice, 1785. Fo. Cont. ptd. translation of verses under each plt. loosely inserted. Cont. hf. mor., worn. (CSK. Aug.22; 18) £500

ZONARAS, Joannes
– **Compendium Historiarum.** Ed.:–Hier. Wolff. Basel, 1557. Lge. fo. Cont. MS. owner's note on title, slightly soiled. Cont. blind-tooled pig-bkd. wd. bds., 2 clasps, worn, slightly wormed. (HK. Nov.18-21; 323) DM 500

ZONCA, Vittorio
– **Novo Treato di Machine et Edificii.** Padua, 1607. 1st. Edn. Fo. Title & 1st. plt. defect. & mntd., both very stained, Alr. badly stained. Limp vell., worn. W.a.f. (S. Jul.27; 114) *Licini.* £320
– – **Anr. Copy.** 2 unnumbered ll. with 3 plts. not called for in list of plts., lacks pp. 59-62 (H2-3) with 1 plt., lower corner of pp. 111/12 torn off & reprd., with sm. part of plt. & 1 letter of text

neatly supplied in MS., some wear & light stains in places. 19th. C. hf. leath. (VG. Oct.13; 174) Fls. 2,000
– – **Anr. Edn.** Padua, 1656. Fo. Title stained in lr. margin, some browning & soiling, last few ll. wormed in lr. fore-corners catching engraved surface of 4 plts. Cont. vell. bds., upr. inside hinge brkn. From libraries of Crosby Gaige & Giorgio di Veroli with bkplts.; from Honeyman Collection. (S. May 20; 3156) *Nador.* £520

ZOOLOGICAL SOCIETY OF LONDON
– **Transactions. Results of the Ruwenzori Expedition, 1905-06.** 1909-10. Vol. XXIX. 4to. Later cl., backstrip & upr. cover detchd. (TA. Mar.19; 570) £85

ZORN, B.
– **Botanolegia Medica.** Berlin, 1714. 1st. Edn. 4to. Lightly browned. Newer hf. leath. (H. May 21/22; 230) DM 480

ZOTENBERG, A.
[–] **Catalogues des Manuscrits Hébreux et Samaritains de la Bibliothéque Impériale.** Paris, 1866. Sm. fo. Hf. leath. (S. Nov.17; 127) *Quaritch.* £140

ZOUGH, Richard
[–] **The Sophister.** 1639. 1st. Edn. 4to. Woodcut border on title cropped, slight foxing. 19th. C. hf. cf. [STC 26133] (C. Nov.19; 172) *Arnold.* £170

ZRITEL' [Spectator]
Ed.:– [Yu. K. Artsybushev]. St. Petersb., 1905; 1906. Nos. 1-6, 9, 11-24 (with extra no. for 24 Nov.); nos. 1 & 2, together 24 iss. only. 4to. Some ll. slightly torn. Disbnd. (SH. Feb.5; 190) *De la Casa.* £50

ZSCHACKWITZ, J.E.
[–] **Leben und Thaten Josephi I. Römischen Kaisers sambt der unter Sr. Majestät Regierung vorgefallenen Reichs-Historie.** Leipzig, 1712. Cont. vell. (R. Oct.14-18; 1209) DM 520

ZSCHOKKE, Hermann
[–] **Ausgewählte Schriften.** Aarau, 1825-28. 1st. Coll. Edn. 40 vols. Cont. hf. leath. (HK. May 15; 5039) DM 2,550

ZSCHOKKE, Johann Heinrich Daniel
– **Die Klassischen Stellen der Schweiz und deren Hauptorte in Originalansichten.** Ill.:– Gust. Adolph Müller, Henry Winkles & others. Karlsruhe, 1842. 1 plt. loose. Orig. linen. (D. Dec.11-13; 1337) DM 1,550
– – **Anr. Edn.** Stuttgart & St. Gallen, [1858]. 4to. Orig. linen. (HK May 12-14; 783) DM 1,400
– **Die Schweiz in Ihren Klassischen Stellen und Hauptorten.** St. Gallen, 1858. Slightly soiled. Cont. hf. leath. (R. Oct.14-18; 2031) DM 1,200
– **Vues Classiques de la Suisse.** Trans.:– E. Haag. Karlsruhe, 1838. 2 pts. in 1 vol. Slightly soiled. Cont. hf. leath. (HK. May 12-14; 784) DM 1,600

ZUALLARDO, Giovanni
– **Il Devotissimo Viaggio di Gerusalemme.** Rome, 1587. 4to. Cont. vell. (P. Oct.2; 1)
Quaritch. £580

ZUALLART, Jean
– **Devotissimo Viaggio de Gerusalemme.** Rome, 1587. 1st. Edn. 4to. Y1 & 4 inserted from anr. copy (?), ll. E2-3, T2, Y4 & Ss1 with blank marginal restorations, repair at upr. margin of Kk4 just touching running head, some sm. rust-holes, engr. at Z4 rubbed, traces of old stains & spotting. Mor., covers with gt. arabesque centrepiece in blind-ruled panel with sm. gt. fleuron cornerpieces, by L. Claessens, with his ticket. Bkplt. of G.J. Arvanitidi. (CNY. Oct.1; 110) $3,000

ZUBLER, Leonhard
– **Das ist, Kurtzer und Grundlicher Bericht, wie nicht Allein aller hand Sonnen Uhren, sampt den XII Himlischen Zeichen ... auffzureissen.** Basel, 1614. Sm. 4to. Colophon dtd. 1615, some dampstaining, 4 engravings & 1 ornament cut into. Bds., worn. From Honeyman Collection. (S. May 20; 3159) *Rogers Turner.* £160
– **Novum Instrumentum Geometricum.–Fabrica et usus Instrumenti Chorographici.** Trans.:– Caspar Waser. [Basel], 1607; 1607. 2 works in 1 vol. Sm. 4to. Some staining & soiling, 2nd. work with last blank lf. used as pastedown. Cont. limp vell., gt., worn & soiled. From Honeyman Collection. (S. May 20; 3158) *Zeitlin & Verbrugge.* £260

ZUCHETTA, Giovanni Battista
- **Arimmetica.** Brescia, 1600. 1st. Edn. Pt. 1, (All publd.). Fo. Lacks blank lf. at end of prelims., tear in H4, occasional browning or staining, a little marginal worming. Cont. vell. bds. From Honeyman Collection. (S. May 20; 3160)
Maggs. £85
- - **Anr. Copy.** Title defect. & reprd., marginal repairs to following 8 ll. touching rule-border on *2, text stained, sig. of Antonio Gozano. Cont. limp vell., worn & stained. Riccardi's copy, with his bkplt.; from Honeyman Collection. (S. May 20; 3161)
De Graeve. £55
- **Prima Parte Della Arimmetica.** Brescia, 1600. 1st. Edn. All publd. Fo. Portion of outer margin of engraved title lacking & reprd., slightly affecting plt., other minor defects to title, some staining & other marks, a few minor paper faults. Cont. vell. (C. Apr.1; 96)
Hopper. £90

ZUCKERT, J.F.
- **Systematische Beschreibung aller Gesundbrunnen und Bäder Deutschlands.** Königsberg, 1776. 2nd. Edn. Stp. on title. Cont. style mod. hf. leath. (R. Oct.14-18; 310)
DM 1,800

ZUCKERT, J.F. (Ed.)
See-SAMMLUNG Der Besten & Neuesten Reisebeschreibungen

ZULIANI, Francesco
- **De Quibusdam Cordis Affectionibus.** Brescia, 1805. 1st. Edn., L.P. Sm. flaw in title, several ll. spotted. Cont. mor., gt. (S. May 5; 150)
Cristani. £70

ZUR GESCHICHTE der Kostüme
Munich, n.d. 4to. A few plts. loose. Orig. cl., brkn. (SH. Oct.9; 27)
Heath. £80

ZURLA, Placido
- **Il Mappamondo di Fra Mauro Camaldolese.** Venice, 1806. Fo. 1 folding facs. map. Old plain wraps., lacks spine. (SG. Oct.2; 386)
$110

ZURLAUBEN, Baron de
- **Histoire Militaire des Suisses . . .** Paris, 1751-53. 8 vols. 12mo. Cont. marb. cf., decor. spines. (HD. Jun.10; 113)
Frs. 2,500
See-LABORDE, Jean Benjamin de & Zurlauben, Baron B.F.A. de

ZUSTO, Giovanni
- **Descrizione Istorica dell'Estrazione della Pubblica nave La Fenice Dal Canale Spignon in cui Giacque cica tre Anni Totalmente Sommersa.** Ill.:- G. Daniotto after G. Cason. Venice, 1789. L.P. 7 folding plts. (Lanckoronska mentions only 5), plts. slightly stained. Mod. cl. From the collection of John A. Saks. (C. Jun.10; 275)
Pilo. £200

ZVI HIRSCH FILIP of Nadworno
- **Zemach Hashem La'zvi.** [Berditchev], [1818]. 1st. Edn., on blue paper. 4to. Tears in title & 3 ll., with loss of text. Hf. leath. (S. Nov.18; 372)
Landau. £50

ZVONAR' [Bell-Ringer]
Ed.:- [A.A. Gol'mstrem]. St. Petersb., 1906. No. 1. Fo. Unbnd. (SH. Feb.5; 170)
Quaritch. £60

ZWEIG, Stephen
- **George Frederick Handel's Resurrection.** Trans.:- Eden & Cedar Paul. Ill.:- Berthold Wolpe. Corvinus Pr., 1938. (32) sigd. 4to. Orig. niger mor. gt., s.-c. (S. Jul.22; 71)
Rota. £210
- **Verwirrung der Gefühle.** Leipzig, 1927. 1st. Edn., (30) Privilege Edn. on Bütten. Minimal staining. Orig. red mor. Printer's mark sigd. by artist. (H. May 21/22; 1883)
DM 650
see-HOLITSCHER, A. & Zweig, Stefan

ZWINGER, Theodor
- **Sicherer und Geschwinder Arzt, oder Neues Artzney-Buch.** Basel, 1725. Cont. vell. (D. Dec.11-13; 246)
DM 950
- **Theatrum Botanicum, Das ist: Neu Vollkommenes Kräuter-Buch . . .** Basel, 1696. Lacks pp. 526/527, wormed in parts at beginning in margin, copper title with sm. faults, pp.261/262 with sm. tear in lower corner, slightly stained in upr. margin, slightly soiled. Cont. hf. leath., later vell. bkd. (HK. May 12-14, 484)
DM 2,200
- - **Anr. Edn.** Basel, 1744. Fo. Cont. cf., brkn. (SG. Oct.9; 259)
$1,500

ZWINNER, E.
- **Blumen-Buch dess Heiligen Landes Palestinae.** Munich, 1661. 4to. 15 (of 18) copperplts., including 3 folding. Cont. vell., spine formerly renewed, slightly soiled at beginning & end. (R. Oct.14-18; 1786)
DM 620

ZYL, Jan van
See-HORST, Tileman van der-ZYL, Jan van

Part II

Printed Maps, Charts & Plans

AA, A.J. Van der
- **Norway.** Leiden, 1729. 'Medium' size. Map, mercantile cartouche. (HL. Apr.1; 1749)   £130

AA, Pierre van der
- **Canada ou Nouvelle France . . .** Leiden, ca.1730. 22.5 x 30cm. Fully cold. map, sm. slit affecting lr. frame line. (CB. Nov.12; 66)   Can. $220
- **La Gueldre.** Ca. 1728. 4to., approximately 28 × 22cm. Uncold. map. (JN. Sep.9; 4001)   £50

ABRAHAM bar Jacob
- **Zot Ladaat Lakol bar daat Derech Hamasaot Arbayim Shanah Bamidbar . . .** Amst., 1712. Double-p. fo. Map, from edn. of the Amst. Hagadah, obverse silked, torn & reprd. at centre fold, trimmed to platemark. (CNY. Oct.9; 18) $2,600

ADMIRALTY CHARTS
- **Kuwait Harbour.** 1867. 'Large'. Chart, some sm. blemishes. (HL. Apr.1; 1726)   £70

AFRICA
- **North Africa, including the Straits of Hercules.** Ca. 1610. 13½ × 18½ inches. Cold. map, from an Ortelius-Hondius atlas, with lge. cold. cartouche of fruits, Latin text on verso. (SG. May 21; 1) $120

AGAS, Ralph
- **Oxonia Antiqua Instaurata sive Urbis & Academiae Oxoniensis Topographica . . .** Ill.:– W. Williams. N.p., 1732. 438 × 507 mm. Hand-cold. engraved map, including 2 coats-of-arms. (S. Jul.19; 45)   Webster. £60

ALLAN, J.
- **Plan shewing the Subdivision of the Petersham Estate.** N.d. Ca. 75 x 63cm. Orig. litho. plan mntd. on linen & in cut tinted mount, proposed railway line indicated & various roads. (JL. Jul.19; 367)   Aus. $100

ALLARD, [Carolus]
- **Planisphaerium Terrestre, sive Terrarum Orbis.** Amst., ca. 1700. 515 × 592mm. Engraved map, flanked by 8 smaller hemisphere maps, all hand-cold. in outl., plus 4 other sm. engrs. F. W.a.f. (S. Jun.29; 22)   Nebenzahl. £420

ALLARD, H.
- **Nova Tabula India Orientalis.** [Amst.], ca. 1640, or later. 445 x 562 mm, hand-cold. in outl., decor., title-cartouche fully cold., short tear in bottom margin touching engraved border. W.a.f. (S. Nov.4; 435)   Terra Australis. £240

AMERICA
- **Etats-Unis de L'Amérique Septentrionale.** Paris, 1785. 22 × 30 inches. Maps,—cold. in outl., engraved cartouche. (SG. Nov.20; 9) $450
- **Map of the Eastern Seaboard of North America.** Nuremb., 1756. 18½ x 20½ ins. Cartouche engr., hand-cold. boundaries, some lines of engraved text in German in upr. left-hand margin, 4 columns of engraved text below. (SG. Aug.21; 258) $250

ANDRICHOMIUS
- **Situs Terrae Promissionis.** Amst., ca. 1650. Uncold. map of the Holy Land. (P. Nov.13; 160)   Weiss. £95

ANTONIADES, C. & Ortelius, Abraham
- **Daniae Regni Typus.** Ca. 1590. Fo. Cold. copper engraved map with 2 painted cartouches. (R. Oct.14-18; 5829)   DM 420

APIAN, Ph. & Ortelius, Abraham
- **Bavariae Delineationis Compendium.** N.d. Ob. fo. Old cold. copper engraved map with painted roll cartouche & cold. arms, soiled, jnt. defect., burst & backed. (R. Oct.14-18; 3687)   DM 560

ARCTIC CIRCLE
- **Engraved Circular Hydrographic chart of the Arctic Regions of Europe, Asia & America.** 14 Feb. 1818. [additions to 1820]. Approximate diameter 606mm. With MS. addition in ink of Bathurst Inlet, Coppermine River, Yellowknife River, Great Slave Lake, etc. W.a.f. (S. Nov.3; 106)   Fisher. £130

ARMSTRONG, Andrew
- **A Map of the County of Northumberland.** 1769. Each sheet 24½ x 19½ inches. Engraved map on 9 sheets, inset town plans of Newcastle & Berwick, marginal tears, stab holes along centre fold of 1 sheet. (CSK. Jul.3; 8)   £160

ARROWSMITH, Aaron
- **Hydrographical Chart of the World.** L., 1811. Fo. 8 folding pts., each of 4 sheets, mntd. on cl., partially cold., slightly soiled. (SPB. Jul.28; 360) $225

ASHBY
- **A Plan of the Batteries Erected before Gibraltar, with the Attacks made by Sea & Land . . . by the Duke de Crillon & Admiral Moreno . . . 1782 in Presence of the Combined Fleets of France & Spain.** 1785. 'Large'. Map, mod. colour, some blemishes. (HL. Apr.1; 1623)   £60

ATLANTIC OCEAN
- **Carte Générale de l'Océan Atlantique Occidentale . . .** [Paris], 1792. 5th. Edn. 25½ × 37 inches. Map. (SG. Nov.20; 19) $170

BAKER, B.
- **Chart of the Coast between Botany Bay & Broken Bay. Surveyed in 1788 & 1789 by Captain John Hunter.** L., 20 Sep. 1792. 73 x 40cm. Shows soundings in the 3 harbours & the settlement at Sydney Cove. (JL. Dec.14; 124)   Aus. $440

BELL, A.
- **A Map of the World showing the Discoveries of Lord Mulgrave & Captain Cook.** N.d. Map in 3 sections. F. (JL. Mar.1; 126)   Aus. $110

BELLIN, Jacques Nicolas
- **Carte du cours du Fleuve de St. Laurent.–Suite du cours du Fleuve de St. Laurent.** [Paris], [1757]. 19 × 30cm.; 19 × 28.5cm. 2 maps, matted, from J.F. de la Harpe's Abregé de l'Histoire Générale des Voyages. (CB. Nov.12; 50)   Can. $130
- **Carte de l'Isle de Nieves.** [Paris], [1758]. 13 × 9 inches. Map, from Description Géographique des Isles Antilles. (SG. May 21; 115) $110
- **Carte Réduite de la Mer du Sud.** Ca. 1753. Reduced chart of the South Sea. (JL. Jul.19; 386)   Aus. $160
- **– – Anr. Edn.** Paris, 1764. 35.5 x 21cm. Cold. map., from [Petit Atlas Maritime], vol. 2. number 64. (JL. Dec.14; 117)   Aus. $150
- **[–] Carte Réduite de St. Laurent Contenant L'Isle de Terre-neuve et Partie de la Coste des Esquimaux. L'Isle Royale, L'Isle St. Jean et celle d'Anticosti . . . Dressée au Dépost des Cartes, Plans et Journaux de la Marine . . .** [Paris], 1754. 555 × 890mm. Engraved map on wtrmkd. paper, bottom corners reprd. (PWP. Apr.9; 154)   Can. $360
- **Carte Réduite des Terres Australes.** Ca. 1753. Map showing Australia joined to both Tasmania & New Guinea. (JL. Jul.19; 384)   Aus. $220

- **Carte Réduite du Globe Terrestre.** 1764. Map from Petit Atlas Maritime, vol. 1, No. 1. (JL. Dec.14; 172)   Aus. $120
- **Carte Réduite du Globe Terrestre showing Nouvelle Hollande with Hypothetical coast line to the East & South coasts.** 1763. Map from Le Petit Atlas Maritime. (JL. Mar.1; 127)   Aus. $150
- **Detroit.** 1764. 'Large'. Map, includes town plan of Detroit, decor. cartouche. (HL. Apr.1; 1801)   £80
- **Gambia.** 1764. 'Large'. 2 maps covering between them course of River Gambia, each with decor. cartouche, trivial foxing. (HL. Apr.1; 1610)   £55
- **Gibraltar.** 1764. 'Large'. Map/town plan, key, decor. cartouche. (HL. Apr.1; 1622)   £70
- **Globe Terrestre. Essay d'une Carte Réduite . . Reduced Map containing the parts of the Known World.** 1748. 51 x 71cm. Map, engraved cartouche with rococco decor., rhumb lines, shows N. Amer. unexplored, Australia shown as New Holland with Queensland joined to New Guinea & Tasmania joined to New South Wales. (JL. Jul.19; 363)   Aus. $363
- **Karte von der Insel Montreal und den Gegenden Umher . . . 1744.** N.d. 21 x 31cm. Map, wormhole touching 1 word, anr. hole reprd. (CB. Nov.12; 51)   Can $100
- **Karte von Neu Frankreich oder Canada.** 1774. Ob. fo. Copper engraved map, folding marbs. (R. Oct.14-18; 5064)   DM 500
- **Mauritius.** 1764. 'Large' Map, compass rose, decor. cartouche. (HL. Apr.1; 1735)   £70
- **Nagasaki.** 1764. 'Large'. Engraved plan of town & port, decor. cartouche, compass rose. (HL. Apr.1; 1725)   £75
- **Partie Occidentale de la Nouvelle France ou du Canada . . . 1755.** [Nurnberg], 1755. 43 x 54cm. Map, cold. in outl., wide margins, stain affecting lr. frame line, 7 place-names underlined in red ink, 5 sm. ink splashes. (CB. Nov.12; 52)   Can. $260
- **Representation de Cours Ordinaire des Vents de Traverse qui Regnent sur les Côtes dans la Grand Mer du Sud.** Ca. 1764. Map. (JL. Jul.19; 385)   Aus. $110
- **St. Helena.** 1764. 'Medium' size. Map, cartouche, mod. colour, printing has slightly off-set, a few trivial blemishes. (HL. Apr.1; 1768)   £65
- **St. Thomas.** 1764. 'Large'. Map, compass rose, cartouche. (HL. Apr.1; 1805)   £60
- **Virgin Islands.** 1764. 'Medium' size. Engraved map, cartouche, a few minor blemishes. (HL. Apr.1; 1804   £80

BENARD
- **Carte de l'Hemisphère Austral. Montrant les Routes des Navigateurs les plus célèbres.** Paris, 1774. Fr. Edn. 53 x 53cm. Map cold. in outl., tables of latitudes & longitudes of Islands etc. in the Pacific. (JL. Mar.1; 171)   Aus.$240

BERRY, William
- **The Dukedom of Pomerania.** Ill.:– after N. Sanson. Ca. 1680-1798. 54.5 x 86.5cm. Engraved map, hand-cold. in outl., some staining, minor surface defects. (BS. Feb.25; 97)   £60

BERTIUS, Petrus
- **Description de la Terre Soubs Australe.** 1618. Map. F. & mntd. (JL. Mar.1; 122)   Aus. $260
- **Newfoundland.** 1609. 'Small'. Map, cartouche. (HL. Apr.1; 1744)   £110

BISWIDDEN in the Parish of Cambron, the land of Sr. John St. Ubyn
Probably 17th. C. 21 x 29 inches. Estate plan, with

key & bird & flora ills., preserved on card. (TA. May 21; 13) £85

BLAEU, Johannes or Jan
– **Anglia Regnum.** Ca. 1650. Hand-cold. map. (P. Dec.11; 182) *Garfunkle.* £160
– **Brasilien.** N.d. Ob. fo. Old cold. copper engraved map, painted heraldic & figure cartouche, stained in upr. margin. (R. Mar.31-Apr.4; 4994) DM 850
– **Brecknock.** 1654. Fo. Map, cold., coats of arms, text on verso. (JN. Apr.2; 619) £65
– **Britannia Ducatus, Duché de Bretaigne.** Mid 17th. C. 15½ x 21 inches. Engraved map, lr. margin dampstained. F. & G. (CSK. Jul.3; 1) £55
– **Buckinghamshire.** 1666. Hf. fo. Map, early colour. (JN. Apr.2; 657) £58
– **Cambridgeshire.** Ca. 1646. Fo. Map, cold., College coats of arms, text on verso. (JN. Apr.2; 660) £135
– – **Anr. Edn.** Ca. 1650. Hand-cold. map, cold. arms. F. & G. (P. Apr.9; 181) *Honniball.* £160
– **Cantium Vernacule Kent.** [1645 or later]. 19 x 23 inches. Engraved map, hand-cold. in outl., dampstains. F. & G. (CSK. Oct.3; 100) £120
– **Cardigan.** Ca. 1646. Fo. Map cold., 2 coats of arms, text on verso. (JN. Apr.2; 617) £75
– **Ceretica Sive Cardiganensis.** Cardiganshire, 1662. 15 x 19½ inches. Cont. cold. map, histor. title cartouche & scale, 3 coats of arms, sailing ships, etc., Fr. text to verso. (TA. May 21; 4) £65
– **Channel Isles.** 1666. Fo. Map, early colour, dampstained in margins. (JN. Apr.2; 577) £85
[–] **Comitatus Brechiniae; Breknoke.** [1648?]. 355 x 485mm. Engraved maps, hand-cold. cartouches & outl., text on verso. F. & G. (SH. Nov.6; 78) *Beynon.* £55
– **Comitatus Dorcestria Sive Dorsettia.** Dorset, ca.1662. 15 x 19¾ inches. Cont. cold. map, histor. title cartouche, 4 coats of arms, 1 blank, sailing ships etc., fold needs repair, Fr. text to verso. (TA. May 21; 1) £110
– **Comitatus Northantonensis.** [1645 or later]. 19 x 16 inches. Engraved map, hand-cold. in outl., stained. F. & G. (CSK. Aug.1; 95) £55
– **Comitatus Northumbria.** [1646 or later]. 16½ x 20 inches. Engraved map, hand-cold. in outl., Dutch text on verso. F. & G. (CSK. Jun.5; 43) £60
– **Comitatus Nottinghamiensis.** Nottinghamshire, ca. 1662. 15 x 19½ inches. Cont. cold. map, histor. title & scale cartouches, Royal coats of arms & 6 others, 2 blanks. (TA. May 21; 2) £85
– **Comitatus Salopiensis Anglice Shrop Shire.** Ca. 1667. 15 x 19½ inches. Cold. map, histor. title & scale cartouches, 4 coats of arms, Fr. text to verso. F. & G. (TA. Feb.19; 59) £62
– **Cumbria.** Ca. 1650. Hand-cold. map, arms. F. & G. (P. Jan.22; 189) *Kidd.* £80
[–] – **Anr. Edn.** [Amst.], [1662]. 409 x 492mm. Engraved map, hand-cold. in outl., histor. title-cartouche & vig. view, scale cartouche, 6 coats of arms decor., fully cold., some details heightened with gold, Spanish text on verso. W.a.f. (S. Nov.3; 147) *Morrison.* £100
– **Darbiensis.** Ca. 1650. Hand-cold. map, cartouche. F. & G. (P. Jan.22; 192) *Kidd.* £90
– **Devon.** Ca. 1650. 555 × 400mm. 400mm. Hand-cold. map, arms, cartouche. (P. May 14; 192d) £90
[–] **Devonia Vulgo Devon-shire.** Ca. 1650. 26 x 21 inches. Hand-cold. map (possibly orig,?), histor. title & scale cartouches, 9 armorials fully cold., Fr. text on verso, 1 sm. orig. printing crease, mntd. (TA. Oct.16; 92) £110
[–] – **Anr. Edn.** [Amst.], [1662]. 390 x 497mm. Engraved map, hand-cold. in outl., histor. title & scale-cartouches, 9 coats of arms, etc. fully cold., Latin text on verso. W.a.f. (S. Mar.30; 37) *Sanders of Oxford.* £110
– **Devonshire.** 1666. Fo. Map, early colour, text on verso, mntd. (JN. Apr.2; 676) £120
[–] **Ducatus Eboracensis, Anglice Yorkshire.** Amst., [1645, or later]. 387 x 500mm. Engraved map, hand-cold. in outl., histor. title & scale cartouches, 3 coats of arms, etc. fully cold., F. W.a.f. (S. Mar.30; 121) *Wood.* £130
[–] – **Anr. Edn.** [Amst.], [1646]. 388 x 501mm. Engraved map, hand-cold. in outl., histor. title & scale cartouches, 3 coats of arms, etc., fully cold., German text on verso. (S. Mar.30; 122) *Map House.* £100
[–] – **Anr. Edn.** [Amst.], [1648]. 387 x 498mm. Engraved map, hand-cold. in outl., histor. title & scale cartouches, 3 coats of arms fully cold., Dutch text on verso. W.a.f. (S. Nov.3; 187) *Radford.* £180
[–] **Ducatus Eboracensis, Pars Borealis. The Northriding of York Shire.** [Amst.], [1648]. 379 x 397mm. Engraved map, hand-cold. in outl., histor. & armorial title cartouche, 16 coats of arms fully cold., Dutch text on verso. W.a.f. (S. Nov.3; 193) *K. Books.* £110
– **Ducatus Eboracensis pars Occidentalis. The Westriding of Yorke Shire.** [Amst.], [1645 or later]. 384 x 498mm. German text on verso, engraved map, hand-cold in outl., scale cartouche, coats of arms, fully hand-cold. (SBA. Mar.4; 139) *Mizon.* £80
[–] – **Anr. Edn.** [Amst.], [1648]. 382 × 497mm. Engraved map, hand-cold. in outl., title & scale cartouches & 8 coats of arms fully cold., Dutch text on verso. W.a.f. (S. Nov.3; 189) *Map House.* £100
[–] – **Anr. Edn.** [Amst.], ca. 1662, or later. 382 x 497mm. Engraved map, hand-cold. in outl., histor. title & scale cartouches, 8 coats of arms fully cold., Latin text on verso, slight staining of top blank margin. W.a.f. (S. Nov.3; 191) *Map House.* £100
– – **Anr. Edn.** N.d. Ob. fo. Old cold. copper engraved map, 3 cold. arms, painted figure cartouche. (R. Mar.31-Apr.4; 5593) DM 500
– **Episcopatus Dunelmensis, Durham.** Ca. 1650. Hand-cold. map, coats-of-arms. (P. Dec.11; 180) *Owen.* £75
[–] **Essexia Comitatus.** [Amst.], [1662, or later]. 416 x 522mm. Engraved map, hand-cold. in outl., cartouches, 9 coats of arms, decor., (fully cold.), Latin text on verso, engr. in text fully cold. W.a.f. (S. Nov.3; 153) *Chapman.* £180
– **Gloucestershire.** Ca. 1650. Hand-cold. map, cartouche, arms. (P. Jan.22; 199) *Lamb.* £80
– **Hertfordshire.** Ob. fo. Old cold. copper engraved map, 3 cold. arms, 2 painted cartouches, stained in upr. margin. (R. Mar.31-Apr.4; 5566) DM 550
– **Holy Island.** N.d. 39.2 x 48cm. Engraved map, hand-cold. in outl., Latin text on verso. (BS. Feb.25; 103) £55
– **Isle of Man.** Ca. 1650. Hf. fo. Map, with text, old colouring. (JN. Apr.2; 575) £100
– **Leicestrensis Comitatvs.** N.d. 380 x 494mm. Engraved map, histor. scale cartouche, arms, hand-cold., slight stain in lr. margin, framed, text on verso. (SKC. Jul.28; 2387) £65
– **Lincolnia Comitatus, Anglis Lincoln-Shire.** [Amst.], [1645, or later]. 384 x 498mm. Engraved map, hand-cold. in outl., text on verso in German, combined title & scale cartouche, coats of arms & decor. features of sailing ships, fully hand-cold. (SBA. Mar.4; 137) *Mizon.* £85
– **Lincolnshire.** N.d. Ob. fo. Old cold. copper engraved map, 12 cold. arms, 1 painted figure cartouche, lightly browned. (R. Mar.31-Apr.4; 5571) DM 1,100
– **Lothian & Linlithgow.** Ca. 1654. Cold. map. F. (PD. Oct.22; 225) £55
[–] **Middle-sexia.** [Amst.], [1645, or later]. 389 x 406mm. Engraved map, hand-cold. in outl., histor. title-cartouche, coat of arms, etc. fully cold. F. W.a.f. (S. Mar.30; 70) *Gilberts.* £100
– – **Anr. Edn.** Ca. 1650. Hand-cold. map, Royal arms. F. & G. (P. Dec.11; 179) *Garfunkle.* £120
– – **Anr. Edn.** Amst., ca. 1650. 410 x 395mm. Uncold. map. (P. Jul.2; 238b) £60
– – **Anr. Edn.** N.d. Ob. fo. Old cold. copper engraved map, cold. arms & painted cartouche, lightly stained in upr. margin. (R. Mar.31-Apr.4; 5579) DM 550
– **Norfolcia.** [1645 or later.] 15 × 20 inches. Engraved map, hand-cold. in outl. F. & G. (CSK. Oct.17; 255) £75
– **Norfolk.** Ca. 1646. Fo., approximately 56 × 43cm. Cold. map, text on verso. (JN. Sep.9; 4225) £95
– **Northumbria.** Ca. 1650. Hand-cold. map, arms. F. & G. (P. Jan.22; 190) *Kidd.* £60
– **Nottinghamshire.** Ca. 1645-62. 38.8 × 50.5cm. Hand-cold. engraved map, with margins. (BS. Feb.25; 83) £65
– **Nova et Accuratissima Totius Terrarum Orbis Tabula.** Ca. 1660. Ob. fo. Cold copper engraved map in 2 hemispheres, allegorical decor. (R. Mar.31-Apr.4; 4800) DM 4,800
– **Praefecturae de Paraiba et Rio Grande** N.d. Ob. fo. Decor. old cold. copper engraved map, browned. (R. Mar.31-Apr.4; 4995) DM 650
[–] **Rvtlandia Comitatus.** N.d. Engraved map, histor. title & scale cartouches, arms, hand-cold. features (some outls., cartouches & arms), 1 tear, a few slight spots. F. (SKC. Jul.28; 2382) £80
– **Salop.** Ca. 1650. Hand-cold. map, arms. F. & G. (P. Jan.22; 191) *Turner.* £90
– **Somersettensis Comitatus Somersett Shire.** Ca. 1640. Approximately 15 × 19¾ inches. Cold. map, histor. title cartouche, scale, 7 coats of arms, sailing ships, etc., Dutch text to verso. (TA. Feb.19; 66) £125
– – **Anr. Copy.** Approximately 15 × 19½ inches. Map, cold. histor. title cartouche, scale, coats of arms, sailing ships, etc., Dutch text on verso., mntd. (TA. Oct.16; 1) £90
– – **Anr. Edn.** Amst., 1645 or later. 30¾ × 23 inches. Hand-cold. engraved map, title & scale cartouches, decor., & coats of arms, Latin text on verso. F. & G. on both sides. (LC. Oct.2; 175) £80
[–] **Suffolcia, Vernacule Suffolke.** [Amst.], [1662]. 381 × 501mm. Engraved map, 12 coats of arms, Fr. text on verso. W.a.f. (S. Mar.30; 107) *J. Holmes.* £100
– **Surria Vernacule Surrey.** Ca. 1650. Hand-cold. map, coats-of-arms. F. & G. (P. Dec.11; 178) *Campbell.* £170
– – **Anr. Edn.** [1659 or later]. 15 × 19½ inches. Engraved map, hand-cold. in outl., Spanish text on verso, slight marginal dampstains. F. & G. (CSK. Feb.6; 2) £150
– **Suthsexia vernacule Sussex.** Ca. 1650. Hand-cold. map, coats-of-arms. F. & G. (P. Dec.11; 177) £200
[–] – **Anr. Edn.** [Amst.], [1662]. 378 × 522mm. Engraved map, hand-cold. in outl., title-cartouche, 6 coats of arms, decor., (fully cold), Latin text on verso, upr. pt. of map dis-cold. W.a.f. (S. Nov.3; 179) *Clark.* £160
– **Virginia Partis Australis, et Floridae Partis Orientalis.** [Amst.], ca. 1640. 17 × 21½ inches. Decor. map, with boundaries cold., cold. ships, compass, 2 coats-of-arms & lge. cartouche, without text on verso, some light stains & spotting. (SG. May 21; 108) $260
[–] – **Anr. Edn.** [Amst.], ca. 1640, or later. Thick paper. 383 × 500mm. Engraved map, hand-cold in outl., historiated title & scale cartouches, 2 coats of arms, 2 compass roses, decors. etc., all fully cold. W.a.f. (S. Nov.3; 73) *Burden.* £150
– – **Anr. Edn.** [Amst.], ca. 1662, or later. 385 × 506mm. Engraved map, hand-cold. in outl., historiated title & scale cartouches, 2 coats of arms, 2 compass roses, decors., all fully cold., Latin text on verso, outer part of blank margin reprd. W.a.f. (S. Nov.3; 74) *Burden.* £140
[–] – **Anr. Edn.** [Amst.], ca. 1663, or later. 384 × 504mm. Engraved map, hand-cold. in outl., 2 compass roses, historiated title & scale cartouches, 2 coats of arms, all fully cold., Fr. text on verso. W.a.f. (S. Nov.3; 75) *Burden.* £140
– – **Anr. Edn.** [Amst.], [1667]. 19 × 22 inches. Hand-cold. map, with cartouches, arms & c., browned. (SG. Nov.20; 129) $400
– – **Anr. Edn.** N.d. Ob. fo. Old cold. copper engraved map, 2 painted figure cartouches, figure & heraldic decor. (R. Mar.31-Apr.4; 5062) DM 950

See–**BLAEU, Willem or Giulielmus Janszoon & Johannes or Jan**
See–**EMMIUS, E. & Blaeu, Willem or Giulielmus Janszoon & Johannes or Jan**
See–**GIGAS, J. & BLAEU Willem or Giulielmus Janszoon & Johannes or Jan**
See–**HENNEBERG, C. & BLAEU, Willem or Giulielmus Janszoon & Johannes or Jan.**
See–**MELLINGER, J. & Blaeu, Willem or Giulielmus Janszoon & Johannes or Jan**
See–**MERCATOR, Gerard & Blaeu, Willem or Giulielmus Janszoon & Johannes or Jan**
See–**MEYER-HUSUM, J. & Blaeu, Willem or Giulielmus Janszoon & Johannes or Jan**
See–**MOLLER, Ch. & Blaeu, Willem or Giulielmus Janszoon & Johannes or Jan**
See–**SCAVENIUS, L. & Blaeu, Willem or Giulielmus Janszoon & Johannes or Jan**
See–**SPRECHER, J.V. Bernegg & Clüver Ph. & Blaeu, Johannes or Jan**

BLAEU, Willem or Giulielmus Janszoon
– **Africae Nova Descriptio.** Ob. fo. Old cold. copper engraved map, figures, 2 scenes, 9 sm. views at head. (R. Mar.31-Apr.4; 4932) DM 1,800
– **Americae Nova Tabula.** [Amst.], ca. 1630, or later. 361 × 463mm. Engraved map, hand-cold. in outl., title-cartouche, etc. fully cold. lacks outer

BLAEU, Willem or Giulielmus Janszoon -contd.
borders of views & figures at top & sides, F. W.a.f. (S. Mar.31; 302) *Burgess*. £160
– – **Anr. Copy**. 16¼ × 21½ inches. Cold. map, border of views & figures, German text on verso, slight soiling. (SPB. Jul.28; 332) $1,700
– – **Anr. Edn**. [Amst.], ca. 1640, or later. 409 × 553mm. Map, hand-cold in outl., title-cartouche, vigs., German text on verso, N.W. corner reprd. & pt. of Eastern margin slightly frayed & discoloured, in both cases touching engraved border, decors., all fully cold. W.a.f. (S. Nov.3; 43) *Levison*. £420
– – **Anr. Edn**. N.d. Old cold. copper engraved map, painted cartouche, figures at side, 9 sm. views at head, browned. (R. Mar.31-Apr.4; 4972) DM 2,300
[–] **Arabia**. [Amst.], [1667, or later]. 417 × 522mm. Engraved map, hand-cold. in outl., historiated title & scale cartouches fully cold., sailing ships partly cold., Fr. text on verso. W.a.f. (S. Nov.4; 376) *Arader*. £210
– **Asia noviter delineata**. [Amst.], [1663]. 410 × 552mm. Engraved map, hand-cold. in out., historiated title-cartouche, decor., (full cold.), Fr. text on verso, wormhole affecting engraved surface. W.a.f. (S. Nov.4; 393) *Nagle*. £220
– – **Anr. Edn**. N.d. Ob. fo. Old cold. copper engraved map, figure decor., 5 scenes at side, 9 sm. views at head. (R. Mar.31-Apr.4; 5068) DM 2,200
– **Bermudas**. Ob. fo. Old cold copper engraved map, 3 painted figure & heraldic cartouches & engraved legend. (R. Mar.31-Apr.4; 4991) DM 1,150
– **Candia olim Creta.–Graecia**. [Amst.], ca. 1650. 19 × 23½ inches. 2 maps, cartouches cold., some spotting, etc. (SG. Nov.20; 27) $200
– **China**. N.d. Ob. fo. Old cold. copper engraved map, painted cartouche & lge. cold. arms. (R. Mar.31-Apr.4; 5091) DM 1,100
– **East-Indies**. Ca. 1660. 'Large'. Cold. map, 3 cartouches, ships, compass-rose, rhumb-lines, from atlas. (HL. Apr.1; 1532) £370
– **Extrima Americae versus Boream**. Amst., [1667]. 44.5 × 56cm. Fully cold. map, from Le Grand Atlas, some browning due to text on verso. (CB. Nov.12; 54) *Can*. $1,300
– **Gran Canaria**. N.d. 38 × 50 cm. Cold. copper engraved map, decor. cartouche. (D. Dec.11-13; 3483) DM 510
– **Guiana sive Amazonum Regio**. Amst., [1630 or later]. 15 × 19½ inches. Partially cold. map. slight stains. F. & G. (SPB. Jul.28; 352) $175
– **India quae Orientalis dicitur, et Insulae Adiacentes**. Amst., 1635. Engraved map, includes the discoveries of Jansz & Cartensz on West Coast of Cape York & the sightings of Hartog, Jacobsen & de Witt around North West Cape, Fr. text on verso. (JL. Jul.19; 305) *Aus*. $700
– – **Anr. Edn**. [Amst.], [1640, or later]. 410 × 501mm. Engraved map, hand-cold. in outl., 3 historiated cartouches, 1 with coat of arms, compass rose, decor., (fully cold.), Fr. text on verso. (S. Nov.4; 440) *Clipstow*. £150
– – **Anr. Edn**. [Amst.], [1667, or later]. 408 × 493mm. Engraved map, hand-cold. in outl., 3 historiated cartouches, 1 with coat of arms, compass rose, decor., (fully cold.), Fr. text on verso. W.a.f. (S. Nov.4; 442) *Clipstow*. £150
– **Insulae Americanae in Oceano Septentrionali cum Terris Adiacentibus**. [Amst.], ca. 1670. 17 × 23 ins. Hand-cold. map. from an atlas, with 3 pict. cartouches, matted. Mntd. to old bd. (SG. May 21; 123) $140
– **Ivnnan Imperii Sinarum Provincia Decimaquinta**. N.d. 40.5 × 49.5 cm. Outl. cold. copper engraved map, title cartouche, topographical explanations & mile indicator. (D. Dec.11-13; 3508) DM 420
– **Magnae Britanniae**. Ca. 1650. Hand cold. map, vig. F. & G. (P. Sep.11; 154) *Weiss*. £150
– **Mappa Aestivarum Insularum, alias Barmudas dictarum**. Amst., ca. 1670, or later. 400 × 522mm. Engraved map, including historiated & armorial title-cartouche, 2 scale-cartouches, compass rose, etc., arms at each end of numbered key across bottom of plt., 1 or 2 perforations in engraved surface, repair at bottom of centre fold, without loss. W.a.f. (S. Nov.3; 97) *Potter*. £240
– **Nova Hispania et Nova Galicia**. [Amst.], ca. 1640, or later. Thick paper. 347 × 482mm. Engraved map, hand-cold. in outl., lge. historiated & armorial tile-cartouche, historiated scale-cartouche, compass rose & sailing ships, all

fully cold., 1 or 2 stains. W.a.f. (S. Nov.3; 56) *Heing*. £100
– **Nova Virginia Tabula**. [Amst.], ca. 1645, or later. 374 × 480mm. Engraved map, hand-cold. in outl., cartouches, coat of arms, decor., fully cold., Fr. text on verso. W.a.f. (S. Nov.3; 70) *Nebenzahl*. £200
– – **Anr. Edn**. [Amst.], [1663]. 372 × 472mm. Engraved map, hand-cold. in outl., cartouches, coat of arms, inset engr., etc., fully cold., Fr. text on verso, slight staining of bottom blank margin. W.a.f. (S. Nov.3; 71) *Burden*. £160
– – **Anr. Edn**. [Amst.], [1665, or later]. 371 × 474mm. Engraved map, including cartouches, coat of arms, inset engr., etc., Dutch text on verso. W.a.f. (S. Nov.3; 72) *Burden*. £120
– – **Anr. Edn**. N.d. Ob. fo. Old cold. copper engraved map, 3 painted cartouches, figure, heraldic decor. (R. Mar.31-Apr.4; 5061) DM 900
– **Regiones sub Polo Arctico**. N.d. Ob. fo. Old cold. copper engraved map, 2 painted figure cartouches & lge. cold arms. (R. Oct.14-18; 3399) DM 700
– **Südafrika**. N.d. Ob. fo. Old cold. copper engraved map, lge. painted figure cartouche. (R. Mar.31-Apr.4; 4965) DM 500
– **Tabula Russiae**. [1635 or later]. 16 × 21½ inches. Engraved map, hand-cold. in outl., insets of Moscow & Archangel, Dutch text on verso, tear along fold, slightly stained. (CSK. Mar.6; 46) £65
– **Venezuela**. Ob. fo. Old cold. copper engraved map, 2 painted cartouches. (R. Mar.31-Apr.4; 5055) DM 450
– **West Indies**. Ca. 1640. 'Large' Map, cold. (probably not early colouring), 3 cartouches, ships & compass-roses. (HL. Apr.1; 1553) £370
See-**GIGAS, J. & Blaeu, Willem or Giulielmus Janszoon & Johannes or Jan**
See-**HENNEBERG, C. & Blaeu, Willem or Giulielmus Janszoon & Johannes or Jan**
See-**MELLINGER, J. & Blaeu, Willem or Giulielmus, Janszoon**
See-**MERCATOR, Gerard & Blau, Willem or Giulielmus Janszoon**
See-**MEYER-HUSUM, J. & Blaeu, Willem or Giulielmus Janszoon & Johannes or Jan**
See-**MOLLER, Ch. & Blaeu, Willem or Giulielmus Janszoon & Johannes or Jan**
See-**SCAVENIUS, L. & Blaeu, Willem or Giulielmus, Janszoon & Johannes or Jan**
See-**SPRECHER, J.V. Bernegg & Clüver Ph. & Blaeu, Willem or Giulielmus Janszoon**

BLAEU, Willem or Giulielmus Janszoon & Johannes or Jan
[–] **Aethiopia Inferior vel Exterior . . .** [Amst.]. ca. 1660. 379 × 484mm. Engraved map, hand-cold. in outl., historiated title-cartouche, decor., (fully cold.), Fr. text on verso. W.a.f. (S. Nov.4; 390) *Ashworth*. £100
– **Comitatus Glatz**. Ca. 1650. 20 × 23½ inches. Cold. map, from an atlas, with armorial cartouche & c. (SG. Nov.20; 102) $110
– **Cypern**. Ob. fo. Old cold. copper engraved map, lge. painted allegorcial cartouche & 2 cold. arms. (R. Mar.31-Apr.4; 5097) DM 1,000
[–] **Cyprus Insula**. [Amst.], ca. 1635, or later. 378 × 506mm. Engraved map, hand-cold. pict. title cartouche, (surface worn), 2 coats of arms, ships & map outl., Dutch text on verso. (SKC. May 19; 373) £85
– – **Anr. Edn**. Ca. 1650. Hand-cold. map, cartouche, vig. sailing ships. (P. Mar.12; 195) *Kay*. £160
– **Danubius, Fluvius Europae Maximus**. N.d. Lge. ob. fo. Old. cold. copper engraved map, 2 lge. painted cartouches, browned at left, some tears & 2 sm. holes backed. (R. Oct.14-18; 3713) DM 8,000
– – **Anr. Copy**. 41 × 96 cm. 2 lge. decor. painted cartouches. (R. Oct.14-18; 3712) DM 1,600
– – **Anr. Copy**. 41 × 96 cm. (R. Mar.31-Apr.4; 3526) DM 1,300
– **Delflandia, Schielandia**. Amst., ca. 1631. 38 × 50 cm. Hand-cold. engraved map, ptd. text on verso, browned. (VG. Oct.28; 348) Fls. 500
– **Dioecesis Stravangriensis**. [Amst.], ca. 1650. 18 × 21 ins. Fully-cold. map, with cartouche, 2 coats-of-arms & ornament. (SG. Nov.20; 28) $175
– **Europa**. Ca. 1650. Hand-cold. map, vigs. of sailing ships, inset town plans & figures in borders, wide margins. F. & G. (P. Feb.19; 142) *Busch*. £170

– **Europa recens descripta**. [1635 or later]. 16 × 22 inches. Engraved map, hand-cold. in outl. Close F. & G. (CSK. May 8; 43) £200
– – **Anr. Edn**. N.d. Ob. fo. Copper engraved map, decor. sides, views at head, painted cartouche. (R. Mar.31-Apr.4; 5162) DM 2,000
– **Franken**. N.d. Ob. fo. Old cold. copper engraved map with painted figure cartouche. (R. Oct.14-18; 3731) DM 430
– **Geldria Ducatus et Zutfania Comitatus**. Amst., ca. 1631. 38 × 50 cm. Engraved hand-cold. map, ptd. Dutch text on verso, slight marginal staining & tears, fold in middle. (VG. Oct.28; 274) Fls. 480
– **Groniga Dominium**. Amst., ca. 1630. 38 × 49 cm. Engraved hand-cold. map, heightened with gold, ptd. Latin text on verso, fold in middle. (VG. Oct.28; 284) Fls. 750
– **Herzogtum Braunschweig und Lüneburg**. N.d. Ob. fo. Old cold. copper engraved map with painted arms cartouche & 6 sm. arms. (R. Oct.14-18; 4350) DM 480
– **Herzogtum Holstein**. N.d. Ob. fo. Old cold. copper engraved map with 2 supplementary maps. (R. Oct.14-18; 4089) DM 480
– **Herzogtum Kleve und Herrschaft Ravenstein**. N.d. Ob. fo. Old cold. copper engraved map with 2 painted figure cartouches & cold. arms. (R. Oct.14-18; 4507) DM 480
– [**Herzogtum Württemberg**]. N.d. Ob. fo. Old cold. copper engraved map with painted figure cartouche & lge. cold. arms. (R. Oct.14-18; 3649) DM 580
– [–] **Anr. Copy**. Browned. (R. Oct.14-18; 3650) DM 430
– **Hollandia Comitatus**. Amst., ca. 1635. 39 × 53 cm. Hand-cold. engraved map, inset map of Texel, Vlieland & Terschelling, ptd. text in Fr. on verso, fold in middle, some names of towns underlined in pen. (VG. Oct.28; 296) Fls. 500
– **The Holy Island**. Ca. 1648. 'Large'. Map, early outl. colour, ornate cartouche, royal coat of arms & galleon, a few minor splits at edge of very wide margins. (HL. Apr.1; 1695) £50
– **Landgrafschaft Hessen**. N.d. Ob. fo. Old cold. copper engraved map with 2 painted cartouches, 2 lge. & 5 sm. cold. arms. (R. Oct.14-18; 4275) DM 530
– **Lutzenburg Ducatus**. Amst., ca. 1640. 38 × 50 cm. Hand-cold. engraved map, ptd. text in Fr. on verso, fold in middle, some names of towns underlined. (VG. Oct.28; 461) Fls. 600
– **Mark und Ravensburg**. N.d. Ob. fo. Old cold. copper engraved map with supp. map: Umgebung Bielefelds & painted arms cartouche. (R. Oct.14-18; 4551) DM 1,700
– **Mediolanum Milano**. After 1706. 20 × 24 inches. Engraved map, laid down, several marginal tears. (CSK. Oct.17; 258) £55
[–] **Nova Belgica & Anglia Nova**. [Amst.], [1635]. 385 × 500mm. Engraved map, hand-cold. in outl., historiated title & scale cartouches, compass roses, decors., Dutch text on verso, slight staining & discolouration. W.a.f. (S. Nov.3; 61) *Arader*. £350
– – **Anr. Edn**. [Amst.], [1663]. 20 × 23 inches. Map, with boundaries, lge. cartouche, scale, etc., all in col., Fr. text on verso, 1 blank corner torn away, some age-browning. (SG. May 21; 15) $800
[–] – **Anr. Edn**. Amst., ca. 1670. 390 × 510mm. Engraved map on wtrmkd. paper with latin text on verso, coastlines hand-cold. thro.-out, decor., ornate title-cartouche, full margins, centre-fold reprd. (PWP. Apr.9; 156) *Can*. $750
– **Nova totius Germaniae Descriptio**. N.d. Ob. fo. Old cold. copper engraved map, caption & painted Reichsadler. (R. Oct.14-18; 3413) DM 850
– **Nova Totius Orbis Terrarum Geographica et Hydrographica Tabula**. 17th. C. Ob. fo. Old cold. copper engraved map, 4 ills. round, allegories of 4 elements, 4 seasons at side, allegories at head & foot, 2 sm. subsidiary maps & 3 cartouches. (R. Mar.31-Apr.4; 4792) DM 7,300
– – **Anr. Copy**. Ob. fo. (R. Oct.14-18; 3370) DM 7,000
– **Novus XVII Inferioris Germaniae Provinciarum Typus**. N.d. Ob. fo. Old cold. copper engraved map with painted figure cartouche & decor, slightly soiled. (R. Oct.14-18; 5347) DM 1,300
– **Oberösterreich**. N.d. Ob. fo. Old cold. copper engraved map, 2 painted figure cartouches & cold. arms. (R. Mar.31-Apr.4; 5739) DM 650

– **[Pfalz].** N.d. Ob. fo. Old cold. copper engraved map with painted cartouche, flag & lge. cold. arms. (R. Oct.14-18; 4892) DM 530
– **Rhenius Fluviorum Europae Celeberrimus.** N.d. 41 × 93 cm. Old cold. copper engraved map with painted figure cartouche & 10 cold arms. (R. Oct.14-18; 4910) DM 2,400
– **[Schwaben].** N.d. Ob. fo. Old cold. copper engraved map with 3 painted cartouches. (R. Oct.14-18; 3592) DM 580
– **[Skandinavien].** N.d. Ob. fo. Old cold. copper engraved map with painted figure cartouche & 2 lge. cold. arms. (R. Oct.14-18; 5830) DM 420
– **Tabula Islandiae.** Amst., n.d. 38 × 49.5 cm. Partly cold. copper engraved map, decor. title & mile indicator, cartouche, wind rose, decor. (D. Dec.11-13; 3472) DM 450
– **Territorio di Verona.** Ca. 1650. Hand-cold. map. Double-glazed. (P. Jun.11; 224) *Dolcetia.* £70
– **Territorium Basiliense.** N.d. Ob. fo. Old cold. copper engraved map, 2 painted figure cartouches. (R. Mar.31-Apr.4; 5857) DM 800
– **Territorium Francofurtensis.** N.d. Ob. fo. Old cold. copper engraved map framed with allegories & costumes & 34 painted arms. (R. Oct.14-18; 4232) DM 2,600
– **Territorium Norimbergense.** N.d. Ob. fo. Old cold. copper engraved map with sm. cold. town plan & 2 painted figure cartouches. (R. Oct.14-18; 3798) DM 480
– **Westfälischer Kreis.** N.d. Ob. fo. Old cold. copper engraved map with painted figure & heraldic cartouche. (R. Oct.14-18; 4644) DM 630
– **Zeelandia Comitatus.** Amst., ca. 1635. 38 × 50 cm. Hand-cold. engraved map, fold in middle, a marginal tear. F. & G. (VG. Oct.28; 338) Fls. 550
– **Zürichgau und Basel.** N.d. Ob. fo. Old cold. copper engraved map with painted cartouche. (R. Oct.14-18; 5823) DM 650
– – **Anr. Copy.** (R. Mar.31-Apr.4; 5891) DM 600
– **Zuydhollandia.** Amst., ca. 1631. 39 × 51 cm. Hand-cold. engraved map, ptd. text in Dutch on verso, fold in middle. (VG. Oct.28; 364) Fls. 520

BLOME, Richard
– **A General Mapp of the Kingdom of Spaine.–A New Mapp of ye Empire of China . . .** L., 1669. Each 14 × 17 inches. 2 maps, with cold. boundaries, cartouches & arms (including those of Sir Thomas Peyton on 2nd. map), some age-browning, etc. (SG. May 21; 16) $110
– **Kent.** L., ca. 1680. 245 × 190mm. Hand-cold. map, F. & G. (P. Jul.2; 238) *Donovan.* £50
– **A New Mapp of Africa.** Ill.:– F. Lamb (engraver) & M. Sanson (designer). [L.], 1669. 18 × 22½ inches. Map, boundaries & cartouche in col., & cold. arms of Hennery, Marquess of Dorchester, some wear at folds, slight spotting. (SG. May 21; 2) $180
– **A New Mapp of America Meridionale.** Ill.:– N. Sanson (designer). L., 1669. 18 × 22 inches. Cold. map, with fully cold. cartouche & arms of the Duke of Albemarle, many sm. decorations, slight fraying at fold & to blank margins. (SG. May 21; 98) $130
– [–] **Paradise or the Garden of Eden (Middle East, etc.).** Ca. 1687. Fo., approximately 56 × 43cm. Uncold. map. (JN. Sep.9; 3760) £50

BOAZIO, Baptista
– **Irlandiae Accurata Descriptio.** Antw., [1606 or later]. 435 × 570mm. Engraved map, hand-cold., including cartouches, coat of arms, sailing ships, sea monsters, etc., Latin text on verso, reprd. at bottom of centre fold, slightly affecting engraved surface, short tear in 1 margin, a few grazes, edges reinforced. W.a.f. (S. Jun.29; 57) *Duyck.* £750
– – **Anr. Edn.** N.d. Ob. fo. Cold. copper engraved map from a later Ortelius Edn. with adress by J.B. Vrinius, 4 painted roll cartouches, cold. arms & figure decor. (R. Oct.14-18; 5531) DM 850

BOHEMIA
N.d. 418 × 541mm. Hand-cold. engraved map, Dutch text on verso. F. & G. on both sides. (SKC. Feb.26; 1543) £140

BONNE
– **Falkland Islands.** 1787. 'Large'. Map, inset maps of S. Georgia & Sandwich Islands, with mod. col. (HL. Apr.1; 1606) £70

BORDONE, [Benedetto]
– **Balearic Islands: Majorca & Minorca.** 1547. 'Small'. Woodcut map, unorig. stippling (period unknown), on reverse is woodcut of Catalonian coast, Ibiza & Formentera. (HL. Apr.1; 1782) £60
– **Jamaica & Cuba.** 1547. 'Small'. Map, in p. of text, on reverse is map of Cuba. (HL. Apr.1; 1719) £155

BOURGOIN, P.
– **Mappe Monde. Carte Universelle de la Terre.** Paris, ca. 1760. 15 × 20 ins. Hand-cold. double-hemisphere copper-plt. map, with engr. & other ornaments surrounding the maps, some minor spotting. (SG. May 21; 143) $250
– – **Anr. Copy.** Hand-cold. map, decor. cartouche & border. (JL. Mar.1; 148) Aus. $150

BOWEN, Emanuel
– **An Accurate Map of the West Indies.** L., ca. 1760. 16 × 18½ inches. Hand-cold. map, with fully-cold. pict. cartouche. (SG. May 21; 111) $160
– **Africa.** 1748. 'Large'. Decorative cartouche. (HL. Apr.1; 1504) £80
– **[Harris Voyages], Southern United States of America & West Indies & Central America.** Ca. 1740. Fo., approximately 56 × 43cm. Cold. map, sm. repairs. (JN. Sep.9; 3603) £50
– **A Map of Discoveries made by Captain William Dampier in the Roebuck, 1699.** N.d. Map showing New Guinea & New Britain. F. (JL. Mar.1; 123) Aus. $120
– **A New & Accurate Map of Louisiana with Part of Florida & Canada . . .** L., ca. 1760. 360 × 430mm. Engraved map, numbered 100, hand-cold. in outls., borders & title cartouche, laid down on card mount, full margins. (PWP. Apr.9; 161) Can. $170
– **A New & Accurate Map of the West Indies . . . Coast of North & South America.** Ca. 1750. Uncold. map. (P. Mar.12; 197) *Radford.* £50
– **A New Map of Georgia . . . Carolina, Florida & Louisiana.** Ca. 1750. Uncold. map. (P. Mar.12; 196) *Radford.* £70
– – **Anr. Edn.** 1764. 'Large'. Map, sm. marginal crease 1 corner. (HL. Apr.1; 1802) £115

BOWEN, Emanuel & Kitchen, Thomas
– **Middlesex.** [1760 or later]. 20½ × 28 inches. Engraved map, hand-cold. in outl. F. & G. (CSK. Apr.10; 1) £100

BOWEN, Thomas
– **Chart of Van Diemen's Land.** L., 1780. Engraved map. (JL. Jul.19; 372) Aus. $120
– **A New & Accurate Map of Asia.** 1777. Map showing New Holland & Whole East coast of Australia as New South Wales discovered 1770. (JL. Jul.19; 383) Aus. $120
– **North Pole.** 1764. 'Large'. Engraved map, decorative cartouche. (HL. Apr.1; 1526) £55
– **The World.** Ca. 1784. Fo. Map, uncold., insets, globes, etc., top left corner reprd. (JN. Apr.2; 13) £52
– **The World including The Discoveries made by Captain Cook.** L., 1789. 44 × 27cm. Map, cold. in outl., Diemen's Land joined to New South Wales. (JL. Mar.1; 192) Aus. $130
See–GIBSON, John & Bowen, Thomas

BRAUN, Georg & Hogenberg, Franz
– **Antequera.** Ca. 1590. Hand-cold. town plan. (P. May 14; 190c) £65
– **Brightstowe [Bristol].** 17th. C. 13¼ × 17¾ inches. Cold. map with ornamental title cartouches, coats of arms, decor., text to verso. F. & G. (TA. Feb.19; 56) £125
– **Bruges.** Ca. 1573. Hand-cold. town plan. In mount. (P. Mar.12; 186) *Dawson.* £65
– **Calaris, Rhodes, Famagusta, Malta.** Ca. 1600. 4 hand-cold. town plans on 1 sheet. F. & G. (P. Mar.12; 192) *Habibis.* £65
– [–] **Cestria vulgo Chester, Angliae Civitatas.** [Cologne], [1598 or later]. 327 × 438mm. Engraved bird's eye view of Chester, Latin text on verso, perforation in title cartouche, coats of arms & decor. feature of men with hunting dogs, hand-cold. F. (SBA. Jul.14; 267) *Nolan.* £80
– [–] **Chester.** [Cologne], [1573, or later]. 325 × 429mm. Engraved plan of bird's eye view of Chester, hand-cold., title cartouche, coats of arms, decor., a few minor defects. (SBA. Dec.16; 274) *Hulme.* £55
– **Civitas Exoniae [Vulgo Excester].** 1587 or later. 12½ × 15¾ inches. Cold. map, 3 coats of arms, decor., etc., Fr. text to verso sm. split to fold. (TA. Feb.19; 81) £105

– – **Anr. Copy.** 12½ × 15¾ inches. Fr. text to verso, sm. split to fold. (TA. May 21; 32) £95
– **Hamburg.** 16th. C. Uncold. town plan, with river & figures in foreground. F. & G. (P. Apr.30; 130) *Map House.* £210
– **Jerusalem.** Cologne, [1572-1618]. Double-p. fo. Fully hand-cold. map from the Civitates Orbis Terrarum, vig. at lower right. (CNY. Oct.9; 13) £620
– **Londinum Feracissimi Anglia Regni Metropolis.** Ca. 1600. Uncold. map. F. & G. (P. Feb.19; 130) *Shires.* £320
– **London.** Ca. 1600. Hand-cold. town plan, with shipping on the Thames & figures in the foreground. F. & G. (P. Mar.12; 191) *Langlois.* £320
– [–] **Mediolanum [Milan].** [Cologne], [1572]. 332 × 478mm. Engraved bird's-eye plan & view, hand-cold., arms, figures, etc., Latin text on verso. W.a.f. (S. Mar.31; 375) *Horbath.* £140
– **Philippeville, Chinay, Mariebourg, Walcourt [Belgium].** Ca. 1596. Fo., approximately 56 × 43 cm. Map, 4 town views, text on verso, cold. (JN. Sep.9; 3896) £60
– **Roterodamum.** Ca. 1588. 28 × 40 cm. Hand-cold. engraved bird's-eye plan, with ptd. text on verso, fold in middle. (VG. Oct.28; 361) Fls. 600
– **Strigonium.** [Cologne]. 1595. 13¾ × 20½ inches. Map, 2 town views, Latin text on verso. F. & G. (SPB. Jul.28; 338) $250
– **Treveris, Cobolentz .., Rotenburg. -Wittenburga, Civitas Francfordiensis, Wismaria, Rostochium.** [Cologne], [1572]. 7 engraved bird's-eye views on 2 plts., hand-cold., Latin text on versos. W.a.f. (S. Mar.31; 378) *Schmidt.* £190

BRION DE LA TOUR, Louis
– **Mappe Monde Géo-Hydrographique.** 1786. 650 × 460mm. Hand cold. map, mntd. (P. Jun.11; 213) *Price.* £100

BRY, Johannes Theodor de
– **Virginia.** Frankfurt, ca. 1628. Sm. fo. Cold. map, 2 sides remargined with neat restoration, Smith derivative from De Bry's German 'America'. (JN. Apr.2; 92) £220

BRYANT, A.
– **Map of the County of Gloucester . . .** 1 Nov. 1824. Narrow lge. fo. (Sheets approximately 26½ × 67 inches). Engraved map in 3 sheets, hand-cold., 5 inset maps, lge. vig., mntd. on linen, 2 sheets detchd., folding into orig. red hr. mor. cl. covers. W.a.f. (S. Jun.29; 2) *Crowe.* £180
– **Map of the County of Oxford.** 1824. Each map approx. 59 × 38 inches. 2 linen-bkd. jointed folding hand-cold. engraved maps (presumably formed from 4 sheets), with vig. of Christ Church, Oxford, key, scale, compass rose, piano-key border, marked 'Proof'. Cont. cf. gt. case. W.a.f. (LC. Jun.18; 195) £100

BUACHE, Philippe
See–DE LISLE, Guillaume & Buache, Philippe

BURE DE BOO, A.J.
– **Svecia, Daria, et Norvegia.** N.d. Ob. fo. Cold. copper engraved map, painted arms cartouche. (R. Mar.31-Apr.4; 5963) DM 550
– – **Anr. Copy.** (R. Oct.14-18; 5861) DM 200

BURGHERS, M.
– **New Map of the Terraqueous Globe according to the Ancient Discoveries & Most General Divisions of it into Continents & Oceans.** Cold. engraved map, in 2 hemispheres, shows western pt. of Australia. (JL. Dec.14; 115) Aus. $230

BURR, David H.
– **City of New York.** N.Y., 1839. 22 × 18 inches. Fully hand-cold. map. Folded in orig. cl. covers. (SG. May 21; 78) $150
– **Maps of New-York Counties.** Ithaca, 1840. Lge. fo. 8 fully-cold. maps. (SG. Nov.20; 31) $180

BYRNE
– **A General Chart exhibiting the Discoveries made by James Cook in this & his 2 Preceding Voyages** . . . 1770. 55 × 94 cm. South Australia marked in approximate outl., East Coast well delineated., outls. hand-cold. (JL. Jul.19; 236) Aus. $100

CAREY, Henry Charles
– **Porto Rico & Virgin Islands.** [Phila.], [1822]. 18 × 22 inches. Hand-cold. map, from the Carey & Lea atlas, extensive text in lr. portion, very slight offsetting. (SG. May 21; 129) $175

CARTE REDUITE du Globe Terrestre
Paris, ca. 1752. Hand-cold. map. (J. Mar.1; 216)
Aus. $100

CARVER, Jonathon
- **A New Map of the Province of Quebec.** L., 1776. 1st. Iss. 49 × 67 cm. Fully cold. map, from Faden's North American Atlas, cartouche, 4 inset maps. (CB. Nov.12; 59)   Can. $950

CARY, John
- **The Eastern Hemisphere.** 1801. Map, shows Cook's tracks & hypothetic South Coast of Australia from Western Port of St. Peter's Islands. (JL. Dec.14; 175)   Aus. $160
- - **Anr. Copy.** (JL. Jul.19; 376)   Aus. $120
- **A New Map of North America.** L., 1806. 20½ × 23¼ inches. Light offsetting. (SG. Aug.21; 247)
$150
- **Western Hemisphere.** L., 1 Aug. 1799. 21 × 25 inches. Fully-cold. circular map. (SG. May 21; 140) $110

CARY, John & George
- **New Plan of London & its Vicinity.** 1836. 29 × 32½ inches. Engraved map, hand-cold. in outl. Folding on cl., in s.-c. with place name index, orig. wraps. (CSK. Jul.10; 20)   £50

CASSINI, A.D.
- **Planispheruim Terrestre.** Leiden, ca. 1720. Ob. fo. Copper engraved map, figure & allegories round. (R. Mar.31-Apr.4; 4823)   DM 2,200

CASSINI, G.M.
- **Europe; Asia; Africa; America; Italy; Naples & Sicily; The World.** Roma, 1788 & 1790. Tall fo. (16½ × 12 inches). Set of 7 double-p. maps, with cold. boundaries & elaborate cartouches, very worn, heavily dampstained thro.-out. Old vell. W.a.f. (SG. May 21; 23) $220

CELLARIUS
- **Hemisphaerium Orbis Antiqui.** 1660. Ob. fo. Old cold. copper engraved map, figure decor. (R. Mar.31-Apr.4; 4869)   DM 800
- - **Anr. Edn.** N.d. Ob. fo. Cold. copper engraved map from Himmelsatlas, allegorical decor. (R. Oct.14-18; 3393)   DM 600

CHETWIND
- **Asia.** 1666. Fo. Uncold. map, sailing ships. (JN. Apr.2; 190)   £70

CLUVERIUS, Phillipus
See–SPRECHER, J.v. Bernegg & Clüverius, Phillipus & Blaeu.

CLUVERIUS, Phillippus & Jansson, Jan or Johannes
- **Italiae Antiquae.** Ca. 1650. 490 × 380mm. Hand-cold. map, cartouche. (P. Apr.30; 148)
Leeuwe. £50

COCCEJO, J.H.
- **Jerusalem aus den Schrifften Josephi ganz neu Vorgestellt.** Ill.:– Christ Weigel. Ca. 1725. 13½ × 18 inches. Hand-cold. plan, extensive captions in German, margins trimmed & reprd. (SG. May 21; 50) $140

COLE, G.
See–ROPER, J. & Cole, G.

COLLINS, Capt. Greenville
- **The River of Thames from London to the Bouy of the Noure.** Ill.:– J. Harris. L., 1723? 24 × 38 inches. Cold. map, from the 'Great Britain's Coasting Pilot', with many decors., 1 sm. tear, & reprd. at centre-fold, pasted to an old bd. (SG. Nov.20; 125) $200

COLTEN
- **Patagonia [& Southern S. America]; South Orkney; Falkland Islands & South Georgia.** 1850. 'Large' 4-pt. map, a few marginal imperfections. (HL. Apr.1; 1607)   £60

COOK, Lieut. James
- **Carte de l'Isle d'Otahiti.** Paris, 1769. 1774. 40×23 cm. Cold. map. (JL. Dec.14; 123)
Aus. $100

COOK, Robert J.
- **Railway Map of England & Wales.** 1866. 212×171 cm. Folding lithographed map, mntd. on linen. Orig. cl. folder. (SH. Oct.9; 265)
Bunsie. £80

CORONELLI, Vicenzo Maria
- **East Indies showing Bay of Diema & New Holland.** Ca. 1696. 46×60 cm. Cold. map, decor.

title with putti & cartouche showing miles & leagues. (JL. Dec.14; 107)   Aus. $350
- **Ireland.** Ca. 1690. Fo. Map, on 2 fo. sheets, lge. cartouche, both uncold. (JN. Apr.2; 597)   £60
- **Isole dell'Indie.** Venice, 1696. Map, hand-cold, decor. title, scale cartouches. (JL. Jul.19; 356)
Aus. $500
- **Jamaica.** 1692. 'Medium' Size. Map, mod. colour. (HL. Apr.1; 1721)   £65
- **Parte Settentrionale (Meridionale) dell' Irlanda.** Venice, [1696-97]. Each sheet approximately 455×610mm. Engraved map in 2 sheets, hand-cold. in outl., 2 armorial title-cartouches, sailing ship, sea monster, etc., fully cold. W.a.f. (S. Jun.29; 58)   Emerald Isle. £110
- **Ristretto de Mediterraneo.** Ca. 1690. 1180×455mm. Hand-cold. map, mntd. (P. Jun.11; 211)   Price. £680
- **Spain & Portugal.** Ca. 1690. Fo. 2 maps, uncold., on 2 folding sheets, lge. cartouches. (JN. Apr.2; 553)   £55

COVENS, Jean
See–HEURDT, J. van & Covens & Mortier
See–SANSON, Nicholas & Jaillot Hubert

COVENS, Jean & Mortier, Corneille
- **Carte de l'Afrique Françoise ou Du Senegal.** N.d. 49.5×61.5 cm. Outl. cold. copper etched map with lge. floral cartouche & mile indicator. (D. Dec.11-13; 3525)   DM 500
- **Hemisphère Occidental.** Amst., ca. 1730. 21 × 26 inches. Fully-cold. circular map. (SG. Nov.20; 134) $180

COVENS, Jean & Mortier, Pierre
- **Carte des Courones du Nord.** N.d. Ob. fo. Old cold, copper engraved map in 2 ll., with painted figure map. (R. Oct.14-18; 5867)   DM 450

CREPY
- **Bermuda & Jamaica.** 1767. 'Medium' size. 2-part map, early colour. (HL. Apr. 1; 1578)
£105
- **Japan.** 1767. 'Medium' Size. Map, early outl. colour, cartouche. (HL. Apr.1; 1724)   £110

CROME, A.F.W. & Schraembl, F.A.
- **Neue Karte von Europea, welche die Merkwürdigsten Produkte und Vornehmsten Handelsplätze nebst den Flächen-Inhalt aller Europäischer Länder in Deutschen Quadrat Meilen enthält.** 1787. 55×71 cm. Cold. copper engraved map. (D. Dec.11-13; 3415)   DM 600

CRUCHLEY, George F.
- **Ordnance Survey of the County Thirty Miles Around London.** Ca. 1840. Hand-cold. folding map on linen. Orig. s.-c. (P. Apr. 9; 173)
Tabor. £75

DANCKERTS, Justus
- **Nova Totius Terrarum Orbis Tabula.** [Amst.], [after 1696]. 17¼×23 inches. Elab. scenic & figural border fully cold, maps cold. in outl., slight staining, repairs on verso, loss to lr. right portion affecting plt., restored & reprd., slight staining. (SPB. Jul.28; 361) $550
- - **Anr. Edn.** Amst., ca. 1700. Approximately 490×580mm. Maps hand-cold. in outl., vigs. hand-cold. (SBA. Oct.21; 254)
Studio Books. £340

DANCKERTS, T.
- **Judaea sive Terra Sancta, quae Israelitarum.** Ca. 1700. 580×520mm. Hand-cold. map, cartouche. (P. Jul.30; 172)   Lawin. £55

D'ANVILLE, Jean Baptiste Bourguignon
- **Amérique Septentrionale.** Paris, 1746. 850×880mm. Lge. 2 sheet engraved map on wtrmkd. paper, hand-cold. in outl. with inset map of Greenland, Hudson & Baffin Bays. (PWP. Apr.9; 163)   Can. $680
- **Europe.** Paris, 1754-60. 22 × 23 inches (each sheet). 3 part map on 6 sheets, with cold. boundaries & cartouches. (SG. Nov.20; 51) $180
- **North America.** Ca. 1760. 865×835mm. Hand-cold. map. cartouches. (P. Jun.11; 241)
Price. £160
- **La Palestine, Les Tribus et Jerusalem.** 1783. 550×425mm. Hand-cold. map, cartouche, centre fold slightly worn. (P. Apr.30; 98a)   Horesh. £80

D'ARCY, Delarochette
- **Colombia Prima: or, South America . . .** Ill.:– Louis Stanislas. L., ca. 1815. Elephant fo. (44¾×33½ inches). Hand-cold. copperplt. folding map. Inserted in orig. cl. s.-c. (PNY. Mar.26; 201)
$100

DE LA ROCHETTE, Louis Stanislas D'Arcy
- **The Dutch Colony of the Cape of Good Hope.** L., 1795. 2nd. Edn. 570×410mm. Engraved map, torn on centre fold, some offsetting. (SSA. Jan.22; 413)   R. 130

DE L'ISLE, Guillaume
- **L'Amérique Septentrionale.** Paris, 1700. Hand-cold. map, cartouche, F. & G. (P. Jun.11; 243)   Price. £130
- **Mappa Totius Mundi.** Augsburg, ca. 1750. Ob. fo. Cold. copper engraved map, in 2 hemispheres, sm. maps in upr. corners, painted figure cartouche. (R. Mar.31-Apr.4; 4831)   DM 850
- **Mappe Monde.** Ca. 1730. Ob. fo. Cold. copper engraved map in 2 hemispheres, sm. maps in corners, figure cartouches at head & at foot. (R. Mar.31-Apr.4; 4824)   DM 1,300
- - **Anr. Edn.** Paris, 1808. Ob. fo. Cold. copper engraved map, in 2 hemispheres, lge. painted cartouche. (R. Mar.31-Apr.4; 4844)   DM 450
- **Orbis Veteribus Noti Tabula Nova.** Paris, 1714. 49cm. diameter. Hand-cold. map, Dutch discoveries in New Holland shown, but no place names. (JL. Mar.1; 196)   Aus. $290
- - **Anr. Copy.** Map, cold. in outl. (JL. Jul.19; 208)   Aus. $160
- - **Anr. Edn.** Amst., ca. 1730. Hand-cold. map. (JL. Jul.19; 322)   Aus. $325

DENMARK
- **Danorum Marca, aut Daniae Regnum.** 1585. Ob. fo. Cold. etched map with figure decor. (R. Oct.14-18; 5827)   DM 2,200

DEPOT DE LA MARINE
- **South Ireland & the British Channel Area.** Ca. 1795. Lge. fo. Chart, cold. (JN. Apr.2; 602)   £65

DEVELOPMENT DE LA ROUTE Faite Autour du Monde par les Vaisseaux du Roy la Bondeuse et Le'Toile
Ca. 1795. Map showing known coastline of New Holland & southern tip of Tasmania & West Coast of New Zealand. F. (JL. Mar.1; 124)
Aus. $140

DEVENTER, J. van
- **Zeeland.** N.d. Ob. fo. Old cold. copper engraved map with painted roll & figure decor, slightly soiled.   (R. Oct.14-18; 5464) DM 1,0

DIECISETTE PROVINCIE DE PAESI BASSI
Rome, G.G. Rossi, 1689. 106×90 cm. Engraved hand-cold. wall map. (VG. Oct.28; 251)   Fls. 780

DONN, Benjamin
- **A Map of the County of Devon.** N.d. Engraved in sections & laid down on 12 sheets of linen. (BS. Feb.25; 372)   £85

DONNE, B.
- **Bristol, Clifton, The Hotwells etc.** 1831. Approximately 29×21 inches. Town plan with vigs., River Avon scene & enumerated keys, uncold., soiled & torn to borders. (TA. Oct.16; 16)
£50

DOPPELMAYER, Johannes & Homann, Johann Baptiste
- **Tabula Selenographica in qua Lunarium Macularum.** Nuremb., n.d. 48.5×58 cm. Cold. copper engraved map in globe form, surrounded by putti & allegoric figures. (D. Dec.11-13; 3409)
DM 450

DOWER, John
- **Colony of New South Wales.** L., 1834. Hand-cold. map. (JL. Mar.1; 213)   Aus. $120
- **Van Diemen's Land.** L., 1842. Hand-cold. map. (JL. Mar.1; 147)   Aus. $100

DRYANDER, J. & Ortelius, Abraham
- **Hassiae Descriptio.** N.d. Fo. Cold. copper engraved map with painted cartouche. (R. Oct.14-18; 4264)   DM 420

DUDLEY, Sir Robert
[-] **Carta Particolare del Peru che Comincia con il Capo di Guanapo e Finisce con il Capo S. Francesco–Carta Particolare del Mare del Zur che Comincia con il Capo S. Francesco . . . e Finisce con il Capo S. Lazaro nella nuova Spagnia.** [Flor.], [1646-61]. Various sizes. 2 engraved maps, with compass roses, sailing ships, etc., some slight spotting, centre folds a little discold. W.a.f. (S. Jun.29; 105)   Potter. £170
[-] **Carta Prima generale d'Affrica e par(t)e d'America.** [Flor.], [1646, or later]. 460×712mm. Engraved map from the Arcano del Mare,

title-cartouche, compass rose, decor. W.a.f. (S. Nov.3; 48) *Sisnet*. £140

DU VAL, Pierre
- Orbis Vetus. Paris, 1677. Map, shows the earliest Dutch discoveries in Australia blended with the mythical reports of Marco Polo. F. & G. (JL. Dec.14; 158) Aus. $340

EGYPT
- Map of Egypt, with part of Arabia & Palestine. Ed.:- Joseph Enouy. L., 12 Aug., 1801. 28 × 20 inches. Fully-cold. map, some dampstaining. (SG. Nov.20; 48) $130

EMMIUS, U. & Blaeu, Willem & Joannes
- Ostfriesland. N.d. Ob. fo. Old cold. copper engraved map with painted figure cartouche & sm. supplementary map & 2 cold. arms. (R. 14-18; 4139) DM 900

EMMIUS, U. & Jansson, Jan or Johannes
- Ostfriesland. N.d. Ob. fo. Old cold. copper engraved map with painted figure cartouche & sm. supp. map & 2 lge. cold. arms. (R. Oct.14-18; 4140) DM 800

ESSEX
L., Lt. Col. Mudge, 1805. Each sheet approx. 665×940mm. Lge. linen-bkd. folding engraved map, hand-cold., on 4 sheets. S.-c. (C. Jul.15; 130) *Traylen*. £80
- - Anr. Edn. N.d. Hand-cold. map, cold. cartouche. F. & G. (P. Jan.22; 213) *Blackburn*. £75

EUROPE
- [Europe, covering South-Eastern Europe, from the Bosphorus North through Russia, & West to the North Sea]. Ca. 1610? 15 × 18 inches. Pict. map. from a Hondius-Ortelius atlas. (SG. May 21; 36) $120

EVANS, G.W.
- Chart of Van Diemen's Land ... J. Souter. 29 Jan., 1822. Engraved chart, hand-cold. in outl., few sm. areas fully cold., in 20 sections. Folding into orig. pull-off. marb. case, worn. W.a.f. (S. Mar.31; 436) *Quaritch*. £400

FADEN, William
- The Country Twenty-Five Miles round London. 1790. Lge. hand-cold. map, dissected on linen. (P. Dec.11; 192) *Harris*. £55
- The United States of North America, with the British Territories & those of Spain. 11th. Feb. 1793. 525×620mm. Engraved map, hand-cold. in outl., principal areas fully cold., pict. title-vig., some very slight offsetting. W.a.f. (S. Nov.3; 50) *Map House*. £100

See-CARVER, Jonathon

FER, Nicolas de
- California. 1700. 'Large'. Map, shows California as an island, early outl. colour, some age staining. (HL. Apr.1; 1800) £270
- Cours du Rhein, depuis Spire jusqu'à Mayence ... 1720. 155×48.5 cm. Cold copper etchg. map, traces of folding, bkd., some defects. (D. Dec.11-13; 3593) DM 1,200
- Le Golfe de Mexique ... La Floride au Nord, Le Mexique ... La Terre Ferme au Sud, Les Antilles ... et Jamaique. Paris, 1717 [or later]. 460×602mm. Engraved map, hand-cold. in outl., some very slight spotting. W.a.f. (S. Jun.29; 137) *Potter*. £130
- Luxembourg. Paris, Ca. 1690. 20 × 27 cm. Copper engraved plan with 3 cartouches. (R. Oct.14-18; 5389) DM 600
- La Principauté de Catalogne. 1714. 46×64 cm. Outl. cold. copper engraved map, rococo cartouche, slightly stained. (D. Dec.11-13; 3484) DM 450
- Quebec, Ville de l'Amérique Septentrionale dans la Nouvelle France avec Titre d'Eveche. Paris, 1705. 11½ × 8 inches. Map. (CB. Dec.9; 15) Cans. $130

FERRARIS, Lieut. Gen. Comte Joseph de
- Carte Chorographique des Pays-Bas Autrichiens. Ill.:- Dupuis. N.p., n.d. Orig. Edn. Map of 25 ll., 35 plts. including title frontis., general map, detailed maps & plan, pasted on cl. (LM. Nov.8; 72) B.Frs. 50,000

FEUILLE, D. de la
- Carte du Duché de Lorraine. 1735. New Edn. Sm. ob. fo. Sm. plan as ill to above title, from Ratelband atlas, old cold. copper engr. with 13 views & plans. (R. Oct.14-18; 5390) DM 900

FLORINI, Matteo
- La Gra Citta di Milano. Early 17th. C. 16×21½ inches. Engraved plan, cut & preserved, soiled. (CSK. Sep.12; 74) £80

FORREST, William, Surveyor
- Lanarkshire. 1813. Cold map. Leath. case, worn. (CE. Nov.20; 149) £66

FOWLER, Charles
- Yorkshire. Leeds, 1834. Each sheet 24 × 29 inches. Engraved map on 4 sheets, hand-cold. in outl. Folding on cl., s.-c., slight staining. (CSK. Jun.5; 29) £50

FREYCINET, L.
- Carte Trigonometrique des Îles Hunter. Paris, 1812. Hand-cold. detailed chart of north west coast of Tasmania & the Hunter Islands. (JL. Mar.1; 219) Aus. $440
- Partie de la Colonie de la Nouvelle-Galles du Sud. Paris, 1825. Hand-cold. map of the Colony with insets of Van Diemens Land & altitude profiles of the route from Sydney to Bathurst & south to near Canberra. (JL. Mar.1; 202) Aus. $210

FRY, Joshua & Jefferson, Peter
- A Map of the Most Inhabited Part of Virginia. Ill.:- T. Jeffreys. L., 1775. 26 × 49 inches. Two part map, with hand-cold. boundaries & lge. pict. cartouche, some creases, right-hand side of top map frayed, affecting extreme edges of engraved portion. (SG. May 21; 40) $650

FULDA
- Plan des Gefechts bei Fulda am 30.11.1759. Ca. 1780. 16×27 cm. Partly cold. copper engraved map. (R. Oct.14-18; 4248) *DM 800*

FUNCK, D.
- [Skandinavien]. N.d. Ob. fo. Old cold. copper engraved map with figure cartouche, fold browned. (R. Oct.14-18; 5833) DM 430

GAGE, Michael Alexander
- The Trigonometrical Plan of the Town & Port of Liverpool. 1835. Lge. engraved plan, in 36 sections, partly hand-cold., very slight offsetting, mntd. on linen, edges bnd. Folded in cont. mor. gt. pull-off case. (SBA. May 27; 338) *Temperley*. £78

GENERAL CHART Exhibiting the Discoveries made by Captain Cook in his First, Second & Third Voyages with the Tracks of Ships under his Command, from Anderson's Account of Cook's Voyages
1780. Map. (JL. Dec.14; 166) Aus. $120

GIBSON, John & Bowen, Thomas
- Botany Bay in New South Wales. 1773. 16.5×13.5cm. Cold. chart of a harbour mainland Australia. (JL. Mar.1; 180) Aus. $190

GIGAS, J. & Blaeu, Willem & Joannes
- Bistum Hildesheim. N.d. Ob. fo. Old cold. copper engraved map with painted cartouche, 1 lge. & 3 sm. mostly cold. arms. (R. Oct.14-18; 4383) DM 480
- Bistum Münster. N.d. Ob. fo. Old cold copper engraved map with painted cartouche & many sm. arms. (R. Oct.14-18; 4566) DM 640
- Bistum Osnabrück. N.d. Ob. fo. Old cold. copper engraved map with cold view, painted cartouches, sm. supp. map, lge. cold. & 7 sm. arms. (R. Oct.14-18; 4414) DM 800
- Bistum Paderborn. N.d. Ob. fo. Old cold. copper engraved map with painted cartouche & 11 sm. arms. (R. Oct.14-18; 4587) DM 800
- Erzbistum Köln. N.d. Ob. fo. Old cold. copper engraved map with painted roll cartouche & many sm. arms. (R. Oct.14-18; 4534) DM 950
- Westphalia Ducatus. N.d. Ob. fo. Old cold. copper engraved map with painted cartouche & 6 sm. arms. (R. Oct.14-18; 4604) DM 850

GOLYATH, C.
- Perfecte Caerte ... van Olinda, de Pharnambuco, Maurits, Stadt ende t'Reciffo. 1648. Ob. fo. Old cold. & gold heightened copper engraved map, 2 views in corners, lightly browned. (R. Mar.31-Apr.4; 4997) DM 900

GOOS, Pieter
- De Custen van Noorwegen tusschen der Neus en Schuitenes. [Amst.], [1650]. 428×525mm. Engraved chart, hand-cold. in outl., title cartouche, compass roses, fully cold. W.a.f. (S. Nov.3; 119) *Norlund*. £110

- Pascaerte ... van America. Ca. 1660. 560×455mm. Hand-cold. map, mntd., cartouche. (P. Jun.11; 215) *Map House*. £500
- Pascaerte van Nieu Nederlandt & Virginies. Ca. 1660. 535×435mm. Hand-cold. sea chart, mntd., vigs. (P. Jun.11; 209) *Map House*. £600
- Pas-Kaarte van de Zuyd-west-kust van Africa, van Capo Negro tot beoosten Cabo de Bona Esperanca.-Pas-Caart van Guinea ... van Cabo Verde tot Cabo de Bona Esperanca. Amst., (1666). Various sizes. 2 engraved charts, hand-cold., including inset chart, etc., on 1st. & title-cartouche on 2nd., repairs to ends of centre fold of 2nd., slightly affecting engraved surface. W.a.f. (S. Jun.29; 123) *Fisher*. £100

GREENLAND
Ca. 1650. 535×430mm. Hand-cold. sea-chart showing Greenland, Iceland, Britain & part of America, slightly browned. (P. May 14; 187a) *Kentish*. £55

GREENWOOD, Charles
- Map of the County of York. Leeds & Wakefield, Robinson, Son & Holdsworth; John Hurst & C. Greenwood. 4 Jun., 1817. 4to. Engraved map in 4 lge. sheets, each sheet in 18 sections, linen-mntd., each sheet extending to 42½in.×36in. 2 pull-off russ. cases, tooled in gt. & blind. W.a.f. (S. Mar.31; 353) *Crowe*. £190
- - Anr. Edn. [1817]. Each sheet approx. 184×75cm. Linen-bkd. engraved folding map, hand-cold., on 3 sheets. Gt. mor. pull-off case. (C. May 20; 125) *Maggs*. £180

GREENWOOD, Charles & John
- Map of the County of Cornwall. 1827. Both 181×93 cm. 2 engraved maps. cold. in outl., mntd. on linen & folded in sections. Cont. cf. case. (SH. May 21; 47) *Crowe*. £90
- Map of the County of Derby. Greenwood, Pringle & Co. 21 Dec.1825. 61 × 46¾ inches, folding to 8vo. Lge. engraved map, hand-cold. vig., lettering partly cold., in 48 sections, linen-mntd. Tree cf. pull-off case gt. W.a.f. (S. Mar.31; 334) *Leviton*. £320
- Map of the County of Devon. 1827. Each 75×24½ inches. Hand-cold. engraved map on 3 sheets, mntd. on cl. & folding. In a cl. case. (CSK. May.8; 16) £70
- Map of the County of Northampton. 1826. 47×54 inches. Folding engraved map with inset view of Peterborough Cathedral, on cl., slight browning. (CSK. Apr.10; 24) £90
- Map of the County of Northumberland. 1828. 75×55 inches. Engraved map, hand-cold. in outl., mntd. on cl., folding. Orig. case. (CSK. Jul.3; 4) £65
- Map of the County of Southampton. 1826. 58×62 inches. Hand-cold. engraved map, mntd. on linen. Cf. case, worn. (SH. Jun.11; 28) *Kentish*. £100
- Map of the County of Surrey. 1 Sep. 1823. 4to. Hand-cold. engraved map in 32 sections, lge. insert engr. of Kew Palace, slightly soiled, a little offsetting, mntd. on linen, edges bnd., folding into cf. pull-off case, extending to 40×48 inches. (S. Dec.9; 414) *Traylen*. £160
- Map of London. 1827. 124×186 cm. Engraved map, cold. in outl., mntd. on linen & folded in sections. Cont. mor. case. (SH. May 21; 48) *Jarndyce*. £140
- - Anr. Edn. 1830. Cold. map, 2 lge. vigs. in 6 sheets, 1 corner slightly defect. (BS. Sep.17; 26) £160

HASIUS
See-HOMANN, Johann Baptist & Hasius

HENNEBERG, K. & Blaeu, Willem & Joannes
- [Ostpreussen]. Ca. 1610. 8.5×12.5 cm. Old cold. copper engraved map from atlas with painted cartouche. (R. Oct.14-18; 4719) DM 630

HENNEBERG, K. & Jansson, Jan or Johannes
- [Ostpreussen]. N.d. Ob. fo. Old cold. copper engraved map with 2 painted cartouches, fold partly backed. (R. Oct.14-18; 4720) DM 560

HENNET, G.
- Map of the County Palatine of Lancaster. 1830. 165×120cm. Partly hand-cold. map, steel-engraved cartouche, scale. Cf. book box. (PL. Sep.18; 91) *Lomax*. £50

HERBERT, L.
- The World on Mercator's Projection-Eastern Part. L., 1812. Map. (JL. Dec.14; 146) Aus. $100

HEURDT, J. van & Covens & Mortier
- Comitatus Meurensis. N.d. Ob. fo. Copper engraved map with old outl. col., with 2 figure & heraldic cartouches. (R. Oct.14-18; 4558) DM 1,600

HOGENBERG, Franz
- Deutschlanndt Germaniae Typus. 1576. Ob. fo. Cold. copper engraved map, 2 painted cartouches & cold. arms, 10 cms. tear bkd. (R. Mar.31-Apr.4; 3269) DM 700
See-BRAUN, Georg & Hogenberg, Franz

HOLE, G.
See-SAXTON, Christopher & Hole, G.

HOLIDAY, Capt.
- A Draft of the Bristol Channel from Holmes to Kings Road. Ca. 1760. 18×22½ inches. Cold. coastal chart. F. & G. (TA. Feb.19; 98) £55
- - Anr. Copy. (TA. May 21; 18) £50

HOMANN, J.C.H.
See-ZOLLMANN, F. & Homann, J.C.H.

HOMANN, Johann Baptist
- Aegyptus Hodierna. Nuremb., ca. 1700. 23 × 20 inches. Hand-cold. copper-plt. map, with lge. engr. to the left. (SG. May 21; 34) $120
- Africa Secundum Legitimas Projectionis Stero Graphica E Regulas . . . Impensis Homannianorum Heredum. Nuremb., 1737. 485×550mm. Engraved map, hand-cold., title cartouche, sm. holes in top margin. (SSA. Jan.22; 414) R. 120
- America Mappa Generalis. 1746. Ob. fo. Old cold. copper engraved map with figure cartouche. (R. Oct.14-18; 5051) DM 470
- Americae Septentrionalis et Meridionalis. ca. 1720. Hand-cold. map. (P. Dec.11; 175) Garfunkle. £250
- Dominia Anglorum in America Septentrionali; Die Gross-Britannische Colonie-Laender in Nord-America. Ca. 1750. 20½ × 24 inches. 4 fully-cold. maps on 1 sheet, lr. margin trimmed to plt. mark. (SG. May 21; 106) $100
- Ducatus Bremae et Ferdae. N.d. 49×56 cm. Cold. copper etching, lge. allegorical cartouche, mile indicator & wind rose. (D. Dec.11-13; 3573) DM 600
- Erzbistum Köln mit Jülich, Berg und der Grafschaft Moers. N.d. Ob. fo. Old cold., copper engraved map with 2 painted figure cartouches. (R. Oct.14-18; 4542) DM 560
- Herzogtum Brabant. N.d. Ob. fo. Painted figure cartouche, lightly browned & fold backed. (R. Oct.14-18; 5263) DM 430
- Herzogtum Holstein. N.d. Ob. fo. Copper engraved map with painted arms cartouche & 4 cold. arms. (R. Oct.14-18; 4094) DM 430
- [Herzogtum Worttemberg]. N.d. Ob. fo. Old cold. copper engraved map in 2 ll., 2 decor. painted figure cartouches, port, sm. views, on both pp., 38 painted arms., not composite. (R. Oct.14-18; 3655) DM 2,000
- Herzogtümer Bremen und Verden. N.d. Ob. fo. Old cold copper engraved map with painted figure cartouche, lightly browned at fold. (R. Oct.14-18; 4059) DM 450
- Holy Land. Ca. 1720. Fo. Map, wash colouring, lge. cartouche. (JN. Apr.2; 238) £130
- Judaea seu Palaestina. N.d. Ob. fo. Old cold. copper engraved map with sm. supp. map & lge. figure cartouche. (R. Oct.14-18; 5134) DM 430
- Mappe Monde que Represente les deux Hemispheres. Nuremb., 1746. 18 × 21 inches. Hand-cold. hemispheric map, with 2 lge. & 6 smaller inset maps & 2 cold. cartouches, many creases. (SG. May 21; 141) $140
- Mississipi seu Provinciae Ludovicianae . . . anno 1687 detectae. [Nuremb.], ca. 1740, or later. 480×570mm. Engraved hand-cold. map, lge. historiated title-cartouche, 2 vigs., 2 sm. repairs on verso, not affecting engraved surface, 1 or 2 paint smears. W.a.f. (S. Nov.3; 51) Burden. £160
- - Anr. Copy. 483×575mm. Repair at bottom of centre fold, just touching engraved border. W.a.f. (S. Nov.3; 52) Nebenzahl. £140
- Nova Anglia, Septentrionali Americae implantata Anglorumque Coloniis florentissima. Nuremb., ca. 1740, or later. 484×576mm. Engraved map, principal areas hand-cold., pict. title-cartouche. W.a.f. (S. Nov.3; 62) Gibbons. £170
- - Anr. Copy. 489×582mm. Sm. perforation affecting engraved surface at top of map. W.a.f. (S. Nov.3; 63) Burden. £140

- - Anr. Edn. N.d. Ob. fo . Old cold. copper engraved map with lge. figure cartouche, 1 brown mark. (R. Oct.14-18; 5075) DM 500
- [Ostpreussen]. N.d. Ob. fo. Old cold. copper engraved map with lge. figure cartouche & port., fold slightly browned & sm. tears backed. (R. Oct.14-18; 4723) DM 440
- [-] Anr. Copy. Old cold. copper engraved map with lge. figure & heraldic cartouche. (R. Oct.14-18; 4722) DM 420
- Pars Vederoviae. Nuremb., ca. 1760. 20 × 24 inches. Hand-cold. copper-plt. map, with inset view & cold. cartouche. (SG. Nov.20; 59) $220
- Plan du Siège de Corfu. ca. 1700. Hand-cold. map, cartouche, 4 inset maps in corners. Maple frame. (P. Dec.11; 161) Dr. Sofu. £85
- Planiglobii Terrestris Cum Utroq Hemisphaerio Caelesti. Nuremb., [1710?]. 19½×22 inches. Fully cold. map, elab. scenic & figural border, repairs to fold & margins on verso, slight wrinkling at fold, slight discolouration. (SPB. Jul.28; 362) $400
- Planiglobii Terrestris . . . Exhibitio. 1720. Ob. fo. Old cold. copper engraved map in 2 hemispheres, 2 sm. maps & allegories at foot. (R. Mar.31-Apr.4; 4822) DM 950
- - Anr. Edn. N.d. Ob. fo. Old cold. copper engraved map in 2 hemispheres surrounded by 2 celestial maps & allegorical decor., slightly soiled, stained, & browned at fold. (R. Oct.14-18; 3377) DM 950
- Principatus et Episcopatus Eistettensis. N.d. Ob. fo. Cold. copper engraved map with 2 lge. figure cartouches & view, soiled, browned at centrefold, sm. tear backed. (R. Oct.14-18; 3722) DM 600
- Principatus Fuldensis. N.d. Ob. fo. Old cold. copper engraved map with figure cartouche, slightly soiled & stain at side. (R. Oct.14-18; 4250) DM 550
- Regiones Mississipi. N.d. Ob. fo. Cold. copper engraved map with 2 painted figure cartouches, slightly soiled. (R. Oct.14-18; 5088) DM 850
- Regionis Mississippi seu Provinciae Ludovicianae Tabula. N.d. Ob. fo. Old cold. copper engraved map with lge. figure cartouche. (R. Oct.14-18; 5069) DM 950
- Regni Mexicani, Ludoviciane, N. Angliae, Carolinae, Virginae . . . Tabula. N.d. Ob. fo. Old cold. copper engraved map with 2 figure cartouches & view, slightly browned at fold. (R. Oct.14-18; 5089) DM 950
- Regni Norvegiae. Nuremb., ca. 1730, or later. 496×582mm. Engraved map, principal areas hand-cold., historiated & armorial title-vig. W.a.f. (S. Nov.3; 120) Norlund. £110
- Scandinavia, complectens Sueciae, Daniae & Norvegiae Regna. N.d. Ob. fo. Old cold. copper engraved map with lge. figure cartouche, lightly browned at fold. (R. Oct.14-18; 5869) DM 430
- Totius Africae Nova Representatio qua praeter diversos in ea Status et Regiones . . . N.d. 52×60 cm. Engraved map, later hand-colouring, centre fold & edges reprd. with cellotape. F. & mntd. (SSA. Apr.22; 292) R. 120
- Totius Americae Novissima Representatio. N.d. Ob. fo. Old cold. copper engraved map, 2 figure cartouches, long tear in fold bkd., slightly soiled. (R. Mar.31-Apr.4; 4978) DM 500
- Virginia, Marylandia et Carolina. Nuremb., ca. 1760. 484×573mm. Engraved map, hand-cold. in outl., principal areas fully cold., lge. pict. title-vig. W.a.f. (S. Nov.3; 53) Nebenzahl. £160
- - Anr. Edn. N.d. Ob. fo. Copper engraved map with old outl. col., lge. figure cartouche & 2 cold arms, slightly browned at fold, 1 sm. tear backed. (R. Oct.14-18; 5093) DM 850
- Westfälischer Kreis. N.d. Lge. fo. Old cold. copper engraved map with figure cartouche, lightly browned at fold. (R. Oct.14-18; 4649) DM 530

HOMANN, Johann Baptist & Hasius
- Asia showing New Guinea. 1744. 50×55 cm. Copper engraved map, late colouring with decor. cartouche. (JL. Mar.1; 120) Aus. $140

HOMANN, Johann Baptist, Heirs of
- Carte de l'Asie Mineure. Nuremb., 1745. 21 × 24½ inches. Cold. map, with Latin text in ornamental border at corner. (SG. Nov.20; 18) $100
- Den Haag. Ca. 1750. Ob. fo. Lge. old cold. copper engraved town plan, uncold. view. (R. Mar.31-Apr.4; 5287) DM 625

- Grundriss und Prospect der Weltberuhmyen Hollandischen Haupt und Handels-Stadt Amsterdam. Nuremb., 1727. 49×56 cm. Engraved plan, cont. hand-colouring, view ptd. below, fold in middle. (VG. Oct.28; 310) Fls. 480
- Map of London on Surroundings. 1741. Inset plan of London. (P. Nov.13; 145) Weiss. £90
- Nouvelle Carte Géographique des Postes D'Allemagne. Ca. 1750. 'Large' (770 × 1015 cm.). Fold-up map on cl., early outl. colour, 2 keys, 3 cartouches, engraving top left corner, some blemishes. (HL. Apr.1; 1613) £150
- Planiglobii Terrestris Mappa Universalis. 1746. Ob. fo. Copper engraved map in 2 hemispheres, surrounded by 6 sm. maps & 2 figure cartouches, slightly soiled, tear in fold reprd. (R. Oct.14-18; 3378) DM 500
- Regionis quae est circa Londinum. 1741. Approximately 505 × 563mm. Engraved map, hand-cold., uncold. panoramic view of L. across bottom of plt., edges reinforced. W.a.f. (S. Jun.29; 48) Miller. £110
- Westphaliae. Ca. 1700. Hand-cold. map, mntd. (P. Apr.30; 143) Fairburn. £55

HONDIUS, Henricus
- Africae Nova Tabula. 1631. Ob. fo. Old cold. copper engraved map, figure, decor., painted cartouche, margins slightly soiled. (R. Mar.31-Apr.4; 4930) DM 500
- - Anr. Copy. Ob. fo. Slightly restored at foot & 2 sm. corners reprd. (R. Oct.14-18; 5005) DM 470
- America Noviter Delineata. 1631. Ob. fo. Old cold. copper engraved map, painted cartouche, 2 sm. maps, margins lightly soiled. (R. Mar.31-Apr.4, 4973) DM 1,700
- - Anr. Edn. [Amst.], [1635]. 18¼×22 inches. Border of views & figures, partially cold., orig. plt. flaw affecting top right corner, 2 slight holes, trimmed to engraved surface, dust-soiled. (SPB. Jul.28; 334) $1,000
- Bermudas. N.d. Ob. fo. Old cold. copper engraved map, 3 painted cartouches & engraved legend at foot, margins slightly soiled. (R. Mar.31-Apr.4; 4992) DM 1,100
- Brasilien. N.d. Ob. fo. Old cold. copper engraved map, 2 sm. supp. maps, 2 painted cartouches, col. strengthened in. parts, margins slightly soiled. (R. Mar.31-Apr.4; 4993) DM 600
- Europa Exactissime Descripta. 1631. Ob. fo. Old cold. copper engraved map, 2 painted figure cartouches, margins soiled. (R. Mar.31-Apr.4; 5160) DM 650
- India quae Orientalis diciture, et Insulae Adiacentes. Amst., 1636. 1st. Edn. Map, hand-cold, Fr. text on verso. (JL. Jul.19; 329) Aus. $630
- Nordamerika. Ob. fo. Old cold. copper engraved map, 2 painted figure cartouches, heavily restored. (R. Mar.31-Apr.4; 5034) DM 850
- Nova Terrarum Orbis. 1630. Hand-cold., map, cartouches, repair in fold. (P. May.14; 191) Price. £320
- Nova Totius Terrarum Orbis Geographica ac Hydrographica Tabula. 1630. Ob. fo. Old cold. copper engraved map, 2 hemispheres, corner medal ports., floral decor. & lge. allegories of 4 elements, slightly restored. (R. Mar.31-Apr.4; 4793) DM 3,600
- Nova Virginiae Tabula. N.d. Ob. fo. Old cold. copper engraved map, 2 painted cartouches, cold. arms & figures, col. restored in parts (R. Mar.31-Apr.4; 5059) DM 800
- Novissima Delflandiae, Schielandiae Tabula. Amst., 1629. 45×56 cm. Hand-cold. engraved map, ptd. text on verso, slightly browned. F. & G. (VG. Oct.28; 362) Fls. 400
- Osnabrugensis Episcopatus. N.d. 37×47.5 cm. Cold. copper engraved map, decor., arms, mile indicator, Fr. text on verso, soiled, margins defect. (D. Dec.11-13; 3584) DM 500
- Poli Artici Descriptio Novissima. N.d. Ob. fo. Old cold. copper engraved map, decor. round, margins slightly soiled. (R. Mar.31-Apr.4; 4863) DM 1,000
- Polus Antarcticus. Ob. fo. Cold. copper engraved map, round, 2 painted roll cartouches, fold with 2 sm. faults restored. (R. Mar.31-Apr.4; 4865) DM 1,100
- South East England. Ca. 1600. Hand-cold. map. F. & G. (P. Jun.11; 221) Campbell. £60
- Venezuela. Amst., ca. 1640. 19×22½ ins. Cold. map, with 2 cartouches & other decors. (SG. Nov.20; 128) $180

See–MERCATOR, Gerard & Hondius, Henricus

HONDIUS, Jodocus
– **Amerika.** N.d. Ob. fo. Old cold. copper engraved map, 2 painted cartouches, figures, fold partly restored. (R. Mar.31-Apr.4; 4971) DM 1,700
– – **Anr. Copy.** Ob. fo. (R. Oct.14-18; 5047) DM 1,400
– **Hispania Nova Descriptio.–Andaluziae Nova Descript.–Hungaria.–Portugalliae.** [Amst.], ca. 1630? Each 18½ × 21 inches. 4 cold. pict. maps, Latin text on versos. (SG. May 21; 51) $425
See–MERCATOR, Gerard & Hondius, Jodocus

HONDIUS, Jodocus & Jansson, H.
– **Africa Nova Tabula.** 1632. Ob. fo. Old cold. copper engraved map, 2 painted cartouches, side figures, 6 sm. views at head. (R. Mar.31-Apr.4; 4931) DM 1,200

HOOGHE, Romain de
– **Carte Maritime de l'Angleterre Depuis les Sorlinques Jusques à Portland** ... Amst., 1693. 24.25×38.5 inches. Hand-cold. engraved chart, elab. dedication cartouche containing view, 2 other inset views, Scilly Isles with decor. surround, compass roses & galleons at sea. F. W.a.f. (LC. Jun.18; 202) £130

HOOGHEYMRAADSCHAP van Rhynland
[Leiden?], [1685-88?]. Fo. Engraved map on 12 double-p. sheets, & mntd. on guards, cold. in red, blue, green & yellow, surround & cartouche on 16 single sheets, with many dedications, & arms of the dedicatees, embellished with cherubs, title on running banner, cold., shields & title in gold, licence by the Staten General for 25 years on 2 sheets, each in surround of cornucopiae, the whole embellished with cherubs, fruit & flowers, at foot of a seated sea-goddess with triton. Cont. mott. cf. gt., strapwork arabesque centre decor. in roll-tool panels on sides, gt. spine, rubbed & corners scuffed. W.a.f. (C. Nov.6; 256) *Menten*. £4,400

HORNEMANN, C.F.
See–PAPEN, A. & Hornemann, C.F.

HOWELL, Reading
– **A Map of Pennsylvania.** Ill.:– J. Trenchard. [Phila.], [1795?]. 19½ × 28 inches. Map, in 2nd. state, copyright notice at lr. right corner, lr. left corner supplied in MS., browned at centre-fold. (SG. Nov.20; 99) $100

HUMBLE, G.
See–SPEEDE, John & Humble, G.

HUNGARY
Ca. 1700. Lge. ob. fo. Engl. copper engraved map, old outl. cold., figure cartouche, views at side, browned & restored. (R. Mar.31-Apr.4; 5813) DM 600

HURTER, Charles & Blaeu
– **Alemannia sive Suevia Superior.** N.d. Ob. fo. Old cold. copper engraved map, 2 painted cartouches. (R. Oct.14-18; 3473) DM 620

HUTCHINGS, W.F.
See–SWIRE, W. & Hutchings, W.F.

INDIA
Muenster?, ca. 1550 345 × 255 mm. Hand-cold. map. (P. Jun.11; 227) *Campbell*. £90
– **India Extra Gangem.** Ca. 1525. 15½ × 20½ inches. Hand-cold. map, from an edn. of Ptolemaeus, Latin text on verso. (SG. May 21; 52) $280

ISLES DES NOUVELLES Hebrides et celle de la Nouvelle Caldonie
Paris, 1788. 34.5 × 23.5 cm. (JL. Dec.14; 119) Aus. $110

JAGER, I.W.
– **Bodensee und Hochrheingebiet.** 1784. Ob. fo. Copper engraved map. (R. Oct.14-18; 3478) DM 450
– **Emsland.** 1784. Ob. fo. Outl. cold. copper engraved map. (R. Oct.14-18; 4361) DM 600

JAILLOT, Hubert
– **La Basse Partie du Cercle du Haut Rhein.** N.d. Ob. fo. Old cold. & partly gold heightened copper engraved map & 2 painted figure cartouches, jnt. slightly reprd. (R. Oct.14-18; 4311) DM 480
– **[Bayrischer Kreis].** 1696. Lge. fo. Old cold. & partly gold heightened copper engraved map with 2 painted figure cartouches. (R. Oct.14-18; 3698) DM 500

– **Le Cercle Eslectoral du Rhein.** N.d. Lge. fo. Old cold. copper engraved map with 2 painted figure cartouches. (R. Oct.14-18; 4917) DM 430
– **Les Duchés de Clèves, de Juliers, les Comptés de Meurs** ... N.d. Ob. fo. Outl. cold. copper engraved map with figure cartouche, in 18 segments mntd. on linen. (R. Oct.14-18; 4513) DM 500
– **[Fränkischer Kreis].** N.d. Ob. fo. Old cold. & partly gold heightened copper engraved map with 2 painted figure cartouches. (R. Oct.14-18; 3737) DM 600
– **Katalonien.** 1696. Ob. fo. Old cold. & partly gold heightened copper engraved map with 2 painted figure cartouches, slightly soiled. (R. Oct.14-18; 5881) DM 550
– **Luxembourg.** Late 18th. C. Ob. fo. Old cold. copper engraved map with painted & partly gold heightened figure cartouche. (R. Oct.14-18; 5400) DM 950
– **Nova Imperii Germanici Descriptio.** N.d. Ob. fo. Old cold. & partly gold heightened copper engraved map, 2 painted figure cartouches. (R. Oct.14-18; 3423) DM 650
– **Nova Scandinaviae.** N.d. Ob. fo. Old cold. copper engraved map with 2 lge. painted & partly gold heightened figure cartouches, slightly soiled, fold brkn. & bkd. (R. Oct.14-18; 5863) DM 600
– **Partie Occidentale de l'Archevesche de Mayence.** N.d. Ob. fo. Old cold. & partly gold heightened copper engraved map with 2 painted figure cartouches, slightly browned at fold. (R. Oct.14-18; 4325) DM 650
– **Partie Occidentale du Palatinat du Rhein.** N.d. Ob. fo. Old cold. & partly gold heightened copper engraved map with 2 painted figure cartouches. (R. Oct.14-18; 4774) DM 500
– **Les Provinces des Pays Bas Catholiques.** 1693. Ob. fo. Old cold. copper engraved map with 2 painted figure cartouches, 1 gold heightened. (R. Oct.14-18; 5405) DM 450
– **[Schwäbischer Kreis].** N.d. Ob. fo. Old cold. & partly gold heightened copper engraved map with painted figure cartouche, slightly stained. (R. Oct.14-18; 3604) DM 700
– **[Skandinavien].** 1696. Ob. fo. Old cold. & partly gold heightened copper engraved map with 2 figure cartouches, sm. stain in fold & backed. (R. Oct.14-18; 5832) DM 500
– **Westfälischer Kreis.** N.d. Lge. fo. Old cold. & partly gold heightened copper engraved map with 2 painted figure cartouches. (R. Oct.14-18; 4648) DM 600
– **Zeeland.** N.d. Ob. fo. Old cold. & partly gold heightened copper engraved map with painted cartouche, slightly browned & soiled. (R. Oct.14-18; 5465) DM 500
See–SANSON, Nicholas & Jaillot, Hubert

JAILLOT, Hubert & Mortier, Pierre
– **[Brabant].** N.d. Lge. ob. fo. Old cold. & partly gold heightened copper engraved map with painted figure cartouche. (R. Oct.14-18; 5261) DM 500
– **Herzogtum Kleve mit Ravenstein und Grafschaft Moers.** N.d. Ob. fo. Old cold. & partly gold heightened copper engraved map with painted figure map. (R. Oct.14-18; 4514) DM 600

JANSSON, Jan or Johannes
– **Albis Fluvius Germaniae Celebris.** N.d. Ob. fo. 2 maps old cold. copper engraved, with 2 painted cartouches, tears backed. (R. Oct.14-18; 4066) DM 460
[–] **Amstelodami celeberrimi Hollandiae Emporii Delineatio nova.** [Amst.], [1657]. 426 × 540 mm. Double-p. engraved bird's-eye plan of the city, 2 coats of arms, tabular keys in Latin & Dutch at sides, decor., Latin text on verso, separated at bottom of centre fold, unc. W.a.f. (S. Nov.4; 286) *Radford*. £150
– **Buckinghamshire & Bedfordshire.** Ca. 1650. Hand-cold. map. (P. Dec.11; 183) *Chelsea*. £80
– **Comitatus Northantonensis.** Northamptonshire, 1646. 1st. Edn. 15½ × 20¼ inches. Uncold. map, histor. title cartouche & scale, Royal coat of arms & 8 other armorials, cherubs, etc., slightly discold. (TA. May 21; 3) £75
– **Essex.** Ca. 1650. Hand-cold. map. (P. Dec.11; 184) *Chelsea*. £110
– **Germaniae Veteris Nova Descriptio.** N.d. Ob. fo. Cold. copper engraved map, 2 painted figure cartouches. (R. Mar.31-Apr.4; 3277) DM 450
– **India Orientalis Nova Descriptio.** Ca. 1630. Ob. fo. Cold. copper engraved map with 3 painted figure cartouches. (R. Oct.14-18; 5119) DM 450

– – **Anr. Edn.** N.d. stated. 29 × 51 cm. Map, hand-cold., decor. cartouche, rhumb lines & compass rose, smaller cartouche with mapmaker's name, anr. cartouche with scale, text on verso. (JL. Jul.19; 364) Aus. $240
– **Insulae Americanae.** Ca. 1650. 525 × 380 mm. Hand-cold. map, vig. sailing ships. (P. May 14; 187c) *Price*. £160
– – **Anr. Edn.** N.d. Ob. fo. Old cold. copper engraved map, 2 painted figure cartouches, sm. stain at lr. fold. F. (R. Mar.31-Apr.4; 4986) DM 450
– **Insulae Sardiniae.** Amst., ca. 1640. Outl. cold. map, sm. tear at foot, guard. (HK. Nov.18-21; 4409) DM 420
– **Insularum Britannicarum–Barkshire.–Cambridge.–Lincoln.–South Wales.–Surrey.** Amst., 17th. C. Each 19 × 22 inches. 6 hand-cold. maps, some darkening & brittleness. All mntd. to old bds. W.a.f. (SG. May 21; 45) $220
– **Island.** N.d. Ob. fo. Old cold. copper engraved map, painted figure cartouche, margins stained. (R. Mar.31-Apr.4; 5926) DM 450
– **Leicestershire.** Ca. 1650. 560 × 440 mm. Hand-cold. map, arms, cartouche. (P. May 14; 192c) *Dawsons*. £55
[–] **Monachium utriusque Bavariae Civitas.** [Amst.], [1657]. 284 × 488 mm. Double-p. engraved perspective view, title-ribbon, a lge. emblematic cartouche with the city arms & enclosing Hoefnagel's dedication, linked to cartouches in bottom corners surmounted by coats of arms, tabular keys at top of the plt., Latin text on verso, separated in lr. pts. of centre fold, without loss of engraved surface, unc. W.a.f. (S. Nov.4; 313) *Loeb*. £230
– **Nova Descriptio Palatinatus Rheni.** N.d. 37.5 × 48 cm. Cold. copper engraved map, decor. cartouche, mile indicator. (D. Dec.11-13; 3590) DM 450
– **Nova et Accurata Poli Arctici et Terrarum Circumjacentium Descriptio.** Amst., ca. 1650? 19 × 22½ inches. Map, with cartouche, some foxing. (SG. Nov.20; 14) $300
– **Nova Hispania et Nova Galica.** [Amst.], [1635]. 19 × 22 inches. Cold. map, with lge. cartouche & other decors., browned. (SG. Nov.20; 75) $425
– **Orbis Terrarum.** Ca. 1640. Ob. fo. Old cold. copper engraved map, decor., painted arms cartouche. (R. Mar.31-Apr.4; 4796) DM 650
– **Palestina sive Terrae Sanctae.** 17th. C. Double-p. fo. Fully hand-cold. (probably by cont. hand) map, from the Atlas, upr. & lr. borders with vigs. (CNY. Oct.9; 17) $2,200
– **Paraguay.** Amst., [1653]. 19 × 22½ ins. Map, cold. in outl., with 1 lge. & 1 sm. decor. cartouche, & other decors., browned. (SG. Nov.20; 97) $140
– **Pernambuco.** Ob. fo. Old cold. copper engraved plan, decor., browned. (R. Mar.31-Apr.4; 4996) DM 1,000
– **[Pfalz].** N.d. Ob. fo. Cold. copper engraved map with painted figure cartouche. (R. Oct.14-18; 4894) DM 500
– **Polus Antarcticus.** Ca. 1645. Fo. Map, cold., surrounded by insets, text on verso. (JN. Apr.2; 3) £185
– – **Anr. Edn.** Ca. 1650. Ob. fo. Old cold. copper engraved map, figures round, slightly browned. (R. Mar.31-Apr.4; 4867) DM 1,000
– **Principatus Walliae Pars Australis Vulgo South Wales.** Amst., 1715. 410 × 520 mm. Engraved hand-cold. map, histor. title & scale cartouches, coat-of-arms, compass roses & decor., all hand-cold., a few spots. F. (SBA. Jul.14; 335) *Morgan*. £50
– **Principatus Walliae Pars Borealis.** 15½ × 20 inches. Engraved map, Latin text on verso, dampstains on margin. F. & G. (CSK. Nov.21; 204) £65
– **Sea-Chart of Great Britain.** Ca. 1650. 555 × 440 mm. Browned. (P. May 14; 187b) £50
– **Territorium Norimbergense.** N.d. 36 × 45 cm. Map & sm. supp. map, decor. cartouche & mile indicator, Fr. text on verso, slightly soiled in parts, middle fold bkd. (D. Dec.11-13; 3552) DM 420
– **Virginia et Florida.** Ca. 1650. 510 × 390 mm. Hand-cold. map, vig. sailing ships. (P. May 14; 194b) £180
– **Virginiae Partis Australia et Floridae Partis Orientalis Nova Descriptio.** N.d. Ob. fo. Old cold. copper engraved map with painted figure cartouche & 2 cold. arms, slightly browned, 1 sm. tear backed. (R. Oct.14-18; 5092) DM 800
See–CLUVERIUS, Phillippus & Jansson, Jan or Johannes

JANSSON, Jan or Johannes -contd.
See–HENNEBERG, K. & Jansson, Jan or Johannes

JANSSON, Jan or Johannes, Schenk, Peter & Valk, G.
– Yorkshire. Ca. 1690. Fo. Map, outl. cold. (JN. Apr.2; 782) £125

JANVIER, Sr.
– L'Amérique. 1784. 660 × 480 mm. Hand-cold. map. (P. Jul.30; 183a) *Davis.* £90

JAPAN
Ca. 1650. 345 × 450 mm. Hand-cold. map, tear in lr. central fold. (P. May 14; 188) *Ashworth.* £70

JAPONICA
Ca. 1640. 445 × 345mm. Hand-cold. map of Japan, vig. sailing ships, wide margins. (P. Jul.30; 174) *Wood.* £130

JEFFERSON, Peter
See–FRY, Joshua & Jefferson, Peter

JEFFREYS, Thomas
– Chart containing the Coasts of California, New Albion & Russian Discoveries to the North with the Penninsula opposite thereto . . . L., 1775. 462 × 1115 mm. Lge. ob. engraved map on wtrmkd. paper, 'R. G. VI', hand-cold. in outl., full margins. (PWP. Apr.9; 165) Can. $560
– The County of York. 1771-72. Lge. fo. Engraved map on 20 sheets, hand-cold. in outl., 6 town plan vigs., elaborate dedication & title cartouches, on guards thro.-out, 2 sheets with tears along centrefold. Cf.-bkd., worn. (CSK. Feb.6; 6) £220
– An Exact Chart of the River St. Laurence from Fort Frontenac to the Island of Anticosti, shewing the Soundings, Rocks, Shoals, etc. with Views of the Lands & all necessary . . . L., 1775. 609 × 947 mm. Lge. engraved map, hand-cold. in outl., title-cartouche on wtrmkd. paper, 1 lf. reprd. (PWP. Apr.9; 164) Can. $520
[-] A New & Correct Map of North America . . . L., 1779. 115 × 110 cm. Map, from the 'American Atlas', orig. cold. in outl., lge. decor. cartouche. (CB. Feb.18; 63) Can. $650
– A New Map of Nova Scotia & Cape Breton Island with the adjacent part of the New England & Canada, Composed from a great number of actual Surveys & other materials . . . L., 1775. 475 × 615 mm. Engraved map on 'L.V.G.' wtrmkd. paper, hand-cold. in outl., with some coast lines heavily cold., lge. margins, some light foxing. (PWP. Apr.9; 166) Can. $320
– St. Lucia. 1779. 'Large'. Map, decorative, mod. colour, enlarged inset of Carenage, a few faults right-hand frame. (HL. Apr.1; 1770) £65

JODE, Gerhardus de
– Carte: Episcopatus Leodiensis . . . Ducatus Bouilonensem . . . Franchimont . . . Ed.:– Iohan a Schilde. Antw., 1593. Fo. Map. (LM. Nov.8; 95) B.Frs. 21,000
– Lutsenbor-gi. 1593. 2nd. Edn. Ob. fo. Copper engraved map from Atlas with roll cartouche & arms, slightly soiled & stained. (R. Oct.14-18; 5392) DM 8,000
– Nouvel Guinea Forma & Situs. 1593. 21.5 × 34 cm. Hand-cold. map, Latin text on verso, lr. hf. of map depicts entirely imaginary N. coast of Australia, vig. decor. F. & G. (JL. Mar.1; 167) Aus. $2,500
– Secundae partis Asiae typis . . . sive Arabia. Ill.:– Jan & Lucas van Doetichum. [Antw.], [1578 or later]. 324 × 504 mm. Map, title-cartouche, Latin text on verso. W.a.f. (S. Jun.29; 132) *Regent Gallery.* £190

JOHNSTON, Alexander Keith
– Australia. Edinb., ca. 1844. Map, shows Dutch discoveries in New Holland but omits Van Diemans Land & New Zealand. (JL. Dec.14; 161) Aus. $150
– – **Anr. Copy.** Hand-cold. litho. map. (JL. Mar.1; 205) Aus. $120
– – **Anr. Edn.** 1860. Map. (JL. Dec.14; 170) Aus. $110

JONGHE, Clement de
– Late 17th Century Engraved Plan & Bird's Eye View of Vienna. Amst., ca. 1690? Approximately 410 × 515 mm. Descriptive text in Dutch along the bottom, armorial cartouche, key. F. (SBA. Oct.21; 253) *Maggs.* £220

KAERIUS, Petrus
– Cambriae Typus. Ca. 1630. Ob. fo. Cold. copper engraved map after H. Lhuyd with 2 painted cartouches & decor. (R. Oct.14-18; 5543) DM 450
– Nova Guinea et Insulae Solominis. Paris, 1602. Map showing earliest Portugese discoveries in this region. (JL. Dec.14; 178) Aus. $120
– Typus Orbis Terrarum. 1689. 19 × 25.5 cm. Cold. copper engraved map in hemispheres, allegories of 4 elements in corners. (R. Oct.14-18; 3372) DM 450

KAYSERL, J.B.H.
– Accurate Vorstellung der Beruhmten Meers-Enge bey Gibraltar . . . N.d. 480 × 575 mm. 5 engraved maps, 4 with ships (some faint), 4 town views, maps & borders hand-cold. F. (SKC. Jul.28; 2377) £65

KEERE, Peter van den
– Barbados. 1676. 'Small'. Miniature map, decor. cartouche & 2 ships. (HL. Apr.1; 1574) £95
– Hampshire. 1662. 'Small'. Miniature map, a few marginal blemishes. (HL. Apr.1; 1653) £55

KENT
L., Camden, Early 17th. C. 385 × 285 mm. Hand-cold. map. (P. Jul.2; 238a) *Donovan.* £110

KEULEN, Johannes van
– Nieuwe Paskaert, van der Kust van Genehoa . . . van Gambia. Amst., ca. 1720. 20 × 24 inches. Fully hand-cold. copper-plt. map, cold. cartouche in upr. left corner, slight tear at top. (SG. May 21; 3) $160
– Nieuwe Paskaart voor en Gedeelte van de Oost-Zee. N.d. Lge. ob. fo. Copper engraved map, lightly soiled. (R. Oct.14-18; 4145) DM 900
– Pas-kaart vande Rivieren Commewinni, Suriname, Suramaca, Cupanama en Courantin. Ca. 1720. 51 × 87.5 cm. Old cold. copper engraved map with 2 painted figure cartouches & supp. map: Mündung des Suriname, slightly soiled & mntd. (R. Oct.14-18; 5062) DM 850

KEUR, P. & J.
– De Betchryvingh van de Reysen Pauli en van de Andere Apostelen. [1648]. Hand-cold. engraved map, border of biblical scenes, extracted from Paradisus Canaan, Dutch text on verso. (CSK. Feb.6; 7) £70

KITCHIN, Thomas
– North America. [L.], ca. 1790. 14 × 15 inches. Hand-cold. copper-plt. map, cartouche in upr. left, some vertical creases. (SG. May 21; 80) $130

LA HARPE, Jean Francoise de
See–BELLIN, Jacques Nicolas

LAPIE, P.
– Océanique Centrale. Paris, 1809. Hand-cold. map, landscape title-cartouche. F. & G. (JL. Mar.1; 240) Aus. $230

LAVAUX, A. de & Leth, H. de
– Allgemeene Kaart van de Colonie of Provintie van Suriname. Amst., mid 18th C. 56 × 83.5 cm & 58 × 87.5 cm. Old cold. copper engraved map with several lge. figure cartouches & heraldic decor. (R. Oct.14-18; 5087) DM 1,900

LEA, Philip
– A Map of the Isle of Wight. Ca. 1689 or later. 14.5 × 19.25 inches. Engraved map, hand-cold. in outl., 4 coats-of-arms, galleons at sea, inset plan of Newport, also with plans of Holy Island, Farne Island, the Isle of Man, & the Islands of Scilly, trimmed to border & laid-down. W.a.f. (LC. Jun.18; 207) £130
– New Mapp of the World. Ca. 1690. Ob. fo. Old cold. copper engraved map in 2 hemispheres, sm. maps round. (R. Mar.31-Apr.4; 4813) DM 3,000

LEFEVRE, F.
– Nouvelle Carte Illustré Suisse . . . Géographie Commerciale et Industriale. Ca. 1860. 60 × 83 cm. Partly cold. steel engraved map, 22 marginal views. (D. Dec.11-13; 3452) DM 800

LE ROUGE, George Louis
– Nouvelle Carte des Côtes des Carolines Septentrionales et Meridionales du Cap Fear à Sud Edisto. Paris, 1777. 395 × 522 mm. Engraved chart, hand-cold. in outl., compass rose & a series of coastal contours fully cold., 2 decors. partly cold., with coastal lines & soundings. W.a.f. (S. Nov.3; 47) *Radford.* £120
– Partie Meridionale de l'Electorat de Hanover. Ca. 1750. Ob. fo. Outl. cold. copper engraved map with lge. view & sm. plans. (R. Oct.14-18; 4370) DM 1,000

– Théâtre de la Guerre en Amérique. Paris, 1777. 27½ × 20 inches. Map, cold. boundaries, lge. inset of the Mississippi Valley, & smaller inset map. (SG. May 21; 7) $275
– – **Anr. Copy.** 25 × 20 inches. Cut into 15 sm. sections & pasted on linen. (SG. Nov.20; 11) $140

LETH, Hendrik de
– A Pocket Map of London, Westminster & Southwark. Amst., 1743. 13 × 19½ inches. Dutch text, Royal & City arms. (C. Jul.15; 73) *Quaritch.* £110

See–LAVAUX, A. de & Leth, H. de

LHUYD, Humphrey
– Cambriae Typus, Wales. Ca. 1600. 510 × 370 mm. Hand-cold. map. F. & G. (P. Jul.30; 171) *Quaritch.* £60
– – **Anr. Edn.** N.d. Ob. fo. Cold. copper engraved map, painted rollwork cartouche. (R. Mar.31-Apr.4; 5589) DM 500

L'ISLE, Guillaume de
– America Septentrionalis. Augsburg, ca. 1700. 452 × 579 mm. Engraved hand-cold. map, histor. title-cartouche, slightly spotted. W.a.f. (S. Nov.3; 54) *Map House.* £100
– Carte de l'Isle de Saint Domingue. Paris, 1725. 18½ × 24½ inches. Hand-cold. map, uncold. cartouche in upr. right. (SG. May 21; 131) $110
– – **Anr. Edn.** Amst., [1741]. 22 × 26 inches. Map, hand-cold. boundaries. (SG. May 21; 116) $110
– Carte de la Louisane et du cours du Mississippi. [Paris], 1745. 21½ × 27½ inches. Map, with cold. boundaries & inset, light foxing. (SG. Nov.20; 72) $300
– Carte des Indes et de la Chine. Amst., ca. 1725. 24 × 25½ inches. Map, boundaries cold., split at centre fold, some marginal tears. (SG. Nov.20; 38) $130
– Hémisphère Septentrional pour voir . . . les Terres Arctiques.–Hémisphère Meridional pour voir . . . les Terres Australes.–Orbis Veteribus noti Tabula Nova. Paris, 1714 [or later]. Various sizes. 3 engraved, circular maps, 3rd. hand-cold. in outl., waterstained in corners, affecting text (titles) of 1st. 2. W.a.f. (S. Jun.29; 140) *Waterloo.* £130

L'ISLE, Guillaume de & Schenk, Pieter
– L'Amérique Septentrionale. 1708. Ob. fo. Old cold. copper engraved map with figure cartouche, sm. fault backed. (R. Oct.14-18; 5079) DM 600

LIVINGSTONE, David
– A Map of a Portion of Central Africa . . . N.d. 76.5 × 84.5 cm. Some tears at folds. (SSA. Jun.18; 346) R. 110

LIZARS, William Home
– Map of Part of New South Wales. Edinb., 1819. Map, showing the earliest routes across the Blue Mountains, vig. of Sydney. (JL. Dec.14; 160) Aus. $260
– – **Anr. Edn.** Edinb., 1824. Hand-cold. map without engraved coastal shading, vig. of Sydney Cove. (JL. Mar.1; 165) Aus. $170
– Map of Van Diemen's Land. Edinb., 1824. Hand-cold. map, engraved vig. of Hobart. (JL. Mar.1; 198) Aus. $120

LOON, Gerard van
– Imperii Sinarum. Amst., ca. 1680. 525 × 485 mm. (P. Jul.2; 233c) £70
– – **Anr. Copy.** 21 × 24 inches. Fully-cold. map, with cartouche, scale & ornaments. (SG. Nov.20; 37) $180
– Orbis Terrarum Nova et accuratissima Tabula. Ca. 1650. Double-p. fo. Map, cold. in outl. (SPB. Oct.1; 268) $1,800

LOTTER, Tobias Conrad
– America Septentrionalis. N.d. Ob. fo. Old cold. copper engraved map with figure cartouche. (R. Oct.14-18; 5082) DM 500
– Pensylvania, Nova Jersey et Nova York. N.d. Lge. fo. Old cold. copper engraved map with lge. figure cartouche. (R. Oct.14-18; 5074) DM 850

LOUIS, Andreas
– Special Retvisende Siöe Kaart fra Cronborg til Höyerups Kierke . . . Ill.:– J.G. Winckler. [?Copen.], [1775]. Each sheet approx. 425 × 560 mm. Engraved chart, lge. pict. title-cartouche with arms & vig., 6 sheets joined, linen mntd. W.a.f. (S. Mar.31; 396) *Schmidt.* £180

MAACOP, G. & Ortelius, Abraham
- Bistümmer Münster und Osnabrück. N.d. Fo. Cold. copper engraved map with painted roll cartouche. (R. Oct.14-18; 4564) DM 530

MAGINI
See–PORRO, Girolamo & Magini

MALLET, Allain Manesson
- Mer de Sud. Paris, 1683. Map from Description de L'Univers. (JL. Dec.14; 165) Aus. $100
- Nouveau Mexique et Californie. Ca. 1685. 155 × 105 mm. Hand-cold. map. (P. Apr.30; 101) *Map House.* £50
- Virginia [Chesapeake Bay area]. 1683. 'Small'. Map, 2 habitations marked & named. (HL. Apr.1; 1803) £55

MALTA
Ca. 1650. 515 × 420 mm. Hand-cold. map, vig. sailing ships, slight tear in lr. fold, inset town plan of Valetta, some browning. (P. May 14; 187) *Kentish.* £60

MAPPE-MONDE
Ed.:– Desnos, L. Paris, 1778. Map with lge. ornate cartouche. F. (JL. Dec.14; 150) Aus. $100

MARIETTE, P.
- Carte Générale des Indes Orientales et des Isles Adiacentes Paris, 1646. Hand-cold. map showing the first Dutch discoveries of Australia at North West Cape & west coast of Cape York, ornate title cartouche, compass rose & sailing ships. (JL. Mar.1; 204) Aus. $480
- Cypern. Ca. 1640. Ob. fo. Outl. cold. copper engraved map, figure cartouche, 2 lge. arms. (R. Mar.31-Apr.4; 5098) DM 550

MARSHALL, G.W.
- Map & Chart of the Muskoka Lakes. Toronto, 1899. 67 × 105 cm. Fully cold. map, backed with linen. Folded into folder. (CB. Feb.18; 168) Can. $160

MEIER-HUSUM, J. & Blaeu, Willem & Joannes
- Schleswig-Holstein. N.d. Ob. fo. Old cold. copper engraved map with 3 painted cartouches, cold. arms & borders with 18 town plans. F. (R. Oct.14-18; 4168) DM 2,500

MEISSNER
- Irakleon. Ca. 1623. 'Small'. Map, tiny trace of stain. (HL. Apr.1; 1703) £50

MELISH, John
- 'Map of Pennsylvania, Constructed from the County Surveys authorised by the State' . . . Ill.:– B. Tanner. Phila., 1822. 1st. Edn. Giant fo., 52 × 77 inches. Copper-engraved hand-cold. folding map, linen-bkd., cl.-trimmed edges. Laid in orig. 3 qtr. roan & marb.-bd. folder, cloth ties. Geological data supplied by William Maclure. (PNY. Oct.1; 347) $2,100
- Plan of Quebec & Adjacent Country . . . during the Siege by General Wolfe in 1759. [Phila.], [1813]. 17 × 21 inches. Partly cold. map, lr. third of sheet with many engraved references, & a sm. view, slight marginal tears. (SG. May 21; 89) $130

MELLINGER, J. & Blaeu, Willem & Joannes
- Herzogtum Lüneburg. N.d. Ob. fo. Old cold. copper engraved map with 2 painted cartouches. (R. Oct.14-18; 4394) DM 420

MERCATOR, Gerard
[-] Aethiopiae Sub Aegypto pars. [1579?]. 15 × 20½ inches. Map, some colouring, ornamental cartouche, decors., discoloured & soiled. (TA. Oct.16; 7) £52
- Africa. Ex Magna Orbis Terrae Descriptione Gerardi Mercatoris. N.d. 38 × 47 cm. Cold. copper engraved map, decorative & mile indicator. Fr. text on verso. (D. Dec.11-13; 3515) DM 500
[-] Africae nova tabula . . . [Amst.], 1631 [but 1633, or later]. 375 × 500 mm. Engraved map, hand-cold. in outl., title-cartouche, decor., fully cold., separated at bottom of centre fold, affecting 1 word. F. W.a.f. (S. Nov.4; 370) *Louman.* £100
- America. 1637. 'Medium' size. Map, cartouche, galleons & sea monsters. (HL. Apr.1; 1509) £130
- America sive India Nova . . . redacta per Michaelem Mercatorem. [Amst.], [1619]. 365 × 457 mm. Engraved circular map, roundels at outer corners, 3 enclosing other maps, 1 the title, all maps hand-cold. in outl., some features & design of flowers & foliage fully cold. Fr. text on verso. W.a.f. (S. Jun.29; 141) *Leycester.* £650

- Anglia Regnum. Ca. 1634. 13½ × 18 inches. Uncold. map, ornamental title cartouche, ship etc., Dutch text to verso, some discolouration. (TA. Feb.19; 82) £56
- Anglia, Scotia et Hibernia. [Amst.], [1595, or later]. Approx. 332 × 412 mm. Engraved map, hand-cold. .in outl., title cartouche fully-cold., Latin text on verso. F. (SBA. May 27; 280a) *Davies.* £120
- Anglia, Scotia et Hibernia.–Anglia Regnum. [Amst.], [1619]. Various sizes. 2 engraved maps, hand-cold. in outl., title-cartouches, etc., fully cold., Fr. text on versos. W.a.f. (S. Jun.29; 151) *Godfrey.* £120
- Arctic. 1637. 'Large'. Map, 3 sm. inset maps. (HL. Apr.1; 1523) £75
[-] Cambriae Typus Auctore Humfredo Lhuydo. [Amst.], [1607, or later]. 344 × 494 mm. Engraved map, hand-cold. in outl., title & scale cartouches, decors. all hand-cold., 1 margin obscured by frame, centre fold split, Latin text on verso. F. (SBA. Dec.16; 276) *Morgan.* £150
[-] - Anr. Edn. [Amst.], [1619]. 346 × 488 mm. Engraved map, hand-cold. in outl., title & scale cartouches, sailing ships, sea monsters, etc., fully cold., Fr. text on verso. W.a.f. (S. Jun.28; 159) *Freeman.* £120
- China Tartariae Pars. N.d. 34.5 × 46 cm. Cold. copper engraved map, title & mile indicator cartouche & religious cartouche, decor., Fr. text on verso. (D. Dec.11-13; 3507) DM 480
- Cyprus Ins. N.d. 35 × 49 cm. Cold. copper engraved map, decor. title & mile indicator cartouche, Fr. text on verso, centre fold lightly torn. (D. Dec.11-13; 3428) DM 550
- D'Escosse. Ca. 1600. (P. Oct.23; 112) *Radford.* £55
[-] Ducatus Holsatiae Nova Tabula. [Amst.], ca. 1640, or later. 380 × 510 mm. Engraved map, 2 inset maps, Latin text on verso, unc. W.a.f. (S. Nov.4; 316) *Bucherkabinett.* £120
- Eboracum, Lincoln, Staffs., . . . Norfolk. 1600. Hand-cold. map. F. & G. (P. Jun.11; 222) *Bailey.* £65
- Emden & Oldenborch Comit. N.d. Ob. fo. Old cold. copper engraved map with painted roll cartouche. (R. Oct.14-18; 4133) DM 560
- England & Wales. Ca. 1608. Fo., approximately 56 × 43 cm. Map, text on verso, orig. colour. (JN. Sep.9; 4095) £70
[-] Exquisita . . . lustrata et iam retecta Freti Magellancici facies. [Amst.], [1619]. 348 × 463 mm. Engraved map, principal features hand-cold., including 3 cartouches (1 enclosing view), seals with pups, compass rose, sailing ships, etc., Fr. text on verso. W.a.f. (S. Jun.29; 145) *Crete.* £110
- Iceland. 1637. 'Medium' size. Map, cartouches, sea monster & Mt. Hekla erupting, light crease in 1 corner. (HL. Apr.1; 1711) £65
- Ins. Ceilan quae Incolis Tenarisin dicitur. N.d. 34.5 × 50 cm. Cold. copper engraved map, title & mile indicator cartouche, wind rose, decor., Fr. text on verso. (D. Dec.11-13; 3506) DM 480
- Insulae Indiae Orientalis Praecipuae, in quibus Moluccae celeberrimae sunt. [Amst.], [1619]. 343 × 475 mm. Engraved map, hand-cold. in outl., cartouches, sailing ships, compass rose, etc., fully cold., Fr. text on verso. W.a.f. (S. Jun.29; 170) *Dawson.* £150
- Iran. 1637. 'Medium' size. Map, 2 cartouches. (HL. Apr.1; 1716) £65
- Island. Ca. 1630. Ob. fo. Cold. copper engraved map with painted cartouche. (R. Oct.14-18; 5853) DM 650
- Islandia. N.d. 28 × 43.5 cm. Cold. copper engraved map, renaissance cartouche, mile indicator & decor., Fr. text on verso. (D. Dec.11-13; 3471) DM 650
- Iuliacensis et Montensis Ducatus. [Amst.], ca. 1640, or later. 376 × 492 mm. Engraved map, cartouche enclosing arms of Gulick & Berghe, histor. title & scale cartouches, Latin text on verso, unc. W.a.f (S. Nov.4; 317) *Schuster.* £160
- Katalonien. N.d. Ob. fo. Old cold. copper engraved map, 2 painted roll-work cartouches. (R. Mar.31-Apr.4; 6003) DM 420
[-] Mappa Aestivarum Insularum, alias Barmudas Dictarum . . . Amst., H. Hondius, ca. 1633, or later. 393 × 516 mm. Engraved map, hand-cold. in outl., title & scale cartouches, etc., fully cold., Fr. text on verso. F. W.a.f. (S. Mar.31; 313) *Quaritch.* £170

[-] - Anr. Edn. Amst., [1647]. 390 × 514 mm. Engraved map, hand-cold. in outl., key to details across bottom of plt. flanked by 2 armorial medallions, latter & title & scale cartouches fully cold., pt. of Virginia & Florida shows in outl., uncold., flaw in paper affecting 1 medallion, some offsetting & discolouration, tear in blank bottom margin. W.a.f. (S. Jun.29; 146) *Waterloo.* £170
- Nordschweiz in der Begrenzung Solothurn-Mulhouse-Bodensee-Zürich. Ca. 1630. Ob. fo. Cold. copper engraved map. (R. Oct.14-18; 5794) DM 430
- [North Pole]. Septentrionalium Terrarum. 1595. Double-p. fo. Map, cold. in outl., slight foxing. F. (SPB. Oct.1; 266) $950
- Orbis Terrae Compendiosa Descriptio. N.p., n.d. 28.5 × 52.5 cm. Cold. copper engraved map, shows old & new world in globe form, armillary sphere & wind rose between, decor., Fr. text on verso. (D. Dec.11-13; 3402) DM 1,800
- [Ostpreussen]. N.d. Ob. fo. Old cold. copper engraved map with painted figure cartouche. (R. Oct.14-18; 4717) DM 600
- Palestine. 1637. 'Medium' size. Map, decorative. (HL. Apr.1; 1753) £80
- Saltzburg Archiepiscopatus. Amst., 1627. 14 × 19½ inches. Map, all edges ragged. (SG. Nov.20; 74) $120
- Scotia Regnum [all Scotland]. Ca. 1600. Map. (P. Oct.23; 111) *Radford.* £70
- Septentrionalium Terrarum Descriptio. [Amst.], [1619]. 365 × 389 mm. Engraved circular map, hand-cold. in outl., including 3 sm. maps in roundels at outer corners (4th. occupied by title), foliate design in intervening spaces fully cold., Fr. text on verso. W.a.f. (S. Jun.29; 135) *Jonsson.* £380
- - Anr. Edn. [Amst.], [1619 or later]. 366 × 394 mm. Engraved circular map, hand-cold. in outl., including 3 sm. maps in roundels at outer corners, some features fully cold., some minimal wear in centre fold, a little discold. F. W.a.f. (S. Jun.29; 47) *Jonsson.* £140
- - Anr. Edn. Ca. 1630. Ob. fo. Cold. copper engraved map, ornamental borders, sm. maps in corners. (R. Oct.14-18; 3401) DM 1,300
- Svecia et Norvegia. N.d. 36 × 47.5 cm. Cold. copper engraved map, Fr. text on verso. (D. Dec.11-13; 3455) DM 600
[-] Tabula Magellanica qua Tierrae del Fuego . . . a F. Magellano detectis. Amst., [1652]. Thick paper. 406 × 525 mm. Engraved map, hand-cold. in outl., historiated title & scale cartouches, armorial dedication cartouche, decors., compass roses, etc., fully cold., short tear in centre fold. W.a.f. (S. Nov.3; 95) *Heinzig.* £160
[-] Terra Sancta quae in Sacris Terra Promissionis ol: Palestina. [Amst.], [1607]. 353 × 492 mm. Engraved map, title & scale cartouches, 1 ship & 1 fish, all hand-cold., Latin text on verso. (SKC. May 19; 377) £100
[-] Venezuela.–Nova Hispania et Nova Galicia. –Terra Firma et Novum Regnum Granatense et Popayan. Amst., [1639]; ca. 1640, or later; ca. 1640, or later. Various sizes. 3 engraved maps, hand-cold. in outl., title & scale cartouches, histor. & armorial on 2nd., compass roses, sailing ships, etc., fully cold., Fr. text on verso of 1st., others with Latin text on versos, papers of 2nd. with flaw round title-cartouche, sm. hole at fold, some discolouration & offsetting on 2nd. & 3rd. W.a.f. (S. Jun.29; 144) *Faupel.* £190
- West Indies. 1637. 'Medium' size. Map, emblem on reverse, cartouche & printer's name (Michael Sparke). (HL. Apr.1; 1552) £65
- Zeelandia Comitatus. [Antw.], ca. 1607. 34 × 50 cm. Engraved hand-cold. map, folded & slightly defect. in middle, a thin spot. F. & G. (VG. Oct.28; 337) Fls. 550

MERCATOR, Gerard & Blaeu, Willem or Guilielmus Janszoon & Johannes or Jan
- Alsatia cum Suntgoia et Brisgoia. N.d. 39.5 × 79 cm. Old cold. copper engraved map, large painted arms cartouche. (R. Oct.14-18; 3453) DM 600
- Helvetiae cum Regionibus Confoederatis. N.d. Ob. fo. Old cold. copper engraved map with 2 painted figure cartouches. (R. Oct.14-18; 5791) DM 900
- Herzogtum Bayern. N.d. Ob. fo. Old cold. copper engraved map with painted figure cartouche. (R. Oct.14-18; 3689) DM 500

MERCATOR, Gerard & Hondius, Henricus
- Irlandiae Regnum. Ca. 1620. 475 × 350 mm. Hand-cold. map. (P. Jul.30; 191) *Malone.* £65

MERCATOR, Gerard & Hondius, Jodocus
- **Africa.** 1689. Ob. fo. Old cold. copper engraved map with painted figure cartouche. (R. Oct.14-18; 5006) DM 650
- **Cypern.** N.d. Ob. fo. Old cold. copper engraved map, 2 painted roll cartouches & figure decor. (R. Mar.31-Apr.4; 5096) DM 800
- - **Anr. Copy.** Cold. copper engraved map with 6 sm. maps & painted cartouche. (R. Oct.14-18; 5109) DM 600
- **Franconia.** 1636. 'Large'. Engraved map, cartouche. (HL. Apr.1; 1617) £120
- **Franken.** 1627. Ob. fo. Old cold. map with 2 painted roll cartouches. (R. Oct.14-18; 3733) DM 420
- **Iaponia.** Ca. 1630. Ob. fo. Old cold. copper engraved map, 2 painted roll cartouches & figures. (R. Mar.31-Apr.4; 5121) DM 1,100
- - **Anr. Copy.** Cold. copper engraved map with 2 painted roll cartouches & figure staffage. (R. Oct.14-18; 5137) DM 1,000
- **Insulae Indiae Orientalis.** Ca. 1630. Ob. fo. Cold. copper engraved map with 3 painted roll cartouches & decor. (R. Oct.14-18; 5118) DM 600
- **Rhineland.** 1632 [1636]. Engl. Edn. 'Large'. Engraved map, from atlas, cartouche, compass-rose. (HL. Apr.1; 1546) £120

MERCATOR, Gerard & Ortelius, Abraham
- **Flandria.** N.d. Ob. fo. Old cold. copper engraved map, cartouche in oval, decor. in corners, painted roll cartouche & figure decor., heavily browned in parts. (R. Oct.14-18; 5297) DM 750

MERCATOR, Gerard & Ptolemaeus, Claudius
- **Arabia.** Ca. 1618. Fo. Map, cold. (JN. Apr.2; 261) £65

MERCATOR, Michael
See–RUMOLD, Gerhard & Mercator, Michael

MERIAN, Matthew
- **India Orientalis et Insulae Adiecentes.** Frankfurt, 1646. Hand-cold. map showing the first Dutch discoveries of Australia, shows western Cape York & North West Cape & includes a decor. cartouche, sailing ships & a sea monster. (JL. Mar.1; 226) Aus. $330
- **[Mannheim].** N.d. Sm. ob. fo. Copper engraved plan. (R. Oct.14-18; 3567) DM 500

MEYER-HUSUM, J.
- **Orbis Vetus cum Origine Gentium.** 1651. Ob. fo. Cold. copper engraved map, figure & decor. baroque, old bkd. (R. Mar.31-Apr.4; 4797) DM 1,000

MEYER-HUSUM, J. & Blaeu, Willem & Joannes
- **Pars Occidentalis Praefecturae Hadersleben.** N.d. Ob. fo. Old cold. copper engraved map with 2 painted figure cartouches. (R. Oct.14-18; 4186) DM 700

MIDDLESEX
Ca. 1640. 410 × 390 mm. Hand-cold. map. F. & G. (P. Jul.2; 240d) *Jaffe.* £100

MINGUET, P.
- **Mapa Universal del Mundo.** Late 18th. C. Outl. cold. copper engraved map, decor. (R. Mar.31-Apr.4; 4838) DM 450

MOLL, Hermann
- **Bermuda.** 1732. 'Medium'. 2-pt. map, upr. hf. Bermuda, lr. hf. pt. of Providence Islands, some marginal staining, barely affecting map proper. (HL. Apr.1; 1577) £95
- **Domina Anglorum in America.** [Nurnberg]., [1759-81?]. 50 × 56 cm. 4 fully cold. maps on 1 sheet. (CB. Nov.12; 61) Can. $200
- **Domina Anglorum in America Septentrionali.** Ca. 1750. 21 × 25 ins. 4 fully-cold. maps on 1 sheet, German text at foot, some repairs. (SG. Nov.20; 126) $150
- **A Map of Mexico or New Spain . . . & Part of California . . .** [L.], [1785]. Approx. 7 × 10 inches. Copperplt. map, cold. in outl., from Bowle's 'Pocket Atlas'. In 12½ × 15½ inch mat, covered with cellophane. (SG. Aug.21; 264) $200
- **A Map of the West Indies or the Islands of America.** L., ca. 1715. 25 × 41 ins. Copper-plt. map, boundaries hand-cold., several insets, some vertical folds, old tape on verso. (SG. May 21; 127) $275
- - **Anr. Edn.** [L.], ca. 1720. 24 × 39 inches. Map, with cold. boundaries & inset views, torn at 1 corner, other slight defects. (SG. Nov.20; 132) $170

- **New & Correct Map of the World.** 1719. 70.5 × 121 cm. Copper engraved decor. map bkd. (D. Dec.11-13; 3401) DM 1,200
- **New Map of Denmark & Sweden.** Ca. 1710. Copper engraved map, old outl. cold., lge. arms cartouche, supp. map & scenes at side, lightly browned, 2 sm. tears & 2 faults bkd. (R. Mar.31-Apr.4; 5968) DM 800
- - **Anr. Edn.** N.d. Lge. ob. fo. Copper engraved map with old outl. cold. with figure cartouche, supp. map & 5 lge. ills. at sides, slightly soiled, sm. tears. (R. Oct.14-18; 5866) DM 600
- **North America.** [L.], n.d. Fo. Double-p. map, cold. in outl., decor. (SPB. Nov.24; 37) $700
- **St. Christopher.** 1732. 'Medium' size. Map, early colour, compass rose, a few faint blemishes. (HL. Apr.1; 1764) £50
- **Südamerika.** N.d. Lge. ob. fo. Copper engraved map with old outl. cold. with figure cartouche & view, browned at folds & backed. (R. Oct.14-18; 5085) DM 450
- **United Provinces of Netherlands.** N.d. Lge. ob. fo. Copper engraved map with outl. cold. with supp. map, 2 sm. town plans, fold brkn. & backed. (R. Oct.14-18; 5333) DM 500

MOLL, J.
- **General & Coasting Trade Winds . . . through ye World.** L., ca. 1730. Map. (JL. Dec.14; 190) Aus. $200

MOLLER, CH. & Blaeu, Willem & Joannes
- **Celeberrimi Fluvii Albis nova delineatio.** 1628. Ob. fo. 2 old maps cold. copper engraved with painted cartouche & cold. arms. (R. Oct.14-18; 4065) DM 650

MORDEN, Robert
- **A New Map of ye World.** L., 1688. Hand-cold., decor. early world hemisphere map. (JL. Mar.1; 238) Aus. $150

MORTIER, Corneille
See–COVENS, Jean & Mortier, Corneille

MORTIER, Pierre
- **Carte Générale de la Caroline.** N.d. Lge. fo. Old cold. copper engraved map, on Jap., cartouche & sm. supp. map, some loss restored. (R. Mar.31-Apr.4; 4998) DM 650
See–HEURDT, J. van & Covens & Mortier
See–JAILLOT, Hubert & Mortier, Pierre
See–SANSON, Nicholas & Mortier, Pierre

MOXON, Joseph
- **Canaan or the Land of Promise.** 1708. Fo., approximately 56 × 43 cm. Uncold. map, repairs. (JN. Sep.9; 3762) £75
- **40 Years travels of Children of Israel [Holy Land & Sinai].** 1708. Fo., approximately 56 × 43 cm. Map, 3 insets, uncold., sm. repair. (JN. Sep.9; 3764) £75
- **Jerusalem plan.** 1708. Fo., approximately 56 × 43 cm. Uncold. map, repair to left & right margins. (JN. Sep.9; 3763) £50
- **Map of all the Earth.** Ca. 1690. Ob. fo. Old cold. copper engraved oval map, 14 scenes round, painted cartouche & cold. arms. (R. Mar.31-Apr.4; 4814) DM 700
- - **Anr. Edn.** Ca. 1700. Hand-cold. figures in border. (P. Oct.23; 109b) *Shirley.* £65
- **World Map.** 1708. Fo., approximately 56 × 43 cm. 14 biblical insets in borders, uncold. (JN. Sep.9; 3503) £62

MUNSTER, Sebastian
- **Africa XXV Nova Tabula.** [1540-45]. 25.2 × 34.2 cm. Woodcut map, full margins. F. (VA. Jan.30; 124) R. 240
- **Description Nouvelle d'Europe** N.d. Sm. ob. fo. Woodcut map. (R. Mar.31-Apr.4; 5151) DM 420
- **Europe.** Ca. 1575. 'Large'. Map, woodcut reversed view, slight blemishing. (HL. Apr.1; 1535) £90
- **Jerusalem.** 16th. C. Map, upr. portion of double-p. fo. sheet from the Cosmographica, woodcut view, ptd. heading & caption in German, fully hand-cold. (CNY. Oct.9; 12) $500
- **Map of England & parts of Ireland.** [1572]. Uncold. W.a.f. (P. Oct.2; 227) *Leave.* £110
- **Map of the Middle-East & Cyprus.** [1572]. Uncold. W.a.f. (P. Oct.2; 225) *Kenton.* £150
- **Map of the Old World.** [1572.] Uncold. W.a.f. (P. Oct.2; 224) *Leave.* £290
- **Northern Netherlands.** 1575. 'Medium' size. Map, woodcut, view of Groningen on reverse. (HL. Apr.1; 1743) £65

- **Palestine & Cyprus.** 1575. 4to., approximately 28 × 22 cm. Cold. map, text on verso. (JN. Sep.9; 3755) £110
- [-] **La Table de la Region Orientale . . . d'Asie.** [?Basle], ca. 1552, or later. Ca. 225 × 340mm. Engraved map, Fr. text on verso, lightly attached to card mount. W.a.f. (S. Mar.31; 413) *Reddui.* £110
- **Tabula Europae IIII.** 1552. Sm. ob. fo. Cold. woodcut map. (R. Oct.14-18; 3406) DM 430
- **Typus Orbis Ptol. Descriptus.** 1552. Sm. ob. fo. Cold. woodcut map. (R. Oct.14-18; 3368) DM 500

NEUBAUER
- **Berlin Stadtplan.** Ca. 1790. 19 × 19 cm. Copper engraved plan with ptd. explanation lf. (R. Oct.14-18; 3859) DM 650

NEW SOUTH WALES with Part of Victoria.
L'pool., 1856. 61 × 52 cm. Map, hand-cold. in outl., inset of Van Dieman's Land. (JL. Jul.19; 209) Aus. $120

NORDEN, John
- **Sussexia.** 1637. Hand-cold. map. F. & G. (P. Jan.22; 201) *Menlove.* £70

NORTH AMERICA
- **A Map of North America, with the European Settlements . . .** Ca. 1750? 15½ × 18 ins. Map, details in col., reprd. on verso, remargined at bottom. (SG. Nov.20; 90) $220
- **New Map of . . . North America.** Balt., 1853. 58 × 62 ins. Cold. wall-map, in wide, elab. floral border, linen-mntd., with rollers, several lge. tears, lge. brown-stains. (SG. Nov.20; 91) $200

OGILBY, John
- **The Road from London to Aberistwith . . . wherein are included the Roads to Oxford & Worcester.** [1675?]. Approximately 444 × 304mm. 3 engraved maps with pict. title-cartouches, various decor. features, partly hand-cold., marginal tear in 1st. but barely affecting plt. (SBA. Oct.22; 701) *Hulme.* £75
- **St. Helena.** 1670. 'Large'. Map, view-type, places indicated by numbers & key reference, galleons, cartouche, compass rose, mod. colour, some slight staining, 3 splits or tears in margin (clear of design). (HL. Apr.1; 1765) £55

ORDNANCE Survey maps of parts of Essex & Kent
1805-05-19. Nos. 1-3 & index. 603 × 910mm. Cl.-bkd. folding engraved maps. Mor. gt. box. (SKC. May 19; 380) £50

ORTELIUS, Abraham
- **Abrahami Patriarchea Peregrinato et Vita.** Late 16th. C. Double-p. fo. Fully hand-cold. map from Latin edn. of Theatrum Orbis Terrarum, border with 22 circular vigs. (CNY. Oct.9; 16) $2,000
- - **Anr. Edn.** N.d. Ob. fo. Cold. copper engraved map with wide border with decor. in sm. medals. (R. Oct.14-18; 5125) DM 1,200
- **Aevi Veteris Geographicus.** 1590. 345 × 310mm. Hand-cold. map. (P. Jun.11; 240) £260
- - **Anr. Copy.** Ob. fo. Cold. copper engraved map with wide ornamental border with sm. maps in corners. (R. Oct.14-18; 3369) DM 650
- **Africae Tabula.** Ca. 1606. Upr. left corner plt. torn. (P. Oct.23; 126) *Radford.* £95
- - **Anr. Edn.** N.d. Ob. fo. Cold. copper engraved map, painted cartouche. (R. Mar.31-Apr.4; 4926) DM 500
- **Americae sive Novi Orbis Descriptio.** Ca. 1580. Cold. copper engraved map, decor. corners, 2 painted figures & 2 cartouches, sm. margin tear bkd. (R. Mar.31-Apr.4; 4970) DM 2,900
- - **Anr. Edn.** [1606]. 355 × 485mm. Engraved map, hand-cold. in outl., sailing ships partly cold., cartouches fully cold., Engl. text on verso, reprd. at bottom of centre fold, slightly affecting engraved surface, in card mount. W.a.f. (S. Jun.29; 24) *Arader.* £450
- - **Anr. Edn.** N.d. 37 × 51 cm. Cold. copper engraved map, decor. renaissance cartouche in oval, floral ornament in corner, bkd., slightly soiled, reprd. tear. (D. Dec.11-13; 3527) DM 1,700
- [-] **Andegavensium Ditionis Vera et Integra Descriptio.** 1579. Fully-cold. map, from an atlas, with lge. decor. cartouche. (SG. Nov.20; 93) $100
- **Angliae et Hiberniae Descriptio.** 1605. Ob. fo. Cold. copper engraved map, with Adresse by J.B. Vrints, 3 painted cartouches & figure decor. (R. Oct.14-18; 5522) DM 1,000

[-] Angliae et Hiberniae.–Angliae . . . Descriptio, Auctore Humfredo Lhuyd. [Antw.] (1st. map), [1606]; [1606]. Various sizes. 1st. map: engraved, Engl. text on verso, hand-cold. in outl., cartouches, sailing ships, arms, allegorical figures, genealogical tables, etc., fully cold., slightly worn in centre fold, in card mount; 2nd. map: engraved, hand-cold. in outl., title-cartouche, sailing ships, etc., fully cold., sm. hole at bottom of centre fold affecting engraved border & 1 word on map, in card mount. W.a.f. (S. Jun.29; 30)
Stephenson. £350

[-] Angliae Regni florentissimi nova Descriptio auctore Humfredo Lhuyd . . . 1573. [Antw.], [1574]. 376 × 467mm. Engraved map, hand-cold., including elab. title & scale cartouches, etc., Latin text on verso, some slight discolouration, lightly hinged to card mount. W.a.f. (S. Nov.3; 134)
Kidd. £100

– **Argonautica.** Ca. 1600. 495 × 345mm. Uncold. map, inset plans. (P. May 14; 194) *Kay.* £100

– **Asiae Nova Descriptio.** Ca. 1580. Ob. fo. Cold. copper engraved map. (R.Mar.31-Apr.4; 5064)
DM 650

– **Austriae Descrip.** Ed.:– W. Lazius. N.d. 35 × 49 cm. Cold. copper engraved map, decor. title & mile indicator cartouche, Fr. text on verso. (D. Dec.11-13; 3446)
DM 500

– **Brabant.** 1591. Ob. fo. Cold. copper engraved map, 3 painted cartouches & sm. supp. maps. (R. Mar.31-Apr.4; 5272)
DM 650

– **[-] Anr. Edn.** N.d. Ob. fo. Old cold. copper engraved map with painted roll cartouche. (R. Oct.14-18; 5260)
DM 650

[-] Cambriae Typus, auctore Humfredo Lhuydo. [Antw.], [1573]. 367 × 491mm. Engraved map, hand-cold. in outl., title-cartouche, sailing ship, sea monster, pts. of England & Ireland, etc., fully cold., Latin text on verso, verso of edges strengthened with paper. In card mount. W.a.f. (S. Jun.29; 56) *Freeman.* £220

[-] – Anr. Edn. [Antw.], [1587, or later]. 367 × 493mm. Engraved map, Latin text on verso, 2 sm. perforations in centre fold. W.a.f. (S. Nov.3; 198)
Radford. £110

– **China.** N.d. Ob. fo. Cold. copper engraved map, 3 painted figure cartouches. (R. Mar.31-Apr.4; 5090)
DM 1,200

– **Culicanae, Americanae Regionis, Descriptio . . . Hispaniolae, Cubae, aliarumque Insularum circumiacentium, Delineatio.** [Antw.], [1592, or later]. 353 × 494mm. Maps of pt. of Mexico & Cuba & other islands, 2 engrs. on 1 plt., Latin text on verso. W.a.f. (S. Nov.3; 100) *Gibbons.* £120

– **Cypern.** Ob. fo. Cold copper engraved map, 2 painted roll cartouches, slightly restored. (S. Mar.31-Apr.4; 5094)
DM 750

[-] Cypri Insulae Nova Descript. [Antw.], [1573, but ca. 1600]. 347 × 492mm. Engraved map, title cartouche, scale cartouche, inset map of Lemnos, & 3 ships, all hand-cold., Latin text on verso. (SKC. May 19; 375)
£140

– **– Anr. Edn.** N.d. Ob. fo. Old cold. copper engraved map with 2 painted roll cartouches & sm. supp. map, slightly soiled. (R. Oct.14-18; 5107)
DM 850

[-] Cyprus Insul, Candia olim Creta. [Antw.], [1570, or later]. 362 × 436mm. 2 engraved maps on 1 sheet, hand-cold., messy, text on verso. (SKC. May 19; 374)
£100

– **Descriptio Germaniae Inferioris.** N.d. Ob. fo. Old cold. copper engraved map, cartouche in oval, decor. in corners, slightly soiled & stained. (R. Oct.14-18; 5346)
DM 950

– **England.** Ob. fo. Old cold. copper engraved map, 2 painted roll work cartouches. (R. Mar.31-Apr.4; 5550)
DM 450

[-] Eryn. Hiberniae . . . nova descriptio. Antw., [1589 or later]. Approximately 350 × 480mm. Engraved map, hand-cold., including cartouches & other features, Latin text on verso, paper a little browned. W.a.f. (S. Jun.29; 65)
Neptune Gallery. £130

– **Europe.** Ca. 1570. Cold. map. Oak frame. (PD. Oct.22; 224)
£55

– **France.** 17th. C. Hand-cold. map. F. & G. (P. Dec.11; 174) *Garfunkle.* £70

– **Frisia Occidentalis.** [Antw.], ca. 1580. 37 × 50 cm. Engraved hand-cold. map, inset map of Frisia in Roman times, ptd. text in Latin on verso, fold in middle. (VG. Oct.28; 263)
Fls. 600

– **Germania.** N.d. Ob. fo. Old cold. copper engraved map, painted cartouche, slightly soiled. (R. Oct.14-18; 3407)
DM 950

– **– Anr. Copy.** Cold copper engraved map, 3 painted rollwork cartouches & arms, 2 wormholes bkd. (R. Mar.31-Apr.4; 3262)
DM 620

– **Graecia Sophiani.** Ca. 1600. 500 × 370mm. Hand-cold. map. (P. Jun.11; 219) *Habibis.* £105

– **Graeciae Universae.** Ca. 1600. Uncold. map. (P. Feb.19; 140)
Kay. £80

– **[Herzogtum Württemberg].** 1579. Ob. fo. Cold. copper engraved map. (R. Oct.14-18; 3648)
DM 650

– **[-] Anr. Edn.** N.d. Fo. Old cold. copper engraved map, with cartouche, slightly soiled. (R. Oct.14-18; 3647)
DM 500

[-] Hispaniae Novae . . . descriptio, 1579. [Antw.], [1598]. 347 × 505mm. Engraved map, hand-cold., including title & scale cartouches, sailing ships, etc., Italian text on verso, 2 sm. wormholes in engraved surface, a few stains & repairs to margins. W.a.f. (S. Jun.29; 142) *Klee.* £100

[-] Hispaniolae, Cubae, Aliarumque Isularem Circumiacientium Delineatio. [Antw.], [1612]. 15 × 20 ins. Map, lge. inset of Western Mexico, Latin text on verso. (SG. May 21; 121)
$200

– **Hollandia Nova Descriptio.** N.d. Ob. fo. Old cold. copper engraved map with painted roll cartouche, decor. & cold. arms, slightly soiled & stained. (R. Oct.14-18; 5332)
DM 1,100

– **Hollandiae Antiquorum Catthorum Sedis Nova Descriptio.** [Antw.], ca. 1570. 35 × 49 cm. Engraved map, ptd. Latin text on verso, browned. (VG. Oct.28; 299)
Fls. 480

– **Hungary.** Ca. 1570. Fo. Map, cold., text on verso. (JN. Apr.2; 482)
£75

– **Iaponiae Insuale Descriptio . . . 1595.** [Antw.], [1598, or later]. 355 × 484mm. Engraved map of Japan, cartouches, decor., Fr. text on verso, 2 sm. wormholes in engraved surface. W.a.f. (S. Nov.4; 404)
Arader. £340

– **Illyricum.** Vienna, 25 Oct. 1572. 18 × 21½ inches. Cold. map, with cartouche including text, slight marginal fraying. (SG. May 21; 81)
$110

– **Indiae Orientalis.** Ca. 1580. 'Large'. 2 cartouches, galleons & sea monsters, a trifle split at centrefold, overall ageing, a little foxing. (HL. Apr.1; 1529)
£300

– **– Anr. Edn.** Ca. 1590. 500 × 350mm. Uncold. map. (P. Jun.11; 232)
Dawson. £220

– **Irland.** N.d. Ob. fo. Old cold. copper engraved map with 2 painted roll cartouches, slightly soiled. (R. Oct.14-18; 5529)
DM 450

– **Island.** N.d. Ob. fo. Cold. copper engraved map, 3 painted roll work cartouches, figure, restored. (R. Mar.31-Apr.4; 5920)
DM 700

– **Islandia.** [Antw.], [1606]. 337 × 494mm. Engraved map, hand-cold. in outl., cartouches, polar bears & ice floes, sea monsters, etc., fully cold., Engl. text on verso, a little worn in centre fold, very slightly affecting engraved surface, in card mount. W.a.f. (S. Jun.29; 29)
Jonsson. £420

– **Karte der Insel, Cyprern.** N.d. Ob. fo. Old cold. copper engraved map, slightly soiled. (R. Oct.14-18; 5106)
DM 650

– **Maris Pacifici.** 1589. Ob. fo. Cold. copper engraved map, 2 painted figure rolls. (R. Oct.14-18; 3397)
DM 2,300

[-] Misniae et Lusatiae. Ca. 1600? 14½ × 10½ inches. Map, from an atlas, with pict. details. (SG. Nov.20; 95)
$120

– **Noblis Hannoniae Comitatus Descrip.** Ill.:– Jacques Surhon. 1579. 15½ × 20 ins. Cold. map, from an atlas, painted. (SG. Nov.20; 123)
$140

[-] Palaestinae sive Totius Terrae Promissionis Nova Descriptio. [Antw.], ca. 1680, or later. 339 × 451mm. Engraved map, title cartouche, further cartouche bordering a Biblical text, 3 ships, all hand-cold., Latin text on verso. (SKC. May 19; 383)
£120

– **Poloniae Finitimarumque Locorum Descriptio.** N.d. 37 × 50 cm. Cold. copper engraved map, renaissance cartouche, decor., mile indicator, Latin text on verso. (D. Dec.11-13; 3448)
DM 650

– **Scandinavia.** Ca. 1590. 490 × 360mm. Uncold. map, vigs. (P. Jun.11; 239) *Map House.* £360

[-] Scotiae Tabula. [Antw.], [1602, or later]. 350 × 471mm. Engraved map, cartouches, decor., Latin text on verso, 2 sm. wormholes in centre fold. W.a.f. (S. Nov.3; 196) *Arader.* £140

[-] Tartariae sive Magni Chami Regni Typus. [Antw.], [1579, or later]. 348 × 469mm. Engraved hand-cold. map, cartouches & other features, Latin text on verso, 2 sm. pieces torn from top blank margin. W.a.f. (S. Nov.4; 419)
Arader. £230

– **– Anr. Edn.** N.d. Ob. fo. Old cold. copper engraved map with 2 painted figure cartouches, slightly soiled, 2 ink stains in 2nd. ill. (R. Oct.14-18; 5138)
DM 600

– **Tartary.** Ca. 1590. 470 × 355mm. Uncold. map. (P. Jun.11; 231)
Dawson. £210

– **La Terre Universelle.–Afrique.–Asie.–Europe.–Espagne.–Egypte.–Angleterre.–Gaule.–Italie.** 1602. 5 × 6½ ins. 9 hand-cold. maps, & various ll. of text, from 'L'Epitome du Théâtre de l'Univers', worming in lr. margin of some maps. (SG. Nov.20; 92)
$375

– **Theatrum Orbis Terrarum.** N.d. Ob. fo. Old cold. copper engraved map, 5 ll., painted cartouche & figurative decor., slightly soiled, partly mntd. (R. Oct.14-18; 3382)
DM 6,500

– **Utriusque Frisiorum . . . Descriptio.** N.d. Ob. fo. Old cold. copper engraved map, painted roll cartouche, soiled. (R. Oct.14-18; 4070)
DM 7,000

– **Zelandicarum Insularum Descriptio.** [Antw.], ca. 1570. 33.5 × 47 cm. Hand-cold. engraved map, ptd. text in Fr. on verso, fold in middle, very slightly browned. (VG. Oct.28; 331)
Fls. 950

See–ANTONIADES, C. & Ortelius, Abraham
See–APIAN, Ph. & Ortelius, Abraham
See–DE VENTER, J. van & Ortelius, Abraham
See–DRYANDER, J. & Ortelius, Abraham
See–MERCATOR, Gerard & Ortelius, Abraham
See–SAXTON, Christopher & Ortelius, Abraham
See–SCHROT, Charles & Ortelius, Abraham
See–SETZNAGEL, M. & Ortelius Abraham
See–STELLA, T. & Ortelius, Abraham
See–VELLEIUS, A. & Ortelius, Abraham
See–ZELL, H. & Ortelius, Abraham

ORTELIUS, Abraham & Vrients
– **England, Wales & Ireland.** 1605. Fo. Map, old colouring, sea monsters, tables, etc., text on verso. (JN. Apr.2; 569)
£610

OTTENS, Joshua
See–SANSON, Nicholas & Ottens, Reiner & Joshua

OTTENS, Reiner
See–SANSON, Nicholas & Ottens, Reiner & Joshua

OTTENS, Reiner & Joshua
– **'Carte des Possessions Angloises & Françoises du Continent de l'Amérique Septentrionale'.?** Amst., 1755. Lge. ob. fo. (19 × 23½ inches.) Hand-cold. copperplt. map, short tear closed at verso with paper. (PNY. Oct.1; 346)
$160

– **Nova Tabula Exhibens Insulas Cubam et Hispaniolam.** Amst., ca. 1750. 20 × 24 inches. Hand-cold. map, with 3 insets. (SG. May 21; 128)
$200

– **South America.** [Argentine & Chile]. 1756. 'Large'. Map, cartouche, galleons, early outl. colour, faint traces of foxing. (HL. Apr.1; 1520)
£60

OVERTON, Henry
– **A New Map of the Whole World.** 1715. 1005 × 1022mm. Engraved map, sailing ships & other features, smaller maps of hemispheres above, constellations, maps of polar regions below, scenes in outer corners & surrounding spaces, the whole hand-cold., some sm. surface flaws, some minor loss of surface, restored, mntd. on linen. (S. Jun.9; 45)
Maggs. £280

OVERTON, John
– **A New & Most Exact Map of America.** [1668]. 423 × 542mm. Engraved map of North, Central & South America, hand-cold. in outl., cartouches, compass roses, etc., cold. W.a.f. (S. Nov.3; 41)
Burns. £750

PAPEN, A. & Hornemann, C.F.
– **Hannover.** 1838. 66.5 × 73 cm. (plan 57 × 56.5). Etched plan with views round, 3 sm. plans in corners, slightly soiled & 1 tear backed. Dedication to Herzog Adolph Friedrich von Cambridge as Vicekönig von Hannover. (R. Oct.14-18; 4366)
DM 3,800

PARADISE, Mount Ararat, & the City of Babel
Ca. 1750. 12 × 16 inches. Cold. map, with inset of 'Astronomical Observations . . .'. (SG. May 21; 82)
$110

PHILIP, George & Son
– **Australia.** L'pool., 1856. 61.5 × 51 cm. Map cold. in outl. (JL. Mar.1; 194)
Aus. $150

PINKERTON, John
- United States of America: Southern Part. Phila., ca. 1810. 21 × 27½ ins. Fully-cold. map, from the 'Modern Atlas', several lge. marginal tears. (SG. Nov.20; 127) $180

PITT, M.
- Bistum Münster. Ca. 1685. Ob. fo. Old cold. copper engraved map with 2 painted cartouches & many sm. arms. (R. Oct.14-18; 4568) DM 580
- Brabant. Ca. 1680. Ob. fo. Cold. copper engraved map, 2 painted figure cartouches & cold. arms. (R. Mar.31-Apr.4; 5274) DM 480
- Erzbistum Köln. Ca. 1685. Ob. fo. Old cold. copper engraved map with 2 painted cartouches & 15 sm. cold. arms. (R. Oct.14-18; 4537) DM 800
- Grafschaft Tirol. Ca. 1685. Ob. fo. Old cold. copper engraved map with 2 painted figure cartouches. (R. Oct.14-18; 5718) DM 520
- Herzogtum Bremen mit Elb- und Wesermündung. Ca. 1685. Ob. fo. Old cold. copper engraved map with 3 painted figure cartouches. (R. Oct.14-18; 4057) DM 500
- Herzogtum Jülich. Ca. 1685. Ob. fo. Old cold. copper engraved map with painted cartouche & cold arms. (R. Oct.14-18; 4490) DM 900
- Herzogtum Kleve und Herrschaft Ravenstein. Ca. 1685. Ob. fo. Old cold. copper engraved map with 2 painted cartouches & cold. arms. (R. Oct.14-18; 4509) DM 500
- Herzogtümer Jülich und Berg. Ca. 1685. Ob. fo. Old cold. copper engraved map with 2 painted cartouches & 2 cold. arms. (R. Oct.14-18; 4491) DM 850
- Insularum Dordracensis ... Descriptio. Ca. 1680. Ob. fo. Cold. copper engraved map, painted cartouche. (R. Mar.31-Apr.4; 5293) DM 500
- Karte des Stadtgebietes Neumarkt. Ca. 1685. Ob. fo. Old cold. copper engraved map with painted figure cartouche & many mostly cold. arms, col. lightly oxidised. (R. Oct.14-18; 3783) DM 430
- Nobilis Saxoniae fl. Visurgis a Brema ad Ostium Maris. Ca. 1685. Ob. fo. 2 superimposed maps, old cold. copper engraved with 2 painted figure cartouches. (R. Oct.14-18; 4188) DM 1,300
- Territorium Francofurtense. Ca. 1685. Ob. fo. Old cold. copper engraved map with 2 painted cartouches & 2 cold. arms, col. very oxidised. (R. Oct.14-18; 4233) DM 500
- Totius Sveviae Novissima Tabula. Ca. 1685. Ob. fo. Painted figure cartouche. (R. Oct.14-18; 3594) DM 500
- Westfälischer Kreis. Ca. 1685. Ob. fo. Old cold. copper engraved map with painted figure cartouche. (R. Oct.14-18; 4346) DM 500
- Wetterau. Ca. 1685. Ob. fo. Old cold. copper engraved map with painted figure cartouche. (R. Oct.14-18; 4337) DM 530
See–WESTENBERG, J. & Pitt, M.

PITT, M. & Swart
- Albius Fluvius Germaniae Celebris. 1685. Ob. fo. Old cold. map, 2 painted cartouches, partly backed. (R. Oct.14-18; 4067) DM 500
- Herzogtum Braunschweig. Ca. 1685. Ob. fo. Old cold. copper engraved map with painted arms cartouche. (R. Oct.14-18; 4354) DM 450
- [Herzogtum Württemberg]. 1685. Ob. fo. Old cold. copper engraved map with painted figure cartouche & lge. cold. arms. (R. Oct.14-18; 3653) DM 450
- Nova Totius Germaniae Descriptio. Ca. 1680 Ob. fo. Cold. copper engraved map, painted cartouche. (R. Mar.31-Apr.4; 3283) DM 500
- Nova Totius Orbis Terrarum Geographica ac Hydrographica Tabula. 1680. Ob. fo. Cold. copper engraved map, decor. border, allegories at side, 2 sm. maps & arms cartouche. (R. Mar.31-Apr.4; 4804) DM 4,400
- Vera Totius Marchionatus Badensis ... Delineatio. 1685. 44.5 × 81 cm. Old cold. copper engraved map, 2 large painted cartouches, not composite. (R. Oct.14-18; 3455) DM 1,800

PLAN OF THE ACTION at Bunker's Hill, on the 17th June 1775
L., n.d. Fo. With overlay ill. troop movements, partially cold. (SPB. Nov.24; 36) $750

PLATTE GRAND VAN GRAVEN-HAGE
1729. Hand-cold. town plan of the Hague. F. & G. (P. Apr.9; 179) Fairburn. £120

POGRABSKI, Andrej
- Poloniae Litvaniae Descriptio. [1570 or later]. 13½ × 19 inches. Hand-cold. engraved map. F. & G. (CSK. Aug.1; 90) £50

POLYNESIE AUSTRALE
Amst., 1808. 45 × 60 cm. Cold. map, showing Australia charted & uncharted, titles in Dutch & Fr. (JL. Mar.1; 119) Aus. $250
[-] – Anr. Copy. (JL. Dec.14; 105) Aus. $240

PORCACCHI, Thomaso
- Iceland. 1590. 'Small'. Map, compass rose, decor. cartouche. (HL. Apr.1; 1710) £55
- Jamaica. 1590. 'Small'. Map, compass rose, ornate cartouche. (HL. Apr.1; 1720) £100
- Mexico City. 1590. 'Small'. Map/view, in p. of text. (HL. Apr.1; 1737) £60
- North America. 1590. 'Small'. Miniature version of map by Zalterie. (HL. Apr.1; 1513) £145
- S. Giovanni [St. Juan]. 1590. 'Small'. Map, sea monsters, etc., depicts Virgin Islands to right top. (HL. Apr.1; 1798) £65
- Temistitan [Mexico City]. 1572. 1st. Edn. 8vo. Map, uncold., with text. (JN. Apr.2; 142) £52
- Turkey: Istanbul. 1590. 'Small'. City plan of Constantinople. (HL. Apr.1; 1792) £70
- The World. 1590. 'Small'. Engraved map, miniature, with Southern continent, America separated from Asia, sea-route shown to North of America & Asia. (HL. Apr.1; 1503) £80
– – Anr. Copy. 'Small'. Miniature map, centred on Atlantic ocean, shows rhumb-lines, in p. of text. (HL. Apr.1; 1502) £70

PORRO, Girolamo
- Europe. 1574. 'Medium' size. Engraved map. (HL. Apr.1; 1534) £75

PORRO, Girolamo & Magini
- America. 1598. 'Medium'. Map. (HL. Apr.1; 1508) £85
- Cyprus. 1620. 'Medium' size. Engraved map, 2 ornate cartouches. (HL. Apr.1; 1600) £70
- Middle East. 1598. 'Medium' size. Copper engraved map, within p. of text. (HL. Apr.1; 1539) £50
- Palestine. 1598. 'Medium' size. Engraved map, 2 cartouches. (HL. Apr.1; 1752) £100
- Palestine, etc. 1620. 4to., approximately 28 × 22 cm. Uncold. map in text. (JN. Sep.9; 3757) £76
- Scandinavia. 1598. 'Medium' size. Map, in p. of text. (HL. Apr.1; 1548) £60
- Switzerland. 1598. 'Medium' size. Engraved map, in p. of text. (HL. Apr.1; 1785) £55

PORT JACKSON
- Map of all those parts of the Territory of New South Wales which have been seen by any person belonging to the Settlement established at Port Jackson in the said Territory. Picadilly, L., 22 Sep. 1792. 54·5 × 41·5 cm. (JL. Dec.14; 127) Aus. $400

PREUSS, Charles
- Topographical Map of the Road from Missouri to Oregon ... Wash., 1846. Map in 7 sections. From liby. of William E. Wilson. (SPB. Apr.29; 193) $275
– – Anr. Edn. [Wash.], [1846]. 16 × 26 inches. Compl. set of 7 maps, some foxing on all. Sewed together. Inscr. on bdg. tape from Senator Dickinson to William J. Dodge. (SG. May 21; 87) $500

PRIDE, T.
- Town of Reading & the County adjacent to the extent of ten miles. 1790. 26 × 35 inches. Engraved map, hand-cold. in outl., mntd. on cl. (CSK. Apr.10; 22) £65

PRIORATA, Gualdo
- Bois Le Duc [now S'Hertogen bosch in the Netherlands]. Vienna, [1672]. 485 × 380mm. Hand-cold. town plan. (P. Apr.9; 161) Fairburn. £65
- Düsseldorf. Vienna, [1672]. 540 × 395mm. Hand-cold. town plan. (P. Apr.9; 162) Map House. £75
- Ratisbona Assediata il di 15 di Maggio 1634. 1672. 695 × 290mm. Uncold. plan, mntd. (P. Jun.11; 214a) Christoph. £250

PTOLEMAEUS, Claudius
- Arabia. Ca. 1545. 12 × 15½ inches. Woodcut map, from Munster's edn. of 'Geography', sm. tears in fold, tape bleed at margins. (SG. Nov.20; 13) $110

- Europae Tabula VIII que continet Sarmatiam Europae & Tauricam Chersonesum. 1541. Ob. fo. Woodcut map, sm. tears at fold backed. (R. Oct.14-18; 5219) DM 600
- Hispania.–Gallia. Ca. 1545. 12 × 15½ inches. 2 woodcut maps, from Munster's edn. of 'Geography', text & woodcut borders on versos, some minor tears. (SG. Nov.20; 82) $180
- Ptolemaisch General Tafel Begreiffend die Halbe Kugel der Welt. N.p., [mid 16th. C.]. 252 × 344mm. Engraved map from Münster's 'Cosmographia', text on verso with heading in German within woodcut. W.a.f. (S. Mar.31; 430) Burgess. £100
- Quarta Europa Tabula. 1511. Ob. fo. Black & red ptd. map. (R. Oct.14-18; 3404) DM 2,900
- Tabula Decima.–Tabula Prima.–Tabula X. 16th. C? 15 × 18 inches; 11 × 14 inches. 3 maps, 1st. 2 fully hand-cold. with Latin texts on versos, 3rd. map from anr. edn. & smaller format (tears at centre-fold & at 1 corner). (SG. Nov.20; 103) $275
- Tabula Moderna Germaniae. 1513. Woodcut map. (R. Mar.31-Apr.4; 3263) DM 3,400
- Tabu[la] Moder[na] Indiae. Early 16th. C. 300 × 445mm. Uncold. map. (P. Jun.11; 226) Dawson. £150
- Tabula Nova Indiae. 1541. Ob. fo. Woodcut Map, lightly browned at fold. (R. Oct.14-18; 5111) DM 500
- Tertia Rheni.–Bohemiae.–Sarmati. Ca. 1545. 12 × 15½ inches. 3 woodcut maps, from Munster's edn. of 'Geography', some tears at fold, cont. ink markings on face of 1st. map. (SG. Nov.20; 83) $180
See–MERCATOR, Gerard & Ptolemaeus, Claudius

PTOLEMAEUS, Claudius & Ruscelli
- World–Ptolemaei Typus. Venetia, 1561. 26 × 19 cm. Cold. map, Latin text on verso, from 'La Geographia Di Claudio Tolomeo Alessandrino'. (JL. Dec.14; 126) Aus. $300

PTOLEMAEUS, Claudius & Sylvanus of Eboli, Bernardus
- World Map. [Venice], [20 Mar. 1511]. Approximately 420 × 555mm. A few sm. repairs at edges, a few stains & slight discolouration, lightly hinged to card mount. W.a.f. (S. Nov.3; 40) Regent. £3,700

QUAD, M.
- Hiberniae Britanicae Insulae nova Descriptio. Eryn. Irlandt. Ill.:– J. Bussemacher. [Cologne], [1600]. 215 × 305mm. Engraved map, medallion port. of Queen Elizabeth I, etc., German text on verso, a few minor stains. W.a.f. (S. Jun.29; 68) Duyck. £220

RAM, Joannes de
- Londini Angliae Regni Metropolis novissima & accuratissima. Amst., ca. 1690. 497 × 585mm. Engraved plan of L. N. & S. of Thames, 2 numbered keys to details, royal arms & city arms borne by putti, ports. of William III & Mary, other decorative features, Panorama of L. across bottom of plt., sm. ink stain in margin, touching panorama. W.a.f. (S. Jun.29; 153) Duyck. £350
– – Anr. Copy. 19½ × 23 inches. Cold. map, histor. armorial, numbered keys , histor. scene to lr. margin with miniatures of the King & Queen & with panorama of the Thames & L. below. F. & G. (TA. Feb.19; 58) £85

RAPIN DE THOYRAS, Paul
- Gibraltar. Ca. 1739. Fo., approximately 56 × 43cm. Uncold. map, long plan/view, sailing ships, etc. (JN. Sep.9; 4033) £50

RAPKIN, J.
- Van Diemens Island or Tasmania. L., 1854. 25 × 33cm. Map, cold. vigs. including Hobart Town. (JL. Dec.14; 120) Aus. $170
See–TALLIS, John & Rapkin, J.

REID
- Vermont. Ca. 1783. Fo. Map, cold. (JN. Apr.2; 108) £65

REINIER & Ottens, J.
- Carte Nouvelle de l'Electorat de Hannover. Amst., 1757. 57 × 50cm. Cold. copper engraved map. (D. Dec.11-13; 3575) DM 700

RENARD, L.
- Nova Totius Terrarum Orbis Tabula. Amst., ca. 1715. Ob. fo. Cold. copper engraved map in 2 hemispheres, 2 sm. pole maps, allegories &

mythological scenes round. (R. Mar.31-Apr.4; 4820) DM 3,700

RENNELL, Maj. James & others
- **Investigation of the Currents: Chart the First. [-] 2nd.; 3rd.; 5th.** 1 Aug. 1832. Various sizes. Together 5 engraved charts in ten sheets, 1st. with 1 imprint cropped, coasts shown in outl., currents & related features shown. W.a.f. (S. Jun.29; 45) *Fisher.* £150

RHODES, Joshua, & Bickham, George
- **A Topographical Survey of the Parish of Kensington: with plans & elevations of the Royal Palace & Gardens, Hyde Park & Knightsbridge.** 22nd. Jul. 1766. Extending to 42 × 104 inches. Lge.-scale plan/perspective view, lge. elab. title-cartouche, numbered key across bottom of plt., the whole mntd. on linen, on ends slightly dust soiled, rolled. W.a.f. (S. Nov.4; 326) *Edmunds.* £370

RIZZI-ZANNONI, Giovanni Antonio
- **Carta Geographica della Sicilia prima o sia Regno di Napoli.** 1769. Each sheet 27 × 18 inches. Engraved map, hand-cold. in outl., on 4 sheets, slight browning. (CSK. Mar.6; 28) £50

ROADES, W.
- **New & Correct Map of Asia.** Ca. 1760. Outl. cold. copper engraved map, figure cartouche, ills., lightly browned. (R. Mar.31-Apr.4; 5075) DM 450

ROBERT DE VAUGONDY, Gilles & Didier
- **La Judée.** Ca. 1750. 645 × 495mm. Hand-cold. map, cartouche, 2 inset plans. F. & G. (P. Jun.11; 250) *Salah.* £60

ROCHETTE, L.S. de la
- **A Chart of the Antilles, or Charibee.** L., 1784. 23 × 20 inches. Decor. hand-cold. map, lacks hf. of left margin, 1 vertical crease. (SG. May 21; 117) $130

ROCQUE, John
- **A Topographical Map of the County of Surrey.** Ill.:- Peter Andrews. Mary Ann Rocque., [1768?]. Fo. Engraved map on 9 double-p. sheets, hand-cold. in outl., engraved title & lge. pict. dedication. Hf. cf. & marb. bds. W.a.f. (C. May 20; 168) *Traylen.* £350

ROSA
- **Battle of Lepanto.** Ca. 1600. 'Small'. Engraved map, cartouche, some minor blemishes. (HL. Apr.1; 1705) £65

ROSSI, G.
See- SANSON, Nicholas & Rossi, G.

ROSSI, Giovanni Giacomo [de]
- **La Scandinavia divisa nelli suoi Regni de Svezia, Danimarc, Norvegia ...** Rome, 1689. 409 × 540mm. Engraved map, hand-cold. in outl., historiated & armorial title-cartouche fully cold. W.a.f. (S. Nov.3; 122) *Riis.* £100

RUMOLD, Gerhard, Jun. & Mercator, Michael
- **Erdteile.** Ca. 1630. Ob. fo. 4 ll. cold. copper engraved map from Mercator & Hondius' Atlas, painted cartouche, America map in wide floral border, sm. supp. maps in corners, Asia map restored & soiled, sm. hole bkd. (R. Oct.14-18; 3384) DM 3,500
- **Orbis Terrae Compendiosa Descriptio.** 1587. Ob. fo. Old cold. copper engraved map in 2 hemispheres, decor. round, slightly browned. F. (R. Mar.31-Apr. 476) DM 3,000

RUSCELLI
- **South America.** 1561. 'Medium' size. Map, based on Gastaldi's map of 1548. (HL. Apr.1; 1518) £65

RUSSELL, J.
- **Map of the Middle States of America.** L., 13 Dec. 1794. 10½ × 19 inches. Map, cold. boundaries, inset of Long Island, slight repair at 1 fold. (SG. May 21; 107) $110

SALZBURG
Ca. 1660? Approximately 380 × 470mm. Hand-cold. map, armorial cartouche, compass, key. F. (SBA. Oct.21; 251) *Galerie Welz.* £220

SANDRART, J.
- **Totius Fluminius Rheni Novissima Descriptio.** Nuremb., Late 17th. C. 37·5 × 103·5cm. Copper engraved map with figure cartouche & 20 views, slightly soiled in centre, partly backed. (R. Oct.14-18; 4915) DM 3,700

SANSON, Nicholas
- **L'Alsace et Duché de Wurtenbergh.** N.d. Ob. fo. Old cold copper engraved map, tear bkd. (R. Oct.14-18; 3465) DM 420
- **Amérique Meridionale.** Paris, 1650. 16 × 22 inches. Copper-plt. map, with faint hand-cold. boundaries, trimmed to margins, & mntd. to old paper, some creases. (SG. May 21; 97) $130
- **Amérique Septentrionale.** Paris, 1669 or later. 22½ × 20¼inches. Map, cold. in outl., matted & framed. (SPB. Jun.22; 87) $600
- **Le Canada, ou Nouvelle France, & c ...** Paris, 1656. 420 × 545mm. Engraved map, hand-cold. in outl., repair in top margin, slightly affecting engraved border. W.a.f. (S. Nov.3; 67) *Arader.* £380
- - **Anr. Copy.** 21¼ × 15½inches. Rebkd., 2 sm. wormholes in lr. margin. (CB. Dec.9; 19) *Can.* $2,600
- - **Anr. Edn.** Ca. 1683. 'Large'. Map, ornate cartouche, slightly discold. (HL. Apr.1; 1582) £55
- **Carte de la Terre des Hébreux ou Israelites.** N.d. 49 × 68cm. Cold. copper engraved map, allegorical cartouche. (D. Dec.11-13; 3502) DM 500
- **Cartes des Pais qui sont situez entre la Moselle la Saare, Le Rhein, et la Basse Alsace.** Paris, 1696. 94 × 59 cm. Cold. copper engraved map, very decor. title cartouche, lge. windrose, (D. Dec.11-13; 3548) DM 700
- **L'Europe.** N.d. Ob. fo. Old cold. copper engraved map, printed figure cartouche. (R. Mar.31-Apr.4; 5178) DM 420
- **Haute Partie de l'Archevesché et Eslectorat de Cologne.** N.d. Ob. fo. Old cold. & partly gold heightened copper engraved map with painted figure cartouche. (R. Oct.14-18; 4539) DM 950
- **L'Hydrographie ou Description de l'Eau.** Paris, 1652. Hand-cold. world map showing pre-Tasman Dutch discoveries in Australia combined with the Mythological reports of Marco Polo. (JL. Mar.1; 224) Aus. $200
- **Les Isles Antilles &c.** Paris, 1656. 18 × 24inches. Copper-plt. map, from an atlas, with hand-cold. boundaries. (SG. May 21; 124) $130
- **Judaea seu Terra Sancta.** 1709. 650 × 465mm. Hand-cold. map, cartouche. (P. Jul.30; 153) *Lowin.* £90
- **Mappo Mondo.** 1684. Ob. fo. Cold. copper engraved map in 2 hemispheres, allegorical figures round. (R. Mar.31-Apr.4; 4811) DM 900
- **Le Nouveau Mexique et La Floride.** Paris, 1656. 311 × 542mm. Engraved map, hand-cold. in outl. W.a.f. (S. Nov.3; 66) *Arader.* £750
- **Orbis Vetus.** Paris, 1657. Ob. fo. Copper engraved map in 2 hemispheres, old outl. cold. (R. Mar.31-Apr.4; 4799) DM 550
- **[Ostpreussen].** 1679. Ob. fo. Old. copper engraved map with painted figure map. (R. Oct.14-18; 4721) DM 430

SANSON, Nicholas & Jaillot, Hubert
- **Archevesché et Eslectorat de Cologne.** N.d. Lge. fo. Old cold. & partly gold heightened copper engraved map with 2 painted cartouches. (R. Oct.14-18; 4538) DM 900
- **Basse Partie de l'Evesché de Munster et le Comté de Bent.** N.d. Ob. fo. Old cold. & partly gold heightened copper engraved map with painted figure cartouche. (R. Oct.14-18; 4569) DM 650
- **Bayrischer Kreis.** 1704. Lge. fo. Old cold. copper engraved map with 2 painted figure cartouches. (R. Oct.14-18; 3699) DM 430
- **Le Cours de Danube.** 1696. 60 × 118cm. Copper engraved map with old cold. outls., lge. figure cartouche, 6 views at foot, sm. tear bkd. (R. Oct.14-18; 3716) DM 1,100
- - **Anr. Copy.** 60 × 118 cm. (R. Mar.31-Apr.4; 3529) DM 1,200
- **Les Dix-Sept Provinces des Pays-Bas.** Paris, 1696. 35 × 21½ inches. Map, elab. cartouche, hand-cold. in outl., slight marginal tears, slight discolouration. (SPB. Jul.28; 353) $325
- **Le Duché de Berg.** N.d. Ob. fo. Old cold. copper engraved map with 2 painted figure cartouches. (R. Oct.14-18; 4464) DM 1,100
- **Le Duché de Westphalie, possedé par l'Electeur de Cologne.** N.d. Ob. fo. Old cold. copper engraved map with 2 painted figure cartouches. (R. Oct.14-18; 4608) DM 900
- **Gueldre Espagnole.** 1701. Ob. fo. Old cold. copper engraved map. (R. Oct.14-18; 4488) DM 610

- **Haute Partie de L'Evesché de Munster.** N.d. Ob. fo. Old cold. & partly gold heightened copper engraved map with 2 painted figure cartouches, lightly wormed at head. (R. Oct.14-18; 4570) DM 700
- **Oost-Frise, ou le Comte d'Emden.** Ca. 1690. Ob. fo. Outl. cold. copper engraved map with 2 cartouches. (R. Oct.14-18; 4144) DM 550
- **Ostfriesland.** N.d. Ob. fo. Old cold. & partly gold heightened copper engraved map with painted figure cartouche, soiled. (R. Oct. 14-18; 4143) DM 800
- **Partie Occidentale de L'Archevesché de Trèves.** Ca. 1690. Lge. fo. Copper engraved map with old outl. col., with 2 cartouches. (R. Oct.14-18; 4860) DM 450
- - **Anr. Edn.** N.d. Ob. fo. Old cold. & partly gold heightened copper engraved map with 2 painted figure cartouches. (R. Oct.14-18; 4993) DM 500
- **Partie Orientale du Palatinat.** N.d. Ob. fo. Old cold. & partly gold heightened copper engraved map, 2 painted figure cartouches. (R. Oct.14-18; 3571) DM 600
- **La Scandinavie.** N.d. Lge. ob. fo. Copper engraved map with old outl. col., 2 painted figure cartouches. (R. Oct.14-18; 5862) DM 430
- **[Schwäbischer Kreis].** 1710. Ob. fo. Cold. copper engraved map with 2 painted figure cartouches. (R. Oct.14-18; 3606) DM 600
- **Téâtre de la Guerre sur le Rhein, Moessele, Mayn & le Necker.** N.d. Ob. fo. Old cold. & partly gold heightened copper engraved map with lge. painted figure cartouche. (R. Oct.14-18; 4234) DM 560
- **The Turkish Empire.** Ca. 1681. 60 × 90cm. Copper engraved map, cold. in outl., title cartouche. (JL. Dec.14; 109) Aus. $390
- - **Anr. Copy.** (JL. Mar.1; 118) Aus. $280

SANSON, Nicholas & Mortier, Pierre
- **Carte Particulière de la Caroline.** Ca. 1690. Ob. fo. Old cold. copper engraved map with cartouche & gold heightened compass rose. (R. Oct.14-18; 5055) DM 1,000
- **Le Cours de la Rivière du Rhin.** N.d. 92 × 56cm. Old cold. & partly gold heightened copper engraved map with 2 painted figure cartouches, not composite. (R. Oct.14-18; 4916) DM 600
- **Partie Orientale de l'Archevesche de Mayence.** N.d. Lge. fo. Old cold. & partly gold heightened copper engraved map with 2 painted figure cartouches. (R. Oct.14-18; 3771) DM 650

SANSON, Nicholas & Ottens, Reiner & Joshua
- **Judaea sive Terra Sancta.** N.d. Ob. fo. Old cold. copper engraved map with lge. painted cartouche with decor. (R. Oct.14-18; 5132) DM 600

SANSON, Nicholas & Rossi, G.
- **L'Ammerica Settentrionale.** 1677. Ob. fo. Outl. cold. copper engraved map with figure cartouche. (R. Oct. 14-18; 5078) DM 7,000
- **Mappa Mondo o Vero Carta Generale del Globe Terrestre.** Rome, 1674. (JL. Mar.1; 162) Aus. $280

SANSON, Robert
- **Apostles Travels (E. Mediterranean).** 1747. Fo. Map, mntd., cold outl., insets of Holy Land, Jerusalem. (JN. Apr.2; 246) £65

SAUTHIER, Claude Joseph & Vaughan, David
- **A Chorographical Map of the Province of New York in America ... reduced from the Original large London Map.** Albany, 1849. 40 × 31 inches. Linen-bkd. (SG. Aug.21; 265) $150

SAXTON, Christopher
- **Cantii, Southsexiae, Suriae, et Middlesexia Comitat.** [1575.] 22 × 16½ inches. Hand-cold. engraved map, slightly stained. F. & G. (CSK. Aug.1; 87) £700
- **Cardigan comitatus pars olim Dimetarum.** [1637]. 263 × 314mm. Engraved map, title cartouche, decor. features of compass rose & sailing ship, hand-cold. F. (SBA. Dec.16; 272) *Harrison.* £50
- **Cestriae Comitatus.** 1577 [but 1579 or later]. 15½ × 20 inches. Engraved map, hand-cold. in outl., sm. tear along fold. F. & G. (CSK. May 8; 39) £800
- **Dunelmensis.** 1576 [but 1579 or later]. 15 × 19½ inches. Engraved map, hand-cold. in outl., a few wormholes. F. & G. (CSK. Jul.3; 19) £300
- **Glamorgan Commitatus.** 1579. 13 × 19 inches. Engraved map, hand-cold. in outl., 1 sm. hole, marginal staining. (CSK. Jan.9; 94) £1,300

SAXTON, Christopher -contd.
- **Lancashire.** 11½ × 12 inches. Hand-cold. map. F. & G. (RBT. Jan.22; 272) £50
- **Staffordiae Comitatus ... 1577.** 1577 [but 1579]. 389 × 498mm. Engraved map, royal arms, Seckford's arms, scale, representation of towns, villages, trees, hills & other features hand-cold., slight spotting. Mntd. on card. W.a.f. (S. Nov.3; 173) *Kentish.* £480
- **Universi Derbiensis Comitatus.** 1577 [but 1579 or later]. 15¼ × 19¼ inches. Engraved map, hand-cold. in outl., marginal spotting slightly affecting engraved surface. F. & G. (CSK. May 8; 40) £550
- **Wiltoniae Comitatus.** 1576 [but 1579 or later]. 16½ × 19 inches. Engraved map, hand-cold. in outl. F. & G. (CSK. May 8; 41) £380
- **– Anr. Edn.** Ill.:– Remigius Hogenberg. [1579]. 415 × 472mm. Engraved map, hand-cold. in outl., histor. & armorial title-cartouche, Seckford's arms, scale, etc. fully cold., F. W.a.f. (S. Mar.31; 348) *Burgess.* £800
- **Wiltshire with Salisbury Citty & Stoneheng Described ...** Philip Lea, 1689 [but ca. 1693]. 415 × 469mm. Engraved map, hand-cold. in outl., 17 coats of arms, inset plan, etc., fully cold. F. W.a.f. (S. Mar.31; 349) *D. Webb.* £160

SAXTON, Christopher & Ortelius, Abraham
- **Anglia Regnum ...** [Paris], J. le Clerc, ca. 1605? 381 × 476mm. Engraved map, hand-cold. in outl. (except Ireland), histor. title-cartouche, 2 other cartouches, coat of arms, etc., fully cold., verso blank, wormed & reprd, bkd. W.a.f. (S. Mar.31; 319) *Burgess.* £100

SCAVENIUS, L. & Blaeu, Willem & Joannes
- **Stavenger Diozese.** N.d. Ob. fo. Old cold. copper engraved map with painted figure cartouche & 2 lge. cold. arms. (R. Oct.14-18; 5870) DM 500

SCHEDEL, Hartmann
- **Destruccio Hierosolime.** Nuremb., 1493. Double-p. fo. Fully hand-cold. map, from Liber Chronicorum, ptd. text & captions in Latin, woodcut view. (CNY. Oct.9; 15) $1,500
- **Deutschland mit den Angrenzenden Ländern Mitteleuropas.** 1493. Latin Edn. Ob. fo. Woodcut map from Weltchronik, sm. faults reprd. (R. Mar.31-Apr.4; 3261) DM 1,700
- **Hierosolima.** Nuremb., 1493. Map on full fo. sheet, from Das Buch der Croniken, woodcut view, ptd. text in German, captions in Latin, fully hand-cold., light soiling & minor dampstaining. (CNY. Oct.9; 14) $520
- **The World.** 1493. Uncold. map. (P. Apr.9; 164) *Burgess.* £920

SCHENCK, Pieter
- **Diverse Orbis Terrae.** Amst., 1706. 20 × 23½ inches. Cold. map, greens oxidized, a few MS. additons to the coast of Alaska, lr. margin with inscr. & dtd. 26 Oct., 1711, margins trimmed. (SPB. Jul.28; 363) $325
- **Plat Ontwerp van Verscheyde Aert-Klooten.** Ca. 1680. Ob. fo. Old cold. copper engraved map in 2 hemispheres, many sm. maps round, fold bkd. (R. Mar.31-Apr.4; 4810) DM 1,700
See–JANSSON, Jan or Johannes, Schenk, Pieter & Valk, G.
See–LISLE, Giullaume de & Schenk, Pieter
See–VALCK, Gerard & Schenk, Pieter
See–VISSCHER, Nicolaus Joannes & Schenk, Pieter

SCHNEIDER, Louis & Weigel, Johann Christoff
- **Die Oestliche Halbkugel.** Nurnberg, 1805. Hand-cold. map, South East Coast of Ulimaroa or New Holland still hypothetical. (JL. Mar.1; 203) Aus. $120

SCHROTEN, Chris.
- **Cliviae, Finitimurumque Locorum verissima Descriptio.** [Antw.], Ortelius, [1570]. 37 × 50cm. Hand-cold. engraved map, ptd. text in Fr. on verso, fold in middle, restored slit in lr. margin, slightly browned. (VG. Oct.28; 446) Fls. 650

SCHROTT, Charles
- **Terra Sancta.** N.d. Ob. fo. Cold. copper engraved map after P. Laicstain from Ortelius, with 2 painted figure cartouches & figure decor. (R. Oct.14-18; 1524) DM 1,100

SCHROTT, Charles & Ortelius, Abraham
- **Geldern und Kleve.** N.d. Ob. fo. Old cold. copper engraved map with painted roll cartouche, slightly soiled, sm. tear backed at fold. (R. Oct.14-18; 4486) DM 650

SEALE
- **North America.** Ca. 1740. Fo. Uncold. map, California on Island, old creases, sm. repair. (JN. Apr.2; 99) £85

SECUNDA ETAS MUNDI
1493. Ob. fo. Woodcut map from Schedelschen Weltchronik, decor, sm. woodcuts at side fold reprd., lower half with text loss. (R. Oct.14-18; 3367) DM 3,100

SEILE, H.
- **Africa.–America.–Asia.–Europe.** 1652. Fo. 4 maps, all cold. & remargined, sm. pts. of maps of Europe & Africa missing, etc. (JN. Apr.2; 5) £75

SENEX, John
- **A New Map of Asia.** [L.], [1719]. 56 × 48cm. Map, cold. in outl., decor. cartouche, inset the Ice Sea, Northern part of New Holland shown. Inscr. to the Right Hon. George Earl of Warrington, etc. (JL. Mar.1; 170) Aus. $360
- **A New Map of Ireland from the latest Observations.** [L.] 1720. 24 × 21½ inches. Hand-cold. engraved map with cartouche & dedication. (GM. Apr.30; 190) £50
- **A New Map of the World** Ca. 1700. Hand-cold. map, worn. F. & G. (P. Nov.13; 148) *Price.* £60
- **North America.** Ill.:– J. Harris. [L.], [1721]. 21 × 23 ins. Map, boundaries lightly cold., with lge. cartouche, browned & spotted. (SG. Nov.20; 8) $275
- **Turkey in Europe [Balkans & Greece].** Ca. 1750. Double fo. Map, cold., strengthened in folds, tears in margin, sm. hole. (JN. Apr.2; 372) £56

SETZNAGEL, M. & Ortelius, Abraham
- **Salisburgensis Iurisdictio** N.d. Ob. fo. Old cold. copper engraved map with lge. view in lower, fold backed, slightly soiled. (R. Oct.14-18; 5701) DM 480

SEUTTER, Matthew
- **Africa.** [1735]. 19 × 25cm. Map, cold. line engraving, slightly dusty. F. (VA. Jan.30; 125) R. 360
- **Amsterdam.** Ca. 1590. 45 × 77.5cm. Old cold. plan including prospectus with allegorical decor. (R. Oct.14-18; 5231) DM 600
- **[Augsburg].** N.d. Ob. fo. Large old cold. copper engraved plan with figure cartouche. (R. Oct.14-18; 3672) DM 850
- **Berlin die ... Haupstatt ...** Augsburg, ca. 1730. 495 × 575mm. Hand-cold. plan, elaborate title-cartouche incorporating royal medallion port., coat of arms, panoramic view of Berlin across bottom of plt. F. W.a.f. (S. Nov.4; 321) *Loeb.* £410
- **Bruxella Belgii Cathol. Ornamentum et Ducatus Brabantiae Metropolis.** 1708. Plan, border of lge. perspective view, plan col. heightened. (LM. Mar.21; 72) B.Frs. 10,000
- **[Erfurt].** 1740. Ob. fo. Cold. copper engraved plan including view 14 × 37·5cm. flanked with allegorical figures. (R. Oct.14-18; 3914) DM 480
- **[Freiburg].** Ca. 1740. Ob. fo. Cold. copper engraved plan flanked with allegories & view. (R. Oct.14-18; 3519) DM 2,200
- **Harlingen.** Ca. 1740. Ob. fo. Old cold. copper engraved plan including view with figure cartouche, decor. & 2 lge. arms, slightly stained. (R. Oct.14-18; 5324) DM 500
- **Ierusalem, cum Suburbiis, prout Tempore Christi floruit.** Augsburg, ca. 1730. 573 × 491mm. Engraved plan, hand-cold., lr. 3rd. of plt. occupied by extensive key, in German, to numbered details. W.a.f. (S. Jun.29; 127) *Cohen.* £220
- **Imperium Romano-Germanicum.** N.d. Ob. fo. Old cold. copper engraved map, 2 figure cartouches, fold backed. (R. Oct.14-18; 3435) DM 500
- **[Landau].** Ca. 1740. Ob. fo. Cold. plan including view, flanked with allegories, sm. brown stain in fold of view. (R. Oct.14-18; 4827) DM 1,800
- **Nova Totius Helvetiae Tabula.** N.d. Ob. fo. Old cold. copper engraved map with lge. figure cartouche & ills. in corners, slightly stained at foot. (R. Oct.14-18; 5801) DM 750
- **[Nürnberg].** N.d. Ob. fo. Old cold. copper engraved plan with allegorical decor. (R. Oct.14-18; 3792) DM 500
- **Prag.** N.d. Ob. fo., 11 × 56cm. Old cold. copper engraved plan with prospectus. (R. Oct.14-18; 5684) DM 700
- **Recens edita Novi Belgii Delineatio.** N.d. Ob. fo. Old cold. copper engraved map with allegorical cartouche & view at foot, fold slightly browned &

sm. fault at head backed, slightly soiled. (R. Oct.14-18; 5073) DM 1,800
- **Regio Canaan, postea Judaea.** N.d. Ob. fo. Old cold. copper engraved map with lge. figure cartouche. (R. Oct.14-18; 5133) DM 600
- **Regio Canaan seu ... Terra Sancta.** Augsburg, ca. 1730. 494 × 573mm. Engraved map, hand-cold. in outl., principal areas fully cold., lge pict. title-vig., sm. inset map, etc. W.a.f. (S. Jun.29; 129) *Whiteson.* £180
- **Les Routes ... France-Italia Antique-Neapolis Regnum Status Ecclesiae.** Ca. 1730. 4 hand-cold. maps. (P. Dec.11; 165) £170
- **Saxoniae Superioris Circulus ...** Augustanus, ca. 1730. 20 × 24ins. Fully-cold. map, with cartouche, sm. tear at lr. end of fold. (SG. Nov.20; 111) $120
- **[Schwäbischer Kreis].** N.d. Ob. fo. Old cold. copper engraved map with figure cartouche, slightly soiled & jnts. sprung & backed. (R. Oct.14-18; 3609) DM 680
- **Suevia Universa, IX Tabulis Delineata.** Ed.:– Jacques Michal. Augsburg, ca. 1730. 140 × 152 cm. Lge. old cold. copper engrd. map in 9 ll., each in 9 segments on linen & folding, light browning. (R. Oct.14-18; 2170) DM 2,000

SEYER, R.
- **Karte des Atlantik zwischen Brasilien, Kanada, Grönland, Norwegen und Kongo.** 1750. Ob. fo. Map, Slightly browned. (R. Oct.14-18; 3390) DM 450

SMITH, William
- **A Delineation of the Strata of England & Wales, with Part of Scotland.** 1 Aug. 1815. 1st. Edn. Approximately 265 × 175cm. Folding hand-cold. engraved map, in 32 sections, mntd. on linen, sm. ink stain, slight dust-soiling, orig. bd. s.-c., worn, hf. mor. case. From Honeyman Collection. (S. May 19; 2862) *Percy.* £1,600

SOCIETY FOR THE DIFFUSION OF USEFUL KNOWLEDGE
- **Australia in 1839.** Ill.:– J. & C. Walker. L., 1840. 38·5 × 32cm. Map, cold. in outl., Victoria shown as Port Phillip. (JL. Mar.1; 179) Aus. $120
- **The Australian Colonies.** L., 1862. 69 × 40cm. Hand-cold. map, list of counties with 37 Queensland counties included, inset maps of the World & Tasmania. (JL. Mar.1; 186) Aus. $150
- **New South Wales.** Ill.:– J. & C. Walker. L., Sep.1, 1833. 33.5 × 38.5cm. 19 counties cold. in outl., inset of Sydney. (JL. Mar.1; 185) Aus. $150
- **– Anr. Copy.** 33.5 × 39cm. (JL. Dec.14; 118) Aus. $130
- **– Anr. Copy.** Map, shows 19 counties hand-cold., inset of Sydney. (JL. Jul.19; 256) Aus. $120
- **Western Australia Containing the Settlements of Swan-River & King George's Sound & Van-Dieman Island.** Ill.:– John & Charles Walker. L., 1833. 31 × 39cm. (JL. Dec.14; 131) Aus. $110

SOUTHERN HEMISPHERE
L'pool., 1856. 50cm. diameter. Map, Hand-cold. in outl. (JL. Jul.19; 258) Aus. $105

SPECHT, C.
- **Carte d'un Très Grand Pays Entre la Nouveau Mexique et la Mer Glaciale.** Utrecht, 1698. 17 × 20½ inches. Cold. map, greens oxidized affecting paper. (SPB. Jul.28; 333) $350

SPEEDE, John
- **Africae described.** [1676, or later]. 393 × 515mm. Engraved map, hand-cold. in outl., cartouche, decor., 8 vig. views of cities & 10 costume figures, fully cold. F. W.a.f. (S. Nov.4; 374) *Bucherkabinett.* £180
- **– Anr. Edn.** N.d. Ob. fo. Copper engraved map, side decors., 8 sm. views above. (R. Mar.31-Apr4; 4929) DM 950
- **America ... Described ... (sic) 1926.** G. Humble, 1626 [but 1631]. 390 × 507mm. Engraved map, hand-cold. in outl., title-cartouche, 8 vig. plans, 10 figures etc., fully cold., Engl. text on verso, sm. repair. W.a.f. (S. Mar.31; 309) *Map House.* £850
- **Asia.** 1626. Hand-cold. map, figures & - town plans round borders, damp stains. F. & G. (P. Jan.22; 193) *Nagel.* £140
- **– Anr. Edn.** 1626 [but 1676, or later]. 394 × 512mm. Engraved map, hand-cold. in outl., vig. city plans & costume figures, etc., fully cold.,

Engl. text on verso. W.a.f. (S. Jun.29; 167) *Nagel.* £190
– **Bedfordshire.** [Overton], [1710]. (P. Oct.23; 120) *Old Hall.* £60
– **Berkshire.** 1627-76. 38·5 × 51cm. Hand-cold. engraved map from the Theatre of the Empire of Great Britain, Engl. text on verso, sm. margins, centre fold defect., other minor defects. (BS. Feb.25; 87) £80
– **Bohemia.** 1626. 418 × 532mm. Engraved map with title cartouche & border on 3 sides of 17 vigs. of figures & views, hand-cold. vigs., cartouche & map outl., Engl. text on verso. F. & G. on both sides. (SKC. Feb.26; 1562) £160
– – **Anr. Edn.** 1626 [but 1627, or later]. 413 × 527mm. Engraved map, hand-cold. in outl., title-cartouche, 7 vig. views, 10 costume fitures in 3 borders fully cold. W.a.f. (S. Nov.3; 238) *Nagle.* £110
– **Britain as it was divided at the tyme of the Englishe-Saxons.** [1614, or later]. 381 × 508mm. Engraved map, hand-cold. in outl., title cartouche, coats-of-arms & 14 fully-cold. vigs. in side margins, text in Engl. on verso, lr. end of centre-fold strengthened. F. (SBA. May 27; 281) *Waite.* £155
– – **Anr. Edn.** [1646]. 15 × 20 inches. Hand-cold. engraved map, lightly dampstained. F. & G. (CSK. May 8; 42) £250
– **Buckingham.** [1676]. 15 & 20 inches. Engraved map, hand-cold. in outl. F. & G. (CSK. May 8; 1) £75
– – **Anr. Copy.** Uncold. map, 2 town plans. F. & double-G. (P. Apr.9; 178) *Honniball.* £70
– **Caernarvon both Shyre & Shire-towne with the ancient Citie Bangor described.** 1610 [but 1614 or later]. 380 × 510mm. Engraved map, hand.-cold., including armorial title-cartouche, inset plans of Bangor & Caernarvon, sailing ships, etc., slight tear reprd. in fold. F. (SBA. Oct.22; 706) *Hulme.* £115
– – **Anr. Edn.** [1676]. 15 × 20 inches. Engraved map hand-cold. in outl. Close F. & G. (CSK. Jun.5; 46) £60
– **Cambridgeshire.** T. Bassett & R. Chiswell, 1610 [but 1676, or later]. 383 × 525mm. Engraved map, hand-cold. in outl., royal coat of arms, 25 coats in borders, 3 other coats, inset plan, 4 figures, etc. fully cold., Engl. text on verso, repair at bottom of centre fold, F. W.a.f. (S. Mar.30; 26) *Edington.* £240
– – **Anr. Copy.** 15 × 20 inches. Engraved map, stained, several sm. tears reprd. F. & G. (CSK. Sep.19; 92) £100
– – **Anr. Edn.** 1611. Hand-cold. map, inset town plan. (P. Sep.11; 129) *Brazier.* £140
– – **Anr. Edn.** Ca. 1611. 38 × 52cm. Map in border of coats of arms of the Colleges, Engl. text on verso. F. & double-G. (O. Jun.3; 46) £210
– – **Anr. Edn.** [1627]. 38.2 × 52cm. Hand-cold. engraved map from the Theatre of the Empire of Great Britain, Engl. text on verso. (BS. Feb.25; 90) £140
– **Cambridgeshire described with . . . the Armes of the Colleges.** 1610 [but 1614, or later]. 385 × 527mm. Engraved map, hand-cold. in outl., royal coat of arms, decor., (fully cold.), slight dust-soiling. F. W.a.f. (S. Nov.3; 143) *Regent Gallery.* £120
– **Channel Islands.** [1676]. Hand-cold. map, F. & double-G. (P. Jun.11; 220) £90
– **The Countie & Citie of Lyncolne Described.** [1710 or later]. 15 × 20½ inches. Engraved map, slightly soiled. (CSK. Jul.3; 13) £65
– **Countie of Leinster.** [1676]. Hand-cold. map, inset plan of Dublin. F. & G. (P. Nov.13; 146) *Kent.* £100
– **The Countye of Monmouth.** 1610. 380 × 508mm. Engraved map with title cartouche, town plan & 3 vigs., partly hand-cold., Engl. text on verso. F. & G. (SKC. Feb.26; 1563a) £80
– – **Anr. Edn.** T. Bassett & R. Chiswell, 1610, [but 1676, or later]. 382 × 508mm. Engraved map, hand-cold. in outl., cartouches, 3 coats of arms, port., inset plan, etc., fully cold., Engl. text on verso. W.a.f. (S. Mar.31; 364) *Burgess.* £100
– **The Countie of Radnor.** [1713.] 18 × 23 inches. Engraved map, hand-cold. in outl. F. & G. (CSK. Oct.3; 107) £60
– **The County Palatine of Chester with that most Ancient Citie described.** [1614, or later]. 380 × 523mm. Engraved map, hand-cold. in outl., title & scale cartouches, coats of arms, inset plan of Chester, decor. F. (SBA. Dec.16; 273) *Nicholson.* £120
– – **Anr. Edn.** T. Bassett & R. Chiswell, [1676, or later]. 389 × 509mm. Engraved map, 13 coats of arms, inset plan, Engl. text on verso, reprd., sm. stain. W.a.f. (S. Mar.30; 30) *Seddon.* £130
– – **Anr. Copy.** 389 × 509mm. W.a.f. (S. Mar.30; 29) *Kidd.* £120
– **The Countie Westmorland & Kendale, the Cheif Toune Described.** [1627 or later]. 38 × 51cm. Map, armorial cartouche, cold. English text on verso. F. (PL. Nov.27; 50) *Leeds Flats.* £90
– **Darbieshire Described.** T. Bassett & R. Chiswell, 1666 [but 1676, or later]. 381 × 507mm. Engraved map, hand-cold. in outl., cartouches, royal arms, etc. fully cold., inset plan, Engl. text on verso, sm. stain. W.a.f. (S. Mar.30; 35) *Kidd.* £140
– **Denbighshire.** 1610 [but 1614, or later]. Approximately 370 × 504mm. Engraved map, principal features hand-cold., title-cartouche, 2 coats of arms, plan of Denbigh inset, sailing ships, etc., all hand-cold. (SBA. Oct.22; 708) *J. Bennett Parry.* £64
– **Devonshire.** [1611]. Hand-cold. map, inset plan. F. & G. (P. Apr.30; 115) *Burgess.* £150
– – **Anr. Edn.** [1614, or later]. 376 × 509mm. Engraved map, slightly torn with some loss of matter at fold. F. (SBA. Oct.22; 333) *Harrison.* £60
– **Dorsetshyre with the Shyre-towne Dorchester Described.** 1610 [but 1611-12]. 382 × 505mm. Map, cartouches, 5 coats of arms, inset plan, Engl. text on verso, 2 sm. stains. W.a.f. (S. Mar.30; 41) *Gilberts.* £150
– – **Anr. Copy.** 383 × 512mm. Engraved hand-cold. map, including title & scale cartouches, 4 coats of arms, inset plan of Dorchester, etc., fully cold., arms heightened with gold, Engl. text on verso, 2 sm. stains affecting the plan & bottom border. W.a.f. (S. Nov.4; 458) *Kidd.* £100
– – **Anr. Edn.** [1614-16]. 13½ × 19½ inches. Engraved map, hand-cold. in outl. F. & G. (CSK. Jan.9; 89) £170
– – **Anr. Edn.** [1676]. Map. (PJ. Dec.5; 58) £80
– – **Anr. Copy.** Hand-cold. map, some stains, F. & G. (P. Sep.11; 143) *Potter.* £70
– – **Anr. Edn.** [1676 or later]. 15¾ × 20½ ins. Hand-cold. engraved map, title with architectonic decors., inset plan of Dorchester, Royal arms, & 3 other coats-of-arms, galleons & monsters at sea, Engl. text on reverse. F. W.a.f. (LC. Feb.12; 238) £110
– – **Anr. Edn.** Early 17th. C. Hand-cold. map, inset plan. F. & G. (P. Sep.11; 152) *Kent.* £110
– **Durham.** [1610]. 37.5 × 50mm. Inset town plan, hand-cold. map. F. & G. (P. May 14; 146) £120
– – **Anr. Edn.** ca. 1611. Hand-cold. map. F. & G, W.a.f. (P. Oct.2; 238) *Goodall.* £190
– **Essex.** 1611. 15 × 20½ inches. Engraved map, sm. tear reprd. (CSK. Apr.10; 45) £110
– – **Anr. Edn.** L., G. Humble, [1611]. Hand-cold. map, inset plan, arms, F. & double-G. (P. Jun.11; 246) *Dawson.* £160
– – **Anr. Copy.** Uncold. map, slight wear centre fold. F. & G. (P. Sep.11; 133) *Brazier.* £100
– – **Anr. Edn.** [1627, or later]. 385 × 514mm. Engraved map, including 8 coats of arms. In card mount. W.a.f. (S. Nov.3; 155) *Tegg.* £140
– – **Anr. Copy.** 385 × 510mm. Inset plan, Engl. text on verso, centrefold reprd. W.a.f. (S. Mar.30; 47) *Burgess.* £100
– – **Anr. Edn.** T. Bassett & R. Chiswell, 1662 [but 1676 or later]. 385 × 511mm. Engraved map, hand-cold. in outl., armorial titled-cartouche, 9 coats of arms, etc. fully cold., Engl. text on verso, F. W.a.f. (S. Mar.30; 46) *A.S. Bale.* £180
– **Europe & the Cheife Cities therin described.** Ill.:– A. Goos (engraver). 1626. Ob. fo. Cold. copper engraved map, side ills., 8 sm. views at head, slightly browned. (R. Mar.31-Apr.4; 5157) DM 2,200
– **Flintshire.** 1610 but 1616, or later. 381 × 508mm. Engraved map, hand-cold. in outl., inset plans of Flint & Saint Asaph, engr. of St. Winifreds Well, all cold., Latin text on verso, 2 sm. rust spots, a few other minor defects, joined in centre. F. (SBA. Dec.16; 275) *Lamb.* £65
– – **Anr. Edn.** L., Bassett & Chiswell, 1676. Uncold. map, inset plans. (P. Jul.2; 244a) *Chapman.* £50
– – **Anr. Edn.** [1676]. Hand-cold. map, 2 inset plans. F. & G. (P. Nov.13; 147) *Kent.* £85
– – **Anr. Edn.** [1676, or later]. Approximately 378 × 505mm. Engraved map, title-cartouche, inset plans of Flint & Saint Asaph, latter in armorial cartouche, engravings of St. Winifrids Well, sailing ships, etc., all hand-cold. (SBA. Oct.22; 742) *Hercules.* £65
– – **Anr. Copy.** 16 × 18 inches. Engraved map, hand cold. in outl. F. & G. (CSK. Oct.3; 103) £60
– **France.** 1626. Hand-cold. map inset town plans & figures in border. F. & G. (P. Dec.11; 164) *Garfunkle.* £90
– – **Anr. Copy.** Ob. fo. Cold. copper engraved map, painted arms cartouche, side figures, 8 sm. views at head. Gold F. (R. Mar.31-Apr.4; 5495) DM 750
– **Glamorgan Shyre.** [1662]. 15½ × 20½ inches. Engraved map, hand-cold. in outl., clean tear along centre fold. F. & G. (CSK. Dec.12; 79) £65
– **Glocestershire . . .** 1610 [but 1614, or later]. 379 × 510mm. Engraved map, hand-cold. in outl., title-cartouche, royal arms, 11 other coats, inset plans of Gloucester & Bristol, etc., fully cold., slight spotting, mostly of blank margins. W.a.f. (S. Nov.3; 157) *Regent Gallery.* £140
– – **Anr. Copy.** 375 × 500mm. Fully cold., Engl. text on verso, reprd., F. W.a.f. (S. Mar.30; 49) *H. Walker.* £100
– – **Anr. Edn.** T. Bassett & R. Chiswell, 1610 [but 1676 or later]. 382 × 513mm. Engraved map, hand-cold. in outl., title-cartouche, royal arms, 13 coats of arms, inset plans, etc. fully cold., Engl. text on verso, some repairs & marginal tears. W.a.f. (S. Mar.30; 48) *Regent Gall.* £100
– – **Anr. Edn.** Ca. 1676. 15 × 20 inches. Uncold. county map with street plans of Bristow & Glocester, alphabetical keys & descriptions, 1 lge. & 11 sm. coats of arms, ills., etc., Engl. text to verso referring to Glocestershire & with a list of its hundreds, brown stain near title. F. & G. to both back & front. (TA. May 21; 21) £105
– – **Anr. Copy.** 15 × 20 inches. Brown stain near title. (TA. Feb.19; 57) £75
– **Guernsey, Jersey, Farne Island & Holy Island.** 1610. 381 × 509mm. 1 engraved sheet with maps hand-cold., short tear reprd., verso with Engl. text also glazed. F. & G. (SKC. Feb.26; 1563) £70
– **Hampshire.** 1611-27. 38 × 51cm. Hand-cold. engraved map from the Theatre of the Empire of Great Britain, Engl. text on verso, with margins, some creasing & minor damage along centrefold. (BS. Feb.25; 89) £120
– – **Anr. Copy.** 38 × 50·5cm. Sm. margins, some nicks along upr. margin & paper loss just outside borderline, other minor defects. (BS. Feb.25; 85) £100
– **Hantshire Described.** T. Bassett & R. Chiswell, [1676, or later]. 376 × 505mm. Engraved map, hand-cold. in outl., title-cartouche, royal arms, 8 coats of arms in borders, & arms on inset plan fully cold., Engl. text on verso, wormed, F. W.a.f. (S. Mar.30; 50) *E. Doherty.* £170
– – **Anr. Edn.** ca. 1710. Map. (P. Oct.23; 128) *Speed.* £110
– – **Anr. Edn.** N.d. Double-p. map hand-cold. in outl., royal arms & armorials, Engl. text on verso, inscr. 'Are to be sold by Thomas Bassett in Fleet Street & Richard Chiswell in St. Pauls Churchyard'. F. (WW. May 20; 18) £185
– **Hartfordshire Described.** [1646]. 15 × 20 inches. Engraved map hand-cold. in outl., reprd. tear on fold. F. & G. (CSK. May 8; 21) £100
– – **Anr. Edn.** T. Bassett & R. Chiswell, [1676, or later]. 383 × 507mm. Engraved map, hand-cold. in outl., inset plans, cartouches, 3 coats of arms & other features fully cold., Engl. text on verso, F. W.a.f. (S. Mar.30; 54) *Stewart.* £190
– **Hertfordshire.** 1611-27. 38 × 51cm. Hand-cold. engraved map from the Theatre of the Empire of Great Britain, Engl. text on verso, sm. margins, some nicks along upr. margin, paper loss just outside borderline, other minor defects. (BS. Feb.25; 86) £80
– **The Invasions of England & Ireland . . .** Roger Rea the Elder & Younger, [1650, or later]. 377 × 513mm. Engraved map, histor. & armorial title-cartouche, coats of arms, Engl. text on verso. W.a.f. (S. Mar.31; 328) *Tooley.* £260
– **Kent.** [1627]. 15 × 20 inches. Engraved map, hand-cold. in outl., marginal tears. (CSK. Mar.6; 5) £220
– – **Anr. Edn.** [1627, or later]. 378 × 505mm. Engraved map, principal features hand-cold., including 10 coats of arms, inset plans, Engl. text on verso, reprd. at bottom of centre fold, slightly affecting engraved surface. W.a.f. (S. Nov.3; 163) *Clark.* £240
– – **Anr. Edn.** Roger Rea the Elder & Younger, [1650, or later]. 377 × 502mm. Engraved map,

SPEEDE, John *-contd.*
hand-cold. in outl., 10 coats of arms & some other features fully cold., plans partly cold., Engl. text on verso, centre fold reprd., F. W.a.f. (S. Mar.30; 59) *Burgess.* £160
– – **Anr. Edn.** T. Bassett & R. Chiswell, [1676, or later]. 379 × 506mm. Engraved map, hand-cold. in outl., 8 coats of arms, inset plans with city arms & some other features fully cold., Engl. text on verso, 2 sm. wormholes, F. W.a.f. (S. Mar.30; 60) *Johnson.* £240
– – **Anr. Copy.** 378 × 492mm. 10 coats of arms, verso blank, tear in blank lower margin, some creasing. W.a.f. (S. Mar.30; 61) *Burgess.* £190
– **The Kingdome of China.** 1626 (but 1627, or later). 392 × 510mm. Engraved map, hand-cold. in outl., title & scale cartouches, sailing ships, 4 vig. views & 8 costume figures all fully cold., Engl. text on verso, separated at bottom of centre fold, minor stains in blank margins. W.a.f. (S. Jun.29; 173) *Nagel.* £240
– – **Anr. Edn.** '1626' [but 1676]. 15½ × 20 inches. Engraved map, torn along fold, light browning. (CSK. Jun.5; 11a) £240
– – **Anr. Edn.** [1676]. 15 × 20½ inches. Engraved map, hand-cold. in outl., Engl. text on verso, tear along centre fold, slight staining. (CSK. Mar.6; 38) £70
– **The Kingdome of Denmarke.** T. Bassett & R. Chiswell. [1676, or later]. 392 × 510mm. Engraved map, hand-cold, in outl., cartouches, 6 vigs., 2 ports., royal arms, 10 figures, etc., fully cold., Engl. text on verso, F. W.a.f. (S. Mar.31; 397) *Jorgenson.* £220
– **The Kingdome of England.** 1610 [but 1614, or later]. 385 × 514mm. Engraved map, hand-cold. in outl., title-cartouche, coat of arms, decor., fully cold., Engl. text on verso. F. W.a.f. (S. Nov.3; 136) *Rayleigh.* £150
– – **Anr. Copy.** 385 × 414mm. Engraved map, hand-cold. in outl., title cartouche, royal coat of arms, 8 figures, etc., fully cold., Engl. text on verso, lr. pt. of centre fold reprd., F. W.a.f. (S. Mar.31; 318) *Potter.* £120
– – **Anr. Edn.** T. Bassett & R. Chiswell, [1676 or later]. 388 × 516mm. Engraved map, title-cartouche, royal arms, 8 figures in borders, Engl. text on verso. W.a.f. (S. Mar.30; 2) *Stephenson.* £160
– – **Anr. Copy.** 388 × 516mm. W.a.f. (S. Mar.30; 1) *Burgess.* £140
– **The Kingdome of Great Britain.** [1611]. Hand-cold. map. F. & double-G. W.a.f. (P. Oct.2; 194) *Goodall.* £360
– **The Kingdome of Irland.** 1662. 384 × 504mm. Engraved map, hand-cold. in outl., historiated title-cartouche, royal arms, costume figures, etc., fully cold., Engl. text on verso. W.a.f. (S. Jun.29; 40) *Emerald Isle.* £160
– **The Kingdom of Persia.** [1676]. 15½ × 20½ inches. Engraved map, torn along fold, marginal soiling. (CSK. Jun.5; 11) £65
– **The Kingdome of Scotland.** William Humbell, 1652. 384 × 512mm. Engraved map, inset map, 2 coats of arms, 4 figures in borders, verso blank. W.a.f. (S. Mar.30; 16) *Map House.* £160
– – **Anr. Edn.** Roger Rea, the Elder & Younger, [1662, or later]. 382 × 509mm. Engraved map, inset map, 2 coats of arms, 4 figures in side borders, Engl. text on verso, bottom of centre fold torn. W.a.f. (S. Mar.30; 17) *Price.* £160
– **A Map of Jamaica–Barbados.** L., [1675]. 17 × 21 ins. Hand-cold. map, from The Theatre of the Empire of Great Britain, Engl. text on verso, some minor tears in lr. portion. (SG. May 21; 126) $170
– – **Anr. Edn.** 1676. 15 × 20 inches. Engraved map, hand-cold. in outl. (CSK. Jul.3; 10) £190
[–] – **Anr. Edn.** T. Bassett & R. Chiswell, [1676, or later]. 385 × 500mm. 2 engraved maps on 1 plt., hand-cold. in outl., armorial title & scale-cartouches, etc. fully cold., Engl. text on verso, F. W.a.f. (S. Mar.31; 316) *Map House.* £150
– **Mappa Aestivarum Insularum . . . A Mapp of the Sommer Ilands once called the Bermudas.** G. Humble, 1626 [but 1627, or later]. 400 × 528mm. Engraved map, title-cartouche, 2 coats of arms, F. W.a.f. (S. Mar.31; 314) *Waterloo Inn.* £170
– **Merionethshire.** [1665]. 14½ × 20 inches. Engraved map, hand-cold. in outl., slight staining. F. & G. (CSK. Mar.6; 3) £50
– **Middle-sex Described . . .** G. Humble, 1610 [but 1627, or later]. 384 × 511mm. Engraved map, hand-cold. in outl., cartouches, inset plans with coat of arms, etc., fully cold., Engl. text on verso, centre fold reprd. W.a.f. (S. Mar.30; 71) *Burgess.* £200
– – **Anr. Edn.** [1611]. 39 × 52.5cm. Hand-cold. map, inset plans, slightly soiled. F. & G. (P. May 14; 184) *Nelson.* £160
– – **Anr. Copy.** Slight wear at centre fold, 2 inset plans. F. & G. in the form of a tray. (P. Mar.12; 185) *Potter.* £70
– – **Anr. Edn.** [1676]. Hand-cold. map. Double G. W.a.f. (P. Oct.2; 196) *Goodall.* £210
– – **Anr. Copy.** 15 × 20 inches. Hand-cold. engraved map, worn along fold, with loss just affecting title. F. & G. (CSK. May 8; 20) £90
– **Montgomeryshire.** [1611]. 15½ × 20 inches. Engraved map, browned, 1 sm. tear. F. & G. (CSK. Mar.6; 2) £75
[–] **A New & Accurate Map of the World . . .** L., ca. 1651. 390 × 510mm. Engraved double-hemispheric map on laid paper with text on verso, hand-cold. overall, northern & southern hemispheres, decor., etc., eclipses & description of John Davis's voyage to discover a north-west passage in 1580, sm. reprd. split lr. cover. (PWP. Apr.9; 168) Can. $2,200
– **New Map, of East India.** [1676]. Hand-cold. map. F. & G. (P. Sep.11; 148) *Marcians.* £170
– **A Newe mape of Germany.** 1626. Hand-cold. map, decor., repair to lr. central fold. F. & G. (P. Dec.11; 191) £210
– – **Anr. Copy.** Ob. fo. Cold. copper engraved map, painted arms cartouche, 5 costume figures at side, 8 sm. views above. (R. Oct.14-18; 3412) DM 2,600
– – **Anr. Copy.** (R. Mar.31-Apr.4; 3272) DM 1,700
– **Newe Mape of Poland.** [1626]. Ob. fo. Decor. cold. copper engraved map with figures at side, 1 arms, port & 6 views at head. (R. Oct.14-18; 5192) DM 1,200
– **A New Mappe of the Romane Empire.** L., Bassett & Chiswell. 1676. Hand-cold. map, figures & plans on borders, F. & G. (P. Jul.2; 236C) *Sloan.* £55
– **New Mappe of ye XVII Provinces of Low Germany.** [1626]. Ob. fo. Cold copper engraved map with painted cartouche & 5 costume figures at sides, 8 sm. views at head. (R. Oct.14-18; 5348) DM 1,200
– – **Anr. Edn.** 1654. 42 × 54cm. Engraved map in border of views & costumes. F., glass brkn. (VG. Oct.28; 248) Fls. 850
– **Norfolk.** Ca. 1614. Uncold. map, inset town plan of Norwich, coats-of-arms. (P. Dec.11; 170) *Powell.* £130
– – **Anr. Edn.** [1627]. 15 × 20½ inches. Hand-cold. engraved map. F. & G. (CSK. Oct.17; 256) £160
– – **Anr. Edn.** 1676. 15½ × 20 inches. Engraved map. F. & G. (CSK. Jul.3; 18) £140
– **The North & East Ridins [sic] of Yorkshire.** J. Sudbury & G. Humbell, 1610 [but 1614, or later]. 390 × 512mm. Engraved map, hand-cold. in outl., title & scale cartouches, 23 coats of arms, inset plans, etc. fully cold., Engl. text on verso, F. W.a.f. (S. Mar.30; 129) *Waggett.* £150
– – **Anr. Edn.** [1676 or later]. 15½ × 20½ inches. Engraved map, hand-cold. in outl., clean tear along centre fold. F. & G. (CSK. Dec.12; 81) £70
– **Northampton.** [1676]. Hand-cold. map, 2 inset town plans, arms, neat repairs. (P. Feb.19; 131) *Honniball.* £60
– **Oxfordshire Described . . .** J. Sudbury & G. Humble, 1610 [but 1627 or later]. 390 × 516mm. Engraved map, hand-cold. in outl., 21 coats of arms, inset plan, etc., fully cold., Engl. text on verso, 2 inscrs. on engd. surface, F. W.a.f. (S. Mar.30; 87) *Cookson.* £190
– – **Anr. Edn.** Henry Overton, 1610 [but 1713, or later]. 384 × 520mm. Engraved map, hand-cold. in outl., 21 coats of arms, inset plan, figures, etc. fully cold., F. W.a.f. (S. Mar.30; 92) *J. Potter.* £260
– – **Anr. Edn.** J. Sudbury & G. Humble, [1614, or later]. 387 × 527mm. Engraved map, hand-cold. in outl., 21 coats of arms, inset plan, etc., fully cold., Engl. text on verso, 4 sm. perforations in engraved surface, lr. margin reprd. W.a.f. (S. Mar.30; 86) *Sanders of Oxford.* £180
– – **Anr. Edn.** T. Bassett & R. Chiswell, [1676, or later]. 390 × 516mm. Engraved map, uncold., few tears & repairs to blank margins, Engl. text on verso. W.a.f. (S. Mar.30; 90) *Kentish.* £140
– – **Anr. Copy.** 390 × 516mm. W.a.f. (S. Mar.30; 88) *Kentish.* £120
– – **Anr. Copy.** 390 × 516mm. Lr. blank margin reprd. W.a.f. (S. Mar.30; 89) *Kentish.* £100
– **Penbrokshyre.** 1610 [but 1612 or later]. 15½ × 20½ inches. Engraved map, hand-cold. in outl., slight wear at lr. fold. F. & G. (CSK. Jul.3; 21) £140
– **A Prospect of the Most Famous Parts of the World; Greece.** 1627-76. 39.7 × 51.2cm. Hand-cold. engraved map, sm. margins. (BS. Feb.25; 93) £140
– **The Province of Connaught.** L., 1610. Map. F. & G. (GM. Apr.30; 200) £150
– – **Anr. Copy.** Cold. map. F. (PD. Oct.22; 221) £120
– – **Anr. Edn.** N.d. 56 × 42cm. Inset plan of the City of Galwaye. F. (PJ. Jun.6; 160) **£95**
– **The Province of Connaugh[t] with the Citie of Galwaye Described.–The Province of Mounster.** 1610 (but 1676 or later). Various sizes. 2 engraved map, hand-cold. in outl., title & scale cartouches, inset plans, etc., fully cold. Engl. text on versos sm. rust hole in surface of 1st. W.a.f (S. Jun.29; 41) *Neptune Gallery.* £160
– **Province of Munster.** 1610. Cold. map. F. (PD. Oct.22; 223) £70
– **The Province of Ulster.** Ca. 1676. 375 × 525mm. Engraved map. title, scale cartouches, view of Enis Kelling, hand-cold., framed, Engl. text on verso. (SKC. Jul.28; 2385) £80
– – **Anr. Edn.** [1676 or later]. 378 × 506mm. Engraved map, some features cold. by hand., including armorial title-cartouche, scale-cartouche, inset engr., etc., Engl. text on verso, minor flaw in engraved surface at bottom of centre fold., some very slight spotting. F. W.a.f. (S. Jun.29; 34) *Emerald Isle.* £120
– – **Anr. Edn.** N.d. Cold. map. F. (PD. Oct.22; 222) £75
– **The Province of Ulster Described.–The Countie of Leinster with the Citie Dublin Described.** 1610 [but 1614 or later]. Various sizes. 2 engraved maps, hand-cold. in outl., title & scale cartouches, inset engr. on 1st. & plan on 2nd., etc., fully cold., Engl. text on versos, both reprd., slightly affecting engraved surface, some marginal tears. W.a.f. (S. Jun.29; 42) *Neptune Gallery.* £190
– **Radnor Described.** [1627]. 15½ × 20½ inches. Engraved map, preserved, slight spotting. F. & G. (CSK. Jun.5; 1) £50
– **Rutlandshire.** [1611]. Hand-cold. map, 2 inset plans, arms. F. & G. (P. Sep.11; 144) *Hunter.* £70
– **Shropshyre.** Ca. 1625. Double-p. fo. Map, cold. in outl. F. (SPB. Nov.25; 115) $200
– **Somerset-shire Described.** J. Sudbury & G. Humble, 1610 [but 1614, or later]. 378 × 506mm. Engraved map, hand-cold. in outl., 8 coats of arms fully cold., inset plan etc. partly cold., Engl. text on verso, centre fold & lr. margin reprd. W.a.f. (S. Mar.30; 101) *D. Burgess.* £100
– – **Anr. Edn.** [1612 or later]. 16 × 20½ins. Hand-cold. engraved map, inset plan of Bath, Royal arms, & 6 other coast-of-arms, galleons at sea, slight tear near border in upr. right-hand corner. F. W.a.f. (LC. Feb.12; 234) £120
– – **Anr. Edn.** 1676. Hand-cold. map, inset plan of Bathe. F. & G. (P. Nov.13; 149) *Kent.* £130
– – **Anr. Edn.** [1676]. Map. (PJ. Dec.5; 57) £95
– **Suffolk.** [1611]. Hand-cold. map, inset plan of Ipswich (some dampstains). F. & G. (P. Jan.22; 196) *Goodall.* £140
– – **Anr. Copy.** F. & G. (P. Feb.19; 132) *Honniball.* £130
– – **Anr. Edn.** [1676]. Hand-cold. map, inset plan of Ipswich, arms. F. & G. (P. Mar.12; 190) *Hall.* £100
– **Surrey.** [1614]. 15½ × 20 inches. Engraved map, hand-cold. in outl. F. & G. (CSK. Oct.3; 102) £120
– **Surrey described & divided into its Hundreds.** 1610 [but 1676, or later]. 382 × 514mm. Engraved map, hand-cold. in outl., cartouches, 9 coats of arms (7 in side borders), inset views fully cold., engraved surface slightly worn at bottom of centre fold. F. W.a.f. (S. Nov.3; 178) *Gibbons.* £200
– **Sussex Described.** J. Sudbury & G. Humble, 1610 [but 1614, or later]. 383 × 507mm. Engraved map, cartouches, 6 coats of arms, inset plan, etc., Engl. text on verso, some boundaries outl. in red crayon, centre fold reprd., stained, old inscr. W.a.f. (S. Mar.30; 112) *Burgess.* £160
– – **Anr. Edn.** G. Humble, [1610, but 1627 or later]. 385 × 508mm. Engraved map, hand-cold. in outl., royal arms, 5 coats of arms, plan, etc.

fully cold., Engl. text on verso, centre fold linen-bkd., 2 tears reprd., F. W.a.f. (S. Mar.30; 113) *Burgess*. £120
– – **Anr. Edn.** 1611. 52 × 39cm. Uncold. map, inset town plan, repairs to both right-hand corners, narrow margins. F. & G. (P. May 14; 184A) *Donovan*. £90
– – **Anr. Edn.** [1611]. Uncold. map. F. & double G. W.a.f. (P. Oct.2; 198) *Davis*. £230
– – **Anr. Edn.** [1676]. Hand-cold. map. Double G. W.a.f. (P. Oct.2; 200) *Menlore*. £190
– – **Anr. Edn.** [1743]. 13½ × 19½ inches. Engraved map, hand-cold. in outl. F. & G. (CSK. Jan.9; 90) £120
– **The Turkish Empire.** L., G. Humble, [1611]. Hand-cold. map, figures & plans on borders, F. & G. (P. Jul.2; 236b) *Sofu*. £100
– – **Anr. Edn.** 1626. Fo. Map with wash colouring, text on verso, signs of restoration. (JN. Apr.2; 206) £140
– **Wales.** [1676, or later]. 381 × 500mm. Engraved map, hand-cold. in outl., coats of arms, compass rose, decor., inset vigs., 12 vig. views in wide side borders, all fully cold., text in Engl. on verso. F. (SBA. Dec.16; 277) *Hulme*. £230
– **Warwickshire.** [1627-76]. 38·5 × 51·5cm. Hand-cold. engraved map from the Theatre of the Empire of Great Britain, sm. margins, a few minor nicks at margin edges. (BS. Feb.25; 91) £95
– **The West Ridinge of Yorkeshyre . . .** J. Sudbury & G. Humbell, 1610 [but 1614, or later]. 380 × 506mm. Engraved map, hand-cold., title cartouche, 7 coats of arms, inset plan, etc. fully cold., Engl. text on verso. W.a.f. (S. Mar.30; 135) *Map House*. £120
– – **Anr. Edn.** [1710]. 15 × 20 inches. Engraved map, hand-cold. in outl., worn along fold. F. & G. (CSK. Jun.5; 3) £95
– – **Anr. Edn.** [1713, or later]. Approximately 380 × 504mm. Engraved map, title cartouche, various coats of arms, inset plan of York, slightly stained. F. (SBA. Oct.22; 663) *Child*. £90
– **Wight Island.** J. Sudbury & G. Humbell, [1614 or later]. 383 × 506mm. Engraved map, hand-cold, in outl., title-cartouche, 4 coats of arms, arms, etc. on inset plans, & other features fully cold., Engl. text on verso. W.a.f. (S. Mar.30; 6) *Shapero*. £100
– **Wilshire [sic].** J. Sudbury & G. Humble, 1610 [but 1614, or later]. 383 × 505mm. Engraved map, hand-cold. in outl., 15 coats of arms, inset plan, etc., fully cold., Engl. text on verso, F. W.a.f. (S. Mar.31; 350) *Doherty*. £140
– – **Anr. Edn.** J. Sudbury & G. Humble, 1610 [but 1616]. 380 × 508mm. Engraved map, hand-cold. in outl., 14 coats of arms, plan, etc. fully cold., Latin text on verso. W.a.f. (S. Mar.31; 351) *Leviton*. £150
– – **Anr. Edn.** Ca. 1611. 380 × 510mm. Engraved map, views of Salisbury & Stonehenge, arms, hand-cold. F., Engl. text on verso. (SKC. Jul.28; 2387) £130
– – **Anr. Edn.** [1614, or later]. 383 × 511mm. Engraved map with town plan, view of Stonehenge & coats of arms, slightly browned, Engl. text on verso. F. & G. (SKC. Feb.26; 1566) £85
– **Worcestershire described.** [1676]. 16 × 21 inches. Engraved map, hand-cold. in outl. F. & G. (CSK. Nov.21; 210) £100
– **York Shire.** J. Sudbury & G. Humble, 1610 [but 1614, or later]. 382 × 507mm. Engraved map, hand-cold. in outl., cartouches, royal arms, etc., fully cold., Engl. text on verso. W.a.f. (S. Mar.30; 131) *Halifax Courier*. £130
– – **Anr. Copy.** 382 × 510mm. Arms, compass rose decor., (fully cold.), lr. pt. of centre fold reprd., slightly affecting engraved surface, some staining & discolouration. F. W.a.f. (S. Nov.3; 195) *Brown*. £125

SPEEDE, John & Humble, G.
– **Italy.** 1626. Old cold. copper engraved map with painted figure cartouche & 1 arms & 4 costume figures at each side, 2 arms & 6 sm. cold. views at head, slightly browned & 10 sm. wormholes, F. (R. Oct.14-18; 5576) DM 850

SPRECHER, J. v Bernegg & Clüver, Ph. & Blaeu
– **Alpinae seu Foederatae Thaetiae Descritio.** N.d. Ob. fo. Old copper engraved map with 4 painted cartouches. (R. Oct.14-18; 5773) DM 1,300

STACKHOUSE, Thomas
– **Eastern Hemisphere.** Ed.:– S. Neele. L., 1 Jun. 1783. 34.5cm. diameter. Hand-cold. map, shows tracks of Cook, Anson & Wallis, Diemens land

joined to New Holland. (JL. Mar.1; 173) Aus. $220

STELLA, T. & Ortelius, Abraham
– **Palaestinae . . . Nova Descriptio.** N.d. Ob. fo. Old cold. copper engraved map with 2 lge. painted roll cartouches & decor., soiled. (R. Oct.14-18; 5123) DM 750

STUMPF, Johann
– **Europa–die erste Tafel.** 1548. Ob. fo. Woodcut map from Schweizerchronik, sm. fault in 1 fold bkd. (R. Mar.31-Apr.4; 5153) DM 450

SUSSEX
Ca. 1650. Hand-cold. map, arms, vig., slightly browned. F. & G. (P. Sep.11; 132) £60

SUTHERLAND, James, Publisher
– **Map of the County of Perth.** Ill.:– Brett & co. after J.S. Kinnefick. N.Y., 1863. 49.5 × 64cm. Folded into 12mo. folder. (CB. Nov.12; 65) Can $220

SWART
See–PITT, M. & Swart

SWIRE, W. & Hutchings, W.F.
– **A Map of the County Palatine of Chester . . .** [1830]. 39 × 52.2 inches (when extended). Hand-cold. engraved map, mntd. on linen, in 36 sections, with key to symbols, lge. inset vig., some slight offsetting. Edges bnd., folding into pull-off mott. cf. case, worn. (S. Jul.27; 46) *Crowe*. £150

TABULA GEOGRAPHICA . . . Europa, Africa, Asia et Circumjacentium Insularum . . .
Ca. 1600. 27.5 × 41.5cm. Map, old traces of folding. (R. Mar.31-Apr.4; 4791) DM 1,000

TALLIS Insularum . . .
– **New Zealand.** 1851. 'Large'. Map, early outl. colour, vigs., tiny stain bottom left margin. (HL. Apr.1; 1748) £65
– **Overland Mail Route to India.** 1543. 'Large'. 2 pt. map covering Europe & Arabia/India, vig. views, from edn. showing additional routes including projected railway to India, etc., entitled 'Overland Routes to India & China', early outl. colour. (HL. Apr.1; 1543) £105
– **Western Australia.** 1851. Map, with view of Perth from Mount Eliza & 2 others in vigs., all cold. (JL. Jul.19; 244) Aus. $100

TALLIS, John & Rapkin, J.
– **British America.–Newfoundland & Nova Scotia. –West Canada.–East Canada.** Ill.:– Warren, Wallis, Fussell & Rogers, etc. Ca. 1850. Map, 14 × 10½ inches. Partly cold., ornamental borders, vigs. (TA. Oct.16; 83) £52
– **Jamaica.** 1851. 'Large'. Map, early outl. colour, vig. views. (HL. Apr.1; 1723) £85
– **New South Wales.** Ill.:– H. Warren, engraved by J. Rogers, map drawn & engraved by J. Rapkin. L. & N.Y., 1851. 25 × 33cm. Counties cold. in outl., cold. vigs. of Coin, Sydney Cove, the Murray River & Xanthorrhaea plant, decor. border, the Gold Diggings cold. yellow. (JL. Mar.1; 184) Aus. $130
– – **Anr. Edn.** N.d. Map, hand-cold. vigs. F. (JL. Mar.1; 128) Aus. $150
– – **Anr. Copy.** Map, with vig. of Sydney Harbour & the Murray, uncold. (JL. Jul.19; 246) Aus. $120

TANNER, B.
– **A Map of the Tennessee Government.** N.Y., [1796]. 9 × 16½inches. Hand-cold. map. (SG. May 21; 103) $180

TANNER, Henry Schenk
– **United States of America.** Phila., 1838. 48 × 60 inches. Map, lge. cartouche, 16 city insets, & inset map of the Oregon & Mandan districts, linen-bkd. Folded in orig. hf. roan folder with ties. (SG. May 21; 102) $800
– **Virginia, Maryland, & Delaware.** Phila., 1820. 22 × 31 inches. Cold. map, some marginal tears. (SG. Nov.20; 131) $100

TAVERNIER
– **Holy Land with Sinai & Egypt.** 1640. Fo. Map, cold. in outl., mntd. (JN. Apr.2; 227) £62

TEESDALE, Henry
– **A Map of the County Palatine of Lancaster Divided into Hundreds of Parishes from an accurate Survey.** 1830. Approximately 1,620 × 1,136mm. Lge. engraved folding map, title cartouche, cold., 48 sections, mntd. on linen, edges

bnd. Folding into cont. tree cf. case. (SBA. Dec.16; 172) *Mortens of Manchester*. £64

TEISERA, L.
– **Japoniae Insulae Descriptio.** 1595. Ob. fo. Cold. copper engraved map, painted cartouche & decor. (R. Mar.31-Apr.4; 5118) DM 1,300

THEVET, A.
– **Europe.** [Paris], [1575]. 352 × 452mm. Engraved map, embellished with sailing ships & other craft, sea monsters, etc., torn & reprd. in N.E. corner & at bottom, slightly affecting engraved surface, tiny perforation in fold, a few stains. W.a.f. (S. Jun.29; 28) *Arader*. £180
– **Quarte Partie du Monde.** [Paris], [1575]. 352 × 452mm. Engraved map, human figures, animals, sailing ships, sea monsters, other decor. features, verso blank, tiny perforation in centre fold, very sm. hole in engraved bottom margin, repair to short tear in E. margin, a few other short tears, 1 or 2 very minor stains. W.a.f. (S. Jun.29; 25) *Arader*. £850
– **Table d'Afrique.** [Paris], [1575]. 353 × 455mm. Engraved map, sailing ships, sea monsters, etc., verso blank, ends of centre fold reprd., with slight loss of engraved surface, a few stains. W.a.f. (S. Jun.29; 27) *Arader*. £240

THOMAS, James
– **Ireland.** L., ca. 1850. 75 × 84 inches. Lge. engraved map, brown-tone on linen, 72 section on 6 pts., with 2 lge. engraved views, scales, star compass, etc. Cont. gt.-stpd. solander case with stp. on lining, 'Dublin, L.M. Strangway's Collection', sm. crease holes, sm. slit in linen between 2 sections, pinholes on blank margins. (PWP. Apr.9; 167) Can. $440

THOMSON
– **Iran.** 1816. 'Large'. Map, early colour. (HL. Apr.1; 1717) £55

THOMSON, John
– **Islands round Britain, Guernsey & Sark, Jersey, Scillies, Isle of Man, Isle of Wight.** 1817. Fo., approximately 56 × 43cm. Cold. map, in 5 insets & 2 views. (JN. Sep.9; 4122) £52
– **Spanish North America.** [Edinb.], ca. 1820. 21 × 25½ inches. Cold. map., number 58 from Thomson's New General Atlas, very light offsetting. (SG. Aug.21; 272) $120

THOMSON, John & Co.
– **Map of the Islands in the Pacific Ocean.** L., 1817. 60 × 49.5cm. Map, cold. in outl., Coast of Holland shown from Solitary Island to Cape Yor, 4 insets Owhyee & Otaheite. (JL. Mar.1; 193) Aus. $130
– **Pacific Islands.** 1817. 'Large'. Map, early colour, 4 enlarged inset maps, faint ageing at centrefold. (HL. Apr.1; 1544) £60

THOMPSON, G.
– **New Map of Europe.** 1789. Lge. ob. fo. Copper engraved map with old outl. col., painted cartouche & 4 etched views, slightly browned & with some sm. tears mntd. on linen. (R. Oct.14-18; 5169) DM 800

THORNTON, John
– **St. Helena.** 1716. 'Large'. Map, cartouche, mileage scale, compass rose, inset of Trinidad Is., some blemishes. (HL. Apr.1; 1766) £145

TIRION, Isaac
– **Algemeene Kaart ven de Westindische Eilanden.** Amst., ca. 1760. 15 × 21 inches. Hand-cold. map. (SG. May 21; 112) $200
– **Nieuwe Kaart van de Grootbritanische Volkplantingen in Noord America.** 1755. Ob. fo. Old cold. copper engraved map. (R. Oct.14-18; 5076) DM 420
– **Nieuwe Kaart van het Oostelykste Deel der Weereld.** Amst., 1753. Map, shows Australian discoveries prior to Cook. (JL. Dec.14; 182) Aus. $190
– – **Anr. Copy.** Hand-cold. map showing New Holland joined to New Guinea & New Hebrides with hypothetical coast lines. (JL. Mar.1; 222) Aus. $160
[–] Quebek De Hoofdstad van Kanada aan de Rivier van St. Laurens. [Amst.], [1769]. 32.5 × 43cm. Fully orig. cold. map, from 'Hedendaagsche Historie of Tegenwooridige Staat van Amerika', recent outl. col. (CB. Feb.18; 65) Can. $160

TREVETHEN, William
– **Americae Descriptio Nova.** 1666 [or later]. 337 × 419mm. Engraved map from Peter Heylyn's

TREVETHEN, William – Americae Descriptio Nova. -contd.
'Cosmography', torn & reprd. W.a.f. (S. Mar.31; 311) *Potter.* £110

TSCHUDI, Aegidius
– Helvetiae Descriptio. N.d. Ob. fo. Cold. copper engraved map, painted cartouche. (R. Mar.31-Apr.4; 5871) DM 900

UTRECHT
– Platte Grond der Stad Utrecht. J. van Schoonhoven, 1778. 970 × 610mm. (P. Jul.2; 239) *Mendes.* £50

VALCK, Gerard
– Novus Planiglobü Terrestris per Utrumque Polum conspectus. Ca. 1690. Ob. fo. Old cold. copper engraved map in 2 hemispheres, in projection, decor. in corners, some sm. margin tears bkd. (R. Mar.31-Apr.4; 4812) DM 1,400
– Pars Borealis Circuli Rhenani. N.d. Old cold. copper engraved map with painted figure cartouche. (R. Oct.14-18; 4301) DM 530
See–JANSSON, Jan or Johannes, Valck, G. & Schenk, Peter

VALCK, Gerard & L.
– America Aurea Pars Altera Mundi. N.d. Ob. fo. Old cold. copper engraved map with figure cartouche tear backed in fold. (R. Oct.14-18; 5049) DM 700

VALCK, Gerard & Schenk, Pieter
– Middlesexiae. Ca. 1650. Hand-cold. map, cartouche. F. & G. (P. Sep.11; 153) *Kent.* £110
– Scenographia Systematis Copernicani. Amst., ca. 1700. 20 × 23 inches. Fully hand-cold. astronomical chart, surrounded by pict. representations, angels, etc. Mntd. to old bd. (SG. May 21; 24) $120

VALGRISI
– Brazil. 1561. 'Medium' size. Map, engraved. (HL. Apr.1; 1580) £75
– British Isles. 1561. 'Medium' size. Map, a few marginal blemishes. (HL. Apr.1; 1624) £155
– Greece. 1562. 'Medium' size. Map, a few marginal blemishes. (HL. Apr.1; 1699) £60
– Iran. 1562. 'Medium' size. Map, based on Gastaldi's map of 1548, a few faint perimeter stains. (HL. Apr.1; 1715) £75
– Northern Atlantic. 1562. 'Medium' size. Based on supposed voyages of the Zeno brothers 1380-87, this copy version with Norway not shown as joined to Greenland. (HL. Apr.1; 1540) £130
– Saudi Arabia. 1562. 'Medium' size. Map, trace of age staining. (HL. Apr.1; 1773) £150
– Scandanavia. 1562. 'Medium' size. Trapezium-shaped map, based on that of Jacob Ziegler first publd. 1532, faint traces of foxing & centrefold & margins. (HL. Apr.1; 1547) £120
– Tierra Nveva. 1561. 'Medium' size. Map, based on Gastaldi's map of 1548, 'Bermuda' island is shown, along with Azores to the east. (HL. Apr.1; 1795) £160
– The World. 1574. 'Medium' size. Double-hemisphere map, first to appear in an atlas, shows America & Asia joined, no Southern continent, details, faint toning at centre fold. (HL. Apr.1; 1501) £175

VAUGONDY, Robert de
– Archipel des Indes Orientales. Paris, 1750. Hand-cold. map, decor. title cartouche & includes northern coast of New Holland. (JL. Mar.1; 234) Aus. $140
– – Anr. Edn. Paris, ca. 1752. Map shows northern coast of Australia according to Tasman, decor. cartouche. (JL. Dec.14; 188) Aus. $180
– Mappe-Monde dressée suivant les Nouvelles Relations et assujetté aux observations astronomiques par ... Découvertés du Capitaine Cook ... Paris, ca. 1757. 4800 × 742mm. Engraved double-hemispheric map, hand-cold. outls. of the continents, title-cartouches & tracks of Cook, Anson, etc. wtrmkd. paper, some light foxing. (PWP. Apr.9; 169) Can. $480
– Orbis Vetus in Utraque Continente. [Paris], 1752. 22 × 29 inches. Double-hemispheric map, with hand-cold. boundaries & ornate cartouche, some marginal tears. (SG. May 21; 142) $300
– – Anr. Edn. Paris, 1755. Lge. decor. map, hand-cold. (JL. Jul.19; 326) Aus. $500
– – Anr. Edn. Ca. 1760. Ob. fo. Cold. copper engraved map with 2 lge. painted figurative cartouches. (R. Oct.14-18; 3380) DM 500

VELLEIUS, A. & Ortelius, Abraham
– Island. N.d. Ob. fo. Cold. copper engraved map with 3 painted cartouches & figure decor. (R. Oct.14-18; 5850) DM 1,600

VENICE
Ca. 1650. Un-cold. town plan. F. & G. (P. Jan.22; 214) *Burlington.* £110

VISSCHER, Nicolaus Joannes
– Asia Nova Delineatio. Amst., [1650-80]. 54 × 43cm. Map cold. in outl., decor. cartouche, Carpentaria & part of Nova Hollandia shown separated from Nova Guinea. (JL. Mar.1; 169) Aus. $525
– Comitatus Zelandiae novissima delineatio. Amst., ca. 1700. 47 × 56 cm. Hand-cold. engraved map, fold, defect., slightly browned & restored in middle. (VG. Oct.28; 336) Fls. 570
– Ducatus Lutzenburgi. Amst., ca. 1698. 46 × 55cm. Hand-cold. engraved map, fold, defect., restored & browned in middle. (VG. Oct.28; 462) Fls. 450
– Exactissima Helvetiae, Rhetiae, Valesiae Tabula. N.d. Ob. fo. Old cold. copper engraved map with 3 painted figure cartouches, old mnt. (R. Oct.14-18; 5796) DM 480
– Europa. 1684-1715. 44.2 × 54.6cm. Hand-cold. engraved map with margins, some foxing. (BS. Feb.25; 104) £100
– Das Herzogtum Schleswig. Ca. 1740. Partly cold. copper engraved map after N. Visscher. (H. Dec.9/10; 730a) DM 560
– Hiberniae Regnum. Amst., ca. 1700. 560 × 738mm. Engraved map, hand-cold. in outl., armorial & pict. title & scale cartouches, etc., fully cold., engraved tables at sides of map. F. W.a.f. (S. Jun.29; 70) *Duyck.* £110
– Hollandia Comitatus. Amst., ca. 1698. 76 × 52cm. Hand-cold. engraved map, fold in middle, slit in fold. (VG. Oct.28; 297) Fls. 480
– Map of Asia from Atlas Major. 1702. Map, 2 cartouches. (JL. Dec.14; 108) Aus. $400
– Novissima et Accuratissima Totius Americae Descriptio. Amst., ca. 1698. 45 × 55cm. Hand-cold. engraved map, folding, defect., browned & restored in middle. (VG. Oct.28; 376) Fls. 500
– Novissima totius Terrarum Orbis Tabula. Amst., ca. 1697. 43 × 54cm. Hand-cold. engraved map, fold in middle, slit in fold (restored), slightly browned, outer margins slightly frayed. (VG. Oct.28; 373) Fls. 1,000
– Orbis Terrarum Tabula. Ca. 1680. Ob. fo. Cold. copper engraved map in 2 hemispheres, allegories in corners. F. (R. May 31-Apr.4; 4806) DM 2,200
– Tabula Ducatus Brabantiae. Amst., Claes Jansz. Visscher. ca. 1698. 47 × 56cm. Hand-cold. engraved map, defect., browned & restored in middle, folded. (VG. Oct.28; 254) Fls. 500
– Terra Sancta. [Amst.], 1659. 462 × 560mm. Engraved map, hand-cold. in outl., principal areas, elab. title-cartouche, decor., (fully cold.), minor marginal repairs with slight loss, bottom & side margins cut close. W.a.f. (S. Nov.4; 363) *Cohen.* £120
– – Anr. Copy. Hand-cold. map, lacks sm. pt. of bottom right corner. (P. Mar.12; 194) *Phelp.* £65

VISSCHER, Nicolaus Joannes & Schenk, Pieter, Jun.
– Herzogtum Holstein. N.d. Lge. ob. fo. Old cold. copper engraved map, tear backed. (R. Oct.14-18; 4094) DM 430
– [Herzogtum Württemberg]. N.d. Lge. fo. Old cold. copper engraved mp with figure cartouche. (R. Oct.14-18; 3654) DM 600
– Superioris Alsatiae, Brisgaviae et Suntgaviae Tabula. N.d. Ob. fo. Old cold. copper engraved map, painted figure cartouche. (R. Oct.14-18; 3488) DM 450

VRIENTS
See–ORTELIUS, Abraham & Vrients

WAGHENAER, Lukas Jansz
[–] The Sea Coastes betweene Dover & Orfordnes, wherein is contiened the most famous River of Thames with all the Sands, Bankes, Flats ... [Amst.], [1588]. 320 × 500mm. Engraved, hand-cold. map, cartouches, coat of arms, compass rose, decors., separated in pt. of centre fold, with some loss of engraved surface, outer corners defect. with some loss of engraved border at lr. corners, 1

or 2 stains. F. W.a.f. (S. Nov.3; 213) *Holley.* £220

WALLIS, J. & E.
– The Panorama of Europe, A New Game. 1815. 18½ × 24½ inches. Hand-cold. engraved views of European cities, mntd. on cl., folding. Orig. s.-c., worn. (CSK. Jul.3; 5) £65

WALLIS, John
– Plan of the cities & of London & Westminster. 1802. 16 × 45 inches. Engraved map, hand-cold. in outl., mntd. on cl. Orig. s.-c., worn. (CSK. Apr.10; 58) £50

WEIGEL, Johann Christoff
See–SCHNEIDER, Louis & Weigel, Johann Christoff

WEILAND, C.F.
– Neu Holland. 1866. German Iss. Map. (JL. Dec.14; 174) Aus. $180

WELLS, Edward
[–] A New Map of the Land of Canaan & Parts Adjoining.–Chorographia Terrae Sanctae ... ex Variis auctoribus ... N.p. (2nd. work), ca. 1700; n.d. Various sizes. 1st. map: engraved map, including inset map & armorial title-cartouche, discold. in centre fold; 2nd. map: engraved map in 2 sheets incorporating lge. inset plan of ancient Jerusalem. W.a.f. (S. Jun.29; 131) *Cohen.* £110
– A New Map of Libya or Old Africa. [1700]. 37 × 49cm. Hand-cold. line engraved map. F. (VA. May 8; 469) R. 120
– A New Map ... Plantations of the English in America. Ca. 1700. Hand-cold. map. F. & G. (P. Jun.11; 245) *Dawson.* £100
– A New Map of Present Asia. Oxford, 1702. 51 × 36.5cm. Map, orig. outl. colouring, cold. Coat of Arms & ornamental cartouches. (JL. Mar.1; 195) Aus. $260

WERELT CAERT
Ca. 1690. Ob. fo. Anon. copper engraved map from a Dutch Bible, 2 hemispheres, allegories in corners, slightly browned, sm. tears mntd. (R. Oct.14-18; 3373) DM 550

WEST INDIES
– A Correct Chart of the Caribbee Islands. L., ca. 1750. 18½ × 25½ inches. Nautical chart, from the English Coast Pilot, minor separations at fold. (SG. May 21; 119) $130
– Stabilimenti de Francesi. Venice, 1785. 14 × 18 inches. Hand-cold. map, with fully-cold. pict. cartouche. (SG. May 21; 133) $325

WESTENBERG, J. & Pitt, M.
– Grafschaft Bentheim. Ca. 1685. Ob. fo. Old cold. copper engraved map with painted cartouche & 7 sm. arms. (R. Oct.14-18; 4342) DM 540

WESTERWALD
– Karte den Militärischen Operationen zwischen Lahn und Sieg 1796. Ca. 1850. Ob. fo. Litho. folding map, cold in part. (R. Oct.14-18; 4994) DM 450

WHISTON, W.
– Holy Land. Ill.:– after Cellarius, Reland, etc. 1737. Fo, approximately 56 × 43cm. Uncold. map, insets of text, Jewish shekel, index, etc., neat repairs at bottom. (JN. Sep.9; 3767) £65

WILKINSON, Robert
– New South Wales, New Zealand, New Hebrides & the Islands Adjacent. L., 1808. Hand-cold. map. (JL. Mar.1; 233) Aus. $100

WILLDAY, G.
– New & Correct Map of the World. L., ca. 1715. Copper engraved map in 2 hemispheres, decor., many sm. maps round, old outl. cold. (R. Mar.31-Apr.4; 4821) DM 3,200

WIT, Frederick de
– Asia Nova Descriptio. N.d. Ob. fo. Cold. copper engraved map, painted figure cartouche, side views, 6 sm. views at head. (R. Mar.31-Apr.4; 5070) DM 1,100
– [Bayrischer Kreis]. N.d. Ob. fo. Old cold. copper engraved map with painted arms cartouche including sm. subsidiary maps. (R. Oct.14-18; 3701) DM 420
– Brabantiae Pars Septentionalis. N.d. Ob. fo. Old cold. copper engraved map with painted figure cartouche, lightly browned, fold backed. (R. Oct.14-18; 5262) DM 450
– Ducatus Geldriae Ruremondana sive Hispanica. Amst., ca. 1680. 48 × 59 cm. Engraved hand-cold.

map, fold in middle, sm. slit in centre of fold, sm. tears in outer margins. (VG. Oct.28; 287) Fls. 480

– **Erzbistum Köln mit den Herzogthümern Jülich und Berg und der Grafschaft Moers.** N.d. Ob. fo. Old cold. copper engraved map with painted arms cartouche, lightly browned at fold. (R. Oct.14-18; 4541) DM 200

– **Germany.** Ca. 1688. Fo., approximately 56 × 43cm. Cold. map, cartouche, browned. (JN. Sep.9; 3950) £110

– **Herzogtum Kleve und Grafschaft Mark.** N.d. Ob. fo. Old cold. copper engraved map with painted arms cartouche, slightly browned at fold. (R. Oct.14-18; 4510) DM 500

– **Herzogtümer Bremen und Verden.** N.d. Ob. fo. Old cold. copper engraved map with painted arms cartouche, fold lightly browned. (R. Oct.14-18; 4058) DM 500

– **Karte der Insel.** N.d. Ob. fo. 6 cold. copper engraved plans with decor. border & cartouche, brkn. at fold & backed. (R. Oct.14-18; 5586) DM 430

– **Luxemburg.** Ca. 1680. Ob. fo. Copper engraved map with old outl. col. with 2 painted cartouches, stained. (R. Oct.14-18; 5398) DM 650

– **Niedersächsicher Kreis.** N.d. Ob. fo. Old cold. copper engraved map with painted arms cartouche, slightly browned at fold. (R. Oct.14-18; 4407) DM 450

– **Nova Africa.** N.d. 430 × 545 mm. Engraved map, 2 histor. cartouches, borders on 3 sides, comprising 8 figures & 6 town views, partly hand-cold., framed. (SKC. Jul.28; 2373) £90

– – **Anr. Copy.** Ob. fo. Cold. copper engraved map, painted figure cartouche, 4 painted figures at sides, sm. cold plans, fold bkd., lightly soiled. F. (R. Mar.31-Apr.4; 4936) DM 1,000

– **Nova et Accurata Totius Europae Descriptio.** N.d. Ob. fo. Cold. copper engraved map, old outl. cold, painted figure cartouche. (R. Mar.31-Apr.4; 5175) DM 420

– **Nova Orbis Tabula.** Ca. 1680. Double-p. fo. Map, cold. in outl. (SPB. Oct.1; 269) $1,700

– – **Anr. Copy.** Ob. fo. Old cold. copper engraved map in 2 hemispheres with sm. maps, corner allegories, slightly restored. F. (R. Mar.31-Apr.4; 4808) DM 3,400

– **Nova totius Westphalia Descriptio.** Amst., [1680]. 467 × 532mm. Engraved map, hand-cold. in outl., title-cartouche, compass rose, etc., fully cold. W.a.f. (S. Nov.3; 243) *Nagle.* £110

– **Novissima et Accuratissima Septentrionalis et Meriodinalis Americae Descriptio.** N.d. Ob. fo. Copper engraved map, surfaces cold., 2 painted figure cartouches. (R. Mar.31-Apr.4; 4976) DM 1,700

– **Poli Arcitici et Cicumjacentium Terrarum** Ca. 1690. Ob. fo. Old cold. copper engraved map, decor., col. oxidised, some sm. faults. (R. Mar.31-Apr.4; 4864) DM 600

– **Regni Sueciae Tabula generalis.** Amst., [1680]. 502 × 575mm. Engraved map, hand-cold. in outl., histor. & armorial title cartouche fully cold. W.a.f. (S. Nov.3; 123) *Gibbons.* £100

– **[Schwäbischer Kreis].** Ob. fo. N.d. Old cold. copper engraved map with cartouche & painted heraldic cartouche & 16 arms. (R. Oct.14-18; 3605) DM 700

– **Septentrionaliora Americae a Groenlandia per Freta Davidis et Hudson ad Terram Novam.** [Amst.], ca. 1730. 490 × 565mm. Engraved map on rag paper laid down on card mount, hand-cold. cartouches, decor. (PWP. Apr.9; 170) £280

– **Totius Europae Littora.** Ca. 1680. Hand-cold. map, some dampstains. Maple frame. (P. Dec.11; 162) *Shirley.* £80

– **Totius Fluminis Rheni Descriptio.** N.d. 23 × 104 cm. Old cold. copper engraved map with 2 painted figure cartouches. (R. Oct.14-18; 4919) DM 700

– **Totius Fluminis Rheni Novissima Descriptio.** N.d. Ob. fo. 2 attached maps from 1 plan, old cold. copper engraved with 2 painted figure cartouches, fold slightly browned. (R. Oct.14-18; 4920) DM 440

WIT, I. de
– **Frisiae.** Ca. 1690. Hand-cold. map. F. & G. (P. Dec.11; 172) *Chelsea.* £75

WORLD. Showing the Latest Discoveries of Captain Cook
L., 1785. 48 × 37 cm. Map, hand-cold. in outl., shows New Holland joined to Van Dieman's Land & Cook's tracks. (JL. Jul.19; 255) Aus. $110

WYLD, James
– **Australia.** N.d. Lge. double fo. Map, cold. in outl., copper-engraved title, insets of the World & Van Dieman's Land. (JL. Jul.19; 243) Aus. $110

ZATTA, Antonio
– **Asia.** 1777. 'Large'. Map, 'oriental' cartouche, early outl. colour. (HL. Apr.1; 1528) £60
– **Balearic Islands.** 1775. 'Large'. Map, early outl. colour, a few insignificant blemishes. (HL. Apr.1; 1783) £50

– **L'Elvezia.** 1781. 415 × 330mm. Cold. map, cartouche. (P. Jul.2; 234) £60
– **Emisfero Terrestre Meridionale.** Venice, 1779. Hand-cold. map. (JL. Mar.1; 142) Aus. $200
– **L'Isola d'Islanda.** 1781. 415 × 325mm. Hand-cold. map. (P. Jul.30; 183d) *Brown.* £60
– **L'Isole Bermuda.** 1778. 445 × 330mm. Hand-cold. map, cartouche. (P. Apr.9; 151) *Map House.* £220
– **Isole Filippine.** 1785. 415 × 325mm. Hand-cold. map. (P. Apr.9; 184e) £110
– **Japan.** 1785. 333 × 420mm. Hand-cold. map. (P. Apr.9; 184c) *Potter.* £120
– **Il Mappamondo.** 1774. 290 × 390mm. Hand-cold. map of the World, vigs. (P. Jul.30; 183c) *Map House.* £95
– – **Anr. Copy.** Map of the World showing Tasmania joined to the rest of Australia & unusual shape to New Zealand. (JL. Dec.14; 171) Aus. $250
– **Mare del Sud.** Venezia, 1765. 420 × 320mm. Hand-cold. map showing Australia & New Zealand, decor., cartouche. (P. Apr.30; 96) *Leycester.* £110
– – **Anr. Edn.** 1776. 'Large'. Map, based on Capt. Cook's discoveries, cartouche, voyages of Cook & Carteret marked, early outl. colour. (HL. Apr.1; 1564) £260
– – **Anr. Copy.** 415 × 315mm. Hand-cold. map, cartouche. (P. Apr.9; 152) *Map House.* £220
– **New Zealand.** 1778. Hand-cold. map, cold. cartouche. (P. Dec.11; 187) *Bonham.* £220
– **North America.** 1785. 420 × 325mm. Hand-cold. map. (P. Apr.9; 184f) *Map House.* £85
– **Philippines.** 1785. Sm. fo. Map, cold., cartouche. (JN. Apr.2; 335) £75
– **Terra de Canaan ou Terra Promessa.** 1785. 420 × 320mm. Hand-cold. map. (P. Jul.30; 181) *Intercol.* £85
– **West Indies.** 1785. 'Large'. Map, cartouche, early outl. colour, a few insignificant paper creases. (HL. Apr.1; 1555) £95

ZELL, H. & Ortelius, Abraham
– **[Ostpreussen].** N.d. Ob. fo. Old cold. copper engraved map with cartouche, slightly soiled. (R. Oct.14-18; 4716) DM 500

ZOLLMANN, F. & Homann, J.C.H.
– **Grafschaft Hanau.** N.d. Ob. fo. Old cold. copper engraved map with view & figure cartouche. (R. Oct.14-18; 4257) DM 550

NOTES

NOTES